KT-413-386

THE SHORTER OXFORD ENGLISH DICTIONARY

THE SHORTER OXFORD ENGLISH DICTIONARY

ON HISTORICAL PRINCIPLES

PREPARED BY

WILLIAM LITTLE

H. W. FOWLER AND JESSIE COULSON

REVISED AND EDITED BY

C. T. ONIONS

THIRD EDITION

COMPLETELY RESET

WITH ETYMOLOGIES REVISED BY

G. W. S. FRIEDRICHSEN

AND WITH REVISED ADDENDA

VOLUME II

MARL–Z

AND ADDENDA

CLARENDON PRESS · OXFORD

Oxford University Press, Walton Street, Oxford OX2 6DP
Oxford New York Toronto
Delhi Bombay Calcutta Madras Karachi
Kuala Lumpur Singapore Hong Kong Tokyo
Nairobi Dar es Salaam Cape Town
Melbourne Auckland
and associated companies in
Beirut Berlin Ibadan Nicosia

Oxford is a trade mark of Oxford University Press

Published in the United States
by Oxford University Press, New York

© *Oxford University Press 1973*

All rights reserved. No part of this publication may be reproduced, stored in a retrieval system, or transmitted, in any form or by any means, electronic, mechanical, photocopying, recording, or otherwise, without the prior permission of Oxford University Press

Plain Edition ISBN 0 19 861126 9
Thumb Index Edition ISBN 0 19 861127 7

First Published February 1933
Reprinted with Corrections March 1933, April 1933
Reprinted 1934. Second Edition 1936. Reprinted 1939
Third Edition 1944. Reprinted with Corrections 1947
Reprinted 1950, 1952, 1955
With Corrections and Revised Addenda 1956
Reprinted with Corrections 1959, 1962, 1964, 1965, 1967, 1968, 1970, 1972
Reset with Revised Etymologies and Addenda 1973, 1974
1975 (With Corrections), 1977, 1978, 1980, 1983, 1984, 1985, 1986

Printed in Great Britain
at the University Printing House, Oxford
by David Stanford
Printer to the University

LIST OF ABBREVIATIONS, SIGNS, ETC.

In this list the abbreviations are printed in the type that is normally used for them, but there are variations for special cases.

a	*ante*, 'before', 'not later than'
a.	adjective
abbrev.	abbreviated, abbreviation (of)
abl.	ablative
Abp.	Archbishop
absol.	in absolute use, absolutely
abstr.	abstract
acc., accus.	accusative
act.	active
adj.	adjective, adjectival
adv.	adverb
advb.	adverbial, -ly
Æol.	Æolic
Aero., *Aeronaut.*	in Aeronautics
AFr.	Anglo-French
Afr.	African
agent-n.	agent-noun
Agric.	in Agriculture
AL.	Anglo-Latin
Alb.	Albanian
Alch.	in Alchemy
Alg.	in Algebra
allus.	allusively
alt.	altered, alteration (of)
alt. f.	altered form of
Amer.	American
Amer. Hist.	in American History
Amer. Ind.	American Indian
anal.	analogy
Anat.	in Anatomy
Anc. Hist., etc.	in Ancient History, etc.
Anglo-Ind.	Anglo-Indian
Anglo-Ir.	Anglo-Irish
Anthrop.	in Anthropology
aphet.	aphetic, aphetized
Apocr.	Apocrypha
app., appar.	apparently
appos.	appositive, -ly
Arab.	Arabic
Aram.	Aramaic
arch.	archaic
Arch., *Archit.*	in Architecture
Archæol.	in Archæology
Arith.	in Arithmetic
Arm.	Armenian
assim.	assimilated, -ation
assoc.	associated, -ation
Astr., *Astron.*	in Astronomy
Astrol.	in Astrology
astrol.	astrological
attrib.	attributive, -ly
attrib. and *Comb.*	in attributive uses and combinations
augm.	augmentative
Austral.	Australian
Av.	Avestic
A.V.	Authorized Version
Bacteriol.	in Bacteriology
BEAUM. & FL.	Beaumont & Fletcher
bef.	before
betw.	between
bibl.	biblical
Biochem.	in Biochemistry
Biol.	in Biology
Biol. Chem.	in Biological Chemistry
B. JONS.	Ben Jonson
Bot.	in Botany
Bot. L.	in Botanical Latin
Bp.	Bishop
Br.	Branch
Braz.	Brazilian
Brit. N. Amer.	British North America
Bulg.	Bulgarian
Byz.	Byzantine
c	*circa*, 'about'
c.	century
Camb.	Cambridge
cap.	capital letter
Cat., Catal.	Catalan
catachr.	catachrestic, -ally
cc.	centuries
Cdl.	Cardinal
Celt.	Celtic
Cent. Dict.	Century Dictionary
CEur.	Common European
Cf., cf.	*confer*, 'compare'
CGmc.	Common Germanic
Chem.	in Chemistry
CHESTERF.	Chesterfield
Ch. Hist.	in Church History
Chin.	Chinese
Chor.	Chorus
Chr. L.	Christian Latin
Chron., *Chronol.*	in Chronology
CIE.	Common Indo-European
Cinemat., *Cinematogr.*	in Cinematography
cl.	clause
Class. Antiq.	in Classical Antiquities
cl. Gr., L.	classical Greek, Latin
cogn., cogn. w.	cognate with
collect.	collective, -ly
colloq.	colloquial, -ism, -ly
Com.	Common
comb.	combining
Comb.	in combination
Comm.	in Commercial usage
Comm. Law	in Commercial Law
comp.	compound
comp., compar.	comparative
Comp. Anat.	in Comparative Anatomy
compl.	complement
Conch., *Conchol.*	in Conchology
concr.	concrete, -ly
conj.	conjunction, conjunctive
conjug.	conjugation
conn.	connected
cons.	consonant
const., const. w.	construed with
constr.	construction
contemp.	contemporary
contempt.	in contemptuous use
contr.	contracted, contraction
Corn.	Cornish
correl.	correlative
corresp.	corresponding
corrupt.	corruption
COTGR.	Cotgrave
CRom.	Common Romanic
Crim.Goth.	Crimean Gothic
Cryst., *Crystall.*	in Crystallography
CSlav.	Common Slavonic
Cursor M.	*Cursor Mundi*
d.	died
Da.	Danish
dat.	dative
D'CHESS	Duchess of
def.	definition
def. art.	definite article
dem., demons.	demonstrative
deriv.	derivation, derivative, -s
derog.	derogatory
dial.	dialect, dialectal, -ly
Dict.	Dictionary
Dicts.	in Dictionaries
dim.	diminutive
dissim.	dissimilated, -ation
dist.	distinguished
distrib.	distributive
Dor.	Doric
DRUMM. of HAWTH.	Drummond of Hawthornden
Du.	Dutch
dub.	dubious
Eccl.	in Ecclesiastical usage
eccl. Gr.	ecclesiastical Greek
Eccl. Hist.	in Ecclesiastical History
eccl. L	ecclesiastical Latin
Econ.	in Economics
ed.	edited by, edition (of)
E.D.D.	*The English Dialect Dictionary*, ed. J. Wright
EE.	Early English
EFris.	East Frisian
e.g.	*exempli gratia*, 'for example'
Egyptol.	in Egyptology
EInd.	East Indian
E. Ind.	in the East Indies
Electr.	in Electricity
Electr. Engin.	in Electrical Engineering
ellipt.	elliptical, -ly
Embryol.	in Embryology
e.midl.	east midland
emph.	emphatic
Eng.	English
Eng. Hist.	in English History
Engin.	in Engineering
Ent., *Entomol.*	in Entomology
Epil.	Epilogue
equiv., equivs.	equivalent, -s
erron.	erroneous, -ly
esp.	especially
etc.	et cetera
Eth.	Ethiopian
Ethnol.	in Ethnology
etym.	etymology
etymol.	etymological
euphem.	euphemistic, -ally
ex.	example
exc.	except
exclam.	exclamation
f.	form of, formation (on), formed (on), from

F.	French
fam.	familiar, -ly
fem.	feminine
ff.	forms, forms of
fig.	in figurative use
Finn.	Finnish
fl.	*floruit*, 'flourished'
Flem.	Flemish
Fo.	(First) Folio edition of Shakespeare's plays
foll.	following, following word or article
Fortif.	in Fortification
Fr.	French
Frank.	Frankish
freq.	frequent, -ly
frequent.	frequentative
Fr. Hist.	in French History
Fris.	Frisian
fut.	future
G.	German
Gael.	Gaelic
Gallo-Rom.	Gallo-Roman
Gaul.	Gaulish
Gen.	General
gen.	general, -ly
gen., genit.	genitive
Geog.	in Geography
Geol.	in Geology
Geom.	in Geometry
Gmc.	Germanic
Goldsm.	Goldsmith
Goth.	Gothic
Gr.	Greek
Gram.	in Grammar
gram.	grammar
Gr. Antiq.	in Greek Antiquities
Gr. Ch.	in the Greek Church
Gr. Hist.	in Greek History
Gr.-L.	Græco-Latin
Heb.	Hebrew
Her.	in Heraldry
Herb.	among herbalists
HG.	High German
Hind.	Hindustani
Hist.	in historical use
hist.	historical
Hort.	in Horticulture
Hydraul. Engin.	in Hydraulic Engineering
hyperbol.	hyperbolically
ib., ibid.	*ibidem*, 'in the same book or passage'
Icel.	Icelandic
Ichth., *Ichthyol.*	in Ichthyology
id.	*idem*, 'the same'
i.e.	*id est*, 'that is'
IE.	Indo-European
imit.	imitative
immed.	immediate, -ly
imper.	imperative
impers.	impersonal
impf.	imperfect
improp.	improper, -ly
incl.	including
incorr.	incorrect
ind., indic.	indicative
indef., indef. art.	indefinite, indefinite article
Indo-Eur.	Indo-European
Indo-Gmc.	Indo-Germanic
inf., infin.	infinitive
infl.	inflected, influenced
instr.	instrumental
int., *interj.*	interjection
interrog.	interrogative, -ly
intr.	intransitive, -ly
Ir.	Irish

Irel.	Ireland
iron.	ironical, -ly
irreg.	irregular, -ly
It.	Italian
J., (J.)	Johnson's *Dictionary*
Jam.	Jamieson's *Scottish Dictionary*
Jap.	Japanese
Jav.	Javanese
joc.	jocular, -ly
Jurisp.	in Jurisprudence
L.	Latin
lang., langs.	language, -s
Langl.	Langland
Lat.	Latin
Law-L.	Law-Latin
Ld.	Lord
LDu.	Low Dutch
Lett.	Lettish
LG.	Low German
Linn.	Linnæus
lit.	literal, -ly
lit. and *fig.*	in literal and figurative use
Lith.	Lithuanian
Liturg.	in liturgical use
Longf.	Longfellow
LXX	Septuagint
Lydg.	Lydgate
m.	masculine
Magn.	in Magnetism
Manuf.	in .. Manufacture
masc.	masculine
Math.	in Mathematics
Maundev.	Maundeville
M.Bret.	Middle Breton
MDu.	Middle Dutch
(M)Du.	Middle and modern Dutch
ME.	Middle English
Mech.	in Mechanics
M.E.D.	*Middle English Dictionary*
Med.	in Medicine
med.L.	mediæval Latin
Metall.	in Metallurgy
Metaph.	in Metaphysics
metath.	metathetic
Meteorol.	in meteorology
Mex.	Mexican
MHG.	Middle High German
midl.	midland
Mil., *Milit.*	in military usage
Milt.	Milton
Min.	in Mineralogy
MIr.	Middle Irish
MLG.	Middle Low German
(M)LG.	Middle and modern Low German
Mme.	Madame
mod.	modern
mod.L.	modern Latin
MSc.	Middle Scottish
MSw.	Middle Swedish
Mus.	in Music
MWelsh	Middle Welsh
Myth., *Mythol.*	in Mythology
n.	neuter, northern, noun
NAfr.	North-African
NAmer.	North American
Nat. Hist.	in Natural History
Nat. Phil., *Nat. Philos.*	in Natural Philosophy
Nat. Sci.	in Natural Science
Naut.	in Nautical language
n. dial.	in northern dialects

N.E.D.	*A New English Dictionary on Historical Principles*
NEFr.	North-eastern French
neg.	negative
n. Eng.	northern English
neut.	neuter
NFris.	North Frisian
N.O.	Natural Order
nom.	nominative
nonce-wd.	nonce-word
north.	northern, in northern dialects
Northumb.	Northumbrian
Norw.	Norwegian
N.S.W.	New South Wales
N.T.	New Testament
num. adj.	numeral adjective
Numism.	in Numismatics
N.W., n.w.	north-west, -western
N.Z.	New Zealand
obj.	object
obl.	oblique
OBret.	Old Breton
OBrit.	Old British
Obs., *obs.*	obsolete
obsc.	obscure, -ly
Obsol.	obsolescent
Obstet. Surg.	in Obstetrical Surgery
occ., occas.	occasional, -ly
OCelt.	Old Celtic
OCorn.	Old Cornish
OE.	Old English (= Anglo-Saxon)
O.E.D.	Oxford English Dictionary
OFr.	Old French
(O)Fr.	Old and modern French
OFris.	Old Frisian
OGael.	Old Gaelic
OHG.	Old High German
OIcel.	Old Icelandic
OIr.	Old Irish
OL.	Old Latin
OLFrank., OLG.	Old Low Frankish, German
OLith.	Old Lithuanian
ON.	Old Norse
ONFr.	Old Northern French
ONorth.	Old Northumbrian
OPers.	Old Persian
opp.	opposed (to)
OPruss.	Old Prussian
Org. Chem., *Organ. Chem.*	in Organic Chemistry
orig.	original, -ly
Ork.	Orkney
Ornith.	in Ornithology
Orthogr.	in Orthography
OS.	Old Saxon
OScand.	Old Scandinavian
OSl., OSlav.	Old Slavonic
OSp.	Old Spanish
OSw.	Old Swedish
O.T.	Old Testament
OW.	Old Welsh
Oxf.	Oxford
Palæogr.	in Palæography
Palæont.	in Palæontology
Palsgr.	Palsgrave
pa. pple.	passive or past participle
parasynth.	parasynthetic
pass.	passive, -ly
pa. t.	past tense
Path., *Pathol.*	in Pathology
perh.	perhaps

pers.	person, -al
Pers.	Persian
Peruv.	Peruvian
Petrog.	in Petrography
pf.	perfect
Pg.	Portuguese
Pharm.	in Pharmacy
Pharm. Chem.	in Pharmaceutical Chemistry
Phil.	in Philosophy
Philol.	in Philology
Philos.	in Philosophy
Phœn.	Phœnician
phonet.	phonetic, -ally
Photogr.	in Photography
phr.	phrase, -s
Phren.	in Phrenology
Phys.	in Physiology
Phys. Chem.	in Physical Chemistry
Physiog.	in Physiography
Physiol.	in Physiology
Physiol. Chem.	in Physiological Chemistry
pl., pl.	plural
poet.	poetical
Pol.	Polish
Pol. Econ.	in Political Economy
Polit.	in Politics
pop.	popular, -ly
pop.L.	popular Latin
poss.	possessive, possible, possibly
post-Aug.	post-Augustan Latin
post-cl.	post-classical Latin
ppl.	participial
pple.	participle
Pr.	Provençal
pr.	present
prec.	preceding word or article
pred.	predicate
predic.	predicative, -ly
Pref.	Preface
pref.	prefix
pre-hist.	prehistoric
prep.	preposition
pres.	present
pret.	preterite
prim.	primitive
priv.	privative
prob.	probably
Promp. Parv.	*Promptorium Parvulorum*
pron.	pronominal, pronounced
pron.	pronoun
pronunc.	pronunciation
prop.	proper, -ly
Pros.	in Prosody
Prov.	Provençal
Prov., prov.	proverb
provb.	proverbial, -ly
Psych., Psychol.	in Psychology
Qo., Qos	Quarto edition, -s
quot., quots.	quotation(s)
q.v.	*quod vide*, 'which see'
R. C. Ch.	in the Roman Catholic Church
rec.	recent
redupl.	reduplicated, -ation(s)
ref.	reference
refash.	refashioned, -ing
refl.	reflexive
reg.	regular
rel.	relative
rel.	related (to)
repl.	replaced, -ing
repr.	representative (of), represented, representing, representation(s)
Rhet.	in Rhetoric
rhet.	rhetorical, -ly
Rom.	Roman, Romance, Romanic
Rom. Antiq.	in Roman Antiquities
Rom. Hist.	in Roman History
Rum.	Rumanian
Russ.	Russian
R.V.	Revised Version
S., s.	South, southern
S. Afr.	South African
S. Amer.	South American
sb.	substantive
Sc.	Scotch, Scots, Scottish
sc., scil.	*scilicet*, 'understand' or 'supply'
Scand.	Scandinavian
Sc. Hist.	in Scottish History
schol. L.	scholastic Latin
Scotl.	Scotland
Sculpt.	in Sculpture
s. dial.	in southern dialects
Seismol.	in Seismology
Sem.	Semitic
Serb.	Serbian
SHAFTESB.	Shaftesbury
SHAKS.	Shakespeare
Shetl.	Shetland
sing.	singular
Sinh.	Sinhalese
Skr.	Sanskrit
sl.	slang
Slav.	Slavonic
Sp.	Spanish
sp.	spelling
spec.	specific, -ally
sp. gr.	specific gravity
Sport.	in Sporting use
Stock Exch.	on the Stock Exchange
str.	strong
subj.	subject, subjunctive
subord. cl.	subordinate clause
subseq.	subsequent, -ly
subst.	substantival, -ly
suff.	suffix
superl.	superlative
Surg.	in Surgery
s.v.	*sub voce*, 'under the word'
S.W., s.w.	South West, south-western
s.w. dial.	in south-western dialect(s)
Sw., Swed.	Swedish
Syd. Soc. Lex.	*The New Sydenham Society's Lexicon*
syll.	syllable(s)
synon.	synonymous
Syr.	Syriac
t.	tense
techn.	in technical use
Telegr.	in Telegraphy
Teut.	Teutonic
Theatr.	in theatrical language
Theol.	in Theology
Tokh.	Tokharian
tr.	translation of
trans.	transitive, -ly
transf.	transferred
transf. and *fig.*	in transferred and figurative use
Trig.	in Trigonometry
Turk.	Turkish
Typog.	in Typography
Tyrol.	Tyrolese
Ukr.	Ukrainian
ult.	ultimate, -ly
unc.	uncertain
unexpl.	unexplained
Univ.	University
unkn.	unknown
U.S.	in the English of the U.S.A.
U.S.(A.)	(the) United States (of America)
usu.	usually
v.	verb
var. (in 'stress var.')	variable
var., vars.	variant, -s (of)
vb.	verb
vbl.	verbal
vbl. sb.	verbal substantive
viz.	*videlicet*, 'namely'
voc.	vocative
Vulg.	the Vulgate
vulg.	vulgar, -ly
W.	Welsh, West
w.	with
west.	western
WFr.	West French
WFris.	West Frisian
WGmc.	West Germanic
WIE.	western Indo-European
W. Ind., *W. Indies*	in the West Indies
wk.	weak
wk. vb.	weak verb
w. midl.	w. midland, w. midland dialect(s)
WORDS.	Wordsworth
WS.	West Saxon
WYCL.	Wyclif
Zool.	in Zoology

SIGNS AND OTHER CONVENTIONS

Before a word or sense

† = obsolete
‖ = not naturalized, alien
¶ = catachrestic or erroneous use

In the etymologies

:– = regular or normal phonetic descendant of
* indicates a word or form not actually found but of which the existence is inferred

The printing of a word in SMALL CAPITALS indicates that further information will be found under the word so referred to.

Roman numbers in small capitals indicate the date by centuries; thus XIV = (in the) fourteenth century.

– before a date indicates that the date so marked is that of the latest recorded use of the word or sense.
In quotations, . . indicates that a word or words have been omitted.

ABBREVIATIONS OF TITLES OF BOOKS OF THE BIBLE

Gen/esis
Exod/us
Lev/iticus
Num/bers
Deut/eronomy
Josh/ua
Judg/es
Ruth
1 Sam/uel
2 Sam/uel
1 K(in)gs
2 K(in)gs
1 Chr/on/icles
2 Chr/on/icles
Ezra
Neh/emiah
Esther
Job
Ps/alms
Prov/erbs
Eccl/es/iastes

S(ong) of S/olomon; Cant/icles
Isa/iah
Jer/emiah
Lam/entations
Ezek/iel
Dan/iel
Hos/ea
Joel
Amos
Obad/iah
Jonah
Mic/ah
Nahum
Hab/akkuk
Zeph/aniah
Hag/gai
Zech/ariah
Mal/achi

1 Esd/ras
2 Esd/ras
Tobit
Judith
Rest of Esther
Wisd/om of Solomon
Eccl(esiastic)us
Baruch
S(ong) of (the) III Ch/ildren
Sus/anna
Bel & (the) Dr/agon
Pr(ayer) of Man/asseh
1 Macc/abees
2 Macc/abees

(St.) Matt/hew
(St.) Mark
(St.) Luke
(St.) John
Acts
Rom/ans

1 Cor/inthians
2 Cor/inthians
Gal/atians
Eph/esians
Phil/ippians
Col/ossians
1 Thess/alonians
2 Thess/alonians
1 Tim/othy
2 Tim/othy
Tit/us
Philem/on
Heb/rews
Ja(me)s
1 Pet/er
2 Pet/er
1 John
2 John
3 John
Jude
Rev/elation

ABBREVIATIONS OF TITLES OF SHAKESPEARE'S WORKS

All's Well	All's Well that Ends Well
Ant. & Cl.	Antony and Cleopatra
A.Y.L.	As You Like It
Com. Err.	The Comedy of Errors
Compl.	A Lover's Complaint
Cor(iol).	Coriolanus
Cymb.	Cymbeline
Ham(l).	Hamlet, Prince of Denmark
1 Hen. IV	The First Part of King Henry IV
2 Hen. IV	The Second Part of King Henry IV
Hen. V	The Life of King Henry V
1 Hen. VI	The First Part of King Henry VI
2 Hen. VI	The Second Part of King Henry VI
3 Hen. VI	The Third Part of King Henry VI
Hen. VIII	The Famous History of the Life of King Henry VIII
(*K.*) *John*	The Life and Death of King John
Jul. C(æs).	Julius Cæsar
Lear	King Lear
L.L.L.	Love's Labour's Lost
Lucr.	The Rape of Lucrece
Macb.	Macbeth
Meas. for M.	Measure for Measure
Merch. V.	The Merchant of Venice
Merry W.	The Merry Wives of Windsor
Mids. N. (*D.*)	A Midsummer-Night's Dream
Much Ado	Much Ado about Nothing
Oth.	Othello, the Moor of Venice
Per.	Pericles, Prince of Tyre
Phœnix	The Phœnix and the Turtle
Pilgr.	The Passionate Pilgrim
Rich. II	The Tragedy of King Richard II
Rich. III	The Tragedy of King Richard III
Rom. & Jul.	Romeo and Juliet
Sonn.	Sonnets
Tam. Shr.	The Taming of the Shrew
Temp.	The Tempest
Timon	Timon of Athens
Tit. A.	Titus Andronicus
Tr. & Cr.	Troilus and Cressida
Twel. N.	Twelfth-Night; or, What You Will
Two Gent.	The Two Gentlemen of Verona
Ven. & Ad.	Venus and Adonis
Wint. T.	The Winter's Tale

KEY TO THE PRONUNCIATION

For a description of the phonetic system employed in this dictionary, see the Introduction, §3, pp. x and xi. The pronunciations given are those in use in the educated speech of southern England (the so-called 'Received Standard'), and the keywords given are to be understood as pronounced in such speech.

I. VOWELS

The symbol ˉ placed over a vowel-letter denotes length.

ORDINARY	LONG	OBSCURE
a as in Fr. à la mode (a la mod)	ā as in alms (āmz), bar (bāɹ)	ă as in amœba (ămī·bă)
‖ai … ayah (ai·ă), saiga (sai·gă)		
‖au … G. frau (frau)		
æ … man (mæn)		æ̆ … accept (æ̆kse·pt), maniac (mē^i·nıæ̆k)
ɑ … pass (pɑs), chant (tʃɑnt)*		
ɑu … loud (lɑud), now (nɑu)		
ɒ … cut (kɒt), son (sɒn)	ɒ̄ … curl (kɒ̄ɹl), fur (fɒ̄ɹ)	ɒ̆ … datum (dē^i·tɒ̆m)
e … yet (yet), ten (ten)	ē^ə … there (ðē^{ə}ɹ), pear, pare (pē^{ə}ɹ)	ĕ … moment (mō^u·mĕnt), several (se·vĕrăl)
		ė … added (æ·dėd), estate (ėstē^i·t)
‖*e* … Fr. attaché (ataʃe)	*ē*^{i} … rein, rain (rē^{i}n), they (ðē^i)	*ĕ* … separate *adj.* (se·părĕt)
‖ę … Fr. chef (ʃęf)	‖ę̄ … Fr. faire (fę̄r)	
	ə̄ … fir (fə̄ɹ), fern (fə̄ɹn), earth (ə̄ɹþ)	ə … *the general obscure vowel, used in the notation of* -er (əɹ), -ous (əs), -sion (ʒən, ʃən), -tion (ʃən)
əi … *I, eye* (əi), bind (bəind)		
‖ə … Fr. coup de grace (kudəgrās)		
i … sit (sit), mystic (mi·stik)	ī^ə … bier (bī^{ə}ɹ), clear (klī^{ə}ɹ)	ĭ … vanity (væ·nĭti)
i … Psyche (səi·k*i*), react (r*i*,æ·kt)	*ī* … thief (þ*ī*f), see (s*ī*)	*ĭ* … remain (r*ĭ*mē^i·n), believe (b*ĭ*l*ī*·v)
o … achor (ē^i·koɹ) morality (moræ·lĭti)	ō^ə … boar, bore (bō^{ə}ɹ), glory (glō^ə·ri)	ŏ … theory (þī·ŏri)
oi … oil (oil), boy (boi)		
o … hero (hī^ə·r*o*), zoology (z*o*,ǫ·lŏdʒi)	‖*ō* … Fr. chose (ʃ*ō*z)	*ŏ* … violet (vəi·*ŏ*lėt), parody (pæ·r*ŏ*di)
	ō^u … so, sow, sew (s*ō*^{u}), soul (s*ō*^{u}l)	
ǫ … what (hwǫt), watch (wǫtʃ)	ǭ … fought (fǭt), walk (wǭk), wart (wǭɹt)	ǫ̆ … authority (ǫ̆þǫ·rĭti)
ǫ, ǫ̀ … got (gǫt), soft (sǫ̀ft)*	*ǭ* … short (ʃ*ǭ*ɹt), thorn (þ*ǭ*ɹn)	*ǫ̆* … connect (k*ǫ̆*ne·kt), amazon (æ·măz*ǫ̆*n)
‖ö … Fr. jeune (ʒön), G. Köln (köln)	‖ȫ … Fr. cœur (kȫr)	
‖*ö* … Fr. peu (p*ö*)	‖*ȫ* … G. Goethe (g*ȫ*tĕ), Fr. jeûne (ʒ*ȫ*n)	
u … full (ful), book (buk)	ū^ə … poor (pū^{ə}ɹ), moorish (mū^ə·riʃ)	ŭ … thankful (þæ·ŋkfŭl)
iu … duration (diurē^i·ʃən)	iū, ^{i}ū pure (piū^{ə}ɹ), lure (l^{i}ū^{ə}ɹ)	iŭ, ^{i}ŭ verdure (və̄·ɹdiŭɹ), measure (me·ʒ^{i}ŭɹ)
u … unto (ɒ·nt*u*), frugality (fr*u*gæ·lĭti)	*ū* … *two* moons (t*ū* m*ū*nz)	*ŭ* … altogether (ǭlt*ŭ*ge·ðəɹ)
i*u* … Matthew (mæ·þi*u*), virtue (və̄·ɹti*u*)	i*ū*, ^{i}*ū* few (fi*ū*), lute (l^i*ū*t)	i*ŭ* … circular (sə̄·ɹki*ŭ*lăɹ)
‖ü … G. Müller (mü·lĕr)		
‖*ü* … Fr. juste (ʒ*ü*st), dune (d*ü*n)	‖*ü* … G. grün (gr*ǖ*n), Fr. pur (p*ǖ*r)	

The incidence of main stress is shown by a raised point (·) after the vowel-symbol, and a secondary stress by a raised double point (:).

II. CONSONANTS

b, d, f, k, l, m, n, p, t, v, z *have their usual English values*

		(FOREIGN)
g as in go (gō^u)	þ as in thin (þin), bath (bɑþ)	ṅ *marks nasalization of the preceding vowel,* as in Fr. environ (aṅviroṅ)
h … ho! (hō^u)	ð … then (ðen), bathe (bē^{i}ð)	n^y … Sp. señor (sen^{y}ō·r)
r … run (rɒn), terrier (te·riəɹ)	ʃ … shop (ʃǫp), dish (diʃ)	χ … G. ach (aχ), Sc. loch (lǫχ)
ɹ … her (hə̄ɹ), farther (fā·ɹðəɹ)*	tʃ … chop (tʃǫp), ditch (ditʃ)	χ^y … G. ich (iχ^y) Sc. licht (liχ^{y}t)
s … see (sī), success (sɒ̆kse·s)	ʒ … vision (vi·ʒən), jeu (ʒö)	γ … G. sagen (zā·γĕn)
w … wen (wen)	dʒ … judge (dʒɒdʒ)	γ^y … G. legen (lē·γ^{y}ĕn), regnen (rē·γ^{y}nĕn)
hw … when (hwen)	ŋ … singing (si·ŋiŋ), ink (iŋk)	
y … yes (yes)	ŋg … finger (fi·ŋgəɹ)	

* The symbols a and ǫ̀ are used to indicate respectively the local or individual variants æ, ā (e.g. in *castle*) and ǫ, ǭ (e.g. in *salt*). For ɹ, see Introduction, § 3, p. x.

Small 'superior' letters are used (*a*) to express the glide element of the diphthongs ē^ə, ī^ə, ō^ə, ū^ə, *e*^{i}, *ē*^{i}, *ō*^{u}, and of the triphthongs ɑu^ə, əi^ə, iū^ə; (*b*) to denote an element that may or may not be present in a local or an individual pronunciation, as (l^i*ū*t) *lute*, (win^{d}mil) *windmill*; (*c*) to indicate the palatal or labial modification of certain consonants (see third column of Consonants above).

A break , is used to indicate syllabic division when necessary to avoid ambiguity.

' indicates that a following l, m, or n is syllabic, as in (ē^i·b'l) *able*, (rū·mătiz'm) *rheumatism*, (ī·t'n) *eaten*.

Marl (māɹl), *sb.* late ME. [– OFr. *marle* (still dial.; repl. in mod. Fr. by *marne*) :– med.L. *margila* (whence also OHG. *mergil*, G. *mergel*), f. (after *argilla* white clay) L. *marga*, said by Pliny to be a Gaulish word.] **1.** A kind of soil consisting principally of clay mixed with carbonate of lime, valuable as a fertilizer. **2.** *poet.* Used generically for: Earth 1590.

1. Red m.: (*a*) m. of a red colour; (*b*) reddle; (*c*) *Geol.* the New Red Sandstone. *Burning m.*: used symbolically, after Milton, in ref. to the torments of hell (*P. L.* I. 296).

Comb.: **m.-grass,** Zigzag Clover, *Trifolium medium*; also Red Clover, *T. pratense*; **-stone** *Geol.*, argillaceous and ferruginous limestone, which lies between the upper and lower Lias of England.

Hence **Marla·ceous, Ma·rly** *adjs.* resembling, composed of, or abounding in m.

Marl (māɹl), *v.*[1] late ME. [f. prec. Cf. med.L. *marlare* (XII).] To apply marl to (ground); to fertilize with marl.

fig. Marl'd with bleaching bones H. COLERIDGE.

Marl (māɹl), *v.*[2] 1425. [– Du. *marlen*, frequent. of MDu. *marren* bind.] *Naut.* To fasten with marline; to secure *together* by a succession of half-hitches; to wind marline or other small stuff round (a rope), securing it with a hitch at each turn. Orig. in **Ma·rl-ing** *vbl. sb.* used *attrib.* in *m.-cord, -line, -twine* = MARLINE.

Marled (māɹld), *ppl. a.* 1603. Chiefly *Sc.* Also **merled.** [Cf. OFr. *merellé.*] Marbled, spotted, streaked. So **Marl** *a.*

Marline (mā·ɹlin). Also **marling,** etc. 1417. [– Du. *marlijn*, f. *marren* bind + *lijn* LINE *sb.*[2], and Du. *marling*, f. *marlen*, frequent. of MDu. *marren* + *-ing* -ING[1].] *Naut.* Small line of two strands, used for seizings.

Marline-spike, marlinspike (mā·ɹlinspəik). 1626. [orig. app. *marling-spike*, f. *marling* vbl. sb. (f. MARL *v.*[2]) + SPIKE *sb.*, the first element being subseq. interpreted as MARLINE *sb.* Cf. LG. *marlspieker.*] **1.** *Naut.* An iron tool tapering to a point, used to separate the strands of rope in splicing, as a lever in marling, etc. **2.** A sailor's name for a tropic bird (*Phaethon*) and a jäger or skua-gull (*Stercorarius*), in allusion to the two long pointed tail-feathers 1867.

Marlite (mā·ɹləit). Also **-yte.** 1794. [f. MARL *sb.* + -ITE[1] 2 b.] *Min.* A variety of marl which resists the action of the air. Hence **Marli·tic** *a.*

Marl-pit (mā·ɹlpit). late ME. [f. MARL *sb.* + PIT *sb.* But cf. AL. *marleputtus* (XIII), which may point to MDu. *marleputte* as the source.] A pit from which marl is dug.

Marmalade (mā·ɹmălēⁱd). 1480. [– Fr. *marmelade* – Pg. *marmelada*, f. *marmelo* quince, dissim. f. L. *melimelum* – Gr. μελίμηλον kind of apple grafted on a quince, f. μέλι honey + μῆλον apple; see -ADE.] **1.** A preserve made by boiling fruits (orig. quinces, now usu. Seville oranges) with sugar. **2.** The fruit of *Lucuma mammosa*; also, the tree itself. Also called *natural m.* 1797.

attrib. **m.-tree,** the mammee-sapota (see sense 2).

Marmarosis (māɹmărōᵘ·sis). 1882. [f. Gr. μάρμαρος marble + -OSIS.] *Geol.* The conversion of limestone into marble by metamorphism. So **Ma·rmarize** *v.* to subject to m. 1893.

Marmolite (mā·ɹmŏləit). 1822. [Referred to Gr. μαρμαίρειν to shine: see -LITE.] *Min.* A laminated serpentine, of a pearly lustre and pale green colour.

Marmoraceous (māɹmŏrēⁱ·ʃəs), *a.* 1822. [f. L. *marmor* MARBLE; see -ACEOUS.] Pertaining to, or like, marble.

Marmorate (mā·ɹmŏreⁱt), *a.* 1537. [– L. *marmoratus*, pa. pple. of *marmorare* overlay with marble, f. *marmor* marble; see -ATE[2].] †**1.** Overlaid with marble. **2.** *Nat. Hist.* Variegated or veined like marble 1826.

Marmoreal (maɹmōᵊ·riăl), *a.* *poet.* and *rhet.* 1798. [f. L. *marmoreus* (f. *marmor* MARBLE) + -AL[1].] **1.** Resembling marble or a marble statue. **2.** Made of marble 1825.

2. Minaret And terrace and m. spire 1880.

Marmorize, *v.* 1897. [f. L. *marmor* marble + -IZE. Cf. Fr. *marmoriser.*] = MARMARIZE.

Marmose (mā·ɹmoᵘs). 1774. [– Fr. *marmose* (Buffon), perh. from colonial Du.] One of several species of small S. Amer. opposums which have only a rudimentary pouch and carry their young on their back.

Marmoset (mā·ɹmŏzet). late ME. [– (O)Fr. *marmouset* (latinized *marmosetus* XIII) grotesque image, little man or boy, (dial.) ape, of unkn. origin.] †**1.** A grotesque figure –1736. **2.** †**a.** In early use: Any small monkey. **b.** Now restricted to the tropical Amer. monkeys of the family *Hapalidæ* (or *Mididæ*), comprising two genera, *Hapale* (the true marmosets) and *Midas* (the tamarins). †**3.** Applied: **a.** to a woman or child; cf. *monkey* –1754. **b.** to a man, as a term of abuse or contempt; cf. *ape*. Occas. (as in OFr.) a favourite. –1825.

2. I have seen her . . as changeful as a marmozet SCOTT.

Marmot (mā·ɹmǫt). 1607. [– Fr. *marmotte*, prob. an altered form of Romansch *murmont* :– Rom. **murem montis* 'mountain mouse'.] A rodent of the genus *Arctomys* or sub-family *Arctomyinæ* of the squirrel family, esp. *A. marmotta*, sometimes called the Alpine marmot. Also applied (with qualification) to other animals of the same or allied genera.

‖**Marocain** (mæ·rŏkeⁱn). 1922. [Fr. *marocain*, f. *Maroc* Morocco.] A dress fabric of wool, silk, or cotton, having a wavy texture.

Maronite (mæ·rŏnəit). 1511. [– med.L. *Maronita*, f. *Maron* name of the Syrian founder of the sect (4th c.); see -ITE[1] 1.] One of a sect of Syrian Christians, dwelling in Lebanon and Anti-Lebanon; orig. Monothelites, but subseq. united with the Roman Church.

Maroon (mărū·n), *sb.*[1] and *a.* 1594. [– Fr. *marron* – It. *marrone* – med. Gr. μάραον.] **A.** *sb.* †**1.** A large kind of sweet chestnut native to Southern Europe; also, the tree bearing this –1699. **2.** [= Fr. *marron.*] A particular kind of brownish-crimson or claret colour 1791. **3.** A firework composed of a small cubical box of pasteboard, wrapped round with twine and filled with gun-powder; it explodes with a report like that of a cannon 1749. **B.** *adj.* Of the colour described in A. 2. 1843.

Maroon (mărū·n), *sb.*[2] 1666. [– Fr. *marron*, †*maron* – Sp. *cimarrón* wild, untamed, run-away slave, f. *cima* peak; see -OON.] **1.** One of a class of Negroes, orig. fugitive slaves, living in the mountains and forests of Dutch Guiana and the West Indies. **2.** A person who is marooned 1883.

Maroon (mărū·n), *v.* 1699. [f. prec.] †**1.** *pass.* or *intr.* To be lost in the wilds. DAMPIER. **2.** *trans.* To put (a person) ashore and leave him on a desolate island or coast (as was done by the buccaneers) by way of punishment 1724. **3.** *transf.* To leave in a position from which one cannot get away: said e.g. of floods 1910. **4.** *Southern U.S.* To camp out for several days on a pleasure party 1777. **5.** To 'hang about' 1808.

4. Marooning differs from pic-nicing in this—the former continues several days, the other lasts but one HALIBURTON. Hence **Maroo·ner,** a pirate; one who is marooned (sense 2); one who goes marooning (sense 4).

†**Maroquin,** *a.* and *sb.* 1511. [– Fr. *maroquin*, orig. an adj. 'pertaining to Morocco', f. *Maroc* Morocco.] **a.** *adj.* (in *m. skins, leather*; also with sense 'made of morocco') = MOROCCO *a.* **b.** *sb.* Morocco leather. –1823.

Marplot (mā·ɹ,plǫt). 1708. [See MAR-.] **a.** *sb.* One who mars or defeats a plot or design by officious interference. Said also of things. **b.** *adj.* That mars or defeats a plot or design 1850.

Marprelate: see MAR-.

Marque (māɹk). 1419. [– Fr. *marque* – Pr. *marca*, f. *marcar* seize as a pledge, perh. ult. f. Gmc. **mark-* MARK *sb.*[1], sign.] †**1.** Reprisals; occas. = *letter of m.* (see 2) –1614. **2. Letter of marque. a.** Usu. pl., *letters of m.* (*and reprisal*). Orig., a licence granted by a sovereign to a subject, authorizing him to make reprisals on the subjects of a hostile state for injuries done to him by the enemy's army. Hence, later, a licence to fit out an armed vessel or privateer and employ it in the capture of the merchant shipping of the enemy's subjects, the holder of letters of marque being entitled by international law to commit against the hostile nation acts which would otherwise have been condemned as piracy. (Abolished in European nations by the Congress of Paris in 1856.) 1447. **b.** A ship carrying letters of marque; a privateer 1800.

Marquee (maɹkī·). 1690. [Spurious sing. form deduced from MARQUISE 3 apprehended as pl. and assim. in ending to -EE[2].] A large tent, as an officer's field-tent, or one used at an entertainment, or the like. Also *attrib.*, as *m. tent*, etc.

Marquetry, marqueterie (mā·ɹkĕtri). 1563. [– Fr. *marqueterie*, f. *marqueter* variegate, f. *marque* MARK *sb.*[1]; see -RY.] Inlaid work, esp. as used for the decoration of furniture.

Marquis, marquess (mā·ɹkwis, -ĕs). [ME. *marchis, markis* – OFr. *marchis*, later alt. to *marquis* after the corresp. Pr. *marques*, Sp. *marqués*; f. Rom. **marca* MARCH *sb.*[3] + **-ese* (see -ESE); prop. adj., sc. *comes* COUNT *sb.*[2] The sp. with *-ess* (XVI) is used by some holders of the title.] **1.** Orig., the title of the ruler of certain territories ('marches' or frontier districts) in various European countries. Later, in Romanic-speaking countries, a mere title indicating rank immediately below that of duke and above that of count. **2.** As an English title it designates a specific degree of the peerage, between those of duke and earl. When a duke is also a marquis, his second title is given by courtesy to his eldest son; thus the eldest son of the Duke of Devonshire is called 'the Marquis of Hartington'. late ME.

Marquisate (mā·ɹkwisĕt). 15.. [f. MARQUIS + -ATE[1], after Fr. *marquisat*, etc.] **1.** The dignity or status of a marquis. Also, †a place from which the title is taken. **2.** In various European countries: The territorial lordship or possessions of a marquis or margrave 1591. So †**Ma·rquisdom,** †**Ma·rquisship.**

‖**Marquise** (maɹkī·z, Fr. markīz). 1706. [Fr., fem. of *marquis.*] **1.** = MARCHIONESS. Only as a title of foreign nobility. 1894. **2.** A kind of pear 1706. **3.** = MARQUEE 1783. **4.** In full *m. ring*: A finger-ring set with a pointed oval cluster of gems 1885.

Marquois (mā·ɹkwoiz). 1788. [alt. of Fr. *marquoir* ruler used by tailors, f. *marquer* MARK *v.* + *-oir* (:– L. *-orium*) -ORY[1]. Sometimes written *Marquoi's, Marquois's*, as if possessive of a proper name.] Used *attrib.* in *m. scale* (*and triangle*), an apparatus for drawing equidistant parallel lines with speed and accuracy.

Marram (mæ·rəm). *local.* 1640. [– ON. *marálmr*, f. *marr* sea + *hálmr* HAULM; chiefly E. Anglian.] **1.** The Sea Reed or Bent Grass (*Psamma arenaria*), which binds together the sands on the shores of N. Europe. Also *m.-grass, sea-m.* **2.** A sand-hill grown over with this grass 1834.

Marrer (mā·rəɹ). late ME. [f. MAR *v.* + -ER[1].] One who mars; a destroyer, injurer, spoiler.

Marriable (mæ·riăb'l), *a.* Now *rare.* 1440. [– (O)Fr. *mariable*, f. *marier* MARRY *v.*; see -ABLE.] That may be married; in early use = MARRIAGEABLE.

Marriage (mæ·redʒ). [ME. *mariage* – (O)Fr. *mariage*, f. *marier* MARRY *v.*; see -AGE.] **1.** The relation between married persons; wedlock. **2.** The action, or an act, of marrying; the ceremony by which two persons are made husband and wife ME. **b.** A wedding feast. *Obs.* or *arch.* ME. **3.** A particular matrimonial union 1473. †**b.** *concr.* A person viewed as a prospective husband or wife; a (good or bad) match –1621. **4.** *transf.* and *fig.* Intimate union. late ME. †**5.** A dowry –1587. **6.** *Cards.* In bezique, etc., the declaration of a king and queen of the same suit 1861.

1. Nor does he dishonour M. that praises Virginity DONNE. Phr. *In m.* (now arch.): in the matrimonial state. *To give, take in m.*: to give, take as husband or wife. *Communal m.* (Anthropol.): the system by which within a small community all the men are regarded as married to all the women; sometimes called *group m.* *Plural m.*: polygamy. **2.** *Civil m.*; a m. performed by an officer of the state, without religious ceremony. *Fleet m.*: see FLEET *sb.*[2] *Scotch m.*: a marriage by a mutual declaration before witnesses, without other formality. **b.** Iesus was called also and his disciples vnto the mariage TINDALE *John* 2:2. **3.** *Cross m.*: the m. of a man to the sister of his sister's husband. **4.** The m. of verse and tune T. HARDY.

attrib. and *Comb.*: **M. Act,** any of the Acts of Parliament regulating marriages, e.g. 4 Geo. IV. c. 76, 6 & 7 Will. IV. c. 85, etc.; **m. articles,** an antenuptial agreement by the parties with respect to rights of property and succession; **m. brokage, brokerage,** consideration given for bringing about a m. (contracts for which are void by English law); **m. licence,** an official permission to marry (in England, a document granted by the ordinary or his surrogate, authorizing a couple to be married without the proclamation of banns); **m. lines,** a certificate of m.; **m. portion,** a portion or dowry, etc., given to a bride at her m.; **m. settlement,** an arrangement made by deed in consideration of an intended m., whereby certain property is secured for the wife, and sometimes also for the children.

Marriageable (mæ·rédʒăb'l), *a.* 1555. [f. prec. + -ABLE.] Of persons: Fit for marriage, of an age to marry. **b.** *transf.*, esp. of the vine 1663. **c.** Of age, etc.: Befitting marriage or the married state 1597.

Marriage-bed. 1590. The bed used by a married couple; hence *transf.* marital intercourse, with its rights and duties.

To defile, violate the m.: to commit adultery.

Married (mæ·rid), *ppl. a.* ME. [f. MARRY *v.* + -ED[1].] **1.** United in wedlock; also *fig.* **2.** Pertaining to persons so united or to matrimony 1588.

1. What says the m. woman? SHAKS. **2.** M. Life; a comedy BUCKSTONE (*title*).

Marrier (mæ·ri,əɹ). 1589. [f. MARRY *v.* + -ER[1].] One who marries (in various senses).

Marron, var. of MAROON *sb.*[1]

‖**Marron glacé** (ma·roṅ gla·se). [Fr., = iced chestnut.] A sweetmeat consisting of a chestnut preserved in sugar.

Marrow[1] (mæ·roᵘ). [OE. *mærh, mærg* (WS. *mearh, mearg*), corresp. to OFris. *merg, merch*, OS. *marg* (Du. *merg*), OHG. *mar(a)g* (G. *mark*), ON. *mergr* :- Gmc. **mazʒam*, **mazʒaz*.] **1.** The soft vascular fatty substance usually contained in the cavities of bones. **b.** The substance forming the spinal cord. Now always *spinal m.* late ME. †**c.** Used (chiefly after L. *medulla*) for: The pith (of a plant); the pulp (of a fruit). Also *m. of wheat* = *medulla tritici* (Vulg.), the finest flour. –1793. **2.** *fig.* **a.** As the type of rich food. late ME. **b.** As the seat of vitality and strength. late ME. **c.** The inmost part. late ME. **d.** The vital part; the essence; the 'goodness'. Often *pith and m.* 1530. **3.** **Vegetable m.: a.** A kind of gourd, the fruit of *Cucurbita ovifera* 1816. **b.** The fruit of the avocado 1763. **4.** A marrow-fat pea 1882.

1. The very m. in my bones is cold DICKENS. **2. a.** My soule shall be satisfied as with m. and fatnesse *Ps.* 63:5. **b.** The pith and m. of manhood 1848. **d.** The very M., Life and Sum of all their Teaching BUNYAN.

attrib. and *Comb.*, as **m. pea** = *marrowfat pea*: **m.-spoon,** a spoon for extracting the m. from bones. Hence **Ma·rrowless** *a.* having no m. (*lit.* and *fig.*). **Ma·rrowy** *a.* of the nature of, or full of, m.

Marrow[2] (mæ·roᵘ). *Obs.* exc. *dial.* 1440. [prob. – ON. *margr* many, fig. friendly, communicative (with special Eng. development).] **1.** A companion, partner, mate. **2.** A husband or wife 1578. **3.** One's equal or like; one's match in a contest 1548. **4.** A thing which makes a pair with another 1674.

2. Busk ye, busk ye, my bony bony bride, Busk ye, busk ye, my winsome m. 1724.

Marrowbone (mæ·roᵘbōᵘn). late ME. [f. MARROW[1].] **1.** A bone containing edible marrow. Also *fig.* **2.** *pl.* Jocularly: The knees. (Rarely *sing.*) 1532. **3.** *pl.* = CROSS-BONES 1832. **4.** *pl.* (*slang.*) Fists as weapons; pugilists 1625. **5.** *attrib.*, as *m.-pie*, etc.

Marrowfat (mæ·roᵘfæt). 1733. [f. MARROW[1] + FAT *sb.*[2]] (More fully *m. pea.*) A kind of large rich pea.

Marrowsky (mărau·ski). 1863. [f. proper name.] A deformed language in which the initial consonants of contiguous words are transposed.

Marry (mæ·ri), *v.* ME. [– (O)Fr. *marier* :- L. *maritare*, f. *maritus* married, husband, usu. referred to IE. **mer-* **mor-*, repr. by various words meaning 'young man', 'young woman'.] **I.** *trans.* **1.** To join in wedlock; to constitute as man and wife according to the laws and customs of a nation. Const. *to*; also *together.* **b.** Said of the priest or functionary who performs the rite. Also *absol.* 1530. **2.** To give in marriage. Said esp. of a parent or guardian. ME. **3.** Said of either contracting party: To take in marriage. (Now the familiar use.) late ME. †**4.** *refl.* and *reciprocal.* –1818. **5.** *transf.* and *fig.* To unite intimately 1526. **b.** *Naut.* To fasten (two ropes) end to end, in such a way that the joining may not prevent their being drawn through a block 1815. Also, to place (two ropes) together so that they may be hauled on at the same time 1867. **c.** *Cards.* In bezique, etc. Of the king or queen, *To be married*: to be declared as held in the same hand with the queen or king of the same suit 1870.

1. The King was maried secreetlie at Chelsey.. to one Jane Seymor 1536. **b.** Come sister, you shall be the Priest, and marrie vs SHAKS. **2.** Good mother, do not m. me to yond foole SHAKS. **3.** He married a Woman of great Beauty and Fortune ADDISON. **4.** Ah me! when shall I m. me? Lovers are plenty; but fail to relieve me GOLDSM. **5.** Soft Lydian Aires, Married to immortal verse MILT.

II. *intr.* **a.** To wed; to take a husband or wife. Const. *with*; occas. *to*. ME. **b.** *transf.* and *fig.* To enter into intimate union; to join, so as to form one 1508.

a. Marrying in hast, and Repenting at leisure 1614. **b.** By that old bridge..where the waters m. TENNYSON.

Marry (mæ·ri), *int. Obs.* exc. *arch.* or *dial.* ME. [orig. the name of the Virgin MARY used as an oath or an ejaculation.] An exclam. of asseveration, surprise, indignation, etc. **a.** Simply. (Often in answering a question: = 'why, to be sure'.) **b.** With interjection or exclamatory phrase 1590.

a. M., hang the idiot..to bring me such stuff GOLDSM. **b.** *M. come up*: used to express indignant or amused surprise or contempt: = 'hoity-toity' 1592. Marrie come vp I trow, Is this the Poultis for my aking bones? SHAKS.

Mars (mɑ̄ɹz). late ME. [– L. *Mars* (stem *Mart-*), app. reduced f. *Mavors* (*Mavort-*).] **1.** The Roman god of war. Often used for: Warfare, warlike prowess, fortune in war. **b.** *allusively.* A great warrior 1569. **2.** *Astron.* The fourth planet in the order of distance from the sun, revolving in an orbit lying between that of the Earth and Jupiter. late ME. †**b.** *Old Chem.* The name of the metal iron –1758. †**c.** *Her.* The name for the tincture gules in blazoning by the names of the heavenly bodies 1572. **d.** = *Mars yellow*: see below 1899.

1. An eye like M., to threaten or command SHAKS. *Mars' hill, hill of M.*, the Areopagus at Athens. **b.** *Rich. II*, II. iii. 101. *Comb.* **M. colours,** as *brown, red, violet, yellow*, pigments prepared from earths, and coloured with iron oxide.

‖**Marsala** (maɹsā·lă). 1806. [Name of a town in Sicily.] (More fully *M. wine.*) A class of white wines resembling light sherry, exported from Marsala.

‖**Marseillais** (marseyę), *a.* (*sb.*) 1686. [Fr., f. *Marseille* Marseilles; see -ESE.] Of or pertaining to (Inhabitants of) Marseilles.

‖**Marseillaise** (marseyę̄z, maɹsĕlē·z). 1826. [Fr., fem. of prec.] The national song of the French Republic, composed by Rouget de l'Isle in 1792; so named from having been first sung in Paris by Marseilles 'patriots'.

†**Marseilles** (maɹsē·lz). 1762. [English name of *Marseille*, a seaport in southern France.] A stiff cotton fabric, similar to piqué. Also *M. quilting.*

Marsh (mɑ̄ɹʃ). [OE. *mersċ, merisċ* = MLG. *mersch, marsch*, MDu. *mersch(e* :- WGmc. **marisk-*, whence med.L. *mariscus*; see MARISH.] A tract of low-lying land, usually flooded in winter and more or less watery at all times.

There were meruaylouse great marshes and daungerous passages LD. BERNERS.

attrib. and *Comb.* **1.** General: *m.-ground, -miasmata*, etc.; *m.-birds, -flies, -herbs*, etc.; *m.-dweller, -dwelling* adj.

2. Special: **m. fever,** malaria fever; **m.-fire, -light,** a will-o'-the-wisp; †**-wall,** a dike.

b. In names of animals inhabiting marshes, as **m. blackbird,** the American red-winged starling, *Agelæus phœniceus*; **m. deer,** a S. American deer, *Cariacus paludosus*; **m. diver,** ? the Water Rail, *Rallus aquaticus*; **-goose,** the greylag goose, *Anser cinereus*; **m. harrier,** the moor buzzard, *Circus æruginosus*; **m. hawk,** the American marsh harrier, *C. hudsonius*; **m. hen,** the moor-hen, *Gallinula chloropus*; *U.S.* applied to other rails, esp. *Rallus elegans* and *R. crepitans*; **m. hog** *Palæont.*, a variety of the pig of which the remains are found in the Swiss lake-villages; **m. quail** *U.S.*, the meadow lark, *Sturnella magna*; **m. worm,** a worm used in angling, called also *blue-head.*

c. In names of plants that grow in marshes, as **m. asphodel,** *Narthecium ossifragum*; **m. bent (grass),** *Agrostis vulgaris*; **m. grass,** any grass that grows in marshy land, *spec.* one of the genus *Spartina*; **m. trefoil** [tr. L. *Trifolium palustre*], the buckbean, *Menyanthes trifoliata.*

Marshal (mā·ɹʃăl), *sb.* ME. [– OFr. *mareschal* (mod. *maréchal*) :- Frankish L. *mariscalcus* (Salic Law) – Gmc. **marχaskalkaz* (OHG. *marahscalh*, G. †*marschalk*, later *marschall*), f. **marχaz* horse (see MARE[1]) + **skalkaz* (OE. *sċealc*) servant. For the development from the designation of a groom to that of a high officer cf. *constable.*] †**1.** One who tends horses; *esp.* a farrier; a shoeing smith –1720. **2.** One of the chief functionaries of a royal household or court; *spec.* a high officer of state in England; now EARL MARSHAL, q.v. ME. **3.** As a title of military rank. †**a.** Orig., A commander, general. Subseq., an officer of a definite rank, which varied according to period and country. –1696. **b.** An officer of the highest rank in certain foreign armies. Often as prefixed title. 1475. †**4.** An officer of a court of law answerable for the charge and custody of prisoners and for the keeping of order, and frequently having the charge of a prison. Also †*M. of the Exchequer, of the King's* (or *Queen's*) *Bench.* (So named as deputies of the M. of England; see 2.) ME. **5.** An officer charged with the arrangement of ceremonies, esp. with the ordering of guests at a banquet, etc. ME. **b.** (More fully *City M.*) An officer of the corporation of the City of London 1632. **6. Knight marshal.** †**a.** A military officer with the functions of a quartermaster. **b.** *Hist.* An officer of the English royal household, who had judicial cognizance of transgressions 'within the king's house and verge', i.e. within a radius of twelve miles from the king's palace. (Abolished in 1846.) 1556. †**7.** = PROVOST-MARSHAL –1633. **8. a.** *Oxford.* The chief of the proctors' 'bull-dogs' 1810. **b.** *Cambridge.* Each of two officials who act as the Vice-Chancellor's messengers, summon meetings, etc. 1800. **9.** *U.S.* 'In America, a civil officer, appointed by the President and a Senate of the United States, in each judicial district, answering to the sheriff of a county. His duty is to execute all precepts directed to him, issued under the authority of the United States' (Webster) 1793. ¶**10.** For *m. court, law*, etc., see MARTIAL *a.*, COURT MARTIAL.

1. Alle maner of werkmen; as goldsmythes, marchallis, smythes of alle forges CAXTON. **4.** *M. of the Admiralty*: an officer of the Court of Admiralty. *Judge's m.*: an official (now usually a barrister) who accompanies a judge on circuit, and is charged with secretarial and other duties. **5.** †*M. of the King's* (or *Queen's*) *house*: = Knight marshal (see 6 b). **9.** *M.-at-Arms*: an official of the House of Representatives corresponding to the English sergeant-at-arms. Hence **Ma·rshalship,** the office of m.

Marshal (mā·ɹʃăl), *v.* late ME. [f. MARSHAL *sb.*] †**1.** *trans.* To tend (horses) as a farrier –1506. **2.** To arrange in proper order at a feast, table, etc. 1450. **3.** *Her.* To combine (two or more coats of arms) in one escutcheon, so as to form a single composition 1572. **4.** To arrange or draw up (soldiers) in order for fighting, exercise, or review; to arrange (competitors) for a race, etc. 1587. Also *transf.* and *fig.* **b.** *refl.* and *intr.* To take up positions in or as in a military array or a procession 1687. **5.** *trans.* To dispose (things, material or immaterial) in methodical order 1550. **b.** *Comm.* To arrange (assets or securities) in the order in which they are available to meet various kinds of claims 1773. **6.** To usher, guide (a person) on his way; to conduct ceremoniously 1586.

4. To command the men to be marshalled into the order that shall bee appointed BARRET. b. The procession was marshalling A. DUNCAN. 5. So to the office in the evening to marshall my papers PEPYS. 6. Thou marshall'st me the way that I was going SHAKS.

Marshalcy (mā·ɹʃălsi). ME. [– AFr. *mareschalcie*, OFr. *mareschaucie* :– Frankish L. *mariscalcia* (AL. *marescalcia* XII), f. *mariscalcus* MARSHAL *sb.* + *-ia* -Y³. As now used, prob. a new formation on MARSHAL *sb.* + -CY.] †1. Farriery –1720. 2. The office, rank, or position of a marshal ME. †3. The military force under the command of a marshal –1748.

Marshalman. Orig. **marshal's man.** 1638. One of a number of men belonging to the royal household and going before the king in processions; also, a similar officer under the marshal of the City of London.

Marshalsea (mā·ɹʃălsi). *Hist.* late ME. [The same word as in other senses is spelt MARSHALCY. In XVI–XVII the word was imagined to be f. MARSHAL *sb.* + SEE *sb.*] A court (abolished in 1849) formerly held by or for the knight marshal, orig. for the purpose of hearing cases between the king's servants. Also, a prison in Southwark under the control of the knight marshal (abolished in 1842).

Marshbanker, etc.: see MOSSBUNKER.

Marsh gas. 1848. Light carburetted hydrogen, CH_4, found in coal-mines and about stagnant pools.

Marshland (mā·ɹʃ,lænd). [OE. *mersćlond*; see MARSH, LAND *sb.*] Marshy country.

Marsh-mallow. [OE. *mersćmealwe.*] (Also *pl.*, const. as *sing.*) A shrubby herb, *Althæa officinalis* (N.O. *Malvaceæ*), which grows near salt marshes, having ovate leaves, pale rose-coloured flowers, and a mucilaginous root. Also, a confection made from this root.

Marsh marigold. 1578. A ranunculaceous plant, *Caltha palustris*, growing in moist meadows and bearing showy golden flowers.

Marshy (mā·ɹʃi), *a.* late ME. [f. MARSH + -Y¹.] Pertaining to or of the nature of a marsh; consisting of or containing marshes or marshland. b. Produced in marshland 1697. Hence **Ma·rshiness.**

Marsipobranch (mā·ɹsipobræŋk). 1872. [Anglicized f. mod.L. *Marsipobranchii*, f. Gr. μάρσιπος pouch (see MARSUPIUM) + βράγχια gills.] One of the *Marsipobranchii*, a class of vertebrates having gills in the form of pouches, and comprising the lampreys and hags. So **Ma:rsipobra·nchiate** *a.* and *sb.*

Marsupial (maɹsiū·piăl). 1696. [– mod.L. *marsupialis*, f. L. *marsupium* pouch, purse (see MARSUPIUM); see -AL¹.] A. *adj.* 1. Pertaining to or resembling a marsupium or pouch. 2. A designation of mammals (including the kangaroos, opossums, etc.) of the family *Marsupialia*, characterized by having a pouch in which to carry their young, which are born imperfect; of or pertaining to this family 1825. b. Connected with this pouch 1819. B. *sb.* A marsupial animal 1835. So **Marsu·pian, Marsu·piate** *adjs.* and *sbs.*

‖**Marsupium** (maɹsiū·piŏm). 1698. [L. – Gr. μαρσύπιον, -σίπιον, dim. of μάρσιπος purse.] A bag or pouch, or something resembling a pouch. *Zool.* a. The bag or pouch of a marsupial. b. A pouch for similar use in certain crustaceans, marsipobranchs, etc. 1843. c. The pecten of the eye of a bird or reptile 1795.

Mart (māɹt), *sb.*¹ 1713. [The second element of FOUMART, q.v.] The marten.

†**Mart,** *sb.*² late ME. [– *Mart-*, stem of L. *Mars* MARS.] = MARS 1, 2. –1636.

Mart (māɹt), *sb.*³ late ME. [– Du. †*mart*, var. of *markt* MARKET.] 1. A fair. *Obs.* or *arch.* †b. *spec.* The German booksellers' fair, held at Easter, orig. at Frankfurt, later at Leipzig –1655. 2. A market-place, market hall, etc. Now *poet.* or *rhet.*, exc. as = 'auction room', and as a tradesman's name for shop. 1590. 3. More widely: A city, region, or locality where things are bought and sold; an emporium. Also *transf.* and *fig.* 1581. †4. Buying and selling; bargaining. Also, a bargain. –1637. †5. *attrib.* as in *m.-time, -town*, etc. –1761.

2. The crowded m., the cultivated plain GOLDSM. 3. She is a m. of nations *Isa.* 23:3. 4. They.. maken a M. of their good name SPENSER.

†**Mart,** *sb.*⁴ 1587. [Alteration of MARQUE, app. infl. by prec.] = MARQUE; in phr. *letter(s*, etc. *of m.* Also *attrib.* –1753.

†**Mart** (māɹt), *v.* 1553. [f. MART *sb.*³; cf. Du., G. *markten* (G. dial. *marten*).] 1. *intr.* To do business at a mart; to chaffer, bargain –1628. 2. *trans.* To traffic in –1788.

2. To sell, and M. your Offices for Gold SHAKS.

‖**Martaban** (mā·ɹtăbæn). 1622. Name of a town in Pegu, used *attrib.* (esp. in *M. jar*) to designate a kind of glazed pottery made there. Hence as *sb.*

Martagon (mā·ɹtăgən). 1477. [– Fr. *martagon* – Turk. *martagān* 'a special form of turban adopted by Sultan Muhammed I; hence the martagon lily' (Redhouse).] The Turk's-cap lily, *Lilium martagon.* Also *Scarlet m.*: the Scarlet Turk's-cap, *L. chalcedonicum.*

Martel (mā·ɹtĕl), *sb.* 1474. [– OFr. *martel* (mod. *marteau*) :– med.L. *martellus*, for L. *martulus*, var. of *marculus*, dim. of late L. *marcus* hammer (see MARCH *v.*²); see -EL.] A hammer; esp. one used in war. Also ‖**M.-de-fer** [Fr. = 'iron hammer'], a weapon which had at one end a pick and at the other a hammer. *Obs.* exc. *Antiq.* Hence †**Ma·rtel** *v. intr.* (*rare*), to hammer SPENSER.

Marteline (ma·ɹtĕlin). 1875. [– Fr. *marteline*, f. OFr. *martel*; see prec.] A small hammer, pointed at one end, used by sculptors and marble-workers.

Martello (maɹte·lo). 1803. [alt., perh. by assoc. with It. *martello* hammer, of the name of Cape *Mortella* in Corsica, where there was a tower of this kind which the English fleet captured in 1794.] *M. tower* (occas. *m.*): a small circular fort with massive walls; usually erected on a coast to prevent the landing of enemies.

Marten (mā·ɹtĕn). [Early forms (XV) *martren, martro(u)n* – MDu. *martren* – OFr. *martrine* marten fur, subst. use (sc. *peau* skin) of *martrin*, f. *martre* – WGmc. **marþr-* (OHG. *mardar*, G. *marder*), extended form of Gmc. **marþuz* (OE. *mearþ*, ON. *mǫrðr*). Cf. FOUMART.] †1. The skins or fur of the marten. Often in *pl.* –1696. 2. An animal of any one of certain species of *Mustela*, yielding a valuable fur. Often differentiated, as **beech-m., stone-m.,** *M. foina*; **pine** (or †**fir**) **m.,** *M. martes*; **American pine m.,** *M. americana.*

Martial (mā·ɹʃăl), *a.* late ME. [– (O)Fr. *martial* or L. *martialis*, f. *Mars, Marti-* MARS; see -AL¹, -IAL.] 1. Of or pertaining to war or battle. b. Of sports, exercises, etc.: Serving as training for warfare. late ME. c. Of music: Appropriate to warfare 1662. 2. Of or pertaining to 'the Army', or the military profession. *Obs.* exc. in COURT MARTIAL. 1470. 3. War-like; brave; valiant; given to fighting. late ME. 4. Characteristic of a warrior 1592. 5. Resembling that of the god Mars. *Cymb.* IV. ii. 310. 6. Of or belonging to the planet Mars 1621. 7. In early *Chem.*: Of or pertaining to iron; containing iron 1684.

1. M. equipage MILT. M. virtues 1872. c. Sonorous mettal blowing M. sounds MILT. 3. Wake the m. spirit in their breasts BRYANT. 4. Go, write it in a m. hand, be curst and briefe SHAKS.

Phr. **Martial law.** a. Military government, by which the ordinary law is suspended, and the military authorities are empowered to arrest and punish offenders at their discretion. †b. = *military law* (MILITARY *a.*). Hence **Ma·rtialism,** warlike qualities. **Ma·rtialize** *v. rare*, to make m. **Ma·rtially** *adv.*

Martialist (mā·ɹʃălist). 1569. [f. MARTIAL *a.* + -IST.] †1. *Astrol.* A person born under the influence of the planet Mars –1686. 2. A military man; one skilled in warfare. Now *rare.* 1576. 3. A Martian. PROCTOR.

Martian (mā·ɹʃăn). late ME. [– OFr. *martien* or L. *Martianus*, f. *Mars, Marti-*; see MARS, -AN, -IAN.] A. *adj.* 1. †a. Having the temperament due to the influence of the planet Mars. b. Of or pertaining to Mars or its supposed inhabitants. †2. Of or pertaining to war or battle –1596. 3. Of or pertaining to the month of March 1623.

3. Gay are the M. Kalends MACAULAY.

B. *sb.* An inhabitant of Mars 1892.

†**Ma·rtiloge.** ME. [– med.L. *martilogium, -legium*, contr. forms of *martyrologium*; see MARTYROLOGE.] A martyrology –1548.

Martin¹ (mā·ɹtin). Also **marten,** etc. 1450. [prob. a use of the name *Martin*, after St. Martin of Tours; see next.] 1. A bird of the swallow family, *Chelidon urbica.* It builds a mud nest on the walls of houses, etc.; hence called **house-martin.** The **sand-m.** or **bank-m.** is *Cotile riparia*; the **purple m.** of N. America is *Progne subis* or *purpurea.* **Bee-m.,** the American king-bird, *Tyrannus carolinensis.* †2. A dupe. [? a different wd.] 1591–1621.

Martin² (mā·ɹtin). 1533. The name of St. Martin bishop of Tours (4th c.) used *attrib.* and in *Comb.* †1. **M. chain,** a sham gold chain. (Cf. 3 b.) BECON. So †*St. M.'s ring.* 2. More fully †**M. dry,** also [Fr.] ‖**M. sec:** a kind of pear, ripe at Martinmas 1664. 3. †a. **St. M.:** St. Martin's day, Martinmas 1533. †b. **St. Martin's:** the parish of St. Martin-le-Grand, London, at one time the resort of dealers in sham jewellery –1618. c. **St. Martin's day,** the 11th of November, Martinmas; (**St.**) **Martin's eve,** the eve of St. Martin's day, 10th November; **St. Martin's Summer,** a season of fine mild weather occurring about Martinmas (SHAKS.).

†**Ma·rtinet**¹. 1460. [– Fr. *martinet*, dim. of proper name *Martin*; see MARTIN¹, -ET.] A name for the martin and the swift –1833.

Martinet² (mā·ɹtinėt). 1523. [– (O)Fr. *martinet* in various unconnected senses, possibly belonging to etymologically distinct words.] 1. A military engine for throwing large stones. *Hist.* 2. *Naut.* One of the leech-lines of a sail 1582.

Martinet³ (māɹtine·t). 1676. [f. General *Martinet*, a French drill-master of the reign of Louis XIV.] †1. The system of drill invented by Martinet. WYCHERLEY. 2. A military or naval officer who is a stickler for strict discipline; hence, any rigid disciplinarian 1779. 3. *attrib.* or *adj.* 1814.

3. A sort of m. attention to the minutiæ and technicalities of discipline SCOTT. Hence **Ma:rtine·tism,** the spirit or action of a m. **Ma:rtine·t(t)ish** *a.* having the characteristics of a m.

Martingale (mā·ɹtiŋgēɪl). 1589. [– Fr. *martingale* (Rabelais) in *chausse à la martingale* kind of hose fastening at the back, which has been derived from mod.Pr. *marte(n)galo*, fem. of *marte(n)gal* inhabitant of *Martigue* in Provence.] 1. A strap or straps fastened at one end to the noseband, bit, or reins, and at the other to the girth, to prevent a horse from rearing or throwing back his head. 2. *Naut.* A rope for guying down the jib-boom to the dolphin-striker; also called *m.-guy, -stay* 1794. b. A dolphin-striker (see DOLPHIN) 1794. 3. A system in gambling which consists in doubling the stake when losing in order to recoup oneself 1815.

3. You have not played as yet? Do not do so; above all avoid a m. if you do THACKERAY.

Martini (maɹtī·ni). 1870. Short for **Martini-Henry** (**rifle**) [f. the names of Frederic *Martini*, Swiss inventor (1832–1897), and A. *Henry*, Scottish gunmaker (died 1894)]: a rifle which combines Henry's seven-grooved barrel with Martini's block-action breech mechanism.

Martinmas (mā·ɹtinmăs). Also †**Martlemas,** etc. ME. [f. MARTIN² + MASS *sb.*¹] 1. The feast of St. Martin, 11 Nov. †2. Used as a derisive appellation. 2 *Hen. IV*, II. ii. 110.

Martlet (mā·ɹtlėt). 1538. [– Fr. *martelet*, alt. of *martinet*; see MARTINET¹.] 1. The swift, *Cypselus apus*, formerly often confused with the swallow and the house-martin. 2. *Her.* An imaginary bird without feet, borne as a charge. Used as a mark of cadency for a fourth son 1550.

Martyr (mā·ɹtəɹ), *sb.* [OE. *martir*, corresp. to OFris., OS., OHG. *martir* – eccl. L. *martyr* – Gr. μάρτυρ, Æolic and late form of μάρτυς, μαρτυρ- witness, (in Christian use) martyr; reinforced in ME. by OFr. *martir, martre* (mod. *martyr*); the sp. was finally assim. to the L. form.] 1. *Eccl.* A designation of honour (connoting the highest degree of saintship) for: One who voluntarily undergoes the penalty of death for refusing to renounce the Christian faith or for obedience to any law or command of the Church. †**b.** Used sarcastically for: One who suffers death in an evil cause –1841. **c.** Used in the etymological sense of: Witness 1642. **2.** One who undergoes death (or great suffering) on behalf of any belief or cause, or through devotion to some object. Const. *to*. 1597. **3.** *hyperbolically*. A constant sufferer. Const. *to* (an ailment, etc.) 1560. **4.** *attrib.*, as *m.-king*, etc. 1532.

1. It was necessary to resist unto blood, to acquire the glorious Privilege of a M. NELSON. **c.** The elect Martyrs and witnesses of their Redeemer MILT. **2.** A M. to Science (*heading*) 1863. **3.** She is a m. to dyspepsia and bad cooking FR. A. KEMBLE. Phr. *To make a m. of*: to subject to inconvenience. *To make a m. of oneself* (joc.): to sacrifice one's inclinations for the sake of gaining credit for doing so.

Martyr (mā·ɹtəɹ), *v.* [f. prec. sb.; OE. (*ġe*)*martyrian*, *-martrian*.] **1.** *trans.* To put to death as a martyr. †**2.** To kill, esp. by a cruel death –1794. **3.** To cause suffering or misery to (*arch.*) ME. †**4.** To mutilate, spoil –1658. **5.** To represent as a martyr. MILT.

1. Tyndale was martyr'd at Fylford HEARNE. **3.** Rack'd with Sciatics, martyr'd with the Stone POPE. To m. anyone with jests 1860. **4.** Time hath so martyred the Records, that [etc.] SIR T. BROWNE.

Martyrdom (mā·ɹtəɹdəm). [OE. *martyrdōm*; see MARTYR *sb.* and -DOM.] **1.** The sufferings and death of a martyr. Also, the act of becoming or condition of being a martyr. **2.** Torment, torture; extreme suffering. late ME.

1. The palm of martirdom for to receyue CHAUCER. *transf.* Social martyrdoms place no saints upon the calendar HELPS.

Martyrize (mā·ɹtĭrəiz), *v.* 1450. [– late L. *martyrizare*, f. *martyr*; see MARTYR *sb.*, -IZE.] **1.** *trans.* To make a martyr of; to martyr. **2.** *intr.* To be or become a martyr (*rare*) 1524. Hence **Ma:rtyriza·tion.**

Martyrly (mā·ɹtəɹli), *a. rare.* 1659. [f. MARTYR *sb.* + -LY[1].] Martyr-like. So **Ma·rtyrly** *adv.*

†**Martyrologe.** 1500. [– Fr. *martyrologe* – med.L. *martyrologium*; see next.] = next –1721.

Martyrology (mā:ɹtĭrǫ·lŏdʒi). 1599. [– med.L. *martyrologium* – eccl. Gr. μαρτυρολόγιον (λόγος account); in sense 2 a distinct word (see -LOGY).] **1.** A list or register of martyrs; a history of martyrs. **2.** The histories of martyrs collectively 1801. Hence **Ma:rtyrolo·gic, -al** *a.* **Martyro·logist,** a writer of m.; one versed in the history of martyrs.

Martyry (mā·ɹtĭri). ME. [– med.L. *martyrium* – Gr. μαρτύριον witness, martyrdom, f. μάρτυρ MARTYR *sb.*] †**1.** Martyrdom; suffering (*rare*) –1677. **2.** A shrine, oratory, or church erected in memory of a martyr; an erection marking the place of a martyrdom or the spot where a martyr's relics lie 1708.

Marvel (mā·ɹvĕl), *sb.* ME. [– (O)Fr. *merveille* :– Common Rom. use as fem. sing. of *mirabilia*, n. pl. of L. *mirabilis* wonderful, f. *mirari* wonder; see MIRACLE, -ABLE.] †**1.** = MIRACLE 1. –1600. **2.** A wonderful or astonishing thing; a wonder ME. **b.** A wonderful example *of* (some quality) 1873. †**3.** A wonderful story –1484. **4.** Astonishment, wonder ME.

2. Marvels still the vulgar love SCOTT. **b.** The house was a m. of neatness and comfort BLACK. **4.** Use lessens m., it is said SCOTT.

Phr. *What m.*, *no m.*: = what wonder, no wonder (*arch.*). **M. of Peru, of the World** = FOUR O'CLOCK 1.

Marvel (mā·ɹvĕl), *v.* Now only *literary.* ME. [– (O)Fr. *merveiller*, f. *merveille*; see prec. sb.] **1.** *intr.* (in *obs.* or *arch.* use also *refl.*, *impers.*, and *pass.*) To be filled with wonder or astonishment. (In mod. use, stronger than *wonder*.) Const. *at*, †*of*, †*on*, †*upon*; *inf.*; also with clause, expressing the object of wonder. **2.** To ask oneself wonderingly. Const. interrog. clause. late ME. †**3.** *trans.* To wonder or be astonished at –1819. †**4.** To cause to wonder –1567.

1. To m. at the inequalities of human destiny TROLLOPE. **2.** I cannot but marvaile from what Sibyl or Oracle they stole the Prophesie of the worlds destruction by fire SIR T. BROWNE. **3.** Let it not be Maruelled, if sometimes they proue Excellent Persons BACON.

Marvellous (mā·ɹvĕləs), *a.* and *adv.* Also (now *U.S.*) **marvelous.** ME. [– OFr. *merveillos* (mod. *merveilleux*), f. *merveille*; see MARVEL *sb.*, -OUS.] **A.** *adj.* Such as to excite wonder; astonishing, surprising. **b.** *spec.* Of poetic material: Concerned with the supernatural 1715. **c.** *The m.*: that which is extravagantly improbable 1749.

Lyke to the Raynbow mervelose unto syght 1471. **c.** The prodigies and the m. of Bible-religion M. ARNOLD.

†**B.** *adv.* In a m. manner or degree –1777. Hence **Ma·rvellous-ly** *adv.*, **-ness.**

Marver (mā·ɹvəɹ), *sb.* 1832. [– Fr. *marbre* MARBLE; workman's approximation to the Fr. pronunc. (marbr).] A polished slab of marble or iron upon which glass-blowers roll and shape the plastic glass while still on the blow-pipe. Hence **Ma·rver** *v.*

Marxian (mā·ɹksiăn), *a.* and *sb.* 1896. Pertaining to or characteristic of, an adherent of, the doctrines of the German Socialist Karl Marx (1818–1883). Also **Ma·rxism, Ma·rxist.**

Mary (mēᵊ·ri). [OE. *Maria*, *Marie*, reinforced in ME. by (O)Fr. *Marie* – eccl. L. *Marīa* – Gr. Μαρία and Μαριάμ – Heb. *miryām* Miriam.] **1.** A female Christian name. The mother of Jesus Christ, commonly called the (Blessed) Virgin Mary, or Saint Mary. Used in asseverations (cf. MARRY *int.*). **2.** *Australian slang.* A native woman 1884.

Comb.: **m.-bud** (*obs.* exc. in echoes of Shaks.), the bud of a marigold. **Mary-lily,** the Madonna lily.

Mary, obs. f. MARROW[1], MARRY.

Marzipan (mā:ɹzipæ·n). 1891. [– G. *marzipan*, earlier *marcipan*, etymol. alt. (quasi *Marci panis* 'Mark's bread') of *marczapan* – It. *marzapane.*] The current form of MARCHPANE, q.v.

Mas. Also **mass, mess.** 1575. [Shortened f. MASTER *sb.*[1]] †**1.** Vulgar shortening of *master*, usually followed by a proper name or official title –1722. **2. Mas John,** applied joc. or contemptuously to a Scottish Presbyterian minister (*arch.*) 1661.

2. These new Mess-Johns in robes and coronets BURKE.

-mas: see MASS *sb.*[1]

Mascagnine (mæskæ·nyəin). Also **-ite.** 1836. [f. Prof. *Mascagni*, its discoverer; see -INE[5].] *Min.* 'Sulphate of ammonium, occurring in crusts and stalactitic forms near volcanoes' (Chester).

Mascle (mɑ·sk'l). ME. [– AFr. *mascle* – AL. *mascula* (also *macula*), alt. of L. *macula* MAIL *sb.*[1] by assoc. with MASK *sb.*[1] Cf. MESH *sb.*] †**1.** = MESH of a net –1696. **2.** *Her.* A charge in the form of a lozenge with a lozenge-shaped opening through which the 'field' appears 1486. **3.** *Antiq.* One of the perforated lozenge-shaped plates of metal coating the military tunic of the 13th c. 1822. Hence **Ma·scled** *a.* covered with mascles.

Mascot (mæ·skǫt). Also **mascotte.** 1884. [– Fr. *mascotte* – mod. Pr. *mascotto*, fem. of *mascot*, dim. of *masco* witch. The word was brought into notice by E. Audran's opera 'La Mascotte', played 29 Dec. 1880.] A person or thing supposed to bring luck. Hence **Ma·scotism, Ma·scotry.**

Masculine (mæ·skiŭlin). late ME. [– (O)Fr. *masculin*, fem. *-ine* – L. *masculinus*, *-ina*, f. *masculus* MALE; see -INE[1].] **A.** *adj.* **1.** Of the male sex; male. Now *rare.* †**2.** Said of inanimate objects to which the male sex was attributed on the ground of some quality, e.g. relative superiority, strength, etc. 1590. **3.** *Gram.* Of or pertaining to the gender to which appellations of males normally belong. late ME. **4.** Pertaining to the male sex; consisting of males 1601. **5.** Having the appropriate excellences of the male sex; virile; vigorous, powerful. Usu. of attributes, actions, or productions 1629. †**b.** Of material things, etc.: Powerful in action –1728. **6.** Of a woman: Having the qualities proper to man 1617.

2. Phr. †*M. hour* (Astrol.): one ruled by a m. planet. †*M. frankincense, gum* = *male incense* (see MALE *a.* 4). **3.** *M. rhyme* (Pros.): in French versification, a rhyme between lines ending in stressed syllables, as opp. to the feminine rhyme ending in *e* mute. Hence *gen.* a 'single' rhyme on a stressed syllable. **4.** M. attyre *Twel. N.* v. i. 257. Hee was soone after slaine in Ireland, and his whole M. race RALEGH. **5.** He proved a stout and m. Prince 1678. **6.** The m. women of the Low Countries vse to make voyages for trafficke 1617.

B. *sb.* **1.** That which is of the male sex 1550. **2.** A person of the male sex 1652. **3.** *Gram.* The masculine gender; a word or form of the masculine gender 1530. **Ma·sculine-ly** *adv.*, **-ness. Masculi·nity,** m. quality or condition; that which is m. **Masculiniza·tion, -ize** *v.*

Masculo- (mæ·skiŭlo), comb. f. L. *masculus* male, as **m.-feminine** *a.* partly masculine and partly feminine, etc.

†**Maselin.** ME. only. [– OFr. *maselin*, also *mazerin*, etc., f. *mazre*, *madre* bowl of maple-wood.] = MAZER 2.

Mash (mæʃ), *sb.*[1] [OE. *māsć* = MLG. *mēsch*, *māsch*, MHG. *meisch* crushed grapes (G. *maisch*) :– WGmc. **maisk-*, of unkn. origin, but perh. rel. to OE. *miscian* mix.] **1.** *Brewing.* Malt mixed with hot water to form wort. **2.** A mixture of boiled grain, bran or meal, etc., given warm as food to horses and cattle. Also qualified, as *bran-m.* (BRAN[1]). 1577. **3.** *gen.* Something reduced to a soft pulp, by beating or crushing, by steeping in water, etc. 1598. **b.** *fig.* A confused mixture; a muddle 1598. **c.** (without article.) Mashed state (*lit.* and *fig.*) 1630.

3. The streets are one m. of snow 1880. **b.** I haue made a faire m. on't B. JONS. **c.** The paper is boiled to m. 1751.

Comb.: **m.-tub, -tun, -vat,** a tub in which malt is mashed; **-wort** (OE. *māsćwyrt*), wort, infused malt.

Mash (mæʃ), *sb.*[2] *slang.* 1882. [f. MASH *v.*[2]] **1.** A person on whom one of the opposite sex is 'mashed'. Also, a 'swell'. **2.** The action of MASH *v.*[2], in *on the m.* 1888.

Mash (mæʃ), *sb.*[3] 1825. [Either f. next, or – Fr. *masse* MACE[1].] A hammer for breaking stones. So **Mash** *v.*[3] 1762.

Mash (mæʃ), *v.*[1] ME. [f. MASH *sb.*[1]] **1.** *Brewing. trans.* To mix (malt) with hot water to form wort. (Also with *up.*) **b.** *dial.* To infuse (tea). Also *intr.* of the tea: To draw. 1845. **2.** To crush, pound, or smash to a pulp. Also with *up.* ME. **3.** To reduce (fruit, potatoes, etc.) to a homogeneous mass by crushing, beating, or stirring 1615. Also *fig.*

3. No cold mutton to hash,..not even potatoes to m. HOOD. Hence **Mashed** (mæʃt) *ppl. a.* (*m. potatoes* 1747).

Mash (mæʃ), *v.*[2] *slang.* (orig. *U.S.*) 1879. [Back-formation from MASHER[2]. In theatrical parlance in U.S. *c*1860 (Barrère and Leland).] **1.** *trans.* To excite sentimental admiration in (one of the opposite sex). **2.** pass. *To be mashed on*: to have such admiration for, to be 'gone' on. Also *intr.* 1883.

Masher[1] (mæ·ʃəɹ). 1500. [f. MASH *v.*[1] + -ER[1].] †**1.** One who mashes (malt) or mixes (wine) –1611. **2.** A machine or vessel for mashing malt, fruit, etc. 1878.

Masher[2] (mæ·ʃəɹ). *slang.* 1882. [prob. f. MASH *v.*[1] (senses 2, 3) + -ER[1].] A fop of affected manners and 'loud' style of dress who frequented music-halls, etc., and posed as a lady-killer. **b.** *U.S.* A man who thrusts himself on women.

Mashie, mashy (mæ·ʃi). 1881. [perh. – Fr. *massue* club.] *Golf.* A golf-club having an iron head with straight sole and face, slightly more lofted than the iron.

Mashlin, dial. f. MASLIN[2].

Mashy (mæ·ʃi), *a.* 1730. [f. MASH *sb.*[1] + -Y[1].] Of the nature of a mash.

‖**Masjid** (mɒ·sdʒid). 1646 (**mesgid**). [– Arab. *masjid*; see MOSQUE.] A mosque.

Mask, *sb.*[1] *Obs.* exc. *dial.* [perh. repr. OE. **masc* (by metathesis *max*), or – cogn. ON. *mǫskve*. See MESH *sb.*, MASCLE.] A mesh.

Mask (mɑsk), *sb.*[2] 1534. [– Fr. *masque* – It. *maschera*, perh. – Arab. *maskara* buffoon, f. *sakira* ridicule.] **1. a.** A covering, usually of velvet or silk (with eye-holes), worn to conceal the face at balls, masquerades, etc. **b.** A screen of wire, gauze, etc. worn on the face for protection 1591. **c.** *Antiq.* The hollow figure of a human head worn by ancient Greek and Roman actors 1705. **d.** A likeness of a person's face in clay, wax, etc.; esp. one made by taking a mould from the face itself. Also *death-m.* 1780. **e.** A grotesque representation of a face worn on festive and other occasions, to produce a humorous or terrifying effect 1837. **2.** *fig.* **a.** A cloak, disguise, pretence 1577. **b.** Something which covers or hides from view 1752. **3.** A masked person 1580. **4.** In techn. uses (see below) 1731.

1. One of the ladies would, and did sit with her m. on PEPYS. **b.** *Mask*,..a face protection to be worn in glass-works or foundries, to protect against radiant heat (Knight). Also = GAS-*mask*. **2. a.** Phr. *Under the m. of, to put on, assume, throw* or *pull off*, or *drop the m.* (*of*), etc. **b.** The new soft-fallen m. Of snow upon the mountains KEATS. **3.** A Masque, armed cap-a-pie DE QUINCEY. **4. a.** *Arch.*, etc. A (grotesque) head or face in stone, used in panels, keystones of arches, etc.; also, in metal on a shield. Also, a kind of corbel the shadow of which is like a man's profile. 1731. **b.** *Hunting.* The face or head of a fox (or otter). 1828. In recent use, the head-skin of any 'big game'. **c.** *Fortif.* A screen to protect men working, to conceal a battery, etc.; also, a casemated redoubt serving as a counter-guard to the caponier 1802. **d.** *Entom.* The enlarged labium of the larval and pupal dragon-fly. Also *Zool.* a formation of the head resembling a mask. 1797. **e.** *Photogr.* A piece of opaque paper used to cover any part of a negative, lantern-slide, or print which it is desired to obscure or shade 1876. **f.** *Surg.* A piece of linen, with holes for the eyes, nose, and mouth, used for applications to the face 1890.

Comb.: **m.-crab**, a crab of the family *Corystidæ*, with mask-like markings on the carapace.

Mask, *v.*[1] *Obs.* exc. *dial.* late ME. [f. MASK *sb.*[1]] *trans.* To mesh, enmesh (*lit.* and *fig.*).

Mask (mɑsk), *v.*[2] *Sc.* 1480. North. var. of MASH *v.*[1]

Mask (mɑsk), *v.*[3] Also **masque.** 1562. [f. MASK *sb.*[2] Cf. Fr. *masquer.*] **1.** *trans.* To cover (the face) with a mask. Chiefly *pass.* To wear a mask. 1588. **b.** *gen.* To disguise 1847. **2.** *transf.* To conceal from view by interposing something 1583. **b.** *Mil.* and *Fortif.* (*a*) To conceal (a battery, a force, etc.) from the enemy's view. (*b*) To hinder (a fortress, an army, etc.) from action by watching it with a sufficient force. (*c*) To hinder the action of a friendly force by standing in the line of its fire. 1706. **3.** *fig.* To disguise (feelings, etc.); to conceal the real nature, intent, or meaning of 1588. †**4.** *intr.* To take part in a masque or masquerade. Also *to m. it.* –1731. †**5.** *intr.* To be or go in disguise. Often *fig.* –1649.

1. The Trompet sounds, be maskt, the maskers come SHAKS. **2.** Masking the Businesse from the common Eye SHAKS. **3.** He has been obliged to m. his pretensions SHERIDAN.

Masked (mɑskt), *ppl. a.* 1585. [f. MASK *sb.*[2] or *v.*[3] + -ED.] **1.** Having or wearing a mask 1637. **b.** Used (often repr. L. *larvatus*, *personatus*) as the specific name of animals having some formation or marking resembling a mask 1840. **c.** *Bot.* Of a corolla: = PERSONATE 1793. **2.** *transf.* and *fig.* Having the real features or character disguised. Also *occas.* Concealed from view. 1585. **b.** *Nosology.* Of diseases, esp. intermittent fevers: not recognizable by the usual criteria 1833. **3.** *Mil.* and *Fortif.* Chiefly in *m. battery*; see MASK *v.*[3] 2 b. 1759.

1. *M. ball* [Fr. *bal masqué*]: a ball at which those taking part wear masks. **b.** The Japan, or M. Pig (*Sus pliciceps* Gray). The M. Crab [= *mask-crab*, MASK *sb.*[2]]. **2.** The m. hypocrisie of this olde foxe 1585.

Masker, masquer (mɑ·skəɹ), *sb.* 1533. [f. MASK *v.*[3] + -ER[1].] One who takes part in a masquerade or masque; a masquerader.

Masker (mɑ·skəɹ), *v. Obs.* exc. *dial.* [OE. **malscrian*, implied in *malscrung* vbl. sb.; app. cogn. w. Goth. **malsks* in *untila-malsks* precipitate.] **a.** *trans.* To bewilder, confuse. **b.** *pass.* To be bewildered.

†**Ma·skery, ma·squery.** 1548. [– Fr. †*masquerie*, f. *masque* MASK *sb.*[2]; see -ERY.] Masking, wearing of masks; a masquerade. Also, masquerader's attire. –1655.

Maskinonge (mæskinǫ·ndʒ, -ǫ·ndʒi). Also **muskellunge,** etc. 1796. [ult. (through Canadian-Fr.) – Ojibwa *mashkinonge*, *mas-*, prob. = great pike or great fish.] A large pike, *Esox nobilior*, inhabiting the Great Lakes of N. America, valued as a food-fish.

Maslin[1] (mæ·zlin). Now *dial.* [OE. *mæstling*, *mæslen*, presumably rel. to MHG. *mess*(*e* brass (early mod. and dial. G. *mess*, *mesch*, *möss*, *mösch*) and cognate words with suffixes, MDu., MHG. *messinc*, *missinc* (Du., G. *messing*).] **1.** A kind of brass. Now only *attrib.* **2.** A vessel made of maslin; now (*dial.*) = *m. kettle* (see 3) OE. **3.** *attrib.* or *adj.* = Made of maslin. Now chiefly in **m. kettle,** a large pan for boiling fruit for preserve.

Maslin[2] (mæ·zlin). (For the numerous variant spellings see O.E.D.) [ME. *mastlyoun* (XIV), *mastylyon* (XV), etc. – OFr. *mesteillon* – Rom. **mistilio*, *-on-*, f. **mistilium* (whence Fr. *méteil*), f. L. *mistus*, pa. pple. of *miscēre* (see MIX *v.*); cf. MDu. *mastelūn* (Du. *masteluin*).] Mixed grain, *esp.* rye mixed with wheat. Also, bread made of mixed corn. †**b.** *fig.* A mixture, medley –1855. **c.** *attrib.*, as *m. bread, corn*; also as *adj.* (*fig.*) mixed, mingled 1544.

Masochism (mæ·zǫkiz'm). 1893. [f. the name of Leopold von Sacher-*Masoch* (1835–1895), Austrian novelist, who described it + -ISM.] A form of sexual perversion in which one finds pleasure in abuse and cruelty from one's associate (cf. SADISM). **Ma·sochist, -i·stic** *a.*

Mason (mē[i]·s'n), *sb.* ME. [Earliest forms (XIII) *machun*, *-oun* – ONFr. *machun*; later *mascun*, *masoun* – OFr. *masson* (mod. *maçon*) :– Rom. **matio*, *-on-* or **macio*, *-on-* (cf. med.L. *machio* Isidore VII; *matio* Reichenau Glosses VIII), prob. – Gmc. **mattjon* (whence OHG. *mezzo*, *steinmezzo*, G. *steinmetz* stonemason), perh. rel. to MATTOCK.] **1.** A builder and worker in stone. **2.** = FREE-MASON 1, 2. 1483.

Comb.: **m.-work,** stone-work, masonry; also in names of insects, etc., which build a nest of sand, mud, or the like; as *m.-ant* (= Fr. *fourmi maçonne*); **m.-bee** (= Fr. *abeille maçonne*), an insect of the genera *Osmia*, *Chalcidoma*, and *Anthophora*; **-spider,** a trap-door spider (*Mygale*); **(free)-mason-wasp,** a solitary wasp, *Odynerus murarius*. Also **m.-shell,** a carrier-shell. Hence **Maso·nic** *a.* of or pertaining to masons or masonry (see MASONRY).

Mason (mē[i]·s'n), *v.* late ME. [– OFr. *maçoner* (mod. *maçonner*), f. *maçon* MASON *sb.*] *trans.* To build of stone (or brick, etc.); to build up or strengthen with masonry. Also with *together*, *out*. †**b.** To build *in* or *into* a wall –1596. Hence **Ma·soned** *ppl. a.*; *spec.* in *Her.* marked with lines representing the joints or divisions between blocks of stone. Also *gen.*

Masonry (mē[i]·s'nri), *sb.* late ME. [– OFr. *maçonerie* (mod. *-nn-*), f. *maçon*; see MASON *sb.*, -ERY. Cf. med.L. *massoneria* (Du Cange).] **1.** The occupation of a mason; the art or work of building in stone. Now *rare*. **2.** *concr.* Work executed by a mason; stone-work. late ME. **3.** = FREEMASONRY 1, 2. 1686. **4.** *attrib.* Composed or built of masonry 1875. Hence **Ma·sonry** *v. trans.* to build or strengthen with m.

Masoola: see MASSOOLA(H.

‖**Masora(h, Massora(h** (mǎsō[ə]·rǎ). 1613. [repr. Heb. *māsōreṯ* (Ezek. 20:37), where it is interpreted 'bond (of the covenant)', f. *'āsar* bind, in post-biblical Heb. in the sense 'tradition', as if f. *māsar* hand down.] The body of traditional information relating to the text of the Hebrew Bible; the collection of critical notes in which this information is preserved.

Masorete, Massorete (mæ·sǒrīt). 1587. [– Fr. *Massoret* and mod.L. *Massoreta*; orig. misapplication of *māsōreṯ* (see prec.), with subsequent assim. of the ending to L. *-eta*, Gr. *-ητης*.] One of the Jewish scholars who contributed to the Masora. Hence **Mas(s)-ore·tic, -al,** *a.* var. **Ma·sorite.**

Masque (mɑsk). 1514. [orig. the same wd. as MASK *sb.*[2]; now differentiated.] **1.** A masquerade, masked ball. [So in Fr.] Now *rare*. **2.** A form of amateur histrionic entertainment, originally consisting of dancing and acting in dumb show, the performers being masked; afterwards including dialogue and song 1562. Also *transf.* and *fig.* **3.** A dramatic composition for this kind of entertainment 1605. †**4.** A set of masquers –1625.

2. *fig.* The M. of Anarchy SHELLEY (*title*). **3.** A Maske presented at Ludlow Castle MILT. (*title of Comus*).

Masque, Masquer, etc.: see MASK, etc.

Masquerade (mɑskĕrē[i]·d), *sb.* 1587. [First in quasi-Sp. forms *mascarado*, *masquerada* (see -ADO), later superseded by *mascarade*, and (with assim. to MASQUE) *masquerade*; – Fr. *mascarade* – It. *mascherata* or Sp. *mascarada*, f. *maschera*, *máscara* MASK *sb.*[2]; see -ADE.] **1.** A masked ball 1597. **b.** *transf.* and *fig.* usually with reference to the fantastic or motley character of a masquerade 1587. **2.** Masquerade dress 1668. **3.** Acting or living under false pretences; false outward show; pretence 1674. **b.** *concr.* A travesty. DISRAELI. †**4.** One who takes part in a masquerade –1727. †**5.** A name for one or more textile fabrics –1714.

3. The smooth tongue's habitual m. CRABBE. **5.** [*Masquerade*, a shot silk of various tints FAIRHOLT.]

Masquerade (mɑskĕrē[i]·d), *v.* 1654. [f. prec. sb.] †**1.** *trans.* To disguise as at a masquerade (*rare*) –1717. **2.** *intr.* To appear or go about in disguise; to pass oneself off under a false character 1692.

Hence **Masquera·der** (*lit.* and *fig.*).

Mass (mæs, mās), *sb.*[1] [OE. *mæsse*, *messe*, corresp. to OFris., OS. *missa*, OHG. *messa*, *missa* (G. *messe*), ON. *messa*. – eccl.L. *missa* (whence also (O)Fr. *messe*, It. *messa*, Sp. *misa*), vbl. sb. f. *miss-*, pa. ppl. stem of *mittere* send, send away (cf. MISSION). The primary meaning is disputed, but many hold that *missa* at first denoted the solemn dimissory formula at the conclusion of a service, *Ite, missa est*, and hence came to be applied to the service itself. The sense 'feast-day' of OE. survives in names of church festivals in *-mas*.] **1.** The Eucharistic service; in post-Reformation use, chiefly that of the R.C. Church. Also, a celebration of the Eucharist having a particular object or intention. **2.** In pre-Reformation use, the sacrament of the Eucharist; subseq., the Eucharist as administered and doctrinally viewed by Roman Catholics OE. **b.** The form of liturgy used in the celebration of the Eucharist. late ME. **3.** A musical setting of those parts of the mass which are usually sung 1597. **4.** Used in oaths. late ME.

1. Suitable masses said for the benefit of his soul SCOTT. Freq. without article, as in phr. *At m.*, (*to go*) *to m.*; *to say, sing, hear, attend m.* Phr. †*Neither m. nor matins*: nothing of very serious import. **High** (or **solemn** or †**great**) **m.,** m. celebrated with the assistance of deacon and subdeacon, with incense and music. **Low** (or †**little**) **m.,** m. said without note and with the minimum of ceremony. **2.** Admitting a real presence in the m. **4.** Phr. *By the m.*; also simply *mass* (often *mess*).

Comb.: **m.-bell,** (*a*) a bell that calls people to m.; (*b*) a bell that is rung during m., a sacring-bell; **-money,** (*a*) offerings of money made at m.; (*b*) money paid to a priest for saying m.

Mass (mæs), *sb.*[2] late ME. [– (O)Fr. *masse* – L. *massa* – Gr. *μᾶζα* barley-cake, perh. rel. to *μάσσειν* knead.] **1.** A coherent body of matter (as dough, clay, metal), not yet shaped; a lump of raw material for moulding, casting, sculpture, etc. Now merged in sense 2. **b.** An amorphous quantity of material used in or remaining after a chemical or other operation; in *Pharmacy*, the substance from which pills are made 1562. †**c.** A plastic substance –1700. **2.** In wider sense: A solid physical object of relatively large bulk. In mod. *Physics*, often contrasted with *molecule* or *atom*. 1440. **b.** *Mining.* A mineral deposit of irregular shape, dist. from a *bed* or *vein* 1855. **3.** A dense aggregation of objects apparently forming a continuous body 1609. **4.** *transf.* and *fig.* **a.** A large quantity, amount, or number 1585. **b.** Applied to an extensive unbroken expanse (of colour, light, shadow, etc.). Also, in *Fine Art*, one of the several main portions distinguishable in a composition. 1662. **c.** A volume or body of sound, esp. when produced by many instruments or voices of the same character 1879. **5.** Of human beings: A compact body; an aggregate in which individuality is lost 1713. **b.** *Mil.* A formation of troops in which the battalions, etc. are arranged one behind another. Opp. to *line*. 1889. **6.** *abstr.* **a.** Solid bulk, massiveness 1602. **b.** *Physics.* The quantity of matter which a body contains; in strict use dist. from *weight* 1704.

1. Of Gold in Masse eight thousand..Cichars HOOKER. 2. The mighty m. of the Finsteraarhorn TYNDALL. 3. There were masses of camellias and azaleas OUIDA. 4. I remember a masse of things, but nothing distinctly SHAKS. Great Masses of Treasure BACON. A m. of evidence TYLOR. Phr. *The (great) m. of*: the greater part or majority of. *The m.*: the generality; the main body. *In the m.*: without distinction of parts or individuals. *To be a* (or *one*) *m. of bruises, faults*, etc. **b.** The effect producible by *masses* of light and shade 1797. **5.** Away with this hurrah of masses, and let us have the considerate vote of single men EMERSON. *The masses*: the lower orders. **6. a.** Gathering m. as it travelled KANE. **b.** Phr. *Centre of m.*: see CENTRE.

attrib. and *Comb.* **a.** *Arch.* 'Arranged in large masses', as *m.-pier*. **b.** *Mil.*, etc. 'Involving masses of people', as *m. drill, vote*. **c.** *Physics*, as *m.-attraction, -moment*. **d.** *Spec.*: **m. meeting,** a large public meeting, usually political (orig. *U.S.*); **m. production,** the production of manufactured articles in large quantities by a standardized process; **m. suggestion,** the influencing of the minds of a large body of people by the suggestion of an idea of general application.

Mass, *v.*[1] Now *rare* or *Obs.* [OE. *mæssian*, f. *mæsse* MASS *sb.*[1]] **1.** *intr.* To celebrate mass; to sing or say mass. **2.** *trans.* To pass *away* (time) at mass 1784.

Mass (mæs), *v.*[2] 1563. [– (O)Fr. *masser*, f. *masse* MASS *sb.*[2]] **1.** *trans.* To form or gather into a mass; to arrange, or bring together, in masses. Also with *up*. 1604. **b.** *Mil.*; also, to concentrate (troops) in a particular place 1861. **2.** *refl.* and *intr.* To collect, or come together in masses 1563.

1. Who mass'd, round that slight brow, these clouds of doom? M. ARNOLD. **b.** Austria is massing troops in Herzegovina 1885.

Massa (mæ·sə). Also **Mas'r.** 1774. Negro corruption of *master*.

Massacre (mæ·săkəɹ), *sb.* 1586. [– (O)Fr. *massacre*, †*maçacre*, etc. shambles, also butchery, of unkn. origin. Spenser stresses *massa·cre*, Shaks. and Marlowe *ma·ssacre*.] **1.** A general slaughter (of human beings; also occas., of wild animals). Also *fig.* †**2.** A cruel or peculiarly atrocious murder –1608.

1. On the late Massacher in Piemont MILT. (*title*). *M. of St. Bartholomew* (earlier †*m. of Paris*): the m. of the Huguenots of France on the 24th of August 1572. *M. of Glencoe*: the m. of the Macdonalds of Glencoe on Feb. 13th, 1692, by the Campbells, under authority from William III. *M. of the Innocents*: see INNOCENT B. 2. **2.** *Rich. III*, IV. iii. 2.

Massacre (mæ·săkəɹ), *v.* 1581. [– (O)Fr. *massacrer*, f. *massacre*; see prec.] **1.** *trans.* To kill indiscriminately (a number of human beings, occas. animals). Also occas. *absol.* **2.** To murder cruelly or violently 1601. †**3.** To mutilate, mangle –1651.

1. These are the Guisians, That seeke to m. our guiltles liues MARLOWE. **2.** Caesar..was masakred with 23. wounds 1606.

Massage (mæsā·ʒ), *sb.* 1876. [– Fr. *massage*, f. *masser* apply massage to, used XVIII by French colonists in India, perh. – Pg. *amassar* knead, f. *massa* dough (MASS *sb.*[2]), but Arab. *massa* touch, handle, *masaḥa* wipe with the hand, stroke, rub, have been suggested; see -AGE.] The application of friction, kneading, etc. to the muscles and joints of the body, in order to stimulate their action and increase their suppleness. Hence **Massa·ge** *v.*

‖**Massasauga** (mæsăsǫ·gă). 1842. [irreg. f. *Missisauga*, (Ojibwa) name of a river in Ontario.] A small N. Amer. rattlesnake of the genus *Crotalophorus* (or *Caudisona*).

Ma·ss-book. OE. [f. MASS *sb.*[1] + BOOK *sb.*] = MISSAL *sb.*[1]

‖**Massé** (mæ·se, mase), *a.* and *sb.* 1873. [Fr., pa. pple. of *masser* make this stroke, f. *masse* MACE[1].] *Billiards.* Applied to a stroke made with the cue held perpendicular.

†**Ma·sser.** [OE. *mæssere*, f. *mæssian* MASS *v.*[1]; see -ER[1].] A priest who celebrates mass; also, one who attends mass. (After OE. only as a term of derision.) –1579.

Masseter (mæsī·təɹ). 1666. [– Gr. μασητήρ, f. μασᾶσθαι chew.] *Anat.* (Usu. *m. muscle*.) The masticatory muscle which passes from the malar bone and zygomatic arch to the ramus of the lower jaw. Hence **Massete·ric** *a.* of or pertaining to the m.; *sb.* a masseteric nerve, muscle, artery, etc.

‖**Masseur** (masör). 1876. [Fr.; f. *masser*; see MASSAGE *sb.*] A man who practises massage. So ‖**Masseuse** (masöz), a woman who practises massage.

Ma·ss-house. *Obs.* exc. *Hist.* 1644. [MASS *sb.*[1]] In 17–18th c. a Protestant term for a Roman Catholic place of worship.

Massicot (mæ·sikǫt). 1472 (*masticot*). [– Fr. *massicot*, †*masticot*, obscurely rel to It. *marzacotto* unguent, Sp. *mazacote* kali, mortar, prob. based on Arab. *mashaḳūnyā* unguent.] Yellow monoxide of lead used as a pigment (cf. LITHARGE).

‖**Massif** (mæ·sif). Also †**-ife.** 1524. [Fr.; subst. use of *massif* MASSIVE *a.*] †**a.** A block or mass of stone. **b.** A large mountain-mass; the central mass of a mountain; a compact portion of a range 1885.

†**Ma·ssily,** *adv.* late ME. [f. MASSY + -LY[2].] Massively –1668. So †**Ma·ssiness.**

Massive (mæ·siv), *a.* late ME. [– Fr. *massif, -ive*, alt. of OFr. *massiz*; see MASSY *a.*, -IVE.] **1.** Forming a large mass; large and heavy or solid. **b.** Of articles of gold or silver: Solid, not hollow or plated. **c.** Of architectural or artistic style: Presenting great masses, solid 1841. **d.** Of the features, head, etc.: Largely moulded or modelled 1843. **2.** *transf.* and *fig.* **a.** Solid, substantial; imposing in scale 1581. **b.** *Psych.* Of a sensation, a state of consciousness: Having large volume or magnitude 1855. **c.** *Path.* Of a disease, etc.:, Affecting a large continuous portion of tissue 1897. **3.** Forming a solid or continuous mass; compact, dense, or (sometimes, merely) uniform in internal structure; existing in compact continuous masses. Now esp. *Min.* applied to minerals not definitely crystalline, and *Geol.* to rocks or formations presenting no structural divisions. 1558.

1. Its ceilings..heavy with m. beams DICKENS. Hence **Ma·ssive-ly** *adv.*, **-ness. Massi·vity.**

Ma·ss-mo:nger. *arch.* 1550. [MASS *sb.*[1]] A contemptuous term for a Roman Catholic. So †**Mass-monging** *vbl. sb.* and *ppl. a.*

‖**Massoola(h** (mæ̆sū·lă). Also **musoola,** etc. 1685. [Of unkn. origin.] A large surf-boat used on the Coromandel coast. Often *m.-boat*.

Ma·ss-penny. *arch.* late ME. [MASS *sb.*[1]] An offering of money made at mass.

Ma·ss-priest. *arch.* OE. [MASS *sb.*[1]] A (Christian) priest.

From the 16th c. chiefly a hostile term for a Roman Catholic priest.

Massy (mæ·si), *a.* Now *rhet.* or *arch.* late ME. [perh. orig. – OFr. *massiz* (whence *massif* MASSIVE) :– pop. L. **massiceus*, f. L. *massa* MASS *sb.*[2]] **1.** Full of substance or mass. **a.** Solid and weighty. Said esp. of the precious metals: Occurring in mass; wrought in solid pieces. †**b.** Having three dimensions –1645. †**c.** Close, compact, dense –1814. **2.** Consisting of a large mass or masses 1587. **b.** Of architecture: Presenting great masses 1819. **3.** Spreading in a mass or in masses 1672. **b.** Of persons and animals: Bulky, large-bodied. late ME. **4.** *transf.* and *fig.* 1588.

1. As a massee vessel of gold WYCLIF *Ecclus.* 50:10. M. old plate SHERIDAN. **c.** The massiest air 1814. **2.** A m. oaken table SCOTT. **3.** Infantry in m. columns ALISON. **4.** A grosse and m. paradox MILT. *Comb. m.-proof* adj. With antick Pillars m. proof MILT.

Mast (mɑst), *sb.*[1] [OE. *mæst* = (M)LG., (M)Du., (O)HG. *mast* :– WGmc. **masta* (ON. *mastr*, etc., being – MLG.) :– IE. **mazdos*, whence poss. L. *malus* mast, OIr. *matan* club.] **1.** A long pole or spar of timber, iron, or steel set upright on a ship's keel, to support the sails. **b.** A piece of timber suitable for a mast 1496. **2.** The tall upright pole of a derrick or similar machine; a climbing pole in a gymnasium; a structure to support a wireless aerial; etc. 1646.

1. The larger masts are composed of several lengths, called *lower m.*, TOPMAST, TOPGALLANT *mast*, and ROYAL *mast*. O.E.D. The tallest Pine Hewn on Norwegian hills, to be the M. Of some great Ammiral MILT. Phr. *Before the m.*: see BEFORE B. 2. *At the m.*: on deck by the mainmast. *To nail one's colours to the m.*, to adopt an unyielding attitude. *To spring, step a m.*: see SPRING, STEP *vbs.*

Comb.: **m.-buoy,** one which carries a m.; **-tree,** a name given to certain tall erect trees.

Mast (mɑst), *sb.*[2] [OE. *mæst* = MLG., MDu., OHG. *mast* :– WGmc. **masta* :– **mazdos*, prob. f. base repr. in MEAT.] **1.** The fruit of the beech, oak, chestnut, and other forest-trees, esp. as food for swine. Rare in *pl.* †**2.** The condition of feeding on mast. Only in phr. *to lie at m.*, *to put to m.* –1664.

1. The Oakes beare M., the Briars Scarlet Heps SHAKS.

Mast (mɑst), *v.* 1627. [f. MAST *sb.*[1]] *trans.* To furnish with masts.

Mastage (mɑ·stėdʒ). *Obs.* exc. *Hist.* 1610. [f. MAST *sb.*[2] + -AGE.] = MAST *sb.*[2] 1. Also, the right of feeding animals on mast.

‖**Mastax** (mæ·stæks). 1855. [Gr., = mouth.] The pharynx of a rotifer.

Masted (mɑ·stėd), *ppl. a.* 1627. [f. MAST *v.* or *sb.*[1] + -ED.] **1.** Furnished with a mast or masts. **2.** Thronged with masts 1757.

Master (mā·stəɹ), *sb.*[1] [OE. *mæġister*, *maġister* (corresp. to OFris. *māster*, (also OS.) *mēster*, (O)HG. *meister*, ON. *meistari*), a CGmc. adoption from L.; reinforced by OFr. *maistre* (mod. *maître*) :– L. *magister*, *magistr-*, usu. referred to *magis* adv. more.]

I. A man having control or authority. †**1.** *gen.* A director, leader, chief, commander; a ruler, governor –1596. Also *transf.* (chiefly of animals). **2.** *spec.* (*Naut.*) **a.** The captain of a merchant vessel; called also †*m.* MARINER. **b.** The officer (ranking next below a lieutenant) entrusted with the navigation of a ship of war. Now styled *navigating officer*. †**c.** *M. and commander*: since 1814 repl. by COMMANDER ME. **3.** An employer; correl. w. *servant, man*; also with *apprentice*. late ME. **b.** Applied to a sovereign in relation to his ministers or officers. Now chiefly *Hist.* 1470. **4.** The owner of a dog, horse, slave, etc. late ME. **5.** The male head of a house or household 1536. **b.** With poss. adj.: (One's) husband (*dial.*) late ME. **6.** A possessor, owner. Now *rare*, exc. in phr. *to be m. of*: to possess; also, occas., to have a mastery of (a subject). late ME. **7.** One who has the control, use, or disposition of something at will. Chiefly *predicative*. ME. **b.** *transf.* of things. late ME. **8.** One who overcomes another, a victor ME. **9.** *Bowls.* = JACK *sb.*[1] II. II.

2. **b.** *Master's mate*, an officer subordinate to but working with the m. of a ship of war. **3.** Who's m., who's man SWIFT. Provb. *Like m., like man.* **4.** An Asse [knoweth] his masters stall COVERDALE *Isa.* 1: 3. **5.** The m. of the house begins first LANE. **6.** I was m. of more than twenty pounds 1785. **7.** The person who really commands the army is your m. BURKE. **b.** Loue is your m. SHAKS.

II. A teacher. **1.** A tutor, preceptor; in later use chiefly a teacher in a school; also, a teacher of an art, a language, etc. OE. **2.** He whose disciple one is in religion, philosophy, art, etc. ME. †**3.** A scholar of authority –1597. **4.** In academic sense, = med.L. *magister*: The holder of a specific degree, originally conveying authority to teach in the university. In Eng. use (until recently) confined to the Faculty of Arts: the full title is in L. *artium magister*, in Eng. *master of arts* (abbrev. M.A. or, now rarely, A.M.). Latterly the degrees of *Master of Science* (M.Sc.), *Master in* or *of Surgery* (*Magister Chirurgiæ*, M.Ch.), have been given in Oxford, etc. late ME. **5.** A workman who is in business on his own account, as dist. from a journeyman; a working man of approved skill; also *transf.* and *fig.* late ME. **6.** An artist of distinguished skill, one who is regarded as a model of excellence in his art 1533. **b.** A work by a master. Now only in *old m.*, and occas. *modern m.* 1752.

1. The village m. taught his little school GOLDSM. French in a fortnight without a M. (*title*) 1856. **2.** My maister Chaucer LYDG. *The (our, his, my) M.*: often applied to Christ. **3.** *M. of the sentences* (*magister sententiarum*), the name given to Peter Lombard, Bishop of Paris in the 12th c., from his book *Sententiarum libri quatuor*, a collection of patristic comments on passages of Scripture. **5.** It is a stroke of a maister CAXTON. **6.** *Old Master*, a master who lived between the 13th and the 16th or 17th centuries. The pictures of the Tuscan and Venetian masters EMERSON. **b.** As a picture-dealer stares at an alleged old m. 1851.

III. As a title of office. **1.** The head of certain colleges (in Oxford, Cambridge, etc.), guilds, corporations, livery companies, hospitals, etc. Formerly also used for GRAND MASTER, *Great master*, the title of the head of a military order. Also as in *master-general*, *m. provincial*, titles of dignitaries of monastic and other religious organizations. **2.** In the designations of certain legal functionaries (see below). late ME. **3. a.** In designations of officials having duties of control, superintendence, or safe-keeping. late ME. **b.** *Mil.* in various titles of command. late ME. †**4.** **Great master.** = GRAND MASTER 1, 2. –1685.

1. *M. of the Temple*: (*a*) *Hist.* the grand master of the Knights Templar; (*b*) the principal clergyman of the Temple Church, London. He was made M. of Balliol Coll. WOOD. **2.** *M. of the* (or *in*) *Chancery*, (*a*) until 1852, one of the twelve assistants to the Lord Chancellor, the chief of whom was M. of the Rolls; (*b*) since 1897, any one of four chief clerks of the Chancery Division of the Supreme Court. *M. of the Court* (*of Common Pleas, of the King's Bench, of the Exchequer*), any one of five officers in each of those courts (now, in the corresponding division of the Supreme Court) charged with the duty of recording the proceedings. *M. of* (*the*) *Faculties*, the chief officer of the Court of Faculties (cf. FACULTY III. b). *M. in Lunacy*, see LUNACY. *M. of the Requests*, see REQUEST. *M. of the Wards* (*and Liveries*), see WARD. **3.** *M. of the* (*King's, Queen's*) *Household*, an officer under the Steward of the Royal Household. *M. of the Jewel-house*, the keeper of the Crown Jewels in the Tower of London. *M. of the* (*King's*) *Music*, an officer of the Royal Household, the conductor of the King's band. *M. of the Robes, of the Wardrobe*, the keeper of the 'great' wardrobe of the King, Queen, or other exalted personage. *M. of* (*the*) *Works* or (now dial.) *Work*, an official who superintends building operations. For *M. of Ceremonies, of the Mint, of Misrule, of the Revels, of the Rolls*, see the second sbs. *M. of the Horse*: (*a*) in England, the title of the third official of the royal household; also rarely *transf.* in joc. use, a head groom or stableman; (*b*) *Antiq.* used as tr. L. *magister equitum*, master of the 'knights', under the Roman republic the title of the commander of the cavalry appointed by a dictator. *M. of the Buckhounds*, the fourth great officer of the household. *M. of hounds*: one who owns, or has the control of, a pack of hounds; usually, the leading member of a hunt who is elected to the office; chiefly = *M. of foxhounds* (abbrev. M.F.H.). Also *m. of beagles, harriers, staghounds*, etc. **b.** *M.* (*General*) *of the Ordnance*, the controller of the Ordnance and Artillery (now, the head of the Board of Ordnance).

IV. As a title of rank or compliment. **1. a.** *sing.* = Sir. Now only in uneducated use. **b.** *pl.* (in later times always *my masters*) = Sirs, gentlemen. Now *arch.* or *rhet.*, chiefly ironical or derisive. ME. **2.** Prefixed to the name or designation of a man. In ordinary use now only *dial.*, but in literature occas. *arch.* or *Hist.*; otherwise repl. by MR. (mi·stəɹ). ME. **3.** Prefixed (esp. by servants and inferiors) to the name of boys and young men not old enough for 'Mr.'. **4.** The heir-apparent to a Scottish peerage (below the rank of earl; formerly, below that of marquis) is often known as **The M. of ——**; the specific designation being usu. identical with the baronial title of the family 1489.

1. Y'are welcome Masters, welcome all SHAKS. **2.** Maister Latymer encouraged Maister Ridley when both were at the stake FOXE. And yet m. Parson must not be called couetous 1625. **3.** Maids, misses, and little m...in a third [coach] SWIFT. Phr. *masters and misses* = young people. **4.** The M. of Ravenswood led the way SCOTT.

V. Attrib. uses. **1.** Used appositively or as *adj.* in the sense 'that is a master'. **a.** As prefixed to designations of persons, now *rhet.*, with implication of imposing greatness ME. **b.** *spec.* denoting (*a*) the leader of a herd of animals, (*b*) the official who has command over others so designated, (*c*) one who is a master, as opp. to an apprentice or journeyman, hence = supremely skilled. **2.** Applied *transf.* as a qualification of things, with the sense 'main', 'principal', 'controlling' ME.

1. a. The master-deuil, Belsabub 1575. The Choice and M. Spirits of this Age SHAKS. **b.** A M.-Pike, that for his Bulk, Beauty, and Strength, was look'd upon to be the Prince of the River R. L'ESTRANGE. A Master-Printer 1683. The king's m. butcher J. GRANT. The French consider the English the master-colonists of the world 1900. **2.** A main Pillar and Master-branch in Englands Grandeur 1667. The lord of irony,—the master-spell BYRON.

Comb.: **m. attendant,** 'an officer in the royal dockyards appointed to assist in the fitting or dismantling, removing or securing vessels of war, etc.' (Smyth); **m. fault** *Geol.*, a fault which governs the configuration of the surrounding area; **m. hand,** (*a*) the hand of a m., the agency of one highly skilled or one possessing commanding power; (*b*) a highly skilled worker; **m. joint** *Geol.*, a principal joint in a rock mass; **m. mariner** (see MARINER); **m. sinew,** a main sinew; *esp.* the tendon of Achilles in man; **m. workman,** a workman thoroughly conversant with his trade; one who employs workmen; also *fig.*

Master (ma·stəɹ), *sb.*[2] 1880. [f. MAST *sb.*[1] + -ER[1] 1.] A ship having (so many) masts, as *three-m.*, etc.

Master (mā·stəɹ), *v.* ME. [f. MASTER *sb.*[1] Cf. OFr. *maistrier*.] **1.** *trans.* To get the better of; to overcome or defeat. **2.** To reduce to subjection; to break, tame (an animal). late ME. **3.** *techn.* To temper or season; to modify. Now only in *Dyeing*, to season or age (dye stuffs), and in *Tanning*, to subject (skins) to the action of an astringent lye. late ME. **4.** To make oneself master of; to acquire complete understanding of (a fact, a proposition), or complete facility in using (an instrument, etc.) 1740. **5.** To rule as a master; to be the master of (a servant, scholar, house, etc.) 1611. †**6.** *trans.* To own, possess –1638. **7.** To address by the style of 'master'. STUBBES.

1. Kings nor authority can m. fate FLETCHER. **2.** The Zebra..could never be entirely mastered GOLDSM. **4.** To m. the difference between 'would' and 'should' 1901. **6.** The wealth That the world masters SHAKS.

Ma·ster-at-a·rms. 1748. *Naut.* Formerly a warrant-officer in the navy who instructed the officers and crew of a ship of war in the exercise of small arms, and acted as principal police officer on board, but now a first-class petty officer doing duty in the latter capacity only. Also *transf.*, the principal police officer on board a ship of the mercantile marine.

Ma·ster-bui:lder. 1557. [MASTER *sb.*[1] II.] **1.** One who is skilled in the art of building, an architect. Chiefly in rhet. use or fig. context. **2.** One who employs workmen in building 1714. **3.** *Naut.* A petty officer formerly employed on the construction of ships 1799.

Masterdom (mā·stəɹdəm). OE. [f. MASTER *sb.*[1] + -DOM.] †**1.** The office of a teacher; the degree of master (of divinity) –ME. **2.** Dominion, supremacy; †victory in battle 1475. †**3.** = MASTERSHIP 3 –1601.

Masterful (mā·stəɹfŭl), *a.* ME. [f. MASTER *sb.*[1] + -FUL.] **1.** Addicted to acting the part of master; imperious, self-willed. Of actions: High-handed, arbitrary. †**b.** *Law.* (chiefly *Sc.*) Of beggars, etc.: Using violence or threats 1474–1754. **2.** Having the capacities of a master; qualified to command. late ME. **b.** Of language, looks, etc.: Indicative of mastery 1824. **3.** = MASTERLY 2. 1613.

1. Yonder m. cuckoo Crowds every egg out of the nest EMERSON. **2. b.** His m., pale face E. B. BROWNING. **3.** Whether pleasing or displeasing to your taste they are entirely m. RUSKIN. Hence **Ma·sterful-ly** *adv.*, **-ness.**

Masterhood (mā·stəɹhu:d). 1454. [f. MASTER *sb.*[1] + -HOOD.] The condition or quality of being a master.

Master-key. 1576. A key that will open a number of different locks.

Masterless (mā·stəɹlės), *a.* late ME. [f. MASTER *sb.*[1] and (sense 2) *v.* + -LESS.] **1.** Having no master. **b.** Vagrant, vagabond. *Obs.* exc. *Hist.* 1471. †**2.** That cannot be mastered; ungovernable –1767.

†**Ma·sterlike,** *a.* and *adv.* 1500. [f. MASTER *sb.*[1] + -LIKE.] **a.** *adj.* Despotic, autocratic, sovereign; authoritative, magisterial; exhibiting masterly ability. **b.** *adv.* In a masterlike manner –1666.

a. I begin to doubt the picture..is not of his making, it is so m. PEPYS.

Masterly (mā·stəɹli), *a.* 1531. [f. MASTER *sb.*[1] + -LY.] †**1.** Belonging to, or characteristic of, a master or lord; usu. in bad sense, arbitrary, despotic; imperious, overbearing –1766. **2.** Worthy of a master or skilled workman; skilfully performed 1666.

2. How m. are the strokes of Virgil! DRYDEN. A small but m. work 1804. M. speeches 1880. Hence **Ma·sterliness.** So **Ma·sterly** *adv.* late ME.

Master-mason. late ME. [MASTER *sb.*[1] II. 5.] **1.** A mason who designs and carries out building in stone or who employs workmen to shape and fit stonework. **2.** A fully qualified freemason, who has passed the third degree 1723.

Masterpiece (mā·stəɹpīs). 1605. [f. MASTER *sb.*[1] + PIECE *sb.*, after Du. *meesterstuk* (adapted in Sc. as *maisterstik* XVI) or G. *meisterstück* piece of work qualifying a craftsman.] **1.** A production surpassing in excellence all others by the same hand; also, a production of masterly skill; a consummate example 1610. †**b.** An action of masterly ability –1715. †**2.** The most important feature, or the chief excellence, of a person or thing –1697.

1. Man is heav'n's Master-piece QUARLES. A m. of assurance FIELDING, of policy FREEMAN. **b.** Confusion now has made his Master-peece SHAKS. **2.** His learning in the law being his m. CLARENDON.

Mastership (mā·stəɹʃip). late ME. [f. MASTER *sb.*[1] + -SHIP. In some senses an Englishing of MASTERY by suffix-substitution.] **1.** The condition of being a master or ruler; dominion, rule, control. †**b.** 'Upper hand', mastery 1573–1829. **2.** The office, function, dignity, or term of office of a 'master' 1455. **b.** The position of a master in or of a school 1806. †**3.** With poss. pron.: The personality of a master. Often abbrev. M. –1622. **4.** The skill or knowledge constituting a master 1607. **b.** The status or degree of a master (in a craft, a university, etc.) 1688. **5.** The existence of masters or employers as the characteristic form of industrial organization 1868.

2. The M. of the Rolls 1873. **3.** How now Signior Launce? what newes with your M.? SHAKS. **4.** M. in tongue-fence; this is the quality of qualities CARLYLE.

Master-singer (mā·stəɹsi:ŋəɹ). Now *rare.* 1810. Anglicization of MEISTERSINGER.

Master-stroke (mā·stəɹstrōᵘk). 1679. [See MASTER *sb.*[1] V. 2; after Fr. *coup de maître*.] **1.** A masterly line or touch (in painting, etc.). Also *transf.* **2.** A surpassingly skilful act (of cunning, policy, etc.); one's cleverest move or device 1711.

2. The steeple..is a master-stroke of absurdity H. WALPOLE.

†**Master-vein.** late ME. [MASTER *sb.*[1] V. 2.] One of the great veins or arteries of the body; *spec.* applied to the saphena –1683.

Master-work (mā·stəɹwɒɹk). 1606. [See MASTER *sb.*[1] V. 2.; after Fr. *chef-d'œuvre*.] **1.** An action or procedure of supreme importance. **2.** A masterpiece 1617. †**3.** A main drain or channel –1789.

Masterwort (mā·stəɹwɒɹt). 1548. [f. MASTER *sb.*[1] + WORT[1], after G. *meisterwurz*.] The umbelliferous plant *Peucedanum* (*Imperatoria*) *ostruthium*, formerly cultivated as a pot-herb, and used in medicine.

Also applied to other genera, as *Astrantia* (Black M.); the goutweed, *Ægopodium podagraria* (English or Wild M.); and the U.S. plants *Angelica atropurpurea* and *Heracleum lanatum*.

Mastery (mā·stəɹi). [ME. *meistrie* – OFr. *maistrie*, f. *maistre* MASTER *sb.*[1] + *-ie* -Y[3].] **1.** The state or condition of being master; authority, sway, dominion; an instance of this. †**b.** Predominance; prevailing character –1642. **2.** 'Upper-hand'; victory. Now only: Victory resulting in the subjection of the vanquished (cf. sense 1). ME. †**3.** Superior force or power –1818. **4.** The skill or knowledge which constitutes a master. *Obs.* or *arch.* exc. with mixture of sense 7. ME. †**5.** An exercise or work of skill or power –1667. †**6.** A competitive feat of strength or skill; esp. in phr. *to try masteries*, to 'try conclusions' –1697. **7.** (*transf.* from 1.) Intellectual command over (a subject of study) 1668. **b.** The action of mastering (a subject) 1797.

1. The Priesthood was not a Maistry, but a Ministry HOBBES. **2.** Four Champions fierce Strive here for Maistrie MILT. **4.** Use maketh Masterie NORTON. **5.** *To do, make, work*, etc. (*a*) m. or *masteries*: to perform a wonderful feat or trick. Ye shul wel seen at eye, That I wol doon a maistrie er I go CHAUCER. *It is great, little, no m.*: it is hard or easy (to do something). **6.** This is but to try Masteries with Fortune BACON. **7.** His m. of English was supreme 1880.

Mast-head, *sb.* (Stress variable.) 1748. [MAST *sb.*[1]] **1.** The head or highest part of a mast, esp. of the lower mast. **2.** A sailor stationed at the mast-head. **3.** *attrib.* as *m.-light*, etc. 1822.

Mast-head, *v.* 1829. [f. the sb.] **1.** *trans.* To send (a sailor) to the mast-head as a punishment. Also *transf.* and *fig.* **2.** To raise (a sail, yard, etc.) to its position on the mast or at the mast-head 1840.

Mastic (mæ·stik). late ME. [– (O)Fr. *mastic* – late L. *mastichum* (Palladius), *masticha*, vars. of L. *mastichē* (Pliny) – Gr. μαστίχη, presumed to be f. μαστιχᾶν (see next), the substance being used as a chewing-gum in the East.] **1.** A gum or resin which exudes from the bark of *Pistacia lentiscus* and some other trees. Now used chiefly in making varnish. **2.** (In full *m. tree.*) An evergreen shrub yielding mastic gum, *Pistacia lentiscus* of the Levant. Applied also to other species of *Pistacia*, and to the W. Indian *Bursera gummifera* and Peruvian *Schinus molle*. late ME. **3.** A timber tree of the W. Indies and Florida, *Sideroxylon mastichodendron* 1657. †**4.** (In full **Herb Mastic.**) The plant *Thymus mastichina* –1836. **5.** A resinous or bituminous cement; also, a lime cement used by builders 1706. **6.** A liquor flavoured with mastic used in Turkey and Greece. **7.** The colour of mastic; a shade of pale yellow 1890.

attrib. and *Comb.*, as *m. gum*, etc.; **m. varnish,** a fine varnish used for varnishing pictures.

Masticate (mæ·stikeˈt), *v.* 1649. [– *masticat-*, pa. ppl. stem of late L. *masticare* – Gr. μαστιχᾶν grind the teeth, rel. to μασᾶσθαι chew, and perh. to synon. L. *mandere*; see -ATE³.] **1.** *trans.* To grind (food) to a pulp with the teeth; to chew. **2.** To crush or knead (rubber) to a pulp 1849. So **Mastica·tion** 1565. **Ma·sticator** (also *attrib.* as *m. muscle*).

Masticatory (mæ·stikătəri). 1611. [– mod.L. *masticatorius*, *-orium*, f. *masticare*; see -ORY¹ and ².] **a.** *adj.* Of, pertaining to, or concerned with mastication; affecting the organs of mastication. **b.** *sb.* A medicinal substance to be chewed 1611.

Masticic (mæsti·sik), **mastichic** (mæsti·kik), *a.* 1845. [f. MASTIC + -IC.] *Chem.* In *m. acid*: an acid resin; the portion (about 90 per cent.) of mastic soluble in alcohol. So **Ma·sticin,** the insoluble residue of mastic 1844.

Masticot, early form of MASSICOT.

Mastiff (mɑ·stif). *Pl.* **mastiffs.** (Also †**mastis,** †**mastie, -y**). ME. [Obscurely repr. OFr. *mastin* (mod. *mâtin*) :– Rom. **mansuetinus*, f. L. *mansuetus* tamed, tame, earlier *mansues*, f. *manus* hand + base of *suescere* accustom.] A large, powerful dog with a large head, drooping ears and pendulous lips, valuable as a watch-dog.

Comb. **m. bat,** a name for bats of the genus *Molossus*.

Masting (mɑ·stiŋ), *vbl. sb.* 1627. [f. MAST *v.* + -ING¹.] **1.** The action or process of fitting with masts. **b.** Masts collectively 1702. **2.** *attrib.* as *m.-sheers*, etc. 1760.

Comb.: **m.-house,** (*a*) a place where masts are made and stored; (*b*) a building furnished with apparatus for fixing masts; **m. pine,** *Pinus strobus*.

‖**Mastitis** (mæstəi·tis). 1842. [mod.L., f. Gr. μαστός breast + -ITIS.] *Med.* Inflammation of the breast.

-mastix (mæ·stiks), repr. Gr. μάστιξ scourge, freq. used in the 17th c. (rarely later), and designating persons violently hostile to some person or class, as *Episcopo-mastix*, etc. Also in titles of books attacking some person, class, institution, etc., as *Histriomastix* [L. *histrio* actor], *Satiromastix*, etc.

Mastless (mɑ·stlės), *a.*¹ 1593. [f. MAST *sb.*¹ + -LESS.] Without a mast or masts.

Mastless (mɑ·stlės), *a.*² [f. MAST *sb.*² + -LESS.] Without mast or acorns. DRYDEN.

Masto- (mæ·sto), used (*Anat.* and *Path.*) **a.** to represent MASTOID *sb.*, in combs. with sense 'pertaining jointly to the mastoid process or bone and some other part of the skull', as *m.-parietal* adj., etc.; **b.** as comb. f. Gr. μαστός breast, in names of diseases of the female breast, as *mastodynia*, *-dyny*, neuralgia of the female breast, etc.

Mastodon (mæ·stŏdǫn). 1813. [– mod.L., f. Gr. μαστός breast + ὀδούς, ὀδοντ- tooth; cf. Fr. *mastodonte* (Cuvier, 1806).] *Palæont.* A large extinct mammal resembling the elephant, characterized by having nipple-shaped tubercles in pairs on the crowns of the molar teeth. Also **Ma·stodont** *sb.* (1826) and *a.*; hence **Mastodo·ntic** *a.*

Mastoid (mæ·stoid). 1732. [– Fr. *mastoïde* (Paré) or mod.L. *mastoides* – Gr. μαστοειδής (ἀποφύσεις μαστοειδεῖς 'mastoid processes', Galen), f. μαστός breast; see -OID.] **A.** *adj.* Shaped like a female breast.

M. process (Anat.), a nipple-shaped, conical prominence of the temporal bone. *M. bone*, a bone of the skull, in fishes and reptiles, homologous with the m. process. *M. cancer* (Path.), a kind of firm carcinomatous growth, the section of which is thought to resemble the boiled udder of the cow 1857.

B. *absol.* as *sb.* = *m. process* or *bone* 1842. **b.** *attrib.* = 'of or pertaining to the m. process', as *m. cell*, *muscle* 1800. Hence **Mastoi·dal** *a.*

Mastoidean (mæstoi·dĭan), *a.* 1841. [f. mod.L. *mastoideus* (f. *mastoides* MASTOID) + -AN.] Of or belonging to the mastoid.

Mastras, -es(s(e, obs. ff. MISTRESS.

Masturbate (mæ·stɒɹbeˈt), *v.* 1857. [– *masturbat-*, pa. ppl. stem of L. *masturbari*, of unkn. origin.] *intr.* and *refl.* To practise self-abuse. So **Masturba·tion** 1766. **Ma·sturbator.**

†**Ma·sty,** *a.* late ME. [f. MAST *sb.*² + -Y¹.] **1.** Producing mast –1630. **2.** Of a swine: Fattened. CHAUCER. **3.** Burly, big-bodied –1886.

Mat (mæt), *sb.*¹ [OE. *matt*, *meatt*, *meatte*, corresp. to MDu. *matte*, OHG. *matta* (Du. *mat*, G. *matte*); WGmc. – late L. *matta*.] **1.** A piece of a coarse fabric of plaited rushes, sedge, straw, bast, etc., used to lie, sit, or kneel upon, to cover floors, walls, plants, etc., and in packing furniture. **2. a.** An article (orig. of this material) placed near a door for persons entering to wipe their shoes upon (= DOOR-*mat*), or similar to those so used 1665. **b.** A thin flat article (orig. made of plaited straw), placed under a dish, plate, or vessel in order to protect the table from heat, etc. Also applied to other similar articles. 1875. **3.** *transf.* A thick tangled mass 1835. **4.** *Naut.* A thick web of rope yarn used to protect the standing rigging from the friction of other ropes 1497. **5.** *Engineering.* = MATTRESS 3. 1884. **6.** *attrib.* 1530.

2. *On the m.* (slang), up for trial, 'in for it'.

Comb.: **m.-grass,** (*a*) *Nardus stricta*, (*b*) *Psamma arenaria*, the marram grass; **-rush,** the bulrush, *Scirpus lacustris*; also = *matweed*; **matweed,** a name for various rush-like grasses.

Mat (mæt), *sb.*² Also **matt.** 1845. [– Fr. *mat*, subst. use of *mat* MAT *a.*] **1.** *Glass-painting.* A layer of colour 'matted' on the glass (see MAT *v.*² b) 1881. **2. a.** *Gilding.* The effect of 'mat' or unburnished gold. **b.** *Metal-work.* A roughened, frosted, or figured groundwork. 1866. **3.** A border of dead gold round a framed picture 1845. **4.** A matting-punch 1890.

Mat (mæt), *sb.*³ 1766. [Short f. MATADOR. Cf. NAP *sb.*³] = MATADOR 2.

Mat (mæt), *a.* Also †**matte, matt.** 1648. [– Fr. *mat*, identical with *mat* MATE *a.*] Of colours, surfaces: Without lustre, dull, 'dead'.

Mat (mæt), *v.*¹ 1549. [f. MAT *sb.*¹] **1.** *trans.* To cover or furnish with mats or matting. **2.** *transf.* To cover with an entangled mass 1577. **3.** To entangle *together* in a thick mass 1577; to make by interlacing 1824. **4.** *intr.* To become entangled *together* 1742.

2. A temple..matted with ivy 1849. **3.** And o'er his eyebrows hung his matted hair DRYDEN.

Mat (mæt), *v.*² 1602. [– Fr. *mater*, f. *mat* MAT *a.*] *trans.* To make (colours, etc.) dull; to give a mat appearance to (gilding, metal, etc.); to frost (glass). **b.** *Glass-painting.* To cover (glass) with a softened layer of colour 1885.

Matachin (mætăʃī·n). *Obs.* exc. *Antiq.* 1578. [– Fr. †*matachin* (now *matassin*) – Sp. *matachin*, prob. – Arab. *mutawajjihin*, active pple. pl. of *tawajjaha* assume a mask, f. *wajh* face.] **1.** A kind of sword-dancer in a fantastic dress. †**2.** A dance performed by matachins. Also *transf.* and *fig.* –1677. **3.** *attrib.*, as *m. dance*, etc. 1584.

2. *fig.* He was taken into seruice..to a base office in his Kitchin; so that (in a kind of Mattacina of humane fortune) Hee turned a Broach, that had worne a Crowne BACON.

Mataco (mæ·tăko). 1834. [prob. S. Amer.] The small three-banded armadillo, *Tolypeutes tricinctus*, which rolls itself up into a ball.

Matador (mæ·tădǭɹ). In senses 2 and 3 usu. **-ore.** 1674. [– Sp. *matador*, f. *matar* kill, f. Pers. *māt* dead. Cf. MATE *a.*] **1.** In Spanish bullfights, the man appointed to kill the bull 1681. **2.** *Cards.* In quadrille and ombre, any of the three best trumps 1674. **3.** *Dominoes.* Any of certain pieces (viz. those whose numbers make up seven, and the double blank) which in a particular form of the game (the *matador game*) can be played at any time 1865.

Matæology (mæti,ǫ·lŏdʒi). 1656. [f. Gr. μάταιος vain + -λογία discourse; see -LOGY.] Vain or unprofitable discourse. So †**Matæolo·gian** 1653.

†**Matæotechny.** 1576. [f. as prec. + τέχνη art.] An unprofitable science –1675.

Match (mætʃ), *sb.*¹ [OE. *ġemæćća* :– **ȝamakjon*, rel. to Gmc. **ȝamakon*, OE. *ġemaca*; see MAKE *sb.*¹]

I. One of a pair. †**1.** A husband or wife, a mate, consort, a lover. Also of animals. –1658. †**2.** One's equal; one's fellow, companion –1571. **3.** †**a.** An antagonist, rival –1593. **b.** A person (occas. a number of persons, a thing) able to contend with another as an equal ME. **4.** A person or thing that equals another in some quality 1470. **5.** A person or thing that exactly corresponds to or forms a pair with another 1474. †Formerly often *pl.*

2. Marry thy m. 1547. **3. a.** M. to m. I haue encountred him SHAKS. **b.** Phr. *To find, meet one's m.*; *to be, prove oneself, a m. for. More than a m. for*: able to overcome. His followers..were no m. for regular soldiers MACAULAY. **4.** I neuer found their matches 1632. **5.** You might by..looking through any Star on the Globe see its M. in Heaven 1674. Extraordinary matches for carriages have sold at 400 dollars per pair 1808.

II. The action of matching. †**1.** A matching of adversaries against each other; a contest viewed with regard to the equality or inequality of the parties –1628. **2.** A competitive trial of skill in which two or more persons or sides are matched against each other; an arrangement for such a contest. Also applied to a contest of animals. 1545. †**3.** A suitable pairing –1748. **b.** A (well or ill) matched pair (or set); two (or more) things which accord (well or ill) in colour, size, etc. 1542. **4.** A matrimonial compact or alliance; esp. one viewed as more or less advantageous 1547. †**b.** The action of marrying; relationship by marriage –1655. **c.** A person viewed with regard to eligibility as a partner in marriage 1586. †**5.** An agreement, an appointment; a compact, bargain –1768.

1. This was a mache vn-mete. late ME. **2.** [He] leaves it a drawn m. 1651. **3. b.** These ribbons are a bad match (*mod.*). **4.** It seems to me a very good m. for her 1866. **b.** *By m.*: in consequence of a marriage; By m., it came to Tremenet RISDON. **c.** He's the great m. of the county MEREDITH. **5.** Phr. *It is a m.* (or, *A m.!*): = 'Agreed', 'Done'. A m., 'tis done SHAKS.

Comb.: **m.-game,** a game (esp. of chess) forming part of a m.; also U.S. = sense II. 2; **-play,** the play in a m.; also in *Golf*, play in which holes, not strokes, are counted; so *m.-player*; **-rifle,** one used in firing competitions: **-rifling** *Gunmaking*, a method of rifling guns to adapt them for long-range shooting in matches; **m. wagon,** a railway wagon run in connection with a break-down crane.

Match (mætʃ), *sb.*² late ME. [– OFr. *meiche*, *mesche* (mod. *mèche*), corresp. to Sp., Pg. *mecha*, It. *miccia*, which have been referred to L. *myxa* (– Gr. μύξα) nozzle of a lamp (in med.L. lamp-wick), with crossing of Rom. **muccare* blow the nose, snuff a wick. For the Eng. development cf. (dial.) *cratch* cradle from (O)Fr. *crèche*, *patch* from OFr. *peche* PIECE.] †**1.** The wick of a candle or lamp –1646. **2.** A wick, cord, or rope of hemp, tow, cotton, etc., so prepared that when lighted at the end it is not easily extinguished, and burns at a uniform rate; used for firing cannon, etc. Also in *Mining*. 1549. **b.** The material of which matches consist; cord, etc., prepared for ignition 1572. **3.** A piece of cord, cloth, paper, wood, etc., dipped in melted sulphur, so as to be readily ignited by the use of a tinder-box, and serving to light a candle, etc. *Obs.* exc. *Hist.* 1519. **b.** A similar article used for fumigation 1703. **4.** A short slender piece of wood, wax taper, etc., tipped with some composition that bursts into flame when rubbed on a rough or specially prepared surface 1831.

4. Phr. *To strike a m.*: to ignite a m. by friction (the verb is borrowed from *to strike a light*). *Paraffin m.*: one having the splints dipped in paraffin. *Safety m.*: one which can be ignited only by striking on a specially prepared surface.
attrib. and *Comb.*, as *m.-box, -girl, -seller*; **m.-paper,** touch-paper; **-paste,** that used for making the heads of matches; **m.-splint, -stick,** the wood of a m.; **-thread,** the thread used as m. for firing guns, etc.; **matchwood,** †(*a*) touchwood; (*b*) wood suitable for match-sticks; (*c*) in phr. (*to break*, etc.) *into matchwood*, into minute splinters.

Match (mætʃ), *a.* 1483. [From the predicative and appositive uses of MATCH *sb.*[1]] That matches; corresponding. *Obs.* exc. *techn.* in certain special collocations, in most of which *match-* may be interpreted as an attrib. use of MATCH *v.*[1], as *m.-gearing, -plane, -plate.*

Match (mætʃ), *v.*[1] late ME. [f. MATCH *sb.*[1]] **1.** *trans.* To join in marriage; to procure a match for. Also *rarely*, †to couple (animals). Const. *to*, †*unto*, *with*. **b.** *intr.* for *refl.* To ally oneself in marriage. Now *rare* exc. *dial.* 1568. †**2.** *trans.* To associate; to put together so as to form a pair or set *with* (another person or thing) –1645. **3.** To encounter as an adversary. Now, to prove a match for. late ME. †**b.** *intr.* To meet in combat *with* –1595. **4.** *trans.* To array or place in opposition *with*; to pit *against* another. Chiefly *refl.* and *pass.* late ME. **5.** To arrange in a suitable or equal pair or set; to provide with an adversary of equal power. Often in *pass.*, *to be well, ill matched.* 1530. **b.** To make to correspond *to* or *with* 1680. **c.** To furnish (boards) with a tongue and a groove, at the edges 1833. **6.** To compare in respect of superiority 1581. †**7.** To regard or treat as equal –1606. **8.** To be equal to, to equal; to be the match or counterpart of. Also *absol.* of two things: To be mutually equal. 1592. **b.** *intr.* To be equal *with*; to correspond, be suitable *to*. Also (*rarely*), to fit *into*. 1567. **9.** *trans.* To furnish with a match 1596. **b.** To compare so as to select one suitable *to*. POPE. †**10.** To procure as a match *Merch. V.* III. i. 81.

1. An idle king..Match'd with an aged wife TENNYSON. **b.** He matched into a most noble and martial family 1647. **2.** *Much Ado* II. i. 111. **3. b.** Strength matcht with strength, and power confronted power SHAKS. **4.** To m. a bauble against the Pantheon DE QUINCEY. **5.** Hounds..match'd in mouth like bels SHAKS. **b.** God doth m. His gifts to man's believing M. ARNOLD. **8.** The event ..cannot..m. the expectation C. BRONTË. Phr. *To m.* (used quasi-adv. or quasi-adj. after a sb.): corresponding in number, size, etc. with what has been mentioned. **9.** I can m. this nonsense JOHNSON. Can you m. me this piece of yellow silk? 1861. Hence **Ma·tchable** *a.* that can be matched; †comparable; †well-suited. †**Ma·tchableness.**

Match (mætʃ), *v.*[2] 1703. [f. MATCH *sb.*[2] Cf. Fr. *mécher* in same sense.] *trans.* To fumigate (wines or liquors, or casks) by burning sulphur matches; now chiefly in *Cider-making.*

Match-board (mæ·tʃbōᵊɹd), *sb.* 1858. [f. MATCH *a.*] *Joinery.* A board which has a tongue cut along one edge and a groove in the opposite edge, so as to admit of being fitted into other similar boards to form one piece with them. Also *collect.* = *match-boarding.*

Hence **Ma·tch-board** *v.* to cover or supply with matchboards. **Ma·tch-boarding,** matchboards fitted together for use.

Matchcoat (mæ·tʃkōᵘt). *Obs.* exc. *Hist.* 1642. [orig. *matchcore*; cf. Ojibwa *manchikōten* woman's skirt; afterwards alt. by popular etymology, as if f. MATCH *sb.*[1] or *v.*[1] + COAT *sb.*] A kind of mantle worn by Amer. Indians, orig. made of fur skins, later of coarse woollen cloth called *match-cloth.*

Matcher (mæ·tʃəɹ). 1611. [f. MATCH *v.*[1] + -ER[1].] **1.** One who matches. **2.** A matching-machine (MATCH *v.*[1] 5 c) 1897.

Matchet (mæ·tʃėt). Also **machet(t)e, †macheto.** 1598. [– Sp. *machete*, f. *macho* hammer :– late L. *marcus.*] A broad and heavy knife or cutlass, used, esp. in Central America and the West Indies, both as a tool and a weapon.

Matchless (mæ·tʃlės), *a.* 1530. [f. MATCH *sb.*[1] + -LESS.] **1.** Without an equal, peerless. **b.** Used as *adv.* 1871. †**2.** That are not a match. SPENSER. Hence **Ma·tchlessly** *adv.*

Matchlock (mæ·tʃlǫk). 1698. [f. MATCH *sb.*[2] + LOCK *sb.*[2]] **1.** An old form of gun-lock in which a match (MATCH *sb.*[2] 2) is placed for igniting the powder. **2.** A musket having a matchlock 1698. **b.** *attrib.* as **matchlock-man** a soldier armed with a matchlock 1782.

Ma·tch-maker[1]. 1639. [f. MATCH *sb.*[1] + MAKER.] **1.** One who brings about a match; one who schemes to bring about marriages. **2.** *Sporting.* One who enters into or arranges a match 1704. So **Ma·tch-making** *vbl. sb.*[1]

Ma·tch-maker[2]. 1643. [f. MATCH *sb.*[2] + MAKER.] One who makes match for guns, or lucifer matches. So **Ma·tch-making** *vbl. sb.*[2]

Mate (mēⁱt), *sb.*[1] [ME. *mat* – (O)Fr. *mat* in *eschec mat* CHECKMATE *sb.*] = CHECKMATE *sb.* 1.

Mate (mēⁱt), *sb.*[2] ME. [– MLG. *mate, gemate* (Flem. *gemaat*, Du. *maat*) = OHG. *gimazzo* :– WGmc. **ʒamato*, f. **ʒa-* Y- (denoting association) + **mat-*, base of MEAT, the lit. sense being 'messmate'. For the sense-development cf. COMPANION *sb.*[1]] **1.** A habitual companion; a fellow-worker or partner. Now only in working-class use. **b.** Used as a form of address by sailors, labourers, etc. 1450. **2.** A suitable associate; an equal. Now only *arch.* 1563. **3.** One of a pair; now *esp.* a suitable partner in marriage 1549. **4.** *Naut.* **a.** An officer (now only on a merchant ship) who sees to the execution of the master's commands, and in his absence takes charge of the ship. Formerly called *master's mate.* 1496. **b.** An assistant to some functionary on board ship, as *boatswain's, cook's, gunner's m.*, etc. 1610. †**c.** In the navy (in full *surgeon's m.*), an assistant to a ship's doctor; in the army, an assistant who acts as dispenser and dresser 1612–1811. **d.** *U.S. Navy.* A subordinate officer having no rank, but taking precedence of all other enlisted men 1890.

2. Ye knew me once no m. For you, there sitting where ye durst not soare MILT. **3.** There shall the vultures also be gathered, euery one with her m. *Isa.* 34:15. **4. b.** The Gunner, and his M. SHAKS.

†**Mate,** *a.* ME. [– (O)Fr. *mat* mated at chess – *māt* in Pers. phr., used in chess, *šāh māt* the king is dead; see CHECKMATE, MATE *sb.*[1]] **1.** Mated at chess –1600. **2.** Overcome, worsted, confounded –1513. **3.** Exhausted, faint –1536. **4.** Downcast, sorrowful –1560.

Mate (mēⁱt), *v.*[1] ME. [– Fr. *mater*, f. *mat* MATE *a.* Cf. med.L. *matare.*] **1.** *trans.* (*Chess.*) To checkmate. Also *absol.* †**2.** *trans.* To overcome, subdue –1590. Also *transf.* †**3.** To nonplus, baffle (a person); to render nugatory (a design) –1670. †**4.** To put out of countenance; to render helpless; to daunt, abash; to stupefy –1827. †**5.** To exhaust, weary; to dull (passion) –1693.

2. *transf.* There is no passion in the minde of man, so weake, but it Mates, and Masters, the Feare of Death BACON. **3.** They mated the Saxons in all their designes SPEED.

Mate (mēⁱt), *v.*[2] 1509. [f. MATE *sb.*[2]] **1.** *trans.* To equal; to vie or cope with; to be a match for. Now *rare.* **b.** *intr.* To claim equality *with* (*arch.*) 1692. **2.** *trans.* To match; to join in marriage; to take or give in marriage 1607. Also *intr.* for *refl.* **3.** *trans.* To pair (animals, esp. birds) for breeding purposes 1601. Also *intr.* **4.** *trans.* To join suitably *with*; to associate, treat as comparable *with* 1593. **5.** *intr.* To keep company *with* 1832.

1. My euer Roiall Master, Dare m. a sounder man then Surrie can be SHAKS. **2.** Thou art mated with a clown TENNYSON. **3.** Pigeons can be mated for life DARWIN. *intr.* These birds do not m. 1877. **4.** On a night, mated to his design DRYDEN.

‖**Maté** (mæ·te). 1717. [Sp. *mate* – Quichua *mati.*] **1.** A gourd, calabash, etc., in which the leaves of maté (see 2) are infused; also *maté-cup.* **2.** An infusion of the leaves of the shrub *Ilex paraguayensis*; Paraguay-tea; also, the shrub itself, and its leaves prepared for infusion 1758. **b.** *attrib.*, as *m. wood*, etc. 1879.

‖**Matelassé** (matəlase). 1882. [Fr., pa. pple. of *matelasser* to quilt, f. *matelas* MATTRESS.] A French dress goods of silk, or silk and wool, having a raised design. Also *attrib.* or *adj.* having a raised pattern like quilting.

Mateless (mēⁱ·tlės), *a.* 1570. [f. MATE *sb.*[2] + -LESS.] Without a mate, or †peer.

‖**Matelote** (matəlot), *sb.* 1730. [Fr., f. *matelot* sailor.] A dish of fish served in a sauce of wine, onions, mushrooms, etc.; also, a dish of viands similarly dressed. Hence **Matelote** *v. trans.* to make into a m.

Mateo-; see MATÆO-.

‖**Mater** (mēⁱ·təɹ). 1594. [L. = MOTHER.] †**1.** The thickest plate of the astrolabe. BLUNDEVIL. **2.** *Anat.* See DURA MATER, PIA MATER. **3.** *Boys'* and *girls' slang.* Used familiarly for *mother.* (Cf. *pater.*) 1864.

‖**Materfamilias** (mēⁱ·təɹfămi·liăs). 1756. [L., f. *mater* + *familias*, old gen. of *familia.*] The mother of a household.

Material (mătīᵊ·riăl). [ME. *materiel* (rare), *-ial* – (O)Fr. *matériel*, †*-ial* – late L. *materialis* (Tertullian; also sb. *-ale*), f. L. *materia* matter; see -AL[1].]

A. *adj.* **1.** *Scholastic Philosophy* and *Theol.* (Opp. to FORMAL.) **a.** Pertaining to matter as opp. to form. †Of number: Concrete. **b.** That is (so and so) merely so far as its 'matter' is concerned 1656. **2.** *Logic.* Concerned with the matter, as dist. from the form, of reasoning. (Opp. to *formal.*) 1628. **3.** Of, pertaining to, or consisting of matter; corporeal ME. **4.** Concerned with or involving matter, its presence, use, or agency 1649. **b.** Usu. coupled with *gross*: Unspiritual 1588. **c.** Relating to the physical aspect of things; concerned with physical progress, bodily comfort, or the like 1843. **5.** Of much consequence; important 1529. **b.** Pertinent, germane, or essential *to* 1603. **c.** *Law*, etc. Of such significance as to be likely to influence the determination of a cause, to alter the character of an instrument, etc. 1581. †**6.** Full of matter, sound information, or sense –1685. †**7.** Bulky, massive, solid –1735.

1. a. *M. cause*: see CAUSE *sb.* 4. **b.** *M. sin*: a wrong action apart from the evil intention necessary to constitute it a sin in the full sense; so *m. heresy, schism*, etc. *M. righteousness*: righteousness as definable by conduct, without regard to its motive. **2.** The m. truth of the Conclusion depends upon the m. truth of the Premises BOWEN. **3.** The m. world BUTLER. **4.** *M. theory* (of heat): the theory that heat is a m. substance ('caloric'). **b.** His gross m. soul DRYDEN. **c.** France..is the country where m. well-being is most widely spread M. ARNOLD. **5.** He would put that which was most Materiall in the Post-script BACON. **c.** A m. witness was wanting 1799. **6.** A materiall foole SHAKS.

B. *sb.* †**1.** *pl.* Things that are material –1605. **2.** The matter from which anything is made. Chiefly *collect. pl.* or *sing.* 1556. **b.** The elements, constituent parts, or substance of something 1642. **3.** Something that can be worked up or elaborated, *esp.* documents, etc. for historical composition; evidence from which a conclusion may be framed 1624. **4.** Tools, apparatus, etc. for performing an action. Now only in *writing materials* (= pen, ink, paper) 1731.

2. Gunpowder..with other materials for kindling fire DE FOE. The raw m. out of which a good army, may be formed MACAULAY. **3.** Their books are m., not literature HOWELLS.

†**Mate·rial,** *v.* 1643. [f. MATERIAL *a.* and *sb.*] **1.** *trans.* To bring into material form. SIR T. BROWNE. **2.** To furnish material for. GLANVILL.

Materialism (mătīᵊ·riăliz'm). 1748. [f. MATERIAL + -ISM, Cf. Fr. *matérialisme.*] **1.** *Philos.* The doctrine that nothing exists except matter and its movements and modifications; also, that the phenomena of consciousness and will are wholly due to the operation of material agencies. **2.** Hence in transf. uses: *esp.* applied to (*a*) theological views supposed to imply a defective sense of the reality of things purely spiritual 1850; (*b*) devotion to material needs or desires; a way of life, opinion, or tendency based entirely upon material interests 1851. ¶**3.** *concr.* The system of material things; the material universe 1817.

2. I fear..you will never rise beyond the grossest everyday m. 1903.

Materialist (mătīᵊ·riălist). 1668. [f. as prec. + -IST. Cf. Fr. *matérialiste.*] **1.** An adherent of the philosophical system known as materialism. **2.** Applied by Berkeley to believers in the objective existence of matter 1705. **3.** One who takes a material view of things 1853. **4.** *attrib.* or *adj.* = MATERIALISTIC.

1. The materialists, who conjoin all thought with extension HUME. *fig.* Those who hold that poetry is an acquirable art,—the materialists of fine literature SOUTHEY. Hence **Mate:riali·stic** *a.* pertaining to, characterized by, or addicted to materialism. **Materiali·stically** *adv.*

Materiality (mătīᵊriæ·lĭti). 1529. [orig. – med.L. *materialitas* material quality or embodiment; in later use (sense 3 and 4) directly f. MATERIAL; see -ITY. Cf. Fr. *matérialité.*] †**1.** That which constitutes the 'matter' of something; opp. to *formality* –1660. **2.** The quality of being material 1570; that which is material; *pl.* things material 1811. **3.** Material aspect or character; mere externality 1599. **4.** The quality of being important for the purpose in hand. Now *legal.* 1644.

2. The decomposition of the rays of light proves their m. G. ADAMS. **4.** Rules which tend to secure the m. of the issue 1824.

Materialize (mătīᵊ·riăləiz), *v.* 1710. [f. MATERIAL *a.* + -IZE.] **1.** *trans.* To make or represent as material; to invest with material attributes. **2.** *Spiritualism.* To cause (a spirit, etc.) to appear in bodily form 1880. **b.** *intr.* To assume a bodily form 1884. **c.** *transf.* To become actual fact; to 'come off' (orig. *U.S.*) 1885. **3.** *trans.* To make materialistic. Also *intr.* to favour materialistic views. 1820.

2. c. Year after year passed and these promises failed to materialise 1891. **3.** The system..tends to m. our upper class, vulgarize our middle class, brutalize our lower class M. ARNOLD. Hence **Materializa·tion,** the giving a material form to; in *Spiritualism,* the appearance of a spirit in bodily form.

Materially (mătīᵊ·riăli), *adv.* 1502. [f. MATERIAL *a.* + -LY².] **1.** Chiefly *Philos.* and *Logic.* With regard to matter as opp. to form. Also, with regard to constituent matter; in respect of material cause. **2.** In, by, with, or in respect of material substance; 'in the state of matter' (J.) 1594. †**3.** Of speaking or writing: Soundly; to the point –1749. **4.** In a material degree; substantially 1654. **5.** In respect of material interests 1871.

1. What is formally correct may be m. false BOWEN. **2.** As he created all Men out of the same matter, they are m. equal 1717. **4.** Short cuts, by ..which the road was m. shortened 1890. So **Mate·rialness.**

‖**Materia medica** (mătīᵊ·riă me·dikă). 1699. [mod.L., tr. Gr. ὕλη ἰατρική (Galen) 'healing material'.] The remedial substances used in medicine; that branch of medical science which treats of these 1811.

fig. What I may call the m. m. of morality TUCKER.

†**Materia·rian,** *a.* and *sb.* [f. late L. *materiarius* (Tertullian, f. *materia* matter) + -AN; see -ARIAN.] Applied to ancient heretics who believed in the eternity of matter. CUDWORTH.

†**Mate·riate,** *a.* 1588. [– schol. L. *materiatus* (also cl. L.; see next), pa. pple. of L. *materiare*; see next, -ATE².] **1.** Composed or consisting of matter; solid, dense –1694. **2.** Involved in matter; said of persons and things 1626–47.

Materiate (mătīᵊ·rieⁱt), *v.* Now *rare* or *Obs.* 1653. [– *materiat-*, pa. ppl. stem of L. *materiare* (in cl. Latin construct of wood, in scholastic use as in sense a below), f. *materia* MATTER *sb.*; see -ATE³.] *trans.* In scholastic use. **a.** To supply or be the matter or material part of; in *pass.*, to be constituted materially *by* something 1680. **b.** To render (a 'form') inherent in a particular 'matter' 1653. So †**Materia·tion** 1646.

‖**Matériel** (materiẹl). 1814. [Fr., subst. use of *matériel* adj. MATERIAL.] **1. a.** The mechanical or material portion of an art; technique. *rare.* **b.** The 'stock-in-trade' for carrying on any business or undertaking. **2.** A collective term for the articles, supplies, machinery, etc. used in an army, navy, or business, as dist. from the *personnel* or body of persons employed 1827.

Maternal (mătɔ̄·ɹnăl), *a.* (*sb.*) 1481. [– (O)Fr. *maternel* or f. L. *maternus*, f. *mater* MOTHER *sb.*; see -AL¹.] **1.** Of or pertaining to a mother or mothers, motherly 1492. **b.** (One's) mother's 1605. **2. a.** That is a mother, or one's mother. Now *rare.* 1513. **b.** Having the instincts of motherhood, motherly 1784. **3.** Inherited or derived from a mother; related through a mother 1656. **4.** Of benevolent organizations: Providing for the requirements of maternity 1856. **5.** *Phys.* Of parts of the placenta: Uterine (opp. to *fœtal*) 1816.

1. Ah! that m. smile! COWPER. **b.** The embrace m., the paternal smack 1894. *M. language*: mother tongue. Now *rare.* **2. b.** M. earth, who doth her sweet smiles shed For all SHELLEY. **3.** Alongside of him stood his m. uncle FREEMAN. Hence **Mate·rnally** *adv.*

Maternalize (mătɔ̄·ɹnăləiz), *v. rare.* 1877. [f. MATERNAL *a.* + -IZE.] *trans.* To make maternal; *absol.* to employ maternal methods.

Maternity (mătɔ̄·ɹnĭti). 1611. [– Fr. *maternité* – med.L. *maternitas*, f. L. *maternus*; see MATERNAL, -ITY.] **1.** The quality or condition of being a mother; motherhood. **b.** Short for *maternity hospital* 1889. **2.** Motherliness 1804. **3.** *attrib.*: **m. hospital,** a hospital for the reception of women during confinement; so *m. nurse, ward,* etc. 1881.

Mateship (mēⁱ·tˌʃip). 1593. [f. MATE *sb.*² + -SHIP.] The condition of being a mate; companionship; †equality.

Matey (mē̆ⁱ·ti), *sb.* 1833. Hypocoristic f. MATE *sb.*² (see -Y⁶).

Ma·tey, *a.* 1915. [f. MATE *sb.*² + -Y¹.] Friendly (*with*); sociable. **Ma·teyness.**

Matfellon (mæ·tfelən). *Obs.* exc. *dial.* late ME. [– OFr. *matefelon*, app. f. *mater* MATE *v.*¹ + *felon* FELON *sb.*²; named from supposed curative properties.] = KNAPWEED.

Math (mɑþ). *Obs.* exc. *dial.* and in AFTERMATH. [OE. *mǣþ*, corresp. to MHG. *māt*, *mād-* (G. *mahd*), f. Gmc. *mæ MOW *v.*¹; see -TH¹.] A mowing; the amount of a crop mowed. (See also LATTERMATH.)

†**Mathe.** [OE. *maþa, maþu*, cogn. w. OS. *matho*, OHG. *mado* (Du., G. *made*), ON. *maðkr* (see MAGGOT), Goth. *maþa* :– Gmc. **maþon*, **maþō*, of obsc. origin.] A maggot, grub, worm –1585.

Mathematic (mæþĭmæ·tik). late ME. [– or f. (O)Fr. *mathématique* or its source L. *mathematicus* – Gr. μαθηματικός, f. μάθημα, μαθηματ- something learned, science, f. *μαθ-, base of μανθάνειν learn; see -IC. As sb. – (O)Fr. *mathématique* – L. *mathematica* (sc. *ars* or *disciplina*) – Gr. μαθηματική (sc. τέχνη or θεωρία), fem. of μαθηματικός. The subst. uses represent different ellipt. or absol. uses of the Gr.-L. adj.] **A.** *adj.* = MATHEMATICAL *a.* Now *rare.* 1549. **B.** *sb.* **1.** = MATHEMATICS. Now *rare.* late ME. †**2.** A mathematician; often, An astrologer –1688.

Mathematical (mæþĭmæ·tikăl). 1522. [f. as prec.; see -ICAL.]

A. *adj.* **1.** Of or pertaining to, relating to, or of the nature of mathematics 1530. **b.** Being what the name imports in mathematics. Chiefly in *m. point.* 1547. **c.** Learned or skilled in, studying or teaching, mathematics 1522. **d.** Used in mathematical operations 1625. **2.** *transf.* Of proofs, certitude, etc.: Resembling what is found in mathematics; rigorously exact 1662. **b.** Constructed with mathematical regularity 1776. †**3.** Astrological –1674. †**4.** GEOMETRICAL –1656.

1. M. Truths LOCKE. **c.** A m. lecturer 1622, student 1839. **d.** *M. instruments*: now usually, the instruments used in drawing geometrical figures. **2.** It will follow with certitude plainly M. HY. MORE. **b.** Straight paths and m. grass-plots 1881. Hence **Mathema·tically** *adv.*

B. *sb.* **1.** *pl.* Mathematical objects (*rare*) 1555. †**2.** *pl.* Mathematics; astrology –1619. †**3.** A mathematician or astrologer –1587.

Mathematician (mæ:þĭmăti·ʃăn). late ME. [– (O)Fr. *mathématicien*, f. L. *mathematicus, mathematica* MATHEMATIC sb. 1 and 2; see -IAN.] One who is versed in mathematics. †**b.** An astrologer. Chiefly *Hist.* –1710.

Mathema·tico-, comb. f. L. *mathematicus*, with sense 'partly mathematical, partly ——'.

Mathematics (mæþĭmæ·tiks), *sb. pl.* 1581. [prob. after Fr. (*les*) *mathématiques* (XVI) – L. n. pl. *mathematica* (Cicero), Gr. τὰ μαθηματικά (Aristotle); see prec., -ICS.] Orig., the collective name for geometry, arithmetic, and certain sciences involving geometrical reasoning, as astronomy and optics. In mod. use, (*a*) the abstract science of quantity, including geometry, arithmetic, algebra, etc. (*pure m.*); (*b*) in a wider sense, those branches of research which consist in the application of this abstract science to concrete data (*applied* or *mixed m.*). Abbrev. **Maths.**

In early use construed as a plural, usu. with *the.* In recent use *the* is commonly dropped, and the sb. construed as a sing., exc. in (*the*) *higher m.*

‖**Mathesis** (măþī·sis). *arch.* late ME. [Late L. – Gr. μάθησις learning, f. base of μανθάνειν learn; cf. prec.] Mental discipline; learning or science, *esp.* mathematical science.

Mad *Mathesis* alone was unconfin'd POPE.

Mathetic (măþe·tik), *a.* 1816. [– Gr. μαθητικός; cogn. w. prec.] Pertaining to learning or scientific knowledge. Also (Bentham) in comb. form **mathetico-.**

Mathurin (mæ·þiurin). Also **Mat(h)urine.** 1611. [From the chapel of St. *Mathurin* at Paris.] A member of the order of regular canons founded (A.D. 1198) by St. John of Matha for the redemption of Christian captives. Also as *adj.*

‖**Matico** (mătī·ko). 1838. [Sp. *yerba Matico* (*yerba* herb; *Matico* dim. of *Mateo* Matthew); said to have been named after a soldier who discovered its styptic properties.] A Peruvian shrub, *Piper angustifolium*; also its leaves.

Matie (mē̆ⁱ·ti). 1858. [– Du. *maatjes* (*haring* herring), earlier *maetgens-, maeghdekins*, f. *maagd* MAID + *-ken* -KIN.] A herring at its best, i.e. when the roe or milt is not fully developed.

Matin (mæ·tin). *Pl.* **matins**; also **mattins.** [Early ME. *matines* – (O)Fr. *matines*, :– eccl.L. *matutinas*, nom. *-inæ* (prob. sc. *vigiliæ* watches); see MATUTINAL.] **I.** In the pl. form. **1.** *Eccl.* **a.** One of the canonical hours of the breviary; properly a midnight office, but occas. recited at daybreak, and followed immediately by lauds. †**b.** Often a term for the whole of the public service preceding the first mass on Sunday –1549. **c.** The order for public morning prayer in the Church of England since the Reformation 1548. **2.** *fig.*, etc. **a.** Chiefly of birds: *To sing* (etc.) *matins*, to sing their morning song (*poet.*) 1530. **b.** A morning duty or performance 1641.

II. †**1.** A morning (*rare*) –1845. **2.** A morning call or song (of birds). *poet.* 1632.

III. *attrib.* and *Comb.* **a.** with *matin*: (*a*) 'pertaining to or used at the time of matins' ME.; (*b*) 'belonging to the early morning, matinal' 1643. **b.** with *matins*: as *matins book, time,* etc..ME.

‖**Mâtin** (matæ̃n). 1774. [Fr.; see MASTIFF.] A large French watch-dog.

Matinal (mæ·tinăl), *a.* Now *rare.* 1803. [– (O)Fr. *matinal*, f. *matin* morning; see MATIN, -AL¹.] Belonging to the morning; early. Also, early-rising, matutinal.

‖**Matinée** (mæ·tineⁱ, Fr. matine). 1880. [Fr. *matinée* morning, what occupies a morning, f. *matin.*] A 'morning' (i.e. afternoon) theatrical or musical performance. *attrib.* as *m. hat.*

Matlo(w (mæ·tlo). *slang.* 1904. [– Fr. *matelot.*] A sailor.

Matrass (mæ·trĕs). 1605. [– Fr. *matras* = Sp. *matraz*, mod.L. *matracium*, of doubtful origin.] A glass vessel with a round or oval body and a long neck, used by chemists for digesting and distilling.

Matriarch (mē̆ⁱ·triăɹk). 1606. [f. L. *mater, matr-*, mother, after PATRIARCH (apprehended as if f. *pater*).] A woman having the status corresponding to that of a patriarch. Now usu. *joc.* Hence **Matria·rchal,** *a.* of or pertaining to a m. or to maternal rule; pertaining to, based on, or of the nature of matriarchy. **Matria·rchate,** a matriarchal community or system.

Matriarchy (mē̆ⁱ·triăɹki). 1885. [f. MATRIARCH, after PATRIARCHY.] That form of social organization in which the mother is the head of the family, and in which descent and relationship are reckoned through mothers.

Matrical (mæ·trikăl, mătrəi·kăl), *a.* 1611. [– late L. *matricalis*, f. *matric-* MATRIX; see -AL¹.] †**1.** Pertaining to the matrix or womb –1651. **2.** Pertaining to the matrix of algæ 1882.

Matrice (mē[i]·tris, mæ·tris). late ME. [– (O)Fr. *matrice* – L. *matrix, -ic-* MATRIX.] †**1.** = MATRIX 1. –1774. †**b.** *transf.* and *fig.* –1698. **2.** *Type-founding.* = MATRIX 4. Now *rare.* 1587. **3.** = MATRIX 3. *rare.* 1855.

Matricidal (mē[i]·trisəi:dal, mæ·tri-), *a.* 1846. [f. MATRICIDE[1] and [2] + -AL[1].] That kills his or her mother.

Matricide[1] (mē[i]·trisəid, mæ·tri-). 1632. [– L. *matricida*; see -CIDE 1.] One who kills his or her mother.

Matricide[2] (mē[i]·trisəid, mæ·tri-). 1594. [– L. *matricidium*; see -CIDE 2.] The action of killing one's mother.

‖**Matricula** (mătri·kiŭlă). 1555. [Late L., dim. of L. *matrix* (see MATRIX); see -CULE.] **1.** A list or register of persons belonging to an order, society, or the like. Also, a certificate of enrolment in this. **2.** *spec.* In the Holy Roman (and the German) Empire: A list of the contingents, in men and money, which the several States were bound to furnish to the empire 1845. *Obs.* exc. *Hist.*

Matricular (mătri·kiŭlăɹ), *a.* 1575. [– med.L. *matricularius* and *-aris*, f. MATRICULA; see -AR[1,2].] **1.** Pertaining to, or of the nature of, a 'matricula' or official register of persons belonging to a university, an association, etc. **b.** (With reference to Germany): Pertaining to the 'matricula' (see prec. 2) 1762. **2.** [as if f. MATRIX; see -ULAR.] Of or belonging to the matrix or womb 1896.

Matriculate (mătri·kiŭlĕt). 1487. [– med. L. *matriculatus*, pa. pple. of *matriculare*; see next, -ATE[1] and [2].] **A.** *ppl. a.* Matriculated. **B.** *sb.* One who has been matriculated 1712.

Matriculate (mătri·kiŭle[i]t), *v.* 1577. [– *matriculat-*, pa. ppl. stem of med.L. *matriculare* enrol, matriculate, f. late L. MATRICULA; see -ATE[3].] †**1.** *trans.* To insert (a name) in a register or official list; usually, to admit or incorporate into a society or body of persons by inserting the name in a register; to enrol (soldiers). †Also *transf.* and *fig.* –1782. †**b.** *occas.* To adopt as a child; to adopt or naturalize (an alien, a foreign custom, book, etc.) –1704. **2.** *spec.* To admit (a student) to a university or college by enrolling his name in the register 1579. **b.** *intr.* To be thus admitted 1851. **3.** *Her.* To record (arms) in an official register 1586.

2. Bentley was matriculated at St. John's College, Cambridge DE QUINCEY. **3.** The Ensigns Armorial..are matriculated in the public registers of the Lyon Office 1809.

Matriculation (mătrikiŭlē[i]·ʃən). 1588. [– med.L. *matriculatio*, f. as prec.; see -ION.] **1.** The action of matriculating (see the vb.). Now chiefly in academic use, formal admission into a university or college. Occas. used for *m. examination.* **2.** *Her.* A registration of armorial bearings 1810.

Matrimonial (mætrimō[u]·niăl), *a.* 1532. [– (O)Fr. *matrimonial* or L. *matrimonialis*, f. *matrimonium*; see next, -AL[1].] **1.** Of or pertaining to matrimony. **2.** Derived from marriage 1577. **3.** Calculated to promote matrimony 1730.

1. He lugged about the m. load 1675. **3.** M. charms FIELDING. Hence **Matrimo·nially** *adv.* according to the manner or laws of matrimony; by right of marriage. So †**Matrimo·nious** *a.* pertaining to marriage MILT.; **-ly** *adv.*

Matrimony (mæ·trimŏni). ME. [– AFr. *matrimonie* = OFr. *matremoi(g)ne* (whence ME. *matermoi(g)ne*) – L. *matrimonium*, f. *mater, matr-* MOTHER; see -MONY.] **1.** The rite of marriage; the action of marrying. †**b.** A marriage; an alliance by marriage –1756. †**c.** The marriage service –1724. **2.** The state or condition of being husband and wife ME. **3.** A game played with a full pack of cards and resembling Pope Joan. Also, the combination of king and queen of trumps in this and other card games 1801. **4.** *slang* and *dial.* A mixture of two comestibles or beverages 1813.

1. Teaching that M. is a Sacrament, giveth to the Clergy the Judging of the lawfulnesse of Marriages HOBBES. *Comb.* **m. vine**, a name for *Lycium barbarum* or *L. vulgare.*

Matrix (mē[i]·triks). *Pl.* **matrixes, matrices** (mē[i]·-, mæ·trisīz). 1526. [– L. *matrix, -ic-* female used for breeding, parent stem, (later) womb, register, roll, f. *mater, matr-* MOTHER, with ending of fem. agent-nouns.] **1.** The uterus or womb. Also occas. used for OVARY. **2.** A place or medium in which something is bred, produced, or developed 1555. **b.** A place or point of origin and growth 1605. **c.** The formative part of an animal organ, e.g. the pulp and capsule of the mammalian tooth 1835. **d.** *Bot.* The body on which a fungus or a lichen grows 1857. **3.** An embedding or enclosing mass; *esp.* the rock-mass surrounding metal (see GANGUE), fossils, gems, and the like 1641. **b.** *Biol.* The substance situated between animal or vegetable cells 1802. **4.** *Type-founding.* A piece of metal, usu. copper, by means of which the face of a type is cast, having the letter stamped on it in intaglio with a punch. Also in stereotyping, the mould of plaster, etc. into which stereotypers' metal is cast. 1626. **b.** *Antiq.* The bed in a slab in which a monumental brass is fixed 1861. **5.** *Math.* A rectangular arrangement of quantities or symbols 1858. **6.** *attrib.* 1598.

1. Every man chylde that fyrst openeth the m. shalbe called holy to the lorde TINDALE *Luke* 2:23.

Matron (mē[i]·trən). late ME. [– (O)Fr. *matrone* – L. *matrona*, f. *mater, matr-* mother.] **1.** A married woman, usually with the accessory idea of rank or dignity. **b.** *Eccl.* A married female saint 1519. **2.** *spec.* A married woman considered as having expert knowledge in matters of pregnancy, etc.; now only in *jury of matrons* 1491. **3.** A (married or unmarried) woman who has official charge of the domestic arrangements of a hospital, school, prison, etc. 1557. **4.** *attrib.* quasi-*adj.* 1667.

1. When Adam and first M. Eve Had ended now their Orisons MILT. **3.** The m. of the Chartreux is about to resign her place JOHNSON. **4.** M. airs 1836. Hence **Ma·tronal** *a.* of, pertaining to, or appropriate to a m.; having the characteristics of a m. 1609. **Ma·tronhood**, the state or condition of being a m. 1836. **Ma·tronly** *a.* like a m.; suitable to a m. 1656. Also as *adv.*

Matronage (mē[i]·trŏnėdʒ). 1771. [f. prec. + -AGE.] **1.** A body of matrons; matrons collectively. **2.** Guardianship by a matron 1771. **3.** The state of being a matron 1870.

1. His exemplary Queen, at the head of the m. of this land BURKE. **2.** Under the m. of the housekeeper 1878.

Matronize (mē[i]·trŏnəiz), *v.* 1754. [f. MATRON + -IZE.] **1.** *trans.* To render matronly. **2.** *intr.* To become or be made a matron 1802. **3.** *trans.* To act as matron to; to chaperon 1807.

Ma·tron-like, *a.* 1575. [See -LIKE.] Like or befitting a matron; matronly.

Matronship (mē[i]·trənʃip). 1550. [See -SHIP.] **1.** The condition of being a matron. **2.** The personality of a matron. In *your, her m.*, used joc. as a title 1591. **2.** The office of matron in a hospital, workhouse, etc. 1843.

Matronymic (mætrŏni·mik), *a.* and *sb.* 1794. [f. L. *mater, matr-* mother, after PATRONYMIC.] = METRONYMIC *a.* and *sb.*

Matross (mătrǫ·s). *Obs.* exc. *Hist.* 1639. [– Du. *matroos* sailor – Fr. pl. of *matelot* sailor.] A soldier next in rank below the gunner in a train of artillery, who acted as a kind of assistant or mate.

Matt, freq. var. of MAT *a.*

‖**Mattamore** (mætămō[ə]·ɹ). 1695. [– Fr. *matamore* – Arab. *maṭmūra*, f. *ṭamara* put underground, bury.] A subterranean habitation, storehouse, or granary.

Matte (mæt). 1839. [– Fr. *matte.*] *Metallurgy.* An impure and unfinished metallic product of the smelting of various ores, esp. those of copper.

Matted (mæ·tėd), *ppl. a.*[1] 1823. [f. MAT *v.*[2]] Dulled, deprived of lustre or gloss.

Matted (mæ·tėd), *ppl. a.*[2] 1607. [f. MAT *v.*[1] + -ED[1].] **1.** Laid or spread with matting or mats. **b.** Made of plaited rushes; of chairs, etc., rush-bottomed 1692. **2.** Of vegetable growths, hair, etc.: Tangled and interlaced, or covered with tangle 1613. **b.** Compressed into the likeness of a mat 1825. **c.** Covered with a dense growth 1791. **3.** Enclosed or wrapt in matting. Also with *up.* 1758.

1. A m. passage 1883. **b.** The ordinary m. chairs DE FOE. **2.** The m. underwood and the rank green grass W. BLACK. **c.** The m. sward BRYANT.

Matter (mæ·təɹ), *sb.* [ME. *materie, mat(i)ere* – AFr. *materie, matere*, (O)Fr. *matière* – L. *materia* (also *-ies*) timber, stuff of which a thing is made, subject of discourse, matter.]

I. In purely physical applications. **1.** The substance, or substances, of which a physical object is made; constituent material. Now only with implication of sense 2 or 4. **2.** Any physical substance not definitely particularized. Often qualified, as in *colouring, fæcal*, etc. *m.* late ME. **3.** *spec.* (= *corrupt m.*) Purulent discharge, pus. late ME. **4.** Physical or corporeal substance in general, as dist. from spirit, soul, mind, etc., and from qualities, actions, or conditions 1626.

1. The m. of the Heavens NEWTON, of the globe MILL. **2.** Milk..deficient in fatty m. 1891. *Grey m., white m.* (of the brain): see the adjs. **4.** M. and Motion cannot think BENTLEY. †*Subtile m.* [tr. L. *materia subtilis*]: Descartes' name for a fluid which he supposed to fill the whole of space.

II. Contrasted with *form.* **1.** *Philos.* In Aristotelian and scholastic use: That component of the essence of any thing or being which has bare existence, but which requires the addition of a particular 'form' (see FORM *sb.* 4 a) to constitute it as determinately existent. late ME. †**b.** = Chaos. BACON. **c.** In Kantian use, applied to that element of knowledge that is supplied by sensation, regarded apart from the 'form' which it receives from the categories of the understanding 1838. **2.** *Theol.* A sacrament is said to have *matter* (as the water in baptism, the bread and wine in the Eucharist) and *form*, which is furnished by certain formulary words ME. **3.** *Logic.* The particular content of a proposition or syllogism, as dist. from its form 1697.

1. Matere is neuer seen wythout fourme TREVISA. *First m.* (= L. *materia prima*, Gr. ἡ πρώτη ὕλη): mere possibility of being. **b.** First he breathed Light vpon the Face of M. or Chaos BACON.

III. Material of thought, speech, or action. **1.** Material for expression; something to say or write ME. †**2.** A theme, topic, subject of exposition –1704. **3.** The substance of a book, speech, or the like; often opp. to the 'manner' in which it is presented. late ME. †**b.** Sense, substance. SHAKS. **4.** That with which a science, art, law, etc. has to do; the subject-matter of a study –1594. **5.** Ground, reason, or cause for doing or being something ME. †**6.** Material cause; that of which something consists or out of which it is developed –1825. **7.** In vague sense, = 'things', 'something'; esp. with qualifying words, things or something of a specified kind, involving or related to a specified thing 1449. **b.** *spec.* in *Law.* Something which is to be tried or proved; statements which come under the consideration of the court 1532. **8. a.** Things printed or written, as *manuscript*, etc. *m.* In *Printing* applied *techn.* to (*a*) the body of a printed work, as dist. from the headings, etc.; in newspapers, the general contents as dist. from the advertisements; (*b*) type set up; (*c*) 'copy'. 1683. **b.** (*Postal*) *m.*: whatever may be sent by post 1891.

1. For I am full of m., the spirit within me constraineth me *Job* 32:18. **2.** Thee, O Queene! the m. of my song SPENSER. **3.** Was euer booke containing such vile m. So fairely bound? SHAKS. **b.** I was borne to speake all mirth, and no m. SHAKS. †*There is m. in it*: it is important. **5.** Phr. †*To seek m.*: to seek a pretext or occasion. **7.** This is rather m. of fact then of Law 1651. **b.** *M. of record*, that which may be proved by some record. *Nude m.*, a naked allegation of a thing done, to be proved only by witnesses.

Phr. *It makes* (later *is*) *no m.* = It is of no consequence; now often shortened to *No m.*, also *What m.?*

IV. A thing, affair, concern; corresp. to L. *res.* **1.** A subject, affair, business ME. **b.** (One's) cause, concern, or affair. *Obs.* or *rare.* ME. **c.** *pl.* Events, affairs, circumstances, etc., understood to refer to a particular occasion, but not further specified 1570. †**d.** *pl.* Occas. used vaguely of concrete things –1826. **2.** *contextually.* A subject of contention, dispute, litigation, or the like. late ME. **3.** With qualification (attribute, or *of* and sb.): A thing, affair, subject, etc. of the kind indicated by the qualification. late

ME. **4.** Used as an indeterminate sb. to which to attach an epithet. late ME. †**5.** With qualifying adj., usu. *small*: A (certain) quantity or amount (*of*) –1772.

1. They order, said I, this m. better in France STERNE. **b.** Manage your matters well T. HOOK. **c.** This seems to be carrying matters too far BLACKSTONE. **d.** She [the landlady]..left the stranger to enjoy in quiet the excellent matters which she had placed before him SCOTT. **3.** *Laughing, money m.*, see the first element. See also MATTER OF COURSE, MATTER OF FACT. *A m. of*: a 'case' of. **4.** Instinct is a great m. SHAKS. Phr. *It is no such m., another m. For that m.*: = 'for the m. of that'. **5.** I..sent a small m. to his wife FIELDING. Phr. *A small m.*, occas. *a m.*, used advb. = Somewhat, slightly.

Phr. *A m. of*: used to qualify a numeral, indicating that it is not literally exact; He had had, as he phrased it, a m. of four wives JOHNSON.

Phr. **The matter:** †**a.** That which is contemplated, intended, or desired. *To the m.*: to the point, relevant(ly); = L. *ad rem.* So *From the m. Much about the m.*: not far from the point. **b.** What actually involves or concerns some person or thing, esp. a circumstance which calls for remedy or explanation; chiefly in *What is the m.?* and the like. *What is the m. with..?* (colloq.) = What is amiss with..? hence (*joc.*) What is the objection to..? **c.** *In the m. of* (= law L. *in re*): in relation to, with regard to; chiefly in *Law.* **d.** *For the m. of that*: as far as that goes.

Matter (mæ·təɹ), *v.* 1530. [f. prec. sb.] **1.** *intr.* To discharge matter or pus; to suppurate. **2.** To be of importance; to signify; chiefly in interrog. and neg. sentences. (Freq. *impersonal.*) Const. *to*; also (*poet. rare*) with *dat.* 1581. **3.** With a neg.: To be concerned about, care for, heed, mind. *Obs.* exc. *dial.* in sense: To approve of, like. 1649. †**b.** *absol.* or *intr.* To care, mind –1729.

2. Nor does it matter a straw whether [etc.] LANDOR. **3.** If it had been out of doors I had not mattered it so much FIELDING.

Matterless (mæ·təɹlės), *a.* 1548. [-LESS.] **1.** Not embodied in matter; immaterial. Now *rare.* †**2.** Devoid of matter, sense, or meaning –1767. **3.** Immaterial, of no importance. Chiefly *dial.* 1650.

1. M. forms H. COLERIDGE. **2.** M. words 1612.

Matter of course. 1739. Something which is to be expected in the natural course of things. **b.** *attrib.* or as *adj.* (written with hyphens): To be expected. Freq. of persons, etc.: Taking things as a matter of course. 1840.

b. The cool matter-of-course manner of this reply DICKENS.

Matter of fact (mæ·təɹəvfæ·kt). 1581. [See MATTER III. 7, IV. 3 and FACT 5.]

A. *sb.* **a.** *Law.* That portion of a subject of enquiry which is concerned with the truth or falsehood of alleged facts; a particular issue of this nature; opp. to *matter of law.* **b.** What pertains to the sphere of fact as opp. to opinion, probability, or inference; something which is of the nature of a fact.

It is either a beleefe of Historie (as the Lawyers speeke, matter of fact:) or else of matter of art and opinion BACON. Phr. *As a m. of fact, in m. of fact*: in point of fact, really.

B. *attrib.* or *adj.* (Usu. hyphened.) Pertaining to, having regard to, or depending upon actual fact; unimaginative, prosaic 1712.

The more Callicles is irritated, the more provoking and matter of fact does Socrates become JOWETT.

Mattery (mæ·təri), *a.* late ME. [f. MATTER *sb.* + -Y[1].] **1.** Full of, forming, or discharging matter; purulent. Now *rare.* †**2.** Full of matter or sense. B. JONS.

Mattins, variant of MATINS.

Matting (mæ·tiŋ), *vbl. sb.*[1] 1682. [f. MAT *v.*[1] and *sb.*[1] + -ING[1].] **1.** In various senses of MAT *v.*[1] **2.** *concr.* A fabric of some coarse material, e.g. coir, bast, hemp, grass, etc., used as a covering for floors or roofs, or as material for packing, for tying plants, etc. Also *Naut.* = MAT *sb.*[1] 4. 1748. **b.** Materials for mats 1847. **3.** *attrib.* 1688.

Matting (mæ·tiŋ), *vbl. sb.*[2] 1688. [f. MAT *v.*[2] + -ING[1].] **1.** The production of a mat surface, in *Chasing, Gilding*, etc. Also, the mat surface itself. **2.** The furnishing (of a picture) with a mat; *concr.* = MAT *sb.*[2] 3. 1864. **3.** *Comb.*, as *m.-punch, -tool* 1877.

Mattock (mæ·tək), *sb.* [OE. *mattuc*, of unkn. origin. The ending appears to be the suffix -OCK.] An agricultural tool used for loosening hard ground, grubbing up trees, etc. It has a socketed steel head, having on one side an adze-shaped blade, and sometimes on the other a kind of pick.

attrib. Born To labour and the mattock-harden'd hand TENNYSON. Hence **Ma·ttock** *v.* to turn *up* with the m.

Mattress (mæ·trės). [ME. *materas* – OFr. *materas* (mod. *matelas*), cogn. with or – It. *materasso*, parallel with OCat. *almatrach*, Sp., Pg. *almadraque* – Arab. *al-maṭraḥ* (AL-[2]) locality, carpet, cushion, seat, bed, f. *ṭaraḥa* throw.] **1.** A case of canvas or other coarse material, stuffed with hair, flocks, straw, or the like, used as a bed or (more commonly) as a support for a bed. Also, any similar appliance, esp. one consisting of wire cloth stretched upon a frame. †**2.** = MAT *sb.*[1] 1. –1706. **3.** *Engineering.* A strong mat of brushwood bound or twisted together, used in layers in the construction of dikes, piers, etc. 1875.

†**Maturant,** *a.* and *sb.* 1661. [– *maturant-*, pr. ppl. stem of L. *maturare*; see next, -ANT.] = MATURATIVE *a.* and *sb.* –1856.

Maturate (mæ·tiureɪt), *v.* 1541. [– *maturat-*, pa. ppl. stem of L. *maturare*, f. *maturus*; see MATURE *a.*, -ATE[3].] **1.** *trans.* (*Med.*) To cause (matter, a boil, etc.) to ripen or suppurate; to 'bring to a head'. Also *absol.* to cause suppuration. Now *rare* or *Obs.* †**2.** To mature, ripen (fruits, liquors, etc.). Also *fig.* –1756. †**3.** To mature, develop (men, hopes, etc.) –1791. †**4. a.** *Alchemy.* To purify and digest (a metal) by maturation; also with *into.* **b.** *Metall.* To bring (an ore) into the metallic state. –1758. †**5.** *intr.* Of fruit: To mature –1756. **6.** Of a pustule: To suppurate 1746.

3. Yeares must m. men to such Functions 1622.

Maturation (mætiurēɪ·ʃən). late ME. [– (O)Fr. *maturation* or med.L. *maturatio*, f. as prec.; see -ION.] **1.** *Med.* The ripening of morbific matter; suppuration; the action of causing this. †**2.** *Alchemy.* The action of converting a baser metal into gold –1671. †**3.** *Physics.* The (supposed) natural ripening or development of material substances by the operation of heat and motion –1753. **4.** Of fruits, juices, etc.: Development to ripeness; also, an instance of this 1621. **b.** Of liquors, etc.: The action of maturing; the process of becoming matured 1605. **5.** The action of coming to full growth and development 1616. **b.** *transf.* and *fig.* (of a plan, work, etc.) 1655. †**6.** The forwarding (of a business, etc.) –1655.

5. b. The germination and m. of some truth J. H. NEWMAN.

Maturative (mătiūə·rătiv). late ME. [– med.L. *maturativus*, f. as prec.; see -IVE. Cf. (O)Fr. *maturatif, -ive*, which may be partly the source.] **A.** *adj.* **1.** *Med.* That causes MATURATION (sense 1); pertaining to or characterized by maturation. †**2.** Having the power or function of maturing (fruits, etc.); of or pertaining to maturation –1685.

1. The m. or suppurative stage [of small-pox] 1858.

B. *sb.* A maturative remedy. late ME.

Mature (mătiūə·ɹ), *a.* 1454. [– L. *maturus* timely, early, f. **matu-* as in MATUTINE, rel. to *mane* early, in the morning.] **1.** Complete in natural development or growth; ripe; full grown; †ready *for* 1599. **2.** Of a person: Fully developed in body and mind. Of qualities, etc.: Fully developed. 1600. **b.** Of or pertaining to maturity or manhood. *Wint. T.* I. i. 27. **3.** (The earliest use.) Of thought or deliberation: Duly prolonged and careful. Of plans, etc.: Formed after due deliberation. 1454. †**4.** Prompt –1672. †**5.** Of an event: Occurring when the time is ripe. Of time: Due. (The opposite of 'premature'.) –1667. **6.** *Med.* In a state of suppuration; ripe 1828.

1. *fig.* For now is love m. in ear TENNYSON. **2.** The yongest Sonne of Priam;..Not yet m., yet matchlesse SHAKS. M. In wisdom COWPER. **3.** Till his plans for revolt were m. 1839. No time for m. and careful reflection 1848. **5.** *Lear* IV. vi. 282.

Hence **Matu·re-ly** *adv.*, **-ness.**

Mature (mătiūə·ɹ), *v.* late ME. [– L. *maturare*, f. *maturus*; see prec. Cf. obs. Fr. *maturer.*] **1.** *trans.* (*Med.*) = MATURATE *v.* 1. **2.** To bring to maturity; to ripen; to bring to full growth. Also *pass.* = 6. 1626. **3.** *transf.* To cause to develop fully; to perfect the development of (a person) mentally and physically 1660. **4.** *fig.* To make ripe or ready; to perfect (a plan, etc.); to bring to a head 1667. †**5.** To forward duly. MARVELL. **6.** *intr.* To come to maturity or perfect development; to grow ripe 1626. Also *transf.* and *fig.* **7.** *Comm.* Of a bill, sum of money, etc.: To become due 1861.

3. His prudence was matured by experience GIBBON. **4.** But these thoughts Full Counsel must m. MILT. **7.** In March as much as 980,000*l.* will m. 1892.

Maturity (mătiūə·rĭti). late ME. [– L. *maturitas*, f. *maturus*; see MATURE *a.*, -ITY. Cf. Fr. *maturité.*] †**1.** Deliberateness of action; mature consideration –1734. †**2.** Due promptness –1670. **3.** The state of being mature; fullness or perfection of development or growth. late ME. **4.** Of immaterial things: The state of being complete, perfect, or ready 1625. **5.** *Comm.* The state of becoming due for payment; the time at which a bill becomes due; also, the bill itself 1815. **6.** The state of an abscess in which the pus is fully formed 1676.

3. Thy full maturitie Of yeares and wisdome DANIEL. A single spreading oak, grown to m. HOGARTH. **4.** Measures..brought to m. 1844. **5.** The period of the date of m. of bills at or after sight 1860. Short-dated maturities 1923.

Matutinal (mætiutəi·năl, mătiū·tinăl), *a.* 1656. [– late L. *matutinalis*, f. L. *matutinus*; see next, -AL[1].] Of or pertaining to the morning, early. Also *rarely*, rising early.

Matutine (mæ·tiutəin), *a.* (and *sb.*) 1445. [– L. *matutinus*, f. *Matuta* goddess of the dawn, rel. to *maturus* MATURE *a.*; see -INE[1].] **1.** Of or pertaining to the morning; occurring in the morning. **b.** Of a star; *spec.* in *Astron.* and *Astrol.*: That rises or is above the horizon before sunrise 1500. †**2.** *sb. pl.* Matins. FULLER. Hence **Ma·tutinely** *adv.* in the morning.

Maty (mēɪ·ti), **mate** (mēɪ·t). *Anglo-Ind.* 1810. [Of unkn. origin.] A native servant, *esp.* an assistant or under-servant.

Maucauco, obs. f. MACACO[2].

Maud (mǭd). 1787. [Of unkn. origin. Cf. Sc. *maldy* (XVI), 'a coarse woollen cloth of grey or mixed colour' (Jamieson).] A grey striped plaid worn by shepherds in the South of Scotland; also a travelling wrap resembling a maud.

Maudle (mǭ·d'l), *v. rare.* 1706. [Back-formation f. MAUDLIN *a.*, taken as pr. pple.] **a.** *trans.* To make maudlin. **b.** *intr.* To talk maudlinly.

Maudlin (mǭ·dlin), *sb.* [ME. *Maudeleyn, Maudelen* (XIV) – (O)Fr. *Madeleine* – eccl. L. *Magdalena* MAGDALEN(E.] †**1.** As proper name: = MAGDALEN 1. –1573. †**b.** *transf.* A penitent resembling Mary Magdalen –1631. **2.** †**a.** = COSTMARY. **b.** The herb *Achillea ageratum.* (Also *sweet m.*) 1460. †**3.** A kind of peach (= MAGDALEN 4); also a kind of pear –1707. **4.** [From the adj.] What is maudlin; weak or mawkish sentiment 1838.

Comb.: †**m. daisy,** the ox-eye daisy: **-wort** (*dial.*) = *m. daisy.*

Maudlin (mǭ·dlin), *a.* 1607. [f. prec. used attrib., in allusion to pictures of the Magdalen weeping.] **1.** Weeping, lachrymose. *Obs.* or *arch.* **2.** Mawkishly emotional; tearfully sentimental 1631. **3.** (First in *maudlin-drunk.*) Used of that stage of drunkenness which is tearful and effusively affectionate 1616.

1. Heraclitus the M. Philosopher BUTLER. **2.** A thousand m. oaths of friendship T. BROWN. **3.** His potations had rendered him somewhat m. 1860.

Comb. **m.-drunk,** in the m. stage of intoxication. Hence **Mau·dlinism,** the state of being maudlin-drunk. **Mau·dlinly** *adv.* in a m. manner.

Maugrabee (mǭ·grăbī). 1704. [– Arab. *maġribīy*, f. *al-maġrib* North West Africa.] An African Moor. So **Mau·grabin,** in same sense. Also *attrib.*

Maugre (mǭ·gəɹ), *sb.* and *prep.* ME. [– (O)Fr. *maugré* (mod. *malgré* prep.), i.e. *mal* bad, evil :– L. *malum* (see MAL-), *gré* pleasure :– L. *gratum*, subst. use of n. of *gratus* pleasing.] †**A.** *sb.* **1.** Ill-will, spite –1542. **2.** The state of being regarded with ill-will. Also, an instance of this. –1560.

Phr. *In* (*the*) *m. of*: in spite of, notwithstanding.

B. *adv.* and *prep.* In spite of, notwithstanding; notwithstanding the power of ME. ¶Used by Spenser for: A curse upon..!

Phr. *M.* (a person's) *teeth, head*: in spite of (his) resistance, notwithstanding all (he) can do.

†**Mau·gre**, *v.* 1597. [– Fr. *maugréer*, f. *maugré* MAUGRE *sb.*] *trans.* To show ill-will to; to defy –1632.

Maukin, var. of MALKIN.

Maul, mall (mǭl), *sb.*[1] [ME. *meall, mal(e* – (O)Fr. *mail* :– L. *malleus* hammer. Cf. MALL[1], MALLET *sb.*[1]] **1.** = MACE[1] 1. Also, a wooden club. *Obs.* exc. *arch.* and *Hist.* **2.** In early use, a massive hammer of any kind. Now, applied to special kinds of heavy hammers or beetles, commonly of wood, used (e.g.) in pile-driving, shipbuilding, etc. late ME. †Also *transf.* and *fig.* after L. *malleus* –1752. †**3.** [f. MAUL *v.*] A heavy blow. BUTLER. †**4.** *Rugby Football.* A mauling or tackling 1867.

Maul (mǭl), *sb.*[2] *dial.* late ME. Var. of MALLOW. (Cf. MAW *sb.*[2])

Maul (mǭl), *v.* ME. [f. MAUL *sb.*[1]] †**1.** *trans.* To beat or strike (with or as with a hammer); to hammer, batter –1633. **b.** *U.S.* To split (rails) with a maul and wedge 1686. †**2.** To strike (a person or animal) with a heavy weapon ME. **3.** To beat and bruise; to maltreat; to knock about 1610. **4.** *transf.* To damage seriously; to shatter, mangle 1692. **5.** *fig.* To injure by criticizing, 'pull to pieces' 1593. **6.** To handle roughly or carelessly 1781. †**7.** *Rugby Football. trans.* To hold (the player holding the ball) and endeavour to wrest it from him 1856.

3. It was proposed..that we should..m. the watch SMOLLETT. **4.** Her larboard side is most terribly mauled 1758. **5.** To vex and m. a ministerial race CRABBE. **6.** He is a man that mauls every truth of God 1847.

Maulstick (mǭ·lstik). Also **mahlstick,** etc. 1658. [– Du. *maalstok*, f. *malen* to paint + *stok* stick.] A light stick with a soft leather ball at the upper end, held by painters in the left hand as a support for the right.

Maumet (mǭ·mėt). *Obs.* exc. *arch.* and *dial.* Also **mammet,** etc. ME. [– OFr. *mahomet* idol; a use of *Mahomet* MAHOMET, due to the mediæval notion that Mohammed was worshipped as a god.] †**1.** A false god; an idol –1647. **2.** A doll, puppet; also, a 'guy'. Now only *dial.* 1494. †Also *fig.* **3.** Applied to a person as a term of abuse. Now *dial.* 1529. †**4.** A kind of pigeon –1835.

2. This is no world To play with Mammets SHAKS. **3.** A whining mammet SHAKS.

Maumetry (mǭ·mėtri). *Obs.* exc. *arch.* Also †**mammitrie,** etc. ME. [f. prec. + -RY.] **1.** The worship of images; idolatry. Also, heathenism. †**2.** Idols collectively –1567. **3.** Islam. late ME.

Maun (mǫn, mǭn), *v.* (*pres. ind.*) *Sc.* late ME. [– ON. *man*, pr. t. of *munu*; see MUN *v.*] Must; = MUN *v.*

Maunche: see MANCHE, MUNCH.

Maund (mǭnd), *sb.*[1] Now *local.* 1459. [– (O)Fr. *mande* – MLG., MDu. *mande* (Du. *mand*) = OE. *mand*, of the survival of which there is no evidence; ult. origin unknown.] **1.** A wicker or other woven basket having a handle or handles. **b.** The contents of a maund 1869. **2.** A measure of capacity varying locally 1545.

‖**Maund** (mǭnd), *sb.*[2] 1584. [Earliest *mana, mao* (XVI) from Pg. – Hindi (Pers.) *man*, perh. ult. – Accadian *manû*, whence also Gr. *μνᾶ*, L. *mina.*] A denomination of weight current in India and Western Asia, varying greatly in value locally. The standard maund of the Indian empire is now = 100 lbs. troy, or 82$\frac{2}{7}$ lbs. avoirdupois.

†**Maund,** *v. Cant.* 1567. [perh. – (O)Fr. *mendier* beg :– L. *mendicare*; see MENDICANT.] To beg –1823.

†**Mau·nder,** *sb.*[1] *Cant.* 1609. [f. prec. + -ER[1].] A beggar –1829. So as vb. = prec. 1611.

Maunder (mǭ·ndəɹ), *sb.*[2] 1880. [f. MAUNDER *v.*] Idle incoherent talk or writing.

Maunder (mǭ·ndəɹ), *v.* 1621. [perh. a use of †*maunder* (see MAUNDER *sb.*[1]), frequent. of MAUND *v.*; see -ER[5].] †**1.** *intr.* 'To grumble, mutter, or growl' –1848. **2.** To move or act in a dreamy, idle, or inconsequent manner 1746. **3.** To ramble or wander in one's talk. Also *trans.* To utter (something) in this manner 1831.

3. Mumbling and maundering the merest commonplaces CARLYLE. Hence **Mau·nderer,** a twaddler.

Maundy (mǭ·ndi). ME. [– OFr. *mandé*, – L. *mandatum* commandment, MANDATE *sb.* See John 13:34 ('Mandatum novum do vobis', the first words of the first antiphon at the ceremony of the pedilavium).] **1.** The ceremony of washing the feet of the poor, performed by royal or other eminent persons on the Thursday before Easter, and commonly followed by the distribution of clothing, food, or money. In England, surviving in the distribution of 'maundy money'. **b.** The dole made at the ceremony 1850. †**c.** *fig.* Almsgiving, largesse –1647. †**2.** The Last Supper –1640. †**3.** A feast. *To make one's m.*: to feast. –1646.

attrib. and *Comb.*, as *m. ale, bread, cup,* things distributed at a m., or *m. man, people, woman,* people receiving them; also, **m. money,** silver money distributed by the royal almoner to poor people on Maundy Thursday at Whitehall; so *m. coin*; **m.-supper** = sense 2; **M.-week,** Holy Week.

Maundy Thursday. 1530. [See prec.] The Thursday next before Easter.

Mauquahog, obs. f. MOHAWK.

Mauresque, var. of MORESQUE.

Maurist (mǭ·rist). 1800. [f. (St.) *Maur* + -IST.] A French Benedictine monk belonging to the congregation of St. Maur, founded in 1618.

Mauser (mau·zəɹ). 1880. [f. the inventor's name.] (More fully *M. rifle.*) A repeating rifle having an interlocking bolt-head and box magazine.

Mausolean (mǭsǒlī·ăn), *a.* 1557. [f. next + -AN.] †**1.** *M. sepulchre, tomb* = MAUSOLEUM. Also *transf.* and *fig.* **2.** Pertaining to, or resembling, mausoleums 1785.

Mausoleum (mǭsǒlī·ǒm). *Pl.* **-lea** (-lī·ă), **-leums.** 1546. [– L. *mausoleum* – Gr. *μαυσωλεῖον*, f. *Μαύσωλος* Mausolus.] **1.** The magnificent tomb of Mausolus, King of Caria, erected in the middle of the 4th c. B.C. at Halicarnassus by his queen Artemisia. **2.** A stately burial-place erected for or by a person of distinction 1600. ¶**b.** *loosely.* A stately tomb 1688. †**3.** = CATAFALQUE 1. –1752.

2. *fig.* The dead, Whose names are mausoleums of the Muse BYRON.

Mauther (mǭ·ðəɹ). *dial.* 1440. [Of unkn. origin.] A young girl; *locally*, a 'great awkward girl'.

‖**Mauvaise honte** (movęz oṅt). 1721. [Fr. lit. = 'ill shame'.] False shame; painful diffidence.

‖**Mauvais sujet** (movę süʒę). 1847. [Fr., = 'bad subject'.] A worthless fellow, a 'bad lot'.

Mauve (mōᵘv). 1859. [– Fr. *mauve* mallow, mauve :– L. *malva* MALLOW.] *sb.* A bright but delicate purple dye obtained from coal-tar aniline; the colour of this. *adj.* Of the colour of mauve.

Mauveine (mōᵘ·vin). 1863. [Fr. *mauve* mallow + -INE[5].] *Chem.* The base of the purple aniline dyes.

Maverick (mæ·vərik). 1872. [f. name of Samuel A. *Maverick* (1803–1870), a Texas cattle-owner who left the calves of his herd unbranded.] **1.** *U.S.* In the cattle-breeding districts, a calf or yearling found without an owner's brand. **2.** *transf.* A masterless person; one who is roving and casual 1892.

Mavis (mēⁱ·vis). Now *poet.* and *dial.* late ME. [– (O)Fr. *mauvis*, obscurely rel. to MBret. *milhuit* (mod. *milfid*) thrush, (O)Corn. *melhuet* lark.] The song-thrush, *Turdus musicus.*

‖**Mavourneen** (măvū·rnīn). Also **-in.** 1800. [– Ir. *mo mhuirnín* (*mo* my, *muirnín*, dim. of *muirn* affection, love; see -EEN[2]).] My darling.

Maw[1] (mǭ). [OE. *maga*, corresp. to OFris. *maga*, MDu. *maghe* (Du. *maag*), OHG. *mago* (G. *magen*), ON. *magi* :– Gmc. **maȝon, -ōn.*] **1.** The stomach; the cavity of the stomach. Now only (exc. *joc.*) the stomach of animals; *spec.* the last of the four stomachs of a ruminant. Also *transf.* and *fig.* **2.** Applied also to: †**a.** The crop of a granivorous bird –1731. **b.** The swim-bladder or sound of a fish. late ME. **3.** The throat, gullet; now chiefly, the jaws or mouth 1530. †**4.** Used (like *stomach*) for: Appetite, inclination –1704.

1. Luckless landsmen's sea-sick maws BYRON. **3.** The hungry m. of a pike 1873. **4.** I have no great M. to that Business, methinks CIBBER.

Maw[2]. Now *dial.* late ME. Var. of MAUL *sb.*[2]

Maw[3] (mǭ). *Obs.* exc. *dial.* 1450. [– ON. *már* = OE. *mǣw*; see MEW *sb.*[1]] A gull, esp. the Common gull, *Larus canus.*

Maw[4] (mǭ). *Obs.* exc. *Hist.* 1548. [Of unkn. origin.] An old game at cards, played with a piquet pack of thirty-six cards, by any number of persons from two to six.

Mawk (mǭk). *Obs.* exc. *dial.* late ME. [– ON. *maðkr*; see MAGGOT.] = MAGGOT.

Mawkin, obs. f. MALKIN.

Maw·kingly, *a. Obs.* exc. *dial.* 1656. [f. *mawking*, MALKIN + -LY[1].] Slovenly.

Mawkish (mǭ·kiʃ), *a.* 1668. [f. MAWK + -ISH[1].] †**1.** Inclined to sickness; without appetite –1836. **2.** Having a nauseating taste; now, having a faint, sickly flavour with little definite taste 1697. **3.** *fig.* Imbued with sickly or false sentiment; lacking in robustness 1702.

1. The dean who us'd to dine at one, Is maukish, and his stomach gone SWIFT. **3.** A m. popularity KEATS. Hence **Maw·kish-ly** *adv.*, **-ness.**

Mawky (mǭ·ki), *a. dial.* 1790. [f. MAWK + -Y[1].] **1.** Maggoty; also, crotchety. **2.** = MAWKISH 1830.

Mawseed (mǭ·sīd). 1730. [Half-translated f. G. dial. *mahsaat, mohsamen*, f. *mah, moh* poppy (literary G. *mohn*) + *saat, samen* seed.] The seed of the opium poppy, *Papaver somniferum.*

Mawworm[1] (mǭ·wǒɹm). 1607. [f. MAW[1] + WORM.] Any worm infesting the stomach or intestines of man and other mammals.

Mawworm[2] (mǭ·wǒɹm). 1850. [prop. with initial capital.] A man who resembles *Mawworm*, a character in Bickerstaffe's play *The Hypocrite*, 1769; a hypocritical pretender to sanctity.

Something of the Maworm spirit, 'I like to be despised' 1850.

‖**Maxilla** (mæksi·lă). *Pl.* **-læ** (-lī). 1676. [L. *maxilla* jaw.] **1.** A jaw or jaw-bone, *esp.* the upper jaw in mammals and most vertebrate animals. **2.** One of the anterior limbs of insects and other arthropods, so modified as to serve the purpose of mastication 1798. Hence †**Maxillar** *a.* = next 1656–1720.

Maxillary (mæksi·lări, mæ·ksilări). 1626. [f. MAXILLA + -ARY[2], after L. *maxillaris.*] **A.** *adj.* **1.** Belonging to, connected with, or forming part of the jaw or jaw-bone, esp. of the upper jaw of vertebrate animals. **2.** Belonging to, connected with, or forming part of the maxillæ of arthropods 1826. **B.** *sb.* = *maxillary bone.*

M. system: the system of classification of insects based on the form of the maxillæ.

Maxilliform (mæksi·lifǭɹm), *a.* 1835. [f. MAXILLA + -FORM.] Formed like a maxilla.

Maxilliped, -pede (mæksi·liped, -pīd). 1846. [f. MAXILLA + L. *pes, ped-* foot.] *Zool.* A 'foot-jaw' (see FOOT *sb.*)

Maxillo-, comb. f. MAXILLA in sense 'pertaining to the maxilla and...; so *m.-mandibular, -palatine, -pharyngeal, -turbinal,* etc.

Maxim[1] (mæ·ksim). late ME. [– Fr. *maxime* or its source med.L. *maxima*, subst. use (for *propositio maxima* 'greatest proposition', Boethius) of fem. of *maximus* great.] †**1.** An axiom; a self-evident proposition assumed as a premiss –1692. **2.** A proposition (esp. in aphoristic or sententious form) expressing some general truth of science or of experience 1594. **b.** *esp.* in *Law* 1567. **3.** A rule or principle of conduct 1579. **4.** *attrib.* 1806.

1. It is urged as an universal M., That Nothing can procede from Nothing BENTLEY. **2.** The m. that knowledge is power 1874. **b.** The m., 'a man's house is his castle' 1893. **3.** Her m. was, that it was time enough to come when she was called HT. MARTINEAU.

Maxim[2] (mæ·ksim). 1885. [f. Sir Hiram S. *Maxim* (1814–1916), the inventor.] In full *M. (machine) gun*: A single-barrelled quick-firing water-cooled machine-gun. Also *M.-Nordenfelt gun*, a modification of this.

†‖**Ma·xima.** 1565. [L., fem. sing. of *maximus*, used *ellipt.* for *maxima propositio, nota.*] **1.** = MAXIM[1] –1594. **2.** *Mus.* = LARGE C. 2.

Maxima, pl. of MAXIMUM.

Maximal (mæ·ksimăl), *a.* 1882. [f. MAXIMUM + -AL[1].] Consisting of, or relating to, a maximum; greatest possible.

Maximalist (mæ·ksimălist). 1909. [f. as prec. + -IST.] Used as an etymological equivalent of BOLSHEVIK, taken as connoting 'extremist'.

Maximite (mæ·ksimait). 1897. [f. Hudson *Maxim*, the inventor + -ITE[1] 4 a.] A smokeless gun-powder composed of gun-cotton, nitroglycerine, and castor oil.

Maximize (mæ·ksimaiz), *v.* 1802. [f. L. *maximus* + -IZE.] **1.** *trans.* **a.** To increase to the highest possible degree. **b.** To magnify to the utmost (in estimation or representation). **2.** *intr.* To maintain the most rigorous or comprehensive interpretation possible of a doctrine or an obligation. Chiefly *Theol.* 1875. So **Ma·ximizer** 1868.

1. a. By this means, appropriate moral aptitude may be maximized BENTHAM. Hence **Maximiza·tion.**

Maximum (mæ·ksimŏm). *Pl.* **maxima,** *rarely* **-ums.** 1740. [– (through Fr.) mod.L. *maximum*, subst. use of n. of L. *maximus*, superlative of *magnus* great.] **1.** *Math.* The greatest of all the values of which a variable or a function is capable; the value of a continuously varying quantity at the point at which it ceases to increase and begins to decrease 1743. **2.** *gen.* The highest attainable magnitude or quantity (of something); a superior limit 1740. **3.** The highest amount (of temperature, barometric pressure, etc.) attained or recorded within a specified period 1850. **4.** A superior limit imposed by authority; esp. in *Fr. Hist.*, a limit of price for corn 1821. **5.** *attrib.* **a.** quasi-*adj.* or *adj.* That is a maximum, or that stands at the maximum; greatest 1834. **b.** Pertaining to a maximum or maxima, as *m. period*; **m. thermometer,** one which records automatically the highest temperature within a given period 1852.

2. The art of conducting a nation to the m. of happiness and the minimum of misery COLQUHOUN. **5. a.** The m. density of average sea-water MAURY.

May (mē[i]), *sb.*[1] *poet.* (*arch.*) ME. [usu. referred to OE. *mǣġ* kinswoman, maid, but perh. – ON. *mær* (gen. *meyjar*) maid = Goth. *mawi* :– Gmc. *maujō, fem. of *mazuz, whence Goth. *magus* boy; see MAIDEN.] A maiden, virgin.

Thow glorie of wommanhede, thow faire m. CHAUCER.

May (mē[i]), *sb.*[2] ME. [– (O)Fr. *mai* :– L. *Maius* (sc. *mensis* month) prop. pertaining to *Maia*, Italic goddess.] **1.** The fifth month of the year in the Julian and Gregorian calendar. **b.** *fig.* Bloom, prime, heyday (*poet.*) 1586. **2.** The festivities of May-day 1506. **3.** Blossoms of the hawthorn (*Cratægus oxyacantha*); hence occas., the tree itself: so called because it blooms in May 1548. **4.** *Cambridge Univ.* **a.** (*sing.* or *pl.*) = *May examination*; **b.** (*pl.*) = *May races* 1852.

1. While the jolly hours lead on propitious M. MILT. *personified.* She came adorned hither like sweet M. SHAKS. **b.** A Prince, In the mid might and flourish of his M. TENNYSON. *May and January*, or *December*: used to describe the marriage of a young woman to an old man. **2.** *Queen of the M., Lady of the M.* (cf. MAY-LADY): a girl chosen to be queen of the games on May-day, being gaily dressed and crowned with flowers. **3.** With blossoms red and white of fallen M. M. ARNOLD.

attrib. and *Comb.*, as *m.-blossom, M.-born, M. moon*, etc.: **M.-drink** [= G. *maitrank*, Du. *meidrank*], white wine medicated with woodruff, drunk in Belgium and northern Germany; **M. examination,** a college examination held at the end of the Easter term at Cambridge; **M. meetings,** meetings of religious and philanthropic societies formerly held annually in M. in Exeter Hall, London, etc.; **M. queen,** the Queen of the M. (see 2); **M. races,** intercollegiate boat-races held in the Easter term at Cambridge (now in June); **M.-term.** Easter term at Cambridge (*colloq.*); **-week,** the week of the M. races at Cambridge.

b. M. beetle, the cockchafer; **M. bird,** the whimbrel, *Numenius phæopus*; *U.S.* the bobolink; **M. fish,** the twait shad, as entering the rivers in **M.**; *U.S.* a killifish, *Fundulus majalis*; **M. parr, peal,** local names for salmon at certain stages of growth; etc.

c. †**M.-blossom,** lily of the valley; **-pop** *U.S.*, the fruit of the passion-flower; also the plant itself; **-rose,** any rose flowering in M.; also the guelder rose, *Viburnum opulus*: **-thorn, -tree,** the hawthorn; **-wort,** *Galium cruciatum*.

May (*mē*[i]; unstressed me[i], mĕ), *v.*[1] *Pa. t.* **might** (mait); **mought** (mō[u]t) now *dial.*, freq. in 16th and 17th c. literary use. [A CGmc. verb belonging by its conjugational form if not by origin to the class of preterite-presents (cf. CAN *v.*[1]). OE. (1st pers. sing.) *mæġ*, corresp. to OFris. *mei*, OS., OHG. *mag* (Du., G. *mag*), ON. *má*, Goth. *mag*. The primary sense is 'have power' (cf. the cogn. MAIN *sb.*[1], MIGHT *sb.*), and the IE. base, **mogh-* **mēgh-*, is repr. also by Gr. μῆχος contrivance, μηχανή MACHINE, OSl. **mogą* I can.] †**I.** As a vb. of complete predication. *intr.* To be strong; to have power or influence; to prevail (*over*) –late ME.

Phr. *If I m.*: if I have any power in the matter.

II. As an auxiliary of predication. **1.** = CAN *v.*[1] II. 2. *Obs.* exc. *arch.* OE. **2.** = CAN *v.*[1] II. 3. OE. **b.** In poetry, *might* sometimes = 'used to', 'would'. KEATS. **c.** *Might* (subj.) is often used *colloq.* (*a*) with pres. inf. to convey a suggestion of action, or a complaint that some action is neglected; (*b*) with perf. inf. to express a complaint that some not difficult act or duty has been omitted 1805. **3.** Expressing permission or sanction: To be allowed (to do something) OE. ¶**b.** *Law.* In the interpretation of statutes, *may* = *shall* or *must* 1728. **4.** Expressing subjective possibility, i.e. the admissibility of a supposition (see quots.) ME. **5.** Uses of the pa. t. subj. in the statement of a rejected hypothesis (or a future contingency deemed improbable) and its consequences (see quots.) OE. **6.** In questions, *may* (or *might*) with inf. is used to render a question less abrupt or pointed 15... **7.** As an auxiliary of the subj. mood. **a.** *May* with inf. serves as a periphrastic subj.: (*a*) in final clauses OE.; (*b*) in rel. clauses with final meaning; (*c*) in clauses depending on *wish, fear* vb. and sb., and the like OE. **b.** In expressions of wish, *may* with inf. has replaced (exc. *poet.* and *rhet.*) the simple pres. subj. 1586. **c.** *Might* is also used to express a wish, esp. one which can hardly be realized. late ME. **d.** *May* with inf. is used to emphasize the uncertainty of what is referred to OE. **8.** With ellipsis of the inf. (see quots.) OE. **9.** For *may well, may as well*, see WELL *adv.* †**10.** In advb. phr. = MAYHAP; **may chance, may-fortune** –1581.

1. We..have endured Sunshine and rain as we might M. ARNOLD. **2.** A soldier may be anything, if brave COWPER. But the reign of Stilicho drew towards its end; and the proud minister might (= 'had opportunity to') perceive the symptoms of his approaching disgrace GIBBON. **c.** 'They might have offered to help us..' said Aunt Ecclesia, pettishly 1894. **3.** May we take your coach to town? I saw it in the hangar THACKERAY. Also with *might* in deferential questions, e.g.: Might I trouble you for the pickles? (*mod.*). **b.** For *may* in the Case of a publick Officer is tantamount to *shall* 1728. **4.** Stick to that truth, and it may (= 'perhaps will') chance to save thee FLETCHER. I dare say, my friend, that you may be (= 'perhaps are') right JOWETT. **5.** Might we (= 'if we might') haue that happinesse..we should [etc.] SHAKS. A Fault which easie Pardon might (= 'would perhaps') receive, Were Lovers Judges DRYDEN. The book is very much what might have been expected from the author 1891. **7. a.** Lest my appearance might draw too many compliments JOHNSON. (*b*) Would I might But euer see that man SHAKS. Be not highminded, but fear..least thou also maist be cut off 1651. **b.** Long may he reigne 1611. **d.** And than he demaunded of his seruauntes what it might be LD. BERNERS. Come what come may SHAKS. **8.** Things must be as they may SHAKS. The Moone shines faire, You may away by Night SHAKS. He that may not as he will, must do as he may 1721.

May (mē[i]), *v.*[2] Now chiefly in vbl. sb. 1470. [f. MAY *sb.*[2]] *intr.* To take part in the festivities of May-day; to gather flowers in May.

‖**Maya** (mā·yă). 1823. [Skr. *māyā.*] Illusion: a prominent term of Hindu philosophy.

May·-apple. *U.S.* 1733. [MAY *sb.*[2]] **1.** An American herbaceous plant, *Podophyllum peltatum*, bearing a yellowish, egg-shaped fruit, which appears in May.

Maybe, may-be (mē[i]·bi), *adv.*, *sb.*, and *a.* late ME. [Shortened from *it may be*; cf. Fr. *peut-être*.] **1.** *adv.* Possibly, perhaps. Occas. used as conj. with *that* (cf. Fr. *peut-être que*). **2.** *sb.* What may be; a possibility 1586. **3.** *adj.* Which are possibly to come 1687.

1. This, may be, was the reason some imagin'd Hell there GLANVILL. **2.** May be is a doubt, but what is must be regarded N. BRETON. **3.** Those may-be years thou hast to live DRYDEN.

May·-bug. 1698. [MAY *sb.*[2]] The cockchafer.

May·-bush. 1579. [MAY *sb.*[2]] **a.** A branch of hawthorn. **b.** The hawthorn or may-tree.

May·-butter. 1584. [MAY *sb.*[2]; cf. Fr. *beurre de mai*.] Unsalted butter preserved in May for medicinal use. Also fig.

Maycock (mē[i]·kǫk). *U.S.* 1588. [Algonquin (Powhattan dialect) *mahcawq*.] A kind of melon.

May·-day. late ME. [MAY *sb.*[2]] The first day of May.

May·-dew. late ME. [MAY *sb.*[2]] Dew gathered in May, supposed to have medicinal and cosmetic properties.

May duke, mayduke (mē[i]·diūk). 1718. [Cf. *May cherry* and *Duke cherry* (Evelyn 1664).] A variety of sour cherry.

Mayflower (mē[i]·flauəɹ). 1626. [f. MAY *sb.*[2] + FLOWER *sb.*] **1.** A flower that blooms in May; used locally for the Cowslip (*Primula veris*), the Lady's Smock (*Cardamine pratensis*), etc. **2.** A variety of apple. EVELYN. **3.** *N. America.* **a.** *Azalea nudiflora.* **b.** The trailing arbutus, *Epigæa repens.* 1838.

May·-fly. 1651. [f. MAY *sb.*[2] + FLY *sb.*[1]] **1.** An insect of the family *Ephemeridæ*; esp. as an angler's name for *Ephemera vulgata* and *E. dania* or either of the corresponding artificial flies. **2.** An insect of the family *Phryganeidæ* or *Sianidæ*; the caddis-fly 1816.

May·-game. 1549. [MAY *sb.*[2]] **1. a.** *pl.* The merrymakings associated with the first of May. **b.** *sing.* A set entertainment in the Mayday festivities. **2.** *transf.* and *gen.* Merry-making, sport, frolic; foolery 1571. **3.** A laughing-stock 1569. **4.** *attrib.*; also as adj. with the sense 'trivial' 1586.

3. What is man but..the spoil of time, the may-game of fortune? QUARLES.

Mayhap (mē[i]hæ·p, mē[i]·hæp), *adv.* Now *arch., rhet.* and *dial.* 1536. [The phr. (*it*) *may hap* (HAP *v.*[1]) taken as one word.] Perhaps, perchance. So **May-happen** *adv.* now *arch.* and *dial.*

Mayhem (mē[i]·hem), *sb.* 1472. [– AFr. *mahem* (whence AL. *mahemium* XII), OFr. *mayhem*, etc.; see MAIM *sb.*] *Old Law.* The crime of maiming a person so as to make him less able to defend himself or annoy his adversary. Also *fig.* Hence **Mayhem** *v. trans.* to inflict m. on 1534.

Maying (mē[i]·iŋ), *vbl. sb.* 1470. [f. MAY *v.*[2]] The celebration of May-day or the month of May.

May·-lady. *Obs.* exc. *Hist.* 1560. [MAY *sb.*[2]] A Queen of the May. Also, a puppet in a May-day game.

May·-lord. 1599. [f. MAY *sb.*[2] + LORD *sb.*] A young man chosen to preside over the festivities of May-day; *transf.* one whose authority is flouted.

‖**Mayonnaise** (me[i]ŏnē[i]·z, Fr. mayonęz). 1841. [– Fr. *mayonnaise*, also *magnonaise*, *mahonnaise*, the latter being prob. fem. of *mahonnais* of Port *Mahon*, capital of Minorca, taken by the duc de Richelieu in 1756.] A sauce consisting of yolk of egg beaten up with oil and vinegar, and seasoned with salt, etc., used as a dressing for salad, cold meat, or fish; also, a dish (of meat, etc.) having this dressing.

Mayor (mē[ə]ɹ). [ME. *mer, mair* – (O)Fr. *maire* :– L. *major* greater, compar. of *magnus* great, used subst. in late L. (cf. MAJOR-DOMO).] The head or chief officer of the municipal corporation of a city or borough.

M. of the Staple: see STAPLE *sb.*[2] *M. of the Palace* (Hist.): = Fr. *maire du palais*, a mod. transl. of med.L. *major domus* (occas. *m. palatii*), the title borne by the prime ministers of the Frankish kingdoms. Hence **May·oral** *a.* pertaining to a m.

or mayoralty. **May·oress,** the wife of a m., or a lady who fulfils the duties belonging to a m.'s wife; female mayor. **May·orship,** the office, position, etc. of a m.

‖**Mayoral** (mayora·l), *sb.* 1598. [Sp., f. *mayor* greater.] A conductor in charge of a train of beasts of burden; also, a head shepherd; *occas.* the conductor of a diligence.

Mayoralty (mē°·rălti). late ME. [– OFr. *mairalté*, f. *maire* MAYOR, after *principalté* (mod. *principauté*).] **1.** The office of a mayor. **2.** The period during which a mayor holds office 1494. **3.** *attrib.* 1573.

Maypole (mēⁱ·pōᵘl). 1554. [f. MAY *sb.*² + POLE *sb.*¹] A high pole, painted with spiral stripes of different colours and decked with flowers, set up on an open space, for the merrymakers to dance round on May-day. *transf.* A lean m. of a man 1871.

Mayweed (mēⁱ·wīd). 1551. [alt. of †*maid-*, *mayde(n)wede*, f. †*maithe*, †*maithen*, OE. *magoþe*, *mæġþa* (obl. cases *magoþan*, *mæġþan*) + WEED *sb.*¹] Stinking Camomile, *Anthemis cotula.* Applied also to other plants resembling this.

Mazame (măzēⁱ·m, masā·me). Also **mazama.** 1791. [– Fr. *mazame* (Buffon) – Mex. *maçame*, pl. of *maçatl* deer, mistaken for a sing.] **1.** A name for various American species of deer; also for the Prong-horn. **2.** The antilopine Rocky Mountain goat, *Oreamnus* or *Haplocerus montanus* 1852.

Mazard (mæ·zăɹd), *sb.*¹ 1601. [alt. f. MAZER, by association of -ER with -ARD.] †**1.** A mazer. **2.** *joc.* (*arch.*) **a.** The head 1602. **b.** The face, 'phiz' 1762. **3.** *slang.* (*Anglo-Irish.*) The 'head' of a coin 1802.

2. a. Knockt about the M. with a Sextons Spade SHAKS. Hence †**Mazard** *v. trans.* to knock on the head B. JONSON.

Mazard (mæ·zăɹd), *sb.*² *dial.* 1578. [perh. a use of prec.] A kind of small black cherry; also *attrib.*, as *m. cherry.*

†**Mazarine,** *sb.*¹ 1673. [perh. attrib. use of the name of Cardinal *Mazarin* (died 1661), or of the Duchesse de *Mazarin* (died 1699).] In early use also *m. dish, plate*: A deep plate, usually of metal –1773.

Mazarine (mæzărī·n), *sb.*² and *a.* 1684. [perh. f. name of Cardinal Jules *Mazarin* (1602–1661) or the Duchesse de *Mazarin* (died 1699).] **1.** In full *m. blue*: A deep rich blue 1686. **2.** A stuff or a garment of this colour 1694. **b.** A London common-councilman; so called from the colour of his gown 1761. **3.** *adj.* Of a mazarine blue colour.

Mazdaism (mæ·zdĕ,iz'm). Also **Mazdeism.** 1871. [f. Avestic *mazda*, name of the good principle (Ahura-mazda, Ormuzd) of ancient Persian theology.] The ancient Persian religion as taught in the Avesta; Zoroastrianism. So **Mazde·an, -æ·an** *a.* pertaining to the religion of the Avesta.

Maze (mēⁱz), *sb.* ME. [f. MAZE *v.*] †**1. The maze.** Delirium, delusion; disappointment. ME. only. †**2. a.** A delusive fancy. **b.** A trick, deception. ME. only. **3.** A state of bewilderment. *Obs.* exc. *dial.* late ME. **4.** A confusing and baffling network of winding and intercommunicating paths; a labyrinth; *occas.* in *pl.*, the windings of a labyrinth. late ME. **b.** A winding movement, esp. in a dance 1610.

3. At this I was put to an exceeding M. BUNYAN. **4.** They walke round about as it were in a round mase SIR T. MORE. *fig.* To lose us in this m. of error SIR T. BROWNE. Phr. *To tread a m.*

Maze (mēⁱz), *v.* ME. [Earliest as pa. pple. *mased* (XIV, also *amased*, *bimased* XIII), f. *mas-*, which is repr. in OE. by *āmasod* (see AMAZE), of which possible cognates are Norw. dial. *mas* exhausting labour, whim, idle chatter, *masa* pass. doze off, and Sw. *mas, masa.*] **1.** *trans.* To stupefy, daze; to put out of one's wits; †to craze. Chiefly in *pass.* Now *arch.* and *dial.* ME. †**2.** *intr.* To be stupefied or delirious; to wander in mind –1568. **3.** *trans.* To bewilder, perplex, confuse 1482. **4.** *intr.* To move in a mazy track 1591. †**b.** *trans.* To involve in a maze; to form mazes upon –1654.

1. Then said the King, 'The man is mazed with fear' MORRIS.

Mazeful (mēⁱ·zfŭl), *a. Obs.* exc. *arch.* 1595. [f. MAZE *sb.* + -FUL.] Bewildering, confounding.

Mazement (mēⁱ·zmĕnt). 1580. [f. MAZE *v.* + -MENT.] A state of stupor or trance. Also = AMAZEMENT.

Mazer (mēⁱ·zəɹ), *sb. Obs.* exc. *Hist.* ME. [– OFr. *masere*, of Gmc. origin, perh. reinforced from MDu. *maeser* maple = OHG. *masar* (G. *maser*) excrescence on a tree, †maple, ON. *mǫsurr* maple, f. *mas-* spot (cf. MEASLE *sb.*).] **1.** A hard wood (? prop. maple) used as a material for drinking-cups. †**b.** The tree yielding this (*rare*) –1547. **2.** A bowl, drinking-cup, or goblet without a foot, orig. made of mazer wood. Often applied to bowls entirely of metal, etc. ME. †**3.** = MAZARD *sb.*¹ 2. –1652. **b.** *transf.* A helmet. SYLVESTER.

2. One of his Shepherds describes a Bowl, or M., curiously Carv'd DRYDEN.

attrib. and *Comb.*; **m. bowl, cup, -dish** = 2; **m. wood** = 1. Hence †**Mazer** *v.* = MAZARD *v.*

Mazurka (măzʊ̄·ɹkă, măzūᵊ·ɹkă). 1818. [– Fr. *mazurka*, G. *masurka* – Pol. *mazurka* woman of the province of *Mazovia.* Cf. POLKA.] **1.** A lively Polish dance resembling the polka; the music is in triple time. **2.** A piece of music composed in the rhythm of this 1854.

Mazy (mēⁱ·zi), *a.* 1579. [f. MAZE *sb.* + -Y¹.] **1.** Resembling or of the nature of a maze; full of windings and turnings. **b.** Moving in a maze-like course 1725. **c.** as *sb. joc.* Short for 'the mazy dance' 1840. **2.** *spec.* (*Min.*) Having convoluted markings 1811.

1. Five miles meandering with a m. motion. . the sacred river ran COLERIDGE. **b.** The m. leveret POPE. Hence **Ma·zily** *adv.* **Ma·ziness.**

M.B. (em bī). 1853. [Abbrev. of 'Mark of the Beast' (see MARK *sb.*¹ III. 2 b, and BEAST *sb.* 5), used joc. with reference to the popular view that this garment was a badge of 'Popery'.] *M.B. waistcoat*: a kind of waistcoat with no opening in front, worn by Anglican clergymen (originally, *c*1840, only by Tractarians).

M.B. (em bī), abbrev. of L. *Medicinæ Baccalaureus* bachelor of medicine.

M.D. (em dī), abbrev. of L. *Medicinæ Doctor* doctor of medicine. Often used *colloq.* for: One holding the M.D. degree, a physician.

Me (mī, mi, mĭ), *pers. pron.*, *1st pers. sing.*, *acc.* and *dat.* [OE. *mē̆* (i) accus., corresp. to OFris. *mi*, OS. *mī*, *mē̆* (Du. *mij*) and further to L. *mē*, Gr. με, ἐμέ, OIr. *mē* (Ir. *mi*), W. *mi*, Skr. *mā*; OE. had also *mec*, corresp. to OFris. *mich*, OS. *mik*, OHG. *mih* (G. *mich*), ON., Goth. *mik* :– IE. **mege* (Gr. ἐμέγε), in which a limiting particle **ge* (Gr. γε at least) is added; (ii) dat., corresp. to OFris. *mi*, *mir*, OS. *mī* (Du. *mij*), (O)HG. *mir*, ON. *mér*, Goth. *mis* :– **mes-*, with suffixed particle of doubtful origin. The base is **me*, on which in all IE. languages the obl. cases of the pronoun of the 1st pers. sing. are formed.] The accus. and dat. form of the pronoun of the first person *I.* **1.** *Accusative*, as direct object. **2.** *Dative.* **a.** As indirect obj.; also (now *rare* exc. *arch.*) in dependence on certain impers. vbs. (cf. MESEEMS, METHINKS, etc.), adjs., and advs. OE. **b.** As dat. of interest (= *for me*), chiefly in commands (*arch.*) OE. **c.** Used expletively in narrative. (The so-called ethical dative.) *arch.* ME. **3.** *Reflexive* (= myself, to or for myself.) Now chiefly *arch.* and *poet.* OE. **4.** For the *nominative* (see quots.) 1500. **5.** In various exclam. uses, without syntactical relation to the context (see quots.) 1589. **6.** quasi-*sb.* Individuality; EGO 1828.

1. Call me not Naomi, call mee Marah *Ruth* 1:20. **2. a.** Will you lend it me? 1898. **b.** Prick me the fellow from the path! M. ARNOLD. **c.** He enters me his name in the book LAMB. **3.** And I awoke, and found me here KEATS. **4.** Oh, the dogge is me, and I am my selfe SHAKS. Is she as tall as me? SHAKS. **5.** Phr. *Ah me! Ay me! Dear me!* Me miserable! (= L. *me miserum!*) MILT. 'Don't you dance?' he said. 'Me?' cried she, embarrassed, 'yes, I believe so' MISS BURNEY. *And me* . . (vulgar) = 'especially considering that I am. .'; And me a widow 1812. **6.** Haunted and blinded by some shadow of his own little Me CARLYLE.

Meach, obs. f. MICHE.

†**Mea·cock.** 1526. [perh. orig. the name of some bird.] **1.** An effeminate person; a coward, weakling –1834. **2.** *attrib.* or *adj.* Effeminate; cowardly –1639.

Mead¹ (mīd). [OE. *medu*, *meodu* = OFris., MLG. (Du.) *mede*, OHG. *metu*, *mitu* (G. *met*), ON. *mjǫðr*, Goth. **midus* (recorded v in Gr. form μέδος) :– Gmc. **meduz* :– IE. **medhu-*, whence Gr. μέθυ wine, Skr. *mádhu* honey, sweet drink.] An alcoholic liquor made by fermenting a mixture of honey and water; also called *metheglin.* **b.** *transf.* esp. U.S., a beverage charged with carbonic acid gas, and flavoured with syrup of sarsaparilla 1890.

attrib. and *Comb.*, chiefly *arch.* or *Hist.*, as *m.-horn*; **m.-bench** (OE. *medubenć*), a seat at a feast when m. was drunk; **-hall** (OE. *meduheall*), a banqueting hall; **-wine,** a home-made 'wine' prepared from m.

Mead² (mīd). Now *poet.* and *dial.* [OE. *mǣd*; see next.] = MEADOW 1. †**b.** Meadow-land –1670.

As it were a mede Al ful of fresshe floures, whyte and rede CHAUCER. Riuers sweete along the meedes TUSSER. *Comb.* **m. grass,** meadow grass.

Meadow (me·doᵘ), *sb.* [repr. OE. *mǣdwe*, etc., obl. cases of *mǣd* (see prec.) :– Gmc. **mǣdwō* :– **mētwá* 'mowed land', f. **mē-* MOW *v.*¹] **1.** Orig., a piece of land permanently covered with grass which is mown for use as hay. In later use extended to include any piece of grass land; and locally applied esp. to a tract of low well-watered ground, usually near a river. **b.** Land used for meadows; meadow land OE. **2.** *N. America.* **a.** A low level tract of uncultivated grass land, esp. along a river or in marshy regions near the sea 1670. **b.** *Beaver m.*: the rich fertile tract of land left dry above a demolished beaver dam 1784. **3.** A feeding ground for fish 1890.

1. Ladie-smockes all siluer white, Do paint the Meadowes with delight SHAKS.

attrib. and *Comb.*, **a.** *m.-croft, -field, -flower*, etc.

b. Prefixed to names of animals as denizens of m. land; as **m. ant,** the small British ant, *Lasius flavus*; **m. chicken,** a name given in N. America to species of Rail or Coot; **m. crake, drake** = CORN-CRAKE; **m. fly,** an American fire-fly; **m. hen** = *meadow chicken*; **m. lark,** (*a*) = TITLARK; (*b*) *U.S.* the grackle, *Sturnella magna*; **m. mouse,** any field vole; **m. mussel,** a mussel found in American salt meadows, *Modiola plicatula*; **m. pipit** = TITLARK; **m. snipe,** (*a*) = *grass-bird* (see GRASS); (*b*) *U.S.* the common American snipe, *Gallinago wilsoni*: **m. vole** = *meadow mouse.*

c. Prefixed to names of plants, to denote varieties or species growing in meadows; often in booknames as tr. L. *pratensis, -ense*, as in *m. barley, clover, trefoil*, etc.; also in **m. beauty,** U.S. name for *Rhexia*; called also *deergrass*; **m. campion, pink,** the Ragged Robin, *Lychnis flos-cuculi*; **m. crocus, saffron,** *Colchicum autumnale*; **m. grass,** any grass of the genus *Poa*, esp. *P. pratensis*; **m. mushroom,** *Agaricus campestris*; **m. rhubarb, rue,** *Thalictrum flavum.* See also PARSNIP, SAXIFRAGE.

d. m. green, lively green, in which the yellow predominates; **m. ground,** (*a*) ground laid down in m.; (*b*) prairie land; **m. ore,** bog iron ore (cf. LIMONITE); **m. thatch,** coarse grass or rush used for thatching.

Hence **Mea·dow** *v.* to devote (land) to the production of grass. **Mea·dowy** *a.* resembling a m.

Meadow-sweet (me·doᵘswīt). 1530. [f. MEADOW *sb.* + SWEET *sb.*] The rosaceous plant *Spiræa ulmaria*, common in moist meadows and along the banks of streams, growing with erect, rigid stems to a height of about two feet, with dense heads of creamy white and highly fragrant flowers. In the U.S., *S. salicifolia.*

†**Mea·dsweet.** late ME. [f. MEAD² + SWEET *sb.*] = prec. –1782.

†**Mea·dwort.** [OE. *medowyrt*, f. *medo* MEAD¹ + *wyrt* WORT¹, plant; possibly the flowers were used for flavouring mead.] = MEADOW-SWEET –1783.

Meagre (mī·gəɹ), *a.* (*sb.*) (*U.S.* **meager.**) [ME. *megre* – AFr. *megre*, (O)Fr. *maigre* (cf. MAIGRE *a.*) :– L. *macer*, *macr-*, rel. to Gr. μακρός long, μακεδνός tall, slender, μῆκος length.] **1.** Of persons, animals, etc.: Lean, thin, emaciated. **2.** Poor, scanty 1501. **b.** Of literary composition or material, ideas, resources, etc.: Wanting in fullness or elaboration 1539. **3.** = MAIGRE *a.* 1705. **b.** *absol.* as *sb.* 'Maigre' diet.

1. Thou art so leane and m. waxen late SPENSER. **2.** Very Maigre, Hungry Soil 1681. The m. banquet LAMB. **b.** The continuation of a m. chronicle D'ISRAELI. A m. and imperfect form of faith J. MARTINEAU. **3.** Phr. *Soup m.*, tr. Fr. *soupe maigre.* **b.** We make m. on Fridays always THACKERAY. Hence **Mea·gre-ly** *adv.*, **-ness.**

†**Meagre** (mī·gəɹ), *v.* 1563. [f. MEAGRE *a.*] *trans.* To make meagre or lean –1807.

Meagre, var. of MAIGRE *sb.*

Meak (mīk). *dial.* 1478. [Of unkn. origin.] An implement with a long handle and crooked iron or blade used to cut down or pull up peas, bracken, etc.

Meaking (mī·kiŋ), *vbl. sb.* 1867. [perh. f. MEAK + -ING[1].] Only in *m. iron*: The tool used by caulkers to pick old oakum out of a vessel's seams.

Meal (mīl), *sb.*[1] [OE. *melu* (*melw-*) = OFris. *mel*, OS. *melo* (Du. *meel*), OHG. *melo* (G. *mehl*), ON. *mjǫl* :– Gmc. **melwam*, f. **mel-* **mal-* **mul-* :– IE. **mel-* **mol-* **mḷ-*, whence OHG., Goth. *malan*, ON. *mala*, L. *molere* grind.] **1.** The edible part of any grain or pulse (usu. exc. wheat) ground to a powder. Also *spec.* in Scotland and Ireland = OATMEAL; in U.S. = *Indian meal* (see INDIAN *a.* 3). *Whole m.*: see WHOLE. **b.** The finer part of the ground grain, in contrast with *bran*. Often *fig.* 1579. **2.** *transf.* A powder produced by grinding (e.g. in *linseed m.*); a powdery substance resembling flour 1549.

Comb.: **m.-beetle,** a coleopterous insect (*Tenebrio molitor*), which infests granaries, etc., and is injurious to flour; **-mite,** the *Acarus farinæ*; **-moth,** either of two species of moth, *Asopia farinalis* and *Pyralis farinalis*, the larvæ of which feed on m. or flour; **-worm,** the larva of the meal-beetle; **-worm beetle** = *meal-beetle*.

Meal (mīl), *sb.*[2] [OE. *mǣl* mark, fixed time, etc., corresp. to OFris. *mēl*, *māl*, OS. *-māl* sign, measure (Du. *maal*), OHG. *māl* time (G. *mal* time, *mahl* meal), ON. *mál* point or portion of time, mealtime, Goth. *mēl* time :– Gmc. **mǣlaz*, *-am*, f. IE. base **mē-* to measure. See -MEAL.] †**1.** A measure –ME. **2.** Any of the customary occasions of taking food at regular times of the day, as a breakfast, dinner, supper, etc. OE. **b.** An occasion of taking food, a repast. Also, the material of a repast. ME. **3.** The quantity of milk given by a cow at one milking; also, the time of milking 1613.

2. Meals, then, ought to be early or late in proportion to the habits of the individual COMBE. **b.** The blackbird, picking food, Sees thee, nor stops his m. M. ARNOLD.

Meal (mīl), *v.*[1] Somewhat *rare*. 1611. [f. MEAL *sb.*[1]] **1.** *trans.* To cover or powder with meal. **2. a.** *trans.* To grind into meal; to reduce to powder. **b.** *intr.* To become reduced to meal or powder. 1669. **3.** *intr.* To yield meal 1799.

Meal (mīl), *v.*[2] 1827. [f. MEAL *sb.*[2]] *intr.* To make a meal; to feed.

†**Meal,** *v.*[3] [Identical with OE. *mǣlan*, f. *māl* spot, stain; see MOLE *sb.*[1]] *trans.* To spot, stain. *Meas. for M.* IV. ii. 86.

-meal, *suffix*, forming advs.; repr. ME. *-mele*, OE. *mǣlum* (in form instr. pl. of *mǣl* MEAL *sb.*[2]), used in combination with sbs. in the sense 'measure, quantity taken at a time', as in DROP-MEAL, INCHMEAL, PIECEMEAL (the only comp. surviving in general use).

Mealie (mī·li). Also (from *pl.*) **milice.** 1853. [– S. Afr. Du. *milie* – Pg. *milho* maize, MILLET, perh. through Bantu.] A S. Afr. name for maize; used chiefly in the *pl.*

Mealing (mī·liŋ), *vbl. sb.* 14... [f. MEAL *sb.*[1] or *v.*[1] + -ING[1].] The action of grinding meal; also, that of finely pulverizing gunpowder. Chiefly *attrib.*

M. stone, a stone used for grinding meal; **m. table,** a slab for mealing gunpowder upon.

†**Mea·lmouth,** *sb.* and *a.* 1546. [f. MEAL *sb.*[1] + MOUTH.] (A) mealy-mouthed (person) –1700. †**Mea·l-mouthed** *ppl. a.* 1570–1686.

Mealy (mī·li), *a.* 1533. [f. MEAL *sb.*[1] + -Y[1].] **1.** Like meal, powdery. Of potatoes when boiled: Forming a dry and powdery mass (opp. to *waxy*). **2.** Containing meal; farinaceous 1591. **3.** Covered with flour 1704. **4.** Covered with or as if with a fine dust or powder. Chiefly in *Bot.* and *Ent.* 1567. **5.** Of colour: Spotty, uneven 1675. **6.** Of complexion: Floury, pale 1838. **7.** Soft-spoken, given to mince matters; mealy-mouthed 1600.

3. The wealthy miller's m. face TENNYSON. **4.** Men like butter-flies, Shew not their mealie wings, but to the Summer SHAKS. **M. bug,** an insect which infests vines and hot-house plants. **5.** A m. bay cob WHYTE MELVILLE. M. prints 1890. **6.** I only know two sorts of boys. M. boys, and beef-faced boys DICKENS. **7.** Bless its m. mouth! CARLYLE. **Mea·liness.**

Mealy-mouthed (mī·li,mau·ðd), *a.* 1572. [Cf. MEALY *a.* 7.] Soft-spoken; not outspoken; afraid to speak one's mind or to use plain terms.

Mealy-mouth'd philanthropies TENNYSON. Hence **Mealy-mouthed-ly** *adv.*, **-ness.**

Mean (mīn), *sb.* ME. [Partly MEAN *a.*[2] used absol.; partly after the similar OFr. use.] **I.** That which is in the middle. **1.** A condition, quality, disposition, course, etc., that is equally removed from two opposite (usu., blamable) extremes; a medium. †**b.** Moderation, measure –1718. †**2.** *Mus.* †**a.** A middle part, esp. the tenor or alto. Also, a person performing that part or the instrument on which it is played. Also *fig.* –1698. †**b.** A name for the second and the third string of a viol or lute. CHAPPELL. †**3.** *Logic.* The middle term of a syllogism. BACON. †**4.** Something interposed or intervening –1593. **5.** *Math.* [= Fr. *moyenne*, ellipt. for *quantité moyenne*.] The term (or in pl., the terms) intermediate between the first and last terms (called the extremes) of a progression of any kind (*arithmetic*(*al*, *geometric*(*al*, *harmonic*(*al m.*) 1571. **b.** An average amount or value; used for *m. pressure, temperature*, etc. 1803.

1. There is a m. in all things SWIFT. **b.** *In a m.*: with moderation; But to speake in a Meane BACON. *To use a m.*: to exercise moderation; Use a m. in sleep and waking CULPEPPER. **4.** Phr. *By means*: through intermediate links (of descent). *Without any m.* (= Fr. *sans moyen*): directly, immediately, unconditionally. *In the m.*: in the meantime.

II. An intermediary agent or instrument. †**1.** A mediator, a 'go-between'. Also in pl. form, with sing. sense and constr. –1612. **2.** That by which some object is or may be attained, or which is concerned in bringing about some result. Often contrasted with *end*. ME. †**3.** An opportunity; in early use *pl.* conditions, terms (of peace) –1613. **4.** *pl.* [= Fr. *moyens*.] (One's) resources; chiefly, (a person's) pecuniary resources; sometimes more explicitly, *means of living, of subsistence*. In absol. sense also = 'money', 'wealth' 1603. †**b.** Formerly construed as sing.; a livelihood (*rare*) –1642. **5.** †**a.** Mediation, intercession; instigation. late ME. **b.** Instrumentality; operation as an instrument, method, or proximate cause. (See below.) late ME.

1. He woweth hire by meenes and brocage CHAUCER. **2.** Yet Nature is made better by no meane, But Nature makes the Meane SHAKS. Phr. *To be the means* (or †*the m.*) *of*. I was the means of this being done 1863. *By fair means*: see FAIR *a.* IV. 3. See also WAYS AND MEANS. *To find* (*the*) *means* (or †*m.*): to find out a way, contrive (now only const. *inf.*). *Means of grace* (Theol.): the sacraments, etc. viewed as the means by which divine grace is imparted to the soul; in Evangelical use often = 'public worship'. *Under the means of grace*: subject to the operation of the means of grace. **4.** Let her haue needfull, but not lauish meanes SHAKS. My means were somewhat broken into TENNYSON. **5. a.** Our Brother is imprison'd by your meanes SHAKS. **b.** Phr. *By all* (*manner of*) *means*: (*a*) in every possible way; (*b*) at any cost, without fail; (*c*) = 'certainly'. *By any* (*manner of*) *means* (or †*m.*): (*a*) in any way, anyhow, at all; †(*b*) by all means. *By no means* (or †*m.*), *by no manner of means* (or †*m.*): (*a*) in no way, not at all; (*b*) on no account. *By this* or *that means* (or †*m.*): (*a*) by means of this or that; in this or that way; thus; (*b*) in consequence, consequently. *By* or *through* (†*the*) *means* (or †*m.*) *of*: (*a*) by the instrumentality of (a person or thing); (*b*) in consequence of, owing to. †*By* (*the*) *means* (*that*): for the reason that, because.

Mean (mīn), *a.*[1] and *adv.*[1] [OE. *mǣne* (rare), ME. *mene*, for OE. *ġemǣne* (ME. *-mene*) = OFris. *gemēne*, OS. *gimēni* (Du. *gemeen*), OHG. *gimeini* (G. *gemein*), Goth. *gamains* :– Gmc. **ʒamainiz*, f. **ʒa-* Y- + **mainiz* :– **moinis* (repr. in **commoinis*, antecedent form of L. *communis* COMMON), f. **moi-*, **mei-* change, exchange.]

I. Common to two or more; possessed jointly. *Obs.* exc. *dial.*

Phr. *In m.*: in common. *To go m.*: to share.

II. Inferior. †**1.** Of persons, etc.: Undistinguished; of low degree; often opp. to *noble* or *gentle*. Also *transf.* –1827. †**b.** Poor, badly off –1776. **c.** Poor in ability, learning, etc. *Obs.* exc. in phr. (*to*) *the meanest understanding*, etc., and as in 3. ME. **d.** (See below). **2.** Of things: †Of little value; inferior –1770; petty; inconsiderable (now *rare*) 1585; low ME.; the reverse of imposing, shabby 1600. **3.** *No m.* —: often = 'no contemptible', applied eulogistically to a person or thing 1596. **4.** Of persons: Ignoble, small-minded 1665. **5.** Penurious, stingy 1755.

1. He bears a lofty spirit in a m. condition BACON. **b.** Thou shalt not steal, though thou be very m. BUNYAN. **c.** Very m. Divines 1738. **d.** Phr. *M. white*: a term of contempt applied to the poor and landless white men in the Southern U.S., who in the days of slavery were regarded by the negroes as inferior to themselves. **e.** *U.S. colloq.* In low spirits or health; poorly, 'seedy' 1848. **2.** The meanest flowret of the vale GRAY. A city of m. streets (*mod.*). Of things in general: poor in quality or condition 1817. **3.** A citizen of no meane citie *Acts* 21:39. **4.** Phr. *To feel m.* (*U.S.*): to feel ashamed of one's conduct. **5.** He is not m. about money GEO. ELIOT. *Comb.*, as *m.-spirited* (1694).

†**B.** *adv.* = MEANLY –1719.

Mean (mīn), *a.*[2] and *adv.*[2] ME. [– AFr. *me*(*e*)*n*, OFr. *meien*, *moien* (mod. *moyen*) :– L. *medianus* MEDIAN.] **A.** *adj.* †**1.** Occupying a middle or an intermediate place. *M. term* (Logic) = 'middle term'. –1822. **b.** *Mus.* Applied to the tenor and alto parts and the tenor clef, as intermediate between the bass and treble –1721. **2.** Intermediate in time; intervening. Now only in *in the m. time, while*. Also MEANTIME, MEANWHILE *advs.* 1464. **3.** *Law.* Intermediate, either in time or status. Usu. spelt MESNE. ME. †**4.** Intermediary –1615. **5.** Intermediate in kind, quality, or degree. Now *rare*. ME. **6.** Not far above or below the average ME. **7.** *Math.* **a.** Of an amount or value: That is an arithmetical mean. Hence used (as in *m. motion, diameter, distance, temperature*, etc.) in concord with a designation of variable concrete quantity, to express the mean value of this. **b.** *M. proportional*: the middle one of three quantities, of which the first has the same ratio to the second as the second has to the third. (Orig. *mean* was the sb.) 1571.

3. The king shal haue the meane issues 1548. M. Lords 1670. **4.** To be m. intercessors and helpers to God 1563. **5.** The meane opinion betweene these is the best 1610. †*M. way* [= L. *via media*]: a middle course (as an escape from a dilemma). **6.** Their Noses of a m. bigness DAMPIER. **7. a.** *M. sun*: a fictitious sun, supposed for purposes of calculation to move in the celestial equator at the mean rate of the real sun. *M.* (*solar*) *time*: the time of day as it would be shown by the 'mean sun' (the time shown by an ordinary correctly regulated clock); so *m. noon*, etc. **b.** *Extreme and m. ratio*: see EXTREME *a.* 1.

B. *adv.* †**1.** Moderately; also, comparatively less –1612. **2.** Intermediately 1548.

Mean (mīn), *v.*[1] Pa. t. and pple. **meant** (ment). [OE. *mǣnan* = OFris. *mēna* signify, OS. *mēnian* intend, make known (Du. *meenen*), (O)HG. *meinen* (now chiefly 'have an opinion') :– WGmc. **mainjan*; f. IE. **mēn-* (see MIND *sb.*).] **1.** *trans.* To have in mind as a purpose; to purpose, design. Chiefly with *inf.* as obj. †**b.** To aim at (*rare*) –1706. **c.** To intend (a remark, etc.) to have a particular reference. Also †absol. *to m. by* = to intend to refer to. 1513. **d.** *intr.* To be (*well, ill*, etc.) intentioned or disposed. Const. *to, by*, or *dat.* ME. **2.** *trans.* To intend to indicate (a certain object), or to convey (a certain sense). Occas. with cl. as obj. OE. **3.** Of things, words, etc.: To have a certain signification; to import; to portend OE. **b.** Of a person: To be of importance *to* (another) 1888.

1. These cut-throates...meant presently to returne MORYSON. Phr. *To m. business*: see the sb. **b.** Who aimeth at the sky Shoots higher much than he that means a tree G. HERBERT. **c.** Did he m. it of any one in particular? (*mod.*). **d.** You seem to m. honestly DE FOE. **2.** The Act does not m. literally what it says 1895. In indignant questions, as *What do you m. by that?* **3.** Neither did hee know what a Disaster meant BACON.

†**Mean,** *v.*[2] Chiefly *Sc.* [OE. *mǣnan*, rel. to MOAN *sb.*] To complain (of) –1800.

Meander (miæ·ndəɹ), *sb.* 1576. [– (partly through Fr. *méandre*) L. *mæander* – Gr. μαίανδρος, appellative use of the name of a winding river in Phrygia.] **1.** *pl.* Sinuous windings; flexuosities. Rarely in *sing.*, the action of winding; one of such windings. Also *transf.* and *fig.* **2.** *pl.* Crooked or winding paths; windings, convolutions 1598. †Also *fig.* †**b.**

sing. A winding course or plan; a labyrinth, maze (*lit.* and *fig.*) –1796. **3.** A circuitous journey or movement; chiefly *pl.* 1631. **4.** *Art.* An ornamental pattern of lines winding in and out or crossing one another rectangularly 1706.

1. The stream loses itself in a distant m. 1796. **2.** *fig.* The meanders of the Law ARBUTHNOT. **3.** So swarming bees..In airy rings, and wild meanders play YOUNG.

Meander (miæ·ndəɹ), *v.* 1612. [f. prec. sb.] **1.** *intr.* Of a stream, etc.: To wind about in its course. **2.** Of a person: To wander deviously or aimlessly 1831.

1. When you shall see in a beautiful Quarto Page, how a neat rivulet of Text shall m. thro' a meadow of margin SHERIDAN.

Meandrine (miæ·ndrin), *a.* 1846. [f. MEANDER *sb.* + -INE[1].] Characterized by windings; said esp. of corals of the genus *Meandrina*, in allusion to the winding convolutions of the surface.

Meandrous (miæ·ndrəs), *a.* 1656. [f. MEANDER *sb.* + -OUS.] Full of windings and turnings; esp. of a river. So †**Mea·ndrian** 1608, **Mea·ndric** 1658, †**Mea·ndry** 1614–1619.

Meaning (mī·niŋ), *vbl. sb.* ME. [f. MEAN *v.*[1] + -ING[1].] **1.** Intention, purpose (*arch.*). **2.** That which is intended to be or actually is expressed or indicated; the signification, sense, import. ME. **b.** The intended sense of a person's words. ME. **c.** In generalized use: Significance 1690.

1. Be ye perfecte in one mynde, and one meanynge TINDALE 1 *Cor.* 1:10. **2.** Difficulties may be raised about the m., as well as the truth, of the assertion BUTLER. What is the m. of all this parade? 1828. The Greeks had sought out the m. of their myths 1885. **b.** Do not misunderstand my m. 1878. **c.** A look so full of m. KINGSLEY. Hence **Mea·ningful** *a.*

Meaning (mī·niŋ), *ppl. a.* 1581. [f. MEAN *v.*[1] + -ING[2].] **1.** Having intention or purpose, as *well m.* **2.** Expressive, significant 1728.

2. 'Had done business with him', said Mr. Barney with a m. look DICKENS. **Mea·ningly** *adv.* late ME.

Meaningless (mī·niŋlės), *a.* 1797. [f. MEANING *vbl. sb.* + -LESS.] Without signification; without purpose. Hence **Mea·ningless-ly** *adv.*, **-ness.**

Meanly (mī·nli), *adv.*[1] 1587. [f. MEAN *a.*[1] + -LY[2].] In a mean manner; poorly; basely, lowlily; shabbily; stingily, illiberally.

To think m. of: to have a mean estimate of.

†**Meanly,** *adv.*[2] late ME. [f. MEAN *a.*[2] + -LY[2].] **1.** In the mean or middling degree or manner; moderately –1763. **2.** Only moderately; hence, indifferently –1707.

Meanness (mī·n,nės). 1556. [f. MEAN *a.*[1] + -NESS.] The condition or quality of being mean; lowliness, insignificance 1583; inferiority; slightness; smallness (also *pl.*) 1556; littleness of character or mind 1660; poorness of appearance or equipment; poverty of execution, design, etc. 1656; niggardliness 1755.

I doubt however whether this Figure be not of a later Date..by the M. of the Workmanship ADDISON.

Meant (ment), *ppl. a.* 1470. [pa. pple. of MEAN *v.*[1]] In senses of the vb. (q.v.).

Mean time, mea·ntime. ME. [prop. two wds. (see MEAN *a.*[2] 2 and TIME *sb.*), and still often so written in the phrases.]

A. *sb.* **1.** *In the mean time.* **a.** During or within the time which intervenes. **b.** Used in adversative or concessive sense: While this is true; still, nevertheless 1633. †**2.** Without prep. = 1 a –1700. **3.** *For the mean time*: so long as the interval lasts. Also predicatively: Intended to serve for the interim. 1480. **4.** *attrib.* BROWNING.

2. The meane time Lady, Ile raise the preparation of a Warre SHAKS. **3.** This order was for the meantime 1897.

B. *adv.* **1.** = *In the mean time*, A. 1 a. 1588. †**2.** = *In the mean time*, A. 1 b. –1681.

Mean while, mea·nwhile. ME. [prop. two wds. (see MEAN *a.*[2] 2 and WHILE *sb.*), and still often so written.] **A.** *sb.* **1.** *In the mean while*: = MEAN TIME A. 1 a. **b.** In adversative or concessive use; cf. MEAN TIME A. 1 b. 1597. †**2.** *The mean while* = 'in the mean while' –1658. **3.** *For the mean while* = 'for the mean time'; see MEAN TIME A. 3. CHAUCER.

B. *adv.* **1.** = *In the mean while*, A. 1 a. 1440. **2.** = *in the mean while*, A. 1 b. 1597.

Meany: see MANY, MEINIE.

Mear(e, var. MARE, MERE *sb.*, *a.*, *v.*

Mease (mīz). 1469. [orig. ME. *meise*, *mayse* (cf. AL. *misa* XII, *meisa* XIII, *maisa* XIV) – OFr. *meise*, *maise* barrel for herrings, of Gmc. origin; cf. MHG. *meise*, MLG., MDu. *mēse*.] A measure for herrings, equal to five 'hundreds' (usu. 'long hundreds').

Measle (mī·z'l), *sb.* [ME. *maseles* pl., prob. – MLG. *masele*, MDu. *masel* pustule, spot on the skin (Du. *mazelen* measles) = OHG. *masala* blood-blister, f. Gmc. **mas-* spot, excrescence (cf. MAZER).] **1.** *pl.* (†in 15th c. also *sing.*). An infectious disease of man (in medical L. called *Rubeola* and *Morbilli*), marked by an eruption of rose-coloured papulæ in irregular circles and crescents, preceded and accompanied by catarrhal and febrile symptoms. The pl. form is now usu. construed as a *sing.* **b.** *pl.* The pustules which mark this disease. late ME. **2.** *pl.* (†formerly also *sing.*) A disease in swine, produced by the scolex of the tapeworm; in later use, a similar disease in other animals. (Due to a misinterpretation of the adj. *mesel* 'leprous' (see next) as used of swine thus affected.) 1587. **b.** The scolex or cysticercus which produces this disease 1863.

1. *German* (formerly also *false*, *French*, *hybrid*) *measles*: a contagious disease (*Roseola epidemica* or *Rubella*) distinct from measles, but like it in some of its symptoms.

†**Mea·sle,** *a.* late ME. [A use of MESEL *a.*, leprous; infl. in spelling by MEASLE *sb.*] Of swine, their flesh: Affected with measles, measly –1652.

Measle (mī·z'l), *v.* 1611. [f. MEASLE *sb.*] **1.** *trans.* To infect with measles. **2.** *transf.* To cover as with measles or spots 1638. **3.** *intr.* To develop the eruption of measles (*colloq.*).

Measled (mī·z'ld), *ppl. a.* ME. [f. MEASLE *sb.*, *a.*, and *v.* + -ED.] **1.** Infected with measles. **2.** Spotted 1634. †**3.** *fig.* Poor, 'scurvy'. NASHE.

Measly (mī·zli), *a.* 1687. [f. MEASLE *sb.* + -Y[1].] **1.** Of, pertaining to, or resembling measles 1782. **2.** = MEASLE *a.* 1687. **3.** Spotty 1876. **3.** *slang.* Poor, of little value 1872.

Measurable (me·ʒ'ŭrăb'l), *a.* ME. [– (O)Fr. *mesurable* – late L. *mensurabilis* MENSURABLE, f. L. *mensurare* MEASURE *v.*; see -ABLE. In sense 3 f. MEASURE *v.*] †**1.** Of persons, etc.: Moderate, temperate; *occas.* modest –1608. **2.** Of moderate size, quantity, duration, or speed. *Obs.* exc. as implied in 3. ME. **3.** That can be measured; of such dimensions as to admit of being measured; *spec.* (of rainfall) not less than $\frac{1}{100}$ inch 1599. †**4.** Characterized by due measure or proportion 1563. †**5.** Regular in movement; metrical, rhythmical –1597. **b.** *Mus.* = MENSURABLE 3. 1614.

1. Of his diete mesurable was he CHAUCER. **3.** Phr. *To come within a m. distance of* [etc.]. **4.** According to the m. distribution of the Holy Ghost 1563. Hence **Mea·surably** *adv.* (late ME.), †moderately; proportionably; in a measure (*U.S.*); to a m. extent.

Measure (me·ʒ'ŭɹ), *sb.* [ME. *mesur(e* – (O)Fr. *mesure* :– L. *mensura*, f. *mens-*, pa. ppl. stem of *metiri* measure; see -URE.]

I. 1. The action or process of measuring, measurement. Now *rare.* **2.** Size or quantity ascertained or ascertainable by measuring. Now chiefly in phr. (*made*) *to m.* (said of garments, etc.; as dist. from *ready-made*) ME. **b.** *techn.* The width of a printed page; the width of an organ pipe 1683. **c.** *Fencing.* The distance of one fencer from another as determined by the length of his reach when lunging or thrusting. Also, in military drill. 1591. †**d.** Duration (of time, of a musical note) –1706. **3.** *fig.* See below. 1650. **4.** An instrument for measuring. **a.** A vessel of standard capacity for dealing out fixed quantities of grain, liquids, some vegetables, coal, etc. ME. **b.** A graduated rod, line, tape, etc. 1555. **5.** A unit or denomination of measurement 1535. **b.** Used for some specific unit of capacity (†or of length) understood from context or usage. Also, such a quantity as is indicated by this unit. ME. **c.** *Chem.* A unit of volume, e.g. of a gas or liquid, usu. indicated by graduations on a tube, etc. Also, the quantity measured by such a unit. 1807. **d.** In mixtures or compositions: A 'part' as estimated by measurement 1837. **6.** A system of measuring, as *linear*, *liquid*, *dry*, *London m.*, etc. ME. **7.** That by which anything is computed or estimated. Chiefly in phr. *to be the m. of.* 1580. **b.** A standard; a criterion, test. Now *rare.* 1641. **8.** *Math.* A quantity which is contained in another some number of times without remainder; a submultiple 1570. **9.** [? *concr.* of sense 2.] A stratum or bed of mineral; now only *pl.* (*Geol.*) in *coal-measures*, *culm m.* 1665.

1. *By m.*: as determined by measuring (not weighing or counting). **2.** Phr. *To know the m. of (a person's) foot*: see FOOT *sb.* Phrases c. *Full*, *good*, *short*, etc. *m.* (see the adjs.). Also *fig.* *To take measures*: to ascertain the different dimensions of a body. So, *to take the m. of* a person for clothes, etc. He that makes Coates for the Moone, had need take m. every noone 1647. **c.** *fig.* Come not within the m. of my wrath SHAKS. **3.** Phr. *To take the m. of*, formerly *to take m. of*: to form an estimate of; now *esp.* to gauge the abilities or character of (a person). **5.** The common m. for tiling is a square of 10 feet GWILT. **b.** Anon wee'l drinke a M. The Table round SHAKS. **7. b.** Man is the m. of all truth Unto himself TENNYSON. **8.** *Common m.* = common divisor (see DIVISOR). Also *fig.* *Greatest common m.* (abbrev. G.C.M.): the greatest quantity that divides each of a number of quantities exactly.

II. Prescribed extent or quantity. †**1.** What is adequate; satisfaction (of appetite, desire, need) –1607. **2.** Proportion; due proportion, symmetry ME. **3.** A limit. Now only in certain phrases, as *to set measures to*, *to know no m.*, etc. ME. †**4.** Moderation, temperance –1667. **5.** A quantity, degree, or proportion (of something), esp. as granted to or bestowed upon a person 1610. **6.** Treatment (of a certain kind) 'meted out' to a person. *Obs.* or *arch.* exc. in *hard m.* 1593.

1. Till either death hath clos'd these eyes of mine, Or Fortune giuen me m. of Reuenge SHAKS. **2.** Phr. *In m. as*: in proportion as. [A Gallicism.] †*To hold m. with*: to be proportionate to. **3.** What measures [can we set] to that anguish? PEARSON. Phr. *Beyond*, *above m.*, also *out of* (*all*) *m.* (arch.): beyond all bounds, excessively. *To keep* or *observe measure(s*: to be restrained in action. †*To keep measures with*: to use consideration towards (a person). *By m.*, *in m.*: to a limited extent, in part. *To fill up the m. of*: to add what is wanting to the completeness of. **5.** Critias..begs that a larger m. of indulgence may be conceded to him JOWETT. Phr. *In a great* or *large m.*: largely. *In some* or *a m.*: in some degree, somewhat. *In the same m.*: to the same extent. **6.** This is hard and vndeserued m. SHAKS.

III. 'Measured' sound or movement. **1.** Poetical rhythm, as measured by quantity or accent; = METRE. Now only *literary.* 1450. **2.** An air, tune, melody. Now *poet.* ME. **3.** *Mus.* **a.** The relation between the time-values of a note of one denomination and a note of the next, determining the kind of rhythm (duple, triple, etc.); hence, the time of a piece of music. (Also called MODE.) 1597. **b.** A group of notes beginning with a main accent, and commonly included between two vertical lines or bars 1667. ¶**c.** Used erron. for L. *modus* as tr. Gr. τρόπος, ἁρμονία; see MODE 1635. **3.** Rhythmical motion, esp. as regulated by music; the rhythm of a movement 1576. **4.** A (grave or stately) dance (*arch.*) 1509.

1. Chaucer's verse seems to consist generally of five measures A. J. ELLIS. *Long m.* (in hymns): see LONG *a.*[1] **2. a.** The triplex, sir, is a good tripping m. SHAKS. **c.** The Lydian m. was appropriated to..songs of sorrow 1776. **3.** Phr. *To keep m.*: to observe exact time. **4.** Where fair Semiramis..Hath trod the measures MARLOWE.

IV. 1. A plan or course of action intended to attain some object 1698. **2.** *spec.* A legislative enactment proposed or adopted 1759.

1. Phr. *To take*, *adopt*, *pursue* (certain) *measures.* Before..any measure of prevention..could be taken 1833. **2.** Measures, and not men, is the common cant of affected moderation '*Junius*' *Lett.*

Measure (me·ʒ'ŭɹ), *v.* ME. [– (O)Fr. *mesurer* – L. *mensurare*, f. *mensura*; see prec.] †**1.** *trans.* To regulate, moderate, restrain –1574. **2.** To ascertain the spatial magnitude or quantity of (something); *properly*, by comparison with some fixed unit ME. **b.** To take (a person's) measure *for* clothes 1836. **c.** *fig.* 1747. **d.** With dimensions or amounts as obj. ME. **e.** *absol.* or *intr.* To take measurements; to use a measuring instrument 1611. **f.** *intr.* (in *pass.* sense). To admit of measurement 1765. **3.** *trans.* Chiefly with *out*: To delimit (*poet.*) 1513. **4.** To have a measurement of (so much) 1671. **5.** To estimate the amount, value, etc. of (an immaterial thing) by comparison with some standard 1667. **6.** To appraise by a certain standard or rule, or by comparison with something else ME. **7.** To be the measure of, or a means of measuring 1590. **b.** *Math.* Of a quantity: To be a measure or submultiple of (another quantity); also †*refl.* †Also *absol.* 1570. **8.** To apportion by measure; to mete *out*. (Also *absol.* or *intr.*) *arch.* ME. **9.** To proportion, adjust (something) *to* an object, or by a standard 1590. †**b.** To be commensurate with –1633. **10.** To bring into competition or comparison *with*. Also *refl.* to try one's strength *against*. 1715. **11.** To travel over, traverse (a certain distance, etc.). Chiefly *poet.* ME. †**12.** To turn into metre –1774.

2. Go, m. earth, weigh air, and state the tides POPE. I. . endeavoured to m. some of the undulations TYNDALL. Phr. *To m.* (†*out*) *one's length*: to fall prostrate. *To m. swords*: *lit.* of adversaries in a duel, to ascertain that their swords are of equal length. Hence, to contend in battle, try one's strength *with*. **d.** He measured sixe measures of barley, and laide it on her *Ruth* 3:15. **4.** *P.R.* I. 210. Phr. *To m. up to* (or *with*): to be comparable *with*; to have necessary or fitting qualifications (chiefly *U.S.*) 1712. **8.** Sermons were measured out with no grudging hand STEPHEN. **9.** M. your desires by your fortune JER. TAYLOR. **11.** For we must m. twentie miles to day SHAKS. Phr. *To m. back*: to retrace (one's steps, etc.). Now *rare*.

Measured (me·ʒ'ŭɹd), *ppl. a.* ME. [f. MEASURE *sb.* and *v.* + -ED.] **1.** In senses of MEASURE *v.* **2.** Consisting of 'measures' or metrical groups; written in metre; metrical 1581. **b.** *gen.* Rhythmical; regular in movement 1633. **c.** *Mus.* = MENSURABLE 3. 1782. **3.** Of language, etc.: Carefully weighed; restrained 1802.

1. Phr. *M. work*, piece-work. **2. b.** Music. . timely echo'd back the m. oar BYRON. A m. tread 1855. **3.** Choice word and m. phrase WORDSW.

Measureless (me·ʒ'ŭɹlės), *a.* ME. [f. MEASURE *sb.* + -LESS.] Having no bounds; immeasurable. **Mea·sureless-ly** *adv.*, **-ness.**

Measurement (me·ʒ'ŭɹmĕnt). 1751. [f. MEASURE *v.* + -MENT.] **1.** The action or an act of measuring; mensuration. **2.** A dimension ascertained by measuring; size or extent measured by a standard 1756. **3.** A system of measuring or of measures 1867.

2. Iron vessels, within the m. allowed by law 1823.

Measurer (me·ʒ'ŭrəɹ). 1552. [f. MEASURE *v.* + -ER[1].] **1.** One who measures or takes measurements; *esp.* one whose duty it is to see that goods or commodities are of the proper measure. Also *fig.* **2.** An instrument for measuring, as a rain-gauge, an hour-glass 1764. **3.** A measuring-worm; = GEOMETER 2.

Measuring (me·ʒ'ŭriŋ), *vbl. sb.* ME. [f. MEASURE *v.* + -ING[1].] The action of MEASURE *v.*

attrib. esp. in the names of vessels and instruments graduated for purposes of measurement, as *m.-chain, -glass, -rod* (also *fig.*), *-tape*, etc.; **m.-wheel,** (1) = HODOMETER; (2) = CIRCUMFERENTOR 2. Phr. **M. cast:** (*a*) *lit.* in the sport of throwing the bar, a throw so nearly equal to another that measurement is required to decide between them (? *Obs.*); (*b*) *fig.* a nice question, a ticklish point; a 'toss-up' (*arch.*).

Mea·suring, *ppl a.* 1570. [f. MEASURE *v.* + -ING[2].] That measures.

M. worm: the larva of a geometrid moth; a geometer or looper 1859.

Meat (mīt), *sb.* [OE. *mete* masc. = OFris. *met(e*, OS. *meti*, ON. *matr*, Goth. *mats* :– Gmc. **matiz* (a parallel **matam* is repr. by OS. *mat*, OHG. *maʒ*), f. **mat-* **met-* measure, METE *v.*[1] Cf. also MAST *sb.*[2]] **1.** Food in general; usually, solid food, in contradistinction to *drink*. Now *arch.* and *dial.* Also *fig.* **b.** The edible part of fruits, nuts, eggs, etc.: the pulp, kernel, yolk and white, etc. Now only *U.S.* exc. in proverbial phrase (see quot.). Also, the animal substance of a shell-fish. ME. †**2.** A kind of food, an article of food, a 'dish' –1726. **3.** The flesh of animals used for food; now chiefly = BUTCHER'S MEAT, excluding fish and poultry ME. **b.** *pl.* Kinds of meat 1693. **c.** In mod. hunting use (*U.S.*), one's quarry or prey 1851. **4.** A meal. Occas. used for dinner. *Obs.* exc. in phrases (see below) ME.

1. *Green m.*: grass or green vegetables used for food or fodder. Thy mete shall be mylk, honye, & wyne ME. *fig.* It is m. and drinke (= a source of intense enjoyment) to me to see a Clowne SHAKS. **b.** Thy head is as full of quarrels, as an egge is full of m. SHAKS. **4.** Phr. *At m.*, †*at m. and meal*: at table, at one's meals. So *after m.*, *before m.* Your Soldiers vse him as the Grace 'fore meate, Their talke at Table, and their Thankes at end SHAKS.

attrib. and *Comb.*, as *m.-broth, -eater, -supper*, etc.; **m.-biscuit,** a biscuit made with concentrated m.; **-earth** *dial.*, good and fertile soil; **-fly,** a bluebottle fly; **m. lozenge,** a lozenge made with concentrated m.; **m. maggot,** the larva of the meat-fly; **-offering,** a sacrifice consisting of food; used in versions of the Bible as tr. Heb. *minḥāh*, an offering of fine flour or parched corn and oil (R.V. 'meal-offering'); **m. tea,** a tea at which m. is served.

Meat (mīt), *v.* Now *dial.* late ME. [f. prec.] **1.** *trans.* To supply with food or provender 1568. **2.** *intr.* To partake of food.

1. Haste then, and meate your men CHAPMAN.

Meatal (mi,ē'·tăl), *a.* 1868. [irreg. f. MEATUS + -AL[1].] Of or pertaining to a meatus.

Meated (mī·tėd), *a.* 1573. [f. MEAT *sb.* + -ED[2].] In Comb. **well-m.,** (*a*) of animals, having plenty of flesh; (*b*) of cheese, rich in nutriment; **open-m.,** of cheese, juicy.

Meath(e, obs. ff. MEAD[1].

Meatless (mī·tlės), *a.* OE. [f. MEAT *sb.* + -LESS.] **1.** Having no food (*arch.*). **2.** Without meat 1845. **b.** Of food: Containing no butcher's meat 1909.

Meato-, used as comb. f. MEATUS, in names of surgical instruments, etc. **Mea·toscope** [-SCOPE], a speculum for examining the urethra near the meatus. **Mea·totome** [Gr. -τόμος], a spring knife for the cutting of a contracted meatus urinarius. **Meato·tomy** [Gr. -τομία], section of the meatus urinarius to make a larger opening.

‖**Meatus** (mi,ē'·tŏs). *Pl.* **meatus** (miē'·tiŭs), **meatuses.** 1665. [L., 'passage, course', f. *meare* go, pass.] †**1.** A channel or tubular passage –1698. **2.** *spec.* in *Anat.* †**a.** = PORE. **b.** With qualification, applied to certain passages in the body. 1665.

2. b. *Auditory m.* (L. *m. auditorius*): the channel of the ear. *Nasal* or *olfactory m.*: the passage of the nose. *Urinary m.*: the external orifice of the urethra.

Meaty (mī·ti), *a.* 1787. [f. MEAT *sb.* + -Y[1].] **1.** Full of meat; fleshy. Also *fig.* (chiefly *U.S.*). **2.** Of or pertaining to meat; having the flavour of meat 1864. Hence **Mea·tiness.**

Meaul, meawl(e, vars. of MIAUL.

Meaw(e, vars. of MIAOW.

Meazle, var. of MESEL (leper).

Mecca (me·kă). 1823. [– dial. var. of Arab. *Makkah*, birthplace of Mohammed, and place of pilgrimage of Moslems.] **1.** Any place which one holds supremely sacred, or which it is the aspiration of one's life to visit. **2.** *attrib.*, in *M. balm, balsam* 1823.

1. Stratford. . is the M. of American pilgrims 1887. Hence **Me·ccan** *a.* and *sb.*

Meccano (mĭkā·no). 1908. Trade name of a set of miniature parts from which engineering models can be constructed.

Mechanic (mĭkæ·nik). late ME. [– (partly through (O)Fr. *mécanique*) L. *mechanicus* – Gr. μηχανικός, f. μηχανή MACHINE; see -IC.]

A. *adj.* **1.** Pertaining to or involving manual labour or skill. Now *rare*. 1549. **2.** Of persons: Having a manual occupation 1549. †**3.** Vulgar, low, base –1762. **4.** Of the nature of, or pertaining to, a machine or machines; worked by machinery. Now *poet.* or *rhet.* 1625. **5.** Worked or working like a machine; acting mechanically. Somewhat *arch.* 1697. †**b.** Involuntary, automatic –1741. **6.** = MECHANICAL *a.* 5. Now *rare* or *Obs.* 1664. †**7.** = MECHANICAL *a.* 6. –1790. †**8.** Skilled in mechanical contrivance –1748.

2. Are the m. and farming classes satisfied? 1837. **3.** *Ant. & Cl.* IV. iv. 32. **4.** *M. powers* or †*faculties*: = *mechanical powers* (see MECHANICAL *a.* 3). **5.** The sad m. exercise, Like dull narcotics TENNYSON.

B. *sb.* †**1.** Manual labour or operation –1605. †**b.** A mechanical art –1691. †**c.** Mechanism. BACON. **2.** A handicraftsman. Formerly often *contemptuous*: A low fellow. Now *rare*. 1562. **3.** A skilled workman, esp. one who makes or uses machinery 1662.

1. c. The fault being in the very frame and Mechanicke of the parts BACON. **2.** *Mechanics' institute* or *institution*: one of a class of societies, established (first in 1823) to afford their members facilities for self-education by classes and lectures. **3.** What is here said of Chymists is applicable to all other Mechaniques HOBBES. The apprentice clings to his foot-rule, a practised m. will measure by his thumb EMERSON.

Mechanical (mĭkæ·nikăl). late ME. [f. L. *mechanicus*; see prec., -ICAL.]

A. *adj.* **1.** Of arts, trades, occupations: Concerned with machines or tools. Hence, **a.** Concerned with the contrivance and making of machines or mechanism. **b.** Concerned with manual operations 1450. †**c.** *transf.* Pertaining to the mere technicalities of a profession or art –1763. **2.** Of persons: Engaged in manual labour; of the artisan class. †Hence, mean, vulgar 1589. †**b.** Practical as opp. to speculative. –1633. **3.** †**a.** Of the nature of a machine or machines. **b.** Now: Acting, worked, or produced by a machine or mechanism. 1567. **4.** Of persons, etc.: Resembling (inanimate) machines or their operations; lacking spontaneity or originality; machine-like; automatic 1607. **5.** Of agencies, principles, etc.: Such as belong to the subject-matter of mechanics (now often opp. to *chemical*) 1626. **b.** *Geol.* Applied to formations in which the ingredients have undergone no chemical change 1833. **6.** Of theories and theorists: Explaining phenomena by mechanical action 1692. **7.** Concerned with or involving material objects or physical conditions 1664. **8.** Pertaining to mechanics as a science 1648; having to do with machinery 1793. **9.** *Math.* Applied to curves not expressible by equations of finite and rational algebraical form; = TRANSCENDENTAL 1727.

1. a. Machine-making. . belongs to a high order of m. art 1872. **b.** Handie-crafte called Arte Mechanicall 1477. **2.** Of mean m. parentage EARL MONM. **3. b.** The m. pianoforte player 1902. Phr. *M. powers* or †*faculties*: the six 'simple machines' (see MACHINE *sb.* 5), the balance, lever, wheel, pulley, wedge, and screw. *M. drawing*: drawing performed with compasses, rulers, etc. *M. construction* (of curves): construction by the use of some apparatus, as dist. from tracing by calculation of successive points. *M. transport* (abbrev. M.T.), the motor branch of the R.A.S.C. **4.** Versification is a thing in a great degree m. HAZLITT. **5.** *M. mixture*, a mixture only separable into its component parts by m. means. **6.** The M. Atheist BENTLEY. The m. theory of slaty cleavage TYNDALL. **8.** M. Engineer 1881.

B. *sb.* **1.** = MECHANIC B. 2. *arch.* 1590. **2.** *pl.* †**a.** The science which relates to the construction of machines. BACON. **b.** Details of mechanical construction (*rare*) 1821.

1. A crew of patches, rude Mechanicals, That worke for bread vpon Athenian stals SHAKS.

Hence **Mecha·nicalism,** the doctrine that phenomena are mechanically caused; m. procedure. **Mecha·nicalize** *v.* **Mecha·nical-ly** *adv.*, **-ness.**

Mechanician (mekăni·ʃən). 1570. [f. MECHANIC + -IAN.] **a.** A mechanic, artisan. Now *rare*. **b.** One skilled in the construction of machinery.

Mecha·nico-, used as comb. f. L. *mechanicus*, with sense 'partly mechanical and partly . . .', as **m.-chemical** *a.*, comprising mechanics and chemistry; (of phenomena) pertaining partly to mechanics and partly to chemistry; **-corpuscular** *a.* epithet of the philosophy which explains all phenomena, material and spiritual, by the movement of atoms according to mechanical laws.

Mechanics (mĭkæ·niks). 1648. [In form a pl. of MECHANIC; see -IC 2.] **a.** Orig. (and still in pop. use): That body of theoretical and practical knowledge which is concerned with the invention and construction of machines, the explanation of their operation, and the calculation of their efficiency. **b.** That department of applied mathematics which treats of motion and tendencies to motion: comprising *kinematics*, the science of abstract motion, and *dynamics* (including *statics* and *kinetics*), the science of the action of forces in producing motion or equilibrium.

Analytical m.: mechanics treated by the differential and integral calculus. *Animal m.*: m.

as applied to the study of the movements of animals.

Mechanism (me·kăniz'm). 1662. [– mod.L. *mechanismus*, f. Gr. μηχανή MACHINE; see -ISM.] **1.** The structure, or mutual adaptation of parts, in a machine or anything comparable to a machine. **2.** *concr.* A system of mutually adapted parts working together; a piece of machinery; the machinery (*lit.* or *fig.*) of some effect 1677. †**3.** Mechanical action –1794. **4.** *Art.* The mechanical execution of a painting, sculpture, piece of music, etc.; technique. (Opp. to *style* or *expression*.) 1843.

1. The m. of society 1833, of movement in the animal frame BAIN, of a door 1867. 2. The m. of a watch 1822, of a flute 1871, of perception and memory 1885. 3. The M. or Necessity of human Actions HARTLEY.

Mechanist (me·kănist). 1606. [f. MECHANIC + -IST.] **1.** †A mechanic; also, a machinist. **2.** One versed in mechanics; a mechanician 1704. **3.** One who holds a mechanical theory of the universe (now *rare*) 1668. Hence **Mechani·stic** *a.* pertaining to mechanics or mechanism. Also, pertaining to mechanical theories in biology or philosophy.

Mechanize (me·kănəiz), *v.* 1678. [f. as prec. + -IZE.] *trans.* To make or render mechanical; to work out the mechanical details of (a design, idea, etc.); *spec.* to substitute mechanical power for man or horse power in (an army, etc.). **Me:chaniza·tion. Me·chanizer** = MECHANIST 3.

‖**Méchant** (meʃaṅ), *a.* Also fem. **-ante** (-āṅt). 1813. [Fr.] Malicious, spiteful.

Mr. Pendennis was wicked, *méchant*, perfectly abominable THACKERAY.

Mechlin (me·klin), *a.* and *sb.* 1483. [f. *Mechlin* (Fr. *Malines*) in Belgium.] †**1.** *M. black*: a black cloth made at Mechlin. **2.** In full *M. lace*: lace produced at Mechlin 1699.

Mechoacan (metʃōᵘ·ăkăn). 1577. [Name of a Mexican province. Often written with a capital M.] **1.** The root of a Mexican species of bindweed, *Ipomæa* (*Batatas*) *jalapa*, formerly used as a purgative; also, the plant itself. Also called *white m.* †**2.** A purgative drug obtained from the roots of *Ipomæa* (*Batatas*) *jalapa* and other similar plants –1768. **3.** *attrib.*, as *m. root*, etc. 1632.

Meconic (mikǫ·nik), *a.* 1819. [f. Gr. μήκων poppy + -IC.] (*Chem.*) *M. acid*: a white crystalline acid obtained from opium. So *m. ether*. Hence **Meconate** (mī·kŏnĕt), a salt of m. acid 1836. So **Meconidine** (mikǫ·nidəin), an amorphous alkaloid found in opium 1871. **Meconin** (mī·kŏnin), a white crystalline neutral compound existing in opium, regarded as an anhydride of meconic acid 1833.

‖**Meconium** (mikōᵘ·niŏm). 1601. [L. (Pliny) – Gr. μηκώνιον, f. μήκων poppy.] †**1.** The inspissated juice of the poppy; opium –1804. **2.** The dark excrementitious substance in the large intestines of the fœtus; hence, the first fæces of a new-born infant 1706.

Medal (me·dăl), *sb.* 1586. [– Fr. *médaille* – It. *medaglia* = OFr. *m(e)aille*, Sp. *medalla* :– Rom. **medallia* :– pop. L. **metallea* (n. pl.), f. L. *metallum* METAL.] †**1.** A metal disc bearing a figure or an inscription, used as a charm or trinket –1674. **2.** A piece of metal, usu. in the form of a coin, with an inscription, or device or figure to commemorate a person, action, or event; also as a distinction awarded to a soldier, a student, etc., for a heroic action, for merit, or for proficiency or skill in any art or subject. In collectors' use, extended to include coins. 1611. †**3.** *fig.* An image, representation (cf. MODEL *sb.*); something beyond the common run (as a medal compared with current coin) –1844. **4.** *attrib.* 1658.

1. *Wint. T.* I. ii. 307. 2. Phr. *The reverse of the m.*: the other side of the question. 3. This little Meddal of God, the Soul of Man HY. MORE.

Comb. **m.-play** *Golf*, play in which the score is reckoned by counting the number of strokes taken for the round by each player.

Medal (me·dăl), *v.* 1822. [f. prec.] *trans.* To decorate or honour with a medal.

Irving went home medalled by the King THACKERAY.

Medalet (me·dălĕt). Also **medallet.** 1789. [f. MEDAL *sb.* + -ET.] A small medal.

Medallic (mĭdæ·lik), *a.* 1702. [f. MEDAL *sb.* + -IC.] Of, pertaining to, or resembling a medal; represented on a medal.

Medallion (mĭdæ·lyən). 1658. [– Fr. *médaillon* – It. *medaglione*, augm. of *medaglia* MEDAL *sb.*] **1.** A large medal. **2.** Anything resembling this; e.g. in decorative work, an oval or circular panel or tablet; a portrait; a decorative design resembling a panel or tablet, as in a carpet, a window, etc. 1762.

2. A medalion of him in marble H. WALPOLE.

Medallist (me·dălist). Also **medalist.** 1682. [f. MEDAL *sb.* + -IST.] **1.** One skilled in medals. **2.** An engraver, designer, or maker of medals 1756. **3.** A recipient of a medal awarded for merit 1797.

3. The Gold Medallists of the year 1898.

Meddle (me·d'l), *v.* ME. [– OFr. *medler*, *mesdler*, var. of *mesler* (mod. *mêler*) :– Rom. **misculare*, f. L. *miscēre* mix. Cf. MELL *v.*] †**1.** *trans.* To mix, mingle; to combine, blend, intersperse. Const. *with*, *together*; also, *among*, *in*, *to*. –1658. †**2.** *intr.* for *refl.* To mingle, combine. Also *refl.* –1610. †**3.** To have sexual intercourse (*with*). Also *refl.* –1655. †**4.** To mingle in fight; to contend –1601. †**5.** *refl.* To busy oneself –1562. **6.** *intr.* To concern oneself; to take part *in*. Now always, to busy oneself or take part interferingly. ME.

2. More to know Did neuer medle with my thoughts SHAKS. 4. *Twel. N.* III. iv. 275. 6. Happie that State wherein the Cobler meddles with his last 1622. Wholly unacquainted with the world in which they are so fond of meddling BURKE. Phr. *Neither make nor m.*: see MAKE *v.* Hence **Me·ddler**, one who meddles. **Me·ddlesome** *a.* given to interfering; **-ly** *adv.*, **-ness. Me·ddlingly** *adv.*

Mede (mīd). late ME. [– L. *Medi* pl. = Gr. Μῆδοι.] A native or inhabitant of Media. *The Law of the Medes and Persians*: see LAW *sb.*[1] I. 1.

Mede, obs. f. MEAD, MEED.

‖**Media** (mī·diă). *Pl.* (in sense 1) **mediæ** (mī·diī). 1841. [L., fem. of *medius* middle used elliptically.] **1.** *Phonetics.* A voiced or 'soft' mute; = MEDIAL *sb.* 2. **2.** *Anat.* The middle tunic or membrane of an artery or vessel 1876.

Media (mī·diă), pl. of MEDIUM.

Mediacy (mī·diăsi). 1853. [f. MEDIATE *a.*; see -ACY.] *Logic* and *Philos.* Mediate state or quality.

Mediæval, medieval (medi,ī·văl, mīdi,ī·văl). 1827. [f. mod.L. *medium ævum* (Melchior Goldast, 1604) 'middle age' + -AL[1]. So *medium tempus* (1586). Cf. Fr. *médiéval* (1874), and earlier MIDDLE-AGE, *middle-aged*.] **A.** *adj.* Of, pertaining to or characteristic of the Middle Ages. Of Art, Religion, etc.: Resembling or imitative of that of the Middle Ages. **B.** *sb.* One who lived in the Middle Ages. **Mediæ-, medie·vally** *adv.*

Mediævalism, medievalism (medi-, mīdi,ī·văliz'm). 1853. [f. prec. + -ISM.] The system of belief and practice characteristic of the Middle Ages; mediæval thought, religion, art, etc.; the adoption of or devotion to mediæval ideals or usages; *occas.* an instance of this. So **Mediæ·-, medie·valist**, one skilled in mediæval history or affairs; one who practises m. in art, religion, etc.

Mediævalize, medievalize (medi-, mīdi,ī·văləiz), *v.* 1854. [f. MEDIÆVAL + -IZE.] *trans.* To make mediæval in character; *intr.* to favour mediæval ideas or usages.

Medial (mī·diăl). 1570. [– late L. *medialis*, f. *medius* MID *a.*; see -AL[1].]

A. *adj.* **1.** Occupying a middle or intermediate position; middle; (of a letter, etc.) occurring in the middle of a word 1721. **2.** Pertaining to a mathematical mean or average 1570. **3.** Of average dimensions; *occas.* of ordinary attainments 1778. **4.** *Mus.* See below. 1809. †**5.** *Phonetics.* (See B. 2.) 1833.

1. M. and paired fins 1880. *M. to*: situated in the middle of. 4. **M. accent,** the fall of a minor third from the dominant or reciting note (Helmore). **M. cadence,** in the eccl. modes, a cadence closing with the mediant of a mode. **M. consonances,** the major sixth and the major third.

B. *sb.* **1.** †**a.** A letter of ordinary height, i.e. having no ascending or descending strokes 1620. **b.** A medial letter; a form of a letter used in the middle of a word 1776. †**2.** *Phonetics.* A voiced mute –1880.

2. Three medials, as they are called, *b*, *g*, *d* GUEST. Hence **Me·dially** *adv.*

Median (mī·diăn), *a.*[1] and *sb.*[1] 1541. [(First in *Anat.*) – Fr. *médiane* (*veine médiane*) or med.L. *medianus* (*mediana vena*) – L. *medianus*, f. *medius* middle; see -AN. As sb. – Fr. †*médiane* or med.L. *mediana* (sc. *vena*) VIII.]

A. *adj.* **1.** Situated in the middle 1645. **2.** Special scientific uses. See below. 1592. **3.** *Statistics.* Used to designate that quantity which is so related to the quantities occurring in a given set of instances that exactly as many exceed as fall short of it 1894.

1. Lower and m. latitudes 1877. 2. *M. artery, nerve, vein* (Anat.): now applied to certain structures in the arm. *M. line*: (*a*) any line in the m. plane; (*b*) (*Bot.*) the midrib of a symmetric leaf; (*c*) (*Geog.*) the line along the middle of the calm belt between the north and south trade winds. *M. lithotomy* (Surg.): the method in which the incision is made through the m. line of the perinæum (opp. to *lateral*). *M. plane*: the plane which divides any body into two equal and symmetrical parts. *M. zone*: a zone along the sea-bottom between 50 and 100 fathoms in depth. 3. The average age of the population of the United States..is twenty-five years; the m. age is twenty-one years 1900.

B. *sb.* **1.** *Anat.* The m. vein, nerve, etc. 1541. **2.** *Math.* Each of the three lines drawn from the angles of a triangle to the middle points of the opposite sides, and meeting in a point within it 1888. **3.** *Statistics.* A median quantity (see A. 3) 1902.

Median (mī·diăn), *a.*[2] and *sb.*[2] 1601. [f. *Media* + -AN, or MEDE + -IAN.] **A.** *adj.* Of or belonging to the ancient kingdom of Media, or the Medes. **B.** *sb.* A Mede 1601.

Mediant (mī·diănt). 1753. [– Fr. *médiante* – It. *mediante*, subst. use of pr. pple. of †*mediare* come between :– late and med.L. *mediare* be in the middle, etc., f. *medius* middle; see MEDIUM.] *Mus.* **a.** In eccl. music: One of the 'regular modulations' of a mode. **b.** In mod. music, the third of any scale, lying midway between the tonic and the dominant. Also *attrib.*

‖**Mediastinum** (mīdiæstəi·nŏm). *Pl.* **-a.** 1541. (Also anglicized **-tine,** 1631–1732). [mod.L., subst. use of med.L. *mediastinus* medial, after L. *mediastinus* low class of slave, f. *medius* MID.] *Anat.* A membranous middle septum or partition between two cavities of the body; esp. that formed by the two inner walls of the pleura, separating the right and left lungs. **Mediasti·nal** *a.* **Mediasti·no-,** comb. form.

Mediate (mī·diĕt), *a.* late ME. [– L. *mediatus*, pa. pple. of *mediare*; see next, -ATE[2].] **1.** Intermediate in position, rank, quality, time, etc. Now *rare.* †**b.** Of a person: Intermediary 1495–1660. **c.** Serving as a means to an end 1502. **2.** Acting or related through an intermediate person or thing; opp. to *immediate*. See below. 1454.

1. After many m. preferments..at last he became Arch-bishop of Canterbury FULLER. 2. *Feudal Law.* Said of a superior and of a tenant or vassal, when the latter holds of the former through a mesne lord. Also *gen.* *M. inference* (Logic): an inference reached through a middle term. *M. knowledge*: knowledge obtained, not by intuition, but by means of inference or testimony. *M. testimony* (Law): secondary evidence. *M. auscultation* (Med.): auscultation performed with the interposition of some object, e.g. a stethoscope, between the body and the ear.

Hence **Me·diate-ly** *adv.* 1526, **-ness** 1704.

Mediate (mī·dieᶦt), *v.* 1542. [– *mediat-*, pa. ppl. stem of L. *mediare*, f. *medius* MID; in part prob. back-formation from the much earlier MEDIATION.] †**1.** *trans.* To divide into two equal parts –1610. **2.** *intr.* To be between; usu., to form a connecting link or a transitional stage between 1642. **3.** To act as an intermediary; to intervene for the purpose of reconciling 1616. **4.** *trans.* 'To effect by mediation' (J.); to procure by intercession 1592. **b.** To settle (a dispute) by mediation 1623. **5.** To be the medium for bringing about (a result) or conveying (a gift, etc.); *pass.* to be communicated or imparted mediately 1630.

2. To m. between the old and the new STANLEY. 3. Bacon attempted to m. between his friend [the Earl of Essex] and the Queen MACAULAY. 4. To m...a suspension of armes BLOUNT. 5. A country

which, like England, mediates the transactions of many others 1861.

Mediation (mīdiēⁱ·ʃən). late ME. [– late L. *mediatio* (f. as prec., see -ION) or f. MEDIATOR.] †**1.** Halving, bisection –1727. **2.** Agency or action as a mediator; the action of mediating between parties at variance; intercession on behalf of another. late ME. **3.** Agency as an intermediary; instrumentality. late ME. **4.** *Mus.* That part of a plainsong or an Anglican chant which lies between the two reciting notes 1845.

2. His [Gregory's] m. appeased the tumult of arms GIBBON. **3.** To seek for peace..through the m. of a vigorous war BURKE.

Mediative (mī·diĕtiv), *a. rare.* 1813. [f. MEDIATE *v.* + -IVE.] That has the quality of mediating; pertaining to mediation.

Mediatize (mī·diătəiz), *v.* 1818. [– Fr. *médiatiser*, f. *médiat*; see MEDIATE *a.* and -IZE.] **1.** *trans. Hist.* In Germany under the Holy Roman Empire: To reduce (a prince or state) from the position of an immediate vassal of the Empire to that of a mediate vassal. Hence, later: To annex (a principality) to another state, leaving to its former sovereign his title, and (usually) some rights of government. Also *fig.* **2.** *intr.* To mediate 1885.

1. His Highness has the misfortune of being a mediatised prince DISRAELI. Hence **Me:diatiza·tion.**

Mediator (mī·dieⁱtəɹ). ME. [– (O)Fr. *médiateur*, †*-our* – Chr. L. *mediator*, which was perh. not formed from L. *mediare* but directly on *medius* MID, after Gr. μεσίτης (f. μέσος) as used in N.T.] **1.** One who mediates (see MEDIATE *v.*). **2.** *Theol.* One who mediates between God and Man; *esp.* Jesus Christ ME. †**3.** A go-between; a messenger or agent –1697. **4.** *Path.* Applied to those constituents of a serum which actively produce hæmolysis 1903. **5.** A variation in the games of ombre and quadrille 1902.

2. For there is one God, and one Mediatour betweene God and men, the man Christ Iesus 1 *Tim.* 2:5. Hence **Me:diato·rial,** †**Mediato·rian** *adjs.* of, pertaining to, resembling, or characteristic of a m. or mediation. **Me·diatorship,** the office of a m. **Me·diatory** *a.* having the function of mediating; pertaining to mediation.

Mediatrix (mīdiēⁱ·triks). *Pl.* **mediatrices** (mīdiĕtrəi·sīz). 1462. [– late L. *mediatrix*, fem. of *mediator*; see prec., -TRIX.] A female mediator. (Often applied to the Virgin Mary.) So **Me·diatress** 1616, **Me·diatrice** [–Fr. *médiatrice*] late ME.

Medic (me·dik). 1659. [– L. *medicus* adj. and sb., f. *medēri* heal. Cf. OFr. *médique* physician, perh. partly the source of the Eng. sb.] **A.** *adj.* = MEDICAL. Only *poet.* 1700. **B.** *sb.* A physician, medical man. *rare* exc. *U.S.* college slang for 'medical student'.

†**Me·dica.** 1577. [– L. *medica*; see MEDICK.] = MEDICK –1753.

Medicable (me·dikăb'l), *a.* 1616. [– L. *medicabilis*, f. *medicare*, *-ari*; see MEDICATE *v.*, -ABLE. In sense 2 – OFr. *medecable*.] **1.** Admitting of cure or remedial treatment. †**2.** Possessing medicinal properties –1666.

Medical (me·dikăl), *a.* (*sb.*) 1646. [– Fr. *médical* or med.L. *medicalis*, f. L. *medicus* physician, f. *medēri*; see MEDIC, -AL¹.] **1.** Pertaining to the healing art or its professors; also, pertaining to 'medicine', as dist. from obstetrics, surgery, etc. **b.** Of diseases: Requiring medical as dist. from surgical treatment or diagnosis 1885. **2.** Curative, medicinal (*rare*) 1646. **3.** *sb.* A student or practitioner of medicine (*colloq.*) 1823.

1. M. Electricity 1778, practice 1799. †**M. finger,** the finger next to the little finger. **M. garden,** a garden for the cultivation of medicinal plants; a 'physic-garden'. *M. man*: a general term, including 'physician' and 'surgeon'. Hence **Me·dically** *adv.*

Medicament (mī-, medi·kămĕnt, me·dikămĕnt), *sb.* 1541. [– Fr. *médicament* or L. *medicamentum*, f. *medicari*; see MEDICATE *v.*, -MENT.] A substance used in curative treatment. Also *transf.* and *fig.* Hence **Medi·cament** *v.* to administer medicaments to. **Me:dicame·ntal** *a.* (now *rare*), of the nature of a m.; medicinal. **Me:dicame·ntally** *adv.* **Me:dicame·ntary** *a.* curative; treating of medicaments.

Medicaster (me·dikæstəɹ). 1602. [– Fr. *médicastre* (XVI) or its source It. *medicastro*; see MEDIC, -ASTER.] A pretender to medical skill; a quack, charlatan.

Medicate (me·dikeⁱt), *v.* 1623. [– *medicat-*, pa. ppl. stem of L. *medicari* administer remedies to, f. *medicus*; see MEDIC, -ATE³.] **1.** *trans.* To treat medically. †**b.** To treat (a thing) with drugs, etc. for any purpose –1775. **2.** To impregnate with a medicinal substance 1707. †**b.** To 'doctor' (liquors, etc.) –1791.

2. The inhalation of steam medicated with terebene 1898. Hence **Medica·tion,** the action of medicating; *concr.* something used for this. **Me·dicative** *a.* curative.

Medicean (medisī·ăn, -tʃī·ăn), *a.* 1610. [f. mod.L. *Mediceus* (f. It. *Medici*, surname) + -AN.] Pertaining to the Medici, a family who ruled Florence during the 15th c. Used as the designation of the library at Florence (otherwise called Laurentian) founded by Lorenzo de' Medici, and of MSS. there preserved; also, of works of art in the Florentine collections.

Medicinable (me·dsĭnăb'l), *a.* late ME. [– OFr. *medecinable*, f. *medeciner*; see MEDICINE *v.* and -ABLE.] **1.** = MEDICINAL. *Obs.* exc. *poet.* or *arch.* Also *fig.* †**2.** Of or belonging to medicine –1607.

Medicinal (mĭdi·sinăl), *a.* (*sb.*) ME. [– (O)Fr. *médicinal* – L. *medicinalis*, f. *medicina*; see MEDICINE, -AL¹.] **1.** Having healing properties or attributes; adapted to medical uses. Const. *against*, *for*. Also *fig.* †**2.** Of or relating to the science or the practice of medicine –1804. **b.** Resembling medicine 1824. **3.** *sb.* A medicinal substance; also, †*pl.* matters pertaining to medical science. late ME.

1. Dire inflammation which no cooling herb Or medcinal liquor can asswage MILT. **2. b.** A m. taste 1824. Hence **Medi·cinally** *adv.*

Medicine (me·ds'n, me·disin, -s'n), *sb.*¹ ME. [– OFr. *medecine*, *-icine* (mod. *médecine*) – L. *medicina*, f. *medicus* physician; see MEDIC. The trisyllabic pronunc. is chiefly Sc. and U.S.] **1.** The science and art concerned with the cure, alleviation, and prevention of disease, and with the restoration and preservation of health. Also, *less widely*, that branch which is the province of the physician; the art of restoring and preserving health by means of remedial substances and the regulation of diet, habits, etc.; dist. from *surgery* and *obstetrics*. **2.** A medicament, esp. one taken internally; also, medicaments generally, 'physic' ME. **b.** *fig.* ME. †**3.** Applied to the philosopher's stone or elixir, to cosmetics, philtres, etc. –1615. **4.** Used to represent the terms applied by Amer. Indians and other savages to any magical object or ceremony; a spell, charm, fetish; occas. = MANITOU 1805. **b.** = *medicine-man* 1817.

2. b. The miserable haue no other m. But onely hope SHAKS. **c.** *To take one's m.* (U.S.): to submit to something disagreeable 1894. **3.** 1 *Hen. IV*, II. ii. 19. *Comb.*: (in sense 2), **m. ball,** a stuffed leather ball used for exercise; **m. seal, stamp,** a name for small cubical or oblong stones with inscriptions in intaglio, found among Roman remains, which seem to have been used by physicians for marking their drugs; **m. tree,** the horse-radish tree; (in sense 4), **m. man,** a magician among the Amer. Indians and other savages.

†**Me·dicine,** *sb.*² 1450. [– (O)Fr. *médecin* or its source med.L. *medicinus* (XIV) physician, subst. use of L. adj. *medicinus* pertaining to a physician (*medicus*).] A medical practitioner –1632.

I haue seen a m. That's able to breath life into a stone SHAKS.

Medicine (me·ds'n, me·disin, -s'n), *v.* 1450. [– (O)Fr. *médeciner*, f. *médecine* MEDICINE *sb.*¹] **1.** *trans.* To cure by means of medicine; to give medicine to. **b.** To bring by medicinal virtue *to.* SHAKS. **2.** *transf.* and *fig.* 1593.

1. b. Not Poppy, nor Mandragora..Shall euer m. thee to that sweete sleepe Which thou owd'st yesterday SHAKS. **2.** Great greefes I see med'cine the lesse SHAKS. So **Mediciner** (*arch.*), a physician, medical man, leech; (*nonce-use*) as tr. Gr. φαρμακεύς poisoner.

Medick (mī·dik). late ME. [– L. *mēdica*, – Gr. Μηδική πόα, lit. 'Median grass'.] Any plant of the genus *Medicago*, esp. *M. sativa*, Purple medick or LUCERNE.

Medico (me·diko). 1689. [– It. *medico* – L. *medicus* MEDIC.] A medical practitioner; also, a medical student. Now *slang* or *joc.*

Medico- (mediko), used as comb. f. L. *medicus* in combs. denoting the application of medical science to various subjects of research, as *m.-botanic(al*, *-electric*, *-legal*, *-psychological*, *-statistical*, etc.

Medicommissure (mīdiko·misiŭɹ). Also **medio-**. 1882. [f. L. *medius* + COMMISSURE.] *Anat.* The middle commissure of the brain.

†**Me·dics,** *sb. pl.* 1663. [pl. of MEDIC; see -IC 2.] The science of medicine –1737.

Mediety (mĭdəi·ĕti). late ME. [– late L. *medietas* half (in cl. L., middle), f. L. *medius* middle; see -ITY, MOIETY.] **1.** †**a.** *gen.* A half –1686. **b.** *spec.* in *Law.* = MOIETY 1661. †**2.** Middle state, position, or quality –1651. †**3.** *Math.* The quality of being a mean between two quantities –1694.

Medieval, etc.: see MEDIÆVAL, etc.

‖**Medine** (medī·n). 1583. [– Fr. †*medin* (Cotgr.) – Arab., ult. f. Sultan *Mu'ayyad*, who first had them struck.] An Egyptian coin corresp. to the Turkish PARA¹.

Medio- (mī·dio), used as comb. f. L. *medius*, with the sense either 'relating to the middle of' (an organ or part), as in *m.-carpal*, *-dorsal*, *-frontal*, etc., or 'in the middle', as in *m.-perforate*; also in **m.-inferior, -posterior** = 'lower middle', 'posterior-middle' (margin).

Mediocre (mī·diōᵘkəɹ), *a.* (*sb.*) 1586. [– (partly through Fr. *médiocre*) L. *mediocris* lit. 'of middle height', f. *medius* MID + *ocris* rugged mountain.] **1.** Of middling quality; neither bad nor good; indifferent. Also *absol.* **2.** *sb.* Only *pl.* Mediocre persons (*rare*) 1834.

1. It is thus that m. people seek to lower great men CARLYLE. So **Me·diocrist,** a person of middling ability 1787.

Mediocrity (mīdiǫ·krĭti). 1450. [– (O)Fr. *médiocrité* – L. *mediocritas*, f. *mediocris*; see prec., -ITY.] **1.** Mean state or condition, mediety. Also, a mean. (Chiefly quasi-techn., with reference to the Aristotelian theory of 'the mean'. Now *rare.*) 1531. †**2.** A middle course in action; moderation, temperance –1774. †**3.** Moderate degree or rate, average quality or amount; tempered condition –1753. †**4.** Moderate fortune or condition in life –1816. **5.** The quality or condition of being mediocre. Now chiefly *disparaging.* 1588. **6.** *concr.* A person of mediocre ability 1694.

1. †*Golden m.* = *golden mean.* **5.** The most important offices in the state were bestowed on decorous and laborious m. MACAULAY. **6.** He is too much a m. CONGREVE.

Medism (mī·diz'm). 1849. [– Gr. μηδισμός, f. μηδίζειν MEDIZE.] **a.** *Gr. Hist.* Sympathy with the Medes. **b.** A word or idiom belonging to the language of the Medes.

†**Meditance.** *rare.* 1612. [f. next; see -ANCE.] Meditation.

Meditant (me·ditănt). *rare.* 1614. [– *meditant-*, pr. ppl. stem of L. *meditari*; see next, -ANT.] **a.** *adj.* Meditating. **b.** *sb.* One who meditates.

Meditate (me·diteⁱt), *v.* 1560. [– *meditat-*, pa. ppl. stem of L. *meditari*, frequent. f. IE. **med-* **mēd-* **mod-* measure (see METE *v.*¹, MODE).] **1.** *trans.* To reflect upon; to study, ponder. Now *rare.* 1580. **b.** To observe with intentness 1700. **2.** To plan by revolving in the mind; to design mentally 1591. †**3.** To think –1609. **4.** *intr.* To exercise the mind in (esp. devotional) thought or contemplation 1560.

1. Him [Rousseau] they study; him they m. BURKE. Phr. *To m. the Muse* (after L. *Musam meditari*, Virg. *Ecl.* i. 2): to occupy oneself in song or poetry. **b.** Like a lion..With inward rage he meditates his prey DRYDEN. **2.** A creature meditating mischief GOLDSM. **4.** And Isaac went out, to m. in the field, at the euentide *Gen.* 24:63. **Me·ditatingly** *adv.*

Meditation (meditēⁱ·ʃən). ME. [– (O)Fr. *méditation* – L. *meditatio*, f. as prec.; see -ION.] **1.** The action, or an act, of meditating; serious and sustained reflection or mental contemplation. **2.** *spec.* in religious use: The continuous application of the mind to the contemplation of some religious truth, mystery, or object of reverence, as a devotional exercise ME. **b.** The theme of one's meditation *Ps.* 119:97. **3.** A discourse, written or spoken, of a meditative character ME.

1. The imperiall Votresse passed on, In maiden m., fancy free SHAKS. **2.** In m. we converse with ourselves; in prayer we converse with God HENRY. **3.** A m. upon a broom-stick SWIFT.

Meditative (me·ditĕtiv, -ēˈtiv), *a.* (*sb.*) 1612. [f. MEDITATE *v.* + -IVE, partly – (O)Fr. *méditatif, -ive.* In senses 4, 5 – late L. *meditativus* (Diomedes, Priscian).] **1.** Inclined or accustomed to meditation 1656. **b.** Inclined to meditate (something specified). Const. *of.* 1876. **2.** Accompanied by, or indicative of, meditation 1756. **3.** Conducive to meditation 1868. †**4.** *Gram.* = DESIDERATIVE 1755. †**5.** *sb.* A desiderative word –1845.

1. His musing m. mind 1683. **2.** M. walks 1756, pulls of a pipe 1903. **Me·ditative-ly** *adv.*, **-ness.**

Meditator (me·diteˈtəɹ). Also **-er.** 1665. [f. MEDITATE *v.* + -OR 2.] One who meditates.

†**Mediterrane,** *a.* and *sb.* late ME. [– OFr. *mediterrain, -an* – L. *mediterraneus*; see next.] = next –1662.

Mediterranean (meditĕrēˈ·niăn), *a.* and *sb.* 1594. [f. L. *mediterraneus* inland, in late L. applied to the Mediterranean Sea, *Mare Mediterraneum*; f. *medius* MID + *terra* land, earth.] **A.** *adj.* **1.** Of land: Midland, inland, remote from the coast; opp. to *maritime.* Also, intermediate (between two areas). 1601. **2.** Of water surfaces: Nearly or entirely surrounded by dry land; land-locked 1594.

1. The more m. parts of Russia BOYLE. **2.** *M. Sea*: proper name of the sea which separates Europe from Africa. var. †**Mediterraneous** *a.*

B. *sb.* **1.** An inland sea or lake; *spec.* the Mediterranean Sea 1652. **b.** *attrib.* or *adj.* Pertaining to the Mediterranean Sea 1599. †**2.** An inhabitant of an inland part 1654.

1. b. *M. fever* = *Malta fever* (see MALTA).

Medium (mī·diŏm). *Pl.* **media, -iums.** 1551. [– L. *medium* middle, midst, med.L. means, subst. use of n. of *medius* MID. Cf. Fr. *médium* (XVI).]

A. *sb.* **1.** A middle quality, degree, or condition. Formerly also, †something intermediate in nature or degree. 1593. †**b.** Moderation –1780. †**c.** A middle course. DE FOE. †**2.** *Logic.* The middle term of a syllogism; hence, a ground of proof –1817. †**3.** A (geometrical or arithmetical) mean; an average 1551–1817. **4.** Any intervening substance through which a force acts on objects at a distance or through which impressions are conveyed to the senses, e.g. air, the ether, etc. Often *fig.* 1595. **b.** Hence, Pervading or enveloping substance; the 'element' in which an organism lives; hence *fig.* one's environment, conditions of life 1865. **5.** An intermediate agency, means, instrument, or channel. Also, intermediation, instrumentality. 1605. **6.** *Painting.* Any liquid vehicle (as oil, water, etc.) with which pigments are mixed for use. Also, any of the varieties of painting as determined by the nature of the vehicle. 1854. **7.** *Theatr.* A screen fixed in front of a gas-jet in order to throw a coloured light upon the stage 1859. **8.** Applied to a person. **a.** *gen.* An agent, mediator 1817. **b.** *Spiritualism.* A person supposed to be the organ of communications from departed spirits 1853.

1. Poesy between the best and worst No m. knows BYRON. **3.** I have reckoned upon a m., that a child just born will weigh 12 pounds SWIFT. **4.** The air, which is the m. of musick and of all sounds 1643. **b.** You cannot thus abstract any man from the social m. by which he is surrounded GROTE. **5.** The proposition is peace. Not peace through the m. of war BURKE. *M. of circulation* or *exchange, circulating m.*: something which serves as the ordinary representative of commercial value, and as the instrument of exchange; usually coins or written promises or orders for the delivery of coins. **8. b.** Attempts to pry by the help of 'mediums' into the book of Fate BRYCE.

B. *attrib.* or *adj.* **1.** Intermediate between two degrees, amounts, qualities, or classes 1796. **b.** A size of paper between royal and demy 1711. †**2.** Average, mean –1800.

1. M. wave *Wireless*, a wave having a wave-length between 100 and 800 metres.

Comb., as *m.-grade, -pace*; *m.-coloured, -sized,* adjs.

Medius (mī·diŏs). 1565. [– L. *medius* middle.] *Mus.* †**1.** = MEAN *sb.* 2. –1758. **2.** In eccl. music = MEDIANT 1782.

Medize (mī·dəiz), *v.* 1629. [– Gr. Μηδίζειν, f. Μῆδοι the Medes; see -IZE.] *intr.* To be a Mede in manners, language, and dress; to side with the Medes. Also *trans.* To make like a Mede.

‖**Medjidie** (medʒī·die). 1856. [Turkish *mecidiye* silver coins, named after the Sultan who first minted them.] **1.** *The M.*: a Turkish order instituted in 1851 by the Sultan 'Abdu'l Majīd. **2.** A Turkish silver coin first minted by the Sultan 'Abdu'l Majīd in 1844, equal to 20 piastres 1882.

Medlar (me·dləɹ). late ME. [– OFr. *medler*, f. **medle*, for **mesdle*, *mesle* :– L. *mespila, -us, -um* – Gr. μεσπίλη, μέσπιλον.] **1.** The fruit-tree *Mespilus germanica.* **b.** Applied to other trees 1718. **2.** The fruit of the medlar tree, resembling a small brown-skinned apple, with a large cup-shaped eye between the persistent calyx-lobes. It is eaten only when decayed. late ME.

1. b. *Neapolitan* or *Oriental M.*, the AZAROLE, *Cratægus azarolus. Japan M.*, the LOQUAT. **2.** You'l be rotten ere you bee halfe ripe, and that's the right vertue of the Medler SHAKS. *Comb.* **m. tree** = 1.

Medle, obs. f. MEDDLE.

Medley (me·dli), *sb.* and *a.* ME. [– OFr. *medlee*, var. of *meslee* MÊLEE :– Rom. **misculata*, subst. use of fem. pa. pple. of med.L. *misculare* MEDDLE *v.*]

A. *sb.* **1.** Combat, conflict; fighting, *esp.* hand-to-hand fighting between two parties of combatants. Now only *arch.* **2.** A combination, mixture; *esp.* a heterogeneous mixture; a mixed company 1440. **3.** A cloth woven with wools of different colours or shades. late ME. †**4.** = MASLIN[1] 1 (*rare*) 1601. **5.** A musical composition consisting of parts or subjects of an incongruous character 1626. **6.** As the title of a literary miscellany 1630.

1. *fig.* In the press and m. of such extremities BURKE. **2.** A wretched M. betwixt Priest and Layman 1683.

B. *adj.* †**1.** Of a mixed colour; motley –1681. **2.** Composed of incongruous parts or elements; mixed, motley 1594. **b.** in CHANCE-MEDLEY.

1. He rood but hoomly in a medlee cote CHAUCER. *M. cloth* = A. 3. Hence **Medley** *v.* to make a m. of; to intermix.

Médoc, Medoc (medǫ·k). 1833. [– Fr., from *Médoc* in S.W. France.] A name for the red wines produced in Médoc.

‖**Medulla** (mĭdɒ·lă). 1643. [L., perh. f. *medius* MID.] **1.** *Anat.* The marrow of bones; also, the spinal marrow. Also, †the substance of the brain. 1651. **b.** (More fully *m. oblongata*: lit. 'prolonged marrow'.) The hindmost segment of the brain 1676. **c.** The central parts of certain organs (esp. the kidney) 1878. **d.** The soft fatty substance which forms the sheath of a nerve 1839. **e.** The pith of mammalian hair. Also, the soft fibrous substance which occupies the axis of the capsule of a growing feather. 1826. **f.** The endosarc of protozoa 1888. **2.** *Bot.* The soft internal tissue of plants 1651. †**3.** *fig.* The 'pith' or 'marrow' of a subject. Often used for: A compendium, abridgement, summary. –1769.

Medullary (mĭdɒ·lări, me·dɒ̆lări), *a.* 1620. [f. prec. + -ARY[2], after L. *medullaris.*] **1.** *Anat.* Of, pertaining to, of the nature of, or resembling marrow. Also, pertaining to the medulla of an organ or part (e.g. *the m. rays in the kidney, the m. sheath of a nerve*); *occas.* pertaining to the *medulla oblongata.* 1677. **b.** *Path.* An alternative epithet for encephaloid or soft cancer 1804. **2.** †**a.** Pertaining to the soft internal substance or pulp (of plants). **b.** *Bot.* Of, relating to, or connected with the pith of plants. 1620.

2. b. *M. rays*: each of the processes in a woody stem connecting the pith with the bark. *M. sheath*: the sheath immediately surrounding the pith. So **Medu·llar** (1541), **Medu·llous** (1578) *adjs.*

Medullated (mĭdɒ·leˈtĕd), *ppl. a.* 1867. [f. MEDULLA + -ATE[2] + -ED[1].] Having a medulla.

Medusa (mĭdiū·să, -ză). late ME. [– L. *Medusa* – Gr. Μέδουσα.] **1.** *Gr. Myth.* One of the three Gorgons, whose head, with snakes for hair, turned him who looked upon it into stone. **2.** *Zool.* (Pl. *medusæ, -as.*) **a.** A soft gelatinous hydrozoan; a jelly-fish. **b.** One of the two types of reproductive zooids in hydrozoans; opp. to *hydroid.* 1758. **c.** *attrib.*, as *m.-bud*, etc. 1846. Hence **Medu·sal** *a.* (*Zool.*), pertaining to, or of the nature of, a m. **Medu·san, Medu·sian** *adjs.* of or pertaining to the medusæ or to medusoid animals; *sbs.* a medusan animal.

Medusa's head. Also, when used attrib., **Medusa head.** 1706. **1.** *Astr.* A cluster of stars, including the bright star Algol, in the constellation Perseus. **2. a.** An ophiuran echinoderm of either of the genera *Astrophyton* and *Euryale*; a basket-fish or sea-basket. **b.** A species of crinoid, *Pentacrinus caput-medusæ.* 1784. **3. a.** A kind of spurge, *Euphorbia caput-medusæ.* **b.** A species of orchid, *Cirrhopetalum medusæ.* **c.** A species of agaric, *Hydnum caput-medusæ.* 1760.

Medusiform (mĭdiū·sifǫɹm), *a.* 1848. [f. MEDUSA + -FORM.] *Zool.* = next, A.

Medusoid (mĭdiū·soid). 1848. [f. MEDUSA + -OID.] **A.** *adj.* Medusa-like. **B.** *sb.* **1.** The medusa-like generative bud of a fixed hydrozoan 1848. **2.** A medusa or medusa-like animal 1882.

Meech, etc., var. f. MICHE, etc.

Meed (mīd), *sb.* [OE. *mēd* = OFris. *mēde*, OS. *mēda, mieda*, OHG. *mēta, mieta* (G. *miete*) :– WGmc. **mēda*, rel. to OE. *meord*, Goth. *mizdō* reward (:– Gmc. **mizdō, -ōn*), and Gr. μισθός.] **1.** In early use: Wages, hire; recompense, reward. Now only *poet.* or *rhet.* in sense: A reward, guerdon; one's merited portion *of* (praise, honour, etc.). †**b.** A gift. SHAKS. ¶**c.** Adjudged character or title (*rare*) 1833. †**2.** Corrupt gain; bribery. ME. only. †**3.** Merit, excellence, worth –1714.

1. He must not flote upon his watry bear.. Without the m. of som melodious tear MILT. **b.** *Timon* I. i. 288. **c.** Pallas and Aphrodite, claiming each This m. of fairest TENNYSON. **2.** He toke mede and money of the Scottis LD. BERNERS.

†**Meed,** *v.* ME. [f. MEED *sb.*] **1.** *trans.* To reward; also, to bribe –1542. **2.** To deserve. HEYWOOD.

†**Mee·dful,** *a.* ME. [f. MEED *sb.* + -FUL.] Deserving of reward –1573. †**Meedfully** *adv.*

Meek (mīk), *a.* [Early ME. *meoc, mec* – ON. **miúkr, mjúkr* soft, pliant, gentle, rel. to Goth. **mūks* in *mūkamōdei* meekness, and (M)LG. *mūke*, MHG. *mūche* (G. dial. *mauche*) malanders.] **1.** †**a.** Gentle, courteous, kind; merciful, indulgent –1009. **b.** (= Vulgate *mansuetus*): Free from self-will; piously humble and submissive; patient and unresentful ME. **c.** Submissive, humble; also, easily 'put upon' ME. †**d.** as *adv.* = *meekly* –1605. **2.** Of animals: Tame, not fierce ME. **3.** In physical applications: Not violent or strong; gentle. *Obs.* or *arch.* ME.

1. a. *Jul. C.* III. i. 255. **b.** In the blest Kingdoms m. of joy and love MILT. *absol.* Blessed are the meeke: for they shall inherit the earth *Matt.* 5:5. Phr. *As m. as a lamb, a maid*, etc., as *Moses.* **d.** *Macb.* I. vii. 17. **3.** *M. mother* (tr. PIA MATER): see MOTHER *sb.*[1] Hence **Mee·k-ly** *adv.*, **-ness.**

†**Meek,** *v.* ME. [f. MEEK *a.*] **1.** *trans.* To make meek in spirit, to humble; *occas.* to appease, mollify –1680. **b.** *refl.* To humble or abase oneself –1583. **2.** *trans.* To tame (an animal) –1653. **3.** *intr.* To become or be meek ME.

Meeken (mī·k'n), *v.* Now *rare.* late ME. [f. MEEK *a.* + -EN[5].] **1.** *trans.* To make meek; to humble, soften, tame; †to mitigate; to bring low, abase. **2.** *intr.* To become meek; to submit meekly (*to* something) 1844.

Meer(e: vars. of MARE[1], MAYOR, MERE, MORE.

Meered: see MERED.

Meerkat (mīᵊ·ɹkæt). 1481. [– Du. *meerkat* = G. *meerkatze* (in OHG. *merikazza*), MLG. *merkatte* lit. 'sea-cat'; perh. orig. alt. of an Oriental name (cf. Hindi *markat*, Skr. *markata* ape) by assim. to words meaning 'sea' and 'cat', with the notion of 'ape from overseas'.] †**1.** A monkey –1559. **2.** A S. Afr. name for two small mammals: **a.** *Cynictis penicillata*, allied to the ichneumon. **b.** The suricate, *Suricata tetradactyla*, which is tamed as a pet. 1801.

Meerschaum (mīᵊ·ɹʃǫm, -ʃəm). 1784. [– G. *meerschaum*, f. *meer* sea + *schaum* foam tr.

Pers. *kef-i-daryā* 'foam of sea', in allusion to its frothy appearance.] **1.** A hydrous silicate of magnesium occurring in soft white clay-like masses. A popular synonym for sepiolite. **2.** (In full *m. pipe.*) A tobacco-pipe with a meerschaum bowl 1799.

Meet (mīt), *sb.* 1831. [f. MEET *v.*] The meeting of hounds and men for a hunt. Also, by extension, a meeting of cyclists, etc.

Meet (mīt), *a.* and *adv.* Now *arch.* ME. [aphet. f. earlier ME. *imete* :- OE. (Anglian) **ġemēte*, (WS.) *ġemǣte* = OHG. *gamāzi* (G. *gemäss*), f. **ʒa-* Y- + **mǣtō* measure, f. * *mǣt-* **met-* measure, METE *v.*[1]; the etymol. sense is 'commensurate'.]

A. *adj.* †**1.** Of proper dimensions; made to fit. Later: Close-fitting, barely large enough. †**2.** Equal *to*, on the same level –1687. **3.** Suitable, fit, proper. Const. *for*, *to*, also *to* with *inf.* **b.** Predicatively: Fitting, becoming, proper. Chiefly in *it is m. that..*, *as* (or *than*) *is m.* ME. †**4.** Mild, gentle –1598.

2. Phr. *To be m. with*: to be even or quits with; You taxe Signior Benedicke too much, but hee'l be m. with you SHAKS. **3.** Not here, O Apollo! Are haunts m. for thee M. ARNOLD. **b.** It is mete and right so to do *Bk. Com. Prayer.*

†**B.** *adv.* In a meet, fit, or proper manner; sufficiently. Also, exactly (in a certain position). –1688.

Meet (mīt), *v.* Infl. **met.** [OE. *mētan* (Northumb. *mǣta*), also *ġemētan* (see Y-) = OFris. *mēta*, OS. *mōtian* (Du. *moeten*), ON. *mœta*, Goth. *gamotjan* :- Gmc. **ʒa|mōtjan*, f. **mōtam* meeting, MOOT *sb.*]

I. *trans.* **1.** To come upon, fall in with, find. Now only *dial.* exc. with person as obj.; otherwise repl. by *m. with.* **2.** To come face to face with or into the company of (a person arriving at the same point from a different direction) ME. **b.** To go to a place at which (a person) arrives, in order e.g. to welcome, communicate with, accompany, or convey (him). Similarly, *to m. a coach*, *a train*, etc. ME. **c.** *transf.* With inanimate things as subj. or obj.: To come into contact, association, or junction with ME. **d.** Of an object of attention: To present itself before, to come under the observation of 1632. **e.** *To m.* a person's *eye*, *gaze*, etc.: to perceive that he is looking at one; also, to submit oneself to his look without turning away 1670. **3.** To encounter or oppose in battle. Also (after Fr. *rencontrer*), to fight a duel with. ME. †**b.** To be even with. FLETCHER. **c.** To oppose, cope or grapple with (something impersonal) 1745. **4.** To come by accident or design into the company of; to come across (a person) in society or business ME. **5.** To encounter, experience (a certain fortune or destiny); to receive (reward, punishment, etc.). Now *rare* or *poet.*, repl. by *m. with.* 1440. **6.** To come into conformity with (a person's wishes, etc.) 1694. **7.** To satisfy (a demand or need). *To m. a bill* (Comm.): to pay it at maturity. 1833.

2. b. I'll m. the seven o'clock train DOYLE. Phr. *To m. half-way*: †to forestall; to respond to the friendly advances of; to make concessions to (a person) in consideration of equal concessions on his part; to come to a compromise with. *To m. trouble halfway*: to distress oneself with anticipations of what may happen. **c.** The gibbet was set up where King Street meets Cheapside MACAULAY. **d.** Phr. *To m. the eye* (*sight*, *view*), *the ear*: to be visible; audible. *To m. the eye of*: to happen to be seen by. **3.** I only with an Oaken staff will m. thee MILT. **c.** The threats of Charles were met by Offa with defiance J. R. GREEN. **4.** I loathe. . the faces that one meets TENNYSON. His medical colleagues refuse to m. him in consultation 1906. Phr. *To be well, happily*, etc., *met.* Also *ellipt.*, *Well met!* (as an expression of welcome). **5.** This generous appeal met no response M. PATTISON. **6.** I will do my best to m. you in the matter 1906. **7.** A remedy which exactly meets the necessities of the case 1884.

II. *intr.* **1.** Of two or more persons: To come face to face, so as to be in each other's presence or company. Often with *together.* Sometimes conjugated with *be.* ME. **b.** Of a society, etc.: To assemble for purposes of conference, business, worship, or the like 1530. †**c.** To keep an appointment –1717. **d.** To arrive at agreement 1851. **2.** To come together in the shock of battle (*arch.*). late ME. **3.** Of inanimate objects: To come into contact ME. **b.** Said of qualities, etc., uniting in the same person, etc. 1581. †**c.** To agree or tally (*rare*) –1823.

1. When shall we three m. againe? SHAKS. **b.** The Parliament will certainly m. on Friday next SWIFT. **3.** Oh, East is East, and West is West, and never the twain shall m. KIPLING. **b.** Thou, the latest-left of all my knights, In whom should m. the offices of all TENNYSON.

Comb. **Meet with.** **a.** = senses I. 1, 5, which it has superseded in common use. †**b.** in various senses (I. 2, 2 c, 3, 3 b, 3 c), most of which are now expressed by *meet.*

Meeten (mī·t'n), *v.* 1807. [f. MEET *a.* + -EN[5].] *trans.* To make meet or fit (*for*).

Meeter (mī·təɹ). 1646. [f. MEET *v.* + -ER[1].] One who attends or takes part in a meeting.

Meeth: var. MEAD[1] (the drink).

Meeting (mī·tiŋ), *vbl. sb.* ME. [f. MEET *v.* + -ING[1]. OE. had *ġemēting* in sense 3.] **1.** In senses of MEET *v.* **2.** Used *euphem.* for a duel 1812. **3.** An assembly of a number of people for entertainment, discussion, or the like 1513. **b.** An assembly of people, in England, of nonconformists, for purposes of worship; now *rare* exc. with reference to the Society of Friends (who apply it also to certain periodical assemblies for discussion and business); also, a dissenting chapel, a meeting-house (surviving in names of buildings as *Old*, *New M.*) 1593. †**4.** = MEETING-PLACE (*poet.*) –1801. **5.** *attrib.* **m.-folks,** dissenters.

1. At Peter's firste metinge with our Savyour Christe 1559. The meetings of the waters 1606. **3.** He was no longer summoned to any m. of the board MACAULAY. **b.** We went to m. at Wells 1774. **4.** 1 *Hen. IV*, III. ii. 174.

Mee·ting-house. 1636. †**1.** A (private) house used for a meeting. WOOD. **2.** A place of worship; in the gen. sense, now only *U.S.* In England, a dissenting place of worship, a conventicle; now usu. disparaging, exc. with reference to Quakers.

Mee·ting-place. 1553. A place in which a meeting occurs or is held; †a meeting-house.

†**Mee·tly,** *a.* ME. [f. MEET *a.* + -LY[1].] **1.** Moderate; of moderate size or quantity –1620. **2.** Fitting, proper, suitable, meet –1633.

Meetly (mī·tli), *adv.* late ME. [f. MEET *a.* + -LY[2].] **1.** Moderately, fairly. (Common in 16th c.) **2.** Fitly, suitably; as is meet 1502.

Meetness (mī·tnės). 1449. [f. MEET *a.* + -NESS.] The condition of being meet; fitness, suitableness.

Meg[1] (meg). 1538. [Sc. var. of MAG *sb.*[1]] Pet form of *Margaret*, used *dial.* to indicate a hoyden, coarse woman, etc. **b.** The great 15th c. gun in Edinburgh Castle was called *Mons Meg*, *Muckle* or *Great Meg*, *Roaring Meg* 1575.

Meg[2] (meg). *slang* and *dial.* 1688. [Of unkn. origin.] †**1.** A guinea –1742. **2.** A halfpenny (cf. MAG *sb.*[2]) 1781.

Mega- (me·gă), bef. a vowel **meg-,** repr. Gr. μεγα-, comb. f. μέγας great, as in: **Megacepha·lic** [Gr. κεφαλή] *a.* large-headed; *spec.* of a skull exceeding 1,450 cubic centimetres. **Me·gadont** [badly f. Gr. ὀδούς, ὀδοντ-] *a.* having large teeth. **Megagame·te,** the larger (or female) of two gametes or conjugating cells. **Me·gaseme** [Gr. σῆμα sign] *a.* having a large orbital index; *spec.* one over 89; *sb.* a m. skull. **Me·gasporange,** ‖**-spora·ngium** (pl. **-ia**), a sporangium containing megaspores. **Me·gaspore** = MACROSPORE. **b.** Prefixed to names of units of measurement, force, etc., with sense 'a million times'; e.g. *megadyne*, *meg(a)erg*, *megavolt*, *megohm*, etc.

Megacosm (me·găkǫz'm). 1617. [f. Gr. μέγας great + κόσμος world, after *macrocosm.*] = MACROCOSM.

Megalithic (megăli·þik), *a.* 1839. [f. Gr. μέγας great + λίθος stone + -IC.] *Antiq.* Consisting or constructed of large stones; *transf.* of a period, a people, etc. Hence **Me·galith,** a stone of great size used in construction or as a monument 1853.

Megalo- (me·gălo), bef. a vowel **megal-,** – Gr. μεγαλο-, comb. f. μέγας great (cf. MEGA-), as in: **Me·galerg** *Physics* = *megerg* (see MEGA- b). **Me·galoblast, -cyte,** a large nucleated red blood-corpuscle occurring in anæmia.

Megalomania (megălomē[i]·niă). 1890. [f. MEGALO- + MANIA.] *Nosology.* The insanity of self-exaltation; the passion for big things. Often *transf.* Hence **Megaloma·niac** *a.* and *sb.* **Megalomani·acal** *a.*

Megalophonous (megălǫ·fŏnəs), *a.* 1819. [f. Gr. μεγαλόφωνος, f. μεγαλο- MEGALO- + φωνή voice, sound; see -OUS.] Grand-sounding SHELLEY.

‖**Megalops** (me·gălǫps). 1855. [mod.L., f. Gr. μεγαλωπός f. μεγαλο- MEGALO- + ὤψ, ὠπ- eye.] *Zool.* A larval stage in the development of crabs (formerly supposed to be a distinct genus), characterized by very large eyes. Also **Megalo·pa** 1815.

Megalosaur (me·gălosǭɹ). 1841. [f. MEGALO- + Gr. σαῦρος lizard.] An animal of the extinct genus *Megalosaurus* (1824) of gigantic lizards. **Megalosau·rian** *a.* and *sb.*

Megaphone (me·găfō[u]n). 1878. [f. MEGA- + -PHONE.] **1.** An instrument for carrying sound a long distance, invented by T. A. Edison. **2.** A large speaking-trumpet 1896.

Megapode (me·găpō[u]d), **-pod** (-pǫd). 1857. [– mod.L. *Megapodius*, f. Gr. μέγας great + πούς, ποδ- foot.] *Ornith.* Any bird of the genus *Megapodius* or family *Megapodiidæ*, a mound-building bird, native of Australia and the Malay Archipelago. **Mega·podan** *a.* and *sb.*

Megarian, -ean (megē[ə]·riăn). 1603. [(1) f. L. *Megara*, Gr. Μέγαρα (neut. pl.), a city in Greece + -IAN; (2) f. L. *Megareus* + -AN.] **A.** *adj.* Pertaining to the school of philosophy founded *c*400 B.C. by Euclides of Megara. **B.** *sb.* One of this school. **Mega·ric** *a.* and *sb.*

Megascope (me·găskō[u]p). 1831. [f. MEGA- + -SCOPE.] A kind of camera obscura or magic lantern for throwing a magnified image upon a screen.

Megascopic (megăskǫ·pik), *a.* 1879. [f. as prec. + -IC.] **1.** = MACROSCOPIC. **2.** Pertaining to a megascope; magnified, as an image 1902.

‖**Megass** (megæ·s). Also **-asse.** 1847. [Of unkn. origin. Cf. BAGASSE.] The fibrous residue after the expression of sugar from the cane. Cf. BAGASSE.

Megatherium (megăþī[ə]·riŏm). *Pl.* **-ia.** 1826. [mod.L. (Cuvier), as if Gr. μέγα θηρίον 'great beast'; see MEGA-.] An extinct genus of huge herbivorous edentates resembling the sloths; one of these. Also *transf.* applied to something huge 1850. Also anglicized **Me·gathere** 1839. Hence **Megathe·rial** *a.* resembling a m.; huge 1894. **Megathe·rian** *a.* of or pertaining to megatheria; *sb.* a m. or kindred animal 1842. **Megathe·rioid** *a.* resembling a m.; *sb.* a megatherioid animal 1839.

Megilp (mĭgi·lp), *sb.* (Many variant spellings.) 1768. [Of unkn. origin.] **1.** A mixture of linseed oil with turpentine or mastic varnish, or the like, employed as a vehicle for oil colours. **2.** A composition used by grainers 1827. Hence **Megi·lp** *v. trans.* to varnish with m.; to give to (oil colours) the quality imparted by m.

Megohm: see MEGA- b.

Megrim[1] (mī·grim). late ME. [– (O)Fr. *migraine*, semi-pop. – late L. see HEMICRANIA.] **1.** Hemicrania; a form of severe headache usually confined to one side of the head; nervous or sick headache; an attack of this. **b.** = VERTIGO 1595. **2.** A whim, fancy, fad 1593. **3.** *pl.* 'Vapours'; low spirits 1633. **4.** *pl.* The staggers 1639.

2. Hee is troubled with a perpetuall migrim; at sea hee wisheth to bee on land, and on land at sea 1631.

Megrim[2] (mī·grim). *dial.* Also **-in.** 1836. [Of unkn. origin.] The scald-fish, *Arnoglossus laterna.*

Meibomian (məibō[u]·miăn), *a.* 1813. [f. *Meibomius* + -AN.] *Anat.* Distinguishing epithet of certain sebaceous glands in the human eyelid, discovered by H. Meibom (Meibomius) of Helmstadt (died 1700).

Meinie (mē[i]·ni). *Obs.* exc. *arch.* ME. [– (O)Fr. *meinée*, *mesnée* = Pr. *mesnada* :- Rom. **mansionata*, f. L. *mansio*, *-on-* MANSION; see -Y[5]. In Eng. partly confused with MANY *sb.*] **1.** A family, household. **2.** A body of retainers, dependents, etc.; a retinue, suite, train ME. †**3.** A company of persons having a common object of association; an army, ship's crew, congregation, etc. –1598. †**4.**

The collection of pieces or 'men' used in the game of chess ME. only. **5.** A multitude of persons; chiefly disparaging, a 'crew', 'set'. Also, the masses. ME. †**6.** Of animals: A herd, drove, flock, etc.; a multitude –1556.

2. They summon'd vp their meiney, straight tooke Horse, Commanded me to follow SHAKS.

Meiocene, var. of MIOCENE.

‖**Meiosis** (məiˌōᵘ·sis). Also †**miosis.** 1577. [mod.L. – Gr. μείωσις, f. μειοῦν lessen, f. μείων less; see -OSIS.] *Rhet.* †**a.** A figure by which the impression is intentionally conveyed that a thing is less in size, importance, etc., than it really is. **b.** = LITOTES 1642.

b. The Words are a *Meiosis*, and import much more than they express SOUTH. Hence **Meio·tic** *a.* 1915.

Meiostemonous (məiˌostī·mŏnəs), *a.* Also **mio-.** 1832. [irreg. f. Gr. μείων less + στήμων, στημον- stamen + -OUS.] *Bot.* Having fewer stamens than petals.

‖**Meistersinger** (məi·stəɹsi:ŋəɹ). 1886. [G. = master-singer.] A member of one of the German artisan guilds of minstrels (14th–16th cent.).

Meith (mīþ). *Sc.* 1513. [app. – ON. *mið* mark, but assoc. with L. *mēta* boundary; see METE *sb.*[1]] A landmark, sea-mark, boundary.

Mekhitarist (me·kitărist). Also **mech-.** 1834. [f. *Mekhitar* + -IST.] **A.** *sb.* One of a congregation of Armenian monks of the R.C. Church originally founded at Constantinople in 1701 by Mekhitar, an Armenian. **B.** *adj.* Of or belonging to these 1874.

Mekometer (mīkǫ·mĭtəɹ). 1894. [f. Gr. μῆκος length + -METER.] An instrument for finding the range for infantry fire.

Melaconite (mĭlæ·kŏnəit). 1850. [Altered from †*melaconise* (1839) – Fr. *mélaconise*, f. Gr. μέλας black + κόνις dust; see -ITE[1] 2 b.] *Min.* An earthy black oxide of copper.

‖**Melada** (melēⁱ·dă). 1875. [Sp., f. *melar* boil sugar a second time, f. *miel* honey.] The sugar and molasses obtained when cane-juice is boiled down to sugar-point.

‖**Melæna** (mĭlī·nă). 1800. [mod.L. – Gr. μέλαινα, fem. of μέλας black.] *Path.* A disease or (in mod. use) symptoms of a disease characterized by the evacuation and vomiting of dark bloody matter. **b.** *concr.* The matter thus discharged 1858.

Melam (me·læm). 1835. [Arbitrary formation (Liebig 1834).] *Chem.* A buff-coloured, insoluble amorphous substance obtained by the distillation of sulphocyanide of ammonium.

Melamine (me·lăməin). Also **-in.** 1835. [Named by Liebig (1834); f. prec. + AMINE.] *Chem.* A crystalline substance obtained by boiling melam with potassic hydrate, or by heating cyanamide to 302° F.; called also *cyanuramide*.

†**Melampod.** Also **-pode.** 1579. [– L. *melampodion* (Pliny) – Gr. μελαμπόδιον black hellebore, f. μέλας, μελαν- black + πούς, ποδ- foot.] Black Hellebore, *Helleborus officinalis* –1656.

‖**Melanæmia** (melănī·miă). 1860. [mod.L., f. Gr. μέλας, μελαν- + αἷμα blood; see -IA[1].] *Path.* A morbid condition, associated with severe forms of malarial fever, in which the blood contains granules and flakes of black or brown pigment. Hence **Melanæ·mic** *a.* 1878.

‖**Melancholia** (melănkōᵘ·liă). *Pl.* **-iæ.** 1814. [Late L.; see MELANCHOLY.] A functional mental disease characterized by extreme depression of spirits. **Melancho·liac** *a.* affected with m.; *sb.* one so affected 1863.

†**Melancho·lian.** ME. [f. MELANCHOLY + -AN.] **A.** *adj.* Having the atrabilious temperament; addicted to 'melancholy' or irascibility. **B.** *sb.* One of an atrabilious temperament or affected with melancholy –1695.

Melancholic (melănkǫ·lik). late ME. [– (O)Fr. *mélancolique* – L. *melancholicus* (Cicero, Pliny) – Gr. μελαγχολικός; see MELANCHOLY *sb.*, -IC.] **A.** *adj.* †**1.** Pertaining to or containing 'melancholy' or 'black bile'; atrabilious. Of food, atmospheric or planetary influences, etc.: Tending to produce melancholy or atrabilious disorder. –1631. **2.** Of persons, etc. †**a.** Having the atrabiliar temperament or constitution. **b.** Constitutionally liable to (or †affected with) depression of spirits; gloomy, melancholy. ME. †**3.** Causing depression of spirits; saddening –1812. †**4.** Expressive of melancholy or sadness –1757. **5.** In mod. use: Pertaining to, or affected with, melancholia 1866.

2. b. Oliver was of the m. temperament MORLEY.

B. *sb.* **1.** †**a.** One who is affected with mental depression. **b.** One suffering from melancholia. 1586. †**2.** Used by Clarendon for: Depression of spirits.

Melancholily (me·lănkǫlili), *adv.* 1536. [f. MELANCHOLY *a.* + -LY[2].] In a melancholy manner. †**Me·lancholiness** 1528–1715.

Melancholious (melănkōᵘ·liəs), *a.* Now *rare.* late ME. [– OFr. *melancolieus*, f. *melancolie*; see MELANCHOLY *sb.*, -OUS.] **1.** Constitutionally inclined to melancholy; †atrabilious in constitution; gloomy. Also, of sounds, etc.: Expressive of melancholy. †**2.** Tending to cause, or of the nature of, atrabilious disorder –1562.

1. This pope..was a fumisshe man and malincolyous 1523.

Melancholist (me·lănkǭlist). Now *rare* or *Obs.* 1599. [f. MELANCHOLY + -IST.] †One of a 'melancholic' constitution; one affected with melancholia.

Melancholize (me·lănkŏləiz), *v.* Now *rare* or *Obs.* 1597. [f. as prec. + -IZE.] To be or become or make melancholy.

Melancholy (me·lănkǫli), *sb.* ME. [–(O)Fr. *mélancolie* – late L. *melancholia* – Gr. μελαγχολία, f. μέλας, μελαν- black + χολή bile; see -Y[3].] †**1.** The condition of having too much 'black bile'; the disease supposed to result from this condition. From the 17th c. onwards used as the name of the mental disease now called technically MELANCHOLIA. –1866. †**b.** *concr.* The 'black bile' itself; one of the four chief fluids or cardinal humours of obsolete physiology –1653. †**2.** Irascibility, sullenness –1595. **3.** Sadness and depression of spirits; gloom or dejection, esp. when constitutional. Often *personified.* ME. †**b.** A vexation –1644. **c.** A state or †(often in *pl.*) mood of melancholy 1586. **d.** A tender or pensive sadness 1614.

2. *John* III. iii. 42. **3.** My minde was troubled with deepe Melancholly SHAKS. Hence loathed M., Of Cerberus and blackest midnight born MILT. **d.** But hail thou Goddes, sage and holy, Hail divinest M. MILT. *Comb.*, as *m.-mad, -sick* adjs., etc.

Melancholy (me·lănkǭli), *a.* 1526. [attrib. use of the sb., the termination of which suggests an adj. formation; cf. *dainty.* Superseded MELANCHOLIOUS.] †**1.** Affected with the disease of melancholy –1732. †**b.** Of or affected by the melancholy 'humour' –1667. †**2.** Irascible; sullen –1604. **3.** Of persons, etc.: Depressed in spirits; sad, gloomy, dejected; *esp.* of a constitutionally gloomy temperament 1579. Also *transf.* (of animals) 1593. **b.** Pensive; sadly meditative 1632. **4.** Suggestive or expressive of sadness, depressing, dismal 1592. **5.** Of a fact, state of things, etc.: Saddening, lamentable, deplorable 1710.

3. There is no more m. creature in existence than a mountebank off duty W. IRVING. *transf.* The mellancholy Owle (Deaths ordinary messenger) NASHE. **b.** Sweet Bird.., Most musicall, most m.! MILT. **4.** M. Bells *Rom. & Jul.* IV. v. 86.

†**Me·lancholy,** *v.* 1491. [– OFr. *melancolier*, f. *melancolie* MELANCHOLY *sb.*] *trans.* To make melancholy –1657.

Melanchthonian (melăŋkþōᵘ·niăn). 1755. [f. Philipp *Melanchthon* (Gr. transl. of G. *Schwarzerd* 'black earth'), a German reformer (1497–1560) + -IAN.] **A.** *adj.* Of or pertaining to Melanchthon or his opinions. **B.** *sb.* A follower of Melanchthon. †**Mela·nchthonist** 1564.

Melanesian (melănī·ʃ[i]ăn). 1849. [f. *Melanesia* (in sense 'the regions of islands inhabited by blacks'), after *Polynesia*, f. Gr. μέλας black + νῆσος island + -AN.] **A.** *adj.* Of or pertaining to Melanesia (a group of islands in the western Pacific), its inhabitants, language, etc. **B.** *sb.* A native of Melanesia; the language of the Melanesians.

‖**Mélange, mel-** (melāŋʒ), *sb.* 1653. [Fr. *mélange*, f. *mêler* mix; see MEDDLE *v.*] **1.** A mixture; usu. a heterogeneous collection, a medley. **2. a.** A dress fabric of cotton chain and woollen weft. **b.** A kind of woollen yarn of mingled colours. So **Melange** *v.* to mix (wool of different colours) 1880; also †**Mela·ngery,** a mixture 1733.

Melanian (mĭlēⁱ·niăn), *a.* 1861. [– Fr. *mélanien*, f. Gr. μέλας, μελαν- black; see -IAN.] *Ethn.* = next 1.

Melanic (mĭlæ·nik), *a.* 1826. [f. Gr. μέλας, μελαν- black + -IC.] **1.** *Ethn.* Having black hair and a dark complexion. **2.** Distinctive epithet of the black pigment occurring in melanosis; hence, affected with melanosis 1847.

Melanin (me·lănin). 1843. [f. Gr. μέλας, μελαν- black + -IN[1].] *Chem.* and *Phys.* The black pigment of melanism; also that of melanosis.

Melanism (me·lăniz'm). 1843. [f. Gr. μέλας, μελαν- black + -ISM.] Darkness of colour resulting from an abnormal development of black pigment in the epidermis, hair, feathers, etc. of animals; opp. to *albinism.* **b.** A melanic variety (of some species) 1863. Hence **Melani·stic** *a.* affected by m. 1874.

Melano- (me·lăno), – Gr. μελανο-, comb. f. μέλας black, as in ‖**Melanode·rma, -de·rmia** [Gr. δέρμα skin; see -IA.] *Path.* = MELASMA.

‖**Melanochroi** (melănǫ·kroˌəi), *sb. pl.* 1866. [mod.L.; formed by Huxley to represent an assumed Gr. μελάνωχροι, f. μέλας, μελαν- black + ὠχρός pale.] *Anthrop.* In Huxley's classification: A subdivision of the *Leiotrichi* or smooth-haired class of mankind, having dark hair and pale complexion. **Melanochro·ic, Melano·chroid, Melano·chrous** *adjs.* pertaining to or resembling the *Melanochroi.*

Melanocomous (melănǫ·kŏməs), *a.* 1836. [f. Gr. μελανοκόμης (f. μέλας, μελανο- + κόμη hair) + -OUS.] Black-haired.

‖**Melanoi,** *sb. pl.* 1866. [Gr. μελανοί, pl. of μελανός = μέλας black.] *Anthrop.* Huxley's name for the black-haired and dark-complexioned division of the LEIOTRICHI.

Melanoid (me·lănoid), *a.* 1854. [f. Gr. μελανοειδής; see MELANO-, -OID.] *Path.* Characterized by the presence of black pigment.

‖**Melanoma** (melănōᵘ·mă). *Pl.* **-mata.** *c* 1830. [mod.L., f. Gr. μέλας, μελαν- + -OMA.] *Path.* A melanotic growth.

Melanose (me·lănōᵘs), *a.* 1823. [irreg. back-formation from next; see -OSE[1].] *Path.* Containing, or of the nature of, the black pigment contained in melanosis.

‖**Melanosis** (melănōᵘ·sis.) *Pl.* **-oses** (-ōᵘ·sīz). 1823. [mod.L., f. Gr. μέλας, μελαν- + -OSIS.] *Path.* **1.** Abnormal development of a black pigment in some tissue. **2.** Black cancer 1834.

Melanotic (melănǫ·tik), *a.* 1829. [Formed after MELANOSIS; see -OTIC.] **1.** *Path.* Characterized by, or of the nature of, melanosis. **2.** *Zool.* = MELANISTIC 1872.

Melanotype (mĭlæ·nŏtəip). 1864. [f. MELANO- + -TYPE.] A kind of FERROTYPE.

Melanous (me·lănəs), *a.* 1836. [f. Gr. μέλας, μελαν- + -OUS.] *Anthrop.* With ref. to hair and complexion: Blackish, dark; *spec.* belonging to the MELANOI.

‖**Melanuria** (melăniūᵊ·riă). 1890. [mod.L., f. MELANO- + -URIA.] *Path.* A condition in which the urine assumes a black or dark blue colour. Hence **Melanu·ric** *a.*[1] 1881.

Melanuric (melăniūᵊ·rik), *a.*[2] 1852. [Based on G. *melanurensäure*, Liebig's alt. of Henneberg's term (1850) *mellanurensäure*, f. *mellan* MELLONE + *uren* a supposed base of urea + *säure* acid.] *Chem.* In *m. acid*, a white chalky powder, obtained by heating urea.

Melaphyre (me·lăfəiᵊɹ). 1841. [– Fr. *mélaphyre* (Brongiart), f. Gr. μέλας black + (*por*)*phyre* PORPHYRY.] *Petrology.* A species of black or dark-coloured porphyry.

‖**Melasma** (mĭlæ·zmă). 1817. [mod.L. – Gr. μέλασμα black spot or dye, ult. f. μέλας black.] *Path.* Excess of black pigment in the skin. Hence **Mela·smic** *a.* 1865.

Melasses, obs. f. MOLASSES.

Melchite (me·lkəit). 1619. [– eccl. L. *Melchitæ* – Byz. Gr. Μελχῖται, repr. Syr. *malkayā* 'royalists' of the party of the Roman Emperor, f. *malkā* king; see -ITE[1] 1.] Orig., the designation applied by the Monophysites to those Eastern Christians in Syria and Egypt who adhered to the orthodox faith as defined by the councils of Ephesus (A.D. 431) and Chalcedon (A.D. 451). Later, applied to those orthodox Eastern Christians who use an Arabic version of the Greek ritual, and esp. to those who have become Uniats.

Meld (meld), *v.* 1897. [– G. *melden* announce, declare (at cards).] *Cards.* In pinocle: = DECLARE (*vb.* 8) in bezique; also *sb.* a group of cards to be melded.

‖**Mêlée** (me·leⁱ, mẹle). 1648. [Fr., earlier *mellée* (whence MELLAY); see MEDLEY.] A mixed fight between two parties of combatants, a skirmish. Also *transf.* a lively debate.

Melene (me·līn). 1848. [f. Gr. μέλισσα bee + -ENE.] *Chem.* An olefine obtained by the distillation of beeswax. Called also **Melissylene.**

Melic (me·lik), *sb.* 1787. [– mod.L. *melica* (Linnæus) – It. *melica* sorghum.] A grass belonging or allied to the genus *Melica.*

Melic (me·lik), *a.* 1699. [– L. *melicus* – Gr. μελικός, f. μέλος song; see -IC.] Of poetry (esp. Gr. strophic odes): Intended to be sung.

‖**Meliceris** (melisīᵊ·ris). *Pl.* **-cerides** (-se·ridīz). 1562. [mod.L. – Gr. μελικηρίς some eruptive disease, f. μελίκηρον honeycomb, f. μέλι honey + κηρός wax.] *Path.* An encysted tumour containing matter which resembles honey. **2.** An affection marked by exudation of viscid honeylike matter 1870. Hence **Meli·ce·ric, Melice·rous** *adjs.* pertaining to a m.

Melicoton(ie, -y, var. ff. MELOCOTON.

†**Me·licrate.** 1563. [– late L. *melicrātum;* – Gr. μελίκρατον, f. μέλι honey + καρ- κεραννύναι mix.] A drink made with honey and water –1775.

Melilite (me·liləit). Also **mell-.** 1796. [– Fr. *mélilite* (Delamétherie, 1795), mod.L. *melilithus*, f. Gr. μέλι honey + *-lite* -LITE.] *Min.* A silicate of calcium, aluminium, and other bases, found in honey-yellow crystals 1821. **2.** = MELLITE (Kirwan).

Melilot (me·lilọt). late ME. [– (O)Fr. *mélilot* – L. *melilotos* – Gr. μελίλωτος sweet kind of clover; f. μέλι honey + λωτός lotus.] A plant of the leguminous genus *Melilotus*, esp. *M. officinalis* or Yellow M., the dried flowers of which were formerly much used in making plasters, poultices, etc.

Melinite (me·linəit). 1886. [– Fr. *mélinite*, f. Gr. μήλινος quince-yellow, f. μῆλον apple, quince; see -ITE¹ 4 a.] A French explosive, said to be composed of picric acid, gun-cotton, and gum arabic.

Meliorate (mī·liŏreⁱt), *v.* 1552. [– *meliorat-*, pa. ppl. stem of late L. *meliorare* improve, f. *melior* better; see -ATE³.] **1.** *trans.* = AMELIORATE *v.* 1. **2.** *intr.* = AMELIORATE *v.* 2. 1654.

1. Religion is to m. the condition of a people JER. TAYLOR. *absol.* Instead of meliorating, it [chastisement *sine causa*] pejorates SEDLEY. Hence **Meliora·tion,** amelioration, improvement. **Me·liorative** *a.* tending to m. **Me·liorator, -er,** one who or that which meliorates.

Meliorism (mī·liŏriz'm). 1877. [f. L. *melior* better + -ISM.] The doctrine, intermediate between optimism and pessimism, which affirms that the world may be made better by human effort. So **Me·liorist,** one who believes in m. 1858. **Meliori·stic** *a.* 1888.

Meliority (mīliọ·rīti). 1578. [– OFr. *meliorité* or med.L. *melioritas*, f. as prec.; see -ITY.] The quality of being better; superiority.

Meliphagous (meli·făgəs), *a.* 1826. [f. mod.L. *Meliphaga*, f. Gr. μέλι honey; see -PHAGOUS.] *Ornith.* Belonging to the *Meliphagidæ* or honey-eating birds.

‖**Melisma** (mĭli·zmă). 1880. [Gr. μέλισμα.] *Mus.* A song, air, or melody, as opp. to recitative or declamatory music.

Melitose (me·litōᵘs). 1861. [f. Gr. μέλι, μελιτ- honey + -OSE¹.] *Chem.* A kind of sugar obtained from the manna of Eucalyptus.

‖**Melituria** (melitiūᵊ·riă). 1863. [f. as prec.; see -URIA.] *Path.* = GLYCOSURIA.

Mell (mel), *sb.*¹ Now only *Sc.* and *dial.* ME. [north. var. of *mall*, MAUL *sb.*¹] A heavy hammer or beetle of metal or wood; †a mace or club; also, a chairman's hammer.

†**Mell** (mel), *sb.*² 1575. [– L. *mel, mell-* honey = Gr. μέλι, μελιτ-.] Honey –1864.

Mell (mel), *v.* Now *arch.* and *dial.* ME. [– OFr. *meller* (mod. *mêler*), var. of *mesler* MEDDLE *v.* Cf. next.] **1.** *trans.* To mix, mingle. Also with *together, up.* **2.** *intr.* for *refl.* To mix, have intercourse *with*, associate ME. †**3.** To copulate –1641. **4.** To mingle in combat ME. **5.** To concern or busy oneself; to deal, treat; to interfere, meddle. Const. *in*, †*of, with.* late ME.

Mellay (me·leⁱ). ME. [– OFr. *mellée*, pa. pple. of *meller* (see prec.); see MÊLÉE, -Y⁵.] **1.** †Contention, fight; *spec.* a close hand to hand fight of two parties or combatants (*arch.*). †**2.** A cloth of a mixture of colours or shades; also, a mixed colour –1593.

1. He rode the m., lord of the ringing lists TENNYSON.

Mellic (me·lik), *a.* 1837. [Shortened from MELLITIC.] In *m. acid* = MELLITIC *acid.*

Melliferous (meli·fĕrəs), *a.* 1656. [f. L. *mellifer* (f. *mel, mell-* honey) + -OUS; see -FEROUS.] Yielding or producing honey.

Mellifluent (meli·flᶦuĕnt), *a.* 1601. [– late L. *mellifluens, -ent-*, f. as next; see -ENT.] = MELLIFLUOUS. Hence **Melli·fluence.**

Mellifluous (meli·fluəs), *a.* late ME. [f. OFr. *melliflue* or its source late L. *mellifluus*, f. *mel, mell-* honey + *fluere* flow; see -OUS.] **1.** Flowing with honey, honey-dropping; sweetened with or as with honey. Now *rare.* 1485. **2.** *fig.* Sweetly flowing, sweet as honey.

2. Saynt Bernard the mellifluous doctor CAXTON. M. and hony-tongued Shakespeare 1598. A m. voyce, as I am true knight SHAKS. Hence **Melli·fluous-ly** *adv.*, **-ness.**

Mellisonant (meli·sŏnănt), *a. arch.* 1634. [f. L. *mel, mell-* honey + *sonans, -ant-*, pr. pple. of *sonare* sound. Cf. AL. *mellisonus.*] Sweet-sounding.

Mellite (me·ləit). 1801. [First in mod.L. *mellites* (Gmelin 1793), f. L. *mel, mell-* honey; see -ITE¹ 2 b.] *Min.* Native mellitate of aluminium, occurring in honey-yellow octahedral crystals. So **Mellitic** (meli·tik) *a.* in *m. acid*, the peculiar acid of mellite 1794; hence **Me·llitate,** a salt of this (formerly *mellate*) 1828.

Mellone (me·loᵘn). Also **mel(l)on.** 1835. [Named by Liebig in 1834; f. *mel-* (as in MELAM) + -ONE.] *Chem.* A compound of carbon and nitrogen obtained as a yellow powder by the action of heat on certain cyanogen-compounds. Hence **Me·llonide,** a compound of mellone with a metal 1845.

Mellow (me·loᵘ), *a.* 1440. [perh. from attrib. use of OE. *melu* (*melw-*), ME. *melow* MEAL *sb.*¹] **1.** Of fruit: Soft, sweet, and juicy with ripeness. **b.** Of landscape, seasons, etc.: Characterized by ripeness 1819. **c.** Of wines, etc.: Well-matured; free from acidity or harshness 1700. **2.** *transf.* Soft; soft and smooth to the touch; orig. and esp. of earth, loamy, rich 1531. **3.** *fig.* Mature, ripe in age. Now chiefly, softened or sweetened by age or experience. 1592. **4.** Of sound, colour, light, etc.: Rich and soft; full and pure without harshness 1668. **5.** Good-humoured, genial, jovial 1711. **6.** Partly intoxicated 1611.

1. M. apples 1806, nuts SCOTT. **b.** Season of mists and m. fruitfulness KEATS. **2.** Hoary Frosts . . will rot the M. Soil DRYDEN. **3.** The m. glory of the Attic Stage M. ARNOLD. **4.** The m. bullfinch THOMSON. The golden harvest, of a m. brown COWPER. **6.** The hateful fellow That's crabbed when he's m. SHERIDAN. Hence **Me·llow-ly** *adv.*, **-ness. Me·llowy** *a.* mellow.

Mellow (me·loᵘ), *v.* 1572. [f. MELLOW *a.*] **1.** *trans.* To render mellow. **2.** *intr.* To become mellow 1594.

1. Wind, Sun and Dews, all . . m. the Land 1707. Age . . Mellows and makes the speech more fit for use COWPER. **2.** His character mellowed and toned down in his later years 1861.

†**Melocoton.** Also †**malacato(o)n, -co-.** 1611. [– Sp. *melocotón* – It. *melocotogno* – med.L. *melum cotoneum* – Gr. μῆλον κυδώνιον 'Cydonian apple'; see COYN, QUINCE.] A peach grafted on a quince –1745.

Melodeon, melodion (mĭlōᵘ·diən). 1858. [In sense 1 quasi-Gr. var. of MELODIUM; in sense 2 perh. f. MELODY after ACCORDION.] **1.** A wind instrument with a key-board, the bellows being moved by pedals worked by the feet; an earlier form of the 'American organ'. **2.** A kind of accordion 1880.

Melodic (mĭlọ·dik), *a.* 1823. [– Fr. *mélodique* – late L. *melodicus* – Gr. μελῳδικός; see MELODY, -IC.] Of or pertaining to melody. Hence **Melo·dically** *adv.* So **Melo·dial** *a.*, **Melo·dially** *adv.* 1818.

Melo·dics. 1864. [See prec. and -IC 2.] The branch of musical science concerned with melody.

Melodious (mĭlōᵘ·diəs), *a.* late ME. [– OFr. *melodieus* (mod. *mélodieux*), = med. L. *melodiosus*; see MELODY, -OUS.] **1.** Characterized by melody; sweet-sounding, tuneful. **2.** Producing melody 1588. **3.** Having a melody 1727.

1. Man . . forges the subtile . . air into wise and m. words EMERSON. **2.** Where like a sweet mellodius bird it sung SHAKS. **Melo·dious-ly** *adv.*, **-ness.**

Melodist (me·lodist). 1789. [f. MELODY + -IST.] **1.** A singer. **2.** A composer of melodies; one skilled in melody 1826.

Melodium (mĭlōᵘ·diŏm). 1847. [f. MELODY, after *harmonium.*] = MELODEON 1.

Melodize (me·lŏdəiz), *v.* 1662. [f. MELODY + -IZE.] **1.** *intr.* To make melody; occas. *joc.*, to play (*on* an instrument). **b.** *transf.* To blend harmoniously *with* 1811. **2.** *trans.* To make melodious 1759. **3.** To compose a melody for (a song) 1881.

Melodrama (me·lŏdrāmă, melŏdrā·mă). 1809. [Alteration of MELODRAME, after DRAMA.] **1.** In early use, a stage-play in which songs were interspersed, and in which orchestral music accompanied the action. Now, a dramatic piece characterized by sensational incident and violent appeals to the emotions, but with a happy ending. **b.** This species of dramatic composition or representation 1814. **2.** *transf.* Incidents, or a story, resembling a melodrama; also, melodramatic behaviour, occurrences, etc. 1814.

1. *attrib.* A m. kitchen, suitable for bandits or noblemen in disguise STEVENSON. **2.** My idea of heaven is that there is no m. in it at all EMERSON. Hence **Melodrama·tic** *a.* having the characteristics of m.; characterized by sensationalism and spurious pathos. **Melodrama·tically** *adv.* **Melodra·matist,** a writer of melodramas. **Melodra·matize** *v.* to make melodramatic; also, to convert the story of (a novel) into a m.

†**Melodrame** (me·lodræm). Also **-dram.** 1802. [– Fr. *mélodrame*, f. Gr. μέλος song, music + Fr. *drame* DRAMA.] = prec.

Melody (me·lŏdi), *sb.* ME. [– (O)Fr. *mélodie* – late L. *melodia* – Gr. μελῳδία singing, choral song, f. μελῳδός musical, f. μέλος song, etc., + ῳδ-; see ODE, -Y³.] **1.** Sweet music; beautiful arrangement of musical sounds; beauty of musical sounds, tunefulness. **b.** *transf.* Musical quality in the arrangement of words 1789. **2.** A series of single notes arranged in musically expressive succession; a tune: = AIR *sb.* III. 1. 1609. **b.** The principal part in a harmonized piece of music. **c.** *transf.* Applied to poems written to be sung to particular melodies 1807. **d.** Applied to pictorial combinations of colour 1830. **3.** That element of musical form which consists in the arrangement of single notes in musical succession; dist. from *harmony* 1727.

1. Whilst all the winds with m. are ringing SHELLEY. Phr. *To make m.* (now *arch.*) **2.** Heard melodies are sweet, but those unheard Are sweeter KEATS. **d.** Studied melodies of exquisite colour RUSKIN. Hence **Me·lody** *v. rare*, to make m., to sing.

Melologue (me·lolọg). 18.. [f. Gr. μέλος song + λόγος speech (see -LOGUE). Cf. Fr. *mélologue* (Berlioz, 1832).] A musical composition in which some of the verses are sung and others recited.

Melon (me·lən). late ME. [– (O)Fr. *melon* :– late L. *melo, melon-*, shortening of *melopepo* – Gr. μηλοπέπων, f. μῆλον apple + πέπων kind of gourd, subst. use of πέπων ripe.] **1.** A name for several kinds of gourds bearing sweet fruit, *esp.* the MUSK M., *Cucumis melo*, and WATER-M., *Citrullus vulgaris.* (Applied both to fruit and plant.) **2.** *Conch.* The shell of a mollusc of the genus *Melo.* Also *m.-shell, -volute.* 1840. **3.** A rounded mass of blubber taken from the top of the head of certain cetaceans 1887. **4.** *U.S. slang.* A large surplus of profits available for distribution to several people; phr. *to cut a m.* 1909. *Comb.*: **m.-beetle,** a beetle of the genus *Diabrotica*, injurious to melons; **-cactus,** any plant of the genus *Melocactus*, so called from the melon-like ridged stems; **-pumpkin,** *Cucurbita maxima* or *C. melopepo*; **-thistle** = *m.-cactus.*

Melophone (me·lofōun). 1859. [f. Gr. μέλος song + -PHONE.] A kind of accordion.

Me·lophonist, a melodist. THACKERAY.

Meloplasty (me·loplæsti). 1883. [f. Gr. μῆλον apple, *poet.* cheek + -PLASTY.] *Surg.* The plastic restoration of a cheek. So **Melopla·stic** *a.* 1848.

‖**Melopœia** (melopī·iă). 1759. [— Gr. μελοποιία, f. μελοποιός maker of songs, f. μέλος + ποι-, ποιεῖν make.] *Antiq.* The art of composing melodies; the part of dramatic art concerned with music.

Melt (melt), *sb.* 1854. [f. MELT *v.*] **1.** The act or operation of melting 1897. **2.** Metal, etc., in a melted condition; the quantity melted at one time.

Melt (melt), *v.* Pa. t. **melted.** Pa. pple. **melted; molten** (mōu·lt'n). [OE. (i) str. vb. *meltan* :- **meltan*; (ii) wk. vb. (Anglian) *meltan*, (WS.) *mieltan* = ON. *melta* digest, malt (grain) :- **maltjan*. The base **melt-* **malt-* (see MALT) **mult-* repr. IE. **meld-* **mold-* **mḷd*, whence Gr. μέλδειν melt, L. *mollis*, Skr. *mṛdus* soft. Cf. MILD, SMELT *v.*]

I. *intr.* **1.** To become liquefied by heat. **b.** *joc.* To perspire excessively 1787. **2.** To be dissolved, e.g. by the agency of moisture OE. **b.** Of clouds, vapour; To dissolve; to break *into* rain ME. **c.** To disappear 1611. **3.** Of a person, his heart, feelings, etc. †**a.** To be overwhelmed with dismay or grief –1611. **b.** To become softened by compassion or love; to dissolve *in* or *into* tears ME. **4.** To dwindle *away* ME. **5.** To filter in, become absorbed *into* ME. **6.** Of sound: To be soft and liquid 1626. **7.** To pass imperceptibly *into* something else 1781.

1. When the snow melts from the Mountaines MORYSON. Phr. *To m. away*: to be destroyed or wasted by being melted. **b.** [Our chariot-horse with heat Must seem to m. CHAPMAN]. **2.** Phr. *To m. in the mouth*: said of food that is extremely tender. **c.** With shriekes She melted into Ayre SHAKS. **3. a.** My soule melteth away for very heuynesse COVERDALE *Ps.* 118[9]: 28. **b.** She melted into a Flood of Tears STEELE. **4.** The body of his party is melting away very fast BURKE. **7.** Downs..That m. and fade into the distant sky COWPER.

II. *trans.* **1.** To reduce to a liquid condition by heat OE. †**b.** To form of molten material. late ME. **2.** To dissolve. late ME. **3.** To make tender, touch the feelings of. late ME. †**4.** To weaken, enervate SHAKS. **5.** To spend, squander (money); to cash (a cheque or bank-note) *slang* 1700. **6.** To blend *with* or *into* 1605.

1. The soring clouds into sad showres ymolt SPENSER. Phr. *To m. down* (also U.S. *up*): to melt (coin, etc.) in order that the metal may be used as raw material. **b.** *Isa.* 40: 19. **3.** Her noble heart was molten in her breast TENNYSON. **4.** *Timon* IV. iii. 256. **5.** I had him arrested before he had time to m. the notes READE. **6.** A grey mist..melted whole mountains into a soft dull grey BLACK.

Melting (me·ltiŋ), *vbl. sb.* late ME. [f. MELT *v.* + -ING[1].] **1.** The action of MELT *v.*; an instance of this. **2.** *concr. pl.* That which has been melted; a substance produced by melting 1558. **3.** *attrib.*, as *m.-furnace*, etc. late ME.

1. †*Surveyor of the Meltings*: the former designation of a certain officer of the mint; hence *the Meltings*, his office.

Comb.: **m.-heat,** the degree of heat required to melt a given substance; **-point,** that point of the thermometer which indicates the melting-heat of any particular solid; **-pot,** a vessel in which metals, etc., are melted; often *fig.* with ref. to remodelling of institutions, etc.

Me·lting, *ppl. a.* late ME. [-ING[2].] That melts; yielding to emotion, tender; (of sound, colour) liquid and soft; that 'melts in the mouth' (esp. of certain pears).

Like unto..m. wax 1577. M. Charitie 2 *Hen. IV*, IV. iv. 32. Albeit vn-vsed to the m. moode *Oth.* V. ii. 349. The m. voice through mazes running MILT. A first-rate m. pear DARWIN. **Me·lting-ly** *adv.*, **-ness.**

Melton (me·ltən). 1823. Name of a town in Leicestershire (more fully Melton Mowbray), a famous hunting centre. Used *attrib.*, esp. in *M. cloth* (also simply **melton**), a stout smooth cloth having the nap cut very close and the face finished without pressing or glossing. Hence **Melto·nian,** *a.* pertaining to Melton Mowbray; *sb.* one who hunts at Melton Mowbray, an adept at hunting 1825.

Mem. Abbrev. of MEMORANDUM 1.

Mem, vulgar var. of MA'AM.

Member (me·mbəɹ), *sb.* [ME. *membre* – (O)Fr. *membre* :- L. *membrum* limb.] **1.** A part or organ of the body; chiefly, a limb, etc. (as opp. to the trunk). *arch.* †**b.** *spec.* (after L.): = 'privy member' –1728. **c.** *Biol.* Any part of a plant or animal viewed with regard to its form and position 1875. **2.** *fig.* chiefly in *m. of Christ, of Satan* ME. **3.** *transf.* Each constituent part of a complex structure. late ME. **b.** *Arch.* 'Any part of an edifice, or any moulding in a collection of mouldings, as those in a cornice, capital, base, etc.' (Gwilt) 1679. **4.** Each individual belonging to a society or assembly. Also formerly, †an inhabitant or native (of a country or city). ME. **b.** *absol.* A person. Now *slang* and *dial.* 1525. †**c.** One who takes part in anything –1604. **5.** One formally elected to take part in the proceedings of a parliament: in full *M. of Parliament* (abbrev. M.P.), in U.S. *M. of Congress* (M.C.) 1454. **6.** A component part, branch, of a political body. late ME. †**7.** A branch (of a trade, art, profession); a branch, species, subdivision of a class –1614. **8.** A section or district of an estate, manor, parish, or the like 1450. **9.** *Math.* **a.** A group of figures or symbols forming part of a numerical expression or formula 1608. **b.** *Alg.* Either side of an equation 1702. **10.** A division or clause of a sentence; a head of a discourse; a branch of a disjunctive proposition 1534. **11.** Each of the items forming a series 1851.

1. *Privy m.* or *members*, †*carnal m.*: the secret part or parts. *The unruly m.* (after *James* 3: 5–8): the tongue. **2.** Wherein I was made a m. of Christe *Bk. Com. Prayer.* **3. b.** In later Gothic the pinnacle became gradually a decorative m. RUSKIN. **4.** Here comes a m. of the common-wealth SHAKS. **c.** All members of our Cause SHAKS. **6.** By estates of the realm they meant members, or necessary parts, of the parliament HALLAM. Hence **Me·mbral** *a.* pertaining to a m.; *Anat.* and *Zool.*, appendicular 1603.

†**Me·mber,** *v.* late ME. [– OFr. *membrer* :- L. *memorare* MEMORATE.] *trans.* = MEMORATE –1589.

Membered (me·mbəɹd), *a.* ME. [f. MEMBER *sb.* + -ED[2].] Having members (of a specified kind or number); divided into members; †consisting of links or segments. **b.** *spec.* in *Her.* Said of a bird, when the legs are of a different tincture from the body 1530.

Membership (me·mbəɹʃip). 1647. [f. MEMBER *sb.* + -SHIP.] **1.** The condition or status of being a member of a society, etc. **2.** The number of members in a particular body 1850.

Membranaceous (membrănē¹·ʃəs), *a.* 1678. [f. late L. *membranaceus*, f. *membrana*; see next, -ACEOUS.] *Nat. Hist.* Membranous. In *Bot.* thin and semi-transparent, like a fine membrane.

Membrane (me·mbreⁱn). 1519. [– L. *membrana* (partly through Fr. *membrane*) 'skin covering a part of the body' (prop. subst. use of fem. of adj. in *-anus* -AN, sc. *cutis* skin), f. *membrum* MEMBER *sb.*] **1.** A thin pliable sheet-like tissue (usually fibrous), serving to connect other structures or to line a part or organ. Also *collect. sing.* = membranous structure. 1615. **b.** *Path.* A morbid formation in certain diseases 1765. **2.** †Parchment; a skin of parchment forming part of a roll 1519.

1. The m. of the nose 1788. The organic basis [of vegetable tissues] is simple m. and fibre 1846. *attrib.* **m.-bone** *Ichthyol.*, a bone originating in membranous tissue. **2.** The third m. of this Roll 1890. Hence **Membra·neous** *a.* = MEMBRANOUS. **Membra·niform** *a.* [-FORM]. **Membra·no-,** comb. form.

Membranous (me·mbrănəs), *a.* 1597. [– Fr. *membraneux*, f. *membrane*; see prec., -OUS.] Consisting of, resembling, or of the nature of membrane. In *Bot.*, thin and more or less translucent. **b.** Of diseases: Pertaining to or involving the formation of a membrane 1875.

‖**Membranula** (membrē¹·niŭlă). Also **-ule.** 1821. [L., dim. of *membrana* MEMBRANE; see -ULE.] A little membrane.

Memento (mĭme·nto). *Pl.* **-oes, -os.** late ME. [imper. of L. *meminisse* remember, redupl. f. root **men-*; see MIND *sb.*] **1.** *Liturg.* Either of two prayers beginning with *Memento* in the Canon of the Mass, in which the living and the dead are commemorated. **2.** A reminder, warning, or hint as to conduct or with regard to future events 1582. **b.** *concr.* An object serving to remind or warn 1580. **3.** Something to remind one of some person or event 1768. ¶**4.** Joc. misused for: **a.** A reverie; hence, a doze; **b.** (One's) memory 1587.

2. Phr. **M. mori** (mōᵊ·rəi). [L. – 'remember that you have to die'.] A warning or (*concr.*) a reminder of death, e.g. a skull 1596. **b.** Rings, deaths heads, and such mementoes FLETCHER.

Memnonian (memnōu·niăn), *a.* 1614. [f. L. *Memnonius* (– Gr. Μεμνόνειος, f. Μέμνων) + -AN.] **a.** Pertaining to the demigod Memnon, said to have erected the palace at Susa; hence, an epithet of Susa or Persia generally. **b.** Having the property of the statue of Memnon at Thebes in Egypt, said to give forth a musical sound when touched by the dawn.

Xerxes,..From Susa his M. Palace..Came MILT.

Memo. (me·mo). 1889. Abbrev. of MEMORANDUM; *colloq.* treated as a word. Cf. MEM.

Memoir (me·mwǫɹ). 1567. [– Fr. *mémoire* masc., a spec. use of *mémoire* fem. MEMORY.] **1.** A note, memorandum; a record –1755. †**2.** In diplomatic and official use: = MEMORANDUM (*rare*). Also *pl.* official reports of business done. –1829. **3.** *collect. pl.* **a.** A record of events, a history treating of matters from the personal knowledge of the writer or with reference to particular sources of information. 1659. **b.** An autobiographical record 1673. **4.** A biography, or biographical notice 1826. **5.** An essay on a learned subject on which the writer has made particular observations. Hence *pl.* the record of the transactions of a learned society. 1680.

3. The following memoirs of my Uncle Toby's courtship STERNE. Hence **Memoirist** (me·mwǭrist), a writer of memoirs, or of a m. **Me·moirism,** the practice of writing memoirs.

‖**Memorabilia** (me:mŏrăbi·liă). 1806. [n. pl. of L. *memorabilis*; see next.] Memorable or noteworthy things.

Memorable (me·mŏrăb'l), *a.* (*sb.*) 1483. [– Fr. *mémorable* or L. *memorabilis*, f. *memorare*; see MEMORATE *v.*, -ABLE.] **1.** Worth remembering; not to be forgotten. **2.** Easy to be remembered 1599. **3.** *sb. pl.* = MEMORABILIA 1611.

1. He nothing common did or mean, Upon that m. scene MARVELL. **2.** *Hen. V*, II. iv. 53. **3.** Recorded..as one of the chiefe memorables in his raigne 1613. Hence **Me:morabi·lity, Me·morableness,** m. quality; also, a person or thing worth remembering. **Me·morably** *adv.* so as to be remembered.

Memorandum (memŏræ·ndŏm), *sb. Pl.* **-anda** (-æ·ndă), **-andums** (-æ·ndŏmz). late ME. [L., neut. sing. of *memorandus*, gerundive of *memorare* bring to mind; see next.] **1.** '(It is) to be remembered': placed at the head of a note of something to be remembered. Now only *legal.* **2.** 'A note to help the memory' (J.); hence a record of events, or of observations, esp. for future use 1542. **b.** *spec.* A record of a pecuniary transaction 1607. **c.** *Law.* The writing in which the terms of a transaction or contract are embodied 1591. **d.** *Diplomacy.* A summary of the grounds for or against an action, the state of a question, etc. 1658. †**3.** An injunction to remember something –1643. †**4.** A reminder; also, a memento, souvenir –1847. **5.** *Comm.* An informal communication, esp. one on paper headed with the word 'Memorandum' and the name and address of the sender. **6.** *attrib.* 1710.

2. c. *Marine Insurance.* A clause in a policy enumerating the articles in respect of which underwriters have no liability. *M. of association*, a document required by law for the registration of a joint-stock company, containing the name of the company, its object, capital, etc. **d.** These deliberations..resulted in the preparation of the so-called Berlin M. 1885. **6. m. cheque,** a cheque given as an acknowledgement of indebtedness, but which is not to be presented for payment until a day agreed upon between the drawer and drawee. Hence **Memora·ndum** *v. trans.* to make a m. of 1805.

†**Me·morate,** *v.* 1623. [– *memorat-*, pa. ppl. stem of L. *memorare*, f. *memor* mindful;

see -ATE[3].] *trans.* To bring to mind; to mention, recount, relate –1686. So †**Memora·tion,** mention; commemoration 1553–1627.

Memorative (me·mŏrătiv), *a.* (*sb.*) 1448. [– (O)Fr. *mémoratif, -ive* or late L. *memorativus* (Priscian), f. as prec.; see -IVE.] **1.** Reminding one of something; commemorative. Now *rare.* †**2.** Of or pertaining to the memory, esp. in *m. faculty, power, virtue* 1481–1706. †**3.** Having a good memory; retentive 1481–1695. †**4.** *sb.* Something to put one in mind of a thing; a memorial 1597–1690.

4. Short sentences and memoratiues, as *Know thy selfe*..and the like 1597.

Memorial (mĭmōᵊ·riăl). late ME. [– (O)Fr. *mémorial* or L. *memorialis* adj. (late L. *memoriale* n. sb., sign of remembrance, memorial, monument), f. *memoria* MEMORY; see -AL[1].] **A.** *adj.* **1.** Preserving the memory of a person or thing, as a statue, a festival, etc. †**2.** Remembered; memorable –1631. **3. a.** Of or pertaining to memory. †**b.** Mnemonic. †**c.** Done from memory. late ME.

1. M. windows 1866. A m. ring 1877. **3. b.** Your Minutes or m. Aids 1745.

B. *sb.* †**1.** = MEMORY. late ME. **2.** A memorial act; *spec.* (*Eccl.*) = COMMEMORATION 2 b. 1468. **3.** Something to preserve the memory of a person, thing, or event, as a statue, a custom, etc. late ME. †**4.** A note or memorandum –1817. **b.** *Law.* An abstract of the particulars of a deed, etc., for registration 1813. **c.** *Scots Law.* A statement of facts drawn up for counsel's opinion. Also, an advocate's brief. 1752. **5.** A record, chronicle, or memoir; now chiefly *pl.*, a record, often containing personal reminiscences 1513. **6.** In diplomatic use: A general designation for various classes of informal state papers 1536. **7.** A statement of facts forming the basis of or expressed in the form of a petition to a person in authority, a government, etc. 1713.

1. The sweet M. of the Just Shall flourish when he sleeps in dust TATE & BRADY. **3.** This also that she hath done, shall be spoken of for a memoriall of her *Mark* 14: 9. **5.** Though of their Names in heav'nly Records now Be no m. MILT. **M. Day** *U.S.* the day set apart for honouring the memory of those who fell in the civil war of 1861–5. Hence **Memo·rialist,** one who presents a m. or writes memorials.

Memorial (mĭmōᵊ·riăl), *v.* 1764. [f. MEMORIAL *sb.*] **1.** *trans.* = MEMORIALIZE 2. 1768. **2.** *intr.* To draw up a memorial; to petition *for* 1764. **3.** *Law.* To enter in a memorandum 1824.

Memorialize (mĭmōᵊ·riăləiz), *v.* 1798. [f. MEMORIAL *sb.* + -IZE.] **1.** *trans.* To commemorate. **2.** To address a memorial to.

‖**Memoria technica** (mĭmōᵊ·riă te·knikă). 1730. [mod.L., repr. Gr. τὸ μνημονικὸν τέχνημα (device, contrivance), whence also AL. *memoria artificialis* (XV).] A system of mnemonics; a mnemonic contrivance.

Memorious, *a. Obs.* or *arch. rare.* 1599. [– OFr. *memorieux* – med.L. *memoriosus*, f. *memoria*; see MEMORY, -OUS.] †**1.** Having a good memory; mindful *of* –1656. **2.** Memorable 1883.

Memorist (me·mŏrist). *rare.* 1682. [f. MEMORY or MEMORIZE *v.*; see -IST.] †**1.** One who prompts the memory. SIR T. BROWNE. **2.** *U.S.* One having a good memory 1872.

‖**Memoriter** (mĭmǫ·ritəɹ), *adv.* 1612. [L., f. *memor* mindful.] From memory, by heart. **b.** as *adj.* Spoken or speaking 'memoriter' 1802.

Memorize (me·mŏrəiz), *v.* 1591. [f. MEMORY + -IZE.] **1.** *trans.* To cause to be remembered, make memorable; also, to preserve the memory of in writing, record. Now *rare.* 1591. **2.** To commit to memory 1856.

1. Except they meane to..m. another Golgotha SHAKS. A Cenotaph to memorise our grave 1822. The R.A. here memorised, was George Daw LAMB.

Memory (me·mŏri). [ME. *memorie, memoire* – OFr. *memorie,* (also mod.) *mémoire* – L. *memoria*, f. *memor* mindful, remembering, redupl. f. on the base **mer-*; see MOURN, -Y[3].] **1.** The faculty by which things are remembered. **2.** This faculty considered as residing in a particular individual. late ME. **3.** Recollection, remembrance. late ME. **b.** An act or instance of remembrance; a recollection 1817. **c.** A person or thing held in remembrance 1842. **4.** The fact or condition of being remembered; 'exemption from oblivion' (J.). late ME. **5.** (Good or bad) posthumous repute 1450. **6.** The length of time over which memory extends 1530. **7.** *Liturg.* A commemoration, esp. of the departed. *Obs.* exc. *Hist.* ME. †**8.** A memorial writing; a record; a history –1730. †**9.** A memorial; a memento –1624. †**10.** A memorial tomb, shrine, chapel, or the like –1691. **11.** *attrib.*, as *m.-picture*, etc. 1642.

1. By the m. it [an idea] can be made an actual perception again LOCKE. Phr. *To commit to m.*: to learn by heart. *Art of m., artificial m.*: mnemonics, a mnemonic system. **2.** I should haue a verie good wit, for I haue but a bad memorie MORLEY. Phr. *Of †good, sane, sound* (etc.) *m.* He was yet in memorie and alyve CHAUCER. **3.** Phr. *From m.*; *to come to* (a person's) *m.*; *to bear, have, keep in m. To draw* or *take into* or *to m.*: to recollect. †*Out of m.*: forgotten. **b.** You put strange memories in my head TENNYSON. **4.** That euer-liuing man of Memorie, Henrie the fift SHAKS. *In m. of, to the m. of*: so as to keep alive the remembrance of. **5.** The memorie of the iust is blessed *Prov.* 10: 7. Phr. *Of blessed, happy, famous* (etc.) *m.*: a formula used after the names of deceased sovereigns, princes, etc. **6.** Phr. *Beyond, within the m.* (*of man*). †*Through all m.*: for all time (MILT.). Law. *Time of* (*legal*) *m.*; Time of m. hath been long ago ascertained by the law to commence from the reign of Richard the first BLACKSTONE. **9.** These weedes are memories of those worser houres SHAKS. Hence **Me·moried** *a.* having a m. (of a specified kind) 1573; fraught with memories 1851.

Memphian (me·mfiăn). 1591. [f. *Memphis* + -AN.] **A.** *adj.* Pertaining to Memphis, a city of ancient Egypt; used vaguely for 'Egyptian'. **B.** *sb.* An inhabitant or native of Memphis; an Egyptian.

Busiris and his M. Chivalrie MILT. So **Memphi·tic** *a.* pertaining to Memphis, or to the dialect of Coptic spoken there 1450. †**Memphi·tical** *a.* 1581.

‖**Mem-sahib** (me·msā,ib). 1857. [f. *mem* = MA'AM + SAHIB.] Used by the natives of India in addressing European women.

Men, pl. of MAN *sb.*

Menace (me·năs), *sb.* [ME. *manas, manace* – L. *minacia* (only pl. in class L.), f. *minax, minac-* threatening, f. base of *minari* threaten.] A declaration or indication of hostile intention, or of a probable evil or catastrophe; a threat. **b.** The action of threatening ME. **c.** Said of a state of things, etc., which threatens danger, etc. 1857.

That M. of committing men to Hell-fire 1664. **b.** The voice of m. and complaint was silent GIBBON. The m. of the skies 1871.

Menace (me·năs), *v.* ME. [– AFr *manasser*, OFr. *menacier* (mod. *menacer*) :– Rom. **minaciare*, f. L. *minacia*; see prec.] **1.** *trans.* To hold out menaces against; to threaten. **2.** *intr.* To utter menaces; to be threatening ME. **3.** *trans.* To threaten to inflict ME. †**4.** To use threateningly. MILT.

1. Your eyes do m. me: why looke you pale? SHAKS. Her life was menaced MACAULAY. **2.** Earth below shook; heaven above menaced BURKE. **3.** Such as m. warre 1621. Hence **Me·naceful** *a.* **Me·nacement. Me·nacer. Me·nacingly** *adv.*

Menad, -ic, var. MÆNAD, -IC.

Ménage, menage (menā·ʒ). Now only as Fr. ME. [– OFr. *menaige, manaige* (mod. *ménage*) :– Rom. **mansionaticum*, f. L. *mansio, -on-* MANSION; see -AGE and cf. MANAGE *sb.*] †**1.** The members of a household; a man's 'meinie' –1490. **2.** The management of a household, housekeeping; hence, a domestic establishment (often semi-*concr.*) 1698.

2. Nothing tended to make ladies so..inefficient in the m. as the study of the dead languages HAN. MORE.

Menage, etc.: see MANAGE, etc.

Menagerie (mĕnæ·dʒĕri). Also †**-ery.** 1712. [– Fr. *ménagerie*, orig. domestic management of cattle, etc., f. *ménage*; see MÉNAGE, -ERY.] **1.** A collection of wild animals in cages or enclosures, esp. one kept for exhibition. Also, the place where they are kept. †**2.** An aviary –1830.

1. *transf.* An old quack doctor named Levett.. completed this strange m. MACAULAY.

Menald (me·năld), *a.* Also †**menild, mennal.** 1611. [perh. f. dial. †*meanel* 'flea-bite', small darker-coloured spot on light-coloured horse, etc. + -ED[2].] Of animals: Spotted, speckled. Of a deer: Of a dappled chestnut. Also *sb.* a deer of this colour.

Mend (mend), *sb.* ME. [Partly aphet. f. *amend* (see AMENDS); partly f. MEND *v.*] †**1.** Recompense, reparation; also, something given as compensation. Usu. *pl.* in form, construed as *sing.* –1816. †**2.** Remedy –1655. **3.** Phr. *On the m.*: recovering; (of affairs, etc.) improving in condition 1802. **4.** An act of mending, a repair; a repaired hole, etc. 1888.

Mend, *v.* ME. [– AFr. *mender*, aphet. f. *amender* AMEND *v.*]

I. To remove or atone for defects. **1.** *trans.* To free (a person, etc.) from sin or fault; to reform; *occas.* to cure *of* (a fault). Now *arch.* or *dial.* exc. in phr. *to m. one's manners, ways,* **b.** *intr.* for *refl.* Now *rare* exc. in provb. *It is never too late to m.* ME. **2.** To remove the defects of (a thing); to correct (what is faulty). Now only *occas.* as transf. of 5. ME. **b.** *intr.* To become less faulty. Of conditions: To improve. ME. **3.** *trans.* To rectify, remedy. remove (an evil); to put right (anything amiss) ME. **b.** *intr.* Of a fault: To undergo rectification. POPE. **4.** *trans.* To make amends or atone for (a misdeed, an injury); also *absol.* *Obs.* exc. in *Least said soonest mended.* ME. **5.** To restore to a complete or sound condition (a road, clothes, furniture, tools, fences, etc.); to repair. Also, to make good (the defective part). Now the prevailing sense. ME. **b.** To adjust, set right. *Obs.* exc. *Naut.* 1515. **6.** *trans.* To restore to health, cure, heal (*arch.*) ME. **b.** *intr.* To recover from sickness 1500. **c.** Of a wound, etc.: To heal. Of a malady: To abate. Now *dial.* 1607.

2. Never think of mending what you write. Let it go COBBETT. **b.** I hope the times will m. HOWELL. **3.** She wolde come, and mende al that was mis CHAUCER. **5.** As they were in the shyppe mendynge their nettes COVERDALE *Mark* 1: 19. Phr. †*To m. the lights*: to trim the lamps, or snuff the candles. *To m. a fire*: to add fuel to it. *To m. a pen*: to cut a worn quill pen so as to make it write properly. **b.** Phr. *To m. sails*, to loose and skin them afresh on the yards. **6. b.** The Queen is slowly mending of her gout SWIFT.

II. Without distinct reference to defect. **1.** *trans.* To improve the condition or fortune of. Now *rare* or *Obs.* exc. *refl.*, to better oneself. ME. †**2.** To improve by additions (*e.g.* wages, prices) –1697. **b.** *intr.* To improve in amount or price 1602. †**c.** *trans.* To supplement –1711. **3.** To improve in quality; to ameliorate (condition, etc.). Now *rare.* 1603. †**b.** *intr.* To improve –1712. **4.** *trans.* To improve upon, surpass, better. Now only *colloq.* to produce something better than. ME.

2. And we will m. thy wages SHAKS. **c.** Wee'll m. our dinner here SHAKS. **4.** In Vshering M. him who can SHAKS.

Phrases, etc. †*God m. all*, a pious wish. *To m. or end*: to improve or put an end to; in early use chiefly = 'to kill or cure'. *To m. the matter, to m. matters*: to improve the state of affairs concerning a person or thing. Often used *ironically*. *To m.* (*one's*) *pace*: to travel faster. †*To m. one's hand*: to improve one's work or conduct. Hence **Me·ndable** *a.* capable of improvement. **Me·nder.**

Mendacious (mendēⁱ·ʃəs), *a.* 1616. [f. L. *mendax, -ac-* (prob. orig. speaking incorrectly or falsely, f. *mendum* defect, fault) + -OUS; see -ACIOUS.] Lying; untruthful; false.

A m. Legend 1616. [The Pagan ages] were not m. and distracted, but in their own poor way true and sane! CARLYLE. **Menda·cious-ly** *adv.*, **-ness.**

Mendacity (mendæ·sĭti). 1646. [– eccl. L. *mendacitas, -tat-*, f. as prec.; see -ITY.] The quality of being mendacious; habitual lying or deceiving; also, a lie or falsehood.

If wee call to minde the m. of Greece SIR T. BROWNE.

Mendelian (mendī·liăn), *a.* 1901. [f. Gregor Johann *Mendel* (1822–84) + -IAN.] *Biol.* Of or pertaining to Mendel, or following his law or theory of heredity. So **Mende·lianism, Mendelism** (me·ndĕliz'm), Mendel's theory of heredity. **Me·ndelist. Me·ndelize** *v. intr.* to exhibit Mendelian characters.

†**Mendiant,** *sb.* and *a.* 1483. [– (O)Fr. *mendiant*, pr. pple. of *mendier* :– L. *mendicare*; see next, -ANT.] = next –1535.

Mendicant (me·ndikănt). 1474. [– *mendicant-*, pr. ppl. stem of L. *mendicare* beg, f. *mendicus* beggar, f. *mendum* fault, blemish; see -ANT.] **A.** *adj.* Begging; given to begging.

Also, characteristic of a beggar. 1613. **b.** *spec.* Applied to those religious orders who lived entirely on alms 1547. **B.** *sb.* A beggar; one who lives by begging 1474. **b.** A begging friar 1530. **c.** Applied to Brahmin, Buddhist, etc. priests who beg for food 1613.

A. M. prophets go to rich men's doors JOWETT. **B.** There is surely a Physiognomy, which those.. Master Mendicants observe, whereby they instantly discover a merciful aspect SIR T. BROWNE.

Mendicate (me·ndike^{i}t), *v. rare.* 1618. [– *mendicat-*, pa. ppl. stem of L. *mendicare*; see prec., -ATE[3].] **1.** *trans.* To ask for like a beggar. **2.** *intr.* To beg (*rare*). Dicts. Hence **Mendica·tion,** begging.

Mendicity (mendi·sĭti). late ME. [– (O)Fr. *mendicité* – L. *mendicitas, -tat-*, f. *mendicus* beggar; see MENDICATE, -ITY.] **1.** The state or condition of a mendicant; beggary. Also, now usually, the existence or numbers of the mendicant class. **2.** The practice of begging 1801. **3.** *attrib.*, as *m. society* 1819.

Me·nding, *vbl. sb.* ME. [f. MEND *v.* + -ING[1].] Amendment (phr. †*on* or *in the m. hand*, see HAND *sb.* I. 4); repair; *colloq.* articles to be repaired, materials (*m. wool*) for repairing.

Mendment (me·ndmĕnt). ME. [aphet. f. AMENDMENT.] **1.** = AMENDMENT; improvement, etc. **2.** Improvement of the soil; *concr.* manure. Now *dial.* 1644.

Mendole (me·ndo^{u}l). 1854. [– It. (Venetian) *mendole* (= Fr. *mendole* – mod. Pr. *mendoulo, mendolo*).] = CACKEREL 1.

Menevian (mĭnī·viăn), *a.* and *sb.* 1865. [f. *Menevia*, med.L. name of St. David's in Wales + -AN.] *Geol.* Name of a very ancient group of rocks found near St. David's, etc.

Me·n-folk(s. 1802. [See MAN *sb.*] **1.** The male sex. **2.** Human beings. MORRIS.

Meng, *v. Obs.* exc. *dial.* [OE. *mengan* = OFris. *menza*, OS. *mengian*, OHG. *mengen* (Du., G. *mengen*), ON. *menga* :– Gmc. **maŋʒjan*, f. **maŋʒ-*; see MINGLE, AMONG.] **1.** *trans.* To mix (*lit.* and *fig.*) **2.** To produce by mixing. late ME. **3.** To stir up; to disturb, trouble, confound. Also *intr.* for *pass.* OE. **4. a.** *trans.* To bring (living creatures) together –ME. **b.** *refl., pass.*, and *intr.* To be singled *together*, or *with, among* others; to be joined in battle; to have sexual intercourse; to be united by marriage –1590. **5.** *intr.* Of things: To be or become mixed OE.

Menhaden (menhē·dən). Also **manhad(d)en.** 1792. [Of Algonquian origin; cf. Narragansett Indian *munnawhatteaûg* menhaden, prob. rel. to *munnohquohteau* he fertilizes, the fish being used by the Indians for manure.] A U.S. fish of the herring family, *Brevoortia tyrannus*, much used for manure and producing a valuable oil.

Menhir (me·nhi^{ə}ɹ). 1840. [– Breton *men hir* (*men, mean* stone, *hir* long) = W. *maen hir*, Corn. *medn hir*.] *Archæol.* A tall upright monumental stone, of varying antiquity, found in parts of Europe, and in Africa and Asia.

Menial (mī·niăl), *a.* (*sb.*) late ME. [– AFr. *menial, meignial*, f. *meinie* MEINIE; see -AL[1].] †**1.** Pertaining to the household, domestic. Also *transf.* –1709. **2.** Of a servant: Forming one of the household; domestic. Now only *contemptuous.* late ME. **3.** Of service: Proper to a menial; servile, degrading 1673. Of temper, spirit, occupations: Sordid 1837. **4.** *sb.* A 'menial' servant (see 2). Now chiefly *contemptuous.* late ME.

2. The labour of a m. servant..adds to the value of nothing ADAM SMITH. **3.** Two other servants for m. offices SWIFT. **4.** A hot m. in a red waistcoat THACKERAY. Hence **Me·nially** *adv.*

Meningeal (mĭni·ndʒiăl), *a.* 1829. [f. *meninges* (see MENINX) + -EAL.] *Anat.* and *Path.* Of or pertaining to the meninges.

M. artery: one of the arteries supplying the dura mater of the brain. So **Meni·ngic** *a.* 1822. **Meni·ngism,** tendency to meningitis 1901.

Mengines, pl. of MENINX.

‖**Meningitis** (menindʒəi·tis). 1828. [mod. L., f. *meninges* (see MENINX) + -ITIS.] *Path.* Inflammation of the membranes of the brain or spinal cord. Hence **Meningi·tic** *a.*

Meningo- (mĭni·ŋgo), comb. f. Gr. μῆνιγξ MENINX = pertaining to the meninx (and another part), as *m.-myelitis.*

‖**Meninx** (mī·niŋks). Chiefly *pl.* **meninges** (mĭni·ndʒīz). 1616. [mod.L. – Gr. μῆνιγξ, μηνιγγ- membrane.] Any of the three membranes enveloping the brain and spinal cord (*viz.* the dura mater, arachnoid, and pia mater).

‖**Meniscus** (mĭni·skŏs). *Pl.* **menisci** (mĭni·səi); also †**meniscusses.** 1693. [mod. L. – Gr. μηνίσκος crescent, dim. of μήνη moon.] A crescent-shaped body. **1.** A crescent moon (*rare*) 1706. **2.** *Optics.* A lens convex on one side and concave on the other, esp. when of true crescent-shaped section (*converging m.*) 1693. **3.** *Physics.* The convex or concave upper surface of a liquid column, caused by capillarity 1812. **4.** *Math.* A figure of the form of a crescent 1885. **5.** *Anat.* A disc-like interarticular fibrocartilage situated in the interior of some joints to adapt the articular surfaces to each other, as in the wrist- and knee-joints 1830. **6.** *attrib.* as *m. lens*, etc. 1704. Hence **Meni·scal, -ate, -oid, -oidal** *adjs.* resembling a meniscus in form.

Meniver(e: see MINIVER.

Mennonist (me·nŏnist). Also †**Menon-.** 1645. [f. as next + -IST.] = next. So **Me·nnonism** 1684.

Mennonite (me·nŏnəit). 1565. [f. *Menno* + -ITE[1] 1.] *Eccl.* A member of a sect of Christians which was founded in Friesland by *Menno* Simons (1492–1559). They are opposed to infant baptism, the taking of oaths, military service, and the holding of civic offices.

Meno- (meno), comb. f. Gr. μήν μηνο- month, used = menses, as in **Me·nopause** (final cessation of the menses) 1872. ‖**Menorrha·gia** (excess) 1776. ‖**Meno·stasis** 1839, **Menosta·tion** 1822 (suppression).

Menology (mĭnǫ·lŏdʒi). Also **menologium.** 1610. [– mod.L. *menologium* – eccl. Gr. μηνολόγιον, f. μήν month + λόγος account; see LOGOS.] **1.** A calendar, esp. of the Greek church, with biographies of the saints. ¶**2.** The part of knowledge relating to the months 1807. So †**Menologe** 1626.

Menow(e, obs. ff. MINNOW.

‖**Mensa** (me·nsă). 1693. [L., = 'table'.] **1.** *Eccl.* The top, or the top slab, of an altar 1848. **2.** The grinding surface of a molar tooth.

Mensal (me·nsăl), *a.*[1] (*sb.*[1]) 1440. [– late L. *mensalis*, f. *mensa* table; see -AL[1].] **1.** Pertaining to or used at the table; table-. **2.** *Sc.* and *Irish Hist.* Applied to land, a church, benefice, etc., set aside for the maintenance of the table: now only with ref. to the R.C.Ch. in Ireland. Also as *sb.* A mensal church or benefice; †the provision of the royal table. 1605. **3.** *Palmistry. M. line*, the 'line of fortune', the table-line 1602.

1. Conversation either mental or m. RICHARDSON.

Mensal (me·nsăl), *a.*[2] and *sb.*[2] 1483. [f. L. *mensis* month + -AL[1].] **A.** *adj.* Monthly 1860. †**B.** *sb.* A monthly account –1526.

Mense (mens), *sb. Obs.* exc. *Sc.* and *n. dial.* 1500. [Sc. pronunc. of MENSK.] Propriety, decorum; neatness, tidiness. So **Mense** *v. trans.* to grace; to be a credit to 1535. Hence **Me·nseful** *a.* proper, decorous; neat; discreet. **Me·nseless** *a.* destitute of decorum, neatness, or propriety.

‖**Menses** (me·nsīz), *sb. pl.* 1597. [L., pl. of *mensis* month.] *Path.* The discharge of blood from the uterus, occurring normally at intervals of a lunar month.

Menshevik (me·nʃĕvik). 1917. [– Russ. *Men'shevik*, f. *mén'shiĭ* less, compar. of *málȳĭ* little. Cf. BOLSHEVIK.] A member of the minority of the Russian Social-Democratic Party at its second conference (London, 1902). Also **Me·nshevism, -ist.**

†**Mensk,** *sb.* ME. [– ON. *mennska* humanity, corresp. to OE. *menniscu* = OS., OHG. *menniskī*, f. Gmc. **mannisk-*; see MANNISH.] **1.** Humanity, kindness; graciousness. ME. only. **2.** Honour, dignity, reverence; *pl.* honours, dignities –1509. So †**Mensk** *v.* to reverence or honour; to grace; to adorn ME. –1470.

Menstrual (me·nstruăl). late ME. [– L. *menstrualis*, f. *menstruus* monthly; see MENSTRUUM, -AL[1].] **A.** *adj.* **1.** Monthly; happening once in a month, varying in monthly periods. Now only *Astr.* 1594. **2.** Of or pertaining to the menses. late ME. †**3.** Pertaining to, or of the nature of, a menstruum 1471. †**4.** Of parts of the body: Produced from the menstrual blood of the mother; opp. to *spermatical.* BACON. **B.** *sb.* †**1.** *pl.* = MENSES –1599. †**2..** *Alch.* The 'menstrual' element (see A. 3, and cf. A. 4) supposed to be added to metal in its conversion into gold –1447.

†**Menstruant,** *a.* [– *menstruans, -ant-*, pr. pple. of late L. *menstruare*; see MENSTRUATE *v.*, -ANT.] Subject to menstruation. SIR T. BROWNE.

†**Menstruate,** *a.* late ME. only. [– late L. (Vulg.) *menstruata* adj. (fem.) and sb., f. *menstruum* + *-ata* -ATE[2].] Menstruous.

Menstruate (me·nstrue^{i}t), *v.* 1658. [– *menstruat-*, pa. ppl. stem of late L. *menstruare*, f. L. *menstrua*; see MENSTRUUM, -ATE[3].] **1.** *intr.* To discharge the menses 1800. **2.** *trans.* To pollute as with menstrual blood. CLEVELAND. Hence **Me:nstrua·tion,** the process of menstruating 1776.

†**Menstrue.** late ME. [– Fr. *menstrue* – L. *menstrua.*] = MENSTRUUM –1684.

Menstruous, *a.* late ME. [– OFr. *menstrueus* or late L. *menstruosus*, f. L. *menstrua*; see next, -OUS.] **1.** Discharging the menses. **2.** Pertaining to the menses 1599. †**b.** Produced from menstrual blood. BACON. †**3.** Defiled with or as with menstrual blood. Hence, in 17th c. often: Horribly filthy or polluted. –1685.

3. All our Righteousnesses are as m. Rags BUNYAN. **Menstru·osity,** the menstrual discharge 1506.

‖**Menstruum** (me·nstruŏm). *Pl.* **menstrua** (me·nstruă). late ME. [L., subst. use of n. of *menstruus* monthly, f. *mensis* month. In cl. L. the sb. (in sense 1) occurs only in the pl. *menstrua.*] †**1.** The menstrual discharge or menses –1726. **2.** A solvent; any liquid agent by which a solid substance may be dissolved 1612.

In alchemy the base metal undergoing transmutation was compared to the seed within the womb in relation to the menstrual blood; hence sense 2.

2. Powerful menstruums are made for its emolition [*sc.* of crystal] SIR T. BROWNE. *fig.* Paradoxes ..are menstruums of friendship, they disintegrate regard 1890.

Mensurable (me·nsiŭrăb'l, me·nʃŭr-), *a.* 1604. [– Fr. *mensurable* or late L. *mensurabilis*, f. *mensurare*; see MENSURATE, -ABLE.] **1.** Capable of being measured; hence, having assigned limits. †**2.** Just, fair 1633. **3.** *Mus.* Having 'measure' and fixed rhythm, with definite duration of notes and rests 1782. Hence **Mensurabi·lity, Me·nsurableness,** m. quality.

Mensural (me·nsiŭrăl, me·nʃŭrăl), *a.* 1609. [– L. *mensuralis*, f. *mensura* MEASURE *sb.*; see -AL[1].] **1.** Pertaining to measure 1651. **2.** *Mus.* = MENSURABLE 3.

Mensurate (me·nsiŭre^{i}t, me·nʃŭr-), *v. rare.* 1653. [– *mensurat-*, pa. ppl. stem of late L. *mensurare*, f. L. *mensura* MEASURE *sb.*; see -ATE[3].] *trans.* To measure.

Mensuration (mensiŭrē^{i}·ʃən, menʃŭrē^{i}·ʃən). 1571. [– late L. *mensuratio*, f. as prec.; see -ION.] **1.** The action, or an act, of measuring. †**b.** Size as measured. COCKER. **2.** *Math.* That branch which gives the rules for finding the lengths of lines, the areas of surfaces, and the volumes of solids 1704. Hence **Mensura·tional** *a.* concerned with m.

-ment (mĕnt), *suffix*, forming sbs. Originally occurring in adopted Fr. words in *-ment*, either repr. L. sbs. in *-mentum*, or formed on the analogy of these by the addition of the suffix to vb.-stems. The resulting sbs. expressed either the result or product of the action of the verb, the means or instrument of the action, or, in late pop.L., and hence in Fr., an act or process. Instances of the two former are *fragmentum* fragment, *alimentum* aliment, *ornamentum* ornament, etc. Many of the Eng. formations are hybrid; e.g. *acknowledgement, atonement, betterment, wonderment*, etc. The suffix has rarely been appended to any other part of speech than a verb, as in *funniment, merriment, oddment.* The letter *y* (after a cons.)

ending a verb is changed to *i* bef. the suffix, as in *accompaniment*.

Ment, pa. pple. of MENG *v.*

Mental (me·ntăl), *a.*[1] late ME. [– (O)Fr. *mental* or late L. *mentalis*, f. *mens, ment-* MIND; see -AL[1].] **1.** Of or pertaining to the mind. **2.** Carried on or performed by the mind 1526. **3.** Concerned with the phenomena of mind 1820.

1. *spec.* Pertaining to, or characterized by, a disordered mind; also as *sb.* **2.** *M. arithmetic*: the art of performing arthmetical operations within the mind, without the aid of written figures, etc. *M. reservation*: see RESERVATION. **3.** M. Science 1860.

Hence **Me·ntally** *adv.* in or as regards the mind.

Mental (me·ntăl), *a.*[2] 1727. [– Fr. *mental*, f. L. *mentum* chin; see -AL[1].] Pertaining to the chin or the mentum.

The second hole in the lower jaw..is named the m. hole BELL.

Mentality (mentæ·lĭti). 1691. [f. MENTAL *a.*[1] + -ITY.] **1.** That which is of the nature of mind or of mental action. **2.** Mental quality, intellectuality 1856. **b.** *loosely*. Mental disposition, outlook 1931.

2. Hudibras has the same hard m. EMERSON.

Mentation (mentēⁱ·ʃən). 1850. [f. L. *mens, ment-* MIND + -ATION. Cf. CEREBRATION.] Mental action, esp. as attributed to the agency of the brain, etc.; also, a product of this, a state of mind.

Menthene (me·nþīn). 1838. [– G. *menthen*, Fr. *menthène*, f. L. *mentha* mint; see -ENE.] *Chem.* A liquid hydro-carbon obtained from peppermint oil.

Menthol (me·nþǫl). 1876. [– G. *menthol* (1861), f. L. *mentha* mint; see -OL.] *Chem.* A crystalline camphor-like substance obtained by cooling various mint-oils.

M. cone or *pencil*: a conical piece of mixed m. and spermaceti, for the relief of facial neuralgia.

Menticulture (me·ntikɒltiŭɹ). 1830. [f. L. *mens, ment-* MIND + *cultura* CULTURE, after *agriculture*.] Cultivation of the mind. **Me:nticu·ltural** *a.*

Mention (me·nʃən), *sb.* ME. [– (O)Fr. *mention* – L. *mentio, -on-*, f. base **men-* of *meminisse* remember.] †**1.** Bearing in mind, consideration. ME. only. **2.** In early use, the action of commemorating in speech or writing. Now, the action, or an act, of incidentally referring to or remarking upon (a person or thing) in spoken or written discourse. ME. †**3.** Indication, evidence; a vestige, trace, remnant –1633.

2. He grows peevish at any m. of business JOHNSON. Phr. *To make m. of* (= Fr. *faire mention de*), now somewhat *arch.* or *literary*, exc. in neg. contexts. I will make m. of thy righteousness, euen of thine onely *Ps.* 71:16. *Honourable m.* (rarely, after Fr. use, *m.* simply): a distinction awarded to exhibited works of art, etc. or to examination candidates that are of exceptional merit, but are not entitled to a prize. **3.** Where he moves in the sea he causeth a m. of his way in the waters. BP. HALL.

Mention (me·nʃən), *v.* 1530. [– Fr. *mentionner*, f. *mention* (see prec.). Cf. med.L. *mentionare*.] **1.** *trans.* To make mention of; to refer to incidentally; to specify by name or otherwise. **b.** To state incidentally (*that*, etc.) 1617. †**2.** *intr.* To speak or make mention *of* –1792.

1. Phr. *Not to m.*: used parenthetically to suggest that the speaker refrains from presenting the full strength of his case. Not to m. several others, Carraciò is said to have assisted Aretine ADDISON. *Don't m. it.*: a colloq. phr. used in deprecating thanks or apology. Hence **Me·ntionable** *a.*

Mento- (me·nto), used as comb. f. L. *mentum* chin, as in **Me:nto-Mecke·lian** *a.*, in *mento-Meckelian bone* or *element*, a small bone formed by the ossification of parts of Meckel's cartilage and the lower labial cartilage.

Mentor (me·ntǫɹ). 1750. [– Fr. *mentor*, appellative use of L. *Mentor* – Gr. Μέντωρ. The name was prob. chosen for its etymol. significance (f. **men-* **mon-* remember, think, counsel; cf. MENTION, MONITOR).] With capital M: Name of the guide and adviser of the young Telemachus; *allusively*, one who fulfils a similar office. Hence, as common noun: An experienced and trusted counsellor.

1. The deep..The only M. of his youth BYRON.

‖**Mentum** (me·ntɒ̆m). 1826. [L., = 'chin'.] **1.** *Anat.* The chin 1855. **2.** *Entom.* A term variously applied to different parts of the labium, esp. the median portion 1826. **3.** *Bot.* A basal projection in certain orchids 1866.

‖**Menu** (me·niu, mənü). 1837. [Fr. *menu* adj. (:– L. *minutus* MINUTE *a.*), used as sb. with the sense of detailed list, etc.] A bill of fare; also, the dishes served.

M. card, the card on which a m. is written.

Mephistopheles (mefistǫ·fĕlīz, -fəl-). Also †**-is, -us.** 1598. [Appears first in the G. *Faustbuch*, 1587, as *Mephostophiles*; of unkn. origin. The now current form *Mephistopheles*, and the abbrev. *Mephisto* come from Goethe's *Faust*.] The evil spirit to whom Faust (in the German legend) sold his soul. Also allusively.

That M. of diplomacy, Talleyrand 1818. Hence **Mephistophelean, -elian,** (me:fistofī·liăn) *adjs.* pertaining to or resembling M. or his actions.

‖**Mephitis** (mĭfəi·tis). 1706. [L. *mephitis* noxious vapour.] A noxious or pestilential emanation, esp. from the earth; a noisome or poisonous stench. So **Mephitic** (mĭfi·tik) *a.* of, pertaining to, or due to m.; offensive to the smell 1623. **Mephitism** (me·fitiz'm), mephitic poisoning of the air 1801. †**Me·phitized** *ppl. a.* charged with m. 1794.

Mer-, used in combs. (chiefly nonce-words) formed after MERMAID, as *mer-child, -folk, -wife*, etc.

Mercantile (mə̄·ɹkăntəil), *a.* 1642. [– Fr. *mercantile* – It. *mercantile*, f. *mercante* MERCHANT; see -ILE.] **1.** Of or belonging to merchants or their trade; commercial. **b.** That deals with commercial affairs 1841. **2.** Engaged in trade or commerce 1645. **3.** Mercenary; also, simply, disposed for bargaining 1756.

1. The Expedition of the Argonauts..was partly m., partly military ARBUTHNOT. Phr. *M. system* (also *m. doctrine, theory*), the system of economic doctrine and legislative policy based on the principle that money alone is wealth. **b.** Leaders of opinion on m. questions MILL. **2.** *M. marine*, the shipping collectively employed in commerce. **3.** The m. bard [*sc.* Dryden] WARTON. Hence **Me·rcantilism,** the m. spirit; commercialism; in *Pol. Econ.* the principles of the m. system. **Me·rcantilist** *sb.* an advocate of the m. system; *adj.* of or pertaining to mercantilism or the m. system.

Mercaptan (mə̄ɹkæ·ptăn). 1835. [f. mod.L. (*corpus*) *mercurium captans* 'catching mercury' (Zeise, 1834).] *Chem.* A sulphur alcohol; any one of a series of compounds resembling the alcohols, but containing sulphur, not oxygen. Hence **Merca·ptal,** a compound of a mercaptan with an aldehyde 1892. **Merca·ptide,** a compound formed by the substitution of a metal for hydrogen in a mercaptan 1835.

Mercat(e, obs. ff. MARKET.

Mercatorial (mə̄ɹkătōᵊ·riăl), *a.* Now *rare*. 1700. [f. L. *mercatorius* (f. *mercator*, f. *mercari* to trade) + -AL[1].] Of or pertaining to merchants or merchandise; mercantile. So †**Mercatory** *a.* FULLER.

†**Mercature.** 1620. [– L. *mercatura*, f. *mercari* to trade; see -URE.] Trading, commerce –1755.

†**Merce,** *v.* 1483. Aphet. f. AMERCE –1661. So †**Me·rcement,** = AMERCEMENT; also doom, adjudged punishment ME. –1598.

Mercenarian (mə̄ɹsĭnēᵊ·riăn). *rare*. 1598. [f. as next + -AN; see -IAN.] = next A. 2, B. 2.

Mercenary (mə̄·ɹsĭnări). late ME. [– L. *mercenarius* adj. and sb., earlier *mercennarius*, f. *merces, merced-* reward, wages; see MERCY, -ARY[1].] **A.** *adj.* **1.** Working merely for monetary or other reward; actuated by self-interest 1532. **b.** Of conduct, etc.: Having the love of lucre for its motive 1532. **2.** Hired; serving for hire. Now only of soldiers serving in a foreign army. 1589. †**b.** Of services, an office, etc.: Salaried, stipendiary. Of a profession, etc.: Carried on for the sake of gain –1782.

1. Such wretches are kept in pay by some m. bookseller GOLDSM. **b.** M. marriages 1837. **2.** They..began..to go ouer to serue as mercenarie soldiers in the Low Countries SIR J. SMYTH.

B. *sb.* †**1.** One who labours merely for hire; a hireling. late ME. –1844. **2.** One who receives payment for his services; now only, a professional soldier serving a foreign power 1523.

2. *fig.* Literary mercenaries, ready to serve under friend or foe 1861.

Mercer (mə̄·ɹsəɹ). ME. [– AFr. *mercer*, (O)Fr. *mercier* :– Rom. **merciarius*, f. L. *merx, merc-* MERCHANDISE; see -ER[2] 2.] A dealer in textile fabrics, esp. silks and other costly materials (in full *silk-m.*). Also *occas.* a small-ware dealer. Hence †**Me·rcership** (*rare*), the trade of a m.

Mercerize (mə̄·ɹsəɹəiz), *v.* 1859. [f. the name John *Mercer* of Accrington, alleged inventor of the process in 1844 + -IZE.] *trans.* To prepare (cotton goods) for dyeing by treating with a solution of caustic potash or soda, or certain other chemicals.

Mercery (mə̄·ɹsəri). [ME. *mercerie* – (O)Fr. *mercerie*, f. *mercier*; see MERCER, -Y[3].] **1.** *collect. sing.* (rarely *pl.*) The wares sold by a mercer. †**2.** *The M.*: The Mercers' Company. Also, the trade in mercery-ware; the part where it is carried on. –1662. **3.** *attrib.* as *m.-ware*. late ME.

2. At the Sign of the Cock, in the M. 1651.

Merchandise (mə̄·ɹtʃăndəiz), *sb.* [ME. *marchaundise* – (O)Fr. *marchandise*, f. *marchand* + *-ise*, repr. L. *-itia* (-ISE[2]). Cf. MERCHANDRY.] †**1.** The action or business of buying and selling commodities for profit; trading; traffic. Also *fig.* **2.** The commodities of commerce; movables which may be bought and sold ME. †**b.** A saleable commodity, an article of commerce –1853.

1. Phr. *To be of good m.*, to be easily marketable. *To make* (*a* or *one's*) *m.*, †to carry on a bargain; also (*arch.*) const. *of* = to traffic in (usu. in bad sense). There [at Rome] Where gainful merchandize is made of Christ CARY. **2.** *Ant. & Cl.* II. v. 104.

Merchandise (mə̄·ɹtʃăndəiz), *v. arch.* late ME. [f. prec.] **1.** *intr.* To trade, traffic; †also, to make merchandise *of*. **2.** *trans.* To buy and sell; to barter; to traffic in 1538.

2. As Roman priests [merchandize] their pardons ROWE. Hence **Me·rchandiser,** a dealer in commodities; one who traffics 1597.

Merchandry (mə̄·ɹtʃăndri). *Obs.* exc. *arch.* late ME. [– OFr. *march(ĕ)anderie*, f. *marchand*; see -ERY, -RY.] = MERCHANTRY 1. Earlier †**Merchandrise, -dy.**

Merchant (mə̄·ɹtʃănt), *sb.* and *a.* [ME. *marchaunt, -and* – O Fr. *march(ĕ)ant*, later and mod. *marchand*, :– Rom. **mercatant-*, pr. ppl. stem of **mercatare*, f. L. *mercari, mercat-* trade, f. *merx, merc-* merchandise.] **A.** *sb.* **1.** One who buys and sells commodities for profit; orig. *gen.*; but early restricted to wholesale traders, esp. those dealing with foreign countries. **b.** A shopkeeper. Now only *Sc.*, *n. dial.*, and *U.S.* late ME. **c.** *slang* One who practises or specializes in some activity (cf. SPEED-*m.*) 1886. †**2.** A supercargo –1681. †**3.** A fellow, 'chap' –1610. †**4.** A trading vessel, merchantman –1740.

1. A wise Marchant neuer aduentureth all his goodes in one ship MORE. *fig.* These wee call Merchants of Light BACON. Phr. †*To play the m. with*: to cheat, get the better of. †*To have* or *put on m.'s ears*: to affect not to hear. **4.** *Temp.* II. i. 5. *attrib.* and *Comb.*: **m.** (formerly †**m.'s) iron,** bar iron in a form suitable for the market, made by heating together and rolling pieces of puddled iron; hence *m. bar, -rolls, train* (= train of rolls); **m. prince** (prob. after *Isa.* 23: 8), a m. of princely wealth.

B. *adj.* **1.** Having relation to merchandise; relating to trade or commerce, esp. in *law-, statute-m.* late ME. **2.** Of a ship: Serving for the transport of merchandise. Hence, of or pertaining to the mercantile marine, as in *m. seaman, service*. (Often hyphened.) late ME. **3.** Of a town: Occupied in commerce. Also, consisting of merchants, as in *guild-m., m.-guild*. 1467.

3. M. citie *Isa.* 23:11.

Merchant (mə̄·ɹtʃănt), *v.* Now *rare*. late ME. [– OFr. *march(ĕ)ander* (mod. *marchander*), f. *marchand* MERCHANT.] **1.** *intr.* To trade as a merchant. †Also, to negotiate; in bad sense, to haggle. **2.** *trans.* To deal in; to buy and sell 1511.

1. I held it not fit, we should m. with our Sovereign 1614. Hence **Me·rchantable** *a.* fit for market; saleable; †of or pertaining to trade; commercial.

Me·rchant-adve·nturer. *Obs.* exc. *Hist.* 1496. = MERCHANT-VENTURER.

†**Me·rchantly,** *a.* 1599. [f. MERCHANT *sb.* + -LY¹.] **a.** Of or pertaining to a merchant. **b.** Huckstering. –1736.

Me·rchantman. 1449. [f. MERCHANT *a.* + MAN.] **1.** = MERCHANT *sb.* 1. *arch.* **2.** A vessel of the mercantile marine 1627.

Merchantry (mɔ̄·ɹtʃăntri). 1789. [f. MERCHANT *sb.* + -RY.] **1.** The business of a merchant; trade, commercial dealings. **2.** Merchants collectively. CARLYLE.

Me·rchant-tai·lor. *Obs.* exc. (with arch. spelling) in 'Company of Merchant Taylors' and the 'Merchant Taylors' School' (London) 1504. [f. MERCHANT + TAILOR.] A tailor who supplies the materials of which his goods are made; a member of the Company of Merchant Taylors. **b.** One educated at Merchant Taylors' School 1877.

Me·rchant-ve·nturer. *Obs.* exc. *Hist.* 1533. A merchant engaged in the dispatch of trading expeditions over sea, and the establishment of factories and trading stations in foreign countries. Hence, a member of an incorporated association of such merchants.

Me·rchet. *Obs.* exc. *Hist.* ME. [– AFr. *merchet* (whence AL. *merchetum* in Domesday Book) = ONFr. *market* MARKET.] A fine paid by a tenant or bondsman to his overlord for liberty to give his daughter in marriage.

†**Merciable,** *a.* ME. [– OFr. *merciable*, f. *merci*; see MERCY, -ABLE.] Merciful –1579.

Mercian (mɔ̄·ɹʃ¹ăn, mɔ̄·ɹsiăn). 1513. [f. med.L. *Mercia*, f. OE. *Merće, Mierće* (pl.) lit. people of 'the march', 'borderers'; see MARCH *sb.*³, -IAN.] **A.** *adj.* Of or belonging to the Old English kingdom of Mercia or its language 1655. **B.** *sb.* **1.** A native or inhabitant of Mercia 1513. **2.** The dialect of Old English spoken in Mercia 1887.

Merciful (mɔ̄·ɹsifŭl), *a.* ME. [f. MERCY + -FUL.] Having or exercising mercy; characterized by mercy.

Blessed be mercyful men, for thei shuln gete mercye WYCLIF *Matt.* 5: 7. **Me·rciful-ly** *adv.*, **-ness.**

†**Me·rcify,** *v. rare.* 1596. [f. MERCY + -FY.] *trans.* To pity, compassionate –1733.

Merciless (mɔ̄·ɹsilės), *a.* late ME. [f. MERCY + -LESS.] Devoid of mercy; showing no mercy; pitiless, unrelenting.

A stern prince, m. in his exactions PRESCOTT. *transf.* M. ridicule STEPHEN. **Me·rciless-ly** *adv.*, **-ness.**

Mercurial (məɹkiū̆ᵊ·riăl), *a.* and *sb.* late ME. [– (O)Fr. *mercuriel* and (as sb., in sense B. 1) *mercurial* or L. *mercurialis*, f. *Mercurius* MERCURY; see -AL¹.] **A.** *adj.* **1.** Of or pertaining to the god Mercury; resembling what pertains to Mercury. Now *rare.* 1599. **2.** Pertaining to (†influenced by) the planet Mercury. late ME. **3.** Of persons: Born under the planet Mercury; having the qualities of such a nativity, as eloquence, ingenuity, aptitude for commerce 1593. **4.** (Hence) Volatile, sprightly, ready-witted. (Now taken as alluding to the properties of the metal mercury) 1647. **5.** Of or pertaining to, consisting of or containing, mercury or quicksilver; (of diseases, etc.) produced by the administration of mercury; (of an organ) showing mercurial symptoms 1657.

1. His Foote Mercuriall: his martiall Thigh, The brawns of Hercules SHAKS. **2.** *M. finger*: the little finger. **4.** The gay, gallant, m. Frenchman DISRAELI.

B. *sb.* †**1.** The plant mercury 1607–1626. †**2.** A person born under the planet Mercury (see A. 3); a lively or sprightly person; also, one addicted to cheating and thieving 1598–1696. **3.** A preparation of mercury used as a drug 1676.

2. The Mercurials with their swiftnesse rush over all things 1650. **3.** The Cure is perform'd by Mercurials outwardly and inwardly 1735. Hence **Mercu·rialism** *Path.*, the condition induced by the absorption of mercury into the body. **Mercuria·lity,** m. condition; †the m. part (of something). **Mercu·rial-ly** *adv.*, **-ness.** So **Mercu·rian** †*a.* and *sb.* = MERCURIAL.

Mercurialist (məɹkiū̆ᵊ·riălist). 1566. [f. prec. + -IST.] †**1.** One under the influence of the planet Mercury –1651; an eloquent or ingenious person; a trader; *occas.* a sharper, a thief –1655. **2.** A medical man who makes free use of mercury 1835.

Mercurialize (məɹkiū̆ᵊ·riăləiz), *v.* 1611. [f. as prec. + -IZE.] †**1.** *intr.* To play the part of a mercurial person –1656. **2.** *trans.* To render mercurial in temper 1862. **3.** To subject to the action of mercury 1843. Hence **Mercu:rializa·tion,** subjection to treatment by mercury; a mercurial process used in the development of photographs.

Mercuric (məɹkiū̆ᵊ·rik), *a.* 1828. [f. MERCURY + -IC.] *Chem.* Said of compounds in which mercury has a valency of two.

M. chloride = CORROSIVE SUBLIMATE; *M. sulphide* = VERMILION.

Mercu·rify, *v.* 1680. [f. MERCURY + -FY.] **1.** *trans.* **a.** *Alch.* To change (a portion of a metallic mass) into the form of mercury. **b.** To extract mercury from (metallic ore). **2.** To combine, treat, or mingle with mercury 1846. Hence **Mercurifica·tion.**

Mercurous (mɔ̄·ɹkiŭrəs), *a.* 1865. [f. MERCURY + -OUS.] *Chem.* Said of compounds in which mercury has a valency of one.

Mercury (mɔ̄·ɹkiŭri), *sb.* ME. [– L. *Mercurius*, f. *merx, merc-* merchandise. The use as a plant-name is Eng. only, suggested by L. (*herba*) *mercurialis* (MERCURIAL B. 1).] **I.** The god (and derived senses). **1.** A Roman deity, early identified with the Greek Hermes, the god of eloquence, skill, trading and thieving, the presider over roads, the conductor of departed souls to the Lower World, and the messenger of the gods; represented as a young man with winged sandals and a winged hat, and bearing the caduceus. **2.** A statue or image of Mercury; *spec.* = HERMA; hence, †a sign-post 1644. **3.** *transf.* **a.** A messenger or news-bearer 1594. **b.** A guide or conductor 1592. †**c.** A dexterous thief. B. JONS. †**d.** A hawker of pamphlets, etc. –1721. **4.** The title of certain journals. †Formerly also *gen.* = newspaper 1643.

1. Now M. indue thee with leasing SHAKS. **3. a.** *Rich. III*, II. i. 88. But what saies shee to mee? be briefe my good shee-Mercurie SHAKS. **4.** Mercuries of furthest Regions BUTLER.

II. The planet. **1.** *Astr.* The planet nearest to the sun, and the smallest of the major planets. late ME. **2.** *Her.* The name for the tincture purpure in blazoning by the names of the heavenly bodies 1562.

III. The metal, etc. **1.** The heavy silver-white liquid metal otherwise called QUICKSILVER. It absorbs other metals, forming amalgams, and is commonly obtained by sublimation from cinnabar, its most important ore. Chem. symbol Hg (*hydrargyrum*). By alchemists represented by the sign of the planet Mercury (☿). late ME. **b.** A preparation of the metal or of one of its compounds (e.g. *m. sublimate*) used in medicine 1699. **c.** The column of mercury in a barometer or thermometer. Also *fig.* 1704. **2.** *Old Chem.* **a.** One of the five elementary 'principles' of which all material substances were supposed to be compounded; also called *spirit* 1471. †**3.** *fig.* as an emblem of sprightliness, volatility, inconstancy, wittiness, etc. –1797.

3. He [Buckingham] was so full of m. that he could not fix long in any friendship or to any design BURNET.

IV. As a plant-name. **1. a.** The pot-herb ALLGOOD, *Chenopodium bonus-henricus* (English, False M.). late ME. **b.** Any plant of the genus *Mercurialis*, esp. *M. perennis* (Dog's M.) 1548.

Hence †**Me·rcury** *v. trans.* to wash with a preparation of mercury B. JONS.

Mercy (mɔ̄·ɹsi). [ME. *merci* – (O)Fr. *merci* :– L. *merces, merced-* pay, recompense, revenue, in Chr. L. used for *misericordia* pity, and *gratiæ* thanks.] **1.** Forbearance and compassion shown by one person to another who is in his power and who has no claim to receive kindness. **b.** *spec.* God's pitiful forbearance towards His creatures ME. **2.** Disposition to forgive; mercifulness ME. **3.** The clemency or forbearance of a conqueror, which he can extend or not as he thinks fit ME. **4.** An act of mercy; esp. one vouchsafed by God to His creatures; a gift of God, a blessing ME. †**5.** = AMERCEMENT –1768. †**6.** Thanks (*rare*) –1500.

1. Phr. *To have m. on, upon,* †*of; to take m. on, show m.*, etc. *In m.* (*to*), in the exercise of m. In m. to him, let us drop the subject '*Junius' Lett.* **b.** Lorde haue mercie vpon vs *Bk. Com. Prayer.* **2.** Phr. *Of* (or †*for*) *one's m.* The taste whereof, God of his mercy giue You patience to indure SHAKS. †*To cry* (*one*) *m.*: to beg for pardon or forgiveness. Hence = 'to beg (one's) pardon'; often *colloq.* with 'I' omitted. Oh, cry you m., sir, I haue mistooke SHAKS. *Mercy* (ellipt.) = 'may God have m.!' Also *m. on us! for m.'s sake! lord-a-m.! m. me!* **3.** Phr. †*To take to* (or *into*) *m.*: to extend pardon to (one who yields at discretion); to give quarter to. †(*To yield*) *to* or *upon m.*, (to surrender) at discretion. †*At m.*: (that has surrendered) at discretion; at the disposal of a victor or superior; on sufferance, liable to interference. The linen of the North, a trade casual, corrupted, and at m. SWIFT. *At the m. of (a person)*: liable to any treatment he may choose to employ. So †*in the m. of; (to leave* or *trust) to the m.* iron. *the tender mercies, of.* Leaving the civil service at the m. of a partisan chief BRYCE. **4.** What a m. it was that I held the ace of spades! 1811.

Phr. *Works of m.* (also †*deeds,* †*duties of m.*, and simply †*mercies*): acts of compassion towards suffering fellow-creatures. *Sisters of M.*, title of a R.C. sisterhood founded at Dublin in 1827; *pop.*, the members of any nursing sisterhood. *House of M.*, a penitentiary or house of refuge.

Comb.: †**m.-stool, -table** = MERCY-SEAT (*fig.*); †**-stroke,** a *coup de grâce.*

Mercy-seat. 1530 (Tindale, *Ex.* 25: 17, after Luther's *Gnadenstuhl*). The golden covering placed upon the Ark of the Covenant and regarded as the resting-place of God. Hence applied to the throne of God in heaven, and to Christ as 'the propitiation for our sins'.

†**Merd.** 1477. [– Fr. *merde* :– L. *merda* dung.] Dung, excrement –1621.

Mere (mīᵊɹ), *sb.*¹ [OE. *mere*, corresp., with variations of gender, to OS. *meri* sea (Du. *meer* sea, pool), OHG. *mari, meri* (G. *meer*), ON. *marr* sea, Goth. *mari-* in *marisaiws, marei* :– Gmc. **mari* :– IE. **mori-* **məri-*, whence OSl. *morje* (Russ. *móre*), L. *mare.*] †**1.** The sea –ME. **2.** A sheet of standing water; a lake, pond. Now chiefly *poet.* and *dial.* OE. †**3.** An arm of the sea –1676. **4.** A marsh, a fen. Now *dial.* ME.

2. Sometimes on lonely mountain-meres I find a magic bark TENNYSON.

Mere, mear (mīᵊɹ), *sb.*² *arch.* and *dial.* Also **meer(e.** [OE. (*ġe*)*mǣre* = MDu. *mēre, meer*, ON. (*landa*)*mæri* landmark :– Gmc. **ʒamairjam*, perh. rel. to L. *murus*, earlier *moerus, moiros* wall.] **1.** A boundary; also, a landmark. **b.** *spec.* A green balk or road, serving as a boundary 1607. **2.** *Derbysh. Lead-mining.* A measure of land containing lead-ore 1653.

Mere (mīᵊɹ), *a.* and *adv.* late ME. [– AFr. *meer* (in legal uses), OFr. *mier* or its source L. *merus* not mixed, pure.] **A.** *adj.* **1.** Pure, unmixed, undiluted. **2.** Performed or exercised by a person or persons specified without the help of any one else; sole. Chiefly *Law*, in *m. motion*, etc. 1444. **3.** *Law. M. right*: right as dist. from possession 1559. †**4.** That is what it is in the full sense of the term; nothing less than; absolute, entire, sheer, perfect, etc. –1775. **5.** That is barely or only what it is said to be; nothing more than 1581.

1. Meere wine ful of the grape HOLLAND. **2.** We were wrong if of our m. motion we..fought with you, and ravaged your land JOWETT. **4.** *Oth.* II. ii. 3. **5.** Decorum's turn'd to m. civility GRAY. The merest nobody 1868.

†**B.** *adv.* = MERELY –1635.

Mere, mear (mīᵊɹ), *v. Obs.* exc. *dial.* OE. [f. MERE *sb.*²] **1.** *trans.* To mark *out* (land) by meres or boundaries. †**2.** *intr.* To abut *upon*; to be bounded *by* –1713.

1. This purchase will..meare and bounde his owne [property] EARL OF CORK.

Mere, obs. var. of MARE.

†**Mered,** *ppl. a.* Also **meered.** 1606. [perh. corrupt.] *The m. question*: either (*a*) the sole (MERE *a.*) ground of dispute; or (*b*) the matter to which the dispute is limited (MERE *v.*). *Ant. & Cl.* III. xiii. 10.

Merel (me·rəl). late ME. [– OFr. *merel* (mod. *méreau*) token coin, counter, f. Rom. **marra* pebbles, shingle (cf. Ladin *mar, mara* pebbles, heap of stone). Cf. AL. *merellus* (XIV).] One of the counters used in the game called *merels*, which is played by two persons (cf. MORRIS *sb.*²).

Merely (mīᵊ·ɹli), *adv.* 1546. [f. MERE *a.* + -LY².] †**1.** Without admixture or qualification –1645. †**2.** Absolutely; altogether –1788; †actually –1601. **3.** Only (what is referred to) and nothing more. Often after *not.* 1580.

1. Such things as are not m., but mixedly Divine 1637. **3.** The multitudes who read m. for the sake of talking JOS. BUTLER.

‖**Merenchyma** (mĕre·ŋkimă). 1839. [mod. L., f. Gr. μέρος part + *-enchyma* in PARENCHYMA.] *Bot.* Tissue consisting of ellipsoidal and spheroidal cells. **Merenchy·matous** *a.*

Meresman (mīᵊ·ɹzmæ̆n). *Obs.* exc. *dial.* 1867. [f. *mere's*, gen. of MERE *sb.*² + MAN.] A man appointed to find out the exact boundaries of a parish, etc.

Merestone (mīᵊ·ɹstōᵘn). *arch.* and *dial.* OE. [f. MERE *sb.*² + STONE.] A stone set up as a landmark.

Meretricious (merĭtri·ʃəs), *a.* 1626. [f. L. *meretricius* (f. *meretrix, -tric-* harlot, f. *merēri* serve for hire) + -OUS.] **1.** Of, pertaining to, befitting, or of the character of a harlot. **2.** Alluring by false show; showily attractive 1633.

2. The style he aims at is gaudy and m. 1846. Hence **Meretri·cious-ly** *adv.*, **-ness.**

‖**Meretrix** (me·rĭtriks). *Pl.* **meretrices** (merĭtrəi·sīz). 1564. [L.; see prec.] A prostitute, harlot.

Merganser (məɹgæ·nsəɹ). 1752. [– mod.L. *merganser* (Gesner, 1555), f. *mergus* diver (water-fowl), (f. L. *mergere* dive; see next) + *anser* goose.] Any bird of the genus *Mergus* or subfamily *Merginæ*, fish-eating ducks of great diving powers, with long narrow serrated bill hooked at the tip, inhabiting the northern parts of the Old World and N. America; esp. *M. merganser*, the common m. or GOOSANDER.

Merge (mɔ̄ɹdʒ), *v.* 1636. [– L. *mergere* dip, plunge. Senses 2 and 3 come through legal AFr. *merger*, earlier translated 'drown'.] †**1.** *trans.* To plunge or sink *in* a (specified) activity, environment, etc.; to immerse –1751. **2.** *Law.* To sink (a lesser estate, title, etc.) in a greater one. Hence *gen.*, to cause (something) to lose its own character or identity in something else. 1728. **3.** *intr.* In *Law*, to be sunk in a greater title, estate, etc. Hence *gen.*, to sink and disappear by absorption *in* or *into* something else. 1726.

2. Their object is to m. all natural and all social sentiment in inordinate vanity BURKE. **3.** Serfdom had merged..into free servitude FROUDE. Hence **Me·rgence,** the action of merging or condition of being merged.

Merger (mɔ̄·ɹdʒəɹ). 1728. [– subst. use of AFr. *merger*; see prec., -ER⁴.] **1.** *Law.* Extinguishment of a right, estate, contract, action, etc. by absorption in another. **b.** *U.S.* The consolidation of one firm or trading company with another 1889. **2.** *gen.* An act of merging; the fact of being merged 1881.

Mericarp (me·rikāɹp). 1832. [– Fr. *méricarpe*, irreg. f. Gr. μέρος part + καρπός fruit. See MERO-¹.] *Bot.* A portion of a fruit which splits away as a perfect fruit; *esp.* each of the two one-seeded carpels which constitute the fruit in umbelliferous plants.

Meridian (mĕri·diăn), *sb.* late ME. [– (O)Fr. *méridien* or L. *meridianus* (in subst. uses L. *meridianum*, sc. *tempus* time, i.e. noon, med.L. *meridiana* noon, siesta), f. *meridies*, nom. f. loc. *meridie*, by dissim. from **mediei die* at midday. In sense 4 ult. for L. *circulus meridianus* meridian circle, tr. Gr. κύκλος μεσημβρινός (f. μεσημβρία, f. μέσος MID, ἡμέρα day).] **1.** Midday, noon. *Obs.* exc. *joc.* **b.** *Hist.* A midday rest or siesta. [tr. med.L. *meridiana.*] 1798. **c.** *Sc.* A midday dram 1818. **2.** The point at which the sun or a star attains its highest altitude 1450. **b.** *fig.* Culmination, full splendour 1613. **c.** The middle period of a man's life; his prime 1645. †**3.** The south –1601. **4.** [Ellipt. for *m. circle* or *line.*] **a.** *Astr.* (More fully *celestial m.*) The great circle (of the celestial sphere) which passes through the celestial poles and the zenith of any place on the earth's surface. **b.** (More fully *terrestrial m.*) The great circle (of the earth) which lies in the plane of the celestial m. of a place, and which passes through the place and the poles; also often applied to that half of this circle that extends from pole to pole through the place. late ME.

So named because the sun crosses it at noon. A globe or map has usually a number of meridians drawn upon it at certain intervals on a parallel from the *first m.*, i.e. the m. (in British maps the m. of Greenwich) conventionally determined to be of longitude 0°.

c. *transf.* (*a*) Occas. applied to any great circle of a sphere that passes through the poles, or to a line, on a surface of revolution, that is in a plane with its axis 1721. (*b*) *Magnetic m.*: the great circle of the earth that passes through any point on its surface and the magnetic poles 1704. **d.** A graduated ring or semicircle of brass in which an artificial globe is suspended 1633. **e.** *attrib.* 1849. **5.** *transf.* and *fig.* A locality or situation having its own particular character; the special character or circumstances of one place, person, etc. as dist. from others. Chiefly in fig. uses of astronomical phr. (see below) 1589.

2. b. I haue touch'd the highest point of all my Greatnesse, And from that full M. of my Glory, I haste now to my Setting SHAKS. **c.** As for her Age, I believe she was near upon the M. 1703. **4. e.** *M. circle*, an astronomical instrument consisting of a telescope carrying a large graduated circle, by which the right ascension and declination of a star may be determined; a transit-circle; **m.-mark,** a mark fixed at some distance due north or south of an astronomical instrument, by pointing at which the instrument is set in the m. **5.** A course of anecdotes..such as suited the m. of the..servants' hall W. IRVING. Phr. *Calculated to* or *for the m. of* = suited to the tastes, habits, capacities, etc. of.

Meridian (mĕri·diăn), *a.* late ME. [– (O)Fr. *méridien* or L. *meridianus*; see prec.] **1.** Of or pertaining to midday or noon. Now *rare* exc. as in 2. **2.** *esp.* Pertaining to the station, aspect, or power of the sun at midday. late ME. **b.** *fig.* Pertaining to the period of greatest elevation or splendour (of a person, state, etc.) 1672. †**c.** Consummate –1734. **3.** Pertaining to a meridian. Chiefly in collocations orig. referable to sense 2. late ME. **b.** Passing along a meridian SIR T. BROWNE. **4.** Southern, meridional (*rare*) late ME.

1. *M. ring*, a ring so marked within the hoop as to serve the purpose of a sun-dial. **2.** Care veils in clouds the sun's m. beam CRABBE. **b.** The year 1713, when Swift was in his m. altitude EARL ORRERY. **c.** M. merit 1728. A. M. Villain NORTH. **3.** *M. circle* = MERIDIAN *sb.* 4. *M. line*: orig. = MERIDIAN *sb.* 4; now usually, a line (on a map, etc.) representing a meridian; also, a line traced on the earth's surface, indicating the course of a portion of a meridian as ascertained by astronomical observations. *M. altitude*; the angular distance between the horizon and the sun at noon, or (in later use) any heavenly body when crossing the meridian. **4.** A stranger..Born far beyond the mountains; but his blood Is all m., as if never fann'd By the black wind that chills the polar flood BYRON.

†**Meridie.** [– L.] Noon. CHAUCER.

Meridional (mĕri·diŏnăl). late ME. [– (O)Fr. *méridional* – late L. *meridionalis*, irreg. f. *meridies* midday, south, after *septentrionalis* SEPTENTRIONAL.] **A.** *adj.* **1.** Southern, southerly. **b.** Characteristic of the inhabitants of the south (of Europe) 1847. †**2.** Pertaining to the noontide position of the sun. *M. line* = MERIDIAN *sb.* 4. –1834. **3.** Pertaining to or characteristic of noonday; chiefly *fig.* Now *rare* or *Obs.* ·1624. **4.** Of or pertaining to a meridian 1555. **b.** Applied to designate markings on a roundish body that lie in a plane with its axis 1658. **B.** *sb.* An inhabitant of the south; esp. of the south of France 1591.

A. 1. The M. people are, for the most part, black and curled 1653. **b.** A dark, m. physiognomy MOTLEY. **3.** This abbey, when in its m. glory 1762. Hence **Meri:diona·lity,** the state of being m. or on the meridian: aspect towards the south. **Meri·dionally** *adv.* north and south; also, in the direction of the poles (of a magnet).

‖**Meringue** (məræ·ŋ). 1706. [– Fr. *meringue*, of unkn. origin.] A delicate confection made of pounded sugar and whites of eggs; *esp.* a small cake made of this. Hence **Meringued** (-æ·ŋgd) *a.*, iced with m.

Merino (mĕrī·no). 1781. [– Sp. *merino*, of disputed origin.] **1.** In full *m. sheep*: A variety of sheep prized for its fine wool, orig. bred in Spain. Also *attrib.* as *m. breed, fleece, wool*, etc. **2.** A soft woollen material like fine French cashmere, orig. of merino wool 1823. **3.** A fine woollen yarn used for hosiery 1886.

Merismatic (merizmæ·tik), *a.* 1849. [– Gr. μέρισμα; -ματ- separated part, f. μερίζειν divide into parts; see -ATIC.] *Biol.* Of cells or tissues. Having the property of dividing into portions by the formation of internal partitions. Of processes: Involving such division.

Meristem (me·ristem). 1874. [irreg. f. Gr. μεριστός divided, divisible, f. μερίζειν, f. μέρος part, with ending after PHLOEM, XYLEM.] *Bot.* The unformed growing cellular tissue of the younger parts of plants; merismatic tissue.

Merit (me·rit), *sb.* ME. [– (O)Fr. *mérite* – L. *meritum* price, value, service rendered, subst. use of pa. pple. n. of *merēre, merēri* earn, deserve, rel. to Gr. μείρεσθαι obtain as a share, μοῖρα share, fate, μέρος part.] †**1.** That which is deserved; due reward or punishment –1706. **2.** The condition or fact of deserving; 'character with respect to desert of either good or evil' (T.). Also *pl.* in same sense. Now *rare.* ME. **3.** The quality of deserving well, or of being entitled to reward or gratitude ME. **b.** *spec.* in *Theol.*, the quality, in actions or persons, of being entitled to reward from God ME. **4.** Excellence, worth. late ME. **5.** Something which entitles to reward or gratitude. Chiefly *pl.*; *spec.* in *Theol.*, good works as entitling to reward from God; also, the righteousness and sacrifice (of Christ) as 'imputed' to sinners ME. **6.** An excellence 1700.

1. Heere men may seen how synne hath his merite! CHAUCER. **2.** Phr. *The merits*, rarely †*the m.* (of a case, question, etc.): chiefly in *Law*, the intrinsic rights and wrongs of the matter. Hence, *to discuss, judge* (a proposal, etc.) *on its merits*, i.e. with regard only to its intrinsic excellences or defects. **3.** The principle of promotion by m. 1881. **4.** A Woman of Merit STEELE. **5.** MILT. *P. L.* III. 290. **6.** Would you ask for his merits? Alas! he had none GOLDSM. Phr. *To make a m. of*: to represent (some action of one's own) as meritorious.

Merit (me·rit), *v.* 1484. [– (O)Fr. *mériter*, f. *mérite* MERIT *sb.*] †**1.** *trans.* To reward, recompense –1611. **2.** = DESERVE *v.* 1 and 2. 1526. **3.** *absol.* or *intr.* To be deserving of good or evil 1599. **4.** *trans.* To earn by meritorious action; *spec.* in *Theol.*, to become entitled to (reward) at the hands of God; also, of Christ, to obtain by his merits (spiritual blessings) for mankind 1543. **5.** *intr.* To acquire merit; to become entitled to reward, gratitude, or commendation. *Obs.* exc. *Theol.* 1526.

2. To do aught may m. praise MILT. He merited ..to be trusted DE FOE. The thing merited confirmation TUCKER. **3.** Die! as thy frailties m. BOWEN. Phr. *To m. well* (*of* a person). **5.** I..am resolved that none shall m. at my Expence SWIFT. So **Me·ritable** *a.* = MERITORIOUS (now *rare*). **Me·ritedly** *adv.*

Me·rit-mo:nger. *contemptuous.* 1552. One who trades in merits; one who seeks to merit salvation or eternal reward by good works.

Meritorious (meritōᵊ·riəs), *a.* late ME. [f. L. *meritorius* (f. *merēre, -ēri* earn, deserve; see MERIT *sb.* and -ORY²) + -OUS.] **1.** Of actions: Productive of merit; serving to earn reward; esp. in *Theol.*, said of good works, penance, etc. †**2.** Of an action or agent: That earns or deserves some specified good or evil. Const. *of.* –1758. **3.** Deserving of reward or gratitude. Now usually: Well-deserving; having merit. (In literary criticism, a term of limited praise.) 1494. †**4.** Merited –1632.

2. *M. cause*: an action or agent that causes by meriting (some good or evil result). His Blood..is the m. cause of mans redemption BUNYAN. **3.** His patience had been most m. HT. MARTINEAU. Hence **Merito·rious-ly** *adv.*, **-ness.**

†**Meritory,** *a.* ME. [– AFr. *meritorie*, (O)Fr. *méritoire*, or L. *meritorius*; see prec., -ORY².] = MERITORIOUS –1523.

Merk(e, var. ff. MARK, MIRK.

Merle (mɔ̄ɹl). 1450. [– (O)Fr. *merle* :– L. *merula*, (post-cl.) *merulus.*] The blackbird, *Turdus merula. arch.*

The m., in his noontide bow'r, Makes woodland echoes ring BURNS.

Merlin¹ (mɔ̄·ɹlin). ME. [– AFr. *merilun*, aphet. f. OFr. *esmerillon* (mod. *émerillon*), augment. of *esmeril* :– Frankish **smeril* = OHG. *smerlo, smiril* (G. *schmerl*).] A small European falcon, *Falco æsalon.*

Merlin². 1644. The name of the soothsayer of the Arthurian legend; used as a title of almanacs, etc.

England's propheticall Merline 1644 (*title*).

†**Me·rling.** ME. [– OFr. *merlenc* (mod. *merlan*), f. L. *merula* some kind of fish + WGmc. *-iŋʒa* -ING³.] The whiting –1736.

Merlion, marlion (mɔ̄·ɹ-. mā·ɹliən). 1553. [perh. var. of MERLIN¹.] *Her.* A bird, identical with MARTLET 2, or with the *merlette* of French heraldry.

Merlon (mɔ̄·ɹlən). 1704. [– Fr. *merlon* – It. *merlone*, augm. of *merlo* battlement.] The part of an embattled parapet between two embrasures; †a similar structure on a battleship.

Mermaid (mɔ̄·ɹmēⁱd). late ME. [f. MERE *sb.*¹ + MAID.] **1.** An imaginary species of beings, supposed to inhabit the sea, and to have the head and trunk of a woman, ending in the tail of a fish or cetacean. †In early use often the SIREN of mythology. **2.** A representation of this, esp. *Her.* 1464. **b.** A shop or inn sign. late ME. **3.** *transf.* †**a.** A siren; in 16–17th c. applied to a prostitute. **b.** *joc.* A woman who is at home in the water 1880.

1. Half-hidden, like a m. in sea-weed KEATS. **2. b.** What things have we seen Done at the M.? BEAUMONT. **3.** *Com. Err.* III. ii. 45.

attrib. and *Comb.*: **m.-fish,** the monk-fish or angel-fish, *Rhina squatina*; **m.'s glove,** (*a*) a British sponge, *Halichondria palmata*, somewhat resembling a glove; (*b*) *pl.* = DEAD-MAN'S FINGERS 2; **m.'s head,** one of the small rounded sea-urchins, as *Spatangus cordatus*; **m.'s purse,** the horny egg-case of a skate, ray, or shark, a sea-purse.

Mermaiden (mɔ̄·ɹmē̆ⁱd'n). Now *rare.* late ME. [f. as prec. + MAIDEN.] = prec. 1, 2.

The cold strange eyes of a little M. M. ARNOLD.

Merman (mɔ̄·ɹmæn). 1601. [f. MERE *sb.*¹ + MAN *sb.*, after MERMAID.] The male of the mermaid.

In *Her.*, the m. (also called *triton* or *Neptune*) is depicted as holding in the right hand a trident, and in the left a conch-shell trumpet.

Mero-¹ (me·ro), bef. a vowel **mer-,** comb. f. Gr. μέρος 'part, fraction', in various technical terms; occas. opp. to HOLO-. **Me·roblast** [Gr. βλαστός, -BLAST], *Biol.* an ovum which is only partly germinal; so **Merobla·stic** *a.* undergoing partial segmentation, as an ovum. **Merohe·dral** [Gr. ἕδρα seat, base], **Me:rosymme·trical, Me:rosystema·tic** *adjs.*, *Cryst.* (of a crystal) having less than the full number of faces of the type of symmetry to which it belongs; so **Merohe·dric** *a.*, **Merohe·drism, Merosy·mmetry. Me·rostome** [Gr. στόμα mouth], *Zool.* an arthropod of the order *Merostomata*; so **Merosto·matous, -o·stomous** *adjs.*

Mero-² (mīᵊ·ro, miᵊrǫ·), comb. f. Gr. μηρός 'thigh', occurring in certain mod. scientific terms. **Me·rocele,** *Path.* femoral hernia; hence **Meroce·lic** *a.* **Merocerite** (-ǫ·sĕrəit) [Gr. κέρας horn], *Zool.* the fourth segment of the antenna of a crustacean; hence **Meroceri·tic** *a.* **Meropodite** (-ǫ·pŏdəit) [Gr. πούς, ποδ- foot], *Zool.* the fourth segment (from the base) of certain limbs of crustaceans; hence **Meropodi·tic** *a.*

‖**Meros** (mīᵊ·rǫs). Also **-us.** 1823. [– Gr. μηρός thigh.] **1.** *Arch.* The plane face between the channels in Doric triglyphs. **2.** *Zool.* A meropodite 1855.

-merous, the ending of the adjs. *dimerous*, etc., used *Bot.* = 'having (a specified number of) parts'. Often written *2-merous, five-merous.*

Merovingian (merŏvi·ndʒiăn). 1694. [– Fr. *mérovingien*, f. med.L. *Merovingi* pl., f. L. form (*Meroveus*) of the name of their reputed founder; see -ING³.] **A.** *adj.* Pertaining to the line of Frankish kings founded by Clovis, and to the kingdoms reigned over by them in Gaul and Germany from A.D. 500 to A.D. 751–2. In *Palæogr.*, applied to the style of handwriting peculiar to that period. **B.** *sb.* A king or other member of this royal line. In *Palæogr.* = Merovingian script.

Merrily (me·rili), *adv.* late ME. [f. MERRY *a.* + -LY².] **1.** In early use: Pleasantly, cheerfully, happily. Now: Joyously, mirthfully, hilariously. †**2.** Jocularly, wittily. –1704. **3.** With alacrity; briskly. Somewhat *arch.* 1530.

1. Full m. the humble Bee doth sing SHAKS. M. danced the Quaker's wife, And m. danced the Quaker 17... **3.** The hare..worked very m., and ..beat a great favourite 1876.

Merriment (me·rimĕnt). 1576. [f. MERRY *a.* + -MENT.] †**1.** Something that makes mirth; a jest; a piece of fooling; *spec.* a brief comic dramatic entertainment –1632. †**b.** Applied as a title to comic pamphlets or the like –1824. **2.** The action (or †an act) of merry-making, or of making merry over something; jocularity; mirth, fun; †a festivity 1588. †**b.** Entertainment. *Mids. N.* III. ii. 146.

1. Your talke replenished with pleasant meriments 1576. **2.** Your flashes of M. that were wont to set the Table on a Rore SHAKS.

Merriness (me·rinės). Now *rare.* ME. [f. MERRY *a.* + -NESS.] The quality or condition of being merry.

Merry (me·ri), *sb.* 1595. [– (O)Fr. *merise* apprehended as a pl.; cf. CHERRY.] A kind of black cherry.

Merry (me·ri), *a.* and *adv.* [OE. *myr(iġ)e* :– Gmc. **murʒjaz* (cf. MIRTH), corresp. to MDu. **merch*, whence *merchte* MIRTH; perh. identical with Gmc. **murʒjaz* short, repr. by OHG. *murgfāri* of short duration, Goth. *gamaurgjan* shorten. For the sense-development cf. ON. *skemta* amuse, f. *skamt* (SCANT), n. of *skammr* short. The standard form with *-e-* repr. a south-eastern development; cf. *left.*] **A.** *adj.* **1.** Of things: Pleasing, agreeable. **b.** Of a saying, jest, etc.: Amusing, diverting. *Obs.* or *arch.*, with mixture of sense 3. 1470. **2.** Of looks or appearance: †Agreeable, bright; hence, expressive of cheerfulness, mirthful (in mod. use merged in sense 3) ME. **3.** Of persons, etc.: Full of animated enjoyment; mirthful, hilarious. Also of disposition: Given to mirth. ME. †**b.** Happy –1634. **c.** Pleasantly amused; hence, facetious. Const. *with, on, upon* (a person). *Obs.* or *arch.* 1607. **d.** Slightly tipsy 1575. **4.** Of times or seasons: Characterized by festivity 1596.

1. Let others then..Extole the merrie Month of May 1567. It was neuer merrie worlde in England, since Gentlemen came vp SHAKS. To mery London, my most kyndly Nurse SPENSER. At the next mery wind tooke shipping HAKLUYT. Phr. *A m. mean*: a happy medium. **b.** The very merriest Passage in the whole Story 1728. **2.** Dark hair, and a m. brown eye HUGHES. **3.** He is melancholy without cause, and m. against the haire SHAKS. Phr. *To make m.* (refl. and intr.): to be festive, to indulge in jollity. *To make m. (over, †with)*: to make fun (of). *The M. Monarch*: Charles II. **c.** I know his Lordship is but m. with me SHAKS. **4.** I wish you a very m. Christmas 1667. **M. dancers, Greek:** see the sbs.

Comb., as *m.-conceited, -hearted, m.-mad* adjs.

B. *adv.* = MERRILY ME.

Merry-andrew, Merry-Andrew (me:ri,-æ·ndru). 1673. [Of unkn. origin.] A buffoon; a clown; prop. (in early use) a mountebank's assistant.

Me·rry-go-round. 1729. **1.** A revolving machine carrying wooden horses or cars, on or in which people ride; a roundabout. **2.** *fig.* A whirl 1856. Hence **Merry-go-rounder,** a 'lark'. DICKENS.

Merry-make (me·rimeⁱk), *sb. arch.* 1579. [f. vbl. phr. *make merry*, with inversion.] = MERRY-MAKING.

Me·rry-make, *v. rare.* 1714. [f. as prec.] *intr.* To make merry; to be festive. So **Me·rry-maker.**

Me·rry-making, *vbl. sb.* 1714. [f. MERRY *a.* + MAKING *vbl. sb.*] The action of making merry; conviviality; also, a convivial entertainment.

Merry man, me·rryman. late ME. **1.** *pl. Merry men*: the companions in arms of a knight, an outlaw chief, etc. **2.** (Chiefly *Mr. Merryman.*) A jester or buffoon 1785.

1. Robyn and his mery men 1510.

Merry-meeting. 1653. A convivial gathering.

Merrythought (me·riþǭt). 1607. [f. MERRY *a.* + THOUGHT *sb.*] The FURCULA or forked bone between the neck and breast of a bird; also called the wishbone.

The name has reference to the custom of two persons pulling the furcula of a fowl until it breaks; the notion being that the one who gets the longer piece will either be married first, or will get any wish he may form at the moment.

Me·rry-totter. *dial.* 1440. [f. MERRY *a.* + TOTTER *sb.*] A see-saw; a swing.

Merse (mers). *Sc.* 1810. [Sc. repr. OE. *mersć* MARSH.] Low flat land, usually beside a river or the sea; marsh.

The Merse is the district between the Lammermoors and the Tweed.

Mersion (mɔ̄·ɹʃən). *Obs.* or *rare.* 1659. [– late L. *mersio*, esp. in eccl. L. of baptism, f. *mers-*, pa. ppl. stem of L. *mergere* dip.] The action, or act, of dipping; *spec.* with reference to baptism.

Merv (mɔ̄ɹv). 1887. [Short for Fr. (*satin*) *merveilleux.*] A silk material for ladies' dresses and dress-trimmings.

Mervail(e, -veil(l(e, obs. ff. MARVEL.

‖**Merveilleux, -euse** (mę̄rveyö, -öz). 1892. [Fr.; see MARVELLOUS.] Names for the extravagantly dressed French fops and fine ladies of the period of the Directory, who affected a revival of the classical costume of ancient Greece.

Merwoman (mɔ̄·ɹwumăn). 1809. [See MER- and cf. G. *meerweib.*] A MERMAID when older or married.

Mes-, comb. f. MESO- before a vowel.

‖**Mesa** (mē·să). *South. U.S.* 1775. [Sp., lit. 'table' :– L. *mensa.*] A high table-land.

Mesaconic (mesăkǫ·nik), *a.* 1854. [f. Gr. μέσος middle + (IT)ACONIC; this acid being intermediate between the itaconic and citraconic acids.] In *m. acid*: an acid, isomeric with itaconic acid, obtained by boiling a weak solution of citraconic acid with nitric acid. Hence **Mesa·conate,** a salt of m. acid.

Mesad (me·sæd), *adv.* 1882. [f. Gr. μέσος middle + -AD II.] = MESIAD.

Mesal (me·săl), *a.* 1882. [f. as prec. + -AL¹.] = MESIAL. Hence **Me·sally** *adv.*

‖**Mésalliance** (mezalyañs). 1782. [Fr., f. *més-* MIS- + *alliance.* Cf. MISALLIANCE.] A marriage with a person of inferior social position.

Mesaraic (mesărē·ik). late ME. [– med.L. *mesaraïcus, -er-* (XIII) – Gr. μεσαραϊκός, f. μεσάραιον, f. μέσον middle + ἀραιά flank, belly; see -IC.] *Anat.* **a.** *adj.* = MESENTERIC. **b.** *sb.* One of the mesaraic veins 1528.

Mesaticephalic (me:săti,sĭfæ·lik), *a.* 1878. [f. Gr. μέσατος (superl. of μέσος) + κεφαλή head + -IC.] = MESOCEPHALIC. So **Me:satice·phalism, Me:satice·phaly,** the condition of being m. **Me:satice·phalous** *a.* = MESATICEPHALIC.

‖**Mescal** (meska·l). Also **mex(i)cal, mezcal.** 1828. [Sp. *mezcal* – Mexican *mexcalli.*] A strong intoxicant distilled from the fermented juice of the American aloe.

‖**Mesdames** (medam). 1573. [Fr., pl. of MADAME.] **1.** The plural of MADAME. **2.** Used as pl. of Eng. MRS. 1792.

Meseems (misī·mz), *impers. v. arch.* Also **meseemeth.** *Pa. t.* **meseemed.** late ME. [orig. two words, *me* dative and *seems* 3rd pers. sing. of SEEM *v.* Cf. METHINKS.] It seems to me. (Used with dependent clause or parenthetically.)

†**Me·sel.** ME. [– OFr. *mesel* leprous, leper – med.L. *mis-, misellus*, in cl. L. *misellus* wretched, wretch, dim. of *miser* wretched; see -EL.] **A.** *adj.* Leprous –1607. **B.** *sb.* **1.** A leper –1550; *fig.* a foul person –1746. **2.** Leprosy; *transf.* an affliction –1530. So †**Me·seled** *ppl. a.* †**Me·selry,** leprosy.

‖**Mesembryanthemum** (mėse:mbriæ·nþĭmŏm, mėz-). 1825. [mod.L., miswritten for **mesembrianthemum*, f. (ult.) Gr. μεσημβρία noon + ἄνθεμον flower.] *Bot.* The typical genus of the N.O. *Mesembryaceæ*; a plant of this genus; a fig-marigold. (The flowers open only for a short time at midday; hence the name.)

‖**Mesencephalon** (mesense·fălǫn). 1846. [f. Gr. μέσος middle + ἐγκέφαλον ENCEPHALON.] *Anat.* The mid-brain. Hence **Mesencepha·lic** *a.*

‖**Mesenchyma** (mese·ŋkimă). Also **-chyme** (me·seŋkəim). 1888. [f. Gr. μέσος (see MES-) + ἔγχυμα infusion.] *Biol.* The cellular tissue which, arising from the hypoblast or the epiblast, constitutes, in some low forms of animal life, the mesoblast. Hence **Mese·nchymal, Mesenchy·matous** *adjs.*

Mesenteric (mesente·rik, mez-), *a.* 1656. [f. MESENTERY + -IC. Cf. Fr. *mésentérique* (XVI).] Pertaining to, connected with, or affecting the mesentery. So **Mesente·rial** *a.* 1605.

‖**Mesenteron** (mése·ntĕrǫn, mez-). 1877. [f. Gr. μέσος (see MES-) + ἔντερον gut, bowel.] The digestive portion of the primitive alimentary canal.

Mesentery (me·sĕntĕri, me·z-). 1547. [– med.L. *mesenterium* – Gr. μεσεντέριον, f. μέσος (see MES-) + ἔντερον intestine.] **1.** *Anat.* A fold of peritoneum which attaches some part of the intestinal canal to the posterior wall of the abdomen 1547. **2.** *Zool.* (*pl.*) The vertical plates which divide the body cavity in actinozoa 1861. vars. **Mesenterium, Mesenterion** (†**Mezentereon**).

Meseraic, -ai(c)k, etc. obs, ff. MESARAIC.

Mesethmoid (mese·þmoid). 1875. [f. MES- + ETHMOID.] *Anat.* The middle ethmoid bone. Also *attrib.* in *m. cartilage.*

Mesh (meʃ), *sb.* 1540. [Early forms also *meish, meash, mash,* the first two indicating a long vowel; prob. – MDu. *maesche* (Du. *maas*), and *masche*, repr. Gmc. **mæsk-* (whence OHG. *māsca*) and **mask-* (whence OE. *max,* **mæsć* net, *mæscre* mesh).] **1.** One of the open spaces or interstices of a net. Also, the similar space in any network, as a sieve. 1558. **b.** *pl.* The threads or cords which bound these; hence, network, netting 1602. **2.** *fig.* Snare, etc. 1540. **3.** *transf.* Network, interlaced structure 1712. **4.** *Machinery.* [f. MESH *v.*] Engagement, or working contact, of the teeth of wheels with each other or with the rack; chiefly in *in* (*into*) *mesh* 1875.

2. Here in her haires The Painter plaies the Spider, and hath wouen A golden m. t'intrap the hearts of men SHAKS. The meshes of diplomacy 1897. *Comb.* **m.-connection,** a method of arranging the coils in a dynamo; **m.-stick,** a stick used to form the m. of nets; **m.-work,** meshes collectively, network. Hence **Me·shy** *a.* consisting of meshes.

Mesh (meʃ), *v.* 1532. [f. MESH *sb.*] **1.** *trans.* To catch in the meshes of a net 1547. **2.** *transf.* and *fig.* To entangle, involve inextricably 1532. **3.** *refl.* and *intr.* (for *refl.* or *pass.*) To become enmeshed or entangled 1589. **b.** *intr.* (*Machinery.*) Of the teeth of a wheel, etc.: To be engaged *with* another piece of machinery or with another toothed wheel 1875.

2. The Flyes by chance mesht in her hayre DRAYTON.

Mesh, var. of MASH.

Meshed (meʃt), *a.* 1664. [f. MESH *sb.* + -ED[2].] **1.** Resembling meshes or network; tangled, intricate; intricately marked. **2.** Having meshes.

Mesiad (mī·ziæd, me·siæd), *adv.* 1803. [f. MESIAL + -AD. Cf. MESAD.] Towards the median line of a body.

Mesial (mī·ziăl, me·siăl), *a.* 1803. [irreg. f. Gr. μέσος middle + -IAL.] = MEDIAN *a.*[1] 2. Also, situated mesially with respect *to*. Hence **Me·sially** *adv.* in a m. position or direction.

Mesityl (me·sitil). 1838. [f. mod.L. *mesita, mesites* (– Gr. μεσίτης go-between) + -YL.] *Chem.* The hypothetical radical of acetone. Hence **Mesitylene** (mĭsi·tilīn), 'a hydrocarbon, isomeric with cumene, produced by the action of sulphuric acid upon acetone' (Watts). **Mesityle·nic** *a.* derived from mesitylene. **Mesity·lic** *a.* derived from or containing m. **Mesi·tylol** = MESITYLENE.

Meslen, etc.: see MASLIN[2].

Mesmerism (me·zmĕriz'm). 1802. [f. name of F. A. *Mesmer*, an Austrian physician (1734–1815) + -ISM.] The doctrine or system according to which a hypnotic state, usu. accompanied by insensibility to pain and muscular rigidity, can be induced by an influence (orig. known as 'animal magnetism') exercised by an operator over the will and nervous system of the patient; the process or practice of inducing this state, the state so induced, or the influence supposed to operate.

So **Mesme·ric, -ical** *a.* pertaining to, characteristic of, producing, or produced by m. 1829. **Me·smerist,** one who practises m.; *occas.* a believer in m. 1840. **Me·smerize** *v. trans.* to subject to the influence of m. 1829; hence **Me:smeriza·tion, Me·smerizer.**

†**Mesnage,** *sb.* [– Fr. †*mesnage*, var. of *ménage* MÉNAGE.] Economical management. JER. TAYLOR. So †**Mesnage** *v.* to 'husband'; to control, manage –1695.

Mesnalty (mī·nălti). 1542. [– law Fr. *mesnalte*, f. *mesne* (see next), after *comunalte* COMMONALTY.] *Law.* The estate or condition of a mesne lord.

Mesne (mīn), *a., sb.,* and *adv.* late ME. [– law Fr. *mesne*, var. of AFr. *meen* MEAN *a.*[1]; for the unetymological *s* cf. DEMESNE.] **A.** *adj.* **1.** *Feudalism.* **a.** *M. lord*: a lord who holds an estate of a superior lord 1614. ¶**b.** *M. tenant*: erron. used for one who holds of a mesne lord 1853. **2.** Occurring or performed at a time intermediate between two dates 1548. **b.** *M. process*: that part of a suit which intervenes between the primary and the final process 1625. **3.** Intermediate, intervening: applied to persons 1810.

2. *M. encumbrance*: an encumbrance with a right of priority intermediate between the dates of two other encumbrances. *M. profits*: the profits of an estate received by a tenant in wrongful possession between two dates. **3.** M. vendors 1810, lessees 1884.

†**B.** *sb.* **1.** = MEAN *sb.* I. 1, II. 2. –1822. **2.** = *M. lord* (see A. 1) –1704.

2. *Writ of m.*: 'an ancient . . writ, which lay when the lord paramount distrained on the tenant paravail; the latter had a writ of m. against the m. lord' (Wharton).

†**C.** *adv.* At a time intermediate (*between* two other times). late ME. –1642.

Meso- (me·so), bef. a vowel occas. **mes-**, comb. form of Gr. μέσος middle, used in scientific terms, many of which have correlates with PRO-, or PROTO-, and META-. **Me·soblast** [-BLAST] *Biol.*, the middle germ-layer of the embryo; hence **Mesobla·stic** *a.* **Mesobra·nchial** *a.* applied to the middle lobe of the branchial region of the carapace of a crab. ‖**Mesocæ·cum** *Anat.* a fold of peritoneum attached to the cæcum. **Me·socarp** [Gr. καρπός fruit] *Bot.* the middle layer of a pericarp. **Mesocepha·lic** [Gr. κεφαλή head] *a.* (*a*) pertaining to the middle region of the head; (*b*) having the cranial cavity of medium capacity or a head of medium proportion; hence **Mesoce·phalism, -ce·phaly.** ‖**Mesoco·lon** *Anat.* a fold of peritoneum attached to the colon; hence **Mesoco·lic** *a.* **Me·soderm** [Gr. δέρμα skin] *Biol.* = *mesoblast*; hence **Mesode·rmal, -de·rmic** *adjs.* **Me·sodont** [Gr. ὀδούς, ὀδοντ- tooth] *a. Anthrop.* and *Entom.* having the teeth of medium size. ‖**Mesoga·ster** [Gr. γαστήρ stomach] *Anat.* = *mesogastrium* (*a*). ‖**Mesoga·strium** *Anat.* (*a*) a fold of peritoneum which attaches the stomach to the dorsal wall of the abdomen; (*b*) the umbilical region; hence **Mesoga·stric** *a. Anat.* pertaining to the mesogastrium; also *Zool.* pertaining to the middle gastric lobe of the carapace of a crab. **Mesogna·thic, -gnathous** [Gr. γνάθος jaw] *adjs., Anthrop.* having the jaws slightly projecting; having a gnathic index between 98 and 103. **Mesoli·thic** [Gr. λίθος stone] *a., Archæol.* belonging to a part of the prehistoric 'stone age' between the Palæolithic and the Neolithic. **Mesona·sal** [see NASAL] *a., Anat.* belonging or relating to the middle of the nose. ‖**Mesono·tum** [Gr. νῶτον back] *Entom.* the dorsal portion of the mesothorax; hence **Mesono·tal** *a.* **Me·sophyll** [Gr. φύλλον leaf] *Bot.* the parenchyma between the epidermal layers of a leaf; hence **Mesophy·llic** *a.* **Me·soplast** [Gr. πλαστός moulded] *Biol.* the nucleus of a cell; hence **Mesopla·stic** *a.* ‖**Mesopo·dium** (also **me·sopod(e)** [Gr. πούς, ποδ- foot] *Zool.* the median region of the foot in molluscs; *Bot.* the intermediate portion of the axis of a phyllopodium; hence **Mesopo·dial** *a.* **Me·sor(r)hine, Mesor(r)hi·nian** [Gr. ῥίς, ῥῖν- nose] *Anthrop., a.* having a somewhat broad but long nose, or a nasal index from 45 to 53; *sb.* a m. person. **Mesosei·smal** [Gr. σεισμός earthquake] *a.* pertaining to the centre of intensity of an earthquake. **Me·soseme** [Gr. σῆμα sign, 'index'] *a., Anthrop.* of skulls: having an orbital index from 84 to 89. ‖**Meso·ste·rnum** *Entom.* the ventral piece of the middle segment of the thorax in insects; *Anat.* the middle portion of the sternum; hence **Mesoste·rnal** *a.* and *sb.* **Mesosysto·lic** *a., Path.* occurring in the middle of the systole. **Me·sotherm** [Gr. θερμός hot] *Bot.* a plant requiring a moderately warm temperature. **Mesotho·rax** *Entom.* the middle ring or segment of the thorax of an insect; hence **Mesothora·cic** *a.*

Mesode (me·soᵘd). 1850. [– Gr. μεσῳδός, f. μεσο- MESO- + ᾠδή ODE.] *Gr. Pros.* A portion of a choral ode, coming between the strophe and antistrophe, without anything to correspond with it. Hence **Meso·dic** *a.*

Mesolabe (me·soleⁱb). 1579. [– L. *mesolabium* (Vitruvius), f. Gr. μεσόλαβος (or -ον), f. μέσος middle + λαβ- base of λαμβάνειν take.] An ancient instrument used for ascertaining mean proportionals between two given lines, and for finding roots of quantities geometrically.

Mesology (mesǫ·lŏdʒi). 1811. [f. Gr. μέσον (taken as = 'medium') + -LOGY.] **1.** The science of means (of attaining happiness). Only in Bentham. **2.** The science of the relations between organisms and their environment 1883.

Mesophragm (me·sŏfræm). 1826. [– mod. L. *mesophragma*, f. Gr. μέσος middle + φράγμα partition.] *Zool.* **a.** *Entom.* The partition that separates the mesothorax from the metathorax. **b.** In Crustacea, the inner prolongation of the capital of an endosternite 1880.

Mesopotamia (mesŏpŏtēⁱ·miă). 1854. [– Gr. μεσοποταμία (sc. χώρα country), f. μέσος middle + ποταμός river.] Name of the tract between the Tigris and the Euphrates. Hence *allusively* of any tract between rivers.

Mesothesis (mesǫ·þĭsis). *rare.* 1812. [f. Gr. μέσος middle + θέσις THESIS.] Something interposed, serving to connect or reconcile antagonistic agencies or principles. So **Mesothe·tic, -ical** *a.* occupying a middle position.

Mesoxalic (mesǫksæ·lik), *a.* 1838. [f. MESO- + OXALIC *a.*] *Chem.* In *m. acid*: a dibasic acid obtained from alloxan. Hence **Meso·xalate,** a salt of m. acid.

‖**Mesozoa** (mesozōᵘ·ă), *sb. pl.* 1877. [mod. L., f. Gr. μεσο- MESO- + ζῷα animals.] *Zool.* Name for forms intermediate in structure between the Protozoa and the Metazoa. Also *sing.* **Mesozo·on,** one of these.

Mesozoic (mesozōᵘ·ik), *a.* 1840. [f. Gr. μεσο- MESO- + ζῳή life + -IC.] *Geol.* Name for the secondary period, intermediate between the Palæozoic and the Cainozoic.

Mesprise, obs. f. MISPRIZE *v.*[1]

‖**Mesquin** (mẹskæṅ), *a.* 1706. [Fr.] Mean, sordid.

†**Mesquita, mesquit**[1]. 1477. [– Sp. *mezquita* and It. *meschita*, ult. – Arab. *masjid*, place of worship, mosque.] = MOSQUE –1665.

Mesquite, mesquit[2] (me·skīt, meskī·t). Also **muskeet,** etc. 1851. [– Mexican Sp. *mezquite.*] **1.** Either of two leguminous trees growing in S.W. North America, *Prosopis juliflora* (honey mesquite), and *P. pubescens* (screw-pod mesquite). **2.** In full *mesquite-grass*: Any grass growing in the neighbourhood of the mesquite tree, esp. the genera *Bouteloua* and *Buchloe* 1851. **3.** *attrib.*, as **m. bean,** the pod of the mesquite tree, etc. 1854.

Mess (mes), *sb.* ME. [– OFr. *mes* portion of food, mod. *mets* (infl. by *mettre* place) :– late L. *missus* course of food, f. *miss-*, pa. ppl. stem of L. *mittere* send (out), put forth.] **I.** Portion of food, etc. **1.** A serving of food; a course of dishes; a prepared dish. Now only *arch.* exc. as in 2. **b.** A quantity (of meat, etc.) sufficient to make a dish. (Now *dial.* and *U.S.*). Also, the quantity of milk given by a cow at one milking 1513. **2.** Applied to a made dish, or to a portion or a kind of liquid, or pulpy food, e.g. milk, broth, porridge, etc. late ME. **b.** A quantity of liquid or mixed food for an animal; a kind of such food 1738. **c.** A concoction, jumble, medley 1828. **3.** A state of confusion or muddle; a condition of embarrassment or trouble 1834. **b.** A dirty or untidy state of things 1851.

1. b. To borrow a messe of Vinegar SHAKS. **2.** *A m. of pottage* (cf. Gen. 25:29–34). Som for a messe of potage, with Esau, careth nat to sell the euerlastyng inheritaunce of heuen 1526. **3.** Phr.

To get into a m. To make a m. of: to bungle (an undertaking).

II. Company of persons eating together. **1.** Orig., each group of four persons (sitting together and helped from the same dishes), into which the company at a banquet was commonly divided. Now only in the Inns of Court, a party of four benchers or four students. Hence, a company of persons who regularly take their meals together. late ME. **b.** In the Army and Navy: Each of the several parties into which a regiment or ship's company is divided, each party taking their meals together 1536. **c.** Without article: The taking of such a meal 1778. **d.** *gen.* = 'Table' (esp. in the sense 'provision of food') 1861. †**2.** *transf.* A set of four persons or things –1661.

1. b. Phr. *To lose the number of one's m.*: to die, be killed. **2.** You three fooles, lackt mee foole, to make vp the messe SHAKS.

Mess (mes), *v.* late ME. [f. MESS *sb.*] **1.** *trans.* To serve up (food); to divide (food) into messes or portions. *Obs.* exc. *dial.* †**2.** To divide (a ship's company) into messes –1690. **3.** *intr.* To take one's meals, esp. as one of a mess; also *rarely* to feed *upon* 1701. **b.** *trans.* To supply with meals 1811. **4.** *intr.* To make a mess; to dabble in water, mud, etc. Also, to 'potter' (const. *about* or with advs. *about*, *away*). 1853. **5.** *trans.* To make a mess of; to dirty, soil (a thing); to muddle (a business). Also with *up*. 1823.

4. I m. about my flowers and read snatches of French MRS. LYNN LINTON. **5.** Lank told him that he had messed the whole business 1901.

Mess, obs. f. MASS *sb.*[1]

Message (me·sėdʒ), *sb.* ME. [– (O)Fr. *message* :– Rom. **missaticum* (in. med.L. IX), f. L. *miss-*; see MESS *sb.*, -AGE.] **1.** An oral or written communication sent from one person to another; also, †intelligence, tidings, news. ¶Often applied to a communication sent by telegraph; hence *transf.* **b.** A divinely inspired communication by a prophet. Also *transf.* 1546. **c.** An official communication from the Sovereign to Parliament, or the like 1625. **2.** The business entrusted to a messenger; a mission, an errand ME. †**3.** One or more messengers or envoys, an embassage –1475.

1. Sometimes from her eyes I did receiue faire speechlesse messages SHAKS. Messages can pass through the brain and the nerves every moment 1884. **b.** Byron and Burns..had a message to deliver 1828. Isaiah's m. is twofold; first ruin and then redemption 1902. **c.** The President, in his m. of the year..referred [etc.] J. M. LUDLOW. **2.** I.. ran messages 1840.

Comb.: **m. stick,** a stick carved with significant marks, used, esp. by Australian aborigines, as a means of communication.

Message (me·sėdʒ), *v.* 1583. [f. MESSAGE *sb.*] **1.** *trans.* To send as a message; to send by messenger; *spec.* to transmit (a sketch, plan, etc.) by means of signalling, telegraphing, etc. **2.** *intr.* To carry a message. DICKENS.

Messageer, -er(e, obs. ff. MESSENGER.

Messalian (mesēⁱ·liăn), **Massalian** (mæsēⁱ·liăn). 1591. [– late Gr. Μεσσαλιανός, Μασσαλιανός, – Syr.; the Gr. writers render the Syrian word εὐχίτης (see EUCHITE) and εὐχόμενος one who prays.] **A.** *sb.* One of an ancient heretical sect, variously identified with the Euchites and with the Hesychasts. **B.** *adj.* Of or pertaining to the Messalians.

Messan (me·săn). *Sc.* Also **-in.** 1500. [– Gael. *measan* = Ir. *measán*, MIr. *mesán*.] A lap-dog; also applied to a person as a term of abuse. Also *m.-dog*, etc.

Messenger (me·sėndʒəɹ). [ME. *messager*, later *messanger* – (O)Fr. *messager*, f. *message*; see MESSAGE, -ER[2] 2. For the intrusive *n* cf. PASSENGER, SCAVENGER, WHARFINGER.] **1.** One who carries a message or goes on an errand; †an envoy, ambassador. **b.** The bearer *of* (a specified message) ME. **c.** *fig.* late ME. †**2.** *esp.* A forerunner, precursor, harbinger. Also *fig.* –1601. **3.** A government official employed to carry dispatches, and, formerly, to apprehend state prisoners; esp. one employed by the Secretaries of State 1535. **4.** An endless rope or chain passing from the capstan to the cable to haul it in. Also, a similar contrivance for hauling in a dredge. 1633. **5.** (In full *m.-bird.*) The secretary-bird 1793.

1. *God's m.*: (*a*) used for ANGEL, q.v.; (*b*) applied to a prophet, or to a clergyman, as charged with a message from God to mankind. **b.** Messengers of Warre SHAKS. **2.** *fig.* Yon grey Lines, That fret the Clouds, are Messengers of Day SHAKS. **3.** *King's* or *Queen's m.*, one who conveys dispatches to or from the Sovereign.

Messet (me·sėt). *dial.* 1631. [perh. alt. f. MESSAN, after dim. ending -ET.] A lap-dog. Also *attrib.*

Messiah (mėsəi·ă, məs-). Also **Messias,** etc. [ME. *Messie* – (O)Fr. *Messie* – L. (Vulg.) *Messias* – Gr. Μεσσίας – Aramaic *m'shīḥā*, Heb. *māshīᵃḥ* anointed, f. *māshaḥ* anoint. The form *Messias* was used in John 1:41 and 4:25 by Wyclif after the Vulgate, and by later translators. The form *Messiah*, invented by the Geneva translators of 1560, as looking more Hebraic than *Messias*, eventually became the only current form.] The Hebrew title (= 'anointed') applied in the O.T. to a promised deliverer of the Jewish nation, hence to Jesus of Nazareth as such deliverer. Hence *transf.* an expected liberator of an oppressed people or country. (Written with capital M.)

Against the Lord and his M. dear MILT. Hence **Messi·ahship,** the character or office of the or a M.

Messianic (mesiæ·nik), *a.* 1834. [– Fr. *messianique*, f. *Messie* MESSIAH, after *rabbinique* RABBINIC.] Of, pertaining to, or relating to the Messiah. Hence **Messia·nically** *adv.* as referring to the Messiah. **Messi·anism,** belief in a coming Messiah.

[Psalm 87] seems clearly Messianic COLERIDGE.

‖**Messidor** (mesidor). 1838. [Fr.; f. L. *messis* harvest + Gr. δῶρον gift.] The tenth month of the French revolutionary calendar.

Messieurs, *sb. pl.* 1624. [– Fr. pl. of MONSIEUR.] **1.** (mesyö) The pl. of MONSIEUR. (As a prefixed title, now usu. abbrev. *MM.*, as in Fr.). **2.** (me·səɹz, me·syəɹz). See MESSRS.

‖**Messire** (mesīr). Now only *Hist.* 1477. [Fr.; repr. the nom. (L. *meus senior*), while *monsieur* represents the accus. (L. *meum seniorem*).] A title of honour (= Sir) prefixed to the name of a French noble of high rank, and later to the names of persons of quality, and members of the learned professions; also used as a form of address.

Mess-John: see *Mas John* (MAS 2).

Messmate (me·smeⁱt). 1746. [f. MESS *sb.* + MATE *sb.*] A companion at meals; one of a mess, esp. of a ship's mess.

Messrs. (me·səɹz). 1779. Abbrev. of MESSIEURS used as pl. of MR.

Messuage (me·swėdʒ). late ME. [– AFr. *messuage*, *mesuage*, prob. orig. misreading of *mesnage* MÉNAGE.] Orig., the portion of land intended as a site for a dwelling-house and its appurtenances. In mod. legal use, a dwelling-house with its outbuildings and curtilage and the adjacent land assigned to its use. *Capital m.*: that occupied by the owner of a property containing several messuages.

They wedded her to sixty thousand pounds, To lands in Kent and messuages in York TENNYSON.

Messy (me·si), *a.* 1843. [f. MESS *sb.* + Y[1].] Of the nature of a mess; untidy. Hence **Me·ssiness.**

Mest(e, obs. ff. MOST.

Mestee: see MUSTEE.

Mester, obs. var. of MISTER *sb.*[1]

‖**Mestizo** (mestī·zo). 1588. [Sp. :– Rom. **mixticius*, f. L. *mixtus*, pa. pple. of *miscēre* mix.] A Spanish or Portuguese half-caste; now chiefly, the offspring of a Spaniard and an American Indian. **b.** *attrib.*, as **m.-wool,** S. American wool from mixed breeds of sheep. So ‖**Mesti·za,** a woman of the mestizo race 1582.

Mestlen, -lin(g, -lyon, obs. ff. MASLIN [1, 2].

Met (met), *sb. Obs.* exc. *dial.* [ME. *met* repr. OE. *met* = OS. *met*, OHG. *mez*, ON. *met* n. pl. weight of a balance :– Gmc. **metam*, f. **met-* measure; see MEET *a.*, METE *v.*[1]] = MEASURE *sb.*

†**Met,** *ppl. a.* late ME. [f. obs. pa. pple. *meten* of METE *v.*[1]] Measured –1460.

Met, pa. t. and pple. of MEET *v.*

‖**Meta** (mī·tă). *Pl.* **metæ** (mī·tī). 1577. [L.] *Rom. Antiq.* One of the conical columns set in the ground at each end of the Circus, to mark the turning-place in a race. Hence *transf.* A boundary.

Meta- (me·tă), *prefix*, bef. a vowel normally **met-** (also bef. *h*, the resulting *meth-* being pronounced meþ), repr. Gr. μετα-, μετ- (μεθ-), occurring separately as the prep. μετά with, after. Its chief senses are: sharing, action in common; pursuit or quest; and *esp.* change (of place, order, condition, or nature), corresp. to L. *trans-*. Occas. it has the sense 'after' or 'behind', as in *metaphrenon* (see 3 below).

1. In supposed analogy to METAPHYSICS (misapprehended as meaning 'the science of that which transcends the physical'), *meta-* has been prefixed to the name of a science, to form a designation for a higher science of the same nature but dealing with ulterior problems. Examples are **Metabiolo·gical** *a.*, **Metache·mistry, Metalo·gic, Metalo·gical** *a.*, **Metamathema·tics, Metapheno·menal** *a.*, **Metaphysio·logy.**

2. *Path.* Used to form adjs. applicable to diseases or symptoms, with the sense 'arising subsequently to.'; e.g **Meta-arthri·tic,** following on gout, **Metapneumo·nic;** etc.

3. *Anat.* and *Zool.* Used to express the notion of 'behind'; also often that of 'hinder', 'hindmost', 'situated at the back'; sometimes correlated with PRO- and MESO-. **Metabra·nchial** [Gr. βράγχια gills], *a.* applied to a division of the carapace of a crab situated behind and to one side of the mesobranchial lobe. ‖**Metacro·mion,** a process of the spine of the scapula behind the acromion in some mammals 1868. ‖**Metane·phron, -ne·phros** [Gr. νεφρός kidney], the hinder division of the typical segmental organ in vertebrates, from which are developed the kidney and the ureter 1877. ‖**Metano·tum** [Gr. νῶτον back], *Entom.* the dorsal part of the metathorax in insects 1836. **Me·taphragm** [Gr. φράγμα partition], *Entom.* the wall that separates the abdomen from the thorax in insects 1826. ‖**Meta·phrenon, -phrenum** [Gr. φρήν midriff], the part of the back that is behind the diaphragm 1621. **Metapneu·stic** [Gr. πνευστικός relating to breathing] *a.*, *Entom.* having a single pair of spiracles situated at the posterior end of the abdomen. ‖**Metapo·physis,** *pl.* **-ses** [APOPHYSIS], a small vertebral prominence 1866. **Me·tapore** [PORE], an orifice in the pia mater covering the fourth ventricle of the brain. ‖**Metaptery·gium,** *Ichth.* the hind-most section of the pterygium in certain fishes 1866. ‖**Metatho·rax,** *Entom.* the hindmost segment of the thorax in insects 1816; so **Metathora·cic** *a.*

4. *Bot.* and *Zool.* Used with the sense 'later', 'subsequent', 'more developed'. **Me·taphase, Meta·phasis,** the separation of the daughter chromosomes in nuclear division. **Me·taphyte,** ‖**Meta·phyton,** a multicellular plant; hence **Metaphy·tic** *a.*

5. *Geol.* In imitation of METAMORPHISM, used irreg. to form words referring to certain specific varieties of metamorphic processes, as **Metache·mic** *a.* applied to chemical metamorphism, etc.

6. In *Chemistry.* **a.** Used to designate compounds derived from, metameric with, or resembling in composition those to the names of which it is prefixed. **Metacre·sol,** one of the three modifications of cresol (*ortho-*, *meta-*, and *paracresol*). **Metage·latin,** a form of gelatin that remains fluid, used in photography. **Metalbu·min, -men,** a form of albumin found in dropsical fluids, etc. 1854. **Meta·ldehyde,** a solid isomeric with aldehyde 1841. **Metape·ctin,** an isomeric form of pectin produced by boiling with dilute acids. More systematically, *meta-* is used to distinguish one class of acids and their corresponding salts from another class (the ORTHO- acids) consisting of the same elements in different proportions, the *meta-* acids containing one, two, or three molecules of water less than the *ortho-* acids: as *metantimonic*, *metapectic*, *metaphosphoric*, *metasilicic*, *metatitanic* acids.

b. In the names of isomeric benzene di-derivatives, *meta-* denotes those compounds in which the two radicals that replace hydrogen in the benzene-ring are regarded as attached to alternate carbon atoms. The number of these is unlimited.

7. *Min.* **a.** Used to designate a mineral that is found along with another or is closely related to it, as in *metabrushite* (a calcium phosphate allied to brushite), etc. **b.** Proposed by Dana to designate minerals produced by metamorphism of sediments, as *metasyenite*, etc.

‖**Metabasis** (metæ·băsis). 1577. [mod.L. – Gr. μετάβασις, related to μεταβαίνειν, f. μετα- META- + βαίνειν go. Cf. BASIS.] A transition, *spec.* in *Rhet.*, from one subject or point to another, in *Med.*, from one remedy, etc. to another. So **Metaba·tic** *a.*, *Rhet.* pertaining to m.

‖**Metabola** (metæ·bŏlă), *sb. pl.* Formerly **metabolia.** 1817. [mod.L. n. pl. f. Gr. μεταβόλος changeable.] *Entom.* A division of insects comprising those which undergo complete metamorphosis.

Metabolic (metăbǫ·lik), *a.* 1743. [– Gr. μεταβολικός changeable; see next.] **1.** Pertaining to or involving transition. **2.** *Biol.* and *Chem.* Pertaining to, involving, characterized or produced by, metabolism 1845. **3.** *Entom.* = METABOLOUS 1882. So **Metabo·lical** *a.*

Metabolism (metæ·bŏliz'm). 1878. [f. Gr. μεταβολή change, f. μεταβάλλειν, f. μετα- META- + βάλλειν throw; see -ISM.] *Biol.* and *Chem.* The process, in an organism or a single cell, by which nutritive material is built up into living matter (*constructive m., anabolism*), or by which protoplasm is broken down into simpler substances to perform special functions (*destructive m., katabolism*). Hence **Meta·bolite,** a product of m. **Meta·bolize** *v.* to affect by m.

Metabolous (metæ·bŏləs), *a.* 1861. [f. Gr. μεταβόλος changeable + -OUS.] *Entom.* Undergoing complete metamorphosis; belonging to the division METABOLA of insects.

Metacarpal (metăkā·ɹpăl). 1739. [f. next + -AL¹.] **a.** *adj.* Of or belonging to the metacarpus. **b.** *sb.* A metacarpal bone 1854.

‖**Metacarpus** (metăkā·ɹpŏs). Also †**Metacarp.** 1676. [mod.L., alt. f. Gr. μετακάρπιον, after CARPUS.] *Anat.* That part of the hand which is situated between the wrist and the fingers: in vertebrates generally, that part of the manus which is situated between the carpus and the phalanges.

Metacentre (me·tăsentəɹ). 1794. [– Fr. *métacentre* (Bouguer, 1746), f. *méta-* META + *centre* CENTRE.] *Hydrostatics* and *Shipbuilding.* The limiting position of the point of intersection between the vertical line passing through the centre of gravity of a floating body when in equilibrium and the vertical line drawn through the centre of buoyancy when the body is slightly displaced; the *shifting centre.* To ensure stable equilibrium this point must be above the centre of gravity. **Metace·ntral, Metace·ntric** *adjs.*

Metacetone (metæ·sĭtōᵘn). 1838. [f. Fr. *métacétone*; see META- 6, ACETONE.] *Chem.* A colourless oil obtained by the distillation of sugar or starch with quicklime.

Metachromatism (metăkrōᵘ·mătiz'm). 1876. [f. META- + Gr. χρῶμα, χρωματ- colour + -ISM.] Change or variation of colour.

Metachronism (metæ·krŏniz'm). 1617. [– med.L. *metachronismus,* abnormally f. Gr. μετάχρονος, -χρόνιος happening later, f. μετα- META- + χρόνος time.] An error in chronology consisting in placing an event later than its real date. (Cf. PARACHRONISM.)

Metacism (me·tăsiz'm). 1844. [– late L. *metacismus,* corruptly – late Gr. μυτακισμός fondness for the letter μ, f. μῦ name of the letter. Cf. ITACISM.] The placing of a word with final *m* before a word beginning with a vowel; regarded as a fault in Latin prose composition.

‖**Metacrasis** (metăkrēⁱ·sis). 1886. [f. META- + CRASIS.] *Geol.* Recombination, denoting changes such as the conversion of mud into a mass of mica, quartz, and other silicates.

Metagastric (metăgæ·strik), *a.* 1877. [f. META- + Gr. γαστήρ belly + -IC.] *Zool.* Applied to portions of the carapace in brachyurous crustaceans situated towards the hinder part of the gastrohepatic area.

Metage (mī·tėdʒ). 1527. [f. METE *v.*¹ + -AGE.] **1.** The action of measuring officially the content or weight of a load of grain, coal, etc.; the duty paid for this.

Metagenesis (metădʒe·nĭsis). 1849. [mod. L.; see META- and GENESIS.] *Biol.* Alternation of generations; alternation between sexual and asexual reproduction. So **Me:tagene·tic** *a. Zool.,* pertaining to, characterized by, or involving m. **Metagene·tically** *adv.*

Metageo·metry. 1882. [See META-.] The geometry of non-Euclidean space. So **Metageo·meter, -me·trical** *a.*

Metagnathous (metæ·gnăþəs), *a.* 1872. [f. Gr. μετά META- + γνάθος jaw + -OUS.] Having the tips of the mandibles crossed.

†**Metagra·mmatism.** 1605. [– Gr. μεταγραμματισμός (Galen), f. μετα- META- + γράμμα γραμματ- letter; see -ISM.] The transposition of letters in a word or phrase; anagrammatism.

Metagraphy (metæ·grăfi). 1872. [f. META- + -GRAPHY.] Transliteration. Hence **Metagra·phic** *a.*

Metagrobolize (metăgrǫ·bŏləiz), *v.* 1653. [– obs. Fr. *metagraboulizer* (Rabelais).] **a.** To puzzle, mystify. **b.** To puzzle out.

‖**Métairie** (metęri). 1817. [Fr., f. *métayer.*] A farm held on the MÉTAYER system.

Metal (me·tăl, me·t'l), *sb.* (and *a.*) Also †**mettle,** etc. ME. [– (O)Fr. *métal,* †*metail* or its source L. *metallum* mine, quarry, metal – synon. Gr. μέταλλον.] **1.** Any member of the class of substances represented by gold, silver, copper, iron, lead, and tin, and orig. confined to these bodies together with certain alloys. In *Chem.* the 'metals' are a division of the 'elements' or simple substances. Of these some possess all the properties, such as high specific gravity and density, fusibility, malleability, etc., formerly viewed as characteristic of a metal, while others possess hardly any of them, the metallic lustre being perhaps the most constant. In pop. lang. not applied when the identity of the element is disguised in combination. **b.** Metallic substance ME. **c.** *pregnantly* for: Precious metal, gold. SHAKS. **d.** *spec.* = CAST-IRON 1794. **e.** *fig., esp.* the 'stuff' of which a man is made 1552. **2.** *Her.* Either of the tinctures or and argent 1450. **3.** = ORE (after Spanish) 1604. †**4.** A mine. JER. TAYLOR. **5.** With qualification: A specific alloy of two or more metals used in an art or trade. Also as short for any of these. 1729. **6.** An object made of metal (see below) 1574. **7.** *Gunnery.* The metal composing the barrel of a gun 1644. **b.** The aggregate number or effective power of the guns on a ship of war 1757. **8.** Material, matter, substance, *esp.* earthy matter 1570. **9.** The material used for making glass, in a molten state 1589. **10.** Hardened clay, shale 1708. **11.** Broken stone used for macadamizing roads or as ballast for a railway. Also *road m.* 1838.

1. †*Noble* or *perfect metals*: gold and silver, as being the only metals that were known to endure any ordinary fire without being 'destroyed'; opp. to *base* or *imperfect metals.* **b.** The hammer breaks mettall, and the fire melts it 1649. **e.** We are.. Mettall, Marcus, steele to the very backe SHAKS. **4.** †Phr. *To condemn to metals* [L. *condemnare ad metalla*]. **5.** *Bath, Britannia, Dutch, white, yellow,* etc. *m.*: see these words. Also BELL-METAL, GUN-METAL, PRINCE'S *metal.* **6.** †**a.** A reflector of a telescope; A very distinct and perfect two-foot m. 1777. **b.** *pl.* The rails of a railway, tramway, etc.; He found the deceased lying on the road, between the 'metals' 1841. **7.** *Line of m.*; an imaginary line drawn along the surface of the m. between the two sights. So *over, undermetal.* **b.** *Heavy m.*: see HEAVY *a.*¹ 5.

attrib. and *Comb.,* as *m.-broker, -bearing* adj., *-yield*; also, **m. bath,** a bath (of mercury, lead, fusible alloys, etc.) used in chemical operations requiring a higher temperature than a water bath can give; **m. bed,** the bed of broken stone in a macadamized road; **m. polish,** a polish used for brightening metals; **m. value,** value (of coin) merely as m.; **-work,** (artistic) work in m.

Metal, *v.* 1617. [f. the sb.] **1.** *trans.* To furnish or fit with metal. **2.** To make or mend (a road) with 'metal' 1806.

‖**Metalepsis** (metăle·psis). 1577. [– L. *metalepsis,* Gr. μετάληψις, f. μεταλαμβάνειν to substitute, f. μετα- META- + λαμβάνειν take.] *Rhet.* A figure mentioned by Quintilian, consisting in the metonymical substitution of one word for another which is itself figurative.

Metaleptic (metăle·ptik), *a.* 1656. [– mod. L. *metalepticus* – Gr., f. μεταλαμβάνειν; see METALEPSIS.] **a.** Participating or acting with: *spec.* applied to muscles. **b.** Pertaining to metalepsis. Hence **Metale·ptically** *adv.* by metalepsis 1655.

Metallic (mĭtæ·lik), *a.* (*sb.*) 1567. [– Fr. *métallique* or L. *metallicus* – Gr. μεταλλικός, f. μέταλλον METAL; see -IC.] **1.** Of, pertaining to, or containing a metal or metals; of the nature of or resembling a metal. **b.** Involving coin as dist. from paper money 1790. **2.** Having the form or outward characters of a metal 1797. **3.** Of a quality: Such as is characteristic of metals (see quots). 1794. **4.** Yielding or producing metal 1689. †**5.** Connected with mining or metallurgy –1834. **6.** *sb pl.* Articles or substances made of or containing metal 1612; *U.S.* powdered metal for lining the bearings of machine shafts 1894.

1. *M. pencil*: one with a tip made of lead or alloy, for writing indelibly on paper with a prepared surface. So *m. book, paper.* **3.** *M. lustre,* the peculiar sheen characteristic of metals. Their deep m. voices (i.e. voices of a harsh unmusical timbre) W. IRVING. M. (i.e. 'coppery') taste 1803. *fig.* With m. beliefs and regimental devotions CLOUGH. So †**Meta·llical** *a.,* **Meta·llically** *adv.*

Metalliferous (metăli·ferəs), *a.* 1656. [f. L. *metallifer* (f. *metallum* + *-fer* bearing); see -FEROUS.] Bearing or producing metal.

Metalline (me·tăləin), *a.* 1471. [– Fr. *métallin,* f. *métal* METAL *sb.*; see -INE¹.] **1.** = METALLIC 1. **b.** Impregnated with metallic substances. Also, of vapours, arising from or produced by metals. 1626. **c.** Made of metal 1575. **2.** Resembling metal in appearance, lustre, etc. 1596. **3.** Metalliferous 1620.

1. The m. salts 1804. **2.** The rocks of a blew metaline colour, like vnto the best steele ore RALEGH.

Metalling (me·tăliŋ), *vbl. sb.* 1819. [f. METAL *v.* (or *sb.*) + -ING¹.] **1.** The process of making or mending roads with metal. Also *concr.* = METAL *sb.* 11. **2.** Metal-work (*rare*). C. T. NEWTON.

Metallist (me·tălist). 1646. [f. METAL *sb.* + -IST.] **1.** One who is skilled in or works in metals. Now *rare.* **2.** An advocate of the use of a particular metal as currency 1886.

Metallize (me·tăləiz), *v.* 1594. [f. METAL *sb.* + -IZE.] **1.** *trans.* To render metallic; to impart a metallic form or appearance to. **2.** To vulcanize 1895. **Metalliza·tion.**

Metallo-, bef. a vowel **metall-,** comb. f. Gr. μέταλλον METAL *sb.*: **Metallochrome** (me·tălokrōᵘm) [Gr. χρῶμα colour], a prismatic tinting imparted to polished steel plates by depositing on them a film of lead oxide. **Metalloscopy** (metălǫ·skŏpi) [-SCOPY], the art of determining by external application what metals or metallic substances act most easily and favourably upon a given person. **Metallothe·rapy** [Gr. θεραπεία], the use of metals in healing or preventing diseases.

Metallography (metălǫ·grăfi). 1721. [f. METALLO- + -GRAPHY. Cf. Fr. *métallographie* (XVI).] **1.** 'A treatise or description of metals' (Bailey). **2.** The science relating to the internal structure of metals 1871. **3.** A printing process akin to lithography, in which metal plates are used instead of stones 1875. Hence **Meta·llograph,** a print produced by m. **Meta:llogra·phic** *a.*

Metalloid (me·tăloid), *a.* (*sb.*) 1832. [f. METAL *sb.* + -OID.] **1.** Having the form or appearance of a metal. Also, of or pertaining to metalloids. 1836. **2.** *sb. Chem.* †**a.** The metallic base of a fixed alkali or alkaline earth –1837. **b.** A non-metallic element. So **Metalloi·dal** *a.*

Metallurgy (me·tălŏɹdʒi). 1704. [f. Gr. μέταλλον metal + -ουργία work, working, as in χειρουργία SURGERY. Cf. Fr. *métallurgie.*] The art of working metals, comprising the separation of them from other matters in the ore, smelting, and refining; often, in a narrower sense, the process of extracting metals from their ores. Hence **Metallu·rgic, -al** *a.* of, pertaining to, or connected with m. **Me·tallurgist,** one who is skilled in m.; a worker in metal 1670.

Metamere (me·tămīᵊɹ). Also **metameron** (mĭtæ·mĕrǫn), *pl.* **-mera.** 1877. [f. Gr. μετα- META- + μέρος part.] *Zool.* One of the several similar segments of which certain bodies, e.g. the crayfish, consist.

Metameric (metăme·rik), *a.* 1847. [f. as prec. + -IC.] **1.** *Chem.* Characterized by metamerism. **2.** *Zool.* Of or pertaining to metameres 1875. Hence **Me·tamer,** *Chem.* a compound which is m. with something else.

Metamerism (metæ·mĕriz'm). 1848. [f. as prec.; see -ISM.] **1.** *Chem.* The condition of those isomeric compounds which, although of the same composition and molecular weight, have different chemical properties. **2.** *Zool.* Metameric segmentation 1877.

Metamorphic (metămǭ·ɹfik), *a.* 1816. [irreg. f. Gr. μετα- META- + μορφή form + -IC; after *metamorphosis.*] **1.** Characterized by metamorphosis or change of form. **2.** *Geol.* Pertaining to, characterized by, or formed by metamorphism. Of a rock or rock-formation: That has undergone transformation by means of heat, pressure, or natural agencies. 1833. **3.** That causes metamorphism or metamorphosis 1853.

2. It is usual to restrict the term 'M. System' to those crystalline schists—Gneiss, Quartz-rock, Mica-schist, and Clay-slate—which underlie all the fossiliferous strata PAGE.

Metamorphism (metămǭ·ɹfiz'm). 1845. [f. as prec. + -ISM.] **1.** *Geol.* The process of change of form or structure produced in a rock by various natural agencies. **2.** The process of metamorphosis (of an insect) 1866.

†**Metamorphize,** *v.* 1591. [f. as prec. + -IZE.] = METAMORPHOSE *v.* –1748.

Metamorphose (metămǭ·ɹfoᵘs, -fǒs), *sb.* 1608. [Anglicized form of METAMORPHOSIS; cf. Fr. *métamorphose.*] = METAMORPHOSIS. Now *rare.*

Metamorphose (metămǭ·ɹfoᵘz, -fǒs), *v.* Also †**-oze.** 1576. [– Fr. *métamorphoser*, f. *métamorphose* sb. – L. *metamorphosis*; see next.] **1.** *trans.* To change in form; to turn *to* or *into* something else by enchantment or other supernatural means. **2.** *gen.* To change the form or character of; to transform. Const. *to, into.* 1576. **3.** To subject to METAMORPHOSIS or METAMORPHISM 1664.

2. Never were a people so metamorphosed. The plain farmer and even the plain quaker is become a soldier BURKE. Hence **Metamo·rphoser.**

Metamorphosis (metămǭ·ɹfǒsis, -mǫɹfōᵘ·sis). *Pl.* **-ses** (-sīz). 1533. [– L. *metamorphosis* – Gr. μεταμόρφωσις, f. μεταμορφοῦν transform, f. μετα- META- + μορφή form; see -OSIS.] **1.** The action or process of changing in form or substance, esp. by magic or witchcraft. **b.** A metamorphosed form 1589. **2.** *transf.* A complete change in the appearance, condition, character of a person, of affairs, etc. 1548. **3. a.** *Physiology.* Change of form in animals and plants, or their parts, during life; esp. in a metabolous insect 1665. **b.** *Morphology.* The modification of organs or structures in form or function (including teratology) 1836. **c.** *Evolution.* Secular change of form 1847. **d.** *Histol.* The change of form which goes on in the elements of living organic structures 1839. **e.** *Chem.* The change of a compound to a new form 1853.

2. His visage changed as from a mask to a face... I know not that I have ever seen in any other human face an equal m. C. BRONTË. **3. a.** A perfect m., such as that of Sphinx, with three well-marked stages, larva, pupa, and imago 1888. var. †**Metamo·rphosy** 1530–1698. Hence **Metamorpho·tic** *a.* pertaining to, based on, or causing m. 1816.

Metaphor (me·tăfǭɹ). 1533. [– (O)Fr. *métaphore* or L. *metaphora* – Gr. μεταφορά, f. μεταφέρειν transfer, f. μετα- META- + φέρειν bear, carry.] The figure of speech in which a name or descriptive term is transferred to some object to which it is not properly applicable; an instance of this.

Those beautiful Metaphors in Scripture, where Life is termed a Pilgrimage ADDISON. We should avoid making two inconsistent metaphors meet on one object. This is what is called *mixed metaphor* L. MURRAY. Hence **Metapho·ric, -al** *a.* **Metapho·rically** *adv.* **Me·taphorist** (*rare*), one who deals in metaphors. **Me·taphorize** *v. trans.* to change metaphorically *into*; to ply with m.

Metaphrase (me·tăfrēⁱz), *sb.* 1607. [– mod. L. *metaphrasis* (also used) – Gr. μετάφρασις, f. μεταφράζειν translate, etc.; see META- and PHRASE *sb.*] †**1.** A metrical translation –1767. **2.** A translation; later, a word-for-word translation as dist. from a paraphrase 1640. Hence **Me·taphrase** *v.* †to translate, esp. in verse 1608–1649; to render into other words 1868.

Metaphrast (me·tăfræst). 1610. [– Gr. μεταφράστης, f. μεταφράζειν translate, f. μετα- META- + φράζειν speak.] One who renders a composition into a different literary form; also, †a translator.

Metaphrastic (metăfræ·stik), *a.* (*sb.*) 1778. [– Gr. μεταφραστικός; see prec. and -IC.] **1.** Of the nature of metaphrase. **2.** *sb. pl.* The art of translation or interpretation 1895. So **Metaphra·stically** *adv.* 1577.

Metaphysic (metăfi·zik), *sb.*[1] late ME. [– (O)Fr. *métaphysique* – med.L. *metaphysica* fem. sing., for earlier n. pl. repr. by METAPHYSICS.] **1.** = METAPHYSICS 1, 1 b. ¶**2.** Something visionary. WARNER.

Metaphysic (metăfi·zik), *a.* and *sb.*[2] 1528. [– scholastic L. *metaphysicus* adj., developed from *metaphysica* sb. pl.; see METAPHYSICS. Cf. (O)Fr. *métaphysique.*] **A.** *adj.* = METAPHYSICAL. Now *rare.* †**B.** *sb.* A metaphysician –1623.

Metaphysical (metăfi·zikăl), *a.* late ME. [f. METAPHYSIC + -AL[1].] **1.** Of, belonging to, or of the nature of, metaphysics; such as is recognized by metaphysics. **b.** Applied with reproach to over-subtle or too abstract reasoning, ideas, etc. 1646. **2.** Based on abstract general reasoning 1647. **3. a.** Applied to what is immaterial, incorporeal, or supersensible 1577. **b.** Supernatural 1590. **4.** Addicted to or fitted for the study of metaphysics 1628. **5.** Of some 17th c. poets: Addicted to witty conceits and far-fetched imagery 1744. **6.** Fantastic 1727.

1. A popular expression, which will not stand a Metaphysicall and strict examination SIR T. BROWNE. **2.** Wars have been waged for points of m. right SCOTT. **4.** The more m. and contemplative East KINGSLEY. **5.** The m. poets were men of learning, and to shew their learning was their whole endeavour JOHNSON. Hence **Metaphy·sically** *adv.* in a m. manner or sense; †supernaturally; †preternaturally.

Metaphysician (metăfizi·ʃăn). 1597. [– Fr. *métaphysicien*, f. *métaphysique* METAPHYSIC; see -ICIAN.] One versed in metaphysics.

Metaphysicize (metăfi·zisəiz), *v.* 1793. [f. METAPHYSIC + -IZE.] **1.** *intr.* To think, talk, or write metaphysically. Also quasi-*trans.* with *away.* **2.** *trans.* To treat metaphysically 1830.

1. He was everlastingly metaphysicising against metaphysics DE QUINCEY. I have metaphysicized away all my senses SOUTHEY.

Metaphysico- (metăfi·ziko), comb. f. METAPHYSIC *a.*, with sense 'partly metaphysical, partly ...'.

Metaphysics (metăfi·ziks), *sb. pl.* 1569. [pl. of METAPHYSIC *sb.*[1], repr. med.L. *metaphysica* neut. pl., med.Gr. (τὰ) μεταφυσικά for Gr. τὰ μετὰ τὰ φυσικά 'the (works of Aristotle) after the Physics' (cf. META- and PHYSICS). From an early period, the word was used as a name for the branch of study, viz. ontology, treated in these works, and hence came to be misinterpreted as meaning 'the science of things transcending what is physical or natural'.] **1.** That branch of speculation which deals with the first principles of things, including such concepts as being, substance, essence, time, space, cause, identity, etc.; theoretical philosophy as the ultimate science of Being and Knowing. (Formerly often *The m.*) **b.** With *of*: The theoretical principles of some particular branch of knowledge 1845. **c.** In inaccurate or extended uses (see quots.) 1727. †**2.** In Marlowe: Occult or magical lore 1590.

1. If such Metaphysiques..be not Vain Philosophy, there was never any HOBBES. **b.** The m. of practical politics 1845. **c.** M. or pneumatics ADAM SMITH. The Philosophy of Mind—Psychology or M., in the widest signification of the terms SIR W. HAMILTON.

Metaplasm[1] (me·tăplæz'm). 1617. [– L. *metaplasmus* (in Quintilian 'rhetorical figure'), Gr. μεταπλασμός, f. μεταπλάσσειν, f. μετα- META- + πλάσσειν to mould.] **a.** *Rhet.* The transposition of words from their usual or natural order. **b.** *Gram.* The alteration of a word by addition, removal, or transposition of letters or syllables. Also, the formation of oblique cases from a stem other than that of the nominative.

Me·taplasm[2]. 1875. [f. META- after *protoplasm.*] *Biol.* That part of protoplasm which contains the formative material.

Me·taplast. 1864. [f. Gr. μεταπλάσσειν; cf. METAPLASM[1].] *Gram.* A noun of which the cases are formed from different stems.

Metapodial (metăpōᵘ·diăl). 1882. [– mod.L. *metapodialis*, f. next.] One of the ‖**Metapodialia** *sb. pl.*, the bones of the metacarpus and metatarsus taken together.

‖**Metapodium** (metăpōᵘ·diǒm). 1853. [mod.L., f. Gr. μετα- META- + πούς, ποδ- foot; see -IUM.] **1.** *Anat.* = METATARSUS 1856. **2.** The posterior lobe of the foot in molluscs.

Metapolitics (metăpǫ·litiks), *sb. pl.* 1784. [META- 1.] Theoretical political science (often *contempt.*). So **Me:tapoli·tical** *a.* **Me:tapoliti·cian,** an adherent of metapolitical theories.

Metapsychics (metăsəi·kiks), *sb. pl.* 1905. [f. META- + PSYCHICS.] The science or study of certain phenomena which are 'beyond the scheme of orthodox psychology'. **Metapsy·chic, -ical** *adjs.* **Metapsy·chism, -ist.**

Metargon (metā·ɹgǫn). 1898. [f. META- + ARGON.] *Chem.* Sir W. Ramsay's name for a supposed gaseous element.

‖**Metasoma** (metăsōᵘ·mă). Also **me·tasome.** 1872. [mod.L., f. Gr. μετα- META- + σῶμα body.] *Zool.* The hinder part of the body in molluscs, or of the abdomen in arthropods. **Me:tasoma·tic** *a.* pertaining to the m.; *Geol.* pertaining to METASOMATOSIS.

‖**Metasomatosis** (me:tăsōᵘmătōᵘ·sis). 1886. [mod.L., f. META- + Gr. σῶμα, σωματ- body + -OSIS.] *Geol.* The transformation of one rock into another of an entirely different kind. Also **Metaso·matism.**

Metastable (me·tăstēⁱb'l), *a.* 1899. [f. META- + STABLE *a.*] *Physics.* Of a state of unstable equilibrium.

‖**Metastasis** (metæ·stăsis). *Pl.* **-ses** (-sīz). 1577. [Late L. – Gr. μετάστασις removal, change, f. μεθιστάναι; see META-, STASIS.] **1.** *Rhet.* A rapid transition from one point to another. **2. a.** *Phys.* and *Path.* The transference of a bodily function, of a pain or a disease, of morbific matter, etc. from one part or organ to another 1663. **b.** *Biol.* The transformation of chemical compounds into other compounds in the process of assimilation by an organism 1875. **3.** *gen.* Transformation (*rare*) 1831.

3. The lamp and oil man, just then beginning, by a not unnatural m., to bloom into a lighthouse-engineer STEVENSON. Hence **Metasta·tic** *a.*

‖**Metasternum** (metăstə̄·ɹnǒm). 1826. [mod.L., f. META- + STERNUM.] **1.** *Entom.* The median ventral piece of the metathorax in insects. **2.** *Anat.* The xiphisternum 1868. Hence **Metaste·rnal** *a.* and *sb.*

‖**Metastoma** (metæ·stǒmă). Also **me·tastome.** 1859. [mod.L., f. Gr. μετα- META- + στόμα mouth.] = LABIUM 2.

‖**Metatarsus** (metătā·ɹsǒs). *Pl.* **-si** (səi). 1676. [mod.L.; see META- and TARSUS.] *Anat.* The group of five long bones of the foot lying between the tarsus and the toes. In birds, the bone which corresponds to tarsus and metatarsus together. **b.** *Entom.* (*a*) The proximal joint of the tarsus. (*b*) The entire tarsus of the hind foot. 1816. Hence **Metata·rsal** *a.* of or belonging to the m.; *sb.* any bone of the m.

‖**Metatheria** (metaþīᵊ·riă), *sb. pl.* 1880. [mod.L., f. Gr. μετα- META- + θηρίον beast; see -IA[2].] *Zool.* Huxley's term for the Marsupials. Hence **Metathe·rian** *a.* belonging to the M.; *sb.* one of these.

Metathesis (metæ·þĭsis). *Pl.* **-ses** (-sīz). 1577. [– late L. (in sense 1) – Gr. μετάθεσις, f. μετατιθέναι transpose, change; see META- and THESIS.] **1.** †**a.** *Rhet.* The transposition of words. **b.** *Gram.* The interchange of position between sounds or letters in a word; the result of this. †**2.** *Path.* **a.** = METASTASIS 2 a. **b.** The transposition of a solid morbific substance from one part to another where it will be less injurious. –1832. **3.** *gen.* Change or reversal of condition 1705. **4.** *Chem.* The interchange of atoms or groups of atoms between two molecules, the structure of the molecules being not otherwise altered 1872.

1. The Assyrian Nipur, which is Nipru, with a mere m. of the two final letters RAWLINSON. So **Metathe·tic, -ical** *a.*

‖**Métayage** (metẹyāʒ). 1877. [Fr.; irreg. f. *métayer*; see next.] A system of land tenure in Western Europe and U.S., in which the farmer pays a proportion (usu. half) of the produce (as rent) to the owner, who furnishes the stock and seed or a part thereof.

‖**Métayer** (metẹye). 1776. [Fr. *métayer* :– med.L. *medietarius*, f. *medietas* half; see MEDIETY, MOIETY.] A farmer who holds land on the *métayage* system. Also *attrib.*, as in *m. system, tenancy.*

‖**Metazoa** (metăzōᵘ·ă), *sb. pl.* 1874. [f. Gr. μετα- META- 4 + ζῷα pl. of ζῷον animal.] Haeckel's term for one of the two great divisions (the other being PROTOZOA) of the animal kingdom, comprising those animals whose bodies consist of many cells. Also sing. **Metazo·on**, one of the m. Hence **Meta-zo·an** *a.* belonging to or characteristic of the M.; *sb.* one of the M. So **Metazo·ic** *a.*

Mete (mīt), *sb.*¹ late ME. [– OFr. *mete* – L. *meta* goal, boundary.] †**1.** A goal –1480. **2.** A boundary, limit; a boundary stone or mark; *esp.* in phr. *metes and bounds*, common in legal use 1471.

Mete (mīt), *sb.*² 1768. [f. METE *v.*¹ Cf. MET *sb.*] Measure.

Mete (mīt), *v.*¹ Infl. **meted, meting.** [OE. *metan* = OFris. *meta*, OS. *metan*, OHG. *mezzan* (Du. *meten*, G. *messen*), ON. *meta*, Goth. *mitan* :– Gmc. **metan*; the IE. base **med-* is repr. also by L. *meditari* MEDITATE, Gr. μέδεσθαι care for, beside **mod-* of L. *modus* MODE, *modius* bushel.] **1.** *trans.* = MEASURE *v.* 2. Now only *poet.* and *dial.* exc. in allusions to Matt. 7:2. **2.** *absol.* or *intr.*; also, to aim at –1649. †**3.** *trans.* = MEASURE *v.* 3. –1819. **4.** = MEASURE *v.* 6 (*arch.*) OE. †**5.** To traverse (a distance). Also *absol.* or *intr.* (and *refl.*) To go, proceed. –1697. **6.** (Often with *out.*) To apportion by measure; to deal out; *esp.* to allot (punishment, reward, etc.) ME.

1. She. .Metes the thin air and weighs the flying sound CRABBE. **2.** *L.L.L.* IV. i. 134. **4.** 2 *Hen. IV*, IV. iv. 77. **6.** I m. and dole Unequal laws unto a savage race TENNYSON.

†**Mete,** *v.*² [OE. *mǣtan* wk. vb.; only Eng.] **1.** *impers. Me mette*: it occurred to me in a dream; I dreamt. Also with *sb.*, as *me mette sweven*, I dreamt a dream. –1643. **2.** *trans.* To dream –1570. **3.** *intr.* To dream (*of*). ME.

Mete, var. of MEAT, MEET, MET.

†**Metecorn.** [OE., f. *mete* MEAT *sb.* + CORN *sb.*¹] An allowance (prop. of corn) made to servants, to inmates of a hospital, etc. –1523.

Metel (mī·tĕl). 1528. [– mod.L. *methel* – Arab. *jawz* (= nut) *māṯil*.] †**a.** *Methelnut*: a narcotic seed described by Avicenna, prob. *Datura stramonium*, the Thorn-apple –1753. **b.** The specific name of the Hairy Thorn-apple, *Datura m.*, used as a name for the plant.

Metely, obs. f. MEETLY *a.* and *adv.*

Metempiric (metempi·rik). 1874. [f. META- + EMPIRIC.] **1.** (Also **Metempirics** constr. as sing.) The philosophy of things outside the sphere of knowledge derived from experience. **2.** One who believes in metempirical philosophy 1881. Hence **Metempi·ricism,** metempirical philosophy. **Metem-pi·ricist.**

Metempirical (metempi·rikăl), *a.* 1874. [f. META- + EMPIRICAL.] Pertaining to matters outside the range of knowledge derived from experience. Also: Maintaining the validity of concepts and opinions based otherwise than on experience.

If then the Empirical designates the province we include within the range of Science, the province we exclude may fitly be styled the M. LEWES. Hence **Metempi·rically** *adv.*

Metempsychose (mete·mpsikōᵘz), *v.* 1594. [f. next.] *trans.* To transfer or translate (a soul) from one body to another. So **Metem-psycho·size** *v.*

Metempsychosis (mete:mpsikōᵘ·sis). *Pl.* **-oses** (-ōᵘ·sīz). 1590. [Late L. – Gr. μετεμψύχωσις, f. μετα- META- + ἐν in + ψυχή soul; see -OSIS. Formerly often stressed *metem-psy·chosis*.] Transmigration of the soul; *chiefly*, passage of the soul of a human being or animal at or after death into a new body of the same or a different species, a tenet of the Pythagoreans, the Buddhists, etc. Also *transf.* and *fig.*

fig. Departed empire has a m., if nothing else has LOWELL. Hence **Metempsycho·sist,** one who believes in m.

‖**Metemptosis** (metemptōᵘ·sis). 1727. [mod.L., f. Gr. μετά after + ἔμπτωσις, f. ἐμπίπτειν fall in or upon.] The solar equation necessary to prevent the calendar new moon from happening a day too late. (Opp. to *proemptosis*.)

‖**Metencephalon** (metense·fălǫn). 1871. [f. META- + ENCEPHALON.] **a.** In Huxley's use: The cerebellum with the pons Varolii. **b.** The after-brain, the last encephalic segment, called *Myelencephalon* by Huxley 1876. Hence **Metencepha·lic** *a.*

‖**Metensomatosis** (metensōᵘmătōᵘ·sis). 1630. [– late L. *metensomatosis* – Gr. μετενσωμάτωσις, f. ἐν IN + σῶμα, σωματ- body; see -OSIS.] Re-embodiment (of the soul); a change of bodily elements.

Meteor (mī·tĭǫɹ). 1471. [– mod.L. *meteorum* – Gr. μετέωρον, subst. use of n. of μετέωρος raised up, lofty, f. μετα- META- + *εωρ-, var. of base of ἀείρειν raise. Cf. (O)Fr. *météore*.] **1.** Any atmospheric phenomenon. Now chiefly *techn.* **2.** *spec.* **a.** A small mass of matter from celestial space, rendered luminous by the heat engendered by collision with the earth's atmosphere; a fire-ball, a shooting star (in 17th c. also †a comet) 1593. **b.** Applied to the aurora borealis, the ignis fatuus, etc. 1592. **c.** *transf.* and *fig.* 1593. **3.** Passing into *adj.* 1711.

1. Atmospheric phenomena were formerly often classed as *aerial* or *airy meteors* (winds), *aqueous* or *watery meteors* (rain, snow, hail, dew, etc.), *luminous meteors* (the aurora, rainbow, halo, etc.), *igneous* or *fiery meteors* (lightning, shooting stars, etc.). O.E.D. **2.** And Meteors fright the fixed Starres of Heauen SHAKS. **c.** I have seen the Meteors of fashion rise and fall JOHNSON. **3.** The m. flag of England CAMPBELL. Bothwell's m. course LANG.

Comb.: **m.-dust,** matter in a state of fine division, supposed to be diffused through interstellar space; **-powder,** a powdered-up alloy which is mixed with steel to form *meteor-steel*; **-steel,** an alloyed steel with a wavy appearance, resembling Damascus steel; **-stone** = *meteoric stone*; also *fig.*; **-stream,** the stream of meteors moving together in the same orbit; **-swarm, -system,** an aggregation of meteoroids pursuing the same orbit.

Meteoric (mītĭ,ǫ·rik), *a.* 1631. [Partly – med.L. *meteoricus*, f. Gr. μετέωρος (see prec.); partly f. METEOR + -IC.] †**1.** Pertaining to the region of mid-air. DONNE. **2.** Meteorological, atmospherical 1830. **b.** *Bot.* Dependent upon atmospheric conditions 1789. **3.** Of, pertaining to, or derived from meteors; consisting of meteors 1812. **4.** *fig.* Transiently brilliant, flashing or dazzling like a meteor; also rapid, swift 1836.

2. M. agents, rain, wind, frost, etc. HERSCHEL. **3.** *M. stone* = METEORITE. *M. paper* = 'natural flannel' (a fibrous texture often found covering meadows after an inundation). *M. steel* = meteor steel. **4.** [Kean's] m. talent 1836. So †**Meteo·ric-al** *a.* Hence **Meteo·rically** *adv.*

Meteorism (mī·tĭ,ǫriz'm). 1843. [– medical L. *meteorismus* (also used), – Gr. μετεωρισμός elevation, f. μετεωρίζειν. Cf. Fr. *météorisme* (Paré).] *Path.* Flatulent distension of the abdomen with gas in the alimentary canal.

Meteorite (mī·tĭ,ǫrəi:t). 1834. [f. METEOR + -ITE¹ 2 b.] A fallen meteor; a mass of stone or iron that has fallen from the sky upon the earth; a meteoric stone. Also (*loosely*), a meteor or meteoroid.

Meteorites, the so-called falling stars,. .follow a perfectly definite track in space TAIT. Hence **Me·teori:tal, Meteori·tic** *adjs.*

Meteorize, *v. Obs.* or *arch.* 1657. [– Gr. μετεωρίζειν elevate, f. μετέωρος; see METEOR and -IZE.] **1.** *trans.* To vaporize, convert into vapour. Also *intr.* Only in Evelyn. **2.** *intr.* To resemble a meteor; to flash, sparkle 1828.

Meteorograph (mī·tĭ,ǫrŏgrɑf). 1780. [– Fr. *météorographe*; see METEOR and -GRAPH.] An apparatus for recording automatically several different kinds of meteorological phenomena at the same time. So **Me·teoro-gram.**

Meteorography (mī:tĭ,ǫrǫ·grăfi). 1736. [f. METEOR + -GRAPHY.] The descriptive science of meteors, or of meteorological phenomena. Hence **Meteorogra·phic, -al** *a.* pertaining to m.

Meteoroid (mī·tĭ,ǫroid). 1865. [f. METEOR + -OID.] **a.** *sb.* A body moving through space, of the same nature as those which when passing through the atmosphere become visible as meteors. **b.** *adj.* Of the nature of a m. Hence **Meteoroi·dal** *a.*

Meteorolite (mī·tĭ,ǫrŏləit). 1802. [– Fr. *météorolithe*; see METEOR, -LITE.] = METEORITE.

Meteorologist (mī:tĭ,ǫrǫ·lŏdʒist). 1621. [orig. f. Gr. μετεωρολόγος; see METEOR, -LOGIST.] One who is skilled in meteorology. So †**Meteoro·loger** 1683. †**Meteorolo·gian** 1614, †**Meteorologi·cian** 1580.

Meteorology (mī:tĭ¹ǫrǫ·lŏdʒi). 1620. [orig. – Gr. μετεωρολογία; see METEOR, -LOGY.] **1.** The study of, or the science that treats of, the motions and phenomena of the atmosphere, esp. with a view to forecasting the weather. **2.** The character, as regards weather, etc., *of* a particular region 1694.

1. In sundry Animals we deny not a kind of natural M., or innate presention both of wind and weather SIR T. BROWNE. **2.** The Climate and M. of Madeira 1850. So **Meteorolo·gic** (1760), **-lo·gical** (1570) *a.* pertaining to or connected with the science of m.; also, pertaining to atmospheric phenomena. **Me:teorolo·gically** *adv.*

Meteoroscopy (mī:tĭ,ǫrǫ·skŏpi). *rare.* 1658. [f. METEOR + Gr. -σκοπία; see -SCOPE, -Y³.] Observation of the stars.

Meteorous (mī·tĭ,ǫrəs, also *poet.* mītī·ǫrəs), *a.* 1667. [f. Gr. μετέωρος raised on high, μετέωρα n. pl. METEOR + -OUS.] = METEORIC.

Meter (mī·təɹ), *sb.*¹ late ME. [f. METE *v.*¹ + -ER¹.] One who measures; a measurer, esp. of land, coal, and other commodities.

Meter (mī·təɹ), *sb.*² 1815. [First in *gas meter* (1815); perh. a use of METER *sb.*¹ suggested by *gasometer* (1790).] **1. a.** (In full *gas-meter*.) An apparatus for automatically measuring and recording the volume of gas supplied.

Usually, the gas is made to pass through receptacles of known capacity, each filling and discharge of one of these being registered by the movement of an index.

b. Any apparatus for automatically measuring and recording the quantity of a fluid or the like flowing through it 1832. **c.** *fig.* A 'gauge', self-acting measure of the fluctuations of anything 1860. **2.** *attrib.*, as *m. box, inspector, rent*, etc. 1882.

1. a. *Dry m.*: one in which no water is used; dist. from the earlier *wet m.* **b.** *Water-m., electric light m.*; also, *ampere-m., voltmeter, watt-m.*, etc. **2. m. mailing machine,** a machine for franking an envelope, etc. (in lieu of the usual postage stamp), and registering the amount (1923); so **m.-mail, (postage) stamp.** Hence **Me·ter** *v. trans.*, to measure by means of a m. *Metered mail* (cf. *meter-mail* above).

Meter: see METRE.

-meter, in use commonly *-o·meter*, and occas. *-i·meter*, a terminal element in names of instruments for automatically measuring something. Early (17th c.) examples are *barometer, hygrometer, thermometer*, repr. mod.L. forms in *-metrum*. In these the ending was intended to represent the Gr. μέτρον measure (see METRE¹); the formation is irregular, as the Gr. word does not occur in comb. with sbs., and would not correctly express 'instrument that measures'. Later, hybrid formations were introduced, some of them imitating the form of Gr. compounds, as *gasometer, galvanometer*, etc., while in others the combining-vowel of the L. first element is retained, as in *calorimeter*, etc. In late formations, as *voltameter, ammeter*, etc., no attempt is made to assimilate the form of the first element to that of a Gr. or L. combining form.

Meterage (mī·tərĕdʒ). 1882. [f. METER *sb.*¹ + -AGE.] Measurement, or the price paid for it.

Metewand (mī·twǫnd). 1440. [f. METE *v.*¹ or MET *sb.* + WAND *sb.*] A measuring-rod. Now *dial.*

fig. A true tochstone, a sure metwand lieth before both their eyes ASCHAM.

Meteyard (mī·tyăɹd). OE. [f. METE *v.*¹ or MET *sb.* + YARD *sb.*²] = prec. Now *dial.* Also *fig.*

Meth, obs. f. MEAD¹.

Methæmoglobin (meþīmoglōᵘ·bin). 1870. [See META- and HÆMOGLOBIN.] *Chem.* A derivative of hæmoglobin obtained by the exposure of an aqueous solution of oxy-hæmoglobin to the air.

Methane (me·þeⁱn). Also **-an.** 1866. [f. METH(YL + -ANE.] *Chem.* Methyl hydride or MARSH-GAS, a colourless odourless gas emanating from stagnant pools, etc., and esp. coal-seams, in which, mixed with air, it forms FIRE-DAMP.

Metheglin (mĭþe·glin). *Obs.* exc. *Hist.* and *dial.* 1533. [– W. *meddyglyn*, f. *meddyg* medicinal (– L. *medicus* MEDICAL) + *llyn* liquor (= Ir. *linn*, Gael. *linne* pool).] A spiced or medicated form of mead, orig. peculiar to Wales.

Methene (me·þīn). 1885. [f. METH(YL + -ENE.] *Chem.* = METHYLENE. Hence **Methenyl** (me·þǐnil), the hypothetical hydrocarbon radical CH. So **Methide** (me·þəid), a combination of methyl with a metal 1868.

Methinks (miþi·ŋks), *impers. v.* Now *arch.* and *poet.* Pa. t. **methought** (miþǭ·t). [OE. *mē þyncþ* (pa. t. *mē þūhte*), where *mē* is dative, and *þyncþ* 3rd pers. sing. of *þyncan* seem, THINK *v.*[1]] It seems to me. (Used with dependent clause or parenthetically.)

Methinkes you are sadder SHAKS. M. a strait canal is as rational at least as a mæandring bridge H. WALPOLE.

Methionic (meþiǫ·nik), *a.* 1842. [f. ME(THYL + Gr. θεῖον sulphur; see -IC.] *Chem.* In *m. acid*: a disulpho-acid obtained from aniline. Hence **Methionate** (meþəi·ŏne[i]t), a salt of this.

Method (me·þǒd). 1541. [– Fr. *méthode* or L. *methodus* – Gr. μέθοδος pursuit of knowledge, mode of investigation, f. μετά (see MID) + ὁδός way.] **I.** Procedure for attaining an object. †**1.** *Med.* The regular systematic treatment proper for the cure of a given disease –1716. **b.** *Hist.* The system of medicine of the 'methodics' or 'methodists' –1790. **2.** A special form of procedure adopted in any branch of mental activity, whether for exposition or for investigation 1586. **3.** A way of doing anything, esp. according to a regular plan 1590. **b.** The methods of procedure in teaching, etc., considered as the object of a branch of study 1848.

2. It is a distinct property of the Comparative Method of investigation to abate national prejudices MAINE. **3.** This is the usual m., but not mine—My way is to begin with the beginning BYRON. **b.** A Manual of M. for Pupil-Teachers (*title*) 1879.

II. Systematic arrangement. **1.** A branch of Logic or Rhetoric which teaches how to arrange thoughts and topics for investigation, exposition, or literary composition 1551. **2.** Orderly arrangement of ideas and topics; orderliness and sequence of thought or expression 1559. **3.** The order and arrangement of a particular discourse, etc. 1591. †**b.** A methodical exposition –1829. †**c.** A summary of the contents of a book –1652. **4.** Orderliness and regularity in doing anything 1611. †**5.** A disposition of things according to a regular plan –1754. **6.** *Nat. Hist.* A system; scheme of classification 1826.

2. Though this be madnesse, Yet there is M. in't SHAKS. **3.** *Verbatim* to rehearse the Methode of my Penne SHAKS. **c.** In what chapter of his bosome? To answer by the m. in the first of his hart SHAKS. **4.** Early hours, and m., and ease, without hurry, will do everything 1754. **6.** *Method* and *System*..have often been..used indifferently to signify the same thing KIRBY and SP.

Methodic (miþǫ·dik). *Obs.* exc. *Hist.* 1541. [– late L. *methodicus* – Gr. μεθοδικός, f. μέθοδος METHOD; see -IC. Cf. Fr. *méthodique* (XVI).] **A.** *adj.* †**1.** Epithet of an ancient school of physicians holding views intermediate between those of the Dogmatic and the Empiric school –1751. **2.** = METHODICAL *a.* 1620. **B.** *sb.* = METHODIST 1. 1541.

Methodical (miþǫ·dikăl), *a.* 1570. [f. as prec.; see -ICAL.] **1.** *Hist.* = METHODIC *a.* 1. 1597. **2.** Characterized by method or order; arranged or disposed with order or regularity 1570. **3.** Of persons, etc.: Acting with or observant of method or order 1664.

3. I find him a most exact and methodicall man PEPYS. Hence **Metho·dical-ly** *adv.*, **-ness.**

Methodism (me·þŏdiz'm). 1739. [f. METHOD + -ISM, after next.] **1.** The system of doctrine, practice, and organization characteristic of the Methodists. **2.** Excessive regard for methods 1856.

2. The Somerset House gentlemen usually introduce their official m. at home 1856.

Methodist (me·þŏdist). 1593. [– mod.L. *methodista*; see METHOD and -IST.] **1.** *Hist.* A physician of the methodic school. In the 17th c. sometimes applied to the regular practitioners of the day. 1598. **2.** One who is skilled in, or attaches importance to, method; one who follows a (specified) method. Now *rare.* 1593. **b.** *Nat. Hist.* One who classifies according to a particular scheme. Also, in Kirby's use, one who prefers an artificial to a natural method of classification. 1753. **3.** *Eccl.* The name given in the 17th c. to a class of Roman Catholic apologists 1686. **4. a.** Orig., a member of the 'Holy Club', established at Oxford in 1729 by John and Charles Wesley and others; later, any of those who sympathized with the evangelistic movement led by the Wesleys and George Whitefield. **b.** In subseq. use, a member of any one of a number of religious bodies which originated from the labours of the Wesleys and Whitefield. 1733. **c.** *transf.* A person of strict religious views (*contempt.*) 1758. **5.** *attrib.* or *adj.* Pertaining to Methodists or Methodism 1751.

4. b. He combines the manners of a Marquis with the morals of a M. W. S. GILBERT. **5.** A M. Preacher WESLEY. Hence **Methodi·stic, -al** *a.* characteristic of or pertaining to Methodism or the Methodists: often *disparaging.* **Methodi·stically** *adv.*

Methodize (me·þŏdəiz), *v.* 1589. [f. METHOD + -IZE.] **1.** *trans.* To reduce to order; to arrange in a methodical manner. **b.** To render (a person) methodical. MME. D'ARBLAY. **2.** *intr.* To talk methodistically. SMOLLETT.

1. He should be taught..to order and methodise his ideas BERKELEY. Hence **Methodiza·tion.**

Methodless (me·þǒdlės), *a.* 1609. [f. METHOD + -LESS.] Devoid of method or order; lacking the habit of order.

Methodology (meþǒdǫ·lŏdʒi). 1800. [– mod.L. *methodologia* (J. F. Buddeus, 1727) or Fr. *méthodologie*; see METHOD, -LOGY.] The science of method; a treatise or dissertation on method. Also *Nat. Hist.* Systematic classification. So **Methodolo·gical** *a.*, **-ly** *adv.* **Methodo·logist,** one who treats method as a science.

Methol (me·þǫl). 1842. [– Fr. *méthol*, f. *méthyle* METHYL; see -OL 1.] *Chem.* A colourless liquid, produced in the distillation of wood.

Methought, pa. t. of METHINKS.

Methoxyl (meþǫ·ksil). 1866. [f. METH(YL + OX(YGEN + -YL.] *Chem.* A hypothetical radical, CH_3O, analogous to hydroxyl.

Methuselah (miþ[i]ū·zělă). Also *corruptly* **Methusalem,** etc. late ME. [bibl. Heb. *m[e]tūšelaḥ.*] The name of one of the pre-Noachian patriarchs, stated to have lived 969 years (Gen. 5:27); hence used as a type of longevity.

Methyl (me·þil). Formerly also **-ule, -yle.** 1844. [– Fr. *méthyle*, G. *methyl*, back-formations from Fr. *méthylène*, G. *methylen* METHYLENE.] *Chem.* The hypothetical radical of the monocarbon series (CH_3), the base of pyroxylic or wood spirit or pyroligneous naphtha, of formic acid, and of a large series of organic compounds.

attrib. and *Comb.*, as *m. compound*; *m. bromide*, etc. Also prefixed (often without hyphen) to the name of an organic compound to express the addition of m. to its composition, or the replacement of hydrogen atoms by equivalents of m., as in *methylaniline*.

Spec. combs.: **m. alcohol,** pyroxylic spirit; **m. green,** a green dye obtained by heating Paris violet with m. chloride; **m. mercaptan,** m. hydrosulphide, CH_3HS; **m. violet,** Paris violet, a reddish-blue coal-tar dye obtained from dimethylaniline.

Methylal (me·þilæl). 1838. [– Fr. *méthylal*, f. *méthyle* METHYL + *al*(*cool* ALCOHOL.] *Chem.* A mobile aromatic liquid obtained by heating methyl alcohol with manganese dioxide and sulphuric acid; occas. used as an anæsthetic.

Methylamine (me·þilăməin). 1850. [f. METHYL + AMINE.] *Chem.* A compound in which one atom of the hydrogen in ammonia has been replaced by methyl.

Methylate (me·þile[i]t), *sb.* 1835. [f. as METHYLIC; see -ATE[1].] *Chem.* A salt formed by the union of methyl with oxygen and a metallic base.

Methylate (me·þile[i]t), *v.* 1865. [f. METHYL + -ATE[3].] *trans.* To mix or impregnate with methyl; usu. to mix (spirit of wine) with pyroxylic spirit, etc., to render it unfit for drinking, and exempt it from the duties imposed on alcohol.

Methylated spirit, containing about ten per cent. of pyroxylic spirit, is the form in which alcohol is most used for industrial purposes.

Methylene (me·þilīn). 1835. [– Fr. *méthylène*, irreg. f. Gr. μέθυ wine + ὕλη wood (see -YL).] *Chem.* A hypothetical radical of the hydrocarbons (CH_2); unknown in the free state, but occurring in many compounds, as *m. hydrate*, etc.

M.-azure, an oxidation product of m. blue; **m.-blue,** a coal-tar colour used in dyeing, and as a bacterioscopic reagent; **m.-violet** = *methyl-violet.*

Methylic (mĭþi·lik), *a.* 1835. [orig. f. METHYL(ENE + -IC; later, f. METHYL + -IC.] *Chem.* Of or pertaining to methyl. Chiefly in names of compounds, in which *methyl* is more commonly used attrib.

Metic (me·tik). 1808. [irreg. – Gr. μέτοικος, f. μετα- (denoting change) + -οικος dwelling, οἰκεῖν dwell.] *Gr. Antiq.* A resident alien in a Greek city, having some of the privileges of citizenship.

Meticulous (mĭti·kiŭləs), *a.* 1535. [f. L. *meticulosus* (Plautus), f. *metus* fear, after *periculosus* PERILOUS; see -OUS.] †**1.** Timid –1674. **2.** Over-careful about minute details 1827.

1. Melancholy and m. heads SIR T. BROWNE. **2.** A stringent and m. discipline 1904. **Meti·culously** *adv.*

‖**Métier** (metye). 1674. [Fr. :– Rom. **misterium*, for L. *ministerium* service (see MINISTRY), assoc. with *mysterium* MYSTERY.] A trade or profession; in Eng. use chiefly *transf.*, a person's 'line'.

Heretic-burning—in fact, 'tis his *m.* BARHAM.

‖**Metif** (mē[i]·tif). 1808. [Fr. *métif* (XVII), alt. f. *metis*, OFr. *mestis* :– Rom. **mixticius* MESTIZO.] The offspring of a white and a quadroon.

Metis (mē[i]·tis). 1839. [– Fr. *métis*; see prec.] The offspring of a white and an American Indian, esp. in Canada.

Metol (me·tǫl). 1893. [– G. *metol*, an arbitrary name.] *Photogr.* A whitish soluble powder (sulphate of methylparamidometacresol) used as a developer.

Metonic (mĭtǫ·nik), *a.* 1696. [f. Gr. Μέτων, name of the Athenian who discovered the cycle; see -IC.] *M. cycle, period,* †*year*: the cycle of 19 Julian years (about 235 lunations) in which the moon returns (nearly) to the same apparent position with regard to the sun, so that the new and full moons occur at the same dates in the corresponding year of each cycle.

Metonym (me·tŏnim). 1826. [Extracted from METONYMY after *paronym/paronymy, synonym/synonymy.*] A word used in a transferred sense.

Metonymy (mĭtǫ·nĭmi). 1562. [First in late L. form *metonymia* – Gr. μετωνυμία lit. 'change of name', f. μετά META- + ὄνομα, Aeol. ὄνυμα name.] *Rhet.* A figure in which the name of an attribute or adjunct is substituted for that of the thing meant, e.g. *sceptre* for *authority.* So **Metony·mical** *a.* pertaining to or involving m. 1579. **Metony·mically** *adv.* by m. 1574.

Metope[1] (me·tŏpi). 1563. [– L. *metopa* – Gr. μετόπη, f. μετά between + ὀπαί holes in a frieze to receive the beam-ends.] *Arch.* A square space between the triglyphs in a Doric frieze. *Demi-, Semi-m.*, the half-space between the corner and the triglyph next the corner.

Metope[2] (me·to[u]p). 1880. [– Gr. μέτωπον forehead.] *Zool.* Applied to the face of a crab. HUXLEY. So **Meto·pic** *a.* of or pertaining to the forehead; (of a skull) having the metopic suture persisting 1878. **Me·topism,** persistence of the frontal suture 1879.

Metoposcopy (metopǫ·skŏpi). 1569. [– Fr. *métoposcopie* (XVI), f. L. *metoposcopus* (whence †*metoposcoper, metoposcopist* XVI) – Gr. μετωποσκόπος, f. μέτωπον forehead; see -SCOPE, -Y[3].] **1.** The art of judging character or of telling a fortune by the forehead or face. **2.** The physiognomical characters of a person's face 1653. Hence **Metoposco·pic, -al** *a.* **Metopo·scopist.**

‖**Metosteon** (metǫ·stĭ,ǫn). 1868. [f. Gr. μετά behind + ὀστέον bone.] *Ornith.* The centre of ossification for the posterior lateral processes of the sternum, behind the pleurosteon. Hence **Meto·steal** *a.*

Metre (mī·təɹ), *sb.*[1] OE. [– (O)Fr. *mètre* – L. *metrum* (which was adopted in OE.) – Gr. μέτρον; f. IE. **mē-* MEASURE + instr. suffix.] **1.** Any form of poetic rhythm, its kind being determined by the character and number of the feet or groups of syllables of which it consists. **2.** Metrical arrangement or method ME. **3. a.** Composition in metre; verse. †**b.** A verse or poem; *occas.* a metrical version. ME. **4.** *Pros.* A metrical group or measure; *spec.* a dipody in iambic, trochaic, and anapæstic rhythms 1880. **5.** *attrib.* as *m. psalm* 1596.

1. Composed in a m. of Catullus TENNYSON. *Common, long, particular, short m.*: see these words. *Peculiar m., proper m.*, a metre used only in a particular hymn, or having no recognized name. **2.** Then arrange this [prose] again into m. WHATELY. **3.** A meter of iiii verses in the Utopian tongue 1556. Those luckless brains That..Indite much m. with much pains COWPER.

Metre (mī·təɹ), *sb.*[2] Also *U.S.* **meter.** 1797. [– Fr. *mètre* – Gr. μέτρον measure; see prec.] The unit of length of the metric system, = 39·37 inches. **b.** *attrib.*, as *m. gauge* 1868.

b. m.-gramme, -ton, etc., the amount of work required to raise a gramme, a ton, etc. one m. in one second.

Metre (mī·təɹ), *v.* late ME. [f. METRE *sb.*[1]] **1.** To compose in or put into metre 1447. **2.** *intr.* To versify. late ME. Hence **Me·tred** *ppl. a.* metrical; also *loosely*, rhythmical.

Metric (me·trik), *a.*[1] and *sb.* 1760. [– L. *metricus* – Gr. μετρικός, f. μέτρον METRE *sb.*[1]; see -IC. With the sb. cf. Fr. *la métrique*, G. *metrik.*] **A.** *adj.* = METRICAL *a.*[1] BLACKIE. **B.** *sb. sing.* and *pl.* The science or art that deals with metre.

Metric (me·trik), *a.*[2] 1864. [– Fr. *métrique*, f. *mètre*, METRE *sb.*[2]] Pertaining to that system of weights and measures of which the metre is the unit.

The system is decimal throughout, and the unit in each of its branches has a definite relation to the metre; e.g. the gramme, the unit of weight, represents the weight of a cubic centimetre of water.

Metrical (me·trikăl), *a.*[1] late ME. [– L. *metricus* relating (1) to measuring, (2) to metre; see METRIC *a.*[1] and -ICAL. Cf. OFr. *metrical.*] **1.** Pertaining or relating to metre or versification; consisting of or composed in metre; having the characteristics of metre. **2.** Relating to, involving, used in, or determined by measurement 1650.

1. The old m. romances WARTON. **2.** *M. geometry*; the science which deals with the comparison and relations of spatial magnitudes. **Me·trically** *adv.*

Metrical (me·trikăl), *a.*[2] 1797. [– Fr. *métrique* METRIC *a.*[2] + -AL[1]; see -ICAL.] **1.** = METRIC *a.*[2] (which is now more usual). **2.** Of lenses or their measurement: Pertaining to the system of which the unit is the 'dioptric', i.e. a focal length of one metre 1879.

Metrician (mĭtri·ʃən). late ME. [f. L. *metricus* METRIC *a.*[1], after *physician.*] †**1.** One who writes in metre –1548. **2.** One who studies or is learned in metre 1835.

Metrification (me:trifikēⁱ·ʃən). 1861. [f. METRIFY; see -FICATION.] The construction of a metrical composition; also, metrical structure.

Metrify (me·trifəi), *v.* 1523. [– OFr. *metre-*, *metrifier* or med.L. *metrificare*, f. L. *metrum* METRE *sb.*[1]; see -FY.] *trans.* To put into metre. Also *intr.* to make verses.

Metrist (me·trist). 1535. [– med.L. *metrista*, f. *metrum* METRE *sb.*[1]; see -IST.] A metrical writer; one skilled in the handling of metre.

Metrology (metrǫ·lŏdʒi). 1816. [f. Gr. μέτρον measure + -LOGY. Cf. Fr. *métrologie* (XVIII).] **a.** A system of weights and measures. **b.** The science of weights and measures. **Metrolo·gical** *a.*

Metromania (metromēⁱ·niă). 1794. [f. Gr. μέτρον METRE *sb.*[1] + -MANIA; after Fr. *métromanie* (XVIII).] A mania for writing verses. Hence **Metroma·niac.**

Metronome (me·trŏnōᵘm). 1815. [f. Gr. μέτρον METRE *sb.*[1] + νόμος law, rule. Cf. Fr. *métronome* (1815).] An instrument used in music for marking the time by means of a graduated inverted pendulum with a sliding weight which can be regulated. Hence **Metrono·mic, -al** *a.* **Metrono·mically** *adv.* **Metro·nomy.**

Metronymic (mītrŏni·mik). 1868. [f. Gr. μήτηρ, μητρ- mother, after PATRONYMIC. Cf. earlier MATRONYMIC.] **A.** *adj.* Derived from the name of a mother or other female ancestor, esp. by the addition of a suffix or prefix indicating descent. Also said of such a suffix or prefix. **B.** *sb.* A m. name.

Metropole (me·trŏpōᵘl). late ME. [– (O)Fr. *métropole*, – late L. *metropolis*; see next.] †**1.** A chief town –1685. **2.** *Eccl.* The see of a metropolitan 1862. So †**Metropolie** 1633–1665.

Metropolis (mĭtrǫ·pŏlis). *Pl.* **-polises.** 1535. [– late L. – Gr. μητρόπολις (Herodotus), f. μήτηρ mother + πόλις city.] **1.** The see of a metropolitan bishop. **2.** The chief town or city of a country; a capital 1590. **b.** A chief centre of some form of activity 1675. **c.** *Nat. Hist.* The district in which a species, group, etc., is most represented 1826. **3.** *Greek Hist.* The parent-state of a colony. Hence *transf.* 1568.

1. Irenaeus was the bishop Lyons, of the m. of Gaul LINGARD. **2.** *The m.*, London as a whole, as dist. from *the City*. **b.** Our m. of law, by which I mean Edinburgh SCOTT.

Metropolitan (metrŏpǫ·lităn), *a.* and *sb.* late ME. [– late L. *metropolitanus*, f. Gr. μητροπολίτης, f. μητρόπολις (see prec.); see -AN.] **A.** *adj.* **1.** Belonging to an ecclesiastical metropolis. Also, pertaining to or characteristic of a metropolitan. 1490. **2.** Of, pertaining to, or constituting a metropolis. Also, belonging to or characteristic of 'the metropolis' (London). 1555. **3.** Belonging to or constituting the mother country 1806. †**4.** *fig.* (from 1 and 2). Principal, chief –1686.

1. *M. bishop* = B. 1. **2.** *M. city* or *town* = METROPOLIS. *M. police*: police pertaining to London as a whole.

B. *sb.* **1.** *Eccl.* [In Gr. μητροπολίτης, in L. *metropolitanus.*] A bishop having the oversight of the bishops of a province; in the West equivalent to *archbishop*; in the Greek church ranking above an archbishop and below a patriarch ME. **2.** A chief town or metropolis 1549. †**3.** *fig.* = METROPOLIS 2 b. –1704. **4.** One who lives in a metropolis; one who has metropolitan ideas 1795. **5.** A citizen of the mother-city of a colony. GROTE.

Hence **Metropo·litanate,** the office or see of a m. bishop.

Metropolite (mĭtrǫ·pŏləit). 1578. [– late L. *metropolita* – Gr. μητροπολίτης, f. μητρόπολις METROPOLIS; see -ITE[1] 1.] **1.** = METROPOLITAN B. 1. †**2.** A metropolis –1635.

Metropolitical (metrŏpŏli·tikăl), *a.* 1541. [f. med.L. *metropoliticus*, f. *metropolita*; see prec., -AL[1].] **1.** *Eccl.* = METROPOLITAN A. 1. **2.** = METROPOLITAN A. 2. 1603. Hence **Metropoli·tically** *adv.*

‖**Metrorrhagia** (mītrorēⁱ·dʒiă). 1856. [mod. L., f. Gr. μήτρα womb + -ραγία breaking forth.] *Path.* Uterine hæmorrhage.

Metroscope (mī·trŏskōᵘp). 1855. [– Fr. *métroscope*, f. Gr. μήτρα womb; see -SCOPE.] **a.** An instrument for examining the uterus. **b.** An instrument for listening to the sounds of the heart of the fœtus during gestation.

Metrotome (mī·trŏtōᵘm). 1856. [f. Gr. μήτρα womb + -TOME[1].] A cutting instrument used in operating on the womb.

-metry (repr. Gr. -μετρία action or process of measuring, f. -μέτρης measurer, μέτρον measure), a terminal element of sbs. correlative to sbs. in -METER, denoting *spec.* the process of measuring by the instrument '—meter'. A few such sbs. represent actual Greek words, as *geometry*, etc., or are formed on the analogy of these, as *aerometry*, etc.; many others, e.g. *calorimetry*, etc., are hybrid formations.

Mettle (me·t'l), *sb.* (and *a.*) Also †**metal.** 1581. [orig. a var. sp. of METAL *sb.*] **1.** Quality of disposition or temperament 1584. **2.** Of a horse, etc.: Natural vigour and ardour; spirit 1596. **3.** Of persons: Ardent or spirited temperament; courage 1581. **4.** *attrib.* or *adj.* Spirited, mettlesome, 'game'. Now *arch.* and *Sc.* 1592.

1. To try the spirit of men, of what m. they are made of ROGERS. **2.** Her [a falcon's] m. makes her careless of danger WALTON. **3.** A Corinthian, a lad of m. SHAKS. Phrases. *To be on* or *upon one's m.*: to be incited to do one's best. *To put* or *set* (a person) *on* or *upon his m.*, *to put to his m.*, *to try* (a person's) *m.*: to test his powers of endurance or resistance.

Hence **Me·ttled, Me·ttlesome** *adjs.* full of m.

Meum (mī·ŏm). 1594. [L., neut. of *meus* mine.] In phr. **Meum and tuum:** 'mine and thine'; what is one's own and what is another's: a pop. phrase used to express the rights of property. Also *m.*, *tuum*; *m. or tuum.*

‖**Meurtrière** (mörtriẹ̄r). 1802. [Fr.; fem. of *meurtrier* murderer, murderous, f. *meurtre.*] A small loophole, large enough to admit the barrel of a rifle, gun, or musket, through which a soldier may fire, under cover.

Meuse, muse (miūs, miūz), *sb.* Now *dial.* 1523. [– OFr. *muce, musse, mouce*, mod. dial. *muche* hiding-place, etc., f. *musser*, *muchier* to hide (whence MICHE *v.*). Cf. MUSET.] **1.** A gap in a fence or hedge through which hares, etc. habitually pass, and through which they run, when hunted, for relief. **b.** *transf.* and *fig.* A loophole or means of escape 1529. **2.** The 'form' of a hare 1611. **Meuse** *v.* to go through a m.

Meuse, Meute, obs. ff. MEWS, MUTE *sbs.*[2,3]

Mew (miū), *sb.*[1] [OE. *mǣw*, corresp. to OS. *mēu* (MLG., MDu. *mēwe*, Du. *meeuw*) :– Gmc. **mai(ʒ)wiz*, rel. to **maixwaz*, whence OHG. *mēh*, ON. *már* (pl. *márvar*, *máfar*).] A gull, *esp.* the common gull, *Larus canus*; a sea-mew.

Mew (miū), *sb.*[2] ME. [– (O)Fr. *mue*, f. *muer* moult, shed horns, in OFr. also change :– L. *mutare* (see MUTATION).] **1.** A cage for hawks, esp. while 'mewing' or moulting. **2.** †**a.** A coop or cage in which fowls, etc. were confined for fattening. **b.** Now *dial.*, a breeding-cage. late ME. **3.** †**a.** A place of confinement –1622. **b.** A secret place; a den. Now *rare.* late ME.

1. They make of the churche, for theyre hawkes a mewe BARCLAY. Phr. *In m.* (rarely *in the m.*): in process of moulting; also *fig.* **3.** Phr. †*In m.*: in hiding or confinement, cooped up.

Mew, *sb.*[3]: see MEW *int.*

Mew (miū), *v.*[1] late ME. [– (O)Fr. *muer*; see MEW *sb.*[2]] **1. a.** *trans.* Of a hawk, etc.: To moult, shed, or change (its feathers). Also in *passive* with the bird as subject. Now only *arch.* †Also *transf.* and *fig.* **b.** *absol.* and *intr.* To moult 1532. †**2.** *trans.* Of a stag: To cast (his horns) ME.

1. His feathers he [Cupid] meweth DRAYTON. As an Eagle muing (? = renewing by the process of moulting) her mighty youth MILTON. **b.** *transf.* One only suit to his backe which now is mewing FLETCHER. **2.** *intr.* When they [deer] cast their heads, they are said to *mew* GOLDSM.

Mew (miū), *v.*[2] late ME. [f. MEW *sb.*[2]] **1.** *trans.* To put a hawk in a mew at moulting time; to keep up 1533. †**2.** To coop *up* (poultry, etc.) for fattening (*rare*) –1639. **3.** To shut up, confine, enclose; to hide, conceal 1450.

1. Merlins, which sometimes she mewed in her own chamber 1640. **2.** *transf. Rich. III*, I. i. 132. **3.** They keep me mew'd up here as they m. mad folkes FLETCHER.

Mew (miū), *v.*[3] ME. [imit.; see next. Cf. MIAOW *v.*] *intr.* Of a cat, sea-birds, etc.: To utter the sound represented by 'mew'. Also *transf.* of a person. **b.** *trans.* To express by mewing 1900.

I heard the white-winged gulls mewing 1902.

Mew (miū), *int.* and *sb.*[3] 1596. [imit.; cf. MIAOW.] **1.** *int.* Used to represent the cry of a cat. Also *sb.* as a name for this. †**2.** Used as a derisive exclamation –1633.

1. I had rather be a Kitten, and cry m. [etc.] SHAKS.

Me-ward(s, orig. *to me ward(s* = towards me: see -WARD and TOWARD, TOWARDS.

Mewl (miūl), *v.* Also †**mule.** 1600. [imit.; cf. MIAUL *v.*] *intr.* **a.** To cry feebly like an infant; to make a whining noise. Also *trans.* with *out.* **b.** To mew like a cat.

Mews (miūz). late ME. [pl. of MEW *sb.*[2]; now construed as sing.] **1.** The royal stables at Charing Cross in London, built on the site where the royal hawks were formerly mewed. Now *Hist.* **2.** A set of stabling grouped round an open yard or alley. Also as *pl.* 1631.

2. Mr. Turveydrop's great room, which was built into a m. at the back DICKENS.

Mexican (me·ksikăn). 1604. [– earlier Sp. *mexicano* (now *mej-*), f. *Mexico*, f. *Mexitli*, one of the names of the Aztec god of war; see -AN.] **A.** *adj.* Of or pertaining to Mexico. In various names of natural and artificial products, etc. as **M. coca**, an American herb, yielding a nutritious fodder. **M. poppy**, *Argemone mexicana*.
B. *sb.* **1.** A native or inhabitant of Mexico 1604. **2.** = *Mexican dollar* (see DOLLAR 4) 1890.

Mezentian (mĭze·nʃăn), *a.* 1837. [f. *Mezentius* + -AN.] Comparable to the action of Mezentius, a mythical Etruscan king, who bound living men to corpses, and left them to die of starvation (Virg. *Æn.* viii. 485–8).

‖**Mezereon, -eum** (mĭzīᵊ·riŏn, -ŏm). 1477. [med.L. *mezereon* – Arab. *māzaryūn* (Avicenna).] **1.** The low shrub *Daphne mezereon*; also called †*Dutch m.* **2.** *Pharm.* The dried bark of the root of this plant, used in liniments 1789. **3.** *attrib.*, as *m. root*, etc. 1626.

‖**Mezuza(h** (mĕzū·ză). *Pl.* **mezuzoth** (mĕzū·zōþ). 1650. [Heb. *mᵉzûzāh*; = 'door-post' (Deut. 6:9, etc.).] Among the Jews, a piece of parchment inscribed on one side with the texts Deut. 6:4–9 and 11:13–21 and on the other with the divine name Shaddai, enclosed in a case and attached to the doorpost.

Mezzanine (me·zănīn). 1711. [– Fr. *mezzanine* – It. *mezzanino*, dim. of *mezzano* middle :– L. *medianus* MEDIAN.] **1.** A low story between two others, usually between the ground floor and the story above. Cf. ENTRESOL. Also *attrib.* in *m. floor, story.* **b.** *Theatr.* A floor beneath the stage. Also *m. floor.* 1859. **2.** A small window, less in height than breadth, occurring in entresols and attics, etc. Also *m. window.* 1731.

‖**Mezza voce** (me·dzaˌvō·tʃe), *adv.* 1775. [It. *mezza* moderate, half + *voce* VOICE.] *Mus.* Prop. *a mezza voce*: With a medium volume of sound.

‖**Mezzo** (me·dzo, -tso), *sb.*[1] 1832. Short for MEZZO-SOPRANO; also *attrib.* as *m. voice.*

‖**Me·zzo**, *sb.*[2] 1886. Short for MEZZOTINT.

‖**Me·zzo**, *a.* 1811. [It., = 'middle, half' :– L. *medius*; see MEDIUM.] *Mus.* In *m. forte* rather loud, *m. piano* rather soft.

‖**Mezzo-rilievo** (me·dzo rilie·vo). *Pl.* **-os.** 1598. [It. *mezzo* half + *rilievo* RELIEF *sb.*] **1.** Half-relief; relief in which the figures project half their true proportions. **2.** *concr.* A sculpture or carving in half-relief 1665.

‖**Mezzo-soprano** (me·dzo soprā·no, me·tso), *sb.* and *a.* 1753. [It.; see MEZZO *a.* and SOPRANO.] *Mus.* **a.** The part intermediate in compass between the soprano and contralto; **b.** a voice of this compass; **c.** a person having such a voice.

Mezzotint (me·tsotint, me·(d)zo-), *sb.* 1738. [Anglicized f. next.] **1.** = MEZZOTINTO 1. *Obs.* or *arch.* **2.** A method of engraving on copper or steel, in which the surface of the plate is first roughened uniformly, the lights and half-lights being then produced by scraping away the 'nap' thus formed, and the untouched parts giving the deepest shadows. Also, a print produced by this process. 1800. Hence **Me·zzotint** *v.* to engrave in mezzotint 1827; **Me·zzotinter** 1763.

‖**Mezzotinto** (medzoti·nto, -ts-), *sb.* and *a.* 1660. [It., f. *mezzo* half + *tinto* tint.] †**1.** A half-tint –1788. **2.** = MEZZOTINT *sb.* 2. 1661.
2. Prince Rupert first shewed me how to grave in Mezzo Tinto EVELYN.

Mho (mōᵘ). 1883. [OHM spelt backwards; proposed by Lord Kelvin.] *Electr.* The unit of conductivity, being the conductivity of a body whose resistance is one ohm. So **Mhometer** (mǫ·mĭtəɹ), an instrument for measuring electrical conductivities.

Mhorr (mǭɹ). Also **m'horr, moh(o)r.** 1833. [Morocco Arabic.] A West African gazelle, having annulated horns. It produces bezoar stones.

Mi (mī). 1529. [orig. the first syllable of L. *mira*; see GAMUT and UT.] The third note in Guido's hexachords, retained in solmization as the third note of the octave. (In Tonic Sol-fa often written *me.*)

M. I. = Mounted Infantry.

Miaow (miau), *int.* and *sb.* 1634. [imit.; cf. Fr. *miaou* and MIAUL.] The cry of a cat, or an imitation of it. Hence **Miaow** *v. intr.* 1632.

Miargyrite (məiˌā·ɹdʒirəit). 1836. [– G. *miargyrit* (H. Rose, 1829), f. Gr. μείων less + ἄργυρος silver + -ITE[1] 2 b.] *Min.* A black sulph-antimonide of silver, which contains less silver than red silver ore.

‖**Mias** (məi·ăs). *sing.* and *pl.* 1840. [Dayak *maias.*] The orang-outang, *Simia satyrus.*

Miascite (məi·ăskəit). Also **-cyte, -kite.** 1854. [– G. *miaszit* (Wuttig, 1814), f. *Miask*, in the Ural Mountains: see -ITE[1] 2 b.] *Petrology.* A rock essentially composed of orthoclase, elæolite, and dark mica.

Miasm (məi·æz'm). 1650. [– Fr. *miasme*; see next.] = next.

‖**Miasma** (məiˌæ·zmă). *Pl.* **mia·smata, mia·smas.** 1665. [Gr. μίασμα defilement, pollution, rel. to μιαίνειν pollute.] Infectious or noxious exhalations from putrescent organic matter; poisonous germs floating in the atmosphere; noxious emanations, *esp.* malaria. Also *fig.* Hence **Mia·smal** *a.* containing miasmatic effluvia or germs. **Miasma·tic, Mia·smic, Mia·smous** *adjs.* having the nature of miasma, malarial.

Miaul (miˌǭ·l), *v.* 1632. [– Fr. *miauler*, of imit. origin.] **1.** *intr.* To call or cry as a cat. **2.** *trans.* To sing with a voice like that of a cat 1862. Hence **Miau·ler.**

Mica (məi·kă). 1684. [– L. *mica* grain, crumb; the mod.L. use in mineralogy (pl. *micæ*) was prob. orig. contextual ('a particle' of..), and the development of the specialized meaning was perh. furthered by assoc. with L. *micare* shine.] *Min.* †**1.** A small plate of talc, selenite, or the like, found in the structure of a rock. In pl. *micæ.* –1803. **2.** Any one of a group of minerals composed essentially of silicate of aluminium combined with the silicates of other bases, e.g. soda, potash, and magnesia, and occurring in small glittering scales in granite, etc., or in crystals characterized by their perfect basal cleavage and their consequent separability into thin, transparent, and usually flexible laminæ 1778.
Comb.: **m.-powder**, a form of dynamite in which the siliceous earth is replaced by m. in fine scales; **-schist, -slate,** a slaty metamorphic rock composed of quartz and m. Hence **Mica·ceous** *a.* containing or resembling m.; pertaining to or of the nature of m.

Mice (məis), pl. of MOUSE.

‖**Micella** (mise·lă). *Pl.* **micellæ** (-ī). 1882. [mod.L., dim. of L. *mica* crumb.] *Biol.* The hypothetical solid molecular aggregate of which Nägeli considered the organized structures of plants to consist. Hence **Mice·llar** *a.*

Michael (məi·kəl). OE. [repr. Heb. *mīkā'ēl*, lit. 'who is like God?' Gr. Μιχαήλ, L. *Michael.*] **1.** The name of one of the archangels. †**2.** = MICHAELMAS. –1622. **3.** As a common Christian name of men ME.
1. *The feast of St. M., St. Michael's day*: Michaelmas. *Order of St. M. and St. George*: an English civil order of knighthood instituted in 1818, now a reward for distinguished services in the colonies and abroad.

Michaelmas (mi·kəlmăs). [OE. *sancte Micheles mæsse* Saint Michael's mass, ME. *Mi(ȝh)elmasse* (XIII), *Mykylmes* (XV); see prec., MASS *sb.*[1]] The feast of St. Michael, 29 Sept., an English quarter-day. Also *attrib.*
Comb.: *M. goose, rent*; **M. daisy,** a sea-starwort, (*a*) wild aster (*Aster tripolium*); (*b*) one of several garden asters bearing masses of purplish flowers; **M. day** = Michaelmas; **M. eve,** the evening before M.; **M. term,** a term or session (beginning soon after M.) of the High Court of Justice in England; and also of Oxford, Cambridge, and other universities. **Old M. day**: the day that was 29 Sept. before the New Style was adopted; from 1900 onwards this has been 12 Oct.

Miche (mitʃ), *v.* Now *dial.* late ME. [app. – OFr. *muchier, mucier* hide; cf. (O)Fr. *musser*, Norm. dial. *mucher*. Cf. MEUSE *sb.*, MOOCH, MUSET.] †**1.** *trans.* To pilfer –1570. **2.** *intr.* To shrink or retire from view; to skulk. Also const. *off.* 1558. **b.** To play truant 1580. So **Mi·cher,** †a secret or petty thief ME. –1823; †one who skulks about for improper or dishonest purposes –1630; a truant (now *dial.*) 1530. †**Mi·chery,** pilfering, thievishness; cheating.

†**Miching malicho.** 1603. Usu. explained as 'skulking mischief' (MICHE *v.*, Sp. *malhecho* misdeed); but form, origin, and meaning are uncertain.
Marry this is Myching Mallico, that meanes Mischeefe *Haml.* III. ii. 146 (1st Qo.).

Mickle (mi·k'l), **muckle** (mɒ·k'l), *a.*, *sb.*, and *adv.* *Obs.* exc. *dial.* and *arch.* [north. and eastern ME. *mikel* (XIII), later north. *mekil* (whence Sc. *meikle*) – ON. *mikele* = OE. *micel* MUCH. The var. ME. *mukel* (XIV), later north. *muckle*, arose from assoc. with *muchel* MUCH.] **A.** *adj.* **1.** = GREAT *a.* **2.** A great quantity or amount of; = MUCH *a.* OE. **B.** *absol.* and *sb.* **1.** The adj. used *absol.* A great quantity or amount; much OE. †**2.** *sb.* Size, stature; bigness –1622. **3.** A large sum or amount. Chiefly in proverb, *Many a little* (or *pickle*) *makes a mickle.* 1599. **C.** *adv.* Greatly; by far OE.

Micklemote, -ġemote (mi·k'lmōᵘt, -gəmōᵘt). [repr. OE. *micel ġemōt*; see MICKLE *a.* and MOOT *sb.*[1]] *OE. Hist.* The great council or parliamentary assembly under the Anglo-Saxon kings.

Micracoustic (məikrăkau·stik). 1683. [In A – Fr. *micracoustique*, f. Gr. μικρός small + ἀκουστικός ACOUSTIC *a.*; in B, direct from the Greek.] **A.** *adj.* Making weak sounds audible 1855. †**B.** *sb.* An instrument which magnifies small sounds –1704.

Micro- (məi·kro), bef. a vowel **micr-**, repr. Gr. μικρο- comb. f. μικρός small.
1. Prefixed to a sb. to indicate relatively small size or extent, as *microbacillus, -bacterium, -gamete*, etc. **Mi·croblast** [-BLAST], *Biol.* = *microcyte.* ‖**Microco·ccus,** *pl.* **-cocci** (-kǫ·ksəi) [Gr. κόκκος berry], *Biol.* any one of a large genus of non-ciliated bacteria. **Mi·crocyte** [-CYTE], *Path.* a minute red blood-corpuscle. **Microfe·lsite,** *Geol.* and *Min.* a form of felsite incapable of resolution under the microscope. ‖**Microlepido·ptera,** *sb. pl.* *Entom.* a collector's term for certain small moths. **Mi·crolite, Mi·crolith** [Gr. λίθος stone], *Petrology*, the microscopic acicular particles contained in the glassy portions of feldspar, hornblende, etc. **Micro·rganism,** *Biol.* a microbe. **Mi·crophyte** [Gr. φυτόν plant], a microscopic plant, *esp.* a bacterium. **Mi·crosome** [Gr. σῶμα body], a name for certain small granules which abound in vegetating cells of protoplasm. **Microzo·ospore,** *Bot.* a minute motile spore.
2. Prefixed to sbs. and derived adjs. to denote 'microscopic' in the sense 'with the microscope', 'revealed by the microscope'; as, **a.** *micro-chemistry* (hence *-chemic* adj., etc.), *-crystallography, -geology* (hence *-geological* adj., *-geologist*), etc., branches of research carried on by means of microscopic examination; **b.** *micro-foliation, -structure*, properties revealed by the microscope; so *micro-crystalline, -granite*; **c.** *micro-section, -slide*, objects prepared for study with the microscope.
3. *Phys.* and *Path.*, in sbs. of mod.L. form in *-ia*, compounded with Gr. names for different parts or unctions of the body, and signifying arrested development of the part or function in question, as ‖**Microphtha·lmia** (also **Mi·crophthalmy**) [Gr. ὀφθαλμός], 'a Disease in the Eyes, the having little Eyes' (Bailey); hence **Microphtha·lmic** *a.* ‖**Micro·psia** [Gr. -οψία kind of vision], the state of vision in which objects appear smaller than natural.
4. Forming adjs. with sense 'containing or possessed of some object or constituent in minute form, quantity, or degree', as **Mi·crodont** [Gr. ὀδούς-, ὀδοντ-], *Anat.* having small or short teeth. **Microphy·llous** [Gr. φύλλον], *Bot.* having small leaves. **Micro·podal, -ic, -ous** [Gr. πούς-, ποδ- foot] small-footed. **Mi·croseme** [Gr. σῆμα sign], (of a skull) having an orbital index below 83. **Microsty·lous** *a.*, *Bot.* having a short style.
5. a. *Physics.* Prefixed to the name of a unit to form a name for one-millionth part of that unit, as *micro-ampere, -coulomb, -farad, -gramme, -litre, -millimetre, -ohm, -volt, -weber.* **b.** *Micro-millimetre*, (*a*) one-millionth of a millimetre; (*b*) *Bot.* one-thousandth of a millimetre.
6. Prefixed to names of instruments, as: **Micro-tasimeter,** an instrument for measuring infinitesimal pressure. **Micro-telephone,** a telephone constructed to render audible very weak sounds.

Microbe (məi·krōᵘb). 1881. Also ‖**micro·bion,** *pl.* **-ia** 1883. [– Fr. *microbe* (Sédillot, 1878), f. Gr. μικρός small + βίος life (used for 'living creature').] *Biol.* An extremely minute living being, whether plant or animal; chiefly applied to the bacteria causing diseases and fermentation. Hence **Micro·bial, Micro·bian, Micro·bic** *adjs.* of or pertaining to microbes; due to microbes.

Microbicide (məikrōᵘ·bisəid). 1885. [f. MICROBE + -CIDE 1.] *Biol.* **A.** *sb.* Something that kills microbes 1887. **B.** *adj.* Microbicidal. Hence **Micro·bicidal** *a.* pertaining to the killing of microbes.

Microbiology (məikrobəi,ǫ·lŏdʒi). 1885. [MICRO- 1.] *Biol.* The science which treats of micro-organisms. Hence **Microbiolo·gical** *a.* **Microbio·logist.**

‖**Microcephalic** (məikrosĭfæ·lik), *a.* 1856. [f. Gr. μικρός small + κεφαλή head.] *Path.* and *Anthropol.* Having an abnormally small head. So **Microce·phalous** *a.* 1840. **Microce·phaly** 1863.

Microcline (məi·krǫkləin). 1849. [– G. *mikroklin* (A. Breithaupt, 1830), f. Gr. μικρός + κλίνειν to incline, as indicating that the angle between its cleavage plane differs a little from 90 degrees.] *Min.* A green and blue variety of feldspar.

Microcosm (məi·krŏkǫz'm). ME. [– Fr. *microcosme* or med.L. *micro(s)cosmus* – Gr. μικρὸς κόσμος little world.] **1.** The 'little world' of human nature; man as an epitome of the 'great world' or universe. **2.** Hence, any community or other complex unity, viewed as an epitome of the world 1562. **b.** A 'miniature' representation *of* 1808. †**3.** *Alch.* The philosopher's stone 1477.

1. The doctrine of a constant analogy between universal nature, or the macrocosm, and that of man, or the m. HALLAM. Hence †**Microcos·mal** *a.*

Microcosmic (məikrokǫ·smik), *a.* 1783. [f. MICROCOSM + -IC.] **1.** Of, pertaining to, or of the nature of a microcosm 1816. **2.** *M. salt* [= L. *sal microcosmicus* (Bergmann)]: a phosphate of soda and ammonia, orig. derived from human urine, and much used as a blow-pipe flux. So **Microco·smical** *a.* 1570.

†**Mi:crocosmo·graphy.** 1606. [f. MICROCOSM + -GRAPHY.] The description of the 'microcosm' or man –1628.

Micrography (məikrǫ·grăfi). 1658. [f. MICRO- 2 + -GRAPHY. Cf. Fr. *micrographie* (XVII).] **1.** The description or delineation of microscopic objects. **2. a.** The art or practice of writing in microscopic characters. **b.** *Path.* Abnormally small handwriting, as a symptom of nervous disorder. 1899. Hence **Micro·grapher,** one addicted to m. **Microgra·phic** *a.* of or pertaining to m.; minutely written (as symptomatic of nervous disorder).

Microlithic (məikroli·þik), *a.* 1872. [f. Gr. μικρός + λίθος stone; see -IC.] *Antiq.* Consisting or constructed of small stones; *transf.* of a period, a people, etc. (opp. to MEGALITHIC).

Micrological (məikrolǫ·dʒikăl), *a.* 1847. [f. MICROLOGY + -ICAL.] **1.** Characterized by minuteness of investigation or discussion 1879. **2.** Of or pertaining to the study of minute objects; belonging to MICROLOGY 2. Hence **Microlo·gically** *adv.*

Micrology (məikrǫ·lŏdʒi). 1656. [– Gr. μικρολογία, f. μικρός small + -λογία; see -LOGY.] **1.** The discussion or investigation of petty affairs; 'hair-splitting'. **2.** (After MICROSCOPE.) That part of science which relates to the examination of minute objects; a treatise on microscopic objects 1849. So **Micro·logist,** one versed in m. (sense 2).

Micromere (məi·kromĭ°ɹ). 1877. [f. MICRO- 1 + Gr. μέρος part.] *Embryology.* The smaller of the two masses into which the vitellus of the developing ovum of *Lamellibranchiata* divides (cf. MACROMERE). Hence **Microme·ral, Microme·ric** *adjs.* of or pertaining to the m.

Micrometer (məikrǫ·mĭtəɹ). 1670. [– Fr. *micromètre,* f. Gr. μικρός small + μέτρον; see -METER.] An instrument for measuring minute objects or differences of dimension. **1.** An astronomical instrument applied to telescopes for measuring very small angular distances. **2.** An instrument applied to the microscope for measuring small objects 1790. **3.** An instrument used in machine-construction, watchmaking, etc., for obtaining extreme accuracy in measurement; also *m. calliper(s, gauge* 1884.

attrib. and *Comb.*, as *m. cell, eye-piece,* etc.; **m. balance,** a balance for ascertaining minute weights, esp. in weighing coins; **m.-microscope,** an apparatus for reading and subdividing the divisions of large astronomical and geodetical instruments; **m. screw,** a screw attached to optical and other instruments for the exact measurement of very small angles. Hence **Microme·tric, -al** *a.* pertaining to or of the nature of a m.; carried on by or resulting from the use of a m. **Microme·trically** *adv.* **Micro·metry,** the measurement of minute objects; the use of the m.

Micron, mikron (məi·krǫn). 1892. [– Gr. μικρόν n. of μικρός small.] The one-millionth part of a metre; denoted by the symbol μ.

Micronesian (məikronī·ʃ'ăn). 1896. [f. *Micronesia* (intended to mean 'the region of small islands'), f. Gr. μικρός + νῆσος + -AN.] **A.** *adj.* Of or pertaining to Micronesia (a group of small islands in the western region of the North Pacific, including the Caroline, Ladrone, Marshall and Gilbert Islands, etc.), its inhabitants, language, etc. **B.** *sb.* A native of Micronesia; the language of the Micronesians.

Microphone (məi·krofōᵘn). 1683. [f. MICRO- + -PHONE.] **1.** An instrument by which small sounds can be intensified. **2.** *spec.* An instrument by means of which the telephone is made to reproduce faint sounds with added intensity 1878. Hence **Micropho·nic** *a.*; *sb. pl.* the science of magnifying sounds. **Micro·phonous** *a.* having the property of augmenting weak sounds.

Microphonograph (məi:krofōᵘ·nŏgrɑf). 1897. [f. as prec. + PHONOGRAPH.] An instrument combining the principles of the microphone and the phonograph, designed for rendering sound audible to deaf-mutes.

Microphotograph (məi:krofōᵘ·tŏgrɑf). 1858. [f. MICRO- + PHOTOGRAPH.] **1.** A photograph reduced to microscopic size. **2.** = PHOTOMICROGRAPH 1860. Hence **Microphotogra·phic** *a.* **Microphotogra·phically** *adv.*

Microphotography (məi:krofŏtǫ·grăfi). 1858. [f. MICRO- + PHOTOGRAPHY.] **1.** The art or process of making microphotographs. **2.** = PHOTOMICROGRAPHY 1858.

Micropyle (məi·kropəil). 1821. [– Fr. *micropyle,* f. Gr. μικρός small + πύλη gate.] **1.** *Bot.* The foramen in the integument of an ovule, by which the pollen penetrates to the apex of the nucleus or radicle. Also, the corresponding external aperture in the mature seed. **2.** *Zool.* A special opening in a female cell for the entrance of the fertilizing cell 1859. Hence **Micropy·lar** *a.*

Microscope (məi·krŏskōᵘp). 1656. [– mod.L. *microscopium,* f. Gr. μικρός; see MICRO-, -SCOPE. Cf. Fr. *microscope.*] **1.** An optical instrument, consisting of a lens or a combination of lenses (or, rarely, also of mirrors) by which objects are so magnified that details invisible to the naked eye are clearly revealed. Also *transf.* and *fig.* **2.** *Astron.* (Also **Microsco·pium.**) A constellation south of Capricorn 1752.

1. *Lucernal, solar, oxy-hydrogen microscopes*: instruments of the nature of the magic lantern, illuminated by a lamp, the sun, and an oxy-hydrogen limelight respectively. *fig.* The critic Eye, that m. of Wit, Sees hairs and pores POPE. Hence **Micro·scopist,** one skilled in the use of the m. **Micro·scopy,** the art or practice of using the m.; the science of the microscopist.

Microscopic (məikrŏskǫ·pik), *a.* 1680. [f. prec. + -IC. Cf. Fr. *microscopique.*] **1.** = MICROSCOPICAL *a.* 1. Now *rare* exc. *fig.* 1779. **2.** Possessing or exercising the functions of a microscope 1680. **3.** So minute as to be invisible or indistinct without the use of a microscope *c*1760.

1. *fig.* A m. self-examination 1850. **2.** Why has not Man a m. eye? For this plain reason, Man is not a Fly POPE. **3.** *fig.* Turner's m. touch RUSKIN.

Microscopical (məikrŏskǫ·pikăl), *a.* 1664. [f. as prec. + -AL¹; see -ICAL.] **1.** Pertaining to the microscope or its use; resembling what pertains to a microscope. **2.** = MICROSCOPIC 3. Now *rare.* 1665. Hence **Microsco·pically** *adv.*

Microseism (məikrosəi·z'm). 1887. [f. Gr. μικρός small + σεισμός shaking, earthquake.] A faint earthquake tremor. So **Microsei·smic, -al** *a.* 1877. **Microsei·smograph,** an instrument for recording microseisms 1881. **Microseismo·logy, -o·metry.**

Microspe·ctroscope. 1867. [f. MICRO- + SPECTROSCOPE.] A combination of the microscope and spectroscope devised for the examination of the absorptive spectrum of very minute quantities of substances.

Microspore (məi·krospōᵊɹ). 1856. [f. MICRO- + SPORE.] **1.** *Bot.* and *Path.* A parasitic fungus which has small spores, characteristic of ring-worm. **2.** *Bot.* One of the small (quasi-male) spores of certain cryptogams; opp. to MACROSPORE 1858. **3.** *Zool.* A spore-like form in Protozoa 1882. So ‖**Micro·sporon** (in sense 1) 1876. **Mi:crospora·nge, -a·ngium** *Bot.* a capsule containing microspores 1881.

Microtome (məi·krŏtōᵘm). 1856. [f. Gr. μικρός + -τόμος -TOME¹.] An instrument for cutting extremely thin sections for microscopic work. **Microto·mic, -al** *a.*, **Micro·tomist, Micro·tomy.**

‖**Microzoa** (məikrozōᵘ·ă), *sb. pl.* In sing. **-zoon** (-zōᵘ·ǫn). 1862. [mod.L., f. Gr. μικρός small + ζῷον animal.] *Zool.* A general name for infusoria, rotifers, etc. Hence **Microzo·al, Microzo·ic** *adjs.* of the nature of, containing, or consisting of m.

Microzyme (məi·krozəim). Also **microzyma** (məikrozəi·mă). 1870. [f. MICRO- 1 + Gr. ζύμη yeast.] *Biol.* A zymotic microbe, to whose presence are attributed epidemic and other zymotic diseases.

Micturition (miktiŭri·ʃən). 1725. [f. pa. ppl. stem of L. *micturire,* desiderative formation on *mict-, minct-,* pa. ppl. stem of *mingere* make water; see -ION] The desire to make water; a morbid frequency in the voiding of urine. Often erron.: The action of making water.

Mid (mid), *a., sb.*¹, and *adv.* [OE. **midd,* only in oblique forms *midde, middes,* etc. (cf. AMID), corresp. to OFris. *midde,* OS. *middi,* OHG. *mitti,* ON. *miðr,* Goth. *midjis* :– Gmc. **miðja-,* **meðja-* :– IE. **medhjo-,* whence also L. *medius,* Gr. μέσσος, later μέσος MESO-.] **A.** *adj.* **1.** Expressing adjectively the sense: (The) middle or midst of. (Now usu. hyphened.) **2.** Occupying a central, medial, or intermediate position. Now usu. superseded by MIDDLE *a.* late ME. **3.** *Phonetics.* Of a vowel-sound: Produced with the tongue or part of it in a middle position, between high and low 1876. **B.** *sb.*¹ *Obs.* exc. *dial.* The adj. used *absol.* = MIDDLE *sb.* ME. †**C.** *adv.* In the middle –1576.

A. 1. The plough was in m.-furrow stayed SCOTT. *Comb.*: *m.-career, -channel, -ocean, -season,* etc. **M.-brain,** the middle segment of the brain: = MESENCEPHALON; **-breast** *Entom.*, the underside of the mesothorax; **-totality** *Astr.*, the middle of the duration of the totality of an eclipse; **-wicket** in *Cricket,* the fieldsman or his position on the off-side; also *m.-wicket off, on* = MID-OFF, MID-ON. The M.-Victorian style of domestic architecture 1902. **2.** In the m.-days of autumn KEATS. *Comb.*: **m.-gut,** the mesenteron; **-iron** *Golf,* an iron with medium loft; also a stroke made with this; **-spoon** *Golf,* a spoon of medium size; **-watch,** the middle watch; **-workings,** workings with other workings above and below in the same mine or colliery.

Mid, *sb.*² 1797. Joc. shortening of MIDSHIPMAN.

†**Mid,** *prep.*¹ (*adv.*). [OE. *mid* (Northumb. *mið*), corresp. to OFris. *mith,* OS. *mid* (Du. *met*), OHG., G. *mit,* ON. *með,* Goth. *miþ,* cogn. with Gr. μετά META-. Superseded XIV by WITH.] = WITH in all senses, except that of 'against' (as in *to fight with*) –ME.

Mid, 'mid (mid), *prep.*² 1808. Poet. aphesis of AMID.

†**Mid-age.** 1440. [f. MID *a.* + AGE *sb.*] = MIDDLE AGE –1757.

Mid air. 1667 (Milton). The tract between the clouds and the part of the atmosphere near the ground: chiefly in phr. *in mid air.*

Midas (məi·dæs). 1568. [– L. *Midas,* Gr. Μίδας.] **1.** The name of a fabled king of Phrygia, whose touch turned everything (including his food) into gold. Apollo gave him ass's ears for being dull to the charm of his lyre. Hence *allusively.* Also *attrib.* **2.** *Midas's ear*: the shell of a gastropod, *Auricula midæ* 1713.

1. Thou gaudie gold, Hard food for M. SHAKS. The M. finger of the State COWPER.

Mid-course. 1513. [f. MID *a.* + COURSE.] The middle of one's or its course.

Midday (mi·dᵢdeⁱ; stress variable). [OE. *middæġ* (MID *a.*, DAY *sb.*).] **1.** The middle of the day; noon. †**2.** The South –1604.

1. Ere mid-day arriv'd in Eden MILT. *attrib.* and *Comb.*, as *m.-devotions, -dinner, -post, -splendour*, etc. Also †**m. devil, fiend,** transl. of Vulg. *dæmonium meridianum* Ps. 90[1]:6, for which the Eng. Bible has 'the destruction that wasteth at noonday'.

Midden (mi·d'n). Now *dial.* (rarely *arch.*). [ME. *mydding*, of Scand. origin; identical with Da. *mødding*, earlier *møgdyng(e*, f. *møg* MUCK + *dynge* heap (cf. DUNG), Norw. dial. *mykjardunge, mitting*.] **1.** A dunghill. Also *fig.* **2.** Short for KITCHEN-MIDDEN 1866.

Middenstead (mi·d'nsted). 1607. [f. MIDDEN + STEAD.] The place where a dunghill is formed; a laystall.

Middest (mi·dėst), *a. superl.* 1590. [f. MID *a.* + -EST.] Most central; in the middle.

Middle (mi·d'l). [OE. *middel, midl-* adj. and (by ellipsis) sb. m. = OFris. *middel* adj., OS. *middil-* in comps. (Du. *middel* adj. and sb.), OHG. *mittil* (G. *mittel* adj. and sb.) :– WGmc. **middila*, f. **middi* :– Gmc. **miðja-* MID + *-il* -LE.] **A.** *adj.* Not in predicative use. **1.** (Orig. in *superl.*) Used of that member of a group or sequence, or that part of a whole, which has the same number of members or parts on each side of it. **b.** Of a point or line: Equidistant from the extremities. late ME. †**c.** Average, mean –1790. **2.** Intermediate, intervening (see quots.) ME. **3.** In partitive concord: = '(The) middle or middle part of; mid.' Now *rare*. OE. **4.** *Philology.* **a.** *Gram.* Intermediate between active and passive: primarily (after Gr. *μέση διάθεσις, μέσον ῥῆμα*), the designation of a voice of Gr. verbs expressing reflexive or reciprocal action or intrans. conditions. **b.** Prefixed (after G. *mittel-*) to the name of a language, to denote a period in its history intermediate between those called *Old* and *New* or *Modern*, as in *Middle-English* (see ENGLISH *sb.*¹ 1 b), etc. **5.** *Geol.* Prefixed to the designation of a formation or period, to denote a subdivision intermediate between two others called 'Upper' and 'Lower' 1838.

1. That m. time of life which is happily tempered with the warmth of youth GOLDSM. *M. brother, sister, son*, etc. (*legal*): the second in age of three brothers, etc. *M. price* (Stock Exchange): the price intermediate between a jobber's buying and selling prices. **2.** They..speed the race, And spurring see decrease the m. space DRYDEN. Men of a m. condition SOUTH. A m. opinion 1782. A man of m. stature SCOTT. **3.** Neuer since the m. Summers spring Met we SHAKS. **5.** M. lias shale 1838.

Special collocations. **m. C** *Mus.*, the note on the first ledger line below the treble stave or above the bass stave; **m. deck,** the deck between the upper and lower decks; **m. distance** (see DISTANCE); **m. ear,** the tympanum; **M. Empire** = *Middle Kingdom*; **m. finger,** the second finger; **m. ground** *Naut.*, a shallow place, formerly a bank or bar; *Painting* = *middle distance*; **M. Kingdom,** a name for the 18 provinces of China proper, or the whole Chinese Empire; **m. line** (*a*) *Naut.*, a line dividing the ship exactly in the middle; (*b*) *Croquet*, the line of hoops placed in the m. of the lawn; **m. passage,** the m. portion (i.e. the part consisting of sea travel) of the journey of a slave carried from Africa to America; **m. pointed** *a. Arch.*, a name for Decorated Gothic; **m. post,** in *Carpentry* = KING-POST; **m. space** *Printing*, a space intermediate in size between 'thick' and 'thin'; **M. States,** the States which originally formed the m. part of the United States, intermediate between New England and the Southern States, namely, New York, New Jersey, Pennsylvania, and Delaware; **M. Temple** (see TEMPLE); **m. term** *Logic*, the term which is common to the premisses of a syllogism, and disappears in the conclusion; **m. tint** *Painting*, 'a mixed tint in which bright colours never predominate' (Fairholt); **m. wall,** a partition wall; **m. watch** *Naut.*, the watch from midnight to 4 a.m.; **m.-weight,** a man of average weight, *esp.* a boxer whose weight is from 11 st. 6 to 10 st. 7; **m. wicket** = *mid-wicket* (see MID *a.*).

B. *sb.* **1.** The middle point or part OE. **2.** = MIDST *sb.* 2. Now only in relation to an action, etc. OE. **3.** The middle part of the human body; the waist OE. **4.** A mean between two extremes ME. †**5.** Something intermediate –1667. **6.** *ellipt.* for various terms, as *middle term, voice* 1818. **7.** *Naut.* = *middle ground* 1702. **8.** *Football.* A return of the ball from one of the wings to mid-field in front of the goal 1899. **9.** (Orig. *m. article.*) A newspaper article on some social, ethical, or literary subject, such as is in some journals placed between the leading articles and the reviews 1862.

1. Canst thou..Murther thy breath in m. of a word? SHAKS. See, there come people downe by the m. of the land *Judg.* 9:37. **2.** I have often been stopped in the middle of a speech JOWETT. **3.** A long Wigg that reaches down to his M. ADDISON. **4.** The rights of men are in a sort of m. BURKE.

Middle (mi·d'l), *v.* 1841. [f. MIDDLE *sb.*] **1.** *Naut.* (*trans.*) To fold or double in the middle. **2.** *techn.* To place in the middle 1883. **3.** *trans.* in *Football.* To return (the ball) from one of the wings to mid-field in front of the goal; to centre. Also *absol.* 1871.

Middle age, *sb.* late ME. **1.** The period between youth and old age. **2.** *The M. Age* (1621), now usu. *the M. Ages* (1722): the period intermediate between 'ancient' and 'modern' times; in early use, from *c*500 to *c*1500; now loosely, the four centuries after A.D. 1000. **3.** *attrib.*, quasi-*adj.* (with hyphen). Belonging to the Middle Ages; mediæval 1753. So **Middle-aged** *a.* of middle age; characteristic of middle-aged people 1676; †mediæval 1710–1845.

Middle class, *sb.* 1812. The class of society between the 'upper' and the 'lower' class. Now usu. *pl.* Also *attrib.* (with hyphen). **b.** Used as *adj.* Characteristic of the middle classes; having the characteristics of the middle classes. (Depreciative.) 1893.

attrib., as in *m. education, life*, etc.; **m. examination,** an early name of the 'local examination' (LOCAL *a.* 2 c); **m. schools,** schools for the middle classes, intermediate between primary schools and the great public schools.

Middle earth. ME. **1.** [Perversion of ME. *middelerd*, alteration of *middenerd* (OE. *middanġeard*).] The earth as placed between heaven and hell. Now only *arch.*, occas. applied to the real world as dist. from fairyland. †**2.** *Sea of middle earth, middle earth sea*, the Mediterranean –1613.

1. That maid is born of middle earth, And may of man be won SCOTT.

Middleman (mi·d'lmæn). 1616. [f. MIDDLE *a.* + MAN *sb.*] †**1.** *Mil.* One of the soldiers in the fifth or sixth rank in a file of 10 deep –1696. **2.** One who takes a middle course 1741. **3.** (Orig. two words.) A person standing in intermediate relation to two parties concerned in some matter of business; usu. in an unfavourable sense. Chiefly applied to traders as intermediate between producers and consumers. 1795. **b.** In Ireland, one who leases land, and sub-lets it again at an advanced rate 1802.

3. The Metcalfes..were middlemen between the vendors and the vendees 1805.

Middlemost (mi·d'lmōᵘst), *a.* Now somewhat *rare*. ME. [f. MIDDLE *a.* + -MOST.] That is in the very middle, or nearest the middle. Now only with ref. to position.

Middler (mi·d'ləɹ). 1531. [f. MIDDLE *a.* + -ER¹.] †**1.** An intermediary, mediator –1675. **2.** The workman who performs the middle one of three operations in the preparation of flax 1847.

Middle way. ME. **1.** A course between two extremes. Cf. mod.L. *via media*. **2.** The middle of the way 1633. **b.** Used *advb.* Half-way, on the way 1568.

Middling (mi·dliŋ), *sb.* 1543. [prob. orig. f. MID *a.* + -LING¹; now the adj. used absol. or ellipt.] †**1.** Something intermediate; a middle term –1620. **2.** *pl.* Pins of medium size 1543. **3.** *pl.* Used as a trade name for the middle one of three grades of goods; e.g. *U.S.* of cotton 1793; of flour or meal 1842. **4.** *U.S.* The portion of a hog between the ham and the shoulder 1859.

Middling (mi·d'liŋ), *a.* and *adv.* 1456. [First in Sc. use; prob. f. MID *a.* + -LING². Cf. OE. *mydlinga* moderately.] **A.** *adj.* †**1.** Intermediate between two things; forming a mean –1767. **2.** Of medium size; moderately large. Now *colloq.* or *vulgar.* 1596. †**b.** Average. HUME. **3.** *Comm.* Used to designate the second of three grades of goods 1550. **b.** Moderately good, mediocre 1652. **4.** Belonging to the middle classes 1692.

3. b. The abundant consumption of m. literature M. ARNOLD. **4.** The m. classes SCOTT. The m. strata of society 1897.

B. *adv.* (Now chiefly *colloq.*) **1.** Moderately, fairly, tolerably 1719. **2.** Fairly well; chiefly *predicatively*, not very well in health 1810.

1. A m. good Anvil DE FOE. **2.** 'How de do?' 'Middling' replies Mr. George DICKENS. Hence **Mi·ddlingly** *adv.*

Middy (mi·di). *colloq.* 1833. [f. MID *sb.*² + -Y⁶.] A midshipman.

Mid-earth. 1559. = MIDDLE EARTH.

Mid-feather.˙ 1748. **1.** *Salt-making.* A partition in a furnace dividing the flue into two chambers. **2.** *Mining.* A support for the centre of a tunnel 1897.

Mid-field. late ME. The middle of the field. Now chiefly in *Football.*

Midge (midʒ). [OE. *myċġ(e*, corresp. to OS. *muggia* (Du. *mug*), OHG. *mucca* (G. *mücke*), ON. *mý* (Sw. *mygg, mygga*):– Gmc. **muʒjaz*, **muʒjōn*, rel. to L. *musca* fly, Gr. *μυῖα*] **1.** A popular name given to many small gnat-like insects; by some restricted to the *Chironomidæ*. **b.** A diminutive person 1796. **2.** The fry of various fishes 1832.

Midget (mi·dʒėt). 1865. [f. MIDGE + -ET.] An extremely small person; *spec.* such a person exhibited as a curiosity; *transf.* anything very small of its kind; also *attrib.* So **Mi·dgety** *a.* very small. JANE AUSTEN.

A little m. of a man MRS. H. B. STOWE.

Mid-heaven. 1594. [MID *a.*] *Astron.* and *Astrol.* **1.** The meridian; the point of the ecliptic on the meridian. **2.** The midst of the heavens 1612.

2. Or how the Sun shall in mid Heav'n stand still MILT.

‖**Midinette** (midine·t). 1909. [Fr., f. *midi* mid-day + *dînette* light dinner.] A Parisian shop-girl, *esp.* a milliner's assistant.

Midland (mi·dlănd). 1555. [f. MID *a.* + LAND.] **A.** *sb.* The middle part of a country. Also *pl.* the middle counties of England. **B.** *adj.* **1.** Situated inland; remote from the sea 1601. **b.** Belonging to the Midlands 1837. **2.** = MEDITERRANEAN *a.* 2. 1579.

1. *M. counties* (of England): the counties south of the Humber and Mersey and north of the Thames, except Norfolk, Suffolk, Essex, Middlesex, Hertfordshire, Gloucestershire, and the counties bordering on Wales. **b. M. dialect,** the dialect spoken in the m. counties. S. Lancashire, the Welsh border, Lincolnshire, and E. Anglia. **2.** *M. sea*, the Mediterranean Sea. O'er the blue M. waters with the gale, Betwixt the Syrtes and soft Sicily M. ARNOLD.

Mid leg. 1500. [MID *a.*] **1.** The middle of the leg. **b.** *advb.* To the middle of the leg 1829. **2.** *Entom.* One of the intermediate or second pair of legs of an insect 1826.

Mid-lent. 1450. [MID *a.*] *M.* (*Sunday*), the 4th Sunday in Lent.

Midmost (mi·dmoᵘst). [alt. (by assoc. with -MOST) of OE., ME. *midmest*, also OE., OFris. *medemest*; for formation and development cf. FOREMOST.] **A.** *adj.* **1.** That is in the very middle. **b.** *absol.* The midmost part. late ME. **2.** In partitive concord: The middle or midst of 1807. **3.** Most intimate. HAWTHORNE.

1. b. From the m. of Ida SWINBURNE. **2.** High in the m. city the horse pours forth from its side Warriors armed BOWEN.

B. *adv.* In the middle or midst 1700. **b.** *prep.* In the middle or midst of 1867.

b. M. the beating of the steely sea MORRIS.

Midnight (mi·dnəit). [OE. *midniht*, f. MID *a.* + NIGHT.] **1.** The middle of the night; 12 o'clock at night. **2.** *transf.* and *fig.* Intense darkness; a period of intense darkness 1593. **3.** *attrib.* Of or pertaining to midnight, occurring at midnight, meeting at midnight. late ME.; dark as midnight 1601.

1. 'Tis now dead m. SHAKS. **2.** The dark m. of papacy 1665. **3.** Survey this M. Scene YOUNG. The m. train from Liverpool-street to Norwich 1905.

attrib. and *Comb.*, as **m. oil,** used *fig.* in phr. *to burn* (etc.) *the m. oil*, to sit up or work after m.; **m. sun,** the sun as seen in the Arctic regions at m.

Wee spend our mid-day sweat, our mid-night oyle QUARLES.

Midnoon (midnūn; stress variable). Now *rare* or *Obs.* 1580. [f. MID *a.* + NOON, after *midday, midnight*, to corresp. to *afternoon, forenoon*.] Midday; noon.

Gentlewoemen..who begin their morning at midnoone LYLY.

Mid-o·ff. 1881. [Short for *mid-wicket off*: see MID *a.*] *Cricket.* A fieldsman on the off-side, in front of the batsman and near the bowler. Also the place where he stands.

Mid-o·n. 1881. [Cf. prec.] *Cricket.* A fieldsman on the on-side, in front of the batsman and near the bowler. Also the place where he stands.

‖**Midrash** (mi·dræʃ). *Pl.* **midrashim** (midrā·ʃīm). 1613. [bibl. Heb. *midrāš* = 'commentary' (2 Chron. 24:27, R. V.), f. root *dāraš* study, in post-biblical Hebrew expound.] An ancient Jewish homiletic commentary on some portion of the Hebrew scriptures, in which allegory and legendary illustration were freely used. Hence **Midra·shic** *a.*

Midrib (mi·drib). 1696. [f. MID *a.* + RIB.] †**1.** In phr. *m. deep*, up to the middle of the ribs (of a horse) –1807. **2.** *Bot.* A principal rib continuous with the petiole extending through the middle of the blade of a leaf 1776. Hence **Mi·dribbed** *ppl. a.*

Midriff (mi·drif). [OE. *midhrif* (= OFris. *midref*), f. **midd* MID *a.* + *hrif* belly = OFris. *hrif, href*, OHG. *href*, of obsc. origin.] **1.** The diaphragm. †**2.** *transf.* A partition –1766.

1. *To shake, tickle the m.*: said of what causes laughter. A sight to shake The m. of despair with laughter TENNYSON.

Mids. [ME. *middes*, evolved from the advs. *in-middes, on-middes* (cf. IN MID, AMIDST; also *to-mids*).] **A.** *sb.* **1.** The middle; the midst. *Obs.* exc. *Sc.* †**2.** A means –1710. **3.** A mean; a middle course, a compromise. *Obs.* exc. *Sc.* 1553. †**B.** *prep.* In the middle of –1611.

Mid-sea. late ME. The open sea.

Mid-season. 1610. †**1.** Noon. SHAKS. **2.** The middle of the season. Also *attrib.* 1882.

Midship (mi·dʃip). 1555. [f. MID *a.* + SHIP.] The middle part of a ship or boat.

Comb.: **m. beam,** the longest beam of a ship, lodged in the m. frame; **m. bend, frame,** that timber or frame in a ship which has the greatest breadth; **m. port,** a porthole in the middle part of a ship.

Midshipman (mi·dʃipmæ̆n). 1601. [f. prec. + MAN. So called because stationed 'amidships' when on duty.] In the navy, a rank intermediate between that of naval cadet and that of sub-lieutenant or in the U.S. navy that of ensign. Hence **Mi·dshipmanship.** COWPER.

Midshipmite (mi·dʃipməit). 1833. A sailor's perversion of MIDSHIPMAN.

Midships (mi·dʃips). 1626. [prob. of LG. origin (Du. *midscheeps*, f. *mid* MID *a.* + *scheeps*, gen. of *schip* SHIP *sb.*[1]; cf. G. *mittschiffs*).] **1.** *sb.* The middle part of a ship. **2.** *adv.* = AMIDSHIPS 1838.

Midst (midst), *sb., adv.,* and *prep.* [ME. *middest*, alt. of †*middes* (XIV), which was evolved from advb. phr. *in middes, on middes*, alterations of *in middan, on middan*, where the prep. governs the dat. of *midde* (see MID *sb.*[1]), or the weak-inflected adj.] **A.** *sb.* **1.** The middle point or part; the centre, middle. *Obs.* or *arch.* **2.** *In the m. of*: Among, amid, surrounded by (a number of things or persons); also, 'in the thick of' (troubles, etc.); during the continuance of (an action, etc.) 1500. **b.** (*In*) *our, your, their m.*: among us, you, etc. 1586 (rare before 19th c.). †**3.** A middle course or term, mean. *Sc.* –1786.

2. In the myddest of lyfe we be in death *Bk. Com. Prayer.* In the m. of an adventure JOHNSON, of peace MACAULAY.

B. *adv.* **1.** In the middle place. Only in Milton's phrase. 1667. **2.** = 'In the midst'. Const. *of. poet. rare.* 1675.

1. Ioyn..to extoll Him first, him last, him m., and without end MILT.

C. *prep.* In the midst of. Commonly written *'midst*, as if aphet. for AMIDST. 1591.

M. others of less note, came one frail Form SHELLEY.

Midstream (mi:dstrī·m). ME. [MID *a.*] The middle of the stream.

Midsummer (mi·dsɒməɹ). [OE. *midsumor*; see MID *a.* and SUMMER.] **1.** The middle of summer; the period of the summer solstice, about June 21st. **2.** = *M. Day* 1530.

attrib. and *Comb.*, as **m. daisy,** *Chrysanthemum leucanthemum*; **M. Day,** the 24th of June, an English quarter-day; **m. madness,** the height of madness; †**m. moon,** the lunar month in which M. Day comes; a time when lunacy is supposed to be prevalent.

Mid-water. 1653. The middle portion of the water vertically.

Red-spotted trout poised in m. HOLMAN HUNT.

Midway (mi·dwē[i]·, *adj.* mi·dwē[i]). OE. [MID *a.*] **A.** *sb.* †**1.** The middle of the way or distance –1770. †**2.** A medium; a middle course, *via media* 1599–1677. **B.** *adj.* **1.** Situated in the middle of the way (*rare* exc. *poet.*) 1605. †**2.** Medium, moderate –1675. **C.** *adv.* In the middle of the way or distance; half-way ME. **D.** *prep.* In the middle of (*rare*) c1798.

A. 3. *U.S.* The entertainment section of an exhibition or fair 1901. (From the inclusion of the 'Midway Plaisance' of Chicago in the grounds of the exposition of 1893).

Mid-week. 1706. [f. MID *a.* + WEEK. Cf. MDu. *middeweke*, MHG. *mittewoche* (G. *mittwoch*), ON. *miðvika* Wednesday.] The middle of the week. In Quaker use, a synonym for Fourth-day or Wednesday.

Midwife (mi·dwəif, *rare colloq.* mi·dif), *sb.* ME. [prob. f. MID *prep.*[1] + WIFE in the sense 'woman' (so †*midwoman* XIII), the notion being 'a woman who is *with* the mother at birth' (cf. the etymol. meaning of *obstetric*).] **1.** A woman who assists other women in childbirth; a female accoucheur. †**2.** = MAN-MIDWIFE –1770. **3.** *fig.* One who or that which helps to produce or bring anything to birth 1593.

1. She [Queen Mab] is the Fairies M. SHAKS. 3. And M. Time the ripen'd Plot to Murder brought DRYDEN.

Midwife (mi·dwəif), *v.* Now *rare.* 1638. [f. prec.] **1.** *trans.* To act as midwife to 1674. **2.** To help in bringing (a child) to the birth by acting the part of a midwife 1638. Also *fig.*

Midwifery (mi·dwifri, *rarely* mi·difri). 1483. [f. MIDWIFE *sb.* + -ERY.] The art or practice of assisting women in childbirth; the department of medical knowledge relating to this; obstetrics.

Midwinter (midwintəɹ; stress variable). OE. [f. MID *a.* + WINTER.] The middle of the winter; *spec.* the winter solstice, Dec. 21st. Also formerly applied to Christmas. **b.** quasi-*adj.* (*fig.*), cold as midwinter 1870. Hence **Midwintry,** *a.*

Mien (mīn). Only *literary.* 1513. [Early forms *men(e, meane, mine*; prob. aphet. f. DEMEAN *sb.*, later assim. to Fr. *mine* look, aspect.] The air, bearing, or manner of a person, as expressing character or mood. †Also *transf.* of a thing. †**b.** Expression (of the face) = Fr. *mine du visage. rare.* 1680–1699.

See..Fops at all corners, lady-like in m. COWPER.

Miff (mif), *sb. colloq.* and *dial.* 1623. [perh. imitative; cf. early mod.G. *muff* int. and sb., a manifestation of disgust.] A petty quarrel; a huff, tiff. Hence **Miff** *a. rare*, out of humour (*with*). **Mi·ffy** *a.* easily offended. Also *transf.* of delicate plants.

Miff (mif), *v.* 1797. [f. MIFF *sb.*] **1.** *trans.* To take offence *with* or *at*. Also *transf.* of a plant, *to m. off*, to go off, fade. **2.** *trans.* To put out of humour 1824.

Might (məit). [OE. *miht*, for *mieht*, non-WS. *mæht* = OFris. *mecht, macht*, OS., OHG. *maht* (Du., G. *macht*), Goth. *mahts* :– Gmc. **maχtiz*, f. **maʒ-* be able; see MAY *v.*[1], -T[1].] **1.** The quality of being able (to do, etc.); operative power. Const. *inf. Obs.* exc. *poet.* **b.** Power, efficacy, virtue (of impersonal agents). *Obs.* exc. *poet.* OE. †**2.** Bodily strength (great or small) –1611. **3.** Great or transcendent power or strength. Now somewhat *rhet.* OE. **4.** Power to enforce one's will. Chiefly in contrast with *right.* ME. †**5.** *pl.* The fifth of the nine orders of angels: = VIRTUE 1 b. –1652.

1. For to be wise and loue, Exceedes man's m. SHAKS. Phr. *With all one's m.*, with all one's powers. **b.** Dead Shepheard, now I find thy saw of m. SHAKS. Phr. †*The fivefold mights*: the five senses. **2.** Their m. hath failed, they became as women *Jer.* 51:30. **3.** Divinest Shakespeare's m. SHELLEY. The m. Of the whole world's good wishes WORDSW. The whole m. of England 1857. **4.** They went to war, preferring m. to right JOWETT.

Might, pa. t. of MAY *v.*[1]

Mightful (məi·tfŭl), *a. arch.* ME. [f. MIGHT + -FUL.] Mighty; †efficacious.

Might-have-been. 1848. [Cf. MAYBE.] That which might have been; a person who might have been greater or more eminent.

Mightily (məi·tili), *adv.* OE. [f. MIGHTY *a.* + -LY[2].] **1.** With great power or strength; with powerful effect; †also, with great effort, vehemently. **2.** In a great degree, to a great extent; greatly 1593 (common 17th–18th c.).

1. Let man and beast..cry m. vnto God *Jonah* 3:8. **2.** I sat m. behind, and could see but little PEPYS.

Mi·ghtiness. late ME. [f. MIGHTY *a.* + -NESS.] The state or condition of being mighty. Also as a title of dignity.

Thinke you see them Great..: Then, in a moment, see How soone this Mightinesse meets Misery SHAKS. *High M.*, a title of dignity; esp. *pl.* = Du. *hoogmogendheden*, the members of the States-General of the United Provinces of the Netherlands; hence *gen.* in ironical use.

Mightless (məi·tlĕs), *a.* Now *arch.* ME. [f. MIGHT + -LESS.] Powerless.

†**Mi·ghtly,** *adv.* [OE. *mihteliće*, var. of *mihtiġlice*.] = MIGHTILY –1744.

Mighty (məi·ti), *a.* and *adv.* [OE. *mihtiġ*; see MIGHT and -Y[1].] **A.** *adj.* **1.** Possessing might or power; potent, strong. Now only *rhet.*, connoting greatness of power. **2.** Of huge proportions; massive, bulky. late ME. **3.** Of things, actions, events, agent-nouns: Very great in amount, extent, or degree. In later use chiefly *colloq.* 1586. **4.** quasi-*sb.* (with *pl.*) A mighty person. Chiefly *pl.* late ME.

1. Fear not, isle of blowing woodland...thou shalt be the m. one yet! TENNYSON. *M. works*, in biblical use (= Gr. δυνάμεις): miracles. **2.** The lone wood and m. hill SCOTT. **3.** A m. flux of blood CULPEPPER. A m. Favourite with the Captain 1743.

B. *adv.* (Qualifying an adj. or adv.) In a great degree; greatly; exceedingly; very. Formerly common *colloq.* (now chiefly ironical and U.S.). ME.

That is all m. fine DICKENS.

†**Migniard,** *a.* and *sb.* 1599. [– Fr. *mignard*, var. by suffix-change of *mignon*; see next, -ARD.] **A.** *adj.* Dainty; mincing; caressing –1653. **B.** *sb.* A courtesan, mistress –1652. So †**Migniardise,** caressing treatment; affected delicacy 1603–1689. †**Migniardize** *v.* to make (language) affected in character; to treat (a person) caressingly 1598–1670.

‖**Mignon** (min[y]oṅ), *a.* Also **-onne** fem. 1556. [Fr.] Small and delicately formed.

Mignonette (minyəne·t). 1721. [– Fr. *mignonnette*, dim. of *mignon*; see prec., -ETTE.] **1.** A plant (*Reseda odorata*) having fragrant blossoms 1798. **b.** The colour of these; greyish green or greenish white 1885. **2.** (More fully *m. lace.*) A light fine kind of lace. *Hist.*

Comb. **m. pepper,** coarsely ground pepper.

‖**Migraine** (migrẹn). 1777. [Fr.; see MEGRIM[1].] = MEGRIM[1] 1. Hence **Migrai·nous** *a.*

Migrant (məi·grănt), *a.* and *sb.* 1672. [– *migrant-*, pr. ppl. stem of L. *migrare*; see -ANT.] **A.** *adj.* Migrating; given to migration. **B.** *sb.* A migratory bird or other animal; a person who migrates 1760.

Migrate (məi·gre[i]t), *v.* 1697. [– *migrat-*, pa. ppl. stem of L. *migrare*; see -ATE[3].] **1.** *intr.* To pass from one place to another. Also *trans.* in *pass.* To be transported. **2.** *intr.* To move from one place of abode to another; *esp.* to leave one's country to settle in another; to remove to another country, town, college, university, etc. 1770. **b.** *Nat. Hist.* Of some animals: To go from one habitat to another; *spec.* of some birds and fishes, to come and go regularly with the seasons 1753. **c.** *fig.* Of inanimate objects: To undergo removal from one place to another 1929.

2. The agricultural labourer is tempted..to m. to a manufacturing town SIR B. BRODIE. **b.** Birds which m. in autumn 1889. Hence **Mi·grative** *a.* migratory. **Migra·tor,** one who migrates; *spec.* a migratory bird.

Migration (məigrē[i]·ʃən). 1611. [– L. *migratio*, f. as prec.; see -ION.] The action, an act, of migrating.

Comb.: **m.-station,** a fixed place for the regular observation of the m. of birds.

Migratory (məi·grătəri), *a.* 1753. [f. MIGRATE *v.* + -ORY^2.] **1.** Characterized by migration; given to migrating; *esp.* of animals, given to periodical migration 1753. **b.** Of a bodily organ, a disease, etc.: Characterized by movement from its normal position; *esp.* in *Histology* of a cell: Given to migration from the blood-vessels to the tissues 1876. **2.** Of or pertaining to migration 1757.
2. The m. passages of the reindeer KANE.

||**Mikado** (mikā·do). 1727. [Jap. *mi* august + *kado* door; cf. 'Sublime Porte'.] The title of the emperor of Japan.

Mike. Colloq. abbrev. of MICROPHONE.

Mil (mil). 1721. [– L. *mille* thousand; in senses 2 and 3 short for L. *millesimum* thousandth.] **1.** *Per mil*: per thousand. **2.** A unit of length used in measuring the diameter of wire, = $\frac{1}{1000}$ of an inch 1891. **3.** *Pharm.* = MILLILITRE 1904.

||**Milady** (milē^i·di). Also **miladi.** 1839. [Fr.; cf. MILORD.] A continental rendering of 'my lady', used in speaking to or of an English gentlewoman.

Milan (mi·lăn, milæ·n). 1464. [– It. *Milano.*] Name of the chief city of Lombardy; used *attrib.* in **M. point,** a fine hand-made lace; **M. steel** (*Hist.*), steel used by the armourers of M. for coats-of-mail, swords, etc. (so *M. hauberk, knife, mail*).

Milanese (milănī·z). 1484. [– It. *Milanese*; see -ESE.] **A.** *adj.* Of or pertaining to Milan, its inhabitants, manufactures, etc. 1756. **B.** *absol.* or as *sb.* **1.** A native or inhabitant of Milan. (Unchanged for pl.) 1484. **2.** *The M.*: the territory of the old duchy of Milan 1715.

Milch (miltʃ), *a.* [ME. *mielche, melche, milche*, repr. OE. _*mielċe_ (cf. *þri|milċe* month of May, in which cows can be milked thrice in the day) :– _*melukjaz_, f. _*meluk-, meolk_ MILK.] Of domestic mammals: Giving milk, kept for milking. †**b.** Applied to a wet-nurse, etc. –1709. †**c.** Applied *transf.* to the eyes when weeping (*Haml.* II. ii. 540).

Mi·lch-cow. late ME. [f. prec.] **1.** A cow giving milk or kept for milking. **2.** *fig.* A source of regularly-accruing profit; *esp.* a person from whom money is easily drawn 1601.

Milched (miltʃt), *ppl. a. local.* 1648. [f. MILCH *a.* + -ED.] In milk; in comb. *new-, old-m.* So **Mi·lcher,** a milch beast 1823.

Mild (məild), *a.* [OE. *milde* = OFris. *milde*, OS. *mildi*, OHG. *milti* (Du., G. *mild*), ON. *mildr*, Goth. *-mildeis, -milds* :– Gmc. _*milðjaz, *milðiz_, f. IE. _*meldh- *moldh- *mḷdh-_, whence L. *mollis* soft, Gr. μαλακός.] **1.** Of persons, their disposition, etc. **a.** Kind, considerate, gracious, merciful; not harsh or severe. Now *rare* or *Obs.* **b.** Applied to God, Christ, and the Virgin Mary. *Obs.* exc. in traditional collocations. **c.** Gentle and conciliatory; not rough or fierce in manners OE. **d.** of rule, punishment, etc. Now chiefly in *comp.*: Less severe 1577. **2.** Of an animal: Tame, gentle; not wild or fierce ME. **3.** Of weather: Calm, fine, and moderately warm. late ME. **4.** Of light, etc.: Softly radiant 1645. **5.** Of a medicine: Operating gently. Of food, tobacco, etc.: Not rough or sharp or strong in taste or odour, not over-stimulating. late ME. **b.** Of ale or beer: Orig., not sour or stale; now, not strongly flavoured with hops (opp. to *bitter*). Also *absol.* = mild ale. 1550. **c.** Of a disease: Not severe or acute 1744. **6.** Of exercise: Gentle, easy 1831. **b.** Used sarcastically to connote tameness or feebleness (in persons or their actions) 1885. **7.** Soft, easy to work (*dial.*) 1852. ¶**8.** Of a slope: Gentle. Of a wood: Not thorny. BYRON. **9.** Used *poet.* = MILDLY 1667.
1. a. So m. a master POPE. b. Ave Maria! maiden m.! SCOTT. c. The mildest man alive SPENSER. His m. eye beams benevolence no more SHELLEY. d. But..why not adopt milder measures? MACAULAY. Phr. *As m. as a dove, as May, as milk,* etc. 2. Among wild Beasts: they at his sight grew m. MILT. 3. A m. September afternoon 1892. 4. M. as a star in water KEATS. 7. Phr. *M. steel*: steel containing only a little carbon, and not readily tempered or hardened. 9. And thus the Godlike Angel answerd milde MILT.
Hence **Mi·ld-ly** *adv.*, **-ness.**

Milden (məi·ld'n), *v.* 1603. [f. MILD *a.* + -EN^5.] To make or become mild or milder.

Mildew (mi·ldiū), *sb.* [OE. *mildēaw, meledēaw* = OS. *milidou* (Du. *meeldauw*), OHG. *militou* (G., with assim. to *mehl* MEAL *sb.*^{1}, *mehltau*), Sw. *mjöldagg*, Da. *meldug*; f. Gmc. _*meliþ_ (Goth. *miliþ*; cf. L. *mel*, Gr. μελι) honey + _*dawwaz_ DEW *sb.*] †**1.** = HONEY-DEW 1. –1658. **2.** A morbid destructive growth of minute whitish fungi on plants. Also, a similar growth on paper, leather, wood, etc., when exposed to damp. Usu. *collect. sing.*; also with *a* and *pl.* ME.
2. *fig.* Neither the blasts of arbitrary power could break them off, nor the m. of servile opinion cause them to wither HALLAM. Hence **Mi·ldewy** *a.*

Mildew (mi·ldiū), *v.* 1552. [f. the sb.] To taint or become tainted with mildew.
Hee..Mildewes the white Wheate SHAKS.

Mile (məil). [OE. *mīl* fem. = MDu. *mīle* (Du. *mijl*), OHG. *mīl(l)a* (G. *meile*), ON. *míla* (prob. f. OE.) :– WGmc. _*mīlja_ – L. *mīlia, millia*, pl. of *mīle, mīlle* thousand.] **1.** Orig., the Roman lineal measure of 1,000 paces, about 1,618 yards. Hence, the British unit of measure derived from this, which has varied considerably at different times and in different localities. The legal mile in the British Empire and the U.S. is now 1,760 yards. (The use of the sing. form with a pl. numeral is now only vulgar or dial.) **b.** A race, or a portion of a race, extending over a mile's length of the course 1901. **c.** *transf.* and *fig.* Chiefly *adv.* in *pl.*, implying a great distance or interval 1588. **2.** Used for its etymol. equivalent in other European languages. late ME. **3.** *attrib.* 1610.
1. c. Villaine and he, be many Miles assunder SHAKS. Phr. *Geographical, geometrical, †maritime, nautic(al m.*: one minute of a great circle of the earth. The British Admiralty fixes it at 6,080 feet. 2. In Italy, Spain, and Portugal, the 'mile' ranges between $\frac{7}{8}$ and $1\frac{1}{4}$ English miles. In Germany, Austria, Holland, and the Scandinavian countries, on the other hand, its values range from about $3\frac{1}{4}$ to over 6 English miles. O.E.D.
Comb. **m.-mark,** a milestone or other object placed to indicate the distance of a m. from the starting-point or from another mark.

Mileage (məi·lėdʒ). Also **milage.** 1754. [f. MILE + -AGE.] **1.** A travelling allowance at a fixed rate per mile. **2.** The aggregate number of miles of way made, used, or travelled over. Also, rate of travel in miles.

Miler (məi·ləɹ). 1891. [f. MILE + -ER^1.] *Sporting slang.* A man or horse specially qualified or trained to run a mile.

Milesian (məilī·ʃăn, mi-, -ʒăn), *a.*^{1} and *sb.*^{1} 1596. [f. L. *Milesius* (Gr. Μιλήσιος) + -AN.] Of or pertaining to (an inhabitant of) Miletus in Asia Minor.
M. tales: a class of short erotic stories current in the 1st century B.C.

Milesian (məilī·ʃăn, mi-, -ʒăn), *a.*^{2} and *sb.*^{2} 1705. [f. *Milesius* (Miledh), a fabulous Spanish king whose sons are said to have conquered Ireland about 1300 B.C.] **A.** *adj.* Of or pertaining to King Milesius or his people; Irish. **B.** *sb.* A descendant of the companions of Milesius. Hence, an Irishman.

Mi·lestone. 1746. [f. MILE + STONE.] A pillar set up on a road or course to mark the miles. Hence **Mi·lestone** *v.*, to mark by or as by milestones.

Milfoil (mi·lfoil). [ME. – OFr. *milfoil* (now *millefeuille*, after *feuille* leaf) :– L. *mīle-, mīllefolium*, f. *mīle, mille* thousand + *folium* leaf (see FOIL *sb.*^{1}), after Gr. μυριόφυλλον (μύριος myriad, φύλλον leaf); the ref. is to the many finely divided leaves.] The common yarrow, *Achillea millefolium*.
Water m., (*a*) the genus *Myriophyllum*; (*b*) the water violet, *Hottonia palustris*.

||**Miliaria** (miliˌē^ə·riă). 1807. [mod.L. use of L. *miliaria*, fem. of *miliarius*; see next.] *Path.* Miliary fever.

Miliary (mi·liˌări), *a.* (*sb.*) 1685. [– L. *miliarius* pertaining to millet, f. *milium* MILLET; see -ARY^1.] **1.** *Phys.* and *Path.* Resembling a millet-seed or an aggregation of millet-seeds. **2.** *Path.* Attended by spots or vesicles resembling millet-seeds or an aggregation of millet-seeds 1737. **3.** *Nat. Hist.* Having numerous small granulations or projections 1760. **4.** *sb. Zool.* A very small tubercle on the integument of some animals 1897.
1. *M. gland*: one of the sebaceous glands of the skin. *M. tubercle*: a greyish-white spherical body about the size of a millet-seed, common in diseased tissues of the lungs, etc. 2. *M. fever*: a fever marked by the presence of a rash resembling measles, with minute vesicles of the form of millet-seed.

||**Milieu** (milyö). 1877. [Fr., f. *mi* (:– L. *medius* MID *a.*) + *lieu* place (:– L. *locus*).] A medium, environment, surroundings.

||**Miliola** (miləi·olă). *Pl.* -æ. 1836. [mod. L., irreg. formed dim. of L. *milium* millet.] *Zool.* A genus of imperforate foraminifera; one of these. So **Mi·lioline** 1873, **Mi·liolite** 1833 *adjs.* and *sbs.*

Militancy (mi·litănsi). 1648. [f. next; see -ANCY.] The condition of being militant.

Militant (mi·litănt). late ME. [– Fr. *militant* or *militant-*, pr. ppl. stem of L. *militare*; see MILITATE *v.*, -ANT.] **A.** *adj.* **1.** Engaged in warfare, warring. **2.** Combative 1603.
1. *Church m.*: see CHURCH *sb.* II. 1. The chirche m., that laboureth here in erthe. late ME. 2. The expenses of the m. Presbyterians 1903. Hence **Mi·litant-ly** *adv.*, **-ness.**
B. *sb.* One engaged in war or strife 1610.

†**Militar(e,** *a.* 1533. [– L. *militaris*; see MILITARY, -AR^1.] Military, martial –1640.
In Militar Commanders and Soldiers, Vaine-Glory is an Essential Point BACON.

Militarism (mi·lităriz'm). 1864. [– Fr. *militarisme*, f. *militaire*; see MILITARY and -ISM.] The spirit and tendencies of the professional soldier; the prevalence of military sentiment and ideals among a people; the tendency to regard military efficiency as the paramount interest of the state. So **Mi·litarize** *v.*

Militarist (mi·litărist). 1601. [f. MILITARY + -IST.] †A soldier (SHAKS.); one who studies military science; now chiefly, one dominated by military ideas, an exponent of militarism.

Military (mi·litări). 1585. [– Fr. *militaire* or L. *militaris*, f. *miles, milit-* soldier + *-aris* -ARY^1.] **A.** *adj.* **1.** Pertaining to soldiers; used or done by soldiers; befitting a soldier. **2.** Of or belonging to an army 1597. **b.** Soldierly 1588. **3.** Having reference to armed forces or to the army; connected with a state of war; dist. from *civil, ecclesiastical,* etc. 1590.
1. The M. profession 1591. M. rules SHAKS., m. obedience MILT., m. music BURNEY. A m. revolution 1843. 2. The Throngs of Militarie men SHAKS. b. He was a man too m. to be warlike KINGLAKE. 3. The public ecclesiastical, military, and maritime jurisdictions BLACKSTONE. Hence **Mi·litarily** *adv.* **Mi·litariness.**
Special collocations. **m. board,** a board dealing with the affairs of the army; **m. chest,** the treasury of an army; **m. engineering,** the art of constructing fortifications, bridges, etc. and the laying and destruction of mines; **m. fever,** enteric or typhus fever; **m. law,** the body of enactments and rules for the government of an army; also, one of these; **m. offence,** one cognizable by a m. court; **m. service** (*Feudalism*), the service in war due from a vassal to his superior; **m. tenure,** a feudal tenure under which a vassal owed his superior certain services in war.
B. *sb.* **1.** Soldiery; soldiers generally. Chiefly, *the m.*; now with pl. vb. 1757. †**2.** A military man –1837.

Militate (mi·litē^{i}t), *v.* 1625. [– *militat-*, pa. ppl. stem of L. *militare* serve as a soldier, f. *miles, milit-* soldier; see -ATE^3.] **1.** *intr.* To serve as a soldier; to take part in warfare. †Also *transf.* and *fig.* **2.** Of things. †**a.** To conflict *with*; also (of speech or action), to be directed *against*. **b.** Of evidence, facts, etc.: To tell *against* (rarely †*for, in favour of*) some conclusion or result 1642. †**3.** *trans.* To fight out (a question) –1762.
1. Men who m. merely for pay K. DIGBY. *fig.* The invisible powers of heaven..seemed to m. on the side of the pious emperor GIBBON. 2. a. Something which militates with any rational plan BURKE. b. Everything may m. for, and nothing m. against, its authenticity 1838.

Militia (mili·ʃă). 1590. [– L. *militia* military service, warfare, war, f. *miles, milit-* soldier; see -IA^1.] †**1.** A system of military discipline, organization, and tactics; the arts of war –1678. †**b.** Military service; warfare –1685. †**2.** The control and administration of the military and naval forces of a country –1647. **3.** A military force; in later use (= Fr. *milice*) a 'citizen army' as dist. from a body of professional soldiers 1590. Also *transf.* and *fig.* **4.** *spec.* A branch of the British military service, forming a part of 'the auxiliary forces' as dist. from the regular army. Also, a similar force raised in British North America. (Constr. either as *sing.* or *pl.*) 1659. **b.** *U.S.* The whole body of men legally amenable to military service 1777. **5.** *attrib.*, as *m. act*, etc. 1655.

1. The Normans had a peculiar M., or Fight, with Bowes and Arrowes RALEGH. **2.** That the m., both by sea and land, might be settled by a bill CLARENDON. **3.** A good m., that is, a certain portion of the people called out in turn to learn the use of arms LD. BROUGHAM. Hence **Mili·tiaman.**

Milk (milk), *sb.* [OE. Anglian *milc*, WS. *meol(o)c*, = OFris. *melok*, OS. *miluk* (Du. *melk*), OHG. *miluh* (G. *milch*), ON. *mjólk*, Goth. *miluks* :– Gmc. **meluks* fem., f. **melk-* :– IE. **melg-* **mlg-*, whence L. *mulgēre*, Gr. ἀμέλγειν.] **1.** An opaque white fluid secreted by the mammary glands of female mammals for the nourishment of their young. †**b.** Milk considered as in process of secretion; hence, lactation –1697. **2.** *fig.* **a.** As the food of infancy; often (after 1 *Cor.* 3:2, etc.) contrasted with '(strong) meat'. late ME. **b.** As a type of what is pleasant and nourishing 1592. **3.** A milk-like juice or sap secreted by certain plants. Cf. LATEX 2. late ME. **4.** A culinary, pharmaceutical, or other preparation of herbs, drugs, or the like, more or less resembling milk. late ME. **5.** The spat of an oyster before its discharge 1858.

1. They'l take suggestion, as a Cat laps milke SHAKS. Phr. *As like as m. to m.* (a Latinism). *In m.*, in a condition to yield m. **2. b.** Aduersities sweete milke, Philosophie SHAKS. Phr. *M. and honey*: (*a*) in the Bible phrase 'flowing with m. and honey' (*Num.* 16:13), hence (*b*) used to express abundance and prosperity. *M. of human kindness* (after Shaks.): compassion characteristic of humane persons. *Spilt m.*: irrecoverable loss or error. **3. b.** *The m. in the cocoa-nut*: a puzzling fact or circumstance, or the explanation of this (*colloq.*, orig. *U.S.*). **4.** *M. of almonds* = ALMOND-MILK. *M. of lime*: hydrate of lime mixed in water. *M. of sulphur*: precipitated sulphur.

attrib. and *Comb.* **1.** General: as *m.-diet, -fat, -porridge*, etc.; *m.-bowl, -cart, -cooler*, etc.; *m.-boy*, etc.; *m.-molar, -tusk*, etc.; *m.-carrier, -seller*, etc.; *m.-faced, -fed*, etc.

2. Special: **m.-abscess,** an abscess occurring in the breasts of women during lactation; **-brother,** a foster-brother; **-cell** *Bot.*, the cell in which the latex of plants is contained; **m. escutcheon,** an area covered by a reversed arrangement of the direction of the hair on the udder and thighs of a milch-cow; **m. factory,** one in which cream is extracted from m.; **-farm,** a dairy-farm; **-fever,** a slight feverish attack which sometimes occurs in women two or three days after childbirth; a similar complaint in milch-cows; **-glass,** an opalescent glass made from cryolite; **-leg,** 'white swelling', a painful swelling of the lower extremities, common after parturition; **-quartz,** an opaque white variety of quartz; **-sickness** *U.S.*, an endemic disease in cattle peculiar to the Western States of America, and sometimes communicated to man through infected meat; **-spot,** a white spot or rash in certain diseases; **-sugar,** sugar of m., lactose; **-thrush** = APHTHA; **-tube** *Bot.*, a laticiferous tube; **-vessel,** (*a*) a dairy utensil for holding m.; (*b*) the udder of a cow; (*c*) *Bot.* one of many tubes in which a milky fluid is secreted; **-walk,** a milkman's round. **b.** Prefixed to names of plants, usu. in the sense 'containing milk', as **m.-grass** = CORN-SALAD; **-parsley,** *Peucedanum palustre*; **m. pea, plant,** a prostrate leguminous plant of the genus *Galactia*, native of the warmer parts of N. America; **-tree,** (*a*) a shrub, *Euphorbia tirucalli*, native of Africa, and naturalized in parts of India; (*b*) any tree yielding a wholesome milky juice, esp. the COW-TREE; (*c*) an apocynaceous tree, *Tanghinia venenifera*, native of Madagascar; **-vetch,** a plant of the leguminous genus *Astragalus*.

Milk (milk), *v.* [OE. *milcian*, f. *milc*; see prec.] **I. 1.** *trans.* To extract milk by handling from the teats of (a cow, goat, ewe, etc.). **b.** To draw (milk). Chiefly *pass.* late ME. †**c.** To obtain milk from by sucking. SHAKS. **2.** *intr.* To yield milk. Now only of cattle. OE. †**3.** *trans.* To suckle –1573.

1. Inprimis She can milke SHAKS. Phr. *To m. the ram, the bull*: *fig.* to engage in an impossible enterprise. **3.** *Macb.* I. vii. 55.

II. *transf.* and *fig.* **1.** *trans.* To drain away the contents of; to 'bleed' pecuniarily; to exploit, turn into a source of (illicit) profit 1526. **2.** To elicit, draw *out* 1628; to drain *away, out of* 1652. **3.** To extract juice, virus, etc. from 1746. **4.** To manipulate as one does the teat 1642. †**5.** To instil with the mother's milk DRYDEN & LEE.

1. He would m. her Purse and fill his own large Pockets 1695. Phr. *To m. the market, street* (U.S. slang): to hold stock in hand so as to make it fluctuate at will, and so yield any financial result desired. *To m. a wire*, to steal the message from it; *to m. a telegram*, to intercept it. **5.** You.. milk'd slow Arts Of Womanish Tameness in my infant Mouth 1682.

Milk-and-water. 1511. Milk diluted with water. †**1.** The colour of milk and water –1571. **2.** Feeble or insipid discourse or mawkish sentiment 1819. **3.** *attrib.* or *adj.* Wishy-washy; insipid, feeble, mawkish 1783.

3. My rascals are no milk-and-water rascals THACKERAY. Hence **Milk-and-wa·terish, -wa·tery** *adjs.*

Milken (mi·lk'n), *a.* Now *rare* or *Obs.* 1570. [f. MILK *sb.* + -EN[4].] **1.** Consisting of milk. **2.** Milk-white 1586.

M. way, race = MILKY WAY. The way of fortune is like the m. way in the skie BACON.

Milker (mi·lkəɹ). 1475. [f. MILK *v.* I. + -ER[1].] **1.** One who or that which milks. **2.** An animal that yields milk, *esp.* a milch-cow. Chiefly with adj., *good, bad*, etc. 1807.

Milkiness (mi·lkinės). 1692. [f. MILKY *a.* + -NESS.] The state of being milky. **b.** Of sidereal and meteorological phenomena: Cloudy whiteness 1791.

fig. Softness and m. of temper TUCKER.

Milk-livered, *a.* 1605. Cowardly, white-livered.

Milk-Liuer'd man, That bear'st a cheeke for blowes SHAKS.

Mi·lkmaid, 1552. [f. MILK *sb.* + MAID.] A woman that milks or is employed in a dairy.

Milkman (mi·lkmæn). 1589. [f. MILK *sb.* + MAN.] A man who sells milk.

Mi·lk-pu·nch. 1704. A drink made of spirits mixed with milk, etc.

Mi·lksop. late ME. [f. MILK *sb.* + SOP *sb.*] †**1.** A piece of bread soaked in milk. †Also *fig.* in *pl.* –1577. **2.** *fig.* An effeminate or spiritless man or youth. late ME.

2. To wedden a Milksope or a coward ape CHAUCER.

Mi·lkstone. 1705. [f. MILK *sb.* + STONE.] A name for various white stones.

Mi·lk-tooth. 1727. [f. MILK *sb.* + TOOTH.] One of a temporary set of teeth in young mammals.

Milkweed (mi·lkwīd). 1706. [f. MILK *sb.* + WEED *sb.*[1]] A name for plants with milky juice.

e.g. the sow-thistle, *Sonchus oleraceus*; the brimstone-wort, *Peucedanum palustre*; the sun-spurge, *Euphorbia helioscopia*; and plants of the N. Amer. genus *Ascelpias*.

Mi·lk-white, *a.* OE. White as milk, pure white. †*M. girdle, way*, the Milky Way.

Milkwort (mi·lkwɒɹt). 1578. [f. MILK *sb.* + WORT[1].] **1.** Any plant of the genus *Polygala*, formerly supposed to increase the milk of nurses; esp. *Polygala vulgaris*. **2.** A primulaceous plant, *Glaux maritima*, common on the sea-coast and in salt marshes 1578. **3.** Any plant of the genus *Euphorbia* 1640.

Milky (mi·lki), *a.* late ME. [f. MILK *sb.* + -Y[1].] **1.** Having the appearance of milk, or of milk and water. Also (chiefly *poet.*) milk-white. **2.** Of or consisting of milk (*rare*) 1552. **3.** Containing, abounding in, or yielding milk 1641. **b.** *Bot.* Yielding milk-like juice 1861. **4.** *transf.* and *fig.* Of persons, etc.: Soft, gentle; in bad sense, timorous, effeminate weakly amiable 1602.

1. With Fleeces m. white (= MILK-WHITE) DRYDEN. The *latex*, or m. fluid 1855. **3.** The milkie fruitfulnesse of the Cow 1641. **4.** Has friendship such a faint and milkie heart, It turnes in lesse then two nights? SHAKS. They made..me (the milkiest of men) a satirist BYRON.

Milky Way. late ME. [f. MILKY *a.* + WAY *sb.*, tr. L. *via lactea*.] **1.** = GALAXY 1. **2.** *fig.* **a.** A path brilliant in appearance, or leading to heaven 1649. †**b.** *poet.* The region of a woman's breast –1730.

Mill (mil), *sb.*[1] [OE. *mylen* m. and fem. :– **mu·lino, -ina*, for late L. *molinum, -ina*, f. L. *mola* grindstone, mill, rel. to *molere* grind (see MEAL *sb.*[1]). For the loss of final *n* cf. the common dial. pronunc. (kil) of *kiln*.] **1.** A building fitted with machinery for grinding corn. Often in *Comb.*, as *water-, wind-, flour-m.* **b.** A mechanical apparatus for grinding corn 1535. **2.** A machine or apparatus for grinding to powder or pulp some solid substance. Also a building fitted with such machinery. Often in comb., as *coffee-, pepper-, paper-m.*, etc. 1560. **b.** An instrument for expressing juices by grinding or crushing; as *cane, cider m.* 1676. **c.** *Sc.* (also in form *mull*) A snuff-box, orig. one in which the tobacco was ground. **3.** Extended to any machine worked by wind or water power in the manner of a corn-mill, though not used for grinding. Subseq. applied to machines for performing certain operations upon material in the process of manufacture: as in *flatting-, fulling-, rolling-, saw-, stamping-m.* late ME. **b.** A machine invented in the 16th c. for the stamping of gold and silver coins. SHAKS. (*m.-sixpence*). **c.** *Calico* and *Bank-note printing*: A steel roller having upon it a pattern which is transferred by pressure to the printing plate 1839. **4.** A building or works fitted with machinery in which a (specific) manufacture is carried on (*cotton-, silk-, silver-m.*, etc.) 1502. **5.** A machine which does its work by rotary motion, esp. a lapidary's mill 1839. **6.** *slang.* Short for TREADMILL 1842. **7.** A pugilistic encounter 1825.

2. *fig.* Gods M. grinds slow; but sure G. HERBERT. Phr. *To draw water to (one's) m.*: to seize every advantage. *To put through the m.*: to cause to pass through a course of labour or experience, esp. an arduous or painful one; so *to go, to have been through the m.*

1. *attrib.* and *Comb.* as *m.-house, -wall.*

2. *Special Comb.*: **m.-bar (iron),** rough bar iron as drawn out by the puddlers' rolls; **-hand,** one employed in a m. or factory; **-head,** (*a*) that part of a horse-mill from which the driving-gear is suspended; (*b*) the head of water which is to turn a m.; **m. ore** *Mining*, metallic ore fit for stamping or crushing; **-run,** (*a*) *Gold Mining*, the work of an amalgamating mill between two 'clean-ups'; (*b*) a mill-race; (*c*) *Mining*, a test of a given quantity of ore by treatment in a m.; **-shaft,** (*a*) a metal shaft used for driving machinery in a m.; (*b*) the tall chimney of a m.; **-stream,** a mill-race; also *fig.*; **-work,** (*a*) the machinery used in mills or factories; (*b*) the designing or erecting of this.

Mill (mil), *sb.*[2] 1791. [Short for L. *millesimum* thousandth part, after CENT. Cf. MIL.] A U.S. money of account, being one-thousandth of a dollar (one-tenth of a cent).

Mill (mil), *v.*[1] 1552. [f. MILL *sb.*[1]] **I. 1.** *trans.* To subject to the operation of a mill; to pass (cloth, etc.) through a fulling-mill; to thicken (cloth, etc.) by fulling; to grind (corn), produce (flour) by grinding, etc. Also, to produce or yield by milling; *intr.* to undergo milling. **2. a.** To stamp (coins) by means of the mill and press 1687. **b.** To flute the edge of (a coin or any piece of flat metal) 1724. **3.** To beat (chocolate, etc.) to a froth *Hist.* 1662.

1. This oval box, well filled With best tobacco finely milled COWPER. **3.** M. the cream till it is all of a thick froth MRS. GLASSE. A second milled and frothed the chocolate DICKENS.

II. *slang.* To beat, strike; to fight, overcome; to smash, break open. Also *intr.* or *absol.* to box. 1700.

Tug..milled away — one, two, right and left THACKERAY.

III. 1. *intr.* Of cattle (in U.S. also of persons): To keep moving round and round in a mass; also, to move in a circle 1888. **2.** *intr.* As a whale: To turn suddenly round 1840.

Mill (mil), *v.*[2] 1567. [perh. a use of prec.] *slang. trans.* To rob, steal.

Mi·llard. *dial.* Also †**mil(le)warde.** [OE. *myle(n)weard*, f. *mylen* MILL *sb.*[1] + *weard* WARD *sb.*, keeper. Cf. the surnames *Millard, Milward.*] = MILLER 1.

Mi·llboard. 1712. [Altered f. *milled board*; see MILLED *ppl. a.*] A kind of stout pasteboard, rolled with high pressure, used for binding, etc.; a piece of this. **b.** A specially prepared 'board' for sketching 1854.

Mi·ll-dam. ME. [f. MILL *sb.*[1]] A dam constructed across a stream to raise its level and make it available for turning a mill-wheel. Also, the entire area covered by the water held in check by the dam.

Milled (mild), *ppl. a.* 1622. [f. MILL *v.*^{1} + -ED^1.] Having been subjected to the action of MILL *v.*^{1}

Mill'd sixpences (cf. *mill-sixpence*, MILL *sb.*^{1} 3 b) 1650. *M. board* = MILLBOARD 1707.

‖**Millefiori** (milifiōᵊ·ri). 1849. [It. *millefiori*, f. *mille* thousand + *fiori* flowers.] A kind of ornamental glass made by fusing together a number of glass rods of different sizes and colours, and cutting the mass into sections; usu. embedded in transparent glass to make paper-weights, etc.

‖**Millefleurs** (milflör). 1849. [Fr. *eau de mille-fleurs*, lit. 'water of a thousand flowers'.] A perfume distilled from flowers of different kinds.

Millenarian (milĭnēᵊ·riăn). 1631. [f. late L. *millenarius* (see next) + -AN; see -ARIAN.] **A.** *adj.* Of or pertaining to the millennium; holding the doctrine of the millennium. **B.** *sb.* A believer in the millennium (in sense 2) 1674. Hence **Millena·rianism,** the doctrine of or belief in the coming of the millennium 1849.

Millenary (mi·lĭnări). 1550. [In sense 1 – late L. *millenarius* consisting of a thousand, commander of a thousand, f. L. *milleni* a thousand each, f. *mille* a thousand; see -ARY^1. In sense 2 – late (eccl.) L. *millenarii* millenarian heretics (Eugippus v/vi).] **A.** *adj.* **1.** Consisting of or pertaining to a thousand (esp. years) 1641. **b.** Commanding one thousand men 1608. **2.** Of or pertaining to the millennium, or those believing in the millennium 1577. Also *transf.* and *fig.*

B. *sb.* **1.** An aggregate of one thousand; *esp.* one thousand years; ten centuries 1550. **2.** An officer in command of a thousand men 1555. **3.** = MILLENARIAN *sb.* 1561.

1. He conceaveth the Elementall frame shall end in the seventh or Sabbaticall m. SIR T. BROWNE.

Millennial (mile·niăl), *a.* 1664. [f. MILLENNIUM + -AL^1.] **1.** Of a thousand years 1807. **2.** Of or pertaining to the millennium 1664.

1. The bloody scroll of our m. wrongs BYRON.

Millennian (mile·niăn), *a.* and *sb.* 1657. [f. as prec. + -AN.] = MILLENARIAN.

†**Millen(n)ist.** 1664. [f. MILLENNIUM + -IST.] A millenarian –1795.

Millennium (mile·niŏm). *Pl.* **-iums,** *occas.* **-ia.** 1638. [– mod.L., f. L. *mille* thousand, after *biennium* (see BIENNIAL).] **1.** A period of one thousand years. Also, a thousandth anniversary. 1711. **2.** The period of one thousand years during which (*Rev.* 20:1–5) Christ will reign in person on earth 1638. **3.** *fig.* A period of happiness and benign government 1820.

1. Let Thy feet, millenniums hence, be set In midst of knowledge TENNYSON.

Millepede (mi·lĭpīd). 1601. [– L. *millepeda* woodlouse, f. *mille* thousand + *pes, ped-* foot.] *Zool.* **1.** Any one of the chilognathan myriapods, with numerous legs usu. placed on each of the segments in double pairs. **2.** Any one of several terrestrial isopod crustaceans, *esp.* the common woodlouse, *Oniscus asellus*; the armadillo, *Armadillo vulgaris*; and the slater, *Porcellio scaber* 1651. **3.** = CENTIPEDE 1705.

Millepore (mi·lĭpōᵊɹ). 1751. [– mod.L. *millepora*, f. *mille* thousand + *porus* passage, PORE *sb.*, or – Fr. *millépore.*] *Zool.* Any one of the *Hydromedusæ* of the genus *Millepora* or of the family *Milleporidæ*, in which the coral-like skeleton is covered with minute pores. Hence **Mi·lleporite,** a fossil m.

Miller (mi·ləɹ). [Late ME. *mulnere, mylnere, miller* prob. (with assim. to MILL *sb.*^{1}) – MLG., MDu. *molner, mulner* (Du. *molnaar, mulder*), in OS. *mulineri*, corresp. to OHG. *mulināri* (G. *müller*), ON. *mylnari* – late L. *molinarius*, f. *molina* MILL *sb.*^{1}; see -ER^1.] **1.** The proprietor or tenant of a corn-mill. **b.** One who works a mill of any kind 1839. **2.** Applied to certain white or white-powdered insects, as the cockchafer, etc., and to certain hairy caterpillars 1668. **3.** *slang.* A pugilist 1812.

1. A myller dusty-poll than dyde come 1515. Prov. *An honest m. hath a thumb of gold*: app. = there are no honest millers; a prov. alluded to by Chaucer and Gascoigne, a thumb of gold being taken to mean one that brings profit to the owner. *Too much water drowned the m.*: = one can have too much of a good thing.

Comb.: **m.-moth,** a white or 'mealy-scaled' moth; so **m.'s soul.**

Millerite^1 (mi·lərəit). *U.S.* 1846. [f. William *Miller* + -ITE^1 1.] A believer in the doctrines of William Miller (died 1849), an American preacher who taught that the coming of Christ and the end of the world were at hand.

Millerite^2 (mi·lərəit). 1854. [– G. *millerit*, named after W. H. *Miller*, professor of mineralogy at Cambridge, 1832–1870; see -ITE^1 2 b.] *Min.* Native sulphide of nickel, usu. occurring in brassy or bronze crystals; capillary pyrites.

Miller's thumb. 1440. [The head of the fish has some resemblance to a thumb. Cf. Prov. s. v. MILLER.] **1.** A small freshwater fish, *Cottus gobio*; the bullhead. **2.** Applied also to: **a.** the whiting-pout, *Gadus luscus*; **b.** *U.S.*, any freshwater sculpin of the genus *Uranidea*; **c.** the Black Goby, *Gobius niger* 1838. **3.** Applied locally to certain small birds, e.g. the Willow Wren 1838.

Millesimal (mile·simăl), *a.* and *sb.* 1719. [f. L. *millesimus* thousandth + -AL^1.] **A.** *adj.* Thousandth; consisting of thousandth parts. Also, of or belonging to a thousand, dealing with thousandths 1741. **B.** *sb.* A thousandth (part).

Millet (mi·lėt). late ME. [– (O)Fr. *millet*, dim. of (dial.) *mil* :– L. *milium* millet.] **1.** A graminaceous plant, *Panicum miliaceum*, native of India, growing three or four feet high, and bearing a large crop of minute nutritious seeds; the seed itself. **2.** Applied to other graminaceous plants, esp. *Sorghum vulgare* (African, Black, Indian, Turkey M.) and *Setaria italica* (Italian or German M.) 1548.

M.-rash, miliary fever; **m.-grass,** the genus *Milium*, esp. *M. effusum*; **m.-seed,** the seed or grain of m.

Milli- (mi·li), comb. f. L. *mille* thousand, used esp. in the metric system to denote the thousandth part of the unit, as *milliampere*; *milliare*, $\frac{1}{1000}$ of an are (154·07 square inches), etc.; †*milli-millesm* (1650), *millistere, millivolt, milliweber*; **millibar,** $\frac{1}{1000}$ of a bar (unit of barometric pressure) 1912.

Milliard (mi·liăɹd). 1823. [– Fr. *milliard*, f. *mille* thousand.] A thousand millions.

Milliary (mi·liări). Also **miliary.** 1610. [– L. *milliarius*, f. *mille* thousand; see MILE, -ARY^1.] **A.** *adj.* Pertaining to the ancient Roman mile of a thousand paces; marking a mile 1700. **B.** *sb.* An ancient Roman milestone 1610.

The miliary column, set up as a centre from which to measure distances 1860.

Milligramme, -gram (mi·ligræm). 1810. [– Fr. *milligramme*; see MILLI-, GRAMME.] In the metric system, a weight equal to $\frac{1}{1000}$ of a gramme, or ·0154 of an English grain.

Millilitre (mi·lilītəɹ). 1810. [– Fr. *millilitre*; see MILLI-, LITRE.] In the metric system, a measure of capacity equal to $\frac{1}{1000}$ of a litre, or ·061 of a cubic inch.

Millimetre (mi·limītəɹ). 1807. [– Fr. *millimètre*; see MILLI-, METRE *sb.*^{2}] In the metric system, a measure of length equal to $\frac{1}{1000}$ of a metre, or ·0393 inch. Also *attrib.* as *m. scale.* Abbrev. *mm.*

Milliner (mi·linəɹ). 1529. [f. MILAN + -ER^1.] **1.** A native or inhabitant of Milan. **2.** †**a.** A vendor of fancy wares and articles of apparel, esp. of those orig. made at Milan, e.g. Milan bonnets, ribbons, gloves, cutlery. **b.** Now, a person (usu. a woman) who makes or deals in women's hats and trimmings (and, formerly, drapery).

No M. can so fit his customers with Gloues SHAKS. A little French M. SHERIDAN.

Millinery (mi·linəri). 1679. [f. prec.; see -ERY.] The articles made or sold by milliners.

Milling (mi·liŋ), *vbl. sb.* 1466. [f. MILL *v.*^{1} + -ING^1.] **1.** The action or process of subjecting something to the operation of a mill, as corn, etc. **b.** The treatment of a substance or material in any kind of mill; e.g. the operation of fulling cloth, rolling metals, crushing minerals, etc. 1617. **2.** *Coining.* The operation of producing a crenation or series of transverse lines on the edge of a coin as a protection against clipping. Now only *concr.* the crenation itself. 1817.

1. *High m.*, milling in which the wheat grain is reduced to flour by successive crackings, or slight and partial crushings, alternating with siftings and sortings of the product, resulting in a flour of extreme whiteness and nutritive quality. *Low m.* milling in which the corn is reduced to flour by a system of mashing, repeated scraping and squeezing, usually attended with some heating of the product, and a single bolting.

Million (mi·lyən). late ME. [– (O)Fr. *million*, prob. – It. †*millione*, now *milione*, f. *mille* thousand + augm. suffix *-one*, -OON.] **1.** The cardinal number equal to a thousand thousands. (Often used for an enormous number.) **b.** As adj. or quasi-adj. (in prose use, always with *a* or prefixed multiplier), followed immediately by a pl. (or collective) noun 1843. **c.** Also used as an ordinal when followed by other numbers, the last of which alone takes the ordinal form 1866. **2.** *ellipt.* **a.** A million coins or units of money of account, *esp.* (in British use) a million pounds or (in the U.S.) dollars. late ME. **b.** *The million*: the multitude; the bulk of the population 1602.

1. Oh, 'giue ye-good-e'vn: heer's a m. of manners SHAKS. He could count his soldiers by the m. 1885. **b.** The roar of a m. cannon BORROW. **2.** Increasing the national debt to near eighty millions Sterling 1790. **b.** The Play I remember pleas'd not the M. SHAKS. *attrib.* **m. act,** an act of parliament authorizing a lottery to be held in 1694 and succeeding years, by which a million pounds was to be raised.

Millionaire (milyənēᵊ·ɹ). 1826. [– Fr. *millionnaire* (formerly also in Engl.), f. *million*; see prec.] A person possessed of a 'million of money', as a million pounds, dollars, francs, etc.; a person of great wealth. So **Millionai·ress,** a female m.

Millionary (mi·lyənări), *a.* and *sb. rare.* 1816. [f. MILLION + -ARY^1, after Fr. *millionnaire* (see prec.).] **A.** *adj.* Possessing millions (of money). **B.** *sb.* = MILLIONAIRE 1834.

Millioned (mi·lyənd), *a.* (? 1600) 1747. [f. MILLION + -ED^2.] **1.** Numbered by the million. **2.** Possessed of millions (of money).

Millionth (mi·lyənþ), *a.* (*sb.*) 1673. [f. MILLION, after HUNDREDTH.] The ordinal number belonging to the cardinal MILLION. Also *absol.*, *attrib.*, and quasi-*sb.*

M. part, one of a million equal parts into which a whole is, or may be, divided.

Milliped, var. of MILLEPEDE.

Mi·ll-lead. 1609. [f. MILL *sb.*^{1} + LEAD *sb.*^{2}] – next.

Mi·ll-leat. 1609. [f. MILL *sb.*^{1} + LEAT.] An artificial channel for the conveyance of water to a mill.

Mi·ll-pond. 1697. The water retained above a mill-dam for driving a mill.

It was quite calm, and the Sea as smooth as a M. 1697. So **Mi·ll-pool** OE.

Mi·ll-post. ME. The post on which a windmill was formerly often supported. Often as a type of something thick and massive; hence *joc.* a massive leg.

Mi·ll-race. 1478. [f. MILL *sb.*^{1} + RACE *sb.*^{1}] The current of water that drives a mill-wheel; also, the channel in which it runs.

Mill-rind (mi·lrəind). 1542. [f. MILL *sb.*^{1} + RIND *sb.*^{2}] The iron which supports the upper millstone of a cornmill, and carries the eye which rests upon the end of the mill spindle. **b.** *Her.* A conventional representation of this.

Mi·ll-round. 1851. The circular path travelled by a mill-horse. Also *fig.*

Millstone (mi·lstōᵘn). OE. **1.** One of a pair of circular stones used for grinding corn in a mill; *Her.* a representation of this. **b.** Stone used or suitable for this 1610. **2.** *fig.* **a.** A heavy burden (cf. *Matt.* 18:6); **b.** a grinding or crushing instrument 1720.

1. *Nether m.*: see NETHER *a.* Phr. *To see far in (into, through) a m.*: to be extraordinarily acute (chiefly ironical). **2. a.** The mill-stone intended for the necks of those vermin..the dealers in corn, was found to fall upon the heads of the consumers BENTHAM. **M. grit** (*Geol.*), a hard siliceous rock belonging to the carboniferous series, and found immediately below the coal-measures.

Mi·ll-wheel. OE. A wheel (esp. a water-wheel) used to drive a mill. **b.** *Her.* A figure of this 1688.

Mi·llwright. 1481. [f. MILL *sb.*^{1} + WRIGHT.] One who designs or sets up mills or mill machinery.

‖**Milor(d** (milō·r). 1824. [Fr. *milord* – Eng. *my lord*; cf. MILADY.] The French designation for an English gentleman.

Milreis (mi·lrēis). 1589. [– Pg. *milreis*, f. *mil* thousand + REIS[1].] A Pg. gold coin and money of account, = 1,000 REIS. Also, a Brazilian silver coin of about half the value, in 1942 replaced by the cruzeiro.

Milt (milt), *sb.* [OE. *milte* and *milt*, corresp. to OFris. *milte*, MDu. *milte* (Du. *milt*), OHG. *milzi* n. (G. *milz* fem.), ON. *milti* :– Gmc. **miltjaz*, **miltjōn*, perh. rel. to **meltan* MELT *v.*] **1.** The spleen in mammals; also, an analogous organ in other vertebrates. Also *transf.* **2.** The roe or spawn of the male fish; the soft roe of fishes 1483. Hence **Milt** *v.* 'to impregnate the roe or spawn of the female fish' (J.). **Mi·lter,** a male fish, esp. in spawning time; also = sense 2.

Miltonian (miltōu·niăn), *a.* 1708. [f. John *Milton* + -IAN.] Of or relating to Milton, or resembling his style or imagery.

Miltonic (miltǫ·nik), *a.* (and *sb.*) 1708. [f. as prec. + -IC.] **A.** *adj.* = prec. **B.** *sb. pl.* Verses of Milton. COWPER. Hence **Milto·nically** *adv.*

Miltonist (mi·ltənist). 1649. [f. *Milton* + -IST.] A follower of Milton in his views on divorce.

Miltwaste (mi·ltweist). 1578. [f. MILT *sb.* + WASTE.] The finger-fern, one of the spleenworts, *Asplenium ceterach.*

Mim (mim), *a. Sc.* and *dial.* 1679. [Imitative of the action of pursing up the mouth. Cf. MUM *sb.*[1]] Demure, primly silent or quiet.

Mime (məim), *sb.* 1616. [– L. *mimus* – Gr. μῖμος.] **1.** *Antiq.* A performer in the dramatic pieces described in sense 4. 1784. **2.** A buffoon; a pantomimist 1616. **3.** *transf.* and *fig.* An imitator 1677. **4.** *Antiq.* A kind of simple farcical drama among the Greeks and Romans, characterized by mimicry; a dialogue written for this. Also *transf.* of modern performances of this kind. 1642.

Mime (məim), *v.* 1616. [f. prec. sb.] **1.** *intr.* To play a part with mimic gesture and action, usu. without words. Also *transf.* and *fig.* **2.** *trans.* To imitate, mimic 1733. Hence **Mi·mer,** a mime, a buffoon.

Mimeograph (mi·mīograf), *sb.* 1889. [irreg. f. Gr. μιμέομαι I imitate + -GRAPH.] An apparatus, invented by Edison, for holding stencils of written pages, from which many copies may be obtained. Hence **Mi·meograph** *v. trans.* to reproduce by means of a m.

‖**Mimesis** (məimī·sis). 1577. [Gr., f. μιμεῖσθαι; see next.] **1.** *Rhet.* A figure of speech whereby the words or actions of another are imitated. **2.** *Biol.* = MIMICRY 2. 1845.

Mimetic (məime·tik), *a.* 1637. [– Gr. μιμητικός, f. μιμεῖσθαι imitate, f. μῖμος MIME *sb.*; see -IC.] **1.** Addicted to or having an aptitude for mimicry or imitation; pertaining to imitation. **2.** Characterized by imitation 1669. **3.** = MIMIC *a.* 3. 1756. **4.** *Biol.* Of animals, etc.: Characterized by mimicry or resemblance in appearance to some other animal or plant, or to some inorganic object. Of appearances or processes: Of the nature of mimicry. 1851. So †**Mime·tical** *a.* (in sense 2) 1617–1764. **Mime·tically** *adv.* 1647.

‖**Mimiambi** (mimiæ·mbəi, məi-), *sb. pl.* 1706. [L. – Gr. μιμίαμβοι pl., f. μῖμος MIME *sb.* + ἴαμβος IAMBUS.] Mimes written in iambic or scazontic verse. So **Mimia·mbic** *a.* 1700; also *sb. pl.* = M. 1845.

Mimic (mi·mik). 1590. [– L. *mimicus* – Gr. μιμικός, f. μῖμος; see MIME *sb.* and -IC.] **A.** *adj.* **1.** †**a.** Exercising the profession of a mime; resembling a mime. **b.** Imitative. 1598. **2.** Of actions, etc. †**a.** Histrionic; hence, hypocritical. **b.** Pertaining to, or of the nature of, mimicry or imitation. 1602. **3.** Imitative as opposed to real. (The word does not now imply any deceptive intention or effect.) 1625.

1. b. Aristotle saith, that Man is the most Mimick of all Animals 1726. **2.** The m. warfare of the opera stage ALISON.

B. *sb.* †A mime, burlesque actor 1590; one who is skilled in mimicry or ludicrous imitation 1599. **b.** 'A mean or servile imitator' (J.); also, something that mimics 1624. Waited on By mimiques, jesters B. JONS. **b.** Cunning is only the Mimick of Discretion ADDISON.

Mimic (mi·mik), *v.* 1687. [f. MIMIC *sb.*] **1.** *trans.* To ridicule by imitating (a person, his manner, etc.) 1697. **2.** To copy with minute accuracy in externals. Chiefly contemptuous. 1687. **3.** To represent imitatively, as by painting, etc. Of things: To resemble closely. 1770. **4.** *Path.* Of a disease: To simulate (another disease) 1744. **5.** *Biol.* To have a mimetic resemblance to (something else) in form or colour 1861.

1. He mocks and mimics all he sees and hears SHELLEY. **2.** Just in the way that monkies m. man 1761. Vice has learned..to mimick Virtue STEELE. **3.** He could m. marble on paper READE.

Mimical (mi·mikăl), *a.* 1603. [f. as MIMIC *a.* + -AL[1]; see -ICAL.] †**1.** = MIMIC *a.* 1. –1693. **2.** †Befitting a mime; pertaining to, characterized by, or of the nature of mimicry 1610. †**3.** = MIMIC *a.* 3. –1693. Hence **Mi·mically** *adv.*

Mimicry (mi·mikri). 1687. [f. MIMIC *sb.* + -RY.] **1.** The action or practice of mimicking; close imitation, either in sport or otherwise, of externals 1709. **b.** An act, instance, or mode of mimicking. Also *concr.* that by which something is mimicked. 1687. **2.** *Biol.* A close external resemblance which a living creature, etc. bears to a different one, or to some inanimate object 1861.

1. As if in mimickry of insect play SOUTHEY. **b.** An Imitation and Mimickry of Good-nature ADDISON.

Mi·miny-pi·miny, *a.* 1815. [Phonetically symbolic; cf. MIM, NIMINY-PIMINY.] Ridiculously affected; finicking. Also *sb.* HAZLITT.

Mimographer (məimǫ·grăfəɹ). 1638. [– L. *mimographus* – Gr. μιμογράφος, f. μῖμος MIME *sb.*; see -GRAPHER.] A writer of mimes.

‖**Mimosa** (mimōu·ză, mimōu·să). *Pl.* **-as,** also L. **-æ.** 1731. [mod.L. (Colin, 1619), app. f. L. *mimus* MIME *sb.* + *-osa*, fem. (sc. *herba, planta*) of *-osus* -OSE[1], and so named from its imitation of animal sensitiveness.] **1.** *Bot.* (A plant of) the genus *Mimosa* of leguminous plants, including the common Sensitive Plant, *M. pudica*: chiefly applied to the latter and to certain trees of the genus *Acacia*, esp. the Australian Wattle-trees. **2.** The bark of these Australian species, used in tanning 1852. **3.** *attrib.*, as **m. gum,** gum arabic (see ARABIC *a.*).

Mimotannic (mimotæ·nik), *a.* 1857. [f. MIMO(SA + TANNIC *a.*] *Chem.* In *M. acid*: a variety of tannic acid found in the mimosa.

‖**Mina**[1] (məi·nă, mi·nă). *Pl.* **-næ** (-nī), **-nas** (-năz). 1579. [L. – Gr. μνᾶ (see MNA); prob. Babylonian.]. **1.** A unit of weight anciently used in Greece, Egypt, etc.; about 1 lb. avoirdupois 1603. **2.** A denomination of money in ancient Greece = 100 drachmas or about £4. (Rendered 'pound' in the N.T.) 1579. **3.** = MANEH 1737.

‖**Mina**[2] (məi·nă). 1769. Also **myna, miner, -or,** etc. [Hindi *mainā.*] Any of several birds of the starling family found in south-eastern Asia, esp. *Acridotheres tristis*, and *Eulabes religiosa*, the common talking starling of India. In Australia applied to species of the genera *Manorhina* and *Myzantha.*

Minacious (minēi·ʃəs), *a.* 1660. [f. L. *minax, -ac-* (f. *minari* threaten) + -OUS.] Menacing, threatening; full of threats or menaces. Hence **Mina·cious-ly** *adv.*, **-ness.**

Minacity (minæ·sĭti). 1656. [f. prec. + -ITY, after *tenacious, tenacity.*] 'Disposition to use threats' (J.); denunciation.

Minaret (mi·năret). 1682. [– Fr. *minaret* or Sp. *minarete*, It. *minaretto* – Turk. *minare* – Arab. *manāra* and *manār* lighthouse, minaret, f. *nār* fire, light.] A tall slender tower or turret, connected with a mosque, surrounded by one or more projecting balconies from which the muezzin calls the people to prayer. Also *transf.* (e.g. *m. of ice*).

Minatory (mi·nătŏri), *a.* and *sb.* 1532. [– late L. *minatorius*, f. *minat-*, pa. ppl. stem of L. *minari* threaten; see -ORY[2].] **A.** *adj.* Threatening, menacing. †**B.** *sb.* A threat, a menace (*rare*) –1686. Hence **Mi·natorily** *adv.* So **Minato·rial** *a.*, **-ly** *adv.* 1847.

‖**Minauderie** (minodri). 1763. [Fr., f. *minauder*, f. *mine* MIEN.] Coquettish airs. The minauderies of the young ladies in the ballrooms THACKERAY.

Mince (mins), *sb.* 1850. [f. MINCE *v.*] Minced meat, esp. as forming a dish.

Mince (mins), *v.* late ME. [– OFr. *mincier* :– Rom. **minutiare*, f. L. *minutia* MINUTIA; dial. vars. with *-ch, -sh* are – OFr. dial. *minchier*. Cf. MINISH.] **1.** *trans.* To cut (meat, etc.) small or into little pieces; **b.** to chop up or grind small with a knife or mincing-machine and cook (*mod.*). **c.** *transf.* To cut (a person) in small pieces 1602. **2.** *transf.* and *fig.* To cut up, subdivide minutely. Also with *up*. 1450. **3.** To make little of, minimize; to disparage; to palliate, extenuate (faults). Now *rare.* 1591. †Also *absol.* **b.** †To report (expressions) euphemistically; to moderate or restrain (one's language) 1599. **4. a.** *trans.* To pronounce with affected elegance, clip (one's words). **b.** *absol.* or *intr.* To speak with affected elegance of pronunciation. 1545. **5.** *intr.* To walk with short steps or with affected nicety; to walk in an affected manner 1562. **b.** *trans.* To perform or express mincingly 1603.

1. The Wife minced a bit of Meat SWIFT. **c.** *Haml.* II. ii. 537. **3.** Wee m. our sins as though they needed no forgivenesse H. SMITH. Phr. *To m. the matter*; in early use, to extenuate it. Now only in neg. contexts, to express oneself delicately or politely: so *to m. matters.* **b.** I know no wayes to m. it in loue, but directly to say, I loue you SHAKS. **5. b.** Behold yond simpring Dame,..that minces Vertue & do's shake the head to heare of pleasures name SHAKS. Hence **Mi·ncer,** one who or that which minces.

Minced (minst), *ppl. a.* late ME. [f. MINCE *v.* + -ED[1].] **1.** Of meat, etc.: Cut up very small. Also *fig.* †**2.** Diminished; mutilated –1707.

Minced meat. 1578. **1. a.** Meat chopped up very small. **b.** = MINCEMEAT 1 b. *rare* or *Obs.* 1762. **2.** *fig.* Anything cut up very small 1649.

Minced-pie. 1607. Now only *U.S.* (*rare*). = MINCE-PIE.

Mi·ncemeat. 1663. [Altered from MINCED MEAT.] **1.** †**a.** = MINCED MEAT 1 a. –1747. **b.** A mixture of currants, raisins, sugar, suet, etc., and sometimes meat, chopped small; used in mince-pies 1845. **2.** *To make m. of* (a person): to cut him up into very small pieces; to annihilate 1663.

Mince-pie·. 1600. [Altered from MINCED-PIE.] A pie containing mincemeat.

Mi·ncing, *vbl. sb.* 1533. [f. MINCE *v.* + -ING[1].] In senses of the vb.

m.-machine, a machine for mincing meat, etc.

Mi·ncing, *ppl. a.* 1530. [f. MINCE *v.* + -ING[2].] That minces; esp. of persons, their speech, gait, etc. Characterized by an affectedly dainty or elegant manner.

Ile..turne two minsing steps Into a manly stride SHAKS. [She] frightened a m. curate out of his life 1887. Hence **Mi·ncingly** *adv.*

Mind (məind), *sb.* [Early ME. *mind(e*, with dial. vars. *münd(e, mend(e*, later *meende*; aphet. f. *imünd*, etc. :– OE. *ġemynd*, corresp. to OHG. *gimunt*, Goth. *gamunds* memory :– Gmc. **ʒamunðiz*, f. *ʒa-* Y- + **mun-*, weak grade of the series **men-* **man-* **mun-* :– IE. **men-* **mon-* **mn* revolve in the mind, think.] **I.** Memory. †**1.** The faculty of memory –ME. **2.** The state of being remembered; remembrance OE. †**3.** That which is remembered *of* (a person or thing); the memory or record *of* –1489. †**4.** The action or an act of commemorating; a commemoration, a memorial OE. †**b.** *spec.* The commemoration of a departed soul, esp. by a requiem said or sung on the day of the funeral in any month or year following –1660. †**5.** Mention, record –1530.

2. Phr. *To have, bear, keep in m.*: to retain in memory; now only, to keep one's attention fixed upon. *To bring, call to m.*: to summon to remembrance. *To be (go, pass) out of m.*: to be forgotten. (*Obs.* exc. in 'Out of sight, out of m.', etc.) *Time out of m.*, used as adv. phr. = from time immemorial. *To put* (a person) *in m.*: to remind. **4. b.** Upon the Anniversary, or the monthly, or weekly minds JER. TAYLOR.

II. Thought; purpose, intention. †**1.** The thought *of* (an object) –1589. **2.** That which a person thinks about any subject or question; one's view or opinion. late ME. **3.** Purpose or intention; desire or wish. *Obs.* exc. in phrases. ME. **4.** Bent or direction of thoughts, desires, inclinations, etc. late ME. **5.** Way of thinking and feeling; moral disposition 1500. **6.** State of thought and feeling as to dejection, fortitude, firmness, etc. 1500.

2. Phr. *To speak one's m.* (*out*): to express one's opinion candidly, to speak plainly. So *to tell* (a person) *one's m.*, *to let* (a person) *know one's m.* *A piece* or *bit of one's m.*: see PIECE *sb.*, BIT *sb.*[2] 4. *To be of a* (specified) *m.*: to hold an opinion. *To be of* (another's) *m.*: to be of his way of thinking. *In my m.*: in my opinion. So *to my m.* *To be of one* or *a m.*: to be unanimous. **3.** Sudden m. arose In Adam, not to let th' occasion pass MILT. Phr. *To know one's own m.*: to form and adhere to a decision. *To make up one's m.*: see MAKE *v.* †*To be of many minds*: to chop and change. *To be in two minds*: to vacillate between two intentions. *To change one's m.*, to alter one's purpose, opinion, disposition, etc. *To have a m.*: to wish, desire, be disposed *to do* something. So, *to have a great, good*, etc., *m.*, *to have no m.*; *to have half a m.*, now = to be strongly disposed or inclined *to do* something. They..thought they could deal as they had a m. to with his property 1895. **4.** Phr. *To set* (*have, keep*) *one's m. on*: to desire to attain or accomplish. *To give one's m. to*: to bend one's energies towards. *To one's m.*: as one would have it to be. Also, *after one's m.* **5.** *Frame of m.*: see FRAME *sb.* II. 5. I would I knew his minde SHAKS. **6.** A turne or two Ile walke To still my beating minde SHAKS.

III. 1. The seat of consciousness, thoughts, volitions, and feelings; also, the incorporeal subject of the psychical faculties; the soul as dist. from the body ME. **b.** Used of God. **c.** Mental or psychical being: opp. to *matter* 1759. **d.** A person regarded abstractly as the embodiment of mental qualities 1580. **2.** In restricted sense: The intellectual powers, as dist. from the will and emotions. Often contrasted with *heart*. ME. **b.** Intellectual quality, mental power 1586. **3.** The normal condition of the mental faculties; one's 'reason', 'wits'. late ME.

1. No Proposition can be said to be in the M... which it was never yet conscious of LOCKE. M. is the mysterious something which feels and thinks MILL. Phr. *On one's m.*: occupying one's (anxious) thoughts. *One's mind's eye*: mental vision, remembrance. **b.** Haunted for ever by the eternal m. WORDSW. **d.** Mindes innocent and quiet take That for an Hermitage LOVELACE. The religious m. of Europe 1883. **2.** ABSENCE, PRESENCE *of m.*: see those wds. **b.** The days of advance, the works of the men of m. TENNYSON. **3.** Phr. (*To be, go*) *out of one's m.*; *to lose one's m.*; *to be in one's right m.*, etc. *Of sound* (or *unsound*) *m.*

Comb.: **m.-cure,** the curing of a disease by the influence of the healer's m. upon the patient's; so **-healing; -reader,** a thought-reader.

Mind (məind), *v.* ME. [f. MIND *sb.*] **1.** *trans.* To put in mind *of* something; to remind. Now *rare*. **2.** To remember; to think of (a past or present object). Now *arch.* and *dial.* late ME. Also *absol.* **b.** In *imper.* To bear in mind. late ME. **c.** *intr.* with *of, on, upon*: To remember. Now *dial.* Also quasi-*refl.* in *I m. me*, etc. (*arch.*). late ME. **3.** To perceive, notice; to have one's attention caught by. *Obs.* exc. *dial.* 1489. **4.** To attend to, give heed to 1559. **b.** *absol.* or *intr.* Chiefly *colloq.* in *imper.* 1806. †**5.** *trans.* To have a mind to; to intend (doing something); also, to plan, provide for (something external to oneself) –1691. **b.** With *inf.* as obj.: To have a mind *to do* something. *Obs.* exc. *dial.* 1513. **6.** To direct or apply oneself to; to practise diligently. late ME. †**b.** To care for –1748. **7.** In neg., interrog., and conditional sentences: (Not) to care for. Hence: (Not) to object to, dislike. 1608. **b.** *absol.* or *intr.* 1786. **8.** To remember and take care *to do* (something), *that* something is done 1641. **9.** To take care of; to take heed (what one does) 1737. **b.** To look out for (something to be avoided). Now only in the imperative, or the like. 1690. Also *absol.* **10.** *trans.* To look after; to have the care of 1694.

1. They m. us of the time When we made bricks in Egypt TENNYSON. **2. b.** Mind to-morrow's early meeting BROWNING. **3.** My Lord you nod, you do not minde the play SHAKS. **4.** Let us take his advice, though he be one only, and not m. the others JOWETT. **b.** So I bar Latin, m. 1806. **5.** What he [the King] minded, he compassed BACON. **6.** Phr. *To m. his book* (colloq.; now obs. or arch.), of a schoolboy, to be diligent in his studies. *To m. one's business*: to prosecute it diligently; hence, *to m. one's own business*: to attend to one's own affairs and leave other people's alone. **7.** Phr. *I should not m.* (something) = I should rather like to have it or do it; *do you* or *would you m.* (doing something)? = be so kind as to do it; *if you don't m.*, if you have no objection. **b.** Phr. *Never m.* = don't let it trouble you, it does not matter; also = it is none of your business. **8.** M. you write DISRAELI. **9.** *M. your eye*, look out, keep your eyes about you. *To m. one's P's and Q's*: see P. **b.** Phr. *If you don't m.* (absol.) = if you are not careful (to avoid something). **10.** Let me m. your pigeons 1884.

Minded (məi·ndėd), *ppl. a.* 1503. [f. MIND *sb.* + -ED[2].] **1.** Having a mind *to do* something; disposed. †**2.** Having a (favourable or hostile) disposition towards a person or thing –1677. **3.** Having a mind of a specified character, as *healthy-, high-*, etc., *m.* 1503.

Minder (məi·ndəɹ). 1650. [f. MIND *sb.* and *v.* + -ER[1].] **1.** One who minds; *esp.* one whose business is to attend to something, as *cattle-, engine-m.* **2.** A child taken care of at a 'minding-school' 1865.

Mindful (məi·ndfŭl), *a.* ME. [f. MIND *sb.* + -FUL.] **1. a.** Taking thought or care *of.* **b.** Having remembrance *of.* TENNYSON. †**2.** Minded, inclined *to do* something –1681.

1. a. What thing is man, that thou art myndeful of him? WYCLIF *Heb.* 2:6. **2.** M. to rest 1681. Hence **Mi·ndful-ly** *adv.*, **-ness.**

Minding (məi·ndiŋ), *vbl. sb.* 1449. [f. MIND *v.* + -ING[1].] **1.** The action of MIND *v.* **2.** *dial.* A reminder 1601.

Comb. †**m.-school,** a dame-school for keeping children out of mischief.

Mindless (məi·ndlės), *a.* OE. [f. MIND *sb.* + -LESS.] **1.** Destitute of mind; unintelligent. Also, †stupefied, insane. **2.** Unmindful, thoughtless, heedless, careless *of* 1547.

1. M. rubbish 1866. **2.** M. of others Lives DRYDEN. Hence **Mi·ndless-ly** *adv.*, **-ness.**

Mine (məin), *sb.* ME. [– (O)Fr. *mine* (perh. f. *miner* MINE *v.*), or f. MINE *v.*] **1.** An excavation made in the earth for the purpose of digging out metallic ores, or coal, salt, precious stones, etc. Also, the place yielding these. **b.** *fig.* An abundant source of supply 1541. **2.** What is mined; mineral or ore. Now only used for iron ore. late ME. **3.** *Mil.* Formerly, a subterranean passage excavated under the wall of a besieged fortress, for the purpose either of getting entrance, or of causing the wall to fall. Later, a subterranean gallery in which gunpowder was placed, for blowing up the enemy's fortifications; the charge of gunpowder so placed. 1483. **4.** In naval warfare, a receptacle filled with dynamite or the like, moored beneath, or floating on or near, the surface of the water to destroy an enemy's vessel. 1483. Also *fig.*

1. b. Her memory was a m.; she knew by heart All Calderon and greater part of Lopé BYRON. **2.** *All-mine*, designating the best quality of pig-iron, made from ore only; *part-m.*, designating that made from ore mixed with cinder.

Comb.: **m. adventure,** a speculation in mines; **m.-adventurer,** one who takes part in a m. adventure; **-dial** (cf. DIAL *sb.* 5); **-dragging,** the operation of dragging a body of water in order to remove submarine or floating mines; **m. field,** a portion of the sea or land in which mines have been laid; **m.-iron, -pig,** pig-iron made from m. or ore, as dist. from *cinder-pig*; **-layer,** a vessel used for laying mines; **-laying,** the operation of laying mines; **-stone, -stuff,** ore, *esp.* ironstone; **-sweeper,** a vessel used for mine-sweeping; **-sweeping** = *mine-dragging*; **-thrower** [tr. G. *minenwerfer*], a trench-mortar; **m. tin,** tin worked out of the lode; **-work,** (*a*) *Mil. pl.* subterranean passages of the nature of mines; (*b*) a system of workings belonging to a m.; **-wo·rker.**

Mine (məin), *poss. pron.* and *a.* [OE. *mīn* = OFris., OS., OHG. *mīn* (Du. *mijn*, G. *mein*), ON. *minn*, Goth. *meins* :– Gmc. **mīnaz*, f. IE. locative **mei* of *me* ME + adj. suffix **-no-*.] The possessive pronoun of the first person sing. **1.** Qualifying a following sb. Now only *arch.* or *poet.* before a vowel or *h*; otherwise repl. by MY, q.v. **2.** Placed after the sb. Now only *arch.* in vocative. ME. **3.** As predicative adj.: Belonging to me OE. **4.** *ellipt.* = MY with the sb. supplied from the context ME. **5.** *absol.* **a.** Those who are mine; chiefly, my family, my kindred OE. †**b.** That which is mine; my property –1596. **c.** *Of m.*: belonging to me: see OF *prep.*

1. Shall I not take m. ease in m. Inne? SHAKS. His, and m. lou'd darling SHAKS. **2.** There, reader m.! 1852. **3.** My doctryne is not myne, but his that hath sent me COVERDALE *John* 7:16. **4.** Your wylle & myne be one 1500. **5. a.** Both I and m. alas would starve 1683. **b.** *Tam. Shrew* II. i. 385.

Mine (məin), *v.* ME. [– (O)Fr. *miner*, perh. orig. Gallo-Rom. deriv. of a Celtic word repr. by Ir., Gaelic *mein* ore, mine, W. *mwyn* ore, †mine.] **1.** *intr.* To dig in the earth; *esp.* in a military sense, to dig under the foundations of a wall, etc. Also, to make subterranean passages. **2.** *trans.* To dig or burrow in (the earth); also, to make (a hole, passage, etc.) underground. late ME. **b.** To make subterranean passages under 1820. **3.** To dig away the foundations of (a wall, fort, etc.); to undermine. Now *rare*. late ME. **4.** In modern warfare; To lay mines (see MINE *sb.* 3) under, for the purpose of destruction 1630. **5.** To obtain (metals, etc.) from a mine. late ME. **6.** *intr.* To dig for minerals, etc.; to make a mine; to work in a mine. late ME. **7.** *trans.* To dig in or penetrate for ore, metals, etc. 1839.

1. The Enemie mined; and they countermined RALEGH. *fig.* To search and m. into that which is not reuealed BACON. **2.** *fig.* He may be said to m. his way into a subject, like a mole HAZLITT. **3.** *fig.* Hee..mines my gentility with my education SHAKS. **4.** The ground is mined and the train is laid 1851. **5.** Lignite..is mined near Brousa 1878. **7.** Lead veins have been traced even further down,..but they have not been mined 1839. Hence **Mi·neable** *a.* capable of being mined.

Miner (məi·nəɹ). [ME. *mynur, minour* – OFr. *minëor, minour* (mod. *mineur*), f. *miner*; see prec., -OR 2.] **1.** One who excavates the ground, or makes subterranean passages; *esp.* one who undermines a fortress, etc.; now *Mil.* a soldier whose work is the laying of mines. *Sappers and Miners*: see SAPPER. **2.** One who works in a mine ME. **3.** A name applied to various burrowing insects or larvæ. (See also LEAF-*miner*.) 1816. **4.** A vessel used for laying mines 1898.

1. *transf.* The mole, the m. of the soil COWPER.

Comb. **m. ant,** see sense 3; **miner's friend,** a name for the Davy safety-lamp; **miner's inch,** see INCH *sb.*[1] 1; also in names of diseases contracted by miners, as *miner's anæmia, elbow, worm*, etc.

Mineral (mi·nĕrăl), *sb.* late ME. [– OFr. *mineral* or med.L. *minerale*, subst. use of n. sing. of *mineralis*, f. *minera* ore – OFr. *miniere* mine :– Rom. **minaria* (in AL. XI), f. **mina*, **minare* MINE *sb.* and *v.*; see -AL[1].] **1.** Any substance which is obtained by mining. In early and in mod. techn. use, the ore (of a metal). †**2.** A mine –1602. **3.** Any natural substance that is neither animal nor vegetable 1602. †**b.** A mineral medicine or poison –1730. **c.** *pl.* = MINERAL WATER(S 1903. **4.** In mod. scientific use, each of the species or kinds of natural inorganic substances 1813.

2. Like some Oare Among a Minerall of Mettels base SHAKS. **b.** *Cymb.* V. v. 50. *attrib.* **m. right,** the right or title to the minerals under a given surface, usu. including the right to mine them.

Mineral (mi·nĕrăl), *a.* 1477. [– Fr. *minéral* or med.L. *mineralis* (XIII), f. *minera*; see prec.] †**1.** Pertaining to mines or mining; (of persons) skilled in mining matters –1706. **2.** Having the nature of a mineral (MINERAL *sb.* 1); obtained by mining 1581. **b.** Impregnated with mineral substances. (See MINERAL WATER.) 1562. **3.** Of material substances: Neither animal nor vegetable; inorganic 1599. **b.** Pertaining to inorganic matter 1876.

Special collocations: **m. candle,** a candle made of paraffin; **m. caoutchouc** = ELATERITE; **m. chameleon** (see CHAMELEON); **m. charcoal,** a charcoal-like substance, often found between layers of coal; **m. coal,** pit-coal, as dist. from charcoal; **m. cotton** = *m. wool*; **m. jelly,** vaseline; **m. kingdom** (see KINGDOM 5); **m. oil,** a general name for petroleum and the oils distilled from it; **m. pitch** = ASPHALT 1; **m. tallow, wax** = OZOCERITE; **m. tar,** a black viscid substance intermediate between petroleum and asphalt; **m. wool,** a fibrous wool-like material made by blowing a jet of air or steam through a stream of liquid slag; slag-wool.

b. in names of various pigments, as *m. black, blue, green, grey, purple, white, yellow*, etc.

†**Mi·neralist.** 1631. [f. MINERAL *sb.* + -IST.] A mineralogist –1796.

Mineralize (mi·nĕrăləiz), *v.* Also **-ise.** 1655. [f. MINERAL *sb.* and *a.* + -IZE.] **1.** *trans.* To transform (a metal) into an ore. **2.** To convert into a mineral substance 1799. **b.** *intr.* for *refl.* To become mineralized 1845. **3.** *trans.* To impregnate with mineral matters

1789. **4.** *intr.* To mineralogize 1792. **5.** *passive.* To be stocked with ore 1890.

2. The bones found in caverns are never mineralised BUCKLAND. **5.** A great quantity of stone, well mineralised, in the level 1890. Hence **Minera·liza·tion.**

Mineralizer (mi·nĕrăləizəɹ). 1795. [f. prec. + -ER¹.] **1.** A substance that combines with a metal to form an ore, as sulphur, arsenic, etc. **2.** The mineral with which a water is impregnated 1799.

Mineralogy (minĕræ·lŏdʒi). 1690. [irreg. f. MINERAL *sb.* + -LOGY.] The science which treats of minerals. Hence **Mineralo·gical** *a.* of or pertaining to m.; used in the study of minerals. **Mineralo·gically** *adv.* **Minera·logize** *v. intr.* to look for or study minerals. So **Minera·logist,** one versed in m. 1646; *Zool.* a carrier-shell 1851.

Mineral water. 1562. **a.** Orig., any natural water impregnated with some mineral substance. Also (with *a* and *pl.*) a kind of such water. **b.** Later, applied also to artificial imitations of such waters, and other effervescent drinks, e.g. soda-water, lemonade, ginger-beer, etc.

Minerva (minɜ̄·ɹvă). late ME. [– L. *Minerva*, earlier *Menerva* :– pre-L. *menes-*wā* (cf. Skr. *manasvin* 'full of mind or sense'), f. *menes- = Skr. *manas* mind, Gr. μένος courage, fury, f. root *men-; see MIND *sb.*] The Roman goddess of wisdom, anciently identified with the Greek Pallas Athene. †**b.** *fig.* Used for: Wisdom, ability. Also with allusion to the myth that Minerva was born from the head of Jupiter. –1734.

†*In spite of M.* (tr. L. *invitâ Minervâ*): contrary to one's natural bent. *Comb.* **M. (machine)** *Printing*, a small platen jobbing machine. **M. press,** a printing-press formerly existing in London; hence, the series of ultra-sentimental novels issued from it *c*1800.

Minerval (minɜ̄·ɹvăl). 1603. [– L. *minerval*, f. *Minerva*; see prec.] A gift given in gratitude by a scholar to a master.

Minery (məi·nəri). 1554. [– med.L. *mineria, minaria*, f. *minare* MINE *v.*] Mining; a place where mining operations are carried on.

Minever, Ming(e, var. MINIVER, MENG.

Mingle (mi·ŋg'l), *sb.* Now *rare.* 1548. [f. MINGLE *v.*] The action of mingling, the state of being mingled; mixture. Also *concr.* a mixture.

Mingle (mi·ŋg'l), *v.* [Late ME. *mengel*, frequent. of MENG *v.*; see -LE 3.] **1.** *trans.* To mix; to combine in a mixture, to blend. **b.** *poet.* To put in as an ingredient. TENNYSON. **2.** To bring together, intersperse (*with* or *among* others), to unite or join in company. Also with *up.* 1450. †**b.** To join (conversation, friendship, etc.) *with* another person. Also *to m. eyes*, look into each other's eyes. –1650. **3.** To concoct, compound 1611. **4.** *intr.* Of things: To join together (or *with* another); to mix, blend 1530. **5.** Of a person: To mix *with* others; to move about *among* or *in* a gathering. Also, to take part with others *in* some action, etc. 1605.

1. I..mengle my drynke with wepynge COVERDALE *Ps.* 101: 9. **b.** Fill the cup, and fill the can! M. madness, m. scorn! 1842. **2.** Both they and their sonnes haue mengled them selues with the daughters of them COVERDALE 1 *Esdras* 8:70. **b.** *Wint. T.* IV. iv. 471. **3.** To m. strong drinke *Isa.* 5:22. **4.** I heard the rack As Earth and Skie would m. MILT. **5.** To m. in society 1870.

Mingle-mangle (mi·ŋg'l,mæ·ŋg'l). 1549. [redupl. of MINGLE *sb.*] A mixture; chiefly, a confused medley (of things or persons). Also *attrib.* or as *adj.* So **Mi·ngle-mangle** *v.*

Mi·nglement. 1674. [f. MINGLE *v.* + -MENT.] The action of mingling; a mixture.

Mingy (mi·ndʒi), *a. colloq.* 1928. [perh. f. M(EAN *a.* + ST)INGY *a.*] Mean, stingy.

Miniaceous (miniēⁱ·ʃəs), *a.* 1688. [f. L. *miniaceus*, f. *minium* native cinnabar, also, red lead; see -ACEOUS.] = MINIATE *a.*

Miniard, -ize: see MIGNIARD, -IZE.

Miniate (mi·niĕt), *a. rare.* 1890. [– L. *miniatus*, pa. pple. of *miniare*; see next, -ATE².] Of the colour of minium or red lead; vermilion-coloured. So **Minia·tous** *a.* 1826.

Miniate (mi·nieⁱt), *v.* 1657. [– *miniat-*, ppl. stem of L. *miniare*, f. *minium*; see MINIUM, -ATE³.] *trans.* To colour or paint with vermilion; to rubricate or (more widely) to illuminate (a manuscript). Also *transf.* Hence **Mi·niator,** a rubricator, an illuminator.

Miniature (mi·niătiŭɹ, mi·nitŭɹ, -tʃəɹ), *sb.* and *a.* 1586. [– It. *miniatura* – med.L. *miniatura*, f. *miniare* rubricate, illuminate; see prec., -URE.] **A.** *sb.* †**1.** The action or process of miniating (see MINIATE *v.*) –1700. **2.** *concr.* An illumination; also, illuminated work in general 1700. **3.** The painting of 'miniatures' (in sense 4 below). Chiefly in phrase *in m.* 1656. **4.** *concr.* A portrait 'in miniature'; a portrait painted on a small scale and with minute finish, usu. on ivory or vellum 1716. **5.** *transf.* and *fig.* A reduced image or representation. Also *occas.* a minutely finished production. 1586. ¶**6.** A lineament. MASSINGER.

5. *In m.*: on a small scale; in brief; That which is correct in m. will be true in the large 1813. *Comb.* **m.-initial,** an ornamental initial having a m. picture painted within it.

B. *adj.* Represented on a small scale 1714.

Hence **Mi·niature** *v. trans.* to embellish with miniatures; to represent or describe in m. **Mi·niaturist,** a miniator; one who paints m. pictures or portraits.

Minié (mi·nie). 1853. [See below.]

M. ball, bullet, an elongated bullet invented by Capt. C. E. Minié of Vincennes, which, when fired, was expanded by the powder contained in an iron cup inserted in a cavity at its base. *M. rifle*, a rifle for firing this bullet.

Minify (mi·nifəi), *v.* 1676. [irreg. f. L. *minor* less, *minimus* least, after *magnify.*] **1.** *trans.* To diminish in importance; to regard or represent (something) as smaller than it is. **2.** To lessen in actual size or importance 1866.

Minikin (mi·nikin), *sb.* and *a.* 1541. [– Du. *minneken*, f. *minne* love + *-ken, -kijn* -KIN.] **A.** *sb.* **1.** A playful or endearing term for a woman or girl. *Obs.* exc. *dial.* †**2.** A thin string of gut used for the treble string of the lute or viol. Also *attrib.*, as *m. string.* –1721. **3.** *transf.* and *fig.* A small or insignificant thing; a diminutive person 1761. **4.** A small kind of pin 1574. **5.** *Printing.* A size of type smaller than 'brilliant' 1890. **B.** *adj.* **1.** Dainty, elegant, sprightly. Now contemptuously: Affected, mincing. 1545. †**2.** Of a voice; Shrill –1608. **3.** Of a thing: Miniature; tiny 1589.

2. For one blast of thy m. mouth, thy sheepe shall take no harme SHAKS.

Minim (mi·nim). late ME. [As sb. repr. various ellipt. uses in med.L. of L. *minimus* least, smallest; as adj. – L. *minimus.* See MINOR.] **A.** *sb.* **1.** *Mus.* The character for a note half the value of a semibreve and double that of a crotchet (now with an open rounded head and a tail); a note of this value. Also *attrib.*, as *m. rest.* **2.** *Calligraphy.* A single down stroke of the pen 1603. **3.** The least possible portion (of something), a jot; †an atom, minute particle 1592. **4.** A creature or thing of the least size or importance 1590. **5.** A friar of the mendicant order (*Ordo Minimorum Eremitarum*) founded by St. Francis of Paula (*c*1416–1507) 1546. †**6.** *Printing.* ? = MINION *sb.*¹ 3. –1818. **7.** The smallest fluid measure, about a drop; the sixtieth part of a fluid drachm. Also, a unit equal to a grain. *attrib.*, as *m.-measure.* 1809.

4. Phr. *M. of nature*, one of the smallest forms of animal life.

B. *adj.* Smallest, extremely small; †atomic 1670.

For man, a m. jot in time and space R. BRIDGES.

So **Mi·nimal** *a.* extremely minute in size; that is the least possible 1666.

Minimalist (mi·nimălist). 1918. [f. MINIMAL + -IST.] Used as an etymological equivalent of MENSHEVIK.

Miniment, obs. f. MUNIMENT.

Minimism (mi·nimiz'm). 1820. [f. L. *minimus* + -ISM.] **1.** Absorption in minute details. COLERIDGE. **2.** *Theol.* The minimizing view of what is involved in a dogma, esp. that of a papal infallibility.

Minimize (mi·niməiz), *v.* 1802. [f. L. *minimus* + -IZE.] **1.** *trans.* **a.** To reduce to the smallest possible amount, extent, or degree. **b.** To estimate at the smallest possible amount. **2.** *intr.* To take the most moderate view possible of what is involved in a dogma 1875. Hence **Minimiza·tion, Mi·nimizer.**

Minimum (mi·nimŏm). *Pl.* **minima** (mi·nimă). 1663. [– L. *minimum*, subst. use of n. of *minimus* least; see MINOR.] **A.** *sb.* †**1.** *Nat. Philos.* The smallest portion into which matter is divisible; an atom. Also, the smallest possible portion of time or space. –1739. **2.** The least amount attainable, allowable, usual, etc. 1676. **3.** *Math.* = *minimum value*: see B. 1743. **4.** The lowest amount or degree of variation (of temperature, a spectrum, etc.) attained or recorded 1823. **5.** *attrib.*, as *m. period* 1860.

1. The imagination reaches a *minimum*, and may raise up to itself an idea, of which it cannot conceive any sub-division HUME. **5. Minimum thermometer,** one which records automatically the lowest temperature since its last adjustment.

B. *adj.* [The sb. used appositively.] That is a minimum 1810.

M. value (of a variable quantity) *Math.*, a value at which it ceases to decrease and begins to increase.

Minimus (mi·nimŏs). *Pl.* **minimi** (mi·niməi). 1590. [– L. *minimus* least; see MINOR.] **A.** *sb.* **1.** A creature of the smallest size. **2.** *Anat.* The fifth digit; the little finger or toe 1881.

1. Get you gone you dwarfe, You *minimus* SHAKS.

B. *adj.* In some schools, appended to the surname of the youngest of several boys having the same. Abbrev. *min., mini.*, or *mins.*

Mining (məi·niŋ), *vbl. sb.* 1523. [f. MINE *v.* + -ING¹.] **1.** The action of MINE *v.* **2.** *attrib.*, as *m.-camp*, etc. 1555.

Comb.: **m.-hole,** a hole bored to receive a blasting-charge in mining; **-ship,** one that carries and lays down submarine mines.

Minion (mi·nyən), *sb.*¹ and *a.* 1500. [– Fr. *mignon* (XV), repl. OFr. *mignot*, f. Gaul. **mino* (cf. OIr. *min* tender, soft) or **mino* (cf. OIr. *min* small) + dim. suffix *-ottus.*] **A.** *sb.* **1.** A beloved object, darling, favourite. **a.** A lover or lady-love; also, a mistress or paramour (*obs.* or *rare*). **b.** One specially esteemed or favoured; a favourite, 'idol'; often *fig.* (now *contempt.*) 1566. **c.** *esp.* A favourite of a sovereign, etc.; an obsequious or servile dependant; a 'creature'; often (now *arch.*) as a form of address 1501. †**2.** A small kind of ordnance of about 3-inch calibre –1894. **3.** *Printing.* (In full *m. type* or *letter.*) A size of type between 'nonpareil' and 'brevier' 1659. **4.** *attrib.* **a.** (sense 1) as *m. maintainer*, etc. 1599. †**b.** (sense 2), as *m.-bore, gun*, etc. –1727.

1. a. What will not a fond lover undertake..for his m.? BARROW. **c.** The king is loue-sicke for his m. MARLOWE. It is no wonder if he helps himself from the city treasury and allows his minions to do so BRYCE.

B. *adj.* Now *rare.* **1.** Dainty, elegant, pretty, neat 1528. **2.** Dearly beloved, favourite, pet 1716.

Hence †**Mi·nionize** *v. trans.* to raise to the position of a m.; *intr.* to play the wanton 1604–1616. †**Mi·nionly** *adv.* delicately, elegantly 1539–1633. †**Mi·nionship,** the position of a m. 1645.

Minion (mi·nyən), *sb.*² 1621. [– Fr. *minion* (Cotgr.), f. L. *minium.*] †**1.** = MINIUM –1654. **2.** Calcined or sifted iron ore 1793.

Minionette (minyəne·t), *sb. U.S.* 1871. [f. MINION *sb.*¹ + -ETTE.] *Printing.* A size of type between nonpareil and minion, used in ornamental borders, etc.

†**Minione·tte,** *a.* 1749. [– Fr. *mignonnette* fem., after MINION *a.*] Small and pretty. H. WALPOLE.

†**Mi·nious,** *a.* [f. L. *minium* + -OUS.] Of the colour of minium, red. SIR T. BROWNE.

Minish (mi·niʃ), *v.* Now only *arch.* [In XIV *menuse, mynusche*, and, with assim. to -ISH², *mynysshe*, – OFr. *menu(i)sier* :– Rom. **minutiare*, f. L. *minutia* MINUTIA; cf. MINCE *v.*] **1.** *trans.* To make fewer or less; to reduce in power, influence, etc. **2.** To remove, withdraw (a portion *of* or *from* something) 1483. Also *absol.* **3.** To depreciate, belittle. late ME. **4.** *intr.* To become less in quantity, number, size, etc. late ME.

1. When they are minished & brought lowe thorow oppression COVERDALE *Ps.* 106[7]: 39. Hence †**Mi·nishment** 1533–1664.

Minister (mi·nistəɹ), *sb.* ME. [– (O)Fr. *ministre* – L. *minister* servant, f. **minis-*, var. of *minus* less, adv. of *minor* MINOR, in formation parallel to the correl. *magister*

MASTER.] †1. A servant, attendant –1781. 2. One who acts as the agent or representative of a superior. Now *rare*. Also with *of*. ME. †b. An officer entrusted with the administration of the law, or attached to a court of justice –1723. †c. An underling –1625. 3. A high officer of state. a. One entrusted with the administration of a department of state 1625. b. A political agent accredited by one sovereign state to another 1709. 4. *Eccl.* a. In the rubrics of the Book of Common Prayer, the clergyman, or any of a number of clergymen, engaged in conducting worship on a particular occasion 1549. b. A person officially charged with spiritual functions in the Christian Church. Now rarely applied to an Anglican clergyman, and chiefly associated with Low Church views; but still usual in non-episcopal communions. ME. c. Applied to non-Christian religious functionaries. *Obs.* exc. *occas.* with reference to Jews. late ME. d. The title of the superior of certain religious orders; also *m. general* 1450. In the Society of Jesus, each of the five assistants of the general 1593.

1. When the seruant [*marg.* minister] of the man of God was risen 2 *Kings* 6:15. *transf.* My tongue. . As Ministre of my wit CHAUCER. 3. What do Ministers (= the Ministry) mean to do? DICKENS. Phr. *M. for, of war, m. for foreign affairs*, etc. 4. b. Renan's appearance is something between the Catholic priest and the dissenting m. GEO. ELIOT. Phr. *M. of religion*, a clergyman of any denomination. Hence **Mi·nistership** 1565.

Minister (mi·nistəɹ), *v.* ME. [– (O)Fr. *ministrer* – L. *ministrare*, f. *minister*; see prec.] I. *trans.* †1. To serve (food or drink) –1662. 2. To furnish, supply, impart (help, etc.). Now only (*arch.* or *literary*) with immaterial obj. late ME. †b. To prompt, suggest. *Meas. for M.* IV. v. 6. †3. To dispense, administer (a sacrament, the elements, etc.) –1816. †4. To apply or administer (something healing); also *absol.* and *fig.* late ME. –1680. †5. To execute or dispense (justice, law); to administer (punishment) –1596. †6. *Law.* To administer (an oath, etc.) –1722. †7. To manage (affairs, etc.) –1541.

2. They m. a singuler helpe and preseruatiue against vnbeleefe and error BACON.

II. *intr.* 1. To serve, wait at table; to render aid or tendance. late ME. 2. To serve or officiate in worship; to act as a minister of the Church ME. 3. To be helpful; also, to be conducive *to* something 1696.

1. The Sonne of man came not to bee ministred vnto, but to m. *Mark* 10:45. 3. To m. to his Necessities 1696. Hence **Mi·nistering** *vbl. sb.* and *ppl. a.* Or ministery, let vs wait, on our ministring *Rom.* 12:7. Are they not all mynistrynge sprêtes? COVERDALE *Heb.* 1:14. When pain and anguish wring the brow, A ministering angel thou! SCOTT.

Ministerial (ministīᵊ·riăl), *a.* (and *sb.*) 1561. [– Fr. *ministériel* or late L. *ministerialis*, f. L. *ministerium* MINISTRY. But app. apprehended as a deriv. of MINISTER *sb.*] 1. Pertaining to, or entrusted with, the execution of the law, or of the commands of a superior 1577. 2. Subsidiary, instrumental 1607. 3. Pertaining to the office, function, or character of a minister of religion 1561. 4. Of or pertaining to a minister of state; siding with or supporting the Ministry as against the Opposition 1655. 5. *sb. Hist.* An executive household officer under the feudal system 1818.

1. Phr. *M. act*: an act which is a necessary part of an official's duty, so that the agent is exempt from responsibility for its consequences. 2. Inferior and ministeriall Arts 1619. 4. M. cries of 'Oh' 1889. Hence **Ministe·rialist,** a supporter of the Ministry in office. **Ministe·rially** *adv.* in a m. manner or capacity; as a minister.

†**Ministral,** *a. rare.* 1727. [– Fr. *ministral*, f. *ministre*; see MINISTER *sb.*, -AL¹.] Pertaining to a minister or agent –1851.

Ministrant (mi·nistrănt). 1667. [– *ministrant-*, pr. ppl. stem of L. *ministrare*; see MINISTER *v.*, -ANT.] A. *adj.* That ministers. Const. *to*. B. *sb.* One who ministers 1818.

A. Thrones and Powers, Princedoms, and Dominations m. MILT.

†**Mi·nistrate,** *v.* 1533. [– *ministrat-*, pa. ppl. stem of L. *ministrare*; see MINISTER *v.*, -ATE³.] 1. *trans.* To administer –1727. 2. *intr.* To minister *to*. BROWNING.

Ministration (ministrēⁱ·ʃən). ME. [– OFr. *ministration* or L. *ministratio*, f. as prec.; see -ION.] 1. The action (*occas.* an act) of ministering or serving. †b. Administration or exercise of (official) functions –1651. †c. Instrumentality –1555. 2. *spec.* Service as a priest or minister; *pl.* the services of ministers of religion 1535. 3. Administration of the sacraments, justice, law, an estate or revenue, etc.; *occas.* executorship (*arch.*). 4. The action of supplying, providing, or giving (something). Const. *of*. 1460.

1. b. Content with the nomination of Magistrates, and publique Ministers, that is to say, with the authority without the m. 1651.

Ministrative (mi·nistrĕtiv), *a.* 1833. [app. f. MINISTER *v.* + -ATIVE.] Pertaining to or of the nature of ministration; affording assistance.

Ministrator (mi·nistreⁱtəɹ). *rare.* 1523. [f. MINISTRATE *v.* + -OR 2 (cf. AL. *ministrator* (eccl.) official XIII); later prob. apprehended as f. MINISTER *v.* + -ATOR.] One who ministers or administers; †a testamentary executor.

Ministress (mi·nistrės). 1600. [f. MINISTER *sb.* + -ESS¹. Cf. Fr. *ministresse*.] A woman who ministers or serves. Also *transf.* and *fig.*

Ministry (mi·nistri). [In XIV *ministerie* – L. *ministerium*; see MINISTER *sb.*] 1. The action of ministering; the rendering of service. Now only in religious use. †2. A mode or kind of service; a function, office –1644. 3. The functions, or any specific function, pertaining to a minister of religion. late ME. b. The ministration of a particular minister 1623. c. The office of minister of the church, or of a religious body or congregation 1824. d. Christian ministers collectively, the clergy (now *rare*) 1561. 4. Agency, instrumentality. Now only with religious colouring. 1581. 5. The body of ministers charged with the administration of a country or state 1710. b. With reference to foreign countries: A ministerial department of government; a minister and his subordinates. Also, the building belonging to such a department. 1877. c. Administration of a minister of state; ministerial term.

1. The perpetual m. of one soul to another TENNYSON. 3. A certain Priest. . was suspended from his m. at the Altar 1635. c. To educate a man for the m. SCOTT. 5. The Cabal M. were in power 1865. c. During Pitt's ministry (*mod.*).

Minium (mi·niɒm). *Obs.* exc. *Hist.* late ME. [– L. *minium* native cinnabar, red lead.] 1. = VERMILION. Also *attrib.* 2. = RED LEAD. Also, †its colour. 1650.

Miniver (mi·nivəɹ). [ME. *meniver, menuver* – AFr. *menuver*, (O)Fr. *menu vair*, i.e. *menu* little (:– L. *minutus* MINUTE), *vair* VAIR.] 1. A kind of fur used as a lining and trimming in ceremonial costume. In 1688 explained as 'plain white fur', and used recently in this sense. 2. †a. The animal from which the fur was supposed to be obtained. b. *dial.* The ermine in its white winter coat. 1665. 3. *attrib.*, as *m. cap*, etc. 1589.

Minivet (mi·nivet). 1862. [Of unkn. origin.] Any bird of the genus *Pericrocotus* of India.

Mink (miŋk). 1466. [Early forms *menks, mynkes*; cf. Sw. *menk, mänk* mink, LG. *mink* otter.] 1. The skins or fur of the animals mentioned in sense 2. 2. A small semi-aquatic stoat-like animal of the genus *Putorius*; orig., the European species *P. lutreola*; now oftener the American *P. vison*, also called *mink-otter* 1624. 3. *attrib.*, as *m.-skin*, etc. 1812.

‖**Minnesinger** (mi·nĭsiŋəɹ). 1825. [G., f. *minne* love + †*singer* (mod. *sänger*) singer.] One of the German lyrical poets and singers of the 12–14th centuries, who chiefly sang of love.

Minnow (mi·noᵘ). late ME. [perh. orig. repr. OE. **mynwe* (beside recorded OE. *myne* 'capito', 'mena'), = OHG. *muniwa* 'capedo' (i.e. L. *capito*), but infl. by ME. *menuse, menise* – OFr. *menuise* :– Rom. **minutia* n. pl. small objects (cf. MINUTIA.] 1. A small cyprinoid freshwater fish, *Leuciscus phoxinus* or *Phoxinus lævis*, common in European streams, ponds etc. Often loosely applied to any small fish; esp. the stickleback (*Gastrosteus*). In the U.S. it is applied similarly, chiefly to cyprinoids; and in Australia to fishes of the genus *Galaxias*. b. *transf.* and *fig.* as a type of smallness 1588. 2. *Angling.* A minnow, real or artificial, used as a bait 1615.

1. b. Phr. *A Triton of* or *among the minnows*: one who appears great from the insignificance of all those around him; Heare you this Triton of the Minnowes? SHAKS. *Comb.* **m.-tansy,** a dish of fried minnows seasoned with tansy.

Mino, obs. f. MINA².

Minoan (minōᵘ·ăn), *a.* and *sb.* 1894. [f. *Minos*, a famous king of Crete + -AN.] Of or pertaining to the prehistoric civilization of Crete (B.C. *c*3000–1400). Also *sb.*

Minor (məi·nəɹ), *a.* and *sb.* ME. [– OFr. *menour* in *freres menours* (med.L. *fratres minores*); in other uses – L. *minor*, which functions as compar. of *parvus* small, and is rel. to *minuere* lessen, Gr. μινύθειν, and μείων less.] A. *adj.* I. *Friar M.*, †*M. Friar*: a Franciscan.

Transl. of med.L. *Fratres Minores*, lit. 'lesser brethren', so named by St. Francis to express the humility he desired them to cultivate. The pl. is now *Friars Minor*.

II. 1. = LESSER (but not followed by *than*.) Opp. to MAJOR. 1654. b. Comparatively small or unimportant. (Not now used with reference to physical magnitude, exc. as this involves importance.) 1623. 2. *Math.* See below 1850. 3. *Logic.* See below 1551. 4. That constitutes the minority. Also rarely in predicative use: In a minority. 1642. 5. *Mus.* a. Applied to intervals smaller by a chromatic semitone than those called *major*; a *m. third*, etc. Hence also to the note distant by a minor interval from a given note. b. Applied to a common chord or triad containing a minor third between the root and the second note; hence to a cadence ending on such a chord. c. Denoting those keys, or that mode, in which the scale has a minor third (and also a minor sixth and seventh). (In naming a key, *minor* follows the letter, as *A minor*.) 1694. d. Minor chords and keys are usually mournful or pathetic; hence various fig. allusions 1869. 6. Following the sb. qualified (see below) 1791.

1. *M. canon, excommunication* (= lesser e.) *orders, prophets*. †*M. Fellow* (Cambridge): a junior Fellow. *M. planet*: one of the asteroids or small planets between Mars and Jupiter. b. The base and m. sort of people SIR T. BROWNE. The m. critic, who hunts for blemishes '*Junius*' *Lett.* *M. operations* (Surg.): those which do not involve danger to life. *M. point* (Football): a try (in the Rugby game). 2. *M. axis* (of an ellipse): the diameter perpendicular to the major or transverse axis. *M. determinant*: a determinant whose matrix is formed from that of another determinant by erasing one or more rows and columns. 3. *M. term*: the subject of the conclusion of a syllogism. *M. premiss, proposition*: that premiss of a syllogism which contains the m. term. 5. d. His conversation was pitched in a m. key BURNAND. 6. *Quint, tierce m.*: see QUINT *sb.*², TIERCE. *Bob-m.* (Bell-ringing): a bob (BOB *sb.*⁵) rung upon six bells. In boys' schools, appended to a surname to distinguish the younger of two boys of the same surname (abbrev. *mi.*). A member of the fifth form, Green minor by name 1852.

III. Under age; below the age of majority. Now *rare*. 1579.

B. *sb.* 1. A Franciscan friar ME. 2. *Logic.* The minor premiss in a syllogism. late ME. 3. = INFANT *sb.*¹ 2. 1612. 4. *Mus.* Short for *m. key, mode*, etc. 1797. Also *fig.* (See A. II. 5 c, d.) 5. *Football.* A minor point 1890. 6. In boys' schools: cf. A. II. 6. 1863.

7. *U.S.* A subsidiary subject of study to which less time is devoted than to a major 1891.

†**Mi·norate,** *v.* 1534. [– *minorat-*, pa. ppl. stem of late (eccl.) L. *minorare* diminish, f. L. *minor*; see prec., -ATE³.] *trans.* To diminish, depreciate –1727. So †**Minora·tion,** a lessening, diminution; mild purgation 1607–1696. †**Mi·norative** *a.* and *sb.* (a) gently laxative (medicine) –1747.

Minorca (minǭ·ɹkă). 1848. [Sp. *Menorca*.] Name of the second in size of the Balearic islands. Used *attrib.*, as *M.-fowl* (also *M.*), a black variety of the domestic fowl introduced from Spain; etc. Hence **Mino·rcan** *a.* of or belonging to M.; *sb.* an inhabitant of M.; also, the language of the Minorcans.

Minoress (məi·nŏrės). *Obs.* exc. *Hist.* [In XIV *menouresse* – OFr. *menouresse*, f.

menour; see MINOR, -ESS¹.] A nun of the second order of St. Francis, known as Poor Clares, whose house outside Aldgate gave its name to the *Minories*, a street in the City of London.

Minorite (məi·nŏrəit). 1537. [f. MINOR + -ITE¹ 1.] **A.** *sb.* **1.** A friar minor or Franciscan. **2.** †**a.** A person of minor rank –1670. **b.** One busied about minor matters. SOUTHEY. **B.** *adj.* Of the order of Friars Minor 1563.

A. 1. Malachias, the minorit or greie frier HOLINSHED.

Minority (məi-, minǫ·rĭti). 1533. [– Fr. *minorité* or med.L. *minoritas*, f. L. *minor*; see MINOR, -ITY.] †**1.** The condition or fact of being smaller, inferior, or subordinate –1751. **2.** The state of being minor or under age; nonage 1547. Also *transf.* and *fig.* (now *rare*). **3.** The smaller number or part; *spec.* the smaller party voting together against a majority 1736. **4.** In voting, the number of votes cast for or by the smaller party 1774.

3. We are a m.; but then we are a very large m. BURKE. **4.** The m. did not reach to more than 39 or 40 BURKE.

Comb.: **m.-report,** a separate report made by those members of a committee, etc., who are unable to agree with the majority; **m. teller,** one who counts for a m.

Minotaur (mi·nŏtǭɹ). late ME. [– OFr. *Minotaur* (mod. *-taure*) – L. *Minotaurus* – Gr. Μινώταυρος, f. Μίνως Minos, king of Crete + ταῦρος bull.] *Gr. Myth.* A fabulous monster, half bull and half man, the son of Pasiphaë, wife of Minos king of Crete, and a bull; he was fed on human flesh. Hence *allusively*.

The Imperial Minotaur [*sc.* Napoleon] 1900.

Minow, obs. f. MINNOW.

Minster (mi·nstəɹ). [OE. *mynster* = OHG. *munistri* (G. *münster*), MDu. *monster*, ON. *mustari* – pop. L. **monisterium* (whence OFr. *moustier*, mod. *moutier*) for eccl. L. *monasterium* MONASTERY.] †**1.** A monastery; a Christian religious house –1513. **2.** The church of a monastery; also *gen.* any large church, *esp.* a collegiate or cathedral church OE. †**b.** *transf.* A temple –1581.

Minstrel (mi·nstrĕl), *sb.* ME. [– OFr. *menestral*, -(*e*)*rel*, *mini-*, entertainer, handicraftsman, servant – Pr. *menest*(*ai*)*ral* officer, attendant, employed person, musician – late L. *ministerialis* official, officer, f. *ministerium*; see MYSTERY², -AL¹.] †**1.** *gen.* A servant having a special function. ME. only. **2.** In early use: Any one whose profession was to entertain his patrons with music, story-telling, buffoonery, etc. In mod. use: A mediæval singer or musician, esp. one who sang or recited heroic or lyric poetry composed by himself or others. ME. **3.** *transf.* Used *poet.* or *rhet.* for a musician, singer, or poet 1718. **4.** Chiefly in *pl.* The designation of certain bands of public entertainers with blacked faces and grotesque costumes, who perform interludes, with songs and music ostensibly of Negro origin 1864.

2. The Lay of the Last M. SCOTT (*title*). **3.** I stood, . . with Thee, Great M. of the Border! WORDSW. Hence **Mi·nstrel** *v.* to sing of, celebrate in song.

Minstrelsy (mi·nstrĕlsi). ME. [– OFr. *menestralsie*, f. *menestrel*; see prec.] **1.** The art or occupation of a minstrel; the practice of playing and singing; now only *poet.* or *rhet.* **2.** A body of minstrels ME. †**3.** *collect.* Musical instruments. Also, a kind of musical instrument. –1523. **4.** Minstrel poetry; *occas.* a body of this 1802.

2. Toforn hym gooth the loude Mynstralcye CHAUCER.

Mint (mint), *sb.*¹ [OE. *mynet*, corresp. (with variation of gender) to OFris. *menote*, *munte*, OS. *munita* (Du. *munt*), OHG. *munizza*, *muniz* (G. *münze*) – WGmc. **munita* – L. *moneta*; see MONEY.] †**1.** A piece of money; money. From 16th c. only *slang.* –1848. **2.** A place where money is coined under public authority. late ME. **b.** A set of machines for coining 1592. **3.** *transf.* and *fig.* A source of invention or fabrication 1555. †**4.** Coinage –1622. **5.** A vast sum (of money); rarely *transf.* a vast amount (of something costly) 1655.

2. *Master of the m.*: the chief officer and custodian of the m. **3.** A man . . That hath a m. of phrases in his braine SHAKS. **5.** He must have lost a m. of money 1833.

Comb.: **m.-bill,** a bill or promissory note issued by the officers of the m. against bullion deposited for coining; **m. condition,** (of a book, picture, etc.) fresh and perfect state as if only just produced; †**m. man,** one engaged or skilled in coining; **m.-mark,** a mark placed upon a coin to indicate the mint at which it was struck; **m.-master,** the master or manager of the mint; **m. price,** the price of bullion as recognized at the m.; so **m. value.**

Mint (mint), *sb.*² [OE. *minte* = OHG. *minza* (G. *minze*) :– WGmc. **minta* – L. *menta*, *mentha* – Gr. μίνθη (also μίνθος), prob. of Mediterranean origin.] **1.** Any aromatic labiate plant of the genus *Mentha*, esp. *M. viridis*, Garden Mint or SPEARMINT. **2.** Applied with defining word to plants of allied genera, e.g. *Calamintha* 1548.

Comb.: **m. julep** (see JULEP 2); **-sauce,** a sauce made of finely chopped m., vinegar, and sugar; usually eaten with roast lamb; **-water,** a cordial distilled from m.

Mint (mint), *v.* 1546. [f. MINT *sb.*¹] **1.** *trans.* To make (coin) by stamping metal. **b.** *fig.* To coin or invent (a word or phrase); in contemptuous use, to invent, fabricate (something counterfeit) 1593. **2.** To convert (bullion) into coin or money. Now *rare.* 1569. **b.** *fig.* To impress (something) with a stamp or character. Also with *out*, *upon*. Also, to stamp (an impress) *upon*. 1664.

1. b. One Happy Phrase, newly minted by the Dr. C. BOYLE.

Mintage (mi·ntĕdʒ). 1470. [f. MINT *v.* or *sb.*¹ + -AGE.] **1.** The action or process (*occas.* the privilege) of coining money; coinage. Also *transf.* and *fig.* (cf. MINT *v.* 1 b). **2.** *concr.* The product of a (particular) mint. Also *transf.* and *fig.* 1638. **3.** The charge or duty for coining 1645. **4.** The stamp impressed on a coin 1634.

1. Coins of Roman m. 1853. A new word of German m. DE QUINCEY.

Minter (mi·ntəɹ). [OE. *mynetere* = OS. *muniteri* (MDu., Du. *munter*), OHG. *munizāri* – late L. *monetarius*, f. *moneta*; see MONEY, -ARY¹.] One who coins or stamps money. Also *fig.*

Minuend (mi·niuend). 1706. [– L. *minuendus* (sc. *numerus*), gerundive of *minuere* diminish.] *Arith.* The number or quantity from which another is to be subtracted.

Minuet (miniue·t). 1673. [– Fr. *menuet*, subst. use of adj. *menuet* small, fine, delicate, dim. of *menu* small; see MENU, -ET.] **1.** A slow, stately dance, in triple measure, for two dancers. **2.** The music used to accompany this dance. Hence, a piece of music in the same rhythm and style, often forming one of the movements of a suite or sonata 1686.

1. I am fit for Nothing but low dancing now, a Corant, a Boreè, Or a Minnuét ETHEREGE. *attrib.* You should do everything, said Lord Chesterfield, in m. time BAGEHOT.

Minum(e, obs. ff. MINIM.

Minunet, obs. f. MIGNONETTE.

Minus (məi·nŏs). 1481. [– L. *minus* 'less', n. of *minor* used as adv.; see MINOR.] **1.** quasi-*prep.* With the deduction of, exclusive of. Cf. LESS *a.* 4, Fr. *moins*, G. *weniger*. **b.** *predicatively* in colloq. use: Short of, without. Hence *occas.* as *adj.* 1813. **2.** As the oral equivalent of the symbol (–), as helping to form a negative quantity, e.g. in '–3', '–*x*', which are read as *minus* 3, *minus x* 1579. **b.** Hence *attrib.* in *minus quantity*, a negative quantity; pop. misused for 'something non-existent' 1863. **c.** *adj.* Of the nature of a minus quantity; also *colloq.* non-existent 1800. **d.** *adv.* and *adj.* Negatively (electrified) 1747. **3.** *sb.* **a.** *Math.* The symbol (–); also *minus sign*. **b.** A subtraction, a quantity subtracted; a loss, deficiency. **c.** A negative quantity. 1654.

1. If all mankind m. one, were of one opinion MILL. **b.** The Englishman got back to civilization m. his left arm 1903. **3. a.** A slatefull of plusses, minusses, *x*, *y*, *z's* 1836.

Minuscule (minɒ·skiul). 1705. [– Fr. *minuscule* – L. *minuscula* (sc. *littera* letter), fem. of *minusculus* rather less, dim. of **minwos*, MINOR; see -CULE.] **A.** *adj.* †**a.** *Printing.* Of a letter: Small, lower-case. **b.** *Palæogr.* Of a letter: Small (see B. b). Also, written in minuscules. 1727. **2.** *gen.* Very small 1893. **B.** *sb.* †**a.** *Printing.* A small or lower-case letter as opp. to a capital. **b.** *Palæogr.* A small letter as opp. to a capital or uncial; the small cursive script developed from the uncial; also, a manuscript in this writing. 1705.

b. The m. arose in the 7th century as a cursive monastic script I. TAYLOR.

†**Mi·nutary,** *a.* [f. MINUTE *sb.* + -ARY¹.] Consisting of minutes (of time). FULLER.

Minute (mi·nit), *sb.* late ME. [– (O)Fr. *minute* – late L. subst. use of L. *minuta*, fem. of *minutus* (see next). Branch I rests ult. on med.L. *pars minuta prima* 'first minute part', the $\frac{1}{60}$ of a unit in the (Babylonian) system of sexagesimal fractions (cf. SECOND *sb.*¹). Branch III depends (perh. through Fr.) on the mediæval use of L. *minuta* (in AL. XIV), which may be for *minuta scriptura* draft in small writing as dist. from the engrossed copy. Branch II is – L. *minutum*, subst. use of n. of *minutus* (MINUTE *a.*) used in various applications in med.L.] **I.** A sixtieth (or other definite part) of a unit. **1.** The sixtieth part of an hour (divided into sixty seconds). Also, one of the lines upon a dial marking the minute spaces. **b.** Vaguely: A short space of time; also, an instant, moment. late ME. **c.** A particular moment; occas. the appointed moment 1598. **2.** *Geom.* The sixtieth part of a degree. (Marked thus ′; as in 5° 12′.) late ME. **3.** *Arch.* The sixtieth or occas. some other part of the MODULE 1696.

1. For the lachesse Of half a Minut of an houre GOWER. **b.** The train will be starting in a m. 1898. **c.** Phr. *The m.* (*that*) . . : as soon as. Hence **Mi·nutely** *a.* and *adv.*¹ (happening) every m.

II. Something small. †**1.** A coin of little value; a mite –1589. †**2.** Something minute; as *pl.* 'small fry'; a detail; something of small value 1515–1670.

2. Let me heare from thee euery m. of Newes B. JONS.

III. A rough draft; a memorandum; a brief summary of events or transactions, esp. (usu. *pl.*) the record of the proceedings of an assembly, committee, etc. 1502. **b.** An official memorandum authorizing or recommending a course, as a *Treasury m.* 1564.

Comb.: **m. bell,** the tolling of a bell at intervals of a m.; **-book,** a book in which minutes are recorded; **-glass,** a sand-glass that runs for a m.; **-gun,** one fired at intervals of a m.; used as a sign of mourning or distress; **-hand,** the longer hand of a time-piece, which indicates the minutes, **-man,** a militiaman, during the American revolutionary period, who was ready to march at a minute's notice (*Hist.*); **-repeater,** a watch which 'repeats' the minutes.

Minute (məiniū·t, miniū·t), *a.* late ME. [– L. *minutus* (whence Fr. *menu* small), pa. pple. of *minuere* make small, diminish.] †**1.** Chopped small. late ME. only. †**2.** Of imposts, etc.: Lesser; esp. in *m. tithes* = 'small tithes' –1696. **3.** Very small in size, amount or degree 1626. **4.** Trifling, petty 1650. **5.** Of investigations, etc.; Very detailed; very precise; very accurate *c* 1680.

3. Very m. changes of temperature GEIKIE. **4.** Those m. philosophers . . are a sort of pirates who plunder all that come in their way BERKELEY. **5.** M. regulations are apt to be transgressed JOWETT. Hence **Minu·te-ly** *adv.*², **-ness.**

Minute (mi·nit), *v.* 1605. [f. MINUTE *sb.*] **1.** *trans.* To time to the minute. **2.** To draft (a document or scheme); to record in a minute or memorandum; to make a minute of the contents of (a document) 1648.

2. To m. the speed of a train SMILES. **2.** Phr. *To m. down*: to make a note of.

‖**Minutia** (məi-, miniū·ʃiă). *Pl.* **-iæ** (-iī). 1751. [L. *minutia* smallness, pl. *minutiæ* trifles, f. *minutus* MINUTE *a.*] A precise detail; a trivial matter or object. Usu. *pl.* So †**Minu·tial** *a.* pertaining to details 1612–1796. **Minu·tiose, -ous** *adjs.* attentive to minutiæ 1819.

Minx (miŋks). 1542. [Of unkn. origin.] †**1.** A pet dog. UDALL. **2.** A pert girl, hussy. Now often playful. 1592. †**b.** A lewd woman –1728.

2. b. This is some Minxes token SHAKS.

Minx, obs. f. MINK.

Miny (məi·ni), *a. rare.* 1611. [f. MINE *sb.* + -Y¹.] **1.** Pertaining to a mine; mineral. **2.** Subterraneous. THOMSON.

Miocene (məi·ŏsīn), *a.* Also **mei-.** 1833. [irreg. f. Gr. μείων less + καινός new, recent.] *Geol.* Epithet of the middle division of the Tertiary strata, and the geological period it represents. Also quasi-*sb.* **Mioce·nic** *a.*

Miserere (mizĕrī·ri). ME. [imper. sing. L. *miserēri* have pity, f. *miser* (see Miser).] The fifty-first Psalm (fiftieth in the Vulgate), beginning *Miserere mei Deus* ('Have mercy upon me, O God'), being one of the Penitential Psalms. **b.** A musical setting of this 1776. **2.** *transf.* A cry for mercy 1610. †**3.** full *M. mei* (mī·əi): a name for the 'iliac passion' (see Ileus 1) –1783. ¶**4.** = Misericord 2 c. 1798.

b. The 'Miserere' of Allegri 1845.

Misericord (mize·rikǭɹd). ME. [– (O)Fr. *misericorde* – L. *misericordia*, f. *misericors* pitiful, f. *miser*, stem of *miserēri* (see prec.) + *cor, cord-* heart.] †**1.** Compassion, pity. Also as *int.* –1705. **2.** *Hist.* and *Antiq.* **a.** An indulgence or relaxation of a monastic rule 1602. **b.** An apartment in a monastery in which such indulgences, esp. as to food and drink, were permitted 1529. **c.** A shelving projection on the under side of a hinged seat in a choir stall, which, when turned up, gave support to one standing in the stall 1515. **3.** A dagger with which the *coup de grâce* was given. late ME. Hence †**Misericordious** *a.* compassionate, merciful.

Miserly (məi·zəɹli), *a.* 1593. [f. Miser *sb.* + -ly[1].] Niggardly, stingy. **Mi·serliness.**

Misery (mi·zĕri). late ME. [– AFr. **miserie*, for (O)Fr. *misère*, or – L. *miseria*, f. *miser*; see Miser, -y[3].] **1.** Wretchedness of outward circumstances; distress caused by privation or poverty. Also with †*a* and *pl.* **2.** Miserable or wretched state of mind; a condition of extreme unhappiness 1535. †**3.** Miserliness –1624. **4.** = Misère (*colloq.*).

1. The m. of unaided poverty Ruskin. *personified*, He gave to Mis'ry all he had, a tear Goldsm. **2.** The miseries of fallen greatness Macaulay. Thou art so full of m., Were it not better not to be? Tennyson.

Misestee·m, *v.* 1611. [Mis-[1] 1. Cf. Fr. *mésestimer*.] *trans.* = Misestimate *v.* So **Misestee·m** *sb.* want of esteem or respect 1850.

Mise·stimate, *v.* 1841. [Mis-[1] 1.] *trans.* To estimate erroneously. So **Mise·stimate** *sb.* 1852. **Misestima·tion** 1809.

Mise·xecute, *v.* 1647. [Mis-[1] 1.] *trans.* To carry out improperly. **Misexecu·tion** 1535.

Misexplai·n, *v.* 1674. [Mis-[1] 1.] *trans.* To explain incorrectly.

Misexposi·tion. 1524. [Mis-[1] 4.] Incorrect exposition.

Misexpre·ss, *v.* 1718. [Mis-[1] 1.] *refl.* To express oneself faultily. So **Misexpre·ssion** 1651. **Misexpre·ssive** *a.* expressing a wrong meaning 1816.

Misfai·th. late ME. [Mis-[1] 4.] Disbelief; mistrust.

Some sudden turn of anger born Of your m. Tennyson.

†**Misfa·ll**, *v.* ME. [Mis-[1] 1. Cf. MLG., MDu., Du. *misvallen*, MHG. *missevallen*, G. *missfallen*.] **1.** *intr.* To come to grief. ME. only. **2.** *impers.* or said of the event: To fall out amiss. *It 'misfell me*: misfortune befell me. –1615.

†**Misfa·re**, *v.* [OE. *misfaran* = OFris. *misfara*, MHG. *missevarn*, ON. *misfara*. See Mis-[1], Fare *v.*[1]] **1.** *intr.* To fare ill, come to grief –1633. **2.** To go wrong; to transgress –1487. So †**Misfa·re** *sb.* going wrong; misfortune –1596.

†**Misfa·shion**, *v.* 1570. [Mis-[1] 1.] *trans.* To put out of shape; to make of a wrong shape –1647. So **Misfa·shioned** *ppl. a.* badly formed, mis-shapen 1500. **Misfa·shioning** *vbl. sb.* disfigurement, deformity 1469.

Misfeasance (misfī·zăns). 1596. [– OFr. *mesfaisance*, f. pr. pple. of *mesfaire* (mod. *méfaire*); see Mis-[2], Feasance. Cf. Malfeasance.] *Law.* A transgression, trespass; *spec.* the improper performance of a lawful act. So **Misfea·sor,** one who commits a m. 1631.

Misfea·ture. 1821. [Mis-[1] 4.] A distorted feature; a bad feature or trait.

†**Misfei·gn**, *v.* [Mis-[1] 1.] *intr.* To feign with a wrong intention. Spenser.

Misfire (misfəiə·ɹ), *v.* 1752. [Mis-[1] 1. Cf. phr. *to miss fire*, Miss *v.* I.] *intr.* Of a gun or its charge: To fail to be discharged. **b.** Said of an internal-combustion engine when its charge fails to ignite or ignites at the wrong time 1905. Hence **Misfi·re** *sb.* a failure to discharge 1839.

Misfit (misfi·t), *sb.* 1823. [f. Mis-[1] 4 + Fit *sb.*[3]] A garment, etc., which does not fit the person it is made for.

[The] shoemaker. .would occasionally have a m. or two on his hands Knight. *transf.* Her mouth. . was an obvious m. for the set of teeth it contained 1862.

Misfi·t, *v.* 1885. [f. Mis-[1] 1 + Fit *v.*[1] or f. prec.] *trans.* and *intr.* To fit badly.

†**Misforgi·ve**, *v.* [Mis-[1] 1.] *trans.* = Misgive 1. Chaucer.

Misfo·rm, *v.* late ME. [Mis-[1] 1.] *trans.* To form amiss; to mis-shape. So **Misforma·tion,** malformation 1822.

Misfo·rtunate, *a.* Now chiefly *Sc.* and *U.S.* 1530. [Mis-[1] 6.] Unfortunate.

Misfortune (misfǭ·ɹtʃən), *sb.* 1502. [f. Mis-[1] 4 + Fortune *sb.*] **1.** Bad fortune; ill-luck; also, an instance of this. **2.** *dial.* and *colloq.* The bearing of an illegitimate child; hence, an illegitimate child 1801.

1. They come in no m. like other folke Coverdale *Ps.* 72:5. Misfortunes seldome come alone 1622. **2.** Phr. *To have* or *meet with a m.* Hence **Misfo·rtuned** *a.* unfortunate 1578.

†**Misfo·rtune**, *v.* 1466. [f. Mis-[1] 1 + Fortune *v.*] **a.** *impers.*, etc.: To happen unfortunately. **b.** *intr.* To happen by mischance *to do* something. **c.** To come to grief. –1615.

Misgive (misgi·v), *v.* 1513. [Mis-[1] 1, 7.] **1.** *trans.* Of one's heart, mind, etc.: To cause (one) to be apprehensive (*that*); to incline to suspicion or foreboding. (The personal obj. was orig. a dat.) **b.** *absol.* or *intr.* To have misgivings 1604. **2.** *intr.* To fail; to go wrong. Of a gun: To miss fire. Chiefly *Sc.* 1579. **3.** *trans.* To bestow amiss; to cite wrongly 1611.

1. So doth my heart mis-giue me, in these Conflicts, What may befall him Shaks. **b.** *Oth.* III. iv. 89.

Misgi·ving, *vbl. sb.* 1601. [f. prec. + -ing[1].] The action of Misgive *v.*; a feeling of mistrust, apprehension, or loss of confidence.

And my misgiuing still Falles shrewdly to the purpose Shaks.

Misgo (misgōᵘ·), *v.* Now *dial.* Pa. t. **-went,** pa. pple. **-gone.** ME. [Mis-[1] 1.] *intr.* To go wrong or astray; to err; to miscarry.

Misgo·tten, *pa. pple.* and *ppl. a.* late ME. [Mis-[1] 2.] **1.** Wrongly acquired; ill-gotten. **2.** = Misbegotten. late ME.

Misgo·vern, *v.* 1440. [Mis-[1] 1.] †**1.** *trans.* To mismanage, misdirect, misconduct –1621. **2.** *trans.* To mismanage the government of (a state, etc.) 1587.

Misgo·vernance. *Obs.* exc. *arch.* late ME. [Mis-[1] 4.] †**1.** Misconduct, misbehaviour –1627. †**2.** Mismanagement, misuse –1678. **3.** Bad government of a country or state 1447.

Misgo·verned, *ppl. a.* late ME. [Mis-[1] 2.] †**1.** Ill-conducted; immoral –1611. †**2.** Unruly; misdirected –1639. **3.** Mismanaged 1834.

2. Rude mis-gouern'd hands Shaks.

Misgo·vernment. late ME. [Mis-[1] 4.] †**1.** Unruly behaviour; misconduct –1665. †**2.** Mismanagement –1777. **3.** Bad government of a country or state; maladministration. Hence, disorder, anarchy (cf. *misrule*) 1592.

†**Misgra·ffed**, *pa. pple.* [Mis-[1] 2.] Grafted amiss; *fig.* badly matched *Mids. N.* I. i. 137.

Misgra·fted, *ppl. a.* [Mis-[1] 2.] Grafted wrongly or unsuitably Warburton.

Misgrou·nded, *ppl. a.* 1598. [Mis-[1] 2.] Falsely grounded; ill-founded.

Misgrow·th. 1647. [Mis-[1] 4.] A distorted or abortive growth.

Misgui·dance. 1640. [Mis-[1] 4.] Misdirection. So †**Misgui·de** *sb.* 1596.

Misgui·de. *v.* late ME. [Mis-[1] 1.] †**1.** *refl.* To go astray; to conduct oneself or manage one's affairs badly –1651. **2.** *trans.* To mismanage, misgovern. Hence (mod. *Sc.*) to treat badly; to injure, spoil 1494. **3.** To misdirect 1509.

3. To. .m. the mind Pope. *absol.* The nobles. . have nearly ceased either to guide or m. Carlyle. Hence **Misgui·dingly** *adv.* in a way to mislead.

Misgui·ded, *ppl. a.* 1490. [Mis-[1] 2.] †**1.** Ill-conducted, immoral –1523. **2.** Misdirected in action or thought; hence, having a wrong purpose or intention 1659.

2. The m. and abus'd multitude Milt.

†**Misgye·**, *v.* late ME. [f. Mis-[1] 1 + *gye* Guy *v.*[1]] *trans.* To misguide; *refl.* to misbehave –1500.

Mishandle (mishæ·nd'l), *v.* 1530. [Mis-[1] 1.] *trans.* To handle badly or improperly; to maltreat, ill-treat.

Mishap (mishæ·p), *sb.* ME. [f. Mis-[1] 4 + Hap *sb.*[1], prob. after OFr. *mescheance* Mischance.] **1.** Evil hap; bad luck. Now *rare.* **2.** An unlucky accident ME.

2. Secure from worldly chaunces and mishaps Shaks.

†**Misha·p**, *v.* ME. [Mis-[1] 1.] **1.** *intr.* Of a person: To meet with mishap. Also, to have the misfortune *to do* something. –1533. **2.** To happen unfortunately –1647. So †**Misha·ppen** *v.* in same senses ME. –1611.

Mishear (mishīə·ɹ), *v.* ME. [Mis-[1] 1.] To hear incorrectly or imperfectly.

Mish-mash (mi·ʃ,mæʃ). 1450. [redupl. of Mash *sb.*[1]] A medley, hodge-podge, jumble.

‖**Mishnah, mishna** (mi·ʃnă). Also †**mischna.** 1610. [Post-Biblical Heb. *mišnāh* (1) repetition, (2) instruction.] The collection of binding precepts or *hᵃlāḵôṯ* (see Halachah) which forms the basis of the Talmud and embodies the contents of the oral law. Also, a paragraph of the mishnah. Hence **Mi·shnic, -al** *a.* pertaining to or characteristic of the m.

Misima·gine, *v.* 1625. [Mis-[1] 1.] *trans.* To imagine wrongly. **Misimagina·tion** 1618.

Misimpre·ssion. 1670. [Mis-[1] 4.] A wrong impression.

Misimpro·ve, *v.* Now *rare.* 1658. [Mis-[1] 7.] **1.** *trans.* To employ wrongly; to abuse, use ill. *Obs.* or *U.S.* **2.** To improve injudiciously 1847. So †**Misimpro·vement,** failure to employ properly, misuse 1644.

Misincli·ne, *v.* [Mis-[1] 1.] To incline in a wrong direction. Bp. Hall. So **Misinclina·tion. Misincli·ned** *ppl. a.* wrongly inclined; disinclined 1716.

Misinfo·rm, *v.* late ME. [Mis-[1] 1.] *trans.* To inform amiss; to give misleadin[g] information (to). So **Misinfo·rmant, -fo·rmer. Misinforma·tion,** the action of mis[informing]; incorrect information 1587.

Misinstru·ct, *v.* 1547. [Mis-[1] 1.] *tran[s.]* To instruct amiss. So **Misinstru·ction** 164[.]

Misinte·lligence. 1639. [f. Mis-[1] 4 + I[n]telligence, prob. after Fr. *mésintelligen[ce]* (xvi).] **1.** Misunderstanding; disagreeme[nt] Now *rare* or *Obs.* **2.** Wrong impression as [to] facts 1779. **3.** Lack of intelligence (*rare*) 18[..]

Misinte·rpret, *v.* 1589. [Mis-[1] 1.] *tra[ns.]* To give a wrong interpretation to. So **Mi[s]interpreta·tion** 1576.

Misjoi·n, *v.* 1540. [Mis-[1] 1.] *trans.* [To] join wrongly, inappropriately, or unsuitab[ly] *spec.* in *Law* (cf. next).

Misjoi·nder. 1852. [Mis-[1] 4.] *Law.* [Im]proper joinder of parties in an action o[r] causes of action in a suit.

Misju·dge, *v.* 1526. [Mis-[1] 1.] *trans.* [To] judge wrongly; to have false opinions of. **Misju·dg(e)ment** 1526.

‖**Miskal** (mi·skăl). 1555. [Arab. *miṯḳā[l]* *ṯaḳala* weigh.] **1.** An Arabian measur[e of] weight, equivalent to 24 carats or abou[t] … dirhems. **2.** In Morocco, a money of acc[ount] 1695.

†**Miskee·p**, *v.* ME. [Mis-[1] 1.] *trans* … keep, guard, or observe badly –1649.

Misken (miske·n), *v.* *Sc.* and *n. dial.* [f. Mis-[1] 1, 7 + Ken *v.*, prob. after … *miskenna* not to recognize (a person) … Misknow.

Were I you, Ranald, I would be for misk… Sir Duncan Scott.

Mi·skin, dial. var. Mixen.

Misknow·, *v.* late ME. [Mis-[1] 1, early use largely Sc.; cf. Misken.] †**1.** Not to know; to be ignorant of –1632. … know badly; to misapprehend, mis… stand 1535. **3.** To fail to recognize, … the identity of (a person). late ME. … refuse to recognize 1483. So **Misk…ledge,** †failure to recognize; also, … knowledge 1533.

Miquelet (mi·kĕlėt). 1670. [– Fr. *miquelet* – Sp. *miquelete, miguelete*, f. Cat. *Miquel*, Sp. *Miguel* Michael.] **a.** In the 17th c., a member of a body of Catalonian banditti who infested the Pyrenees. **b.** Later, a Spanish guerrilla soldier during the Peninsular War; also, a member of a corps of French irregulars raised for service against the Spaniards. **c.** In mod. Spain, a soldier of certain local regiments, chiefly employed on escort duties.

‖**Mir** (mīr). 1877. [Russ.] A Russian village community.

Mirabelle (mirăbe·l). 1706. [– Fr. *mirabelle*.] A variety of plum.

†**Mira·bilis.** 1673. = Aqua mirabilis –1687.

Mirabilite (miræ·biləit). 1854. [– G. *mirabilit*, f. mod.L. (*sal*) *mirabilis*, Glauber's name for his salt; see -ite[1] 2 b.] *Min.* Native sodium sulphate (Glauber's salt).

†**Mi·rable,** *a.* and *sb.* 1450. [– L. *mirabilis*, f. *mirari* wonder; see -able. Cf. OFr. *mirable*. In B, after eccl. L. (Vulg.) *mirabilia*.] **A.** *adj.* Wonderful, marvellous –1606. **B.** *sb.* Something wonderful –1653.

Miracle (mi·răk'l), *sb.* late OE. [– (O)Fr. *miracle* – L. *miraculum* object of wonder, f. *mirari, -are* look at, wonder, f. *mirus* wonderful.] **1.** A marvellous event exceeding the known powers of nature, and therefore supposed to be due to the special intervention of the Deity or of some supernatural agency; chiefly, an act (e.g. of healing) exhibiting control over the laws of nature, and serving as evidence that the agent is either divine or is specially favoured by God. **2.** *transf.*, *esp.* as applied hyperbolically to an unusual achievement or event. late ME. **b.** *concr.* A wonderful object, a marvel. late ME. †**3.** A miraculous story; a legend. Chaucer. **4.** = *Miracle play* ME.

1. This is againe the second m. that Iesus did *John* 4:54. **2.** O M.! He blushes! Dryden. The radium 'miracle' 1903. Phr. *To a m.*: marvellously well 1643. **b.** A m. of worth Daniel, of rare device Coleridge, of ingenuity (*mod.*). **3.** Chaucer *Sir Thopas* Prol. 1.

attrib. and *Comb.*, as *m.-monger*, etc.; **m. play,** one of the mediæval dramatic representations based on the life of Our Lord and the legends of the Saints 1602; **m. player, -playing** [from sense 4] late ME.

Miracle (mi·răk'l), *v.* 1611. [f. the sb.] **a.** *refl.*? To be revealed by miracle. *Cymb.* IV. ii. 29. **b.** *intr.* To work miracles.

Miraculize (miræ·kiŭləiz), *v.* 1711. [f. next + -ize.] *trans.* To consider as miraculous.

Miraculous (miræ·kiŭləs), *a.* 1502. [– (O)Fr. *miraculeux* or med.L. *miraculosus*, f. *miraculum*; see Miracle, -ous.] **1.** Of the nature of a miracle; beyond the agency of natural laws; supernatural. †**b.** Concerned with miracles –1845. **2.** *transf.*, etc. Resembling a miracle; extraordinary; marvellous; astonishing 1573. **3.** Of things (formerly also of persons): Having the power to work miracles; wonder-working 1596.

1. This strength M. yet remaining in those locks Milt. *Sams.* 587. **3.** His word is more then the m. Harpe Shaks. Hence **Mira·culous-ly** *adv.*, **-ness.**

‖**Mirador** (miradǭ·ɹ). Also **-dore.** 1670. [Sp., f. *mirar* look.] A watch-tower; also, a belvedere on the top of a Spanish house.

Mirage (mirā·ʒ). 1812. [– Fr. *mirage*, f. *mirer*, refl., be reflected or mirrored; – L. *mirare*; see Miracle, -age.] An optical illusion, common in hot countries, and esp. in sandy deserts, arising from the reflection of an object at some distance, often giving the false appearance of a sheet of water.

fig. A moist m. in desert eyes Tennyson.

Mirbane (mə̄·ɹbeⁱn). 1857. [– Fr. *mirbane*, of unkn. origin.] *Essence, oil of m.*, nitrobenzol used in perfumery.

Mire (məiəɹ), *sb.* [ME. *müre, myre* – ON. *mýrr* :– **miuzjō*, f. Gmc. **meus-* **mus-* Moss.] **1.** A piece of wet, swampy ground; a boggy place. Also *gen.* swampy ground, bog. **2.** Wet or soft mud, slush, dirt. (Cf. 2 *Pet.* 2:22.) ME. **b.** A mass of dirt 1871.

1. Fig. phr. *To bring, drag, lay, leave, stick in the m.*; *to find oneself in the m.* Honest water, which nere left man i' th' m. Shaks. **2. b.** Until a stumble, and the man's one m.! Browning. *Comb.* **m.-crow,** the laughing gull, *Larus ridibundus.*

†**Mire,** *a.* late ME. [f. prec.] Miry –1656.

Now that the Fields are dank, and ways are m. Milt.

Mire (məiəɹ), *v.* late ME. [f. Mire *sb.*] **I.** *trans.* **1.** To plunge or set fast in the mire. (Chiefly *pass.*) 1559. **b.** *fig.* To involve in difficulties. late ME. **2.** To bespatter with mire or filth; to defile (*lit.* and *fig.*) 1508.

1. Some of them were mired in it [a slough] 1752. **2.** Smeer'd thus and mir'd with infamie Shaks.

II. *intr.* To sink in the mire, be bogged 1607.

Paint till a horse may myre upon your face Shaks.

Mirific (məiri·fik), *a.* *rare.* 1490. [– Fr. *mirifique* – L. *mirificus*, f. *mirus* wonderful + *-ficus* (see -fic).] Doing wonders; exciting astonishment; marvellous. So †**Miri·fical** *a.* 1603–1829. **Miri·fically** *adv.*

Miriness (məiə·rinės). 1608. [f. Miry *a.* + -ness.] Miry condition or quality.

Mirk, Mirky, etc., var. ff. Murk, etc.

Mirror (mi·rəɹ), *sb.* [ME. *mirour* – OFr. *mirour* (mod. *miroir*, f. var. *mirēoir*) :– Rom. **miratorium*, f. *mirat-*, pa. ppl. stem of L. *mirari, -are* wonder, look at; see -or 3.] **I.** Literal uses, etc. **1.** A polished surface, now usu. of glass coated with tin amalgam or silver, which reflects images of objects; a looking-glass. **b.** *transf.* Applied to water (chiefly *poet.*) 1595. **2.** *spec.* **a.** A magic glass or crystal ME. †**b.** A small glass formerly worn in the hat by men and at the girdle by women. B. Jons. **3.** *Optics.* A polished surface, either *plane, convex,* or *concave,* that reflects rays of light; a speculum 1728.

1. And in her hand she held a mirrhour bright Spenser. *fig.* To hold as 'twer the Mirrour up to Nature Shaks. **3.** *Burning m.*: a concave m. which concentrates the sun's rays at a focus, and causes them to set fire to objects.

II. Fig. uses. **1.** That which gives a faithful reflection of anything. late ME. **b.** Used of a person (*poet.*) 1563. **2.** That which exhibits something to be imitated; an exemplar. Now *rare.* ME. †**b.** Hence of persons: A paragon –1785. †**c.** A warning –1633.

1. The stage. .the mirrour of life Johnson. **b.** Mirrour of Poets, Mirrour of our Age Waller. **2.** Sir Tristram. .the m. of chivalry 1801. **b.** Our m. of ministers of finance Burke.

III. a. *Arch.* A small oval ornament resembling a mirror in shape 1847. **b.** *Ornith.* The speculum of a bird's wing.

attrib. and *Comb.*, as *m.-silverer, -surface*, etc.; also **m. carp,** the looking-glass carp, *Cyprinus carpio*; **-plate,** a plate of glass suitable for a m.; **-writing,** writing which appears as though viewed in a m., reversed writing (a characteristic of aphasia).

Mirror (mi·rəɹ), *v.* 1820. [f. prec. sb.] *trans.* To reflect in the manner of a mirror.

Mirth (mə̄ɹþ). [OE. *myriġþ* (cf. MDu. *merchte*) :– Gmc. **murʒiþō*, f. **murʒjaz* Merry; see -th[1].] †**1.** Pleasurable feeling; joy, happiness –1696. **2.** Rejoicing, *esp.* manifested rejoicing; merry-making; jollity ME. †**3.** A diversion, sport, entertainment –1606. **4.** Merriment, hilarity; in early use, fun, ridicule. late ME. †**b.** Put for: The object of one's mirth –1708.

2. Be large in m., anon wee'l drinke a Measure The Table round Shaks. **3.** To giue a Kingdome for a M. Shaks. **4.** I was borne to speake all m., and no matter Shaks. **b.** He's all my Exercise, my M., my Matter Shaks.

Mirthful (mə̄·ɹþfŭl), *a.* ME. [f. Mirth + -ful.] **1.** Full of mirth; gladsome, hilarious; expressive of mirth. **b.** Of places, seasons, etc.: Characterized by rejoicing 1450. **2.** Of things: Amusing. Shaks.

1. Each m. lout The ale-house seeks Clare. A m. jest Crabbe. **b.** M. bower or hall Keble. Hence **Mi·rthful-ly** *adv.*, **-ness.**

Mirthless (mə̄·ɹþlės), *a.* late ME. [f. Mirth + -less.] Joyless; sad, dismal. Hence **Mi·rthless-ly** *adv.*, **-ness.**

Miry (məiə·ri), *a.* late ME. [f. Mire *sb.* + -y[1].] **1.** Of the nature of mire, swampy. **2.** Abounding in mire, muddy 1440. **3.** Covered with mud or mire 1496. **4.** *fig.* Dirty; despicable 1532.

1. Marishes and myrie bogs Spenser. **2.** M. roads 1833. **4.** A m. business 1877.

‖**Mirza** (mī·ɹzā). 1613. [Pers. *mīrzā*, for *mīrzād*, f. *mīr* prince (– Arab. *'amīr* Ameer) + *zāde* born.] In Persia: **a.** A royal prince; as a title, placed after the name. **b.** Title of honour prefixed to the name of an official or a man of learning.

†**Mis,** *a.* ME. [Partly the prefix Mis-[1] (4) used as a separate word; partly a reduced form of Amiss.] Bad; wrong; wicked. In predicative use: Amiss. –1556. So †**Mis** *adv.* wrongly; badly; amiss.

Mis- (mis), *prefix*[1], repr. OE. *mis-* = OFris., OS. *mis-*, OHG. *missa-, missi-* (Du. *mis-*, G. *miss-*), ON. *mis-*, Goth. *missa-* :– Gmc. **missa-*.

The hyphen is now employed chiefly in new or rarely used formations, and in words like *mis-say mis-cite*, etc.

The predominant meaning of the prefix is that of 'amiss', 'wrong(ly)', 'bad(ly)', 'improper(ly)', 'mistaken(ly)'.

In early ME. many new compounds were made, some of which appear to have been suggested by French formations with *mes-* (see Mis-[2]); a word like *misjudge* has prob. a double origin, being partly of native formation, and partly an adaptation of OFr. *mesjuger*. The most prolific period for the formation of *mis-* compounds was the 17th c., when writers such as Bacon, Donne, and Bp. Hall employed them largely.

In OE. *mis-* was prefixed to vbs., active and passive pples., nouns of action and condition, and adjs. In ME. its composition with agent-nouns and adverbs followed as a matter of course.

1. Prefixed to verbs, with the meaning 'amiss', 'badly', 'wrongly', 'perversely', 'mistakenly'; as †*misact*, Misdo, Mislead, Mislike, etc. **b.** In the 14th-16th c., in some words, as Misdeem, etc., *mis-* took the force of 'unfavourably', and in Misbode, Misdoubt, etc., it intensified the notion of uneasy feeling contained in the vb. These new senses and combs., however, are now *arch.* or *dial.*

2. Prefixed to pples. and ppl. adjs. with the same meaning as in 1; as *misbound, misbuilt.*

3. Similarly prefixed to vbl. sbs., as *misaccenting.*

4. Prefixed to nouns of action, condition, and quality, with the meaning 'bad', 'wrong', 'erroneous', 'perverse', 'misdirected'; as *misaccentuation, misappraisement, misattribution, misproposal.*

5. Prefixed to agent-nouns; as *misprofessor.*

6. Prefixed to adjs. with the sense of 'wrongly', 'erroneously', 'perversely'; as *misconvenient.*

7. Expressing negation (of something good or desirable); = Dis-, In-, or Un-; as *misadvertence.*

8. Prefixed to words denoting something wrong or bad, serving as an intensive; as *misdemeriting.*

9. *Mis-* was often substituted for *dis-* (and even *des-*); hence the dial. *misdain* (after *disdain*), *miscry* for *descry.*

Mis- (mis), *prefix*[2], in compounds adopted from French represents OFr. *mes-* (mod. *més-, mes-, mé-*) :– Rom. **minus-*, a use of L. *minus* (see Minus) in the senses 'bad(ly)', 'wrong(ly)' 'amiss', and with neg. force, in comb. with verbs, adjs., and nouns. Examples are Misadventure, Mischance, Mischief, Miscreant.

Misaccou·nt, *v.* late ME. [Mis-[1] 1.] *trans.* To misreckon, misjudge –1655.

Misaddre·ss, *v.* 1648. [Mis-[1] 1.] *trans.* To address wrongly or impertinently.

Misadventure (misădve·ntiŭɹ, -tʃəɹ). [ME. *misaventure* – OFr. *mesaventure*, f. *mesavenir* turn out badly (f. *mes-* Mis-[2] + *avenir* :– L. *advenire*; cf. Advent), after *aventure* Adventure.] **1.** Ill-luck, bad fortune. Usu.: A piece of bad fortune; a mishap. **2.** *Law.* Homicide committed accidentally by a person in doing a lawful act, without intention of hurt; now chiefly in phr. *homicide* or *death by m.* 1509. Hence †**Misadve·ntured** *a.* unfortunate. Shaks.

Misadve·nturous, *a.* Now *rare.* late ME. [orig. – OFr. *mesaventureux*; later f. Misadventure + -ous.] Unfortunate.

Misadvi·ce. 1632. [Mis-[1] 4.] Wrong advice.

Misadvi·se, *v.* late ME. [Mis-[1] 1.] †**1.** *refl.* To take a wrong counsel; to act unadvisedly –1602. **2.** *trans.* To advise wrongly 1548. So †**Mis-advi·sed** *ppl. a.* ill-advised; injudicious.

†**Misaffe·ct,** *v.* 1586. [Mis-[1] 1, 7.] **1.** *trans.* To affect injuriously –1650. **2.** To dislike –1641.

†**Misaffe·cted,** *ppl. a.* 1621. [Partly f. prec. + -ed[1], partly f. Mis-[1] 2 + Affected.] **1.** Affected by illness or disease –1694. **2.** Ill-disposed, disaffected –1645.

Misaffe·ction. Now *rare* or *Obs.* 1621. [Mis-[1] 4.] **1.** Perverted affection; disaffection. **2.** Physical disorder; disease 1673.

†**Misalle·ge,** *v.* 1559. [Mis-[1] 1.] *trans.* To cite falsely as supporting one's contention –1684. So †**Misallega·tion** 1633–1647.

Misalli·ance. 1738. [f. Mis-^{1} 4 + Alliance, after Fr. *mésalliance.*] An improper alliance, association, or union; *esp.* a Mésalliance.

Misanthrope (mi·sænþrōᵘp). 1683. (In 16–17th c. **misant(h)ropos,** *pl.* **-pi.**) [– Fr. *misanthrope* (Rabelais), mod.L. *misanthropus*, Gr. μισάνθρωπος, f. μισ(ο-, comb. form of base of μισεῖν hate, μῖσος hatred + ἄνθρωπος man.] A man-hater; one who distrusts men and avoids them. **b.** as *adj.* = next 1757.
So **Misanthro·pic** (1762), **-al** (1621) *a.* characterized by misanthropy; man-hating. **Misanthro·pically** *adv.* **Misa·nthropist** = Misanthrope 1656. **Misa·nthropize** *v. intr.* to be a misanthrope; to hate mankind 1846. **Misa·nthropy,** hatred of mankind; the condition of a misanthrope 1656.

Misapply (misăpləi·), *v.* 1571. [Mis-^{1} 1.] *trans.* To make a wrong application of. So **Misapplica·tion** 1607.

Misappre·ciate, *v.* 1828. [Mis-^{1} 1.] *trans.* To fail to appreciate rightly; to make a wrong estimate of. So **Misapprecia·tion,**

Mi:sapprehe·nd, *v.* 1646. [Mis-^{1} 1.] *trans.* To apprehend wrongly; to misunderstand. So **Mi:sapprehe·nsion** 1629. **Mi:sapprehe·nsive** *a.* 1646.

Misappro·priate, *v.* 1857. [Mis-^{1} 1.] *trans.* To appropriate to wrong uses; chiefly, to apply dishonestly to one's own use. So **Mi:sappropria·tion** 1794.

Misarra·nged, *pa. pple.* and *ppl. a.* 1848. [Mis-^{1} 2.] Wrongly arranged. So **Misarra·ngement** 1784.

Misarray·. [Mis-^{1} 4.] Disarray. Scott.

Misaventeur, -ur(e, etc.: obs. ff. Misadventure.

Misbapti·ze, *v.* 1610. [Mis-^{1} 1.] **1.** *trans.* To misname. **2.** To baptize wrongly. Keats.

†**Misbea·r,** *v.* ME. [f. Mis-^{1} 1 + Bear *v.*^{1}] *refl.* To misconduct oneself –1502.

Misbecome (misbĭkɒ·m), *v.* 1530. [Mis-^{1} 1.] *trans.* To fail to become; to suit ill. So **Misbeco·ming** *ppl. a.* unbecoming, unsuitable. **Misbeco·ming-ly** *adv.*, **-ness.**

†**Misbe·de,** *v.* [OE. *misbēodan*, f. *mis-* Mis-^{1} 1 + *bēodan* (see Bid *v.* A).] *trans.* To ill-use; to injure, abuse. Also *intr.* const. *till.* –1496.
Or who hath yow misboden, or offended? Chaucer.

Misbege·t, *v. rare.* ME. [Mis-^{1} 1.] *trans.* To beget unlawfully.

Misbego·tten, *ppl. a.* and *sb.* Also **misbegot.** 1546. [Mis-^{1} 2.] **A.** *adj.* **1.** Unlawfully begotten; illegitimate; bastard 1554. Also *transf.* and *fig.* **2.** Used as a term of opprobrium 1571. **B.** *sb.* A bastard; also, as a term of abuse (cf. A. 2). Now only *dial.*, in form *misbegot.* 1546.
A. 1. That m. diuell Falconbridge Shaks. **2.** Such a m. beast Southey.

Misbeha·ve, *v.* 1451. [Mis-^{1} 1.] *refl.* and (later) *intr.* To conduct oneself improperly; to behave wrongly. So **Misbeha·ved** *ppl. a.* ill-behaved. Shaks. **Misbeha·viour,** bad behaviour 1486.

Misbelief (misbĭlī·f). ME. [Mis-^{1} 4, 7.] **1.** Erroneous religious belief. **2.** *gen.* False opinion or notion. late ME. †**3.** Want of belief; incredulity –1653. Hence †**Misbelieved** *a.* infidel, heathen; incredulous.

Misbelieve, *v.* late ME. [Mis-^{1} 1, 7.] **1.** *intr.* To believe amiss; to hold an erroneous belief. †**2.** *trans.* Not to believe; to disbelieve –1728. Hence **Misbelie·ver,** a heretic or infidel. **Misbelie·ving** *ppl. a.* heretical.

Misbesee·m, *v.* 1598. [Mis-^{1} 1.] = Misbecome.

Misbestow·, *v.* 1532. [Mis-^{1} 1.] *trans.* To bestow wrongly or improperly. So **Misbestow·al,** wrong bestowal.

Misbi·rth. *rare.* 1648. [Mis-^{1} 4.] = Abortion.

Misbo·de, *v. rare.* 1626. [Mis-^{1} 1.] *trans.* To forebode (something evil). So **Misbo·ding** *vbl. sb.* and *ppl. a.*

Misboden, pa. pple. of Misbede.

Misborn (misbǭ·ɹn), *ppl. a.* Now *rare.* OE. [Mis-^{1} 2.] **1.** Prematurely born; abortive. Hence, mis-shapen. **2.** Born out of wedlock; hence, base-born 1590.

Misca·lculate, *v.* 1697. [Mis-^{1} 1.] *trans.* To calculate or reckon wrongly. Also *absol.* or *intr.* Hence **Miscalcula·tion.**

Miscall (mis,kǭ·l), *v.* late ME. [Mis-^{1} 1.] **1.** *trans.* To call by a wrong name. **2.** To call by a bad name; to call (a person) names; to revile. Now *dial.* 1449.
2. By opprobrious Epithets we m. each other Sir T. Browne.

Miscarriage (mis,kæ·rėdʒ). 1614. [f. next + -age.] †**1.** Misbehaviour –1682. †**b.** An instance of this –1829. **2.** Mismanagement (of a business); failure (of an enterprise, etc.). Now *rare.* 1651. **b.** An instance of this; a failure; a mistake. Now *rare*, exc. in *m. of justice.* 1614. †**c.** Mishap, disaster –1776. †**d.** An unfortunate lapse *into.* H. Walpole. **3.** Untimely delivery (of a woman): usu. taken as synonymous with *abortion* 1662. **4.** The failure (of a letter, etc.) to reach its destination 1650.
2. The m. of the late King's counsels Burnet. **c.** If I should meet with any..m. in the voyage De Foe.

Miscarry (mis,kæ·ri), *v.* ME. [– OFr. *mescarier*; see Mis-^{2}, Carry.] †**1.** *intr.* To come to harm, misfortune, or destruction; to perish –1749. †**b.** *pass.* in same sense –1666. †**2.** *intr.* and *refl.* To go wrong or astray; to behave amiss –1732. **3.** *intr.* Of a person: To fail in one's purpose or object 1612. **4.** Of a business, design, etc.: To go wrong; to be a failure. †Also *pass.* 1607. †**b.** Of plants, seeds, etc.: To be abortive; to fail. Also *transf.* –1740. **5.** To be delivered prematurely *of* a child 1527. †**b.** Said of the child. Shaks. **6.** *intr.* Of a letter, etc.: To fail to reach its proper destination 1613. †**7.** *trans.* To cause (a person) to go wrong; to lead astray –1700.
1. The great ships bringing corne from Siria and Egipt..doe seldome miscarrie 1601. **4.** When a great action miscarrieth, the blame must be laid on some Fuller. **6.** The Cardinals Letters to the Pope miscarried Shaks.

†**Misca·st.** *sb.* [Mis-^{1} 4.] Miscalculation. Sandys.

Misca·st, *v. Obs.* exc. *dial.* late ME. [Mis-^{1} 1.] **1.** *trans.* To cast with evil intent. **2.** To miscalculate. Also *absol.* 1598. **3.** To mislay. P. Holland.

Miscegenation (mi:sĭdʒĭnēⁱ·ʃən). 1864. [irreg. f. L. *miscēre* mix + *genus* race + -ation.] Mixture of races; *esp.* the sexual union of whites with Negroes.

†**Miscellana·rian.** [f. Miscellany + -arian.] A writer of miscellanies. Shaftesb.

†**Miscellane,** *a.* and *sb.* 1600. [– L. *miscellaneus*; see Miscellaneous.] **A.** *adj.* Mixed; miscellaneous –1658. **B.** *sb.* A mixture, medley, miscellany. (Cf. Maslin^{2}.) –1664.

‖**Miscellanea** (misĕlēⁱ·nĭ,ă). 1571. [n. pl. of L. *miscellaneus* (see next).] A collection of miscellaneous literary compositions, notes, etc.; a literary miscellany.

Miscellaneous (misĕlēⁱ·nĭ,əs), *a.* 1637. [f. L. *miscellaneus*, f. *miscellus* mixed, f. *miscēre* Mix; see -eous.] **1.** With sing. sb.: Of mixed composition or character. With pl. sb.: Of various kinds. **2.** Of persons: Having various qualities or aspects: many-sided. †Also, general (as opp. to *technical*). 1646.
1. A m. rabble, who extol Things vulgar Milt. My second boy..received a sort of m. education Goldsm. M. volumes of Manuscripts 1899. **2.** A M. Writer Shaftesb. Hence **Miscella·neously** *adv.*, **-ness.**

Miscellany (mi·sĕlăni, mise·lăni), *sb.* 1599. [– (with assim. to -y^{3}) Fr. *miscellanées* fem. pl., or L. Miscellanea.] **1.** A mixture, medley. †*M. madam*: a female dealer in miscellaneous articles. B. Jons. **2.** *pl.* Miscellaneous pieces brought together to form a volume 1615. **3.** The volume containing such miscellaneous pieces 1638.
3. The Bible, in fact, is a 'miscellany' — a very various one 1873. Hence **Misce·llanist,** a writer of miscellanies. So †**Miscellany** *a.* = Miscellaneous 1629–1804.

Mischance (mis,tʃɑ·ns), *sb.* ME. [– OFr. *mesch(e)ance*, f. *mescheoir*; see Mis-^{2}, Chance *sb.*] **1.** Ill-luck, ill-success. In early use, disaster. **2.** A piece of bad luck, a mishap; †*spec.* an accidental mutilation ME.
1. Beholding all his own m., Mute Tennyson. **2.** Phr. *By m.*: by an unlucky accident. Hence **Mischa·nceful** *a.* unlucky.

Mischa·nce, *v. Obs.* or *arch.* 1542. [Mis-^{1} 1.] **1.** *intr.* To happen unfortunately 1552. **2.** *pass.* To be unfortunate.

Mischa·rge, *v.* Now *rare.* 1571. [Mis-^{1} 1.] *trans.* To charge wrongly or falsely. So **Mischa·rge** *sb.* a mistake in charging, as in an account 1828.

Mischief (mi·stʃif), *sb.* ME. [– OFr. *meschief, -chef* (mod. *méchef*), f. *meschever*; see Mischieve.] †**1.** Evil plight; misfortune; distress; in ME. often, need, poverty –1679. †Also with *a* and *pl.* **2.** Harm or evil as wrought by a person or a particular cause 1480. **b.** An injury so wrought. Now only in *collect. pl.* = 'evil consequences', and in phr. *to do oneself a m.* late ME. **3.** *Law.* A condition in which a person suffers a wrong or is under some disability 1596. **4.** †**a.** A disease or ailment. **b.** In medical parlance, a morbid condition not further defined. 1552. **5.** Hurtful character or influence. Now *rare* or *Obs.* 1646. †**6.** Evil-doing –1611. **7.** A cause or source of harm or evil; a worker of mischief; also, one who acts in a vexatious or annoying manner 1586. **8.** Vexatious or annoying action or conduct. Also, a tendency to or disposition for such conduct. 1784.
2. The devil is seldom out of call when he is wanted for any m. De Foe. Phr. *To make m.*: to create discord, e.g. by talebearing. **b.** Thy tongue deuiseth mischiefes *Ps.* 52:2. **3.** Hee tooke his graunt subiect to that mischiefe Bacon. Better a m., then an inconvenience 1670. **4. b.** When the m. is confined to the lung 1899. **5.** The m. of the precedent 1803. Phr. *The m. (of..) is (that)*: the most unfortunate or vexatious part of the matter. **6.** O full of all subtilty and all mischiefe *Acts* 13:10. **8.** He..had more m. than ill-will in his composition W. Irving.
Phrases, chiefly expletive and imprecatory. *A m. on..! A m. take..! To play the m.* (= 'the devil') (*with*). So in *What* (*how*, etc.) *the m...?* Also *to go to the m.*

Mischief (mi·stʃif), *v. arch.* 1440. [f. Mischief *sb.*] = Mischieve *v.* 1, 3, 3 b.

Mischiefful (mi·stʃif,fŭl), *a.* Now *dial.* ME. [f. as prec. + -ful.] †**1.** Disastrous –1470. **2.** Full of mischief; mischievous 1541.

Mi·schief-ma:ker. 1710. One who makes mischief, esp. by talebearing. So **Mi·schief-ma:king** *vbl. sb.* and *ppl. a.*

Mischieve (mistʃī·v), *v.* Now *dial.* or *arch.* ME. [– OFr. *meschever*, f. *mes-* Mis-^{2} + *chever* Cheve *v.*] †**1.** *intr.* To suffer harm or injury; to come to grief, miscarry –1604. **2.** *trans.* To bring to destruction or ruin. late ME. **3.** To inflict injury or loss upon 1475. **b.** To do physical harm to. late ME. †**4.** To abuse, slander –1785.

Mischievous (mi·stʃivəs), *a.* ME. [– AFr. *meschevous*, f. OFr. *meschever* Mischieve; see -ous. Till 1700, stressing on the second syllable was common.] †**1.** Unfortunate, disastrous; *occas.* of persons, miserable, poverty-stricken –1583. **2.** Of persons and animals, or their dispositions: Producing or designing mischief or harm. Now *rare.* 1473. **3.** Of things, events, actions: Fraught with mischief or harm; having harmful effects. late ME. **4.** Of persons, etc.: Characterized by acts of playful malice or petty annoyance 1676.
2. *Jul. C.* II. i. 33. **3.** A m. fallacy Lowell. **4.** M. de Voltaire had..a big Ape, of excessively m. turn; who used to throw stones at the passers-by Carlyle. Hence **Mi·schievous-ly** *adv.*, **-ness.**

Mischoi·ce. 1684. [Mis-^{1} 4.] Wrong choice.

Mischoo·se, *v.* ME. [Mis-^{1} 1.] *trans.* and *intr.* To choose wrongly.

†**Mischri·sten,** *v.* [Mis-^{1} 1.] = Misbaptize 1. Donne.

Miscible (mi·sib'l), *a.* (*sb.*) 1570. [– med.L. *miscibilis* (xiii), f. L. *miscēre* mix; see -ible.] Capable of being mixed (*with* something). †**b.** *sb.* A substance that will mix with another –1678. **Miscibi·lity.**

Mis-cite (mis,səi·t), *v.* 1591. [Mis-^{1} 1.] *trans.* To cite incorrectly. **Mis-cita·tion** 1634.

Misco·lour, *v.* 1809. [Mis-^{1} 1.] *trans.* To give a wrong colour to (facts, etc.); to misrepresent.

†**Misco·mfort,** *sb.* ME. [Mis-^{1} 7.] = Discomfort *sb.* 2 –1526. So †**Misco·mfort** *v.* to trouble, distress –1483.

Mi:scomprehe·nd, *v.* 1813. [Mis-^{1} 1.] *trans.* To misunderstand. So **Mi:scomprehe·nsion.**

Mi:scomputa·tion. 1647. [Mis-^{1} 4.] Misreckoning. So †**Miscompute** *sb.* Sir T. Browne; *v.* 1672.

Misconcei·t, *sb. arch.* 1576. [Mis-^{1} 4.] = Misconception. So **Misconcei·t** *v.* to have a false idea of; to think erroneously (that ...) 1595.

Misconcei·ve, *v.* late ME. [Mis-^{1} 1.] **1.** *intr.* To have a false conception or entertain wrong notions (*of*). Also with clause, †to suspect. **2.** *trans.* To mistake the meaning of 1597.
2. To yeeld them..reasonable causes of those things, which, for want of due consideration heretofore, they misconceiued Hooker. Hence **Misconcei·ver.**

Misconce·ption. 1665. [Mis-^{1} 4.] The action or an act of misconceiving; a notion resulting from misconceiving.

Misco·nduct, *sb.* 1710. [Mis-^{1} 4.] **1.** Bad management; mismanagement. Often quasi-*spec.*, malfeasance. **2.** Improper conduct. Often *spec.* in the sense of 'adultery'. 1729. †**b.** *pl.* Instances of misconduct –1857.

Miscondu·ct, *v.* 1755. [Mis-^{1} 1.] **1.** *trans.* To mismanage. **2.** *refl.* To misbehave oneself 1883.

Misconje·cture, *sb. rare.* 1646. [Mis-^{1} 4.] Erroneous conjecture. So **Misconje·cture** *v.* (*rare*) 1626.

Misco·nsecrated, *ppl. a.* 1634. [Mis-^{1} 2.] Consecrated to a wrong purpose; improperly consecrated. So **Misconsecra·tion** 1664.

Misconstru·ct, *v.* 1637. [Mis-^{1} 1.] †**1.** Chiefly *Sc.* = Misconstrue –1795. **2.** To construct badly. De Quincey.

Misconstru·ction. 1513. [Mis-^{1} 4.] **1.** The putting of a wrong construction on words or actions. **2.** Faulty or bad construction (*rare*) 1819.

Misconstrue (-kǫ·nstru, -kǫ̆nstrū·), *v.* late ME. [Mis-^{1} 1.] **1.** *trans.* To put a wrong construction on (words or actions); to mistake the meaning of (a person). **2.** To infer wrongly. Scott.
1. Thou misconstrewest al the good which the bountiful prouidence of God doth vnto thee 1587. Hence **Misconstruable** *a.* **Misconstruer.**

Miscontent, *a. arch.* and *dial.* 1489. [f. Mis-^{1} 6, 7 + Content *a.*] Not content; dissatisfied; ill-pleased. So †**Misconte·nted** *a.* **Misconte·ntment** (*arch.*).

†**Misconti·nuance.** 1540. [AFr.; see Mis-^{2}.] *Law.* Continuance by unlawful process –1771.

Misco·py, *sb.* 1881. [Mis-^{1} 4.] An error in copying. So **Misco·py** *v.* to copy incorrectly 1825.

Miscorre·ct, *v.* 1697. [Mis-^{1} 1.] *trans.* To correct wrongly. So **Miscorre·ction** 1685.

Miscou·nsel, *sb.* 1496. [Mis-^{1} 4.] Wrong advice. So **Miscou·nsel** *v.* to counsel wrongly 1389.

Miscou·nt, *v.* late ME. [Mis-^{1} 1.] **1.** *trans.* To misreckon 1548. **2.** *intr.* To make a wrong calculation. **3.** To regard erroneously (*as*). Tennyson. So **Miscou·nt** *sb.* a wrong reckoning 1586.

Miscreance (mi·skri,ăns). Now *arch.* late ME. [– OFr. *mescreance* (mod. *mécréance*); see Mis-^{2}, Creance *sb.*] False belief or faith; misbelief. So **Mi·screancy** in same sense; also villainy, depravity (cf. Miscreant 2).

Miscreant (mi·skri,ănt). ME. [– OFr. *mescreant* (mod. *mécréant*) misbelieving, unbelieving, pr. pple. of *mescroire* (mod. *mécroire*) disbelieve, f. *mes-* Mis-^{2} + *croire* :– L. *credere*; see -ant.] **A.** *adj.* **1.** Misbelieving; unbelieving, infidel. Now *arch.* **2.** Depraved, villainous, base 1593.
1. Al m. Painyms, all false Jewes, al false heretikes More. **2.** The..miscreantest rakehells in Italy 1593.
B. *sb.* **1.** A misbeliever; an unbeliever, infidel. late ME. **2.** A vile wretch; a villain, rascal 1590.

Miscrea·te, *v. rare.* 1603. [Mis-^{1} 1.] *trans.* To create amiss. So **Mi·screate, Miscrea·ted** *pa. pples.* and *ppl. adjs.* created or formed unnaturally or improperly; misshapen (also as an abusive epithet) 1585. **Miscrea·tion** 1852. **Miscrea·tive** *a.* 1819.

Miscre·dit, *v.* 1554. [Mis-^{1} 7.] To disbelieve.

Miscree·d. *poet.* 1821. [Mis-^{1} 4.] A mistaken creed.

Mis-cue·, *sb.* 1873 (**miss cue**). [f. Mis-^{1} 4 (or stem of Miss *v.*) + Cue *sb.*^{3}] *Billiards.* A failure to strike the ball properly with the cue. So **Mis-cue·** *v.* to make a m.

Misda·te, *v.* 1586. [Mis-^{1} 1.] *trans.* To affix a wrong date to; to date wrong. So **Misda·te** *sb.* a wrong date 1858.

Misdea·l, *v.* 1481. [f. Mis-^{1} 1 + Deal *v.*, in sense 1 after Du. *misdeelen.*] †**1.** *intr.* To distribute unfairly. Caxton. **2.** To act improperly 1561. **3.** *Cards.* To make a mistake in dealing; usu. *intr.*, but occas. *trans.* 1850. So **Misdea·l** *sb.* (*Cards*) an error in dealing 1850. **Misdea·ling** *vbl. sb.*

Misdeed (misdī·d). [OE. *misdǣd* = OHG. *missitāt*, Goth. *missadeþs*; see Mis-^{1}, Deed.] An evil deed; a wrong action; a crime. †In ME. *collect.* = misdoings.
He was woundid for oure mysdede Chaucer.

Misdee·m, *v.* Now chiefly *arch.* and *poet.* ME. [Mis-^{1} 1. Cf. ON. *misdœma.*] †**1.** *trans.* To judge unfavourably, think evil of –1767. †**2.** *intr.* To think ill (*of*) –1671. **3.** To be mistaken in one's view of. late ME. **b.** *trans.* To suppose (a person or thing) erroneously to be (something else); to mistake *for* 1667. **4.** To form a wrong judgement (*of*); to hold a mistaken opinion ME. **b.** To suppose mistakenly 1596. †**5.** *trans.* To have a suspicion or inkling of –1607. †**6.** *intr.* To suspect something evil (or that ...) –1600.
2. What but thy malice mov'd thee to m. A righteous Job? Milt.

Misdeli·ver, *v.* 1858. [Mis-^{1} 1.] To deliver wrongly; to hand down improperly. So **Misdeli·very,** wrong delivery.

Misdemea·n, *v.* 1494. [f. Mis-^{1} 1 + Demean *v.*^{1}] **1.** *refl.* To misconduct oneself †**2.** *trans.* To misuse. Sir H. Finch.

Misdemeanant (misdĭmī·nănt). 1819. [f. Misdemean + -ant.] A person convicted of a misdemeanour. **b.** *transf.* A person guilty of misconduct 1886.

Misdemea·nour, -or. 1487. [Mis-^{1} 4.] **1.** Evil behaviour, misconduct. Now *rare.* 1494. **b.** An instance of this; a misdeed, offence 1494. **2.** *Law.* One of a class of indictable offences deemed less heinous than felonies 1487. †**3.** A misdemeanant –1812.
2. This general definition comprehends both crimes and misdemesnors; which, properly speaking, are mere synonymous terms Blackstone. Phr. *High m.*: a crime of a heinous nature, next to high treason.

†**Misdepa·rt,** *v.* [Mis-^{1} 1.] *trans.* To distribute unfairly. Chaucer.

Misderi·ve, *v.* 1649. [Mis-^{1} 1.] †**1.** *trans.* To divert into a wrong channel. Bp. Hall. **2.** To assign a wrong derivation to 1817.

Misdescri·be, *v.* 1827. [Mis-^{1} 1.] *trans.* To describe inaccurately. **Misdescri·ption.**

Misdese·rt. *Obs.* or *arch.* 1596. [Mis-^{1} 4.] Ill-desert.

Misdevo·tion. 1612. [Mis-^{1} 4.] Wrong or misdirected devotion.

†**Misdi·ght,** *pa. pple.* late ME. [Mis-^{1} 2.] Ill-clothed; badly furnished or prepared; ill-treated –1607.

Misdire·ct, *v.* 1603. [Mis-^{1} 1.] *trans.* To give a wrong direction to (a jury, a blow, etc.).
In the hurry of a trial the ablest judge may mistake the law, and misdirect the jury Blackstone.

Misdire·ction. 1768. [Mis-^{1} 4.] **1.** The action of misdirecting or the condition of being misdirected; direction to a wrong address. **2.** A wrong direction or course 1861.

Misdo (misdū·), *v.* [OE. *misdōn*; see Mis-^{1} 1 and Do *v.*] **1.** *intr.* To do evil or wrong. Now *rare* or *Obs.* **2.** *trans.* To do amiss OE. †**3.** To harm, injure, wrong –1597. †**4.** To put out of existence. Also *refl.* –1619.
1. I have misdone; and I endure the Smart Dryden. **2.** All is forgyuen that was mysse done 1440. Hence **Misdo·er,** a wrong-doer, evil-doer.

Misdo·ing, *vbl. sb.* ME. [Mis-^{1} 3.] Wrong-doing, evil-doing; also *Law*, improper performance of an act. **b.** A misdeed. Chiefly in *pl.* 1543.
Forgyve thou all my mysdoynge Coverdale.

Misdou·bt, *sb.* Now *arch.* and *dial.* 1592. [Mis-^{1} 4.] Apprehension of evil; hence *gen.* mistrust, suspicion.
Change m. to resolution Shaks.

Misdou·bt, *v.* Now c
1540. [f. Mis-^{1} 1 + Do
have doubts as to the
reality of. **b.** with cla
that..; to have doubts
2. To have doubts ab
honesty, etc. of (a perso
misgivings in regard to,
1563. **4.** To fear or susp
occurrence of (something
fear or suspect (that som
the case) 1596. **b.** *refl.* an
to have suspicions *of. Ob*
1. I will never m. the piety
2. I doe not m. my wife Sha
hath bin limed in a bush, W
misdoubteth euery bush Sha
won't like it 1885.

†**Misdou·btful,** *a.* 1575.
cious –1596.

†**Misdrea·d,** *sb.* [Mis-^{1} 4
Shaks.

Mise (mīz, məiz), *sb.* 14
action of setting, expenses
tion (whence med.L. *misa*,
pple. of *mettre* place, set :–
later (iv onwards) put, pla
penses or costs –1492. **2.** A
or tribute made to secure
munity, as (*a*) by the people o
Lord Marcher, king, or pri
inhabitants of the Count
Chester on a change of e
settlement by agreement;
Amiens and *M. of Lewes*, bet
and his barons 1700. **4.** *Law.*
writ of right 1544. Hence **M**
rate for the m. 1673.

Misease (misī·z), *sb. arch.*
mesaise, f. *mes-* Mis-^{2} + *aise*
tress; misery; extreme suffer
fort. †**2.** Lack of the means of
ty, destitution –1490. Hence †
in want; troubled, distressed –

Mise·ducate, *v.* 1827. [Mi
To educate wrongly. So **M**
1624.

‖**Mise-en-scène** (mīzansę̄n)
Mise, Scene.] Staging of a play

Misemploy·, *v.* 1609. [Mis
To employ amiss. So **Mise**
1597.

†**Mise·nter,** *v.* 1551. [Mis-^{1} 1
enter erroneously. So **Mise·ntr**

†**Misentrea·t, -intrea·t,** *v.*
1.] *trans.* To treat badly; to ill-u

Miser (məi·zəɹ), *a.* and *sb.*
miser wretched, unfortunate.]
Wretched –1612. **2.** [attrib. us
Miserly; avaricious. *arch.* or *dial.*
2. The m.-spirit eyes the spendthrift
B. *sb.* **1.** A miserable or wretche
wretch. *Obs.* (*arch.* in Scott.) 154
who lives miserably in order to hoa
Also, an avaricious person, a nigga
2. As some lone m., visiting his stor
his treasure, counts, recounts it o'er G

Miserable (mi·zĕrăb'l), *a.* and
[– (O)Fr. *misérable* – L. *miserabilis*
f. *miserari* be pitiful, f. *miser*; see pre
A. *adj.* **1.** Of persons: Wretchedly
Now often in somewhat trivial sense:
edly uncomfortable. 1526. **2.**
wretchedly poor. *Obs.* exc. as merg
1585. **3.** Of events, etc.: Fraught with
causing wretchedness 1500. **4.** Of
Pitiable; despicable; paltry, sorry, po
5. Miserly, mean, stingy. Now *dia*
†**6.** Compassionate –1630.
1. O m. Mankind, to what fall Degraded
3. I haue past a m. night, So full of f
Dreames Shaks. **4.** M. geuers of comforte
Coverdale *Job.* 16:2. M. tea 1900.
B. *sb.* A miserable person; one wh
extreme unhappiness or great want
Hence **Mi·serableness.** So **Mi·se**
adv. late ME.

†**Misera·tion.** late ME. [– L. *mise*
f. *miserat-*, pa. ppl. stem of *miserari*
prec., -ion. Cf. OFr. *miseration* (xii).]
compassion, mercy –1638.

‖**Misère** (mizēᵊ·ɹ, Fr. mizę̄r). 1830. [Fr
poverty, Misery.] *Cards.* A declaration
which the caller undertakes not to tak
trick.

Mislay (mislēi·), *v.* late ME. [MIS-[1] 1.] **1.** *trans.* To place wrongly; to misplace; to err in placing (a thing). Now *rare.* **2.** To lay (a thing) by accident where it cannot readily be found 1614. †**3.** To allege incorrectly BACON.

1. The Fault is generally mislaid upon Nature LOCKE. 2. I cannot conceive what possesses me.. to m. papers SCOTT.

Mislead (mislī·d), *v.* *Pa. t.* and *pple.* **misled.** [OE. *mislǣdan*; see MIS-[1] 1 and LEAD *v.*[1]] **1.** *trans.* To lead astray in conduct; to lead into error. †**b.** *refl.* To misconduct oneself. ME. only. †**2.** To mismanage –1494. **3.** To lead in the wrong direction 1575.

1. By ambition far misled SCOTT. *absol.* What can they teach, and not m.? MILT. 3. Are you not hee, That..misleade night-wanderers? SHAKS.

Mislea·rn, *v.* 1678. [MIS-[1] 1.] *trans.* To learn badly.

Mislen, var. of MASLIN[2].

Misli·ke, *sb.* ME. [f. MISLIKE *v.*] †**1.** The opposite of pleasure; discomfort; unhappiness. ME. only. **2.** Dislike (*of*), distaste (*for*), objection (*to*). Now *rare.* Also with *a* and *pl.* 1557. †**3.** Disaffection, disagreement –1654. †**4.** Wasting in animals or plants; sickliness, disease –1622.

2. Julian's m. of the rising faith TRENCH.

Misli·ke, *v.* Now chiefly *literary* or *dial.* [OE. *mislīcian*; see MIS-[1] 1 and LIKE *v.*[1]] **1.** *trans.* To displease. †**2.** *intr.* To be displeased; in ME. also, to be uneasy –1642. **3.** *trans.* To be displeased at; to dislike 1513. †**4.** *intr.* To grow sickly; to waste away –1606.

1. *absol.* That pleaseth well, and This as much mislikes DRAYTON. 3. 'Tis not my speeches that you do m.: But 'tis my presence that doth trouble ye SHAKS. Hence **Misli·king** *vbl. sb.* = MISLIKE *sb.*

Mislin, var. of MASLIN[2], MISTLETOE.

†**Misli·ve,** *v.* OE. [MIS-[1] 1.] *intr.* To live a bad life –1579. Hence **Misli·ver** (*rare* or *Obs.*), an evil liver 1436.

Mislo·dge, *v.* 1676. [MIS-[1] 1.] *trans.* To lodge in a wrong place; †to mislay.

Mislu·ck, *sb.* Chiefly *Sc.* 1623. [MIS-[1] 4.] Misfortune. **Mislu·ck** *v.* meet with misfortune.

Misly, obs. f. MIZZLY.

Misma·ke, *v.* Now *Sc.* late ME. [MIS-[1] 1.] **a.** *trans.* To make badly. †**b.** To unmake, depose. **c.** *refl.* To disturb oneself.

Misma·nage, *v.* 1690. [MIS-[1] 1.] *trans.* and *intr.* To manage badly or wrongly. So **Misma·nagement** 1668. **Misma·nager** 1683.

Misma·rk, *v.* 1535. [MIS-[1] 1.] *trans.* To mark wrongly. Also in pa. pple., having wrong markings.

Misma·rry, *v.* 1892. [MIS-[1] 1.] *trans.* To marry unsuitably (*lit.* and *fig.*). So **Misma·rriage** 1817.

Misma·tch, *v.* 1599. [MIS-[1] 1.] *trans.* To match badly, esp. in marriage; *pass.* to be ill-mated. So **Misma·tch** *sb.* a bad match 1606.

Misma·ted, *pa. pple.* and *ppl. a.* 1825. [MIS-[1] 2.] Ill-matched, unsuitably allied.

Mismea·sure, *v.* 1742. [MIS-[1] 1.] *trans.* To measure or estimate incorrectly. So **Mismea·surement.**

Misme·tre, *v.* late ME. [f. MIS-[1] 1 + METRE *v.*] *trans.* To spoil the metre of.

Misna·me, *v.* 1500. [MIS-[1] 1.] **1.** = MISCALL 1. 1537. †**2.** = MISCALL 2. –1632.

Misnomer (misnōu·məɹ), *sb.* 1455. [– AFr., subst. use of OFr. *mesnom(m)er*, f. *mes-* MIS-[2] + *nommer* :– L. *nominare*, f. *nomen* name; see -ER[4].] **1.** *Law.* A mistake in naming a person or place. **2.** *gen.* The use of a wrong name or term 1635. **3.** A wrong name or designation 1657.

2. The City which, by a m., is called the Metropolis 1882. 3. My name of Epic's no m. BYRON. Hence **Misno·mer** *v. trans.* to misname 1740.

Misnu·mber, *v.* 1614. [MIS-[1] 1.] *trans.* To number incorrectly.

Miso- (məiso, miso), bef. a vowel usu. **mis-**, repr. Gr. μισο- (μισ-), comb. f. root of μισεῖν to hate, μῖσος hatred. Cf. PHILO-.

Miso·gamy [Gr. γάμος marriage], hatred of marriage 1656; so **Misoga·mic** *a.*, **Miso·gamist.** **Miso·gynist** [Gr. γυνή woman], a woman-hater 1620; so **Mi·sogyne** = m.; **Misogy·nic, -ous, -istic, -istical** *adjs.*; **Miso·gynism, Miso·gyny.** **Miso·logy** [-LOGY], hatred of discussion or knowledge 1833; so **Miso·logist, Mi·sologue.** **Misone·ism** [Gr. νέος new], hatred of novelty 1886; hence **Misone·ist; Misonei·stic** *a.* **Misothe·ism** [Gr. θεός god], hatred of God or gods 1846; so **Misothe·ist, Misothei·stic** *a.*

Misobse·rvance. *rare.* 1496. [MIS-[1] 4.] Failure to observe rules or conditions properly. So **Misobse·rve** *v.*

†**Misopi·nion.** 1545. [MIS-[1] 4.] An erroneous opinion –1680.

Miso·rder, *sb.* Now *rare.* late ME. [MIS-[1] 4.] = DISORDER *sb.*

†**Miso·rder,** *v.* 1494. [MIS-[1] 1.] **1.** *trans.* To put into disorder; to disturb, confuse –1597. **2.** To ill-treat, ill-use –1575. **3.** *refl.* To misbehave –1740.

1. 2 *Hen. IV*, IV. ii. 33.

Mispay·, *v.* ME. [– OFr. *mespaier*; see MIS-[2] and PAY *v.*[1]] †**1.** *trans.* To displease, dissatisfy –1493. **2.** To pay by mistake 1698.

Misperfo·rm, *v.* 1656. [MIS-[1] 1.] *trans.* To perform improperly. So **Misperfo·rmance.**

Mispersua·de, *v.* Now *rare* or *Obs.* 1597. [MIS-[1] 1.] *trans.* To persuade wrongly or into error. So **Mispersua·sion** 1594.

Mispickel (mi·spikĕl). 1683. [– G. *mispickel.*] *Min.* Arsenopyrite.

Mispla·ce, *v.* 1551. [MIS-[1] 1.] **1.** *trans.* To put in a wrong place or in wrong hands 1594. †**b.** *absol.* To misplace one's words. SHAKS. **2.** To set (one's affections) on a wrong object; to place (one's confidence) amiss; †to spend (time) unprofitably 1638.

1. b. *Meas. for M.* II. i. 90. 2. Munificence misplaced COWPER. So **Mispla·cement** 1655.

Misplaced (misplēi·st), *ppl. a.* 1595. [MIS-[1] 2.] Put in a wrong place; devoted to a wrong object; out-of-place, ill-timed.

M. acts of foolery LAMB.

Misplea·d, *v. rare.* 1676. [MIS-[1] 1. Cf. AFr. *mespleder.*] *trans.* To plead wrongly or falsely. So **Misplea·ding** *vbl. sb.* a mistake in pleading 1532.

Mispoi·nt, *v.* Now *rare* or *Obs.* 1542. [MIS-[1] 1.] †**a.** To point with the wrong finger. **b.** To punctuate wrongly; to mispunctuate.

Misprai·se, *v.* Now *rare.* ME. [MIS-[1] 1, 7.] **1.** *trans.* To dispraise, blame. **2.** To praise amiss 1631.

Mispri·nt, *v.* 1494. [MIS-[1] 1.] *trans.* To print incorrectly. So **Mi·sprint** *sb.* 1818.

Misprisal (misprəi·zăl). *rare.* 1620. [f. MISPRIZE *v.*[1] + -AL[1] 2.] Contempt, disdain, scorn.

Misprision[1] (mispri·ʒən). late ME. [– AFr. *mesprisioun* = OFr. *mesprison* error, wrong action or speech, f. *mesprendre* (mod. *méprendre*), f. *mes-* MIS-[2] + *prendre* take.] **1.** *Law.* A wrong action or omission; *spec.* a misdemeanour or neglect of duty on the part of a public official. **2.** The mistaking one thing, etc., for another; a mistake (*arch.*) 1588.

1. *M. of treason, of felony*: orig., an offence or misdemeanor akin to treason or felony, but not liable to the capital penalty. Later misunderstood as meaning only concealment of a person's knowledge of treasonable actions or designs. Also *transf.* in pop. use. 2. The m. of this passage has aided in fostering the delusive notion HARE.

Misprision[2] (mispri·ʒən). *arch.* 1586. [f. MISPRIZE *v.*[1] after prec.] **a.** Contempt, scorn. **b.** Failure to appreciate or recognize as valuable.

That dost in vile m. shackle vp My loue SHAKS.

Misprize (misprəi·z), *v.*[1] 1481. [– OFr. *mesprisier* (mod. *mépriser*), f. *mes-* MIS-[2] + *priser* PRIZE *v.*[1]] *trans.* **a.** To despise, contemn, scorn. **b.** To fail to appreciate.

a. *Much Ado* III. i. 52. b. It sorrows me that you misprise my love HEYWOOD. Hence **Mispri·ze** *sb.*[1] = MISPRISION[2] (*rare*) 1590.

†**Mispri·ze,** *v.*[2] 1485. [f. OFr. *mespris*, pa. pple. of *mesprendre* commit a crime (mod. *se méprendre* be mistaken); see MIS-[2], PRIZE *v.*[1]] **1.** *intr.* To commit an offence –1500. **2.** *trans.* To mistake, misunderstand –1657.

2. Monsieur Gaspar..misprise me not B. JONS. Hence †**Mispri·ze** *sb.*[2] mistake SPENSER.

Mispronou·nce, *v.* 1593. [MIS-[1] 1.] *trans.* To pronounce incorrectly.

They mispronounc't and I mislik't MILT. So **Mispronuncia·tion** 1539.

Mispropo·rtioned, *ppl. a.* 1552. [MIS-[1] 2.] Badly or wrongly proportioned. So **Mispropo·rtion** *sb.* lack of proportion 1825. **Mispropo·rtion** *v. trans.* 'to join without due proportion' (J.).

Misproud (misprau·d), *a. arch.* ME. [MIS-[1] 6.] Wrongly or wickedly proud; arrogant.

Mispu·nctuate, *v.* 1849. [MIS-[1] 1.] To punctuate incorrectly. **Mispunctua·tion** 1807.

Misquo·te, *v.* 1596. [MIS-[1] 1.] *trans.* To quote incorrectly.

Looke how we can, or sad or merrily, Interpretation will m. our lookes SHAKS. So **Misquota·tion,** inaccuracy in quoting; an incorrect quotation 1773.

Misra·te, *v.* Now *rare.* 1624. [MIS-[1] 1.] *trans.* To estimate wrongly.

Misrea·d, *v.* 1809. [MIS-[1] 1.] *trans.* To read or interpret wrongly.

Misreci·te, *v.* 1572. [MIS-[1] 1.] *trans.* To recite incorrectly; to give a wrong account of. So **Misreci·tal** 1539.

Misre·ckon, *v.* 1524. [MIS-[1] 1.] **1.** To reckon incorrectly; to miscalculate, miscount. †**2.** *trans.* To present an incorrect account to –1654. So **Misre·ckoning** *vbl. sb.* 1540.

Misrela·te, *v.* 1621. [MIS-[1] 1.] *trans.* To relate or recount incorrectly. So **Misrela·tion;** also **Misrela·ted** *ppl. a.* wrongly related or connected.

Misreli·gion. *rare.* 1623. [MIS-[1] 4.] False religion.

Misreme·mber, *v.* 1533. [MIS-[1] 1.] *trans.* To remember wrongly; to have an imperfect recollection of. Now chiefly *dial.* to forget. So **Misreme·mbrance** (*rare*) 1542.

Misre·nder, *v.* 1661. [MIS-[1] 1.] *trans.* To render or interpret incorrectly.

Misrepo·rt, *sb.* ME. [MIS-[1] 4.] †**1.** Evil report; ill repute –1697. **2.** False or erroneous report, as of the actions, etc., of a person 1530.

Misrepo·rt, *v.* late ME. [MIS-[1] 1.] **1.** *trans.* To report erroneously; to give a false account of the statements or opinions of. †**2.** To speak ill of; to slander –1625.

Mi:srepresе·nt, *v.* 1647. [MIS-[1] 1.] *trans.* To represent improperly or imperfectly; to give a false account of. So **Mi:srepresenta·tion** 1647. **Mi:srepresе·ntative** *a.* not properly representative (*of*) 1736.

Misru·le, *sb.* late ME. [MIS-[1] 4.] †**1.** Disorderly conduct; ill-regulated life; excess –1613. **2.** Bad government (of a state, etc.); misgovernment; a state of disorder, anarchy, or rebellion. late ME.

Lord (also *Abbot, Master*) *of M.*: one chosen to preside over the Christmas games and revels in a great man's house (*Hist.*); also *transf.* and *fig.*

Misru·le, *v.* ME. [MIS-[1] 1.] †**1.** *trans.* To manage or control badly –1530. **2.** To rule (a country, etc.) badly. late ME.

†**Misru·ly,** *a.* late ME. [f. MIS-[1] 6 + RULY *a.*] Disorderly; unruly –1598.

Miss (mis), *sb.*[1] [OE. *miss* loss, corresp. to MLG., MHG. *misse* (Du. *mis*), ON. *missa, missir.*] **I.** Loss, lack. (Cf. MISS *v.* IV.) **1.** The fact or condition of missing or being without; loss, lack, privation. Const. *of* or *genitive.* 1470. †**b.** Observable lack –1722. **2.** Disadvantage or regret occasioned by loss, absence, or privation *of* a person or thing ME.

1. At Carthage, the misse of so great a person was diuersly construed RALEGH. 2. Phr. *To feel the m. of; there is no* (*great*) *m. of.* Now *dial.* or *vulgar.*

II. Wrong, mistake. (Cf. MISS *v.* V.) †**1.** Wrong; offence, injury; a wrong, misdeed –1616. †**2.** Error, mistake. ASCHAM.

2. Without any great misse in the hardest pointes of Grammer 1568.

III. Failure to hit or attain. (Cf. MISS *v.* I.) **1.** Failure to hit something aimed at 1555. **2.** Failure to obtain or achieve something. Now *rare.* 1609. **3.** *Printing.* The omitting to lay on a sheet in feeding a printing-machine 1888.

1. Provb.: *A m. is as good as a mile*: failure by however little is still failure. *To give a m.* (Billiards): to avoid hitting the object ball, esp. in playing for safety. The opponent is said *to score a m.*

Miss (mis), *sb.*[2] 1666. [Clipped form of MISTRESS; cf. MAS.] **1.** A kept mistress. Less commonly, a whore. *Obs.* exc. *dial.* 1675. **2.**

As a title of an unmarried woman or girl 1666. **3.** With ellipsis of the proper name. Not now in educated use. 1667. **4.** A young unmarried woman; a girl, *esp.* a schoolgirl; in mod. use, often connoting squeamishness or sentimentality. (In literary English use now only playful or contemptuous.) 1667.

2. *The Misses Smith, the Miss Smiths*: alternative forms of the pl., of which the former is grammatically the more proper. *Miss Smith*: normally the eldest (unmarried) daughter of the family. **3.** Is it m. or the cash of mamma you pursue? BYRON. 'I beg your pardon, Miss', said she [a maidservant] 1850. **4.** Under the tyranny of some small m. of two or three 1885. Hence **Mi·ssish** *a.* like a m.; hence, affected, prim, squeamish, or sentimental. **Mi·ssishness.**

Miss (mis), *sb.*[3] 1767. [perh. a use of prec., or of MISS *sb.*[1]; cf. KITTY[3].] *Cards.* An extra hand for which any of the players may discard his own.

Miss (mis), *v.* [OE. *missan* = OFris. *missa*, (M)LG., (M)Du. *missen*, (O)HG. *missen*, ON. *missa* :– Gmc. **missjan*, f. *missa-*; see MIS-[1].] **I.** *trans.* To fail to hit, meet, or light upon. **1.** To fail to hit (something aimed at). **b.** Occas., of a missile, a blow, etc.: To pass by without touching 1749. **2.** Not to hit upon (the right path) 1547. **3.** To fail to obtain footing on (a step, plank, etc.) 1550. **4.** To fail to meet (a person). Also occas. *intr.* for *reciprocal.* 1589.

1. Mark like this Was Bertram never known to m. SCOTT. †*To m. the cushion*: to miss the mark; to make a mistake, err. *To m. one's aim, one's* (or *the*) *mark* (fig.): see MARK *sb.*[1] II. 3. d. absol. *Hit or m.*: see HIT *v.* **2.** *To m. one's way.* **3.** Blind with rage she miss'd the plank, and rolled In the river TENNYSON. **4.** I wonder how I missed you NASHE. Then we missed: now we meet MEREDITH.

Phrases. **To m. fire.** Of firearms: To fail to go off. Hence *fig.* to be unsuccessful. **To m. stays** (*Naut.*): To fail in an attempt to go about from one tack to another. Also *fig.*

II. *trans.* To fail to attain. **1.** To fail to get; to come short of, go without ME. **b.** Not to have the satisfaction of hearing, seeing, or witnessing (something) 1841. **2.** To fail to do, achieve, or accomplish (something). late ME. **3.** To escape, avoid. Now only *dial.*, exc. with adv. 1526. **4.** To let slip (an opportunity, etc.) 1628; to fail to catch (a train, etc.) 1823. **5.** To fail to see; to fail to 'catch' or understand 1588.

1. Since the time I missed the solicitor's place BACON. **b.** I would not have missed the speech.. for a great deal JOWETT. **2.** To m. a stroke at billiards 1888. **5.** I sat so high and far off that I missed most of the words PEPYS.

III. *trans.* To omit. **1.** To omit, leave out. Also with *out.* 1530. **2.** To omit the performance of; to fail to keep (an appointment); to omit to be present at 1598.

1. To m. one of the responses SCOTT. **2.** I never missed chapel RUSKIN.

IV. *trans.* To be without; lack; want. †**1.** To be without, lack; to cease to have, lose. Also with *away.* –1677. †**b.** Contextually, to do without –1637. **2.** To discover the absence of ME. **3.** To feel the want of 1470.

1. b. We cannot misse him; he do's make our fire [etc.] SHAKS. **2.** One morn I missed him on the custom'd hill GRAY. **3.** Milton was too busy to much m. his wife JOHNSON.

V. *intr.* †**1.** To go wrong, make a mistake, err –1754. †**2.** To be lacking –1828. †**3.** To come to an end, give out, fail –1529. **4.** To be unsuccessful. Now *arch.* or *Obs.* 1592. **5.** Of crops, etc.: To be abortive (*dial.*) 1615.

1. Starres are poore books, and oftentimes do misse G. HERBERT. **2.** 1 *Sam.* 25:7. **3.** Til the day gan misse CHAUCER.

Miss of —. Chiefly *Obs.* or *arch.* = senses I. 1, 4, 5; II. 1–4; IV. 1. **M. on** —. To fail to hit upon. LAMB.

Miss, obs. f. MASS *sb.*[1]

Missal (mi·săl), *sb.*[1] ME. [– *missale*, subst. use of n. sing. of eccl. L. *missalis* pertaining to the Mass, f. *missa* MASS *sb.*[1]; see -AL[1].] The book containing the service of the Mass for the whole year; a mass-book. ¶**b.** Vaguely: A Roman Catholic book of prayers, esp. when illuminated 1651.

attrib., etc., as **m. caps** (*Printing*), a style of fancy letter, used sometimes as initials to Old English or Black letter.

Missal (mi·săl), *a.* (*sb.*[2]) 1466. [– eccl. L. *missalis*; see prec.] Of or pertaining to the Mass; mass-.

Mis-say (misˌsēⁱ·), *v. arch.* Pa. t. and pple. **mis-said** (misˌse·d). [MIS-[1] 1.] **1.** *trans.* To speak evil of or against; to slander, vilify. Now *arch.* and *poet.* †**b.** To say with evil intent –1614. †**2.** *intr.* To speak evil –1596. **3.** *trans.* To say wrongly. Now *rare.* late ME. **b.** *intr.* To say something wrong or amiss. late ME.

1. Far liefer had I fight a score of times Than hear thee so m. me and revile TENNYSON.

Mis-see, *v.* 1591. [MIS-[1] 1.] To see imperfectly; to take a wrong view of.

Mis-see·m, *v.* Now *rare.* late ME. [MIS-[1] 1.] *trans.* To misbecome.

Missel (mi·sĕl). [OE. *mistel* (1) basil, (2) mistletoe = OHG. *mistil* (G. *mistel*), Du. *mistel*, ON. *mistil-*; of unkn. origin.] †**1.** Mistletoe –1670. **2.** Short for MISSEL-BIRD, -THRUSH. 1845.

Mi·ssel-bird. Now *dial.* 1626. [f. prec.] = MISSEL-THRUSH.

Misseldin(e, obs. ff. MISTLETOE.

Mi·ssel-thrush. 1774. [f. MISSEL.] A species of thrush, *Turdus viscivorus*, which feeds on the berries of the mistletoe.

Mis-se·nd, *v.* late ME. [MIS-[1] 1.] *trans.* To send to a wrong place or person.

Mis-se·rve, *v.* Now *rare.* ME. [In early use – OFr. *messervir* (MIS-[2]); later f. MIS-[1] 1 + SERVE *v.*] **1.** *trans.* To serve badly or unfaithfully. †**2.** *intr.* To miss fire –1685.

Mis-set (misˌse·t), *v.* ME. [MIS-[1] 1.] **1.** *trans.* To misplace. †**2.** To put out of humour, 'upset' (*Sc.*) –1818.

Miss-fi·re. 1811. [f. phr. *to miss fire.*] = MISFIRE *sb.*

Mis-shape (misʃēⁱ·p), *sb.* Now *rare.* 1465. [MIS-[1] 4.] A bad or deformed shape or figure; deformity. Also, a mis-shapen body or person.

Mis-shape (misʃēⁱ·p), *v.* 1450. [MIS-[1] 1.] *trans.* To shape ill; to give a bad form to; to deform. *lit.* and *fig.*

Figures monstrous and mis-shap'd POPE.

Mis-shapen (misʃēⁱ·p'n), *ppl. a.* late ME. [f. MIS-[1] 2 + *shapen* pa. pple. of SHAPE *v.*] Having a bad or ugly shape; ill-shaped; deformed.

The m. hairy Scandinavian troll EMERSON. *fig.* Crooked and m. minds FLORIO. Hence **Missha·pen-ly** *adv.*, **-ness.**

Mis-shea·thed, *ppl. a.* [MIS-[1] 2.] Sheathed by mistake. *Rom. & Jul.* V. iii. 205.

Missible (mi·sib'l), *a. rare.* 1789. [– Fr. †*missible* or med.L. *missibilis*, f. L. *miss-*; see MISSION, -IBLE.] Capable of being sent.

†**Missi·ficate,** *v.* 1641. [– *missificat-*, pa. ppl. stem of med. (eccl.) L. *missificare*, f. L. *missa* MASS *sb.*[1] + *-ficare*; see -FY.] *intr.* To perform Mass –1694. So †**Missifica·tion** [see -FICATION] 1641.

Missile (mi·səil, mi·sil), *a.* and *sb.* 1606. [– L. *missilis* (n. sing. *missile* as sb.), f. *miss-*; see MISSION, -ILE.] **A.** *adj.* Capable of being thrown; adapted to be discharged from the hand or from a machine or engine; chiefly in *m. weapon* 1611. **b.** Applied to weapons that discharge arrows, bullets, etc. 1819.

We bend the bow, or wing the m. dart POPE. **b.** Their long-bows, slings, and other m. weapons SCOTT.

B. *sb.* **1.** A missile object or weapon, as a stone, an arrow, a bullet 1656. **2.** *pl.* = L. *missilia, res missiles*, largess (i.e. sweets, perfumes, etc.) thrown by the Roman emperors to the people 1606.

Mi·ssing, *ppl. a.* 1530. [f. MISS *v.* + -ING[2].] **1.** Not present; not found; absent; gone. **2.** That fails to hit 1586.

1. Moses was in the Mount, and m. long MILT. The ship is what is called a m. ship, i.e. has been so long on the voyage that the owner has reason to suspect that she has met with some casualty 1848.

Special collocations: **m. link,** (*a*) something lacking to complete a series; (*b*) *Zool.* a hypothetical type assumed to connect two related types; *esp.* a hypothetical intermediate form between the anthropoid apes and man; also applied to an animal (or person) supposed to resemble this.

Mission (mi·ʃən), *sb.* 1598. [– Fr. *mission* or L. *missio*, f. *miss-*, pa. ppl. stem of *mittere* send; see -ION.] †**1.** The action or an act of sending –1698. **2.** A sending or being sent to perform some function or service; *Theol.* the sending of the Second or Third Person of the Trinity by the First, or of the Third by the Second, for the production of a temporal effect 1609. **3.** *Eccl.* The action of sending men forth with authority to preach the faith and administer the sacraments; hence, authority given by God or the Church to preach 1613. **4.** A body of persons sent to a foreign country to conduct negotiations, watch over interests, etc. 1626. **5.** A body of persons sent out by a religious community to convert the heathen; also, to spiritualize various classes of people 1622. **6.** A permanent establishment of missionaries in a country; a particular field of missionary activity; a missionary post or station 1769. **b.** *transf.* An organization in a particular district for the conversion of the people 1800. **7.** A special course of religious services, sermons, etc., organized in connection with a particular church or parish for this purpose 1772. **8.** The commission of a messenger, envoy, or agent; now *esp.* the errand of a political mission 1671. **9.** (A person's) vocation or work in life. Also *transf.* attributed to things. Occas. *trivial* or *contempt.* 1805. **10.** *attrib.*, as *m. church, house, work*, etc. 1792.

1. *Tr. & Cr.* III. iii. 189. **2.** The M. of the Comforter 1846. **3.** Christ..in the M. first of his Twelve, and after of his Seventy 1641. Men..who, so far from having any Orders or M., had not so much as Baptism CHALLONER. **5.** Like zealous Missions, they did care pretend Of souls in show, but made the gold their end DRYDEN. *Home, city, police-court m.* **6.** They..To the nearest m. sped and ask'd the Jesuit's aid SOUTHEY. **8.** How to accomplish best His end of being on Earth, and m. high MILT. A M. to the King of Dahomey 1863. **10. b.** *U.S.* Denoting a style of architecture, furniture, etc. characteristic of the Spanish Roman Catholic missions in California.

Mission (mi·ʃən), *v.* 1692. [f. prec. sb.] **1.** *trans.* To send on a mission; to give (a person) a mission to perform. Chiefly in *pass.* **2.** To conduct a religious mission among (a people) or in (a district) 1772. Also *intr.*

Missionary (mi·ʃənări), *a.* and *sb.* 1644. [– mod.L. *missionarius* (XVII), whence also Fr. *missionnaire*, f. L. *miss-*; see MISSION *sb.*, -ARY[1].] **A.** *adj.* **1.** Of or pertaining to missions; engaged in a mission; proper to one sent on a mission; occupied in or characterized by mission-work. **2.** That is sent out or forth. Now *Obs.* or *poet.* 1691.

1. *M. box*: a box for contributions towards the funds of a m. society.

B. *sb.* **1.** A person who carries on missionary work, esp. among the heathen 1656. **2.** An agent or emissary; esp. one sent on a political mission. Now *rare* or *Obs.* 1693. †**3.** A missionary establishment –1761.

1. Phr. *Home m.*: a person (usu. a layman) employed to labour in the spiritual instruction of the poor. *City m.*: one so employed amongst the poor of a city; so *town m. Police-court m.*: a person employed to attend a police-court, and to work for the spiritual and moral benefit of those brought before it. *transf.* The fanatic missionaries of sedition GIBBON.

Missioner (mi·ʃənəɹ). 1654. [f. MISSION + -ER[1].] One sent on a mission, a missionary. In mod. use chiefly, one who conducts a parochial mission.

The pope enjoined his m. to remove the pagan idols GOLDSM. *fig.* A m. of peace and order in every parish BURKE.

Missionize (mi·ʃənəiz), *v.* 1826. [f. MISSION *sb.* + -IZE.] *intr.* To do missionary work. Also *trans.*

Missis, missus (mi·sis, -iz, mi·sŏs). *dial.* and *vulgar.* 1837. [Slurred pronunc. of MISTRESS. The oral equivalent of MRS. (q.v.).] **1.** Wife 1839. **2.** Used by servants (usu. without article) in speaking of their mistresses.

1. *The missis*: used by a man in speaking of his own or another man's wife. Hence **Mi·ssis** *v.* to address as 'Mrs.' DICKENS.

Missish (mi·siʃ), *a.* 1795. [f. MISS *sb.*[2] + -ISH[1].] Characteristic of a miss; affected or sentimental.

Missive (mi·siv), *a.* and *sb.* 1466. [– med.L. *missivus* (in *litteræ missivæ*), f. L. *miss-*; see MISSION *sb.*, -IVE. Cf. Fr. *missive* (XVI) in *lettre missive.*] **A.** *adj.* **1.** *Letter m., m. letter.* Usu. pl. *letters m.* or †*missives.* †**a.** *gen.* An epistle sent from one person to another –1710. **b.** A letter or letters sent by a superior authority to a particular person or body of persons, conveying a command, recommendation, or permission. Now chiefly, a letter from the sovereign to a dean and chapter nominating a person to be elected bishop. (See CONGÉ D'ÉLIRE.) 1466. †**2.** = MISSILE *a.* –1809. †**3.** That is sent –1830.

1. b. A letter missiue Vnder the Kynges signett 1487. **2.** Now with their m. weapons onely..but with their drawne swords KNOLLES.

B. *sb.* **1.** A written message; a letter. Occas. *spec.* = A. 1. Now usu. an official letter, or high-flown for 'letter'. late ME. **2.** *Scots Law.* A document in the form of a letter interchanged by the parties to a contract 1561. †**3.** A messenger (*rare*) –1649. †**4.** Something hurled or thrown; *esp.* a missile weapon –1809.

1. Mysterious missives, sealed with red 1885. **3.** Missiues from the King, who all-hail'd me Thane of Cawdor SHAKS.

Mis-so·rt, *v.* 1581. [MIS-[1] 1.] *trans.* To sort badly.

Mis-sou·nd, *v.* 1500. [MIS-[1] 1.] **1.** *intr.* To sound amiss. **2.** *trans.* To mispronounce.

Mis-spea·k, *v.* ME. [MIS-[1] 1.] †**1.** *intr.* To speak wrongly or improperly; to speak evil –1613. †**2.** *trans.* To speak evil of –1584. **3.** To speak incorrectly or improperly (*rare*) 1593. So **Mis-spee·ch,** †evil-speaking; incorrect speaking ME.

Mis-spe·ll, *v.* 1655. [MIS-[1] 1.] *trans.* To spell incorrectly. Hence **Mis-spe·ll, -spe·lling** *sbs.* a bad spelling.

Mis-spe·nd, *v.* late ME. [MIS-[1] 1.] *trans.* To spend amiss or wastefully. So †**Mis-spe·nse, -e·nce,** improper or wasteful expenditure 1591–1788. **Mis-spent** *ppl. a.* ill-spent, wasted 1500.

Mis-sta·te, *v.* 1650. [MIS-[1] 1.] *trans.* To state erroneously. So **Mis-sta·tement** 1790.

Misstay·, *v.* 1885. [f. phr. *to miss stays* (see MISS *v.* I. *Phrases*).] *intr.* Of a ship: To miss stays. Also *sb.* 1878.

†**Mis-ste·p,** *v.* late ME. [MIS-[1] 1.] *intr.* To take a wrong step; to go astray –1598. So **Mis-ste·p** *sb.* a wrong step; a FAUX PAS 1855.

Mis-sty·le, *v. rare.* 1604. [MIS-[1] 1.] *trans.* To style or term incorrectly.

†**Mis-succee·ding,** *vbl. sb.* 1661. [MIS-[1] 3.] Ill-success FULLER. †**Mis-succe·ss** 1656.

Mis-sui·t, *v.* 1618. [MIS-[1] 1.] *trans.* To suit ill.

Mis-swo·rn, *ppl. a.* 1506. [MIS-[1] 2.] **a.** Forsworn. **b.** Whose name has been taken in vain.

Missy (mi·si), *sb.* 1676. [f. MISS *sb.*[2] + -Y[6].] An affectionate or playful form of MISS. Occas. *contempt.*

Missy, var. of MISY. *Obs.*

Mist (mist), *sb.*[1] [OE. *mist* = (M)LG., (M)Du. *mist*, Icel. *mistur*, Norw. dial., Sw. *mist* :– Gmc. **mixstaz*, f. **miz-* (cf. Du. *miggelen*, WFris. *miggelje* drizzle) :– IE. **migh-* **meigh-*, as in Gr. ὀμίχλη mist, fog.] **1.** Vapour of water precipitated in very fine droplets, smaller and more densely aggregated than those of rain. **b.** *transf.* A cloud (of small particles) resembling a mist; a haze or haziness; hence *fig.* of time, etc. 1785. **2.** Dimness of eyesight; a filmy appearance before the eyes caused by disorders of the body or by tears OE. **3.** Applied to immaterial things conceived as dimming, obscuring, or blurring OE. †**4.** An atmosphere of doubt –1715.

1. Whan the moysture of the dewe stryketh upwarde agayne, it maketh a myste 1530. *Scotch m.*: a thick, soaking mist characteristic of the Scottish hills. **b.** Times..half shrouded in the m. of legend FREEMAN. **2.** O'er her meek eyes came a happy m. TENNYSON. **3.** The mists Of despondency and gloom M. ARNOLD. Phr. *Mists of death, deathly mists.*

Comb.: **m.-bow,** a fog-bow (FOG *sb.*[2]); **-flower,** a plant of the tropical American genus *Conoclinium.*

†**Mist,** *sb.*[2] late ME. [perh. a use of prec. infl. by *mystic*, etc.; cf. MISTY *a.*[2]] Things spiritual or mystical. *In m.*: mystically. –1667. (MILT. *P. L.* v. 435.).

Mist (mist), *v.* [OE. *mistian*, f. *mist* MIST *sb.*[1]] **1.** *intr.* To be or become misty; (of the eyes, outlines, etc.) to become dim, obscure, or blurred. **2.** *trans.* To cover or obscure with or as with mist; to bedim (the eyes) with tears. late ME.

1. When thy gold breath is misting in the west KEATS. **2.** He sits Misted with darknes like a smoaky roome 1598.

Mistakable (mistēⁱ·kăb'l), *a.* 1646. [f. MISTAKE *v.* + -ABLE.] Capable of being mistaken, misapprehended, or misunderstood. Hence **Mista·kableness. Mista·kably** *adv.*

Mistake (mistēⁱ·k), *sb.* 1638. [f. next.] *prop.* A misconception of the meaning of something; *hence*, an error or fault in thought or action.

The great m. of expecting too much of life 1856. *gen.* Infallibility is an absolute security of the understanding from all possibility of m. in what it believes TILLOTSON. Phr. †*A m. of*: a misconception as to. †*Under a m.*: under a misapprehension. *By m.*: mistakenly. *And no m.*: undoubtedly; used *colloq.* to emphasize a preceding statement. Also used attrib., (*and-*) *no-m.* = undoubted. The real old original and no-mistake nobility THACKERAY.

Mistake (mistēⁱ·k), *v.* ME. [– ON. *mistaka* take in error, refl. miscarry (Sw. *misstaga* be mistaken), f. *mis-* MIS-[1] + *taka* TAKE. Cf. OFr. *mesprendre* (see MISPRIZE *v.*[2]), which has prob. infl. the meaning.] †**1.** *trans.* To take wrongfully, wrongly, or in error –1631. †**2.** *intr.* To transgress, offend –1822. **3.** To err in the choice of. late ME. **4.** *trans.* To misunderstand the meaning or †character of (a person). late ME. **5.** To take (an opinion, statement, action, purpose, etc.) in a wrong sense 1496. **6.** *intr.* To make a mistake; to be in error; to take a wrong view 1581. †**7.** *trans.* To suppose erroneously to be or to do ... –1736. **8.** *To mistake* (a person or thing) *for* (another): to suppose erroneously the former to be the latter 1611. **9.** To take to be somebody or something else 1590. †**10.** To commit an error in regard to (a date, etc.); to perform (an action) at a wrong time –1734.

3. Phr. *To m. the* or *one's road* (*way*); *to m. one's mark.* **4.** Why, thou whorson Asse, thou mistak'st me SHAKS. **5.** The judge may m. the law *'Junius' Lett.* **6.** Oh, cry you mercy sir, I haue mistooke SHAKS. You're mistaken I dare say DICKENS. **7.** Lest I should be mistaken to vilify Reason 1736. **8.** She [a hen] mistakes a Piece of Chalk for an Egg, and sits upon it in the same manner ADDISON. **9.** Phr. *There's no mistaking* = it is impossible not to recognize. There was no mistaking the fact DICKENS. Hence **Mista·kingly** *adv.*

Mistaken (mistēⁱ·k'n), *ppl. a.* 1597. [pa. pple. of prec. vb.] †**1.** Wrongly supposed to be so. **2.** Of persons: Taking a wrong view 1601. **3.** *transf.* of their opinions, actions, etc.: Wrongly conceived or carried out; erroneous 1676.

2. I think him honest, though m. *'Junius' Lett.* **3.** A m. feeling of loyalty FREEMAN. Hence **Mista·ken-ly** *adv.*, **-ness.**

Misteach (mistī·tʃ), *v.* [OE. *mistǣcan*; see MIS-[1] 1 and TEACH *v.*] *trans.* To teach or instruct badly or wrongly. So **Mistaught** (mistǭ·t), *ppl. a.* 1552.

Mistell (miste·l), *v.* late ME. [MIS-[1] 1.] †**1.** To miscount –1647. **2.** To relate incorrectly; †to misinform 1565.

†**Miste·mper,** *v.* 1547. [f. MIS-[1] 1 + TEMPER *v.*] *trans.* To disturb or disorder –1642.

Miste·mpered, *ppl. a. Obs.* or *arch.* 1506. [MIS-[1] 2.] **1.** Badly mixed. **2.** Disordered, deranged 1541. **3.** Of weapons: Tempered for an evil purpose. *Rom. & Jul.* I. i. 94.

Mister (mi·stəɹ), *sb.*[1] *Obs.* exc. *arch.* or *dial.* ME. [– AFr. *mester*, OFr. *mestier* (mod. MÉTIER) :– Rom. **misterium*, for L. *ministerium*; see MYSTERY[2].] †**1.** Handicraft, trade; profession, craft –1613. †**2.** Office, business, function. ME. only. †**3.** Occupation. ME. only. †**4.** Need –1768.

Comb. †**m. man, misters** (genitive) **man:** a craftsman. Phr. like *all mister* (*men*), *what mister* (*man*) were subsequently misapprehended as = 'of all (what, etc.) class(es, kind(s'; hence *arch.* and *dial.*

Mister (mi·stəɹ), *sb.*[2] 1551. [Weakened form of MASTER *sb.*[1] originating from reduced stress in proclitic use. Cf. MISTRESS.] **1.** Title of courtesy prefixed to the surname or Christian name of a man, and to designations of office or occupation. The oral equivalent of MR. (q.v.). **b.** The word 'mister' (Mr.) as a prefix or title 1758. **2.** = SIR (or less respectful than that title). Now only *vulgar.* 1760.

1. b. They never spoke to us without putting M. to our Names GOLDSM. **2.** 'Good morning, mister', said Dominicus HAWTHORNE.

†**Mi·ster,** *v.*[1] Chiefly *Sc.* ME. [f. MISTER *sb.*[1]] **1.** *intr.* To be necessary or needful –1715. **2.** *trans.* To have need of, require –1722. **3.** *intr.* To have need (*of*) –1572.

1. As for my name, it mistreth not to tell SPENSER.

Mi·ster, *v.*[2] 1742. [f. MISTER *sb.*[2]] *trans.* To address or speak of as 'Mr.'

'Pray, don't m. such fellows to me', cries the Lady FIELDING.

Miste·rm, *v.* 1579. [MIS-[1] 1.] *trans.* To apply a wrong term or name to.

Mistery: see MYSTERY[2].

Mistful (mi·stfŭl), *a.* 1599. [f. MIST *sb.* [1] + -FUL.] Full of mist; obscured by or as by mist.

Misthi·nk, *v.* ME. [f. MIS-[1] 1 + THINK *v.*[2]] †**1.** *intr.* To have sinful thoughts –1615. **2.** To think mistakenly 1530. **3.** *trans.* To have a bad opinion of. Also *intr.* const. *of.* 1593. **4.** With cogn. obj.: To think bad thoughts 1618. So **Misthou·ght,** erroneous thought or notion; mistaken opinion 1596.

Misthrive (misþrəi·v), *v.* 1567. [MIS-[1] 7.] *intr.* To be unsuccessful; not to thrive.

‖**Mistico** (mi·stiko). 1801. [Sp., perh. ult. – Arab. *musattah* armed vessel.] A Mediterranean coasting vessel having two sails.

†**Misti·de,** *v.* [OE. *mistīdan*; see MIS-[1] 1 and TIDE *v.*] **1.** *intr.* To happen amiss or unfortunately –ME. **2.** To have misfortune. CHAUCER.

Mistigris (mi·stigris). 1882. [– Fr. *mistigri* knave of spades.] The name of the blank card in a variety of draw poker; hence, the game in which it is used.

Mistime (mistəi·m), *v.* [OE. *mistīmian*; see MIS-[1] 1 and TIME *v.*] †**1.** *intr.* Of the event: To happen amiss. Of the person: To come to grief. –late ME. **2.** To time wrongly or improperly; to do or perform at a wrong time; to miscalculate the time of. late ME.

†**Mi·stion.** 1612. [– L. *mistio*, *-on-*, f. *mist-*, pa. ppl. stem of *miscēre* mix. Cf. OFr. *mistion.*] Mixtion, mixture –1680.

Mistitle (mistəi·t'l), *v.* 1618. [MIS-[1] 1.] *trans.* To give a wrong title or name to.

Mistle, obs. f. MISSEL, MIZZLE.

Mistletoe (mi·z'ltoᵘ, mi·s'ltoᵘ). [OE. *misteltān* (= ON. *mistilteinn*), f. *mistel* mistletoe (see MISSEL) + *tān* twig (= Du. *teen* withe, OHG. *zein* rod, ON. *teinn* twig, spit, Goth. *tains* twig).] A parasitic plant of Europe, *Viscum album*, growing, in Britain, on the apple-tree, rarely on the oak, and bearing a whitish berry, from which a birdlime is prepared. It was held in veneration by the Druids, esp. when found growing on the oak. Also applied to various allied plants.

The m. is still hung up in farm-houses and kitchens at Christmas: and the young men have the privilege of kissing the girls under it W. IRVING. *Comb.* **m. thrush,** the missel-thrush, *Turdus viscivorus.*

Mistral (mi·străl, mistrā·l). 1604. [– Fr. *mistral* – Pr. *mistral* :– L. *magistralis* (sc. *ventus* wind) MAGISTRAL; *lit.* 'master-wind'.] A violent cold north-east wind experienced in the Mediterranean provinces of France, etc.

Mistransla·te, *v.* 1532. [MIS-[1] 1.] *trans.* To translate incorrectly. **Mistransla·tion** 1694.

†**Mistrea·ding,** *vbl. sb.* 1596. [MIS-[1] 3.] A mis-step; a misdeed –1772.

Mistreat (mistrī·t), *v.* 1453. [MIS-[1] 1.] *trans.* To treat badly or wrongly; to ill-treat, maltreat. So **Mistrea·tment** 1716.

Mistress (mi·strės). [ME. *maistresse* (XIV) – OFr. *maistresse* (mod. *maîtresse*), f. *maistre* MASTER *sb.*[1] + *-esse* -ESS[1]. Forms in *mis-* (due to light stress) are recorded from XV; cf. MISTER *sb.*[2]] **I. 1.** A woman who has the care of or authority over servants or attendants, and, in early use, of children or young women. **2.** The female head of a household or of an establishment of any kind. late ME. **3.** A woman who has power to control or dispose *of* something. Now *rare* exc. in *one's own m.*, *m. of the situation*, etc. late ME. †**4.** The female governor of a state, etc. –1785. **b.** Also of countries, etc. late ME. †**5.** A woman, a goddess, a virtue, passion, etc., having dominion over a person or regarded as a protecting or guiding influence –1677. †**6.** A woman, or personified thing, regarded as the authoress, creatress, or patroness of an art, religion, a state of life, etc. –1708. **7.** A female possessor or owner 1551. **8.** A woman who has mastered any art, craft, or subject 1484. **9.** A woman who is loved and courted by a man. (Now only in unequivocal contexts.) 1509. **10.** A woman who illicitly occupies the place of a wife. late ME.

1. As the eyes of a maiden [look] vnto the hand of her mistresse *Ps.* 123: 2. **2.** The m. of a family must be ever watchful MRS. CHAPONE. **3.** You are your own m. 1794. **b.** *transf.* Such a lord is Love, And Beauty such a m. of the world TENNYSON. **4. b.** Rome now is m. of the whole World, sea and land, to either pole B. JONS. **7.** Phr. *To be m. of*: to have in her possession or at her disposal; also, to be perfectly acquainted with (a subject). **9.** I giue thee this For thy sweet Mistris sake, because thou lou'st her SHAKS.

II. A female teacher, instructress; now only, one engaged in a school, or teaching a special subject, as music, etc. late ME.

III. As a title. **1.** Used vocatively; = MADAM, MA'AM. *Obs.* exc. *arch.* late ME. **2.** As a title of courtesy. Now *Obs.* or *dial.* 1461. **b.** *transf.* and *joc.* 1577. **3.** In the title of certain Court offices 1710.

1. Studies my Ladie? Mistresse, looke on me SHAKS. **2.** So, here is m. Stella again SWIFT. M. Gilpin (careful soul!) COWPER. **b.** Mistris line, is not this my Ierkin? SHAKS. **3.** *M. of the Robes*: a lady of high rank, charged with the care of the Queen's wardrobe.

IV. Techn. **1.** *Bowls.* = JACK *sb.*[1] II. 11. Often *fig.* 1586. **2.** A lantern used in coal-mines 1851.

1. So, so, rub on, and kisse the mistresse SHAKS.

Mistressly (mi·strěsli), *a.* 1748. [-LY[1].] **1.** Belonging to the mistress of a household. RICHARDSON. **2.** [after MASTERLY 2.] Like one who is a mistress in her art 1786.

2. I did see the new bust of Mrs. Siddons, and a very m. performance it is indeed H. WALPOLE.

Mi·stress-piece. Now *rare.* 1648. [f. MISTRESS after *masterpiece*.] A feminine masterpiece.

Mi·stress-ship. 1460. [f. MISTRESS + -SHIP.] **1.** Authority of one in the position of a mistress 1581. †**2.** A style of address; always in *your m.* –1632. **3.** The post of mistress in a school 1891.

Mistrial (mistrəi·ăl). 1628. [MIS-[1] 4.] A trial vitiated by some error. Also, *U.S.*, an inconclusive trial, as where the jury cannot agree.

Mistri·st, *sb.* and *v.* *Obs.* or *dial.* late ME. = MISTRUST.

†**Mistrow·**, *v. north.* ME. [– ON. *mis-trúa*, f. MIS-[1] + *trúa* (see TROW *v.*).] = MISTRUST *v.* –1480. So †**Mistrow·** *sb.* ME.

Mistrust (mistrɒ·st), *sb.* late ME. [MIS-[1] 7.] Lack of trust or confidence; suspicion, distrust. **Mistru·stless** *a.* unsuspecting 1586.

Mistrust (mistrɒ·st), *v.* late ME. [f. MIS-[1] 7 + TRUST *v.*, prob. after OFr. *mesfier* (mod. *méfier*).] **1.** *trans.* Not to trust (a person); to suspect the actions, intentions, motives, etc. of. Also *refl.* **2.** To have doubts about (a thing); to doubt the truth, validity, or genuineness of. late ME. †**3.** To suspect the existence or anticipate the occurrence of (something evil) –1728. **b.** To suspect *that* something has happened or will happen (now *rare*). late ME. **4.** *intr.* To be distrustful, suspicious, or without confidence. late ME.

1. I will neuer m. my wife againe SHAKS. **2.** For my part I am ever ready to m. a promising title GOLDSM. **3.** They were all asleepe mistrusting to harme FLORIO. Hence **Mistru·stingly** *adv.*

Mistru·stful, *a.* 1529. [f. MISTRUST *sb.* + -FUL.] Full of mistrust; wanting in confidence; distrustful, suspicious. Const. *of.* †**b.** *transf.* Causing mistrust 1592.

b. Or stonish'd as night-wanderers often are, Their light blown out in some m. wood SHAKS. Hence **Mistru·stful-ly** *adv.*, **-ness.**

Mistry·st, *v. Sc.* and *north.* 1816. [MIS-[1] 1, 7.] **1.** *trans.* To fail to keep an engagement with. **2.** *pass.* To be perplexed.

Mistu·ne, *v.* 1504. [MIS-[1] 1.] *trans.* To tune wrongly; to make discordant; to perform (music) out of tune.

Misturn (mistɔ̄·ɹn), *v.* ME. [MIS-[1] 1. Partly after OFr. *mestourner*.] *trans.* and *intr.* To turn in a wrong direction.

Mistu·tored, *ppl. a.* 1757. [MIS-[1] 2.] Badly instructed or brought up.

Misty (mi·sti), *a.*[1] [OE. *mistiġ*, f. *mist* MIST *sb.*[1] + -Y[1].] **1.** Covered with mist; accompanied or characterized by mist; consisting of mist. **b.** Clouded, blinded, or blurred as if by mist 1590. **2.** *fig.* Obscure; vague, indistinct. late ME. **b.** Of persons: Clouded in intellect 1822.

1. And Iocond day Stands tipto on the mistie Mountaines tops SHAKS. **2.** The Philosopher..is so hard of vtterance, and so mistie to bee conceiued, [etc.] SIDNEY. A m. recollection TYLOR. Hence **Mi·sti-ly** *adv.*, **-ness.**

†**Mi·sty,** *a.*[2] late ME. [A use of prec. for L. *mysticus*. Cf. MIST *sb.*[2]] Mystical, spiritual –1570.

Mi:sundersta·nd, *v.* ME. [MIS-[1] 1.] Not to understand rightly; to take in a wrong sense; to misinterpret the actions, etc. of (a person).

To be great is to be misunderstood. EMERSON.

Mi:sundersta·nding, *vbl. sb.* 1449. [MIS-[1] 3.] **1.** Failure to understand; misconception, misinterpretation. **2.** Dissension, disagreement 1642.

2. Some little pique or m. between them GEO. ELIOT.

Misusage (misyū·sédʒ). Now *rare.* 1532. [MIS-[1] 4.] †**1.** Misconduct –1579. **2.** Ill-usage; maltreatment 1554. **3.** Wrong use, misuse 1567.

Misuse (misyū·s), *sb.* late ME. [MIS-[1] 4.] **1.** Wrong or improper use; misapplication. †**2.** Ill-usage. SHAKS. †**3.** Evil custom or conduct –1604.

1. Artful m. of the confidence of others 1866. **2.** 1 *Hen. IV*, I. i. 43. **3.** *Oth.* IV. ii. 109.

Misuse (misyū·z), *v.* late ME. [MIS-[1] 1. Cf. OFr. *mesuser*.] **1.** *trans.* To use or employ wrongly or improperly; to misapply. **2.** To maltreat, ill-use 1540. †**b.** To violate –1540. †**3.** *refl.* To misconduct oneself 1532–1581. †**4.** To speak evil of; to revile, deride –1633. †**5.** To deceive –1601.

1. I haue misvs'd the Kings Presse damnably SHAKS. **2.** Who misuses a dog would m. a child TENNYSON. **5.** Proofe enough, to m. the Prince, to vexe Claudio SHAKS. Hence **Misu·ser**[1], one who misuses 1548.

Misuser[2] (misyū·zəɹ). 1625. [– OFr. *mesuser*, inf. as sb.; see -ER[4].] *Law.* Unlawful use of a liberty or benefit such as may lead to its forfeiture.

Misva·lue, *v.* 1626. [MIS-[1] 1.] *trans.* To value falsely or wrongly; to misesteem. So **Misvalua·tion.**

Ignored or misvalued during his life 1900.

Misve·nture. Now *arch.* 1563. [MIS-[1] 4.] An unfortunate venture; a misadventure.

Misvou·ched, *pa. pple.* and *ppl. a.* 1626. [MIS-[1] 2.] **1.** Alleged wrongly. BACON. **2.** Not well vouched for 1876.

†**Miswa·ndered,** *ppl. a.* 1590. [MIS-[1] 2.] In which one has gone astray –1620. †**Miswa·ndering** *ppl. a.* going astray. late ME. –1645.

†**Misway·.** [MIS-[1] 4.] A wrong path. CHAUCER.

Miswe·dded, *a.* [MIS-[1] 2.] Unsuitably married; *transf.* of a marriage MILT.

†**Miswee·n,** *v.* 1590. [MIS-[1] 1.] **1.** *intr.* To have a wrong opinion –1640. **2.** *trans.* To think wrongly of –1749.

†**Miswe·nd,** *v.* ME. [MIS-[1] 1.] To lead or go astray (*lit.* and *fig.*) –1723.

Misword (miswɔ̄·ɹd), *sb.* Now *dial.* ME. [MIS-[1] 4. Cf. MIS *a.*] A harsh, angry, or cross word.

Mis-wo·rd, *v.* 1883. [MIS-[1] 1.] *trans.* To word incorrectly. So **Mis-wo·rding** *vbl. sb.* wrong wording 1680.

Miswo·rship, *sb.* 1626. [MIS-[1] 4.] Wrong or false worship. So **Miswo·rship** *v. trans.* to worship amiss. **Miswo·rshipper.**

Miswrite (misrəi·t), *v.* OE. [MIS-[1] 1.] *trans.* To write incorrectly.

†**Miswrou·ght,** *pa. pple.* ME. [MIS-[1] 2.] Done amiss; manufactured badly –1626.

†**Mi·sy.** 1601. [– L. *misy* (Pliny) – Gr. μίσυ.] **1.** A kind of mushroom or truffle. HOLLAND. **2.** *Min.* Copiapite, or some related species –1775.

Misyoke (misyōᵘ·k), *v.* 1645. [MIS-[1] 1.] *trans.* To yoke (in marriage) unsuitably. Also *intr.*

Miszea·lous, *a.* 1617. [MIS-[1] 6.] Wrongly zealous.

Mitch-board (mi·tʃboᵊɹd). 1883. [perh. f. *mitch* = *miche* forked shaft for a pump, Sc. dial. *mitch* support for a mast when lowered. Cf. G. *micke* fork of a branch, Du. *mik* forked stick.] *Naut.* A support for a boom, yard, etc., when not in use.

Mite[1] (məit). [OE. *mīte* = MLG., MDu. *mīte* (Du. *mijt*), OHG. *mīza* gnat :– Gmc. *mītōn*.] In early use, any minute insect or arachnid. Now usually restricted to certain genera of the order *Acarida* of arachnids, and chiefly applied to the cheese-mite, *Tyroglyphus* (formerly *Acarus*) *domesticus*.

Mite[2] (məit). ME. [– MLG., MDu. *mīte* :– Gmc. **mītōn*, prob. identical with prec.] **1.** Orig., a Flemish copper coin of very small value. From the 14th c., used as tr. L. *minutum* (Vulg.), Gr. λεπτόν in Mark 12: 43, where two 'mites' are stated to make a 'farthing' (Gr. κοδράντης, L. *quadrans*); hence pop. = 'half-farthing'. **b.** *fig.* An immaterial contribution, but the best one can do, to some object or cause (see *Mark* 12: 43) 1650. †**2.** A small weight: *spec.* one twentieth of a grain troy –1738. **3.** A minute particle or portion; a tiny fragment. Now *colloq.* or *vulgar.* 1608. **4.** *fig.* A jot, whit. Now *colloq.* late ME. **5.** A very small object; often, a tiny child 1594.

1. And there came a poore wyddowe, and put in two mytes, which make a farthinge COVERDALE *Mark* 12: 43. **b.** It may not be amiss to contribute my m. of advice BERKELEY. **5.** A m. of a boy DICKENS.

Miter: see MITRE.

Mithras (mi·þræs), **Mithra** (mi·þrā). 1585. [L. *Mithras*, *Mithres* = Gr. Μίθρας – OPers. *Mithra*, = Skr. *Mitra*, one of the gods of the Vedic pantheon.] A god of the ancient Persians, in later times often identified with the sun. Hence **Mithra·ic** *a.* of or connected with M. or his worship. **Mi·thraism. Mi·thraist.**

Mithridate (mi·þrideᶦt). Also †‖**Mithrida·tum.** 1528. [– med.L. *mithridatum*, altered from late L. *mithridatium*, orig. neut. of *Mithridatius* adj., pertaining to Mithridates, f. L. *Mithri-*, *Mithradates*, Gr. Μιθρι-, Μιθραδάτης. Cf. Fr. *mithridate*.] **1.** *Old Pharmacy.* A composition in the form of an electuary, regarded as a universal antidote against poison and infectious disease. Hence any similar antidote. Also *transf.* and *fig.* **2.** In full *m. mustard*, a name for the plants *Lepidium campestre* and *Thlaspi arvense*. Also *Bastard m. mustard*: candy-tuft. 1597. Hence, **Mi·thridatism,** immunity from a poison induced by administering gradually increased doses of it 1851. **Mi·thridatize,** *v. trans.* to produce mithridatism in 1866.

Mithridatic (miþridæ·tik), *a.* 1649. [– L. *mithridaticus* – Gr. Μιθριδατικός, f. Μιθριδάτης; see prec., -IC.] **1.** Of or pertaining to Mithridates VI, king of Pontus. **2.** Of or pertaining to mithridate 1847. **3. a.** Resembling Mithridates or his alleged immunity from poisons; pertaining to mithridatism 1868.

Mitigable (mi·tigăb'l), *a.* 1677. [– med.L. *mitigabilis*, f. *mitigare*; see MITIGATE *v.*, -ABLE.] Capable of being mitigated.

Mitigant (mi·tigănt), *a.* and *sb.* *rare.* 1541. [– *mitigant-*, pr. ppl. stem of L. *mitigare*; see next, -ANT.] **A.** *adj.* Mitigating, lenitive. **B.** *sb.* A lenitive 1865.

Mitigate (mi·tigeᶦt), *v.* late ME. [– *mitigat-*, pa. ppl. stem of L. *mitigare*, f. *mitis* mild, gentle; see -ATE[3].] **1.** *trans.* To render (a person, etc.) milder; to appease, mollify. Now *rare.* **2.** To render (anger, etc.) less violent; to appease 1494. **3.** To alleviate (a disease, an evil). late ME. **4.** To abate the rigour of (a law) 1532. **5.** To reduce the severity of (a punishment, etc.) 1533. **b.** To render (a custom, etc.) more humane 1835. **6.** To moderate (heat, cold, etc.) 1611. **7.** To palliate (an offence) 1719. **8.** With a quality as obj.: To moderate (the severity, rigour, etc., *of* something) 1571. **9.** *intr.* To become mitigated; to grow milder or less severe (*rare*) 1633.

2. To m. the king's anger PRESCOTT. **3.** The swelling of his woundes to m. SPENSER. **5.** Those hard censures..are to be mitigated BURTON. **b.** Christianity first mitigated, and then abolished slavery 1835. **8.** We could greatly wish that the rigor of this their opinion were alayed and mitigated HOOKER. Hence **Mi·tigative** *a.* lenitive; *sb.* a soothing remedy. **Mi·tigator. Mi·tigatory** *a.* tending or serving to m.; *sb.* something which serves to m.

Mitigation (mitigē¹·ʃən). late ME. [– (O)Fr. *mitigation* or L. *mitigatio*, f. as prec.; see -ION.] **1.** The action of mitigating or the state of being mitigated. **b.** quasi-*concr.* A circumstance that mitigates 1729. †**2.** A qualification (of words or statements) –1709.
1. Without any m. or remorce of voice SHAKS. In m. of damages BLACKSTONE.

†**Mi·ting.** 1440. [f. MITE² + -ING³.] A diminutive creature. Used in endearment or contempt –1585.

Mitis (mī·tis). 1885. [Named by the inventor of the process, P. Östberg of Stockholm; app. f. L. *mitis* mild, in the sense of *mild steel* (see MILD *a.* 7).] *Metall.* In *m. casting*: a method of increasing the fluidity of molten iron by adding a minute quantity of aluminium to the charge in the crucible; also, a casting produced by this process. So *m.-metal, process*, etc.

‖**Mitosis** (mitōᵘ·sis). *Pl.* **-oses** (-ōᵘ·sīz). 1888. [mod.L., f. Gr. μίτος thread; see -OSIS.] *Biol.* The process of division of the nucleus of a cell into minute threads. Hence **Mito·tic** *a.* pertaining to, characterized by, or exhibiting m.

‖**Mitraille** (mitray, mitrē¹·l), *sb.* 1868. [Fr. *mitraille*, OFr. *mi(s)traille* small money, pieces of metal; a var. of OFr. *mitaille*, f. *mite*; cf. MITE².] Fragments of iron, heads of nails, etc. shot in masses from a cannon; now *spec.* small shot fired from a mitrailleuse. So **Mitrai·lle** *v.* to assail with m. (*rare*) 1844.

‖**Mitrailleur** (mitrayǒr). 1869. [Fr., agent-n. f. *mitrailler* fire mitraille.] = MITRAILLEUSE.

‖**Mitrailleuse** (mitrayǒz). 1870. [Fr., fem. of prec.] A breech-loading machine-gun with a number of barrels fitted together, so arranged that it can discharge small missiles simultaneously or in rapid succession.

Mitral (məi·trăl), *a.* and *sb.* 1610. [– mod. L. *mitralis*, f. L. *mitra* MITRE *sb.*¹; see -AL¹. So Fr. *mitral* (XVIII).] **A.** *adj.* **1.** Of, pertaining to, or resembling a mitre. **2.** *Anat.* **M. valve:** the left auriculo-ventricular valve of the heart, so called from its shape. Also called *bicuspid valve*. 1705. **b.** *Anat.* and *Path.* Of or pertaining to the m. valve 1853. **B.** *sb.* = *M. valve* 1835.

Mitre (məi·təɹ), *sb.*¹ Also (now *U.S.*) **miter.** late ME. [– (O)Fr. *mitre* – L. *mitra* – Gr. μίτρα belt, turban, perh. of Asiatic origin.] **1. a.** *Antiq.* As tr. Gr. μίτρα, L. *mitra*: A headband worn by ancient Greek women; also, a kind of headdress common among Asiatics, considered by the Romans a mark of effeminacy when worn by men. ¶Used by Chapman and Pope as tr. Homeric μίτρη, a belt or girdle 1611. †**b.** Applied by travellers to the turban worn by certain Asiatic peoples, and the like 1585–1638. **2.** A sacerdotal head-dress. **a.** *Heb. Antiq.* The ceremonial turban of the high priest. late ME. **b.** *Eccl.* A bishop's tall cap, deeply cleft at the top, the outline of the front and back having the shape of a pointed arch: part of the insignia of a bishop in the Western Church, and worn also by certain abbots, etc. late ME. **c.** Used as the symbol of the episcopal office or dignity. late ME. **d.** *Her.* The representation of a mitre 1610. **3.** A name of taverns and hotels 1608. **4.** *Conch.* A mitre-shell 1840.
2. c. Learning being..reckon'd a very ordinary Qualification for yᵉ M. HEARNE. **3.** *attrib.* A right Miter supper MIDDLETON.
attrib. and *Comb.*: **m.-mushroom,** an edible mushroom (*Helvella crispa*), so called from the shape of the pileus; **-shell,** any species of marine univalve shells of the genus *Mitra*.

Mitre (məi·təɹ), *sb.*² Also (now *U.S.*) **miter.** 1678. [perh. transf. use of prec.] **1.** In Joinery, etc.: A joint (also *m.-joint*) in which the line of junction bisects the angle (usu. a right angle) between the two pieces. **2.** Short for *mitre square* 1678. **3.** Short for *mitre-wheel* 1844. **3.** = GUSSET 2. 1882.
1. *Keyed m.*: a mitre-joint strengthened by the insertion of keys (see KEY *sb.*¹ III. 1). *Lapped m.*: a combination of the lap and m. joints.
Comb.: **m.-arch,** the curve formed by the m. or junction of two curved surfaces, as in groining, etc.; **-bevel** = *mitre square*; **-block, -board,** (*a*) a joiner's mitre box; (*b*) = *mitre shooting-board*; **m. box,** a joiner's template with kerfs or guides for the saw in cutting mitre-joints; **-dovetail, dovetailing,** a combination of the m. and dovetail joints; **-gauge,** a gauge for determining the angle of a mitre; **-joint** (see sense 1); **m. shooting-board,** a shooting-board used in chamfering the edges of wood; **m. square,** a square with the blade set at an angle of 45° for striking lines on something to be mitred; **-valve,** a puppet valve having its face and seat inclined 45° to its axis; **-wheel,** each of a pair of bevelled cog-wheels, the axes of which are at right angles, and which have their teeth set at an angle of 45°.

Mitre (məi·təɹ), *v.*¹ late ME. [f. MITRE *sb.*¹] *trans.* To confer a mitre upon. Chiefly in pa. pple. *mitred*, invested *with* something by way of mitre.

Mitre (məi·təɹ), *v.*² Also (now *U.S.*) **miter.** 1731. [f. MITRE *sb.*²] **1.** *trans.* To join with a mitre-joint; to cut or shape to a mitre. Also with *away, up*. **b.** *intr.* To meet in a mitre-joint 1820. **2.** *Needlework.* To make an angle in (a straight strip or band, etc.) by cutting out a three-cornered piece and uniting the resulting edges 1880.
1. *To m. the square*: to bisect the angle of a joint.

Mitred (məi·təɹd), *ppl. a.* late ME. [f. MITRE *sb.*¹ and *v.*¹ + -ED.] **1.** Entitled or privileged to wear a mitre. **2.** Wearing or adorned with a mitre. late ME. **3.** Formed like a mitre; having a mitre-shaped apex; *Nat. Hist.* in specific names (= mod.L. *mitratus*) 1547.
1. *M. abbot* (= med.L. *abbas mitratus*): an abbot invested by the pope with the privilege of wearing a mitre; *m. abbey*, an abbey ruled by a mitred abbot.

Mitre-wort (məi·təɹwɒɹt). 1845. [f. MITRE *sb.*¹ + WORT¹.] Any plant of the genus *Mitella*.
False mitre-wort: a plant of the genus *Tiarella*.

Mitriform (məi·trifǭɹm), *a.* 1824. [f. MITRE *sb.*¹ + -FORM.] **a.** *Bot.* Shaped like a mitre: applied to the calyptra of mosses, etc. **b.** *Conch.* Shaped like a mitre-shell.

Mitring (məi·t'riŋ), *vbl. sb.* 1731. [f. MITRE *v.*² + -ING¹.] The action of MITRE *v.*²; also *concr.* the shaped end of a piece prepared to be mitred with another.
Comb. **m.-machine,** any machine for mitring neatly and accurately.

Mitt (mit). Also **mit.** Chiefly in *pl.* 1765. Shortened form of MITTEN.

Mitten (mi·tən). [Late ME. *mytayne* (XIV) – (O)Fr. *mitaine* = Pr. *mitana* (cf. med.L. *mitan(n)a* :– Rom. **medietana* (sc. *muffula*) 'skin-lined glove cut off at the middle', f. L. *medietas* half.] **1.** A covering for the hand, differing from a glove in having no fingers, but only a thumb; worn either for warmth or protection. Also (now *dial.*) applied to a thick winter glove. **2.** A sort of glove of lace or knitted work covering the forearm, wrist, and part of the hand 1755.
1. Phr. *To handle without mittens*; to treat unmercifully. **2.** Phr. *To get the m.*: of a lover, to be dismissed; hence, to be dismissed from any office or position. Hence **Mi·ttened** *a.* furnished with, or wearing, mittens.

†**Mi·ttent,** *a.* 1661. [– *mittent-*, pr. ppl. stem of L. *mittere* send; see -ENT.] *Path.* Said of the organ or part supposed to send peccant 'humours' to another –1684.

‖**Mittimus** (mi·timǒs), *sb.* 1443. [L., = 'we send', the first word of the writ in Latin.] †**1.** *Law.* A writ for removing records from one court to another –1559. **2.** *Law.* A warrant directed to the keeper of a prison, ordering him to receive into custody and hold in safe-keeping, until delivered in due course of law, the person sent and specified in the warrant 1591. **3.** *colloq.* A dismissal from office; a notice to quit (*dial.*) 1596. **4.** *joc.* A magistrate 1630.
2. No words, Sir; a Wife, or a M. 1728. **3.** Phr. *To get one's m.*: to be dismissed; also, to get one's 'quietus'. **4.** Nay, 'tis but what old M. commanded SHERIDAN. Hence **Mi·ttimus** *v.* to commit to jail by a warrant.

Mity (məi·ti), *a.* 1681. [f. MITE¹ + -Y¹.] Full of or abounding in mites; said esp. of cheese.

Mix (miks), *sb.* 1586. [f. MIX *v.*] Chiefly *colloq.*: A muddle, mess; also, a state of being mixed or confused.

Mix (miks), *v.* Pa. t. and pple. **mixed** (mikst). 1480. [Back-formation from pa. pple. *mixed*, var. of †*mixt* – (O)Fr. *mixte* (spec. in AFr. law-phr. *accioun mixte* action partly real, partly personal) – L. *mixtus*, pa. pple. of *miscēre* mingle, mix, rel. to Gr. μίσγειν, μιγνύναι.] **1.** *trans.* To put together (two or more substances, groups, or classes) so that the particles or members of each are more or less evenly diffused among those of the rest; to mingle, blend. Also with *with*. **b.** With immaterial obj. 1597. †**c.** To put in as an ingredient, to intersperse. Const. *to*. –1742. **d.** To prepare (a compound) by putting ingredients together 1592. **e.** *hyperbolically.* To confound 1667. **2.** *intr.* = to be mixed. Also, to admit of being mixed; to go (well or badly) along with 1632. **3.** *trans.* To unite (persons) in dealings or acquaintance. Chiefly *refl.* and *pass.* Now *rare*. 1535. **4.** *intr.* To have intercourse *with* (occas. *among*); to take part *in* 1667. **b.** To have sexual intercourse *with* 1615. **c.** To join battle. DRYDEN. **5.** *trans.* and *intr.* To cross in breeding 1737.
1. Aufidius, myxt heddy wyne, and honey all in one 1566. Oxygen gas and sulphurous acid gas probably combine when simply mixed together 1811. **b.** Brothers, you mixe your Sadnesse with some Fear SHAKS. **d.** Had'st thou no poyson mixt? SHAKS. **e.** MILT. *P.L.* VII. 215. **2.** Her dear idea mixes with every scene of pleasure GOLDSM. **4.** To m. in the best society 1872.

Mix up. **a.** *trans.* To m. intimately, to m. *with* something else. **b.** In immaterial applications. Now only: To m. irrelevantly or unsuitably; to confuse. **c.** To associate *with* (inferior or bad company): to connect *with*, involve *in* (something 'shady'). Chiefly *refl.* and *pass.*

Mixed, †**mixt** (mikst), *ppl. a.* 1448. [See prec. *Mixt* being taken as an Eng. pple. in *-t*, was alternatively spelt with *-ed*, whence the vb. MIX.] **1.** *Law.* Formerly applied to an action which partook of the nature both of a real and of a personal action. **2.** In senses of MIX *v.* 1530. **3.** Of a company of persons: Not select, containing persons of doubtful character or status 1611. **4.** Of sciences: Involving matter; not pure or simply theoretical. Now *rare* exc. in *m. mathematics*. 1641. **5.** Comprising both sexes 1644. **6.** *colloq.* Muddled; *esp.* muzzy with drink 1872. **7.** *Phonetics.* Of a vowel sound: Intermediate between *high* and *low*; pronounced with the tongue in a flattened position 1867.
2. Unbounded liberty of the press..is one of the evils attending..mixt forms of Government HUME. **5.** *M. school*, one in which boys and girls are taught together. *M. bathing.*
Spec. collocations: †**m. angle,** a mixtilinear angle; **m. marriage,** a marriage between persons of different races or religions; **m. metal,** an alloy; **m. metaphor,** the combination of inconsistent metaphors in one figure; **m. number,** the sum of an integer and a fraction; **m. train,** a railway train made up of both passenger-carriages and goods-wagons; formerly also a train carrying different classes of passengers. Hence **Mi·xed-ly** *adv.*, **-ness.**

Mixen (mi·ksən). Now *dial.* or *arch.* [OE. *mixen* :– **mixsinnja*, f. Gmc. **mixsa-*, parallel to **mixstuz*, whence OS., OHG., G. *mist*, Goth. *maihstus* dung, f. **miȝ* make water (OE. *miċġe, migga* urine, OE. *mīgan*, LG. *mīgen*, ON. *mīga* urinate).] **1.** A dunghill; also, a compost-heap used for manure. **2.** A term of abuse for a woman (*dial.*) 1764.

Mix·er. 1611. [f. MIX *v.* + -ER¹.] One who or that which mixes. **b.** orig. *U.S.* A person in respect of his capacity for mixing with others; esp. *a good m.* 1896.

Mix-Hellene (mikshelī·n). 1856. [– Gr. μιξέλλην; see MIXO- and HELLENE.] A person of mixed Greek and barbarian blood.

Mixo- (mi·kso), repr. Gr. μιξο-, f. root of μιγνύναι, with the sense 'mixed', as **Mixo·gamous** [Gr. γάμος] *a.*, *Ichth.* (of fishes) given to promiscuous pairing; **Mixo·gamy,** the condition of being mixogamous; etc.

Mixolydian (miksoli·diăn), *a.* 1589. [f. Gr. μιξο-λύδιος half-Lydian; see MIXO- and LYDIAN.] *Mus.* **a.** The highest in pitch of the modes in ancient Greek music. **b.** The fourth of the 'authentic' ecclesiastical modes, having G for its final and D for its dominant.

†**Mixt,** *sb.* 1589. [– L. *mixtum*, n. of *mixtus*; see MIXED *ppl. a.*] **1.** A substance consisting of different elements mixed together; esp. in *Old Chem.*, a compound –1805. **2.** In immaterial applications: A compound –1647.

†**Mixt,** *v.* 1526. [Inferred from the pa. pple. *mixt* (see MIXED *ppl. a.*).] = MIX *v.* –1609.

Mixtilinear (mikstili·niăɹ), *a.* 1702. [f. L. *mixtus* mixed, after *rectilinear*.] Formed or bounded partly by straight, partly by curved lines. So **Mixtili·neal** *a.*

†**Mixtion.** late ME. [– (O)Fr. *mistion* – L. *mixtio*, also *mistio*, *-on-*, f. *mixt-*, *mist-*, pa. ppl. stem of *miscēre* MIX; see -ION.] = MIXTURE 1, 2, 3, 5. –1757.

Mixture (mi·kstiŭɹ, -tʃəɹ). 1460. [– Fr. *mixture* or its source L. *mixtura*, f. *mixt-*; see prec., -URE.] **1.** The action, process, or fact of mixing or becoming mixed; also, an instance of this 1530. **b.** Mixed state or condition 1597. **2.** *concr.* A product of mixing 1460. **3.** *spec.* **a.** A medicinal preparation of two or more ingredients mixed together. In *Pharmacy*, now applied to potions or liquid medicines. 1592. **b.** A cloth of variegated fabric, as *Heather, Oxford m.* 1722. **c.** A blend of tea, tobacco, snuff, etc. 1840. **d.** Gas or vaporized oil mixed with air, forming the explosive charge in an internal-combustion engine 1894. **4.** The mechanical mixing of two substances as dist. from (*chemical*) *combination*; also *concr.* the product of such a mixing, as dist. from a *compound* 1797. **b.** A fluid containing some foreign substance in suspension; opp. to *solution* 1765. **5.** The action or an act of adding as an ingredient; the presence of a foreign element in the composition of something; quasi-*concr.* an amount or proportion of something foreign that has been added; admixture. *Without m.*: unmixed, pure. 1526. **6.** *Mus.* In full *m.-stop*: An organ-stop comprising several ranks of pipes, used in combination with the foundation-stops 1688.

1. b. There was a m. of company SWIFT. **2.** A fatal m. of weakness and temerity 1732. **3. a.** What if this m. do not worke at all? SHAKS. **5.** The same shall drinke of the wine of the wrath of God, which is powred out without m. into the cup of his indignation *Rev.* 14: 10.

Mizen, mizzen (mi·z'n). 1465. [Early forms *mesan, meson, -eyn* (XV) – Fr. *misaine* (now fore-sail, fore-mast) – It. *mezzana*, subst. use of fem. of *mezzano* middle; forms with *mi-, my-* appear in XVI.] *Naut.* **1.** (Also **mizen-sail.**) A fore-and-aft sail set on the after side of the mizen-mast. Often synonymous with SPANKER. **2.** = MIZEN-MAST. Now *rare.* 1583. **3.** *attrib.*, as *m.-boom* 1485.

Mi·zen-mast. 1420. The aftermost mast of a three-masted ship. So **Mi·zen-to·p,** the 'top' of a mizen-mast; a platform just above the head of the lower mizen-mast 1667. **Mi·zen-topga·llant-mast,** the mast above the mizen-topmast 1864. **Mi·zen-to·pmast,** the mast next above the lower mizen-mast 1626. **Mi·zen-to·psail,** the sail set on the mizen-topmast 1626. **Mi·zen-yard,** the yard on which the mizen-sail is extended 1485.

Mizmaze (mi·zmeⁱz). 1547. [Varied redupl. of MAZE *sb.*] †**1.** A labyrinth or maze. Chiefly *fig.* –1794. **2.** Mystification. Chiefly *dial.* 1604.

Mizzle (mi·z'l), *sb. Obs.* or *dial.* 1490. [f. MIZZLE *v.*¹] Slight or drizzling rain, drizzle.

Mizzle (mi·z'l), *v.*¹ *dial.* 1483. [prob. – LG. *miseln* = Du. dial. *miezelen*, WFlem. *mizzelen, mijzelen*, frequent. formation (see -LE) on the LG. base found in Du. dial. *mies|regen* drizzle, *miezig*, LG. *misig* drizzling.] **1.** *intr.* (*impers.*) To drizzle. †**2.** *trans.* Of a cloud (also *impers.*): To send down in a drizzling shower –1592. **Mi·zzly** *a.* 1566.

Mizzle (mi·z'l), *v.*² *slang.* 1781. [Of unkn. origin.] *intr.* To disappear suddenly; *imper.* = be off!

Mizzy (mi·zi). *dial.* [ME. *misy*; cf. OE. *mēos* moss, bog.] A quagmire.

‖**Mna.** 1603. [Gr. μνᾶ.] = MINA¹.

‖**Mneme** (nī·mi). 1913. [Gr. μνήμη 'memory'.] *Psychol.* Capacity for retaining after-effects of experience or stimulation.

Mnemonic (nimǫ·nik). 1753. [– med.L. *mnemonicus* – Gr. μνημονικός, f. μνήμων, μνημον- mindful, f. μνᾱ-, base of μνᾶσθαι remember.] **A.** *adj.* **1.** Intended to aid the memory; pertaining to mnemonics. **2.** Of or pertaining to memory 1825.

2. The m. power of the late Professor Porson 1825.

B. *sb.* **a.** A mnemonic device. **b.** = MNEMONICS. 1858. So **Mnemo·nical** *a.* = A. 1. **Mnemo·nically** *adv.* **Mnemoni·cian, Mne·monist,** one versed in mnemonics. **Mnemo·nics** *sb. pl.* [see *-ics*, -IC 2], the art of assisting the memory, esp. by artificial aids; a system of precepts intended to aid the memory 1721. Also **Mne·motechny** (-te:kni), mnemonics 1845.

Mo (mōᵘ), *adv.*, quasi-*sb.*, and *a.* †Also **moe.** *Obs.* exc. *Sc.* and *n.* (**mae**). [OE. *mā* = OFris. *mā(r, mē(r*, OS., OHG. *mēr* (MDu. *mee*, G. *mehr*), ON. *meir*, Goth. *mais* :– Gmc. **maiz* :– IE. *meis*, with compar. ending *-is* (cf. L. *magis* and see BETTER); cf. MORE, MOST.] †**A.** *adv.* **1.** In or to a greater degree, extent, or quantity –ME. **2.** Longer, further, again. Chiefly qualified by *any, no, none*; *ever, never.* –1812. **B.** quasi-*sb.* †**1.** A greater number; more of the kind specified –1684. **2.** Others of the kind specified OE. **C.** *adj.* = MORE *a.* OE.

A. 2. Gent'lest fair, mourne, mourne no moe FLETCHER. **B. 2.** And besides which axioms, there are divers moe BACON.

Mo (mōᵘ). 1896. Colloq. abbrev. of MOMENT.

-mo (mōᵘ), the final syllable of terms derived from the abl. sing. masc. of L. ordinal numerals which denote book sizes by the number of leaves into which the sheet of paper has been folded, e.g. *duodecimo, sextodecimo*, which are read as *12mo, 16mo*; so *thirty-twomo, 32mo.*

‖**Moa** (mōᵘ·ă). 1842. [Maori.] A giant extinct flightless bird of New Zealand, *Dinornis gigantea*, allied to the kiwi.

Moabite (mōᵘ·ăbəit), *sb.* and *a.* late ME. [– L. (Vulg.) *Moabita* (Gr. Μωαβίτης, repr. Heb. *mô'ābî*), f. *Moab* + -ITE¹ 1.] **A.** *sb.* One of the people of Moab, which bordered on the territory of the trans-Jordanic Israelites. In 16–17th c. applied opprobriously to Roman Catholics. **B.** *adj.* Pertaining to Moab or the Moabites 1870.

The M. stone, a monument erected by Mesha king of Moab c850 B.C., furnishing the earliest known inscription in the Phoenician alphabet. Hence **Mo·abitish** *a.*

Moan (mōᵘn), *sb.* [ME. *mone*, repr. OE. **mān* :– Gmc. **main-*, whence **mainjan*, ME. *mene* (MEAN *v.*²), which was repl. by MOAN *v.*] **1.** Complaint, lamentation; a complaint, lament. Now apprehended as a transf. use of 2. †**b.** A state of grief or lamentation –1631. **2.** In mod. use: A low mournful murmur (less deep than a groan) indicative of physical or mental suffering 1673. **b.** *transf.* of the plaintive sound produced by the wind, water, etc. 1813.

1. A carpenter. . made such pitiful m. to be taken in DE FOE. **b.** Thy mirth shall turne to moane SHAKS. **2.** M. of an enemy massacred TENNYSON. **b.** The brooklet's m. SCOTT. The m. of the adjacent pines TYNDALL.

Moan (mōᵘn), *v.* 1548. (earlier possible exx. are doubtful). [f. prec.] **1.** *trans.* To complain of, lament; to bewail 1548. †**b.** *refl.* To bewail one's lot –1642. †**2.** To condole with (a person) –1669. **3.** *intr.* To make complaint or lamentation. Const. *of, for.* Now *arch.* or *poet.* 1593. **4.** *intr.* To utter a moan or moans 1724. **b.** *transf.* of inanimate things 1805. **5.** *trans.* To utter moaningly.

1. This man was greatly moaned of the people STOW. **3.** And what is life, that we should m.? TENNYSON. **4.** In bed she moaning lay WORDSW. **b.** Though the harbour bar be moaning KINGSLEY. **5.** Fair Madeline began to weep And m. forth witless words KEATS. Hence **Moa·ningly** *adv.*

Moanful (mōᵘ·nfŭl), *a.* 1573. [f. MOAN *sb.* + -FUL.] **1.** Full of moaning; expressing lamentation or grief. Now somewhat *rare.* 1586. †**2.** Causing lamentation –1662. Hence **Moa·nfully** *adv.*

Moat (mōᵘt), *sb.* [ME. *mot(e*, identical with MOTE *sb.*², with transference of sense as in *ditch, dike, dam.*] **1.** *Fortif.* A deep and wide ditch surrounding a town, castle, etc., usually filled with water. **2.** A pond, lake; *esp.* a fish-pond. *Obs.* exc. *dial.* 1463.

1. The siluer sea, Which serues it in the office of a wall, Or as a Moate defensiue to a house SHAKS.

Moat (mōᵘt), *v.* late ME. [f. MOAT *sb.*] *trans.* To surround with or as with a moat, ditch, or trench. Also with *about, in, round.*

The torrent broke down the quays. . We were moated into our house all day H. WALPOLE.

Mob (mǫb), *sb.*¹ 1688. [abbrev. of MOBILE *sb.*²] **1.** The disorderly and riotous part of the population, the rabble; a tumultuous crowd bent on lawlessness. **2.** The lower orders; the uncultured or illiterate as a class; the masses 1691. †**3.** Without *the* –1789. **4.** A promiscuous assemblage of people. In Australian use, without disparaging implication, a crowd. 1688. **b.** *transf.* and *fig.* of things, etc. *Obs.* exc. *Austral.* 1728. **5.** *slang.* A gang of thieves or pickpockets working together 1843.

1. When mobs were roaring themselves hoarse for 'Wilkes and liberty' GREEN. **2.** The m. of the great cities. . is hostile to us DUFF. **3.** I saw the street. . full of m. DE FOE. **4.** The M. of Gentlemen who wrote with Ease POPE. A m. of steady men 1890. **b.** She sees a M. of Metaphors advance POPE. **5.** *Swell m.*, a class of pickpockets who dress stylishly.

Comb. **m. law,** 'law' imposed and enforced by a m.

Mob (mǫb), *sb.*² *Obs.* exc. *Hist.* 1665. [var. of MAB.] †**1.** *Cant.* A strumpet –1697. †**2.** A négligé attire –1712. **3.** = MOB-CAP 1748.

†**Mob,** *v.*¹ 1664. [Cf. prec. and MOBLE *v.*] *trans.* To muffle the head of (a person); to dress untidily –1837.

To m. (it), to go a-mobbing: to go in disguise to the unfashionable part of a theatre, etc. Hence, to frequent low company.

Mob (mǫb), *v.*² 1709. [f. MOB *sb.*¹] **1.** *trans.* To attack in a mob; to crowd round and molest; to throng. Also, to force *into* something by such action. **2.** *intr.* To congregate in a mob; also *to m. it* 1711. **3.** *trans.* To mix *up* with a mob. TENNYSON.

Mobbish (mǫ·biʃ), *a.* 1695. [f. MOB *sb.*¹ + -ISH¹.] Resembling a mob; disorderly, tumultuous. Also, †appealing to the mob; vulgar, clap-trap.

His m. fallacious way of arguing 1711. An irregular and m. appearance SCOTT.

Mobble: see MOBLE.

Mob-cap. 1812. [f. MOB *sb.*²] An indoor cap worn by women in the 18th and early 19th c.

A mob-cap; I mean a cap,. .with side-pieces fastening under the chin DICKENS.

Mobile (mōᵘ·bil), *sb.*¹ 1549. [– Fr. *mobile* (in *premier mobile, etc.* – L. *mobile* adj. neut.; see MOBILE *a.*] †**1.** *First, grand, great, principal m.*, anglicized forms of PRIMUM MOBILE (*lit.* and *fig.*) –1797. **2.** *Metaph.* A body in motion or capable of movement. Now *rare.* 1676.

Mobile (mōᵘ·bilĭ), *sb.*² *arch.* 1676. [Short for L. *mobile vulgus* the excitable crowd.] The populace, rabble, MOB.

Yᵉ mobele was very rud to yᵉ Dutch Imbasidor 1679.

Mobile (mōᵘ·bəil, -il), *a.* 1490. [– (O)Fr. *mobile* – L. *mobilis*, f. *mo-*, *movēre* MOVE; see -ILE.] **1.** Capable of movement; movable 1490. **b.** Of a limb, etc.; Movable; not fixed, free 1828. **c.** Of a fluid: That has its particles capable of free movement. **d.** Of a cell, molecule, etc.: Free; not adnate or fixed 1871. **2.** Characterized by facility of movement. **a.** Of features: Easily changing in expression 1851. **b.** Of persons: Wanting in stability; also, versatile 1855. **3.** *Mil.* Of troops: That may be rapidly moved from place to place 1879.

1. †*M. spirits*, the 'spirits' by which the motor impulses were supposed to be transmitted to the muscles. **2. a.** The thin m. lips. . picture the inner soul of the man GREEN. **b.** Women's minds are by nature more m. than those of men, less capable of persisting long in the same continuous effort MILL.

Mobiliary (mobi·liări), *a.* 1682. [– Fr. *mobiliaire*, f. L. *mobilis* movable; see -ARY¹.] **1.** In the Channel Islands: Relating to movable property. **2.** *Mil.* Pertaining to mobilization 1888.

Mobility¹ (mobi·lĭti). 1490. [– (O)Fr. *mobilité* – L. *mobilitas*, f. *mobilis*; see MOBILE *a.*, -ITY.] The quality or condition of being mobile.

Nature not having given that m. to the eyes of flies BOYLE. To promote the m. of labour and capital 1889.

Mobility² (mobi·lĭti). 1690. [f. MOBILE *sb.*², MOB *sb.*¹, after *nobility.*] The mob; the lower classes.

Mobilization (mōᵘ:biləizēⁱ·ʃən). 1799. [– Fr. *mobilisation*, f. *mobiliser*; see next, -ATION.] The action or process of mobilizing. **1.** *Law.* The conversion of real or immovable property into personal or movable property. **2.** *Mil.* and *Naval.* The mobilizing (an army, a fleet, etc.) 1866.

Mislay (mislēi·), *v.* late ME. [MIS-[1] 1.] **1.** *trans.* To place wrongly; to misplace; to err in placing (a thing). Now *rare.* **2.** To lay (a thing) by accident where it cannot readily be found 1614. †**3.** To allege incorrectly BACON.

1. The Fault is generally mislaid upon Nature LOCKE. **2.** I cannot conceive what possesses me.. to m. papers SCOTT.

Mislead (mislī·d), *v. Pa. t.* and *pple.* **misled.** [OE. *mislǣdan*; see MIS-[1] 1 and LEAD *v.*[1]] **1.** *trans.* To lead astray in conduct; to lead into error. †**b.** *refl.* To misconduct oneself. ME. only. †**2.** To mismanage –1494. **3.** To lead in the wrong direction 1575.

1. By ambition far misled SCOTT. *absol.* What can they teach, and not m.? MILT. **3.** Are you not hee, That..misleade night-wanderers? SHAKS.

Mislea·rn, *v.* 1678. [MIS-[1] 1.] *trans.* To learn badly.

Mislen, var. of MASLIN[2].

Misli·ke, *sb.* ME. [f. MISLIKE *v.*] †**1.** The opposite of pleasure; discomfort; unhappiness. ME. only. **2.** Dislike (*of*), distaste (*for*), objection (*to*). Now *rare.* Also with *a* and *pl.* 1557. †**3.** Disaffection, disagreement –1654. †**4.** Wasting in animals or plants; sickliness, disease –1622.

2. Julian's m. of the rising faith TRENCH.

Misli·ke, *v.* Now chiefly *literary* or *dial.* [OE. *mislīcian*; see MIS-[1] 1 and LIKE *v.*[1]] **1.** *trans.* To displease. †**2.** *intr.* To be displeased; in ME. also, to be uneasy –1642. **3.** *trans.* To be displeased at; to dislike 1513. †**4.** *intr.* To grow sickly; to waste away –1606.

1. *absol.* That pleaseth well, and This as much mislikes DRAYTON. **3.** 'Tis not my speeches that you do m.: But 'tis my presence that doth trouble ye SHAKS. Hence **Misli·king** *vbl. sb.* = MISLIKE *sb.*

Mislin, var. of MASLIN[2], MISTLETOE.

†**Misli·ve**, *v.* OE. [MIS-[1] 1.] *intr.* To live a bad life –1579. Hence **Misli·ver** (*rare* or *Obs.*), an evil liver 1436.

Mislo·dge, *v.* 1676. [MIS-[1] 1.] *trans.* To lodge in a wrong place; †to mislay.

Mislu·ck, *sb.* Chiefly *Sc.* 1623. [MIS-[1] 4.] Misfortune. **Mislu·ck** *v.* meet with misfortune.

Misly, obs. f. MIZZLY.

Misma·ke, *v.* Now *Sc.* late ME. [MIS-[1] 1.] **a.** *trans.* To make badly. †**b.** To unmake, depose. **c.** *refl.* To disturb oneself.

Misma·nage, *v.* 1690. [MIS-[1] 1.] *trans.* and *intr.* To manage badly or wrongly. So **Misma·nagement** 1668. **Misma·nager** 1683.

Misma·rk, *v.* 1535. [MIS-[1] 1.] *trans.* To mark wrongly. Also in pa. pple., having wrong markings.

Misma·rry, *v.* 1892. [MIS-[1] 1.] *trans.* To marry unsuitably (*lit.* and *fig.*). So **Misma·rriage** 1817.

Misma·tch, *v.* 1599. [MIS-[1] 1.] *trans.* To match badly, esp. in marriage; *pass.* to be ill-mated. So **Misma·tch** *sb.* a bad match 1606.

Misma·ted, *pa. pple.* and *ppl. a.* 1825. [MIS-[1] 2.] Ill-matched, unsuitably allied.

Mismea·sure, *v.* 1742. [MIS-[1] 1.] *trans.* To measure or estimate incorrectly. So **Mismea·surement.**

Misme·tre, *v.* late ME. [f. MIS-[1] 1 + METRE *v.*] *trans.* To spoil the metre of.

Misna·me, *v.* 1500. [MIS-[1] 1.] **1.** = MISCALL 1. 1537. †**2.** = MISCALL 2. –1632.

Misnomer (misnōu·məɹ), *sb.* 1455. [– AFr., subst. use of OFr. *mesnom(m)er*, f. *mes-* MIS-[2] + *nommer* :– L. *nominare*, f. *nomen* name; see -ER[4].] **1.** *Law.* A mistake in naming a person or place. **2.** *gen.* The use of a wrong name or term 1635. **3.** A wrong name or designation 1657.

2. The City which, by a m., is called the Metropolis 1882. **3.** My name of Epic's no m. BYRON. Hence **Misno·mer** *v. trans.* to misname 1740.

Misnu·mber, *v.* 1614. [MIS-[1] 1.] *trans.* To number incorrectly.

Miso- (məiso, miso), bef. a vowel usu. **mis-**, repr. Gr. μισο- (μισ-), comb. f. root of μισεῖν to hate, μῖσος hatred. Cf. PHILO-.

Miso·gamy [Gr. γάμος marriage], hatred of marriage 1656; so **Misoga·mic** *a.*, **Miso·gamist.** **Miso·gynist** [Gr. γυνή woman], a woman-hater 1620; so **Mi·sogyne** = m.; **Misogy·nic, -ous, -istic, -istical** *adjs.*; **Miso·gynism, Miso·gyny.** **Miso·logy** [-LOGY], hatred of discussion or knowledge 1833; so **Miso·logist, Mi·sologue.** **Misone·ism** [Gr. νέος new], hatred of novelty 1886; hence **Misone·ist; Misonei·stic** *a.* **Misothe·ism** [Gr. θεός god], hatred of God or gods 1846; so **Misothe·ist, Misothei·stic** *a.*

Misobse·rvance. *rare.* 1496. [MIS-[1] 4.] Failure to observe rules or conditions properly. So **Misobse·rve** *v.*

†**Misopi·nion.** 1545. [MIS-[1] 4.] An erroneous opinion –1680.

Miso·rder, *sb.* Now *rare.* late ME. [MIS-[1] 4.] = DISORDER *sb.*

†**Miso·rder**, *v.* 1494. [MIS-[1] 1.] **1.** *trans.* To put into disorder; to disturb, confuse –1597. **2.** To ill-treat, ill-use –1575. **3.** *refl.* To misbehave –1740.

1. 2 *Hen. IV*, IV. ii. 33.

Mispay·, *v.* ME. [– OFr. *mespaier*; see MIS-[2] and PAY *v.*[1]] †**1.** *trans.* To displease, dissatisfy –1493. **2.** To pay by mistake 1698.

Misperfo·rm, *v.* 1656. [MIS-[1] 1.] *trans.* To perform improperly. So **Misperfo·rmance.**

Mispersua·de, *v.* Now *rare* or *Obs.* 1597. [MIS-[1] 1.] *trans.* To persuade wrongly or into error. So **Mispersua·sion** 1594.

Mispickel (mi·spikĕl). 1683. [– G. *mispickel.*] *Min.* Arsenopyrite.

Mispla·ce, *v.* 1551. [MIS-[1] 1.] **1.** *trans.* To put in a wrong place or in wrong hands 1594. †**b.** *absol.* To misplace one's words. SHAKS. **2.** To set (one's affections) on a wrong object; to place (one's confidence) amiss; †to spend (time) unprofitably 1638.

1. b. *Meas. for M.* II. i. 90. **2.** Munificence misplaced COWPER. So **Mispla·cement** 1655.

Misplaced (misplēi·st), *ppl. a.* 1595. [MIS-[1] 2.] Put in a wrong place; devoted to a wrong object; out-of-place, ill-timed.

M. acts of foolery LAMB.

Misplea·d, *v. rare.* 1676. [MIS-[1] 1. Cf. AFr. *mespleder.*] *trans.* To plead wrongly or falsely. So **Misplea·ding** *vbl. sb.* a mistake in pleading 1532.

Mispoi·nt, *v.* Now *rare* or *Obs.* 1542. [MIS-[1] 1.] †**a.** To point with the wrong finger. **b.** To punctuate wrongly; to mispunctuate.

Misprai·se, *v.* Now *rare.* ME. [MIS-[1] 1, 7.] **1.** *trans.* To dispraise, blame. **2.** To praise amiss 1631.

Mispri·nt, *v.* 1494. [MIS-[1] 1.] *trans.* To print incorrectly. So **Mi·sprint** *sb.* 1818.

Misprisal (misprəi·zăl). *rare.* 1620. [f. MISPRIZE *v.*[1] + -AL[1] 2.] Contempt, disdain, scorn.

Misprision[1] (mispri·ʒən). late ME. [– AFr. *mesprisioun* = OFr. *mesprison* error, wrong action or speech, f. *mesprendre* (mod. *méprendre*), f. *mes-* MIS-[2] + *prendre* take.] **1.** *Law.* A wrong action or omission; *spec.* a misdemeanour or neglect of duty on the part of a public official. **2.** The mistaking one thing, etc., for another; a mistake (*arch.*) 1588.

1. *M. of treason, of felony*: orig., an offence or misdemeanor akin to treason or felony, but not liable to the capital penalty. Later misunderstood as meaning only concealment of a person's knowledge of treasonable actions or designs. Also *transf.* in pop. use. **2.** The m. of this passage has aided in fostering the delusive notion HARE.

Misprision[2] (mispri·ʒən). *arch.* 1586. [f. MISPRIZE *v.*[1] after prec.] **a.** Contempt, scorn. **b.** Failure to appreciate or recognize as valuable.

That dost in vile m. shackle vp My loue SHAKS.

Misprize (misprəi·z), *v.*[1] 1481. [– OFr. *mesprisier* (mod. *mépriser*), f. *mes-* MIS-[2] + *priser* PRIZE *v.*[1]] *trans.* **a.** To despise, contemn, scorn. **b.** To fail to appreciate.

a. *Much Ado* III. i. 52. **b.** It sorrows me that you misprise my love HEYWOOD. Hence **Mispri·ze** *sb.*[1] = MISPRISION[2] (*rare*) 1590.

†**Mispri·ze**, *v.*[2] 1485. [f. OFr. *mespris*, pa. pple. of *mesprendre* commit a crime (mod. *se méprendre* be mistaken); see MIS-[2], PRIZE *v.*[1]] **1.** *intr.* To commit an offence –1500. **2.** *trans.* To mistake, misunderstand –1657.

2. Monsieur Gaspar..misprise me not B. JONS. Hence †**Mispri·ze** *sb.*[2] mistake SPENSER.

Mispronou·nce, *v.* 1593. [MIS-[1] 1.] *trans.* To pronounce incorrectly.

They mispronounc't and I mislik't MILT. So **Mispronuncia·tion** 1539.

Mispropo·rtioned, *ppl. a.* 1552. [MIS-[1] 2.] Badly or wrongly proportioned. So **Mispropo·rtion** *sb.* lack of proportion 1825. **Mispropo·rtion** *v. trans.* 'to join without due proportion' (J.).

Misproud (misprau·d), *a. arch.* ME. [MIS-[1] 6.] Wrongly or wickedly proud; arrogant.

Mispu·nctuate, *v.* 1849. [MIS-[1] 1.] To punctuate incorrectly. **Mispunctua·tion** 1807.

Misquo·te, *v.* 1596. [MIS-[1] 1.] *trans.* To quote incorrectly.

Looke how we can, or sad or merrily, Interpretation will m. our lookes SHAKS. So **Misquota·tion,** inaccuracy in quoting; an incorrect quotation 1773.

Misra·te, *v.* Now *rare.* 1624. [MIS-[1] 1.] *trans.* To estimate wrongly.

Misrea·d, *v.* 1809. [MIS-[1] 1.] *trans.* To read or interpret wrongly.

Misreci·te, *v.* 1572. [MIS-[1] 1.] *trans.* To recite incorrectly; to give a wrong account of. So **Misreci·tal** 1539.

Misre·ckon, *v.* 1524. [MIS-[1] 1.] **1.** To reckon incorrectly; to miscalculate, miscount. †**2.** *trans.* To present an incorrect account to –1654. So **Misre·ckoning** *vbl. sb.* 1540.

Misrela·te, *v.* 1621. [MIS-[1] 1.] *trans.* To relate or recount incorrectly. So **Misrela·tion**; also **Misrela·ted** *ppl. a.* wrongly related or connected.

Misreli·gion. *rare.* 1623. [MIS-[1] 4.] False religion.

Misreme·mber, *v.* 1533. [MIS-[1] 1.] *trans.* To remember wrongly; to have an imperfect recollection of. Now chiefly *dial.* to forget. So **Misreme·mbrance** (*rare*) 1542.

Misre·nder, *v.* 1661. [MIS-[1] 1.] *trans.* To render or interpret incorrectly.

Misrepo·rt, *sb.* ME. [MIS-[1] 4.] †**1.** Evil report; ill repute –1697. **2.** False or erroneous report, as of the actions, etc., of a person 1530.

Misrepo·rt, *v.* late ME. [MIS-[1] 1.] **1.** *trans.* To report erroneously; to give a false account of the statements or opinions of. †**2.** To speak ill of; to slander –1625.

Mi:srepresent, *v.* 1647. [MIS-[1] 1.] *trans.* To represent improperly or imperfectly; to give a false account of. So **Mi:srepresenta·tion** 1647. **Mi:srepresentative** *a.* not properly representative (*of*) 1736.

Misru·le, *sb.* late ME. [MIS-[1] 4.] †**1.** Disorderly conduct; ill-regulated life; excess –1613. **2.** Bad government (of a state, etc.); misgovernment; a state of disorder, anarchy, or rebellion. late ME.

Lord (also *Abbot, Master*) *of M.*: one chosen to preside over the Christmas games and revels in a great man's house (*Hist.*); also *transf.* and *fig.*

Misru·le, *v.* ME. [MIS-[1] 1.] †**1.** *trans.* To manage or control badly –1530. **2.** To rule (a country, etc.) badly. late ME.

†**Misru·ly**, *a.* late ME. [f. MIS-[1] 6 + RULY *a.*] Disorderly; unruly –1598.

Miss (mis), *sb.*[1] [OE. *miss* loss, corresp. to MLG., MHG. *misse* (Du. *mis*), ON. *missa, missir.*] **I.** Loss, lack. (Cf. MISS *v.* IV.) **1.** The fact or condition of missing or being without; loss, lack, privation. Const. *of* or *genitive.* 1470. †**b.** Observable lack –1722. **2.** Disadvantage or regret occasioned by loss, absence, or privation *of* a person or thing ME.

1. At Carthage, the misse of so great a person was diuersly construed RALEGH. **2.** Phr. *To feel the m. of; there is no (great) m. of.* Now *dial.* or *vulgar.*

II. Wrong, mistake. (Cf. MISS *v.* V.) †**1.** Wrong; offence, injury; a wrong, misdeed –1616. †**2.** Error, mistake. ASCHAM.

2. Without any great misse in the hardest pointes of Grammer 1568.

III. Failure to hit or attain. (Cf. MISS *v.* I.) **1.** Failure to hit something aimed at 1555. **2.** Failure to obtain or achieve something. Now *rare.* 1609. **3.** *Printing.* The omitting to lay on a sheet in feeding a printing-machine 1888.

1. Provb.: *A m. is as good as a mile*: failure by however little is still failure. *To give a m.* (Billiards): to avoid hitting the object ball, esp. in playing for safety. The opponent is said *to score a m.*

Miss (mis), *sb.*[2] 1666. [Clipped form of MISTRESS; cf. MAS.] **1.** A kept mistress. Less commonly, a whore. *Obs.* exc. *dial.* 1675. **2.**

As a title of an unmarried woman or girl 1666. **3.** With ellipsis of the proper name. Not now in educated use. 1667. **4.** A young unmarried woman; a girl, *esp.* a schoolgirl; in mod. use, often connoting squeamishness or sentimentality. (In literary English use now only playful or contemptuous.) 1667.

2. *The Misses Smith, the Miss Smiths*: alternative forms of the pl., of which the former is grammatically the more proper. *Miss Smith*: normally the eldest (unmarried) daughter of the family. **3.** Is it m. or the cash of mamma you pursue? BYRON. 'I beg your pardon, Miss', said she [a maidservant] 1850. **4.** Under the tyranny of some small m. of two or three 1885. Hence **Mi·ssish** *a.* like a m.; hence, affected, prim, squeamish, or sentimental. **Mi·ssishness.**

Miss (mis), *sb.*[3] 1767. [perh. a use of prec., or of MISS *sb.*[1]; cf. KITTY[3].] *Cards.* An extra hand for which any of the players may discard his own.

Miss (mis), *v.* [OE. *missan* = OFris. *missa*, (M)LG., (M)Du. *missen*, (O)HG. *missen*, ON. *missa* :– Gmc. **missjan*, f. *missa-*; see MIS-[1].] **I.** *trans.* To fail to hit, meet, or light upon. **1.** To fail to hit (something aimed at). **b.** Occas., of a missile, a blow, etc.: To pass by without touching 1749. **2.** Not to hit upon (the right path) 1547. **3.** To fail to obtain footing on (a step, plank, etc.) 1550. **4.** To fail to meet (a person). Also occas. *intr.* for *reciprocal*. 1589.

1. Mark like this Was Bertram never known to m. SCOTT. †*To m. the cushion*: to miss the mark; to make a mistake, err. *To m. one's aim, one's* (or *the*) *mark* (fig.): see MARK *sb.*[1] II. 3. d. absol. *Hit or m.*: see HIT *v.* **2.** *To m. one's way.* **3.** Blind with rage she miss'd the plank, and rolled In the river TENNYSON. **4.** I wonder how I missed you NASHE. Then we missed: now we meet MEREDITH.

Phrases. **To m. fire.** Of firearms: To fail to go off. Hence *fig.* to be unsuccessful. **To m. stays** (*Naut.*): To fail in an attempt to go about from one tack to another. Also *fig.*

II. *trans.* To fail to attain. **1.** To fail to get; to come short of, go without ME. **b.** Not to have the satisfaction of hearing, seeing, or witnessing (something) 1841. **2.** To fail to do, achieve, or accomplish (something). late ME. **3.** To escape, avoid. Now only *dial.*, exc. with adv. 1526. **4.** To let slip (an opportunity, etc.) 1628; to fail to catch (a train, etc.) 1823. **5.** To fail to see; to fail to 'catch' or understand 1588.

1. Since the time I missed the solicitor's place BACON. **b.** I would not have missed the speech.. for a great deal JOWETT. **2.** To m. a stroke at billiards 1888. **5.** I sat so high and far off that I missed most of the words PEPYS.

III. *trans.* To omit. **1.** To omit, leave out. Also with *out.* 1530. **2.** To omit the performance of; to fail to keep (an appointment); to omit to be present at 1598.

1. To m. one of the responses SCOTT. **2.** I never missed chapel RUSKIN.

IV. *trans.* To be without; lack; want. †**1.** To be without, lack; to cease to have, lose. Also with *away.* –1677. †**b.** Contextually, to do without –1637. **2.** To discover the absence of ME. **3.** To feel the want of 1470.

1. b. We cannot misse him; he do's make our fire [etc.] SHAKS. **2.** One morn I missed him on the custom'd hill GRAY. **3.** Milton was too busy to much m. his wife JOHNSON.

V. *intr.* †**1.** To go wrong, make a mistake, err –1754. †**2.** To be lacking –1828. †**3.** To come to an end, give out, fail –1529. **4.** To be unsuccessful. Now *arch.* or *Obs.* 1592. **5.** Of crops, etc.: To be abortive (*dial.*) 1615.

1. Starres are poore books, and oftentimes do misse G. HERBERT. **2.** 1 *Sam.* 25:7. **3.** Til the day gan misse CHAUCER.

Miss of —. Chiefly *Obs.* or *arch.* = senses I. 1, 4, 5; II. 1–4; IV. 1. **M. on —.** To fail to hit upon. LAMB.

Miss, obs. f. MASS *sb.*[1]

Missal (mi·săl), *sb.*[1] ME. [– *missale*, subst. use of n. sing. of eccl. L. *missalis* pertaining to the Mass, f. *missa* MASS *sb.*[1]; see -AL[1].] The book containing the service of the Mass for the whole year; a mass-book. ¶**b.** Vaguely: A Roman Catholic book of prayers, esp. when illuminated 1651.

attrib., etc., as **m. caps** (*Printing*), a style of fancy letter, used sometimes as initials to Old English or Black letter.

Missal (mi·săl), *a.* (*sb.*[2]) 1466. [– eccl. L. *missalis*; see prec.] Of or pertaining to the Mass; mass-.

Mis-say (mis,sē[i]·), *v. arch.* Pa. t. and pple. **mis-said** (mis,se·d). [MIS-[1] 1.] **1.** *trans.* To speak evil of or against; to slander, vilify. Now *arch.* and *poet.* †**b.** To say with evil intent –1614. †**2.** *intr.* To speak evil –1596. **3.** *trans.* To say wrongly. Now *rare.* late ME. **b.** *intr.* To say something wrong or amiss. late ME.

1. Far liefer had I fight a score of times Than hear thee so m. me and revile TENNYSON.

Mis-see, *v.* 1591. [MIS-[1] 1.] To see imperfectly; to take a wrong view of.

Mis-see·m, *v.* Now *rare.* late ME. [MIS-[1] 1.] *trans.* To misbecome.

Missel (mi·sĕl). [OE. *mistel* (1) basil, (2) mistletoe = OHG. *mistil* (G. *mistel*), Du. *mistel*, ON. *mistil-*; of unkn. origin.] †**1.** Mistletoe –1670. **2.** Short for MISSEL-BIRD, -THRUSH. 1845.

Mi·ssel-bird. Now *dial.* 1626. [f. prec.] = MISSEL-THRUSH.

Misseldin(e, obs. ff. MISTLETOE.

Mi·ssel-thrush. 1774. [f. MISSEL.] A species of thrush, *Turdus viscivorus*, which feeds on the berries of the mistletoe.

Mis-se·nd, *v.* late ME. [MIS-[1] 1.] *trans.* To send to a wrong place or person.

Mis-se·rve, *v.* Now *rare.* ME. [In early use – OFr. *messervir* (MIS-[2]); later f. MIS-[1] 1 + SERVE *v.*] **1.** *trans.* To serve badly or unfaithfully. †**2.** *intr.* To miss fire –1685.

Mis-set (mis,se·t), *v.* ME. [MIS-[1] 1.] **1.** *trans.* To misplace. †**2.** To put out of humour, 'upset' (*Sc.*) –1818.

Miss-fi·re. 1811. [f. phr. *to miss fire.*] = MISFIRE *sb.*

Mis-shape (misʃē[i]·p), *sb.* Now *rare.* 1465. [MIS-[1] 4.] A bad or deformed shape or figure; deformity. Also, a mis-shapen body or person.

Mis-shape (misʃē[i]·p), *v.* 1450. [MIS-[1] 1.] *trans.* To shape ill; to give a bad form to; to deform. *lit.* and *fig.*

Figures monstrous and mis-shap'd POPE.

Mis-shapen (misʃē[i]·p'n), *ppl. a.* late ME. [f. MIS-[1] 2 + *shapen* pa. pple. of SHAPE *v.*] Having a bad or ugly shape; ill-shaped; deformed.

The m. hairy Scandinavian troll EMERSON. *fig.* Crooked and m. minds FLORIO. Hence **Mis-sha·pen-ly** *adv.*, **-ness.**

Mis-shea·thed, *ppl. a.* [MIS-[1] 2.] Sheathed by mistake. *Rom. & Jul.* V. iii. 205.

Missible (mi·sib'l), *a. rare.* 1789. [– Fr. †*missible* or med.L. *missibilis*, f. L. *miss-*; see MISSION, -IBLE.] Capable of being sent.

†**Missi·ficate,** *v.* 1641. [– *missificat-*, pa. ppl. stem of med. (eccl.) L. *missificare*, f. L. *missa* MASS *sb.*[1] + *-ficare*; see -FY.] *intr.* To perform Mass –1694. So †**Missifica·tion** [see -FICATION] 1641.

Missile (mi·səil, mi·sil), *a.* and *sb.* 1606. [– L. *missilis* (n. sing. *missile* as sb.), f. *miss-*; see MISSION, -ILE.] **A.** *adj.* Capable of being thrown; adapted to be discharged from the hand or from a machine or engine; chiefly in *m. weapon* 1611. **b.** Applied to weapons that discharge arrows, bullets, etc. 1819.

We bend the bow, or wing the m. dart POPE. **b.** Their long-bows, slings, and other m. weapons SCOTT.

B. *sb.* **1.** A missile object or weapon, as a stone, an arrow, a bullet 1656. **2.** *pl.* = L. *missilia, res missiles*, largess (i.e. sweets, perfumes, etc.) thrown by the Roman emperors to the people 1606.

Mi·ssing, *ppl. a.* 1530. [f. MISS *v.* + -ING[2].] **1.** Not present; not found; absent; gone. **2.** That fails to hit 1586.

1. Moses was in the Mount, and m. long MILT. The ship is what is called a m. ship, i.e. has been so long on the voyage that the owner has reason to suspect that she has met with some casualty 1848.

Special collocations: **m. link,** (*a*) something lacking to complete a series; (*b*) *Zool.* a hypothetical type assumed to connect two related types; *esp.* a hypothetical intermediate form between the anthropoid apes and man; also applied to an animal (or person) supposed to resemble this.

Mission (mi·ʃən), *sb.* 1598. [– Fr. *mission* or L. *missio*, f. *miss-*, pa. ppl. stem of *mittere* send; see -ION.] †**1.** The action or an act of sending –1698. **2.** A sending or being sent to perform some function or service; *Theol.* the sending of the Second or Third Person of the Trinity by the First, or of the Third by the Second, for the production of a temporal effect 1609. **3.** *Eccl.* The action of sending men forth with authority to preach the faith and administer the sacraments; hence, authority given by God or the Church to preach 1613. **4.** A body of persons sent to a foreign country to conduct negotiations, watch over interests, etc. 1626. **5.** A body of persons sent out by a religious community to convert the heathen; also, to spiritualize various classes of people 1622. **6.** A permanent establishment of missionaries in a country; a particular field of missionary activity; a missionary post or station 1769. **b.** *transf.* An organization in a particular district for the conversion of the people 1800. **7.** A special course of religious services, sermons, etc., organized in connection with a particular church or parish for this purpose 1772. **8.** The commission of a messenger, envoy, or agent; now *esp.* the errand of a political mission 1671. **9.** (A person's) vocation or work in life. Also *transf.* attributed to things. Occas. *trivial* or *contempt.* 1805. **10.** *attrib.*, as *m. church, house, work*, etc. 1792.

1. *Tr. & Cr.* III. iii. 189. **2.** The M. of the Comforter 1846. **3.** Christ..in the M. first of his Twelve, and after of his Seventy 1641. Men..who, so far from having any Orders or M., had not so much as Baptism CHALLONER. **5.** Like zealous Missions, they did care pretend Of souls in show, but made the gold their end DRYDEN. *Home, city, police-court m.* **6.** They..To the nearest m. sped and ask'd the Jesuit's aid SOUTHEY. **8.** How to accomplish best His end of being on Earth, and m. high MILT. A M. to the King of Dahomey 1863. **10. b.** *U.S.* Denoting a style of architecture, furniture, etc. characteristic of the Spanish Roman Catholic missions in California.

Mission (mi·ʃən), *v.* 1692. [f. prec. sb.] **1.** *trans.* To send on a mission; to give (a person) a mission to perform. Chiefly in *pass.* **2.** To conduct a religious mission among (a people) or in (a district) 1772. Also *intr.*

Missionary (mi·ʃənări), *a.* and *sb.* 1644. [– mod.L. *missionarius* (XVII), whence also Fr. *missionnaire*, f. L. *miss-*; see MISSION *sb.*, -ARY[1].] **A.** *adj.* **1.** Of or pertaining to missions; engaged in a mission; proper to one sent on a mission; occupied in or characterized by mission-work. **2.** That is sent out or forth. Now *Obs.* or *poet.* 1691.

1. *M. box*: a box for contributions towards the funds of a m. society.

B. *sb.* **1.** A person who carries on missionary work, esp. among the heathen 1656. **2.** An agent or emissary; esp. one sent on a political mission. Now *rare* or *Obs.* 1693. †**3.** A missionary establishment –1761.

1. Phr. *Home m.*: a person (usu. a layman) employed to labour in the spiritual instruction of the poor. *City m.*: one so employed amongst the poor of a city; so *town m. Police-court m.*: a person employed to attend a police-court, and to work for the spiritual and moral benefit of those brought before it. *transf.* The fanatic missionaries of sedition GIBBON.

Missioner (mi·ʃənəɹ). 1654. [f. MISSION + -ER[1].] One sent on a mission, a missionary. In mod. use chiefly, one who conducts a parochial mission.

The pope enjoined his m. to remove the pagan idols GOLDSM. *fig.* A m. of peace and order in every parish BURKE.

Missionize (mi·ʃənəiz), *v.* 1826. [f. MISSION *sb.* + -IZE.] *intr.* To do missionary work. Also *trans.*

Missis, missus (mi·sis, -iz, mi·sŏs). *dial.* and *vulgar.* 1837. [Slurred pronunc. of MISTRESS. The oral equivalent of MRS. (q.v.).] **1.** Wife 1839. **2.** Used by servants (usu. without article) in speaking of their mistresses.

1. *The missis*: used by a man in speaking of his own or another man's wife. Hence **Mi·ssis** *v.* to address as 'Mrs.' DICKENS.

Missish (mi·siʃ), *a.* 1795. [f. MISS *sb.*[2] + -ISH[1].] Characteristic of a miss; affected or sentimental.

Missive (mi·siv), *a.* and *sb.* 1466. [– med.L. *missivus* (in *litteræ missivæ*), f. L. *miss-*; see MISSION *sb.*, -IVE. Cf. Fr. *missive* (XVI) in *lettre missive.*] **A.** *adj.* **1.** *Letter m., m. letter.* Usu. pl. *letters m.* or †*missives.* †**a.** *gen.* An epistle sent from one person to another –1710. **b.** A letter or letters sent by a superior authority to a particular person or body of persons, conveying a command, recommendation, or permission. Now chiefly, a letter from the sovereign to a dean and chapter nominating a person to be elected bishop. (See CONGÉ D'ÉLIRE.) 1466. †2. = MISSILE *a.* –1809. †3. That is sent –1830.

1. b. A letter missiue Vnder the Kynges signett 1487. 2. Now with their m. weapons onely..but with their drawne swords KNOLLES.

B. *sb.* 1. A written message; a letter. Occas. *spec.* = A. 1. Now usu. an official letter, or high-flown for 'letter'. late ME. 2. *Scots Law.* A document in the form of a letter interchanged by the parties to a contract 1561. †3. A messenger (*rare*) –1649. †4. Something hurled or thrown; *esp.* a missile weapon –1809.

1. Mysterious missives, sealed with red 1885. 3. Missiues from the King, who all-hail'd me Thane of Cawdor SHAKS.

Mis-so·rt, *v.* 1581. [MIS-[1] 1.] *trans.* To sort badly.

Mis-sou·nd, *v.* 1500. [MIS-[1] 1.] 1. *intr.* To sound amiss. 2. *trans.* To mispronounce.

Mis-spea·k, *v.* ME. [MIS-[1] 1.] †1. *intr.* To speak wrongly or improperly; to speak evil –1613. †2. *trans.* To speak evil of –1584. 3. To speak incorrectly or improperly (*rare*) 1593. So **Mis-spee·ch**, †evil-speaking; incorrect speaking ME.

Mis-spe·ll, *v.* 1655. [MIS-[1] 1.] *trans.* To spell incorrectly. Hence **Mis-spe·ll, -spe·lling** *sbs.* a bad spelling.

Mis-spe·nd, *v.* late ME. [MIS-[1] 1.] *trans.* To spend amiss or wastefully. So †**Mis-spe·nse, -e·nce**, improper or wasteful expenditure 1591–1788. **Mis-spent** *ppl. a.* ill-spent, wasted 1500.

Mis-sta·te, *v.* 1650. [MIS-[1] 1.] *trans.* To state erroneously. So **Mis-sta·tement** 1790.

Misstay·, *v.* 1885. [f. phr. *to miss stays* (see MISS *v.* I. *Phrases*).] *intr.* Of a ship: To miss stays. Also *sb.* 1878.

†**Mis-ste·p**, *v.* late ME. [MIS-[1] 1.] *intr.* To take a wrong step; to go astray –1598. So **Mis-ste·p** *sb.* a wrong step; a FAUX PAS 1855.

Mis-sty·le, *v. rare.* 1604. [MIS-[1] 1.] *trans.* To style or term incorrectly.

†**Mis-succee·ding**, *vbl. sb.* 1661. [MIS-[1] 3.] Ill-success FULLER. †**Mis-succe·ss** 1656.

Mis-sui·t, *v.* 1618. [MIS-[1] 1.] *trans.* To suit ill.

Mis-swo·rn, *ppl. a.* 1506. [MIS-[1] 2.] a. Forsworn. b. Whose name has been taken in vain.

Missy (mi·si), *sb.* 1676. [f. MISS *sb.*[2] + -Y[6].] An affectionate or playful form of MISS. Occas. *contempt.*

Missy, var. of MISY. *Obs.*

Mist (mist), *sb.*[1] [OE. *mist* = (M)LG., (M)Du. *mist*, Icel. *mistur*, Norw. dial., Sw. *mist* :– Gmc. **mixstaz*, f. **mīʒ-* (cf. Du. *miggelen*, WFris. *miggelje* drizzle) :– IE. **migh-* **meigh-*, as in Gr. ὀμίχλη mist, fog.] 1. Vapour of water precipitated in very fine droplets, smaller and more densely aggregated than those of rain. b. *transf.* A cloud (of small particles) resembling a mist; a haze or haziness; hence *fig.* of time, etc. 1785. 2. Dimness of eyesight; a filmy appearance before the eyes caused by disorders of the body or by tears OE. 3. Applied to immaterial things conceived as dimming, obscuring, or blurring OE. †4. An atmosphere of doubt –1715.

1. Whan the moysture of the dewe stryketh upwarde agayne, it maketh a myste 1530. *Scotch m.*: a thick, soaking mist characteristic of the Scottish hills. b. Times..half shrouded in the m. of legend FREEMAN. 2. O'er her meek eyes came a happy m. TENNYSON. 3. The mists Of despondency and gloom M. ARNOLD. Phr. *Mists of death, deathly mists.*

Comb.: **m.-bow**, a fog-bow (FOG *sb.*[2]); **-flower**, a plant of the tropical American genus *Conoclinium.*

†**Mist**, *sb.*[2] late ME. [perh. a use of prec. infl. by *mystic*, etc.; cf. MISTY *a.*[2]] Things spiritual or mystical. *In m.*: mystically. –1667. (MILT. *P. L.* v. 435.).

Mist (mist), *v.* [OE. *mistian*, f. *mist* MIST *sb.*[1]] 1. *intr.* To be or become misty; (of the eyes, outlines, etc.) to become dim, obscure, or blurred. 2. *trans.* To cover or obscure with or as with mist; to bedim (the eyes) with tears. late ME.

1. When thy gold breath is misting in the west KEATS. 2. He sits Misted with darknes like a smoaky roome 1598.

Mistakable (mistē[1]·kăb'l), *a.* 1646. [f. MISTAKE *v.* + -ABLE.] Capable of being mistaken, misapprehended, or misunderstood. Hence **Mista·kableness. Mista·kably** *adv.*

Mistake (mistē[1]·k), *sb.* 1638. [f. next.] *prop.* A misconception of the meaning of something; *hence*, an error or fault in thought or action.

The great m. of expecting too much of life 1856. *gen.* Infallibility is an absolute security of the understanding from all possibility of m. in what it believes TILLOTSON. Phr. †*A m. of*: a misconception as to. †*Under a m.*: under a misapprehension. *By m.*: mistakenly. *And no m.*: undoubtedly; used *colloq.* to emphasize a preceding statement. Also used attrib., (*and-*) *no-m.* = undoubted. The real old original and no-mistake nobility THACKERAY.

Mistake (mistē[1]·k), *v.* ME. [– ON. *mistaka* take in error, refl. miscarry (Sw. *misstaga* be mistaken), f. *mis-* MIS-[1] + *taka* TAKE. Cf. OFr. *mesprendre* (see MISPRIZE *v.*[2]), which has prob. infl. the meaning.] †1. *trans.* To take wrongfully, wrongly, or in error –1631. †2. *intr.* To transgress, offend –1822. 3. To err in the choice of. late ME. 4. *trans.* To misunderstand the meaning or †character of (a person). late ME. 5. To take (an opinion, statement, action, purpose, etc.) in a wrong sense 1496. 6. *intr.* To make a mistake; to be in error; to take a wrong view 1581. †7. *trans.* To suppose erroneously to be or to do ... –1736. 8. *To mistake* (a person or thing) *for* (another): to suppose erroneously the former to be the latter 1611. 9. To take to be somebody or something else 1590. †10. To commit an error in regard to (a date, etc.); to perform (an action) at a wrong time –1734.

3. Phr. *To m. the* or *one's road* (*way*); *to m. one's mark.* 4. Why, thou whorson Asse, thou mistak'st me SHAKS. 5. The judge may m. the law *'Junius' Lett.* 6. Oh, cry you mercy sir, I haue mistooke SHAKS. You're mistaken I dare say DICKENS. 7. Lest I should be mistaken to vilify Reason 1736. 8. She [a hen] mistakes a Piece of Chalk for an Egg, and sits upon it in the same manner ADDISON. 9. Phr. *There's no mistaking* = it is impossible not to recognize. There was no mistaking the fact DICKENS. Hence **Mista·kingly** *adv.*

Mistaken (mistē[1]·k'n), *ppl. a.* 1597. [pa. pple. of prec. vb.] †1. Wrongly supposed to be so. 2. Of persons: Taking a wrong view 1601. 3. *transf.* of their opinions, actions, etc.: Wrongly conceived or carried out; erroneous 1676.

2. I think him honest, though m. *'Junius' Lett.* 3. A m. feeling of loyalty FREEMAN. Hence **Mista·ken-ly** *adv.*, **-ness.**

Misteach (mistī·tʃ), *v.* [OE. *mistǣćan*; see MIS-[1] 1 and TEACH *v.*] *trans.* To teach or instruct badly or wrongly. So **Mistaught** (mistǭ·t), *ppl. a.* 1552.

Mistell (miste·l), *v.* late ME. [MIS-[1] 1.] †1. To miscount –1647. 2. To relate incorrectly; †to misinform 1565.

†**Miste·mper**, *v.* 1547. [f. MIS-[1] 1 + TEMPER *v.*] *trans.* To disturb or disorder –1642.

Miste·mpered, *ppl. a. Obs.* or *arch.* 1506. [MIS-[1] 2.] 1. Badly mixed. 2. Disordered, deranged 1541. 3. Of weapons: Tempered for an evil purpose. *Rom. & Jul.* I. i. 94.

Mister (mi·stəɹ), *sb.*[1] *Obs.* exc. *arch.* or *dial.* ME. [– AFr. *mester*, OFr. *mestier* (mod. MÉTIER) :– Rom. **misterium*, for L. *ministerium*; see MYSTERY[2].] †1. Handicraft, trade; profession, craft –1613. †2. Office, business, function. ME. only. †3. Occupation. ME. only. †4. Need –1768.

Comb. †**m. man, misters** (genitive) **man**: a craftsman. Phr. like *all mister* (*men*), *what mister* (*man*) were subsequently misapprehended as = 'of all (what, etc.) class(es, kind(s'; hence *arch.* and *dial.*

Mister (mi·stəɹ), *sb.*[2] 1551. [Weakened form of MASTER *sb.*[1] originating from reduced stress in proclitic use. Cf. MISTRESS.] 1. Title of courtesy prefixed to the surname or Christian name of a man, and to designations of office or occupation. The oral equivalent of MR. (q.v.). b. The word 'mister' (Mr.) as a prefix or title 1758. 2. = SIR (or less respectful than that title). Now only *vulgar.* 1760.

1. b. They never spoke to us without putting M. to our Names GOLDSM. 2. 'Good morning, mister', said Dominicus HAWTHORNE.

†**Mi·ster**, *v.*[1] Chiefly *Sc.* ME. [f. MISTER *sb.*[1]] 1. *intr.* To be necessary or needful –1715. 2. *trans.* To have need of, require –1722. 3. *intr.* To have need (*of*) –1572.

1. As for my name, it mistreth not to tell SPENSER.

Mi·ster, *v.*[2] 1742. [f. MISTER *sb.*[2]] *trans.* To address or speak of as 'Mr.'

'Pray, don't m. such fellows to me', cries the Lady FIELDING.

Miste·rm, *v.* 1579. [MIS-[1] 1.] *trans.* To apply a wrong term or name to.

Mistery: see MYSTERY[2].

Mistful (mi·stfŭl), *a.* 1599. [f. MIST *sb.*[1] + -FUL.] Full of mist; obscured by or as by mist.

Misthi·nk, *v.* ME. [f. MIS-[1] 1 + THINK *v.*[2]] †1. *intr.* To have sinful thoughts –1615. 2. To think mistakenly 1530. 3. *trans.* To have a bad opinion of. Also *intr.* const. *of.* 1593. 4. With cogn. obj.: To think bad thoughts 1618. So **Misthou·ght**, erroneous thought or notion; mistaken opinion 1596.

Misthrive (misþrəi·v), *v.* 1567. [MIS-[1] 7.] *intr.* To be unsuccessful; not to thrive.

‖**Mistico** (mi·stiko). 1801. [Sp., perh. ult. – Arab. *musattah* armed vessel.] A Mediterranean coasting vessel having two sails.

†**Misti·de**, *v.* [OE. *mistīdan*; see MIS-[1] 1 and TIDE *v.*] 1. *intr.* To happen amiss or unfortunately –ME. 2. To have misfortune. CHAUCER.

Mistigris (mi·stigris). 1882. [– Fr. *mistigri* knave of spades.] The name of the blank card in a variety of draw poker; hence, the game in which it is used.

Mistime (mistəi·m), *v.* [OE. *mistīmian*; see MIS-[1] 1 and TIME *v.*] †1. *intr.* Of the event: To happen amiss. Of the person: To come to grief. –late ME. 2. To time wrongly or improperly; to do or perform at a wrong time; to miscalculate the time of. late ME.

†**Mi·stion.** 1612. [– L. *mistio*, *-on-*, f. *mist-*, pa. ppl. stem of *miscēre* mix. Cf. OFr. *mistion.*] Mixtion, mixture –1680.

Mistitle (mistəi·t'l), *v.* 1618. [MIS-[1] 1.] *trans.* To give a wrong title or name to.

Mistle, obs. f. MISSEL, MIZZLE.

Mistletoe (mi·z'ltoᵘ, mi·s'ltoᵘ). [OE. *misteltān* (= ON. *mistilteinn*), f. *mistel* mistletoe (see MISSEL) + *tān* twig (= Du. *teen* withe, OHG. *zein* rod, ON. *teinn* twig, spit, Goth. *tains* twig).] A parasitic plant of Europe, *Viscum album*, growing, in Britain, on the apple-tree, rarely on the oak, and bearing a whitish berry, from which a birdlime is prepared. It was held in veneration by the Druids, esp. when found growing on the oak. Also applied to various allied plants.

The m. is still hung up in farm-houses and kitchens at Christmas: and the young men have the privilege of kissing the girls under it W. IRVING. *Comb.* **m. thrush**, the missel-thrush, *Turdus viscivorus.*

Mistral (mi·străl, mistrā·l). 1604. [– Fr. *mistral* – Pr. *mistral* :– L. *magistralis* (sc. *ventus* wind) MAGISTRAL; *lit.* 'master-wind'.] A violent cold north-east wind experienced in the Mediterranean provinces of France, etc.

Mistransla·te, *v.* 1532. [MIS-[1] 1.] *trans.* To translate incorrectly. **Mistransla·tion** 1694.

†**Mistrea·ding**, *vbl. sb.* 1596. [MIS-[1] 3.] A mis-step; a misdeed –1772.

Mistreat (mistrī·t), *v.* 1453. [MIS-[1] 1.] *trans.* To treat badly or wrongly; to ill-treat, maltreat. So **Mistrea·tment** 1716.

Mistress (mi·strés). [ME. *maistresse* (XIV) – OFr. *maistresse* (mod. *maîtresse*), f. *maistre* MASTER *sb.*[1] + *-esse* -ESS[1]. Forms in *mis-* (due to light stress) are recorded from XV; cf. MISTER *sb.*[2]] I. 1. A woman who has the care of or authority over servants or attendants, and, in early use, of children or young women. 2. The female head of a household or of an establishment of any kind. late ME. 3. A woman who has power to control or dispose *of* something. Now *rare* exc. in *one's own m.*, *m. of the situation*, etc. late ME. †4. The female governor of a state, etc. –1785. b. Also of countries, etc. late ME. †5. A woman, a goddess, a virtue, passion, etc., having dominion over a person or regarded as a protecting or guiding influence –1677. †6. A woman, or personified thing, regarded as the authoress, creatress, or patroness of an art, religion, a state of life, etc. –1708. 7. A female possessor or owner 1551. 8. A woman who has mastered any art, craft, or subject 1484. **9.** A woman who is loved and courted by a man. (Now only in unequivocal contexts.) 1509. **10.** A woman who illicitly occupies the place of a wife. late ME.

1. As the eyes of a maiden [look] vnto the hand of her mistresse *Ps.* 123: 2. **2.** The m. of a family must be ever watchful MRS. CHAPONE. **3.** You are your own m. 1794. **b.** *transf.* Such a lord is Love, And Beauty such a m. of the world TENNYSON. **4. b.** Rome now is m. of the whole World, sea and land, to either pole B. JONS. **7.** Phr. *To be m. of*: to have in her possession or at her disposal; also, to be perfectly acquainted with (a subject). **9.** I giue thee this For thy sweet Mistris sake, because thou lou'st her SHAKS.

II. A female teacher, instructress; now only, one engaged in a school, or teaching a special subject, as music, etc. late ME.

III. As a title. **1.** Used vocatively; = MADAM, MA'AM. *Obs.* exc. *arch.* late ME. **2.** As a title of courtesy. Now *Obs.* or *dial.* 1461. **b.** *transf.* and *joc.* 1577. **3.** In the title of certain Court offices 1710.

1. Studies my Ladie? Mistresse, looke on me SHAKS. **2.** So, here is m. Stella again SWIFT. M. Gilpin (careful soul!) COWPER. **b.** Mistris line, is not this my Ierkin? SHAKS. **3.** *M. of the Robes*: a lady of high rank, charged with the care of the Queen's wardrobe.

IV. Techn. **1.** *Bowls.* = JACK *sb.*[1] II. 11. Often *fig.* 1586. **2.** A lantern used in coal-mines 1851.

1. So, so, rub on, and kisse the mistresse SHAKS.

Mistressly (mi·strěsli), *a.* 1748. [-LY[1].] **1.** Belonging to the mistress of a household. RICHARDSON. **2.** [after MASTERLY 2.] Like one who is a mistress in her art 1786.

2. I did see the new bust of Mrs. Siddons, and a very m. performance it is indeed H. WALPOLE.

Mi·stress-piece. Now *rare.* 1648. [f. MISTRESS after *masterpiece.*] A feminine masterpiece.

Mi·stress-ship. 1460. [f. MISTRESS + -SHIP.] **1.** Authority of one in the position of a mistress 1581. **†2.** A style of address; always in *your m.* –1632. **3.** The post of mistress in a school 1891.

Mistrial (mistrəi·ăl). 1628. [MIS-[1] 4.] A trial vitiated by some error. Also, *U.S.*, an inconclusive trial, as where the jury cannot agree.

Mistri·st, *sb.* and *v. Obs.* or *dial.* late ME. = MISTRUST.

†Mistrow·, *v. north.* ME. [– ON. *mis-trúa*, f. *mis-* MIS-[1] + *trúa* (see TROW *v.*).] = MISTRUST *v.* –1480. So **†Mistrow·** *sb.* ME.

Mistrust (mistrɒ·st), *sb.* late ME. [MIS-[1] 7.] Lack of trust or confidence; suspicion, distrust. **Mistru·stless** *a.* unsuspecting 1586.

Mistrust (mistrɒ·st), *v.* late ME. [f. MIS-[1] 7 + TRUST *v.*, prob. after OFr. *mesfier* (mod. *méfier*).] **1.** *trans.* Not to trust (a person); to suspect the actions, intentions, motives, etc. of. Also *refl.* **2.** To have doubts about (a thing); to doubt the truth, validity, or genuineness of. late ME. **†3.** To suspect the existence or anticipate the occurrence of (something evil) –1728. **b.** To suspect *that* something has happened or will happen (now *rare*). late ME. **4.** *intr.* To be distrustful, suspicious, or without confidence. late ME.

1. I will neuer m. my wife againe SHAKS. **2.** For my part I am ever ready to m. a promising title GOLDSM. **3.** They were all asleepe mistrusting to harme FLORIO. Hence **Mistru·stingly** *adv.*

Mistru·stful, *a.* 1529. [f. MISTRUST *sb.* + -FUL.] Full of mistrust; wanting in confidence; distrustful, suspicious. Const. *of.* **†b.** *transf.* Causing mistrust 1592.

b. Or stonish'd as night-wanderers often are, Their light blown out in some m. wood SHAKS. Hence **Mistru·stful-ly** *adv.*, **-ness.**

Mistry·st, *v. Sc.* and *north.* 1816. [MIS-[1] 1, 7.] **1.** *trans.* To fail to keep an engagement with. **2.** *pass.* To be perplexed.

Mistu·ne, *v.* 1504. [MIS-[1] 1.] *trans.* To tune wrongly; to make discordant; to perform (music) out of tune.

Misturn (mistɒ̄·ɹn), *v.* ME. [MIS-[1] 1. Partly after OFr. *mestourner.*] *trans.* and *intr.* To turn in a wrong direction.

Mistu·tored, *ppl. a.* 1757. [MIS-[1] 2.] Badly instructed or brought up.

Misty (mi·sti), *a.*[1] [OE. *mistiġ*, f. *mist* MIST *sb.*[1] + -Y[1].] **1.** Covered with mist; accompanied or characterized by mist; consisting of mist. **b.** Clouded, blinded, or blurred as if by mist 1590. **2.** *fig.* Obscure; vague, indistinct. late ME. **b.** Of persons: Clouded in intellect 1822.

1. And Iocond day Stands tipto on the mistie Mountaines tops SHAKS. **2.** The Philosopher..is so hard of vtterance, and so mistie to bee conceiued, [etc.] SIDNEY. A m. recollection TYLOR. Hence **Mi·sti-ly** *adv.*, **-ness.**

†Mi·sty, *a.*[2] late ME. [A use of prec. for L. *mysticus.* Cf. MIST *sb.*[2]] Mystical, spiritual –1570.

Mi:sundersta·nd, *v.* ME. [MIS-[1] 1.] Not to understand rightly; to take in a wrong sense; to misinterpret the actions, etc. of (a person).

To be great is to be misunderstood. EMERSON.

Mi:sundersta·nding, *vbl. sb.* 1449. [MIS-[1] 3.] **1.** Failure to understand; misconception, misinterpretation. **2.** Dissension, disagreement 1642.

2. Some little pique or m. between them GEO. ELIOT.

Misusage (misyū·sėdʒ). Now *rare.* 1532. [MIS-[1] 4.] **†1.** Misconduct –1579. **2.** Ill-usage; maltreatment 1554. **3.** Wrong use, misuse 1567.

Misuse (misyū·s), *sb.* late ME. [MIS-[1] 4.] **1.** Wrong or improper use; misapplication. **†2.** Ill-usage. SHAKS. **†3.** Evil custom or conduct –1604.

1. Artful m. of the confidence of others 1866. **2.** 1 *Hen. IV*, I. i. 43. **3.** *Oth.* IV. ii. 109.

Misuse (misyū·z), *v.* late ME. [MIS-[1] 1. Cf. OFr. *mesuser.*] **1.** *trans.* To use or employ wrongly or improperly; to misapply. **2.** To maltreat, ill-use 1540. **†b.** To violate –1540. **†3.** *refl.* To misconduct oneself 1532–1581. **†4.** To speak evil of; to revile, deride –1633. **†5.** To deceive –1601.

1. I haue misvs'd the Kings Presse damnably SHAKS. **2.** Who misuses a dog would m. a child TENNYSON. **5.** Proofe enough, to m. the Prince, to vexe Claudio SHAKS. Hence **Misu·ser**[1], one who misuses 1548.

Misuser[2] (misyū·zəɹ). 1625. [– OFr. *mesuser*, inf. as sb.; see -ER[4].] *Law.* Unlawful use of a liberty or benefit such as may lead to its forfeiture.

Misva·lue, *v.* 1626. [MIS-[1] 1.] *trans.* To value falsely or wrongly; to misesteem. So **Misvalua·tion.**

Ignored or misvalued during his life 1900.

Misve·nture. Now *arch.* 1563. [MIS-[1] 4.] An unfortunate venture; a misadventure.

Misvou·ched, *pa. pple.* and *ppl. a.* 1626. [MIS-[1] 2.] **1.** Alleged wrongly. BACON. **2.** Not well vouched for 1876.

†Miswa·ndered, *ppl. a.* 1590. [MIS-[1] 2.] In which one has gone astray –1620. **†Miswa·ndering** *ppl. a.* going astray. late ME. –1645.

†Misway·. [MIS-[1] 4.] A wrong path. CHAUCER.

Miswe·dded, *a.* [MIS-[1] 2.] Unsuitably married; *transf.* of a marriage MILT.

†Miswee·n, *v.* 1590. [MIS-[1] 1.] **1.** *intr.* To have a wrong opinion –1640. **2.** *trans.* To think wrongly of –1749.

†Miswe·nd, *v.* ME. [MIS-[1] 1.] To lead or go astray (*lit.* and *fig.*) –1723.

Misword (miswɒ̄·ɹd), *sb.* Now *dial.* ME. [MIS-[1] 4. Cf. MIS *a.*] A harsh, angry, or cross word.

Mis-wo·rd, *v.* 1883. [MIS-[1] 1.] *trans.* To word incorrectly. So **Mis-wo·rding** *vbl. sb.* wrong wording 1680.

Miswo·rship, *sb.* 1626. [MIS-[1] 4.] Wrong or false worship. So **Miswo·rship** *v. trans.* to worship amiss. **Miswo·rshipper.**

Miswrite (misrəi·t), *v.* OE. [MIS-[1] 1.] *trans.* To write incorrectly.

†Miswrou·ght, *pa. pple.* ME. [MIS-[1] 2.] Done amiss; manufactured badly –1626.

†Mi·sy. 1601. [– L. *misy* (Pliny) – Gr. μίσυ.] **1.** A kind of mushroom or truffle. HOLLAND. **2.** *Min.* Copiapite, or some related species –1775.

Misyoke (misyōᵘ·k), *v.* 1645. [MIS-[1] 1.] *trans.* To yoke (in marriage) unsuitably. Also *intr.*

Miszea·lous, *a.* 1617. [MIS-[1] 6.] Wrongly zealous.

Mitch-board (mi·tʃboᵊɹd). 1883. [perh. f. *mitch* = *miche* forked shaft for a pump, Sc. dial. *mitch* support for a mast when lowered. Cf. G. *micke* fork of a branch, Du. *mik* forked stick.] *Naut.* A support for a boom, yard, etc., when not in use.

Mite[1] (məit). [OE. *mīte* = MLG., MDu. *mīte* (Du. *mijt*), OHG. *mīza* gnat :– Gmc. *mītōn.*] In early use, any minute insect or arachnid. Now usually restricted to certain genera of the order *Acarida* of arachnids, and chiefly applied to the cheese-mite, *Tyroglyphus* (formerly *Acarus*) *domesticus.*

Mite[2] (məit). ME. [– MLG., MDu. *mīte* :– Gmc. **mītōn*, prob. identical with prec.] **1.** Orig., a Flemish copper coin of very small value. From the 14th c., used as tr. L. *minutum* (Vulg.), Gr. λεπτόν in Mark 12: 43, where two 'mites' are stated to make a 'farthing' (Gr. κοδράντης, L. *quadrans*); hence pop. = 'half-farthing'. **b.** *fig.* An immaterial contribution, but the best one can do, to some object or cause (see *Mark* 12: 43) 1650. **†2.** A small weight: *spec.* one twentieth of a grain troy –1738. **3.** A minute particle or portion; a tiny fragment. Now *colloq.* or *vulgar.* 1608. **4.** *fig.* A jot, whit. Now *colloq.* late ME. **5.** A very small object; often, a tiny child 1594.

1. And there came a poore wyddowe, and put in two mytes, which make a farthinge COVERDALE *Mark* 12: 43. **b.** It may not be amiss to contribute my m. of advice BERKELEY. **5.** A m. of a boy DICKENS.

Miter: see MITRE.

Mithras (mi·þræs), **Mithra** (mi·þră). 1585. [L. *Mithras, Mithres* = Gr. Μίθρας – OPers. *Mithra*, = Skr. *Mitra*, one of the gods of the Vedic pantheon.] A god of the ancient Persians, in later times often identified with the sun. Hence **Mithra·ic** *a.* of or connected with M. or his worship. **Mi·thraism. Mi·thraist.**

Mithridate (mi·þrideⁱt). Also †‖**Mithrida·tum.** 1528. [– med.L. *mithridatum*, altered from late L. *mithridatium*, orig. neut. of *Mithridatius* adj., pertaining to Mithridates, f. L. *Mithri-*, *Mithradates*, Gr. Μιθρι-, Μιθραδάτης. Cf. Fr. *mithridate.*] **1.** *Old Pharmacy.* A composition in the form of an electuary, regarded as a universal antidote against poison and infectious disease. Hence any similar antidote. Also *transf.* and *fig.* **2.** In full *m. mustard*, a name for the plants *Lepidium campestre* and *Thlaspi arvense.* Also *Bastard m. mustard*: candy-tuft. 1597. Hence, **Mi·thridatism,** immunity from a poison induced by administering gradually increased doses of it 1851. **Mi·thridatize,** *v. trans.* to produce mithridatism in 1866.

Mithridatic (miþridæ·tik), *a.* 1649. [– L. *mithridaticus* – Gr. Μιθριδατικός, f. Μιθριδάτης; see prec., -IC.] **1.** Of or pertaining to Mithridates VI, king of Pontus. **2.** Of or pertaining to mithridate 1847. **3. a.** Resembling Mithridates or his alleged immunity from poisons; pertaining to mithridatism 1868.

Mitigable (mi·tigăb'l), *a.* 1677. [– med.L. *mitigabilis*, f. *mitigare*; see MITIGATE *v.*, -ABLE.] Capable of being mitigated.

Mitigant (mi·tigănt), *a.* and *sb. rare.* 1541. [– *mitigant-*, pr. ppl. stem of L. *mitigare*; see next, -ANT.] **A.** *adj.* Mitigating, lenitive. **B.** *sb.* A lenitive 1865.

Mitigate (mi·tigeⁱt), *v.* late ME. [– *mitigat-*, pa. ppl. stem of L. *mitigare*, f. *mitis* mild, gentle; see -ATE[3].] **1.** *trans.* To render (a person, etc.) milder; to appease, mollify. Now *rare.* **2.** To render (anger, etc.) less violent; to appease 1494. **3.** To alleviate (a disease, an evil). late ME. **4.** To abate the rigour of (a law) 1532. **5.** To reduce the severity of (a punishment, etc.) 1533. **b.** To render (a custom, etc.) more humane 1835. **6.** To moderate (heat, cold, etc.) 1611. **7.** To palliate (an offence) 1719. **8.** With a quality as obj.: To moderate (the severity, rigour, etc., *of* something) 1571. **9.** *intr.* To become mitigated; to grow milder or less severe (*rare*) 1633.

2. To m. the king's anger PRESCOTT. **3.** The swelling of his woundes to m. SPENSER. **5.** Those hard censures..are to be mitigated BURTON. **b.** Christianity first mitigated, and then abolished slavery 1835. **8.** We could greatly wish that the rigor of this their opinion were alayed and mitigated HOOKER. Hence **Mi·tigative** *a.* lenitive; *sb.* a soothing remedy. **Mi·tigator. Mi·tigatory** *a.* tending or serving to m.; *sb.* something which serves to m.

Mitigation (mitigēⁱ·ʃən). late ME. [– (O)Fr. *mitigation* or L. *mitigatio*, f. as prec.; see -ION.] **1.** The action of mitigating or the state of being mitigated. **b.** quasi-*concr.* A circumstance that mitigates 1729. †**2.** A qualification (of words or statements) –1709.

1. Without any m. or remorce of voice SHAKS. In m. of damages BLACKSTONE.

†**Mi·ting.** 1440. [f. MITE[2] + -ING[3].] A diminutive creature. Used in endearment or contempt –1585.

Mitis (mī·tis). 1885. [Named by the inventor of the process, P. Östberg of Stockholm; app. f. L. *mitis* mild, in the sense of *mild steel* (see MILD *a.* 7).] *Metall.* In *m. casting*: a method of increasing the fluidity of molten iron by adding a minute quantity of aluminium to the charge in the crucible; also, a casting produced by this process. So *m.-metal*, *process*, etc.

‖**Mitosis** (mitōᵘ·sis). *Pl.* **-oses** (-ōᵘ·sīz). 1888. [mod.L., f. Gr. μίτος thread; see -OSIS.] *Biol.* The process of division of the nucleus of a cell into minute threads. Hence **Mito·tic** *a.* pertaining to, characterized by, or exhibiting m.

‖**Mitraille** (mitray, mitrēⁱ·l), *sb.* 1868. [Fr. *mitraille*, OFr. *mi(s)traille* small money, pieces of metal; a var. of OFr. *mitaille*, f. *mite*; cf. MITE[2].] Fragments of iron, heads of nails, etc. shot in masses from a cannon; now *spec.* small shot fired from a mitrailleuse. So **Mitrai·lle** *v.* to assail with m. (*rare*) 1844.

‖**Mitrailleur** (mitrayö̆r). 1869. [Fr., agent-n. f. *mitrailler* fire mitraille.] = MITRAILLEUSE.

‖**Mitrailleuse** (mitrayö̆z). 1870. [Fr., fem. of prec.] A breech-loading machine-gun with a number of barrels fitted together, so arranged that it can discharge small missiles simultaneously or in rapid succession.

Mitral (məi·trăl), *a.* and *sb.* 1610. [– mod. L. *mitralis*, f. L. *mitra* MITRE *sb.*[1]; see -AL[1]. So Fr. *mitral* (XVIII).] **A.** *adj.* **1.** Of, pertaining to, or resembling a mitre. **2.** *Anat.* **M. valve:** the left auriculo-ventricular valve of the heart, so called from its shape. Also called *bicuspid valve*. 1705. **b.** *Anat.* and *Path.* Of or pertaining to the m. valve 1853. **B.** *sb.* = *M. valve* 1835.

Mitre (məi·təɹ), *sb.*[1] Also (now *U.S.*) **miter.** late ME. [– (O)Fr. *mitre* – L. *mitra* – Gr. μίτρα belt, turban, perh. of Asiatic origin.] **1. a.** *Antiq.* As tr. Gr. μίτρα, L. *mitra*: A headband worn by ancient Greek women; also, a kind of headdress common among Asiatics, considered by the Romans a mark of effeminacy when worn by men. ¶Used by Chapman and Pope as tr. Homeric μίτρη, a belt or girdle 1611. †**b.** Applied by travellers to the turban worn by certain Asiatic peoples, and the like 1585–1638. **2.** A sacerdotal head-dress. **a.** *Heb. Antiq.* The ceremonial turban of the high priest. late ME. **b.** *Eccl.* A bishop's tall cap, deeply cleft at the top, the outline of the front and back having the shape of a pointed arch: part of the insignia of a bishop in the Western Church, and worn also by certain abbots, etc. late ME. **c.** Used as the symbol of the episcopal office or dignity. late ME. **d.** *Her.* The representation of a mitre 1610. **3.** A name of taverns and hotels 1608. **4.** *Conch.* A mitre-shell 1840.

2. c. Learning being..reckon'd a very ordinary Qualification for yᵉ M. HEARNE. 3. *attrib.* A right Miter supper MIDDLETON.

attrib. and *Comb.*: **m.-mushroom,** an edible mushroom (*Helvella crispa*), so called from the shape of the pileus; **-shell,** any species of marine univalve shells of the genus *Mitra*.

Mitre (məi·təɹ), *sb.*[2] Also (now *U.S.*) **miter.** 1678. [perh. transf. use of prec.] **1.** In Joinery, etc.: A joint (also *m.-joint*) in which the line of junction bisects the angle (usu. a right angle) between the two pieces. **2.** Short for *mitre square* 1678. **3.** Short for *mitre-wheel* 1844. **3.** = GUSSET 2. 1882.

1. *Keyed m.*: a mitre-joint strengthened by the insertion of keys (see KEY *sb.*[1] III. 1). *Lapped m.*: a combination of the lap and m. joints.

Comb.: **m.-arch,** the curve formed by the m. or junction of two curved surfaces, as in groining, etc.; **-bevel** = *mitre square*; **-block, -board,** (*a*) a joiner's mitre box; (*b*) = *mitre shooting-board*; **m. box,** a joiner's templet with kerfs or guides for the saw in cutting mitre-joints; **-dovetail, dovetailing,** a combination of the m. and dovetail joints; **-gauge,** a gauge for determining the angle of a mitre; **-joint** (see sense 1); **m. shooting-board,** a shooting-board used in chamfering the edges of wood; **m. square,** a square with the blade set at an angle of 45° for striking lines on something to be mitred; **-valve,** a puppet valve having its face and seat inclined 45° to its axis; **-wheel,** each of a pair of bevelled cog-wheels, the axes of which are at right angles, and which have their teeth set at an angle of 45°.

Mitre (məi·təɹ), *v.*[1] late ME. [f. MITRE *sb.*[1]] *trans.* To confer a mitre upon. Chiefly in pa. pple. *mitred*, invested *with* something by way of mitre.

Mitre (məi·təɹ), *v.*[2] Also (now *U.S.*) **miter.** 1731. [f. MITRE *sb.*[2]] **1.** *trans.* To join with a mitre-joint; to cut or shape to a mitre. Also with *away*, *up*. **b.** *intr.* To meet in a mitre-joint 1820. **2.** *Needlework.* To make an angle in (a straight strip or band, etc.) by cutting out a three-cornered piece and uniting the resulting edges 1880.

1. *To m. the square*: to bisect the angle of a joint.

Mitred (məi·təɹd), *ppl. a.* late ME. [f. MITRE *sb.*[1] and *v.*[1] + -ED.] **1.** Entitled or privileged to wear a mitre. **2.** Wearing or adorned with a mitre. late ME. **3.** Formed like a mitre; having a mitre-shaped apex; *Nat. Hist.* in specific names (= mod.L. *mitratus*) 1547.

1. *M. abbot* (= med.L. *abbas mitratus*): an abbot invested by the pope with the privilege of wearing a mitre; *m. abbey*, an abbey ruled by a mitred abbot.

Mitre-wort (məi·təɹwɒɹt). 1845. [f. MITRE *sb.*[1] + WORT[1].] Any plant of the genus *Mitella*.

False mitre-wort: a plant of the genus *Tiarella*.

Mitriform (məi·trifǭm), *a.* 1824. [f. MITRE *sb.*[1] + -FORM.] **a.** *Bot.* Shaped like a mitre: applied to the calyptra of mosses, etc. **b.** *Conch.* Shaped like a mitre-shell.

Mitring (məi·t'riŋ), *vbl. sb.* 1731. [f. MITRE *v.*[2] + -ING[1].] The action of MITRE *v.*[2]; also *concr.* the shaped end of a piece prepared to be mitred with another.

Comb. **m.-machine,** any machine for mitring neatly and accurately.

Mitt (mit). Also **mit.** Chiefly in *pl.* 1765. Shortened form of MITTEN.

Mitten (mi·tən). [Late ME. *mytayne* (XIV) – (O)Fr. *mitaine* = Pr. *mitana* (cf. med.L. *mitan(n)a* :– Rom. **medietana* (sc. *muffula*) 'skin-lined glove cut off at the middle', f. L. *medietas* half.] **1.** A covering for the hand, differing from a glove in having no fingers, but only a thumb; worn either for warmth or protection. Also (now *dial.*) applied to a thick winter glove. **2.** A sort of glove of lace or knitted work covering the forearm, wrist, and part of the hand 1755.

1. Phr. *To handle without mittens*; to treat unmercifully. 2. Phr. *To get the m.*: of a lover, to be dismissed; hence, to be dismissed from any office or position. Hence **Mi·ttened** *a.* furnished with, or wearing, mittens.

†**Mi·ttent,** *a.* 1661. [– *mittent-*, pr. ppl. stem of L. *mittere* send; see- ENT.] *Path.* Said of the organ or part supposed to send peccant 'humours' to another –1684.

‖**Mittimus** (mi·timŏs), *sb.* 1443. [L., = 'we send', the first word of the writ in Latin.] †**1.** *Law.* A writ for removing records from one court to another –1559. **2.** *Law.* A warrant directed to the keeper of a prison, ordering him to receive into custody and hold in safekeeping, until delivered in due course of law, the person sent and specified in the warrant 1591. **3.** *colloq.* A dismissal from office; a notice to quit (*dial.*) 1596. **4.** *joc.* A magistrate 1630.

2. No words, Sir; a Wife, or a M. 1728. 3. Phr. *To get one's m.*: to be dismissed; also, to get one's 'quietus'. 4. Nay, 'tis but what old M. commanded SHERIDAN. Hence **Mi·ttimus** *v.* to commit to jail by a warrant.

Mity (məi·ti), *a.* 1681. [f. MITE[1] + -Y[1].] Full of or abounding in mites; said esp. of cheese.

Mix (miks), *sb.* 1586. [f. MIX *v.*] Chiefly *colloq.*: A muddle, mess; also, a state of being mixed or confused.

Mix (miks), *v.* Pa. t. and pple. **mixed** (mikst). 1480. [Back-formation from pa. pple. *mixed*, var. of †*mixt* – (O)Fr. *mixte* (spec. in AFr. law-phr. *accioun mixte* action partly real, partly personal) – L. *mixtus*, pa. pple. of *miscēre* mingle, mix, rel. to Gr. μίσγειν, μιγνύναι.] **1.** *trans.* To put together (two or more substances, groups, or classes) so that the particles or members of each are more or less evenly diffused among those of the rest; to mingle, blend. Also with *with*. **b.** With immaterial obj. 1597. †**c.** To put in as an ingredient, to intersperse. Const. *to*. –1742. **d.** To prepare (a compound) by putting ingredients together 1592. **e.** *hyperbolically.* To confound 1667. **2.** *intr.* = to be mixed. Also, to admit of being mixed; to go (well or badly) along with 1632. **3.** *trans.* To unite (persons) in dealings or acquaintance. Chiefly *refl.* and *pass.* Now *rare.* 1535. **4.** *intr.* To have intercourse *with* (occas. *among*); to take part *in* 1667. **b.** To have sexual intercourse *with* 1615. **c.** To join battle. DRYDEN. **5.** *trans.* and *intr.* To cross in breeding 1737.

1. Aufidius, myxt heddy wyne, and honey all in one 1566. Oxygen gas and sulphurous acid gas probably combine when simply mixed together 1811. b. Brothers, you mixe your Sadnesse with some Fear SHAKS. d. Had'st thou no poyson mixt? SHAKS. e. MILT. *P.L.* VII. 215. 2. Her dear idea mixes with every scene of pleasure GOLDSM. 4. To m. in the best society 1872.

Mix up. a. *trans.* To m. intimately, to m. *with* something else. **b.** In immaterial applications. Now only: To m. irrelevantly or unsuitably; to confuse. **c.** To associate *with* (inferior or bad company): to connect *with*, involve *in* (something 'shady'). Chiefly *refl.* and *pass.*

Mixed, †**mixt** (mikst), *ppl. a.* 1448. [See prec. *Mixt* being taken as an Eng. pple. in *-t*, was alternatively spelt with *-ed*, whence the vb. MIX.] **1.** *Law.* Formerly applied to an action which partook of the nature both of a real and of a personal action. **2.** In senses of MIX *v.* 1530. **3.** Of a company of persons: Not select, containing persons of doubtful character or status 1611. **4.** Of sciences: Involving matter; not pure or simply theoretical. Now *rare* exc. in *m. mathematics.* 1641. **5.** Comprising both sexes 1644. **6.** *colloq.* Muddled; *esp.* muzzy with drink 1872. **7.** *Phonetics.* Of a vowel sound: Intermediate between *high* and *low*; pronounced with the tongue in a flattened position 1867.

2. Unbounded liberty of the press..is one of the evils attending..mixt forms of Government HUME. 5. *M. school*, one in which boys and girls are taught together. *M. bathing.*

Spec. collocations: †**m. angle,** a mixtilinear angle; **m. marriage,** a marriage between persons of different races or religions; **m. metal,** an alloy; **m. metaphor,** the combination of inconsistent metaphors in one figure; **m. number,** the sum of an integer and a fraction; **m. train,** a railway train made up of both passenger-carriages and goods-wagons; formerly also a train carrying different classes of passengers. Hence **Mi·xed-ly** *adv.*, **-ness.**

Mixen (mi·ksən). Now *dial.* or *arch.* [OE. *mixen* :– **mixsinnja*, f. Gmc. **mixsa-*, parallel to **mixstuz*, whence OS., OHG., G. *mist*, Goth. *maihstus* dung, f. **mīʒ* make water (OE. *miċġe*, *migga* urine, OE. *mīgan*, LG. *mīgen*, ON. *miga* urinate).] **1.** A dunghill; also, a compost-heap used for manure. **2.** A term of abuse for a woman (*dial.*) 1764.

Mix·er. 1611. [f. MIX *v.* + -ER[1].] One who or that which mixes. **b.** orig. *U.S.* A person in respect of his capacity for mixing with others; esp. *a good m.* 1896.

Mix-Hellene (mikshelī·n). 1856. [– Gr. μιξέλλην; see MIXO- and HELLENE.] A person of mixed Greek and barbarian blood.

Mixo- (mi·kso), repr. Gr. μιξο-, f. root of μιγνύναι, with the sense 'mixed', as **Mixo·gamous** [Gr. γάμος] *a.*, *Ichth.* (of fishes) given to promiscuous pairing; **Mixo·gamy,** the condition of being mixogamous; etc.

Mixolydian (miksoli·diăn), *a.* 1589. [f. Gr. μιξο-λύδιος half-Lydian; see MIXO- and LYDIAN.] *Mus.* **a.** The highest in pitch of the modes in ancient Greek music. **b.** The fourth of the 'authentic' ecclesiastical modes, having G for its final and D for its dominant.

†**Mixt,** *sb.* 1589. [– L. *mixtum*, n. of *mixtus*; see MIXED *ppl. a.*] **1.** A substance consisting of different elements mixed together; esp. in *Old Chem.*, a compound –1805. **2.** In immaterial applications: A compound –1647.

†**Mixt,** *v.* 1526. [Inferred from the pa. pple. *mixt* (see MIXED *ppl. a.*).] = MIX *v.* –1609.

Mixtilinear (mikstili·nĭăɹ), *a.* 1702. [f. L. *mixtus* mixed, after *rectilinear*.] Formed or bounded partly by straight, partly by curved lines. So **Mixtili·neal** *a.*

†**Mixtion.** late ME. [– (O)Fr. *mistion* – L. *mixtio*, also *mistio*, *-on-*, f. *mixt-*, *mist-*, pa. ppl. stem of *miscēre* MIX; see -ION.] = MIXTURE 1, 2, 3, 5. –1757.

Mixture (mi·kstiŭɹ, -tʃəɹ). 1460. [– Fr. *mixture* or its source L. *mixtura*, f. *mixt-*; see prec., -URE.] **1.** The action, process, or fact of mixing or becoming mixed; also, an instance of this 1530. **b.** Mixed state or condition 1597. **2.** *concr.* A product of mixing 1460. **3.** *spec.* **a.** A medicinal preparation of two or more ingredients mixed together. In *Pharmacy*, now applied to potions or liquid medicines. 1592. **b.** A cloth of variegated fabric, as *Heather, Oxford m.* 1722. **c.** A blend of tea, tobacco, snuff, etc. 1840. **d.** Gas or vaporized oil mixed with air, forming the explosive charge in an internal-combustion engine 1894. **4.** The mechanical mixing of two substances as dist. from (*chemical*) *combination*; also *concr.* the product of such a mixing, as dist. from a *compound* 1797. **b.** A fluid containing some foreign substance in suspension; opp. to *solution* 1765. **5.** The action or an act of adding as an ingredient; the presence of a foreign element in the composition of something; quasi-*concr.* an amount or proportion of something foreign that has been added; admixture. *Without m.*: unmixed, pure. 1526. **6.** *Mus.* In full *m.-stop*: An organ-stop comprising several ranks of pipes, used in combination with the foundation-stops 1688.

1. b. There was a m. of company SWIFT. **2.** A fatal m. of weakness and temerity 1732. **3. a.** What if this m. do not worke at all? SHAKS. **5.** The same shall drinke of the wine of the wrath of God, which is powred out without m. into the cup of his indignation *Rev.* 14:10.

Mizen, mizzen (mi·z'n). 1465. [Early forms *mesan, meson, -eyn* (XV) – Fr. *misaine* (now fore-sail, fore-mast) – It. *mezzana*, subst. use of fem. of *mezzano* middle; forms with *mi-, my-* appear in XVI.] *Naut.* **1.** (Also **mizen-sail.**) A fore-and-aft sail set on the after side of the mizen-mast. Often synonymous with SPANKER. **2.** = MIZEN-MAST. Now *rare.* 1583. **3.** *attrib.*, as *m.-boom* 1485.

Mi·zen-mast. 1420. The aftermost mast of a three-masted ship. So **Mi·zen-to·p,** the 'top' of a mizen-mast; a platform just above the head of the lower mizen-mast 1667. **Mi·zen-topga·llant-mast,** the mast above the mizen-topmast 1864. **Mi·zen-to·pmast,** the mast next above the lower mizen-mast 1626. **Mi·zen-to·psail,** the sail set on the mizen-topmast 1626. **Mi·zen-yard,** the yard on which the mizen-sail is extended 1485.

Mizmaze (mi·zme^{i}z). 1547. [Varied redupl. of MAZE *sb.*] †**1.** A labyrinth or maze. Chiefly *fig.* –1794. **2.** Mystification. Chiefly *dial.* 1604.

Mizzle (mi·z'l), *sb. Obs.* or *dial.* 1490. [f. MIZZLE *v.*^{1}] Slight or drizzling rain, drizzle.

Mizzle (mi·z'l), *v.*^{1} *dial.* 1483. [prob. – LG. *miseln* = Du. dial. *miezelen*, WFlem. *mizzelen, mijzelen*, frequent. formation (see -LE) on the LG. base found in Du. dial. *mies|regen* drizzle, *miezig*, LG. *misig* drizzling.] **1.** *intr.* (*impers.*) To drizzle. †**2.** *trans.* Of a cloud (also *impers.*): To send down in a drizzling shower –1592. **Mi·zzly** *a.* 1566.

Mizzle (mi·z'l), *v.*^{2} *slang.* 1781. [Of unkn. origin.] *intr.* To disappear suddenly; *imper.* = be off!

Mizzy (mi·zi). *dial.* [ME. *misy*; cf. OE. *mēos* moss, bog.] A quagmire.

‖**Mna.** 1603. [Gr. μνᾶ.] = MINA^{1}.

‖**Mneme** (nī·mi). 1913. [Gr. μνήμη 'memory'.] *Psychol.* Capacity for retaining after-effects of experience or stimulation.

Mnemonic (nimǫ·nik). 1753. [– med.L. *mnemonicus* – Gr. μνημονικός, f. μνήμων, μνημον- mindful, f. μνᾱ-, base of μνᾶσθαι remember.] **A.** *adj.* **1.** Intended to aid the memory; pertaining to mnemonics. **2.** Of or pertaining to memory 1825.

2. The m. power of the late Professor Porson 1825.

B. *sb.* **a.** A mnemonic device. **b.** = MNEMONICS. 1858. So **Mnemo·nical** *a.* = A. 1. **Mnemo·nically** *adv.* **Mnemoni·cian, Mne·monist,** one versed in mnemonics. **Mnemo·nics** *sb. pl.* [see *-ics*, -IC 2], the art of assisting the memory, esp. by artificial aids; a system of precepts intended to aid the memory 1721. Also **Mne·motechny** (-te:kni), mnemonics 1845.

Mo (mō^{u}), *adv.*, quasi-*sb.*, and *a.* †Also **moe.** *Obs.* exc. *Sc.* and *n.* (**mae**). [OE. *mā* = OFris. *mā(r, mē(r*, OS., OHG. *mēr* (MDu. *mee*, G. *mehr*), ON. *meir*, Goth. *mais* :– Gmc. **maiz* :– IE. *meis*, with compar. ending *-is* (cf. L. *magis* and see BETTER); cf. MORE, MOST.] †**A.** *adv.* **1.** In or to a greater degree, extent, or quantity –ME. **2.** Longer, further, again. Chiefly qualified by *any, no, none; ever, never.* –1812. **B.** quasi-*sb.* †**1.** A greater number; more of the kind specified –1684. **2.** Others of the kind specified OE. **C.** *adj.* = MORE *a.* OE.

A. 2. Gent'lest fair, mourne, mourne no moe FLETCHER. **B. 2.** And besides which axioms, there are divers moe BACON.

Mo (mō^{u}). 1896. Colloq. abbrev. of MOMENT.

-mo (mō^{u}), the final syllable of terms derived from the abl. sing. masc. of L. ordinal numerals which denote book sizes by the number of leaves into which the sheet of paper has been folded, e.g. *duodecimo, sextodecimo*, which are read as *12mo, 16mo*; so *thirty-twomo, 32mo.*

‖**Moa** (mō^{u}·ă). 1842. [Maori.] A giant extinct flightless bird of New Zealand, *Dinornis gigantea*, allied to the kiwi.

Moabite (mō^{u}·ăbəit), *sb.* and *a.* late ME. [– L. (Vulg.) *Moabita* (Gr. Μωαβίτης, repr. Heb. *mô'ābî*), f. *Moab* + -ITE^{1} 1.] **A.** *sb.* One of the people of Moab, which bordered on the territory of the trans-Jordanic Israelites. In 16–17th c. applied opprobriously to Roman Catholics. **B.** *adj.* Pertaining to Moab or the Moabites 1870.

The M. stone, a monument erected by Mesha king of Moab c850 B.C., furnishing the earliest known inscription in the Phoenician alphabet. Hence **Mo·abitish**) *a.*

Moan (mō^{u}n), *sb.* [ME. *mone*, repr. OE. **mān* :– Gmc. **main-*, whence **mainjan*, ME. *mene* (MEAN *v.*^{2}), which was repl. by MOAN *v.*] **1.** Complaint, lamentation; a complaint, lament. Now apprehended as a transf. use of 2. †**b.** A state of grief or lamentation –1631. **2.** In mod. use: A low mournful murmur (less deep than a groan) indicative of physical or mental suffering 1673. **b.** *transf.* of the plaintive sound produced by the wind, water, etc. 1813.

1. A carpenter..made such pitiful m. to be taken in DE FOE. **b.** Thy mirth shall turne to moane SHAKS. **2.** M. of an enemy massacred TENNYSON. **b.** The brooklet's m. SCOTT. The m. of the adjacent pines TYNDALL.

Moan (mō^{u}n), *v.* 1548. (earlier possible exx. are doubtful). [f. prec.] **1.** *trans.* To complain of, lament; to bewail 1548. †**b.** *refl.* To bewail one's lot –1642. †**2.** To condole with (a person) –1669. **3.** *intr.* To make complaint or lamentation. Const. *of, for.* Now *arch.* or *poet.* 1593. **4.** *intr.* To utter a moan or moans 1724. **b.** *transf.* of inanimate things 1805. **5.** *trans.* To utter moaningly.

1. This man was greatly moaned of the people STOW. **3.** And what is life, that we should m.? TENNYSON. **4.** In bed she moaning lay WORDSW. **b.** Though the harbour bar be moaning KINGSLEY. **5.** Fair Madeline began to weep And m. forth witless words KEATS. Hence **Moa·ningly** *adv.*

Moanful (mō^{u}·nfŭl), *a.* 1573. [f. MOAN *sb.* + -FUL.] **1.** Full of moaning; expressing lamentation or grief. Now somewhat *rare.* 1586. †**2.** Causing lamentation –1662. Hence **Moa·nfully** *adv.*

Moat (mō^{u}t), *sb.* [ME. *mot(e*, identical with MOTE *sb.*^{2}, with transference of sense as in *ditch, dike, dam.*] **1.** *Fortif.* A deep and wide ditch surrounding a town, castle, etc., usually filled with water. **2.** A pond, lake; *esp.* a fish-pond. *Obs.* exc. *dial.* 1463.

1. The siluer sea, Which serues it in the office of a wall, Or as a Moate defensiue to a house SHAKS.

Moat (mō^{u}t), *v.* late ME. [f. MOAT *sb.*] *trans.* To surround with or as with a moat, ditch, or trench. Also with *about, in, round.*

The torrent broke down the quays...We were moated into our house all day H. WALPOLE.

Mob (mǫb), *sb.*^{1} 1688. [abbrev. of MOBILE *sb.*^{2}] **1.** The disorderly and riotous part of the population, the rabble; a tumultuous crowd bent on lawlessness. **2.** The lower orders; the uncultured or illiterate as a class; the masses 1691. †**3.** Without *the* –1789. **4.** A promiscuous assemblage of people. In Australian use, without disparaging implication, a crowd. 1688. **b.** *transf.* and *fig.* of things, etc. *Obs.* exc. *Austral.* 1728. **5.** *slang.* A gang of thieves or pickpockets working together 1843.

1. When mobs were roaring themselves hoarse for 'Wilkes and liberty' GREEN. **2.** The m. of the great cities..is hostile to us DUFF. **3.** I saw the street..full of m. DE FOE. **4.** The M. of Gentlemen who wrote with Ease POPE. A m. of steady men 1890. **b.** She sees a M. of Metaphors advance POPE. **5.** *Swell m.*, a class of pickpockets who dress stylishly.

Comb. **m. law,** 'law' imposed and enforced by a m.

Mob (mǫb), *sb.*^{2} *Obs.* exc. *Hist.* 1665. [var. of MAB.] †**1.** *Cant.* A strumpet –1697. †**2.** A négligé attire –1712. **3.** = MOB-CAP 1748.

†**Mob,** *v.*^{1} 1664. [Cf. prec. and MOBLE *v.*] *trans.* To muffle the head of (a person); to dress untidily –1837.

To m. (it), to go a-mobbing: to go in disguise to the unfashionable part of a theatre, etc. Hence, to frequent low company.

Mob (mǫb), *v.*^{2} 1709. [f. MOB *sb.*^{1}] **1.** *trans.* To attack in a mob; to crowd round and molest; to throng. Also, to force *into* something by such action. **2.** *intr.* To congregate in a mob; also *to m. it* 1711. **3.** *trans.* To mix *up* with a mob. TENNYSON.

Mobbish (mǫ·biʃ), *a.* 1695. [f. MOB *sb.*^{1} + -ISH^{1}.] Resembling a mob; disorderly, tumultuous. Also, †appealing to the mob; vulgar, clap-trap.

His m. fallacious way of arguing 1711. An irregular and m. appearance SCOTT.

Mobble: see MOBLE.

Mob-cap. 1812. [f. MOB *sb.*^{2}] An indoor cap worn by women in the 18th and early 19th c.

A mob-cap; I mean a cap,..with side-pieces fastening under the chin DICKENS.

Mobile (mō^{u}·bil), *sb.*^{1} 1549. [– Fr. *mobile* (in *premier mobile, etc.* – L. *mobile* adj. neut.; see MOBILE *a.*] †**1.** *First, grand, great, principal m.*, anglicized forms of PRIMUM MOBILE (*lit.* and *fig.*) –1797. **2.** *Metaph.* A body in motion or capable of movement. Now *rare.* 1676.

Mobile (mō^{u}·bili), *sb.*^{2} *arch.* 1676. [Short for L. *mobile vulgus* the excitable crowd.] The populace, rabble, MOB.

Y^{e} mobele was very rud to ye Dutch Imbasidor 1679.

Mobile (mō^{u}·bəil, -il), *a.* 1490. [– (O)Fr. *mobile* – L. *mobilis*, f. *mo-, movēre* MOVE; see -ILE.] **1.** Capable of movement; movable 1490. **b.** Of a limb, etc.; Movable; not fixed, free 1828. **c.** Of a fluid: That has its particles capable of free movement. **d.** Of a cell, molecule, etc.: Free; not adnate or fixed 1871. **2.** Characterized by facility of movement. **a.** Of features: Easily changing in expression 1851. **b.** Of persons: Wanting in stability; also, versatile 1855. **3.** *Mil.* Of troops: That may be rapidly moved from place to place 1879.

1. †*M. spirits*, the 'spirits' by which the motor impulses were supposed to be transmitted to the muscles. **2. a.** The thin m. lips..picture the inner soul of the man GREEN. **b.** Women's minds are by nature more m. than those of men, less capable of persisting long in the same continuous effort MILL.

Mobiliary (mobi·liări), *a.* 1682. [– Fr. *mobiliaire*, f. L. *mobilis* movable; see -ARY^{1}.] **1.** In the Channel Islands: Relating to movable property. **2.** *Mil.* Pertaining to mobilization 1888.

Mobility^{1} (mobi·līti). 1490. [– (O)Fr. *mobilité* – L. *mobilitas*, f. *mobilis*; see MOBILE *a.*, -ITY.] The quality or condition of being mobile.

Nature not having given that m. to the eyes of flies BOYLE. To promote the m. of labour and capital 1889.

Mobility^{2} (mobi·līti). 1690. [f. MOBILE *sb.*^{2}, MOB *sb.*^{1}, after *nobility.*] The mob; the lower classes.

Mobilization (mō^{u}:biləizē^{i}·ʃən). 1799. [– Fr. *mobilisation*, f. *mobiliser*; see next, -ATION.] The action or process of mobilizing. **1.** *Law.* The conversion of real or immovable property into personal or movable property. **2.** *Mil.* and *Naval.* The mobilizing (an army, a fleet, etc.) 1866.

Mobilize (mōᵘ·biləiz), *v.* 1838. [– Fr. *mobiliser*, f. *mobile*; see MOBILE *a.*, -IZE.] **1.** *trans.* To render movable or capable of movement; to bring into circulation. **2.** *Mil.* To prepare (an army or fleet) for active service 1853. **b.** *intr.* (for *pass.*) To undergo mobilization 1878.

Moble, mobble (mǫ·b'l), *v.* *Obs.* exc. *dial.* 1603. [frequent. f. MOB *v.*[1]; see -LE. Cf. MABBLE *v.*] *trans.* To muffle (one's) head or face. Chiefly with *up*.

But who, O who had seene the mobled Queene? *Haml.* (Qos.) II. ii. 524.

Mobocracy (mǫbǫ·krăsi). 1754. [f. MOB *sb.*[1]: see -CRACY.] **1.** Government by a mob. **2.** The mob as a ruling body 1754.

2. The shopocracy in the pit, and the m. in the gallery 1856. So **Mo·bocrat**, a demagogue 1798. **Mobocra·tic** *a.* 1775.

Mobsman (mǫ·bzmæn). 1851. [f. *mob's*, genitive of MOB *sb.*[1]] **1.** One of a mob 1868. **2.** (In full *swell m.*) A member of the swell mob (see MOB *sb.*[1] 5).

Moccasin (mǫ·kăsin). 1612. [– Powhatan *mo·ckasin*, Ojibwa *ma·kisin*; other dialects have the stress on the second syll., e.g. Narragansett *moku·ssin*, Micmac *mku·ssun*.] **1.** A kind of foot-gear made of deerskin or other soft leather, worn by N. Amer. Indians, trappers, backwoodsmen, etc. **2.** [perh. a distinct word.] In full **M. snake:** a venomous crotaline snake, *Ancistrodon piscivorus*, of the Southern U.S. *Highland* or *Upland M.*, the Cottonmouth, *A. atrofuscus*, a similar snake inhabiting the dry land and mountainous regions. 1791.

M. flower, plant, U.S. name for the genus *Cypripedium* (Lady's Slipper); **yellow m.,** *C. pubescens*. Hence **Mo·cassined** *a.*

Mocha[1] (mōᵘ·kă). 1679. [prob. identical with the place-name MOCHA[2]. Now written with capital M.] **1.** (Also *M. stone, pebble.*) A variety of chalcedony resembling or identical with moss-agate. **2.** One of several geometrid moths, esp. of the genus *Ephyra* 1775.

Mocha[2] (mōᵘ·kă). 1773. [Name of an Arabian port at the entrance of the Red Sea.] In full. *M. coffee*: a fine quality of coffee; orig. that produced in the Yemen province, in which Mocha is situated.

Moche, obs. f. MUCH *sb.*, *a.*, and *adv.*

Mochel(l, -il(l, obs. ff. MICKLE.

Mock (mǫk), *sb.* Now *rare* or *arch.* 1440. [f. MOCK *v.*] **1.** An act of mocking or derision. **b.** Mockery 1568. **2.** Something deserving of scorn 1489. **3.** The action of mocking or imitating; *concr.* an imitation, a counterfeit 1646.

1. He..called me boye, and gave me many a mocke 1509. Phr. *To make a m. of*: to bring into contempt.

Mock (mǫk), *a.* (Not used predicatively.) 1548. [Partly f. prec., partly f. stem of MOCK *v.* in comb. with an object. The hyphen is still often used in the collocations of the adj. with sbs.] Prefixed to a sb.; = sham, counterfeit, imitation, pretended.

I feare me some be rather mocke gospellers then faythful ploughmen LATIMER. That superior Greatness and Mock-Majesty, which is ascribed to the Prince of the fallen Angels ADDISON. A m. trial in which the enemies were judges THIRLWALL.

Spec. collocations (usu. hyphened): **m. auction,** a Dutch auction (see AUCTION *sb.* 3); also, a fraudulent auction, in which confederates bid briskly in order to elicit genuine bids; **-lead** = BLENDE; **-moon** = PARASELENE; **-rainbow,** a secondary rainbow (see RAINBOW); **-sun** = PARHELION. Also in names of culinary preparations, as **m.-duck, -goose,** a piece of pork from which the crackling has been removed, baked with a stuffing of sage and onions (*colloq.*); **-venison,** leg of mutton long hung, cooked after the manner of venison. **b.** In names of plants, as **m.-orange,** (*a*) the common syringa, *Philadelphus coronarius*; (*b*) the Carolina cherry-laurel, *Prunus caroliniana*; (*c*) the Australian native laurel, *Pittosporum undulatum*. **c.** In names of birds, as **m.-nightingale,** the Blackcap, the Sedge-warbler.

Comb. **a.** with adjs. and advs. with sense 'counterfeitly'. Chiefly implying humorous or ludicrous simulation, as in MOCK-HEROIC. **b.** With a vb., with joc. sense 'pretendingly', as *mock-knight*.

Mock (mǫk), *v.* [Early forms *mokke, mocque, mok* (XV) – OFr. *mo(c)quer*, (mod. *se moquer de* laugh at) deride, jeer :– Rom. **moccare*, f. **mok-*, repr. by It. dial. *moka*, Sp. *mueca* grimace, Pg. *moca* derision.] **1.** *trans.* To hold up to ridicule; to deride 1450. **b.** To defy; to set at nought 1558. **c.** *fig.* of impersonal things 1667. **2.** *intr.* To act or speak in derision; to jeer, scoff; to flout. Const. *at*, †*with*. 1450. †**b.** To jest –1611. **3.** *trans.* To impose upon; to befool; to tantalize 1470. **4.** To ridicule by imitation of speech or action. (The current colloq. use.) Hence, to mimic, counterfeit. 1595. †**b.** To simulate, make a false pretence of. SHAKS.

1. M. not a Cobler for his black thumbs FULLER. **b.** Let's mocke the midnight Bell SHAKS. **c.** A perishing That mocks the gladness of the Spring WORDSW. **2.** I wil mocke when your feare commeth *Prov.* 1:26. **b.** *Gen.* 19:14. **3.** Behold, thou hast mocked me, and told mee lies *Judg.* 16:10. **4.** Prepare To see the Life as liuely mock'd, as euer Still Sleepe mock'd Death SHAKS. He mocks and mimics all he sees and hears 1822. **b.** 3 *Hen. VI*, III. iii. 255. Hence **Mo·ckable** *a.*

†**Mockado** (mǫkā·do). 1543. [app. a perversion of It. †*mocaiardo* mohair.] A kind of cloth much used for clothing in the 16th and 17th centuries. Also *attrib.*, as *m. doublet*, etc. –1660. **b.** *fig.* as the type of an inferior material. Also *attrib.* or *adj.*: Trumpery, inferior. –1741.

b. Fustian, or m. Eloquence 1621.

†**Mo·ckage.** 1470. [f. MOCK *v.* + -AGE.] (Very common in 16th and 17th c.) = MOCKERY 1 and 2. –1686.

Mo·ck-bird. 1649. [f. MOCK *sb.* + BIRD *sb.*] = MOCKING-BIRD.

Mocker (mǫ·kəɹ). 1477. [f. MOCK *v.* + -ER[1].] One who or that which mocks or scoffs. **b.** A mocking-bird 1773.

Mockery (mǫ·kəri). late ME. [– (O)Fr. *moquerie*, f. *moquer*; see MOCK *v.*, -ERY.] **1.** Derision; a derisive utterance or action. **b.** A subject or occasion of derision 1560. **2.** Mimicry; a counterfeit representation; an unreal appearance. Now only, an impudent simulation. 1599. **3.** Ludicrously or insultingly futile action 1602. **4.** *attrib.*, as *m. King* 1593.

1. Wherefore was I to this keene m. borne? SHAKS. **b.** Genius will have become a m., and virtue an empty shade HAZLITT. **2.** Hence horrible shadow, Vnreal mock'ry hence SHAKS. The m. of a trial 1872. **3.** It is as the Ayre, invulnerable, And our vaine blowes malicious M. SHAKS.

Mo:ck-hero·ic, *a.* and *sb.* 1711. [f. MOCK *a.*] **A.** *adj.* Imitating in a burlesque manner the heroic style. **B.** *sb.* A burlesque imitation of the heroic style 1728.

Mo·cking-bird. 1676. [f. *mocking* ppl. a.] **1.** An Amer. passerine song-bird of the genus *Mimus*, esp. *M. polyglottus*, characterized by its habit of mimicking the notes of other birds. **2.** Applied to other birds having a similar aptitude; esp. the Sedge-warbler and the Blackcap 1779.

Mockingly (mǫ·kiŋli), *adv.* 1545. [f. *mocking* ppl. a. + -LY[2].] In a mocking manner.

†**Mo·cking-stock.** 1526. [f. *mocking* vbl. sb. + STOCK.] A laughing-stock –1833.

Mock turtle. 1763. [MOCK *a.*] **1.** Calf's head dressed with sauces and condiments so as to resemble turtle. **2.** (In full, *Mock turtle soup.*) A soup made (usu. of calf's head) in imitation of turtle soup 1783.

‖**Moco** (mōᵘ·ko). 1834. [Tupi *mocó.*] The rock cavy, *Cavia rupestris*.

Mod., abbrev. for MODERN, MODERATO.

Modal (mōᵘ·dăl), *a.* (*sb.*) 1569. [– med.L. *modalis*, f. L. *modus*; see MODE, -AL[1].] **1.** Pertaining to mode or form as opp. to substance 1625. **2.** *Law.* Of a legacy, contract, etc.: Containing provisions defining the manner in which it is to take effect 1590. **3.** *Mus.* Pertaining to mode 1597. **4.** *Logic.* Of a proposition: Involving the affirmation of possibility, impossibility, necessity, or contingency; or, according to others, a proposition in which the predicate is affirmed or denied of the subject with any kind of qualification. Of a syllogism: Containing a modal proposition as a premiss. 1569. **5.** *Gram.* **a.** Of or pertaining to mood; performing the function of a mood. **b.** Of a particle: Denoting proposition (see sense 4) 1725. Hence **Mo·dally** *adv.*, with ref. to mode or manner.

Modalism (mōᵘ·dăliz'm). 1859. [f. prec. + -ISM.] The Sabellian doctrine that the distinction in the Trinity is 'modal' only, i.e. that the Father, the Son, and the Holy Spirit are merely three different modes of manifestation of the Divine nature. So **Mo·dalist** 1832. **Modali·stic** *a.*

Modality (modæ·lĭti). 1545. [– med.L. *modalitas*, f. *modalis*; see MODAL, -ITY.] **1.** The quality or fact of being modal; state or condition in respect of mode or manner. Now *rare*. **2.** *Logic.* **a.** In the scholastic logic, the fact of being a model proposition or syllogism. Also, the modal qualification. 1628. **b.** In Kant, etc., that feature of a judgement which causes it to be classed as problematic, assertory, or apodictic 1836.

Mode (mōᵘd). late ME. [In branch I – L. *modus* measure, etc., f. IE. **mod-* **med-*; see METE *v.*[1]. In branch II – Fr. *mode* fem. – L. *modus* (with change of gender due to final *e*); the Fr. word (= fashion) was adopted into Eng. in XVII.] **I. 1.** *Mus.* †**a.** A tune, air. **b.** A kind or form of scale; a particular scheme or system of sounds. (*a*) In ancient Greek music: Each of the scales (Dorian, Phrygian, Lydian, etc.), according to one or other of which a piece of music in the diatonic style was composed 1674. (*b*) In mediæval church music: Each of the scales in which PLAINSONG was composed; beginning on different notes of the natural scale, and thus having the intervals (tones and semitones) differently arranged 1721. (*c*) In mod. music: Each of the two classes (*major* and *minor*) of keys, having the intervals differently arranged. Formerly sometimes = KEY *sb.*[1] II. 5 b. 1721. †**2.** *Gram.* = MOOD *sb.*[2] 1520–1843. **3.** *Logic.* [= med.L. *modus*, tr. Gr. τρόπος.] **a.** = MOOD *sb.*[2] 1. 1532. **b.** The character of a modal proposition; each of the four kinds into which modal propositions are divided (see MODAL 4) 1852. **4.** A way or manner of doing or being; a method of procedure 1667. **5.** A form, manner, or variety. Now *rare* exc. in *m. of life* and similar uses. 1661. **6.** *Philos.* **a.** A manner or state of being of a thing; a thing considered as possessing certain non-essential attributes. **b.** An attribute or quality of a substance 1677. **7.** *Mus.* In mensurable music, the proportion (3 or 2) of a long to a large or a breve to a long, determining the rhythm of a piece. Now *Hist.* 1667.

4. A regular m. of bringing to an amicable adjustment..any questions which might hereafter arise WELLINGTON. **5.** Every m. of life has its conveniences JOHNSON. The m. of superstition which prevailed in their own times GIBBON. Heat considered as a M. of Motion TYNDALL (*title*). **6.** **a.** That a Spirit is not an Accident or M. of Substance, all in a manner profess GLANVILL. *Mixed m.*: a mode formed by the combination of different simple ideas.

II. 1. A prevailing fashion or custom, practice or style 1645. **2.** Conventional usage in dress, manners, habit of life, etc., esp. among persons of fashion 1692. **3.** *The m.*: the fashion for the time being (*arch.*) 1649. †**4.** = ALAMODE 4. 1751–(*Hist.*).

1. Larding of meat after the m. of France HOWELL. **3.** The m. she fixes by the gown she wears YOUNG. What do you take to be the most fashionable age about town? Some time ago, forty was all the m. GOLDSM.

Model (mǫ·dĕl), *sb.* 1575. [– Fr. †*modelle*, now *modèle* – It. *modello* :– Rom. **modellus*, for L. MODULUS.] **I.** Representation of structure. †**1.** An architect's set of designs for a projected building; hence a similar set of drawings representing an existing building. Also occas. a delineation of a ground-plan. –1714. †**b.** *transf.* A summary, epitome, or abstract –1772. **2.** A representation in three dimensions of some projected or existing structure, or of some material object, showing the proportions and arrangement of its parts 1610. **b.** *fig.* Something that accurately resembles something else. *Obs.* exc. *dial.* in *the* (*very*) *model of*. 1593. †**3.** A mould; something that envelops closely. SHAKS. †**4.** A small portrait. Hence confused with MEDAL. –1658. **5.** An object or figure made in clay, wax, etc., and intended to be reproduced in more durable material 1686.

1. When we meane to build, We first suruey the Plot, then draw the Modell SHAKS. **2.** *Working m.*, one so constructed as to imitate the movements of the machine represented.

II. Type of design. **1.** Design; style of structure or form; pattern, build, make 1593.

†2. Scale of construction; allotted measure; the measure of a person's ability –1675. **3.** Of a violin, viol, etc.: Curvature of surface 1836.

1. *The* (*New*) *M.* (Hist.): the plan for the reorganization of the Parliamentary army, passed in 1644–1645. **b.** In dressmaking, etc., any article made by a recognized designer; any copy of such an article; also, a motor car, etc. of a particular design. **2.** Thus much (considering the modell of the whole worke) is sufficient HOBBES.

III. An object of imitation. **1.** A person, or work, that is proposed or adopted for imitation 1639. **2.** A person who poses for artists and art-students 1691. **b.** A mannequin 1904. **3.** A perfect exemplar *of* some excellence 1700.

1. I then resolved some m. to pursue, Perused French critics, and began anew GAY. **3.** Mr. Gray thought the narrative of Thucydides the m. of history 1805.

attrib. and *Comb.* Serving as, or suited to be, a model, exemplary; as *m. lodging-house, m. dwellings. Spec.* **m.-drawing,** in art-teaching, drawing in perspective from solid figures; **-room,** a room for the storage or exhibition of models of machinery, etc. Hence **Mo·dellist,** a maker of models.

Model (mǫ·dĕl), *v.* 1604. [f. prec. sb., after Fr. *modeler.*] †**1.** *trans.* To present as in an outline; to portray in detail –1667. **2.** To produce in clay, wax, or the like (a figure or imitation of anything) 1665. **3.** To give shape to (a document, argument, etc.) 1625. **b.** To form after a particular model. Usu. const. *after, on, upon.* 1730. †**4.** To organize (a community, a government, etc.) –1842. †**5.** To train or mould (a person) to a mode of life; also, to make a tool of –1734. **6.** To act or pose as a model (III. 2, b) 1927.

1. Cease dreames,..To modell forth the passions of to morrow DRUMM. OF HAWTH. MILT. *P.L.* VIII. 79. **3.** Budgets..modelled too much on..free-trade principles 1885. **b.** He modelled his court on that of Nádir Sháh ELPHINSTONE. Hence **Mo·deller** 1603.

†**Mo·delize,** *v.* 1599. [f. MODEL *sb.* + -IZE.] *trans.* To model –1810. Hence **Modelizing** *ppl. a.* formative.

Modelling (mǫ·dĕliŋ), *vbl. sb.* 1799. [f. MODEL *v.* + -ING¹.] The action or art of making models; the art of making a model in clay or wax to be copied in more durable materials by the sculptor or founder; the representation of solid form in sculpture, or of material relief and solidity in painting.

attrib., as *m.-clay, -stick, -tool, -wax.*

Modena (mǫ·dĭnă). 1822. [Name of an Italian city.] A deep purple colour.

Moder, obs. f. MOTHER.

Moderantism (mǫ·dĕrăntiz'm). *Obs.* exc. *Hist.* 1793. [– Fr. *modérantisme*, f. *modérant*, pr. pple. of *modérer* – L. *moderari*; see MODERATE *v.*, -ANT, -ISM.] In France, during the Revolution, and later, the doctrines and spirit of the Moderate party in politics. So **Mo·derantist.**

Moderate (mǫ·dĕrĕt), *a.* and *sb.* late ME. [– L. *moderatus*, pa. pple. of *moderari, -are*; see next, -ATE².] **A.** *adj.* **1.** Exhibiting moderation; avoiding extremes; temperate in conduct or expression. **2.** Not strongly partisan 1644. **b.** Hence (now usu. with initial capital) used as the designation of various parties and their views; see B. below 1753. **3.** Fairly large or good; tolerable. Now, mediocre, scanty. late ME. **b.** Of physical processes, etc.: Not intense, violent, or rigorous. Of the voice: Neither loud nor low. late ME. Of prices, charges: Not high 1904.

1. Sound sleepe commeth of m. eating *Ecclus.* 31: 20. **2.** The temptation to a Prime Minister is to appoint only 'moderate' men 1889. **b.** The M. clergy..were very unpopular 1848. **3.** There's not so much left to furnish out a m. Table SHAKS. The rest are very m. productions PUSEY. **b.** Winde that is m. and not contraryouse to Shypmen. late ME. Bake them in a m. oven 1769. **Mo·derate-ly** *adv.*, **-ness.**

B. *sb.* One who holds moderate opinions in politics, religion, etc. Hence (now usu. with initial capital), a member of any party customarily called 'Moderate'; e.g. in the French Revolution, applied to the Girondins. 1794. **b.** In the Church of Scotland in the 18th and early 19th c., a member of that party which held lax views on doctrine and discipline. **c.** In recent municipal politics (opp. to *Progressive*): A member of the party hostile to undertakings involving large expenditure 1894.

Moderate (mǫ·dĕrēˈt), *v.* late ME. [– *moderat-*, pa. ppl. stem of L. *moderari, -are* reduce, abate, control, f. **moder-* :– **modes-* (whence *modestus* MODEST), parallel with **modos, modus* MODE; see -ATE³.] **1.** *trans.* To render less violent, intense, rigorous, or burdensome; †to reduce (a fine, charge, etc.). **b.** *intr.* for *refl.* To become less violent, etc. Now *rare.* 1678. †**2.** *trans.* To regulate, restrain, control, rule –1808. †**b.** To adjust, arrange; to modify –1630. **3.** In academic and Eccl. use: To preside over (a deliberative body) or at (a debate, etc.) 1577. **b.** *intr.* To act as moderator; to preside 1581. †**4.** *trans.* To settle as an arbitrator –1744. †Also *absol.* or *intr.* To act as mediator or arbitrator –1756.

1. I..advise you to m. your demands 1732. **b.** Fortunately the weather moderated 1897. **2.** The woman was ordayned..to gouerne and m. the house at home 1615. **3. b.** Phr. *To moderate* (*in*) *a call*; in the Scottish Presbyterian churches, to preside over a meeting of a congregation for signing a call to a minister-elect; hence, to sign such a call. **4.** It passeth mine abilitie to m. the question CAREW. Endeavouring to m. between the rival Powers SWIFT.

Moderation (mǫdĕrēˈ·ʃən). late ME. [– (O)Fr. *modération* – L. *moderatio*, f. as prec.; see -ION.] **1.** The action or an act of moderating (see prec.). Now *rare* or *Obs.* **2.** The quality of being moderate; now *esp.*: avoidance of extremes; self-control, temperance; occas. clemency. late ME. **3.** *pl.* In the Univ. of Oxford, the 'First Public Examination' for the degree of B.A., conducted by the Moderators (see MODERATOR 4 a). Colloq. abbrev. MODS. 1858.

1. What is all Virtue but a M. of Excesses? SOUTH. **2.** Can you write with sufficient m., as 'tis called, when one suppresses the one half of what one feels or could say on a subject? LAMB. Phr. *In m.*: in a moderate manner or proportion.

Moderatism (mǫ·dĕrĕtiz'm). 1795. [f. MODERATE *a.* and *sb.* + -ISM.] The doctrines or policy of any of the parties known as 'Moderate'; addiction to moderate views or courses of action. So **Mo·deratist** 1716.

‖**Moderato** (mǫdĕrā·to). 1724. [It.; cf. MODERATE.] *Mus.* A direction: At a moderate pace or tempo. Abbrev. *Mod.*

Moderator (mǫ·dĕrēˈtəɹ). late ME. [– L. *moderator* ruler, director, f. *moderat-*; see MODERATE *v.*, -OR 2. Cf. Fr. *modérateur* (XV).] †**1.** A ruler, governor, director –1867. **2.** An arbiter, umpire, judge; a mediator 1560. **3.** A presiding officer or president, *esp.* (U.S.) one elected to preside over a 'town meeting' 1573. **4.** In academic use: **a.** A public officer formerly appointed to preside over the disputations prescribed in the University schools for candidates for degrees. Now (*a*) at Cambridge, one of the officers who preside over the examination for the Mathematical Tripos; (*b*) at Oxford, an examiner for Moderations. 1573. **b.** At Dublin, a candidate for the degree of B.A. who passes with first-class (Senior) or second-class (Junior) honours 1838. **5.** In the Presbyterian churches: A minister elected to preside over any one of the eccl. bodies, *e.g.* the congregation, the presbytery, etc. 1563. **6.** One who or that which makes moderate 1621. **b.** (Occas. *modérateur.*). A mechanical contrivance for regulating something, esp. the supply of oil to the wick in a lamp; also short for *m.-lamp* 1851.

4. a. As he was abroad in the schooles, so wuld neds seme a m. at home too in the haul G. HARVEY. **6.** Hope, that sweet m. of passions as Simonides calls it BURTON.

attrib., in names of certain structures exercising a regulating action, as *m.-band, -ligament.* **M.-lamp,** a lamp with a moderator (sense 6 b). Hence **Mo·deratorship,** the function, office, or position of a m. †**Moderatress,** †**Moderatrix,** a female m.

Modern (mǫ·dəɹn), *a.* and *sb.* 1500. [– (O)Fr. *moderne*, or its source late L. *modernus* (VI), f. L. *modo* just now, after L. *hodiernus* of today (f. *hodie* today).] **A.** *adj.* †**1.** Now existing –1752. **2.** Of or pertaining to the present and recent times; originating in the current age or period 1585. **b.** *Geol.* and *Zool.* Belonging to a comparatively recent period in the life-history of the world 1823. **c.** Prefixed to the name of a language to designate that form of the language that is now in use, in contrast to any earlier form. **d.** *M. languages*: (the study of) the better-known living literary languages of Europe (sometimes merely French and German) 1838. **e.** Applied (in contradistinction to *classical*) to subjects of school instruction other than the ancient languages and literature 1862. **3.** Characteristic of the present and recent times; not antiquated or obsolete 1590. †**4.** Every-day, ordinary, commonplace. (Freq. in Shaks.) 1591–1610.

2. *M. History*: history of the times subsequent to the Middle Ages. **c.** *M. English*: see ENGLISH *sb.* 1 b. **e.** Phr. *M. school, m. side*: a school or part of a school in which m. subjects are chiefly or exclusively taught. *Modern Greats* (colloq.): the honour school of philosophy, politics, and economics at the University of Oxford. **3.** He is indeed the Pattern of m. Foppery 1676. **4.** The Justice,..Full of wise sawes and moderne instances SHAKS.

B. *sb.* (Chiefly *pl.*) **1.** One who belongs to the present time or a modern epoch 1585. **2.** One whose tastes or opinions are modern 1897.

1. Some in ancient books delight; Others prefer what moderns write M. PRIOR. So **Mode·rnity. Mo·dern-ly** *adv.*, **-ness.**

Modernism (mǫ·dəɹniz'm). 1737. [f. MODERN *a.* + -ISM.] **1.** A usage expression, or peculiarity of style, etc., characteristic of modern times. **2.** Modern quality of thought, expression, workmanship, etc.; sympathy with what is modern 1830. **3.** A mode of theological inquiry according to which the Bible and the doctrines of the Church are examined in the light of 'modern thought' 1907. (Cf. MODERNIST 3.)

1. ['Its'] is a comparative m. in the language EARLE.

Modernist (mǫ·dəɹnist). 1588. [f. as prec. + -IST. Cf. mod.L. *modernista* (Luther), Fr. *moderniste.*] †**1.** A modern –1592. **2.** A supporter or follower of modern ways or methods; in the 18th c., a maintainer of the superiority of modern over ancient literature 1704. **3.** An adherent of modernism (in sense 3) 1907.

3. Applied orig. to members of the R.C.Ch. whose opinions were condemned in the encyclical *Pascendi gregis* of Pope Pius X 'de modernistarum doctrinis', 8 Sept. 1907.

Modernize (mǫ·dəɹnəiz), *v.* 1741. [– Fr. *moderniser*, f. *moderne*; see MODERN *a.*, -IZE.] **1.** *trans.* To make or render modern; to give a modern character or appearance to. **2.** *intr.* To adopt modern customs, habits, etc. (*rare*) 1753.

1. I have taken the liberty to m. the language FIELDING. The King has decided to have Windsor Castle thoroughly modernised 1901. Hence **Mo:derniza·tion** 1770. **Mo·dernizer** 1732.

Modest (mǫ·dėst), *a.* 1565. [– (O)Fr. *modeste* – L. *modestus* keeping due measure, f. **modes-* (see MODERATE *v.*) + **-tos*, pa. ppl. suffix.] †**1.** Well-conducted, orderly; not domineering –1652. **2.** Having a humble estimate of one's own merits; unobtrusive, retiring, bashful; (of actions, etc.) proceeding from or indicating these qualities 1595. **3.** Of women: Decorous in manner and conduct; not forward or lewd; 'shamefast'. Hence (in later use also of men), scrupulously chaste. 1591. **4.** Of demands, statements, estimates: Not excessive 1601. **5.** Of things: Unpretentious in appearance, style, amount, etc. 1770.

2. You are so m., that me thinks I may promise to grant it before it is asked WALTON. *fig.* Wee, m., crimson-tipped flow'r BURNS. **3.** The m. matron, and the blushing maid GOLDSM. **4.** By a m. Computation [etc.] ADDISON. **5.** The village preacher's m. mansion GOLDSM. Hence **Mo·destly** *adv.* 1548, **-ness** 1546.

Modesty (mǫ·dėsti). 1531. [– (O)Fr. *modestie* or L. *modestia*, f. *modestus* MODEST *a.*; see -Y³.] †**1.** Moderation; freedom from excess; self-control; clemency –1781. **2.** The quality of being modest (see MODEST *a.*) 1553. **3.** Womanly propriety of behaviour; scrupulous chastity of thought, speech, and conduct 1565. **b.** A kind of veil to cover the bosom. In full *m.-bit, -piece.* 1713. **4.** Unpretentious character (of things) 1906.

1. *Jul. C.* III. i. 213. **2.** An Excess of M. obstructs the Tongue ADDISON. **3.** By my modestie (the iewell in my dower) SHAKS. **4.** The m. of their homes 1906.

Modicum (mǫ·dikŏm). 1470. [– L. *modicum* little way, short time, n. sing. of *modicus* moderate, f. *modus* MODE.] **1.** A small quantity or portion (of food, money, etc.). †**2.** Applied joc. to a person of small size; also, to a woman (cf. *piece, bit*). –1632.

1. A small M. of good Wine 1725. *gen. Tr. & Cr.* II. i. 74.

Modifiable (mǫ·difəi,ăb'l), *a.* 1611. [f. MODIFY *v.* + -ABLE.] That can be modified. Hence **Mo:difiabi·lity, Mo·difiableness.**

Modification (mǫdifikēⁱ·ʃən). 1502. [– (O)Fr. *modification* or L. *modificatio*, f. *modificat-*, pa. ppl. stem of *modificari, -are*; see MODIFY *v.*, -FICATION.] **1.** The action of modifying; a limitation, restriction, qualification 1603. †**2.** *Philos.* Determination of a substance into a particular mode or modes of being. (Merged in 3.) –1837. †**b.** One of the particular forms into which a substance or entity is differentiated –1841. **3.** The action of making changes in an object without altering its essential nature; the state of being thus changed; partial alteration 1774. **4.** The result of such alteration; a modified form or variety 1669. **5.** *Scots Law.* Assessment, etc. (see MODIFY *v.* 5) 1485. **6.** *Gram.* **a.** Qualification of the sense of one word, phrase, etc. by another; an instance of this 1727. **b.** Alteration of a vowel by umlaut; an instance of this 1845.

3. Sir, a partial repeal, or..a *m.*, would have satisfied a timid, unsystematic, procrastinating Ministry BURKE. 4. All the parts of a plant..are mere modifications of a leaf 1867.

Modificative (mǫ·difikeⁱtiv), *a.* and *sb.* 1661. [– med.L. *modificativus*, f. as prec.; see -IVE, -ATIVE. Cf. Fr. *modificatif, -ive.*] **A.** *adj.* That modifies. **B.** *sb.* Something that modifies; a modifying word or clause.

Modificatory (mǫ·difikeⁱtŏri), *a.* 1824. [f. L. *modificator*; see -ORY².] Modifying; tending to modify.

Modify (mǫ·difəi), *v.* late ME. [– (O)Fr. *modifier* – L. *modificare, -ari*, f. *modus* MODE; see -FY.] †**1.** To limit, restrain; to assuage –1546. **2.** To make less severe, rigorous, or decided; to tone down. late ME. **3. a.** *Philos.* To give (an object) its particular modality or form of being 1643. †**b.** *gen.* To distinguish by investing with specific characteristics. (Merged in 4.) –1777. **4.** To make partial changes in; to alter without radical transformation 1780. **5.** *Scots Law.* To assess, award (a payment); *esp.* to determine the amount of (a parish minister's stipend) 1457. **6.** *Gram.* **a.** To qualify the sense of (a word, phrase, etc.) 1727. **b.** To change (a vowel) by umlaut 1845.

2. I..prayed hym..that he wold..modefyen his vengeaunce, and to with-drawe his Iugement 1426. Upon the whole I conceive that it would be best for the court to m. their sentence WELLINGTON. 4. The Crown must either assent to or reject bills in Parliament, but cannot m. them 1863. **Mo·difier** 1583.

Modillion (modi·lyən). 1563. [– Fr. *modillon*, †*modiglion* – It. *modiglione* :– Rom. **mutellio, -on-*, f. **mutellus*, for L. *mutulus* MUTULE.] *Arch.* A projecting bracket placed in series under the corona of the cornice in Corinthian, Composite, and Roman Ionic orders.

‖**Modiolus** (modəi·ŏlŏs). 1823. [L. *modiolus* nave of a wheel, dim. of MODIUS.] *Anat.* The conical axis around which the cochlea of the ear winds. Hence **Modi·olar** *a.*

Modish (mōᵘ·diʃ), *a.* 1660. [f. MODE + -ISH¹.] **1.** Of persons: Following the mode or prevailing fashion (usu. with a suggestion of disparagement). **2.** Of things: Conforming to the mode; also, fashionable 1663.

Very common in 17th–18th c.; now somewhat *arch.*

1. The m. Hypocrite endeavours to appear more vicious than he really is, the other kind of Hypocrite more virtuous ADDISON. 2. A good velvet cloak..and other things m. PEPYS. Hence **Mo·dish-ly** *adv.* 1665, **-ness** 1676.

‖**Modiste** (modist). 1852. [Fr., f. *mode* fashion; see MODE.] One who makes or deals in articles of fashion; a milliner, dressmaker.

‖**Modius** (mōᵘ·diŏs). *Pl.* **-ii** (-iəi). late ME. [L. *modius*, whence Fr. *muid.*] *Antiq.* **1.** A Roman corn-measure, equal to about a peck. Also, in the Middle Ages, a measure of capacity of varying size. **2.** A tall cylindrical head-dress with which certain deities are represented in ancient art 1800.

Mods (mǫdz). 1858. Colloq. abbrev. of *Moderations*; see MODERATION 4.

Modular (mǫ·diŭlăɹ), *a.* 1798. [– mod.L. *(ratio) modularis* (R. Cotes, 1722), f. L. *modulus*; see MODULUS, -AR¹.] Of or pertaining to a module or modulus.

Modulate (mǫ·diŭleⁱt), *v.* 1557. [– *modulat-*, pa. ppl. stem of L. *modulari* measure, adjust to rhythm, make melody, f. *modulus*; see MODULUS, -ATE³.] **1.** *trans.* To set or regulate; to adjust; to soften, temper, tone down 1623. **2.** *spec.* To attune (the voice, sounds, etc.) to a certain pitch or key; to vary in tone; to give tune or melody to. Const. *to*, †*unto.* 1615. **3. a.** To sing, intone (a song). **b.** *intr.* To play (*on* an instrument). *rare.* 1557. **4.** *Mus. intr.* To pass from one key *to* or *into* another. (Also said of the key.) 1721.

2. Is it credible that any person could m. her voice so artfully as to resemble so many voices? BROOME. *fig.* He [Bentley] would not stop to m. a tuneless sentence DE QUINCEY.

Modulation (mǫdiulēⁱ·ʃən). late ME. [– L. *modulatio*, f. as prec.; see -ION. Cf. (O)Fr. *modulation.*] **1.** The action of regulating, toning down, etc. (see prec. 1) 1531. **2.** The action of inflecting the voice or an instrument musically 1543. **3.** The action of singing or making music; an air or melody. Now *rare.* late ME. **4.** *Mus.* †**a.** Management of melody and harmony in a particular mode or key. Also a chord or succession of notes, an air or melody. –1797. **b.** In mod. use: The action of passing from one key to another; a change of key 1696. **5.** *transf.* Harmonious use of language in writing 1759. **6.** *Arch.* The proportioning of the parts of an order by the module 1665.

2. With the same gentle m. of voice as when he spoke to Seth GEO. ELIOT. 3. The profaner but more lively m. of *Voulez vous danser, Mademoiselle* T. L. PEACOCK. 5. The regulation of figures, the selection of words, the m. of periods JOHNSON.

Modulator (mǫ·diŭleⁱtəɹ). 1500. [f. MODULATE *v.* + -OR 2.] **1.** One who or that which modulates. **2.** A chart used in the tonic sol-fa system, showing the relations of tones and scales 1862.

Module (mǫ·diul). 1586. [– Fr. *module* or its source L. *modulus*; see next. The earliest senses show confusion of the word with MODEL.] †**1.** = MODEL *sb.* II. 2. –1681. **2.** †**a.** The plan in little of some large work. Cf. MODEL *sb.* I. 1. –1695. †**b.** = MODEL *sb.* I. 2. –1661. †**c.** *poet.* A mere image –1608. †**d.** *poet.* = MODEL *sb.* III. 1. –1598. **3.** A standard or unit for measuring 1628. **4.** *Arch.* In the classic orders, the unit of length by which the proportions of the parts are expressed; usu. the semidiameter of the column at the base of the shaft 1664.

2. c. Come, bring forth this counterfet m. SHAKS. 3. Not made..by measure or m. 1712.

‖**Modulus** (mǫ·diŭlŏs). *Pl.* **-li** (-ləi), **-luses.** 1563. [L., dim. of *modus* measure; see -ULE.] †**1.** *Arch.* = MODULE *sb.* 4. **2.** *Math.* **a.** A number by which Napierian logarithms must be multiplied in order to obtain the corresponding logarithms in another system (usu. that with base 10) 1753. **b.** A constant multiplier, coefficient, or parameter involved in a given function of a variable 1843. **c.** A measure of a quantity which depends upon two or more other quantities. In rec. use chiefly, the absolute value of a complex quantity. 1845. **3.** *Physics* and *Mech.* A constant indicating the relation between the amount of a physical effect and that of the force producing it 1807.

‖**Modus** (mōᵘ·dŏs). *Pl.* (*rare*) **modi** (mōᵘ·dəi); (in sense 3) **moduses.** 1618. [L.; see MODE.] **1.** Mode or manner of operation 1648. †**2.** *Philos.* (*m. essendi* or *existendi*) = MODE I. 6. –1679. **3.** (*m. decimandi*) A money payment in lieu of tithe 1618.

3. The spiritual person who still took his tithe-pig or his *modus* GEO. ELIOT.

Phr. (mod.L.): **m. agendi,** the mode in which a thing acts or operates; **m. operandi,** the way in which a thing, cause, etc., operates; the way in which a person goes to work; **m. vivendi,** a mode of living; i.e. a working arrangement between contending parties, pending settlement of matters in dispute.

†**Mo·dy,** *a.* 1701. [f. MODE + -Y¹.] Modish –1771.

Moe, var. Mo more; obs. f. MOW.

Moeble, obs. f. MOBILE; var. MOBLE.

Mœso-Goth (mī·sogǫþ). 1818. [– mod.L. *Mœsogothi* pl., f. L. *Mœsi* (Pliny) the people of *Mœsia* (= mod. Bulgaria and Serbia) + *Gothi*; see GOTH.] A member of the Gothic tribe that inhabited Mœsia in the 4th–5th c. A.D. So **Mœso-Gothic** (mīsogǫ·þik). [late L. *Mœsogothicus*] *a.* pertaining to the Mœso-Goths or their language; *sb.* the M. language.

Moët (mo,ę). 1841. [f. *Moët et Chandon* of Rheims.] The name of a kind of champagne.

‖**Mofette** (mofe·t). 1822. [Fr. – It. (Naples) *mofetta* = Sp. *mofeta.*] An exhalation of mephitic gas escaping from a fissure; also, a fissure from which such exhalations escape.

‖**Mofussil** (mofɒ·sil). *Anglo-Ind.* 1781. [Hindustani *mufaṣṣil* – Arab. *mufaṣṣal*, pa. pple. of *faṣṣala* divide, separate.] **1.** In India, the country as dist. from the 'Presidency'; the rural localities as dist. from the chief station. **2.** *attrib.* Rural, provincial 1836.

1. Thus if, in Calcutta, one talks of the M., he means anywhere in Bengal out of Calcutta 1886.

Mogul (mogɒ·l, mōᵘ·gɒl). 1588. [– Arab., Pers. *muġal, muġūl*, a mispronunc. of MONGOL.] **A.** *sb.* **1.** A Mongol or Mongolian; *spec.* in *Hist.* (*a*) A follower of Baber, who founded the Mongol empire in Hindustan in 1526; (*b*) a follower of Genghis Khan in the 13th c. 1601. **2.** *The Great* or *Grand M.*, also *the M.*: designation among Europeans of the emperor of Delhi, whose empire at one time included most of Hindustan; the last nominal emperor was dethroned in 1857. 1588. **b.** *transf.* A great personage; an autocratic ruler 1678. **3.** *pl.* Playing cards of the best quality; so called from the picture of the Great Mogul on the wrappers 1842.

2. b. I don't deny your sister comes the M. over us DICKENS. 3. [A case in which the plaintiff applied for an injunction to restrain the defendant from using the Great Mogul as a stamp upon his cards, was decided in 1742.]

B. *adj.* Of, pertaining or relating to, the Moguls, or the Mongol empire in India 1617.

Moguntine (mogɒ·ntin), *a.* 1641. [f. late L. *Moguntia*, ancient name of Mainz, where printing was invented by Gutenberg; see -INE¹.] Of or pertaining to Mainz in Germany; also, belonging to the art of printing.

Mohair (mōᵘ·hēəɹ). 1619 (earlier **mocayare** 1570). [ult. – Arab. *mukayyar* cloth of goat's hair, lit. 'select, choice', pa. pple. of *kayyara* choose; later assim. to *hair.* Cf. MOIRE.] **1.** Prop., a kind of fine camlet made from the hair of the Angora goat, sometimes watered. Also yarn made from this hair. Now often, an imitation of true mohair, made usu. of a mixture of wool and cotton. 1570. **2.** A garment made of such material 1673. **3.** The hair of the Angora goat 1753. †**4.** *slang.* A soldier's nickname for a civilian 1785. **5.** *attrib.*, as *m.* (*boot*)*laces.*

Mohammed (mohæ·mĕd). 1615. The name (repr. Arab. *Muḥammad*) of the founder of the Moslem religion. (See MAHOMET.)

Mohammedan (mohæ·mĕdăn). 1681. [f. prec. + -AN. Repl. older MAHOMETAN and now largely superseded by Moslem or Muslim.] **A.** *adj.* Of or relating to Mohammed, or to his doctrine. **B.** *sb.* A follower of Mohammed: one who professes Islam 1777. Hence **Moha·mmedanism** 1815, †**Moha·mmedism,** Islam 1614–1850.

‖**Moharram, mu-** (mohɒ·rŏm). 1861. [Arab. *muḥarram*, name of the first Islamic month.] **a.** The first month of the Moslem year, containing thirty days. **b.** A Shiite festival held during the first 10 days of this month.

Mohawk (mōᵘ·hǫk). Also †**Mohock,** etc. 1638. [From the native name.] **1.** One of a tribe of N. Amer. Indians, formerly supposed to be cannibals. **2.** The language of the Mohawks 1754. **3.** *Skating.* A step or stroke from any edge in one direction to the same edge on the other foot in an opposite direction 1880.

Mohican (mōᵘ·ikăn, mohī·kăn). Also **-egan.** 1766. [From the native name.] **A.**

adj. Of or pertaining to the Mohicans. **B.** *sb.* One of a warlike tribe of N. Amer. Indians of the Algonquin stock, formerly occupying the western part of Connecticut and Massachusetts. Also, the language of this tribe.

‖**Moho** (mōᵘ·ho). 1848. [Maori.] An extinct ralline bird, *Notornis mantelli*, of New Zealand.

Mohock (mōᵘ·hǫk). Also **-awk,** etc. 1711. [transf. use of *mohock* MOHAWK; now differentiated in spelling.] One of a class of aristocratic ruffians who infested the streets of London by night in the 18th c.

Mohoohoo. 1849. [Native name.] The white rhinoceros of Bechuanaland.

‖**Mohur** (mōᵘ·həɹ). 1621. [Pers. *muhr* seal, cogn. w. Skr. *mudrā* seal.] The chief gold coin of British India, worth 15 rupees.

Moider: see MOITHER.

Moidore (moi·dōᵊɹ). 1711. [– Pg. *moeda d'ouro* 'coin of gold' (*moeda* MONEY, *ouro* :– L. *aurum* gold).] A gold coin of Portugal, formerly current in England. Later, used as a name for the sum of 27*s.*, its value.

Moiety (moi·ĕti, -ĭti). 1444. [Late ME. *moite, moitie* – OFr. *moité,* (also mod.) *moitié* :– L. *medietas, -tat-*; see MEDIETY.] **1.** A half; esp. in legal or quasi-legal use. **2.** *loosely.* One of two (or more) parts into which something is divided; †one's share 1596. †**b.** *Contextually.* A small part –1650. **3.** *joc.* One's 'better half', i.e. a wife (rarely, a husband). (So Fr. *moitié.*) 1737.

1. The moitie or half pairte of the mannor 1545. **2.** The Southern and greater M. of this Island FULLER. **3.** The Lady with a skeleton m. in the old print LAMB.

Moil (moil), *sb.*[1] *arch.* and *dial.* 1612. [f. MOIL *v.*] **1.** Toil, drudgery; freq. in *toil and m.* **2.** Turmoil, confusion 1855.

1. This night his weekly m. is at an end BURNS.

Moil, *sb.*[2] 1871. [Of unkn. origin.] *Mining.* A tool for cutting ground accurately.

Moil (moil), *v.* late ME. [– OFr. *moillier* wet, moisten, paddle in mud (mod. *mouiller*) :– Rom. **molliare*, f. L. *mollis* soft.] **1.** *trans.* To wet, moisten; to soil, bedaub. *Obs.* exc. *dial.* and *arch.* †**2.** *intr.* To make oneself wet and muddy; to wallow in mire –1599. **3.** To toil, drudge; esp. in *to toil and m.* 1548. †**4.** *trans.* To weary; to harass, worry. Chiefly *pass.* –1869.

1. *fig.* Thou. . doest thy mynd in durty pleasures moyle SPENSER. **3.** To toyle and moyle for worldly drosse 1580. **4.** *refl.* But 'e tued an' moil'd 'issen deäd TENNYSON.

Moile, var. of MULE[1] and [2].

‖**Moire** (mwār, m(w)ōᵊɹ). 1660. [Fr. *moire,* later form of *mouaire* (XVII) – MOHAIR.] Orig., a kind of watered mohair; later, any watered fabric; *esp.* a watered or clouded silk. Also **M. antique.**

‖**Moiré** (mware, m(w)ōᵊ·rēⁱ). 1818. [Fr., pa. pple. of *moirer* give a watered appearance to.] **A.** *adj.* Of silk: Watered. Of metals: Having a watered or clouded appearance. 1823. **B.** *sb.* **1.** A variegated or clouded appearance like that of watered silk; esp. on metals. ¶**2.** Used erron. for MOIRE 1851.

Moist (moist), *a.* (and *sb.*) late ME. [– OFr. *moiste* (mod. *moite*), perh. :– Rom. **muscidus* mouldy, (hence) wet, alt. of L. *mucidus* (cf. MUCUS) by assoc. with *musteus* new, fresh, f. *mustum* MUST *sb.*[1]] **1.** Slightly wet; damp, humid. **b.** Of a season, climate, etc.: Wet; rainy 1481. †**2.** Of plants, fruits, etc.: 'Juicy, succulent' (J.); fresh as opp. to dried –1611. †**b.** New, not stale or worn. CHAUCER. †**3.** Yielding moisture; that brings rain or moisture; containing water, etc. –1704. †**4.** Liquid; watery –1611. **5.** Associated or connected with liquid or tears. *spec.* Of diseases, etc.: Marked by a discharge of matter, phlegm, etc. 1562. **b.** *Med.* Of sounds heard in auscultation: Suggesting the presence of liquid 1843. †**6.** *absol.* or *sb.* That which is moist; moisture. Also, moist quality. –1742.

1. Haue you not a m. eye? a dry hand?. . a white beard?. . and wil you cal your selfe yong? SHAKS. Like the red-rose bud m. with morning-dew THOMSON. **b.** One somer is softe and moyste, And another is drye and wyndy CAXTON. **2.** Nor [shall he] eate m. grapes, or dried *Num.* 6:3. **b.** A draughte of moyste and corny Ale CHAUCER. **3.** Ere twice. . M. Hesperus hath quench'd her sleepy Lampe SHAKS. **4.** The m. waies of the sea they saild CHAPMAN. **6.** Who. . Bear his swift errands over m. and dry MILT. Hence **Moi·stful** *a. rare.* 1591. **Moi·stless** *a.* 1592. **Moi·stly** *adv.* **Moi·stness.**

Moist, *v. Obs.* exc. *dial.* late ME. [f. prec.] *trans.* = MOISTEN *v.*

Now no more The iuyce of Egypts Grape shall moyst this lip SHAKS.

Moisten (moi·s'n), *v.* 1580. [f. MOIST *a.* + -EN[5].] *trans.* and *intr.* To make or become moist.

Phr. *To m. the lips, throat,* etc., with ref. to quenching thirst. *To m. one's clay* (see CLAY *sb.*). *fig.* It moistened [= softened] not his executioner's heart with any pity FULLER. Hence **Moi·stener.**

Moisture (moi·stiŭɹ, moi·stʃəɹ), *sb.* late ME. [alt., by substitution of suffix, of OFr. *moistour* (mod.Fr. *moiteur*), f. *moiste.* See MOIST *a.*, -URE.] †**1.** Moistness; the quality or state of being moist or damp –1794. **2.** Water or other liquid diffused in small quantity through air as vapour, or through a solid substance, or condensed upon a surface. late ME. †**b.** The liquid part of a body. In mediæval philosophy, the 'humours'. –1732. †**3.** Liquid in general –1741.

2. Some fell vpon a rocke, and as soone as it was sprung vp, it withered away, because it lacked m. *Luke* 8:6. Snow is not the only solid form in which atmospheric m. is precipitated HUXLEY. **b.** I cannot weepe: for all my bodies moysture Scarce serues to quench my Furnace-burning hart SHAKS. Hence †**Moi·sture** *v.* to moisten; to make wet or damp; also *intr.* 1471–1610. **Moi·stureless** *a.* 1828.

Moisty (moi·sti), *a.* late ME. [f. MOIST *a.* + -Y[1].] †**1.** Of ale: New. CHAUCER. **2.** Moist, damp: usu. coupled with *misty.*

Moither (moi·ðəɹ), *v. dial.* Also **moider.** 1674. [Of obsc. origin.] **1.** *trans.* To worry, bother, fatigue. Chiefly *pass.* and *refl.* **2.** *intr.* To talk incoherently; to wander in one's mind 1839. **3.** *intr.* To labour hard 1828.

Mokado(u)r, vars. of MUCKENDER.

Moke[1] (mōᵘk). *dial.* 1604. [Assumed sing. of *mokes* :– OE. *max* net; see MESH.] A mesh of a net. Also *pl.* wicker-work.

Moke[2] (mōᵘk). *slang* and *dial.* 1848. [prob. derived from a proper name applied to the ass.] A donkey. Also *transf.* = DONKEY 2.

‖**Mola** (mōᵘ·lă). 1601. [L.] A fleshy mass occurring in the womb; a false conception.

Molar (mōᵘ·lăɹ), *a.*[1] and *sb.* 1541. [– L. *molaris* of a mill, *sb.* millstone, grinder tooth, f. *mola* millstone; see -AR[1]. Cf. Fr. *molaire,* AFr. *dentz moellers.*] **A.** *adj.* **1.** Grinding, serving to grind; applied *spec.* to the back teeth of mammals 1626. **2.** Of or pertaining to a molar tooth 1831. **B.** *sb.* A molar or grinding tooth; a grinder 1541.

True m., a m. tooth in the adult which is not preceded by a deciduous or milk-molar. *False m.*, a m. tooth which has replaced a milk-tooth. So **Mo·lary** *a.* = A. 1. 1826.

Molar (mōᵘ·lăɹ), *a.*[2] 1862. [f. L. *moles* mass; see -AR[1].] Pertaining to mass; acting on or by means of large masses of matter. Often opp. to *molecular.*

‖**Molasse** (molas). 1796. [Fr.] *Geol.* A soft coherent greenish sandstone of Miocene age, esp. that found between the Alps and the Jura.

Molasses (molæ·sėz). (Properly *pl.*, construed as *sing.*) 1570. [– Pg. *melaço* :– late L. *mellaceum* must, subst. use of n. sing. of **mellaceus* (cf. -ACEOUS), f. L. *mel, mell-* honey.] The thick viscid syrup drained from raw sugar in the process of manufacture. In U.S. used promiscuously with *treacle.*

Our lading, which was Sugar, Dates, Almonds, and Malassos or sugar Syrrope HAKLUYT.

Mold, Mold-: see MOULD, MOULD-.

Mole (mōᵘl), *sb.*[1] [OE. *māl*, corresp. to MLG. *mēl*, OHG. *meil, meila*, Goth. **mail* :– Gmc. **mailam*, **mailō*, whence also OE. *mǣlan*, OHG. *meilen* stain.] †**1.** A discoloured spot, esp. on cloth, linen, etc. –1825. **2.** *spec.* A spot or blemish on the human skin; in mod. use, an abnormal pigmented prominence on the skin, sometimes hairy. late ME. †**b.** *fig.* A fault; a distinguishing mark –1743.

2. My father had a moale vpon his brow SHAKS.

Mole (mōᵘl), *sb.*[2] [Late ME. *molle, mulle, mole,* prob. – MDu. *mol, moll(e,* (M)LG. *mol, mul*, repr. in an early latinized Frank. form *muli* pl.] **1.** Any one of the small mammals of the family *Talpidæ*; *esp.* the common mole, *Talpa europæa*, a small animal having a velvety fur, usu. blackish, very small but not blind eyes, and very short strong fore-limbs for burrowing and excavating. **2.** *transf.* and *fig.* One who works in darkness 1601. **b.** One who sees imperfectly 1610. **3.** The borer of a mole-plough 1805. **4.** *pl.* Moleskin trousers. Also *m. trousers.* 1890. **5.** The colour of moleskin 1908.

1. While Moles the crumbled Earth in Hillocks raise GAY. As blind as a m. BENTLEY. **2.** Well said old M., can'st worke i' th' ground so fast? SHAKS.

attrib. and *Comb.*: as *m.-catcher*; **m.-cast,** a mole-hill; **-cricket,** any fossorial orthopterous insect of the genus *Gryllotalpa*; **-plough,** a plough in which a pointed iron shoe makes an underground channel resembling the track of a mole, to serve as a drain; **-rat,** (*a*) any myomorphic rodent of the family *Spalacidæ*; (*b*) *dial.* the common m.

Mole (mōᵘl), *sb.*[3] 1548. [In sense 1 – L. *moles* fem., mass. In senses 2 and 3 – Fr. *môle* masc. – L. *moles.*] †**1.** A great mass; the collective mass of any object –1711. **2.** A massive structure, esp. of stone, serving as a pier or breakwater, or joining two places separated by water. Hence, the water-area within the mole; an artificial harbour. 1548. †**3.** *Antiq.* A Roman form of mausoleum –1818.

3. The m. of Adrian GWILT.

†**Mole,** *sb.*[4] 1547. [– L. *mola* (Gr. *μύλη*).] *Antiq.* A cake made of grains of spelt coarsely ground and mixed with salt (*mola salsa*), strewn on the victims at sacrifices –1697.

Mole, *sb.*[5] 1611. [– Fr. *môle* – L. MOLA.] = MOLA.

†**Mole,** *v.* Chiefly *dial.* late ME. [f. MOLE *sb.*[1]] *trans.* To spot, stain, discolour –1818.

†**Mo·lebut.** *rare.* 1598. [– Fr. *molebout.*] The sun-fish, *Orthagoriscus mola* –1736.

Molecular (mǫle·kiŭlăɹ), *a.* 1823. [f. next + -AR[1].] Pertaining to, consisting of, or concerned with molecules; acting or inherent in the molecules of a substance. *M. heat, weight*: see the sbs. Hence **Molecula·rity, Mole·cularly** *adv.*

Molecule (mǫ·lĭkiūl, mōᵘ·lĭkiūl). 1794 (earlier in L. form, 1678–1800). [– Fr. *molécule* – mod.L. *molecula*, dim. of L. *moles* MOLE *sb.*[3]; see -CULE.] **1.** *Physics* and *Chem.* One of the minute discrete particles of which material substances are conceived to consist. In modern chemistry the molecules of any element or compound are assumed to be of uniform size and mass, representing the smallest portions into which the substance can be divided without losing its chemical identity. **2.** In pop. use: A small particle 1799.

1. A group of atoms drawn and held together by what chemists term affinity, is called a m. TYNDALL.

Mole-head. 1585. [f. MOLE *sb.*[3] + HEAD *sb.*] = PIER-HEAD.

Mo·le-hill, molehill. late ME. [f. MOLE *sb.*[2]] A small mound, or occas. a ridge, of earth thrown up by moles in burrowing.

Phr. *To make a mountain (out) of a mole-hill*: to make too much of a small difficulty or grievance.

Molendinar. 1820. [– med.L. *molendinarius*, f. *molendinum* mill. (In Glasgow pron. molĕndī·năr.)] **A.** *adj.* Of or concerning a mill or miller. **B.** *sb.* A molar tooth. SCOTT. So **Mole·ndinary** *a.* and *sb.*

Moleskin (mōᵘ·lskin). 1668. [f. MOLE *sb.*[2] + SKIN.] **1.** The skin of the mole used as a fur. **2.** A strong, soft, fine-piled cotton fustian, the surface of which is shaved before dyeing 1803. **3.** *pl.* Trousers, etc., made of moleskin (in sense 2) 1836.

Mole·st, *sb. Obs.* exc. *arch.* ME. [– OFr. *moleste*, subst. use of L. *molestus* troublesome; see next.] Trouble, injury.

Molest (mole·st), *v.* late ME. [– OFr. *molester* or L. *molestare* trouble, annoy, f. *molestus* troublesome, perh. rel. to *moles* MOLE *sb.*[3]] †**1.** *trans.* To cause trouble to; to vex, annoy, put to inconvenience –1726. †**b.** Of disease: To afflict –1696. **2.** To meddle with (a person) injuriously or with hostile intent 1494.

2. No protestant. . ought. . to be forc'd or molested for religion MILT. Hence **Mole·ster.**

Molestation (mōᵘlĕstēⁱ·ʃən, mǫl-). late ME. [– (O)Fr. *molestation* – med.L. *molestatio*, f. *molestat-*, pa. ppl. stem of L *molestare*; see prec., -ION.] **1.** The action of molesting or condition of being molested; annoyance, disturbance; †vexation. **2.** With *a* and *pl.*: A trouble, annoyance, vexation; *concr.* a cause of annoyance. Now *rare.* late ME.

Molestful (mole·stfŭl), *a.* Now *rare.* 1596. [f. MOLEST *sb.* or *v.* + -FUL.] Troublesome.

Molewarp, obs. f. MOULDWARP.

‖**Molimen** (moləi·men). *Pl.* **molimina** (moli·mină). 1865. [L., f. *moliri* make an effort.] *Phys.* and *Path.* An effort by which the system endeavours to perform any natural function, esp. *menstrual m.*, the straining to bring about the catamenia.

Molinary (mōu·linări), *a. rare.* 1774. [f. late L. *molina* mill + -ARY[1].] Of or pertaining to the grinding of corn.

Moline (moləi·n). 1562. [prob. repr. AFr. **moliné*, f. *molin* (mod. Fr. *moulin*) mill; see MILL *sb.*[1] -Y[5].] *Her.* **A.** *adj.* Of or resembling the expanded and curved extremities of a mill-rind. **B.** *sb.* = *Cross moline* 1777.

Cross m., a cross each of the arms of which terminates in two expanded and curved branches resembling the extremities of a mill-rind.

Molinism[1] (mǫ·liniz'm). 1669. [f. Luis *Molina*, a Spanish Jesuit (1535–1600) + -ISM.] The doctrine of Molina that the efficacy of grace depends simply on the will which freely accepts it. So **Mo·linist**[1] 1655.

Molinism[2] (mǫ·liniz'm). 1720. [f. Miguel de *Molinos*, a Spanish priest (1627–1696) + -ISM.] Quietism. Hence **Mo·linist**[2] 1868.

Moll (mǫl), *sb.* 1567. [Pet-form of *Mary.* Cf. MOLLY.] **1.** A female personal name. **2.** A prostitute 1604.

†**Moll,** *a. rare.* 1474. [– OFr. *mol* (mod. *mou, mol*, fem. *molle*) :– L. *mollis* soft.] **1.** Soft. CAXTON. **2.** *Mus.* In *B moll*, ♭ *moll* = flat. (Also BEMOL.) –1667.

Molla(h, var. of MULLAH.

Molleton (mǫ·lĕtǫn). 1858. [– Fr. *molleton*, f. *mollet*, dim. of *mol* (see prec.).] = SWANSKIN.

Mollify (mǫ·lifəi), *v.* late ME. [– Fr. *mollifier* or L. *mollificare*, f. *mollis* soft; see -FY.] **1.** *trans.* To render soft or supple. Now *rare.* **2.** To soften in temper or disposition; to appease. late ME. †**b.** *intr.* To become softened; to relent –1823. †**3.** To abate the violence of (passions; also heat, cold, etc.); to relieve (care) –1833. **4.** To lessen the harshness of (laws, etc.); to abate the rigour of (demands); also, to euphemize. Now *rare.* 1523.

2. I must m. him with money 1667. **4.** Now mince the Sin, And mollifie Damnation with a Phrase DRYDEN. Hence **Mo·llifiable** *a.* 1611. **Mollifica·tion.** late ME. **Mo·llifier** 1592.

‖**Mollities** (mǫli·ʃi,iz). 1604. [L., f. *mollis* soft.] †**a.** *fig.* Effeminacy. **b.** *Med.* Softening 1835.

Mollitious (mǫli·ʃəs), *a. rare.* 1646. [f. prec. + -OUS.] Luxurious, sensuous.

Mollusc, mollusk (mǫ·lŏsk). 1783. [– Fr. *mollusque* – mod.L. *mollusca*; see next.] *Nat. Hist.* An animal belonging to the Mollusca.

‖**Mollusca** (mǒlʊ·skă), *sb. pl.* 1783. [mod. L. *mollusca* (Jonston, 1650), n. pl. of L. *molluscus* (used in fem. sing. of a soft nut and in n. sing. of a fungus), f. *mollis* soft.] *Zool.* **a** Applied by Linnæus to a heterogeneous group of invertebrates, comprising the Echinoderms, Hydroids, Annelids, and naked Mollusca. **b.** Now (mainly after Cuvier), a phylum, comprising soft-bodied unsegmented animals (usu. having a hard shell) of the five classes Amphineura (chitons), Gastropoda (limpets, snails, etc.), Scaphopoda (tooth-shells), Cephalopoda (cuttlefish, etc.), and Lamellibranchia (oysters, mussels, etc.). Hence **Mollu·scan** *a.* **Mollu·scoid** *a.*; *sb.* one of the **Molluscoi·dea,** also **-oida,** a division (now discarded) comprising the Polyzoa, Brachiopoda, and Tunicata.

Molluscous (mǒlʊ·skəs), *a.* 1813. [In sense 1, f. prec. + -OUS; in sense 3 f. mod.L. *molluscum* kind of soft tumour.] Of or belonging to the Mollusca; *fig.* flabby, invertebrate.

Molly (mǫ·li). 1719. [f. MOLL *sb.* 1 + -Y[6].] **1.** (With capital M.) A familiar pet-form of *Mary*; occas. applied to a prostitute. **2.** An effeminate man or boy; a milksop. Also *Miss Molly.* 1754.

Comb. **M. cotton-tail** *U.S.* = *cotton-tail.*

Molly-coddle (mǫ·likǫd'l), *sb.* 1833. [f. MOLLY + CODDLE *v.*[2]] One who coddles himself or is coddled; an effeminate man. **Mo·lly-coddle** *v.* to coddle or cocker up 1867.

Molly Maguire (mǫ·limăgwəiə·ɹ). 1867. [See MOLLY; *Maguire* is a common Irish surname.] A member of a secret society formed in Ireland in 1843 for the purpose of resisting the payment of rent. Also *transf.* A similar society formed in the mining districts of Pennsylvania.

Moloch (mōu·lǫk). 1661. [– late L. (Vulg.) *Moloch* – Gr. Μόλοχ, Μολόχ – Heb. *mōlek*, held to be alt. of *melek* (king), by substitution after the Captivity of the vowels of *bōšet* shame.] **1.** The name of a Canaanite idol, to whom children were sacrificed as burnt offerings (*Lev.* 18:21); in Milton, one of the devils. Hence, an object to which horrible sacrifices are made. 1667. **2.** The Australian thorn-lizard or thorn-devil, *Moloch horridus*, one of the most grotesque and hideous of reptiles 1845. **3.** A Brazilian monkey, *Callithrix moloch* 1875.

1. M., horrid King besmear'd with blood Of human sacrifice, and parents tears MILT. Hence **Mo·lochize** *v.* to sacrifice as to M. TENNYSON.

Molosses, obs. f. MOLASSES.

Molossian (mǒlǫ·siăn). *Hist.* 1592. [f. L. *Molossia* = Gr. Μολοσσία, f. Gr. Μολοσσός; see -AN.] **A.** *adj.* Of or pertaining to Molossia, a country in Epirus; esp. *M. dog, hound*, a kind of mastiff 1649. **B.** *sb.* An inhabitant of Molossia.

‖**Molossus** (mǒlǫ·sǒs). Also **molo·ss** (1731). 1586. [L., = Gr. Μολοσσός Molossian used subst.; see prec.] *Prosody.* A foot of three long syllables.

Molt: see MELT *v.*; obs. f. MOULT.

Molten (mōu·lt'n), *ppl. a.* ME. [Strong pa. pple. of MELT *v.*] **1.** Liquefied by heat. (Now only of bodies that require great heat to melt them; not, e.g., of wax or ice.) **2. a.** Of metal, etc.: That has been melted (and again solidified). **b.** Of an image, etc.: Produced by melting and running into a mould.

1. I am as hot as m. Lead SHAKS. *fig.* The m. passion of Burke 1884. **2. b.** They made a m. calf COVERDALE *Exod.* 32:4. Hence **Mo·ltenly** *adv.* like what is m.

Molucca (mǒlʊ·kă). 1681. [Appears in Fr. (1522) as *Isles Moluques*, in It. (1598) as *Isole Moluche*, and in XVII Sp. and Pg. as *Maluco, islas Malucas* and *Molucas.*] The name (*the Moluccas, the M. Islands*) of a group of islands (also called the Spice Islands) situated in the Eastern Archipelago; used *attrib.* in **M. bean,** the fruit of a species of BONDUC, *Guilandina bonducella*; etc.

Moly (mōu·li). 1567. [– L. *moly* – Gr. μῶλυ, rel. to Skr. *mūlam* root.] **1.** *Myth.* A fabulous plant having a white flower and a black root, endowed with magic properties, said by Homer to have been given by Hermes to Odysseus as a charm against the sorceries of Circe. **2.** Applied to various plants supposed to be identical with the moly of Homer; *esp.* the wild garlic, *Allium moly* 1597.

Molybdate (moli·bdĕt). 1794. [f. as MOLYBDIC *a.*; see -ATE[4].] *Chem.* A salt of molybdic acid.

†**Molybdena** (mǫlibdī·nă). 1693. [– L. *molybdæna* – Gr. μολύβδαινα angler's plummet, f. μόλυβδος lead.] **a.** Applied vaguely to various salts or ores of lead. **b.** An older name for MOLYBDENITE. **c.** From c1790 to c1820 occas. used for MOLYBDENUM.

Molybdenite (moli·bdĕnəit). 1796. [f. prec. + -ITE[1] 4 b.] †**a.** *Chem.* An artificial sulphide of molybdenum. **b.** *Min.* Disulphide of molybdenum occurring in tabular bluish-grey crystals.

Molybdenum (mǫlibdī·nǒm, moli·bdĭnǒm) 1816. [mod.L., alt. of *molybdena* after the names of other elements in *-um*; cf. -IUM.] *Chem.* A metallic element (symbol Mo) occurring in combination, as in molybdenite, wulfenite, etc. When separated it is a brittle, almost infusible silver-white metal, permanent at ordinary temperatures, but rapidly oxidized by heat.

Molybdic (moli·bdik), *a.* 1796. [f. MOLYBDENA + -IC.] **a.** *Min.* Containing or derived from molybdenum. **b.** *Chem.* Applied to compounds containing molybdenum in its higher valency; esp. in *m. acid.*

Molybdite (moli·bdəit). 1868. [f. MOLYBDENA + -ITE[1] 4 b.] *Min.* Trioxide of molybdenum occurring in yellow capillary crystals or incrustations.

Molybdous (moli·bdəs), *a.* 1796. [f. MOLYBDENA + -OUS.] *Chem.* Applied to compounds into which molybdenum enters in its lower valency, as opp. to MOLYBDIC.

Mom. *U.S.* 1911. Shortened f. MOMMA.

Mome[1] (mōum). *Obs.* exc. *arch.* 1553. [Of unkn. origin.] A blockhead, dolt, fool.

Mome[2]. 1563. Anglicized f. MOMUS.

Moment (mōu·mĕnt), *sb.* ME. [– (O)Fr. *moment* – L. *momentum* (i) movement, moving power, (ii) importance, consequence, (iii) moment of time, particle :– **movimentum*, f. *movēre* MOVE; see -MENT.] **1.** A point of time, an instant. †**2.** In the 17–18th c. occas. used for SECOND –1767. †**3.** A small particle –1754. †**b.** *Math.* An infinitesimal increment or decrement of a varying quantity –1743. **4.** Importance, weight. Now only in *of* (*great, little*, etc.) *m.* 1522. †**5.** Cause or motive of action; determining influence or consideration –1691. **6.** A definite stage or turning-point in a course of events 1666. **7.** *Mech.* Applied, with qualifying words, to certain functions serving as the measure of some mechanical effect depending on two different factors 1830. **8.** One of the elements of a complex conceptual entity. (After Ger. use.) 1863.

1. We shall all be chaunged and that in a m. and in the twincklynge of an eye TINDALE 1 *Cor.* 15:52. Phr. *The m.*: occas. in pregnant sense, the fitting or favourable m. *For the m.*: so far as the near future is concerned; also, during the brief space referred to. *One m.*: ellipt. for 'wait' or 'listen one m.' *On the spur of the m.*: see SPUR. *The m.*: ellipt. for 'the m. when' or 'that'. *This m.*: used advb. for (*a*) immediately; (*b*) hardly a m. ago. *To the m.*: with exact punctuality; also, for the exact time required. **3.** *To the m.*: to the smallest detail. **4.** Things which appear at first view of little m. BURKE. **7.** *The m. of a force* or *a velocity* about a point, the product of the length of the directed line representing the force or the velocity, multiplied by the length of the perpendicular from the point. *M. of a couple*, the product of either of the two equal forces into the length of the arm. *M. of inertia* of a body about any axis, the sum of the products of the mass of each particle of the body into the square of its least distance from the axis. *M. of momentum* of a rotating body, the product of momentum into the distance from the axis. **8.** Being and not-Being are the elements or moments of Becoming FERRIER. *Comb.* **m.-axis** *Physics*, a line indicating by its length and direction respectively the m. and the direction of a couple. Hence †**Moment** *v.* to time precisely. FULLER.

Momental (mome·ntăl), *a.* 1606. [– late L. *momentalis*; see prec., -AL[1].] †**1.** Momentary –1646. **2.** *Math.* Of or pertaining to momentum, as *m. ellipse*, etc. 1877.

1. Not one momentall minute doth she swerue BRETON. Hence †**Mome·ntally** *adv.* from moment to moment; for a moment 1612–1646.

†**Momenta·neous,** *a.* 1610. [f. late L. *momentaneus* (f. *momentum* MOMENT) + -OUS.] **1.** Momentary –1801. **2.** Instantaneous –1793. **3.** Pertaining to an infinitesimal division of time 1708.

†**Momentany,** *a.* 1508. [– Fr. *momentané*, – L. *momentaneus*; see prec., -Y[5].] Pertaining to the moment; transitory; evanescent –1726.

Momentary (mōu·mĕntări), *a.* 1526. [– L. *momentarius*, f. *momentum*; see MOMENT *sb.* and -ARY[1].] **1.** Lasting but for a moment; transitory. **2.** Short-lived; ephemeral 1587. **3.** Recurring at every moment. Now *rare.* 1745. †**4.** Instantaneous –1847. †**5.** *Math.* Pertaining to an infinitesimal portion of time –1833. **6.** quasi-*adv.* POPE.

1. His Griefs are M., and his Joys Immortal STEELE. **2.** Born like a m. fly, To flutter, buzz about, and die 1762. **3.** A dealer in the fine arts in m. fear of a spunging-house 1799. Hence **Mo·mentarily** *adv.* for a moment; at every moment; †instantly 1654.

Momently (mōu·mĕntli), *adv.* 1676. [f. MOMENT *sb.* + -LY[2].] **1.** Every moment. **2.** At any moment; on the instant 1775. **3.** For a single moment 1868.

Momentous (moᵘme·ntəs), *a.* 1652. [f. MOMENT *sb.* + -OUS.] †**1.** Having motive force. **2.** Of moment; important, weighty 1656. **3.** Of persons: Having influence or importance. Now *rare.* 1667.
2. There remaineth a second objection, which is the more m. 1656. Hence **Mome·ntous-ly** *adv.*, **-ness.**

Momentum (moᵘme·ntŏm). *Pl.* **-ta.** 1699. [– L. *momentum*; see MOMENT *sb.*] †**1.** = MOMENT *sb.* 3 b. 1735. †**2.** 'Impulsive weight' (J.); force of movement –1817. †**3.** *Mech.* = MOMENT *sb.* 7. 1839. **4.** *Mech.* The 'quantity of motion' of a moving body, measured by the product of the mass into the velocity 1699. Hence, in pop. use, impetus gained by movement 1860. **5.** = MOMENT *sb.* 8. 1829.
4. *fig.* That m. of ignorance, . . presumption, and lust of plunder, which nothing has been able to resist BURKE.

Mo·mma. *U.S. colloq.* 1895. = MAMMA[1].

Mommer, etc., var. of MUMMER, etc.

‖**Momus** (mōᵘ·mŏs). Occas. *pl.* **Momi, Momusses, Momus's.** 1563. [L. *Momus*, Gr. Μῶμος, personification of μῶμος ridicule.] A Greek divinity, the god of ridicule; hence, a fault-finder, a captious critic. *A daughter, disciple, son of M.*, a wag, buffoon.

Mona (mōᵘ·nă). 1774. [– Sp., Pg., It. *mona* monkey (whence mod.L. specific name).] A small, long-tailed African monkey, *Cercopithecus mona.*

Monachal, monacal (mǫ·năkăl), *a.* 1587. [– (O)Fr. *monacal* or eccl. L. *monachalis*, f. *monachus* MONK; see -AL[1].] Of or pertaining to a monk or monastic life; monastic; monkish.

Monachism (mǫ·năkiz'm). 1577. [f. L. *monachus* MONK + -ISM.] **1.** The monastic system or principle; monasticism. †**2.** A monkish characteristic. MILT. So **Mo·nachist** *a.* favouring m.

Monacid (mǫnæ·sid), *a.* 1862. [MONO- 2.] *Chem.* Having the power of saturating one molecule of a monobasic acid.

Monad (mǫ·næd). Also †**-ade.** 1615. [– Fr. *monade* or its source late L. *monas, monad-* – Gr. μονάς, -αδ- unit, f. μόνος alone; see -AD.] **1.** The number one, unity; an arithmetical unit. Now only *Hist.* with reference to the Pythagorean or other Greek philosophies. **b.** Applied to the Deity 1642. **2.** An ultimate unit of being; an absolutely simple entity 1748.
Chiefly used with reference to the philosophy of Leibnitz (1646–1716), according to which the universe of existence consists of entities without parts, extension, or figure, and possessing, in infinitely varied degrees, the power of perception.
3. *Biol.* A hypothetical simple organism, assumed as the first term in the genealogy of living beings 1835. **4.** *Zool.* A protozoon of the genus *Monas*, or, more widely, of the order *Monadidea* or the class *Flagellata* 1836. **5.** *Chem.* An element or radical which has the combining power of one atom of hydrogen 1865. **6.** quasi-*adj.* = MONADIC 1846.
Comb. **m.-deme** (DEME[2] 2); *m. atom, element,* etc.

‖**Monadelphia** (mǫnăde·lfiă). 1753. [mod. L. (Linn., 1735), f. Gr. μόνος one + ἀδελφός brother + -IA[1].] *Bot.* The sixteenth class in the Linnæan Sexual System, comprising plants with hermaphrodite flowers having the stamens united in one bundle. Hence **Mo·nadelph,** a plant of this class. **Monade·lphian, Monade·lphous** *adjs.*

Monadic (mǫnæ·dik), *a.* 1788. [– Gr. μοναδικός composed of units, f. μονάς, μοναδ-; see MONAD, -IC.] **1.** Composed of monads or units; pertaining to or of the nature of a monad; existing singly. Also quasi-*sb.*, that which is so composed. **2.** *Chem.* Of the nature of a monad; univalent 1872. **3.** Relating to monadism 1862. **Mona·dical** *a.* in sense 1. 1642.

Monadiform (mǫnæ·difǭɹm), *a.* 1862. [f. MONAD; see -FORM.] *Biol.* Having the form of a monad.

Monadism (mǫ·nădiz'm). 1875. [f. MONAD + -ISM.] The theory of the monadic nature of matter or of substance generally; the doctrine of monads, esp. that of Leibnitz.

Monadology (mǫnădǫ·lŏdʒi). 1732. [– Fr. *monadologie* (Leibnitz); see MONAD and -LOGY.] The doctrine of monads.

Monal: see MONAUL.

Monamide (mǫ·nămɘid). 1861. [f. MON(O)- + AMIDE.] *Chem.* An amide formed by the displacement of one of the three hydrogen atoms of ammonia.

Monamine (mǫ·nămɘin). 1859. [f. as prec. + AMINE.] *Chem.* An amine formed by the exchange of one of the three hydrogen atoms of ammonia for a basic radical.

‖**Monandria** (mǫnæ·ndriă). 1753. [mod.L. (Linn., 1735), f. Gr. μόνανδρος having one husband (f. μόνος + ἀνδρ- male, taken in the sense 'stamen'); see -IA[1].] *Bot.* The first class in the Linnæan Sexual System, comprising all plants having hermaphrodite flowers with but one stamen or male organ. Hence **Mona·ndrous** *a.* 1806.

Monandry (mǫnæ·ndri). 1855. [f. MONOGAMY after *polygamy, polyandry.*] The custom of having only one husband at a time.

Monarch (mǫ·năɹk), *sb.* 1450. [– (O)Fr. *monarque* or late L. *monarcha* – Gr. μονάρχης, more freq. μόναρχος, f. μόνος alone; see MONO-, -ARCH.] **1.** Orig., a sole and absolute ruler of a state. In mod. use, a sovereign bearing the title of king, queen, emperor, or empress, or the like. (Now more or less rhet., exc. in techn. use.) **b.** *transf.* and *fig.* 1581. **2.** A very large red and black butterfly 1893.
1. He is reputed as absolute a monarch as any other in India SIR T. HERBERT. **b.** Come thou M. of the Vine, Plumpie Bacchus SHAKS. Mont Blanc is the m. of mountains BYRON. Hence **Mo·narch** *v. intr.* to act the m.: also *to m. it.*

Monarch (mǫ·naɹk), *a.* 1884. [f. Gr. μόνος single + ἀρχή beginning; cf. DIARCH.] *Bot.* Arising from only one point of origin, as the woody tissue of a root.

Monarchal (mǫ̆nā·ɹkăl), *a.* 1586. [– OFr. *monarchal* or med.L. *monarchalis*; see prec., -AL[1].] **1.** Of, belonging to, or befitting a monarch 1592. **2.** Having the status or exercising the functions of a monarch 1586. **3.** Ruled by a monarch; monarchical. Now *rare* or *Obs.* 1586.
1. Satan, whom now transcendent glory rais'd Above his fellows, with M. pride . . thus spake MILT. **3.** Nations m. and aristocratical LANDOR.

Monarchess (mǫ·năɹkės). Now *rare.* 1595. [f. MONARCH *sb.* + -ESS[1].] A female monarch.

Monarchial (mǫ̆nā·ɹkiăl), *a.* 1600. [f. MONARCH + -IAL, or MONARCHY + -AL[1]. Cf. OFr. *monarchial.*] = MONARCHAL *a.*

Monarchian (mǫ̆nā·ɹkiăn). 1765. [– late L. *monarchiani* pl. (Tertullian), f. *monarchia*; see MONARCHY, -AN.] **A.** *sb.* One of those heretics in the 2nd and 3rd centuries who denied the doctrine of the Trinity, interpreting ἡ μοναρχία τοῦ Θεοῦ 'the monarchy of God' (a current designation for monotheism), as implying this. **B.** *adj.* Of or belonging to the Monarchians or to Monarchianism 1847. Hence **Mona·rchianism,** the antitrinitarian doctrine of the Monarchians.

Monarchic (mǫ̆nā·ɹkik), *a.* 1612. [– Fr. *monarchique* or med.L. *monarchicus* (XIV) – Gr. μοναρχικός, f. μόναρχος; see MONARCH, -IC.] **1.** Of a government: Having the characteristics of monarchy. Now usu. MONARCHICAL. 1624. **2.** Of or belonging to a monarchy; favouring monarchy 1647. **3.** Of or pertaining to a monarch or monarchs. Now *rare* or *Obs.* 1612.

Monarchical (mǫ̆nā·ɹkikăl), *a.* 1576. [f. as prec.; see -ICAL.] **1.** Of the nature of a monarchy; *esp.* of government, vested in a monarch 1589. **2.** = MONARCHIC *a.* 2. 1628. **3.** = MONARCHIC *a.* 3. 1576. **4.** Having undivided rule; †autocratic 1618. Hence **Mona·rchically** *adv.*

Monarchism (mǫ·năɹkiz'm). 1838. [– Fr. *monarchisme*, f. *monarchie*; see MONARCHY, -ISM.] The principles of monarchical government; attachment to monarchy. So **Mo·narchist,** an advocate of monarchy 1647.

Monarchize (mǫ·năɹkɘiz), *v.* 1592. [f. MONARCH *sb.* + -IZE.] **1.** *intr.* To perform the office of monarch; to rule absolutely. Also *to m. it.* **2.** *trans.* †**a.** To rule over as a monarch –1621. **b.** To make a monarchy of 1660.
1. Allowing him a breath, a little Scene, To M., be fear'd, and kill with lookes SHAKS.

†**Mona·rcho.** 1588. [repr. It. *monarca* MONARCH.] **1.** The title assumed by an insane Italian who fancied himself emperor of the world; hence *transf.* –1634. **2.** Used derisively for MONARCH. Marston.

Monarchy (mǫ·năɹki). late ME. [– (O)Fr. *monarchie* – late L. *monarchia* – Gr. μοναρχία rule of one, f. μόναρχος MONARCH.] †**1.** Undivided rule by a single person; absolute power –1876. **2.** A state ruled by a monarch; also, the rule or government exercised by a monarch. late ME. **3.** Monarchical rule 1638. †**4.** The territory of a monarch (*rare*) –1699.
1. Gregory VII . . claimed the m. of the world 1876. **2.** *Absolute* or *despotic m.*, government in which the will of the monarch is absolute. *Constitutional m.* (see CONSTITUTIONAL *a.* 4). *Elective m.*, one in which the monarch is elected. *Hereditary m.*, one in which the monarch succeeds by heredity. *Limited m.* (see LIMITED). **3.** The very institution of m. was repulsive to them BUCKLE. *fig.* The M. of right Reason STEELE.

‖**Monas** (mǫ·næs). *Pl.* **monades** (mǫ·nădīz). 1568. [Gr. μονάς; see MONAD.] = MONAD.

Monasterial (mǫnăstīᵊ·riăl), *a.* late ME. [– late and med.L. *monasterialis*, f. eccl. L. *monasterium*; see next, -AL[1].] Belonging to or of the nature of a monastery. Hence **Monaste·rially** *adv.* like a monk.

Monastery (mǫ·năstəri). late ME. [– eccl. L. *monasterium* (IV) – eccl. Gr. μοναστήριον, f. Gr. μονάζειν live alone, f. μόνος alone.] A place of residence of a community (now almost exclusively, of monks) living secluded from the world under religious vows.

Monastic (mǫ̆næ·stik), *a.* (and *sb.*). 1600. [– (O)Fr. *monastique* or late L. *monasticus* – Gr. μοναστικός, f. μονάζειν; see prec., -IC.] **1.** Pertaining to or characteristic of monks, nuns, friars, and the like, or monasteries. **2.** *Bookbinding.* Epithet of a method of finishing by tooling without gold; = 'antique' 1880. **3.** *sb.* A member of a monastic order; a monk 1632.
1. To forsweare the ful stream of yᵉ world, and to liue in a nooke meerly Monastick SHAKS. So **Mona·stical** *a.* pertaining to m. life. late ME.; **-ly** *adv.*

Monasticism (mǫnæ·stisiz'm). 1795. [f. MONASTIC + -ISM.] The monastic system.

Monatomic (mǫnătǫ·mik), *a.* 1848. [f. MON(O)- + ATOM + -IC.] *Chem.* Containing one atom; consisting of molecules each containing one atom. Also used for: Univalent. So **Mona·tomism,** m. quality or condition.

Monaul (mǫnǭ·l). Also **monal, minaul,** etc. 1769. [Hind. *munāl* or *monāl.*] Anglo-Indian name for the Impeyan pheasant.

Monaxial (mǫnæ·ksiăl), *a.* 1880. [f. MON(O)- + L. *axis* + -AL[1], after AXIAL.] *Bot.* and *Zool.* Having only one axis; developing along a single line.

Monazite (mǫ·năzɘit). 1836. [– G. *monazit* (Breithaupt, 1829), f. Gr. μονάζειν be solitary, on account of its rarity; see -ITE[1] 2 b.] *Min.* Phosphate of the cerium metals, found in reddish or brownish crystals.

‖**Mondaine** (mondẹn). 1908. [Fr.; cf. MUNDANE.] A woman belonging to the world of fashion.

Monday (mɒ·ndeⁱ, -di). [OE. *mōnandæġ*, corresp. to OFris. *mōne(n)dei*, MLG., MDu. *mān(en)dach* (Du. *maandag*), OHG. *mānatag* (G. *Montag*), ON. *mánadagr*; f. MOON + DAY, tr. late L. *lunæ dies* 'day of the moon' (after Gr. ἡμέρα Σελήνης), of which the var. *lunis dies* gave OFr. *lunsdis* (mod. *lundi*).] The second day of the week.
But soft What day is this? M., my Lord SHAKS. **Black M.,** (*a*) a name for Easter M.; (*b*) *school slang*, the first school-day after a vacation. **Saint M.,** used with reference to the practice among workmen of being idle on M., as a consequence of drunkenness on Sunday; chiefly in *to keep Saint M.* 1753. Hence **Mo·ndayish** *a.* affected with the indisposition, often felt by clergymen on Monday, resulting from Sunday's work 1804.

‖**Monde** (mõnd). 1765. [Fr., = 'world'. Cf. BEAU-MONDE.] The world of fashionable people; society. Also, the set in which one moves.

Mondial (mǫ·ndiăl), *a.* 1918. [– Fr. *mondial* – eccl. L. *mundialis* (Tertullian), f. *mundus* world; see -IAL.] World-wide.

Mone, obs. f. MOAN, MOON.

Monest, obs. f. MONISH *v.*

Monetary (mɒ·nĭtări, mǫ·n-), *a.* 1802. [– Fr. *monétaire* or late L. *monetarius*, f. L. *moneta* MINT *sb.*¹; see -ARY¹.] **1.** Of or pertaining to the coinage or currency. **2.** Pertaining to or concerned with money, pecuniary 1860.

1. *M. unit*, the standard unit of value of a country's coinage. **2.** Deep in great m. transactions 1865.

Moneth(e, obs. ff. MONTH.

Monetize (mɒ·nĭtəiz, mǫ·n-), *v.* 1880. [– Fr. *monétiser*, f. L. *moneta*; see next, -IZE.] *trans.* To give a standard value to (a metal) in the coinage of a country; to put into circulation as money. So **Monetiza·tion** 1864.

Money (mɒ·ni), *sb. Pl.* **moneys** (mɒ·niz). [ME. *money(e, -ei(e, mone* – OFr. *moneie* (mod. *monnaie* change) :– L. *moneta* mint (in Rome), money, orig. epithet of Juno, in whose temple (also so named) the mint was housed.] **1.** Current coin; metal stamped in pieces as a medium of exchange and measure of value. **b.** Hence, anything serving the same purposes as coin. late ME. **c.** In mod. use applied indifferently to coin and to such promissory documents representing coin (esp. bank-notes) as are currently accepted as a medium of exchange. See PAPER MONEY. 1819. **2.** (With *pl.*) A particular coin or coinage. Also, a denomination of value representing a fraction or a multiple of the value of some coin; in full, *money of account*. late ME. **3.** Coin in reference to its purchasing power; hence, possessions or property viewed as convertible into money ME. **b.** as a commodity in the market 1687. **4.** *pl.* Prop. = 'sums of money', but often = the sing. (sense 3). Now chiefly in legal or quasi-legal use, or as an archaism. late ME.

1. I will giue thee the worth of it in m. 1 *Kings* 21:2. *fig.* Words are wise mens counters, they do but reckon by them: but they are the mony of fooles HOBBES. †*White m.*: standard silver coin. **c.** In international commerce..a good bill [*sc.* of exchange] is good m. 1903. **3.** Wealth and m... are, in common language, considered as in every respect synonymous ADAM SMITH. **b.** The value of m. must be judged, like every thing else, from it's rate at market BURKE. **4.** You come to me, and you say, Shylocke, we would haue moneyes SHAKS. From Shaks. onwards the use of the pl. for the sing. has been attributed to Jews, whose pronunc. is sometimes ridiculed by the spelling 'monish'.

Phrases. *M. makes the mare to go*; *m. is the sinews of war*; *time is m.*; etc. *For love or m.*: see LOVE *sb.* (*So and so*) *for my m.* (colloq.) = 'is what I desire or like', 'is my choice', 'give me..'. *To make m.*: to acquire or earn m. *To coin m.*: to make m. rapidly. (*It is*) *not everybody's* or *every man's m.*: not what everybody would find worth its price. *There is m. in* (*something*): m. can be made out of it.

attrib. and *Comb.*: **m.-bill**, a bill in Parliament for granting supplies; **-broker**, a money-dealer; **-clause**, a clause (in a parliamentary bill) for granting supplies; **-column**, (*a*) a portion of a page marked off by vertically ruled lines for figures denoting sums of money; (*b*) the column of a newspaper devoted to the money-market; **-dealer**, one who deals in m. in the way of exchange, banking, lending, etc.; so **-dealing** *vbl. sb.*; **-jobber**, a dealer in m. or coin; **-market**, the sphere of operation of the dealers in loans, stocks, and shares; **-monger**, a dealer in money, esp. in the way of lending it; hence **-mongering**, †**-monging** *vbl. sb.* and *ppl. a.*; **-order**, an order for payment of a specified sum, issued at one post-office and payable at another (in British use restricted to what is pop. called a *post-office order*, as dist. from a *postal order*); †**-scrivener**, one whose business it is to raise loans, put money out at interest, etc., on behalf of his clients; **-spider** = next (*a*); also, a spider of the genus *Salticus*; **-spinner**, (*a*) a small spider, *Aranea scenica*, supposed to bring good luck in money or other matters to the person over whom it crawls; (*b*) one who makes great sums by speculation or usury.

Money (mɒ·ni), *v.* late ME. [In sense 1 – Fr. *monnayer*; in other senses f. MONEY *sb.*] **1.** *trans.* To coin or mint (money). *rare.* †**2.** To supply with money; hence, to bribe –1625. **3.** To dispose of for money (*rare*) 1611.

Mo·neyage. *Hist.* 1747. [– Fr. *monnayage* (OFr. *moneage*), f. *monnayer* MONEY *v.*; see -AGE.] 'A payment by the moneyers for the privilege of coining; otherwise explained as a payment by the subjects to prevent loss by the depreciation or change of coinage' (Stubbs).

Mo·ney-bag. 1565. **1.** A bag for holding money. In pl. often joc. for 'wealth'. **2.** *transf. pl.* A person notable as having or loving money 1818.

Mo·ney-bound, *a. joc.* 1825. [After *weather-bound*.] Detained by want of money.

Mo·ney-box. 1585. A box for money; *esp.* a closed box into which coin is dropped through a slit.

Mo·ney-cha:nger. late ME. One whose business it is to change money at a fixed rate.

Moneyed (mɒ·nid), *a.* Also **monied.** 1457. [f. MONEY *sb.* + -ED².] **1.** Having money, rich in money. *M. man* often *spec.* = CAPITALIST. **2.** Consisting of money, derived from money 1790. **3.** *M. interest*: interest in money as a possession; a class of persons having such interest. (Cf. *landed interest.*) 1711. **4.** *U.S.* Of a company, etc.: Having power to deal in money 1872.

1. The monied men and leaders of commerce RUSKIN. **2.** The monied resources of the State 1835.

Moneyer (mɒ·niəɹ). ME. [– OFr. *mon(n)ier, -oier* (mod. *monnayeur*) :– late L. *monetarius*; see MINTER.] †**1. a.** A money-changer. ME. only. **b.** A money-dealer, banker, capitalist 1706. **2.** One who coins money; a minter. Now chiefly *Hist.* late ME.

2. The Provost and Company of Moneyers 1668.

Mo·ney-grub. 1768. [Cf. GRUB *sb.*] One who is sordidly intent on amassing money. So **Mo·ney-gru:bber. Mo·ney-gru:bbing** *vbl. sb.* and *ppl. a.*

Mo·ney-lender. *c* 1780. One whose business is lending money at interest. So **Mo·ney-lending** *vbl. sb.* and *ppl. a.*

Moneyless (mɒ·nilės), *a.* ME. [-LESS.] Without money.

Mo·ney-ma:ker. late ME. †**1.** A minter, moneyer –1523. **2.** One who gains and accumulates money; one intent on getting money 1864. So **Mo·ney-making** *vbl. sb.* acquisition of wealth; *ppl. a.* occupied in, or intent on, acquiring wealth; also (of things) lucrative.

Money matter. 1552. [MATTER *sb.* IV. 3.] An affair turning upon money. Chiefly *pl.*, the financial side of things.

Money's-worth. 1588. [WORTH *sb.*] **1.** Something recognized as worth money or equivalent to money 1604. **2.** Full value for money paid or to be paid. (Now chiefly with poss. pron.)

Mo·ney-wort. 1578. [After the old L. name *Nummularia*.] The plant *Lysimachia nummularia* or Herb Twopence, which has roundish glossy leaves. Also, a book-name for *Anagallis tenella* and other plants.

Mongcorn (mɒ·ŋkǫɹn). *Obs.* exc. *dial.* ME. [f. ME. *mong* mixture + CORN *sb.*¹] 'Mixed corn' = MASLIN².

Monger (mɒ·ŋgəɹ). [OE. *mangere* (= OHG., ON. *mangari*) agent-n., f. *mangian* (= OS. *mangon*, ON. *manga*) :– Gmc. **manʒōjan*, f. L. *mango* dealer, trader; see -ER¹.] A dealer, trader, trafficker. Now *rare*, exc. as the second element in compounds, as *cheesemonger, fishmonger, ironmonger*. Since 16th c., chiefly, one who carries on a petty or disreputable traffic, as *fashion-m., mass-m., news-m., scandal-m.*, etc.

Mongering (mɒ·ŋgəriŋ), *vbl. sb.* 1846. [f. MONGER + -ING¹.] Trading, trafficking. Chiefly used as a second element in compounds. So **Mo·ngering** *ppl. a.*, **Mo·ngery.**

Mongol (mǫ·ŋgǫl). 1738. [Native name, said to be f. *mong* 'brave'. Cf. MOGUL.] **A.** *sb.* One of an Asiatic race now chiefly inhabiting Mongolia, between China proper and Siberia; also more widely, a Mongolian. **B.** *adj.* Pertaining to or characteristic of the Mongols, their country, or language; Mongolian 1763.

Mongolian (mǫŋgōᵘ·liăn). 1738. [f. MONGOL + -IAN.] **A.** *adj.* **1.** = MONGOL *a.* **2.** *Anthropology.* Belonging to the yellow-skinned straight-haired type of mankind 1828. **3.** Applied to a type of idiot resembling the Mongols in physiognomy 1892. **B.** *sb.* A native of Mongolia; the language of the Mongols; one of the Mongolian race of mankind (see A. 2) 1846. So **Mongo·lic** *a.* and *sb.* 1834.

Mongoloid (mǫ·ŋgǫloid), *a.* (and *sb.*) 1868. [f. MONGOL + -OID.] **1.** Belonging to that one of the five principal races of mankind which prevails over the vast region lying east of a line drawn from Lapland to Siam. HUXLEY. **2.** = MONGOLIAN *a.* 3. 1899. **3.** *sb.* One of the Mongoloid race 1868.

Mongoose, mungoose (mǫ·ŋgūs, mɒ·ŋgūs). 1698. [– Marathi *mangūs*.] **1.** An ichneumon, *Herpestes griseus*, common in India, and able to kill venomous snakes unharmed. Also applied to other ichneumons (subfamily *Herpestinæ*). **2.** A species of lemur or maki, *Lemur mongoz* 1758.

Mongrel (mɒ·ngrĕl), *sb.* and *a.* 1486 (**mengrell**). [app. f. base **menʒ-* **manʒ-* **monʒ-* mix (see MENG *v.*) + -REL.] **A.** *sb.* **1.** A dog of no definable breed, resulting from various crossings. †**b.** Applied to persons as a term of contempt. (Cf. *cur.*) –1764. **2.** An animal or plant resulting from the crossing of different breeds or kinds; restricted by some to the result of the crossing of varieties (opp. to *hybrid*) 1677. **3.** A person not of pure race. Chiefly *disparaging*. 1542.

2. The parents of mongrels are varieties, and mostly domestic varieties DARWIN. *fig.* Though his two faculties of Serving-man and Solliciter, should compound into one m. MILT.

B. *adj.* (the sb. used attrib. and appositively). **1.** Of dogs: That is a mongrel 1576. **b.** As an abusive epithet for a person 1605. **2.** In wider use, of animals and plants 1635. **3.** Of persons: Of mixed race. Chiefly *disparaging*. 1606. **4.** *transf.* That is 'neither one thing nor the other'. Chiefly *contempt.* 1581. **b.** Applied to a word or a dialect 1610.

1. b. A Knaue, a Rascall,..and the Sonne and Heire of a Mungrill Bitch SHAKS. **4.** These Mungrell Pamphlets (part true, part false) FULLER. Hence **Mo·ngrelism,** the condition of being m. or hybrid. **Mo·ngrelize** *trans.* to make m. in race, etc.

'Mongst (mɒŋst), *prep. poet.* 1590. Aphet. f. AMONGST.

Monial (mōᵘ·niăl). ME. [– OFr. *moinel* (mod. *meneau*), subst. use of *moi(e)nel* adj. middle, f. *moien* (see MEAN *a.*²) + *-el* -AL¹.] *Arch.* Now *Antiq.* A mullion.

Monied, var. of MONEYED.

Monilated (mǫnileⁱ·tėd), *ppl. a.* 1877. [f. L. *monile* necklace + -ATE² + -ED¹.] *Anat.* = next.

Moniliform (mǫni·lifǭɹm), *a.* 1802. [– Fr. *moniliforme*, or – mod.L. *moniliformis*, f. L. *monile* necklace; see -FORM.] Of the form of a necklace; having contractions at regular intervals; consisting of protuberances suggesting a string of beads.

Moniment, obs. f. MONUMENT.

Monish (mǫ·niʃ), *v.* ME. Now *rare.* [– OFr. *monester*, aphet. f. *amonester*; see ADMONISH.] To admonish. Hence **Mo·nisher. Mo·nishment** (*arch.*).

Monism (mǫ·niz'm). 1862. [– mod.L. *monismus*, f. Gr. μόνος single; see MONO-, -ISM.] *Philos.* **a.** The doctrine that only one being exists. **b.** A general name for those theories which deny the duality (i.e. the existence as two ultimate kinds of substance) of matter and mind 1876. **c.** The doctrine that there is only one Supreme Being, as opp. to the belief in a Good and an Evil Principle as co-ordinate powers 1872.

b. Thus materialism and idealism or spiritualism are both species of m.; the name, however, is often applied specifically to a third variety, viz. the doctrine that physical and psychical phenomena are alike manifestations of a reality which cannot be identified with either matter or mind. O.E.D. So **Mo·nist,** one who holds a doctrine of m. (in any sense) 1836. **Moni·stic** *a.*, **Moni·stically** *adv.*

Monition (mŏni·ʃən). late ME. [– (O)Fr. *monition* – L. *monitio, -on-*, f. *monit-*, pa. ppl. stem of *monēre* advise, warn; see -ION, -ITION.] **1.** †**a.** Instruction. **b.** Warning. Also, a warning. **2.** A warning of the presence or imminence of something (now only, of some impending danger). late ME. **3.** An official or legal intimation or notice 1460. **b.** A formal notice from a bishop or an eccl. court admonishing a person to refrain from a specified offence 1509. **c.** In those courts which use the civil law process, a process in the nature of a summons 1840.

1. Sage monitions from his friends His talents to employ for nobler ends SWIFT. 2. The first monitions of the impending catastrophe occurred in 63 A.D. 1906. Hence **Moni·tion** *v. Eccl. Law.*, to warn by a m.

Monitor (mǫ·nitǫ̆ɹ), *sb.* 1546. [– L. *monitor*, f. as prec.; see -OR 2.] **1.** One who (or that which) admonishes another as to his conduct. Now somewhat *arch.* †Also (*rare*), an instigator. 1596. **2.** A senior pupil in a school, with special duties, esp. that of keeping order, and occas. of acting as teacher to a junior class 1546. **3.** Something that reminds or gives warning 1655. **†4.** = BACK-BOARD 4. –1831. **5.** A lizard of the family *Monitoridæ* or *Varanidæ*, inhabiting Africa and Australia, supposed to give warning of the vicinity of crocodiles 1826. **6.** An ironclad having a very low freeboard and one or more revolving turrets containing great guns; so called from the name given by Captain Ericsson, its inventor, to the first vessel of the sort 1862. **7.** *U.S.* (In full *m. roof* or *top.*) A raised part of a roof (e.g. in a railway-carriage), with openings for light and ventilation. Hence *m.-car.* 1871. **8.** A jointed nozzle used in hydraulic mining, which may be turned in any direction 1881.

1. In this [*sc.* religion] you need not be a M. to the King BACON. Conscience, this once able m.,—placed on high as a judge within us STERNE. Hence **Mo·nitor** *v. trans.* to guide as a m. KEATS. **Monito·rial** *a.* monitory; of, pertaining to, or performed by monitors in schools. **Monito·rially** *adv.* **Mo·nitorship. Mo·nitress,** a female m.

Monitory (mǫ·nitəri). 1450. [– L. *monitorius*, f. as prec.; see -ORY[2].] **A.** *adj.* **1.** Giving or conveying a warning; admonitory. **b.** *M. letter* = B. 2. 1696. **2.** *M. lizard* = MONITOR *sb.* 5. 1810. **B.** *sb.* **†1.** An admonition –1677. **2.** A letter containing an admonition or warning, esp. one issued by a bishop or pope 1624.

A. 1. He heard the m. growl [of a mastiff] WORDSW.

Monk (mɒŋk). [OE. *munuc* = OFris. *munek*, OS. *munik* (Du. *monnik*), OHG. *munih* (G. *mönch*), ON. *múnkr*; Gmc. – pop. L. **monicus*, for late L. *monachus* (cf. **monisterium* MINSTER) – late Gr. μόναχος, subst. use of adj. 'single, solitary', f. μόνος alone.] **1.** A member of a community of men living apart from the world under vows of poverty, chastity, and obedience, according to a rule. (Cf. *friar.*) **2.** As the name of certain animals, esp. with reference to the cowl or hood of a monk; see also SEA-MONK 1713. **3.** As the name of various objects in certain arts and crafts 1683.

1. Black m., a Benedictine; also, a Black or Augustinian canon; **†gray m., white m.,** a Cistercian m. But all Hoods, make not Monkes SHAKS. The object of a m. was to make a good man of himself, the object of a friar was to do a good work among others 1889. **2.** *Tropidorhynchus Corniculatus*..Its bare head and neck have also suggested the names of 'Friar Bird', 'Monk', 'Leather Head', etc. J. GOULD. **3.** The Sheet Printed on has a black blotch on it: Which Blotch is called a M. MOXON. A round-faced pestle, called a M. 1763. The piece of agarick used to communicate the fire to the powder is called the m. 1834.

Comb.: **m.-bat,** the *Molossus nasutus* of Jamaica, etc.; **M.-Latin,** the corrupt Latin used by monks; **m.-seal,** a white-bellied seal inhabiting the Mediterranean; **m.'s rhubarb,** a species of dock, esp. *Rumex patientia* and *R. alpinus.*

Monkdom (mɒ·ŋkdəm). 1862. [f. prec. + -DOM.] The condition of a monk; monks collectively; the domain of monks.

Monkery (mɒ·ŋkəri). Chiefly *contempt.* 1536. [f. MONK + -ERY.] **1.** The state, condition, or profession of monks; monastic life, monasticism. **2. a.** A body of monks; a monastery 1549. **b.** Monks collectively; also, the monks (of a particular place) 1552. **3.** *pl.* Monkish practices or paraphernalia 1624. **4.** Conduct or practice characteristic of monks (esp. in the Middle Ages) 1649.

1. You quote not one line from any Father in the third century, in favour of m. WESLEY. **2. a.** A long residence..in courts, monkeries, and barracks 1852.

Monkey (mɒ·ŋki), *sb.* *Pl.* **†monkies, monkeys.** 1530. [Of unkn. origin; a possible source has been suggested in LG. **moneke*, dim. of Rom. **monno, -a*, repr. by Fr. *†monne*, It. *monna*, Sp., Pg. *mono, -a*, which has been referred to Turk. *maymun* ape.] **I. 1.** An animal of any species of the group of mammals closely allied to and resembling man, and ranging from the anthropoid apes to the marmosets; any animal of the order *Primates* except man and the lemurs. In a more restricted sense, the term is taken to exclude the anthropoid apes and the baboons. **2.** *transf.* **a.** One who resembles a monkey; *esp.* a mimic 1589. **b.** A term of playful contempt, chiefly of young people 1604. **3. a.** A young hare. *dial.* **b.** A sheep. *Australian.* 1881.

1. His Monkie..tore his Principall Note-Booke all to pieces, when by chance it lay forth BACON. *Howling m.*, a m. of the genus *Mycetes.* **2. b.** Well, little monkeys mine, I must go write; and so good-night SWIFT.

II. †1. A kind of gun or cannon –1663. **2.** A machine consisting of a heavy hammer or ram working vertically in a groove and used in pile-driving, etc. Also, the ram itself and the hook by which it is raised. 1750. **3.** Applied to various receptacles for liquor; *esp.* a globular earthenware water-vessel with a straight upright neck 1834. **4.** *Betting-slang.* £500; in America, $500. 1832.

Phrases (colloq. and slang). *To suck* (or *sup*) *the m.*: (*a*) to drink from the bottle; hence, to tipple; (*b*) to drink out of a cocoa-nut emptied of milk and filled with spirit; (*c*) to drink spirits from a cask through a straw or tube inserted in a small hole. *My monkey's up*: I am angry or enraged. So *to get one's m. up, to put* (a person's) *m. up.*

attrib. and *Comb.*: **m.-block,** 'a small single block strapped with a swivel; also, those nailed on the topsail-yards of some merchantmen, to lead the bunt-lines through' (Smyth); **-board,** a footboard at the back of a vehicle for a footman or conductor to stand on; **-boat,** (*a*) a small boat used in docks and on the Thames; **-engine,** a pile-driver having a ram moving in a wooden frame; **-gaff** *U.S.*, a small gaff on some large merchant-vessels, placed above the spanker-gaff; **-jacket,** a short close-fitting jacket, such as is worn by sailors; **-rail,** a supplementary rail above the quarter-rail; **-shines** *pl., U.S. slang*, monkey-like tricks or antics; **monkey('s)-tail,** a short iron bar used in training naval guns; a lanyard attached to the end of a lever; **m. tricks,** mischievous tricks 1780; **-wrench,** a wrench or spanner having a movable jaw.

b. m.-bread, the fruit of the baobab tree; also, the tree; **-cup,** the pitcher-plant, genus *Nepenthes*; **-flower,** the genus *Mimulus*; **m. nut,** a name for the pea-nut, *Arachis hypogæa*; **-puzzle,** the puzzle-monkey, *Araucaria imbricata.*

Mo·nkey, *v.* 1859. [f. prec.] **1.** *trans.* **a.** To ape the manners of, mimic. **b.** To mock, make a jest of. **2.** *intr.* To play mischievous or foolish tricks 1886.

Mo·nkey-face. 1598. A (human) face like a monkey's. So **Mo·nkey-faced** *a.*

Monkeyfy (mɒ·ŋkifəi), *v.* Also **†monkify.** 1761. [f. MONKEY *sb.* + -FY.] To make like a monkey; to make ridiculous-looking.

Monkeyish (mɒ·ŋkiˌiʃ), *a.* 1621. [f. MONKEY *sb.* + -ISH[1].] Like a monkey in imitativeness or mischievousness. **Mo·nkeyishness.**

Mo·nkeyism. 1845. [f. MONKEY *sb.* + -ISM.] Monkey-like character or behaviour.

Mo·nkey-pot. Also **monkey's pot. 1.** The woody seed-vessel of the Brazilian tree *Lecythis ollaria*; the tree itself. **2.** A vessel used in tropical countries for cooling water 1897.

†Monkeyro·ny. 1773. Alteration of MACARONI (sense 2) –1786.

Mo·nk-fish. 1610. [f. MONK.] **1.** The Angel-fish, *Squatina angelus.* **2.** The Angler, *Lophius piscatorius* 1666.

Monkhood (mɒ·ŋkhud). OE. [f. MONK + -HOOD.] The state or profession of a monk; monasticism; monks collectively.

Monkish (mɒ·ŋkiʃ), *a.* 1546. [f. MONK + -ISH[1].] **1.** Of or belonging to monks; monastic. **b.** That is a monk 1697. **c.** Used or done by monks 1612. **2.** Resembling a monk or what pertains to a monk 1577. **3.** Characteristic of monks or the monastic system. Chiefly *depreciatory.* 1570.

1. b. An old M. author 1697. **c.** M. Latin 1761. **2.** A thinne lippe, and a little m. eye 1602. Hence **Mo·nkishness.**

Monkly (mɒ·ŋkli), *a.* Now *rare.* OE. [f. MONK + -LY[1].] Of or pertaining to a monk or monks; monastic.

Monkship (mɒ·ŋkʃip). 1620. [f. MONK + -SHIP.] The monastic system; monks collectively. With *poss. pron.* The personality of a monk.

Monk's-hood, monkshood (mɒ·ŋkshud). 1578. [From likeness of form.] **1.** A plant of the genus *Aconitum*, esp. *A. napellus.* **2.** Applied to species of the genus *Delphinium* (Larkspur) and to *Dielytra cucullaria* 1597.

Monmouth (mɒ·n-, mǫ·nməþ). *Hist.* 1599. The name of an English county town (formerly regarded as part of Wales), used *attrib.* **1.** *M. cap*: a flat round cap formerly worn by soldiers and sailors. **2.** *M. cock*: a military 'cock' of the hat 1711–1769.

1. The Welchmen..wearing Leekes in their M. caps SHAKS.

Mono- (mǫno, mǫ̆nǫ·), bef. a vowel often **mon-**, repr. Gr. μονο-, comb. f. μόνος alone, only, single, occurring in a number of words adopted from existing Greek compounds (as MONARCH, MONOGAMY, MONOPOLY), and hence used to form words independently of a Greek original. In recent formations *mono-* is often combined (instead of UNI-) with a Latin element, and occas. prefixed to an English word. Many of these words have correlatives in DI- *pref.*[2], TRI-, POLY-, etc.

1. General words: **Monoca·rdian** [Gr. καρδία] *a.*, having a single auricle and ventricle to the heart, as fishes and reptiles. **Monoci·liate(d** *adjs.*, *Zool.* having a single cilium. **Monoco·ndylar, -condy·lian, -condy·lic** [Gr. μονοκόνδυλος] *adjs.*, *Zool.* having one occipital condyle, as the skull of birds and reptiles. **Monocro·tic, Mono·crotous** [Gr. κρότος beat] *adjs.*, *Phys.* of a pulse, having a single beat, not DICROTIC. **Mo·nocyst** *Path.* a tumour consisting of a single cyst. **Monoda·ctyl(e, Monoda·ctylous** [Gr. δάκτυλος finger] *adjs.*, *Zool.* having only one finger, toe, or claw; in Crustacea = SUBCHELATE. **Monoga·stric** [Gr. γαστήρ stomach] *a.*, *Anat.* having only one stomach or digestive cavity. **Mo:noïde·ism,** concentration of the mind upon one idea; esp. as a form of monomania. **Mono·latry,** worship of one out of many gods. **Monomeni·scous** *a.*, applied to those eyes, in invertebrates, that have only one lens. **Mono·merous** [Gr. μέρος part] *a.* *Entom.* consisting of only one member or joint; *Bot.* applied to flowers having one member in each whorl. **Monope·talous** *a.*, of a flower, having the corolla in one piece or the petals united so as to form a tube. **Mo·nophase** *a.*, *Electr.* exhibiting a single phase. **Monophyle·tic** [Gr. φυλετικός, f. φυλέτης tribesman] *a.*, pertaining to one family or race or to descent from a single prototypal form. **Monophy·llous** [Gr. φύλλον leaf] *a.*, of a calyx, consisting of one leaf. **Monophy·odont** [Gr. φύειν to generate + ὀδούς, ὀδοντ- tooth] *a.*, having only one set of teeth. **Mo·noplast, -plastid** [Gr. πλαστός formed], *Biol.* a single or simple cell; an organism or stage of an organism consisting of such; hence **Monopla·stic** *a.* ||**Monople·gia** [Gr. πληγή stroke], *Path.* paralysis of one part or limb only; hence **Monople·gic** *a.* **Mono·pody** [Gr. πούς, ποδ- foot], *Pros.* a measure consisting of a single foot. **Monopo·lylogue** [POLY- + -LOGUE], an entertainment in which one actor sustains many characters. **Monopsy·chism** [Gr. ψυχή soul], the theory that all souls are one; the unity of souls thus asserted. **Monopyre·nous** [Gr. πυρήν fruit-stone] *a.*, *Bot.* having but one stone or kernel; said of fruits. **Mo·norail,** a railway with carriages running on a single rail. **Monose·palous** *a.*, *Bot.* prop., having one lateral sepal only; but misused for *gamosepalous.* **Monosi·phonous** *a.*, *Bot.* having a single siphon; applied to certain Algæ. **Monospe·rmous** [Gr. σπέρμα] *a.*, *Bot.* having only one seed. **Mono·stichous** [Gr. στίχος row] *a.*, *Zool.* consisting of a single layer or row. **Mo·nostyle** [Gr. στῦλος pillar], *Arch.* having or consisting of a single shaft, pillar, or column; so **Monosty·lar** *a.* **Monosymme·trical** *a.*, *Bot.* of flowers, fruits, etc.: divisible into exactly similar halves in one plane only. **Monothe·cal** [Gr. θήκη case, box] *a.*, *Bot.* having only one loculament or cell; applied to anthers. **Mono·tomous** [Gr. τομή cutting] *a.*, *Min.* having a cleavage distinct only in a certain direction. **Monozo·ic** [Gr. ζῷον animal] *a.*, *Zool.* applied to a spore which produces one sporozoite.

2. *Chem.* Used in the names of compounds to signify the presence of a single atom or combining equivalent of the element or radical indicated by the word to which *mono-* is prefixed; as in **Monoba·sic** [BASE *sb.*[1]] *a.*, having one base, or one atom of a base; of an acid, containing one atom of replaceable hydrogen. **Monoca·rbon** *a.*, containing or derived from one atom of carbon. **Monoste·arin,** that species of stearin formed from glycerin by the replacement by stearyl of one only of the three OH groups.

Monocarpellary (mǫ:nokā·ɹpėlări), *a.* 1863. [f. MONO- + CARPEL + -ARY[2].] *Bot.* Having or consisting of a single carpel.

Monocarpic (mǫnokā·ɹpik), *a.* 1849. [f. MONO- + Gr. καρπός fruit + -IC.] *Bot.* Of a plant: Bearing fruit only once (and then dying). So **Mo·nocarp**, a m. plant 1846.

Monocarpous (mǫnokā·ɹpəs), *a.* 1731. [In sense 1, f. as MONOCARPELLARY; in sense 2, f. as prec.; see -OUS.] **1.** *Bot.* = MONOCARPELLARY. **2.** *Bot.* = MONOCARPIC 1830.

Monocephalous (mǫnose·fǎləs), *a.* 1845. [f. Gr. μονοκέφαλος one-headed (f. μόνος MONO- + κεφαλή head) + -OUS.] Having only one head. Applied **a.** to a fruit or ovary which has but one head or summit; **b.** to a plant which has its flowers disposed in a single head or umbel.

†**Monoceros** (mǒnǫ·sěrǫs). [ME. *monoceros*, *-on* (XIV) – OFr. *monoceros*, *-on* – L. *monoceros* (Pliny) – Gr. μονόκερως, f. μόνος MONO- + κέρας horn.] **1.** The UNICORN –1749. **2.** A fish having one horn, as the saw-fish, sword-fish, or narwhal –1825.

Monochlamydeous (mǫnoklǎmi·dǐəs), *a.* 1830. [f. mod.L. *Monochlamydeæ*, f. Gr. μόνος MONO- + χλαμύς, χλαμυδ- cloak; see -EOUS.] *Bot.* Having only one floral envelope; having a single perianth; belonging to the division *Monochlamydeæ*.

Monochloro- (mǫnoklōᵊro). Also **mono-chlor-.** 1855. [See MONO- 2 and CHLORO-.] *Chem.* Comb. form, expressing the presence in a compound of one equivalent of chlorine, as *monochloracetic acid*, etc.

Monochord (mǫ·nǒkǫɹd). late ME. [– (O)Fr. *monocorde* – late L. *monochordon* – Gr. μονόχορδον, subst. use of n. of μονόχορδος having a single string, f. μόνος MONO- + χορδή string (see CHORD *sb.*[1]).] **1.** A musical instrument composed of a sound-board with a single string; used for the mathematical determination of musical intervals. **2.** A mediæval musical instrument with several strings and bridges for the production of a combination of sounds. *Obs.* exc. *Hist.* late ME. **3.** A harmonious combination of sound; hence *fig.* harmony, agreement. Now *rare.* late ME.

Monochromatic (mǫnǒkromæ·tik), *a.* 1822. [f. MONO- + CHROMATIC.] **1.** Of or presenting one colour only; applied *spec.* to light of one wave-length. **2.** Executed in monochrome 1823.

1. *M. lamp*, a lamp which produces a m. light. Hence **Monochroma·tically** *adv.*

Monochrome (mǫ·nokrōᵘm), *sb.* (and *a.*). 1622. [In sense 1 – med.L. *monochroma*, evolved from Gr. (L.) μονοχρώματος of one colour; in 2, 3 – Fr. *monochrome* – Gr. μονόχρωμος of one colour, a by-form of μονοχρώματος.] **1.** A painting executed in different tints of one colour. **2.** Representation in one colour; esp. in phr. (to paint, etc.) *in m.* Hence occas., the being in one colour, a tract of one colour. 1851. **3.** *adj.* Having only one colour; executed in one colour 1849.

2. One cold monotonous m. of gray FERGUSSON. Hence **Monochro·mic, -al** *a.* = MONOCHROME *a.* **Mo·nochro:mist,** a painter in m. **Monochro·mous** *a.* **Mo·nochro:my,** the art of painting in m.

Monocle (mǫ·nǫk'l). 1858. [– Fr. *monocle*, subst. use of adj. 'one-eyed' – late L. MONOCULUS.] A single eye-glass.

Monoclinal (mǫnoklǝi·năl), *a.* 1858. [f. Gr. μόνος MONO- + κλίνειν to bend + -AL[1].] *Geol.* Applied to strata that dip in one and the same direction. So **Mo·nocline,** a m. fold 1879.

Monoclinic (mǫnokli·nik), *a.* 1868. [f. as prec. + -IC.] *Cryst.* Having one of the axial intersections oblique.

Monoclinous (mǫnoklǝi·nəs), *a.* 1828. [f. Fr. *monocline*, or mod.L. *monoclinus*, f. Gr. μόνος MONO- + κλίνη bed; see -OUS.] **1.** *Bot.* Having both stamens and pistils in the same flower; hermaphrodite. **2.** *Geol.* = MONOCLINAL 1882.

Monocotyledon (mǫ:nokǫtilī·dǫn). 1727. [– mod.L. *monocotyledon*, f. Gr. μόνος MONO- + κοτυληδών; see COTYLEDON.] *Bot.* A flowering plant having one cotyledon or seed-leaf. The Monocotyledons, or Endogens, constitute one of the two great classes of flowering plants. Hence **Monocotyle·donous** *a.*, having a single cotyledon; belonging to the class of Monocotyledons 1770.

Monocracy (mǒnǫ·krăsi). 1651. [f. MONO- + -CRACY; see next.] Government by a single person, autocracy.

Monocrat (mǫ·nǒkræt). 1792. [– Gr. μονοκρατής ruling alone; see MONO-, -CRAT.] *U.S. Hist.* A partisan of monocracy; a nickname given c1790 by Jefferson to members of the Federalist party, because they sided with England against France. Hence **Monocra·tic** *a.*

Monocular (mǒnǫ·kiŭlaɹ), *a.* 1640. [f. late L. *monoculus* (see MONOCULUS) + -AR[1].] **1.** Having only one eye, or the use of only one. Now *rare.* **2.** Of or pertaining to one eye only; adapted to one eye 1858.

1. He had..catch'd M. Trouts 1696. **2.** M. vision 1858. Hence **Monocula·rity,** m. condition. **Mono·cularly** *adv.* with the use of one eye only.

Monocule (mǫ·nokiul). *rare.* 1771. [– Fr. †*monocule* (now *monocle*) or late L. MONOCULUS.] A creature with one eye only (e.g., the Cyclops). Also, a member of the Linnæan genus MONOCULUS.

Monoculous (mǒnǫ·kiŭləs), *a.* 1656. [f. L. *monoculus* (see next) + -OUS.] One-eyed.

‖**Monoculus** (mǒnǫ·kiŭlǒs). 1440. [Late L., f. Gr. μόνος MONO- + L. *oculus* eye, after Gr. μονόφθαλμος.] **1.** A one-eyed being. **2.** A Linnæan genus of minute crustaceans; a member of this genus 1752.

Monocycle (mǫ·nǒsǝik'l). 1869. [f. MONO- + CYCLE *sb.*] A velocipede having only one wheel.

Monocyclic (mǫnosi·klik, -sǝi·klik), *a.* 1882. [f. Gr. μόνος MONO- + κύκλος circle + -IC.] *Bot.* and *Zool.* Having or consisting of a single circle or whorl of parts.

Monodelph (mǫ·nǒdelf). 1842. [– Fr. *Monodelphe*, f. mod.L. *Monodelphia*, f. μόνος MONO- + δελφύς womb.] *Zool.* A mammal of the subclass *Monodelphia*, characterized by a single uterus and vagina, and comprising all mammals except the monotremes and marsupials. So **Monode·lphian, Monode·lphic, Monode·lphous** *adjs.*

Monodic (mǒnǫ·dik), *a.* 1818. [– Gr. μονῳδικός, f. μονῳδός; see MONODY and -IC.] Pertaining to or of the nature of monody. In *Music*, characterized by the predominance of one part or melody, to which the other parts merely furnish harmonies.

Monodist (mǫ·nǒdist). 1751. [f. MONODY + -IST.] One who writes or sings a monody. So **Mo·nodize** *v. trans.* to make the subject of a monody. COLERIDGE.

Monodrama (mǫ·nodrāmă). Also †**-dram(e.** 1793. [f. MONO- + DRAMA.] A dramatic piece for a single performer. Hence **Mo:nodrama·tic** *a.*

Monody (mǫ·nǒdi). 1623. [– late L. *monodia* – Gr. μονῳδία, f. μονῳδός singing alone, f. μόνος MONO- + *ῳδ- in ᾠδή (see ODE); see -Y[3].] **1.** In Greek literature: **a.** A lyric ode sung by a single voice; an ode sung by one of the actors in a tragedy (as dist. from the chorus); hence, a mournful song or dirge. **b.** A funeral oration. GIBBON. **2.** A poem in which the mourner bewails some one's death 1637. **3.** Monotonous sound POE.

2. In this M. the Author bewails a learned Friend, unfortunately drown'd MILT.

‖**Monœcia** (mǫnī·ʃiă). 1753. [mod.L. (Linn.), f. Gr. μόνος MONO- + οἶκος house; cf. DIŒCIA.] *Bot.* The twenty-first class in the Sexual System of Linnæus, comprising plants which have the stamens and pistils in separate flowers, but on the same plant.

Monœcious (mǫnī·ʃ[i]əs), *a.* 1761. [f. prec. + -OUS.] **1.** *Bot.* **a.** Of phanerogams: Having unisexual male and female flowers on the same plant; belonging to the class MONŒCIA. **b.** Of cryptogams: Having both male and female organs on the same individual 1861. **2.** *Zool.* Having the two sexes in one individual; hermaphrodite 1826. So **Monœ·cism** 1875.

‖**Monogamia** (mǫnogēˈ·miă, -gæ·miă). 1760. [mod.L. (Linn.) use of late L. *monogamia* 'single marriage', MONOGAMY.] *Bot.* The sixth order in the nineteenth class (*Syngenesia*) of the Linnæan Sexual System, containing species which bear solitary flowers in which the anthers are united. Hence **Mo·nogam,** a plant of this order 1828.

Monogamist (mǒnǫ·gămist). 1651. [f. Gr. μονόγαμος marrying only once (f. μόνος MONO- + γάμος marriage) + -IST.] **1.** 'One who disallows second marriages' (J.); also, one who is debarred from second marriage after the death of the first spouse; opp. to *digamist*. **2.** One who practises or favours monogamy (sense 2), as opp. to *bigamist* or *polygamist* 1731. **3.** quasi-*adj.* 1875.

Monogamy (mǒnǫ·gămi). 1612. [– Fr. *monogamie* – eccl. L. *monogamia*, Gr. μονογαμία, f. μονόγαμος (see prec.).] **1.** The practice or principle of marrying only once; opp. to *digamy*. Now *rare.* **2.** The condition, rule, or custom of being married to only one person at a time (opp. to *bigamy* or *polygamy*) 1708. **3.** *Zool.* The habit of living in pairs, or having only one mate 1785. Hence **Monoga·mian, Monoga·mic** *adjs.* of or pertaining to m.; monogamous. **Mono·gamous** *a.* practising m.; of or pertaining to m.

Monogenesis (mǫnodʒe·nĭsis). 1864. [– mod.L.; see MONO- and GENESIS.] *Biol.* **a.** Development of all living things from a single cell, or of all human beings from a single pair. **b.** Asexual reproduction. **Monogene·tic** *a.* 1873.

Monogenic (mǫnodʒe·nik), *a.* 1893. [f. Gr. μόνος MONO- + γένος kind, origin (see -GEN) + -IC.] **1.** Math. *M. function*: a function which has a single differential coefficient. **2.** *Biol.* Of or pertaining to monogenesis; monogenetic 1897. **Mono·genous** *a.* 1866.

Monogenism (mǒnǫ·dʒĭniz'm). 1865. [f. MONO- + -GEN + -ISM.] The doctrine of MONOGENY. So **Mono·genist,** one who maintains this doctrine 1857.

Monogeny (mǒnǫ·dʒĭni). 1865. [f. MONO- + -GENY.] The (theoretical) origination of mankind from one common pair of ancestors; also, *loosely*, monogenism.

Monoglot (mǫ·nǒglǫt). 1830. [– Gr. μονόγλωττος, f. μόνος MONO- + γλῶττα tongue.] **A.** *adj.* **1.** That speaks, writes, or understands only one language. **2.** Written in only one language 1890. **B.** *sb.* One who knows only one language 1894.

Monogony (mǒnǫ·gǒni). 1873. [f. Gr. μόνος MONO- + -γονία begetting.] *Biol.* Asexual propagation: opp. to *amphigony*.

Monogram (mǫ·nǒgræm). 1610. [In sense 1 – L. *monogrammus*; in sense 2 – Fr. *monogramme* – late L. *monogramma*, f. Gr. *μονόγραμμος; see MONO-, -GRAM.] †**1.** A picture drawn in lines without shading or colour; a sketch –1843. **2.** A character composed of two or more letters interwoven together, the letters being usually the initials of a person's name 1696.

2. *The Christian m.* or *m. of Christ*, the combination (☧) of the first two letters of Χριστός (Christ). Hence **Mo:nogramma·tic, -al** *a.* of, pertaining to, or in the style of, a m.

Monograph (mǫ·nǒgraf), *sb.* 1821. [repl. earlier MONOGRAPHY, prob. because the form in -Y[3] suggested an abstract sense (cf. *telegraph* and *telegraphy*).] **1.** Orig., a separate treatise on a single species, genus, or larger group of plants, animals, or minerals. (Often with const. *of.*) Hence *gen.* a separate treatise on a single object or class of objects. ¶**2.** Misused for MONOGRAM 2. 1849.

1. A M. of Fossil Crustacea 1876, on Poe 1880. Hence **Mo·nograph** *v.* to write a m. on; to discuss in a m. **Mono·grapher,** a writer of a m.

Monography (mǒnǫ·grăfi). 1773. [– mod. L. *monographia*, f. *monographus* (Linn.) writer of a treatise on a single genus or species; see MONO-, -GRAPHY.] = MONOGRAPH 1.

‖**Monogynia** (mǫnodʒi·niă). 1760. [mod.L. (Linn.), f. *monogynus* (see MONO-, -GYNOUS) + -IA[1].] *Bot.* The first order in each of the first thirteen classes of the Linnæan Sexual System, comprising plants having flowers with only one pistil. Hence **Monogyn** (mǫ·nodʒin). **Monogy·nian, Monogy·nic, Mono·gynous** *adjs.* having only one pistil; belonging to the order *Monogynia*.

Monogyny (mǒnǫ·dʒini). 1876. [f. MONO- + Gr. γυνή woman, wife; see -Y[3].] The practice of mating with only one female, or marrying only one wife. (Cf. MONANDRY.)

Monoicous (mǒnoi·kəs), *a.* 1822. [f. mod.L. *monoicus*, Fr. *monoïque*, (irreg. f. Gr. μόνος MONO- + οἶκος house) + -OUS. Cf. MONŒCIOUS.] *Bot.* **a.** = MONŒCIOUS 1. Now *rare* or *Obs.* **b.** Applied by Darwin to those polygamous plants which have the three sexual varieties together on the same individual; opp. to *trioicous*.

Monoline (mǫ·nŏləin). 189.. [f. MONO- + LINE *sb.*²] **1.** Name for one of the printing machines which cast a line at a time. Cf. LINOTYPE. **2.** = *monorail* (see MONO- 1) 1903.

Monolith (mǫ·nŏliþ). 1848. [– Fr. *monolithe* – Gr. μονόλιθος, f. μόνος MONO- + λίθος stone; see -LITE, -LITH.] **A.** *sb.* A single block of stone, esp. one shaped into a pillar or monument. **B.** *adj.* Of the nature of a monolith 1850. Hence **Mo·nolithal** (*rare*), **Monoli·thic** *adjs.* formed of a single block of stone; consisting of or relating to monoliths.

Monologist (mŏnǫ·lŏdʒist). 1625. [f. MONOLOGUE + -IST. Cf. DIALOGIST.] †**1.** One who repeats the same word. **2.** One who soliloquizes; also, one who monopolizes the conversation 1711. So **Mono·logize** *v. intr.* to talk in monologue.

Monologue (mǫ·nŏlǫg), *sb.* 1668. [– Fr. *monologue*, 'one that loues to heare himselfe talke' (Cotgr.); cf. late Gr. μονόλογος speaking alone. See MONO-, -LOGUE.] **1.** 'A scene in which a person of the drama speaks by himself' (J.); contrasted with *chorus* and *dialogue*. Also, in mod. use, a dramatic composition for a single performer. **b.** *gen.* Literary composition of this nature 1668. **2.** Talk or discourse of the nature of a soliloquy 1859.

1. The m. in Hamlet 1872. **b.** He also gives you an account of himself..in m. DRYDEN. So **Monolo·gic, -al** *a.* **Mo·nologue** *v. intr.* **Mo·nologuist**, also **-logueist**, one who talks or performs in m. **Mo·nologuize** *v.* to monologize.

Monology (mŏnǫ·lŏdʒi). 1608. [f. MONO- + -LOGY, after prec.] †**a.** A monologue. **b.** The habit of monologizing.

b. Coleridge persisted in m. through his whole life DE QUINCEY.

Monomachy (mŏnǫ·măki). 1582. [– late L. *monomachia* – Gr. μονομαχία single combat; see MONO-, -MACHY.] A single combat; a duel. So **Mono·machist**, one who fights in single combat. DE QUINCEY.

Monomania (mǫnomē¹·niă). 1823. [– Fr. *monomanie* (see MONO-), with assim. to the terminal element -MANIA.] Insanity on one subject only.

b. I call it quite my m., it is such a subject of mine DICKENS. Hence **Monoma·niac** *sb.* one who suffers from m.; also *adj.* **Mo:nomani·acal** *a.*

Monomark (mǫ·nomāɹk). 1925. [f. MONO- + MARK *sb.*¹] One of a system of registered marks (letters and figures) identifying articles, goods, addresses, etc.

Monometallic (mǫnomĭtæ·lik), *a.* 1877. [f. MONO- + METALLIC, after *bimetallic*.] Pertaining to, involving, or using a standard of currency based upon one metal. Hence **Monome·tallism**, the m. system or standard of currency. **Monome·tallist**, one who advocates monometallism.

Monometer (mŏnǫ·mĭtəɹ). 1847. [– late L. *monometer* adj. (Priscian) – Gr. μονόμετρος adj.; see MONO-, METRE *sb.*¹] *Pros.* A line consisting of one metre.

Monometric (mǫnome·trik), *a.* 1837. [f. Gr. μόνος MONO- + μέτρον measure + IC.] *Cryst.* = ISOMETRIC. 3

Monomial (mŏnōᵘ·miăl). 1706. [f. MONO- after *binomial*.] *Alg.* (An expression) consisting of one term only.

Monomorphous (mǫnomǭ·ɹfəs), *a.* 1839. [f. Gr. μόνος MONO- + μορφή form + -OUS.] Having only one form throughout development. So **Monomo·rphic** *a.* 1880.

Monomyary (mǫnomai·ări), *a.* and *sb.* 1835. [f. mod.L. *Monomyaria* n. pl. (f. Gr. μόνος MONO- + μῦς muscle) + -ARY¹.] **A.** *adj.* Belonging to the group *Monomyaria* of bivalves, having only one adductor muscle. **B.** *sb.* A bivalve of this group 1842. So **Monomya·rian** *a.* and *sb.* 1837.

Mononomial (mǫnonōᵘ·miăl), *a.* and *sb.* 1844. A more correct form of MONOMIAL.

Monophthong (mǫ·nŏfþǫŋ). 1620. [– Gr. μονόφθογγος adj., f. μόνος MONO- + φθόγγος sound.] A single vowel sound. **Monophtho·ngal** *a.* consisting of a m. **Monophtho·ngize** *v. trans.* to convert into a m.

Monophysite (mŏnǫ·fisəit), *sb.* (*a.*) 1698. [– eccl. L. *Monophysita* – eccl. Gr. Μονοφυσίτης, f. μόνος MONO- + φύσις nature; see -ITE¹ 1.] *Eccl. Hist.* A heretic who believes that there is only one nature in the person of Jesus Christ. Hence **Monophysi·tic, -al** *a.* pertaining to the Monophysites or their heresy. **Mono·physitism.**

Monoplane (mǫ·noplein). 1910. [f. MONO- + PLANE *sb.*³] An aeroplane having one plane.

Monopode (mǫ·nopōᵘd). 1816. [– L. *monopodius* adj., *-ium* sb. – late Gr. μονοπόδιος adj., -ιον sb., f. μόνος MONO- + πούς, ποδ- foot; see -IUM.] **1.** A creature having only one foot; *spec.* one of a race of men fabled to have only one foot, with which they shaded themselves from the heat of the sun (see Pliny *Nat. Hist.* VII. ii.) **2.** = MONOPODIUM 1890.

‖**Monopodium** (mǫnopōᵘ·diǒm). 1875. [mod.L., f. as prec.] *Bot.* A single axis which extends at the apex, producing in succession lateral structures beneath it. **Monopo·dial** *a.*

Monopolism (mŏnǫ·pŏliz'm). 1881. [f. MONOPOLY + -ISM.] The system of monopolies.

Monopolist (mŏnǫ·pŏlist). 1601. [f. MONOPOLY, or synon. †*monopole* (XVI) + -IST.] One who monopolizes or possesses a monopoly; one who favours monopoly.

transf. The monopolists of political power BRIGHT. Hence **Monopoli·stic** *a.*

Monopolize (mŏnǫ·pŏləiz), *v.* 1611. [f. as prec. + -IZE.] **1.** *trans.* To get into one's hands the whole stock of (a commodity); to gain or hold exclusive possession of (a trade); to engross. **2.** *transf.* and *fig.* To obtain exclusive possession or control of 1628.

2. This fellow, Hawk, is monopolising your niece DICKENS. Hence **Mono:poliza·tion** 1727. **Mono·polizer** 1629.

Monopoly (mŏnǫ·pŏli). 1534. [– L. *monopolium* – Gr. μονοπώλιον, -πωλία, f. μόνος MONO- + πωλεῖν sell.] **1.** Exclusive possession of the trade in some commodity. **2.** An exclusive privilege (conferred by the sovereign or the state) of selling some commodity or trading with a particular place or country 1596. **3.** *transf.* and *fig.* Exclusive possession, control, or exercise of something 1643. **4.** A thing which is the subject of a monopoly 1838. **5.** A trading company that has a monopoly 1871. **6.** *attrib.*, as *m. price*, etc. 1625.

1. Suffer not thies ryche men to bye vp all,..and with theyr monopolye to kepe the market alone as please them 1551. **2.** The m. of the right to print the Bible in England is still possessed by the Universities of Oxford and Cambridge, and her Majesty's printer for England 1875. **3.** Neither side has a m. of right or..wrong FREEMAN. **4.** The culture..of tobacco was made a Crown m. G. DUFF.

‖**Monopteros** (mŏnǫ·ptĕrǫs). Also †**-on.** 1706. [subst. use of L. *monopteros* adj. – Gr. μονόπτερος having one wing, f. μόνος MONO- + πτερόν wing.] *Arch.* A temple consisting of a single circle of columns supporting a roof. Hence **Mono·pteral** *a.* 1823.

Monoptote (mǫ·nǫptoᵘt). 1612. [– late L. *monoptotus* – late Gr. μονόπτωτος with but one case, f. μόνος MONO- + πτωτός falling, cogn. w. πτῶσις case.] A noun occurring in a single oblique case (as L. *astu*).

Monorhine (mǫ·norəin), *a.* Also **monorrhine.** 1890. [f. mod.L. *Monorhina*, f. Gr. μόνος MONO- + ῥίς, ῥιν- nose.] *Zool.* Having a single nasal passage; belonging to the group *Monorhina* of vertebrates, comprising the lampreys and hags. Also **Mo·norhinal, Mo·norhinous** *adjs.*

Monorhyme, -rime (mǫ·norəim). 1731. [– Fr. *monorime* (XVII), f. *mono*- MONO- + *rime* RHYME, RIME.] **A.** *sb.* A poetical composition or passage in which all the lines have the same rhyme. **b.** *pl.* Lines forming a 'tirade' with one rhyme. **B.** *adj.* Having a single rhyme 1833.

Monostich (mǫ·nostik). 1577. [– late L. *monostichum*, *-ium* (Ausonius) – Gr. μονόστιχον, subst. use of n. of μονόστιχος adj.; see MONO-, STICH.] *Pros.* A poem or epigram consisting of but one metrical line.

Monostrophic (mǫnostrǫ·fik), *a.* (and *sb.*) 1671. [– Gr. μονοστροφικός, f. μονόστροφος adj., f. μόνος MONO- + στροφή recurring metrical scheme, STROPHE; see -IC.] *Pros.* Consisting of repetitions of one and the same strophic arrangement; *sb. pl.* monostrophic verses.

Monosyllabic (mǫ:nosilæ·bik), *a.* 1824. [f. MONO- + SYLLABIC. Cf. Fr. *monosyllabique* (XVIII).] **1.** Of a word: Consisting of one syllable 1828. **2.** Consisting of monosyllables or of a monosyllable 1824. **3.** Of a person: Uttering only monosyllables 1870.

2. The Chinese, and other m. tongues 1824. Throwing out a m. hint to his cattle GEO. ELIOT. So †**Monosylla·bical** *a.* 1686–1776, **-ly** *adv.*

Monosyllabism (mǫnosi·lăbiz'm). 1804. [f. MONOSYLLAB(LE + -ISM.] Addiction to the use of monosyllables; the quality of being monosyllabic.

Monosyllable (mǫnosi·lăb'l). 1533. [f. MONO- + SYLLABLE, prob. after L. *monosyllabon*, pl. *monosyllaba* (sc. *verba*) in Quintilian.] **A.** *sb.* A word of one syllable. **B.** *adj.* = MONOSYLLABIC *a.* 1, 2. *rare.* 1589.

Phr. *To speak* (*answer*, etc.) *in monosyllables*: to speak with intentional curtness; to answer little but 'yes' or 'no'.

‖**Monotessaron** (mǫnote·sărǫn). 1831. [f. (erron. after *diatessaron*) Gr. μόνος single. (Cf. med.L. *monotessaron* (Du Cange).] = DIATESSARON 3.

Monothalamic (mǫnoþălæ·mik), *a.* 1870. [f. as next + -IC.] *Bot.* Of a fruit: Formed from one pistil or flower.

Monothalamous (mǫnoþæ·lămǝs), *a.* 1816. [f. Gr. μόνος MONO- + θάλαμος (see THALAMUS) + -OUS.] *Bot.* and *Zool.* Having only one chamber; unilocular: as the chambered shells of foraminiferous and gasteropodous molluscs.

Monotheism (mǫ·noþī,iz'm). 1660. [f. Gr. μόνος MONO- + θεός god + -ISM.] The doctrine that there is only one God. So **Mo·notheist**, an adherent of m. **Mo:nothei·stic, -al** *a.* **Mo:nothei·stically** *adv.*

Monothelete (mŏnǫ·þĭlīt). 1850. *Theol.* A more correct form of MONOTHELITE. So **Mo:nothele·tian** *a.*, etc.

Monothelism (mŏnǫ·þĭliz'm). *rare.* 1685. [f. next + -ISM.] = MONOTHELITISM.

Monothelite (mŏnǫ·þĭləit). late ME. [– med.L. *monothelita* – late Gr. μονοθελήτης, f. Gr. μόνος MONO- + θελητής, agent-n. f. θέλειν will.] **A.** *sb.* An adherent of the 7th c. heretical sect which maintained that Christ has only one will. **B.** *adj.* Of or pertaining to the Monothelites or their doctrine 1619. Hence **Monotheli·tic** *a.* **Mono·thelitism.**

Monotint (mǫ·notint). 1886. [f. MONO- + TINT.] Representation in a single colour; also, a picture in only one colour. Chiefly in phr. *in m.*

Monotone (mǫ·notoᵘn). 1644. [– mod.L. *monotonus* adj. – late Gr. μονότονος; see MONO-, TONE *sb.* Earliest as sb., the use of which is peculiar to English.] **A.** *adj.* = MONOTONOUS *a.* 1 (rarely 2) 1769.

As lulling as the m. waves KINGLAKE.

B. *sb.* **1.** The utterance of a number of successive syllables without change of tone 1644. **2.** Sameness of style in writing; something composed in such a style 1871. **3.** *fig.* A monotonous continuance or recurrence *of* something 1856.

1. *transf.* Tolling, tolling, tolling In that muffled m. POE. Hence **Mo·notone** *v.* to recite, sing, speak in one unvaried tone. **Monoto·nic, -al** *a.* relating to or uttered in a m.; **-ly** *adv.* **Mono·tonist**, one who speaks monotonously; one who harps on one subject; one who loves monotony.

Monotonous (mŏnǫ·tŏnəs), *a.* 1778. [f. prec. + -OUS.] **1. a.** Of sound or utterance: Having little or no variation in tone or cadence. **b.** Producing but one tone or note; as the drum, etc. 1811. **2.** *transf.* and *fig.* Lacking in variety; wearisome through continued sameness 1791.

2. The m. smoothness of Byron's versification MACAULAY. Dull straight streets of m. houses GREEN. Hence **Mono·tonous-ly** *adv.*, **-ness.**

Monotony (mŏnǫ·tŏni). 1706. [– Fr. *monotonie* – late Gr. μονοτονία, f. μονότονος MONOTONE *a.*] The quality of being monotonous. **1.** Sameness of tone or pitch; want of variety in cadence or inflexion; occas. quasi-*concr.* a monotone 1724. **2.** *transf.* and *fig.* Wearisome sameness of effect; lack of interesting variety.

2. At sea, everything that breaks the m. of the surrounding expanse, attracts attention W. IRVING.

‖**Monotremata** (mǫnotrī·mătă), *sb. pl.* 1833. [mod.L., n. pl. of *monotrematus* adj., f. Gr. μόνος MONO- + τρῆμα, τρηματ- perforation, hole.] *Zool.* The lowest Order of Mammalia, having only one opening or vent for the genital, urinary, and digestive organs.

The Order comprises the duck-billed platypus (*Ornithorhynchus paradoxus*) and several species of spiny ant-eaters. Hence **Monotre·matous** *a.* **Mo·notreme** *a.* and *sb.* 1835.

Monotriglyph (mǫnotrəi·glif), *a.* 1706. [– L. *monotriglyphos* (Vitruvius) – Gr. *μονοτρίγλυφος* adj.; see MONO-, TRIGLYPH.] *Arch.* Having only one triglyph in the space over an intercolumniation, as the entablature in the Doric order.

Monotype (mǫ·notəip). 1882. [f. MONO- + TYPE.] **1.** A print from a metal plate on which a picture is painted. Also, the process of producing such prints. **2.** Trade-name of a composing-machine which first casts, and then sets up the type by means of a perforated paper roll which has been previously produced on another part of the machine. (Cf. LINOTYPE, MONOLINE.) 1895.

Monotypic (mǫnoti·pik), *a.* 1874. [f. mod. L. *monotypus* (f. Gr. *μόνος* MONO- + *τύπος* TYPE) + -IC.] Having or containing only one type or representative. So **Mono·typous** *a.* 1856.

Monoxide (mǫnǫ·ksəid). 1869. [f. MONO- 2 + OXIDE.] *Chem.* An oxide containing one equivalent of oxygen.

Monoxy-, monox-. 1863. [f. MONO- 2 + OXY(GEN.] *Chem.* Comb. form, expressing the presence in a compound of one equivalent of oxygen.

‖**Monoxylon** (mǫnǫ·ksilǫn). *Pl.* **-la.** Also in mod.Gr. form †**monoxylo.** 1555. [– Gr. *μονόξυλον*, neut. of *μονόξυλος*; see next.] A canoe or boat made from one piece of timber. Also **Mono·xyl(e.**

Monoxylous (mǫnǫ·ksiləs), *a.* 1863. [f. L. *monoxylus* (– Gr., f. *μόνος* + *ξύλον* wood, timber) + -OUS.] Made out of a single piece of wood; also, using one piece of wood to make a boat or coffin, etc. So **Monoxy·lic** *a.*

Monroeism (mŏnrōᵘ·iz'm). 1896. [f. James *Monroe*, president of the U.S. 1817–1825.] The 'Monroe doctrine' (see DOCTRINE). So **Monroe·ist,** a supporter of this.

‖**Monseigneur** (moṅseṅyör). *Pl.* **messeigneurs** (męsęnyör). 1600. [Fr., *mon* my + *seigneur* lord.] **1.** A French title given to persons of eminence, esp. to princes, cardinals, archbishops, and bishops. Abbrev. *Mgr.* †The title conferred since the time of Louis XIV upon the Dauphin of France. 1610. †**2.** Used for MONSIGNOR –1660.

‖**Monsieur** (mosyö, məsyö). 1500. [Fr., orig. two words, *mon* my, *sieur* lord.] **1.** The title of courtesy prefixed to the name, surname, or nobiliary title of a Frenchman; now = Eng. 'Mr.', except that it is also applied to any title of rank. In English often used in speaking of Europeans other than Frenchmen. Abbrev. *M.* (the forms *Mons.*, *Mons*[r]. are not now in use in France). See also the pl. MESSIEURS. 1512. **2.** Used (*a*) in speaking to or of a Frenchman; (*b*) in literal renderings of French speech 1588. **3.** *Hist.* A title of the second son or next younger brother of the King of France 1572. **4.** A Frenchman generally. Now *rare* or *Obs.* 1500.

1. *transf.* Mounsieur Cobweb, good Mounsier get your weapons in your hand SHAKS. **4.** Now I would pray our Monsieurs To thinke an English Courtier may be wise, And neuer see the Louure SHAKS. Hence †**Monsieurship** 1579–1673.

‖**Monsignor, -ore** (mǫnsi·nyǫr, -nyǭre). *Pl.* **monsignori** (-nyǭ·ri). 1635. [It. *Monsignore* (shortened *-signor*), formed after Fr. MONSEIGNEUR; see SIGNOR.] An honorific title bestowed upon prelates, officers of the Papal court and household, etc.

Monsoon (mǫnsū·n). 1584. [– early mod. Du. †*monssoen*, †*monssoyn* (mod. *moesson*, infl. by Fr. forms) – Pg. *monção*, †*moução* – Arab. *mawsim* fixed season, f. *wasama* to mark.] **1.** A seasonal wind prevailing in southern Asia, blowing approximately from the south-west in summer (*wet* or *rainy m.*), and in winter from the north-east (*dry m.*). **b.** The rainy season which accompanies the south-west monsoon 1747. **2.** *transf.* Any wind which has periodic alternations. Cf. TRADE-WIND. 1691.

Monster (mǫ·nstəɹ), *sb.* ME. [– (O)Fr. *monstre* – L. *monstrum*, orig. a divine portent or warning, f. *monēre* warn.] **A.** *sb.* †**1.** A prodigy, a marvel –1710. **2.** A malformed animal or plant; a misshapen birth, an abortion. Cf. MONSTROSITY. ME. **3.** An imaginary animal, either partly brute and partly human, or compounded of elements from two or more animal forms; e.g. the centaur, sphinx, minotaur, wyvern. late ME. **4.** A person of inhuman cruelty or wickedness; a monstrous example *of* (some particular vice) 1556. **5.** An animal of huge size; hence, anything of vast proportions 1530.

2. The princes keep favourite dwarfs. The Emperor and Empress have two of these little Monsters LADY M. W. MONTAGU. *fig.* The non-Christian religions are not to the wise man mere monsters M. ARNOLD. **3.** *transf.* You'l draw A faultless M. which the world ne're saw 1682. **4.** These monsters of inhumanity ADDISON. **5.** I condempne thee to be ·xxviii· yeres a m. in y[e] see 1533.

B. *adj.* Of extraordinary size; gigantic, huge, monstrous 1839.

The phrase 'monster meeting' was due to me F. ROGERS (*c* 1842).

Mo·nster, *v. rare.* 1605. [f. prec. sb.] **1.** *trans.* To make a monster of. **2.** To exhibit as a monster, or as something wonderful 1607.

1. *Lear* I. i. 223. **2.** I had rather haue one scratch my Head i' th' Sun,..then idly sit To heare my Nothings monster'd SHAKS.

Monstrance (mǫ·nstrăns). ME. [– med.L. *monstrantia*, f. *monstrant-*, pr. ppl. stem of L. *monstrare* show, f. *monstrum*; see MONSTER *sb.*, -ANCE.] †**1.** Demonstration, proof. ME. only. **2.** *R. C. Ch.* **a.** An open or transparent vessel of gold or silver in which the host is exposed 1506. **b.** A receptacle for the exhibition of relics 1522. So †**Monstral,** †**Monstrant,** †**Mo·nstre** *sbs.* (in sense 2).

Monstrosity (mǫnstrǫ·siti). 1555. [– late L. *monstrositas*, f. *monstrosus* MONSTROUS; see -ITY.] **1.** An abnormality of growth; *concr.* a part or organ that is such; also occas. = MONSTER *sb.* 2. **2.** = MONSTER *sb.* 3. 1643. **3.** The condition or fact of being monstrous 1656. Also *transf.* and *fig.*

2. *fig.* The Multitude..confused together, make but one great beast, and a m. more prodigious then Hydra SIR T. BROWNE.

Monstrous (mǫ·nstrəs), *a.* 1460. [– OFr. *monstreux* or L. *monstrosus*, f. *monstrum*; see MONSTER *sb.*, -OUS.] †**1.** Deviating from the natural order; unnatural –1736. **2.** Abnormally formed; malformed 1597. **3.** Having the nature or appearance of a monster (see MONSTER *sb.* 3) 1540. **b.** Abounding in monsters. *poet.* 1637. **4.** Of unnaturally huge dimensions; gigantic, enormous 1500. **5.** Outrageously wrong or absurd 1573. **6.** Atrocious, horrible 1560. †**7.** As an exclam. = 'astounding' –1693. †**8.** As a colloq. or affected intensive –1825. **b.** quasi-*adv.* 'Mighty'. Now *rare* or *Obs.* 1587.

1. An atheist, a man in my opinion m. LYLY. More m. Tales have oft amus'd the Vulgar 1701. **2.** A man in shape, immane, and monsterous CHAPMAN. **3.** Their m. Idol DE FOE. **b.** Where thou..under the whelming tide Visit'st the bottom of the m. world MILT. **4.** In bulk as huge As whom the Fables name of m. size, Titanian,.. Briarios..or that Sea-beast Leviathan MILT. **5.** Wilt thou tell a m. lie? SHAKS. **6.** Thou m. slanderer of heauen and earth SHAKS. **7.** O m.! eleuen Buckrom men growne out of two? SHAKS. **8.** A m. favourite of George's 1782. **b.** She's a m. shocking dresser MISS BURNEY. Hence **Mo·nstrous-ly** *adv.*, **-ness.** So †**Mo·nstruous.** late ME. –1727; †**Monstruo·sity,** †**Mo·nstruous-ly** *adv.*, †**-ness.**

Mont, obs. f. MOUNT.

‖**Montagnard** (moṅtanʸar). 1879. [Fr., f. *montagne*; see MOUNTAIN and -ARD.] *Hist.* A member of the MOUNTAIN (sense 5).

Monta(i)gne, obs. ff. MOUNTAIN.

‖**Montaña** (mǫnta·nʸă). 1840. [Sp., mountain.] In Spanish-American countries: A forest of considerable extent; *spec.* the name of the part of Peru east of the Andes.

Montane (mǫ·nteⁱn), *a.* 1863. [– L. *montanus*, f. *mons, mont-*; see MOUNT *sb.*, -ANE.] = MOUNTAIN II. a. b.

Montanism (mǫ·ntăniz'm). 1597. [f. *Montanus* (see below) + -ISM.] The tenets of a heretical Christian sect, founded in Phrygia by Montanus in the 2nd century. Montanus claimed for himself and two female associates prophetic inspiration. The tenets of the sect were millenarian and severely ascetic. So **Mo·ntanist,** a believer in M. 1449; as *adj.* = **Montani·stic,** †**-al** *a.* of or relating to M. **Mo·ntanize** *v. intr.* to follow the doctrines of the Montanists.

†**Montant.** *rare.* Also **montanto.** 1598. [– Fr. *montant* 'an upright blow, or thrust' (Cotgr.).] A 'downright' blow or thrust. *Merry W.* II. iii. 27.

Montant, early form of MUNTIN.

‖**Montbretia** (mǫntbrī·ʃⁱă). 1899. [mod.L., after A. F. E. Coquebert de *Montbret*, a French botanist (1780–1801); see -IA¹.] A genus of iridaceous plants, bearing bright orange-coloured flowers; a plant of this genus.

Monte (mǫ·nte). Also **monty.** 1850. [– Sp. *monte* mountain; heap of cards left after each player has his share.] A Spanish game of chance, played with a pack of forty-five cards.

Three-card m., a game of Mexican origin, played with three cards only, of which one is usu. a court-card.

Monteith (mǫ̆nti·þ). Also †**monteigh,** †**-éff, -eth.** 1683. [Named, according to Anthony Wood, after a certain 'Monsieur Monteigh'.] *Antiq.* A punch-bowl with a scalloped brim, also used for cooling and carrying glasses.

Montem (mǫ·ntem). *Obs.* exc. *Hist.* 1743. [From L. *ad montem*, 'to the Hill'.] A festival (orig. annual, later triennial) formerly celebrated by the scholars of Eton, who went in fancy costumes to 'Salt Hill', a mound near Slough, and there collected money from the bystanders, to support at King's College, Cambridge, the senior colleger of the school.

‖**Montero** (mǫntēᵊ·ro). Also **montera,** etc. 1611. [Sp. *montera*, f. *montero* hunter, lit. 'mountaineer', f. *monte*; see MOUNT *sb.*¹] A Spanish hunter's cap with a spherical crown and a flap. Also *m. cap.*

Montgolfier (mǫntgǫ·lfiəɹ; Fr. moṅgolfye). 1784. [Named after the brothers J. M. and J. E. *Montgolfier* of Annonay, France, its inventors.] A balloon raised by heated air instead of gas; a fire-balloon. (In full *M. balloon.*)

Month (mɒnþ). [OE. *mōnaþ* = OFris. *mōnath, mōn(a)d*, OS. *mānoth* (Du. *maand*), OHG. *mānōd* (G. *monat*), ON. *mánuðr*, Goth. *mēnōþs* :– Gmc. **mǣnōþ(az)*, rel. to **mǣnon* MOON *sb.*] A measure of time corresponding to the period of revolution of the moon. **1.** Any one of the twelve portions into which the conventional year is divided. More explicitly *calendar m.* **2.** *Astr.* **a.** (In full *Lunar m.*) The period in which the moon makes a complete revolution relatively to some point, either fixed or movable OE. **b.** *Solar m.*: the twelfth part of the solar year; the time occupied by the sun in passing through one of the signs of the zodiac OE. **3.** A space of time, either (*a*) extending from any day to the corresponding day of the next calendar month (called 'a calendar month'), or (*b*) containing 28 days (often miscalled a 'lunar month') OE. **b.** Used as an indefinite measure of time, esp. in *pl.*, a long while 1601. †**4.** *pl.* = MENSES –1694.

2. a. Usually the term denotes the *synodical month*, i.e. the period from one new moon to the next, the length of which is 29 days, 12 hours, 44 minutes, 2·7 seconds. The other kinds of lunar month (the lengths of which are all between 27 and 28 days) are the *anomalistic, sidereal, tropical*, and *nodical months*: see those adjs. O.E.D. **3.** A m. in law is a lunar m., or twenty-eight days, unless otherwise expressed BLACKSTONE. The Word 'Month' to mean Calendar Month, unless words be added showing Lunar Month to be intended *Act* 13–14, *Vict.* c. 21. **b.** 'Dead', he answered. 'When?' 'Months back.' MEREDITH. Phrases. *M. by m.*: in each successive m. *M. after m.*: each m. as a sequel to the preceding (without suggestion of continuity). *From m. to m.*: continuously from one m. to the next. *M. of Sundays* (colloq.): an indefinite period. *This day m.*: at a time a m. after the day indicated.

Monthly (mɒ·nþli), *a.* and *sb.* 1572. [f. MONTH + -LY¹.] **A.** *adj.* **1.** Done or recurring once a month or every month 1647. **b.** = MENSTRUAL *a.* 2. 1612. **2.** Pertaining to a month; payable every month 1572. **3.** Continued for a month. Now *rare.* 1589.

1. The m. parcel from London LYTTON. **2.** A m.

salary 1843. **3.** Minutes ioyes are monthlie woes GREENE.

Spec. collocations. †**m. mind** = MONTH'S MIND; **m. nurse,** one who attends a woman during the first month after child-birth; **m. rose (tree),** the Indian or China rose, supposed to flower every month.

B. *sb.* **1.** *pl.* = MENSES (*vulgar*). 1872. **2.** A magazine, etc. published once a month 1856.

Monthly (mɒ·nþli), *adv.* 1533. [-LY².] Once a month; in each or every month; month by month.

Month's mind. 1466. **1.** *Eccl.* The commemoration of a deceased person by the celebration of masses, etc., on a day one month from the date of his death. **2.** An inclination, a fancy, a liking. Also (rarely) *To be in a month's mind,* to have a strong expectation. *Obs.* exc. *dial.* 1580.

Monticle (mǫ·ntik'l). 1490. [– Fr. *monticule*; see next.] A small mountain or hill.

Monticule (mǫ·ntikiul). 1799. [– Fr. *monticule* – late L. *monticulus,* dim. of *mons, mont-* MOUNT *sb.*¹; see -CULE.] **1.** = MONTICLE. **b.** *spec.* A small conical mound produced by a volcanic eruption 1833. **2.** *Anat.* and *Zool.* A minute eminence (on an animal, etc.) 1874.

‖**Monton** (mǫ·ntǫn). 1858. [Sp., = 'heap', f. *monte* MOUNT *sb.*¹; see -OON.] *Mining.* A heap of ore; a batch under the process of amalgamation.

Montross, obs. f. MATROSS.

Monture (mǫ·ntiŭɹ). 1831. [– Fr. *monture,* f. *monter* to MOUNT; see -URE.] A mounting or setting; the manner in which anything is set or mounted.

Monture: see MOUNTURE.

Monument (mǫ·niŭmĕnt), *sb.* ME. [– (O)Fr. *monument* – L.*monu-, monimentum,* f. *monēre* remind; see -MENT.] †**1.** A sepulchre, place of sepulture –1658. **2.** A written document, record; a legal instrument. (Occas. confused with *muniment.*) 1440. †**b.** A piece of information given in writing –1650. **3.** An indication, evidence, or token (of some fact). Now *rare.* 1605. †**b.** A mark, indication; a portent –1657. **c.** *U.S. Law.* Any object fixed permanently in the soil and used as a means of ascertaining the location of a tract or a boundary 1828. **4.** Anything that by its survival commemorates a person, action, period, or event 1530. **b.** An enduring evidence or example 1675. **5.** A structure, edifice, or erection intended to commemorate a notable person, action, or event 1602. **b.** A structure of stone or other material erected over the grave or in church, etc., in memory of the dead 1588. †**c.** A carved figure, effigy SHAKS.

1. In that dim M. where Tybalt lies SHAKS. **2.** This discourse..I have transcribed from the original, and put it among the monuments in the end of the book 1709. **3. b.** *Tam. Shr.* III. ii. 97. **4. b.** It may be considered as a m. of the taste and skill of the authors HAZLITT. **5.** *The M.*: a Doric column 202 feet high in the City of London, built to commemorate the great fire of London 1666. **b.** Honours shall gather round his m. *'Junius' Lett.* **c.** You are no Maiden but a m. SHAKS. Hence **Mo·nument** *v. trans.* to cause to be perpetually remembered; to record on, or furnish with, a m. (*nonce-uses*) 1606.

Monumental (mǫniume·ntăl), *a.* 1601. [f. prec. + -AL¹.] **1.** Pertaining to a monument, or to monuments in general 1604. **2.** Serving as a monument, or †as a memento 1601. **3.** Like a monument 1606. **4.** *transf.* Of literary works, etc.: Massive and permanent. Also, *loosely,* vast, stupendous. 1658. **5.** Historically prominent; remaining conspicuous 1844.

1. Press'd with a Load of M. Clay! POPE. **2.** Hee hath giuen her his monumentall Ring SHAKS. **3.** Pine, or m. Oake MILT. **4.** His m. obtuseness GEO. ELIOT. A truly m. work 1894. **5.** That gallery of m. men SWINBURNE. Hence **Monume·ntally** *adv.* by way of a monument; in a m. degree.

-mony, *suffix,* occurring only in sbs. adopted from Latin; repr. L. *-monia* in *acrimony, ceremony,* etc., and L. *-monium* in *matrimony, parsimony,* etc.

Moo (mū), *v.* 1549. [imit.] *intr.* Of a cow, etc.: To low. Of a person: To make the sound 'moo'. Hence **Moo** *sb.* 1789.

Moo, obs. f. MO, more.

Mooch, mouch (mūtʃ), *v.* Now *slang* and *dial.* 1460. [prob. – OFr. *muchier* (Norman dial. *mucher*) hide, skulk, perh. of Gaulish origin. Cf. MICHE *v.*] †**1.** *intr.* ?To pretend poverty. **2.** To play truant 1622. **3.** *intr.* To loaf, skulk, or hang *about*; to slouch *along* 1851. **4.** *trans.* To pilfer, steal 1862. Hence **Mooch, mouch** *sb.* (esp. *on the m.*), **Moo·cher, mou·cher.**

Mood¹ (mūd). [OE. *mōd,* corresp. with variety of gender to OFris., OS. *mōd* (Du. *moed*), OHG. *muot* (G. *mut*), ON. *móðr* anger, grief, Goth. *mōþs, mōd-* anger, emotion :– Gmc. **mōðaz,* **mōðam,* of unkn. origin.] †**1.** Mind, heart, thought, feeling – late ME. †**2.** *spec.* Courage, anger 1600. **3.** A frame of mind or state of feelings OE. **b.** *pl.* Fits of variable or unaccountable temper 1859.

2. Who, in my moode, I stab'd vnto the heart SHAKS. **3.** Fortune is merry, And in this m. will giue vs any thing SHAKS. Phr. *In a m.* (*for* something), *in the m.* (*to do* something) disposed.

Mood² (mūd). 1569. [alt. of MODE by assoc. with prec.] **1.** *Logic.* Any one of the classes into which each of the four figures of valid categorical syllogisms is subdivided with reference to the quality and quantity of the constituent propositions. **2.** *Gram.* Any one of the groups of forms in the conjugation of a verb which serve to indicate the function in which the verb is used; i.e. whether it expresses a predication, a command, a wish, or the like; that quality of a verb which depends on the question to which of these groups its form belongs 1573. **3.** *Mus.* †**a.** = MODE 7. –1782. †**b.** = MODE 1 b. –1844.

3. b. Anon they move In perfect Phalanx to the Dorian m. Of Flutes and soft Recorders MILT. *transf.* That strain I heard was of a higher m. MILT.

Mooder, obs. f. MOTHER *sb.*¹

Moody (mū·di), *a.* [OE. *mōdiȝ,* f. MOOD¹ + -Y¹.] †**1.** Brave, bold, proud, high-spirited –1755. †**2.** Proud, haughty; head-strong, stubborn, wilful –1460. †**3.** Angry, wrathful –1697. **4.** Subject to moods; ill-humoured, gloomy, sullen, melancholy 1593. **b.** Applied to humour, thought, action, etc. 1593. **c.** Expressive of ill humour 1596.

3. Angry Jove..the m. sire DRYDEN. **4.** The Iews, a headstrong, m., murmuring race DRYDEN. **b.** M. Madness laughing wild GRAY. **c.** Maiestie might neuer yet endure The m. Frontier of a seruant brow SHAKS. Hence **Moo·dily** *adv.* **Moo·diness.**

Mool(l)a(h, obs. ff. MULLAH.

‖**Moolvee** (mū·lvi). 1625. [Urdu *mulvī* – Arab. *mawlawīy,* orig. adj., judicial, used subst. in the sense of *mawlā* MULLAH, of which it is a derivative.] A Moslem doctor of the law; in India, a complimentary term among Moslems for a teacher of Arabic, or any learned man.

Moon (mūn), *sb.* [OE. *mōna* = OFris. *mōna,* OS. *māno* (Du. *maan* fem.), OHG. *māno* (G. *mond*), ON. *máni,* Goth. *mēna* :– Gmc. **mǣnon,* rel. to **mǣnōþ-* MONTH; referred ult. to IE. base **mē-,* as in L. *metiri* MEASURE *v.,* the moon being the star by which time is measured.] **1.** The satellite of the earth; a secondary planet, whose light, derived from the sun, is reflected to the earth, and serves to dispel the darkness of the night. **b.** Since the disappearance of OE. grammatical genders, the moon has been treated as feminine; in poetry it is sometimes, after classical example, identified with various goddesses. **2.** The moon as visible during one (lunar) month, spoken of as a distinct object from that of another month. Similarly, with qualifying words: The moon as shining at a particular time or place, etc. See also FULL MOON, NEW MOON, etc. OE. **3.** With ref. to the moon's position above the earth, etc.; often quasi-personified ME. **4.** An appearance in the sky resembling a moon OE. **5.** A figure or representation of the moon, either crescent-shaped or circular; a moon-shaped marking, ornament, or vessel. late ME. **6.** The satellite of a planet 1665. **7.** *poet.* = MOONLIGHT. late ME. **8.** The period from one new moon to the next; a lunation, lunar month; *gen.* a month. late ME. †**9.** *The m.* **a.** *Alch.* Silver. **b.** *Her.* Argent. –1651. †**10.** = LUNE 2. –1642.

1. To wexe and wane..As dooth the faire whyte mone CHAUCER. The minde of men chaungeth as the mone HAWES. *Mean m.* (Astr.): an imaginary m., supposed to move uniformly in the ecliptic, completing its circuit in the same time as the actual m. *Calendar, ecclesiastical m.*: an imaginary m. used in determining the date of Easter. Provb. *To believe that the m. is made of green cheese*: to believe an absurdity. *Minion of the m.* = MOON-MAN 1. **2.** Phr. *There is a (no) m.* = the m. is visible (not visible) at the time and in the place referred to. *The old m. in the new moon's arms* (or *lap*): the appearance of the m. during the first quarter in which the dark portion of the orb is made more or less luminous by earth-light. **3.** 'Tis like the howling of Irish Wolues against the Moone SHAKS. While over head the M. Sits Arbitress MILT. He was a mere child in the world, but he didn't cry for the m. DICKENS. Phr. *To shoot the m.* (slang): to make a moonlight flitting. **4.** *John* IV. ii. 182. **5.** Precious oils In hollow'd moons of gems TENNYSON. **6.** And other Suns.. With thir attendant Moons MILT. **7.** White in the m. the long road lies A. E. HOUSMAN. **8.** This is the m. of roses, The lovely and flowerful time HENLEY.

attrib. and *Comb.*: **m.-blink,** a temporary evening blindness caused by sleeping in the moonshine in tropical climates; **-bow,** a lunar rainbow; **-culminating** *ppl. a.,* applied to such stars (used in calculating longitude) as culminate with the m. and are near its parallel of declination; **-daisy,** the ox-eye daisy, *Chrysanthemum leucanthemum*; **-dog,** a dog that bays the m.; **-glade** *U.S.,* the track made by moonlight on water; **-madness,** lunacy; **-month,** a lunar month; **-rainbow,** a lunar rainbow; **-trefoil,** *Medicago arborea.*

Moon (mūn), *v.* 1601. [f. prec.] **1. a.** *trans.* To expose to the rays of the moon. **b.** *intr.* To shine as a moon; to move as a satellite. **2.** *intr.* To move or look listlessly or aimlessly *about, along, around,* etc., as if moonstruck. *colloq.* 1848. **b.** *trans.* To pass away (the time) in a listless manner 1876. **3.** To hunt by moonlight 1898.

1. *refl.* The huge man..not sunning, but mooning himself—apricating himself in the occasional moon-beams DE QUINCEY. **2.** I mooned up and down the High-street T. HUGHES.

Moo·nbeam. 1590. A ray of moonlight.

Moo·n-blind, *a.* 1668. **1.** Of horses: Suffering from moon-eye. †**2.** *fig.* Purblind –1757. **3.** Suffering from blindness brought on by sleeping exposed to the moon's rays 1830. Hence **Moo·n-blindness.**

Moo·n-calf. 1565. [perh. after G. *mondkalb* (Luther); cf. G. *mondkind,* MLG. *maanenkind* 'moon-child'.] †**1.** An abortive shapeless fleshy mass in the womb; a false conception (regarded as produced by the influence of the moon) –1658. **b.** A misshapen birth. *Obs.* or *arch.* 1610. **c.** A congenital idiot; a born fool 1620. **2.** A mooning, absent-minded person 1613.

Moo·n-dial. 1686. A dial for showing the hours of the night by the moon.

Mooned (mūnd, *poet.* mū·nĕd), *ppl. a.* 1550. [f. MOON *sb.* or *v.* + -ED.] †**1.** Lunatic. CHEKE. **2.** Crescent-shaped; also, having moon-shaped markings 1607. **3.** Attended by or associated with the moon 1629. **4.** Moonlit. LYTTON.

2. Th' Angelic Squadron..sharpning in m. hornes Thir Phalanx MILT. **3.** M. Ashtaroth MILT.

Mooner (mū·nəɹ). 1576. [f. MOON *sb.* or *v.* + -ER¹; in sense 1 rendering mod.L. *lunarius.*] †**1.** A kind of watch-dog –1688. **2.** One who moons about 1848.

Moo·n-eye. 1607. [f. MOON *sb.* + EYE *sb.*; in sense 1 tr. late L. *oculus lunaticus* (Vegetius).] **1.** *Farriery.* (Usu. *pl.*) An eye affected with intermittent blindness (attributed to the moon's influence); also, moon-blindness. **2.** The cisco 1884.

Moo·n-eyed, *ppl. a.* 1610. [f. prec. + -ED².] **1.** *Farriery.* Affected with the disease of moon-eye; moon-blind. †**b.** Purblind; squint-eyed –1785. †**2.** Having eyes that see well at night –1817. **3.** Having round, wide-open eyes, as a terrified person 1790.

Moo·n-fern. 1671. = LUNARY *sb.* b.

Moo·n-fish. 1646. A name for various fishes resembling, or having parts that resemble, the moon; e.g. the sunfish (*Orthagoriscus mola*), the opah.

Moo·n-flower. 1787. **1.** The moon-daisy. **2.** A tropical plant, *Ipomœa bonanox,* that blooms at night, having large fragrant white flowers. *U.S.*

Moong, mung (mūŋ, mɒŋ). 1800. [Hindi *mūng.*] A species of vetch, *Phaseolus mungo,* common in India; also, its fibre, of which mats are made.

Moonish (mū·niʃ), *a. Obs.* or *arch.* late ME. [f. MOON *sb.* + -ISH[1].] Resembling or characteristic of the moon; influenced by the moon; changeable, fickle.

At which time would I, being but a m. youth, greeue, be effeminate, changeable SHAKS.

Moonless (mū·nlės), *a.* 1508. [f. MOON *sb.* + -LESS.] Without a moon; not lit up by the moon.

Moonlight (mū·nləit), *sb.* and *a.* late ME. [f. MOON *sb.* + LIGHT *sb.*] **A.** *sb.* **1.** The light of the moon. †**2.** A moonlight landscape –1778. †**3.** = MOONSHINE 3. –1829. **B.** *attrib.* or *adj.* Accompanied by, bathed in, moonlight; moonlit; done by moonlight 1584.

B. *M. flit, flitting*: the removal of household goods by night to avoid paying rent.

Moonlight (mū·nləit), *v.* 1887. [Back-formation from MOONLIGHTER.] **a.** *pass.* To be attacked by moonlighters. **b.** *intr.* To engage in moonlighting.

Moonlighter (mū·nləitəɹ). 1882. [f. MOONLIGHT *sb.* + -ER[1].] One who engages in moonlighting or commits a moonlighting outrage.

Moonlighting (mū·nləitiŋ), *vbl. sb.* 1881. [f. as prec. + -ING[1].] **1.** The performance by night of an expedition, or of an illicit action. **2.** *spec.* In Ireland, the perpetration by night of outrages on tenants who incurred the hostility of the Land League 1882.

Moonlit (mū·nlit), *a.* 1817. [f. MOON *sb.* + LIT *ppl. a.*] Lit up by the moon; flooded with moonlight. So **Moo·n-litten** *a. poet.*

†**Moo·n-man.** 1608. **1.** A night-walker; one who robs by night 1632. **2.** A gipsy –1700. **3.** A dweller in the moon –1847.

Moonraker (mū·nrēⁱkəɹ). 1787. [f. MOON *sb.* + RAKER[1].] **1.** A native of Wiltshire. (See quot.) **2.** *Naut.* A sail above the sky-sail 1867.

1. Wiltshire Moonrakers. Some Wiltshire rusticks,..seeing the figure of the moon in a pond, attempted to rake it out GROSE. Hence **Moo·n-raking** *vbl. sb. fig.* pursuing vain thoughts, woolgathering.

Moo·nrise. 1728. [f. MOON *sb.* + RISE *sb.*] The rise of the moon. Also, The East.

Moo·nseed. 1739. [f. MOON *sb.* + SEED *sb.*, after mod.L. *menispermum.*] A plant of the genus *Menispermum* (having lunate seeds).

Moo·nset. *poet.* 1845. [f. MOON *sb.*, after *sunset.*] The setting of the moon.

‖**Moonshee, munshi** (mū·nʃi). 1622. [Urdu *munshī* – Arab. *munšī'* writer, author.] A native secretary or language-teacher in India.

Moonshine (mū·nʃəin). late ME. [f. MOON *sb.* + SHINE *sb.*] **1.** = MOONLIGHT *sb.* 1. Now *rare* or *poet.* †**b.** *transf.* (*joc.*) A month. *Lear* I. ii. 5. **2.** Foolish or visionary talk, ideas, plans, etc. 1468. **3.** Smuggled or illicit spirit. *dial.* 1785. †**4.** as *adj.* Moonlit; (of persons) active by moonlight or at night –1831.

2. As for all this talk about Federalism, it is m. 1887. **Moo·nshiner** *U.S.*, a distiller of m. (sense 3).

Moonshiny (mū·nʃəini), *a.* 1602. [f. prec. + -Y[1].] **1.** = MOONLIGHT *a.* **2.** White as moonlight 1825. **3.** Of the nature of moonshine; vain, unreal 1880.

3. Unsubstantial emptinesses and m. illusions 1884.

‖**Moonsif(f, munsif** (mū·nsif). 1812. [Urdu – Arab. *munṣif* just, honest.] A native judge in India.

Moonstone (mū·nstōun). 1632. [f. MOON *sb.* + STONE *sb.*, after L. *selenites*, Gr. σεληνίτης (λίθος) SELENITE.] A translucent stone (a variety of feldspar) having a pearly lustre, used as a gem.

Moonstruck (mū·nstrɒk), *ppl. a.* 1674. [f. MOON *sb.* + STRUCK; cf. Gr. σεληνόβλητος, -πληκτος.] **1.** Mentally affected or deranged (through the supposed influence of the moon); in early use = lunatic; now, distracted or dazed. **2.** = MOON-BLIND 3; also, made unsuitable for food, as fish, by the moon's influence 1846.

1. And Moon struck madness, pining Atrophie MILT. So **Moo·n-stricken** *ppl. a.*

Moonwort (mū·nwɒɹt). 1578. [f. MOON *sb.* + WORT[1], after late L. *lunaria* LUNARY *sb.*; cf. Du. *maankruid.*] = LUNARY *sb.*

Moony (mū·ni), *a.* 1586. [f. MOON *sb.* and *v.* + -Y[1].] **1.** Of or belonging to the moon; like the moon; like that of the moon. **2.** Moon-shaped; †lunate; hence, bearing a crescent as an emblem or ensign; circular 1591. **3.** Illuminated by the moon; resembling moonlight 1648. **4.** Given to mooning; stupidly dreamy 1848.

2. The M. Standards of proud Ottoman 1591. **4.** Casting upon the reflection of his white neckcloth a pleased m. smile THACKERAY.

Moor (mūəɹ, mōəɹ), *sb.*[1] [OE. *mōr* waste land, marsh, mountain, corresp. to OS. *mōr* marsh, (M)Du. *moer*, (M)LG. *mōr* (whence G. *moor*), OHG. *muor* :– Gmc. **moraz*, **moram*, perh. rel. to MERE *sb.*[1]] **1.** A tract of unenclosed waste ground; now usu., a heath. Also, a tract of ground preserved for shooting. †**2.** A marsh –1787. **3.** *dial.* The soil of which moorland consists; peat 1596. **4.** *Cornwall.* **a.** A moor or waste land where tin is found; hence *m.-house, -tin, -works.* **b.** A quantity of ore in a particular part of a lode, as a 'moor' of tin. 1602.

1. Could you on this faire Mountaine leaue to feed, And batten on this Moore? SHAKS. The moors thrown on the market for the year hung heavily on hand at first 1886.

attrib. and *Comb.*, as *m.-dike, -keeper*; *m.-bred* adj.; **m.-ball,** a sponge-like ball formed by the threads of a freshwater alga, *Conferva ægagropila*; **-band,** a hard substratum of the soil found in moorland, consisting of clay, iron ore, and small stones, and impervious to moisture; called also **m.-band pan; -coal,** a friable variety of lignite; **-evil,** a kind of dysentery in sheep and cattle; **-hag** = *peat-hag* (see PEAT[1]); **-pan** = *moor-band*; **-sickness** = *moor-evil.*

b. In names of plants: **m.-berry,** any plant of the genus *Vaccinium*; **m. myrtle,** bog myrtle, *Myrica gale*; **-palm,** any of several cotton-grasses or sedges growing on moors, or their flower-heads; the catkin of the dwarf sallow; **-wort,** *Andromeda polifolia.*

c. In names of animals: **m.-bird** (esp. the grouse); **m. buzzard, harrier, hawk,** the marsh harrier, *Circus æruginosus*; **m. coot,** the common gallinule or water-hen, *Gallinula chloropus*; **m. game,** the red grouse, *Lagopus scoticus*; also rarely, the black grouse, *Tetrao tetrix*; **m.-tetter, -tit, -titling,** (*a*) the stone-chat, *Pratincola rubicola*; (*b*) the meadow-pipit, *Anthus pratensis.*

Moor (mūəɹ, mōəɹ), *sb.*[2] [Late ME. *More*, – (O)Fr. *More*, (mod.) *Maure*, L. *Maurus*, med.L. *Morus* – Gr. Μαῦρος.] **1.** In *Ancient History*, a native of Mauretania, a region corresponding to parts of Morocco and Algeria. Later, one belonging to the people of mixed Berber and Arab race, Moslem in religion, who in the 8th c. conquered Spain. As late as the 17th c., the Moors were supposed to be mostly black or very swarthy (though 'white Moors' were known), and hence the word was often used for 'Negro'. **2.** A Moslem, esp. one living in India 1588.

1. Ethiopes, which we nowe caule Moores, Moorens, or Negros 1555.

Moor (mūəɹ, mōəɹ), *sb.*[3] 1750. [f. MOOR *v.*] An act of mooring.

Moor (mūəɹ, mōəɹ), *v.* 1495. [Early mod. *more*, prob. – (M)LG. *mōren*; cf. OE. *mǣrels*, *mārels* mooring-rope, MDu. vbs. *māren*, *mēren* (Du. *meren*), *moeren.*] **1.** *trans.* To secure (a ship, boat, etc.) in a particular place by means of chains or ropes, fastened either to the shore or to anchors. **2.** *absol.* and *intr.* **a.** To anchor 1627. **b.** Of a ship: To be made secure by means of anchors 1697.

1. A ship may be either moored by the head..or by the head and stern FALCONER. **2. a.** Two cables is the least, and foure cables the best to more by CAPT. SMITH. **b.** At length on Oozy ground his Gallies m. DRYDEN. Hence **Moo·rage,** the action of mooring; the condition of being moored; a place for mooring; also, money paid for the use of moorings 1648.

Moo·r-cock. ME. [f. MOOR *sb.*[1] + COCK *sb.*[1]] The male of the red grouse. Also occas. the blackcock.

Mooress (mūə·rės, mōə·rės). 1611. [f. MOOR *sb.*[2] + -ESS[1].] A female Moor.

Moo·r-fowl. 1506. [f. MOOR *sb.*[1] + FOWL.] **1.** *Sc.* The red grouse, *Lagopus scoticus.* **2.** *South Carolina.* The ruffed grouse 1791.

Moo·r-hen. ME. [f. MOOR *sb.*[1] + HEN.] **1.** The Water-hen, *Gallinula chloropus.* **2.** The female of the red grouse, *Lagopus scoticus.*

Mooring (mūə·riŋ, mōə·riŋ), *vbl. sb.* late ME. [f. MOOR *v.* + -ING[1].] **1.** The action of MOOR *v.* **2.** *concr.* (Usu. *pl.*) The rope, chain, etc. by which a floating object is made fast; also the object to which it is moored 1744. **3.** *pl.* The place where a vessel can be moored 1758. **4.** *attrib.*, as *m.-mast* (for an airship).

2. *fig.* The tempest which had driven him from his domestic m. was followed by a fitful calm 1854.

Moorish (mūə·riʃ, mōə·riʃ), *a.*[1] late ME. [f. MOOR *sb.*[1] + -ISH[1].] †**1.** Of soil: Boggy, swampy –1820. †**b.** Of water: Such as is found in bogs –1640. **2.** Of or pertaining to a moor; abounding in moors or moorland; having the characteristics of a moor 1546. **3.** Growing on moors 1612.

2. M. Skiddaw and far-sweeping Saddleback RUSKIN.

Moorish (mūə·riʃ, mōə·riʃ), *a.*[2] late ME. [f. MOOR *sb.*[2] + -ISH[1].] **1.** Of or pertaining to the Moors. **2.** Moslem. Now only *colloq.* in Southern India and Ceylon. 1613.

1. The greatest peculiarity in the M. architecture is the horse-shoe arch 1797. (Cf. MORESQUE.)

Moorland (mūə·ɹlænd, mōə·ɹ-). OE. [f. MOOR *sb.*[1] + LAND *sb.*] **1.** Uncultivated land; in mod. use, land abounding in heather; a moor. **2.** *attrib.* or *adj.* Of the nature of or pertaining to moorland; inhabiting moorland 1612. Hence **Moo·rlander,** one who lives in a m.; *spec.* one who lives in the Moorlands of Staffordshire 1646.

Moorman[1] (mūə·ɹ-, mōə·ɹmæn). 1687. [f. MOOR *sb.*[1] + MAN *sb.*] **1.** One who lives on a moor 1790. **2.** An official who has charge of a moor.

Moorman[2]. 1698. [f. MOOR *sb.*[2] + MAN *sb.*] = MOOR *sb.*[2]; in India, a Moslem.

Moor-pout (mūə·ɹpaut, mōə·ɹ-). 1506. [f. MOOR *sb.*[1] + *pout*, dial. var. of POULT *sb.*] A young grouse.

†**Moors,** *a.* and *sb. Anglo-Ind.* 1767. [– Du. *Moorsch* MOORISH.] Urdu or Hindustani –1840.

Moorstone (mūə·ɹ-, mōə·ɹstōun). 1600. [MOOR *sb.*[1]] **1.** A kind of granite found chiefly in Cornwall. **2.** A slab of this 1698.

‖**Mooruk** (mūə·ruk). 1860. [From its cry.] A kind of cassowary, *Casuarius bennetti.*

‖**Moory** (mūə·ri), *sb.* 1605. [prob. native adj. formation from *Moor* = Moslem (see MOOR *sb.*[2]).] A kind of Indian cloth.

Moory (mūə·ri, mōə·ri), *a.* late ME. [f. MOOR *sb.*[1] + -Y[1].] **1.** Marshy, fenny; growing in a marsh or fen. **2.** Of, pertaining to, or like a moor; abounding in heath 1794.

1. With winged course ore Hill or moarie Dale MILT.

Moose (mūs). 1613. [– Narragansett *moos.*] A cervine animal native to N.America closely allied to, or identical with, the European Elk (*Alces malchis*). Also *m. deer.*

attrib. and *Comb.*, as *m.-flesh, -track, -trail*, etc.; **m. bird** *U.S.*, the Canada jay, *Garrulus canadensis*; **m. call,** a trumpet of birch bark used by hunters in calling moose; **m.-wood,** (*a*) striped maple, *Acer pennsylvanicum*; (*b*) leatherwood; **m. yard,** an area in which the snow is trodden down by moose, where they remain together in winter.

Moot, *sb.* [Early ME. *mōt, imōt* :– OE. *mōt* and *ġemōt* :– Gmc. *(ʒa)*mōtam*; cf. MDu. *moet*, (also mod.) *gemoet*, MHG. *muoze* meeting, attack, ON. *mót*, and MEET *v.*] †**1.** *gen.* Meeting, encounter –1470. **2.** An assembly of people, esp. one forming a court of judicature; a meeting, also the place where a meeting is held. *Obs.* exc. *Hist.* OE. †**3.** Litigation; an action at law; a plea; accusation –1609. †**4.** Argument; disputation; talking –1676. **5.** *Law.* The discussion of a hypothetical case by students at the Inns of Court for practice; also, a case of this kind. 1531.

2. In the Anglo-Saxon moots may be discerned the first germs of popular government in England 1885. **5.** A m. was held last night in the hall of Gray's-inn on the following question 1876.

Comb.: **m. court,** a court at which students argue imaginary cases for practice; **m.-stow** *Hist.*, the place where a m. was held.

Moot (mūt), *a.* 1577. [f. attrib. use of MOOT *sb.*] That can be argued; debatable; not decided, doubtful.

M. case, primarily, a case for discussion in a 'moot'; hence, a doubtful case. Those who are.. quite prepared to discuss m. and difficult points 1899.

Moot (mūt), *v.* [OE. *mōtian*, f. *mōt* MOOT *sb.*] †**1. a.** *intr.* To speak, to converse –1644. †**b.** *trans.* To say, to utter –1585. †**2. a.** *intr.* To argue, to plead, to discuss, esp. in a law case. In later use, *esp.* to debate an imaginary case of law (see MOOT *sb.*[1] 5) –1652. †**b.** *trans.* To argue (a point, case, etc.) –1796. **3.** *trans.* To raise (a point, subject, etc.) for discussion 1685.

2. a. He talkes Statutes as fiercely, as if he had mooted seuen yeers in the Inns of Court 1628. Hence **Moo·table** *a.* **Moo·ted** *ppl. a.* brought forward for discussion; also *U.S.* = MOOT *a.* **Moo·ter,** †one who discusses a m. case –1827; one who proposes a question, etc. 1844.

Moot, obs. f. MOTE *sb.* and *v.*

Moot hall. late ME. [f. MOOT *sb.* + HALL.] A hall in which a moot is held.

The hall in which the assizes are held at Carlisle, still goes by the name of the mote, or moot-hall 1794.

Moo·t-hill. 1609. [f. MOOT *sb.* + HILL *sb.*] *Antiq.* A hill on which moots or assemblies were held.

†**Moo·t-house.** [OE. *mōthūs.*] = MOOT HALL –1677.

†**Moo·tman.** 1602. [f. MOOT *v.* + MAN *sb.*] A law student of an Inn of Court; a student who argues a moot case –1797.

Mop (mǫp), *sb.*[1] 1496. [First in naut. use in form †*mapp(e* XV, which survived dial. as *map(p*; later *mop* (XVII); ult. connection with L. *mappa* (see NAPKIN) is possible, but the immed. source remains obscure.] **1.** A bundle of coarse yarn or cloth fastened at the end of a stick, used in cleaning floors, etc. **2.** *transf.* Applied to instruments resembling a mop 1869. **3.** A thick mass (of hair, etc.) 1616.

1. Now Moll had whirl'd her M. with dext'rous Airs SWIFT.

attrib. and *Comb.*, as **m.-brush,** a round paint-brush with a short thick head; **-head,** (*a*) the head of a m.; (*b*) a thick head of hair resembling a m.; also, a person having a m. of hair.

Mop (mǫp), *sb.*[2] 1581. [Goes with MOP *v.*[1]] A grimace, esp. one made by a monkey. Chiefly in *mops and mows.*

†**Mop,** *sb.*[3] 1589. [Of unkn. origin.] In *whiting-m., gurnard-m.*, a young whiting or gurnard. Also *fig.* –1758.

Mop (mǫp), *sb.*[4] *dial.* 1677. [perh. short for *mop-fair*, a hiring fair, at which the maids carried mops or brooms in token of the capacity in which they wished to engage.] A local name for the annual gathering at which servants are hired; a statute fair.

Mop (mǫp), *v.*[1] 1567. [perh. imit. of the pouting of the lips; prob. of LG. origin (cf. Du. *mop* pug-dog, *moppen* be surly, pout).] *intr.* To make a grimace. Chiefly in phr. *to mop and mow.*

Mop (mǫp), *v.*[2] 1709. [f. MOP *sb.*[1]] **1.** *trans.* To rub with a mop; to wipe with or as with a mop. Also with *out.* **2.** To wipe sweat, tears, etc., from (the face, brow, etc.). Also *rarely* with *up.* 1840.

1. *To m. the floor with* (slang): said of a combatant in whose hands his opponent is helpless.

M. up: to absorb, wipe up, with or as with a mop; to absorb, get hold of (profits, etc.); to make an end of, slaughter.

Mope (mōᵘp), *sb.* 1540. [In sense 1 *mope* (XVI), earlier †*moppe* (XIV), with †*mop(p)ish* bewildered (XIV), perh. of Scand. origin; cf. OSw. *mopa* befool, Sw. dial. *mopa* look discontented, sulk, Da. *maabe* be stupid or unconscious; in other senses f. next.] †**1.** A fool –1788. **2.** One who mopes; a gloomy, listless person 1693. **3.** *pl. The mopes*: depression of spirits 1825.

Mope (mōᵘp), *v.* 1568. [rel. to MOPE *sb.*] **1.** *intr.* To be in a state of bewilderment; to go about or act aimlessly. *Obs.* exc. *dial.* **2.** To be dull, dejected, and spiritless 1590. Also quasi- *trans.* with *away* 1791. **3.** *trans.* To make dull, dejected, or melancholy. Now only *refl.* and in *pass.* 1602.

1. *Hen. V*, III. vii. 143. **2.** Here I sit moping all the live-long Night STEELE. **3.** My father is moped to death for want of you both 1803.

Mope-eyed (mōᵘ·pˌəi·d), *a.* 1606. [f. stem of MOPE *v.* (see sense 1).] Purblind, short-sighted.

Mopish (mōᵘ·piʃ), *a.* 1621. [f. MOPE *v.* + -ISH[1].] Given to moping; causing moping; dejected. Hence **Mo·pish-ly** *adv.*, **-ness** 1598.

Moplah (mǫ·plă). *Anglo-Ind.* 1787. [– Malayālam *māppila.*] One of the Moslem inhabitants of Malabar, descended from Moors and Arabs who have settled on that coast, and married Malabar women.

Mopoke (mōᵘ·pōᵘk). **morepork** (mōᵊ·ɹpōᵊɹk). 1827. [Imitative of the bird's note.] Name in New Zealand of an owl, the *Spiloglaux novæ-zealandiæ*, in Tasmania of the night-jar, *Podargus cuvieri*, and in Australia of various birds. Also, the note of the bird.

Moppet (mǫ·pėt). 1601. [f. †*moppe* baby, rag doll (XV) + -ET.] **1.** An endearing term for a baby, a girl, etc.; a darling. Also, a gaily dressed woman (*contempt.*). †**2.** A rag doll (*rare*) 1755.

Moppy (mǫ·pi), *a.* 1725. [f. MOP *sb.*[1] + -Y[1].] Resembling (as thick as) a mop.

†**Mops.** 1565. [Cf. MOPPET.] A term of endearment for a young girl –1654.

Mopstick (mǫ·pstik). 1710. [f. MOP *sb.*[1] + STICK.] The handle of a mop.

Mopus[1] (mōᵘ·pŏs). *Obs.* exc. *dial.* 1700. [f. MOPE *sb.*] A mope; a dull stupid person.

Mo·pus[2]. *slang.* 1769. [Cant word of unkn. origin.] Usu. in *pl.* Money.

Mopy (mōᵘ·pi), *a.* 1827. [f. MOPE *v.* + -Y[1].] Given to or causing moping.

Moquette (mǫke·t). 1762 (**mocketto**). [– Fr. *moquette*, said to be alt. of *mocade* MOCKADO.] A fabric with a velvety pile, used for carpeting and upholstery.

‖**Mora**[1] (mōᵊ·ră). 1569. [L. *mora* delay.] **1.** *Sc. Law.* Negligent delay. †**2.** A delay (*rare*) –1677. **3.** (Pl. *moræ.*) A unit of metrical time equal to a short syllable 1832.

‖**Mora**[2], **morra** (mǫ·ră). 1706. [It. *mora*; origin unkn.] A popular game in Italy in which one player guesses the number of fingers held up simultaneously by another player. A similar game in China. (Cf. LOVE *sb.* 9.)

‖**Mora**[3] (mōᵊ·ră). *Pl.* **moras.** 1838. [– Gr. μόρα, f. μορ-, μερ- divide.] *Gr. Hist.* One of the (orig. six) divisions of which the Spartan army consisted.

‖**Mora**[4] (mōᵊ·ră). 1826. [Shortened from Tupi *moiratinga*, f. *moira* tree + *tinga* white.] A lofty tree, *Mora excelsa*, found in British Guiana and Trinidad.

Moraine (mŏrēⁱ·n). 1789. [– Fr. *moraine* – Savoyard It. *morena*, f. southern Fr. *mor(re* muzzle, snout :– Rom. **murrum*; see MORION[1].] An accumulation of débris from the mountains carried down and deposited by a glacier.

Lateral, terminal m. a deposit at the side or at the end of a glacier respectively. *Medial m.*, a deposit between two conjoining glaciers. **b.** In rock-gardening, a raised border or ridge of stones, etc. on which plants are grown. **Morai·nal, Morai·nic** *adjs.*

Moral (mǫ·răl), *sb.* late ME. [subst. use of MORAL *a.*; but also infl. by late L. *morale* n. sing., *moralia* n. pl., Fr. *moral, morale* (see MORALE).] **1.** *pl.* (earlier †*sing.*) Used as tr. L. *Moralia* pl. as the title of writings by St. Gregory the Great, Plutarch, Seneca, etc. **2.** The moral teaching (of a fable, an occurrence, etc.); also in phr. *to point a m.* 1500. **b.** That part of a fable, etc., which points the moral meaning 1560. †**c.** Meaning, import –1841. †**3.** A symbolical figure –1599. ¶**b.** Vulgarly confused with *model.* Counterpart, double. Chiefly in *the very m. of*...1757. **4.** = MORALITY 4 b. *Obs.* exc. *Hist.* 1578. †**5.** (A person's) moral principles or practice –1820. ‖**b.** The condition (of troops, etc.) as to discipline and confidence. [Fr.; pronounced (moral).] 1883. **6.** *pl.* In early use: †(A person's) moral qualities or endowments. Now, Moral habits or conduct; also *spec.*, sexual conduct. 1613. **7.** *pl.* Moral science; ethics. Chiefly construed as *sing.* Now *rare.* 1651. **8.** *slang.* A moral certainty 1861.

2. To point a m., or adorn a tale JOHNSON. **c.** *Tam. Shr.* IV. iv. 79. **3.** *Hen. V*, III. vi. 40. **b.** He's the very m. (as the old women call it) of Sir John 1850. **6.** The morals of Sedley were such as, even in that age, gave great scandal MACAULAY. **7.** In morals the action is judged by the intention SWINBURNE.

Moral (mǫ·răl), *a.* ME. [– L. *moralis* (Cicero, *De Fato* II. i, rendering Gr. ἠθικός ETHIC *a.*), f. *mos, mor-* custom (pl. *mores* manners, morals, character); see -AL[1].] **1.** Of or pertaining to character or disposition; of or pertaining to the distinction between right and wrong, or good and evil, in relation to actions, volitions, or character; ethical. **b.** Of knowledge, opinions, judgements, etc.: Relating to the nature and application of the distinction between right and wrong 1500. **c.** *Moral sense*: the power of apprehending the difference between right and wrong, esp. when viewed as an innate faculty of the human mind. So *m. faculty.* 1699. **d.** Of feelings: Arising from the contemplation of an action, character, etc., as good or bad 1768. **e.** Of concepts or terms: Involving ethical praise or blame 1845. **2.** Concerned with virtue and vice, or the rules of right conduct, as a subject of study. late ME. **3.** †**a.** Of a writer, etc.: That enunciates moral precepts –1742. **b.** Of a literary, pictorial, or dramatic work: That deals with the ruling of conduct; that conveys a moral; also, †allegorical, emblematical. late ME. **c.** Of a literary work: Good in moral effect 1671. **4.** *Moral law*: the body of requirements in conformity to which virtuous action consists; one of these requirements. Opp. to 'positive' or 'instituted' laws. late ME. **5.** Of rights, obligations, etc.: Founded on the moral law. Opp. to *legal.* 1690. **6. a.** Of actions: Subject to the moral law; having the property of being right or wrong 1594. **b.** Of an agent, etc.: Capable of moral action 1736. **7.** Pertaining to or operating on the character or conduct of human beings; acting through or upon the moral sense 1597. **b.** Applied to the indirect effect of some action or event (e.g. a victory or defeat) in producing confidence or discouragement, and the like 1835. **8.** Of, pertaining to, or concerned with the morals (of a person or a community) 1794. **9.** Of persons, etc.: Conforming to the rules of morality; morally good 1638. **b.** Virtuous with regard to sexual conduct 1803. **c.** Of a tale, etc.: Not ribald or vicious. late ME. **10.** Used to designate that kind of probable evidence which rests on a knowledge of character and of the general tendencies of human nature; often more loosely applied to all evidence which is merely probable 1646.

1. *M. virtue*: tr. L. *virtus moralis*, Gr. ἀρετὴ ἠθική (Aristotle), (an) excellence of character or disposition, as dist. from *intellectual virtue* (ἀρετὴ διανοητική). *M. virtue* is occas. restricted to such virtues as may be attained without the aid of religion. **b.** A correct m. judgment GEO. ELIOT. **2.** *M. philosophy*: the part of philosophy which treats of the virtues and vices, the criteria of right and wrong, the formation of virtuous character, and the like; ethical philosophy, ethics. Formerly used more widely, including psychology and metaphysics. So, in recent use, *m. science.* At Cambridge, etc. *m. sciences* is used as a comprehensive name for all that is now commonly understood by 'philosophy'. Also *attrib.*, as in *m. sciences tripos. M. theology*: the practical part of ethics treated as a branch of theology; the part of theological learning which is concerned with cases of conscience. **3. a.** O m. Gower this boke I directe To the CHAUCER. **b.** *Moral play* (*Obs.* exc. *Hist.*) = MORALITY 4 b. **4.** The m. law must be the law of the perfect man H. SPENCER. **5.** The sense of m. responsibility in connexion with the use of capital MORLEY. **6. b.** Every creature possessing mind is a m. agent 1868. **7.** I wonder that thou..goest about to apply a morall medicine to a mortifying mischiefe SHAKS. There is now very little m. hold which the latter [the clergy] possess COBBETT. The moral-force men and the physical-force men 1851. *M. courage*: courage to encounter odium, disapproval, or contempt, rather than depart from what is right; dist. from *physical courage.* **b.** *M. victory*: a defeat or an indecisive result claimed as a victory on account of its moral effects. **8.** The m. interests of society 1848. **9.** A m., sensible, and well-bred man COWPER. **10.** In Matters of Faith, an exceeding great Probability is called a m. Certainty WATTS.

Phr. *M. sense* or *interpretation*: orig., interpretation of events recorded in Holy Scripture as typical of something in the life of the Christian soul; †hence *transf.* applied to the moral of a fable, etc.

Moral (mǫ·răl), *v. rare.* 1600. [f. prec.] = MORALIZE *v.*

‖**Morale** (mŏrā·l; as Fr. moral). 1752. [Fr., fem. of *moral* used subst.; in sense 2 = Fr. *moral* sb. masc. (cf. MORAL *sb.* 5 b).] **1.** Morality, morals: moral principles or practice; moral teaching 1812; moral aspect 1834. **2.** Moral condition; conduct, behaviour; esp. with regard to confidence, discipline, etc. Said of a body of troops, etc. 1831.

2. The *morale* of the troops is excellent 1870.

Moralism (mǫ·răliz'm). 1828. [f. MORAL + -ISM.] **1.** Addiction to moralizing; (with *pl.*) an act of moralizing. **2.** The practice of a natural system of morality; morality not spiritualized 1850.

Moralist (mǫ·rălist). 1621. [f. MORAL + -IST.] **1.** One who practises morality. **2.** A teacher of morals; a moral philosopher 1639. **3.** A merely moral man. (Cf. MORALISM 2.) 1649.

1. And many a holy text around she strews, That teach the rustic m. to die GRAY. **Morali·stic** *a.*

Morality (mŏræ·lĭti). late ME. [– (O)Fr. *moralité* or late L. *moralitas*, f. L. *moralis*; see MORAL *a.*, -ITY.] †**1.** Knowledge of moral science. late ME. only. **2.** *pl.* Moral qualities or endowments. late ME. **3.** Moral discourse or instruction; a moral exhortation. Now chiefly in disparaging sense, moralizing. late ME. †**b.** Moral sense or interpretation (see MORAL *a.*); also, the moral (of a fable, etc.) –1623. †**4.** A literary or artistic production inculcating a moral lesson; a moralizing commentary; a moral allegory –1649. **b.** *Hist.* Name for the species of drama (popular in the 16th c.) in which some moral or spiritual lesson was inculcated, and in which the chief characters were personifications of abstract qualities 1765. **5.** Moral science 1449. **b.** *pl.* Points of ethics, moral principles or rules 1605. **c.** A particular system of morals 1680. **d.** Ethical aspect (of a question) 1869. **6.** The quality or fact of being moral 1592. **7.** Moral conduct; usu. good moral conduct 1609. **b.** A mock-title for one who assumes airs of virtue 1672.

1. Of moralitee he [*sc.* Seneca] was the flour CHAUCER. **2.** A saint..in her moralities BYRON. **3.** Quaint monkish moralities and scriptural quotations 1877. **5.** I am bold to think, that m. is capable of demonstration, as well as mathematicks LOCKE. **c.** The m. of the Gospel had a direct influence upon the politics of the age FREEMAN. **6.** Instances..of genius and m. united in a lawyer..are distinguished by their singularity *'Junius' Lett.* **7.** We do not look in great cities for our best m. JANE AUSTEN.

Moralize (mǫ·răləiz), *v.* 1450. [– (O)Fr. *moraliser* or med.L. *moralizare*, f. as prec.; see -IZE.] **1.** *trans.* To interpret morally or symbolically; to point the moral of; to make (an event, etc.) the subject of moral reflection. †**2.** Of an event: To exemplify the moral of (a fable, etc.) –1611. †**b.** To supply (a poem) with a moral –1754. **3.** *intr.* To indulge in moral reflection; to found a moral (*on* or *upon* an event, etc.) 1525. **b.** *trans.* To change the condition or aspect of (a person or thing) by moral discourse or reflection. Const. *into, out of.* 1722. **4.** To make moral; to affect the moral quality of (actions, feelings) 1592. **5.** To improve the morals of 1633.

1. But what said Iaques? Did he not m. this spectacle? SHAKS. **2.** I speake..onely to shewe how it doth m. this Prouerbe, That where the Body is, the Eagles will Resort 1601. **3.** No one can m. better after a misfortune has taken place W. IRVING. **b.** To m. Affliction into Use 1722. **4.** Good and bad Stars m. not our Actions SIR T. BROWNE. **5.** To M. the Stage 1723. Hence **Moraliza·tion, Mo·ralizer. Mo·ralizingly** *adv.*

Morally (mǫ·răli), *adv.* late ME. [f. MORAL *a.* + -LY².] †**1.** In a moral sense –1509. **2.** In respect of moral conduct; from the point of view of ethics; with reference to moral responsibility 1449. **3.** Virtuously 1540. **4.** On grounds of moral evidence; according to the normal human judgement, or to reason and probability (cf. VIRTUALLY 1 b) 1615.

2. A government is m. bound to keep itself in existence KINGSLEY. **3.** To live m. DRYDEN. **4.** It being m. sure, that the Earl of Essex would put himself in their way CLARENDON.

Morass (mŏræ·s). 1655. Now *literary* exc. in the West Indies (pron. mǫ·rəs). [– Du. *moeras*, †-*asch*, alt., by assim. to *moer* MOOR *sb.*¹, of MDu. *maras, marasch* – (O)Fr. *marais* MARISH.] A wet swampy tract, a bog, marsh; *occas.*, boggy land.

attrib. and *Comb.*, as **m. ore,** bog iron ore; **m.-weed** *West Ind.*, the aquatic plant hornwort, *Ceratophyllum demersum*. Hence **Mora·ssy** *a.*

Morat (mōᵊ·ræ̆t). 1807. [– med.L. *moratum* (XII), whence OFr. *moré, moret*, f. L. *morus* mulberry; see -ATE¹.] *Antiq.* A drink made of honey and flavoured with mulberries.

Moration (morē̆ⁱ·ʃən). *rare.* 1650. [– L. *moratio*, f. *morat*-, pa. ppl. stem of *morari* to delay, f. *mora* delay; see -ION.] Delay, tarrying.

‖**Moratorium** (mǫrătōᵊ·riŏ̆m). 1875. [mod. L., subst. use of n. sing. of late L. (legal) *moratorius*, f. *morat*-; see prec., -ORY¹.] *Law.* A legal authorization to a debtor to postpone payment for a certain time. So **Mo·ratory** *a.* authorizing delay in payment.

Moravian (mŏrē̆ⁱ·viăn), *sb.*¹ and *a.*¹ 1577. [f. med.L. *Moravia* Moray (– Gael. *Muireibh*) + -AN.] **A.** *sb.* An inhabitant of Moray, in Scotland. **B.** *adj.* Of or pertaining to Moray 1897.

Moravian (mŏrē̆ⁱ·viăn), *sb.*² and *a.*² 1616. [f. *Moravia* (med.L., f. *Morava* the river March), part of the Austro-Hungarian empire, G. *Mähren*; see -AN.] **A.** *sb.* **1.** An inhabitant of Moravia. GIBBON. **2.** A member of a Protestant sect, founded in Saxony by emigrants from Moravia, and holding Hussite doctrines 1746. **B.** *adj.* **1.** Of or pertaining to Moravia 1616. **2.** Of or belonging to the sect of the Moravians 1745. Hence **Mora·vianism.**

Moray (mōᵊ·reⁱ, mŏrē̆ⁱ·). *U.S.* 1624. [– Pg. *moreia* :– L. *muræna*; see MURÆNA.] Any tropical species of eel of the family *Murænidæ*.

Morbid (mǭ·ɹbid), *a.* 1656. [– L. *morbidus*, f. *morbus* disease; see -ID¹.] **1.** Of the nature of or indicative of disease; also, †morbific. †**b.** Of persons or animals, their parts, etc.: Diseased, unhealthy –1846. **2.** Of mind, ideas, etc.: Unwholesome, sickly. Hence of persons: Given to morbid feelings or fancies. 1834.

1. Of m. hue his features THOMSON. **b.** *M. anatomy*: the anatomy of diseased organs or structures. **2.** The m. German fancies which proved so fatal to Carlyle RUSKIN. Hence **Mo·rbid-ly** *adv.*, **-ness** 1668.

‖**Morbidezza** (mǫrbide·tsa). 1624. [It., f. *morbido* morbid.] *Painting.* Life-like delicacy in flesh-tints.

Morbidity (mǫɹbi·dĭti). 1721. [f. MORBID *a.* + -ITY.] **1.** The quality or condition of being morbid; a morbid state or symptom; *pl.* morbid characteristics. **2.** *Med.* Prevalence of disease; the sick rate in a district 1882.

Morbific (mǫɹbi·fik), *a.* 1652. [– Fr. *morbifique* or mod.L. *morbificus*, f. *morbus*; see -FIC.] Causing disease. ¶**b.** Occas. misused for: Caused by disease 1658. So †**Morbi·fical** *a.* 1620–1694. **Morbi·fically** *adv.*

Morbillous (mǫɹbi·ləs), *a.* 1775. [– med.L. *morbillosus*, f. *morbillus* pustule, f. L. *morbus* disease; see -OUS.] *Path.* Of or pertaining to measles.

‖**Morbleu** (morblö̆). 1664. [Fr.; euphem. alt. of *mort Dieu* 'God's death'.] A comic oath; usu. attributed to French speakers.

†**Morbo·se,** *a.* 1691. [– L. *morbosus*, f. *morbus*; see -OSE¹.] Proceeding from disease, causing disease, unhealthy –1765. Hence †**Morbo·sity** 1646–1689. So †**Mo·rbous** *a.* 1651–1684.

‖**Morbus** (mǭ·ɹbŏ̆s). L., = disease, as in CHOLERA *m.*

‖**Morceau** (morso). 1751. [Fr.; see MORSEL *sb.*] A short literary or musical piece.

‖**Morcellement** (morsęlmaṅ). 1848. [Fr., f. *morceler* break in pieces, f. OFr. *morcel* MORSEL; see -MENT.] Division (*spec.* of land or property) into small portions.

Mordacious (mǫɹdē̆ⁱ·ʃəs), *a.* Now *rare.* 1650. [f. L. *mordax, mordac-* (f. *mordēre* bite) + -IOUS.] **1.** Biting; given to biting 1777. †**2.** Of substances: Pungent, caustic –1684. **3.** Of sarcasm, etc.: Biting, keen 1650. Hence **Morda·ciously** *adv.*

Mordacity (mǫrdæ·sĭti). 1601. [– Fr. *mordacité* or L. *mordacitas*, f. as prec.; see -ITY.] **1.** Propensity to biting 1677. **2.** 'Biting' or mordant quality.

2. He ieasteth, but without mordacitie c1630.

Mordant (mǭ·ɹdănt), *sb.* late ME. [– (O)Fr. *mordant* (see next) used subst.] †**1.** An instrument that bites or holds fast; e.g. a tag of metal at the end of the pendant of a girdle –1500. **2.** *Dyeing.* A substance used for fixing colouring matters on stuffs 1791. **b.** *Gilding.* An adhesive compound for fixing gold-leaf 1825. **3.** *Etching.* The fluid used to 'bite in' the lines on the plate 1878.

Mordant (mǭ·ɹdănt), *a.* 1474. [– (O)Fr. *mordant*, pr. pple. of *mordre* bite :– Rom. **mordere*, for L. *mordēre*; see -ANT.] Biting. **1.** Of sarcasm (hence of speakers, etc.): Caustic, incisive. **2.** Corrosive. Now *rare.* 1601. **3.** That causes pain or smart. Of pain: acute, burning. 1845. **4.** Serving to fix colouring matter or gold-leaf 1825. Hence **Mo·rdancy,** sarcastic force; incisiveness 1656.

Mordant (mǭ·ɹdănt), *v.* 1836. [f. MORDANT *sb.*] *Dyeing.* To impregnate with a mordant.

Mordent (mǭ·ɹdent). Also **mordente** (mǫɹde·nte). 1806. [– G. *mordent* – It. *mordente*, subst. use of pr. pple. of *mordere* bite (see MORDANT *a.*); so called in allusion of the force of the 'attack'; see -ENT.] *Mus.* A grace consisting in the rapid alternation of a note with the one immediately below it. Also applied to other graces.

†**Mo·rdicant,** *a.* 1597. [– Fr. †*mordicant*, pr. pple. of *mordiquer* – late and med.L. *mordicare* gripe, f. L. *mordax, mordac-*, f. *mordēre* bite; see -ANT.] Biting, sharp, pungent –1834. Hence †**Mo·rdicancy,** m. quality; also, a biting irritation 1693–1699.

†**Mordica·tion.** late ME. [–(O)Fr. *mordication* or late L. *mordicatio*, f. *mordicat*-, pa. ppl. stem of *mordicare*; see prec., -ION.] A biting, burning, or gnawing sensation or pain –1684. So †**Mordicative** *a.*, biting, sharp, pungent. late ME. –1634.

†**Mordishee·n.** *Anglo-Ind.* 1598. [– Pg. *mordexim* – Marathi *moḍachī.*] Cholera –1787.

More, *sb.*¹ *Obs.* exc. *dial.* [OE. *more, moru*, corresp. to OS. *morha*, MLG. *more*, OHG. *mor(a)ha* (MHG. *mor(h)e, mörhe*, G. *möhre*) :– Gmc. **morχōn*.] A root; a tree-stump; †*fig.* 'root', origin. †**b.** A plant. SPENSER.

More (mōᵊɹ), *a.* (*sb.*²) and *adv.* [OE. *māra* (fem., n. *māre*) = OFris. *māra*, OS. *mēro* (MDu. *mēre*, repl. in mod. Du. by *meerder*), OHG. *mēro* (G. *mehr*, with compar. suffix *mehrere* several), ON. *meire*, Goth. *maiza* :– Gmc. **maizon*, f. **maiz* (see MO *adv.*).] **A.** *adj.* **1.** Greater. **2.** [Modelled on the older use of Mo with partitive genitive.] Existing in greater quantity, amount, or degree; a greater quantity or amount of. late ME. **3.** (With sb. in *pl.*) A greater number of..1584; existing in greater numbers, more numerous (now only in pred. use) 1565. (Not in A.V. or Shaks.) **4.** Additional to the quantity or number expressed or implied; further. Now *rare* exc. as preceded by an indef. or num. adj., e.g. *any more, two more*, etc.; and in arch. phrases like *without more ado.* ME.

1. Hit semed moche m. Then I had any Egle seyne CHAUCER. Lets flye to some strong Cittadell, For our m. safety 1632. Phr. *The m. part. (The) more's the pity. The m. fool you.* **2.** Perchance my Lord, I shew m. craft then loue SHAKS. **3.** M. things are wrought by prayer Than this world dreams of TENNYSON. They that be with us are m. than they that be with them R.V. 2 *Kings* 6:16. **4.** Oliver..basin and spoon in hand, said..'Please, sir, I want some m.' DICKENS.

B. *absol.* and quasi- *sb.* †**1.** Used *absol.* in the sense 'greater' –1646. **2.** Something that is more; a greater quantity, amount, degree, etc. OE. **b.** Used predicatively: Something of greater importance or magnitude 1484. **3.** (With pl. construction.) A greater number *of* the class specified; also, a greater number of persons 1629. **4.** An additional quantity, amount, or number ME.

1. Phr. †*M. and less* = persons of all ranks (*Macb.* v. iv. 12). **2.** Where m. is meant then meets the ear MILT. The m. I saw of my guide the m. I liked him TYNDALL. 91 acres, m. or less (= approximately) of excellent..land 1798. **b.** Phr. *To be m.*: to count for m.; The individual withers, and the world is m. and m. TENNYSON. **4.** This Answer Proteus gave, nor m. he said DRYDEN. Hints haunt me ever of a m. beyond CLOUGH. Phr. *Of which m. anon.* Now *arch.* or *joc. And m.*: indicating an indefinite addition to what has been mentioned.

C. *adv.* **1.** In a greater degree, to a greater extent ME. **b.** Forming the comparative of most adjs. and advs. of more than one syllable and of all of more than two syllables ME. **c.** Formerly prefixed pleonastically to the comparative of the adj. or adv. *Obs.* exc.

arch. ME. **2.** Phr. *M. or less*: in a greater or less degree; to a greater or less extent. Hence with negative: (Not) at all. ME. **3.** Qualifying a predicate or a predicative adjunct as being applicable in a greater degree *than* another ME. **4.** Additionally, in addition. **a.** In neg., interrog., or hypothetical contexts: Further, longer, again OE. **b.** Besides, moreover ME. **5.** *More than* before adjs., advs., vbs., and descriptive sbs., indicates that the word thus qualified is inadequate to the intended meaning 1553. **b.** *Neither m. nor less than*: exactly, precisely, (that) and nothing else 1460. **6.** Used conjunctionally to introduce a clause or sentence of the nature of an important addition. Now only *arch.* chiefly in *nay m.*, rarely (*and*) *m.* late ME. †**7.** quasi-*prep.* = PLUS 1. –1706.

1. The m. he explains, the m. I am puzzled BERKELEY. **b.** He finds Rest m. agreeable than Motion STEELE. **c.** But Paris was to me M. lovelier than all the world beside TENNYSON. Phr. *The m.* = the rather, the more so (*because*, etc.) **2.** Lawyers..that are m. or less passionate according as they are paid for it ADDISON. **3.** M. dead than alive 1834. **4. a.** Hee..sent forth the doue, which returned not againe vnto him any m. *Gen.* 8:12. **b.** Ile not offend thee with a vaine teare m. B. JONS. **5.** My much m. than disrespect for the Jamaica Committee RUSKIN. **6.** We are betroathd: nay m., our mariage howre..Determin'd of SHAKS. Phr. *M. by token*: see TOKEN *sb.* **7.** That Number m. one 1706.

†**More,** *v.* ME. [f. MORE *a.*] *trans.* and *intr.* To increase –1483.

More, var. MOHUR; obs. f. MOOR.

-more (mōᵊɹ), *suffix*, forming advs. of place (rarely of time) in the comparative degree. Chiefly appended to advs. having already the comparative ending *-er*, as in *furthermore*, etc.

Moreen (mŏrī·n). 1691. [perh. fancifully f. MOIRE.] A stout woollen or woollen and cotton material either plain or watered, used for curtains, etc.

Morel[1] (more·l). ME. [– OFr. *morele* (mod. *morelle*) = med.L. *morella, maurella* (XIII); prob. fem. of *morel* (mod. *moreau*) = med.L. *morellus* dark brown (of horses) :– Rom. **maurellus* – L. *Maurus* MOOR *sb.*[2]] A name for kinds of NIGHTSHADE; chiefly the Black Nightshade (*petty m.*).

Morel[2] (more·l). 1611. [app. – Fr. †*morelle*; see MORELLO.] A morello cherry.

Morel[3] (more·l). 1672. [– Fr. *morille* – Du. *morilje*, rel. to OHG. *morhila* (G. *morchel* fungus).] An edible fungus of the genus *Morchella*, esp. *M. esculenta*.

Morello (mŏre·lo). Also † **-a.** 1648. [Of It. form and presumably a use of *morello*, fem. *-a* blackish :– med.L. *mo-, maurellus*, f. L. *Maurus* MOOR *sb.*[2]; see MOREL[1].] A dark-coloured kind of cherry with a bitter taste.

‖**More·na.** [Sp., fem. of *moreno* dark-complexioned.] A brunette. PEPYS.

†**Mo·reness.** late ME. [f. MORE *a.* + -NESS.] **1.** The condition of being greater than another. late ME. only. **2.** Plurality –1674.

Moreover (mōᵊrōᵘ·vəɹ), *adv.* Now only *literary*. late ME. [f. MORE *adv.* + OVER *adv.*] †**1.** In the phr. *And yet more over* = 'that is not all' –1526. **2.** Introducing an additional statement: Besides, further. (Often following *and*, occas. *but*.) late ME. †**b.** Governing a clause: Besides *that*. *Haml.* II. ii. 2.

2. More ouer there was no water for the multitude TINDALE *Num.* 20:2.

Morepork, var. of MOPOKE.

Moresco (more·sko). 1551. [– It. *moresco* (cf. next), f. *Moro* MOOR *sb.*[2]; see -ESQUE.] **A.** *adj.* Of or pertaining to the Moors; Moorish. **B.** *sb.* **1.** A Moor 1577. †**2.** The Moorish language –1678. **3.** A morris-dance 1625.

Moresque (more·sk). 1611. [– Fr. *moresque* – It. *moresco*; see prec., -ESQUE.] **A.** *adj.* Moorish in style or ornamental design. **B.** *sb.* **1.** Arabesque ornament 1727. **2.** A Moorish woman 1895.

†**Morfound,** *v.* late ME. [– (O)Fr. *morfondre* chill through, f. *morve* mucus + *fondre* melt, FOUND *v.*[2]] *intr.* and *pass.* Of horses, etc.: To take a thorough chill, to be benumbed with cold –1720. Hence †**Morfound** *sb.* 1523–1725.

Morganatic (mǭɹgǟnæ·tik), *a.* 1727. [– Fr. *morganatique*, G. *morganatisch*, or their source med.L. *morganaticus*, evolved from phr. *matrimonium ad morganaticam*, of which the last word is prob. based on Gmc. **morgangeba* (G. *morgengabe*) = OE. *morgenġifu* (f. *morgen* MORN + **geƀ-* GIVE) gift made by husband to wife on the morning after consummation of the marriage and relieving him of further liability.] Epithet of a kind of marriage between a man of exalted rank and a woman of lower station in which it is provided that neither the wife nor her children shall share the dignities or inherit the possessions of her husband; also, occas., used of the marriage of a woman of superior rank to a man of inferior station. Hence **Morgana·tically** *adv.*

Morgay (mǭ·ɹgēⁱ). Also **-ghi.** 1672. [– Cornish *morgi*, f. *mōr* sea + *ci* dog.] The Dog-fish, esp. the lesser spotted Dog-fish.

‖**Morgen** (mǭ·rgən). 1674. [Du. and G. *morgen*, app. = 'area of land that can be ploughed in one morning'.] A measure of land in Holland and the Dutch colonies, equal to about two acres. Also in Prussia, Norway, and Denmark, a measure of land now equal to about two-thirds of an acre.

Morgenstern (mǭ·ɹgənstɔ̄ɹn). 1637. [– G. *morgenstern*, lit. 'morning star'.] *Antiq.* A club with a head set with spikes (cf. MORNING STAR 2).

†**Morglay.** ME. [perh. – W. *mawrgleddyf* (or a cogn. form), f. *mawr* great + *cleddyf* sword. Cf. CLAYMORE.] The sword belonging to Sir Bevis; hence, a sword (1582–1647).

‖**Morgue**[1] (mǭɹg, morg). 1599. [Fr.; of unkn. origin.] A haughty demeanour, haughty superiority, pride.

An amiable family, and with nothing at all of the English *morgue* M. ARNOLD.

‖**Morgue**[2] (mǭɹg, morg). 1821. [Presumed to be identical with prec., the Fr. word having passed through the intermediate sense of 'place in a prison where prisoners were examined on entry'.] Name of a building in Paris, in which the bodies of persons found dead are exposed for identification. Hence (esp. in U.S.), any building used for the same purpose.

†**Mo·rian.** 1500. [Early mod. E. *Morien*, – OFr. *Morien*, f. *More* MOOR *sb.*[2]; see -IAN.] **A.** *adj.* Moorish; hence, black, dark –1597. **B.** *sb.* A Moor, blackamoor, Negro –1657.

Moribund (mǫ·ribɒnd). 1721. [– L. *moribundus*, f. *mori* die.] **A.** *adj.* At the point of death; in a dying state. **B.** *sb.* A dying person 1835.

A. *fig.* The wail of a m. world CARLYLE. Hence **Moribu·ndity.**

Morice, obs. f. MORRIS *sb.*[1] and *v.*

Morigerate (mori·dʒĕrĕt), *a. rare.* 1533. [– L. *morigeratus*, pa. pple. of *morigerari*, f. *morigerus*; see next, -ATE[2].] Complying, obedient. So **Morigera·tion,** obedience, compliance 1605.

Morigerous (mori·dʒĕrəs), *a.* 1600. [f. L. *morigerus* (f. *mos, mor-* custom, humour + *gerere*; after phr. *morem gerere* humour a person) + -OUS.] Obedient, compliant, submissive. Const. *to*.

Morillon[1] (mori·lən). 1664. [– Fr. *morillon*, OFr. *moreillon* (XIII), f. *mor* dark brown, whence *morel* adj.; see MOREL[1].] A variety of vine; also, its fruit.

Morillon[2] (mori·lən). 1678. [– Fr. *morillon*, app. identical with prec.] The female or young of the Golden-Eye (*Clangula glaucion*).

Morin (mōᵊ·rin). 1837. [– Fr. *morine*, f. L. *morus* (in mod.L. name of a genus formerly including the fustic-tree); see -IN[1].] *Chem.* A yellow colouring matter obtained from fustic.

Morindin (mori·ndin). 1848. [f. mod.L. *Morinda* (f. L. *morus* mulberry-tree + *Indus* Indian), a cinchonaceous genus of plants, the bark of which yields red and yellow dyes + -IN[1].] *Chem.* A yellow crystalline colouring matter.

‖**Moringa** (mori·ŋgă). 1753. [mod.L.] The ben-nut tree (BEN *sb.*[3]).

Morion[1] (mǫ·riən). 1554. [– Fr. *morion* – Sp. *morrion*, f. *morro* :– Rom. **murrum* round object. Cf. MORAINE.] *Antiq.* A kind of helmet, without beaver or visor, worn in the 16th and 17th c.

The soldiers of the guard With musquet, pike, and m. SCOTT.

Morion[2] (mǫ·riən). 1748. [– Fr. *morion* – *morio(n*, false reading for L. *mormorion* (Pliny).] *Min.* Black smoky quartz.

Morisco (mori·sko). 1550. [– Sp. *Morisco*, f. *Moro* MOOR *sb.*[2] Cf. MORESCO.] **A.** *adj.* Of or pertaining to the Moors; Moorish. **B.** *sb.* **1.** A Moor, *esp.* one of the Moors in Spain 1550. **2.** Arabesque ornament 1727. **3.** A morris-dance 1561. †**b.** A morris-dancer. 2 *Hen. VI*, III. i. 365. So †**Morisk** *a.* and *sb.*

Morkin (mǭ·ɹkin). [Late ME. *mortkyn* = AFr. *mortekine* (XV), alt. (infl. by -KIN) of OFr. *mortecine* – late L. (Vulg.) *morticina* carrion, subst. use of n. pl. of L. *morticinus* that has died, f. *mors, mort-* death.] A beast that dies by disease or accident.

Morling (mǭ·ɹliŋ). Also **mortling.** 1448. [app. formed after MORKIN by substituting -LING for -KIN.] **1.** Wool taken from the skin of a dead sheep. (*Obs.* exc. in schedules to Acts of Parliament.) Opp. to *shorling*. †**2.** = MORKIN –1753.

†**Mo·rmal.** late ME. (Chaucer). [– OFr. *mortmal* (= med.L. *malum mortuum*), f. *mort* dead + *mal* evil.] An inflamed sore, esp. on the leg –1685.

‖**Mormaor** (mǫɹmē·ǒɹ). Also **maormor.** 1807. [– Gael. *mormaer*, mod. *mòrmhaor*, app. f. *mòr* great + *maor* bailiff, steward.] In ancient Scotland, a high steward of a province.

†**Mo·rmo.** 1605. [– Gr. μορμώ a hideous she-monster.] A hobgoblin, bugbear –1738.

Mormon (mǭ·ɹmən). 1837. [f. *Mormon*, the alleged author of 'The Book of Mormon'.] **1.** A member of a religious body, calling itself 'The Church of Jesus Christ of the Latter-day Saints', having its headquarters at Salt Lake City, Utah, U.S.A., and founded in 1830 at Manchester, New York, by Joseph Smith on the basis of supposed divine revelations contained in 'The Book of Mormon'.

The best known feature of the sect is the practice of polygamy; but this is not countenanced by the Book of Mormon or the law of the U.S.

Hence **Mo·rmondom,** Mormons collectively, their territory, or their usages. **Mo·rmonism,** the religious doctrines of the Mormons 1834. **Mo·rmonite** *sb.* a M. 1833; *adj.* of or pertaining to the Mormons.

Morn (mǭɹn). [OE. *morgen*, inflected *mor(g)n-* = OFris. *morgen, morn*, OS., OHG. *morgan* (Du., G. *morgen*) :– Gmc. **murʒanaz*. The typical developments of OE. *morgen* were: *morʒen, morwen; morun, moren, morn; morwe, moru*, MORROW.] **1.** Dawn, sunrise. Only *poet.* **b.** The east 1642. **2.** The early part of the day; morning. Now chiefly *poet.* OE. **3.** The next morning. Hence = MORROW 2. OE.

1. While the still m. went out with Sandals gray MILT. Phr. *Northern m.*: the aurora borealis TENNYSON. **2.** One m. I miss'd him on the custom'd hill GRAY. **3.** He wad be glad if I wad eat a reisted haddock..at breakfast wi' him the m. SCOTT.

Morne (mǭɹn), *sb.* 1494. [– Fr. *morne* in same sense, f. *morner* blunt (a lance), f. *morne* blunted, dull; see next.] *Antiq.* The rebated head of a tilting lance.

‖**Morne** (mǫrn), *a.* 1844. [(O)Fr. *morne*, f. OFr. **morner* be sad – Frankish **mornōn* MOURN *v.*] Dismal, dreary.

A silence m. and drear AYTOUN.

‖**Morné** (mǭɹne), *a.* 1722. [Fr.; pa. pple. of *morner* blunt; see MORNE *sb.*] *Her.* Said of a lion rampant represented as having no tongue, teeth, or claws.

Morning (mǭ·ɹniŋ), *sb.* (and *a.*) [ME. *morwening, morning*, f. *morwen* MORN + -ING[1], after EVENING.] **I. 1.** Orig., the time of the approach or beginning of morn. In mod. use: The early part of the day-time, ending at noon or at the hour of the midday meal. **b.** The portion of the day extending to the fashionable dinner time 1745. Now *Obs.* or *arch.* **c.** *fig.* The beginning, or early part 1595. **2.** With qualifying adj. denoting the kind of weather, etc., prevailing, or the pleasure, etc., experienced during the morning. late ME. **3.** *poet.* The dawn, daybreak; the light of dawn. Often *personified*. 1593. **4.** A morning draught, taken before breakfast. Chiefly *Sc.* 1718. **b.** 'A slight repast taken at rising' (Jam.). *dial.* 1818.

1. The m. weares, 'tis time we were at Church SHAKS. *In the morning*, appended to an hour-date, means between midnight and noon; = *a.m.* c. In the m. of my victories 1595. 2. In a Frosty M. 1678. *Good m.*: see GOOD *a.* III. 1. *M., noon, and night* = all the day, incessantly. *All (the) m.* (*Of* or *on*) *mornings, in* or *of a m.* (*dial.*): habitually in the m. *This m.*: the m. of to-day. 3. See how the M. opes her golden Gates SHAKS. *Northern m.*: the aurora borealis 1836.

II. *attrib.* (and quasi-*adj.*) Existing, prevailing, or taking place in the morning 1535. **b.** In poetry, *morning* adj. often connotes vaguely the attributes possessed in the morning, or the fact that morning is the time referred to 1590. **c.** Of things intended to be worn in the morning 1620.

Your loue is like a mornynge cloude, & like a dew y^t goeth early awaye COVERDALE *Hosea* 6:4. b. The m. Larke SHAKS. The Schoole-boy with his.. shining m. face SHAKS. c. A loose Morning-dress 1700. A man's m. suit 1896.

Comb.: **m. call**, a visit paid during the 'morning' (*i.e.* afternoon); **m.-gun**, a gun fired from the admiral's ship, or at a military post or camp, to announce day-break; **-land**, the East, the Orient; **-office**, morning prayer; **m. prayer,** (*a*) prayer said in the m.; (*b*) the Anglican service of matins; **-room**, a room used as a sitting-room during the early part of the day; **-sickness**, nausea occurring in the morning, one of the earlier symptoms of pregnancy.

Mo·rning-gift. 1597. *Antiq.* A mod. rendering of OE. *morgenġifu* (see MORGANATIC) or its equivalents = a gift made by the husband to the wife on the morning after the consummation of the marriage.

Mo·rning-glory. 1836. [f. MORNING + GLORY *sb.*] An American convolvulaceous plant, *Ipomœa purpurea*; also applied to other species of *Ipomœa*, and allied plants.

Morning star. 1535. **1.** = LUCIFER 1. Also *gen.* a star or planet that is visible in the morning. **b.** *fig.* Applied (after *Rev.* 22:16) to Christ; also, to any person who is regarded as the precursor of a figurative 'dawn' 1567. **2.** *Antiq.* = MORGENSTERN 1684.

1. The bright morning Star, Dayes harbinger MILT. b. John Wickliffe, the morning star of the Reformation 1732.

Mo·rning-tide. Now *poet.* 1530. [f. MORNING + TIDE *sb.*] The morning, or early part of the day.

Morning-watch. 1535 (Coverdale). [f. MORNING + WATCH *sb.*] **1.** The last of the (three or four) watches into which the night was divided by the Jews and Romans. **2.** *Naut.* The watch between 4 and 8 a.m.; the men on duty at that time 1840.

Mo·rnward(s, *adv. poet. rare.* 1850. [f. MORN + -WARD(S.] Towards the morning; eastward.

‖**Moro** (mō·ro). 1886. [Sp., = MOOR *sb.*²] A Moslem Malay of the southern Philippine Islands.

Moroccan (mŏrǫ·kăn), *a.* and *sb.* 1860. [f. next + -AN.] Of or pertaining to (an inhabitant of) Morocco.

Morocco (mŏrǫ·ko). Formerly also **Marocco,** etc. 1634. [– It. *Marocco*, corresp. to Sp. *Marruecos*, Fr. *Maroc* – Arab. *Marrākeš* Marrakesh.] **1.** Used *attrib.* in the sense 'of or pertaining to or made in Morrocco'; as in *M. cherry, gum*, etc. 1664. **b.** *M. leather*: see 2. So *M. hides, skins.* 1716. **2.** (In full *morocco-leather.*) Leather made (orig. in Morocco and the Barbary States, and now in Europe) from goatskins tanned with sumac. Also, a leather in imitation of this, made from sheepskins and lambskins, etc., used chiefly in shoemaking. 1634. **b.** *attrib.*, as *m. bindings* 1817.

2. **French m.,** an inferior Levant m., having a smaller and less prominent grain. **Levant m.,** a high-grade m., with a large grain, properly made from the skin of the Angora goat. **Persian m.,** see PERSIAN *a.*

†**Morology** (morǫ·lŏdʒi). 1596. [– Gr. μωρολογία, f. μωρός foolish; see -LOGY.] Foolish talking –1656.

Moron (mō^ə·rǫn). 1912. [– Gr. μωρόν, n. of μωρός foolish.] A person whose intellectual development is arrested.

Morone, incorrect var. MAROON *sb.*¹, *a.*

Morose (mŏrō^u·s), *a.*¹ 1565. [– L. *morosus* peevish, etc., f. *mos, mor-* manner; see MORAL *a.*, -OSE¹.] **1.** Sour-tempered, sullen, gloomy, and unsocial. †**2.** Scrupulous, fastidious –1696.

1. He was a man of very m. manners, and a very sowr aspect CLARENDON. *transf.* The m. climate A. LANG. 2. He was a very m. interpreter 1695. Hence **Moro·se-ly** *adv.*, **-ness** 1653.

Morose (mŏrō^u·s), *a.*² *rare.* 1644. [– late L. *morosus*, f. L. *mora* delay: see -OSE¹.] **1.** *Casuistry.* Chiefly in the phr. *m. delectation*, the habit of dwelling with enjoyment on evil thoughts. So *m. thoughts.* **2.** *Civil Law.* Chargeable with negligent delay 1875.

Morosity (morǫ·sĭti). Now *rare.* 1534. [– L. *morositas*, f. *morosus*; see MOROSE *a.*¹, -ITY. Cf. Fr. *morosité* (XVII).] Moroseness.

Morosoph (mō^u·rŏsǫf). 1693. [First recorded in Urquhart, tr. Fr. *morosophe* (Rabelais, c1526), but cf. †*morosophist* (1610), †*morosophy* (1594), and Sir T. More's latinized *morosophus* (1519); – Gr. μωρόσοφος, f. μωρός foolish + σοφός wise.] †**a.** In Rabelais: A 'wise fool', jester. **b.** A foolish pedant.

Moroxite (morǫ·ksəit). 1814. [– G. *moroxit*, f. Gr. μόροξος a kind of pipeclay; see -ITE¹ 2 b.] *Min.* A crystallized form of apatite, found in Norway and Finland.

Morphean (mǫɹfī·ăn, mǭ·ɹfiăn), *a.* 1694. [f. MORPHEUS + -AN.] Of or pertaining to MORPHEUS; sleepy, drowsy.

‖**Morpheus** (mǭ·ɹfiŭs). late ME. [L.; Ovid's name for the god of dreams, the son of Sleep, as if – Gr. *Μορφεύς, f. μορφή form.] The god of dreams (or, pop., of sleep). Hence (irreg.) **Morphe·tic** *a.* pertaining to sleep. MME. D'ARBLAY.

†**Morphew** (mǭ·ɹfiu). late ME. [Earliest as *morphe* (XIV–XVI) – med.L. *morphea* (XII), (mod.L. *morphœa*), of unkn. origin. Cf. Fr. †*morfée*, mod. It. *morfea.*] A leprous or scurfy eruption –1835. Also *fig.*

Morphia (mǭ·ɹfiă). 1818. [– mod.L. *morphia*, alt. of *morphium* (named by W. Sertürner after *opium*), f. MORPHEUS. See -IA¹.] *Chem.* = MORPHINE.

Morphic (mǭ·rfik), *a.* 1868. [f. Gr. μορφή; see -IC.] *Biol.* Of or pertaining to form; morphological.

Morphine (mǭ·ɹfin), *sb.* Also **-in.** 1828. [– G. *morphin* (Sertürner 1816); see MORPHIA, -INE⁵.] *Chem.* The most important alkaloid narcotic principle of opium, largely used in medicine to alleviate pain. **b.** *attrib.*, as *m. habit*, etc.

Hence **Mo·rphine** *v. trans.*, to drug with m. **Mo·rphinism,** the effect of m. on the human system; the practice of injecting m. into the system. **Mo·rphinist,** one who takes m. to excess.

Morphinomania (mǭ·ɹfinomē^i·niă). 1887. [f. prec.; see -MANIA.] *Nosology.* Uncontrollable craving for morphine or opium. Hence **Morphinoma·niac,** one affected with m. Also **Morphioma·nia** 1882, **-ma·niac.**

‖**Morphoge·nesis.** 1890. [mod.L., f. Gr. μορφή shape; see -GENESIS.] *Biol.* The origination of morphological characters. So **Morphogene·tic** *a.* 1880, **Morpho·geny** 1879.

Morphography (mǫɹfǫ·grăfi). 1856. [f. Gr. μορφή + -GRAPHY.] The scientific description of form; descriptive morphology; also, the phenomena which this deals with. Hence **Morpho·grapher. Morphogra·phic, -al** *a.*

Morphology (mǫɹfǫ·lŏdʒi). 1830. [f. Gr. μορφή + -LOGY.] The science of form. **1.** *Biol.* That branch of biology which deals with the form of animals and plants, and the structures, homologies, and metamorphoses which govern or influence that form. **2.** *Philol.* That branch of grammar which is concerned with inflexion and word-formation 1869. **3.** *gen.* 1885. Hence **Morpholo·gic, -al** *a.* of, pertaining to, or derived from m.; of or pertaining to the history of form 1830. **Morpholo·gically** *adv.* **Morpho·logist** 1845.

Morphon (mǭ·ɹfǫn). Also **-one.** *Pl.* (badly formed) **-ontes.** 1873. [– G. *morphon* (pl. *-onten*), explained by Haeckel as f. Gr. μορφή form + ὄν being.] *Biol.* A morphological individual, element, or factor.

Morphosis (mǫɹfō^u·sis). *Pl.* **-ses** (sīz). 1675. [– Gr. μόρφωσις a shaping, f. μορφοῦν [illegible] shape, f. μορφή shape; see -OSIS.] †**1.** Fo[illegible] figure, configuration –1676. **2.** *Bot.* [illegible] manner or order of development of an o[illegible]

or organism 1857. So **Morpho·tic** *a.* formative; contributory to organic structure 1876.

Morra, var. of MORA².

Morrice, obs. f. MORRIS.

Morricer (mǫ·risəɹ). [f. *morrice* MORRIS *sb.*¹ + -ER¹.] A morris-dancer. SCOTT.

Morris (mǫ·ris), *sb.*¹ 1500. [orig. in *mor(e)ys dance*; subst. use of var. of MOORISH *a.*² (cf. MORRIS-PIKE), perh. after Flem. *mooriske dans*, Du. *moorsche dans*; cf. G. *moriskentanz*, Fr. *danse moresque.*] **1.** = MORRIS-DANCE 1512. **2.** A body of morris-dancers 1500. **3.** *transf.* and *fig.* 1547. **4.** *attrib.*, as *m. feast*, etc. **m. bell,** one of the small metal bells attached to the clothing of morris-dancers. 1560.

1. Footing the M. about a May pole 1589. 3. Gulls in an aëry morrice Gleam and vanish and gleam HENLEY.

Morris (mǫ·ris), *sb.*² *Obs.* exc. *Hist.* 1590. [Perversion of *merels*; see MEREL.] The game of 'merels'. Chiefly *nine men's* (*peg*) *m.*

Morris (mǫ·ris), *sb.*³ 1769. [f. William *Morris* of Holyhead.] An elongated flat eel-like fish formerly named *Leptocephalus morrisii*, but now taken to be the immature young of the conger-eel. Also *Anglesea m.*

Morris, morrice (mǫ·ris), *v.* 1725. [f. MORRIS *sb.*¹] **1.** *intr.* To dance. †**2.** *slang.* To decamp. Also with *off.* –1838.

2. I think the Welshman must *morris* COWPER.

Mo·rris-dance. 1458. [See MORRIS *sb.*¹] A grotesque dance performed by persons in fancy costume, usu. representing characters from the Robin Hood legend. Hence, any similar mumming performance. Also, a representation of this dance. Hence **Mo·rris-dancer** 1507.

Morris-pike (mǫ·ris,pəik). *Obs.* exc. *Hist.* 1487. [f. *morys*, obs. var. of MOORISH *a.*² Cf. MORRIS *sb.*¹] A form of pike supposed to be of Moorish origin.

Morris tube. 1884. [f. Richard *Morris* (d. 1891), the inventor.] A small-bore rifle barrel capable of being inserted in a large-bore rifle for shooting practice.

Morrow (mǫ·ro^u), *sb.* Now only *literary* and *dial.* [ME. *morwe, -ewe, -owe, moru*; see MORN and, for the phonology, SORROW *sb.*] **1.** = MORN 1, MORNING 1; occas. = GOOD MORROW 1. *Obs.* exc. *dial.* **2.** The day next after the present, or any specified day ME. **3.** *transf.* and *fig.*, esp.: The time immediately following a particular event 1586. **4.** *attrib.* (now only *poet.*), as *m. day*, (*a*) the next day; (*b*) daybreak ME.

1. Wel loved he by the morwe a sop in wyn CHAUCER. 2. Care not then for the morow, for the morow shall care for it self COVERDALE *Matt.* 6:34. *The m.*, freq. used advb. = on the following day. 3. Let them sleepe on, Till this stormy night be gone, And th' eternall m. dawne CRASHAW. Hence **Mo·rrow** *v. intr.* to dawn.

†**Mo·rrow-mass.** 1440. The first mass of the day –1635.

†**Mo·rrow-tide.** ME. = MORNING-TIDE –1520.

Morse (mǫɹs), *sb.*¹ late ME. [– OFr. *mors* – L. *morsus* bite, catch, f. *mors-*, pa. ppl. stem of *mordēre* bite.] The clasp or fastening of a cope.

Morse (mǫɹs), *sb.*² 1475. [Caxton has *mors marine* corresp. to Fr. *morce marin* (XVI), of which the immed. source is unknown; ult. – Lappish *moršša*, whence Finnish *morsu*, Russ. *morzh.*] The sea-horse or walrus, *Trichechus rosmarus.*

Morse (mǫɹs), *sb.*³ The name of the American electrician S. F. B. *Morse* (1791–1872), the inventor (1837) of the recording telegraph, and of the alphabet (in which the letters are expressed by dots and dashes) used for sending messages by this instru[illegible]ment: used *attrib.*, as in *M. Code*, etc[illegible] also *ellipt.* as *sb.* = 'M. telegrap[illegible]

Morsel (mǭ·ɹsĕl), *sb.* ME[illegible] (mod. *morceau*), dim. of [illegible] -EL.] **1.** A bite; a[illegible] piece of food [illegible] snack 147[illegible] small[illegible]

1598; (with *out*) to distribute in small quantities 1855.

Mo·rsing, *vbl. sb. Sc. Obs.* exc. *Hist.* 1552. [f. †*mors* vb., aphet. f. Fr. *amorcer* prime (a gun).] The action of priming (a gun). Also *attrib.*, as *m.-horn, -powder*; *m.-hole*, touch-hole.

†**Mo·rsure.** late ME. [– (O)Fr. *morsure* – late L. *morsura*, f. *mors-*, pa. ppl. stem of L. *mordēre* bite.] The action of biting; a bite –1819.

Mort (mǭɹt), *sb.*[1] ME. [– (O)Fr. *mort* :– L. *mors, mort-* death; in 3 prob. – (O)Fr. *mort* MORT *a.*] †**1.** Death, slaughter –1590. **2.** *Hunting.* The note sounded on a horn at the death of the deer 1500. **b.** The death, the kill (*arch.*). KINGSLEY. **3.** The skin of a sheep or lamb that has died a natural death. Also *m. skin* (*dial.*) 1495.

2. And then to sigh, as 'twere The M. o' th' Deere SHAKS. *Comb.*: **m.-cloth** *Sc.*, a funeral pall; also, fees paid for the use of it; **m. safe** *Sc.*, an iron frame placed over a coffin or at the entrance to a grave as a protection against resurrectionists; †**m. stone,** a stone on which the bearers of a dead body rested the coffin.

Mort, *sb.*[2] *local.* 1530. [Of unkn. origin.] The salmon in its third year.

Mort (mǭɹt), *sb.*[3] *Cant.* Also **mot.** 1561. [Cant word of unkn. origin.] **a.** A girl or woman, as KINCHIN-, *walking m.*, etc. **b.** A harlot, loose woman 1567.

Mort (mǭɹt), *sb.*[4] 1694. [perh. alt. of synon. north. dial. *murth* (– ON. *mergð* multitude, f. *margr* many) by assoc. with *mortal* excessive(ly).] A great quantity or number; a great deal. Usu. const. *of*; rarely *absol.* Also *pl.*

Here's a m. o' merrymaking, hey? SHERIDAN.

†**Mort,** *a.* late ME. [– (O)Fr. *mort* (fem. *morte*) dead – L. *mortuus*, pa. pple. of *mori* die.] Dead –1658.

Mortal (mǭ·ɹtăl), *sb.* 1526 (Tindale). [f. MORTAL *a.*] **1.** Mortal thing or substance. 1 *Cor.* 15:53. **2.** One who is mortal 1567. **b.** Used playfully for 'person'. In neg. contexts emphatic for '(any) one', '(no) one'. 1718.

2. Lord, what fooles these mortals be! SHAKS. **b.** She dared not trust such a treasure to m. READE.

Mortal (mǭ·ɹtăl), *a.* late ME. [– OFr. *mortal*, latinized var. of OFr. (also mod.) *mortel* or directly – L. *mortalis*, f. *mors, mort-* death; see -AL[1].] **1.** Subject to death, destined to die. **2.** Causing death, deadly, fatal. Const. *to*. Now only of diseases, wounds, and blows. late ME. †**b.** Of a season or region: Characterized by many deaths –1803. **3. a.** Of war, a battle, etc.: Fought to the death. late ME. **b.** Of an enemy: Implacable. late ME. **c.** Of enmity, hatred, etc.: Pursued to the death, unappeasable; deadly. late ME. **4.** Of pain, grief, fear, etc.: Deadly in its effects. Often used hyperbolically. late ME. **5.** Of sin: = DEADLY *a.* 5. Opp. to *venial*. late ME. **6.** Pertaining to or accompanying death 1542. **7.** *transf.* (from sense 1.) Of or pertaining to man as a creature destined to die; relating to humanity. late ME. **8.** In colloq. or slang uses. **a.** Extremely great 1716. **b.** As an emphatic expletive (with *any, every*, or a neg.) 1609. **c.** *slang.* Long and tedious 1820. **9.** *adv.* = MORTALLY. Extremely, excessively (*dial.* and *vulgar*) late ME.

1. For what wears out the life of m. men? M. ARNOLD. **2.** A m. wound SCOTT. *fig.* A m. defect in their constitution PALEY. **3. a.** The shocking Squadrons meet in m. Fight DRYDEN. **b.** *fig.* The mortallest enemy unto knowledge SIR T. BROWNE. **c.** *fig.* A Tribe of Egotists for whom I have always had a m. Aversion ADDISON. **4.** The marriage gave m. offence to his father M. ARNOLD. **5.** Mans m. crime MILT. **6.** This Fellow has a good m. Look—place him near the Corps STEELE. **7.** When we haue shuffel'd off this mortall coile [SH]AKS. **8. a.** I was a m. sight younger then [DICK]ENS. **b.** We may eat any m. thing we like [...] For three m. hours SCOTT. **9.** Missis was [...] THACKERAY. †**Mo·rtalness** 1530.

[...] (mǫɹtæ·lĭti). ME. [– (O)Fr. [...]ortalitas, f. *mortalis*; see prec., [...]ndition of being mortal or [...]ortal nature or existence. [...]v. Now *rare* or *Obs.* [...]a large scale, as by [...] a visitation of [...]The number of deaths in a given area or period, from a particular disease, etc.; death-rate 1645. †**c.** Death (of individuals) –1772. **d.** Mortal remains 1827. **3.** Of a sin: The quality of being mortal 1532. **4.** *attrib.*, as *m. bill, returns, table* 1665.

1. Never did man put off m. with a braver courage 1644. **2.** Years of dearth..are generally among the common people years of sickness and m. ADAM SMITH. **b.** *Bill of mortality*: see BILL *sb.*[3] **c.** 1 *Hen. VI*, IV. v. 32.

Mortalize (mǭ·ɹtăləiz), *v.* 1633. [f. MORTAL *a.* + -IZE.] *trans.* To make mortal.

Mortally (mǭ·ɹtăli), *adv.* late ME. [f. MORTAL *a.* + -LY[2].] **1.** So as to cause death; †(to fight) to the death. **2.** In reference to hatred, jealousy, fear, etc.: Bitterly, intensely. late ME. **3.** In the way of mortal sin (see MORTAL *a.* 5) 1526. **4.** *colloq.* Extremely, exceedingly. (Cf. MORTAL *a.* 8, 9.) 1759.

Mortancestry (mǫɹtæ·nsĕstri). 1471. *Scots. Law.* Corrupt Sc. form of MORT D'ANCESTOR.

Mortar (mǭ·ɹtəɹ), *sb.*[1] ME. [Partly – AFr. *morter*, (O)Fr. *mortier* :– L. *mortarium* (to which the Eng. sp. was finally assim.); partly – LG.; cf. MLG. *mortēr* (Du. *mortier*).] **1.** A vessel of a hard material (e.g. marble), having a cup-shaped cavity, in which ingredients are pounded with a pestle. Also *transf.* **2.** A bowl of wax or oil with a floating wick, and later a kind of thick candle, used esp. as a night-light. *Obs.* exc. *Hist.* ME. **3.** orig. †*m.-piece*: A short piece of ordnance with a large bore and with trunnions on its breech for throwing shells at high angles 1558. **b.** *transf.* A contrivance for firing pyrotechnic shells or bombs and for throwing a life-line 1669. †**4.** = MORTIER 1604–1686.

2. For, by this morter which that I see brenne, Knowe I ful wel that day is not far henne CHAUCER. **3. b.** The rocket and m. apparatus.. has frequently done good service where a lifeboat would have been useless 1873.

Comb.: **m.-bed,** (*a*) see BED *sb.* II. 5 a; (*b*) the bed on which the ore is crushed in a stamp-mill; †**-piece** (see 3); **m. vessel,** a class of gun-boat for mounting sea-service mortars.

Mortar (mǭ·ɹtəɹ), *sb.*[2] [– AFr. *morter* = (O)Fr. *mortier* (see prec.), with transference of meaning from the vessel to the substance produced in it, as already in Latin. Cf. MDu., MHG. *morter*, (with dissim.) *mortel* (Du. *mortel*, G. *mörtel*).] A mixture of cement (or lime), sand, and water, used to make the joints between stones and bricks in building; also for plastering, etc.

Phr. *Bricks and m.*, (*a*) the essential materials used in building; (*b*) used colloq. for 'houses' or 'house property'. *fig.* A trowel or two of biographic m. CARLYLE.

Comb.: **m.-bed,** the layer of m. between courses of brickwork or masonry; **-liquid** = GROUT *sb.*[2] Hence **Mo·rtary** *a.*

Mortar (mǭ·ɹtəɹ), *v.* late ME. [f. prec.] *trans.* To plaster with mortar; to fix or join with or as with mortar.

Mo·rtar-board. 1854. [f. MORTAR *sb.*[2] + BOARD *sb.*] **1.** A board for holding mortar 1876. **2.** A pop. name for the academic or college cap with its projecting square top 1854.

Mort d'ancestor (mǫɹdæ·nsĕstəɹ). ME. [– AFr. *mordancestre, mort d'auncestre* 'ancestor's death'.] *Old Law.* The term applied to an assize brought by the right heir against one who wrongfully took possession of his inheritance on the death of his ancestor.

Mortgage (mǭ·ɹgĕdʒ), *sb.* late ME. [– OFr. *mortgage* 'dead pledge', f. *mort* dead + *gage* GAGE *sb.*[1]; AL. *mortuum vadium* (XII).] *Law.* The conveyance of real or personal property by a debtor (called the *mortgagor*) to a creditor (called the *mortgagee*) as security for a money debt, with the proviso that the property shall be reconveyed upon payment to the mortgagee of the sum secured within a certain period. Also applied to the deed effecting this, the rights conferred on the mortgagee, and the condition of being mortgaged.

'The general object of mortgage is to secure a money debt by making it a charge on land, so that, if the debt be not paid by a time agreed upon between the parties, the creditor may sell the land and pay himself out of the proceeds' (*Encycl. Brit.* s.v.). For the etymological meaning formerly current see COKE *On Litt.* 205.

fig. They will purchase the hollow happiness of the next five minutes, by a m. on the independance and comfort of years HAZLITT. Phrases. †*In m.*: mortgaged. *To lend on m.*: to advance (money) on the security of property, esp. land or houses.

b. *attrib.*, as *m. debt, deed, money, term*, etc.

Mortgage (mǭ·ɹgĕdʒ), *v.* 1467. [f. prec.] *trans.* To make over (property, esp. land or houses) as security for a money debt, on condition that if the debt be discharged the grant shall be void. **b.** *fig.* To pledge; to make liable; *esp.* to establish a claim in advance upon (an income or the like); hence *pass.* to be attached or pledged (*to* something) in advance 1588.

b. Mortgaging their lives to Covetise SPENSER. And I my selfe am morgag'd to thy will SHAKS. Hence **Mo·rtgageable** *a.* **Mortgagee** (mǭɹgĕdʒī·) 1584, **Mo·rtgager, Mortgago·r** (mǭɹgĕdʒǭ·ɹ) 1559. (See MORTGAGE *sb.*)

Mortice, variant of MORTISE.

‖**Mortier** (mortye). 1727. [Fr.; see MORTAR *sb.*[1]] A cap formerly worn by high officials in France.

Mortiferous (mǫɹti·fĕrəs), *a.* Now *rare.* 1535. [f. L. *mortifer* (f. *mors, mort-* death) + -OUS; see -FEROUS.] Bringing or producing death; deadly. **b.** *transf.* Bringing spiritual death 1542. Hence **Morti·ferous-ly** *adv.*, **-ness.**

Mortific (mǫɹti·fik), *a. rare.* 1651. [– eccl. L. *mortificus*, f. as prec.; see -FIC. Cf. OFr. *mortifique*.] Death-producing; deadly.

Mortification (mǫɹtifikēⁱ·ʃən). late ME. [– (O)Fr. *mortification* – eccl. L. *mortificatio* (Tertullian), f. *mortificat-*, pa. ppl. stem of *mortificare*; see next, -ION.] **1.** In religious use: The action of mortifying the flesh or its lusts by the practice of austere living, esp. by the self-infliction of bodily pain or discomfort. **2.** *Path.* The death of a part of the body while the rest is living; gangrene, necrosis 1555. †**3.** Destruction of vital or active qualities; devitalization –1770. †**4.** *Old Chem.* Alteration of the form of metals, etc.; destruction or neutralization of the active qualities of chemical substances –1678. **5.** *Sc. Law.* The act of disposing of property for religious, or, since the Reformation, for charitable or public purposes. Also, property so given. (Cf. MORTMAIN.) 1471. **6.** The feeling of humiliation caused by a disappointment, a slight, or an untoward accident. Also, an instance of this; a cause or source of such humiliation. 1692.

1. He destroyed his health by his austerity and mortifications 1848. Phr. *M. of the body, of sin*, etc. **5.** Thomas Moodie's m. for building a kirk in Edinburgh 1685. **6.** He continued to offer his advice daily, and had the m. to find it daily rejected MACAULAY.

Mortify (mǭ·ɹtifəi), *v.* late ME. [– (O)Fr. *mortifier* – eccl. L. *mortificare* kill (Tertullian), subdue (the flesh), f. L. *mors, mort-* death; see -FY.] †**1.** *trans.* To deprive of life; to kill. Also, to make as if dead; to render insensible. –1692. †**b.** *intr.* for *pass.* To lose vitality –1707. †**2.** *trans.* To kill (in transf. and fig. senses); to destroy the vitality, vigour, or activity of; to neutralize; to deaden; to dull, etc. –1711. †**3.** *Old Chem.* To alter or destroy the outward form of; to hinder the operation of (spirits) by mixing with other things –1704. **4.** To bring into subjection (the body, etc.) by self-denial, abstinence, or bodily discipline. late ME. †**b.** To render dead to the world and the flesh –1581. †**c.** *absol.* or *intr.* To practise mortification; to be an ascetic –1842. **5.** *trans. Sc. Law.* To dispose of (property) by mortification 1498. †**6.** *Cookery.* To make (raw meat, game, etc.) tender by hanging, keeping, etc. Also *intr.* for *pass.* –1790. **7.** *pass.* and *intr. Path.* To become mortified or gangrenous. Also (rarely) *trans.*, to render mortified. late ME. **8.** *trans.* To cause to feel humiliated; to cause (a person) mortification (freq. in *pass.*) 1691.

1. The Lord mortifieth, and quykeneth WYCLIF 1 *Sam.* 2:6. **2.** The knowledge of future evils mortifies present felicities SIR T. BROWNE. **3.** This quik-silver wol I mortifye CHAUCER. **4.** Mortifie therfore youre members which are on the erth TINDALE *Col.* 3:5. **c.** Imagine him mortifying with his barrel of oysters in dreary solitude JANE AUSTEN. **7.** The wound..began to mortifie and grow blacke 1603. **8.** I could easily forgive his pride, if he had not mortified mine JANE AUSTEN.

Hence **Mo·rtified** *ppl. a.* **Mo·rtified-ly** *adv.*, **-ness. Mo·rtifier. Mo·rtifyingly** *adv.*

Mortise, mortice (mǭ·ɹtis), *sb.* [Late ME. *mortais, -eis* (XV) – OFr. *mortoise* (mod. *mortaise*) = Sp. *mortaja* – Arab. *murtazz* fixed in.] **1.** A cavity or hole into which the end of some other part of a framework or structure is fitted so as to form a joint; also, a groove or slot for the reception of a rope, an adjustable pin, etc. **2.** *spec.* in *Carpentry*, etc. The counterpart of a TENON; a cavity, usu. rectangular in shape, cut in the surface of a piece of timber, etc., to receive the shaped end or tenon of another piece 1440. **3.** *nonce-use* [from the vb.] State of being mortised. TENNYSON.

2. *M. and tenon, tenon and m.*, as the component parts of a particular kind of joint; hence, a joint composed of a m. and tenon. Also *collect.* as a method of joining material.

attrib. and *Comb.*: **m. clamp,** a clamp mortised at the ends; **m. gauge,** a carpenter's tool for scribing parallel lines for mortises; **m.-hole** = sense 1; *fig.* an obscure place; **-joint,** a m. and tenon joint; **m. lock,** one made for insertion in a m. cut in the edge of the lock-rail of a door; **m. wheel,** a cast-iron wheel having cogs of wood set into mortises.

Mortise, mortice (mǭ·ɹtis), *v.* 1440. [f. prec. sb.] **1.** *trans.* To fasten or join securely; *spec.* in *Carpentry*, etc., to join with a mortise; to fasten *into* or *to* by means of mortise and tenon; to secure (a tenon) with a mortise. Also *intr.* for *pass.* **2.** To cut a mortise in; also with *through* 1703.

1. Maiestie..is a massie wheele..To whose huge Spoakes, ten thousand lesser things Are mortiz'd and adioyn'd SHAKS.

Mortlake (mǭ·ɹtlēⁱk). *Obs.* exc. *Hist.* 1682. Name of the Surrey town used *attrib.* in *M. hangings, tapestry*, a kind of tapestry woven there in the reigns of James I and Charles I.

Mortling, var. of MORLING.

Mortmain (mǭ·ɹtmēⁱn). 1450. [– AFr., OFr. *mortemain* – med.L. *mortua manus* (XIII) 'dead hand', i.e. *mortua*, fem. of L. *mortuus* dead, *manus* hand; the term may be intended as a metaphor for 'impersonal ownership'.] *Law.* The condition of lands or tenements held inalienably by an ecclesiastical or other corporation. **b.** A licence of mortmain 1567. **c.** *transf.* and *fig.*

The M. Act: the statute 9 Geo. II, cap. 36, passed in 1736, imposing restrictions on the devising of property to charitable uses; also, the title of various later statutes. *Licence of M.*: an instrument conveying the permission of the king to alienate property in m. **b.** A Mortmaine to found a Colledge 1655.

†**Mo·rtress.** late ME. [– OFr. *mortreux*, pl. of *morterel*, kind of milk soup.] A kind of soup or pottage, made either of bread and milk or of various kinds of meat –1626.

Mortuary (mǭ·ɹtiu̯ări). late ME. [As sb. orig. – AFr. *mortuarie* – med.L. *mortuarium*, n. sing. of L. *mortuarius* (whence the Eng. adj.; cf. Fr. *mortuaire*), f. *mortuus* dead; see -ARY¹.] **A.** *sb.* **1.** A customary gift formerly claimed by the incumbent of a parish from the estate of a deceased parishioner. late ME. †**b.** A fine payable to certain ecclesiastical dignitaries on the death of a priest within their respective jurisdictions –1778. †**2.** A funeral; obsequies –1613. **3.** A dead-house. Also, a place specially prepared for the temporary reception of a corpse. 1865.

1. *attrib.* Tithe-Pig, and m. Guinea POPE.

B. *adj.* **1.** Of or belonging to the burial of the dead 1514. **2.** Of, concerned with, or depending upon death; reminiscent of death 1540.

1. He carried me with him as often as he could to these m. ceremonies SCOTT. **2.** A m. ring 1855.

‖**Morula** (mǫ·rŭlă). 1874. [mod.L., dim. of L. *morum* mulberry.] *Embryol.* Haeckel's term for that stage of development of an ovum in which it has become completely segmented.

Morw(e, Morwening(e, obs. ff. MORROW, MORNING.

Mosaic (mŏzē·ik), *sb.* and *a.*¹ late ME. [– Fr. *mosaïque* – It. †*mosaico, musaico* – med.L. *mosaicus, musaicus*, obscurely f. late Gr. μουσεῖον, μουσίον mosaic work (see MUSEUM), whence late L. (*opus*) *museum* and *musivum*.] **A.** *sb.* **1.** The process of producing pictures or patterns by cementing together small pieces of stone, glass, etc. of various colours; pictures or patterns thus produced; the constructive or decorative material of these. late ME. **b.** Applied to work analogous to mosaic or resembling it, as *wood, wool m.*, etc. 1727. **2.** A piece of mosaic work 1678. **3.** *transf.* and *fig.* in certain scientific uses 1877.

1. *transf.* MILT. *P. L.* IV. 700. **2.** *fig.* He [Pitt in 1766] made an administration, so checkered..; a cabinet so variously inlaid; such a piece of diversified M.;..that it was indeed a very curious show BURKE.

B. *adj.* **1.** Pertaining to that form of art described in A. 1; produced by this method 1585. **2. M. vision:** the manner of vision of the compound eye of an arthropod 1880; so *m. theory*. **3.** *Biol.* Pertaining to or exhibiting alternative characters of both parents.

1. *fig.* Let the m. brain of old Burton give forth the workings of this strange union CARLYLE. *M. wool-work*: a kind of work used in rugs, carpets, etc., in which coloured threads are arranged side by side so that the cross-section shows a pattern resembling that of mosaic. So *m. carpet*, etc.

Hence **Mosa·icist,** a worker, or dealer, in m. 1847. **Mosa·icked** *a.*, also **mosaiced,** ornamented with, or composed of, m. work 1849.

Mosaic (mŏzē·ik), *a.*² 1662. [– Fr. *mosaïque* or mod.L. *Mosaicus*, f. *Moses*; see -IC.] Of, pertaining, or relating to Moses the lawgiver of the Hebrews, or the writings, etc. attributed to him.

M. law, the ancient law of the Hebrews, contained in the Pentateuch.

Mosa·ic, *v. rare.* 1839. [f. MOSAIC *sb.*] **1.** *trans.* To adorn with mosaics. **2.** To combine as if into a mosaic; also, to produce by so doing 1841.

†**Mosa·ical,** *a.*¹ 1586. [f. as MOSAIC *a.*¹; see -ICAL.] = MOSAIC *a.*¹ –1687. Hence **Mosa·ically** *adv. rare.* 1614.

Mosaical (mŏzē·ikăl), *a.*² 1563. [f. as MOSAIC *a.*²; see -ICAL.] **1.** Pertaining to or resembling what is Mosaic. †Formerly also often = MOSAIC *a.*² †**2.** *M. rod*: a divining rod –1778.

Mosaic gold. 1746. [f. MOSAIC *a.*¹ and *sb.*] **1.** [tr. late L. *aurum musivum*.] A disulphide of tin. **2.** = ORMOLU 1839.

Mosaic work. Now *rare.* 1606. **1.** = MOSAIC *sb.* 1. **2.** = MOSAIC *sb.* 2. 1687.

Mosaism (mōᵘ·ze̜iz'm). 1845. [– mod.L. *Mosaismus*, f. *Moses*; see -ISM.] The religious system, laws, and ceremonies prescribed by Moses; adherence to these.

‖**Mosasaurus** (mōᵘsăsǭ·rŏs). Also **Moso-, Mosæ-.** *Pl.* **-i.** 1830. [mod.L., f. *Mosa* the river Meuse + Gr. σαῦρος lizard.] *Palæont.* A genus of large extinct marine reptiles, combining the characters of a saurian reptile with those of a snake. First discovered near Maestricht (on the Meuse) in 1780. Hence **Mo·sasaur,** a reptile of the genus *Mosasaurus*. **Mosasau·rian** *a.* of or pertaining to the m.; belonging to the sub-order *Mosasauria*; *sb.* a reptile of this sub-order. **Mosasau·roid** *a.*

Moschatel (mǫskăte·l). 1732. [– Fr. *moscatelle* – It. *moscatella*, f. *moscato* musk.] *Bot.* A small herb (*Adoxa moschatellina*), having pale-green flowers with a musky smell, found in shady places: freq. *tuberous m.*

Mosel(l, obs. ff. MUZZLE.

Moselle (moze·l). 1687. [– Fr. name (– G. *Mosel*, in L. *Mosella*) of a river which joins the Rhine at Coblentz.] In full *M. wine*: a dry white wine, produced near the Moselle.

Moses (mōᵘ·zĭz). 1528. [– eccl. L. *Mōses*, *Mōÿses*, eccl. Gr. Μωσῆς, Μωυσῆς – Heb. *Mōšeh*.] **1.** Applied allusively to some one resembling Moses, esp. as lawgiver or leader. **b.** Used as an oath or expletive 1855. †**2. a.** A kind of boat used in the West Indies. **b.** *M. boat*: a kind of boat used in Massachusetts 1706–1775.

Comb. **Moses' rod,** a divining-rod.

Mosk, var. of MOSQUE; obs. f. MUSK.

Moslem, Muslim (mǫ·slĕm, mǫ·z-, mɒ·s-, mɒ·zlim), *sb.* and *a.* 1615. [– Arab. *muslim*, active pr. pple. of *aslama*; see ISLAM.] **A.** *sb.* One who professes Islam. (Pl. **Moslems,** occas. **Moslemin, Moslem.**) **B.** *adj.* Of or pertaining to the Moslems 1777. Hence **Mo·slemize** *v.* 1845.

Mosque (mǫsk). late ME. [The earliest forms (*moseak, -ache* XIV) are of obsc. origin; the present form is a shortening (XVII) of *mosquee* (XVI) – Fr. *mosquée* – It. *moschea* (whence also G. *moschee*) ult. – Arab. *masjid* place of worship, mosque.] A Moslem temple or place of worship.

The m.: those who worship in mosques; the body of Moslems.

Mosquito (mǫskī·to). 1583. [– Sp., Pg. *mosquito*, dim. of *mosca* :– L. *musca* fly.] **1.** A gnat of several different species of the genus *Culex* (esp. *C. mosquito*) and allied genera, the female of which punctures the skins of animals, and sucks their blood, by means of a long proboscis. **2.** *attrib.*, as *m.-bite* 1805.

1. Howbeit the Muskitto or Gnats pestered us extreamly 1665.

Comb.: **m.-bar** *U.S.*, a kind of m.-net; **-blight,** a plant-bug of the East Indian genus *Helopeltis*; **-fly, -gnat** (= sense 1); **-hawk** *U.S.*, any dragon-fly which preys upon mosquitoes; **-net,** a net (of lace, gauze, etc.) to keep off mosquitoes; so **-netting**; so **m.-canopy, -curtain.**

b. M. craft, small light vessels adapted for rapid manœuvring. So **m. fleet,** a fleet of such vessels; **m.-built** *a.*, said of a light vessel adapted for being rapidly manœuvred.

Moss (mǫs), *sb.* [OE. *mos* = MLG., MDu. *mos* bog, moss (Du. *mos*), OHG. *mos* (G. *moos*) :– Gmc. **musam*, rel. to ON. *mosi* wk. masc. bog, moss, and ult. to L. *muscus* moss.] **I.** A bog, swamp, or morass; a peat-bog. (Chiefly *Sc.* and *n. dial.*) **b.** Wet spongy soil; bog 1596. **II.** The plant. **1.** Any of the small herbaceous cryptogamous plants constituting the class *Musci*, some characteristic of bogs, others growing in crowded masses on the surface of the ground, or on stones, trees, etc. In pop. language often extended to small cryptogams of other orders, esp. lichens and lycopods, etc. ME. **b.** With *a* and *pl.*: A species or kind of moss 1562. **2.** With defining word 1597. **3.** *transf.* An excrescence or incrustation resembling moss; *esp.* the mossy covering of the stalk and calyx of the moss rose 1607. **4.** Short for MOSS ROSE 1837.

II. 1. Hence, ancle-deep in m. and flow'ry thyme, We mount again COWPER. Provb. *A rolling stone gathers no m.*: i.e. a man who is constantly changing from place to place or calling to calling will never grow rich. **b.** On high Benmore green mosses grow SCOTT. **2. American m.,** the dried stems of Florida m., used in upholstery; **black m.** = *Florida moss*; **Canary m.,** *Parmelia perlata*, a lichen used for dyeing; **Florida m.,** *Tillandsia usneoides*; **snake m.,** club-moss, *Lycopodium clavatum*; **white m.,** a name for various lichens. Also BOG-*moss*, CLUB-MOSS, ICELAND *moss*, etc., q.v.

Comb. **1.** In sense I. **a.** In names of plants growing in bogs: as **m.-berry,** the cranberry, *Vaccinium oxycoccos*; **-corn,** the silverweed, *Potentilla anserina*; **-rush,** goose-corn, *Juncus squarrosus*; **-whin,** *Genista anglica*.

b. Spec. comb.: **m.-earth,** earth composed of, or largely mixed with, peat; **-flow,** a semi-fluid part of a bog or morass; **-oak,** oak-wood preserved in a black state in peat-bogs, etc., bog-oak; also, a seat made of this.

2. In sense II. 1. Spec. comb.: **m.-agate,** a variety of agate containing brown or black moss-like dendritic forms; **-animal, -animalcule,** a bryozoon or polyzoon; **m. campion,** a dwarf, perennial, tufted moss-like plant (*Silene acaulis*) with purple flowers, growing in northern latitudes; **-carder,** also **-carder bee,** *Bombus muscorum*, a variety of humble-bee; **-coral** = *moss-animalcule* (see above); **m. pink,** a species of phlox (*Phlox subulata*), with dark purple flowers, growing on rocky hills and sandy soils in the central U.S.; **-starch** = LICHENIN.

Moss (mǫs), *v.* late ME. [f. MOSS *sb.*] †**1.** *intr.* To become mossy –1654. **2.** To gather moss (chiefly in gerund *mossing*) 1700. **3.** *trans.* **a.** To cover with a growth of moss 1600. †**b.** To roof with moss –1722.

2. Sam. Stocks came a mossing 1700. **3. a.** An old Oake, whose bows were moss'd with age SHAKS.

Mo·ss-back. *U.S.* 1872. [f. MOSS *sb.* + BACK *sb.*¹; perh. orig. a perversion of next.] **1.** = next. **2.** *slang.* **a.** During the U.S. civil war, one who hid himself to avoid conscription for the Southern army 1872. **b.** One 'behind the times'; an extreme conservative 1885.

Mossbunker (mǫ·sbɒŋkəɹ). Also **moss-banker,** etc. *U.S.* 1792. [Earlier *marsbancker* (XVII), *mosbanker* (XVIII) – Du. *marsbanker*, of unkn. origin.] The menhaden.

Mo·ss-grown, *a.* late ME. [f. MOSS *sb.* + GROWN.] Overgrown with moss. **b.** *fig.* Antiquated.

Mo·ss-hag. *Sc.* 1816. [f. MOSS *sb.* + HAG *sb.*[4]] A pit or hole from which peat has been dug.

Moss rose. 1731. [MOSS *sb.*] A garden variety of the cabbage rose, *Rosa centifolia*; so called from the moss-like growth on its calyx and stalk.

Mo·ss-trooper. 1651. [MOSS *sb.* I.] One of the freebooters who infested the mosses of the Scottish Border, in the middle of the 17th c. **b.** *transf.* A bandit or raider 1701.

Mossy (mǫ·si), *a.* 1558. [Alteration of obs. or dial. *mosy* (= OE., ME. *mos* + *-y*), after MOSS *sb.*] **I.** *Sc.* and *dial.* Marshy, boggy, peaty 1596. **II. 1.** Overgrown or covered with moss, abounding in moss. Also of a fountain, spring, etc.: Encircled with moss; issuing from a moss-grown rock, etc. 1565. **2.** As if covered with moss; downy, velvety 15.. **3.** Resembling moss: as down, etc. 1558.

II. 1. And every bird lulled on its m. bough SHELLEY. Where thou sittest by thy m. spring R. BRIDGES. **3.** A mossie beard 1585. Hence **Mo·ssiness.**

Most (mō^{u}st), *a.* (*sb.*) and *adv.* [OE. *māst* (late Northumb.) = OFris. *māst*, *maest*, OS. *mēst* (Du. *meest*), (O)HG. (*meist*), ON. *mestr*, Goth. *maists* :– Gmc. **maistaz*, f. base of **maiz* MO + **-ista-* -EST.] **A.** *adj.* **I. 1.** = GREATEST *a.* in various applications. *Obs.* exc. in phr. *for the m. part*: usually; in the main. **2.** With *sb.* in *pl.*: The greatest number of; the majority of OE. **3.** Existing in the greatest quantity, amount, or degree; the greatest amount or quantity of. late ME.

1. The m. noumber shall have the choice and election 1579. The sence of death is m. in apprehension SHAKS. †*M. master*: ruler, commander; also, one who is 'master' in a contest, etc. **2.** Party loyalty is strong enough, with m. people BRYCE. **3.** Have not I the m. Reason to complain? SWIFT.

II. *absol.*(quasi-*sb.*) **1.** Absol.uses of sense I. 1. The greatest persons (or, rarely, things). Usu. assoc. w. *least*. Now only *poet.* in *m. and least* = 'all without exception'. ME. **2.** The greatest amount or quantity OE. **3.** (Construed as *pl.*) The greatest number. Now usu. without the article. 1470.

1. Enuenoming the hearts of m. and least 1600. **2.** This is really the m. that I can concede (*mod.*). Phr. *To make the m. of*: (*a*) To employ to the best advantage; (*b*) To treat with the greatest consideration; (*c*) To exhibit at the best or worst. **At most, at the m.** A qualifying phr., indicating that the attached amount, number, or quantity is the largest admissible; or that a statement expresses not less, but probably more, than the truth. **3.** Portraits, m. of them of persons now dead BURKE. A gentleman..who felt the infirmities of age at an earlier period than m. do 1791.

B. *adv.* **1.** As a superl. of comparison: In the greatest degree; to the greatest extent OE. **2.** As an intensive superlative qualifying adjs. and advs.: In the greatest possible degree 1508. †**3.** Mostly; for the most part –1734. **4.** Almost, nearly. Now *dial.* and *U.S.* 1584.

1. He..thought it m. for his honor & profite 1548. The m. dogged of fighters 1892. My m. extremest time of misery (now only *poet.*) 1881. **2.** Oh horrible, Oh horrible, m. horrible SHAKS. *M. Christian*, *M. Honourable*, etc., see the adjs. **3.** He took m. to silence,..yet, when he did speak, it was much to the purpose NORTH. **4.** M. everybody's here THACKERAY.

Comb.: †**mostwhat** *adv.*, for the most part, also quasi-*adj.*, the greater part of; †**mostwhen** *adv.*, on m. occasions; †**mostwhere** *adv.*, in most places.

-most (mō^{u}st, mǒst, məst), *suffix*, forming adjs. in the superl. degree, is an altered form of OE. *-mest*, a combination of two distinct Gmc. superl. suffixes, *-mo-* and *-isto-* -EST. The OE. superlatives in *-mest* descended from Gmc., except *midmest* MIDMOST, are formed not on adjs. but on prepositional or demonstrative stems; e.g. *æftemest* (see AFTERMOST), *formest* or *fyrmest* FOREMOST, *inmest* INMOST, *ūtmest* or *ȳtmest* UTMOST, etc. On the analogy of these older words, *-mest* was in OE. used to form the superlatives of several adjs. of local and temporal meaning, as *lætmest*, *ēastmest*, etc. In late OE. the adjs. in *-mest* were regarded as compounds of *mǣst* MOST, and were often spelt *-mæst*. In the 15th and 16th c. the suffix *-most* (taken as = MOST *a.*) was added to many comparatives in *-er*, as in *furthermost*, *hindermost*, etc. In subsequent formations, with the single exception of *bettermost*, the application of the suffix has been restricted to words denoting position in place, time, or serial order, as in OE.

Moste, obs. f. MUST *sb.* and *v.*, MOIST *a.*

Mostic(k, obs. vars. of MAULSTICK.

Mostly (mō^{u}·stli), *adv.* 1594. [f. MOST *a.* + -LY[2].] **1.** For the most part. †**2.** In the greatest degree; most –1768.

†**Mot**[1]. 1586. [– Fr. *mot* word, saying = It. *motto* (see MOTTO) :– Gallo-Rom. **mottum*, alt. f. *muttum* uttered sound, rel. to (colloq.) *muttire* to murmur.] A motto –1659.

And Tarqvins eye maie read the m. a farre, 'How he in peace is wounded not in warre' SHAKS.

‖**Mot**[2] (mo). 1813. [Fr.; see prec.] A witty saying. **M. juste,** the precise expression for the meaning intended.

Mot: see MORT *sb.*[3]

Mote (mō^{u}t), *sb.*[1] [OE. *mot*, corresp. to WFris., Du. *mot* sawdust, dust of turf (in MDu. *steenmot*, *turfmot*), of unkn. origin. The present form (ME. *moot*) descends from OE. obl. case-forms (*mott*, repr. the uninflected form, survived till XVIII).] **1.** A particle of dust; *esp.* one of the specks seen floating in the sunbeam; an irritating particle in the eye or throat. †**b.** A minute particle, an atom; a trifle –1725. †**c.** = ATOM 2. –1601. †**2.** A spot, a blemish –1711.

1. As the gay motes that people the Sun Beams MILT. **b.** Phr. †(*Not*) *a m.*: (not) a jot. **2.** *Hen. V*, IV. i. 189.

Mote (mō^{u}t), *sb.*[2] *Obs.* exc. *Hist.* [ME. *mote* – OFr. *mote*, *motte* clod, hillock, mound, castle, etc. (mod. Fr. *motte* clod, mound). See MOAT *sb.*, orig. the same word.] **1.** A mound, eminence, hill, esp. as the seat of a camp, city, castle, fort, etc.; also, an embankment. **2.** A barrow, tumulus 1513.

Mote, moot, *sb.*[3] *Obs.* exc. *arch.* ME. [– Fr. *mot* (see MOT[1]), similarly used.] *Hunting.* A note of a horn or bugle.

Mote (mō^{u}t), *v. arch.* [A WGmc. and Gothic preterite-present verb: OE. *mōt*; see MUST *v.*[1]] **1.** = MAY *v.*[1] II. 1–4. ¶**b.** Used as pa. t. (esp. by confusion in the 16th c. with *mought*, pa. t. of MAY *v.*[1]) = *might*, *could* –1765. **c.** In wishes, forming a periphrastic subj.: = MAY *v.*[1] II. 7 b. ME. **2.** = MUST *v.*[1] II. 1. OE. ¶**b.** Used erron. as pa. t. 1596.

1. Nor m. my shell awake the weary Nine BYRON. **b.** SPENSER *F.Q.* IV. ii. 8. **c.** *Amen.* So m. it be 1775. **2.** I merueylle moche of thy wordes that I m. dye in bataille MALORY. **b.** Sith he mought needs sail by Judaea HY. MORE.

Mo·ted, *a.* 1821. [f. MOTE *sb.*[1] + -ED[2].] Full of motes.

Mo·te-hill. 1682. *Antiq.* = MOTE *sb.*[2] 1.

Motet (mote·t). late ME. [– (O)Fr. *motet*, dim. of *mot* MOT[1]; cf. med.L. *motetus*, *-um*; see -ET.] *Mus.* †**a.** A melody. **b.** A vocal composition in harmony, set usually to words from Scripture, for church use 1597.

The boy and I again to the singing of Mr. Porter's mottets PEPYS.

Moth (mǫþ), *sb.* [OE. *moþþe* (also *mohðe*); obsc. rel. to synon. MLG., MDu. *motte* (Du. *mot*), (M)HG. *motte*, ON. *motti*.] **1.** A small nocturnal lepidopterous insect of the genus *Tinea*, which breeds in cloth, furs, etc., on which its larva feeds; a clothes-moth. In early use applied to the larva. From the 16th c. taken to denote primarily the insect in its winged state, and applied to any nocturnal lepidopterous insect of similar appearance. **b.** *fig.* Something that eats away, gnaws, or wastes silently and gradually 1577. **c.** In allusion to the insignificance of the moth, or to its liability to be attracted by the flame of a candle to its own destruction 1596. †**d.** Applied vaguely to various kinds of 'vermin', as lice, bugs, cockroaches –1748. **e.** (Also with cap.) Trade name of a type of light aeroplane 1926. **2.** *Entom.* Any insect of that one of the two great divisions of the *Lepidoptera* which includes the 'moths' in the older sense 1753.

1. The Moath breedeth upon Cloth;..It delighteth to be about the Flame of a Candle BACON. **b.** The Corruptions and Mothes of Historie, which are Epitomes BACON. **2.** CODLING-*m.*, HAWK-M., etc. q.v.

attrib. and *Comb.*: **m.-blight,** various species of homopterous insects of the genus *Aleurodes*, which are destructive to plants; **-gnat,** a dipterous insect of the family *Psychodidæ*; **-hunter,** (*a*) one who hunts for moths; (*b*) the Nightjar; **-worm,** the larva of a m. Hence **Moth** *v. intr.* to hunt for moths (chiefly in gerund *mothing*).

Mo·th-eaten, *pa. pple.* and *a.* late ME. Eaten away or destroyed by moths. Often *fig.*

Mother (mɒ·ðəɹ), *sb.*[1] [OE. *mōdor* = OFris., OS. *mōdar* (Du. *moeder*), OHG. *muotar* (G. *mutter*), ON. *móðir* :– Gmc. **mōðar-* (cons.-stem) :– IE. **māte·r-*, whence also L. *māter*, Gr. (Doric) μάτηρ, (Attic, Ionic) μήτηρ, OSl. *mati* (*mater-*), OIr. *māthir* (Ir., Gael. *máthair*), Skr. *mātṛ*, *mātar-*, Tokh. *mācar*.] **I. 1.** A woman who has given birth to a child; *gen.* a female parent. **2.** *fig.* Applied to things regarded as giving birth, or standing in the relation of a mother, e.g. a condition that gives rise to another, the Church, Nature, one's native country, one's university OE. **3.** A woman who exercises control like that of a mother, or who is looked up to as a mother. late ME. **4.** A term of address for, or a prefix to the surname of, an elderly woman of the lower class. late ME.

1. Cybele, M. of a hunderd gods MILT. *transf.* All my m. came into my eyes, And gaue me vp to teares SHAKS. **2.** Ydelnes, moder of all vyces 1463. Earth all-bearing M. MILT. The Good of M. Church 1726. Scotland, my auld, respected Mither! BURNS. Nature, a m. kind alike to all GOLDSM. Aqueous vapour is the great m. of clouds 1868. **3.** The glorius Virgine, the Mothir 1563. They call me Lady Abbess, or M. at the least, who address me SCOTT. **4.** *M. Carey's Chicken*, *Goose*: see CHICKEN, GOOSE. *M. Hubbard*: a kind of cloak (named after the person in the nursery rhyme). *M. Shipton*: a legendary 'prophetess' of the 16th c.; also, a moth, *Euclidea mi* (the *Shipton moth*).

II. Techn. uses. †**1.** After L. *mater*. *Anat.* *Hard m.* = DURA MATER; *godly*, *meek*, *mild*, *soft m.* = PIA MATER –1615. **2.** = *mother-liquor*, *-water* 1611. **3.** (More fully, *artificial m.*) An apparatus for rearing chickens artificially 1807. **III.** †**1.** The womb –1706. **2.** Hysteria. Also *fits of the m.* *Obs.* or *arch.* late ME. **IV.** Quasi-adj. **1.** Used *appos.* = 'that is a mother' ME. **2. a.** Simple attrib. (more or less *rhet.*): as *m. arms*, etc. late ME. **b.** with the sense 'inherited or learned from one's mother', 'native', as in MOTHER TONGUE, and the like 1603.

IV. 1. The M. Cow DRYDEN. The Mother-goddess Cybele 1904. O dear Britain! O my M. Isle! COLERIDGE. A 'primary' or 'mother-vesicle' 1885.

Comb.: **m.-city** = METROPOLIS in various senses; †**m. fit** = 'fit of the mother' (sense III. 2); **m. idea** [= Fr. *idée mère*], the fundamental idea (e.g. of a literary work, etc.); **m. liquid, liquor** = the liquid left after crystallization, e.g. of sea-salt; **-lye,** the mother liquor of an alkali; **m. maid, maiden,** the Virgin Mary; **m.'s mark,** a nævus; **mothers' meeting,** a (periodical) meeting of mothers connected with a parish or congregation, for instruction and counsel; **m. queen** = QUEEN-MOTHER; also applied to a queen-bee; **m. right,** (*a*) = MATRIARCHY; (*b*) the custom by which dynastic succession passes only through the female line; **m. ship,** a ship having charge of one or more torpedo boats; **m. stone,** the matrix of a mineral; also, a stone from which other minerals are derived by structural or chemical change; **-water** = *mother liquor*.

Mother (mɒ·ðəɹ), *sb.*[2] 1538. [corresp. in form and sense to MDu. *moeder* (Du. *moer*), G. *mutter* MOTHER *sb.*[1], and in use to Fr. *mère* (*de vinaigre*) and Sp., It. *madre*.] †**1.** Dregs, scum –1870. **2.** *spec.* (In full *m. of vinegar*.) A ropy mucilaginous substance produced in vinegar during acetous fermentation by a mould-fungus called *Mycoderma aceti* 1601. †**3.** *M. of grapes*: = MARC –1725.

Mother (mɒ·ðəɹ), *v.*[1] 1542. [f. MOTHER *sb.*[1]] **1.** *trans.* To be the mother of, give birth to (*lit.* and *fig.*) 1548. **2.** To take care of as a mother 1863. **3.** To acknowledge the maternity of (a child) 1622. **4.** Const. *on*, *upon*. To attribute the maternity of (a child) to (a woman) 1542. **5.** To find a mother for (a lamb or calf). Also const. *upon*. 1844.

3. That the Queen, to have put lady Elizabeth besides the Crown, would have mothered another bodies Child; but King Philip scorn'd to father it 1679. 4. *fig.* Many venerable repartees were mothered on her 1907.

Mother (mʊ·ðəɹ), *v.*[2] 1718. [f. MOTHER *sb.*[2]] *intr.* To become mothery.

Mother-church. ME. **1.** †**a.** A parish church, as dist. from a chapel of ease –1688. **b.** The principal or original church of a country, region, or city. late ME. **2.** A church (i.e. body of Christians) of which another church is an offshoot; also, the original church from which all others have sprung 1574.

1. b. The mother church of the whole land, the church of Christ at Canterbury FREEMAN. ¶See also MOTHER *sb.*[1] I. 2 quot. 1726.

Mother country. 1587. **1.** A country in relation to its colonies. **2.** One's native country 1595.

Mothercraft (mʊ·ðəɹkraft). 1914. [f. MOTHER *sb.*[1] + CRAFT.] The craft or art of caring for young children as a mother.

Mother earth. 1586. The earth as the mother of its productions and inhabitants; also (in somewhat joc. use), the ground.

He..With bloudy mouth his mother earth did kis SPENSER.

Motherhood (mʊ·ðəɹhud). 1473. [-HOOD.] **1.** The condition or fact of being a mother; the status of a mother. **b.** The feeling or love of a mother 1593. **2.** Mothers collectively 1835.

Mothering (mʊ·ðəriŋ), *vbl. sb.* 1648. [f. MOTHER *v.*[1] and *sb.*[1] + -ING[1].] **1.** Motherly care and supervision 1868. **2.** The custom of visiting parents and giving or receiving presents on Mid-lent Sunday, hence called *M. Sunday*.

2. Ile to thee a Simnell bring, 'Gainst thou go'st a m. HERRICK.

Mo·ther-in-law. 1440. [See -IN-LAW.] **1.** The mother of one's husband or wife. **2.** = STEPMOTHER. Now incorrect. 1482.

1. The everlasting Din of Mothers-in-law 1688.

Motherland (mʊ·ðəɹlænd, -lǎnd). 1711. [f. MOTHER *sb.*[1] + LAND *sb.*] **a.** A country as the producer of anything. **b.** One's native country.

Motherless (mʊ·ðəɹlės), *a.* OE. [f. MOTHER *sb.*[1] + -LESS.] Having no mother.

Mo·therlike, *a.* and *adv.* 1530. [f. MOTHER *sb.*[1] + -LIKE.] Like a mother.

Motherly (mʊ·ðəɹli), *a.* [OE. *mōdorlić*; see MOTHER *sb.*[1], -LY[1].] **1.** Of or pertaining to a mother (*rare*). **2.** Befitting a mother ME. **3.** Resembling a mother 1530.

3. A brisk, wholesome, m. body 1882. Hence **Mo·therliness.** **Mo·therly** *adv.* in a m. manner.

Mo·ther na·ked, *a.* late ME. [Cf. MDu. *moeder naect* (Du. *-naakt*), MHG. *muoternacket* (G. *mutternackt*).] As naked as at birth.

Mother of pearl. 1510. [In early use also *mother perle*, tr. Fr. †*mère perle*, corresp. to It., Sp. *madreperla*, Du. *paarlmoer*, G. *perlmutter*.] = NACRE.

Mother of thyme. 1597. Wild thyme.

Mother's son. ME. A man. Chiefly in phr., *every mother's son*.

Mother tongue. late ME. [In sense 1 *mother* was orig. the uninflected genitive.] **1.** One's native language. **2.** An original language from which others spring 1645.

Mother wit. 1529. [Earlier *moderis wytte*, 1440.] Native or natural wit; common sense.

Mo·therwort. late ME. [f. MOTHER *sb.*[1] (sense III. 1) + WORT[1].] A name for plants formerly supposed to be valuable in diseases of the womb; now chiefly *Leonurus cardiaca*; formerly also the mugwort, *Artemisia vulgaris*.

Mothery (mʊ·ðəri), *a.* 1709. [f. MOTHER *sb.*[2] + -Y[1].] Mouldy, feculent.

Moth mullein. 1578. [After mod.L. *blattaria*, f. *blatta* moth.] The plant *Verbascum blattaria*.

Mothy (mǫ·þi), *a.* 1596. [f. MOTH *sb.* + -Y[1].] Infested by moths.

‖**Motif** (moti·f). 1848. [Fr.; see MOTIVE.] **1.** In art and literature, a distinctive feature or element of a design or composition; a particular type of subject; also, the dominant idea of a work; *Mus.* a leading figure or short phrase, a subject or theme; see also LEITMOTIV. **2.** *Dress-making.* An ornament of lace, braid, or the like, sewn separately on a dress 1882. ¶**3.** Often used instead of MOTIVE, in order to avoid the suggestion of volition associated with the Eng. word 1874.

Motific (mo[u]ti·fik), *a.* 1822. [f. L. *motus* motion + -FIC.] Producing motion.

Motile (mō[u]·til), *a.* 1864. [f. as prec., after *mobile*.] *Biol.* Exhibiting, or capable of, motion. So **Moti·lity** 1834.

Motion (mō[u]·ʃən), *sb.* late ME. [– (O)Fr. *motion* – L. *motio, -on-*, f. *mōt-*, pa. ppl. stem of *movēre* MOVE *v.*; see -ION.] **1.** The process of moving; the condition of a body (point, line, etc.) when at each successive instant it occupies a different position in space. Also, An instance, kind, or variety of this process or condition. **b.** *Philos.* (now only *Hist.*) *Motion* (Gr. κίνησις) was formerly applied to all kinds of change, the term *local motion* being used to distinguish change of place 1678. **2.** Change of place in an animate body or its parts; an instance of this, a movement 1588. **b.** Capability of moving (as the property of an animate body) 1603. **c.** The action of moving the body in walking, running, etc. Also, gait, carriage. 1598. †**d.** Bodily exertion (tending to fatigue); *pl.* = bodily exercises –1695. **3.** An act of moving the body (or its members); a change of posture; a gesture; †a grimace, antic 1608. **b.** A step, gesture, or other movement acquired by drill and training (e.g. in *Fencing*) 1601. **c.** *Mil.* Each of the several successive actions of a prescribed exercise of arms 1635. **4.** Commotion, agitated condition (e.g. of water); shaking, oscillation (of a ship, a vehicle). †Also, a political commotion; agitation (of the mind or feelings). late ME. **5.** *pl.* Movements on the part of a person or body of persons, when pursuing an affair; *esp.* the movements of an army in the field. Now *rare.* 1674. **6.** The action of moving, prompting, or urging (a person to do something, etc.); a proposal, suggestion; an instigation, prompting, or bidding. *Obs.* in general sense. late ME. **7.** *spec.* **a.** A proposition formally made in a deliberative assembly 1579. **b.** *Law.* An application made to a court or judge by a party to an action or his counsel, to obtain some rule or order of court necessary to the progress of the action 1726. †**8.** An inward prompting or impulse; a desire or inclination (*to* or *towards*). Also, an emotion. –1726. †**b.** *spec.* A working of God in the soul –1772. **9.** The involuntary action of the intestines, leading to discharge of their contents; an evacuation of the bowels. Also, chiefly in *pl.*, that which is evacuated; the fæces. 1598. **10.** *Mus.* †**a.** Movement (quick or slow); tempo –1752. **b.** (*a*) The melodic progression of a voice or voice-part: dist. as *conjunct* and *disjunct*. (*b*) The progression of two or more parts with relation to each other: dist. as *similar, parallel, contrary, oblique*, and *mixed*. 1731. †**11. a.** A puppet-show –1678. **b.** A puppet. Also applied contempt. to a person. –1689. **12.** A piece of mechanism which itself moves, or which sets other pieces moving or modifies their motion; †the MOVEMENT of a watch 1605.

1. *M. of* ROTATION, *of* TRANSLATION; see those words. *Laws of M.*: see LAW *sb.*[1] III. 1. Diogenes confuted him who denyed there was any m., by saying nothing but walking before his eyes FULLER. **2.** To retard the m. of the heart and circulating fluids 1799. **b.** Devoid of sense and m. MILT. **d.** His violent m. going up Shotover Hill on foot WOOD. **3.** Speaking or mute all comliness and grace Attends thee, and each word, each m. formes MILT. Phr. *To make a m.* or *motions*: to beckon, invite by gestures (*to do* something). **4.** But in a minute she 'gan stir, With a short uneasy m. COLERIDGE. **5.** Phr. *To make a m.*: to begin to move in some particular direction or with some specified purpose; About an Hour after they made a M. to attack us again DE FOE. **7. a.** The M. being made, and the Question being put STEELE. **8.** Phr. *Of* (†*upon*) *one's own* (or †*proper*) *m.* = of one's own accord. Now *arch.* **9.** Shall I loose my Doctor? No, hee giues me the Potions and the Motions SHAKS. **11. a.** Then hee compast a M. of the Prodigall sonne SHAKS.

Phrase. **In motion. a.** *lit.* In a state of moving or of being moved. Opp. to *at rest*. Phr. *To put* (*set*) *in m.* **b.** *fig.* In a state of activity, excitement, commotion, or the like.

Comb.: **m.-bar,** a guide-bar in a steam-engine; **-block,** the guide which forms a connection between the piston-rod and connecting-rod; **m. picture** = MOVING *picture*; **-work,** the mechanism for moving the hands of a watch or clock.

Motion (mō[u]·ʃən), *v.* 1476. [f. MOTION *sb.*] †**1.** *trans.* To propose, move, bring forward –1823. †**b.** To propose or recommend (a person) for employment, or as a partner in marriage –1694. †**c.** To petition or suggest to (a person) –1544. †**2.** *intr.* or *absol.* To make a proposal, bring forward a motion, offer a plan (*rare*) –1839. **3.** *trans.* To direct or guide by a gesture or movement 1787. **4.** *intr.* †**a.** To make a movement as if *to do* something 1747–1803. **b.** To make a movement or gesture in order to direct or guide 1788.

2. MILT. *P. L.* IX. 229. **3.** She motioned him..to be silent L. HUNT. **4. a.** She..motioned to depart 1803. **b.** She..motioned to him to stand by her side 1897. Hence †**Mo·tioner,** one who motions, proposes, or instigates; also *transf.* of things –1665.

Motionless (mō[u]·ʃənlės), *a.* 1599. [f. MOTION *sb.* + -LESS.] Having no movement; incapable of motion. **Mo·tionlessness** 1817.

Motitation (mō[u]titē[i]·ʃən). *rare.* 1641. [f. *motitat-*, pa. ppl. stem of L. *motitare* (Gellius), frequent. of *movēre* MOVE *v.*; see -ION.] A quivering movement.

Motive (mō[u]·tiv), *sb.* [ME. *motyf, -yve* (XIV) – (O)Fr. *motif*, subst. use of the adj.; see next.] †**1.** Something moved; a motion, proposition; esp. in *to move* (or *make*) *a m.* –1652. **2.** That which moves or induces a person to act in a certain way; a desire, fear, reason, etc., which influences a person's volition: also often applied to a result or object which is desired. late ME. †**b.** A moving or exciting cause –1727. †**3.** A mover, instigator, promoter –1681. †**4.** A moving limb or organ. (Only in Shaks.) **5.** In art and literature: = MOTIF 1. 1851.

2. By M., I mean the whole of that which moves, excites, or invites the Mind to Volition 1754. **b.** *Oth.* IV. ii. 42. **4.** The slauish motiue of recanting feare [i.e. the tongue] SHAKS. **5.** A great composition always has a leading emotional purpose, technically called its m., to which all its lines and forms have some relation RUSKIN. *Leading m.*: see LEADING *ppl. a.* Hence **Mo·tiveless** *a.* having no m.

Motive (mō[u]·tiv), *a.* 1502. [– (O)Fr. *motif, -ive* – late L. *motivus*, f. *mōt-*, pa. ppl. stem of L. *movēre* MOVE *v.*; see -IVE.] **1.** That moves or tends to move a person to a course of action. Now somewhat *rare.* **2.** Having the quality of initiating movement; productive of physical or mechanical motion; *spec.* in Physics, etc. 1578. **b.** Of nerves = MOTOR *a.* 2. 1668. **3.** Concerned with or having the quality of initiating action 1569. †**4.** Of the limbs: Concerned with the faculty of motion or locomotion 1541–1835.

1. Those..whose m. principles are selfish 1858. **2.** *M. energy*: see ENERGY 6. *M. power*, moving or impelling power (so also *m. force*); also, the mechanical energy (as steam, electricity, air, etc.) used to drive machinery. **3.** Public reputation is a m. power DISRAELI. **4.** The m. parts of animals SIR T. BROWNE. Hence **Moti·vity,** the power of initiating motion; in *Dynamics*, kinetic energy.

Motive (mō[u]·tiv), *v.* 1650. [f. MOTIVE *sb.*; in later use after Fr. *motiver* (XVIII).] **1.** *trans.* To give or supply a motive to; to be the motive of; also *pass.*, to be prompted by (something) as a motive. **2.** In *pass.*, of incidents in a drama, etc.: To be provided with a motive to render them credible 1858.

2. His malice must be motived in some satisfactory way 1858.

‖**Motivo** (moti·vo). 1789. [It.; see MOTIVE *sb.*] *Mus.* = MOTIF (by which it has now been superseded).

Motley (mǫ·tli), *a.* and *sb.* [Late ME. *mottelay, -ley* (XV), perh. – AFr. **motelé*, f. MOTE *sb.*[1] (but the formation remains obscure).] **A.** *adj.* **1.** Diversified in colour; variegated; parti-coloured; chequered. **b.** esp. of a fool's dress. Hence *m. fool.* 1600. **2.** *transf.* and *fig.* Composed of elements of diverse or varied character 1687. †**3.** Varying in character or mood; changeable in form –1755.

1. M. dresses of black and white 1851. **b.** I met a foole i' th Forrest, A m. Foole SHAKS. **2.** M. images POPE. A motly crew 1748.

B. *sb.* †**1.** A cloth of a mixed colour; a mixture –1617. **2.** A variegated, chequered, or mixed colour; also *transf.* and *fig.* an incongruous mixture 1440. **3.** A parti-coloured dress worn by the professional fool or jester, freq. in phr. *to wear m.*; hence, allusively, foolery, nonsense. *A piece of m.*, a fool. *Obs.* exc. *Hist.* 1600. **b.** A fool, jester 1600.

1. *transf.* The fresshe hawethorn In whyte motle, that so swote doth smelle LYDG. **3.** A worthy foole: Motley's the onely weare SHAKS. **b.** I haue..made my selfe a m. to the view SHAKS. Hence **Mo·tley** *v. trans.* to make m. or parti-coloured in hue; to diversify in character; to mix incongruously. **Mo·tleyness,** m. condition or quality 1819.

Motmot (mǫ·tˌmǫt). 1837. [mod.L.; app. imit. of the bird's note.] A bird of the family *Momotidæ*, native of Mexico and S. America.

Moto-, irreg. repr. L. *mot-* (as in MOTION, etc.): used *Anat.* as in **m.-sensitive** *a.*, composed of motor and sensitive nerve-fibres; and in combs. as †*motocycle* = MOTOR *c.*, etc.

Motograph (mōᵘ·tǒgrɑf). 1877. [f. MOTO- + -GRAPH.] A receiver for an electric telegraph or telephone, invented by Edison.

Motor (mōᵘ·tɔɹ). 1586. [– L. *motor* mover, later in philos. use, f. *mōt-*; see MOTIVE *a.*, -OR 2. Prob. partly after Fr. *moteur.*] **A.** *sb.* **1.** One who or something which imparts motion; an agent or force that produces mechanical motion. **2. a.** *Anat.* A muscle which moves a particular part of the animal frame. **b.** A nerve whose function it is to excite muscular activity in a particular part of the animal body. 1808. **3.** An apparatus for employing some natural agent or force for the impulsion of machinery; a machine that supplies the motive power for the propulsion of a carriage or vessel. In recent use also in a narrower sense excluding steam engines. 1856. **b.** Short for MOTOR CAR. 1900. **4.** *Math.* An operator or quantity which represents the displacement of a rigid body 1873. **5.** *attrib.*, designating a vehicle driven by a motor, as *m. bicycle, boat, cab, cycle* 1894; connected with a motor car or motoring, as *m.-coat, -horn, -road*, etc. 1902; **m.-bandit,** a thief who uses a motor car in his depredations.

1. †*First* or *prime m.* [= med.L. *primus motor*] = PRIMUM MOBILE 1; (*b*) applied (allusively) to God, as the cause of the motion of the heavens; (*c*) the first instigator, or the chief director, e.g. of a plot, etc.; (*d*) the part that initiates motion in a piece of mechanism, etc.

B. *adj.* [After Fr. *moteur, motrice.*] **1.** Giving, imparting, or producing motion 1872. **2.** *Phys.* Of nerves (opp. to *sensory*), muscles, etc.: Conveying or imparting an impulse which results or tends to result in motion. So *m. area* (*region, zone*): that part of the cortex of the brain from which motor impulses are directed to the various parts of the animal body. 1824. **3.** Of or pertaining to motor nerves 1878. Hence **Mo·tor** *v. trans.*, to convey in a motor car; *intr.* to travel in a motor car 1896.

Mo·tor car. 1895. [MOTOR *sb.* 5.] **1.** A carriage propelled by a motor, for use on ordinary roads. **2.** *U.S.* A motor-driven car on an electric railroad.

Motorial (motōᵊ·riăl), *a.* 1843. [app. f. MOTOR *adj.* + -IAL, after *sensorial.*] Of or pertaining to motion; *spec.* of or pertaining to a motor nerve; motor.

Motorist (mōᵘ·tərist). 1896. [f. MOTOR *v.* + -IST.] One who motors, esp. habitually.

Mo·torize, *v.* 1918. [f. MOTOR *sb.* + -IZE.] *trans.* To provide with motor vehicles or traffic; to convert into a motor-driven vehicle.

Mo·tor-man. 1890. [f. MOTOR *sb.*] The driver of a motor vehicle; *spec.* the hired driver of a public motor-driven conveyance.

Motory (mōᵘ·təri), *a.* 1691. [– late L. *motorius*, f. L. *motor*; see MOTOR, -ORY^2.] **1.** *Phys.* = MOTOR *a.* 2, 3. **2.** *gen.* That causes motion 1799.

1. The m. Muscles RAY.

Motte (mǫt). *U.S.* Also **mot(t.** 1844. [app. a use of Fr. *motte* mound. See MOTE *sb.*^{2}] A clump of trees in a prairie.

‖**Mottetto** (mǫte·to), *pl.* **-ti.** 1644. [It.; see MOTET.] = MOTET b.

Mottle (mǫ·t'l), *sb.* 1676. [prob. a back-formation from MOTLEY *a.*] **1.** One of a number of spots or blotches by which a surface is variegated. **2.** The arrangement of such spots or blotches forming a mottled surface 1858. **b.** A woollen yarn of variegated colour 1887. So **Mo·ttle** *a.* mottled, now only in Combs. e.g. *m.-faced* (Dickens).

Mottle (mǫ·t'l), *v.* 1676. [f. as MOTTLE *sb.*] *trans.* To mark or cover with spots or blotches; *spec.* in *Soap-making*, to impart a mottled appearance to white soap by the addition of chemicals. Hence **Mo·ttled** *ppl. a.* dappled with spots or blotches; marked with spots, streaks, or patches of different colour.

Mo·ttler. 1839. [f. prec. + -ER^1.] **a.** A workman who mottles soap. **b.** A house-painter's brush for mottling.

Motto (mǫ·to). *Pl.* **-os, -oes.** 1589. [– It. *motto* = Fr. *mot*; see MOT^1.] **1.** Orig., a word, sentence, or phrase attached as a legend to an 'impresa' or emblematical design. Hence, more widely, a short sentence or phrase inscribed on some object, and expressing an appropriate reflection or sentiment; also, a proverbial or pithy maxim adopted by a person as his rule of conduct. **b.** *spec.* in *Her.* A significant word or sentence usually placed upon a scroll, occas. having some reference to the name or exploits of the bearer, to the charges upon the shield or to the crest, but more often expressing merely a pious aspiration or exalted sentiment 1600. **c.** The poetical lines contained in a motto-kiss or paper cracker. Also U.S. = *m.-kiss.* **3.** A short quotation (or original passage) prefixed to a literary work or to one of its parts, and expressing some idea appropriate to its contents 1711. **4.** *Mus.* A recurrent phrase 1891.

1. 'Nitor in adversum' is the m. for a man like me BURKE. **b.** *Festina Lente*—'Hasten slowly', or 'On slow', is the M. of the Onslow family CUSSANS. *Comb.* **m.-kiss,** a sweetmeat wrapped in fancy paper, having a m. or scrap of poetry enclosed with it. Hence **Mo·ttoed** *a.* inscribed with a m. †or legend 1608.

Motty (mǫ·ti), *a. Sc.* 1599. [f. *mot*, Sc. pronunc. of MOTE *sb.*^{1} + -Y^1.] Containing motes.

‖**Motu proprio** (mōᵘ·tiu prǫ·prio). 1847. [L., = of one's own motion.] A papal rescript of which the provisions are decided on by the pope personally.

Mouch, variant of MOOCH.

‖**Moucharaby** (muʃa·răbi). 1884. [Fr.; – Arab. *mašrabiyya.*] In northern Africa, an external balcony enclosed with latticework.

‖**Mouchoir** (muʃwar). 1690. [Fr.] A handkerchief.

‖**Moue** (mū). 1850. [Fr.; see MOW *sb.*^{2}] A pout.

Mouedhin, var. of MUEZZIN.

Moufflon (mū·flǫn). 1774. [– Fr. *mouflon* (Buffon) – It. *muflone* – Rom. **mufro, -on-*.] A wild sheep, esp. *Ovis musimon*, native of the mountainous regions of southern Europe.

Mought(e, obs. pa. t. of MAY *v.*^{1}

‖**Mouillé** (muye). 1833. [pa. pple. of Fr. *mouiller* wet, moisten.] *Romance Philol.* Of a consonant, chiefly *l*, also *n, r*: Palatalized or 'fronted', changed into (lʸ *and hence* y, nʸ, rʸ).

‖**Moujik, muzhik** (mū·ʒik). 1568. [Russ. *muzhik* peasant.] **1.** A Russian peasant. **2.** (In full *m. blouse, coat.*) A loose fur cape for ladies' wear 1897.

Moul, *v. Obs.* or *dial.* [– ON. **mugla* grow mouldy; see MOULD *sb.*^{4}] To grow or make mouldy.

Mould (mōᵘld), *sb.*^{1} Also (now *U.S.*) **mold.** [OE. *molde* = OFris. *molde*, (M)Du. *moude*, OHG. *molta*, ON. *mold*, Goth. *mulda* :- Gmc. **moldō*, **muldō*, f. **mul-* (**mel-* **mal-*) pulverize, grind (cf. OE. *myl*, MDu. *mul, mol* dust, and MEAL *sb.*^{1}).] **1.** Loose, broken, or friable earth; hence, the surface soil, which is easily broken up. Also *pl.* (now only *dial.*) lumps or clods of earth. **2.** The earth of the grave. Also *pl.* Now only *poet.* or *dial.* OE. **3.** The upper soil of cultivated land; garden-soil; *spec.* soil rich in organic matter and suitable for the cultivation of plants ME. **4.** Earth as the material of the human body. *Obs.* or *poet.* ME. †**5.** The ground regarded as a surface or as a solid stratum –1624. **6.** The world on which we dwell. Also, the land of a particular region. *Obs.* or *poet.* OE.

2. When Spring with dewy fingers cold Returns to deck their hallowed mold COLLINS. **3.** *Leaf-m.*, *vegetable m.* (see these words). **4.** *Man of m.*: a mortal man. Be mercifull great Duke to men of m. SHAKS. (Occas. misunderstood as 'men of parts or distinction', and so used by some mod. writers.) **6.** The fairest knight on Scottish mold SCOTT.

Mould (mōᵘld), *sb.*^{2} Now *dial.* [OE. *molda, -e* = MDu. *moude*, rel. to Skr. *mūrdhán* highest point, head.] The top or dome of the head; also the fontanelle in an infant's head.

Mould (mōᵘld), *sb.*^{3} Also (now *U.S.*) **mold.** [ME. *mold(e*, app. metathetic alteration of OFr. *modle* (whence mod.Fr. *moule*) :- L. MODULUS.] **I. 1.** A pattern by which something is shaped; e.g. the templet used by a shipbuilder, mason, bricklayer, or plasterer. **2.** A hollow form or matrix into which fluid or plastic material is cast or pressed and allowed to cool or harden so as to take a particular shape or pattern. late ME. **b.** *gen.* A modelled surface from which an impression can be taken 1530. **3.** *spec.* in *Cookery.* A hollow utensil of metal or earthenware used to give a shape to puddings, jelly, etc. Also, a pudding, etc., shaped in a mould. 1573. **4.** *transf.* and *fig.* 1557. †**b.** Said of the body with reference to its clothes –1639. †**5.** A model, a pattern –1618. **6.** A frame or body on or round which a manufactured article is made; e.g. the frame on which a sheet of paper, a basket, a hurdle (etc.) is made 1655. **7.** A package of leaves of gold-beater's skin between which gold-leaf is placed for beating 1727. **8.** *Photo-engraving.* The gelatine which receives the impression from the negative and from which the copper plate is taken; also, the metal plate itself 1875.

2. The liquid Ore he dreined Into fit moulds prepar'd MILT. Phr. *To break the m.*: *fig.* to render impossible the repetition of a certain type of creation. **4.** Phr. *To be cast in a* (certain) *m.*: to have a certain form or character. **b.** *Macb.* I. iii. 145. **5.** The glasse of Fashion, and the m. of Forme SHAKS.

II. Imparted form or make; result of moulding. **1.** Distinctive nature as indicative of origin; esp. of persons, native constitution or character ME. **2.** The form or shape of an animal body, or (less usually) of something inanimate. Now *techn.* (among cattle- or stud-breeders); otherwise *rhet.* 15.. **b.** *concr.* Bodily form, body. Chiefly *poet.* 1579. †**3.** The form or structural type or model of a building or ship –1774. †**4.** Style, fashion, mode –1656. **5.** That which is moulded or fashioned (*rare*) 1667. **6.** *Arch.* A moulding or group of mouldings belonging to a particular member of a building 1480. **7.** *Geol.* An impression made in earth by the convex side of a fossil shell 1748. **8.** = *m. candle* 1797.

1. Merchants.., That trade in mettall of the purest m. MARLOWE. A character of a finer m. JOWETT. **2. b.** Whom doth she behold?..His vital presence? his corporeal m.? WORDSW.

Comb. **m. candle,** a candle made in a m. (as dist. from a dip-candle); **m.-loft** *Shipbuilding*, a room on the floor of which the plans of a ship are drawn at full size.

Mould (mōᵘld), *sb.*^{4} Also (now *U.S.*) **mold.** late ME. [prob. developed from †*mould*, †*mouled*, pa. pple. of *moule*, *muwle* MOUL *v.* – ON. **mugla*, rel. to synon. ON. *mygla.*] A woolly or furry growth (consisting of minute fungi) which forms on substances that lie for some time in moist warm air. As a disease of the hop plant = FEN *sb.*^{2}

A man that hates cheese must call me fool for loving blue mold MANDEVILLE. *fig.* The m. of time 1829.

Mould (mōᵘld), *a.* (orig. *ppl.*) *Obs.* exc. *dial.* ME. [f. MOUL *v.* + -ED^1.] Mouldy.

Mould (mōᵘld), *v.*^{1} Also (now *U.S.*) **mold.** 1530. [f. MOULD *sb.*^{1}] **1.** *trans.* †To bury; to cover (plants) with mould; to earth *up.* †**2.** *To m. away*: to moulder, crumble away –1633.

Mould (mōᵘld), *v.*^{2}. Also (now *U.S.*) **mold.** late ME. [f. MOULD *sb.*^{3}] **1.** *trans.* To mix or knead (dough, bread); now *techn.*: To shape into loaves. †**2.** To mix (ingredients) to form a paste –1652. †**b.** *fig.* To mix *up* (*with*) –1855. **3.** To shape; to fashion, form, model. Chiefly *poet.* 1475. **4.** To shape (fluid or plastic matter) in or as in a mould 1573. **5.** *transf.* and *fig.* To create, produce, or form *out of* certain elements or material, or *upon* a certain pattern; also, to plan, design. Also with *up*. 1603. **6.** To bring into a particular shape or form; to shape or model the character or style of. Const. *into, to*. 1605. **7.** *intr.* and *refl.* (now *rare*). To assume a certain form; to shape itself (*into*) 1612. **8.** *trans. Ship-building.* To give a particular mould to (a vessel); to shape timbers with moulds 1570.

3. Two louely berries molded on one stem SHAKS. **4.** In harden'd orbs the school-boy moulds the snow GAY. **5.** They say best men are moulded out of faults SHAKS. **6.** Logic was beginning to m. human thought JOWETT. Hence **Mou·ldable** *a.* 1626.

Mould (mōᵘld), *v.*^{3} Also (now *U.S.*) **mold.** 1460. [f. MOULD *sb.*^{4} or f. MOUL *v.* by addition of excrescent *-d*.] **1.** *trans.* †**a.** To allow to become mouldy. **b.** To cause to contract mould. **2.** *intr.* To become mouldy or covered with mould 1530. **b.** *transf.* and *fig.* of things that lie unused 1547.

2. b. The Grecians..were not wont to suffer bookes of worth to lye moulding in Kings Libraries BIBLE *Transl. Pref.* ¶ 6.

Mould-board (mōᵘ·ldbōᵊɹd). Also (now *U.S.*) **mold-.** 1508. [f. MOULD *sb.*^{1} + BOARD *sb.*; replacing earlier *moldbred* (BRED *sb.*).] The board or metal plate in a plough, which turns over the furrow-slice.

Moulder (mōᵘ·ldəɹ), *sb.* Also (now *U.S.*) **molder.** 1440. [f. MOULD *v.*^{2} + -ER^{1}.] **1.** One who moulds dough or bread. **2. a.** One who makes moulds for casting. **b.** One who moulds clay into bricks. 1535. †**3.** An instrument for moulding –1823.

Moulder (mōᵘ·ldəɹ), *v.* Also (now *U.S.*) **molder.** 1531. [perh. f. MOULD *sb.*^{1} + -ER^{5}; but adoption from Scand. is more likely (cf. Norw. dial. *muldra* crumble).] **1.** *intr.* To turn to dust by natural decay; to waste away; to crumble. Also with *away, down*. **2.** *transf.* To dwindle. Said chiefly of armies. Also with *away*. Now *rare* or *Obs.* 1674. **3.** *trans.* To cause to crumble, fall to pieces, or decay. Also with *away, down*. Now *rare* or *dial.* 1649.

1. When statues m., and when arches fall PRIOR. *fig.* Never man, I think, So moulder'd in a sinecure as he TENNYSON. **2.** If he had sat still the other great army would have mouldered to nothing CLARENDON. **3.** *transf.* How many men have we seene Molder and crumble away great Estates DONNE. Hence **Mou·ldery** *a.* crumbly 1600.

Mouldiness (mōᵘ·ldinės). 1577. [f. MOULDY *a.* + -NESS.] The condition of being mouldy; often *concr.* mould.

Mou·lding, *vbl. sb.*^{1} 1699. [f. MOULD *v.*^{1} + -ING^{1}.] The earthing-*up* of plants.

Mou·lding, *vbl. sb.*^{2} ME. [f. MOULD *v.*^{2} + -ING^{1}.] **1.** The action of MOULD *v.*^{2} **b.** Bodily form. SCOTT. **2.** *concr.* A moulded object 1727. **3.** *spec.* (*Arch.*, etc.) An ornamental variety of contour given to stone-, wood-, or metal-work, effected by means of carving or the application of pieces in relief; material shaped and prepared in this way.

Moulding-board. ME. [f. prec.] *Baking.* A board on which dough or paste is kneaded and shaped.

Mouldwarp (mōᵘ·ldwǫɹp). Now chiefly *n. dial.* ME. [prob. – MLG. *moldewerp* (whence Du. *muldvarp*) = OHG. *multwurf*, a WGmc. compound of *moldō MOULD *sb.*^{1} and *warp- throw, WARP *v.*] = MOLE *sb.*^{2}

Mouldy (mōᵘ·ldi), *a.* Also (now *U.S.*) **moldy.** late ME. [f. MOULD *sb.*^{4} + -Y^{1}.] Overgrown or covered with mould; hence, mouldering or mouldered. **b.** Of, consisting of, or resembling mould (*rare*) 1579.

Hee liues vpon mouldie stew'd Pruines SHAKS. *fig.* Away you mouldie Rogue, away SHAKS. Pretty m. health STEVENSON.

‖**Moulin** (mulæṅ). 1860. [Fr., a mill.] A nearly vertical well or shaft in a glacier, formed by the surface water falling through a crack in the ice, and gradually scooping out a deep chasm.

Moulinet (mū·line·t). 1662. [– Fr. *moulinet*, dim. of *moulin* mill; see -ET.] **1.** A winch. **2.** *Fencing.* A circular swing of a sword or sabre 1875.

Moult (mōᵘlt), *sb.* Also (now *U.S.*) **molt.** 1815. [f. MOULT *v.*] The action of moulting in birds, or (*transf.*) in reptiles, crustacea, etc.

Moult (mōᵘlt), *v.* [ME. *moute, mowte*, later *molt* (XVI), *moult* (XVII); repr. OE. *mutian = MLG., MDu. *mūten* change, moult, OHG. *mūzzōn* (G. *mause(r)n*); WGmc. – L. *mutare* change. The intrusion of *l* is on the analogy of *fault*, etc., and the mod. pronunc. is based on the new spelling.] †**1.** *intr.* Of feathers: To be shed in the process of change of plumage. Also with *off*. Hence loosely of hair. –1647. **2.** Of birds: To shed or cast feathers in changing plumage 1440; also *trans.* with feathers as obj. 1530.

2. *transf.* The youthful crayfish 'moult', or shed their shells 8 times in their first twelvemonth of life 1902; *trans. Ham.* II. ii. 306; *fig.* I moulted my stick to-day H. WALPOLE.

†**Mou·lten,** *ppl. a.* [irreg. strong pa. pple. of prec.] Having moulted. SHAKS.

A moulten Rauen 1 *Hen. IV*, III. i. 152.

Moulten, obs. f. MOLTEN.

Moun, obs. f. MAY *v.*^{1}, MOUNT *sb.*^{2}

Mound (maund), *sb.*^{1} ME. [– (O)Fr. *monde* :– L. *mundus* world.] †**1.** The world; the earth as man's abode. ME. only. **2.** An orb or ball of gold, etc., repr. the glóbe of the earth; often surmounting a crown, or forming part of the insignia of royalty. Also *Her.* a figure of this, as a bearing; often used as including the cross which commonly surmounts it.

Mound (maund), *sb.*^{2} 1551. [perh. f. the somewhat earlier MOUND *v.*, but the origin of this is unknown.] **1.** A hedge or other fence bounding a field or garden. Now only *dial.* †**b.** *fig.* A boundary –1742. **2.** *Mil.* = MOUNT *sb.*^{1} 2 a. Hence *gen.* an embankment, a dam. Now *rare.* 1558. **3.** An artificial elevation of earth or stones; *esp.* the earth heaped up upon a grave 1726. **b.** A natural elevation resembling a heap or pile of earth; a hillock 1810. **4.** *spec.* **a.** A pile of fuel for roasting ores. **b.** The heap of earth, dead leaves, etc., built by megapodes for their eggs. **c.** *Archæol.* An elevation produced upon a land surface by the natural burial of an abandoned city. **d.** A kind of earthwork formerly constructed by natives of parts of N. America. **e.** = KITCHEN-MIDDEN. 1839.

1. This great gardin, compast with a m. SPENSER. **2.** The mounds and dykes of the low fat Bedford level BURKE. **3.** A church-yard's dreary mounds CLARE.

attrib. and *Comb.*: **m.-bird** = next (*b*); **-builder**, (*a*) one of a prehistoric race of American Indians, who erected immense burial and fortification mounds 1841; (*b*) any of the megapode birds which deposit their eggs in a mound 1880; **-burial** *Archæol.*, the practice of burying beneath a m. or cairn; **-dweller,** a primitive man who dwelt in a rudely erected m.; so **-dwelling.**

Mound (maund), *v.* 1515. [See prec.] **1.** *trans.* To enclose or bound with a fence. Also *absol.* or *intr.*, to make fences. *Obs.* exc. *dial.* **2.** To enclose, bound, or fortify with an embankment 1600. **3.** To heap up in a mound or hillock 1859.

Mounseer (maunsīᵊ·ɹ). *arch.* 1641. An illiterate or derisive anglicized pronunciation of MONSIEUR.

Mount (maunt), *sb.*^{1} [OE. *munt* (reinforced in ME. from (O)Fr. *mont*) :– L. *mons, mont-* mountain.] **I. 1.** In early use, a mountain, lofty hill; from 17th c. in prose use *esp.* a more or less conical hill of moderate height rising from a plain; a hillock. Now chiefly *poet.* exc. in proper names of mountains or hills, and in *the Sermon on the M.* When prefixed abbrev. *Mt.* **2.** *Mil.* **a.** A substantial work of earth or other material, thrown up to resist an attack or to advance an assault. *Obs.* exc. *Hist.* 1558. †**b.** = CAVALIER *sb.* 4. Also *fig.* –1721. †**3.** An artificial mound of earth, stones, etc.; *esp.* a raised piece of ground, or walk, in a garden –1813. Also *transf.*

1. *fig.* I have a m. of mischiefe clogs my soule 1602. **2.** I..will lay siege against thee with a m., and I will raise forts against thee *Isa.* 29:3. **3.** At the End of both the Side Grounds, I would haue a M. of some Pretty Height..to looke abroad into the Fields BACON.

II. In transf. uses. †**1.** [After It. *monte.*] A bank –1765. **2.** *Palmistry.* One of the fle[...] prominences on the palm of the hand by [...] development of which palmists profes[...]

ascertain the degree of influence exercised by a particular planet 1644.

1. †**Mount of piety, mount piety,** a rendering of It. *monte di pietà*, Fr. *mont-de-piété*, in Italy and France, a pawnbroking establishment instituted and carried on by the State for the purpose of affording loans to the poor at low interest.

Mount (maunt), *sb.*^{2} ME. [f. MOUNT *v.* Cf. Fr. *monte*, which may be the source of some of the senses.] †**1.** = AMOUNT *sb.* –1651. **2.** An act of mounting (*rare*); a manner of mounting 1486. **3.** That in or on which anything is mounted, fitted, supported, or placed; a mounting, fitting, or setting; *spec.* (*a*) the margin surrounding a picture, or the cardboard on which a drawing is mounted; (*b*) *pl.* the metal ornaments serving as borders, edges, or guards to the angles and prominent parts of 18th c. furniture, etc.; (*c*) the glass slip with its adjuncts used to preserve objects for examination under the microscope. 1739. **b.** Of a fan: (*a*) The pieces of wood, ivory, etc. forming the frame or support. (*b*) The silk, paper, etc. forming the surface of the fan. 1811. **4.** *colloq.* A horse, etc., provided for a person's riding 1856. **5.** An opportunity or occasion of riding; hence, an undertaking to ride or an act of riding (a horse) in a race 1856.

4. A good high-bred dromedary is as comfortable a m. as can be desired 1885.

Mount (maunt), *v.* [ME. *munt(e, mont(e* – OFr. *munter*, (also mod.) *monter* :– Rom. *montare, f. *mont-* (see MOUNT *sb.*^{1}); for the sense cf. Fr. *amont* uphill, upstream, and AMOUNT *v.*, with which *mount* was synon. XIV–XVIII.] **I.** *intr.* **1.** To go upwards, ascend. Also with *up*. **b.** Of the blood: To rise into the cheeks. Also, of the effects of wine: To go to the head. 1625. **2.** *fig.* **a.** To ascend to a higher level in rank, estimation, power, excellence, completeness, etc. late ME. **b.** To ascend or go back in date (*arch.*) 1796. **3.** To get upon the back of a horse, etc., for the purpose of riding. Const. *on, upon,* †*to*. 1509. **4.** To get up *on* something; e.g. a platform, a stage 1642. **5.** To rise in amount; to increase by addition. Chiefly with *up*. late ME. †**6.** To amount *to* a certain sum, number, or quantity –1738. **7.** *slang.* To swear or give false evidence for payment 1789.

1. Doth the Aegle mounte vp..at thy commaundement? COVERDALE *Job* 39:27. They causyd the mynstrell to m. vp on yᵉ ladder LD. BERNERS. [The chamois] always m. or descend in an oblique direction GOLDSM. **2. b.** For the antiquity of which [method] we must m. up to Celsus 1803. **3.** Wel father in Gods name, m. on my shoulder, I pray you 1582. **5.** The debts of the Crown mounted to four times its annual income J. R. GREEN.

II. *trans.* **1.** To ascend or climb up (a hill, etc.); to ascend (a river, stair) 1500. **2.** To get upon the back of (a horse, etc.) for the purpose of riding 1599. **3.** To get upon, for copulation. Now only *colloq.* of animals. 1592. **4.** To get upon or into, from below 1698.

1. Phr. *To m. a breach*: to ascend it for the purpose of assault or attack. The stayres That m. the Capitoll SHAKS. **4.** The Boy accordingly mounted the Pulpit ADDISON.

III. *trans.* in causative uses. †**1.** To cause to ascend or rise: to raise. Also with *up*. –1766. †**2.** In various *fig.* or non-material uses (see quots.) –1796. **3.** To set or place upon an elevation. Now only with *on, upon*. 1567. **4.** To set on horseback; to help into the saddle; also, to furnish with a saddle-horse. In *pass.*, to be seated on horseback. 1603. **5.** *Mil.* **a.** To raise (guns) into position 1539. **b.** Of a fort, a ship: To have (cannon) in position 1748. **c.** *pass.* To be provided *with* cannon 1662. **d.** To raise the muzzle [...] (a gun) 1545. **e.** To post for defe[...] observation. Hence *to m.* (†*the*[...]) go on duty as a guard. Also [...] To put in position for us[...] to fix on a mount[...] 1712. **7.** To put [...] as wearing [...] *arch.* 18[...]

1. [...]

we see more than the ancients, because we are mounted upon their shoulders J. H. NEWMAN. **4.** He was..excellently well mounted, on a very gallant horse 1662. **6.** The paste used for 'mounting' water-colour paintings 1859. He mounted his rod, and tried casting in shallow water 1895. **b.** In theatrical parlance..'The piece was excellently mounted' 1874. **7.** I expect he has mounted a pair of leather breeches W. IRVING.

Mountain (mau·ntėn). ME. [– OFr. *montaigne* (mod. *-agne*) :– Rom. **montania* or *-ea*, fem. sing. or n. pl. (quasi 'mountainous region') of adj. **montanius, -eus*, f. L. *mons, mont-* MOUNT *sb.*[1]] **I. 1.** A natural elevation of the earth's surface, rising notably above the surrounding level. See also HILL *sb.* 1. **b.** *poet.* Used in *pl.* as the type of a region remote from civilization 1601. **2.** *transf.* A huge heap or pile; a towering mass 1450. **3.** *fig.* A quantity or amount of impressive proportions 1592. **4.** (In full *m. wine.*) A variety of Malaga wine, made from grapes grown on the mountains 1710. **5.** *The Mountain* [Fr. *la Montagne*]: an extreme party led by Robespierre and Danton in the first French Revolution, so called because it occupied the most elevated position in the chamber of assembly 1799.

1. That chain of majestic mountains [*sc.* the Sussex Downs] G. WHITE. Mountains formed in the volcanic way are almost always conical GEIKIE. Phr. *To run* (etc.) *mountains high*, said hyperbolically of high seas DE FOE; cf. *mountain-high* adj. 1693. **b.** *Twel. N.* IV. i. 52. **2.** †*M. of ice* = ICEBERG.

II. *attrib.* passing into *adj.* **a.** Of or belonging to mountains; situated in or on mountains; consisting of mountains. late ME. **b.** Born in or inhabiting mountains; having one's abode in mountains; coming from the mountains 1591. **c.** Used in the mountains 1848. **d.** Resembling a mountain; huge, enormous 1656.

a. Your m. air is sweet 1865. **b.** The m.-boar on battle set SCOTT. **c.** M.-chaises 1897. **d.** Me all thy M. Waves have press'd TATE & BRADY.

Comb.: **m. artillery, m. battery,** (a battery of) light guns for use in mountainous countries; so **m.-gun, -howitzer; m. chain** (CHAIN *sb.* 4); **m. cure,** the cure of disease (esp. tuberculous) by residence at high elevations; **m. dew,** Scotch whisky; **m. railway; m. range; m. sickness,** a malady caused by breathing the rarefied air of m. heights; **m. wine** (see I. 4 above).

b. In the names of minerals, etc. [chiefly after G. compounds of *berg-*]: **m. cork, flesh, leather, paper, wood,** descriptive names for varieties of asbestos; **m. crystal** = ROCK-CRYSTAL; **m. flour, meal,** (*a*) a recent freshwater deposit consisting of the siliceous frustules of diatoms; (*b*) a white cotton-like variety of calcite occurring as an efflorescence on rocks; **m. limestone** *Geol.*, a thick massive limestone belonging to the carboniferous series; **m. milk,** a soft spongy variety of carbonate of lime.

c. Prefixed to the names of many animals found in upland districts: as, **m. cat,** a catamount or catamountain; **m. eagle,** the golden eagle, *Aquila chrysaëtus*; **m. hare,** the alpine hare, *Lepus variabilis*, native of the northern parts of both hemispheres; **m. lion** = PUMA; **m. panther,** (*a*) = OUNCE *sb.*[2] 2; (*b*) = PUMA.

d. In names of plants, etc., growing in elevated situations: as, **m. cowslip,** a herbaceous plant, *Primula auricula*, native of the Swiss Alps; **m. ebony,** a leguminous tree of the genus *Bauhinia*, having dark-coloured and hard wood; also, the wood; **m. mint,** †(*a*) calamint, (*b*) the U.S. genus *Pycnanthemum*; **m. pine,** a dwarf alpine pine, *Pinus pumilio*, native of Europe; **m. rose,** the rhododendron.

Mountain ash. 1597. The tree *Pyrus* (formerly *Sorbus*) *aucuparia*, characterized by its delicate pinnate leaves and masses of bright scarlet berries; the rowan-tree. In N. America applied to the native species, *Pyrus americana* and *P. sambucifolia*.

Mountaineer (mauntėnīə·ɹ), *sb.* 1610. [f. MOUNTAIN + -EER[1].] **1.** A native of or dweller among mountains. **2.** A member of the 'Mountain' (see MOUNTAIN I. 5) 1802. **3.** A ...ntain-climber 1860. Hence **Mountain-** ... *intr.* to be a mountain-climber; usu. ... and *ppl. a.*

...**ner.** 1598. [f. as prec. + -ER[1].] ... –1744.

...**ette** (mauntėne·t). 1586. [– ... dim. of *montagne*; see ...] A small mountain; a ...

... **1.** Purging flax, ...ANTHUS 1. 1807.

Mountain-green. 1727. [After G. *berggrün.*] †**1.** *Min.* = MALACHITE –1841. **2.** Name of a colour 1796.

Mountainous (mau·ntėnəs), *a.* 1601. [f. MOUNTAIN + -OUS; partly after Fr. *montagneux*; see -OUS.] **1.** Characterized by, abounding in, or of the nature of mountains. **2.** Mountain-like; huge, enormous. Now *rare.* 1607. †**3.** Inhabiting mountains; hence, barbarous –1703. †**4.** Derived from mountains –1801.

2. The two m. cheek-bones of the house-keeper FIELDING. **3.** Ignorant and Mountanous People BACON. Hence **Mou·ntainous-ly** *adv.*, **-ness.**

Mountainy (mau·ntėni), *a.* Now *dial.* 1613. [f. MOUNTAIN + -Y[1].] Having or belonging to mountains.

Mountant (mau·ntănt), *sb.* 1886. [f. MOUNT *v.* + -ANT, after Fr. *montant.*] An adhesive paste for mounting photographs, etc.

†**Mountant,** *a.* 1525. [– Fr. *montant*, pr. pple. of *monter* MOUNT *v.*; see -ANT.] Mounting, rising –1812.

Mountebank (mau·ntĭbæŋk), *sb.* 1577. [– It. *montambanco, montimbanco*, for *monta in banco* 'mount (imper.) on a bench'; see MOUNT *v.*, BANK *sb.*[2] and cf. rare OFr. *montenbancque.*] **1.** An itinerant quack who from a platform appealed to his audience by means of stories, tricks, juggling, and the like, often with the assistance of a professional clown. **2.** *fig.* An impudent charlatan 1589. **3.** *appos.* (quasi-*adj.*) That is a mountebank; characteristic of a mountebank 1603.

1. Men..will often preferre a Mountabanke or Witch, before a learned Phisitian BACON. **2.** The Mountebanks and Zanies of Patriotism COLERIDGE. Hence **Mou·ntebankery,** action, or an act, which bespeaks a m. **Mou·ntebankish** *a.*

Mou·ntebank, *v.* 1602. [f. prec.] †**1.** *trans.* To prevail over (a person) by mountebank persuasion –1702. †**2.** To transform by mountebank trickery. DE FOE. **3.** *intr.* To play the mountebank. Usu. with *it.* 1602.

Mounted (mau·ntėd), *ppl. a.* 1582. [f. MOUNT *v.* + -ED[1].] **1.** Elevated (*lit.* and *fig.*). **2.** Seated or appointed to serve on horseback 1598. **3.** Set up for use, as cannon. Of a fort, ship, etc.: Furnished (*with* cannon). 1639.

2. While M. Infantry are footmen trained for purposes of mobility to ride a horse or bicycle, M. Rifles are horsemen trained to fight on foot 1901.

Mounter (mau·ntəɹ). 1609. [f. MOUNT *v.* + -ER[1].] **1.** *gen.* One who ascends. **2.** One whose business it is to mount, fit, or set (anything) in order 1747.

Mounting (mau·ntiŋ), *vbl. sb.* late ME. [f. MOUNT *v.* + -ING[1].] **1.** The action of MOUNT *v.* **2.** *concr.* **a.** Something that serves as a mount, support, or setting to anything 1618. †**b.** *sing.* and *pl.* *Mil.* A soldier's outfit or kit –1722.

1. *attrib.* **m.-block,** a block of stone from which to mount on horseback. **2. a.** *Hilt*, the head or m. of a sword 1767.

†**Mou·nture.** ME. [– Fr. *monture*, OFr. *monteüre*, f. *monter* MOUNT *v.*, with sp. assim. to Eng.; see -URE.] **1.** A horse, etc., for riding –1600. **2.** = MOUNTING 2. –1575. †**3.** *Mil.* The angle at which a gun is elevated –1692.

†**Mou·nty.** 1586. [– (O)Fr. *montée*, pa. pple. fem. of *monter* MOUNT *v.*; see -Y[5].] *Falconry.* The action, or an act, of rising in pursuit of the quarry –1657.

Mourn (mōᵊɹn), *v.* [OE. *murnan*, corresp. to OS. *mornon, mornian*, OHG. *mornên* be anxious, ON. *morna* pine away, Goth. *maurnan* be anxious.] **I.** *intr.* **1.** To feel sorrow, grief, or regret; to sorrow, grieve, lament. †**b.** Of animals: To pine –1784. **c.** *fig.* Of a plant or flower. †Also, to droop, hang down. 1626. **2.** *esp.* To lament the death of some one. Const. *for.* ME. **b.** To show the conventional signs of grief for a period following a person's death; *esp.* to put on mourning 1530. **3.** Of a dove: = MOAN *v.* 4. 1535.

1. In all euyll thou mayst fynde cause to mourne and sorowe 1526. I mourned for the iniquitie 1 *Esd.* 8:72. **2.** A widow bird sate mourning for her love SHELLEY. **b.** We mourne in black, why m. we not in blood? SHAKS. **3.** The dove mourned in the pine SHELLEY.

II. *trans.* **1.** To grieve or sorrow for (something); to lament, deplore, bewail OE. **2.** To lament, grieve, or sorrow for, to express grief for (some one dead) 1526. **3.** To utter in a sorrowful manner 1607.

1. Mourning, in others, our own miseries 1586. **2.** Here comes his Body, mourn'd by Marke Antony SHAKS. **3.** Where the love-lorn Nightingale Nightly to thee her sad Song mourneth well MILT.

Mourner (mōᵊ·ɹnəɹ). late ME. [f. prec. + -ER[1].] **1.** One who mourns or grieves; *spec.* one who mourns the death of a friend, etc.; one who attends a funeral out of respect or affection for the deceased. †**b.** One employed or hired to attend funerals –1741. **2.** *Indian m.*: the sad-tree 1597.

1. *Chief m.*: the nearest relative present at a funeral. When..the mourners go aboute the stretes COVERDALE *Eccles.* 12:2.

Mournful (mōᵊ·ɹnfŭl), *a.* 1542. [f. MOURN *v.* + -FUL.] **1.** Denoting, exhibiting, or expressive of mourning or deep sorrow. **2.** Feeling or oppressed with deep sorrow 1579.

1. He shook his head with an intensely m. air DICKENS. **2.** Thou wilt the m. Spirit chear WESLEY. Hence **Mou·rnful-ly** *adv.*, **-ness.**

Mourning (mōᵊ·ɹniŋ), *vbl. sb.* ME. [f. MOURN *v.* + -ING[1].] **1.** The action of MOURN *v.* Also with *a* and *pl.* **2.** *spec.* The feeling or the expression of sorrow for a death; also, a lament ME. **3.** The wearing of black clothes, etc., as a manifestation of sorrow for the death of a friend. Also, the period during which they are worn. 1532. **b.** An instance of this. Now *rare.* 1611. **4.** The dress (now usu. black) worn by mourners. Also occas. applied to the black draperies placed on buildings, etc. on occasions of mourning. 1654.

1. The mournynges of soch as be in captiuyte COVERDALE *Ps.* 101[2]:20. **2.** The noise of the m. of a mighty nation TENNYSON. **3. b.** And he made a m. for his father seuen days *Gen.* 50:10. **4.** Pray desire Mrs. Taylor to inform me what m. I should buy for my mother and Miss Porter JOHNSON. *Deep m.*: complete or full m.; so HALF-M. (†*second m.*). *In m.* (as adjectival phr.): wearing the garments indicative of grief. So *To go* or *put into m.*; *to be out of m.*, etc.

attrib. and *Comb.*: **m.-band,** a strip of black cloth or crape worn round the sleeve of a coat or round the hat in token of bereavement; **m. border,** a black border on note-paper, envelopes, etc., used by persons who are in m.; **m. coach,** (*a*) a black coach, usually draped in black, used by a person in mourning *Hist.*; (*b*) a closed carriage used by mourners at a funeral; **-paper,** note-paper with a black edge; **-ring,** a ring worn as a memorial of a deceased person.

Mou·rning, *ppl. a.* OE. [f. MOURN *v.* + -ING[2].] That mourns; sorrowing, lamenting; characterized by or expressive of grief.

Spec. collocations: **m. bride,** a pop. name for the sweet scabious, *Scabiosa atropurpurea*; **m. dove,** the common American or Carolina turtle-dove, *Zenaidura carolinensis*; **m. warbler,** an American warbler, *Geothlypis philadelphia*; **m. widow,** a European geranium, *Geranium phæum.* Hence **Mou·rningly** *adv.* 1519.

Mournival (mōᵊ·ɹnivăl). Now only *Hist.* 1530. [– Fr. *mornifle* (XVI), (now) slap, taunt; of unkn. origin.] *Cards.* **1.** A set of four aces, kings, queens, or knaves, in one hand. †**2.** *transf.* A set of four (things or persons) –1711.

Mouse (maus), *sb. Pl.* **mice** (məis). [OE. *mūs*, pl. *mȳs* = OFris., OS., OHG. *mūs* (Du. *muis*, G. *maus*), ON. *mús*; Gmc. and IE. **mūs-* is repr. also by L. *mūs*, Gr. μῦς.] **I. 1.** An animal of any of the smaller species of the genus *Mus* of rodents; e.g. the house mouse, *M. musculus*, the field or wood mouse, *M. sylvaticus*, the harvest mouse, *M. minutus*. **b.** Popularly applied to animals of other genera having some resemblance to mice, esp. the shrews (*Sorex*) and the voles (*Arvicola*) OE. **2.** As a type of something small or insignificant. Chiefly after Horace. 1584. †**3.** As a playful term of endearment –1798. **4.** *techn.* Applied to things resembling a mouse in shape, etc. **a.** *Naut.* (*a*) A kind of ball or knob, wrought on the collars of stays by means of spun-yarn, to prevent the running eye from slipping. (*b*) = MOUSING *vbl. sb.* 2 a (*concr.*). 1750. **b.** A match used in firing a mine or a gun 1867. **5.** *slang.* A lump or discoloured bruise, *esp.* a black eye 1854.

1. Phr. *Drunk, mum, mute, quiet, still*, etc., *as a m.* (†*in a cheese*). *M. and man*, every living thing. **2.** The mountain travail'd, and brought forth A scorned m.! B. JONS. tr. *Horace, Art P.* 199. **3.** *Haml.* III. iv. 183.

II. †**1.** A muscle. *Obs.* in gen. sense. –1561. **2.** *spec.* Applied variously to certain muscular parts of meat. Now only *dial.* 1584.

attrib. and *Comb.*: **m.-bird,** any bird of the African genus *Colius*; **-hawk,** (*a*) a hawk that devours mice; (*b*) the short-eared owl or hawk-owl, *Asio brachyotus*; **m. lemur,** any small Madagascan lemur of the genus *Chiroyaleus*; **-mark,** a birth-mark resembling a mouse.

Mouse (mauz), *v.* ME. [f. MOUSE *sb.*] **1.** *intr.* To hunt for or catch mice; said esp. of a cat or an owl. **2.** *transf.* and *fig.* To hunt or search industriously or captiously: to go or move *about* softly in search of something, to prowl. Also with *around, along.* 1575. **b.** *trans.* To hunt for patiently and carefully. Also with *out. U.S.* 1864. †**3.** *trans.* To handle as a cat does a mouse; to tear, bite –1647. †**b.** To pull about good-naturedly but roughly –1691. **4.** *Naut.* To put a mouse (see MOUSE *sb.* I. 4a) on (a stay); to secure (a hook) with a mouse 1769.

2. Mousing for faults 1778. Phr. *To m. over* (a book): to study eagerly. *U.S.* **3.** *John* II. i. 354.

Mou·se-colour, *sb.* (*a.*). 1606. **1.** A colour like that of the common mouse; a dark grey with a yellowish tinge. **2.** *attrib.* or *adj.* Mouse-coloured 1716. **Mouse-coloured** *a.* 1687.

Mou·se-deer. Also **moose-.** 1836. [Both forms are app. corruptions of *musk-deer.*] The Chevrotain (*Tragulus meminna*), native of Ceylon and Java.

Mouse-dun. late ME. **a.** *adj.* Mouse-coloured. **b.** *sb.* Mouse-colour.

Mou·se-ear. ME. [tr. med.L. *auricula muris*, Gr. μυοσωτίς; see MYOSOTE.] A name for various plants mostly with soft hairy leaves, as *Hieracium pilosella* (also *m. hawkweed*), various species of *Cerastium* (also *m. chickweed*), and of *Myosotis* (as the forget-me-not), and *Sisymbrium thaliana* (also *m. cress*). So **Mouse-eared** *a.* having leaves resembling a mouse's ear: *spec.* in *m. chickweed, hawkweed* (see above) 1789.

Mou·se-hole. late ME. A hole used by a mouse for passage or abode; a hole only big enough to admit a mouse.

Mou·se-hunt[1]. *Obs.* exc. *dial.* 1481. [– MDu. *muushont* weasel, f. *muus* mouse + *hont* dog (see HOUND *sb.*[1]).] A weasel, also *gen.* an animal that hunts mice.

Mouse-hunt[2]. *rare.* 1828. [HUNT *sb.*[2]] A hunt for mice.

Mou·se-pea. *Obs.* exc. *dial.* [OE. *mūse-pise.*] The Heath-pea (*Lathyrus macrorrhizus*); also the Meadow Vetchling (*L. pratensis*).

Mouser (mau·zəɹ, -səɹ). late ME. [f. MOUSE *v.* or *sb.* + -ER[1].] An animal that catches mice, e.g. a cat, an owl. Also *fig.*

Mou·setail. 1548. [f. MOUSE *sb.* + TAIL *sb.*[1]] †**1.** The stonecrop, *Sedum acre* –1611. **2.** A plant of the genus *Myosurus*, esp. *M. minimus*, from the shape of its seed receptacle 1578.

Mousetrap (mau·s,træp). *Pl.* **mousetraps,** also †**mice-traps.** 1475. [f. MOUSE *sb.* + TRAP *sb.*[1]] A trap for catching mice.

transf. The house..is too small, a mere mousetrap 1839. *Comb.* **m.-switch** *Electr.*, an automatic switch moved by a spring which is released when the current through a controlling magnet falls below a certain limit.

Mousing (mau·ziŋ), *vbl. sb.* 1832. [f. MOUSE *v.* + -ING[1].] **1.** The action of MOUSE *v.* 1856. **2.** *Naut.* **a.** The action of fastening spun-yarn or rope, etc., round the point and shank of a hook; *concr.* the rope or yarn so fastened; **b.** The action of making a mouse on a rope; *concr.* the mouse so made 1832. **3.** *attrib.*, as *m. hook*, etc. 1856.

Mousing (mau·ziŋ), *ppl. a.* 1605. [f. as prec. + -ING[2].] That hunts or catches mice. **b.** *transf.* Prying, prowling, rapacious, inquisitive 1692.

Mousle (mau·z'l), *v. arch.* Also **mouzle.** 1662. [frequent. of MOUSE *v.* after *tousle.*] *trans.* To pull about roughly.

‖**Mousquetaire** (muskətē̆r). 1706. [Fr.; see MUSKETEER.] **1.** *Fr. Hist.* Orig. a foot-soldier armed with a musket; in the 17th and 18th c. a member of either the Grey or White and the Black Mousquetaires (so called from the colour of their horses), which formed part of the king's household troops. They were all of noble birth, and were famous as dandies. **2.** Applied *attrib.* to certain styles of articles of female attire, as in *m. cloak, cuff*, etc. Also short for *m. glove* [1850 *à la m.*], 1883.

‖**Mousse** (mūs). 1892. [Fr., = moss.] *Cookery.* A sweet made of whipped cream frozen.

‖**Mousseline** (muslīn). 1696. [Fr.; see MUSLIN.] **1.** French muslin; also, a dress of this. (Often short for *m. de laine.*) **b. M. de laine** ('muslin of wool'), a dress-material, orig. all wool, but later of wool and cotton, printed with various patterns. **c. M. de soie** ('muslin of silk'), a thin silk fabric resembling muslin 1850. **2.** A thin blown glass-ware with ornamentation resembling muslin or lace. Also, a wine-glass of this. 1862.

Moustache (mustɑ·ʃ, mŏs-). Also (now *U.S.*) **mustache.** 1585. [– Fr. *moustache* fem. – It. *mostaccio, mostacchio*; see MUSTACHIO.] **1.** The hair which grows upon the upper lip of men: either (*a*) that on both sides, or (*b*) that on one side of the lip, as a single moustache, or as a 'pair of moustaches'. **2.** *Zool.* Hair or bristles, resembling a moustache, round the mouth of certain animals 1605.

1. And he twirl'd his m. with so charming an air,—His moustaches I should say, because he'd a pair BARHAM. *Old m.* [tr. Fr. *vieille moustache*]: an old soldier.

Comb.: **m.-cup,** a cup with an arrangement to protect the m. when drinking; **m. monkey,** a W. African monkey, *Cercopithecus cephus.* Hence **Mousta·ched** *a.*

Mousy (mau·si), *sb.* Also **-ie.** 1693. [f. MOUSE *sb.* + -Y[6].] Playful dim. of *mouse.*

Mousy (mɑ ·si), *a.* Also **-ey.** 1812. [f. MOUSE *sb.* + -Y[1].] **1.** Resembling a mouse, its colour, smell, etc. 1859. **2.** As quiet as a mouse 1812. **3.** Infested with mice 1871.

Mouth (mauþ), *sb.* [OE. *mūþ* = OFris. *mūth*, later *mund*, ON. *munnr, muðr*, Goth. *munþs* :– Gmc. **munþaz* :– IE. **mn̥tos*, corresp. to L. *mentum* chin. For the loss of *n* in OE., etc., cf. *five, other, tooth, uncouth.*] **I. 1.** The external orifice in an animal body which serves for the ingestion of food, together with the cavity to which this leads, containing the apparatus of mastication and the organs of vocal utterance. **b.** In expressions like *a good, bad, hard*, etc. *m.*, used with ref. to a horse's readiness to feel and obey the pressure of the bit. Hence *abstr.* of a horse: Capability of being guided by the bit. 1727. **2.** As the receptacle of food, or with ref. to swallowing, devouring, taste, etc. OE. **b.** A person viewed only as a consumer of food 1550. **3.** As the instrument of speech or voice. (In this use *tongue* is more usual.) OE. **4.** The orifice of the mouth considered as part of the face OE.

1. He was thrust in the m. with a Speare SHAKS. Mouths that gaped TENNYSON. Phr. †*To draw one's m.*: to extract a tooth. PEPYS. **b.** A horse that has no m. 1791. **2.** Phr. *The m. waters* (*after, at* something), (it) *makes* (*one's*) *m. water*, referring to the flow of saliva caused by the anticipation of appetizing food; also *fig. To open ones m. wide*, to ask a high price. See also HAND TO MOUTH. **b.** *Useless m.*, one who does no work but has to be fed. **3.** You must borrow me Gargantuas m. first: 'tis a Word too great for any m. of this Ages size SHAKS. I had the relation from his own m. DE FOE. Phr. *By word of m.*: orally; often opp. to 'by writing'. (*To condemn a person*) *out of his own m.* (Luke 19:22): by the evidence of his own words. *With one m.*, with one voice; unanimously. (A Hebraism.) Now *rare. To open one's m.*: to begin speaking. *To close, shut one's m.*: to refrain from speaking. *To stop* (a person's) *m.*: to keep (him) from talking. *To put words into another's m.* = to tell him what to say. *To put* (a speech) *into a person's m.*: to represent him as having uttered it. *To take the words out of another's m.*: to say what he was about to say. *To make a poor m.*, to plead poverty. *To give m.*: (of a hound) to bark or bay vehemently, also *transf.* of a person. **4.** Hir m. ful smal, and ther-to softe and reed CHAUCER. Phr. *Down in the m.*, having the corners of the m. turned downwards, as a sign of dissatisfaction; dejected, dispirited. *To laugh* (*on*) *the wrong side of one's m.*, in early use to laugh in a forced manner; now, to lament instead of laughing. *To make a* (*wry, ugly, hard*, etc.) *m.*, or *mouths*: to express disapproval, derision, etc., by putting awry one's m.; of an animal, to menace with the m.; also *fig.* to refuse to believe or accept. Const. *at, upon.*

II. Transf. applications to persons. **1.** A spokesman. *Obs.* exc. in renderings of foreign modes of speech. 1563. †**2.** *slang.* A silly person; a dupe –1823.

1. I was but the m. of the rest, and spoke what they have dictated to me PEPYS.

III. Applied to things resembling a mouth. **1.** The opening of anything, e.g. a bottle, a furnace, a beehive, a cave, etc.; also *fig.* of the pit of Hell ME. **2.** The outfall of a river; the entrance to a haven, valley, etc. OE. **3.** The opening out of a tube, passage, drain, burrow, and the like; the hole or aperture of various natural or artificial structures 1582. **4.** The fork between the open jaws of scissors, pincers, or a vice; the working edge of a tool 1576. †**5.** A mouthpiece –1821.

attrib. and *Comb.*: with the meaning 'coming from the m. only and not from the heart', as *m.-charity, -friend, -honour*; also **m.-filling** *a. fig.* (of an oath, compliment, etc.), that fills the m., bombastic, inflated; **-footed** *a.*, having a foot-jaw (see FOOT *sb.*); **m. pipe** *Organ-building*, an organ pipe having an oblong opening, called the *mouth*, at the junction of the body with the foot, a flue-pipe; **m.-wash,** a therapeutic wash for the m.

Mouth (mauð), *v.* ME. [f. prec.] **1.** *trans.* To pronounce, speak; to give utterance to. *Obs.* exc. *arch.* **2.** *trans.* To utter in a pompously oratorical style, or with great distinctness of articulation; to declaim. Also with *out.* 1602. **3.** *intr.* To use a pompous or affected style of utterance; to declaim. Also *to m. it.* 1602. **4.** *trans.* To put or take (something) in the mouth; to seize with the mouth; to press (a thing) with the mouth or lips. late ME. **5.** To train the mouth of (a horse); to accustom to the use of the bit 1533. †**6.** *intr.* (*contempt.*) To join lips (*with*); to kiss –1693. **7.** To make mouths; to grimace 1827. **8.** Of a river: To disembogue (*in, into*) 1598.

1. He that knows not how to m. a curse QUARLES. **2.** He..mouths a sentence, as curs m. a bone CHURCHILL. **3.** Nay, and thoul't m., Ile rant as well as thou SHAKS. **4.** *Haml.* IV. ii. 20. **6.** *Meas. for M.* III. ii. 194.

Mouthed (mauðd), *a.* ME. [f. MOUTH *sb.* + -ED[2].] **1.** Having a mouth, or such-and-such a mouth or mouths. †**2.** Gaping, open-mouthed –1649.

1. A many-m. chorus 1905.

Mouther (mau·ðəɹ). 1822. [f. MOUTH *v.* + -ER[1].] One who mouths; a boastful or declamatory speaker.

Mouthful (mau·þful). 1530. [f. MOUTH *sb.* + -FUL.] A quantity that fills the mouth; as much as a mouth can take in at one time; hence, a small quantity. Also *transf.* said esp. *colloq.* of a long name which 'fills' the mouth when uttered.

Mouth glue. 1573. Glue (orig. a preparation of isinglass) to be used by moistening with the tongue.

Mouthless (mau·þlės), *a.* OE. [f. MOUTH *sb.* + -LESS.] Having no mouth.

Mouth-organ. 1668. **1.** A musical instrument operated by the mouth; e.g. a pan-pipe, a jews'-harp. **2.** *Zool.* One of the appendages forming the mouth (of an insect, crustacean, etc.) 1863.

Mou·th(-)piece. 1683. **1.** A piece placed at or forming the mouth (of a receptacle, organ-pipe, etc.). **2.** Something to put in the mouth: e.g. the part of a musical instrument, a pipe, etc., which is placed between the lips. Also, that part of a bit which crosses the horse's mouth. 1727. **3.** One who speaks on behalf of another or others 1805.

3. The thing called the Cabinet is nothing more than the mouth-piece of the Boroughmongers COBBETT.

Mouthy (mau·ði), *a.* 1589. [f. MOUTH *sb.* + -Y[1].] Characterized by railing, ranting, or the use of bombastic language.

He..was prone to be m. and magniloquent W. IRVING.

Mouton. late ME. [– OFr. *mouton* sheep; see MUTTON.] **1.** (mū·tọn) A French gold coin of the 14th–15th c., bearing the figure of the Lamb of God (whence the name). *Hist.* **2.** (mutoṅ) A spy quartered with an accused person to obtain evidence against him 1804.

‖**Moutonnée** (mutone), *a.* 1872. [Fr. (in *roche moutonnée*), fem. pa. pple. of *moutonner*, f. *mouton* sheep; see MUTTON.] *Geol.* Rounded like a sheep's back; said of rocks shaped by glacial action.

Movable, moveable (mū·văb'l). late ME. [– OFr. *movable*, f. *moveir* MOVE; see -ABLE.] **A.** *adj.* †**1.** Apt or disposed to movement –1705. †**2.** *fig.* Changeable, fickle, inconstant –1682. **3.** Capable of being moved; not fixed in one place or posture. late ME. **4.** Of property: Admitting of being removed or displaced; applied to 'personal' as opp. to 'real' property. In *Sc. Law*, opp. to HERITABLE *a.* late ME. **5.** Changing from one date to another every year. late ME. **6.** *Semitic Gram.* Of certain letters, etc.: Pronounced; not 'quiescent' 1837.

2. The moeuable poeple [orig. *mobile vulgus*] CHAUCER. **3.** This moveable structure of shelves COWPER. The clinical history of the movable (= FLOATING) kidney 1878. **5.** *M. feast*: an eccl. festival which, being always on the same day of the week, varies in date from year to year; also *transf.* and *joc.* Breakfast is a m. feast with us (*mod.*).

B. *sb.* †**1.** In the Ptolemaic astronomy: Any of the nine concentric revolving spheres of the heavens. Chiefly in *First* or *highest m.* = PRIMUM MOBILE. late ME. **2.** *pl.* Personal property; property that is capable of being moved, as dist. from real or fixed property (as land, houses, etc.). In *Sc.* and *Civil Law*, opp. to 'heritable' property. 1440. **3.** An article of furniture that may be removed from the building in which it is placed; opp. to *fixture*. Now chiefly in *pl.* 1523. †**4.** Something capable of being set in motion; *spec.* any part of the works of a watch –1779. †**5.** A person given to movement or change –1658.

2. *Rich. III*, III. i. 195. **3.** I wrote to you..for my movables BYRON. Hence **Movabi·lity, Mo·vableness. Mo·vably** *adv.*

Move (mūv), *sb.* 1439. [f. MOVE *v.*] †**1.** A proposal; motion (*rare*). **2.** *Chess*, etc. The moving or changing of position of a piece in the regular course of the game; the manner in which a piece is allowed to be moved; (a player's) turn to move 1656. **b.** *fig.* A device, trick; an action calculated to secure some end 1812. **3.** An act of moving from a stationary position; a beginning of movement or departure; esp. in phr. *to make a m.* 1827. **4.** A change of house or place of sojourn 1853.

2. *The m.*: the right to make the first move in the game (so in *pawn and m.* in chess, with reference to odds). **b.** *A* (*good, bad*, etc.) *m.*: a (prudent, etc.) step or proceeding. *To be up to every m. on the board*: to be cunning, smart, wide-awake, experienced. **3.** Directly there was a m., the ladies went to bed 1856. *On the m.*: travelling, moving about. *To get a m. on* (orig. *U.S.*), to hurry up.

Move (mūv), *v.* ME. [– AFr. *mover* = OFr. *moveir* (mod. *mouvoir*) :– L. *movēre*.] **I.** *trans.* **1.** To change the position of; to shift, remove; *occas.* to dislodge or displace (something fixed). Also to *m. away, along*, etc. **b.** *Chess*, etc. To change the position of (a piece) in course of play 1474. **c.** To bring or apply (something) to –1611. †**d.** To raise (one's hat, cap) or bow as a gesture of salutation –1825. Cf. II. 2 c below. **2.** To put or keep in motion; to shake, stir, or disturb. late ME. **3.** To change the position or posture of (one's body or any member). late ME. †**4.** To put forth, utter (sound) –1674. **5.** *Med.* To cause (the bowels) to act; also *absol.* Also *intr.* of the bowels = to be moved, to act. 1700. **6.** To stir up or excite (an emotion, appetite, etc.) in a person; to provoke (laughter, contradiction). late ME. **7.** To stir up, commence (strife, war, etc.). Now *rare* or *Obs.* ME. **8.** To affect with emotion; to excite *to* (laughter or tears). Often *spec.* to affect with tender or compassionate emotion. ME. **9.** To prompt, actuate, or incline *to* (an action) or *to do* (something) ME. †**10.** To urge (a person) *to* (an action) or *to do* (something); to apply or appeal to. late ME. **11.** To make a formal application, suit, or request to (the sovereign, a court, Parliament, etc.). Const. *for*. Cf. MOTION *sb.* 7 b. 1683. †**12.** To propose or suggest (something to be done); to prefer (a request); to lodge (a complaint); to propound (a question, etc.), mention (a matter). Const. *to* (a person). late ME. **13.** *spec.* †**a.** To plead (a cause etc.) in a court: to bring (an action at law) –1641. **b.** To propose (a resolution, etc.) formally in a deliberative assembly. Also with *clause*. 1452.

1. But none myght stere the swerd nor meue hit MALORY. **b.** My liege, I m. my bishop TENNYSON. **c.** Deut. 23:25. **2.** *To m. heaven and earth*: to make unheard-of efforts (*to do* something). **3.** She moved her lips..but could not speak T. HARDY. **6.** To moue wilde laughter in the throate of death? SHAKS. **8.** And Iesus mooued with compassion, put foorth his hand, and touched him *Mark* 1:41. Phr. *To m. to anger, wrath*, etc. **9.** What reason shou'd thy Mind to Marriage move? DRYDEN. *absol.* I feare these stubborn lines lack power to moue SHAKS. Phr. *The spirit moves me*: a phrase orig. in Quaker use, referring to the Holy Spirit; now = 'I feel impelled or in the humour (*to do* something)'. **11.** The Bank now moved the Court..for..a reversal of the verdict 1885. **13. b.** Your Lordship would undertake to m. the Address PITT. I moved first that the L. Chancellor be brought to the barre 1621.

II. *intr.* **1.** To go, advance, proceed, pass from one place to another, esp. deliberately. Also with advs., as *about, away*, etc. ME. **b.** Of an army, etc.: To go forward, march. Also, to quit one's position. ME. **c.** *transf.* late ME. **d.** *Chess*, etc. (*a*) Of a piece: To be transferred from one position to another in the course of the game; (*b*) Of a player: To make a move 1474. **e.** To change one's abode 1707. **f.** Of goods: To change hands, find buyers 1759. **2.** Of living beings: To change position or posture, to exhibit motion. Freq. with neg. = not to stir. ME. **b.** To dance. Also with cogn. obj. Now *rare*. 1594. **c.** To raise the hat, bow in salutation (now *provincial*) 1594. **3.** Of inanimate objects: To suffer change of position or posture; to be stirred. late ME. **b.** Of a piece of machinery: To turn, work, revolve. late ME. **4.** Of animate beings: To live, 'have one's being', esp. *in* a particular sphere. Also *transf.* and *fig.* of things. ME. **5.** To take action, proceed (*in* an affair). Also with cogn. obj. (fig.) *to m. a step*. late ME. †**6.** To proceed, originate *from* –1676. **7.** *To m. for*: to make a request, proposal, or application for (something) 1638.

1. Katie never ran: she moved To meet me TENNYSON. Phr. *M. on*: a policeman's order to a person who stands too long in one place; also *trans.* to order to move on. **b.** Anon they m. In perfect Phalanx to the Dorian mood MILT. **c.** Then the tale Shall m. on soberly KEATS. **e.** *To m. about*, etc., to keep changing one's abode. *To m. in*, to take possession of a new domicile. **2.** He heareth not, he stirreth not, he moueth not SHAKS. Nor would his lips M. HENLEY. **c.** At least we m. when we meet one another DICKENS. **3.** Then m. the trees, the copses nod TENNYSON. **4.** The little world in which she moved DISRAELI. **5.** God moves in a mysterious way His wonders to perform COWPER. I would urge parents to m. in the matter LUBBOCK. **7.** I moved for a physician to be sent to her from Oxford 1707. Hence **Mo·veless** *a.* having no movement; immovable, fixed 1578. **Mo·veless-ly** *adv.*, **-ness.**

Movement (mū·vmĕnt). late ME. [– OFr. *movement* (mod. *mouvement*) – med.L. *movimentum*, f. *movēre*; see MOVE *v.* and -MENT. Rare between XIV and XVIII; not in Shaks., A.V., or Milton's poetry.] **1.** The action or process of moving (see MOVE *v.*). Also, a particular act or manner of moving. **b.** *Mil.* and *Nav.* A tactical or strategical change of position 1784. **c.** Chiefly *pl.*: Actions, activities, doings of a person or body of persons 1833. **2.** *concr.* (*Mech.*) (*a*) The moving mechanism of a watch or clock; (*b*) a particular part or group of parts in a mechanism serving some special purpose 1678. **3. a.** A moving (of the mind) towards or from some object; an impulse of desire or aversion, an act of volition. Now *rare*. 1456. **b.** In a poem or narrative: Progress of incidents, development of plot; the quality of having plenty of incident, or of carrying on the interest of the reader 1838. **c.** *Fine Art.* In a painting, etc., the quality of suggesting that the figures represented are moving. Also, in *Arch.*, harmonious variety in the lines and ornamentation of a building. 1773. **4. a.** *Mus.* (*a*) The manner in which a piece or a passage moves; variously applied to melodic progression (now usu. MOTION *sb.* 10 b), 'tempo', and rhythm. (*b*) A principal division of a musical work, as a sonata or symphony, having a distinctive structure of its own. 1771. **b.** *Prosody.* Rhythmical or accentual character 1871. **5.** A series of actions and endeavours by a body of persons, tending more or less continuously towards some special end; as *the Oxford m.* (see OXFORD), *the Labour m.* 1828. **b.** *The m.* = *m. party* 1831. **c.** The way in which things are moving at a particular time or in a particular field 1846. **6.** *Comm.* Activity in the market for some commodity. Also, a rise or fall in price. 1886.

1. There was a general m. toward the door 1894. **c.** The police watched the movements of the mob 1908. **3. a.** I blush'd in my turn; but from what movements I leave to the few who feel to analyse STERNE. **4. b.** The orderly and majestic m. of the Roman hexameter 1887. **5.** Oxford is the home they say of movements, and Cambridge of men 1885. Phr. *In the m.* [after Fr. *dans le mouvement*]: 'in the swim', in the prevalent direction or tendency of things. **6.** An upward m. in stocks 1895.

attrib. and *Comb.*, as **m. cure** = *kinesipathy* (see KINESI-); **m. party** [after Fr. *le parti du mouvement*], the 'liberal' or innovating party in the first half of the 19th c.

Mover (mū·vəɹ). late ME. [f. MOVE *v.* + -ER[1].] **1.** One who moves or sets in motion. Applied *esp.* to God; also *First M.* **2.** Something which sets in motion or actuates 1586. **b.** A machine or mechanical agency which imparts motion 1654. **3.** One who incites to action; one who promotes or originates (an action, etc.) 1497. **b.** One who moves a proposal in a deliberative assembly 1737. **4.** A person or thing that moves or is in motion. Now chiefly of an animal. 1592. **5.** *Chess.* With prefixed numeral, denoting a problem in which the king is to be mated in the specified number of moves 1900.

1. Oh thou eternall mouer of the heauens SHAKS. **2.** Phr. *First m.*, in mediæval astronomy = *first motor*, PRIMUM MOBILE. **b.** *First* or *prime m.*: an initial source, natural or mechanical, of motive power. **3.** Providence, which I humbly recognize as the first m. of your thoughts in my favour DE FOE. **4.** Though elegant in form, this buck is but a poor m. 1895.

Movie (mū·vi). orig. *U.S.* 1913. [f. MOV(ING *picture* + -IE, -Y[6].] A cinematograph picture: usu. *pl.* cinema pictures, 'the cinema'.

Moving (mū·viŋ), *ppl. a.* late ME. [f. MOVE *v.* + -ING[2].] **a.** That moves. **b.** That originates or actuates 1489. **c.** That touches the feelings or affects the mind 1591.

a. M. picture, a cinematograph picture or film 1899. **M. plant**, the Indian plant, *Meibomia gyrans*, the leaflets of which are in constant motion. **M. staircase, stairway**, an escalator. **b.** He was a m. spirit in fun and mischief 1902. **c.** The gentle spirit of mouing words SHAKS. I..begged, by all that was m., to be delivered out of the Dungeon SWIFT. Hence **Mo·ving-ly** *adv.*, **-ness.**

Mow (mau), *sb.*[1] Now chiefly *dial.* or *U.S.* [OE. *mūga, mūha, mūwa*, corresp. to ON. *múgi* swath, (also *múgr*) crowd; of unkn. origin.] **1.** A stack of hay, corn, beans, peas, etc.; also, a heap of grain or hay in a barn. Cf. HAYMOW. **2.** A place in a barn where hay or corn is heaped up 1755. †**3.** A heap or pile; also, a mound, hillock –1681.

Mow (mau, mōᵘ), *sb.*[2] Now *literary* or *dial.*; in Scot. pron. (mau). ME. [prob. – OFr. *moe*, (also mod.) *moue* †mouth, †lip, pouting; otherwise – MDu. *mouwe*, which may be the source of the OFr. word.] A grimace; *esp.*, a derisive grimace.

Phr. *Mops and mows* (see MOP *sb.*[2]), *mocks and mows, mows and mocks.*

Mow (mōᵘ), *v.*[1] *Pa. t.* **mowed;** *pa. pple.* **mowed, mown.** [OE. *māwan* str. vb. (in other WGmc. langs. weak), repr. by OFris. *mēa*, MDu. *maeien* (Du. *maaien*), OHG. *māen* (G. *mähen*), f. **mǣ-* (see MEAD[2]).] **1.** *trans.* To cut down grass, corn, etc. in a field, etc. with a scythe or a machine: with (*a*) corn, etc. or (*b*) field, etc. as obj. **b.** *absol.* or *intr.* **2.** *transf.* and *fig.* To sweep down in battle; to destroy or kill indiscriminately or in great numbers; now usu. with *down*; also with cognate obj. ME.

1. The hay of our town is almost fit to be mowed SWIFT. **b.** Like an ill Mower, that mowes on still, and neuer whets his Syth BACON. **2.** To m. whole Troops, and make whole Armies fly POPE. The rifle mowed them down as they approached 1884.

Mow (mau), *v.*[2] Now *dial.* late ME. [f. MOW *sb.*[1]] *trans.* To put in mows. Also with *up*.

Mow (mau, mōᵘ), *v.*[3] late ME. [f. Mow *sb.*[2]] *intr.* To make mouths or grimaces.

Mowburn (mōᵘ·bɒɹn), *v.* 1707. [Back-formation from next.] *intr.* Of hay, corn, etc.: To heat and ferment through being stacked too green.

Mow·burnt, *a.* 1548. [f. Mow *sb.*[1] + BURNT *ppl. a.*] Of hay, corn, etc.: Spoilt by becoming overheated in the mow.

Mowe, obs. f. MAY *v.*[1], MEW *sb.*[2], MOVE *v.*, Mow.

Mower (mōᵘ·əɹ). late ME. [f. Mow *v.*[1] + -ER[1].] **1.** One who cuts grass, etc. with a scythe. **2.** A mowing-machine 1852.

Mowing (mōᵘ·iŋ), *vbl. sb.* 1494. [f. Mow *v.*[1] + -ING[1].] **1.** The action of Mow *v.*[1] **b.** *concr.* The quantity of grass cut at one time; also *pl.* grass removed by mowing 1764. **2.** *U.S.* Land on which grass is grown for hay 1786. *attrib.* and *Comb.*, as *m.-machine*, etc.; **m. grass,** grass reserved for mowing.

Mown (mōᵘn), *ppl. a.* OE. [pa. pple. of Mow *v.*[1]] Cut down with a scythe or mowing-machine. Cf. NEW-MOWN.

Moxa (mǫ·ksă). 1677. [– Jap. *mokusa* (phonetically mǫ·ksa), contr. f. *moe kusa* burning herb.] **1.** The downy covering of the dried leaves of *Artemisia moxa*; esp. as prepared for burning on the skin as a counter-irritant for gout, etc. Also, the plant. **2.** Any substance used like moxa for burning on the skin 1833.

‖**Moya** (mōᵘ·ya). 1830. [Former name of a mountain near Quito.] *Geol.* Volcanic mud.

Moyen (moi·ĕn), *sb.* and *a. Obs.* exc. *Sc.* 1440. [– OFr. *moien* sb. and adj., (mod. *moyen*); see MEAN *a.*[2]] **A.** *sb.* A means; means, resources; mediation; instrumentality. †**B.** *adj.* Middle 1481–1550.

Moyl(e see MOIL, MULE.

Mozarab (mozæ·răb). Also **Mozarabe, Muzarab.** 1753. [– Sp. *Mozarabe* (in med.L. pl. *Mozarabes*) – Arab. *mustaʿrib* 'would-be Arab', active pr. pple. of desiderative conjugation f. *ʿarab* the Arabs.] *Hist.* In Spain under Moorish rule: One of those Christians who, on condition of owning allegiance to the Moorish king, and conforming to certain Moorish customs, were allowed the exercise of their own religion. So †**Mozarabite** 1537. **Moza·rabic** *a.* 1706.

Moze (mōᵘz), *v.* 1505. [perh. a derivative of MOSS *sb.* (in the sense of 'nap'; cf. MOSS *sb.* 3).] = GIG *v.*[3]

Mozzetta, mozetta (moze·tă, ‖mǫtsę·tta). 1774. [It. *mozzetta*, dim. of *mozza*; see AMICE[2].] *Eccl.* A cape with a small hood, worn by the Pope and other dignitaries of the R. C. Ch.

M.P. 1809. Abbrev. for 'Member of Parliament'. Pl. *M.P.'s*, occas. *M.P.s.*

Mr. 1447. [orig. an abbrev. of MASTER.] †**1.** In the 16th and 17th c. used for MASTER –1674. **2.** As a prefixed title, now pronounced (mi·stəɹ), or (mistəɹ, m'stəɹ). The regular abbrev. of MISTER *sb.*[2] 1, which is now used only occas. (chiefly *joc.*). For pl. *Messrs.*, MESSIEURS 2, is used. 1447. **b.** Prefixed to a foreign name. Now *rare.* 1601.

1. I refused the Title of Mr. of Arts 1674. **2.** All the lettres of Mʳ. Secretary 1524. 'Mr. Justice—', the style of a Judge of the Supreme Court. Mr. Chairman, Mr. President, Mr. Mayor, etc., forms used now only vocatively.

Mrs. 1582. [orig. an abbrev. of MISTRESS.] †**1.** In the 17th c. often written for MISTRESS –1679. **2.** As a prefixed title of courtesy. Now pronounced (mi·sis, mi·siz); cf. MISSIS. **a.** Prefixed to the surname of a married woman who has no superior title 1582. †**b.** In the 17th and 18th c. prefixed to the name of an unmarried lady or girl –1791.

MS., abbrev. of L. *manu scriptum* MANUSCRIPT.

Often pron. (em es), e.g. [He] drew forth an MS. (Byron).

MSS., used (1) as pl. of prec., and (2) as adj. in concord with a pl. sb.; (3) erron. for MS.

Mt., abbrev. of MOUNT *sb.*[1]

Mucate (miū·kĕt). 1815. [f. MUCIC + -ATE[4].] *Chem.* A salt of mucic acid.

Mucedin (miū·sidin, miusī·din). 1871. [f. L. *mucedo* mucus (in mod.L. 'mould') + -IN[1].] *Chem.* A nitrogenous substance, one of the constituents of gluten. So **Mucedinous** (-se·d-) *a. Bot.* having the character of mould or mildew 1857.

Much (mɒtʃ), *a.*, quasi-*sb.*, and *adv.* [Early ME. *muche, moche, meche, miche,* shortened from *muchel, mochel, mechel, michel*; see MICKLE.] **A.** *adj.* †**1.** = GREAT *a.*, in various applications –1697. **2.** A great quantity or amount of, existing or present in great quantity ME. **3.** With agent-noun: that is much in the habit of performing the action 1711.

1. *M. Burstead, M. Wenlock*, names of English villages. †*M. deal*: a great part; also *advb.* largely. **2.** There is m. truth in that remark of yours JOWETT. A pale yellow sun. .showed the m. dirt of the place KIPLING. Phr. *M.* (ironically, = *no*) *good may it do you. Too m.*: see TOO. **3.** Your long and m. talkers hated him LAMB.

B. *absol.* and quasi-*sb.* †**1.** Used *absol.* in the sense 'great'. Only in *m. and lite, m. and little* = all (people) without exception. ME. only. **2.** A great deal, a great quantity. Provb. *M. will have more.* ME.

2. He who drinks m. is a Slave to himself 1710. There was room for m. of thoughtful consultation FREEMAN. Phr. *By m.*: by a great deal. *To think m. of*: see THINK *v. To make m. of*: see MAKE *v.* II. 9, III. 2. *To be m.*: chiefly neg., (not) to be important or conspicuous, esp. in a specified relation. It was also m., that one that was so great a Louer of Peace should bee so happy in Warre BACON. *Not to be m. to look at*: to be of unattractive appearance. You are not m. to look at DICKENS. *To think* (*it*) *m.* (with *inf.*): to regard as important or onerous; to be shy of (doing something).

C. *adv.* **1.** In a great degree; to a great extent; greatly ME. **b.** = VERY. *Obs.* exc. with *like.* 1449. **c.** Used ironically for 'not at all' 1590. **d.** *Not much*: not likely, certainly not (*colloq.*). **2.** Pretty nearly 1560. **3.** For a large part of one's time 1755.

1. For my part, I don't m. like it GOLDSM. **2.** *M. as, m. of an age, of a muchness, of a size, of a piece.* All of them left the World m. as they found it TEMPLE. It was m. about that time 1704.

Muchel(e, etc.: see MICKLE, etc.

Muchly (mɒ·tʃli), *adv.* Now *joc.* 1621. [f. MUCH *a.* + -LY[2].] Much, exceedingly.

Muchness (mɒ·tʃnės). late ME. [f. MUCH *a.* + -NESS.] †**1.** Large size or bulk; also, size, magnitude (large or small) –1631. **2.** Greatness in quantity, number, or degree. late ME.

Phr. *Much of a m.*: much of the same importance or value; very much alike (*colloq.*).

†**Mu·chwhat,** *sb.* and *adv.* ME. [f. MUCH *adv.* + WHAT *pron.*] **a.** *sb.* Many matters. **b.** *adv.* Greatly; nearly, almost; just; pretty much, pretty well –1701 (very common in 17th c.).

b. Much-what in like manner as before GLANVILL.

Mucic (miū·sik), *a.* 1809. [– Fr. *mucique*, f. L. *mucus*; see MUCUS and -IC.] *Chem.* In *m. acid*: an acid formed by the action of dilute nitric acid upon various kinds of gum. *M. ether*, an ether obtained from *m. acid.*

Mucid (miū·sid), *a. rare.* 1656. [– L. *mucidus*, f. *mucēre* be mouldy; see -ID[1].] Mouldy, musty. So **Mu·cidous** *a.* 1866.

Muciferous (miusi·fĕrəs), *a.* 1842. [f. L. *mucus* MUCUS; see -FEROUS.] Secreting or conveying mucus. So **Muci·fic** *a.* producing mucus 1848. **Mu·ciform** *a.* resembling mucus 1848.

Mucigen (miū·sidʒĕn). 1876. [f. as prec. + -GEN.] *Chem.* The substance of the granules forming a mucous cell.

Mucigenous (miusi·dʒĕnəs), *a.* 1886. [f. as prec. + -OUS.] **a.** Producing mucus. **b.** Of the nature of mucigen.

Mucilage (miū·silėdʒ). late ME. [– (O)Fr. *mucilage* – late L. *mucilago, -agin-* musty juice, f. L. *mucus* MUCUS.] **1.** A viscous substance obtained from the roots, seeds, etc., of plants by maceration in water. Also *pl.* in same sense. **b.** *transf.* A viscous mass, a pulp 1657. **c.** *spec.* Chiefly *U.S.* The adhesive in England commonly called 'gum' 1880. **2.** A viscous lubricating fluid (e.g. mucus, synovia) in animal bodies 1600. **3.** *Bot.* A gummy secretion present in various parts of vegetable organisms 1677. **Mu·cilage** *v.* to stick with or as with m.

Mucilaginous (miūsilæ·dʒinəs), *a.* 1646. [– med.L. *mucilaginosus*, f. L. *mucilago*; see prec., -OUS. Cf. (O)Fr. *mucilagineux.*] **1.** Having the nature or properties of mucilage; soft, moist, and viscous. Also, pertaining to or characteristic of mucilage. **2.** Containing or secreting mucilage 1689.

2. *M. glands*: the fringed vascular folds of the synovial membrane. **Mucila·ginous-ly** *adv.*, †**-ness.**

Mucin (miū·sin). Also **-ine.** 1846. [– Fr. *mucine*, f. L. *mucus* MUCUS; see -IN[1].] *Phys.* The nitrogenous principle of mucus. Hence **Mu·cinous** *a.*

Mucinogen (miusi·nŏdʒĕn). 1886. [f. MUCIN + -GEN.] *Phys.* = MUCIGEN.

Muciparous (miusi·părəs), *a.* 1835. [See MUCUS and -PAROUS.] Producing mucus.

Muck (mɒk), *sb.*[1] [prob. of Scand. origin and – forms rel. to ON. *myki, mykr* dung, Da. *møg*, †*mwgh, mug, mog, møk,* Norw. *myk*, f. Gmc. **muk-* **meuk-* soft (see MEEK), poss. repr. in OE. *hlōs* (pigsty) *moc.*] **1.** Farm-yard manure. Now chiefly *dial.* †**2.** *fig.* Contemptuously applied to money –1710. **3.** Unclean and soiling matter; dirt, filth; also, anything disgusting. Now *colloq.* late ME. **4.** *dial.* or *colloq.* An uncleanly or untidy condition 1766. **5.** *attrib.*, as *m. cart*, etc.

2. Moyling for mucke and trash 1633. **3.** The m. doctors give you 1899. *fig.* You rank stark M. o' th' World DRYDEN.

Comb.: **m.-bar,** iron roughly shaped into bars by being passed once through the rolls; **-iron,** crude puddled iron ready for squeezing or rolling; **-wet** *a.* wet as m.

Muck (mɒk), *sb.*[2] 1687. [The second syllable of AMUCK taken erron. as a sb.] In *to run a m.* = 'to run AMUCK'. Hence, an act of running amuck.

Muck, *v.* late ME. [f. MUCK *sb.*[1] Cf. ON. *moka* to shovel (manure).] **1.** *trans.* To free from muck. **2.** To dress with muck, to manure 1440. **3.** *trans.* To make dirty; to soil. Now *vulgar.* 1832. **b.** *fig. slang.* To make a 'mess' of 1899.

Phr. *To m. about*: to go aimlessly about (*colloq.*).

Muckender (mɒ·kĕndəɹ). *Obs.* exc. *dial.* [Late ME. *mokedore*, prob. – s.w. dial. equiv. of Fr. *mouchoir*, f. *moucher* clear the nose :– pop. L. **muccare*; cf. mod.Pr. *moucadour*, Sp. *mocador, -dero* pocket-handkerchief. For the intrusive *n* cf. *colander.*] A handkerchief. †Also, a table-napkin; a bib.

†**Mu·cker,** *sb.*[1] 1483. [f. MUCK *v.* + -ER[1].] **1.** A scavenger –1790. **2.** A money-grubber –1584.

Mucker (mɒ·kəɹ), *sb.*[2] *slang.* 1852. [f. MUCK *sb.*[1] + -ER[1].] A heavy fall, as in the muck; a 'cropper'.

To come, go a m.: chiefly *fig.*, to come to grief.

Mucker (mɒ·kəɹ), *sb.*[3] *U.S. slang.* 1890. [prob. – G. *mucker* sulky person, etc.] **a.** A fanatic or hypocrite. **b.** A rough, coarse person.

Mucker (mɒ·kəɹ), *v.*[1] *Obs.* exc. *dial.* ME. [perh. f. MUCK *sb.*[1] + -ER[5].] *trans.* To hoard (money, goods). Hence **Mu·ckerer.**

Mucker (mɒ·kəɹ), *v.*[2] *slang.* 1861. [f. MUCKER *sb.*[2]] **a.** *intr.* To 'come a mucker'; to come to grief. **b.** *trans.* To ruin (one's chances).

†**Mu·ckibus.** *vulgar.* [joc. formation from MUCK *sb.*[1]] Tipsy, fuddled. H. WALPOLE.

Muckle, dial. var. of MICKLE.

Mu·ckna. 1780. [Hindustani.] A male elephant without, or with only rudimentary, tusks.

Mu·ck-rake, *sb.* 1684. A rake for collecting muck. In literary use only *fig.* (after Bunyan *Pilgr.*). **Mu·ck-rake,** *v. intr.*, **-raker.**

Mucksy (mɒ·ksi), *a. dial.* 1666. [f. MUCK *sb.*[1] + -SY (cf. *tricksy*, etc.).] Mucky, dirty.

Mu·ckworm. 1598. [f. MUCK *sb.*[1] + WORM.] **1.** A worm or grub that lives in muck. **2.** *fig.* in various applications; *esp.* **a.** a money-grubber 1598; **b.** = GUTTER-SNIPE 2 b. 1859.

Mucky (mɒ·ki), *a.* 1538. [f. MUCK *sb.*[1] + -Y[1].] **1.** Dirty, filthy, muddy. †**b.** *fig.* Applied to money, also to a miserly person –1652. **2.** Consisting of or resembling muck 1570.

1. b. Mynded to prefer oure muckye monie. . before the ioyse of heauen LATIMER. Hence **Mu·ckiness.**

Muco- (miū·ko), used as comb. f. MUCUS, to indicate the presence of mucous matter.

Mu·cocele *Path.*, a mucous dilatation of the lachrymal gland or of the vermiform appendix. **Muco-pu·rulent** *a.*, of the nature of, characterized by the presence of, both mucus and pus.

Mucoid (miū·koid), *a.* 1849. [f. Mucus + -oid.] Resembling mucus.

M. degeneration: transformation of cells or intercellular substance into a substance containing mucin.

‖**Mucor** (miū·kǫɹ). 1818. [L., f. *mucēre* be mouldy; see -or 1.] *Bot.* A plant belonging or allied to the genus *Mucor* of fungi, orig. including all the mould-plants.

Mucoso- (miukōᵘ·so), comb. f. L. *mucosus* mucous in adjs. with sense 'partly mucus and partly —', as **m.-calca·reous** *a.*, consisting of mucus and lime; etc.

Mucous (miū·kəs), *a.* 1646. [– L. *mucosus*, f. *mucus*; see Mucus, -ous. Cf. Fr. *muqueux*.] **1.** Containing, consisting of, or resembling mucus; slimy. **2.** Characterized by the presence of mucus 1825. **3.** *Bot.* Covered with a viscous secretion or with a coat readily soluble in water 1839.

2. *M. râle*, a sound indicating a m. condition of the lungs.

Spec. collocations: **M. membrane**, the lining membrane of those cavities of the body which communicate with the exterior, continuous with the skin and secreting a fluid containing mucus. **M. tissue**, gelatinous connective tissue. **Muco·sity** 1684.

‖**Mucro** (miū·kro). *Pl.* **mucrones** (miukrōᵘ·nīz), **mucros.** 1646. [L. *mucro* point.] *Zool.* and *Bot.* A sharp point or process, as of a leaf or shell.

Mucronate (miū·krŏnĕt), *a.* 1776. [– L. *mucronatus* (Pliny), f. *mucro, -on-* point; see -ate².] Terminating in a point; esp. *Bot.* abruptly terminated by a hard short point. So **Mu·cronated** *a.* 1657. Hence **Mu·cronately** *adv.*

Mucronulate (miukrǫ·niŭlĕt), *a.* 1829. [– mod.L. *mucronulatus*, f. *mucronula*, f. L. *mucron-* Mucro; see -ule.] Having a small sharp point. **Mucro·nulated, Mucro·nulatous** *adjs.*

Muculent (miū·kiŭlĕnt), *a.* 1656. [– late L. *muculentus*, f. L. *mucus*; see next, -ulent.] Slimy, mucous.

Mucus (miū·kŏs). 1661. [– L. *mucus* mucus of the nose, cogn. w. Gr. *μύσσεσθαι*, *μυκτήρ* nose, nostril; cf. L. *emungere*.] **1.** A viscid or slimy substance not miscible with water, secreted by the mucous membrane of animals. **2.** *Bot.* A gummy or glutinous substance soluble in water; found in all plants 1839. **3.** A viscid substance exuded by certain animals, esp. the slime of fishes 1835. **4.** *attrib.*, as *m. duct*, etc. 1835.

Mud (mʋd), *sb.*¹ [ME. *mode, mudde*, prob. – MLG. *mudde* (LG. *mudde, mod, mōde, māde*; cf. Du. *modden* dabble in mud), MHG. *mot* (G. dial. *mott*) bog, bog-earth, peat.] **1.** Wet and soft soil or earthy matter; mire, sludge. **b.** *pl.* Tracts of mud on the margin of a tidal river 1883. **c.** *Geol.* A mixture of finely comminuted particles of rock with water, of varying consistency; usu. either deposited from suspension in water, or ejected from volcanoes. Also *pl.* kinds of mud. 1878. **2.** *fig.* **a.** As a type of what is worthless or polluting 1563. †**b.** The lowest or worst part of anything; the lowest stratum; the dregs –1856.

1. b. Herons — which feed on the muds left by the tide 1897. **2. b.** Defoe said in his wrath, 'the Englishman was the m. of all races' Emerson. Phr. *As clear as m.*: said in mockery of something by no means clear. *To fling* or *throw m.*: to make disgraceful imputations. *To stick in the m.*: see Stick *v.*¹

attrib. and *Comb.* **1.** General: as, *m. colour*; *m.-exhausted*, etc., adjs.; *m.-slinging, -throwing*.

2. Special: **m.-bath,** a medicinal bath of heated m.; **-boat,** (*a*) a board with sides, used for crossing tidal m. for the purpose of shooting sea-birds; (*b*) a barge for carrying away m. dredged from a river or bar; **-drum,** a cylindrical chamber attached to a boiler to collect the sediment and mud in the water for removal; **-flat,** a stretch of muddy land left uncovered at low tide; **mudguard,** a guard over the wheel of a cycle or other vehicle, serving as a protection against m.; **-lava,** volcanic m. (= Moya); **m. pie,** m. or wet earth formed by children in the shape of a pie; **-quake** *joc.*, an earthquake in Holland (H. Walpole); **-scow,** a flat mud-boat; **m. sill,** the lowest sill of a structure, usually embedded in the soil; hence *fig.* (*U.S.*) a person of the lowest class of society; **-stone** *Geol.* shale readily reduced to mud by the action of frost; **m. volcano,** a volcano which discharges m. instead of lava.

b. In names of animals: **m. bass,** a small fresh-water sun-fish (*Acantharchus pomotis*) of U.S.; **m.-cat, catfish** *U.S.*, names given to several species of catfish; **m. crab,** a crab of the genus *Panopæus*: **m. dab,** the winter flounder, *Pseudopleuronectes americanus*; **-dauber,** a wasp of the genus *Pelopæus* that builds its nest of m.; **-devil** = Hellbender 1; **m. eel** = *mud iguana*; **-hen,** a moor-hen, rail, gallinule, or coot; **m. iguana,** the siren, *Siren lacertina*; **m. minnow,** any fish of the family *Umbridæ*; **m. puppy** *U.S.*, the axolotl, the hellbender, and other salamanders; **-terrapin, -tortoise, -turtle** *U.S.*, a turtle which lives in the m. or muddy water, esp. species of *Trionychidæ* and *Emydidæ*; **-worm,** a worm that lives in the m., *esp.* one of the *Limicolæ*; also *fig.* applied contemptuously to a person.

c. In names of plants; **m.-rush, -sedge,** various cyperaceous plants; **-wort,** any herb of the genus *Limosella*, esp. *L. aquatica*.

Mud (mʋd), *sb.*² 1477. [– Du. *mudde, mud* = OS. *muddi*, OHG. *mutti*, G. *mutt*; – L. Modius bushel. Cf. Mutchkin.] A Du. measure of capacity, a hectolitre.

Mud (mʋd), *v.* Now *rare.* 1593. [f. Mud *sb.*¹] **1.** *trans.* To make (water, liquor) turbid by stirring up the mud or sediment at the bottom. Also *fig.* **2.** To cover or plaster with mud 1632. **3.** To bury in mud. Shaks. **4.** *intr.* Of eels, etc.: To lie dormant in the mud 1606.

Mudar, madar (mŏ·dā·ɹ). 1819. [– Hindi *madār*.] **a.** E. Indian name for shrubs of the genus *Calotropis*, esp. *C. gigantea*, the root-bark of which yields a diaphoretic medicine and the inner bark of the stem a strong silky fibre known as yercum. **b.** The medicinal product of the root. Hence **Mu·darine,** a bitter principle obtained from the root-bark of the m.

Muddle (mʋ·d'l), *sb.* 1818. [f. Muddle *v.*] **1.** A muddled condition; confusion; intellectual bewilderment. Also, a bungle, mess. **2.** A confused assemblage 1865.

1. *To make a m. of*: to bungle.

Muddle (mʋ·d'l), *v.* 1596. [perh. – MDu. *moddelen*, frequent. of *modden*; see Mud *sb.*¹, -le.] **1.** *intr.* To bathe or wallow in mud or muddy water. *Obs.* exc. *arch.* 1607. **b.** To grub in the soil; to do dirty work; also †*fig.* (*rare*) 1756. **2.** *trans.* To make muddy. Now *rare.* 1624. **b.** *transf.* To destroy the clearness of (colours) 1596. **3.** To confuse, bewilder, esp. with drink. Also, to render (speech) confused or indistinct. 1687. **4.** To mix up blunderingly, to confuse *together* 1836. **b.** To bungle, mismanage (an affair); also, to render (accounts) unintelligible by want of method 1885. **5.** *intr.* To busy oneself in a confused, unmethodical, and ineffective manner 1806. **6.** *trans.* with *away*. To waste, get rid of (money, time, etc.) without clearly knowing how 1827.

2. Where they mudled the Water and Fished after Marvell. **3.** Their old Master seems to have had his Brains so muddled Bentley. **4.** My Critic has muddled it together in a most extraordinary manner J. H. Newman. **5.** He meddled or rather muddled with literature W. Irving.

Phr. *To m. about*: to potter about, busy oneself aimlessly. *To m. on*: to get along in a haphazard way through makeshifts. *To m. through*: to attain one's end in spite of blunder upon blunder. Hence **Mu·ddler** 1884.

Mu·ddle-hea:ded, *a.* 1759. [f. Muddle *sb.* or *v.* + -ed.] Having a muddled head; characteristic of one with a muddled head; stupid, confused. So **Mu·ddle-head,** a m. person. **Muddlehea·dedness.**

Muddy (mʋ·di), *a.* late ME. [f. Mud *sb.*¹ + -y¹.] **1.** Abounding in mud; turbid or foul with mud; covered or bespattered with mud 1526; resembling mud 1737. **2.** Living or growing in mud 1598. **3.** Of a liquid: Not clear, thick, turbid 1618. **4.** *transf.* **a.** Not clear in colour. Of light: Dull, smoky. 1590. **b.** Of the voice: Thick 1841. **5.** Not clear in mind; muddled 1611. **6.** Of style, thought, etc.: Obscure, vague, confused 1611. **7.** Morally impure or dirty. Now *rare.* late ME.

1. M. marysshes 1555. **2.** M. weeds Shelley. **3.** M. coffee and scorched toast Mrs. Carlyle. **5.** Cold hearts and m. understandings Burke. **6.** The present m. French transcendentalism Thackeray. **7.** She is a muddie queane, a filthy beast 1603. Hence **Mu·ddily** *adv.* **Mu·ddiness.**

Muddy (mʋ·di), *v.* 1601. [f. Muddy *a.*] To make or become muddy.

Mu·d-fish. 1502. Any of several fishes which frequent muddy water or burrow in the mud; *esp.* the common European loach, bowfin, lepidosiren, and mud minnow.

‖**Mudir** (mudīᵊ·ɹ). 1864. [Turk. use of Arab. *mudīr* active, pr. pple. of *'adāra* direct, manage.] In Turkey, the governor of a village or canton; in Egypt, the governor of a province.

Hence **Mudi·rate,** ‖**Mudi·rieh,** the territory, also the official head-quarters, of a m.

Mudlark (mʋ·dlāɹk). 1796. [f. Mud *sb.*¹ + Lark *sb.*¹] **1.** *colloq.* One who dabbles, works, or lives in mud; *esp.* a gutter-child, street arab. **2.** A pipit (*local*) 1882.

‖**Muezzin** (mu,e·zin). Also **mueddin,** etc. 1585. [– dial. var. (with *zz*) of Arab. *mu'aḏḏin* pr. pple. of *'aḏḏana* call to prayer, f. *'uḏn* ear.] In Moslem countries, a public crier who proclaims the regular hours of prayer (cf. Minaret).

†**Muff,** *sb.*¹ 1590. [– Du. *mof*, contempt. name for a Westphalian.] A depreciative term for a German or Swiss –1656.

Muff (mʋf), *sb.*² 1599. [– Du. *mof*, shortening of MDu. *moffel, muffel* (corresp. to Fr. *moufle*, It. *mufla*) – med.L. *muff(u)la*, of unkn. origin.] **1.** A covering (usu. of fur and of cylindrical shape) into which both hands are thrust from opposite ends to keep them warm. A similar covering for the feet (*foot-m.*). †**2.** = Mitten 2. –1749. **3.** A tuft of feathers on the head of some domestic fowls 1809. **4.** *techn.* **a.** *Glass-manuf.* A cylinder of blown glass for flattening out into a plate 1875. **b.** *Mech.* A short hollow cylinder surrounding an object, or used to connect two adjoining pipes 1875.

Muff (mʋf), *sb.*³ *colloq.* 1837. [Of unkn. origin. Cf. WFlem. *moef*, of similar meaning.] **1.** Orig., one who is awkward or stupid in some athletic sport. Hence = Duffer *sb.*² 1. **2.** [Prob. from Muff *v.*¹] A failure; anything bungled; *spec.* in any game at ball, failure to hold a ball that comes into one's hands 1871.

1. A tremendous m. in the hunting-field 1880. Hence **Mu·ffish** *a.* **Mu·ffism.**

Muff (mʋf), *sb.*⁴ *dial.* 1831. [perh. a use of Muff *sb.*², from the ring of outstanding feathers round the neck. But cf. Du. *mof* greenfinch.] The whitethroat, *Sylvia cinerea*.

Muff, *v.*¹ *colloq.* and *slang.* 1841. [f. Muff *sb.*³] *trans.* To make a muddle or mess of, to bungle; to miss (a catch or ball) at cricket, etc. Also *intr.*, to miss catches, to act bunglingly.

Muff, *v.*² 1868. *trans.* = Muffle *v.* 5.

Muffetee (mʋfĕtī·). 1706. [app. irreg. f. Muff *sb.*²] **1.** A muffler worn round the neck. *Obs.* exc. *dial.* **2.** A worsted cuff worn on the wrist 1808.

Muffin (mʋ·fin). 1703. [Of unkn. origin.] **1.** A light, flat, circular, spongy cake, eaten toasted and buttered at breakfast or tea. Formerly (now *dial.*) applied to other kinds of tea-cake. **2.** A kind of flat earthenware or china plate 1864.

Comb.: **m.-bell,** the bell rung by a muffin-man; **-face** *slang*, an expressionless countenance; **-man,** a man who sells muffins. Hence **Muffinee·r,** a small castor with a perforated top for sprinkling sugar or salt on muffins; also, a covered dish to keep muffins hot 1806.

Muffle (mʋ·f'l), *sb.*¹ 1570. [In branch I app. f. Muffle *v.*; in II. and III. – Fr. *moufle*.] **I. 1.** = Muffler 1 a. *rare.* **2.** Something that muffles or deadens sound 1734. **3.** Muffling effect; muffled sound 1886. **II.** A receptacle, placed within a furnace, for heating substances without exposure to the direct action of the fire; spec. in *Chem.*, *Metall.*, and *Ceramics* 1644. **III. 1.** = Muffler 2 a. 1747. **2.** = Mitten 1 and 2. 1808.

Mu·ffle, *sb.*² 1601. [– Fr. *mufle*, of unkn. origin.] The thick part of the upper lip and nose of ruminants and rodents.

Muffle (mʋ·f'l), *v.* late ME. [perh. aphetic f. OFr. **amoufler*, *enmoufler*, f. *en-* En- + *moufle* thick glove (cf. Muff *sb.*²).] **1.** *trans.* To wrap or cover up or enfold esp. so as to conceal, also for warmth and protection from the weather. †2. To prevent from seeing by covering up the head (or eyes); to blindfold; also *fig.* –1700. **3.** To restrain (a person) from speaking by wrapping up his head 1570. **4.** To wrap up (oars, a drum, bell, etc.) so as to deaden the sound 1761. **b.** To deaden (a sound). Chiefly in *passive.* 1832. **5.** To render (glass) semi-opaque by giving it a crinkled surface 1908.

1. The Duke of Suffolk, muffled vp in ragges? SHAKS. *fig.* M. your false loue with some shew of blindnesse SHAKS. **4.** The drums were muffled with black cloth 1806. **b.** The panther's roar came muffled TENNYSON.

Muffler (mʊ·fləɹ). 1535. [f. prec. + -ER[1].] **1. a.** A sort of kerchief or scarf formerly worn by women to cover part of the face and the neck. *Obs.* exc. *Hist.* †**b.** A bandage for blindfolding a person –1621. **c.** A wrap or scarf (usu. of wool or silk) worn round the neck for warmth 1594. **d.** *fig.* Something that muffles or disguises 1633. **2. a.** A boxing-glove 1755. **b.** A glove or mitten 1824. **c.** A leather glove for lunatics who tear up their clothes. DICKENS. **3.** Something to deaden sound; *spec.* a piece of mechanism to deaden the noise of escaping gases, etc., a silencer; in a pianoforte, a felt strip which is inserted between the hammers and strings by depressing the soft pedal 1856.

1. Mufflers.., which they call Masks 1694. **b.** *Hen. V,* III. vi. 33. **c.** Very unwell. Went to meeting with my m. 1787.

‖**Mufti**[1] (mʊ·fti). 1586. [Arab. *muftī*, active pr. pple. of *'aftā* to give a FETWA or decision on a point of law.] A Moslem priest or expounder of the law; in Turkey restricted to the official head of the religion of the state (formerly often †*Grand M.*) and his deputies.

Mufti[2] (mʊ·fti). 1816. [perh. facetious use of prec.] **1.** Plain clothes worn by any one who has a right to wear a uniform; esp. *in m.* **2.** A civilian; one who wears mufti 1833.

Mug (mʊg), *sb.*[1] 1570. [prob. of Scand. origin (cf. Norw. *mugge*, Sw. *mugg* pitcher with handle, of uncertain connections).] **1.** *dial.* Any (large) earthenware vessel or bowl; also, a pot, jug, or ewer. **2.** A drinking-vessel, usu. cylindrical, with or without a handle 1664. **b.** A mug with its contents; the liquid in a mug 1682. **3.** A cooling drink 1633.

Mug (mʊg), *sb.*[2] *slang.* 1708. [prob. transf. use of prec., drinking-mugs being frequently made to represent a grotesque face.] The face or mouth.

Mug (mʊg), *sb.*[3] *slang.* 1859. [perh. transf. use of prec. with ref. to stupid looks.] A stupid person; a muff, duffer; a card-sharper's dupe.

Mug (mʊg), *sb.*[4] *slang.* 1853. [f. MUG *v.*[3]] **1.** An examination. **2.** One who mugs or reads hard 1888.

Mug, *v.*[1] *dial.* ME. [prob. of Scand. origin; cf. ON. *mugga* mist, drizzle (whence Eng. dial. *mug* mist, drizzle), Norw., Sw. dial. *mugg* mould, mildew, prob. rel. to MUCUS.] To drizzle.

Mug, *v.*[2] *slang.* 1855. [f. MUG *sb.*[2]] *Theatr.* **a.** *intr.* To 'make a face'; to grimace. **b.** *To m. up*: to paint one's face; to make up.

Mug, *v.*[3] *slang.* 1848. [Of unkn. origin.] *intr.* To read hard, to 'grind'; *trans.* to get *up* (a subject).

‖**Mugger** (mʊ·gəɹ). Also **-ur, -ar.** 1844. [Hindi *magar.*] The broad-nosed crocodile of India.

Mugget (mʊ·gėt). *Obs.* exc. *dial.* 1481. [Of unkn. origin.] The intestines of a calf or sheep, as an article of food; †a dish made of these –1677.

Muggins (mʊ·ginz). 1865. [perh. the surname *Muggins*, with allusion to MUG *sb.*[3]] **1.** *slang.* A fool, simpleton 1873. **2. a.** A children's game of cards 1865. **b.** A game of dominoes in which the players count by fives 1881.

Mu·ggish, *a. rare.* 1655. [f. dial. *mug* mist, drizzle + -ISH[1]. Cf. MUG *v.*[1]] Damp, musty.

Muggletonian (mʊg'lĭtōᵘ·niăn). 1670. [f. *Muggleton* + -IAN.] **A.** *sb.* A member of the sect founded *c* 1651 by Lodowicke Muggleton and John Reeve, who claimed to be the 'two witnesses' of Rev. 11: 3–6. **B.** *adj.* Belonging to this sect.

Muggy (mʊ·gi), *a.* 1731. [f. dial. *mug* mist, drizzle (see MUG *v.*[1]) or f. MUG *v.*[1] + -Y[1].] **1.** Mouldy, moist, damp, wet. *Obs.* exc. *dial.* **2.** Of weather, a day, etc.: Damp, close and warm 1746. **b.** Stifling 1820.

2. Weather quite m. MISS BURNEY. **b.** The 'muggy' smell so generally noticeable in lodging houses and barrack-rooms 1906. Hence **Mu·gginess.**

Mu·g-house. 1685. [MUG *sb.*[1]] An ale-house, beer-house.

Mugient (miū·dʒiĕnt), *a. rare.* 1646. [– *mugient-*, pr. ppl. stem of L. *mugire* bellow; see -ENT.] Lowing, bellowing. Hence †**Mu·giency,** a bellowing 1646.

Mugweed (mʊ·gwīd). *dial.* late ME. [f. *mug-* (in MUGWORT) + WEED *sb.*[1]] **a.** Mugwort, *Artemisia vulgaris.* **b.** Crosswort, *Galium cruciata*; also *golden m.*

Mugwort (mʊ·gwʊɹt). [OE. *mucgwyrt*, f. base of MIDGE + WORT[1].] **1.** The plant *Artemisia vulgaris,* formerly also called *motherwort.* Also applied to wormwood, *A. absinthium*, etc. **2.** = MUGWEED b. 1796.

Mugwump (mʊ·gwʊmp), *sb. U.S.* 1832. [– Natick (Algonquin) *mugquomp* great chief.] **1.** *joc.* A great man, a 'boss'. **2.** An Independent in politics; *spec.* a Republican who refused to support the nominee of the party for president in the 1884 election. Hence **Mu·gwump** *v. intr.* to play the part of a m. **Mu·gwumpery, Mu·gwumpism. Mu·gwumpish** *a.*

Muhammad, etc.: var. MOHAMMED, etc.

Muir, Sc. var. of MOOR *sb.*[1]

Mulatto (miulæ·to). 1595. [– Sp. (and Pg.) *mulato* young mule, hence, one of a mixed race, obscurely f. *mulo* MULE[1].] **A.** *sb.* One who is the offspring of a European and a Negro; hence, any half-breed resembling a mulatto. **B.** *adj.* Belonging to the class of mulattos; of the colour of a m.; tawny 1622. So †**Mula·tta** [– Sp. *mulata*] 1622–1828. **Mula·tress** [– Fr. *mulâtresse*], a female m. 1845.

Mulberry (mʊ·lbĕri). [OE. *mōrberie*, **murberie*, ME. *murberie*, corresp. to Du. *moerbezie*, OHG. *mōr-*, *murberi* (MHG. *mūlber*, G. *maulbeere*); f. **mor* – L. *morum* mulberry, *morus* mulberry-tree + BERRY *sb.*[1]; the dissimilation of *r..r* to *l..r* is evidenced XIV (Trevisa).] **1.** The fruit of any tree of the genus *Morus*, *esp.* the Black Mulberry, *M. nigra*; also, the tree. **3.** Applied to plants or trees of other genera; e.g. the Blackberry. Also PAPER-*m.* 1672. **3.** A dark purple colour like that of mulberries. Also as *adj.* = m.-coloured. 1837.

3. If ever there was a wolf in a m. suit, that ere Job Trotter's him DICKENS.

Comb.: *m.-faced*, etc.; also **m. bush,** a children's game, with a ditty 'Here we go round the mulberry-bush'; **m. germ, mass** = MORULA; **m. rash,** a name given to the rash of typhus fever.

Mulch (mʊlʃ), *sb.* 1657. [subst. use of *mulsh* adj. soft, (dial.) of 'soft' weather, rel. to (dial.) *melsh* mellow, soft, mild :– OE. *mel(i)sć*, *mylsć*, f. **mel-* **mul-* (see -ISH[1]), whence also MHG. *molwic*, G. *mollig*, *mollecht*, *molsch*, *mulsch* soft, OHG. *molawēn* be soft, cogn. with L. *mollis* tender.] Half-rotten straw; in *Gardening*, a mixture of wet straw, leaves, loose earth, etc., spread on the ground to protect the roots of newly planted trees, etc. Hence **Mulch** *v. trans.* to cover with m. 1802.

Mulct (mʊlkt), *sb.* 1591. [orig. *mult(e* – L. *mulcta*, *multa*; see next. Cf. Fr. †*mulcte*, earlier *multe.*] **1.** A fine imposed for an offence. Also *occas.* a compulsory payment. **2.** A penalty of any kind 1619. Hence †**Mu·lctary** *a.* of the nature of a fine 1695. †**Mu·lctuary** *a.* that punishes by a fine; punishable by a fine 1613–1689.

Mulct (mʊlkt), *v.* 1483. [orig. *multe* – Fr. †*multer*, *mulcter* – L. *mulctare*, prop. *multare*, f. *mulcta*, *multa* fine, amercement.] **1.** *trans.* To punish (a person, †an offence) by a fine. †Also *occas.* to subject to a penalty of any kind. **2.** To deprive or divest *of* 1748.

Mule[1] (miūl). [ME. *mule*, etc. – OFr. *mul* m., *mule* fem. :– L. *mulus* m., *mula* fem. OE. *mūl* was prob. inherited from a Gmc. adoption f. L.] **1.** The offspring of a he-ass and a mare. Also, pop., the offspring of a she-ass and a stallion (techn. called a HINNY). (Without good grounds, the mule is a proverbial type of obstinacy.) **2.** *transf.* **a.** A stupid or obstinate person 1470. **b.** One who is 'neither one thing nor the other' B. JONS. **3.** A hybrid plant or animal; *esp.* a mule canary 1727. **4.** *techn.* **a.** A kind of spinning jenny invented by S. Crompton 1797. **b.** *Numism.* A coin presenting two obverse types, or two reverse types, or types which do not correspond 1884. **c.** An electric tractor for drawing vessels through canals.

1. She was as obstinate as a m. on that point 1809. *attrib.* and *Comb.*: **m. armadillo,** *Dasypus septemcinctus* or *hybridus*; **m.-bird, m. canary,** a cross between a canary and another finch, esp. the goldfinch; **m. deer,** *Cariacus macrotis*, on account of its mule-like ears; **m. jenny** = sense 4 a; **m. twist, yarn,** yarn spun on a m.

Mule[2] (miūl). late ME. [– Fr. *mule* fem., slipper, *mules* pl., chilbains.] †**1.** A chilbain on the heel; also, later, a sore on a horse's heel –1720. **2.** A kind of slipper or shoe 1562.

Muleteer (miūlĕtīᵊ·ɹ). 1538. [– Fr. *muletier*, f. *mulet*, dim. of OFr. *mul* (which it superseded); see MULE[1], -ET, -EER.] A mule-driver.

Muley (miū·li). Also **mulley.** 1573. [var. of Sc. and Anglo-Irish *moiley*, f. *moil* adj. – Ir. *maol*, and the equivalent W. *moel*, lit. 'bald'.] **A.** *sb.* **1.** Name for a hornless cow. (Now common in U.S.) Also used for any cow (*dial.*). **2.** *U.S.* A muley saw (see B. 2) 1864. **B.** *adj.* **1.** Of cattle: Hornless 1885. **2.** *U.S.* (*Mech.*) In **m. axle,** a car axle having no collars at the ends of the journals; **m. saw,** a stiff long saw which is not stretched in a gate or sash, but has guide-carriages called *m.-heads* 1872.

Muliebrity (miuli,e·brĭti). *rare.* 1592. [– late L. *muliebritas*, f. *muliebris*, f. *mulier* woman; see -ITY.] Womanhood; the characteristics or qualities of a woman.

†**Mulier** (miū·liəɹ). late ME. [repr. AFr. *mulieré*, (AL. *mulieratus* XII), f. *mulier*, OFr. *moiller* wife – L. *mulier* woman.] **A.** *adj.* Of a child: Born in wedlock, legitimate; also in *Eccl. Law*, legitimatized by marriage –1642. **B.** *sb.* A legitimate child; a child born in wedlock –1766. Hence †**Mu·lierly** *adv.* (begotten or born) in wedlock; legitimately 1506–1586. †**Mu·lierty,** the condition of being a legitimate issue 1628. var. †**Muliery** –1572.

Mulierose (miū·li,ĕrōᵘs), *a. rare.* 1721. [– L. *mulierosus*, f. *mulier* woman; see -OSE[1].] Fond of women. So **Mu:liero·sity** 1656.

Mulish (miū·liʃ), *a.* 1751. [f. MULE[1] + -ISH[1].] Characteristic of, or resembling, a mule; intractable, stubborn. Hence **Mu·lish-ly** *adv.*, **-ness.**

Mull (mʊl), *sb.*[1] *Obs.* exc. *dial.* [ME. *mul*, *mol* – (M)Du. *mul*, *mol*, cogn. with OE. *myl* dust, ON. *moli* crumb, *mylja* crush, f. **mul-* (cf. MEAL *sb.*[1]); see MULLOCK.] Something reduced to small particles; dust, ashes, mould, rubbish.

Mull (mʊl), *sb.*[2] *Sc.* late ME. [In Gael. *maol*; in Icel. *múli*, perh. identical with *múli* snout = OHG. *mūl* (G. *maul*) snout.] In Scotland, a promontory or headland.

Mull (mʊl), *sb.*[3] 1640. [– Du. *mul*, etymologically = MULL *sb.*[1]] The lowest of the four qualities of Dutch madder. Also **m.-madder.**

Mull (mʊl), *sb.*[4] *Sc.* 1771. See MILL *sb.*[1] 2 c.

Mull (mʊl), *sb.*[5] 1798. Shortened f. MULMULL.

Mull (mʊl), *sb.*[6] *colloq.* or *slang.* 1821. [perh. f. next. Cf. MUFF *sb.*[3] 2, *v.*[1]] A muddle, mess. Chiefly in phr. *to make a m. of.*

Mull (mʊl), *v.*[1] *Obs.* exc. *dial.* late ME. [f. MULL *sb.*[1]] *trans.* To grind to powder, pulverize; to crumble.

†**Mull,** *v.*[2] *rare.* 1607. [Of unkn. origin.] *trans.* To dull, stupefy –1687.

Mull (mʊl), *v.*[3] 1607. [Of unkn. origin.] *trans.* To make (wine, beer, etc.) into a hot drink with the addition of sugar, spices, beaten yolk of egg, etc.

Mull (mʊl), *v.*[4] 1862. [f. MULL *sb.*[6]] **1.** *trans.* (*Athletics.*) To make a failure of. **2.**

intr. To work (*over*) mentally; to cogitate, ruminate, ponder. *colloq. U.S.* 1879.

Mullah (mɒ·lă). 1613. [– Pers., Turk., Urdu *mullā* – Arab. *mawlā*.] A Moslem title for one learned in theology and sacred law.

Mullein (mɒ·lėn, -in). late ME. [– OFr. *moleine* (mod. *molène*) – Gaulish **melena* (*melinus* 'color nigrus') sb. *fem.*, corresp. to Breton *melen*, W. *melyn* yellowish.] **1.** Common name of various species of the genus *Verbascum*, herbaceous plants with woolly leaves and an erect woolly raceme of yellow flowers; esp. *V. thapsus*, Common or Great (Torch) M. **2.** Short for *mullein moth* 1868.

attrib. and *Comb.*: **m. foxglove,** a wild plant of the U.S., *Seymeria macrophylla*; **m. moth, shark,** a moth, *Cucillia verbasci*, whose larva feeds upon the m. plant; **m. tea,** an infusion of m. leaves.

Muller (mɒ·ləɹ), *sb.* late ME. [perh. – AFr. **moloir* (cf. OFr. *moloir* adj. serving to pound or grind), f. *moldre* grind; cf. -ER[2] 3.] A stone with a flat base or grinding surface, used, in conjunction with a grinding stone or slab, in grinding painters' colours, apothecaries' powders, etc. Also, **m.-stone. b.** Applied to mechanical contrivances for grinding or crushing 1858. Hence **Mu·ller** *v. trans.* to grind with a m.

Müllerian (mülī°·riăn), *a.* 1875. [f. Joh. *Müller* (1801–1858), a German physiologist + -IAN.] In *M. duct*, each of a pair of ducts in a vertebrate embryo, which in the female become oviducts or Fallopian tubes.

Mullet[1] (mɒ·lėt). 1440. [ME. *molet, mulet* – OFr. *mulet*, dim. f. L. *mullus* red mullet – Gr. μύλλος, rel. to μέλας black.] **1.** A name for any fish of **a.** the genus *Mullus*, family *Mullidæ*, of which the Red mullet (*M. barbatus*) is the type; **b.** the genus *Mugil*, family *Mugilidæ*, of which the Grey mullet (*M. capito*) is the best-known species. **2.** Applied to fish of other genera, as Black m., *Menticirrus nebulosus*, the American king-fish, etc. 1880.

1. Mullets, Sous'd in high-countrey wines B. JONS.

Mullet[2] (mɒ·lėt). late ME. [– AFr. *molet*, (O)Fr. *molette* rowel, dim. of *meule* millstone :– L. *mola* grindstone.] *Her.* A figure of a star, having five (or more) straight points. Given as a mark of cadency for a third son.

†**Mu·llet**[3]. late ME. [– Fr. *molet*.] *pl.* A kind of pincers or tweezers –1634. Hence †**Mu·llet** *v.* to treat with these 1649.

Mulley, var. of MULEY.

Mulligatawny (mɒ:ligătǭ·ni). 1784. [– Tamil *milagu-tannīr* 'pepper-water' (Yule).] An East Indian highly seasoned soup. Also *m. soup.* **b.** *M. paste*, a curry paste used for flavouring this soup 1858.

Mulligrubs (mɒ·ligrɒbz), *sb. pl.* 1599. [Arbitrary.] A state of depression of spirits; a fit of megrims or spleen; in early use in phr. (*in*) *her, his*, etc. *mulligrubs*; hence joc., stomach-ache or colic.

Whose dog lyes sicke o' th m.? FLETCHER.

Mullion (mɒ·lyən). 1567. [Metathetic alt. of ME. *munial* MONIAL, as the contemp. MUNNION is an assim. form (*n..l* to *n..n*).] *Arch.* A vertical bar dividing the lights in a window, esp. in Gothic architecture; also, a similar bar in screen-work.

attrib. and *Comb.* **m. window** = mullioned window. Hence **Mu·llioned** *a.*

Mullock (mɒ·lək). late ME. [f. MULL *sb.*[1] + -OCK.] **1.** Rubbish, refuse matter. Now only *dial.* **2.** *Austral.* Rock which does not contain gold; also, the refuse from which gold has been extracted 1864.

Mulmull (mɒ·lmɒl). 1619. [– Hindi *malmal*.] A thin variety of muslin. Cf. MULL *sb.*[5]

†**Mulse.** 1533. [– L. *mulsum*, n. pa. pple. of *mulcēre* sweeten.] A liquor made of honey mixed with water or wine; hydromel, mead. Also *m.-water*. –1661.

Multangular (mɒltæ·ŋgiŭlaɹ), *a.* (*sb.*). Also **multi-.** 1677. [– med.L. *multangularis*; see MULTI-, ANGULAR.] **A.** *adj.* Having many angles: polygonal. **B.** *sb. rare.* A polygon 1766. **Multa·ngular-ly** *adv.*, **-ness.** So †**Multa·ngulous** *a.* 1659–1680.

Multa·nimous, *a. rare.* 1854. [f. MULTI- after *magnanimous*.] Having a many-sided mind.

Multarti·culate, *a. rare.* Also **multi-.** 1681. [f. MULTI- + ARTICULATE.] *Zool.* Having many articulations or joints.

Multeity (mɒltī·ĭti). 1814. [f. L. *multus* after *hæcceity*, etc.] The quality of being many; manifoldness.

Multi- (mɒ·lti), occas. bef. a vowel **mult-,** comb. f. L. *multus* much, many. (The L. compounds were chiefly parasynthetic, as *multicaulis* many-stalked.)

1. Forming parasynthetic adjs. with the sense 'having many..', having sometimes corresponding forms in POLY-. **a.** In scientific and technical use: as *multia·xial*, having many axes or lines of growth, *-camerate* (chambers), *-capsular*, *-carinate(d* (keels), *-cellular* (cells), *-central*, *-cipital* (heads), *-costate* (ribs), *-cuspid(ate* (cusps), *-dentate* (teeth), *-digitate* (fingers), *-dimensional*, *-floral*, *-florous* (flowers), *-foliate* (leaves), *-jugate*, *-jugous* (pairs of leaflets), *-lineal*, *-linear*, *-lobar*, *-lobate*, *-lobed*, *-locular*, *-loculate(d* (cells), *-nodal*, *-nodate*, *-nodous*, *-nuclear*, *-nucleate(d*, *-polar*, *-radiate(d* (rays), *-ramose*, *-ramous* (branches), *-septate* (septa or partitions), *-siliquose* (pods), *-striate* (striæ or streaks), *-tubercular*, *-ate* (tubercles), *-tubular* (tubes). **Multise·rial, -se·riate,** arranged in many series or rows. **Multivo·ltine** [It. *volta* time, turn], (of a silkworm) producing several broods a year.

b. In general use (mostly nonce-wds.): as *multifaced*. **Multiflu·vian** [L. *fluvius*], having many rivers flowing into it. **Multili·ngual,** using, characterized by, or written in, many languages. **Multino·minal,** †**-no·minous,** having many names. **Multiti·tular,** having many titles.

2. Prefixed to a sb. either with adjectival sense = 'multiple, manifold', or with adverbial sense = 'in many ways or directions'. **Mu·lticycle,** (*a*) a cycle having more than three wheels; (*b*) a cycle for two or more riders. **Mu·ltifoil,** a foil (in a window) of more than five divisions. **Multiloca·tion,** location in many places at the same time. **Mu:ltimillionai·re,** one who is worth two or more millions of money.

3. Prefixed to a sb. forming a compound used attrib. with the force of a parasynthetic adj. **Mu·lticharge,** (of a gun) capable of containing several charges. **Mu·lticoil,** possessing more than one coil. **Mu·lti-cy:linder** (of an engine) having three or more cylinders. **Mu·ltispeed,** (of a motor) of several (usu. definite) speeds.

Mu·lti-colour, *sb.* and *a.* 1849. [MULTI- 2, 3.] **1. a.** The condition of being many-coloured. **b.** *pl.* Many or various colours 1901. **2. a.** *attrib.* Applied to printing in many colours or a machine for such printing 1884. **b.** *adj.* Many-coloured 1881. **Multi-coloured** *a.*, of many colours 1845.

Multifarious (mɒltifē°·riəs), *a.* (*sb.*). 1593. [f. L. *multifarius* (Gellius) + -OUS.] **1.** Having great variety; (with pl. sb.) many and various. **b.** *Bot.* Arranged in many rows, as leaves (*rare*) 1838. **2.** *Law.* 'Improperly joining in one bill distinct matters, and thereby confounding them' (Story) 1838. **3.** *sb.* In Kantian philosophy = MANIFOLD *sb.*[1] 2 a. 1819.

1. That m. thing called a state BURKE. Hence **Multifa·rious-ly** *adv.*, **-ness.**

Multiferous (mɒlti·fĕrəs), *a. rare.* 1656. [f. L. *multifer* + -OUS; later – mod.L. *multiferus*; see MULTI-, -FEROUS.] Bearing much or many; fruitful.

Multifid (mɒ·ltifid), *a.* 1731. [f. MULTI- after earlier BIFID, TRIFID (XVII). Cf. L. *multifidus*.] *Bot.* and *Zool.* Having many divisions; cleft into many parts.

A simple, bifid, or m. fold of the integument HUXLEY. So **Multi·fidous** *a.*, said esp. of feet 1646.

Mu·ltifold, *a.* 1806. [f. MULTI- + -FOLD, after *manifold*.] Manifold.

Multiform (mɒ·ltifǭɹm), *a.* and *sb.* 1603. [– Fr. *multiforme* or L. *multiformis*: see MULTI- and -FORM.] **A.** *adj.* Having many forms, shapes, or appearances; of many and various forms or kinds. **B.** *sb.* That which is multiform. Also, multiform character, multiformity 1849.

A. The m. brogue, which salutes the ears of a traveller in..New-York 1817. So **Multifo·rmity,** diversity or variety of form 1589. **Multifo·rmous** *a.* multiform 1670.

Multila·teral, *a.* 1696. [– late L. *multilaterus* (Boethius), med.L. *multilateralis* (Duns Scotus); see MULTI-, LATERAL.] = MANY-SIDED 1, 2.

Multi·loquy. 1542. [– L. *multiloquium*, f. *multi-* much + *loqui* speak.] Much speaking, talkativeness.

So **Multi·loquence** 1760; **Multi·loquent** (1656), **-lo·quious** (1640), **-loquous** (1664) *adjs.*, given to much talking.

Multinomial (mɒltinōᵘ·miăl), *a.* and *sb.* 1608. [f. MULTI- 1, after *binomial*.] *Alg.* **A.** *adj.* Of an expression: Consisting of many (i.e. more than two) terms connected by the signs + or −. **B.** *sb.* A m. expression 1674.

Multi·parous, *a.* 1646. [f. mod.L. *multiparus*: see MULTI- and -PAROUS.] **1.** Bringing forth many young at a birth; characterized by such parturition. **2.** Of or pertaining to, or that is, a **Multi·para** (a woman who has borne more than one child) 1860. **3.** *Bot.* Applied to a cyme that has many axes 1880. So **Multipa·rient** *a.* (in sense 1). 1822. Hence **Multipa·rity** 1890.

Multipartite (mɒltipā·ɹtəit), *a.* 1721. [– L. *multipartitus*: see MULTI- and PARTITE *a.*] Divided into many parts; having many divisions.

Multiped, -pede (mɒ·ltiped, -pīd), *sb.* and *a.* Now *rare.* 1601. [– L. *multipeda* sb., *multipes* adj., f. *multus* MULTI- + *pes, ped-* foot.] **A.** *sb.* A many-footed creature; †*spec.* a woodlouse. **B.** *adj.* Many-footed 1736.

Multiple (mɒ·ltip'l), *a.* and *sb.* 1647. [– Fr. *multiple* – late L. *multiplus* = cl. L. *multiplex* (see MULTIPLEX).] **A.** *adj.* **1.** *Math.* That is a multiple (see B. 1); †that is some multiple *of* 1714. **2.** Consisting of or characterized by many parts, elements, or individual components; manifold. With pl. sb.: Many and various. 1647. **3.** In techn. use; esp.

a. *Astron. M. star*: a cluster of stars forming apparently one system 1850. **b.** *Electr. M. arc*: a compound electric circuit. *M. telegraphy*: a system by which many messages may be sent over the same wire 1873. **c.** In the Kantian philosophy: That is a manifold (*rare*) 1839.

1. *M. proportion, ratio*: the proportion or ratio existing between a quantity and some multiple of it, or between several multiples of it. *Law of m. proportions* (Chem.): the generalization that whenever elements combine together in several proportions, the proportions in which the one element unites with the other invariably bear a simple relation to one another. Thus 1 part by weight of hydrogen unites with 8 parts by weight of oxygen, forming water, and with 16 or 8 × 2 parts of oxygen, forming peroxide of hydrogen. **2. M. shop, store:** one of several shops of the same kind under one and the same management, situated in different localities.

B. *sb.* **1.** *Math.* A quantity which contains another quantity some number of times without remainder. Thus 4 is a multiple of 2; 6 of 2 and of 3. 1685. Also *fig.* **2.** In the Kantian philosophy: = MANIFOLD *sb.*[1] 2 a. 1839.

1. *Least common m.* (L.C.M.): the least quantity that contains two or more quantities some number of times without remainder: e.g. 12 is the L.C.M. of 2, 3, and 4.

Mu:ltiplepoi·nding (pi·ndiŋ). 1693. [See POIND *v.*] *Sc. Law.* An action raised by the holder of a fund or property to which there are several claimants, who are thereby required to come together and settle their claims in court.

Multiplex (mɒ·ltipleks), *a.* and *sb.* 1557. [– L. *multiplex*, f. *multus* MULTI- + *-plex* = -FOLD.] **A.** *adj.* †**1.** *Math.* **a.** *M. to, of*: that is some multiple of –1690. †**b.** *M. proportion*, multiple proportion –1788. **2.** = MANIFOLD *a.* 1, 2; MULTIPLE *a.* 2, 3. 1676. **B.** *sb.* †**1.** *Math.* = MULTIPLE *sb.* 1. –1695. **2.** = MULTIPLE *sb.* 2. 1836.

Mu·ltipliable, *a.* 1625. [f. MULTIPLY *v.* + -ABLE.] Capable of being multiplied.

Multiplicable (mɒ·ltiplikăb'l), *a.* 1471. [– OFr. *multiplicable* or med.L. *multiplicabilis* – L. *multiplicare*; see MULTIPLY, -ABLE.] = prec. Hence **Mu:ltiplicabi·lity** 1677.

Multiplicand (mɒ:ltiplikæ·nd, mɒ·ltiplikænd). 1594. [– med.L. *multiplicandus* (sc. *numerus*), gerundive of L. *multiplicare*; see MULTIPLY.] *Math.* The quantity to be multiplied; correl. to *multiplier*.

Multiplicate (mɒ·ltiplikĕt, mɒlti·plikĕt), *a.* and *sb.* Now *rare.* late ME. [– L. *multiplicatus*, pa. pple. of *multiplicare*; see MULTIPLY, -ATE[2]. As sb. (XIX) f. MULTI- after *duplicate*, etc.] **A.** *adj.* †Multiplied, increased; manifold; multiplex. **B.** *sb.* **a.** *In m.*: in many exactly corresponding copies or reproductions. **b.** One of such copies. 1858. So †**Mu·ltiplicated** *pa. pple.* folded many times 1638.

Multiplication (mɒ·ltiplikēⁱ·ʃən). late ME. [– (O)Fr. *multiplication* or L. *multiplicatio*, f. *multiplicat-*, pa. ppl. stem of *multiplicare*; see MULTIPLY, -ION.] **1.** The act or process of multiplying; the state of being multiplied. Now *rare* exc. as coloured by sense 3. **2.** Propagation of animals and plants. late ME. **3.** *Math.* The process of finding the quantity produced (see PRODUCT) by taking a given quantity (the *multiplicand*) as many times as there are units in another given quantity (the *multiplier*); or, in the case of a fractional multiplier, of finding the same fraction of the multiplicand as the mulipliер is of unity. late ME. **b.** In *Higher Algebra*: The successive application of operators 1843. †**4.** *Alch.* The art of 'multiplying' –1696. **5.** *Bot.* Increase in the number of whorls or of organs in a whorl 1849.

1. M. of words in the body of the Law, is m. of ambiguity HOBBES. One of the peculiarities which distinguish the present age is the m. of books JOHNSON. Repeated transcription involves m. of error 1881. **2.** Multiplicacioun and encrese of men and children in þe norþ TREVISA.

attrib.: **m. table**, a table of products of factors taken in pairs, usually beginning 'twice one are two' (2 × 1 = 2) and going up to some assumed limit. Also †*table of m.*

Multiplicative (mɒ·ltiplikĕtiv), *a.* and *sb.* 1653. [– late L. *multiplicativus* (Boethius), f. as prec.; see -IVE.] Tending, or having the power, to multiply or increase. **b.** *Gram.* Applied to numerals that express 'so many times'. Also *sb.*, a m. numeral. 1727.

Multiplicator (mɒ·ltiplikeⁱtǫɹ). 1542. [– late L. *multiplicator* (Boethius), f. as prec.; see -OR 2.] **1.** *Math.* = MULTIPLIER 2. Now *rare* or *obs.* **2.** *Elect.* and *Magn.* = MULTIPLIER 4. 1823. **b.** In a galvanometer, a flat coil of conducting wire for multiplying the effect of the current 1884.

†**Multipli·cious**, *a.* 1617. [app. f. L. *multiplex, -plic-* + -OUS; see -IOUS. Cf. med. L. *multiplicus.*] Multiplex –1713. Hence †**Multipli·ciously** *adv.*

Multiplicity (mɒltipli·sĭti). 1587. [– late L. *multiplicitas*, f. as prec.; see -ITY.] **1.** Multiplex quality or condition; manifold variety. **b.** In the Kantian philosophy = MANIFOLD *sb.*[1] 2 a. 1839. **2.** *The m. of*: the great number of. So *a, such (a), this*, etc. *m. of*. 1598.

2. Such m. of words he hath 1598.

Multiplier (mɒ·ltiplǝiˌǝɹ). late ME. [f. MULTIPLY *v.* + -ER[1].] **1.** One who or a thing which multiplies something 1470. **2.** *Math.* The quantity by which another (the *multiplicand*) is multiplied 1542. †**3.** One who performs the alchemical process of multiplication; hence, a false coiner –1560. **4.** *Electr.* and *Magn.* An instrument used for multiplying or increasing by repetition the intensity of a force, current, etc. so as to make it appreciable or mensurable 1823. **5.** *Angling.* A kind of reel by which the speed at which the fishing-line is gathered in at each turn of the handle is accelerated; also *multiplying-reel* 1867. **6.** An arithmometer for multiplying 1875.

Multiply (mɒ·ltiplǝi), *v.* ME. [– (O)Fr. *multiplier* – L. *multiplicare*, f. *multiplic-*, stem of MULTIPLEX.] **1.** *trans.* To cause to become much, many, or more; to make many or manifold. Now *rare* exc. as coloured by sense 5. **b.** To adduce a large number of (instances, etc.) 1716. †**c.** To increase the intensity of; *occas.* to magnify optically –1651. **2.** *intr.* To become of great number or quantity; to be increased by accumulation or repetition ME. **3.** *trans.* To increase (a family, etc.). by procreation (freq. in *pass.*); †to cause (the earth) to become populous. *Obs.* or *arch.* –1784. **b.** To breed (animals); to propagate (plants) 1471. **4.** *intr.* To increase in number by natural generation ME. **5.** *trans.* (*Math.*) To operate upon (a *multiplicand*) with a *multiplier* so as to produce a *product* having the same ratio to the multiplicand as the multiplier has to unity. In *Higher Algebra*, to apply an operator to (an operand). late ME. **b.** *intr.* To perform the process of multiplication 1579. †**6.** *Alch.* (*trans.* and *intr.*) To increase the precious metals, as by transmutation of the baser metals. Also *intr.* (for *pass.*) said of the precious metals. late ME.

1. Swete wordes multiplien & encressen frendes CHAUCER. Phr. *To m. words*: †(*a*) to be loquacious; (*b*) to be verbose. *To m. evil upon evil*: to add evil to evil. **c.** Wee M. Smells, which may seeme strange BACON. **2.** The flame increased—multiplied—at one point after another KINGSLEY. **4.** As for my Cats, they multiply'd DE FOE. **5.** Phr. *To m.* (one quantity) *into*, †*in* (another); *to m.* (two quantities) *together*: to find the product of the two quantities. **6.** Upon Nature thei falsely lye For Mettalls doe not Multiplie 1477.

Multiply (mɒ·ltipli), *adv.* 1881. [f. MULTIPLE + -LY[2].] In a multiple manner; *spec.* in *Math.*

Mu·ltiplying-glass. 1628. †**1.** A magnifying-glass –1680. **2.** A toy consisting of a concave glass or lens, the surface of which is cut into numerous facets so as to give as many reflections of the object observed 1671.

Multipotent (mɒlti·pŏtent), *a.* *rare.* 1606. – L. *multipotens, -ent-*; see MULTI-, POTENT.] Having much power.

Multipre·sence. 1614. [f. MULTI- + PRESENCE after contemp. *omnipresence.*] The fact or faculty of being present in many places at once. So **Multipre·sent** *a.*

The multi-presence of Christ's body BP. HALL.

Multisect (mɒ·ltisekt), *a.* 1826. [f. MULTI-, after *insect.*] *Entom.* Of an insect: Divided into numerous segments. So **Mu·ltisect** *v.* 1862.

Multisonant (mɒlti·sŏnănt), *a.* *rare.* 1656. [f. MULTI- + SONANT.] Having many sounds; sounding much. So **Multi·sonous** *a.*

Multitude (mɒ·ltitiūd). ME. [– (O)Fr. *multitude* – L. *multitudo, -tudin-*, f. *multus*; see -TUDE.] **1.** Numerousness; great number. Also, number whether great or small. **2.** A great number, a host, a crowd (*of* persons or things). Often *ellipt.* = m. of men, etc. in question. ME. **b.** *pl.* Great numbers, hosts, crowds 1596. †**c.** A great quantity (*of* something) –1777. **3.** A large gathering of people; a throng. late ME. **4.** With *the*: 'The many', the populace, the common people 1535.

1. Euen as the sand that is vpon the Sea-shore in m. *Josh.* 11:4. **2.** A m. of actions done by a m. of men HOBBES. **b.** Multitudes of words bring much error 1683. **c.** All this..m of misery CHATHAM. **3.** A Multitude's a Bulky Coward 1682. **4.** The many-headed M. SHAKS.

Multitudinous (mɒltitiū·dinǝs), *a.* 1605. [f. L. *multitudo* (see prec.) + -OUS.] **1. a.** with pl. sb.: Existing in multitudes; very numerous 1629. **b.** with collect. sb.: Consisting of a multitude 1606. **c.** with sing. sb.: Existing in a multitude of forms; having many elements or features; arising from or involving a multitude 1656. **d.** Said of the ocean or any mass of water with reference to its great bulk or to its innumerable ripples 1605. **e.** Crowded (*with*). *poet.* 1820. **2.** Of or pertaining to the multitude. *Cor.* III. i. 156.

1. a. The m. Pagans and Idolaters 1650. **b.** A more m. brood of sectaries HALLAM. **c.** The m. moan and wail of the lost spirits KINGSLEY. **d.** This my Hand will rather The m. Seas incarnardine SHAKS. **e.** To live In a home m. with herds BROWNING. So **Multitu·dinary** *a.* (*rare*) 1846. **Multitu·dinism,** the principle which places the interests of multitudes before those of individuals, esp. in religion 1860. Hence **Multitu·dinous-ly** *adv.*, **-ness.**

Multivalent (mɒlti·vălĕnt), *a.* 1872. [See MULTI- 1.] *Chem.* Having many degrees of valency. Hence **Multi·valence, -ency.**

Multivalve (mɒ·ltivælv), *a.* and *sb.* 1753. [– mod.L. *multivalvis* (cf. Linnæus's division *Multivalvia*); see MULTI-, VALVE.] *Zool.* and *Bot.* Having many valves; *sb.* a m. shell or animal having such a shell. Hence **Mu·ltivalved, Multiva·lvular** *adjs.*

Multivarious (mɒltivēᵊ·riǝs), *a.* Now *rare.* 1620. [f. MULTI- + L. *varius* (see VARIOUS *a.*), as tr. Gr. πολυποίκιλος much-variegated.] Manifold and diverse.

Multivious (mɒlti·viǝs), *a.* 1656. [– L. *multivius* (f. *multus* MULTI- + *via* way) + -OUS.] Having many ways; going in many directions.

Multivocal (mɒlti·vŏkăl), *a.* and *sb.* 1810. [f. MULTI-, after *univocal, equivocal.*] Susceptible of many meanings; *sb.* a m. word.

An ambiguous or m. word COLERIDGE.

Multocular (mɒltǫ·kiŭlăɹ), *a.* 1713. [f. MULTI- after MONOCULAR.] Having many eyes.

‖**Multum** (mɒ·ltɒm). 1820. [perh. a use of L. *multum* much.] *Brewing.* An extract of quassia and liquorice, used by brewers as an adulterant. *Hard m.*, a preparation of *Cocculus indicus*, similarly used.

‖**Multum in parvo** (mɒ·ltŏm in pā·ɹvo). 1732. [L., = 'much in little'.] A great deal in a small compass. Also *attrib.*, as 'm.-in-p. pocket-knife'.

Multungulate (mɒltɒ·ŋgiŭlĕt), *a.* and *sb.* 1839. [– mod.L. *multungulatus*, f. L. *multus* MULTI- + *ungula* hoof; see -ATE[2].] Having more than two hoofs; *sb.* a m. animal.

Multure (mɒ·ltiŭɹ, -tʃǝr). ME. [– OFr. *molture, moulture* (mod. *mouture*) :– med. L. *molitura*, f. *molit-*, pa. ppl. stem of *molere* grind; see MILL *sb.*[1], -URE.] A toll in kind paid to the miller for grinding corn; the right to exact this. Hence **Mu·lturer,** one who pays toll for the grinding of his corn at a mill.

Mum (mɒm), *sb.*[1], *int.*, and *a.* late ME. [imit.; goes with MUM *v.*] **A.** *sb.* †**1.** An inarticulate sound made with closed lips. Also, in neg. or hypothetical context = '(not) the slightest word'. –1651. **2.** Refusal to speak, silence (*colloq.*) 1562. †**3.** A silent person –1808. **B.** *int.* = 'Hush!' 'silence!' 'not a word!' Also in *m.'s the word.* late ME. **C.** *adj.* Strictly silent or secret. Sometimes quasi-*adv.*, as *to stand m.*, etc. (*colloq.*). 1521.

B. No more woords, but m. & stand a while aside 1568.

Mum (mɒm), *sb.*[2] Now chiefly *Hist.* 1640. [– G. *mumme.*] A kind of beer originally brewed in Brunswick.

I thinke you'r drunk With Lubecks beere or Brunswicks M. 1640.

Mum (mɒm), *sb.*[3] 1823. [Shortened f. MUMMY *sb.*[2]] A pet name for 'mother'.

Mum (mɒm), *v.* late ME. [Goes with MUM *sb.*[1]; cf. MLG. *mummen*, Du. *mommen.*] †**1.** *trans.* To silence; to put to silence –1654. †**2.** *intr.* To make an inarticulate sound with closed lips; hence, to keep silence –1637. †**3.** To whisper –1680. **4.** To act in dumb show; to play as a mummer 1530.

4. When a whole People goes mumming and miming CARLYLE.

Mum, vulgar var. of MA'AM.

Mumble (mɒ·mb'l), *v.* [ME. *momele*, frequent. formation on MUM *v.*; see -LE. Cf. LG. *mummelen*, Du. *mommelen, mummelen.*] **1.** *intr.* To speak indistinctly or with the lips partly closed; to mutter. **2.** *trans.* To utter in low or indistinct tones 1440. **3.** *intr.* and *trans.* To chew or bite softly, as with toothless gums (now *rare*) ME. †**4.** To maul, maltreat. Also, to bungle. –1753.

1. So tottered, muttered, mumbled he, till he died BROWNING. **2.** By one meanes or other, he learned to m. a Masse 1626. **3.** Sitting..alone, mumblyng on a crust 1561. And Gums unarm'd to m. Meat in vain DRYDEN. **4.** Mr. Fox mumbled the Chancellor and his lawyers H. WALPOLE.

Comb.: †**M.-matins,** a Romish priest: †**m.-news,** a tale-bearer. Hence **Mu·mble** *sb.* an act of mumbling. **Mu·mbler. Mu·mblingly** *adv.*

Mumbo Jumbo (mɒ:mboˌdʒɒ·mbo). 1738. [Of unkn. origin.] **1.** A grotesque idol said to have been worshipped by certain tribes of Negroes. **2.** *transf.* An object of senseless veneration 1847.

†**Mu:mbu·dget.** 1564. [perh. orig. the name of some children's game in which silence was required. Cf. next.] = MUM *int.*, *a.*, and *sb.*[1] –1663.

(Quoth she) Mum budget BUTLER *Hud.* I. iii. 208.

Mumchance (mɒ·mtʃans), *sb.* and *a.* 1528. [– MLG. *mummenschanze, -scanze, -kanze* game of dice, masked serenade (= MDu. *mommecanse*), f. *mummen* (see MUMMER) + *schanz* – (O)Fr. *chance* CHANCE.] **A.** *sb.* †**1.** A dicing game resembling hazard –1656. †**2.** Masquerade; mumming –1591. **3.** In similative phrases: One who acts in dumb show. Hence, one who has nothing to say; a dummy. 1694. **B.** *adj.* Silent; tongue-tied (*arch.* and *dial.*) 1681.

A. Phr. †*To play m.*: *fig.* or *allusively*, to preserve a dogged silence. **B.** Poor Twenty Ninth of February that had sate all this while m. at the side-board LAMB.

Mummer (mɒ·məɹ). 1440. [– OFr. *momeur*, f. *momer* act in dumb show, rel. to *momon* mask, Sp. *momo* grimace; perh. of Gmc. origin (cf. MDu. *momme*, Du. *mom* mask, MLG. *mummen* mask, disguise; also MUM *v.*); see -ER² 3.] †1. One who mutters or murmurs –1548. 2. †An actor in a dumb show; one who takes part in a mumming 1502. b. *slang*, etc. A 'play-actor' 1840.

2. Grave mummers! sleeveless some, and shirtless others POPE.

Mummery (mɒ·məɹi). 1530. [– (O)Fr. *momerie*; see prec., -ERY.] 1. A performance of mummers. 2. *transf.* 'Play-acting'. Often applied contempt. to religious ritual. 1549.

1. Your Fathers..Disdain'd the M. of Foreign Strollers 1719. 2. Those rags of Popish mummeries 1864.

Mummify (mɒ·mifəi), *v.* 1628. [f. MUMMY *sb.*¹ + -FY, after Fr. *momifier*.] 1. *trans.* To make into a mummy; to preserve by embalming and drying. Also, to dry into the semblance of a mummy. Also *transf.* and *fig.* 2. *Path.* (chiefly in pa. pple.) To shrivel or dry up (tissues, etc.) 1857. **Mummifica·tion** 1800.

Mumming (mɒ·miŋ), *vbl. sb.* 1465. [f. MUM *v.* + -ING¹.] The action of disguising oneself; *spec.* the action of taking part in the representation of a mummers' play. Chiefly in phr. *to go a mumming*. Also, a performance of mummers. b. *transf.* and *fig.* Often with contempt. ref. to religious ceremonial 1528.

Mummy (mɒ·mi), *sb.*¹ late ME. [– OFr. *mumie*, (also mod.) *momie* – med.L. *mumia* – Arab. *mūmiyā* embalmed body, f. *mūm* wax.] 1. A medicinal preparation of the substance of mummies (see 3); hence, an unctuous liquid or gum used medicinally. *Obs.* exc. *Hist.* (formerly also in med.L. form). †b. *joc.* Dead flesh –1622. c. A pulpy substance or mass. Chiefly in *to beat*, etc. *to a m.* (earlier, *to m.*). 1601. 2. In transf., etc., uses. †a. A sovereign remedy –1671. b. A medicinal bituminous drug obtained from the East 1601. †c. *Gardening.* A kind of wax used in grafting, etc. –1789. d. A rich brown bituminous pigment 1854. 3. A dead body embalmed (according to the ancient Egyptian or other method) as a preparation for burial 1615. b. A human or animal body desiccated by exposure to sun or air. Also applied to a frozen carcase found in prehistoric ice. 1727. c. *Stock Exchange slang*: *pl.* Egyptian securities 1903.

1. *fig.* This universal medicine made of church m. is to cure all the evils of the state BURKE. b. *Merry W.* III. v. 18. 3. *fig.* The old theological dogmas had become mere mummies 1876.

Comb.: **m.-case**, the case of wood, etc. (usu. decorated with hieroglyphics) in which Egyptian mummies were enclosed; **-pits** *pl.*, the catacombs in which the Egyptian mummies were interred; **-wheat**, a variety of wheat cultivated in Egypt, and said to have been grown from grains found in mummy-cases. **Mu·mmiform** *a.* 1856. **Mu·mmy** *v.* to mummify 1620.

Mummy (mɒ·mi), *sb.*² 1839. [Childish var. of MAMMY.] A child's word for mother.

Mu·mmy-cloth. 1843. 1. The cloth in which Egyptian mummies were wrapped. 2. *U.S.* A trade name for certain modern fabrics more or less resembling the material of mummy-cloths. Also *momie-cloth*. 1886.

Mump, *sb.* 1592. [Symbolic of the movements of the lips in making a 'mouth'.] †1. A grimace –1635. 2. *pl.* See MUMPS *sb. pl.*

Mump (mɒmp), *v.*¹ 1586. [Goes with prec. Cf. Icel. *mumpa* take into the mouth, *mumpaskælur* grimace, Du. *mompen*, *mompelen* mumble in utterance, G. *mumpfeln*, *-en* mumble in eating.] †1. *trans.* To utter imperfectly; to mumble, mutter. Also with *out*. –1773. 2. *intr.* †a. To grimace with the lips; to grin. Also *transf.* and *fig.* –1754. b. To assume a demure or miserable aspect of countenance; to be silent or sullen; to sulk, mope (*arch.*) 1610. 3. a. *intr.* To mumble with the gums; to move the jaws as if munching food; to munch, nibble. *Obs.* exc. *dial.* 1596. †b. *trans.* To chew with toothless gums –1838.

1. Old men,..Who m. their passion GOLDSM. 2. b. It is better to enjoy a novel than to m. STEVENSON. 3. When he mumped or spoke, they [*sc.* his nose and chin] approached one another like a pair of nut-crackers SMOLLETT.

Mump (mɒmp), *v.*² *colloq.* (orig. *slang*). 1651. [prob. – Du. *mompen* cheat.] †1. *trans.* To overreach, cheat. Const. *of*, *out of*. –1734. 2. a. *intr.* To beg; †to sponge on others. b. *trans.* To obtain by begging or sponging. c. To visit (a house) in the course of a begging round. 1673.

2. One prince came mumping to them annually with a lamentable story about his distresses MACAULAY. Hence **Mu·mper**, a beggar.

Mumpish (mɒ·mpiʃ), *a.* 1721. [f. MUMP *sb.* or *v.*¹ + -ISH¹.] Sullenly angry; depressed.

†**Mumps**, *sb.* 1598. [perh. short for MUMPSIMUS 1 b., or connected with MUMP *v.*] A term of contempt or mock endearment for a woman –1695.

Mumps (mɒmps), *sb. pl.* 1598. [Plural of MUMP *sb.*] 1. (const. as *sing.*). An acute specific contagious disease characterized by inflammation and swelling of the parotid and salivary glands. 2. A fit of melancholy or ill temper; sulks 1599.

Mumpsimus (mɒ·mpsimɒ̆s). 1530. [In allusion to the story (in Richard Pace *De Fructu*, 1517) of an illiterate English priest who, when corrected for reading 'quod in ore *mumpsimus*' in the Mass, replied, 'I will not change my old mumpsimus for your new sumpsimus.'] †1. One who obstinately adheres to old ways; an ignorant and bigoted opponent of reform –1553. ¶b. As a vague term of contempt: An old fogey –1815. 2. A traditional custom, etc., obstinately adhered to however unreasonable it may be 1545. 3. *attrib.*, quasi-*adj.* Stupidly conservative 1680.

3. The m., and 'well as we are' people SYD. SMITH.

Mun, *v. north.* and *midl.* ME. [– ON. *muna*, f. the base of MIND *sb.*; the var. *man* of the pres. sing. gave dial. MAUN.] Const. inf. without *to*: Must; †formerly occas. = shall.

Munch (mɒnʃ), *v.* late ME. [imit.; cf. *crunch*, *scrunch*.] 1. *trans.* To eat with noticeable action of the jaws, as cattle chewing fodder, etc. Also with *up*. 2. *intr.* and *absol.* Also with *away*. 1530. b. To work the jaws up and down, as old toothless people do in talking. DICKENS.

1. I could m. your good dry Oates SHAKS. 2. *Macb.* I. iii. 5. Hence **Munch** *sb.* an act of munching.

Munchausen (mɒnˌtʃǭ·zən). The name of Baron Munchausen, the hero of a narrative of extravagant adventures, written in English by the German Rudolf Erich Raspe (1785); hence, an extravagantly mendacious story of adventure. Hence **Munchau·senism** 1850.

Mundane (mɒ·ndeⁱn), *a.* 1475. [– (O)Fr. *mondain* – late L. *mundanus*, f. *mundus* world; see -ANE.] 1. Belonging to this world (i.e. the earth); worldly; earthly. b. Belonging to the world as dist. from the church; secular (*rare*) 1848. 2. Pertaining to the universe; cosmic 1642. 3. *Astrol.* Pertaining to the horizon and not to the ecliptic or zodiac; chiefly in *m. aspect*, *parallel* 1687. 4. *Nat. Hist.* Found in all parts of the world. DARWIN.

1. Entangled with the birdlime of fleshly passions and m. vanity 1652. 2. *M. soul*, *spirit*: the *anima mundi* of the Platonists 1642. *M. era*, an era reckoned from the time of the creation of the world 1838. Hence **Mu·ndane-ly** *adv.*, **-ness. Mundanity** (-æ·n-), worldliness (now *rare*).

†**Munda·tion.** 1633. [– late (eccl.) L. *mundatio*, f. *mundat-*, pa. ppl. stem of L. *mundare* cleanse, purify, f. *mundus* clean; see -ION.] The action of cleansing; cleansed state –1755. So **Mu·ndatory** *a.*, cleansing (*rare*) 1706; *sb.* a means or implement of cleansing; a purificator 1674.

Mundic (mɒ·ndik). 1671. [prob. Celtic Cornish.] Cornish miners' name for pyrites.

Mundify (mɒ·ndifəi), *v.* Now *rare* or *Obs.* late ME. [– (O)Fr. *mondifier* or late L. *mundificare*, f. L. *mundus* clean; see -FY.] 1. *trans.* To cleanse, purify (*lit.* and *fig.*) 1504. 2. *trans.* In medical use: To free (the body, blood, etc.) from noxious matter; to cleanse, deterge. late ME. Hence **Mundifica·tion** 1543. †**Mundificative** *a.* and *sb.* late ME. –1727. †**Mu·ndifier** 1603–1727.

Mundil, var. of MANDIL, turban.

Mundu·ngus. 1637. [joc. use of Sp. *mondongo* tripe, etc.] †1. Offal, refuse (*rare*) –1834. 2. Bad-smelling tobacco 1641.

2. Clouds of vile m. vapour SCOTT.

‖**Munga** (mɒ·ŋgă). 1843. The bonnet monkey.

Mungcorn(e, var. ff. MONGCORN.

Mungo¹ (mɒ·ŋgo). 1738. [var. of *mungos* MONGOOSE.] †1. = MONGOOSE 1 –1845. 2. *M.-root* (also *mungo*): the plant *Ophiorrhiza mungos*, a supposed antidote against the poison of snakes 1738.

†**Mu·ngo**². 1769. [Name of a Negro in Bickerstaffe's *The Padlock* (1768).] A typical name for a black slave. Hence, a Negro. –1839.

Mungo³ (mɒ·ŋgo). Also **mongoe.** 1857. [perh. a use of Sc. Christian name *Mungo*, in Yorkshire often applied to dogs, with allusion to *mung*, *mong* mixture.] Cloth made from devilled woollen rags; like shoddy, but of a better quality.

Mungoos(e, Mungos, var. ff. MONGOOSE, MUNGO¹.

Mungrel(l, -il(l, obs. ff. MONGREL.

Municipal (miuni·sipăl), *a.* and *sb.* 1540. [– L. *municipalis*, f. *municipium* MUNICIPIUM, f. *municeps*, *-cip-*, f. *munia* civic offices + *capere* take; see -AL¹.] A. *adj.* 1. Pertaining to the internal affairs of a state as dist. from its foreign relations (now *rare*). b. *transf.* Belonging to one place only; having narrow limits 1631. 2. Pertaining to the local self-government or corporate government of a city or town 1600. 3. *Roman Hist.* Of or pertaining to a MUNICIPIUM; hence, contempt., provincial 1618.

1. M. or civil law: that is, the rule by which particular districts, communities, or nations are governed BLACKSTONE. Phr. *M. rights*, *jurisdiction*, etc. 2. M. charters 1864. A m. tramway 1898.

B. *sb.* 1. *Roman Hist.* An inhabitant of a municipium (tr. L. *municeps*) 1727. ‖2. [Fr.; short for *garde municipale*.] A member of the Municipal Guard, a body of soldiers under the control of the municipality of Paris 1837. Hence **Muni·cipalism**, m. or local patriotism; m. institutions generally; also, preference for the m. principle in local government. **Muni·cipalist**, an advocate of m. action or control; also, one skilled in m. administration. **Muni·cipally** *adv.* with regard to a municipality or to m. affairs.

Municipality (miuːnisipæ·lĭti). 1790. [– Fr. *municipalité*, f. *municipal*; see prec., -ITY.] 1. A town, city, or district possessed of privileges of local self-government, also applied to its inhabitants collectively. 2. The governing body of such a town or district 1795. 3. A MUNICIPIUM 1805. 4. Government on municipal principles. E. A. FREEMAN.

4. Here [in Italy] was m. on its grandest scale 187..

Municipalize (miuni·sipălǝiz), *v.* 1880. [f. MUNICIPAL *a.* + -IZE.] *trans.* To bring under municipal ownership or control; to endow with municipal institutions. Hence **Municipaliza·tion.**

‖**Municipium** (miŭnisi·piɒ̆m). *Pl.* **municipia.** 1720. [L., f. *municeps*, *-cip-*; see MUNICIPAL.] *Roman Antiq.* A city whose citizens had the privileges of Roman citizens. var. †**Muni·cipy** (*rare*) 1579.

†**Muni·fic**, *a.* 1754. [– L. *munificus*, f. *munus* gift; see -FIC.] = MUNIFICENT. So †**Munifi·cal** *a.* 1603.

Munificence (miuni·fisĕns). 1555. [– Fr. *munificence* or L. *munificentia*, f. *munificent-*; see next, -ENCE.] The quality of being munificent; splendid or princely generosity. So †**Muni·ficency** 1504–1651.

Munificent (miuni·fisĕnt), *a.* 1583. [– L. *munificent-*, used as stem of *munificus*; see MUNIFIC, -ENT.] Splendidly generous in giving; (of actions, gifts) characterized by splendid generosity.

Think it not enough to be Liberal, but M. SIR T. BROWNE. Hence **Muni·ficently** *adv.*

†**Munifience.** 1596. [Badly f. MUNIFY + -ENCE.] Fortification, defence. SPENSER.

†**Mu·nify**, *v.* 1603. [irreg. f. L. *munio* (*munire*) + -FY.] To fortify; to provide with defences –1635.

Muniment (miū·nimĕnt). late ME. [– (O)Fr. *muniment* – L. *munimentum* (in med.L.) title-deed, f. *munire* fortify, secure; see -MENT.] **1.** A document, e.g. a title-deed, etc., preserved as evidence of rights or privileges. Chiefly in *collect. pl.* **2.** Anything serving as a means of defence or protection. Now *rare.* 1546. †**b.** *pl.* Things with which a person or place is provided; furnishings –1852. **3.** *attrib.*, as *m.-room*, etc.; also **m. deed,** a title-deed 1656.

2. We cannot spare the coarsest m. of virtue EMERSON.

Muni·te, *v. Obs.* exc. *Hist. Pa. pple.* †**munyte,** †**munite.** late ME. [– *munit-*, pa. ppl. stem of L. *munire* fortify; see prec.] *trans.* To fortify, strengthen, protect.

Munition (miuni·ʃən), *sb.* 1533. [– (O)Fr. *munition* – L. *munitio*, f. *munit-*; see prec., -ION.] †**1. a.** The action of fortifying or defending, fortification (*lit.* and *fig.*). **b.** *concr.* Anything that serves as a defence or protection 1533. **2.** *sing.* and *pl.* = AMMUNITION *sb.* 1. Often *munition(s of war.* 1533.

1. With what m. he did fortifie His heart DANIEL. Hence **Muni·tion** *v.* to supply with munitions of war 1578; to furnish (a room) *rare* 1877; to work in a munition-factory 1916. **Muni·tioner,** one who has the custody of ammunition; (also **Munitionee·r**) a worker in a munition-factory.

Munity (miū·nĭti). Now *rare.* 1467. [– AFr., OFr. *munité* or med.L. *munitas* (in 'charta immunitatis'), equivalent of *immunitas*, after *munitio* muniment, deed, charter. Cf. IMMUNITY.] A granted right or privilege.

‖**Munjeet** (mɒndʒī·t). 1813. [Bengali *manjīṭh.*] The Bengal Madder, *Rubia cordifolia* (formerly *Munjista*); the roots of this plant used in dyeing.

Munjistin (mɒndʒi·stin). 1863. [f. mod.L. *Munjista* (see prec.) + -IN[1].] *Chem.* An orange colouring matter contained in munjeet.

Munnion (mɒ·nyən). 1593. [See MULLION.] *Arch.* = MULLION.

Munshi, Munsif: see MOONSHEE, MOONSIFF.

Muntin (mɒ·ntin). Also **-ing.** 1611 (**mountan**). [By-form of earlier *mountant* (XV), *montant* – Fr. *montant*, pr. pple. of *monter* MOUNT *v.*] *Building.* A central vertical piece between two panels, the side pieces being called *stiles*.

Muntjak (mɒ·ntdʒæk). 1798. [– Sunda *minchek.*] A small Asiatic deer of the genus *Cervulus*, esp. *C. muntjak* of Java.

Muntz (mɒnts). [Patented 1832; name of G. F. *Muntz*, of Birmingham, inventor.] *M. metal*: an alloy of copper and zinc used esp. for sheathing the bottoms of ships.

Muræna, murena (miurī·nă). 1555. [– L. *muræna, murena* sea-eel, lamprey – Gr. μύραινα, also σμύραινα, a fem. formation on μῦρος, σμῦρος sea-eel. Cf. MORAY.] In early use, a kind of eel mentioned by ancient writers. Now usually, a fish of the genus *Muræna*, the type of the family *Murænidæ* or Eels. Hence **Muræ·noid** *a.* belonging to the family *Murænidæ* of fishes; *sb.* a m. fish 1803.

Murage (miūᵊ·rėdʒ). Now *Hist.* late ME. [– OFr. *murage*, in med.L. *muragium*, f. Fr. *mur* MURE *sb.*; see -AGE.] A toll or tax levied for the building or repairing of the walls of a town. Also the right of levying such a toll.

Mu·ral, *sb.* 1471. [orig. *murail* (XV) – (O)Fr. *muraille* :– Rom. **muralia*, repr. L. *muralia* n. pl. of *muralis* (see next) taken as fem. sing.; see -AL[1].] **1.** A wall –1555. **2.** [f. next.] A mural decoration.

Mural (miūᵊ·răl), *a.* 1546. [– (O)Fr. *mural*, – L. *muralis*, f. *murus* wall; see -AL[1].] **1.** Of, pertaining to, or resembling a wall 1586. **2.** Placed, fixed, or executed on a wall 1561. †**b.** Of a fruit-tree: Growing against, and fastened to, a wall. Also of the fruit. –1731. **3.** *Phys.* and *Path.* Belonging to or connected with the wall of the body or of any of its cavities. Cf. PARIETAL. 1884.

1. And soon repaird Her m. breach MILT. Lofty unbroken m. precipices 1880. **M. crown** (*Roman Antiq.*): an embattled crown, conferred upon the soldier who first scaled the wall of a besieged town. So *m. coronet, garland, wreath*, etc. Hence, any embattled crown. **2.** The m. tablets to the memory of departed rectors 1837. *M. arch* (Astr.): a wall or arch to which is attached an instrument (*m. arc, circle, quadrant*, etc.) for observing meridian altitudes.

Murder (mɔ̄·ɹdəɹ), *sb.* Also (now *dial.* and *Hist.* or *arch.*) **murther.** [OE. *morþor* (ME. *morþre, murþre*) = Goth. *maurþr* :– Gmc. **murþram*, f. IE. **mrt-*, repr. also by Gmc. **mortam* (whence OE., OS., ON. *morð*, (O)HG. *mord*, Du. *moord*); reinforced in ME. by OFr. *murdre* (mod. *meurtre*) – Gmc., whence the establishment of the forms with *u* and *d.*] **1.** The most heinous kind of criminal homicide; an instance of this. In *Eng. Law*, defined as the unlawful killing of a human being with malice aforethought; often *wilful m.* **b.** Often applied to a death-sentence, killing of men in war, or any action causing destruction of human life, which is regarded as morally wicked, whether legal or not. *Judicial m.*: see JUDICIAL *a.* 1. 1551. †**2.** Without moral reprobation: Terrible destruction of life –1590. **3.** As a cry or exclam. of real or pretended alarm 1470.

1. There was..one called Barrabas, which in the vproure had committed murthur COVERDALE *Mark* 15:7. *M. in the first degree* (U.S.): i.e. where there are no extenuating circumstances; opp. to *m. in the second degree.* Provb. *M. will out*: i.e. cannot be hidden. *The m. is out*: said when something is suddenly revealed or explained. **b.** Condemn them for the Murther of Socrates STILLINGFL. **3.** *To cry blue m.* (slang): to make an extravagant outcry.

Murder (mɔ̄·ɹdəɹ), *v.* Also (now *dial.*) **murther.** ME. [A new formation on the sb., not continuous with OE. (*ā-, for-, of-*) *myrþrian.*] **1.** *trans.* To kill (a human being) unlawfully with malice aforethought; to kill wickedly, inhumanly, or barbarously. **b.** To slaughter in a terrible manner, to massacre ME. **c.** *absol.* To commit murder. Now *rare.* 1535. **2.** To spoil by bad execution, representation, pronunciation, etc. 1644. **3.** To consume (time) unprofitably 1712.

1. Hamilton murdered the old man in cold blood MACAULAY. *fig.* Macbeth does murther Sleepe, the innocent Sleepe SHAKS. **2.** The Sense too oft is murder'd by the Sound 1693. **3.** It kills time, or rather murders it, this company-keeping SCOTT.

Murderer (mɔ̄·ɹdərəɹ). ME. [Partly f. prec. + -ER[1]; partly – AFr. *mordreour, murdreour*, agent-n. f. *mordrer* = prec.] **1.** One who murders or is guilty of a murder. †**2.** A small cannon or mortar used to clear the decks when an enemy boards a ship; a *murdering piece* 1497–1704. Hence **Mu·rderess** 1588.

Murderous (mɔ̄·ɹdərəs), *a.* 1535. [f. MURDER *sb.* + -OUS.] **1.** Of persons: †Guilty of murder; capable of or bent on murder. Also *transf.* of weapons, physical agents, etc. **2.** Of the nature of, characteristic of, or involving murder 1593.

1. Stay murtherous villaines SHAKS. The Murd'rous King MILT. **2.** A murd'rous deede SHAKS. Where..the brown Indian marks with m. aim GOLDSM. Hence **Mu·rderous-ly** *adv.*, **-ness.**

†**Mure,** *sb.* 1471. [– (O)Fr. *mur* :– L. *murum*, acc. of *murus* wall.] A wall –1651.

Mure (miūᵊɹ), *v.* late ME. [– (O)Fr. *murer*, f. *mur* (see prec.).] *trans.* = IMMURE *v.* 1, 2; also, to block *up*, or build up (a door, gate, etc.) with bricks and mortar, stones, etc.

The fiue Kings are mured in a caue *Josh.* 10, *heading.*

†**Mu·renger.** Also **muringer.** 1506. [orig. *murager* (AL. *muragiarius* XIV), f. MURAGE + -ER[2]; cf. *messenger, passenger.*] An officer whose duty it was to keep the walls of a city in repair –1815.

Murex (miūᵊ·reks). *Pl.* **murices** (miūᵊ·risīz), also **murexes.** 1589. [– L. *murex*, perh. rel. to Gr. μύαξ sea-mussel.] A kind of shell-fish, which yields a purple dye. Hence **Mu·rexan** *Chem.* purpuric acid 1838. **Mu·rexide,** purpurate of ammonia 1838.

Muriate (miūᵊ·riĕt), *sb.* 1790. [– Fr. *muriate*, f. *muriatique* MURIATIC. See -ATE[4].] *Chem.* Old name, still current *Comm.*, for CHLORIDE.

Muriate (miūᵊ·rieit), *v. rare.* 1699. [f. L. *muria* brine + -ATE[3].] *trans.* To pickle in brine.

Muriated (miūᵊ·riĕtėd) *ppl. a.* 1789. [f. MURIATE *sb.* or *v.* + -ED.] †**a.** *Chem.* Combined with chlorine. *M. iron, lead*, etc. = chloride of iron, etc. **b.** Impregnated with a chloride or chlorides.

Muriatic (miūᵊriæ·tik), *a.* 1675. [– L. *muriaticus* pickled in brine, f. *muria* brine; see -ATIC.] †**1.** Pertaining to, of the nature of, consisting of, or containing brine 1830. **2.** *Chem.* Applied to substances obtained from the sea, as in *m. acid*, hydrochloric acid (now *Comm.*): †*m. salt*, a chloride; †*m. ether*, chloric ether.

Muricate (miūᵊ·rikĕt), *a.* 1661. [– L. *muricatus* shaped like the murex, f. *murex, muric-*; see MUREX, -ATE[2].] *Bot.* and *Zool.* Furnished with sharp points, studded with short hard excrescences. So **Mu·ricated** *a.* 1707.

Muricoid (miūᵊ·rikoid), *a.* 1890. [f. as prec. + -OID.] *Zool.* Resembling a murex or some part of a murex.

Mu·riform, *a.* 1832. [f. L. *murus* wall + -FORM.] *Bot.* Applied to cellular tissue suggesting resemblance to courses of bricks in a wall.

Murine (miūᵊ·rəin, -rin). 1607. [– L. *murinus*, f. *mus, mur-* mouse; see -INE[1].] **A.** *adj.* Resembling a mouse; of or belonging to the family *Muridæ* or the sub-family *Murinæ.* **B.** *sb.* A member of this family or sub-family 1879.

Murk, mirk (mɔ̄ɹk), *sb.*[1] [prob. of Scand. origin (ON. *myrkr* sb. and adj. = OS. *mirki* adj.) rather than OE. *mirce, myrce*, sb. and adj. though this may have preserved k of an original **kw*, as in *þicce* THICK.] **1.** Darkness (*lit.* and *fig.*). Now chiefly *Sc.* **2.** Thick or murky air or vapour ME.

1. Ere twice in murke and occidentall dampe Moist Hesperus hath quench'd her sleepy Lampe SHAKS.

Murk (mɔ̄ɹk), *sb.*[2] 1676. [perh. var. of MARC.] = MARC.

Murk, mirk (mɔ̄ɹk), *a.* Now *dial.* (*Sc.*) and *poet.* or *arch.* [prob. – ON. *myrkr* adj. = OS. *mirki*, OE. *myrce, mirce* adj.; see MURK *sb.*[1]] Deficient in light, dark; dark in colour.

M. Monday *Sc.*, the day of the great solar eclipse of 29 Mar. (= 8 April N.S.) 1652. *fig.* Mirk despair Made me think life was little worth RAMSAY. Hence **Mu·rkness, mi·rkness.**

Murk, mirk (mɔ̄ɹk), *v.* ME. [f. prec. Cf. ON. *myrkva* grow dark (possibly the source).] †**1.** *intr.* To grow dark –1633. **2.** *trans.* To darken, obscure (*lit.* and *fig.*) ME.

Murky (mɔ̄·ɹki), *a. rare* bef. 17th c. ME. [f. MURK *sb.*[1] + -Y[1].] **1.** Of places: Dark and gloomy. **2.** Of darkness, the atmosphere: Thick and heavy. **3.** Sullen, 'dark'.

1. Hell is m. SHAKS. **2.** So sented the grim Feature, and upturn'd His Nostril wide into the murkie Air MILT. Hence **Mu·rkily** *adv.* **Mu·rkiness.**

Murmur (mɔ̄·ɹmɔ̆ɹ), *sb.* late ME. [– (O)Fr. *murmure* or L. *murmur* rumbling noise, murmur; see next.] **1.** Subdued continuous sound; an instance of this. Now *rare* exc. in *the m. of* (a brook, the waves, etc.). **b.** *Path.* A sound of this kind heard in auscultation 1833. **2.** †**a.** Muttered or indistinct complaint, grumbling, or repining. **b.** An instance of this. late ME. †**3.** Rumour. *In m.*: 'whispered about'. –1772. **4.** A softly spoken word or sentence; subdued or nearly inarticulate speech 1674. **b.** *Phonetics.* Applied to the utterance of voiced sounds 1669.

1. All the live m. of a summer's day M. ARNOLD. **2.** Some discontents there are; some idle murmurs DRYDEN. **4.** What billing, exchanging stolen glances, and broken murmurs? GOLDSM. **b.** *m.-vowel*, the vowel (ə). Hence **Mu·rmurous** *a.* accompanied by m.; abounding in or characterized by murmurs; †complaining. **Mu·rmurous-ly** *adv.*, **-ness.**

Murmur (mɔ̄·ɹmɔ̆ɹ), *v.* late ME. [– (O)Fr. *murmurer* – L. *murmurare*, corresp. to Gr. μορμύρειν, Skr. *marmaras* noisy, and with variation OHG. *murmurōn, -ulōn* (G. *murmeln*), Du. *murmelen* burble.] **1.** *intr.* To produce or emit a low continuous sound. **2.** To complain in low muttered tones; to grumble. Often with *at, against.* 1474. **3.** *trans.* To utter (sounds, words) in a low voice and indistinctly 1535.

1. They murmureden as dooth a swarm of Been CHAUCER. **2.** The peple m. and ryse agayn theyr lord CAXTON. **3.** The Pharisees heard that the people murmured such things concerning him *John* 7:32. Hence †**Murmura·tion,** murmuring. late ME. –1687. **Mu·rmurer** 1526. **Mu·rmuringly** *adv.* 1611.

Murphy (mɔ̄·ɹfi). *slang.* 1811. [Use of a common Irish surname.] A potato.

Murphy('s) button. *Surg.* 1895. A device invented by J. B. Murphy, an American surgeon, for reuniting the parts of an intestine after complete severance.

†**Murr.** late ME. [prob. of symbolic origin.] A severe form of catarrh –1756.

‖**Murra** (mɒ·ră). Also **murrha, myrrha.** 1598. [L. *murra* = late Gr. μόρρια.] *Rom. Antiq.* A substance of which precious vases and other vessels are made.

Murrain (mɒ·rėn), *sb.* and *a.* ME. [– AFr. *moryn*, (O)Fr. *morine*, †*moraine*, f. stem of *mourir*, †*morir* :– Rom. **morire*, for L. *mori* die.] **A.** *sb.* †**1.** Plague, pestilence –1613. **2.** An infectious disease in cattle. late ME. †**3.** Flesh of animals that have died of disease; also, dead flesh, carrion –1610. †**4.** Mortality (usu., by pestilence); *occas.* slaughter –1632. **5.** *attrib.*, as *m. cattle*, etc. 1490. †**B.** *adj.* Ill-conditioned, 'plaguy'. Also quasi-*adv.* 'confoundedly'. –1728.

A. 1. Phr. †*A m. of (it), m. meet them, m. on (one)*, may a m. or pestilence fall on (some one). *With a m., what a (the) m.*, etc.: exclamations of anger. **2.** *transf.* The m. among bees is very rare 1657.

Murre (mɒ̄ɹ). 1602. [Of unkn. origin.] **a.** Any of several guillemots; **b.** the razor-billed auk. So **Murrelet** (mɒ̄·ɹlėt), a small species of auk.

Murrey (mɒ·ri), *sb.* and *a.* Now *Hist.* or *arch.* late ME. [– OFr. *moré* adj. and sb., *morée* sb. – med.L. *moratus, morata*, f. L. *morum* mulberry; see -Y[5].] (Of) the colour of the mulberry; purple-red; also, cloth of this colour.

M. and blue were the colours of the house of York 1834.

Murrhine (mɒ·rin, -əin), *a.* and *sb.* Also **my-.** 1579. [– L. *murr(h)inus*, f. *murra*; see MURRA, -INE[1].] Made of or pertaining to murra. *M. glass*: a mod. fancy name for a delicate ware brought from the East, and made of fluor-spar. *sb.* A m. vase.

Murrion, Murry, Murther, Murza: see MORION[1], MURRAIN, MORAY, MURDER, MIRZA.

Mus, obs. f. MOUSE.

‖**Musa** (miū·ză). *Pl.* **-æ, -as.** Also 16–17th c. **muse.** 1578 (**musa, mose**). [mod.L., f. Arab. *mawza.*] In early use, the plantain or banana tree. Now only *Bot.*, a plant of the genus including the plantain tree (*M. paradisiaca*), the banana.

Hence **Musa·ceous** *a.* pertaining to the N.O. *Musaceæ* (typical genus *Musa*) 1852.

Musang (miusæ·ŋ). 1783. [– Malay *musang* wild cat.] An E. Indian palm-civet (*Paradoxurus hermaphroditus*).

Mus.B., Mus.Bac. Abbrev. of mod.L. *Musicæ Baccalaureus* 'bachelor of music'.

Muscadel, var. of MUSCATEL.

‖**Muscadin** (müskadæ̃n). 1794. [Fr.; *muscadin* musk-comfit used transf.] A Parisian term for: A dandy, exquisite. Hence applied in contempt to the members of a moderate party in the French Revolution (about 1794–6), composed chiefly of young men of the upper middle class.

Muscadin (mɒ·skădəin, -in). 1517. [perh. Eng. formation on Pr. *muscat*, fem. *muscade* (see MUSCATEL) + -INE[4].] **1.** In full *m.-wine.* = MUSCATEL 1. *Obs.* exc. *Hist.* **2.** In full *m. grape.* The name of varieties of grape having the flavour or odour of musk; also, a vine bearing a variety of this grape 1611.

‖**Muscæ** (mɒ·si). 1753. [L., nom. pl. of *musca* fly.] Specks which appear to float before the eyes; in full *muscæ volitantes* (vǫlitæ·ntīz).

Muscal(l)onge, var. ff. MASKINONGE.

Muscardine (mɒskā·ɹdin). 1846. [– Fr. *muscardine.*] A disease of silkworms, caused by a vegetable parasite or fungus. Hence **Mu·scardined** *a.*

‖**Muscari** (mɒskēᵊ·ri, -rəi). 1597. [mod.L.] A genus of plants of the hyacinth tribe of *Liliaceæ*; a plant of this genus, esp. *M. botryoides*, the grape hyacinth.

Muscat (mɒ·skæt). 1578. [– (O)Fr. *muscat* – Pr. *muscat*, f. *musc* MUSK; see -ATE[1].] **1.** In full *m. wine.* = MUSCATEL 1. **2.** In full *m. grape.* = MUSCADINE 2. 1655. †**3.** A kind of peach; also, a kind of pear –1741. **4.** A fungus, *Agaricus albellus* 1887.

Comb. **m. rose** [Fr. *rose muscate*], the musk-rose.

Muscatel, muscadel (mɒskăte·l, -de·l). late ME. [– OFr. *muscadel, muscatel* (cf. It. *-dello, -tello*, Sp., Pg. *-tel*) – Pr. **muscadel*, dim. of *muscat*; see prec.] **1.** A strong sweet wine made from the muscat or similar grape. **2.** = MUSCADINE 2. 1517. **3.** *pl.* In full *m. raisins.* Raisins prepared from the muscatel grape, Malaga raisins 1652.

‖**Muschelkalk** (mu·ʃəlkalk). 1833. [G., f. *muschel* mussel + *kalk* lime.] *Geol.* A limestone bed belonging to the red sandstone formation of Germany.

Muscid (mɒ·sid), *a.* (*sb.*) 1895. [f. mod.L. *Muscidæ*, f. *musca* fly; see -ID[3].] *Entom.* Of or pertaining to the dipterous family *Muscidæ*, or flesh-flies; *sb.* one of these.

Muscle (mɒ·s'l). 1533. [– (O)Fr. *muscle* – L. *musculus*, dim. of *mus* mouse, from the fancied similarity of the form of some muscles.] **1.** *Anat.* and *Phys.* Any one of the contractile fibrous bands or bundles, having the function of producing movement in the animal body. **2.** *collect.* The muscles collectively; muscular substance or tissue 1781. **b.** Used in ref. to the exercise of the muscles, esp. as opposed to the mind 1850.

1. *Not to move a m.*: to be perfectly motionless. *Comb.*: **m. sensation, m. sense** = *muscular sensation, sense* (see MUSCULAR *a.* 1). Hence **Mu·scle** *v.*, *to m. in(to* (U.S.): to force one's way in(to. **Mu·scled** *a.* (chiefly with adj. or adv. prefixed). **Muscly** (mɒ·s'li), *a.* composed of muscle, exhibiting great muscular development (*rare*) 1594.

†**Muscle:** see MUSSEL.

†**Mu·scling.** 1709. [f. MUSCLE + -ING[1].] The delineation or representation of the muscles in Painting or Sculpture –1720.

Muscology (mɒskǫ·lŏdʒi). 1818. [– mod.L. *muscologia*, f. L. *muscus* moss; see -LOGY.] = BRYOLOGY. So **Musco·logist.**

Muscose (mɒ·skōᵘs), *a.* 1707. [– L. *muscosus*, f. *muscus* moss; see -OSE[1].] Moss-like.

Muscovado (mɒskŏvā·do). 1619. [– Sp. (*azúcar*) *mascabado.* Cf. Fr. *moscouade*, †*mascovade.*] In full *m. sugar*: Raw or unrefined sugar obtained from the juice of the sugar-cane by evaporation and draining of the molasses.

Muscovite (mɒ·skŏvəit), *sb.*[1] and *a.* Now *Hist.* or *arch.* 1537. [– mod.L. *Muscovita*, f. *Muscovia* MUSCOVY; see -ITE[1] 1.] **A.** *sb.* A native or inhabitant of Muscovy; a Russian. **B.** *adj.* Of or pertaining to Muscovy or its inhabitants, Russian 1601. Also †**Musco·-vian** 1555–1691.

Muscovite (mɒ·skŏvəit), *sb.*[2] 1862. [f. the name *Muscovy* (*glass*); see -ITE[1] 2 b.] *Min.* Common mica.

Muscovy (mɒ·skŏvi). 1573. [– Fr. †*Muscovie*, now *Moscovie*, – mod.L. *Moscovia*, f. Russ. *Moskvá* Moscow.] The name of the principality of Moscow, applied to Russia generally. **I.** Used attrib. or quasi-*adj.* in the name of things belonging to, produced in, or obtained from Muscovy, as **M. hide, leather,** Russia leather; †**M. glass,** common mica; also, occas., = TALC. **II.** Uses due to misinterpretation or perversion of designations connected with MUSK *sb.* **1.** A species of Crane's-bill or Geranium, *Erodium moschatum* 1688. **2.** = MUSK-RAT 1. 1693. **3. Muscovy duck.** = MUSK-DUCK 1. 1657.

Muscular (mɒ·skiŭlăɹ), *a.* 1681. [f. MUSCULOUS by substitution of suffix -AR[1].] **1.** Of or belonging to muscle or the muscles 1685. **2.** Composed of or of the nature of muscle 1681. **3.** Characterized by muscle, having well-developed muscles 1736.

1. *M. feeling, sensation*: feeling or sensation which accompanies the action of the muscles. *M. sense*: the faculty of m. sensation, popularly regarded as a particular application of the sense of 'touch'. M. sound, or the resonance attending sudden m. contraction [of the heart] 1837. M. rheumatism 1896. **3.** The spreading Shoulders, m., and broad THOMSON. Phr. *M. Christianity*: applied since about 1857 to a variety of Christian opinion and practice (associated with the writings of Charles Kingsley) which lays stress upon the importance of a healthy condition of body as conducive to morality and true religion. So **Muscula·rity,** the quality or state of being m. 1681. **Mu·scularize** *v.* to make m. **Mu·scularly** *adv.*

Musculation (mɒskiulēⁱ·ʃən). 1857. [– Fr. *musculation*, f. L. *musculus*; see MUSCLE, -ATION.] **a.** The function of muscular movement. **b.** The disposition or arrangement of muscles.

Musculature (mɒ·skiŭlătiŭɹ). 1875. [– Fr. *musculature*, f. as prec.] The muscular system of the whole body or of one of its organs.

Muscule, obs. f. MUSCLE, MUSSEL.

Musculo- (mɒ·skiŭlo), comb. f. L. *musculus* MUSCLE, usu. in sense 'pertaining to muscle and . . .', as *m.-arterial, -cutaneous, -ligamentous, -tendinous* adjs.

†**Mu·sculous,** *a.* 1541. [– (O)Fr. *musculeux* or L. *musculosus*, f. *musculus*; see MUSCLE, -OUS.] = MUSCULAR –1775.

Mus.D., Mus.Doc. 1786. Abbrev. of mod.L. *Musicæ Doctor*, doctor of music.

Muse (miūz), *sb.*[1] late ME. [– (O)Fr. *muse* or L. *musa* – Gr. μοῦσα.] **1.** *Myth.* (Now usu. w. capital.) One of nine sister-goddesses, the offspring of Zeus and Mnemosyne (Memory), regarded as the inspirers of learning and the arts, esp. of poetry and music, and represented as young and beautiful virgins. **b.** In classical poetry *the muse* is often invoked as if there were only one 1629. **2.** (With or without capital.) **a.** Chiefly with possessive: The inspiring goddess of a particular poet. Hence, his particular genius, style, or spirit. late ME. **b.** *The M.*: poetry personified, as an object of devotion. So *the Muses*: the liberal arts, polite literature. 1755. **c.** *transf.* One under the guidance of a Muse, a poet 1604.

1. In modern use Clio is the Muse of history, Thalia of Comedy, Melpomene of tragedy, Euterpe of music, Terpsichore of dancing, and Urania of astronomy. The other names, Erato, Polyhymnia, and Calliope, are not so frequently mentioned in modern literature. So songe the myghty M., she That cleped ys caliope CHAUCER. **2. a.** As though my muze were mute and durst not sing GASCOIGNE. Foole saide My m. to mee, looke in thy heart and write SIDNEY. **b.** And strictly meditate the thankles M. MILT. The votaries of the northern muses JOHNSON. **c.** That attenuated but majestic m. Mrs. Montagu 1905.

Muse (miūz), *sb.*[2] *arch.* 1475. [f. MUSE *v.*] †**a.** The action of musing; profound abstraction. **b.** A fit of abstraction; now only in *sing.* †**c.** *To be at a m.*: to 'wonder' (*whether*, etc.).

a. He..was fill'd With admiration, and deep M. to heare Of things so high and strange MILT.

†**Muse,** *sb.*[3] See MUSA.

Muse (miūz), *v.* ME. Now *literary.* [– (O)Fr. *muser* †meditate, waste time, trifle :– Rom. **musare*, presumably rel. to med.L. *musum* (see MUZZLE *sb.*), but the sense-development is not obvious.] **1.** *intr.* To be absorbed in thought; to ponder; also *trans.* (now *rare*) to ponder over, reflect upon, contemplate. **2.** *intr.* With dependent question: To be at a loss to discover, wonder *what, how*, etc. Now *rare.* late ME. **3.** To be astonished, wonder, marvel (now *rare, poet.*) ME.; †also *trans.* to marvel at 1567–1610. **4.** *intr.* To gaze meditatively *on, upon.* ME. †**5.** To mutter (discontentedly); to grumble, complain. late ME. –1598; also *trans.* late ME. only. **b.** *trans.* To say or murmur meditatively 1834.

1. Whyle I was thus musynge, the fyre kyndled COVERDALE *Ps.* 38: 3. **2.** Whyle men mused what the matter ment MORE. **3.** Do not m. at me my most worthy Friends SHAKS. I m. my Lord of Gloster is not come SHAKS. I cannot too much m. Such shapes SHAKS. **4.** The mind..Is left to m. upon the solemn scene WORDSW. **5.** *Merry W.* v. v. 253. Hence **Mu·ser. Mu·singly** *adv.*

Muse: see MEUSE.

Museful (miū·zfŭl), *a.* 1618. [f. MUSE *sb.*[2] + -FUL.] Absorbed in thought; pensive.

Full of m. Mopings DRYDEN. Hence **Mu·sefully** *adv.* 1885.

Mu·seless, *a. pedantic.* 1644. [f. MUSE *sb.*[1] + -LESS, after Gr. ἄμουσος.] Without learning; uncultured.

The m. cry of the multitude RUSKIN.

Musellim (muse·lim). 1687. [– Turk. *mütesellim*, commonly pronounced *musellim*, tax officer, f. Arab. *mutasallim*, lit. payer.] A Turkish officer, the lieutenant of a pasha.

Muset (miū·zėt). *Obs.* exc. *dial.* (**mussit**). 1592. [– OFr. *mucette, mussette* hiding-place, dim. of *muce, musse*; see MEUSE, MICHE.] = MEUSE *sb.* 1.

Musette (miuze·t). late ME. [– (O)Fr. *musette*, dim. of OFr. *muse* bagpipe; see -ETTE.] **1.** A kind of bagpipe. **2.** A soft pastoral air imitating the sound of the bagpipe; a dance for this music 1726. **3.** A reed stop on an organ 1825. **4.** A small kind of oboe 1880.

Museum (miuzī·ǝ̆m). Also †**musæum.** 1615. [– L. *museum* library, study – Gr. μουσεῖον seat of the Muses, subst. use of n. of μουσεῖος, f. μοῦσα MUSE *sb.*[1]] **1. a.** *Hist.* (with capital M.) The university building erected at Alexandria by Ptolemy Soter. †**b.** *gen.* A building or apartment dedicated to the pursuit of learning or the arts; a study; a library –1760. **2.** A building used for storing and exhibiting objects illustrative of antiquities, natural history, art, etc. 1683.

2. The *Museum* or *Ashmole's Museum*, a neat Building in the City of Oxford 1706. *fig.* Miss Blanche..had quite a little m. of locks of hair in her treasure-chest THACKERAY. *attrib.* **m.-piece,** a piece worthy of exhibition in a m.; a very fine example; also, in derogatory sense, an antiquated or outdated specimen.

Mush (mɒʃ), *sb.*[1] 1671. [app. a var. of MASH *sb.*[1]] **1.** *N. Amer.* A kind of porridge made with meal (chiefly of maize) boiled in water or milk. **2.** Anything soft and pulpy 1824.

2. *fig.* Stewed into m., hearing a popular preacher 1856.

Mush (mɒʃ), *sb.*[2] *slang.* 1821. [Shortened f. MUSHROOM *sb.*] **1.** An umbrella. **2.** A small cab-proprietor 1887.

Mush (mɒʃ), *v. Sc.* 1578. [perh. – OFr. *moucher* cut, trim.] *trans.* 'To cut out with a stamp, to nick or notch' (Jam.).

Musha (mɒ·ʃă), *int.* 1831. [– Ir. *muise*, var. of. *máiseadh*, i.e. *má* if, *is* is, *eadh* it.] An exclam. of strong feeling used by Irish speakers.

Mushroom (mɒ·ʃrum), *sb.* [Late ME. *musseroun, musheron*, by assim. *musherom* (XVI) – (O)Fr. *mousseron* – late L. *mussirio, -ion-* (Anthimus).] **1.** In early use, a fungus of any of the larger 'umbrella-shaped' species. Now, the common edible fungus, *Psalliota* (*Agaricus*) *campestris*, and closely resembling species. Some apply *mushroom* to the edible fungi, and *toadstool* to the poisonous. The mushroom is a proverbial type of rapid growth. **2.** *fig.* **a.** A person or family that has suddenly sprung into notice; an upstart. Also applied to a city, institution, etc. 1593. †**b.** A contemptible person –1769. **3. a.** *slang* (disused). An umbrella 1856. **b.** *colloq.* A low-crowned circular hat, *esp.* a lady's straw hat with down-curving brim 1865. **4.** = *mushroom-colour* 1884. **5.** *attrib.* or quasi-*adj.*, esp. with sense 'upstart', 'ephemeral' 1599.

2. a. Sheffield is an old oak; Birmingham is a m. BENTHAM. **5.** A Mushrome Love sprung from a transitory View SAVAGE.

Comb.: **m. anchor,** a mooring anchor having a saucer-shaped head upon a central shaft; **m.-colour,** a pale pinkish colour resembling that of a m.; **m.-†coral, -stone** = FUNGITE; **-ring** = FAIRY-RING; **m. spawn,** the vegetative mycelium of mushrooms, usu. embedded in an earthy matrix.

Mushroom (mɒ·ʃrum), *v.* 1893. [f. prec.] *intr.* Of rifle-bullets: To expand and flatten (*out*). **b.** *U.S.* Of fire: To spread outwards 1903. **c.** *trans.* To cause (a bullet) to 'mushroom'.

Mu·shrooming, *gerund* and *pr. pple.* 1894. [f. prec. + -ING[1].] Gathering mushrooms.

Mushy (mɒ·ʃi), *a. colloq.* 1876. [f. MUSH *sb.*[1] + -Y[1].] Soft, pulpy; also *fig.* Hence **Mu·shiness.**

Music (miū·zik). ME. [– (O)Fr. *musique* – L. *musica* – Gr. μουσική, subst. use (sc. τέχνη art) of fem. of μουσικός of a Muse or the Muses, concerning the arts, poetry, literature, f. μοῦσα MUSE *sb.*[1]] **1.** That one of the fine arts which is concerned with the combination of sounds with a view to beauty of form and the expression of thought or feeling; also, the science of the laws or principles by which this art is regulated. **2.** Sounds in melodic or harmonic combination, whether produced by voice or instruments. late ME. **b.** *transf.* Applied, e.g., to the song of birds, the murmur of running water, etc., *spec.* the cry of hounds on seeing the chase. Also in ironical collocations. 1590. **3.** Musical composition 1607. †**4.** A piece of music composed or performed –1674. **5.** A company of musicians; the company of musicians attached to a military force; a 'band of music' (see BAND *sb.*[3] 4). [Cf. Fr. *musique.*] *Obs.* exc. in military or court use. 1586. **6.** Musical instruments (now *dial.*) 1661. **7.** The written or printed score of a musical composition; such scores collectively; musical composition as represented by graphic symbols 1770. **8.** *U.S. colloq.* Liveliness; excited wrangling; diversion; sport 1859.

1. Considered as an art, music has two distinct branches, the art of the composer and that of the executant. The word is often used with special ref. to the executive branch, and to instrumental execution rather than vocal O.E.D. **2.** Musick has Charms to sooth a savage Breast CONGREVE. *fig.* I shall now be kil'd, Even with the musick of her voice DAVENANT. He murmurs near the running brooks A m. sweeter than their own WORDSW. Phr. *Rough m.*: noisy uproar; *esp.* a din produced by knocking together pots, pans, kettles, etc. for purposes of annoyance 1708. **b.** Clashing of swords was then daily musicke in every street 1617. **3.** Phr. *To set to m.*: to provide (a poem, etc.) with m. to which it may be sung. **4.** *Cymb.* II. iii. 44. **5.** He says many of the musique are ready to starve PEPYS. **6.** She plays the M. without one sensation but the feel of the ivory at her fingers KEATS.

Phr. (*colloq.*). *To face the m.*, to face boldly the consequences of one's actions 1850.

attrib. and *Comb.*, as *m.-desk, -lesson, -master, -rack, -room, -stand*, etc.; **m.-book,** a book containing music-scores; **-box,** †(*a*) a barrel-organ; (*b*) = *musical box* (see MUSICAL *a.*); (*c*) *joc.*, a pianoforte; **-demy,** a white thick soft paper, used by music publishers for printing music, 21 by 14½ inches; **m. gallery,** a gallery in a church or hall for the accommodation of the musicians; **-hall,** a hall used for musical performances; *spec.* (since about 1885) a hall licensed for singing, dancing, and other entertainments exclusive of dramatic performances; also *attrib.*; **-loft,** a gallery for musicians; *spec.* an organ-loft; **-paper,** paper ruled for writing m. upon; **-pen,** a pen having five points for drawing at one time the five lines of the musical stave; †**-shell,** one of several species of gasteropodous molluscs of the family *Volutidæ*, having markings on the shell resembling written music; **m.-stool,** a stool (usu. with adjustable seat) for one who plays on the piano. Hence **Mu·sicless** *a.*

Musical (miū·zikăl), *a.* (and *sb.*) late ME. [– (O)Fr. *musical* – med.L. *musicalis*, f. L. *musica*; see prec., -AL[1].] **A.** *adj.* **1.** Of or belonging to music. **2.** Having the nature of music; tuneful, melodious, harmonious; pleasing in sound, euphonious. Of sounds: Having the nature of 'tones', as dist. from mere 'noises'. late ME. **3.** Fond of or skilled in music. late ME. **4.** Set to or accompanied by music 1685.

2. The musicall confusion Of hounds and eccho in coniunction SHAKS.

Spec. collocations: **m. box,** a mechanical m. instrument consisting of a revolving toothed cylinder working upon a resonant comb-like metal plate; **m. chairs,** a game in which a number of players march to music round a smaller number of chairs and each try to secure a seat when the music stops; **m. chime,** a set of bells arranged to play a tune, a carillon; **m. clock,** a clock which produces short tunes at regular intervals; **m. glasses** = HARMONICA 1 a, b; **m. ride,** a kind of equestrian dance executed by the Life or Horse Guards to the accompaniment of music; **m. shell** = *music-shell*; **m. snuff-box,** a snuff-box containing a small m. instrument worked by machinery.

B. *sb.* A musical party 1823. Also in Fr. form **musicale.** *U.S.* 1883. Hence **Musica·lity,** m. quality or character. **Mu·sical-ly** *adv.*, **-ness.**

Musician (miuzi·ʃăn). late ME. [– (O)Fr. *musicien*, f. *musique*; see MUSIC, -IAN.] **1.** One skilled in the science or practice of music. **2.** A professional performer of (esp. instrumental) music. Also *transf.* and *fig.* 1450.

Musicens (whiche encludeth singing and plaieng) 1555. Hence **Musi·cianly** *a.* characteristic or worthy of a skilled m. 1864.

Musicianer (miuzi·ʃănǝɹ). Now chiefly *Irish.* 1540. [f. prec. + -ER[1].] = MUSICIAN.

Musico- (miū·ziko), comb. f. L. *musicus*, as in *m.-dramatic* adj., etc.

Musimon, obs. f. MUSMON.

Musit, var. of MUSET.

†**Mu·sive,** *a.* and *sb.* 1506. [– Fr. *musif, -ive* – late L. *musivus*, in *opus musivum* mosaic work.] **A.** *adj.* = MOSAIC *a.*[1] 1. –1813. **B.** *sb.* = MOSAIC *sb.* 1. – 1658.

Musk (mɒsk), *sb.* late ME. [– late L. *muscus* (Jerome) – Pers. *mušk, mišk*, perh. – Skr. *mushká* scrotum (the shape of the musk-deer's musk-bag being similar).] **1.** An odoriferous reddish-brown substance secreted in a gland or sac by the male musk-deer. It is used as the basis of many perfumes, and in medicine as a stimulant and antispasmodic. Also applied occas. to substances of similar odour secreted by certain other animals. **b.** An artificial preparation imitating musk 1658. **2.** An animal which produces 'musk', now usu. the MUSK-DEER, sometimes called *Tibet* (or *pouched*) *m.*; also applied to other animals resembling this or possessing a musky smell 1470. **3.** A name for plants having a musky odour, esp. *musk-plant* (*b*) 1731. **b.** Short for *m. apple, pear* 1708.

1. They lefte a very sweete sauour behynde them sweeter then muske 1555. **b.** Animall-musk, seems to excell the vegetable SIR T. BROWNE. **2.** In the m. the fur is thick and elastic, fit for a cold country 1879. **3.** Close in a bower of hyacinth and m. KEATS.

attrib. and *Comb.* **a.** In names for the receptacle in the musk-deer, etc., which contains the musk, as *m.-bags, -gland, -pod, -sac.*

b. In the names of plants having a musky odour, as **m. carnation,** the clove-gillyflower; **m. cranesbill, geranium,** *Erodium moschatum*; **m. crowfoot, root,** *Adoxa moschatellina*; **m.-flower** = *musk-plant* (*b*); **-hyacinth,** one of the grape-hyacinths, *Muscari moschatum*; **-mallow,** (*a*) *Malva moschata*; (*b*) = *musk-plant* (*a*); **m. orchis,** *Herminium monorchis*; **m.-plant,** †(*a*) *Hibiscus abelmoschus*; (*b*) *Mimulus moschatus*; (*c*) = *musk-mallow* (*a*); **-rose,** a rambling rose, *Rosa moschata*, having fragrant white flowers; **-seed,** the seed of *Hibiscus abelmoschus*; **m. thistle,** the thistle *Carduus nutans.*

c. In the names of varieties of fruits having a musky smell or taste, as *m. apple, pear*, etc.

d. In the names of animals having a musky odour as †**m.-beaver** = MUSK-RAT 1; **-beetle,** a longicorn beetle, *Callichroma moschata*; **-bison, -buffalo** = *m.-ox*; **-kangaroo,** a very small, rat-like, arboreal kangaroo, *Hypsiprymnodon moschatus*; **-mole,** a Mongolian mole, *Scaptochirus moschatus*; **-ox,** a ruminant of Arctic America, *Ovibos moschatus*; **-shrew,** the Indian musk-rat (see MUSK-RAT 2); **-tortoise, -turtle,** a small American freshwater turtle, *Aromochelys odorata*; **-weasel,** any viverrine carnivore.

Musk, *v. rare.* 1632. [f. MUSK *sb.*] *trans.* To perfume with or as with musk.

Muskadel(l, Muskalinge, etc., **Muskat,** var. MUSCATEL, MASKINONGE, MUSK-CAT.

†**Mu·sk-cat.** Also †**musket, -at,** etc. 1551. The animal from which musk is got; usu., the MUSK-DEER. Cf. CIVET-CAT. –1794. **b.** *transf.* applied as a term of reproach to a fop; also to a courtesan 1566–1777.

†**Mu·sk-cod.** 1599. [COD *sb.*[1]] **1.** The bag or gland containing musk 1672–1721. **2.** *transf.* A scented fop –1634.

Mu·sk-deer. 1681. A small hornless ruminant (*Moschus moschiferus*) of Central Asia, the male of which yields the perfume called 'musk' (see MUSK *sb.* 1). Also, a chevrotain.

Mu·sk-duck. 1774. **1.** A tropical American duck, *Cairina moschata*, erron. called the *Muscovy* and *Barbary duck*. **2.** An Australian duck, *Biziura lobata*, so called from the musky odour of the male 1834.

Musked (mɒskt), *a.* Now *rare.* 1576. [f. MUSK *sb.* or *v.* + -ED.] Flavoured or perfumed with musk; tasting like musk. (Often in names of plants and fruits, transl. mod.L. *moschatus.*)

Muskellunge, var. MASKINONGE.

Musket[1] (mɒ·skėt). *Obs.* exc. *Hist.* late ME. [– ONFr. *musket, mousquet*, OFr. *mou(s)chet, moschet*, now *émouchet*. Ult. origin unc. Cf. med.L. *muscetus.*] The male of the sparrowhawk.

Musket[2] (mɒ·skėt). 1587. [– Fr. *mousquet* (Brantôme), †*-ette* – It. *moschetto, -etta* (formerly) bolt from a cross-bow, f. *mosca* fly :– L. *musca.*] A hand-gun carried by infantry soldiers. (Orig. applied to the match-lock gun, and now usu. restricted to obsolete kinds of infantry gun, as dist. from the rifle.)

Muskettes and calleevers and holebertes shall be provided for this company 1587.

Comb.: **m.-arrow,** a short arrow discharged from a m.; **-rest,** a forked staff to support the heavy m. formerly in use; **m. shot,** (*a*) shot fired from a musket, a musket-ball, (*b*) the range of a musket; **-slit,** a slit in a wall through which a m. may be fired. Hence **Musketee·r** *Hist.*, a soldier armed with a m. 1590.

Musketo(e, obs. ff. MOSQUITO.

Musketoon (mɒskėtū·n). *Obs.* exc. *Hist.* 1638. [– Fr. *mousqueton* – It. *moschettone*,

f. *moschetto* MUSKET²; see -OON.] A kind of musket, short and with a large bore; a soldier armed with this.

Musketry (mɒ·skĕtri). 1646. [– Fr. *mousqueterie*, f. *mousquet*; see MUSKET² and -ERY, -RY.] **1.** Muskets collectively. **2.** The fire of muskets 1756. **3.** The art or science of manipulating small arms 1854. **4.** Musketeers 1772.

Musk melon. 1573. [f. MUSK *sb.*] The MELON, *Cucumis melo*. (Applied both to fruit and plant.)

Mu·sk-rat. 1620. **1.** A large aquatic rodent, *Fiber zibethicus*, common throughout N. America, so called from its musky smell. Also called MUSQUASH. **b.** The fur or skin of the musk-rat 1879. **2.** Applied to other rat-like animals having a musky odour; as the musk-kangaroo, the musk-shrew, the DESMAN, etc. 1681.

Mu·sk-root. 1844. Any of several plants having strong-scented roots, as moschatel, spikenard, sumbul; also, a drug obtained from the root of sumbul.

Mu·sk-tree. 1848. Any of several Australian trees or shrubs having a musky smell, as *Marlea vitiensis*, *Olearia argophylla* (Silver-leaved M.), and *O. viscosa* (Dwarf M.).

Mu·sk-wood. 1725. Any of several trees having a musky smell, as *Trichilia moschata* and *Guarea trichilioides* of the West Indies, and the Australian silver-leaved musk-tree; the wood of any of these.

Musky (mɒ·ski), *a.* 1610. [f. MUSK *sb.* + -Y¹.] Smelling or tasting of musk, or somewhat like musk; scented with musk. Hence **Mu·skiness.**

Muslim: see MOSLEM.

Muslin (mɒ·zlin). 1609. [– Fr. *mousseline* – It. *mussolina*, *-ino*, f. *Mussolo*, the town of Mosul in Mesopotamia, where muslin was formerly made; see -INE¹.] **1.** General name for the most delicately woven cotton fabrics, used for ladies' dresses, curtains, hangings, etc. Also, a garment of this. **b.** *U.S.* Any of various coarser and heavier cotton goods, used for shirts, bedding etc. 1872. **2.** *slang.* 'The fair sex'. *A bit of m.*, a woman or girl. 1823. **3.** *Naut. slang.* 'Canvas', sails 1822. **4.** *attrib.* or *adj.* Made or consisting of muslin 1684.

Muslinet (mɒzline·t). Also **-ette.** 1787. [f. MUSLIN + -ET.] A thick variety of muslin; used for infants' clothing, etc.

Musmon (mɒ·smǫn). Also †**musi-.** 1601. [– L. *musimo* (Pliny), late Gr. μούσμων (Strabo).] = MOUFFLON.

‖**Musnud** (mɒ·snɒd). 1763. [Urdu *masnad*, – Arab. *misnad*, f. *sanada* lean against.] A seat made of cushions, esp. one used as a throne by native princes of India.

Musquash (mɒ·skwǫʃ). 1624. [– Algonquian word.] The musk-rat, or its fur (1884). *attrib.* and *Comb.*, as **m. root**, Water Hemlock, *Cicuta maculata*.

Musquaw (mɒ·skwǭ). 1861. [Cree Indian.] An American name for the Black Bear.

Musque(e)to, etc., **Musquet,** var. MOSQUITO, MUSKET.

†**Mu·srol.** 1551. [– Fr. *muserolle* – It. *museruola*, f. *muso* muzzle.] The nose-band of a bridle –1833.

Muss (mɒs), *sb.*¹ *Obs.* exc. *dial.* 1591. [Of unkn. origin.] A game in which small objects are thrown down to be scrambled for.

Muss (mɒs), *sb.*² *dial.* and *U.S.* 1843. [app. var. of MESS *sb.*] **1.** A disturbance, row 1848. **2.** A state of untidiness; a muddle, mess. Hence **Muss** *v. trans.* to make untidy; to crumple, ruffle; to smear, mess; to entangle, confuse 1850.

Mussel (mɒ·s'l). [OE. *muscle*, *muxle*, *musle* (– L. *musculus*), superseded by MLG. *mussel*, MDu. *mosscele* (Du. *mossel*), = OHG. *muscula* (G. *muschel*) – Rom. **muscula*, alt. f. L. *musculus*, dim. (see -CULE) of L. *mus* mouse; sp. with *-sk-* survived till XVII, but *-ss-* occurred XV.] **1.** A bivalve mollusc belonging to either of the two families *Mytilacea* (Sea Mussels) and *Unionacea* (Freshwater Mussels). **2.** A fossil bivalve shell found in ironstone bands in coal 1834.

attrib. and *Comb.*, as **m. band** *Geol.*, a bed of clay ironstone containing fossil bivalve shells, anthracosia, etc.; **m.-bank, -bed,** a layer of mussels at the bottom of the sea; **m. digger** *U.S.*, a name for the California grey whale; **m. plum,** a dark purple variety of plum; **m. scale,** an insect having the shape of a small mussel-shell, which attacks the bark of apple-trees.

Mu·ssel-shell. OE. The shell of a mussel. **b.** One who gapes like a mussel-shell. *Merry W.* IV. v. 29.

†**Mu·ssitate,** *v.* 1626. [– *mussitat-*, pa. ppl. stem of L. *mussitare*, frequent. of *mussare* mutter; see -ATE³.] *intr.* To mutter –1721. So †**Mussita·tion** 1649–1891.

‖**Mussuck** (mɒ·sɒ̆k). *Anglo-Ind.* 1610. [Hindi *maçak.*] A leather water-bag.

Mussulman (mɒ·sǒlmæ̆n), *sb.* and *a.* *Pl.* **-mans.** *Catachr. pl.* **-men.** 1563. [– Pers. *musulmān*, prop. adj. f. *muslim* MOSLEM.] (A) Moslem. Hence **Mu·ssulmanic,** †**Mu·ssulmanish** *adjs.* = M.; **Mu·ssulmanism** (now *rare*), Islam; ‖**Mussulmanlik,** the M. faith, Islam; †**Mu·ssulmans** *Anglo-Ind.*, the Urdu language. So **Mu·ssulwoman,** a female M. (*joc.*) 1668.

Mussy (mɒ·si), *a.* *U.S.* 1859. [f. MUSS *sb.*² + -Y¹.] Untidy, rumpled, tousled. Hence **Mu·ssiness.**

Must (mɒst), *sb.*¹ [OE. *must* = (O)HG. *most* – L. *mustum*, subst. use of n. of *mustus* new, fresh.] **1.** New wine; grape-juice unfermented or before fermentation is complete. Also *new m.* †**b.** *In (the) m., on the m.*: said of wine in process of fermentation 1533–1700. **2.** †**a.** Any juice or liquor undergoing or prepared for undergoing alcoholic fermentation. late ME. –1708. **b.** The pulp of apples or pears after the juice has been pressed out in making cider or perry (*dial.*) 1670. †**3.** A variety of cider-apple 1664–1707.

1. Will put newe muste into old bottelles UDALL. *fig.* Els the Jewes might haue..preferred the old wine of Moses lawe, aboue the new m. of the doctrine of Christ 1563.

Must (mɒst), *sb.*² 1602. [Back-formation from MUSTY.] Mustiness; mould.

Must, *sb.*³ 1603. The verb MUST used as a noun.

Must is for kings, And low obedience for low underlings DEKKER.

Must (mɒst), *a.* and *sb.*⁴ Also **musth.** 1871. [– Urdu *mast* – Pers. *mast*, lit. 'intoxicated'.] **A.** *adj.* Applied to male animals, as elephants and camels, in a state of dangerous frenzy to which they are subject at irregular intervals. Phr. *To go m.* **B.** *sb.* The condition or state of being 'must'; an elephant in must 1878.

Must (mɒst), *v.*¹ [OE. *mōste*, pa. t. of *mōt* (see MOTE *v.*), = OFris. *mōt*, OS. *mōt*, *muot* (Du. *moet*), OHG. *muoȥ* find room or opportunity, may, must (G. *muss*), Goth. *gamōtan* find room, rel. to MLG. *mōte*, OHG. *muoȥa* (G. *musse*) leisure :– Gmc. **mōtō*, of unkn. origin.] †**I.** The pa. t. of MOTE *v.*, in senses 1 and 2. –1471. **II.** Used as a pres. tense, and hence (under certain conditions) as a pa. tense, corresponding to this. **1.** Expressing necessity: Am (is, are) obliged or required to; have (has) to; it is necessary that (I, you, he, it, etc.) should : = MOTE *v.* 2. ME. **b.** Used to express a fixed or certain futurity. *I m.* = I am fated or certain to . . ., I shall certainly or inevitably . . . late ME. **c.** In expressions like *I m. say* = I cannot help saying. Also in explanatory clauses, as *you m. know* or *understand* = you ought to be informed, I would have you know. 1563. **d.** As a pa. tense: Was obliged, had to; it was necessary that (I, he, it, etc.) should. (Now only in oblique narration, and when the speaker has in his mind what might have been said or thought at the time.) 1691. **e.** As a pa. or historical pres. tense with ref. to some foolish or annoying action or some untoward event. Now *colloq.* late ME. **2.** In the 1st pers., *must* often expresses an insistent demand or a firm resolve on the part of the speaker. Hence also in the 2nd and 3rd persons, rendering sentiments imputed to others. late ME. **3.** As *must* has no pa. pple., the need of a past conditional is supplied by placing the principal verb in the perfect infinitive; as, *I m. have seen* (*done*) *it* 1460. **4.** Expressing the inferred or presumed certainty of a fact; either (with present inf.) relating to the present time, as in *you m. be aware of this* = I cannot doubt that you are aware of this; or (with perf. inf.) relating to the past, as in *he m. have done it* = it is to be concluded that he did it 1652. **5.** In *m. not* the negative has the same effect as if it belonged to the following infinitive 1583. **6.** Elliptical uses. **a.** With ellipsis of a verb of motion (now *arch.*) late ME. **b.** With ellipsis of infinitive to be supplied from the context ME.

1. Tom, you m. go with us to [etc.] SWIFT. **b.** He m. increace: and I muste decreace TINDALE *John* 3:30. **c.** I m. beg to be absolved from the promise JOWETT. **d.** He could not bear to be idle..he m. always be doing something 1894. **e.** Just when I was busiest, that bore C. m. come in and waste three hours (*mod.*). **2.** I m., and will go DRYDEN. Let us leave this room, if you m. laugh 1798. **3.** If he had looked he m. have seen the light of the approaching train 1896. **4.** This m. have been a sad shock to the poor disconsolate parent GOLDSM. **5.** You m. not meruaile Helen at my course SHAKS. **6. a.** His work is done, the minister m. out SWIFT. **b.** I have not spoken to the king One word; and one I m. Farewell! TENNYSON.

Must, *v.*² *Obs.* exc. *dial.* 1530. [Back-formation from MUSTY.] *intr.* and *trans.* To become, or make, musty or mouldy.

Mustache: see MOUSTACHE.

Mustachio (mustɑ·ʃo, mɒ̆s-). *Pl.* **mustachios** (-ʃoz). 1551. [– Sp. *mostacho* and its source It. *mostaccio* (cf. med.L. *mustacia*), based ult. on Gr. μύσταξ, μυστακ- upper lip, moustache.] = MOUSTACHE 1, 2; *transf.* esp. †the whiskers of a cat; †the awn or bristles of certain grasses 1591–1790. Hence **Mustachioed** *a.* moustached.

Mustang (mɒ·stæŋ). 1808. [app. blending of Sp. *mestengo* (now *mesteño*) and *mostrenco*, both applied to wild or masterless cattle, the former being f. *mesta* (:– L. *mixta*, subst. use of fem. pa. pple. of *miscēre* mix) association of graziers, who appropriated wild cattle that attached themselves to the herds.] **1.** The wild or half-wild horse of Mexico, California, etc. Also *m. pony.* **2.** In full *M. grape*: A small red grape, *Vitis candicans*, of Texas 1854.

Mustard (mɒ·stăɹd). ME. [– OFr. *mo(u)starde* (mod. *moutarde*) = Pr., Cat., Pg., It. *mostarda*, Rum. *mostar*, f. Rom. **mosto*, L. *mustum* MUST *sb.*¹; prop. applied to the condiment as orig. prepared by making the ground seeds into a paste with must.] **1.** The seeds of the plant mustard (see 2) ground or pounded to a powder, sometimes called *flour of m.*; also, this substance as made into a paste, and used as a condiment, or applied to the skin as a poultice or plaster. **2.** Any of the cruciferous plants yielding these seeds, forming the Linnæan genus *Sinapis*, but now included in the genus *Brassica*; esp. *B. nigra*, the black (or brown) mustard, and *B. alba*, the white mustard ME. **b.** Applied with defining word to various other (chiefly cruciferous) plants resembling mustard in appearance, taste, etc. 1597.

2. *M. and cress*: the plants white mustard and cress (*Lepidium sativum*) used in the seed-leaf as a salad-herb. **b. Poor man's m.,** hedge-garlic. **Wild m.,** (*a*) charlock, *Brassica arvensis*; (*b*) *Raphanus raphanistrum.*

Comb.: **m. beetle,** a small black beetle (*Phædon armoraciæ*) destructive to mustard plants; †**m.-bowl,** a wooden bowl in which mustard seed was pounded, proverbially referred to as the instrument for producing stage thunder; **-gas,** a variety of poison gas; **-oil,** an oil obtained from mustard seed; **-pot,** a pot or cruet for holding table m.; **m.-shrub,** a West Indian shrub, *Capparis ferruginea*, the berries of which have a pungent flavour; **-tree,** the m. of the N.T., described as a 'tree' (see next 1).

Mustard seed. late ME. **1.** The seed of mustard.

The 'mustard seed' (κόκκος σινάπεως,) of the N.T., spoken as of producing a 'tree' (*Matt.* 13:31), is prob. the seed of the black mustard (*Brassica nigra*), which in Palestine grows to a great height. †**2.** = MUSTARD 2. –1681. **3.** *U.S.* A very fine shot used in shooting birds to minimize injury to the plumage 1884.

Mustee (mɒ·stī), **mestee** (mestī·). 1699. [– Sp. *mestizo* (pronounced mestī·þo); see MESTIZO.] The offspring of a white and a quadroon; also, loosely, a half-caste.

Musteline (mɒ·stĭləin). 1656. [– L. *mustelinus* of or belonging to a weasel, f. *mustela* weasel; see -INE¹.] **A.** *adj.* Of, pertaining to, or characteristic of the subfamily *Mustelinæ* of weasels; *spec.* of the brown tawny colour of the summer fur of the weasel. **B.** *sb.* A m. animal 1891.

Muster (mɒ·stəɹ), *sb.*[1] [Late ME. *mostre, moustre* – OFr. *moustre* (later in latinized form *monstre*, mod. *montre*) repr. Rom. sb. f. **mostrare* :– L. *monstrare* show.] †**1.** The action, or an act, of showing; manifestation; exhibition, display –1661. **2.** A pattern, specimen, example. Now only *Comm.*, a pattern, sample. late ME. **3.** An act of mustering soldiers, sailors, etc.; an assembling of men for inspection, ascertainment of numbers, introduction into service, exercise, or the like. Phr. *To make, take a m.* late ME. **4.** The number of persons or things mustered or assembled on a particular occasion; an assembly, collection. late ME. **5.** A muster-roll 1565. **6.** *Muster out*: the action of 'mustering out'; discharge from service. *U.S.* 1892.

1. They begin to make some m. and shew of their learning 1581. **2.** In mod. use confined to certain particular branches of commerce or particular localities (used, e.g. in the Sheffield cutlery trade, and by British merchants in Asia) O.E.D. A few musters of new Teas have been shewn 1879. **3.** They took a m. and found their Army amounted to four thousand Foot, and six hundred Horse 1726. Phr. *To pass m.*: orig. *Mil.* To undergo m. or review without censure; hence *transf.* and *fig.* to bear examination or inspection, to come up to the required standard, to be above, or go free from, censure; to succeed, be accepted (*as* or *for* the possessor of certain qualities). *False m.*: a fraudulent presentation at a m., or a fraudulent inclusion in a muster-roll, of men who are not available for service. Formerly often *fig.* **4.** A tolerable m. of amateurs and boxing gentry 1810. **5.** I..got put down upon the m. DICKENS.

attrib. and *Comb.*: **m.-book,** a book in which muster-rolls are transcribed 1587; **m.-master,** an officer who was responsible for the accuracy of the muster-roll (now *Hist.*) 1579; **m.-roll,** a register of the officers and men in an army or ship's company (also *fig.*) 1605.

†**Muster,** *sb.*[2] 1466. Short for MUSTERDEVILLERS –1549.

Muster (mɒ·stəɹ), *v.* ME. [– OFr. *mo(u)strer* (mod. *montrer*) :– L. *monstrare* show.] †**1.** *trans.* To show, display, exhibit; to show up, report, tell, explain –1622. †**b.** *intr.* for *refl.* To show, to appear, to be displayed; to make a (good, bad, etc.) appearance –1597. **2.** *trans.* To collect or assemble (*primarily* soldiers) for ascertainment of numbers, inspection, exercise, display, or introduction into service. late ME. **b.** *intr.* for *refl.* Of an army, etc.: To come together for inspection, exercise, or preparation for service 1450. †**c.** *trans.* To enlist, enroll –1748. **d.** To call the roll of. Now chiefly *Naut.* 1670. **e.** Of an army, etc.: To comprise, to number 1837. **3.** To collect, bring together (persons or things); *esp.* to bring forward from one's own stores 1586. **b.** *fig.* To summon, gather up (one's thoughts, courage, strength, etc.) 1588. **4.** *intr.* To assemble, gather together in a body 1603. **5.** *trans.* To 'take stock of' 1625. **6.** *intr.* To pass muster *for.* LAMB.

2. How busy he was in mustering, how diligent in setting forward HALL. I then in London,..Muster'd my Soldiers SHAKS. **b.** *fig.* A field of fancies musterd in my mynd 1611. **c.** We being not knowne, not muster'd Among the Bands SHAKS. **d.** Phr. *To m. in* (U.S.): to m. (a watch) at the time of duty. *To m. in (into) (the) service* (U.S.): to enroll as recruits. *To m. out (of service)* (U.S.): to summon together in order to discharge from service; to pay off (soldiers). **3.** All the Hands we could m...were but twelve 1743. **b.** Muster your Wits, stand in your owne defence SHAKS. Mustring all her wiles MILT. **4.** Oh, heauens Why doe's my bloud thus m. to my heart? SHAKS. **5.** Mustering cattle 1875.

Phr. **Muster up. a.** To bring together (troops) for battle, etc. **b.** *fig.* To summon up, gather up, marshal.

a. In Oxfordshire shalt m. vp thy friends SHAKS. **b.** She had mustered up courage to speak to him 1893.

†**Musterdevillers.** (Many variant spellings.) 1400. [f. *Mouster(de)villers*, old form of the name of Montivilliers, Normandy.] A grey woollen cloth –1564.

Musty (mɒ·sti), *a.* (and *sb.*) 1530. [perh. alt. of MOISTY by assoc. with MUST *sb.*[1]] **1. a.** Spoiled with damp; moist and fetid. **b.** Having the rank odour or taste of mouldy substances 1530. **2.** *fig.* **a.** Spoiled with age; stale; antiquated 1592. **b.** Of persons: Dull, 'mouldy', antiquated 1637. **3.** Ill-humoured, peevish, sullen. *Obs.* exc. *dial.* 1620. †**4.** *sb.* A kind of snuff having a musty flavour. STEELE.

1. Old m. papers 1693. Unsavoury smells of m. hay DICKENS. **b.** Do not all Houses and Places glow m...if the Air be any way prevented by Window-shutters..? 1683. Sour milk and m. eggs 1891. **2. a.** Some old m. laws 1683. **b.** A m. moralist FIELDING. Hence **Mu·stily** *adv.* **Mu·stiness.** †**Mu·sty** *v.* to become or make m. or mouldy 1631–1707.

Mutable (miū·tăb'l), *a.* and *sb.* late ME. [– L. *mutabilis*, f. *mutare* change, see -ABLE.] **A.** *adj.* **1.** Inconstant in mind, will, or disposition; fickle; unsettled, variable. Now *rare.* **2.** Liable or subject to change or alteration. **b.** *Gram.* Subject to mutation 1707.

1. The m. mynde of quene Elyzabeth 1548. **2.** The Use of Clothes continues, though the Fashion of them has been m. STEELE.

B. *sb.* A mutable consonant 1821.

[Letters] capable of aspiration, or mutables 1843. Hence **Mutabi·lity, Mu·tableness** (now *rare*). **Mu·tably** *adv.*

Mutage (miū·tėdʒ). 1839. [– Fr. *mutage*, f. *muter*; see MUTE *v.*[4], -AGE.] The process of muting wine.

Mutant (miū·tănt), *a.* and *sb.* 1901. [– *mutant-*, pr. ppl. stem of L. *mutare* change; see -ANT.] *Biol.* (A form) resulting from mutation.

Mutate (miutē[i]·t), *v.* 1818. [Back-formation from next.] **a.** *intr.* To undergo change; *Gram.* to undergo mutation. **b.** *trans.* (*Gram.*) To cause mutation of.

Mutation (miutē[i]·ʃən). late ME. [– L. *mutatio*, f. *mutat-*, pa. ppl. stem of *mutare* change; see -ATION. Cf. (O)Fr. *mutation*, which may be partly the source.] **1.** The action or process of changing; alteration, change. **2.** *Mus.* In mediæval solmization: The change from one hexachord to another involving a change of the syllable applied to a given note 1597. **3.** *Philol.* **a.** In the Celtic langs., a change of an initial consonant, depending on the character of the preceding word 1843. **b.** In Germanic langs., modification of an accented vowel under the influence of a following vowel (*i, u, a/o*) or consonants *j* (= *y*), *w*; umlaut. 1875. **4.** *Biol.* Used (in contrast to *variation*) for the kind of change which results in the production of a new species. Hence quasi-*concr.* a species resulting from this process. 1894.

1. O world! But that thy strange mutations make vs hate thee Life would not yeelde to age SHAKS.

attrib. **Mutation stop,** an organ-stop whose pipes produce tones a fifth or a major third above the proper pitch of the key struck, or above one of its octaves.

‖**Muta·tis muta·ndis,** *adv. phr.* 1498. [L.] 'Things being changed that have to be changed', i.e. with the necessary changes.

Mutative (miū·tătiv), *a.* 1743. [– med.L. *mutativus*, f. *mutat-*; see MUTATION, -IVE.] Of, pertaining to, or characterized by mutation or sudden variation.

Mutch (mɒtʃ). *dial.* and *Sc.* 1473. [– MDu. *mutse* (Du. *muts*), corresp. to (M)HG. *mütze*, shortened by-forms of MDu. *amutse, almutse* – med.L. *almucia* AMICE[2].] †**1.** *Sc.* A night covering for the head –1831. **2.** A cap or coif, usu. of linen, worn by women and young children 1634.

Mutchkin (mɒ·tʃkin). *Sc.* late ME. [– early mod.Du. *mudseken* (now *mutsje*), dim. of *mudde*; see MUD *sb.*[2], -KIN.] A measure of capacity for liquids, etc.; the fourth part of the old Scots pint, or about three-quarters of an imperial pint.

Mute (miūt), *a.* and *sb.*[1] late ME. [Early forms *muet, mewet, muwet* (two syll.) – (O)Fr. *muet*, dim. formation on OFr. *mu* :– L. *mutus*. In XVI permanently assim. to L.] **A.** *adj.* **1.** Not emitting articulate sound; silent. **2.** Destitute of the faculty of speech; dumb. late ME. **b.** Applied to the lower animals 1667. **3.** Temporarily bereft of the power of speech 1483. **4.** Of things or action: Not characterized by speech or vocal utterance 1599. **5.** *Gram.* and *Phonetics.* **a.** Of a consonant: Produced by an entire interruption of the passage of breath, or by the complete closure of the organs of the mouth; 'stopped' 1589. **b.** Of a letter: Not pronounced, silent 1638. **6.** *Sporting.* Not giving tongue (said of hounds while hunting) 1677. **7.** Said of metals that do not ring when struck 1806.

1. Phr. *To stand m. (of malice)*: in *Law*, to refuse deliberately to plead. Some m. inglorious Milton here may rest GRAY. *transf.* The groves are still and m.! SCOTT. *M. swan*: the common swan, *Cygnus olor.* **2. b.** Oaths..seem to be considered as the only language the m. creation can comprehend 1845. **3.** M. with wonder I stood 1887. **4.** M. solemn Sorrow, free from Female Noise DRYDEN. *transf.* The jurisdiction of the magistrate was m. and impotent GIBBON. **6.** Phr. *To run m.*: to follow the chase without giving tongue. Hence **Mu·te-ly** *adv.*, **-ness.**

B. *sb.*[1] **1.** *Phonetics.* An element of speech formed by a position of the vocal organs such as stops the breath, or entirely interrupts the sound; a stopped consonant, a 'stop' 1530. **2.** A person precluded by nature, mutilation, or employment from the exercise of speech. **a.** A person dumb by nature or as a result of mutilation. **b.** An actor on the stage whose part is performed only in dumb show 1579. **c.** In oriental countries: A dumb house-servant or janitor 1599. †**d.** *Law.* One who refuses to plead to an indictment –1738. **e.** A professional attendant at a funeral 1762. **3.** *Mus.* **a.** A clip of metal, wood, or ivory that can be placed over the bridge of a violin or the like to deaden the resonance without affecting the vibration of the strings 1811. **b.** A pad that can be inserted into the bell of a metal wind-instrument to muffle the sound 1841.

1. Mutes (*mutæ*), these letters *b, c, d, g, h, k, p, q, t*, are so called, because they have no sound, without the assistance of a vowel BLOUNT. **3. c.** Our graue Like Turkish m., shall haue a tongueless mouth SHAKS. *Comb.* **m.-closure** (*Phonetics*), closure of the oral passage so as to form a m.

†**Mute,** *sb.*[2] 1575. [f. MUTE *v.*[1] Cf. Fr. *émeut.*] The action of 'muting'; *concr.* (*sing.* and *pl.*) dung (of birds) –1820.

†**Mute,** *sb.*[3] ME. [– OFr. *muete*, (also mod.) *meute* :– pop.L. **movita*, f. L. *movēre* MOVE.] A pack of hounds –1688; also, the cry of hounds working (ME.).

Mute (miūt), *sb.*[4] *dial.* 1843. [Of unkn. origin.] A kind of mule.

Mute (miūt), *v.*[1] *Obs.* exc. *dial.* 1450. [– OFr. *meutir* (later †*mutir*), aphetic of *esmeutir*, earlier *esmeltir*, (mod. *émeutir*), f. Frank. **smeltjan* SMELT *v.* (MDu. *smelt* bird's fæces).] Of a bird, esp. a hawk; **a.** *intr.* To void the fæces. **b.** *trans.* To discharge as fæces. Hence **Mu·ting** *vbl. sb.*, also *concr.* 'droppings'.

†**Mute,** *v.*[2] 1570. [perh. – L. *mutire* murmur.] *intr.* To murmur –1655.

Mute (miūt), *v.*[3] 1861. [f. MUTE *a.*] *trans.* To deaden or subdue the sound of; *spec.* in *Mus.*, to muffle the sound of (a musical instrument).

Mute (miūt), *v.*[4] 1839. [– Fr. *muter.*] *trans.* To check the fermentation of (must).

Mutic (miū·tik), *a.* 1777. [– L. *muticus* awnless.] = MUTILATE *a.* 2. **a.** *Bot.* Without a point or beard. **b.** *Entom.* Wanting spines. So **Mu·ticous** *a.* 1856.

Mutilate (miū·tile[i]t), *a.* 1532. [– L. *mutilatus*, pa. pple. of *mutilare*; see next, -ATE[2].] **1.** Of a human body, a limb, and other things: Mutilated (in senses 1 and 2 of next). *Obs.* exc. *poet.* **2.** *Nat. Hist.* Deficient in some part common to the species or to closely related species, or possessing it only in an imperfect or modified form 1760.

Mutilate (miū·tile[i]t), *v.* 1534. [– *mutilat-*, pa. ppl. stem of L. *mutilare* cut or lop off, f. *mutilus* maimed; see -ATE[3].] **1.** *trans.* To deprive (a person or animal) of a limb or organ of the body; to cut off or otherwise destroy the use of (a limb or organ) 1562. **2.** To render (a thing, e.g. a record, etc.) imperfect by cutting off or destroying a part 1534.

1. The Greeks..mutilated the slain THIRLWALL. **2.** I wil not in any worde wyllinglye mangle or mutilate that honourable mans worke MORE. Hence **Mu·tilator,** also †**-er,** one who mutilates.

Mutilation (miūtilē[i]·ʃən). 1525. [– late L. *mutilatio*, f. as prec.; see -ION. Cf. (O)Fr. *mutilation.*] The action of mutilating; deprivation of a limb or of an essential part. **b.** *spec.* Castration 1727.

†**Mutilous,** *a.* 1649. [f. L. *mutilus* (see MUTILATE *v.*) + -OUS.] Of things: Mutilated, imperfect –1707.

†**Mutine**, *sb.* and *a.*[1] 1560. [– (O)Fr. *mutin* adj. and sb., f. *muete* (mod. *meute*) :– Rom. **movita* movement; see MUTE *sb.*[3]] **1.** Popular tumult; rebellion, mutiny –1600. **2.** A mutineer –1604. **3.** *adj.* Mutinous –1598.

‖**Mutine** (mütin), *a.*[2] 1870. [Fr., fem. of *mutin* adj.; see prec.] Of a girl's or woman's looks; Rebellious, unsubmissive.

†**Mutine**, *v.* 1555. [– Fr. *mutiner*, f. *mutin*; see MUTINE *sb.*] **1.** *intr.* To rebel, mutiny –1692. Also *fig.* **2.** *trans.* To incite to revolt –1613. Hence †**Mutiner** = next 1569.

Mutineer (miūtinīᵊ·ɹ), *sb.* 1610. [– Fr. *mutinier* (XVI), f. *mutin*; see MUTINE *sb.*, -EER[1].] One who mutinies. **Mutinee·r** *v.* to mutiny.

Mutinize (miū·tinəiz), *v.* Now *arch.* 1605. [f. MUTINE *sb.* + -IZE.] †**a.** *intr.* To mutiny. **b.** *trans.* To cause mutiny in.

Mutinous (miū·tinəs), *a.* 1578. [f. MUTINE *sb.* + -OUS.] **1.** Given to mutiny, rebellious; †turbulent –1621. **b.** *transf.* and *fig.* of the elements, passions, etc. 1610. **2.** Of the nature of or proceeding from mutiny; characterized by or expressing mutiny 1592. **3.** = MUTINE *a.*[2] 1882.

1. The m. humour of the Camp SIR T. HERBERT. **b.** I haue..call'd forth the mutenous windes SHAKS. **2.** For the late license of printing all m. and seditious discourses was not yet in fashion 1647. Hence **Mu·tinous-ly** *adv.*, **-ness.**

Mutiny (miū·tini), *sb.* 1567. [f. MUTINE *v.* or *sb.* + -Y[3].] **1.** Open revolt against constituted authority; now chiefly *spec.* revolt of soldiers or sailors against their officers; behaviour subversive of discipline 1579. **b.** A mutinous revolt 1581. **c.** In attrib. uses; now often with sense 'that took part in or was present during the Indian Mutiny' 1731. †**2.** Discord, contention; a state of discord, a dispute, quarrel –1667.

1. Hear a rumour of the Goorkha corps..in open m., and refusing to march 1857. **b.** *The Indian M.*, a revolt of the native troops of Bengal in 1857–1858. **c.** *M. Act*, an Act, passed annually from 1689 to 1879, dealing with offences against discipline in the military and naval forces, etc., now embodied in the Army Act, 1881. I was a M. baby, as they call it KIPLING. **2.** *Rom. & Jul.* I. v. 82.

Mutiny (miū·tini), *v.* 1584. [f. prec.] **1.** *intr.* To commit the offence of mutiny; to rise in revolt *against* (rarely †*upon*); to refuse submission to discipline or obedience to the lawful command of a superior, esp. in the military and naval services. †**b.** To contend (*with*); to quarrel –1603. †**2.** *trans.* To cause to mutiny or rebel *against* –1648.

1. *fig.* The powers of pleasure m. for employment JOHNSON. **b.** My very haires do m.: for the white Reproue the browne for rashnesse, and they them For feare SHAKS.

Mutism (miū·tiz'm). 1824. [– Fr. *mutisme*, f. L. *mutus*; see MUTE *a.*, -ISM.] The state or condition of being mute or a mute.

Muto- (miū·to), used as comb. form of L. *mutare* to change: **Mu·tograph**, an apparatus for taking a series of photographs of objects in motion; hence **Mu·tograph** *v. trans.* **Mu·toscope**, an apparatus for exhibiting a scene recorded by the mutograph; hence **Mutosco·pic** *a.*

Mutt (mɒt). *slang* (orig. *U.S.*). 1910. [abbrev. of *mutton-head.*] An ignorant blunderer; a blockhead; *contempt.* a small dog.

Mutter (mɒ·təɹ), *v.* late ME. [frequent. formation (see -ER[5]) on a base **mut-*, repr. also in MUTE *a.*; cf. G. dial. *muttern.*] **1.** *intr.* To speak in low and barely audible tones, with the mouth nearly closed. **b.** *esp.* To murmur, complain, grumble (*against, at*) 1548. **c.** *transf.* To make a low rumbling sound, as thunder 1797. **2.** *trans.* To utter with imperfect articulation and in a low tone. Also *fig.* to express or say in secret. late ME.

1. Seeke..vnto wizards that peepe and that m. *Isa.* 8:19. **b.** The worthie magistrate Moses was muttered against ABP. SANDYS. **2.** There are a kinde of men, So loose of Soule, that in their sleepes will m. Their Affayres SHAKS. Hence **Mu·tter** *sb.*, the act of muttering, **Mu·tterer, Mu·tteringly** *adv.*

Mutton (mɒ·t'n). [ME. *moto(u)n* – OFr. *moton* (mod. *mouton*) :– med.L. *multo, -on-*, prob. of Gaul. origin (cf. OIr., Ir. *molt* ram, Gael. *mult* wether, W. *mollt*, Corn. *mols*, Breton *maout* sheep).] **1.** The flesh of sheep, as food. **2.** A sheep, esp. one intended to be eaten. Now only *joc.* ME. **b.** The carcase of a sheep. *Obs.* or *arch.* 1607. **3.** *slang.* Food for lust; loose women, prostitutes. Also *laced m.* (see LACED *ppl. a.*[1]). late ME. †**4.** Short for *mutton-candle* (see below) –1859.

1. They..had a breast of m. and a pint of wine SWIFT. **2.** Pious men, Like muttons in a pen THACKERAY. Phr. *As dead as m.*: quite dead. *To take* (or *eat*) *a bit of* (or *one's*) *m. with*: to dine with. *To return to one's muttons* (joc.), to return to the matter in hand (after Fr. *revenons à nos moutons*).

Comb.: **m.-bird**, any of several petrels and shearwaters of the genera *Œstrelata* and *Puffinus* of the South Seas; **-broth; -candle**, a candle made of mutton-fat; **-fist** *slang*, a large red coarse hand, or a person having such a hand; **-ham**, a leg of mutton cured like a ham; **-head** *colloq.*, a dull, stupid person; hence **-headed** *a.*; †**-monger** *slang*, a whoremonger; a great eater of mutton; a sheep-stealer; **-wood**, a composite tree (*Olearia colensoi*) of New Zealand; so called because it grows on islands frequented by mutton-birds.

Mu:tton-cho·p. 1720. A piece of mutton (usually one rib with the end chopped off, together with half the vertebra to which it is attached) for broiling or frying.

Mutton-chop (*whisker*): a side whisker shaped like a mutton-chop, i.e. roundish at one end and narrow and prolonged at the other.

Mu·tton-fish. 1735. **1.** A name for various American and W. Indian sea-fish, esp. the eel-like *Zoarces anguillaris*. **2.** *Austral.* An ormer 1882.

Muttony (mɒ·t'ni), *a.* 1858. [f. MUTTON + -Y[1].] Having the qualities of mutton.

Mutual (miū·tiuăl), *a.* 1477. [– (O)Fr. *mutuel*, f. L. *mutuus* borrowed, mutual :– **moitwos*, f. **moi-* change, as in *mutare*; see MUTABLE, -AL[1].] **1.** Of relations, feelings, actions: Possessed, entertained, or done by each towards or with regard to the other; reciprocal. **b.** Qualifying personal designations of relationship, friendship, or hostility 1562. **c.** *transf.* Pertaining to or characterized by some (implied) mutual action or relation 1848. **2.** Respective; belonging to each respectively 1548. †**3.** Of intercourse: Intimate –1749. **4.** Pertaining to both parties; common. (Now regarded as incorrect.) 1591. †**5.** Responsive –1850.

1. M. fear is the only solid basis of alliance JOWETT. Phr. *M. admiration society*: a coterie of persons who over-estimate each other's merits 1858. **b.** Kings And subjects, m. foes SHELLEY. **c.** *M. terms, principles*: name for a business arrangement in which exchange of services takes the place of money payments 1848. **2.** The time would not allow them to enter into minute details of their m. adventures 1796. **4.** Mr. Hobhouse was desirous that I should express our m. opinion of Pope BYRON. Our m. friend Mr. Wright SCOTT. **5.** Who then could guess If ever more should meet those m. eyes! BYRON. Hence **Mu·tual-ly** *adv.*, **-ness.**

Mutualism (miū·tiuăliz'm). 1863. [f. MUTUAL *a.* + -ISM.] **1.** The doctrine that individual and collective well-being is attainable only by mutual dependence. **2.** *Biol.* A condition of symbiosis in which two associated organisms contribute mutually to the well-being of each other 1876. So **Mu·tualist**, an advocate of m. 1892; *Biol.* one of two organisms which mutually live on each other 1876.

Mutuality (miūtiu,æ·lĭti). 1586. [f. MUTUAL *a.* + -ITY.] **1.** The quality or condition of being mutual; reciprocity. **b.** *Law.* A condition of things under which two parties are mutually bound to perform certain reciprocal duties 1845. **2.** Interchange of acts of goodwill; intimacy 1604. **3.** *Biol.* The rendering of mutual service by organisms in the condition of symbiosis 1876.

Mutualize (miū·tiuăləiz), *v.* 1812. [f. MUTUAL *a.* + -IZE.] *trans.* and *intr.* To make or become mutual. Hence **Mutualiza·tion.**

Mutuary (miū·tiu,ări). 1839. [– L. *mutuarius*, f. *mutuus* borrowed; see -ARY[1].] *Civil Law.* The borrower in a contract of mutuum.

†**Mu·tuate**, *v.* 1548. [– *mutuat-*, pa. ppl. stem of L. *mutuari* borrow, f. *mutuus*; see MUTUAL *a.*, -ATE[3].] *trans.* To borrow –1716. So †**Mutua·tion** 1604–1827. †**Mutuati·tious** *a.* borrowed 1625–1813.

Mutule (miū·tiul). 1563. [– Fr. *mutule* (XVI), f. L. *mutulus* modillion.] *Arch.* A block projecting under the corona of the Doric cornice, corresp. to the modillion of other orders.

†**Mu·tuum.** 1486. [– L. *mutuum* loan, n. of *mutuus* borrowed; see MUTUAL.] *Civil Law.* A contract under which such things are lent as are consumed in the use, on condition that they are restored in kind and of the same quantity and quality –1839.

Muzarab(ic, var. ff. MOZARAB(IC.

Muzhik, var. of MOUJIK.

Muzz (mɒz), *sb. slang.* Also **muz.** 1788. [Goes with next.] One who 'muzzes' over books.

Muzz (mɒz), *v. slang.* 1775. [Of unkn. origin. Cf. MUG *v.*[3]] **1.** *intr.* To study intently; to 'mug'. Const. *over.* **2.** *trans.* To render 'muzzy'; to fuddle (cf. MUZZLE *v.*[2]) 1787.

Muzzle (mɒ·z'l), *sb.* [ME. *mosel* (XIV) – OFr. *musel* (mod. *museau*) :– Gallo-Rom. **musellum*, dim. of med.L. *musum* (cf. MUSE *v.*), of unkn. origin.] **I. 1.** The projecting part of an animal's head which includes the nose and mouth. **2.** That end of a fire-arm from which the shot is discharged; *spec.* in a cannon, the part extending from the astragal to the extreme end mouldings 1566. †**3.** The nozzle of a pair of bellows. SWIFT. **4.** *Agric.* The clevis or bridle of a plough 1765.

1. *transf.* Of a black m., and long beard, beware DRYDEN. **2.** *Charged* (*crammed*) *to the m.*: loaded, filled, or stuffed *with*. The boy..crammed to the m. with lies MEREDITH.

II. An arrangement of straps or wires, put over an animal's mouth to prevent it from biting, eating, or rooting. late ME. **b.** An ornamental piece of armour covering a horse's nose 1860.

A moosle that letteth dogges to bite 1556. *fig.* So to enure Rome to the snaffle, and break the Senate to the musle 1644.

Comb.: **m.-loader**, a gun that is loaded at the m. (opp. to *breech-loader*); so **-loading** *ppl. a.*; **-sight**, a sight placed at or near the m. of a gun; **m. velocity**, the velocity at which a projectile leaves the muzzle of a gun.

Mu·zzle, *v.*[1] late ME. [f. MUZZLE *sb.*] **1.** *intr.* To thrust out the muzzle or nose; to feel, smell, or root about with the muzzle 1489. **2.** *trans.* To bring the muzzle or snout close to 1600. †**b.** To root about or amongst –1733. †**c.** 'To fondle with the mouth close. A low word' (J.). –1708. **3.** To put a muzzle on (an animal or its mouth) 1470. †**4.** *transf.* To muffle. late ME; *Sc.* to veil, mask (the face) 1457–1590. **5.** To restrain from speaking 1531. **6.** *Naut.* †**a.** *To lie muzzled*: (of a ship) to remain inactive. **b.** In yachting use: To take in (a sail). 1697.

1. If we euer be like swine, muzling in the ground HIERON. **2.** The Bear comes directly up to Him, Muzzles, and Smells to him R. L'ESTRANGE. **3.** Thou shalt not mosell the mouth of the oxe TINDALE 1 *Cor.* 9:9. *fig.* My dagger muzzel'd SHAKS. **5.** What establishment can m. its fools and lunatics SYD. SMITH.

Mu·zzle, *v.*[2] *dial.* 1796. [app. connected with MUZZ *v.* and MUZZY.] **a.** *trans.* To make 'muzzy'; to fuddle. **b.** *intr.* To drink to excess 1828.

Muzzy (mɒ·zi), *a. colloq.* and *dial.* 1727. [Of unkn. origin. Cf. prec.] **1.** Dull, stupid, spiritless, gloomy; also, mentally hazy. Of times, places: Dully, gloomy. **b.** *transf.* Blurred 1832. **2.** Stupid with excess of liquor 1775.

1. A damn'd m. dinner at Boodle's 1770. His view of the past will be rather m. THACKERAY. **b.** The execution..is vague and m. 1867. **2.** His m., whiskified brain THACKERAY. Hence **Mu·zzily** *adv.* **Mu·zziness.**

My (məi, *unstressed* mi), *poss. adj.* [Early ME. *mi*, reduced form of *min* (see MINE *poss. pron.*), used orig. bef. consonants except *h*, and becoming later the poss. adj. of the 1st pers. sing. in prose use.] **1.** Of or belonging to me. The poss. genitive of I *pron.* **b.** Used with vague application. Also with ethical force in certain idiomatic collocations. 1592. **2. a.** Prefixed affectionately, compassionately or familiarly, to certain terms of address, as *my boy, my friend, my man, my good fellow*, also *my son, my daughter* (but, as a rule, not to other terms of relationship, as *father, mother*, etc., used vocatively) ME. **b.** *esp.* in *my dear* (*dearest*), *my love*, etc. 1807. **c.** Prefixed to the name of the person addressed 1732. **3.** In ejaculations, as *my eye! my word!* etc. (see these words); *my God!* used to express strong feeling or excitement; whence (ellipt.) *My!*

or *Oh, my!* which is common (esp. *U.S.*) as a mild exclam. of surprise; also *Oh-my* vb., to say 'Oh, my!' 1707.

1. My time will now be my own GIBBON. b. I brought down my bird every shot 1808. 2. c. Awake, my St. John! POPE. 3. My, what a race I've had! 'MARK TWAIN'. The servant maids.. were listening and..oh-mying over the bargains 1893.

Myal (məi·ăl). 1774. [perh. of W. Afr. origin.] Only in attrib. use denoting persons or things associated with the practice of **Myalism** (1843), a kind of sorcery practised esp. by the natives of the W. Indies. Hence **My·alist** 1851.

||**Myalgia** (məi,æ·ldʒiă). 1860. [mod.L., f. Gr. μῦς muscle + -αλγία, ἄλγος pain.] *Path.* Pain in the muscles; muscular rheumatism. Hence **Mya·lgic** *a.*

Myall[1] (məi·ăl). 1835. [Native name: in Bigambel (Dumaresque River) *mail* the blacks (*namail* a black).] A wild·aboriginal of Australia.

Myall[2] (məi·ăl). 1845. [Native name: in Kamilaroi (Hunter River) *maiāl*.] An Australian acacia or its wood, esp. *Acacia pendula* or *A. homalophylla* (which yields a useful hard scented wood).

||**Myasthenia** (məi,ăsþī·niă). 1856. [mod. L., f. Gr. μῦς muscle + ἀσθένεια weakness.] Muscular weakness. Hence **Myasthe·nic** *a.*

||**Mycelium** (məisī·liŏm). 1836. [mod.L., f. Gr. μύκης mushroom, after *epithelium.*] *Bot.* The vegetative part of the thallus of fungi, consisting of white filamentous tubes (hyphæ); the spawn of mushrooms. Hence **Myce·lial, Myce·lian** *adjs.* consisting of or characterized by m. **Myce·lioid** *a.* resembling or having the structure of m.

Mycenæan (məisīnī·ăn). 1797. [f. L. *Mycenæus* (f. *Mycenæ*) + -AN.] **A.** *adj.* Of or belonging to Mycenæ, an ancient Greek city in the Argive plain, and esp. its civilization, culture, art, etc. **B.** *sb.* A native or inhabitant of Mycenæ.

||**Mycetes** (məisī·tīz), *sb. pl.* 1876. [mod.L., – Gr. μύκητες, pl. of μύκης mushroom, fungus.] *Biol.* The group of organisms known as microbes. Hence **Myce·tic** *a.*

Myceto- (məisī·to, məisĭtǫ·), bef. a vowel **mycet-**, comb. f. Gr. μύκης mushroom. **Myceto·logy**, the science of fungi. ||**Mycetozo·a**, a group of fungoid organisms, consisting chiefly of the Myxomycetes; also **Mycetozo·an**, ||**-zo·on**, a member of this group.

||**Mycetoma** (məisĭtōu·mă). 1874. [mod.L.; see prec., -OMA.] *Path.* A fungoid disease of the foot (or hand). Hence **Myceto·matous** *a.*

Myco- (məi·ko), irreg. comb. form (for MYCETO-) of Gr. μύκης mushroom, as in **mycodextrin, -inulin, -protein**, substances occurring in certain fungi; also **Myco·logy**, that branch of botany which treats of fungi; hence **Mycolo·gic, -al** *a.*, **-ly** *adv.*, **Myco·logist; Myco·phagy**, the eating of fungi or mushrooms; hence **Myco·phagist.**

||**Mycoderma** (məikodɔ̄·ɹmă). Also **my·coderm.** 1846. [mod.L.; see MYCO-, DERMA.] The pellicle which forms on the surface of liquors during alcoholic fermentation ('mother of vinegar'); hence as the name of a genus of fermentation-fungi. Hence **Mycode·rmatoid, -de·rmatous, -de·rmic** *adjs.*

||**Mycosis** (məikōu·sis). 1876. [f. Gr. μύκης mushroom + -OSIS.] *Path.* A disease caused by parasitic fungi in any part of the body. Hence **Myco·tic** *a.*

Mycterism (mi·ktĕriz'm). *rare.* 1593. [– Gr. μυκτηρισμός, f. μυκτηρίζειν sneer at, f. μυκτήρ nose.] A gibe or scoff.

Mydaleine (məidēi·lī,in). 1887. [f. Gr. μυδαλέος dripping, wet + -INE[5].] *Physiol. Chem.* A poisonous ptomaine obtained from putrid flesh and herring brines.

||**Mydriasis** (midriēi·sis). 1805. [L. – Gr. μυδρίασις.] *Path.* Excessive dilatation of the pupil of the eye. Hence **Mydria·tic** *a.*

||**Myelencephalon** (məi:ĕlense·fălǫn). 1866. [f. Gr. μυελός, -όν marrow + ENCEPHALON.] *Anat.* **a.** The cerebro-spinal axis or system (Owen). **b.** The medulla oblongata (Huxley). So **Myelencepha·lic** *a.* pertaining to or connected with the m. 1866.

Myelin, -ine (məi·ĕlin). 1867. [– G. *myelin*, f. Gr. μυελός marrow; see -IN[1], -INE[5].] **1.** *Chem.* Virchow's term for a fatty substance obtainable from various animal tissues (e.g. brain-substance, yolk of egg), and also from some vegetable tissues. **2.** *Anat.* The medullary sheath of nerve-fibres, or white substance of Schwann 1873.

Myelitis (məi,ĕləi·tis). 1835. [– mod.L., f. Gr. μυελός marrow + -ITIS.] Inflammation of the spinal cord. Hence **Myeli·tic** *a.*

Myelo- (məi·ĕlo, məi,ĕlǫ·), bef. a vowel **Myel-**, comb. f. Gr. μυελός, -όν marrow. **My·elocœle** [Gr. κοῖλος hollow], the cavity of the myelon or spinal cord. **Myeloge·nic** *a.* originating in the bone marrow. **Myelo·pathy**, disease of the spinal cord; hence **Myelopa·thic** *a.*

Myeloid (məi·ĕloid), *a.* 1857. [f. Gr. μυελός marrow + -OID.] Resembling or pertaining to marrow.

||**Myiasis** (məi,iēi·sis). 1837. [mod.L., f. Gr. μυῖα fly + -ASIS.] *Path.* Injury inflicted by dipterous larvæ on the human body.

||**Mylodon** (məi·lŏdǫn). 1839. [mod.L., f. Gr. μύλη, μύλος molar, prop. mill, millstone + ὀδούς, ὀδοντ- tooth. Cf. MASTODON.] A genus of gigantic extinct sloths from the Pleistocene, having teeth more or less cylindrical. So **My·lodont** *sb.* and *a.*

Mylohyoid (məilohəi·oid), *a.* and *sb.* 1838. [– mod.L. *mylohyoideus* (also used earlier), f. Gr. μύλη, -ος (see prec.) + ὑοειδής HYOID.] Applied to a flat triangular muscle extending from the lower jaw to the hyoid bone.

Myna: see MINA[2].

||**Mynheer** (mainhē·r, mənē·r). 1652. [Du. *mijnheer*, f. *mijn* my + *heer* lord, master.] The Dutch equivalent of 'sir', 'Mr.'; hence, a Dutchman.

Myo- (məi·o), comb. f. Gr. μῦς (gen. μυός) muscle. ||**Myoco·mma** (pl. **-co·mmata, -co·mmas**) [Gr. κόμμα segment], one of the divisions of the muscular system of lower vertebrates. **Myodyna·mics** *sb. pl.*, that branch of physiology which treats of muscular contraction. ||**Myofibro·ma**, a tumour consisting of muscular and fibrous tissue. **Myoge·nic** *a.* produced by or arising in the muscles. **Myo·pathy** [-PATHY], any affection of the muscles. **Myophy·sics**, the physics of muscular action. **Myopo·lar** *a.* relating to muscular polarity. **Myosarco·ma**, a sarcoma partly composed of muscular tissue. **My·oscope** [-SCOPE], an instrument for observing muscular contraction.

||**Myocardium** (məi,okā·ɹdiŏm). 1866. [mod.L., f. Gr. μυο- MYO- + καρδία heart; see -IUM.] The muscular substance of the heart. Hence **Myoca·rdial** *a.* Also **My:ocardi·tis**, inflammation of the m.; whence **My:ocardi·tic** *a.*

Myograph (məi·ŏgrɑf). 1867. [f. MYO- + -GRAPH.] An instrument for taking tracings of muscular contractions and relaxations. Hence **Myogra·phic, -al** *a.* So **My·ogram**, a tracing made by a m. 1890.

Myology (məi,ǫ·lŏdʒi). 1649. [– mod.L. *myologia*; see MYO-, -LOGY.] That branch of anatomy which treats of muscles. **b.** A myological description; the myological features of an animal. Hence **Myolo·gic, -al** *a.* **Myo·logist.**

||**Myoma** (məi,ōu·mă). 1875. [mod.L., f. Gr. μῦς muscle + -ωμα (after *sarcoma*).] *Path.* A tumour composed of muscular tissue. Hence **Myo·matous** *a.*

Myomorph (məi·ŏmǭɹf). 1887. [– mod. L. *Myomorpha*, f. Gr., μῦς, μυ(ο)- mouse + μορφή shape.] *Zool.* A rodent of the division *Myomorpha* (including mice, rats, dormice, etc.). So **Myomo·rphic** 1880, **-mo·rphine** 1898 *adjs.*

Myope (məi·oup). 1728. [– Fr. *myope* (XVI) – late L. *myops*, *myop-* – Gr. μύωψ, μυωπ-, f. μύειν shut + ὤψ eye.] A short-sighted person. So ||**Myo·pia, My·opy**, short-sightedness. Hence **Myopic** (məi,ǫ·pik) *a.*; **My·opism**, myopia.

Myosin (məi·ŏsin). Also **-ine.** 1869. [f. Gr. μῦς muscle + -OSE[2] + -IN[1].] *Chem.* The chief ingredient of the clot formed on coagulation of muscle-plasma.

||**Myosis** (məi,ōu·sis). 1819. [f. Gr. μύειν to shut the eyes + -OSIS.] *Path.* Contraction of the pupil of the eye. Hence **Myotic** (məi,ǫ·tik) *a.* pertaining to or causing m.; *sb.* an agent which causes m.

Myosote (məi·ŏsōut). 1879. [– L. *myosotis* – Gr. μυοσωτίς, f. μυός, gen. of μῦς mouse + οὖς, ὠτ- ear.] The forget-me-not, *Myosotis palustris.*

Myotome (məi·ŏtōum). 1846. [f. MYO- + -TOME.] **1.** *Anat.* A muscular segment or metamere 1856. **2.** *Surg.* An instrument for dividing muscle. So **Myoto·mic** *a.* pertaining to myotomy or a m. 1856.

Myotomy (məi,ǫ·tŏmi). 1676. [– mod.L *myotomia*; see MYO-, -TOMY.] Dissection, anatomy, or surgical division of muscles.

Myria- (mi·riă), rarely **myrio-**, bef. a vowel **myri-**, comb. f. Gr. μυριάς MYRIAD (or μυρίοι countless, μύριοι 10,000). **1.** With the meaning 'ten thousand', in names of weights and measures of the metric system: **My·riagram(me, -litre, -metre, My·riare** = 10,000 grammes, litres, metres, ares. 1804. **2.** With the meaning 'very numerous'; **Myriaca·nthous** *a.* [Gr. ἄκανθος thorn], having very many spines; etc. 1856.

Myriad (mi·riăd). 1555. [– late L. *myrias*, *-ad-* – Gr. μυριάς, -αδ-, f. μυρίος countless, innumerable, pl. μυρίοι 10,000. Cf. Fr. *myriade* (XVII); see -AD.] **A.** *sb.* **1.** As a numeral: Ten thousand. **2.** *transf.* (*pl.*) Countless numbers, hosts (*of*) 1555. **b.** *sing.* in same sense 1850. **3.** *absol.* Countless numbers of men, animals, or inanimate things (indicated contextually) 1559. **b.** *sing.* in same sense 1718.

2. Their myriads of horses WELLINGTON. 3. Who ..Cloth'd with transcendent brightness didst outshine Myriads though bright MILT.

B. *adj.* Existing in myriads; countless. Chiefly *poet.* 1800. **b.** with *sing. sb.* Consisting of myriads. Also, having a myriad phases. 1817.

The City's moonlit spires and m. lamps SHELLEY. b. The m. mind of Shakespeare 1854. *Comb.*, as *m.-handed, -minded* adjs. Hence **My·riadfold** *a.* countless in number or aspects; *sb.* only advb., with indef. article: *A m.*, an infinite amount. **My·riadth** *a.* that is a very minute part of a whole.

Myriapod (mi·riăpǫd). Also **myrio-**. 1826. [– mod.L. *Myriapoda*; see MYRIA-, -POD.] **A.** *adj.* Having very numerous legs; *spec.* pertaining to or having the characteristics of the class *Myriapoda* of arthropodous animals, comprising the centipedes and millipedes. **B.** *sb.* One of these.

Hence **Myria·podan, Myria·podous** *adjs.* = MYRIAPOD *a.*

||**Myrica** (mirəi·kă). 1706. [L. – Gr. μυρίκη.] **1.** The tamarisk. **2.** A Linnæan genus of shrubs including the bog myrtle, *M. gale* 1797.

Comb. **m.-tallow, -wax** = myrtle wax.

Myricin (mirəi·sin, mi·-, məiə·risin). Also **-ine.** 1821. [f. prec. + -IN[1].] *Chem.* That part of bees-wax which is insoluble in boiling alcohol.

Myrio-: see MYRIA-.

Myriologue (mi·riŏlǫg). 1824. [– mod. Gr. μυριολόγιον, corrupt f. μοιρολόγιον, f. μοῖρα fate + λόγος speech.] An extemporaneous funeral song, composed and sung by a woman. Hence **Myriolo·gical** *a.* So **Myrio·logist**, one who sings or composes a m.

Myriorama (miriŏræ·mă, -ā·mă). 1824. [f. MYRIO-, after *panorama*.] A picture made of a number of separate sections which are capable of being combined in numerous ways so as to form different scenes. **b.** An entertainment consisting of a series of views 1901.

Myristic (məi-, miri·stik), *a.* 1848. [f. med.L. (*nux*) *myristica*, Linnæan generic name of the nutmeg-tree, f. Gr. μυρίζειν anoint.] *Chem.* In *m. acid*: a fatty acid found in nutmeg-oil and other vegetable and animal fats. Hence **Myri·state**, a salt of m. acid. **Myri·stin**, the glyceride of m. acid. **Myri·stone**, a crystalline substance obtained by the distillation of calcium myristate.

Myrmeco- (mɔ̄·ɹmĭko, -kǫ·, məɹmī·ko), comb. form of Gr. μύρμηξ, μυρμηκ- ant; as in: **Myrmecolo·gical** *a.*, pertaining to myrmecology. **Myrmeco·logy**, the scientific study of ants; whence **Myrmeco·logist. Myrmeco·phagous** *a.* ant-eating. **Myrmeco·philous** *a.* applied to insects that live in ant-hills or to plants that are cross-fertilized by ants.

Myrmecoid (mə̄·ɹmīkoid), *a. rare.* 1861. [- Gr. μυρμηκοειδής, f. μύρμηξ ant; see -OID.] Ant-like.

Myrmicine (mə·ɹmisəin), *a.* 1881. [- mod.L. *Myrmicinæ*, f. *Myrmica*: see -INE[1].] *Entom.* Of or belonging to the sub-family *Myrmicinæ* of stinging ants.

Myrmidon (mə̄·ɹmidən). late ME. [- L. *Myrmidones* pl. - Gr. Μυρμιδόνες, acc. to legend orig. created from ants (μύρμηκες).] **1.** (With capital M.) One of a warlike race of men inhabiting Thessaly, who followed Achilles to the siege of Troy (*Il.* ii. 684). **b.** Used of Achilles himself. *Tr. & Cr.* I. iii. 378. **2.** *transf.* A faithful follower or servant. Now chiefly *joc.* 1610. **3.** In derogatory sense: An unscrupulously faithful attendant or hireling; a hired ruffian 1649.

2. Now, my myrmidons, fall on 1698. **3.** *M. of the law, of justice*: applied contempt. to a policeman, bailiff, or other inferior administrative officer of the law. Bow-street myrmidons BYRON. Hence **Myrmido·nian** *a.* 1624.

Myrobalan (məirǫ·bălăn). late ME. [- (O)Fr. *myrobalan* or its source L. *myrobalanum* - Gr. μυροβάλανος, f. μύρον balsam, unguent + βάλανος acorn, date, ben-nut.] **1.** The astringent plum-like fruit of species of *Terminalia*, e.g. *T. bellerica* (see BELLERIC), *T. chebula* (see CHEBULE), *T. citrina*; formerly used medicinally, but now chiefly in dyeing, tanning, and ink-making. **2.** A variety of plum 1664.

Myronic (məirǫ·nik), *a.* 1840. [- Fr. *myronique* (Bussy), f. Gr. μύρον unguent, perfume; see -IC.] In *m. acid*, an acid obtained from black mustard. Hence **My·ronate**, a salt of m. acid.

Myrosin (məiə·rǒsin). Also **-ine, -yne.** 1840. [- Fr. *myrosyne* (Bussy), f. as prec. (with inserted *s*); see -INE[5].] *Chem.* A nitrogenous ferment contained in the seeds of black mustard.

Myrrh[1] (mǝ̄ɹ). [OE. *myrra, myrre*, corresp. to OS. *myrra* (Du. *mirre*), OHG. *myrra* (G. *myrrhe*), ON. *mirra*; Gmc. = L. *myrrha* - Gr. μύρρα, of Semitic origin (cf. Arab. *murr*, Aram. *mūrā*); reinforced in ME. from OFr. *mirre* (mod. *myrrhe*).] **1.** A gum-resin produced by several species of *Commiphora* (*Balsamodendron*), esp. *C. myrrha* (see 2); used for perfumery and as an ingredient in incense. Also *Med.* the tincture made from this. **†2.** Any shrub or tree that yields the gum-resin, esp. *Commiphora* (*Balsamodendron*) *myrrha* -1634.

1. Often with ref. to *Matt.* 2: 11. **2.** With Groves of myrrhe, and cinnamon MILT.

Comb.: **m. resin**, a resin obtained from m. by alcohol; **m.-seed**, a book-name for *Myrospermum pubescens*. Hence **Myrrhed** (mǝ̄ɹd) *ppl. a.* mixed or sprinkled with m. (*rare*) 1450. **My·rrhy** *a.* smelling like m. 1842.

Myrrh[2] (mǝ̄ɹ). 1597. [- L. *myrris* - Gr. μυρρίς.] Sweet Cicely, *Myrrhis odorata.*

Myrrhine: see MURRHINE.

My·rrh-tree. late ME. [MYRRH[1].] = MYRRH[1] 2.

†Myrt. late ME. [- L. *myrtus*; see MYRTLE. Cf. (O)Fr. *myrte*.] = MYRTLE -1615.

Myrtaceous (məɹtē[i]·ʃəs), *a. Bot.* 1835. [- mod. L. *Myrtaceæ*, fem. pl. of L. *myrtaceus* (Celsus), f. *myrtus*; see prec., -ACEOUS.] Belonging to the N.O. *Myrtaceæ*, of which the myrtle is the type.

Myrtiform (mǝ̄·ɹtifǭɹm), *a.* 1840. [f. L. *myrtus* myrtle + -FORM.] Of the shape of a myrtle-berry; in *m. caruncle, fossa.*

Myrtle (mǝ̄·ɹt'l). late ME. [- med.L. *myrtilla, -us* (whence OFr. *myrtille, -il*), dim. of L. *myrtus, -a* - Gr. μύρτος.] **†1.** The fruit or berry of the myrtle tree -1732. **2.** A plant of the genus *Myrtus*, esp. *M. communis*, the Common Myrtle, a shrub having shiny evergreen leaves and white sweet-scented flowers, now used chiefly in perfumery. The myrtle was held sacred to Venus and is used as an emblem of love. Also applied with qualifying word to allied or similar plants, esp. of the genus *Myrica*, as *bog m.*, *Dutch m.*, Sweet Gale, *Myrica gale.* 1562. **3.** Short for *myrtle-green* 1884.

2. I will plant in the wildernes..the M., and the Oyle tree *Isa.* 41: 19. The Sweet Gale or Bog M., ..the badge of the Campbells 1866.

attrib. and *Comb.*, as *m. wreath*, etc.; **m. bird** (U.S.), *Dendroica* (*Silvicola*) *coronata*, which feeds on the berries of the candleberry m.; **m. green,** a shade of green like that of m. leaves; **m. wax,** wax produced by the candleberry m.

My·rtle-berry. 1579. **a.** The fruit of the myrtle (*Myrtus*). **b.** The bilberry or whortleberry. **c.** *Myrtle-berry wax* = myrtle wax.

Myself (məise·lf, mise·lf), *pron.* OE. [orig. ME *acc.-dat. pron.* + SELF, q.v. The transition from *meself* to *miself, myself* was prob. due, partly to unstressing of the vowel of *me*, partly to the analogy of *herself*, in which *her* was felt as a possessive genitive.] **I.** Emphatic uses. **1.** In apposition with *I*: In my own person; for my part. **2.** By ellipsis of *I*, *myself* comes to be used as a nominative. (As simple subject, now only *poet.*) ME. **3.** Substituted for ME as the object of a verb or governed by a prep. ME. **4.** (passing into *sb.*) My being or personality; my own or very self 1526.

1. I my selff will fight agaynst you COVERDALE *Jer.* 21: 5. **2.** Ther was also a Reve and a Millere, ..A Maunciple, and m. CHAUCER. M. when young did eagerly frequent Doctor and Saint FITZ-GERALD. One of our party and m. started on an expedition 1866. **3.** To m., mountains are the beginning and the end of all natural scenery RUSKIN. **4.** †*Another m.* [after L. *alter ego*]: a second self. *To be m., to feel like m.*: to be, or feel as if I were, in my normal condition of body or mind.

II. Reflexive uses. As direct or indirect obj., in acc. and inf. const., or in dependence on a prep. (Orig. only emphatic refl., but now in gen. use, repl. the refl. *me*, which is now only *arch.*) OE.

I very often walk by m. in Westminster Abbey ADDISON.

Mystacal (mi·stăkăl), *a.* 1888. [f. Gr. μύσταξ, μυστακ- (see MOUSTACHE) + -AL[1].] Resembling a moustache. So **Mysta·cial** *a.* 1782.

Mystagogue (mi·stăgǫg). 1550. [- Fr. *mystagogue* or L. *mystagogus* - Gr. μυσταγωγός, f. μύστης initiated person + ἀγωγός leading, f. ἄγειν lead.] A teacher of mystical doctrines; *orig.*, to candidates for initiation into the Eleusinian or other mysteries. Hence **Mystagogic** (-gǫ·dʒik), **-al** *a.* pertaining to a m. or mystagogy; **-ly** *adv.* **My·stagogy,** interpretation of mysteries; initiation, or instruction preparatory to initiation, in mysteries.

Mysterial (mistĭə·riăl), *a.* Now *rare.* 1529. [- late L. *mysterialis*, f. *mysterium* MYSTERY[1]; see -AL[1].] Mysterious; †mystical. So **†Myste·rially** *adv.* late ME. only.

Mysteriarch (mistĭə·riăɹk). 1656. [- eccl. L. *mysteriarches* - Gr. μυστηριάρχης, f. μυστήριον MYSTERY[1]; see -ARCH.] One who presides over mysteries.

Mysterious (mistĭə·riəs), *a.* 1616. [- Fr. *mystérieux*, f. *mystère* MYSTERY[1]; see -IOUS.] **1.** Full of, or wrapt in, mystery; of obscure origin, nature, or purpose. **2.** Of persons: **†a.** Dealing with or versed in mysteries; using occult arts. **b.** Whose movements are full of mystery; delighting in mystery 1620. **3.** That is due to a mystery. MILT. *P.L.* viii. 599.

1. God moves in a m. way His wonders to perform COWPER. A few m. words having been exchanged 1797. It is a m. sea, that has baffled for centuries the research of navigators 1853. **2. b.** Sheila.. romantic and m., and believes in..dreams 1874. Hence **Myste·rious-ly** *adv.*, **-ness.**

Mysterize (mi·stərəiz), *v. rare.* 1650. [f. MYSTERY[1] + -IZE.] **a.** *trans.* To interpret mystically. SIR T. BROWNE. **b.** *intr.* To make mysteries of things 1845.

Mystery[1] (mi·stəri). ME. [- AFr. *misterie (OFr. *mistere*, mod. *mystère*) or immed. - the source, L. *mysterium* - Gr. μυστήριον secret thing or ceremony, f. *μυσ- as in μύστης initiated one, μυστικός MYSTIC.] **I.** Theological uses. **†1.** *In* (*his*) *m.*: mystically -1628. **2.** A religious truth known only by divine revelation; usu. a doctrine of the faith involving difficulties which human reason is incapable of solving. late ME. **3.** A religious ordinance or rite, *esp.* a sacramental rite of the Christian religion; *spec.* (*pl.*) the Eucharist; *occas.* the consecrated elements 1506. **4.** An incident in the life of our Lord or of the Saints regarded as having a mystical significance. Hence, each of the fifteen divisions of the rosary corresponding to the 'mysteries of redemption' 1655.

2. By the misterye of thy holy incarnacion,.. Good Lorde deliuer vs 1549.

II. Other uses. **1.** A hidden or secret thing; something beyond human knowledge or comprehension; an enigma ME. **†b.** A personal secret -1617. **c.** A political or diplomatic secret; a secret of state. *Obs.* exc. as a use of the gen. sense. 1618. **2.** In generalized sense. **a.** The condition of being secret or obscure; mysteriousness. Also, mysteries collectively. 1601. **b.** The behaviour or attitude of mind of one who makes a secret of things (often intrinsically unimportant) 1692. **†3.** Mysterious reason; mystic meaning -1687. **4.** An action or practice about which there is some secrecy; a trade or other secret. Now often *trivial.* 1594. **5.** Chiefly *pl.* In ancient religious systems, certain secret rites to which only the initiated were admitted 1643. **b.** The secrets of freemasonry 1738. **6.** Used (after Fr. *mystère*, med.L. *mysterium*) as a name for the miracle-play. (Often erron. referred to MYSTERY[2] on the ground that the miracle-plays were often acted by the trade guilds.) 17... **7. a.** A kind of fly for salmon fishing 1867. **b.** A kind of cake or pudding 1889.

1. The M. of Edwin Drood DICKENS (*title*). **b.** *Haml.* III. ii. 382. Phr. *To make a m. of*: to treat as a secret in order to make an impression. **2. a.** A Science without m. is unknown; a Religion without m. is absurd H. DRUMMOND. Phr. *Wrapped in m.*

Comb.: **m.-man,** a conjuror, a medicine-man; **-play** = sense II. 6; **-ship,** an armed and camouflaged merchantman used to decoy submarines in the war of 1914–1918; = Q-BOAT.

Mystery[2] (mi·stəri). late ME. [- med.L. *misterium* (see MISTER *sb.*[1]), contr. of L. *ministerium* (see MINISTRY), by assoc. with *mysterium* (see prec.).] **†1.** Service, occupation; office, ministry -1533. **2.** Handicraft; craft, art; (one's) trade or calling (*arch.*) late ME. **†b.** Skill, art -1661. **3.** A trade gild or company (*arch.* or *Hist.*). late ME.

2. That noble Science or M. of the healing mans body 1612. Phr. *Art and m.*: a formula in indentures of apprenticeship to a trade. **3.** President of the m. of the workers in iron SCOTT.

Mystic (mi·stik). late ME. [- (O)Fr. *mystique* or L. *mysticus* - Gr. μυστικός f. μύστης initiated one, f. μύειν close (of eyes, lips), μυεῖν initiate; see -IC.] **A.** *adj.* **1.** Spiritually allegorical or symbolical. Also = MYSTICAL *a.* 1, but now somewhat rhet. **2.** Pertaining to the ancient religious mysteries, etc.; occult, esoteric 1615. **†3.** Secret, concealed -1697. **4.** Pertaining to or connected with that branch of theology which relates to the direct communion of the soul with God. Now *rare.* 1639. **5.** Of hidden meaning or nature; enigmatical 1631. **b.** In recent use: Inspiring an awed sense of mystery 1842.

1. The m. Dove Hovering His gracious brow above KEBLE. **2.** The m. rites of Demeter 1835. **5.** Foole, thou didst not understand The mystique language of the eye nor hand DONNE. **b.** An arm Clothed in white samite, m., wonderful TENNYSON.

B. *sb.* **†1.** Mystical meaning or representation. Only ME. **2.** Orig., a 'mystic doctor', an exponent of mystical theology; also, one who maintains the importance of this. Hence: One who seeks by contemplation and self-surrender to obtain union with or absorption into the Deity, or who believes in the spiritual apprehension of truths inaccessible to the understanding 1679. **3.** *occas.* One initiated into mysteries 1859.

2. Those mysticks who would discard the passions of hope and fear 1714. **3.** This was the meaning of the founders of the mysteries when they said, 'Many are the wand bearers but few are the mystics' JOWETT.

Mystical (mi·stikăl), *a.* 1471. [f. as prec.; see -ICAL.] **1.** Having a certain spiritual character or import by virtue of a connection or union with God transcending human comprehension: said esp. with ref. to the Church as the Body of Christ, and to sacramental ordinances 1529. **b.** (Spiritually) allegorical or symbolical 1500. **2.** Of dark import, obscure meaning, or occult influence. Now *rare* or *Obs.* 1500. **†b.** Of a person: Obscure in speech or style -1626. **3.** Connected with occult rites or practices 1577. **†4.** = MYSTIC *a.* 3. –1687. **5.** = MYSTIC *a.* 4. Also, pertaining to mystics or mysticism. 1613.

1. The churches mysticall repast G. HERBERT. **b.** The m. horseman in the Apocalypse 1861. **2.** That m. needle which mariners talk of SCOTT. **3.** 'Tis the sunset of life gives me m. lore, And coming events cast their shadows before CAMPBELL. **5.** With my ascetick course of life I joined the reading all the Misticall Authors I could find BURNET. Hence **My·stical-ly** *adv.*, **-ness.**

Mysticete (mi·stisīt). 1801. [– mod.L. *mysticetus* – Gr. μυστίκητος (in old edd. of Aristotle *Hist. Anim.* III. xii. where mod. edd. read ὁ μῦς τὸ κῆτος).] **1.** The Arctic Right Whale, *Balæna mysticetus.* **2.** A whalebone whale 1876.

Mysticism (mi·stisiz'm). 1736. [f. MYSTIC + -ISM.] **1.** The opinions, mental tendencies, or habits of thought and feeling, characteristic of mystics; belief in the possibility of union with the Divine nature by means of ecstatic contemplation; reliance on spiritual intuition as the means of acquiring knowledge of mysteries inaccessible to the understanding. **2.** As a term of reproach. **a.** Applied loosely to any religious belief associated with self-delusion and dreamy confusion of thought. **b.** Sometimes applied to philosophical or scientific theories which assume occult qualities or mysterious agencies of which no rational account can be given. 1763.

Mysticize (mi·stisəiz), *v.* 1680. [f. MYSTIC *a.* + -IZE.] *trans.* To render mystical; to give a mystic meaning to.

My·stico-, comb. f. Gr. μυστικός MYSTIC, with sense 'partly mystical and partly ——', or 'mystically', as *mystico-religious* adj.

Mystification (mi:stifikēⁱ·ʃən). 1815. [– Fr. *mystification*, f. *mystifier*; see MYSTIFY *v.*², -FICATION.] The action of mystifying a person; an instance of this; the condition or fact of being mystified.

Special pleading of advocates, whose main talent is quibbling and m. 1826. So **My·stificator** [– Fr. *mystificateur*] *rare.* 1823.

Mystify (mi·stifəi), *v.*¹ *rare.* Also †**mist-.** 1734. [f. MIST *sb.*¹ or MISTY *a.*¹ + -FY.] Only in pa. pple.: Beclouded; befogged (*lit.* and *fig.*).

Mystify (mi·stifəi), *v.*² Also **mist-.** 1814. [– Fr. *mystifier*, irreg. f. *mystère* MYSTERY¹ or *mystique* MYSTIC; see -FY. Cf. prec.] **1.** To bewilder; to play on the credulity of; to hoax, humbug. **2.** To wrap up or involve in mystery; to make mystical; to interpret mystically 1829. **3.** To involve in obscurity; to obscure the meaning or character of 1827.

1. Puebla was to choose his words — to hint at dark intrigues — to m. the council 1873. **2.** The fabulous age, in which vulgar fact becomes mystified, and tinted up with delectable fiction W. IRVING. **3.** We abhor those who m. it [*sc.* the Gospel] SPURGEON.

Myth (miþ). Also †**mythe.** 1830. [– mod. L. MYTHUS, late L. *mythos* – Gr. μῦθος.] **1.** A purely fictitious narrative usually involving supernatural persons, actions, or events, and embodying some popular idea concerning natural or historical phenomena. Often used vaguely to include any narrative having fictitious elements. **2.** A fictitious or imaginary person or object 1849.

1. It is chronicled in an old Armenian m. that the wise men of the East were none other than the three sons of Noe 1899. **2.** Parliamentary control was a m. 1888.

Mythic, -al (mi·þik, -ăl), *a.* 1669. [– late L. *mythicus* – Gr. μυθικός, f. μῦθος; see prec., -IC, -ICAL.] **1.** Of the nature of, consisting of, or based on a myth or myths. **b.** *transf.* Having no foundation in fact 1870. **2.** Existing only in myth 1678. **3.** Of writers, their methods: Dealing with or involving the use of myths 1874.

1. A tradition, perhaps true, perhaps mythical, grew up, of Homer's blindness GLADSTONE. To reject the Gospels themselves as mythic 1881. **b.** Her influence is mythical DISRAELI. **3.** The grave Thucydides, least mythical of historians 1888.

Hence **My·thically** *adv.* in a mythical manner; by means of myths 1847. **My·thicism,** the principle of attributing a mythical character to narratives of supernatural events 1840. **My·thicist,** an exponent of mythicism or mythical theories 1871. **My·thicize** *v. trans.* to turn into myth; to interpret mythically 1840.

My·thico-, comb. f. Gr. μυθικός MYTHIC, with sense 'mythical and —'.

Mythism (mi·þiz'm). 1848. [f. MYTH *sb.* + -ISM.] = MYTHICISM. So **My·thist** 1840. **My·thize** *v.* 1851.

Mytho- (məi·þo, mi·þo, miþǫ·, məiþǫ·), comb. f. Gr. μῦθος MYTH. **Mythoge·nesis,** the production of myths. **Mytho·gony** [Gr. -γονία creation], the study of the origin of myths. **Mytho·grapher,** a writer or narrator of myths. **Mytho·graphy,** representation or expression of myths. **Mythopœ·ic, -poe·tic,** [Gr. ποιεῖν make] *adjs.* myth-making or relating to the making of myths. **Mythopo·em,** a mythical poem; **Mythopo·etry,** mythological poetry; so **Mythopo·et.**

Mythologer (miþǫ·lŏdʒəɹ). 1610. [– Fr. *mythologue* (XVI) – Gr. μυθολόγος; see MYTHO-, -LOGER.] A mythologist. So **Mytholo·gian** (*rare*) 1613.

Mythologic, -ical (miþŏlǫ·dʒik, -ăl), *a.* 1614. [– late L. *mythologicus* – Gr. μυθολογικός, f. μυθολογία; see MYTHOLOGY, -IC, -ICAL. Cf. Fr. *mythologique.*] Of or belonging to mythology or myths; mythical. Hence **Mytholo·gically** *adv.*

Mythologist (miþǫ·lŏdʒist). 1631. [f. MYTHOLOGY + -IST, or f. MYTHOLOGER by substitution of suffix.] **1.** A writer of myths 1642. **2.** One versed in myths or mythology.

Mythologize (miþǫ·lŏdʒəiz), *v.* 1603. [– Fr. *mythologiser*; see next, -IZE.] †**1.** *trans.* To interpret (a story, fable) with regard to its mytholigical features –1727. **2.** *intr.* To relate a myth or myths; to construct a mythology 1609. **b.** *trans.* To relate (something fictitious) (*rare*) 1851. **3.** To represent or express mythologically (*rare*) 1678. **4.** To make mythical; to convert into myth or mythology 1847.

1. This Parable was immediately mythologised. The Whale was interpreted to be Hobbes's *Leviathan* SWIFT. Hence **Mytho·logizer** (*rare*).

Mythology (miþǫ·lŏdʒi). late ME. [– Fr. *mythologie* or late L. *mythologia* – Gr. μυθολογία; see MYTHO-, -LOGY.] †**1.** The exposition of myths –1656. †**b.** Symbolical meaning (of a fable, etc.) –1734. **2.** A mythical story (*rare*). †Formerly: A parable, allegory. 1603. **b.** *gen.* without article 1646. **3.** A body of myths, esp. that belonging to the religious literature or tradition of a country or people 1781. **4.** That department of knowledge which deals with myths 1836.

1. b. Those [*sc. Whig* and *Tory*] were the Appellatives; but the M. was Seditious and Loyal NORTH. **2. b.** The Heathen Religion is mostly couched under M. SWIFT. **3.** The M...of the Iliad 1830. **4.** The science of comparative m. 1864.

‖**Mythus** (məi·þŏs). 1825. Also in form **mythos** (1753). [mod.L.; see MYTH.] = MYTH 1.

‖**Mytilus** (mi·tilŏs). 1817. [L. *mytilus* (*mitulus, mutulus*) = Gr. μύτυλος.] A genus of bivalves, now comprising the marine mussels. Hence **My·tiloid** *a.* mussel-like; belonging to the family *Mytilidæ*; *sb.* a member of this family; a mussel 1847.

Myxinoid (mi·ksinoid), *a.* (*sb.*) 1846. [f. mod.L. *Myxine* (Linn.), app. alt. of Gr. μυξῖνος slime-fish, f. μύξα slime; see -OID.] Pertaining to (a fish of) the family *Myxinidæ* (typical genus *Myxine*) of cyclostomous fishes.

Myxo- (mi·kso), bef. a vowel **myx-**, comb. f. Gr. μύξα slime, mucus: as in ‖**Myxœde·ma,** a disease characterized by swelling due to infiltration of gelatinous fluid into the tissues; hence **Myxœde·matous, -œde·mic** *adjs.* ‖**My:xomyce·tes** *sb. pl.*, the slime-moulds or slime-fungi; hence **Myxomyce·tous** *a.* **My·xopod** [Gr. πούς, ποδ- foot], a protozoan possessing pseudopodia.

‖**Myxoma** (miksōᵘ·mă). *Pl.* **myxo·mata.** 1870. [mod.L., f. Gr. μύξα mucus, after *sarcoma*; see -OMA.] *Path.* A tumour consisting of mucous or gelatinous tissue. Hence **Myxo·matous** *a.*

Myzont (məi·zǫnt), *a.* and *sb.* 1882. [– μυζοντ-, pr. ppl. stem of Gr. μύζειν suck.] *Zool.* = MARSIPOBRANCH, MARSIPOBRANCHIATE *a.* and *sb.*

‖**Myzostoma** (məizǫ·stŏmă). Also anglicized **myzostome.** 1876. [mod.L., f. Gr. μύζειν suck + στόμα mouth.] *Zool.* One of an order of small parasitic worms, having disc-like bodies provided with suckers. Hence **Myzosto·matous, Myzo·stomous** *adjs.*

N

N (en), the fourteenth letter of the modern, and thirteenth of the ancient Roman alphabet, represents historically, and is in form derived from, the Greek *nū* and the Semitic *nun.* It usually denotes a voiced nasal consonant with front closure (the point of the tongue touching the teeth or the fore part of the palate). The sound is in certain positions a sonant or vowel, here denoted by (ʼn), as in *bidden* (bi·dʼn). It is silent only in a few cases at the end of syllables after *l* and *m*, as *kiln, damn, hymn, column,* etc.

Before (g) and (k), *n* may also represent a nasal with back tongue-closure, here denoted by (ŋ), as in *finger* (fi·ŋgəɹ), *think* (þiŋk). When not followed by these sounds this back-nasal is expressed by the digraph *ng* as in *hang* (hæŋ), etc.

In ME. the *n* of the indef. article *an* is often transferred to a following word beginning with a vowel, as in *newt, nickname.* A similar transference takes place with the *n* of *min, myn* my, and *þin, thyn* thy: see NAIN, NAUNT, etc.

I. 1. The letter used to represent the sound OE. **b.** In *Printing* used as a unit of measurement (often *en*; cf. EM); also *n.-quadrat* 1683. **2.** Used to indicate that the name of a person is to be inserted by the speaker or reader OE. **3.** Used to denote one of a series of things, a point in a diagram, etc. 1677. **4.** In *Math.* used to indicate an indefinite number. *To the* n^{th} (*power*), to any required power; hence *fig.* to any extent 1852. **5.** *n-declension*, the 'weak' declension of Gmc. nouns and adjs., in which the stem ends in *n*; so *n-stem, n-plural* 1843. **6.** *N-rays* (orig. *n-rays*), N^1*-rays* (orig. n_1*-rays*), forms of radiation having opposite effects; named from the initial letter of Nancy, at which University the *N-rays* were discovered 1903.

II. Abbrevs. **a.** Miscellaneous. N. = various proper names, as Nicholas, Naomi, etc.; N (*Chem.*) = nitrogen; n. (*Gram.*) = noun, neuter, nominative; n.b. = no ball; n.d. = no date; N.F. = Norman French; N.O. = Natural Order; n.p. = (*a*) new paragraph; (*b*) no place; N.S. (*Banking*) = not sufficient. **b.** N. = North; in points of the compass and London postal districts, as N.E., NE. = North-east, etc.; N.B. = North Britain (Scotland), North British; N.C. = North Carolina. **c.** N. = New, as in N.B. = New Brunswick; N.E.D. = (A) New English Dictionary (on Historical Principles); N.J. = New Jersey; N.S. = New Style; N.T. = New Testament. **d.** N. = National, as in N.S.P.C.C. = National Society for the Prevention of Cruelty to Children; N.U.R. = National Union of Railwaymen; N.U.T. = National Union of Teachers. See also N.B., N.C.O.

n-, in OE. and ME., the negative particle *ne* in combination with a word beginning with a vowel, *h*, or *w*, as *nam*, am not, *nis*, is not, etc.

†**Na,** *adv.*¹ and *conj.* [OE. *nā*, f. *ne* NE + *ā* ever (see A *adv.* and O *adv.*), giving normally *nā* in northern ME. and Sc., and *nō* (see NO *adv.*) in midland and southern dialects.] Not; nor –1786.

Na (nā), *adv.*² *Sc.* and *n. dial.* ME. [repr. OE. *nā* (see prec.), and corresp. to the midland and southern No.] No, in answer to a question, to express dissent, etc.

Na (nă), *adv.*³ *Sc.* and *n. dial.* 1714. [Enclitic form of NO *adv.* 'not', with obscuration of vowel owing to the absence of stress.] Not. Used chiefly with auxiliary verbs, as *canna, dinna* (= don't), *hasna*, etc.

Naam (nām). [OE. *naam, nām* – ON. *nám*, related to *niman* take, NIM.] *Hist. Law.* The act of taking another's goods by way of distraint; the goods thus taken.

Nab (næb), *sb.*¹ Chiefly *n.* and *Sc.* late ME. [– ON. *nabbr* and *nabbi* projecting peak or knoll.] **1.** A jutting out part of a hill or rock; a peak or promontory; a summit. **2.** A projection or spur on the bolt of a lock 1677.

†**Nab,** *sb.*² *Obs. Cant.* 1673. [perh. a use of prec.; cf. NOB *sb.*¹, KNOB *sb.* 4.] A hat –1754.

Nab (næb), *v. slang* or *colloq.* 1678. [Of unkn. origin; parallel to synon. and contemp. NAP *v.*³] **1.** *trans.* To catch and take into custody; to apprehend, arrest. **2.** To snatch or seize (a thing); to steal 1814.

Nabal (nēⁱ·băl). 1604. [See 1 Sam. 25:3 ff.] A churlish or miserly person.

Nabob (nēⁱ·bǫb). 1612. [– Pg. *nababo* or Sp. *nabab*– Urdu *nawwāb* deputy governor; see NAWAB.] **1.** Title of certain Moslem officials, who acted as deputy governors of provinces or districts in the Mogul Empire; an official thus designated; a governor of a town or district in India. **2.** *transf.* A person of great wealth; *spec.* one who has returned from India with a large fortune 1764.

2. Dawdling, like a bilious old n. at a watering place MACAULAY. Hence **Na·bobess,** a female n. 1767. **Na·bobship,** the office or rank of a n.; a district governed by a n. 1753.

Nabs (næbz). 1790. [Of unkn. origin; cf. NIBS, and *my nobs* (XVI) = my darling.] *His nabs*, he; *my nabs*, my friend; myself.

‖**Nacelle** (năse·l). 1909. [Fr. :– late L. *navicella*, dim. of *navis* ship.] The framework of an aeroplane or dirigible containing the engine, controlling gear, and propellers.

†**Nache.** ME. (**nage**); 1523 (**nache**). [– OFr. *nache*, *nage*; see AITCH-BONE.] The point of the rump in an ox or cow; the rump.

Nacre (nēⁱ·kəɹ). 1598. [– (O)Fr. *nacre*, prob. of oriental origin.] **1.** The pinna or sea-pen, or other shell-fish yielding mother-of-pearl. **2.** A smooth, shining, iridescent substance forming the inner layer in many shells; mother-of-pearl 1689. Hence **Na·cred** *a.* faced with, having the hues of, n. 1755. **Na·creous** *a.* consisting of n.; resembling n. in substance or in hues 1819.

†**Nad(de,** had not; see NE and HAVE *v.* –1480.

Nadder, Naddre, etc., obs. ff. ADDER.

Nadir (nēⁱ·dəɹ). late ME. [– (O)Fr. *nadir*, corresp. to Sp., It. *nadir*– Arab. *naẓīr* opposite to, over against, opposite point. In sense 2 used ellipt. for *naẓīr as-samt* opposite to the zenith.] *Astron.* †**1.** A point in the heavens diametrically opposite to some other point, esp. to the sun. Const. *of* and *to*. –1738. **2.** The point of the heavens diametrically opposite to the zenith; the point directly under the observer 1495. **3.** *transf.* The lowest point (*of* anything); the place or time of greatest depression or degradation 1793.

3. The seventh century is the *nadir* of the human mind in Europe HALLAM. **Na·diral** *a. rare* 1891.

Nae(-), Sc. var. of NA(-) = NO(-).

‖**Nævus** (nī·vŏs). *Pl.* **nævi** (nī·vəi). 1835. Also (17th c.) anglicized **næve.** [L.] *Path.* A hypertrophied state of the blood-vessels of the skin, forming spots or elevations of a red or purplish colour, usu. congenital; a mole. Hence **Næ·void** *a.* of the nature of a n.

Nag (næg), *sb.*[1] late ME. [Of unkn. origin; cf. Du. *neg(ge.*] A small riding horse or pony. †**b.** *transf.* as a term of abuse –1606.

Nag (næg), *sb.*[2] 1894. [f. next.] The act of nagging.

Nag (næg), *v.* 1828. [Also *gnag*, *knag*; of dial. origin; perh. of Scand. or LG. origin, (cf. Norw., Sw. *nagga* gnaw, nibble, irritate), LG. (*g*)*naggen* (XV) irritate, provoke).] **1.** To be persistently worrying or irritating by continued fault-finding, scolding, or urging. **2.** *trans.* To assail or annoy (a person) in this manner. 1840. Also **nagnag.**

1. It's no good my mother nagging at me TROLLOPE. **2.** Is it pleasing..to have your wife nagnagging you because she has not been invited? THACKERAY. Hence **Na·gging** *vbl. sb.* and *ppl. a.*

‖**Nagari** (nā·gărī). 1776. = DEVANAGARI.

Naggy (næ·gi), *a.* 1697 (**knaggie**). [f. NAG *v.* + -Y[1].] Given to nagging.

Nagor (nēⁱ·gǫɹ). 1780. [Arbitrary alteration by Buffon of *nanguer*, a species of antelope formerly recognized.] The Senegal antelope, *Cervicapra redunca*.

Nagualism (næ·gwăliz'm, næ·wăl-). 1883. [– Quechua *naual* wizard + -ISM.] A system of superstition practised by a secret sect formerly existing in Central America.

Naiad (nəi·ăed, nēⁱ·æd). 1610. [– L. *Naïas*, *Naïad-* – Gr. Ναϊάς, Ναϊαδ-, rel. to νάειν flow.] *Myth.* One of a number of beautiful young nymphs imagined as living in, and being the tutelary spirits of, rivers and springs; a river nymph. Also **Naïd** (nēⁱ·id) [L. *Naïs*, Gr. Ναΐς] –1717.

You Nimphs cald Nayades of yᵉ windring brooks SHAKS. Also **Naiades** (nəi·ădīz, nēⁱ·ădīz), *sb. pl.* ME. The flowry-kirtl'd Naiades MILT.

Naiant (nēⁱ·ănt), *a.* 1562. [– AFr. **naiant* = OFr. *noiant*, pr. pple. of *noier*, *noer* swim (mod. *noyer* drown) = It. *nuotare* :– Rom. **notare*, for L. *natare*.] *Her.* Swimming.

‖**Naib** (nā·ib, nēⁱ·ib). 1682. [Arab. *nā'ib* deputy; see NAWAB.] A deputy governor; a deputy.

‖**Naïf** (naif), *a.* Now *rare*. 1598. [Fr.; see NAÏVE.] = NAÏVE.

‖**Naik** (nā·ik, nēⁱ·ik). 1588. [– Urdu *nā'ik* – Hindi *nāyak* chief, officer :– Skr. *nāyaka* leader.] **1.** An Indian title of authority; a governor. **2.** A military officer; in later use, a corporal of native infantry 1787.

Nail (nēⁱl), *sb.* [OE. *næġ(e)l* = OFris. *neil*, OS., OHG. *nagal* (Du., G. *nagel*), ON. *nagl* :– Gmc. **naʒlaz*. IE. base **nogh-* or **noqh-* is repr. also by Lith. *nāgas* nail, claw, Gr. ὄνυξ, L. *unguis*. The applications to measure of land and cloth (see III) are of uncertain origin.] **I. 1.** A hard, oval-shaped, protective covering of modified epidermis, formed upon the upper tip of the fingers and toes in Man and the Quadrumana, and answering to the claws and hoofs of other animals and birds. **b.** A similar growth on the toes of beasts and birds; a claw or talon OE. **2.** Anything resembling a nail in shape or colour; *esp.* a nail-like excrescence, situated on the upper mandible of certain soft-billed birds. late ME.

1. A scoldyng woman, whose weapon is onely her toungue and her nayles HALL.

Phrases. *A n.* or *nail's breadth* (cf. L. *transversum unguem*), the smallest amount. *To bite, blow, pare one's nails*. *From the tender n.* (tr. L. *de tenero ungui*, Hor. *Odes* III. vi. 24), from early youth. *To the* or *a n.* (tr. L. *ad unguem*, Hor. *Sat.* I. v. 32), to a nicety, to perfection. *Tooth and n.*: see TOOTH.

II. A small spike or piece of metal (gen. with a point and a broadened head, so as to be easily driven in by a hammer), used to fix one thing firmly to another, or as a peg, or occas. as an ornament; rarely, a wooden peg (cf. *tree-n.*) OE.

As a nayle, the moo knockes it hath the more sure it is fixed 1526. *fig.* The countless nails that rivet the chains of habit LAMB. Provb. *One n. drives out another*. The nails of the Cross..were converted by the emperor into a helmet LECKY.

Phrases. *To hit the* (*right*) *n. on the head*, to hit the mark, to say or do exactly the right thing. *To drive the n. home*, to push a matter to a conclusion. *A n. in one's* (*its*) *coffin*, something that contributes to the end of the person or thing referred to. *On the n.* (cf. SUPERNACULUM), on the spot, at once. Chiefly of making money payments. *Hard as nails*, in perfect condition; extremely obdurate, callous, etc. *Right as nails*, quite right.

III. 1. = CLOVE *sb.*[3]; †also, a measure of land. Now only *south. dial.* late ME. **2.** A measure of length for cloth; $2\frac{1}{4}$ inches, or the sixteenth part of a yard 1465.

attrib. and *Comb.*, as *n.-brush*, *-scissors*, etc.; **n. rod,** a strip or rod of iron from which nails are cut. Hence **Nai·lless** *a.* destitute of nails.

Nail (nēⁱl), *v.* [OE. *næġlan*, f. prec. Cf. Goth. *nagljan*.] **I. 1.** *trans.* To fix or fasten (a person or thing) with nails *on* or *to* something else. **2. a.** To pierce or drive through with a nail or nails. Now *rare* or *Obs.* **b.** To fix or fasten with nails. Also with *about*, *in*, *together*, etc. ME. **c.** To stud with (or as with) nails; to mark by driving in a nail (*rare*) late ME. †**d.** *Mil.* To spike (a cannon) –1781. **3.** *Nail up*: **a.** To close up firmly by fixing with nails 1530. **b.** To affix at some height by means of nails; to fasten with nails to a wall, etc. 1630. †**c.** *Mil.* = 2 d. –1781. **4.** *Nail down*, to fix down with nails; to fix down the lid of (a box) in this way 1669.

1. He was nailed to the tre ME. The royal anathema was nailed on the Episcopal gate at London D'ISRAELI. He called to his coachman.. to wait as if nailed to the spot MEREDITH. Phr. *To n. one's colours to the mast*, to adopt an unyielding attitude. *To n. to the counter*, to expose as false or spurious (as shopkeepers deal with bad coin). *To n. to the barndoor*, to exhibit after the manner of dead vermin. **2. b.** He is now deed, and nayled in his chest CHAUCER. **c.** Those Stars which n. Heav'ns pavement 1648.

II. 1. To fix, make fast, as by means of nails; to secure. Now *rare* or *Obs.* late ME. **2.** To fix (a person or thing) firmly *to* something; e.g. *to* or *on* the ground, etc., with a weapon 1590. **b.** To fix, or keep (one) fixed, *to* or *in* a certain place, position or occupation 1611. **c.** To fix or fasten (the eyes, mind, etc.) *to* or *on* the object of one's attention 1591. **3.** To fix or pin one *down* to something 1615. **4.** *slang*. **a.** To secure; to succeed in catching or getting hold of (a person or thing); to steal 1760. **b.** To catch (one) in some fix 1766.

2. To whose Fingers their Money is as it were glued and nailed 1691. **b.** Those Whose headaches n. them to a noonday bed COWPER. **c.** I cannot n. my mind to one subject of contemplation SCOTT. **4. a.** [He] insisted on nailing me for dinner before he would leave me THACKERAY. Hence **Nai·ler,** a nail-maker; one who drives in nails 1440; *slang*, a marvellously good specimen; a very skilful hand *at* something 1818. **Nai·ling** *ppl. a.* fixing like a nail; *slang*, excellent, splendid 1883.

Nailery (nēⁱ·ləri). 1798. [f. NAILER; see -ERY.] A place or workshop where nails are made.

Nai·l-head. 1683. [f. NAIL *sb.* + HEAD *sb.* II. I.] **1.** The head of a nail. **2.** An ornament shaped like the head of a nail 1836. **b.** *attrib.*, with *moulding*, *ornament*, *pattern* 1845.

2. The n. being an ornament easily cut, was much used in almost all periods of Norman work PARKER. So **Nai·l-headed** *a.* 1801.

Nain (nēn), *a.* *Sc.* ME. [The erron. division of *min own* as *my nown*, hence also *his nown*, *her nown*, survives in northern dial. as *nain*, etc.] (One's) own. Hence **Nainse·l', -se·ll,** (one's) own self; *her nainsel'*, a phr. supposed to be used by Highlanders in place of the 1st pers. pron.

‖**Nainsook** (nēⁱ·nsuk). 1804. [Urdu (Hindi) *nainsukh*, f. *nain* eye + *sukh* pleasure.] A cotton fabric, a kind of muslin or jaconet, of Indian origin.

‖**Naïs** (nēⁱ·is). *Pl.* **naïdes** (nēⁱ·idīz). 1697. [L. *Naïs*, Gr. Ναΐς; see NAIAD.] **1.** *Mythol.* = NAIAD. **2.** *Zool.* A small fresh-water worm allied to the earthworm 1835.

Naissant (nēⁱ·sănt), *a.* 1572. [– (O)Fr. *naissant*, pr. pple. of *naître* be born :– Rom. **nascere*, f. L. *nasci*; see NASCENT.] **1.** *Her.* Of animals: Issuing from the middle of the fesse or other ordinary. **2.** That is in the act of springing up, coming into existence, or being produced (*rare*) 1885.

Naïve (na,ī·v, nā·īv, nē·īv), *a.* Also **naive.** 1654. [– (O)Fr. *naïve*, fem. of *naïf* (see NAÏF) :– L. *nativus* NATIVE.] Characterized by unsophisticated or unconventional simplicity or artlessness. Hence **Nai·vely** *adv.* 1705.

‖**Naïveté** (naivte, nē·īvti). 1673. Also **naïvety** (1708). [Fr.; see prec. and -TY[1].] The condition or quality of being naïve; a naïve remark, etc.

He had a sort of n. and openness of demeanour SCOTT.

‖**Naja** (nēⁱ·dʒă, nēⁱ·yă). 1753. [mod.L., f. Hindi *nāg* snake.] A genus of highly venomous snakes, comprising the species *N. tripudians* of India and *N. haje* of Africa; the Indian or African cobra; a snake of either of these species.

Naked (nēⁱ·kėd), *a.* and *sb.* [OE. *nacod* = OFris. *naked*, *-et*, MLG., MDu. *naket* (Du. *naakt*), OHG. *nackut* (G. *nackt*), ON. *nǫkkviðr*, Goth. *naqaþs*, *-ad-* :– Gmc. **naquaðaz*, **-eðaz*, rel. to L. *nudus*, Skr. *nagnás*.] **A.** *adj.* **I. 1.** Unclothed; stripped to the skin. **b.** Of a horse or ass: Unsaddled, bare-backed OE. **2.** Of parts of the body: Not covered by clothing; bare, exposed ME. **3.** Destitute of clothing (implying wretchedness). Also *occas.* of animals: Stripped of the usual warm covering. OE. **b.** Bare of means (*rare*) 1625. †**4.** Without weapons (or armour); unarmed –1787. **b.** Defenceless, unprotected; open *to* assault or injury 1560.

1. To bed he goes; and Jemy euer used to lye n., as is the use of a number 1608. **b.** A n. man on a n. horse is a fine spectacle DARWIN. **2.** There is my Dagger, And heere my n. Breast SHAKS. *transf.* He..Had gazed on Nature's n. loveliness SHELLEY. Phr. *N. bed*, orig. a bed in which the occupant slept entirely n.; later used with ref. to the removal of the ordinary wearing apparel. Now *arch.* **3.** Poore n. wretches..That bide the pelting of this pittilesse storme SHAKS. **4. b.** Left n. to infinite temptations 1688.

II. 1. Of a sword, etc.: Not covered by a sheath OE. **2.** Free from concealment or reserve; straightforward. Now *rare*. ME. **3.** Uncovered, stripped of all disguise or concealment. late ME. **b.** Plain, obvious, clear 1589.

1. In her right hand a n. poniard 1634. **2.** By this n. confession of my life 1652. *The n. truth*, the plain truth, without concealment or addition. **3.** Nakid is helle beforn hym WYCLIF *Job* 26:6. **b.** Chamberlayne laid his plan, in all its n. absurdity, before the Commons MACAULAY.

III. †**1.** Bare, destitute, or devoid *of* something; unoccupied, blank –1822. **2.** Of physical objects or features: Lacking some natural or ordinary covering, as vegetation, foliage 1549. **3.** Lacking the usual furniture or ornament. late ME. **4.** Unprotected, exposed 1607. **5.** *Bot.* **a.** Of parts of a plant: Having no covering, leaves, hairs, etc. 1578. **6.** *Zool.* Destitute of hair or scales; not defended by a shell 1769.

1. The maritine Townes..being left halfe n. of defence 1632. **2.** Sea-beaten rocks and n. shores COWPER. Let birds be silent on the n. spray SPENSER. Huge precipices of n. stone MACAULAY. Phr. *N. fallow*, a bare fallow, one on which no crop at all is grown. *transf.* Wild swans struggling with the n. storm SHELLEY. **3.** Some forlorne and n. Hermitage SHAKS. *N. flooring*, the timbers which support the flooring boards. **4.** I always felt it on the n. nerve BURKE. *N. light*, one not placed with a case. *N. fire*, one not closed in any contrivance.

IV. 1. Left without any addition; not overlaid with remarks or comments OE. **b.** Not otherwise supported or confirmed; (chiefly in legal use) not supported by proof or evidence. late ME. **2.** *N. eye*, the eye unassisted by any aid to vision. So *n. sight*. 1664.

1. He chooses to suppose..a n. possibility BURKE. The n. facts BLACKSTONE. **b.** A n. and bare promise of affiance 1555. For the evidence of these designs, Mr. Hastings presents his own n. assertion 1817.

B. *sb.* †**1.** *Art. The n.*: the nude 1735–1815. **b.** The face or plain surface (of a wall, etc.) 1726. †**2.** *Art.* A nude figure 1622–1675. Hence **Na·ked-ly** *adv.*, **-ness.**

Naker (nēⁱ·kəɹ). Current in 14th c.; now *Hist.* ME. [– OFr. *nacre, nacaire* = It. *nacchera* (cf. med.L. *nacara*, med. Gr. ἀνάκαρα) – Arab. *nakkāra* drum.] A kettle-drum.

Pypes, trompes, nakers, and clariounes CHAUCER.

†**Nale,** In phr. *at þe nale, atte nale*, for *at þen ale, atten ale*; see ALE 2.

†**Nam,** am not: see NE, BE *v.* OE. –1576.

Namaycush (næ·mekʊʃ). 1785. [Amer. Indian; in Cree *numākoos*, Ojibwa *namēgoss*.] The great lake trout (*Cristivomer namaycush*) of N. America.

Namby-pamby (næ·mbiˌpæ·mbi), *a.* and *sb.* 1745. [Formed fancifully on the name of *Ambrose* Philips (died 1749), who wrote pastorals ridiculed by Carey (in *Namby Pamby* 1726) and Pope (*Dunc.* iii. 319).] **A.** *adj.* **1.** Of style, actions, etc.: Weakly sentimental, insipidly pretty. **2.** Of persons: Inclined to affected daintiness, of a weak or trifling character 1774.

2. She was a namby-pamby milk-and-water affected creature THACKERAY.

B. *sb.* **1.** That which is marked by affected prettiness and feeble sentimentality 1764. **2.** A namby-pamby person 1885. Hence **Na·mby-pa·mbyism** 1834.

Name (nēⁱm), *sb.* [OE. *nama, noma* = OFris. *nama, noma*, OS., OHG. *namo* (Du. *naam*, G. *name*), ON. *nafn, namn*, Goth. *namo* :– Gmc. **namōn, -on.* Cogn. forms occur in all IE. languages, as in L. *nomen*, Gr. ὄνομα, Skr. *nāman*.] **I. 1.** The particular combination of vocal sounds employed as the individual designation of a single person, animal, place, or thing. **2.** The specific word or words (term) used to denote a member of a particular class of beings or objects OE.

1. Peter Simple, you say your n. is? SHAKS. God needeth not to distinguish his Celestiall servants by names HOBBES. Phr. *To keep one's n. on, take one's n. off, the books of a college or hall*: (in Oxford and Cambridge use) to continue to be, cease to be, an actual member of the college or hall. **2.** Now foloys the naamys of all maner of hawkys 1486. There is a Fault, which, tho' common, wants a N. STEELE. *To call names*: see CALL *v.* III.

II. In pregnant senses, chiefly of biblical origin. **1.** The name (sense 1) of God or Christ, regarded as symbolizing the divine nature or power OE. **2. a.** The name of a person as implying his individual characteristics. late ME. **b.** The name (sense 1) of a person or group of persons, as implying all the individuals that bear it; those having a certain name; hence, a family, clan, people. late ME. **3.** The name (sense 1) of a person as mentioned by others with admiration or commendation; hence, the fame or reputation involved in a well-known name ME. **b.** One whose name is well known (*rare*) 1611. **4.** The reputation *of* some character or attribute ME. **b.** With *a* and *adj.* late ME. **c.** (Usu. in phr. *to get* or *make* (*oneself*) *a n.*) A distinguished name. late ME. **5.** Without article: Repute, fame, distinction. Now *rare*. late ME. **6.** One's repute or reputation, etc.; esp. *one's* (*good*) *n.* ME. **7.** The mere appellation in contrast to the person or thing; reputation without correspondence in fact. late ME.

1. Thee we adore Eternal N. WESLEY. **2. a.** By the hand Of that black N., Edward, black Prince of Wales SHAKS. **b.** All the clans hostile to the n. of Campbell were set in motion MACAULAY. **3.** Some to the fascination of a n. Surrender judgment hoodwinked COWPER. Phr. *Of no n.*, without (*a*) *n.*, implying obscurity. **b.** I am become a n.; For always roaming..Much have I seen and known TENNYSON. **4. b.** A good N., for good and faire dealing BACON. **5.** Phr. *Of* (*great*, etc.) *n.*, noted, distinguished, famous. Authors of illustrious n...Are sadly prone to quarrel COWPER. **6.** I love you so well that your good n. is mine TENNYSON. **7.** Christian in n., and infidel in heart COWPER.

Phrases. **By name. a.** Used with verbs of naming or calling, or, later, simply added to the proper appellation of a person, as *a spy, John Jones by n.* **b.** With vbs. of summoning, or mentioning, or in enumeration of individuals. **c.** With *know*. (*a*) Individually. (*b*) By repute only; not personally. **In one's n., in the n. of** one. **a.** In phr. expressing invocation of or devotion to the persons of the Godhead. This, in the N. of Heauen, I promise thee SHAKS. **b.** In adjurations, orig. solemn, but latterly freq. trivial; What in the n. of fortune have they been doing to you? 1861. **c.** Denoting that one acts as deputy for another; or implying that the action is done on account of or on behalf of some other person or persons. Hence, by contrast, *in one's own n.* †**d.** = Under the character or designation of, as. **e.** Indicating the assigned ownership of a thing, as *consols standing in the n. of A. B., deceased*. **By the n. of,** called or known by, having, the n. of. Now *colloq.* and *U.S.* So *of the n. of*. **To** one's **n.** (colloq.), belonging to one.

attrib. and *Comb.*, as *n.-giver*; 'bearing a name', as *n.-card, -plate*, etc.; 'named after, or giving a n. to, one', as *n.-saint, -sire*, etc.; **n.-part,** the part in a play from which it takes its n.

Name (nēⁱm), *v.* [OE. (*ȝe*)*namian*, of WGmc. extent; a new formation on the sb. in late ME. replaced ME. *nemne*, OE. *nemnan* :– **namnjan*.] **I. 1.** *trans.* To give a name or names to; to call by some name. **2.** To call by some title or epithet OE. †**b.** To allege or declare (a person or thing) *to be* something –1647. **3.** To call (a person or thing) by the right name 1450.

1. Then one of them shal n. the childe, and dippe him in the water *Bk. Com. Prayer*. A Son.. Whom she brought up and Comus nam'd MILT. **2.** Ye shalbe named the prestes of the Lorde COVERDALE *Isa.* 61:6. **3.** *Temp.* I. ii. 335. I'm sure I've seen that bonie face, But yet I canna n. ye BURNS.

II. 1. To nominate, assign, or appoint (a person) to some office, duty, or position OE. **2.** To mention or specify (a person or persons, etc.) by name OE. **b.** Of the Speaker of the House of Commons: To indicate (a member) by name as guilty of disorderly conduct or disobedience to the chair 1792. **c.** *Name!* Used in parliamentary practice, etc., to demand that a member be 'named', or that the name of some person alluded to by a speaker shall be given 1817. **3.** To mention, speak of, or specify (a thing) by its name or usual designation. late ME. **b.** To make mention of, to speak about (a fact, etc.); to cite as an instance; to give particulars of 1542. **4.** With cogn. obj. late ME. **5.** To mention or specify as something desired or decided upon; to appoint or fix (a sum, time, etc.) 1593.

1. Such persons, as shalbe named to be iustices of peace 1542. **2.** Now n. the rest of the Players SHAKS. Phr. *To n. on* (or *in*) *the same day* or *in the same breath* (*with*), to bring into comparison or connection. Only in neg. and interrog. sentences. **c.** Loud cries of hear, hear, name, name, order *Parl. Deb.* 279. 1817. **3.** N. not Religion, for thou lou'st the Flesh SHAKS. **b.** The measures we have named were only part of Henry's legislation GREEN. He names the price for ev'ry office paid POPE. **4.** When tongues speak sweetly, then they n. her name SHAKS. **5.** Phr. *To n. the day*, of a woman, to fix her wedding day 1748.

Nameable (nēⁱ·măb'l), *a.* 1840. [f. prec. + -ABLE.] That admits of being named.

Na·me-child. 1845. [f. NAME *sb.* + CHILD.] One called after, or named out of regard for, another.

Name-day (nēⁱ·mˌdēⁱ). Also **name's-day.** 1721. [f. NAME *sb.* + DAY *sb.*] **1.** The day of the saint whose name one bears. (Used chiefly with ref. to continental sovereigns.) **2.** *London Stock Exch.* The day before the account-day, on which the buyers of shares or stock pass to the sellers tickets setting forth the names into which they are to be transferred 1902.

Nameless (nēⁱ·mlės), *a.* ME. [f. NAME *sb.* + -LESS. Senses 5–8 are chiefly *poet.* or *rhet.*] **1.** Not possessed of a (distinguished) name; unknown by name; obscure, inglorious. **b.** Not mentioned by name 1535. **2.** Left unnamed in order to avoid giving offence, or the like. late ME. †**3.** Of a book, letter, etc.: Anonymous –1822. **4.** Of a person: Anonymous, unknown 1591. **5.** Bearing no legitimate name 1593. **b.** Having no name 1638. **6.** Of tombs, etc.: Bearing no name or inscription 1655. **7.** Inexpressible, indefinable 1591. **8.** Unutterable; horrible, abominable 1611.

1. To be namelesse in worthy deeds exceeds an infamous history SIR T. BROWNE. **b.** N. in dark oblivion let them dwell MILT. **2.** On the authority of one who shall be n. JOWETT. **4.** A certain n. Socinian was the Author of them STILLINGFL. **5.** Blur'd with namelesse bastardie SHAKS. **b.** Iles for the greatest part namelesse and numberlesse 1638. **7.** A n. sense of fear SHELLEY. **8.** A flood of n. sensualities LIDDON. Hence **Na·meless-ly** *adv.*, **-ness** 1847.

Namely (nēⁱ·mli), *adv.* ME. [f. NAME *sb.* + -LY².; rendering L. *nominatim* by name, expressly, in detail.] †**1.** Particularly –1700. **2.** To wit; that is to say; videlicet 1450. †**b.** With *as*. For example –1653.

1. Returning thanks..for many blessings and favors..And, n., for the enjoyment of the Gospel 1700. **2.** That thou hast not prayed for, haue I geuen the also, n., ryches, and honoure COVERDALE 1 *Kings* 3:13. **b.** Almost all things, as namelie butter, cheese, fagots 1583.

Namer (nēⁱ·məɹ). 1627. [f. NAME *v.* + -ER¹.] One who, or that which, gives a name or names.

Namesake (nēⁱ·msēⁱk). 1646. [prob. orig. said of persons or things coupled together 'for the *name*('*s*) *sake*'.] A person or thing having the same name as another.

Nammo(re, Na-mo(re, obs. ff. NO MO, NO MORE.

Nandu (næ·ndu). Also **-dou.** 1835. [– Tupi-Guarani *nhandú, ñandú*.] A variety of ostrich (*Rhea americana*) peculiar to S. America.

Nankeen (nænkī·n), *sb.* (and *a.*) Also **-kin.** 1755. [f. *Nankin* or *Nanking*, 'southern capital', in the province of Kiangsu in China. Cf. PEKIN.] **1.** A kind of cotton cloth, orig. made at Nanking from a yellow variety of cotton, but now from ordinary cotton dyed yellow. **b.** With *pl.* A kind of this cloth 1781. **2.** *attrib.* or *adj.* Made of nankeen 1774. **b.** *pl.* Trousers made of nankeen 1806. **3.** A yellow or pale buff; the colour of nankeen. Also *attrib.* 1775. **4.** A kind of Chinese porcelain 1781.

1. *N. cotton*, the variety of cotton from which nankeen cloth was originally made. **3.** *N. bird, crane*, or *night-hawk, n. hawk*: names of Australian birds.

Nanny (næ·ni). Also **nan(n)a.** 1864. [Appellative use of pet-form of the female name *Ann*(*e*; see -Y⁶.] A child's name for a nurse; a children's nurse.

Nanny-goat (næ·niˌgōᵘt). 1788. [As prec.; cf. BILLY-GOAT.] A she-goat (*colloq.*). Also ellipt. **Nanny.**

Nantz (nænts), *sb.* (and *a.*) Now *arch.* 1684. [From *Nantes* in France, where made.] (Often *right N.*) Brandy.

‖**Naos** (nē·ǫs). 1775. [Gr. ναός temple.] A temple; the inner cell or sanctuary of a temple.

Nap (næp), *sb.*¹ ME. [f. NAP *v.*¹] A short

light sleep, *esp.* during the day. Phr. *To take a n.*

Nap (næp), *sb.*² late ME. [– MLG., MDu. *noppe* (whence G., Da. *noppe*), rel. to MLG., MDu. *noppen* trim by shearing the nap. For the change of vowel cf. STRAP *sb.*] **1.** orig. The rough layer of projecting threads or fibres on the surface of a textile fabric, requiring to be smoothed by shearing; in later use, the surface given to cloth by artificial raising of the short fibres, with subsequent cutting and smoothing; the pile. **b.** With *pl.* A cloth having a nap on it 1771. **2.** *transf.* A surface resembling the nap of cloth 1591. **3.** The smooth and glossy surface of a beaver, felt, or silk hat 1727.

1. *fig.* To dresse the Common-wealth, and turne it, and set a new n. vpon it SHAKS.

Nap (næp), *sb.*³ 1820. [abbrev. of *Napoleon.*] **1.** = NAPOLEON 1. **2.** A card game, in which each player receives five cards, and calls the number of tricks he expects to win; one who calls five is said to *go N.*, and to *make his N.* if he wins them all 1879. **b.** *To go n.*, to stake all one can, to speculate heavily 1884.

Nap (næp), *v.*¹ [OE. *hnappian*, rel. to OHG. *(h)naffezan* slumber, of unkn. origin.] *intr.* To sleep lightly for a brief time.

Phr. *To take* or *catch (one) napping*, to find (one) asleep; also *fig.* to take unawares or off one's guard.

Nap (næp), *v.*² 1483. [– MLG., MDu. *noppen*; see NAP *sb.*²] †**1.** *trans.* To trim (cloth) by shearing the nap –1582. **2.** To furnish with a nap; to raise a nap on 1620.

Nap, *v.*³ *Cant* and *slang.* 1673. [See NAB *v.*, KIDNAP *v.*] = NAB *v.*

Napæa (năpī·ă). *rare.* 1612. [– L. *Napæa* – Gr. Ναπαία, fem. of ναπαῖος, f. νάπη wooded dell.] A nymph haunting wooded dells.

Nape (nēⁱp). ME. [Of unkn. origin.] The back of the neck; that part which contains the first cervical vertebra. **b.** esp. in phr. *the n. of the neck* ME.

‖**Napellus** (năpe·lŏs). 1626. [med.L. *napellus*, f. L. *napus* turnip; see -EL.] *Bot.* The common aconite; monk's-hood, wolf's-bane.

Naperer (nēⁱ·pərəɹ). *Obs.* exc. *Hist.* 1450. [f. NAPERY + -ER¹. Cf. med.L. *napparius* XII.] The person having charge of the royal table linen.

Napery (nēⁱ·pəri). ME. [– OFr. *naperie* – *nape*; see NAPKIN, -ERY.] **1.** Household linen, esp. table linen. †**2.** The charge of the royal linen; the office of naperer –1628. †**3.** The making up or manufacture of personal or household linen (*rare*) –1650.

Naphtha (næ·fþă, næ·pþă). 1572. [– L. *naphtha* (Pliny) – Gr. νάφθα, also νάφθος, of oriental origin.] A name orig. applied to an inflammable volatile liquid (a constituent of asphalt and bitumen) issuing from the earth in certain localities; now applied to most of the inflammable oils obtained by dry distillation of organic substances, esp. coal, shale, and petroleum. Also *attrib.*, as *n.-fuel*, *-lamp.* Hence **Na·phthous** *a.*

Naphthalene (næ·fþălīn). Also **-in(e.** 1821. [f. NAPHTHA + *-l-* + -ENE; named by Kidd (1821).] *Chem.* A white crystalline substance, of peculiar smell and pungent taste, usually obtained as a product in the distillation of coal-tar. Also *attrib.* with names of colours. So **Naphtha·lic** 1837.

Naphthalize (næ·fþăləiz), *v.* 1842. [f. as prec. + -IZE.] *trans.* To mingle, saturate, or impregnate with naphtha.

Naphthol (næ·fþǫl). 1849. [f. NAPHTHA + -OL.] *Chem.* One of two phenols of naphthaline, distinguished as α (*or* alpha) and β (*or* beta) naphthol; the latter is employed in the cure of skin-diseases, etc.

Na·phthyl. 1866. [f. as prec. + -YL.] *Chem.* The monatomic radical of naphthylamine.

Naphthy·lamine. Also **-in.** 1857. [f. as prec. + AMINE.] *Chem.* A crystalline substance produced by the action of ammonium sulphide, or acetic acid, on an alcoholic solution of nitro-naphthaline.

Napierian (nēⁱpīᵊ·riăn), *a.* 1816. [f. John *Napier* (see next) + -IAN.] Invented by Napier (see LOGARITHM).

Napier's bones. 1658. Narrow slips of bone, ivory, wood, etc., divided into compartments marked with certain digits, and used to facilitate the variations of multiplication and division according to a method invented by John Napier of Merchiston (1550–1617). Also occas. called *Napier's rods.*

Napiform (nēⁱ·pifǫɹm), *a.* 1846. [f. L. *napus* turnip + -FORM.] Having the shape or appearance of a turnip; esp. *Bot.* of roots.

Napkin (næ·pkin). late ME. [f. (O)Fr. *nappe* linen cloth :– L. *mappa* MAP (for the change of *m* to *n* cf. Fr. *natte* :– L. *matta* MAT, *nèfle* :– L. *mespilus*) + -KIN.] **1.** A square piece of linen, used at meals to wipe the fingers or lips, or to serve certain dishes on; a serviette. **b.** A small towel 1687. **2.** A (pocket-)handkerchief. Now only *Sc.* and *n. dial.* 1530. **3.** A triangle or folded square of absorbent material wrapped round a baby's waist, with the point brought forward between the legs.

2. *To hide, lay up, wrap up*, etc. *in a n.*, in allusion to Luke 19:20. *Comb.* **n.-ring,** a ring placed on a table-napkin when rolled up to distinguish it. Hence †**Na·pkin** *v.* to wrap *up* or hide in or as in a n. –1680.

Naples (nēⁱ·pl'z). 1507. The name of a city in Southern Italy, used to designate various things in some way associated with it. †**1.** As an epithet of venereal disease (cf. NEAPOLITAN *a.*) –1656. **2. N. yellow,** a yellow pigment in the form of a fine powder, prepared from antimony, and orig. manufactured at Naples; also, the colour of this 1738.

Napless (næ·plės), *a.* 1596. [f. NAP *sb.*² + -LESS.] Having no nap; worn threadbare.

The Naples Vesture of Humilitie SHAKS.

Napoleon (năpōᵘ·liŏn). 1814. [– Fr. *napoléon*, f. Christian name of certain Emperors of the French, esp. *Napoleon I* (1769–1821).] **1.** A gold coin issued by Napoleon I, of the value of twenty francs. **2.** A make of long or high boot 1853. **3.** = NAP *sb.*³ 2. 1876. Hence **Napoleo·nic** *a.* connected with or characteristic of Napoleon. **Napoleo·nically** *adv.* **Napo·leonist,** an adherent of N. or of the Napoleonic dynasty; also *attrib.* = Napoleonic. **Napo·leonize** *v.* to govern in the style of N.

Napoo (napū·). 1915 (orig. army slang). [– Fr. *il n'y en a plus* there's nothing left.] There is or was nothing to be done; no good!

‖**Nappe** (næp). 1906. [Fr. 'table-cloth'.] **1.** The sheet of water falling over a weir, etc. **2.** *Geol.* A recumbent fold or anticline 1927.

Nappy (næ·pi), *a.*¹ Now *rare.* 1499. [– MDu. *noppigh*, or MLG. *noppich*, f. *noppe* NAP *sb.*²] Having a nap; downy, shaggy.

Nappy (næ·pi), *a.*² 1529. [prob. transf. use of prec.] **1.** Of ale, etc.: Having a head, foaming; heady, strong. **2.** Slightly exhilarated by drink 1721. Hence **Na·ppy** *sb.* ale.

Napu (nā·pu). 1820. [– Malay *nāpu.*] The musk-deer of Java and Sumatra.

Nar, *a. Obs.* exc. *n. dial.* [OE. *nēarra* etc., compar. of *nēah* NIGH; but in ME. perh. partly – ON. *nærri.*] Nearer. Also *adv.* [– ON.], nearer, near.

Narceine (nā·ɹsīˌin, -əin). Also **-in.** 1834. [– Fr. *narcéine* (Pelletier, 1832), f. Gr. νάρκη numbness; see -INE⁵.] *Chem.* A bitter crystalline alkaloid obtained from opium, sometimes used in medicine instead of morphia. var. **Narceia** (-ī·ă).

Narciss (naɹsi·s). 1586. [– L. *Narcissus* or Fr. *Narcisse.*] = NARCISSUS.

Narcissism (naɹsi·siz'm). 1921. [f. *Narcissus*, in Gr. myth. name of a beautiful youth who fell in love with his own reflection and pined away; see -ISM.] A morbid self-love or self-admiration.

Narcissus (naɹsi·sŏs). *Pl.* **narcissi, -cissuses.** 1548. [– L. *narcissus* – Gr. νάρκισσος, said to be f. νάρκη numbness, in ref. to the narcotic effects produced by it.] *Bot.* A genus of the order *Amaryllidaceæ*, containing many species; a plant of this genus; now esp. *Narcissus poeticus*, a bulbous plant, bearing a heavily scented single white flower with an undivided corona edged with crimson and yellow.

Narcosis (naɹkōᵘ·sis). 1693. [– Gr. νάρκωσις, f. ναρκοῦν benumb; see -OSIS.] *Path.* The production of a narcotic state; the operation or effects of narcotics upon the system; a state of insensibility.

Narcotic (naɹkǫ·tik), *sb.* late ME. [– (O)Fr. *narcotique* or med.L. *narcoticus*, sb. *-icum* – Gr. ναρκωτικός, sb. -ικόν, f. ναρκοῦν benumb, stupefy, f. νάρκη numbness, stupor; see -OTIC.] *Med.* A substance which when swallowed, inhaled, or injected into the system induces drowsiness, sleep, stupefaction, or insensibility, according to its strength and the amount taken.

Narcotic (naɹkǫ·tik), *a.* 1601. [– (O)Fr. or med.L.; see prec.] **1.** Of substances, etc.: Having the effect of inducing stupor, sleep, or insensibility. **b.** *transf.* of persons, actions, etc.: Producing sleep or dullness 1751. **2.** Of the nature of narcosis 1661.

1. b. Silly and n. lecturers 1888. So **Narco·tical** *a.* soporific 1587; **-ly** *adv.* 1654.

Narco:tico-a·crid, *a.* and *sb.* 1829. [f. *narcotico*, as comb. form of NARCOTIC *a.* Cf. Fr. *narcotico-âcre.*] *Med.* (A poison) possessing both narcotic and acrid properties.

Narcotine (nā·ɹkŏtin, -əin). 1823. [– Fr. *narcotine* (Derosne, 1803); see NARCOTIC *a.*, -INE⁵.] *Chem.* A bitter crystalline alkaloid derived from opium, sometimes used in medicine.

Narcotism (nā·ɹkŏtiz'm). 1831. [f. NARCOTIC *a.* + -ISM. Cf. Fr. *narcotisme.*] **1.** The condition produced by narcotics; a state of somnolence or insensibility. **b.** The method of producing insensibility by narcotics 1843. **2.** A morbid inclination to sleep 1843. **3.** *transf.* The narcotic influence *of* something 1867. So **Na·rcotist,** one addicted to the use of narcotics.

Narcotize (nā·ɹkŏtəiz), *v.* 1843. [f. NARCOTIC *a.* + -IZE.] **1.** *trans.* To drug or render insensible with a narcotic. **2.** *transf.* To dull or deaden 1864. Hence **Narcotiza·tion.**

Nard (nāɹd). late ME. [– L. *nardus* – Gr. νάρδος, of Semitic origin. Cf. OFr. *narde* (mod. *nard*).] **1.** An aromatic balsam used by the ancients, derived from the plant of the same name (see sense 2 and cf. SPIKENARD). **2.** An aromatic plant, esp. that yielding the ointment used by the ancients (supposed to be *Nardostachys jatamansi*) 1591.

1. Marie took a pound of oynement spikenard, or trewe nard, precious WYCLIF *John* 12:3.

Nardoo (naɹdū·, nā·ɹdū). Also **-du.** 1861. [Native Australian.] **1.** The sporocarp of the plant *Marsilea quadrifolia*, used as food by the Australian aborigines; the flour made from this. **2.** The plant itself, also called *clover-fern* 1864.

‖**Nardus** (nā·ɹdŏs). Now *rare.* OE. [L.; see NARD.] Nard, spikenard (the ointment and plant).

Nare (nēᵊɹ). Now only *arch.* late ME. [– L. *naris* (usu. in pl. *nares*; see next).] A nostril –1663; *spec.* of a hawk 1486.

‖**Nares** (nēᵊ·rīz). 1693. [L., pl. of *naris* (see prec.), related to OE. *nasu* nose.] *Anat. pl.* The nostrils or nasal passages. Hence **Na·rial** *a.* 1870.

Narghile, nargileh (nā·ɹgile). Also **-gilly.** 1839. [– (partly through Fr. *narghileh*, *narguilé*) Pers. (Turk.) *nārgīleh*, f. Pers. *nārgīl* coco-nut, of which the receptacle for the tobacco was made.] An Oriental tobacco-pipe in which the smoke passes through water before reaching the mouth; a HOOKAH.

Narrate (nĕrēⁱ·t), *v.* [First recorded in 1656; stigmatized as Sc. by S. Richardson and Johnson; not in gen. Engl. use before XIX; – *narrat-*, pa. ppl. stem of L. *narrare* (f. *gnarus* knowing), or back-formation from NARRATION; see -ATE³.] *trans.* To relate, recount, give an account of. Also *absol.*

In narrating interesting facts, his comments.. often fatigue by their plenitude 1788. So **Narra·tor** 1611. **Na·rratory** *a.* of a narrative nature 1586. **Narra·tress, -trix** 1798.

Narration (nĕrēⁱ·ʃən). late ME. [– (O)Fr. *narration* or L. *narratio*, f. as prec.; see -ION.] **1.** The action of relating or recounting, or the fact of being recounted; an instance of this. In early use esp. in phr. *to make n.* **b.** That which is narrated; a story, narrative, account. late ME. **2. a.** *Rhet.* That part of an oration in which the facts of the matter are stated 1509. †**b.** The narrative part of a poem; a narrative passage in a drama 1586–1783.

1. [Dante] the great master of laconic n. LOWELL. **b.** The following N. is a sufficient Testimony of the Truth of this Observation STEELE.

Narrative (næ·rătiv), *sb.* 1561. [– Fr. †*narratif, -ive* sb., subst. use of the adj.; see next.] **1.** *Sc. Law.* That part of a deed or document which narrates the relevant or essential facts. **2.** An account or narration; a tale, recital (of facts, etc.) 1566. **3.** (Without article.) The practice or act of narrating; something to narrate 1748.

2. He shall find me ready to maintain the truth of my n. '*Junius*' *Lett.* **3.** To have frequent recourse to n. betrays great want of imagination CHESTERF.

Narrative (næ·rătiv), *a.* 1605. [– Fr. *narratif, -ive* adj. – late L. *narrativus*, f. *narrat-*; see NARRATE *v.*, -IVE.] **1.** That narrates; occupied or concerned with, having the character of, narration. †**2.** Garrulous, talkative –1826.

1. The *Paradise Lost* is an Epic or N. Poem ADDISON. **2.** Mr. John Smith (called Narrative Smith) 1681. Hence **Na·rratively** *adv.*

Narrow (næ·ro͡u), *a.* and *sb.* [OE. *nearu* (stem *nearw-*) = OS. *naru* (MDu. *nare, naer*, Du. *naar*) :- Gmc. **narwaz* (repr. in MHG. *narwe*, G. *narbe*, MLG. *nar(w)e* scar, subst. use of adj.), of which no certain cogns. are known.] **A.** *adj.* **1.** Having little breadth or width in comparison with the length. **b.** *Phonetics.* Of vowels, in contrast to *wide* or *open* 1844. **2.** Of restricted extent or size. *N. house*, the grave. OE. **b.** Lying or pressing close OE. **3.** Limited or restricted in range or scope or amount; of slight dimensions or extent 1523. **b.** Of time, brief (*rare*) 1611. **4.** Parsimonious, mean (now *dial.*); lacking in sympathy; narrow-minded, illiberal ME. **5.** Characterized by close or exact scrutiny ME. **b.** *transf.* of the eyes, etc. partly with ref. to near-sightedness 1577. **6.** Involving or marked by close approximation to something expressed or implied; near, close; (of an escape) barely effected 1551. **7.** *Comb.* as *n.-hearted, -leaved, -necked, -shouldered, -sighted, -souled, -spirited* adjs.

1. The streets are for the most part n. and winding 1756. Phr. *The n. way*; Strait is the gate, and n. is the way, which leadeth unto life *Matt.* 7:14. *N. cloth*, cloth under 52 inches wide. *N. front* (Mil.): a battalion, &c. is said to assume a n. front, when it goes from line into column 1802. *N. goods*, braid, ribbons, and the like. *N. work*, excavations 3 yards in width and under. **b.** Each of the vowels..is either *n.* or *wide*, according as the tongue and uvula are tense..or relaxed SWEET. **2.** The place where we dwell..is to narow for vs COVERDALE 2 *Kings* 6:1. **b.** Life, within a n. ring Of giddy joys comprised COWPER. **3.** The question is yet driuen to a narrower issue HOOKER. Let me rather have a n. estate and wide soul 1688. **4.** Archibald..was n. in his ordinary expenses JOHNSON in *Boswell.* I daily find more Instances of this n. Party-Humour ADDISON. The days of cold hearts and n. minds MACAULAY. A n. oligarchy MACAULAY. **5.** Seeking to make a narrower inquiry SMOLLETT. **b.** Looking into her eyes with his n. gaze GEO. ELIOT. **6.** What's a n. squeak, a close shave, to such as I am? 1860.

B. *sb.* **1.** A narrow place, or thing; the narrow part of something. Now *rare.* ME. **2.** *spec.* Chiefly in *pl.* **a.** A narrow part of a strait or river, a pass or valley (chiefly *U.S.*); a street 1633. **b.** *Mining.* A narrow gallery 1850.

1. *fig.* When it came to the n. of any question he would still profess himself conquered by Mr. Hooker's reason 1702.

Na·rrow, *adv.* Now *rare.* [OE. *nearwe*, f. *nearu* NARROW *a.*] †**1.** Closely, strictly –1460. †**2.** Carefully, keenly –1596. **3.** Narrowly, in various senses ME.

3. Phr. *To fall n.*, to fall short. *To go n.*, of a horse, to keep the legs too close together.

Narrow (næ·ro͡u), *v.* [OE. *nearwian*, f. *nearu* NARROW *a.*; but in ME. (XIII) f. the adj.] **1.** *intr.* To become narrower; to diminish, contract. **2.** *trans.* To make narrower; †also *fig.* to constrict, constrain OE. **b.** To contract, reduce 1674. **c.** To drive into a narrow space, press closely 1814.

1. Following up The river as it narrow'd to the hills TENNYSON. **2.** She narrowed her lids slightly O. W. HOLMES. **b.** He has here pretty well narrowed the field of taxation BURKE. **c.** Tho' the gathering enemy n. thee TENNYSON. Hence **Na·rrower.** **Na·rrowing** *vbl. sb.* the action of the vb.; a narrowed place or part.

Narrow-eyed, *a.* 1599. [f. NARROW *a.* 1 and 5 + EYED *ppl. a.*] Having narrow eyes.

Narrow gauge. 1841. A gauge of less than 4 ft. 8½ in. (as opp. to the BROAD GAUGE); formerly, the gauge of 4 ft 8½ in.

Narrowly (næ·ro͡uli), *adv.* [OE. *nearulīće*, f. *nearu* NARROW *a.* + *-līće* -LY²; but later f. the adj.] **1.** With close attention or scrutiny. **2.** In a contracted or confined manner OE. †**3.** †**a.** Barely, scarcely. ME. only. **b.** Only just (escape, miss) 1560. †**4.** Closely –1707. **5.** Illiberally; strictly 1708.

1. I watched him n. for Six and Thirty Years 1709. **3. b.** One [arrow] very n. missed my left eye SWIFT.

Narrow-minded, *a.* 1625. [f. NARROW *a.* 4 + MINDED *ppl. a.*] Lacking in breadth of mind; incapable of or not given to broad views or wide sympathy. Hence **Narrow-mi·nded-ly** *adv.*, **-ness.**

Narrowness (næ·ro͡unės). 1530. [f. NARROW *a.* Cf. OE. *nearunes.*] The fact or quality of being narrow.

Narrow seas. late ME. [NARROW *a.* 1.] The channels separating Great Britain from the Continent and from Ireland.

Sterne Falconbridge commands the Narrow Seas SHAKS.

Narthex (nā·ɹþeks). 1673. [– L. *narthex* – Gr. νάρθηξ giant fennel, stick, casket, and eccl. (as below).] *Archæol.* A vestibule or portico stretching across the western end of some early Christian churches, divided from the nave by a wall, screen, or railing, and set apart for women, catechumens, etc.

Narw(e, obs. ff. NARROW.

Narwhal (nā·ɹhwăl). 1658. [– Du. *narwal* – Da. *narhval* (whence also G. *narwal*, Fr. *narval*), f. *hval* WHALE, rel. obscurely to ON. *náhvalr* (f. *nár* corpse, with ref. to the colour of the skin.] A delphinoid cetacean (*Monodon monoceros*) inhabiting the Arctic seas, having only two teeth, one (or both) of which develops into a spirally-twisted straight horn; the sea-unicorn.

Nary (nēə·ri), *a.* 1836. *U.S.* and *dial.* [var. of NE'ER A.] Neither; no; not a.

Nasal (nēⁱ·zăl), *sb.* 1480. [In sense 1 – OFr. *nasal* – med.L. *nasale* (XII), subst. use of n. of the adj.; see next; otherwise f. next.] **1.** A nose-piece on a helmet. **2.** A nasal letter or sound 1669. **3.** *Anat.* A nasal bone 1854.

Nasal (nēⁱ·zăl), *a.* 1656. [– Fr. *nasal* or med.L. *nasalis*, f. L. *nasus* nose; see -AL¹.] **1.** Of or pertaining to the nose; used in connection with the nose (1875). **2.** Of speech-sounds: Produced, more or less, by means of the nose 1669. **b.** Characterized by the presence of sounds so produced 1669.

1. Phr. *N. artery, bone, cartilage*, etc., *n. douche, speculum*, etc. **2.** In n. sounds, such as *m*, the passage of the nose is left open SWEET. **b.** Odious as a n. twang Heard at conventicle COWPER. Hence **Nasa·lity,** the quality of being n.; an instance of this. **Na·sally** *adv.*

Nasalize (nēⁱ·zăləiz), *v.* 1846. [f. NASAL *a.* + -IZE.] **a.** *intr.* To speak through the nose. **b.** *trans.* To utter with a nasal sound. Hence **Na:saliza·tion.**

Nascency (næ·sĕnsi). 1682. [– L. *nascentia*; see next and -ENCY.] The process or fact of being brought into existence; birth.

Nascent (næ·sĕnt), *a.* 1624. [– *nascent-*, pr. ppl. stem of L. *nasci* be born; see -ENT.] **1.** In the act of being born or brought forth. **2.** *transf.* In the act or condition of coming into existence; just beginning to form, grow, develop, etc. 1706.

1. Food for the n. larvæ 1816. **2.** Imagination.. reigns in all n. societies of men GRAY. That cartilage in truth is only n. or imperfect bone PALEY. Phr. *N. state*, the state of coming into existence, beginning to form, etc.; *Chem.* the condition of an element at the moment of liberation from a compound.

Naseberry (nēⁱ·zbĕri). 1698. [– Sp., Pg. *néspera* MEDLAR, with assim. to BERRY.] A W. Indian tree (*Sapota achras*) which yields an edible fruit called the Sapodilla plum.

Nash-gab, -gob. *Sc.* and *n. dial.* 1816. [f. dial. *nash* impertinence + GAB *sb.*³, GOB *sb.*²] Impertinent talk; a pert or gossiping person.

Nasiform (nēⁱ·zifǫɹm), *a. rare.* 1752. [f. L. *nasus* nose + -FORM.] Nose-shaped.

Naso- (nēⁱ·zo), mod. comb. form of L. *nasus* nose, used **a.** in terms relating to the nose in conjunction with some other part, as *n.-frontal, -lachrymal, -palatal, -pharyngeal*, adjs.; also *n.-pharyngitis, -pharynx*, etc. †**b.** in terms denoting nasal sounds, as *n.-guttural.*

Nasturtium (năstɒ̆·ɹʃɒ̆m). Also (corruptly) **-tian** (-ʃən). 1570. [– L. *nasturtium*, named, acc. to Pliny, from its pungency ('nomen accepit a narium tormento').] **1.** A genus of cruciferous plants having a pungent taste, including the Watercress (*N. officinale*); also, a plant belonging to this genus. Now only *Bot.* **2.** A trailing plant of the S. American genus *Tropæolum*, cultivated in gardens for its showy orange-coloured flowers; Indian Cress. (Now usu. denoting the larger species *Tropæolum majus*, but at first applied to *T. minus*, both introduced from Peru.) 1704.

Nasty (na·sti), *a.* late ME. [Origin unkn.] **1.** Foul, filthy, dirty, unclean, esp. to a disgusting degree; offensive through filth or dirt. Also, morally filthy, obscene 1601. **2.** Offensive to smell or taste; nauseous 1548. **3.** Disagreeable, unpleasant 1634. **b.** Difficult to deal with, dangerous; rather serious 1828. **4.** Ill-natured, 'disagreeable' (*to* another) 1825.

1. The nastie filthinesse of the nation in generall MORYSON. The greatest heap of n. language that perhaps ever was put together 1731. **2.** For one good smell by the river's side, there be ten n. ones MARRYAT. **3.** It is a cursed n. morning FIELDING. **b.** This is a n. ditch we are coming to 1875. A n. blow on the finger 1883. **4.** 'He's a n. stuck-up monkey,..' said Mrs. Squeers DICKENS. Lest the headstrong William might turn n. 1874. N. little tricks 1888. *absol.* The cheap and n. 1884. Hence **Na·stily** *adv.* **Na·stiness** 1611.

Nasute (neⁱ·siut, năsiū·t), *a.* 1653. [– L. *nasutus*, f. *nasus* nose.] †**1.** Keen-scented, sagacious –1707. **2.** *Zool.* Nose-shaped. Having a large nose or prominent nostrils 1884.

Natal (nēⁱ·tăl), *a.* late ME. [– L. *natalis* adj. and sb., f. *nat-*, pa. ppl. stem of *nasci* be born; see -AL¹.] †**1.** Presiding over nativities. CHAUCER. **2.** Of places: Native. Chiefly *poet.* late ME. **3.** Of or pertaining to (one's) birth; connected with one's birth 1447.

2. He sought his n. mountain-peaks divine SHELLEY. **3.** *N. hour* or *day*, the hour or day of one's birth.

†**Natali·tial,** *a.* 1611. [f. L. *natalitius* (f. *natalis* NATAL) + -AL¹.] Belonging to or connected with one's birth or birthday –1679. So †**Natali·tious** *a.* 1646–1669.

Natality (nătæ·lĭti). 1483. [f. NATAL *a.* + -ITY. In recent use – Fr. *natalité.*] **1.** Birth (*rare*). **2.** Birth-rate 1888.

Natant (nēⁱ·tănt), *a.* 1707. [– *natant-*, pr. ppl. stem of L. *natare*, frequent. of *nare* swim, float; see -ANT.] Swimming, floating.

Natation (nătēⁱ·ʃən). 1542. [– L. *natatio*, f. *natat-*, pa. ppl. stem of *natare*; see prec., -ION.] The action or art of swimming; also, †that which swims or floats. Hence **Nata·tional** *a.*, **Nata·tionist.**

‖**Natatores** (nēⁱtătōə·rīz). 1823. [L., pl. of *natator* swimmer, f. as prec.; see -OR 2.] *Ornith. pl.* An order of birds adapted for swimming, including ducks, geese, swans and pelicans.

Natatorial (nēⁱtătōə·riăl), *a.* 1816. [f. as next + -AL¹.] **1.** Of or belonging to swimming. **b.** Of organs: Adapted for swimming 1823. **2.** Characterized by swimming; *esp.* in *Ornith.* of the *Natatores* 1839.

Natatory (nēⁱ·tătəri), *a.* 1799. [– late L. *natatorius*, f. L. *natator*; see NATATORES, -ORY².] **1.** Of organs: Adapted for swimming or floating. **2.** Of or belonging to swimming 1836. **3.** Characterized by swimming 1887.

3. Nereus..With his n. daughters 1895.

Natch-bone. *rare.* 1613. [var. of NACHE.] = AITCH-BONE.

Nates (nēⁱ·tīz), *sb. pl.* 1681. [– L. *nates*, pl. of *natis* rump, buttock.] *Anat.* and *Med.* **1.** The buttocks, haunches 1706. **2.** The anterior and larger pair of the optic lobes (*corpora quadrigemina*) of the brain 1681.

Natheless, nathless (nēⁱ·plės, næ·plės), *adv.* (and *prep.*). Now only *arch.* [f. OE. *nā*

NA *adv.*[1] + *þe* THE *adv.* + *lǣs* LESS *adv.*] Nevertheless. **b.** *prep.* In spite of, notwithstanding *(rare)* 1567.

†**Nathemo(re,** *adv.* OE. [f. as prec. + MO(RE.] Never the more –1596.

‖**Natica** (næ·tikă). 1840. [mod.L., perh. f. med.L. *natica* buttock, f. L. *natis*; see NATES.] *Zool.* A genus of carnivorous sea-snails; a snail of this genus.

Nation (nēi·ʃən), *sb.* ME. [– (O)Fr. *nation*, †*nacioun* – L. *natio, -on-* breed, stock, race, f. *nat-*, pa. ppl. stem of *nasci* be born, see -ION.] **I. 1.** A distinct race or people, characterized by common descent, language, or history, usu. organized as a separate political state and occupying a definite territory. †**b.** People of a particular nation –1818. **c.** In mediæval universities, a body of students belonging to a particular district, country, or group of countries; still retained in the universities of Glasgow and Aberdeen in connection with the election of the Rector 1664. †**d.** A country, kingdom *(rare)* –1668. †**2.** Without article: Nationality –1641. **3.** *The n.*, the whole people of a country 1602.

1. In Switzerland four languages are spoken; yet the Swiss certainly make one n. FREEMAN. *transf.* The famous Nations of the dead SIR T. BROWNE. **b.** It being express in his orders not to permit any n...to come on shore and stay there DE FOE. **2.** Though he were a Fleming by Nation, yet was hee not separated from the interest of France 1641.

The nations: **a.** *biblical*, the heathen nations, the Gentiles. **b.** *poet.*, the peoples of the earth collectively. *Law of nations*: see LAW *sb.*[1] 4. *League of Nations*: see LEAGUE *sb.*[2] 1 b.

II. 1. †**a.** A family, kindred, clan –1584. **b.** A tribe of N. American Indians 1763. †**2.** A particular class, kind, or race of persons or of animals –1781.

1. b. The sachems and warriors of the Six Nations 1775. **2.** All the barbarous n. of scholemen ASCHAM. The scaly Nations of the Sea profound DRYDEN.

Nation (nēi·ʃən), *adv., a., int. dial.* and *U.S.* 1785. A euphemistic abbr. of DAMNATION 3. Cf. *darnation, tarnation.*

National (næ·ʃənăl), *a.* and *sb.* 1597. [– Fr. *national*, f. *nation*; see NATION *sb.*, -AL[1].] **A.** *adj.* **1.** Of or belonging to a or the nation; affecting or shared by the nation as a whole. **b.** Of troops: Maintained by a nation 1842. **c.** Of or belonging to the French Government during the time of the first Republic 1793. **2.** Characteristic or distinctive of a nation 1625. **3.** Strongly upholding one's own nation or countrymen 1711. **b.** Devoted to the interests of the nation as a whole 1801.

1. N. corruption must be purged by n. calamities BOLINGBROKE. **2.** That an unsavoury odour is gentilitious or n. unto the Jews SIR T. BROWNE. It is of great consequence to preserve a n. character 1778. **3.** He is intensely n...He believes that the Scots are the finest race in the world 1871.

Spec. collocations: **n. council, debt** (see the sbs.); **n. anthem,** a hymn adopted by a people and used (esp. on public occasions) as an expression of national and patriotic sentiment (in the British Empire, 'God save the King'); **N. Assembly,** an assembly consisting of representatives of a nation; spec. †*(a)* = *General Assembly* (see ASSEMBLY); *(b)* a synod of the Church in a particular nation; *(c)* the first of the revolutionary assemblies of France, in session 1789–91; also applied at various times to the popular assembly, and now to the two houses, the Senate and the Chamber of Deputies, when in joint session; *(d)* the deliberative and legislative body created by the Church of England Assembly (Powers) Act, 1919; **n. bank,** a bank associated with the national finances; *U.S.* one whose circulating notes are secured by U.S. bonds deposited with the government; **n. church,** *(a)* a church consisting of a nation; *(b)* a church established by law in a particular nation; **n. guard,** an armed force existing in France at various times between 1789 and 1871; **n. insurance,** a scheme organized by the state for the compulsory insurance of employed persons against sickness or unemployment; **N. Republicans,** *U.S.*, an early name for the Whig party; **n. school,** one of the schools established by the **National Society,** founded in 1811 to promote the education of the poor.

B. *sb.* †**1.** One who supports national, not party, interests –1768. **2.** *pl.* (after Fr. *nationaux*): Persons belonging to the same nation; (one's) fellow-countrymen 1887. Hence **Na·tional-ly** *adv.*, **-ness.**

Nationalism (næ·ʃənăliz'm). 1844. [f. NATIONAL *a.* + -ISM.] **1.** Devotion to one's nation; a policy of national independence. **b.** *spec.* The programme of the Irish Nationalist party 1885. **2.** A form of socialism, based on the nationalizing of all industry 1892.

Nationalist (næ·ʃənălist). 1715. [f. as prec. + -IST.] An adherent or supporter of nationalism; an advocate of national rights, etc. **b.** *spec.* One who advocates the claims of Ireland to be an independent nation 1846. Hence **Nationali·stic** *a.*

b. The Nationalists, in short, are to call the tune and the people of this country to pay the piper 1893.

Nationality (næʃənæ·lĭti). 1691. [f. NATIONAL + -ITY.] **1.** National quality or character. **2.** National feeling 1772. **3.** The fact of belonging to a particular nation 1828. **4.** Separate existence as a nation; national independence or consolidation 1832. **5.** A nation 1832.

1. Ancient British n. received into itself a Roman n. 1854. I have little faith in that quality in literature which is commonly called n. LOWELL. **2.** He could not but see in them that n. which I should think no liberal minded Scotsman will deny BOSWELL.

Nationalize (næ·ʃənăləiz), *v.* Also **-ise.** 1800. [– Fr. *nationaliser* (1794); see NATIONAL, -IZE.] **1.** *trans.* To render national in character. **2.** To naturalize; to admit into, or make part of, a nation 1809. **b.** *intr.* To become naturalized 1891. **3.** To bring under the control of, to make the property of, the nation 1869.

1. He took what may be called cosmopolitan traditions,..and nationalized them LOWELL. **3.** It is a perfectly intelligible proposition that all the land in the kingdom ought to be 'nationalized' 1881. Hence **Na:tionaliza·tion.**

Nationalty (næ·ʃənălti). 1812. [f. NATIONAL *a.* + -TY[1], after *personalty*, etc.] National property.

Nationhood (nēi·ʃənhud). 1850. [f. NATION *sb.* + -HOOD.] The state or fact of being a nation.

Native (nēi·tiv), *sb.* 1450. [Earliest in sense 1 – AL. *nativus, nativa* XII (see NEIF), subst. use of med.L. *nativus* adj. (see next). In later use sometimes directly from the adj.] **1.** One born in bondage; a born thrall. Now only *Hist.* **2.** *Astrol.* One born under a particular planet or sign 1509. **3.** One born in a place; or, *legally*, one whose parents have their domicile in a place 1535. **b.** In Australia, a white person born in the country 1861. **4.** One of the original or indigenous inhabitants of a country; now *esp.* one belonging to a non-European or uncivilized race 1603. **5.** An animal or plant (†or mineral) indigenous to a locality 1690. **b.** An oyster altogether or partially reared in British waters; now *spec.* those reared in artificial beds 1818. †**6.** *pl.* Fellow-countrymen –1655. **7.** Native place (or country). Now only *dial.* 1604.

2. Nebulous Stars..being joyn'd with the Luminaries to afflict a N. with blindness 1679. **3.** He speaks English like a n. LYTTON. **4.** Columbus ..continued to interrogate all the natives 1777. **5. b.** A newly-opened oyster-shop,..with natives laid one deep in circular marble basins in the windows DICKENS.

Native (nēi·tiv), *a.* late ME. [– (O)Fr. *natif, -ive* or L. *nativus* produced by birth, innate, natural, f. *nat-*, pa. ppl. stem of *nasci* be born; see -IVE.] **I. 1.** Belonging to, or connected with, a person or thing by nature; inherent, innate. **b.** Natural *to* a person or thing 1533. **c.** Natural. Now *rare.* 1509. **2.** Left in a natural state; *esp.* untouched by art; unadorned, simple 1560. **3.** That was the place or scene of one's birth. Also const. *to.* 1500. **b.** Original, parent 1590. **4.** Belonging to, or natural to, one by reason of the circumstances of one's birth.

1. So angelik was her natyf beute, That lyke thing immortal seemyd she CHAUCER. **b.** If there is a thing specially n. to religion, it is peace and union M. ARNOLD. **2.** If..sweetest Shakespear.. Warble his n. Wood-notes wild MILT. Mere Words,..used only as they serve to betray those who understand them in their n. sense STEELE. **3.** Say..the cause Why thou departedst from thy natiue home? SHAKS. **b.** Is this the way I must return to n. dust? MILT. **4.** The Language I haue learn'd these forty yeares (My natiue English) now I must forgo SHAKS. A..people, tenacious of their n. liberty 1801.

II. 1. Connected with one by birth or race; closely related. Now *rare.* 1470. †**2.** Being what one is by right of birth; natural, rightful –1593. **3.** Of metals, etc.: Occurring naturally in a pure or uncombined state; also used to describe a mineral occurring in nature, as opp. to a similar substance formed artificially. So *n. rock.* 1695. **b.** *transf.* Applied to the state or form of such substances 1753.

2. The Head is not more Natiue to the Heart.. Then is the Throne of Denmark to thy Father SHAKS. **3.** *Rich. II*, III. ii. 25. **b.** Substances.. found in the bowels of the earth, in their n. state GOLDSM.

III. 1. Born in a particular place or country; belonging to a particular race, district, etc., by birth. In mod. use, *spec.* with connotation of non-European (cf. NATIVE *sb.* 4). 1470. **2.** Of indigenous origin, production, or growth 1555. **3.** Of or belonging to the natives of a particular place 1796.

1. Be caus I am a natyff Scottis man 1470. Are you natiue of this place? SHAKS. **2.** Trade is twofold, viz. N., and Forein 1670. It is rather a difficult matter to define what is a n. oyster 1865. *N. bear* (the KOOLAH), *bustard, cat, dog* (= DINGO-), *hen, rabbit, turkey*: names of Australian animals and birds. *N. bread*, an underground fungus (*Mylitta australis*) eaten by Australian aborigines. **3.** Living in the n. houses 1897. Hence **Na·tive-ly** *adv.*, **-ness.**

Native-born, *a.* 1500. [f. prec. + BORN *ppl. a.*] Belonging to a particular place or country by birth; sometimes *spec.* applied to persons of immigrant race born in a colony.

Nativism (nēi·tiviz'm). 1856. [f. as prec. + -ISM; with sense 2 cf. Fr. *nativisme.*] **1.** (Chiefly *U.S.*) Prejudice in favour of natives against strangers; the practice or policy of giving effect to this. **2.** *Philos.* The doctrine of innate ideas 1887. So **Na·tivist,** one who favours n. in either sense.

Nativity (năti·vĭti). ME. [– (O)Fr. *nativité* – late L. *nativitas, -tat-* (Tertullian), f. L. *nativus*; see NATIVE *a.*, -ITY.] **1.** The birth of Christ, of the Virgin Mary, or of St. John Baptist. Also, a picture representing the Nativity. **2.** The festival of the birth of Christ; Christmas. Also, that of the birth of the Virgin Mary, Sept. 8, or of St. John Baptist, June 24. ME. **3.** Birth. late ME. **4.** A horoscope. late ME. **5.** Birth as determining nationality 1592. Now *rare.*

1. At the time of his n...there was peace amongst all nations ABP. SANDYS. **3.** I haue serued him from the houre of my Natiuitie to this instant SHAKS. *fig.* Plagiary had not its N. with Printing SIR T. BROWNE. **5.** He owed this to his Scotch n. 1821.

Natrolite (næ·troləit, nēi·-). 1805. [f. NATRON + -LITE; named by Klaproth, 1803.] *Min.* A hydrous silicate of aluminium and sodium.

Natron (nēi·trŏn). 1684. [– Fr. *natron* – Sp. *natrón* – Arab. *naṭrūn, niṭrūn* – Gr. νίτρον NITRE. Cf. ANATRON.] Native sesquicarbonate of soda, occurring in solution or as a deposit (mixed with other substances) in various parts of the world. **b.** *attrib.* in *n. lake* 1821.

Natterjack (næ·təɹdʒæk). 1769. [perh. f. prec. (from its loud croak) + *jack* (see JACK III), applied dial. to newts and flies.] A British species of toad (*Bufo calamita*), having a light yellow stripe down the back.

Nattier (næ·tiəɹ). 1918. [The name of a French painter, Jean Marc *Nattier* (1685–1766).] *N. blue*: a variety of blue.

Natty (næ·ti), *a.* 1785. [orig. dial. or slang; rel. obscurely to NEAT *a.*; see -Y[1].] Neatly smart; spruce, trim; exhibiting dainty tidiness, taste, or skill.

A n. spark of eighteen 1806. His uncle used to.. arrange the n. curl on his forehead THACKERAY. Hence **Na·ttily** *adv.* **Na·ttiness.**

Natural (see next), *sb.* 1509. [subst. use of next, in some senses after Fr. *naturel* sb. Sense I. 2 is peculiar to Eng.] **I.** †**1.** A native of a place or country –1657. **2.** *arch.* One naturally deficient in intellect 1533.

2. She..is not quite a n., that is, not an absolute idiot MME. D'ARBLAY.

II. †**1.** *pl.* Natural gifts or powers of mind (or body) –1678. †**2.** *In* one's *pure naturals* (after med.L. *in puris naturalibus*): not altered or improved in any way; also, in a perfectly naked state –1737. †**3.** *pl.* Natural things or objects –1738. **4.** *Mus.* **a.** A natural note 1609. **b.** The sign ♮ used to cancel a preceding sharp or flat, and give a note its 'natural' value 1797. **c.** One of the white keys on a pianoforte, etc. 1880. **5.** In the card-game of vingt-et-un, an ace and a ten dealt in the first instance, making exactly 21. 1849.

Natural (næ·tʃŭrăl, næ·tiŭrăl), *a.* ME. [Earlier *naturel* – (O)Fr. *naturel*, †*natural* – L. *naturalis*, f. *natura*; see NATURE, -AL[1].] **I. 1.** Of law and justice: Based upon the innate moral feeling of mankind; instinctively felt to be right and fair. **2.** Constituted by nature. late ME. **b.** *Bot.* Applied spec. to Jussieu's arrangement of plants according to the likeness they bear to each other, in contrast with the sexual system of Linnæus, and to the orders, families, etc. resulting from this arrangement 1803. **3.** Taking place or operating in accordance with the ordinary course of nature 1477. **4.** In a state of nature, without spiritual enlightenment 1526. **5.** Having a real or physical existence, as opp. to what is spiritual, intellectual or fictitious; pertaining to the physical (as opp. to the spiritual) world 1526. **6.** Existing in, or formed by, nature; not artificial 1568. **b.** Of vegetation: Self-sown or planted. Also of land: Not cultivated. 1526. **7.** Life-like 1581. **b.** Simple, unaffected, easy 1607. **c.** Not disfigured or disguised 1800.

1. Man, yf he be brought vp in corrupt opynyon, hath no perceyuance of thys n. law 1538. N. justice required that the loss..should be recouped by the other party 1883. **2.** *N. day*, i.e. twenty-four hours. *N. year*, the period occupied by the earth in making its revolution round the sun; the solar year. *N. number*, one without fractions; also, an actual number as dist. from a logarithm. *N. note, key*, etc. (*Mus.*): opp. to *sharp* or *flat*. *N. scale*, the scale of C major, so called as having no accidentals. **3.** It was no naturall eclypse CAXTON. We were come into a more convenient and naturall temperature 1604. So likewise yong men..die by naturall death as well as old men doe 1576. **4.** For the naturall man perceaveth not the thyngs off the sprete off god TINDALE 1 *Cor.* 2:14. *N. religion*, 'the Things knowable concerning God and our Duty by the Light of Nature' (Watts). *N. theology*, a theology based upon human reasoning, apart from revelation. **5.** Which is the naturall man, And which the spirit? SHAKS. **6.** A fertile plain, watered by the n. and artificial channels of the Tigris GIBBON. 'Natural' sticks—that is, those cut from the stem with the bark on 1878. *N. wig*, one made of human hair. **7. b.** Just put all thought of yourself aside and be n. 1863.

II. 1. Present by nature; innate; not acquired or assumed. late ME. **2.** Normally connected with, or pertaining to, a person or thing; consonant with the nature or character of the person or thing. late ME. **b.** Coming easily or spontaneously *to* one 1589. **c.** Naturally arising from the circumstances of the case 1667. **3.** Standing in a specified relationship to another person or thing by reason of the nature of things or the force of circumstances 1516. †**b.** Natural-born –1656. †**4.** Native (country or language) –1661. †**5.** *N. parts* or *places*, the genitals –1754.

1. The n. love of life SWIFT. †*N. parts*, native ability, apart from learning –1771. **2.** The n. recoil of superstition is scepticism 1850. *N. life*, used chiefly (and now only) with ref. to the duration of this life. **b.** Phr. *To come n. to*, to be a n. action for (one). **c.** Som n. tears they drop'd, but wip'd them soon MILT. **3.** My naturall enemy death 1516. **b.** Whom should hee follow, but his naturall King? SHAKS.

III. †**1.** Of children: Legitimate –1741. †**b.** Similarly *n. father, brother*, etc. –1641. **c.** In later use, that is such by nature only; hence, illegitimate, bastard 1586. **2.** Having a specified character by nature; esp. in *n. fool*, †*idiot*. late ME. †**3.** Native-born –1665. **4.** Having natural feeling; kindly. Now *rare.* 1470.

1. Not one of his naturall children, yet brought up with his other children 1599. **b.** My selfe.. They take for Naturall Father SHAKS. **c.** He was never married, but had n. daughters 1817. **2.** Thou [art] a naturall Coward, without instinct SHAKS. **3.** Good and naturall English words 1579. **4.** I pray you to be a good and naturall modre unto hyr 1530.

IV. Dealing or concerned with, relating to, nature as an object of study or research, as *n. science*. late ME.

Some N. Observations made..in Shropshire 1707. The three branches of the N. Sciences 1840. *N. philosophy*, the study of n. bodies as such and of the phenomena connected with them; physics. So *N. philosopher*, a physicist. Hence **Na·turally** *adv.* in a n. manner. **Na·turalness.**

Na·tural-born, *a.* 1583. [f. prec. + BORN *ppl. a.*] Having a specified position or character by birth; esp. with *subject*.

Na·tural Hi·story. 1555. [HISTORY *sb.* 4.] **1.** A work dealing with the properties of natural objects, plants, or animals; a scientific account *of* any subject on similar lines. **2.** The aggregate of facts relating to the natural objects *of* a place, or the characteristics *of* a class of persons or things. Also *transf.* 1593. **3.** orig., The systematic study of all natural objects, animal, vegetable, and mineral; now restricted to the study of animal life, usu. in a popular manner 1662.

1. That Natural History, which he wrote of all plants BACON. **2.** Another incident in natural history..is..Toads eat larks! 1816.

Naturalism (næ·tʃŭrăliz'm, næ·tiŭ-). 1641. [f. NATURAL + -ISM. In sense 2 after Fr. *naturalisme* (XVIII).] **1.** Action arising from, or based on, natural instincts (†also with *pl.*); a system of morality or religion having a purely natural basis. **2.** *Philos.* A view of the world, and of man's relation to it, in which only the operation of natural (as opp. to supernatural or spiritual) laws and forces is assumed 1750. **3.** A style or method, in literature and art, characterized by close adherence to nature 1850. **4.** Adherence to what is natural 1865.

3. The Gothic n. advancing gradually from the Byzantine severity RUSKIN. **4.** Goethe's profound, imperturbable n. M. ARNOLD.

Naturalist (næ·tʃŭrălist, næ·tiŭ-). 1587. [– Fr. *naturaliste* (1527); partly f. NATURAL *a.* + -IST.] **1.** One who studies natural, in contrast to spiritual, things; an adherent of, or believer in, naturalism. **b.** One who follows the light of nature, as contrasted with revelation 1608. **2.** One who studies, or is versed in, natural science; a physicist. Now *rare* or *Obs.* 1587. **b.** *spec.* One who makes a special study of animals or plants. (A less precise term than *zoologist, botanist*, etc.) 1600. **c.** A dealer in cage animals, dogs, etc.; also, a taxidermist 1863. **3.** A representative of naturalism in art or literature 1784. **4.** *adj.* Naturalistic 1830.

2. b. A lion; of whom the n. writeth [etc.] 1600.

Naturalistic (nætʃŭrăli·stik, næt̆iŭ-), *a.* 1840. [f. prec. + -IC.] **1.** In accordance with the doctrine of naturalism; of the nature of, characterized by, naturalism 1860. **2.** Aiming at a faithful representation of nature in art or literature 1849. **3.** Of or belonging to natural history 1859. **Naturali·stically** *adv.*

Naturality (nætʃŭræ·lĭti, nætiŭ-). Now *rare.* 1533. [– (O)Fr. *naturalité* – late L. *naturalitas, -tat-*; see NATURAL *a.*, -ITY.] †**1.** Natural character or quality –1651. †**2.** Naturalness –1678. **3.** Natural feeling or conduct. In later use *Sc.* 1628. **4.** An illustration drawn from natural things 1649.

Naturalize (næ·tʃŭrăləiz, næ·tiŭ-), *v.* 1571. [– Fr. *naturaliser*; see NATURAL *a.* and -IZE.] **I. 1.** *trans.* To admit (an alien) to the position and rights of citizenship; to invest with the privileges of a native-born subject. **2.** To introduce (a word, practice, thing, etc.) into a country or into common use 1593. **3.** To introduce (animals or plants) to places where they are not indigenous, but in which they may flourish under the same conditions as those which are native 1708. **4.** *intr.* (or *refl.*) To become naturalized; to settle down in a natural manner 1660.

1. By their naturalizing Men of all Countries, they have laid the beginnings of many great advantages 1667. *fig.* Persons..not naturalized by conversion..from another religion to this DONNE. **2.** The yard was naturalized as an English measure 1866. **3.** Our Melons, our Peaches..are Strangers among us,..naturalized in our English Gardens ADDISON.

II. †**1.** *trans.* To make natural or familiar (*to*); occas. to familiarize –1742. **2. a.** To free from conventionality 1603. **b.** To free from the supernatural or miraculous 1647. **3.** To pursue the studies of a naturalist 1787.

1. *All's Well*, I. i. 223. Custom has naturalized his Labour to him SOUTH. **2. a.** Were I of the trade I would n. Arte, as much as they Artize nature FLORIO. So **Na:turaliza·tion,** the action of naturalizing; the fact of being naturalized 1578.

Nature (nē[i]·tʃŭı, nē[i]·tiŭı), *sb.* ME. [– (O)Fr. *nature* – L. *natura*, f. *nat-*, pa. ppl. stem of *nasci* be born; see -URE.] **I. 1.** The essential qualities of a thing; the inherent and inseparable combination of properties essentially pertaining to anything and giving it its fundamental character. **2.** The inherent and innate disposition or character of a person (or animal) ME. **b.** The general inherent character or disposition of mankind. More fully *human n.* 1526. **3.** With *a* and *pl.* An individual character, disposition, etc., considered as a kind of entity in itself; hence, a person or thing of a particular quality or character. late ME. **b.** *Artillery.* A class or size of guns or shot 1813.

1. The Passion of Love in its N. has been thought to resemble Fire ADDISON. You have twice had warning of the fleeting n. of riches 1832. **2.** Men may change their Climate, but they cannot their N. STEELE. GOOD NATURE, ILL NATURE, SECOND NATURE: see those phrases. **b.** A just and lively image of human n. DRYDEN. Men have a physical as well as a spiritual n. 1878. It's only human n. to do that (*mod.*). **3.** There are some Natures in the World who never can proceed sincerely in Business TEMPLE.

Phr. *Of* (a certain) *n.*; A plan of this n. 1765. *Of* or *in the n. of*; A Peace is of the n. of a Conquest SHAKS. *In the n. of things, of the case*; It is, in the n. of the case, probable that [etc.] PALEY. *By n.*, in virtue of the very character or essence of the thing or person; He..ordained thy will By n. free, not over-rul'd by Fate MILT.

II. 1. The vital or physical powers *of* man; the strength or substance *of* a thing ME. †**2. a.** Semen. **b.** The menses. –1607. †**3.** The female pudendum, esp. that of a mare –1750.

III. 1. The inherent dominating power or impulse (in men or animals) by which action or character is determined, directed, or controlled. (Sometimes personified.) late ME. **b.** Natural feeling or affection. Now *dial.* 1605. **2.** The inherent power or force by which the physical and mental activities of man are sustained. (Sometimes personified.) late ME. **b.** The vital functions as requiring to be supported by nourishment, etc. 1460.

1. 'Twas N., sir, whose strong behest Impelled me to the deed COWPER. *Law of N.*: see LAW *sb.*[1] I. 9 c. *Light of N.*: see LIGHT *sb.* 6 b. *Against n.*, contrary to what n. prompts, unnatural, immoral, vicious. **b.** Stop vp th' accesse, and passage to Remorse, That no compunctious visitings of N. Shake my fell purpose SHAKS. **2.** Tir'd nature's sweet restorer, balmy sleep! YOUNG. **b.** When with meats & drinks they had suffic'd Not burd'nd N. MILT.

IV. 1. The creative and regulative physical power which is conceived of as operating in the physical world and as the immediate cause of all its phenomena. late ME. **b.** Personified as a female being. (Usu. with capital.) late ME. **c.** Contrasted with medical skill or treatment in the cure of wounds or diseases 1597. **d.** Contrasted with art (see ART *sb.* I. 2.). Also, naturalness. 1704. **2.** The material world, or its collective objects or phenomena, the features and products of the earth itself, as contrasted with those of human civilization 1662.

1. That common saying, that God and N. the minister of God doe nothing without cause 1594. **b.** Flowres which only Dame N. trauels with SIR T. HERBERT. **c.** N., in desperate diseases, frequently does most when she is left entirely to herself BURKE. *Against*, or *contrary to, n. Debt of n.*, etc.: see DEBT *sb. Course of n.*: see COURSE *sb.* 13. *Law(s) of n.*: see LAW *sb.*[1] III. 1. *In n.*, in the actual system of things, in real fact. **2.** To enjoy cool n. in a country seat COWPER. *In n.*, anywhere; at all. *The* or *a state of n.*: (*a*) the moral state natural to man, as opp. to a state of grace; (*b*) the condition of man before the organization of society; (*c*) an uncultivated or undomesticated condition; (*d*) physical nakedness. *attrib.* and *Comb.*, as *n.-cure, -study, -worship*; **n.-god,** one of the powers or phenomena of n. personified as a god; so **-being, deity; -people,** people in a primitive state of culture; **-spirit,** a spirit supposed to reside in some natural element or object.

†**Na·ture,** *v.* late ME. [– OFr. *naturer* or med.L. *naturare*, f. *natura* NATURE *sb.*] *intr.* in pres. pple. or ppl. a. *naturing* [after

med.L. *natura naturans*]: Creative, and giving to each thing its specific nature –1694.

Natured (nēⁱ·tʃŭɹd, nēⁱ·tiŭɹd), *ppl. a.* 1577. [f. NATURE *sb.* + -ED².] Having a (good, ill, etc.) nature or disposition.

Nature-printing. 1855. [Cf. G. *natur-(selbst)druck.*] The method or process of producing a print of a leaf, etc., by means of the mark made by the object itself, under pressure, on a prepared plate. **Nature-print** *v.* and *sb.*

Na·turize, *v. rare.* 1607. [f. NATURE *sb.* + -IZE. Cf. NATURE *v.*] *trans.* To invest with a specific nature.

†**Nau·frage.** 1480. [– Fr. *naufrage* – L. *naufragium* for **navifragium*, f. *navis* + *frag-*, *frangere* break.] Shipwreck (*lit.* and *fig.*) –1755.

Naught (nǭt), *sb.*, *a.*, and *adv.* [OE. *nāwiht*, *nāwuht*, *nauht*, f. *nā* (see NA *adv.*², NO *adv.*³) + *wiht* WIGHT *sb.* Cf. NOUGHT.] **A.** *sb.* **1.** Nothing, nought. (Now *arch.*) †**2.** Wickedness, evil, moral wrong, mischief –1656. †**b.** That which is wrong in method –1658. **3.** With *a* and *pl. Arith.* A cipher, a nought 1649. **b.** (From B. 2.) One who is bad 1657.

1. God made them and mans generacion of n. 2 *Macc.* 7: 28. Phr. *To bring, come, go to n. To set at n., set n. by*: see SET *v.* †*To call all to n.*, to abuse or decry vehemently. *To be n.*, to efface oneself, to keep quiet or withdraw. Usu. in im er. **2.** Phr. *To do n.*

B. *adj.* [orig. the sb. in predic. use.] **1.** Of no worth or value; good for nothing; worthless, bad, poor OE. †**b.** Of no legal value; invalid –1660. †**c.** Bad in condition or quality –1813. †**2.** Morally bad; wicked –1740. †**b.** Immoral; vicious –1693. †**3.** Injurious, hurtful; unlucky –1658. †**4.** Lost, ruined –1826.

1. Tom sings well; but his Luck's n. SWIFT. **b.** The election is..n. and voide 1632. **c.** Which [figges] can not be eaten because they are n. *Bible* (Douay) *Jer.* 24:3. **2.** But if thine eye be n.; thy whole body shall be darksome N.T. (Rhem.) *Matt.* 6:23. **4.** Be gone, away, All will be n. else SHAKS.

C. *adv.* †**1.** [orig. the accus. of the sb. used advb.] Not. OE. –late ME. †**2.** [From B.] Badly, wrongly –1625.

Naughty (nǭ·ti), *a.* late ME. [f. NAUGHT *sb.* + -Y¹.] †**1.** Having or possessing naught; poor, needy. late ME. only. **2.** †**a.** Of persons: Morally bad, wicked –1699. **b.** Of children: Given to doing wrong, esp. through waywardness or disobedience. Also used playfully of older persons. 1633. **3.** Of actions, places, things, etc.: Characterized by moral badness or wickedness; bad, wrong, blameworthy, improper. In mod. use applied playfully. 1536. †**4.** Bad, inferior, not up to the usual standard or quality –1799.

2. b. Go, get you gone, you n. girl, you are well enough SWIFT. **3.** Naughtie and Pestilent bokes should be burned 1560. This naughtie world 1620. It was very n. of her, she felt aware 1871. **4.** 'Tis a naughtie night to swimme in SHAKS. Hence **Nau·ghtily** 1552. **Nau·ghtiness** 1541.

Naughty pack. *Obs.* exc. *dial.* 1530. [PACK *sb.*¹ 4.] †A woman (or man) of bad character –1743. **b.** *dial.* A naughty child 1828.

‖**Naumachia** (nǭmēⁱ·kiă). *Pl.* **-iæ**, **-ias.** 1596. [L. – Gr. ναυμαχία, f. ναῦς ship + μάχη fight; see -IA¹.] **1.** A mimic sea-fight. **2.** A place specially constructed for the exhibition of mock sea-fights 1617.

Naunt (nānt). Now *dial.* or *arch.* 1621. [var. of AUNT, with *n* transferred from *myn* 'mine'; see N.] Aunt.

‖**Nauplius** (nǭ·pliŏs). *Pl.* **-plii** (-pliəi). 1836. [L. *nauplius* kind of shellfish, or *Nauplius* – Gr. Ναύπλιος, a son of Poseidon.] †**a.** O. F. Müller's name for a supposed genus of crustaceans. **b.** A larval stage of development in some of the lower crustaceans 1869.

Nausea (nǭ·siă, nǭ·ʃiă). 1569. [– L. *nausea*, *nausia* – Gr. ναυσία, ναυτία seasickness, nausea, f. ναῦς ship.] **1.** A feeling of sickness, with loathing of food and inclination to vomit. **b.** Sea-sickness. (The orig. sense.) 1771. **2.** *transf.* A strong feeling of disgust or loathing 1619. **3.** That which causes sickness or loathing 1654.

2. Sated to n. as we have been with the doctrines of Sentimentality CARLYLE.

Nau·seant. 1846. [f. NAUSEATE *v.* + -ANT.] *Med.* A substance which produces nausea. *adj.* Producing nausea 1864.

Nauseate (nǭ·sĭ,eⁱt, nǭ·ʃĭ,eⁱt), *v.* 1640. [– *nauseat-*, pa. ppl. stem of L. *nauseare*, f. *nausea*, after Gr. ναυσιᾶν; see NAUSEA, -ATE³.] **1.** *trans.* To reject (food, etc.) with loathing or nausea 1646. **2.** To affect with nausea; to create a loathing in 1654. **3.** *intr.* To become affected with nausea, to feel sick (*at* something) 1640.

1. *fig.* The Prince began to n. the match, and to meditate all honourable evasions 1654. **2.** It nauseated their very Stomachs, made them sick when they thought of it DE FOE. **3.** *fig.* He cannot but hate that in himself, which he nauseates at in another 1657. Hence **Nau·seatingly** *adv.* 1883. **Nausea·tion,** the action of nauseating, or state of being nauseated 1628.

Nauseous (nǭ·səs, nǭ·ʃⁱes), *a.* 1604. [– L. *nauseosus*, f. *nausea*; see NAUSEA, -OUS.] †**1.** Inclined to nausea; fastidious (*rare*) –1678. **2.** Causing nausea or squeamishness; also, later, highly unpleasant to the taste or smell 1612. **3.** *fig.* Loathsome, disgusting; highly offensive 1663.

2. Cured by remedies in themselves very n. and unpalatable DICKENS. **3.** All affectation of talking piously is quite n. 1751. **Nau·seous-ly** *adv.*, **-ness.**

Nautch (nǭtʃ), *sb.* Also **notch, na(t)ch.** 1796. [– Urdu (Hindi) *nāch* – Prakrit *nachcha* – Skr. *nṛitja* dancing, f. *nṛit* dance.] **1.** An East Indian exhibition of dancing, performed by professional dancing-girls. **b.** A nautch girl. BROWNING. **2.** *attrib.*, as *n. dancer*, *girl* 1809.

Nautic (nǭ·tik), *a.* 1613. [– Fr. *nautique* or L. *nauticus* – Gr. ναυτικός, f. ναύτης sailor, f. ναῦς ship; see -IC.] *adj.* Nautical. (Chiefly in poetic or dignified use.)

Nautical (nǭ·tikăl), *a.* 1552. [f. as prec. + -AL¹; see -ICAL.] **1.** Pertaining to seamen or to the art of navigation. **b.** In special applications, as *n. almanac*, *day*, *distance*, *mile*, etc. (see quots. and the various sbs.) 1765. **2.** *absol.* A nautical person or writer 1840.

1. My n. enthusiasm fairly got the better of me 1834. **b.** *N. almanac*, a year-book containing information for the use of mariners. *N. Day.* This day commences at noon, twelve hours before the civil day SMYTH. The rhumb-line intercepted between any two places through which it passes, is called their *n. distance* OGILVIE. **Nau·tically** *adv.* 1835.

Nautilus (nǭ·tilŏs). *Pl.* **-i** (-əi); also **-uses.** 1601. [– L. *nautilus* – Gr. ναυτίλος sailor, nautilus, f. ναύτης (see NAUTIC).] **a.** In full, *Paper Nautilus*, the argonaut, a small dibranchiate cephalopod, the female of which is protected by a very thin, single-chambered, detached shell, and has webbed dorsal arms which it was formerly believed to use as sails. **b.** In full, *Pearly Nautilus*, a tetrabranchiate cephalopod (*N. pompilius*) found in the Indian and Pacific Oceans, having a beautiful chambered shell with nacreous septa; also, any related fossil species.

a. Learn of the little N. to sail, Spread the thin oar, and catch the driving gale POPE. The paper-shelled n. 1753. **b.** *attrib.* A fairy cup made out of a N. shell SCOTT. Hence **Nau·tilite** (*Palæont.*), a fossil n. 1748. **Nau·tiloid** *a.* resembling the n. in form; *sb.* a nautiloid mollusc 1847.

Naval (nēⁱ·văl), *a.* 1593. [– L. *navalis*, f. *navis* ship; see -AL¹. Cf. (O)Fr. *naval.*] **1.** *N. crown*: (*a*) the crown or garland given by the Romans to one who had distinguished himself in a sea-fight; (*b*) the form of crown used as a badge in the navy. **2.** Of or pertaining to, connected with, characteristic of, used in, the navy (†or shipping); (of persons) serving in the navy 1602. **3.** Fought, gained, sustained, carried out, etc. by means of ships or a navy 1606. **b.** Consisting of, or based on the possession of ships of war 1617.

2. *N. officer*: (*a*) an officer in the navy (see OFFICER *sb.*); (*b*) *U.S.*, an officer whose duty it is to receive copies of all manifests and entries in the Custom-House. *N. stores*, all those articles or materials made use of in shipping or in the navy; also *spec.*, the different resinous products of trade. *Royal N.* (*Volunteer*) *Reserve* (see RESERVE *sb.*); abbrev. R.N.(V.)R. **3.** Lest..the Seamen should be forgetful and unfitting for n. warfare 1660. Beaks of ships in n. triumph borne 1700. **b.** The N. Strength of this Realm 1720. The n. power of Carthage 1869. Hence **Na·vally** *adv.* 1816.

Nave (nēⁱv), *sb.*¹ [OE. *nafu* and *nafa*, corresp. to MDu. *nave* (Du. *naaf*), OHG. *naba* (G. *nabe*), ON. *nǫf* :– Gmc. **nabō* :– IE. **nobhā*, repr. also by Skr. *nābhis* nave, navel; see NAVEL.] The central part or block of a wheel, into which the end of the axle-tree is inserted, and from which the spokes radiate; = HUB.

Nave (nēⁱv), *sb.*² 1649. [– med.L. spec. use of L. *navis* ship, whence (O)Fr. *nef*, Sp., It. *nave* (in both senses); so G. *schiff*, Du. *schip* ship, nave.] The body of a church, from the inner door to the choir or chancel, usually separated from the aisles by pillars.

Navel (nēⁱ·v'l), *sb.* [OE. *nafela* = OFris. *navla*, *naula*, (M)LG., MDu. *navel*, OHG. *nabalo* (G. *nabel*), ON. *nafli* :– Gmc. **nabalon*, based on IE. **nobh-* (cf. NAVE *sb.*¹), **onobh-*, repr. also by L. *umbo* boss of shield, Gr. ὀμφαλός navel, boss.] **1.** A rounded depression, with a raised centre, situated on the abdomen at the point where the umbilical cord was originally attached; the umbilicus. **2.** The centre or central point of anything, e.g. of a country, sea, forest, etc. late ME. †**3.** The nave of a wheel (*rare*) –1624.

1. Launcelot..smote hym on the sholder and clafe hym to the nauel MALORY. **2.** Within the navil of this hideous Wood..a Sorcerer dwels MILT.

attrib. and *Comb.*, as *n.-knot*, *-vein*, etc.; **n.-gall,** a gall in the middle of a horse's back; **n. orange,** a large variety of orange, having a navel-like formation at the top; **-point** *Her.*, the point next below the fesse point; **n.-string,** the umbilical cord; **n.-wort,** various plants, esp. *Cotyledon umbilicus*. Hence **Navel** *v.* in *pa. pple.* situated in the middle 1818.

Navew (nēⁱ·viu). Now *rare.* 1533. [– OFr. **naveu*, earlier *navel*, mod. dial. *naveau* :– L. *napus* kind of turnip; see NEEP.] The rape (*Brassica napus*) or coleseed (*B. campestris*).

‖**Navicula** (năvi·kiŭlă). 1853. [L., dim. of *navis* ship; see next.] *Eccl.* An incense-boat.

Navicular (năvi·kiŭlăɹ), *a.* and *sb.* 1541. [– Fr. *naviculaire* or late L. *navicularis*, f. *navicula*, dim. of *navis* ship; see -CULE, -AR¹.] **A.** *adj.* **1.** *N. bone*, the scaphoid bone of the hand (*rare*), or the corresponding bone in the foot lying between the astragalus and cuneiform bones. **b.** *Farriery.* Connected with the navicular bone of a horse's foot, esp. *n. joint*, *disease* 1828. **2.** Pertaining to, connected with, boats –1721. **3.** Having the form of a (small) boat 1774. **4.** *N. fossa*, (*a*) the depression between the helix and anthelix of the ear; (*b*) the anterior portion of the urethra 1816.

3. The name of this, and of all the n. shrines was Baris J. BRYANT. The n. goddess of Egypt was called Isis 1816. Glumes n., entire 1806.

B. *ellipt.* passing into *sb.* = Navicular bone (1816), disease (1888): see above.

Navigable (næ·vigăb'l), *a.* 1527. [– Fr. *navigable* or L. *navigabilis*, f. *navigare*; see NAVIGATE *v.*, -ABLE.] **1.** Admitting of being navigated, affording passage for ships or boats. **2.** Of ships: Capable of navigation; seaworthy (*rare*) 1535. **b.** Of balloons: Dirigible 1903.

1. Yf the North sea were not nauigable by reason of extreme cold and Ise 1553. An incomparable great iland..nauigable round about 1625. At Lechlade..the Thames ceases to be n. 1878. Hence **Navigabi·lity** 1846, **Na·vigableness** 1720.

Navigate (næ·vigeⁱt), *v.* 1588. [– *navigat-*, pa. ppl. stem of L. *navigare*, f. *navis* ship + *-ig-*, comb. stem of *agere* drive; see -ATE³.] †**1.** *intr.* To go from one place to another in a ship or ships, to sail. **2.** *trans.* To sail over, on, or through (the sea, a river, etc.) 1646. **3.** To sail, direct, or manage (a ship) 1670. **4.** Of vessels (now *rare*): **a.** *intr.* To sail; to ply 1758. **b.** *trans.* To sail on or over (the sea, etc.) 1858. **5.** To manage, direct the course of (aircraft) 1784.

1. In the Summer you may n. as you please CHESTERF. **2.** Drusus..was the first who navigated the Northern Ocean 1705. *fig.* The number of vehicles which n. the streets 1845. **3.** Want of hands to n. his ships 1758. **4. b.** Ships destined to n. the icy seas 1878.

Navigation (nævigēⁱ·ʃən). 1527. [– (O)Fr. *navigation* or L. *navigatio*, f. as prec.; see -ION.] **1.** The action of navigating; the action or practice of passing on water in ships or other vessels 1533. **2.** The art or science of directing the movements of vessels on the sea, including more esp. the methods of determining a ship's position and course by the principles of geometry and nautical astronomy 1559. **3.** An expedition or journey by water. Now *rare*. 1527. †**4.** *concr.* The means of navigation; shipping. In later use *U.S.* –1850. †**5.** Shipping business –1720. **6.** †**a.** A passage or course by which one may sail –1654. **b.** A canal or other waterway (now *dial.*) 1720.

1. Phr. *Aerial n.*, the science, art, or practice of sailing or floating in the air; aeronautics. *Inland n.*, communication by means of canals and navigable rivers. **2.** My Father now and then sending me small Sums of Money, I laid them out in learning N. SWIFT. **3.** Their N. was short, and favoured with gentle windes 1632. **4.** *Macb.* IV. i. 54.

attrib., as *n. season*; **n. act** or **law**, a legal enactment regulating n. or shipping; **n. coal**, steam coal. Hence **Naviga·tional** *a.*

Navigator (næ·vigeⁱtǫɹ). 1590. [– L. *navigator*, f. as prec.; see -OR 2.] **1.** One who navigates; a sailor or seaman, esp. one skilled in the art of navigation; one who conducts explorations by sea. **2.** A labourer employed in the work of excavating and constructing a canal (cf. NAVIGATION 6 b), or, in later use, any similar kind of earthwork. Now usu. NAVVY. 1775.

2. Seven old navigators (as canal-men are called in the midland counties) SOUTHEY.

Navvy (næ·vi), *sb.* 1832. [abbrev. of prec. 2.] **1.** A labourer employed in the excavation and construction of earthworks, such as canals, railways, drains, etc. **2.** A machine for excavating earth; a *steam n.* 1877.

Hence **Na·vvy** *v.*, to do navvy's work.

Navy (nēⁱ·vi). ME. [– OFr. *navie* ship, fleet – Rom. **nāvia* for pop. L. *nāvia* ship, boat, collect. formation on L. *navis* ship; see -Y³.] †**1.** (Without article.) Ships or shipping –1473. **2.** A fleet; a number of ships collected together, esp. for purposes of war. Now *poet.* and *rhet.* ME. **3.** The whole of the ships of war belonging to a nation or ruler considered collectively with all the organization necessary for their command and maintenance; a regularly organized and maintained naval force 1540. **b.** The officers and men serving in a particular navy 1648. **4.** *ellipt.* Navy blue 1884.

2. The nauee of Yram, the which bare gold of Oofer WYCLIF 1 *Kings* 10:11. **3.** Alfred the Great was the founder of the English n. 1840. Phr. *The king's (queen's) n., the Royal n.*, †*n. royal.* **b.** The Indian n. now consists of 150 officers 1845.

attrib. and *Comb.*, as *n. man, revolver, surgeon*, etc.; **n. agent**, one who manages the business affairs of naval officers; **n. bill**, a bill issued by the Admiralty in place of ready-money payment, or drawn by a naval officer on the Admiralty; **n. blue**, a dark blue, the colour of the British naval uniform; **N. Board**, a former name for the Admiralty; **N. League**, a body founded in 1895 with the object of arousing national interest in the British N.; **N. List**, an official publication containing a list of the officers of the Navy, and other nautical information; †**N. Office**, the Admiralty building; **n. register**, *U.S.* = *Navy List*; **n. yard**, a government dockyard (now (*U.S.*).

‖**Nawab** (năwǭ·b). 1758. [Urdu *nawwāb*, var. of *nuwwāb*, pl. of (Arab.) *nā'ib* deputy.] = NABOB.

†**Nawle**, obs. f. AWL.

Nay (nēⁱ), *v. Obs.* exc. *arch.* late ME. [– OFr. *neier* (mod. *nier*) :– L. *negare*, or, later, f. NAY *adv.* Cf. DENY, RENAY.] **1.** †To refuse (ME. only); to give a refusal to (a person) 1592. †**2. a.** To deny (a matter) –1560; †**b.** *intr.* To say nay –1680.

Nay (nēⁱ), *adv.* and *sb.* [ME. *nei, nai* (Orm *naȝȝ*) – ON. *nei*, f. *ne* NE + *ei* AY, AYE. Cf. NO *adv.*³] **A.** *adv.* **1.** A word used to express negation, dissent, denial, or refusal, in answer to some statement, question, command, etc. (In older use *nay* (like *yea*) was usu. employed when the preceding statement, etc., contained no negative; otherwise *no*.) Now *arch.* or *dial.* **2.** Used to introduce a more precise or forcible term or statement than that which precedes 1585.

1. Phr. *To say n.*: (*a*) To make denial or refusal. (*b*) To deny or refuse (one); to forbid, prohibit. Also, to refuse (a thing) *to* one. (*c*) To express dissent or contradiction. **2.** I have weighty, nay unanswerable reasons MISS BURNEY.

B. *sb.* An utterance of the word 'nay'; a negative reply or vote; a denial, refusal, or prohibition ME.

He would have no n. at God's hands 1643. Phr. †*It* (*there*, etc.) *is no n.* = 'It cannot be denied'. Also simply *no n.* †*Without n.*, beyond doubt, assuredly.

Nay-say, *sb.* 1631. [f. NAY *adv.* + SAY *sb.*] Refusal, denial. So **Nay-say** *v.* to refuse (one). *dial.* and *arch.* 1773.

†**Nay·ward.** *rare.* [f. NAY *sb.* + -WARD.] *To the n.*, towards denial or unbelief. *Wint. T.* II. i. 64.

Nayword (nēⁱ·wǝ̄ɹd). 1598. [Of unkn. origin.] **1.** A watchword or catchword (*rare*). **2.** A byword, a proverb 1601. Now *dial.*

1. *Merry W.* II. ii. 131. **2.** *Twel. N.* II. iii. 146.

Nazarene (næzărī·n). ME. [– Chr. L. *Nazarenus* – Gr. Ναζαρηνός (Mark 1:24), f. Ναζαρέτ Nazareth.] **A.** *adj.* **1.** Of or belonging to Nazareth (*rare*). **2.** Belonging to the sect of the Nazarenes 1689. **B.** *sb.* **1.** A native of Nazareth 1611. **b.** A follower of Jesus of Nazareth; a Christian. (So called esp. by Jews and Moslems.) late ME. **2.** *pl.* An early Jewish-Christian sect, allied to the Ebionites. var. **Nazare·an.** 1689.

B. 1. He shalbe called a N. *Matt.* 2:23. **b.** The very name of N. Was wormwood to his Paynim spleen BYRON.

Nazarite¹ (næ·zărəit). 1535. [f. Chr. L. *Nazaræus* – Gr. Ναζαραῖος (Matt. 2:23) + -ITE¹ 1.] = prec. sb.

Nazarite² (næ·zărəit). Also **-irite.** 1560. [f. Chr. L. *Nazaræus* (LXX Ναζιραῖος), f. Heb. *nāzīr*, f. *nāzar* separate or consecrate oneself; see -ITE¹ 1.] Among the ancient Hebrews, one who took certain vows of abstinence (see *Numbers* 6).

To drinke wine..was a pollution both of the Nazarites and Priestes 1585. Hence **Na·zariteship, Nazari·tic** *a.*, **Na·zaritish** *a.*, **Na·zaritism.**

Naze (nēⁱz). 1774. [app. inferred from place-names.] A promontory or headland.

‖**Nazi** (nā·tsi, nā·zi). 1930. [repr. pronunc. of *Nati-* in G. *Nationalsozialist.*] A member of the German National Socialist party.

N.B. (en bi), abbrev. of NOTA BENE.

N.C.O., = NON-COMMISSIONED *officer.*

Ne, *adv.* and *conj. arch.* [OE. *ne, ni* (see NAY, NO *adv.*¹) = OFris., OS., OHG. *ni, ne*, ON. *né*, Goth. *ni*; corresp. to L. *ne-* (as in *nefas, nullus, numquam*), Lith., OSl. *ne*, Skr. *na.*] = NOT *adv.* †Also as *n-* comb. w. a vb., as *nadde* had not, *nam* am not.

1. A youth Who ne in virtue's ways did take delight BYRON. Phr. †*Ne were, ne had..been*, were it not, had it not been (for). **2.** They nentende nyght nor day But vnto merthe LYDG.

B. *conj.* = NOR. *arch.* or *Obs.* OE. †**b.** = Nor, and..not, neither –1618.

1. *Ne..ne* (sometimes) = neither..nor. Now only *arch.* Ne could we laugh, ne wail COLERIDGE.

Neaf, obs. f. NIEVE, fist.

Neal (nīl), *v. Obs.* exc. *dial.* 1538. [aphet. f. ANNEAL *v.*] *trans.* = ANNEAL *v.* 2, 4. Also †*intr.* to undergo the process of annealing –1684.

Neanderthaloid (niæ·ndəɹtā·loid), *a.* 1887. [See def. and -OID.] Having the characteristics of a skull of very low type found at Neanderthal in Rhenish Prussia in 1857; characterized by this type of skull. So **Nea·nderthal** *man*, etc.

Neap (nīp), *sb.*¹ *n. dial.* and *U.S.* 1553. [perh. of Scand. origin; cf. Norw. dial. *neip* a forked pole, etc.] **1.** The pole or tongue of a cart. (Now *U.S.*). **2.** A three-legged rest used to support the shaft of a vehicle 1691.

Neap (nīp), *a.* and *sb.*² [OE. *nēp* in *nēpflōd*; then not recorded till XV. Of unkn. origin.] **1.** *N. tide*, a tide occurring shortly after the first and third quarters of the moon, in which the high-water level stands at its lowest point. **2.** *absol.* A neap tide 1584.

1. *N. season*, the time of n. tide. **2.** High springs and dead Neapes 1627.

Neap (nīp), *v.* 1652. [f. prec.] **1.** *intr.* Of tides: To become lower, to tend towards the neap. Also *pass.* **2.** *To be neaped*, of a vessel: to be left aground on the height of a spring-tide 1704.

Neapolitan (niăpǫ·lităn). late ME. [– L. *Neapolitanus*, f. *Neapolites* (see -ITE¹ 1), f. Gr. Νεάπολις 'New Town'; see -AN.] **A.** *adj.* Belonging or native to, distinctive or characteristic of, connected with, Naples 1592.

†*N. disease*: see NAPLES 1. *N. ice*, one made in layers of different flavours. *N. violet*, a double sweet-scented variety of viola. *N. yellow*, Naples yellow.

B. *sb.* An inhabitant or native of Naples. ME.

Near (nīᵊɹ), *a.* ME. [f. NEAR *adv.*²] **1.** Closely related by blood or kinship. **2.** Close, intimate, familiar 1523. **3.** With ref. to animals or vehicles: Left (as opp. to †*far, off*, = right): horses, etc., being usu. mounted, led, or approached from the left side 1453. **4.** Close at hand; not distant 1565. **5.** Of a road: Short, direct. (Chiefly in *compar.* and *superl.*) 1579. **6.** Close, narrow 1548. **7.** Closely affecting or touching one 1605. **8.** Niggardly, mean 1616.

1. They are her neere kinsewomen *Lev.* 18:17. **2.** Your neere friends and familiar companions 1576. **3.** The track of the left or n. wheel 1842. **4.** When we look at a n. object with both eyes BERKELEY. *N. distance*, the part of a scene between foreground and background. *N. point*, a point, at a distance of about 4 or 5 inches from the eye, within which clear vision is no longer possible without optical assistance. *N. work*, work involving proximity of the eye to the object. **6.** It was a n. race 1856. **7.** Euery minute of his being thrusts Against my neer'st of Life SHAKS. **8.** A good-natured man, but reckoned n. 1753. **Nea·rness.**

Near (nīᵊɹ), *v.* 1513. [f. NEAR *adv.*² or *a.*] **1.** *intr.* To draw or come near, to approach. **2.** *trans.* To draw near to, to approach. †Also, to be near. 1610.

1. Still it ner'd and ner'd COLERIDGE. **2.** Keep off, I charge thee neere me not HEYWOOD.

Near (nīᵊɹ), *adv.*¹ (and *prep.*) *Obs.* exc. *dial.* [OE. *nēar*, etc., compar. of *nēah* NIGH *adv.*, corresp. to OFris. *niar*, OS. *nāhor* (Du. *naar* to, for, after), OHG. *nāhor*, Goth. *nehwis* :– Gmc. **nēxwiz*, **nēxwōz*. Superseded in gen. use by the new formation *nearer* (XVI).] †**I.** In advb. (or prepositional) use. With verbs of motion. Nearer or closer (to a place, point, or person). Freq. governing a noun in the dative –1596.

Pardon me, I will come no n. 1596. *No n. !* (or *n. !*) Naut.: a command to the helmsman to come no closer to the wind.

II. In predic. use after the subst. vb. (Freq. with dative or *to*.) **1.** Nearer in space or time, †in relationship OE. **2.** Nearer to one's end or purpose. (Only in neg. and interrog. clauses; *dial.*) late ME.

1. The nere to the churche, the ferther from God 1562. The neere in blood, the neerer bloody SHAKS. **2.** Phr. *Never the n.* (common 1560–1625).

Near (nīᵊɹ), *adv.*² (and *prep.*) [ME. *ner, nere* – ON. *nær*, prop. compar. of *ná* = OE. *nēah* NIGH *adv.*, but also used as a positive. Cf. NAR *adv.*] **I.** Used absol. (without *to* or dependent sb.). **Denoting proximity.* **1.** To, within, or at a short distance; to, or in, close proximity. **b.** *Naut.* Close to the wind 1634. **2.** Of time: Close at hand ME. **3.** Closely connected with one by kinship or intimacy. late ME.

1. Things n. seem further off; farst off, the nearst at hand H. MORE. N. is my shirt, but nearer is my skin ! 1890. Phr. *Far and n.* (see FAR *adv.*), properly meaning 'farther (off) and nearer (at hand)'. **b.** *No Nearer!* = *No near* (see NEAR *adv.*¹). **2.** My heart failed me as the time drew n. MRS. CARLYLE. Phr. *N. upon*, close upon a particular time. **3.** In company with one 'n. and dear' 1826. Phr. *N. akin* or *of kin* (see AKIN *adv.* and KIN).

***Denoting approximation in degree or amount.* **4.** Within a (very) little, almost. (Now usu. expressed by NEARLY.) ME. **5.** With negatives: (Not) by a great deal or a long way, (not) anything like, (not) nearly. Usu. followed by *so.* 1447. **6.** Closely, esp. in respect of pressure or touching, of resemblance, connection, scrutiny, etc. Now *rare.* 1456. **7.** In phr. *as n. as* (one can, etc.) 1538. †**8.** Narrowly, only by a little (*rare*) –1819.

4. They appear to have been pretty n. of an Age 1696. It cost us n. a Fortnight's Time DE FOE. I am n. upon eighty years of age LANDOR. **5.** He is nothing neere so much delighted 1638. **6.** His

Majesty had another Exception against the Duke, which touched him as n. CLARENDON. The nearer it [tragedy] approaches the reality,..the more perfect is its power BURKE.

***Denoting manner.* **9.** Thriftily; parsimoniously, meanly 1625. **10.** With the legs close together 1710.

10. A Horse that goes wide before, and n. behind 1737.

II. Followed by *to* (or †*unto*). **1.** Close *to* a place, thing, or person, in respect of space, or *to* a point in time ME. **2.** Closely related *to* one by kinship, etc., esp. in *n. and dear* 1450. **3.** Close *to* something in respect of likeness or correspondence 1548. **4.** *To go n. to* (with inf.), to be on the point of, almost to succeed in (doing something). Also const. gerund. 1593.

1. Neere vnto the said plaine are diuers woods and forrests 1600. Phr. †*To come* or *go n. to*, to touch closely. **3.** The case that comes nearest to this of those I have seen NORTH. **4.** It would go n. to break her heart 1889.

III. Governing a sb. (passing into *prep.*). **1.** Close to or upon (a place, person, thing, point of time, state or condition) ME. †**2.** Intimate with (one) –1660. **3.** Close to (a thing or person) in point of similarity or achievement 1585. Latterly chiefly *U.S.*, as in *n. beer*.

1. Our Coffee-house is n. one of the Inns of Court STEELE. I must have gone very n. convincing him 1825. The time draws n. the birth of Christ TENNYSON. The hope was n. fulfilment 1902. *fig.* I thinke we came neere you when wee saide you loued LYLY. Phr. *To lie, come,* or *go n.* (one, the heart, etc.), to touch or affect deeply. **2.** 2 *Hen. IV*, v. i. 81. **3.** Their language..is nearer the Latine, then the Italian 1632.

Near by, *adv.* and *a.* late ME. [NEAR *adv.*[2] and BY *adv.*] **A.** *adv.* **1.** Close at hand. **2.** Nearly, almost. *Sc.* 1456. **B.** *adj.* (*near-by, nearby*) Neighbouring. orig. *U.S.* 1858.

Nearctic (nīˌā·ɹktik), *a.* 1858. [f. NEO- + ARCTIC *a.*] *Zool.* Comprising, or pertaining to, the temperate and arctic parts of N. America, in respect of the distribution of birds, etc.

Near East. 1869. [NEAR *a.* 4.] The south-eastern part of Europe; the Balkan States together with Asia Minor. Hence **Near-Ea·stern** *a.*, **-Ea·sterly** *adv.*

Near hand, *adv., prep.,* and *a.* Now only *Sc.* and *dial.* ME. [NEAR *adv.*[2] and HAND *sb.*] **A.** *adv.* **1.** Close at hand, close by. †**b.** At close quarters (*rare*) –1670. **2.** Nearly, almost ME. **B.** *prep.* Near to, close to. ME.

Nearly (nīᵊ·ɹli), *adv.* 1540. [f. NEAR *a.* + -LY[2].] **1.** In a near manner; closely; intimately. **2.** Particularly 1562. **3.** Almost, all but 1683.

1. To be n. acquainted with the people of different countries can happen to very few JOHNSON. **2.** This..I only mention, because it so n. touches myself SWIFT. **3.** I languished here for n. three weeks GOLDSM. Phr. *Not..n.*, nothing like.

Near-sighted, *a.* 1686. [f. NEAR *a.* + SIGHT *sb.* + -ED[2].] Short-sighted. Hence **Near-si·ghtedness** 1811.

Neat (nīt), *sb.* [OE. *nēat* = OFris. *nāt, naet,* OS. *nōt* (Du. *noot*), OHG. *nōȥ* (obs. or dial. *noss, nos*), ON. *naut* :– Gmc. **nautam*, f. **naut- *neut- *nut-* make use of, enjoy, whence also OE. *nēotan*, etc.] **1.** *sing.* An animal of the ox-kind; an ox or bullock, a cow or heifer. Now *rare* or *arch.* **2.** (†*pl.* or) *collect.* Cattle OE.

1. A savage Bull.., he was a gallant-looking n. MORRIS. **2.** The Steere, the Heyefer, and the Calfe, Are all call'd N. SHAKS. *appos.* Every kind of n. cattle 1805.

Neat (nīt), *a.* and *adv.* 1542. [– (O)Fr. *net* :– L. *nitidus* shining, clean, f. *nitēre* shine. Cf. NET *a.*] **A.** *adj.* **I.** †**1.** Clean. Also const. *from.* –1632. †**2.** Clear, bright –1797. **3.** Of liquors: Pure; *spec.* undiluted 1579. **b.** Of other substances (*rare*) 1651. **4.** Free from any reductions; clear, net. (Now usu. NET.) 1599. **b.** Exact, precise. Now *dial.* 1682.

2. Fresh springing wells as christall neate SPENSER. **3.** I was obliged to drink rum; it wouldn't ha done to ha drunk the water n. 1851. **4.** A n. sum, to cover all expenses 1817.

II. †**1.** Of persons: Inclined to refinement or elegance; trim or smart in apparel –1656. **2.** Characterized by elegance of form without unnecessary embellishment; of agreeable but simple appearance; nicely made or proportioned 1549. **3.** Of language, style, etc.: Well expressed; *esp.* brief, clear, and to the point; cleverly or smartly put or phrased 1586. **b.** Of preparations, cookery, etc.: Dainty, elegant, tasteful. Now *rare.* 1611. **c.** Cleverly done 1598. **4.** Inclined to tidiness 1577; skilful and precise 1612. **5.** Put or kept in good order, tidy 1596.

1. Still to be n., still to be drest, As you were going to a feast B. JONS. **2.** Many n. houses and pleasant seats there be in the country FULLER. The furniture was n. 1888. **3.** A n. speech by one Pym 1621. **b.** A very n. and curious Banquet SIR T. HERBERT. **c.** A n. and happy turn to give the subject DICKENS. **4.** He was n. and methodical in all small matters 1885. **5.** A tradesman's books should always be kept clear and n. 1745.

B. *adv.* Neatly 1665. Hence **Nea·tly** *adv.* in a n. manner or style. **Nea·tness.**

Neaten (nī·t'n), *v.* 1898. [f. NEAT *a.* + -EN[5].] *trans.* To make neat, *esp.* in needlework.

Neath, 'neath (nīþ), *prep. dial.* and *poet.* 1787. [Aphetic of BENEATH; see ANEATH.] Beneath.

Neat-handed, *a.* 1632. [NEAT *a.*] Deft in handling things; dexterous. Hence **Neat-ha·ndedness** 1839.

Neatherd (nī·tˌhōɹd). late ME. [f. NEAT *sb.* + HERD *sb.*[2]] One who has the care of neat cattle, a cowherd.

Nea·t-house. Also **neats'.** 1440. [f. NEAT *sb.*] **1.** A house or shed in which cattle are kept. **2.** A locality near Chelsea Bridge, where there was a celebrated market garden. Also *pl.* 1632.

Neatify (nī·tifəi), *v.* Now *rare* or *Obs.* 1601. [f. NEAT *a.* + -FY, after *beautify.*] *trans.* To make neat, to purify.

Neat's foot. 1579. [f. NEAT *sb.*] The foot of an ox, used as an article of food 1595. **b.** *attrib.* in **neat's-foot oil,** an oil obtained from the feet of neat cattle.

Neat's leather. 1530. [f. NEAT *sb.*] Leather made from the hides of neat cattle.

Neat's tongue. 1596. [f. NEAT *sb.*] An ox-tongue, used as an article of food.

Silence is onely commendable In a neats tongue dri'd SHAKS.

Neb (neb). Now chiefly *north.* and *Sc.* [OE. *nebb* = ON. *nef, nefj-*, rel. to MLG., MDu. *nebbe* (Du. *nebbe, neb*) :– Gmc. **nabja-*. Cf. NIB *sb.*] **1.** The beak or bill of a bird. **b.** The mouth (of a person) 1611. **2.** The nose; the snout of an animal OE. **3.** The point or nib of a pen (or pencil) 1599. **b.** Any projecting part or point; a peak, tip, spout, etc. 1584.

‖**Ne·bbuk.** Also **nabk.** 1846. [Arab. *nabḳ, nabaḳ, nabiḳ* the fruit of the lote-tree, or the tree itself.] The Christ's Thorn, *Zizyphus spina-christi*, or its fruit.

‖**Nebula** (ne·biŭlă). *Pl.* **-æ** (-ī). 1661. [L. *nebula* mist, vapour, rel. to Gr. νεφέλη cloud.] **1. a.** A film upon, or covering, the eye; *spec.* a clouded speck or spot on the cornea causing defective vision. **b.** A cloudy or flocculent appearance 1805. **2.** *Astron.* An indistinct cloud-like cluster of distant stars, or a luminous patch of supposed gaseous or stellar matter lying beyond the limits of the solar system 1727. **3.** Mist 1894.

Nebular (ne·biŭlăɹ), *a.* 1837. [f. prec. + -AR[1].] **1.** *N. hypothesis* or *theory*, the theory, propounded by Kant and elaborated by Herschel and Laplace, which supposes a nebula to be the first state of the solar and stellar systems. **2.** Consisting of, concerned with, or relating to a nebula or nebulæ 1856.

Nebule[1] (ne·biul). late ME. [Anglicized f. NEBULA.] **1.** A cloud; a mist or fog. **2.** *Astron.* A nebula 1830.

Nebule[2] (ne·biul). 1823. [app. due to misapprehension of next.] *Arch.* A moulding of a wavy or serpentine form.

Nebulé (ne·biule), **nebuly** (ne·biuli), *a.* Also **-ée.** 1550. [– Fr. *nébulé* – med. L. *nebulatus*, f. L. NEBULA; see -ATE[2], -Y[5].] **1.** *Her.* Of a wavy or serpentine form, like the edges of conventional clouds; represented in the form of a cloud. **2.** *Arch.* Of mouldings: see NEBULE[2] 1842.

Nebulium (nībiū·liŏm). 1898. orig. **nebulum.** [f. NEBULA + -IUM.] *Chem.* An element the existence of which is inferred from certain green lines in the spectra of gaseous nebulæ.

Nebulize (ne·biŭləiz), *v. rare.* 1872. [f. NEBULA + -IZE.] **1.** *trans.* To reduce to a mist or spray. **2.** *intr.* To become nebulous or indefinite 1891. Hence **Ne·bulizer,** an instrument for converting a liquid into a fine spray, esp. for medical purposes 1874.

Nebulose (ne·biŭlōᵘs), *a.* late ME. [– L. *nebulosus*; see NEBULA and -OSE[1].] Cloudy, misty, indistinct (*lit.* and *fig.*). **b.** Clouded, cloudlike 1826.

Nebulosity (nebiŭlǫ·sĭti). 1761. [– Fr. *nébulosité* or late L. *nebulositas*, f. L. *nebulosus*; see next, -ITY.] **1.** Nebulous or indistinctly luminous appearance; a faintly luminous patch or mass. **b.** Nebulous state or form; nebulous matter 1833. **2.** Cloudiness; indistinctness 1809.

1. b. *fig.* He had been a mere n. whom she had never distinctly outlined T. HARDY.

Nebulous (ne·biŭləs). *a.* late ME. [– Fr. *nébuleux* or L. *nebulosus*; see NEBULA, -OUS.] **1.** Cloudy, foggy, misty, dank (*rare*). **2.** *Astron.* **a.** *N. star*, a small cluster of indistinct stars, or a star which is surrounded by a luminous haze 1679. **b.** Of the nature of a nebula or nebulæ; consisting of, abounding in, nebulæ 1784. **3.** Cloud-like 1805. **b.** *fig.* Hazy, vague, formless 1831. **4.** Clouded in colour; turbid 1820.

3. b. N. disquisitions on Religion CARLYLE. Hence **Ne·bulous-ly** *adv.*, **-ness.**

Necessarian (nesĕsēᵊ·riăn). 1777. [f. NECESSARY + -IAN; see -ARIAN.] A believer in necessity; a necessitarian. **b.** *attrib.* or as *adj.* 1795. Hence **Necessa·rianism,** necessitarianism 1840.

Necessarily (ne·sĕsărili), *adv.* 1488. [f. as prec. + -LY[2].] †**1.** (Senses now merged in 3.) Unavoidably –1710; indispensably –1748. **2.** As a necessary result or consequence 1509. **3.** Of necessity; inevitably 1562. So **Ne·cessariness,** indispensability (now *rare*) 1551.

Necessary (ne·sĕsări), *a.* and *sb.* late ME. [– AFr. **necessarie* ((O)Fr. *nécessaire*) or L. *necessarius*, f. *necesse* (*esse, habēre*) (be, consider) necessary; see -ARY[1].] **A.** *adj.* **I. 1.** Indispensable, requisite, needful; that cannot be done without. Also const. *to* or *for* (a person or thing) and with *inf.* †**b.** Commodious, convenient (*rare*) –1548. **2.** Of servants, etc.: Rendering (certain) necessary or useful services, as *n. woman. Hist.* **3.** Of actions: Needful to be done 1601.

1. Which wife is not..called an impediment or n. evil 1577. Since light so n. is to life MILT. Phr. *N. house*, a privy. So *n. place, stool, vault.* Now *dial.* **3.** Still doubting if that deed Be just which is most n. SHELLEY.

II. 1. Inevitably determined or fixed by predestination or natural laws; happening or existing by an inherent necessity. late ME. **b.** Of mental concepts or processes: Inevitably resulting from the constitution of things or of the mind itself 1551. **c.** Inevitably produced by a previous condition of things 1860. **2.** Of actions: Determined by force of nature or circumstances. late ME. **b.** Enforced by another; compulsory 1655. **3.** Of agents: Impelled by the action of circumstances upon the will; having no independent volition 1690.

1. b. The ideas of space and time are called in philosophy n. ideas 1878. **2.** The n. action, where all the motives are on one side 1855. **3.** They all agree, that man is not a free but a n. agent WESLEY.

B. *sb.* **1.** A necessary thing; an essential or requisite ME. **2.** A necessary house (*dial.*) 1756. **3.** With *the.* That which is needful; *spec.* the necessary funds or money *colloq.* 1772.

1. She denied herself every n. MME. D'ARBLAY. The money to buy the necessaries of their household 1875.

Necessitarian (nĭsesitēᵊ·riăn). 1798. [f. NECESSITY + -ARIAN; cf. NECESSARIAN.] One who maintains that all human action is necessarily determined by antecedent causes, as opposed to one who believes in the freedom of the will. Hence **Necessita·rianism** 1854.

Necessitate (nĭse·siteⁱt), *v.* 1628. [– *necessitat-*, pa. ppl. stem of med.L. *necessitare* compel, constrain, f. *necessitas*; see NECES-

SITY, -ATE [3]. Cf. (O)Fr. *nécessiter*.] **1.** *trans.* To bring (a person) under some necessity; to compel, oblige, or force. (Chiefly in *pass.*) Now *rare* (freq. in 17th c.). **2.** To render necessary; *esp.* to demand, require, or involve as a necessary condition or result 1628. †**3.** To reduce (a person) to want or necessity –1700.

1. Each boy is necessitated to decide and act for himself 1779. Necessitated by weak health to the regularity and the quiet of a monk PATER. **2.** Assumptions..such as the received theology necessitates M. ARNOLD. **3.** The King..being necessitated for Money 1700. Hence **Necessita·tion,** the action of necessitating; the result of this 1652.

Necessitous (nĭse·sitəs),*a.* 1611. [– Fr. *nécessiteux*, or f. NECESSITY + -OUS.] **1.** Placed or living in a condition of necessity; poor, needy. **2.** Characterized by necessity or poverty 1639.

1. A greedy and n. publick BURKE. *absol.* The ambitious hoped for kingdoms; the greedy and the n. for plunder CHESTERF. **2.** In n. circumstances 1885. Hence **Nece·ssitous-ly** *adv.*, **-ness.**

Necessitude (nĭse·sitiūd). Now *rare.* 1612. [– L. *necessitudo*, f. *necesse* necessary; see -TUDE.] †**1.** A relation or connection between persons –1653. **2.** Necessity, need 1677.

1. Between Parents and their children there is so great a necessitude JER. TAYLOR.

Necessity (nĭse·sĭti). late ME. [– (O)Fr. *nécessité* – L. *necessitas*, f. *necesse* necessary; see -ITY.] **I.** †**1. a.** The fact of being inevitably fixed or determined –1568. †**b.** The constraining power *of* something –1533. **2.** Constraint or compulsion having its basis in the natural constitution of things; *esp.* such constraint conceived as a law prevailing throughout the material universe and within the sphere of human action. late ME. **b.** Differentiated as *absolute, conditional, logical, moral, natural, philosophical, physical* 1587. **3.** The constraining power of circumstances; a condition of things compelling to a certain course of action. late ME. †**4.** A necessary piece of business; a necessary act –1676. †**b.** Something unavoidable. SHAKS. **5. a.** An unavoidable compulsion or obligation of doing something. Also with *inf.* Now *rare.* 1630. **b.** An imperative need *for* or †*of* something 1673. **6.** The fact of being indispensable; the indispensableness *of* some act or thing 1597.

2. Who can..breake the chayne of strong necessitee SPENSER. **b.** Physical n. has its origin in the established order and laws of the material universe 1840. **3.** I know the rigour of political n.; but I see here, as little of n...as of propriety BURKE. Phr. *Work of n.*, something which cannot possibly or naturally be left undone. *Of n.*: Necessarily. *Phrases and proverbs.* To maken vertu of necessite CHAUCER. N...hath no law 1614. N. is the Mother of Invention 1658. **4. b.** 2 *Hen. IV*, III. i. 92. **5. b.** He..produced a n. of private conversation JOHNSON. **6.** The n. of adopting some measures to subsist their armies WELLINGTON.

II. 1. †**a.** What is necessarily required; necessaries –1650. **b.** A necessary thing 1481. **2.** The condition of being necessitous; want, poverty 1475. **3.** A situation of hardship or difficulty; a pressing need or want. (Chiefly in *pl.*) 1450. †**4.** Want *of* a thing –1754.

2. Necessities sharpe pinch SHAKS. They will not ask whether his n. be a sufficient title HOBBES. **3.** The necessities of the mother country 1775.

Neck (nek), *sb.*[1] [OE. *hnecca*, corresp. to OFris. *hnecka, necke*, MDu. *nac, necke* (Du. *nek*), OHG. (*h*)*nac* (G. *nacken* nape), ON. *hnakki* nape :– Gmc. **χnak(j)*- repr. IE. **knok*-.] **I. 1.** That portion of the body lying between the head and shoulders; †in early use the nape of the neck. **b.** The cervical vertebræ. Chiefly in phr. *to break the n.* ME. **2. a.** The flesh of the neck of an animal, esp. of beef or mutton 1603. **b.** That part of a garment which covers, or lies next to, the neck 1530.

1. He would..make two Fellows who hated, embrace and fall upon each other's N. STEELE. **b.** I had as liefe thou didst breake his necke as his finger SHAKS. Without regard for the safety of their own necks 1893. **2. a.** Eight to a n. of mutton—is not that your commons 1603.

II. In fig. or allusive expressions, implying subjugation, submission, resistance, †the imposition of a burden or charge; or with allusion to hanging or beheading. late ME.

Wilt thou set thy foot o' my necke SHAKS. Let his N. answere for it SHAKS. *Oth.* v. ii. 170. Sturdiest Oaks Bow'd thir Stiff necks MILT.

Phrases. *In, on,* or *upon the n. of,* on the top of. Now only *dial. To break the n. of,* to counteract the chief force or main effect of; to finish the main part of. *N. and heels* = neck and crop. Now *dial. N. and crop,* bodily, altogether. *N. or nothing* (occ. *nought*), expressing determination and readiness to take all risks; also *attrib.* of persons or actions. *N. and n.*, of horses, etc.: keeping abreast; also *fig.*; *attrib.* close, near. *To get it in the n.* (slang), to sustain a severe blow, as of defeat, reprimand, etc.

III. In transf. uses. **1.** The narrow part *of* some passage, cavity, or vessel, *esp.* the part of a bottle next the mouth ME. **2.** Of natural formations, or artificial structures: A pass between hills or mountains; the narrow part *of* a mountain pass; a narrow channel or inlet; the narrow part *of* a sound; *Fortif.* The narrow part *of* a bastion or embrasure; an isthmus or narrow promontory; a narrow stretch of wood, ice, etc. 1555. **3.** A narrow or constricted part in any manufactured article; a connecting part between two portions of a thing 1598. **b.** The part of a violin, etc., connecting the head and the body 1611. **c.** *Arch.* The lower part of a capital, lying immediately above the astragal terminating the shaft of the column 1624. **d.** In cannon, (*a*) the narrow part connecting the cascabel with the breech; (*b*) the part immediately behind the swell of the muzzle 1753. **4. a.** *Bot.* A neck-like part in plants 1672. **b.** Excessive elongation of stem or stalk 1882. **5.** *Anat.* **a.** The small circular depression where the base of a tooth ends and the roots begin 1732. **b.** A constricted part in a bone 1726.

Combs.: **n.-cell** *Bot.*, a cell forming (part of) the n. in the archegonium of ferns or bryophytes; **-fillet**, in cannon, a fillet on the breech, next to the n. of the cascabel; **-mould(ing)** *Arch.*, a moulding on the n. of a capital; **-twister** *U.S. slang*, a kind of drink; **-wear,** collars and ties.

Neck, *sb.*[2] *s.w. dial.* late ME. [Of unkn. origin.] The last handful or sheath of corn cut at harvest-time.

Neck (nek), *v.* Now only *techn.* or *dial.* 1450. [f. NECK *sb.*[1] Cf. Du. *nekken* kill.] **1.** *trans.* To strike on the neck, esp. so as to stun or kill; to behead; to pull the neck of (a fowl). **b.** *intr.* (*U.S.*) To indulge in intimate hugging and kissing. **2.** To make or clear the neck of (a drain) 1844. **3.** *pass.* or *intr.* To break off at the head 1828. **4.** To reduce the diameter of, by planing, etc. 1873.

Ne·ck-band. 1446. [f. NECK *sb.*[1]] **1.** A band for the neck. **2.** The part of a garment encircling the neck 1591.

†**Ne·ck-beef.** 1662. [f. NECK *sb.*[1]] Beef from the necks of cattle, which is of poor quality. Hence *transf.* of anything inferior and cheap. –1812.

Ne·ck-bone. ME. [f. NECK *sb.*[1]] The bone (or †nape) of the neck; a cervical vertebra.

Ne·ckcloth. 1639. [f. NECK *sb.*[1]] A cloth worn round the neck; a cravat. Now *rare.* **b.** *transf.* The hangman's rope 1836.

Necked (nekt), *a.* late ME. [f. NECK *sb.*[1] + -ED[2].] **1.** Having a neck *like* something specified, or of a specified kind. **2.** Having a neck 1841.

Neckerchief (ne·kəɹtʃif). late ME. [f. NECK *sb.*[1] + KERCHIEF.] A kerchief worn about the neck. So **Ne·ckercher** (now *dial.*). So **Neck-ha·ndkerchief** 1642.

Necking (ne·kiŋ), *sb.* 1804. [f. NECK *sb.*[1] + -ING[1].] *Arch.* The part of a column lying between the capital and the shaft.

Necklace (ne·klės), *sb.* 1590. [f. NECK *sb.*[1] + LACE *sb.*] **1.** An ornament of precious stones, precious metal, beads, etc. worn round the neck. †**b.** A lace or ribbon for the neck; a neck-tie –1740. **2.** *transf.* A noose or halter 1616. **3.** *Naut.* A chain or strop round a mast 1860. **4.** *attrib.* applied to certain plants or woods having features resembling strings of beads, as *n.-tree.*

Necklace (ne·klės), *v.* 1702. [f. prec.] **1.** *trans.* and *intr.* To form into a necklace. **2.** *trans.* To surround with, or as with, a necklace 1763.

Necklet (ne·klėt). 1865. [f. NECK *sb.*[1] + -LET.] A closely fitting ornamental band for the neck.

Ne·ck-piece. 1611. [f. NECK *sb.*[1]] **1.** The part of a garment next the neck. **b.** A piece of armour, cloth, etc., covering the neck 1752. **2.** Of meat: The part of the carcass between the shoulder and the head 1818.

Ne·ck-tie. 1838. [f. NECK *sb.*[1]] A narrow band of woven or knitted material placed round the neck and tied or knotted in front.

Ne·ck-verse. 1450. [f. NECK *sb.*[1]] A Latin verse printed in black-letter (usu. the beginning of *Ps.* 51) formerly set before one claiming benefit of clergy (see CLERGY), by reading which he might save his neck. Now only *Hist.* †Also in *transf.* or *fig.* uses –1659.

Ne·ckweed. 1562. [f. NECK *sb.*[1]] †**1.** The plant hemp (with ref. to the use of hempen rope for hanging persons) –1681. **2.** *U.S.* An American weed, *Veronica peregrina* or Purslane Speedwell, formerly supposed to be of service in scrofulous affections, whence the name 1846.

Necro- (nekro), *occas.* **necr-**, comb. f. Gr. νεκρός dead body or person, occurring in compounds either of Gr. origin, as NECROPOLIS, etc., or of modern formation, as NECROBIOSIS, etc.; also **necro·latry,** worship of the dead; **necro·phagous,** feeding on dead bodies or carrion; **ne·crophore,** a burying-beetle, one belonging to the genus *Necrophorus*; **necro·scopy,** examination of bodies after death; **necro·tomy,** the dissection of dead bodies; the excision of dead bone or tissue.

‖**Necrobiosis** (nekrobəiōᵘ·sis). 1880. [mod. L., f. NECRO- + Gr. βίος life; see -OSIS.] *Path.* The process of decay or death in tissues of the body; the gradual degeneration and death of a part through suspended or imperfect nutrition; an instance of this. So **Necrobio·tic** *a.* 1875.

Necrology (nekrǫ·lŏdʒi). 1727. [In sense 1 – med.L. *necrologium* (whence Fr. *necrologe* XVII); with sense 2 cf. Fr. *necrologie* (XVIII); see NECRO-, -LOGY.] **1.** An ecclesiastical or monastic register containing entries of the deaths of persons connected with, or commemorated by, the church, monastery, etc. **b.** A death-roll 1854. **2.** An obituary notice 1799. Hence **Necrolo·gic, -al** *a.* obituary; **-ally** *adv.* **Necro·logist,** one who writes an obituary notice. **Ne·crologue,** an obituary notice.

Necromancer (ne·kromænsəɹ). Earlier **nigro-.** [ME. *nigromauncer(e* – OFr. *nigromansere*, f. *nigromancie*; see NECROMANCY, -ER[2] 2.] One who practises necromancy; more generally, a wizard, magician.

Necromancy (ne·kromænsi). Earlier **nigro-.** [ME. *nigro-*, etc. – OFr. *nigromancie* – Rom. (med.L.) *nigromantia*, alt., by assoc. with *niger, nigr-* black, of late L. *necromantia* – Gr. νεκρομαντεία, f. νεκρός + μαντεία; see NECRO-, -MANCY; refash. XVI as in Fr. after L. and Gr.] **1.** The pretended art of revealing future events, etc., by means of communication with the dead; more generally, magic, enchantment, conjuration. Also with *a* and *pl.* **2.** Applied, after Gr. and L. use, to the part of the Odyssey describing Ulysses' visit to Hades 1601.

1. You by your N. have disturb'd him, and rais'd his Ghost MARVELL. Love, with all his necromancies, fled 1849.

Necromantic (nekromæ·ntik), *a.* and *sb.* 1574. [– late L. *necromanticus* or med.L. *nigromanticus*; see prec., -MANTIC. Cf. Fr. †*nigromantique* adj.] **A.** *adj.* **1.** Given to the practice of necromancy. **2.** Of, belonging to, or used in necromancy or magic; performed by necromancy 1590. **b.** *transf.* Magical, wonderful 1630. **B.** *sb.* A necromancer –1652. †**Necromantical** *a.*, **-ly** *adv.*

Ne·cronite. 1819. [f. NECRO- + -(N)ITE; see -ITE[1] 2 b.] *Min.* A variety of orthoclase, giving out a fetid smell when broken or struck.

Necropolis (nekrǫ·polis). *Pl.* **-ises.** 1819. [– Gr. νεκρόπολις, f. νεκρός corpse + πόλις city.] A cemetery; freq. used as the name of cemeteries in or near cities. **b.** An old or prehistoric burying-place 1850.

Necropsy (nekrǫ·psi). 1856. [f. NECRO- after AUTOPSY.] **1.** A post-mortem examination, an autopsy. **2.** Surgical investigation of a dead body 1881.

Necrose (nekrōᵘ·s, ne·kroᵘs), *v.* 1873. [f. NECROSIS. Cf. Fr. *nécroser*.] *Path. intr.* To mortify; to become affected with necrosis.

Necrosed (nekrōᵘ·st, ne·kroᵘst), *ppl. a.* 1830. [f. NECROSIS + -ED². Cf. Fr. *nécrosé* (prec.).] *Path.* Mortified, affected by necrosis.

‖**Necrosis** (nekrōᵘ·sis). 1665. [mod.L. – Gr. νέκρωσις state of death, f. νεκροῦν kill, mortify, f. νεκρός corpse; see NECRO-, -OSIS.] **1.** *Path.* The death of a circumscribed piece of tissue; mortification, esp. of the bones. **2.** *Bot.* Canker; a drying and dying of the branch of a tree, beginning with the bark and eating inwards 1866. So **Necro·tic** *a.* **Ne·crotize** *v. intr.* to become affected with n.

Nectar (ne·ktăɹ). 1555. [– L. *nectar* – Gr. νέκταρ.] **1.** *Class. Myth.* The drink of the gods. Cf. AMBROSIA. Also *fig.* **2.** *transf.* **a.** Any delicious wine or other drink 1583. **b.** The sweet fluid or honey produced by plants, esp. as collected by bees 1609.

1. But might I of Jove's n. sup, I would not change for thine B. JONS. Hence **Necta·rean** *a.* **Ne·ctared** *a.* filled, flavoured, or impregnated with n.; deliciously sweet or fragrant (*lit.* and *fig.*). **Necta·reous** *a.* consisting of n. **Necta·reous-ly** *adv.*, **-ness.** **Nectari·ferous** *a.* bearing or producing n. **Ne·ctarous** *a.* resembling n.

Nectarine (ne·ktărin, -īn), *sb.* 1616. [prob. a sb. use of next.] A variety of the common peach, with a thinner and downless skin and a firmer pulp.

Nectarine (ne·ktărin), *a.* 1611. [f. NECTAR + -INE¹.] Of the nature of, sweet as, nectar.

‖**Nectarium** (nektēᵊ·riŏm). Pl. **-ia.** 1753. [mod.L.; see NECTAR, -ARIUM.] = NECTARY 2.

Nectary (ne·ktări). 1759. [– mod.L. *nectarium*; see NECTAR, -ARY¹.] **1.** *Bot.* The organ or part of a flower or plant which secretes honey. **2.** *Entom.* A wart-like tube on the body of an aphis, from which 'honeydew' is exuded 1890.

Nectocalyx (nektǫkēⁱ·liks). *Pl.* **-calyces.** 1859. [mod.L., f. Gr. νηκτός swimming (f. νήχειν swim) + CALYX.] *Zool.* The swimming-bell which forms the natatory organ in many hydrozoans. So **Ne·ctosac,** the interior of a n. (also called *nectocyst*); **Ne·ctosome,** the upper portion of a siphonophore, bearing the natatory organs. **Ne·ctostem,** the axis of a series of nectocalyces. Hence **Nectoca·lycine** *a.* of the nature of, resembling or pertaining to, a n.

Nedder, obs. f. ADDER.

Neddy (ne·di). 1790. [dim. of *Ned,* pet-form of the Christian name *Edward*; see -Y⁶.] **1.** A donkey. **2.** *Cant.* A life-preserver 1864.

‖**Née** (nēⁱ), *ppl. a.* 1835. [Fr., pa. pple. fem. of *naître*.] Born; used in adding a married woman's maiden name, as, Madame de Staël, *née* Necker.

Need (nīd), *sb.* [OE. *nēd* (WS. *nied, nȳd*), = OFris. *nēd, nāth,* OS. *nōd* (Du. *nood*), OHG. *nōt* (G. *not*), ON. *nauð, neyð,* Goth. *nauþs* :- Gmc. **nauðiz,* **nauþiz*.] **1.** †**1.** Violence, constraint or compulsion, exercised upon or by persons –ME. **2.** Necessity arising from the facts and circumstances of a case. Chiefly in phr. *if* (etc.) *n. require, if n. be* (or *were*), *there is no n.* OE. **3.** In predic. use: Necessary, needful. Now *rare.* OE. **4.** Imperative call or demand for the presence, possession, etc., *of* something OE. **5.** A condition of affairs placing one in difficulty or distress; a time of difficulty or trouble OE. **6.** A condition marked by the lack or want of some necessary thing, or requiring some extraneous aid or addition OE. **b.** A state of extreme want or destitution ME.

2. Repeat this if N. be WESLEY. There was no n. of you to confess it 1845. *To have n. to,* to be under a necessity to do something, to require to. †Also with omission of *to,* and with *that. Had n. to,* would require to, ought to. So with omission of *to*; The Portuguese had n. have the stomachs of ostriches BECKFORD. 3. Some Reformed Churches..have..made themselves much poorer than was n. 1849. 4. The n. of further securities against the royal power GREEN. Phr. *To have n. of* (†*to,* †*unto*) the thing required. †Const. with direct object: To need, require; Here he had n. All circumspection MILT. Phr. *To have n.,* to be in straits or in want. Now *rare* or *Obs.* 5. I thank you for lending me a hand at my n. BUNYAN. Phr. *At n.*; Sir William of Deloraine, good at n. SCOTT. 6. The great n. of her heart compelled her to [etc.] GEO. ELIOT. *Prov.* A friend in n. is a friend indeed. **b.** When n. crept in, love walked out 1847.

II. †**1.** A matter requiring action to be taken; a piece of necessary business. In later use chiefly *pl.* Also *good n.,* good service –1508. †**b.** Chiefly *pl.* One's errands or business –1550. **2.** A particular point or respect in which some necessity or want is present or is felt OE.

2. Servile subjection to daily needs 1874. †*At a n.,* in an emergency or crisis. So †*in a n.* †*For a n.,* in an emergency.

Need (nīd), *v.* [OE. *nēodian* (rare), f. *nēod* desire, var. of *nied* NEED *sb.*] **1.** *intr.* †**1.** *It needs,* it is needful or necessary. Usu. const. with *that* or inf., and occas. without *it.* –1765. **2.** *There needs,* there is need for (some thing or person) 1440. †**b.** *What needs..?* What need is there for (something)? –1662. **c.** *It needs,* it requires 1839. **3.** *impers.* Of things: To be needful or necessary 1526.

2. There needes no such Apologie SHAKS. **c.** It needs heaven-sent moments for this skill M. ARNOLD. 3. But little learning needs in noble blood DRYDEN.

II. †**1.** To be needful or necessary *to* a person, or *to* some end or purpose –1496. †**2.** Impersonally: **a.** To be necessary for (one) *to* do something –1590. †**b.** So *What need(s..?* Why should (one)? –1597.

2. **b.** What nedeth me then to laboure eny more for wyszdome? COVERDALE *Eccles.* 2:15.

III. †**1.** To have need *of* (also *to*) a thing –1598. **2.** *trans.* To stand in need of, to require. late ME. **b.** *intr.* To be in need or want. late ME. **3.** To be under a necessity or obligation *to* do something. late ME. **b.** With omission of *to,* when the clause has the forms *it* (*he, I,* etc.) *need not,* (*why*) *need* (*it,* etc.)? 1470.

2. Pickwick needed no second invitation DICKENS. **b.** Betere is to dyen, than to neden WYCLIF *Ecclus.* 40:29. 3. Vice..to be hated, needs but to be seen POPE. **b.** I n. hardly ask again JOWETT. Hence **Nee·ded** *ppl. a.* required. **Nee·der.**

†**Need,** *adv.* [OE. *nēde,* etc., orig. the instrumental case of *nēd* NEED *sb.*] Of necessity, necessarily, etc. –1732.

Nee·dfire. 1535. [f. NEED *sb.* + FIRE, prob. repr. an OE. *niedfȳr* = OS. *nōdfȳr,* MLG. *nōtvūr,* MHG. *nōtviur* (G. *notfeuer*) in sense 2.] †**1.** *Sc.* Spontaneous combustion. Only in phr. *to take n.* –1669. **2.** Fire obtained from dry wood by means of violent friction, formerly used as a means of curing disease among cattle 1633. **3.** A beacon or bonfire 1805.

Needful (nī·dfŭl), *a.* (and *sb.*) ME. [f. NEED *sb.* + -FUL.] **1.** Of persons: Needy, necessitous. Now *rare.* **2.** Of circumstances, occasions, etc.: Characterized by need or necessity. Now rare. ME. **3.** Requisite, necessary. Also const. *to* or *for* the person or thing concerned. ME. **4.** *The n.,* what is necessary or requisite 1709. **b.** *colloq.* The necessary funds; money, cash 1774. **5.** *sb.* A necessary thing 1856.

2. Why..hydest [thou] thy face in that neadeful tyme of trouble *Bible* (Cranmer) *Ps.* 10:1. 3. We myght doo any nedeful busynesse upon the Sunday 1545. Phr. *It is n. that* or *to* (with inf.). 4. To live I must have 'the n.' C. BRONTË. Hence **Nee·dful-ly** *adv.*, **-ness.**

†**Nee·dham.** 1573. Name of a small town (Needham Market) near Ipswich in Suffolk, used punningly with allusion to NEED *sb.*; hence, need, poverty, beggary –1661.

They are said to be in the high way to N. who do hasten to poverty FULLER.

Needle (nī·d'l), *sb.* [OE. *nǣdl* = OFris. *nēdle,* OS. *nādla, nāthla,* MLG. *nālde,* OHG. *nādala* (Du. *naald,* G. *nadel*), ON. *nál* (:- **naðl*), Goth. *nēþla* :- Gmc. **nēþlō* :- **nētlā,* f. **nē-* sew, repr. also by L. *nēre* spin, Gr. νῆμα thread.] **I. 1.** A small and slender piece of polished steel having a fine point at one end and at the other a hole or eye (see EYE *sb.*) for thread; used in sewing. **b.** *transf.* A needlewoman (*rare*) 1834. **2. a.** A piece of magnetized steel (orig. a needle in sense 1) used as an indicator of direction (in later use as a part of the COMPASS), or in connection with magnetic or electric apparatus, e.g. the telegraph. late ME. Also *ellipt.* = needle telegraph. **b.** A small strip of gold or silver of known fineness used with a touchstone in testing the purity of other pieces of those metals 1469. **c.** The tongue of a balance 1589. **3. a.** A pointed instrument used in engraving or etching 1662. **b.** *Surg.* A long slender pointed instrument used in operations; the end of a hypodermic or other syringe; a pointed electrode used in surgical electrolysis 1727. **c.** In breech-loading fire-arms, a slender steel pin which ignites the cartridge by impact 1853. **4. a.** A knitting or netting pin 1719. **b.** One of the parallel pieces of wire in a stocking frame or in the Jacquard loom 1839. **5.** *Mining.* A sharp-pointed copper or brass rod with which a small hole is made through the stemming to the cartridge in blasting operations 1839.

1. *Sharp as a n.*: see the adj. *Pins and needles*: see PIN *sb. fig.* Catherine ran infinite pins and needles of speech into them READE. Phr. *To look for,* or *seek, a n. in a meadow, haystack, bottle* (*truss* or *bundle*) *of hay,* to attempt a hopeless task. *Needle's eye,* denoting the smallest possible opening or space, chiefly with ref. to *Matt.* 19:24, etc. 2. **a.** *Magnetic n.,* a magnetized rod turning on a pivot, as in a mariner's compass; so *mariner's n.* 3. **d.** The thin pointed piece of metal, wood, etc., that receives and transmits the vibrations set up by a revolving gramophone disc 1902.

II. 1. A pillar or obelisk. late ME. **2.** A sharp-pointed mass of rock; *esp.* in *pl.* as the name of those to the west of the Isle of Wight. late ME. **3.** A beam of wood, *esp.* one used as a temporary support for a wall during underpinning 1471. **4.** *Chem.* and *Min.* A crystal or spicule resembling a needle in shape 1712. **5.** One of the leaves of the fir and pine trees 1798. **6.** *slang. The n.,* a fit of irritation or nervousness 1887.

Comb.: **n.-bath,** a shower-bath with a very fine and strong spray; **-bolt,** the bolt which carries the n. in a needle-gun; **-book,** a needle-case shaped like a book; **-case,** a case in which needles are kept; **-dial,** a dial bearing a n. in an electrical apparatus; **-furze** or **gorse,** *Genista anglica*; **-lace,** lace made with the n., as opp. to bobbin-lace; **-syringe,** a sharp-pointed hypodermic syringe; **-telegraph,** a telegraph in which the n. is employed as an indicator; **-worm,** a small worm parasitic in horses.

Needle (nī·d'l), *v.* 1715. [f. prec.] **1.** *trans.* To sew or pierce with (or as with) a needle. **b.** To penetrate; to pierce or thread (one's way); to underpin with needle-beams, etc. 1820. **2.** *intr.* **a.** To form acicular crystals. **b.** To pass through, or in and out, like a needle. **c.** To use the needle, to sew. 1780.

Nee·dle-fish. 1601. [NEEDLE *sb.* I. 1.] A name for various fishes; esp. the pipe-fish or gar-fish.

Nee·dleful 1611. [NEEDLE *sb.* I. 1.] The amount of thread which is put into a needle at one time.

Nee·dle-gun. 1865. [NEEDLE *sb.* I. 3 c.] A gun in which the cartridge is exploded by the impact of a needle.

Nee·dle-point. 1700. [NEEDLE *sb.* I. 1.] **1.** The point of a needle; also *transf.* **2.** Point-lace made with the needle 1869. So **Nee·dle-pointed** *a.* 1599. Chiefly *fig.*

Needler (nī·dləɹ). ME. [f. NEEDLE *sb.* + -ER¹.] A needle-maker.

Needless (nī·dlės), *a.* ME. [f. NEED *sb.* + -LESS.] †**1.** In quasi-advb. use: Without any compulsion or necessity; needlessly –1475. **2.** Not needed; unnecessary, useless ME. (Common from *c*1570.) †**3.** Having no want; not in need –1668.

2. The message was n. MACAULAY. Beware of.. questions which raise n. doubts 1880. 3. *A.Y.L.* II. i. 46. Hence **Nee·dless-ly** *adv.*, **-ness.**

Nee·dlestone. 1820. [– G. *nadelstein*.] *Min.* A name formerly given to minerals having needle-like crystals, as natrolite and scolecite.

Nee·dlewoman. 1611. [NEEDLE *sb.* I. 1.] A woman who works with the needle; a sempstress. Also with qualification, as *good, bad.*

Nee·dlework. late ME. [f. NEEDLE *sb.* I. 1.] **1.** Work done with the needle; sewing, embroidery, or fancy work. †**b.** *pl.* Pieces or kinds of this –1748. So **Nee·dleworker** 1611.

Needly (nī·dli), *a. rare.* 1671. [f. NEEDLE *sb.* + -Y[1].] Resembling a needle or needles.

†**Nee·dly,** *adv.* [OE. *nēodlīće*; see NEED *sb.*, -LY[2].] Necessarily; of necessity –1647.

Needment (nī·dmĕnt). 1590. [f. NEED *sb.* or *v.* + -MENT.] **1.** *pl.* Things needed; *esp.* personal necessaries carried as luggage. **2.** *pl.* Needs, requirements 1603.

1. Carrying each his needments tied up in a pocket-handkerchief WORDSW.

Needs (nīdz), *adv.* [OE. *nēdes*, finally superseding NEED *adv.*; see NEED *sb.*, -S.] Of necessity, necessarily. Now chiefly with *must* (colloq. often iron. implying foolish or perverse insistence).

Stooping down as n. he must Who cannot sit upright COWPER. The Squire must n. have something of the old ceremonies observed on the occasion W. IRVING. She shall go, if n. must BROWNING.

†**Nee·dsly,** *adv.* 1449. [f. as prec. + -LY[2].] Of necessity. (Usu. with *must.*) –1656.

Needy (nī·di), *a.* ME. [f. NEED *sb.* + -Y[1].] **1.** Of persons: Poor, necessitous. †**b.** In need *of* a thing (*rare*) –1601. **2.** Of circumstances: Characterized by poverty or need 1574. †**3.** Needful, necessary –1608.

1. What time the pore and nedye are releved 1560. The n. Cheat, The poor and friendless Villain POPE. **2.** In his needie shop a Tortoyrs hung SHAKS. **3.** *Per.* I. iv. 95. Hence †**Nee·dily** *adv.* **Nee·diness.**

Neeld, obs. and dial. f. NEEDLE.

Neem (nīm). 1824. [– Hindi *nīm*, Skr. *nimba.*] An E. Indian tree, the margosa.

Neep (nīp). *Sc.* and *n. dial.* [OE. *nǣp*.–L. *napus.* Cf. TURNIP.] A turnip.

Neer, obs. f. NEAR.

Ne'er (nēᵊɹ), *adv. dial.* or *poet.* ME. [contr. f. NEVER, as *e'er* for *ever.*] **1.** Never. **b.** *Sc.* Euphem. for *deil*, devil. SCOTT. **2.** *Ne'er the less* = NEVERTHELESS ME.

Ne'er a, *adj. phr. dial.* or *poet.* Also **narrow a, narra.** late ME. [f. prec. + A *adj.*[2]] Never a, not a, no.

Ne'er-do-well, *sb.* and *a.* Also *Sc.* and *n.* **-weel.** 1737. **A.** *sb.* One who never does, and never will do, well; a good-for-nothing. **B.** *adj.* Good-for-nothing, worthless 1773.

Neeze (nīz), *v.* Now *Sc.* and *n. dial.* [– ON. *hnjósa* = OHG. *niosan*, MLG. *niesen* (G. *niesen*, Du. *niezen*), of imit. origin. Cf. FNESE.] To sneeze. Hence **Nee·zing** *vbl. sb.* (*n.-powder*).

‖**Nef** (nef, nef). 1687. [Fr. = ship, nave; see NAVE *sb.*[2]] †**1.** The nave of a church –1775. **2.** An incense-boat 1867.

Nefandous (nĭfæ·ndəs), *a. Obs.* or *arch.* 1640. [f. L. *nefandus*, f. *ne* not + *fandus*, gerundive of *fari* speak; see -OUS.] Not to be spoken of; unmentionable, abominable.

Many n. crimes 1640. A most n. error 1827.

Nefarious (nĭfēᵊ·riəs), *a.* 1604. [f. L. *nefarius* (Cicero), f. *nefas* wrong, wickedness, f. *ne-* not + *fas* divine permission, command, or law; see -OUS.] Wicked, iniquitous, villainous. So **Nefa·riously** *adv.* 1599.

Negate (nĭgē[i]·t), *v.* 1623. [– *negat-*, pa. ppl. stem of L. *negare* say no, deny, f. *neg-*, var. of *nec* (cf. NE and NEGLECT *v.*); see -ATE[3].] *trans.* To deny, negative; to deny the existence of; to destroy, nullify, render ineffective. (Freq. in recent use.)

Negation (nĭgē[i]·ʃən). 1530. [– (O)Fr. *négation* or L. *negatio*, f. as prec.; see -ION.] **1.** The action of denying or of making a statement involving the use of 'no', 'not', 'never', etc. Also const. *of.* **b.** An instance of this; a refusal or contradiction; a denial 1576. **c.** *Logic.* Opp. to AFFIRMATION 3. 1570. **2.** The absence or opposite of something which is actual, positive, or affirmative 1642. **3.** A negative or unreal thing, a nonentity; a thing whose essence consists in the absence of something positive 1707.

1. This is the n. of God erected into a system of Government GLADSTONE. **2.** Death is nothing more than the n. of life FIELDING. Hence **Nega·tional** *a.* negative, using or involving n. 1865. **Nega·tionist,** one who denies accepted beliefs without advancing anything positive in their place 1856.

Negative (ne·gătiv), *sb.* late ME. [– (O)Fr. *négative* (XIII) or late (and med.) L. *negativa* (sc. *sententia, propositio*) subst. use of fem. of adj. *negativus*, f. as prec.: see -IVE.] **1.** †**a.** A negative command, a prohibition –1581. **b.** A negative statement or proposition; a negative mode of stating anything 1567. **c.** A negative reply; †a denial or refusal 1571. **2.** A negative word or particle; a negative term 1567. †**3.** A right of veto –1796. †**b.** A negative or adverse vote –1743. **4.** *Photogr.* A print made on prepared glass or other transparent substance by the direct action of light, in which the lights and shadows of nature are reversed, and from which positive prints are made 1853.

1. a. The text Deut. 6 hath the negative, Thou shalt serue no strange gods 1581. **b.** I am not bound to prove a n. *'Junius' Lett.* xliv. (1788) 252. **c.** Dreading a n. COWPER. **2.** If your foure negatiues make your two affirmatiues, why then the worse for my friends SHAKS. Phr. *The negative*: The side, position, or aspect of a question which is opposed to the affirmative or positive. *In the n.*: †(*a*) In the face of, in opposition to, something. †(*b*) On the negative side of a question. (*c*) In favour of or with the effect of rejecting a proposal or suggestion. (*d*) With denial or negation; negatively; of a negative character.

Negative (ne·gătiv), *a.* late ME. [– (O)Fr. *négatif, -ive* or late L. *negativus*; see prec.] **I.** †**1.** Of persons: Making denial of something –1736. **2.** Expressing, conveying, or implying negation or denial 1509. **b.** *spec.* in *Logic*, of propositions, etc., or names 1551. **3. a.** Of commands, etc.: Prohibitory 1526. **b.** Expressing refusal; refusing consent to a proposal or motion 1535. **c.** Able to impose a veto (now *rare*) 1648.

1. *Wint. T.* I. ii. 274. **2.** There are two n. conclusions which seeme necessary 1649. **b.** Names, called N.; which are notes to signifie that a word is not the name of the thing in question HOBBES. A n. proposition..asserts a difference or discrepancy JEVONS. **3. b.** They..yealded to his request, notwithstanding my negatiue voyce 1576. **c.** Denying me any power of a N. voice as King *Eikon Bas.* vi (1662) 20.

II. 1. Characterized by the absence of distinguishing features; devoid of positive attributes 1565. **2.** In *Algebra*, denoting quantities which are to be subtracted from other quantities, or from zero; marked by the sign –. 1673. **b.** *N. sign*, the sign – used to mark a negative quantity 1704. **3.** Applied to the kind of electricity produced by friction upon resin, wax, gutta-percha, etc., as dist. from that produced by rubbed glass, which is called *positive* 1755. **b.** Characterized by the presence or production of negative electricity 1799. **4.** Extending or reckoned on the other side of the point from which the positive is measured, or in an opposite direction to that regarded as positive 1802. **5.** *Photogr.* Characterized by a reversal of the lights and shadows of the object, scene, etc. 1840.

1. A man who..was thought to be made choice of only for his n. qualities CLARENDON.

Comb.: **n. crystal,** (*a*) a crystal in which the index of refraction is greater for the ordinary than the extraordinary ray; (*b*) a crystalliform cavity in a mineral mass; **n. eye-piece,** one consisting of two plano-convex lenses, the convex sides of both being turned towards the object-glass. Hence **Ne·gative-ly** *adv.*, **-ness. Negati·vity,** the fact or quality of being n. 1860.

Negative (ne·gătiv), *v.* 1706. [f. prec.] **1.** *trans.* **a.** *U.S.* To reject (a person proposed for some office). **b.** *U.S.* To veto (a bill, etc.) 1749. **2.** To reject, set aside (a proposal, motion, etc.); to refuse to entertain or countenance 1778. **3.** To disprove; to show to be false 1790; to deny, contradict 1812. **4.** To neutralize 1837.

2. Resolutions..were negatived without a division 1812. Taxation..implies compact, and negatives any right to plunder COLERIDGE. **3.** All our reasonings seemed to be negatived by the results 1853.

Negatory (ne·gătŏri), *a.* 1580. [– Fr. *négatoire* or late L. *negatorius*; see NEGATE *v.*, -ORY[2].] Of the nature of negation.

Neger (nī·gəɹ). *Sc.* and *n. dial.* 1568. [– Fr. *nègre* – Sp. *negro* NEGRO.] A Negro.

Neglect (nĭgle·kt), *sb.* 1588. [f. NEGLECT *v.*, partly after L. *neglectus*, f. as next.] **1.** The fact of disregarding, slighting, or paying no attention to, a person, etc.; the fact or condition of being so treated; †a slight. **b.** Disregard *of*, or with respect to, something; †indifference 1597. **2.** Want of attention to what ought to be done; negligence. Also const. *of.* 1591. **b.** An omission or oversight (now *rare*) 1638.

1. Rescue my poor remains from vile n. PRIOR. **2.** Everybody fancies that his own n. will do no harm JOWETT. **b.** A province..gradually recovering from the effects of Mahratta ravages and neglects 1845. **Negle·ctful** *a.* careless; **-ly** *adv.*; **-ness** 1644.

Neglect (nĭgle·kt), *v.* 1529. [– *neglect-*, pa. ppl. stem of L. *neglegere* disregard, slight, f. *neg-*, var. of *nec* (see NE) + *legere* choose.] **1.** *trans.* To disregard; to pay little or no respect or attention to; to slight. **2.** To fail to bestow proper attention or care upon 1538. **3.** To fail to perform, render, discharge (a duty), or take (a precaution) 1533. **4.** With *inf.* To omit through carelessness *to do* something 1548.

1. That noble discourse had been neglected by the generation to which it was addressed MACAULAY. **2.** Their own education..has been neglected JOWETT. **4.** If they n. To punish crime SHELLEY. Hence **Negle·ctable** *a.* **Negle·ctedly** *adv.* **Negle·cter, -or.** †**Negle·ctingly** *adv.* †**Negle·ction,** negligence, neglect. †**Negle·ctive** *a.* (common in 17th c.), neglectful, inattentive.

‖**Négligé** (ne·gliʒe[i], negliʒe). 1835. [Fr., pa. pple. of *négliger* neglect.] Free and easy attire as worn by women, esp. before 'dressing'; also, a loose gown worn by women on certain informal occasions.

Negligee. *Obs.* or *Hist.* 1756. [– Fr. *négligé*; see prec. In sense 1 pron. (neglidʒi).] **1.** A kind of loose gown worn by women in the 18th c. **2.** A necklace of irregular beads 1841.

Negligence (ne·glidʒĕns). ME. [– (O)Fr. *négligence* or L. *negligentia*, f. as next; see -ENCE.] **1.** Want of attention to what ought to be done or looked after; lack of proper care in doing something. †**b.** Neglect –1778. **2.** An instance or act of inattention or careless behaviour. late ME. **3.** A careless indifference, as in appearance or costume, or in literary or artistic style; in later use esp. with suggestion of an agreeable absence of artificiality or restraint. late ME.

1. The deceased was also guilty of n. or of want of reasonable care contributing to the accident 1884. **b.** *Haml.* IV. v. 134. **2.** Our synnes, negligences, and ignoraunces 1549. **3.** Nothing is so modish as an agreeable N. ADDISON.

Negligent (ne·glidʒĕnt), *a.* late ME. [– (O)Fr. *négligent* or – *negligent-*, pr. ppl. stem of L. *negligere* (for *neglegere*); see NEGLECT *v.*, -ENT.] **1.** Of persons: Inattentive to what ought to be done; neglectful. Also const. *of.* **b.** Indifferent 1440. **2.** Of actions, conduct, etc.: Characterized by or displaying negligence or carelessness 1500.

1. To better him if he be n., to be like him if he be diligent 1581. **2.** O n. and heedlesse Discipline SHAKS. Hence **Ne·gligently** *adv.*

Negligible (ne·glidʒib'l), *a.* 1829. [– Fr. †*négligible*, f. *négliger* NEGLECT *v.*; see -ABLE, -IBLE and cf. *negligeable* (also – Fr.).] Capable of being neglected or disregarded.

Negotiable (nĭgōᵘ·ʃiăb'l), *a.* 1758. [f. NEGOTIATE *v.* 3 + -ABLE. Cf. Fr. *négociable.*] **1.** Of bills, drafts, cheques, etc.: Capable of being negotiated; transferable or assignable in the course of business from one person to another. **2.** Admitting of being crossed, ascended, etc. 1880.

1. The funds and other n. securities MILL. **2.** That this [path] was n. was evident 1880. Hence **Negotiabi·lity,** n. quality 1828.

Negotiate (nĭgōᵘ·ʃie[i]t), *v.* 1599. [– *negotiat-*, pa. ppl. stem of L. *negotiari* carry on business, f. *negotium* business, f. *neg*, var. of *nec* + *otium* leisure, see -ATE[3].] **1.** *intr.* To confer (*with* another) for the purpose of arranging some matter by mutual agreement; to discuss a matter with a view to a settlement or compromise. †**b.** To traffic –1759. **2.** *trans.* To deal with, manage, or conduct (a matter, etc., requiring skill or consideration) 1619. **b.** To arrange for, bring about (something) by means of negotiation 1721. **3.** To transfer or assign (a bill, etc.) to another in return for something of equal value, to convert into cash or notes; to get or give value for (bills, cheques, etc.) in money 1682. **b.** To carry out, as a business or monetary transaction 1809. **4.** (Orig. *Hunting.*) To clear (a hedge or fence); to succeed in getting round, over, or through (an obstacle, etc.) 1862.

1. Both parties were now willing to n. with the view of gaining time BUCKLE. 2. To n. this affair we sent a Turk 1703. b. It was impossible..to n. a sale of their effects PRESCOTT. 3. When I paid it by these securities, you pledged yourself not to n. them LEVER. 4. The first fence I negotiated successfully 1862. Hence **Nego·tiant, Nego·tiator,** †a trader; one who negotiates (a matter, bills, loans, etc.). **Nego·tiatress, -trix,** a female negotiator.

Negotiation (nɪ̆gōᵘʃiēⁱ·ʃən). Also **-oci-**. 1579. [– L. *negotiatio*, f. as prec.; see -ION. Cf. (O)Fr. *négotiation*.] **1.** †**a.** A business transaction –1662. †**b.** Trading, traffic –1669. **2.** A course of treaty with another (or others) to bring about some result, esp. in affairs of state. Freq. in *pl.* 1579. **3.** The action or business of negotiating with others 1597. **4.** The action of getting over or round some obstacle by skilful manœuvring 1885.

1. b. The Phenicians..possessed themselves of the sea coasts, the better to carry on their n. 1669. 2. The long n. of a political marriage was terminated by a war 1828. 3. The established channels of peaceable n. WELLINGTON.

†**Nego·tious,** *a. rare.* 1603. [– L. *negotiosus* busy, f. *negotium* business; see -OUS.] Involving, or given to, occupation or business –1656.

Negress (nī·grės). 1786. [– Fr. *négresse*; see NEGRO, -ESS[1].] A female Negro.

Negrillo (nɪ̆gri·lo). 1853. [– Sp., dim. of NEGRO.] **a.** A little Negro. **b.** One of a race of dwarfish Negroes living in Central or Southern Africa 1866.

Negrito (nɪ̆grī·to). 1840. [– Sp., dim. of NEGRO.] One of a diminutive negroid race existing in the Malayo-Polynesian region; esp. one of the Aëtas in the Philippine Islands.

Negro (nī·gro). 1555. [– Sp., Pg. *negro* :- L. *niger, nigr-* black.] **I.** An individual (esp. a male) belonging to the African race of mankind, which is distinguished by a black skin, black woolly hair, flat nose, and thick protruding lips. Also *transf.* in various uses.

Phr. †*To wash a n.*, to attempt an impossible task (*rare*, chiefly 17th c.). *Comb.* **negro's head,** the Ivory Palm.

II. *attrib.* (passing into *adj.*). **1.** With names of persons: Belonging to the race of Negroes; black-skinned 1594. **2.** Consisting of, inhabited by, of or belonging to, a Negro or Negroes 1652.

1. I bought me a N. Slave DE FOE. *N. minstrels*: a troupe of comic entertainers, having blackened hands and faces, who sing plantation songs in the manner of American negroes. 2. A N. School 1740. Abyssinia and the N. countries 1841.

In spec. uses, as **n. ant,** a blackish ant; **n. corn,** the Turkish millet or dhurra; **n. monkey,** a black monkey of the Malay Peninsula, Java, etc. (*Semnopithecus maurus*).

Negro-head. 1839. **1.** A strong black plug tobacco. **2.** An inferior quality of india-rubber 1881.

Negroid (nī·groid). 1859. [f. NEGRO; see -OID.] **A.** *adj.* Of a Negro type. **B.** *sb.* A person of a Negro type 1859. Hence **Negroi·dal** *a.*

Negrophil (nī·grofil). Also **-phile.** 1803. [f. NEGRO + -PHIL or – Fr. *négrophile.*] A friend of the Negroes; one who favours the advancement of Negro interests or rights. So **Negro·philism** 1865. **Negro·philist** 1842.

Negrophobia (nīgrofōᵘ·biă). 1833. [f. NEGRO + -PHOBIA.] Intense dislike of the Negro. **Negropho·biac** *a.* **Negro·phobist.**

‖**Negus**[1] (nī·gǒs). 1594. [Amharic *n'gus*, kinged, king.] Title of the supreme ruler of Abyssinia.

Negus[2] (nī·gǒs). 1743. [Inventor's name, Col. Francis *Negus* (died 1732).] Wine (esp. port or sherry) and hot water, sweetened, and flavoured with lemon and spice.

Neif (nīf). Now only *Hist.* 1532. [– AFr. *neif, nief* = OFr. *naïf*; see NAÏF, NAÏVE.] One born in a state of bondage; occas. *spec.* a female serf.

Neigh (nēⁱ), *sb.* 1513. [f. next.] The natural cry or call of the horse.

Neigh (nēⁱ), *v.* [OE. *hnǣgan* = MDu. *neyen* (Du. dial. *neijen*), MHG. *nēgen*, of imit. origin.] **1.** *intr.* Of a horse: To utter its characteristic cry. **2.** *trans.* To utter in or as in neighing 1623.

1. *transf.* Adultery neighing at his neighbour's door COWPER.

Neighbour (nēⁱ·bəɹ), *sb.* [OE. *nēahġebūr*, *nēahhebūr*, f. *nēah* NIGH + *ġebūr* BOOR; corresp. MDu. *nagebuer*, OHG. *nāhgibūr*; cf. OS. *nābūr*, MLG., MDu. *nabur*, MHG. *nāchbūr* (G. *nachbar*); also ON. *nábúi* (Sw., Da. *nabo*), f. *ná* NEAR + *búa* dwell.] **1.** One who lives near or next to another; e.g. in an adjoining house, or in the same street or village. **b.** More widely, in echoes of Biblical passages (as Luke 10:27) ME. **2. a.** (Chiefly *pl.*) One who dwells in an adjacent town, district, or land. Also applied to the rulers of adjacent countries. OE. **b.** A person or thing which is in close proximity to another 1567. **3.** In *attrib.* use, passing into *adj.* Living or situate near or close to some other person or thing. Now *rare* with names of persons and abstract sbs. 1530.

1. Come, neighbours, we must wag COWPER. Near neighbors are seldom good ones 1790. b. The name of n. containeth..also those whom we know not, yea, and our enemies 1570. 2. a. Nowe that he possesseth Lorayne, he shall be their nere n. 1560. b. *fig. Rich. III*, IV. ii. 43. 3. Our Neighbour-Shepheard's Sonne SHAKS. The Neighbor roome SHAKS. All our Neighbour-States 1668.

Neighbour (nēⁱ·bəɹ), *v.* 1586. [f. prec.] **I.** *intr.* **1.** Of persons: To live near or close *to* a person, place, etc.; to border *upon*. Also freq. with *near*. Now *arch.* **2.** Of things or places: To lie near or close (*to* or *upon* something else); to be contiguous *with* 1592. **3.** To be on neighbourly terms with others 1820.

1. Let us..beare affection..unto such as N. at any time neere unto us 1615. 2. A copse that neighbours by SHAKS. 3. The Welsh won't n. with them BORROW.

II. *trans.* **1.** To lie next or close to, border upon 1586. **b.** To approach 1859. **2. a.** To bring near *to* something 1662. **b.** To place in conjunction *with* something 1791.

1. He seemed..to suck in fresh vigour from the soil which he neighboured LAMB. *Neighboured by* or *with*, (*a*) having (some person or thing) as near neighbour or close at hand; (*b*) brought or placed near *to* some person or thing. 2. a. The barbarous Scythian..shall to my bosome Be as well neighbour'd SHAKS.

Neighboured (nēⁱ·bəɹd), *ppl. a.* 1562. [f. NEIGHBOUR *sb.* or *v.* + -ED.] Having neighbours or surroundings (of a specified kind).

Neighbourhood (nēⁱ·bəɹhud). 1449. [f. NEIGHBOUR *sb.* + -HOOD.] **1.** Friendly relations between neighbours; neighbourly feeling or conduct. **2.** The quality, condition, or fact of being neighbours or lying near to something; nearness 1567. **3.** The vicinity, or near situation, *of* something 1577. **4.** Resort or haunt of persons near one; company; neighbours 1596. **5.** A community; a certain number of people who live close together 1625. **6.** The people living near to a certain place 1686. **b.** A district, freq. considered in ref. to the character or circumstances of its inhabitants 1697.

1. There is a Law of N. which does not leave a man perfect master on his own ground BURKE. Phr. The rules of *good n.* 2. Then the prison and the palace were in awful n. LYTTON. 3. Phr. *In the n. of*, somewhere about. 4. Immediate n. I have none, save one family 1800. 6. b. The back slums of his ferocious n. DISRAELI. 7. *attrib.*, as *n. meeting, party, school.*

Nei·ghbouring, *ppl. a.* 1601. [f. NEIGHBOUR *v.* + -ING[2].] That neighbours; lying or living near, adjacent.

The n. monarchies BURKE. A n. bush 1863.

Neighbourly (nēⁱ·bəɹli), *a.* 1558. [f. NEIGHBOUR *sb.* + -LY[1].] **1.** Characteristic of a neighbour or neighbours; friendly, kindly. **2.** Of persons: Inclined to act as neighbours; situated as neighbours 1612.

1. He hath a n. charitie in him SHAKS. 2. Farmers as a rule are n. 1886. Hence **Nei·ghbourliness.** So **Nei·ghbourly** *adv.* after the manner of neighbours 1525.

Nei·ghbourship. 1456. [f. as prec. + -SHIP.] **1.** The state or fact of being a neighbour; nearness, propinquity. Also *pl.* **2.** Neighbourly relations 1456.

Neither (nəi·ðəɹ, nī·ðəɹ), *adv.* (*conj.*) and *a.* [ME. *naiđer, neiđer*, alt., after EITHER, of *nauther*, etc.; see NOUTHER, NOWTHER.] **A.** *adv.* (*conj.*) **1.** Introducing the mention of alternatives or different things, about each of which a negative statement is to be made. See quots. **2.** = Nor, nor yet; and not, also not. Now used only when the alternatives are expressed in clauses or sentences. 1462. **3.** Used to strengthen a preceding negative; = Either 1551. †**b.** Without a preceding negative –1742.

1. *Neither..nor.* Quarter was to be n. taken nor given MACAULAY. Phr. *N. here nor there*: see HERE *adv.* With another neg., usu. preceding. Now *rare.* Christianity abrogated no duty.. neither for Jew nor Gentile 1849. With two sing. subjects and pl. vb. N. search nor labour are necessary JOHNSON. *Neither..or.* Engaging to spare n. trouble or expence 1786. †*Neither.. neither.* N. alwaies, n. to euery one, n. of euery sort 1620. 2. If there are no teachers, n. are there disciples JOWETT. 3. There were no books n. DISRAELI. b. *Com. Err.* V. i. 94.

B. 1. *adj.* Not the one or the other. late ME. **2.** *absol.* as *pron.* ME. †**b.** *N. of both, of either* –1633. †**c.** Not any one, none (of more than two) –1846. **d.** With pl. vb. 1611.

1. Nothing n. way SHAKS. 2. N. of his visitors saw him 1870. b. *L. L. L.* V. ii. 459. c. Matter, Form, and Accidents; n. of which can be the Aristotelick Nature CUDWORTH. d. N. of us are the proper judges 1781.

‖**Nek.** *S. Afr.* 1834. [Du., = neck.] A neck between two hills.

Nekton (ne·ktọn). 1895. [– G. *nekton* – Gr. νηκτόν, n. of νηκτός swimming, f. νήχειν swim. Cf. PLANKTON.] Free-swimming organic life: opp. to *benthos* and *plankton.*

Nelly (ne·li). 1823. [perh. the feminine name.] A large sea-bird (*Ossifraga gigantea*) of the petrel group.

Nelson (ne·lsən). 1889. [app. from a proper name.] In *double, half, quarter n.*, etc., designations of holds in *Wrestling.*

‖**Nelumbium** (nɪ̆lɒ·mbiŏm). 1857. [mod.L. (de Jussieu, 1789), f. Singhalese *nelumbu* or *nelum*; see -IUM.] *Bot.* A genus of water-beans (also called *Nelumbo*), to which the lotus of Egypt and Asia belongs.

‖**Nemathecium** (nemăþī·ʃiŏm). *Pl.* **-ia.** 1830. [mod.L. (Agardh), f. Gr. νῆμα thread + θήκη box, sheath, etc.; see -IUM.] *Bot.* A warty protuberance developed in some of the florideous algæ, usu. containing tetraspores. Hence **Nemathe·cial** *a.*

Nemathelminth (nemăþe·lminþ). 1890. [f. Gr. νῆμα, νήματ- thread + ἕλμινς, ἑλμινθ- worm.] *Zool.* One of that class of worms which includes the nematodes and related forms.

Nemato- (ne·măto), comb. form of Gr. νῆμα, νήματος thread; as in **Ne·matoblast,** *Biol.* a blastema which develops into a spermatozoon. **Ne:matoca·lyx,** *Zool.* a calyx containing nematocysts, occurring in some *Hydromedusæ*; hence **Ne:matoca·lycine** *a.* **Ne:matoce·ratous** [Gr. κέρας horn] *a.*, *Entom.* having filiform antennæ. **Ne·matocyst,** *Zool.* a small cell in the external layer of jelly-fishes and other cœlenterates, containing a thread capable of being ejected and of producing a stinging sensation; a lasso-cell or thread-cell. **Ne·matogen,** *Biol.*, in Dicyemids, the form which produces a filiform embryo; hence **Ne:matoge·nic, Nemato·genous** *adjs.* **Ne·matognath** [Gr. γνάθος jaw], *Zool.* a fish of the sub-order *Nematognathi*; a catfish; also **Ne:mato·gnathous** *a.* **Ne·matophore,** *Zool.* a special cup-shaped process of the cœnosarc in certain hydrozoans, having nematocysts at the extremity; hence **Nemato·phorous** *a.*

Nematode (ne·mătōᵘd), *a.* and *sb.* 1861. [See NEMATO- and -ODE.] **1.** *adj.* Of worms: Pertaining to the class *Nematoda* or *Nematoidea*, comprising those of a cylindrical or slender thread-like form (chiefly parasitic in animals and plants), such as the common round-worm, maw-worm, etc. **2.** [Partly *attrib.* uses of 3.] Pertaining to, or characteristic of worms of this class 1866. **3.** *sb.* A nematode worm 1865. **Ne·matoid** *a.* and *sb.*

Nem. con. 1588. Abbrev. of L. phr. *nemine contradicente* 'no one dissenting or opposing', without a dissentient voice.

Nemean (nɪ̆mī·ăn, nī·mĭăn), *a.* 1588. [f. L. *Nem(e)æus, Nemēus* – Gr. Νεμεαῖος, Νέμεος, f. Νεμέα; see -AN.] Of or belonging to Nemea, a wooded district near Argos in Greece. **1.** *N. lion*, a lion killed by Hercules at Nemea. **2.** *N. games* or *festival*, a Greek festival, held at Nemea in the second and fourth years of each Olympiad 1656.

Nemertean (nĭmə̄·ɹtĭăn), *sb.* and *a.* 1861. [– mod.L. *Nemertes* (Cuvier) – Gr. Νημερτής, name of a sea-nymph; see -EAN.] = NEMERTINE *sb.* and *a.*

Neme·rtid. 1870. [f. as prec. + -ID³.] A nemertean form. Also *attrib.* or as *adj.*

Nemertine (nĭmə̄·ɹtəin). 1851. [f. as prec. + -INE¹.] **A.** *adj.* Belonging to the class of flat-worms (chiefly marine) known as *Nemertina, Nemertida,* or *Nemertea,* usu. having an elongated, very contractile body, and often brilliantly coloured. **B.** *sb.* A flat-worm of the class *Nemertina*; a ribbon-worm 1875.

Nemesia (nĭmī·ʒ¹ă). 1886. [mod.L. (Vertenet, 1803), f. Gr. νεμέσιον used by Dioscurides (IV. 28) to denote an allied plant; see -IA¹.] A plant of a S. African genus of flowering plants, a few species of which are cultivated as hardy annuals.

Nemesis (ne·mĭsis). 1553. [– Gr. νέμεσις righteous indignation (also personified), f. νέμειν deal out what is due, rel. to νόμος custom, law.] **1.** The goddess of retribution; hence, one who avenges or punishes. **2.** Retributive justice; an instance of this 1597.

2. Guilt..produces a fear of the divine N. 1733.

‖**Nemophila** (nĭmǫ·filă). Also *erron.* **-phyl(l)a.** 1838. [mod.L. f. Gr. νέμος glade + -φιλος -PHIL; see -A 2.] *Bot.* A genus of ornamental herbaceous annuals (N.O. *Hydrophyllaceæ*), esp. *N. insignis*; a plant of this genus.

Nemoral (ne·mŏrăl), *a. rare.* 1656. [– Fr. *némoral* or L. *nemoralis*, f. *nemus, nemor-* grove; see -AL¹.] Of, living in, or frequenting groves or woods.

Nenuphar (ne·niufāɹ). 1425. [– med.L. *nenuphar* (whence also Fr. *nénufar*) – Arab. and Pers. *nīnūfar, nīlūfar* – Skr. *nīlōtpala* blue lotus, f. *nīla* blue (see NIL¹) + *utpala* lotus, water-lily.] A water-lily, esp. the common white or yellow species.

Neo- (nī·o), comb. form of Gr. νέος new (as in νεόγαμος newly married), common in recent use as a prefix to adjs. and sbs.

1. a. In combs. denoting a new or modern form of some doctrine, belief, practice, language, etc., or designating those who advocate, adopt, or use it, as *N.-Anglican, -Christian, -Darwinian,* etc.; *N.-Anglicanism, -Christianity, -Darwinianism,* etc. **b.** *Chem.* designating certain more recently discovered varieties of isomeric hydrocarbons, as *n.-paraffins.* **c.** *Geol.* denoting the most recent division of a period, as *N.-cambrian, -devonian,* etc. **d.** In terms denoting sciences or scientists that deal with recent forms of animals and plants, as *neo-botany, -botanist.* **2.** In misc. combs., as **Neoa·rctic** *a.* = NEARCTIC. **Ne·ocene** *a. Geol.* belonging to the later Tertiary (Miocene and Pliocene). **Neogæan, -gean** (nī,ŏdʒī·ăn) *a.*, of or pertaining to the New World or western hemisphere. **Neogra·phic** *a.*, of the nature of, pertaining to, a new system of writing or spelling. **Neomo·rphism,** the process of change into a new form.

Neocomian (nī,okō^u·miăn), *a.* and *sb.* 1843. [– Fr. *Néocomien* (Thurmann, 1832), f. *Neocomium* (f. Gr. νέος new + κώμη village), latinized form of *Neuchâtel*.] Belonging to or characteristic of the series of lower cretaceous rocks found at Neuchâtel in Switzerland; *sb.* the Neocomian series or period 1888.

Neodamode (ni,ǫ·dămō^ud). 1808. [– Gr. νεοδαμώδης, f. νέος new + δᾶμος, δῆμος people.] *Gr. Antiq.* Among the ancient Spartans, an enfranchised Helot. Chiefly *attrib.*

Neodymium (nī:odi·miŏm). 1886. [f. NEO- and DIDYMIUM.] *Chem.* A rare metallic element separated from praseodymium in 1885 by Auer von Welsbach.

Neolithic (nī,oli·þik), *a.* 1865. [f. Gr. νέος (see NEO-) + λίθος stone + -IC.] *Archæol.* Of or belonging to the later stone age, characterized by the use of ground or polished stone implements and weapons.

Neologian (nī,olō^u·dʒiăn). 1831. [f. NEOLOGY + -AN.] **A.** *adj.* **1.** Inclined towards theological neologism 1833. **2.** Of the nature of, marked by, neologism (sense 2) 1831.

2. The n. article about German divinity MACAULAY.

B. *sb.* A neologist (sense 2) 1846.

Neolo·gic, -al, *a.* 1754. [– Fr. *néologique*; see NEOLOGY, -IC, -ICAL.] Of the nature of, characterized by, neologism (sense 2) 1827.

Neologism (ni,ǫ·lŏdʒiz'm). 1800. [– Fr. *néologisme*; see NEOLOGY and -ISM.] **1.** The use of, or the practice of using, new words. **b.** A new word or expression 1803. **2.** Tendency to, adoption of, novel (rationalistic) views in theology or matters of religion 1827.

1. b. Scotticisms, neologisms..dance through each page 1803.

Neologist (ni,ǫ·lŏdʒist). 1785. [= Fr. *néologiste*; see NEOLOGY and -IST.] **1.** One who invents or uses new words or forms. **2.** One who rationalizes in theology or religious matters 1827.

2. The Neologists of the present day deny that the miracles took place in the manner related in the sacred record J. H. NEWMAN.

Neologize (ni,ǫ·lŏdʒəiz), *v.* 1846. [– Fr. *néologiser*: see NEOLOGY and -IZE.] **1.** *intr.* To invent or use new words or phrases. **2.** To introduce or accept new theological doctrines 1882.

Neology (ni,ǫ·lŏdʒi). 1797. [– Fr. *néologie*; see NEO-, -LOGY.] = NEOLOGISM 1 and 2.

‖**Neomenia** (nī,omī·niă). late ME. [eccl. L. – Gr. νεομηνία, f. νέος new NEO- + μήνη moon.] In Gr. and Jewish antiq., the time of the new moon, the beginning of the lunar month; also, the festival held at that time.

Neon (nī·ǫn). 1898. [– Gr. νέον, neut. of νέος new.] *Chem.* An atmospheric gas discovered in 1898; symbol Ne.

Neonomian (nī,onō^u·miăn). 1692. [f. Gr. νέος NEO- + νόμος law, after ANTINOMIAN.] *sb.* One who maintains that the Gospel is a new law taking the place of the old or Mosiac law. *adj.* Pertaining to the assertion of a new law. Hence **Neono·mianism.**

Neophyte (nī·ŏfəit). Also **-phite.** 1451. [– eccl.L. *neophytus* – Gr. N.T. νεόφυτος (1 Tim. 3:6) 'newly planted', f. νέος NEO- + φυτόν plant.] **1.** A new convert, esp. with ref. to the primitive Christian Church. **2.** One who is newly initiated into anything; a novice 1599.

2. *attrib.* A certain neophite and girlish trepidation 1883. **Ne·ophytic, -phytish** *adjs.* **Ne·ophytism.**

Neoplasm (nī·oplæz'm). 1864. [f. NEO- + Gr. πλάσμα formation; see PLASM, PLASMA.] *Path.* A new formation of tissue in some part of the body; a tumour. So **Neopla·sma** (*pl.* **-ata**). **Neopla·stic** *a.*

Neoplatonic (nī,oplătǫ·nik), *a.* 1836. [f. NEO- + PLATONIC *a.*] Of or pertaining to Neoplatonism or the Neoplatonists. Hence **Neoplato·nically** *adv.* So **Neoplatoni·cian** *a.* Neoplatonic 1831; *sb.* a Neoplatonist 1842.

Neoplatonism (nī,oplē^i·tŏniz'm). 1845. [f. NEO- + PLATONISM; cf. Fr. *néo-platonisme.*] A philosophical and religious system, chiefly consisting of a mixture of Platonic ideas with Oriental mysticism, which originated at Alexandria in the 3rd c., and is esp. represented in the writing of Plotinus, Porphyry, and Proclus. **Neopla·tonist** 1837.

Neossine (ni,ǫ·səin). 1849. [f. Gr. νεοσσός young bird + -INE⁵.] The substance of which the edible birds' nests of the East are made, being a mucus secreted by the salivary glands of a genus of swifts (*Collocalia*). Hence **Neo·ssidine.**

Neoteric (nī,ote·rik). 1577. [– late L. *neotericus* adj. and sb. – Gr. νεωτερικός, f. νεώτερος, compar. of νέος new; see -IC.] **A.** *adj.* Recent, new, modern. **B.** *sb.* A modern; esp. a modern writer or author 1598.

A. Our n. sages 1876. The n. fashion of spending a honeymoon on the railway MEREDITH. **B.** A landscape of a justly admired n. LAMB.

Neoterism (ni,ǫ·tĕriz'm). 1851. [– Gr. νεωτερισμός, f. νεωτερίζειν make innovations; see prec., -ISM.] The use of new words or phrases; a new term or expression. So **Neo·terist; Neoteri·stic** *a.*; **Neo·terize** *v.*

Neotro·pical, *a.* 1858. [f. NEO- + TROPICAL.] Including, belonging to, or characteristic of, Tropical and South American as a zoogeographical region.

‖**Neoza** (ni,ō^u·ză). 1832. [Bhutanese *neosa, niosa.*] *N. pine,* a Himalayan pine (*Pinus gerardiana*), the cones of which contain edible seeds.

Neozoic (nī,ozō^u·ik), *a.* 1854. [f. NEO- 1. c, after PALÆOZOIC.] *Geol.* **1.** Post-palæozoic (comprising both Mesozoic and Cainozoic). **2.** = CAINOZOIC 1873.

‖**Nepenthe** (nĭpe·nþi). 1596. [alt., after It. *nepente,* of NEPENTHES.] **1.** = NEPENTHES 1. **b.** *Med.* A drink possessing sedative properties 1681. **2.** The plant supposed to supply the drug 1623.

1. A crystal glass, Mantling with bright N. SHELLEY.

‖**Nepenthes** (nĭpe·nþīz). 1580. [– L. *nepenthes* (Pliny) – Gr. νηπενθές (Odyssey iv. 221, qualifying φάρμακον drug), n. of νηπενθής banishing pain, f. νη- not + πένθος grief.] **1.** A drug of Egyptian origin mentioned in the Odyssey as capable of banishing grief or trouble from the mind; hence, any drug or potion having this power; also, occas. the plant supposed to yield the drug. **2.** A genus of plants (chiefly East Indian) in which the leaves have the form of pitchers; the Pitcher-plant 1747.

1. Where is..that herbe N. that procureth all delights? LYLY.

Nephalism (ne·făliz'm). *rare.* 1861. [– late Gr. νηφαλισμός, f. νηφάλιος sober.] Teetotalism. So **Ne·phalist.**

Nepheline (ne·fĕlin). Also **-in.** 1814. [– Fr. *népheline* (Haüy, 1800), f. Gr. νεφέλη cloud, because its fragments are rendered cloudy by immersion in nitric acid; see -INE⁵.] *Min.* A double silicate of aluminium and sodium, occurring chiefly in volcanic deposits in Italy. var. **Ne·phelite.**

Nephelo-, comb. form of Gr. νεφέλη; as in **Nep:helodo·meter,** an instrument for ascertaining the distances of the clouds. **Nephelo·meter,** an instrument to register the comparative cloudiness of the sky.

Nephew (ne·viu, ne·fiu). [ME. *neveu* – (O)Fr. *neveu,* also ONFr. *nevu, nevo* :– L. *nepos, nepot-* grandson, nephew, descendant.] **1.** A brother's or sister's son; also, the son of a brother- or sister-in-law. **b.** *euphem.* The illegitimate son of an ecclesiastic 1587. †**2.** A niece –1585. †**3.** A grandson –1699. †**4.** A descendant –1676.

1. 'Mr. Jones your nephew, sir!'..'He is indeed.. my own sister's son' FIELDING. **b.** More papal 'nephews' had been stalled and mitred in the English Church DIXON. **3.** Ye had your nevewes, sonnes of your chyldren, maryed LD. BERNERS. **4.** Thy children's children & nephews to come 1597. Hence **Ne·phewship** 1647.

Nephology (nefǫ·lŏdʒi). 1890. [f. Gr. νέφος cloud + -LOGY.] That department of meteorology which treats of clouds.

Nephoscope (ne·foskō^up). 1881. [f. Gr. νέφος cloud + -SCOPE.] An instrument used to determine the altitude, velocity, and direction of clouds.

‖**Nephralgia** (nĕfræ·ldʒiă). 1800. [mod.L., f. Gr. νεφρός kidney + -αλγία, f. ἄλγος pain.] *Path.* Pain in, or neuralgia of, the kidneys. Hence **Nephra·lgic** *a.*

Nephridium (nĕfri·diŏm). *Pl.* **-dia.** 1877. [mod. L., for Gr. νεφρίον, dim. of νεφρός kidney; see -IUM, and cf. *gonidium,* etc.] *Zool.* A primitive excretory organ in the lower invertebrates, analogous in function to the kidney, but also, in some forms of Mollusca, used in reproduction. Hence **Nephri·dial** *a.* 1884.

Nephrite (ne·frəit). 1794. [– G. *nephrit* (Werner, 1780), f. Gr. νεφρός, in allusion to its supposed efficacy in kidney disease; see -ITE¹ 2b, and cf. JADE *sb.*²] *Min.* The mineral jade.

Nephritic (nĕfri·tik), *a.* 1580. [– late L. *nephriticus* (Celsus) – Gr. νεφριτικός, f. νεφρῖτις; see next, -IC.] **1.** Of pains, etc.: Affecting, having their seat or origin in, the kidneys; renal. †**2.** Of medicines, etc.: Helping to cure affections of the kidneys –1799. **3.** Affected with pain or disease in the kidneys 1656.

1. Chronic n. disease 1859. **2.** Garlick is.. Nephritick 1710. †*N. wood,* a wood of which the infusion (*n. tincture*) was formerly used as a remedy in diseases of the kidney. †*N. stone,* jade, nephrite –1811. **3.** N. patients 1834.

Nephritis (ne –frəi·tis). 1580. [– late L. *nephritis* (Cæl. Aur.) – Gr. νεφρῖτις – νεφρός kidney; see -ITIS.] *Path.* Inflammation of the kidneys.

Nephro- (ne·fro, nĕfrǫ·), comb. form of Gr. νεφρός kidney; as in **Nephrodi·nic** *a.*, of molluscs, discharging the genital products by means of nephridia. **Nephrolithi·asis,**

disease caused by the presence of renal calculi. **Nephroli·thic** *a.*, pertaining to calculi in the kidney. **Nephro·logy**, the scientific study of the kidneys and their diseases. **Nephro·rrhaphy**, the suturation of a displaced kidney in its normal place. **Nephro·stoma, Ne·phrostome**, a funnel-shaped ciliated aperture in a primitive kidney.

Nephrotomy (néfrǫ·tŏmi). 1696. [f. NEPHRO- + -TOMY.] *Surg.* Incision of the kidney, esp. for renal calculus. So **Nephro·tomize** *v.* 1825.

‖**Ne plus ultra** (nī plɒs ɒ·ltrǎ). †Also **ne plus.** 1638. [L. '(let there) not (be) more (sailing) beyond', alleged to have been inscribed on the Pillars of Hercules.] **1.** A command to go no further; also, an impassable obstacle or limitation 1661. **2.** The furthest point reached or capable of being reached 1638. **b.** *esp.* The point of highest attainment; the highest pitch *of* some quality, etc.; the acme, culmination 1696.

2. b. The populace..have arrived at their *ne plus ultra* of insolence 1760.

Nepotal (ne·pŏtǎl), *a.* 1837. [f. NEPOT(ISM + -AL[1].] Of the nature of, belonging or pertaining to, a nephew or nephews.

Nepotic (nėpǫ·tik), *a.* 1847. [f. as prec. + -IC.] **a.** Inclined to, of the nature of, nepotism. **b.** Holding the position of a nephew.

To set bounds..to the personal or n. ambition of the ruling pontiff MILMAN.

Nepotism (ne·pŏtiz'm). 1670. [– Fr. *népotisme* – It. *nepotismo*, f. *nepote* NEPHEW; see -ISM.] The practice, on the part of the Popes or other ecclesiastics (and hence of other persons), of showing special favour to nephews (or other relatives) in conferring offices; unfair preferment of nephews, etc., to other qualified persons.

This n. of the Bishop who made a maintenance for his kinsfolk out of the estates of the Church FREEMAN. So **Ne·potist**, one given to n. 1837.

Neptune (ne·ptiūn). late ME. [– Fr. *Neptune* or L. *Neptunus*.] **1.** *Rom. Myth.* The god of the sea, corresponding to the Greek *Poseidon*; also *transf.* the sea or ocean. **2.** A remote planet of the solar system, discovered by Galle in 1846. **3.** A large brass or copper pan used in trade with African natives 1833.

1. *Neptune's cup* (or *goblet*): **a.** A species of coral; **b.** A kind of sponge (*Thalassema neptuni*).

Neptunian (neptiū·niǎn). 1656. [f. L. *Neptunius*, f. *Neptunus* + -AN. Cf. Fr. *Neptunien*.] **A.** *adj.* **1.** Pertaining to the sea-god Neptune, or to the sea (*rare*). **2.** *Geol.* Resulting from, produced by, the action of water. (Opp. to *volcanic* or *plutonic*.) 1794. **b.** Based upon the view that certain geological formations are due to the action of water 1802. **3.** Of or belonging to the planet Neptune 1849. **B.** *sb.* = NEPTUNIST 2. 1799.

Neptunist (ne·ptiunist). 1593. [f. NEPTUNE + -IST.] †**1.** A nautical person (*rare*) –1597. **2.** An asserter of the Neptunian origin of certain geological formations 1802.

†**Nere**, were not; see NE and BE *v.* –1600.

Nereid (nīᵊ·rī,id). Also erron. **Neread.** 1513. [– L. *Nereïs*, *Nereïd-* – Gr. Νηρηΐς, Νηρεΐς, -ιδ-, f. Νηρεύς name of an ancient sea-god; see -ID.] **1.** *Myth.* A daughter of Nereus; a sea-nymph. **2.** *Zool.* An errant annelid of the family *Nereidæ*; a sea-centipede 1840.

1. Behold the Nereids under the green sea SHELLEY.

Nere·idean. *rare.* 1835. [f. mod.L. *Nereideæ*, f. L. *Nereid-* NEREID; see -EAN.] *Zool.* A nereid or similar marine annelid.

‖**Nereides** (nīrī·idīz, nīᵊ·rī,idīz), *sb.. pl.* late ME. [L., pl. of *Nereïs* NEREID.] Nereids.

Nere·idous, *a.* 1839. [f. NEREID + -OUS.] *Zool.* Resembling a nereid; belonging to the *Nereidæ*.

‖**Nereis** (nīᵊ·rī,is). 1752. [L.; see NEREID.] *Zool.* †**1.** A medusid (*rare*) –1813. **2.** The typical genus of the *Nereidæ*; the sea-centipede 1797.

‖**Nerita** (nĭrəi·tǎ). *Pl.* **-æ**, also **-as.** 1748. [L. – Gr. νηρίτης sea-mussel, f. Νηρεύς; see NEREID.] *Zool.* A genus of gasteropod molluscs; a mollusc of this genus. So **Nerite** (nīᵊ·rəit), 1708.

Nerka (nō·ɹkǎ). 1764. [Native name.] The blueback salmon (*Oncorhynchus nerka*) of Alaska and Kamchatka.

Neroli (nīᵊ·rŏli). 1676. [– Fr. *néroli* – It. *neroli*, said to be from the name of its discoverer, an Italian princess.] An essential oil distilled from the flowers of the bitter orange. Also *n. oil, oil of n.*

Neronian (nĭroᵘ·niǎn), *a.* 1598. [– L. *Neronianus*, f. C. Claudius *Nero*, Roman Emperor A.D. 54–68; see -IAN.] **1.** Characteristic of, resembling that (or those) of, Nero; exhibiting his tyranny, cruelty, or depravity. **2.** Of, pertaining to, or connected with, the emperor Nero or his times 1650. So **Nero·nic** *a.*

Nerval (nō·ɹvǎl), *a.* 1636. [– Fr. *nerval* or L. *nervalis*; see NERVE *sb.*, -AL[1].] Of, relating to, or affecting the nerves; neural.

†**Ne·rvate,** *v.* 1682. [app. f. NERVE *sb.* 2, 3 or NERVE *v.* 2, 3 + -ATE[3].] *trans.* To nerve, support, strengthen –1792.

Nervation (nəɹvēⁱ·ʃən). 1841. [– Fr. *nervation*, f. *nerver*; see NERVE *sb.*, -ATION.] *Bot.* The disposition of the nerves in leaves, insects' wings, etc. So **Ne·rvature** 1866.

Nerve (nōɹv), *sb.* late ME. [– L. *nervus* sinew, bowstring, rel. to Gr. νεῦρον sinew, nerve, and to L. *nēre* spin. Cf. Fr. *nerf*.] **I. 1.** A sinew or tendon. Now *poet.*, exc. in phr. *to strain every n.*, to make the utmost exertion. **2.** *fig.* in *pl.* Those things, parts, or elements, which constitute the main strength or vigour *of* something. Also *sing.* in same sense. 1603. **3.** Strength, vigour, energy 1605. **4.** A sinew or tendon used for some practical purpose, esp. *poet.* [after L. use], a bow-string 1674. **5. a.** *Bot.* One of the ribs of fibro-vascular matter extending through the parenchyma of a leaf; esp. the midrib 1585. **b.** *Entom.* = NERVURE 1833.

2. Agamemnon, Thou..Nerue and Bone of Greece SHAKS. Money, which is the N. and Sinew of War 1726. Prosperity had relaxed the nerves of discipline GIBBON. **3.** Mightiest deeds Above the n. of mortal arm MILT.

II. 1. A fibre or bundle of fibres arising from the brain, spinal cord, or other ganglionic organ, capable of stimulation by various means, and serving to convey impulses (esp. of sensation and motion) between the brain, etc., and some other part of the body 1606. **b.** In non-scientific use, with ref. to feeling, courage, etc. 1601. **c.** A disordered nervous system; nervousness 1890. **2.** Nervous fibre 1839. **3.** Courage or coolness in danger 1809. **b.** *colloq.* Impudent boldness or assurance 1899.

1. b. We soldiers need nerves of steel! BROWNING. **d.** Phr. *To get on one's nerves*: to be a worry or annoyance to one. **3.** O iron n. to true occasion true! TENNYSON *attrib.* and *Comb.*, as *n.-racking, -shaking, -shattering*, etc.; **-cell**, one of the cells composing the cellular element of nervous tissue; **-centre**, a group of ganglion-cells closely connected with one another and associated in performing some function; **-deafness**, deafness due to disorder of the acoustic nerve; **-fibre**, the fibrous matter composing the nervous system, or one of the thread-like units of this; **-knot**, a ganglion.

Nerve (nōɹv), *v.* 1749. [f. NERVE *sb.*] **1.** *trans.* To give strength or vigour to (the arm, etc.). **2.** To imbue with courage, to embolden 1810.

2. *refl.* He hath nerved himself, And now defies them BYRON.

Nerved (nōɹvd), *ppl. a.* 1800. [f. NERVE *sb.* + -ED[2].] **1.** *Bot.* Of leaves: Having a nerve or nerves; ribbed. **2.** In *Comb.* Having nerves of a specified kind or number, as *five-, full-, weak-n.*

Nerveless (nō·ɹvlės), *a.* 1735. [f. NERVE *sb.* + -LESS.] **1.** Wanting nerve, incapable of effort, weak, inert 1742. **2.** Characterized by lack of vigour or energy 1735. **3. a.** *Bot.* and *Entom.* Having no nervures 1796. **b.** *Anat.* and *Zool.* Having no nerves 1862.

1. His old right hand lay n., listless, dead KEATS. **1.** Sad o'er all, profound dejection sat, And n. fear 1735. Lord Byron retains the same n. and pointless kind of blank verse 1822. Hence **Ne·rveless-ly** *adv.*, **-ness.**

Nervine (nō·ɹvəin). 1661. [In sense 1 – med.L. *nervinus* belonging to a sinew (XV); in medical use – Fr. *nervin* (XVIII) in some senses; see NERVE *sb.*, -INE[1].] **A.** *adj.* †**1.** Used for the sinews. **2.** Having the quality of acting on the nerves, relieving nervous disorders 1718. **B.** *sb.* A medicine that acts upon the nerves; a nerve-tonic 1730.

Nervo-, comb. f. L. *nervus* NERVE, as in **n.-muscular** *a.*, concerned with both nerves and muscles; etc.

Nervose (nō·ɹvoᵘs), *a.* late ME. [– L. *nervosus* sinewy, vigorous, etc.; see NERVE *sb.*, -OSE[1].] **1.** Pertaining to or affecting the nerves (†or sinews). *rare.* **2.** *Bot.* = NERVED 1. 1753. Hence **Nervo·sity** 1611.

Nervous (nō·ɹvəs), *a.* late ME. [– L. *nervosus*; see prec., -OUS.] †**1.** Affecting the sinews. ME only. **2.** Sinewy, muscular; vigorous, strong. late ME. **3.** Of writings, arguments, speakers, etc.: Vigorous, forcible; free from weakness and diffuseness 1637. †**4.** Sinewy, tendinous –1796; †resembling a sinew in texture; strong –1762. †**5.** *Bot.* Nerved –1776. **6.** Full of nerves 1659. **7.** Of or belonging to the nerves 1665. **b.** Affecting the nerves; characterized by a disordered state of the nerves 1734. **c.** Pertaining to the nerves 1804. **8.** Of medicines, etc.: Acting upon the nerves or nervous system 1718. **9.** Of persons: Suffering from disorder of the nerves; also, excitable, easily agitated, timid 1740. **10.** Characterized by agitation of the nerves 1775.

2. The n. strength and weight of one of the muscular armourer's [hands] SCOTT. **3.** Whatever is short should be n., masculine, and compact COWPER. **6.** The retina, or the n. coat of the eye 1855. **7.** The brain and spinal cord are termed the n. centres 1848. *N. system*, the complex of nerves and nerve-centres. 1665. **b.** A severe n. fever ensued 1869. **c.** Modern n. physiology 1877. **8.** The gentle fair on n. tea relies CRABBE. **9.** The ladies were too narvous to venture further than the entrance to the cavern 1763. **10.** With all the eagerness of the most n. irritability JANE AUSTEN. Hence **Ne·rvous-ly** *adv.*, **-ness.**

Nervure (nō·ɹviŭɹ). 1816. [– (O)Fr. *nervure*, f. *nerf*; see NERVE *sb.*, -URE.] **1.** *Entom.* One of the slender hollow tubes forming the framework of the wings of insects. **2.** *Bot.* A principal vein of a leaf 1842.

Nervy (nō·ɹvi), *a.* 1607. [f. NERVE *sb.* + -Y[1].] **1.** Vigorous, sinewy, full of strength. Now *poet.* **2.** Boldly courageous. (*rare*). 1882. **b.** *slang.* Coolly or impudently confident 1897. **3.** *colloq.* Having disordered nerves; easily excitable, hysterical, 'jumpy' 1906.

1. Death, that darke Spirit, in 's neruie Arme doth lye SHAKS.

Nescience (ne·ʃⁱěns, nī·-). 1612. [– late L. *nescientia*, f. *nescire*; see next, -ENCE.] Absence of knowledge, ignorance.

The ignorance and involuntary n. of men JER. TAYLOR. There was in Adam a n. of many things MANNING.

Nescient (ne·ʃⁱěnt, nī·-) 1626. [– *nescient-*, pr. ppl. stem of L. *nescire*, f. *ne* not + *scire* know; see -ENT.] **A.** *adj.* Ignorant. Chiefly const. *of.* **b.** Agnostic 1876. **B.** *sb.* An agnostic 1872.

Nese. Now only *Sc.* [Early ME. *neose, nese*, perh. = MLG, MDu. *nese*; the relationship to NOSE is obscure.] The nose.

Nesh (neʃ), *a.* (and *adv.*). Now *dial.* [OE. *hnesće* = Du. (XVI) *nesch, nisch* soft (of eggs), damp, sodden, foolish, Goth. *hnasqus* soft, tender; ult. origin unkn.] **1.** Soft in texture or consistency; in later use, tender, succulent, juicy. **2. a.** Slack, negligent OE. **b.** Timid; faint-hearted. late ME. †**3.** Tender, mild, kind –1530. **4.** Delicate, weak; unable to endure fatigue or exposure; sensitive to cold. (Prevailing mod. dial. use.) OE. **Ne·shness.**

Ness (nes). [OE. *næs(s, nes(s, næsse*, corresp. to LG. *nesse*, ON. *nes*, rel. to OE. *nasu, næs-* NOSE.] A promontory.

-ness, *suffix*, OE. *-nes(s, -nis(s* = OFris. *-nesse, -nisse*, OS. *-nessi, -nissi* (Du. *-nis*), OHG. *-nessi, -nissi, -nassi* (G. *-nis*), Goth. *-nassus*; f. *n (of str. pa. pples.) + *-*assus*, f. *-*atjan* verbal suffix). **1.** In OE. *-nes* is most usu. attached to adjs. and pa. pples. to form sbs. expressing a state or condition, as *biternes*. The same formation is frequent in all periods of the language. Formations from compound adjs. are also common, as *selfconceitedness*, etc.; and even from adjectival phrases, as *used-upness, up-to-*

dateness. The latter, however, and also formations on pronouns, adverbs, etc., as *I-ness, everydayness*, etc., are seldom in serious use. **b.** Used absol. in *pl.* 1775. **2.** In particularized use compounds in *-ness* are often concr. in sense; similarly in titles of dignity as *highness, holiness*, and in WILDERNESS, WITNESS.

1. b. Cleverness and contentedness, and all the other good nesses LOWELL.

Nesslerize (ne·slĕrəiz), *v.* 1881. [f. the name *Nessler* + -IZE.] *Chem. intr.* To employ Nessler's reagent as a test for ammonia in water.

Nest (nest), *sb.* [OE. *nest* = (M)Du., (O)HG. *nest* :- IE. **nizdo-*, whence also L. *nidus*, OIr. *net* (mod. *nead*), W. *nyth* nest, Skr. *nīḍá* resting-place; f. **ni* down (cf. NETHER) + **sed-* SIT.] **1.** The structure made, or the place selected, by a bird for laying and incubating its eggs and sheltering its unfledged young. **b.** A place or structure used by animals or insects as an abode or lair or as a spawning or breeding place. late ME. **2.** A place in which a person (or personified thing) finds rest or has residence; a lodging, home, bed, etc.; a secluded or snug retreat OE. **b.** A receptacle 1589. **3.** A place of habitual residence or resort of thieves, robbers, pirates, etc. late ME. **b.** A haunt *of* crime, vice, etc. 1576. **4.** A brood, swarm, colony of birds, insects, or other animals 1470. **b.** A collection of people, esp. of the same class or frequenting a common resort 1589. **5.** A collection of similar objects; also *fig.* of immaterial things 1642. **6.** A set or series of similar objects, *esp.* of such as are contained in the same receptacle, or fit one within the other according to size 1521. **7.** *Min.* An isolated deposit of a mineral or metal occurring in the midst of other formations 1725.

1. The mery foulis in thair n. DUNBAR. The proverbe sayes, 'That it is an evill birde, will file its owne n.' 1599. **b.** Fore-warning winde Did seeme to say, seeke not a Scorpions N. SHAKS. **2.** Like some poore man's n. SPENSER. The lightest wind was in its n. SHELLEY. **3.** The hill-fortress became a mere n. of robbers FREEMAN. **b.** Gold, which is..The neast of strife 1576. **4.** That n. of Hornets POPE. **b.** Should I call the whole university of Oxford a n. of fools 1721. [The Americans] are a sad n. GEO. III. **5.** Born and bred in some hideous n. of alleys 1875. **6.** One N. of Drawers 1704. *attrib.* **nest-box,** (*a*) a box containing others of graduated sizes packed in a n.; (*b*) a box provided for a domestic fowl or other bird to lay its eggs in.

Nest (nest), *v.* ME. [f. prec.] **1.** *intr.* Of birds, etc.: To make or have a nest or abode in a particular place. **b.** To engage in nest-building 1774. **2.** To settle or lodge as in a nest 1591. **3.** In *pa. pple.* Settled, established, in or as in a nest 1599. **b.** Packed one inside another 1870. **c.** Used for making nests *in* 1883. **4.** *intr.* To go bird's-nesting 1896.

1. I have..seen them nesting in the Borough 1773. **2.** Where better could her love then here have nested? 1633. *refl.* A Rabble of Pirats n. themselves in Salla 1652. **3.** The side hills are well wooded, and nested among them are some delightful country-houses 1834. **c.** Chestnuts nested in by song birds STEVENSON.

Ne·st-egg. 1606. [f. NEST *sb.* + EGG *sb.*] **1.** A real or artificial egg left in a nest to induce the hen to go on laying there. **2.** Something serving as an inducement or decoy 1678. **3.** A sum of money put by as a reserve or serving as the nucleus of a fund 1700.

2. Books and money laid for shew, Like nest-eggs to make clients lay BUTLER. **3.** A nice little n. of five hundred pounds in the bank RUSKIN.

Ne·stful. 1598. [f. NEST *sb.* + -FUL.] The quantity (of eggs or young) that a nest can contain.

Nestle (ne·s'l), *v.* [OE. *nestlian* = MLG., (M)Du. *nestelen* (cf. OE. *nistl(i)an*, MHG. *nistelen*); see prec., -LE 3.] **1.** *intr.* = NEST *v.* 1. **b.** To lodge or settle as in a nest. late ME. †**2.** To take up one's abode, to settle or squat in a place –1797. Also *refl.* (now *rare*) 1547. **3.** Of persons: To settle down comfortably, as in a nest 1687. **b.** To draw or press *close*, or near, *to* a thing or person, esp. in an affectionate manner 1709. **4.** Of things or qualities: To lie half hidden or embedded in some place or thing 1788. **b.** Of dwellings, etc.: To lie snugly in some situation 1842. **5.** *trans.* To push *in*, to press, rest, or settle (one's head, etc.) in a snug or affectionate manner 1696. **6.** To place in, or as in, a nest; to provide with a nesting-place; to set in a secure place. *lit.* and *fig.* 1548.

1. The birdes nestled in hir branches 1545. **2.** If they can n. in the country for any time..they cannot fail of profiting of the discontents BURKE A gentleman..who had nestled himself in an English borough 1826. **3.** She nestled luxuriously among the cushions 1883. Nestling closer to him in the dark corner 1863. **4. b.** Large groves of palm trees, among which nestled small hamlets 1884. **6.** Trees..which serve to n. and pearch all sorts of birds EVELYN. The words had nestled their venomous life in her GEO. ELIOT.

Nestle-cock. Now only *dial.* 1626. [f. NESTLE *v.* + COCK *sb.*[1]] The last-hatched bird, or weakling of a brood; hence, a mother's pet; a spoilt or delicate child.

Nestling (ne·s(t)liŋ). late ME. [f. NEST *sb.* + -LING[1], or NESTLE *v.* + -ING[3], perh. after MDu. *nestelinc* (mod. *-ling*).] A young bird which is not yet old enough to leave the nest.

Nestor (ne·stǫɹ). 1588. [– Gr. Νέστωρ.] Name of a Homeric hero famous for his age and wisdom, applied allusively to an old man.

Nestorian (nestō^ə·riăn), *a.* and *sb.* 1449. [– late L. *Nestorianus*, f. *Nestorius*; see next, -AN, -IAN.] Pertaining to, characteristic of or professing, an adherent of, Nestorianism.

Nesto·rianism. 1612. [f. NESTORIAN + -ISM.] *Theol.* The doctrine of Nestorius (patriarch of Constantinople, deposed in 431) according to which distinct divine and human persons are to be attributed to Christ.

Net (net), *sb.*[1] [OE. *net(t* = OFris. *net(te*, OS. *netti, net*, (M)Du. *net*, MLG., MDu. *nette*, OHG. *nezzi* (G. *netz*), ON. *net*, Goth. *nati*.] **1.** An open-work fabric of twine or strong cord, forming meshes of a suitable size, used for catching fish, birds, etc. Freq. specialized, as *bag-, beach-, cast(ing)-, dip-, dredge-, drift-, fishing-, trawl-n.*, etc.; *herring-, mackerel-, rabbit-, sparrow-n.*, etc. **b.** *fig.* A moral or mental snare, trap, or entanglement OE. **c.** *transf.* A spider's web OE. **2.** An open-work fabric of mesh-work, of various materials, used for covering, protecting, confining, holding, etc. OE. **3.** A piece of fine mesh-work used as a veil, or to confine the hair 1483. **b.** A kind of machine-made lace composed of small meshes. 1832. **4.** Something resembling a net; a reticulation or network; in recent *Math.*, a system of intersections of lines, curves, etc. 1594.

1. b. Skill'd to..draw Hearts after them tangl'd in Amorous Nets MILT. Not only was the town..a mere n. of peril for their lives STEVENSON. **2.** *At the nets* (Cricket): on a pitch enclosed by nets which prevent the escape of balls, used for practice in batting. Their wickets at the nets were as a rule very poor 1889. **3. b.** Her mob-cap was of spotted n. 1862. *attrib.* **net-ball,** a team-game in which the object is to score by throwing a ball through a hoop from which a network depends.

Net, *sb.*[2] Now *rare.* [OE. *nette* = OFris. *nette*, ON. *netja*; a deriv. of NET *sb.*[1]] The omentum.

Net (net), *a.* Also **nett.** ME. [– Fr. *net*, fem. *nette*; see NEAT *a.*] **1.** †**a.** Of persons: Trim, smart, esp. in dress (*rare*) –1562. **b.** Of things: Neat, smart (*rare*) 1637. **2.** †Clean; bright, clear –1609. **b.** Pure, unadulterated, unmixed (*rare*) 1713. **3.** Of amounts: Free from, or not subject to, any deduction 1500. **b.** Sold at, based upon, net prices 1893.

2. Her brest all naked, as nett yvory SPENSER. **b.** N. Natural French Wine 1713. **3.** The 'n. effective power'..of an engine 1840. **b.** A book sold at 12*s.* becomes under the n. system 10*s.* n. 1804.

Net (net), *v.*[1] 1593. [f. NET *sb.*[1]] **1.** *trans.* **a.** To cover with, to hem *in*, close *round*, as with a net 1607. **b.** To pen in by means of nets 1847. **2. a.** To take, catch, or capture (people, fish, birds, etc.) with or as with a net 1801. **b.** To fish (a river, etc.) with a net; to set nets in 1843. **3.** *intr.* To make nets or network; to occupy oneself with netting 1674. **b.** *trans.* To make (a thing) by the process of producing network 1789. **4.** *trans.* and *absol.* In games: To send (a ball) into the net 1906.

1. a. To leave his favourite tree..after..netting it to keep off the birds MISS EDGEWORTH. **2. a.** One or two of Plutarch's touches..had netted her fancy MEREDITH. **3.** I often..see you..sitting netting in your parlour 1789. **b.** I had more purses netted then Than I could hope to fill HOOD.

Net, *v.*[2] 1758. [f. NET *a.* 3.] **1.** *trans.* To gain as a net sum or as clear profit. **2.** To bring in as a profit or net sum 1786.

1. By the new plan..he can n. a full profit of £4 per acre 1862.

Nether (ne·ðəɹ), *a.* [OE. *neoþera, niþera* = OFris. *nithera, nethera*, OS. *nithiri* (Du. *neder* in comps.), MLG. *ned(d)er*, OHG. *nidari, -eri, -iri* (G. *nieder*), ON. *neðri*; f. Gmc. **niþar* (repr. by OE. *niþer*, etc.) down, downwards = Skr. *nitarām*, f. *ni-* down, with compar. suffix.] Lower, under (in contrast to *higher, over*, or *upper*).

The hornèd Moon, with one bright star Within the n. tip COLERIDGE. The great reservoirs of melted matter..in the n. regions 1830. His n. person was rendered conspicuous by a pair of dingy small-clothes 1835. An uneasy gnawing of the n. lip LYTTON. *N. millstone* (or *stone*), now only in fig. or allusive use. His heart is as strong as a stone and as hard as the n. milstone BIBLE (Genev.) *Job.* 41:14.

Ne·therlander. 1610. [– Du. *Nederlander*, f. *Nederland*; see -ER[1].] An inhabitant or native of the Netherlands (formerly including Flanders and Belgium). So **Ne·therlandian** (*rare*), **Ne·therlandish** *adjs.* 1600.

Ne·thermore, *a.* and *adv.* *Obs.* or *arch.* late ME. [f. NETHER *a.* + -MORE.] *adj.* Nether, lower, inferior.

Ne·thermost, *a.* ME. [f. as prec. + -MOST.] Lowest, undermost, furthest down. From the n. fire..Thy servant deliver J. H. NEWMAN.

Ne·therstock. *Obs.* exc. *Hist.* 1565. [f. as prec. + STOCK.] A stocking.

‖**Netsuke** (ne·tsukē). Also **-ké.** 1883. [Japanese.] A small piece of ivory, wood, etc., carved or decorated, worn by the Japanese as a bob or button on the cord by which articles are suspended from the girdle.

Ne·tting, *sb.* 1567. [f. NET *sb.*[1] or *v.*[1] + -ING[1].] **1.** *Naut.* A coarse network of small ropes used for various purposes, as to prevent boarding, stow hammocks or sails in, etc. **2.** Nets or network used for various purposes 1846.

2. Cover the beds..with n. to keep off the birds.

Ne·tting, *vbl. sb.* 1801. [f. NET *v.*[1] + -ING[1].] **1.** The making of a net or nets, *spec.* a kind of fancy work in which a network fabric is made with needles. **2.** The action or the right of fishing with a net 1875.

Nettle (ne·t'l), *sb.* [OE. *net(e)le, netel* = OS. *netila*, MLG. *net(t)ele*, MDu. *netele* (Du. *netel*), OHG. *nezzila* (G. *nessel*), OSw. *netla*, ODa. *næt-, nædlæ*, Icel. *netla* :- Gmc. **natilōn*, deriv. (see -LE) of base of OHG. *nazza*, Icel. *nötu* (*gras*).] A plant of the genus *Urtica*, of which the species *U. dioica*, the Common or Great Nettle, and *U. urens*, the Small Nettle, grow profusely on waste ground, waysides, etc., and are covered with stinging hairs. **b.** attrib., *n.-bed, -beer*, etc.

1. The Greek, Italian, or Roman Nettle is *U. pilulifera*. With distinctive epithets the name of *nettle* is also given to a number of plants belonging to other genera, as *blind, dead, deaf, red, white nettle*; *bee-, hedge-, wood-nettle*.

In groping flowers wyth Nettels stong we are 1563. *fig.* Out of this N., Danger; we plucke this Flower, Safety SHAKS.

Comb.: **n. battery,** one of the stinging organs of a hydrozoon; **-bird, -creeper,** the Whitethroat and the Golden Warbler, which nest among nettles; **-rash,** an exanthematous eruption on the skin, appearing in patches like those produced by the 'sting' of a n.; **-wort,** (*a*) a spurgewort of the genus *Acalypha*; (*b*) a plant of the n. family.

Nettle (ne·t'l), *v.* late ME. [f. NETTLE *sb.*] **1.** *trans.* To beat or 'sting' with nettles. **b.** (Also *absol.*) To 'sting' as a nettle does 1858. **2.** To irritate, vex, pique 1562. **b.** In *pa. pple.* Const. *at, by, with*, etc. late ME. **3.** To prick or stir up; to incite 1592.

1. 1 *Hen. IV*, I. iii. 240. **2.** This last discourse nettled me DE FOE. **b.** He beyng netteled with these uncurteous..prickes and thornes HALL. Hence **Ne·ttler** (Milton), **Ne·ttling** *vbl. sb.* and *ppl. a.*

Nettle. Var. of *Knettle*, KNITTLE.

†**Ne·ttle-cloth.** 1539. [f. NETTLE *sb.* Cf.

G. *nesseltuch.*] Cloth made of nettle-fibres –1626.

Ne·ttle-tree. 1548. **1.** A tree of the genus *Celtis*, belonging to the natural order *Ulmaceæ*, esp. *C. australis*, the European, and *C. occidentalis*, the N. American species. **2.** An Australian tree of the genus *Laportea*, esp. the Giant Nettle (*L. gigas*) and Small-leaved Nettle (*L. photiniphylla*) 1849.

Netty (ne·ti), *a.* Now *rare.* 1628. [f. NET *sb.*¹ + -Y¹.] Net-like; made of net.

Network (ne·twɒɹk). 1560. [f. NET *sb.*¹ + WORK *sb.*] **1.** Work in which threads, wires, or the like, are arranged in the form of a net; *esp.* a light fabric made of netted threads. **2.** (With *a* and *pl.*) A piece of work having this form 1590. **b.** *transf.* Of structures in animals and plants 1658. **c.** A complex system of rivers, canals, railways, wireless transmitting stations, etc. 1839. **3.** *attrib.* Made of or resembling network 1601.

1. I do give to my said aunte one suyte of networke 1575. **2.** *fig.* Their law is a n. of fictions EMERSON. **c.** The Northmen..had surrounded their whole camp with a n. of trenches FREEMAN. **3.** A Gold and Silk Net-work purse JOHNSON.

‖**Neuma** (niū·mă). *Pl.* **neu·mata, neu·mæ.** 1776. [med.L.; see next.] *Mus.* = next.

Neume, neum (niūm). 1440. [– (O)Fr. *neume* – med.L. *neuma*, *neupma* – Gr. πνεῦμα breath.] *Mus.* **1.** In plainsong, a prolonged pause or group of notes sung to a single syllable, esp. at the end of a melody. **2.** One of a set of signs orig. employed to indicate the structure of a melody 1843.

Neur-, var. of NEURO-, used bef. vowels (and *h*), as in **Neuradyna·mia,** nervous debility, neurasthenia. **Neurarthro·pathy,** disease of the joints in which the nerves are affected. **Neura·xis,** the nervous axis of the body; the brain and spinal column. **Neury-pno·logy,** that branch of science which deals with the phenomena of hyponotism.

Neural (niūᵊ·răl), *a.* 1839. [f. Gr. νεῦρον nerve + -AL¹.] **1.** *Anat.* Pertaining or relating to, or connected with, the nerves; *spec.* pertaining to the cerebro-spinal system of vertebrates (as opp. to *hæmal*). Freq. in *n. arch, canal, cavity, spine, tube*, etc. **b.** Situated on, or inclining to, that side of the body in which the central nervous axis lies 1861. **2.** *Phys.* Relating to, or occurring in the nerves as organs which convey sensation or impulse 1864. **3.** *Path.* Affecting the nerve-tissues or nervous system; nervous 1883.

Neuralgia (niuræ·ldʒ'ă). 1822. [– mod.L., f. Gr. νεῦρον nerve + ἄλγος pain; see -IA¹.] *Path.* An affection of one or more nerves (esp. of the head or face), causing pain which is intermittent but frequently intense; an instance of this. Hence **Neura·lgic** (niuræ·ldʒik) *a.*

Neurapophysis (niūᵊrăpǫ·fisis). *Pl.* **-phy-ses** (-fisīz). 1839. [f. NEUR- + APOPHYSIS.] *Anat.* **1.** (Chiefly in *pl.*) One or other of the two processes of a vertebra which form the neural arch. **2.** The spinous process arising from the bony elements which compose the neural arch; the neural spine 1870. Hence **Neurapophy·sial** *a.*

Neurasthenia (niūᵊræsþī·niă). 1856. [f. as prec. + ASTHENIA.] *Path.* An atonic condition of the nervous system; functional nervous weakness; nervous debility. Hence **Neurasthenic** (-sþe·nik), *a.* caused by, affected with, symptomatic of, neurasthenia; *sb.* a person suffering from this 1884.

Neuration (niurēⁱ·ʃən). 1826. [irreg. f. Gr. νεῦρον nerve + -ATION, after NERVATION.] = NERVATION.

Neurectomy (niure·ktŏmi). 1856. [f. NEUR- + -ECTOMY.] *Surg.* The operation of excising a nerve.

Neurenteric (niūᵊrente·rik), *a.* 1884. [f. NEUR- + ENTERIC.] *Anat.* Connected with the nervous and intestinal systems. *N. canal*, a prolongation of the neural canal behind the notochord into the archenteron in some vertebrate embryos.

Neuridine (niūᵊ·ridəin). Also **-in.** 1887. [f. Gr. νεῦρον nerve + -ID⁴ + -INE⁵.] *Chem.* A non-poisonous ptomaine of a gelatinous nature, chiefly occurring as a product of putrefaction.

Neurilema (niūᵊrilī·mă), **neurilemma** (-le·mă). 1825. [orig. f. Gr. νεῦρον nerve + εἴλημα covering; subseq. taken as f. Gr. λέμμα husk, skin. Cf. Fr. *névrilème* (Bichat, 1801).] *Anat.* **a.** The delicate membranous outer sheath of a nerve. **b.** The sheath of a nerve-funiculus, the perineurium.

Neurility (niuri·lĭti). 1860. [f. NEUR- + -ILE + -ITY; see -ILITY.] The power of a nerve to transmit impulse or sensation.

Neurine (niūᵊ·rəin). Also **-in.** 1839. [f. NEUR- + -INE⁵.] **1.** *Anat.* Nerve-substance or tissue; the matter contained in the nerve-tubes. **2.** *Chem.* **a.** A poisonous alkaloid or ptomaine, derived from putrefying flesh, etc.; choline. **b.** An alkaloid produced with the former, and differing very slightly from it in chemical composition, but more actively poisonous. 1869.

Neuritis (niurəi·tis). 1840. [f. Gr. νεῦρον nerve + -ITIS.] *Path.* Inflammation of a nerve or nerves. Hence **Neuri·tic** *a.*

Neuro- (niūᵊ·ro), comb. form of Gr. νεῦρον nerve, used chiefly in *Anat.* and *Path.* terms as in **Neu·roblast,** an embryonic nucleated cell from which the nerve-fibres originate. **Neuro-ce·ntral** *a.*, connected with the centrum and neural arch of a vertebra, esp. in *neurocentral suture.* **Neu·rocœle** (-sīl), the central cavity of the cerebro-spinal system. **Neuro·graphy,** scientific description of the nerves. **Neuroke·ratin,** a substance closely resembling keratin, found in certain nerve-tissues. **Neurole·mma** = NEURILEMA. **Neu·romere,** a part or segment of the nervous system; hence **Neuro·merous** *a.*, characterized by a segmented nervous system. **Neuromu·scular** *a.*, relating or belonging to both nerve(s) and muscle(s). **Neu·ropath,** a person subject to, or affected by, nervous disease. **Neuro-patho·logy,** the study of nervous diseases and their treatment; hence **Neuropatho-lo·gical** *a.* **Neurophysio·logy,** the physiology of the nervous system. **Neu·ropore,** an exterior orifice in the neural canal of some embryos. **Neuropsy·chic** *a.*, pertaining to the nervous and psychic functions. **Neuro-psycholo·gical** *a.*, dealing with psychology in relation to the nerves. **Neuroske·leton,** *Anat.* the endoskeleton; so **Neuroske·letal** *a.* **Neuroto·xin,** a substance having a poisonous effect on the nerves; so **Neuro-to·xic** *a.* **Neurova·scular** *a.*, having both a nervous and a vascular character.

Neuroglia (niurǫ·gliă). 1873. [f. NEURO- + late Gr. γλία glue; named by Virchow.] *Anat.* The delicate connective tissue found in the great nerve-centres, and in the retina; the reticular or sustentacular tissue.

Neurolite (niūᵊ·rŏləit). *Min.* 1836. [f. NEURO- + -LITE.] A variety of pinite with fibrous texture.

Neurology (niurǫ·lŏdʒi). 1681. [– mod.L. *neurologia* – mod. Gr. νευρολογία (Willis 1664); see NEURO-, -LOGY. Cf. Fr. *névrologie* XVII.] The scientific study or knowledge of the anatomy, functions, and diseases of the nerves and the nervous system. Hence **Neurolo·gical** *a.* **Neuro·logist** 1832.

Neuroma (niurōᵘ·mă). *Pl.* **-mata.** 1839 [f. Gr. νεῦρον nerve + -OMA.] *Path.* A tumour growing upon a nerve or in nerve-tissue. Hence **Neuro·matous** *a.*

‖**Neuron** (niūᵊ·rǫn). Also **-one.** 1884. [Gr. νεῦρον sinew, cord, nerve.] **1.** The cerebro-spinal axis. **2.** A process of a nerve-cell 1896. **3.** A nerve-cell with its appendages 1896. Hence **Neuro·nic** *a.*

Neuropathy (niurǫ·păþi). 1857. [f. NEURO- + -PATHY.] Nervous disease; a case of this. Hence **Neuropa·thic** *a.*, relating to, caused or distinguished by nervous disease or functional weakness of the nervous system. **Neuro·pathist,** one who makes a special study of nervous diseases.

Neuropod (niūᵊ·rŏpǫd). 1856. [f. NEURO- + -POD.] *Zool.* An annulose or invertebrate animal, in which the limbs or motor organs are on the neural aspect of the body. Hence **Neuro·podous** *a.*

Neuropodium (niūᵊropōᵘ·diŏm). 1870. [mod.L., f. NEURO- + Gr. πόδιον, dim. of πούς foot.] *Zool.* The lower, ventral, or neural branch of a parapodium. Hence **Neuro-po·dial** *a.*

‖**Neuroptera** (niurǫ·ptĕră), *sb. pl.* 1752. [mod.L., f. NEURO- + Gr. πτερόν wing; see -A 4.] *Entom.* An order of insects, having four membranous transparent wings, with reticulate neuration. Hence **Neuro·pter,** an insect of this order. **Neuro·pterous** *a.*

Neurosis (niurōᵘ·sis). *Pl.* **-ses.** 1776. [– mod.L., f. NEURO- + -OSIS.] **1.** *Path.* A functional derangement arising from disorders of the nervous system, esp. such as are unaccompanied by organic change. **2.** *Psychol.* A change in the nerve-cells of the brain resulting in morbid psychic activity 1871.

Neurotic (niurǫ·tik), *sb.* 1661. [subst. use of next. Cf. contemp. HYPNOTIC *sb.*] **1.** *Med.* A drug having a (bracing) effect upon the nervous system. **2.** A neurotic person 1896.

Neurotic (niurǫ·tik), *a.* 1775. [orig. f. Gr. νεῦρον nerve, after *hypnotic*, etc.; in mod. use f. after NEUROSIS; see -OTIC.] **1.** Acting upon, or stimulating, the nerves. **2.** Of the nature of, marked by, neurosis or nervous disorder 1873. **3.** Of persons: Affected by neurosis; having disordered nerves 1887.

3. The n. woman is sensitive, zealous, managing 1887.

Neurotomy (niurǫ·tŏmi). 1704. [– mod.L. *neurotomia*; see NEURO- and -TOMY.] *Surg.* The section of a nerve, for the purpose of producing sensory paralysis. So **Neuro·-tomist,** one who practises or studies n.; *fig.* a dissector of feelings or emotions.

Neuter (niū·təɹ), *a.* and *sb.* late ME. [– (O)Fr. *neutre* or its source L. *neuter*, f. *ne-* not + *uter* either of two. Cf. NEITHER.] **A.** *adj.* **1.** *Gram.* **a.** Of gender: Neither masculine nor feminine. Hence also, later, of parts of speech, etc. **b.** Of a verb: Neither active nor passive; intransitive 1530. **c.** *N. passive*, semi-deponent 1530. **2.** = NEUTRAL *a.* Now *rare* or *arch.* Phr. *To stand n.* 1525. **3.** Belonging to neither of two specified or usual categories 1591. **4. a.** *Bot.* Having neither pistils nor stamens; asexual 1785. **b.** *Entom.* Sexually undeveloped, sterile 1816.

1. The n., or feigned gender: whose notion conceives neither sex B. JONS. **2.** It was a n. town indifferent to both 1560. As to these matters I shall be impartial, though I cannot be n. STEELE.

B. *sb.* **1.** *Gram.* **a.** A neuter verb 1530. **b.** A neuter noun or adjective 1611. **2.** A neutral thing (*rare*) 1522. **3.** One who holds himself neutral 1556. **4. a.** *Entom.* A sexually undeveloped female insect; a mature worker 1797. **b.** A castrated animal 1900.

3. Must we stand dubious and neuters between both BENTLEY. Which knows no n., owns but friends or foes BYRON. Hence **Neu·ter** *v. trans.* to castrate.

Neutral (niū·trăl), *sb.* and *a.* 1449. [– Fr. †*neutral* or L. *neutralis* (Quintilian), f. *neuter, neutr-*; see prec., -AL¹.] **A.** *sb.* **1.** One who remains neutral between two parties or sides; a subject of a neutral state, etc. **2.** A neutral salt 1822.

1. b. A position of the parts in a gear mechanism in which no power is transmitted 1914. Hence **Neu·tralism,** maintenance of neutrality. **Neu·tralist,** one who maintains a neutral attitude 1623.

B. *adj.* **1.** Of rulers, states, etc.: Not assisting either party in the case of a war between other states 1549. **b.** Belonging to a power which remains inactive during hostilities; exempted or excluded from the sphere of warlike operations 1711. **2.** Taking neither side in a dispute; indifferent 1551. **b.** Belonging to neither party or side 1564. **3.** Belonging to neither of two specified or implied categories; occupying a middle position between two extremes 1567. **b.** Undefined, vague 1805. **c.** Having no decided colour; of a bluish or greyish appearance 1821. **4. a.** *Chem.* Neither acid nor basic; not distinguished by either acid or alkaline reaction 1661. **b.** *Optics.* Having or indicating none of the phenomena of polarization 1813 **c.** *Electr.* Neither positive nor negative 1837. **d.** *Mech.* Lying at the point where the forces of extension and compression meet and are in equilibrium 1845. **5.** = NEUTER *a.* 4. 1747.

1. b. N. goods..are not liable to capture under enemy's flag 1878. **2.** While sagely n. sits thy silent friend SMOLLETT. **3. b.** Miss Merry was elderly and altogether n. in expression GEO. ELIOT. **c.** The most remote distance becomes a mass of n. colour 1821. **4. c.** *N. temperature*, that at which no current is produced by two metals arranged to exhibit thermo-electric force. *N. point*, the point of temperature at which a given pair of metals have the same thermo-electric power. Hence **Neu·trally** *adv.*

Neutrality (niutræ·liti). 1480. [– (O)Fr. *neutralité* or med.L. *neutralitas*, f. L. *neutralis*; see prec., -ITY.] **1.** (With *the*.) The neutral party or powers in a dispute or war. Now only *Hist.* **2.** A neutral attitude between contending parties or powers; abstention from taking any part in a war between other states 1494. **b.** The condition of being inclined neither way; absence of decided views, feeling, or expression; indifference 1561. **3.** An intermediate state or condition 1570. **b.** *Chem.* The fact or state of being neutral 1880.

1. The association of the Northern States in 1780, known by the name of the armed N. SCOTT. **2.** England set aside the balanced n. of Elizabeth GREEN. The n. of the port of Lisbon WELLINGTON. **b.** Those Readers that can iudge of the truth of a historie and the newtrallitie of the writer 1600.

Neutralize (niū·trăləiz), *v.* 1665. [orig. (sense 1) – med.L. *neutralizare*; in mod. use – Fr. *neutraliser*; see NEUTRAL, -IZE.] **†1.** *intr.* To remain neutral (*rare*). **2.** *trans.* **a.** *Chem.* To render neutral. Also refl. 1759. **b.** *Electr.* To render electrically inert 1837. **3.** To counterbalance; to render ineffective by an opposite force or effect 1795. **4.** To exempt or exclude (a place) from the sphere of war-like operations 1856.

2. a. The solution was . . neutralized by sulphuric acid FARADAY. **3.** The very nature of our academic institutions . . neutralizes a taste for the productions of native genius HAZLITT. **4.** The Black Sea is neutralised 1856. Hence **Neutraliza·tion** (in senses 2–4) 1808. **Neu·tralizer** 1843.

Neutral-tinted, *a.* 1879. Of a neutral tint (see NEUTRAL *a.* 3 c).

Neutro- (niū·tro), comb. form of NEUTRAL *a.*, as in **Neu·trophil(e** *a.*, that can be stained with neutral solutions; *sb.* a cell that may be so stained. **Neu:tro-sa·line** *a.*, *Chem.* that possesses the properties of a neutral salt.

Neutron (niū·trǫn). 1921. [f. NEUTRAL *a.* 4 c; after ELECTRON² and PROTON.] *Physics.* A subatomic electrically neutral particle of mass very slightly greater than that of a proton.

‖Névé (neve). 1853. [Swiss Fr. *névé* glacier :– Rom. **nivatum*, f. L. *nix, niv-* snow.] **1.** = FIRN. **2.** A field or bed of frozen snow 1884.

†Ne·ven, *v.* ME. [– ON. *nefna*, also *nemna*, f. *nafn, namn*; see NAME *sb.*] **1.** *trans.* To name –1513. **2.** To mention, give an account of –1529. **3.** With cognate obj.: To utter –1520.

Never (ne·vəɹ), *adv.* [OE. *nǣfre*, f. *ne* NE + *ǣfre* EVER.] **I. 1.** At no time, on no occasion. (Formerly often with *ne, no, none*, etc.) **b.** With *after, before, since, yet*, etc. OE. **c.** Repeated for emphasis 1605. **d.** In emphatic denial, or expressing surprise 1836. **2.** Not at all, in no way. late ME. **3.** *Never a*: not a, no . . at all ME. **4.** *Never so*, in conditional clauses, denoting an unlimited degree or amount OE. **5.** *Never the*, followed by a comparative: None the, not at all the (better, etc.) ME.

1. Serpent like, . . That bowes the Grasse, but neuer makes no path 1632. A braver n. drew a sword; A wiser n. SCOTT. Provb. *N. is a long word* (or *day*). **b.** The fact was n. before observed TYNDALL. **c.** *Lear* v. iii. 308. **d.** This almost caused Jemima to faint with terror. 'Well, I n.', said she THACKERAY. **2.** Phr. *N. you fear* (or *mind*). *N. mind. N. any* or *one*, no one, none at all. **3.** You have n. a shirt on DE FOE. Phr. *†N. a deal*, not a bit; see DEAL *sb.*¹ So *n. a whit*: see WHIT. *N. a one*, not (a single) one. **4.** Sufficient for a whole host, be it neuer so great BIBLE *Transl. Pref.* **5.** I am n. the wiser, nor the more able to account for Temple's letter GRAY. Phr. *N. the less, nevertheless*, no less, not in any way less, by no means less. So *N. the more, neverthemore.*

II. In attrib. phrases, formed with inf., or with pa. pples. and pres. pples. (hyphened) as *n. enough to be admired, n. to be forgotten*; *n.-ended, -satisfied*; *n.-ceasing, -dying, -ending, -fading*. Also *Never Never* (*Land* or *Country*), in Australia, the unpopulated northern part of Queensland; the desert country of the interior.

Nevermo·re, *adv.* ME. [f. NEVER + MORE *adv.*] Never again, at no future time.

He never more henceforth will dare set foot In Paradise MILT. Weep now or n. 1845.

†Never the lat(t)er, *adv.* ME. [See NEVER 5 and LATER, LATTER *advs.*] = next –1652.

Ne:verthele·ss, *adv.* ME. [See NEVER 5, THE *adv.*, LESS *adv.*] Notwithstanding; none the less.

They, knowing them to be evil, n. indulge in them JOWETT.

New (niū), *a.* and *sb.* [OE. *niwe, nīowe, nēowe* = OFris. *nȳ, nī*, OS. *niuwi, nigi*, MLG. *nige, nie*, MDu. *nieuwe, nuwe, nie* (Du. *nieuw*), OHG. *niuwi* (G. *neu*), ON. *nýr*, Goth. *niujis* :– Gmc. **neujaz* :– IE. **newjos*, repr. by Gr. (Ionic) *νεῖος*, Gaul. *Novio-* (in place-names); also by L. *novus*, Gr. *νέος* NEO-, Skr. *návas*.] **A.** *adj.* **I. 1.** Not existing before; now made, or brought into existence, for the first time. **b.** Of a novel kind ME. **2.** Not previously known; now known for the first time OE. **b.** Strange, unfamiliar (*to* one) 1595. **3.** Starting anew OE.; fresh, further, additional 1576; restored after demolition, decay, disappearance, etc. OE. **4.** Other than the former or old; different, changed OE. **5.** Used with *the* as a distinguishing epithet, implying some difference or change of nature or character OE.

1. To morow is a new day 1520. N. Discov'ries DRYDEN. **b.** Newe-fashioned cloathes I loue to weare, Newe tires, newe ruffes 1611. **2.** We . . curious are to hear, What happ'ns n. MILT. Seeking n. countries DE FOE. Tell not as n. what everybody knows COWPER. The n. acquaintance soon became a guest COWPER. **b.** Alacke, how n. Is husband in my mouth SHAKS. **3.** As the Sun is daily n. and old SHAKS. A motion for a n. trial 1818. A n. cause of displeasure MACAULAY. **4.** For in Christ Iesu nether circumcision auayleth eny thinge at all nor vncircumcision; but a n. creature TINDALE *Gal.* 6:15. He must turne the leafe, and take out a n. lesson 1577. N. Lords, n. lawes CAPT. SMITH. Fresh Woods, and Pastures n. MILT. A n. classification of birds 1849. **5.** The olde doctryne and ye newe COVERDALE. According to the newe fashion 1590. It was in New-France 1687. From N. Orleans to the mouth of the Missouri 1833. The 'n. diplomacy' 1898. *New woman*, a woman who has 'advanced' ideas on women's rights 1894. *N. learning, Testament, World*, etc.; see the sbs.

II. 1. Of recent origin or growth; †young; freshly made, produced, or grown; not yet used or worn. Also (now *rare*) of events or points of time: Recent, not long ago. OE. **2.** Having or retaining the qualities of a fresh or recent thing; showing no decline or decay. In later use esp. *ever n.* ME. **3.** Having but recently come into a certain state, position, or relationship OE. **b.** Fresh *from* some place, state, or operation 1700. **4.** That has just recently risen to notice; not belonging to a noted family 1611.

1. She semede lyk a rose newe Of colour CHAUCER. As with n. Wine intoxicated both They swim in mirth MILT. The n. red sandstone 1845. Provb. *N. brooms sweep clean. New rich* (tr. Fr. *nouveau-riche*): one who has recently attained to wealth: usu. with connotation of ostentation or vulgar show. Similarly, since the war of 1914–1918, *n. poor.* **2.** Heav'ns last best gift, my ever n. delight MILT. **3.** Newe soldiors and nouices of warre 1590. The Government was n. to office 1884. **b.** N. from her sickness 1700. **4.** A n. man, as I am styled in Rome 1611. Hence **New·ness,** the state, fact, or quality of being new.

B. *absol.* or as *sb.* **1.** That which is new OE. **2.** *The n. of the moon*, the time at which the moon is n. (see NEW MOON). Now *rare* or *obs.* late ME. **3. Of new. †a.** Of late; newly –1728. **†b.** Afresh, over again –1865. **†c.** By new arrangement, appointment, etc. –1658.

1. As in the arts, so also in politics, the n. must always prevail over the old JOWETT. **2.** Shooe him in the n. of the moone 1610.

†New, *v.* [OE. *nīwian*, f. *nīwe* NEW *a.* Cf. OS. *niwian*, OHG. *niwōn*, ON. (*endr-*)*nýja*, Goth. (*ana*)*niujan*.] To make or become new; to renew (itself) –1569.

New (niū), *adv.* [OE. *nīwe*, f. the adj.] **†I.** In ordinary advb. uses. **1.** Newly, recently –1610. **2.** Anew, afresh –1615.

1. Euen before this truce, but n. before SHAKS. **2.** I Richards body haue interred n. SHAKS. Phr. *N. and n.*, ever anew, over and over.

II. Preceding, and in later use hyphened with the qualified word. **1.** Newly, recently, freshly ME. **2.** With pa. pples. used predicatively in the sense of 'Anew, afresh'. (Also in Cotgr. to render Fr. pa. pples. in *re-*.) ME. **b.** Placed after a noun or pronoun 1593. **3.** With active forms of trans. vbs., in the same sense. (Also in Cotgr. to render Fr. vbs. in *re-*.) 1442. **4.** With pres. pples. of intr. vbs. used attrib., as *n.-appearing*, etc. 1594.

1. The new-gathered Mulberries 1620. New-departed Souls KEN. As sullen as a beast new-caged TENNYSON. **2.** Some [verses] . . I have entirely new express'd POPE. **b.** Me thinkes I am a Prophet n. inspir'd SHAKS. **3.** She had new-whitened the house all below stairs PEPYS.

New-blown, *ppl. a.* 1667. [f. NEW *adv.* II. 1 + BLOWN *ppl. a.*²] Of flowers: Newly opened.

fig. Converting the sweet Flow'r of new blown Hope To deadly Night-Shade 1740.

New-born, *ppl. a.* ME. [NEW *adv.* II. 1.] **1.** Just born. **2.** Born anew; regenerated.

1. Where is the new borne kynge of the Iues? COVERDALE *Matt.* 2:2. *fig.* His newborn virtues COWPER. **2.** *fig.* The number of the new-born increased WESLEY.

New-coined, *ppl. a.* 1598. [NEW *adv.* II. 1.] Freshly coined; newly made or invented; as, *new-coined words.*

New-come, *ppl. a.* and *sb.* OE. [NEW *adv.* II. 1.] **A.** *ppl. a.* Newly arrived; but lately come. **B.** *sb.* A new or recent arrival; a novice. Now *rare* or *arch.* 1577. So **New-co:mer,** a new arrival 1592.

New-create, *v.* 1604. [NEW *adv.* II. 3.] *trans.* To create anew.

Newel (niū·ĕl). 1611. [ME. *nowel* – OFr. *nouel, noel* knob :– med.L. *nodellus*, dim. of *nodus* knot.] **1.** *Arch.* The pillar forming the centre from which the steps of a winding stair radiate; †one of the stones forming this. **2.** The post at the head or foot of a stair supporting the hand-rail 1833. **3.** *attrib.*, as *n.-staircase*, etc. 1798.

1. *Open* or *hollow n.*, a central open space or well in a winding stair. Hence **New·elled** *a.* 1677.

New E·nglander. 1637. [f. *New England* (so named by Capt. John Smith in 1616) + -ER¹.] An inhabitant or native of New England, comprising the six north-eastern states of the U.S. So **New E·nglish,** of or pertaining to New England.

New-fallen, *a.* 1592. [NEW *adv.* II. 1.] **1.** Newly or recently fallen. **†2.** Newly fallen to one –1600. **3.** Newly dropped; new-born 1684.

1. As apt as new-fall'n snow takes any dint SHAKS. **2.** *A. Y. L.* v. iv. 182.

Newfangle (niūfæ·ŋg'l), *a.* and *sb.* Now *dial.* [ME. *newefangel*, f. *newe* adv. of NEW *a.* + *-fangel*, repr. OE. **fangol* 'inclined to take', from the stem *fang-* FANG *v.*¹; see -LE.] *adj.* = NEW-FANGLED. *sb.* A new thing or fashion; a novelty 1520. Hence **Newfa·ngle** *v.* to make newfangled. **Newfa·ngleness** (*rare* or *Obs.*).

Newfangled (niūfæ·ŋg'ld), *a.* 1470. [f. prec. + -ED¹.] **1.** Very fond of novelty or new things. **2.** New-fashioned, novel (*depreciatory*) 1533.

1. These new fangled Christians 1659. **2.** Gorgeous apparell and new fangled fashions 1598. Hence **Newfa·ngledness** 1549.

New-fashioned, *ppl. a.* 1611. [NEW *adv.* II. 1.] Made after a new fashion; of a new type or of recent invention.

New-found, *a.* 1496. [NEW *adv.* II. 1.] Newly found or invented; recently discovered. **b.** Of lands, islands, etc., esp. with ref. to America or certain parts of it (as in next) 1509.

Newfoundland (niufau·ndlǣnd, niū·fəndlǣnd, niu:faundlæ·nd). 1585. The name of a large island at the mouth of the river St. Lawrence used attrib., esp. in *N. dog.*, a large breed of dog, noted for its sagacity, good temper, strength, and swimming powers. *N. fish*, codfish.

Newfoundlander (niufau·ndlĕndəɹ). 1611. [Cf. prec. and -ER¹.] **1.** A native or inhabitant of Newfoundland. **2.** A ship belonging to Newfoundland 1801. **3.** A Newfoundland dog 1806.

New-furnish, *v.* 1611. [NEW *adv.* II. 3.] *trans.* To refurnish.

Newgate (niū·gĕt). 1596. Name of a

celebrated London prison (pulled down in 1902), used attrib. as **N. fashion,** etc.; also **N. bird,** a gaol-bird; **N. Calendar,** a former publication containing accounts of prisoners in N.; **N. frill** or **fringe,** a fringe of beard worn under the chin; **N. knocker,** a lock of hair twisted back from the temple to the ear, worn by costermongers, etc. Hence **New·gatory** *a.* belonging to N. (with pun on *nugatory*).

Newish (niū·iʃ), *a.* 1570. [f. NEW *a.* + -ISH¹.] Somewhat new.

New-laid, *ppl. a.* 1528. [NEW *adv.* II. 1.] Of eggs: Newly or freshly laid.

New light: see LIGHT *sb.* 6 c, quots.

Newly (niū·li), *adv.* OE. [f. NEW *a.* + -LY².] **1.** Very recently or lately. **2.** Anew, afresh OE. **3.** In a new fashion 1553.

1. The Infante Cardinal..being dead but n. EVELYN. A Ladies head newly dress'd for a Ball 1676. **2.** She was n. planked inside and out 1876. **3.** A word n. or fancifully applied 1885.

Newmanism (niū·măniz'm). 1838. [f. John Henry *Newman* (1801–1890) + -ISM.] The views on theological and ecclesiastical matters put forward by Newman while a member of the Anglican Church; the principles involved in Newman's teaching. So **New·manite,** a follower of Newman 1837.

Newmarket (niū·maːɹkėt, niū̆mā·ɹkėt). 1685. Name of a town (east of Cambridge) famous for its horse-races, used *attrib.* or *ellipt.* **1.** *attrib.* with *condition, cut, tail*; also **N. coat,** a long, close-fitting coat, orig. worn for riding; **N. greyhound,** a greyhound of a speedy, yet stout, breed. **2.** *ellipt.* A Newmarket coat 1843. **3.** A card-game in which the object is to play the same cards as certain duplicates which are exhibited and on which stakes are laid 1840.

New moon. OE. [NEW *a.* I. 3.] **1.** The moon when first seen as a slender crescent shortly after its conjunction with the sun. **2.** The time when the new moon appears; also *Astron.* the time at which the moon is in conjunction with the sun. **b.** = NEOMENIA. OE.

1. The new moone..Wi' the auld moone in hir arme 17... **2.** A few hours after 'new moon', the moon appears a little to the east of the sun as a thin crescent 1864.

New-mown, *ppl. a.* 1470. [NEW *adv.* II. 1, 2.] Freshly cut, just mown, as, *n. hay.*

News (niūz), *sb.* (*pl.*) late ME. [pl. of NEW *a.*, after OFr. *noveles*, pl. of *novele* (mod. *nouvelle*) NOVEL; or after med.L. *nova*, pl. of *novum* new thing, subst. use of *novus* NEW.] †**1.** New things, novelties –1565. **2.** Tidings; new information of recent events; new occurrences as a subject of report or talk. late ME. **b.** Construed as *sing.* 1566. **3.** The newspaper(s); a newspaper. Now *rare.* 1738.

1. Not for a vayne and curious desiere to see newes 1551. **2.** There are bad n. from Palermo SHELLEY. **b.** The next n. was that I was in the water 1897. Provb. *No n., good n. Ill n. fly fast.* †*No n.*, nothing new. *In the n.*, in the public eye. *attrib.* and *Comb.*: **n.-agent,** a regular dealer in newspapers and periodicals; **-boat,** a boat which puts out to passing vessels to receive and communicate news; †**-book,** a small newspaper; **-boy,** a boy who sells newspapers in the streets, or delivers them; **-editor,** on a daily newspaper, the editor in charge of the telegraphic news; **-print,** (*a*) newspapers; (*b*) printing-paper for newspapers; **-reel,** a cinema film giving the news of the day; **-room,** a reading-room set apart for newspapers; **-sheet,** = SHEET *sb.*¹ 6 d; **-stand,** a stall for the sale of newspapers; **news-vendor,** a newspaper seller. Hence **News** *v. trans.* to tell or spread as n. Now *dial.* **New·sless** *a.* devoid of n.

New-set, *v.* 1709. [NEW *adv.* II. 3.] *trans.* To set afresh or in a new fashion. So **New-set,** *ppl. a.* 1553.

New·s-le:tter. *Hist.* 1674. A letter specially written to communicate the news of the day, common in the late 17th and early 18th c.; also, a printed account of the news (sometimes with blanks left for private additions).

New·s-man. 1596. **1.** A bearer or collector of news; a news-writer. Now *arch.* **2.** A man who sells or delivers newspapers 1796.

New·smo:nger. 1592. One who collects and retails news.

Newspaper (niū·speⁱːpəɹ). 1670. [f. NEWS *sb.* Cf. Du. *nieuwspapier.*] A printed, now usu. daily or weekly, publication containing the news, advertisements, literary matter, and other items of public interest.

New·s-wri:ter. 1700. One who writes up the news for the information of others; in early use, a writer of news-letters.

Newsy (niū·zi), *a.* 1832. [f. NEWS + -Y¹.] Full of news; given to retailing news. Hence **New·siness.**

Newt (niūt). late ME. [For *ewt* (with *-n* from *an*: see N), var. of *evet* EFT *sb.* The change of *f, v* to *w* is unusual, but cf. the name *Pewsey, Pusey*, from OE. *Pefesig*; with the var. *neuft* (B. Jonson) cf. *ewft* (Spenser).] Any of certain aquatic salamanders (*Triton* or *Triturus*).

Newtonian (niutōᵘ·niăn). 1713. [f. Sir Isaac *Newton* (1642–1727) + -IAN.] **A.** *adj.* **1.** Devised, discovered, or suggested by Newton; pertaining to, or arising from, the theory of the universe propounded by Newton. **2.** Resembling, characteristic of, accepting the views of, Newton 1742. **3.** Of telescopes, their parts, etc.: Of the kind devised by Newton 1761.

1. The N. theory of gravitation 1830. **2.** Men of N. capacity MORLEY. **3.** An excellent N. reflector 1872.

B. *sb.* A follower of Newton; one who accepts the N. system 1741. Hence **Newto·nianism,** the N. system.

New-Year. Also **New year, Newyear.** ME. [f. NEW *a.* + YEAR.] **1.** The coming year; the commencement of another year; the first few days of a year. **2.** *attrib.* as *New-year day*, etc. late ME.

1. Phr. *New-year's day* (in U.S. also with ellipse of *day*), the first day of the year. So *New-year's eve, morn, morrow, tide.*

New Yo·rker. 1796. [-ER¹.] A native or inhabitant of the state or city of New York.

New Zea·lander. 1791. [-ER¹.] **a.** One of the aborigines of New Zealand; a Maori. **b.** A European settler in New Zealand. **c.** A native or inhabitant of New Zealand.

Nexal (ne·ksăl), *a. Rom. Law.* 1886. [f. L. *nexus* or *nexum* bond, obligation + -AL¹.] Characterized by the imposition of servitude as a penalty on a defaulting debtor.

Next (nekst), *a., sb.,* and *adv.* [OE. *nēhsta*, WS. *nīehsta* = OFris. *neeste*, OS. *na(h)isto* (Du. *naaste*), OHG. *nāhisto* (G. *nächste*), ON. *nǽstr, nǽsti*; superl. of NIGH; see -EST.] **A.** *adj.* and *sb.* **I.** In attrib. use, or absol. as *sb.* †**1.** Lying nearest in place or position –1710. **2.** Of persons: Living nearest to one; happening to be nearest at a particular time. Now *rare* or *Obs.* OE. **3.** Nearest in relationship or kinship. Also *absol.* in *the n. of* (one's) *blood, kin,* etc. OE. †**4.** Closest to hand, most convenient –1679; of ends, causes, etc., least remote –1754. **5.** Of periods of time: Immediately following or preceding. Also const. *after.* OE. **b.** Of persons, things, occasions, etc.: Coming directly after another in point of time. late ME. **c.** *ellipt.* with omission of *letter, number,* etc. 1629. **6.** Immediately succeeding or preceding in respect of position, order, arrangement, value, birth, etc. OE.

1. †*The n. way*, the shortest, most convenient or direct way. *fig.* I speake the truth the n. waie SHAKS. **3.** Thou art the nexte kynsman COVERDALE *Ruth* 3:9. The widow, or n. of kin BLACKSTONE. *N. friend*, nearest friend or relative; *spec.* in Law, one who represents any person who is not able to appear *sui juris*, in a suit at law. **4.** Extremity makes the n. the best remedy FULLER. **5.** The n. morning of the skirmish of the Boyn 1711. What is written on public affairs in one week may be..obsolete..the n. 1859. **b.** Have him peach'd the n. Sessions GAY. **c.** To be continued in our n. 1893. **6.** When Gabriel to his n. in power thus spake MILT. In the n. place, the chairs should be dusted 1756. *N. best*, second-best.

II. In predic. use or following the sb. **1.** Nearest in place or position OE. †**b.** *transf.* of help, accidents, etc. –1568. **2.** Of days, etc.: Immediately following; coming directly after (the time in question) ME. **3.** Immediately following (or going *before*) in order or succession ME. **4.** Nearest in respect of kinship, intimacy, or other such relationship ME. **b.** Nearest *after* or *to* (another) in rank or excellence 1535. **5. Next to,** the nearest approach to; very nearly, almost 1656.

1. In the parish n. adjoining 1765. [She] drew a chair n. to her MISS BURNEY. **2.** The end of February n. CARLYLE. **3.** Thammuz came n. behind MILT. *What n.?* an exclam. of surprise. **4. b.** Phr. *N. after, n. to*, used in loose apposition to the person or thing spoken of; He was, n. after Lucy,..by far the best news-gatherer of the country side MISS MITFORD. **5.** Phr. *To get n. to* (U.S.): to become acquainted with. So *To put n. to*: to acquaint (one) with. 1896.

III. Governing a sb. (orig. in dative). Nearest to in respect of situation, rank, condition, character, etc. OE. **b.** In loose apposition ME.

One n. himself in power, and n. in crime MILT. All of them..wear Drawers n. their Skin 1687. **b.** The thing that..I loue best, n. my wyfe and children 1568.

B. *adv.* †**1.** Last, on the last occasion. –ME. **2.** In the next place; immediately thereafter ME. **3.** On the first future or subsequent occasion 1536.

2. Hippias the sage spoke n. JOWETT. **3.** When he n. doth ride abroad May I be there to see COWPER.

Next door. 1485. [NEXT *a.* I. 1.] **1.** The (door of the) nearest or adjoining house. **2.** In advb. use. **a.** Very close or near *to* (a state, condition, etc.); almost amounting *to* (something) 1529. **b.** In or at the next house (*to* a person or place) 1579. **3.** *attrib.* as *ne·xt-door neighbour* 1749.

1. The girl from next door but one DICKENS. **2. a.** To be next Door to Starving DE FOE. **b.** The Armenian lady next door 1863.

Ne·xtly, *adv.* Now *rare.* 1584. [f. NEXT *a.* + -LY².] In the next place; next.

‖**Nexus** (ne·ksŏs). 1663. [L., f. *nectere, nex-* bind.] **1.** A bond or link; a means of connection. **2.** A connected group or series 1858.

1. Cash Payment..the universal sole n. of man to man CARLYLE. *Causal n.*, the necessary connection between cause and effect.

Niagara (nəiˌæ·gără). 1799. [Name of a N. American river, on which there is a famous waterfall.] A cataract, torrent, deluge. Hence **Niaga·rean, -ian** *adjs.* resembling N.

‖**Niaiserie** (niˌēⁱ·zəri). 1657. Now *rare.* [Fr., f. *niais* simple.] Foolish or silly simplicity; an instance of this.

Niata (niā·tă). 1868. [Native name.] A dwarf variety of cattle bred in S. America. Hence **Niatism** (nəi·ătiz'm), dwarfed condition.

Nib (nib), *sb.* 1585. [prob. – MDu. *nib* or MLG. *nibbe*, var. of *nebbe* beak; see NEB.] **1.** = NEB 1, 2. **2.** = NEB 3. 1611. **b.** A separate pen-point, for fitting into a pen-holder 1837. **c.** Each of the divisions of a pen-point 1840. **3.** = NEB 3 b. 1713. **4.** *dial.* **a.** *pl.* The two short handles projecting from the shaft or snead of a scythe 1673. **b.** The pole or draught-tree of an ox-cart or timber-carriage 1808. **5.** *pl.* Pieces of crushed cocoa-beans 1842. **6.** A lump or knot in wool or raw silk 1879.

Nib, *v.*¹ *Obs.* exc. *dial.* 1558. [app. related to NIBBLE *v.*] †**1.** *trans.* To peck, pick, prick –1645. **2.** *intr.* and *trans.* To nibble. Now *dial.* 1613.

Nib, *v.*² 1757. [f. NIB *sb.*] *trans.* To mend the nib of (a pen).

Nibble (ni·b'l), *sb.* 1658. [f. next.] The act or fact of nibbling; an instance of this, esp. of a fish at a bait. **2.** A quantity (of grass) sufficient for a nibble 1838.

Nibble (ni·b'l), *v.* 1460. [prob. of LDu. origin; cf. LG. *nibbeln*, also *gnibbeln, knibbeln* gnaw = Du. *knibbelen* gnaw, murmur, squabble, parallel to *knabbelen*, whence KNABBLE *v.*] **1.** *trans.* To take little bites of (a thing); to bite away little by little. **2.** *intr.* To take little bites; to eat or feed in this fashion 1582. **b.** To carp (*at* something), to make trifling criticisms 1591. **3.** *slang.* To catch, nab; to pilfer 1608.

1. Some, clambring..N. the bushie shrubs SPENSER. All my baits nibbled off, And not the fish caught 1617. **2.** To let them play and n. with the bait a while MILT. Hence **Ni·bbler. Ni·bblingly** *adv.*

Nibbling (ni·bliŋ), *vbl. sb.* 1590. [f. prec. + -ING¹.] **1.** The action of the verb; an instance of this; a portion nibbled. **2.** *techn.* The gradual reduction of the edge of a piece of glass to a circular form before it is ground for a lens 1850.

Ni·blick. 1862. [Of unkn. origin.] A golf club, with a stiff shaft and a round heavy head, used to take the ball out of a bad lie.

Nibs. *slang.* 1821. [Of unkn. origin; see NABS.] = NABS.

Nicæan (nəisī·ăn), *a.* and *sb.* 1706. [f. *Nicæa* (see NICENE) + -AN.] = NICENE *a.* and *sb.*

Nicaragua (nikăræ·giuă). 1703. [Name of a republic in Central America.] *N. wood*, a red dye-wood similar to Brazil wood, obtained from species of *Cæsalpinia*; peach-wood.

Niccolite (ni·kǒləit). 1868. [f. mod.L. *niccolum* NICKEL + -ITE[1] 2 b.] *Min.* Native arsenide of nickel; copper-nickel, nickeline.

Nice (nəis), *a.* ME. [– OFr. *nice* silly, simple :– L. *nescius* ignorant, f. *nescire*; see NESCIENT.] †**1.** Foolish, stupid –1560. †**2.** Wanton, lascivious –1606. †**3.** Strange, rare –1555. †**4.** Tender, delicate, over-refined –1720. †**5.** Coy, (affectedly) modest; shy, reluctant –1676. **6.** Difficult to please or satisfy; fastidiously careful, precise, or punctilious; 'particular'. Now *rare* or *arch.* 1551. **7.** Requiring or involving great precision, accuracy, or minuteness 1513. **8.** Not readily apprehended, difficult to decide, determine, or distinguish; minutely or delicately precise 1513. †**9.** Slender, thin; unimportant, trivial –1604. **10.** †**a.** Critical, doubtful –1710. **b.** Delicate, needing tactful handling 1617. **11.** Able to discriminate in a high degree, finely discriminative 1586. **b.** Delicate in manipulation 1711. **12.** Minutely or carefully accurate; finely poised or adjusted 1599. **13.** Of food: Dainty, appetizing 1712. **14.** *colloq.* Agreeable; delightful 1769. **b.** *To look n.*, to have an agreeable, attractive, or pretty appearance 1793. **c.** Kind, considerate, or pleasant (to others) 1830. **d.** In ironical use. Also *n. and.* 1846. **e.** In negative contexts: Refined, in good taste c1860.

2. *L. L. L.* III. i. 24. *Ant. & Cl.* III. xiii. 180. **4.** He..was of so n. and tender a composition, that a little rain or wind would disorder him CLARENDON. **5.** Ere..The n. Morn on th' Indian steep From her cabin'd loop hole peep MILT. †Phr. *To make it n.*, to display reluctance, make a scruple –1677. *John* III. iv. 138. **6.** The Parliament is alwayes very n. and curious on this point 1661. Some people are more n. than wise COWPER. I should..not be too n. about the means 1887. **7.** N. philosophical experiments 1822. **8.** One of the nicest problems for a man to solve 1847. The nicer shades of meaning 1870. **9.** *Oth.* III. iii. 15. *Jul. C.* IV. iii. 8. **10.** 1 *Hen. IV*, IV. i. 48. **b.** The nicest political negociations 1777. **11.** A n. observer of mens actions and manners 1617. A n. pallate in good liquor had made my landlord a favourite companion 1755. A n. sense of elegance and form 1845. **12.** Despight his n. fence, and his actiue practise SHAKS. Weigh arguments in the nicest intellectual scales 1875. **13.** You must give us something very nice, for we are used to live well JANE AUSTEN. **14.** The n. long letter which I have..received from you JANE AUSTEN. How n. it must be to be able to get about in cars, omnibuses and railway trains again! 1897. **c.** 'Not n. of Master Enoch', said Dick T. HARDY. **d.** You'll be n. and ill in the morning D. JERROLD. Hence **Ni·cely** *adv.* **Ni·ceness.**

Nicene (nəi·sīn, nəisī·n), *a.* late ME. [– late L. *Nicenus*, *Nicænus*, f. *Nicea*, *Nicæa*, Gr. Νίκαια, name of a town in Bithynia.] **1.** *N. Council*, one or other of two Church Councils held at Nicæa, the first in the year 325 to deal with the Arian controversy, and the second in 787 to consider the question of images. **2.** *N. Creed*, the creed used in the Eucharistic services of the Eastern and the Western Church, being that received at Constantinople in A.D. 381 (except for the Western addition of the FILIOQUE, q.v.), which is an expanded form of the formula set forth by the Council of Nicæa, A.D. 325. 1567. **3.** Connected with, originating from, relating to, the Nicene Council(s) 1597. Hence **Nice·nian, Nice·nist.**

Nicety (nəi·sėti). ME. [– OFr. *niceté*; see NICE *a.*, -TY[1].] **I.** †**1.** Foolish conduct; wantonness –1483. †**2.** Reserve, shyness, coyness –1757. †**3.** Excessive refinement or elegance in dress or manner of living –1652. **4.** Scrupulosity, punctiliousness 1693; fastidiousness 1723. **5.** Precision, accuracy, minuteness 1660. **6.** The quality of requiring consideration or management; delicacy, difficulty, subtlety 1707. **b.** The point in which precision is required or which is difficult to hit 1727.

2. Pride and Ignorance..preferring nicity before health 1652. N. and affectation; which is no more but modesty depraved into a vice DRYDEN. **4.** Such as had a N. in their Sense of Honour STEELE. Those who can distinguish with the utmost n. the boundaries of vice and virtue JOHNSON. My own n., and the n. of my friends, have made me..an idle, helpless being JANE AUSTEN. **6.** The question..is one of considerable n. and difficulty 1845.

II. 1. Something choice, elegant, or dainty, *esp.* something to eat (now *rare* or *Obs.*) late ME. **2.** A nice or minute distinction; a subtle point in theory or practice 1589. **b.** A minute point or detail 1649.

1. Niceties do little towards filling the bellies of a hungry family 1793. Clean linen and other niceties of apparel HAWTHORNE. **2.** Theological niceties 1880. **b.** Young women..do not know the niceties of legal proof 1875.

Niche (nitʃ), *sb.* 1611. [– (O)Fr. *niche*, f. *nicher* (OFr. *-ier*) make a nest, nestle :– Rom. **nidicare*, f. L. *nidus* nest.] **1.** A shallow, ornamental recess or hollow in a wall, to contain a statue or other decorative object. **2.** A small vaulted recess or chamber made in the thickness of a wall, or in the ground 1662. **3.** *fig.* **a.** A place or position adapted to the character, or suited to the merits, of a person or thing 1726. **b.** A place of retreat or retirement 1725.

1. You have the blessed Virgin and a Child sitting in a Nitch STEELE. **3. a.** The work fills a n. of its own and is without competitor 1869.

Niche (nitʃ), *v.* 1752. [f. the sb., in some senses perh. partly – Fr. *nicher*; see prec.] **1.** *trans.* (in *pass.*) To place (an image, etc.) in a niche or similar recess 1757. **2.** To place in some recess or nook; to ensconce 1752. **3.** *refl.* To settle or ensconce (oneself) quietly or comfortably 1824.

1. A waxen Virgin niched in a little box against the wall 'MARK TWAIN'. **2.** Niched between two bouncing lasses, he had commenced acquaintance with them 1847. **3.** Here Dolly loved to retreat and n. herself down in a quiet corner 1878.

Nichil, early form of NIHIL.

Nicholas (ni·kǒlăs). [Name of an early Christian saint (died A.D. 326), bishop of Myra in Lycia, patron of scholars, esp. of school-boys.] †**1.** *St. Nicholas' bishop*, a boy-bishop elected by choir-boys or scholars on St. Nicholas' Eve (Dec. 5) 1501–5. **2.** *St. Nicholas' clerks*: †**a.** Poor scholars 1489–1581. **b.** Highwaymen (now only *arch.*) 1570.

2. b. If they meete not with S. Nicolas Clarks, Ile giue thee this necke SHAKS.

Nick (nik), *sb.*[1] 1483. [perh. f. the verb.] **I. 1.** A notch, groove, or slit in something; an incision, indentation. **b.** *Printing.* A notch made on one side of the shank of a type, serving as a guide to the compositor in setting 1683. **2.** A notch used as a means of keeping a score: hence †reckoning, account 1483. **3.** A gap in a range of hills 1793. **4.** A cut; the act of cutting 1816.

1. *spec.* The Notch or N., in the Arrow for the Bowstring to go in 1688. A n. is the mark cut in the mandible of a swan to distinguish its ownership 1842. **2.** He lou'd her out of all nicke SHAKS.

II. †**1.** A pun –1589. **2.** In the game of hazard: A throw which is either the same as the main, or has a fixed correspondence to it 1635.

III. 1. *The* (*very*) *n.*: **a.** The critical moment. Chiefly used in phr. *in* (†*at, upon*) *the n.* 1577. Now *in the* (*very*) *n. of time* 1643. †**b.** The exact point aimed at; the mark –1656. **2.** The precise moment or time of some occurrence or event 1645. **3.** (With *a* and *pl.*) A critical point or moment. Now *rare.* 1628.

1. a. Married..they would have been, if I had not come just in the n. 1774. He had changed sides at the very n. of time DICKENS. **2.** In the very n. Of giving up BROWNING.

Nick (nik), *sb.*[2] 1643. [prob. abbrev. of the name *Nicholas*, but no reason for such an application is known.] The devil. Usu. *Old N.*

You..made us laugh with your conceit, being always conceited as Old N. 1886.

Nick (nik), *v.* 1523. [Of unkn. origin.] **I. 1.** *trans.* To make a nick or notch in; to cut in nicks or notches; to indent 1530. **b.** To score by means of a notch or notches on a stick or tally. Also with *up, down*, and in fig. use. 1523. **2.** To cut into or through; to cut short 1592. **b.** To fashion or mark out by cutting 1605. **3.** To make an incision at the root of (a horse's tail) in order to make him carry it higher; also with *horse* as obj. 1737.

1. b. I'll get a knife and n. it down, that Mr. Neverout came to our House SWIFT. **3.** Prosecuted..for 'nicking' two hackneys and a chestnut mare 1896.

II. †**1.** To tally with, resemble, suit exactly –1702. †**2.** To hit off or fit *with* (or *in*) an appropriate name –1693. **b.** To nickname. *Obs.* exc. as *nonce-wd.* 1605. **3. a.** *To n. it*, to make a hit; to guess rightly 1624. **b.** To hit, arrive at with precision; to hit *off* neatly or precisely 1673. **4.** To hit (the proper time, season, etc. for something) 1664. **b.** To catch (a boat, train, etc.) 1841. **5.** *slang.* To catch, take unawares; to nab, nail. Now *spec.* of the police. 1622. **b.** To steal 1869.

2. I have so nickt his Character in a Name as will make you split 1687. **b.** Goodith.., by which name King Henry the first was nicked in contempt CAMDEN. **3. a.** Have I not nick'd it, tutor? MASSINGER. **b.** You just nicked my palate LAMB. **4.** I had nicked my time, and..I embarked 1843. **5.** All my pals got nicked, and I chucked it 1893.

III. †**1.** In the game of hazard: To win against (the others) by casting a nick –1684. **2.** To make (a winning cast) at hazard; to get as a nick; to throw the nick of (a certain number) 1598. †**3.** To trick, cheat; to defraud *of*, do out *of* –1818. **4.** *intr.* In hunting, racing, etc.: To cut in. Also with past, up, etc. 1852.

3. He was nick'd of three pieces of cambrick GAY. **4.** [He is] always nicking and skirting SURTEES.

IV. Of breeding stocks: To unite, couple 1865.

Nickar, early form of NICKER *sb.*[3]

Nickel (ni·k'l), *sb.* 1775. [abbrev. of G. *kupfernickel*, mining name of the copper-coloured ore (niccolite) from which nickel was first obtained by A. F. von Cronstedt in 1751. The second element is G. *nickel* dwarf, mischievous demon, the name being given to the ore because it yielded no copper in spite of its appearance.] **1.** A hard, silvery-white lustrous metallic element, usu. occurring in combination with arsenic or sulphur and associated with cobalt; it is malleable and ductile, and resistant to oxidation, and is used principally in alloys. Symbol Ni. **2.** *U.S. colloq.* †**a.** A one-cent piece partly made of nickel –1858. **b.** A five-cent piece (containing one part of nickel to three of copper) 1883.

attrib., in **n. bloom, green, ochre** = ANNABERGITE; **n. silver**, an alloy similar to German silver; **n. steel**, an alloy of iron with n. Hence **Ni·ckel, Ni·ckelize** *vbs. trans.*, to coat with n. **Ni·ckelic** *a.* pertaining to, or containing, n. **Ni:ckeli·ferous** *a.* containing or yielding n. **Ni·ckeline** *sb.* = NICCOLITE; *a.* consisting of n. **Ni·ckelous** *a.* containing n.

Nicker, *sb.*[1] 1669. [f. NICK *v.* + -ER[1].] †**1.** One who cheats at play –1714. †**2.** One who fits a thing neatly MARVELL. **3.** One who hits in throwing; *spec.* early in the 18th c., one of the disorderly youths who made a practice of breaking windows by throwing coppers at them 1716. **4.** One who, or that which, nicks or cuts 1810; *spec.* that part of a centre-bit which cuts the circle of the hole made by the tool 1846.

Nicker (ni·kəɹ), *sb.*[2] 1675. = KNICKER[1].

Nicker (ni·kəɹ), *sb.*[3] Also **-ar.** 1696. [perh. native name.] The hard seed of the bonduc tree; also = NICKER-TREE.

Ni·cker, *v.* Chiefly *Sc.* and *north. dial.* 1774. [Imitative.] **1.** *intr.* To neigh. **2.** To laugh loudly or shrilly. Also *trans.*

Ni·cker-tree. 1707. [See NICKER *sb.*[3]] = BONDUC.

Nicking (ni·kiŋ), *vbl. sb.* 1551. [f. NICK *v.* + -ING[1].] **1.** The action of notching or cutting. **b.** A notch or indentation; a cutting or set of cuts 1844. **2.** The action of hitting (upon) or striking 1668.

1. b. *Nicking*, the cutting made by the hewer at the side of the face. *Nickings* is the small coal produced in making the n. 1881.

Nick-nack. 1692. Var. of KNICK-KNACK.

Nickname (ni·knē¹m), *sb.* 1440. [For EKE-NAME, with *n* from *an* (see N).] A name added to, or substituted for, the proper name of a person, place, etc., usu. in ridicule or pleasantry. **b.** A familiar form of a Christian name 1605.

He unfortunately got the N. of the Squeaking Doctor ADDISON. **b.** A wery good name it [*sc.* Job] is; only one, I know, that ain't got a n. to it DICKENS.

Ni·ckname, *v.* 1536. [f. the sb.] **1.** *trans.* To call by an incorrect name; to misname. †**b.** To mention by mistake (*rare*) –1665. **2.** To give a nickname to (one); to call by a nickname 1567.

1. You lispe, and n. Gods creatures SHAKS. **b.** *L. L. L.* v. ii. 349. **2.** They were soon nicknamed Methodists WESLEY.

Nicol (ni·kəl). 1838. [f. William *Nicol*, its inventor (died 1851).] *Optics.* A prism of Iceland spar, so constructed as to transmit only the extraordinary ray of doubly refracted light. (Also freq. *Nicol's prism.*)

Nicolaitan (nikǫlē¹·tăn). 1526. [f. Gr. Νικολαΐτης, f. personal name Νικόλαος + -AN.] *sb.* A member of an early Christian party or sect mentioned in Rev. 2: 6, 15, the precise nature of which is uncertain. *adj.* Held by the Nicolaitans 1864. So †**Nicolaite** *sb.* –1586.

‖**Nicotia** (nikōᵘ·ʃ¹ă). 1830. [mod.L., f. *nicot-* (see NICOTIANA) + -IA¹.] **a.** Nicotianin. **b.** Nicotine.

†**Nico·tian,** *sb.*¹ 1577. [– Fr. *nicotiane* (XVI), f. *Nicot*; see NICOTIANA.] The tobacco-plant –1673.

Nicotian (nikōᵘ·ʃ¹ăn), *a.* and *sb.*² 1825. [f. *nicot-* (see next) + -IAN.] **A.** *adj.* Of or pertaining to tobacco; arising from the use of tobacco. **B.** *sb.* **1.** = NICOTIANIN 1840. **2.** A tobacco-smoker O. W. HOLMES.

‖**Nicotiana** (nikōᵘʃiē¹·nă, -tiā·nă). 1600. [mod.L. (sc. *herba*), f. Jacques *Nicot*, French ambassador at Lisbon, who introduced tobacco into France in 1560.] **1.** The tobacco-plant. **2.** A genus of plants (chiefly American) of the nightshade family, to which the tobacco-plant (*N. tabacum*) belongs 1846.

Nicotianin (nikōᵘ·ʃ¹ănin). Also **-ine.** 1838. [f. prec. + -IN¹.] *Chem.* A camphorous bitter substance, extracted from tobacco.

Nicotic (nikǫ·tik), *a.* 1857. [f. *nicot-* (see NICOTIANA) + -IC.] *Chem.* Of or pertaining to nicotine, esp. in *N. acid.*

Nicotina (nikǒtəi·nă). 1838. [f. *nicot-* (see NICOTIANA) + -INA.] *Chem.* = next.

Nicotine (ni·kǒtīn, ni·kǒtĭn). Also **-in.** 1819. [– Fr. *nicotine*, f. mod.L. *nicotiana* (sc. *herba*) tobacco-plant; see NICOTIAN *sb.*¹, NICOTIANA, -INE⁵.] A poisonous alkaloid forming the essential principle of tobacco, from which it is obtained as an oily liquid. Hence **Nicoti·nian** *a.* = NICOTIAN *a.* **Ni·cotinism,** a diseased condition produced by the excessive use of tobacco. **Ni·cotinize, Ni·cotize,** *vbs. trans.* to drug or saturate with n.

Nictate (ni·ktē¹t), *v.* 1691. [– *nictat-*, pa. ppl. stem of L. *nictare* blink; see next, -ATE³.] *intr.* To wink. Only in *nictating membrane*; see NICTITATE *v.* Hence **Nicta·tion.**

Nictitate (ni·ktitē¹t), *v.* 1822. [– *nictitat-*, pa. ppl. stem of med.L. *nictitare*, frequent. of L. *nictare* blink; see prec., -ATE³.] *intr.* Of the eyelids: To wink (*rare*). Hence **Ni·ctitating** *ppl. a.*, in *nictitating membrane*, a third or inner eyelid present in many animals, serving to protect the eye from dust, etc., and to keep it moist 1713. So **Nictita·tion** 1784.

Nidamental (nəidămĕ·ntăl), *a.* 1835. [f. L. *nidamentum* (see NIDUS, -MENT) + -AL¹.] **1.** *Zool.* Serving as a receptacle for the ova of molluscs or other marine animals; forming a collection of ova. **2.** Serving as a nest or nests 1879.

Ni·ddering, *sb.* and *a.* Also **nider-.** 1596. [Erroneous form of NITHING, originating in the early printed text (1596) of William of Malmesbury, by misreading *niðing* as *nid'ing* (= nidering). The modern currency of the word is due to Scott.] *sb.* A base coward or wretch. *adj.* Base, cowardly, vile 1848.

Nide (nəid). 1679. [– Fr. *nid* or L. *nidus* nest; see NYE.] A brood or nest of pheasants. Also *transf.* of geese. Now only *arch.*

Nidificate (ni·difikē¹t), *v.* 1816. [Back-formation from NIDIFICATION.] *intr.* To make a nest.

All the Birds of Prey..n. in lofty situations 1835. So **Nidifica·tion,** the operation of nest-building; the manner in which this is done 1658.

Nidify (ni·difəi), *v.* 1656. [– L. *nidificare*, f. *nidus* nest; see -FY. Cf. Fr. *nidifier.*] *intr.* To build a nest or nests.

Nid-nod, *v.* 1787. [redupl. f. NOD *v.*] To nod repeatedly.

Nidor (nəi·dǭɹ). Now *rare.* 1619. [– L. *nidor.*] The smell of animal substances when burned, roasted, or boiled; †a strong odour of any kind.

Nidorous (nəi·dŏrəs), *a.* Now *rare.* 1626. [– late L. *nidorosus* (see prec., -OUS) or f. NIDOR + -OUS.] Of smells: Resembling that of cooked or burnt animal substances; strong and unpleasant. **b.** Applied to stomachic eructations 1651.

Nidulant (ni·diŭlănt), *a.* Now *rare.* 1797. [– *nidulant-*, pr. ppl. stem of L. *nidulari*, f. *nidus* nest; see -ANT.] Nestling; embedded in pulp or cotton, or in a berry.

‖**Nidus** (nəi·dǒs). *Pl.* **nidi** (nəi·dəi), **niduses** (nəi·dǒsėz). 1742. [L.; see NEST *sb.*] **1. a.** *Zool.* A nest or place in which insects, snails, etc., deposit their eggs. **b.** *Bot.* A place or substance in which spores or seeds develop 1796. **c.** *Phys.* and *Path.* A place of origin or development *for* some state or substance 1804. **d.** *fig.* A source or place of origin 1807. **2.** A place in which something is formed, deposited, settled, or located 1778. **3.** A collection *of* eggs, tubercles, etc. 1822.

1. c. The mammary gland seems to be the n. for this diseased action ABERNETHY. **d.** The Sorbonne, formerly the n. of pedantry 1817.

Niece (nīs). ME. [– (O)Fr. *nièce* :– pop.L. **neptia*, for L. *neptis*, corresp. to Skr. *naptīs*, Lith. *neptė̃*, Gmc. **niptiz*, whence OE. *nift* (current till XV), OFris., OHG. *nift*, MDu. *nichte* (whence G. *nichte*), Du. *nicht*, ON. *nipt*. Cf. NEPHEW.] **1.** †**a.** A grand-daughter, or more remote female descendant (Common down to *c*1600). **b.** A daughter of one's brother (brother-in-law) or sister (sister-in-law). †**2.** A female relative –1508.

1. b. His neece by the sister's side 1673.

Niellated (ni·elē¹tėd), *ppl. a.* 1886. [– It. *niellato*, pa. pple. of *niellare*, f. NIELLO.] Inlaid in niello.

‖**Niello** (ni₁e·lo), *sb. Pl.* **-i, -os.** 1816. [– It. *niello* :– L. *nigellus*, dim. of *niger* black.] **1.** A black composition, consisting of metallic alloys, for filling in engraved designs on silver or other metals. **b.** Ornamental work in niello 1842. **2.** A specimen of niello work 1840. **3.** An impression on paper of the design which is to be filled with niello 1854. Hence **Nie·llist,** a worker or artist in n. **Nie·llo** *v.* inlay with n. **Nie·lloed** *ppl. a.*

Nietzschean (nī·tʃiăn), *a.* and *sb.* 1914. [f. the name of the German philosopher Friedrich Wilhelm *Nietzsche* (1844–1900) + -AN.] Pertaining to or characteristic of Nietzsche or his philosophy of the *Übermensch* (see SUPERMAN). So **Nie·tzscheanism, Nie·tzscheism.**

Nieve (nīv), **nief** (nīf). Now *dial.* or *arch.* [ME. *neve* – ON. *hnefi*, *nefi*, which has no known cognates.] A clenched hand, a fist.

Giue me your neafe, Mounsieur Mustardseed SHAKS.

Nifle (nəi·f'l). Now *dial.* late ME. [perh. – med.L. NICHIL, infl. by *trifle*, with which it is often combined.] A trifle; †a trifling or fictitious tale. (Common *c*1550–1650.)

‖**Nigella** (nəidʒe·lă). late ME. [L., fem. of *nigellus*; see NIELLO.] *Bot.* A genus of ranunculaceous plants, having numerous black seeds, esp. the Fennel-flower (*N. sativa*) and Love-in-a-mist (*N. damascena*); also, the seeds of this used for medicinal purposes.

Niggard (ni·găɹd), *sb.* and *a.* late ME. [Alteration, with substitution of suffix -ARD, of earlier †*nigon* (XIV–XVI), f. †*nig* (XIII–XVII); prob. of Scand. origin; cf. NIGGLE.] **A.** *sb.* **1.** A mean, stingy, or parsimonious person; a miser. **2.** *dial.* A false bottom for a grate, to economize fuel. Also *n. iron.* 1688.

1. The negard then saith to his money.., my god arte thou 1510. Be niggards of advice on no pretence, For the worst avarice is that of sense POPE.

B. *adj.* **1.** Miserly, parsimonious, mean; unwilling to give or spend anything. late ME. **2.** Of actions and qualities; Niggardly, ungenerous 1672. **3.** Scanty 1751.

1. N. with pence and lavish with millions BENTHAM. Hence †**Ni·ggardise,** niggardliness. **Ni·ggard-ly** *adv.* in a n. manner; **-ness.**

Niggardly (ni·găɹdli), *a.* 1561. [f. prec. *sb.* + -LY¹.] **1.** Having a niggard's nature; close-fisted, stingy; sparing 1571. **2.** Of actions, qualities, etc.: Characteristic of a niggard; mean, miserly 1561. **3.** Such as a niggard would give; meanly small; scanty 1599.

1. The Israelites..were perpetually slack or n. in the service of Jehovah M. ARNOLD. **3.** The niggardliest mouse of biefe will cost him sixpence 1599. Hence **Ni·ggardliness.**

Nigger (ni·gəɹ). 1786. [Later form of NEGER.] **1.** A Negro. (Colloq. and usu. contempt.) Also *transf.* of members of other dark-skinned races. **2.** The black caterpillar of the turnip saw-fly 1840. **3.** *attrib.* (or *adj.*). **a.** Belonging to the Negro race; black-skinned. Also *n.-minstrel*; see NEGRO. 1836. **b.** Of, or belonging to, occupied by, Negroes. Also *transf.* 1834. **c.** The name of a colour 1914.

3. a. He was about to be serenaded by a n.-minstrel 1883. Hence **Ni·ggerdom, Ni·ggerish** *a.*

Ni·ggerhead. 1859. [f. prec. + HEAD *sb.*] Applied to various black or dark-coloured roundish objects. (Cf. NEGRO-HEAD.)

A clump or tussock of vegetation (*U.S.*), the black or rough head of some plants (*Austral.*); *Min.* a dark-coloured nodule or boulder; = NEGRO-HEAD 1.

Niggle (ni·g'l), *v.* 1599. [app. of Scand. origin, corresp. both in form and meaning to Norw. *nigla*, with the vars. *nagla* and *nugla.*] **1.** *intr.* To work, or do anything, in a fiddling way; to spend time unnecessarily on petty details; to keep moving *along*, in a fiddling or ineffective manner. †**2.** Of girls: To be restless or fidgety from wantonness –1809.

1. Take heed, daughter, You n. not with your conscience MASSINGER. When I have nobody at all at my place but workmen;..I n. after them up and down MME. D'ARBLAY. Hence **Ni·ggled** *ppl. a.* over-elaborated 1884. **Ni·ggler** 1862. **Ni·ggling** *ppl. a.*, trifling, petty, finicking. **Ni·ggly** *a.*

Nigh (nəi), *adv.*, *a.*, and *sb.* [OE. *nēah*, *nēh*, corresp. to OFris. *nei*, *nī*, OS., OHG. *nāh* (Du. *na*, G. *nah*), ON. *ná-*, Goth. *nēhw-* (*nēhw* prep., *nēhwa* adv.); Gmc. of unkn. origin. Orig. compared, as *ān* adv., *nēar* NEAR *adv.*, as an adj., *nēarra*, ME. *ner* NAR *a.* The relationship of these forms to the positive becoming obscured, they were replaced by *nigher*, *nighest.*] = NEAR *adv.* and *a.* (which in all senses has taken the place of *nigh* exc. in arch. or dial. use.) **Denoting proximity in place, time*, etc. **I.** *adv.* With dependent dative (passing into *prep.*), or followed by *to*.

There came other shippes..nye vnto yᵉ place COVERDALE. Neuer harme,..Come our louely Lady nye SHAKS. A Ship..N. Rivers Mouth or Foreland MILT.

II. *adv.* Used absol. as complement or predicate (passing into *adj.*) OE.

Now is your husband nie SHAKS. So saying, he drew n. MILT. The hour is n. 1866. Phr. *N. at hand* (see HAND *sb.*). †*N. and far* (cf. FAR *adv.*).

III. *adj.* In attrib. use.

Is there any nigher way to lead unto damnation? 1547. Signe of n. battail, or got victory SPENSER. The n. trace-chain of the n. horse 1844.

***Denoting approximation in degree or amount.* **IV.** *adv.* **1.** Nearly, almost, all but OE. †**2.** Nearly, closely –1587. **3.** Near or close (to), in respect of attainment, resemblance, †likelihood, etc. ME. **4.** as *adj.* Close, near; parsimonious 1555.

1. Thenne the quene was nyghe oute of her wytte MALORY. I gave nie five times five assaultes 1559. **2.** For I am shave as nye as is a frere CHAUCER. **3.** Her sarcasms and self-will..go n. to confirm it L. HUNT.

Nigh (nəi), *v.* Now *rare.* ME. [f. NIGH *adv.*] **1.** *trans.* To go, come, or draw near to; to approach closely. **2.** *It nighs*: It draws *to* or *towards* a time. *Obs.* or *arch.* ME. **3.** *intr.*

To draw or come near *toward* or *to* a person, place, etc. ME. **4.** To go, come, or draw near; to approach ME.

2. When it nigh'd to Christmas tide 1821. **4.** Now day is doen, and night is nighing fast SPENSER.

Nigh by, *adv.* (and *a.*) late ME. [f. NIGH *adv.* + BY; cf. NEAR BY.] †**1.** *adv.* Nearly, almost (*rare*) –1448. **2.** Near to; near at hand 1500.

Nigh hand, *adv.* OE. [f. NIGH *adv.* + HAND *sb.*; cf. NEAR HAND.] **1.** Near or close at hand; close by. **b.** Governing a *sb.* Near, close to ME. **2.** Almost, nearly ME.

2. Wasn't it enough for you to nigh-hand kill one of my horses? 1842.

Nighly (nəi·li), *adv.* [OE. *nēahlīće*; see NIGH *adv.*, -LY².] **1.** Nearly, almost. †**2.** Nearly, closely –1691. †**3.** Niggardly –1579.

Nighness (nəi·nės). late ME. [f. NIGH *a.* + -NESS.] The quality or state of being NIGH.

The nighnes of blood which they be of unto hym 1471.

Night (nəit), *sb.* [OE. *niht*, Angl. *næht*, *neaht* = OFris., MDu. *nacht*, OS., OHG. *naht* (Du., G. *nacht*), ON. *nátt*, *nótt*, Goth. *nahts* :– IE. **nokt-*, repr. also by L. *nox*, *noct-*, Gr. *νύξ*, *νυκτ-*, Skr. *náktā*, *náktis*.] **1.** The period of darkness between day and day; that part of the natural day (of 24 hours) during which no light is received from the sun; the time between sunset and sunrise or dusk and dawn. **b.** The darkness which prevails during this time; the dark 1855. **2.** The close of daylight ME. **3.** With *a* and *pl.* One of the intervals of darkness between two days OE. **4.** With possessive pronouns: The particular night on which a person performs some duty (†receives visitors, etc.). Also *n. out*, the evening on which a domestic servant is free to go out. 1525. **b.** The kind of night one has had, or usually has 1667.

1. Yᵉ nyghte..gyueth triews to alle labours, and by slepyng maketh swete alle peynes and traueylles CAXTON. Phr. *As black, dark*, etc., *as n.* *Personified* (*as a female being*). They must for aye consort with blacke browd n. SHAKS. *fig.* Yet hath my n. of life some memorie SHAKS. Dido.. clos'd her Lids at last, in endless N. DRYDEN. **b.** I heard The shrill-edged shriek..divide the shuddering n. TENNYSON. **2.** *Mids. N.* III. ii. 275. **3.** Now will he lie ten nights awake caruing the fashion of a new dublet SHAKS. A Crown..Brings sleepless nights MILT. The missing of an Opera the first N. ADDISON. *Christmas*, *first*, *Midsummer*, *wedding n.*, etc.; see these words. Phr. *To make* (or *have*) *a n. of it*, to spend the n. in enjoyment or revelling. *A n. out*: a night spent away from home, esp. in amusement. **4.** Her annual n. (= benefit n.) DICKENS. **b.** My nights are very restless and tiresome JOHNSON.

Phrases. **a.** Adverbial. *N. and day*, always, continually. *N.* (*n*)*or day*, by n. or by day. *All*, or *the whole, n.* (*long*), throughout the n. **b.** Prepositional. *By n.*, during the n., in the night-time. *By n. and day*, always, at any time. *At n.*, at nightfall, in the evening. Also designating the hours of darkness, esp. up to midnight. †*On nights*, by n. (habitually). Also A-NIGHTS, *o'* and *in nights*. So *At nights*, *of nights*. *On* (*upon*), *in*, or *of the n.*, by n., during the n. Now only with *in*.

attrib. and *Comb.* **1.** General: as *n.-bringing*, etc.: *n. clad*, *-enshrouded*, etc.; *n.-black*, *-swift*, etc.; in sense of 'by n.', 'during the n.', as *n.-blowing*, *-warbling*, etc.; *n.-angling*, etc.; *n.-fallen*, *-scented*, etc.; in senses 'of n.', 'existing, prevailing, taking place, etc., during the n.', as *n.-air*, *-attack*, *-brawl*, *-fears*; with sense '(intended to be) worn or used during the n.', as *n.-attire*, *-bell*; with sense 'acting, or on duty or abroad, during the n.', as *n.-attendant*, *-brawler*, *-nurse*, *-porter*; so *n. duty*. Also with names of animals, birds, plants, etc., as *n.-dog*, *-moth*, *-warbler*, *-weed*, *-willow-herb*.

2. Spec.: as **n.-bag,** a travelling bag containing necessaries for the n.; **-blue,** a dyestuff giving a blue which retains its colour under artificial light; **-boat,** a passenger-boat which travels by n.; **-cart,** a cart for removing night-soil; **-chair,** a commode for use by n.; **-cloud,** the form of cloud known as *stratus*; **-club,** a club frequented during the night hours, esp. for drinking and dancing; **-eyed** *a.*, capable of seeing in the night-time; **-fire,** a fire kindled at, or for the n.; **-line,** a line with baited hooks set to catch fish by n.; **-rider,** one who rides on horseback by night, esp. *U.S.* one who damaged tobacco plantations; **-school,** a school held in the evening, esp. for those who have ceased to attend a day-school; **-sight,** = NYCTALOPIA; **-singer,** a bird that sings by n.; *spec.* the sedge-warbler; **-soil,** excrementitious matter removed by night from cesspools, etc.; **-stick,** *U.S.* a strong stick carried by a policeman at night; **-sweat,** profuse perspiration occurring during the n., symptomatic of certain diseases; **-wanderer,** one who or that which wanders by n.; one who is travelling by n. (SHAKS. and MILT.); so **-wandering,** *ppl. a.*; **-water,** water which collects or is stored during the n.

Night (nəit), *v.* ME. [f. the sb.] **1.** *intr.* To spend or pass the night; to remain or lodge for the night. Now *rare.* †**2.** *impers.* To grow dark –1520. †**3.** *pass.* To be overtaken by night –1641.

Ni·ght-bird. 1546. [f. NIGHT *sb.* + BIRD.] **1.** A bird of nocturnal habits; *esp.* the owl or the nightingale 1608. **2.** *transf.* One who goes about at night, *esp.* a night-thief.

Ni·ght-bli:ndness. 1754. [f. NIGHT *sb.* + BLINDNESS.] *Path.* = NYCTALOPIA. So **Ni·ght-blind** *a.* 1898.

Ni·ght-cap. late ME. [f. NIGHT *sb.* + CAP *sb.*¹] **1.** A covering for the head, worn esp. in bed. **2.** An alcoholic drink taken immediately before going to bed to induce sleep 1818.

1. *transf.* They say in Wales, When certain Hills have their Night-caps on, they mean mischief BACON.

Ni·ght-ce:llar. 1743. [f. NIGHT *sb.* + CELLAR *sb.*] A cellar serving as a low-class tavern or place of resort during the night.

Ni·ght-clothes. 1602. [f. NIGHT *sb.* + CLOTHES.] **1.** Such garments as are worn in bed. †**2.** Négligé or informal dress worn in the evening –1751.

2. My Lady Castlemaine, who looked prettily in her night-clothes PEPYS.

Ni·ght-crow. Now *arch.* ME. [f. NIGHT *sb.* + CROW *sb.*¹] A bird supposed to croak or cry in the night and to be of ill omen; prob. an owl or a nightjar. Also *transf.* of persons.

Ni·ght-dress. 1712. [f. NIGHT *sb.* + DRESS *sb.*] A night-gown or other dress worn in bed.

Ni·ghted, *ppl. a.* 1604. [f. NIGHT *v.* + -ED¹.] **1.** Made dark or black as night SHAKS. **2.** Benighted 1640.

†**Ni·ghtertale.** Chiefly *north.* and *Sc.* ME. [prob. – ON. *náttarþel* (f. *náttar*, gen. of *nátt* NIGHT *sb.* + *þel* groundwork, stuff, etc.) with assimilation to *tale* reckoning.] Night-time, the night. Only in phr. *by*, *on*, *a* (etc.) *n.* –1670.

Ni·ghtfall. 1611. [f. NIGHT *sb.* + FALL *sb.*¹] **1.** The coming on of night; the time of dusk 1700. **2.** That which falls at night (*rare*) 1611.

Ni·ght-glass. 1779. [f. NIGHT *sb.* + GLASS *sb.*] *Naut.* A short refracting telescope for use at night.

Ni·ght-gown. late ME. [f. NIGHT *sb.* + GOWN *sb.*] **1.** A dressing-gown. Now only *Hist.* †**2.** A kind of gown worn by ladies in the 18th c., orig. as an evening dress –1778. **3.** A long, loose, light garment worn by women or children in bed 1822.

Ni·ght-hag. Now *rare.* 1666. [f. NIGHT *sb.* + HAG *sb.*¹] A female demon supposed to ride the air by night; the nightmare.

Ni·ght-hawk. 1611. [f. NIGHT *sb.* + HAWK *sb.*¹] **1.** A name for various birds; esp. the Nightjar or Goatsucker. **2.** *fig.* One who seeks his prey by night 1818.

Nightingale (nəi·tiŋgēⁱl). [ME. *nihtingale* (XIII), alt. of *nihtegale*, OE. *nihtegala* = OS. *nahta-*, *nahtigala* (Du. *nachtegaal*), OHG. *nahta-*, *nahtigala* (G. *nachtigall*), ON. *nǽtrgali*; f. Gmc. **naχt(i)-* NIGHT + **ʒalan* sing.] A small reddish-brown or tawny migratory bird, *Daulias* (*Luscinia*) *luscinia*, celebrated for the sweet song of the male heard by night during the breeding season. Applied with qualification to other sweet-singing birds. **b.** *Dutch n.*, a frog 1769.

1. The lorn n. Mourns not her mate with such melodious pain SHELLEY. *transf.* His voice..was so naturally musical, that..honest Tom Southerne used always to call him [Pope] The little n. 1751.

Ni·ghtjar. 1630. [f. NIGHT *sb.* + JAR *sb.*¹] A name for the GOATSUCKER, from the peculiar whirring noise which the male makes during the period of incubation. Also applied to other birds of the genus *Caprimulgus* 1712.

Ni·ghtless, *a.* 1613. [f. NIGHT *sb.* + -LESS.] Having no night.

Ni·ght-light. 1648. [f. NIGHT *sb.* + LIGHT *sb.*] **1.** The faint light which is perceptible in the night. **2.** A light which burns or shines during the night 1839. **b.** A short thick candle, a wick, etc., designed to burn during the night, e.g. in sick-rooms, etc. 1844.

Ni·ght-long, *a.* and *adv.* 1850. [f. NIGHT *sb.* + LONG *a.*] **1.** *adj.* That lasts or has lasted the whole night. **2.** *adv.* During the whole night 1870.

Nightly (nəi·tli), *a.* [OE. *nihtlić*; see NIGHT *sb.* and -LY¹.] **1.** Coming or happening by night; done by night. **b.** Happening every night 1705. **2.** Of or pertaining to the night; used by night; acting by night ME. **b.** Dark as, or with, night; resembling night 1602.

2. Some pilgrim..With many a tale repays the n. bed GOLDSM. **b.** Good Hamlet cast thy n. colour off SHAKS.

Nightly (nəi·tli), *adv.* 1457. [f. NIGHT *sb.* + -LY².] **1.** Every night. **2.** At or by night; during the night 1592.

1. The clamorous Owle that n. hoots SHAKS. **2.** When the blue wave rolls n. on deep Galilee BYRON.

Ni·ghtman. 1606. [f. NIGHT *sb.* + MAN *sb.*] A man employed during the night to empty cesspools, etc., and to remove night-soil.

Nightmare (nəi·tmēᵊɹ), *sb.* ME. [f. NIGHT *sb.* + MARE².] **1.** A female monster supposed to settle upon people and animals in their sleep producing a feeling of suffocation. **2.** A feeling of suffocation or great distress felt during sleep, from which the sleeper vainly tries to free himself; a bad dream producing these or similar sensations 1562.

1. *fig.* For weeks past this n. of war has been riding us THACKERAY. **2.** A good remedy agaynst the stranglyng of the nyght mare 1562. *attrib.* A n. sleep CARLYLE. *fig.* Quilp was a perpetual nightmare to the child DICKENS. Hence **Ni·ght-mare** *v. trans.* to beset as by a n. Also *fig.*

Ni·ght-owl. 1513. [f. NIGHT *sb.* + OWL *sb.*] An owl which flies especially by night.

Ni·ght-piece. 1605. [f. NIGHT *sb.* + PIECE *sb.*] A painting or picture representing a night-scene.

Ni·ght-rail. Now only *Hist.* or *dial.* 1552. [f. NIGHT *sb.* + RAIL *sb.*¹] A loose wrap, dressing-gown, or negligee.

Ni·ght-ra:ven. Now only *poet.* [OE. *nihthræfn*; see NIGHT *sb.* and RAVEN *sb.*] A nocturnal bird, variously identified as a night-owl, night-heron, or night-jar, or imagined as a distinct species.

Where brooding darkness spreads his jealous wings, And the night-Raven sings MILT.

Ni·ght-sea:son. *arch.* 1535. [f. NIGHT *sb.* + SEASON *sb.* II.] Night-time.

Nightshade (nəi·tʃēⁱd). [OE. *nihtscada*, corresp. to MLG., MDu. *nachtschade*, OHG. *nahtscato* (G. *nachtschatten*); app. f. NIGHT *sb.* + SHADE *sb.*, prob. with allusion to the poisonous or narcotic properties of the berries.] **1. a.** A plant of the genus *Solanum*, esp. *S. nigrum* (Black N.), with white flowers, and black poisonous berries, or *S. dulcamara* (Woody N.), with purple flowers, and bright red berries. **b.** A plant of the genus *Atropa*, Deadly N. or BELLADONNA. **2.** Used with specific names to denote species of *Solanum*, *Atropa*, etc. 1839.

2. Enchanter's N. (see ENCHANTER). **Sleeping** or **Sleepy N.** = *Deadly N.* **Stinking N.,** Henbane. **Three-leaved N.,** a N. Amer. plant (*Trillium*), having simple stems with three leaves at the top.

Ni·ght-shift. 1710. [f. NIGHT *sb.* + SHIFT *sb.*] †**1.** A shift worn by women at night –1727. **2.** A shift, or gang of workmen, employed during the night 1839; the time the shift lasts 1860.

Ni·ght-shirt. 1857. [f. NIGHT *sb.* + SHIRT *sb.*] A long shirt worn by men or boys in bed.

Ni·ght-spell. late ME. [f. NIGHT *sb.* + SPELL *sb.*¹] †**1.** A spell used against harm by night –1674. **2.** A spell used to cause harm by night 1589.

Ni·ght-tide. late ME. [f. NIGHT *sb.* + TIDE *sb.*] **1.** Night-time. **2.** A tide of the sea occurring at night 1795.

Ni·ght-time. late ME. [f. NIGHT *sb.* + TIME *sb.*] The time between evening and morning; the time of night or darkness.

Ni·ght-wa:lker. 1447. [f. NIGHT *sb.* + WALKER *sb.*¹] **1.** One who walks about by night, esp. with criminal intentions; a bully or thief. Now *rare.* (Common in 17th c.) †**b.** A prostitute –1825. **2.** An animal that moves about by night 1686. So **Ni·ght-walking** *vbl. sb.* and *ppl. a.*

Ni·ght-watch. OE. [f. NIGHT *sb.* + WATCH *sb.*] **1.** A watch or guard kept during the night; the time such a watch is kept. **2.** The person or persons keeping such a watch. late ME. **3.** One of the (three or four) watches into which the night was divided by the Jews and Romans; hence, any similar period. Usu. in *pl.* ME.

3. I..meditate on thee in the night-watches *Ps.* 63:6. So **Ni·ght-watcher; -watching** *vbl. sb.* and *ppl. a.*

Ni·ght-wa:tchman. 1874. [f. NIGHT *sb.* + WATCHMAN.] A watchman who is on duty by night.

Ni·ght-work, *sb.* 1594. [f. NIGHT *sb.* + WORK *sb.*] Work done, or to be done, during the night.

Nighty (nəi·ti). 1895. [f. NIGHT-DRESS or NIGHT-GOWN + -Y[6].] A familiar (orig. nursery) name for a night-gown or night-dress.

Nigrescent (nəigre·sĕnt, nig-), *a.* 1755. [– *nigrescent-*, pr. ppl. stem of L. *nigrescere* grow black, f. *niger* black; see -ESCENT.] Blackish, somewhat black. So **Nigre·scence,** the process of becoming black; blackness; *spec.* darkness of hair, eyes, or complexion 1856.

Nigrify (ni·grifəi), *v.* 1656. [In mod. use f. L. *niger* black + -FY.] *trans.* To blacken.

Nigrine (ni·grəin). Also **-in.** 1805. [f. L. *niger* black + -INE[5].] *Min.* A black ferruginous variety of rutile.

Nigritian (nigri·ʃ[i]an). 1733. [f. *Nigritia* (see def.) + -AN.] **A.** *adj.* Of or belonging to Nigritia, a region nearly co-extensive with the Sudan, the home of the most pronounced types of the Negro race; of or belonging to the Negro race. **B.** *sb.* An inhabitant of Nigritia 1881.

Nigritude (ni·gritiūd). 1651. [– L. *nigritudo*, f. *niger, nigr-*; see -TUDE.] Black; *concr.* a black thing.

Nigromancer, -mancy, etc.; see NECRO-.

Nigrosine (ni·grŏsin). Also **-in.** 1892. [f. L. *niger* black + -OSE[2] + -INE[5].] *Chem.* A blue-grey or blue-black colouring matter derived from aniline hydrochlorate.

‖**Nigua** (ni·gwă). 1622. [Sp.] The chigoe or jigger.

‖**Nihil** (nəi·hil). 1579. Earlier **Nichil** (1500). [L. *nihil*, in med.L. *nichil* nothing.] **1.** A thing of no worth or value (*rare*). **2.** *Law.* The return made by the sheriff to the exchequer in cases where the party named in the writ had no goods on which a levy could be made 1629.

Nihilism (nəi·(h)iliz'm). 1817. [f. L. *nihil* nothing + -ISM; in philos. uses after G. *nihilismus* (F. H. Jacobi 1799); extended to the political sense after Fr. *nihilisme* (Russ. *nigilizm*).] **1.** Negative doctrines in religion or morals; total rejection of current religious beliefs or moral principles. **2.** *Philos.* A form of scepticism, involving the denial of all existence 1836. **3.** The doctrines or principles of the Russian Nihilists 1868.

Nihilist (nəi·(h)ilist). 1836. [f. as prec. + -IST; in philos. use after G. *nihilist* (Jean Paul 1804), Fr. *nihiliste* (1793); extended to the political sense after Fr. *nihiliste* (1793).] **1.** One who professes nihilism in philosophy or religion. **2.** A member of a Russian revolutionary party professing extreme anti-social principles 1871. Hence **Nihili·stic** *a.*

Nihility (nəihi·lĭti). 1678. [– med.L. *nihilitas*, f. L. *nihil* nothing; see -ITY. Cf. Fr. †*nihilité*.] The quality or state of being nothing; non-existence, nullity. **b.** With *a* and *pl.* A mere nothing; a non-existent thing 1765.

Nil[1]. Now *rare* or *Obs.* 1597. [– Arab. – Pers. *nīl*; see ANIL.] **1.** The indigo plant; indigo dye 1598. **2.** A species of convolvulus with blue flowers.

‖**Nil**[2]. 1833. [L., contr. f. NIHIL.] Nothing.

Nilgai (nī·lgai). 1882. [– Hindi *nīlgāī*, f. *nīl* blue + *gāī* cow; see NYLGHAU.] = NYLGHAU.

Nill (nil), *v.* Now *arch.* [OE. *nyle* (pres. tense) = OFris. *nil, nel*; f. NE + *wile* WILL *v.*[1]] **1.** *intr.* To be unwilling, not to will. **b.** In the phrases *n. he, will he*; *nilling, willing*, etc. ME. **2.** *trans.* Not to will (a thing); to refuse; to negative, etc. OE.

1. If I may rest, I nill live in sorrowe SPENSER. **b.** Nylle he wille he, he shalle put forthe his honde 1440. **2.** So as to will what he wills..and to n. what he nills 1708. Hence †**Nill** *sb.* a disinclination or aversion to something –1677.

Nilometer (nəilǫ·mĭtəɹ). 1707. [– Gr. Νειλομέτριον, after words in -METER.] A graduated pillar or the like, to show the height to which the Nile rises during its annual floods.

Nilot (nəi·lǫt). 1893. [f. *Nile* + -OT[2], or – Gr. Νειλώτης.] A native inhabitant of the banks of the Upper Nile.

Nilotic (nəilǫ·tik), *a.* 1653. [– L. *Niloticus*, – Gr. Νειλωτικός, f. Νεῖλος the Nile; see -OTIC.] Of or pertaining to the Nile, the Nile region, or its inhabitants or languages.

Nim, *v.* Now only *arch.* [OE. *niman* = OFris. *nima*, OS. *niman* (Du. *nemen*), OHG. *neman* (G. *nehmen*), ON. *nema*, Goth. *niman* :– Gmc. **neman*, rel. to Gr. νέμειν deal out, distribute, possess, occupy.] †**1.** *trans.* To take, in various senses –1566. †**2.** *intr.* To betake oneself, to go –1430. **3.** *trans.* To steal, filch, pilfer 1606. Also *intr.* (Common in 17th c.)

3. The thieuing knaue the purse he nimbly nims 1630.

Nimb (nimb). 1849. [– L. NIMBUS. Cf. Fr. *nimbe.*] A nimbus or halo. Hence **Nimbed** *a.*

Nimble (ni·mb'l), *a.* (and *adv.*) [ME. *nemel* (XIII), later *nemble, neam(b)le*, app. repr. OE. *nǣmel* quick at seizing, f. **nǣm-* **nem-* take, NIM; superseded by *nymel* (XV), later *nymble*, which may repr. either a phonetic development or an OE. **nimol* (cf. *numol* grasping, biting); see -LE. For the intrusive *b* cf. THIMBLE.] †**1.** Quick at comprehending or learning; hence wise –1483. **2.** Quick and light in movement or action; agile, active, swift ME. **3.** Of the mental faculties, etc.: Quick in devising, designing, etc.; acute, alert 1589. **b.** Of persons: Quick or ready-witted 1604. **c.** Cleverly or smartly contrived 1602. **4.** Quick or ready *at* or *in* (or *to* do) something 1591. †**5.** Quasi-*adv.* Nimbly 1568.

2. Now see him mounted once again Upon his n. steed COWPER. The 'n. ninepence' being considered 'better than the slow shilling' 1851. **3. b.** A n. dialectician 1893.

Comb.: *n.-fingered, -footed, -witted* adjs.; also **n.-come-quick** *a.*, of rapid growth. Hence **Ni·mble** *v.* †*trans.* to make n.; *intr.* to move nimbly. Now *rare* or *Obs.* **Ni·mbling** *vbl. sb.* and *ppl. a.* **Ni·mbleness. Ni·mbly** *adv.*

Nimbus (ni·mbŏs). *Pl.* **nimbi** (*rare*). 1616. [– L. *nimbus* rain, cloud, aureole.] **1.** A bright cloud, or cloudlike splendour, imagined as investing deities when they appeared on earth. **2.** *Art.* A bright or golden disc surrounding the head, esp. of a saint. Cf. AUREOLE 2, HALO *sb.* 2. 1727. **3.** *Meteorol.* A rain-cloud 1803.

1. *transf.* The romantic old castle surrounded by the n. of both history and romance 1881. **2.** At Venice, one only knows a fisherman by his net, and a saint by his n. RUSKIN. **3.** A rainy south-wester..was now spreading with its black n. over the bay 1856. Hence **Ni·mbused** *a.* 1852.

Nimiety (niməi·ĕti). 1564. [– L. *nimietas*, f. *nimis* too much; see -ITY.] Excess, redundancy; an instance of this.

Ni·miny-pi·miny. 1801. [Jingling formation based on NAMBY-PAMBY; cf. MIMINY-PIMINY.] Mincing, affected; lacking in force or spirit.

A n. creature, afraid of a petticoat and a bottle STEVENSON.

Nimious (ni·miəs), *a.* 1485. [f. L. *nimius*, f. *nimis* too much; see -OUS.] Overmuch, excessive. Now chiefly as a Sc. legal term.

Nimmer (ni·məɹ). ME. [f. NIM *v.* + -ER[1].] One who takes. **b.** A pilferer, a thief 1608.

Nimrod (ni·mrǫd). 1545. [– Heb. *Nimrōd* valiant, strong; see Gen. 10:8, 9.] †**1.** A tyrant –1697. **2.** A great hunter 1712.

Nincom, -cum, abbrev. ff. NINCOMPOOP.

Nincompoop (ni·nkǫmpūp). 1676. [The earliest forms suggest deriv. from a proper name, such as *Nicholas* or *Nicodemus* (cf. Fr. *nicodème* simpleton) + the word repr. by †*poop* cheat, befool (XVI–XVII); alt. of the first syll. to *nin-* is prob. due to NINNY.] A fool, blockhead, simpleton, ninny.

An old Ninny hammer, a Dotard, a N. 1713.

Nine (nəin), *a.* and *sb.* [OE. *nigon* = OFris. *nigun*, OS. *nigun, -on* (Du. *negen*) :– **niʒun*, var. of Gmc. **niwun* (repr. by OHG. *niun*, G. *neun*, ON. *níu*, Goth. *niun*) :– IE. **(e)newn̥*, repr. by L. *novem*, Gr. ἐννέα, Skr. *návan*.] The cardinal number next after eight; symbols 9 or ix. **A.** *adj.* **1.** In concord with sb. expressed. (Also coupled with a higher cardinal numeral, as *n. and twenty.*) **2.** With sb. unexpressed OE. **b.** Of the hour of the day 1548.

1. When I was crown'd, I was but n. moneths old SHAKS. **2.** Fancies..too greene and idle For Girles of n. SHAKS. N. of the strongest men of his band SCOTT. I started at n. next morning BORROW. *The N.*, the nine Muses. **b.** *N. o'clock*, attrib. with ref. to the left-hand position of the hour hand at that time. It was a '9 o'clock wind'..It blew from the left side of the rifleman 1894.

Phrases. *A n. days' wonder*, in ref. to the time a novelty is said to hold attention; also applied to an event of temporary interest. *N. times* (etc.) *out of ten*, in the great majority of cases. *Possession is n. points of the law*: see POSSESSION.

Comb., as *n.-feet, -foot, -hole, -pound*, etc.; *n.-year-old* sb. and adj.; *n.-lived, -tailed*, etc.; *n.-pounder*; also **n.-bark,** an Amer. shrub, *Spiræa opulifolia*, having many layers of bark; **nine-men's morris**; see MORRIS *sb.*[2]

B. *sb.* **1.** The number nine; the figure or symbol representing this. late ME. **2. a.** *Cards.* A card marked with nine pips 1599. **b.** A set of nine persons, players, etc. 1860. **3.** *Long n.*: **a.** A nine-pounder gun 1799. **b.** *U.S.* A kind of cigar 1837. **4.** (*Up*) *to the nines* (rarely *nine*), to perfection 1787.

4. When she's dressed up to the nines for some grand party T. HARDY.

Nine-eyed (nəi·n,əid), *a.* 1694. Having nine eyes. †**1.** As an opprobrious epithet (*rare*) –1703. **2.** *Nine-eyed eel*, the lamprey. Sc. 1810. So **Nine-eyes** (*dial.*) 1841.

Ninefold (nəi·nfōᵘld). OE. [f. NINE + -FOLD.] **A.** *adj.* **1.** Nine times as great or numerous. **2.** Consisting of nine folds or parts. Also (with sb. in *pl.*): Nine in number 1594. **B.** *sb.* An attendant company of nine 1605.

A. 1. A n. woe remains behind HOOD. **2.** N. harmony MILT. **B.** *Lear* III. iv. 126.

C. *adv.* To nine times the number 1849.

Nine-holes. 1573. **a.** A game in which the players endeavour to roll small balls into nine holes made in the ground, each hole having a separate scoring value. **b.** A similar game played with a board having nine holes or arches.

Ni·ne-ki:ller. 1801. [tr. Du. *negendooder* or G. *neuntöter*.] The butcher bird or shrike (*Lanius excubitor* or *L. borealis*).

Ninepence (nəi·npĕns). 1606. **1.** The sum of nine pence. **2.** A coin of the value of nine pence. (In former English use applied to the Irish shilling. In U.S. a name for the Sp. real = 12½ cents.) 1663.

1. Phr. *As right as n.* 1890. **2.** *Nimble n.*: see NIMBLE *a.*

Ninepenny (nəi·npĕni), *sb.* and *a.* 1826. **A.** *sb.* A coin equal in value to nine pennies 1830. **B.** *adj.* **1.** Of the value of ninepence 1894. **2.** *N. marl* = Nine men's morris 1826.

Ninepins (nəi·npinz), *sb. pl.* 1580. [PIN *sb.* IV. 2.] **1.** A game in which nine 'pins' are set up to be knocked down by a ball or bowl thrown at them. **2.** The pins with which this game is played; also sing. one of these 1664. **3.** *attrib.* as *n. alley, yard* 1756.

Nineteen (nəintī·n, nəi·ntīn), *a.* (and *sb.*) [OE. *nigontȳne* = OFris. *niogentena*, OS. *nigentein* (Du. *negentien*), OHG. *niunzehan* (G. *neunzehn*), ON. *nítján*; see NINE, -TEEN.] The cardinal number composed of nine and ten; symbols 19 or xix. **1.** In concord with sb. expressed. **2.** With sb. understood ME. †**3.** = Nineteenth –1523.

2. Phr. *To talk* (*run*) *n. to the dozen*: to talk, or run on, at a great rate.

Nineteenth (nəintī·nþ, nəi·ntīnþ), *a.* and *sb.* [OE. *nigontēoþa*, etc., whence ME. *nintethe*, superseded by *nintenthe*; see prec., -TH[1].] The ordinal numeral corresponding to the cardinal NINETEEN. **A.** *adj.* In concord with sb. expressed or understood.

1. *The n. hole*: the convivial gathering place of golfers after play on the course.

B. *sb.* **a.** A nineteenth part. **b.** *Mus.* An interval of two octaves and a fifth. 1597. **Ninetee·nthly** *adv.* in the n. place; also as *sb.*

Nine-tenths. 1812. Nine parts out of ten; also *loosely*, nearly the whole of any number or amount.

Ninetieth (nəi·ntiėþ), *a.* (*sb.*) OE. [f. next + *-eth*, -TH¹.] The ordinal number corresponding to the cardinal NINETY.

Ninety (nəi·nti), *a.* and *sb.* [OE. *niʒontiʒ*; see NINE, -TY².] **1.** The cardinal number equal to nine tens, represented by 90 or xc. Also with omission of sb., and in comb. with numbers below ten (ordinal and cardinal), as *ninety-one, ninety-first*, etc. **2.** *The nineties*: The numbers between n. and a hundred; *esp.* the years between n. and a hundred in a particular century or in a person's life 1883.

Ninevite (ni·nĭvəit). 1550. [– eccl. L. *Ninivitæ* pl., f. *Ninive* Nineveh; see -ITE¹ 1.] An inhabitant of Nineveh.

Ninny (ni·ni). 1593. [Appellative use of *Ninny*, pet-form of *Innocent*, with prefixed *n-* (cf. *Ned*, NEDDY and -Y⁶.] A simpleton; a fool.

Ni·nny-ha:mmer. 1592. [app. f. prec.] A simpleton.

‖**Ninon** (nī·non̈). 1913. [Fr.; pet form of *Anne.*] A light semi-transparent silk material.

Ninth (nəinþ), *a.* and *sb.* [ME. *niʒon þe* (XII), a new formation superseding OE. *niʒoþa*; see NINE, -TH¹. Cf. SEVENTH.] The ordinal numeral corresponding to the cardinal NINE. **A.** *adj.* **1.** With sb. expressed or understood. **b.** The ninth day (*of* a month) 1596. **2.** *N. part* or *deal*, one of the nine equal parts into which a thing may be divided OE. **B.** *sb.* **1.** = Ninth part ME. **2.** *Mus.* The interval of an octave and a second; a tone at this interval 1591. **b.** (Also *n. chord*) A chord of the dominant seventh with the ninth added.

1. Find one n...of £57. 15*s.* 1870. Hence **Ni·nthly** *adv.* in the n. place; *sb.* the n. head of a sermon.

Niobate (nəi·ŏbeⁱt). 1845. [f. NIOBIUM + -ATE⁴.] *Chem.* A salt of niobic acid.

Niobe (nəi·ŏbī). 1589. [– Gr. Νιόβη.] In Greek myth., the name of the daughter of Tantalus, who was changed into stone while weeping for her children; hence *transf.* and *fig.*

Haml. I. ii. 149. Hence **Niobe·an** *a.* 1847.

Niobic (nəiōᵘ·bik), *a.* 1845. [f. NIOBIUM + -IC 1 b.] *Chem.* Of or pertaining to, derived from, niobium; esp. in *n. acid, oxide.*

Niobite (nəi·ŏbəit). 1854. [f. next + -ITE¹ 2 b and 4 b.] **1.** *Min.* = COLUMBITE. **2.** *Chem.* A niobic salt 1866.

Niobium (nəiōᵘ·biŏm). 1845. [f. NIOBE, daughter of Tantalus + -IUM; named by H. Rose, who rediscovered it in the tantalites of Bavaria.] *Chem.* A metallic element, occurring in tantalite and other minerals. Symbol Nb. Hence **Nio·bous** *a.* derived from n. (denoting a lower degree of oxidation than *niobic*).

Nip, *sb.*¹ 1549. [f. NIP *v.*¹] **I. 1.** The act of nipping; a pinch; a sharp bite 1551. **b.** *Naut.* Pressure exerted by ice on the sides of a vessel; the crushing effect of this 1850. **c.** *Naut.* The grip of a rope where it is twisted round something; the part of a rope held fast in this way 1841. **2.** A sharp saying, or comment; a slight rebuke, or sarcasm. Now somewhat *rare.* 1549. **3.** A check to vegetation caused by cold; the quality in wind or weather which produces this 1614. **4.** *N. and tuck* (U.S.), neck and neck, a close thing 1832.

1. b. On the following morning we sustained a slight 'n.', caused by the ice setting rapidly in towards us 1878. **2.** Many a shrewd n. has he in old days given to the Philistines, this editor M. ARNOLD.

II. †**1.** A cutpurse or pickpocket –1700. **2.** In wool- or silk-combing apparatus, a piece of mechanism which catches and carries forward the material 1884. **III.** A small piece pinched off something; a fragment, little bit 1606.

Nip, *sb.*² 1796. [prob. short for NIPPERKIN.] †**a.** A half-pint of ale –1824. **b.** A small quantity of spirits, usu. less than a glass 1869.

Nip, *v.*¹ late ME. [prob. of LDu. origin; cf. †Sc. *gnip* (XIV), †*knip* (XVI).] **I.** *trans.* **1.** To compress or catch between two surfaces or points; to pinch, squeeze sharply. †**b.** To close up (a glass vessel) by pressing together the heated end of the neck or tube –1665. **c.** *Naut.* Of ice: To squeeze or crush (the sides of a vessel) 1853. **2.** To pinch *off.* late ME. **3.** To check the growth or development of (something), as by pinching off the buds or shoots of a plant 1581. **4.** Of cold: To affect painfully or injuriously 1548. †**5.** To censure –1720. **6.** To touch (one) closely; to vex. Now *rare.* 1553. **7.** To snatch or seize smartly. Chiefly *dial.* or *slang.* 1560. **b.** *slang.* To arrest 1566.

1. They doe bite and with their teeth n. one another 1585. **2.** The small shoots..must be nipt off 1707. Phr. *To n. in the bud*, to arrest or check at the very beginning. **4.** The wind blew keenly, nipping the features DICKENS. **6.** Not a word can bee spoke, but nips him somewhere 1633. **7.** Phr. *To n. a bung* (slang), to cut a purse.

II. *intr.* **1.** To give a nip or pinch; to cause or produce pinching 1460. †**2.** *Cant.* To pick pockets, to steal –1634. **3.** *slang.* To move rapidly or nimbly 1825. Const. with *in, out, up*, etc.

3. 'N. in, sir', said the driver 1889.

Nip, *v.*² 1887. [f. NIP *sb.*²] **1.** *intr.* To take nips of liquor. **2.** *trans.* To take (liquor) in nips 1897.

Nipa (nī·pă, nəi·pă). 1588. [Sp., Pg. – Malay *nīpah.*] †**1.** A kind of toddy obtained from the spadix of the nipa palm (see 2) –1616. **2.** A kind of palm (*Nipa fruticans*), native to the coasts and islands of the Indian seas; also, the foliage of this plant 1839.

Nipper (ni·pəɹ), *sb.* 1535. [f. NIP *v.*¹ + -ER¹.] **I. 1.** One who nips (see NIP *v.*¹). **b.** *U.S.* The Cunner. and the Bluefish 1888. †**2.** *Cant.* A thief or pickpocket –1785. **3.** A boy who assists a costermonger, carter, or workman 1851. **b.** *slang.* A boy, lad 1872.

1. I offre my backe vnto yᵉ smyters, and my chekes to the nyppers COVERDALE *Isa.* 50:5. **3. b.** The mind of the East End 'nipper' is equal to most emergencies 1892.

II. 1. *pl.* An instrument, usu. made of iron or steel, having two jaws by which a thing may be seized and held firmly, or cut through, by pressure on the handles; forceps, pincers, pliers. Freq. *a pair of nippers.* 1541. **b.** *slang.* Pince-nez 1876. **2.** (Usu. in *pl.*) **a.** One of the incisors of a horse 1621. **b.** One of the great claws or chelæ of the Crustacea 1769. **3.** *Naut.* **a.** A piece of braided cordage used to prevent a cable from slipping 1627. **b.** A thick woollen mitten or glove used by codfishers to protect their wrists and hands 1897.

Nipper (ni·pəɹ), *v.* 1794. [f. NIPPER *sb.*] *Naut.* To secure (a rope) by means of crossturns; to fasten with nippers.

Nipperkin (ni·pəɹkin). Now *rare.* 1671. [rel. to LDu. *nippen* sip, whence G. *nippen*, Da. *nippe.*] **1.** A measure or vessel for liquors, containing half a pint or less 1694. **2.** The quantity contained in such a measure; a small quantity of wine, ale, or spirits. In later use chiefly *Sc.* 1671.

Nipping, *ppl. a.* 1547. [f. NIP *v.*¹ + -ING².] That nips; sharp, biting; checking growth, blighting. So **Ni·ppingly** *adv.* 1542.

†**Nippitate,** *sb.* Also **-ato, -atum, -aty.** 1575. [Of unkn. origin.] Good ale or other liquor of prime quality and strength –1693. Hence †**Nippitate** *a.* strong, good –1634.

Nipple (ni·p'l), *sb.* 1530. [Early forms also *neble, nible*, perh. dim. of NEB, NIB point; see -LE.] **1.** The small prominence in which the ducts of the mammary gland terminate externally in nearly all mammals of both sexes; esp. that of a woman's breast; a teat. **b.** *transf.* A cover to protect the nipple while a child is sucking; also, the teat of a nursing-bottle 1661. **2.** Something resembling a nipple in function and form 1573. **b.** A prominence such as marks the outlet of any secretory gland 1713. **c.** A projection of any kind having the appearance of a nipple 1839. **3.** A short perforated piece made upon, or screwed into, the breech of a muzzle-loading gun, on which the percussion cap is fixed and exploded 1822.

1. *fig.* He infected the Universitie, from which he suck'd no milk but poysoned her nipples FULLER. *Comb.* **ni·pplewort**, a common wayside annual (*Lapsana communis*). Hence **Nipple** *v.* to furnish with or as with a n. or nipples 1882.

Nippy (ni·pi), *a.* (*sb.*) 1575. [f. NIP *v.*¹ + -Y¹.] **1.** Of a nipping nature or disposition: see the vb. **2.** *slang.* Sharp, quick, nimble 1853. **B.** *sb.* [Registered trade-mark of Messrs. J. Lyons & Co., Ltd.] A waitress in a Lyons restaurant 1924.

‖**Nirvana** (nəɹvā·nă). Also **-wana.** 1836. [– Skr. *nirvāṇa*, subst. use of n. pa. pple. of *nirvā* be extinguished, f. *nis* out + *vā-* blow (see WIND *sb.*).] In Buddhist theology, the extinction of individual existence, or the extinction of all desires and passions and attainment of perfect beatitude.

†**Nis,** is not; see NE and BE *v.* –1586.

‖**Nisi** (nəi·səi). 1817. [L., 'unless'.] *Law.* A limiting term added to such words as *decree, order*, or *rule*, to indicate that these are not absolute or final, but are to be valid or take effect unless some cause is shown, or reason arises, to prevent this.

‖**Nisi prius** (nəi·səi prəi·ŏs). 1468. [L., 'unless previously'.] *Law.* A writ directed to a sheriff commanding him to provide a jury at the Court of Westminster on a certain day, unless the judges of assize previously come to the county from which the jury is to be returned 1495. **b.** The clause in such a writ beginning with these words 1543. **c.** The authority or commission to try causes conferred by this clause on judges of assize 1596. **2.** An action tried under a writ of this kind 1468. **3.** The trial or hearing of civil causes by judges of assize; court-business of this kind. Hence *Cause, Court, Justice*, etc., of *Nisi Prius.* 1543. **4.** *attrib.* as *Nisi Prius Court, sitting* 1734.

†**Nist,** for *ne wist*, knew not; see NE and WIT *v.* –1447.

‖**Nisus** (nəi·sŏs). 1699. [L., f. *niti* to endeavour.] Effort, endeavour, impulse.

This *Nisus* of the Mind to free the Body 1741.

Nit. [OE. *hnitu* = MLG., MDu. *nēte* (Du. *neet*), OHG. (*h*)*niz* (G. *niss, nisse*) :– WGmc. **χnito* :– IE. **knidā* (cf. Gr. κονίς, κονιδ- dust).] **1.** The egg of a louse or other insect parasitic on man or animals; the insect itself in a young state. †**2.** Applied to persons in contempt or jest –1632.

2. Thou Flea, thou N., thou winter cricket thou SHAKS. Phr. *As dead as a n.*

Ni·t-grass. 1847. [f. prec.] *Bot.* A species of grass, so called from its small nit-like flowers.

Nithing (nəi·ðiŋ). Now only *arch.* or *Hist.* [Late OE. *niþing* – ON. *niðingr*, f. *nið* contumely, libel, insult = OE. *nīþ* enmity, malice, affliction, OFris., OS., OHG. *nīd* (Du. *nijd*, G. *neid* envy), Goth. *neiþ*; see -ING³. Cf. NIDDERING.] **1.** A vile coward; an abject wretch; a villain of the lowest type. **2.** *N.-post* or *stake*, a post or stake set up as a form of insult to a person 1847.

Nitid (ni·tid), *a.* 1656. [– L. *nitidus*, f. *nitēre* shine; see -ID¹.] Bright, shining, glossy (*lit.* and *fig.*).

Nitraniline (nəitræ·niləin). 1846. [f. NITRE *sb.* + ANILINE.] *Chem.* Nitro-aniline.

Nitrate (nəi·trĕt), *sb.* 1794. [– Fr. *nitrate* (1787); see NITRE, -ATE⁴.] *Chem.* **1.** A salt produced by the combination of nitric acid with a base, or a compound formed by the interaction of nitric acid and an alcohol. **2.** *ellipt.* Potassium nitrate or sodium nitrate used as a fertilizer 1846. **3.** *attrib.*, as *n. deposit*; *n. bath, Photogr.* the solution of n. of silver into which the plate to be developed is placed.

Nitrate (nəi·treⁱt), *v.* 1872. [See NITRE and -ATE³.] *Chem.* To treat, combine, or impregnate with nitric acid.

Nitrated (nəi·treⁱtėd), *ppl. a.* 1694. [f. prec. + -ED¹.] **1.** Chemically treated with nitric acid (†or nitre). **2.** Impregnated with nitre 1799. **3.** Manured with nitrate of soda or potash 1841.

Nitratine (nəi·trătin). 1849. [f. NITRATE *sb.* + -INE⁵.] *Min.* Native sodium nitrate.

Nitre (nəi·təɹ). late ME. [– (O)Fr. *nitre* – L. *nitrum* – Gr. νίτρον, of Semitic origin. Cf. NATRON.] **1.** †**a.** Natron. **b.** Potassium nitrate; saltpetre. †**c.** A supposed nitrous element in the air or in plants –1796. **2.** Used allus.: **a.** In sense 1 a, in echoes of Jer. 2:22. 1587. **b.** In sense 1 b, with ref. to the use of saltpetre in gunpowder. 1649. **3.** *Cubic n.*, sodium nitrate 1782. **4.** *attrib.* as *n.-bed, -pit*, etc.

2. a. Let them take much snow and n., yet of themselues can they neuer be cleane 1612. **b.** Som tumultuous cloud Instinct with Fire and N. MILT. **4. N.-bush,** a species of *Nitraria*, a genus of plants so named because first noticed near Siberian nitreworks. (*Sweet*) *spirits of n.*: see SPIRIT.

Ni·triary. *rare.* 1839. [– Fr. *nitrière*; see NITRE and -ARY[1].] An artificial nitre-bed.

Nitric (nəi·trik), *a.* 1794. [– Fr. *nitrique* (1787); see NITRE, -IC.] Of, pertaining to, derived from, nitre. (In *Chem.* dist. from NITROUS; see -IC 1 b.)

N. acid, a highly corrosive and caustic acid (HNO_3), which is usu. obtained by treating potassium nitrate or sodium nitrate with sulphuric acid, and in its pure state is a clear colourless liquid with an acrid taste; as used in the arts for dissolving metals, etc., it is known as *aquafortis*. *N. oxide*, a colourless gas (formerly also called *nitrous gas* or *air*) obtained by the action of nitric acid on metals, esp. copper. *N. ether*, a compound obtained by the interaction of ethyl alcohol and nitric acid, also called *ethyl nitrate*.

Nitride (nəi·trəid). 1850. [f. NITRE + -IDE.] *Chem.* A compound of nitrogen with another element or radical.

Nitrify (nəi·trifəi), *v.* 1828. [– Fr. *nitrifier* (1777); see NITRE, -FY.] **1.** *trans.* To convert into, impregnate with, nitre; to make nitrous. **2.** *intr.* To turn to nitre; to become nitrous 1884. Hence **Ni·trifi:able** *a.* capable of being nitrified. **Ni:trifica·tion,** the process of nitrifying; the process of impregnating with nitric acid.

Nitrile (nəi·tril). Also **-yle, -il.** 1848. [f. NITRE + -ILE.] *Chem.* A cyanogen compound of an alcohol radical, in which the alkyl grouping is directly attached to carbon and in which the nitrogen atom may be regarded as trivalent.

Nitrite (nəi·trəit). 1800. [f. NITRE + -ITE[1] 4 b.] *Chem.* A compound produced by the combination of a base or an alcohol with nitrous acid.

Nitro- (nəi·tro), comb. form. of Gr. νίτρον (as in νιτροποιός making nitre).

a. In names of acids, denoting the combination of nitric with an organic acid, as **nitromuria·tic acid,** nitrohydrochloric acid, *n.-trityric, -sulphuric.* **b.** In names of chemical compounds or groupings, denoting the presence of the nitro-grouping NO_2 in place of hydrogen, as *n.-aniline,-benzoate*; **nitromu·riate,** a compound (*of* a base) produced by treatment with nitromuriatic acid. **nitro-pru·sside,** one of a series of salts obtained by the action of nitric acid upon ferrocyanides. **nitro-su·lphate,** a compound (*of* a base) produced by the action of nitrosulphuric acid.

c. In certain names of minerals, as **nitro-ca·lcite,** native calcium nitrate; **nitroglau·berite,** a compound of sodium nitrate and sodium sulphate; **nitroma·gnesite,** native magnesium nitrate.

d. In miscellaneous combs., as **n.-a·cid,** a compound of nitric with an organic acid; **-be·nzide, -be·nzol** = NITROBENZENE; **-ce·llulose,** a compound of nitric acid and cellulose; **-co·mpound,** a compound substance resulting from the action of nitric acid; **-explo·sive,** an explosive prepared by means of nitric acid; **-pow·der,** a gunpowder prepared by means of nitric acid; **-su·bstitute,** a compound in which nitrogen peroxide is substituted for hydrogen.

Nitrobenzene (nəitrobe·nzīn). 1868. [NITRO- b.] *Chem.* A poisonous yellowish liquid, smelling like oil of bitter almonds, which is used in the preparation of aniline.

Ni·troform. 1866. [f. NITRO- d + -FORM.] *Chem.* A colourless crystallizable substance, with a bitter taste and unpleasant smell, which readily inflames and detonates.

Nitrogen (nəi·trŏdʒĕn). 1794. [– Fr. *nitrogène* (Chaptal 1790); see NITRO- and -GEN 1.] *Chem.* A 'permanent' gas (symbol N), without colour, taste, or smell, which forms about four-fifths of the atmosphere. Hence **Nitro·genize** *v. trans.* to combine with n. 1897. **Nitro·genized** *ppl. a.*, combined or furnished with n. 1843. **Nitro·genous** *a.* containing, having the nature of, n. 1828.

Nitroglu·cose. 1858. [NITRO- b.] A compound produced by the action of nitro-sulphuric acid on cane or grape sugar, used esp. in photography.

Nitroglycerine, -in (nəitrogli·sĕrin). 1857. [NITRO- d.] A violently explosive substance obtained by adding glycerine to a mixture of nitric and sulphuric acids.

Nitrohydrochlo·ric, *a.* 1836. [NITRO- a.] *Chem.* In *n. acid*, a mixture of nitric and hydrochloric acids, forming a powerful solvent, also called *nitromuriatic acid* and *aqua regia*.

Nitrolic (nəitrǫ·lik), *a.* 1892. [f. NITRE + -OL + -IC.] *Chem.* In *n. acids*, acids formed by the action of nitrous acid on any of the sodium derivatives of primary nitro-paraffins.

Nitrolim (nəi·trŏlim). Also **-lime.** 1909. [f. NITRO- + LIME *sb.*[1]] Cyanamide of calcium, used with other constituents, as a fertilizer.

Nitroma·nnite. 1857. [f. NITRO- d.] An explosive crystalline substance, obtained by treating mannite with nitric and sulphuric acids.

Nitrometer (nəitrǫ·mĭtəɹ). 1828. [f. NITRO- d + -METER.] An instrument for determining the amount of nitrogen or some of its compounds in a substance.

Nitroso- (nəitrōᵘ·so), *Chem.*, used as comb. form to indicate the presence of a nitrosyl (NO), as in *n.-compound, -derivative, -substitution*, and in specific names such as *n.-naphthaline* (*-ene*), *-phenol.*

Nitrosyl (nəi·trŏsil). 1866. [See prec. and -YL.] *Chem.* The grouping NO.

Nitrous (nəi·trəs), *a.* 1601. [– L. *nitrosus*, later – Fr. *nitreux*; see NITRE, -OUS. The mod. chem. uses date from XVIII.] Having the nature or qualities of nitre; impregnated with nitre. **b.** Mixed or impregnated with nitre so as to form an explosive compound 1667. †**c.** As an epithet applied to the air, on the supposition that it was charged with particles of nitre –1784.

N. acid, an acid having n. properties; in later use *spec.* an acid (HNO_2) which contains less oxygen than *nitric acid*. *N. gas*, a mixture of oxides of nitrogen, such as is obtained when most metals are acted on by nitric acid in the presence of air. *N. oxide*, a colourless gas (nitrogen protoxide, N_2O), which when inhaled produces exhilaration (hence called *laughing gas*) or anæsthesia. *N. salt*, a salt containing nitre.

Nitroxyl (nəitrǫ·ksil). 1869. [f. NITRO- + OX(IDE + -YL.] *Chem.* The grouping NO_2.

Ni·tta. 1797. [Native name.] *Bot.* A West African tree (*Parkia africana* or *biglandula*), bearing pods which contain edible pulp and seeds.

Nitty (ni·ti), *a.* Now *rare.* 1570. [f. NIT + -Y[1].] Full of, abounding or infested with, nits.

Niveous (ni·vĭ,əs), *a.* 1623. [– L. *niveus*, f. *nix, niv-* snow; see -OUS.] Snowy, resembling snow.

Nix. 1833. [– G. *nix* masc.] A water-elf. (Cf. next.)

Nixie (ni·ksi). 1816. [– G. *nixe* fem.; see prec.] A female water-elf; a water-nymph.

‖**Nizam** (nizā·m). 1768. [Urdu and Turk. *niẓām* – Arab. *niẓām* order, arrangement; in sense 1 short for *niẓam-al-mulk* 'government of the kingdom'.] **1.** The hereditary title of the rulers of Hyderabad belonging to the dynasty founded by Asaf Jāh, Subahdar of the Deccan, 1713–1748. **2.** The Turkish regular army; the men, or one of the men, composing this 1840.

No., Nº. 1583. Abbrev. of L. *numero* in number, abl. sing. of *numerus* = NUMBER *sb.* I. 4 and read as *number*; later, perh. after Fr. *numéro* (– It., Sp. *numero*), standing for 'number' (so-and-so). Also pl. *Nos.* 'numbers'.

No (nōᵘ), *a.* ME. [Reduced form of *nān, nōn* NONE *a.*, orig. used only bef. consonants.] **I. 1.** Not any. **2.** Qualifying a noun and adj. in close connection, usu. implying that an adj. of an opposite meaning would be more appropriate ME. **b.** Preceded by *the* or personal pronoun. Now only with *no small* or *little.* 1559. **3.** Qualifying a sb. in the predicate: Not (a). late ME. **b.** *hyperbolically.* Hardly any 1837. **4.** Qualifying a verbal sb. or gerund in the predicate, denoting the impossibility of the action specified 1560.

1. There is no neede of any such redresse SHAKS. Provb., No news, good news. *No one*, nobody. (See ONE.) **2.** This one prayer yet remains,..No long petition MILT. **b.** Falsfinge..the scriptures, to the no small admiration of all the learned readers 1559. **3.** He chose a wife..who..was no chicken SMOLLETT. **b.** The mare will get there in no time 1891. **4.** There's no accounting for tastes, sir THACKERAY.

II. In combination with sbs. or adjs. **1. a.** Denoting that the thing (or person) in question cannot properly be called by that name, as *no-faith, no-marriage*, etc. 1565. **b.** Denoting entire absence of the thing named 1603. **2.** In attrib. phrases: **a.** Denoting objection or opposition to the thing in question, as *no-popery man*, etc. 1825. **b.** Denoting absence of the thing named, as *no-confidence vote* 1832. **3.** In parasynthetic combs., as *no-coloured, -shaped*, etc. 1836; *no-trumper*, a hand at bridge on which one declares 'no trumps'.

1. Frightened with certain no-persons called ghosts FIELDING. **b.** Walking in the Middle Temple..to get them a Stomach to their No-dinners 1700. **2. a.** Just in his..'no-nonsense' style L. HUNT. **b.** A real, genuine, no-mistake Osiris O. W. HOLMES. **3.** He was a brown-whiskered, white-hatted, no-coated cabman DICKENS.

No (nōᵘ), *adv.*[1] [Two forms: (1) repr. OE. *nō*, f. *ne* NE + *ō* always, var. of *ā*, A *adv.*, O *adv.* (2) Southern and midl. representatives of OE. *nā* NA *adv.*[1]] = NOT. **1.** In ordinary uses. Now only *Sc.* **2.** Expressing the negative in an alternative choice, possibility, etc. (Usu. *whether..or no.*) late ME.

1. Alas! it's no thy neebor sweet, The bonie Lark BURNS. **2.** I am uncertain whether or no to notice..some of his previous exploits 1813.

No (nōᵘ), *adv.*[2] [OE. *nā* identical with NA *adv.*[1]] With comparatives: Not any, not at all (better, etc.). See also NO LESS, NO MO(RE.

They now no longer enjoyed the Ease of Mind.. in which they were formerly happy STEELE.

No (nōᵘ), *adv.*[3] and *sb.* ME. [Southern and midl. form of NA *adv.*[2]] **A.** *adv.* **1.** A word used to express a negative reply to a question, request, etc., or to introduce a correction of an erroneous opinion or assumption. (Cf. NAY *adv.*) **2.** Repeated for the sake of emphasis or earnestness 1500. **3.** Introducing a more emphatic or comprehensive statement, followed by *not*, or *nor*. late ME. **b.** Introducing a correction or contradiction 1616.

1. Art thou the Prophet? And he answered: No COVERDALE *John* 1:21. *ellipt.* Then I propose the question in Parliamentary form, 'Aye or no' GLADSTONE. **2.** I answered..'No, no, Sir; that will not do' BOSWELL. **3.** Who spake no slander, no, nor listened to it TENNYSON. **b.** That class of persons was composed of men—no, he could not call them men..—of individuals 1825.

B. *sb.* **1.** An utterance of the word *no*; an instance of its use; a denial 1575. **b.** A negative vote or decision 1589. **2.** *pl.* Those who vote on the negative side in a division 1657.

1. Russet yeas, and honest kersie noes SHAKS. The Everlasting No CARLYLE. **2.** The ayes proved 138 and the noes 129 1669.

Noachian (no,ē·kiăn), *a.* 1678. [f. *Noach* = *Noah* + -IAN.] Of or relating to the patriarch Noah or his time, esp. *N. deluge*, the Flood. So **Noa·chic** *a.* 1722.

Noah's Ark (nōᵘ·əz,ā·ɹk). 1611. [See *Gen.* 6:14, etc.] **1.** The ark in which Noah and his family, with the animals prescribed, were saved from the Flood. **b.** A toy consisting of an ark-shaped box, filled with figures of Noah, his family, and the animals 1846. **2.** Anything suggestive of the Ark in respect of size, shape, etc., *esp.* a large, cumbrous, or old-fashioned trunk or vehicle 1829. **3.** A small bivalve mollusc (*Arca noæ*) 1713. **4.** A cloud-formation somewhat resembling the outline of a ship's hull 1787.

1. b. Noah's Arks, in which Birds and Beasts were an uncommonly tight fit DICKENS. **2.** The barouche will hold us all. It is a regular Noah's Ark MISS BRADDON. *Noah's nightcap*, the eschscholtzia.

Nob (nǫb), *sb.*[1] *slang.* 1700. [perh. a var. of KNOB *sb.*] **1.** The head. **2.** In *Cribbage*, the knave of the same suit as the turn-up card, counting one to the holder; esp. in phr. *one for his n.* 1821.

Nob (nǫb), *sb.*[2] *slang.* Also *Sc.* **knabb, nab.** 1755. [In XVIII Sc. *nab, knab,* the local pronunc. of which may have suggested *nob* to the southerner.] A person of some wealth or social distinction.

Nob, *sb.*[3] 1774. Var. of KNOB *sb.*

Nob, *v. Boxing slang.* 1812. [f. NOB *sb.*[1] 1.] **1.** *trans.* To strike (one) on the head. **2.** *intr.* To deliver blows on the head 1812.

No ball, no-ball, *sb.* 17.. [f. NO *a.* + BALL *sb.*[1]] **1.** The words used by an umpire at cricket to signify that the ball has not been bowled in accordance with the rules of the game. **2.** A ball not bowled in accordance with the rules 1884. Hence **No-ball** *v. trans.* to condemn as a no-ball; to declare a bowler to have delivered a no-ball.

Nobble (nǫ·b'l), *v. slang.* 1847. [prob. var. of (dial.) *knobble,* var. of *knubble* knock, beat, f. KNUB, var. of KNOB + -LE.] **1.** *trans.* To tamper with (a horse) as by drugging or laming it, in order to prevent it from winning a race. **b.** To secure (a person, etc.) to one's own side or interest by bribery or other underhand methods 1865. **2.** To steal 1854. **3.** To seize, catch 1877. Hence **No·bbler,** one who nobbles horses 1854.

Nobby (nǫ·bi), *a. slang.* 1810. [f. NOB *sb.*[2] + -Y[1].] Belonging to, or characteristic of, the 'nobs'; extremely smart or elegant. Hence **No·bbily** *adv.*

Nobiliary (nobi·liări), *a.* 1762. [– Fr. *nobiliaire*; see NOBLE *a.*, -ARY[1].] Of or pertaining to the nobility.

N. particle, the preposition (as Fr. *de,* G. *von*) forming part of a noble title. He was frankly proud of..n. rank 1889.

†**Nobilitate** (nobi·litēˈt), *v.* 1538. [– *nobilitat-,* pa. ppl. stem of L. *nobilitare,* f. *nobilis*; see NOBLE *a.*, -ATE[3].] = ENNOBLE *v.* in various senses –1699. **b.** To raise (one) to noble rank –1763. Hence †**Nobilita·tion,** the action of ennobling –1775.

Nobility (nobi·lĭti). late ME. [– (O)Fr. *nobilité* or L. *nobilitas,* f. *nobilis*; see NOBLE *a.*, -ITY.] **1.** The quality of being noble in respect of excellence, value, or importance. Now *rare.* **b.** Nobleness or dignity of mind or character 1595. **2.** The quality, state, or condition of being noble in respect of rank or birth 1440. **3.** (With *the.*) The body of persons forming the noble class in any country or state 1530. **4.** (With *a.*) A noble class; a body of nobles 1612.

1. b. They say base men being in Loue, haue then a Nobilitie in their Natures, more then is natiue to them SHAKS. **2.** Their Merchants who are grown rich..buy their N. ADDISON. **3.** A street where many of the n. reside JOHNSON. **4.** A great.. Nobilite addeth maiesty to a Monarch, but diminisheth power BACON.

Noble (nōᵘ·b'l), *a.* and *sb.* ME. [– (O)Fr. *noble* – L. *nobilis,* for earlier *gnobilis* (cf. IGNOBLE), f. **gnō-* KNOW; see -BLE.] **A.** *adj.* **1.** Illustrious or distinguished by position, character, or exploits. (Now merged in 2 and 3.) **b.** Of actions: Illustrious, great 1470. **2.** Illustrious by rank, title, or birth; belonging to, or forming, the nobility of a country or state ME. **b.** Pertaining to, connected with, a person or persons of high rank. late ME. **3.** Having high moral qualities or ideals; of a great or lofty character; proceeding from, characteristic of, indicating or displaying, greatness of character or moral superiority 1503.

1. b. What poore an Instrument May do a N. deede SHAKS. **2.** More faire and famous it is to be made, then to be borne N. 1631. **b.** At your n. pleasure SHAKS. **3.** This was the Noblest Roman of them all SHAKS. Whether 'tis Nobler in the minde to suffer The Slings and Arrowes of outragious Fortune SHAKS. A zeal worthy of a nobler cause 1831.

II. 1. Distinguished by splendour, magnificence, or stateliness of appearance; of impressive proportions or size ME. **2.** Having qualities or properties of a very high or admirable kind ME. **b.** Of precious stones, metals, or minerals. late ME. **c.** Of parts of the body, *spec.* of those without which life cannot be maintained, as the heart, lungs, etc. late ME. **d.** Of hawks. (See IGNOBLE *a.*) 1614. **3.** Splendid, admirable ME. **4.** *The n. science (of defence), the n. art,* the art of (†fencing, or) boxing 1588.

1. Being past Rochester, this n. riuer goeth to Chatham 1577. **2.** Highly dangerous it is for those, that have been us'd to the most generous Wines, suddenly to abandon those N. liquors 1725. **b.** The three first [Gold, Platina, Silver] and Quicksilver commonly called N. and Perfect metals 1796. **3.** See that there be a n. supper provided SHERIDAN. *Comb.,* as *n.-couraged, -hearted, -looking* adjs.

B. *sb.* **1.** A member of the nobility ME. **2.** A former English gold coin, first minted by Edward III, having the current value of 6*s.* 8*d.* (or 10*s.*). Also *Angel, George, Rose, Thistle n.,* for which see these words. Hence †**No·ble** *v.* to ennoble –1621.

Nobleman (nōᵘ·b'lmæn). 1526. [f. NOBLE *a.* + MAN.] **1.** One of the nobility; a peer. **b.** Formerly, a nobleman's son as a member of the University of Oxford or Cambridge 1682. **2.** *pl.* The superior pieces in the game of chess 1680. Hence **No·blemanly** *a.* 1809.

Noble-minded, *a.* 1586. [f. NOBLE *a.* + MIND *sb.* + -ED[2].] Possessed of or characterized by a noble mind, magnanimous. So **Noblemi·ndedness** 1583.

Nobleness (nōᵘ·b'lnės). late ME. [f. NOBLE *a.* + -NESS.] **1.** The state or quality of being NOBLE. †**b.** With personal pronouns as a title –1772.

1. We must prove the n. of the delights, and thence the n. of the animal RUSKIN.

Noblesse (noble·s). ME. [– (O)Fr. *noblesse,* f. *noble*; see NOBLE *a.*, -ESS[2].] (Frequent down to the 17th cent., later re-adopted from Fr.) **1.** Noble birth or condition. **2.** The nobility; persons of noble rank 1598.

1. The n. of his Ancestours is forgotten JER. TAYLOR. **2.** That advantage..which the n. of France would never suffer in their peasants DRYDEN.

Noblewoman (nōᵘ·b'lwumăn). 1575. [Cf. NOBLEMAN.] A woman of noble birth or rank.

Nobly (nōᵘ·bli), *adv.* ME. [f. NOBLE *a.* + -LY[2].] **1.** With noble courage or spirit; gallantly, bravely. **2.** Splendidly, magnificently ME. **3.** In the condition or status of a noble; as or like a noble; esp. *n. born* 1591.

1. Patriots have toiled, and in their country's cause Bled n. COWPER. **2.** There I was stopped and dined mighty n. at a good table PEPYS. **3.** Thinking it better to be n. remembered than n. born RUSKIN.

Nobody (nōᵘ·bǫdi). ME. [f. NO *a.* + BODY *sb.* III. 2. Written as two words from XIV to XVIII, and with hyphen in XVII and XVIII.] **1.** No person; no one. **b.** Followed by *they, their,* or *them* 1548. **2.** A person, or persons, of no importance, authority, or position 1581. **b.** So with *a* and *pl.* 1583.
sb. III. 2. Written as two words from the 14th to the 18th c., and with hyphen in the 17th and 18th.] **1.** No person; no one. **b.** Followed by *they, their,* or *them* 1548. **2.** A person, or persons, of no importance, authority, or position 1581. **b.** So with *a* and *pl.* 1583.

1. And whan they came to the vttemost ende of yᵉ tentes, beholde, there was no body COVERDALE 2 *Kings* 7:5. **b.** N. ever put so much of themselves into their work 1874. **2. b.** Which exasperates somebodies who feel they are treated as nobodies 1899.

Nocake (nōᵘ·kēˈk). *U.S.* 1634. [Narragansett *nokehick,* Natick *noohkik* maize.] Indian corn parched and pounded into meal.

Nocent (nōᵘ·sĕnt), *a.* and *sb.* Now *rare* or *arch.* late ME. [– L. *nocens, nocent-,* pr. pple. of *nocēre* hurt; see -ENT.] **A.** *adj.* **1.** Harmful, injurious, hurtful 1485. **2.** Guilty; criminal 1566. **B.** *sb.* A guilty person 1447.

A. 2. The innocent and the n. 1678. Hence **No·cently** *adv.*

Nock (nǫk), *sb.*[1] late ME. [perh. the same word as next.] **1.** *Archery.* **a.** orig., One of the small tips of horn fixed at each end of a bow and provided with a notch for holding the string (*obs.*); in later use, the notch cut in this or in the bow itself. **b.** A small piece of horn fixed in the butt-end of an arrow, provided with a notch for receiving the bowstring; also, the notch itself 1530. Hence **Nock** *v.* to provide (a bow or arrow) with a n.; to fit (the arrow) to the bowstring.

Nock (nǫk), *sb.*[2] 1794. [– MDu. *nocke* (Du. *nock*), whence also G. *nock.*] *Naut.* In sails: The foremost upper corner of boomsails, and of staysails cut with a square tack.

Noct-, comb. form of L. *nox, noct-,* night, used in words based on L. *ambulare* to walk, as **Nocta·mbulant** *a.*, night-walking. **Nocta·mbulation, Nocta·mbulism,** somnambulism. **Nocta·mbulist,** a somnambulist; hence **Nocta·mbulistic** *a.* **Nocta·mbulous** *a.*, given to night-walking.

Nocti-, comb. form of L. *nox, noct-,* night, as in **Nocti·dial** [L. *dies* day] *a.*, comprising a night and a day.

‖**Noctiluca** (nǫktilˈū·kă). *Pl.* **-lucæ** (-lˈū̆sī). 1680. [L. *noctiluca* moon, lantern, f. *nox, noct-* night + *lucēre* shine.] †**1.** A species of phosphorus –1738. **2.** *Zool.* A marine animalcule, of a nearly spherical shape, which produces a phosphorescent appearance in the sea 1855. Hence **Noctilu·cin(e,** the light-giving substance in phosphorescent animalcules. **Noctilu·cous,** *a.* (*rare*) phosphorescent.

Noctivagant (nǫkti·văgănt), *a.* (and *sb.*). 1620. [f. L. *noctivagus* (NOCTI-, *vagari* wander) + -ANT; perh. infl. by †*vagant* wandering.] Wandering by night. Also **Nocti·vagous** 1801. So †**Noctivaga·tion,** wandering by night, esp. as an unlawful practice subject to a fine –1678.

No·ctograph. 1864. [f. L. *nox, noct-,* night; see -O-, -GRAPH.] A writing-frame for a blind person.

‖**Noctua** (nǫ·ktiuă). 1840. [L. *noctua* night-owl.] *Entom.* A moth of the genus *Noctua.*

Noctuid (nǫ·ktiuˌid). 1880. [f. mod.L. *Noctuidæ*; see prec. and -ID[3].] *Entom.* **a.** *adj.* Belonging to the family of moths named *Noctuidæ.* **b.** *sb.* A noctuid moth.

Noctule (nǫ·ktiul). 1771. [– Fr. (Buffon), – It. *nottola* bat; hence mod.L. *noctula.*] *Zool.* The largest British species of bat (*Vesperugo noctula*); the great bat.

Nocturn (nǫ·ktɒɹn). ME. [– (O)Fr. *nocturne* or eccl. L. *nocturnus, -um,* subst. use of L. *nocturnus* pertaining to the night, f. *nox, noct-* NIGHT.] *Eccl.* **1.** One of the divisions, usu. three, of the office of matins. †**2.** Any of the seven portions into which the Psalms were divided for recitation 1549.

Nocturnal (nǫktɒ̄·ɹnăl), *a.* and *sb.* 1485. [– late L. *nocturnalis* (cf. *diurnalis* DIURNAL), f. L. *nocturnus*; see prec., -AL[1].] **A.** *adj.* **1.** Of or pertaining to the night; done, held, or occurring by night. **2.** *Zool.* **a.** Active during the night 1726. **b.** Capable of vision by night 1840.

1. In this dismal gloom of n. peregrination JOHNSON. **2. a.** The hedge hog is a n. animal PENNANT.

B. *sb.* **1.** An astronomical instrument for taking observations by which to ascertain the hour of the night, etc. 1627. **2.** A night-walker; a night-hag (*arch.*) 1693. Hence **Noctu·rnally** *adv.*

Nocturne (nǫ·ktɒɹn). 1862. [– Fr. *nocturne*; see NOCTURN.] **1.** *Mus.* An instrumental composition of a dreamy character, expressive of sentiment appropriate to evening or night. **2.** *Painting.* A night-piece, night-scene 1880.

2. I can't thank you too much for the name 'Nocturne' as the title for my moonlights WHISTLER.

Nocuous (nǫ·kiuˌəs), *a.* 1635. [– L. *nocuus,* f. *nocēre* hurt; see -OUS. Cf. *innocuous.*] Noxious, hurtful; venomous, poisonous.

Nod (nǫd), *sb.* 1540. [f. next.] **1.** A short, quick inclination of the head used as a sign, esp. of salutation, assent, or to direct attention to something. **b.** A sign of this kind conveying a command, or expressive of absolute power 1567. **2.** An involuntary forward movement of the head in one who has fallen asleep or is drowsy; hence, a nap 1610.

1. A Look or a N. only ought to correct them, when they do amiss LOCKE. [The] smirk..was converted into a familiar n. MISS BURNEY. **b.** In Turkey, where the sole n. of the despot is death 1787. **2.** *transf.* Even Homer had his nods now and then 1793. *The land of Nod,* sleep. [A pun on the place-name, *Gen.* 4:16.]

Nod (nǫd), *v.* late ME. [perh. of LG.

origin; the nearest corresp. form is MHG. *notten* (in mod. G. *notteln*) move about, shake.] **I. 1.** *intr.* To make a quick inclination of the head, esp. in salutation, assent, or command. **2.** To let the head fall forward with a quick, short, involuntary motion when drowsy or asleep 1562. **b.** To be momentarily inattentive; to make a slip or mistake. In echoes of Horace *Ars Poet.* 359 (*dormitat Homerus*). 1677. **3.** To swing or sway from the perpendicular, as if about to fall 1582. **4.** To bend or incline downward or forward with a swaying movement 1606.

1. N. to him, Elues, and doe him Curtesies SHAKS. **2.** She would be seen..to n. a little way forward, and stop with a jerk DICKENS. **b.** Homer nods; and the duke of Bedford may dream BURKE. **3.** If ancient Fabricks n., and threat to fall DRYDEN. *fig.* A later Empire nods in its decay SHELLEY. **4.** Green hazels o'er his basnet n. SCOTT.

II. 1. *trans.* To incline (the head) 1553. **2.** To signify by, to say with, a nod 1713. **3.** To invite, send, or bring, by a nod 1606. **4.** To cause to bend or sway KEATS.

1. Some noddes their hedde at euery sentence 1553. **2.** He nodded assent GEO. ELIOT. **3.** Cleopatra Hath nodded him to her SHAKS.

Nodal (nōu·dăl), *a.* 1831. [f. NODE + -AL[1].] Pertaining to, of the nature of, a node or nodes, in various senses.

N. line or *point*, a line or point of absolute or comparative rest in a vibrating body or surface; cf. NODE 5 a. *N. point*, a stopping- or starting-point; a point constituting a node of any kind.

Nodated, *ppl. a. rare* or *Obs.* 1710. [f. L. *nodatus*, pa. pple. of *nodare* knot + -ED[1].] Knotted.

Nodding (nǫ·diŋ), *vbl. sb.* 1495. [-ING[1].] The action of the verb NOD, esp. in *n. acquaintance*, a slight acquaintance (*with* a person), extending no further than recognition by a nod 1711.

Nodding (nǫ·diŋ), *ppl. a.* 1590. [-ING[2].] **1.** That nods. **2.** *Bot.* (and *Entom.*) Bent or curved downward 1776.

1. The n. Violet SHAKS. The n. promontories SHELLEY.

Noddle (nǫ·d'l), *sb.* late ME. [Of unkn. origin.] **1.** †**a.** The back *of* the head –1676. **b.** The back *of* the neck. Now *dial.* 1564. **2.** *absol.* †**a.** The back of the head. **b.** The head or pate. (Colloq. or joc.) late ME. **3.** The head as the seat of mind or thought. (Colloq., and usu. playful or contempt.) 1579.

2. b. Many a sharp rap with the rolling-pin have I had over my n. THACKERAY. **3.** Slatternly girls, without an idea inside their noddles! TROLLOPE.

Noddle (nǫ·d'l), *v.* 1733. [freq. of NOD *v.*; see -LE.] **1.** *trans.* To nod (the head) quickly or slightly. **2.** *intr.* To nod or shake the head. (Now *dial.*) 1734.

1. The bishop..noddling his head, and beating time with his foot T. L. PEACOCK.

Noddy (nǫ·di), *sb.*[1] 1530. Formerly also **noddypeak, noddypoll.** [prob. subst. use of †*noddy* adj. foolish, silly (XVI-XVII), perh. f. NOD *v.* + -Y[1].] **1.** A fool, simpleton, noodle. **2.** A soot-coloured sea-bird (*Anous stolidus*) of tropical regions, having the figure of a tern, but with shorter wings and tail less forked 1578.

Noddy (nǫ·di), *sb.*[2] 1589. [Origin obscure.] **1.** A card-game resembling cribbage. Also *n.-fifteen.* Now *rare.* †**2.** The knave in various card-games. Also *knave n.* –1799.

Noddy (nǫ·di), *sb.*[3] 1639. [perh. f. NOD *v.*] **1.** A light two-wheeled hackney-carriage, formerly used in Ireland and Scotland. **2.** An inverted pendulum fitted with a spring which tends to restore it to a vertical position 1846.

Node (nōud). 1572. [– L. *nodus* knot.] **1.** A knot or complication; an entanglement. **2.** A knot, knob, or protuberance on a root, branch, etc. 1582. **b.** *Bot.* The point of a stem from which the leaves spring 1835. **3. a.** *Path.* A hard tumour; a knotty swelling or concretion, esp. on a joint affected by gout or rheumatism 1610. **b.** Any knot, lump, or knotty formation 1753. **4.** *Astr.* One of the two points at which the orbit of a planet intersects the ecliptic, or in which two great circles of the celestial sphere intersect each other 1665. **5. a.** A point or line of absolute or comparative rest in a vibrating body 1831. Cf. NODAL *a.* **b.** A central point in any complex or system 1869. **6.** *Geom.* A point at which a curve crosses itself; a double or multiple point 1850.

4. *Ascending* and *descending n.*: see the adjs. Hence **No·dous** *a.* full of knots, knotty.

Nodi-, comb. form of L. *nodus* knot, NODE, as in **Nodi·ferous** *a.*, bearing nodes.

Nodical (nōu·dikăl), *a.* 1839. [f. NODE 4 + -ICAL.] *Astr.* Of or pertaining to the nodes. *N. month*: the mean time of revolution from ascending node to ascending node.

Nodosarian (nōu·dosēə·riăn). 1858. [f. mod.L. *Nodosaria* (see def.) + -AN.] **a.** *adj.* Belonging to a family (*Nodosaria*) of vitreous-shelled foraminifera, the individuals of which are composed of a rectilinear succession of similar chambers. **b.** *sb.* An individual of this family. So **Nodo·sarine** *a.* and *sb.*

Nodose (nodōu·s), *a.* 1721. [– L. *nodosus*; see NODE and -OSE[1].] Knotty; furnished with, or characterized by, knot-like swellings.

Nodosity (nodǫ·sĭti). 1601. [– late L. *nodositas*, f. *nodosus*; see prec., -ITY.] **1.** The state or quality of being nodose or knotty 1611. **2.** A knotty swelling or protuberance.

Nodular (nǫ·diŭlăɹ), *a.* 1794. [f. NODULE + -AR[1].] **1.** *Min.* and *Geol.* Having the form of, occurring in, nodules. **2.** Of zoophytes: Having nodes on the stem 1846. **3.** *Path.* Of the nature of, characterized by, knotty tumours 1872.

Nodulated (nǫ·diŭlēɪtĕd), *a.* 1835. [f. NODULE + -ATE[3] + -ED[1].] Furnished with, characterized by, nodular growths. So **Nodula·tion,** the process of becoming n., or the result of this.

Nodule (nǫ·diul). 1600. [– L. *nodulus*, dim. of *nodus* knot; see -ULE. Cf. Fr. *nodule.*] †**1.** A small quantity of some medicinal substance tied up in a bag –1756. **2.** *Min.* and *Geol.* A small rounded lump of some mineral or earthy substance 1695. **3.** *Bot.* A small node or knot in the stem or other part of a plant 1796. **4.** *Anat.* **a.** The anterior segment of the inferior vermis of the cerebellum in the fourth ventricle 1839. **b.** A small knot or knotty tumour in some part of the body 1845. Hence **Nodulo·se, no·dulous,** *adjs.* Having little knots or knobs 1828.

‖**Nodus** (nōu·dŏs). *Pl.* **nodi.** late ME. [L., = knot.] †**1.** *Path.* = NODE 3a. –1706. **2.** A knotty point, a difficulty or complication 1727.

2. The whole n. may be more of a logical cobweb, than any actual material perplexity CARLYLE.

‖**Noel** (nōue·l). Also **noël.** 1811. [Fr.] = NOWEL.

Noesis (no,ī·sis). 1881. [– Gr. νόησις, f. νοεῖν, f. νόος mind, thought.] **a.** The sum-total of the mental action of a rational animal. MIVART. **b.** An intellectual view of the moral and physical world 1905.

Noetian (no,ī·ʃiăn), *sb.* and *a.* 1585. [– eccl. L. *Noetiani* pl. (Augustine), f. *Noetus*, a native of Smyrna and presbyter of the church in Asia Minor (*c* A.D. 230).] **A.** *sb.* A follower of Noetus in acknowledging only one person (the Father) in the Godhead. **B.** *adj.* Of, pertaining or relating to, Noetus or Noetianism 1719. Hence **Noe·tianism,** the heresy of Noetus 1874.

Noetic (no,e·tik), *a.* and *sb.* 1644. [– Gr. νοητικός, f. νοητός intellectual, f. νοεῖν think, perceive, f. νοῦς, νόος mind.] **A.** *adj.* **1.** Of or pertaining to the mind or intellect; characterized by, or consisting in, intellectual activity. **2.** Originating or existing in the mind or intellect; purely intellectual or abstract 1810. **3.** Given to intellectual speculation 1882.

1. The n. faculty, intellect proper, or place of principles SIR W. HAMILTON. **3.** The new Oriel sect was declared to be N., whatever that may mean MOZLEY.

B. *sb.* **1.** A science of the intellect. Also *pl.* 1825. **2.** That which has a purely intellectual existence or basis 1854. **3.** A member of the noetic school (see A. 3) 1882.

3. The Noetics knew nothing of the philosophical movement which was taking place on the continent M. PATTISON.

Nog (nǫg), *sb.*[1] 1611. [Of unkn. origin.] A peg, pin, or small block of wood serving for various purposes; chiefly *techn.* Also, a knag or stump on a tree or branch.

Nogs, the same as Wood Bricks...The term is chiefly used in the north of England GWILT. *Nog*, square bits of wood piled to support the roof of coal mines 1856.

Nog (nǫg), *sb.*[2] 1693. [Of unkn. origin.] A kind of strong beer, brewed in East Anglia.

Nog, *v.* 1711. [f. NOG *sb.*[1]] **1.** *trans.* To secure by nogs or pegs. **2.** To build with timber-framing and brick 1805.

Noggin (nǫ·gin). 1630. [Of unkn. origin.] **1.** A small drinking vessel; a mug or cup. **2.** A small quantity of liquor, usu. a quarter of a pint 1693. **3.** *attrib.*, as *n.-bottle, -stave* 1663.

Nogging (nǫ·giŋ). Also **-in.** 1825. [f. NOG *sb.*[1] or *v.* + -ING[1].] (Usu. *brick-n.*) Brickwork built up between wooden quarters or framing. **b.** *N.-pieces*, horizontal pieces of wood nailed to the quarters to strengthen the work in brick-nogging.

No-go. Also **no go.** 1870. [The phr. *no go* used subst.; see GO *sb.*] An impracticable situation; an impasse; an indecisive contest.

No·how, *adv.* 1775. [f. NO *a.* + HOW *adv.* Cf. SOMEHOW, ANYHOW.] **1.** In no manner, by no means; not at all. **b.** In uneducated speech freq. with another negative. **2.** In no particular manner or condition; with no distinctive appearance or character 1779.

1. b. That don't dovetail n. READE.

Noil (noil). 1623. [prob. in earlier use and – OFr. *noel* :– med.L. *nodellus*, dim. of L. *nodus* knot.] *pl.* and *sing.* The short pieces and knots of wool combed out of the long staple.

Noint, 'noint, aphetic forms of ANOINT *v.*

Noise (noiz), *sb.* ME. [– (O)Fr. *noise* outcry, hubbub, disturbance, noisy dispute = Pr. *nausa* noisy confusion :– L. *nausea* sea-sickness; see NAUSEA.] **1.** Loud outcry, clamour, or shouting; din or disturbance. †**2.** Common talk, rumour; also, evil report, scandal –1734. **3.** A loud or harsh sound of any kind; a din ME. **b.** Sounds of this kind collectively 1450. **4.** In neutral sense, a sound of any kind (defined by the context). late ME. **5.** An agreeable or melodious sound. Now *rare.* ME. †**b.** A company or band of musicians –1668.

1. Who is that at the doore y[t] keeps all this n. SHAKS. I wish you'd hold your n.! DICKENS. Phr. *Without n.*, in a quiet manner; without display, privately. **2.** All agree in the n. of more plotts 1655. **3.** I never heard any one make such a n. on a piano MISS BRADDON. **b.** Preferring quiet and solitude to the n. of a great town BERKELEY. **5.** A n. like of a hidden brook In the leafy month of June COLERIDGE. **b.** A whole n. of fiddles at his heels DRYDEN.

Phr. *To make* (or †*keep*) *a n.* (in other than literal senses): **a.** To talk much or loudly *about* a thing. **b.** To be much talked of (*arch.*). **c.** *To make a n. in the world*, to attain to notoriety or renown. *The* (or *a*) *big n.*: a person of importance (orig. *U.S.*).

Noise (noiz), *v.* late ME. [f. prec., or – OFr. *noisier, noiser* make a noise, quarrel, wrangle.] **1.** *trans.* To report, rumour, spread (*abroad*). Now somewhat *rare.* †**2.** To spread a report concerning (a person, etc.); *esp.* to speak ill of –1530. **3.** *intr.* **a.** To talk loudly or much *of* a thing. late ME. **b.** To make a noise or outcry. late ME.

1. Hit is noysed that ye loue quene Gueneuer MALORY. They have noyzed and bruted abrode most shameful sklaunders 1555. **3. a.** A plan, much noised of in those days CARLYLE. **b.** Noising loud and threatening high MILT. Hence **Noi·seful** *a.* full of noise; noisy.

Noiseless (noi·zlĕs), *a.* 1601. [f. NOISE *sb.* + -LESS.] Silent, quiet; making no stir or commotion.

Th' inaudible, and noiselesse foot of time SHAKS. Hence **Noi·seless-ly** *adv.*, **-ness.**

Noisette[1] (nwaze·t). 1837. [f. Philippe *Noisette*, who first introduced it.] A variety of rose, being a cross between a common China rose and a musk-rose.

Noisette[2] (nwaze·t). 1891. [– Fr. *noisette*, dim. of *noix* nut; see -ETTE.] A small piece of meat rolled up and filled with stuffing.

Noisome (noi·sŏm), *a.* late ME. [f. NOY *sb.* or *v.* + -SOME[1].] **1.** Harmful, injurious, noxious. **2.** Ill-smelling 1577. **3.** Disagreeable, offensive 1440.

1. He shall deliuer thee from the snare of the fouler: and from the n. pestilence BIBLE *Ps.* 91:3. **2.** Nasty streets, noisom Ditches 1678. **3.** Such a n. thing as a collection of postage stamps 1899. Hence **Noi·some-ly** *adv.* (*rare*), **-ness.**

Noisy (noi·zi), *a.* 1693. [f. NOISE *sb.* + -Y¹.] **1.** Making, or given to making, a loud noise; clamorous, turbulent. **2.** Full of, characterized by, noise 1693.

1. A n. crowd DRYDEN. **2.** A filthy and n. market MACAULAY. Hence **Noi·sily** *adv.* **Noi·siness.**

Nold(e, would not, see NILL *v.*

‖**Nolens volens** (nōᵘ·lenz vōᵘ·lenz). 1593. [L. pr. pples. of *nolle* be unwilling, *velle* be willing.] Willing or unwilling, willy-nilly.

No less, *adv.* and *a.* ME. [NO *adv.*² + LESS *a.*] Not less, as much, in various uses.

‖**Noli me tangere** (nōᵘ·ləi mī tæ·ndʒĕrī). late ME. [L., 'touch me not', occurring in the Vulgate, *John* 20:17; cf. sense 5.] **1.** *Path.* Any of several ulcerous cutaneous diseases of the face, esp. lupus and rodent ulcer. **2.** *Bot.* A species of balsam, so called from the forcible expulsion of its ripe seeds (see TOUCH-ME-NOT). Now only as part of the full botanical name, *Impatiens noli (me) tangere.* 1563. **3.** A person or thing that must not be touched or interfered with 1475. **4.** A warning or prohibition against meddling or interference, etc. 1634. **5.** A painting representing the appearance of Christ to Mary Magdalen 1680.

3. Mr. Wormwood, the *noli-me-tangere* of literary lions LYTTON. **4.** Every dish,..carrying a 'noli me tangere' on the face of it 1806. *attrib.* A sort of *noli me tangere* manner DE QUINCEY.

Noll (nōᵘl). Now *dial.* [OE. *knoll* = MDu. *nolle,* OHG. *hnol* top, summit, crown of head.] **1.** The top or crown of the head; the head generally; the noddle. †**b.** *transf.* A (dull, drunken, etc.) person –1600. †**2.** The nape of the neck; the back of the head –1720.

1. The nappy Ale makes many a drunken N. 1626.

‖**Nolle prosequi** (nǫ·lĭ prǫ·sĕkwəi). 1681. [L., 'to be unwilling to pursue'.] *Law.* An entry made upon the record of a court, when the plaintiff or prosecutor abandons part, or all, of his suit or prosecution against a defendant. Abbrev. **Nol(le pros;** also **Nolle** *sb.* and *v. U.S.*

Nolt (nōᵘlt, nǫlt). *Sc.* 1470. [Graphic var. of NOWT.] = NEAT *sb.* 2, NOWT 1.

‖**Nom** (noṅ). 1679. [Fr., 'name'.] Used in expressions denoting a pseudonym, a false or assumed name; esp. **a.** *Nom de guerre* (noṅ də gęr), lit. 'war-name', a name assumed by, or assigned to, a person engaged in some action or enterprise. **b.** *Nom de plume* (noṅ də plüm), lit. 'pen-name', a name assumed by a writer 1823.

‖**Noma** (nōᵘ·mă). 1834. [mod.L. for L. *nome* (Pliny) – Gr. νομή, f. νέμειν, νομ- feed.] *Path.* A gangrenous ulceration of the cheek or vulva, occurring mainly in young children.

Nomad (nǫ·mæd, nōᵘ·mæd), *sb.* and *a.* 1587. [– Fr. *nomade* – L. *Nomas,* pl. *Nomades* – Gr. νομάς, νομαδ- roaming about, esp. for pasture, pl. Νομάδες pastoral people, f. *nom- *nem-, νέμειν pasture; see NIM, -AD.] **1.** One of a race or tribe which moves from place to place to find pasture; hence, one who lives a wandering life. **2.** *attrib.* or *adj.* **a.** Living as a nomad; nomadic 1798. **b.** Belonging to or characteristic of nomads 1835. Hence **No·madism,** the practice, fact, or state of living a wandering life 1841. **No·madize** *v. intr.* to live, or roam about, as nomads 1799.

Nomade (nǫ·mēⁱd, nōᵘ·mēⁱd), *sb.* and *a.* 1775. [var. of prec.; in later use prob. after Fr.] = NOMAD 1. 1775. **2.** *attrib.* or *adj.* **a.** = NOMAD 2 a. 1817. **b.** = NOMAD 2 b. 1819.

Nomades (nǫ·mădīz), *sb. pl.* Now *rare.* 1555. [– L. *Nomades;* see NOMAD.] **a.** The nomad tribes or peoples mentioned by ancient writers. **b.** Such tribes as move about from place to place.

Nomadic (nomæ·dik), *a.* 1799. [– Gr. νομαδικός, f. νομαδ- NOMAD; see -IC.] **1.** Characterized by, or leading, a wandering life. **2.** Peculiar to, distinctive of, a wandering people or manner of life 1825. So **Noma·dical** *a.*, **-ly** *adv.*

No man. OE. [f. *none,* NO *a.* + MAN *sb.*] No one, nobody.

No man's land: a piece of waste, or unowned, land; in early use as the name of a plot of ground, lying outside the north wall of London, and used as a place of execution. Also *Naut.*, a space amidships used to contain any blocks, ropes, tackles, etc. necessary on the forecastle; *Mil.*, an unoccupied space between fronts of opposing forces.

Nomarch (nǫ·maɹk). 1656. [– Gr. νομάρχης or νόμαρχος, f. νομός NOME *sb.*¹; see -ARCH.] †**1.** A local ruler or governor (*rare*) –1678. **2.** The governor of an ancient Egyptian nome 1846. **3.** The governor of a modern Greek nomarchy 1880.

Nomarchy (nǫ·maɹki). 1803. [– Gr. νομαρχία; see prec., -ARCHY.] One of the provinces into which modern Greece is divided.

‖**No·mbril.** 1562. [Fr., = the navel.] *Her.* That point on an escutcheon which lies midway between the true centre (or fesse point) and the base point. Occas. vaguely alluded to as the centre of the escutcheon.

Nome (nōᵘm), *sb.*¹ 1727. [– Gr. νομός, f. νέμειν divide.] One of the thirty-six territorial divisions of Ancient Egypt.

Nome (nōᵘm), *sb.*² 1753. [– Gr. νόμος; see prec.] An ancient Greek form of musical composition.

†**Nome,** *sb.*³ 1665. [– Fr. *nôme,* second element in *binôme,* etc.; see BINOMY.] *Math.* A member of a compound quantity –1738.

Nomenclate (nōᵘ·mĕnklēⁱt), *v. rare.* 1801. [Back-formation from NOMENCLATURE.] *trans.* To assign a name or names to; to call by a certain name.

Nomenclator (nōᵘ·mĕnkleⁱtǫɹ). 1585. [– L. *nomenclator* one who names (senses 2, 3), f. *nomen* name + *calare* call.] †**1.** Used as the title of books containing lists of words; hence, a vocabulary –1707. **2.** *Rom. Antiq.* **a.** A servant or dependant who had to inform his master or patron of the names of persons, esp. when canvassing for office. **b.** A steward or usher who assigned or indicated the places at a banquet 1601. **3.** One who announces, or communicates to another the names of persons or guests 1599. **4.** One who gives or invents names for things; *esp.* in a classification of natural objects 1644.

Nomenclature (nōᵘ·mĕnklēⁱtiŭɹ, nome·nklĕtiŭɹ, -tʃəɹ), *sb.* 1610. [– Fr. *nomenclature* – L. *nomenclatura* (Pliny), f. *nomenclator;* see prec., -URE.] **1.** A name, appellation, designation. Now *rare.* **2.** A list or collection of names or particulars; a catalogue, a register 1635. †**b.** A glossary, a vocabulary –1745. **3.** The system or set of names for things, etc., commonly employed by a person or community 1664. **b.** The terminology of a science 1789. **c.** The collective names given (or to be given) to places in a district or region 1828. **4.** (Without article.) Names or designations forming a set or system 1785. **5.** (With *a* and *pl.*) A particular set or system of names or designations 1809.

2. He rank't in the N. of Fooles 1635. **3. c.** The n. of the frozen regions 1828. Hence **Nomencla·tural** *a.* relating to, or concerned with, n. **Nomenclature** *v.* to name or designate 1803.

Nomic (nǫ·mik), *a.* 1727. [f. Gr. νόμος NOME *sb.*² + -IC.] Pertaining to, having the character of, Greek musical nomes.

Nominal (nǫ·minăl), *a.* and *sb.* late ME. [– Fr. *nominal* or L. *nominalis,* f. *nomen, -in-* NAME; see -AL¹.] **A.** *adj.* **1.** *Gram.* Of the nature of, or pertaining to, a noun or nouns (*rare*). **2.** Belonging or pertaining to the nominalists; holding views akin to these (*rare*) 1528. **3.** Of the nature of, consisting in, pertaining or relating to, a name or names (as opp. to things) 1620. **4.** Existing in name only, as dist. from *real* or *actual;* merely named, stated, or expressed, without ref. to reality or fact 1624. **5. a.** Consisting of, containing, or giving names 1802. **b.** Assigned to a person by name 1882.

3. *N. definition,* a statement of all the marks which are connoted in the name of the concept. **4.** Thus..blindly adopting n. pleasures, I lost real one's CHESTERF. An action for mere n. damages 1799. **5. a.** A n. list of the officers and crew of the gunboat Wasp 1884. **b.** The shares are still n., and the original subscribers, as well as subsequent holders are liable on them 1882. Hence **No·minally** *adv.*, by name; in name, as opp. to *really.*

B. *sb.* **1.** A nominalist. Now *rare* or *Obs.* 1519. **2.** *Mus.* A note giving its name to a scale 1811.

Nominalism (nǫ·minăliz'm). 1836. [– Fr. *nominalisme* (1752); see NOMINAL B. 1, -ISM.] The view which regards universals or abstract concepts as mere names, without any corresponding realities.

Nominalist (nǫ·minălist). 1654. [– Fr. *nominaliste* (1752); see NOMINAL A. 2, -IST.] One who maintains or accepts the doctrine of nominalism. Hence **Nominali·stic** *a.* 1863.

Nominate (nǫ·minĕt), *pa. pple.* and *ppl. a.* 1485. [– L. *nominatus,* pa. pple. of *nominare;* see next, -ATE².] **A.** *pa. pple.* †**1.** Named, entitled –1567. †**2.** Nominated, appointed –1648. **B.** *ppl. a.* **1. a.** Having a special name. **b.** Mentioning a particular name. 1818. **2.** Nominated to an office. Chiefly *Sc. Law.* 1681.

Nominate (nǫ·mineⁱt), *v.* 1545. [– *nominat-,* pa. ppl. stem of L. *nominare* name, f. *nomen, -in-* name; see -ATE³.] **1.** *trans.* To call by the name of; to call, name, designate. Now somewhat *rare.* †**b.** To provide with a name –1697. **2.** To mention or specify by name. Now somewhat *rare.* 1593. **3.** To name, fix, appoint, specify. Now *rare.* 1564. **4.** To appoint (a person) by name to some office or duty 1560. **b.** To enter or put up the name of (one) as a proper person or candidate for election 1601.

1. Those animals whom we are pleased to n. 'the lower creation' 1868. **3.** Let the forfeite Be nominated for an equall pound Of your faire flesh SHAKS. **4. b.** We are thinking to augment our Club, and I am desirous of nominating you JOHNSON.

Nomination (nǫminēⁱ·ʃən). late ME. [– (O)Fr. *nomination* or L. *nominatio,* f. as prec.; see -ION.] †**1.** The action of mentioning by name –1665. †**b.** The action of appointing or the fact of being appointed (*rare*) –1753. **2.** The action (or right) of appointing a person by name to some office or duty 1454. **b.** The action of proposing as a candidate, or as a suitable person to be elected 1601. **3.** The fact or position of being nominated; freq. in phr. *to put in n.*, to nominate 1494. †**4.** Name, designation, denomination –1794. **5.** Assignation of a name or names 1552; designation by a certain name 1865.

2. He had absolute power over every n. to an English benefice FROUDE. **b.** The n. of a member for South Lancashire 1861. **3.** The commons yesterday, after they expelled Mr. Wollaston, had in n. some others 1699.

Nominative (nǫ·minătiv), *a.* and *sb.* late ME. [– (O)Fr. *nominatif, -ive* or L. *nominativus* (sc. *casus* case, Varro), tr. Gr. ὀνομαστική (sc. πτῶσις case); f. as prec.; see -IVE.] **A.** *adj.* **1.** Gram. *N. case,* that case which belongs to the subject of a finite verb (or of a participle in the absolute construction) or to a word referring thereto. **b.** Of or pertaining to the (or a) nominative case 1824. **2.** Nominated; appointed by nomination 1660. **3.** Bearing the name of a person 1872. **B.** *sb.* **1.** The nominative case 1620. *N. of address,* the vocative. **2.** A word in the nominative case; a form which is the nominative case of a word 1668. **b.** A subject (*to* a verb) 1824. Hence **Nominati·val** *a.* of or pertaining to the n. case 1843.

Nominator (nǫ·mineⁱtǫɹ). 1659. [– late L. *nominator,* f. as prec.; see -OR 2, -ATOR.] One who nominates to office or for election.

Nominee (nǫminī·). 1688. [f. NOMINATE *v.*; see -EE¹.] **1.** The person who is named in connection with, or as the recipient of, an annuity, grant, etc. 1697. **2.** One who is nominated for some office.

†**No mo,** *sb.* and *a.* [f. OE. *nā* NO *adv.*² + *mā* MO *sb.* and *a.*] No more (in number) –1813.

Nomo-, – Gr. νομο-, comb. form of νόμος law, as in **Nomo·cracy,** a system of government based on a legal code; the rule of law in a community. **Nomo·grapher** [Gr. νομογράφος], (*a*) a writer of laws, a legislator; (*b*) one skilled in nomography. **Nomo·graphy** (*a*) a treatise on laws; (*b*) the logic of the will (Bentham); (*c*) the expression of law in a written form. **Nomo·logy,** (*a*) the science of the laws of mind; (*b*) that part of Botany which relates to the laws which govern the variations of organs; (*c*) the inductive science of law.

No more, *sb., a.,* and *adv.* [f. OE. *nā* NO *adv.*² + MORE *sb.*² Cf. NO LESS.] **A.** *sb.*

Nothing more or further. **B.** *adj.* Not any more; no further. late ME. **C.** *adv.* **1.** No longer. (Passing into 2.) ME. **b.** As predicate: No longer existent; departed, dead 1601. **2.** Never again; nevermore ME. **3.** To no greater extent; in no greater degree. **4.** just as little; neither.

1. b. Cassius is no more SHAKS. **3.** Eche of them . . spared no thynge, no more than yf the Kynge of Englande had bene there in proper persone LD. BERNERS. **4.** You are not yong, no more am I SHAKS.

†**No·mothete.** *rare.* 1586. [– Gr. νομοθέτης.] A lawgiver or legislator –1641. Hence **Nomothe·tic, -al** *a.* law-giving; legislative 1619.

-nomy, a second element in compounds, repr. Gr. -νομία (related to νόμος law, νέμειν distribute) as in *autonomy, economy,* etc.; also in words formed after these, as *geonomy, zoonomy,* etc.

‖**Non** (nǫn). 1551. [L., 'not'.] The first word in many Latin phrases; see Main words.

Non- (nǫn), *prefix,* formerly often written separate, used to express negation. The earlier formations were either directly adopted from, or modelled upon, AFr. compounds in *noun-* = OFr. *non-, nom-* (mod.Fr. *non-*) :– L. *non* 'not' used as a prefix. It appears first in English towards the end of the 14th c. in *non-power* (Chaucer, Langland, Wyclif), and *non-residence, nonsuit* (Wyclif). In the majority of the compounds of *non-* the hyphen is usu. retained; but it is commonly omitted in a few, such as *nonconformist, nonentity, nonsense,* in which the etymological meaning has been lost sight of. Normally the prefix receives only secondary stress, but it has the main stress in *nonage, nonchalant, nondescript, nonsense.*

1. Prefixed to nouns of action, condition, or quality, as *non-acquaintance* = want of acquaintance, *non-adherence* = the condition or quality of not being adherent, *non-attendance* = failure or neglect to attend, *non-compliance* = failure or refusal to comply. **2.** Prefixed to agent-nouns and designations of persons and objects, as *non-abstainer* = one who is not an abstainer or does not abstain, *non-accent* = absence or lack of accent. **3.** Prefixed to adjectives, as *non-absorbable* = not absorbable, that cannot be absorbed. **4.** Prefixed to a sb. (or vbl. sb.) forming a phrase used attrib., as *non-church* people. **5.** Prefixed to an infinitive, as *non-act* = not to act, to refuse, neglect, or omit to act; also in attrib. phr., as *non-skid* tyre, *non-stop* train. **6.** Prefixed to ppl. adjs., as *non-articulated* = not articulated, *non-budding* = not budding, that does not bud. **b.** Prefixed to combs. formed with ppl. adjs., as *non-slave-grown* commodities. **7.** Prefixed to gerunds and vbl. sbs., as *non-accompanying* = failure or neglect to accompany. **8.** Prefixed to adverbs, as *non-contentiously* = not contentiously. See also Main words.

Non-abi·lity. 1477. [NON- 1.] Inability, incapacity; *spec.* inability to commence a suit at law.

Non-a·ccess. 1799. [NON- 1.] *Law.* Impossibility of access for sexual intercourse, as in the case of a husband being abroad or at sea.

Nonage (nǭᵘ·nėdʒ). late ME. [– AFr. *nounage* = OFr. *nonage,* f. *non-* (see NON-) + *age* AGE *sb.*] **1.** The condition of being under age; the period of legal infancy; minority. **2.** *fig.* The period of immaturity 1584.

1. He had passed a riotous n. STEVENSON. **2.** Nations outgrew their spiritual n. FARRAR.

Nonagenarian (nǫnădʒĭnēᵊ·riăn). 1804. [f. L. *nonagenarius* (f. *nonageni* ninety each); see -IAN, -ARIAN.] **A.** *adj.* Ninety years old, or between ninety and a hundred. **B.** *sb.* A person of such age.

Nonagesimal (nǫnădʒe·simăl). 1704. [f. L. *nonagesimus,* ordinal of *nonaginta* ninety; see -AL¹.] **1.** *adj.* In *n. degree, point:* that point of the ecliptic which is highest above the horizon at any given time, being 90° above the point at which the ecliptic intersects the horizon. **2.** *sb.* The nonagesimal degree 1789.

Nonagon (nǫ·năgǫn). 1688. [irreg. f. L. *nonus* ninth, after *hexagon.* Cf. OFr. *nonogone.*] *Geom.* A figure having nine angles; an enneagon.

Nonane (nǭᵘ·neⁱn). 1868. [f. L. *nonus* ninth + -ANE 2.] *Chem.* A hydrocarbon (C_9H_{20}), being the ninth of the methane series.

Non-appea·rance. 1475. [NON- 1.] Failure or neglect to appear, *esp.* in a court of law, as a party to a suit or as a witness.

Non-a·rcking, *ppl. a.* Also **-arcing.** 1895. [f. NON- 6 + ARC 5.] *Electr.* Of a metal: That does not form a voltaic arc or allow it to be formed.

Nonary (nǭᵘ·nări), *a.* 1666. [irreg. f. L. *nonus* ninth + -ARY¹, after *denary,* etc.] *Arith. N. scale:* a scale of notation having nine as its basis 1870.

‖**Non-assumpsit** (nǫn ăsɒ·mpsit). 1631. [L., 'he did not undertake'.] *Law.* A plea in an action of assumpsit by which the defendant denies that he made any promise or undertaking.

‖**Non avenu** (nonavnü). 1840. [Fr., f. *avenir* happen.] Not having happened.

Nonce (nǫns). [orig. in ME. phrases **for þan ane, *for þan anes,* the latter of which was altered by wrong division (see N) to *for þe nanes, nones,* lit. = for the one (thing, occasion, etc.).] **1. For the nonce: a.** For the particular purpose; expressly. *Obs.* exc. *dial.* ME. **b.** In ME. poetry used as a metrical tag, with no special meaning. **c.** For the occasion; hence, for the time being; temporarily 1589. **2.** *At the very n.:* at the very moment 1855. **3.** *attrib.* **nonce-word,** a word apparently used only for the nonce (see O.E.D. vol. I, p. xxx); so *nonce-use,* etc.

1. A Cook they hadde with hem for the nones, To boille the chiknes with the mary-bones CHAUCER. **c.** I therefore made a virtue of necessity, and was a good Catholic for the n. 1859.

Nonchalance (nǫ·nʃălăns; as Fr., nońʃalań). 1678. [– (O)Fr. *nonchalance,* f. *nonchalant;* see next, -ANCE.] The condition of being nonchalant.

Nonchalant (nǫ·nʃălănt; as Fr., nońʃalań), *a.* 1734. [– (O)Fr. *nonchalant,* f. *non* NON- + pr. pple. of *chaloir* be concerned.] Wanting in warmth of feeling; lacking in enthusiasm or interest; indifferent. Hence **No·nchalant-ly** *adv.*, **-ness.**

No·n-claim. 1488. [– AFr. *nounclaim;* see NON- 1 and CLAIM *sb.*] *Law.* Failure or neglect to make a claim within the time limited by law.

Non-coll. *colloq.* Short for next.

Non-colle·giate. 1683. [NON- 2, 3.] **A.** *adj.* Not belonging to a college; belonging to the body of students (in certain universities) not attached to any college or hall (*scholares nulli collegio vel aulæ ascripti*). Also, occas. of a university. Not having a collegiate system. 1874. **B.** *sb.* One not educated or trained in a college; one of a non-collegiate body.

Non-com. 1883. Colloq. abbrev. of *non-commissioned officer.*

Non-co·mbatant. 1811. [NON- 2.] One who is not a combatant, as a civilian in time of war; *spec.* in the army and navy, one whose duties do not include that of fighting, as a surgeon, purser, or chaplain.

Non-commi·ssioned, *a.* 1703. [NON- 6.] **1.** Of officers of the army (†and navy): Not holding a commission. **2.** Of a ship: Not put in commission 1868.

Non-commi·ttal, *sb.* (*a.*) 1836. [NON- 1.] Refusal to commit oneself to a particular view or course of action. (orig. *U.S.*) **b.** *attrib.* or *adj.* Characterized by such refusal; (*esp.* of words and actions) implying neither consent nor dissent 1851. Hence **Non-commi·ttally** *adv.* 1885.

Non-commu·nicant, *sb.* (*a.*) 1598. [NON- 2.] One who is not a communicant or does not communicate (e.g. at a particular service); in the 17th c. often *spec.,* one who did not communicate according to the rites of the Church of England. So **Non-commu·nicating** *vbl. sb.* and *ppl. a.*

‖**Non compos mentis** (nǫn kǫ·mpǫs me·ntis). 1607. [L., 'not master of one's mind'.] Not *compos mentis;* not in one's right mind. Also as *sb.* Abbrev. **Non co·mpos** 1628.

Non-compou·nder. 1651. [NON- 2.] One who does not compound; *spec. Hist.* one of that section of the Jacobites which desired the restoration of James II without imposing any conditions on him.

Non-con. 1681. Abbrev. of NONCONFORMIST.

Non-conde·nsing, *ppl. a.* 1841. [NON- 6.] Applied to a kind of steam-engine in which the steam on leaving the cylinder is not condensed in a condenser but is discharged into the atmosphere.

Non-conductor. 1759. [NON- 2.] *Physics.* A substance or medium that does not permit the passage of any form of energy (as heat or electricity). Hence **Non-conductibi·lity,** the quality or condition of being a non-conductor 1844. **Non-condu·cting** *ppl. a.* that is a non-conductor 1771. **Non-condu·ction** 1828.

Nonconfo·rming, *ppl. a.* 1646. [NON- 6.] = NONCONFORMIST *attrib.*

Nonconformist (nǫnkǫ̆nfǭ·ɹmist). 1619. [NON- 2.] **1. a.** (Usu. with capital N.) Orig., one who, while adhering to the doctrine of the Church of England, refused to conform to its discipline and practice. Now *Hist.* **b.** Later, a member of a religious body which is separated from the Church of England; in mod. use, usu. = Protestant Dissenter. **c.** *gen.* One who does not conform to the doctrine or discipline of an established church 1672. †**2.** One who does not conform to a particular practice or course of action –1685. **3.** *attrib.* or *adj.* 1641.

1. b. I suppose the Nonconformists value themselves tho upon their Conscience and not their numbers 1672. **3.** The minimum demand of the great N. party is the . . abdication of Mr. Parnell 1890. *N. conscience,* the views held to be characteristic of Nonconformists esp. as affecting their attitude on public affairs.

Nonconformity (nǫnkǫ̆nfǭ·ɹmĭti). 1618. [NON- 1.] **1.** Refusal to conform to the doctrine, discipline, or polity of an established church, orig. and now *esp.* of the Church of England; the principles and practice of Nonconformists; in mod. use, usu. = Protestant dissent. Also, Nonconformists as a body. (Usu. with capital N.) **2.** Want of conformity or refusal to conform to a rule, practice, or requirement. Const. *to, with.* 1682. **3.** Want of correspondence, agreement, or adaptability between persons or things 1672.

2. The . . sufferings caused by n. to the laws of life 1879.

Non-conta·gion. 1808. [NON- 1.] *Med.* The condition or property of being non-contagious. So **Non-conta·gious** *a.*

No·n-content. 1778. [NON- 2. See CONTENT *a.* 3 c.] **a.** In the House of Lords, one who votes 'Not content'. **b.** One who is not content 1860.

Non-contradi·ction. 1836. [NON- 1.] The absence of contradiction; in Logic, *principle* or *law of non-contradiction* = 'principle of contradiction' (see CONTRADICTION 4, quot.).

Nonda (nǫ·ndă). 1847. [Native name.] A rosaceous tree, *Parinarium nonda,* of north-eastern Australia, yielding an edible fruit.

Nondescript (nǫ·ndĭskript). 1683. [f. NON- 3 + DESCRIPT *ppl. a.*] **A.** *adj.* †**1.** *Nat. Hist.* Of a species, etc.: Not hitherto described. Also *transf.* –1820. **2.** Not easily described or classified; that is neither one thing nor another 1806.

2. Those n. animals that are neither boys nor young men 1876.

B. *sb.* †**1.** *Nat. Hist.* A species, etc., that has not been hitherto described. Also *transf.* –1817. **2.** A person or thing that is of no particular class or kind 1811.

1. *transf.* A valuable addition of nondescripts to the . . known classes, genera and species, which . . beautify the *hortus siccus* of dissent BURKE.

Nondo (nǫ·ndo). 1860. A tall, umbelliferous plant, *Ligusticum actæifolium,* found in North America.

None (nǭᵘn), *sb.* 1656. [– (O)Fr. *none* (Sp., It. *nona*) – L. *nona* (sc. *hora* hour); see NOON, NONES.] †**1.** *N. of the day:* the third quarter of the day, from 3.0 p.m. to 6.0 p.m. **2.** = NONES 2. 1845.

None (nɒn), *pron., a.,* and *adv.* [OE. *nān* = OFris. *nen,* ON. *neinn;* f. *ne* NE + *ān* ONE *a.*] **A.** *pron.* **1.** No one, not any (one), of a number of persons or things. Also, neither *of* two (now *dial.*) **2.** No one, no person, nobody. Also *n. other*, no other person (now *arch.*). OE. **b.** *pl.* No persons. (Now the commoner usage.) OE. †**c.** *N. other*, no other thing (or course); nothing else –1645. **3.** *ellipt.* Not any (such thing or person as that mentioned) OE. **b.** In predicative use, denoting lack of the essential qualities of the thing or person mentioned OE. **c.** *N. of*, not in the least 1571. **4.** No part or amount of some thing, quality, etc. ME.

1. N. of these however are known to us GOLDSM. He was n. of your hesitating half story-tellers LAMB. His understanding was n. of the clearest 1888. **2.** There is n. like her, n. TENNYSON. **b.** N. have all; all must have some 1641. **c.** Sir, this is n. other but the hand of God CROMWELL. **3.** It seems to be a much greater Affront..to have an ill opinion of him, than to have n. at all 1718. **c.** It was n. of my business DE FOE. **4.** Of that there's n., or little SHAKS.

B. *adj.* Not any; = No *a.* 1. Now *arch.* (In later use only bef. vowels and *h*, and after 1600 usu. repl. by *no.*) OE. **b.** Followed by *other*. Now *arch.* OE. **c.** Placed after (or separated from) the noun OE.

To render grants of n. effect 1801. **b.** I have n. other disease, than a swelling in my legs SWIFT. **c.** Remedy there was n. HOBBES.

C. *adv.* **1.** With comparatives: †**a.** = No *adv.*² (*rare*) –1691. **b.** With *the*: In no way, to no extent 1799. †**2.** *Or n.*, or no, or not. (Common in Chaucer). –1452. **3.** By no means, not at all. Now usu. followed by *so* or *too*. 1651.

1. b. The children n. the less knew their love RUSKIN. **3.** Their merits are n. too liberally recognised 1885.

None, obs. var. of OWN (see N) –1679.

Non-effe·ctive. 1756. [NON- 3.] **A.** *adj.* **1.** Producing no effect 1862. **2.** Of soldiers and sailors: Not fit or qualified for active service 1802. **3.** [attrib. use of B.] Pertaining to, consisting of, connected with non-effectives or their maintenance 1756. **B.** *sb.* A soldier or sailor who is not fit or qualified for active service 1800.

Non-effi·cient, *a.* (*sb.*) 1863. [NON- 3.] Of volunteers: Not efficient; not having acquired a certificate of efficiency. Also *sb.*

Non-ego (nǫnī·go, -e·go). 1829. [NON- 2.] *Metaph.* All that is not the ego or conscious self; the object as opp. to the subject. Hence **Non-egoi·stical** *a.*

Non-ele·ct, *a.* 1674. [NON- 3.] Not elect (chiefly in the theological sense). Usu. *absol.* So **Non-ele·ction** 1651.

†**Non-ele·ctric.** 1739. [NON- 3.] **a.** *adj.* Not electric; incapable of developing electricity when excited by friction –1797. **b.** *sb.* A non-electric substance –1832.

†‖**Non-ens** (nǫne·nz). *Pl.* **none·ntia** (-e·nʃ'iă). 1603. [med.L. *non ens* sb., f. L. *non* not, *ens* ENS.] Something which has no existence; a nonentity –1803.

Nonentity (nǫne·ntĭti). 1600. [– med.L. *nonentitas* non-existence; see NON- 1, ENTITY.] **1.** The quality or condition of not being or existing; non-being, non-existence 1643. **2.** A non-existent thing; hence, a thing existing in the imagination only; a figment, a nothing 1600. **b.** What does not exist 1655. **3.** A person or thing of no consequence or importance 1710.

3. He was an atom, a n., a very worm, and no man LYTTON.

Nones (nōᵘnz). late ME. [In sense 1 – (O)Fr. *nones* – L. *nonæ*, acc. *nonas*, fem. pl. of *nonus* ninth, f. *novem* nine; in sense 2 pl. of NONE *sb.*, after *mattins, lauds, vespers*.] **1.** *Rom. Antiq.* The ninth day (by inclusive reckoning) before the Ides of each month, being thus the 7th of March, May, July, and October, and the 5th of all other months. **2.** *Eccl.* A daily office, orig. said at the ninth hour of the day (about 3 p.m.), but in later use sometimes earlier 1709.

Non-esse·ntial. 1751. [NON- 3.] **a.** *adj.* Not essential (in various senses). **b.** *sb.* A thing that is not essential or of the utmost consequence 1806.

‖**Non est** (nǫn e·st). 1870. = next.

‖**Non est inventus** (nǫn est inve·ntǒs). 1475. [L., 'he was not found'.] *Law.* The answer made by the sheriff in the return of the writ when the defendant is not to be found in his bailiwick. In 16–17th c. often allusively.

Nonesuch (nɒ·nsɒtʃ). 1590. [f. NONE *pron.* and *a.* + SUCH *a.* See also NONSUCH, now the usual form. Suggested partly by NONPAREIL.] **I. 1.** An unmatched or unrivalled thing 1590. **b.** A person who has no equal; a paragon 1647. †**2.** The most eminent person or thing *of* some class, kind, place, etc. –1670. †**3.** *adj.* Unequalled, incomparable –1715.

1. The Scripture itself..presenteth Solomon's [temple] as a N., or peerless structure FULLER.

II. *spec.* **1.** The Scarlet Lychnis 1597. **2.** = NONSUCH II. 1. 1762.

Nonet (noᵘne·t). 1865. [– It. *nonetto* (also used), f. *nono* ninth; see -ET.] *Mus.* A composition for nine instruments or voices.

Non-Eucli·dean, -ian, *a.* 1874. [NON- 3.] Not Euclidean or in accordance with the principles of Euclid.

Non-Euclidean geometry: a system involving the study of the consequences which follow from denying (or merely dispensing with) any of the assumptions on which the Euclidean system is founded. *Non-Euclidean space*: the kind of space with which this geometry deals.

Non-exi·stence. 1646. [– med.L. *non-existentia*; see NON- 1, EXISTENCE.] **1.** The condition of being non-existent; non-being, nonentity. **2.** A non-existent thing. Also (indefinitely) that which has no existence.

1. Some I never heard of; tho' that is no Argument of their Non-Existence 1728.

Non-exi·stent. 1658. [f. NON- 3; cf. prec., NON-ENS.] **a.** *adj.* Not existent or having existence 1682. **b.** *sb.* A person or thing that does not exist.

Non-feasance (nǫnfī·zăns). 1596. [NON- 1.] Omission of some act which ought to have been done. (Dist. from MALFEASANCE, MISFEASANCE.)

Non-gre·mial. 1841. [NON-2.] A non-resident member (of the university of Cambridge). Also in *n. examinations*, an early name for the 'local' examinations –1865.

Nonillion (nǫni·lyən). 1690. [– Fr. †*nonillion* (XVI), f. L. *nonus* ninth, after *billion*, etc.] The ninth power of a million, denoted by 1 followed by 54 ciphers. In American use, an octillion multiplied by 1000, denoted by 1 followed by 30 ciphers.

Non-importa·tion. 1770. [NON- 1.] Neglect or refusal to import. **b.** *attrib.* in *non-importation agreement* or *act*, applied to various agreements or acts made by the American colonial governments (from 1768 to 1774) to prevent the importation of goods from Great Britain and her colonies.

Non-i·ntercourse. 1809. [NON- 1.] Want of intercourse. **b.** *attrib.* in *non-intercourse act*, in *U.S. Hist.*, an Act of 1809 prohibiting ships from France and Great Britain from entering American ports.

Non-interfe·rence. 1830. [NON- 1.] Failure or refusal to interfere, *esp.* in politics.

Non-interve·ntion. 1831. [NON- 1. So in Fr.] Absence of intervention; in international politics, systematic non-interference by a nation in the affairs of other nations except where its own interests are directly involved.

Non-intru·sion. 1840. [NON- 1.] Absence of intrusion; *spec.* in the Church of Scotland, applied to the principle of resisting the intrusion by patrons of unacceptable ministers upon objecting congregations.

Nonius (nōᵘ·niǒs). 1750. [mod.L. name of Pedro *Nuñes*, a Portuguese mathematician (1492–1577).] A contrivance for the graduation of mathematical instruments, invented by Nuñez and described by him in his work *De Crepusculis* (A.D. 1542). Often erron. used for the VERNIER, which is an improved form of the Nuñez instrument.

Non-joi·nder. 1833. [NON- 1.] *Law.* The omission to join, as a party to a suit.

Non-ju·rant. 1696. [f. NON-JUROR; see -ANT and cf. JURANT.] *Hist.* **A.** *adj.* That is a non-juror; belonging to or characteristic of non-jurors. **B.** *sb.* = NON-JUROR 1702. Hence **Non-ju·rancy,** the condition of being a non-juror; the principles of the non-jurors 1715.

Non-ju·ring, *ppl. a.* 1691. [irreg. f. NON-JUROR; see -ING².] *Hist.* Refusing the oath of allegiance; belonging to the party of non-jurors.

Non-juror, nonjuror (nǫn,dʒūᵊ·rəɹ). 1691. [NON- 2.] *Hist.* One of the beneficed clergy who refused to take the oath of allegiance in 1689 to William and Mary.

Non-jury. 1897. [NON- 4.] *attrib.* in *non-jury action, case,* an action or case not requiring a jury.

‖**Non liquet** (nǫn ləi·kwėt). 1605. [L., 'it is not clear'.] A condition of uncertainty as to whether a thing is so or not; *spec.* in *Law*, a verdict given by a jury in a doubtful case, deferring the matter to another day for trial.

Non-me·mber. 1650. [NON- 2.] One who is not a member. So **Non-me·mbership.**

Non-me·tal. 1866 [NON- 2.] *Chem.* A non-metallic element. So **Non-meta·llic** *a.* not metallic; *Chem.* that is not a metallic element 1815.

Non-mo·ral, *a.* 1866. [NON- 3.] Not moral; having no moral standard; wanting in moral instinct or sense.

Keats..the most absolutely non-moral of all serious writers SWINBURNE. So **Non-mora·lity.**

Non-na·tural. 1621. [NON- 3.] **A.** *adj.* †**1.** *Non-natural things* [medical L. *res non-naturales*] = 'non-naturals' (see B) –1738. **2.** Not belonging to the natural order of things; not according to or dependent upon nature 1826. **3.** Not in accordance with the natural meaning 1844.

3. The word 'wife' is taken in a non-natural sense 1884.

B. *sb. pl. Old Med.* The six things necessary to health, but liable, by abuse or accident, to become the cause of disease, *viz.* air, meat and drink, sleep and waking, motion and rest, excretion and retention, the affections of the mind 1708.

Non-nece·ssity. 1594. [NON- 1.] The condition of being unnecessary; absence of necessity.

‖**Non nobis** (nǫn nōᵘ·bis). 1475. The first words of the psalm (part of 113 in the Vulgate) beginning *Non nobis, Domine, non nobis* 'Not unto us, O Lord, not unto us', used as an expression of gratitude or thanksgiving for mercies vouchsafed.

Nonny-nonny (nǫ·ni,nǫ·ni). *Obs.* exc. *arch.* 1533. A meaningless refrain, formerly often used to cover indelicate allusions.

Non-obe·dience. 1582. [NON- 1.] Neglect of obedience; failure to obey.

‖**Non obstante** (nǫnǫbstæ·nti). late ME. [med.L. *non obstante* (XIII), 'not being in the way', orig. agreeing with a sb. in the abl. absol. construction, e.g. *non obstante veredicto* 'notwithstanding the verdict'.] †**1.** as *adv.* or *prep.* Notwithstanding –1653. **2.** as *sb.* (*Law.*) The first two words of a clause formerly used in statutes and letters patent, which conveyed a licence from the king to do a thing notwithstanding any statute to the contrary (*non obstante aliquo statuto in contrarium*); hence, a clause of this nature. Now *Hist.* 1444. †**3.** *transf.* and *gen.* **a.** A dispensation from or relaxation of a law or rule. Const. *on, of, to.* **b.** An exception to a rule –1742. †**c.** *With a non obstante to*: notwithstanding –1710.

2. King Henry the 3, though he at first detested ..these..*Non-obstantes* in Popes Bulls..yet at last he began to imitate them PRYNNE.

Nonoic (nonōᵘ·ik), *a.* 1891. [f. L. *nonus* ninth, after *octoic*.] *Chem.* The ninth in the series of fatty acids.

Nonpareil (nǫnpăre·l). 1477. [– Fr. *nonpareil*, f. *non* NON- + *pareil* like; see PAREIL *a.* and *sb.*] **A.** *adj.* Having no equal; peerless. **B.** *sb.* **1.** A person or thing having no equal; something unique 1479. **2.** *Printing.* A size of type intermediate between emerald and ruby (in America between minion and agate) 1647.

This line is printed in nonpareil type.

3. A kind of comfit 1697. **4.** A kind of apple 1731. **5. a.** A small beautifully coloured finch of the southern U.S., *Cyanospiza* (*Emberiza*) *ciris*. **b.** The rose parrakeet, *Platycercus eximius*. 1758. **6.** A name for several moths 1778.

Non-pay·ment. late ME. [NON- 1.]

Failure or neglect to pay; the condition of not being paid.

Non-perfo·rmance. 1509. [NON- 1.] Failure or neglect to perform or fulfil a condition, promise, etc.; the condition of not being performed.

‖**Non placet, non-placet** (nǫn plē̆ⁱ·sėt). 1589. [L.; see NON and PLACET.] The Latin for 'it does not please' (*scil.* me, us), being the formula used in university and ecclesiastical assemblies in giving a negative vote; hence, as *sb.*, a negative vote in such an assembly, and †*gen.* an expression of dissent or disapproval. Hence **Non-pla·cet** *v. trans.* to vote *non placet* upon (a proposition); to throw out (a measure).

Nonplus (nǫ·nplɒs). 1582. [f. L. phr. *non plus* not more, no further. Cf. obs. Fr. *mettre à non-plus* to nonplus.] **A.** *sb.* A state in which no more can be said or done; inability to proceed; a state of perplexity or puzzle. Usu. in phr. *to be at* (rarely *in*) *a n.* = to be nonplussed; *to put, bring, drive, reduce to a n.* = NONPLUS *v.* **b.** *At a n.*: unprepared (*rare*) 1803.

1. I have done! any man, that can, go further! I confess myself at a non-plus BEAUM. & FL. **b.** He can never find our larder at a n. MAR. EDGEWORTH.

†**B.** *adj.* [app. short for *at a n.*] At a nonplus; perplexed, embarrassed –1631.

No·nplus, *v.* 1591. [f. prec.] *trans.* To bring to a nonplus or standstill; to perplex. **b.** With a thing as obj.: To render ineffective or inoperative 1640.

In which [*sc.* wrangling] his Parts were so accomplisht, That right, or wrong, he ne'r was nonplust BUTLER. Hence **No·nplussed** *ppl. a.*

‖**Non plus ultra** (nǫn plɒs ɒ·ltrǎ). 1678. [L. = 'not more beyond'. So used in Fr. (from XVII).] = NE PLUS ULTRA 2 b.

‖**Non possumus** (nǫn pǫ·siumɒ̆s). 1883. [L., 'we can not'.] A statement or answer expressing inability to move in a matter.

Non-profi·ciency. 1592. [NON- 1.] Failure to make progress or improve. So **Non-profi·cient** [NON- 2], one who fails to make progress or improve.

Non-pros (nǫnprǫ·s). 1675. *Law.* Abbrev. of next. Hence **Non-prossed** (nǫnprǫ·st) *pa. pple.* (said of the suit or of the plaintiff).

Non-prosequitur (nǫnproᵘse·kwitǒɹ). 1768. [L., 'he does not prosecute'.] *Law.* A judgement entered against a plaintiff in a suit in which he does not appear to prosecute.

Non-re·gent. Now *Hist.* 1504. [f. NON- 2 + REGENT *sb.* 3, after AL. *non regens* (XIV).] A master of arts whose regency has ceased. Also *attrib.* or as *adj.*

Non-regula·tion. 1845. [NON- 4.] Applied to provinces in India in which the ordinary laws are not in force.

Non-re·sidence. late ME. [– AL. *non-residentia* (XIV); see NON- 1, RESIDENCE.] **1.** Systematic absence of a clergyman from his benefice or charge. **2.** *transf.* and *gen.* The fact of not residing in a particular place 1583. So †**Non-re·sidency** –1696.

Non-re·sident, *a.* 1530. [NON- 3.] **1.** Of a clergyman: Not residing where his official duties require him to reside; culpably absent from his benefice or charge. **2.** *transf.* and *gen.* Not residing on one's estate; not resident in a particular place 1540.

1. The non-resident and plurality-gaping Prelats MILT. So **Non-re·sident** *sb.* one who is n. (in both senses) 1583.

Non-reside·ntial, *a.* 1898. [NON- 3.] Not residential, as a college or university.

Non-resi·stance. 1643. [NON- 1.] The practice or principle of not resisting authority, even when it is unjustly exercised. Now only *Hist.* with ref. to the *doctrine of non-resistance* as held in England in the 17th c. (Cf. *passive obedience.*) Also *gen.* (const. *to*).

Non-resi·stant. 1702. [NON- 2, 3.] **a.** *adj.* Not resistant; †pertaining to or involving the doctrine of non-resistance. **b.** *sb.* One who does not resist authority or force (occas. = NON-COMBATANT); one who holds or practises the doctrine of non-resistance 1850. So **Non-resi·sting** *ppl. a.* (= sense a).

Nonsense (nǫ·nsěns), *sb.* 1614. [f. NON- 2 + SENSE *sb.*, after Fr. *nonsens* (XV).] **1.** That which is not sense; words which make no sense or convey absurd ideas; also, absurd or senseless action. (Often used exclamatorily.) **2.** Absurdity, nonsensicalness 1630. **3.** Unsubstantial or worthless stuff or things 1638. **4.** A meaning that makes no sense 1650.

1. For learned N. has a deeper Sound, Than easy Sense, and goes for more profound BUTLER. 'It's all stuff and n.' said the little lady 1894. *No n.*: no foolish or extravagant conduct; no humbug. Chiefly in phr. *stand no n.* (also used as adj.). **4.** How easy it is to a Caviller to give a new Sense, or a new N. to any thing POPE.

attrib. and *Comb.*, as **n.-book,** a book of n. or nonsense verses; **n. verses,** verses consisting of words and phrases arranged without regard to the sense 1822. **b.** That is n.; full of n.; †formerly often used as *adj.* = Nonsensical; as *a n. sculpture*, etc.

Nonsensical (nǫnse·nsikǎl). 1655. [f. prec. + -ICAL.] **A.** *adj.* That is nonsense; of the nature of, or full of, nonsense; absurd. Also of persons. **B.** *sb.* A nonsensical, absurd, or trifling thing 1842. Hence **Nonse·nsical-ly** *adv.*, **-ness.**

‖**Non sequitur** (nǫn se·kwitǒɹ). 1533. [L., 'it does not follow'.] An inference or conclusion which does not follow from the premisses. Also *transf.* and *fig.*

Non-soci·ety. 1851. [NON- 4.] *attrib.* Not belonging to a society; *spec.* (now *rare*) applied to non-union workmen or establishments.

Non-subscri·ber. Now *Hist.* 1599. [NON- 2.] **1.** One who refuses to subscribe to an undertaking, a creed, etc. **2.** One who does not pay a subscription 1713. So **Non-subscri·ption,** refusal or failure to subscribe (e.g. to a religious creed) 1736.

Non-substa·ntial, *a.* 1836. [NON- 3.] *Philos.* Not substantial. Hence **Non-substa·ntialism,** the theory that there is no substance underlying phenomena; = NIHILISM 2. Also **Non-substa·ntialist,** one who holds the doctrine of non-substantialism; = NIHILIST 1.

Nonsuch (nǫ·nsɒtʃ). 1620. [var. of NONESUCH, and now the usual form.] **I.** = NONESUCH I. 1–3. **II. 1.** A species of Lucern, *Medicago lupulina*. Also called *black n.* 1668. **2.** A variety of apple (†and pear) 1676.

Nonsuit (nǫ·nsiūt), *sb.* late ME. [– AFr. *no(u)nsuit*; see NON- 1, SUIT *sb.*] *Law.* orig., The cessation of a suit resulting from the voluntary withdrawal of the plaintiff; in mod. use, the stoppage of a suit by the judge, when, in his opinion, the plaintiff fails to make out a legal cause of action or to bring sufficient evidence.

†**No·nsuit,** *a.* 1476. [app. – pa. pple. formed after words like *execute*. Cf. AFr. *nounsuy.*] *Law.* Non-suited –1817.

No·nsuit, *v.* 1531. [f. NONSUIT *sb.* or *a.*] *Law. trans.* To subject to a nonsuit. †Also *transf.* and *fig.* –1714.

Non-te·nure. 1574. [– AFr. *nountenure*, AL. *nontenura* (XIII); see NON- 1, TENURE.] *Old Law.* A plea in bar to a real action, in which the defendant said that he did not hold the land.

†**Non-term.** 1607. [NON- 1.] The time of vacation between two terms; the cessation of term; hence *gen.*, a period of inaction –1824.

Nontronite (nǫ·ntrǒnəit). 1832. [– Fr. *nontronite* (Berthier, 1827), f. *Nontron* (in France); see -ITE[1] 2 b.] *Min.* A pale-yellow variety of chloropal.

†**Non u·ltra.** 1672. [L., 'not beyond'.] = NE PLUS ULTRA 2, 2 b. –1704.

Non-u·nion, *a.* 1863. [NON- 4.] Not belonging to a trade-union; also, manufactured by non-union men. So **Non-u·nionist,** one who does not belong to a trade-union 1861. **Non-u·nionism,** the principles of non-unionists.

Non-u·ser. 1565. [– AFr. *nounuser (= AL. *non usus*); see NON- 1, USE *v.*, -ER[4].] *Law.* Neglect to use a right, by which it may become void.

Non-va·scular, *a.* 1857. [NON- 3.] *Anat.* Destitute of vessels for the circulation of fluids.

Nonyl (nǫ·nil). 1866. [f. L. *nonus* ninth + -YL.] *Chem.* The ninth in the series of alcohol radicals of the general formula C_nH_{2n+1}. So **No·nylene,** a hydrocarbon produced in the decomposition of lime soap; whence **Nonyle·nic** *a.* **Nony·lic** *a.*, pertaining to or derived from n.

Noodle (nū·d'l), *sb.*[1] 1753. [Of unkn. origin.] A simpleton. Hence **Noo·dledom,** noodles collectively; foolishness; an instance of this.

Noodle, *sb.*[2] 1779. [– G. *nudel*, of unkn. origin.] A strip or ball of dough made with wheat-flour, and eggs, and served in soup. Also *attrib.* in **n.-soup.**

Nook (nuk), *sb.* [ME. *nok(e* (earliest in *four nokede* four-cornered, square, *c*1200), of unknown origin.] **1.** A corner of a square or angular thing, or of a figure bounded by straight lines. Now *rare.* **b.** A corner of land; a small triangular field 1603. **c.** A headland or promontory; also, a piece of land projecting from one division into another and terminating in a point. Now *rare.* 1487. **2.** An interior angle formed by the meeting of two walls or the like; a corner in a room or other enclosed space. late ME. **b.** A small or out-of-the-way corner ME. **c.** A secluded or sheltered spot among natural scenery 1555. **d.** A small or sheltered creek or inlet 1582. **3.** An outlying, remote, or secluded part of a country, region, etc., or of the world. late ME.

1. The lamb was slung in the n. of his plaid 1897. **c.** He wants my poor little Farm, because it makes a N. in his Park-wall ARBUTHNOT. **2.** There were so many nooks and corners in the..room 1877. **b.** I write in a n. that I call my *boudoir* COWPER. **c.** In the deep Trosachs' wildest n. SCOTT. **d.** *Temp.* I. ii. 227. **3.** While yet a n. is left Where English minds and manners may be found COWPER.

Comb.: **n.-rib,** *Arch.* a rib in the corner of a vault; **-shaft,** *Arch.* a shaft in the internal angle formed by the meeting of two contiguous faces in a compound archway; **-window,** a window in the corner of a room next the fireplace. Hence **Noo·kshotten** *a.* running out into corners or angles (now *arch.* or *dial.*) 1599.

Nook (nuk), *v. rare.* 1611. [f. prec.] **a.** *intr.* To hide in a corner. **b.** *trans.* To chip *off*, so as to form corners. **c.** To conceal.

Noology (no,ǫ·lǒdʒi). 1811. [f. Gr. νόος mind + -LOGY.] The science of the understanding. Hence **Noolo·gical** *a.* pertaining to n. **Noo·logist,** one who refers the origin of certain ideas to the mind itself and not to experience.

Noon (nūn), *sb.* [OE. *nōn*, corresp. to OS. *nōn(e*, (M)Du. *noen*, OHG. *nona* (G. *none*), ON. *nón*; – L. *nōna* (sc. *hora* hour), fem. sing. of *nonus* ninth; cf. NONE *sb.*, NONES.] †**1.** The ninth hour of the day, reckoned from sunrise according to the Roman method, or about 3 p.m. –1420. †**b.** *Eccl.* The hour or office of NONES –1561. **2.** Twelve o'clock in the day; mid-day. (The change is probably due to anticipation of the eccl. office.) ME. **b.** *transf.* The most important hour of the day 1712. **3.** The time of night corresponding to mid-day; midnight. Chiefly in phr. (*the*) *n. of night.* 1603. **b.** The place of the moon at midnight 1605. **4.** The culminating point 1600. **5.** *attrib.*, as **n.-beam,** etc., 1461.

2. The heat, bustle, and activity of n. DICKENS. *fig.* In the broad n. Of public scorn SHELLEY. **b.** It is 5 o'clock, the n. in Pall Mall THACKERAY. **3.** Night hath climbed her peak of highest n. TENNYSON. **b.** To behold the wandring Moon, Riding near her highest n. MILT. **4.** Thou oft Amidst thir highth of n., Changest thy countenance MILTON. *Comb.* **n.-flower,** a name given to plants of the genus *Mesembryanthemum*, and to the Goat's beard (*Tragopogon pratensis*).

Noon (nūn), *v. U.S.* 1806. [f. prec.] *intr.* (also with *it.*) To halt or rest at noon; to stop for, or partake of, the mid-day meal.

Noonday (nū·ndeⁱ). 1535. [f. NOON *sb.* + DAY *sb.* Cf. ONorw. *nóndagr.*] The middle of the day; mid-day.

Nooning (nū·niŋ). Now *U.S.* 1460. [f. NOON *sb.* + -ING[1] 1.] **1.** Noontide. **2.** A noonday meal 1652. **3.** A rest at noon 1552. **b.** An interval in the middle of the day, esp. for rest or food 1865.

Noo·n-light. 1598. [f. NOON *sb.* + LIGHT *sb.*] The light of noon; the brightest or clearest light of the day.

Noontide (nū·ntəid). [OE. *nōntīd* = MDu. *noentijd*, MHG. *nōn(e)zīt*; see NOON *sb.*, TIDE *sb.*] **1.** The time of noon; mid-day. **2.**

transf. The middle *of* night; the position *of* the moon at midnight 1560. **b.** *fig.*, esp. the culminating point *of* something 1578.

1. The noontide's hush and heat and shine E. B. BROWNING. *attrib.* The Noone-tide Sun SHAKS. **2. b.** A Poor Relation—is..a preposterous shadow, lengthening in the n. of your prosperity LAMB.

Noose (nūs, nūz), *sb.* 1600 (?1450.) [Late ME. *nose*, perh. – OFr. *nos, nous*, nom. sing. and acc. pl. (:– L. *nōdus, -ōs*) of *no, nou*, later *noud*, mod. *nœud*.] **1.** A loop, with a running knot, which tightens as the string or rope is pulled, as in a snare, lasso, hangman's halter, etc.; a loop, a folding or doubling of a string or rope. *Running n.*: see RUNNING *ppl. a.* **2.** *fig.* **a.** The marriage tie 1600. **b.** A snare or bond 1624.

Noose (nūs, nūz), *v.* 1600. [f. prec.] **1.** *trans.* To secure as by a noose; to ensnare. **2.** To hang; to put to death by hanging 1673. **3.** To capture by means of a noose; to cast a noose round 1748. **4.** To make a noose on (a cord); to place *round* in a noose; to arrange like a noose or loop 1814.

1. He, that loves at first sight, nooses himself by vows 1710. **3.** G. had..noosed the animal with his lasso 1843.

Nopal (nōᵘ·păl). 1730. [– Fr. (– Sp.) *nopal* – Mex. *nopalli* cactus.] An American species of cactus (*Nopalea coccinellifera*) cultivated for the support of the cochineal-insect; a plant of this kind; a prickly pear. 1808.

Nopalry (nōᵘ·pălri). Also **-ery.** 1783. [f. prec. + -RY, after Sp. *nopalera*, Fr. *nopalerie, nopalière*.] A plantation of nopals where the cochineal-insect is bred.

Nope[1] (nōᵘp). 1611. [app. a var. of ALP[2], OLP; see N.] The Bullfinch.

Nope[2], *U.S.* pron. of NO *adv.*[3] 1.

Nor (nǭɹ), *conj.*[1] ME. [contr. of NOTHER, as OR *conj.*[2] is of OTHER.] **1.** A negative particle co-ordinating two or more words, phrases, or clauses between which there is an alternative. **a.** Where a negative other than *neither* qualifies the first alternative (the normal conj. being now *or*); †formerly the second alternative might be qualified by another negative. **b.** Where the alternative is emphasized by prefixing *neither* to the first member. (The main current use.) **c.** *arch.* Introducing both alternatives (*nor..nor* = *neither..nor*). **d.** *arch.* Without preceding negative. **2.** and..not.

1. a. She could not heare, nor speake, nor understand SPENSER. It requires no rhymes nor no certain number of feet or syllables CHESTERF. **b.** Quarter was to be neither taken nor given MACAULAY. **c.** Nor shapes of men nor beasts we ken COLERIDGE. **d.** A heart his words nor deeds can daunt BYRON. **2.** Away! nor weep! BYRON.

Nor, *conj.*[2] *Sc.* and *dial.* late ME. [Of unkn. origin.] Than.

I know better nor you GEO. ELIOT.

Nor', abbrev. f. NORTH. late ME.

Norbertine (nǭ·ɹbəːtin, -əin), *sb.* and *a.* 1674. [f. *Norbert* (1092–1134), founder of the order + -INE[1].] A member of (pertaining to) the Premonstratensian order.

No·rdenfelt. 1880. Name of a Swedish engineer, used *attrib.* and *absol.* to designate a kind of machine-gun invented by him.

Nordhausen (nǭ·ɹdhauz'n). 1849. The name of a town in Saxony, used *attrib.* as a designation of fuming sulphuric acid, orig. made there.

Nordic (nǭ·ɹdik), *a.* 1898. [– Fr. *nordique* (J. Deniker, 1898), f. *nord* NORTH; see -IC.] Of or pertaining to the type of northern Germanic peoples represented by the blond dolichocephalic inhabitants of Scandinavia and the north of Britain. Also *sb.*

†**Nore**, obs. var. of *nor'*, NORTH. 1612.

Norfolk (nǭ·ɹfək). [OE. *Norðfolc* 'North people'.] Name of an English county, used *attrib.* to designate things peculiar to or characteristic of the district. **b.** *spec.* **N. capon,** a red herring; **N. dumpling, turkey,** a native or inhabitant of N.; **N. jacket,** a loosely fitting jacket with a waist-belt (1866); **N. plover,** the Stone Curlew.

Norfolk Howard (nǭ·ɹfək hau·əɹd). 1865. [In the *Times* of 26 June, 1862, one Joshua Bug declared in due form that he had assumed the name of Norfolk Howard.] A bed-bug. *slang.*

‖**Noria** (nōᵊ·riă). 1792. [Sp. *noria* – Arab. *nā'ūra*.] A device for raising water, used in Spain and in the East, consisting of a revolving chain of pots or buckets which are filled below and discharged when they come to the top.

Norimon (nǭ·rimǭn). 1616. [– Jap. *norimono*, f. *nori* to ride + *mono* thing; cf. KAKEMONO.] A kind of litter or palanquin used in Japan.

Norite (nōᵊ·rəit). 1878. [f. *Nor(way* + -ITE[1] 2 b.] *Geol.* and *Min.* A variety of gabbro or granite.

Norland (nǭ·ɹlănd). 1578. [Reduced f. NORTHLAND.] The north-country; the land in the north. **b.** *attrib.* Belonging to the north 1578. Hence **No·rlander,** a northerner 1716.

Norm (nǭɹm). 1821. [Anglicized f. next.] A rule or authoritative standard.

‖**Norma** (nǭ·ɹmă). Also *pl.* **normæ** (nǭ·ɹmī). 1676. [L. *norma* carpenter's square, pattern, rule.] **1.** = NORM. **2.** One of the southern constellations 1840.

Normal (nǭ·ɹmăl), *a.* and *sb.* 1530. [– Fr. *normal* or L. *normalis* made according to the square, right (angle), in med.L. regular (monast.), mod.L. perpendicular; see prec., -AL[1].] **A.** *adj.* **1.** Right (angle), rectangular (*rare*) 1650. **b.** Standing at right angles; perpendicular 1696. **2.** According to or squaring with a norm; constituting, conforming to, not deviating or differing from a type or standard; regular, usual 1828. **b.** *Chem.*, in spec. uses (see quots. in O.E.D.) 1857. **3.** *N. school* [after Fr. *école normale*], a school for the training of teachers 1834.

B. *sb.* **1.** *Geom.* A perpendicular; a straight line at right angles to the tangent or tangent plane at any point of a curve or curved surface 1727. **2.** *Physics.* The average or mean of observed quantities 1859. **3.** The usual state or condition 1890. **b.** *ellipt.* Normal temperature 1896. Hence **No·rmalcy** (orig. *U.S.*), **Norma·lity,** n. character or state. **No·rmally** *adv.*

Normalize (nǭ·ɹmăləiz), *v.* 1865. [f. NORMAL *a.* + -IZE.] *trans.* To make normal or regular. Also *absol.* Hence **Normaliza·tion,** the action or process of making normal.

Norman (nǭ·ɹmăn), *sb.*[1] and *a.* ME. [– (O)Fr. *Normans, -anz*, pl. of *Normant* (mod. *-mand*) – ON. *Norðmaðr*, pl. *-menn*, which was adopted as OE. *Norþmann*, pl. *-menn*, **Norman*, pl. *Normen*, OHG. *Nordman* (Du. *Noorman*, G. *Normanne*); see NORTH, MAN.] **A.** *sb.* **1. a.** A native or inhabitant of Normandy; one belonging to the mixed Scandinavian and Frankish race there settled. **2.** = Norman-French (see B. 3 b) 1646. **B.** *adj.* **1.** Belonging or pertaining to the Normans 1589. **2.** *N. Conquest*, the conquest of England in 1066 by the Normans under William I. 1605. **3.** *Norman-English* or *-Saxon.* English as spoken by the Normans, or as influenced by them (*rare*) 1589. **b.** *Norman-French*, the form of French spoken by the Normans, or the later form of this in English legal use (Law French) 1605. **4.** The distinctive epithet of a form of architecture, or its details, developed by the Normans, and employed in England after the Conquest 1772.

1. The rage of building fortified castles..among the N. princes 1797. Hence **Normane·sque** *a.* suggestive of the N. style of architecture 1844. **No·rmanism,** prevalence of N. rule or characteristics; tendency to favour or copy the Normans 1647. **No·rmanize** *v.* **1.** *intr.* to adopt the N. tongue or manners 1623. **2.** *trans.* to make N. 1861. **Norma·nnic** *a.* of or belonging to the Normans 1710.

Norman (nǭ·ɹmăn), *sb.*[2] 1769. [= Du. *noorman*, G. *normann*.] *Naut.* A short wooden bar, thrust into one of the holes of the windlass in a merchant-ship, whereon to fasten the cable (FALCONER).

Normative (nǭ·ɹmătiv), *a.* 1880. [– Fr. *normatif, -ive*; see NORMA and -ATIVE.] Establishing a norm or standard.

No·rmoblast. 1890. [f. *normo-*, as comb. form of L. NORMA + -BLAST.] *Path.* A nucleated red blood-corpuscle of a normal size.

Norn (nǭɹn). 1770. [– ON. *norn*, of unkn. origin.] One of the female Fates of Scandinavian mythology.

No·rna. 1840. Latinized form of prec.

Norroy (nǭ·roi). †Also **Norrey.** 1470. [– AFr. **norroi*, f. (O)Fr. *nord* NORTH + *roi* king.] Title of the third King of Arms, with jurisdiction north of the Trent.

Norse (nǭɹs), *sb.* and *a.* 1598. [– Du. *noorsch*, var. of *noordsch*, f. *noord* NORTH + *-sch* -ISH[1].] **A.** *sb.* **1.** A Norwegian. Now only as collect. sing. = Norwegians. **2.** The Norwegian tongue 1688. **B.** *adj.* Norwegian; from, or belonging to, Norway 1768. Hence **No·rseland,** Norway. **No·rseman,** a Norwegian.

A. 2. *Old N.*, the language of Norway and its colonies down to the 14th c. (sometimes loosely used to include early Swedish and Danish).

Norsk, *a.* and *sb.* 1851. [– Scand. *norsk*.] = prec.

North (nǭɹþ), *adv.*, *sb.*, and *a.* Abbrev. *nor'* in *nor'(nor')east*, etc. [OE. *norþ* = OFris. *north, noerd*, OS. *norð* (Du. *noord*), (O)HG. *nord*, ON. *norðr*; Gmc., of unkn. origin.] **A.** *adv.* **1.** Towards or in the north (see B). Also with additions, as *n. by east*, etc. **2.** quasi-*sb.* without article = B. 1. ME.; also = northerliness.

1. There is one [river] that commeth due n. CAPT. SMITH. This Bay lieth N. and South CAPT. SMITH. Phr. †*Too far n.* (slang), too clever, too knowing. **2.** Most Conquests have gone from N. to South HUME. *By n.*: (see BY *prep.* 1 d).

B. *sb.* (Usu. with *the*.) **1.** That one of the four cardinal points which lies on the left-hand of a person facing due east ME. **2.** The northern part of a country or region; *spec.* **a.** of England (beyond the Humber), Great Britain, Scotland, or Ireland; the North Country ME. **b.** Of Europe: The northern lands 1579. **c.** *U.S.* The northern States bounded on the south by Maryland, the Ohio river, and Missouri, in which there was no slaveholding 1835. **3.** The north wind. Chiefly *poet.* ME. **b.** A north wind, esp. *pl.* those which blow in the West Indies 1699.

1. The Magnetic N. (= north magnetic pole), almost always, differs from the true (= north pole) 1812. **2. a.** The..gray metropolis of the N. TENNYSON. **b.** A multitude, like which the populous N. Pour'd never from her frozen loyns MILT. **3.** I will speake as liberall as the N. SHAKS.

C. *adj.* [Developed partly from OE. *norð-* in compounds.] **1.** Of, belonging to, or lying towards the north; situated on the north side OE. **b.** Facing the north 1642. **c.** Of a northern type 1820. **2.** Of the wind: Blowing from the north ME.

1. The N.-Welch MILT. N.-Britain 1708. Did ever any North-American bring his hemp to England for this bounty? FRANKLIN. Thy Master staies for thee at the N. gate SHAKS. **b.** A North-window is best for Butteries and Cellars FULLER. **2.** When I was born, the wind was n. SHAKS. Hence **North** *v. rare. intr.* of the wind: to begin to blow from the north; to veer towards the north.

North abou·t. 1710. *Naut.* By a northerly route, *spec.* round the north of Scotland.

North Bri·ton. 1708. [NORTH *a.* 1.] A native of Scotland; a Scot.

North cou·ntry. ME. [NORTH *a.* 1.] The northern part of any country; *spec.* of England (beyond the Humber) or Great Britain; the country or region towards the north. Also *attrib.* Hence **North-cou·ntryman,** a native of the north of England.

North-east (nǭɹþ,ī·st, *attrib.* nǭ·ɹþ,īst), *adv.*, *sb.*, and *a.* OE. [f. NORTH and EAST.] **A.** *adv.* **1.** In the direction lying midway between north and east. **2.** quasi-*sb.* With preps., as *on, from, at* OE. **B.** *sb.* **1.** The direction, or point of the horizon, lying midway between north and east. late ME. **2.** The north-east wind. Now chiefly *poet.* late ME.

2. The wynd Tiffonyk, that is clepid north eest, or wynd of tempest WYCLIF *Acts* 27:14.

C. *adj.* **1.** Of the wind: Blowing from the north-east. late ME. **2.** Situated in or towards the north-east 1440.

2. *North-east passage*, a passage for vessels along the northern coasts of Europe and Asia, formerly thought of as a possible course for voyages to the East.

North-ea·ster. 1774. [f. as prec. + -ER[1].] A wind blowing from the north-east.

North-ea·sterly, *a.* and *adv.* 1739. [f. NORTH + EASTERLY.] **A.** *adj.* Blowing from, lying towards, the north-east 1743. **B.** *adv.* From or towards the north-east 1739.

North-ea·stern, *a.* 1841. [f. NORTH + EASTERN.] Pertaining to the north-east; lying on the north-east side.

North-ea·stward, *adv.*, *a.*, and *sb.* 1553. [f. NORTH-EAST + -WARD.] **A.** *adv.* Towards the north-east. **B.** *adj.* Situated towards the north-east 1766. **C.** *sb.* The north-east quarter 1892. Hence **North-ea·stwardly** *a.* blowing from, situated or leading towards, the north-east; *adv.* towards the north-east.

North-end. [OE. *norðende*, f. *norð* NORTH + *ende* END *sb.* In later use f. NORTH *a.*, and properly unhyphened, exc. when used *attrib.*] The northern end or extremity of anything.

Norther (nǭ·ɹðəɹ), *sb.* 1844. [f. NORTH + -ER[1].] A northerly wind; esp. a strong and cold north wind, which blows in autumn and winter, over Texas, Florida, and the Gulf of Mexico.

Norther (nǭ·ɹðəɹ), *v.* 1628. [f. NORTH *adv.* + -ER[5].] *intr.* Of the wind: To shift or veer northward.

Northerly (nǭ·ɹðəɹli), *a.* 1551. [f. NORTH; cf. *easterly*, etc.] **1.** Situated towards the north; northern. **2.** Of the wind: Blowing from the northward 1555. So **No·rtherly** *adv.* to the northward; on the north side. Hence **No·rtherliness.**

Northern (nǭ·ɹðəɹn), *a.* and *sb.* [OE. *norþerne*; cf. OS. *northrōni-wind*, OHG. *nordrōni*, ON. *norðrœnn.*] **A.** *adj.* **1.** Of persons or peoples: Living in, originating from, the north, esp. of England or of Europe. **b.** *U.S.* Belonging to the northern States 1836. **2.** Of the wind: Blowing from the north OE. **3.** Of things: Pertaining to, found in, characteristic of, the north. late ME. **b.** In the specific designations of animals or plants 1860. **4.** Lying or situated to the north; having a position relatively north 1590. **5.** Taking place or carried on in the north 1589.

2. That northren wynde is euer redy and destinat to all euell 1480. **3. b.** *N. diver*, the common loon (*Urinator imber* or *Colymbus torquatus*). *N. spy*, an American apple. **4.** *N. star* = NORTH STAR. *N. Lights*, the Aurora Borealis. **5.** A northerne progresse 1669.

B. *sb.* **1.** A native of the north 1774. Hence **No·rthern** *v.* to become more n. **No·rtherner,** a native or inhabitant of the n. part of any country, *esp.* (*U.S.*) of the n. States 1840. **No·rthernly** *a.* (now *rare*), northerly; †also as *adv.* **No·rthernmost** *a.* most northerly; furthest north.

Northing (nǭ·ɹþiŋ), *vbl. sb.* 1669. [f. NORTH + -ING[1].] **1.** (Chiefly *Naut.*) Progress or deviation towards the north made in sailing or travelling; difference in latitude due to moving northwards. Freq. in phr. *to make* (so much) *n.* **2.** Of heavenly bodies: Apparent movement towards the north 1808.

Northland (nǭ·ɹþlænd). [OE. *norðland* (see NORTH *a.*).] The northern part of a country, etc.; also *pl.* the lands lying in the north.

North-light. 1706. **1.** (Usu. *pl.*) = *northern lights* (NORTHERN A. 4). Now *rare.* **2.** Light coming from the north 1870.

2. The equable north-light of the artist LOWELL.

Northman (nǭ·ɹþmǣn). [OE. *Norþmann*; see NORMAN *sb.*[1]] (Chiefly *pl.*) An inhabitant or native of Norway or of Scandinavia.

No·rthmost, *a.* Now *rare.* OE. [See -MOST.] Most northerly, northernmost.

North-north-east, *adv.* late ME. [= Du. *noordnoordoost*, etc.] In the direction lying midway between north and north-east. Also as *sb.* and *adj.*

North-north-west, *adv.* late ME. [= Du. *noordnoordwest*, etc.] In the direction lying midway between north and north-west. Also as *sb.* and *adj.*

North Sea. OE. [Cf. MDu. *Nort, Noortzee* (Du. *Noordzee*), G. *Nordsee*, Da. *-sö*, Sw. *-sjö.*] **1.** The proper name of certain seas in northern Europe; now only, 'the German Ocean' (bounded by Great Britain, Scandinavia, and Holland) ME. †**2.** *pl.* The seas of the northern hemisphere –1726.

North star. [Late ME. *north sterre.*] The pole-star.

Northu·mber. Now *rare* or *Hist.* [OE. *Norðhymbre*, f. *norð-* NORTH + *Humbre* the Humber.] *pl.* The ancient inhabitants of Northumbria, or England north of the Humber.

Northumbrian (nǭɹþɒ·mbriǎn). 1612. [f. prec. + -IAN.] **A.** *adj.* Of or pertaining to Northumbria or Northumberland 1622. **B.** *sb.* **1.** An inhabitant or native of ancient Northumbria or modern Northumberland 1612. **2.** The northern dialect of ancient Northumbria or modern Northumberland 1845.

Northward (nǭ·ɹþwəɹd, *Naut.* nǭ·ɹþəɹd), *adv.*, *sb.*, and *a.* See also NORWARD. late OE. [f. NORTH + -WARD.] **A.** *adv.* **1.** Towards the north; in a northern direction. **2.** quasi-*sb.* = next 1864.

1. I am going N. for a while JOHNSON. On the Downs n. of Brighton 1885. **2.** To n. of Bautzen forty miles 1865.

B. *sb.* That direction or part which lies to the north (of a place or thing) 1624. **C.** *adj.* That moves or looks northward 1597. Hence **No·rthwardly** *adv.* in a n. direction; *adj.* having a n. situation or direction; (of the wind) blowing from the n.

No·rthwards, *adv.* and *sb.* OE. [f. NORTH + -WARDS.] Northward.

North-west (nǭɹþwe·st, *Naut.* nǫɹwe·st; see NOR'-WEST), *adv.*, *sb.*, and *a.* OE. [f. NORTH and WEST.] **A.** *adv.* **1.** In the direction lying midway between north and west. **2.** quasi-*sb.* = next. late ME. **B.** *sb.* The direction or part lying midway between north and west; *spec.* the North-west Territories of Canada. late ME. **C.** *adj.* **1.** Of the wind: Blowing from the north-west. late ME. **2.** Pertaining to the north-west; situated in the north-west part of a country, etc. 1827.

N. Passage, a passage for vessels along the north coast of America, formerly thought of as possible for navigation between the Atlantic and the Pacific.

North-we·ster. 1737. [f. prec. + -ER[1].] **1.** A wind or gale blowing from the north-west. **2.** = NOR'WESTER 2. 1830.

North-we·sterly, *a.* 1611. [f. NORTH-WEST, after WESTERLY.] **a.** Of the wind: Blowing from the north-west. **b.** Tending north-west.

North-we·stern, *a.* 1612. [Cf. WESTERN.] Situated or extending towards the north-west.

North-we·stward, *adv.* and *sb.* late ME. [f. NORTH-WEST + -WARD.] **a.** *adv.* In a north-westerly direction; towards the north-west. **b.** *sb.* = NORTH-WEST *sb.* 1796. Hence **North-we·stwardly** *a.* and *adv.*

Norward (nǭ·ɹwəɹd). 1618. Also *Naut.* **nor'ard** (nǫ·rəɹd). [f. *nor'* NORTH + -WARD.] **a.** *adv.* Northward. **b.** *sb.* The northern part or region 1618.

a. Nor'ard of the Dogger (*title*) 1887.

Norway (nǭ·ɹwe[i]). 1674. [Late OE. *Norweġ* – ON. *Norvegr*, f. *norðr* NORTH + *vegr* WAY, (in place-names) region.] Name of one of the Scandinavian countries, used *attrib.*, as in *N. fir, spruce*, etc.; *N. haddock, lobster, rat*, etc.; *N. deal, skiff, yawl*, etc.

Norwegian (nǫɹwī·dʒǎn). 1605. [– med. L. *Norvegia* (– ON. *Norvegr*; see prec.) + -AN. The *w* is from NORWAY.] **A.** *adj.* Of or pertaining to Norway; belonging to, found in, Norway 1607.

The tallest Pine Hewn on N. hills MILT.

B. *sb.* **1.** A native of Norway 1599. **2.** The language of Norway 1605. **3.** *U.S.* A kind of fishing-boat 1872.

Nor'-west. late ME. Reduced f. NORTH-WEST *a.* and *sb.*

Nor'-we·ster. 1703. [Reduced f. NORTH-WESTER.] **1.** A wind or gale from the north-west. **2.** A glass of strong liquor 1840. **3.** An oilskin hat; a sou'wester 1851.

Norweyan (nǫɹwē[i]·ǎn), *a.* 1605. [f. NORWAY + -AN.] Norwegian SHAKS.

Nose (nōuz), *sb.* [OE. *nosu* = OFris. *nose*, MDu. *nōse, nuese* (Du. *neus*). Related forms are OE. *nasu*, OHG. *nasa* (G. *nase*), ON. *nasar* pl., nom. sing. *nǫs*; L. *nares* pl. nostrils, *nās(s)us* nose, Skr. *nás.*] **I. 1.** That part of the head or face in men and animals which lies above the mouth and contains the nostrils. Also, the analogous part in lower forms of animal life. **2.** The organ of smell. late ME. **b.** The sense of smell; a (good, bad, etc.) faculty of smell or power of tracking by scent ME. **c.** Smell, odour (*dial.*) 1894. **3.** As an organ by which speech-sounds may be produced or affected. Chiefly in phr. *in* or *through the n.* 1530. **4.** *A n. of wax*, a person or thing easily moulded or influenced 1532. **5.** *slang.* A spy or informer 1812.

1. His n. on the sodaine bled LODGE. Phr. *Parson's n.*, the rump of a fowl. **2. b.** *fig.* He was a gentilman of a longe n...Thys Shyryffe was a couetuouse man LATIMER. **3.** He..pays as he speaks..—through the n. DICKENS.

Phrases (more or less fig.). *To make a long n.* (see LONG *a.*[1]). †(*In*) *spite of one's n.*, notwithstanding one's opposition 1675. *To count*, or *tell, noses*, denoting the counting of supporters, deciding by mere numbers. **b.** *Under one's* (*very*) *n.*, often implying that an action is done in defiance of a person, or without his perceiving it. **c.** *To cut off one's n.*, to do something to one's own hurt or loss. *To follow one's n.*, to go straight forward, be guided by instinct. *To hold one's n.*, to compress the nostrils between the fingers and thumb in order to avoid perceiving a bad smell. *To poke, put*, or *thrust one's n.*, to poke or pry *into* something. *To turn up one's n.*, to show disdain. **d.** *To bite* or *snap one's n. off*, to answer snappishly. *To put one's n. out of joint*, etc., to displace or supplant one; to spoil one's plans; to throw one out. **e.** *To pay through the n.*, to pay excessively.

II. In transf. uses. **1. a.** The open end of a pipe or tube; the muzzle of a gun, the nozzle of a pair of bellows, etc. 1598. **b.** The beak of an alembic, retort, or still 1651. **2.** The prow, bow, or stem of a ship or boat 1538. **b.** The corresponding part of an airship, aeroplane, torpedo, etc. 1899. **3.** A prominent or projecting part; the point or extremity of anything 1592. **b.** A projecting part of a shell 1681. **c.** *Arch.* The projecting part or edge of a moulding, stair-tread, or mullion 1815.

2. One of the Gallies lost her N. with a shot 1613. **3.** The Lode-stone that alwaies holdeth his n. to the North LYLY.

attrib. and *Comb.*: **n.-ape**, the proboscis-monkey; **-cap**, a metal cap on the n. of a gun-stock; **-dive**, the forward and downward plunge of an aeroplane, etc.; also *vb.*; **-leaf**, the foliaceous appendage of the nostrils in some bats; **-monkey** = *nose-ape*; **-rag**, a pocket handkerchief (*slang*); **-tube**, a tube for feeding a patient through the n.; **-worm**, the larva of the sheep-bot.

Nose (nōuz), *v.* 1577. [f. the sb.] **I.** *trans.* **1.** To perceive the smell of (something); to discover or notice by the sense of smell. **b.** To scent or smell *out* (*lit.* and *fig.*) 1630. †**2.** To confront, face, or oppose (a person, etc.) in an impudent or insolent manner. (Cf. BEARD *v.* 3.) –1824. **3.** To utter with a nasal twang; to sing through the nose 1643. **4.** To rub with the nose; to press the nose close to (something) 1777. **b.** To examine with the nose; to put the nose close to (a thing) in examining 1851.

1. *fig.* Nosing a job in every Ministerial move 1893. **2.** A sort of national convention..nosed parliament in the very seat of its authority BURKE. **3.** It makes far better musick when you n. Sternhold's..meeter 1643. **4.** Lambs are glad Nosing the mother's udder TENNYSON.

II. *intr.* **1.** To sniff, to smell. Also with *about* or *round* 1783. **b.** To pry or search (*after* or *for* something) 1648. **2.** To push with the nose 1891. **3.** Of strata or veins: To dip in, run *out* 1879.

1. *fig.* That fellow's still nosing round here with his gun 1895. **2.** A steamer slowly noseing round off the wharf-cranes 1891.

No·se-bag. 1796. [f. NOSE *sb.*] A bag to contain provender for a horse, suspended from the horse's head by straps fitted to the open end.

No·se-band. 1611. [f. NOSE *sb.* + BAND *sb.*[2]] The lower band of a bridle, passing over the nose, and attached to the cheek-straps.

No·se-bleed. late ME. [f. NOSE *sb.* + stem of BLEED *v.*] **1.** An old name for the plant Milfoil or Yarrow. **2.** A bleeding at the nose 1852.

Nosed (nōuzd), *a.* 1440. [f. NOSE *sb.* + -ED[2].] **1.** Having a nose of a specified shape.

b. (Also *well-n.*) Keen-scented 1604. **2.** Having a prominent nose, as *Nosed Monkey* 1896.

Nosegay (nō^u·zge^i). late ME. [f. NOSE *sb.* + GAY *sb.* 2.] A bunch of flowers or herbs, esp. sweet-smelling flowers; a bouquet, a posy. **b.** A perfume or scent (*spec.* one artificially prepared); an odour, smell 1855.

1. *transf.* The country is one big n. W. MORRIS.

Noseless (nō^u·zlės), *a.* late ME. [f. NOSE *sb.* + -LESS.] Lacking or deprived of a nose.

No·se-piece. 1611. [f. NOSE *sb.*] **1. a.** A part of a helmet or turban serving as a guard for the nose; a nasal. **b.** A nose-band for a horse 1865. **2.** *Optics.* The part of a microscope to which the objective (or object-glass) is attached 1867.

No·se-pipe. 1784. [f. NOSE *sb.*] **1.** A pipe, or piece of piping, forming a nose or terminal to another pipe, a vessel, etc. **2.** *spec.* The blast-pipe nozzle inside the tuyère of a blast furnace 1839.

Noser (nō^u·zəɹ). 1852. [f. NOSE *sb.* + -ER[1].] **1.** A strong head wind; *esp.* in phr. *a dead n.*

No·se-ring. 1778. [f. NOSE *sb.*] **1.** A ring fixed in an animal's nose. **2.** A ring-shaped ornament worn in the nose 1839.

†**No·se-smart.** 1589. [f. NOSE *sb.* + SMART, after L. *nasturtium*.] The plant Cress –1755.

Nose-thirl, †-thrill, -tril. ME. [f. NOSE *sb.* + THIRL *sb.*, a new comb. in place of OE. *nospyr(e)l* NOSTRIL.] = NOSTRIL.

†**No·se-wise,** *a.* 1566. [f. NOSE *sb.* + WISE *a.*, perh. after Du. *neuswijs*, LG. *näsewis*, G. *naseweis*.] **1.** Conceited; clever in one's own opinion –1787. **2.** Keen-scented –1630.

Nosey, nosy (nō^u·zi). 1620. [f. NOSE *sb.* + -Y[1].] **A.** *adj.* **1.** Having a large nose. **2.** Smelly 1836. **3.** *slang.* Inquisitive, prying 1910. **B.** *sb.* One who has a large nose. (Used as a nickname.)

A. 3. *N. Parker*, an inquisitive person. **B.** *sb.* Had heer'd of the Duke of Wellington; he was Old N. 1851.

Nosing (nō^u·ziŋ). 1771. [f. NOSE *sb.* + -ING[1].] The rounded edge of a bench, or of a step projecting over the riser; also, a metal shield for the same; the prominent edge of a moulding or drip.

Noso- (nǫ·so, nǒsǫ), comb. form of Gr. νόσος disease, as in †**No·socome** [– Fr. – L. *nosocomium*, Gr. νοσοκομεῖον], a hospital (URQUHART *Rabelais*); hence **Nosoco·mial** *a.*; **Noso·graphy** [-GRAPHY], systematic description of diseases, hence **-gra·phic, -ical** *adjs.* **Nosopoe·tic** *a.*, producing or causing disease.

Nosology (nǒsǫ·lǒdʒi). 1721. [– mod.L. *nosologia*, f. Gr. νόσος disease; see -LOGY.] **1.** A classification or arrangement of diseases. **b.** The list of known diseases 1839. **2.** Systematic classification or investigation of diseases; that branch of medical science which deals with this 1727. **3.** The special character of a particular disease, or the views current with regard to this 1825. Hence **Nosolo·gical** *a.* of, pertaining to, or dealing with, n. **Noso·logist,** one occupied with, or versed in, n.

Nostalgia (nǫstæ·ldʒiă). 1770. [– mod.L. *nostalgia* (1688, rendering G. *heimweh*), f. Gr. νόστος return home + ἄλγος pain; see -IA[1].] A form of melancholia caused by prolonged absence from one's country or home; severe homesickness. Also **Nosta·lgy.** Hence **Nosta·lgic** *a.* of the nature of, caused by, n.; home-sick.

Nostoc (nǫ·stǫk). 1650. [Invented by Paracelsus.] *Bot.* A genus of unicellular *Algæ*, having the cells arranged in rows which intertwine with each other and form a gelatinous mass; *esp.* the ordinary species of this, *N. commune*, formerly believed to be an emanation from the stars. **b.** An individual plant of this genus 1851.

Nostradamus (nǫstrădē^i·mǒs). 1668. [Latinized form of the name of Michel de *Nostredame*, a French physician (1503–1566) who published a collection of prophecies in 1555.] One who professes to foretell future events; a seer like Nostradamus.

Nostril (nǫ·stril). [OE. *nospyrl*, *nosterl* (= OFris. *nosterl*), f. *nosu* NOSE + *pyr(e)l* hole; see THIRL.] One of the external openings in the nose of vertebrates; an analogous opening in other animals.

fig. phr. Our judgments stink in the nostrils of the people BURKE.

Nostrum (nǫ·strǒm). 1602. [– L. *nostrum*, neut. sing. of *noster* our.] **1.** A medicine, or medical application, prepared by the person recommending it; *esp.* a quack remedy, a patent medicine. **2.** A special device for improving or accomplishing something; *esp.* a pet scheme of political or social reform 1749.

1. The owner of a n. of some kind, called a patent food 1883. **2.** Another party's n. is, more churches, more schools, more clergymen KINGSLEY. *Comb.*, as **n.-monger** (now *rare* or *Obs.*).

Nosy, var. NOSEY.

Not (nǫt), *a.* and *sb.* Now *dial.* [OE. *hnot*, of unkn. origin.] †**1.** Close-cropped, short-haired –1633. **2.** Of sheep or cattle: Hornless, polled 1587. **b.** *sb.* A hornless sheep 1834. †**3.** Of wheat or barley: Awnless, beardless –1680.

1. A not-heed hadde he, with a broun visage CHAUCER. *Comb.* as *n.-headed*, *-pated* adjs.

†**Not,** *v.*[1] 1530. [f. prec.] *trans.* To clip or cut short (the hair or beard) –1674.

†**Not,** *v.*[2], **note.** OE. For *ne wot* know(s) not; see NE and WIT *v.* –1614.

Not (nǫt), *adv.* and *sb.* ME. [Reduced form of *noht*, *noȝt* NOUGHT.] The ordinary adverb of negation. **1.** Modifying an ordinary verb. **a.** Following the verb. Now *arch.* **b.** Preceding the verb. Chiefly *poet.* late ME. **2.** Following an auxiliary verb. Also in the form **n't**, usu. written as one word with the verb. ME. Also *ellipt.* in replies. **3.** Following the verb *to be*. Also as *n't*. late ME. **b.** With ellipse of vb. esp. after *if*, or in replies. late ME. **4.** Preceding an infinitive or gerundial clause 1440. **5.** †**a.** Used redundantly after vbs. of forbidding, dissuading, or preventing –1677. **b.** Coupled with other negatives, or repeated. Now *dial.* or *vulgar.* late ME. **6.** Preceding a sentence, clause, or word. **a.** In introductory phrases, as *not but (that)*, *not that*, etc. ME. **b.** Placed first for the sake of emphasis. late ME. **c.** In contrast with a following *but* 1579. **d.** Emphasizing a pronoun after a neg. statement, or in a reply 1625. **7.** With terms of number or quantity ME. **8.** After *or*, *if*, or *as*, with ellipse of words expressed or implied in the preceding clause. late ME. **9.** Denoting contrast or opposition to what precedes, with or without *and* 1471. **10.** With advs. or advb. phrases 1475. **b.** Modifying adjs. or pples. in agreement with a preceding sb. or pronoun 1529. **c.** With neg. adjs. or advs., implying the affirmative term 1657.

1. a. They wyst n. what folke they were CAXTON. **2.** I'll n. offend thee with a vain tear more B. JONS. You mustn't tell me anything 1895. *ellipt.* 'You've seen this before?' 'No, n. that I can remember' (*mod.*). **3.** This is n. the cause of a king, but of kings BURKE. It isn't true 1895. **b.** Fame if n. doublefac't is double-mouth'd MILT. **4.** I knew neither what to do, or what n. to do DE FOE. **6. a.** N. that I lou'd Cæsar lesse, but that I lou'd Rome more SHAKS. **b.** Yet n. the more Cease I to wander MILT. **c.** Which were borne, n. of blood,..but of God *John* 1:13. **d.** He is no Witch, n. he DEKKER. **7.** He spoke n. a Word DE FOE. Phr. *N. a little*, a good deal. **8.** Shall we give battle..or n. DE FOE. If virtue is of such a nature, it will be taught; and if n., n. JOWETT. **9.** They are in heauen and n. here *Bk. Com. Prayer.* **10.** N. once or twice..The path of duty was the way to glory. TENNYSON. **b.** You have got to be regarded as n. quite right in your head 1889. **c.** A certain air of dignity, n. unmingled with insolence 1900.

B. *sb.* The word 'not'; a negation or negative 1601.

They still doe returne us a n. 1608.

Comb. **n.-self** = NON-EGO.

‖**Nota bene** (nō^u·tă bī·ni). 1721. [L., 'mark well'.] Mark well, observe particularly. (Abbrev. N.B.) **b.** Used substantively 1731.

Notability (nō^{u}tăbi·lĭti). late ME. [– (O)Fr. *notabilité* or late and med.L. *notabilitas*, f. *notabilis*; see next, -ITY.] **1.** †**a.** A notable fact or circumstance –1470. **b.** A notable or prominent person 1851. **2.** The quality of being notable; esp. housewifely industry or management 1786. Now *dial.*

1. b. Various other little notabilities of the neighbourhood KINGSLEY. **2.** Mary has infected me with her n., and I'm going to work Mama a footstool MRS. GASKELL.

Notable (nō^u·tăb'l), *a.*, *sb.*, and *adv.* ME. [– (O)Fr. *notable* – L. *notabilis*, f. *notare*; see NOTE *v.*[2], -ABLE.] **A.** *adj.* **1.** Deserving of note, esp. on account of excellence, value, or importance; remarkable, striking, eminent. **2.** †**a.** Attracting notice; conspicuous –1621. **b.** Noticeable, perceptible. Now *Chem.* 1551. **3.** †**a.** Of men: Industrious, business-like –1732. **b.** Of women: Capable, managing, bustling; active in household management and occupations. Now *dial.* 1718. **c.** Connected with household management and industry 1787.

1. Acts of n. Oppression and Injustice STEELE. You have mingled many Unworthies among them, rather Notorious than N. FULLER. **3. b.** A n. Woman, who was thoroughly sensible of the intrinsick Value of Time 1718.

B. *sb.* **1.** A noteworthy fact or thing (*rare*) 1483. **b.** A person of eminence or distinction 1815. **2.** *pl. Hist.* A number of prominent men from the various estates of the realm of France, summoned by the king as a deliberative assembly in times of emergency 1568.

1. The notables of the town were fast assembling SCOTT. **2.** From the very commencement of the revolution, at the first meeting of the notables 1792. Hence **No·tableness. No·tably** *adv.*

‖**Notandum** (notæ·ndǒm). Also *pl.* **notanda.** 1605. [L., neut. gerundive of *notare* to NOTE.] An entry or jotting of something to be specially noted; a memorandum, note.

Notarial (notē^ə·riăl), *a.* 1482. [f. NOTARY + -AL[1].] **1.** Of or belonging to a notary. **b.** Characteristic of notaries 1828. **2.** Drawn up, framed, or executed by a notary 1622. Hence **Nota·rially** *adv.* 1847.

Notary (nō^u·tări). ME. [– L. *notarius* short-hand writer, clerk, f. *nota* NOTE; see -ARY[1].] †**1.** A clerk or secretary to a person –1711. **2.** A person publicly authorized to draw up or attest contracts, etc., to protest bills of exchange, etc., and discharge other formal duties ME. **b.** More fully *n. public*, *public* (or †*common*), *n.* 1494. †**3.** A noter or observer –1685.

1. *fig.* O comfort-killing Night,..Dim register and n. of shame SHAKS. **2. b.** Protest is..made by a N. Publick in the presence of two credible Witnesses 1682.

Notation (notē^i·ʃən). 1570. [– (O)Fr. *notation* or L. *notatio*, f. *notat-*, pa. ppl. stem of *notare*; see NOTE *v.*[2], -ION.] †**1.** The explanation of a term in accordance with its etymology; the primary sense of a word. (Common in 17th c.) –1690. **2.** A note or annotation. Now *rare.* 1584. **3.** The action of taking or making note of something (*rare*) 1646. **4.** The process or method of representing numbers, quantities, etc., by a system of signs; hence, any set of symbols or characters used to do this; *e.g.* in *Arith.* and *Algebra*, *Music*, etc. 1706.

1. If we may Admit that Gentleman's N. of a Libell (a Lie because False, and a Bell because Loud) 1690. **4.** The ecclesiastical n. of the Greek Church..is supposed to have originated in the Greek accents 1876.

Not-being. 1586. [NOT *adv.*] Absence of being; non-existence.

[In the philosophy of Hegel] Being and not being are thus declared to be identical 1880.

Notch (nǫtʃ), *sb.* 1577. [– AFr. *noche* (XIV), perh. f. **nocher*; see next.] **1.** A V-shaped indentation or incision in an edge or across a surface. **2.** A nick made on a stick, etc., as a means of keeping a score or record 1580. **b.** A run in cricket. Now *rare.* 1737. **3.** *U.S.* A narrow defile through mountains; a deep narrow pass 1649. **4.** An opening; a break or breach 1789.

2. Upon the Sides of this square Post, I cut every Day a N. with my Knife DE FOE. *fig.* Its prices are at the lowest notch (*U.S.*). **3.** About half way between the N. of the Mountain and Hartford 1718.

Comb.: **n.-board,** a board grooved to receive the ends of the steps in a stair; **-wing,** a name of various moths.

Notch (nǫtʃ), *v.* 1597. [– AFr. **nocher* (rel. to *anoccer* add a notch to); cf. L. *inoccare* harrow in (which may have been used transf. for making a score or notch), and rare ME. *oche* vb. ('Morte Arthure'), OFr.

oche, osche (mod. *hoche*), f. *o(s)chier* (*hocher*) = Pr. *oscar* nick, notch.] **1.** *trans.* To cut (hair) unevenly (*rare*) –1747. **2.** To make notches in; to cut or mark with notches 1600. **b.** To shape *into* (some form) by making notches 1768. **3.** To score or record by means of notches. Also with *up* and *down*. 1623. **b.** To score (a run, etc.). Now *rare*. 1837. **4.** To fix, secure, or insert, by means of notches 1768. **b.** To chop *off*, cut *out* 1820. **5.** To fit the arrow to the bow-string; to nock 1635.

2. He scotcht him, and notcht him like a Carbinado SHAKS. **3.** We notched the votes down on three sticks LOWELL. **4.** *fig.* The houses were notched, as it were, into the side of the steep bank SCOTT. **5.** His bow is bent, and he has notch'd his dart QUARLES. Hence **Notched** *ppl. a.*; *spec.* in *Bot.*, coarsely dentate or serrate; in *Zool.*, having notches or incisions.

Notching (nǫ·tʃiŋ), *vbl. sb.* 1611. [f. prec. + -ING[1].] **1.** The action of making notches, esp. in carpentry as a method of joining timbers. **2.** A notch or notch-like incision 1842.

Note, *sb.*[1] *Obs.* exc. *n. dial.* [OE. *notu*, related to NEAT *sb.* and NOWT.] **1.** Use, usefulness, profit, advantage. **b.** *dial.* The milk given by a cow; the period of giving milk; the condition of a cow when giving, or beginning to give, milk after calving 1728. **2.** Office; employment, work OE.

Note (nō^{u}t), *sb.*[2] ME. [– (O)Fr. *note* – L. *nota* a mark.] **I. 1. a.** A written character or sign, expressing the pitch and duration of a musical sound. **b.** A key of a pianoforte, etc. 1848. **2.** A single tone of definite pitch, as produced by a musical instrument or by the human voice in singing ME. **b.** With ref. to the song, etc. of birds. late ME. **3.** A strain of music, a melody. In later use only *poet.* ME. **b.** The musical call or song of a bird ME. **4.** A cry, call, or sound of a bird or fowl ME. **5.** *transf.* 1483.

2. First rehearse this song by rote, To each word a warbling n. SHAKS. **b.** Where birds..Sit sweetly tuning of their noates together 1613. **3.** The pealing anthem swells the n. of praise GRAY. **b.** The deep mellow crush of the wood-pigeon's n. CAMPBELL. **4.** The n. of the carrion crow.., a note-call of danger 1866. **5.** We can catch clearly enough the n. of extreme..self-dependence 1877. Phr. *To change* (*one's*) *n.*: To alter (one's) way of speaking or thinking.

II. 1. A mark, sign, token, or indication *of* some quality, condition, or fact; a characteristic or distinguishing feature. late ME. **b.** *Theol.* One of certain characteristics by which the true Church may be known; a sign or proof of genuine origin, authority, and practice 1555. **2.** A stigma or reproach. Const. *of*. Now *rare*. 1531. **3.** An objective sign, or visible token or mark, which serves to identify or distinguish a person, thing, or condition. Now *rare*. 1577. **4.** A sign or character (other than a letter) used in writing or printing; a mark *of* interrogation, etc. 1529.

1. These are the notes of the 'Neo-paganism', which began a good hundred years ago 1891. **b.** How comes subjection to the Pope to be..an essential n. of the Church? WESLEY.

III. 1. *Law.* An abstract of essential particulars relating to transfer of land by process of FINE, which was engrossed and placed on record 1483. **2.** A brief record or abstract of facts written down to assist the memory, or to serve as a basis for a fuller statement; also *transf.* a mental impression of something. (Usu. *pl.*) 1548. **b.** A brief memorándum of topics for a discourse on any subject. (Usu. *pl.*) 1693. **3.** An annotation appended to a passage in a writing or book 1560. **4.** A brief statement of particulars or of some fact; †a bill 1587. **5.** A short or informal letter 1594. **b.** A formal diplomatic communication 1796. **c.** Short for NOTE-PAPER 1883. **6.** A written promise to pay a certain sum at a specified time. Also *n. of hand.* 1683. **7.** A bank-note, or similar promissory note passing current as money 1696.

2. And 'tis out of these Notes that my Observations are compiled 1695. Phr. *To make*, or *take*, *a n.* or *notes*. *To compare notes*: see COMPARE *v.*[1] 2. **b.** He spoke for more than an hour without a n. FROUDE. **3.** I found two other volumes.., enriched with manuscript notes LAMB. **4.** Heere is now the Smithes n., for Shooing, And Plough-Irons SHAKS. **5.** Not a n., not a line did I receive in the mean time JANE AUSTEN.

IV. 1. Distinction, mark, importance; reputation. Now *Obs.* or *arch.* 1538. **2.** Notice, regard, or attention 1598. **b.** Information; intimation (*rare*) 1598.

1. A young writer struggling into n. MACAULAY. Phr. *Of n.*, of distinction; notable. **2.** Phr. *To take n. of*; No one took n. of me THACKERAY. *attrib.*, as *n.-case*, etc.

†**Note,** *v.*[1] [OE. *notian*, f. *notu* NOTE *sb.*[1]] *trans.* To use, make use of (something) –1560.

Note (nō^{u}t), *v.*[2] ME. [– (O)Fr. *noter* – L. *notare*, f. *nota* NOTE *sb.*[2]] **I. 1.** *trans.* To mark carefully; to give heed or attention to; to notice, perceive. **2.** To mention separately or specially among other items committed to writing. late ME. **3.** To set down in writing; to put down as a memorandum. late ME. So with *down* 1669.

1. I received your lordship's letter, and as the merchants say, n. the contents BURKE. **2.** Which thing the Evangelist notes as one of the criticall passages of his Passion 1646. **3.** Ile n. you in my Booke of Memorie SHAKS.

II. †**1.** To denote, or signify (something) –1573. †**b.** To indicate; to point *out*, set or show *forth* –1813. **2. a.** To mark (a book, words, etc.) with a musical score (*rare*) 1440. †**b.** To distinguish by a mark –1725. **c.** To annotate 1809. †**3. a.** To affix to (one) the stigma or accusation *of* some fault, etc. –1680. †**b.** To mark or brand *with* some disgrace or defect –1652. †**c.** To stigmatize for some reason –1601.

1. b. Distinguish all betimes, with branding Fire; To n. the Tribe, the Lineage, and the Sire DRYDEN. **2. b.** *To n. a bill*, is when a public notary goes as a witness, or takes notice, that a merchant will not accept or pay it CHAMBERS. **3. c.** *Jul. C.* IV. iii. 2.

No·te-book. 1579. [f. NOTE *sb.*[2] + BOOK.] A book reserved for or containing notes or memoranda.

Noted (nō^{u}·tėd), *ppl. a.* ME. [f. NOTE *v.*[2] + -ED[1].] **1.** That is specially noticed; hence, distinguished, famous. **2.** Provided with a musical score; having musical notation 1700. Hence **No·tedly** *adv.* markedly; particularly 1603.

Noteless (nō^{u}·tlės), *a.* 1616. [f. NOTE *sb.*[2] + -LESS.] **1.** Devoid of note; undistinguished, unnoticed. **2.** Unmusical; unharmonious; voiceless 1721.

1. Let her walke Saint-like, notelesse, and unknowne DEKKER.

Notelet (nō^{u}·tlėt). 1824. [f. NOTE *sb.*[2] + -LET.] A short note or communication.

No·te-pa:per. 1849. [f. NOTE *sb.*[2] III. 5 + PAPER *sb.*] Paper of the various sizes now generally used for correspondence. (Also *ellipt.* **note.**)

Noter (nō^{u}·təɹ). 1491. [f. NOTE *v.*[2] + -ER[1].] †**1.** A writer of the musical score in MSS. **2.** One who takes or writes notes 1589.

Noteworthy (nō^{u}·twɒ̄ɹðĭ), *a.* 1552. [f. NOTE *sb.*[2] + WORTHY *a.*] Worthy of notice; remarkable. Hence **No·teworthily** *adv.* **No·teworthiness.**

No·ther, *adv.* and *conj.* *Obs.* exc. *dial.* [ME. *nōþer*, repr. OE. **nōþer*, var. of *nawþer*, contr. of *nāhwæþer*, f. *nā* (see NO *adv.*[1]) + *hwæþer* WHETHER. Cf. NOUTHER.] = NEITHER, NOR.

Nothing (nɒ·þiŋ), *sb.* and *adv.* [OE. *nān þing*; see NO *a.*, THING. Cf. NOUGHT.] **A.** *sb.* **1.** Not any (material or immaterial) thing; nought. **2.** With dependent genitive: No part, share, etc., *of* some thing (or person) OE. **3.** A thing (or person) not worth reckoning, considering, or mentioning. late ME. **4.** *Arith.* That which is not any number, and possesses neither quantity nor value; the character representing this; NOUGHT. late ME. **5.** That which is non-existent. Also personified 1535. **b.** Denoting extinction or destruction 1590. **6.** With *a* and *pl.* **a.** A non-existent, a comparatively insignificant or worthless, thing; a trifling event 1607. **b.** A trivial or trifling remark 1601. **c.** A person of no note; a nobody 1611. †**7.** = NOTHINGNESS 1, 2, 3 (*rare*) –1682.

1. Without whom nothyng is strong, n. is holy *Bk. Com. Prayer.* Ther's n. ill can dwell in such a Temple SHAKS. A fellow whom all the world knew to have N. in him FIELDING. Many..were heretics, or n. at all J. H. NEWMAN. Provbs. *N. venture, n. win.* *N. great is easy.* **2.** N. of him that doth fade SHAKS. Yet had his aspect n. of severe DRYDEN. **3.** Knowledge is n. compared with doing J. H. NEWMAN. **4.** *fig.* Now thou art an O without a figure, I am better then thou art now, I am a Foole, thou art n. SHAKS. **5.** Phr. *To dance on n.*: see DANCE *v.* 3. *To n.*, denoting the final point, stage, or state of the process of destruction, dissolution, etc. **6.** The little nothings of occupied life leave a man no time for his duty 1850. **b.** To his gay nothings, n. was replied BYRON. Phr. *A new n.*, a worthless novelty. Now *dial.* *No n.*, n. at all. *colloq.*

Phrases, etc. *Neck or n.*, see NECK *sb.*[1] *N. else* (*but* or *than*): see ELSE *adv.* *N. but* (or *except*): see BUT *conj.* *N. doing* (slang), ellipt. formula expressing refusal or failure to do something. *One has*, or *there is*, *n. for it but*, denoting absence of any alternative course. *N.*, *if not*.., above everything. *For n.*: †**a.** by no means; on no consideration; **b.** in vain, to no purpose; **c.** causelessly; **d.** gratuitiously. *N. to*: **a.** of no consequence *to* one; **b.** not to be compared *to* some other person or thing. *To make n. of*: **a.** to make light of; **b.** (with *can*) to be unable to do anything; to fail to comprehend or solve. *To come to n.*, to have no result; to break down, fail. *To have n. to do with* (a thing or person): see DO *v.* IV. Also *ellipt.* *All to n.*, to the fullest extent (*arch.*). *N. off* (*Naut.*): an order not to let the ship fall off from the wind.

B. *adv.* Not at all, in no way OE.

I praise nothyng the knowlege of myne auncesters LD. BERNERS. †Phr. *to make n.*, not to be *of* consequence *to*, not to tell *for* or *against* –1727. To a shadie bank..He led her n. loath MILTON. The bird was n. the worse for what it had undergone SOUTHEY. *N. like* (see LIKE *a.* 2): in no way approaching (another thing) in size or quality; also advb. = not nearly, and *absol.* far from it. *N. near*: cf. NEAR *adv.*[2] 5. *N. worth*, of no value (now *rare*).

Nothingarian (nɒþiŋē^{ə}·riăn). 1789. [f. NOTHING + -ARIAN.] One who holds no religious belief. Hence **Nothinga·rianism.**

Nothingism (nɒ·þiŋiz'm). 1742. [f. as prec. + -ISM.] **1.** A triviality, a trifle. **2.** = NIHILISM 1. 1809. **3.** = NIHILISM 2. 1890.

No·thingness. 1631. [f. as prec. + -NESS.] **1.** The condition or state of being nothing; non-existence; also, that which is non-existent. **b.** The cessation of consciousness or of life 1813. **2.** The worthlessness or vanity *of* something 1646. **b.** That which has no value; the condition of being worthless 1654. **3.** Utter insignificance 1652. **4.** A non-existent thing; a state of non-existence or worthlessness; a thing of no value, etc. 1652.

1. A thing of beauty is a joy for ever:..it will never Pass into n. KEATS. **b.** The first dark day of n. BYRON. **2.** A sarment upon the n. of good works..was preached SMOLLETT.

No-tho·roughfare. 1809. A way, lane, etc., from which there is no exit at one end; a cul-de-sac.

Notice (nō^{u}·tis), *sb.* 1483. [– (O)Fr. *notice* – L. *notitia* being known, acquaintance, knowledge, notion, f. *notus* known.] **1.** Intimation, information, intelligence, warning. Also with *pl.* **b.** A sign, placard, etc., conveying some intimation or intelligence 1805. **2.** Formal intimation or warning of something 1594. **b.** An intimation by one of the parties to an agreement that it is to terminate at a specified time, *esp.* with ref. to quitting a house, lodgings, or employment 1837. **3.** Heed, cognizance, note, attention 1597. **4.** A brief mention in writing; *spec.* in mod. use, a paragraph or article on a newly published book, a review 1840.

1. Of these..I thought fit to give thee this n. WALTON. Phr. *To give* (and *to have*) *n.* *At short n.*, with little time for preparation. So *at ten minutes' n.*, etc. **2.** I had the lease of the house, and the n. to quit lying at my disposal MRS. CARLYLE. **b.** The girl was under n. 1887. **3.** The author speaks ..of her debt, as a thing scarcely worthy of n. BURKE. **4.** That brilliant n. of some..book of verses 1872. Phr. *To take n.* (const. *of*), to give heed, bestow attention; *spec.* of babies, to show signs of intelligent observation.

Notice (nō^{u}·tis), *v.* 1450. [f. prec. Little used bef. *c*1750.] †**1.** *trans.* To notify, intimate –1627. **2.** To make mention of; to remark upon; to speak of (something observed) 1611. **b.** To point out, make mention of, *to* one 1627. **3.** To take notice of; to perceive, observe 1757. **4.** To treat (a person) with attention and civility; to recognize or acknowledge. Now *rare*. 1746. **5.** To serve with a notice; to give notice to 1850.

2. b. She looked so much better that Sir Charles

noticed it to Lady Harriet MRS. GASKELL. **3.** I could n. a turbidity gathering in the air TYNDALL. **5.** The men, about forty in number, were 'noticed' on Friday 1880. Hence **No·ticeable** *a.* worthy of notice; capable of being noticed 1796. **No·ticeably** *adv.* remarkably 1855.

Notifiable (nōᵘ·tifəiăb'l), *a.* 1889. [f. NOTIFY *v.* + -ABLE.] That should be notified to some authority, *esp.* of diseases.

Notify (nōᵘ·tifəi), *v.* late ME. [– (O)Fr. *notifier* – L. *notificare*, f. *notus* known; see -FY.] †**1.** *trans.* To take note of, observe –1678. **2.** To make known, publish, proclaim; to announce. late ME. †**3.** To indicate, denote –1727. **4.** To give notice to; to inform. (Common in U.S. since 1700.) 1440.

2. The king therefore notified to the country his intention of holding a parliament MACAULAY. **4.** Peter notified him, through his first minister, that he was to attend the ceremony 1843. So **No:tifica·tion,** the action of notifying; an intimation, a notice. **No·tified** *ppl. a.* (now *dial.*) celebrated, notorious. **No·tifier.**

Notion (nōᵘ·ʃən). 1567. [– L. *notio* conception, idea, f. *not-*, pa. ppl. stem of *(g)noscere* know; see -ION.] **I. 1.** A general concept under which a particular thing or person may be classed; a term expressive of such a concept. Chiefly with *under*. †**b.** A character, relation, form, etc., in which anything is conceived, mentioned, or exists –1651. †**2.** The connotation *of* a term –1713.

1. *Under the n. of*, under the concept, category, or designation of; I travelled..under the n. of a Japanese converted to Christianity 1764.

II. 1. An idea or concept 1605. †**2.** Understanding, mind, intellect –1667. **3.** An idea, view, opinion, theory, or belief 1603. **4.** An inclination, disposition, or desire to do something specified; a fancy for something 1746. Now *rare*. **5.** A product of invention 1700. **6.** *U.S.* **a.** *pl.* Wares of various kinds forming a miscellaneous cargo 1805. **b.** *pl.* Small wares, *esp.* cheap useful ingenious articles 1830.

1. Her n. of a joke is not very delicate JOHNSON. How he first Learned of the complication, I've no n. 1878. *First* and *second notions* = *First* and *second intentions* (see INTENTION II. 2). *General n.*, (see GENERAL *a.* 5c). **2.** *Lear* I. iv. 245. The Quaker N. of the Light within 1697. At Winchester College, a characteristic expression, tradition, custom, etc. current in the school. **4.** Gloucestershire people have no n. of dying with hunger COBBETT. **5.** Machines for flying in the air, and other wonderful notions EVELYN.

Notional (nōᵘ·ʃənăl), *a.* 1597. [– Fr. †*notional*, *-el* or med.L. *notionalis*, f. *notio*; see prec., -AL¹.] **1.** Of knowledge, etc.: Purely speculative; not based upon fact or demonstration. †**b.** Of persons: Given to abstract speculation; holding merely speculative views –1772. **2.** Of things, relations, etc.: Existing only in thought; imaginary 1629. **3.** Of the nature of, pertaining or relating to, a notion or idea 1861.

1. A n. work as distinguished from an experimental work M. ARNOLD. **2.** Meere notionall is their [gems] value; which is in the Opinion, not in the Thing 1629. Hence **No·tionalist,** a speculative thinker; a theorist. **No·tionally** *adv.* speculatively, theoretically. **No·tionist** (now *rare*), one who holds extravagant or whimsical opinions.

No·tionate, *a.* *Sc.* and *U.S.* 1859. [f. NOTION *sb.* + -ATE²; cf. *opinionate.*] Full of notions, fanciful; also, headstrong.

Notitia (noᵘti·ʃiă). 1700. [– L. *notitia* knowledge, in late and med.L. also list, account, etc., f. *notus* known.] †**1.** Literary particulars. HEARNE. **2.** An account or list; now *spec.* a register of ecclesiastical sees or districts 1797.

Noto- (nōᵘ·to), comb. form of Gr. νῶτον back, as in **Notobra·nchiate** *a.* having dorsal branchiæ or gills 1870; **Notone·cta** [Gr. νήκτης swimmer] *Entom.* a species of water-beetle which swims on its back; the boat-fly 1638.

Notochord (nōᵘ·tŏkǭɹd). 1848. [f. prec. + CHORD.] *Biol.* A cartilaginous band or rod forming the primitive basis of the spinal column in vertebrates. Hence **Notocho·rdal** *a.*

Notogæa (nōᵘtŏdʒī·ă). 1868. [f. Gr. νότος south wind + γαῖα earth, land.] A large zoological region, comprising the Australian, New Zealand, and Neotropical regions. Hence **Notogæ·al, -gæ·an, -gæ·ic** *adjs.*

Notopodium (nōᵘtopōᵘ·diŏm). 1870. [mod. L., f. NOTO- + Gr. πόδιον, dim of πούς foot; see -IUM.] *Biol.* The upper or dorsal branch of a parapodium. Hence **Notopo·dial** *a.*

Notoriety (nōᵘtŏrəi·ėti). 1592. [– Fr. *notoriété* or med.L. *notorietas*, f. *notorius*; see next, -ITY.] **1.** The state or character of being notorious; the fact of being publicly or commonly known. **2.** A well-known or celebrated person 1837.

1. He had been raised..to n. such as has for low and bad minds all the attractions of glory MACAULAY.

Notorious (nŏtōᵊ·riəs), *a.* 1548. [– med.L. *notorius* (cf. late L. *notoria* notice, news, *notorium* information, indictment), f. L. *notus* known; see NOTION, -ORIOUS.] **1.** Of facts: Well known; forming a matter of common knowledge 1555. **2.** Of places, persons, etc.: Well or widely known (now *rare*); †famous 1555. **b.** Such as is generally, openly, or publicly known. Now *rare*. 1584. †**3.** Conspicuous; obvious, evident –1770. **4.** Used attrib. with designations of persons, deeds, etc., which imply condemnation: Well known, noted (as being of this kind) 1548. **5.** Noted *for* some bad practice, quality, etc.; unfavourably known or spoken of 1579.

1. Men..who deny the most n. facts JOHNSON. Phr. *It is n. that* [etc.]. **2. b.** The Privy Council, whom the law recognised as the sworn and n. Councillors of the Crown 1863. **4.** Declarit tratouris and notorius rebellis 1574. His mean suberfuge renders him more contemptible than his n. untruth 1807. **5.** You n. stinkardly beareward B. JONS. These books were perfectly n. PALEY. Hence **Noto·rious-ly** *adv.*, **-ness.**

Notornis (notǭ·ɹnis). 1848. [f. Gr. νότος south + ὄρνις bird.] *Ornith.* A New Zealand flightless bird, now rare or extinct, related to the coots and rails.

Notothere (nōᵘ·toþīᵊɹ). 1881. [Anglicized f. mod.L. *nototherium*, f. Gr. νότος south + θηρίον beast.] *Palæont.* An extinct marsupial of great size found in post-tertiary formations.

Not-out, *a.* 1891. *Cricket.* The phrase 'not out' (see OUT *adv.*) used attrib. to designate a batsman (his score, etc.) whose innings either is unfinished or is ended only by his side going out.

‖**Notum** (nōᵘ·tŏm). 1877. [mod.L. – Gr. νῶτον back.] The dorsal part of the thorax in insects.

‖**Notus** (nōᵘ·tŏs). *poet.* late ME. [L. – Gr. Νότος.] The south wind.

Notwithstanding (nǫtwiðstæ·ndiŋ, -wiþ-), *prep.*, *adv.*, and *conj.* ME. [f. NOT *adv.* + *withstanding*, pres. pple. of WITHSTAND *v.*, after (O)Fr. *non obstant*, L. NON OBSTANTE.] **A.** *prep.* **1.** Despite, in spite of. **2.** Following *this*, *that*, or a sb., after OFr. absolute participial construction *ce non obstant*, etc. 1490.

1. N. all her sodaine quips SHAKS. **2.** These n., His hair and wrinkles will betray his age MASSINGER.

B. *adv.* Nevertheless, still, yet 1440.

He saw that it would come to pass n. SOUTHEY.

C. *conj.* Although 1449. **b.** Followed by *that* with dependent clause 1584.

N. objections may lie against some parts of her Liturgy,..her doctrines are exclusively scriptural WORDSW. **b.** N. that it were once burned by the D. of Burgundie 1596.

‖**Nougat** (nū·ga). 1827. [– Fr. *nougat* – Pr. *nogat*, f. *noga* nut + *-at* :– L. *-atum* -ATE¹.] A sweetmeat composed chiefly of sugar and almonds (or other nuts).

Nought (nǭt), *sb.*, *a.*, and *adv.* [OE. *nōwiht*, f. NE + *ōwiht* OUGHT *sb.*¹, var. of *āwiht* AUGHT *sb.*² Cf. NAUGHT, NOT.] **A.** *sb.* **1.** = NOTHING A. 1. (Now only literary.) †**2.** Nothingness –1711. **b.** *Arith.* = NOTHING A. 4. late ME. **3.** With *a* and *pl.* **a.** A thing or person of no worth or value; a mere nothing ME. **b.** *Arith.* A cipher 1660.

1. I am n., I have n., I desire n. 1665. **2.** He comaundide, and thingis weren maad of nouȝt WYCLIF *Ps.* 32[3]. Phr. *To bring, come, go*, etc., *to n.* †*N. worth*, worth nothing, of no value. †*A thing of n.*, a mere nothing. *For n.*: †in vain, to no purpose; without payment; gratis. *To set at n.*: to despise, defy, scorn, disregard. **3. b.** *Noughts and crosses*: a game played with a figure containing (usu.) nine spaces which are filled alternately by the two players with noughts and crosses, the object being to get a row of one or the other.

B. *adj.* [Cf. NAUGHT *a.*, the more usual form.] †**1.** Of material things: Bad in condition or of their kind –1728. †**b.** Of actions, etc.: Bad, wicked –1607; immoral, vicious –1550. **2.** Good for nothing. late ME. †**3.** Injurious *to*, bad *for*, a thing or person. Also without const. –1690.

1. 'Tis too plain, the Materials are n. SWIFT.

C. *adv.* [orig. the accus. of the sb.] **1.** To no extent; in no way; not at all OE. †**2.** = NOT *adv.* –1724.

1. Vertues are laide aside, and n. accounted off 1568.

Nou·ghty, *a.* ME. *Obs.* exc. *Sc.* [f. prec. sb. + -Y¹.] = NAUGHTY.

†**Nould,** would not: see NILL *v.* 1579–1742.

Noumenon (nau·mĕnǫn). Pl. **noumena.** 1798. [– G. *noumenon* (Kant) – Gr. νοούμενον, n. of pr. pple. pass. of νοεῖν apprehend, conceive. Introduced by Kant in contrast to *phenomenon.*] *Metaph.* In Kantian philosophy: An object of purely intellectual intuition, devoid of all phenomenal attributes. Hence **Nou·menal** *a.* relating to, consisting of, noumena; given only by intuition; not phenomenal. **Nou·menally** *adv.* in a noumenal aspect.

Noun (naun). late ME. [– AFr. *noun* = OFr. *nun*, *num* (mod. *nom*) :– L. *nomen.*] *Gram.* **1.** A word used as the name of a person or thing. In older grammars including *nomen substantivum* and *nomen adjectivum* (see 2 and 3). **2.** *N. substantive* = sense 1. late ME. **3.** *N. adjective* = ADJECTIVE B. 1530. Hence **Nou·nal** *a.*

†**Nourice.** [ME. *nurice* – OFr. *nurice*, etc. (mod. *nourrice*) :– late L. *nutricia* (Jerome), fem. of L. *nutricius*, f. *nutrix*, *-ic-* (wet-)nurse, f. *nutrire* (see next).] A nurse –1768.

Nourish (nɒ·riʃ), *v.* ME. [– OFr. *noriss-*, lengthened stem (see -ISH²) of *norir* (mod. *nourrir*) :– L. *nutrire* feed, foster, cherish.] **I.** †**1.** *trans.* To bring up, rear, nurture (a child, an animal) –1618. †**2.** To allow (one's hair) to grow –1807. †**3.** To promote the growth of, tend or cultivate (plants, etc.) –1792.

1. He..left the yonger [daughter] styll in Englande, wheras she had been brought vp and norisshed 1523.

II. †**1.** = NURSE *v.* 1 –1551. **b.** To sustain (a person or living thing) with food or proper nutriment ME. **c.** To supply (a thing) with whatever is necessary for growth, formation, or proper condition. late ME. **2.** To provide with food and sustenance. Now *rare*. late ME. **3.** *absol.* To afford nutriment –1667.

1. b. The human body can be nourished on any food EMERSON. **c.** The mountain slopes which n. the glacier TYNDALL. **2.** And thou shalt dwell in the land of Goshen.., And there wil I n. thee *Gen.* 45:11. **3.** Sheepes Milke is sweeter, and nourisheth more 1577.

III. 1. To promote or foster (a feeling, habit, etc.) in or among persons ME. **b.** To cherish or nurse (a feeling) in one's own heart or mind 1560. **2.** To maintain, encourage, strengthen (one's heart, mind, etc.) in or with something. late ME.

1. Freedom nourishes self-respect 1837. **b.** Clodius..nourishing an implacable hate against Cicero FROUDE. **2.** A man, who nourished his spirit with the contemplation of ancient heroes JAS. MILL. Hence **Nou·rishable** *a.* capable of affording, susceptive of, nourishment. **Nou·risher,** one who, or that which, nourishes; a nourishing agent. **Nou·rishing** *ppl. a.*, nutritious.

Nourishment (nɒ·riʃmĕnt). late ME. [f. NOURISH *v.* + -MENT (repl. next). Cf. OFr. *norrissement.*] **1.** That which nourishes or sustains; aliment, food. **2.** The action, process, or fact of nourishing 1485.

1. No Dressing they require..; The Soil it self due N. supplies DRYDEN. *transf.* More substantial literary n. than could be..packed into so portable compass RUSKIN.

Nou·riture. Now *rare* or *Obs.* late ME. [ME. *noriture*, etc. – OFr. *nore-*, *noriture* etc. (mod. *nourriture*), f. *norir*; see NOURISH, -TURE. Cf. NURTURE *sb.*] **1.** Nourishment, sustenance, food. †**2.** Nurture, upbringing –1647.

‖**Nous** (naus). 1678. [Gr. νοῦς mind.] **1.** *Gr. Philos.* Mind, intellect. **2.** *colloq.* or *slang.* Intelligence, common sense, gump-

tion. (Occas. written in Greek letters.) 1706.
2. I think his doing so exhibits considerable n. in a brute 1847.

Nousel, Nousle, var. ff. NUZZLE *v.*[1] and *v.*[2]

Nouther, nowther, *pron., a., adv., conj.* Now *dial.* [OE. *nowþer*, contr. of *nōhwæþer*, f. *nō* (see NO *adv.*[1]) + *hwæþer* whether. Cf. NOTHER.] **A.** †**1.** *pron.* Neither (of two) –1596. †**2.** *adj.* Neither. ME only. **B.** *adv.* and *conj.* **1.** = NEITHER A. 1. ME. †**b.** = NOR –1596. **2.** = NEITHER A. 3. ME.

Nov., abbrev. of NOVEMBER.

‖**Nova** (nōᵘ·vă). *Pl.* **novæ** (nōᵘ·vī). 1877. [L., fem. sing. of *novus* new.] *Astr.* A new star or nebula.

Novaculite (novæ·kiŭləit). 1796. [f. L. *novacula* razor + -ITE[1] 2 b.] *Min.* A hard argillaceous slate used for hones.

Novate (novēⁱ·t), *v. rare.* 1611. [– *novat-*, pa. ppl. stem of L. *novare* make new, f. *novus* new; see -ATE[3].] *trans.* To replace by something new; *spec.* in (Roman) law, to replace by a new obligation, debt, etc.

Novatian (novēⁱ·ʃⁱăn), *sb.* and *a.* 1449. [– eccl. L. *Novatiani* (pl.), f. *Novatianus* (see def.).] **A.** *sb.* A member of the sect founded by Novatianus, a Roman presbyter in the middle of the 3rd c. (see quots.) Chiefly *pl.* **B.** *adj.* Of or pertaining to Novatianus or the sect of Novatians 1630.

A. The Novatians, excepting their peculiar error, of denying reconciliation to those that fell in persecution, held other things in common with Catholiques CHILLINGW. Hence **Nova·tianism. Nova·tianist.**

Novation (novēⁱ·ʃən). 1533. [– late L. *novatio*, f. L. *novat-*; see NOVATE *v.*, -ION. So (O)Fr. *novation* in sense 2.] **1.** The introduction of something new; an innovation. Now *rare.* **2.** *Law.* The substitution of a new debtor, creditor, contract, etc., in place of an old one 1682.

Novator (novēⁱ·təɹ). 1644. [– L. *novator*, f. as prec.; see -OR 2.] An innovator.

Novel (nǫ·vĕl), *sb.* 1460. [In senses 1 and 2 – OFr. *novelle* (mod. *nouvelle*) = It. *novella* :– L. *novella*, n. pl. (construed as sing.) of *novellus*, f. *novus* new; in senses 3 and 4 directly – It. *novella*, orig. fem. (sc. *storia* story) of *novello* new. In sense 5 – late L. *novella* (sc. *constitutio*), usually in pl. *novellæ*.] †**1.** Something new; a novelty –1719. †**2.** *pl.* News, tidings –1724. †**b.** *sing.* A piece of news –1736. **3.** (Chiefly in *pl.*) One of the short stories contained in such works as the *Decameron* of Boccaccio, the *Heptameron* of Marguerite of Valois, etc.; a short story of this type 1566. **4.** A fictitious prose narrative of considerable length, in which characters and actions representative of real life are portrayed in a plot of more or less complexity 1643. **b.** This type of literature. (Formerly without article; now with *the.*) 1757. **5.** *Roman Law.* A new decree or constitution, supplementary to the Codex, *esp.* one of those made by the Emperor Justinian 1612.

2. Ready to bring his Maister Nouels and tidinges, whether they be true or false 1561. **4.** This is no mere amatorious n. MILT. **b.** England has hardly received the honour she deserves as the birthplace of the modern n. 1871.

Novel (nǫ·vĕl), *a.* late ME. [– OFr. *novel* (mod. *nouvel, nouveau*) :– L. *novellus*, f. *novus* new.] **1.** †**a.** New, young, fresh (*rare*) –1616. **b.** Recent; of recent origin –1727. **2.** New; of a new kind or nature; strange; hitherto unknown 1475.

1. b. *N. disseisin*: disseisin of a fresh or recent date. **2.** A style of decoration more n. than elegant 1870. *N. constitution* = NOVEL *sb.* 5.

Novelese (nǫvĕlī·z). 1900. [f. NOVEL *sb.* 4 + -ESE; cf. *journalese.*] The style of language characteristic of inferior novels.

Novelette (nǫvĕle·t). 1780. [f. as prec. + -ETTE.] **1.** A short novel. **2.** *Mus.* A pianoforte piece of free form containing a variety of themes, e.g. the *Novelletten* of Schumann 1893.

Novelism (nǫ·vĕliz'm). 1626. [f. NOVEL *sb.* + -ISM.] †**1.** Innovation, novelty –1703. **2.** Novel-writing 1828.

Novelist (nǫ·vĕlist). 1583. [f. NOVEL *sb.* + -IST; sense 2 – Fr. *nouvelliste*) (XVII).] †**1.** An innovator; one who favours novelty –1727. (Common in 17th c.) †**2.** A newsmonger, news-carrier –1764. **3.** A writer of novels 1728.

Novelize (nǫ·vĕləiz), *v.* 1625. [f. NOVEL *sb.* + -IZE.] **1.** †**a.** *trans.* To make new or novel –1660. **b.** *intr.* To introduce novelty 1823. **2.** To convert into the form or style of a novel 1828.

2. Attempts to n. history 1833.

Novelty (nǫ·vĕlti). late ME. [– OFr. *novelté* (mod. *nouveauté*); see NOVEL *a.*, -TY[1].] **1.** A new or unusual thing or occurrence. Also *the n.*, the newest thing. †**b.** A new matter of report or talk. (Usu. in *pl.*) –1595. **c.** An innovation 1576. **2.** Novel or unusual character *of* something. late ME. **3.** The quality or state of being novel; that which is novel, new, or hitherto unknown 1484.

1. They are curious, and great louers of nouelties 1632. **2.** The n. of these amusements interested me 1841. **3.** Any thing which has the least appearance of N. 1728.

November (nove·mbəɹ). Abbrev. **Nov.** ME. [– (O)Fr. *novembre* – L. *November*, also *Novembris* (sc. *mensis* month), f. *novem* nine.] The eleventh month of the year, containing 30 days.

‖**Novena** (novī·nă). 1745. [– med.L. *novena*, f. *novem* nine, after L. *novenarius* of nine days.] *R.C.Ch.* A devotion consisting of special prayers or services on nine successive days.

Novenary (nǫ·vĕnări). 1577. [– L. *novenarius*, f. *novem* nine; see -ARY.] **A.** *adj.* Pertaining to, or consisting of, the number nine (*rare*) 1603. **B.** *sb.* **1.** An aggregate or set of nine 1577. **2.** = prec. 1818.

Novennial (nove·niăl), *a.* 1656. [– late L. *novennis* (f. *novem* nine + *annus* year), after *biennial*, etc.] Happening or recurring every ninth year.

Novercal (novɜ̄·ɹkăl), *a.* 1623. [– L. *novercalis*, f. *noverca* step-mother, f. *novus* new; see -AL[1].] Characteristic of, or resembling, a stepmother.

Novice (nǫ·vis). ME. [– (O)Fr. *novice* m. and fem. – L. *novicius, -icia*, f. *novus* new; see -ICE.] **1.** *Eccl.* One who has entered a religious house and is under probation. **b.** A new convert 1526. **2.** One who is new to the circumstances in which he is placed; a beginner, tyro ME. **3.** *attrib.* 1530. **b.** Appositive, as *n. hand*, etc. 1605.

1. He then assumes the dress of the Order, a cassock and bands, and becomes a n. 1859. **2.** Though they came to us under the name of Veterans [they] proved to be ignorant Novices 1726.

No·viceship. 1620. [f. NOVICE + -SHIP.] = NOVITIATE 1. 1639. **b.** = NOVITIATE 3. 1620.

Novilu·nar, *a. rare.* 1686. [f. med.L. *noviluna* (late L. *-ium*; f. L. *novus* new + *luna* moon), after LUNAR.] Of or pertaining to the new moon.

Novitiate, noviciate (novi·ʃⁱĕt). 1600. [– Fr. *noviciat* or med.L. *noviciatus*; see NOVICE, -ATE[1].] **1.** The probationary period of a novice. **b.** *transf.* and *fig.*. The state or time of being a novice or beginner; time of initiation, apprenticeship, or probation 1610. **2.** A novice in a religious order 1655. **b.** A beginner, tyro 1734. Now *rare* or *Obs.* **3.** The quarters occupied by novices; a place where novices are trained 1626. **4.** *attrib.* as *n. chapel*, etc. 1704. **b.** Appositive, as *n. candidate*, etc. 1775.

†**Novi·tious,** *a.* 1619. [– L. *novitius* (med. L. *novicius* novice, convert), f. *novus* new; see -ITIOUS[1].] **1.** Having the character of novices. SCLATER. **2.** Of recent origin –1669. So **Novi·tial** *a.*, characteristic of a novice (*rare*) 1700.

No·vity. Now *rare* or *Obs.* 1460. [– OFr. *novité* – L. *novitas, -tat-*, f. *novus* new; see -ITY.] †**1.** An innovation; a novelty –1692. **2.** Novelty, newness 1569.

‖**Novodamus** (nōᵘvodē·mŏs). 1768. *Sc. Law.* [L. *de novo damus* 'we grant anew'.] A charter containing a clause (also called 'of n.') by which the superior grants afresh the matters described in the dispositive clause.

†**No·vum.** 1588. [– L. *novem* nine. Cf. Fr. (XVII) and Pg. *quinquenove* (said to have been introduced from Flanders) = L. *quinque* five + *novem* nine.] An old game at dice played by five persons, the two principal throws being nine and five –1621.

Now (nau), *adv., conj., sb.,* and *a.* [OE. *nū* = OS. *nū* (Du. *nu*), OHG. *nū* (G. *nun*, with advb. *n* added), ON., Goth. *nū*; CIE. adv. of time, repr. also by L. *num, nunc*, Gr. νυ, νῦν, Skr. *nū, nūnám.*] **I. 1.** At the present time or moment. **b.** Under the present circumstances; in view of these facts 1508. **2.** In the time directly following on the present moment; immediately OE. **3.** In the time directly preceding the present moment. Now only in *just now* or (poet.) *even now.* OE. **4.** At the time spoken of or referred to; by this time 1548. **5.** *Now.. now*, used to introduce antithetical clauses, phrases, or words. late ME. **b.** So *now.. then, now,.. and again* (arch.), etc. 1593.

1. They will be our lords, as they are n. M. ARNOLD. Phr. (*It's*) *n. or never*, this is the moment to act, or not at all. **b.** I can believe anything n. MRS. STOWE. **2.** I am in a hurry, and must go n. JOWETT. **3.** The good Man whom I have just n. mentioned ADDISON. **4.** The war was n. practically concluded 1874. **5.** N. vsed in this sence, n. in that 1620. **b.** His walk was n. quick, and again slow JOHNSON.

Phrases. †*As n.*, at this time. *N. and again, anon, †eft, †n.*, at one time and another, from time to time. *N. and* (also †*or*) *then*, occasionally, fitfully, at intervals. So *Every n. and then* (or *again*).

II. 1. In sentences expressing a command or request, with the purely temporal sense weakened or effaced. Later also with ellipse of verb. OE. **b.** So *Now then.* (Freq. in mod. use.) OE. **2.** Used to introduce a noteworthy point in an argument or proof, etc. OE. **b.** Inserted parenthetically, or at the end of a clause, with similar force OE. **3.** Used ellipt., esp. at the beginning of a clause 1450. **4.** as *conj.* Since, seeing that; as...now OE. **b.** So *now that* 1530.

1. N. your Counsels, For I am at my wits end FLETCHER. **b.** 'N. then,' said Amyas, 'to breakfast' KINGSLEY. **2.** N. this was bad enough,..but this was not all DICKENS. **b.** There's a wise young woman, n. 1760. **3.** N., n., Ringwood has him WALTON. N. for it, Sneak; the enemy's at hand 1764. **4.** N. they are oppress'd with trauaile, they..cannot vse such vigilance As when they are fresh SHAKS.

III. 1. With preps., as *by, ere, for, or, till, unto, now* OE. **b.** *From now* (*forth, forward*, etc.) ME. **2.** as *sb.* The present time. late ME. **3.** A present point or moment of time 1630.

1. And for n. Ile leave ye FLETCHER. **b.** From n. till Doomsday KINGSLEY. **2.** N. is an atome, it will puzzle the skill of an angell to divide FULLER. Plant the great hereafter in the n. 1851. **3.** An everlasting N. reigns in nature EMERSON. Man ever with his N. at strife LOWELL.

IV. *attrib.* or *adj.* Present, of the present time 1444. (Common in 17th c.)

The dreadful treatment of the n. King BURKE.

Now-a-day, *adv.* late ME. [Cf. next and ADAY.] = next.

Now-a-days (nau·ădeⁱz), *adv.* late ME. [f. NOW *adv.* + ADAYS 2. Now freq. written as one word.] At the present day, in these times. Also *attrib.* and as *sb.*

Guineas are scarce now-a-days 1833. *sb.* The Phisitians of now a dayes 1647.

Noway (nōᵘ·weⁱ), *adv.* ME. [f. NO *a.* + WAY *sb.*] In no way or manner; not at all; by no means.

Noways (nōᵘ·weⁱz), *adv.* [Early ME. *nanes wei(e)s*, i.e. gen. sing. of NONE *a.* and WAY *sb.*; in later use only the second element retains its inflexion.] = prec.

Nowch(e, obs. ff. OUCH, clasp.

Nowed (nū·ėd, naud), *a.* 1572. [– Fr. *noué* knotted + -ED[1]; see NOWY.] *Her.* Knotted; tied in a knot.

Nowel[1] (nōᵘe·l). late ME. [– OFr. *nouel, noel* (mod. *noël*), obscure var. of *nael, neel* :– L. *natalis* (sc. *dies* day) NATAL.] **1.** A word shouted or sung as an expression of joy at Christmas. (Retained in Christmas carols.) †**2.** The feast of Christmas; Christmastide –1599.

Now·el.[2] late ME. [var. of NEWEL.] †**1.** = NEWEL 1 –1688. **2.** *Founding.* The core or inner part of a mould for casting large hollow objects 1864.

Nowhere (nōᵘ·hweᵊɹ), *adv.* OE. [f. NO *adv.* + WHERE *adv.*] **1.** In or at no place; not anywhere. **b.** To no place ME. **2.** In no work or author ME. **3.** as *sb.* A non-existent place; absence of all place 1831.

1. He was n. to be seen 1797. **b.** Mr. C. was minded to go n. this summer MRS. CARLYLE. Phrases. *N. near* or †*nigh*, not nearly, not by a long way. *To be n.* (colloq.): **a.** To be badly beaten (in a race, contest, etc.); to be out of the running. Also *transf.* **b.** *U.S.* To be utterly at a loss; to be ignorant.

No whit, *adv. arch.* 1530. [See WHIT *sb.*] Not at all, not the least.

Nowhither (nōu·hwiðəɹ), *adv.* OE. [f. No *adv.* + WHITHER *adv.*] To no place; nowhere.

Nowise (nōu·wəiz), *adv.* late ME. [f. No *a.* + WISE *sb.*] In no way or manner; not at all.

Nowt (naut). *Sc.* and *n. dial.* ME. [– ON. *naut*, corresp. to OE. *nēat* NEAT *sb.*] **1.** *pl.* Cattle, oxen. **2.** *sing.* An ox, a bullock. late ME. **b.** *transf.* A stupid, coarse, or clumsy person 1806. **3.** *attrib.* late ME.

Nowt(h, dial. and obs. forms of NOUGHT.

Nowy (nau·i), *a.* 1562. [– OFr. *noé* (mod. *noué*), pa. pple. of *noer*, *nouer* knot :– L. *nodare*, f. *nodus* knot; see -Y^{5}. Cf. NOWED.] *Her.* †**1.** = NOWED *a.* **2.** Having a projection or curvature in or near the middle.

‖**Nox** (nǫks). 1567. [L.] Night. (Chiefly *poet.*)

No·xal, *a.* 1605. [– late L. *noxalis*, f. L. *noxa* hurt, damage; see -AL^{1}.] *Civil Law.* Relating to damage or injury done by a person or animal belonging to another, or to an action in respect of this.

Noxious (nǫ·kʃəs), *a.* 1612. [– L. *noxius*, f. as prec.; see -OUS.] Injurious, hurtful, harmful; unwholesome. Hence **No·xious-ly** *adv.*, **-ness.**

†**Noy,** *sb.* ME. [Aphetic f. ANNOY *sb.*] Annoyance, trouble –1611.

†**Noy,** *v.* ME. [Aphetic f. ANNOY *v.*] **1.** *trans.* To annoy, trouble, vex, harass; to harm or injure –1609. **2.** *refl.* and *intr.* To vex oneself, to grieve –1587. **3.** *absol.* To cause annoyance or harm –1573.

1. I ymagyn with myself whiche wayes they myght take to n. our enemyes most T. CROMWELL.

‖**Noyade** (nwaya·d), *sb.* 1819. [Fr., f. *noyer* drown :– L. *necare* kill without a weapon, (later) drown, f. *nex*, *nec-* slaughter; see -ADE.] The execution of persons by drowning, as practised by Carrier at Nantes in 1794. Hence **Noyade** *v.* and **Noyading** *vbl. sb.* 1837.

†**Noy·ance.** ME. Aphetic f. ANNOYANCE –1670.

‖**Noyau** (nwa·yo). 1797. [Fr., earlier *noiel* kernel :– Rom. **nucale*, subst. use of n. of late L. *nucalis*, f. *nux*, *nuc-* nut.] A liqueur made of brandy flavoured with the kernels of certain fruits.

†**Noy·ful,** *a.* late ME. [f. NOY *sb.* + -FUL.] Annoying; also noxious –1618.

†**Noy·ous,** *a.* ME. [Aphetic f. ANNOYOUS *a.*] Vexatious, troublesome –1675.

Nozzle (nǫ·z'l). 1608. [f. NOSE *sb.* + -LE.] **1.** A socket on a candlestick or sconce, for receiving the lower end of the candle. Now *rare.* **2.** A small spout, mouthpiece, or projecting aperture; a short terminal pipe or part of a pipe, as the nose of a pair of bellows, etc. 1683. **b.** Applied to parts of a steam-engine, *esp.* the steam-port, or the part of the cylinder enclosing this, and the exhaust-pipe or the adjustable end of this 1839. **3.** *slang.* The nose 1771. **4.** A small nose or beak; a projecting part or end 1850.

‖**Nuance** (niū·āṅs). 1781. [Fr., f. *nuer* show variations of shades of colour like clouds, f. *nue* cloud :– pop. L. **nube*, L. *nubes*; see -ANCE.] **1.** A slight or delicate variation in expression, feeling, opinion, meaning, etc. **2.** A shade of colour; a slight difference in shade or tone 1856. **3.** A delicate gradation in musical expression 1879.

1. The more expert one were at *nuances*, the more poetic one should be H. WALPOLE.

Nub (nɒb). 1594. [var. of KNUB.] †**1.** = KNUB 2. (*rare*) –1759. **2.** A knob or protuberance; a lump 1727. **3.** *U.S.* The point of a story or matter 1859.

Nubble (nɒ·b'l). 1818. [dim. of prec. Cf. KNOBBLE (XV).] A small knob or lump.

‖**Nubecula** (niubī·kiŭlă). *Pl.* **-læ.** 1699. [L., dim. of *nubes* cloud; see -CULE.] **1.** *Path.* **a.** A cloudy formation in urine. **b.** A speck or small cloud in the eye 1727. **2.** *Astron.* One or other of the Magellanic Clouds 1842.

Nubian (niū·biăn). 1727. [– med.L. *Nubianus*, or f. med.L. *Nubia*, f. L. *Nubæ* – Gr. Νοῦβαι, the name of the people.] **A.** *adj.* **1.** Pertaining or belonging to the country of Nubia. **2.** In specific names of animals 1879. **B.** *sb.* **1.** A native of Nubia; a Nubian slave 1788. **2.** A Nubian horse 1790. **3.** The Nubian language 1855.

Nubiferous (niubi·fĕrəs), *a.* 1656. [f. L. *nubifer*, f. *nubes* cloud; see -FEROUS.] Cloud-bringing.

Nubilate (niū·bileit), *v.* 1691. [– *nubilat-*, pa. ppl. stem of L. *nubilare* be or make cloudy, f. *nubila* (n. pl.), f. *nubes* cloud; see -ATE^{3}.] *trans.* To cloud; to obscure; to render less clear or transparent.

Nubile (niū·bil), *a.* 1642. [– L. *nubilis*, f. *nubere* be married to (a man); see -ILE.] **1.** Of females: Marriageable. **2.** Of age: Admitting of, suitable for, marriage 1831. Hence **Nubi·lity** 1813.

Nubilous (niū·biləs), *a.* Now *rare.* 1533. [– L. *nubilosus* or f. *nubilus*, f. *nubes* cloud; see -OUS.] **1.** Cloudy, foggy, misty. **2.** *fig.* Obscure, indefinite.

‖**Nucellus** (niuse·lɒs). 1882. [mod.L., app. meant as a dim. of *nucleus*.] *Bot.* The essential part of an ovule, containing the embryo-sac.

‖**Nucha** (niū·kă). late ME. [– med.L. *nucha* medulla oblongata – Arab. *nukā*ᶜ spinal marrow, medulla.] *Anat.* †**a.** The spinal chord. **b.** The nape of the neck. Hence **Nu·chal** *a.* of, belonging or pertaining to, the nape of the neck 1833. var. †**Nuche** (*rare*) –1601.

Nuci- (niū·si), comb. form of L. *nux*, *nuc-* nut, as in **Nuci·ferous** *a.* bearing nuts. **Nu·ciform** *a.* nut-shaped. **Nuci·vorous** *a.* nut-eating.

Nuclear (niū·kliăɹ), *a.* 1846. [f. NUCLEUS + -AR^{1}.] **1.** Having the character or position of a nucleus; like a nucleus; constituting a nucleus. Chiefly in *Biol.* or *Astron.* **2.** Of or belonging to a nucleus 1880.

1. A nucleolated n. cell 1846. The n. parts of the sun 1881. So **Nu·cleary** *a.* of the nature of a nucleus. **Nu·cleate** *a.* nucleated.

Nucleate (niū·klieit), *v.* 1864. [– *nucleat-*, pa. ppl. stem of late L. *nucleare*, become kernelly or hard, f. *nucleus* kernel; see -ATE^{3}.] **1.** *trans.* To form (anything) into, bring together as, a nucleus. **2.** *intr.* To form a nucleus; to collect about a nucleus 1883. So **Nu·cleated** *ppl. a.* having a nucleus, as a *n. cell*; clustered together 1843.

Nu·cleifo:rm, *a.* 1840. [f. NUCLE(O- + -FORM.] Having the form of a nucleus; tuberculated.

Nuclein (niū·kliin). Also **-ine.** 1878. [f. NUCLEUS + -IN^{1}, after G. *nuklein.*] *Chem.* The principal constituent of cell-nuclei.

Nucleo- (niū·klio), comb. form of L. *nucleus*, used in a number of compounds, chiefly biological, as *n.-albumin*, *-proteid*, etc. **Nu·cleobranch,** *Zool.* a mollusc of the order *Nucleobranchiata*; a Heteropod 1851. **Nu·cleoplasm,** *Biol.* nuclear protoplasm 1882.

‖**Nucleolus** (niuklī·ŏlɒs). Pl. **-li.** 1845. [late L., dim. of NUCLEUS.] *Biol.* A small nucleus; *esp.* a minute rounded body within the nucleus of a cell in animal and vegetable substance; also, a paranucleus. Also **Nu·cleole** 1864. Hence **Nucle·olar** *a.* of the nature of, pertaining to, a n. **Nu·cleolated** *a.* furnished with a n.

Nucleus (niū·kliɒs), *sb. Pl.* **nuclei** (niū·kliəi) and **nucleuses.** 1704. [– L. *nucleus* nut, kernel, inner part, var. of *nuculeus*, f. *nucula*; see NUCULE.] **I. 1.** *Astr.* The more condensed portion of the head of a comet. Also *fig.* †**2.** A supposed interior crust of the earth –1727. **3.** A central part or thing around which other parts or things are grouped, collected, or compacted; that which forms the centre of some aggregate or mass 1762. **b.** esp. *Bot.* and *Zool.* 1829. **c.** *Archæol.* A block of flint or other stone from which early implements have been made 1869.

3. Some extraneous body, which becomes the n. of the calculus 1797. About 700 individuals.. were the n. of his colony of Georgia 1798. A very fair collection of modern books.., the n. of a library 1875. Hence **Nu·cleal** *a.* pertaining to, having the form or position of, a n. 1840.

‖**Nuculanium** (niūkiulēi·niɒm). 1819. [mod. L., irreg. f. L. *nucula* NUCULE.] **1.** An indehiscent fleshy fruit. **2.** A hard nut-like case in the interior of a fleshy fruit, enclosing several seeds 1849.

Nucule (niū·kiul). 1819. [– L. *nucula*, dim. of *nux*, *nuc-* nut; see -ULE. Cf. Fr. *nucule.*] **1.** One of the seeds of a nuculanium; a nutlet; a small stone or seed. **2.** The female organ of reproduction in the cryptogamic tribe *Chara* 1830.

Nuddle (nɒ·d'l), *v.* Now *dial.* 1640. [Of unkn. origin. Cf. dial. *nud* in same sense; cf. also *nuzzle.*] **1.** *intr.* †**a.** To push with the nose; to press close to the ground in this way; to grovel –1661. **2.** *trans.* To squeeze, press 1875.

Nude (niūd). 1531. [– L. *nudus* bare, naked. In B *sb.* 2 after Fr. *nu.*] **A.** *adj.* **1.** *Law.* **a.** Of statements, promises, etc.: Not formally attested or recorded. **b.** Of persons, esp. *n. executor*: An executor, etc., in trust 1590. **2.** Naked, bare; without covering; devoid of furniture or decorations 1866. **b.** Of the human figure, etc.: Naked, undraped 1873.

1. a. *N. contract* or *pact*: a bare contract or promise, without any consideration. **2. b.** The medals..bear..on their obverse the n. bust of that Empress 1879.

B. *sb.* **1.** A nude figure in painting or sculpture 1708. **2.** With *the.* The undraped human figure; the representation of this in the arts 1760. **b.** The condition of being undraped 1856.

2. Modern chalk drawings, studies from the n. BROWNING.

Nudge (nɒdʒ), *v.* 1675. [Of unkn. origin; perh. in much earlier use and rel. to Norw. dial. *nugga*, *nyggja* push, rub.] **1.** *trans.* To touch or push (one) slightly with the elbow to attract attention. **2.** *intr.* To give a push or thrust 1825. Hence **Nudge** *sb.* 1826.

Nudi- (niū·di), comb. form of L. *nudus* NUDE *a.*, as **Nudibra·chiate** *a. Zool.* of polyps, having arms or tentacles covered with cilia.

Nudibranch (niū·dibræŋk). 1844. [– Fr. *nudibranche* (Cuvier); see NUDI-, BRANCHIÆ Cf. next.] *Zool.* A mollusc of the order *Nudibranchiata*, having naked gills and no shell. Also *attrib.* or as *adj.* So **Nudibra·nchial** *a.* **Nudibra·nchian** = next 1839.

Nudibra·nchiate. 1836. [– mod.L. *Nudibranchiata*; see NUDI-, BRANCHIATE.] *Zool.* **A.** *adj.* Of molluscs: Having naked branchiæ; belonging to the *Nudibranchiata.* **B.** *sb.* A mollusc of this order.

Nudist (niū·dist). 1931. [f. NUDE + -IST.] An adherent of the cult of the nude.

Nudity (niū·dĭti). 1611. [– (O)Fr. *nudité*, or late L. *nuditas*, *-at-*, f. *nudus* NUDE; see -ITY.] **1.** The condition or fact of being naked or nude; a nude or naked state. **2.** A nude figure, *esp.* as represented in the arts 1662. †**3.** *pl.* The private parts when exposed –1769.

1. In another [plate] the august n. of Downing-Street is made interesting 1900. **2.** Fat Graces and other plump nudities by Rubens HAWTHORNE.

Nugacious (niugēi·ʃəs), *a.* Now *rare.* 1652. [f. L. *nugax*, *-ac-* trifling + -OUS; see -ACIOUS.] Trivial, trifling, of no moment.

Nugacity (niugæ·sĭti). Now *rare.* 1593. [– late L. *nugacitas*, f. as prec.; see -ITY, -ACITY.] **1.** Trifling, triviality, futility. **2.** A trifling or frivolous idea 1653.

Nugatory (niū·gătəri), *a.* 1603. [– L. *nugatorius*, f. *nugat-*, pa. ppl. stem of *nugari* trifle, f. *nugæ* jests, trifles; see -ORY^{2}.] **1.** Trifling, worthless. **2.** Of no force, invalid; useless, futile, inoperative 1605.

2. Those provisions of the edict..were contrived so artfully as to be nearly n. PRESCOTT. *N. payment*, one involving an immediate and formal loss, i.e. the payment of money, in return for which no service is rendered. Hence **Nu·gatoriness.**

Nugget (nɒ·gĕt). 1852. [perh. dim. of s.w.

dial. *nug* lump, block, unshapen mass, of unkn. origin; see -ET.] **1.** A rough lump of native gold. **2.** A lump of anything 1860. **3.** *Austral.* A small compact beast or runt 1852. Hence **Nu·gget(t)y** *a.*

Nugi- (niū·dʒi), comb. form of L. *nugæ*, as in **Nu·gifying** *ppl. a.* productive of mere trifling; etc.

Nuisance (niū·săns). late ME. [– OFr. (now arch.) *nuisance* hurt, f. *nuis-*, stem of *nuire* injure :– L. *nocēre*; see -ANCE.] **1.** Injury, hurt, harm, annoyance. (In later use only as implying sense 2 or 2 b.) **2.** Anything injurious or obnoxious to the community, or to the individual as a member of it, for which some legal remedy may be found 1464. **b.** More widely; Anything obnoxious to the community or individual by offensiveness of smell or appearance, by causing obstruction or damage, etc. 1661. **c.** Applied to persons 1695. **d.** An obnoxious practice, institution, state of things, etc. 1820. **e.** A source of annoyance 1831.

2. All such Lotteries are..declared to be Common Nusances 1710. *Commit no n.*: an injunction to the public not to defile a place. **b.** The n. of the smoke of London EVELYN. **c.** He is a sort of privileged n. SCOTT. **e.** The other set,..who go little into parties, and vote balls a n. LYTTON. Hence **Nui·sancer,** one who causes a n. BLACKSTONE.

Null (nɒl), *a.* 1563. [– (O)Fr. *nul*, fem. *nulle*, or L. *nullus*, *-a* no, none, f. *ne* not + *ullus* any, f. *unus* one.] **1.** Void, of no legal or binding force; of no efficacy, invalid. **2.** Of no value or importance; insignificant 1790. **b.** Devoid of character or expression 1850. **3.** Amounting to nothing, non-existent 1761.

1. If such consent from the father was wanting, the marriage was n. BLACKSTONE. Phr. *N. and void* 1669. **2. b.** Faultily faultless, icily regular, splendidly n. TENNYSON. **3.** The combined effect..is thus n. 1866. *N. method* (Electr.), a method in which the thing to be observed is the non-existence of some phenomenon; called also *zero method.*

Null (nɒl), *v.* 1643. [f. NULL *a.*, after *annul*, perh. after med.L. *nullare*, Fr. †*nuller.*] †**1.** To reduce to nothing –1722. **2.** To annul, cancel, make void 1643.

2. The first election he nulled, because its irregularity was glaring BURKE.

‖**Nulla bona** (nɒ·lă bōᵘ·nă). 1807. [L., 'no goods'.] The return made by a sheriff upon an execution when the party has no goods to be distrained.

‖**Nullah** (nɒ·lă). *Anglo-Ind.* Also **nulla.** 1776. [Hindi *nālā* brook, ravine.] A river or stream; a watercourse, river-bed, ravine.

Nullification (nɒlifikē¹·ʃən). 1630. [f. NULLIFY; see -FICATION.] †**1.** Reduction to nothing DONNE. **2.** The action of rendering null or of no effect 1808. **b.** *U.S.* The action, on the part of a State legislature, of refusing to allow a general law to be enforced within the State 1799.

2. His accession..was ushered in by the n. of his father's will 1839.

Nullifidian (nɒlifi·diăn). 1564. [f. med.L. *nullifidius*, f. *nulli-*, comb. form of L. *nullus* no, none + *fides* faith; see -AN, -IAN.] **A.** *sb.* **1.** One of no faith or religion; a sceptic in religious matters. **2.** *transf.* A disbeliever 1668. **B.** *adj.* Having no faith or belief 1627.

Nullifier (nɒ·lifəi,əɹ). 1832. [f. next + -ER¹.] One who nullifies; *spec.* in *U.S. Hist.*, one who maintained the right of nullification on the part of any State.

Nullify (nɒ·lifəi), *v.* 1595. [f. NULL *a.*; see -FY.] **1.** *trans.* To render legally null and void; to annul, cancel. **2.** To make of no value, use, or efficacy; to efface completely 1609.

2. They had long learnt to n. what they professed to defend 1876.

‖**Nullipara** (nɒ·lipără). 1872. [mod.L., f. *nulli-*, comb. form of L. *nullus* no, none + *-para*, fem. of *-parus*; see -PAROUS.] A female who has never given birth to a child. Hence **Nullipa·rity; Nulli·parous** *a.*

Nullipore (nɒ·lipōᵊɹ). 1840. [f. L. *nullus* (see prec.) + PORE *sb.*] A form of marine vegetation having the power of secreting lime like the coral polyp.

Nullity (nɒ·lĭti). 1570. [– (O)Fr. *nullité* or med.L. *nullitas*, f. L. *nullus* no, none; see -ITY.] **1.** The fact of being legally null and void; invalidity. Also (with *a* and *pl.*), an instance of this; a fact or circumstance causing invalidity. **2.** An act or thing which is null or invalid 1624. **3.** The condition of being null or nought; a state of nothingness 1589. **4. a.** A mere nothing 1591. **b.** Of persons: A nonentity 1657.

1. A petition for n. of marriage on the ground of imperfect publication of the banns 1865. The n. of all proceedings taken in contravention of them STUBBS. **2.** The Court declared the deed a n. 1891. **4. a.** Such a mere n. is time, to a creature to whom God gives a feeling heart COWPER. **b.** Such a miserable n., and husk of a man BROWNING.

Numb (nɒm), *a.* (and *sb.*) [Late ME. *nome(n*, pa. pple. of NIM *v.* take, seize. For the parasitic *b* cf. THUMB.] **1.** Deprived of feeling, or of the power of movement, *esp.* through cold 1440. **b.** Helpless, incapable 1802. **2.** Of the nature of numbness 1641. **3.** *sb.* A cold which numbs fish 1888.

1. Leaning long upon any Part maketh it Numme, and as we call it, Asleep BACON. **2.** †*N. palsy*, paralysis 1772. Hence **Nu·mb-ly** *adv.* 1895, **-ness** 1571.

Numb (nɒm), *v.* 1602. [f. prec., or back-formation from *numbed* ppl. a.; cf. the earlier BENUMB.] *trans.* To make numb.

For lazy Winter nums the lab'ring Hand DRYDEN.

Number (nɒ·mbəɹ), *sb.* [ME. *numbre*, etc. – AFr. *numbre*, (O)Fr. *nombre* :– L. *numerus.*] **I. 1.** The sum or aggregate *of* any collection of individual things or persons. **b.** *pl.* The title of the fourth book in the Bible, containing a census of the Israelites. late ME. **2.** A sum or total of abstract units ME. **b.** In *pl.* as a subject of study or science. late ME. **c.** A symbol or figure, or collection of these, which represents graphically an arithmetical total; a ticket or label bearing such signs 1837. **3.** The particular mark or symbol, having an arithmetical value, by which a person or thing has a place assigned to it in a series. late ME. **4.** Prefixed to a numeral, as *number two* or No. 2 (see NO.), to designate things or persons by the place assigned to them in an arithmetical series. late ME. **5.** A single numbered part or issue of a book or periodical publication 1757. **b.** One of a collection of songs or poems 1878. **c.** A part or division of an opera, oratorio, etc. 1881.

1. The n. of fools is infinite SOUTHEY. **2.** I hope good lucke lies in odde numbers SHAKS. Phr. *Golden n.*: see GOLDEN *a.* **b.** The science of numbers JOHNSON. **c.** A strange specimen of the human race..with a brass label and n. round his neck DICKENS. **3.** To 'take' a Policeman's 'n.' 1880. Phr. *To lose the n. of one's mess*, to die, to perish. *One's n. is up* (colloq.): one is doomed to die or to come to disaster. **4.** N. twenty-two wants his boots DICKENS. *N. one*, one's self, one's own person and interests; *esp.* in *to look after*, or *take care of, n. one.* **5.** The old back numbers of periodicals 1851. Phr. *Back n.* (fig.), an antiquated, out-of-date person or thing. *In numbers*, in a series of separate parts published at intervals.

II. 1. The full tale or count of a collection, company, or class of persons. Also *pl.* ME. **b.** The body or aggregate of persons specified 1529. **2.** A (large, small, etc.) collection or company *of* persons or things ME. **3.** A certain (usu. a considerable) company, collection, or aggregate *of* persons or things ME. **4.** *pl.* A (great, infinite, etc.) multitude or aggregate of persons or things. late ME. **b.** Many persons, etc. 1597. **c.** In contexts denoting superiority derived from numerical preponderance 1638.

1. Hell, her numbers full, Thenceforth shall be for ever shut MILT. Is gratitude in the n. of a man's virtues? CHATHAM. **2.** An infinite nombre of grassehoppers came flieng into Germany 1560. A considerable n. are employed in..workshops 1895. **3.** He..kept himself by keeping a n. of bees 1860. The testimony of a n. is more cogent than the testimony of two or three 1833. **4.** The French have lost immense numbers of men WELLINGTON. **b.** There are numbers in this city who live by writing new books 1760. **c.** They overpowered the foreigners by force of numbers 1861.

III. 1. That property of things according to which they can be counted or enumerated ME. **b.** *Phren.* The faculty of numbering or calculating 1835. **2.** In phrases denoting that persons, things, etc., have not been, or cannot be, counted ME. **3.** *In n.*: in sum total; altogether ME.

1. A child..perceives a difference between many and few; and that difference it is taught to call n. 1762. **2.** A shout Loud as from numbers without n. MILT.

IV. †**1.** Quantity, amount (*rare*) –1720. **2.** *Gram.* The property in words of denoting that one, two, or more persons or things are spoken of; the special form of a word by which this is expressed. late ME. †**3.** Conformity, in verse or music, to a certain regular beat or measure; rhythm –1667. **4.** *pl.* **a.** Musical periods or groups of notes 1579. **b.** Metrical periods or feet; hence, lines, verses 1588.

2. There are two numbers, the singular speaking of one, the plurall of moe 1591. **3.** MILT *P.L.* IV. 687. **4.** In Musickes Numbers my Voyce rose and fell DRAYTON. **b.** I lisped in numbers, for the numbers came POPE. Hence **Nu·mberless** *a.* innumerable 1573.

Number (nɒ·mbəɹ), *v.* ME. [– (O)Fr. *nombrer* :– L. *numerare*, f. *numerus*; see prec.] **1.** *trans.* To count, to ascertain the number of (individual things or persons). †**b.** To compute, calculate, reckon, measure –1794. **2.** To enumerate, reckon *up.* Also *absol.* late ME. **b.** To fix the number of; to reduce to a definite number; to make few in number; to bring to a close. (Chiefly in passive.) late ME. †**c.** To collect, up to a certain number –1611. **3.** To check, control, or verify the number of; to count or tell *over.* Also *absol. poet.* †**b.** To count out or pay *down* (money) –1725. **c.** To apportion (one's days) with care 1535. **4.** To count, reckon, or class among certain persons or things. Chiefly const. *among, in, with.* late ME. **5.** To assign or attach a number to (a thing); *spec.* to distinguish by a number. late ME. **6.** To have lived, or to live (so many years) 1590. **7.** To comprise in a number; to have or comprise (so many things or persons) 1645. **b.** To equal, amount to 1842.

1. To n. the Votes HOBBES. **b.** Have you nombred the distaunce bytwene the sonne and the moone? 1530. **2. b.** The Sands are numbred, that makes vp my Life SHAKS. **c.** N. thee an armie, like the armie that thou hast lost 1 *Kings* 20:25. **3. c.** O teach vs to nombre oure dayes, that we maye applie our hertes vnto wyszdome COVERDALE *Ps.* 89:5. **4.** Make them to be noumbred with thy sainctes *Bk. Com. Prayer.* **5.** The houses were not numbered MACAULAY. **6.** Of as able bodie as when he number'd thirty SHAKS. **7.** Otranto numbered twenty-two thousand inhabitants FREEMAN. **b.** The crew and passengers numbered 33. 1883. Hence **Nu·mberer** 1594.

Numb-fish. 1711. [f. NUMB *a.*] The Electric Ray or Torpedo, which numbs by the electric shocks emitted by it.

Numbles (nɒ·mb'lz). Now only *arch.* ME. [– OFr. *numbles, nombles* :– L. *lumbulus*, dim. of *lumbus* loin; see HUMBLES, UMBLES.] Certain of the inward parts of a deer, etc., as used for food. Also, in early use, part of the back and loins of a hart.

‖**Numdah** (nɒ·mda). *Anglo-Ind.* 1876. [– Urdu *namdā*, f. Pers. *namad* felt, carpet, rug.] A kind of felt or coarse woollen cloth; a saddlecloth or pad made of this. Var. **Nu·mnah** 1859.

Numen (niū·mĕn). 1628. [– L. *numen*, rel. to *-nuere* nod, Gr. νεύειν incline the head.] Deity, divinity; divine or presiding power or spirit.

Numerable (niū·mĕrăb'l), *a.* 1570. [– L. *numerabilis*, f. *numerare*; see NUMBER *v.*, -ABLE. Cf. OFr. *numérable.*] Capable of being numbered.

Numeral (niū·mĕrăl). 1530. [– late L. *numeralis* (Priscian), f. *numerus* number; see -AL¹. Cf. Fr. *numéral* (XV).] **A.** *adj.* **1.** Expressing or denoting number. **2.** Belonging or appertaining to number 1607.

1. *One* is a n. adjective 1824. N. characters are either letters; or figures, otherwise called digits 1727.

B. *sb.* **1.** A word expressing a number 1530. **2.** A figure or character (or a group of these) denoting a number 1686.

1. Cardinal, Ordinal, and Indefinite Numerals 1872. **2.** The letters of the alphabet themselves came to be used as numerals.

Numerary (niū·mĕrări), *a.* 1726. [– med.L. *numerarius* (in late L. as sb. = arithmetician, accountant), f. L. *numerus*;

see NUMBER *sb.*, -ARY[1].] **1.** *Eccl.* Of a canon: Forming one of the regular number. **2.** Of or pertaining to a number or numbers 1742.

Nu·merate, *v. rare.* 1721. [– *numerat-*, pa. ppl. stem of L. *numerare*; see NUMBER *v.*, -ATE[3].] *trans.* To number, reckon. Also *absol.* Hence **Nu·merative** *a.* pertaining to numeration or numbering.

Numeration (niūmĕrē¹·ʃən). late ME. [– L. *numeratio* payment, late and med.L. = numeration, numbering, f. as prec.; see -ION.] **1. a.** A method or process of numbering, or computing. **b.** Without article: Calculation; the assigning of number to things 1596. **2.** The action, process, or result of ascertaining the number *of* people, etc. 1533. **3.** *Arith.* The art of expressing any number in words that is already given in figures 1542.

1. a. If..time is a n. of motion 1837. **b.** That progress of Science, which is to destroy Wonder, and in its stead substitute Mensuration and N. CARLYLE. **2.** To make an exact n. of the inhabitants of Ireland, distinguishing their religion BURKE. **3.** *N. table*, a table showing the value of figures according to their place in a system of notation.

Numerator (niū·mĕre¹tǫɹ). 1542. [– Fr. *numérateur* or late L. *numerator*, f. as prec.; see -OR 2.] **1.** *Arith.* †**a.** The word(s) or figure(s) by which the number of things or persons in question is denoted. **b.** The number written above the line in a vulgar fraction, which shows how many of the specified parts of a unit are taken 1575. **2.** One who or that which numbers 1675.

Numeric (niume·rik), *a.* and *sb.* 1663. [In sense 2 f. L. *numerus* + -IC. The sense-history and origin of 1 are obscure.] †**1.** *adj.* Identical –1727. **2.** *sb.* Any number, proper or improper fraction, or incommensurable ratio 1879.

Numerical (niume·rikăl), *a.* 1624. [f. med. L. *numericus* (see NUMBER *sb.*, -IC) + -AL[1]; cf. -ICAL.] **1.** Pertaining to number; of the nature of, according to, number; etc. 1628. **b.** Of figures: Denoting a number 1706. **c.** In respect of numbers 1812. **d.** Characterized by the use of ordinary figures expressive of number 1840. †**2.** Particular, individual (*rare*) –1699. †**3.** With *same*: Individual, identical. So with *very*. –1716.

1. Tickets in a N. Order 1712. **b.** The Brahmans were the original inventors of those n. symbols MAX-MÜLLER. **c.** Nikostratus..was not afraid of this n. superiority 1849. **d.** An equation is n. or algebraical according as its coefficients are numbers or algebraical symbols 1881. **3.** This is that very n. Lady, with whom I am in love DRYDEN. Hence **Nume·rically** *adv.* with respect to number; by means of numbers.

Nu·merist. *rare.* 1646. [f. L. *numerus* + -IST.] One who concerns himself with numbers.

Numerosity (niūmĕrǫ·sĭti). 1589. [– late L. *numerositas*, f. L. *numerosus*; see next, -ITY.] **1.** The state of being numerous; condition in respect of number 1611. **2.** Rhythmic quality.

Numerous (niū·mĕrəs), *a.* 1586. [– L. *numerosus*, f. *numerus* number; see -OUS.] **1.** Qualifying a sing.: abundant, copious; comprising many units. Now *rare.* **b.** Consisting of many individuals 1647. **c.** Coming from or pertaining to large numbers 1832. Now *rare.* **2.** Qualifying a pl.: Many 1622. †**3.** Containing many individuals; thronged, crowded –1831. **4.** Consisting of 'numbers' or rhythmical periods; measured, rhythmical 1589.

1. A n. Acquaintance STEELE. **b.** He exalted allmost all of his own n. Family CLARENDON. **c.** That n. voice which we designate as 'Public Opinion' 1841. **2.** Contriving presses to put my books up in; they now growing n. PEPYS. **4.** Eloquence..in Prose or n. Verse MILT. Hence **Nu·merous-ly** *adv.*, **-ness.**

Numismatic (niūmizmæ·tik), *a.* and *sb.* 1792. [Fr. *numismatique*, f. L. *numisma*, *-mat-*, var. (infl. by *nummus* coin) of *nomisma* – Gr. νόμισμα current coin, f. νομίζειν have in use; see -ISM, -ATIC.] **1.** Of, pertaining or relating to, coins or coinage. **2.** Consisting of coins 1851. **3.** *sb. pl.* The study of coins and medals 1829. Hence **Numisma·tically** *adv.* **Numismati·cian, Numi·smatist,** a student of coins. **Numismato·logy,** the science of numismatics; whence **Numismato·logist.**

Nummary (nɒ·mări), *a.* 1603. [– L. *nummarius*, f. *nummus* coin; see -ARY[1].] **1.** Pertaining or relating to money or coinage. **2.** Dealing with coins or money 1695.

Nummular (nɒ·miŭlăɹ), *a.* 1846. [f. L. *nummulus*, dim. of *nummus* coin + -AR[2].] *Path.* Coin-shaped, *esp.* of sputa.

Nummulary (nɒ·miŭlări), *a.* 1767. [See prec. and -ARY[1].] Nummary.

Nu·mmulated, *ppl. a.* 1873. *Path.* [f. L. *nummulus* (see prec.) + -ATE[2] + -ED[1].] = NUMMULAR.

Nummulite (nɒ·miŭləit). 1811. [f. as NUMMULAR + -ITE[1] 2a.] *Zool.* A genus of fossil foraminiferous cephalopods belonging to the order *Polythalamia*, found in the Tertiary strata; an individual of this genus. Hence **Nummuli·tic** *a.* (*Geol.*), containing, or formed of, nummulites.

†**Nump(s.** 1611. [of unkn., prob. symbolic, origin.] A silly or stupid person –1730.

Numskull (nɒ·mskɒl). 1717. [f. NUMB *a.* + SKULL *sb.*] **1.** A blockhead, thick-head, dolt 1724. **2.** The head, pate, noddle, *esp.* that of a dull person 1717.

1. He considered them to be numskulls, and little better than idiots TROLLOPE. So **Nu·mskulled** *a.* slow-witted; stupid 1706.

Nun (nɒn). [OE. *nunne* = OHG. *nunna* (MHG., G. dial. *nunne*), ON. *nunna*, beside ME. *nonne* (partly – OFr. *nonne*) = MDu. *nonne* (Du. *non*), G. *nonne* – eccl. L. *nonna*, fem. of *nonnus* monk, orig. titles given to elderly persons.] **1.** A woman devoted to a religious life under certain vows; usu., one who has vowed poverty, chastity, and obedience, and who lives in a convent under a certain rule. †**b.** A priestess or votaress of some pagan deity –1698. **2.** The name of various birds: **a.** The Blue Titmouse, *Parus cæruleus* 1589. **b.** The Smew, *Mergus albellus* 1666. **c.** A variety of domestic pigeon having a veil of white feathers covering its head 1725. **3.** A species of moth 1832.

1. For my Daughters..They shall be praying Nunnes, not weeping Queenes SHAKS. *attrib.* and *Comb.*, as †**nun's flesh,** a cold or ascetic temperament; **nun's thread,** a fine white sewing-cotton, such as is used by nuns; **nun's veiling,** a soft thin woollen material.

Nun-bird. 1881. [f. prec.] A South American puff-bird of the genus *Monacha.*

Nun-buoy. 1703. [f. obs. *nun* child's top.] *Naut.* A buoy of circular shape in the middle and tapering towards each end.

‖**Nunc dimi·ttis.** 1552. [L., first words of the Song of Simeon in Luke 2:29.] **1.** The canticle beginning with these words. **2.** Permission to depart; departure, dismissal 1621.

1. The sweetest Canticle is, *Nunc dimittis*; when a Man hath obtained worthy Ends, and Expectations BACON. Phr. *To sing* (one's) *nunc dimittis*, to declare oneself contented to depart from life or from some occupation.

†**Nunce.** 1566. [Anglicized form of NUNCIO or *nuntius* NUNTIUS, or – Fr. *nonce.*] = NUNCIO. –1712.

Nuncheon (nɒ·nʃən). Now *dial.* [ME. *non(e) shench*, f. *non* NOON + *shench* draught, cup (OE. *sćenć*, rel. to *sćenćan* :– Gmc. **skaŋkjan* give to drink.] A slight refreshment of liquor, etc., orig. taken in the afternoon; a light refreshment taken between meals; a lunch.

Nunciate (nɒ·nʃ¹e¹t). 1596. [irreg. f. L. *nuncius* or *nunciare*, perh. after *legate.*] One who or that which announces; a messenger, nuntius.

Nunciature (nɒ·nʃ¹ătiūəɹ). 1652. [– It. *nunziatura*, f. *nunzio* NUNCIO.] The office or the period of office of a papal nuncio.

Nuncio (nɒ·nʃio). 1528. [– It. †*nuncio*, †*nuntio* (mod. *nunzio*) – L. NUNTIUS messenger.] **1.** A permanent official representative of the Roman See at a foreign court. **2.** A messenger 1601. **3.** A member of the Polish diet 1684.

Nuncius (nɒ·nʃ¹ɒs). *rare.* 1613. [– L. *nuncius*, var. of NUNTIUS.] A messenger.

Nuncle. 1589. Now *dial.* Var. of UNCLE with *n* transferred from *myn*; see N.

Nuncupate (nɒ·nkiupe¹t), *v.* 1550. [– *nuncupat-*, pa. ppl. stem of L. *nuncupare* name, designate, declare; see -ATE[3].] †**1.** To express (a vow) in words –1788. **2.** To declare (a will) orally 1677. †**3.** To dedicate (a work) *to* some one –1656. So **Nuncupa·tion** (in senses 1–2).

Nuncupative (nɒ·nkiupē¹tiv, nɒnkiū·pătiv), *a.* (and *sb.*). 1546. [– late and med.L. *nuncupativus*, f. as prec.; see -IVE.] **1.** Of wills: Oral, not written. **2.** Denoting nuncupation; designative (*rare*) 1619.

1. Soldiers and sailors..when on service, may make n. wills 1883. Hence **Nuncupatively** *adv.*

†**Nuncupatory,** *a.* 1603. [– med.L. *nuncupatorius*, f. as prec.; see -ORY[2].] **1.** Nuncupative, oral –1704. **2.** Dedicatory –1679.

Nundinal (nɒ·ndinăl), *a.* (and *sb.*). 1656. [– Fr. *nundinal*, in *lettres nundinales*, f. †*nundine*; see NUNDINE, -AL[1].] Pertaining to a fair or market; connected with the Roman nundines.

N. letter, a letter of the alphabet (A to H) attached to each day of the Roman n. period.

Nundina·tion. 1623. [– L. *nundinatio*, f. *nundinat-*, pa. ppl. stem of *nundinari* attend or hold market, f. *nundinæ*; see next, -ION.] Traffic, trade, buying and selling; sale.

Nundine (nɒ·ndəin). Also *pl.* 1533. [– L. *nundinæ* fem. pl., f. *novem* nine + *dies* day.] Among the ancient Romans, a market-day held every eighth (by Roman reckoning, ninth) day.

Nunky (nɒ·ŋki), pet form of NUNCLE 1798.

Nunnation (nɒnē¹·ʃən). 1776. [– mod.L. *nunnatio*, f. *nūn* Arabic name of letter *n*; see -ATION.] **1.** The addition of a final *n* in the declension of Arabic nouns, denoted by doubling the vowel sign. **2.** The addition of inorganic *n* in Middle English forms 1838.

Nunnery (nɒ·nəri). ME. [– AFr. **nonnerie*, f. *nonne* NUN; see -ERY.] **1.** A place of residence for nuns; a building in which nuns live under religious rule and discipline; a convent. **b.** *transf.* A house of ill fame 1593. **2.** A company of nuns 1651.

1. Get thee to a Nunnerie SHAKS.

Nunnish (nɒ·niʃ), *a.* 1570. [f. NUN + -ISH[1].] Pertaining to a nun; nun-like.

‖**Nuntius** (nɒ·nʃ¹ɒs). *Pl.* **nuntii** (-ʃi,əi). 1605. [L.; cf. NUNCIUS.] = NUNCIO.

Nuphar (niū·făɹ). 1845. [– Arab. – Pers. *nūfar*, reduced f. *nīnūfar*; see NENUPHAR.] The yellow water-lily.

Nuptial (nɒ·pʃăl), *a.* and *sb.* 1490. [– Fr. *nuptial* or L. *nuptialis*, f. *nuptiæ* wedding, f. *nupt-*, pa. ppl. stem of *nubere*; see NUBILE, -IAL.] **A.** *adj.* Of or pertaining to marriage or the marriage ceremony.

She..at last fixed the n. day JOHNSON.

B. *sb.* Marriage, wedding. (Usu. in pl.) 1555.

1. The nuptials were solemnised according to Persian usage 1840. *sing.* The N. was no sooner celebrated, than he repented it 1654.

Nuptiality (nɒpʃi,æ·lĭti). 1789. [f. prec. + -ITY.] **1.** *pl.* Nuptial ceremonies 1863. **2.** Conjugal character.

Nuragh (nūə·ræg). 1828. [Sardinian.] A massive stone tower of ancient date, of a type peculiar to Sardinia.

Nurse (nɒ̄ɹs), *sb.*[1] late ME. [Reduced f. ME. *norice*, *n(o)urice*; see NOURICE.] **1.** A woman employed to suckle, and take charge of, an infant, a WET NURSE; also, one who has general charge of a young child or children, a DRY NURSE. **b.** *transf.* One who takes care of, looks after, or advises another. late ME. **c.** *fig.* That which nourishes or fosters some quality, condition, etc. 1526. **2.** A person, usu. a woman, who attends or waits upon the sick; now *esp.* one trained for this purpose 1590. **3.** *Forestry.* A tree set in a plantation to protect smaller or newly planted ones from wind or cold 1788. **4.** *Entom.* A sexually imperfect member of a community of bees, ants, etc., upon whom devolves the care of the young brood 1818. **5.** *Zool.* An individual in the asexual stage of metagenesis 1845.

1. Shal I go, and call the a n. of the Hebrues women, to nurse ye the childe? COVERDALE *Exod.* 2:7. The nurse's legends are for truths receiv'd DRYDEN. **c.** Time is the N., and breeder of all good SHAKS. Phr. *At n.*, in the care of a n. *To put to n.*, to commit to the care of a n. Also *fig.*, e.g. of estates in the hands of trustees. **2.**

The n. sleeps sweetly, hired to watch the sick COWPER. *N.-housemaid*, a maid who combines the duties of a nursemaid and a housemaid.

Nurse (nɒ̄ɹs), *sb.*[2] 1499. [perh. a var. of HUSS, with added (*a*)*n* (see N 2); assim. to prec.] A dog-fish or shark (of various species). So *n.fish, -hound, -shark.*

Nurse (nɒ̄ɹs), *v.* 1526. [alt. of †*nurish*, †*norsh* NOURISH *v.* assim. to NURSE *sb.*[1]] **1.** Of a woman: To suckle, and otherwise attend to, or simply to take charge of (an infant) 1535. **b.** *intr.* To act as wet-nurse 1789. **2.** In *pass.* **a.** To be reared or brought up in a certain place 1526. **b.** To be brought up under certain conditions, *in* a certain environment, etc. 1601. **3.** To foster, tend, cherish (a thing); to promote the growth or development of 1542. **b.** To supply (plants) with warmth and moisture; to tend or cultivate carefully 1594. **c.** To manage (land) economically 1745. **d.** To cherish (a feeling, etc.) in one's own heart 1763. **e.** To assist or cause (a thing) to develop *into* a certain form, or *to* a certain size 1775. **4.** To bring or rear *up* with care 1603. **5.** To wait upon, attend to (a person who is ill) 1736. **b.** To try to cure (an illness) by taking care of oneself. Also with *away*. 1785. **c.** *intr.* To perform the duties of a sick-nurse 1861. **6.** To clasp (the knee, etc.) in one's hands 1849. **b.** To hold caressingly or carefully, *esp.* in the arms or on the lap 1850. **c.** To sit close to, as if taking care of (a fire) 1857. **7.** *slang.* **a.** To keep close to (a rival omnibus), so as to interfere with its custom 1858. **b.** To impede (a horse) in a race, by surrounding it with other and slower ones 1893. **8. a.** To keep in touch with (a constituency) in order to obtain votes 1869. **b.** To assist (a business house) so as to prevent its bankruptcy 1890. **9.** *Billiards.* To keep (the balls) together in order to make a series of cannons 1869.

1. So is it..comly for the own mother to nource her own childe 1546. **2.** For we were nurst upon the self-same hill MILT. **b.** O Lady, nursed in pomp and pleasure! COLERIDGE. **3.** To n. with tender care the thriving arts COWPER. **b.** I.. live in Oak'n bowr, To n. the Saplings tall MILT. **c.** He nursed what property was yet left to him SCOTT. **d.** He could n. his injuries for many years 1879. **5.** The arrangements for nursing the sick have greatly improved in recent times 1881. **b.** My cold..has returned, and I am nursing it before I sail 1813. **6. b.** They..drove home again, Francesca nursing a Dying Gladiator in terra-cotta 1887. **8. a.** To n. the borough cost him £500 a year at least 1869.

Nu·rse-child. 1560. [NURSE *sb.*[1]] A foster-child.

†Nu·rse-father. 1564. [f. NURSE *sb.*[1] or *v.*] A foster-father. Chiefly *fig.* –1714.

Nu·rsemaid. 1657. [NURSE *sb.*[1]] A young woman employed as maid to attend to little children.

Nu·rse-mother. Now *rare.* 1579. [f. NURSE *sb.*[1] or *v.*] A foster-mother.

Nu·rser. late ME. [f. NURSE *v.* + -ER[1].] One who, or that which, nurses, fosters, or encourages.

Nursery (nɒ̄·ɹsəri). ME. [prob. – AFr. **noricerie*, f. *norice* NOURICE; see -ERY.] **†1.** Fosterage, upbringing, breeding; nursing –1671. **2.** The apartment which is given up to infants and young children with their nurse 1499. **3.** A practice, institution, etc., in or by which something is fostered or developed 1509. **b.** A place, sphere, etc., in which people are trained or educated; a school *of*, or *for*, certain professions, etc. 1581. **†c.** A theatre established in London for the training of young players –1683. **4.** A piece of ground in which young plants or trees are reared until fit for transplantation; †a collection of such plants. Now usu., a nursery-garden. Also *transf.* and *fig.* 1565. **5.** A place which breeds or supports animals 1661; a pond for rearing fish 1771. **b.** Of ants, etc.: The cells in which the larval and nymphal insects attain maturity 1797. **c.** A place or part in which any form of animal life is developed 1871. **6.** A race for two-year-old horses 1883. **7.** *Billiards.* A series (of cannons) made by keeping the balls close together 1869.

1. *Lear* I. i. 126. **2.** He is taught from the N., that he must inherit a great Estate SWIFT. **3.** That all subordinate treasuries, as the nurseries of mismanagement..ought to be dissolved BURKE. **4.** *fig.* Ye sacred Nurseries of blooming Youth! WORDSW. *attrib.* and *Comb.*, as (in sense 2), *n.-governess, school*, etc.; (in sense 4), *n.-garden, -gardener*, etc.

Nu·rseryman. 1672. [f. prec.] One who owns, or works in, a nursery for plants.

Nu·rse-tree. 1805. [NURSE *sb.*[1]] **1.** A tree planted to protect others. **2.** A tree supporting a parasitic plant 1857.

Nu·rsing, *vbl. sb.* 1532. [f. NURSE *v.* + -ING[1].] **1.** The action of NURSE *v.* **2.** *attrib.*, as *n.-chair*; *n. home*, a small private hospital.

Nu·rsing, *ppl. a.* 1535. [f. NURSE *v.* + -ING[2].] **1.** That nurses, or tends like a nurse, as *n.-father, n.-mother*, a foster-father, -mother. **2.** That is being nursed, as, *a n. baby* (*rare*) 1860.

Nursle (nɒ̄·ɹs'l), *v.* 1596. *rare.* [var. of *nousle* NUZZLE *v.*[2], assim. to NURSE *v.*] **1.** *trans.* = NUZZLE *v.*[2] 2. **2.** To nurse, foster, cherish 1652.

Nursling, nurseling (nɒ̄·ɹsliŋ). 1557. [f. NURSE *v.* + -LING[1], after *suckling*.] **1.** An infant or child in relation to its nurse 1607. Also *transf.* **2.** *attrib.*, as *n. babe*, etc. 1793.

1. I was his nursling once and choice delight MILT. *transf.* Forms more real than living man, Nurslings of immortality SHELLEY.

Nurture (nɒ̄·ɹtiŭɹ, -tʃəɹ), *sb.* ME. [– OFr. *nourture*, contr. of *noureture*; see NOURITURE.] **1.** Breeding, upbringing, training, education (received or possessed by one). Now *rare.* **†b.** Moral training or discipline –1637. **2.** That which nourishes; nourishment, food. late ME. **3.** The bringing-up *of* some one; tutelage; fostering care 1676.

1. His father in his youthe had taught him good n. LD. BERNERS. **b.** Who so despiseth wisedome, and n., he is miserable *Wisdom* 3:11. **2.** Your lovers feeble eyes you feed, But sterve their harts that needeth nourture most SPENSER. Hence **Nu·rtural** *a.* 1922.

Nurture (nɒ̄·ɹtiŭɹ, -tʃəɹ), *v.* ME. [f. prec.] **1.** *trans.* To feed or nourish; to rear. **b.** *transf.* To foster, cherish 1828. **2.** To bring up, train, educate 1526. **†b.** To discipline, chasten –1636.

1. By his Grandsyre nourisht up And nurtred from a boye 1575. **b.** To n. a secret affection 1872. **2.** They nurter the yonge wemen for to love their husbandes TINDALE *Titus* 2:4. **b.** He that spareth the rod, hateth his childe; but he that loveth him doth instantly n. him BIBLE (Douay) *Prov.* 13:24. Hence **Nu·rturer.**

Nut (nɒt), *sb.* [OE. *hnutu* = MLG. *note*, MDu. *note, neute* (Du. *noot, neut*), OHG. (*h*)*nuz* (G. *nuss*), ON. *hnot* :– Gmc. **χnut-*.] **I. 1.** A fruit which consists of a hard or leathery (indehiscent) shell enclosing an edible kernel; the kernel itself. **†2.** A cup formed from the shell of a coco-nut mounted in metal; also, one made of other materials to resemble this –1580. **3.** In allusive contexts 1562. **4.** In allusions to the difficulty of cracking hard-shelled nuts: **a.** A difficult question or problem 1545. **b.** A difficult undertaking; a person hard to deal with or conciliate 1662. **5.** *slang.* The head (of a person) 1858. **6.** A 'swell', dandy. *slang.* 1904. (Jocularly spelt and pronounced *knut.*)

3. More noise than nuts LONGF. They can't shoot for nuts 1899. **4. a.** He especially liked his mental nuts 1858. **b.** Fortified towns are hard nuts to crack FRANKLIN. **5.** Phr. *Off one's n.*, out of one's mind, insane. Phrases. †*Nuts to* (a person), a source of pleasure to one. *To be* (*dead*) *nuts on* or *upon*, to set great store upon, to be devoted to, or delighted with (a person or thing). *slang.*

II. 1. A small metal projection upon a spindle (of a clock, etc.) furnished with teeth, and engaging in a cog-wheel; a small spur-wheel. late ME. **†2.** A projection from the lock of a cross-bow, serving to detain the string until released by the trigger –1674. **3.** A small block of wood, iron, etc., pierced, and wormed with a female screw; used to make a bolt fast or adjust it 1611. **b.** The portion of a wooden printing-press in which the screw plays 1642. **c.** The contrivance at the lower end of a violin-bow, or the like, by which the horse-hair may be relaxed or tightened 1662. **4.** *Naut.* Either of two projections on the square part of the shank of an anchor, to secure the stock in its place 1627. **5.** *Mus.* The fixed bridge formed by a slight projection or ridge at the upper end of the strings of the violin, guitar, etc. 1698.

III. †1. The glans penis –1758. **†2.** = POPE'S EYE –1682. **b.** *dial.* The pancreas; also, part of the caul 1816. **3.** *pl.* Coal in small lumps 1859. **4.** A small rounded biscuit or cake. Only in *doughnut, gingerbread* or *spice nut*, q.v.

attrib. and *Comb.*, as **N.-Monday**, the first Monday in August, locally observed as a holiday; **n.-palm**, an Australian palm (*Cycus media*) which bears edible nuts; **n.-pine**, a species of pine (*Pinus sabiniana*) indigenous to N. America.

Nut, *v.* 1604. [f. prec.] To seek for, or gather nuts; *esp.* in phr. *to go* (*a*) *nutting.*

Nutant (niū·tănt), *a.* 1751. [– *nutant-*, pr. ppl. stem of L. *nutare*; see next, -ANT.] Drooping, pendent.

Nuta·te, *v. rare.* 1880. [– *nutat-*, pa. ppl. stem of L. *nutare*, f. base of *-nuere* nod; see -ATE[3].] *intr.* To droop or bend downwards; chiefly in **Nuta·ting** *ppl. a.*

Nutation (niutē[i]·ʃən). 1612. [– L. *nutatio*, f. as prec.; see -ION.] **1.** The action of nodding the head; an instance of this. **2.** *Astr.* A slight oscillation of the earth's axis; now *spec.* that by which the pole of the equator would describe a small ellipse in 19 years and which actually renders its motion round the pole of the ecliptic (see PRECESSION) wavy instead of circular 1715. **b.** The oscillation of a top in spinning 1879. **3.** Curvature in the stem of a growing plant 1789.

Nu·t-brown, *a.* (and *sb.*). ME. [f. NUT *sb.*] **1.** Of the colour of a ripe hazel-nut; brown as a nut; of a warm reddish-brown colour. **2.** *absol.* as *sb.* **a.** Ale 1828. **b.** A brown colour like that of nuts 1883.

1. The Nutbrowne mayd 1500. Good Nut-browne-Ale and Tost DAVENANT. **2. b.** Her hair was of a soft nut-brown 1883.

Nu·t-crack. 1570. Now *vulgar.* [f. NUT *sb.*] = NUT-CRACKER 1.

Nu·t-cracker. 1548. [f. NUT *sb.*] **1.** An instrument for breaking the shells of nuts. Now usu., (*a pair of*) *nut-crackers*. **b.** Used *attrib.* and *Comb.* to describe the appearance of nose and chin produced by the want of teeth 1700. **2.** A brown corvine bird (*Nucifraga caryocatactes*), common in various parts of Europe, but rare in Britain 1758.

1. b. She is a toothless, nutcracker jawed old woman 1818.

Nu·t-gall. 1595. [f. NUT *sb.* + GALL *sb.*[3]] A gall produced upon the Dyer's Oak (*Quercus infectoria*), used esp. as a dye-stuff.

Nu·t-grass. 1830. [f. NUT *sb.*] A variety of sedge (*Cyperus hydra*, also *C. phymatodes*), so called from its tuberous roots.

Nuthatch (nɒ·t,hætʃ). ME. [f. NUT *sb.* The second element is conn. w. HACK *v.*[1], HAG *v.*[1], and HATCH *v.*[2]] A small creeping bird belonging to the genus *Sitta*, so named from the way in which it breaks nuts to feed on the kernel. The common British species is *S. cæsia.*

Nu·t-hook. 1500. A hooked stick used when nutting, to pull down the branches of the trees. **†b.** Applied to a beadle, constable, etc. –1658.

Nu·tjobber. Now *dial.* 1544. [JOBBER[1].] = NUTHATCH.

Nu·tlet. 1856. [f. NUT *sb.* + -LET.] A small nut.

Nutmeg (nɒ·tmeg). ME. [Partial tr. of AFr. **nois mugue*, for OFr. *nois mug*(*u*)*ede* (also *musguete*, now *noix muscade*) :– Rom. **nuce muscata* 'musk-smelling nut' (L. *nux* NUT, *muscus* MUSK).] **1.** A hard aromatic seed, of spheroidal form, obtained from the fruit of an evergreen tree (*Myristica fragrans* or *officinalis*), indigenous to the East Indian islands, used as spice and in medicine. **2.** Used to denote colour or appearance 1610.

1. *N.-tree*, the tree which produces the n. **2.** A Roan or N. colour'd Mare 1745. *N. liver*, a diseased condition of the liver, also called *red atrophy.*

Comb., as *n.-grater*; **n.-apple**, the fruit of the nutmeg-tree, containing the mace and n.; **-bird**, *Munia punctulata*, also called *Cowry-bird*; **n. butter**, a solid fatty reddish-brown substance, obtained by grinding the refuse nutmegs to a fine powder; **-flower**, *Nigella sativa*, of Egyptian origin; **-pigeon**, a white pigeon (*Carpophaga ænea*), common in the Indo-Burmese countries, Ceylon, and the Andamans; **-wood**, the wood of the Palmyra palm, *Borassus flabelliformis*. Hence

Nu·tmegged *a.* flavoured with n.; *Path.* affected with red atrophy.

Nu·t-oil. 1664. Oil obtained from nut-kernels, esp. those of the hazel and walnut, used in the manufacture of paints, varnishes, etc.

Nutria (niū·triă). 1836. [– Sp. *nutria* otter.] The skin or fur of the coypu of S. America.

Nutrient (niū·triĕnt), *a.* and *sb.* 1650. [– *nutrient-*, pr. ppl. stem of L. *nutrire* nourish; see -ENT.] **1.** Serving as nourishment; nutritious 1661. **2.** Conveying or providing nourishment 1650. **3.** *sb.* A nutritious substance 1828.

Nutrify (niū·trifəi), *v.* 1509. [f. L. *nutrire* nourish + -FY.] **a.** *trans.* To nourish. **b.** *intr.* To supply nutriment.

Nutriment (niū·trimĕnt). 1541. [– L. *nutrimentum*, f. *nutrire* nourish; see -MENT.] That which nourishes; nourishing food.

Our dayly and special nutrimentes of breade and wyne 1558. *fig.* Is not Virtue in Mankind The N., that feeds the Mind? SWIFT. Hence **Nutrime·ntal** *a.* having the qualities of nutriment; nutritious; also, conveying nourishment.

Nutrition (niutri·ʃən). 1551. [– (O)Fr. *nutrition* or late L. *nutritio*, f. *nutrit-*, pa. ppl. stem of L. *nutrire* nourish; see -ION.] **1.** The action or process of supplying, or of receiving, nourishment. **2.** Food, nutriment 1603.

1. *fig.* The N. of a Common-wealth consisteth, in the Plenty and Distribution of Materials conducing to Life HOBBES. Hence **Nutri·tional, Nutri·tionary** *adjs.*

Nutritious (niutri·ʃəs), *a.* 1665. [– L. *nutritius, -icius*, f. *nutrix, nutric-* nurse; see -ITIOUS¹.] Serving as or supplying nourishment. Hence **Nutri·tious-ly** *adv.*, **-ness.**

Nutritive (niū·tritiv), *a.* and *sb.* late ME. [– Fr. *nutritif, -ive* – med.L. *nutritivus*, f. as NUTRITION; see -IVE.] **1.** Having the property of nourishing; nutritious. **2.** Of, pertaining to, or concerned in, nutrition. late ME. **3.** Giving or providing nourishment 1548. **4.** *sb.* A nourishing article of food 1440. Hence **Nu·tritive-ly** *adv.*, **-ness.**

†**Nu·triture.** 1557. [– late L. *nutritura*, f. as prec.; see -URE.] **1.** Nourishment, nutrition –1740. **2.** Fostering; careful bringing up –1684.

Nu·tshell. ME. [f. NUT *sb.* + SHALE *sb.*, SHELL *sb.*] **1.** The hard exterior covering within which the kernel of a nut is enclosed. **2.** As an example of something without value, or of something extremely small ME. **3.** In phrases denoting great condensation, brevity, or limitation 1693. **b.** With *in.* In a few words 1831.

2. O God, I could be bounded in a n., and count my selfe a King of infinite space SHAKS. I have sometimes heard of an Iliad in a Nut-shell SWIFT. **3. b.** There, sir, is political economy in a n. T. L. PEACOCK.

Nutter (nʊ·təɹ). 1483. [f. NUT *sb.* or *v.* + -ER¹.] One who gathers nuts.

Nu·tting, *vbl. sb.* 1824. [f. NUT *v.* + -ING¹.] The action of gathering nuts.

Nu·t-tree. late ME. A tree that bears nuts; *esp.* the hazel (*Corylus avellana*).

Nutty (nʊ·ti), *a.* 1662. [f. NUT *sb.* + -Y¹.] **1.** Abounding in, or productive of, nuts. **2.** Nut-like; having a taste like nuts 1836. **b.** Pleasant, full of flavour 1823. **3.** *slang.* Amorous, fond; enthusiastic. Usu. const. *upon* (a person). 1821. **4.** *slang.* Smart, spruce 1823; 'swell', dandyish 1913.

2. b. Mr. Blackmore's characteristic, leisurely, n. humor 1894. **4.** The beak wore his nuttiest wig 1839.

Nu·t-weevil. 1802. [f. NUT *sb.* + WEEVIL.] *Entom.* A small beetle (*Balaninus nucum*), which deposits its eggs in green hazel- and filbert-nuts.

‖**Nux vomica** (nʊks vǫ·mikă). 1578. [med. L., f. *nux* nut + fem. of *vomicus*, f. *vomere* to vomit.] **1.** The seed contained in the pulpy fruit of an E. Indian tree (*Strychnos nux-vomica*), which yields the poison strychnia. **2.** The tree itself 1876.

‖**Nuzzer** (nʊ·zəɹ). 1776. [Urdu (Pers., Arab.) *naḏr* gift, f. Arab. *naḏara* he vowed.] In India, a present made by an inferior to a superior. So **Nuzzera·na.**

Nuzzle (nʊ·z'l), *v.*¹ late ME. [f. NOSE *sb.* + -LE 3; orig. perh. back-formation on †*noseling* with the nose to the ground (see -LING²), but perh. infl. later by Du. *neuzelen* poke with the nose, f. *neus* nose.] **I.** *intr.* †**1.** To bring the nose towards the ground; to grovel. ME. only. **2.** To burrow or dig with the nose; to thrust the nose into the ground or anything lying on it 1530. **3.** To poke or push with the nose *in* or *into* something 1592. **b.** With *at, about, against* 1603. **c.** Of dogs: To snuff or poke with the nose 1806. **d.** To poke with the fingers (*rare*) 1806. **4.** To nestle, lie snug in bed 1601. **b.** To nestle on or close to some part of a person 1611. **c.** To lie close *together* or *with* another 1708.

2. Like sows nuzzling for acorns T. HARDY. **3. b.** The Lambs riggle and nussle at their dugs 1657. **4.** 'Twixt the sheete and pillow I nuzled in 1601.

II. *trans.* **1. a.** To root *up* with the nose or snout 1613. **b.** To touch or rub with the nose 1812. **2.** To thrust in (the nose or head) 1594.

1. b. Twenty whale-boats were nuzzling a sand-bank KIPLING.

Nuzzle (nʊ·z'l), *v.*² Now *rare.* 1519. [perh. f. as prec., but connection of sense is obscure.] †**1.** *trans.* To accustom (a dog or hawk) to attack other animals or birds –1688. †**2.** To train, educate, nurture (a person) *in* some opinion, habit, etc. Freq. with *up.* –1686. †**3.** To bring up, rear, educate –1645. **4.** To nurse, to cherish fondly; to provide with a snug place of rest (cf. prec. I. 4) 1581.

†**Nyas,** *sb.* (and *a.*) 1495. [See EYAS.] **1.** An EYAS –1575. **2.** Applied allusively to persons –1616.

‖**Nychthemeron** (nikþī·mĕrǫn). 1682. [– Gr. νυχθήμερον, neut. of νυχθήμερος lasting for a day and a night, f. νύξ, νυκτ- night + ἡμέρα day.] A period of twenty-four hours, consisting of a day and a night.

Nyctalope (ni·ktălōᵘp), *sb.* and *a.* 1601. [– Gr. νυκτάλωψ, -ωπ- NYCTALOPS. Cf. Fr. *nyctalope* sb. and adj. (XVI).] (One) affected with nyctalopia.

‖**Nyctalopia** (niktălōᵘ·piă). 1684. [Late L., f. Gr. νυκτάλωψ; see next, -IA¹. Cf. HEMERALOPIA.] **a.** Night-blindness; recurrent loss of vision after sunset. **b.** Inability to see clearly except by night; day-blindness. So **Ny·ctalopy.**

‖**Nyctalops** (ni·ktălǫps). *rare.* 1661. [L. – Gr. νυκτάλωψ, f. νύξ, νυκτ- night + ἀλαός blind + ὤψ eye.] †**1.** Nyctalopia –1738. **2.** One affected with nyctalopia 1818.

Nycti- (ni·kti), repr. Gr. νυκτι-, a comb. form (properly locative) of νύξ, νυκτ- night, used in a few scientific terms, chiefly zoological as *Nyctiardea*, the nycticorax.

‖**Nycticorax** (nikti·kǒræks). 1688. [Late L. – Gr. νυκτικόραξ, f. νύξ, νυκτ- night + κόραξ raven.] The night-heron. (Cf. *night-raven.*)

Nyctitropic (niktitrǫ·pik), *a.* 1880. [f. NYCTI- + Gr. τρόπος turn; cf. *heliotropic.*] *Bot.* Turning in a certain direction at night.

Nycto- (ni·kto), repr. Gr. νυκτο-, comb. form of νύξ, νυκτ- night, as in *Nyctophilus*, a genus of bats; *nyctophobia*, dread of the night or of darkness; etc.

Nye (nəi). Now *dial.* 1470. [– OFr. *ni* (mod. *nid*) :– L. *nidus* NEST.] A brood (of pheasants). Cf. EYE *sb.*²

Nylghau (ni·lgǭ). 1770. [– Hind. – Pers. *nīlgāw*, f. *nīl* blue + *gāw* Cow *sb.* See NILGAI.] A large short-horned Indian antelope, the adult male of which is of a bluish- or iron-grey colour, and has a tuft of hair on the throat.

Nymph (nimf). late ME. [– OFr. *nimphe* (mod. *nymphe*) – L. *nympha* – Gr. νύμφη bride, nymph, rel. to L. *nubere.*] **1.** *Myth.* One of a class of semi-divine beings, imagined as beautiful maidens inhabiting the sea, rivers, fountains, hills, woods, or trees, or attending on superior deities. **b.** *transf.* A stream, river 1591. **2.** *poet.* A young and beautiful woman; hence, a maiden, damsel 1584. **3.** A pupa 1577.

1. There is a gentle N. not farr from hence, That with moist curb sways the smooth Severn stream MILT. **2.** But soft, what nimphs are these? SHAKS. **Nymph-like** *a.* and *adv.*

‖**Nympha** (ni·mfă). *Pl.* **nymphæ** (ni·mfī). 1601. [L. – Gr. νύμφη bride, nymph.] **1.** = NYMPH 3. **2.** *pl. Anat.* The labia minora of the vulva, situated within the labia majora 1693.

‖**Nymphæa** (nimfī·ă). Also **nymphea.** 1562. [L. – Gr. νυμφαία, fem. of νυμφαῖος sacred to the nymphs.] The common white or yellow water-lily; a genus of aquatic plants including these and other species.

†**Ny·mphal,** *sb.*¹ [– late L. *nymphalis* adj.; see NYMPH, -AL¹.] Used by Drayton as the name of each division of his *Muses' Elysium.*

Nymphal (ni·mfăl), *a.* (and *sb.*²). 1656. [f. as prec.] **A.** *adj.* **1.** Belonging to a nymph; consisting of nymphs. **2.** Of the nature of, pertaining to, a pupa 1864. **3.** Including or belonging to the water-plants related to *Nymphæa* 1846. **B.** *sb.*² **1.** [– Fr. *nymphale.*] A name for a class of butterflies 1797. **2.** A plant belonging to the nymphal alliance 1846.

Nymphean (nimfī·ăn), *a.* 1758. [f. Gr. νυμφαῖος + -AN.] Of or belonging to a nymph or nymphs; nymph-like.

Nymphiparous (nimfi·părəs), *a.* 1835. [f. NYMPH + -PAROUS.] *Entom.* Of insects: Producing nymphæ or pupæ.

Nympholepsy (ni·mfǒlepsi). 1775. [f. next, after *epilepsy.*] A state of rapture supposed to be inspired in men by nymphs; hence, an ecstasy or frenzy, esp. that caused by desire of the unattainable. So ‖**Nymphole·psia.**

Nympholept (ni·mfǒlept), *sb.* and *a.* 1813. [– Gr. νυμφόληπτος caught by nymphs, f. νύμφη nymph + λαμβάνειν take.] **1.** *sb.* One who is inspired by a violent enthusiasm, esp. for an unattainable ideal. Also const. *of.* **2.** *adj.* Inspired by such enthusiasm 1902. Hence **Nymphole·ptic** *a.*

‖**Nymphomania** (nimfǒmēⁱ·niă). 1775. [mod.L.; see NYMPH, -MANIA.] *Path.* A feminine disease characterized by morbid and uncontrollable sexual desire. Hence **Nymphoma·niac** *a.* and *sb.*

‖**Nymphon** (ni·mfǫn). 1855. [– Gr. νυμφών bride-chamber, f. νύμφη bride.] *Zool.* A species of sea-spider.

Nymphotomy (nimfǫ·tǒmi). 1704. [– mod.L. *nymphotomia*, f. Gr. νύμφη (see NYMPHA 2) + -τομία -TOMY.] *Surg.* Excision of the nymphæ.

‖**Nystagmus** (nistæ·gmǒs). 1822. [mod.L. – Gr. νυσταγμός nodding, drowsiness, f. νυστάζειν nod, be sleepy.] An involuntary oscillation of the eyeball, usually lateral, especially common among miners. Hence **Nysta·gmic** *a.*

O

O (ōᵘ), the fifteenth letter in the English alphabet, and the fourth vowel letter. O was the fourteenth letter in the ancient Roman alphabet, corresponding in form and value to the ancient Greeks O, derived from the sixteenth letter of the Phœnician and ancient Semitic alphabet.

The normal sound of short *o* in modern English is (ǫ), low- (or mid-) back-round-wide; but it frequently stands for (ʊ), as in son, doth, or (ʊ̄), as in word; and in unaccented syllables sinks to (ə), as in nation. When original short *o* comes before *r* final, or *r* + cons., as in *or, for, corn, sort,* it is now lengthened into the corresponding long sound ǭ; a later lengthening has taken place, chiefly in the South, before certain cons. groups, as in *cloth, cross, off, soft,* here represented by ǫ̇.

The normal sound of long *o*, as in no, toe, bone, is the quasi- or imperfect diphthong (ōᵘ); but before *r*, as in bore, choral, story, the sound is that of the open quasi-diphthong (ǭᵊ).

I. 1. The letter. Pl. *Os*, O's, *os*, o's (oes). *O per se*, the letter O forming by itself a word. **b.** The sound of the letter, the vowel-sound *o*. **2.** Used to indicate serial order and distinguish things in a series, as the 'quires' or sheets of a book, etc.

3. In *Logic*, = a particular negative. **4.** In *Chem.*, the symbol for Oxygen.

II. *Abbreviations.* **a.** O. = various proper names, as *Oliver, Olivia*, etc. **b.** = 'old', as in OE., Old English; OF., Old French; OHG., Old High German; ON., Old Norse; OS., old style; O.T., Old Testament. **c.** = 'Order', as in D.S.O., Distinguished Service Order; O.M., Order of Merit; O.S.B., Order of Saint Benedict, etc. **d.** = 'Officer', as in O.B.E., Officer of the British Empire; O.C., Officer Commanding; O.T.C., Officers' Training Corps. **e.** O.K.: see in alphabetical position. O.P. (*a*) (also o.p.) 'opposite the prompter side' in a theatre, also *attrib.*; (*b*) 'overproof'; (*c*) (also o.p., *o.p.*) in booksellers' catalogues, 'out of print'.

O (ōᵘ), *sb.*[1] ME. [From resemblance in shape to the letter O.] **1.** The Arabic zero or cipher; hence, a cipher, a mere nothing 1605. **2.** (*Pl.* **oes.**) Anything round, as a circle, round spot, orb ME.

1. Now thou art an O without a figure. . thou art nothing SHAKS. **2.** *Mids. N.* III. ii. 188. *Giotto's O*, the perfect circle, said to have been thrown off free hand by Giotto, the Florentine painter (1266–1336).

O', O, *sb.*[2] 1730. [Ir. *ó, ua*, OIr. *au*; see OY.] A prefix of Irish patronymic surnames, as *O'Connell*, etc. Hence, a person whose surname begins with *O'*.

Ireland her O's, her Mac's let Scotland boast FIELDING.

†**O,** *adv.* [OE. *ā*; cf. A *adv.*, AY *adv.*] Ever, always.

†**O, oo,** *numeral adj.* ME. reduced form of *on, oon* [:– OE. *ān*], ONE, used in south. and midl. bef. a cons. Cf. A *adj.*[1] –1678.

O flessh they been, and o flessh as I gesse Hath but oon herte, in wele and in distresse CHAUCER. Then Christian stept a little a to-side [= at o side] BUNYAN.

O, o' (*o, ŏ,* ə), *prep.*[1] ME. [Worn down f. ON *prep.*, used bef. a cons.; cf. A *prep.*[1]] = ON *prep.*, in various senses; in early use including the sense 'in'. Now only in some *arch.* or traditional phrases.

Cupid hath clapt him oth' shoulder SHAKS.

O, o' (*o, ŏ,* ə), *prep.*[2] ME. [Worn down f. OF *prep.*, used bef. a cons.; cf. A *prep.*[2]] = OF. In form o', still used *arch., dial., colloq.*; e.g. in *six o'clock*; also in *John o' Groats, Jack o' lantern*, etc.

O (ōᵘ), *int.* (*sb.*[3], *v.*) ME. [A natural exclam., expressive of sudden feeling.] **A.** *interj.* **1.** Standing bef. the sb. in the vocative relation. **2.** In other connections, or without construction, expressing, according to intonation, appeal, entreaty, surprise, pain, lament, etc. (In 17th and 18th c., often written OH; but see OH.) ME. **3.** In ballads (chiefly *Sc.*) added after the rhyme-word at the end of a line 1724.

1. O Lord, our God, arise 1742. **2.** O that I had wynges like a doue COVERDALE *Ps.* 54[55]:6. O mee most wretched man! 1610. O, but we all live beyond our incomes 1837. It's O for a manly life in the camp! WHITMAN. **3.** The wintry sun the day has clos'd, And I'll awa to Nanie, O. BURNS.

B. as *sb.* **1.** The interj. considered as a word. So **O me, O dear,** etc., 1609. **2.** pl. *O's of Advent*, the seven Advent Anthems, each containing a separate invocation of Christ beginning with *O*, as *O Sapientia* (O Wisdom), *O Adonai*, etc. ME.

1. O me no O's, but hear B. JONS.

-o-, terminal vowel of combining forms of words, being the usual connective orig. in ethnic names, and, later, in scientific terms generally; it is affixed, not only to terms of Greek origin, but also to those derived from Latin (Latin compounds of which would have been formed with *-i-*.). Instances are *concavo-; chloro-; cumulo-; politico-; joco-; serio-*.

1. Primarily *-o-* qualifies adverbially the adj. to which it is prefixed; as in Gr. λευκόχλωρος 'whitely green', pale green; mod.L. *ovato-cordatus* 'ovately heart-shaped', cordate with ovate modification; *Anglo-Norman*, Norman as modified in England. **2.** Hence, used to express, shortly, almost any manner of relation between two components. *Franco-German*, orig. 'German of a French sort', may even mean 'French in conflict with German'; *Græco-Latin*, 'common to Greek and Latin'; *pneumogastric*, 'communicating with both lungs and stomach', etc. **3.** Appearing frequently bef. *-cracy, -graphy, -logy, -meter, -o-* tends to be permanently associated with these elements; cf. *shop-ocracy*, 'the last new *-ology*', 'galvanometers. . and other *-ometers* without number', and the like.

-o (oᵘ), the final syllable of an abbreviated form, as in *hippo, photo*; an addition to a word or the first part of a word forming a colloq. or slang equiv., as in *ammo, beano, compo*; a meaningless ending, as in *blotto, doggo*, (*like*) *billy-o, cheerio, right(y)-o*.

Oad, obs. f. WOAD.

Oaf (ōᵘf). *Pl.* **oafs**; also 9 **oaves.** 1625. [Varying at first with OUPH and *aufe* (see AUF), *aulfe*, the earliest sense of which was 'elf', 'goblin'; see ELF.] An elf's child; a changeling left by the elves or fairies; hence, a misbegotten, deformed, or idiot child; a half-wit, dolt, booby. So **Oa·fish** *a.* 1610.

Oak (ōᵘk). [OE. *āc* (pl. *ǣc*) = OFris., MLG. *ēk* (Du. *eik*), OHG. *eih* (G. *eiche*), ON. *eik* :– Gmc. **aiks* (cons.-stem); ult. connections unknown. There is no CIE. word for this tree.] **1.** Name of a forest tree, *Quercus robur* (now divided into two sub-species, *Q. pedunculata* and *Q. sessiliflora*, DURMAST), noted for its timber, and bearing a fruit or species of mast called the ACORN; thence extended to all species of *Quercus*, trees or shrubs; the common species in N. America being *Q. alba*, the white oak, and *Q. macrocarpa*, the bur oak. **b.** With defining adjective, applied to other species of *Quercus* 1727. **2.** In Eng. versions of the Bible, used also to render Heb. *ēlāh*, the terebinth tree. late ME. **3.** With qualification, applied to trees or plants in some way resembling the oak 1551. **b.** In Australia, applied to trees of the genus *Casuarina* ('Native Oak') 1802. **4.** The wood of the oak. Hence allusively, with ref. to its hardness and enduring qualities. late ME. **b.** As the material of a ship OE. **c.** *Univ. colloq.* An oaken door; esp. in phr. *to sport one's o.*, to shut the outer door of one's rooms as a sign that one is engaged 1785. **5.** The leaves of the oak. late ME. **6.** *The Oaks*: a race for three-year-old fillies, founded in 1779, and run at Epsom on the Friday after the Derby. (So called from an estate near Epsom.)

1. Our Dance of Custome, round about the Oke Of Herne the Hunter SHAKS. **b. Black** or **Dyer's O.,** *Q. tinctoria* = QUERCITRON. **Blue O., Mountain White O.,** *Q. douglassii* of California. **Bur, Mossy-cup,** or **Overcup O.,** *Q. macrocarpa* of N. America. **Chestnut O.,** *Q. sessiliflora*, and in N. America, *Q. prinus* and other species having leaves like the chestnut. **Cork O.,** *Q. suber*, a native of southern Europe and northern Africa, the bark of which furnishes cork. **Evergreen O.** = HOLM-OAK. **Italian O.,** *Q. æsculus* of southern Europe, having edible acorns. **Kermes-oak,** *Q. coccifera*, in which the kermes insect lives. **Live O.,** a name for *Q. virens*, and other American species. **Scarlet O.,** *Q. coccinea* of N. America, so called from the colour of its foliage in autumn. **Turkey O.,** *Q. cerris* of southern Europe; in America, *Q. catesbæi*. **Weeping O.,** *Q. lobata* of Western U.S. **White O.,** *Q. alba*, a large American tree, occas. called in England *Quebec o.* **O. of Bashan,** *Q. ægilops*. **3. Dwarf O., Ground O.,** various species of *Teucrium*. **O. of Cappadocia,** *Ambrosia maritima*. **O. of Jerusalem** or **Paradise,** *Chenopodium botrys*, having leaves jagged like those of an o. **Poison O.,** species of sumach. **4.** With thunders from her native o. She quells the floods below COWPER. Phr. *Heart of o.*: see HEART *sb.* IV. 3. **5.** Our custom of wearing o. on the twenty-ninth of May 1772.

Combs.: **O.-bark,** the bark of the o., used in tanning and as an astringent; **-beauty,** a moth (*Biston* or *Amphidasis prodromaria*), the larva of which feeds on the o.; **-button** = next; **-gall,** a gall or excrescence produced on species of o. by the punctures of gall-flies; *spec.* a gall-nut used in making ink; **-leather,** a fungus found on old oaks, and somewhat resembling white kid-leather; **-lungs,** lung-wort; **-pest,** an insect (*Phylloxera rileyi*) which infests oaks in the U.S.; **-spangle,** a kind of flattened fungus-like gall, occurring on the lower side of oak-leaves; **-wart,** an oak-gall.

Oak-apple (ōᵘ·kˌæ:p'l). late ME. **1.** A globular form of oak-gall; *spec.* the bright-coloured spongy gall formed on the leaf-bud of the common British oak. **2.** In Australia, the young cone of the SHE-OAK 1889.

attrib., as **Oak-apple day,** the 29th of May, the day of the Restoration of Charles II, when oak-apples or oak-leaves have been worn in memory of his hiding from his pursuers in an oak, on the 6th of Sept., 1651.

Oaken (ōᵘ·kĕn), *a.* ME. [f. OAK + -EN[4].] **1.** Made of the wood of the oak. (Now often repl. by 'oak' used *attrib.*) **2.** Of, pertaining to, or forming part of the oak. *Obs.* or *arch.* (repl. by 'oak' used *attrib.*) 1450. **3.** Formed of oak leaves or twigs (*arch.*) 1605. **4.** Consisting of oak-trees (*arch.* and *poet.*) 1638.

1. An o. chest 1820. **3.** Hee comes the third time home with the O. Garland SHAKS. **4.** With breezes from our o. glades TENNYSON.

Oakling (ōᵘ·kliŋ). 1664. [f. OAK + -LING[1].] A young or small oak; an oak sapling.

Oak-tree (ōᵘ·ktrī). OE. = OAK 1.

Oakum (ōᵘ·kŏm). [OE. *ācumbe, ācum(b)a*, (var. of *ǣcumbe, ǣcuma*), lit. 'off-combings'.] †**1.** The coarse part of the flax separated in hackling; hards, tow. OE. only. **2.** Loose fibre, obtained by untwisting and picking old rope; used esp. in caulking ships' seams, etc. The picking of oakum was formerly a common employment of convicts and inmates of work-houses. 1481.

Oar (ōᵊɹ), *sb.* [OE. *ār* = ON. *ár* :– Gmc. **airō*; perh. ult. rel. to Gr. ἐρετμός oar, ἐρέτης rower, ἐρέσσειν row, τριήρης TRIREME.] **1.** A stout pole, widened and flattened at one end into a blade, used as a lever to propel a boat. (See SCULL, SWEEP.) **b.** In ref. to slaves or criminals compelled to row in galleys; see GALLEY *sb.* 1. 1711. **2.** *fig.* Anything that serves, like an oar, as a means of propulsion in the water 1586. **3.** *transf.* **a.** A rowing-boat 1611. **b.** An oarsman 1608. **4.** A stick, pole, or paddle, with which anything is stirred 1743.

1. Phrases. *To put in one's o.*, to interfere in another's business. *To rest, lie, on one's oars*, to lean on the handles of one's oars; *fig.* to take things easy. **b.** To condemn Criminals. . to the O. 1711. **2.** *transf.* The Oars or finny feet of Water-Fowl SIR T. BROWNE. **3. a.** *Pair of oars*, a boat rowed by two men. **b.** He was a capital o. at Eton 1861.

Comb. **o.-fish,** a name for fishes of the family *Regalecidæ*, esp. *Regalecus banksii*, from their compressed oar-like bodies.

Oar, *v.* 1610. [f. prec.] **1.** *trans.* To propel with or as with oars; to row. **2.** *intr.* To row; to advance, as if propelled by oars. Also with *it.* 1647. **3.** *trans.* To make (one's way) as with oars 1801. **4.** To move (one's hands, etc.) like oars 1882.

1. He. . oared Himselfe with his good armes. . To th' Shore SHAKS. **3.** Now oaring with slow wing her upward way SOUTHEY.

Oarage (ōᵊ·rėdʒ). 1762. [f. OAR *sb.* + -AGE.] **1.** The action of oars; movement of limbs like that of oars. **2.** Apparatus of the nature of oars; outfit of oars; rowing apparatus 1828.

Oared (ōᵊɹd), *a.* 1590. [f. OAR *sb.* + -ED[2].] Provided with oars; also in comb., as *four-oared*, etc.

Oarlock (ōᵊ·ɹlǫk). [OE. *ārloc*, f. *ār* OAR + *loc* LOCK *sb.*[2] Cf. ROWLOCK.] = ROWLOCK.

Oarsman (ōᵊ·ɹzmăn). 1824. [f. *oar's* possess. of OAR + MAN; formerly *oarman* (1608).] A 'man of the oar'; a rower. Hence **Oa·rsmanship.** So **Oa·rswoman.**

Oary (ōᵊ·ri), *a.* 1667. [f. OAR *sb.* + -Y[1].] **a.** Of the nature of, or having the function of, an oar or oars; oar-like. **b.** Furnished with oars; oared.

a. The Swan. . with Oarie feet MILT.

Oasis (oˌēⁱ·sis, ōᵘ·ăsis). *Pl.* **oases** (-īz). 1613. [– late L. *oasis* – Gr. ὄασις (Herodotus), presumably of Egyptian origin. The pronunc. *o·asis* is chiefly Sc. and U.S.] A name of the fertile spots in the Libyan desert; hence *gen.* A fertile spot in the midst of a desert.

fig. My one O. in the dust and drouth Of city life TENNYSON.

Oast (ōᵘst). [OE. *āst* = WFris. *iest*, MLG. *eist* (Du. *eest*) :– Gmc. **aistaz*, for **aiþtaz*, f. IE. base **aidh-* burn.] †**a.** *orig.* = KILN. **b.** Later, A kiln for drying malt or hops, now *spec.* for drying hops.

Comb. **o.-house,** a building containing a kiln for drying hops; the whole structure composing a kiln.

Oat (ōᵘt); usu. in pl. **oats** (ōᵘts). [OE. *āte*, pl. *ātan*, peculiar to Eng. and of unkn. origin. App. *oat* denoted primarily an individual grain; cf. *groat, groats.*] **1.** *pl.* The grains of a hardy cereal (see sense 2) forming an article of food for men and also a chief food of horses; usu. collectively, as a species of grain. **2.** The cereal plant *Avena sativa*, which yields this grain. **a.** Usu. in *pl.*, collectively, as a crop. ME. **b.** In *sing.* (*rare*). late ME. **3.** *sing.* and *collect. pl.* Applied to wild species of *Avena* (called also *Oat-grass*); esp. the **Wild O.,** *Avena fatua*, a tall grass resembling the cultivated oat. **False O.,** the Oat-like Grass, *Arrhenatherum*. OE. **4.** *transf.* (*poet.*). A pipe made of an oaten straw, as a pastoral instrument of music. [After L. *avena*.] 1637.

3. Phr. *To sow one's wild oats*: to commit youthful excesses or follies (usu. implying subsequent reform). **4.** That strain I heard was of a higher mood: But now my Oate proceeds MILT.

Comb.: **o.-grass,** a grass of the genus *Avena*; sometimes also applied to those of allied genera, as *Arrhenatherum, Bromus*; **-pipe, -reed,** a musical instrument made of an oat-straw.

Oat-cake. 1588. [f. OAT + CAKE *sb.*] = CAKE *sb.* 1 b.

Oaten (ōu·t'n), *a.* late ME. [f. OAT + -EN^{4}.] **1.** Composed of the grain of oats, or of oatmeal. **2.** Made of the straw or stem of an oat. late ME. **3.** Of or belonging to the oat as a plant 1588.

1. They did eate..oten bread P. HOLLAND. **2.** Rural ditties..Temper'd to th' O. Flute MILT. **3.** When Shepheards pipe on O. strawes SHAKS.

Oath (ōuþ), *sb.* *Pl.* **oaths** (ōuðz). [OE. *āþ* = OFris. *ēth, ēd*, OS. *ēth* (Du. *eed*), (O)HG. *eid*, ON. *eiðr*, Goth. *aiþs* :– Gmc. **aiþaz*.] **1.** A solemn appeal to God (or to something sacred) in witness that a statement is true, or a promise binding; an act of swearing; a statement or promise corroborated by such an appeal, or the form of words in which such a statement or promise is made. **b.** Loosely applied to an asseveration not involving a ref. to God or anything sacred 1600. **2.** A careless use of the name of God or Christ, or of something sacred, in asseveration or imprecation, or a formula of words involving this; an act of profane swearing; a curse ME.

1. *To take (an) o.*, to utter, or bind oneself by, an o.; to swear; also *to make (an) o. On* or *upon o.*, under the obligation of an o.; as having made an o. BIBLE *o.*, BODILY *o.*, BOOK *o.*, CORPORAL *o.*; see those words. **b.** *A. Y. L.* IV. i. 192–3. Hence **Oath** *v.* to utter an oath or oaths, to swear. Also *to o. it.*

Oatmeal (ōu·tmīl). late ME. [f. OAT + MEAL *sb.*^{1}] Meal made from oats. Also *attrib.*

†**Ob,** *sb.* 1588. [From *ob.*, abbrev. of *objection*, used in conjunction with *sol.* = *solution*, in old books of divinity.] In phr. *Ob(s) and sol(s)* = objection(s) and solution(s); scholastic or subtle disputation –1660.

†**Ob.** ME. Abbrev. of OBOLUS, used for a halfpenny –1631.

1 *Hen. IV*, II. iv. 590.

Ob., abbrev. of L. *obiit* died; used before the date of a person's death.

Ob-, *pref.* The Lat. prep. *ob* 'towards, against, in the way of', becoming, in comb. with vbs. and their derivs., *oc-* before *c-*, *of-* before *f-*, *op-* before *p-*, and app. *o-* before *m-* (in *omittere*). In Eng. use, *ob-* (*oc-, of-, op-, o-*) occurs **1.** In combs. already formed in L.; rarely in words formed in Eng. itself on L. elements; e.g. *obduce, obdurate, obedience, object, obversion, occident, occur, opponent, opposite*, etc. **2.** In mod. scientific Latin, and hence in Eng., in Botany, etc., *ob-* is prefixed to adjs. in the sense 'inversely', or 'in the opposite direction', as in *obcordatus* (Linn.) OBCORDATE, *obconical, obimbricate, oblanceolate, obovoid, obvallate, obvolute*, etc.

In this use, apparently the prefix represents the *ob-* of L. *obverse* OBVERSELY, and is short for that word.

Obambulate (ǫbæ·mbiŭleˡt), *v. rare.* 1614. [– *obambulat-*, pa. ppl. stem of L. *obambulare* walk about, f. *ob-* OB- 1 + *ambulare* walk; see -ATE^{3}.] *intr.* To walk about. So **Obambula·tion.**

‖**Obbligato** (ǫbligā·to, obbligā·to), *a.* (*sb.*). Often **Obligato.** 1794. [It., 'obliged', 'obligatory'.] *Mus.* **1.** That cannot be omitted; applied to a part essential to the completeness of a composition (or to the instrument on which such a part is played); esp. to an accompaniment having an independent value. Opp. to *ad libitum*. Also *transf.* forced, compulsory. **2.** *sb.* An obbligato part or accompaniment 1845.

Obcordate (ǫbkǭ·ɹdĕt), *a.* 1775. [OB- 2.] *Nat. Hist.* Inversely cordate; heart-shaped, with the apex serving as the base or point of attachment.

Obdiplostemonous (ǫbdiploˌstī·mŏnəs), *a.* 1880. [OB- 2.] *Bot.* Diplostemonous with the disposition of the two stamen-whorls reversed; having the stamens of the outer whorl opposite to, and those of the inner whorl alternate with, the petals. Hence **Obdiploste·mony.**

†**Obdu·ce,** *v.* 1657. [– L. *obducere* draw over, cover over, f. *ob-* OB- 1 + *ducere* lead, draw.] *trans.* To cover, envelop –1709.

†**Obdu·ction.** 1578. [– L. *obductio* covering, veiling, f. *obduct-*, pa. ppl. stem of *obducere*; see prec., -ION.] The action of covering or enveloping –1656.

Obduracy (ǫ·bdiurăsi). 1597. [f. OBDURATE *a.* + -ACY.] The state or quality of being obdurate; obstinacy; persistent hardness of heart.

Obdurate (ǫ·bdiurĕt, ǭbdiūᵊ·rĕt), *a.* late ME. [– L. *obduratus*, pa. pple. of *obdurare*, f. *ob-* OB- 1 + *durare* harden, f. *durus* hard; see -ATE^{2}.] **1. a.** Hardened in evil; insensible to moral influence. **b.** Unyielding, relentless, hard-hearted, inexorable 1586. †**2.** Physically hardened or hard –1784.

1. a. The o. conscience of the old sinner SCOTT. **b.** Women are soft, milde, pittifull, and flexible; Thou, sterne, o., flintie, rough, remorselesse SHAKS. *fig.* They have joined the most o. consonants without one intervening vowel SWIFT. Hence **Obdurate-ly** *adv.*, **-ness.**

Obdurate (ǫ·bdiureˡt, ǭbdiūᵊ·reˡt), *v.* 1540. [f. prec., or – *obdurat-*, pa. ppl. stem of L. *obdurare*; see prec., -ATE^{3}.] *trans.* **To** make morally obdurate (see prec.) So **Obdura·tion,** the action of hardening or condition of being hardened 1494.

†**Obdure** (ǭbdiūᵊ·ɹ), *a.* 1608. [f. OB- 1 + L. *durus* hard, after *obdurare*; see next.] = OBDURATE *a.* –1860. Hence †**Obdu·re-ly** *adv.*, †**-ness.**

Obdure (ǭbdiūᵊ·ɹ), *v.* Now *rare* or *Obs.* 1598. [– L. *obdurare*; see OBDURATE *a.*] *trans.* = OBDURATE *v.* So **Obdu·red** *ppl. a.* = OBDURATE *a.* 1. 1585.

Obe (ōub). 1835. [– Gr. ὠβά.] *Gr. Hist.* A village or district in ancient Laconia; a subdivision of an original φυλή or clan.

‖**Obeah** (ōu·biă), **obi** (ōu·bi), *sb.* 1764. [West African.] **1.** An amulet, charm, or fetish used by Negroes for magical purposes 1796. **2.** A kind of pretended sorcery or witchcraft practised by the Negroes in Africa, and formerly in the West Indies 1764. **3.** *attrib.*, as *obeah* (or *obi*) *-man*, a Negro sorcerer, etc. 1764. Hence **O·beah, o·bi** *v. trans.* to bewitch by o.; **O·beahism** the practice of or belief in o.

Obedience (ŏbī·diĕns). ME. [– (O)Fr. *obédience* – L. *obedientia*, f. *obedient-*; see next, -ENCE.] **1.** The action or practice of obeying; the fact or character of being obedient. **2.** The fact or position of being obeyed, or of having others subject to one; command, authority. (Now esp. of the authority of the Church of Rome.) ME. **b.** *transf.* A sphere of authority or dominion, esp. ecclesiastical 1635. **3.** = OBEISANCE 3. Now *arch.* and *dial.* 1503. **4.** In a monastic or conventual establishment: Any office, official position, or duty, under the abbot or superior; the particular office or duty of any inmate of a convent; also, the cell, room, or place appertaining or appropriate to such an office; = med.L. *obedientia* (see Du Cange) 1700.

1. To bee brought vppe in the o. of Lawes 1602. *fig.* A heavy body falls to the ground in o. to the law of gravitation 1902. *Passive o.* (*a*) (opp. to *active o.*) an obedience in which the subject suffers without resistance or remonstrance; (*b*) unqualified obedience to commands, whether reasonable or unreasonable, lawful or unlawful. **2.** The two Houses decided..to return to the o. of the Papal See GREEN. **b.** All the English land-owners within William's o. FREEMAN. The clergy and the laity of the Roman obedience (*mod.*).

Obedient (obī·diĕnt), *a.* (*sb.*) ME. [– OFr. *obédient* – L. *obediens, -ent-*, pr. pple. of *obedire* OBEY; see -ENT.] **1.** That obeys; submissive to the will of a superior; doing what one is bidden; subservient; dutiful. **b.** Conventionally used as an expression of courtesy, *esp.* in phr. *your o. servant* 1548. †**2.** *Astrol.* Of signs of the zodiac, etc.: Subject; see OBEY *v.* 4. –1391. **3.** *fig.* (chiefly of things or involuntary agents): Moving or yielding as actuated or affected by something else. late ME. †**4.** *sb.* One who is subject to authority; a subordinate –1662.

1. Such delight hath God in Men O. to his Will MILT. **3.** Floating..o. to the streame SHAKS. Hence **Obe·diently** *adv.*

Obediential (obīdiˌe·nʃăl), *a.* 1619. [– med.L. *obedientialis*, f. L. *obedientia*; see OBEDIENCE, -AL^{1}. Cf. Fr. *obédientiel*.] Of, pertaining to, of the nature of, or characterized by obedience. (Chiefly *Theol.*; now *rare* or *Obs.* in gen. sense.)

Obedientiary (obīdiˌe·nʃări). 1536. [– med.L. *obedientiarius*, f. *obedientia*; see -ARY^{1}.] †**1.** A person practising obedience; one owning allegiance; a subject; a liegeman –1603. **2.** A member of a conventual establishment charged with any duty or 'obedience'. (See OBEDIENCE 4.) 1794.

Obeisance (obēˡ·săns). late ME. [– (O)Fr. *obéissance*, f. *obéissant*, pr. pple. of *obéir* OBEY; see -ANCE.] †**1.** = OBEDIENCE 1. –1660. †**2.** *The o.* (of any one): = OBEDIENCE 2. –1678. †**b.** = OBEDIENCE 2 b. –1616. **3.** A respectful salutation; a bow or curtsy. Often in phr. *to do, make, pay, o.* (Chiefly literary, and often *arch.*) late ME. **4.** Respectfulness of manner or bearing, deference; homage, submission. (In mod. use, regarded as *fig.* from 3.) late ME.

3. He made a low Obeysance 1640. **4.** A Throne to which conquered Nations yielded Obeysance STEELE.

Obeisant (obēˡ·sănt), *a.* ME. [– (O)Fr. *obéissant*; see prec., -ANT.] **1.** = OBEDIENT 1, *Obs.* exc. as in 2. **2.** Showing respect or deference; servilely obedient, obsequious 1642.

‖**Obelion** (obī·liǫn). 1878. [mod.L., f. Gr. ὀβελός spit + Gr. dim. ending -ιον; see -IUM.] *Anat.* A point on the sagittal suture, between the parietal foramina. Hence **Obe·liac** *a.*

Obelisk (ǫ·bĕlisk, -ĭ-). 1569. [– L. *obeliscus* small spit, obelisk – Gr. ὀβελίσκος, dim. of ὀβελός spit, pointed pillar.] **1.** A tapering shaft of stone, usu. monolithic, and square or rectangular in section, with a pyramidal apex; a type of monument specially characteristic of ancient Egypt. **b.** A natural formation resembling an obelisk, e.g. a mountain peak, a cypress tree, etc. 1845. **2.** A mark (either – or ÷) used in ancient MSS. to point out a spurious, corrupt, or doubtful word or passage (= OBELUS); in mod. use applied to the mark † used in printing for marginal references, foot-notes, etc. (= DAGGER *sb.* 5). *Double o.*, the double dagger (‡). 1583. Hence **Obeli·scal** *a.*

Obelize (ǫ·bĭləiz), *v.* 1611. Also *erron.* **obolize.** [– Gr. ὀβελίζειν mark with a critical obelus; see OBELUS, -IZE.] *trans.* To mark (a word or passage) with an obelus or obelisk; to condemn as spurious or corrupt.

‖**Obelus** (ǫ·bĭlŏs). *Pl.* **obeli** (-ləi). late ME. [L. *obelus* spit, critical obelus – Gr. ὀβελός spit, obelisk, critical mark.] = OBELISK 2.

Obese (obī·s), *a.* 1651. [– L. *obesus* that has eaten himself fat, stout, plump, f. *ob-* OB- 1 + *esus*, pa. pple. of *edere* eat.] Very fat or fleshy; corpulent. Hence **Obe·se-ly** *adv.*, **-ness.**

Obesity (obī·sĭti, obe·sĭti). 1611. [– Fr. *obésité* or L. *obesitas*, f. *obesus*; see prec., -ITY.] The condition of being obese; corpulence.

‖**Obex** (ōu·beks). 1611. [L. *obex, obic-* barrier, bolt, f. *obicere* cast in front of, f. *ob-* OB- 1 + *jacere* cast.] **1.** An impediment, obstacle. Now *rare* or *Obs.* **2.** *Anat.* A thickening of the ependyma of the fourth ventricle of the brain at the point of the *calamus scriptorius* 1892.

Obey (ŏbēˡ·), *v.* [ME. *obeie* – (O)Fr. *obéir* – L. *obedire, obœdire*, f. *ob-* OB- 1 + *audire* hear.] **1.** *trans.* (orig. *intr.* with *dat. obj.*). **a.** To be obedient to. **b.** To comply with, perform (a command, etc.) late ME. **c.** To submit to, subject onself to (a principle, authority, etc.). Now *rare* or *arch.* late ME.

d. *fig.* To act as compelled by (a thing, agency, force, impulse, etc.); to be actuated by 1598. †**2.** *intr.* To be obedient *to* or *unto* (= 1) –1667. **3.** *intr.* or *absol.* To do what one is commanded; to submit; to be obedient. late ME. **b.** *fig.* of a thing 1567. **4.** *intr. Astrol.* Said of certain signs of the zodiac in relation to others (called *commanding* or *sovereign signs*), or of planets when in such signs. late ME. †**5.** To do obeisance to, bow to –1650.

1. a. The highe powers shuld be alweys obeid 1529. **b.** The ladies obeying the summons, came up in a group GOLDSM. **c.** What obeyes Reason, is free MILT. **d.** He marks how well the ship her helm obeys BYRON. **2.** His seruants ye are to whom ye o. *Rom.* 6:16. To their Generals Voyce they soon Obey'd MILT. **3.** Will he o. when one commands? TENNYSON. **b.** To speak I tri'd..My Tongue obey'd MILT. **4.** *Obeying Signs*, the Southern, or last six Signs of the Zodiac are so called 1679. Hence **Obey·able** *a.* that can, or should, be obeyed. **Obey·er**, one who obeys. **Obey·ingly** *adv.*

†**Obfirm**, *v.* 1563. [– L. *obfirmare*, *off-*, render firm or steadfast, f. *ob-* OB- 1 + *firmare* strengthen, f. *firmus* strong.] *trans.* To make firm (in bad sense); to confirm (*in* an evil course, error, etc.); to make stubborn; to harden –1686. Hence †**Obfirma·tion**, confirming or being confirmed in evil; obduracy.

Obfuscate (ǫbfʊ̆skēⁱt), *v.* 1536. [– *obfuscat-*, pa. ppl. stem of late L. *obfuscare*, f. *ob-* OB- 1 + *fuscare* darken, *fuscus* dark; see -ATE³.] **1.** *trans.* To darken, obscure (physically); to deprive of light or brightness; to eclipse. Now *rare.* 1650. †**2.** *fig.* To darken or obscure to the mind; to deprive of lustre or glory, throw into the shade –1702. **3.** To dim (the sight); to obscure (the understanding, judgement, etc.); to stupefy, bewilder (a person) 1577.

1. Atmospheres..so dense..as may suffice to o... the Light of the Star 1734. **3.** He was obfuscated with brandy and water 1893. Hence **Obfusca·tion**, obfuscating; the being obfuscated; *transf.* something that obfuscates. So **Obfu·scate** *ppl. a.* Now *rare* or *Obs.* 1531.

‖**Obi**¹, **obi-man**, etc.: see OBEAH.

‖**Obi**² (ōᵘ·bi). 1802. [Jap. *ōbi* belt.] A brightly coloured sash worn round the waist by Japanese women and children; any similar sash.

Obit (ǫ·bit, ōᵘ·bit). *Obs.* exc. *Hist.* Also freq. **obiit.** late ME. [– (O)Fr. *obit* – L. *obitus* going down, setting, death, f. *obit-*, pa. ppl. stem of *obire* go down, perish, die (for *mortem obire* meet death), f. *ob-* OB- 1 + *ire* go. Cf. EXIT.] **1.** †**a.** Death, decease (of a particular person) –1694. **b.** An obituary notice (*arch.*) 1459. **2.** †**a.** Funeral rites, obsequies. (Also in *pl.*) –1708. **b.** A yearly (or other) service in commemoration of, or on behalf of the soul of, a deceased person on the anniversary or other mind-day of his death. *Obs.* exc. *Hist.* late ME.

2. b. Obits, Dirges, Masses are not said for nothing 1670.

†**O·bital**, *a.* and *sb.* 1690. [f. prec. sb. + -AL¹.] **1.** *adj.* Recording or commemorating a death or deaths, or the celebration of obits (see prec. 2 b) –1715. **2.** *sb.* An obituary WOOD.

Obiter (ǫ·bitəɹ), *adv.* and *adj.* 1573. [L. adv., orig. two words, *ob iter*, by the way.] **A.** *adv.* By the way, in passing, incidentally. **b.** *esp.* in the phr. **Obiter dictum** [L., (a thing) said by the way]: in *Law.* An expression of opinion on a matter of law, given by a judge in court, but not essential to his decision, and therefore not of binding authority; hence *gen.* Any incidental statement or remark 1812. **B.** quasi-*adj.* (after *obiter dictum*). Made or uttered by the way; incidental 1767.

Obitual (obi·tiu,ăl), *a.* and *sb. rare.* 1706. [f. L. *obitus* OBIT + -AL¹; cf. *habitual.*] **1.** *adj.* = OBITAL 1. **2.** *sb.* = OBITAL 2, OBITUARY A 1. 1812.

Obituary (obi·tiu,ări), *sb.* and *a.* 1706. [– med.L. *obituarius* adj. and sb., f. *obitus*; see OBIT and -ARY¹.] **A.** *sb.* **1.** A register of deaths, or of obit days. **2.** A notice or announcement of a death or deaths, esp. in a newspaper; usu. comprising a brief biography of the deceased 1738. **B.** *adj.* Relating to or recording a death (usu. with a biographical sketch of the deceased); esp. *o. notice* 1828.

Object (ǫ·bdʒĕkt), *sb.* late ME. [Partly subst. use of OBJECT *ppl. a.*; but in philosophical senses – med. schol.L. *objectum*, lit. thing thrown before (the mind). In branch II rendering L. *objectus*, thus properly a distinct wd.] **I.** From L. *objectum*, pl. *objecta*. †**1.** A statement introduced in opposition; an objection –1617. †**2.** Something 'thrown' or put in the way as an obstacle; a hindrance –1564. **3.** Something presented to the sight or other sense; a material thing; *spec.* the thing or body observed by means of an optical instrument, or represented in drawing or perspective. late ME. **b.** Something which on being seen excites admiration, horror, amusement, commiseration, etc.; in colloq. use a person or thing of pitiable or ridiculous aspect 1588. **4.** That to which action, thought, or feeling is directed; the thing (or person) to which something is done or about which something acts or operates (= Schol. *materia circa quam*). Const. *of* (the action, etc. or agent). 1586. **5.** The thing aimed at; purpose, end 1597. **6.** *Metaph.* A thing of which one thinks or has cognition, as correlative to the thinking or knowing *subject*; something regarded as external to the mind; the non-ego; also extended to include states of the ego, or of consciousness, as thought of 1651. **7.** *Gram.* A substantive word, phrase, or clause, 'governed by' a verb. Also, the word 'governed by' a preposition. 1729.

3. Þe obiect of the eye is all þᵗ may be seen, & al þᵗ maye be herde is obiect to the herynge TREVISA. **b.** Some poor objects will be sent thither in hopes of relief BUTLER. **4.** He..will be deemed a proper o. of public charity 1773. **5.** How quickly Nature falls into reuolt, when Gold becomes her Obiect? SHAKS. **7.** *O. clause*, a clause or subordinate sentence forming the object of a verb, as in 'we know (that) he is alive'. *Direct o.*, the word or phrase 'governed' by a transitive verb. *Indirect o.* of a (trans. or intr.) verb. ¶*No o.*: a matter of indifference (e.g. *distance no o.*).

II. [= L. *objectu-s* (*u*-stem).] †**1.** The fact of throwing itself or being thrown in the way (*rare*) –1555. †**2.** = OBJECTION 3. –1616.

2. Reason flyes the obiect of all harme SHAKS. *Comb.*: **o.-ball** (*Billiards, Croquet*, etc.), the ball at which the player aims his own ball; **-finder,** a contrivance for registering the position of an o. on a mounted microscopic slide, so as to find it again; **-lens** = OBJECT-GLASS; **-lesson,** a lesson about a material o. conveyed by actual examination of the o.; *fig.* something that exemplifies some principle in a concrete form: so *o. teaching*; **-plate** (*Microscopy*), the plate upon which the object to be examined is placed; **-staff** (*Surveying*), a levelling-staff. Hence **O·bjectless** *a.* devoid of an object or objects, *esp.* aimless, purposeless; so **O·bjectless-ly** *adv.*, **-ness.**

†**Obje·ct**, *ppl. a.* late ME. [– L. *objectus*, pa. pple. of *obicere*; see next.] **1.** Thrown or put in the way; exposed (to injury or any influence, or to sight) –1650. **b.** Opposite; also *fig.* opposed, contrary –1613. **2.** Objected, charged (*against* a person) –1529.

Object (ŏbdʒe·kt), *v.* late ME. [– *object-*, pa. ppl. stem of L. *obicere*, f. *ob-* OB- 1 + *jacere* throw; or – L. *objectare* (cf. Fr. *objecter*).] **1.** *trans.* To put over against or in the way of something; to expose *to*. *Obs.* or *arch.* 1578. **b.** To put in the way or interpose, as an obstacle or hindrance to progress, or a defence from attack. *Obs.* or *arch.* 1548. †**c.** To expose *to* danger, etc. –1677. **2.** To place (something) before the eyes, etc., or the mind. *Obs.* or *arch.* 1534. **3.** To bring forward as a reason, ground, or instance; to adduce. *Obs.* or *arch.* 1536. **4.** To urge as an objection (*to, unto, against*). late ME. **5.** To attribute to any one as a fault or crime. Const. *to, against* (†*upon*, indirect obj.). 1469. †**6.** *trans.* To impute, attribute (*to*) –1776. **7.** *intr.* To state an adverse reason; now often merely: To express or feel disapproval. late ME. **b.** with *to* (occas. *against*, rarely *at*) or *inf.*: To bring forward a reason against: now usu.: To express, or merely to feel, disapproval of; to have an objection *to*, dislike. (The chief current sense.) 1513. †**c** *intr.* To bring an accusation. *Acts* 24:19.

1. He commanded him to be objected to a hungry and an enraged Lyon 1654. **b.** Pallas to their eyes The mist objected POPE. **2.** Whose temperance was of proof against any meat objected to his appetite FULLER. **4.** Bryant objects this very circumstance to the authenticity of the Iliad 1830. **5.** When God afflicted Job, he did o. no sin to him HOBBES. **7.** I think I'll have a smoke, if you don't o. (*mod.*). **b.** We o. to the argument on scientific grounds 1869. Hence †**Obje·ctable** *a.* that may be objected, or urged as an objection (*against* or *to*); that may be objected to –1885. **Obje·cted** *ppl. a.* placed opposite, presented to the view or perception. *Obs.* or *arch.*

O·bject-glass. 1665. [OBJECT *sb.* I. 3.] The lens or combination of lenses in a telescope, microscope, etc., which is situated nearest to the object. (Cf. EYE-GLASS 3.)

Objectify (ŏbdʒe·ktifəi), *v.* 1836. [f. OBJECT *sb.* + -FY.] *trans.* To make into, or present as, an object, esp. an object of sense; to render objective. Hence **Obje:ctifica·tion**, the action of objectifying or condition of being objectified; an instance of this.

Objection (ŏbdʒe·kʃən). late ME. [– OFr. *objection* or late L. *objectio*, f. as OBJECT *v.*; see -ION.] **1. a.** The action of stating something in opposition to a person or thing. **b.** That which is objected; †an accusation against a person; an adverse reason, argument, or contention. Now often merely: An expression, or feeling, of disapproval, disagreement, or dislike (esp. in phr. *to have an* or *no o.*). **c.** A document in which an objection is stated. †**2.** *transf.* and *fig.* An adverse action, an assault –1586. **3.** Presentation to the view or to the mind, or that which is so presented; representation, offer –1649.

1. b. I have no o. to join with you in the enquiry 1875. Phr. *To take o.*, to bring forward a reason against something, or merely to object. Hence **Obje·ctionable** *a.* open to o.; now often, unacceptable, unpleasant. **Obje·ctionableness. Obje·ctionably** *adv.*

Obje·ctivate, *v.* 1873. [f. OBJECTIVE *a.* + -ATE³. Cf. Fr. *objectiver.*] *trans.* = OBJECTIFY. So **Obje:ctiva·tion** = OBJECTIFICATION.

Objective (ŏbdʒe·ktiv), *a.* and *sb.* 1620. [– med.L. *objectivus* (Occam; cf. adv. *objective* in Duns Scotus); so Fr. *objectif*; see OBJECT *sb.*, -IVE.] **A.** *adj.* †**1.** *Philos.* Pertaining or considered in relation to its object; constituting, or belonging to, an object of action, thought, or feeling; 'material', as opp. to *subjective* or 'formal' –1675. †**b.** Of or pertaining to the object or end as the cause of action; *o. cause* = final cause: see CAUSE *sb.* I. 4. –1678. **2.** *Philos.* Used of the existence or nature of a thing as an object of consciousness (as dist. from *subjective*). †**a.** Opp. to *subjective* in the older sense = 'in itself': Existing as an object of consciousness; considered only as presented to the mind –1744. **b.** Opp. to *subjective* in the modern sense: That is the object of perception or thought, as dist. from the perceiving or thinking subject; hence, that is, or is regarded as, a 'thing' external to the mind; real 1647. **3.** *transf.* (from 2 b) **a.** Of a person, a writing, work of art, etc.: Treating of outward things or events; regarding things from an objective standpoint. (Occas., after mod. G. *objektiv*: Treating a subject so as to exhibit the actual facts, not coloured by the feelings or opinions of the writer.) 1855. **b.** *Med.* Applied to symptoms 'observed by the practitioner, in distinction from those which are only felt by the patient' (*Syd. Soc. Lex.*) 1877. **4.** With *to*: That is the object of sensation or thought. In *Metaph.* Related as object to subject (see OBJECT *sb.* 6). 1762. **5.** *Perspective.* That is, or belongs to, the object of which the delineation is required 1706. **6.** Applied to the lens or combination of lenses in an optical instrument which is nearest to the object (*o. glass*; now usu. OBJECT-GLASS, or simply *objective*) 1753. **7.** *Gram.* Expressing or denoting the object of an action; *spec.* applied to that case in mod. English in which a noun or pronoun stands when it is the object of a verb, or is governed by a preposition; also to the relation of such noun or pronoun to such verb or preposition 1763. **8.** *O. point*: orig. *Mil.* the point towards which the advance of troops is directed; hence *gen.* the point aimed at 1864. **9.** Characterized by objecting 1814.

2. a. This confession was the o. foundation of faith; and Christ and his Apostles, the subjective JER. TAYLOR. Natural phænomena are..such as we see and perceive them: Their real and o. natures are, therefore, the same BERKELEY. **b.** In the philosophy of mind, subjective denotes what is referred to the thinking subject, the Ego; o. what belongs to the object of thought, the Non-Ego 1853. This [Christ's resurrection] was an historic o. fact FARRAR. **3.** The book [Robinson Crusoe]..is, to use a much-abused word, eminently o.; that is, the circumstances are drawn from a real study of things as they are 1855. To complete the survey of the actualities of party politics by stating in a purely positive, or as the Germans say 'objective', way, what the Americans think about..their system BRYCE. **8.** The city of Meshed being my o. point 1893.

B. *sb.* (the adj. used ellipt.) **1.** Short for *o. glass* (see A. 6) 1835. **2.** *Gram.* Short for *o. case* (see A. 7) 1861. **3.** Short for *o. point* (see A. 8); also *fig.* something aimed at, an object or end 1881. Hence **Obje·ctively** *adv.* in an o. manner or relation (usu. opp. to *subjectively*). **Obje·ctiveness, Objecti·vity,** the quality or character of being o.

Objectivism (ǫ̆bdʒe·ktiviz'm). 1872. [f. OBJECTIVE *a.* + -ISM.] The tendency to lay stress upon what is objective or external to the mind; the philosophical doctrine that knowledge of the non-ego is prior in sequence and importance to that of the ego; the character (in a work of art, etc.) of being objective. So **Obje·ctivist,** one who holds the doctrine of o. (also *attrib.*).

Obje·ctivize, *v.* 1856. [f. OBJECTIVE *a.* + -IZE.] *trans.* To render objective.

Objectize (ǫ·bdʒėktaiz), *v.* 1668. [f. OBJECT *sb.* + -IZE.] *trans.* To make into an object, objectify. So **Objectiza·tion.**

Object-matter. 1652. [= OBJECT *ppl. a.* + MATTER *sb.*] †**1.** Matter presented to view or to be employed as a means GAULE. **2.** The matter that is the object of some action or study. (Usu. *subject-matter*) 1836.

Objector (ǫ̆bdʒe·ktəɹ). 1640. [f. OBJECT *v.* + -OR 2.] One who objects or makes an objection to something.

A conscientious o. to vaccination 1899.

Objicient (ǫ̆bdʒi·ʃ[i]ĕnt). 1864. [– L. *objiciens, -ent-*, pr. pple. of *obicere*; see OBJECT *v.*, -ENT.] One who objects; an opponent of a motion or proposition.

Objurgate (ǫ·bdʒɒɹge[i]t), *v.* 1616. [– *objurgat-*, pa. ppl. stem of L. *objurgare*, f. *ob-* OB- 1 + *jurgare* quarrel, scold, f. *jurgium* quarrel, strife; see -ATE[3].] *trans.* To chide, scold. Also *absol.* or *intr.* Hence **Objurga·tion,** chiding, scolding. **Obju·rgative, Obju·rgatory** *adjs.* **Obju·rgatorily** *adv.*

‖**Oblata** (ǫblē[i]·tă), *sb. pl. Hist.* 1658. [L., subst. use of n. pl. of *oblatus*; see next.] *Law.* Old debts, or offerings made to the king by any of his subjects, which, if not paid, were put in the sheriff's charge.

Oblate (ǫ·ble[i]t), *sb.* 1756. [– Fr. *oblat* – med.L. *oblatus*, subst. use of pa. pple. of L. *offerre* OFFER.] A person solemnly devoted to a monastery or to a religious work; *spec.* a member of a congregation or order devoted to a specific work.

Oblate (ǫblē[i]·t, ǫ·ble[i]t), *a.* 1696. [– mod.L. *oblatus*, f. *ob-* OB- 1 + *latus*, as in L. *prolatus* PROLATE *a.*] *Geom.* Flattened at the poles; said of a spheroid produced by the revolution of an ellipse about its shorter axis. Opp. to *prolate*. Hence **Oblate-ly** *adv.*, **-ness.**

Oblation (ǫ̆blē[i]·ʃən). late ME. [– (O)Fr. *oblation* or late and eccl. L. *oblatio*, f. *oblat-*, pa. ppl. stem of L. *offerre* OFFER; see -ION.] **I.** In religious senses. **1.** The action of solemnly offering something (e.g. a sacrifice, thanksgiving, etc.) to God or to a deity. **2.** The action of offering the elements of bread and wine to God in the Eucharist; also, the whole service of the Eucharist 1450. **3.** That which is offered to God or to a deity; an offering, sacrifice; a victim. late ME. †Also *transf.* **4.** The presentation of something to God for the services of the Church, or other pious uses; that which is so presented 1455.

1. Therfore will I offre in his dwellinge, the oblacion of thankes geuynge COVERDALE *Ps.* 26[7]:6. **2.** *The great o.* (Liturg.), that in which the consecrated elements are presented as sacramentally the body and blood of Christ. **3.** Hee..shall bring his o. vnto the Lord *Lev.* 7:29. **4.** We humbly beseech thee most mercifully to accept our alms and oblations *Bk. Com. Prayer.*

II. In general uses. **1.** The action of offering or presenting 1595. †**2.** A subsidy or tax; a gift to the king –1668. Hence **Obla·tional** *a.* **Obla·tionary** *sb. Eccl.* one who receives the oblations at the celebration of the Eucharist; *adj.* having the function of receiving the oblations. †**Obla·tioner,** one who makes an o.

Oblatory (ǫ·blătəri), *a.* 1611. [– Fr. †*oblatoire* or med.L. *oblatorius*, f. as prec.; see -ORY[2].] Pertaining to oblations.

†**Oble·ctate,** *v. rare.* 1611. [– *oblectat-*, pa. ppl. stem of L. *oblectare* delight, f. *ob-* OB- 1 + *lectare*, frequent. of *lacere* entice; see -ATE[3].] *trans.* To delight, please, rejoice –1621. †So **Oblecta·tion,** delight, pleasure, enjoyment 1508.

Obley (ǫ·bli). [ME. *uble, obly* – OFr. *ublee, oubleie, oblie* (mod. *oublie*) :– eccl. L. *oblata*, subst. use of fem. pa. pple. of L. *offerre*. Cf. OBLATION.] †**1.** An offering, oblation. ME. only. **2.** An altar-bread or wafer. Now *Hist.* ME.

Obligant (ǫ·bligănt). 1754. [– L. *obligans, -ant-*, pr. pple. of *obligare*; see OBLIGE, -ANT.] *Sc. Law.* One who binds himself, or is legally bound, to pay or perform something.

Obligate (ǫ·bligĕt), *ppl. a.* late ME. [– L. *obligatus*, pa. pple. of L. *obligare*; see OBLIGE, -ATE[2].] †**1.** Bound by oath, law, or duty; obliged –1539. **2.** *Biol.* That is of necessity such. *O. parasite*, an organism of necessity parasitical. 1887.

Obligate (ǫ·blige[i]t), *v.* 1541. [– *obligat-*, pa. ppl. stem of L. *obligare*; see OBLIGE, -ATE[3].] **1.** To bind (a person) by a moral or legal tie. Chiefly in *pass.* 1668. **2.** To make (a thing) a security; to pledge, pawn, mortgage –1890. **3.** = OBLIGE *v.* III. 1, 2. (In later use chiefly *dial.* and *U.S. colloq.*) 1692. **b.** To render (conduct, etc.) obligatory 1879.

1. Every contract..by which a debtor is obligated to pay any tax BRYCE. **3. b.** An interest in him beyond what gratitude obligated 1879.

Obligation (ǫbligē[i]·ʃən). ME. [– (O)Fr. *obligation* – L. *obligatio*, f. as prec.; see -ION.] **1.** The action of binding oneself by oath, promise, or contract to do or forbear something; a binding agreement; also, that to which one binds oneself, a formal promise. **2.** *Law.* An agreement, enforceable by law, whereby a person or persons become bound to the payment of a sum of money or other performance; the document containing such an agreement; *esp.* in Eng. Law, a written contract or bond under seal containing a penalty with condition attached. Also, the right created or liability incurred by such an agreement, document, or bond. late ME. **3.** Moral or legal constraint, or constraining force or influence; the condition of being morally or legally obliged or bound; a moral or legal tie binding to some performance; the binding power of a law, moral precept, duty, contract, etc. 1602. **4.** Action, or an act, to which one is morally or legally obliged; one's bounden duty, or a particular duty. Occas.: An enforced or burdensome task or charge. 1605. **5. a.** The fact or condition of indebtedness for a benefit or service received 1632. **b.** A benefit or service done or received 1618. †**6.** Legal liability –1758.

1. Of the obligacyon made bytwene god and us 1526. **3.** Bound In filiall O., for some terme To do obsequious Sorrow SHAKS. What o. lay on me to be popular? BURKE. *Of o.*, obligatory. *Day of o.*, a day on which it is of obligation for the faithful to abstain from work and to attend divine service. **4.** The o. of tribute BRYCE. **5. a.** They return benefits..because o. is a pain JOHNSON. **b.** When a kindly face greets us, though but passing by,..we should feel it as an o. LAMB. Phr. *To be, put, under an o.*

Obligato, var. of **Obbligato.**

Obligatory (ǫ·bligătəri, ǫ̆bli·gătəri), *a.* ME. [– late L. *obligatorius*, f. as prec.; see -ORY[2].] **1.** Imposing obligation, binding legally or morally; of the nature of an obligation; that must be done. Const. *on, upon* (†*to*, †*of*). 1502. **2.** Creating or constituting an obligation ME. **3.** *Biol.* = OBLIGATE *ppl. a.* 2. 1896.

1. There are situations.. in which, therefore, these duties are o. BURKE. **2.** *Writing* (*bill*, etc.) *o.* = OBLIGATION 2. Hence **O·bligato:rily** *adv.* **O·bligato:riness.**

Oblige (ǫ̆bləi·dʒ), *v.* ME. [– (O)Fr. *obliger* – L. *obligare* bind around or up, bind by oath or other tie; pledge, impede, restrain, f. *ob-* OB- 1 + *ligare* bind. Formerly pronounced ǫ̆blī·dʒ (XVI–early XIX).] **I. 1.** *trans.* To bind (a person) by an oath, promise, contract, or any moral or legal tie (*to* a person or a course, or *to do* a thing). Now only in *Law.* Also *refl.* †**2.** To make (lands, property, a possession) a guarantee or security for the discharge of a promise or debt; to pledge, pawn, or mortgage –1750. **3. a.** Of an oath, promise, law, command, etc.: To bind (a person) *to* some action or conduct, or *to do* something; also, *to* a person (*obs.* exc. in *Law*). late ME. **b.** With simple obj.: To be binding on (a person, conscience). Also *absol.* late ME.

1. It has been commonly suppos'd, That a Father could o. his Posterity to that Government of which he himself was a Subject LOCKE. The town council obliged themselves to his son to build that aisle to his memory 1890. **3. b.** You say they are no Laws unless they o. the Conscience MARVELL. *To be obliged*: to be bound by a legal or moral tie.

II. †**a.** *trans.* To make (any one) subject or liable *to* a bond, penalty, or the like –1649. **b.** *refl.* To render oneself liable to punishment (L. *se obligare*). Now only *Civil Law.* late ME.

III. 1. *trans.* To bind or make indebted (†*to* oneself) by conferring a benefit or kindness; to gratify *with* or *by doing* something; to do a service to, confer a favour on. Said also of the service, kindness, etc. 1567. **b.** *absol.* To confer a favour; *esp.* to favour a company (with some performance). *colloq.* 1735. **2.** *pass.* To be bound *to* a person by ties of gratitude; to owe or feel gratitude. Now said freq. in ref. to small services, or formally, as in ordering goods from a tradesman, etc. 1548. †**3.** *trans.* (vaguely) To gratify, charm –1709.

1. Your early attention to this application will much o., Sir, your very faithful and obedient servant 1796. O. me with the milk DICKENS. **b.** He 'obliged' at the pianoforte 1897. **2.** I told them I was very much obliged to them for their Good-will 1726.

IV. 1. *trans.* To constrain, esp. by moral or legal force or influence 1632. **2.** To render imperative 1638.

1. Self-preservation obliged the people to these severities DE FOE. Hence **O·bligable** *a.*, **Obli·ged-ly** *adv.*, **-ness. Obli·ger,** one who imposes or confers an obligation.

Obligee (ǫbləidʒī·). 1559. [f. prec.; see -EE[1].] **1.** *Law.* One to whom another is bound by contract; the person to whom a bond is given. (Correl. to *obligor.*) **2.** One who is under obligation for benefits received 1610.

Obligement (ǫ̆bləi·dʒmĕnt). 1584. [f. OBLIGE *v.* + -MENT.] **1.** = OBLIGATION 2. *Obs.* exc. in *Civil Law.* **2.** Obligation (moral or legal); obligation for benefits received; a kindness, favour 1611.

2. This I would endure, And more, to cancel my obligements to him DRYDEN.

Obliging (ǫ̆bləi·dʒiŋ), *ppl. a.* 1632. [f. OBLIGE *v.* + -ING[2].] That obliges. **1.** That imposes obligation; obligatory. Now *rare.* 1638. **2.** Of persons, etc.: Ready to do services or favours 1632. **b.** Of actions, words, etc.: Courteous, civil, polite 1635.

2. Keppel had a sweet and o. temper MACAULAY. Hence **Obli·ging-ly** *adv.*, **-ness.**

Obligor (ǫbləidʒǭ·ɹ). 1541. [f. OBLIGE *v.* + -OR 2.] *Law.* One who binds himself to another by contract; the person who gives a bond or obligation. (Correl. to *obligee.*)

†**Obliquate,** *v. rare.* 1670. [– *obliquat-*, pa. ppl. stem of L. *obliquare*, f. *obliquus*; see next, -ATE[3].] *trans.* To bend aside, twist obliquely –1736. So †**Obliqua·tion,** a bending obliquely; a twisting awry.

Oblique (ǫ̆blī·k), *a.* (*sb.*) late ME. [– (O)Fr. *oblique* – L. *obliquus*, f. *ob-* OB- 1 + obscure element.] **1.** Having a slanting direction or position; declining from the vertical, or from the horizontal; diverging from a given straight line or course. **2.** Spec. uses. **a.** *Geom.* Of a line, a plane figure, or a surface: Inclined at an angle other than a right angle. Of an angle: Either greater or less than a right angle. Of a solid, as a cone, cylinder, or prism: Having its axis not perpendicular to the plane of its base. 1571. **b.** Astron. *O. sphere*, the celestial or terrestrial sphere when its axis is oblique to the horizon of the place; which it is at any part of the earth's surface except the poles and the equator. *O. ascension, descension*: see ASCENSION 3, DESCENSION 5. *O. horizon*, one which is oblique to the celestial equator. 1503. **c.** *Anat.* Parallel neither to the long axis of the body or limb, nor to its transverse section; esp. of certain muscles, etc. 1615. **d.** *Bot.* Of a leaf: Having unequal sides 1835. **e.** *Cryst.* = MONOCLINIC 1878. **f.** *Naut. O. sailing*: the movement of a ship when its course makes an o. angle with the meridian. 1706. **g.** *O. perspective*: see PERSPECTIVE. **3.** *fig.* Not going straight to the point; indirect. late ME. **b.** Of an end, result, etc.: Indirectly aimed at 1528. **4.** Deviating from right conduct or thought 1576. **5.** *Gram.* **a.** *O. case*, any case except the nominative and vocative (and occas., the accusative). **b.** Of speech or narration: see INDIRECT *a.* 3 (L. *oratio obliqua*) 1530. **6.** *Mus. O. motion*: when one part remains without moving while another ascends or descends. (Opp. to *similar* and *contrary*.) 1811. **B.** *sb.* An oblique muscle.

1. If straight thy track, or if o. [*rhymes* strike], Thou know'st not TENNYSON. **2. a.** *O. hyperbola*, one the asymptotes of which are not at right angles to one another. **3.** All censure of a man's self is o. praise JOHNSON. **b.** For that the love we bear our friends..Hath in it certain o. ends DRAYTON. **4.** There are persons to be found..who grow rich and great..by various o. and scandalous ways 1770. **5. b.** There is scarcely a single o. sentence throughout St. John's Gospel 1882. Hence **Obli·que-ly** *adv.*, **-ness.**

Oblique (ǒblī·k), *v.* 1775. [– Fr. *obliquer* march in an oblique direction, f. *oblique* OBLIQUE *a.*] †**1.** *trans.* To turn in a sidelong direction. **2.** *intr.* To advance obliquely, esp. (*Mil.*) by making a half-face to the right or left and then marching forward 1787. **b.** Of a line, etc.: To slant at an angle SCOTT.

1. When her love-eye was fixed on me,..her eye of duty was finely obliqued SHERIDAN.

Obliquity (ǒbli·kwĭti). late ME. [– (O)Fr. *obliquité* – L. *obliquitas*, f. *obliquus*; see OBLIQUE *a.*, -ITY.] **1.** The quality of being oblique; degree of this 1551. **2.** *fig.* Deviation from moral rectitude, sound thinking, or right practice; a delinquency, a fault, an error. late ME. †**3.** Deviation from directness in action, conduct, or speech; a method that is not straightforward –1818.

1. The o. of the eye, which is proper to the Chinese and Japanese DARWIN. *O. of the ecliptic*, the inclination of the plane of the ecliptic to that of the equator. **2.** The perversnesse and o. of my will DONNE. **3.** The obliquities of Eastern negotiation 1818. Hence **Obli·quitous** *a.* mentally or morally perverse.

Obliterate (ǒbli·tĕrĕt), *ppl. a.* 1598. [– L. *oblit(t)eratus*, pa. pple. of *oblit(t)erare*; see next, -ATE².] **1.** Blotted out; obliterated. Now only *poet.* **2.** *Entom.* Applied to the markings on insects, when the borders of spots fade into the ground-colour, etc. 1826.

Obliterate (ǒbli·tĕreit), *v.* 1548. [– *oblit(t)erat-*, pa. ppl. stem of L. *oblit(t)erare* strike out, erase, f. *ob-* OB- + *lit(t)era* LETTER; see -ATE³.] **1.** *trans.* To blot out (anything written, etc.) so as to leave no distinct traces; to erase, delete, efface 1611. **b.** To cause to disappear (anything perceived by the senses) 1607. **2.** To efface, wipe out (a memory, etc.); to do away with, destroy (qualities, characteristics, etc.) 1548. **3.** *Phys.* and *Path.* To efface, close up, or otherwise destroy (esp. a duct or passage, the cavity of which disappears by contraction and adhesion of the walls). Also *intr.* for *refl.* 1813.

2. He designed to o. and extinguish the memory of heathen antiquity and authors BACON. Hence **Oblitera·tion**, effacement, extinction. **Obli·terative** *a.* tending to o.

Oblivion (ǒbli·viən). late ME. [– (O)Fr. *oblivion* – L. *oblivio, -on-*, f. stem *obliv-* of *oblivisci* forget.] **1.** The state or fact of forgetting; forgetfulness. **b.** Heedlessness, disregard 1470. **c.** Intentional overlooking, esp. of political offences 1564. **2.** The state or condition of being forgotten. late ME.

1. Make us drinke Lethe..; That for two daies o. smother griefe MARSTON. **b.** Among our crimes o. may be set DRYDEN. **c.** *Act* or *Bill of O.*, an act or bill granting a general pardon for political offences; in *Eng. Hist.* spec. applied to the Acts of 1660 and 1690, exempting those who had taken arms against Charles II and William III respectively from the consequences of their deeds. **2.** A question..which ought to have been buried in o. 1769. Hence **Obli·vionize** *v. trans.* to consign to o.

Oblivious (ǒbli·viəs), *a.* late ME. [– L. *obliviosus*, f. *oblivio*; see prec., -OUS.] **1.** That forgets; forgetful; unmindful. Const. *of.* ¶**b.** *erron.* Unconscious 1862. **2.** Of or pertaining to forgetfulness; attended by or associated with oblivion 1563.

1. The slow formality of an o. and drowsy exchequer BURKE. **b.** He was frequently o. of what was passing around him 1862. **2.** Some sweet Obliuious Antidote SHAKS. Hence **Obli·vious-ly** *adv.*, **-ness.**

Obliviscence (ǫblivi·sĕns). 1774. [f. *obliviscent-*, pr. ppl. stem of L. *oblivisci* forget; see -ENCE.] Forgetfulness.

†**Oblocu·tion.** late ME. [– late L. *oblocutio*, f. *oblocut-*, pa. ppl. stem of L. *obloqui* contradict; see LOCUTION. Cf. OFr. *oblocution.*] Evil-speaking, obloquy, slander –1731.

Oblong (ǫ·blǫŋ), *a.* and *sb.* late ME. [– L. *oblongus* somewhat long, oblong, elliptical, f. *ob-* OB- 1 + *longus* long.] **A.** *adj.* Elongated in one direction (usu. as a deviation from an exact square or circular form); having the chief axis longer than the transverse diameter; *spec.* in *Geom.*, rectangular with the adjacent sides unequal. **b.** Of a sheet of paper, page, book, panel, postage stamp, etc.: Rectangular with the breadth greater than the height; as an *o.* (opp. to an *upright*) *octavo* 1888. Also in *Comb.*

O. spheroid, a prolate spheroid.

B. *sb.* An oblong figure, or something oblong in form; *spec.* in *Geom.*, a rectangle of greater length than breadth 1608.

Xenophon then moved..that the march should be in a hollow o., with the baggage in the centre GROTE. Hence **Oblo·ngo-**, used in *Bot.* as comb. form of *oblong* adj. in sense 'with o. extension'.

Oblongatal (ǫblǫŋgēi·tăl), *a.* 1885. [f. mod.L. *oblongatus*, as in *medulla oblongata*, f. L. *oblongus* OBLONG; see -ATE², -AL¹.] Of or pertaining to the medulla oblongata, the hindmost segment of the brain.

Oblongated (ǫ·blǫŋgeitĕd), *ppl. a.* 1706. [f. as prec. + -ED¹.] Prolonged; in *o. marrow*, the medulla oblongata.

Obloquy (ǫ·blŏkwi). 1450. [– late L. *obloquium* contradiction, f. *ob-* OB- 1 + *loqui* speak.] **1.** Evil-speaking against a person or thing; abuse, detraction. †Formerly also with *an* and *pl.* **b.** The condition of being spoken against; bad repute; reproach, disgrace 1469. †**2.** *transf.* A cause of detraction or reproach; a disgrace –1621.

1. They had to..hold their convictions in the face of o. 1867. **b.** And undergo the perpetual o. of having lost a Kingdom CLARENDON. **2.** *All's Well* IV. ii. 44. So **Obloquious** (ǫblōᵘ·kwiəs), *a.* characterized by o.

Obmutescence (ǫbmiute·sĕns). 1646. [f. L. *obmutescere* (f. *ob-* OB- 1 + *mutescere* grow mute) + -ENCE.] A becoming (wilfully) mute; the action of obstinately remaining mute. So **Obmute·scent** *a.* remaining mute 1876.

Obnoxious (ǒbnǫ·kʃəs), *a.* 1581. [– L. *obnoxiosus* or, f. *obnoxius* exposed to harm, subject, liable, f. *ob-* OB- 1 + *noxa* hurt, injury; see -IOUS.] **1.** Exposed to harm; subject or liable to injury or evil of any kind. Const. *to*, †*inf.*, or †*simply.* 1597. †**2.** Liable to punishment or censure; reprehensible –1774. †**3.** Answerable, amenable (*to* some authority); dependent, subject; hence, submissive, obsequious. Const. *to.* –1754. †**4.** With *to*: Exposed to the (physical) action or influence of; open *to* –1671. ¶**5.** *erron.* (by confusion with *noxious*): Hurtful, injurious –1683. **6.** That is an object of aversion or dislike; *occas.* giving offence, acting objectionably. (The chief current use, app. assoc. with *noxious.*) Const. *to.* 1675.

1. The time of Youth is most O. to forget God 1677. We are o. to so many Accidents ADDISON. **2.** A late work has appeared to us highly o. in this respect GOLDSM. **3.** An existence that is not dependent upon or o. to any other 1722. **6.** Carlyle..is becoming very o. now that he has become popular E. FITZGERALD. Hence **Obno·xious-ly** *adv.*, **-ness.**

Obnubilate (ǫbniū·bileit), *v.* 1583. [– *obnubilat-*, pa. ppl. stem of L. *obnubilare* cover with clouds or fog; see -ATE³.] *trans.* To darken as with a cloud; to overcloud, obscure. Hence **Obnubila·tion,** obscuration; *spec.* clouding of the mind or faculties.

Oboe (ōᵘ·boi, ōᵘ·bōᵘ). 1700. [– It. *oboe* (three syll.) – Fr. *hautbois* HAUTBOY.] **1.** = HAUTBOY 1. 1794. **2.** Name of a reed-stop in an organ, with metal pipes, giving a penetrating tone 1700. Hence **O·boist,** a performer on the o.

Obol (ǫ·bǒl). 1670. [Anglicization of OBOLUS.] = OBOLUS 1.

O·bolary, *a. nonce-wd.* [f. L. *obolus* + -ARY¹.] That contributes an obolus; or, Possessing only oboli, impecunious. LAMB.

Obole (ǫ·boᵘl). 1656. [– (O)Fr. *obole* – L. *obolus*; see next.] A small French coin orig. of silver, later of billon, in use from 10th to 15th c. = ½ a denier; also called *maille.*

‖**Obolus** (ǫ·bǒlǒs). *Pl.* **-li** (-ləi). 1531. [L. – Gr. ὀβολός, var. of ὀβελός OBELISK.] **1.** A silver (later, bronze) coin of ancient Greece, = ⅙ of a drachma, or about 1½*d.* English 1579. **2.** Applied to the French OBOLE, and to other (small) coins formerly current in Europe; also any small coin. Cf. OB. †**3.** *Apothecaries' Weight.* A weight of 10 grains, or half a scruple –1661.

Obovate (ǫbˌōᵘ·vĕt), *a.* 1785. [OB- 2.] *Nat. Hist.* Inversely ovate; egg-shaped with the broader end upmost or forward. **b.** In comb. with adj., as *o.-cuneate, -lanceolate* 1806.

Obreption (ǫbre·pʃən). 1611. [– Fr. *obreption* or L. *obreptio, -on-*, f. *obrept-*, pa. ppl. stem of *obrepere* creep up to, steal upon, f. *ob-* OB- 1 + *repere* creep; see -ION.] The obtaining of something by craft or deceit, *spec.* in *Eccl.* and *Sc. Law*, of a dispensation, gift, etc. by false statement. (Opp. to *subreption.*)

Obreptitious (ǫbrepti·ʃəs), *a.* 1611. [f. late L. *obrepticius* (f. as prec.) + -OUS; see -ITIOUS¹.] Characterized by obreption; containing a false statement made for the sake of obtaining something.

Obrogate (ǫ·brŏgeit), *v. rare.* 1656. [– *obrogat-*, pa. ppl. stem of L. *obrogare*, f. *ob-* OB- 1 + *rogare* ask, supplicate, propose a law, introduce a bill; see -ATE³.] To repeal (a law) by passing a new one.

Obscene (ǒbsī·n), *a.* 1593. [– Fr. *obscène* or L. *obscenus, obscænus* ill-omened, abominable, disgusting, indecent, orig. a term of augury.] **1.** Offensive to modesty or decency; expressing or suggesting lewd thoughts 1598. **2.** Offensive to the senses or the mind; disgusting, filthy. *arch.*

1. The rabble of Comus..reeling in o. dances MACAULAY. **2.** In rags o. decreed to roam POPE. So **Obsce·ne-ly** *adv.* 1588, **-ness** 1637.

Obscenity (ǒbsī·nĭti, ǒbse·nĭti). 1608. [– L. *obscænitas*, f. *obscænus*; see prec., -ITY. Cf. Fr. *obscénité.*] Obscene quality or character: **a.** Indecency, lewdness (esp. of language); in *pl.* obscene words or matters. †**b.** Foulness, loathsomeness; in *pl.* foul acts, dirty work –1807.

a. Worse..then the worst obscenities of heathen superstition MILT. **b.** Slovenly cooks, that after their obscenities never wash their bawdy hands BURTON.

Obscurant (ǫbskiūə·rănt), *sb.* and *a.* 1799. [= G. *obscurant* (XVIII) – L. *obscurans, -ant-*, pr. pple. of *obscurare*; see OBSCURE *v.*, -ANT.] **A.** *sb.* One who obscures; one who strives to prevent inquiry, enlightenment, or reform. **B.** *adj.* That obscures or darkens; of or belonging to an obscurant 1878. Hence **Obscu·rantism** [cf. G. *obscurantismus*, (XVIII)], the practice or principles of those who strive to prevent enlightenment or the progress of knowledge 1834; **Obscu·rantist** *sb.* and *a.* = OBSCURANT 1838.

Obscuration (ǫbskiurēⁱ·ʃən). 1471. [– L. *obscuratio, -on-*, f. *obscurare* darken, f. *obscurus*; see OBSCURE *v.*, -ATION.] **1.** The action of obscuring, darkening, or clouding over; obscured or dimmed state or condition; in *Astron.*, occultation, eclipse. **2.** *fig.* The darkening or dimming of intellectual light, of the mental vision, of the sense of words, of truth, etc. 1611.

1. *transf.* Our old dramatists are full of such obscurations..of the *th*, making *whe'r* of *whether* LOWELL. **2.** The o. of religion is superstition 1879.

Obscure (ǫ̆bskiūᵊ·ɹ), *a.* (*sb.*) late ME. [– (O)Fr. *obscur*, latinized form of earlier *oscur*, *escur* :– L. *obscurus* dark.] **1.** Devoid of light; dim; hence, gloomy, dismal. **2.** Of, pertaining to, or frequenting the darkness; hence, eluding sight 1605. **3.** Of colour, etc.: Dark, sombre; in later use, dingy, dull 1490. **4.** Indistinct, undefined; hardly perceptible to the eye; faint, 'light' 1593. **b.** Indistinctly perceived, felt, or heard 1597. **5.** Of a place: Hidden, retired; remote from observation 1484. **6.** Inconspicuous, undistinguished, unnoticed 1555. **b.** Of persons, their station, etc.: Unknown to fame; humble, lowly 1548. **7.** *fig.* Not manifest to the mind or understanding; hidden, doubtful, vague, uncertain 1432. **b.** Of words, statements, etc.: Not perspicuous; hard to understand. Also, of a speaker or writer. 1495.

1. His lampe shall be put out in o. darkenesse *Prov.* 20:20. *O. rays*, the dark or invisible heat-rays of the solar spectrum. **2.** The o. Bird clamor'd the liue-long Night SHAKS. **3.** An o. Yellow 1662. **4. b.** E..where it endeth, and soundeth o. and faintly JONSON. **5.** They pursue, even such as me, into the obscurest retreats BURKE. **6.** The small and o. beginnings of great political institutions 1854. **b.** Their homely joys, and destiny o. GRAY. **7.** The Cause and seat of this Disease, which is often o. 1732. **b.** A darke, o., and crabbed style 1573. Hence **Obscu·re-ly** *adv.*, **-ness** (now *rare*).

B. *sb.* **1.** Obscurity, darkness; the 'outer darkness' 1667. **2.** Indistinctness of outline or colour 1792.

1. Who shall..through the palpable o. find out His uncouth way MILT.

Obscure (ǫ̆bskiūᵊ·ɹ), *v.* late ME. [f. OBSCURE *a.*, or the corresp. L. *obscurare*, OFr. *obscurer* (earlier *oscurer*; cf. prec.).] †**1.** *trans.* To make obscure or dark, to involve in darkness; to dim 1547. **2.** To dim the lustre or glory of; to outshine 1548. **3.** To hide from view 1604. †**b.** *intr.* (for *refl.*) To hide oneself –1632. **4.** To conceal from knowledge or observation; to keep dark; to disguise. Also *refl.* 1530. **5.** To render vague or unintelligible 1584.

1. Cynthia for shame obscures her silver shine SHAKS. *transf.* In modern English speech, vowels are regularly obscured in syllables that have neither primary nor subordinate stress *O.E.D.* Introd. **2.** To deface and o. Godes glory LATIMER. **5.** This language..serves not to elucidate, but to disguise and o. MILL.

Obscurity (ǫ̆bskiūᵊ·rĭti). late ME. [– (O)Fr. *obscurité* – L. *obscuritas*, f. *obscurus*; see OBSCURE *a.*, -ITY.] **1.** The quality or condition of being obscure; darkness 1456. **2.** The quality or condition of being unknown or inconspicuous 1619. **b.** An inconspicuous or unknown person 1822. **3.** The quality or condition of not being clearly known or comprehended 1474. **4.** Unintelligibleness 1538. **b.** An obscure point; an unintelligible speech or passage. late ME.

1. We waite for light, but behold obscuritie *Isa.* 59:9. **2.** Suffering Worth Lost in o. THOMSON. **3.** The thought is enuoluped in obscurete CAXTON. **4.** One of the most pernicious effects of haste is o. JOHNSON. **b.** The obscurities of early Greek poets 1875.

Obsecrate (ǫ·bsĭkreⁱt), *v. rare, pedantic.* 1597. [– *obsecrat-*, pa. ppl. stem of L. *obsecrare* entreat, beseech (orig. by the name of the gods), f. *ob* for the sake of + *sacrare* hold sacred; see -ATE³.] *trans.* To entreat earnestly, as in the name of something sacred; to supplicate (a person); to beg (a thing).

Obsecration (ǫbsĭkrēⁱ·ʃən). late ME. [– L. *obsecratio, -on-*, f. as prec.; see -ION.] **1.** Earnest entreaty; occas. in orig. L. sense, entreaty made in the name of something sacred. **b.** *Rhet.* A figure by which the orator implores the assistance of God or man 1609. **2.** *spec.* One of the suffrages or prayers of the Litany beginning with the word 'by' (L. *per*) 1877.

Obsequies: see OBSEQUY².

Obsequious (ǫ̆bsī·kwiəs), *a.* 1450. [– L. *obsequiosus*, f. *obsequium*; see OBSEQUY¹, -OUS.] **1.** Compliant with the will of another; prompt to serve, please, or follow directions; obedient; dutiful. Now *rare.* †**b.** Through association with OBSEQUY²: Dutiful in manifesting regard for the dead; proper to obsequies –1674. **2.** Servilely compliant; fawning, cringing, sycophantic 1602.

1. Was no man so obsequyous and seruiceable TINDALE. **b.** Bound In filiall Obligation..To do o. Sorrow SHAKS. **2.** Following him out, with most o. politeness DICKENS. So **Obse·quious-ly** *adv.*, 1599, **-ness** 1447.

†**O·bsequy¹.** late ME. [– L. *obsequium* compliance, f. *ob-* OB- 1 + *sequi* follow. Partly from Fr. †*obsèque* obedience (XV).] Ready compliance with the will of another; deferential service; obsequiousness.

Obsequy²; now always in pl. **obsequies** (ǫ·bsĭkwiz). late ME. [– AFr. *obsequie(s* = OFr. *obsèque(s* (mod. *obsèques*) – med.L. *obsequiæ*, prob. alt. of L. *exsequiæ* (see EXEQUY), by assoc. with *obsequium* dutiful service (see prec.).] Funeral rites or ceremonies; a funeral. Sometimes including or denoting commemorative rites or services.

sing. Silent obsequie and funeral train MILT. *pl.* See perform'd their Fun'ral Obsequies DRYDEN. Hence **Obse·quial** *a.*

Observable (ǫ̆bzō·ɹvăb'l), *a.* and *sb.* 1608. [f. OBSERVE + -ABLE. Cf. Fr. †*observable* = sense 1, L. *observabilis* = sense 3.] **1.** That must or may be observed, attended to, or kept. **2.** Noticeable, perceptible 1646. **3.** Noteworthy; formerly, †Remarkable, notable 1609. †**B.** *sb.* A noteworthy thing, fact, or circumstance. Chiefly in *pl.* –1822.

1. Forms o. in social intercourse H. SPENCER. **2.** A marked change in public sentiment became at once o. 1874. **3.** We met with nothing very o. JOHNSON. **Obse·rvably** *adv.*

Observance (ǫ̆bzō·ɹvăns). ME. [– (O)Fr. *observance* – L. *observantia*, f. *observant-*, pr. ppl. stem of *observare*; see OBSERVE, -ANCE.] **I. 1.** The action or practice of observing (a law, duty, ceremony, custom, rule, method, etc.). Const. *of*, †*to*. late ME. **b.** The keeping of a prescribed ritual. late ME. **2.** A customary rite, custom ME. **b.** An ordinance to be observed; *esp.* the rule of a religious order; *spec.* of the Observants or stricter Franciscans. late ME.

1. A Custome More honour'd in the breach, then the obseruance SHAKS. **b.** For to doon his obseruaunce to May CHAUCER. **2.** Superstitious observances..will not..mend matters with us 1729.

II. Respectful or courteous attention, dutiful service. (Rarely const. *of*.) *arch.* ME.

He compass'd her with sweet observances TENNYSON.

III. †**1.** Observant care, heed –1660. **2.** The action of paying attention; notice; watching 1600. Now *rare.*

1. *Haml.* III. ii. 21. **2.** I passed, And pried, in every place, without o. MASSINGER.

Observancy (ǫ̆bzō·ɹvănsi). 1567. [– L. *observantia*; see prec., -ANCY.] **1.** The quality of being observant or observing; †the action of observing. **2.** Respectful or obsequious attention. *arch.* 1601. **3.** A House of the Observant Order. BROWNING.

Observant (ǫ̆bzō·ɹvănt), *a.* and *sb.* 1460. [– Fr. *observant* (formerly as sb.), pr. pple. of *observer*; see OBSERVE, -ANT.] **A.** *adj.* **1.** Attentive in observing a law, custom, principle, etc. Const. *of*. 1608. †**2.** Showing respect, honour, or deference; assiduous in service; obsequious. Const. *of*, *to*. –1743. **3.** Heedful 1627. **4.** Attentive in marking; quick to perceive. Const. *of* (†*on*). 1602.

1. O. of the little niceties of phrase and manner 1829, of contracts 1834. **3.** Scrupulously o. to avoid offending the prince GOLDSM. Hence **Obse·rvantly** *adv.*

B. *sb.* †**1.** One who observes a law, etc. –1613. **2.** *spec.* A member of that branch of the Franciscan order which observes the strict rule; the other branch being the Conventuals 1460. †**3.** A dutiful servant –1617.

3. *Lear* II. ii. 109.

Observantine (ǫ̆bzō·ɹvăntin, ǫbzəɹvæ·ntin). 1646. [– Fr. *Observantin*, f. *observant*; see prec., -INE¹.] = OBSERVANT B. 2.

Observation (ǫbzəɹvēⁱ·ʃən). late ME. [– L. *observatio, -on-*, f. *observat-*, pa. ppl. stem of *observare*; see OBSERVE, -ION. Cf. (O)Fr. *observation*.] **1.** = OBSERVANCE I. 1. Now *rare* or *Obs.* 1533. †**2.** = OBSERVANCE I. 2. –1718. †**3.** = OBSERVANCE II. –1721. †**4.** = OBSERVANCE III. 1. –1673. **5.** = OBSERVANCE III. 2. 1557. **b.** The faculty or habit of taking notice 1605. **c.** Attention to presages or omens; an act of augury or divination. (Now only in general sense.) 1605. **d.** *Mil.* The watching of a fortress, of an enemy's movements, etc. 1836. **6.** The action or an act of observing scientifically a phenomenon in regard to its cause or effect, or phenomena in regard to their mutual relations, these being observed as they occur in nature (and so opp. to *experiment*); also, the record of this 1559. **b.** *spec.* The taking of the altitude of the sun (or other heavenly body), in order to find the latitude or longitude; the result obtained 1559. **7.** Observed truth or fact; a rule or maxim gathered from experience. Now *rare.* 1600. **8.** A remark in speech or writing in ref. to something observed 1593.

1. The o. of the Sabbath MACAULAY. **4.** *Temp.* III. iii. 87. **5.** They were..in less danger of o. MRS. RADCLIFFE. **b.** Men of narrow o. BACON. **d.** *Army* (*corps*, etc.) *of o.*, a force employed in watching an army of the enemy. **6.** O...without experiment..can ascertain sequences and co-existences, but cannot prove causation MILL. **b.** *To work an o.*, to ascertain the latitude or longitude by means of calculations based on the sun's altitude. **7.** *A. Y. L.* II. vii. 41. **8.** Tut, that's a foolish obseruation SHAKS.

attrib. and *Comb.*, as *o.-balloon*, *-post*, etc.: **o.-car,** an open railway carriage, or one with glass sides; **-mine,** a mine (originally) fired from an observing station. Hence **Observa·tional** *a.* of or pertaining to (scientific) o.

Observative (ǫ̆bzō·ɹvătiv), *a.* 1611. [f. OBSERVATION + -IVE, on the anal. of *conservation, conservative*, etc.] Of or pertaining to observation; observant, heedful. Now *rare.*

†**O·bservator.** 1502. [– Fr. *observateur* and L. *observator*, f. *observat-*; see OBSERVATION, -OR 2.] = OBSERVER –1798.

Observatory (ǫ̆bzō·ɹvătəri), *sb.* 1676. [– mod.L. *observatorium* (Newton, 1686), perh. after Fr. *observatoire*; f. as prec.; see -ORY¹.] **1.** A building or place for making observations of natural phenomena; esp. for astronomical, meteorological, or magnetic observations. **2.** A position or building affording an extensive view 1695. **3.** (*nonce-use.*) A place of observation. STEVENSON.

1. The new Observatorie in Greenewich Park EVELYN.

Obse·rvatory, *a.* 1864. [f. OBSERVATION + -ORY², on the anal. of *conservation, conservatory* adj. (etc.).] Of or pertaining to scientific observation, as, *o. work.*

Observe (ǫ̆bzō·ɹv), *v.* late ME. [– (O)Fr. *observer* – L. *observare* watch, attend to, guard, f. *ob-* OB- 1 + *servare* watch, keep.] **I. 1.** *trans.* To adhere to or abide by in practice (anything prescribed or fixed). **b.** To adhere to, follow (a method, rule, etc.) 1548. **2.** To hold or keep to (a manner of life or conduct, a habit); to maintain (a quality, state, etc.). late ME. **3.** To celebrate duly (a religious rite, fast, festival, etc.) 1526.

1. They..o. Circumcision PURCHAS. **b.** In ordinary writing and speaking this rule is seldom observed 1870. **2.** The people o. a dead silence 1843. **3.** Ye shall o. the feast of unleavened bread *Exod.* 12:17.

II. †To treat with ceremonious respect or reverence; to worship, honour; to court; to humour –1754.

Jul. C. IV. iii, 45.

III. †**1.** To give heed to (a point); to take care *that* something be done, or *to do* something –1793. **2.** To regard with attention; to watch 1567. **b.** *spec.* To inspect for purposes of divination; to watch or take note of (presages or omens). late ME. **c.** *Mil.* To watch (a fortress, the enemy's movements, etc.); also *absol.* or *intr.* 1611. **d.** *absol.* or *intr.* To make observations 1604. †3. *trans.* To watch for in order to avail oneself of (a proper time, an opportunity) –1642. **4.** To notice, remark, perceive, see (a thing or fact) 1560. **5.** To perceive or learn by scientific inspection (without the aid of experiment) 1559. **b.** *spec.* To make an observation (see OBSERVATION 6 b) in order to determine the altitude of (the sun, etc.), to ascertain (the latitude or longitude, etc.); also *absol.* or *intr.* 1559.

1. If we obserue to doe all these Commandements *Deut.* 6:25. **2. d.** He has not observed on the nature of vanity who does not know that it is omnivorous BURKE. **5.** *absol.* When, as in astronomy, we endeavour to ascertain these causes by simply watching their effects, we *observe* 1879.

IV. To say by way of remark; to mention in speech or writing 1605. **b.** *absol.*, or *intr.* with *on* or *upon*: To make an observation, to comment (on) 1613. Hence **Obse·rve** *sb.* † = OBSERVATION 5, 6, 7. –1830; = OBSERVATION 8. *Sc.* 1711. **Obse·rvedly** *adv.* notably. **Obse·rvership,** the office of Observer. **Obse·rving** *ppl. a.* that observes; observant; engaged in scientific observation. **Obse·rvingly** *adv.*

Observer (ǫ̆bzə̄·ɹvəɹ). 1555. [f. prec. + -ER¹.] **1.** One who observes or keeps a law rule, custom, practice, method, etc. †**2.** An obsequious follower –1633. **3.** One who watches, marks, or takes notice. (A frequent title of newspapers.) 1581. **b.** One who accompanies the pilot of a flying machine to make military or other observations 1914. **4.** One who observes phenomena scientifically; occas. the official title of the person in charge of an observatory 1795.

1. Suppos'd to be a conceal'd o. of the Jewish law 1721. **3.** He is a great Obseruer, and he lookes Quite through the Deeds of men SHAKS. **b.** *Mil.* One who makes observations, esp. in connection with the firing of artillery 1903.

Obsess (ǫ̆bse·s), *v.* 1503. [– *obsess-*, pa. ppl. stem of L. *obsidēre* sit down before, f. *ob-* OB- 1 + *sedēre* sit.] †**1.** *trans.* To sit down before (a fortress, the enemy); to besiege, invest –1647. **2.** Of an evil spirit: to beset (a person); to haunt; to actuate from without 1540. **3.** *transf.* To beset like a besieging force or an evil spirit; in mod. use *esp.* to haunt and trouble as a 'fixed idea' 1531.

Obsession (ǫ̆bse·ʃən). 1513. [– L. *obsessio*, f. as prec.; see -ION. Cf. Fr. *obsession.*] †**1.** The action of besieging; investment, siege –1638. **2.** Actuation by the devil or an evil spirit from without; the fact of being thus actuated 1605. **3.** *transf.* The action of any influence, notion, or 'fixed idea', which persistently assails or vexes 1680.

2. These cases belong rather to o. than possession, the spirits not actually inhabiting the bodies, but hanging or hovering about them 1871. **3.** The thought of death began to haunt him till it became a constant o. 1893. Hence **Obse·ssional** *a.* **Obsessionist. Obse·ssive** *a.*

Obsidian (ǫ̆bsi·diăn). 1656. [– erron. L. *obsidianus*, in edd. of Pliny for *obsianus*; so called from its resemblance to a stone found in Ethiopia by one *Obsius* (erron. *Obsidius*); see -IAN.] *Min.* A dark-coloured vitreous lava or volcanic rock, of varying composition, resembling common bottle-glass; volcanic glass 1796. **b.** Also *o. stone* (*lapis Obsi*(*di*)*anus*).

Obsidional (ǫ̆bsi·diŏnăl), *a.* 1430. [– L. *obsidionalis*, f. *obsidio*, *-on-* siege, f. *obsidēre*; see OBSESS *v.*, -AL¹.] **1.** Of or pertaining to a siege. **2.** *fig.* Besetting 1879.

1. *O. crown* (*coronet, garland, wreath*), tr. L. *corona obsidionalis*, a wreath of grass or weeds conferred as a mark of honour upon a Roman general who raised a siege. *O. coins*, coins struck in a besieged city to supply the want of current coins.

†**Obsi·gnate,** *v.* 1653. [– *obsignat-*, pa. ppl. stem of L. *obsignare* seal, seal up, f. *ob-* OB- 1 + *signare* mark, seal, SIGN; see -ATE³.] *trans.* To seal; to mark as with a seal; to ratify or confirm formally –1677. So †**Obsi·gn** *v.* 1554–1670.

Obsignation (ǫbsignē¹·ʃən). Now *rare.* 1568. [– L. *obsignatio*, f. as prec.; see -ION.] The action of sealing; formal ratification or confirmation as by sealing.

Obsignatory (ǫ̆bsi·gnătəri), *a.* Now *rare.* 1630. [f. OBSIGNATION + -ORY².] Having the function of, or pertaining to, obsignation; ratifying or confirming as with a seal.

Obsolesce (ǫbsŏle·s), *v. rare.* 1873. [– L. *obsolescere* grow old, etc., inchoative form of **obsolēre*, f. *ob-* OB- 1 + *solēre* be accustomed.] *intr.* To be obsolescent; to fall into disuse.

Obsolescence (ǫbsŏle·sĕns). 1828. [f. as next; see -ENCE.] **1.** The process of becoming obsolete. **2.** *Biol.* The gradual disappearance or atrophy of an organ or part, esp. from disuse 1852.

Obsolescent (ǫbsŏle·sĕnt), *a.* 1755. [– *obsolescent-*, pr. ppl. stem of L. *obsolescere*; see OBSOLESCE, -ENT.] **1.** Becoming obsolete; going out of use or date. **2.** *Biol.* Gradually disappearing; imperfectly or slightly developed; said of an organ, structure, or mark, which was formerly fully developed or well-marked 1846.

1. The stronghold of o. opinions 1863.

Obsolete (ǫ·bsŏlīt), *a.* (*sb.*) 1579. [– L. *obsoletus* grown old, worn out, pa. pple. of **obsolēre*, repr. by inchoative *obsolescere* OBSOLESCE.] **1.** That is no longer practised or used; discarded; out of date. **2.** Worn out; effaced through wearing down, atrophy, or degeneration 1832. **3.** *Biol.* Indistinct; not clearly marked; very imperfectly developed 1760. **B.** *absol.* or *sb.* One who or that which is out of date or has fallen into disuse 1748.

1. Olde and o. wordes 1579. One o. ironclad 1884. **2.** Cases of o. tubercle 1897. Hence **O·bsolete** *v.* (now *rare*), *trans.* to render or account o.; to disuse. **O·bsolete-ly** *adv.*, **-ness. Obsole·tion,** the action of becoming or condition of being o. **O·bsoletism,** an o. term, phrase, custom, etc.; obsoleteness.

Obstacle (ǫ·bstăk'l). ME. [– (O)Fr. *obstacle* (earlier *ostacle*) – L. *obstaculum*, f. *obstare* stand in the way, f. *ob-* OB- 1 + *stare* stand; see -ACLE.] **1.** A hindrance, impediment, obstruction. †**2.** Resistance, objection; in phr. *to make o.*, to offer opposition –1632.

1. He should remove the O. which prevented the Use of his Sight STEELE. *Comb.*, as **o.-race,** a race in which impediments have to be surmounted.

Obstetric, -al (ǫ̆bste·trik, -ăl), *adjs.* 1742. [– mod.L. *obstetricus*, for L. *obstetricius*, f. *obstetrix*, *-tric-* midwife, lit. 'a woman who is present, i.e. to receive the child', f. *obstare*; see prec., -TRIX, -IC, -ICAL.] Of or pertaining to a midwife or accoucheur, or to midwifery as a branch of medical practice.

Obstetrical toad, the nurse-frog, *Alytes obstetricans.* So **Obste·trically** *adv.* 1759.

†**Obste·tricate,** *v.* 1623. [– *obstetricat-*, pa. ppl. stem of eccl. L. *obstetricare* (Tertullian), f. L. *obstetrix*; see prec., -ATE³.] **1.** *intr.* To act as midwife; to aid in childbirth –1809. **2.** *trans.* To help the delivery of. Chiefly *fig.* –1741. So †**Obstetrica·tion** (*rare*) 1615–1823.

Obstetrician (ǫbstĕtri·ʃăn). 1828. [f. OBSTETRICS + -ICIAN, after *physician*, etc.] One skilled in obstetrics; an accoucheur.

Obstetrics (ǫ̆bste·triks). 1819. [pl. of OBSTETRIC; see -IC 2.] The branch of medical practice which deals with parturition, and its antecedents and sequels; the practice of midwifery.

Obstinacy (ǫ·bstinăsi). late ME. [– med. L. *obstinacia*, f. *obstinatus*; see next, -ACY. Partly f. next.] The quality or condition of being obstinate; stubbornness, persistency; *spec.* of a disease. Rarely in neutral or good sense. **b.** With *an* and *pl.* An act or instance of this 1628.

1. O. in a bad cause, is but constancy in a good SIR T. BROWNE. [He] adhered to his own opinion with his usual o. 1769. The o. of the disease 1808. **b.** An o. against the Laws HOBBES. So **O·bstinance, O·bstinancy** (*rare*).

Obstinate (ǫ·bstinĕt), *a.* (*sb.*) ME. [– L. *obstinatus*, pa. pple. of *obstinare* persist, f. *ob-* OB- 1 + **stan-* (cf. DESTINE); see -ATE².] **1.** Pertinacious in adhering to one's own course; not yielding to argument, persuasion, or entreaty; inflexible, headstrong, self-willed. Rarely in neutral or good sense. **2.** Unyielding, rigid, stiff; *spec.* of a disease, etc., not yielding readily to treatment; stubborn 1638. **B.** *sb.* A stubborn or inflexible person 1502.

1. The o. Man does not hold Opinions, but they hold him 1680. **2.** An o. sleeplessness JOHNSON, diarrhœa 1871. So **O·bstinate** *v.* (now *rare*), to render o.; to cause to persist stubbornly. Also *refl.* (= Fr. *s'obstiner*). **O·bstinate-ly** *adv.*, **-ness.** †**Obstina·tion,** obstinacy.

Obstipation (ǫbstipē¹·ʃən). 1597. [alt. of CONSTIPATION by substitution of prefix.] The action of blocking or stopping up; *Med.* extreme constipation. So †**Ob·stipate** *v.* (*rare*) –1702.

Obstreperous (ǫ̆bstre·pĕrəs), *a.* 1600. [f. L. *obstreperus* (f. *obstrepere* make a noise against) + -OUS.] **1.** Characterized by great noise or outcry, esp. in opposition; clamorous; vociferous. **2.** Turbulent or unruly, esp. in resistance 1657.

1. They [ravens] sate all night, Beating the ayre with their o. beakes B. JONS. The most careless and o. merriment JOHNSON. **2.** Becoming remarkably o. when thwarted 1874. Hence **Obstre·perous-ly** *adv.*, **-ness.**

†**Obstri·nge,** *v. rare.* 1528. [– L. *obstringere*, f. *ob-* OB- 1 + *stringere* tie, bind.] *trans.* To put under obligation; to bind –1660. So **Obstri·ction,** obligation.

Obstruct (ǫ̆bstrɒ·kt), *v.* 1611. [– *obstruct-*, pa. ppl. stem of L. *obstruere* build against, block up, f. *ob-* OB- 1 + *struere* pile, build.] **1.** *trans.* To block, close up, or fill (a way or passage) with obstacles or impediments; to render impassable or difficult of passage. **2.** To interrupt or render difficult the passage or progress of; to impede, hinder, or retard (a person or thing in its motion) 1655. **3.** *fig.* To stand in the way of, or persistently oppose the progress or course of (proceedings, or a person or thing in a purpose or action); to impede, retard, withstand, stop 1647. **4.** To interrupt, shut out (the sight or view of) 1717.

1. The door is now so obstructed with Stones 1703. **2.** The Wind..obstructs the coming of any letters from Holland 1688. **2.** I don't know if it be just thus to o. the union of man and wife GOLDSM. *To o. process* (in *Law*): to commit the punishable offence of intentionally hindering the officers of the law in the execution of their duties. **4.** There was nothing to o. the view GEO. ELIOT.

Obstruction (ǫ̆bstrɒ·kʃən). 1533. [– L. *obstructio*, *-on-*, f. as prec.; see -ION. Cf. Fr. *obstruction* (XVI).] **1.** The action of obstructing; the condition of being obstructed; frequently in ref. to passages, organs, cr functions of the body; *esp.* the ill-condition produced by constipation of the bowels. **2.** *fig.* The hindering or stopping of the course, performance, or doing of anything; *spec.* the persistent attempt to stop the progress of business, e.g. in the House of Commons 1656. **3.** Anything that stops or blocks a way or passage, or hinders or prevents progress; an obstructing obstacle 1597.

1. This does make some o. in the blood: This crosse-gartering SHAKS. He advanced without further o. to the capital 1841. O. of the Eustachian tube 1844. *Cold o.*, stoppage of the vital functions, the condition of the body in death. **2.** That practice of talking against time which has more recently become famous under the name of o. 1880. **3.** The great o. to generosity in our nature is jealousy 1876.

Comb., **o.-guard,** a bar, etc. fixed in front of a railway engine to remove an o. from the rails. Hence **Obstru·ctionist,** one who advocates or systematically practises o. 1846; so **Obstru·ctionism.**

Obstructive (ǫ̆bstrɒ·ktiv), *a.* (*sb.*) 1611. [f. OBSTRUCT *v.* + -IVE.] **A.** *adj.* **1.** Obstructing; tending to obstruct; causing impediment. Const. *of, to.* **2.** Of, pertaining to, or of the nature of obstruction of the bowels or of any bodily duct or passage 1620.

1. Academies may be said to be o. to energy and inventive genius M. ARNOLD.

B. *sb.* **1.** An obstructive agent, instrument, or force; a hindrance 1642. **2.** One who obstructs, esp. in parliamentary business 1856.

1. Episcopacy..was instituted as an o. to the diffusion of Schisme and Heresy JER. TAYLOR. Hence **Obstru·ctive-ly** *adv.*, **-ness. Obstru·ctivism.**

Obstructor (ǫ̆bstrɒ·ktəɹ). 1649. [f. OBSTRUCT + -OR 2.] One who or that which obstructs; a hinderer; an opponent of progress.

Obstruent (ǫ·bstruĕnt), *a.* and *sb.* 1669. [– *obstruent-*, pr. ppl. stem of L. *obstruere*;

see OBSTRUCT, -ENT.] **A.** *adj.* Obstructing; *Med.* closing up the ducts or passages of the body 1755. **B.** *sb.* Something that obstructs, an obstruction; *Med.* a medicine which closes the orifices of ducts or vessels, or the natural passages of the body.

Obstupefy (ǫbstiū·pǐfəi), *v.* 1613. [f. L. *obstupefacere*, after STUPEFY.] *trans.* To stupefy, esp. mentally. So †**Obstu·pefact** *a.*, **-fa·ction, -fa·ctive** *a.*

Obtain (ǫbtē¹·n), *v.* [Late ME. *obteine*, *-tene* repr. tonic stem of (O)Fr. *obtenir* – L. *obtinēre*, f. *ob-* OB- 1 + *tenēre* hold.] **1.** *trans.* To procure or gain, as the result of purpose and effort; hence, generally, to acquire, get. Also *absol.* †**2.** To gain, win (a battle or other contest) –1649. **3.** *intr.* To gain the day, prevail; to succeed, prosper. *Obs.* or *arch.* late ME. **4.** To attain to, get as far as, reach, gain. *Obs.* or *arch.* 1477. †**b.** with *inf.* To attain or come *to be*, *to do*, etc.; to succeed in doing something –1703. †**5.** To hold; to possess; to occupy. (A Latin sense.) –1710. **6.** *intr.* To prevail; to be in force or in vogue; to hold good, have place, subsist, exist. 1618.

1. Blessed are the mercifull: for they shall obteyne mercy TINDALE *Matt.* 5:7. Obtaining Pardon by Mony, or other rewards HOBBES. **3.** This, though it failed at present, yet afterwards obtained SWIFT. **5.** He who obtains the Monarchy of Heav'n MILT. **6.** Laws of nature which universally o. 1764. Hence **Obtai·nable** *a.* **Obtai·nal** (*rare*) 1803, **Obtai·nment**, the action of getting. **Obtai·ner.**

Obtected (ǫbte·ktėd), *ppl. a.* 1816. [f. L. *obtectus*, pa. pple. of *obtegere* cover over + -ED¹.] *Entom.* **a.** Covered by a neighbouring part. **b.** Of pupæ: Having the limbs, etc., of the future insect indistinctly discernible through the outer covering (opp. to *coarctate*); in later use occas. including *coarctate*. Also said of the metamorphosis in which such pupæ occur.

Obtemper (ǫbte·mpəɹ), *v.* 1450. [– (O)Fr. *obtempérer* – L. *obtemperare* obey, f. *ob-* OB- + *temperare* qualify, temper, restrain oneself; see TEMPER *v.*] *trans.* To comply with, submit to, obey; now only in *Sc. Law*, to obey (a judgement or order of a court). †**b.** *intr.* with *to* –1584.

Obtemperate (ǫbte·mpěre¹t), *v.* late ME. [– *obtemperat-*, pa. ppl. stem of L. *obtemperare*; see prec., -ATE³. Cf. TEMPERATE *v.*] *trans.* and *intr.* = prec.

†**Obte·nd**, *v.* 1573. [– L. *obtendere* spread in front of, f. *ob-* OB- 1 + *tendere* stretch.] **1.** *trans.* To put forward as a statement, reason, etc.; to pretend –1700. **2.** To hold out; to present in opposition; to oppose –1725.

Obtenebrate (ǫbte·nǐbre¹t), *v.* 1611. [– *obtenebrat-*, pa. ppl. stem of eccl. L. *obtenebrare*, f. *ob-* OB- 1 + L. *tenebrare* darken; see -ATE³.] *trans.* To overshadow, darken. Hence **Obtenebra·tion**, the action of overshadowing; being overshadowed.

Obtention (ǫbte·nʃən). 1624. [– late L. *obtentio* (Jerome), f. *obtent-*, pa. ppl. stem of L. *obtinēre* OBTAIN; see -ION. In later use – Fr. *obtention* (XVI).] The action of obtaining; obtainment.

Obtest (ǫbte·st), *v.* 1548. [– L. *obtestari* call to witness, protest by, f. *ob* on account of + *testari* bear witness, call upon as witness. Cf. OFr. *obtester*.] **1.** *trans.* To adjure; to beg earnestly, beseech, supplicate (a person *that* .., or *to do* something). **2.** *intr.* or with dependent clause: **a.** To make earnest supplication or entreaty. **b.** To call heaven to witness, to protest 1650.

2. Obtesting Deputies o. vainly CARLYLE.

Obtestation (ǫbtestē¹·ʃən). 1531. [– L. *obtestatio*, f. *obtestat-*, pa. ppl stem of *obtestari*; see prec., -ION. Cf. OFr. *obtestation*.] **1.** A beseeching by some sacred name; supplication. **2.** The action of calling (the Deity, etc.) to witness 1555.

†**Obtre·ct**, *v.* Also **obtract.** 1596. [– L. *obtrectare* disparage, detract from, f. *ob-* OB- + *tractare* drag, haul.] *trans.* To detract from, to disparage, decry –1617. So †**Obtrecta·tion**, detraction, slander 1563. †**O·btrectator**, detractor. late ME.

Obtrude (ǫbtrū·d), *v.* 1555. [– L. *obtrudere*, f. *ob-* OB- 1 + *trudere* thrust.] **1.** *trans.* To thrust forth; to eject, push out. Also *refl.* 1613. **2.** To thrust forward forcibly or unduly; to thrust (a matter, person, etc.) *upon* any one. Const. *on*, *upon*, *into* (†*to*, *unto*). 1555. Also *refl.* **b.** *intr.* (for *refl.*) To be or become obtrusive; to intrude, force oneself 1579.

2. A man of low birth.., obtruded on them..by the king for their general FULLER. Subordinate officials, who..obtruded themselves into matters beyond their office 1847. **b.** Let us not o. Upon her sorrows' holy solitude 1844. Hence **Obtru·der.**

Obtruncate (ǫbtrɒ·ŋke¹t), *v.* 1623. [– *obtruncat-*, pa. ppl. stem of L. *obtruncare* cut off, lop away, f. *ob-* OB- 1 + *truncare* cut off, maim; see -ATE³.] *trans.* To top, decapitate. So **Obtrunca·tion.**

Obtrusion (ǫbtrū·ʒən). 1579. [alt., by substitution of prefix, of INTRUSION.] **1.** The action of obtruding (anything) into any space or place, or against anything else 1847. **2.** The importunate thrusting of some one or something (upon one, or upon one's attention); also *concr.* something thus thrust upon one 1641. **b.** The forcing of oneself or one's company upon any one.

2. Disturbed by the o. of new ideas JOHNSON.

Obtrusive (ǫbtrū·siv), *a.* 1667. [– *obtrus-*, pa. ppl. stem of L. *obtrudere* (see OBTRUDE) + -IVE.] **1.** Projecting so as to be in the way 1842. **2.** Forward, unduly prominent.

2. Not obvious, not o., but retir'd, The more desirable MILT. Hence **Obtru·sive-ly** *adv.*, **-ness.**

Obtund (ǫbtɒ·nd), *v.* late ME. [– L. *obtundere* beat against, blunt, dull, f. *ob-* OB- 1 + *tundere* beat.] *trans.* To blunt, deaden, dull, render obtuse (the faculties, physical qualities, etc.). Chiefly in medical use.

The sense of smell is obtunded 1872.

Obtundent (ǫbtɒ·ndėnt), *a.* and *sb.* 1842. [– *obtundent-*, pr. ppl. stem of L. *obtundere*, or f. OBTUND *v.* + -ENT.] **a.** *adj.* Dulling sensibility. **b.** *sb.* A substance used to do this; a demulcent.

Obturate (ǫ·btiure¹t), *v.* 1628. [– *obturat-*, pa. ppl. stem of L. *obturare* stop up, f. *ob-* OB- 1 + *turare* close up; see -ATE³.] *trans.* To stop up, close, obstruct.

Obturation (ǫbtiurē¹·ʃən). 1610. [– late (eccl.) L. *obturatio*, f. as prec.; see -ION. Cf. Fr. *obturation*.] The action of stopping up; obstruction of an opening or channel; *spec.* in *Gunnery* (see next, 2 b).

Obturator (ǫ·btiure¹təɹ). 1727. [– med.L. *obturator* obstructor, f. as prec.; see -OR 2. Cf. Fr. *obturateur* (Paré).] Something that stops up. **1.** *Anat.* (usu. *attrib.*) Name of a membrane (**o. membrane**, or **o. ligament**) which closes the thyroid foramen; applied also to structures connected with this. **2.** An artificial device for stopping an opening. *spec.* **a.** *Surg.* A plate, etc., for closing an opening of the body, esp. an abnormal opening, as in cleft palate. **b.** *Gunnery.* A gas-check. **c.** A shutter of a photographic camera. 1862.

1. O. foramen, a large opening in the os innominatum, representing the division between the ischium and pubis. **O. muscles**, two muscles (*o. externus* and *o. internus*) serving for rotation, etc., of the thigh. **O. nerve**, a branch of the lumbar plexus, having twigs distributed to the hip and knee joints and various muscles of the thigh.

Obtusangular (ǫbtius,æ·ŋgiŭlăɹ), *a.* Now *rare* or *Obs.* 1680. [f. OBTUSE *a.*, after *rectangular*.] = *Obtuse-angled.*

Obtuse (ǫbtiū·s), *a.* 1509. [– L. *obtusus*, pa. pple. of *obtundere* OBTUND.] Blunt; opp. to *acute*. **1.** *lit.* Of a blunt form; not sharp or pointed; *esp.* in *Nat. Hist.* of parts or organs of animals or plants 1589. **2.** *Geom.* Of a plane angle: Greater than a right angle; exceeding 90° 1570. **3.** *fig.* Indistinctly felt or perceived; dull 1620. **4.** Not acutely sensitive or perceptive; stupid, insensible 1509.

1. A blow with an o. weapon 1767. **2.** *O. cone*, a cone of which the section by a plane through the axis has an o. angle at the vertex. *O. hyperbola*, a hyperbola lying within the o. angles between its asymptotes. **3.** I..felt an o. pain..in my stomach 1790. **4.** O. in his understanding, but kind and faithful in his disposition SCOTT. *Comb.*, as **o.-angled** *a.*, having an o. angle or angles; also in *Nat. Hist.*, with another adj., expressing a combination of forms, as **o.-ellipsoid.** Hence **Obtu·se-ly** *adv.*, **-ness.**

Obtusi- (ǫbtiū·si), comb. form of L. *obtusus* OBTUSE, as in **Obtusifo·lious** *a.*, having obtuse leaves; etc.

Obtusity (ǫbtiū·sǐti). 1805. [f. OBTUSE *a.* + -ITY.] The quality of being obtuse, obtuseness; dullness, stupidity.

His combined conceit and o. POE.

Obumbrate (ǫbɒ·mbrĕt), *a.* *rare.* 1513. [– L. *obumbratus*, pa. pple. of *obumbrare*; see next, -ATE².] †**a.** Overshadowed, darkened –1632. **b.** *Entom.* Concealed under some overhanging part, as the abdomen in some spiders 1826.

Obumbrate (ǫbɒ·mbre¹t), *v.* Now *rare.* 1526. [– *obumbrat-*, pa. ppl. stem of L. *obumbrare*, f. *ob-* OB- 1 + *umbrare* shade, f. *umbra* shadow; see -ATE³.] **1.** *trans.* To overshadow; to shade, darken; to obscure. ¶**2.** Misused for ADUMBRATE 3. 1632.

So **Obumbra·tion** (now *rare*) late ME.

‖**Obus** (obüs, -z). 1871. [Fr.] A howitzer shell.

Obvention (ǫbve·nʃən). 1459. [– (O)Fr. *obvention* or late L. *obventio* revenue, f. *obvent-*, pa. ppl. stem of *obvenire* come in the way of, happen to, f. *ob-* OB- 1 + *venire* come; see -ION.] That which comes to one incidentally; in *Eccl. Law*, an (occasional) incoming fee or revenue.

†**Obve·rsant**, *a.* 1579. [– *obversant-*, pr. ppl. stem of L. *obversari* take position over against, f. *obversus*; see OBVERSE *a.*, -ANT.] Standing over against, opposite; also, placed in front of; hence, familiar, well-known –1754.

Obverse (ǫ·bvɜ̄ɹs), *a.* and *sb.* 1656. [– L. *obversus*, pa. pple. of *obvertere* turn towards, f. *ob-* OB- 1 + *vertere* turn.] **A.** *adj.* **1.** Turned towards or against; opposite. **2.** Of a figure: Narrower at the base or point of attachment than at the apex or top; *spec.* in *Nat. Hist.* Also in *comb.* = obversely, OB- 2, as *obverse-lunate*. 1826. **3.** Answering to something else as its counterpart 1875. **B.** *sb.* **1.** That side of a coin, medal, seal, etc. on which the head or principal design is struck; the opposite of *reverse* 1658. **2.** The face or side of anything intended to be presented to view; *front* as opp. to *back* 1831. **b.** *fig.* The counterpart of any fact or truth 1862. **3.** *Logic.* A proposition obtained by OBVERSION 1870.

B. 2. b. Here you have the two sides—the science of medicine, and its o., the practice of witchcraft 1862. Hence **Obve·rsely** *adv.* in an o. form or manner; with an adj. of shape = OB- 2.

Obversion (ǫbvɜ̄·ɹʃən). 1864. [irreg. f. OBVERSE + -ION, after VERSION.] **1.** The action of turning towards some person or thing. **2.** *Logic.* A form of immediate inference in which, by changing the quality, from one proposition another is inferred having a contradictory predicate 1870.

Obvert (ǫbvɜ̄·ɹt), *v.* 1623. [– L. *obvertere*, f. *ob-* OB- 1 + *vertere* turn.] †**1.** *trans.* To turn (something) towards; to place fronting –1781. †**2.** To turn (a thing) in a contrary direction –1657. **3.** *Logic.* To change the quality of (a proposition) in the way of OBVERSION 1870.

Obviate (ǫ·bvi,e¹t), *v.* 1567. [– *obviat-*, pa. ppl. stem of late L. *obviare* meet in the way, prevent, f. *ob-* OB- + *via* way; see -ATE³. Cf. (O)Fr. *obvier*.] †**1.** *trans.* To meet, encounter; hence, to withstand, oppose –1702. **2.** To meet and dispose of or do away with; to prevent by anticipatory measures 1598.

2. The remedies and means to o. these dangers CROMWELL. So **Obvia·tion**, prevention. late ME.

Obvious (ǫ·bviəs), *a.* 1586. [f. L. *obvius*, f. *obviam* in the way; see prec., -OUS.] **1.** Lying or standing in the way; placed in front of or over against; fronting. *Obs.* or *arch.* 1594. †**2.** Open *to* (action or influence); liable –1772. †**3.** Coming in one's way; frequently met or found –1772. **4.** Plain and open to the eye or mind, perfectly evident; palpable 1635. **b.** *Zool.* Plainly visible, evident, as *an o. marking* or *stripe*; opp. to *obscure*.

1. No more rejoycing in the o. Light DRAYTON. **2.** The Pedant is so o. to Ridicule STEELE. **4.** Things present are o. to the sense, things to come to our Reason only HOBBES. It appears o. to me, that one or the other of those two great men.. must be minister BURKE. **c.** quasi-*sb.*, *The obvious*: that which is obvious. Hence **O·bviously** *adv.*, **-ness.**

Obvolute (ǫ·bvŏliut), *a.* 1760. [– L. *obvolutus*, pa. pple. of *obvolvere*; see next.] *Bot.* Applied to a vernation in which two leaves are so folded in the bud that half of one enrolls half of another.

Obvolve (ŏbvǫ·lv), *v. rare.* 1623. [– L. *obvolvere*, f. *ob-* OB- 1 + *volvere* roll.] *trans.* To wrap round, muffle up; to disguise. So **Obvolu·tion** (*rare*), the wrapping of a bandage round a limb; also, †a fold or twist 1578.

Obvolvent (ŏbvǫ·lvĕnt), *a.* 1857. [f. OBVOLVE + -ENT.] Wrapping round; *Entom.* curving inward or downward.

‖**Oca** (ōᵘ·kă). 1604. [Sp. – Peruv. *occa.*] Either of two S. Amer. species of *Oxalis*, *O. crenata* and *O. tuberosa*, cultivated for their edible tubers.

Ocarina (ǫkărī·nă). 1877. [– It. *ocarina*, f. *oca* goose (with ref. to its shape); see -INA[1].] A musical instrument consisting of an egg-shaped terracotta body with a whistle-like mouthpiece and finger-holes.

Occamist (ǫ·kămist). 1550. [f. name *Occam* or *Ockham* + -IST.] A disciple or follower of William of Occam (early 14th c.), the 'Invincible Doctor', who revived the tenets of the Nominalists. Hence **O·ccamism,** the doctrine or system of the Occamists 1837.

Occamy (ǫ·kămi). 1596. [A corrupt form of *alcomye, alcamy* ALCHEMY.] A metallic composition imitating silver.

Occasion (ŏkēⁱ·ʒən), *sb.* late ME. [– (O)Fr. *occasion* or L. *occasio, -ion-* juncture, opportunity, motive, reason, (later) cause, f. *occas-*, pa. ppl. stem of *occidere* go down, set, f. *ob-* OB- 1 + *cadere* fall; see -ION.] **I. 1.** A favourable juncture of circumstances; an opportunity. **b.** Personified (see FORELOCK *sb.*[2] 2). 1592. **2.** = CAUSE *sb.* I. 3. late ME. **†b.** A pretext, an excuse –1649. **3.** = CAUSE *sb.* I. 1. Const. *of*, †*that.* late ME. **b.** A subsidiary or incidental cause. Dist. from *cause* = 'efficient cause' (CAUSE *sb.* I. 4). 1605. **c.** A person who (*esp.* incidentally) brings about something 1548. **†d.** The action of causing or occasioning. Also *transf.* That which is caused or occasioned. –1600. **†4.** That which gives rise to discussion or consideration; the subject treated –1651.

1. Phr. *To take o.*, to take advantage of an opportunity (to do something); I took o. to go up and to bed in a pet PEPYS. **2.** †*Evil o.*, inducement to sin, 'offence', 'stumbling-block' (= Gr. σκάνδαλον in N.T.) TINDALE. **3.** *To give o. to*, to give rise to, to occasion; A mistake which had given o. to a burst of merriment JOHNSON. **b.** It [medicine] considereth causes of diseases, with the occasions or impulsions BACON. **d.** By the occasyon of duke Huon of Burdeaux, he had loste .iiii. of his nephues BERNERS.

II. 1. Necessity or need arising from a juncture of circumstances. Const. *for* (†*of*) or *inf.* 1576. **†b.** A particular, esp. a personal, need, want, or requirement. Chiefly in *pl.* = needs, requirements. –1807. **2.** Necessary business; a matter, piece of business, business engagement. Chiefly *pl.*, affairs, business. Now *arch.* 1594. **†b.** *pl.* Necessities of nature –1789.

1. When he had o. to be seene, He was but as the Cuckow is in Iune, Heard, not regarded SHAKS. **b.** *Merch. V.* I. i. 139. **2.** Such as pass on the seas vpon their lawfull occasions 1662 *Bk. Com. Prayer.*

III. †1. A juncture of circumstances (in itself); an event, incident, circumstance –1649. **†b.** *gen.* The course of events or circumstances SHAKS. **2.** A particular casual occurrence or juncture; the time at which something happens; a particular time marked by some occurrence or by its special character. †Formerly occas.: A case, an instance. 1568. **3. a.** A religious function; in Scotland, a Communion service. *arch.* or *Obs.* 1789. **b.** A special ceremony or celebration; a 'function', an 'event'. Chiefly *colloq.* 1860.

1. b. With-hold thy speed, dreadfull O. SHAKS. **2.** Vpon the next o. that we meete SHAKS. On the o. of her marriage with Mr. —. 1902. **3. b.** It was a great o. 1902.

Phrases. *On* or *upon o.*, as o. or opportunity arises. *On* or *upon o. of*, in casual connection with. *For* (*on, upon*) *one's o.*, on one's account, for one's sake.

Occasion (ŏkēⁱ·ʒən), *v.* 1530. [f. prec.; = Fr. *occasionner.*] **†1.** *trans.* To give occasion to (a person); to induce; also, to do this habitually; hence, to habituate, accustom –1684. **2.** To be the occasion or cause of (something); to cause, bring about, esp. in an incidental or subsidiary manner 1596. **†3.** *Occasioned by*, in consequence of –1725.

2. I occasioned much mirth with a ballet I brought with me PEPYS. **3.** Some of which.. were drowned, unable to swim to shore occasioned by age 1634. So **Occa·sioner** (now *rare*), one who or that which occasions 1452.

Occasional (ŏkēⁱ·ʒənăl), *a.* (*sb.*) 1568. [f. OCCASION *sb.* + -AL[1]. Cf. med.L. *occasionalis* (XIII).] **†1.** That happens casually or incidentally; casual –1654. **2.** Happening or operating on some particular occasion; limited to specific occasions; arising out of, required by, or made for, the occasion 1631. **b.** Of an article of use, building, piece of furniture, etc.: Made or constructed for the occasion; adapted for use on special occasions 1760. **c.** Of persons: Acting or employed for the occasion or on particular occasions 1759. **3.** Taking place, occurring, or met with now and then 1630. **4.** Serving as the occasion or incidental cause. Rarely const. *of.* 1646. **B.** *sb.* An occasional workman, etc. (cf. CASUAL B. 3.) 1892.

2. His o. going from the Sermon, being forced thereunto by the Extremity of the Toothach 1677. *O. Conformity*, a phr. applied after 1700 to the practice of persons who, in order to qualify themselves for office, received the Sacrament according to the rites of the Church of England, and afterwards during their office were present at any dissenting meeting for worship. *O. Conformist*, one who practised this. **b.** A loo, or o. table 1875. **c.** The o. soldier is no match for the professional soldier. MACAULAY. *O. speaker, writer*, etc., one who makes speeches for particular occasions or writes o. verses, pamphlets, etc. **3.** An o. raid upon his neighbour's moveables 1881. **4.** *O. cause* (*Metaph.*), (*a*) a secondary cause whereby or whereupon the primary cause comes into operation; (*b*) in the Cartesian philosophy: see next. Hence **Occa:siona·lity,** the quality or fact of being o. **Occa·sionally** *adv.*, †on occasion; †incidentally; now and then.

Occasionalism (ŏkēⁱ·ʒənăliz'm). 1842. [f. prec. + -ISM, after G. *occasionalismus.*] The doctrine of the Cartesian philosopher Geulincx which accounted for the interaction of mind and matter by supposing that on occasion of every volition God produces a corresponding movement of the body and on occasion of every affection of the body a corresponding idea, mind and body thus standing to each other in the relation of occasional causes. So **Occa·sionalist** 1776.

†Occa·sionate, *v.* 1545. [– *occasionat-*, pa. ppl. stem of late and med.L. *occasionare*, f. *occasio*; see OCCASION, -ATE[3].] *trans.* = OCCASION *v.* 1, 2. –1647.

Occident (ǫ·ksidĕnt). Chiefly *poet.* late ME. [– (O)Fr. *occident* – L. *occidens, -ent-* setting, sunset, west, subst. use of pr. pple. of *occidere* go down, set; see OCCASION *sb.*, -ENT.] **1.** That quarter of the sky in which the sun and other heavenly bodies set, or the corresponding region of the earth; the west. Now *rare.* **2.** Western countries, the West; i.e. orig., the countries of Western Europe, or of Europe as opp. to Asia and the Orient; also, now, America. late ME.

1. His [the sun's] bright passage to the O. SHAKS.

Occidental (ǫkside·ntăl), *a.* and *sb.* late ME. [– (O)Fr. *occidental* or L. *occidentalis*, f. as prec.; see -AL[1].] **A.** *adj.* **1.** Belonging to, situated in, or directed towards the Occident; of or in the west, western, westerly. **2.** Belonging to, found in, or characteristic of, western countries or regions of the earth (i.e. usu. those west of Asia); belonging to or situated in the West; Western 1553. **3.** Applied to precious stones of inferior value and brilliancy, as opp. to ORIENTAL *a.* 4. 1747.

1. *All's Well* II. i. 166. *fig.* Vpon the setting of that bright Occidentall Starre, Queene Elizabeth of most happy memory BIBLE, *Transl. Ded.* [With allusion to 2.]

B. *sb.* **†a.** A western country or region; *the o.*, the west 1829. **b.** A native or inhabitant of the West 1857. Hence **Occide·ntalism,** o. quality, style, character, or spirit; the customs, institutions, etc. of Western nations. **Occide·ntalist,** one who favours Western customs, modes of thought, etc.; one who studies the languages and institutions of Western nations. **Occidenta·lity, Occide·ntalize** *v.* to render o. **Occide·ntally** *adv.*

Occipital (ǫksi·pităl), *a.* (*sb.*) 1541. [– Fr. *occipital* – med.L. *occipitalis, -ale*, f. *occiput*; see OCCIPUT, -AL[1].] **1.** Belonging to, or situated in or on, the occiput or back part of the head. Chiefly *Anat.*, as *o. artery, bone, condyle*, etc. **2.** Having a large occiput 1873. **B.** *sb.* **a.** The occipital bone. **b.** The occipital muscle. **c.** *pl.* A pair of occipital plates on the head of some serpents. 1758.

1. *O. bone*, the bone forming the last part of the cranium between the parietal and temporal bones. *O. muscle*, the hinder part of the occipito-frontalis muscle. Hence **Occi·pitally** *adv.*

Occipito- (ǫksi:pito), bef. a vowel occas. **occipit-,** used in *Anat.* as comb. form of OCCIPUT, in adjs. expressing a relation or connection between the occiput and another part, and denominating a ligament, muscle, measurement, etc.: as, **o. -a·xial, -a·xoid,** pertaining to the occiput and the axis vertebra; **-fro·ntal,** pertaining to, or extending between, the back of the head and the forehead; also *ellipt*, as *sb.*, the *o.-frontal muscle* or *occipitofrontalis*, the large flat muscle of the scalp; **-ma·stoid,** pertaining to the occiput and the mastoid process, etc.

Occiput (ǫ·ksipɒt). late ME. [– L. *occiput, -pit-*, f. *ob-* OB- 1 + *caput* head.] Chiefly *Anat.* The back or hinder part of the head. **b.** The occipital bone of the skull 1578.

†Occi·sion. ME. [– (O)Fr. *occision* – L. *occisio*, f. *occis-*, pa. ppl. stem of *occidere*, f. *ob-* OB- 1 + *cædere* cut (down), kill, slay; see -ION.] Killing, slaying; slaughter –1677.

Occlude (ǫklū·d), *v.* 1597. [– L. *occludere*, f. *ob-* OB- 1 + *claudere* close.] **1.** *trans.* To shut or stop up, obstruct (a passage), close (a vessel or opening). **2.** To prevent the passage of (a thing) by placing something in the way; to shut in, out, or off 1623. **b.** *Chem.* Of certain metals, etc.: To absorb and retain (gases) within their substance 1866. **3.** *Dentistry.* To cause the cusps of (the upper and lower teeth) to fit together; also *intr.*

So **Occlu·dent** *a.* having the property of occluding; *sb.* something having this property.

Occlusal (ŏklū·zăl), *a.* 1904. [f. OCCLUSION (sense 3) + -AL[1].] *Dentistry.* Of or pertaining to occlusion of the teeth.

Occlusion (ŏklū·ʒən). 1645. [f. *occlus-*, pa. ppl. stem of L. *occludere*; see prec., -ION.] **1.** The action of occluding or fact of being occluded; stopping up, closing. (Chiefly scientific). **2.** *Chem.* The retention of gases in the pores of metals or other substances 1866. **3.** *Dentistry.* The bringing of the opposing surfaces of the teeth of the two jaws into contact 1902.

Occlusor (ŏklū·sǫɹ). 1877. [f. OCCLUSION + -OR 2.] Something that occludes; chiefly *Anat.*, a structure which closes an opening. Also *attrib.*, as *o. muscle*, etc.

Occult (ŏkɒ·lt), *a.* 1533. [– L. *occultus*, pa. pple. of *occulere*, f. *ob-* OB- 1 + **celere* CONCEAL.] Hidden (*lit.* and *fig.*). **1.** Hidden (from sight); concealed. Now *rare* or *Obs.* 1567. **b.** Applied to a line drawn in the construction of a figure, but not forming part of the finished figure; also to a dotted line 1669. **2.** Secret; communicated only to the initiated 1533. **3.** Not apprehensible by the mind; recondite, mysterious 1545. **b.** Imperceptible by the senses. Now *rare* or merged in prec. 1650. **c.** Applied to physical qualities discoverable only by experiment, or to those whose nature was unknown and unexplained; latent; also *transf.* experimental. *Obs.* exc. *Hist.* or as merged in 3. 1652. **4.** Of the nature of or pertaining to those sciences involving the knowledge or use of the supernatural (as magic, alchemy, astrology, theosophy, and the like); also *transf.* magical, mystical 1633.

1. We two will stand beside that shrine, O., withheld, untrod ROSSETTI. **3. c.** The Aristotelians give the name of o. qualities..to such qualities.. as they supposed to lie hid in bodies, and to be the unknown causes of manifest effects NEWTON. Hence **Occu·ltism**, the doctrine, principles, or practice of 'occult' science (see sense 4); mysticism. **Occu·ltist**, one versed in, or believing in, occultism; a mystic. **Occu·lt-ly** *adv.*, **-ness.**

Occult (ǫkɒ·lt), *v.* 1527. [– L. *occultare*, frequent. of *occulere*; see prec.] *trans.* To hide, conceal; to cut off from view by interposing some other body. Now chiefly in scientific or techn. use. **b.** *spec.* in *Astron.* said of one heavenly body (as the moon, or a planet) hiding another (as a star, etc.) by passing in front of it 1764. Hence **Occu·lted** *ppl. a.*, hidden, concealed. **Occu·lting** *ppl. a.*, that occults; *spec.* in lighthouses, applied to a light cut off from view for a few seconds at regular intervals.

Occultation (ǫkɒ̆ltēⁱ·ʃən). late ME. [– Fr. *occultation* or L. *occultatio*, f. *occultare*; see prec., -ION.] **1.** Hiding, concealment; the fact of being cut off from view by something interposed. Now only scientific or techn. **2.** *Astron.* †**a.** The disappearance of a star in the sun's rays when in an apparent position near that of the sun. **b.** The concealment of one heavenly body by another passing between it and the observer. (Also, the concealment of a heavenly body behind the body of the earth; so in *circle of perpetual o.*; see CIRCLE *sb.* I. 2.) 1551. **c.** *fig.* Disappearance from view or notice 1825.

1. The Light will be under o. three times in quick succession every Minute 1882. **2. c.** The prospect of the coming o. of personally disagreeable authors 1892.

Occupance (ǫ·kiŭpăns). *Sc. rare.* 1814. [f. OCCUPANT; see -ANCE.] = next, 1.

Occupancy (ǫ·kiŭpănsi). 1596. [f. as prec.; see -ANCY.] **1.** The condition of being an occupant; = OCCUPATION 1, 2. **2.** The fact of occupying or taking up (space) 1833. **3.** = OCCUPATION 4. 1826.

1. O. is the taking possession of those things, which before belonged to nobody. This..is the true ground and foundation of all property BLACKSTONE.

Occupant (ǫ·kiŭpănt). 1596. [– Fr. *occupant* or L. *occupans, -ant-*, pr. pple. of *occupare*; see OCCUPY, -ANT.] A person occupying or holding in actual possession (property, esp. land, or an office or position); an occupier 1622. **b.** *Law.* One who takes possession of something having no owner, and so establishes a title to it 1596.

Occupation (ǫkiŭpēⁱ·ʃən). ME. [– AFr. *ocupacioun* (sense 1) = (O)Fr. *occupation*,– L. *occupatio*, f. *occupat-* pa. ppl. stem of *occupare*; see OCCUPY, -ION.] **1.** The action of taking possession, esp. of a place or of land; seizure, as by military conquest, etc.; entrance upon possession ME. **2.** Actual holding or possession, esp. of a place or of land; rarely, also, of an office or position; tenure; occupancy. late ME. **3.** The taking up of space or time (*rare*) 1460. **4.** The being occupied with, or engaged in something; that in which one is engaged; employment, business ME. **b.** with *pl.* A particular action or course of action in which one is engaged; an employment, business, calling ME. †**c.** *spec.* Handicraft; trade –1607. †**5.** Use, employment (*of* a thing) –1703.

1. Its inhabitants must have possessed the art of working in metals before the Roman o. 1893. **2.** During his o. of the house and land 1902. Phr. *Army of o.*, an army left to occupy a newly conquered country or region until the conclusion of hostilities or establishment of a settled government. **3.** Stooping down in complete o. of the foot-path JANE AUSTEN. **4. b.** Farewell: Othello's Occupation 's gone SHAKS. **c.** *Cor.* IV. vi. 97. *attrib.*, as **o. disease,** a disease incidental to one's occupation; **o. franchise,** the right to vote at a parliamentary election as a tenant or occupier; **o. bridge, road,** a bridge, road, for the use of occupiers of the land. **Occupa·tional** *a.*, pertaining to one's or an occupation.

Occupier (ǫ·kiŭpəi,əɹ). late ME. [orig. (sense 1) – AFr. *occupiour*; otherwise f. OCCUPY + -ER¹.] **1.** One who takes, or (more usu.) holds possession; a holder, occupant. †**2.** One who uses, employs, or deals in (something); one who follows (a specified occupation) –1611. †**b.** *esp.* One who employs money or goods in trading; a trader, dealer, merchant –1611.

2. All my Auncestours were occupiers of husbandry 1577. **b.** He will..Lie faster than ten city occupiers Or cunning tradesmen 1611.

Occupy (ǫ·kiŭpəi), *v.* ME. [– AFr. **occupier*, for (O)Fr. *occuper* – L. *occupare* seize, f. *ob-* OB- 1 + *capere* seize. Almost entirely disused in XVII and most of XVIII, app. because of its vulgar employment in sense 8.] †**1.** *trans.* To take possession of, seize. *Obs.* in *gen.* sense. –1614. **b.** *spec.* To take possession of (a place) by settling in it, or by conquest, etc. ME. **2.** To hold possession of; to hold (a position or office). late ME. **b.** To reside in, tenant. late ME. †**c.** *intr.* or *absol.* To hold possession or office; to dwell, reside; to stay, abide –1535. **3.** *trans.* To take up, use up, fill (space or time); also in weakened sense, To be in or at (a place or position) ME. **4.** To employ, busy, engage (a person, or the mind, attention, etc.). Often in *pass.*; also *refl.* ME. †**5.** To make use of, use (a thing) –1774. †**6.** *trans.* To employ oneself in, carry on; to follow or ply as one's business or occupation –1660. Also †*intr.* –1653. †**7.** *trans.* To employ (money or capital) in trading; to lay out, invest, trade with; to deal in. [L. *occupare pecuniam.*] –1773. †**b.** *intr.* To trade, deal –1650. †**8.** *trans.* and *intr.* To deal with sexually; to cohabit –1660.

1. b. Glencoe was to be occupied by troops MACAULAY. **2.** A married woman is now to o. the same position as her Saxon ancestress 1883. **3.** Thanne wolde it occupie a someres day CHAUCER. The voyage..has occupied thirty days 1875. **4.** Whatever subject o. discourse COWPER. I occupied myself with my instruments 1860. **6.** They that go downe to the see in shippes, & occupie their busynesse in greate waters COVERDALE *Ps.* 106[7]:23. **7.** *Ezek.* 27:9. **b.** Occupye tyll I come TINDALE *Luke* 19:13.

Occur (ǒkɔ̄·ɹ), *v.* 1513. [– L. *occurrere* run to meet, present itself, befall, f. *ob-* OB- 1 + *currere* run.] †**1.** *intr.* To run to meet a person, to run up (to the spot); to run against, to meet, encounter –1695. †**b.** *trans.* (by ellipsis of prep.) To meet, encounter; to oppose, resist –1767. **2.** *intr.* To present itself; to 'turn up' or appear 1516. **b.** To come into one's mind. Const. *to.* 1626. **3.** To happen, befall, take place 1549.

1. Bodies..have..a certain and determinate motion according to..the resistance of the bodies they occurr with BENTLEY. **2.** That name doth often occurre in olde evidences CAMDEN. Marble also occurs here HAWTHORNE. **b.** It could not but o. to me that you would be agreeably surprised 1809. **3.** To Mrs. Orme she told all that had occurred TROLLOPE.

Occurrence (ǒkɒ·rĕns). 1539. [orig. prob. for *occurrents* (cf. ACCIDENCE); later f. OCCURRENT (see -ENCE). Cf. Fr. *occurrence* (XV), med.L. *occurrentia* (Du Cange).] **1.** The fact of occurring 1725. **2.** That which occurs or is met with, or presents itself; now with *an* and *pl.*: An event, incident 1539.

1. Landslips are of frequent o. GEIKIE. **2.** The chief Occurrences of my Life STEELE.

Occurrent (ǒkɒ·rĕnt), *a.* and *sb.* Now *rare.* 1513. [– Fr. *occurrent* or L. *occurrens, -ent-*, pr. ppl. stem of *occurrere*; see OCCUR, -ENT.] **A.** *adj.* That occurs, presents itself, or happens; occurring; current. Sometimes *spec.* Incidental. **B.** *sb.* **1.** = OCCURRENCE 2. (Now *Obs.* or a rare archaism.) 1523. †**b.** *transf.* A narration of what has happened; *pl.* news –1655. †**2.** A person or thing that meets or runs against one –1615.

1. There is neither aduersary, nor euill o. 1 *Kings* 5:4.

Ocean (ōᵘ·ʃăn), *sb.* (*a.*) [ME. *occean(e* – OFr. *occean, -ane* (mod. *océan*) – L. *oceanus* – Gr. ὠκεανός orig. the great river (ῥόος Ὠκεανοῖο, Ὠκεανὸς Ποταμός, Homer) encompassing the disc of the earth; hence, the great outer sea, as opp. to the Mediterranean.] **1.** The vast body of water on the surface of the globe, which surrounds the land; the main or great sea. (Down to *c*1650, commonly **ocean sea,** representing L. *mare oceanum*, OFr. *occeanne mer*, in which *oceanum*, *occeanne* are adjs.) **2.** One of the main areas into which this body of water is divided geographically, as the *Atlantic*, *Pacific*, *Indian*, *Arctic*, and *Antarctic Oceans.* late ME. **3.** *transf.* and *fig.* An immense or boundless expanse of anything; *hyperbolically*, a very great or indefinite quantity 1590.

1. The deck it was their field of fame, and O. was their grave CAMPBELL. **2.** *German O.*, a former name of the North Sea; As the Atlantic and German Oceans unite at this point, a frightful tide runs here 1814. **3.** An o. of troubles 1642. Ale flowed in oceans for the populace MACAULAY. *attrib.* and *Comb.*, as *o. bed, isle, monster, nymph,* etc.; *o. line, liner, power, scout, steamer,* etc.; *o.-sundered* adj.; *o.-wide* adj.; also **o. greyhound,** a swift o. steamer; **o.-lane,** a lane or track across the o.; *esp.* one prescribed for o. steamers; **o.-river, -stream,** the great stream anciently supposed to encompass the earth; **o. tramp,** a term applied to all sea-going steamships (outside the regular liners) which earn their freight solely by cargo-carrying.

Oceania (ōᵘʃi,ēⁱ·niă). 1849. [mod.L. – Fr. *Océanie* (Malte Brun, *c*1812), f. L. *oceanus*, after *Asia*, etc.] A general name for the islands of the Pacific and its adjacent seas. So **Ocea·nica** 1832.

Oceanian (ōᵘʃi,ēⁱ·niăn), *a.* and *sb.* 1831. [– Fr. *océanien*, f. *océan* OCEAN; see -IAN.] **A.** *adj.* Of or pertaining to the Pacific Ocean and its islands, or to Oceania generally. **B.** *sb.* A native of Oceania; a Polynesian 1831.

Oceanic (ōᵘʃi,æ·nik), *a.* 1656. [f. OCEAN + -IC, perh. partly – Fr. *océanique* (XVI).] **1.** Of or pertaining to, situated or living in or by, the ocean; flowing into the ocean. **2.** Ocean-like; vast COLERIDGE. **3.** = OCEANIAN A. 1842.

1. Gulls, petrels, and other o. birds 1772.

Oceanid (osī·ănid). *Pl.* **-ids, -ides** (ōᵘsi,æ·nidīz). 1869. [– Gr. ὠκεανίς, pl. -ιδες, Fr. *Océanide* (1732); see -ID³.] **1.** *Gr. Myth.* A nymph of the Ocean, one of the daughters of Oceanus and Tethys. **2.** *pl.* Marine mollusca, as dist. from *Naiades* or 'Fresh-water shells'.

Oceanography (ōᵘ:ʃiănǫ·grăfi). 1883. [f. OCEAN + -GRAPHY, after G. *oceanographie* (*c*1880).] That branch of physical geography which treats of the ocean, its form, physical features, and phenomena; = THALASSOGRAPHY. So **Oceano·grapher. Ocea:nogra·phic, -al,** *adjs.*

Ocellar (ose·lăɹ), *a.* 1889. [f. L. OCELLUS + -AR¹.] **1.** Of or pertaining to the ocelli or small simple eyes of insects or other Arthropoda 1891. **2.** *Petrography.* Applied to that structure of rocks in which minute individual components of one mineral are arranged in radiating aggregations round another.

Ocellate (ose·lĕt, ǫ·sĕlĕt), *a.* 1857. [– L. *ocellatus*, f. *ocellus* eyelet; see -ATE².] = next.

Ocellated (ose·l-, ǫ·séleⁱtéd), *a.* 1713. [f. as prec. + -ED¹.] **1.** Marked with an ocellus or ocelli; having eye-like spots. **2.** Formed like a small eye; said of a small round spot surrounded by a ring of a different colour 1828.

1. The O. Turkey of Honduras 1864.

Ocelli-, comb. form of L. *ocellus* eyelet, as in **Ocelli·ferous** *a.*, ocellated, **Oce·lliform** *a.*, having the form of an ocellus or little eye; etc.

‖**Ocellus** (ose·lɒ̆s). *Pl.* **ocelli** (əi). 1819. [L., dim. of *oculus* eye.] **1.** A little eye or eyelet; *spec.* **a.** One of the simple eyes of insects and some other Arthropoda; a stemma. **b.** The simple eye or visual spot of Mollusca, Hydrozoa, etc. **c.** One of the facets or segments of a compound eye. (Usu. in *pl.*) **2.** A coloured spot surrounded by a ring or rings of different colour, as found on some feathers, etc.; an eye-like spot, an eyelet 1826.

Ocelot (ōᵘ·silǫt). 1774. [– Fr. (Buffon), shortening of Mexican *tlalocelotl*, f. *tlalli* field + *ocelotl* tiger, jaguar.] A Central and South American feline quadruped (*Felis pardalis*), about three feet in length; the prevailing colour is grey, marked with numerous elongated fawn spots edged with black; the under parts are whitish with black markings; also called *tiger-cat*, *leopard-cat*.

Och (ox), *int. Irish* and *Sc.* 1528. [– Ir., Gael. *och*; cf. OHONE.] An exclamation of surprise, regret, or sorrow; oh! also *och how!* alas!

Ochlocracy (ǫklǫ·krăsi). 1584. [– Fr. *ochlocratie* or mod.L. – Gr. ὀχλοκρατία, f. ὄχλος crowd; see -CRACY.] Government by the mob; mob-rule. Hence **O·chlocrat. Ochlocra·tic, -al** *adjs.*; **-ally** *adv.*

Ochraceous (okrēⁱ·ʃəs), *a.* 1776. [f. L. *ochra* OCHRE + -ACEOUS.] = OCHREOUS 1, 2.

Ochre, ocher (ōᵘ·kəɹ), *sb.* late ME. [– (O)Fr. *ocre* – L. *ochra* (Pliny) – Gr. ὤχρα, f. ὠχρός pale yellow, ὦχρος paleness.] **1.** A native earth, or class of earths, consisting of a mixture of hydrated oxide of iron with varying proportions of clay in impalpable subdivision; varying in colour from light yellow to deep orange or brown. Much used as pigments. **b.** As a pigment; also the colour of this; esp. a pale brownish yellow. late ME. **2.** Applied to the earthy pulverulent oxides of other metals, as *antimony, bismuth, chrome, tantalic, tungstic o.* 1863. **3.** *slang.* Money, in allusion to the colour of gold coin 1854.

3. If I was flush of the o., I tell yer I'd make the thing hum 1890. Hence **O·chre, ocher** *v. trans.* to colour, mark, or rub with o.; chiefly in *pa. pple.* **O·chreish** *a.* ochreous.

Ochreous (ōᵘ·kri,əs), *a.* 1728. [f. mod.L. *ochreus* + -OUS.] **1.** Of the nature of, containing, or abounding in ochre. **2.** Of the colour of ochre; *spec.* of a light brownish yellow 1750.

2. A brown, bricky, o. tone, never bright RUSKIN.

Ochro- (ōᵘkro), comb. form of Gr. ὤχρα, ὠχρός (OCHRE), as in **Ochroleu·cous** *a.* [Gr. ὠχρόλευκος, yellowish-white; etc.

Ochrous (ōᵘ·krəs), *a.* Also (*U.S.*) **ocherous.** 1757. [f. OCHRE + -OUS.] = OCHREOUS.

Ochry, ochery (ōᵘ·kri, ōᵘ·kəri), *a.* 1567. [f. OCHRE, OCHER + -Y¹.] = OCHREOUS 1, 2.

Ochymy, var. of **Occamy.**

-ock, *suffix*, forming dims., as in *bullock, hillock; haddock, paddock, pollock*; also *buttock, tussock*, etc. In *bannock, hassock*, etc., *-ock* appears to be of different origin.

o'clock: see CLOCK *sb.*¹

-ocracy, the suffix *-cracy* with connective -o-; also, as a nonce-word, 'the rule of any class'. So **-ocrat.** See -CRACY, -CRAT.

‖**Ocrea** (ǫ·kriă). Also erron. **ochrea.** *Pl.* **-æ.** 1830. [L., = a greave or legging.] **a.** *Bot.* (*a*) A sheath or tube round a stem or stalk formed by the lateral cohesion of two or more stipules; (*b*) The thin sheath surrounding the seta in mosses. **b.** *Zool.* An investing part or growth similar to this; the 'boot' of a bird (see next).

Ocreate (ǫ·kriĕt), *a.* Also erron. **ochreate.** 1830. [f. prec. + -ATE².] **1.** Wearing or furnished with an *ocrea*, greave, or legging; booted. **2.** *Ornith.* Booted; having the tarsal envelope fused into a continuous ocrea or boot, as thrushes, nightingales, redbreasts, etc. **3.** *Bot.* Having the stipules united by cohesion into a sheath surrounding the stem 1830.

Oct-, form of OCTA-, OCTO-, bef. a vowel.

Oct., abbrev. of OCTAVO, OCTOBER.

Octa- (ǫ·ktă) – Gr. ὀκτα-, comb. form of ὀκτώ eight. **b.** In *Chem. octa-, oct-* (occas. *octo-*) indicates the presence of eight atoms or units of an element or radical, as in *octacarbon, octachloride*, etc.

Octachord (ǫ·ktăkǭɹd), *a.* and *sb.* Also **octo-.** 1760. [– L. *octachordos* adj., late L. *octachordon* (Boethius) – Gr. ὀκτάχορδος -ον, f. ὀκτα- OCTA- + χορδή string.] **A.** *adj.* **a.** Having eight strings. **b.** Relating to a scale of eight notes. **B.** *sb.* **a.** A series of eight notes, as the ordinary diatonic scale. **b.** A musical instrument having eight strings. 1776. Hence **Octacho·rdal** (**octo-**) *a.*

Octad (ǫ·ktæd). 1801. [– late L. *octas, octad-* – Gr. ὀκτάς, ὀκταδ-, f. ὀκτώ eight; see -AD.] **1.** A group or series of eight; *spec.* in ancient systems of notation: A group or series of eight characters corresponding to successive powers of ten (analogous to the groups of six figures marking millions, billions, etc. now used). **2.** *Chem.* An element or radical that has the combining power of eight units, i.e. of eight atoms of hydrogen 1877. Hence **Octa·dic** *a.*

Octagon (ǫ·ktăgǭn), *sb.* and *a.* 1656. [– L. *octa-, octogonos* adj., *-gonum* sb. (Vitruvius) – Gr. ὀκτάγωνος, -γωνον, f. ὀκτα- OCTA-; see -GON.] **A.** *sb. Geom.* A plane figure having eight angles and eight sides. Hence applied to material objects, as a fortification, of this form or section. **B.** *adj.* = OCTAGONAL 1679.

Octagonal (ǫktæ·gŏnăl), *a.* 1571. [orig. *octogonal* (so Fr.), – mod.L. *octogonalis*; see prec. and -AL¹.] Of the form of an octagon; eight-sided. So **Octa·gonally** *adv.* late ME.

Octahedrite (ǫktăhī·drəit, -he·drəit). Also **octo-.** 1805. [f. OCTAHEDRON + -ITE¹ 2 b.] *Min.* Native dioxide of titanium, occurring in crystals of octahedral and other related forms; also called ANATASE.

Octahedron (ǫktăhī·drǭn, -he·drǭn). Also **octo-.** *Pl.* **-ons** or **-a.** 1570. [– Gr. ὀκτάεδρον, subst. use of n. of ὀκτάεδρος adj. eightsided, f. ὀκτα- OCTA-; see -HEDRON. Cf. late L. *octahedrum*, med.L. *octa(h)edrum*, Fr. *octaèdre.*] *Geom.* A solid figure contained by eight plane faces; usu., one contained by eight triangles; *spec.* the *regular o.*, one of the five regular solids, contained by eight equal equilateral triangles. Hence *gen.* Any material body, esp. a crystal, of this form. Hence **Octahedral** (ǫktăhī·drăl, -he·drăl), **-ic** *adjs.* having the form of an o.; of or belonging to an o.

Octamerous (ǫktæ·mĕrəs), *a.* Also **octo-.** 1864. [f. Gr. ὀκταμερής in eight parts; see OCTA-, -MEROUS.] **a.** *Bot.* Having the parts of the flower in series of eight. (Often written 8-*merous.*) **b.** *Zool.* Having the radiating parts or organs eight in number, as an actinoid zoophyte.

Octameter (ǫktæ·mĭtəɹ), *a.* and *sb.* Also **octo-.** 1828. [f. OCTA- (OCTO-) after *hexameter, pentameter.*] *Pros.* **A.** *adj.* Consisting of eight measures or feet. **B.** *sb.* A verse containing eight feet.

B. 'March: an Ode' [by Swinburne], is the only instance in the language of a poem written in octometers 1889.

‖**Octandria** (ǫktæ·ndriă). 1753. [mod.L., f. Gr. ὀκτώ eight + ἀνδρ- (ἀνήρ) male; see -IA¹.] *Bot.* A class in the Linnæan Sexual System, comprising plants with eight stamens. Hence **Octa·ndrous** *a.* 1830.

Octane (ǫ·ktēⁱn). 1872. [f. OCT(A-, OCT(O- + -ANE 2.] *Chem.* The paraffin of the octacarbon series (C_8H_{18}). So **O·ctene** (-īn) [-ENE], the olefine of the same series (C_8H_{16}), also called *octylene*; **O·ctine** (-əin) [-INE⁵], the hydrocarbon of the same series (C_8H_{14}) homologous with acetylene or ethine; **Octo·ic** *a.*, applied to fatty acids, etc., of the same series, as *o. acid* ($C_8H_{16}O_2$).

†**O·ctangle,** *a.* and *sb.* 1613. [– L. *octangulus* eight-angled, f. *octo* eight + *angulus* ANGLE *sb.*²] **A.** *adj.* Octagonal. **B.** *sb.* An octagon. –1726. So **Octa·ngular** *a.* octagonal.

Octant (ǫ·ktănt). 1661. [– L. *octans, octant-* half-quadrant (Vitruvius), f. *octo* eight.] **1.** The eighth part of a circle; *i.e.* either (*a*) an arc, forming one-eighth of the circumference, or (*b*) one-eighth of the area of a circle, contained within two radii at an angle of 45°. 1750. **b.** Each of the eight parts into which a solid figure or body (*e.g.* a sphere), or the space around a central point, is divided by three planes (usu. mutually at right angles) intersecting at the central point 1790. **2.** *Astron.* That point in the apparent course of a planet at which it is 45° distant from another planet, from the sun, or from some particular point; *spec.* each of the four points at which the moon is 45° from conjunction with or opposition to the sun, or midway between the syzygies and quadratures 1661. **3.** An instrument in the form of a graduated eighth of a circle, used for making angular measurements, esp. in astronomy and navigation 1731.

‖**Octapla** (ǫ·ktăplă). Also anglicized **octaples.** 1684. [– Gr. ὀκταπλᾶ, n. pl. of ὀκταπλοῦς eight-fold, after HEXAPLA.] A text consisting of eight versions, esp. of the Scriptures, in parallel arrangement.

Octarchy (ǫ·ktaɹki). 1799. [f. Gr. ὀκτώ eight, after HEPTARCHY; see -ARCHY.] A government by eight rulers; applied by some historians (instead of HEPTARCHY) to the kingdoms established by the Angles and Saxons in Britain.

Octastich (ǫ·ktăstik). 1577. [– Gr. ὀκτάστιχος of eight verses; see OCTA-, STICH.] A group of eight lines of verse.

Octastichous (ǫktæ·stikəs), **octo-,** *a.* 1870. [f. as prec. + -OUS.] *Bot.* Having eight leaves in the spiral row, and thus eight vertical rows in the phyllotaxis.

Octastyle (ǫ·ktăstəil), *a.* and *sb.* Also **octo-.** 1706. [– L. *octastylus* adj. (Vitruvius) – Gr. ὀκτάστυλος (στῦλος pillar).] *Arch.* **A.** *adj.* Having eight columns in front or at the end, as a building. **B.** *sb.* A building or portico having eight columns.

Octateuch (ǫ·ktătiūk). Also **octo-.** 1677. [– late L. *octateuchus* (Cassiod.) – Gr. ὀκτάτευχος containing eight books (τεῦχος book). Cf. PENTATEUCH.] The first eight books of the Old Testament collectively; the Pentateuch, together with Joshua, Judges, and Ruth.

Octave (ǫ·ktĕv), *sb.* (*a.*) Also in sense 1 (*pl.*) †**utaves,** †**utas** (see also UTAS). ME. [– (O)Fr. *octave*, superseding semi-pop. *oitieve, utave* (see UTAS) – L. *octava* (sc. *dies* day), fem. of *octavus* eighth, f. *octo* eight.] **1.** *Eccl.* (Formerly always in *pl.*) **a.** The eighth day after a festival. **b.** The period of eight days beginning with the day of a festival. **c.** *transf.* A period of festivity 1597. **2.** A group of eight lines of verse; a stanza of eight lines (*spec.* = OTTAVA RIMA) = OCTET 2. 1586. **3.** *Mus.* (Formerly EIGHTH. Occas. abbrev. 8ve.) **a.** The note eight diatonic degrees above (or below) a given note (both notes being counted), which is produced by vibrations of twice (or half) the rate. Hence, any of the notes at successive intervals of eight degrees above or below a given note (*second o., third o.*, etc.). **b.** The interval between any note and its octave; an interval comprising five tones and two diatonic semitones. **c.** A series of notes, or keys of an instrument, extending through this interval. **d.** A note and its octave played or sung together. 1656. **e.** An organ-stop sounding an octave higher than the ordinary pitch; more usu. called *principal* 1716. **4.** A group or series of eight 1806. **5.** *Fencing.* (In full *o. parade.*) The position of parrying or attacking in the low outside line with the hand in supination (cf. *seconde*) 1771. **6.** A small wine-cask containing the eighth part of a pipe, or 13½ gallons 1880.

1. *In the octaves* = med.L. *in octavis* 'on the eighth day' of a festival. **c.** 2 *Hen. IV*, II. iv. 22. **2.** With monefull melodie it continued this octaue SIDNEY. **3.** *Consecutive octaves, hidden octaves*: see the adjs. **4.** *Law of octaves* (*Chem.*), the 'periodic law' as orig. stated by its discoverer Newlands 1887.

attrib. (or *adj.*) and *Comb.*: **o. flute,** (*a*) a small flute sounding an o. higher than the ordinary flute, a piccolo; (*b*) a flute-stop on an organ sounding an o. higher than the ordinary pitch; †**o. rime** = OTTAVA RIMA; **o. stanza,** a stanza of eight lines.

Octavo (ǫktēⁱ·vo). Abbrev. **8vo** or **oct.** 1582. [L., abl. of *octavus* eighth, in the phr. *in octavo* in an eighth (*sc.* of a sheet); Fr. *in-octavo* sb.] **1.** The size of a book, or page, when the sheets are so folded that each leaf is one-eighth of a whole sheet. Orig. in L. phr. *in octavo*, subseq. treated as Eng. prep. and sb. **2.** A book or volume *in octavo* 1712. **3.** *attrib.* or *adj.*, as in 'octavo edition' = edition *in o.* 1704.

2. Imparting his lucubrations to the world in the shape of one or two octavos 1854.

Octennial (ǫkte·niăl), *a.* 1656. [f. late L. *octennium* period of eight years (f. *octo* eight + *annus* year) + -AL¹; cf. *biennial*, etc.] Of or pertaining to a period of eight years; occurring, or lasting, during eight years; recurring every eighth year. Hence **Octe·nnially** *adv.* once in eight years.

Octet, octette (ǫkte·t). 1864. [– It. *ottetto*, or its derivative G. *oktett*; assim. to OCTA-, OCTO-, and *duet, quartet.*] **1.** *Mus.* A composition for eight singers or voices. **b.** A company of eight singers or players who perform together. **2.** A group of eight lines of verse; *spec.* the first eight lines of a sonnet 1879. **3.** *gen.* A group of eight 1894.

Octile (ǫ·ktəil), *a.* and *sb.* 1690. [– mod.L. *octilis*, f. *octo* eight, after *quintilis*, etc. Cf. Fr. *octil.*] **A.** *adj.* Said of the 'aspect' of two planets distant 45° (= ⅛ of a circle) from each other. **B.** *sb.* = Octile aspect, OCTANT 2. 1690.

Octillion (ǫkti·lyən). 1690. [– Fr. *octillion* (La Roche XVI), f. L. *octo* eight, after *million*; see BILLION.] The eighth power of a million, denoted by 1 followed by 48 ciphers. (In U.S., following later French usage, the ninth power of a thousand, denoted by 1 and 27 ciphers.) Hence **Octi·llionth.**

Octine (*Chem.*): see under OCTANE.

Octingentenary (ǫktindʒe·ntīnări, -dʒentī·nări). *rare.* 1893. [f. L. *octingenti* eight hundred, after *centenary.*] The eight-hundredth anniversary of an event.

Octo- (bef. a vowel **oct-**), comb. form of L. *octo*, and occas. of Gr. ὀκτώ eight. (The Gr. form is usu. ὀκτα-, OCTA-.) **Octoda·ctyl, -da·ctylous** *adjs. Zool.* [Gr. δάκτυλος digit], having eight digits. **O·ctofid** *a.* [L. *-fidus* = cleft], divided into eight segments, as a calyx or corolla. **O·ctofoil** *a.* [after *trefoil*, etc.: see FOIL *sb.*[1]], *sb.* an ornamental figure consisting of eight leaves or lobes; *adj.* eight-lobed (also **O·ctofoiled**). **Octo·gamy** [after *bigamy*], the marrying of eight spouses. **O·ctoglot** *a.* [Gr. γλῶττα, γλῶσσα tongue], written in eight languages. **Octola·teral** *a.* [LATERAL] eight-sided, formed of eight straight lines. **Octora·dial, -ra·diate, -ra·diated** *adjs.* [L. *radius* ray], having eight rays. **O·ctospore** *Bot.* [SPORE], each of the eight carpospores produced by certain algæ; so **Octo·sporous** *a.*, producing eight spores. **Octo·valent** *a.* [L. *valentem* having value], *Chem.* having the combining power of eight atoms of hydrogen; octadic.

October (ǫktōᵘ·bəɹ). [Late OE. *october* – L. *october*, *-bris* (with or without *mensis* month), f. *octo* eight (cf. *December, November, September*); ME. *octobre* – (O)Fr. *octobre* was superseded by the L. form.] **1.** The tenth month of the year (as now reckoned). **2.** Ale brewed in October 1708.

1. Bright O. was come, the misty-bright O CLOUGH.

Octodecimo (ǫktode·simo). 1795. [For *in octodecimo*, from L. *octodecimus* eighteenth, as in *octavo*, etc.] The size of a book or page when each leaf is one-eighteenth of a whole sheet; a book of this size. Abbrev. 18mo.

‖**Octodon** (ǫ·ktŏdǫn). 1841. [mod.L., f. Gr. ὀκτώ eight + ὀδούς, ὀδοντ- tooth; for the form cf. MASTODON.] **a.** A genus of S. Amer. rodents, resembling rats. **b.** A genus of coleopterous insects.

Octogenarian (ǫ:ktoˌdʒĭnēᵊ·riăn), *a.* and *sb.* 1815. [f. L. *octogenarius*, f. *octogeni* eighty each, + -AN.] **A.** *adj.* Of the age of eighty; also *transf.* of or belonging to a person eighty years old 1818. **B.** *sb.* A person eighty years old 1815.

A. Blind old Dandolo! Th' o. chief BYRON. Hence **Octogena·rianism.** So **Octo·genary** *a.* and *sb.* (now *rare*) 1696.

‖**Octogynia** (ǫktoˌdʒi·niă). Also **octa-**. 1760. [mod.L., f. Gr. ὀκτώ eight + γυνή female + -IA[1].] *Bot.* A Linnæan order of plants comprising those with eight pistils. Hence **Octogy·nious, Octo·gynous** *adjs.*

Octoic, *a.* (*Chem.*): see under OCTANE.

Octonary (ǫ·ktonări), *a.* and *sb.* 1535. [– L. *octonarius* containing eight, f. *octoni* eight at a time, f. *octo* eight. Cf. med.L. *octonarium*, in sense B.] **A.** *adj.* Pertaining to the number eight; consisting of eight; proceeding by eights 1615. **B.** *sb.* A group of eight, an ogdoad; a group or stanza of eight lines of verse (esp. used of the 119th Psalm) 1535.

Octopartite (ǫktopā·ɹtəit), *a.* 1752. [f. OCTO- after *tripartite, quadripartite.*] Divided into or consisting of eight parts; as, an †*o. indenture.*

Octoped (ǫ·ktŏped). Also **-pede.** 1822. [f. L. *octo* eight + *pes, ped-* foot.] An eight-footed animal or thing.

Octopod (ǫ·ktŏpǫd), *sb.* and *a.* 1826. [– ὀκτωποδ-, stem of Gr. ὀκτώπους; see next, -POD.] **A.** *sb.* An animal having eight feet; *spec.* an octopus, or other member of the suborder *Octopoda* of cephalopods 1835. **B.** *adj.* Eight-footed. So **Octo·podan** *a.* and *sb.*, **Octo·podous** *a.*

Octopus (ǫ·ktŏpŏs, ǫktōᵘ·pŏs). *Pl.* **octopodes** (ǫktōᵘ·pŏdīz), **octopuses.** 1758. [– mod.L. *octopus* – Gr. ὀκτώπους (usually ὀκτάπους; cf. L. *octipes*), f. ὀκτώ eight + πούς foot.] A genus of cephalopod molluscs, characterized by eight 'arms' surrounding the mouth and provided with suckers; a (large and formidable) individual of this genus.

fig. We are the very o. of nations 1882.

Octoroon (ǫktŏrū·n). 1861. [f. L. *octo* eight, after QUADROON.] A person having one-eighth negro blood; the offspring of a quadroon and a white; sometimes used of other mixed races.

Octosyllabic (ǫ:ktosilæ·bik), *a.* and *sb.* 1771. [f. late L. *octosyllabus*, in late Gr. ὀκτασύλλαβος, f. Gr. ὀκτώ, ὀκτα- eight + συλλαβή, L. *syllaba* syllable; cf. SYLLABIC.] **A.** *adj.* Consisting of eight syllables (chiefly in *Pros.* of a verse or line of poetry); composed of lines of eight syllables each. **B.** *sb.* A verse or line of eight syllables 1842.

A. The o. measure of the Lady of the Lake LOCKHART.

Octosyllable (ǫktosi·lăb'l), *sb.* and *a.* 1775. [f. L. *octosyllabus*, after *syllable.*] **A.** *sb.* = prec. B; also, a word of eight syllables. **B.** *adj.* = prec. A.

‖**Octroi** (oktrwa, ǫ·ktroi). Also †**octroy.** 1614. [Fr., f. *octroyer*; see next.] †**1.** A privilege granted by government, esp. an exclusive right of trade, etc. –1721. **2.** A tax levied on certain articles on their admission into a town (esp. in France) 1714. **b.** The barrier at which the tax is paid; also, the service, or body of officers, collecting it 1861.

Octroy (ǫ·ktroi), *v.* 1480. [– Fr. *octroyer* grant (earlier *ot(t)-*) :– Gallo-Rom. **auctoricare*, med.L. *auctorizare* AUTHORIZE.] *trans.* To concede, grant, accord; said of a government or appointed authority.

Octuor (ǫ·ktiuˌǫɹ). 1864. [Fr., irreg. f. L. *octo* eight, after *quatuor* four (in *Mus.* = *quartet*).] = OCTET 1.

Octuple (ǫ·ktiup'l), *a.* (*sb.*) 1603. [– Fr. *octuple* or L. *octuplus*, f. *octo* eight + *-plus*, as in *duplus* DOUBLE.] **A.** *adj.* Eightfold; eight times as much as..; composed of eight. **B.** *sb.* That which is eight times something else, or consists of eight parts 1692. Hence **O·ctuple** *v. trans.* to increase eightfold.

Octyl (ǫ·ktil). 1866. [f. OCT(A-, OCT(O- + -YL.] *Chem.* The hydrocarbon radical of the octacarbon series (C_8H_{17}); sometimes called *capryl.* Also *attrib.*, as *o. alcohol*, etc. (Earlier named *octylia.*) So **O·ctylene** = *Octene* (see under OCTANE); **Octy·lic** *a.* of or pertaining to o., as *octylic acid, alcohol*, etc. 1857.

Ocular (ǫ·kiŭlăɹ), *a.* and *sb.* 1503. [– Fr. *oculaire* – late L. *ocularis*, f. L. *oculus* eye; see -AR[1].] **A.** *adj.* **1.** Of, belonging to, or connected with the eye as a bodily organ; seated in, or in the region of, the eye. *spec.* in *Entom.* Pertaining to the compound eye of an insect (dist. from *ocellar*). **b.** Used for, applied to, or relating to the eye 1599. **c.** Of the nature, form, or function of an eye 1640. **d.** Expressed by the eye 1627. **2.** Belonging to the action of the eye, and hence to the sense of sight; visual 1575.

1. b. O. remedies 1661. **d.** The o. dialect needs no dictionary EMERSON. **2.** Phr. *O. inspection, testimony, demonstration.*

B. *sb.* **1.** The eye-piece of a telescope, microscope, etc. 1835. **2.** Joc. for 'ocular organ', 'eye' 1825. Hence **O·cularly** *adv.* 1646.

Ocularist (ǫ·kiŭlărist). 1866. [– Fr. *oculariste*, f. *oculaire* OCULAR; see -IST.] A maker of artificial eyes.

Oculate (ǫ·kiŭlĕt), *a.* 1549. [– L. *oculatus*, f. *oculus* eye; see -ATE[2].] †**1.** Possessed of eyes or sight; sharp-sighted; observant –1660. **2.** *Nat. Hist.* Having eye-like spots or holes resembling eyes 1656. So **O·culated** *a.*, in sense 2.

O·culiform, *a.* 1828. [f. L. *oculus* eye + -FORM.] Having the form of an eye; eye-like.

Oculist (ǫ·kiŭlist). 1615. [– Fr. *oculiste*, f. L. *oculus* eye; see -IST.] One versed in the knowledge or treatment of the eyes; a physician or surgeon who treats diseases and affections of the eye. Hence **Oculi·stic** *a.*

Oculo- (ǫ·kiŭlo), bef. a vowel **ocul-,** comb. form of L. *oculus* eye (see -O-); as in **Oculomotor** (-mōᵘ·tǫɹ) *a.*, serving to move the eye; epithet of the third pair of cranial nerves, which supply most of the muscles of the eyeballs; *sb.* the oculomotor nerve; **Oculonasal** (-nēⁱ·zăl) *a.*, belonging or relating to the eye and the nose; etc.

‖**Oculus** (ǫ·kiŭlŏs). Pl. **oculi** (-əi). [L., eye.] †**1.** *O. Christi*: (*a*) wild sage; (*b*) *Inula o.-c.* –1658. †**2.** *O. mundi*, hydrophane –1796. **3.** *Nat. Hist.* **a.** An eye; *spec.* a compound eye, as in insects (dist. from *ocellus*). **b.** A spot resembling an eye; an ocellus. 1857. **4.** *Bot.* A leaf-bud; cf. EYE *sb.*[1] III. 1 a. 1727. **5.** *Arch.* **a.** A large circular window at the west end of a church. **b.** A round hollowed stone. 1848.

Ocydrome (ǫ·sidroᵘm). 1895. [– mod.L. *Ocydromus* (Wagler, 1830) – Gr. ὠκύδρομος swift-running.] *Ornith.* A bird of the genus *Ocydromus*, native of New Zealand, incapable of flight.

Ocypode (ǫ·sipoᵘd), *a.* and *sb.* 1864. [– mod.L. *Ocypoda*, f. Gr. ὠκύπους, ὠκυποδ- swift-footed.] *Zool.* **A.** *adj.* Belonging to the genus *Ocypoda* or family *Ocypodidæ* of crabs. **B.** *sb.* A crab of this genus or family; a sand-crab or racing-crab. Also **Ocypodan** (ǫsi·pŏdăn) *a.* and *sb.*

Od[1], **'od** (ǫd). Also **odd.** 1598. A minced form of *God* (GOD *sb.*), very frequent in XVII and early XVIII. Now *arch.* and *dial.* **1.** Used interjectionally, by way of asseveration. Still *dial.* 1695. **b.** In imprecations and exclamatory phrases, as *od rat it* (*'drat it*), *od save's*, etc. Still *dial.* 1749. **2.** The possessive *'od's* (*od's, odds*, etc.) occurs like *God's* in many exclams. 1598. **b.** In *od's me, od's my life, od's my will*, and the simple *'od's, odds* it has been suggested that *'s* is for *save* 1598.

1. Od, ye are a clever birkie! SCOTT. **b.** Fools! 'od rot 'em! 1812. **2.** 'Ods pittikins:can it be sixe mile yet? SHAKS. Odzooks, I'm a young Man CONGREVE.

Od[2] (ǫd, ōᵘd). 1850. [Arbitrary term.] A hypothetical force held by Baron von Reichenbach (1788–1869) to pervade all nature, manifesting itself in certain persons of sensitive temperament, and exhibited esp. by magnets, crystals, heat, light, and chemical action, and held to explain the phenomena of mesmerism and animal magnetism. Also *attrib.* as *od force*, etc. (Cf. ODYL.) Hence **O·dic** *a.* **Odize** (ǫ·dəiz, ōᵘ·dəiz) *v. trans.* to charge with odic force. **b.** Forming the second element in various derivatives, as *biod* the 'od' of animal life, *thermod* heat 'od', etc.

‖**Oda** (ōᵘ·dă). 1625. [– Turk. *ōtah, ōdah* chamber, hall.] A room in a harem; *transf.* the inmates of such a room.

Odal (ōᵘ·dăl), *sb.* (*a.*) 1839. [– Norw. *odal* property held by inheritance :– ON. *óðal* = OE. *æþel, ēþel, ōþel*, OS. *ōðil*, OHG. *uodal*, f. Gmc. **ōþ-* **āþ-*, whence also OE. *æþele* noble (cf. ATHELING). Cf. UDAL.] Land held in absolute ownership without service or acknowledgement of any superior, as among the early Teutonic peoples. Chiefly *attrib.* See also UDAL.

‖**Odalisque** (ōᵘ·dălisk). 1681. [– Fr. *odalisque* – Turk. *ōdaliq*, f. *ōdah* (see ODA) + *-liq* affix expressing function.] A female slave or concubine in an Eastern harem, esp. in the seraglio of the Sultan of Turkey.

Odaller (ōᵘ·dălǝɹ). 1860. [f. ODAL + -ER[1].] A free possessor by odal tenure; = UDALLER.

Odd (ǫd), *a.* (*sb.*) and *adv.* [ME. *odde* – ON. *odda-* in comb. in *odda-maðr* (acc. *-mann*) third man, odd man, who gives the casting vote, in which *odda-* is genitive or comb. form of *oddi* 'point, angle, triangle', whence 'third or odd number'.] **A.** *adj.* **I.** With ref. to number. **1.** Of an individual: That is one in addition to a pair, or remaining over after division into pairs. **2.** Of a number: Having one left over as remainder when divided by two; opp. to *even.* late ME. **b.** Numbered with or known by such a number. late ME. **c.** *absol.* as *sb. The odd*, uneven number 1589. **3.** Added to a 'round number', and thus becoming virtually an indefinite cardinal number of lower denomination than the round number named. late ME. **b.** *ellipt.* denoting age, the word 'years' being understood (*colloq.*) 1845. **4.** Used to denote a surplus over a definite sum, or a remainder of lower denomination of money, weight, or measure. late ME.

1. *O. man*, the third (fifth, etc.) man in a body of arbitrators, a committee, etc., who, in case of an equal division of opinion, may give a casting vote. *O. trick*, in whist, the thirteenth trick, after each side has won six. 2. This is the third time: I hope good lucke lies in odde numbers SHAKS. Phr. *O. and (or) even* (dial. *odds or evens*): a game of chance. 3. Two hundred and o. men 1748. Fleeced of seventy o. dollars 1793. b. At sixty o., love, most of the ladies of thy orient race have lost the bloom of youth THACKERAY. 4. The proceeds..amounted to 47 *l.* o. MARRYAT.

II. Transf. senses. 1. That exists or stands alone; single, sole, solitary, singular. Now only *dial.* ME. †2. Singular in valour, worth, merit, or eminence. (Comp. *odder, oddest.*) –1698. †3. Not even, accordant, or conformable; uneven, discrepant –1596. †b. (*rare*) At odds (*with*) –1606. 4. Extraneous or additional to what is reckoned or taken into account; hence, Not belonging to any particular total, set, or group; unconnected; irregular; casual. Also in weakened sense, esp. with indef. adjs., as *some o.* (= 'some or other'), *any o.* (= 'any chance', 'any stray'). *O. ends, o. things*, odds and ends (see ODDS). 1450. *O. job*, occasional employment; hence *o. job man*. b. Of a place: Out of the way 1576. c. Of an interval of time: Occurring casually 1644. d. Not forming part of a regular course of work, as *o. job*; whence *o. jobber*, and similarly *o. man, lad, hand*, etc. 1859. e. Forming part of an incomplete pair or set 1746. †f. Extra –1602. 5. Extraordinary, strange. (Comp. *odder, oddest.*) 1592. b. Of persons, their actions, etc.: Peculiar; eccentric 1588. c. Of material things: Fantastic, grotesque 1613.

1. *An o. one* (n. dial.), a single one, one only. 2. He was an Odde man indeed, for all the Popish party could not match him with his equal in Learning and Religion FULLER. 3. b. *Tr. & Cr.* IV. v. 265. 4. A few o. observations FIELDING. c. To pick up knowledge at o. moments 1893. e. Two o. volumes of Swift 1764. f. *Haml.* V. ii. 185. 5. If she be mad..Her madnesse hath the oddest frame of sense SHAKS. b. The village people thought her o., and were a little afraid of her 1882. c. It is the oddest carriage in the world DICKENS.

B. *sb.* (the adj. used ellipt.) a. An odd thing; that which is odd 1830. b. *Golf. The o.*; the stroke which one player has played more than his adversary 1881.

Comb.: **o.-come-short**, a short length of cloth forming the end of a piece; an odd remainder or fragment; **o.-man-out**, a mode of singling out, by tossing, counting, or the like; **o.-pinnate** *a.*, pinnate (as a leaf) with an odd terminal leaflet. Hence **O·dd-ly** *adv.*, **-ness**.

O·ddfe:llow. 1811. [A fanciful name: cf. ODD *a.* II. 5 b.] A member of a secret society, fraternity, or order, organized under this name, for social and benevolent purposes.

Oddity (ǫ·dĭti). 1713. [f. ODD *a.* + -ITY.] 1. The quality or character of being odd; strangeness, singularity 1750. 2. An odd trait, a peculiarity 1713. 3. a. An odd person 1748. b. Something odd; a fantastic object; a strange event 1834.

2. All people have their oddities DISRAELI. 3. a. This ridiculous o. danced up to the table at which we sat SMOLLETT.

Oddments (ǫ·dmĕnts), *sb. pl.* 1780. [f. ODD *a.* + -MENT, after *fragment.*] Odds and ends; esp. articles belonging to broken or incomplete sets, as offered for sale.

Odds (ǫdz). 1500. [app. pl. of ODD *a.* taken subst.: cf. *news*. Usu. construed as a singular bef. XIX.] 1. (?) Odd or unequal things; inequalities; hence *to make odds even*, to do away with inequalities. 2. = DIFFERENCE *sb.* 1. Now *rare*. 1542. b. The amount by which one quantity or thing exceeds or falls short of another; difference 1548. c. Difference in the way of detriment or benefit 1642. 3. = DIFFERENCE *sb.* 3. Chiefly in *at odds* 1587. 4. Difference in favour of one of two contending parties; balance of advantage 1574. †b. Superior position, advantage –1750. c. Equalizing allowance given to a weaker competitor or side. Also *fig.* 1591. 5. In *Betting*, advantage conceded by one of the parties in proportion to the assumed chances in his favour 1597. 6. 'Chances' or balance of probability in favour of something happening or being the case, esp. in *it is o.* (*that, but*), now usu. *the o. are* 1589. 7. **O. and ends**, odd remnants, miscellaneous articles or things (cf. *odd ends*: ODD *a.* II. 4) 1746.

1. *Meas. for M.* III. i. 41. 2. I ken nae o. o' her this many a year GALT. b. It [a bill] was retained by the o. of two voices 1671. c. Phr. *What's the o.? It is* or *makes no o.* (colloq.). 4. *At o.*, with the balance of advantage for or against one. c. Each side feels that it cannot allow any o. to the other 1888. 5. Phr. *To give* (*lay*, etc.) *o.*, to offer a wager on terms favourable to the other party; *to take o.*, to accept such a wager. 6. *By all o.*, in all probability.

Ode (ōᵘd). 1588. [– Fr. *ode* – late L. *oda, ode* – Gr. ᾠδή, Attic form of ἀοιδή song, lay, f. ἀείδειν sing.] 1. a. orig., A poem intended to be sung; e.g. the Odes of Pindar, etc. *Choric Odes*, the songs of the chorus in a Greek play, etc. b. In mod. use: A rhymed (rarely unrhymed) lyric, often in the form of an address; usu. dignified or exalted in subject, feeling, and style, but sometimes simple and familiar, and rarely extending to 150 lines. 2. *Gr. Ch.* Each of the nine Scripture canticles; also, each song or hymn of a series called the *canon of the odes* 1881.

1. O run, prevent them with thy humble o., And lay it lowly at his blessed feet MILTON.

-ode, *formative suffix*, repr. Gr. -ώδης, -ώδες adj.-ending = 'like, of the nature of', contr. from -οειδής = -o- final of root or comb. vowel + -ειδής like; e.g. λιθώδης stony, etc. Hence Eng. sbs. in *-ode*, in the sense of 'something of the nature of' that expressed by the first element; e.g. *geode*, etc. (Not the same as *-ode* = Gr. ὁδός way, in *anode, cathode*, etc.)

Odelet (ōᵘ·dlėt). 1589. [f. ODE + -LET. Cf. Fr. *odelette* (XVI).] A short or little ode.

‖**Odeum** (odī·ŏm). *Pl.* **odea** (odī·ă). 1682. [– Fr. *odéum* or L. *odeum* – Gr. ᾠδεῖον, f. ᾠδή singing (see ODE).] Among the ancient Greeks and Romans, a roofed building, akin to a theatre, for vocal and instrumental music; also, a modern hall, etc., for musical performances.

Odinism (ōᵘ·diniz'm). 1848. [f. *Odin* + -ISM.] The worship of *Odin*, called the *All-father*, the chief deity of Norse mythology, corresp. to the OE. Woden; the pre-Christian mythology and religious doctrine of the ancient Scandinavian people. So **Odi·nian Odi·nic, Odini·tic** *adjs.* of or pertaining to Odin or Odinism; **O·dinist**, a votary of Odin; a student of O.; also *attrib.* or *adj.*

Odious (ōᵘ·diəs), *a.* late ME. [– OFr. *odious, odieus* (mod. *odieux*) – L. *odiosus*, f. *odium*; see next, -OUS.] Deserving of hatred, hateful; causing or exciting repugnance, disagreeable, offensive, repulsive.

You told a Lye, an o. damned Lye SHAKS. The unhappy woman..whose image became more o. to him every day GEO. ELIOT. Hence **O·dious-ly** *adv.*, **-ness**.

Odium (ōᵘ·diŏm). 1602. [– L. *odium* hatred, f. *odi* I hate.] 1. Hatred, dislike, aversion, detestation: a. as a quality of the subject 1654. b. as a condition affecting the object 1602. 2. Odiousness; opprobrium 1678.

1. The universal o. against him 1654. b. To avoid yᵗ o. vnder wᶜʰ I lye 1691. 2. When the o. of the transaction shall be forgotten SCOTT. Phr. *Odium theologicum* (mod.L.), the hatred which proverbially characterizes theological dissensions. Hence, by imitation, *odium æstheticum, medicum, musicum*, etc.

Odometer, etc.: see HODOMETER, etc.

‖**Odontalgia** (ǫdǫntæ·ldʒiă). Also †**-algy.** 1651. [– Gr. ὀδονταλγία toothache.] Toothache. So **Odonta·lgic** *a.* of or pertaining to toothache; *sb.* a medicine for toothache.

Odonto-, bef. a vowel **odont-**, comb. form of Gr. ὀδούς, ὀδοντ- tooth, as in **Odo·ntocete** (-sīt) [Gr. κῆτος whale] *a. Zool.* (of a cetacean) having teeth instead of whalebone, opp. to *mysticete*; *sb.* a toothed cetacean; hence **Odontoce·tous** *a.* **Odonto·geny** [-GENY], the generation or origin and development of the teeth; hence **Odontoge·nic** *a.* **Odo·ntolite** [Gr. λίθος stone], a fossil tooth; with lapidaries, a fossil tooth or other bone coloured blue by mineral impregnation, occurring in tertiary strata. **Odontosto·matous, Odonto·stomous** [Gr. στομα(τ-) mouth] *adjs.*, having jaws which bite like teeth; mandibulate (as an insect).

Odontoblast (odǫ·ntŏblast). 1878. [f. prec. + -BLAST.] A tooth-cell that produces dentine; any tooth-secreting cell. Hence **-bla·stic** *a.*

‖**Odontoglossum** (odǫ:ntoglǫ·sŏm). 1880. [mod.L., f. Gr. ὀδούς (see ODONTO-) + γλῶσσα tongue.] *Bot.* A genus of orchids having flowers of great size and beautiful colours; also, a plant or flower of this genus.

Odontograph (odǫ·ntŏgrɑf). 1838. [f. ODONTO- + -GRAPH.] An instrument for marking or setting out the teeth of gear-wheels.

Odontography (ǫdǫntǫ·grăfi). 1840. [f. ODONTO- + -GRAPHY.] A description, or history, of the teeth. Hence **Odontogra·phic** *a.*

Odontoid (odǫ·ntoid), *a.* and *sb.* 1797. [– Gr. ὀδοντοειδής tooth-like; see ODONTO- and -OID. Cf. Fr. *odontoïde* (XVII).] A. *adj.* 1. Resembling or formed like a tooth; tooth-like. 2. (*attrib.* use of B.) Of or belonging to the odontoid process, as *o. ligament, tubercle* 1840.

1. *O. process* (*o. peg*), a tooth-like projection from the body of the axis or second cervical vertebra of certain mammals and birds; when this process does not coalesce with the body of the axis, as in *Ornithorhynchus* and many reptiles, it is sometimes called the *o. bone*.

B. *sb.* The odontoid process 1854.

Odontology (ǫdǫntǫ·lŏdʒi). 1819. [f. ODONTO- + -LOGY. Cf. Fr. *odontologie.*] The science which treats of the structure or development of the teeth. So **Odontolo·gic, -al** *adjs.*, **-ally** *adv.* **Odonto·logist** 1788.

Odontophoran (ǫdǫntǫ·fŏrăn), *a.* and *sb.* 1877. [f. mod.L. *Odontophora* (see next); see -AN.] *Zool.* A. *adj.* Of or belonging to the *Odontophora*, or division of molluscs having an odontophore. B. *sb.* A mollusc of this group.

Odontophore (odǫ·ntŏfoᵊɹ). 1870. [– Gr. ὀδοντοφόρος bearing teeth; see ODONTO-, -PHORE.] *Zool.* A ribbon-like or strap-like structure covered with teeth, forming the masticatory organ of certain molluscs; the lingual ribbon or 'tongue'. So **Odonto·phoral** *a.* of or pertaining to an o.; also, ODONTOPHORAN *a.* **Odonto·phorous** *a.* possessing an o.

‖**Odoom** (odū·m). 1887. [Ashanti *odúm.*] A W. African timber tree (*Chlorophora excelsa*).

Odorant (ōᵘ·dŏrănt), *a.* Now *rare*. 1465. [– *odorant*, pr. pple. of (O)Fr. *odorer* – L. *odorare* give a smell or fragrance to; see ODOUR, -ANT.] = ODOROUS, ODORIFEROUS.

Odorate (ōᵘ·dŏrėt), *a.* Now *rare*. 1626. [– L. *odoratus*, pa. pple. of *odorare* perfume, scent, f. *odor*; see ODOUR, -ATE².] Scented, fragrant.

Odoriferous (ōᵘdŏri·fĕrəs), *a.* late ME. [f. L. *odorifer* (f. *odor* ODOUR) + -OUS; see -FEROUS.] 1. That bears or diffuses scent or smell; odorous; *rarely*, ill-smelling. 2. *fig.* Sweet; 'fragrant' 1577.

1. The o. & swete vyolettes of all obedyence 1497. Hence **Odori·ferous-ly** *adv.*, **-ness.**

Odorous (ōᵘ·dŏrəs), *a.* 1550. [f. L. *odorus* fragrant (f. *odor* ODOUR) + -OUS.] Emitting a smell or scent; odoriferous; more usu., sweet-smelling; fragrant.

An o. Chaplet of sweet Sommer buds SHAKS. With scents o., spirit-soothing sweets COWPER. Hence **O·dorous-ly** *adv.*, **-ness.**

Odour, odor (ōᵘ·dəɹ). ME. [– AFr. *odour*, OFr. *odor, odur* (mod. *odeur*) – L. *odor, odor-* smell, scent.] 1. That property of a substance that is perceptible by the sense of smell; scent, smell; occas. *spec.* sweet scent; fragrance. 2. *transf.* A substance that emits a sweet smell or scent; a perfume; *esp.* incense, spice, ointment, etc. *arch.* or *Obs.* late ME. 3. *fig.* a. 'Fragrance'; 'savour' ME. b. (*Good* or *bad*) Repute, favour, estimation 1847.

1. The effluvium or odor of Steel SIR T. BROWNE. The lime at dewy eve Diffusing odours COWPER. 2. Thy Myrtles strow, thy Odours burn PRIOR. 3. a. No o. of religious intolerance attaches to it 1873. b. Hartlib was in good odor during the days of the commonwealth 1864. Phr. **Odour of**

sanctity (Fr. *odeur de sainteté*): a sweet or balsamic odour stated to have been exhaled by the bodies of eminent saints at their death, or when exhumed, and held to attest their saintship; hence, *fig.*, reputation for holiness; occas. used ironically. Hence **O·dourless** *a.* without o. or scent.

Odyl (ōu·dil, ǫ·dil). Also **-yle.** 1850. [f. OD[2] + Gr. ὕλη material; see -YL.] = OD[2]. Hence **Ody·lic** *a.* **O·dylism,** the doctrine of o. or od. **O·dylize** *v. trans.* to subject to or affect with o.

Odyssey (ǫ·disi). 1601. [– L. *Odyssea* – Gr. Ὀδύσσεια, f. Ὀδυσσεύς Ulysses, a king of Ithaca.] **1.** One of the two great epic poems of ancient Greece, attributed to Homer, which describes the ten years' wanderings of Odysseus on his way home to Ithaca after the fall of Troy. **2.** *fig.* A long wandering or series of travels 1889. Hence **Odyssean** (ǫdisī·ăn) *a.*

œ (at first, and now often, written separately *oe*) reproduces in modern Eng. the usual L. spelling of Gr. οι, which often in med.L., and in Romanic, was treated like simple *ē*. In words that have come into Eng. through med.L. or Fr., or other Romanic langs., Eng. has usu. a simple *e*, as in *economy*, Fr. *économie*, L. *œconomia*, Gr. οἰκονομία; but in recent words derived immed. from L. or Gr., *œ*, *oe* is usu. retained. This *œ*, being orig. a diphthong and subsequently a long vowel, is usu. pronounced as 'long *e*' (ī), rarely as 'short *e*' (e); when changed to *e*, it submits to the same usages as ordinary *e* from Gr. and L.

Œcist (ī·sist), **œkist** (ī·kist). Also **oikist.** 1846. [– Gr. οἰκιστής f. οἰκίζειν settle (a colony), f. οἶκος house, dwelling.] The founder of an ancient Greek (rarely a modern) colony.

Œcoid (ī·koid). Also **oikoid.** 1892. [f. Gr. οἶκος house; see -OID.] *Biol.* The colourless stroma of a red blood-corpuscle.

‖**Œcology,** etc., earlier var. ECOLOGY, etc.

Œconomic, -nomy: see ECONOMIC, etc.

Œcumenic (īkiume·nik), *a.* 1588. [– late L. *œcumenicus* – Gr. οἰκουμενικός of or belonging to ἡ οἰκουμένη 'the inhabited (earth)', the whole world.] = next.

Œcumenical (īkiume·nikăl), *a.* Also **ecumenical** (now more usual). 1563. [f. as prec. + -AL[1]; see -ICAL.] **1.** *Eccl.* Belonging to or representing the whole (Christian) world, or the universal church; general, universal, catholic; *spec.* applied to the general councils of the early church, and (in mod. use) of the R. C. Church; also assumed as a title by the Patriarch of Constantinople; formerly sometimes applied to the Pope of Rome. **2.** *gen.* Universal, general, world-wide 1607. Hence **Œcume·nicalism,** the theological system or doctrine of the œcumenical councils. **Œcume·nically** *adv.*

Œcumenicity (īkiŭmėni·sĭti). Also **ec-.** 1840. [f. ŒCUMENIC + -ITY; see -ICITY.] Œcumenical character.

‖**Œdema** (idī·mă). Also **edema.** late ME. [– late L. *œdema* – Gr. οἴδημα, -ματ-, f. οἰδεῖν swell.] *Path.* A swelling due to effusion of watery fluid into the intercellular spaces of connective tissue. **Œde·matose** *a.* = next.

Œdematous (idī·m-, ide·mătəs), *a.* Also **oid-, ed-.** 1646. [f. Gr. οἰδηματ- (see prec.) + -OUS.] Pertaining to, of the nature of, or having œdema. Hence **Œde·matously** *adv.*

Œdipean (īdipī·ăn, *U.S.* ed-), *a.* 1621. [irreg. f. ŒDIPUS; see -EAN.] Pertaining to, or like that of, Œdipus; clever at guessing a riddle.

Œdipus (ī·dipŏs, *U.S.* ed-). 1557. [– Gr. Οἰδίπους, Οἰδιποδ-, lit. 'swollen-footed', proper name.] Name of the Theban hero who solved the riddle propounded by the Sphinx; hence, one who is clever at guessing riddles.

I am not Oedipus inough, To vnderstand this Sphynx B. JONS. *Œ. complex*: a psychoanalyst's term for an infantile fixation on the mother.

‖**Œil-de-bœuf** (öydəböf). 1826. [Fr., lit. 'ox-eye'.] **1.** = BULL'S EYE 6. 1849. **2.** Name of a small octagonal vestibule lighted by a small round window in the palace at Versailles; hence *transf.* and *fig.*

Œillade. 1592. Now *arch.* [(In early use anglicized as *oeyliad, eliad, illiad*; now only as Fr.); – Fr. *œillade*, f. *œil* eye, after It. *occhiata*, f. *occhio* eye; see -ADE.] A glance of the eye, *esp.* an amorous glance, ogle. *Lear* IV. v. 25.

Œillet, œlet: see **Oillet.**

Œnanthic (inæ·nþik), *a.* 1838. [– L. *œnanthē* – Gr. οἰνάνθη (f. οἴνη vine + ἄνθη blossom, etc.) a vine-shoot or bud, vine-blossom, vine; see -IC.] *Chem.* Having the characteristic odour of wine.

Œ. acid, an acid (or mixture of acids) $C_{14}H_{26}O_2 + H_2O$, obtained from œnanthic ether. *Œ. ether*, a mobile oily liquid, the source of the peculiar odour of wines, obtained by distillation of wine-lees. So **Œna·nthol,** œnanthylic aldehyde, furnished by the destructive distillation of castor oil. **Œna·nthyl,** $C_7H_{15}O$, the hypothetical radical of œnanthylic acid and its derivatives. **Œnanthy·lic** *a.*, in *œ. acid*, $C_7H_{14}O_2$, a transparent colourless oil, having an unpleasant odour like that of cod-fish. **Œna·nthylate,** a salt of œnanthylic acid.

Œno- (īno), occas. **oino-** (oino), comb. form of Gr. οἶνος wine, as in **Œnology** (inǫ·lŏdʒi), the knowledge or study of wines; so **Œno·lo·gical** *a.*, **Œno·logist. Œnomania** (īnomēi·niă), **oino-** [MANIA], (*a*) dipsomania; (*b*) delirium tremens; hence **Œnoma·niac. Œnometer** (inǫ·mĭtəɹ) [-METER], an alcoholometer. **Œnophilist** (inǫ·filist) [Gr. -φιλος, a lover of wine. **Œnothionic** (-þəi,ǫ·nik) *a.* [Gr. θεῖον sulphur], *Chem.* in *Œnothionic acid*, an acid ($C_2H_6SO_4$) obtained by treating alcohol with sulphuric acid; *ethylsulphuric* or *sulphovinic acid.*

Œnolic (īnǫ·lik), *a.* 1860. [f. Gr. οἶνος wine; see -OL, -IC.] *Chem.* in *Œ. acid*, any of a series of weak tannin-like acids forming the colouring matter of wine.

Œnomel (ī·nomel). Also †**oino-.** 1574. [– late L. *œnomeli* (later *-melum*) – Gr. οἰνόμελι, f. οἶνος wine + μέλι honey.] A mixture of wine and honey, used by the ancient Greeks.

fig. Those memories..Make a better œ. E. B. BROWNING.

O'er (ōəɹ), formerly **ore,** poet. and dial. contr. of OVER, dating from XVI.

Œsophageal (īsofæ·dʒiăl), *a.* Also **eso-.** 1807. [irreg. f. *œsophagus* + -AL[1]; cf. *œsophagal* (XVIII), PHARYNGAL, PHARYNGEAL.] Of, belonging to, or connected with the œsophagus. So **Œso·phagal, Œsopha·gean, Œsopha·giac** *adjs.* in same sense.

Œsophagitis (īsofădʒəi·tis). 1857. [f. ŒSOPHAGUS + -ITIS.] *Path.* Inflammation of the œsophagus.

Œsophago- (īsǫ·făgo), bef. a vowel **œsophag-,** comb. form. of Gr. οἰσοφάγος, ŒSOPHAGUS, as in **Œsophagectomy** (-e·ktŏmi) [Gr. ἐκτομή excision], excision of a portion of the œsophagus. **Œsophago·tomy** [Gr. -τομία], incision into the œsophagus; etc.

Œsophagus (īsǫ·făgŏs). Also **eso-.** late ME. [Earliest form *ysophagus* (XIV–XVI) – med.L. *yso-*, *isophagus* (XIII), cf. OFr. *ysophague* (XIV); the current sp. is mod.L. – Gr. οἰσοφάγος, of which the first element is unknown, and the second appears to be -φαγος eating (see -PHAGOUS), but Aristotle says that the organ gets its name from its length and its narrowness.] The tube or canal extending from the mouth to the stomach, and serving for the passage of food and drink; the gullet.

‖**Œstrum** (ī·strŏm, *U.S.* e·s-). 1656. [med.L., var. of next.] = next.

‖**Œstrus** (ī·strŏs, *U.S.* e·s-). 1697. [L. – Gr. οἶστρος gad-fly, breeze, also sting, hence frenzy.] **1.** *Entom.* A genus of dipterous insects of which the larvæ are parasitic in the bodies of various animals; an insect of this genus or of the family *Œstridæ*; a gad-fly or bot-fly. **2.** *fig.* Something that stings or goads one on, a stimulus; vehement impulse; frenzy 1850. **b.** *Physiol.* A vehement bodily appetite; *spec.* sexual orgasm; the rut of animals 1890.

2. The Impetus, the Lyrical œstrus, is gone E. FITZGERALD.

Of (ǫv, ŏv, əv), *prep.* See also O *prep.*[2] [OE. *of*, orig. stressless var. of *æf* (surviving only as prefix), corresp. to OFris. *af, of*, OS. *af*, MLG., MDu. *ave, af*, OHG. *aba* adv. and prep., MHG. *abe, ab* (Du. *af*, G. dial. *ab*), ON. *af*, Goth. *af* (:– **ab*) :– Gmc. adv. and prep. **ab*(*a*) :– IE. **ap*, **apo*, repr. also by L. *ab*, Gr. ἀπό, Skr. *ápa* away from, down from; cf. A *prep.*[2], O *prep.*[2], OFF.] *General Signification.* The primary sense was *away, away from*, a sense now obsolete. Hence *of* was naturally used in the expression of the notions of removal, separation, privation, derivation, origin or source, starting-point, spring of action, cause, agent, instrument, material, etc. Its scope was enlarged, even in OE., by its employment to render L. *ab, de*, or *ex*, in constructions where the native idiom would not have used it; and by its employment from the 11th c. as the equivalent of Fr. *de*, which not merely represented L. *de* in its prepositional uses, but had come to be the Common Romanic, and so the French, substitute for the genitive case.

I. Of *motion, direction, distance.* **1.** Indicating a point of time, etc. from which something begins or proceeds. *Obs.* exc. in archaic expressions, and in such phrases as *of late, of recent years, of old, of yore*, which have come to have the sense of 'during', 'in the course of' the time indicated. OE. **2.** Away from, out of (see quots.). OE. **b.** *U.S.* In expressing the time: = To *prep.* II. 1 b. 1879.

1. One that I brought vp of a puppy SHAKS. **2.** *North of, south of*, etc., *within* (a mile, an hour, an ace, etc.) *of, wide of, back of* (U.S.), *backwards of* (arch.), *upwards of* (an amount); see these words.

II. Of *liberation* and *privation.* Expressing separation from or of a property, possession, or appurtenance. **1.** In the construction of trans. etc. vbs.; as, *to cure, heal*, etc.; *to cleanse, purge*, etc.; *to free, rid of*, etc.; *to deprive, strip of*, etc. OE. **2.** In the construction of intrans. vbs.; as, *to recover*, †*lack*, etc. *of* ME. **3.** In the constr. of adjs.; as, *whole (of a wound); clean, quit, rid*, etc.; *bare, barren, void*, etc. *of* OE.

1. What little town..Is emptied of its folk this quiet morn KEATS. **2.** I thinke it lacks of twelue SHAKS. **3.** I am poor of thanks SHAKS.

III. Of *origin* or *source.* Indicating the person or thing whence anything originates, comes, is acquired or sought OE.

I hope you will not take it ill of me, that I offer my advice 1755. Of English parents, and of a good English family of clergymen, Swift was born in Dublin THACKERAY. You expect too much of your sister DICKENS. There was one child of the marriage 1885.

IV. Of the *source* or *starting-point of action, emotion*, etc.; *motive, cause, ground, reason.* **1.** Out of, from, as an outcome, expression, or consequence of OE. **b.** *Of oneself*, by one's own motion, spontaneously, unaided OE. **2.** Indicating the cause, reason, or ground of an action, occurrence, fact, feeling, etc. OE. **3.** After an adj. or sb., indicating that which causes or gives rise to the quality, feeling, or action: Because of, on account of. ME.

1. Phr. *Of one's own accord, of choice, course, one's own knowledge, necessity, one's own good pleasure, purpose, right*, etc. **b.** The Goats..would many of them come of themselves to be milked 1707. **2.** All women labouryng of chylde *Bk. Com. Prayer.* How can wee excuse ourselues of negligence? BIBLE *Transl. Pref.* 1611. I am dying of fatigue 1843. **3.** We were dead of sleepe SHAKS. I wish him ioy of her SHAKS. Sick of inaction MACAULAY.

V. Indicating the *agent* or *doer.* **1.** Introducing the agent after a passive vb. (Now usu. repl. by BY, but still in literary use.) OE. **2.** Indicating the doer of something characterized by an adj., as *it was kind of you* (= a kind thing done by you) *to help him.* Used with an adj. and sb., as *a cruel act, an odd thing*, etc.; a qualified pa. pple., as *ill done*, etc.; now only with an adj. alone, as *good, bad, rude, silly*, etc. (Usu. followed by *to do* something.) 1532. **3.** After a sb., expressing the relation of doer, or that of maker or author (= *subjective genitive*) ME.

1. Being warned of God in a dreame *Matt.* 2:12. A wretch forsaken of God and man 1869. **2.** It was most absurd of you to offer it 1887. **3.** He had the secret approbation of his prince FROUDE. The Iliad of Homer. The phonograph of Edison 1902.

VI. Indicating *means* or *instrument* OE.

They live of bread made of pith of trees PURCHAS. It was pouring of rain 1824.

VII. Indicating the *material* or *substance* of which anything is made or consists, or the class of which anything is an example OE.

Will you make an Asse o' me? SHAKS. On Beds of Violets blew MILT. That scamp of a [=

scampish] husband of hers THACKERAY. Living quite as hard a life of it RUSKIN. A distance of over 700 yards 1896. A house of cards. The name of John. The hour of eleven. A state of rest (*mod.*). Phr. *To make much of, the best of.*

VIII. Indicating the *subject-matter of thought, feeling,* or *action,* i.e. that about which it is exercised: Concerning, about, with regard to, in reference to OE. **1.** After vbs. OE. **2.** After sbs. *Obs.* or *arch.* ME. **3.** After adjs. 1489.

1. Thus it fortuned of this adventure LD. BERNERS. Of Mans First Disobedience..Sing Heav'nly Muse MILT. To observe the young prince, and to inform himself of his character 1861. **2.** Mr. Hobbs, in his Discourse of Human Nature ADDISON. **3.** The same observations are true of all other contracts 1886.

IX. Representing an original *genitive dependent on a vb. or adj.* **1.** In the construction of vbs. ME. **2.** In the construction of adjs.

Many of these involve a sb., which may be taken as the subject of the genitive relation; e.g. *hopeful of,* having hope of, *envious of,* having envy of, etc.; others are verbal derivs., e.g. *expressive of* = that expresses ME.

1. Haue merci of me ME. As for the earthquake, I heard not of it 1575. Shakespear..availed himself of the old Chronicles HAZLITT. Resolutions which perhaps no single member in his heart approves of 1888. **2.** The Generous Youth.. studious of the Prize DRYDEN. Symbolic of the place and people too BROWNING.

X. Expressing the relation of the *objective genitive.* **1.** After a vbl. sb. in *-ing* ME. **2.** After what was formerly a vbl. sb. governed by *in* or *a,* but is now identified with a present pple. Now *dial.* or *vulgar.* 1563. **3.** After a noun of action OE. **4.** After an agent-n. ME.

1. For the auoydinge of strife 1551. We must cease throwing of stones either at saints or squirrels RUSKIN. **2.** They being altering of the stage PEPYS. **3.** The betrayal of a secret 1873. **4.** I am a great eater of beefe SHAKS.

XI. Indicating that *in respect of* which a quality is attributed, or a fact is predicated.

Infirme of purpose SHAKS. Of able Body, sound of Limb and Wind DRYDEN. He is.. fifty-three years of age 1843. He is rather hard of hearing 1902.

XII. Indicating a *quality* or other mark, *time, place,* etc., by which a person or thing is characterized. (For OE. genitive; Fr. *de;* = *genitive of quality or description.*)

Sonne be off good chere TINDALE *Matt.* 9:2. Are you of fourescore pounds a yeere SHAKS. One Vice, but of a minute old SHAKS. Four Misses all pretty much of a size RICHARDSON. She was all of a muck of sweat GOLDSM. Is it the hour of prayer? 1816. A boy of fourteen DICKENS. The haven of their desire R. V. *Ps.* 107:30 *margin.*

XIII. In *partitive* expressions; indicating things or a thing of which a part is expressed by the preceding words.

More than any of his predecessours 1523. The fairest of her Daughters Eve MILT. That sacred head of thine MILT. This was..a false step of the ..general's DE FOE. It is what I desire of all things BERKELEY. As though of hemlock I had drunk KEATS. Shakespeare was of [= one of] us BROWNING. He had not been sworn of the Council MACAULAY. Whatever of best he can conceive RUSKIN. My person was indeed of [= one of, something of] the shortest 1878. Had three sons, of whom Thomas married twice 1888. The most dogged of fighters, the most dangerous of enemies 1892. There were only five of us 1902.

XIV. In the sense *Belonging* or *pertaining to*: expressing possession and its converse: 'the owner of the house', 'the house of the owner'. **1.** Belonging to a place, time, or thing OE. **2.** Belonging to a person, etc. ME. **3.** Belonging to an action or the like, as that to which it relates 1534.

1. Men of Nynyue WYCLIF *Matt.* 12:41. Justice of the Kinges Bench. late ME. Don Quixote of the Mancha 1612. He was not of an age, but for all time! B. JONS. Gideon the Judge of Israel 1662. One side of the barricadoes 1756. Companions of his exile 1844. A man of that time THACKERAY. A thing of the near future 1885. **2.** I am glad you understand the reason of it 1559. But yet the pitty of it, Iago SHAKS. The tomb of England's first martyr 1886. **3.** The weather is the solitary topic of conversation 1886.

XV. Indicating a *point or space of time.* **1.** At some time during, in the course of, on. Now only *colloq.,* in *of an evening, of a morning,* and the like. OE. **b.** Occas. the genitival *-s* is retained; perh. often understood as pl. 1740. **2.** During, for (a space of time). (In later use only with a neg.) *Obs.* or *arch.* late ME. **3.** *Of old, of yore, of late, of late years*: In or during the time specified (but prob. orig. in sense I. 1.) late ME.

1. Of a Thursday my dear Father and Mother were marry'd RICHARDSON. **b.** Shut up by himself of nights LAMB. **2.** Not seeing or hearing from him of a long time 1760. **3.** The duties have been very much lightened of late years 1885.

XVI. In *locative* and other obsolete uses. *esp.* **1.** In sense *on. Obs., colloq.,* or *vulgar.* late ME. †**b.** esp. with *side, hand, part,* etc. –1779. **2.** In sense *in.* Mostly *Obs.* late ME. **3.** In sense *with.* Mostly *Obs.* 1523.

1. She might send him of an errand WESLEY. **b.** Six banks of paddles, three banks of a side 1779. **2.** I have just been mortified enough of all conscience GOLDSM. **3.** What do you want of Padre Francisco! LONGF.

XVII. Phr. **1. a.** *Of* followed by a sb. forms attrib. or advb. phrases; as, *of age, of a certainty, of choice, of course, of necessity, of right, of a truth,* etc.: see the sbs. **b.** *Of* followed by an adj. (or advb.) formerly formed advb. phrases [cf. Fr. *de loin, de nouveau,* etc.] *Obs.* exc. in *of a sudden,* or as repr. by worn-down forms in *a-* (*afar, afresh, alight, anew*). ME. **2.** *Of* forms the last element of many prepositional phrases: e.g. *because of; by means of, by reason of; for fear of; in behalf of, in case of, in consequence of, in face of, in lieu of, in respect of, in spite of, instead of; on account of, on behalf of, on condition of, on the point of;* etc. See the sbs.

Of-, *prefix,* the prepositional adv. OF, OFF in comb. corresp. to OS. *af-,* ON. *af-,* Goth. *af-,* OHG. *ab-;* L. *ab-* Gr. ἀπο-, Skr. *apa-,* forming compounds of different ages.

1. In vbs. and their derivs. of Germanic or OE. age, retained in ME., but now obs.

2. In later combs. of OE. and ME. age, the sense of the particle is usu. 'off'. In the 16th c., *of-* in this connection passed imperceptibly into *off-,* the form in later combinations.

Off (ǫf), *adv., prep., adj.,* and *sb.* OE. [orig. the same word as OF, *off* being at first a variant spelling, which was gradually appropriated to the emphatic form, i.e. to the adv. and the prepositional senses closely related to it. *Of* and *off* were not completely differentiated till after 1600.] **A.** *adv.* **I. 1.** To a distance, away, quite away. Also expressing resistance to motion towards; as in *ward off,* etc. **b.** *Naut.* Away from land, or from the ship; also, away from the wind 1610. **c.** *ellipt.* Gone off, just going off. Also *fig.* fallen or falling asleep. 1791. **2.** At a distance, distant. Also in AFAR *off,* FAR *off.* 1500. **b.** *fig.* Distant or remote in fact, nature, character, feeling, thought, etc. *Obs.* or *arch.* (except U.S.). 1555. **3.** Expressing separation from attachment, contact, or position on; as in *to break, cast, cut, put, shake, take off,* etc. OE. **b.** with ellipsis of pa. pple. = *come, cut, fallen off;* esp. *put* or *taken off* as clothes ME. **4.** So as to interrupt continuity or cause discontinuance; as in *break off, leave off, declare off,* etc. ME. **b.** Discontinued; no longer in operation or going on 1752. **c.** *transf.* Of a person: Disengaged, done *with* 1710. **5.** To the end; entirely, completely; as *to clear off, drink off, pay off, polish off, work off* 1440. **6.** In the way of abatement, diminution, or decay; as in *to fall off, cool off, go off;* also, *to be off* 1632. **7.** In all senses, *off* may be followed by *from;* formerly, and still *dial.,* by *of* 1526.

1. Quilp..took himself off DICKENS. **b.** Phr. *Nothing off,* to bring the ship's head nearer to the wind. **c.** I'm off for the Red Sea 1822. **2.** A street or two off FIELDING. **3.** Let it stew..then strain it off 1756. *fig.* Will. laught this off at first ADDISON. **b.** With some of his clothes on, and some off DE FOE. **4.** Upon Saturday..they break off work sooner by an hour 1657. To turn the gas off 1902. **b.** When football is 'off' and cricket not yet 'on' 1901. **c.** It is best to be off wi' the old love, Before you be on wi' the new SCOTT *'Old Song'.* **d.** Away from work or duty, as *a day off* 1893. **5.** To pay off the mortgage 1818. **7.** Stand or syt a good waye of from the fyre 1542. A fall off of a Tree SHAKS.

II. Phr. etc. **1.** BUY, COME, DASH, GET, GO, LOOK, MARK, PALM, PASS, RATTLE, TAKE OFF, etc.: see those verbs. **2.** Used with ellipsis of *come, go, take,* etc. *Off with* = take or put off. ME. **b.** *Off!* = stand off! be off! *Off with you!* = be off! 1594. **3.** *Right off, straight off*: straightway, forthwith. **4.** In *well, ill, better, worse, badly, comfortably off,* etc., *off* = '-circumstanced', '-conditioned', esp. as regards the means of life. Rarely *attrib.* or *adj.* 1733. **5.** *Either off or on,* either one way or another. See also OFF AND ON. 1549.

B. *prep.* **I.** Of motion or direction. **1.** Away from, down from, up from, so as no longer to lie, rest, or lean on OE. **2.** Of source: From the hands, charge, or possession of; esp. with *take, buy, borrow, hire,* and the like. Also expressed by FROM. 1535. **3.** Of material or substance: with *dine, eat,* etc. Now *rare.* 1815. **4.** Of deduction, etc.: From 1833.

1. A man falling off a ladder H. WALPOLE. **2.** She admitted borrowing the 1 *l.* off the plaintiff 1897. **3.** He always..eats a supper off pork steaks, nearly raw 1815. **4.** To get something taken off the price 1902.

II. Of position. **1.** Away from being on; not on; no longer on 1688; *fig.* of a condition; not engaged in or upon, disinclined for 1681. **2.** Distant from (*lit.* and *fig.*) 1627. **b.** *Naut.* To seaward of; opposite or abreast of to seaward; also, away from (the wind). See also OFFSHORE. 1669. **3.** *ellipt.* Opening or turning out of 1845. **4. From off:** = sense I. 1. late ME.

1. As soon as the dew is off the ground 1759. *fig.* To be off one's feed 1816. I have been off my head ever since the blow fell 1894. Phr. *To be off duty.* **2.** Two Miles off this Town ADDISON. **b.** The Stagg Rocks off the Lizard 1726. **3.** Thoroughfares off Cheapside and Cornhill 1851. **4.** Would I might never stirre from off this place SHAKS.

C. *adj.* [The adv. used attrib.] **1.** More distant, farther, far 1856. **b.** *Naut.* Farther from the shore; seaward 1666. **2.** *spec.* **a.** Of horses and vehicles: Right, as opp. to the *near* or left side, on which the driver walks, the rider mounts, etc. Hence *off horse* (of a pair), *off foot, leg, wheel,* etc. (Often hyphened.) 1675. **b.** *Cricket.* Applied to that side of the wicket, or of the field, opposite to that on which the batsman stands 1850. **3.** Lying off from, leading out of the main part 1851. **b.** *Off chance, off-chance,* a remote chance 1861. **4.** Said of a day, evening, season, etc., when one is 'off work', The precise meaning depends on the context. (Occas. hyphened.) 1848. **5.** In ref. to the sale of beer, etc.: Short for 'off the premises', as in *off licence, sale, consumption,* etc. 1891.

1. It is on the 'off' side of the spectator 1902. **b.** Our masts fell all over the off side 1726. **2.** Silver Blaze with his..mottled off fore leg 1894. **3. b.** There was an off-chance he might go back on the whole idea STEVENSON. **4.** That in future all such meetings be held on 'off days' in preference to 'market days' 1897.

D. *sb.* [the adj. used absol. or ellipt.] **1.** The condition or fact of being off 1669. **2.** *Cricket.* = Off side: see C. 2 b. *Comb.* **Off-drive,** a drive to the off. 1857.

Off, *v.* 1882. [From (chiefly colloq. or illiterate) uses of OFF *adv.*; cf. *to* IN, *to* BACK.] **1.** *intr.* To make off. (*illiterate.*) 1895. **2.** *Naut.* Of a ship: To move off from shore. In pr. pple. *offing.* **3.** *To off with,* to take off instantly. *illiterate* or *joc.* 1892.

Off-, *prefix.* In earlier times written *of-* (see OF- *pref.* 2). In verbs, the stress is now usu. upon the root; in the other classes (2–4) on *off-.*

1. with vbs., *off-* (ME. *of-*) enters into quasi-combination, chiefly as a separable particle, like G. *ab-* in *ab-reisen, ab-schreiben,* etc. In the pples. the adv. is still sometimes put first, and is then sometimes hyphened to the vb. Late examples are *off-drive, off-load,* etc.

2. with pres. and pa. pples, forming adjs. (stress on *off*) as *o·ff-bitten, off-standing,* etc.

3. with vbl. sbs. and nouns of action, forming sbs., sometimes concrete (stress on *off*): *o·ff-setting, off-break* (a break off), *off-look,* etc. See also Main words.

4. with other sbs., usu. with the sense 'lying or leading off from the main trunk', etc.: as in *o·ff-branch, off-spur, off-stream.*

Offal (ǫ·făl). late ME. [– (M)Du. *afval* extremities of animals cut off, giblets, trotters, shavings, refuse, f. *af* OFF + *vallen* FALL *v.,* with assim. to the corresp. Eng. elements; cf. G. *abfall* – Du. or LG.] **1.** That which falls, or is thrown off, as chips, dross, etc.; refuse, waste; also *pl.,* scraps of waste stuff or refuse. Now only *techn.* or *dial.* = *o. corn* or *wheat, o. leather, o. wood.* †**b.** In collect. sing. and pl.: Crumbs, leavings; relics, remnants –1786. **2. a.** The parts cut off in dressing the carcase of an animal killed for food; orig., the entrails; now, as a trade term, including the head and tail, the kidneys, heart, tongue, liver, and other parts. †Formerly also in *pl.* late ME. **b.** Contemptuously: Putrid flesh; carrion; also, opprobriously, the bodies or limbs of the slain 1581. **3.** In the fish trade: Low-priced or inferior fish as opp. to those called *prime* 1859. **4.** Refuse in general; rubbish, garbage. Now chiefly *sing.* 1598. **5.** *fig.* Refuse, off-scourings, dregs, scum. Chiefly in *collect. sing.* 1581. **6.** *attrib.* or *adj.* **a.** *lit.* (See preceding senses.) 1596. **b.** *fig.* Outcast; worthless; vile. Now esp. *dial.* 1605.

2. b. Nigh burst With suckt and glutted o. MILT. **3.** Plaice, haddock, cod, ling, etc. come under the technical name of o. 1887. **5.** What trash is Rome? What Rubbish, and what Offall? SHAKS. **6. b.** He's an o. creatur as iver come about the primises GEO. ELIOT.

Off and on, *adv. phr.* (*adj.*) 1535. [OFF *adv.* I. 4, I. 1 c, II. 5.] **1.** With interruption and resumption of action; intermittently, now and again. **2.** *Naut.* On alternate tacks 1608. **b.** Used prepositionally 1708.

1. I..slept off and on..all the way to Crewe 1860. **2. b.** To stand off and on shore 1769.

B. *predicatively* or as *adj.* Sometimes off and sometimes on; intermittent; vacillating 1583.

Off-cast, offcast (ǫ·fkɑst), *ppl. a.* and *sb.* 1571. [f. OFF *adv.* + *cast*, pa. pple. of CAST *v.*] **A.** *ppl. a.* Cast off, rejected. **B.** *sb.* A thing or person that is cast off or rejected (*lit.* or *fig.*). 1587.

Off-chance: see OFF *a.* 3 b.

O·ff co·lour, o·ff-co·lour, *phr.* and *a.* orig. *U.S.* 1860. [OFF *prep.* II. 1.] Of precious stones: Not of the right colour. Hence *fig.* (*a*) Improper, 'doubtful' (*U.S.*); (*b*) out of order, in poor health, 'not up to the mark'.

Off-corn (ǫ·fkǭɹn). 1573. [OFF *adv.* I. 1.] Waste or 'offal' corn.

Offcut (ǫ·fkɒt). 1663. [f. OFF *adv.* 3 (cf. also OFF- *pref.* 3) + CUT *v.*] Something that is cut off. In *Printing*, a piece cut off a sheet to reduce it to the proper size; also, a part cut off the main sheet and folded separately, as in a sheet of duodecimo.

Offence (ǫ̆fe·ns). late ME. Also U.S. **offense.** [ME. *offens, offense* – (O)Fr. *offens* – L. *offensus* annoyance, and (O)Fr. *offense* – L. *offensa* striking against, hurt, wrong, displeasure; both L. forms f. *offens-*, pa. ppl. stem of *offendere*; see next.] †**1.** In Biblical use: Striking the foot against, stumbling. *lit.* and *fig.* (*rare*) –1611. **2.** A stumbling-block; an occasion of unbelief, doubt, or apostasy. late ME. **3.** Attack, assault, late ME. †**4.** Hurt, harm, injury, damage –1705. †**b.** Feeling of being hurt, pain –1674. **5.** The act or fact of offending, wounding the feelings of, or displeasing, another; usu. viewed as it affects the person offended; hence, **b.** Offended or wounded feeling. late ME. †**c.** Disfavour –1601. †**6. a.** Offensiveness. **b.** An offensive object, quality, feature, or state of things; a nuisance. –1660. **7.** A breach of law, duty, propriety, or etiquette; a transgression, sin, wrong, misdemeanour, or misdeed. Const. *against.* late ME. **b.** *spec.* in *Law.* 1780.

1. *Isa.* 8:14. **2.** The o. of the Cross shall be my proudest boast 1865. **3.** Phr. *Arms of o.*, offensive weapons. **4.** *Jul. C.* IV. iii. 201. **b.** They leave an o. in the ear 1674. **5.** As full of Quarrell, and o. As my yong Mistris dogge SHAKS. Unfortunately, o. is usually taken where o. is meant 1882. Phr. *To give o. to*, to offend; *to take o.*, to be offended, to take umbrage; *without o.*, without giving or taking o. **6. b.** *All's Well* II. iii. 270. **7.** Phr. *To commit* (†*do, make*) *an o.*; What o. hath this man made you, Sir? SHAKS. **b.** *Offence, crime*; act of wickedness. It is used as a *genus*, comprehending every crime and misdemeanor; or as a *species* signifying a crime not indictable, but punishable summarily, or by the forfeiture of a penalty WHARTON. Hence **Offe·nceless** *a.* (chiefly *poet.*), without o.; unoffending, inoffensive; **-ly** *adv.*

Offend (ǫ̆fe·nd), *v.* ME. [– OFr. *offendre* or its source L. *offendere*, f. *ob* (see OB- *pref.*) + *-fendere* (only in comps.). Cf. prec.] **I. 1.** To stumble morally; to commit a sin, crime, or fault; to transgress. Const. *against*, †*to*, †*unto*. late ME. †**2.** *trans.* To sin against; to wrong (a person); to violate (a law, etc.) –1651. †**3.** In Biblical use: To be a stumbling-block to (a person); to cause to stumble or sin –1658. †**b.** *intr.* To be caused to stumble –1611.

1. We haue offended agaynst thy holy lawes *Bk. Com. Prayer.* Great wits sometimes may gloriously o. POPE. **2.** *Meas. for M.* III. ii. 16. **3.** Yf thy hande offende the cut hym of TINDALE *Mark* 9:43. **b.** If meate make my brother to o. 1 *Cor.* 8:13.

II. †**1.** *trans.* To attack, assail; also *absol.* to act on the offensive –1744. †**2.** To strike so as to hurt; to give (physical) pain to; to harm –1758. **3.** To vex, annoy, displease, anger; now *esp.* To excite personal annoyance, resentment, or disgust in (any one). (Now the chief sense.) late ME.

3. The rankest compound of villanous smell, that euer offended nostrill SHAKS. *To be offended*: to be displeased, vexed, or annoyed. Now, usu., To feel hurt, take offence; He was highly offended at being passed over 1902. Hence **Offe·ndedly** *adv.* in an offended manner. **Offe·nder,** one who offends; in *Law*, one who commits an OFFENCE (sense 7 b).

†**Offe·nsion.** late ME. [– OFr. *offension* – L. *offensio* injury, offence, stumbling-block, f. *offens-*; see OFFENCE, -ION.] **1.** = OFFENCE 4–7. –1582. **2.** Stumbling; striking against some obstacle –1656. **b.** Spiritual stumbling, or the occasion of it WYCLIF.

Offensive (ǫ̆fe·nsiv), *a.* (*sb.*) 1547. [– Fr. *offensif, -ive* or med.L. *offensivus*, f. as prec.; see -IVE. As *sb.* after Fr. *l'offensive*, after It. *l'offensiva.*] **1.** Pertaining or tending to attack; aggressive; adapted or used for purposes of attack; characterized by attacking. Opp. to *defensive.* †**2.** Hurtful, injurious –1813. **3.** Giving, or of a nature to give, offence; displeasing; annoying; insulting 1576. **4.** Causing unpleasant sensations; now, nauseous, repulsive 1594. †**5.** Of the nature of a transgression –1649. **B.** *sb.* [absol. use of 1.] *The offensive*: the position or attitude of attack; aggressive action 1720.

1. O. and defensive arms GIBBON. **2.** Water Fowl are o. to the Stomach sometimes 1732. **3.** Like an offensiue wife, That hath enrag'd him on, to offer strokes SHAKS. The Prussians are very insolent, and hardly less o. to the English than to the French 1815. **4.** Permitting o. smells to emanate from certain drains 1886. **B.** Haphazard o. is one thing; judicious o. quite another 1879. **Offe·nsive-ly** *adv.*, **-ness.**

Offer (ǫ·fəɹ), *sb.* late ME. [f. OFFER *v.* Cf. Fr. *offre.*] **1.** An act of offering (see OFFER *v.* 3, 4); a presenting for acceptance; a proposal to give or do something. **b.** *ellipt.* A proposal of marriage. *arch.* 1548. **c.** The act of making a bid for something 1550. **d.** The condition of being offered; in *Comm.* the fact of being offered for sale 1794. **2.** *concr.* That which is offered. Now *rare* or *Obs.* 1548. **3.** An essay at doing something, or a show of this; the act of aiming at something, an aim. Now *rare* or *Obs.* 1581. **b.** A knob or bud showing on a stag's antler 1884.

1. A virtuous Woman should reject the first O. of Marriage ADDISON. **b.** It was owing to her never having had an o. W. IRVING. **c.** The proprietor does not bind himself to accept the highest or any o. 1890. **d.** Very little barley on o. 1881. **3.** One sees in it a kind of O. at Modern Architecture ADDISON.

Offer (ǫ·fəɹ), *v.* [OE. *offrian* sacrifice, bring an offering = OFris. *off(a)ria*, OS. *offron* (Du. *offeren*), ON. *offra*; an early Gmc. adoption of L. *offerre* present, offer, bestow (in Christian use, spec. present in sacrifice), f. *ob-* OB- 1 + *ferre* bring. The OE. word was reinforced from (O)Fr. *offrir*, which brought in the primary senses.] **1.** *trans.* To present (something) to God (or to a deity, saint, etc.) as an act of worship or devotion; to sacrifice. Also with *up*. Const. *to* or †simple dative. **b.** *absol.* To present a sacrifice or offering; to make a donation as an act of worship OE. †**2.** *gen.* To give, make presentation of (*spec.* to a superior as an act of homage). Const. as in 1. –1568. **3.** To tender for acceptance or refusal; to hold out (a thing) to a person to take if he will. (The prevailing sense.) late ME. †**b.** with *obj. cl.* To make the proposal, suggest (*that* something be done) –1727. **c.** *absol.* To make a proposal; to make an offer of marriage, to 'propose'. *arch*, 1596. **d.** *Comm.* To present for sale 1632. **4.** with *inf.* To propose, or express one's willingness (to do something), conditionally on the assent of the person addressed. late ME. **5.** To make an attempt to inflict or deal (violence, or injury of any kind) 1530. **b.** with *inf.* To essay, try, endeavour. Now *arch.* or *lit.* 1540. **c.** *intr.* with *at*: To make an attempt at or upon. Now *rare* or *Obs.* 1611. **6.** *trans.* To bring forward or propound 1583. **7.** Of a thing: To present (to sight, notice, etc.); to furnish 1576. **b.** *intr.* for *refl.* To present itself; to occur 1601.

1. After having washed myself, and offered up my Morning Devotions ADDISON. **b.** So many as are disposed, shall o. unto the poore mennes boxe *Bk. Com. Prayer.* **3.** I o. thee three things; chuse thee one of them 2 *Sam.* 24:12. I o. no apology 1875. Phr. *To o. battle*, etc. (cf. sense 5). **4.** I offered to go to the king DE FOE. **5.** Every man offerith hym wronge 1530. **b.** I knocke your costarde if ye o. to strike me 1553. **c.** He did not o. at coming in MRS. CARLYLE. **6.** On this I wish to o. a few remarks 1902. **7.** Each age offers its characteristic riddles 1892. **b.** Taking the first path that offered, we soon galloped out of the forest 1809. Hence **O·fferer.**

Offering (ǫ·fəriŋ), *vbl. sb.* [OE. *offrung*, f. *offrian*; see prec., -ING[1].] **1.** The action of OFFER *v.*; *esp.* sacrifice; oblation. **2.** *concr.* **a.** A sacrifice; an oblation OE. **b.** Something offered to a person; a present, a gift 1440.

1. The kynges that made offryng to oure lord whan he was born. late ME. **2.** Plucking the intrailes of an O. forth SHAKS. *Burnt-, drink-, free-will-, thank-o.*, etc.; see under their first elements. **b.** Crowns of gold, the offerings of grateful cities GIBBON.

Offertory (ǫ·fəɹtəri). late ME. [– eccl. L. *offertorium* place of offering (Isidore), oblation, f. late L. *offert-* (cf. *offertor* offerer III), for *oblat-* (cf. OBLATION); see -ORY[1] and cf. (O)Fr. *offertoire.*] **1.** An anthem sung or said in the Latin Mass immediately after the Creed, while the offerings of the people are made, and the unconsecrated elements are placed on the altar; the Scriptural sentences read or sung in the corresponding part of the English Communion Service (the *o. sentences*). **2.** That part of the Mass or Communion Service at which offerings are made; the offering of these, or the gifts offered; also *spec.* the anticipatory oblation. 1539. **3.** *transf.* †**a.** The offering *of* anything, esp. to God –1684. **b.** Short for *o. money*, properly, money collected at the o.; hence, a collection of money made at any religious service 1862. **4.** *attrib.* 1563.

Off-hand, offhand (see below), *adv.* and *adj. phr.* 1694. [f. OFF *prep.* + HAND *sb.*] **A.** *adv.* (ǫ·fhæ·nd). At once, straightway, forthwith; extempore.

He..would..speak very neatly o. in Latin 1711.

B. *adj.* (*attrib.* ǫ̀·fhæ:nd; *pred.* ǫ̀:fhæ·nd). **1.** Of action, speech, etc.: Done or made off-hand (see A); unpremeditated, extemporaneous, impromptu; free and easy, unstudied, unceremonious 1719. **2.** *transf.* Of persons: Doing or saying things off-hand, unceremonious, curt, brusque 1708.

1. Speaking in his rapid, off-hand way DICKENS. **2.** They are painfully off-hand with me T. HARDY. So **O·ff-ha·nded** *a.* = B.; whence **O:ff-ha·ndedly** *adv.*, **-ness.**

Office (ǫ·fis), *sb.* ME. [– (O)Fr. *office* – L. *officium*, orig. performance of a task, in med.L. also office, rite, divine service; :- **opificium*, f. *opus* work + *facere*, *-fic-* Do *v.*] **1.** Something done toward any one; a service, kindness, attention. (Chiefly with qualification.) late ME. **2.** †**a.** *gen.* Duty towards others; a moral obligation. **b.** Duty attaching to one's station, position, or employment; business; function, one's part. ME. †**c.** Performance of a duty or function, service, etc. –1621. **3.** = FUNCTION *sb.* 3. ME. †**b.** The proper action of an organ or faculty –1656. **4.** A position to which certain duties are attached, esp. a place of trust, authority, or service under constituted authority ME. **b.** In absolute sense: Official position or employment; *spec.* that of a minister of state ME. **c.** Personified, or denoting an office-holder, or office-holders as a body 1602. **5.** A ceremonial duty or service; a religious or social observance; *esp.* obsequies; now chiefly in *last office(s)*. late ME. **6.** *Eccl.* **a.** The daily service of the Roman breviary (more fully *Divine O.*); in the Ch. of England, Morning and Evening Prayer. *To say o.*, to recite the Divine O. **b.** The introit, sung at the beginning of the Mass or Holy Communion; also, the service of the Mass or Holy Communion. **c.** Any occasional service, as the *O. for the Dead, of Baptism*, etc. ME. **7.** An official inquest concerning any matter that entitles the king to the possession of land or chattels: = *Inquest of O.*, INQUEST 1. **8.** A place for the transaction of business; often including the staff, or denominating their department. Applied to the room or department in which the clerical work of an establishment is done; also to that in which the business of any department of a large concern is conducted, as the *booking-o., goods o., inquiry o.*, etc. at a railway station. Formerly used of the court of an eccl. official, as still of a police court (*police o.*). late ME. **b.** Sometimes transferred from the place of business to the company, etc., there established, as in *Assurance* or *Insurance O.* (cf. *the Post O.*) 1646. **c.** (With capital O.) With defining adj., etc.: The quarters of a government department, as the *Colonial, Home O.*, etc.; the staff engaged in carrying on the business of the department. See FOREIGN, HOME, WAR, etc.; also POST OFFICE. 1707. **d. Holy Office** (*R. C. Ch.*): = INQUISITION 3. 1727. **9.** *pl.* The parts of a house specially devoted to household work or service; the kitchen and its appurtenances: often including outhouses, the barns and cowhouses of a farm, etc. 1548. **b.** *sing.* A privy 1727. **10.** *slang.* A hint, signal, or private intimation 1803.

1. I would I could doe a good o. betweene you SHAKS. *Ill o.*, a disservice. **2.** Doe you your o., or giue vp your Place SHAKS. **3.** The o. of the arteries is to lead the blood from the heart into all the parts of the body 1830. **b.** *Oth.* III. iv. 113. **4.** The O. of Corouner. late ME. **b.** Phr. *To take o., leave o.*, etc. *Jack in (out of) o.*: see JACK *sb.*[1] IV. 3. **c.** The insolence of O. SHAKS. **5.** I.. will be first to render thee the decent offices due to the dead SCOTT. **6. c.** The O. ensuing is not to be used for any that die unbaptized *Bk. Com. Prayer.* **7.** *To find an o.*, to return a verdict showing that the king is entitled to the possession of lands or chattels. *O. found*, a verdict having this effect. **8.** His O. keeps your Parchment fates entire POPE. The 'Pall Mall Gazette' had its offices..in Catherine street THACKERAY. **10.** Phr. *To give* (or *take*) *the o.* **11.** attrib. *o.-holder, -seeker.*

†**O·ffice**, *v.* 1449. [f. prec. sb.] **1.** *intr.* = OFFICIATE *v.* 1. –1502. **2.** To appoint to, or place in, office –1763. **3.** *slang.* To 'give the office' to (a person); see prec. sb. 10. –1819.

Office-bearer (ǫ·fisbēᵊ:rəɹ). 1645. One who bears or holds office; an officer.

Officer (ǫ·fisəɹ), *sb.* ME. [– AFr. *officer*, (O)Fr. *officier* – med.L. *officiarius*, f. *officium*; see OFFICE *sb.*, -ER² 2.] †**1.** One to whom a charge is committed, or who performs a function; a minister; an agent –1669. **2.** One who holds an office, post, or place. **a.** One who holds a public, civil, or ecclesiastical office; a servant or minister of the king; a functionary authoritatively appointed or elected to exercise some public, municipal or corporate function. In early use, applied esp. to persons administering law or justice. ME. †**b.** A person engaged in the management of the domestic affairs of a great household or collegiate body, of a private estate –1611. **c.** A person holding the office of president, treasurer, secretary, etc. of a society or institution; an office-bearer 1711. **3.** *spec.* A petty officer of justice or of the peace; a bailiff, catchpole; a constable; †a jailer; †an executioner *c*1500. **4.** A person occupying a position of authority in the army, navy, air force, or mercantile marine; *spec.* one holding a commission in the army, navy, or air force 1565. **5.** A member of a grade in some honorary orders 1846.

1. MILT. *Comus* 218. **2. a.** Medical O. for the Workhouse 1860. The great officers of the household..furnish the king with the first elements of a ministry of state STUBBS. Phr. *O. of (at) arms*, a herald, pursuivant. **b.** *Twel. N.* II. v. 53. **3.** The Theefe doth feare each bush an O. SHAKS. **4.** *General, non-commissioned, staff o.*, etc.; see these words. *O. of the day, Orderly o.*, an officer who is in charge of the arrangements of a military force or post on a given day. *O. of the deck*, the o. temporarily in charge of the deck of a vessel, and responsible for the ship's management. See also FLAG OFFICER, PETTY OFFICER, WARRANT OFFICER. Hence **O·fficership**, the position or rank of an officer; a staff of officers 1775.

Officer (ǫ·fisəɹ), *v.* 1670. [f. prec. sb.] **1.** *trans.* **a.** To furnish with officers. **b.** To command, or direct as an officer: esp. in *pass.* **2.** *transf.* To command; to lead, conduct, manage; to escort 1838.

1. The French must have been very badly officered 1852.

Official (ǒfi·ʃăl), *sb.* ME. [Partly – (O)Fr. *official*, partly subst. use of next (XVI).] **1.** *Eccl.* In the Ch. of Eng., the presiding officer or judge of an archbishop's, bishop's, or archdeacon's court; now usu. styled *O. Principal* ME. **2.** One who holds a public office; as a *government, municipal*, or *railway o.* 1555.

Official (ǒfi·ʃăl), *a.* 1533. [– L. *officialis*, f. *officium* OFFICE; see -AL¹.] †**1.** Performing some office or service; subservient *to* –1667. **2.** Of or pertaining to an office, post, or place 1607. **3.** Of persons: Holding office; employed in some public capacity 1833. **4.** Derived from, or having the sanction of, persons in office; hence, authorized, authoritative 1854. **b.** *Med.* Authorized by the pharmacopœia; officinal 1884. **5.** Having the manner or air usual with persons in office; formal, ceremonious 1882.

1. The Oesophagus,..a part officiall unto Nutrition SIR T. BROWNE. Phr. *O. member*, a bodily organ which serves the needs of a higher organ. **2.** O. documents 1842. *O. arms* (*Her.*), arms representing those of an office or dignity, as those of a city, as used by the Mayor, etc. **3.** The heavy footfall of the o. watcher of the night DICKENS. **4.** The o. definition of a charity 1898. **5.** Handing it with o. solemnity MISS BRADDON. Hence **Offi·cialdom**, o. routine; the domain of officials; officials collectively. (Often in hostile sense.) **Offi·cialism**, official system or routine; officials collectively or in the abstract. (Often = *red tape, red tapeism*). **Offi·cially** *adv.* in an o. manner or capacity. **Offi·cialize** *v.* to render o., give an o. character to; to bring under o. control 1887. **Offi:cializa·tion.**

Officiality (ǒfiʃiˌæ·līti). 1662. [In sense 1 – (O)Fr. *officialité* or med.L. *officialitas* (XIII), in late L. official duty; later f. OFFICIAL *a.* + -ITY.] **1.** The office or dignity of an eccl. official (OFFICIAL *sb.* 1); the court of such, or its quarters. *Obs.* exc. *Hist.* **2.** = OFFICIALISM (*rare*) 1841. **b.** An official post, notice, duty, etc. 1843.

Officiant (ǒfi·ʃiănt). 1740. [– med.L. *officians, -ant-*, subst. use of pr. pple. of *officiare* say Mass; see OFFICIATE *v.*, -ANT.] An officiating priest or minister.

Officiary (ǒfi·ʃiări), *sb.* 1545. [In I – med.L. *officiarius* official, agent, etc. (X). In II – med.L. **officiarium*; see OFFICER, -ARY¹.] **I. 1.** An officer or official (*rare*). **2.** A body of officers; an official body *U.S.* 1888. **II.** A division of a Highland estate, in charge of a ground officer 1799.

Officiary (ǒfi·ʃiări), *a.* 1612. [– med.L. *officiarius* adj.; see prec., -ARY¹.] Of a title, etc.: Attached to or derived from an office held. Of a dignitary: Having a title or rank derived from office.

Officiate (ǒfi·ʃieˈt), *v.* 1631. [– *officiat-*, pa. ppl. stem of med.L. *officiare* perform divine service (IX), f. *officium*; see OFFICE, -ATE³.] To discharge an office. **1.** *intr.* To discharge the office of a priest 1641. †**b.** *trans.* To perform, celebrate (a religious service or rite); to exercise (a spiritual charge or function) –1718. **2.** *intr.* To perform the duties attaching to an office or place, or any particular duty or service 1683. †**3.** *trans.* To perform the duties of (an office or place); to execute, do (a duty or charge, business) –1727. †**4. a.** *trans.* To minister, supply. **b.** *intr.* To minister, be subservient. –1667.

2. His unmarried daughter, who officiated as his private secretary 1841. **4. a.** MILT. *P. L.* VIII. 22. Hence **Officia·tion**, performance of a religious, ceremonial, or public duty. **Offi·ciator.**

‖**Officina** (ǫfisəi·nă). 1835. [L., = workshop, etc.; contr. of *opificina*, f. *opifex* workman.] Workshop; place of production.

Officinal (ǒfi·sinăl), *a.* (*sb.*) 1693. [– med.L. *officinalis*, f. *officina*; see prec., -AL¹. In med.L. *officina* was applied to a store-room of a monastery, in which medicines, etc. were kept.] **1.** Of a herb, plant, drug, etc.: Used in medicine or the arts. Of a medical preparation: Kept in stock in apothecaries' shops; made according to the pharmacopœia. Of a scientific name: Adopted by the Pharmacopœia. (Recently repl. by OFFICIAL *a.* 4 b.) 1720. **2.** Of or pertaining to a shop; 'shoppy' (*rare*) 1751. **B.** *sb.* An officinal drug or medicine 1693. Hence **Offi·cinally** *adv.* in o. use; according to the pharmacopœia.

Officious (ǒfi·ʃəs), *a.* 1565. [– L. *officiosus* (or Fr. *officieux*), f. *officium* OFFICE; see -IOUS.] †**1.** Doing or ready to do kind offices; obliging, kind –1827. †**2.** Dutiful; zealous in doing one's duty –1770. **b.** Of a thing: Serving its purpose, efficacious (*rare*) 1618. **3.** Unduly forward in proffering services; doing, or prone to do, more than is asked or required; pragmatical, meddlesome 1602. †**4.** Pertaining to an office or business, official; hence, formal –1852. **5.** *Diplomacy.* As opp. to *official*: Having an extraneous relation to official matters or duties; having the character of a friendly communication, or informal action, on the part of a government or its representatives 1852.

1. They were tolerably well-bred; very o., humane, and hospitable BURKE. †*O. lie* (L. *mendacium officiosum*): a lie told as an act of kindness to further another's interests. **2.** The o. daughters pleas'd attend AKENSIDE. **3.** Wolsey, that slye, o., and too Lordly Cardnall 1602. One of those o., noisy little men who are always ready to give you unasked information DISRAELI. **5.** Feelers put out in the o. press 1866. Hence **Offi·cious-ly** *adv.*, **-ness.**

Offing (ǫ·fiŋ). 1627. [perh. f. OFF *adv.* + -ING¹.] **1.** The part of the visible sea distant from the shore or beyond the anchoring ground. **2.** Position at a distance off the shore 1688. Also *transf.*

1. At Two this day..the Generals discovered Trump..in the Offen 1666. **2.** Phr. *To gain, get, keep, make, take an o.*

Offish (ǫ·fiʃ), *a. colloq.* 1842. [f. OFF *adv.* + -ISH¹. Cf. *uppish*.] Inclined to keep aloof; distant in manner. Hence **O·ffishness.**

Offlet (ǫ·fˌlėt). 1838. [f. OFF- 3 + LET *v.*¹; cf. *inlet, outlet*.] A channel or pipe for letting water off.

Off licence: see OFF C. 5.

Off-load (ǫ·fˌlōᵘd), *v. S. Afr.* 1850. [f. OFF- 1 + LOAD *v.*, after Du. *afladen*. Cf. *outspan*.] *trans.* To unload.

Offprint, off-print (ǫ·fˌprint). 1885. [f. OFF- 3 + PRINT; cf. Du. *afdruk*.] A separately printed copy of an article, etc., which orig. appeared as part of a larger publication.

O·ff-re:ckoning. Usu. in *pl.* 1687. [f. OFF- 3 + RECKONING *vbl. sb.* Cf. Du. *afreckening*, G. *abrechnung* deduction, settlement of accounts.] A deduction; formerly, in the British army, the name of a special account between the government and the commanding officers of regiments in ref. to the clothing, etc. of the men.

O·ffsa:ddle, off-saddle, *v. S. Afr.* 1863. [f. OFF- 1 + SADDLE *v.*, after Du. *afzadelen*.] *trans.* To take the saddle off (a horse) for a rest, feeding, etc.; also *absol.*; *transf.* to make a break in a journey.

Offscouring (ǫ·fskauᵊ:riŋ). 1526. [OFF- 3.] **1.** The action of scouring off 1896. **2.** That which is scoured off; filth or defilement cleaned off and cast aside; refuse, rubbish (*lit.*, in *pl.* of things, and *fig.* in *collect. sing.* (after 1 Cor. 4:13) or *pl.* of persons) 1526.

2. *fig.* White people, who are generally the dregs and offscourings of our colonies 1775.

Offscum (ǫ·fskʊm). 1579. [f. OFF- 3 + SCUM *sb.*] That which is skimmed off; scum, dross, refuse. Also *fig.* that which is rejected as vile or worthless (usu. of persons, in *collect. sing.* or *pl.*).

Offset (ǫ·fset), *sb.* 1555. [f. OFF- 3 + SET. Cf. SET-OFF.] **1.** The act of setting off; outset, start. **2.** A short lateral offshoot from the stem or root of a plant, serving for propagation. Also *transf.* and *fig.* 1664. **b.** *spec.* A person or tribe, springing collaterally from a specified family or race; a 'scion' 1711. **c.** A 'spur' of a mountain range 1833. **3.** Something that 'sets off' something else 1675. **4.** Something 'set off' against something else; anything that counterbalances, compensates, or makes up for something else; a set-off 1769. **5.** *Surveying.* A short distance measured perpendicularly from a main line of measurement, as from the straight line joining the two ends of an irregular boundary, to a point (*e.g.* an angle) in the boundary, in order to calculate the area of the irregularly bounded part 1725. **6.** *Arch.* A horizontal or sloping break or ledge on the face of a wall, pier, etc., formed where the portion above is reduced in thickness 1721. **7.** A bend made in a pipe to carry it past an obstruction. **8.** *Printing*, etc. The accidental transfer of undried ink from one surface to another, esp. to an opposite page. 1888. **b.** (Also *o. process*, etc.), a method of printing from a rubber surface to which a drawing or design has been transferred 1918.

Comb. **o.-pipe:** cf. 7 above; **-sheet** (*Printing*), = *set-off sheet*; see SET-OFF; **-staff** (*Surveying*), a rod used in measuring offsets.

Offset (ǫ·fse·t), *v.* Chiefly *U.S.* 1792. [f. OFF- 1 + SET *v.*] **1.** *trans.* To set off as an equivalent *against* something else. Also said of the equivalent: To counterbalance, compensate. **2.** *intr.* To spring, branch off, or project as an offset *from* something else 1853. **b.** *trans.* To furnish with an offset (see prec. 7) 1889. **3.** *Printing.* = *set off* j (SET *v.*) 1888.

Offshoot (ǫ·fʃūt). 1674. [OFF- 3.] A lateral shoot or branch from the stem or main part of a plant, or anything material, as a mountain-range, a street 1814. **b.** *fig.* A collateral branch or descendant from a (specified) family or race 1710. **c.** A derivative 1801.

1. Stunted offshoots of felled trees 1814. **b.** An o. of the great house which had already given Dukes to Florence 1874.

Off shore, o·ff-sho·re, *adv. phr.* (*adj.*) 1720. [f. OFF *prep.* + SHORE *sb.* Opp. to IN SHORE.] **1. a.** In a direction away from the shore. **b.** At some distance from the shore 1745. **2.** *adj.* (*attrib.* ǫ·fˌʃōᵊɹ). **a.** Moving or directed away from the shore 1839. **b.** Situated, existing, or operating at a distance from the shore 1883.

1. a. The wind blowing off shore DE FOE. **2. a.** The off-shore tack 1860. **b.** The off-shore fisheries 1883.

Off side, o·ff-si·de, *phr.* 1845. [f. OFF *prep.* + SIDE.] Away from one's own side; on the wrong side, *i.e.* in Football, Hockey, etc., between the ball and the opponent's goal (the specific meaning varying in the different games). Also *attrib.* or as *adj.* (ǫ·fˌsəid).

Offspring (ǫ·fˌspriŋ). [OE. *ofspring*, f. *of* OF 'from' + *springan* SPRING. A formation peculiar to Eng.] **1.** Children or young (more widely, descendants); progeny, issue. Applied without indef. art. to a number, or to one; with indef. art. always collective, as *a numerous o.* (Rarely of plants.) **b.** Rarely in *pl.*: †(*a*) = children or descendants; (*b*) in collective sense = progenies, broods, families 1548. **c.** *fig.* In relation to place of birth or origin 1695. **2.** *fig.* Produce, product; issue, outcome, result; 'fruit' 1609. **†3.** Descent, derivation, origin –1715. **†b.** *transf.* Family, race, stock; ancestry –1612. **†4.** Source, original –1604.

1. c. And there Euphrates her soft Off-spring arms DRYDEN. **2.** The law of nations . . is the o. of modern times 1826.

Offtake (ǫ·fˌtēᶦk). 1793. [f. OFF- 3 + TAKE *sb.*] **1.** The action of taking off; *spec.* the taking of commodities off the market 1885. **2.** A deduction 1793. **3.** A channel by which, or place where, something is taken off 1839.

Offu·scate, *ppl. a.* Now *rare.* 1603. [var. of earlier OBFUSCATE; see next.] = OBFUSCATE *ppl. a.*

Offu·scate, *v.* Now *rare.* 1586. [Assimilated var. (see OB- 1) of OBFUSCATE *v.*] = OBFUSCATE *v.* So **Offusca·tion** = OBFUSCATION 1502.

Offward (ǫ·fwǫɹd), *adv.* 1563. [f. OFF *adv.* + -WARD.] In a direction or position off or away from something; *spec.* (*Naut.*) away from the shore. Also quasi-*sb.* in phr. *to the o.* 1600.

Oft (ǫft), *adv.* and *a.* Now *arch.*, *poet.*, or *dial.*; repr. in ordinary use by OFTEN. [OE. *oft* = OFris. *ofta*, OS. *oft(o*, OHG. *ofto* (G. *oft*), ON. *opt*, *oft*, Goth. *ufta*; Gmc. adv. of obscure origin.] **A.** *adv.* = OFTEN A. Compared *ofter* (*arch.* and *dial.*), †*oftest*. **b.** Usu. hyphened to a ppl. adj. used *attrib.*, as *oft-told*. (In this construction still frequent.) 1586.

Many's the time and o. GOLDSM. Much in sorrow, o. in woe, Onward, Christians, onward go! 1806.

†B. *adj.* = OFTEN B. (Chiefly with *vbl. sbs.*) –1671.

Warn'd by o. experience MILT.

Often (ǫ·f'n), *adv.* and *a.* ME. (first in northern texts *c*1300). [ME. *oftē* (XII) extended form of OFT, and by further extension (prob. after *selden* SELDOM) *often* (*oftin* XIV).] **A.** *adv.* **1.** Many times; frequently. Opp. to *seldom*. Compared *oftener*, *oftenest*. **2.** In many instances; in cases frequently occurring. late ME. **3.** Usu. hyphened to a ppl. adj. used *attrib.* 1601.

1. Seldom contented, o. in the wrong DE FOE. **2.** A good character is o. worth [= it often happens that a good character is worth] a great deal of money JEVONS. **3.** At often-recurring intervals 1877.

B. *adj.* (The adv. used with sbs.) Done, made, happening, or occurring many times; frequent. Now *arch.* 1450.

Vse a lytell wyne for thy stommakes sake, and thyne o. diseases TINDALE 1 *Tim.* 5:23. *Comb.* With nouns denoting time, as **-while, -s** = OFTENTIME, -S. Hence **O·ftenness,** frequency (now *rare*).

O·ftentime, *adv. rare.* late ME. [An extended form of OFT-TIME.] Variant of next. Also *adj.*

Oftentimes (ǫ·f'nˌtəimz), *adv.* Now only *arch.* or *literary.* late ME. [An extended form of earlier OFT-TIMES.] Many times; frequently, often.

O·ft-ti:me, *adv. Obs.* or *arch.* late ME. [f. OFT *adv.* + TIME, replacing obs. *oftsithe.*] = next. Also *adj.*

Oft-times, ofttimes (ǫ·ftˌtəimz), *adv.* Now *arch.* and *poet.* late ME. [f. OFTEN + pl. of TIME *sb.*, after †*oftsithes.*] = OFTENTIMES.

Ogdoad (ǫ·gdoˌĕd). 1621. [– late L. *ogdoas*, *-ad-* – Gr. ὀγδοάς, -αδ-, f. ὄγδοος eighth, ὀκτώ eight; see -AD.] **a.** The number eight. **b.** A group, set, or series of eight; *spec.* in *Gnosticism*, a group of eight divine beings or æons; also, the heavenly region.

Ogee (ōᵘdʒī·, ōᵘ·dʒī). Occas. written **OG** or **O.G.** late ME. [prob. reduced form of *ogive*, perh. through the pl. form *ogi(v)es.*] *Arch.* and *Joinery.* **†1.** = OGIVE 1. –1611. **2.** A moulding consisting of a continuous double curve, convex above and concave below; a cyma reversa. In cross-section, its outline is a sort of *S* shape. 1677. **b.** Any curve or line having this form 1851. **c.** Short for *o. arch*, *plane* 1667.

attrib., etc., as **o. arch,** an arch formed by the union of two contrasted ogees meeting at its apex; so **o. doorway, o. window,** etc., a doorway, etc. having the form of an o. arch; **o. moulding** = OGEE 2; **o. plane,** a joiner's moulding-plane with an o. sole. Hence **Ogee'd, ogee·d** *a.* furnished with an o. or ogees; having the form of an o.

Ogham, ogam (ǫ·găm). 1627. [– OIr. *ogam*, *ogum* (gen. *oguim*), mod.Ir. *ogham*, pl. *-uim*, Gael. *oghum*, a name conn. with its mythical inventor *Ogma.*] **1.** An alphabet of twenty characters used by the ancient British and Irish; the system of writing, or an inscription written, in such characters; also, one of the characters themselves 1677. **2.** An obscure mode of speaking used by the ancient Irish. **3.** *attrib.*, as *o. alphabet*, *inscription*, etc. 1784. Hence **Oghamic, ogamic** (ǫ·gămik, ogæ·mik) *a.* of or pertaining to o.; consisting of oghams 1876. var. **Ogmic.**

Ogival (oᵘdʒəi·văl, ōᵘ·dʒivăl), *a.* (*sb.*) 1841. [f. next + -AL¹ or – Fr. *ogival.*] **1. a.** Having the form or outline of an ogive or pointed ('Gothic') arch. **b.** Characterized by ogives 1855. **B.** *sb.* An ogival head of a shot 1868.

Ogive (ōᵘ·dʒəi·v, oᵘdʒəi·v). ME. [– Fr. *ogive*, of unkn. origin.] *Arch.* **1.** The diagonal groin or rib of a vault, two of which cross each other at the centre. **2.** A pointed (= 'Gothic') arch 1841. **3.** *attrib.*, as *o. window*, etc. 1842. Hence **Ogived** *a.* consisting of an o. or ogives; having the form of an o. or ogee.

Ogle (ōᵘ·g'l), *sb.* 1700. [f. or cogn. w. the vb.] **1.** An eye; usu. *pl.* the eyes. Orig. *Vagabonds' cant*, in early 19th c. in *Pugilistic slang*, etc. **2.** An amorous glance; an ocular invitation to advances 1711.

Ogle (ōᵘ·g'l), *v.* 1682. [orig. cant; prob. of LDu. origin; cf. LG. *oegeln*, frequent. of *oegen* look at, also early mod.Du. *oogheler*, *oegeler* flatterer, *oogen* cast sheep's eyes at. See -LE.] **1.** *intr.* To cast amorous or coquettish glances. **b.** *trans.* To turn or bring by ogling 1712. **2.** *trans.* To eye amorously; to 'make eyes' at 1698. **3.** To keep one's eyes upon; to eye 1820.

1. He sighs and ogles so, that it would do your heart good to see him 1713. **2.** As soon as the Minuet was over, we ogled one another through our Masques ADDISON. **3.** He stood ogling the wreck through his binocular 1891. Hence **O·gler. O·gling** *vbl. sb.* the throwing of amorous or languishing glances; also the glance itself.

Ogpu (ǫ·gpu). 1927. [Made up of the initials of *Otdelénie Gosudárstvennoĭ Politicheskŏĭ Uprávȳ* Department of State Political Directorate.] A state department in the Russian Republic, taking the place of the Cheka.

-ography: the element -GRAPHY preceded by the connective -o-; used also as *sb.* like -OLOGY.

Ogre (ōᵘ·gəɹ). 1713. [– Fr., (first used by Perrault in his *Contes*, 1697); of unknown origin.] In folk-lore and fairy tales, a man-eating monster, usu. represented as a hideous giant; hence, a man likened to such a monster.

He's the most hideous, goggle-eyed creature, . . quite an o. DICKENS. Hence **O·greish, o·grish** *a.* resembling, or characteristic of, an o. **O·greism,** the character or practices of ogres. **O·gress¹,** a female o.

Ogress². 1572. [perh. alt. of *oglys* 'gonestonys', i.e. gun-stones (Book of St. Albans, 1486), of unkn. origin.] *Her.* A representation of a cannon-ball as a bearing; = PELLET *sb.* 3.

Ogygian (odʒi·dʒiăn), *a.* 1834. [f. L. *Ogygius*, Gr. Ὠγύγιος (f. personal name Ὠγύγης) + -AN.] Of or pertaining to the mythical Attic or Bœotian king Ogyges; of obscure antiquity; of great age.

O. deluge, a famous flood said to have taken place in the reign of Ogyges.

Oh (ōᵘ), *int.* (*sb.*) 1534. [var. of O – Fr. *oh*, L. *oh.*] An exclam. expressing emotion of various kinds; now chiefly used when the exclam. is detached from what follows, and esp. as a cry of pain or terror, or in expression of shame, derisive astonishment or disapprobation, in which case it is often repeated as *Oh! oh!* 1548. **B.** *sb.* The exclam. *Oh*, as a name for itself. So *Oh dear*, *Oh fie*, etc.

Oh sleep! it is a gentle thing COLERIDGE. **B.** Never-ending ohs and ahs 1820. Hence **Oh** *v. intr.* to exclaim 'Oh!'; *trans.* to greet with 'Oh!' Also **Oh-oh** *v.*

Ohm (ōᵘm). 1870. [f. Georg Simon *Ohm*, German physicist (1787–1854), who determined mathematically the law of the flow of electricity (*Ohm's law*).] *Electr.* The unit of electrical resistance; the resistance of a column of mercury of a constant section of one square millimetre and of a length of 106·3 centimetres, at the temperature of melting ice. Hence **Oh·mad** = OHM 1866; **Ohm-a·mmeter,** an instrument for measuring electrical current and resistance; **Oh·mic** *a.*, pertaining to or measured by the o.; **Oh·mmeter,** an instrument for measuring electrical resistance in ohms.

Oho (ohōᵘ·), *int.* ME. [Combining O with HO *int.*¹] An exclam. expressing surprise, taunting, exultation, etc.

Ohone (ohōᵘ·n), *int.* (*sb.*) 1480. [– Gael., Ir. *ochòin*. Cf. OCH.] Oh! alas! A Sc. and Ir. exclam. of lamentation.

Oh yes: see OYEZ.

-oid (oid, oˌid), *suffix* – mod.L. *-oides*, Gr. -οειδής, i.e. *-o-* of prec. element or connective + -ειδής 'having the form of', 'like', f. εἶδος form; cf. L. *-i-formis* (see -FORM). In Eng. the prevalent pronunc. is with the diphthong (oi) as in *void*. Largely used in scientific terms, formed on Gr. (rarely L.) words. These are primarily adjs.; but also (as occas. in Gr.) sbs.

Examples:—(adjs.) Anat. *adenoid, thyroid*, etc.; Zool. *anthropoid, simioid*, etc.; Bot. *ovoid, scorpioid*.

(sbs.) Math. *cycloid, rhomboid, spheroid*, etc.; Astron. *asteroid*; Chem. *albuminoid, alkaloid*, etc.; Bot. *fucoid*; Zool. *zooid*.

-oidal. When the form in *-oid* is a sb., an adj. is formed in *-oidal* (see -AL[1]), as *conchoidal, rhomboidal*; so *alkaloidal, asteroidal, fucoidal*, etc.

‖**Oidium** (o,i·diŏm). 1836. [mod.L., f. Gr. ᾠόν egg + -ιδιον dim. suffix; see -IUM.] *Bot.* Link's name for a genus of parasitic fungi, comprising species now viewed as the conidial stage of various fungi of the family *Erysipheæ*; they cause various diseases. *spec.* The species *O. tuckeri* (*Erysiphe tuckeri*), or the disease of the vine produced by this; grape-mildew.

Oil (oil), *sb.* [ME. *oli(e, oile* – AFr., ONFr. *olie*, OFr. *oile* (mod. *huile*) – L. *oleum* (olive) oil; see OLIVE.] **1.** A substance having the following characters (or most of them): viz. those of being liquid at ordinary temperatures, of a viscid consistence and characteristic unctuous feel, lighter than water and insoluble in it, soluble in alcohol and ether, inflammable, chemically neutral. **a.** without *an* or *pl.*; orig. usu. = OLIVE-OIL ME. **b.** with *an* and *pl.*, indicating a kind or different kinds. late ME.

The oils are divided into three classes: (1) *Fatty* or *fixed oils* (see FATTY, FIXED), of animal or vegetable origin, which are chemically triglycerides of fatty acids, and produce a permanent greasy stain on paper, etc.; these are either *drying oils*, which by exposure absorb oxygen and thicken into varnishes, or *non-drying oils*, which by exposure ferment; they are used as lubricants, as illuminants, in making soap, etc. (2) *Essential* or *volatile oils* (see ESSENTIAL *a.*), chiefly of vegetable origin, which are acrid and limpid, and form the odoriferous principles of plants, etc.; they are hydrocarbons, or mixtures of hydrocarbons with resins, etc., and are used in medicine, perfumery, and (occas.) in the arts. (3) *Mineral oils*, which are mixtures of hydrocarbons, and are used chiefly as illuminants.

†**c.** *Old Chem.* One of the supposed five 'principles' of bodies –1741. **2.** In the names of the various kinds, unlimited in number. See below. late ME. **3.** In fig. and allusive uses. ME. **4.** = OIL-COLOUR. Often in pl. *oils*. 1663. **b.** *colloq.* An oil-painting. Chiefly in *pl.* 1890. **5.** *colloq.* abbrev. of OILSKIN. Chiefly in *pl.* 1891.

1. (*a*) The five foolish virgins..begd oyle JER. TAYLOR. *Holy o.*: o. used in religious or sacred rites, as the anointing of priests or kings, extreme unction, etc. **2.** (*a*) With the name of the source following *oil of*, as *o. of almonds, amber, eucalyptus, lavender*, etc. (*b*) With name of source, etc., preceding *oil*, as *cod-liver o., cottonseed o., linseed o., olive o.*, etc.; *hair o., salad o.* (see these words); **animal o.,** any o. obtained from an animal body; spec. *Dippel's animal o.*, an oil prepared by distillation from stag's horns, etc. and used in medicine; **dead o.** (see DEAD); **sweet-o.** = OLIVE-OIL. **3.** Oile of gladnesse. late ME. Phr. *To add* (*put*) *o. to the fire, flames*, etc., to aggravate fury, passion, etc.; to 'add fuel to the flame'. *To smell of o.*, to bear marks of laborious study; *to burn the midnight o.*, to study late into the night. *To pour o. upon the waters*, etc., to appease disturbance; in allusion to the effect of o. on water in agitation. *To strike o.* (U.S.), *lit.* to reach the o. (petroleum) in sinking a shaft for it; hence *fig.* to hit upon a means of growing rich quickly. †*O. of angels* (ANGEL 4), gold employed in gifts or bribes; *o. of birch, hazel, holly, hickory o., strap o.*, a flogging (with a birch-rod, hazel-stick, etc.).

attrib. and *Comb.* **1.** General: as *o.-bath, -box, -brush*, etc.; *o.-tank, -vat, -vessel*, etc.; *o.-factory, -well*, etc.; *o. gas, spirit*; *o.-engine, -lamp, -motor, -stove*; *o.-bearing, -refining* adjs.; *o.-atomizer, -refiner*, etc.; *o.-dried* (dried of o., having the o. dried up), *-driven, -fed*, adjs.; *o.-yellow* adj.

2. Special: **o.-beetle,** a beetle of the genus *Meloe*, which exudes an oily liquid when alarmed; **-bird,** name for various birds yielding o., esp. the GUACHARO, *Steatornis caripensis*: **-bush** [BUSH *sb.*[2]], a socket containing o. in which an upright spindle runs; **-can; -cellar,** (*a*) a cellar for storage of o.; (*b*) a small reservoir for o. in a piece of machinery; **-cup,** a small vessel to hold o. for lubricating, either portable, or attached to the machinery and acting automatically; **-derrick,** a derrick or frame used in boring for o.; **-field,** an area occupied by oil-bearing strata; **-garden,** a garden of olives grown for o.; **-gauge** (*-gage*), an oleometer; **-gland,** a gland which secretes o.; *spec.* the uropygial or coccygeal gland in birds, which secretes the o. with which they preen their feathers; **-meal,** ground linseed cake; **-paint** = OIL-COLOUR; **-painting,** (*a*) the action, or art, of painting in oils; (*b*) a picture painted in oils; **-palm,** a species of palm yielding o.; esp. *Elæis guineensis*, which yields palm-oil; **-paper,** paper made transparent or waterproof by soaking in o.; **-press,** an apparatus for expressing o. from fruits, seeds, etc.; so **-presser; -sand,** a stratum of sandstone yielding o.; **-shark,** any species yielding o., esp. *Galeorhinus zyopterus* of California; **-sheet,** a sheet made of oil-skin or oil-paper; **-spring,** a spring of mineral o. (with or without admixture of water); **-stock,** *Eccl.* a vessel for containing holy o.; **-test, -tester,** a contrivance for ascertaining the flash-point, burning-point, lubricating quality, etc., of oils. See also OIL-BAG, etc. Hence **Oilless** (oi·l,lės) *a.* containing no o.; not lubricated, or not requiring to be lubricated, with o. 1787.

Oil, *v.* late ME. [f. prec.] **1.** *trans.* †**a.** = ANOINT *v.* 2. –1764. **b.** To smear or lubricate with oil 1440. **2.** *fig.* 1602. **3.** To convert (butter or grease) into oil by melting 1759. **b.** *intr.* To become of the consistency of oil 1741. **4.** *intr.* Of a ship: To take in a supply of oil 1906.

1. b. Phr. *To o. the wheels* (also *fig.*). *To o. out* (in *Painting*), to moisten (for retouching) with a thin coating of oil. **2.** Error, oiled with Obsequiousness,..has often the Advantage of Truth 1716. *To o. the hand* (*fist*), to bribe. Also with the person as obj. *To o. one's tongue*, to adopt or use flattering speech. **3. b.** Take Care the Butter do not o. 1741.

Oi·l-bag. 1713. **a.** A sac or gland in an animal which secretes or contains oil. **b.** A bag for expressing oil. **c.** A bag to contain oil for any purpose.

Oilcake (oi·l,kēⁱk). 1757. The cake or mass of rapeseed, cottonseed, linseed, etc., which is left after the oil has been expressed; used as a fattening food for cattle or sheep, or as manure.

Oilcloth (oi·l,klǫþ). 1697. A general name for any fabric prepared with oil, so as to be rendered waterproof. **a.** = OILSKIN. **b.** A canvas painted or coated with a preparation containing a drying oil, used for table-cloths, floor-cloths, etc. 1803.

Oi·l-co:lour. 1539. 'Colour' or paint made by grinding a pigment in oil. (Chiefly in *pl.*)

Oiled (oild), *ppl. a.* 1535. [f. OIL *v.* + -ED[1].] **1.** Smeared, or lubricated with oil 1550. **b.** Soaked, ground, or preserved in oil 1535. **c.** Impregnated with oil, as *o. cloth* = OILCLOTH, *o. silk*, etc. 1624. **2.** Melted into oil 1769. **3.** Having taken alcohol; drunk (*slang*) 1916.

Oiler (oi·ləɹ). 1846. [f. OIL *sb.* or *v.* + -ER[1].] **1.** One who, or that which, oils. Also *fig.* **2.** An oil-driven vessel 1915.

Oilery (oi·ləri). 1864. [f. OIL *sb.* + -ERY; cf. Fr. *huilerie*.] The business, establishment, or stock of an oilman.

Oillet (oi·lėt). late ME. [– OFr. *oillet* (mod. *œillet*), dim. of *oil, oeïl* eye. Repl. by EYELET.] †**1.** = EYELET *sb.* 1. –1627. **2.** = EYELET *sb.* 2. Now only *Hist.* late ME. **3.** *attrib.*, as *o.-hole* = EYELET-HOLE. 1530.

Oilman (oi·lmæ̆n). 1440. **1.** A manufacturer of or dealer in oil. **2.** One who oils machinery.

Oi·l-mill. late ME. A machine in which seeds, fruits, etc., are crushed or pressed to extract oil; a factory where oil is expressed by such machines.

Oi·l-nut. 1707. A name for various nuts and large seeds which yield oil; also for the plants producing them.

spec. **a.** the Castor-oil Plant, *Ricinus communis*; **b.** the N. American Butternut, *Juglans cinerea*; **c.** the N. American Buffalo-nut or Elk-nut; **d.** the Oil Palm, *Elæis guineensis*.

Oi·l-seed. 1562. Any seed yielding oil, e.g. linseed, rapeseed, mustard-seed.

spec. **a.** that of the Castor-oil Plant, *Ricinis communis*; **b.** that of *Guizotia oleifera*, an E. Indian Composite plant, the oil of which is used for lamps and as a condiment; **c.** that of the False Flax, *Camelina sativa* (*Siberian oil-seed*); **d.** cottonseed (also attrib. *oil-seed cake*).

Oi·lskin. 1812. Cloth made waterproof by being treated with oil; a piece, or garment, of such cloth 1816. **b.** Often *attrib.* (made of oilskin) 1812.

Oilstone (oi·l,stōᵘn), *sb.* 1585. A smooth and fine-grained whetstone, the rubbing-surface of which is lubricated with oil; the stone of which such whetstones are made. Hence **Oi·lstone** *v. trans.* to sharpen on an o.

Oi·l-tree. 1611. Name for trees, etc., yielding oil; as the Castor-oil plant, the Illupi, and the Oil Palm.

Oily (oi·li), *a.* (*adv.*) 1528. [f. OIL *sb.* + -Y[1].] **1.** Of or of the nature of oil; having the consistence or appearance of oil. *O. acid* = FATTY acid. **2.** Containing oil; smeared or covered with oil; greasy, fat 1597. **3.** *fig.* 'Smooth' in manner or (esp.) speech; subservient; bland, unctuous; 'slippery' 1598.

2. This oyly Rascall is knowne as well as Poules SHAKS. He mopped his o. pate BROWNING. **O. grain, †corn,** the seed of *Sesamum orientale*. **3.** What had this o. scoundrel..to do with it? 1894. Hence **Oi·lily** *adv.* **Oi·liness.**

Oino-: see ŒNO-.

†**Oint,** *v.* ME. [– OFr. *oint*, pa. pple. of *oindre* :– L. *ung(u)ere*; see ANOINT.] *trans.* = ANOINT *v.*

Ointment (oi·ntmĕnt). [alt., after OINT *v.*, of earlier †*oi(g)nement* – OFr. *oignement* :– pop. L. **unguimentum*, f. L. *unguentum* UNGUENT; see prec., -MENT.] An unctuous preparation, used chiefly for application to the skin; an unguent.

O.K. Orig. U.S.; initials of *Old Kinderhook* (near Albany), name of the birthplace of a Democratic candidate, Martin Van Buren, used first as a slogan and passing into a term of approval, being interpreted as standing for *oll korrect* 'all correct'.

‖**Oka, oke** (ōᵘ·kă, ōᵘk). 1625. [– It. *oca*, Fr. *oque* – Turk. *okka* – Arab. *'ūḳiya*, prob. – (through Syriac) Gr. οὐγκία – L. *uncia* OUNCE *sb.*[1]] A Turkish and Egyptian measure of weight, = about 2¾ lb. English; also, a measure of capacity, = about ⅚ of a quart.

Okapi (okā·pi). 1900. [Mbuba (Congo).] A bright-coloured, partially striped ruminant of Central Africa, having points of likeness to the giraffe, the deer, and the zebra, discovered by Sir Harry Johnston in 1900.

Okenite (ōᵘ·kĕnəit). 1828. [G. *okenit*, f. Lorenz *Oken*, a German naturalist; see -ITE[1] 2 b.] *Min.* A hydrous silicate of calcium, usu. forming a tough fibrous mass, of a whitish colour, and subtransparent. Also called *dysclasite*.

‖**Okimo·no.** 1888. [Japanese.] A small carved ornament worn by the Japanese.

Ok(k)er, obs. f. OCHRE.

‖**Okro, okra** (ǫ·kro, ǫ·kră). 1707. [app. W. African.] A tall malvaceous plant, *Hibiscus* or *Abelmoschus esculentus*, the young mucilaginous capsules or 'pods' of which are used as an esculent vegetable and for thickening soup; the stem furnishes a fibre suitable for ropes; also the pods = GUMBO 1. a.

-ol, *suffix*, in chemical terms. **1.** The termination of *alcohol*, used to form the names of substances which are alcohols in the wider sense (ALCOHOL 5), or compounds analogous to alcohol; e.g. *methol, naphthol, phenol*, etc. **2.** From *phenol* the ending has been transferred to bodies belonging to the group of phenols, (which are alcohols), as *cresol, thymol*, etc., and to some phenol derivs., as *creosol, veratrol*, etc. **3.** Occas. *-ol* is a deriv. of L. *oleum* oil; in which case it is more systematically written *-ole*; e.g. *furfurol*, etc.

Ola, var. of OLLA[2], palm-leaf.

Olacaceous (ōᵘlăkēⁱ·ʃəs), *a.* 1895. [f. mod. L. *Olacaceæ*, f. late L. *olax* odorous; see -ACEOUS.] *Bot.* Pertaining to the order *Olacaceæ* of tropical trees or shrubs.

‖**Olam** (ōᵘlă·m). 1872. [Heb., perh. properly 'that which is hidden'.] A vast period of time, an age.

-olater, -olatry (see -O-), the forms in which -LATER, -LATRY usu. occur.

Old (ōᵘld), *a.* (*adv., sb.*) [OE. *ald* (WS. *eald*) = OFris., OS. *ald* (Du. *oud*), (O)HG. *alt* :– WGmc. **alđa* (cf. Goth. *alþeis* old :– **alþijaz*); pa. ppl. formation (cf. COLD) on the base of OE. *alan*, ON. *ala* nourish, Goth. *alan* grow up, rel. to L. *alere* nourish.] **I. 1.** That has lived long; far advanced in years or life. (Opp. to *young*; less emphatic than *aged*.) **b.** Having the characteristics of age 1832. **c.** Used disparagingly; esp. *colloq.* and *slang.* 1508. **2.** *transf.* Characteristic of old persons; of or pertaining to advanced life. Also *absol.* and *attrib.* ME. **3.** Of a thing: Having existed long, long-made, that has been long in use. (Opp. to *new.*) Hence, Worn out, decayed, dilapidated, shabby, stale, etc.; also, Discarded after long use, disused. OE. **4.** Of (any specified) age or length of existence; e.g. *How o.? Ten days o.* When used *attrib.*, usu. hyphened to *old* (*year* being used instead of *years*), as in a *two-year-old sheep*, etc. These attrib. forms are also used *absol.* as sbs.; e.g. *a flock of two-year-olds.* OE. **b.** The expression '*x* years old' may be preceded by a prep., as if it were a sb. phrase = 'the age of *x* years'; e.g. *a child of ten years old* ME. **5.** *fig.* Of long practice and experience *in* something; experienced, skilled OE. **6.** In colloq. use: = Great, plentiful, excessive, 'grand'. Now only after *good, grand, high*, and the like. 1440. **b.** Technically applied to a lens of high magnifying power 1667.

1. An olde Gentleman called M. Erasmus 1568. My o. bones akes SHAKS. An o. oak COWPER. *The o.* (pl.), o. people; so *o. and young, young and o.* (sc. *people*). **b.** An o. head upon very young shoulders 1837. **c.** *O. bloke, buffer, cat, codger, fogy* (see these wds.). **2.** *O. age*, the latter period of life; also *absol.* and *attrib.*, as in *o.-age pension*, etc. Abraham died in a good o. age *Gen.* 25:8. **3.** Neither do men put new wine into o. bottles *Matt.* 9:17. Pale sherry, o. port, and cut and come again THACKERAY. Phr. *Any o...*, any..whatever (*slang*). **4. b.** I was made a King, at nine months olde SHAKS. **5.** Vane, young in yeares, but in sage counsell o. MILT. O. in vices 1853. O. sailors JOWETT. *O. bird*, a person who has become knowing through experience, *spec.* an experienced thief; *o.* FILE, SOLDIER, STAGER. **6.** Yonders o. coile at home SHAKS. A high o. time 1898.

II. 1. a. Dating far back into the past; made or formed long ago. Also *poet.* of elemental forces, etc.: Primeval. OE. **b.** In personal or other particular ref.: That has been long such; not new or recent OE. **c.** Known or familiar from of old OE. **2.** Used as an expression of familiarity, as in the colloq. *o. boy, chap, fellow, man*; also, with names of places which one has long known. Often in *good o.*, a familiar expression of appreciation. 1588. **3.** Applied to the devil, **a.** orig. in ref. to his primeval character; in OE. *se ealda feond* and *se ealda* (= 'the old one') OE. **b.** also in jocular names of the devil, as in *the o. one, the o.* GENTLEMAN (*in black*); *o.* HARRY, NICK, SCRATCH, etc. 1668.

1. O. fashions please me best SHAKS. An o. and haughty Nation proud in Arms MILT. **b.** To pay up o. scores 1840. An o. friend of your father JOWETT. **c.** One of his o. tricks SHELLEY. Travelling over o. ground 1865. **2.** From scenes like these o. Scotia's grandeur springs BURNS. Take another tumbler, o. man 1890. Good o. Camel Corps 1898. **3. a.** *O. dragon, serpent, enemy, adversary*, etc.

III. 1. Of or pertaining to the distant past; ancient, bygone, olden. (Opp. to *modern.*) OE. **b.** Relating to or dealing with past times OE. **c.** Proper to antiquity or a bygone age; antique ME. **d.** Renowned in (classical) history; esp. in poetry, as an epithet with proper names 1631. **2.** Belonging to an earlier period (of time, one's life, etc.) or to the earlier or earliest of two or more; possessed, occupied, practised, etc., at a former time. (Opp. to *new.*) OE. **b.** That was or has been (the thing designated) at a former time 1571. **3.** Of earlier date, prior in time or occurrence, former, previous OE. **b.** With names of countries: Known or inhabited at an earlier period. 1647.

1. The Prophets o., who sung thy endless raign MILT. The 'good old times' W. IRVING. **b.** O. annals SHELLEY. **c.** What they call the o. blue, the shade seen in enamelling 1899. **d.** To glide adown o. Nilus SHELLEY. **2.** New Presbyter is but O. Priest writ Large MILT. The o. order changeth, yielding place to new TENNYSON. **b.** An o. pupil of mine 1847. **3.** How slow this o. Moon wanes SHAKS. *O. Year's Day*, the last day of the o. year. *O. style*: see STYLE. *O. Christmas Day, O. May-day, O. Michaelmas-day*, etc., these days according to the computation of o. style. **b.** *O. England, O. France, O. Spain* (opp. to the American colonies of *New England, France, Spain*; now only *Hist.*), and similarly in mod. colonial use, *the o. country, o. home* = Great Britain. *The O. Dominion*: see DOMINION. *O. World*, the Eastern Hemisphere, as opp. to the New World of America.

B. *sb.* (the adj. used ellipt.) †**1.** = Old man, old woman -1532. **2.** *pl.* (*olds*). Old ones; old persons, etc. 1883. **3.** *pl.* (*olds*). Hops more than two and less than four years old 1892. **4.** = ELD 4. Chiefly in *men, times, days*, etc. *of o.* late ME. **b.** advb. phr. *Of o.*: of old time, long since, formerly; also, From old days, for a long time (before now). late ME.

4. Then remembred I the tymes of olde, & the yeares that were past COVERDALE *Ps.* 76[7]:5. **b.** You alwaies end with a Iades tricke, I know you of o. SHAKS.

C. *Old-* in Comb. **1. a.** With another adj., in antithetic relation, as *o.-new, o.-young.* **b.** With pr. pple., as *o.-looking.* **c.** With a pa. pple., in advb. sense 'of old, long, anciently', as *o.-acquainted, -established*, adjs. **2.** Parasynthetic combinations: **a.** general, as *o.-blooded* (having o. blood), *o.-faced, -sighted*, etc., adjs.; hence *o.-sightedness* (= presbyopia). **b.** based on a phrase, as *o.-bachelorish, o.-boyish, o.-fogyish, o.-fogyism*, etc. **3.** With a sb. (or its equivalent) forming an attrib. phrase, as *o.-book, o.-life, o.-Roman, o.-school*, etc. See also OLD-TIME, OLD-WORLD.

Special combs., etc.: **o.-clo·thes-man,** a dealer in o. or second-hand clothes; **-clo·thes-shop,** a shop for the sale of o. clothes; **o. gentleman:** see II. 3 b; **o. hand,** (*a*) one who has experience in any business, one skilful in doing something (see HAND *sb.*); (*b*) one who has been a convict; also *attrib.*; **O. Squaw** = OLD-WIFE 2; **o.-style** *a.*, belonging to the o. style, old-fashioned; **O. Tom,** a kind of strong gin. Hence **O·ldish** *a.* somewhat o. **O·ldness.**

Olden (ōᵘ·ldĕn, -d'n), *a.* late ME. [f. OLD *sb.* + -EN⁴.] Belonging to a bygone time; ancient, old; esp. in phr. 'the o. time' (Shaks. *Macb.* III. iv. 75). *literary* and *arch.*

Olden (ōᵘ·ld'n), *v. rare.* 1827. [f. OLD *a.* + -EN⁵.] **1.** *intr.* To grow old, to age. **2.** *trans.* To cause to grow old, to age 1850.

1. She had oldened..as people do who suffer silently great mental pain THACKERAY.

Older (ōᵘ·ldəɹ), *a.* ME. [f. OLD *a.* + -ER³.] The later 'levelled' comparative of OLD, which has superseded the earlier ELDER, q.v., except in special uses. So **O·ldest** *a. superl.* (cf. ELDEST).

Deposits of older date 1863. Our oldest reformation is that of Magna Charta BURKE. He is the older of the two sons, but not the eldest child (*mod.*).

Old-fangled, *a.* 1842. [f. after *new-fangled*; cf. FANGLE.] Old-fashioned. Hence **Old-fa·ngledness.**

Old-fashioned, *a.* 1604. [See FASHIONED *ppl. a.*] **1.** Antiquated in form or character. **2.** Attached to old fashions or ways 1687. **3.** Having the ways of a grown-up person; hence, precocious, knowing. Chiefly *dial.* 1844.

1. Good, old-fashioned, long skirts 1897. **2.** Old-fashioned men of wit and pleasure ADDISON. **3.** The little fellow..was an old-fashioned boy DICKENS.

Old maid. 1530. **1.** An elderly spinster; usu. connoting habits characteristic of such a condition. **2.** A bivalve mollusc of the family *Myidæ*, also called Gaper 1865. **3.** A simple round game at cards 1844. Hence **Old-mai·dish, -mai·denish, -mai·denly** *adjs.* **Old-mai·dery, Old-mai·dism,** the habits or characteristics of an old maid.

Old man. ME. **1.** *lit.* A man advanced in years. **b.** As a term of affectionate familiarity; see OLD *a.* II. 2. **c.** = Husband; father; 'boss' (*vulgar*). 1854. **2.** *Theol.* Unregenerate human nature (cf. *Old* ADAM). late ME. **3.** The Rainbird of Jamaica (*Hyetornis pluvialis*) 1694. **4.** In Australia: A full-grown male kangaroo 1828. **5.** A name of the Southernwood (*Artemisia abrotanum*); perh. from its hoary foliage 1824. **6.** *Mining.* An old vein or working which has been long abandoned; also, oreless stuff 1653. **7.** *Old Man of the Sea*, a person or thing that cannot be shaken off, in allusion to the story of Sinbad the Sailor.

Comb. in plant names, as *old man's beard*, (*a*) a name of the epiphytic plant *Tillandsia usneoides*; (*b*) the Traveller's Joy, *Clematis vitalba*; (*c*) the Strawberry Saxifrage, *Saxifraga sarmentosa*; (*d*) the South European Composite *Geropogon.*

Oldster (ōᵘ·ldstəɹ). 1829. [f. OLD *a.* + -STER, after *youngster.*] One who is no longer a youngster (*colloq.*); *spec.* (*Naut.*) a midshipman of four years' standing.

O·ld-time, *a.* Also **-times.** 1824. Of, belonging to, or characteristic of the olden time. So **Old-ti·mer** (chiefly *U.S.*) 1882.

Old wife, old-wife. ME. **1.** An old woman. Now usu. disparaging. **2.** The Long-tailed Duck (*Harelda glacialis*) 1634. **3.** A name of various fishes, esp. of the family *Labridæ* (wrasse), *Sparidæ* (sea-bream), and *Clupeidæ* (alewife and menhaden) 1588.

1. *Old wives' fable, story, tale*, a trivial story such as is told by garrulous old women.

Old woman. late ME. **1.** *lit.* A woman advanced in years; hence, A person compared to an old woman; a man of timid and fussy character. **b.** = Wife ('my old woman'); mother (*vulgar*). 1825. **2.** A cap or cowl to prevent a chimney from smoking 1861.

1. *Old woman's fable, tale, story*: see prec. Hence **Old-wo·man-ish, -ly** *adjs.*

Old-world (ōᵘ·ld,wǭɹld), *a.* 1712. [The phr. *old world* used attrib.; see WORLD.] **1.** Of or pertaining to the old world or ancient order of things; characteristic of bygone times. **2.** Of or pertaining to the Old World, as opposed to the New World or America.

1. She watched the simple pastoral old-world life around her 1876.

Oleaceous (ōᵘli,ēⁱ·ʃəs), *a.* 1857. [f. mod.L. *Oleaceæ*, f. *olea* olive-tree; see -ACEOUS.] *Bot.* Belonging to the N.O. *Oleaceæ*, comprising trees and shrubs chiefly of temperate regions; the typical genus is *Olea*, the Olive.

Oleaginous (ōᵘli,æ·dʒinəs), *a.* 1634. [– (O)Fr. *oléagineux*, f. L. *oleaginus* oily, f. *oleum* oil; see -OUS.] Having the properties of, or containing oil; oily, fatty, greasy. **b.** Producing oil 1696. Hence **Olea·ginousness.**

Oleander (ōᵘli,æ·ndəɹ). 1548. [– med.L. *oleander, oliandrum.* Cf. Fr. *oléandre* (XV).] An evergreen poisonous herb, *Nerium oleander* (N.O. *Apocynaceæ*), a native of the Levant, with leathery lanceolate leaves, and handsome red or white flowers; rose-bay. Hence, any shrub of the genus *Nerium*, as *N. odorum*, the sweet o.

Oleandrine (ōᵘli,æ·ndrəin). 1885. [f. prec. + -INE⁵.] *Chem.* A yellow, poisonous, bitter alkaloid, the active principle of the leaves, etc. of the oleander.

Oleaster (ōᵘli,æ·stəɹ). late ME. [– L. *oleaster*, f. *olea* olive-tree; see -ASTER.] **a.** The true Wild Olive (*Olea oleaster*). **b.** A small tree of the genus *Elæagnus*, with fragrant yellow flowers, and reddish-brown inedible fruit; wild olive.

Oleate (ōᵘ·li,ĕt). 1831. [f. OLE(IC + -ATE⁴.] *Chem.* and *Pharm.* A salt of oleic acid; also applied to pharmaceutical preparations composed of alkaloids or metallic oxides or salts, dissolved in this.

‖**Olecranon** (ōᵘlĭ,krēⁱ·nǫn). 1727. [– Gr. ὠλέκρανον shortened from ὠλενόκρανον, head or point of the elbow, f. ὠλένη elbow + κρανίον head.] *Anat.* The apophysis at the upper end of the ulna, forming the bony prominence at the elbow. Hence **Olecra·nal, Olecra·nial, Olecra·nian** *adjs.*

Olefiant (ōᵘ·lĭfəi,ănt, olĭ·fiănt), *a.* 1797. [– Fr. (*gaz*) *oléfiant* (1795); in form pr. pple. of a vb. **oléfier* make oily, f. L. *oleum* OIL + *-fier* -FY.] *Chem.* Making or forming oil; only in *O. gas*: the name orig. given to what is now called ETHYLENE (C_2H_4), from its forming with chlorine an oily liquid ('Dutch oil', 'D. liquid').

Olefine (ōᵘ·lĭfin). Also **-in.** 1860. [f. prec. with ending -INE⁵.] *Chem.* Name for the series of hydrocarbons homologous with olefiant gas or ethylene, having the general formula C_nH_{2n}; forming with chlorine and bromine oily dichlorides and dibromides analogous to Dutch liquid (see prec.). Also *attrib.*, as *o. series.*

Oleic (olĭ·ik, ōᵘ·li,ik), *a.* 1819. [f. L. *oleum* oil + -IC.] *Chem.* Pertaining to or derived from oil; *spec.* in *O. acid*: one of the fatty acids ($C_{18}H_{34}O_2$) occurring in most fats, and a constituent of most soaps; also called *elaic acid*; in *pl.* extended to the series of acids to which this belongs. *O. ether*: a general name for the oleates of hydrocarbon radicals, esp. oleate of ethyl, $C_{18}H_{33}(C_2H_5)O_2$.

Oleiferous (ōuli,i·fĕrəs), *a.* Also *erron.* **oliferous.** 1804. [f. L. *oleum* oil + -FEROUS.] Producing oil.

Olein (ōu·li,in). 1838. [– Fr. *oléine* (Chevreul), f. L. *oleum* oil + *-ine* -IN[1], after *glycerine.*] **1.** *Chem.* The trioleate of glyceryl, $C_3H_5(C_{18}H_{33}O_2)_3$, a widely diffused natural fat, obtained as a colourless oily liquid, solidifying at –6° C.; also called *elain.* In *pl.* applied to the oleates of glyceryl or glycerides of oleic acid in general; the above being distinguished as *triolein.* **2.** *Comm.* Any liquid oil obtained by pressure from partly solid oils 1893.

Oleo (ōu·lio). 1884. **1.** Commercial contr. for OLEOMARGARINE, esp. in U.S. sense of artificial butter or MARGARINE. **2.** *O. oil* (esp. U.S.) = OLEOMARGARINE 1893. **3.** Short for OLEOGRAPH.

Oleo- (ōulio), used **a.** as comb. form of L. *oleum* oil; as in **O·leodu:ct** [after *aqueduct*], a duct for conveying oil from an oil-well or oil-field. **O·leopte:ne** [Gr. πτηνός winged, volatile] = ELÆOPTENE. **b.** as comb. form of *oleic, olein,* as in OLEOMARGARINE.

Oleograph (ōu·liŏgraf). 1880. [f. OLEO- + -GRAPH.] A picture printed in oil-colours in imitation of an oil-painting. Hence **O:leogra·phic** *a.* So **Oleo·graphy** 1873.

Oleomargarine (ōu:lio,mā·ɹgărīn, -dʒ-, -in). 1873. [f. OLEO- b + MARGARINE. Often mis-pronounced (-mā·ɹdʒərīn).] A fatty substance obtained by extracting the liquid portion from clarified beef fat by pressure, and allowing it to solidify; with the addition of butyrin, etc., it forms a substitute for natural butter, formerly sold as *butterine,* but now legally called *margarine.*

Oleoresin (ōu:lio,re·zin). 1853. [f. OLEO- + RESIN.] **a.** A natural mixture of a volatile oil and a resin; a balsam. **b.** A mixture of an oil (fixed or volatile) and a resin or other active substance, artificially obtained by evaporation from an ether tincture. Hence **O:leore·sinous** *a.*

Oleraceous (ǫlĕrēi·ʃəs), *a.* 1682. [f. L. (*h*)*oleraceus* (f. (*h*)*olus,* (*h*)*oler-* pot-herb) + -OUS; see -ACEOUS.] Of the nature of or obtained from a pot-herb.

Olfaction (ǫlfæ·kʃən). 1846. [f. *olfact*(*ive* (f. L. *olfactus* smell + -IVE) + -ION. Cf. Fr. *olfaction.*] The action of smelling or the sense of smell.

Olfactory (ǫlfæ·ktəri), *a.* and *sb.* 1658. [– L. **olfactorius* (repr. by *olfactoria, -orium* nosegay), f. *olfactare,* frequent. of *olfacere* smell (trans.), f. *olēre*; see -ORY[2].] **A.** *adj.* Of or pertaining to the sense of smell; concerned with smelling. **B.** *sb.* An organ of smelling 1823. Hence **Olfa·ctorily** *adv.*

‖**Olibanum** (oli·bănŏm). late ME. [med. L., ult. repr. Gr. λίβανος frankincense tree, incense (of Semitic origin; cf. Heb. *lᵉbônāh* incense), perh. through Arab. *al-lubān* (AL-[2]).] An aromatic gum resin obtained from trees of the genus *Boswellia*; formerly used as a medicine, but now chiefly as incense.

Olibene (ǫ·libīn). 1881. [f. prec. + -ENE.] *Chem.* A volatile oil $C_{10}H_{16}$, obtained from olibanum.

Olid (ǫ·lid), *a.* 1680. [– L. *olidus* smelling, f. *olēre* smell; see -ID[1].] Having a strong disagreeable smell; fetid.

Oligandrous, etc.: see OLIGO-.

Oligarch (ǫ·ligāɹk), *sb.* 1610. [– Gr. ὀλιγάρχης, f. ὀλίγος few; see -ARCH.] A member of an oligarchy; one of a few holding power in a state. Hence **O·ligarchal, Oliga·rchic, -al** *adjs.* of, pertaining to, or of the nature of an oligarchy; carried on, administered or governed by an oligarchy; supporting or advocating oligarchy. **Oliga·rchically** *adv.* **O·ligarchize** *v. trans.* to convert into an oligarchy; to subject to an oligarchy.

Oligarch (ǫ·ligāɹk), *a.* 1884. [f. Gr. ὀλίγος few + ἀρχή origin.] *Bot.* Proceeding from few points of origin, said of the primary xylem (or wood) of the root.

Oligarchy (ǫ·ligāɹki). 1577. [– (O)Fr. *oligarchie* or med.L. *oligarchia* – Gr. ὀλιγαρχία, f. ὀλιγάρχης; see OLIGARCH *sb.*] Government by the few; a form of government in which the power is confined to a few persons or families; the body of persons composing such a government.

An ignoble o. founded on the destruction of the crown, the church, the nobility, and the people BURKE.

Oligist (ǫ·lidʒist). 1828. [Named 1801 (*oligiste*) by Haüy, – Gr. ὀγίλγιστος least.] *Min.* More fully *o. iron*: A variety of native iron sesquioxid or hæmatite so called as containing less iron than the magnetic oxide. So **Oligi·stic, -al** *adjs.*

Oligo- (ǫ·ligo), bef. a vowel **olig-,** comb. form of Gr. ὀλίγος small, little, pl. few, in forming nouns and adjs., e.g. ὀλιγόκαρπος with little fruit, oligocarpous; etc. Hence **Oliga·ndrous,** *a. Bot.,* having fewer than twenty stamens.

‖**Oligochromæ·mia** [Gr. χρῶμα colour, αἷμα blood], deficiency of hæmoglobin in the red blood-corpuscles. ‖**Oligocythæ·mia** [Gr. κύτος a hollow, αἷμα blood], deficiency of the red corpuscles of the blood; so **Oligocythæ·mic** *a.* **Oligo·merous** [Gr. μέρος part], *a. Bot.,* having fewer divisions than is normal; so **Oligo·mery. Oligoside·ric** [Gr. σίδηρος iron], *a.* containing only a small proportion of iron]. **Oligosi·derite,** a stony meteorite containing a small proportion of iron. **Oligosylla·bic** [Gr. ὀλιγοσύλλαβος] *a.,* having less than four syllables. **Oligosy·llable,** a word of less than four syllables.

Oligocene (ǫ·ligosīn), *a.* 1859. [f. Gr. ὀλίγος OLIGO- + καινός new, recent.] *Geol.* Of certain Tertiary strata; Of an intermediate age between the Eocene and Miocene formations.

Oligochæte, -chete (ǫ·ligokīt), *a., sb.* 1876. [f. mod.L. *Oligochæta,* f. OLIGO- + Gr. χαίτη mane, taken as 'bristle'.] **A.** *adj.* Belonging to the *Oligochæta,* one of the divisions of the *Chætopoda* (see CHÆTOPOD), including the earthworms and lugworms; so called from the small number of their bristly foot-stumps or parapodia. **B.** *sb.* A worm of this division.

Oligoclase (ǫ·ligoklēis). 1832. [Named 1826 f. OLIGO- + Gr. κλάσις fracture; because thought to have a less perfect cleavage than albite.] *Min.* A lime- and soda-felspar resembling albite, occurring either in crystals or massive.

Olio (ōu·lio), 1643. [alt. of Sp. *olla* (Pg. *olha*) (o·lʸa) :– Rom. **olla,* for L. *ōlla* pot, jar (cf. OLLA[1]); with substitution of *-o* as in -ADO for *-ada.*] **1.** A dish of various meats and vegetables, stewed or boiled together, and highly spiced; hence, Any dish containing a variety of ingredients, a hotchpotch. Now *Obs.* or *arch.* **2.** *fig.* A hotchpotch, farrago, medley 1648. **b.** A collection of various pieces, as engravings, verses, etc.; a miscellany; a musical medley 1655.

1. Such a soup, or ollio..is much in vogue 1763. **2.** An o. of all ages and all countries DISRAELI.

O·liphant. *arch.* ME. [– OFr. *olifant.*] Obs. f. ELEPHANT, occas. retained by mod. writers in sense 'horn of ivory': see ELEPHANT 2b.

Olitory (ǫ·litŏri), *a.* and *sb.* Now *rare.* 1658. [– L (*h*)*olitorius,* f. (*h*)*olitor* kitchen gardener, f. *holus* pot-herbs; see -ORY[1] and [2].] **A.** *adj.* Of or pertaining to pot-herbs, or to the kitchen garden. †**B.** *sb.* **1.** A pot-herb, a culinary vegetable EVELYN. **2.** A kitchen garden –1793.

‖**Oliva** (olǝi·vă). 1839. [L. *oliva* olive.] **1.** *Zool.* A genus of gasteropod molluscs; a member of this genus; an olive-shell (see OLIVE *sb.*[1] 5). **2.** *Anat.* The olivary body 1892.

Olivaceo- (ǫlivēi·ʃio), comb. form of next.

Olivaceous (ǫlivēi·ʃəs), *a.* 1776. [f. OLIVE + -ACEOUS.] Of a dusky green colour with a tinge of yellow; olive-green.

Olivary (ǫ·livări), *a.* 1541. [– L. *olivarius* pertaining to olives, f. *oliva* OLIVE; see -ARY[1].] Shaped like an olive. Chiefly *Anat.*

O. body, each of two oval prominences of nerve-matter, one on each side of the medulla oblongata. Also applied to parts of or connected with the o. body.

Olive (ǫ·liv), *sb.*[1] ME. [– (O)Fr. *olive* – L. *oliva* – Gr. *ἐλαίϝα, rel. to *ἔλαιϝον OIL.] **1.** An evergreen tree, *Olea europæa,* esp. *O. sativa,* with narrow entire leaves, green above and hoary beneath, and axillary clusters of small whitish four-cleft flowers; cultivated in the Mediterranean countries chiefly for its fruit and the oil thence obtained. **b.** Extended to the whole genus *Olea,* and to various trees and shrubs allied to or resembling the olive 1577. **2.** The fruit or 'berry' of *Olea sativa,* a small oval drupe, bluish-black when ripe, with bitter pulp abounding in oil, and hard stone; valuable for its oil, and also eaten pickled in an unripe state. late ME. **3.** A leaf, branch, or wreath of the common olive, an ancient emblem of peace; hence allusively. late ME. **b.** A child (= OLIVE-BRANCH 2); also *attrib.* 1803. **4.** Olive-wood. late ME. **5.** A gasteropod mollusc of the genus *Oliva* or family *Olividæ*; or its shell, of an elongated oval form and fine polish; an olive-shell 1776. **6.** *Cookery.* (*pl.*) A dish composed of thickish slices of beef or veal, rolled up with onions and herbs, and stewed in brown sauce 1598. **7.** A button, etc., of the shape of an olive, for fastening a garment by means of a loop of braid. **8.** *Anat.* The olivary body 1899. **9.** = Olive colour 1662.

1. b. Wild O., the wild variety of the common o. (= OLEASTER a), or any wild species of *Olea*; also applied to various trees and shrubs resembling this. **2.** The ripe Oliues overturne the stomach, and cause wambling therein 1579. **3.** The three nook'd world Shall beare the Oliue freely SHAKS.

B. *adj.* **a.** Of the colour of the unripe fruit of the olive, a dull somewhat yellowish-green. late ME. **b.** Also, applied to a yellowish brown or brownish yellow, in complexions 1634. **c.** Also, of the colour of the foliage of the olive, a dull ashy green with silvery sheen.

attrib. and *Comb.*: **o.-acanthus,** in decorative art, an ornamental form of acanthus leaf with lobes each resembling an olive leaf; **-berry** = sense 2; **o.-cautery,** a cautery with an oval head; **-crown,** a wreath of o. (as a token of victory); **o. pie,** a pie made with veal olives (see 6); **-shell** = sense 5.

Olive (ǫ·liv), *sb.*[2] 1541. [Of unkn. origin.] Local name of the Oyster-catcher (*Hæmatopus ostrilegus*).

O·live-branch. ME. **1.** *lit.* A branch of an olive-tree. **b.** As an emblem of peace; hence *fig.* anything offered in token of peace and goodwill. Also in allusion to Gen. 8:11. ME. **2.** usu. *pl.* (in allusion to Ps. 128:3 (4).) Children. (Now *joc.*) 1605.

Olivenite (oli·vĕnəit, ǫ·livenəit). 1820. [f. G. *oli·ven-* in *oli·ven-erz* (Werner, 1789) olive-ore + -ITE[1] 2b.] *Min.* A native arsenate of copper, occurring in crystals or masses, usu. of olive-green colour.

Oliver (ǫ·livəɹ). 1846. [perh. f. the personal name *Oliver.*] A small tilt-hammer worked with the foot; used esp. in the shaping of nails, bolts, etc.

Oliver, in *a Roland for an O.*: see ROLAND.

Oliverian (ǫlivīə·riăn), *sb.* and *a.* 1658. [f. *Oliver,* proper name + -IAN.] **A.** *sb.* A partisan of Oliver Cromwell; a Cromwellian; puritan. **B.** *adj.* Cromwellian; puritanical 1704.

Olivet (ǫ·livet). *Obs.* exc. as in b. ME. [– L. *olivetum* olive-grove.] †An olive-grove –1610. **b.** The Mount of Olives, the scene of the Ascension; hence allusively.

Olivetan (ǫlivī·tăn). 1691. [f. Monte Oliveto near Siena, the site of the mother convent; see -AN.] One of an order of monks founded in 1313 by John Tolomei of Siena, and subjected to the Benedictine rule.

O·live-woo:d. 1681. **1.** The wood of the common olive, *Olea europæa.* **2.** Any tree of the genus *Elæodendron* (N.O. *Celastraceæ*), furnishing an ornamental wood 1866.

Olivil (ǫ·livil). 1810. [– Fr. *olivile,* f. *olive.*] *Chem.* A crystalline substance obtained from the gum of the olive tree.

Olivine (ǫ·livəin, -in). Also **-in.** 1794. [f. L. *oliva* OLIVE; see -INE[5].] *Min.* A variety of CHRYSOLITE, chiefly of olive-green colour, occurring in eruptive rocks and in meteorites. Also *attrib.* = **Olivi·nic** *a.*

Olla[1] (ǫ·lă). 1622. [– Sp. *olla*; see OLIO.] **1.** In Spain, etc., an earthen jar or pot used for cooking, etc.; also, a dish of meat and vegetables cooked in this; hence = OLIO 1,

OLLA PODRIDA. **2.** In parts of the U.S. formerly Spanish: A large porous earthen jar for keeping drinking-water cool 1851.

‖**Olla**². 1622. [– Pg. *olla* – Malayalam *ōla*.] = CADJAN 2.

‖**Ollamh, ollav** (ǫ·lăv). Also **ollave, ollam.** 1723. [– Ir. *ollamh* (o·lav, with nasal *v*), OIr. *ollam*, learned man, doctor.] *Ir. Antiq.* A learned man; a rank equal to that of a doctor or professor in a university.

Olla podrida (ǫ:lă podrī·dă). 1599. [– Sp., = 'rotten pot', f. *olla* (see OLLA¹) and *podrida* = L. *putrida* putrid.] **1.** = OLIO 1. **2.** = OLIO 2. 1634.

-ology, Ology (ǫ·lŏdʒi), *suffix* and quasi-*sb.* 1786. **1.** *suffix.* The form in which the suffix -LOGY (Gr. -λογία) usu. occurs, the *o* belonging to the prec. element (see -O-); hence regularly used in mod. formations. *-ology* is added directly to some sbs., as in *sexology, thyroidology.* So **-olo·gic(al, -o·logist;** cf. -LOGIC, -LOGICAL, -LOGIST. **2.** quasi *sb.* Any science or department of science 1811.

2. Maid-servants, I hear people complaining, are getting instructed in the 'ologies' CARLYLE.

Olp, dial. var. of ALP²: cf. NOPE.

Olympiad (oli·mpiæ̆d). late ME. [– Fr. *Olympiade* or L. *Olympias, -ad-* – Gr. Ὀλυμπιάς, -αδ-, f. Ὀλύμπιος, adj. of Ὄλυμπος OLYMPUS; see -AD.] A period of four years reckoned from one celebration of the Olympic games to the next, by which the ancient Greeks computed time, the year 776 B.C. being taken as the first year of the first Olympiad.

Olympian (oli·mpiăn), *a.* and *sb.* 1593. [f. L. *Olympus* + -IAN, or f. OLYMPIC by substitution of suffix.] **A.** *adj.* **1.** Of or belonging to Olympus; heavenly, celestial 1603. **2.** = OLYMPIC A. 1593.

1. Above th' O. Hill I soare MILT.

B. *sb.* **1.** A native or inhabitant of Olympia; an athlete who took part in the Olympic games 1606. **2.** An inhabitant of Olympus; one of the greater gods of ancient Greek mythology; *spec.* (*the O.*) Zeus or Jupiter 1843.

Olympic (ŏli·mpik), *a.* and *sb.* 1610. [– L. *Olympicus* – Gr. Ὀλυμπικός, orig. 'of Olympus', later 'of Olympia'.] **A.** *adj.* Of or belonging to Olympia in Elis (see prec.), in which the most famous games of ancient Greece (the *Olympic games*) were celebrated in honour of the Olympian Zeus. **B.** *sb.* An Olympic game; usu. in *pl.* Also *transf.* and *fig. c* 1640.

A. *O. games*, also, a quadrennial international contest at various places, the first at Athens in 1896.

Olympus (ŏli·mpŏs). 1580. [– L. *Olympus* – Gr. Ὄλυμπος name of several lofty mountains.] A mountain in the north of Thessaly, the fabled abode of the greater Greek gods; hence, heaven as the divine abode.

-oma, *suffix*, mod.L. – Gr. -ωμα as in ῥίζωμα RHIZOMA, σάρκωμα SARCOMA, τρίχωμα TRICHOME, φύλλωμα PHYLLOME, f. vbs. in -οῦσθαι, as ῥιζοῦσθαι take root. **1.** Used in sbs. denoting some formation or member of the nature of that denoted by the radical part: now superseded by -OME as RHIZOME. **2.** Used in names of tumours or other abnormal growths.

Omander (omæ·ndəɹ). 1843. [Of unkn. origin.] Name of an E. Indian ebony obtained from the tree *Diospyros ebenaster*; akin to calamander.

‖**Omasum** (omē¹·sŏm). 1706. [L., 'bullock's tripe'.] The third stomach of a ruminant; the *psalterium* or manyplies.

Ombre (ǫ·mbəɹ, Sp. o·mbre). 1660. [– Sp. *hombre* (:– L. *hominem*, nom. *homo* man); cf. Fr. (*h*)*ombre* chief player at hombre, and the game itself.] **1.** A card-game played by three persons with forty cards; very popular in 17th–18th c. **2.** The player at this game who undertakes to win the pool 1724.

Ombro-, comb. form of Gr. ὄμβρος shower of rain: as in **Ombro·logy** [see -LOGY], the branch of meteorology that deals with rain. **Ombro·meter** [see -METER], a rain-gauge.

-ome, *suffix* = -OMA 1 and 2, but now general only in *Bot.* e.g. CAULOME, PHYLLOME, RHIZOME.

Omega (ōᵘ·mĭgă, ōᵘme·gă). 1526. [Gr. ὦ μέγα, i.e. 'great O'.] **1.** The last letter of the Greek alphabet 1656. **2.** *transf.* The last of a series; the last word; the end or final development 1526. **3.** *attrib.* 1880.

2. *Alpha and O.*: see ALPHA 1.

Omelet, omelette (ǫ·mlėt). 1611. [(also *aumelet, am(m)ulet, amlet*) – Fr. *omelette*, also †*aume-*, †*amelette*, metath. alt. of †*alumette*, by-form of †*alumelle*, †*alemel(l)e*, f. *lemele* blade of a sword or knife, by wrong analysis of *la lemel(l)e* (– L. *lamella*, dim. of *lamina* thin plate of metal). The omelette is presumed to have been named from its thin flat shape.] A dish consisting of eggs whipped up, seasoned, and fried; often varied by the addition of other ingredients.

Prov. You can't make an o. without breaking eggs.

Omen (ōᵘ·mĕn), *sb.* 1582. [– L. *omen, omin-*, earlier (acc. to Varro) **osmen*, which was pop. assoc. with *ōs* mouth (cf. ORAL), whence the sense 'word of good or bad augury'.] Any phenomenon or circumstance supposed to portend good or evil; a prophetic sign, prognostic, augury. **b.** Without *an* and *pl.*: Foreboding; prognostication 1742.

1. Far be that O. from vs [= L. *absit omen!*] HEYWOOD. **b.** Birds of evil o. 1876. Hence **O·men** *v. trans.* to presage, prognosticate, forebode. **O·mened** *a.* having an o., as *happy-omened*, etc.

‖**Omentum** (ome·ntŏm). *Pl.* **-a.** 1547. [L.] *Anat.* A fold or duplication of the peritoneum connecting the stomach with the liver, spleen, colon, etc.; the caul.

Three divisions of the omentum are commonly recognized: the *gastro-colic* or *greater o.* descending over a part of the intestines from the lower border of the stomach to the transverse colon; the *gastro-hepatic, hepato-gastric*, or *lesser o.* extending from the liver to the smaller curvature of the stomach; the *gastro-splenic o.* connecting the cardiac end of the stomach with the spleen. Hence **Ome·ntal** *a.* of, pertaining to, or situated in the o. 1758.

‖**Omer** (ōᵘ·məɹ). 1611. [bibl. Heb. *'ōmer.*] **1.** A Hebrew measure of capacity equal to the tenth part of an ephah, or $5\frac{1}{10}$ pints Imperial measure. (Cf. GOMER¹, HOMER².) **2.** A sheaf; *spec.* the sheaf of the wave-offering 1860.

2. *Counting of the O.*, the formal enumeration by Jews of the days from the eve of the 2nd day of the Passover till Pentecost. (see Leviticus 23:15, 16.)

-ometer (ǫ·mĭtəɹ), the element -METER preceded by *-o-*, belonging to the prec. element, or merely connective (see -O-). Also as quasi-*sb.*

†**O·minate,** *v.* 1582. [– *ominat-*, pa. ppl. stem of L. *ominari, -are* prognosticate, f. *omen, omin-*; see OMEN, -ATE³.] **1.** *trans.* To prognosticate from omens, to augur, forebode –1742. **b.** *intr.* To have or utter forebodings –1667. **2.** *trans.* To be a prognostic of, to portend –1827. **b.** *intr.* To be or serve as an omen –1702. Hence †**Omina·tion,** prognostication, foreboding.

Ominous (ǫ·minəs, ōᵘ·m-), *a.* 1589. [– L. *ominosus*, f. *omen, omin-* OMEN; see -OUS.] **1.** Of the nature of an omen, presaging events to come, portentous 1592. †**2.** Of good omen; fortunate –1662. **3.** Of ill omen, inauspicious 1589. **b.** Marked by evil omens, disastrous 1634. **c.** Of doubtful or menacing aspect 1877.

3. An o. shake of the head supplied the remainder of the sentence 1871. **c.** In the dimness or coruscation of o. light RUSKIN. Hence **O·minous-ly** *adv.*, **-ness.**

Omissible (omi·sĭb'l), *a.* 1816. [f. *omiss-*, pa. ppl. stem of L. *omittere* OMIT + -IBLE.] Capable of being omitted.

Omission (omi·ʃən). late ME. [– (O)Fr. *omission* or late L. *omissio*, f. as prec.; see -ION.] **1.** The action of omitting, or fact of being omitted; also, an instance of this 1555. **2.** The non-performance or neglect of action or duty; an instance of this.

1. To supply the o. in the preceding narrative PALEY. **2.** His faults to me seem only great omissions PEPYS.

Omissive (omi·siv), *a.* 1629. [f. *omiss-* (see prec.) + -IVE.] Characterized by neglecting to perform, or leaving out.

Omit (omi·t), *v.* late ME. [– L. *omittere*, f. *ob-* OB- 1 + *mittere* send, let go.] **1.** *trans.* To leave out, not to insert or include. **2.** *trans.* To fail or forbear to use or perform; to let alone, pass over, neglect, leave undone 1533. †**b.** To leave disregarded, take no notice of SHAKS. †**3.** To let go –1646.

1. So moche as they omitted or lefte vnsayd 1526. **2.** He will o. nothynge, that consereuth hys dewtie 1560. Some people . . did not o. publicly to attend the worship of God DE FOE. **b.** 2 *Hen. IV*, IV. iv. 27. Hence **Omi·tter.**

‖**Omlah** (ǫ·mlā). *E. Ind.* 1778. [– Arab. *'umalā'.*] In northern India, A body or staff of native officials in a civil court.

‖**Ommatidium** (ǫmăti·diŏm). *Pl.* **-ia.** 1888. [mod.L., f. Gr. ὄμμα, ὀμματ- eye + dim. suff. -ιδιον; see -IUM.] *Zool.* A structural element of the eyes of Invertebrates; *e.g.* one of the simple eyes which make up the compound eye of an insect. Hence **Ommati·dial** *a.*

Omneity (ǫmnī·ĭti). *rare.* 1638. [f. L. *omni-s, omne* all + -ITY, prob. immed. – schol. L. **omneitas* (after *hæceitas, seitas*, etc.).] The condition of being all; 'allness'.

So nothing became something and O. informed Nullity into an Essence SIR T. BROWNE.

Omni- (ǫmni), comb. form of L. *omnis* all, used in L. in forming compound adjs., and in Eng. in a multitude of words formed on L. models, or to supply a latinized equivalent to an Eng. compound in ALL-, as in: **Omnibene·volent** *a.* benevolent towards all; so **Omnibene·volence,** universal benevolence. **Omni·parent** [see PARENT] *a.*, producing or bringing forth all things. **Omnipa·rient** *a.* = prec. **Omni·parous** [L. *-parus* producing] = *omniparent.* **Omnipa·tient** *a.*, patient of everything; having unlimited endurance. **Omniperci·pient** *a.*, perceiving all things; so **Omniperci·pience. Omnipre·valent** *a.*, prevailing everywhere.

Omniana (ǫmni,ē¹·nă). 1807. [f. L. *omnis* all, *omnia* all things + -ANA.] Notes or scraps of information about everything; '*ana*' of all kinds.

Omnibus (ǫ·mnibŏs), *sb.* and *a.* 1829. *Pl.* **-buses.** See also BUS. [– Fr. *omnibus* (1828), also *voiture omnibus* carriage for all (L. *omnibus*, dat. pl. of *omnis* all).] **A.** *sb.* **1.** A four-wheeled public vehicle for carrying passengers, usually covered and freq. with seats on the roof as well as inside, plying on a fixed route; (also *hotel o.*) a vehicle conveying guests between a hotel and the railway station; (also *private* or *family o.*) a vehicle provided by a railway company, etc., for conveying a party and its luggage to or from a station. **2.** = *Omnibus-box*: see B. 1848. **3.** A man or boy who assists a waiter at an hotel, etc. 1888.

1. The new vehicle, called the o., commenced running this morning [4 July] from Paddington to the City 1829. **2.** Having just arrived from the o. at the Opera THACKERAY.

B. *adj.* Serving for several distinct objects at once; comprising a large number of items 1854.

Phr. *O. bill, clause, order, faculty. O. box*, name of a large box on the pit tier in some theatres and opera-houses, appropriated to a number of subscribers. *O. train* [after Fr. *train omnibus*], a railway train stopping at all stations on the route. *O. bar, wire*, etc. (*Electr.*), one through which the whole current passes. *O.* (*book*), a volume containing several stories, etc. (usu. by a single author) published at a low price to be within the reach of all.

Omnifarious (ǫmnifēᵊ·riəs), *a.* 1653. [f. late L. *omnifarius* (OMNI-; cf. *multifarius*) + -OUS.] Of all kinds and forms; exceedingly various.

Omnific (ǫmni·fik), *a.* 1667. [f. *omni-* OMNI- + -FIC 'maker of all things', after *omnipotent*, etc.] All-creating. *P.L.* VII. 217.

Omniform (ǫ·mnifǭɹm), *a.* 1647. [– late L. *omniformis*, f. *omni-* OMNI- + *forma* shape; see -FORM.] Of all forms or shapes; taking any or every form. So **Omnifo·rmity,** the quality of being omniform; the being of all forms 1644.

Omnify (ǫ·mnifəi), *v.* 1622. [f. OMNI- + -FY, after *magnify*.] †**1.** *trans.* To make everything of; to account as all in all –1668. **2.** To render universal 1810.

Omnigenous (ǫmni·dʒĭnəs), *a.* 1650. [f.

L. *omnigenus* (f. OMNI- + *genus* kind) + -OUS.] Of all kinds.

Omnipotence (ǫmni·pŏtĕns). 1566. [– late L. *omnipotentia*, f. L. *omnipotens*; see next, -ENCE. Cf. Fr. *omnipotence* (XVI).] The quality of being omnipotent; almightiness. **a.** *strictly*, as an attribute of deity; hence God himself = 'the Omnipotent'. **b.** *gen.* as an attribute of persons or things; hence *transf.* an omnipotent force or agency 1590.

a. The Right of Gods Soveraignty is derived from his O. HOBBES. **b.** The O. of an Ordinance of Parliament, confirmed all that was this way done CLARENDON. So †**Omni·potency** 1470.

Omnipotent (ǫmni·pŏtĕnt), *a.* ME. [– (O)Fr. *omnipotent* – L. *omnipotens, -ent-*; see OMNI-, POTENT *a.*[1]] **1.** Almighty, infinite in power, as a deity. **2.** *gen.* All-powerful; having unlimited or very great power, force, or influence 1598. **b.** *joc.* Capable of anything; unparalleled 1596. **3.** *absol.* or as *sb.* An omnipotent being; *spec.* (with *the*) the Almighty, God 1601.

1. As helpe me verray god o. CHAUCER. **2.** O o. Loue SHAKS. **b.** 1 *Hen. IV*, I. ii. 121. **3.** Who durst defie th' O. to Arms MILT. Hence **Omni·potently** *adv.*

Omnipresence (ǫmni,pre·zĕns). 1601. [– med.L. *omnipresentia*; see OMNI-, PRESENCE.] The fact or quality of being omnipresent.

Next to God's Eternitie follows his Immensitie or O., which denotes his presence in althings and al spaces 1677. The o. of casualties..threatened all projects with futility GEO. ELIOT.

Omnipresent (ǫmni,pre·zĕnt), *a.* 1610. [– med.L. *omnipresens, -ent-*; see OMNI-, PRESENT *a.*] Present at the same time in all places; everywhere present. Often *hyperbolical.*

The bird is o. 1867. God is not ubiquitous, but o. 1885. Hence **Omnipre·sently** *adv.*

Omniscience (ǫmni·ʃĕns, -iĕns). 1612. [– med.L. *omniscientia*; see OMNI-, SCIENCE.] **a.** Strictly: Infinite knowledge; hence *transf.* the omniscient Being, the Deity. **b.** *hyperbolically.* Universal knowledge 1845.

b. [Said of Whewell] 'Science is his forte, o. is his foible' SYD. SMITH.

Omniscient (ǫmni·ʃĕnt, -iĕnt), *a.* 1604. [– med.L. *omnisciens, -ent-*; see OMNI-, SCIENT *a.*; repl. earlier †*omniscious* – med.L. *omniscius.*] **1.** Knowing all things. Often *hyperbolical* (cf. prec.) **2.** *absol.* or as *sb.* An omniscient being or person; *spec.* (with *the*) the Deity, God 1794.

1. By no means trust to your own judgement alone; for no man is o. BACON. So †**Omni·scious** *a.* 1588–1728.

O:mnisuffi·cient, *a. Obs.* or *rare.* 1543 [f. OMNI- + SUFFICIENT.] All-sufficient, all-sufficing. So **O:mnisuffi·ciency.**

Omnium (ǫ·mniŏm). 1760. [– L., 'of all (things, sorts)', gen. pl. of *omnis* all. In sense 1, also, *omnium gatherum.*] **1.** *Stock Exch.* The aggregate amount of the parcels of different stocks and other considerations, formerly offered by Government in raising a loan, for each unit of capital (= £100) subscribed. **b.** Colloq. applied to other combined stocks the constituents of which can be dealt with separately. **2.** (with allusion to prec.) One's 'all'. 1766.

1. In the loan of 36,000,000 *l.* contracted for in June, 1815, the o. consisted of 130 *l.* 3 per cent. reduced annuities, 44 *l.* 3 per cent. consols, and 10 *l.* 4 per cent. annuities for each 100 *l.* subscribed MᶜCULLOCH.

Omnium gatherum (ǫ·mniŏm gæ·ðərŏm). *colloq.* Also hyphened. 1530. [f. L. OMNIUM + *gatherum*, quasi-Latin for 'a gathering'.] A gathering of all sorts; a miscellaneous collection (of persons or things); a medley.

Such an omnium gatherum as the inhabitants of a new settlement 1830.

Omnivorous (ǫmni·vŏrəs), *a.* 1656. [f. L. *omnivorus*; see OMNI-, -VOROUS.] All-devouring; that feeds on all kinds of food.

fig. He has not observed on the nature of vanity, who does not know that it is o. BURKE. Hence **Omni·vorous-ly** *adv.*, **-ness.**

Omo-hyoid (ōᵘmo,hai·oid), *a.* (*sb.*) 1840. [f. Gr. ὦμος shoulder + HYOID.] *Anat.* Relating to, or connecting, the shoulder and the hyoid bone. Also as *sb.* the omohyoid muscle.

‖**Omophagia** (ōᵘmofē·dʒiă). 1706. [– Gr. ὠμοφαγία (whence in late L.), f. ὠμός raw; see -PHAGY.] The eating of raw food, esp. raw flesh. So **Omophagic** (ōᵘmofæ·dʒik), **Omophagous** (omǫ·făgəs) *adjs.* eating, or characterized by the eating of, raw flesh. **Omophagist** (omǫ·fădʒist), an eater of raw flesh.

Omoplate (ōᵘ·mŏpleⁱt). Also **-plat** (-plæt). 1597. [– Gr. ὠμοπλάτη, f. ὦμος shoulder + πλάτη broad surface, blade. Cf. Fr. *omoplate* XVI.] The shoulder-blade, scapula.

Omostegite (omǫ·stīdʒəit). 1870. [f. Gr. ὦμος shoulder + στέγη covering, roof + -ITE[1] 3.] *Anat.* The posterior part of the carapace, covering the thorax, in certain crustaceans.

‖**Omosternum** (ōᵘmostə·ɹnŏm). 1868. [f. Gr. ὦμος shoulder + STERNUM.] *Comp. Anat.* A cartilage, or an ossification of such cartilage at the anterior extremity of the sternum. Often applied to the membrane bone overlying the front end of the sternum, and more properly called *episternum* or *interclavicle.*

†**O·mphacine,** *a.* (*sb.*) 1548. [f. Gr. ὀμφάκινος made of unripe grapes, olives, etc., f. ὄμφαξ unripe (grape, berry): see -INE[2].] In *oil o.*, an oily liquid expressed from unripe olives. Also as *sb.* = oil o. –1712.

Omphacite (ǫ·mfăsəit). 1828. [– mod. G. *omphazit* (Werner, 1812), f. Gr. ὄμφαξ (see prec.) + -ITE[1] 2b.] *Min.* A leek-green mineral, allied to pyroxene.

Omphalitis (ǫmfălǝi·tis). 1857. [f. Gr. ὀμφαλός navel + -ITIS.] *Med.* Inflammation of the navel.

Omphalo- (ǫmfălo), bef. a vowel **omphal-**, comb. form of Gr. ὀμφαλός navel, boss, hub. **O·mphaloce:le** (-sīl) [Gr. κήλη tumour, etc.], umbilical hernia. **O·mphaloma:ncy** [Gr. μαντεία], divination, by the number of knots on the umbilical cord at birth, of the number of future children of the mother. **O:mphalo-mesente·ric** *a.*, *Anat.* Pertaining to, or connecting, the navel and the mesentery. **O:mphalopsy·chic** (-səi·kik) *a.*, **O:mphalo·psychite** [Gr. ψυχή], one of a sect of quietists who practised gazing at the navel as a means of inducing hypnotic reverie.

‖**Omphalodium** (ǫmfălōᵘ·diŏm). 1839. [mod.L., f. Gr. ὀμφαλώδης navel-like, f. ὀμφαλός; see -ODE, -IUM.] *Bot.* The centre of the hilum of a seed, through which the nourishing vessels pass. So **O·mphalode.**

‖**Omphalos** (ǫ·mfălǫs). 1850. [– Gr. ὀμφαλός navel, etc.] **1.** *Gr. Antiq.* **a.** A boss on a shield, etc. 1857. **b.** A sacred stone, of a rounded conical shape, in the temple of Apollo at Delphi, fabled to mark the central point of the earth 1850. **2.** *gen.* and *fig.* A central point or portion, centre, hub 1855.

‖**Omrah** (ǫ·mrā). 1621. [– Urdu *'umarā'* – pl. of Arab. *'amīr* AMEER.] A lord or grandee of a Moslem court, esp. that of the great Mogul.

On (ǫn), *prep.* [OE. *on*, orig. unstressed var. of *an* = OFris. *an*, OS., OHG. *ana, an* (Du. *aan*, G. *an*), ON. *á*, Goth. *ana* (see ANA-), rel. to Gr. ἀνά, ἄνα on, upon, Skr. *ā* up, Av. *ana*, OSl. *na.*] **I.** Of position. [OE. *on* with dative.] Of local position outside of, but close to or near, any surface. **1.** Above and in contact with, above and supported by; upon. **2.** Expressing contact with any surface, whatever its position OE. **3.** In proximity to; close to, beside, near, at OE. **4.** Expressing position with ref. to a place or thing; esp. with *side, hand, bow* (of a ship), and words of direction implying 'side', as *front, back, rear*; *north, south, east, west*, etc. Hence in many fig. and transf. uses of *hand, part, side, behalf*, etc. OE.

1. A citee putt on a hill may nat be hid WYCLIF *Matt.* 5 : 14. All these hostages took a solemn oath on the gospels 1785. On life's tempestuous sea CRABBE. A colonel on half-pay 1843. During his residence on the Continent MACAULAY. On the horns of a dilemma 1894. Phr. *On one's feet, knees, legs, back, face, on tiptoe, on all fours. On foot, on horseback, on an ass, on the wing*, etc. Phr., more or less fig., *On the bench, on the cards, on the carpet, on 'Change, on the fence, on the market, on the nail, on the parish, on the rack, on the shelf, on the spot, on the streets, on the stump, on tenterhooks, on the throne, on the way*; also, *on a level, on an equality, on a par*; see the respective sbs. **2.** On Shrubs they browze DRYDEN. Isabella on its music hung KEATS. Phr. *To hang, stick on a wall*; *a fly walking on the ceiling*; *blisters on the soles of his feet*; also, *a coat on his back, shoes on his feet.* **3.** Detained long at the Douane on the Italian frontier 1832. Burton-on-Trent, Clacton-on-Sea 1902. **4.** It was agreed on all hands 1747. The numbers on either side 1838.

†**II.** Of position *within.* Within the limits or bounds of; = IN *prep.* –1485.

III. Of time, or action implying time. **1.** Indicating the day of an occurrence, treated as a unit of time; so with *night, morning*, etc. *On the instant*, instantly. OE. **b.** = Close upon, touching upon. Also in *on time* (U.S.) = exactly at the (right, etc.) time, punctual(ly) 1843. **2.** Followed by a noun of action, etc., expressing the occasion of what is stated 1593.

1. Presented to A. B. on the occasion of his wedding 1902. **b.** It is now just on post-time CARLYLE. **2.** On hearing this = when (and because) I heard this, I changed my plans 1902.

IV. Of order, arrangement, manner, state. **1.** Indicating physical arrangement or grouping; = *in* (a row, a heap, pieces). *Obs.* or *arch.* OE. **2.** Indicating manner; = *in. Obs.* exc. in archaic phrases, as *on this wise.* OE. **3.** Of state, condition, action (see quots.) OE.

1. There lyeth nine little Ilands on a row PURCHAS. **2.** The byrthe off Christe was on thys wyse TINDALE *Matt.* 1:18. Phr. *On the cheap, on the sly, on the square*: see CHEAP C., etc. **3. a.** with a sb., as *on fire, on live, on sleep, on the tap* (now usu. *in*, occas. *on*, often *a-*, now written in comb. (*afire, alive, asleep*); **b.** with noun of action, as *on loan, on sale, on the look-out, on the move, run, wane, on the watch, on the make, on the drink, on the spree*, etc. (in these *on* is still normal); **c.** formerly with vbl. sb. as *on singing, on building* (*Obs.* or *arch.*, the vbl. sb. now functioning as a pres. pple., with *on* omitted, as 'the ark was building'). Workmen on strike 1876. On our best behaviour 1886.

V. Indicating non-material basis, ground, or footing. (fig. extension of I.) **1.** Indicating the ground, basis, or reason of action, opinion, etc. OE. **2.** Indicating that which forms the basis of income, taxation, borrowing, betting, profit, or loss 1697.

1. He..was convicted on evidence which would not have satisfied any impartial tribunal MACAULAY. Phr. *On account* (*of*), *on pretence, on purpose*; *on terms*; *on an* (or *the*) *average, on the whole*: see the sbs. **2.** The king borrowed considerable sums on his jewels 1753. Six to four on Leader 1764. The interest on the debentures 1885. The margin of profit on the sales 1902.

VI. Of motion or direction towards a position. **1.** On to OE. **b.** Indicating accumulative addition, or repetition 1611. **c.** Of continued motion: *On one's way, on a journey*, etc.; also *on an errand, a message.* See these sbs. **2.** Against, towards OE. **3.** Of aspect or direction towards OE. **4.** Into, unto, to (some action, etc. Now *rare.*) OE. **5.** Indicating the person or thing to which action, feeling, etc. is directed, or that is affected by it ME. **b.** Indicating the object of desire and the like. Also *ellipt.* = bent on, set on. ME. **c.** Indicating the bank, banker, or person to whom a cheque is directed, and by whom it is payable; in *to draw on, a cheque*, etc. (*drawn*) *on* 1671. **6.** Indicating a person or thing to which hostile action is directed; against. late ME. **7.** In regard to, in reference to, with respect to, as to OE. **b.** Expressing the object to which mental activity is directed; after such verbs as *think, consider, reflect*, etc. Also after derived sbs., as *thought*, etc. OE. **c.** After *speak, write*, etc. q.v.; after *book, article, lecture*, etc., or an author's name; also ellipt. in titles and the like. late ME.

1. He threw the coins on the table. They fixed placards on the walls. A blow on the head (*mod.*). Phr. *To lay hold on, seize on*: see these vbs. **b.** With ruin upon ruin, rout on rout MILT. **2.** He bears his Rider headlong on the Foe DRYDEN. He drew his knife on her and attacked her 1894. **3.** *ellipt.* Feeling that I was on him, I pulled 1888. Phr. *To smile on, turn one's back on.* **4.** Dauid.. fell on slepe BIBLE (Great) *Acts* 13:36. Facts which ought to have put him on enquiry 1885. **5.** On them she workes her will to uses bad SPENSER. The decision..which is binding on us 1883. Phr. *Eager, keen, mad, bent, determined, set, gone*, etc. *on. ellipt.* Their mind was so on their worke 1623. There was no doubt that the trout were 'on' worms 1904. **6.** Phr. *To complain, inform, tell, 'peach' on*; also *an attack, assault*, etc., *on.* Ay, 'twas he that told me on her first SHAKS. **7.** The appellants had failed on the main question 1885. **b.** The sleepless nights in which he meditated on the trophies of Miltiades 1838. **c.** Laplace's Book on the Stars CARLYLE. Coke on Littleton 1902.

VII. Other senses, obs., arch., or dial. (All these orig. belonged to branches I–V.) **†1.** After verbs of *winning, gaining, taking* (by force) := from. Here orig. belonged vbs. of *wreaking* or *taking vengeance, avenging*, etc., still construed with *on* –1671. **†2.** Indicating that to which a quality has relation: In respect of –1703. **†3.** In uses now expressed by AT (esp. *on a price* or *rate*) –1794. **4.** In uses now expressed by OF. Now *dial.* and *vulgar.* ME.

VIII. 1. *On* is used in the construction of verbs like *depend; attend, wait; follow; believe, rely; feed, live*; also after the direct object, with *beget, bestow; spend, waste; congratulate; pride, value* oneself; or as a second construction, e.g. to *condole, consult with* a person *on* something. See these vbs. **2.** *On* was formerly frequent in connections in which *a-* is now usual; e.g. *on back* (= aback), *on broche, on wry*, etc.

¶ *On* is used in U.S. in senses where English usage would have another preposition or expression, such as 'at, of, about, regarding, dealing with'.

On (ǫn), *adv.* (*a., sb.*). [OE. *an, on*: see prec. In mod. Eng. often an elliptic use of the prep. = on something understood.] **A.** *adv.* **1.** In the position of being in contact with, or supported by, the upper surface of something. **2.** Into the position defined in 1. OE. **3.** In the position of being attached to or covering any surface, esp. the body; on the body, as clothing or a limb ME. **4.** Into the position defined in 3. OE. **b.** *ellipt.* in *on with* = put on 1485. **5.** In a direction towards something, at; as *to* LOOK *on.* **6.** Towards something in the way of approach. late ME. **7.** Directed towards, or in a line *with*, something 1804. **8.** *Cricket.* To the on side 1882. **9.** Onward, forward in space or time OE. **b.** *ellipt.* = Go on, advance. late ME. **10.** Gone onward or ahead; in advance in space or time 1872. **b.** *Cricket*, etc.: Ahead of the opposite side 1884. **c.** *slang.* The worse for drink 1802. **11.** With onward movement or action; continuously; as *to speak on*, etc. OE. **12.** Into action or operation; as *thrash on*, proceed to thrash. late ME. **13. a.** Of persons: Engaged in some function or action; on the stage, the field, etc. 1541. **b.** Of things: In progress; in a state of activity 1605. **c.** Having a wager on (something) 1812. **d.** Ready or eager for or to do what is proposed (*colloq.*). **14.** Used idiomatically with many verbs; e.g. *to carry, catch, come on*, etc.: see the vbs.

1. Then to the well-trod stage anon, If Jonsons learned Sock be on MILT. **2.** They also set a..ham on BYRON. **3.** He had a clean Shirt on ADDISON. *Mod. slang*, Keep your hair on! **4.** He immediately drew on his Boots ADDISON. **b.** I will..on with the monk's cowl DISRAELI. **6.** It was getting on for two 1885. **7.** *Broadside on, face on, stem on*, etc., with the face, stem, etc. directed to the point of contact. **9.** They passe on through the cittie HOLLAND. From that day on, centaurs and men are foes HOBBES. **b.** On, Stanley, on SCOTT. **10.** It was now well on in the afternoon 1872. **11.** Now say on Diggon SPENSER. **12.** It came on to rain 1832. **13. a.** Supposing a slow bowler has been 'on' for some time 1888. **b.** There was a considerable sea on 1873. The water was not on 1902. **d.** If there's going to be a fight, I'm on (*mod.*).

B. *adj.* (Cf. OFF C.). **1.** *Cricket.* Applied to that side of the wicket on which the batsman stands, or to the corresponding part of the field 1851. **2.** In ref. to the licensed sale of liquors: Short for 'on the premises'; opp. to OFF C. 5. Often hyphened, as *on-licence* 1891. **C.** *sb. Cricket.* = On side; see B. 1. *attrib.* in *on drive, on-drive*, a drive to the on side 1881.

On-, *prefix*, unstressed form of OE. *an, on* ON, *adv., prep.*, in comb. with verbs and their derivs., and sometimes with other sbs.

1. Old verbal compounds, as *oncnáwan* to recognize, ACKNOW.

2. Later verbal compounds or collocations of adv. and verb; as **†on-become**, to befall, happen; **on-draw**, to draw on; **†on-take**, to take on, assume, behave; etc. In these the union of elements is incomplete, though less so in the inf. and pples.

3. With pr. and pa. pples. forming adjs., as *o·n-carrying* (= carrying on), etc.

4. With vbl. sbs. and nouns of action, forming sbs. (sometimes concrete), as *on-bringing* (= bringing on), etc., (which can be formed at pleasure); **on-go**, going on, progress, advance; **on-roll**, etc.; also *on-goer*, etc. See also ON-LOOKER, etc.

‖**Onager** (ǫ·nădʒəɹ). *Pl.* **-gers, -gri.** ME. [L. – Gr. ὄναγρος = ὄνος ἄγριος the wild ass; also both in Gr. and L. in sense 2.] **1.** A wild ass; *spec.* the species *Equus onager* (E. *hemippus*) of Central Asia. **2.** An ancient and mediæval engine of war for throwing stones 1609.

Onagraceous (ǫnăgrēⁱ·ʃəs), *a.* 1845. [f. mod.L. *Onagraceæ*, f. L. *onager, onagr-* (see prec.); see -ACEOUS.] *Bot.* Belonging to the N.O. *Onagraceæ*, of which *Œnothera* is the typical genus. So **Onagrad** (ǫ·nāgræd), a plant of this order.

On and off, *adv. phr.* (*sb.*) 1823. = OFF AND ON, q.v.; also in more general sense (see ON *adv.*, OFF *adv.*). **b.** *attrib.* **c.** *sb.* A putting on and taking off; intermittent action.

A siege which lasted on and off for twenty years 1889. Hence **On-and-off** *v.*, (*a*) *intr.* to sail on alternate tacks on and off the shore; (*b*) *trans.* to leap on and then off.

Onanism (ōᵘ·năniz'm). 1727. [– Fr. *onanisme* or mod.L. *onanismus*, f. *Onan* (*Gen.* 38:9); see -ISM.] Self-abuse, masturbation.

Once (wɒns), *adv.* (*conj., a., sb.*) [ME. *ānes, ōnes*, gen. of *ān, ōn* ONE (see -S), superseding *ēnes*. The final *s* retained its voiceless sound and *c*1500 began to be repl. by *ce*, as in *hence, ice, mice, thrice, twice.*] **A.** *adv.* **1.** In strict sense: One time only. (Without any ref. to *when.*) **†b.** Firstly –1596. **2.** At any one time; ever, at all, only, merely. (Chiefly in conditional and neg. statements). ME. **†3.** *emphatically.* Once for all. Hence, To sum up; in short –1667. **4.** At one time in the past; formerly. Also *once upon a time.* late ME. **5.** At some future time; one day. Now *rare.* late ME. **6.** *Once removed*, removed by one degree of relationship 1601. **7.** Usu. hyphened to a ppl. or other adj. standing before its sb. 1668.

1. I..have read it more than o. GARRICK. *Prov.* O. bit, twice shy. **2.** *If o., when o.*, if ever, when ever; *not o.*, never. If we o. lose sight of him we shall never set eyes on him again 1902. **4.** The o. famous doctrine of divine right BRYCE. O. upon a time there were gods only, and no mortal creatures JOWETT. **6.** The relationship of second cousin o. removed 1882. **7.** Seek we thy once-loved home? CAMPBELL.

Phr. **a.** *O. or twice*, a few times; *o. and again*, twice (or oftener). *O. again, o. more. O. for all* (*for always*, etc.), once as a final act; once and done with. So *o. and away. O. in a way*, as an exceptional instance; rarely. *O. in a while*, at long intervals; very occasionally. *Once-over* (U.S.), a single rapid inspection. **b.** (arising from the sense *one time*). AT ONCE. *For o.*, for one occasion. *For o. and all, for o. and away, for o. in a way*; cf. **a.** *This, that o.*: this or that time only. Hence **Oncer** (wɒ·nsəɹ), one who attends church only once on Sundays.

B. as *conjunctive adv.* = When once, if once; as soon as. (So *o. that.*) 1761.

O. I have stamped it there, I lay aside my doubts for ever SHERIDAN.

C. *ellipt.* (quasi-*adj.* and *sb.*). **1.** quasi-*adj.* **a.** = Done or performed once 1548. **b.** That once was; former. Now *rare.* 1691. **2.** quasi-*sb.* Doing a thing once, going once, etc. 1623.

1. a. O. Harrowing is generally enough 1739. **b.** The o. enemies 1880. **2.** O. a week is enough for me 1902.

‖**Oncidium** (ǫnsi·diǒm). 1882. [mod.L., f. Gr. ὄγκος barb of an arrow, angle; so called from the form of the lower petal; see -IUM.] *Bot.* A large genus of American orchids, one of the best known being the Butterfly-plant (*O. papilio*).

Onco-, comb. form of Gr. ὄγκος mass, bulk, in mod.Gr. also tumour; used in a few technical terms of medical science. **Oncograph** (ǫ·ŋkograf) [-GRAPH], an instrument, used in connection with the *oncometer*, for recording variations in the size of an organ. **Onco·logy** [-LOGY], that part of medical science which relates to tumours; hence **Oncolo·gical** *a.* **Onco·meter** [-METER], an instrument for measuring variations in the size of an organ; hence **Oncome·tric** *a.* **Onco·tomy** [Gr. -τομία cutting], incision into, or excision of, a tumour.

Oncome (ǫ·nkɒm). 1898. [f. ON- + COME *v.*; cf. *to come on.*] = next.

O·n-coming, *sb.* 1844. [See ON-.] Coming on; advance. So **O·n-coming** *ppl. a.*

Oncost (ǫ·nkǫst). 1480. [– (M)Du. *onkosten* pl., f. *on-* + *kost* COST *sb.*[2]] **†1.** (in form *uncost.*) Additional or incidental expenses –1795. *Sc.* **b.** In general use: Overhead expenses or costs 1912. **2.** *attrib.* or *adj.* Applied (esp. among miners) to work done on time wages. *O. men*, (also *oncosts*), men who work on such terms 1886.

‖**On dit** (oṅ di). 1826. [The Fr. phr. *on dit* = 'it is said', used as a sb.] An item of gossip; something reported on hearsay.

I thought it was a mere *on dit* DISRAELI.

One (wɒn, wŏn, wən, *dial.* and *vulgar* ən), *numeral a., pron., sb.* [OE. *ān* = Fris. *ān, ēn*, OS. *ēn* (Du. *een*), (O)HG. *ein*, ON. *einn*, Goth. *ains* :– Gmc. **ainaz* :– IE. **oinos*, whence also OL. *oinos*, L. *unus*. By XV, *on, oon* had developed locally an initial *w*, which survives in the standard pronunciation.] **I.** As simple numeral. **1.** The lowest of the cardinal numbers; the number of a single thing without any more, the addition of another to which makes *two.* **2.** Joined to the tens (*twenty, thirty*, etc.), *one* orig. always preceeded (*one-and-twenty*, etc.), but now often follows (*twenty-one*, etc.). So with the ordinals: *one-and-twentieth*, now usu. *twenty-first.* OE. **3.** Used before collective numerals (*dozen, score, hundred*, etc.), and fractions (*half, third*, etc.), with more precise or definite force than *a, an*; and so also in legal phraseology, etc. ME. **4.** Occas. put for *first.* late ME. **5.** *absol.* (with abstract conception of number) late ME. **6.** Hence, as *sb.* with pl., Unity; a unit; a single thing, or the abstract number denoting a single thing 1542. **b.** A single person, thing, example, etc. 1840. **c.** The symbol or figure (1. I. i) denoting unity (*mod.*). **d.** *colloq.* (now *number one*) = Oneself, one's own interest 1567.

1. We say o. book, o. page, o. line, etc.; all these are equally units BERKELEY. The principle of 'o. man, o. vote' 1891. *ellipt.* The one-and-sixpenny packet contains 100 varieties 1871. Phr. *Like o. o'clock*, vigorously, quickly. *Train due at o. twenty-five* (1 hr. 25 m.). *To go o. better* (orig. = to play a better card). **2.** Phr. *O. or two* = a very few, a small number of. **3.** The price of labour..is fully one-third less COLERIDGE. Three one-hundred guinea cups 1896. In the year of our Lord, One thousand, eight hundred, and ninety-nine (*mod.*). **4.** Isaiah, chapter fifty-one. *In the year o.* (joc.), a long while ago, time out of mind. **5.** Twenty to o. then, he is ship'd already SHAKS. O. from twenty leaves nineteen 1902. **6. b.** Afterwards, sauntering by ones and twos, came the village maidens THACKERAY. **c.** A row of ones (*mod.*). **d.** Humbly endeavouring to reform Number o. DARWIN.

II. Emphatic numeral. **1.** One in contrast to two or more; one only; a single OE. **2. a.** *pred.* Single, individual ME. **b.** *absol.* or as *sb.* ME. **3.** One at least, one at any rate (as dist. from 'none at all') 1481.

1. The o. and onlye way to the wealthe of a communaltye 1551. **2. a.** The action is neither o., entire, nor great 1789. **b.** The Good or O. BERKELEY. **3.** That's o. comfort, however 1765.

III. In pregnant senses. **1.** One made up of many components, a united OE. **b.** *pred.* (esp. = united in marriage) 1590. **2.** One in continuity; uniformly the same; one and the same ME. **3.** One in substance; identical; the same OE. **4.** One in kind; the same in quality or nature ME. **b.** *pred.* The same; the same thing. Often *all o.* late ME. **5.** One in mind, feeling, intention, or bearing; at one ME.

1. All of them with o. voice vehemently assented JOWETT. **b.** We have been both o. these two Months STEELE. **2.** God remains for ever o. and the same BERKELEY. **3.** He is made o. with Nature SHELLEY. **4.** Be of o. mynde TINDALE 2 *Cor.* 13:11. **b.** All is O. to Him, to make an Angell, or an Ant 1631. **5.** Addington and I are o. again PITT.

IV. In a particularizing or partitive sense. **1.** One from amongst others; a particular, an individual. **a.** *attrib.* OE. **b.** absol. with *of*; formerly with gen. pl.; rarely without either, as in *to make o.*, to form one of a company OE. **2.** In antithesis to *one* in the sense of 'another' OE. **3.** In antithesis to ANOTHER,

OTHER, *others*; with or without sb. following. *O. and another*, more than one, two or more in succession. OE. **4.** Of two things, now usu. *the one* *the other* (rarely in poetry without *the*) OE. **b.** When *the one* and *the other* refer severally to two things previously named, they are by some taken as = *the former* and *the latter*, by others as = *the latter* and *the former*. **5.** *reciprocally*, of two or more: one another (formerly, of two, *one* *other*, and *the o.* *the other*), *one* being grammatical subject, and *another* object, as they met *one another*, they spoke *one to another*, now usu. *to one another*, in which the grammatical relation is lost sight of, and *one another* becomes a kind of reflexive pron., with objective and possessive but no nominative case. ME.

1. a. Ae dreary, windy, winter night BURNS. *O. day*, on a particular day in the past; on some undefined day in the future; I hope to see them o. day all put downe 1588. **b.** O. of his Friends came and proposed to him, to make o. at a Feast 1686. **2.** O. foote in sea, and o. on shore SHAKS. Phr. **One by one** (also *o. after o.*), formerly *o. and o.*, *by o. and o.*, = o. after another, o. at a time, singly. **3.** What's o. man's meat is another man's poison FIELDING. Phr. *O. with another*, (*a*) together (*obs.* or *arch.*); (*b*) on the average. **4.** The o. shall be taken and the other left *Luke* 17:35. Phr. *The o. and the other* = both (= Fr. *l'un et l'autre*). **b.** A Side for the Banquet and a Side for the Household; The O. for Feasts and Triumphs, the Other for Dwelling BACON. The nobility and the clergy, the o. by profession, the other by patronage, kept learning in existence BURKE. **5.** Yf ye shall haue loue won to another TINDALE *John* 13:35. Cudgel-Players, who were breaking o. another's Heads 1711.

V. Indef. pron. (with genitive *one's*). **1.** Some one, a certain one, an individual, a person (L. *quidam*). A following pronoun referring to *one* is in the 3rd pers. sing. ME. **2.** Any one of everybody; any one whatever; including (or specially meaning) the speaker himself; 'you, or I, or any o.'; a person, a man; we, you, people, they (= OE. *man*, ME. *me*, G. *man*, Fr. *on*). Poss. *one's*, obj. *one*; reflexive ONESELF (formerly *one's self*); also formerly and still occas. *his, him, himself*. (The pl. prons. *their, them, themselves*, formerly in general use, are now considered ungrammatical.) In this sense *one* is quite toneless (wən), proclitic or enclitic. 1477.

1. Oon Martyn luther a frere 1521. O. that lou'd not wisely, but too well SHAKS. O. with a beard 1825. He is not o. to take this lying down (*mod.*). **2.** Why, may o. aske? SHAKS. If o. propose any other end unto himself 1650. One's brothers and sisters are a part of one's self 1834.

VI. Pronominal or substantival form of *a*, *an*. (With pl. *ones*.) **1.** An absol. form of *a*, to avoid repeating a sb.; A person or thing of the kind already mentioned ME. **2.** Added after *the, this*; *any, every, many* (*a*), etc., and (in certain phrases) after *a*; also after ordinary adjs. preceded by any of these or (in pl.) alone; in the sense of: A thing or person, pl. things or persons, of the kind in question OE. **3.** After pronominal and other adjs., without contextual ref. = Person, body, persons ME.

1. He rents a house, but I own o. I have forgotten an umbrella; I think I must buy o. 1902. Phr. *O. of these days*, some time or other. **2.** Ne'er a o. to be found B. JONS. The ones you mention. That o. on the table. This o. will do. (*mod.*). **3.** The Consultations of the great Ones and Governours 1665. Come along, young 'un 1857. *Any o., every o., many a o., some o., such a o.; little ones, the Holy O., the Evil O.*, etc.: see under these words.

VII. Obs. uses. †**1.** = indef. article A, AN –1552. †**2.** *One* was formerly used with superlatives, as 'one the fairest toun' = 'a town, the fairest one', 'the one fairest town' –1613.

1. My sayde lorde was oon faytheful man 1514. **2.** He is o. The truest manner'd SHAKS.

Phr. **One and all,** every one individually and jointly. **In o.:** (*a*) in or into one place, company, or mass; together; (*b*) in unison, agreement, or harmony. Now *arch.* (*c*) in one shot or stroke; at one go. **Into o.** = *In one* (*a*). **Ones:** see ONCE.

Combs. **1.** General. **a.** attrib. phrases (unlimited in number), as *o·ne-act, -book, -clause, -year*, etc. Also *o·ne-by-o:ne, o·ne-o'clock*. **b.** Compound adjs., as *o·ne-year-o:ld*. **c.** Parasynthetic formations on such phrases as those in **a.** by adding *-ed* (also unlimited in number) as *o·ne-a:rmed, -roomed, -storied*, etc. **d.** Parasynthetic formations in *-er* (see -ER[1] 1), as *one-decker, one-pounder*.

2. Special: **o·ne-co:loured** *a.*, of uniform colour throughout; **one-man** *a.*, consisting of, exercised, managed, or done by, one man only; **one-manual; one-pair** *a.* (in full, *one pair of stairs*), situated above one 'pair' or flight of stairs, i.e. on the first floor; **one-time** *a.*, that was so at one time or formerly, 'sometime'; **one-way** *a.*, applied to a plough which turns the furrows in one direction; also to a street in which traffic is allowed to go in one direction only, and to the traffic in such a street; **one-while** *a.*, or *adv.* = *one-time*.

One (wɒn), *v.* Now *rare*. [ME. *ōnen, ānen* (cf. OE. *ġeānian*); f. prec.] *trans.* To make into one; to unite.

-one, *Chem.* formative suffix. [Gr. -ωνη feminine patronymic.] **a.** An ending used unsystematically in forming the names of chemical derivatives, as in *acetone, mellone, quinone*. 1848. **b.** In Hofmann's systematic nomenclature, the formative of the names of hydrocarbons of composition C_nH_{2n-4}, as in *propone* C_3H_2, *quartone* C_4H_4, etc. 1866.

O·ne-berry. 1548. †**a.** Herb Paris, *Paris quadrifolia* –1789. **b.** = HACKBERRY 2. *U.S.*

One-eyed, *a.* OE. **1.** Having only one eye; blind in one eye. **2.** *fig.* (*derogatory*) Wanting in an essential quality; *U.S.* unfair 1833.

Onefold (wɒ·nfōᵘld), *a.* 1844. [f. ONE + -FOLD.] **1.** Consisting of one member or constituent; single; simple. **2.** Simple in character; single-minded 1882.

O·ne-ha:nded, *a.* 1440. **1.** Having only one hand, or only one capable of use. **2.** Used, worked, or performed with one hand 1611.

2. The one-handed alphabet 1837. A one-handed catch 1894.

O·ne-horse, *a.* 1750. **1.** Drawn, or worked, by a single horse (as a vehicle, etc.); having or using only one horse. **2.** *fig.* (*U.S. colloq.*) On a small scale; petty; of limited resources or capacity 1854.

2. A country-clergyman, with a one-story intellect and a one-horse vocabulary O. W. HOLMES.

One-ideaed, -idea'd (wɒ·n,əidī·ăd), *a.* 1849. Having, or possessed by, a single idea.

Oneiro- (onəiᵊro), also **oniro-,** bef. a vowel **oneir-,** comb. form of Gr. ὄνειρος a dream. **Oneirology** (ǫnirǫ·lŏdʒi) [Gr. ὀνειρολογία; see -LOGY], the science or subject of dreams, or of their interpretation; so **Oneiro·logist,** one versed in this. **Onei·romancy** [see -MANCY], divination by dreams. **Oneiroscopy** (-ǫ·skŏpi) [Gr. ὀνειροσκόπος an interpreter of dreams], examination or interpretation of dreams; so **Oneiro·scopist,** one versed in this.

Oneirocritic, oniro- (onəiᵊrokri·tik), *sb.* 1614. [– Gr. ὀνειροκριτικός pertaining to the interpretation of dreams; see -IC.] **1.** A judge or interpreter of dreams 1652. **2.** (Usu. in *pl.*) The art of interpreting dreams. So **Oneirocri·tical, oniro-** *a.*; **-ly** *adv.* Hence **Oneirocri·ticism, oniro-,** the art of interpreting dreams.

One-legged (wɒ·n,legd, -le:gĕd), *a.* 1842. **1.** Having only one leg 1883. **2.** *fig.* That is only a half-measure; one-sided 1842.

†**O·nement.** ME. [f. ONE *v.* + -MENT; an early instance of the addition of the Romanic suffix *-ment* to an Eng. vb. Cf. the later ATONEMENT.] **1.** Physical union, conjunction. WYCLIF. **2.** = ATONEMENT 1, 2. –1598.

Oneness (wɒ·n,nĕs). [f. ONE + -NESS. Cf. OE. *ānnes*.] **1.** The quality of being one in number, singleness. **b.** Uniqueness 1715. **2.** The quality of being one body or whole; integrity, unity OE. **3.** The fact of forming one whole; combination, unity, union 1657. **4.** Sameness, identity; unchangingness 1611. **5.** Unity of mind, feeling, or purpose; agreement, harmony, concord ME.

1. Our God is one, or rather very onenesse, and meere unitie HOOKER. **2.** The solidarity and o. of humanity WHITTIER. **3.** The closest human o., of husband and wife PUSEY.

Oner (wɒ·nəɹ). *slang* or *colloq.* Also **one-er.** 1840. [f. ONE + -ER[1].] **1.** *slang.* A person or thing of a unique kind; a prime one. **b.** *spec.* A heavy blow 1861. **2.** *colloq.* A person or thing in some way denoted or characterized by the number one 1889.

1. She is such a o. at eating THACKERAY. **b.** A o. on his ears 1885.

Onerary (ǫ·nĕrări), *a.* (*sb.*) *rare.* 1658. [– L. *onerarius*, f. *onus, oner-* burden; see -ARY[1]. In B. = *oneraria* (Cicero) ship of burden.] **A.** *adj.* Fitted for the carriage of burdens. **B.** *sb.* A ship of burden, transport.

†**O·nerate,** *v.* 1453. [– *onerat-*, pa. ppl. stem of L. *onerare*, f. *onus, oner-* load, burden; see -ATE[3].] *trans.* To load, burden, charge, oppress (*lit.* and *fig.*) –1726.

Onerous (ǫ·nĕrəs), *a.* late ME. [– (O)Fr. *onéreux*, †*-ous* – L. *onerosus*, f. as prec.; see -OUS.] Of the nature of a burden; burdensome, oppressive; of the nature of a legal obligation.

Worldly cares and o. business BURTON. In *o. consideration, grant*, etc. (Sc. Law.), done or given for value received; opp. to *gratuitous*. Hence **O·nerous-ly** *adv.*, **-ness.**

Oneself (wɒnse·lf), *pron.* Also **one's self.** 1548. [orig. **one's self,** after *my self*, etc.; assim. later to *himself, itself*. The corresponding possess. is *one's own*.] **1.** Emphatic use: A person's self; himself or herself (including or meaning the speaker or writer) 1621. **2.** Reflexive use: objective case of ONE V. 2. (In this sense often stressless.) 1548.

1. One might wear the articles one's-self DICKENS. **2.** To be pleased with o. is the surest way of offending every-body else LYTTON.

One-sided (wɒ·n,səi·dĕd; stress var.), *a.* 1793. [Parasynthetic f. *one side*; see ONE *Combs.* 1 c; partly after G. *einseitig*.] **1.** Relating to, considering, or dealing with only one side; partial 1833. **2. a.** Leaning to one side; larger or more developed on one side than on the other 1845. **b.** Unilateral 1793. **c.** Existing or occurring on one side only 1864.

1. A one-sided report of a trial 1885. **2. a.** Tom's face begins to look very one-sided—there are little queer bumps on his forehead HUGHES. So **One-si·ded-ly** *adv.*, **-ness** 1831.

One-step (wɒ·nstep), *sb.* 1911. [f. ONE *a.* + STEP *sb.*] A dance in two-four time, danced by couples and characterized by various walking steps; also the music for this. Hence **O·nestep** *v.*

On-going (ǫ·ngōᵘ:iŋ). 1825. [ON- 4.] **1.** *pl.* = Goings-on (see GOING *vbl. sb.*) **2.** *sing.* The action of going on; proceeding, continued movement (*rare*) 1890.

1. Milton had to describe the ongoings of angels 1856.

Onhanger (ǫ·nhæ:ŋəɹ). 1848. [ON- 4.] A hanger-on: see HANGER[2] 5 a.

Onion (ɒ·nyən), *sb.* [ME. *unyon, oyn(y)on* – AFr. *union*, (O)Fr. *oignon* :– Gallo-Rom. **unione*, L. *unio*, rustic equiv. of L. *cæpa* CHIVE.] **1. a.** The edible rounded bulb of *Allium cepa*, consisting of close concentric coats, and having a pungent flavour and smell; used as a culinary vegetable from the earliest times. **b.** The plant *Allium cepa* itself (N.O. *Liliaceæ*). **2.** Applied to varieties of the above or other species of *Allium*, as **Rock** or **Welsh O.,** a bulbless species (*A. fistulosum*) cultivated for its leafy tops; the chibol; **Wild O.** (U.S.), *A. cernuum*, etc.; also to plants of other genera, mostly bulbous 1548. †**3.** A bunion –1846 **4.** The head (*slang*) 1922.

1. Who would ask for her opinion Between an oyster and an o.? PRIOR. He'll be rampant. .at his child being lost; and the beef and the inguns not done! HOOD. **4.** Phr. *Off one's onion*.

attrib. and *Comb.*, as **o.-couch, -grass, -twitch,** a species of wild oat (*Avena elatior*), so called from the rounded nodes of the root-stock; **-eyed** *a.*, having the eyes full of tears; **-shell,** name for various molluscan shells of rounded form, as those of species of *Ostrea, Lutraria*, and *Mya*. Hence **O·niony** *a.* 1838.

O·nion, *v.* 1755. [f. prec. sb.] **1.** *trans.* To flavour with onions. **2.** To apply an onion to; to produce (tears) by the application of an onion 1763.

Oniro-: see ONEIRO-.

Onliness (ōᵘ·nlinĕs). Now *rare.* ME. [f. ONLY *a.* + -NESS.] **1.** The fact or condition of being alone. **2.** The fact or character of being the only one of its kind; uniqueness 1633.

On live, *phr.*, earlier form of ALIVE.

Onlooker (ǫ·nlu:kəɹ). 1606. [f. ON- 4 + LOOKER.] One who looks on; a spectator.

O·nlooking, *ppl. a.* 1663. [ON- 3.] That looks on; looking at something.

Only (ō^u·nli), *a.* [OE. *ānlić*, late var. of *ǣnlić* corresp. to MLG. *einlīk*, MDu. *een(e)lijc*; see ONE, -LY¹.] **1.** One; solitary, lonely. Now only *dial.* **2.** One (or, by extension, two or more) of which there exist no more, or no others, of the kind OE. **b.** In later use, in ref. to relationship, also preceded by *an*, and used with a pl.; as *an o. child, o. children* 1670. †**c.** *absol.* = only one, only ones –1693. **3.** Single, one. Now *rare.* 1485. †**4.** (The thing in question) acting alone; mere, sole –1856. †**b.** Placed between a demonstrative or possessive adj. or poss. case and its sb., or bef. a sb. followed by an *of*-phrase; referring to the sb. as thus qualified –1741. **5.** Unique in quality, rank, etc.; peerless, pre-eminent. Now only as hyperbolic use of 2, = 'the only one to be counted, reckoned, or considered' OE.

2. The onely ruler of princes *Bk. Com. Prayer.* These two passages are the o. ones in which Plato makes mention of himself JOWETT. **b.** An o. son, sir, might expect more indulgence GOLDSM. **3.** Phr. *One o.*, o. one, one and no other; This country hath one o. deanery 1630. **4.** The onely odour of quicksilver killeth lice 1544. **b.** At the charges & only expenses of these. vi. abbeyes HOLINSHED. **5.** Your onely Iigge-maker SHAKS.

Only (ō^u·nli), *adv., conj.* (*prep.*) [ME. *onliche* (XIII), *-like* (cf. MDu. *eenlike*); partly alt. of OE. *ǣnlīće*, after the adj., partly developed from prec. uses of the adj.; see ONE, -LY².] **A.** *adv.* **1.** As a single or solitary thing or fact. *Only* may be (*a*) dist. from *more*, or (*b*) opp. to any *other*. **b.** *Only* was formerly, and in speech is still, often placed away from the word or words limited by it; this is now avoided in careful writing 1483. †**2.** By or of itself alone, without anything else –1801. †**3.** Singularly, uniquely, specially, pre-eminently –1611. **4.** Idiomatic uses. **a.** The sense 'no more than' often passes into 'as much as'; = JUST *adv.* 5. (Cf. G. *nur.*) 1838. **b.** *O. not* = all but, little else than 1779. **c.** Not before, not till. (*Only* may precede or follow the word or phrase expressing time.) 1676. †**d.** *O. but, but o.*: (*a*) = only, merely; (*b*) except only –1711. **e.** *O. too* (*true*, etc.): see TOO.

1. I will haue nothing else but onely this SHAKS. I have been o. twice 1805. In one o. of the casements 1838. **b.** Luke is o. with me CAXTON. I o. asked the question from habit JOWETT. **4. a.** He is coming. .if you will o. wait JOWETT. **b.** I was o. not a boy JOHNSON. **c.** *O. just*, no longer ago than the immediate past; I have o. just received it 1902.

B. *conjunctive adv., conj.* (*prep.*) **1.** The only thing to be added being; with this restriction, drawback, or exception only; but (*adversative*); on the other hand. late ME. **2.** Except. Now only *dial.* †**b.** Introducing a clause: Except that, were it not that –1802.

1. The flowers are lovely; o., they have no scent (*mod.*). *O. that*, except that, were it not that; O. that I know you don't love bustle, I should wish you were here 1771. **2.** *O. for*, except for, but for; O. for my tea, I should have had the head-ache 1811.

O·nly-bego·tten, *a.* 1450. Begotten as an only child; tr. L. *unigenitus*, Gr. μονογενής.

Onocentaur (ǫnoˌse·ntǫɹ). 1567. [– late L. *onocentaurus* – Gr. ὀνοκένταυρος, f. ὄνος ass + κένταυρος CENTAUR.] *Myth.* A fabulous creature, a centaur with the body of an ass.

Onomancy (ǫ·nŏmænsi). 1602. [– med.L. **onomantia*, whence also Fr. *onomancie*, It. *onomantia*, irreg. f. Gr. ὄνομα name + *-mantia* -MANCY. Cf. ONATOMANCY.] Divination from names or the letters of a name. Hence **Onoma·ntic, -al** *adjs.* of or pertaining to o.; practising o.

Onomastic (ǫnomæ·stik), *a.* and *sb.* 1609. [– Gr. ὀνομαστικός; see next, -IC.] **A.** *adj.* Of, relating to, or connected with a name or names, or with naming; consisting of or dealing with names 1716. **b.** Used in ref. to the autograph subscription of a legal document (of which the body is in the handwriting of another person) 1802. †**B.** *sb.* A writer of an onomasticon; a vocabularist, a lexicographer –1716. So †**Onoma·stical** *a.* = A.

‖**Onoma·sticon.** 1710. [– Gr. ὀνομαστικόν, subst. use (sc. βιβλίον book) of n. of ὀνομαστικός pertaining to naming, f. ὄνομα name.] A vocabulary or alphabetic list of proper names, esp. of persons. Formerly used of a vocabulary of names or nouns, or even of a general lexicon.

Ono·mato-, = Gr. ὀνοματο-, comb. form of ὄνομα, gen. ὀνόματος name.

Onomatology (onǫmătǫ·lŏdʒi). *rare.* 1847. [f. ONOMATO- + -LOGY.] The science of the formation of names or terms; terminology. So **Onomato·logist,** one versed in o. 1695.

†**Ono·matoma:ncy.** 1652. [app. – Fr. †*onomatomancie* (Rabelais); see ONOMATO-, -MANCY.] = ONOMANCY –1727.

Onomatop, -ope (onǫ·mătǫp, -tō^up). 1828. [abbrev. f. next.] A word formed by onomatopœia.

‖**Onomatopœia** (onǫ:mătopī·a, ǫ:nŏmæ-). 1577. [Late L. – Gr. ὀνοματοποιία making of words, f. ὀνοματοποιός, f. ὄνομα, ὀνοματο- name + -ποιος -making (see POET).] **1.** The formation of a name or word by an imitation of the sound associated with the thing or action designated; this principle as a force in the formation of words; echoism. **b.** A word so formed 1842. **2.** *Rhet.* The use of naturally suggestive words, sentences, and forms for rhetorical effect 1860.

2. A good instance of o. in 'Paradise Lost' (Bk. II. 879) TENNYSON. Hence **Ono:matopœ·ic, -al** *adjs.* of, pertaining to, or characterized by o., esp. as applied to the origin of names or words; imitative; echoic; **-ally** *adv.* 1860.

‖**Ono:matopoë·sis** (-poˌī·sis). Also **-poiesis.** 1864. [– Gr. ὀνοματοποίησις the making of a name, f. ὀνοματοποιεῖν.] The naming of a thing, etc., from the sound associated with it; onomatopœia. So **Ono:matopoe·tic** *a.* onomatopœic 1847. **Ono:matopoe·tically** *adv.* 1866.

Onrush (ǫ·nrɒʃ). 1844. [f. ON- 4 + RUSH *sb.*] The act of rush on; impetuous forward movement.

Onset (ǫ·nset), *sb.* 1513. [f. ON- 4 + SET *sb.*¹] **1.** An act of setting on (an enemy); an attack, assault. **b.** (Without article.) Attack, assault 1667. **2.** The action, or an act, of beginning some operation; commencement, start 1561.

1. These troops had to bear the first brunt of the o. MACAULAY. *fig.* The o. of a fever 1789. **b.** Achiev'd By sudden o. MILT. **2.** There is surely no greater Wisedome, then well to time the Beginnings, and Onsets of Things BACON.

†**Onse·t,** *v.* 1602. [f. ON- 2 + SET *v.*] *trans.* To make an onset upon; to set upon, attack –1648. Hence **O·nse:tter,** one who incites; one who makes an onset; *spec.* in *Coal-mining*, a workman who puts the corves or tubs into the cage at the bottom of the shaft.

On side, *phr.* 1887. In Football, Hockey, etc.: One's proper side; the opposite of OFF SIDE, q.v. Also *attrib.*

Onslaught (ǫ·nslǭt). 1625. [Early forms also *anslaight*, *onslat* – early MDu. *aenslag* (mod. *aan-*), f. *aan* ON + *slag* blow, stroke, rel. to *slagen* strike (see SLAY *v.*); with assim. to †*slaught* (cf. SLAUGHTER *sb.*). Not evidenced in XVIII, and app. revived by Scott.] Onset, attack; *esp.* a vigorous or destructive assault or attack..

By Siege or O., to invest The Enemy 1663. The fierce o. upon that Government 1859.

Onstead (ǫ·nstėd). *Sc.* and *n. dial.* 1666. [f. ON- + STEAD place, station, etc.] A farmhouse, with its outhouses, a farmstead; now sometimes *spec.* the offices, as dist. from the farmer's house.

On to, onto (ǫ·ntu), *prep.* 1581. [ON *adv.* + TO *prep.*, having the same relation to *on* as *into* has to *in.*] To a position on or upon (or one that is expressed by these preps.).

Please you walk forth O. the Terrace KEATS. Assisting Mr. Pickwick o. the roof DICKENS.

Onto, on to, obs. (14–16th c.) form of UNTO.

Onto-, comb. form of Gr. ὄν, ὀντ- being, neut. pr. pple. of εἶναι to be. See below.

Ontogenesis (ǫntodʒe·nīsis). 1875. [f. ONTO- + Gr. γένεσις birth.] *Biol.* The origin and development of the individual living being (as dist. from *phylogenesis*). Hence **O:ntogene·tic** *a.* of, pertaining to, or characteristic of o.; relating to the development of the individual being. **O:ntogene·tically** *adv.* with ref. to o.

Ontogeny (ǫntǫ·dʒĭni). 1872. [f. ONTO- + -GENY. Cf. prec.] **1.** = prec. **2.** The history or science of the development of the individual being; embryology 1874. Hence **Onto·genist,** one versed in o.

Ontology (ǫntǫ·lŏdʒi). 1721. [– mod.L. *ontologia* (Jean le Clerc 1692), f. Gr. ὀντο- ONTO-; see -LOGY. Cf. Fr. *ontologie.*] The science or study of being; that department of metaphysics which relates to the being or essence of things, or to being in the abstract. So **Ontologic, -al** (ǫntolǫ·dʒik, -ăl), *adjs.*, of or pertaining to, or of the nature of, o.; metaphysical. *Ontological argument, proof* (for the existence of God), the *a priori* argument that the existence of the idea of God of necessity involves the objective existence of God.

‖**Onus** (ō^u·nǒs). 1640. [L. *onus* burden.] A burden, charge, responsibility.

Onus probandi (L. phrase), the burden of proving; the obligation of proving an assertion, allegation, or charge which rests on one who makes it.

Onward (ǫ·nwǫ̆ɹd), *adv.*, *a.* late ME. [f. ON *adv.* + -WARD; after *inward, forward*, etc.] **A.** *adv.* (Formerly occ. with *of*; e.g. *o. of one's journey.*) **1.** = ON *adv.* 9. 1532. †**2.** Provisionally; *spec.* on account, 'in advance'; as an 'earnest' –1555. **3.** = ON *adv.* 10. late ME. Now *rare* or *arch.*

1. O. still his way he takes GRAY. From. .the times of Philo and four centuries o. 1839. **3.** My greefe lies o. and my ioy behind SHAKS.

B. *adj.* **1.** Of motion, etc.: Directed onward or forward. Rarely of a thing: Moving onward, advancing. 1674. †**2.** Situated in front or in advance; advanced –1644.

1. Resuming his o. course W. IRVING. **2.** To discover o. things more remote from our knowledge MILT. Hence **O·nwardness,** advance, progression, progress 1548.

Onwards (ǫ·nwǫɹdz), *adv.* 1600. [f. prec. with advb. *-s*; see -WARDS.] = ONWARD A.

Ony, Sc. etc. f. ANY.

‖**Onycha** (ǫ·nikă). late ME. [L. = Gr. ὄνυχα, accus. of ὄνυξ ONYX; in med.L. *onic(h)a*, treated as indecl., or as fem. of 1st decl. The form *onycha*, being app. not recognized as the accus. of *onyx*, was treated by mediæval writers as a distinct word; hence in Eng. versions of the Bible (Exod. 30:34).] One of the ingredients in the incense used in the Mosaic ritual; the operculum of a species of *Strombus*, or other marine mollusc, which emits a penetrating aroma when burnt.

‖**Onychia** (oni·kiă). 1857. [mod.L., f. Gr. ὄνυξ, ὀνυχ- nail; see -IA¹.] *Path.* Inflammation of the matrix of the nail, or of the adjacent part of finger or toe.

Onychomancy (ǫ·nikoˌmæ:nsi). 1652. [f. Gr. ὀνυχο-, comb. form of ὄνυξ ONYX + -MANCY.] Divination from the finger-nails.

Onychophorous (ǫnikǫ·fŏrəs), *a.* 1857. [f. as prec.; see -PHOROUS.] *Zool.* Bearing nails or claws; applied to a group (*Onychophori*) of ophidian reptiles having rudimentary hind limbs, and to an order (*Onychophora*) of myriapods comprising the single genus *Peripatus*, having two chitinoid claws on each limb. So **Onycho·phoran** *a.* and *sb.*

Onymous (ǫ·niməs), *a. rare.* 1775. [Extracted from ANONYMOUS.] Having or bearing a name.

Onyx (ō^u·niks, ǫ·niks). ME. [Earliest form *oniche*, later *onix*; from XVIII *onyx*. – OFr. *oniche, onix* – L. acc. *onycha*, nom. *onyx* – Gr. ὄνυξ, ὄνυχα nail, claw, onyx stone.] **1.** A variety of quartz allied to agate, consisting of plane layers of different colours; much used for cameos. †**2.** = ONYCHA. *Ecclus.* 24:15. **3.** *Path.* An opacity of the lower part of the cornea of the eye, caused by an infiltration of pus behind it or between its layers, and resembling a finger-nail 1706.

attrib. and *Comb.*, as **o.-marble,** a stalagmitic limestone or marble, having a banded structure like o.; also called †*onychite* or *oriental alabaster.*

Oo- (ō^uˌo), bef. a vowel **o-,** comb. form of Gr. ᾠόν egg, ovum, used in scientific, chiefly biological, terms. **Oœcium** (oˌī·ʃiŏm) [Gr. οἰκίον a little house], a bud-like sac in which the ova are received and fertilized, in certain

Polyzoa; hence **Oœ·cial** *a.* **Oo·gamous** *a.* [Gr. γάμος + -OUS], *Biol.* applied to organs which reproduce (or to reproduction) by union of dissimilar (male and female) cells. **Oogenesis** (ōu,o,dʒe·nĭsis) [GENESIS], the production or development of an ovum; so **Oogenetic** (ōu:o,dʒĭne·tik) *a.*, **Oogeny** (o,ǫ·dʒĭni) = *oogenesis*. **Oophyte** (ōu·ŏfəit) [Gr. φυτόν plant] = OOPHORE. **O·osperm** [SPERM], **a.** *Zool.* a fertilized ovum; **b.** *Bot.* = OOSPORE. **O·osphere** [Gr. σφαῖρα sphere], *Bot.* the female reproductive cell, esp. in the Thallophytes or lower Cryptogams, which when fertilized becomes an *oospore*. **Oostegite** (o,ǫ·stĭdʒəit) [Gr. στέγειν cover; see -ITE[1] 3], an egg-case in some Crustacea, formed by an expansion of the limbs of certain somites; hence **Oostegitic** (o,ǫ·stĭdʒi·tik) *a.* ‖**Ootheca** (ōu,oþī·kă) [Gr. θήκη case], an egg-case in certain invertebrate animals; also, a sporangium; **Oothe·cal** *a.*

Oobit: see WOUBIT.

Oodles (ū·d'lz). *U.S.* 1869. [Of unkn. origin.] 'Heaps.'

Oof (ūf). *slang.* 1885. [Shortening of *ooftisch*, Yiddish for G. *auf tisch*, i.e. *auf dem tisch(e* on the table, said of money laid on the table in gambling.] Money. Also in the fuller form **Oo·ftish.** Hence **Oof-bird,** a supplier of money. **Oo·fless** *a.* **Oo·fy** *a.*

‖**Oogonium** (ōu,ogōu·niŏm). 1867. [f. Oo- + Gr. γόνος generation; see -IUM.] *Bot.* The female reproductive organ in the Thallophytes or lower Cryptogams, usu. a rounded cell or sac containing one or more *oospheres*.

Ooidal (o,oi·dăl), *a.* 1836. [f. Gr. ᾠοειδής egg-shaped + -AL[1].] Resembling an egg; oval.

‖**Oolakan, -chan** (ū·lăkăn). Also **ou-, eu-.** 1836. [Native name.] The candle-fish (*Thaleichthys pacificus*) of north-western America. Also *attrib.*, as *o. oil.*

Oolite (ōu·ŏləit). 1802. [– Fr. *oölithe*, mod. L. *oolites*; see Oo-, -LITE.] **1.** *Min.* A concretionary limestone composed of small rounded granules, like the roe of a fish, each consisting of carbonate of lime around a grain of sand as a nucleus; roe-stone. **2.** *Geol.* The name of an important series of fossiliferous rocks of this character, lying between the Chalk, or the Wealden, and the Lias; sometimes applied to the whole series of limestones, sandstones, and clays, to which these belong; now usu. included, with the Lias, in the Jurassic system 1816. **3.** *attrib.*, as *o. formation*, etc. 1813. Hence **Ooli·tic** *a.* of the structure of o.; pertaining to the O. formation.

Oology (o,ǫ·lŏdʒi). 1831. [– Fr. *oölogie*, mod.L. *oologia*; see Oo-, -LOGY.] **a.** The study of, or a description of, birds' eggs, esp. in regard to their external appearance. **b.** The practice of collecting birds' eggs. Hence **Oolo·gic, -al** *adjs.*; **-ly** *adv.* **Oo·logist,** one versed in o.; a collector of birds' eggs.

‖**Oolong** (ū·lǫŋ). Also **ou-.** 1852. [Chinese *wulung*, f. *wu* black + *lung* dragon.] A dark variety of cured tea.

‖**Oomiak** (ū·miæk). 1769. Also **umiak, ooniak.** 1769. [Eskimo.] A large Eskimo boat for women and children, propelled by paddles.

-oon, the form usu. taken in Eng. by Fr. final *-on* in words stressed on the final syllable, adopted XVI–XVIII, as Fr. *dragon*, Eng. *dragoon* (corresp. to *-on* in old adoptions, as *baron, felon*, and mod. borrowings, as *chignon*); and hence by the Fr. suffix *-on*, = It. *-one*, Sp. *-on*, L. *-o, -onem*, forming in L. masculine appellatives as *naso* big-nosed man. Examples of adopted words are *balloon, buffoon, cartoon, quadroon*; *-oon* is rare as an Eng. formative, as in *spittoon*.

Oons (ūnz), *int.* Now *rare.* 1593. [Worn-down f. *wounds* (= *God's wounds*.).] = ZOUNDS.

‖**Oopak, oopack** (ū·pæk). 1858. [Chinese *u-pak*, Cantonese dial. form of *Hu-peh*, a central province of China.] A variety of black tea.

Oophore (ōu·ŏfoəɹ). 1875. [f. Oo- + -PHORE.] *Bot.* That stage, or form of a plant, in the higher Cryptogams (ferns, mosses, etc.) which, in the alternation of generations, bears male and female organs; the 'sexual generation'; also called *oophyte*. Opp. to *sporophore* or *sporophyte*.

Oophorectomy (ōu:ofore·ktŏmi). 1872. [f. Oo- + -PHORE (cf. Gr. ᾠοφόρος bearing eggs) + -ECTOMY, as a parallel form of OVARIOTOMY.] *Surg.* Excision of the ovary.

Oophoridium (ōu:ofori·diŏm). Also **oophorid.** 1835. [f. Oo- + Gr. -φορος bearing + *-idium* = Gr. -ιδιον, dim. ending; see -IUM.] *Bot.* A name for the macrosporangia (or loosely, the macrospores) of certain *Lycopodiaceæ*.

Oophoritis (ōu:oforəi·tis). 1872. [f. Oo- + -PHORE + -ITIS.] *Path.* Inflammation of the ovary.

‖**Oorali** (*u*rā·li). 1880. Var. of WOORALI.

‖**Oosporangium** (ōu:osporæ·ndʒiŏm). Also **o·ospora:nge.** 1857. [f. Oo- + SPORANGIUM.] *Bot.* **a.** Thuret's term for the unilocular zoo-sporangium of certain fucoid Algæ (Phæosporeæ). **b.** A case or sac containing an oospore.

Oospore (ōu·ŏspōəɹ). [f. Oo- + SPORE.] *Bot.* The fertilized female cell or oosphere, esp. in the lower Cryptogams, which forms the germ of a future plant.

Ootocoid (o,ǫ·tŏkoid), *a.* and *sb.* 1863. [– mod.L. *Ootocoidea* (n. pl.), f. Gr. ᾠοτόκος oviparous; see -OID.] *Zool.* **a.** *adj.* Belonging to the *Ootocoidea*, a division of mammals comprising the marsupials and monotremes. **b.** *sb.* One of the *Ootocoidea*. Also **Ootocoi·dean** *a.* and *sb.*

Ooze (ūz), *sb.*[1] [OE. *wōs*, corresp. to MLG. *wōs(e* scum, ON. *vás* (MSw. *oss, os, oos*, MDa. *oss, oess, voos*). Sense 3 is from OOZE *v.* Now assoc. with OOZE *sb.*[2]] †**1.** Juice, sap –1450. **2.** *techn.* The liquor of a tan-vat; an infusion of oak-bark, sumach, or the like 1575. **3.** The act or fact of oozing; exudation; gentle flow; also, that which oozes; a sluggish stream 1718.

Comb. (from 2) **o.-calf,** calf-skin through which the dye has been forced by mechanical means, used for the uppers of boots and shoes, and by bookbinders.

Ooze (ūz), *sb.*[2] [OE. *wāse* = OFris. *wāse*, ON. *veisa* stagnant pool, puddle. For the vocalism cf. *two, who, womb*; for the loss of *w* cf. prec. and dial. *ood, ool, ooman* for *wood, wool, woman*.] **1.** Wet mud or slime; esp. that in the bed of a river or estuary. **b.** A stretch of mud; a mudbank; a marsh or fen, etc. 1500. **2.** *Ocean-sounding.* White or grey calcareous matter, covering vast tracts of the ocean-floor 1860.

1. The ose or salt water mudde 1602. *fig.* Fishing a manuscript out of the o. of oblivion LOWELL.

Ooze (ūz), *sb.*[3] *Obs.* or *rare.* 1555. [Of unkn. origin.] Seaweed.

Ooze (ūz), *v.* [ME. *wōsen*, f. *wōse* OOZE *sb.*[1] 1, 2.] **1.** *intr.* Of moisture: To pass slowly or in small quantities through the pores of a body; to exude, to percolate. **b.** Of a substance: To exude moisture. late ME. **2.** *transf.* and *fig.* To pass as through pores, and so slowly, gradually, or imperceptibly. Often with *out, away.* 1775. **3.** *trans.* To emit (moisture, etc.) slowly and gradually. Often with *out.* late ME.

1. I saw the water o. in at several crannies SWIFT. **2.** Your valour has oozed away SHERIDAN. Rumours began to o. out 1867. **3.** His doe-skin boots were oozing out water MRS. CARLYLE.

‖**Oozoa** (ōu,ozōu·ă), *sb. pl.* 1881. [mod.L., f. Gr. ᾠόν egg + ζῷα, pl. of ζῷον animal; see -A 4.] *Zool.* A synonym of PROTOZOA. Hence **Oozo·an** *a.* and *sb.*

Oozy (ū·zi), *a.* [In 1 and 2 late ME. *wosie*, f. *wose* mud, OOZE *sb.*[2]; in 3 a later formation related to OOZE *v.*] **1.** Of water: Charged with ooze or mud; muddy. **2.** Composed of or resembling ooze, having the consistency of wet mud or slime. Of a sea-bottom: Consisting of ooze. 1563. **3.** Exuding moisture; damp with exuded or deposited moisture 1714. **b.** Slimy or damp; said of seaweed 1742.

2. And bid the weltring waves their o. channel keep MILT. **3.** The floor of the dungeon o. with wet HAWTHORNE. Hence **Oo·zily** *adv.* **Oo·ziness.**

Op-, the form of the L. prefix OB- bef. *p*, as in *oppose*, etc.

Opacity (opæ·sĭti). 1560. [– Fr. *opacité* – L. *opacitas*, f. *opacus* OPAQUE.] **1.** The state of being in shadow; darkness, obscurity; an instance of this 1611. **b.** The condition of not reflecting light 1794. **2.** The quality or condition of being impervious to light; non-translucency 1634. **b.** *transf. Acoustic o.*, imperviousness to waves of sound 1871. **3.** *fig.* **a.** Darkness of meaning. **b.** Denseness or obtuseness of intellect; *concr.* one in whom this is embodied. 1560.

Opacous (opēi·kəs), *a.* Now *rare.* 1621. [f. L. *opacus* OPAQUE + -OUS.] = OPAQUE *a.* Hence **Opa·cous-ly** *adv.*, **-ness.**

Opah (ōu·pă). 1750. [West African.] A rare fish of the North Atlantic (*Lampris guttatus*), of the mackerel family, conspicuous for its brilliant colour. Also called King-fish, Moon-fish.

Opal (ōu·păl). 1591. [– Fr. *opale* or L. *opalus* (Pliny), prob. ult. (like late Gr. ὀπάλλιος) – Skr. *upalas* precious stone.] **1.** An amorphous form of hydrous silica, somewhat resembling quartz, but in some species exhibiting a delicate play of colour; these when cut are valuable as gems. **2.** = OPALINE *sb.* 2. 1889. **3.** *attrib.* or *adj.* Of or resembling the opal or that of the opal, opalescent 1649.

1. *fig.* Thy minde is a very Opall SHAKS. *Common o.*, a milk-white or bluish variety, with reflexion of green, yellow, and red; *fire* or *sun o.*, a rich hyacinth-red variety from Mexico; *harlequin, precious*, or *noble o.*, a variety exhibiting a rich play of prismatic colours, which flash from minute fissures apparently striated with microscopic lines. See also CACHOLONG, GIRASOL, HYALITE.

Opalesce (ōupăle·s), *v.* 1819. [f. OPAL + *esce*; see -ESCENT.] *intr.* To exhibit a play of colours or iridescence like that of the opal.

Opalescent (ōupăle·sĕnt), *a.* 1813. [f. OPAL + -ESCENT.] Exhibiting a play of colours or iridescence like that of the opal. So **Opale·sque** *a.* 1863. **Opale·scence,** the quality of being o. 1805.

Opaline (ōu·pălin, -əin), *a.* and *sb.* 1784. [f. OPAL + -INE[1].] **A.** *adj.* Opalescent; of the nature of opal. **B.** *sb.* **1.** Occas. applied to a variety of yellow chalcedony which presents an opaline semi-opacity 1861. **2.** A semi-translucent glass; also called *milk-glass* 1875. **3.** An opaline colour, surface, or expanse 1871.

Opalize (ōu·păləiz), *v.* 1811. [f. OPAL + -IZE.] **1.** *intr.* To opalesce. **2.** *trans.* To make iridescent like an opal. Chiefly in **O·palized** *ppl. a.*

O·paloty:pe. 1873. [f. OPAL + -TYPE.] A positive photograph on opal glass.

Opaque (opēi·k), *a.* (*sb.*) late ME. [(Formerly often *opake*) – L. *opacus*, partly through Fr. *opaque*, whence the current sp.] **1.** †Lying in shadow; darkened, obscure –1775. **b.** Of a body or surface: Not reflecting or emitting light; not lustrous, dull 1794. **2.** Impermeable to light; hence, impenetrable to sight 1641. **3.** *fig.* **a.** Hard to make out; obscure 1761. **b.** Impervious to reason, dense, obtuse 1850. **B.** *sb.* **a.** Something opaque; a medium or space through which light cannot pass 1742. **b.** A shade for the eyes 1900.

1. b. The planets are all opake, or dark bodies 1794. **3. a.** The o. but authentic Commons Journals CARLYLE. **b.** Too o. to understand her husband's jeers 1882. **B. a.** The light began to penetrate the dim o. of his understanding 1824. Hence **Opa·que-ly** *adv.*, **-ness.**

-opathy: see -PATHY.

Ope (ōup), *a.* and *sb.* ME. [Reduced from OPEN; cf. *awake(n*, etc.] = OPEN *a.* and *sb.*

Ope (ōup), *v.* late ME. [Reduced from OPEN *v.* after prec.] To open. Chiefly *poet.*

Oped his young eye to bear the blaze of greatness GRAY.

Opeidoscope (opəi·dŏskoup). 1873. [f. Gr. ὄψ, ὀπ- voice + εἶδος form + -SCOPE.] An instrument consisting of a tube closed at one end by a tense membrane, having attached to its centre a small mirror, to show the musical vibration caused by speaking or singing at the open end.

Opelet (ōu·plĕt). 1860. [irreg. f. OPE *a.* + -LET.] A name of a sea-anemone, *Anemonia sulcata*, so called because the tentacles cannot be retracted.

Open (ōᵘ·p'n), *sb.* late ME. [Partly vbl. sb. f. OPEN *v.*; partly ellipt. use of OPEN *a.*] **I. 1.** = OPENING *vbl. sb.* 2; an aperture 1470. **2.** = OPENING *vbl. sb.* 5. Now *arch.* 1711.

2. Perhaps this may leave an o. to sarcasm 1757.

II. sb. use of OPEN *a.* †**1.** Open, unconcealed, or plainly seen condition –1646. **2. a.** *The o.*: the open space. (*a*) The part of the country not enclosed; (*b*) Ground without buildings, trees, etc.; (*c*) The open water, in sea or river; (*d*) The open air 1624. **b.** An open or clear space 1796. **3.** *Stock Exchange.* The open market 1898.

1. *Hen. VIII*, III. ii. 405. **2. a.** The soldier is taught how to attack in the o. 1880. Raspberries ..grown in the o. 1893.

Open (ōᵘ·p'n), *a.* (*adv.*) [OE. *open* = OFris. *open*, OS. *opan* (Du. *open*), OHG. *offan* (G. *offen*), ON. *opinn* :– Gmc. **upanaz*, having the form of a strong pa. pple. f. UP.] **I.** Physical senses. **1.** Of a door, gate, etc.: Not 'put to', not closed or shut; 'up', set up, so as to allow free passage through. Also said of a doorway or other passage. **2.** Of a containing space, a house, box, etc.: Having its gate, door, lid, or some part of its enclosing boundary drawn aside or removed; not shut up OE. **b.** Hence, Free of entrance to all (or *to* persons specified) OE. **3.** Of a space: Not shut in; unenclosed, unwalled, unconfined. See also OPEN AIR. OE. **b.** Hence, of a battle: Fought in the open (not in a fortress, etc.), and so with full forces 1548. **4.** Not covered over or covered in; esp. in *o. boat, carriage* OE. **5.** Uncovered; bare, exposed OE. **6.** Unclosed, expanded, spread out ME. **7.** Of a line, texture, etc.: Having spaces between its parts; containing interstices, gaps, holes, or unoccupied spaces; perforated, porous 1625. **8.** Of a passage or space: Unobstructed, clear. Of a country: Free from wood, buildings, etc. Of a river, port, etc.: Free from ice. ME. **b.** Of the bodily passages: Not obstructed; *esp.* of the bowels 1562. **9. a.** Of the soil: Unbound; loose, permeable. **b.** Of weather, etc.: Free from frost, as an *o. winter*. 1615. **10.** *Naut.* †**a.** Looking unobstructedly *upon* or *to*. **b.** Seen with an opening between; clear, detached. 1478. **11.** *techn.* **a.** *Mus.* Of an organ-pipe: Not closed or shut at the top. Of a string: Not stopped by a finger. Hence, of a note. Produced by such a pipe or string, or on a wind-instrument without the aid of a slide, key, or piston. 1674. **b.** Of sounds: Uttered with the mouth open. *spec.* Of vowels: Produced with a wider opening of the oral cavity than those called *close*; e.g. *open o.* and *e* (= ǒ, ě), *close o* and *e* (= ō, ē). 1485. **c.** Of a syllable: Ending in a vowel 1871.

1. The windows..were left o. SWIFT. The door burst o. FIELDING. **2.** His head was split o. with a blow 1887. Standing beside the o. grave 1902. **b.** The old universities are o. to all 1891. **3.** The fields then being o. and champain BACON. The Enemy..sent a strong Party into an o. Village 1704. *O. grate, o. fireplace*, one in which the whole of the fire is visible. **b.** We our forts and lines forsake, To dare our British foes to o. fight 1706. **4.** A drive in an o. carriage and four 1854. **5.** Sow Alaternus Seeds in..o. Beds EVELYN. **6.** An o. letter in his hand TROLLOPE. **7.** Phr. *O. order* (*Mil.*), a formation in which the individual men are three or more yards apart; (*Naval*), a formation in which the individual ships are more than a cable's length apart. *O. harmony* (*Mus.*), a harmony in which the chords are separated by wide intervals. **8.** The Ice being broke, the Sound is again o. for the Ships STEELE. The Preservation of O. Spaces 1896. **10.** I found myself o. to the northern shore DE FOE.

II. Non-physical senses. **1.** Exposed to the mental view; patent, plain, easy to understand. Now only in *to lay o.*, to lay bare, 'expose'. OE. **2.** Exposed to general view or knowledge; public. Of persons: Acting in public or without concealment. OE. **3.** Not confined or limited to a few; that may be used, shared, or competed for without restriction 1460. **4.** Exposed, liable, or subject *to* 1450. **5.** Unreserved, frank, candid 1513. **6.** Free in giving. Now chiefly in *o. hand, o.-handed.* 1597. **7.** Of a question, etc.: Not finally settled; undecided; hence, uncertain 1562. **8.** Of a thing, course of action, etc.: Not closed against access; accessible, available. Const. *to* (a person). 1526. **9.** Of a person: Accessible to appeals, offers, emotions, or ideas; impressionable; amenable *to* (pity or reason) 1672.

1. A foole layeth o. his folly *Prov.* 13:16. **2.** Cleombrotus he treated with o. contempt 1844. **3.** *O. champion*, one who has been successful in an unrestricted championship. **4.** It seem o. to doubt 1891. **5.** One Monarch wears an honest o. Face DRYDEN. **6.** A Hand O. (as Day) for melting Charitie SHAKS. **7.** O. POLICY, VERDICT: see these words. Certain questions brought before Parliament are treated as 'open' questions; that is, questions on which Ministers in Parliament are allowed to take opposite sides without resigning 1863. **8.** There are three..courses o. to us 1883. **9.** Those whose intelligence is quickest, openest, most sensitive M. ARNOLD. I am o. to offers 1902.

Phrases, etc. *With o. arms* (sense I. 6), with arms outspread to receive; hence, with great willingness of reception. *In o. court*, in the public court of justice, before the judge and the public. *O. ear*, an attentive ear. *O. eye*, an unclosed, hence an observant or watchful eye. *O. letter*, a letter addressed to an individual but published as a matter of general interest. *With o. mouth*, with mouth open to speak; also, gaping with wonder, etc.; open-mouthed. *To keep o. doors, house*, or *table*, to provide hospitality for all comers. See also sbs. and Main words.

Comb. **a.** With a sb., forming an *attrib.* phr., as *o.-fire, -house, -view*, etc. See also Main words. **b.** Parasynthetic combs. in *-ed* (unlimited in number), as *o.-armed, -fronted, -sleeved, -windowed* (hence *o.-windowedness*). **c.** Special combs.: **o.-cast, -cut**, in *Mining*, an o. working; **-faced** *a.*, having a frank or ingenuous face; hence *open-facedness*; **-hearth**, a hearth of the reverberatory type; see HEARTH 3 b; also *attrib.*; **-minded** *a.*, accessible to new arguments or ideas, hence *open-mindedness*; **o. note**, a musical note having an open head.

†**B.** *adv.* = Openly ME. *Twel. N.* III. iii. 37.

Open (ōᵘ·p'n), *v.* [OE. *openian* = OS. *opanon* (Du. *openen*), OHG. *offanōn* (G. *öffnen*); f. OPEN *a.*] **I.** *trans.* **1.** To move or turn (a door, gate, etc.) away from its closed position, so as to admit of passage. Also *absol.* **2.** To make (a building, box, or enclosed space) open (OPEN *a.* I. 2); to break open, unclose, undo; to provide free access to or egress from ME. **b.** With the purpose as the main notion: To render accessible *to* (persons or the public) or *for* (some purpose) 1560. **c.** To declare open to public use by a formal ceremony 1889. **3.** To spread apart, widen, expand, unroll, extend. Also *absol.* with ellipsis of object, as 'to o. (a book) at a page', etc. OE. **4.** To make an opening in; to cut or break into ME. **b.** To make, produce, or cause (an opening or open space of some kind) ME. **5.** To loosen. (In various shades of meaning.) 1683. **6.** To clear of obstruction or hindrance; to make (a road) free for passage. Chiefly *fig.* ME. **7.** To uncover, lay bare, expose to view, display OE. **8.** *Naut.* To come in sight of, get an open view of, by rounding or passing an intervening object 1628. †**9.** To reveal, disclose, declare, make known. *Obs.* exc. as in b. –1804. **b.** *esp.* To disclose or divulge (one's mind, feelings, designs, etc.); *refl.* to unbosom oneself ME. †**10.** To unfold the sense of; to expound –1720. **11.** To expand, enlarge, enlighten (the mind or heart) ME. **12.** To render available for settlement, use, intercourse, etc. Usu. *o. up.* 1617. **13.** To begin, start, commence 1693. **14.** *legal.* To state (a case) to the court, as a preliminary to adducing evidence; esp. to speak first in a case, a privilege of the affirmative side. 1621. **15.** To undo, recall, or set aside (a judgement, settlement, sale, etc.) so as to leave the matter open to further action, discussion, or negotiation 1792.

1. Huy had opened its gates to the French MACAULAY. O., in the King's name LYTTON. **2.** Why, then the world's mine Oyster, which I, with sword will o. SHAKS. Shall we o. another bottle? (*mod.*). **b.** *Mod.* To o. a shop, store, branch of a bank, registry office, etc. **3.** He too had a library, although he never opened a book 1783. *absol.* I will take the first stanza, on which I have chanced to o., in the Lyrical Ballads COLERIDGE. **4.** Who stooping op'nd my left side, and took From thence a Rib MILTON. Phr. *To o. ground*, to break up the surface of ground, as by ploughing, etc. **b.** Alpheus bold..With his trident..opened a chasm In the rocks SHELLEY. Phr. *To o. trenches*, to dig trenches in besieging: see TRENCH. **5.** All kinds of manures o. the soil 1765. The leading troop..opens its ranks 1796. **6.** Thou op'nst Wisdoms way, And giv'st access MILT. The bowels should be well opened at the onset by a brisk purgative 1897. **7.** Herbs of every leaf.. Op'ning their various colours MILT. **8.** Taking care not to o. the Obelisk on the slope of the North Head 1858. **9.** Nor o. it to others that he was Messias 1548. **b.** I have opened my mind unto you BUNYAN. **11.** My eyes had been opened, and my heart with them RUSKIN. **12.** Phr. *To o. land, to o. a country to trade.* **13.** Phr. *To o. an account, o. the ball, o. fire*, etc.: see the sbs. **14.** Phr. *To o. pleadings*, in a trial before jury, to state briefly the substance of the pleadings. **15.** The mortgagor is entitled to open the foreclosure on the usual terms 1877.

II. *intr.* (Sometimes for *refl.*, sometimes *ellipt.* or *absol.* use of the trans.) **1.** To become open, unshut, or unclosed. Hence, generally, to come apart or asunder, so as to admit of passage, disclose a vacant space, display the interior or contents; (of an abscess) to burst and discharge. OE. **2. a.** Of a door, etc.: To serve as a passage *to* or *into* 1760. **b.** Of a room or space: To have an opening or passage *to, into, out of*, etc. 1615. Also **c.** To have its opening, or outlet *towards*, to lie open *to* 1697. **3.** To expand, extend, spread apart. Also *o. out.* late ME. **b.** *fig.* To expand in intellect or sympathy 1709. **4.** To become disclosed or revealed, to begin to appear; to expand to the view, to become more and more visible 1708. **b.** *Naut.* To appear distinct or separate 1745. **5.** To speak out; to speak explicitly, explain. Now *rare.* 1641. **6.** Of hounds: To give tongue, begin to cry when in pursuit on a scent; hence, contemptuously, of men. late ME. **7.** To begin; to start operations. In theatrical parlance, To make a début, to begin a season or tour. Often *ellipt.*, for *o. fire.* 1716.

1. My wound opened again with riding DE FOE. Law offices opened at eight o'clock in those days 1870. **2. b.** A library, opening through a greenhouse on to a lawn 1801. **c.** A valley opening to the sea shore 1839. **3.** MILTON *P. L.* VI. 481. **b.** All Hearts begin to o. STEELE. **4.** The stainless sky Opens beyond them like eternity SHELLEY. **5.** When I opened, I found that this man was willing to o. too COBBETT. **6.** *Merry W.* IV. ii. 209. **7.** A battery of eight guns opened on the fleet 1894. Our school opens next Monday 1902.

With advs. in specialized senses. **Open out.** *trans.* **a.** To unfold, unpack. **b.** To develop. **c.** To disclose, reveal, display or offer to mental view. *intr.* **d.** = sense II. 3. **e.** = sense II. 5. **O. up.** (*Up* thus added to *Open* often merely strengthens or gives emphasis, esp. in the senses following.) **a.** *trans.* To open to view, access, use, passage, or traffic; to lay open (a question previously untouched); to bring to light, disclose, raise and leave open. **b.** *intr.* To become open to passage, view, enterprise, etc. (by the removal of obstructions).

Phr. *To o. a* (or *the*) *door to*: to give access or free course to. *To o. one's eyes*, to take notice, regard; to stare with astonishment. *To o. a person's eyes*, to cause him to see, to make him aware of facts. *To o. one's mouth*, i.e. in order to swallow or eat, or (also *one's lips*) to speak; *not to o. one's lips*, to be absolutely silent.

Open air, open-air. 1526. **1.** *O·pen a·ir.* The unconfined atmosphere; hence, the unconfined space outside buildings, etc., usu. exposed to the weather. **2.** *attrib.* (usu. *o·pen-ai:r*). Existing, carried on, performed in, or characteristic of the open air 1860.

1. A Jesuit preaching in the o. BERKELEY. **2.** The hygienic and dietetic arrangements and especially the o. treatment 1896.

O·pen-bill. 1837. A bird of the genus *Anastomus*, allied to the stork, found in Africa and Asia; so called because the mandibles of its bill when shut are in contact only at the ends, leaving an open space in the middle.

O·pen-brea·sted (stress var.), *a.* 1594. Now *Obs.* or *arch.* **a.** Having the breast exposed. **b.** Of a garment: Not covering the breast 1599.

Open door. 1526. A door standing open; hence used *fig.* to typify free admission or access, freedom of admission. **b.** *International Politics.* Admission to a country, esp. for commercial intercourse, open to all upon equal terms. Used esp. with ref. to Chinese ports. 1856.

1. b. *attrib.* Coöperation between this republic and Great Britain as to the furtherance of the open door policy 1898.

Opener (ōᵘ·p'nəɹ). 1548. [f. OPEN *v.* +

-ER¹.] One who or that which opens; †an aperient.

Open-eyed (ōᵘ·p'n,əi·d; stress var.), *a.* 1601. **1.** Having the eyes open; awake, vigilant. **b.** Done with the eyes open 1876. **2.** Having the mental 'eyes' or perceptive powers alert 1648.

1. Open-ey'd Conspiracie His time doth take SHAKS.

Open field. 1780. An unenclosed field; undivided arable land. Chiefly *attrib.* in *open-field system* by which the arable land of a village was planned out into a number of unenclosed portions or strips and distributed among the villagers.

O·pen-ha·nded (stress var.), *a.* 1601. [Parasynthetic f. *open hand*; see -ED².] *lit.* Having an open hand. **a.** Free in giving, liberal, generous. †**b.** Ready to receive gifts –1785. Hence **O:penha·nded-ly** *adv.*, **-ness.**

O·pen-hea·rted (stress var.), *a.* 1611. [Parasynthetic f. *open heart*; see -ED².] **1.** Disposed to communicate thoughts or feelings; not reserved, frank. **2.** Accessible to noble emotions; full of kindly feeling 1617. So **O:penhea·rted-ly** *adv.*, **-ness.**

Opening (ōᵘ·p'niŋ, ōᵘ·pniŋ), *vbl. sb.* ME. [f. OPEN *v.* + -ING¹.] **1.** The action of OPEN *v.* Also with adv. as *o. out, o. up.* **2.** A gap, hole, or passage; an aperture ME. **b.** A bay, gulf, or other more or less wide indentation of the land 1719. **c.** The width of an arch between its pillars 1739. **3.** *U.S.* A tract of ground over which trees are wanting or thinly scattered, in the midst of forest tracts 1704. **4.** The action of beginning; commencement 1712. **b.** *spec.* The statement of a case made by counsel preliminary to adducing evidence 1660. **c.** *Chess.* A mode of beginning a game; *spec.* a definite sequence of moves for the purpose of establishing a line of defence or attack 1735. **5.** An opportunity; a vacancy in connection with any business or profession 1793.

1. A confused noise of the o. of hounds BERKELEY. The opening-up of a market 1887. **4.** The days which..preceded the o. of the session MACAULAY. **5.** She might have made him miss one or two openings in life 1855.

O·pening, *ppl. a.* late ME. [f. as prec. + -ING².] That opens, in various senses. **1.** That renders open; *spec.* aperient. **b.** That opens or commences, initial; introductory. **2.** That becomes open; unclosing, unfolding, etc.

1. b. It was the o. day of the exhibition 1882. **2.** The o. eyelids of the morn MILTON.

Openly (ōᵘ·p'nli), *adv.* OE. [f. OPEN *a.* + -LY².] **1.** Without concealment; in public; publicly. **2.** Frankly, unreservedly ME. †**3.** Manifestly; clearly, plainly –1682.

1. My loue to ye, Shall shew it selfe more o. hereafter SHAKS.

Open-mouthed (ōᵘ·p'nmau·ðd; stress var.), *a.* 1470. [Parasynthetic f. *open mouth*; see -ED².] **1.** Having the mouth open; having an open mouth; hence, rapacious, in full cry, etc. 1532. **b.** Of a vessel or the like: Having a wide mouth 1660. **2.** Gaping, as with astonishment or surprise 1593. **3.** Clamorous, vociferous. Now *rare* or *arch.* 1470.

Openness (ōᵘ·p'n,nės). 1530. [f. OPEN *a.* + -NESS.] **1.** The quality or condition of being OPEN. **2.** Absence of dissimulation, secrecy, or reserve; candour, sincerity 1611.

Open sesame (ōᵘ·p'n se·sămi). 1826. [See SESAME.] The magic words by which, in the tale of Ali Baba and the Forty Thieves, the door of the robbers' cave was made to fly open; hence, any irresistible means of securing immediate admission.

That universal key, that *open sesame*, a bribe 1837.

†**O·pen-ti:de.** ME. [See TIDE *sb.* I.] = next –1744.

O·pen ti:me. 1483. The time during which anything is open: *spec.* †**a.** The time after harvest when cattle might be turned into the open fields. †**b.** The time out of Lent when no fast is imposed. **c.** That which is not close time for fish, etc.

O·pen-wo:rk. 1812. [See OPEN *a.* I. 7.] **1.** Any kind of work with interstices in its substance, as in open-work of iron, etc.; *esp.* such work in knitting, netting, embroidery. **2.** *Mining.* Excavation open to the surface 1881.

Opera (ǫ·pĕră). 1644. [– It. *opera* (whence also Fr. *opéra*) :– L. *opera* labour, work produced, fem. collect. sb. f. *opus, oper-* work.] **1.** A dramatic performance in which music forms an essential part, consisting of recitatives, arias, and choruses, with orchestral accompaniment and scenery; also, a dramatic or musical composition intended for this, a libretto or score. **2.** (Usu. *the o.*) As a branch of dramatic art 1759. **b.** With qualification denoting a particular branch or kind 1711.

1. Phr. *At* or *to the o.*, including the notion of the place (cf. *at the play*). **2. b.** *Comic o.* (see COMIC A. 1); *grand o.* (see GRAND A. 8); *o. bouffe* (= Fr. *opéra bouffe*, also ellipt. *bouffe*, and in It. form *opera buffa*), comic o., esp. an operatic extravaganza.

Comb.: **o.-cloak,** a cloak of rich material worn by ladies at the opera or in going to evening parties, dances, etc.; **-girl,** (*a*) a girl or woman who dances in the ballet of an o.; (*b*) *pl.* a greenhouse plant, *Mantisia saltatoria*, called also DANCING-GIRLS; **-glass, -glasses,** a small binocular for use at theatres, etc.; **-hat,** a hat suitable for use at the o.; *spec.* a crush-hat; **-house,** a theatre for the performance of operas.

Operable (ǫ·pĕrăb'l), *a.* 1646. [– late and med.L. *operabilis*, f. L. *operari*; see OPERATE *v.*, -BLE. In mod. use f. OPERATE *v.*] †**1.** Practicable –1677. **2.** *Med.* That admits of being operated upon 1904. Hence **O:perabi·lity.**

Operameter (ǫpĕræ·mĭtəɹ). 1829. [irreg. f. L. *opera* works + -METER.] *Mech.* A device for registering the number of revolutions made by a shaft, axle, or wheel, the strokes of a piston, the copies delivered from a printing-press, etc.

Operancy (ǫ·pĕrănsi). *rare.* 1810. [f. OPERANT; see -ANCY.] The quality or condition of being operant; operation.

Operand (ǫ·pĕrænd). 1886. [– L. *operandum*, n. gerundive of *operari* OPERATE *v.*] *Math.* A quantity or symbol to be operated on.

Operant (ǫ·pĕrănt). 1602. [– *operant-*, pr. ppl. stem of L. *operari*; see next, -ANT.] **A.** *adj.* That operates; operative. **B.** *sb.* One who, or that which, operates 1700; an operative (LAMB).

Operate (ǫ·pĕreᶦt), *v.* 1606. [– *operat-*, pa. ppl. stem of L. *operari* work, bestow labour upon, f. *opus, oper-* work; see -ATE³.] **I.** *intr.* **1.** To be in working, exercise influence, produce an effect, act. **2.** Of persons: To bring force or influence to bear *on* or *upon*. Now *rare* or *arch.* 1650. **3.** Of drugs, medicines, etc.: To produce the desired effect; to act 1706. **4.** To perform a practical operation or series of operations; see OPERATION 5. Const. *on, upon.* 1674. **b.** *Surg.*: see OPERATION 6. 1799. **c.** *Mil.* and *Naval*: see OPERATION 7. 1808. **d.** To deal or speculate in stocks or shares; to buy and sell commodities as a broker 1859.

1. The revolutionary spirit, ceasing to o. in politics MACAULAY. **2.** He knew the Highland chieftans well, and how to o. on them 1790. **4. d.** A bull in the same jargon, is one who operates for a rise 1859.

II. *trans.* **1.** To effect by the exertion of force or influence; to bring about, accomplish 1637. **2.** To cause or actuate the working of; to work (a machine, etc.). Chiefly *U.S.* 1864. **3.** To direct the working of; to manage, conduct, work (a railway, business, etc.); to carry out, direct to an end (an undertaking, etc.) Chiefly *U.S.* 1880.

1. Now plotting to o. the ruine of the Protestant Religion MILT. **2.** The cost of operating the cars 1886. **3.** The..Company o. a large foundry 1891.

Operatic, †-ical (ǫpĕræ·tik, -ăl), *adjs.* 1730. [irreg. f. OPERA after *dramatic, dramatical*; see -IC, -ICAL.] Pertaining to, or of the nature of, opera. Hence **Opera·tically** *adv.*

Operating (ǫ·pĕreᶦtiŋ), *vbl. sb.* 1674. [f. OPERATE *v.* + -ING¹.] The action of OPERATE *v.*; an instance of this, an operation.

attrib. and *Comb.*, as *o. room*; **o.-table,** one on which a patient is operated upon; **-theatre,** a room constructed for surgical operations before a class.

Operation (ǫpĕrēᶦ·ʃən). late ME. [– (O)Fr. *opération* – L. *operatio*, f. as OPERATE *v.*; see -ION.] †**1.** Action, performance, work –1567. **2.** Working; exertion of force, energy, or influence; the way in which anything works. late ME. **b.** The condition of being in working 1818. **3.** Power to operate or work; efficacy, influence, virtue, force. Now chiefly of legal instruments. 1509. **b.** The effect produced; influence *on* something. Now *rare* or *Obs.* 1605. **4.** A particular form or kind of activity; an active process 1594. **5.** The performance of something of practical or mechanical nature, e.g. as a scientific experiment or demonstration. late ME. **b.** A (speculative) business transaction. orig. *U.S.* 1863. **6.** *Surg.* An act or series of acts performed upon an organic body with the hand alone or by means of an instrument, to remedy deformity or injury, cure or prevent disease, or relieve pain 1597. **7.** *Mil.* and *Naval.* A series of warlike or strategic acts; a movement 1749. **8.** *Math.* The action of subjecting a number or quantity to any process whereby its value or form is affected 1713. **9.** The action of operating a machine, engine, railway, business, etc. 1872.

2. There are divers manners off operacions and yet but one God which worketh all thynges TINDALE 1 *Cor.* 12:6. The o. of the condenser pump is very simple 1824. **b.** Phr. *In o., to come into o.* **3.** He cannot..enlarge, in his own favour, the legal or equitable o. of the instrument 1884. **4.** By the operations of the mind we understand every mode of thinking of which we are conscious 1785. **7.** Phr. *Line of operations*, the line an army follows to attain its objective point 1867. Hence **Opera·tional** *a.* (esp. with reference to sense 7).

Operative (ǫ·pĕrătiv), *a.* and *sb.* 1598. [– late L. *operativus*, f. as prec.; see -IVE. Cf. (O)Fr. *opératif, -ive.*] **A.** *adj.* **1.** Characterized by operating; exerting force, energy, or influence; productive *of* something; in operation 1603. **2.** Productive of the intended or proper effect; effectual, efficacious 1598. **3.** Concerned with manual or mechanical work; practical 1624. **4.** Pertaining to surgical operations 1783. **5.** Of a person: Engaged in work or production, active 1824. **6.** Engaged in production as a workman or artisan, working. (Now perh. the sb. used *attrib.*) 1831.

1. The strongest and most o. sense of duty would not satisfy you 1879. **2.** Fraud was an o. instrument in the hands of this aspiring general 1818. **3.** In Architecture, as in all other O. Arts, the End must direct the Operation 1624. **6.** Members of the o. class C. BRONTË.

B. *sb.* **1.** One who operates or works in any branch of industry, trade, or profession; a worker 1809. **2.** A workman in any industrial art; an artisan, mechanic. Also *attrib.* 1827. Hence **O·perative-ly** *adv.*, **-ness.**

Operator (ǫ·pĕreᶦtəɹ). 1597. [– late L. *operator*, f. as prec.; see -OR 2. Cf. (O)Fr. *opérateur.*] One who operates. **1.** One who does or effects something; a worker, an agent 1611. **2.** One who performs the practical or mechanical operations belonging to any process, business, or investigation; a person professionally or officially so engaged 1597. **3.** One who performs surgical operations; an operating surgeon or dentist 1597. †**b.** A quack manufacturer of drugs, etc. –1710. **4.** One who carries on financial operations in stocks, shares, or commodities 1828. **5.** One who works a machine, telegraph, etc. 1870. **6.** One who works a business, undertaking, etc. *U.S.* 1877. **7.** *Math.* A symbol indicating an operation or series of operations, and itself subject to algebraical operation 1855.

Opercle (opə̄·ɹk'l). 1597. [– L. *operculum* cover, etc.; see -CULE.] †**1.** A cover, covering –1597. **2.** *Nat. Hist.* = OPERCULUM 1840.

Opercular (opə̄·ɹkiŭlăɹ), *a.* 1830. [f. OPERCULUM + -AR¹.] *Nat. Hist.* Of, pertaining to, or of the nature of an operculum; characterized by the presence of an operculum.

Operculate (opə̄·ɹkiŭleᶦt), *a.* (*sb.*). 1775. [f. OPERCULUM + -ATE².] *Nat. Hist.* **A.** *adj.* Furnished with or having an operculum; effected by means of an operculum. **B.** *sb.* An operculate mollusc. In the pl. the L. form **Operculata** is usual. 1856.

Operculi-, comb. form of L. *operculum*, as

in **Operculi·ferous** *a.*, having an operculum, operculate; **Ope·rculiform** *a.*, having the form of an operculum; **Oper-culi·genous** *a.*, producing an operculum; said of the metapodium of gastropods.

Operculum (opɔ̄·ɹkiŭlŏm). *Pl.* **-la.** 1713. [– L. *operculum*, f. *operire* cover, close, parallel formation to *aperire* open (see APERTURE); see -CULE.] An organ or structure forming or resembling a lid or cover; *spec.* **1.** *Zool.* **a.** The gill-cover of a fish 1752. **b.** The plate which serves to close the aperture of the shell of some molluscs when the animal is retracted; also, the flap or lid in sessile cirripeds 1777. **c.** Applied to various other lid-like parts and organs 1713. **2.** *Bot.* The lid of the capsule in mosses; also, the lid of the pitcher in *Nepenthes*, and the conical limb of the calyx of *Eucalyptus* 1788. **3.** *Anat.* In the brain, the principal covering of the insula or island of Reil, which overlaps the gyri operti from above 1889.

Operetta (ǫpĕre·tă). 1770. [– It. *operetta*, dim. of *opera*; see OPERA, -ETTE.] A short (orig. one-act) light opera.

Operose (ǫ·pĕrōᵘs), *a.* 1670. [– L. *operosus*, f. *opus*, *oper-* work; see -OSE[1].] **1.** Made or done with, attended by, or involving much labour; laborious; elaborate 1683. **2.** Of a person: Laborious; industrious, busy.

1. Browne might himself have obtained the same conviction by a method less o. JOHNSON. 2. An o. Compiler of History 1734. So **O·pero:sely** *adv.* 1668, **-ness** 1664. **Opero·sity,** laboriousness 1623.

Ophicalcite (ǫfikæ·lsəit). 1846. [f. Gr. ὄφις serpent + CALCITE.] *Min.* A species of rock composed of a mixture of serpentine and crystalline limestone (calcite).

Ophicleide (ǫ·fikləid). Also **-cleid.** 1834. [– Fr. *ophicléide* (1811), f. Gr. ὄφις serpent + κλείς, κλειδ- key.] A musical wind-instrument of powerful tone, a development of the ancient 'serpent', consisting of a conical brass tube bent double, with keys, forming the bass or alto to the key-bugle; also, a performer on this. **b.** A powerful reed-stop on the organ, now usu. called *tuba* 1842.

‖**Ophidia** (ofi·diă), *sb. pl.* 1802. [mod.L. *Ophidia*, f. Gr. ὄφις, ὀφιδ- serpent + -IA[2].] *Zool.* An order of Reptiles containing the snakes or serpents.

Ophidian (ofi·diăn), *a.* and *sb.* 1813. [f. prec. + -AN.] **A.** *adj.* **1.** *Zool.* Belonging to the order *Ophidia*. **2.** Pertaining or relating to, or resembling that of, a snake or serpent; snake-like 1883. **B.** *sb.* *Zool.* A reptile of the order *Ophidia*; a snake or serpent 1832.

‖**Ophidium** (ofi·diŏm). 1706. [Latinized form of *ophidion* (Pliny) – Gr. ὀφίδιον 'a fish resembling the conger', dim. of ὄφις, ὀφιδ- serpent; see -IUM.] *Zool.* A genus of acanthopterygian fishes with elongated bodies; a fish of this genus. So **Ophi·dioid** *a.* (*sb.*) belonging to (a fish of) the group *Ophidioidea*, of which O. is the typical genus.

Ophio-, comb. form of Gr. ὄφις serpent, as in ‖**Ophioglo·ssum** [Gr. γλῶσσα] *Bot.* the genus of ferns containing the adder's tongue, the type of the sub-order *Ophioglossaceæ*. **Ophio·later** [Gr. -λατρης], a serpent-worshipper. So **Ophio·latrous** *a.* given to serpent-worship. **Ophio·latry. Ophio·logy** [-LOGY], that branch of zoology which treats of serpents. Hence **Ophiolo·gic, -al** *adjs.*, **Ophio·logist. O·phioma:ncy** *rare* [Gr. μαντεία -MANCY], divination by means of serpents 1753.

Ophiomorph (ǫ·fiŏmǭɹf). [f. OPHIO- + Gr. μορφή form.] *Zool.* An amphibian of the order *Ophiomorpha* or *Ophiomorphæ* (also called *Apoda*, *Gymnophiona*, and *Ophiobatrachia*); a limbless serpentiform amphibian; a cæcilian. So **Ophiomo·rphic, Ophiomo·rphous** *adjs.* having the form of a serpent or snake; *spec.* of or pertaining to the *Ophiomorpha*; **Ophiomo·rphite,** an old name for fossil ammonite shells, from their snake-like appearance; a snake-stone.

‖**Ophiophagus** (ǫfiǫ·făgəs). *Pl.* **-gi** (dʒəi). 1555. [L. *Ophiophagi* (Pliny) – Gr. Ὀφιοφάγοι snake-eaters.] **1.** A serpent-eater. **2.** *Zool.* A genus of very venomous serpents allied to the cobra, inhabiting the East Indies, and feeding upon other snakes. One species is *O. elaps*, the HAMADRYAD 1883. So **Ophio·phagous** *a.* eating or feeding upon serpents 1650.

Ophir (ōᵘ·fəɹ). 1595. [Heb. *'ôpîr*.] The name of a place or region mentioned in the O.T., whence fine gold was obtained; its locality is uncertain.

Ophite[1] (ǫ·fəit). 1617. [– L. *ophites* (Pliny), – Gr. ὀφίτης (sc. λίθος) serpentine stone, f. ὄφις serpent; see -ITE[1] 2 b.] *Min.* Name for various eruptive or metamorphic rocks, usu. green, and having spots or markings like a serpent; serpentine; serpentine marble. Also *attrib.* Hence **Ophi·tic** *a.*[1] 1883.

Ophite[2] (ǫ·fəit). 1692. [– late L. *Ophitæ* (Tertullian) – Gr. Ὀφῖται, pl. of Ὀφίτης, f. ὄφις serpent; see -ITE[1] 1.] A member of a 2nd century sect, who worshipped the serpent as an embodiment of divine wisdom. Hence **Ophi·tic** *a.*[2] 1865.

‖**Ophiuchus** (ǫfi,iū·kŏs). 1658. [L. *ophiuchus* – Gr. ὀφιοῦχος, f. ὀφιο- OPHIO- + -εχος holding.] One of the ancient constellations, figured as a man holding a serpent; also called *Serpentarius*.

Ophiuran (ǫ·fi,iūᵊ·răn), *a.* and *sb.* 1836. [f. mod.L. *Ophiura*, f. Gr. ὄφις serpent + οὐρά tail, in ref. to the long snake-like arms; see -AN.] *Zool.* **A.** *adj.* Belonging to the genus *Ophiura*, family *Ophiuridæ*, or class *Ophiuroidea* of echinoderms. **B.** *sb.* A starfish of this genus, family, or class; a brittle-star or sand-star. So **O·phiure** (= B); **Ophiu·rid** *a.* and *sb.*; **Ophiu·roid** *a.* and *sb.*

‖**Ophryon** (ǫ·friǫn). 1878. [mod.L., f. Gr. ὀφρύς eyebrow.] *Anat.* That point in the forehead at the middle of the line joining the upper margins of the orbits of the eyes.

Ophthalmia (ǫfþæ·lmiă). late ME. Also †**Ophthalmy** (1543–1865). [– late L. *ophthalmia* (Boethius) – Gr. ὀφθαλμία, f. ὀφθαλμός eye; see -IA[1].] *Path.* Inflammation of the eye, esp. of the conjunctiva of the eye; ophthalmitis.

Ophthalmic (ǫfþæ·lmik), *a.* and *sb.* 1605. [– L. *ophthalmicus* – Gr. ὀφθαλμικός of or pertaining to the eye, f. ὀφθαλμός eye; see -IC.] **A.** *adj.* **1.** Pertaining or relating to the eye, ocular; connected with the eye, as a nerve, etc.; affecting the eye, as a disease 1727. **2.** Good for diseases of the eye; that treats such maladies; that performs, or is used for, operations on the eye 1605. **3.** Affected with ophthalmia 1845.

1. The o. artery 1831. 2. A competent o. surgeon 1871.

B. *sb.* (the adj. used absol.) **1.** A medicine or remedy for diseases of the eye 1653. **2.** The ophthalmic or orbital nerve 1727.

Ophthalmite (ǫfþæ·lməit). 1877. [f. Gr. ὀφθαλμός eye + -ITE[1] 3.] *Zool.* The stalk on which the eye is borne in podophthalmous Crustacea; the ophthalmic peduncle, eye-stalk.

Ophthalmitis (ǫfþælməi·tis). 1822. [mod. L., f. Gr. ὀφθαλμός + -ITIS.] Inflammation of the eye, ophthalmia; *spec.* inflammation involving all the structures of the eye.

Ophthalmo- (ǫfþæ·lmo), comb. form of Gr. ὀφθαλμός eye. See Main words.

Ophthalmology (ǫfþælmǫ·lŏdʒi). 1842. [f. OPHTHALMO- + -LOGY.] The scientific study of the structure, functions, and affections of the eye. So **Ophthalmolo·gical** *a.*, **-ly** *adv.* 1839. **Ophthalmo·logist** 1834.

Ophthalmometer (ǫfþælmǫ·mitəɹ). 1864. [f. as prec. + -METER.] An instrument devised by Helmholtz for measuring the curvatures of the (living) eye by means of images reflected in it. So **Ophthalmome·tric** *a.* relating to ophthalmometry. **Ophthalmo·metry,** measurement of the eye.

Ophthalmoscope (ǫfþæ·lmoskoᵘp). 1857. [f. as prec. + -SCOPE.] An instrument for inspecting the interior of the eye, esp. the retina. So **Ophthalmosco·pic, -al** *adjs.* of or pertaining to the o. or its use; **-ly** *adv.*

Ophthalmoscopy (ǫfþælmǫ·skŏpi). 1730. [f. as prec. + -SCOPY.] †**1.** A branch of physiognomy, by which character is inferred from the appearance of the eyes –1828. **2.** Inspection of the interior of the eye; the use of the ophthalmoscope 1864.

Opiane. [f. OPIUM + *-ane* as var. of *-ine*.] Obs. synonym of narcotine. Hence chemical terms in *opian-*: **Opia·nic** *a.*, formed from narcotine; as in *o. acid* ($C_{10}H_{10}O_5$), *o. ether* ($C_{10}H_9 . C_2H_5 . O_5$). **O·pianyl** $C_{10}H_9O_4$, the radical of opianic acid and its derivs.

Opiate (ōᵘ·piĕt), *a.* and *sb.* 1543. [– med.L. *opiatus* adj., *opiatum* sb. (XIII), f. *opiat-*, pa. ppl. stem of *opiare*, f. L. *opium*; see OPIUM, -ATE[2].] **A.** *adj.* Made with or containing opium; hence, inducing sleep; narcotic, soporiferous. **b.** *fig.* Inducing drowsiness or inaction 1626.

The Pastoral Reed Of Hermes, or his o. Rod MILT.

B. *sb.* Any medicine containing opium and having the quality of inducing sleep; a narcotic.

fig. [He] began to lull my conscience with the opiates of irreligion JOHNSON.

Opiate (ōᵘ·pieᶦt), *v.* 1611. [– *opiat-*, pa. ppl. stem of med.L. *opiare* (see prec.); in mod. use f. OPIUM + -ATE[3].] **1.** *trans.* To stupefy or put to sleep by means of opium; to narcotize. **b.** *fig.* To dull the sense or sensibility of 1762. **2.** To mix or impregnate with opium. Chiefly in **Opiated** *ppl. a.* 1611.

Opinable (opəi·năb'l, †ǫ·pinăb'l), *a.* Now *rare* or *Obs.* 1456. [– L. *opinabilis*, f. *opinari* OPINE; see -ABLE. Cf. Fr. †*opinable*.] †**1.** That is a matter of opinion; disputable –1546. **2.** Capable of being opined or held as an opinion 1603.

†**Opi·native,** *a.* 1530. [– late L. *opinativus*, f. *opinat-*, pa. ppl. stem of L. *opinari*; see OPINION, -ATIVE. Cf. Fr. †*opinatif, -ive*.] **1.** Opinionative –1660. **2.** Conjectural –1829.

Opine (opəi·n), *v.* 1557. [– L. *opinari* think, believe. Cf. Fr. *opiner*.] **1.** *intr.* or with *obj. cl.*: To express an opinion; to say that one thinks (so and so) 1598. **b.** *esp.* To express a formal opinion, *e.g.* in council, etc. Now *rare*. 1557. **2.** To hold an opinion, or to hold as one's opinion; to think, suppose. **a.** *trans.* (usu. with *obj. cl.*) 1611. **b.** *intr.* 1656.

1. Mr. Squeers yawned fearfully, and opined that it was high time to go to bed DICKENS. 2. b. You may o. upon everything under the sun M. PATTISON. Hence **O·pinant, Opi·ner,** one who opines 1611. †**Opina·tion,** an opinion 1611–1687.

†**Opinia·strous,** *a.* [f. Fr. †*opiniastre* (now *opiniâtre*) + -OUS; see OPINION, -ASTER.] Opinionated. MILTON.

Opiniated (ŏpi·ni,eᶦtĕd), *ppl. a.* 1589. [Presumably f. a shortened stem of L. *opinio* OPINION + -ATE[2] + -ED[1]. Cf. next] †**1.** Having a conceited opinion *of* –1719. **2.** Opinionated 1597.

Opiniative (ŏpi·niĕtiv), *a.* Now *rare*. 1574. [f. as prec. + -IVE. Cf. Fr. †*opiniatif*, med.L. *opiniativus* (XIV).] = OPINATIVE 1. Hence **Opi·niative-ly** *adv.*, **-ness.**

†**Opinia·tre, opinia·stre,** *a.* and *sb.* 1591. [– Fr. †*opiniastre*, now *opiniâtre*; see OPINIASTROUS.] **A.** *adj.* Opinionated. **B.** *sb.* An opinionated person 1603. So †**Opinia·tre** *v.* 1652–1777. †**Opinia·trety, -a·strety,** the character of being o. 1619.

Opi·ning, *vbl. sb.* 1656. [f. OPINE *v.* + -ING[1].] The formation or expression of opinion; an opinion, a notion.

Opinion (ŏpi·nyən), *sb.* ME. [– (O)Fr. *opinion* – L. *opinio, -on-*, f. stem of *opinari* think, believe; see -ION.] **1.** What one opines; judgement resting on grounds insufficient for complete demonstration; belief of something as probable or as seeming to one's own mind to be true. (Dist. from *knowledge*, *conviction*, or *certainty*; occas. = belief.) **b.** What is generally thought about something. Often qualified by *common*, *general*, *public*, *vulgar*. late ME. **2.** (With *an* and *pl.*) What one thinks about a particular thing, subject, or point; a judgement formed; a belief, view, notion. (Sometimes denoting a systematic belief, and then = *conviction*.) ME. **3.** The formal statement by an expert or professional man of what he thinks, judges or advises upon a matter submitted to him; considered advice 1470. **4.** Estimation, or an estimate, *of* a person or thing.

late ME. **b.** *spec.* Favourable estimate, esteem. (Now only with neg., or such adjs. as *great.*) 1597. †**c.** Self-conceit, arrogance, dogmatism; or, in good sense, self-confidence. SHAKS. †**5.** What is thought of one by others; standing; reputation, repute, character, credit (*of* being so and so, or *of* possessing some quality) –1705. †**6.** Expectation; apprehension –1658.

1. O. in good men is but knowledge in the making MILT. Phr. *In my o.*, as I think, as it seems to me. *A matter of o.*, a disputable point. **b.** Nothing is so easily cheated, nor so commonly mistaken, as vulgar O. 1689. This..stupid idol, o. 1753. **2.** How long halt ye between two opinions? 1 *Kings* 18:21. Dr. Macleod had always the courage of his opinions 1876. Phr. *Pious o.*, a belief commonly accepted, but not enjoined as matter of faith. Hence *transf.*, A belief cherished in the mind, but not insisted on in practice. *To be of o.*, to hold the belief or view; to opine: often with *that*... **3.** Barristers in England advise on the law by giving an o. on a case stated 1888. **4.** I haue bought Golden Opinions from all sorts of people SHAKS. **b.** She is a selfish, hypocritical woman, and I have no o. of her JANE AUSTEN. **5.** 1 *Hen. IV*, v. iv. 48. Hence †**Opi·nion** *v. trans.*, to hold the opinion, or hold as an opinion; to think, suppose 1555–1839.

†**Opi·nionate,** *a.* 1553. [f. OPINION + -ATE², perh. after OFr. *opinionné.*] **1.** Based on opinion, or held in the way of opinion; supposed, fancied –1661. **2.** = OPINIONATED 3. –1658.

Opinionate (ŏpi·nyŏneᶦt), *v.* Now *rare.* 1603. [f. OPINION + -ATE³, perh. after OFr. *opinionner.*] **1.** *trans.* and *intr.* = OPINE *v.* 2. 1621. †**2. a.** *trans.* To express as a formal opinion. **b.** *intr.* = OPINE *v.* 1. –1677. **3.** *refl.* To become or be opinionated or obstinate. *Obs.* exc. in pa. pple.; see next. 1603.

Opinionated (ŏpi·nyŏneᶦtėd), *ppl. a.* 1601. [f. OPINIONATE *a.*, perh. after OFr. *opinionné*; see -ATE², -ED¹.] †**1.** = OPINIONED 1. –1645. †**2.** Possessed of a particular (*esp.* a favourable) opinion *of* –1739. **3.** Thinking too highly of one's opinion; conceited or obstinate in opinion 1601. **b.** Obstinate, self-willed (in general sense) 1649.

Opinionative (ŏpi·nyŏneᶦtiv), *a.* 1547. [f. OPINION + -ATIVE.] †**1.** = OPINIONATE *a.* 1. –1702. **b.** Relating to, or consisting in, opinion; doctrinal (as dist. from *practical*) 1638. **2.** = OPINIONATE *a.* 2. 1547. So **Opi·niona:tive-ly** *adv.*, **-ness.**

Opinioned (ŏpi·nyənd), *a.* Now *rare.* 1584. [f. OPINION *sb.* + -ED².] **1.** Having a (specified) opinion; holding the opinion, or of opinion (*that*..). Also in comb., as *ill-o.* **2.** Thinking highly *of* oneself or one's own qualities, conceited *of* 1612. **3.** Opinionated 1649.

2. He's so opinion'd of his own Abilities, that he is ever designing somewhat DRYDEN.

Opinionist (ŏpi·nyənist). 1623. [f. as prec. + -IST.] †**1.** A holder of some peculiar opinion; a sectary, a faddist –1760. **b.** *Ch. Hist.* One of a 15th c. sect who held that only those Popes who practised voluntary poverty were true vicars of Christ 1693. **2.** The holder of any specified opinion 1630.

Opisometer (ǫpisǫ·mĭtəɹ). 1872. [f. Gr. ὀπίσω backwards + -METER.] An instrument for measuring curved lines, as on a map, consisting of a small wheel turning on a screw fixed in a rod or frame.

Opistho- (opi·sþo), bef. a vowel **opisth-**, comb. form of Gr. ὄπισθεν behind, as in **Opisthoglyphic** (-gli·fik), **Opisthoglyphous** (-ǫ·glifəs) [f. mod.L. *Opisthoglyphia* neut. pl., f. Gr. γλυφή carving], *adjs. Zool.* belonging to the division *Opisthoglyphia* of snakes, having grooves on the posterior teeth. **Opisthomous** (-ōᵘ·məs) [f. mod.L. *Opisthomi* (pl.), f. Gr. ὦμος shoulder], *a. Ichthyol.* belonging to the division *Opisthomi* of teleostean fishes, having the scapular arch separate from the skull. **Opisthopulmonate** (-pɒ·lmŏnĕt) [L. *pulmo, pulmon-* lung], *a. Zool.* applied to those pulmonate or air-breathing gastropod molluscs which have the pulmonary sac behind the heart.

Opisthobranchiate (-bræ·ŋki,ĕt), *a.* (*sb.*) 1854. [– mod.L. *Opisthobranchiata* = *Opisthobranchia* n.pl., f. OPISTHO- + Gr. βράγχια gills; see -ATE².] *Zool.* Belonging to the order *Opisthobranchiata* or *Opisthobranchia* of gastropod molluscs, comprising aquatic forms having the gills behind the heart. **b.** *sb.* An opisthobranchiate gastropod. So **Opi·sthobranch** (-bræŋk), in same senses 1851.

Opisthocœlous (-sī·ləs), *a.* 1872. [f. OPISTHO- + Gr. κοῖλος hollow + -OUS.] *Comp. Anat.* Applied to vertebræ the bodies of which are concave posteriorly; dist. from *procœlous* and *amphicœlous.* Also **Opisthocœlian** (-sī·liăn), *a.*; and as *sb.* 1854.

‖**Opistho·domos.** 1706. [Gr., f. ὀπισθο- behind + δόμος house, room.] *Gr. Antiq.* An apartment at the back of an ancient Greek temple, corresponding to the vestibule in front.

Opisthograph (opi·sþograf), *sb.* (*a.*) 1623. [– Gr. ὀπισθόγραφος; see OPISTHO- and -GRAPH.] *Gr.* and *Rom. Antiq.* A manuscript written on the back as well as the front of the papyrus or parchment; also, a slab inscribed on both sides. **b.** *adj.* = *Opisthographic.* So **Opisthogra·phic, -al** *adjs.* written or inscribed upon the back as well as the front. **Opistho·graphy,** the practice of writing on both sides; *concr.* writing of this kind.

Opisthotic (ǫpisþǫ·tik, -ōᵘtik), *a.* (*sb.*) 1870. [f. OPISTH(O- + Gr. οὖς, ὠτ- ear, ὠτικός of the ear.] *Comp. Anat.* Epithet of one of the otic or periotic bones, situated at the back of the ear; in mammals, fused with the other otic bones, and forming that part of the petrosal bone which contains the auditory chamber. **b.** *sb.* The opisthotic bone.

‖**Opisthotonos** (ǫpisþǫ·tŏnǫs). Also **-us.** 1657. [– late and med.L. *opisthotonus* – Gr. ὀπισθότονος drawn backwards (cf. ὀπισθοτονία tetanic recurvation), f. ὄπισθεν OPISTHO- + -τονος stretched.] *Path.* Spasm of the muscles of the neck, back, and legs, in which the body is bent backwards; a form of tetanus. So **Opisthoto·nic** *a.* 1623.

Opium (ōᵘ·piŏm), *sb.* late ME. [– L. *opium* (Pliny) – Gr. ὄπιον 'poppy juice, opium', dim. of ὀπός vegetable juice, which has been referred to an IE. base **ăp-* water; cf. (O)Fr. *opium.*] The inspissated juice of a species of poppy (*Papaver somniferum*), obtained from the unripe capsules by incision and spontaneous evaporation, of a reddish-brown colour, heavy smell, and bitter taste; valuable as a sedative and narcotic drug, and much used as a stimulant and intoxicant, esp. in the East.

fig. There is no antidote against the O. of time SIR T. BROWNE.

Comb.: **o. den,** a public room, of low or mean character, kept as a resort of opium-smokers; **o. habit,** the habit of eating or smoking o. as a stimulant or intoxicant; **o. plant, o. poppy,** the white poppy. Hence **O·pium** *v. trans.* to treat with o.

‖**Opobalsamum** (ǫpobæ·lsămŏm). late ME. Also anglicized **Opoba·lsam.** [L. – Gr. ὀποβάλσαμον, f. ὀπός juice + βάλσαμον the balsam-tree.] The balsam or oleoresin called Balm of Gilead or Balm of Mecca; see BALM *sb.* **b.** The tree producing this, a species of *Balsamodendron* 1737.

Opodeldoc (ǫpŏde·ldǫk). 1656. [In the work of Paracelsus (*oppodeltoch*) applied to various medical plasters and believed to have been invented by him (*a*1541). For the ending cf. NOSTOC.] †**1.** *orig.* The name used by Paracelsus for medical plasters of various kinds –1733. **2.** Now applied to various kinds of soap liniment; *esp.* to that (*Linimentum saponis*) of the British Pharmacopœia, a solution of soap in alcohol, with camphor, oils of origanum, and rosemary added 1733.

-opolis, comb. form of -POLIS, Gr. πόλις city.

Opopanax (opǫ·pănæks). late ME. [– L. *opopanax* (Pliny) – Gr. ὀποπάναξ (Dioscorides), f. ὀπός juice + πάναξ: see PANACEA.] **1.** A fetid gum-resin obtained from the root of *Opopanax chironium*; formerly of repute in medicine. **2.** In *Perfumery,* applied to a gum-resin obtained from *Balsamodendron kataf* 1895. **3.** Short for *Opopanax-tree.*

attrib. and *Comb.*, as **o. soap,** soap perfumed with o. (sense 2); **o.-tree** (*Acacia farnesiana*), the Sponge-tree of the Southern U.S., West Indies, etc.

Oporto (wine): see PORT *sb.*⁶

Opossum (ŏpǫ·sŏm). 1610. [– Virginian Indian *āpassŭm* (cf. Ojibwa *wābassim*). Cf. POSSUM.] **1.** General name of the small marsupial mammals of the American family *Didelphyidæ*, mostly arboreal, some (genus *Chironectes*) aquatic, of nocturnal habits, with an opposable thumb on the hind foot, and tail usu. prehensile; esp. *Didelphys virginiana,* the common opossum of the U.S. (Colloq. shortened to POSSUM, q.v.) **2.** Extended to various small or moderate-sized marsupials; *esp.* the common name in Australia and Tasmania of those of the subfamily *Phalangistinæ*, more properly called Phalangers 1777.

attrib. and *Comb.*, as **o.-mouse,** the Pygmy Flying Phalanger of Australia; **-shrimp,** a shrimp of the genus *Mysis* or family *Mysidæ*, so called from the brood-pouch in which the female carries her eggs.

Oppidan (ǫ·pidăn), *a.* and *sb.* 1540. [– L. *oppidanus* belonging to a town (other than Rome), f. *oppidum* (fortified) town; see -AN.] **A.** *adj.* Of or belonging to a town, or to the town (as opp. to the country); civic; urban 1643. †**b.** Pertaining to a university town, as opp. to the university itself –1831. **B.** *sb.* **1.** An inhabitant of a town 1540. †**2.** A 'townsman', as opp. to a 'gownsman'; also, a student not resident in a college –1696. **3.** At Eton College: A student not on the foundation (who boards in the town); dist. from *colleger* 1557.

†**Oppi·gnorate, oppi·gnerate,** *v.* 1622. [f. *oppignorat-, -erat-,* pa. ppl. stem of L. *oppignorare, -erare* to pledge.] *trans.* To pawn, pledge –1857.

Oppilate (ǫ·pileᶦt), *v.* 1547. [– *oppilat-,* pa. ppl. stem of L. *oppilare* stop up, f. *ob-* OB- 1 + *pilare* ram down, stop up; see -ION.] *trans.* To stop or block up, obstruct. So **Oppila·tion,** the action of stopping up or obstructing, or condition of being obstructed; an obstruction. **O·ppilative** *a.* obstructive, constipating.

†**Oppo·ne,** *v.* 1513. [– L. *opponere*, f. *ob-* OB- 1 + *ponere* place.] = OPPOSE –1671.

Opponency (ǫ̆pōᵘ·nĕnsi). 1727. [f. next; see -ENCY.] **1.** Antagonism, opposition. **2.** The action or position of the opponent in an academical disputation as an exercise for a degree. *Obs.* exc. *Hist.* 1730.

Opponent (ǫ̆pōᵘ·nĕnt), *a.* and *sb.* 1536. [– L. *opponens, -ent-,* pr. pple. of *opponere,* f. *ob-* OB- 1 + *ponere* place; see -ENT.] **A.** *adj.* **1.** Standing over against; opposing 1728. **2.** Antagonistic, adverse, contrary, opposed. Const. *to,* †*against.* 1647. **3.** *Anat.* Said of a muscle (*opponens*) of the hand in man and some quadrumana, which opposes a lateral digit to one of the other digits. Also of the digit itself. 1842. **B.** *sb.* **1.** One who maintains a contrary argument in a disputation; correl. to *respondent. Obs.* exc. *Hist.* 1536. **2.** An antagonist, adversary 1615.

2. I had already run my o. through the sword arm LYTTON.

Opportune (ǫ·pǫɹtiun, ǫpǫ̆ɹtiū·n), *a.* late ME. [– (O)Fr. *opportun*, fem. *-une* – L. *opportunus* (orig. of wind) driving towards the harbour, (hence) seasonable (cf. *Portunus* protecting god of harbours), f. *ob-* OB- 1 + *portus* harbour, PORT *sb.*¹ Cf. IMPORTUNE *a.*] **1.** Adapted to an end or purpose or the circumstances of the case; fit, suitable, appropriate; convenient. **2.** Of an event, action, or thing: Fitting in regard to time or circumstances, seasonable; now chiefly. Timely, well-timed. late ME. †**3.** Advantageous, useful –1658.

1. *Temp.* IV. i. 26. **2.** Most o. to her neede, I haue A Vessell rides fast by SHAKS. **3.** It is o. to look back upon old Times, and contemplate our Forefathers SIR T. BROWNE. Hence **Opportune-ly** *adv.* late ME., **-ness** 1727.

Opportunism (ǫ·pǫ̆ɹtiuniz'm, ǫpǫ̆ɹtiū·niz'm). 1870. [f. prec. + -ISM after It. *opportunismo*, Fr. *opportunisme*, etc.; terms first of Italian, and later of French, politics.] In politics, the policy of doing what is presently expedient, as opp. to rigid adherence to party principles; often used to imply sacrifice of principles or an undue spirit of accommodation to present circumstances. So **O·pportunist,** one who professes or practises o.; also *attrib.*

Opportunity (ǫpǭɹtiū·nĭti). late ME. [– (O)Fr. *opportunité* – L. *opportunitas*, f. *opportunus*; see OPPORTUNE, -ITY.] **1.** The quality or fact of being opportune; timeliness, opportuneness. Now chiefly with ref. to the L. phrase 'felix opportunitate mortis'. 1531. **2.** A time, juncture, or condition of things favourable to an end or purpose; occasion, chance. late ME. †**3.** Convenience or advantageousness of site or position –1781.

1. A death which, for its swiftness and its o., he might well have desired PATER. **2.** I am not a little pleased with the O. of running over all the Papers STEELE. In national history o. is as powerful as purpose STUBBS. **3.** Hull, a town of great strength and opportunitie both to sea and land affaires MILT.

Opposable (ǫ̆pōᵘ·zăb'l), *a.* 1667. [f. OPPOSE *v.* + -ABLE.] **1.** Capable of being opposed, withstood, or placed in opposition *to* (*rare*). **2.** Of a digit, esp. the thumb: Capable of being opposed to, or applied so as to meet, another 1833. Hence **Opposabi·lity,** o. quality 1863.

Oppose (ǫ̆pōᵘ·z), *v.* late ME. [– (O)Fr. *opposer*, based on L. *opponere*; see OPPONENT, POSE *v.*[1] Repl. OPPONE *c*1600.] **I.** ME. uses. †**1.** *trans.* = APPOSE *v.*[1] 1. –1607. **2.** *absol.* and *intr.* To put objections or hard questions. *Obs.* exc. *Hist.* late ME.

II. Modern uses. **1.** *trans.* To set (a thing) over against, place directly before or in front. Const. *to*, †*against*. 1593. †**b.** To expose, subject –1605. **2.** To contrast; to put in rhetorical or ideal opposition (*to*) 1579. **3.** To set (something) against by way of hindrance, check, or resistance; to place as an obstacle; also, to set or place (a person) as an antagonist 1596. †**4.** *refl.* and *intr.* To set oneself in opposition, contend *against*, act in opposition *to* –1717. **5.** *trans.* To stand or lie over against (something); to look towards; face, front. Now *rare*. 1608. **6.** To set oneself against (a person or thing); to withstand, resist, combat; to stand in the way of, obstruct 1596. Also *absol.* **b.** To contest. SHELLEY.

1. Her Grace sate downe..opposing freely The Beauty of her Person to the People SHAKS. **b.** *Lear* IV. vii. 32. **2.** Memory and imagination, though we sometimes o. them, are nearly allied JOWETT. **3.** I do o. My patience to his fury SHAKS. **6.** The world does not o. religion as such J. H. NEWMAN. *absol.* Or to take Armes against a Sea of troubles, And by opposing end them SHAKS. Hence **Oppo·seless** *a. poet.* and *rhet.*, not to be opposed, irresistible 1605.

Opposer (ǫ̆pōᵘ·zəɹ). 1483. [f. OPPOSE *v.* + -ER[1].] **1.** One who 'opposes' the defender of a thesis in an academical disputation. *Obs.* exc. *Hist.* **2.** = OPPONENT B. 2. 1601.

Opposing (ǫ̆pōᵘ·ziŋ), *ppl. a.* 1608. [f. OPPOSE *v.* + -ING[2].] That opposes.

As up the o. hills they slowly creep WORDSW. All these parts of our constitution..are balanced as o. interests BURKE.

Opposite (ǫ·pŏzit), *a.*, *sb.* (*adv.*, *prep.*) late ME. [– (O)Fr. *opposite* – L. *oppositus*, pa. pple. of *opponere*; see OPPONENT.] **A.** *adj.* **1.** Placed or lying over against something on the other or farther side of an intervening line, space, or thing; contrary in position. Const. *to*, *from*, †*against*. **b.** *Bot.* (*a*) Situated in pairs on opposite sides of an axis or intervening body, as leaves on a stem; (*b*) Situated in front of an organ so as to come between it and its axis, as a stamen in front of a sepal or petal. Opp. to *alternate*. 1707. **2.** Turned or moving the other way; contrary, reverse 1594. **3.** Contrary in nature, character, or tendency. Const. *to*, *from*. 1580. **b.** With *the*: that is opposed to something else; the contrary, the other (of two related things of different character.) 1638. †**4.** Antagonistic, adverse, hostile. Const. *to*, *against*. –1737.

1. At the o. side of the glacier was the Aiguille Verte TYNDALL. *O. number*, either of two persons or things who occupy corresponding positions in parallel bodies, enterprises, etc. **2.** We started in o. directions (*mod.*). **3.** Self love takes a clean o. way, from that of charity 1650. **b.** The o. Sex ADDISON. **4.** Be o. with a kinsman, surly with seruants SHAKS.

B. *sb.* [The adj. used *absol.*] †**1.** = Opposite point, esp. of the heavens –1604. †**b.** Opposite aspect. MILT. **2.** That which is opposite; an object, fact, or quality, that is the reverse of something else; often in *pl.*, things the most different of their kind 1549. **b.** *Logic.* An opposite term or proposition; †a contrary argument 1588. **3.** An antagonist, adversary, opponent. Now *rare* or *Obs.* late ME.

2. The most extreme opposites have some qualities in common JOWETT. **3.** The opposites of this day's strife SHAKS.

C. *adv.* In an opposite position or direction 1817.

Several hon. gentlemen sat o. (*mod.*).

D. *prep.* [*ellipt.* for *o. to.*] Over against; facing or fronting on the other side 1758.

We knelt down o. each other LANDOR. Hence **O·pposite-ly** *adv.*, **-ness.**

Oppo:siti-, comb. form of L. *oppositus* opposite, used chiefly in botanical adjs., as **Oppositifo·lious,** (*a*) having opposite leaves, (*b*) situated opposite a leaf (as a peduncle or tendril). **Oppositipe·talous, Oppositise·palous.**

Opposition (ǫpŏzi·ʃən). late ME. [– (O)Fr. *opposition* – L. *oppositio*, f. *opposit-*, pa. ppl. stem of *opponere*; see OPPOSITE, -ION.] **1.** The action of setting opposite or against 1602. **b.** *spec.* Cf. OPPOSABLE *a.* 2. 1899. **2.** Position over against something; opposite situation or direction 1667. **3.** *Astrol.* and *Astron.* The relative position of two heavenly bodies when exactly opposite to each other as seen from the earth's surface, their longitude then differing by 180°; *esp.* the position of a heavenly body when opposite to the sun. late ME. **4.** The action of placing one thing in contrast with another; the condition of being opposed or contrasted; contrast, contradistinction, antithesis 1581. †**b.** *Rhet.* A contrast of positions or arguments; a contrary position or argument; a counter-proposition, objection –1678. **c.** *Logic.* The relation between two propositions which have the same subject and predicate but differ in quantity or quality or both 1697. **5.** Contrary or hostile action, antagonism, resistance; the fact or condition of being opposed, hostile, or adverse 1588. †**b.** Encounter, combat –1655. **6.** *concr.* A political party opposed to that in office; *esp.* the party opposed to the administration in the British Parliament or other legislative body 1704. **b.** *transf.* Any party or body of opponents 1781. **7.** *attrib.*, as *o. benches, cheer, newspaper*, etc. 1801.

1. *Haml.* V. ii. 178. **2.** Phr. *In o.* (*to*), facing, fronting. **4.** In the English Chronicles..the o. is made between 'French' and 'English' FREEMAN. **c.** *Contradictory, Contrary, Subcontrary, Subaltern O.*; see these words. **5.** A disagreeable man will often dissent from you from the mere love of o. 1868. Phr. *In o.*, in the position of being opposed to the administration; They are in O. and not in office 1895. **6.** Hear, hear, from the O., and laughter from the Ministerial benches 1817. Hence **Opposi·tional** *a.* **Opposi·tionist,** one who professes or practises o.; *esp.* a member of the parliamentary o.; also *attrib.* or as *adj.*

Oppositive (ǫ̆pǫ·zĭtiv), *a.* 1622. [– med.L. *oppositivus* (in sense 2), f. as prec.; see -IVE.] †**1.** = OPPOSITE A. 1, 1 b. –1857. **2.** Characterized by opposing or contrasting; adversative. So **Oppo·sitive-ly** *adv.*, **-ness.**

Oppress (ǫ̆pre·s), *v.* ME. [– (O)Fr. *oppresser* – med.L. *oppressare*, f. *oppress-*, pa. ppl. stem of L. *opprimere*, f. *ob-* OB- 1 + *premere* PRESS.] **1.** *trans.* †To press injuriously upon or against; to press down by force; to crush, trample down, smother, crowd –1781. **b.** *esp.* To bear down in battle; to overwhelm with numbers. Now *rare*. late ME. **c.** *fig.* Of sleep, etc.: To overpower, weigh down. (Chiefly *poet.*) 1582. **2.** To lie heavy on, weigh down, crush (the feelings, mind, spirits, etc.) late ME. †**3.** To put down, suppress; to crush, overwhelm (a person); to put an end to (a thing or state of things, feeling, etc.) –1829. †**b.** To suppress, keep out of sight –1560. **4.** To keep under by tyrannical exercise of power; to load or burden with cruel or unjust impositions or restraints; to tyrannize over. late ME. †**5.** Of an enemy, circumstances, etc.: To bear heavily upon; to reduce to straits; to harass, distress –1611. †**6.** *trans.* To come upon unexpectedly, take by surprise. (So L. *opprimere.*) –1603. †**7.** To force, ravish. (So L. *opprimere.*) –1613. **8.** *Her.* = DEBRUISE *v.* 2. Chiefly in *pa. pple.* 1572.

1. Fear to put on his hat, lest he should o. his foretop RICHARDSON. **b.** Opprest with multitudes he greatly fell ADDISON. **c.** Until the poppied warmth of sleep oppress'd Her soothed limbs KEATS. **2.** The Weary World of Waters between us oppresses the imagination LAMB. **4.** The powerful citizens oppressed the weak THIRLWALL. *absol.* That the man of the earth may no more o. *Ps.* 10:18.

Oppression (ǫ̆pre·ʃən). ME. [– (O)Fr. *oppression* – L. *oppressio*, f. as prec.; see -ION.] **1.** The action of oppressing or condition of being oppressed. late ME. **2.** The feeling of being oppressed or weighed down; bodily or mental uneasiness or distress. late ME. **3.** Exercise of power in a tyrannical manner; cruel treatment of subjects, inferiors, etc.; the imposition of unjust burdens.

1. There gentle sleep..with soft o. seis'd My droused sense MILT. **2.** Dreams, Agitations, and Oppressions, that Excess in Diet occasions in the Night 1748. **3.** There is not a word in our language which expresses more detestable wickedness than *oppression* 1729.

Oppressive (ǫ̆pre·siv), *a.* 1627. [– Fr. *oppressif, -ive* – med.L. *oppressivus*, f. as prec.; see -IVE.] **1.** Of the nature of oppression; unjustly burdensome, harsh, or merciless. **2.** Characterized by oppressing, disposed to oppress 1712. **3.** Having the quality of oppressing or weighing heavily on the mind, spirits, or senses; depressing; overpowering 1712.

1. The o. taxation of the provinces 1861. **2.** The yoke of an o. aristocracy 1845. **3.** A bright, o., sultry morning LYTTON. Hence **Oppre·ssive-ly** *adv.*, **-ness.**

Oppressor (ǫ̆pre·səɹ). late ME. [– AFr. *oppressour* = (O)Fr. *oppresseur*, f. *oppresser* OPPRESS; see -OUR, -OR 2. Cf. AL. *oppressor* in same sense.] **1.** One who oppresses; *esp.* one who harasses with unjust or cruel treatment. **2.** Anything that oppresses 1723.

1. I have been no avaricious o. of the people BACON.

Opprobrious (ǫ̆prōᵘ·briəs), *a.* late ME. [– late L. *opprobriosus*, f. L. *opprobrium* (naturalized as †*opprobry* XV); see next, -OUS.] **1.** Of words, language: Conveying injurious reproach; contumelious, abusive. Of persons: Using contumelious or abusive language. **2.** Associated with disgrace; infamous, shameful. Now *rare*. 1510.

1. The multitude pressed round the King's coach, and insulted him with o. cries MACAULAY. **2.** Neither did any thing seeme o. out of which there might arise commoditie and profit HOOKER. Hence **Oppro·brious-ly** *adv.*, **-ness.**

Opprobrium (ǫ̆prōᵘ·briŏm). 1656. [– L. *opprobrium* infamy, reproach, f. *ob-* OB- 1 + *probrum* shameful deed, disgrace, subst. use of n. of *probrus* disgraceful.] **1.** The disgrace attached to conduct considered shameful; the imputation of this disgrace; infamy, reproach 1683. **2.** Something that brings disgrace.

1. Great o. has been thrown on her name 1862. **2.** That o. of Mankind..who now calls himself our Protector CLARENDON. So †**Oppro·bry** –1795.

Oppugn (ǫ̆piū·n), *v.* late ME. [– L. *oppugnare*, f. *ob-* OB- 1 + *pugnare* to fight.] †**1.** *trans.* To fight against, attack, besiege –1860. **2.** *fig.* To call in question (a state of things), controvert (a statement, belief, etc.) 1529. **b.** Of things: To run counter to. Now *rare*. 1584. **c.** *intr.* To fight, contend, oppose 1591.

2. Then and afterwards he openly oppugned Popery 1734. **b.** When Law and Conscience.. seem to oppugne one another, the written Law should be preferr'd HOBBES. So **Oppugnance, -nancy** (ǫ̆pv·gnăns, ǫ̆pv·gnănsi), opposition, antagonism, conflict. **Oppugnant** (ǫ̆pv·gnănt), *a.* opposing, antagonistic, contrary, repugnant. **Oppugna·tion,** attack, assault; opposition; also *fig.* **Oppu·gner** (ǫ̆piū·nəɹ), one who oppugns.

Opsimathy (ǫpsi·măþi). *rare*. 1656. [– Gr. ὀψιμαθία, f. ὀψιμαθής, f. ὀψι- late + μαθ- learn; see -Y[3].] Learning acquired late. So **O·psimath,** one who begins to learn late in life 1883.

Opsiometer (ǫpsi,ǫ·mĭtəɹ). 1842. [f. Gr. ὄψις sight + -METER.] = OPTOMETER.

Opsonin (ǫ·psŏnin). 1903. [Discovered by A. E. Wright and S. R. Douglas (*Proc. Royal Soc.* LXXII. 366); f. Gr. ὀψώνιον victuals, provisions + -IN[1].] A substance present in blood serum which acts upon bacteria so as to render them subject to phagocytosis. Hence **Opso·nic** *a.*, **O·psonize** *v.* to affect by means of opsonins, **-iza·tion.**

Opt (ǫpt), *v.* 1877. [– Fr. *opter* – L. *optare* choose, desire, frequent. of **opere*. Cf. ADOPT.] *intr.* To make choice (*between* alternatives); to decide (*for* one of two alternatives).

Optation (ǫptēi·ʃən). 1577. [– L. *optatio*, f. *optat-*, pa. ppl. stem of *optare*; see OPT, -ION.] The action of wishing; a wish or desire. **b.** *Rhet.* The expression of a wish under the form of an exclam.

Optative (ǫ·ptătiv, ǫptēi·tiv). 1530. [– Fr. *optatif, -ive* – late L. *optativus*, f. as prec.; see -IVE.] The first pronunc. is normal, but the second prevails in Eng. schools and colleges.] **A.** *adj.* **1.** *Gram.* Having the function of expressing wish or desire. **2.** Characterized by desire or choice; expressing desire. **B.** *sb. Gram.* The optative mood; an optative form of a verb 1530.

A. 1. *O. mood*: that mood or form of the verb, of which a prominent function is the expression of wish or desire, as in Gr. μὴ γένοιτο, 'may it not happen!' Hence **Optatively** *adv.* in an o. manner or sense, in expression of a wish; in the o. mood.

Optic (ǫ·ptik). 1541. [– (O)Fr. *optique* or med.L. *opticus* (XII) – Gr. ὀπτικός, f. ὀπτός seen, visible, f. stem ὀπ- (in ὄψομαι I shall see, etc.); see -IC.] **A.** *adj.* **1.** Of or pertaining to sight; visual. (Now *rare* or *Obs.* in general sense.) 1599. **2.** *Anat.* Pertaining to or connected with the eye as the organ of sight, or with the sense of sight as a function of the brain; esp. in the names of bodily parts or structures. (Also in *Path.* and *Surg.*) 1541. **3.** = OPTICAL 2, 3. *Obs.* or *arch.* 1569. **4.** = OPTICAL 4. Chiefly in the phr. (now *arch.*) *o. glass*, a lens, or an instrument having a lens, esp. a telescope. 1607. **5.** = OPTICAL 2. 1664.

2. O. nerve, the second cranial nerve on each side, which enters the eyeball and terminates in the retina; they are the nerves of the special sense of sight. **O. thalamus,** each of two large masses of nerve-matter in the brain, one on each side of the third ventricle. **4.** The moon, whose orb Through o. glass the Tuscan artist views MILT. **5. O. angle,** (*a*) the angle between the two lines from the extremities of an object to the eye, being the angle under which it is seen, or the visual angle; (*b*) the angle between the optic axes of the eyes when directed to the same object; (*c*) the angle between the optic axes of a biaxial doubly-refracting crystal. **O. axis,** (*a*) the straight line through the centres of the pupil and crystalline lens, the axis of the eye; (*b*) a line in a doubly-refracting crystal such that a ray of light passing in the direction of it suffers no double refraction.

B. *sb.* **1.** The organ of sight, the eye; chiefly in *pl.* (Formerly learned and elegant, afterwards pedantic, now joc.) 1620. **†b.** Short for *optic nerve*; *fig.* visual power –1718. **†2.** An 'optic glass'; an eye-glass, lens, magnifying glass; a microscope or telescope –1800. **†3.** = OPTICIAN 1. –1675. **†4.** The science of sight and light, OPTICS –1869.

Optical (ǫ·ptikăl), *a.* 1570. [f. prec. + -AL[1]; see -ICAL.] **1.** Of, pertaining or relating to, the sense of sight; visual; ocular. (Now chiefly in special connections, e.g. *an o. illusion.*) **2.** Of or pertaining to sight in relation to the physical action of light upon the eye; hence, Pertaining or relating to light, esp. as the medium of sight; belonging to optics 1570. **3.** Treating of, or skilled in, optics 1570. **4.** Constructed to assist the sight; acting by means of sight or light; devised according to the principles of optics 1748.

2. O. axis = *optic axis* (see OPTIC A. 5). **4.** *O. square*, reflecting instrument used by surveyors and others for laying off lines at right angles to each other. Hence **O·ptically** *adv.*

Optician (ǫpti·ʃăn). 1687. [– Fr. *opticien*, f. med.L. *optica* OPTICS; see -ICIAN.] **1.** One versed in optics. Now *rare* or *Obs.* **2.** A maker of or dealer in optical instruments 1737.

O·ptico-, comb. f. Gr. ὀπτικός OPTIC, as in **O.-che·mical** *a.*, relating to optics and chemistry conjointly; **O.-pa·pillary** *a.* belonging to the optic papilla.

Optics (ǫ·ptiks). 1579. [pl. of OPTIC *a.*, used subst. to render med.L. *optica* n. pl. – Gr. τὰ ὀπτικά optics; see -ICS.] The science of sight or of the medium of sight, i.e. light; that branch of physics which deals with the properties and phenomena of light. Now always construed as singular.

Optimacy (ǫ·ptimăsi). Now *rare.* 1579. [– mod.L. *optimatia*; see next, -ACY. Repl. later by *aristocracy*.] **1.** Government, or a government, by the upper classes in a state; aristocracy; also, a state so governed 1594. **2.** The upper classes in a state; the aristocracy.

Optimate (ǫ·ptimĕt). 1611. [– L. *optimas*, as adj. aristocratic, as sb. pl. *optimates* aristocrats; f. *optimus* best. Chiefly in pl., **optimates** (ǫptimēi·tīz).] A member of the patrician order in Rome; *gen.* a noble or aristocrat.

‖**Optime** (ǫ·ptimĭ). 1755. [– L. adv. = 'best', 'very well', from the phr. *optime disputasti* 'you have disputed very well'.] One who has been placed in the second or third division, called respectively senior and junior optimes, in the Mathematical Tripos at Cambridge.

Optimism (ǫ·ptimiz'm). 1759. [– Fr. *optimisme* (1737 in 'Mémoires de Trévoux', in an account of Leibniz), f. L. *optimum*, subst. use of n. of *optimus* best.] **1.** The doctrine propounded by Leibniz, that the actual world is the 'best of all possible worlds', being chosen by the Creator as that in which most good could be obtained at the cost of the least evil. Also applied to other doctrines of like effect. **b.** Applied to any view which supposes that good must ultimately prevail over evil in the universe 1841. **2.** The character or quality of being for the best 1795. *rare.* **3.** Disposition to hope for the best or to look on the bright side of things under all circumstances 1819.

1. Voltaire's Candide, written to refute the system of o. BOSWELL. **b.** The young reformer's social simplicity, his dreams, his optimisms 1888. **3.** 'Let it be cheerful' said he, with his gay o. 1881.

Optimist (ǫ·ptimist), *sb.* (*a.*) 1766. [f. as prec. + -IST.] **1.** One who holds or believes in the metaphysical principle of optimism 1783. **2.** One disposed, under all circumstances, to hope for the best 1766. **B.** *adj.* Optimistic 1863.

2. I have always observed that good physicians are optimists 1895. **B.** The o. governess..who, when the weather was very bad, was still thankful because it was better than none at all 1865. Hence **Optimi·stic, -al** *adjs.* **Optimi·stically** *adv.* So **O·ptimize** *v.*

‖**Optimum** (ǫ·ptimŏm). 1879. [L., subst. use of n. of *optimus* best.] *Biol.* That degree or amount of heat, light, food, moisture, etc. most favourable for growth, reproduction, or other vital process. Also *attrib.* Best or most favourable.

Option (ǫ·pʃən). 1604. [– Fr. *option* or L. *optio*, f. stem of *optare*; see OPT, -ION.] **1.** The action of choosing; choice. Also *transf.* A thing that is or may be chosen. **2.** Power or liberty of choosing; a freedom of choice 1633. **3.** The right which an archbishop formerly had on the consecration of a bishop, of choosing one benefice within the see of the latter, to be in his own patronage for the next presentation. (Abolished in 1845.) 1701. **4.** The privilege (acquired on some consideration) of executing or relinquishing, as one may choose, within a specified period a commercial transaction on terms now fixed; esp. that of calling for the delivery (a *call*), or making delivery (a *put*), or both (a *double option*), within a specified time, of some particular stock or produce at a specified price and to a specified amount 1755.

1. Plantation..must proceed from the o. of the people, else it sounds like an exile BACON. **2.** He [Peel] had no o. about accepting [office]—his sovereign sent for him, and he must come 1850. A sentence of imprisonment without the o. of a fine (*mod.*).

Optional (ǫ·pʃənăl), *a.* 1765. [f. prec. + -AL[1].] **1.** That is a matter of choice; depending on choice or preference; not obligatory 1792. **2.** Leaving something to choice.

1. Even this burthen was o., not compulsory 1818. **2.** Original writs are either o. or peremptory BLACKSTONE. **B.** *sb. U.S.* An o. subject of study 1857.

Opto-, from Gr. ὀπτός 'seen, visible', used as comb. form with the notion of 'sight, vision', or 'optic'. See Main words.

Optogram (ǫ·ptŏgræm). 1878. [f. OPTO- + -GRAM.] Kühne's term for the image formed on the retina by the action of light, which may be rendered permanent by chemical means.

Optologist (ǫptǫ·lŏdʒist). 1903. [f. OPTO- + -LOGIST.] A sight-testing optician. So **Opto·logy, Optolo·gical** *a.*

Optometer (ǫptǫ·mĭtəɹ). 1738. [f. OPTO- + -METER.] A name of various instruments for testing vision; *esp.* one for measuring the refractive power of the eye and thus testing long- or short-sightedness. Hence **Opto·metrist, Opto·metry.**

Optophone (ǫ·ptofoun). 1923. [f. OPTO- + -PHONE.] An instrument to enable the blind to read printed type by the medium of sound.

Opulence (ǫ·piŭlĕns). 1510. [– L. *opulentia*, f. *opulent-*; see next, -ENCE.] Wealth, riches, affluence. Also *transf.* and *fig.*

Opulent (ǫ·piŭlĕnt), *a.* 1601. [– L. *opulens, -ent-* or *opulentus*, f. **ops-*, pl. *opes* resources, wealth (cf. OPUS, COPIOUS); see -ULENT.] **1.** Rich, wealthy, affluent. **b.** Yielding great wealth 1664. **2.** *transf.* and *fig.* Rich in some respect: **a.** in mental wealth; **b.** in material possessions; **c.** in physical development; plump [from Fr.]. 1791. **3.** Of flowers, etc.: Rich in blossom, tint, or fragrance; splendid 1863.

1. I shall be strangely unfortunate if I meet not with some o. widow 1704. **2.** Her braided o. hair 1863. **3.** Or beast or bird or fish, or o. flower TENNYSON. Hence **O·pulent-ly** *adv.*

‖**Opuntia** (opɒ·nʃiă). 1601. [L. *Opuntia* (sc. *herba*), a plant growing about the Locrian city Opus (acc. *Opuntem*) in Greece; taken as a generic name.] A large genus of cactaceous plants; also, the fruit of a plant of this genus; the Prickly Pear or Indian Fig.

‖**Opus** (ǫ·pŏs, ōu·pŏs). 1809. [L. *opus* work, pl. *opera*.] A work, a composition; *esp.* a musical composition or set of compositions as numbered among the works of a composer in order of publication. Abbrev. *Op.*

O. magnum or *magnum o.*: a L. expression signifying 'great work', frequent in Eng. use, esp. in ref. to a large or important literary work.

Opuscule (opɒ·skiul). 1656. [– (O)Fr. *opuscule* – L. *opusculum*, dim. of *opus* work; see OPUS, -CULE.] A small work; esp. a literary or musical work of small size. var. ‖**Opu·sculum** (pl. **-ula**).

Or (ǭɹ), *sb.* 1562. [– (O)Fr. *or* :– L. *aurum* gold.] *Her.* The tincture gold or yellow in armorial bearings. **b.** *Or moulu, or molu*; see ORMOLU.

Or (ǭɹ, ǫɹ). *adv.*[1] (*prep., conj.*[1]) *arch.* and *dial.* [Late Northumb. OE. *ār* early, ME. (in Scandinavianized areas) *ār*, later *ōr* – ON. *ár* = OE. *ǣr* ERE.] **†A.** *adv.* **I.** As a positive. Early; = AIR *adv.* 2, ERE A. 1.–ME. **II.** As comparative. **1.** Earlier, sooner; = ERE A. 2. ME. only. **2.** Formerly, before; = AIR *adv.* 1, ERE A. 4. –1500.

B. *prep.* **1.** Before (in time); = ERE B. 1. ME. **b.** Confused with the conjunctive *or ere* (C. 1 d) for *or e'er, or ever*, but used simply as = ere, before 1629. **2.** Bef. an adv. of time taken subst., as *long, now*, etc., forming an advb. phrase; = ERE B. 2. 1450.

1. To dye or their day 1509. **b.** The Shepherds on the Lawn, Or ere the point of dawn, Sate simply chatting in a rustick row MILTON.

C. *conj.* (or *conjunctive adv.*). **1.** Of time: Before. **†a.** in conjunctional phrases *or than, or that*; see ERE C. 1 –1721. **b.** *Or* alone, in same sense ME. **c.** with the addition of *ever, e'er* (adding emphasis). late ME. **d.** *Or ere*, for *or e'er*, or ever; see B. 1 b. 1568. **2.** Of preference: Sooner than; = ERE C. 2. ME.

1. b. Wil you drink or you go, or wil you go or you drinke? 1553. **c.** Thou accursed Spirit! damned or ever thou wert born! WESLEY. **d.** *Lear* II. iv. 288.

Or (ǭɹ, ǫɹ) *conj.*[2] (*adv.*[2]) ME. [Reduced form of the obs. OTHER *conj.* *Or* is properly the conjunction, not the associated adv. (see sense 2), which continued to be *other*, or *outher*, = mod. Eng. *either* (in *either..or*), though *or..or* also occurs.] **1.** *gen.* A particle co-ordinating two (or more) words, phrases, or clauses, between which there is an alternative. **b.** When singular subjects (sb. or pron.) are co-ordinated by *or*, the tendency is for the vb. and following pronouns to be plural, when the mutual exclusion of the singular subjects is not emphasized 1601. **2.** The alternative expressed by *or* is emphasized by prefixing to the first member, or adding after the last, the associated adv. EITHER, formerly OTHER or OUTHER ME. ¶**b.** For *or* occurring after *neither*, see these words and *nor* 1523. **c.** *Or* is used after *whether*; see WHETHER ME. **3.** *Or..or* in the sense of *either..or* is now poetic ME. †**b.** *Or..or* occurs with alternative questions; = *whether..or*. (*Or* alone = 'whether' is rare, prob. repr. L. *an*.) –1734. **4.** After a primary statement or an exhortation, *or* appends a secondary alternative; = otherwise, else; in any other case; if not ME. **5.** *Or else* (also formerly *orels*): = or if not, or otherwise; = sense 4; see ELSE 4. ME. **6.** *Or* connects two words denoting the same thing: = otherwise called, that is (= L. *vel, sive*) ME.

1. Did you send a verbal or a written message? 1776. A vine or two 1861. You may walk ten or even twelve miles without finding one 1903. **b.** If Tintoret or Giorgione are at hand RUSKIN. Mr. Darwin or Barnum would claim him as their own 1874. **2.** You may take either the medal or its value 1903. **b.** An horse that had neither good eyes or feet 1691. **3.** Or let us glory gain, or glory give POPE. **b.** Tell me where is fancie bred, Or in the heart, or in the head SHAKS. **4.** Awake, arise, or be for ever fall'n MILT. **6.** The Tame or House Spider 1608.

Or-, *pref.*, freq. in OE., and occas. in ME., now surviving in ORDEAL, and perh. in ORT. OE. *or-* was the stressed form (used in nominal compounds), corresp. to OFris., OS. *ur-*, *or-* (Du. *oor-*), OHG. *ur-*, *ir-*, *ar-* (G. *ur-*), ON. *or-*, *ur-*, *ǫr-*, Goth. *us-*, *ur-*; orig. an adv. and prep., meaning 'out'.

-or, a termination of words, and form of various suffixes, of L. origin.

In AFr. the sound arising from Latin *ō* became (*ū*) and came *c*1300 to be written *ou* (*onour*). The earliest adopted words in ME. had *o* or *u* (*onor, onur*), but the regular representation after 1300 was with *ou* (*onour, honour*). At the Renaissance, many of the *-our* words were conformed to the L. in *-or*; and nearly all words taken then or later from L. were spelt *-or*. In Great Britain *-our* is still written in many of the words left unchanged in the 16th c., but American usage favours *-or* in all.

1. -or (formerly often *-our*), repr. ultimately *L. -or, -orem*, in nouns of condition derived from verbal stems, as *error, horror, liquor, tenor, torpor, tremor*, etc.

2. -or (formerly *-our*), repr. L. *-or, -orem* of agent-nouns, formed on stems identical with the supine stems of vbs. Of these there are: **a.** Those repr. L. agent-nouns other than those in *-ātor, -ētor, -itor, ītor*; as *actor, author, confessor, doctor, inventor, tutor*, etc. **b.** Agent-nouns in L. *-ātor, -ētor, -itor, -ītor* were regularly reduced from *-ātōrem*, etc., through *-edor* to OFr. *-eör, -eür*, AFr. *-eour*, which became in ME. *-our*, and in Fr. *-eur*, and thus fell together with those from simple *-orem* in **a.** Such are *conqueror, donor, emperor* (*imperatorem*), *juror, solicitor, vendor*, etc. Also, *saviour* (AFr. *sauveöur* :– OFr. *salveör, salvedor*, L. *salvatorem*), which has preserved the vowel bef. *-our*. Similar are agent-nouns formed in Fr. or AFr. on the vb.st em, as *purveyor, surveyor, tailor, warrior* (AFr. *werreyour*, f. *werreier* to war). **c.** Agent-nouns in *-ātor, -ētor, -itor, ītor, -ūtor*, adopted in later times in Fr., or in Eng., retain *t*, appearing in Fr. as *-ateur, -iteur*, etc., and have now in Eng. the same written form as in L., e.g. *administrator, creator, creditor*, etc. Some of these, from OFr. or AFr., had formerly *-our*, as *creatour, creditour*, etc.; others of later formation, immed. from L., have had the *-or* form from the first. **d. -or** is sometimes an alteration of another suffix, as of L. *-arius*, Fr. *-ier*, AFr. *-er*, in *bachelor, chancellor*, or of Eng. *-er* :– OE. *-ere*, in *sailor*. The frequent occurrence of ME. *-our*, mod. *-or*, in legal terms denoting the person acting, as opp. to the person acted upon in *-é, -ee*, e.g. *lessor, lessee*, has given it a kind of professional character; cf. *sailor, sailer*.

3. -or (-our) sometimes represents Fr. *-oir*, as *manor*, OFr. *manoir, maneir*, L. *manēre*; *mirror*, Fr. *miroir*, L. **miratorium*; *parlour*, Fr. *parloir*, L. **parabolatorium*.

4. -or, repr. ME. = AFr. *-our*, Fr. *-eur*, L. *-or, -orem*, a var. of *-ior*, suffix of the comparative degree of adjs., in *major, minor*. See -IOR.

Ora[1] (ō°·ră). *Hist.* [OE., app. – ON. *aurar* pl.; commonly regarded as – L. *aureus* golden.] **1.** A Danish money of account, reckoned in Domesday Book as = 20 pence. **2.** A measure of weight, used in Domesday Book for the ounce 1610.

‖**Ora**[2] (ō°·ră). 1826. [L., = border, brim, coast, etc.] *Entom.* The inflexed or inferior lateral margin of the prothorax.

Orach, orache (ǫ·rătʃ). late ME. [XV *arage, orage*, XVI *arache*, etc. – AFr. *arasche*, OFr. *arache, arrace* (mod. *arroche*) :– L. *atriplex*. *-plic-* (or some intermediate form between this and its source) – Gr. ἀτράφαξυς -ις.] A plant of the genus *Atriplex*, N.O. *Chenopodiaceæ*; esp. the Garden Orach or Mountain Spinach (*A. hortensis*).

Oracle (ǫ·răk'l), *sb.* ME. [– (O)Fr. *oracle* – L. *oraculum*, f. *orare* speak, plead, pray; see -CLE.] **I. 1.** *Gr.* and *Rom. Antiq.* The agency or medium by which a god was supposed to speak; the mouthpiece of the deity; the place or seat of such agency, at which divine utterances were believed to be given. **2.** A response, often ambiguous or obscure, given usu. by a priest or priestess of a god, at the shrine or seat of the deity 1598.

1. The Oracles are dumm MILT. Phr. *To work the o.*, to influence the agency or medium; to obtain the response desired by influence or manœuvring behind the scenes; also (*slang*), to raise money 1863. **2.** An o. was procured exactly suited to the purpose of the leaders of the expedition THIRLWALL.

II. *transf.* **1.** A vehicle or medium of divine communication. **a.** The holy of holies in the Jewish Temple; also, the mercy-seat within it 1440. **b.** One who or that which expounds or interprets the will of God 1548. **2.** Divine revelation; a message divinely inspired; also, *pl.* the sacred scriptures (from Rom. 3:2). late ME.

1. a. Sion Hill..and Siloa's Brook that flowd Fast by the O. of God MILT. **b.** In his company Ione the Puzel, whom he used as an o. and a southsaier 1548. **2.** The oracles or sayinges of God 1548.

III. *fig.* **1.** Something reputed to give oracular replies or advice 1625. **b.** Something regarded as an infallible guide or indicator, esp. when its action is mysterious, as a chronometer, a compass 1726. **2.** A person reputed or affecting to be infallible 1596. **3.** A wise utterance; an authoritative and infallible declaration; undeniable truth 1569. **4.** A prognostication 1596.

1. b. He called it [a watch] his o., and said it pointed out the time for every action of his life SWIFT. **2.** I am sir O., And when I ope my lips, let no dog barke SHAKS. **3.** His Words were received as Oracles 1701. Hence **O·racle** *v. trans.* to utter as an o., *intr.* to speak as an o.

Oracular (ŏræ·kiŭlăɹ), *a.* 1631. [f. L. *oraculum* + -AR[1].] **1.** Of or pertaining to an oracle; that is the seat or medium of an oracle, or of direct divine communications 1678. **2.** Of the nature of an oracle 1631. **b.** Mysterious, ambiguous, or sententious, like the ancient oracles 1736. **c.** Ominous, portentous 1820. **3.** Of a person: That delivers oracular responses; also *transf.* 1821. **4.** Delivered, uttered, or decreed by an oracle 1820.

2. Whatever he said or wrote was considered as o. by his disciples MACAULAY. **b.** He opened his lips, with an o. shake of the head 1845. **3.** The o. press lays down the law 1863. Hence **Ora·cular·ly** *adv.*, **-ness.**

Oraculous (ŏræ·kiŭləs), *a.* Now *rare* or *Obs.* 1610. [f. as prec. + -OUS, perh. after contemp. *miraculous*. Cf. Fr. †*oraculeux*.] = ORACULAR.

Urim and Thummim, those o. gems On Aaron's breast MILT. He grows on a sudden o. and infallible JOHNSON. Hence **Ora·culous-ly** *adv.*, **-ness.**

Oraison, obs. f. ORISON.

Oral (ō°·răl), *a.* (*sb.*) 1625. [– late L. *oralis*, f. L. *ōs*, *ōr-* mouth; see -AL[1].] **1.** Uttered in spoken words; transacted by word of mouth: spoken, verbal 1628. **2.** Using speech only, *esp.* for the instruction of the deaf and dumb 1870. **3.** Of or pertaining to the mouth 1656. **4.** Done or performed with the mouth, as the organ of eating and drinking 1625. **B.** *sb.* Short for *oral examination, sound*, etc. 1876.

1. As for orall Traditions, what certaintie can there be in them? BP. HALL. **2.** An o. school 1880. **3.** *O. cavity*, (*a*) the cavity of the mouth; (*b*) in haustellate insects, the hollow on the lower surface of the head, from which the haustellum or sucking-mouth protrudes. **b.** *Phonetics.* Uttered through the mouth, with the nasal passage closed. **4.** The orall eating and drinking of Christ in the Sacrament 1625. **B.** The Orals, short or long, in Feel, Fill, Tulle, Full, Fool 1887. So **O·ralism,** the instruction of deaf-mutes by 'lip-language' 1883. **O·ralist** 1867. **O·rally** *adv.*, by, through, or with the mouth 1608.

Orang (ŏræ·ŋ). 1778. = ORANG-OUTANG.

Orange (ǫ·rĕndʒ), *sb.*[1], *a.* [ME. *orenge* – OFr. *orenge* in *pomme d'orenge* (XIV), later and mod. *orange*; ult. – Arab. *nāranj* – Pers. *nārang* (whence also Sp. *naranja*, etc.).] **A.** *sb.* **1.** The fruit of a tree (see sense 2), a large globose, many-celled berry (HESPERIDIUM) with subacid juicy pulp, enclosed in a tough rind externally of a bright reddish yellow (= orange) colour. **2.** In full *orange-tree*: An evergreen tree (*Citrus aurantium*), a native of the East; it produces fragrant white flowers, and the fruit mentioned in sense 1. (Also applied to allied species, or subspecies, as *C. bigaradia, C. bergamia*; see quots.) 1615. **3.** Applied to various plants, or their fruit, mostly from some apparent resemblance in flower or fruit to the orange-tree 1817. **4.** = SEA ORANGE, a large orange-coloured holothurian (*Lophothuria fabricii*) of globose shape 1753. **5.** In full *orange-colour*: The reddish-yellow colour of the orange. Also, a pigment of this colour. 1587. **6.** *Her.* A roundel tenné (tawny-coloured) 1562.

1. *Blood* (*-red*), *Malta* or *Maltese O.*, a red-pulped variety. *Jaffa* or *Joppa O.*, a lemon-shaped and very sweet kind. *Navel O.*, a nearly seedless variety from Brazil, etc., having the rudiment of a second fruit embedded in its apex. *Clove, Noble*, or *Mandarin O.* = MANDARIN. *Tangerine O.*: see TANGERINE. The fruit of the *Citrus bigaradia* is called the *Bitter, Horned*, or *Seville O.*; and that of the *C. bergamia, Bergamot O.* or BERGAMOT[1]. Phr. *To squeeze* or *suck an o.*, to extract all the juice from it; *fig.* to take all that is profitable out of anything. *Oranges and lemons*, a nursery game, in which a ditty beginning with these words is sung. **3. Native o.** (*Australia*), (*a*) the orange-thorn, an orange berry with a leathery skin, about one inch and a half in diameter; (*b*) the small native pomegranate, *Capparis mitchelli.* **Quito O.,** *Maclura aurantiaca*, a species of nightshade in colour, fragrance, and taste resembling an o. See also MOCK-ORANGE.

attrib. and *Comb.* **1.** General: as *o.-bloom, -grove*, etc.; *o.-girl, -merchant*, etc.; *o.-wine*; *o.-grower*; *o.-shaped* adj.

2. Special: **o.-aphis,** a black aphis (*Siphonophora citrifolii*) that infests the orange-tree; **-jelly,** (*a*) a jelly flavoured with orange-juice and orange-peel; (*b*) a variety of swede turnip; **-marmalade,** see MARMALADE; **-oil,** the essential oil obtained from the rind of the o.; **-scale,** any scale-insect which infests the orange-tree; esp. *Aspidiotus aurantii.*

B. *adj.* Of the colour of an orange (see A. 5) 1542.

Comb. In names of orange-coloured varieties of apples or pears, as *o.-bergamot, -musk, -pear, -pippin*; also in names of plants, animals, etc. of this colour (more or less), as **o. bat,** the *Phinonycteris aurantia*, inhabiting northern Australia, the male of which has fur of a bright orange; **o.-cowry,** a large handsome cowry (*Cypræa aurantia*) of a deep yellow colour; **-grass,** *Hypericum sarothra*, having minute deep-yellow flowers; **o. lily,** *Lilium croceum*; **o. thorn;** see A. 3, quots.

Orange (ǫ·rĕndʒ), *sb.*[2] 1558. **1.** Name of a town on the river Rhone in France, formerly the capital of a small principality of the same name, from which the princes of Orange-Nassau, the ancestors of William III of England, took their title. In Eng. Hist., 'William of Orange' is an appellation of William III. **b.** *attrib.* Of or belonging to the Orange family or dynasty in Holland 1647. **2.** *Eng. Hist.* (*attrib.*) Applied to the ultra-Protestant party in Ireland, in ref. to the secret society of Orangemen formed in 1795; cf. ORANGEMAN 1796.

The members of 'The Orange Lodge' of Freemasons in Belfast and their adherents were known as 'Orange boys' and 'Orangemen'. The name of the lodge probably had ref. to William of Orange, or to the use of orange badges at the anniversary celebrations of his memory. Hence, no doubt, the use of 'Orange' as a party name.

Orangeade (ǫréndʒēⁱ·d). 1706. [f. ORANGE *sb.*[1] + -ADE, after *lemonade*.] A drink composed of orange and lemon juice diluted with water and sweetened. Also, now, an aerated water of an orange tint.

†**Orangea·do.** 1599. [Cf. Sp. *naranjada* conserve of oranges, Fr. *orangeat*; see -ADO.] Candied orange-peel –1796.

O·range-blo:ssom. 1786. The white fragrant blossom of the orange-tree. Worn by brides in wreaths, trimmings, etc., or carried in bouquets at the marriage ceremony.

O·range-flow:er. 1626. = prec.
Comb. **orange-flower water,** the aqueous solution of orange-flowers; the fragrant watery distillate left over in the preparation of neroli oil.

Orang(e)ism (ǫ·réndʒiz'm). 1823. [f. ORANGE *sb.*[2] + -ISM.] The system and principles upheld by the Orange Association; the principle of Protestant political ascendancy in Ireland.

Orangeman (ǫ·réndʒ₁mæ̆n). 1796. [f. ORANGE *sb.*[2] + MAN.] A member of a political society formed, in 1795, for the defence of Protestantism and maintenance of Protestant ascendancy in Ireland; see ORANGE *sb.*[2]

Orangery (ǫ·réndʒ₁ri, ǫ·réndʒĕri). 1664. [In sense 1 – Fr. *orangerie*, f. *oranger* orange-tree; see -ERY 2.] **1.** A place appropriated to the cultivation of orange-trees. †**2.** A scent extracted from the orange-flower; also, snuff scented with this –1744.

O·range-taw:ny, *a.* and *sb.* 1575. **A.** *adj.* Of a dull yellowish brown colour; tan-coloured with a tinge of orange. **B.** *sb.* As the name of a colour or a fabric.

Orangite (ǫ·réndʒəit). 1851. [Named, 1851, from its colour. See -ITE[1] 2 b.] *Min.* An orange variety of thorite.

Orang-outang (ǒræ·ŋ₁utæ·ŋ). Also **orang-utan** (ōᵊ·răŋ₁ū·tăn). 1699. [alt. of Malay *ōrang ūtan* wild man, prob. through Du. *orangutan*, *oerangoetan*.] *Zool.* An anthropoid ape, *Simia satyrus*, of arboreal habits, inhabiting Borneo, Sumatra, and formerly Java; the male exceeds 4 feet in height and has very long arms. The *Lesser Orang-utan* is *S. morio* of Borneo.

‖**Orarion** (orēᵊ·riǫn). 1772. [Græcized f. next.] In the Greek Church, the deacon's stole.

‖**Orarium** (orēᵊ·riǒm). 1706. [L., a napkin, f. *os, or-* mouth, face; see -ARIUM.] **a.** The earlier name of the stole; *spec.* in the Greek Church = ORARION. **b.** The scarf attached to a pastoral staff 1814.

Orate (ŏrēⁱ·t, ōᵊ·reⁱt), *v.* 1600. [f. *orat-*, pa. ppl. stem of L. *orare* speak, plead. Formed anew in U.S. *c* 1860, as a back-formation from *oration*.] *intr.* †**1.** To pray; to plead. **2.** To act the orator; to hold forth, 'speechify'. Now usu. joc. or sarcastic.
1. A Rhetorician, whose businesse is to o. and persuade 1669.

Oration (ŏrēⁱ·ʃən), *sb.* late ME. [– L. *oratio* discourse, speech, (eccl.) prayer, f. as prec.; see -ION.] **1.** A prayer or petition to God; orison. Now only *Hist.* **2.** A formal speech or discourse; *esp.* one delivered in connection with some particular occasion 1502. **3.** Speech, language; now only in *Gram.*, in 'direct' and 'oblique o.'
2. The greatest orations of the first orators of any age, Demosthenes and Æschines 1844.

Ora·tion, *v. colloq.* 1633. [f. prec. sb.] *intr.* To orate; to 'speechify'.

Orator (ǫ·rătəɹ). late ME. [– AFr. *oratour* = (O)Fr. *orateur* – L. *orator, oratōr-* speaker, pleader, f. *orat-*; see ORATE, -OR 2.] †**1.** An advocate, a spokesman; *spec.* a professional advocate –1650. †**2.** A petitioner or suppliant. (Commonly used in subscribing a letter or petition to a superior.) –1727. **b.** *Law.* The plaintiff or petitioner in a bill or information in chancery or equity (now *U.S.*). **3.** One who delivers a speech or oration in public; esp. an eloquent public speaker. late ME. †**4.** One sent to plead or speak for another; an ambassador, envoy, or messenger –1673. **5.** *Public O.*: an officer of the Universities of Oxford and Cambridge, whose functions are to speak in the name of the University on State occasions; to go in person, when required, to plead the cause of the University; to write suitable addresses, letters of congratulation or condolence; to introduce candidates for honorary degrees, and to perform other like duties 1614.
3. I come not (Friends) to steale away your hearts, I am no o., as Brutus is SHAKS. Som O. renound In Athens or free Rome MILTON.

Oratorial (ǫrătōᵊ·riăl), *a.* Now *rare.* 1546. [In sense 1 f. L. *oratorius* (f. *orator* ORATOR + *-ius*; see -ORY[2]) + -AL[1]. In sense 2 referred to ORATORIO.] **1.** Of, pertaining to, or proper to an orator. **2.** Of or pertaining to an oratorio 1811. Hence **Orato·rially** *adv.*

Oratorian (ǫrătōᵊ·riăn). 1644. [f. L. *oratorius* of or pertaining to an orator, *oratorium* place of prayer, ORATORY *sb.*[1] + -AN.] **A.** *adj.* †**1.** = ORATORIAL 1. –1734. **2.** Of or pertaining to the ORATORY (*sb.*[1] 3) 1862. **B.** *sb.* A father or priest of an oratory; *spec.* a member of the Oratory of St. Philip Neri, or other similar society (see ORATORY *sb.*[1] 3) 1656.

Orato·ric, *a.* 1656. [f. L. *orator* ORATOR + -IC, after *historic, rhetoric*.] = next.

Oratorical (ǫrătǫ·rikăl), *a.* 1619. [f. as prec. + -AL[1]; see -ICAL.] †**1.** = ORATORIAN *a.* 2. **2.** Of, pertaining to, or characteristic of an orator or oratory; rhetorical; also, according to the rules of oratory; characteristic of a professional advocate 1634. **3.** Given to the use of oratory 1801.
2. O. Discourses 1702. **3.** Americans are an o. race 1898. Hence **Orato·rically** *adv.*

Oratorio (ǫrătōᵊ·rio). 1727. [– It. *oratorio* – eccl. L. *oratorium* ORATORY *sb.*[1] Named in XVI from the musical services in the church of the Oratory of St. Philip Neri in Rome, these being virtually examples of the older mystery play adapted to a religious service.] A form of extended musical composition, of a semi-dramatic character, usu. founded on a scriptural theme, sung by solo voices and a chorus, to the accompaniment of a full orchestra, without the assistance of action, scenery, or dress.

O·ratorize, *v.* 1620. [f. ORATOR *sb.* + -IZE.] *intr.* To play the orator; to deliver an oration. Now usu. joc. or contemptuous: to 'speechify'.

O·ratorship. [See -SHIP.] The position or office of orator; esp. in *Public O.*, the office of Public Orator in a University.

Oratory (ǫ·rătəri), *sb.*[1] ME. [– AFr. *oratorie* = (O)Fr. *oratoire* – eccl.L. *oratorium*, subst. use (sc. *templum* temple) of n. of *oratorius*, f. *orat-*; see ORATE, -ORY[1].] **1.** A place of prayer; a small chapel; a room or building for private worship. Also in ref. to Jewish or pagan worship. †**2.** A faldstool at which a worshipper kneels –1771. **3.** The name of certain religious societies in the R.C. Church; orig. and esp. the *O. of St. Philip Neri* or *Congregation of the Fathers of the O.*, a society of priests living in community without vows, constituted at Rome in 1564.
1. In Temples hallowed for publique vse and not in priuate Oratories HOOKER.

Oratory (ǫ·rătəri), *sb.*[2] 1586. [– L. *oratoria* (Quintilian), subst. use (sc. *ars* art) of fem. of *oratorius*, f. *orator*; see ORATOR, -ORY[1].] **1.** The art of the orator or of public speaking; the art of speaking eloquently; rhetoric 1593. **2.** The delivery of orations or speeches; rhetorical or eloquent language.
1. That part of o., which relates to the moving of passions SWIFT. **2.** It is seldom that o. changes votes 1849.

Oratress (ǫ·rătrės). 1586. [f. ORATOR + -ESS[1].] A female orator, †petitioner, or †plaintiff.

Orb (ǭɹb), *sb.*[1] 1526. [– L. *orbis* ring, round surface, disc.] **I.** A circle and deriv. senses. **1.** A circle, or anything of circular form, as a circular disc, etc. Now *rare.* 1590. **2.** *Astrol.* The space on the celestial sphere within which the influence of a planet, star, or 'house' is supposed to act 1727. †**3.** *Astron.* The plane of the orbit of a planet, etc.; also, the orbit or path –1674. †**4.** A cyclical period, a cycle –1742.
1. And I serue the Fairy Queene, To dew her orbs vpon the green SHAKS. **3.** Instruct the planets in what orbs to run POPE.

II. A sphere and deriv. senses. **1.** *Old Astron.* Each of the concentric hollow spheres supposed to surround the earth and to carry the planets or stars with them in their revolution; see SPHERE. *Obs.* exc. *Hist.* 1526. **2.** Anything of spherical or globular shape 1597. **3.** A general name for the heavenly bodies (sun, moon, planets, or stars), in sense either of 'globe', or of 'disc'. Chiefly *poet.* or *rhet.* 1596. †**b.** *spec.* The earth; cf. L. *orbis terrarum* –1667. **4.** The eye-ball; the eye. *poet.* and *rhet.* 16.. **5.** The globe surmounted by a cross forming part of the regalia; also called *mound*, formerly *globe, ball* 1702. **6.** *fig.* †**a.** A 'sphere' of action or activity; rank, station. (Often with ref. to sense II. 1.) –1757. **b.** (from II. 2 or 3.) An organized or collective whole; a rounded mass; a 'world' 1603.
2. What a hell of witchcraft lies In the small o. of one particular tear! SHAKS. **3.** The O. of Day GRAY. **b.** *Twel. N.* III. i. 43. **4.** These eys..thir seeing have forgot, Nor to thir idle orbs doth sight appear MILT. **6. a.** Evangelists of an higher Orbe then..Bishops 1644. *Comb.* **o.-fish,** an East Indian fish (*Chætodon* or *Ephippius orbis*).

Orb, *sb.*[2] 1500. [– AFr. *orbe*, AL. *orba*, perh. – subst. use of fem. of L. *orbus* deprived, devoid (of), rel. to ORPHAN. Cf. Fr. *mur orbe* blind wall.] *Arch.* Blank or blind window; hence plain stone panel, blank panel.

Orb (ǭɹb), *v.* 1600. [f. ORB *sb.*[1]] **1.** *trans.* To enclose in, or as in, an orb or circle 1645. **2.** To form or gather into an orb, disc, or globe; to round out 1600.
1. Yea Truth and Justice then Will down return to men, Orb'd in a Rain-bow MILTON.

Orbed (ǭɹbd, *poet.* ǭ·ɹbėd), *a.* 1597. [f. ORB *sb.*[1] and *v.* + -ED.] **1.** Formed into, or having the form of, an orb; rounded; arched. Also *fig.* **2.** In comb., as *full-o.* (having a full orb), etc. 1667.

Orbicular (ǫɹbi·kiŭlăɹ), *a.* (*sb.*) late ME. [– late L. *orbicularis*, f. L. *orbiculus*, dim. of *orbis* (see ORB *sb.*[1], -CULE); see -AR[1].] **A.** *adj.* **1.** Round as a circle or disc; circular, of circular plan or section. **b.** *Anat.* and *Zool.* Applied to structures of circular or discoidal form; *spec.* to those muscles (*sphincters*) surrounding, and having the function of closing, natural apertures of the body, as the sphincters of the mouth, eyelids, etc. (Also in L. form *orbicularis.*) 1615. **c.** *Bot.* Of circular outline, as leaves, etc. 1731. **2.** Spherical, globular. Sometimes *loosely*, Having a rounded or convex (as opp. to a flat) surface. late ME. **3.** *fig.* Full-orbed, rounded, complete 1673. **4.** *Nat. Hist.* Combined with other adjs. of form; (*esp.* in *Bot.* of leaves), as *o.-cordate, -ovate*, etc. 1847. **5.** *O. bone* (*os orbiculare*), a very small bone of the middle ear, at the end of the incus, and articulating with the stapes 1706.
1. Quite through his bright o. targe CHAPMAN. **3.** The household ruin was thus full and o. DE QUINCEY.
B. *sb. Anat.* An orbicular muscle. See A. 1. b. Also in L. form *orbicularis.* 1872. Hence **Orbicula·rity,** o. form or character. **Orbi·cular-ly** *adv.*, **-ness** (*rare*).

Orbiculate (ǫɹbi·kiŭlĕt), *a.* 1760. [– L. *orbiculatus*, f. *orbiculus*; see prec., -ATE[2].] = ORBICULAR. Chiefly in *Nat. Hist.* So **Orbi·culated** *a.*

Orbiculato-, comb. f. L. *orbiculatus*, ORBICULATE, in sense 'orbiculately—', as *o.-ordate*, etc.

Orbit (ǭ·ɹbit). 1548. [– L. *orbita* wheel-track, course, path (of the moon), in med.L. eye-cavity, subst. use of fem. (sc. *via* way) of *orbitus* circular, f. *orbis, orb-* ORB *sb.*[1]] **1.** *Anat.* The bony cavity containing the eye and its muscles, glands, etc.; the eye-socket. **b.** *Zool.* The border of, or part surrounding, the eye in a bird, insect, etc. 1774. ¶**c.** (By confusion with ORB *sb.*[1] II. 4.) The eye-ball; the eye 1728. **2.** *Astron.* The path of a heavenly body; the curved path described by a planet or comet round the sun, by a satellite about its primary, etc. (Rarely = *the ecliptic.*) 1696. ¶**b.** Confused with *orb*; see ORB *sb.*[1] II. 1, 3, 6. 1727.

1. c. Or roll the lucid o. of an eye YOUNG. **2.** *fig.* The backslidings of my aunt Dinah in her o. did the same service in establishing my father's system 1759. Hence **O·rbital** *a.* of, belonging to, or connected with an o.; taking place in an o., as *o. revolution.*

Orbitar (ǭ·ɹbităɹ), *a.* (*sb.*) 1741. [– Fr. *orbitaire* (Paré), f. *orbite*; see ORBIT, -AR[1].] *Anat.* = ORBITAL; var. **O·rbitary. B.** *sb.* The zygomatic suture 1782.

Orbitelous (ǭɹbitī·ləs), *a.* 1857. [f. mod.L. *orbitelus,* Fr. *orbitèle,* f. L. *orbis* circle + *tela* web; see -OUS.] *Zool.* Applied to those spiders which spin circular webs, as the garden-spider. So **O·rbitele,** an o. spider.

O·rbito-, comb. form of L. *orbita* ORBIT, usu. in sense 'relating to the orbit along with (some other part)', as *o.-nasal, -temporal* adjs., etc.

Orbitolite (ǫɹbi·tŏləit). 1859. [In mod.L. *orbitolites,* f. *orbita* ORBIT + Gr. λίθος stone; see -LITE.] The fossil shell of a foraminifer of the genus *Orbitolites.*

Orbitosphenoid (ǭ:ɹbitoˌsfī·noid). 1854. [f. ORBITO- + SPHENOID.] **A.** *adj.* Belonging to the orbit and the sphenoid bone; applied to a small bone or bony process forming part of the eye-socket, and (in man) constituting the lesser wing of the sphenoid bone. **B.** *sb.* The o. bone or process. So **O:rbito-sphenoi·dal** *a.* = prec. A.

Orby (ǭ·ɹbi), *a. rare* and *poet.* 1611. [f. ORB *sb.*[1] + -Y[1].] Of the form of an orb; moving as in a circle, 'coming round'; of the nature of, or pertaining to, a heavenly body.

Orc, ork (ǭɹk). 1590. [In sense 1 – Fr. *orque* or L. *orca* kind of whale (Pliny).] **1.** A cetacean of the genus *Orca,* family *Delphinidæ*; esp. the killer (*O. gladiator* Gray). Formerly applied to more than one vaguely identified sea-monster. 1611. **2.** Occas. more vaguely (cf. L. *Orcus,* Rom. *orco,* and see OGRE): A devouring monster, an ogre 1590. Also (in sense 1) **O·rca.**

Orcadian (ǫɹkēⁱ·diăn), *a.* and *sb.* 1661. [f. L. *Orcades* the Orkney Islands + -IAN.] **A.** *adj.* Of or pertaining to Orkney. **B.** *sb.* A native or inhabitant of Orkney.

Orcanet (ǭ·ɹkănėt). 1548. [– OFr. *orcanette,* altered from *arcanette,* dim. of *arcanne,* for OFr. *alcanne* – med.L. *alkanna,* whence ALKANET.] = ALKANET.

Orcein (ǭ·ɹsiˌin). 1838. [Altered from ORCIN.] *Chem.* A red colouring-matter ($C_7H_7NO_3$) obtained from orcin by the action of ammonia and oxygen, and existing in the dye called orchil.

Orchard (ǭ·ɹtʃəɹd). [OE. *ortġeard, orċġeard, orċe(a)rd* garden, orchard = Goth. *aurtigards* garden (cf. *aurtja* γεωργός, and OHG. *kaorzōn* cultivate). The first element repr. L. *hortus* garden; the second YARD *sb.*[1]] †**a.** Formerly, in general sense, A garden, for herbs and fruit-trees. **b.** Now, an enclosure for the cultivation of fruit-trees.

attrib. and *Comb.*, as **o. grass,** any grass grown in an o., *esp.* in U.S., the Cock's-foot Grass, *Dactylis glomerata*; **-house,** a glass house for the protection of fruit that is delicate, or is wanted early; **o. oriole,** a N. Amer. oriole (*Icterus spurius*) which hangs its nest from the boughs of fruit and other trees.

O·rcharding. 1664. [f. prec. + -ING[1].] **1.** The cultivation of fruit-trees in orchards. **2.** *concr.* Land laid out and planted with fruit-trees. (Chiefly Amer.) 1721.

O·rchardist. 1794. [f. as prec. + -IST.] One who cultivates an orchard.

Orchestic (ǫɹke·stik), *a.* and *sb.* 1842. [– Gr. ὀρχηστικός, f. ὀρχηστής dancer; see -IC.] **A.** *adj.* Of or pertaining to dancing. **B.** *sb.* (more freq. in pl.) The art of dancing 1850.

Orchestra (ǭ·ɹkėstră). 1606. [– L. *orchestra* – Gr. ὀρχήστρα, f. ὀρχεῖσθαι dance. Formerly stressed *orche·stra.*] **1.** *Gk. Theatre.* A large semicircular space in front of the stage, where the chorus danced and sang. **2.** That part of a theatre or other building assigned to the band or chorus of singers 1724. **3.** The company of musicians themselves; a company of performers of concerted instrumental music in a theatre, concert-room, etc. 1720. **b.** *transf.* The set of instruments played by such a company of musicians 1834.

3. c. Also *o. chairs, stalls* (U.S.), that part of a theatre known in England as the 'stalls' (STALL *sb.*[1] 4 c). Hence **Orchestral** (ǫɹke·străl, ǭ·ɹkės-trăl) *a.*

Orchestrate (ǭ·ɹkėstreⁱt), *v.* 1880. [f. prec. + -ATE[3], perh. after Fr. *orchestrer.*] *trans.* To compose or arrange for an orchestra; to score for orchestral performance. Hence **Orchestra·tion,** the action or art of orchestrating; the style in which a piece of music is orchestrated; instrumentation of orchestral music. **O·rchestrator.**

Orchestre, -ter (ǭ·ɹkėstəɹ, *formerly* ǫɹke·s-təɹ). 1623. [– Fr. *orchestre* – L. *orchestra.*] = ORCHESTRA.

Orchestric (ǫɹke·strik), *a.* 1786. [f. ORCHESTRA + -IC.] **1.** Better ORCHESTIC, q.v. **2.** Orchestral 1839.

Orchestrina (ǭɹkėstrī·nă). Also **-ino.** 1838. [f. ORCHESTRA + -INA[1], after *concertina,* etc.] †**a.** An instrument of the keyboard kind, imitating various other musical instruments. **b.** A mechanical instrument resembling a barrel-organ, intended to imitate the effect of an orchestra. So **Orche·strion** [cf. *accordion*].

Orchid (ǭ·ɹkid). 1845. [Introduced by Lindley; f. mod.L. *Orchideæ* or *Orchidaceæ*; see ORCHIDEOUS and -ID[2].] Any plant of the orchis family (*Orchidaceæ* or *Orchideæ*), a large Natural Order of monocotyledons, distinguished by having one, or rarely two, sessile anthers, united with the pistil (*gynandrous*) into a central body called the *column,* and containing pollen coherent in masses (*pollinia*); the flowers have three sepals and three petals, and are often remarkable for brilliancy of colour or grotesqueness of form.

Orchidaceous (ǭɹkidēⁱ·ʃəs), *a.* 1838. [f. mod.L. *Orchidaciæ,* substituted by Lindley for the earlier *Orchideæ*; see ORCHIDEOUS, -ACEOUS.] **1.** Belonging to the N.O. *Orchidaceæ,* ORCHID. **2.** Resembling an orchid, esp. in being showy 1864.

Orchidean (ǫɹki·diăn), *a. rare.* 1821. [f. mod.L. *Orchideæ* (see ORCHIDEOUS) + -AN.] Belonging to the *Orchideæ,* orchidaceous; pertaining to or characteristic of an orchid.

Orchideous (ǫɹki·diəs), *a.* 1818. [f. mod. L. *Orchideæ* (Linnæus, 1751), irreg. f. *orchid-,* wrongly assumed stem of L. *orchis* – Gr. ὄρχις testicle; see -OUS.] Belonging to the *Orchideæ* or natural order of plants akin to the genus *Orchis*; orchidaceous.

Orchido-, assumed comb. form of Gr. ὄρχις (the etym. form being *orchio-*); usu. taken as if repr. ORCHID; as in **Orchido·logist,** one versed in orchidology; **Orchido·logy,** that branch of botany which deals with orchids; etc.

Orchil (ǭ·ɹtʃil). 1483. [– OFr. *orcheil, orcele, orseil* (mod. *orseille*), perh. to be referred ult. to L. *herba urceolaris* plant for polishing glass pitchers (Pliny), f. *urceolus,* dim. of *urceus* pitcher. See ARCHIL.] **1.** A red or violet dye prepared from certain lichens, esp. *Roccella tinctoria.* **2.** The lichen *Roccella tinctoria,* or other species from which the dye is obtained 1758.

Orchilla (ǫɹtʃi·lă), **orchella** (ǫɹtʃe·lă). 1703. [– It. *orcello,* OSp. *orchillo* (mod. *archilla*); see ORCHIL.] **1.** = prec. 1. **2.** (usu. *o.-weed.*) = prec. 2. 1772.

Orchis (ǭ·ɹkis). 1562. [– L. *orchis,* the plant – Gr. ὄρχις testicle, also the plant ὄρχις (so called from the usual shape of the tubers). See ORCHID.] The typical genus of *Orchidaceæ* or Orchids, comprising terrestrial herbs of temperate regions, with tuberous root (usu. having two tubers), and erect fleshy stem bearing a spike of flowers, usu. purple or red, with spurred lip; any plant of this genus, or (pop.) of other genera resembling this. **b.** With defining word (sometimes denoting an insect, etc., which the flower resembles): as BEE O., BUTTERFLY O., FINGER O., FLY O., etc. 1785.

Where. .far descried High tower'd the spikes of purple orchises M. ARNOLD.

‖**Orchitis** (ǫɹkəi·tis). 1799. [f. Gr. ὄρχις testicle + -ITIS.] *Path.* Inflammation of the testicle. Hence **Orchi·tic** *a.*

Orchotomy (ǫɹkǫ·tŏmi). Also **orchio-.** 1753. [– Gr. ὀρχοτομία, f. ὄρχις testicle; see -TOMY.] *Surg.* Excision of the testicles; castration.

Orcin (ǭ·ɹsin). Also **-ine.** 1840. [– mod. L. *orcina,* f. stem of It. *orcello* ORCHIL; see -IN[1].] *Chem.* A colourless crystalline substance ($C_7H_8O_2$ + H_2O) obtained from the various kinds of orchilla-weed, turning red, brown, or yellow, in contact with air, or when treated with various compounds. Cf. ORCEIN.

Ordain (ǫɹdēⁱ·n), *v.* [ME. *ordeine* – AFr. *ordeiner* = OFr. *ordener* (tonic stem *ordein-*), later *-oner* (mod. *-onner*) – L. *ordinare,* f. *ordo, ordin-* ORDER *sb.*] **I.** To put in order, arrange, make ready, prepare. †**1.** *trans.* To arrange in regular order; to array, marshal, order –1581. †**2.** To set or keep in proper order; to regulate, direct, conduct –1489. †**3.** To arrange the order or course of –1681. **4.** To set up (something) to continue in a certain order; to institute. Now *arch.* ME. †**5.** To plan, devise, contrive –1526. †**6.** To put in order (for a purpose); to prepare, equip; to furnish –1548. †**7.** To dispose (aright) –1502. †**8.** *intr.* To make preparation –1533.

6. He hath. .ordened his arowes to destroye COVERDALE *Ps.* 7:13.

II. To appoint, decree, destine, order. †**1.** *trans.* To appoint to a charge, duty, or office –1809. †**b.** Const. *to do* something; *to* (*on, upon*) some office, etc. –1676. **2.** *Eccl.* To appoint or admit ceremonially to the ministry of the Christian Church; to confer holy orders upon ME. †**3.** To appoint or assign (*to* or *for* a special purpose, etc.) –1618. **4.** Of the Deity, fate, etc.: To decree, predestine, destine. Also *absol.* or *intr.* ME. **5.** To decree as a thing to be observed; to enact ME. **b.** *absol.* or *intr.* To appoint, command ME. **6.** = ORDER *v.* II. 2. *Obs.* or *arch.* late ME. †**7.** = ORDER *v.* II. 3. –1621.

1. Wherefore are magistrates ordayned, but that the tranquillitie of the commune weale maye be confirmed? LATIMER. **2.** I am a young Clergyman, Ordained the very Last Ember-Week 1718. **4.** The moment. .which God had ordained from the beginning 1865. The path we are ordained to tread LYTTON. **5.** That which is ordained by law they term lawful and just JOWETT. **7.** Afterward he ordeined a boat made of one tree. .and went to sea in it HAKLUYT. Hence **Ordai·nable** *a.* **Ordai·ner. Ordai·nment,** the action or fact of ordaining.

‖**Ordalium** (ǫɹdēⁱ·liŏm). 1599. Med.L. adaptation of the word *ordāl,* ORDEAL; in Eng. use in XVII.

Ordeal (ǭ·ɹdiăl, ǭ·ɹdīl). [OE. *ordāl, ordēl* (whence AL. *ordalium, ordela, -elum*) = OFris. *ordēl,* OS. *urdēli* (Du. *oordeel*), OHG. *urteili* (G. *urteil*) judgement, judicial decision :– Gmc. **uzdailjam,* corresp. to OE. *ādǣlan,* OS. *ādēljan,* OHG. *ar-, irteilen* (G. *urteilen*), adjudge as one's share, decide, give judgement :– **uzdailjan* share out, f. **uz-* out (OR- *pref.*) + **dailjan* DEAL *v.*] **1.** An ancient Teutonic mode of trial, in which a suspected person was subjected to some physical test fraught with danger, e.g. the plunging of the hand in boiling water, the carrying of hot iron, walking barefoot and blindfold between red-hot plough-shares, etc., the result being regarded as the immediate judgement of the Deity. **2.** *fig.* Anything which severely tests character or endurance; a trying experience, a trial 1658.

attrib. and *Comb.*, as *o. fire,* etc.; **o.-bean,** the poisonous CALABAR-BEAN.

Order (ǭ·ɹdəɹ), *sb.* [ME. *ordre* – (O)Fr. *ordre,* earlier *ordene* – L. *ordo, ordin-* row, series, course, array, rank (of soldiers), class, degree, captaincy, command, (eccl.) rank in the Church, rel. to *ordiri* begin, *ornare* ADORN.] **I.** Rank generally; a rank, grade, class. **1.** A rank, row, series. *Obs.* or *arch.* 1563. **b.** *Arch.* A series of mouldings 1845. **2.** A rank of the community; a social division, grade, or stratum; *esp.* in *higher, lower orders* ME. **b.** A definite rank in the state. late ME. **c.** Rank in the abstract. *poet.* 1667. **3.** A body of persons of the same profession, occupation, or pursuits, regarded as a separate class in the community. late ME. **4.** A class, group, kind, or sort, of persons, beings, or things, having its rank in a scale of being, or importance, or distinguished from others by nature or character 1736.

2. That part of the Catechism is written for the lower orders 1893. **b.** The most High and Sacred O. of Kings 1683. **3.** The spirit of the whole clerical o. rose against this injustice MACAULAY. **4.** He possessed talents of a high o. DISRAELI.

II. Rank in specific departments. **1.** Each of the nine ranks or grades of angels, viz. seraphim, cherubim, thrones, dominations, principalities, powers, virtues, archangels, angels ME. **2.** *Eccl.* **a.** A grade or rank in the Christian ministry, or in an eccl. hierarchy ME. **b.** The rank, status, or position of a clergyman or ordained minister of the Church. Now always *pl.*, more fully *holy orders.* ME. **c.** The conferment of holy orders, the rite of ordination ME. **3. a.** A religious society or fraternity (as of monks, nuns, friars) living under a rule; as *the Benedictine* or *Franciscan o.* ME. **b.** A fraternity of knights bound by a common rule of life, and having a combined military and monastic character; as *the Teutonic O., the O. of Knights Templars*, etc. late ME. **4.** An institution, generally founded by a sovereign, or prince of high rank, for the purpose of rewarding meritorious service by the conferring of a dignity. late ME. **b.** The badge or insignia of such a dignity 1533. **5.** *Arch.* A system of parts subject to certain uniform established proportions; esp. in *Class. Arch.*, applied to modes of architectural treatment founded upon the proportions of columns and the kind of their capitals, with the relative proportions and amount of decoration used in their entablatures, etc. 1563. **6.** *Math.* The degree of complexity of any analytical or geometrical form, equation, expression, operator, or the like, as denoted by an ordinal number (first, second, third, . ., *n*th) 1706. **7.** *Nat. Hist.* One of the higher groups in the classification of animals, vegetables, or minerals, forming a subdivision of a *class*, and itself subdivided into families, or into genera and species 1760.

2. a. *Holy orders*: in the R.C.Ch., those of bishop, priest, deacon, and (since 12th c.) subdeacon; in the Anglican and Eastern Ch., only those of bishop, priest, and deacon. *Minor orders*: in the R.C.Ch., those of acolyte, exorcist, reader, and door-keeper, in the Eastern Ch., subdeacon, reader, and sometimes singer. **b.** The Pope has pronounced against the validity of Anglican orders 1903. Phr. *To take orders*, to be ordained. *In orders*, in the position of an ordained clergyman. *In deacon's orders, in priest's* or *full orders.* **c.** Those five commonly called Sacraments, that is to say, Confirmation, Penance, Orders, Matrimony, and Extreme Unction *Art. Religion* xxv. **3. a.** It was the Friar of Orders gray 1596. **b.** The hospytelers and Templars were two fygtinge orders 1550. That fair O. of my Table Round TENNYSON. **4.** The honourable Ordre of the Gartier. late ME. **b.** To whom he will carry the O. of the Black Eagle 1710. **5.** *The five Orders of Classical Architecture*, the Tuscan, Doric, Ionic, Corinthian, and Composite, rising above each other in relative height, lightness, and decoration. Of these the Doric, Ionic, and Corinthian are the original Greek orders, the Tuscan and Composite, Roman modifications or varieties. **6.** *A fluxion of the second order* is a fluxion of a fluxion; *an infinitesimal of the second order* is one infinitely smaller than one of the first order. The degree of a quantic in the variables *x, y, z* . . is generally spoken of as its o. 1895. **7.** *Natural O.* (of plants), a group consisting of genera or families naturally allied in general structure, as opp. to an O. in an artificial system (e.g. the Sexual System of Linnæus), the members of which agree only in some single characteristic which may be unimportant.

III. Sequence, disposition. **1.** Sequence or succession in space or time; succession of acts or events; the course or method of occurrence or action ME. **2.** Formal disposition or array, late ME. **b.** The condition in which everything is in its proper place, and performs its proper functions. late ME. **c.** *Mil.* Equipment for a particular purpose, as *marching o.* 1837. †**3.** Disposition of measures for some purpose; suitable action –1827. †**4.** Regular or customary mode of procedure –1715. **5.** The fixed arrangement found in the existing constitution of things; a natural, moral, or spiritual system in which things proceed according to definite laws ME. **6.** *Liturgiology.* A stated form of divine service, etc., prescribed by eccl. authority or custom; the service so prescribed. late ME. **7.** *spec.* (from III. 4.) The prescribed or customary mode of proceeding in debates or discussions, or in the conduct of public meetings, etc., or conformity with the same 1782. **8.** (= *civil* or *public o.*) The maintenance and observance of law or constituted authority; law-abiding state; absence of insurrection, riot, turbulence, or crimes of violence 1483. **9.** State or condition generally (qualified as *good, bad*, etc.); normal, healthy, or efficient condition 1568. **10.** *Mil.* The position in which a rifle is held as a result of the command to 'order arms'; see ORDER *v.* 1. 1847.

1. Stand not vpon the o. of your going, But go at once SHAKS. He has inverted the natural o. 1799. **2.** The crevasses are . . apparently without law or o. in their distribution TYNDALL. **b.** O. is Heav'n's first Law POPE. His love of o. made him always the most regular of men 1882. **3.** *Meas. for M.* II. ii. 25. Phr. *To take o.*, to take measures, make arrangements. **5.** The old o. changeth, yielding place to new TENNYSON. The existence of an invisible o. of things 1878. Phr. *O. of nature, of things, of the world, moral o., spiritual o.*, etc. **6.** The O. of Confirmation *Bk. Com. Prayer.* **7.** Here Gen. Manners called Sir Francis to o. 1812. Phr. *O. of business, to rise to a point of o., the speaker* or *motion is not in o.*, or *is out of o.* See also *O. of the day*, in V. **8.** Peace and o. were maintained by police regulations of German minuteness and strictness M. PATTISON. **9.** The Ships were all in prime O., all lately rebuilt 1743.

IV. The action or an act of ordering. †**1.** The action of putting or keeping in order; regulation, control –1690. **2.** An authoritative direction, injunction, mandate; an instruction 1548. **3.** *spec.* **a.** *Law.* A decision of a court or judge, made or entered in writing; in the Supreme Court, a direction other than a final judgement 1726. **b.** *Banking*, etc. A written direction to pay money or deliver property, given by a person legally entitled to dispose thereof 1673. **c.** *Business.* A direction to make, provide, or furnish anything, at the responsibility of the person ordering; a commission to make purchases, supply goods, etc. *A large o.* (slang), a large demand, proposal, etc. **d.** A pass for admission, without payment or at a reduced price, to a theatre, etc., or to a museum, park, private establishment, or the like 1763.

2. Grumio gaue o. how it should be done SHAKS. The Agamemnon was under orders to strengthen the China fleet 1884. **3. a.** An o. to pay 2*s.* a month was made 1903. **b.** I will send a Post-Office o., in repayment 1846. **c.** Poets indeed are not made 'to o.' BAGEHOT. Boots and shoes ready made, or to o. 1903.

V. Phrases and Combinations.

O. of the day. **a.** In a legislative body, the business set down for debate on a particular day (= Fr. *l'ordre du jour*). **b.** Specific commands or notices issued by the commanding officer to his troops. **c.** *colloq.* The prevailing rule or custom of the time. **In order: a.** In proper sequence or succession. **b.** In proper condition; in obedience to constituted authority or usage. **c.** Appropriate to or befitting the occasion; suitable. **d.** *In* (or *on*) *short o.* (also *quick o.*): without delay, immediately *U.S.* **In o. to:** †**a.** In reference to; for the sake of. **b.** With a view to the bringing about of (something), for the purpose of (some prospective end). Now only const. inf. *In o. that*: to the end that. **Out of o.:** Not in proper sequence, orderly arrangement, or settled condition; not in proper or normal condition of action, mind, bodily health, etc.

Comb.: **o. clerk,** a clerk who enters business orders; **o. form,** a partially blank form to be filled up in giving a business order; **o.-paper,** a paper on which questions, etc., coming in the o. of the day, in a legislative assembly, are entered; **-word** (Fr. *mot d'ordre*), the military pass-word, a watchword. Hence **O·rderless** *a.* devoid of o. or method; disorderly 1596.

Order (ǭ·ɹdəɹ), *v.* [ME. *ordre*, f. prec.] **I. 1.** *trans.* To give order or arrangement to; to put in order; *spec.* to draw up in order of battle, to array. *arch.* **2.** To set or keep in order or proper condition; to dispose according to rule; to regulate, govern, manage; to settle 1509. **b.** *refl.* To conduct oneself, behave. Now *arch.* 1535. **c.** Of the Deity, etc.: To ordain 1642. †**3.** To make ready, prepare (for a purpose) –1722. †**4.** To bring into order or submission to lawful authority; hence, to correct, chastise –1667. †**5.** To treat, deal with, manage (in a specified manner) –1799.

1. He ordred his battail, like a man expert in marciall science 1548. Phr. *To o. arms* (*Mil.*): to bring a firearm into a position in which it is held vertically against the right side, the butt on the ground. **2.** They o., said I, this matter better in France STERNE. **b.** To ordre myselfe lowlye and reuerentlye to al my betters *Bk. Com. Prayer.* **c.** It was ordered otherwise, and doubtless wisely FROUDE.

II. 1. To give orders for (something to be done); to bid, command, direct; to prescribe medically 1550. **2.** To give orders to, command, direct (a person, *to do* something, etc.) 1628. **b.** *ellipt.* To command or direct (a person) to go or come *to, into, upon* (a place, etc.), *away, here, home, out*, etc. 1667. **3.** To give an order for; to direct (a thing) to be furnished or supplied 1836.

1. The doctor had ordered as much fresh air as possible 1891. In U.S., also with ellipse of *to be.* These things were ordered delivered to the army 1781. **2. b.** He . . was ordered to a warmer climate 1898. **3.** What have you ordered for dinner? 1903.

III. *Eccl.* To admit to holy orders; to ordain; formerly also, to admit or institute to a benefice. *arch.* ME. Hence **O·rderer, O·rdering** *vbl. sb.* the action of the vb.

O·rder-book. 1833. [f. ORDER *sb.* + BOOK.] A book in which orders are entered. *spec.* **a.** In the army, a book in which the orderly sergeants enter general and regimental orders. **b.** In the navy, a book kept on a man-of-war for recording occasional orders of the commander. **c.** In the House of Commons, a book in which motions to be submitted to the House must be entered. **d.** In business, a book in which the orders of customers are entered.

Orderly (ǭ·ɹdəɹli), *a.* and *sb.* 1577. [f. ORDER *sb.* + -LY[1].] **A.** *adj.* **1.** Arranged or disposed in order; exhibiting system or method; regular. **b.** Of persons: Regular, methodical 1830. †**2.** Conformable to established order or rule; regular –1637. **3.** Observant of order, rule, or discipline; well-conducted, well-behaved 1598. **4.** *Mil.* Pertaining to orders or their issue; charged with the conveyance or execution of orders 1723. **5.** Pertaining to the system of keeping the streets clean 1851.

1. We were . . tied together, and thus advanced in an o. line TYNDALL. **3.** Elections are now conducted in an o. manner 1884. **4.** *O. book*, a book kept in a regiment or company, for the entry of general or regimental orders. *O. man* = B. 1, 2. *O. officer*, the officer of the day; rarely = B. 1. *O. room*, the office and court of the commanding officer. **5.** *O. bin*, a street box for the reception of refuse. So **O·rderliness** 1571.

B. *sb.* **1.** A non-commissioned officer or private soldier attending upon a superior officer to carry orders or messages 1800. **2.** An attendant in a military or other hospital, charged esp. with the maintenance of order and cleanliness 1809.

Orderly (ǭ·ɹdəɹli), *adv.* 1477. [f. ORDER *sb.* + -LY[2].] **1.** In order; in due order or course. Now *rare.* **2.** According to established order or rule; duly; in a well-conducted manner 1509.

1. I thought it good . . to wryte the same orderly vnto the (good Theophilus) COVERDALE *Luke* 1:3.

Ordinal (ǭ·ɹdinăl), *a.* (*sb.*[1]) late ME. [– late L. *ordinalis* denoting order in a series, f. *ordo, ordin-* ORDER; see -AL[1].] †**1.** Conformable to order, rule, or custom; orderly –1496. **2.** Marking position in an order or series, as *first, second, third*, etc.; opp. to CARDINAL 1599. **3.** *Nat. Hist.* Of or pertaining to an order of animals or plants, or to natural order in general 1822. **4.** Relating to, or consisting of, a row or rows 1892. **B.** *sb.* An ordinal number (see 2) 1591.

Ordinal (ǭ·ɹdinăl), *sb.*[2] late ME. [– med.L. *ordinale*, subst. use of n. sing. of *ordinalis* (sc. *liber* book); see prec. Cf. MANUAL *sb.*] †**1.** A book containing rules, or a body of rules or regulations –1674. **2.** A book setting forth the order of the services of the Church, or of any one of them, as they existed before the Reformation; a service-book. late ME. **3.** A book prescribing the rules to be observed, and containing the form of service to be used, in the ordination of deacons and priests, and the consecration of bishops 1658.

Ordinance (ǭ·ɹdinăns). ME. [– OFr. *ordenance* (now *ordonnance*) – med.L. *ordinantia*, f. L. *ordinare* ORDAIN; see -ANCE. Cf. ORDNANCE, ORDONNANCE.] †**1.** Arrangement in ranks or rows; esp. battle-array; also, a host in array –1601. **2.** Disposition (of things or matters) according to rule; arranged condition; order. *Obs.* exc. as in b. late ME. **b.** = ORDONNANCE 1. 1460. †**3.** Provision; a preparatory step or measure; hence, provision *of* (something) –1612. †**b.** Apparatus, furniture –1611. **4.** The action of ordering or regulating; control, disposal. *arch.* ME. **b.** A dispensation, decree, or appointment of Providence or of Destiny *arch.* ME. †**c.** Ordained place, condition, course, etc. –1601. **5.** Authoritative direction how to act; system of government, polity, or discipline. *Obs.* or *arch.* ME. **6.** An authoritative direction, decree, or command; e.g. of a sovereign, a local body, etc. **7.** A practice or usage authoritatively enjoined or prescribed, *esp.* a religious or ceremonial observance. late ME. **b.** Applied esp. to the sacrament of the Lord's Supper 1830.

2. b. Verrio's invention is admirable, his ordnance full and flowing EVELYN. **3.** Great ordynance of gunnes the kynge let make 1500. **4.** I putte me hoolly in youre disposicion and ordinaunce CHAUCER. **b.** Let Ord'nance Come as the Gods fore-say it SHAKS. **c.** *Jul. C.* I. iii. 66. **6.** According to Thy blessed Word and o. *Bk. Com. Prayer.* The Acts of the Long Parliament after 1641 were at first called *Ordinances*; one of these was the *Self-denying O.* of 1645, ordaining that no member of parliament should thenceforth hold any civil or military office. O.E.D. **7.** Candidates of this sacred O. [Confirmation] 1704.

Ordinand (ǭ·ɹdinænd). 1842. [– L. *ordinandus*, gerundive of *ordinare* ORDAIN.] A candidate for ordination.

Ordinant (ǭ·ɹdinănt), *a.* and *sb.* *rare.* late ME. [In XV – OFr. *ordinant*, pr. pple. of *ordiner*; in mod. use – pr. pple. of L. *ordinare*; see ORDAIN, -ANT.] **A.** *adj.* That arranges, regulates, or directs. **B.** *sb.* One who confers holy orders 1842.

Ordinarily (ǭ·ɹdinărili), *adv.* 1532. [f. ORDINARY *a.* + -LY².] †**1.** In conformity with rule; as a matter of regular occurrence –1695. **2.** In most cases; usually, commonly 1555. **3.** To the usual extent 1697. **4.** As is normal or usual 1831.

2. Of a more blew colour than Lead o. is 1691. **3.** Phr. *More than o.*, exceptionally; I am more than o. anxious to do Justice to the Persons 1709.

Ordinary (ǭ·ɹdinări), *sb.* ME. [– AFr., OFr. *ordinarie* (later and mod. *ordinaire*, whence ME. and Sc. *ordinar*) – med.L. *ordinarius* (sc. *judex* judge, etc.), and in n. sing. *ordinarium*; see next.] **I.** Applied to a person or staff of persons. **1.** *Eccl.* and *Common Law.* One who has, of his own right and not by deputation, immediate jurisdiction in eccl. cases, as the archbishop in a province, or the bishop or bishop's deputy in a diocese. **2.** *Civil Law.* A judge having authority to take cognizance of cases in his own right and not by delegation; *spec.* in Scotland, one of the five judges of the Court of Session who constitute the Outer House (= *Lord Ordinary*, ORDINARY *a.* 2); in *U.S.*, a judge of a court of probate 1607. **3.** The chaplain of Newgate prison, whose duty it was to prepare condemned prisoners for death. *Obs.* exc. *Hist.* 1700. †**4.** A courier conveying dispatches or letters at regular intervals; hence, post, mail. (= Fr. *ordinaire*) –1730. **5.** Chiefly in phr. *in ordinary* (of a ship), laid up or out of commission 1754.

II. Rule, ordinance, ordinal. (= med.L. *ordinarius, ordinarium.*) †**1.** A formula or rule of action; an ordinance, regulation, prescript –1594. **2.** A rule prescribing, or book containing, the order of divine service; the form for saying mass; the service of the mass, or that part preceding and following the canon 1494.

III. Something ordinary, regular, or usual. (From the adj. in Fr. or Eng.) †**1.** Customary fare; a regular daily allowance of food; hence, an allowance of anything (= Fr. *ordinaire*) –1668. **2.** A public meal regularly provided at a fixed price in an eating-house or tavern; also, formerly, the company frequenting this 1589. **b.** An eating-house where such meals are provided; a dining-room in such a building 1590. **c.** In parts of U.S.: A tavern or inn of any kind 1774. **3.** *Her.* A charge of the earliest, simplest, and commonest kind, e.g. Chief, Pale, Bend, Bend-Sinister, Fesse, Bar, Chevron, Cross, Saltire 1610. **4. a.** Ordinary condition, course, run, degree; ordinary state of health, etc. 1581. **b.** An ordinary thing or person (*rare*) 1624. **5.** Applied to various things of the most usual type; e.g. an ordinary share, as dist. from preference shares, etc. 1552.

1. Giue him his ordinarie of Oats 1616. **2.** He kept a daily O. (thanks being the only shot his guests were to pay) FULLER. **b.** The unwholsome ayre of an Eightpenny Ordinarie 1631. **4. a.** *The o.*, what is customary or usual. Now *colloq.*, as in adj. phr. *out of the o.*, unusual. I see no more in you then in the o. Of Natures sale-worke SHAKS. Phr. *In o.* added to official designations: app. a modification of the simple *ordinary* (see ORDINARY *a.* 3 b), and opp. to *extraordinary*, as *chaplain-in-o.* to his Majesty, *physician-in-o.* to the Prince of Wales.

Comb. **o. table,** the table at which an o. was served and which was afterwards cleared for gambling; hence, a gambling-table or gambling-house.

Ordinary (ǭ·ɹdinări), *a.* (*adv.*) 1460. [– L. *ordinarius* orderly, usual, f. *ordo, ordin-* ORDER *sb.*; see -ARY¹.] †**1.** Conformable to order or rule; regular; orderly, methodical –1639. **2.** Of a judge: Having regular jurisdiction, not deputed, *esp.* empowered *ex officio* to take cognizance of eccl. or spiritual cases. Of jurisdiction, etc.: Exercised *ex officio.* 1483. **3.** Regular, normal, customary, usual 1460. **b.** Of officials, persons employed, etc.: Belonging to the regular staff or class of such. Now mostly *-in-ordinary*: see ORDINARY *sb.* 1555. †**4.** Of common occurrence; frequent; abundant –1725. †**b.** Customary, usual. Chiefly predicative. –1794. **5.** Of the usual kind, not singular or exceptional. Often *depreciatory*: Commonplace, somewhat inferior; also (now *dial.* or *colloq.*) ordinary-looking, 'plain' 1590. †**6.** Not distinguished by rank or position; of low degree; common, vulgar, unrefined –1741. †**B.** *adv.* In an ordinary manner; ordinarily –1798.

2. *Judge o.*: (*a*) the judge of the Court for Divorce; (*b*) in Scotland, the sheriff of a county. **3.** In o. life we use a great many words with a total disregard of logical precision JEVONS. Phr. *More than o.*: (*a*) more in number or amount than is usual; (*b*) with adj. or sb., To a greater degree than is usual, exceptional; also *advb.* unusually, exceptionally. *Obs., arch.,* or *dial.* So *greater, better,* (etc.) *than o.* **5.** *O. seaman*, one not expert; dist. from *able seaman.* His Books are very mean and o. HEARNE. Hence **O·rdinariness.**

Ordinate (ǭ·ɹdinĕt), *a.* and *sb.* late ME. [– L. *ordinatus*, pa. pple. of *ordinare*; see ORDAIN, -ATE² and ¹.] **A.** *ppl. a.* and *adj.* Now *Obs.* or *rare.* †**I.** Construed as *pa. pple.* Ordered, disposed; ordained, destined, appointed –1649. **II.** Construed as *adj.* †**1.** Conformed to order or rule; observant of order; orderly, regular –1678. **2.** *Entom.* Arranged in a row or rows 1826.

Phr. *O. proportion* (*Math.*), a proportion in which the terms are in regular order. *O. line* = B. Hence †**O·rdinately** *adv.* –1763.

B. *sb. Geom.* (Formerly more fully *o. applicate.*) **a.** Any one of a series of parallel chords of a conic section, in relation to the diameter which bisects each of them; now usu. applied to half the chord (i.e. the line from the curve to the bisecting diameter), orig. called the *semi-o.* Hence, **b.** A straight line drawn from any point parallel to one of the co-ordinate axes, and meeting the other. (Correl. to ABSCISSA.) 1537.

Ordinate (ǭ·ɹdineᵗt), *v.* 1562. [– *ordinat-*, pa. ppl. stem of L. *ordinare*; see prec., -ATE³.] †**1.** *trans.* = ORDAIN *v.* II. 2. –1597. **2.** To order, regulate, control, govern, direct. Now *rare* or *Obs.* 1595. **3.** To institute, establish, ordain, predestine. Now *rare* or *Obs.* 1610. **4.** To co-ordinate 1882.

Ordination (ǭɹdinēⁱ·ʃən). late ME. [– (O)Fr. *ordination* or L. *ordinatio*, f. as prec.; see -ION.] The action of ordaining. **I.** The action of ordering, arranging, or disposing in ranks or order; ordered condition; an arrangement or disposition 1658. **b.** Classification in orders 1656. **II.** The action of ordaining, or conferring holy orders; admission to the ministry of the Church; the fact of being ordained. late ME. **III. 1.** The action or fact of ordaining or decreeing, esp. as a divine action 1460. †**b.** Destination (*to* an end or purpose); destined function or disposition –1829. †**2.** That which is ordained; an ordinance, decree –1656.

1. The quality of transparency is given, by a wise o. of Providence, to the fluid substance of water 1794.

Ordinative (ǭ·ɹdinĕtiv), *a.* 1605. [– late L. *ordinativus*, f. as prec.; see -IVE.] Having the character or function of ordaining, ordering, determining, or regulating; of the nature of ordination or ordering. Now *rare.*

Ordinee (ǭɹdinī·), *a.* and *sb.* [In ME. – OFr. *ordiné*, pa. pple. of *ordiner* ORDAIN; in mod. use formed anew; see -EE¹.] †**A.** *adj.* Admitted to holy orders, or into a religious order; ordained. ME. only. **B.** *sb.* An ordained clergyman; now, usu., a newly-ordained deacon ME.

Ordnance (ǭ·ɹdnăns). late ME. [contr. of *ordenance*, ORDINANCE.] †**1.** = ARTILLERY 1. –1644. **2.** Engines for discharging missiles. **a.** = ARTILLERY 2. ME. †**b.** With *pl.* A large gun, piece of ordnance –1629. †**c.** The artillery as a branch of the army –1786. **3.** The branch of the public service concerned with the supply of military stores and materials, the management of the artillery, etc. 1485. †**4.** Occas. var. of ORDINANCE in other senses. **5.** *attrib.*, as *o. officer, stores,* etc. 1800.

2. *Piece of o.*: see PIECE. **b.** Gunners spunge your Ordinances CAPT. SMITH. **3.** *Board of O.*, a board, partly military and partly civil, which had the management of all affairs relating to the artillery, engineers, and the matériel of the Army. It was dissolved in 1855, most of its functions as regards matériel being now discharged by the *Army Ordnance Department.*

Ordnance Survey: The official survey of Great Britain and Ireland, undertaken by the Government, and originally carried out under the direction of the Master-General of the O. Hence **o.-datum,** the datum-line or level to which all heights are referred in the O. Survey, being 12½ feet below Trinity High-water mark, and 4½ feet above Trinity Low-water mark; **o. map,** a map prepared by the Survey.

‖**Ordo** (ǭ·ɹdo). 1849. [L., = row, series, order.] *Eccl.* An ordinal, directory, or book of rubrics; an office or service with its rubrics.

Ordonnance (ǭ·ɹdŏnăns, ‖ordonā·ns). 1644. [– Fr. *ordonnance*, alt. of OFr. *ordenance*, after (O)Fr. *ordonner*; see ORDINANCE *sb.*] **1.** Systematic arrangement, esp. of literary material, architectural parts or features, or the details of a work of art; a plan or method of composition; an order of architecture. **2.** In ref. to France, etc.: An ordinance, decree, law, or by-law 1756.

Ordovician (ǭɹdovi·ʃ'ăn), *a.* 1887. [f. L. *Ordovices*, name of an ancient British tribe in North Wales + -IAN.] *Geol.* The name of a series of rocks, including part of the Lower Silurian of Murchison; applied also to the age in which these strata were deposited.

Ordure (ǭ·ɹdiŭɹ). late ME. [– (O)Fr. *ordure*, f. *ord* filthy :– L. *horridus* HORRID; see -URE.] **1.** Filth, dirt. Formerly also in *pl. arch.* Also *fig.* of foul language, etc. **2.** Excrement, dung. Formerly also in *pl.* late ME.

Ore (ōᵊɹ). OE. [Two types: (1) ME. *oor(e, oure, ure* repr. OE. *ōra* unwrought metal (corresp. to Du. *oer*, LG. *ūr*, of unkn. origin); (2) ME. *ōre* repr. OE. *ār* = OS., OHG. *ēr*, ON. *eir*, Goth. *aiz* :– Gmc. **aiz* :– **ajiz*, corresp. to L. *æs* crude metal, bronze, money. Thus the mod. Eng. word app. derives its sense from OE. *ōra*, but its form from OE. *ār.*] **1.** A native mineral containing a precious or useful metal in such quantity, etc., as to make its extraction profitable. **b.** With *an* and *pl.* A quality or kind of ore OE. **2.** Metal, esp. precious metal. Chiefly *poet.* 1639.

1. *fig.* The good Yeoman is a Gentleman in O. FULLER. **2.** Let others toil to gain the sordid o. 1763.

attrib. and *Comb.*, as **o. body,** a body or connected mass of ore in a mine, as a vein, bed, pocket, etc.; **-hearth,** a form of small reducing furnace made of cast iron, used in lead-smelting; a Scotch or blast hearth.

Ore, O're, Ore-, obs. ff. *o'er*, OVER, OVER-.

Oread (ōᵊ·riæd). late ME. [– L. *Oreas*, *Oread-* – Gr. Ὀρειάς, Ὀρειαδ-, f. ὄρος mountain; see -AD.] *Gr.* and *Lat. Myth.* A mountain-nymph.

Like a Wood-Nymph light O. or Dryad MILT.

Orectic (ore·ktik), *a. rare.* 1779. [– Gr. ὀρεκτικός appetitive, f. ὀρεκτός, f. ὀρέγειν stretch out, grasp after, desire.] **a.** *Philos.* Of, pertaining to, or characterized by appetite or desire; appetitive. **b.** *Med.* Having the quality of stimulating appetite or desire.

Oreide (ōᵊ·ri,id). 1875. [– Fr. *oréide*, f. *or* gold. Cf. OROIDE.] A kind of brass resembling gold in colour, etc., used for imitation jewellery.

‖**Oreodon** (orī·ŏdǫn). 1877. [mod.L. f. Gr. ὄρος, ὀρε-ος mountain + ὀδούς, ὀδοντ- tooth: named by Leidy in 1851. For the ending, cf. MASTODON.] *Palæont.* A genus of extinct ruminant mammals, typical of the family *Oreodontidæ*, the remains of which are found in the miocene tertiary formations of the western U.S. Hence **Ore·odont, -do·ntine** *adjs.*

Oreography, -ology, etc., var. ORO-GRAPHY, etc.

Ore-weed (ōᵊ·ɹwīd). *local.* 1586. [f. *ore*, earlier *wore*, *woore* seaweed (see WARE *sb.*[1]) + WEED *sb.*[1]] Seaweed.

Orexin (ore·ksin). 1891. [f. Gr. ὄρεξις desire, appetite + -IN[1].] *Chem.* The hydrochlorate of phenyl-dihydro-quinazolin, a colourless, odourless crystalline substance, used as a stomachic.

Orfe (ǭɹf). 1688. [– G. *orfe*, Fr. †*orfe*; cf. L. *orphus* (Pliny) – Gr. ὀρφός sea-perch.] A golden-yellow variety of the ide (*Leuciscus idus*), acclimatized in England in the 19th c.

Orgal(l, obs. var. of ARGOL[1].

Organ (ǭ·ɹgăn), *sb.* OE. [– OFr. *organe*, *orgene* (mod. *orgue*) – L. *organum* instrument, engine, musical instrument, (eccl.) church organ – Gr. ὄργανον, f. IE. *worg- *werg- WORK; cf. ORGY.] **I.** A musical instrument. †**1.** Applied vaguely in a general sense to various musical (esp. wind) instruments –1667. **2.** *spec.* A musical instrument, consisting of a number of pipes, supplied with *wind* or compressed air by means of bellows, and sounded by means of keys, which on being pressed down admit the wind to the pipes by opening valves or *pallets*. late ME. †**b.** Formerly in *pl.* denoting a single instrument. (The L. sing. had also the sense 'pipe'. With *the organs* cf. *the bagpipes*, *the pipes*.) –1825. †**c.** Also called *a pair*, or *set, of organs* –1714. **d.** Applied, with distinctive epithets, to the separate groups of stops (*partial organs*), each with its own keyboard, which make up an organ 1606. **3.** Applied to other musical instruments, as in *Dutch o.* 1825. **b.** = BARREL-*organ* 1840. **c.** A keyboard wind-instrument with metal reeds; a reed-organ. *American o.*: a reed-organ in which the air is drawn inwards to the reeds. 1880.

2. d. A complete o. may be said to consist of five parts: choir o., great o., swell o., solo o., and pedal o... A large o. therefore consists of a number of small organs differing in quality of tone, and so arranged as to be under the control of one performer. STAINER & BARRETT.

II. A part or member of an animal or plant body adapted by its structure for a particular vital function, as seeing, hearing, speaking, digestion, respiration, etc. late ME. **b.** The human organs of speech or voice collectively; the larynx and its accessories as used in singing. (Somewhat *rare.*) 1601. **c.** *Phrenology.* One of the regions of the brain held to be the seat of particular mental faculties or tendencies 1806. **d.** Used in the names of special structures in the animal body, denominated after their discoverers 1877.

1. The parts of our body, by which we perceive any thing, are those we commonly call the organs of sense 1656. **b.** Thy small pipe Is as the maidens o., shrill, and sound SHAKS. **d.** *O. of Corti*, a complicated structure in the cochlea of the ear, supposed to be the essential auditory apparatus.

III. A means of action or operation, an instrument, a 'tool'; a person, body of persons, or thing by which some purpose is carried out or some function performed (*arch.*) 1548. **b.** A mental or spiritual faculty regarded as an instrument of the mind or soul 1656. **c.** An instrument, means, or medium of communication, or of expression of opinion; *spec.* applied to a newspaper or journal which is the mouthpiece of a particular party, cause, movement, or pursuit 1788.

1. An enchanteresse, an orgayne of the deuill, sent from Sathane 1548. **b.** Faith,—Belief,—is the o. by which we apprehend what is beyond our knowledge 1836. **c.** A newspaper which was generally considered throughout India to be the o. of the Government 1853.

attrib. and *Comb.*, as **o.-bird,** a name for the S. Amer. *Cyphorhinus cantans* and a Tasmanian species of *Gymnorhina*, from their notes; **-blower,** a person who works the bellows of an o.; also a mechanical contrivance for the same purpose; **-cactus,** the giant cactus, *Cereus giganteus*, from the shape of its stem resembling an organ-pipe; **-grinder,** an itinerant street musician who turns the handle of a barrel-organ (see GRIND *v.*); so *organ-grinding* adj. and sb.; **-harmonium,** a large harmonium of elaborate construction or powerful tone, adapted to take the place of an o.; **-loft,** a loft or gallery in which an o. is placed; **-point** (*Mus.*) = PEDAL-POINT; **-stop,** a stop or set of pipes of the same quality of tone, in an o.

O·rgan, *v. rare.* 1652. [f. ORGAN *sb.*] †**1.** *trans.* To furnish with an organ or organs –1681. **2.** To play on an organ 1827.

Organdie (ǭ·ɹgăndi). 1835. [– Fr. *organdi*, of unkn. origin.] A very fine and translucent kind of muslin.

Organic (ǫɹgæ·nik), *a.* 1517. [– Fr. *organique* (*Anat.* XIV) – L. *organicus* – Gr. ὀργανικός pertaining to an organ, instrumental, f. ὄργανον ORGAN; see -IC.] **1.** Serving as an organ; instrumental. Now *rare.* **2.** Done by means of instruments; mechanical 1885. **3.** *Phys.* Of or pertaining to the bodily organs; vital; *spec.* in *Path.* of a disease, Producing or attended with alteration in the structure of an organ; structural (opp. to *functional*) 1706. **4.** Having organs, or an organized physical structure (of animals or plants). Opp. to *inorganic.* 1778. **b.** *Chem.* Applied to a class of compound substances which naturally exist as constituents of organized bodies (animals or plants), or are formed from compounds which so exist, as in *o. acid, base, compound, molecule, radical*; all these contain or are derived from hydrocarbon radicals, hence *O. Chemistry* is the chemistry of the hydrocarbons and their derivs. 1827. **5.** Belonging to the organization or constitution (bodily or mental) of a living being; constitutional; fundamental. **b.** Structural. 1796. **c.** *Philol.* Belonging to the etymological structure of a word; not secondary or fortuitous (often opp. to *analogical*) 1845. **6.** Of, pertaining to, or characterized by connection or co-ordination of parts in one whole; organized; systematic 1850. **b.** *U.S.* Organizing, constitutive, as *o. act, law* 1849. **7.** Organ-like 1609.

1. Those o. arts which enable men to discourse and write MILT. **4.** These rocks contain no o. remains 1813. I have used it [organic nature] almost as an equivalent of the word 'living' HUXLEY. **5.** My o. indolence BURNEY. **6.** Consciousness is..a membered or o. whole, every part of which exists only in and through its relation to the rest 1880. So †**Orga·nical** *a.*, in all senses 1521–1837. Hence **Orga·nically** *adv.* 1662.

Organicism (ǫɹgæ·nisiz'm). 1853. [See -ISM.] **1.** The doctrine that organic structure is merely the result of an inherent property in matter to adapt itself to circumstances 1883. **2.** *Path.* The doctrine of the localization of disease which refers it to a material lesion of an organ.

Organific (ǭɹgăni·fik), *a.* 1840. [f. ORGAN + -FIC.] Having the property or power of forming organs or organized structures; formative, organizing.

Organism (ǭ·ɹgăniz'm). 1664. [In sense 1 f. ORGANIZE *v.* + -ISM; senses 2 and 3 – Fr. *organisme.*] **1.** Organic structure; organization. Now *rare.* **2.** An organized or organic system; a whole consisting of dependent and interdependent parts, compared to a living being 1768. **3.** An organized body, consisting of mutually connected and dependent parts constituted to share a common life; the material structure of an individual animal or plant 1842.

1. The advantagious O. of the Eye 1701. **2.** Paul first taught us to speak of society as an o. 1900. Hence **Organi·smal** *a.*

Organist (ǭ·ɹgănist). 1591. [– Fr. *organiste* (XV) or med.L. *organista* (XIII); see ORGAN, -IST.] **1.** One who plays an organ, e.g. at the services in a church. †**2.** A maker of organs –1653. **3.** A W. Indian song-bird, a species of *Euphonia*, esp. *E. musica.* Also *o. tanager.* 1882.

Organizable (ǭ·ɹgănəizăb'l), *a.* 1679. [f. ORGANIZE *v.* + -ABLE.] Capable of being organized; *spec.* in *Biol.* Capable of being converted into organized or living tissue. Hence **O:rganizabi·lity.**

Organization (ǭ:ɹgănəizēⁱ·ʃən, -izēⁱ·ʃən). late ME. [f. ORGANIZE + -ATION; in early use, and sense 3, – med.L. *organizatio* (XIII).] **1.** The action of organizing, or condition of being organized, as a living being; also, the way in which a living being is organized; the structure of an organized body (animal or plant), or of any part of one; bodily (*rarely* mental) constitution. **b.** The fact or process of becoming organized or organic; in *Path.* conversion into living tissue 1804. **c.** *concr.* An organized structure, body, or being; an organism 1707. **2.** *gen.* The action of organizing 1816. **b.** The condition of being organized; the mode in which something is organized; systematic arrangement for a definite purpose 1790. **c.** *concr.* An organized body, system, or society 1873. **3.** *Mediæval Mus.* The singing of the ORGANUM 1782.

1. That being then one Plant, which has such an O. of Parts in one coherent Body LOCKE. **c.** Choice organisations—natures framed to love perfection GEO. ELIOT. **2.** The o. of a service of transport was then proceeded with 1897. **b.** The Turks arrived in Europe with an o. wholly military 1832.

Organize (ǭ·ɹgănəiz), *v.* late ME. [– (O)Fr. *organiser* – med.L. *organizare*; see ORGAN, -IZE.] **1.** *trans.* To furnish with organs; to give an organic structure to; to form into a living being or living tissue. Usu. in *pa. pple.* **b.** *intr.* for *refl.* To become organic 1880. **2.** *gen.* To form into a whole with interdependent parts; to give a definite and orderly structure to; to systematize; to arrange or 'get up' something involving united action 1632. **3.** *Mus.* To sing the ORGANUM to a plain-song 1782.

1. Some Cheese Mites we could see (as little..as a Mustard-seed) yet perfectly shap'd and organiz'd 1664. **2.** The several orders..so organized and so acting..they were the people of France BURKE. To o. a procession, a demonstration (*mod.*). Hence **O·rganizer,** one who organizes 1849.

Organo-, comb. form of Gr. ὄργανον ORGAN; as in: **O:rganometa·llic** *a.*, *Chem.* applied to compounds in which an organic radical is directly combined with a metal. **O:rganopla·stic,** having the property of forming or producing the bodily organs. **O:rganotherapeu·tics, -the·rapy,** the treatment of disease by the administration of portions of certain animal organs or of extracts of them.

O:rganoge·nesis. 1859. [f. ORGANO- + -GENESIS.] *Biol.* = next, a. So **O:rganogene·tic** *a.* organogenic.

Organogeny (ǭɹgănǫ·dʒĕni). 1844. [f. ORGANO- + -GENY.] *Biol.* **a.** The production or development of the organs of a plant. **b.** The department of biology dealing with this. So **O:rganoge·nic** *a.* **Organo·genist.**

Organography (ǭɹgănǫ·grăfi). 1559. [f. ORGANO- + -GRAPHY.] **1.** A description of instruments –1674. **2.** The description of the organs of living beings; structural anatomy, esp. of plants 1806. So **O:rganogra·phic, -al** *adjs.* **Organo·graphist.**

Organology (ǭɹgănǫ·lŏdʒi). 1814. [f. ORGANO- + -LOGY.] **1.** The department of biology which treats of the organs of living beings, in ref. to their structure and functions 1842. **2.** Phrenology 1814. So **O:rganolo·gical** *a.*, **-o·logist.**

‖**Organon** (ǭ·ɹgănǫn). 1590. [– Gr. ὄργανον instrument, organ, etc.; the title of Aristotle's logical treatises = 'instrument' of all reasoning; cf. ORGANUM.] †**1.** A bodily organ, esp. as an instrument of the soul or mind –1629. **2.** An instrument of thought or knowledge; *esp.* a system of rules or principles of demonstration or investigation; spec. title of the logical writings of Aristotle 1643.

O·rgan-pi·pe. late ME. [f. ORGAN *sb.* + PIPE *sb.*[1]] **1.** One of the pipes of an organ 1440. **2.** *transf.* Applied to things resembling the pipes of an organ; e.g. *pl.* to basaltic columns closely placed 1861. **3. Organ-pipe coral:** see CORAL *sb.* 1 b. 1833.

1. *fig.* The Thunder (That deepe and dreadfull Organ-Pipe) pronounc'd The name of Prosper SHAKS.

‖**Organum** (ǭ·ɹgănɒ̆m). 1614. [L. – Gr.; see ORGANON.] **1.** = ORGANON 1. **b.** = ORGANON 2; esp. in the title of Bacon's *Novum Organum*, i.e. New Instrument for scientific investigation 1856. **2.** *Mediæval Mus.* A part sung as an accompaniment below or above the melody or plain-song, usu. at the interval of a fourth or fifth; also, *loosely*, this method of singing in parts. (Also called DIAPHONY.) 1782.

Organzine (ǭ·ɹgănzīn), *sb.* 1699. [– Fr. *organsin* – It. *organzino*, of unkn. origin.] Silk thread, formed of several strands twisted together in the contrary direction to that in which their component filaments are twisted. Also *o. silk*. Hence **O·rganzine** *v.* to make into o.; *intr.* to twist threads of silk so as to form o.

Orgasm (ǭ·ɹgæz'm). 1684. [– Fr. *orgasme* or mod.L. *orgasmus* – Gr. ὀργασμός, f. ὀργᾶν swell as with moisture, be excited.] **1.** Violent excitement of feeling; rage, fury; a paroxysm of excitement or rage 1763. **2.** *Physiol.* Excitement in an organ or part, accompanied with turgescence; *spec.* the height of venereal excitement in coition 1684. Hence **Orga·stic** *a.*

Orgeat (ǭ·ɹdʒiăt, ‖orʒa). 1754. [– Fr. *orgeat* – Pr. *orjat*, f. *ordi* barley :– L. *hordeum*.] A syrup or cooling drink made orig. from barley, later from almonds, and orange-flower water.

‖**Orgia:** see ORGY.

Orgiastic (ǭɹdʒiæ·stik), *a.* 1698. [– Gr. ὀργιαστικός, f. ὀργιαστής, f. ὀργιάζειν celebrate orgies; see -IC.] Belonging to, or characterized by orgies; marked by licentiousness or dissolute revelry. So **Orgia·stical** *a. rare.*

‖**Orgueil.** ME. [– AFr. *orguil* (Gower), OFr. *orgoill, orguill* (mod. *orgueil*) :– Frankish **urgōli* pride.] Pride, haughtiness. *Obs.* exc. as alien.

Orgulous (ǭ·ɹgiŭləs), **orgillous** (ǭ·ɹgiləs), *a. arch.* ME. [– OFr. *orguillus*, AFr. *-ous* (mod. *orgueilleux*); see prec., -OUS.] Proud, haughty. **b.** Splendid. **c.** Swelling, violent.

Orgy, orgie (ǭ·ɹdʒi); chiefly in pl. **orgies** (ǭ·ɹdʒiz), †**orgia.** 1589. [In pl. *orgies* – Fr. *orgies* – L. *orgia* – Gr. ὄργια n. pl. 'secret rites', also in L. 'secret frantic revels'; f. IE. **worg-* **werg-* WORK; see -Y[3] (Cf. ORGAN). The sing. is used mainly in sense 3.] **1.** *Gr.* and *Rom. Antiq.* Secret rites practised in the worship of various deities; *esp.* those connected with the festivals in honour of Dionysus or Bacchus, celebrated with extravagant dancing, singing, drinking, etc. **2.** *transf.* Applied to any rites, ceremonies, or secret observances 1598. **3.** Feasting or revelry; wild or dissolute revels; debauchery; often in *sing.* A drunken or licentious revel 1703.

1. The Thracian Matrons,..With Furies, and Nocturnal Orgies fir'd DRYDEN. **2.** *P.L.* I. 415. **3.** The worship of the beautiful always ends in an o. DISRAELI. *fig.* That o. of blood and arrogance—the European tyranny of Bonaparte 1883.

-o·rial, a compound suffix, consisting of -AL, L. *-alis*, added to L. *-ori-* in *-orius, -a, -um* (see -ORY). The termination is orig. adjectival (substantival only by ellipsis). In sense, adjs. in *-orial* are usu. identical with those in *-ory*, but the former are preferred where there is a sb. in *-ory* (e.g. *purgatory, purgatorial*).

‖**Oribi, orebi** (ǫ·rĭbi). 1795. [Cape Du., app. from Hottentot.] A small species of S. African antelope (*Antilope* or *Ourebia scoparia* or *Scopophorus ourebi*).

Orichalc (ǫ·rikælk). Also in L. form **orichalcum.** 1590. [– L. *orichalcum* – Gr. ὀρείχαλκον, lit. 'mountain-copper'. In later L. made into *aurichalcum*, as if 'golden copper'.] Some yellow ore or alloy of copper, highly prized by the ancients; perh. brass.

Oriel (ō[ə]·riĕl). ME. [– OFr. *oriol, eurieul* passage, gallery, of unkn. origin; so med.L. *oriolum* (XIII) porch, anteroom, upper chamber.] †**1.** A portico, corridor, balcony, etc. –1500. **b.** In Cornwall (*orrel*), a porch or balcony at the head of an outside stair 1880. **2.** A large recess with a window, of polygonal plan, projecting from the outer face of a building, usu. in an upper storey, and either supported from the ground or on corbels ME. **b.** for *o. window*. (Occas. used vaguely for *stained-glass window*.) 1805.

2. That small excursion out of gentlemen's halls in Dorsetshire..is commonly called an orial FULLER. **b.** The moon on the east o. shone SCOTT.

attrib. and *Comb.* (from 2), as *o. casement*, etc.; **o. window,** the window of an 'oriel'; a projecting window in an upper storey. **b.** *Oriel College* (Oxford) derives its name from a messuage called, in the reign of Henry III, *La* (or *Le*) *Oriole*, the origin of which name is unknown.

Oriency (ō[ə]·riĕnsi). Now *rare.* 1652. [f. ORIENT *a.*; see -ENCY.] 'Orient' quality; brilliancy, lustre.

Orient (ō[ə]·riĕnt). late ME. [– (O)Fr. *orient* – L. *oriens, orient-* rising, rising sun, east, pr. pple. of *oriri* rise; see -ENT.] **A.** *sb.* (In sense 1 and 2 usu. with cap.) **1.** That region of the heavens in which the sun rises, or the corresponding region of the world, or quarter of the compass; the east. Now *poet.* or *rhet.* **2.** Eastern countries, or the eastern part of a country; the East; usu., those countries east of the Mediterranean or of Southern Europe, the countries of South-western Asia or of Asia generally (cf. ORIENTAL A. 3); occas., in mod. Amer. use, Europe or the Eastern Hemisphere. Now *poet.* or *literary*. late ME. **3.** Rising (of the sun, or the daylight); sunrise, dayspring, dawn. Now *rare* or *Obs.* 1582. **4.** Short for 'pearl of orient' or 'orient pearl' 1831. **5.** The peculiar lustre of a pearl of the best quality 1755.

1. Lo! in the o. when the gracious light Lifts up his burning head SHAKS. **2.** Sicily, Greece, will invite, and the O. 1849. Phr. *Pearl of O.*: = o. pearl, oriental pearl; a pearl from the Indian seas; hence, a brilliant or precious pearl. **3.** *fig.* His life having set in the o. of his age and hopes DRUMM. OF HAWTH.

B. *adj.* **1.** Situated in or belonging to the east; eastern, oriental. Now *poet.* 1450. **2.** Applied to pearls, etc., of superior value and brilliancy, as coming anciently from the East; often a vague epithet: Precious; brilliant, lustrous, sparkling. late ME. **b.** Hence, of other things: Brilliant, lustrous, radiant, resplendent; occas. (after A. 3), Shining like the dawn, bright red (*arch.*) late ME. **3.** Rising, as the sun or daylight 1598.

1. When the Sun..Pillows his chin upon an O. wave MILT. **2.** He nowe shyneth as doth an o. stoone 1494. **b.** Banners..With O. Colours waving MILT. **3.** *fig.* The o. moon of Islam SHELLEY.

Orient (ō[ə]·rient), *v.* 1727. [– Fr. *orienter* place facing the east, f. *orient* east; see prec.] **1.** *trans.* To place or arrange (anything) so as to face the east; *spec.* to build (a church) with the longer axis due east and west, and the chancel or chief altar at the east end; also, to bury with the feet to the east. **b.** By extension: To place with the four faces towards the four points of the compass; to place in any particular way with respect to the cardinal points; also, to determine the bearings of (anything) relatively to the points of the compass 1842. **2.** *fig.* To adjust, correct, or bring into defined relations, to known facts or principles; *refl.* to put oneself in the right position or relation; also, to ascertain one's bearings. Now more usu. ORIENTATE. 1850. **3.** *intr.* To turn to the east, or (by extension) towards any specified direction 1896.

2. Mistress Kitty..presently began orienting herself, and getting ready to make herself agreeable O. W. HOLMES.

Oriental (ō[ə]ri,e·ntăl). late ME. [– (O)Fr. *oriental* or L. *orientalis*; see ORIENT *sb.*, -AL[1].] **A.** *adj.* **1.** Belonging to, or situated in, the east, eastern, easterly; *spec.* in *Astrol.* said of a heavenly body when in the eastern part of the sky, *esp.* of a planet when seen in the east before sunrise. †**2.** Belonging to or situated in the east of a country or place, or of the earth –1669. **3.** *spec.* Belonging to, found in, or characteristic of, the countries east of the Mediterranean; belonging to Asiatic countries; also, belonging to the east of Europe, or of Christendom (as the *O. Church*); Eastern. (Usu. with capital O.) 1425. **4.** Of pearls and precious stones, and hence (formerly) of other things: = ORIENT B. 2, 2 b. late ME.

3. O. sore, an ulcerous skin-disease occurring in the East, also called *Aleppo boil, Aleppo ulcer*, etc. **4.** *O. amethyst, O. emerald, O. topaz* (respectively purple, green, and yellow varieties of sapphire).

B. *sb.* †**1.** An oriental pearl or other gem; see A. 4. –1750. †**2.** *pl.* Oriental languages; see A. 3. 1734. **3.** A native or inhabitant of the East; i.e. usu., an Asiatic 1701.

3. A solemn, bearded, turbanded, and robed O. BURTON. Hence **Orie·ntalism,** o. character, style, or quality; with *pl.* an o. trait or idiom; o. scholarship. **Orie·ntalist,** = B. 3; one versed in o. languages and literature. **Orienta·lity,** the quality or condition of being o. **Orie·ntally** *adv.* in an o. manner or position 1649.

Orie·ntalize, *v.* 1823. [f. ORIENTAL *a.* + -IZE.] **1.** *trans.* To make oriental. **2.** *intr.* **a.** To become oriental in character. **b.** To play the oriental 1829. Hence **Orientaliza·tion.**

Orientate (ō[ə]·riĕntē[i]t), *v.* 1849. [prob. back-formation f. ORIENTATION.] = ORIENT *v.*

To o. exactly his present mode of thought 1884.

Orientation (ō[ə]riĕntē[i]·ʃən). 1839. [app. f. ORIENT *v.* + -ATION.] **1.** The action of orienting (see ORIENT *v.* 1). **b.** Position or arrangement (of a natural object or formation) relatively to the points of the compass or to other parts of the same structure; the 'lie' of a thing. In *Chem.*, the relative positions of the atoms or radicals in complex molecules. 1875. **c.** Transference eastwards. **2.** The action of turning to or facing the east, the eastward position 1875. **3.** The action of ascertaining, or fact of knowing, the relative position of anything or of oneself; *spec.* in *Zool.* the faculty by which birds and other animals find their way back to a place after going or being taken to a place distant from it (as in homing pigeons and migratory birds) 1868. **4.** *fig.* (from various senses): Adjustment, position, or aspect with regard to anything; determination of one's bearings in relation to circumstances, ideas, etc. 1870.

1. The o. of churches is from the rites of Etruscan augury 1881. **3.** Psychical disturbance, marked by apathy,..variable temper, delusions, imperfect o. 1899. **4.** The double o., one towards God, the other towards the world BARING-GOULD.

†**O·riently,** *adv.* 1515. [f. ORIENT *a.* + -LY[2].] In an 'orient' manner; brilliantly; clearly –1664. So †**O·rientness** –1661.

Orifice (ǫ·rifis). 1541. [– (O)Fr. *orifice* – late L. *orificium*, f. *ōs, ōr-* mouth + *fic-*, var. of *facere* make, do.] An opening or aperture, which serves as, or has the form of, a mouth, as of a tube, of the stomach, bladder, etc., of a wound; the mouth of any cavity, a perforation or vent.

The mountain resembled Ætna, being bored through the top with a monstrous o. ADDISON.

Oriflamme (ǫ·riflæm). 1475. [– (O)Fr. *oriflambe, -flamme*, in med.L. *auriflamma*, f. *aurum* gold + *flamma* FLAME.] **1.** The sacred banner of St. Denis, a banderole of two (or three) points, of red or orange-red silk, attached to a lance, which the early kings of France used to receive from the hands of the abbot of St. Denis, on setting out for war. **2.** *transf.* and *fig.* **a.** Any banner or ensign, material or ideal, that serves as a rallying point for a struggle, etc. 1600. **b.** Something which suggests the Oriflamme of St. Denis by its colouring, conspicuous position, etc. 1862.

2. a. And be your o. to-day the helmet of Navarre! MACAULAY. **b.** The new-bathed Day With o. uplifted o'er the peaks GEO. ELIOT.

Origan (ǫ·rigăn). Now *rare.* late ME. [– (O)Fr. *origan* – L. *origanum*; see next.] A plant of the genus *Origanum*, esp. Wild Marjoram (*O. vulgare*); formerly also applied to other aromatic labiates, as Pennyroyal (*Mentha pulegium*).

‖**Origanum** (ǒri·gǎnǒm). ME. [– L. – Gr. ὀρίγανον, perh. f. ὄρος mountain + γάνος brightness, joy, pride.] A genus of labiates, with aromatic leaves; comprising Wild Marjoram (*O. vulgare*), Sweet Marjoram (*O. marjorana*), Pot Marjoram (*O. onites*), Dittany of Crete (*O. dictamnus*), etc.

Origenist (ǫ·ridʒěnist). 1546. [-IST.] A follower of Origen of Alexandria (*c*185–253), or a holder of some one of the special doctrines attributed to him, among which were a threefold sense (literal, moral, and mystical) in Scripture, the pre-existence of souls, and the probable ultimate salvation of all men and of the fallen angels. So **O·rigenism.**

Origin (ǫ·ridʒin). 1563. [– Fr. *origine* or L. *origo, origin-*, f. *oriri* rise.] **1.** The act or fact of arising from something; derivation, rise; beginning of existence in ref. to its source or cause. **b.** Of a person: Descent, parentage 1605. **2.** That from which anything arises, springs, or is derived 1604. **b.** *Anat.* The place at which a muscle, nerve, etc. arises; the root of a nerve in the brain or spinal cord 1691. **c.** *Math.* A fixed point from which measurement or motion commences; *spec.* the point of intersection of the axes in Cartesian co-ordinates, or the pole in polar co-ordinates. [= Fr. *origine.*] 1723.

1. Phr. *Certificate of o.*, a custom-house document certifying the place of o. of a commodity imported. The O. and Commencement of this greefe SHAKS. **b.** A distinguished man of humble o. 1903. **2.** We hoped..to be able to examine the glacier to its o. TYNDALL.

Original (ǒri·dʒinǎl), *a.* and *sb.* ME. [– (O)Fr. *original* or L. *originalis*, f. *origin-*; see prec., -AL[1]. Cf. Fr. *originel* in some of the senses.] **A.** *adj.* **1.** Of or pertaining to the origin of something; that existed at first, or has existed from the first; primary; initial, first. **b.** *transf.* That is such from the beginning, or by birth; 'a born..' *rare* 1720. **2.** That is the origin or source of something; primary; originative. (Now usu. merged in 1.) late ME. **b.** *spec.* Applied to anything in relation to that which is a representation or reproduction of it 1631. **3.** Produced by or proceeding from some thing or person directly; underived, independent 1792; first-hand 1700. **4.** Such as has not been done or produced before; novel or fresh in character or style 1756. **b.** *transf.* Of a person: Capable of original ideas or actions; inventive, creative 1803.

1. I am as sory, as if the originall fault had beene my fault 1592. Phr. *O. sin* (Theol.): the innate depravity of man's nature, held to be inherited from Adam in consequence of the Fall. (Opp. to *actual sin.*) **2.** The rote and orygynall fountaine of all synne BIBLE 1551 *Rom.* Prol. O. and documentary authorities 1861. Phr. †*O. writ* (in *Law*): a writ issuing from the Court of Chancery, which formed the beginning or foundation of a real action at common law. **b.** The O. Texts are not corrupted 1659. It may be a misprint; you had better examine the o. document 1903. **3.** There is a certain quality about an o. drawing which you cannot get in a woodcut RUSKIN. **4.** Even on..Aristotle's Ethics he could throw an o. light 1882. **b.** A great o. genius struggling with unequal conditions of knowledge JOWETT.

B. *sb.* **1.** = ORIGIN 1. Now *rare* or *arch.* late ME. **b.** Of persons: = ORIGIN 1 b. Now *rare* or *arch.* 1555. †**c.** Beginning, earliest stage –1753. **2.** = ORIGIN 2; an originator, an author. Now *rare* or *arch.* in gen. sense. late ME. **b.** *Law.* = *O. writ*: see A. 2. 1450. **3.** A thing (or person) in relation to something else which is a copy, imitation, or representation of it; the pattern, archetype. late ME. **4.** A work of literature or art that is not a copy or imitation; an original portrait 1683. **5.** A person who acts in an original way; a singular, odd, or eccentric person 1676. **6.** †**a.** *pl.* Original elements –1667. **b.** *pl.* Original inhabitants, members, etc. *rare.* 1703.

1. The Circus and Amphitheatre..all owe their o. to the Theatre 1726. **2.** Spangled Heav'ns, a Shining Frame, Their great O. proclaim ADDISON. **3.** The resemblance is more visible in the o. than in our translation PALEY. Cunobelin, the o. of Shakspere's Cymbeline 1892. **4.** There are no absolutely undoubted originals of Queen Mary SCOTT. **5.** This boy is a real o. M. ARNOLD. Hence **Ori·ginally** *adv.*

Originality (ǒridʒinæ·lǐti). 1742. [– Fr. *originalité*, f. *original*; see prec., -ITY.] The quality or fact of being original. **b.** with *pl.* An original trait, act, remark, etc. 1854.

Originant (ǒri·dʒinǎnt), *a.* (*sb.*) 1647. [f. ORIGINATE + -ANT.] **A.** *adj.* Originating. **B.** *sb.* Originating agent or influence 1892.

Originary (ǒri·dʒinǎri), *a.* (*sb.*) Now *rare.* 1594. [– late and med.L. *originarius*, f. L. *origin-*; see ORIGIN, -ARY[1]. Cf. (O)Fr. *originaire.*] **A.** *adj.* †**1.** That originates *from* (*of*) the thing or place in question; derived *from*; aboriginal, native. **2.** = ORIGINAL A. 2. 1638.

1. A Natif of Coventry, tho' o. of Cheshire 1716. †**B.** *sb.* An aboriginal, a native –1716.

Originate (ǒri·dʒineɪt), *v.* 1653. [– *originat-*, pa. ppl. stem of med.L. *originare*, f. as prec.; see -ATE[3].] **1.** *trans.* To give origin to, cause to arise or begin, initiate 1657. **2.** *intr.* To take its origin or rise, have its beginning; to spring, be derived. Const. *from, in, with.* 1775. **b.** *Anat.*, etc. To have its origin (locally); to arise (*in* or *from*) 1799.

1. Men..who have originated remarkable religious movements 1878. **2.** The fire originated in the chemical room 1885. So **Origina·tion**, the action or fact of originating 1647; *spec.* †derivation (of a word) 1641–1741. **Ori·ginative** *a.* having the quality or power of originating; productive, creative. **Ori·ginator.**

‖**Ori·llion, oreillon.** 1647. [– (O)Fr. *orillon, oreillon*, f. *oreille* ear; see -OON.] *Fortif.* A part of the defence of a bastion; a projecting tower at the shoulder of a bastion.

Orinasal (ōᵊrinē·zǎl), *a.* (*sb.*) 1862. [f. L. *ori-*, comb. form of *os, or-* mouth + NASAL.] Pertaining to the mouth and nose; *spec.* of a vowel: Pronounced with the oral and nasal passages both open, as the 'nasal' vowels in French. **B.** *sb.* An orinasal vowel.

Oriole (ōᵊ·rioᵘl). 1776. [– med. and mod.L. *oriolus* – OFr. *oriol* :– L. *aureolus*, f. *aureus* golden, f. *aurum* gold.] **1.** A bird of the genus *Oriolus*, esp. *O. galbula* (the Golden Oriole), a summer visitor to Europe, with plumage of a rich yellow and black; also, any bird of the family *Oriolidæ*. **2.** A bird of the genus *Icterus*, as the Baltimore Oriole (*I. baltimore*), the Orchard Oriole (*I. spurius*); or any bird of the family *Icteridæ* or subfamily *Icterinæ*, peculiar to America, mostly with similar coloration; also called *hangnests* or *hangbirds* 1792.

Orion (ǒrəi·ǒn). late ME. [– L. *Orion* – Gr. Ὠρίων orig. name in Gr. myth. of a mighty hunter slain by Artemis.] *Astron.* A large and brilliant constellation south of the zodiac, figured as a hunter with belt and sword. *Orion's hound*, the dog-star, Sirius (S.E. of Orion).

Great O. sloping slowly to the West TENNYSON. Hence **Ori·onid**, one of a system of meteors whose radiant point is in O. 1876.

-o·rious, a compound suffix forming adjs., consisting of -OUS (L. *-osus*), added to L. *-ori-* in *ori-us, -a, -um* (see -ORY). The sense is either the same as, or closely akin to, that of adjs. in -ORY.

Orismology (ǫrizmǫ·lǒdʒi). *rare.* 1816. [For **horismology*, f. Gr. ὁρισμός definition + -LOGY.] A name for the explanation of technical terms, or for such terms collectively; terminology. Hence **Orismolo·gic, -al** *adjs.*

Orison (ǫ·rizən, -sən). *arch.* [ME. *ureisun, oreison, oriso(u)n* – AFr. *ur-*, OFr. *oreison, orison* (now *oraison*) :– L. *oratio, -on-* speech, ORATION.] A prayer. (In later use chiefly in *pl.*) **b.** Without *an* or *pl.* The action of praying, prayer. Now *rare.* ME.

Nimph, in thy Orizons Be all my sinnes remembred SHAKS.

Orison, -soun, -sont(e, obs. ff. HORIZON.

-o·rium, *suffix*, neut. sing. ending of L. adjs. in *-orius* (see -ORIOUS, -ORY), used subst. in sense 'place for or belonging to, thing used for', as in *auditorium* place for hearing, *prætorium* general's tent, etc. The Eng. form of these words is -ORY; but some of the L. words have been taken into historical or learned use, as *sanatorium, scriptorium*, and after these others have been formed as scientific terms.

Orle (ǭɹl). 1572. [– (O)Fr. *orle*, also †*ourle* (cf. mod. *ourlet* hem), f. *ourler* to hem :– Rom. **orulare*, f. **orula*, dim. of L. *ora* edge, border, prob. f. *ōs, ōr-* mouth.] *Her.* A narrow band of half the width of the bordure, following the outline of the shield, but not extending to the edge of it 1610. **b.** A band of small charges arranged round the shield orlewise. Hence *in o.*, said of subordinate charges thus borne. 1572. **c.** The chaplet or wreath round the helmet of a knight, bearing the crest 1834.

Orleanist (ǭ·ɹliǎnist). 1848. [– Fr. *Orléaniste*, f. local name *Orléans*; see next and -IST.] In French politics: An adherent of the princes of the house of Orleans, descended from the Duke of Orleans, younger brother of Louis XIV, whose descendant Louis Philippe reigned as King of the French. Also *attrib.* or as *adj.* So **O·rleanism**, the political principles of the Orleanists.

Orleans (ǭ·ɹliǎnz). 1664. [Name of a city in France.] **1.** A variety of plum. **2.** A fabric of cotton warp and worsted weft, brought alternately to the surface in weaving 1844.

Orlop (ǭ·ɹlǫp). 1467. [– (M)Du. *overloop*, f. *overloopen* run over; see OVER-, LEAP.] orig. The single floor or deck with which the hold of a ship was covered in, which, by the successive addition of one, two, or three complete decks above, became the lowest deck of a ship of the line; occas. applied to the lowest deck of a steamer, etc.

Ormer (ǭ·ɹməɹ). 1672. [– Channel Islands Fr. *ormer* = Fr. *ormier* :– L. *auris maris* 'ear of the sea' (so called from its resemblance to the ear).] The Sea-ear, a species of univalve mollusc, *Haliotis tuberculata*, specially abundant in Guernsey, where it is used as food. Hence any species of *Haliotis*.

Ormolu (ǭ·ɹmǒlū). 1765. [– Fr. *or moulu* 'ground gold', i.e. *or* gold, *moulu* pa. pple. of *moudre* grind.] orig., Gold or gold-leaf ground and prepared for gilding brass, bronze, or other metal; hence, gilded bronze used in the decoration of furniture, etc. Now, An alloy of copper, zinc, and tin, having the colour of gold. **b.** *attrib.* and *Comb.*, as *o. clock*; **o.-varnish**, a copper, bronze, or imitation-gold varnish, also called 'Mosaic gold'.

Ornament (ǭ·ɹnǎměnt), *sb.* [ME. *urnement, ournement* – AFr. *urnement*, OFr. *o(u)rnement* (mod. *orne-*) – L. *ornamentum* equipment, ornament, f. *ornare* adorn; see -MENT. Refash. after L. from XV.] †**1.** Any adjunct or accessory; equipment, furniture, attire, trappings –1747. **b.** *Eccl.* The accessories or furnishings of the Church and its worship, e.g. vestments, plate, organs, bells, etc. late ME. **2.** Anything used, or serving to adorn; a decoration, embellishment. late ME. **b.** A person who adorns his sphere, time, etc. 1573. **3.** The action of adorning or fact of being adorned; adornment, decoration (*lit.* or *fig.*): that in which this consists 1596. **b.** Mere adornment; outward show. SHAKS.

1. b. *Ornaments rubric*, the rubric immediately before the Order for Morning and Evening Prayer in the Book of Common Prayer, which refers to the 'ornaments' to be used in the Church. **2.** This O. of Knighthood [the garter] SHAKS. *fig.* The o. of a meek and quiet spirit 1 *Pet.* 3:4. **b.** Thos singular men, the late ornaments of Cambridg and the glori of Pembrook Hal 1573. **3.** There was no beauty..either of artful o., or natural wildness 1817. **b.** *Merch. V.* III. ii. 97. Hence **Orname·ntal** *a.* of the nature of, or serving as, an o.; decorative; *sb. pl.* things that are ornamental (as opp. to *essentials*). **Orname·ntalism**, the principle or practice of being o. **Orname·ntalist. Orname·ntally** *adv.*

Ornament (ǭ·ɹnǎment), *v.* 1720. [f. prec.] *trans.* To furnish with ornament; to adorn, embellish. Hence **O:rnamenta·tion**, the action or process of ornamenting; the state of being adorned; ornament in general. **O·rnamenter. O·rnamentist**, a professional decorator.

Ornate (ǫɹnē·ɪt), *ppl. a.* late ME. [– L. *ornatus*, pa. pple. of *ornare* adorn; see -ATE[2].] †**1.** as *pa. pple.* Adorned, ornamented (*with*) –1771. **2.** as *adj.* Ornamented; elaborately adorned or embellished 1503. **b.** Of literary or oratorical style: Embellished with choice language or flowers of rhetoric. late ME.

2. Femal of sex it seems, That so bedeckt, o., and gay, Comes this way sailing Like a stately Ship

MILT. **b.** In diction Virgil is o. and Homer simple GLADSTONE. Hence **Ornate·ly** *adv.*, **-ness.**

†**Orna·te,** *v.* 1495. [– *ornat-*, pa. ppl. stem of L. *ornare*; see prec., -ATE[3].] *trans.* To adorn, embellish –1651.

Ornature (ǭ·ɹnătiŭɹ). *rare.* 1538. [– Fr. *ornature* – late L. *ornatura*, f. as prec.; see -URE.] Ornamentation, embellishment.

‖**Ornis** (ǭ·ɹnis). 1861. [– G. *ornis* – Gr. ὄρνις bird. (Introduced c1859).] = AVIFAUNA.

Ornithic (ǫɹni·þik), *a.* 1854. [– Gr. ὀρνιθικός bird-like, f. ὄρνις bird.] Of, or pertaining to, birds; characteristic of birds; avian. **b.** Dealing with or skilled in birds 1876.

Ornithichnite (ǭɹniþi·knəit). 1836. [– mod.L. *ornithichnites* (also much used), f. Gr. ὄρνις, ὀρνιθ- bird + ἴχνος track; see -ITE[1] 2 a, ICHNITE.] A fossil footprint of a bird or bird-like reptile.

Ornitho-, bef. a vowel **ornith-,** repr. Gr. ὀρνιθο-, ὀρνιθ-, comb. form of ὄρνις bird, as in ὀρνιθο-φάγος bird-eating, etc. Used in Eng. to form many scientific terms; as ‖**Ornitho-de·lphia** [Gr. δελφύς womb], *Zool.* = MONOTREMATA. **Orni·tholite** [-LITE], a fossil of a bird or part of a bird. **Ornitho·pterous** [Gr. πτερόν feather, wing], *a.* having wings like a bird. **Ornitho·tomy** [Gr. -τομια cutting; see -TOMY], dissection of birds; the anatomy of birds. See also Main words.

Ornithology (ǭɹniþǫ·lŏdʒi). 1706. [– mod.L. *ornithologia*, f. Gr. ὀρνιθολόγος treating of birds; see prec. and -LOGY. Cf. Fr. *ornithologie.*] The branch of zoology which deals with birds, their nature and habits. (By Fuller used for 'the Speech of Birds'.) So **Ornitholo·gic, -al** *adjs.* of or pertaining to o. 1802. **Ornitho·logist,** one versed in o.; a student of birds 1677.

Ornithomancy (ǭ·ɹniþomæːnsi). 1652. [– Gr. ὀρνιθομαντεία augury; see ORNITHO-, -MANCY.] Divination by means of the flight and cries of birds; augury.

Ornithopod (ǭ·ɹniþopǫd). 1888. [– mod. L. *Ornithopoda* n. pl.; see ORNITHO-, -POD, -A 4.] **A.** *adj.* Having feet like those of a bird; belonging to the *Ornithopoda*, a group or order of extinct saurians, containing herbivorous *Dinosauria*. **B.** *sb.* A member of this group. So **Ornitho·podous** *a.*

‖**Ornithorhynchus** (ǭːɹniþori·ŋkǒs, ǫɹnəiþo-). 1800. [f. ORNITHO- + Gr. ῥύγχος bill.] An aquatic mammal of Australia, the duck-billed platypus or duck-mole (*O. paradoxus* or *anatinus*), the only species of its genus or family in the order *Monotremata*; it has glossy dark-brown fur, webbed feet and bill like a duck's; it lays eggs with a flexible shell.

Ornithosaurian (-sǭ·riăn), *a.* and *sb.* [f. mod.L. *Ornithosauria* n. pl., f. ORNITHO- + Gr. σαῦρος lizard; see SAURIAN.] *Palæont.* = PTEROSAURIAN.

Ornithoscelidan (-se·lidăn), *a.* (*sb.*) 1876. [f. mod.L. *Ornithoscelida* n. pl., f. ORNITHO- + Gr. σκέλος leg; see -IDAN.] *Palæont.* Of or belonging to the *Ornithoscelida*, a sub-class or order of extinct reptiles of Mesozoic and Tertiary age, which approached birds in the form of the hinder legs and the pelvic arch. **B.** *sb.* A member of this order.

Ornithoscopy (ǭɹniþǫ·skŏpi). 1840. [– Gr. ὀρνιθοσκοπία augury; see ORNITHO-, -SCOPY.] Observation of birds for the purpose of divination; augury.

Orocentral (ōᵊrose·ntrăl), *a.* 1884. [irreg. for *oricentral, f. L. *os, or-* mouth + CENTRAL.] Occupying the centre of the oral side (of an echinoderm).

Orography (orǫ·grăfi), **oreography** (ǫri,ǫ·g-). 1846. [f. Gr. ὄρος, ὀρε- mountain + -GRAPHY. *Orography* is now usual.] That branch of physical geography which deals with the formation and features of mountains; the description of mountains. So **Orogra·phic, -al** *adjs.* 1802.

‖**Orohippus** (ǫrohi·pǒs). 1877. [mod.L., f. Gr. ὄρος mountain + ἵππος horse.] A genus of fossil quadrupeds found in the Eocene beds of North America, held to be an ancestral form of the horse.

Oroide (ōᵊ·ro,id). 1875. [app. alt. of OREIDE, with assim. to -OID.] An alloy of copper and zinc, having the colour of gold.

Orology (orǫ·lŏdʒi), **oreology** (ǫri,o·l-). 1781. [f. Gr. ὄρος, ὀρε- mountain + -LOGY.] The scientific study of mountains.

Oronoco, -ooko (ōᵊronōᵘ·ko, -ū·ko). 1706. [Origin unkn.: app. unconnected with the river Orinoco.] A variety of tobacco from Virginia.

Orotund (ōᵊ·rotǫnd), *a.* (*sb.*) 1792. [f. L. phrase *ore rotundo* lit. 'with round mouth', with well turned speech (Horace 'Ars Poetica' 323), with reduction of *ore ro-* to *oro-*.] Of the voice or utterance: Full, clear, and stronger than ordinary speech; also, contemptuously, magniloquent, inflated, pompous. **b.** *ellipt.* as *sb.* (*sc.* voice, utterance).

Orphan (ǭ·ɹfăn), *sb.* and *a.* 1483. [– late L. (Vulgate) *orphanus* – Gr. ὀρφανός without parents, bereft, rel. to L. *orbus* bereft.] **A.** *sb.* One deprived by death of father or mother, or (usu.) of both; a fatherless or motherless child 1484.

fig. They..Are orphans of the earthly love and heavenly E. B. BROWNING. *Orphan's Court*, a probate court in some states of the U.S., having jurisdiction over the estates and persons of orphans. **O.-asylum, -hospital, -house,** an orphanage.

B. *adj.* Bereaved of parents; fatherless or motherless, or both 1483. Hence **O·rphan, O·rphanize,** *vbs.* to make an o. of. **O·rphancy, O·rphanhood,** †**O·rphanism,** the condition or position of an o.

Orphanage (ǭ·ɹfănėdʒ). 1579. [f. prec. sb. + -AGE.] **1.** The state of being an orphan. **2.** An institution or home for orphans 1865.

Orpharion (ǭɹfărəi·ǫn). 1593. [Fusion of the names Orpheus and Arion.] A large instrument of the lute kind with from six to nine pairs of metal strings played with a plectrum; much used in the 17th c.

Orphean (ǫɹfī·ăn), *a.* and *sb.* 1593. [f. L. *Orphēus* (– Gr. Ὀρφεῖος, f. Ὀρφεύς) + -AN.] **A.** *adj.* Of or relating to Orpheus, as musician and singer, who was said to move rocks and trees by the music of his lyre; hence, melodious, entrancing, like his music. **B.** *sb.* An adherent of the Orphic philosophy 1818.

A. With other notes then to th' O. Lyre I sung of Chaos and Eternal Night MILT.

Orpheonist (ǭ·ɹfĭŏnist). 1860. [– Fr. *orphéoniste*, f. *Orphéon*, name of a school of vocal music established at Paris in 1833, and called after Orpheus.] A member of an *Orphéon*; a choral singer.

Orphic (ǭ·ɹfik), *a.* (*sb.*) 1678. [– L. *Orphicus* – Gr. Ὀρφικός, f. Ὀρφεύς; see -IC.] **A.** *adj.* **1.** Of or connected with Orpheus, or the mysteries, writings, or doctrines associated with his name; hence, oracular. **2.** Of the nature of the music of Orpheus; melodious, ravishing 1817. **B.** *sb.* An Orphic song or hymn; chiefly in *pl.* 1855.

A. 2. An o. song indeed, A song divine of high and passionate thoughts COLERIDGE.

Orphism (ǭ·ɹfiz'm). 1880. [f. prec. + -ISM.] The system of mystic philosophy embodied in the Orphic poems, and taught to the initiated in the Orphic mysteries. So **O·rphist.**

Orphrey, orfray. (ǭ·ɹfreⁱ, -fri). [Falsely inferred sing. from ME. *orphreis* taken as pl. – OFr. *orfreis* (mod. *orfroi*) – med.L. *aurifrisium*, alt. of *auriphrygium* gold embroidery, i.e. *aurum Phrygium* 'Phrygian gold' (cf. L. *Phrygia chlamys* embroidered mantle, *phrygio* embroiderer in gold).] **1.** Gold embroidery, or any rich embroidery; with *an* and *pl.*, a piece of richly embroidered stuff. Now only *Hist.* or *arch.* **2.** An ornamental strip or band, esp. on an eccl. vestment, often richly embroidered. late ME.

Orpiment (ǭ·ɹpimĕnt). ME. [– (O)Fr. *orpiment* – L. *auripigmentum*, f. *aurum* gold + *pigmentum* PIGMENT.] A bright yellow mineral substance, the trisulphide of arsenic, also called Yellow Arsenic, found native in soft masses resembling gold in colour; also manufactured by the combination of sulphur and arsenious oxide; used as a pigment under the name of King's Yellow.

O. is the original ARSENIC (sense 1 a) of the ancients. Also called *Yellow O.* to distinguish it from the so-called *Red O.* = REALGAR, disulphide of arsenic.

Orpine, orpin (ǭ·ɹpin). late ME. [– OFr. *orpine* yellow arsenic, presumably shortening of *orpiment*. In sense 2 – (O)Fr. *orpin*; cf. AL. *orpina.*] †**1.** = ORPIMENT 1548–1725. **2.** A succulent herbaceous plant, *Sedum telephium*, well-known in the cottage garden; from its tenacity of life, pop. called *Live-long*.

O·rpington. 1887. [f. *Orpington* in Kent.] Name of a breed of poultry.

Orrery (ǫ·rəri). 1713. [Named after Chas. Boyle, Earl of O., for whom one was made.] A piece of mechanism devised to represent the motions of the planets about the sun by means of clockwork.

Orris[1] (ǫ·ris). 1545. [Early forms *oreys, oris, arras* (XVI), unexpl. alt. of IRIS.] **1.** A plant of the genus *Iris*, esp. *I. germanica* and *I. florentina*; the flower-de-luce 1626. **2.** Short for *orris-root, -powder*.

Comb.: **o.-powder,** powdered orris-root; **-root,** the rhizome of three species of Iris (*I. florentina, I. germanica, I. pallida*), which has an odour like that of violets; used as a perfume and in medicine.

Orris[2] (ǫ·ris). 1701. [In XVIII *or(r)ice, -ace*; poss. alt. of *orfris* ORPHREY.] A name given to lace of various patterns in gold and silver; embroidery made of gold lace.

Orse·llic, *a.* 1848. [app. f. Fr. *orseille* ORCHIL + -IC.] *Chem.* In *o. acid*, a crystalline solid, $C_{16}H_{14}O_7 + 2\,H_2O$, obtained from S. African and S. American lichens. So **O·rsellate,** a salt of o. acid. **Orselli·nic acid,** a crystalline substance, $C_8H_8O_4 + H_2O$, obtained by the action of baryta water on erythrin.

Ort (ǭɹt). Usu. in pl. **orts.** late ME. [– (with pl. suffix) MLG. *ort-e* refuse of food = early mod. Du. †*ooræte* (cf. Sw. dial. *oräte* refuse fodder, LG. *orten, verorten* leave remains of food or fodder), perh. f. *o(o)r-* out (as in ORDEAL) + *eten* EAT.] Fragments of food left over from a meal; refuse fodder; scraps, leavings; also *fig. To make orts of*, to undervalue.

Let him haue time a beggers orts to craue SHAKS.

Orthian (ǭ·ɹþiăn), *a.* 1751. [f. Gr. ὄρθιος upright, high-pitched + -AN.] Applied to a style of singing, or tune, of very high pitch.

Orthid (ǭ·ɹþid). 1861. [f. mod.L. *Orthidæ*, f. *Orthis*, f. Gr. ὀρθός straight; see -ID[3].] A member of the *Orthidæ*, or genus *Orthis*, of fossil bivalves.

Orthite (ǭ·ɹþəit). 1817. [– G. *orthit* (Berzelius, 1817), f. Gr. ὀρθός straight; see -ITE[1] 2 b.] *Min.* A variety of ALLANITE, found in long slender crystals, or straight masses. Hence **Orthi·tic** *a.*

Ortho- (bef. a vowel occas. **orth-**), comb. form of Gr. ὀρθός, used sometimes in the physical sense 'straight', sometimes in the ethical sense 'right, correct'.

1. In technical words generally: **O·rthocentre,** *Geom.* the point at which the perpendiculars from the vertices of a triangle to the opposite side intersect. **Orthodia·gonal,** *Cryst.* (*a*) *sb.*, that lateral axis in the monoclinic system which is at right angles to the vertical axis; (*b*) *adj.*, belonging to or in the line of this axis (opp. to *clinodiagonal*). **O·rthodome** [DOME *sb.* 5 b], *Cryst.* a dome parallel to the orthodiagonal in the monoclinic system. **Orthopi·nacoid,** *Cryst.* one of the principal planes in the monoclinic system, parallel to the vertical axis and the orthodiagonal; hence **Orthopinacoi·dal** *a.* **Orthopy·ramid,** *Cryst.* in the monoclinic system a pyramid lying between the orthodomes and the zone of unit pyramids. **Orthosymme·tric** *a., Cryst.* symmetric about two, or three, axes at right angles to each other; *spec.* = ORTHORHOMBIC. **Ortho·to·mic** [Gr. -τόμος cutting], *a. Math.* intersecting at right angles.

2. In *Chemistry.* **a.** *Ortho-* is used to distinguish one class of acids and their salts from another denoted by the prefix *meta-*, which contain the same elements in different proportions, the *meta-* acid containing a molecule of H_2O less than the *ortho-* acid, the *ortho-* salt being also the more basic and the *meta-* salt the less basic. Thus *orthophosphoric acid* H_3PO_4, *metaphosphoric acid* HPO_3; *sodium orthophosphate* Na_3PO_4, *sodium metaphosphate* $NaPO_3$. **b.** With the names of isomeric benzene di-derivatives, *ortho-* is applied to those in which two consecutive hydrogen atoms are replaced by another element or radical, as dist. from *meta-* and *para-* derivatives, in which the two atoms are not consecutive, but unsymmetrically or symmetrically dispersed respectively. Examples: *orthodibromobenzene, orthopropylphenol.*

Orthocephalic (ǭːɹþosĭfæ·lik), *a.* 1865. [f. ORTHO- 'right, correct' + Gr. κεφαλή head + -IC.] *Ethnol.* Applied to skulls of which the breadth is from about $\frac{7}{10}$ to $\frac{4}{5}$ of the length (intermediate between *brachycephalic* and *dolichocephalic*); or, according to some, of which the height is from $\frac{7}{10}$ to $\frac{3}{4}$ of the length, or of which the height is $\frac{4}{5}$ of the breadth. So **Orthoce·phalous** *a.* **Orthoce·phaly,** the condition of being o.

‖**Orthoceras** (ǫɹþǫ·sĕræ̂s). *Pl.* **orthocerata** (ǭːɹþosĕrēⁱ·tă). 1830. [f. ORTHO- 'straight' + Gr. κέρας, pl. κέρατα horn.] *Palæont.* An extinct genus of cephalopods, having long straight chambered shells; a fossil shell of this genus. Hence **Ortho·ceran** *a.*

Orthoceratite (ǭɹþose·rătəit). Also in L. form **orthoceratites** (ǭːɹþoserătəi·tīz). 1754. [f. as prec. + -ITE¹ 2 a.] A shell of the genus *Orthoceras* or family *Orthoceratidæ*; also, an animal of this genus or family.

Orthochromatic (ǭːɹþoˌkromæ·tik), *a.* 1887. [f. ORTHO- 'correct, proper' + Gr. χρωματικός CHROMATIC.] *Photogr.* Representing colours in their correct relations, i.e. without exaggerating the deepness of some and the brightness of others (as in ordinary photography). So **Orthochromatism** (-krōᵘ·mătiz'm), the condition of being o. **Orthochro·matize** *v.*

Orthoclase (ǭ·ɹþŏkléⁱs). 1849. [f. ORTHO- 'straight, right' + Gr. κλάσις breaking, cleavage.] *Min.* Common or potash feldspar, a silicate of aluminium and potassium, occurring in crystals or masses of various colours, characterized by two cleavages at right angles to each other. So **Orthocla·stic** *a.* having cleavages at right angles to each other.

Orthodox (ǭ·ɹþŏdǫks). 1581. [– eccl. L. *orthodoxus* – Gr. ὀρθόδοξος right in opinion, f. ὀρθός straight, right + δόξα opinion, f. base of δοκεῖν seem, rel. to L. *decet* (see DECENT).] **A.** *adj.* **1.** Holding correct, i.e. currently accepted, opinions, *esp.* in theology 1611. **2.** Of opinions or doctrines: Right, correct, true; in accordance with what is authoritatively established as the true view or right practice; *orig.* in theological and eccl. doctrine 1581. **3.** Conventional; approved 1838. **4.** (*With capital.*) Specific epithet of the Eastern Church, which recognizes the headship of the Patriarch of Constantinople, and of the historical churches of Russia, Serbia, Rumania, etc., which recognize each other as of the same communion; the historical representative of the churches of the ancient East, commonly called the *Greek Church* 1772.

1. Men falsely called o. and divines 1722. **2.** To maintain the precepts of the o. faith JAS. I. I am well aware, how much my sentiments differ from the o. opinions of one or two principal patriots SWIFT. **3.** The o. half-hour had expired LYTTON. **4.** The epithet 'Orthodox' was orig. assumed to distinguish it [the Eastern Church] from the various divisions of the Eastern Church, e.g. the Jacobite or Monophysite, Nestorian, etc.,..; but it is sometimes used by historical writers as opposed to 'Catholic'. O.E.D.

B. *sb.* An orthodox person. **b.** A member of the orthodox Eastern Church. 1587.

Was he an Heretick, or an Orthodoxe? 1641. Hence †**O·rthodoxal** *a.* †**Orthodoxa·stical** *a.*, in senses A. 1, 2. **Orthodo·xical** *a.* (now *rare*), **-ly** *adv.* **O·rthodoxism,** †orthodoxy; in derogatory sense, the treating orthodoxy as the important feature of religion. **O·rthodox-ly** *adv.*, **-ness.**

Orthodoxy (ǭ·ɹþŏdǫksi). 1630. [– late L. *orthodoxia* – late (eccl.) Gr. ὀρθοδοξία right opinion, sound doctrine, f. ὀρθόδοξος; see prec., -Y³.] The quality or character of being orthodox; belief in or agreement with what is, or is currently held to be, right, esp. in religious matters. **b.** with *pl.* An orthodox belief or opinion 1871.

Lanfranc was again present as the champion of o. FREEMAN. *Feast of O.*, in the Greek Church, a festival celebrated on the first Sunday in Lent, called *O. Sunday.*

Orthoepy (ǫɹþōᵘ·ĭpi). 1668. [– Gr. ὀρθοέπεια correctness of diction, f. (ult.) ὀρθός ORTHO- + ἔπος, ἐπε- word.] **1.** That part of grammar which deals with pronunciation. **2.** Correct or customary pronunciation 1801.

2. Formerly they regulated their orthography by their o. 1830. So **Orthoepic** (e·pik), **-al** *adjs.*, **-ly** *adv.* **Ortho·epist.**

Orthognathic (ǭɹþognæ·þik), *a.* 1849. [f. as ORTHOGNATHOUS + -IC.] = ORTHOGNATHOUS.

Orthognathous (ǫɹþǫ·gnăþəs), *a.* 1853. [f. ORTHO- 'straight' + Gr. γνάθος jaw + -OUS.] *Ethnol.* Straight-jawed; having the jaws not projecting beyond the vertical line drawn from the forehead; having a facial angle of about 90°. Said of the skull; also of persons. So **Ortho·gnathism,** the condition of being o.

Orthogonal (ǫɹþǫ·gŏnăl), *a.* 1571. [– med.L. *orthogonalis* (whence also Fr. *orthogonal* XVI), f. late and med.L. *orthogonus* right-angled; see -AL¹.] *Geom.* Right-angled, rectangular.

O. projection, projection in which the rays are at right angles to the plane of projection. Hence **Ortho·gonally** *adv.* at right angles.

Orthographic (ǭɹþogræ·fik), *a.* 1668. [In sense 1 f. ORTHO- 'straight, right'; see -GRAPHIC. In sense 2 f. ORTHOGRAPHY + -IC.] **1.** Epithet of a kind of perspective projection, used in maps, etc., in which the point of sight is supposed to be at an infinite distance, so that the rays are parallel. **2.** Pertaining to orthography; belonging to correct spelling in general; correct in spelling 1868.

Orthogra·phical, *a.* 1589. [f. as prec.; see -ICAL.] **1.** = prec. 2. **2.** = prec. 1. 1706.

Orthogra·phically, *adv.* 1617. [f. prec. + -LY².] **1.** In relation to spelling or orthography. **2.** On the principle of orthographical projection 1669.

Orthography (ǫɹþǫ·grăfi). 1450. [Early form *ortografy* – OFr. *ortografie,* later *-graphie* (mod. *orthographie*) – L. *orthographia* – Gr. ὀρθογραφία; see ORTHO-, -GRAPHY.] **1.** Correct spelling; spelling according to accepted usage; the way in which words are conventionally written. (By extension) Any mode or system of spelling. **b.** That part of grammar which treats of the nature and values of letters and of their combination; the subject of spelling 1616. **2.** Orthographic projection. **b.** A representation in orthographic projection or section; a vertical elevation. 1645.

1. When we use the word 'orthography', we do not mean a mode of spelling which is true to the pronunciation, but one which is conventionally correct 1873. Hence **Ortho·grapher, Ortho·graphist,** one skilled in o. **Ortho·graphize** *v. intr.* to follow or apply o.; *trans.* to spell (a word) correctly.

Orthology (ǫɹþǫ·lŏdʒi). *rare.* 1619. [– Gr. ὀρθολογία correctness of language; see ORTHO-, -LOGY.] Correct speaking; that part of grammar which deals with the correct use of words. So **Ortho·loger. Ortholo·gical** *a.*

Orthometry (ǫɹþǫ·mĕtri). *rare.* 1775. [f. ORTHO- + -METRY; cf. *orthoepy, orthology.*] The art of correct versification.

Orthomorphic (ǭɹþomǭ·ɹfik), *a. rare.* 1882. [f. ORTHO- + Gr. μορφή form + -IC.] Preserving the original shape of infinitesimal parts; applied to a class of map-projections in which small areas retain their correct shapes 1882.

Orthopædy, -pedy (ǭ·ɹþŏpīdi). 1840. [– Fr. *orthopédie,* f. *ortho-* ORTHO- + Gr. παιδεία rearing of children.] The curing or correcting of deformities in children, or in persons generally; orthopædic surgery. Hence **Orthopæ·dic, -pedic, -al** *adjs.* **Orthopæ·dics, -ped-,** orthopædy. **O:rthopæ·dist, -pedist,** an orthopædic surgeon.

‖**Orthopnœa** (ǭɹþopnī·ă). 1657. [L. (Pliny) – Gr. ὀρθόπνοια, f. (ult.) ὀρθός upright + πνοή breathing, breath, πνεῖν breathe.] *Path.* A form of asthma or dyspnœa in which breathing is possible only in an upright position. So **Orthopno·ic, -pnœic,** *adjs.* affected with o. 1601.

Orthopraxy (ǭ·ɹþopræksi). *rare.* 1852. [f. ORTHO- + Gr. πρᾶξις action.] **1.** Rightness of action; practical righteousness; correct practice. **2.** Orthopædic surgery 1865.

‖**Orthoptera** (ǫɹþǫ·ptĕră), *sb. pl.* 1826. [mod.L., n. pl. of *orthopterus,* f. Gr. ὀρθός straight + πτερόν wing.] *Entom.* An order of Insects, distinguished by more or less coriaceous and usu. straight and narrow fore wings, broad longitudinally-folded hind wings, and incomplete metamorphosis; comprising the cockroaches, walking-stick insects, crickets, grasshoppers, etc. Hence **Ortho·pteral, Ortho·pterous** *adjs.* belonging to the order *O.* **Ortho·pterist,** a student of *O.*

Orthoptic (ǫɹþǫ·ptik), *a.* (*sb.*) 1881. [f. ORTH(O- 'straight' + Gr. ὀπτικός of or pertaining to sight.] **1.** *Fire-arms.* (*adj.* and *sb.*) Name for an opaque disc perforated with three small holes, through one of which the rifleman looks in taking aim. **2.** *Math.* *O. locus*: the locus of intersection of tangents to any curve at right angles to each other 1882.

Orthorhombic (ǭɹþorǫ·mbik), *a.* 1868. [f. ORTHO- + RHOMBIC.] *Cryst.* Applied to that system of crystalline forms in which the three axes are mutually at right angles and unequal; also called *rectangular, prismatic, trimetric,* or *orthosymmetric.*

Orthoscopic (ǭɹþoskǫ·pik), *a.* 1875. [f. ORTHO- + Gr. -σκοπος viewing; see -IC.] Having or producing correct vision; free from, or constructed to correct, optical distortion.

Orthospermous (ǭɹþospə̄·ɹməs), *a.* 1859. [f. ORTHO- 'straight' + Gr. -σπερμος having seeds, f. σπέρμα seed; see -OUS.] *Bot.* Having straight seeds or fruits, as certain Umbelliferæ; also said of the seeds.

Orthostichy (ǫɹþǫ·stiki). 1875. [f. ORTHO- + Gr. στίχος row, rank, line + -Y³.] *Bot.* A vertical row or rank; an arrangement of lateral members (e.g. of leaves) inserted on an axis or stem one directly above another. Hence **Ortho·stichous** *a.*

Orthotone (ǭ·ɹþotoᵘn), *a.* (*sb.*) 1882. [– Gr. ὀρθότονος, f. ὀρθός (ORTHO-) + τόνος tone, accent.] *Pros.* Having its own accent as an independent word; accented; *spec.* said of a word ordinarily unaccented when it retains or takes an independent accent. **B.** *sb.* An orthotone word.

Orthotropal (ǫɹþǫ·trŏpăl), *a.* 1832. [f. as ORTHOTROPOUS + -AL¹.] *Bot.* = ORTHOTROPOUS.

Orthotropic (ǭɹþotrǫ·pik), *a.* 1886. [f. as prec. + -IC.] *Bot.* Growing vertically upwards or downwards, as a root or stem. So **Ortho·tropism,** o. condition.

Orthotropous (ǫɹþǫ·trŏpəs), *a.* 1819. [f. ORTHO- + *-tropous* in *atropous, homotropous.*] *Bot.* **a.** = ATROPOUS. **b.** = HOMOTROPOUS. So **Ortho·tropy,** o. condition.

Ortolan (ǭ·ɹtŏlăn). 1656. [– Fr. *ortolan* – Pr. *ortolan* gardener – L. *hortulanus,* f. *hortulus* (pl. garden grounds), dim. of *hortus* garden; so named because it frequents gardens.] A small bird, a species of bunting (*Emberiza hortulana*), highly esteemed for its delicate flavour; the garden-bunting. Also called *o. bunting.*

Applied in America and the West Indies to two other birds, also esteemed as table delicacies, viz. the bobolink (*Dolichonyx oryzivorus*), and the soree or sora rail (*Porzana carolina*) 1666.

Orvietan (ǫɹviˌī·tăn). *Obs.* exc. *Hist.* 1676. [– Fr. *orviétan,* or It. *orvietano,* f. *Orvieto* in Italy, where the inventor was born.] A composition, formerly held to be an antidote against poisons; 'Venice Treacle'. Hence *gen.* and *fig.* An antidote.

Orvieto (orviĕ·to). 1860. [From *Orvieto*; see prec.] A white wine made near the city of Orvieto.

Ory (ōᵊ·ri), *a.* 1549. [f. ORE + -Y¹.] Of the nature of, containing, or resembling ore; metallic.

-ory¹, formerly **-orie,** a suffix forming sbs., originating in ONFr. and AFr. *-orie* = Central Fr. *-oire,* as in *glorie, gloire,* repr. L. *-oria,* and subseq. *-orium,* as in *oratoire,* ORATORY¹; these also took in Eng. the form *-orie,* later *-ory,* which thus came to be the normal Eng. repr. of L. *-oria, -orium,* Fr. *-oire.* The most numerous of these are adaptations of L. neuter sbs. in *-orium,* from adjs. in *-orius* (see -ORY²). These usu. denote a place or instrument used in some process, as *directory, dormitory, refectory,* etc.; but occas. they have other senses, as *promontory, territory.* In a few words *-ory* is the suffix *-y* added to an agent-noun in *-or*, e.g. *rectory* (the seat of a rector).

-ory², formerly **-orie**, a suffix forming adjs. (whence also sbs.), originating in AFr. *-ori*, *-orie*, OFr. *-oir*, *-oire*, and repr. L. *-orius*, *-a*, *-um*, = the adj. formative *-i-us* added to derivative sbs. in *-or*, chiefly agent-nouns in *-tor*, *-sor* (see -OR), but sometimes app. from the cognate ppl. stem in *-t-*, *-s-*; e.g. *accusator-i-us*, *suasor-i-us*. Instead of *-ory*, the Eng. adj. has often -ORIAL, less frequently -ORIOUS.

Orycterope (ori·ktĕrōᵘp). 1836. [– Fr. *oryctérope* – mod.L. *Orycteropus* (-pod-), f. Gr. ὀρυκτήρ digger + πούς, ποδ- foot. Now usu. in L. form.] *Zool.* A mammal of genus *Orycteropus*; = AARD-VARK.

Orycto-, comb. form of Gr. ὀρυκτός dug up, used in mod. compounds, with the sense of 'fossil' or 'mineral'; as **†Orycto·gnosy** [Gr. γνῶσις knowledge], mineralogy; so **†Oryctogno·stic** *a.* **†Orycto·graphy** [-GRAPHY], descriptive mineralogy.

Orycto·logy. Now *rare.* 1753. [f. prec. + -LOGY, prob. after Fr. *oryctologie.*] The science of 'fossils'; **a.** mineralogy; **b.** palæontology. So **Oryctolo·gical** *a.* **Orycto·logist.**

Oryx (ǫ·riks). late ME. [– L. *oryx* – Gr. ὄρυξ stonemason's pickaxe, applied to an antelope or gazelle having pointed horns.] **a.** The ancient name of an antelope of northern Africa, perh. *O. leucoryx* or *O. beisa*. **b.** In mod. *Zool.*, a genus of African antelopes, of large size, with long pointed horns; one of these. The S. African species is *O. capensis*, the gemsbok.

‖**Os¹** (ǫs). 1548. [L. *os*, pl. *ossa.*] The Latin word for bone, commonly used in *Anat.* in the mod.L. names of particular bones.

‖**Os²** (ǫs). 1737. [L. *ōs*, pl. *ōra.*] The Latin word for mouth, used in *Anat.* in naming the mouths or entrances of certain passages; esp. *os uteri*, the mouth or orifice of the uterus.

Os: see OSAR.

Osage (ōᵘ·sėdʒ). 1817. [Name of a group of Sioux Indians.] In *O. orange*, an ornamental American plant, *Toxylon pomiferum*, orig. found in the country of the O. Indians; also short for this, and in other attrib. uses (*o. plant*).

Osar (ōᵘ·saɹ). 1854. [– Sw. *åsar*, pl. of *ås* ridge (of a roof or hill), a 'rigg'. In Eng. use sometimes *os*, pl. *osar*, but usu. *osar* as sing., with pl. *osars.*] *Geol.* A term for certain narrow ridges or mounds of gravel which occur in glaciated regions, essentially the same as the *kames* of Scotland and the *eskars* of Ireland, but much more elongated.

Oscheo- (ǫskio), bef. a vowel **osche-**, comb. form of Gr. ὄσχεον scrotum; in med. and surg. terms, as **O·scheocele** [Gr. κήλη tumour], scrotal hernia.

Oscillate (ǫ·sileᶦt), *v.* 1726. [– *oscillat-*, pa. ppl. stem of L. *oscillare* swing; see -ATE³.] **1.** *intr.* To swing backwards and forwards, like a pendulum; to vibrate; to move to and fro between two points. **b.** *loosely.* To move or travel to and fro 1865. **c.** To set up electrical oscillations 1913; esp. in wireless telephony; of a receiving apparatus, to 'howl' 1926. **2.** *fig.* To fluctuate between two opinions, principles, purposes, etc.; to vary between two limits 1797. **3.** *trans.* To cause to swing or vibrate to and fro 1766.

1. b. Miss Lavinia, oscillating between the kitchen and the opposite room, prepared the dining-table in the latter chamber DICKENS. **2.** Human nature oscillates between good and evil JOWETT. Hence **O·scillative, O·scillatory** *adjs.*

O·scillating, *ppl. a.* 1743. [f. prec. + -ING².] Swinging or moving to and fro, vibrating. **b.** *spec.* Applied to machines or parts of them characterized by the oscillatory motion of some part or parts, which in other cases are fixed.

b. *O. cylinder*, a cylinder in a steam-engine mounted on trunnions and oscillating through a small arc, so that the piston-rod can follow the movements of the crank. *O. engine*, one having an o. cylinder.

Oscillation (ǫsilēᶦ·ʃən). 1658. [– L. *oscillatio*, f. as OSCILLATE; see -ION.] **1.** The action of oscillating; a swinging to and fro like that of a pendulum; a periodic movement to and fro, or up and down. **b.** In *Acoustics*, occas. = vibration; occas. = BEAT *sb.*¹ 6. *rare.* **c.** (Usu. *pl.*) Esp. in wireless telephony, applied to (high-frequency) alternations of electric currents. **2.** *fig.* Alternating variation, fluctuation, wavering; *Math.* the variation of a function between limits 1798. So **O·scillator** *spec.* a machine to produce oscillations; also, a form of wireless transmitter 1898.

‖**Oscillatoria** (ǫsilătōᵊ·riă). 1861. [mod.L. (fem. sing.), f. as prec. + *-oria*; see -ORY¹.] *Bot.* A genus of confervoid Algæ, typifying the N.O. *Oscillatoriaceæ*, growing in dense slimy tufts, in running or stagnant water, and exhibiting an oscillatory or wavy motion.

Oscillograph (ǫ·silograf). 1904. [f. *oscillo-*, used as comb. f. of OSCILLATE + -GRAPH.] An instrument for recording or indicating electrical oscillations. Hence **O·scillogram.** Similarly **O·scilloscope** [see -SCOPE].

‖**Oscines** (ǫ·siniz), *sb. pl.* 1621. [L. *oscines*, pl. of *oscen* singing bird, divining bird, f. *ob-* OB- 1 + *canere* sing.] **1.** *Rom. Antiq.* The birds from whose notes or voices auguries were taken, e.g. the raven, owl, etc. **2.** *Ornith.* The 'Song-birds', containing those families of the *Insessores* or Passerine birds which possess true song-muscles, forming a complicated and effective musical apparatus. **O·scine, O·scinine** (-əin) *adjs.* belonging to the *O.*

Oscitancy (ǫ·sitănsi). 1619. [f. as OSCITANT; see -ANCY.] **1.** Drowsiness; dullness; negligence, inattention. **b.** (with *pl.*) An instance of this 1677. **2.** Yawning; gaping with sleepiness 1717.

1. I judge it rather the Historians oscitancie, and supine negligence 1658.

Oscitant (ǫ·sitănt), *a.* Now *rare* or *Obs.* 1625. [– *oscitant-*, pr. ppl. stem of L. *oscitare* gape; see -ANT.] Gaping from drowsiness, yawning; hence, drowsy, dull, negligent.

Southey..has been strangely o., or..has not understood the sentences COLERIDGE.

Oscitation (ǫsitēᶦ·ʃən). 1547. [– L. *oscitatio*, f. *oscitat-*, pa. ppl. stem of L. *oscitare* gape; see -ION.] **1.** The action of yawning or gaping from drowsiness. **2.** The condition or fact of being drowsy, listless, inattentive, or negligent; an instance of this 1656.

Osculant (ǫ·skiulănt), *a.* 1826. [f. OSCULATE *v.* 3 + -ANT.] Situated between and connecting two things; intermediate; *spec.* in *Nat. Hist.* applied to two species, genera, or families, that are united by some common characters, and to an intermediate species, genus, or group, which unites in itself the characters of two groups 1826.

Oscular (ǫ·skiŭlăɹ), *a.* 1828. [Sense 1 f. L. *osculum* kiss; sense 2 f. OSCULUM 2; sense 3 f. OSCULATE *v.* 4; see -AR¹.] **1.** Of or belonging to the mouth or to kissing. **2.** *Zool.* Of or pertaining to the osculum of a tapeworm, or of a sponge 1881. **3.** *Math.* Pertaining to a higher order of contact than the first (cf. next 4) 1869.

1. *O. muscle* (*musculus oscularis*), the *orbicularis oris* or sphincter muscle of the lips, the kissing muscle.

Osculate (ǫ·skiŭleᶦt), *v.* 1656. [– *osculat-*, pa. ppl. stem of L. *osculari* kiss, f. *osculum* little or pretty mouth (cf. -CULE), kiss, hypocoristic dim. of *ōs* mouth; see -ATE³.] **1.** *trans.* To kiss (*rare*). **2.** *trans.* To bring into close contact 1671. **3.** *intr.* To come into close contact or union; to have close contact with each other. In *Nat. Hist.* To have contact through an intermediate species or genus (cf. OSCULANT) 1737. **4.** *Math. trans.* To have contact of a higher order with, esp. the highest contact possible for two loci; to have three or more coincident points in common with; *intr.* (for *refl.*) to osculate each other; as two curves, two surfaces, or a surface and a curve 1727. So **O·sculatory** *sb.* a representation of Christ or the Virgin, formerly kissed by the priest and people during Mass. **O·sculatory** *a.* characterized by kissing; *Math.* osculating; of or belonging to osculation.

Osculation (ǫskiulēᶦ·ʃən). 1658. [– L. *osculatio*, f. as prec.; see -ION.] **1.** The action of kissing, a kiss. **2.** Close contact. **a.** *gen.* **b.** *Anat.* The mutual contact of blood-vessels. **c.** *Geom.* Contact of a higher order; the fact of touching at three or more coincident points (see prec. 4). 1669.

Oscule (ǫ·skiul). 1835. [f. L. *osculum*; see next.] A little mouth or mouth-like aperture; *spec.* = next 2.

‖**Osculum** (ǫ·skiŭlǒm). *Pl.* **-a.** 1612. [L.; see OSCULATE *v.*] **1.** A kiss. **2.** *Zool.* **a.** A mouth or 'flue' of a sponge. **b.** Occas. applied to the pit-like suckers on the head of a tapeworm by which it attaches itself. 1727.

-ose¹, a suffix repr. L. *-osus*, forming adjs. from sbs., with the meaning 'full of', 'abounding in'; e.g. *annosus* full of years, *religiosus* scrupulous. As a living suffix *-osus* came down to Eng. as -OUS (ME. also *-ows*), which survives with pron. (-əs). A few words in *-ose* after L. have taken their place in the language, as *bellicose*, *jocose*, *morose*, etc. Where *-ous* and *-ose* forms are both in use, e.g. in *acinous*, *acinose*, those in *-ose* are more or less technical. Nouns of state from these adjs., as from those in *-ous*, end in *-osity*, as *verbosity*.

-ose², *Chem.*, a suffix originating in the ending of the word *glucose*, and employed in forming the names of the related carbohydrates, *saccharose* and *cellulose*, with the isomers of these three, as *dextrose*, *lævulose*, etc.

Osiandrian (ōᵘsiæ·ndriăn). 1565. [f. personal name *Osiander* (see def.) + -IAN.] One of the German Protestant followers of Andreas Hosemann (latinized *Osiander*, 1498–1552), who held that the Atonement of Christ was wrought by the power of His divine and not of His human nature. Also **Osia·ndrist.**

Osier (ōᵘ·ʒᶦəɹ), *sb.* (*a.*) ME. [– (O)Fr. *osier*; masc. form corresp. to fem. (dial.) *osière* :– med.L. *auseria* (VIII), which has been referred to Gaulish **auesa* river-bed (whence Breton *aoz*).] **1.** A species of Willow (*Salix viminalis*); much used in basket-work; also other species used for the same purpose; one of the shoots of a willow. **2.** *attrib.* or *adj.* Of, belonging to, or made of osiers; covered with osiers 1578.

1. Who will make a staff of an o.? FULLER. **2.** On list'ning Cherwell's o. banks reclin'd 1750.

Comb.: **o.-ait, -isle**, a small islet in a river overgrown with osiers; **-bed, -holt**, a place where osiers are grown for basket-making. Hence **O·siered** *a.* covered or adorned with osiers; twisted like osiers. **O·siery**, osiers in the mass; articles made of osiers; an osier-bed.

Osirian (osəiᵊ·riăn), *a.* 1849. [f. proper name *Osiris* (see def.) + -IAN.] Of or pertaining to Osiris, the Egyptian deity personifying the power of good and the sunlight. So **Osi·ride, Osiri·dean** *adjs.*

-osis, *suffix*, repr. Gr. -ωσις, originating in the addition of the general suffix -σις, forming verbal nouns of action or condition, to derivative vbs. in -ό-ω from adj. or sb. stems or combining forms in ο-; e.g. μεταμόρφωσις, f. μεταμορφόω, f. μετά + μορφή form. Many such words were also formed directly from the sbs. or adjs. themselves, e.g. ἐξόστωσις exostosis, f. ἐξ out + ὀστέον bone. Many of these Greek terms have passed through Latin into English, e.g. *apotheosis*, *metamorphosis*, rhetorical terms, as *meiosis*, etc., and esp. medical terms, as *sclerosis*, *thrombosis*, etc. On the analogy of these last, others have been freely formed from Gr. elements, as *chlorosis*, *trichinosis*; less frequently from Latin, as *tuberculosis*.

-osity, *compound suffix* of sbs. = Fr. *-osité*, L. *-ositat-*; see -OSE¹, -OUS, and -ITY.

Osmanli (ǫsmæ·nli), *a.* and *sb.* 1813. [f. *Osman*, the Turk. pronunc of Arab. *ʻuṯmān* (see OTTOMAN) + adj. suffix *-li.*] **A.** *adj.* = OTTOMAN 1843. **B.** *sb.* An OTTOMAN.

Osmazome (ǫ·smăzōᵘm, ǫ·z-). 1819. [– Fr. *osmazôme*, irreg. f. Gr. ὀσμή scent + ζωμός soup, sauce.] *Chem.* That part of the aqueous extract of meat which is soluble in alcohol and contains those constituents of the flesh which determine its taste and smell. Hence **O:smazoma·tic, -o·matous** *adjs.*, of the nature of o.

||**Osmeterium** (ǫsmīˈtīᵊriŏm, ǫz-). *Pl.* **-ia.** Also **osma-.** 1816. [mod.L., f. Gr. ὀσμᾶσθαι to smell + -τήριον formative suffix, = 'instrument', 'organ', 'thing used'; see -IUM.] *Entom.* An organ or apparatus adapted to emit a smell or odour; *spec.* a forked process borne by some caterpillars on the segment immediately behind the head, from which they can emit a disgusting odour.

Osmiamic (ǫsmi,æˑmik, ǫz-), *a.* 1873. [f. OSMIUM + AMIC.] *Chem.* In *O. acid*: A dibasic acid, $H_2Os_2N_2O_5$, an acid amide of osmium. Its salts are **O·smiamates.**

Osmic (ǫˑsmik, ǫˑz-), *a.* 1842. [f. OSMIUM + -IC.] *Chem.* Containing osmium; applied to compounds in which osmium is quadrivalent, as *o. chloride* $OsCl_4$, *o. oxide*, OsO_2. *O. acid*, a name given to *osmium tetroxide* OsO_4. Its salts are **O·smiates.**

Osmio-, comb. form of OSMIUM, in names of chemical compounds in which osmium and another element enter into combination with a third, as *osmio-cyanide*.

Osmious (ǫˑsmiəs, ǫˑz-), *a.* 1849. [f. OSMIUM + -OUS.] *Chem.* Containing osmium; applied to compounds in which osmium is divalent, as *o. chloride* $OsCl_2$. (Formerly to the *trichloride*, etc.)

Osmite (ǫˑsməit, ǫˑz-). 1849. [f. OSMIUM + -ITE[1] 4 b.] *Chem.* A salt of osmious acid.

Osmium (ǫˑsmiŏm, ǫˑz-). 1804. [f. Gr. ὀσμή odour + -IUM; so called (S. Tennant, 1804) from the pungent and peculiar smell of the tetroxide.] One of the metals of the platinum group, generally found, associated with platinum, in the alloy iridosmine. Chem. symbol Os; atomic wt. 190·8.

Osmo-[1], repr. Gr. ὀσμο-, comb. form of ὀσμή smell, odour; as in **Osmo·logy,** the study of smells, a treatise on odours; etc.

Osmo-[2], repr. Gr. ὠσμός push, thrust, impulse, used as comb. form of OSMOSE. **Osmo·meter,** an instrument for exhibiting the force of osmotic action. **Osmo·metry,** measurement of osmotic force.

Osmose (ǫˑsmōᵘs, ǫˑz-). 1854. [The common element of the words *endosmose* and *exosmose*, taken as a generalized term (by Graham, 1854); cf. Gr. ὠσμός push.] The tendency of fluids separated by porous septa to pass through these and mix with each other; the action of this passage and intermixture; diffusion through a porous septum or membrane.

Osmosis (ǫsmōᵘˑsis, ǫz-). 1867. [Latinized form of prec.; cf. -OSIS.] = prec. Hence **Osmo·tic** *a.* of, pertaining to, or caused by o. **Osmo·tically** *adv.* by osmotic action.

Osmund[1] (ǫˑzmŏnd). [ME. *osemond* (in AL. *osemondum* XIII), prob. – MLG. *osemunt*, reinforced later from OSw. *osmunder*, ODa. *osmund*; of unkn. origin.] A superior quality of iron formerly imported from the Baltic regions, for the manufacture of arrow-heads, fish-hooks, etc. With pl., a bar of this. Also, *o. iron*, *o. bar*.

Osmund[2] (ǫˑsmŏnd, ǫˑz-). ME. [– AFr. *osmunde* (in AL. *osmunda* XIII), (O)Fr. *osmonde*, of unkn. origin.] †**1.** A name formerly given to various ferns –1611. **2.** Now, the 'Flowering Fern', *Osmunda regalis* Linn., having large bipinnate fronds with terminal panicles of sporangia; also called *Osmund Royal, Royal Fern, King Fern.* **b.** Also as the Eng. name of the genus (of which six species are known). 1578.

Osmundaceous (ǫsmŏndēⁱˑʃəs, ǫz-). 1857. [f. mod.L. *Osmundaceæ*; see prec. and -ACEOUS.] *Bot.* Of or belonging to the *Osmundaceæ*, one of the principal subdivisions of the N.O. *Polypodiaceæ*, the type of which is the genus *Osmunda*.

†**Osnaburg.** 1545. [f. *Osnabrück* (in later Eng. corruptly *Osnaburg*) in North Germany.] A kind of coarse linen originally made in Osnabrück –1862.

Oso-berry (ōᵘˑso,beːri). 1884. [f. Sp. *oso* bear (:– L. *ursus*) + BERRY.] The blue-black drupe of *Nuttallia cerasiformis*, a shrub or small tree of western North America. Also, the shrub.

||**Osphradium** (ǫsfrēⁱˑdiŏm). 1883. [mod. L. – Gr. ὀσφράδιον strong scent, dim. of ὀσφρά smell; see -IUM.] *Zool.* The olfactory organs of some molluscs, consisting of a collection of elongated sense-cells over each gill. Hence **Osphra·dial** *a.*

Osprey (ǫˑspreⁱ). late ME. [– OFr. *ospres*, repr. obscurely L. *ossifraga* OSSIFRAGE.] **1.** A large diurnal bird of prey, *Pandion* (*Falco*) *haliaëtus*; also called sea-eagle, fishing-eagle, fish-hawk. **2.** A milliner's name for an egret plume worn as an ornament on a lady's hat or bonnet. (App. erron. assoc. w. *spray*.) 1885.

Ossature (ǫˑsătiŭɹ). 1879. [– Fr. *ossature*, f. L. *os* bone (see OS[1]), after *curvature* CURVATURE.] **1.** The arrangement of the bones of the skeleton. *rare.* 1885. **2.** *Arch.* The skeleton or framework that supports any structure, as the beams of a roof, or the metal frame of a glass window.

Osse, oss (ǫs), *v.* Now *dial.* late ME. [Of unkn. origin.] †**1.** *trans.* To signify as an omen; to prophesy; to wish good luck. Also *absol.* or *intr.* –1606. **2.** *dial.* To give augury of what one is going to be or do, to shape well or ill for something; hence, to show signs of being about (to do something).

†**Osse, oss,** *sb.* 1600. [app. f. prec.] A word of omen, a presage; a wishing of good luck. (Almost peculiar to Ph. Holland, as tr. L. *omen*.) –1611.

Ossein (ǫˑsi,in). Also **-ine.** 1857. [f. L. *osseus* bony + -IN[1].] *Chem.* Bone-cartilage; the organic gelatinous principle in true bony tissue; the embryonic tissue which develops into bone by the deposit of mineral salts.

Osselet (ǫˑsĕlĕt, ǫˑslĕt). 1686. [– (O)Fr. *osselet*, f. *os* bone; see -LET.] **1.** A little bone, an ossicle; one of the small bones of the carpus or tarsus. **2.** The cuttle-bone, pen, or calamary of some cephalopods 1849.

Osseo- (ǫˑsio), comb. form of L. *osseus* OSSEOUS, as in **Osseo-fi·brous** *a.* consisting of osseous combined with fibrous tissue.

Osseous (ǫˑsiəs), *a.* 1682. [f. L. *osseus* (f. *os, oss-* bone) + -OUS; see -EOUS.] **1.** Of, consisting of, or of the nature of bone; bony; ossified 1707. **2.** Having a bony skeleton, teleostean 1828. **3.** Abounding in fossil bones 1823. **4.** *fig.* Hard or firm as bone 1682.

||**Osseter** (oseˑtəɹ). 1887. [– Russ. *osëtr* sturgeon.] *Zool.* A species of sturgeon, *Acipenser güldenstädtii*.

Ossianic (ǫsi-, ǫʃiæˑnik), *a.* 1808. [f. *Ossian*, anglicized form of *Oisin* (oʃin), name of a legendary Gaelic bard whose poems Macpherson claimed to have collected and translated.] Of or pertaining to Ossian or to the poems ascribed to him; of the style or character of Macpherson's rhythmic prose rendering of these poems; hence, magniloquent, bombastic.

Ossicle (ǫˑsik'l). 1578. [– L. *ossiculum*; see next.] **1.** A small bone; a small piece of bony substance; as, the *auditory ossicles* in the tympanic cavity of the ear. **2.** A small plate, joint, etc. of chitinous or calcareous substance in the animal framework; e.g. one of the plates or skeletal elements of a starfish or other echinoderm 1852.

||**Ossiculum** (ǫsiˑkiŭlŏm). *Pl.* **-a.** 1706. [L., dim. of *os, oss-* bone; see -CULE.] A little bone; an ossicle; the †stone of a fruit.

Ossiferous (ǫsiˑfĕrəs), *a.* 1823. [f. as prec.; see -FEROUS.] Containing or yielding bones.

Ossific (ǫsiˑfik), *a.* 1676. [f. as prec. + -FIC.] Bone-forming; becoming or making bone; ossifying. *O. centre*, a centre of ossification.

Ossification (ǫːsifikēⁱˑʃən). 1697. [– Fr. *ossification*, f. as prec.; see -FICATION.] **1.** The formation of bone; the process of becoming bone; the condition of being ossified. **2.** *concr.* A bony formation or concretion; bone as a formation 1705.

1. O. of the arteries is most commonly the lot of old age 1830. *Centre of o.*, the point at which cartilage or connective tissue begins to ossify. Hence **O·ssified** *ppl. a.* made into bone; hardened like bone.

Ossifrage (ǫˑsifrĕdʒ). 1601. [– subst. uses of L. *ossifragus, -fraga* bone-breaking, f. as prec. + **frag-*, f. *frangere* break. Cf. OSPREY.] **1.** The Lammergeyer or Geir Eagle. **2.** The Osprey or fish-hawk 1658.

1. The Eagle, and the O. [*R.V.* gier eagle], and the Ospray *Lev.* 11:13.

Ossify (ǫˑsifəi), *v.* 1713. [– Fr. *ossifier*, f. as prec.; see -FY.] **1.** *intr.* To become bone; to change from soft tissue into bone. **2.** *trans.* To convert into bone; to harden. (Chiefly in *passive*.) 1721.

1. *fig.* The natural instinct of veneration had ossified into idolatry FROUDE. **2.** *fig.* Our phrases, often repeated, o. the very organs of intelligence 1860.

Ossivorous (ǫsiˑvŏrəs), *a.* 1676. [f. as prec.; see -VOROUS.] Bone-devouring; feeding upon bones; in *Path.* bone-destroying.

Ossuary (ǫˑsiu,ări). 1658. [– late L. *ossuarium*, f. *ossu*, var. of *os* (earlier *oss*) bone; see -ARY[1].] A receptacle for the bones of the dead; a charnel-house; a bone-urn. **b.** *transf.* A bone-cave, or deposit formed largely of bones 1861. **c.** *fig.* That in which relics of the dead past are preserved 1872. **d.** *attrib.* or as *adj.* 1857.

The earth had confounded the ashes of these Ossuaries SIR T. BROWNE.

Osteal (ǫˑstiăl), *a.* 1877. [f. Gr. ὀστέον bone + -AL[1].] Of or pertaining to bone; *spec.* of the quality of sound produced by the percussion of bone.

Ostein, -ine (ǫˑsti,in). 1854. [f. Gr. ὀστέον bone + -INE[4]; cf. *dentine*.] *Anat.* The substance of bone, bony tissue, bone as a tissue.

Osteitis (ǫsti,əiˑtis). Also **ostitis.** 1839. [f. Gr. ὀστέον bone + -ITIS.] *Path.* Inflammation in the substance of a bone.

Ostend (ǫsteˑnd), *v.* Now *rare.* 1450. [– L. *ostendere* stretch out to view; see next.] *trans.* To show, reveal; to manifest, exhibit.

Ostensible (ǫsteˑnsĭb'l), *a.* 1762. [– Fr. *ostensible* – med.L. *ostensibilis*, f. *ostens-*, pa. ppl. stem of *ostendere* (see prec.), f. *obs-* OB- 1 + *tendere* stretch; see -IBLE.] †**1.** That may be shown; hence, presentable; also, made to be shown –1828. †**2.** Open to public view; conspicuous, ostentatious –1828. **3.** Declared, avowed, professed; put forth as actual or genuine; often opp. to 'actual', 'real', and so = merely professed, pretended 1771.

2. The outward and o. workings of this complicated mechanism 1828. **3.** My o. errand on this occasion was to get measured for a pair of shoes C. BRONTË. Hence **Ostensibi·lity. Oste·nsibly** *adv.*

Ostension (ǫsteˑnʃən). 1474. [– (O)Fr. *ostension* – L. *ostensio*, f. as prec.; see -ION.] †**1.** The action of showing; exhibition; manifestation –1789. **2.** *Eccl.* The action of holding forth the Eucharistic elements to the sight of the people 1607.

Ostensive (ǫsteˑnsiv), *a.* 1605. [– late L. *ostensivus* (Boethius), f. as prec.; see -IVE.] **1.** Manifestly or directly demonstrative; *spec.* in *Logic*, Setting forth a general principle manifestly including the proposition to be proved. **2.** = OSTENSIBLE *a.* 3. 1782.

1. *O. reduction*, reduction by the direct processes of conversion, permutation, and transposition, as opp. to indirect reduction. Hence **Oste·nsively** *adv.*

Ostensory (ǫsteˑnsəri). Also (in Fr., It., or L. forms) **-oir, -orio, -orium.** 1722. [(Earlier in foreign forms *ostensorio, -orium, -oir*) – med.L. *ostensorium*, f. as prec.; see -ORY[1].] A monstrance.

Ostent[1] (ǫsteˑnt). Now *rare.* 1563. [– L. *ostentum* (pl. *-a*) something shown, prodigy, subst. use of pa. pple. n. of *ostendere*; see OSTENSIBLE.] A sign, portent, wonder, prodigy.

The Night waxed wan, As though with an awed sense of such o. T. HARDY.

Ostent[2] (ǫsteˑnt). Now *rare.* 1596. [– L. *ostentus* showing, display, f. *ostent-*, pa. ppl. stem of *ostendere*; cf. prec.] **1.** The act of showing; manifestation; display, appearance. **2.** Vainglorious display, ostentation 1598.

1. *Merch. V.* II. viii. 44. **2.** Thou proud Achilles with thy great o. 1609.

Ostentate (ǫˑstĕnteⁱt), *v.* Now only *U.S.* 1540. [– *ostentat-*, pa. ppl. stem of L. *ostentare*; see next, -ATE[3].] *trans.* To make a show of, show off, display boastfully.

Ostentation (ǫstĕntēⁱˑʃən). late ME. [– (O)Fr. *ostentation* – L. *ostentatio*, frequent. of *ostendere*; see OSTENT[2], -ION.] †**1.** The presaging of future events; a presage; a portent, prodigy (*rare*) –1607. **2.** The action of showing; an exhibition, display (*of* something). *Obs.* or *arch.* 1534. **†b.** Mere show, appearance; false show, pretence –1649. **3.** Pretentious parade, vainglorious 'showing off' 1450.

2. Finck to ride-out reconnoitering. . and to make motions and ostentations (= DEMONSTRATION 6) CARLYLE. **3.** Hence o. here, with tawdry art, Pants for the vulgar praise which fools impart GOLDSM.

Ostentatious (ǫstĕntēⁱ·ʃəs), *a.* 1658. [f. prec. + -OUS, -IOUS. Has displaced the earlier *ostentative, ostentatory, ostentive, ostentous.*] **1.** Characterized or marked by ostentation; unduly conspicuous; boastful; pretentious. **2.** Conspicuous, showy. *Obs.* (or blending with 1). 1713.

1. His Religion was sincere, not o. ADDISON. They are not, like the Mohammedans, o. in their prayers LIVINGSTONE. So **Ostenta·tious-ly** *adv.*, **-ness.**

Osteo- (ǫ·stio), bef. a vowel also **oste-**, comb. form of Gr. ὀστέον bone, in many derivatives, chiefly anatomical.

‖**Osteoarthri·tis**, now usually **Ostearthri·tis** [Gr. ἀρθρῖτις gout], inflammation of the bones of a joint. **O·steoblast** [Gr. βλαστός bud, germ], Gegenbaur's term for granular corpuscles found in all developing bone as the active agents of osseous growth; hence **Osteobla·stic** *a.* ‖**Osteo·clasis** [Gr. κλάσις fracture], fracture of a bone to correct a deformity; dissolution or destruction of bone tissue. **O·steoclast** [G. *osteoklast*, f. Gr. κλαστός broken], (*a*) Kölliker's term for the many-nucleated cells, found in growing bone, and concerned with the absorption of osseous tissue in the formation of the medullary spaces in cartilage; (*b*) a surgical instrument for effecting osteoclasis. ‖**Osteoco·lla** [Gr. κόλλα glue] a deposit of carbonate of lime forming an incrustation on the roots and stems of plants. **O·steocope,** also ‖**Osteo·copus** [Gr. ὀστεοκόπος, f. κόπος fatigue], violent wearing pain in the bones, esp. of syphilitic origin; syphilitic rheumatism; hence **Osteoco·pic** *a.* **Osteoge·nesis** [Gr. γένεσις GENESIS], the origination or formation of bone. **Osteo·graphy** [-GRAPHY], description of the bones; descriptive osteology. **O·steolite** [Gr. λίθος stone], compact earthy calcium phosphate, resembling lithographic stone. ‖**Osteo·ma,** *pl.* **-ata** [Gr. -ωμα, as in *carcinoma*, etc.], *Path.* a tumour composed of osseous tissue. ‖**Osteomala·cia, -mala·kia** [Gr. μαλακία softness], softening of bones due to the disappearance of earthy salts; also called *malacosteon.* **O·steomancy** [-MANCY], divination from bones. ‖**O:steomyeli·tis** [Gr. μυελός marrow], inflammation of the marrow of a bone. **O·steophyte** [Gr. φυτόν a growth], an osseous outgrowth, a bony excrescence; hence **Osteophy·tic** *a.* **O·steoplasty** [Gr. πλαστός moulded; see -PLASTY], the transplanting of a piece of bone with its periosteum to fill up a gap; hence **Osteopla·stic** *a.* ‖**O:steosclero·sis** [Gr. σκλήρωσις induration], hardening of a bone. **O·steotome** [Gr. -τομος that cuts], *Surg.* any instrument for cutting or dividing bone.

Osteoid (ǫ·sti,oid), *a.* 1847. [f. OSTE(O- + -OID.] Resembling bone; bony, osseous.

Osteologic, -al (ǫ:stiolǫ·dʒik, -ăl), *adjs.* 1777. [f. next; see -AL¹, -ICAL.] **1.** Pertaining to, dealing with, or relating to osteology. **2.** Of or pertaining to the objects of osteology, i.e. to bones, their structure, etc.; coming within the sphere of osteology 1794.

Osteology (ǫstiǫ·lŏdʒi). 1670. [– mod.L. *osteologia* (1573 Jasolinus); see OSTEO-, -LOGY. Cf. Fr. *ostéologie.*] **1.** The science which treats of bones; that branch of anatomy which deals with the structure, genesis, and disposition of bones. **b.** A treatise on the bones 1713. **2.** *transf.* The objects of this science; the bony structure of an animal 1833. So **Osteo·logist**, one versed in o.

Osteometry (ǫsti,ǫ·métri). 1878. [f. OSTEO- + -METRY.] The measurement of bones; that part of zoömetry (or *esp.* anthropometry) which has to do with the proportions of the different bones.

Osteopathy (ǫstiǫ·păþi). 1857. [f. OSTEO- + -PATHY. In sense 2, after *homœopathy, allopathy.*] **1.** Disease or affection of the bones. **2.** A theory of disease and method of cure which assumes that deformation of the skeleton and consequent interference with the adjacent nerves and blood-vessels are the cause of most diseases 1897. Hence **Osteopath** (ǫ·stiopæþ), one who practises o.; **Osteopa·thic** *a.*; **Osteopa·thically** *adv.*; **Osteo·pathist**, a believer in or practiser of o.

‖**O:steosarco·ma.** 1807. [f. OSTEO- + SARCOMA.] *Path.* **1.** Sarcoma in the bone; a disease of the bone in which a fleshy, medullary, or cartilaginous mass grows within it. **2.** A sarcoma which undergoes osseous transformation 1878.

Osteotomy (ǫsti,ǫ·tŏmi). 1844. [f. OSTEO- + -TOMY.] **a.** *Anat.* Dissection of the bones. **b.** *Surg.* The cutting of a bone in order to correct a deformity, etc.

‖**Osteria** (ostĕrī·a). 1605. [It., f. *oste* HOST *sb.*²] An inn or hostelry in Italy or an Italian-speaking country.

Ostiary (ǫ·stiări). late ME. [– L. *ostiarius*, f. *ostium* opening, river mouth, door, f. *ōs* mouth; see -ARY¹.] *Eccl.* A door-keeper, esp. of a church; the lowest of the minor orders of the R.C.Ch. Also in L. form *ostiarius.*

Ostiole (ǫ·stiōᵘl). Also irreg. **osteole;** and in L. form. 1835. [– L. *ostiolum*, dim. of *ostium* door; see prec.] A small orifice or opening; esp. *Bot.* the orifice or opening in the conceptacles and perithecia of certain algæ and fungi, through which the spores are discharged; also, openings of the stomata or breathing pores.

Osti·tis, var. of OSTEITIS.

‖**Ostium** (ǫ·stiŏm). *Pl.* **ostia.** 1665. [L. = opening, river mouth, door.] **†1.** The mouth of a river –1695. **2.** *Anat.* Applied to the openings of the ventricles and pulmonary arteries, the Fallopian and Eustachian tubes, the urethra, etc., in the animal body 1877.

Ostler (ǫ·slər). late ME. [var. sp. of HOSTLER, restricted since XVI to this sense.] A man who attends horses at an inn; a stableman, a groom. Also *attrib.*, as *o.-boy.* Hence **O·stleress,** a female o.

Ostlerie, -rye, obs. ff. HOSTELRY.

Ostmen (ōᵘ·stmĕn), *sb. pl. Hist.* late ME. [– ON. *Austmenn*, pl. of *Austmaðr*; see EAST, MAN.] Name given in Ireland and Iceland to invaders or settlers from Denmark and Norway.

Ostracean (ǫstrēⁱ·ʃiăn), *a.* and *sb.* 1835. [f. mod.L. *Ostracea* or *-eæ*, pl., the family of bivalve molluscs containing the oyster (f. Gr. ὀστράκεος, f. ὄστρακον earthen vessel, tile, shell of oyster, etc.) + -AN; see -ACEAN.] **a.** *adj.* Belonging to the *Ostracea* or oyster family, ostraceous. **b.** *sb.* A member of the *Ostracea*, an oyster. So **Ostra·ceous** *a.* of or pertaining to the *Ostracea*; of the nature of an oyster.

‖**Ostracion** (ǫstrēⁱ·siǫn). 1658. [mod.L. – Gr. ὀστράκιον, dim. of ὄστρακον hard shell.] *Ichth.* A genus of fishes having their bodies covered with juxtaposed hexagonal plates; a trunk-fish or coffer-fish.

Ostracism (ǫ·străsiz'm). 1588. [– Fr. *ostracisme* or mod.L. *ostracismus* – Gr. ὀστρακισμός, f. ὀστρακίζειν; see OSTRACIZE, -ISM.] **1.** A method of temporary banishment practised in Athens, etc., by which a too popular or powerful citizen was sent into exile for ten (later five) years; so called because it was effected by voting with potsherds or tiles, on which was written the name of the person proposed to be exiled; hence, Temporary banishment or expatriation in general. **2.** *fig.* Banishment by general consent; exclusion from society, favour, or common privileges 16. .

1. By the o. a citizen was banished without special accusation, trial or defence GROTE. **2.** The social o. of a heretic 1870.

Ostracite (ǫ·străsəit). 1653. [– L. *ostracites*, a stone mentioned by Pliny – Gr. ὀστρακίτης earthen, testaceous, f. ὄστρακον shell.] A fossil shell of a species or genus allied to the oyster.

Ostracize (ǫ·străsəiz), *v.* 1649. [– Gr. ὀστρακίζειν, f. ὄστρακον shell, tile, potsherd; see -IZE.] **1.** *trans.* (*Gr. Hist.*) To banish by voting with potsherds; see OSTRACISM 1. 1850. **2.** *fig.* To banish or expel as by ostracism; to exclude from society, favour, or common privileges.

2. Ostracised from society because of the drunken and violent habits of his wife 1890.

Ostraco-, bef. a vowel **ostrac-,** comb. form of Gr. ὄστρακον hard shell; as in **O·straco·de:rm** [Gr. ὀστρακόδερμος] *a.*, having a bony integument or external skeleton; *sb.* an ostracoderm fish; so **O:stracode·rmal, -mous** *adjs.*

Ostracode (ǫ·străkōᵘd), *a.* and *sb.* 1865. [– Gr. ὀστρακώδης testaceous, f. ὄστρακον shell; see -ODE.] **a.** *adj.* Belonging to the *Ostracoda* or *Ostracopoda*, an order of entomostracous crustaceans. **b.** *sb.* A member of the *Ostracoda.* So **Ostraco·dal, Ostraco·dous** *adjs.*

Ostracon, -kon (ǫ·străkǫn). *Pl.* **-ca, -ka** (-kă). 1885. [– Gr. ὄστρακον potsherd.] Any inscribed fragment of pottery or limestone such as those found in Upper Egypt.

Ostreaceous (ǫstri,ēⁱ·ʃəs), *a.* 1678. [f. L. *ostrea* oyster + -ACEOUS.] Of the nature of the oyster or its shell; proper to an oyster; oyster-like; ostraceous.

Ostreger, ostringer (ǫ·strĕdʒəɹ, ǫ·strindʒəɹ). [– OFr. *ostruchier, austruchier*, based on *ostour* (mod. *autour*) hawk :– Gallo-Rom. *auceptore*, alt. form (by assoc. with L. *avis* bird) of *acceptore*, for L. *accipiter*. For *ostringer*, cf. *messenger*, etc.] A keeper of goshawks.

Ostrei-, ostreo-, comb. forms of L. *ostrea*, *ostreum*, and Gr. ὄστρεον oyster. Hence: **O·streiform** *a.*, having the form of an oyster or of oysters. **O·streophage** (-feⁱdʒ), **Ostreophagist** (-ǫ·fădʒist) [Gr. -φάγος eating], one who or that which eats or feeds upon oysters; so **Ostreo·phagous** *a.*

Ostreiculture (ǫ·stri,ikɒ:ltiŭɹ). Also erron. **ostr(e)a-, ostreo-, ostri-.** 1861. [f. OSTREI- + CULTURE.] The artificial breeding of oysters for the market. Hence **O:streicu·ltural** *a.* **O:streicu·lturist.**

Ostrich (ǫ·stritʃ). [ME. *ostrice, -iche, -ige* – OFr. *ostrice, -iche, -usce* (mod. *autruche*) :– Rom. **avistruthius*, f. L. *avis* bird + late L. *struthio* – Gr. στρουθίων ostrich, f. στρουθός sparrow, ostrich.] **1.** A very large ratite bird, *Struthio camelus*, the only species of the genus *S.* and the family *Struthionidæ*, inhabiting the sandy plains of Africa and Arabia; it is the largest of existing birds.

There is much ref. in proverb and allusion to its indiscriminate voracity and its liking for hard substances, which it swallows to assist the gizzard in its functions; its supposed want of regard for its young; and the practice attributed to it of burying its head in the sand when pursued, through incapacity to distinguish between seeing and being seen.

b. Applied to the rhea of South America, a ratite bird resembling the ostrich; more fully *American o.* 1813. **2.** *attrib.* Of or pertaining to an ostrich or ostriches; ostrich-like 1494.

1. Cruel, as an o. in desert WYCLIF *Lam.* 4:3. Twil digest a Cathedral Church as easilie, as an Estritch a two penie nail 1589. **2.** Whole nations, fooled by falsehood, fear, or pride, Their ostrich-heads in self-illusion hide MOORE.

Comb.: **o.-farm,** a farm on which ostriches are reared for the sake of their plumes; **-farming; -fern,** the fern *Onoclea struthiopteris* (*S. germanica*); **-tip,** the tip of an ostrich-feather.

O·strich-fea:ther. 1460. A feather of an ostrich, *esp.* one of the long curly quill-feathers of the wings or tail used as a personal ornament or for decorative purposes.

Ostrich-plume. 1637. **1.** An ostrich-feather, or a bunch of two or three feathers. **2.** *attrib.* Applied to a variety of Chrysanthemum 1891.

Ostringer: see OSTREGER.

Ostrogoth (ǫ·strogǫþ). 1647. [– late L. pl. *Ostrogothi*, f. Gmc. **austro-*, whence OHG., OS. *ōstar*, ON. *austr* eastward (see EAST) + L. *Gothus* Goth.] An East Goth; a name given to the division of the Teutonic race of Goths which conquered Italy, and in 493, under Theodoric, established a kingdom which continued till 555. Hence **Ostrogo·thian, Ostrogo·thic** *adjs.*

-ot, *suffix*¹, repr. Fr. *-ot*, orig. dim., but the dim. force is often lost, as in *ballot, chariot, parrot*, etc. It is not a living suffix in Eng.

-ot, *suffix*², repr. Fr. *-ote*, L. *-ota*, Gr. -ώτης, expressing nativity, as Ἠπειρώτης Epirot, native of Epirus, in which use it is often represented by -OTE. It occurs also in *helot, idiot, patriot, zealot*, and a few other sbs. of Greek origin.

Otacoustic (ōᵘtăkū·stik, -ăkau·stik), *rare.* 1643. [f. Gr. οὖς, ὠτ- ear + ἀκουστικός ACOUSTIC.]

An instrument to assist hearing, as an ear-trumpet. So ‖**Otacou·sticon.**

Otaheite apple (ōᵘtăhī·ti æ·p'l). 1814. [Named after *Otaheite*, or *Tahiti*, one of the Society Islands.] The fruit of *Spondias dulcis*, a native of Java, the Moluccas, and the Society Islands; it is of a golden yellow colour, the rind tasting like turpentine, and the pulp having the flavour of pine-apple.

Otalgia (oᵘtæ·ldʒiă). 1657. [– Gr. ὠταλγία ear-ache, f. οὖς ὠτ- ear + ἄλγος pain.] Neuralgic pain in the ear. Hence **Ota·lgic** *a.*

Otary (ōᵘ·tări). 1847. [– mod.L. *otaria*, f. Gr. οὖς, ὠτ- ear.] An eared seal; a member of the *Otariidæ*, a family of pinnipeds having very small external ears, which includes the fur seals and sea lions.

O.T.C. = Officers' Training Corps.

-ote, *suffix*, another form of -OT², as in *Candiote*, a native of Candia.

Otheoscope (ōᵘ·þioskoᵘp). 1877. [f. Gr. ὠθεῖν push + -SCOPE.] A modification of the radiometer, devised by Sir W. Crookes, in which the black or driving surface is stationary, while the cooling surface is movable.

Other (ɒ·ðəɹ), *adj. pron.* (*sb.*). [OE. *ōþer* = OFris. *ōther*, OS. *ōðar*, *andar*, OHG. *andar* (Du., G. *ander*), ON. *annarr*, Goth. *anþar* :– Gmc. **anþeraz* :– IE. **ánteros* (compar. formation with *-*teros*), whence the orig. sense of alteration (cf. ALTER); parallel to Skr. *ántaras* different.] **A.** *adj.* †**1.** One of the two, the one (of two); L. *alter* –1596. **2.** The remaining (person, thing, or group) of two; later, also, of three or more. Usu. preceded by *the* or an equivalent word (e.g. *his other foot*). OE. **b.** *Every o.*, every second, every alternate 1480. †**3.** That follows the first; second (of two or more). *Obs.* (exc. as in quots.) OE. **4.** With plural sb. = the remaining, the rest of the; L. *ceteri* OE. **5.** Existing besides, or distinct from, that already mentioned or implied; not this, not the same, different in identity; further, additional OE. **b.** In this sense, *other* may be construed with *than* ME. **6.** Different (in kind or quality). Const. *than* (*from*, †*but*). ME. †**7.** Used to characterize things as of a different kind from those previously mentioned; e.g. *other sinful men* = other men, who are sinful –1699.

1. Her o. leg was lame SPENSER. **2.** Phr. *On the o. hand*: see HAND *sb.* But (O poore Glouster) Lost he his o. eye? SHAKS. **b.** A committee every o. week SWIFT. **3.** Phr. *The o. day*: †(*a*) orig. the second day, the next day; †(*b*) the preceding day, yesterday; (*c*) a day or two ago, recently. So *the o. night*, *week*, etc. They played a match the o. day against a local club 1885. **4.** Satan..With Head up-lift above the wave,..his other Parts besides Prone on the Flood MILT. **5.** It may chance of wheat, or of some o. graine 1 *Cor.* 15:37. We have o. evidence.. how deeply he had drunk..at classic fountains GLADSTONE. Phr. *O. such* (arch.): now usu. *such other(s)*. *O. six*, etc. (arch. or dial), ambiguous: = the (or an) other six, or six other(s), etc. *O. the king's enemies* (arch.), ambiguous: = others, (who are) the king's enemies, or other enemies of the king. **b.** Gratuities o. than money 1866. **6.** It could not be o. than pleasant to me COLERIDGE. **7.** *Other sinful men* now means only 'others of such men as are sinful'.

B. *absol.*, *pron.*, or *sb.*

I. *absol.* †**1.** One of the two, the one; L. *alter* –ME. **2.** *The o.*: The remaining one of two; later, of three or more. (Esp. contrasted with (*the*) *one*.) OE. †**b.** Instead of 'the other', the simple *other* was formerly used after *each*, *either*, *neither*, *whether* (occas. after *one*, *none*) –1657. †**c.** The simple *other* was formerly used in the sense 'each preceding one (in turn)' –1694. **3.** *pl.* The remaining ones, the rest; L. *ceteri* OE. **4.** absol. use of A. 5, the sb. being expressed in the context: **a.** *sing.* One besides ME. **b.** *pl.* (formerly *other* :– OE. *óþre*, *-u*) Other things or persons of the kind mentioned OE.

2. One Monarch wears an honest open Face,.. That o. looks like Nature in Disgrace DRYDEN. **b.** Priest and people interchangeably pray each for o. 1657. Phr. *Each other*, as in *they help each other*, i.e. each [helps] the other. **c.** Euery Letter he hath writ, hath disuouch'd o. SHAKS. **3.** Awaking when the o. doe SHAKS. The cave where the others lay DE FOE. **4. a.** Some time or o. we may be at leisure ADDISON. Ten years ago I used your soap; since when I have used no o. (*mod.*). **b.** I know two o. of his works J. H. NEWMAN. The very place, of all others, where it is most likely to be of real service 1877.

II. *pron.* **1. a.** *sing.* = Another person; some one else; any one else OE. **b.** *pl.* (formerly *other*; cf. B. I. 4 b.) Other persons OE. **2.** = Another thing; something else, anything else; *no* or *none o.*, nothing else. *Obs.* or *arch.* OE. **3.** In reciprocal sense: = Each other, one another. In later use only *Sc.* late ME.

1. a. Euery one taketh before o., his owne supper 1 *Cor.* 11:21. It is plain..she likes some o. 1811. **b.** I have pleased some and displeased o. 1607. Others indeed may talk BERKELEY. **2.** This is none o., but the house of God *Gen.* 28:17. He thought he could not do o. than send the two prisoners for trial 1895. **3.** Nae doubt but they were fain o' ither BURNS.

III. *sb. Philos.* That which (in relation to something already mentioned) constitutes the other part of the universe of being, and is thus the counterpart or double of the former; e.g. the *non-ego* is the 'other' of the *ego*, Creation of the Creator, etc. 1863.

Other (ɒ·ðəɹ), *adv.*¹ ME. [advb. use of prec., sometimes due to ellipsis.] = OTHERWISE B. 1.

It is impossible to refer to them..o. than very cursorily 1883.

†**Other**, *conj.* and *adv.*² [The OE. word for 'or', *oððe*, earlier *oðða*, was superseded *c* 1130 by *oðer*, the source of which is conjectural.] **A.** *conj.* The earlier form of OR *conj.*² Const. *simply*, or preceded by *other*, *whether* –1574. **B.** *adv.* **1.** Placed before two (or more) words, phrases, or clauses connected by *other* or *or*, so that *other*..*other*.., and (later) *other*..*or*.. was equivalent to mod. Eng. *either*..*or*..: see EITHER B. 3. –1588. **2.** Following an alternative clause with *or* (*rare*). ME. only. **3.** = Whether (*rare*) 1523.

Othergates (ɒ·ðəɹgeⁱts), *adv.* and *adj. Obs.* exc. *dial.* ME. [f. OTHER *a.* + GATE *sb.*² 5, with advb. genitive *-es*; see -S *suffix.*] **A.** *adv.* In another way, otherwise, differently. †**B.** *adj.* Of another fashion or kind, different –1669.

A. If he had not beene in drinke, hee would haue tickel'd you other gates then he did SHAKS.

Otherguess (ɒ·ðəɹges), *a.* Now only *colloq.* 1632. [Reduction of *othergets* from prec., spelt after *guess.*] = prec. B.

†**Otherguise**, *a.* 1653. [Alteration of prec. by folk-etymology, after *guise.*] = prec. –1755.

Otherness (ɒ·ðəɹnės). 1587. [f. OTHER *a.* + -NESS.] The quality of being other; difference, diversity. **b.** *transf.* The fact of being other; something that is other 1821.

Other some, †**othersome**, *a.* and *pron.* Now *arch.* or *dial.* ME. [OTHER *a.*, SOME *pron.* or *a.*] *adj.* Some other; *pron.* Some others.

Otherways (ɒ·ðəɹweⁱz), *adv. Obs.* exc. *dial.* ME. [f. OTHER *a.* + -WAYS.] = OTHERWISE.

Otherwhere (ɒ·ðəɹhwēᵊɹ), *adv.* Also hyphened or as two words. ME. [f. OTHER *a.* + WHERE; cf. *somewhere.*] In another place; elsewhere 1541. **b.** To another place. late ME. **c.** quasi-*sb.*, esp. with *some*, *any*, etc. (better written separately, *some other where* = some other place) ME.

Otherwhile (ɒ·ðəɹhwəil), *adv.* Now *rare* or *dial.* Also hyphened, or as two words. ME. [f. OTHER *a.* + WHILE *sb.*] **1.** At one time or other; at times; sometimes, now and then, occasionally. †**b.** quasi-*sb.* in *every otherwhile* (prop. three words), every now and then –1736. **2.** At another time, or at other times. Chiefly as *correl.* to *sometime* or an equiv. Now *arch.* late ME.

Otherwhiles (ɒ·ðəɹhwəilz), *adv.* Now *rare* or *dial.* ME. [f. as prec. with advb. genitive *-s*, (see -S); in later times often felt as pl.] †**1.** = prec. 1. –1787. **2.** = prec. 2. 1460.

Otherwise (ɒ·ðəɹwəiz), *sb. phr.*, *adv.*, *adj.* OE. [orig. OE. *on ōðre wisan* in other manner, ME. *oþre wise*, at length written *otherwise*; cf. *in any wise*, *anywise*, etc.: see WISE *sb.*¹] **A.** Phr. with *wise*, manner, way, as distinct sb., e.g. *in other wise* (arch.).

To be led any o. than blindly BURKE.

B. *adv.* **1.** In another way, or in other ways; differently. Const. *than.* ME. **2.** In another case; in other circumstances; if not; else. late ME. **3.** In other respects 1594. †**4.** On the other hand (*rare*) –1673. **5.** *And, or o.*, and, or the opposite or the reverse 1895.

1. God saw o. PUSEY. **2.** I went at once; o. I should have missed him 1903. **3.** The best men o. are not alwayes the best in regard of societie HOOKER.

C. Adjectival uses. **1.** In another state or condition; not so; different; other. late ME. **2.** as *adj.* That would otherwise be..; that would otherwise exist 1600.

1. Some [scholars] are wise, and some are o. 1680. **2.** At the table aboue all others their o. equals 1600.

Other world, o·ther-world, *sb.* and *a.* 1884. [OTHER *a.* 2.] **1.** A world other than this: **a.** The world to come. **b.** The spirit-land of many non-Christian peoples. **c.** The world of idealism, poetry, or romance. 1888. **2.** *attrib.* Unearthly; heavenly.

2. That sweet other-world smile TENNYSON. Hence **O·therwo·rldliness**, devotion to the other world, or to the interests of a future life, *esp.* morbid, ascetic, or selfish spirituality; the quality attributed to an ideal world. **O·ther-wo:rldly** *a.* devoted to the concerns of the world to come, or the world of mind.

Othman. 1813. = OTTOMAN *a.* and *sb.*¹

Otic (ōᵘ·tik, ǫ·tik), *a.* 1657. [– Gr. ὠτικός, f. οὖς, ὠτ- ear; see -IC.] *Anat.*, *Path.* Of, belonging to, or relating to the ear; auricular.

-otic (ǫ·tik), compound suffix, repr. ult., through Fr. *-otique*, L. *-oticus*, Gr. *-ωτικος*, f. sbs. in *-ωτ-ης* or adjs. in *-ωτ-ος* (from vbs. in *-όω*) + *-ικός* -IC. Adjs. in -OTIC go in sense with sbs. in -OSIS, as *amaurotic*, of, pertaining to, or affected with *amaurosis*; so *hypnotic*, *narcotic*, etc. Exceptions are *erotic*, *exotic*, etc., which are otherwise derived, and *chaotic*, formed by analogy.

Otiose (ōᵘ·ʃⁱōᵘs), *a.* 1794. [– L. *otiosus*, f. *otium* leisure; see -OSE¹.] **1.** At leisure or at rest; unemployed, idle; indolent 1850. **2.** Having no practical result; sterile; nugatory 1794. **b.** Superfluous, useless 1837.

1. An o. support of the Government 1850. Reposing with a vague and o. belief on the traditionary doctrines 1853. **2.** Such stories..as require..nothing more than an o. assent PALEY. **b.** The number of o. lines..which swell the piece out 1866. Hence **O·tio:se-ly** *adv.*, **-ness.**

Otiosity (ōᵘʃiǫ·sĭti). 1483. [Earlier *ociosity* – Fr. †*ociosité* (XV), f. *ociose* – L. *otiosus* (see prec.); see -ITY.] The condition or state of being otiose.

‖**Otitis** (oᵘtəi·tis). 1799. [mod.L., f. Gr. οὖς, ὠτ- ear + -ITIS.] *Path.* Inflammation of the ear. Hence **Oti·tic** *a.*

‖**Otium** (ōᵘ·ʃiŏm). 1729. The Latin word for 'leisure, ease'; used esp. in the phrase *otium cum dignitate*, dignified leisure or ease.

Oto- (ōᵘ·to), bef. a vowel **ot-**, repr. Gr. ὠτο-, comb. form of οὖς, ὠτ- ear, an element of medical and other scientific words.

Otoco·nia [Gr. κονία or κόνις dust], term for the white pulverulent dust in the inner ear, the aggregation of which forms an otolith. **Oto·conite** = OTOLITH. **O·tocrane** [Gr. κρανίον the skull], the auditory capsule, the portion of the petrous bone which encloses the organ of hearing; hence **Otocra·nial, Otocra·nic** *adjs.* **O·tocyst** [Gr. κύστις bladder], term for the auditory vesicle or organ of hearing in some of the Invertebrata; hence **Otocy·stic** *a.* **O·tolite** [-LITE] = OTOLITH. ‖**Otorrhœ·a** [Gr. ῥοία a flow], purulent discharge from the ear. **Oto·steal** [Gr. ὀστέον bone], *a.* relating to the auditory ossicle.

Otolith (ōᵘ·tŏliþ). 1835. [f. OTO- + -LITH.] *Anat.* and *Physiol.* An ear-stone; one of the calcareous bodies found in the inner ear of vertebrates and some invertebrates; in fishes often of great size. Hence **Otoli·thic, -li·tic** *adjs.*

Otology (oᵘtǫ·lŏdʒi). 1842. [f. OTO- + -LOGY.] That branch of science which treats of the ear, its anatomy, functions, and diseases; a treatise on the ear. Hence **Oto·logist**, an ear-specialist. **Otolo·gical** *a.*

Otoscope (ōᵘ·tŏskoᵘp). 1849. [f. OTO- + -SCOPE.] **1.** A modification of the stethoscope for auscultation of sounds in the ear. **2.** An optical instrument for inspection of the cavity of the ear 1853. Hence **Otosco·pic** *a.* **Oto·scopy**, the use of the o.

Ottar, var. of ATTAR, OTTO.

‖**Ottava** (ottā·vă). 1820. [It. = eighth, octave.] **1.** *Mus.* An octave. (Usu. abbrev. 8*va.*) 1848. **2.** *O. rima* (rī·ma). An Italian stanza of eight 11-syllabled lines, rhyming as *a b a b a b c c*; the Byronic adaptation has English heroic lines of ten syllables.

Otter (ǫ·tə̆ɹ), *sb.* [OE. *otr, ot(t)or* = MLG., Du. *otter*, OHG. *ottar* (G. *otter*), ON. *otr* :- Gmc. **otraz* :- IE. **udros*, repr. by Skr. *udrás*, Gr. ὕδρος water-snake, ὕδρα HYDRA.] **1.** An aquatic fur-bearing carnivorous mammal (*Lutra vulgaris*) feeding chiefly on fish, having fin-like legs, webbed feet, and long horizontally flattened tail, which enable it to swim and turn in the water with remarkable rapidity. **b.** Applied to other species of *Lutra*, and allied genera 1781. **2.** The fur or skin of any species of otter. late ME. **3.** A tackle consisting of a float with line and a number of hooks 1851.

1. An O., sir Iohn? Why an O.? *Fal.* Why? She's neither fish nor flesh SHAKS. **b. American O.,** *L. canadensis.* **Sea O.,** *L.* (*Enhydris*) *marina*, which inhabits the American shores of the North Pacific. *attrib.* and *Comb.*, as **o.-dog, -hound,** a dog of a breed used for hunting the o.; **-shell,** any bivalve shell of the genus *Lutraria*; **-spear,** a spear used in hunting otters. Hence **O·tter** *v. intr.* to hunt the o., to fish with the 'o.' tackle (see sense 3).

Otter, var. of OTTO, ATTAR.

Otto (ǫ·to). Also formerly **otter, ottar.** 1639. An altered form of *ottar, otter*, vars. of Pers. *'aṭṭar* ATTAR, in *attar* or *otto of roses*, the fragrant essence of roses. **b.** Hence, *joc.*, in *o. of whisky.* THACKERAY.

Ottoman (ǫ·tŏmăn), *a.* and *sb.*[1] 1600. [- Fr. *Ottoman*, It. *Ottomano*, med.L. *Ottomanus*, med. Gr. Ὀθωμανοί, f. Arab. *'uṭmānī* adj. of proper name *'uṭmān.* See OSMANLI.] **A.** *adj.* Of or belonging to the Turkish dynasty founded *c* 1300 by Othman or Osman I, the branch of the Turks to which he belonged, or the Turkish empire ruled by his descendants; Turkish (of the dominions of the Sultan).

O. Porte, the court or palace of the Sultan; the Turkish government; also called the Porte or Sublime Porte.

B. *sb.* A Turk of the family or tribe of Othman or Osman; a Turkish subject (of the Sultan); an OSMANLI; a Turk in the usual political sense 1605.

It is too late to change, in general use, the familiar Ottomans for the more accurate Osmans or Osmanli 1854. Hence **Ottoma·nic** *a.* and *sb.*

Ottoman (ǫ·tŏmăn), *sb.*[2] 1806. [- Fr. *ottomane* (XVIII), fem. of *ottoman* adj.; cf. prec.] **1.** A cushioned seat like a sofa, but without back or arms; or a small article of the same kind used as a low seat or footstool. **2.** A kind of fabric of silk, or silk and wool 1883.

†O·ttomite. Also **Otta-.** 1604. [f. OTTOM(AN + -ITE[1].] = OTTOMAN *sb.*[1] -1818.

Ottrelite (ǫ·trĕləit). 1812. [f. *Ottrez*, in Belgium, where found; see -LITE.] *Min.* A hydrous silicate of aluminium, iron, and manganese, found in greyish to black crystalline scales 1844.

‖**Ouabaio, wabaio** (wabai·o). 1890. The Somali name of the plant *Acocanthera schimperi*, the juice of which is used to poison arrows. Hence **Ouabaïn, wabaïn** (wabā·in), the glucoside $C_{31}H_{48}O_{12}$, obtained from this plant, in action and composition closely resembling strophanthin.

Ouakari, var. of WAKARI, S. Amer. monkey.

‖**Oubliette** (ublię·t). 1819. [Fr., usu. pl. *oubliettes*, f. *oublier* forget; see -ETTE.] A secret dungeon, access to which was gained only through a trapdoor above; often having a secret pit below, into which the prisoner might be precipitated.

Forgotten like one in the oubliettes of the Bastille 1872.

Ouch (autʃ), *sb.* Now only *arch.* or *Hist.* [ME. *ouche*, arising from misdivision of *a nouche* (cf. *adder*) - OFr. *nosche, nouche* - OFrank. (= OHG.) *nuskja* buckle, clasp, perh. of Celtic origin.] **1.** A clasp, buckle, or brooch (often set with precious stones); hence, a clasped necklace, bracelet, or the like; also, a buckle or brooch worn as an ornament. **2.** The gold or silver setting of a precious stone 1481.

1. Most rich and precious Ouches and Brouches 1563. **2.** Make them [ii stones] to be set in ouches of gold 1551 *Exod.* 28:11. Hence **Ouch** *v. trans.* to set or adorn with, or as with, ouches.

Ought (ǭt), *sb.*[1] (*pron.*), *adv.*, var. of AUGHT *sb.*[2]

Ought, *sb.*[2] 1678. [OUGHT *v.* III used as a noun.] That which is denoted by the verb *ought*; duty, obligation.

Ought, *sb.*[3] *illiterate.* 1844. ['A nought' divided as 'an ought'.] = NOUGHT in sense 'cipher'.

Ought (ǭt), *v.* [OE. *āhte*, ME. *ōhte, oȝte, oughte*, pa. t. of *āgan*, ME. *oȝen, owen* OWE. This partly retains a past sense; but as an auxiliary of predication it has become indefinite as to time; see Branch III, and B.] **A.** as finite verb; properly pa. t. of OWE. **I.** Pa. t. of OWE *v.* in sense 'to have or possess'; possessed, owned. *Obs.* -1670. **II.** Pa. t. of OWE *v.* in its existing sense. **1.** Had to pay; owed. *Obs.* or *dial.* ME. **†b.** *absol.* Was in debt (*to*) -1610. **†2.** *fig.* Owed, had to repay (an ill turn, shame, etc.) -1694. **†b.** Bore (ill or good will, a grudge, a spite, regarded as something yet to be paid or rendered); occas. nearly = showed, rendered (favour, allegiance, etc.) -1678. **†3.** Was indebted or beholden for; owed -1568.

1. He..sayde this other day, You o. him a thousand pound SHAKS. **2. b.** He highly inveighed against many gentlemen..that o. him no homage, as persons disaffected 1678.

III. As auxiliary of predication. The general verb to express duty or obligation of any kind, strictly used of moral obligation, but also expressing what is befitting, proper, correct, or naturally expected. Only in pa. t. (indic. or subj.), which may be either past or present in meaning. (The only current use in standard Eng.) **a.** In past sense: = Owed it to duty; was (were) under obligation (*to do* something). Now only in dependent clause, corresp. to a pa. t. in principal clause; *he said you ought* = he said it was your duty. ME. **b.** In present sense: = Am (is, are) bound or under obligation. (The most frequent sense. Formerly expressed by the pres. t., OWE *v.* III. 1.) ME. **c.** With past sense indicated by a following perf. infin. with *have*; *you o. to have known* = it was your duty to know, you should have known. (The usual modern idiom.) 1551.

a. He did not think that the defendant o. to be kept in prison any longer 1892. **b.** The precedent o. to be followed 'JUNIUS'. **c.** We haue left vndone those thinges whiche we oughte to haue done *Bk. Com. Prayer.*

IV. The pa. pple. *ought* (*aught*) was formerly in literary, and is still in dial. and vulgar use, to form the perfect tense or passive voice of OWE *v.*: **a.** Owed; **b.** Possessed (*mod. Sc.*); **c.** Been obliged (*illiterate*) ME.

b. I would give half of what I am aught, to know if it is still in existence SCOTT. **c.** He hadn't o. to have done it (*mod.*).

B. as present stem, with inflexions (*oughted, oughting*, etc.). *Obs.* or *dial.* **†1.** = A. III, OWE *v.* III. 1. -1654. **2.** *Sc.* To have to pay; = OWE *v.* II. 1. 1552. **3.** *Sc.* To possess; = OWN *v.* 1. 1800.

2. We aught him the siller SCOTT. **3.** There's naebody but you and me that o. the name STEVENSON. Hence **Ou·ghtness** [f. sense III], that quality of an action that is expressed by 'ought'; moral obligatoriness (*rare*).

Ouija (wī·ya, -dʒa). 1904. [- Fr. *oui* yes + G. *ja* yes.] A board used with a planchette for obtaining messages in spiritualistic séances. (Now a registered trade-mark.)

Ouistiti, var. of WISTITI, S. Amer. monkey.

Ounce (auns), *sb.*[1] [ME. *unce* - OFr. *unce* (mod. *once*) :- L. *uncia* twelfth part of a pound or foot (cf. INCH *sb.*[1]), f. *unus* ONE, prob. intended orig. to express a unit.] **1.** A unit of weight; orig., as still in Troy weight, the twelfth of a pound, but in avoirdupois the sixteenth of the pound. **b.** *loosely.* usu. A small quantity. late ME. **c.** *fig.* of imponderable things 1526. **2.** Used to render *onza*, a coin of Spain (= £3 12*s.*) and Sicily (= 10*s.* 3½*d.*) 1799. **3.** *attrib.* Of the weight of one ounce or (in comb.) so many ounces 1846.

1. The Troy o. consists of 480 grains, and is divided into 20 pennyweights; the avoirdupois o. contains 437·5 grains, and is divided into 16 drams; *Fluid o.*, a measure of capacity, containing an avoird. o. of distilled water at 62° Fahr. O.E.D. **b.** My sweete o. of mans flesh, my in-conie Iew SHAKS. **c.** An o. of mothers wit is worth a pound of Clergy RAY.

Ounce (auns), *sb.*[2] ME. [- AFr. **unce*, OFr. *once*, beside *lonce* (the *l* of which was taken for the def. art.), corresp. to It. *lonza*, repr. Rom. **luncia*, f. L. *lynx, lync-* LYNX.] **1.** A name orig. given to the common lynx, subseq. to various other moderate-sized feline beasts, vaguely identified. **2.** *Zool.* A feline beast (*Felis uncia*), also called *mountain-panther*, and *snow-leopard*; it resembles the leopard in marking 1774. **†b.** Applied to the Cheetah or Hunting Leopard -1821.

Ouph(e (auf). 1623. [var. of AUF(E, OAF; perh. a typographical or scribal error for *auph* or *oaph.*] = AUFE.

Strew good lucke (Ouphes) on euery sacred roome SHAKS.

Our (auəɹ), *pron.* [Com. Gmc.: see below.] **A.** *personal pron.* [OE. *ūre* (*ūsser, ūser*), gen. pl. (of 'US') of the 1st pers. pron., = OFris., OS. *ūser*, OHG. *unsēr*, ON. *vár*, Goth. *unsara.*] The genitive pl. of the first personal pronoun: = Of us. *Obs.* (exc. in some phrases, as *in our midst, on our behalf*, and with sense of the objective genitive, as *in our despite, our dismissal, our accusers*, and the like). late ME.

B. *poss. pron.* [As pron. adj. OE. *ūre* (declined like adj. in *-e*) = OFris. *ūse*, OS. *unsa* (Du. *onze, ons*), OHG. *unsēr* (G. *unser*), ON. *várr*, Goth. *unsar.*] **1.** Of or belonging to us, i.e. to the speakers, or the speaker and those whom he speaks for or includes. The possess. adj. corresponding to WE, US; expressing the genitive of possession; also the objective genitive, as *in our defence, our Maker*, etc.; see A. OE. **b.** Of the body of Christians, as *Our Lord*, etc., or of humanity, as *Our Father* OE. **c.** In imperial or royal use, instead of *my* ME. **d.** In vaguer sense: With whom or which we have to do; whom we have in mind; of whom (or which) we are speaking; of the writer and his readers, or merely of the writer. Cf. WE. 1612. **†2.** *absol.*: = OURS -1641. **3. Our Father.** The 'Lord's Prayer': = PATERNOSTER 1882.

1. 'Gainst us, our lives, our children, and our heirs SHAKS. **c.** Geven at Laterane the tenth yere of our popedome 1568. **d.** If we should each kill our man 1612. We must now introduce our reader to the..fisher's cottage SCOTT.

-our, *suffix* (repr. AFr. *-our*, OFr. *-or, -ur, -eör, -eür*, mod.Fr. *-eur*), the earliest spelling of the suffix -OR.

Ourali, var. of WOURALI.

Ourang-outang, -utang, ff. ORANG-OUTANG.

Ourano-: see URANO-.

Ourn (auəɹn), *poss. pron. dial.* late ME. [f. OUR, *poss. pron.*, as in HERN, HISN, etc., app. by form-association with *my, mine, thy, thine.* These *-n* forms are midland and southern.] = OURS.

Ours (auəɹz), *poss. pron.* ME. [In form a double possessive, f. poss. pron. *ur, ure* OUR + *-es*; of north. origin.] The absol. form of the possessive pronoun OUR, used when no sb. follows: Our one, our ones; that or those belonging to us. **b.** *Of ours*: see OF XIII. ME.

He and al his is owris 1533. Ours..is 'a time of loud disputes and weak convictions' MORLEY. **b.** Let us close those wide mouths of ours CARLYLE.

Ourself (auəɹse·lf), *pron.* ME. [A parallel formation to next, with *self* instead of *selves.*] Emphatic and reflexive pronoun, corresponding to *we, us*; orig. = OURSELVES, but later differentiated, so as to be used mostly where *we* refers to a single person or is not definitely plural; e.g. in royal, divine, or editorial utterance, or when used indef. in the sense of *one, oneself.* **1.** *emphatic.* **a.** Standing alone as subject, as object, or predic. *poet.* or *arch.* late ME. **b.** In apposition with *we* or *us.* late ME. **2.** *reflexive*, as direct or indirect obj. ME.

1. a. Which our selfe haue granted SHAKS. Were you sick, o. Would tend upon you TENNYSON. **b.** What touches vs our selfe shall be last seru'd SHAKS. **2.** We..found ourself running among the first DICKENS.

Ourselves (auəɹse·lvz), *pron. pl.* 1495. [The orig. construction was nom. *wē selfe*, acc. *ūs selfe*, dat. *ūs selfum*; whence ME. *us selven.* Bef. 1500, *our(e selfs, our selves* became the standard form; cf. *yourselves*, etc., and see SELF.] **1.** *emphatic.* **a.** Standing alone as subject, as object, or after *be, become*, or the like 1591. **b.** In apposition with *we* or (rarely) *us* 1526. **2.** *reflexive*, as direct or indirect object 1495.

1. a. Our selues will heare Th' accuser SHAKS. **b.** The light..that we have attained vnto our selues BIBLE *Transl. Pref.* **2.** To see oursels as others see us BURNS.

-ous, *suffix*, repr. L. *-osus* (*-a, -um*), forming adjs., with the sense 'abounding in, full of, characterized by, of the nature of'. In Anglo-Fr. and early ME. the forms were the same as in early OFr., e.g. *coveitos, -us, envios, -us*, but the vowel was soon identified with OE. long *ū*, and like it written after 1300 *ou* (*covetous, envious*), the spelling ever since retained, though the sound has passed through (*-ūs, -us*, -us) to (-ɒs, əs). Thus *-ous* became the established type of the suffix, and its addition has become the ordinary mode of anglicizing L. adjs. of many kinds, esp. those in *-eus, -ius, -uus, -er, -ris, -ax, -ox, -oci-endus, -ulus, -vorus, -orus*, e.g. *aqueous, conscious, arduous, alacritous, hilarious, capacious, ferocious, stupendous, garrulous, omnivorous, sonorous*.

b. The compound form *-eous* is sometimes a corruption of another suffix, e.g. in *righteous, courteous, gorgeous*; sometimes, e.g. in *bounteous, duteous*, etc., results from the addition of *-ous* to another suffix.

c. In *Chem.*, adjs. in *-ous* indicate acids and other compounds containing a larger proportion of the element indicated by the stem than those expressed by an adj. in *-ic*; e.g. *cuprous* oxide, *ferrous* salts, *sulphurous* acid, etc.; see -IC 1 b.

d. Nouns of quality from adjs. in *-ous* are usu. formed in *-ousness*, as *covetousness*; those from L. *-osus* have often also forms in *-osity*, as *curiosity*, etc.; but this termination more often accompanies adjs. in -OSE[1].

Ousel, var. OUZEL.

Oust (aust), *v.* 1588. [– AFr. *ouster* = OFr. *oster* (mod. *ôter*) take away, remove :– L. *obstare* oppose, hinder.] **1.** *trans. Law.* To eject, dispossess, disseise; to deprive *of* a corporeal or incorporeal hereditament. **b.** To exclude, bar, take away (a right, privilege, etc.) 1656. **2.** *transf.* To eject from any place or position. Const. *of, from*, or with double obj. 1668. **b.** To drive (a thing) out of use or fashion 1865.

1. Farmers were ousted of their leases made by tenants in tail BLACKSTONE. **2.** It was altogether impossible to o. him from command 1868. **b.** The..waggons were built on those ancient lines whose proportions have been ousted by modern patterns T. HARDY.

Ouster (au·stəɹ). 1531. [– law AFr. *ouster*, subst. use of the infin. (prec.); see -ER[4].] *Law.* Ejection from a freehold, etc., deprivation of a corporeal or incorporeal hereditament; now implying a wrongful dispossession.

‖**Ouster-le-main.** 1485. [– law AFr. *ouster la main*, in med.L. *amovere manum* remove the hand; see prec.] *Feudal Law.* A livery of land out of the sovereign's hands, on a judgement given for one who has pleaded that the sovereign has no title to hold it; also, a judgement or writ granting such livery. **b.** The delivery of lands out of a guardian's hands on a ward's coming of age.

Out, *sb.* 1717. [The adv. OUT, used subst. as a name for itself, or elliptically with some sb. understood.] **1.** Short for *outside*. **2. a.** *pl.* The party which is out of office; usu. opp. to the *ins* 1764. **b.** = OUTSIDE A. 6. 1844. **c.** *pl.* In games: The side that is not playing; in *Cricket*, that is not in; also, the players, on either side, who are not taking part in the scrimmage at Rugby football 1895. **3.** An excursion, outing (*dial.*) 1762. **b.** *Outs and ins*, more usu. *ins and outs*; see IN *sb.* 2. 1773. **4.** *Printing.* An omission 1784. **5.** *pl.* Amounts paid out; rates and taxes (*local*) 1884. **6.** *U.S.* A blemish, flaw 1885.

2. d. *At outs* (U.S.): at odds, at variance 1901.

Out (aut), *a.* ME. [OUT *adv.* used attrib. by ellipsis of a pple. (as *lying*, etc.), or by taking the predic. use of the adv. as adj., or by resolution of compounds with *out-* (e.g. out-worker, out worker).] **1.** External, exterior. Now usu. *outer, outside, external*, or written in comb., as *out-edge*, OUTSIDE. †**2.** Outlying, or at a distance outside some place in question –1726. **3.** In cricket, football, etc.: Played *out*, or away from the home ground; played in the outer parts of the field. (Often hyphened.) 1884. **4.** Beyond the usual or normal (size) 1883.

2. In the o. Parts of his Diocess 1726. Phr. *O. isle* (*o. island*), an isle or island lying away from the mainland. (Often hyphened.) **4.** She was 'rather an o. size', as they say in the Duchy 1894.

Out, *v.* [OE. *ūtian* = OFris. *utia*, OHG. *uzōn*; newly formed XIV (Chaucer) and later.] **1.** *trans.* To put out, drive out, eject, reject, get rid of, dismiss, oust (*from* a place, office, possession, etc.); to do out or deprive (*of* a possession). Now *Obs.* exc. *dial.* **b.** To put out, extinguish, blot out, abolish. *Obs.* exc. *dial.* 1502. **c.** *slang.* (orig. pugilistic): To 'knock out' or disable (an opponent); hence, To render insensible, or kill, by a blow 1896. †**2.** To set out, expose (for sale, etc.) –1670. **3.** To disclose, exhibit; to speak out, vent. *Obs.* exc. *dial.* ME. **4.** *intr.* [From the ellipt. use in OUT *adv.* I. 13.] **a.** To go out, esp. on a pleasure excursion. Also *to o. it* (colloq.) 1846. **b.** *To o. with*: To come out with; to utter (*colloq.*) 1802.

1. Outed of iurisdiction 1602. **4. a.** With that he ups and he outs 1894. **b.** He outs with his lie SPURGEON.

Out (aut), *adv.* [OE. *ūt* = OFris., OS. *ūt* (Du. *uit*), OHG. *ūz* (G. *aus*), ON. *út*, Goth. *ūt*; Gmc. adv. rel. to Skr. prefix *ud-* out (cf. Gr. ὕστερος later :– **udteros*).] **I.** Of motion or direction. **simply*. **1.** Expressing motion or direction from within a space, or from a point considered as a centre. **b.** Implying distribution and division; esp. with *deal, portion, serve, share*, and the like 1535. **2.** Away from some recognized place; e.g. the land, the shore, one's own country; away, to a distance OE. **3.** So as to project or extend beyond the general surface or limits; as in *to hang, jut, shoot*, or *stick out*. *To hold out*: see HOLD *v.* 1535. **b.** Expressing extension or prolongation (in space or time). late ME.

1. The children of the kyngedome shalbe caste oute into vtter darcknes 1551 BIBLE *Matt.* 8:12. General Adams' horse struck o. and kicked me on the shin 1854. I will look o. a book for her 1903. *To call one o.* (see CALL *v.*), *come o., have one o.*, i.e. to a duel. **b.** The great Empire of his Father was parcelled o. into members 1652. **2.** The Freight and Assurance o. and home STEELE. **3.** The room..built o. to serve as a library 1896. **b.** To lengthen o. the period of life GOLDSM.

***in pregnant and transf. uses.* **4.** Expressing removal from its position when *in* OE. **5.** From one's normal or equable state of mind, or ordinary course of action. See PUT *out*. 1588. **b.** From one's harmonious relations. See also FALL *out*. 1530. **6.** So as to be no longer alight or burning; as *to do, go, put out*. late ME. **b.** From being in existence or activity; as *to die, give, go, kill o.* 1523. **7.** To an end ME. **b.** Completely, quite, outright ME. **8.** To an issue, explicit result, or solution; as *to make, find, puzzle, work out*; *to help out*; *to come, fall, turn out* 1534. **9.** To the full, complete, or utmost degree; as in *to deck, fit, rig out* 1555. **10.** From a contained or quiescent state into one of activity, accessibility, or manifestation; as *to break* or *burst out, to open out* OE. **11.** Into utterance of sound; aloud; as *to call, cry, shout, speak out*. late ME. **b.** In the way of disclosure; openly ME. **12.** Into public notice, publicity, or publication; from the printing-press 1542. **b.** Of a person: Into society; into work or service 1782. **13.** With ellipsis of intr. vb. (*go, come*, etc.); hence functioning as a verb without inflexion. late ME. **b.** So *Out with* = have out, bring out ME. **14.** With ellipsis of trans. vb. (*put, bring*, etc.) 1819.

4. Mr. Wood sat..laughing his sides o. THACKERAY. Hanmer got..run o. after a splendid hit 1843. The former member was turned o. 1903. **5.** Neither he nor any other sensible man puts himself o. about new books 1887. **b.** Wine made them fall o. 1637. **6.** A Candle goes half o. in the Light of the Sun ADDISON. **7.** The match to be played o. 1746. Phr. *To fight it o., talk it o. To have it o.*, to bring it to a finish. **8.** Worke o. youre awne saluacion with feare and tremblynge TINDALE *Phil.* 2:12. **10.** The stars come o. M. ARNOLD. **11.** Come hither Herald..And read o. this SHAKS. **b.** If things come o., we should keep counsel 1637. **12.** Not yet set o. in Print ASCHAM. **b.** My sister in town bringing o. a young sister-in-law 1849. **13.** O., damned spot: o., I say SHAKS. Murder will o. 1887. **b.** O. with your cambric, dear ladies, and let us all whimper together THACKERAY.

II. Of position. (Senses corresponding to those in I, as indicating the position resulting from the motion there expressed.)

simply*. **1. Expressing position or situation beyond the bounds of, or not within, a space, etc. late ME. **b.** Not 'in'; in the open air 1440. **c.** Away from home; on an expedition, esp. in arms 1605; *mod.* on strike. **2.** Away or at a distance from some recognized place; abroad in a distant country OE. **b.** Away from the land or shore. late ME. **3.** Projecting; protruding; *spec.* through a rent in the clothing, as *out at elbows, heels*, etc. 1553. **b.** Unfurled, displayed, as a flag, etc. 1720. **4.** Without; on the outside; externally ME.

1. If the River had been o., and the Fields under Water SIR T. BROWNE. My sword was already o. 1843. Obliged to call in money that he had lying o. 1903. **c.** Most of the miners are 'out' 1890. **d.** Phr. *To be out for* (something) (orig. *U.S.*): to have all one's attention, energies, etc., directed towards securing or doing (something); so *to be out to* (do something) 1889. **4.** *Merry W.* v. v. 60.

***in pregnant and transf. uses.* **5.** Removed from its own place or position. *O. of joint*: see JOINT *sb.* I. 1. ME. **b.** Not in office 1605. **c.** No longer in the game, or *in* (IN *adv.* II. 2 c); in Cricket, dismissed from the wickets 1746. **d.** No longer in prison 1885. **6.** †**a.** At fault; nonplussed, puzzled –1681. **b.** Mistaken, in error 1641. **c.** Short for *out of practice, time, tune*, etc. 1588. **d.** At variance, no longer friendly 1565. **7.** Out of pocket; in default; minus (a sum) 1632. **8. a.** No longer burning or alight; extinguished ME. **b.** No longer in vogue; not in season, as game, etc. 1660. **9.** No longer current or lasting; at an end ME. **10.** Become visible; manifest, apparent; (of a plant) in leaf, in flower 1573. **11.** Made known, no longer a secret 1713. **12.** Made public; in circulation; published (as a book, etc.) 1625. **b.** Of a girl or young woman: **a.** Introduced into society; **b.** At work, in domestic service 1814. **c.** In existence 1857.

5. I feare (sir) my shoulder-blade is o. SHAKS. **b.** Court newes..who's in, who's o. SHAKS. **d.** He's o. now on ticket-of-leave 1885. **6. a.** I haue forgot my part, And I am o. SHAKS. **b.** If the captain is not o. in his reckoning 1887. **c.** One string.., which was a little o. 1837. **d.** Launcelet and I are o. SHAKS. **8.** When the Funeral Pyre was o. and the last Valediction over SIR T. BROWNE. **b.** Jewels are quite o. at present GOLDSM. **9.** Before the week was o., he had been duly installed 1885. **10.** The trees are all o. MACAULAY. **12. b.** They are not o., you know, till after the Easter ball MRS. GASKELL. **c.** Fanny was the worst casuist o. 1859.

III. Besides the preceding senses, *out* is used idiomatically with many verbs; e.g. to BEAR *out*, CLEAN *out*, EKE *out*, FACE *out*, etc., which see under the vbs. themselves.

Phr. **Out and about.** Going out and going about, as after an illness, etc. **O. and away.** By far; beyond all others. **O. and home. a.** To a place at a distance, and home again. **b.** *attrib.* Played alternately on their own ground and that of their opponents. **O. and in. a.** Out of a place and in again; in and out. **b.** Outside and inside.

Out, *prep.* ME. [prep. use of the adv. for the usual OUT OF.] **1.** = OUT OF 1. *Obs.* or *arch.* **2.** Outside beyond the limits of, beyond (*lit.* and *fig.*). *Obs.* or *dial.* ME.

1. Whan that the sunne o. the south gan weste CHAUCER. **2.** Both within and o. that Wall SHAKS.

Out, *int.* late ME. [f. OUT *adv.* (see sense I. 13).] **1.** As an imperative exclam., with ellipsis of the vb.; see OUT *adv.* I. 13. **2.** An exclam. of lamentation, abhorrence, or indignant reproach (*arch.* or *dial.*) late ME.

2. O., o., (Lucetta) that wilbe illfauord SHAKS. *O. upon* (*on*), arch. or dial. phr. expressing abhorrence or reproach (cf. *fie upon*.); They crie, O upon him Heretike, to the fyre with hym 1560.

Out- in *comb.* is used with sbs., with vbs. and their derivatives, and with other adverbs.

A. Forming sbs. **I.** In comb. with ordinary sbs. (Stress on *out*. The separation or hyphening of the two elements is in many cases optional.) **1.** In the sense 'Outlying, situated outside the bounds, or remote from the centre'; also, 'outside the house, out of doors'; as *out-district*, OUTFIELD, OUTHOUSE, OUTLAND, OUTPORT, *-village*, *-yard*, etc. **2.** In the sense 'Living, residing, or engaged outside (a house, hospital, borough, city, country, etc.); as *out-dweller*, OUT-PATIENT, -PENSIONER, *-pupil*, *-student*, etc.; also in sense 'external, foreign', as †*out-folk*, *-merchant*, *-people*. **3.** In the sense 'Exterior, external, outward' (one or other of which words would now in most cases be substituted); as in OUTLINE, OUTSIDE; also *out-bough*, *-branch*, *-edge*, *-end*, *-layer*, *-limit*, *-list*, *-porch*, etc. **4.** In the sense 'Out of office', as *out-party* 1817. **5.** In the sense 'Leading out', as *out-path*, *-trail*, *-way*.

II. In comb. with nouns of action, agent-nouns, and verbal sbs., cogn. w. or derived from the simple vb. followed by *out*. **1.** With nouns of action; as OUTBREAK [cf. *break out*], OUTBURST, OUTCOME, *outgush*, *outjet*, etc.; also *outvoyage*, etc. **2.** With agent-nouns; as OUTFITTER, OUTPUTTER, etc. **3.** With vbl. sbs. in *-ing*; as OUTGOING, etc.

B. Forming *adjs.* (Stress on *out.*) **1.** With ppl. adjs. in *-ing* (OE. *-ende*), from pres. pples.; as *outbreaking* [cf. *break out*], *outlying*, *outstanding*, etc. **2.** With ppl. adjs. in *-ed*, *-en*, etc. (from pa. pples.); as OUTBOUND, OUTCAST, etc.; also *out-flung*, *-pointed*, *-pushed*, etc. **3.** With a sb. (as obj. of *out* prep.), forming adjs., meaning 'Out of or outside the thing named'; as OUT-COLLEGE, OUTDOOR, etc. **4.** Parasynthetic derivatives from phrases in which *out* mostly means 'projecting, protruding', forming adjs.; as *out-kneed*, *-lipped*, *-shouldered*, etc.

C. *Out-* in comb. forming verbs. (Stress on the second element.) **I.** Separable or syntactic combinations. (In ME. prop. two words; in mod. use, more or less, *habitual nonce-wds.*, made up each time.) **1.** With intrans. vbs., in the same sense as the simple vb. followed by *out*; as OUTBREAK, *outflash out-flow*, *outgive*, etc. late ME. **2.** With trans. vbs., in the same sense as the simple vb. followed by *out*. **a.** With the force of: Out, away; out of existence; out of a socket or place, loose; outward, so as to project; forth; into the open, into manifestation; as OUTBEAR, *out-cast*, OUTPOUR, etc. **b.** With the force of 'completely, thoroughly', 'to a finish'; as OUTPLAY; also *out-tire*, etc. late ME. **3.** Forming trans. vbs. with the sense 'to put or drive out by means of' the action expressed in the simple vb. (cf. *bow out*, *crowd out*, etc.); as *outhiss*, *outjeer*, *outjest*.

II. Compound vbs. in *out-*, with the trans. force of exceeding or going beyond some thing or person in some action. **Formed on verbs*. **1.** To pass beyond, exceed (a defined point, a limit in time, space, degree, etc.), by or in the action expressed by the simple vb.; as OUTGROW (2), OUTLAST, OUTPASS, *out-reign*, OUTRUN, etc. 1603. **2.** To surpass, excel or outdo (a person, etc.) in the action of the simple vb. The number of these compounds is unlimited, Examples are: *out-bellow*, OUTBID, *out-bloom*, *outclimb*, *outdance*, OUTDO, *outflash*, *outgive*, *outglare*, *outjuggle*, *outlabour*, *outlie*, OUTLIVE, *outlove*, *outpace*, *outplan*, *outplay*, *outpray*, *outpreach*, *outreign*, *outroar*, OUTRUN, *outsoar*, *outsparkle*, *outspeed*, *outstrike*, *outswear*, *outsweeten*, *out-trot*, etc. **b.** To get the better of, defeat, beat, in some reciprocal action or contest; as OUTBALANCE, OUTBRAVE, *outmate*, *outpeer*, *outpoise*, OUTRIVAL, *outscold*, 1600. **c.** To overcome or defeat by the action expressed by the simple verb; as *out-baffle*, *outfrown*, *outhector*, *outreason*, *outroar*, etc. **3.** To exceed or do more than is expressed by the simple vb.; as *outlas* to load more than Atlas, *outbeggar* to more than beggar, etc. late ME.

***Formed on adjectives*. **4.** To exceed or surpass in the quality expressed by the adj.; as *out-active*, *-black*, *-swift*, etc. 1605.

****Formed on sbs*. **5.** On names of qualities, actions, or objects: To exceed in the quality or action, or in ref. to the thing, expressed by the sb.; as *outlove*, *outlustre*, *outmeasure*, OUTNUMBER, OUTRANGE, *out-value*, *outvoice*, etc. **6.** On names of persons, actors, agents: To excel, surpass, or outdo in executing the office, or acting the part characteristic of the person or agent in question; as OUTFOOL, OUTGENERAL, etc. **7.** Hence (cf. prec. senses 2–6), esp. with proper names of persons, nations, sects, etc., in the sense of 'to outdo the person, etc., in question in his special attribute'. The classical example is Shakespeare's OUT-HEROD *Herod*. Other examples are *out-Darwin*, *-Quixote*, *-Zola*, etc. See also Main words.

Out-a·ct, *v.* 1644. [OUT- C. II. 2.] *trans.* To surpass in acting or performing; to excel, outdo.

Garrick says 'She so much outacted him it is time for him to leave the stage' 1776.

Out and out, ou·t-and-ou·t. *adv. phr.* (*a.*) ME. [Cf. OUT *adv.* I. 7.] Thoroughly, completely, entirely; downright. **b.** *adj.* Complete, unqualified 1813.

She was wyckyd oute and oute. late ME. **b.** They're the out-and-outest young scamps 1868. Hence **Ou·t-and-ou·ter**, a thorough or perfect type of his or its kind (*colloq.* or *slang*) 1812.

Out-a·rgue, *v.* 1748. [OUT- C. II. 2.] *trans.* To get the better of in argument.

†**Outas, outes.** *Obs.* exc. *dial.* [Early ME. *uthēs*, app. repr. an OE. **ūthǣs*, f. *ūt* out + *hǣs* command; see HEST *sb.*] = OUTCRY *sb.* 1.

Out-a·sk, *v. dial.* 1642. [OUT- C. I. 2 b.] *trans.* To 'ask' the banns of marriage of (a couple) in church for the last time 1719.

Out-ba·bble, *v.* 1649. [OUT- C. I. 2, II. 2.] *trans.* **a.** To babble out. **b.** To exceed in babble or noisy talk.

Ou·tback, *adv. Austral.* 1890. [f. OUT *adv.* + BACK *adv.*] Out in or to the back settlements or back-country. Also as *adj.* (1900) and *sb.* (1907).

Outbalance (autbæ·lăns), *v.* 1644. [OUT- C. II. 2 b.] = OUTWEIGH *v.*

Outbear (autbēᵊ·ɹ), *v.* ME. [OUT- C. I. 2, II. 2.] **1.** *trans.* To carry forth. **2.** *Naut.* To carry more sail than; hence, to outsail 1691.

Outbi·d, *v.* 1587. [OUT- C. II. 2, 1.] **1.** *trans.* To outdo in bidding; to offer a higher price than. **2.** *fig.* To outdo in any quality, statement, etc. 1597.

Outblaze (autblēⁱ·z), *v.* 1711. [OUT- C. I. 1, II. 2.] **1.** *intr.* To blaze forth, burst out with ardour. **2.** *trans.* To surpass in blazing; *fig.* to outshine in brilliancy 1742.

Outblu·sh, *v.* 1634. [OUT- C. II. 2.] *trans.* To outdo in blushing, to surpass in rosy colour.

Outblu·ster, *v.* 1748. [OUT- C. I. 3, II. 2 b, c.] **1.** *trans.* To drive or do out of by blustering. **2.** To outdo in blustering, to get the better of by bluster 1863.

Outboard (au·tbōᵊɹd), *a.*, *adv.* 1823. [f. OUT- B. 3 + BOARD *sb.* Cf. INBOARD.] **A.** *adj.* **a.** Situated on the outside of a ship or boat, as *o. motor*. **b.** Outward from the median line of a ship 1893. **B.** *adv.* **a.** In a direction outward from a ship's side, or laterally away from the centre of a ship 1836. **b.** Of position: Outside a ship or boat; nearer to the outside than something else 1869.

†**Ou·tborn**, *a.* (*sb.*) 1450. [OUT- B. 2.] Born out of the country; of foreign birth. **B.** *sb.* A foreigner. –1550.

Ou·t-bound, *a.* 1598. [OUT- B. 2.] Outward bound.

Out-bra·g, *v.* 1565. [OUT- C. II. 2.] *trans.* To outdo in bragging; to go beyond in boastful talk.

Outbrave (autbrēⁱ·v), *v.* 1589. [OUT- C. II. 2 b.] **1.** *trans.* To face defiantly. **2.** To surpass in daring 1596. **b.** To outdo in beauty, finery or splendour of array; cf. BRAVERY 3. 1589. **c.** To outrival (in any quality) 1589.

2. b. The Lillies of the field outbraued him 1597.

Outbra·zen, *v.* 1681. [OUT- C. I. 2 b, II. 2 + BRAZEN *v.*] **1.** *trans.* To face out defiantly or impudently. **2.** To outdo in unabashedness 1702.

Outbreak (au·tbrēⁱk), *sb.* 1602. [OUT- A. II. 1.] **1.** A breaking out; an eruption; an outburst of hostilities, of disease, etc. **2.** *Geol.* An outcrop; the emergence of a rock or stratum 1797. **3.** An insurrection 1849.

1. The flash and out-breake of a fiery minde SHAKS.

Outbreak (autbrēⁱ·k), *v.* OE. [OUT- C. I. 1.] *intr.* To break out. Now only *poet.*

Outbreathe (autbrī·ð), *v.* 1559. [OUT- C. I. 1, 2.] *trans.* To breathe out; to emit as breath. Now *poet.* Also *intr.* or *absol.*

Outbreathed (autbre·pt), *ppl. a.* 1597. [f. OUT- + BREATH + -ED.] Put out of breath. Now *poet.*

Outbuild (-bi·ld), *v.* 1742. [OUT- C. II. 2, 1, I. 2.] **1.** *trans.* To surpass in building or durability of building; also, *catachr.* to over-build. **2.** To build out (*poet.* and *rhet.*) 1847.

Ou·t-bui:lding. 1626. [OUT- A. I. 1.] A detached building, subordinate and accessory to a main building; an out-house.

Out-bu·rn, *v.* late ME. [OUT- C. I. 2, II. 2, 1.] **1.** *intr.* To burn out or away. **2.** *trans.* To burn longer than 1742.

2. Lamps which outburn'd Canopus TENNYSON.

Outburst (au·tbɒ̄ɹst), *sb.* 1657. [OUT- A. II. 1.] **1.** An act of bursting out; an outbreak, explosion (of feeling, indignation, etc.). **2.** = OUTBREAK *sb.* 2. 1708.

1. Tom was a little shocked at Maggie's o. GEO. ELIOT.

Ou·t-by, -bye, *adv.* (*adj.*) *Sc.* and *north.* late ME. [f. OUT *adv.* + BY *adv.*] Out a little way; outside the house, abroad, in the open air; to the outside (of a house, farm, etc.).

Outcast (au·tkɑst), *sb.* ME. [subst. use of next.] **1.** A person 'cast out' or rejected; a pariah; an exile; a homeless vagabond. **2.** Refuse, offal; a plant thrown out from a garden. late ME.

1. I am a worme and no man: a very scorne of men and the o. of the people COVERDALE *Ps.* 21[2]:6.

Outcast (au·tkɑst), *ppl. a.* late ME. [OUT- B. 2.] **1.** Of persons: Abject, socially despised; later, Cast out from home and friends; hence, forsaken, homeless, and neglected. **2.** Of things: Rejected, discarded 1560.

1. I all alone beweep my o. state SHAKS.

Ou:tca·ste, *v.* 1867. [f. OUT- + CASTE *sb.* 2, 4, after prec.] *trans.* To put (a person) out of his caste; to cause to lose caste. So **Ou·tcaste** *sb.* one who has lost his caste; one of no caste; *adj.* of no caste.

Outcasting (au·tkɑ:stiŋ), *vbl. sb.* late ME. [OUT- A. II. 3.] The action of casting out; ejection; rendering outcast.

Outclass (autklɑ·s), *v.* 1870. [OUT- C. II. 5.] *Sporting.* To beat (a rival) so completely as to put him virtually out of the same class; to leave 'nowhere' in a race or contest.

transf. As a liar, I out-classed every man on board 1893.

Ou·t-clea:ring, *vbl. sb.* 1875. [OUT- A. II. 1.] *Banking.* The sending out of bills of exchange and cheques to the clearing-house for settlement; hence, the bills and cheques collectively thus sent out to be cleared; the converse of IN-CLEARING.

Ou·t-co:llege, *a.* 1861. [OUT- B. 3.] Not residing within the walls of a college; applied chiefly to members of a college who reside or lodge outside.

Outcome (au·tkɒm), *sb.* ME. [OUT- A. II. 1.] †**1.** The act or fact of coming out; *Sc.* the time of year when days begin to lengthen –1715. **2.** That which comes out of something; visible or practical result, effect, or product. (orig. *Sc.* app. made Eng. by Carlyle.) 1788. **3.** An outlet 1885.

2. We do the man's intellectual endowment great wrong, if we measure it by its mere intellectual o. CARLYLE.

Outcrop (au·tkrǫp), *sb.* 1805. [OUT- A. II. 1.] *Mining* and *Geol.* The cropping out of a stratum or vein at the surface; the edge of the stratum or vein thus cropping out. **b.** *fig.* A coming into outward manifestation 1864.

Ou·tcrop, *v.* 1845. [f. prec. sb.] *intr.* **a.** *Mining* and *Geol.* To crop out (see CROP *v.*), as a stratum or vein. **b.** *fig.* To come out casually 1856. Hence **Ou·tcropper**, a miner who works an outcrop.

Outcry (au·tkrəi), *sb.* late ME. [OUT- A. II. 1.] **1.** The act of crying out; loud clamour; noise, uproar; hence, an emphatic protest. **2.** A public sale to the highest bidder; an auction. *Obs.* or *local.* 1600.

Outcry·, *v.* late ME. [OUT- C. I. 1, 2, II.

2.] †1. a. *intr.* To cry out. b. *trans.* To cry aloud, make an outcry; to proclaim. –1654. 2. To cry louder than; to shout down 1530.

Outda·re, *v.* 1593. [OUT- C. II, 2, 2 c.] 1. *trans.* To overcome by daring; to outbrave, defy. 2. To dare more than 1607.

Outda·zzle, *v.* 1705. [OUT- C. II. 2.] *trans.* To outdo in brilliancy; to outshine.

Outdi·stance, *v.* 1857. [OUT- C. II. 2 b.] *trans.* To outstrip (in a race; hence, in any competition or career.)

Outdo (autdū·), *v.* ME. [OUT- C. I. 2, II. 2, 2 c.] †1. *trans.* To put out. (In ME. two wds.) –1603. 2. To exceed in doing; to excel, surpass, beat; to be superior to 1607. b. To defeat, overcome; to exhaust 1677.

2. Wherein the Grauer had a strife With Nature, to out-doo the life B. JONS.

Ou·t-door, ou·tdoor, *a.* 1765. [OUT- B. 3.] 1. That is done, exists, lives, or is used, out of doors, or in the open air. 2. Relieved or administered outside or apart from residence in a workhouse, etc.; as *o. pension, relief* 1833. 3. Applied to the outward or down stroke of a Cornish pumping engine 1875.

Ou:tdoo·rs, *adv.* 1844. [OUT *prep.*] Out of doors; in the open air; also as *sb.* = OUT-OF-DOOR B.

Ou·tdraught. 1857. [OUT- A. II. 1.] An outward draught of air; the 'back-wash' of a wave.

Outdri·nk, *v.* 1593. [OUT- C. I. 2 b, II. 2.] *trans.* a. To drink (anything) out or up, drink dry. b. To drink more than.

Outdri·ve, *v.* ME. [OUT- C. I. 2, II. 2.] †1. *trans.* To drive out, expel. (Prop. two wds.) ME only. 2. To drive faster than 1611. 3. *Golf.* To drive farther than 1906.

Outer (au·təɹ), *a.* (*sb.*[1]) late ME. [A new comparative formed on OUT, instead of UTTER from OE. *ūterra, uttra. Outer* is not followed by *than.*] 1. That is farther out than another (distinguished as *inner*), exterior; farther from the centre or inside; hence, relatively far out; external; of or pertaining to the outside. 2. Said of the objective or physical as opp. to the subjective or psychical world. late ME.

1. But the children of the kingdom shall be cast out into o. darkness *Matt.* 8:12. 2. Phr. *O. man*, the body (after *inner man*); hence joc., personal appearance, dress (so *o. woman*). *O. world*, the material world outside that familiar or known; also, people generally, outside one's immediate circle.

B. *ellipt.* as *sb.* In rifle-shooting, that part of the target outside the circles surrounding the bull's eye; hence, a shot that hits this part 1862.

Outer (au·təɹ), *sb.*[2] 1898. [f. OUT *v.* + -ER[1].] *Pugilism.* A knock-out blow.

Outermost (au·təɹmōst), *a.* (*adv.*) 1857. [f. OUTER *a.* + MOST, after *innermost, uppermost.*] Farthest out from the inside or centre; most outward; most external; extremest. b. as *adv.* In the most outward position 1858.

Beyond the o. part of the o. Heaven 1665.

Outfa·ce, *v.* 1529. [OUT- C. II. 2 b, c.] 1. *trans.* To outdo in facing or confronting; to look (a person) out of countenance; to stare down; hence, to put out of countenance generally. 2. To brave, defy 1574. †3. To give the lie to boldly or defiantly –1686. †b. To maintain boldly or impudently to the face of (a person), *that*, etc. –1678. †4. To brazen out –1692.

1. See if thou canst out-face me with thy lookes SHAKS. 2. They..o. you with an eye that challenges inquiry 1870.

Ou·tfall. 1629. [OUT- A. II. 1.] The outlet or mouth of a river, drain, sewer, etc., where it falls into the sea, lake, etc.

†Ou·tfangthie:f. [repr. *ūtfangenne þēof 'out-caught thief', corresp. to *infangenne þēof* INFANGTHIEF, q.v.] *OE. Law.* Orig., the lord's right to pursue a thief (at least when the latter was 'his own man') outside his own jurisdiction, bring him back to his own court for trial, and keep his forfeited chattels on conviction. By the 13th c. its meaning had become conjectural.

Out-field, outfield (au·tfīld). 1637. [OUT- A. I. 1.] 1. The outlying land of a farm; esp. in Scotland, the outlying land which is either unenclosed and untilled moorland or pasture, or was formerly cropped from time to time without being manured. b. An outlying field 1676. 2. In *Cricket* and *Baseball*: The part of the field most remote from the batsman 1895. b. = OUT-FIELDER 1884.

1. *fig.* Words are enclosures from the great o. of meaning TRENCH. *O. and infield system*: see INFIELD.

Ou·t-fie:lder. 1893. [OUT- A. I. 1.] The player or fielder who stands in the out-field; see prec. 2. So **Ou·t-fie:lding** *vbl. sb.*

Outfi·ght, *v.* 1643. [OUT- C. II. 2 b.] To fight better than.

Outfit (au·tfit), *sb.* 1769. [OUT- A. II. 1.] 1. The act of fitting out or furnishing with requisites; *ellipt.* = expenses of fitting out. 2. The articles and equipment required for an expedition, journey, etc.; a set of things for any purpose. orig. *U.S.* 1787. 3. A travelling party or a party in charge of cattle, etc.; a person along with his conveyance, his tools, or the like *U.S.* 1872.

2. *fig.* Man's mental and moral o. 1872.

Ou·tfit, *v.* 1840. [f. prec. sb.] *trans.* To provide with an outfit, to fit out. Also *intr.* for *refl.* or *pass.* So **Ou·tfitter**, *spec.* a dealer in outfits for travelling, athletic sports, etc.

Outfla·me, *v.* 1839. [OUT- C. II. 2, I. 1.] a. *trans.* To surpass in blaze or brilliancy. b. *intr.* To flame out, burst into blaze. *poet.*

Outflank (autflæ·ŋk), *v.* 1765. [OUT- C. II. 2 c, 1.] 1. *trans.* To extend or get beyond the flank of the opposing army. b. *fig.* To 'get round', get the better of 1773. 2. To lie or extend beyond (the flank). Also *intr.* 1796.

1. b. We were outflanked by the law 1773.

Ou·tflow, *sb.* 1800. [OUT- A. II. 1.] 1. The act or fact of flowing out, efflux 1839. b. The amount that flows out 1875. 2. *fig.* Any outward movement analogous to the outflowing of water 1800.

Outfly·, *v.* 1591. [OUT- C. I. 1, II. 1, 2.] 1. *intr.* To fly out (*poet.*) 1599. 2. *trans.* To outstrip or surpass in flight; to fly beyond or past 1591.

1. Out-flew Millions of flaming swords MILT.

Outfoo·l, *v.* 1638. [OUT- C. II. 2, 2 c.] *trans.* To outdo in folly or fooling; to overcome by fooling.

Outfoo·t, *v.* 1737. [OUT- C. II. 2, 5.] *trans.* To surpass in footing it; to outpace; to outstrip in dancing, running, or sailing; to outrun.

Ou·tgate, *sb.* (*adv.*) Now *Sc.* and *n. dial.* ME. [OUT- A. II. 1.] 1. The action of going out; exit, egress; debouching. 2. An outlet; *fig.* a way of escape or deliverance 1456.

Outge·neral, *v.* 1767. [OUT- C. II. 6.] *trans.* To outdo or defeat in generalship; to get the better of as by superior military skill.

Ou·tgo, *sb.* 1640. [OUT- A. II. 1.] 1. The fact of going out, or that which goes out; *spec.* outlay; opp. to *income.* 2. The action of going out; outflow 1858.

Outgo (autgō[u]·), *v.* OE. [OUT- C. I. 1, II. 2, 1.] 1. *intr.* To go out, go forth. (In OE. and ME. usu. two wds.) *Obs.* or *rare.* 2. *trans.* To go faster than; to outdistance (*arch.*) 1530. 3. To go beyond (a point, bounds, etc.); to exceed, surpass; to outdo 1553.

Ou·tgo:er. late ME. [OUT- A. II. 2.] One who goes out (see GO *v.*); esp. one who goes out of a place, office, or tenancy.

Ou·tgo:ing, *vbl. sb.* ME. [OUT- A. II. 3.] 1. The action or fact of going out or forth. †2. A passage or way of exit or egress –1609. b. †The outer limit; the upper termination of an inclined stratum. late ME. 3. (Usu. *pl.*) Outlay, expenses, charges 1622.

1. Men that go out of the bath and drynke muche wyne after theyr outgoyng 1562. 2. b. The coast of Manasseh also was on the north side of the river, and the outgoings of it were at the sea *Josh.* 22:9.

Ou·tgo:ing, *ppl. a.* 1633. [OUT- B. 1.] That goes out; issuing, outflowing. b. Going out from office, position, or possession.

Outgrow (autgrō[u]·), *v.* 1594. [OUT- C. II. 2, 1, I. 1.] 1. *trans.* To grow faster than; to grow taller or bigger than. 2. To grow out of, to become too large for (clothes, etc.) 1691. 3. *fig.* To leave behind in the process of growth or development 1665.

2. 'I doubt they'll o. their strength', she added GEO. ELIOT. 3. Even our gray heads o. not those errors which we have learn't before the Alphabet 1665.

Outgrowth (au·tgrō[u]þ). 1837. [OUT- A. II. 1.] The process of growing out; that which grows out of or from anything; an offshoot; an excrescence. b. *fig.* Of things immaterial: A natural product 1850.

b. Primogeniture is not a natural o. of the family 1857.

Ou·t-guard. 1623. [OUT- A. I. 1, 3.] A guard placed at a distance outside the main body of an army, an advanced guard, an outpost.

Outhaul (au·tˌhǭl). 1840. [OUT- A. II. 1.] *Naut.* A rope used for hauling out a sail upon a spar; opp. to *inhaul.* So **Ou·thau:ler** 1793.

Outher (au·ðəɹ, ǭ·ðəɹ), *adv.* (*conj.*) Now *dial.* ME. [The neuter or uninflected form of *outher* pron. = EITHER.] An early equivalent of EITHER B. 2.

Out-Herod (autˌhe·rǫd), *v.* 1602. [OUT- C. II. 7.] *To out-Herod Herod*: to outdo Herod in violence; hence, to outdo in any excess of evil or extravagance.

Haml. III. ii. 16.

Outhouse (au·tˌhaus). ME. [OUT- A. I. 1.] A house or building, belonging to and adjoining, and subsidiary to, a dwelling-house; e.g. a stable, barn, wash-house, etc.

Outing (au·tiŋ), *vbl. sb.* 1440. [f. OUT *v.* + -ING[1].] 1. The action of putting or driving out. Now *rare* or *Obs.* 2. An airing, excursion, pleasure-trip. Orig. *dial.* 1786.

Outjo·ckey, *v.* 1714. [OUT- C. II. 2 b, c.] *trans.* To get the better of by adroitness or trickery.

Ou·tkeeper. 1875. [OUT- A. II. 2.] An instrument used with the surveyor's compass, to keep tally in chaining.

Outland (au·tlænd), *sb.* and *a.* OE. [OUT- A. I. 1.] A. *sb.* 1. A land that is outside, a foreign land. (Now only a poetic archaism.) †2. The outlying land of an estate or manor. In OE. and feudal tenure, that part which the lord granted to tenants. (Opp. to INLAND 1.) –1848. †3. *Out-lands*: the outlying lands of a province, district, or town. *Amer. Colonies.* –1731. B. *adj.* [In origin an attrib. use of the sb.] 1. Of or belonging to another country; foreign, alien. Now *poet.* or *arch.* late ME. 2. *Sc.* Outlying 1791.

Outlander (au·tlændəɹ). 1605. [f. prec. + -ER[1], after Du. *uitlander*, G. *ausländer.*] A man of foreign nationality; a foreigner, alien, stranger. (Now *poet.*, or a literary revival.) b. In ref. to S. African politics, a rendering of Du. *uitlander*, as applied, before the war of 1899–1902, to aliens settled or sojourning in the South African Republic 1892.

Outlandish (autlæ·ndiʃ), *a.* [OE. *ūtlendisć*, f. *ūtland* OUTLAND A. 1; see -ISH[1].] 1. Foreign, alien; not native or indigenous. *arch.* 2. Foreign-looking, of foreign fashion; unfamiliar, strange; odd, bizarre, uncouth 1596. 3. Out-of-the way, remote; far removed from civilization (now usu. derogatory) 1869.

1. But kynge Salomon loued many o. women COVERDALE 1 *Kings* 11:1. 2. They were dressed in a quaint o. fashion W. IRVING. 3. Living in such an o. place T. HARDY. Hence **Outla·ndishly** *adv.*, **-ness.**

Outlast (autla·st), *v.* 1573. [OUT- C. II. 1, 2.] *trans.* To last longer than or beyond; to exceed in duration; to survive.

Outlaugh (autla·f), *v.* 1477. [OUT- C. II. 2, 2 c.] †1. *trans.* To laugh down, deride –1790. 2. To outdo in laughing 1672.

Outlaw (au·tlǭ), *sb.* [Late OE. *ūtlaga* – ON. *útlagi*, f. *útlagr* outlawed, banished, f. *út* OUT + *lagu, *lǫg* LAW.] One put outside the law and deprived of its benefits and protection; one under sentence of OUTLAWRY. b. More vaguely: An exile, a fugitive ME.

Outlaw (au·tlǭ:), *v.* [Late OE. *ūtlagian*, f. *ūtlaga*; see prec.] 1. *trans.* To put outside the law; to proscribe; †to exile, banish; to declare an outlaw. 2. To deprive of legal force. Now only in U.S. 1647.

1. *fig.* Charite is outelawed amonge hom WYCLIF.

Outlawry (au·tlǭri). late ME. [In early forms repr. AFr. *utlagerie*, AL. *utlagaria* (XI), f. OE. *ūtlaga* (whence AL. *utlaga* XI) + Rom. suffix *-erie* -ERY, -RY. In anglicized form *outlawry* from XIV.] **1.** The action of putting a person out of the protection of the law, or the legal process by which a person is or was proclaimed or made an outlaw; the condition of one so outlawed. †In early use, often = exile, banishment. **2.** Disregard or defiance of the law 1869.

Outlay (au·tlēⁱ), *sb.* 1798. [OUT- A. II. 1.] The act or fact of laying out or expending; expenditure (of money upon something). Orig. *Sc.* and *dial.*

Outlay (autlēⁱ·), *v.* 1555. [OUT- C. I. 2.] **1.** *trans.* To lay out; to spread out, display. Now *rare* or *poet.* **2.** To lay out (money), expend 1802.

Ou·tleap, *sb.* ME. [OUT- A. II. 1.] An act of leaping out; an escape, sally, or excursion; an outburst (*lit.* and *fig.*).

Outlea·p, *v.* 1600. [OUT- C. II. 1, 2, I. 1.] **1.** *trans.* To leap over or beyond. **2.** To surpass in leaping 1629. **3.** *intr.* To leap out or forth (*poet.*) 1850.

Outlet (au·tlėt). ME. [OUT- A. II. 1.] **1.** A place or means of issue; a vent; a passage out, an exit. Also *transf.* and *fig.* **2. a.** A place into which anything is let out; *spec.* a pasture into which cattle are let out. **b.** A field, yard, or other enclosure attached to a house. 1752. †**3. a.** The outlying parts; the environs of a town. **b.** The suburban streets or roads passing into the country. –1771. **4.** Discharge, escape by outflow (*lit.* and *fig.*) 1640. **5.** *attrib.*, as *o.-pipe*, etc. 1762.

1. Like the Caspian Sea, receiving all, and having no Out-let FULLER.

Outle·t, *v. Obs.* or *rare.* 1592. [OUT- C. I. 2.] *trans.* To let out, give egress to, pass forth.

Outlie·, *v.* 1873. [f. OUT- C. II. 1 + LIE *v.*¹] *trans.* To lie beyond or on the outside of.

Ou·tli:er. 1610. [OUT- A. II. 2.] **1.** One who lies (i.e. sleeps or lodges) out, i.e. in the open air, or away from his place of business, etc. 1676. **b.** An outsider 1690. **c.** An outlying deer, etc. 1658. **2. a.** A boulder 1610. **b.** *Geol.* A portion of a geological formation lying *in situ* at a distance from the main body, the intervening part having been removed by denudation 1833. **c.** *gen.* An outlying portion or member of anything 1849.

2. c. Great mountain outliers, isolated or branching from the central chain RUSKIN.

†**Outligger, outlicker.** 1481. [f. OUT- A. II. 2 + *ligger*, f. *lig*, dial. form of LIE *v.*¹; lit. 'outlier'; cf. Du. *uitligger*. See *outrigger*.] *Naut.* **1.** A spar projecting from a vessel to extend some sail, or to make a greater angle for some rope, etc. 1626. **2.** = OUTRIGGER 2. –1755.

Outline (au·tləin), *sb.* 1662. [f. OUT- A. I. 3.] **1.** *pl.* The lines, real or apparent, by which a figure is defined or bounded in the plane of vision; the sum of these lines forming the contour of a figure. **b.** *sing.* The contour thus defined 1828. **2.** A sketch or drawing in which an object is represented by lines of contour without shading 1735. **3.** A rough draft or sketch in words; a description omitting details 1759. **b.** in *pl.* The main features of any subject; the general principles 1710. **4.** *attrib.*, as *o.-map*, *-stitch*, etc. 1859.

1. b. He..beheld in the distance the black o. of a gallows SCOTT. 2. *In o.*, with only the o. drawn, represented, or visible. 3. b. His Drama at present has only the Out-lines drawn STEELE. Hence **Outli·near** *a.* of the nature of an o.

Outline (au·tləin), *v.* 1790. [f. prec. sb.] **1.** *trans.* To draw or trace the exterior line of; to draw in outline. **b.** To indicate or define the outline of 1817. **2.** To sketch in general terms 1855.

2. The scheme outlined in Mr. Bright's speech 1880.

Outlive (autli·v), *v.* 1472. [OUT- C. II. 2, 1.] **1.** *trans.* To live longer than; to survive; also, to live longer than (a thing) lasts. **b.** To outlast 1597. **2.** To live through or beyond (a specified time) 1657. **b.** To pass through (a certain state or experience); to outgrow 1641. †**3.** *intr.* To survive SHAKS. **4.** *trans.* To excel in (virtuous) living 1883.

1. Asham'd his Country's freedom to out-live 1695. 2. b. They have outlived the age of weakness JOHNSON.

Outlook (au·tluk), *sb.* 1667. [OUT- A. II. 1.] **1.** The act or practice of looking out; vigilant watch (*lit.* and *fig.*) 1815. **2.** A place from or by which a view is obtained; a lookout 1667. **3.** The view or prospect from a place or point 1828. **b.** A mental view or survey 1742. **c.** The prospect for the future 1832. **4.** *attrib.*, as *o. post*, etc. 1851.

1. Jackdaws..on the out-look for plunder 1862. 3. c. My political o. is very gloomy MACAULAY.

Outloo·k, *v.* 1595. [OUT- C. II. 2 c.] *trans.* To look or stare down; to outstare. *John* V. ii. 115.

Outlying (au·tləi:iŋ), *ppl. a.* 1663. [OUT- B. 1.] **1.** Lying or situated outside certain limits; hence *fig.* extrinsic, extraneous. Of a beast: That makes its lair outside a park or enclosure. **2.** Lying at a distance from the centre of an area; remote, out-of-the-way; living at a distance from centres of population 1689.

2. Some of these out-lying Parts of the World 1689.

Outmanœu·vre, -ver, *v.* 1799. [OUT- C. II. 2.] *trans.* To outdo in manœuvring; to get the better of by superior strategy.

Outma·rch, *v.* 1647. [OUT- C. II. 2.] *trans.* To outdo in marching, to march faster or farther than; to march so as to leave behind.

Outma·tch, *v.* 1603. [OUT- C. II. 2 b.] *trans.* To be more than a match for; to outdo.

Outmoded (autmōᵘ·dėd), *ppl. a.* 1903. [f. OUT *adv.* II. 8. b + MODE II. 1 + -ED¹, after Fr. *démodé*.] Out of fashion, obsolete.

Outmost (au·tmōᵘst, -məst), *a.* ME. [var. of *utmest* UTMOST, which it gradually supplanted as superlative of *out*.] **1.** Most outward, farthest out; outermost. **b.** Hence, Most remote, farthest off, utmost 1561. †**2.** *ellipt.* The utmost point, degree, or limit; esp. in phr. *to the outmost* –1692.

Outmo·ve, *v.* 1635. [OUT- C. II. 2, 2 b.] †**1.** *trans.* To surpass or exceed in moving –1761. **2.** To defeat by a move, as in chess 1860.

Outness (au·tnės). 1709. [f. OUT *adv.* or *adj.* + -NESS.] The quality, fact, or condition of being external, esp. to the percipient or to the mind; externality.

Outnu·mber, *v.* 1670. [OUT- C. II. 5.] *trans.* To number more than.

Out of (au·tǫ̆v, -əv), *prep. phr.* OE. [orig., and still in writing, two words, viz. OUT *adv.* followed by OF *prep.* (in its primary sense = from).] **1.** Of motion or direction: From within, from. **2.** Of position: Not in or within, outside ME. **b.** Deprived or destitute of, without 1599. **c.** Taken or derived from (*spec.* of a foal in ref. to its dam). late ME. **3.** With *sb.*, used attrib. as adj. phr., as *out-of-bounds*, *out-of-joint*, *out-of-pocket*, *out-of-the-world*, *out-of-work* (also *sb.*); also derivatives of these, as *out-of-jointness*, *out-of-the-worldish*.

1. This house..wil I cast awaye out of my presence COVERDALE 2 *Chron.* 7:20. Nothing can be made out of nothing SHAKS. Out of my doore, you Witch, you Ragge..out, out SHAKS. He quotes it out of Pliny 1662. Every body is going out of town H. WALPOLE. As you come only out of compliment to me WELLINGTON. His majesty ..was thought by the physicians to be out of danger MACAULAY. He fairly laughed the Bill out of the House 1872. 2. So I were out of prison, and kept Sheepe I should be merry as the day is long SHAKS. He is but Four Miles dwelling out of Cambridg 1625. He is placed quite out of their hearing ADDISON. The Church of England is intirely out of the Dispute STEELE. To shut up the shops one day out of the seven 1866. It was expected that the meeting..would be a little out of the ordinary 1893. Our horses being out of condition 1893. b. These English are shrowdly out of Beefe SHAKS. c. Both grandsons of Eclipse and both out of Herod mares 1881. 3. Every raw, peevish, out-of-humoured, affected fop 1675. Out-of-work and sick allowances 1887.

Ou·t-of-da·te, *adj. phr.* 1628. [f. prec. 3 + DATE *sb.*] That continues to exist beyond its proper date or time; obsolete.

Ou·t-of-door, -doo·rs, *adj.* and *sb. phr.* 1800. [The advb. phr. *out-of-door(s* (see DOOR) used attrib. or subst.; in the attrib. use *out-of-door* is usual. See OUT OF 3.] **A.** *adj.* **1.** That is outside the house, in the open air; done or grown in the open air; for use outside the house. **2.** *spec.* **a.** Outside the Houses of Parliament; **b.** Carried on or given outside a workhouse, as *out-of-door relief* 1802. **B.** *sb.* (the adj. used ellipt.) The world outside the house; the open air 1856.

Ou·t-of-fa·shion, *adj. phr.* 1623. [OUT OF 3.] That is no longer in fashion or fashionable.

Out-office (au·tˌǫ:fis). 1624. [f. OUT- A. I. 1. + OFFICE *sb.* 9.] An outside building forming one of the offices of a mansion, farmhouse, etc.; an outhouse.

Ou·t-of-the-way·, *adj. phr.* 1704. [The advb. phr. *out of the way* (see WAY *sb.*), used attrib.] **1.** Remote from any frequented route; remote from any centre of population, secluded 1797. **2.** Seldom met with, far-fetched; hence, extraordinary, odd 1704.

2. Out-of-the-way humours and opinions—heads with some diverting twist in them—please me most LAMB.

Ou·t-pa:rish. 1577. [OUT- A. I. 1.] **a.** A parish lying outside the walls of a city or town, though belonging to it. **b.** An outlying parish.

Outpass (autpɑ·s), *v.* late ME. [OUT- C. II. 1, 2.] **1.** *trans.* To pass out of (bounds), beyond (a limit). **2.** *fig.* To go beyond (in any quality) 1594.

Ou·t-pa:tient. 1715. [OUT- A. I. 2.] A patient who receives treatment at a hospital without being an inmate; opp. to *in-patient*. Also *attrib.*, as *o. department*, *treatment*.

Ou·t-pe:nsion, *sb.* 1711. [OUT- A. I. 2.] A pension given without the condition of residence in a charitable institution. So **Ou·t-pe:nsion** *v. trans.* to pension out. **Ou·t-pe:nsioner,** a non-resident pensioner; opp. to *in-pensioner* 1706.

Outpoi·nt, *v.* 1883. [OUT- C. I. 2, II. 2.] **1.** *Yachting.* To outdo in pointing; to sail closer to the wind than. **2.** *Boxing, etc.* To beat on points.

Ou·tpo:rt. 1642. [OUT- A. I. 1, 5.] **1.** A port outside a city or town; in England, a term including all ports other than that of London. **2.** A port of embarkation or exportation 1790.

Outpost (au·tpōᵘst). 1757. [OUT- A. I. 1.] A post at a distance from the body of an army; a detachment placed at a distance from a force, when halted, to guard against surprise. Also *transf.* and *fig.* Also *attrib.*

Outpour (au·tpōᵊɹ), *sb.* 1864. [OUT A. II. 1.] The act of pouring out; that which pours out, an overflow.

Outpour (autpōᵊ·ɹ), *v.* 1671. [OUT- C. I. 2, 1.] **1.** *trans.* To pour out, send forth in or as in a stream. (Chiefly *poet.*) **2.** *intr.* To flow out as in a stream 1861. Hence **Ou·t-pou:ring** *vbl. sb.* the action of pouring out; an effusive or impetuous utterance. (Chiefly *pl.*)

Output (au·tput). 1839. [OUT- A. II. 1.] The act or fact of putting or turning out; production; the quantity or amount produced; the product of any industry or exertion, viewed quantitatively; the result given to the world. (Orig. a techn. or local term of iron-works, coal-mines, etc.) **b.** *Physiol.* Applied to the waste material expelled from the body by the lungs, skin, and kidneys; as opp. to the *income* or material taken into the system 1883.

Hence **Ou·tputter,** one who turns out some industrial product; a producer 1902.

Ou·t-qua:rter. 1651. [OUT- A. I. 1, 3.] *Mil.* usu. in *pl.* A station or quarter (cf. QUARTER *sb.*) away from the head-quarters of a regiment.

Outrage (au·treⁱdʒ), *sb.* ME. [– (O)Fr. *outrage*, f. OFr. *outrer* exceed (bounds, etc.), exaggerate, f. *outre* beyond :– L. *ultra*; see ULTRA-, -AGE. Cf. OUTRANCE.] †**1.** The passing beyond bounds, want of moderation, intemperance; excess. Rarely with *an* and *pl.* –1590. †**b.** Excess of boldness; foolhardiness; presumption –1553. **2.** Extravagant, violent, or disorderly action; passionate behaviour; fury; disorder; insolence. Also rarely with *an* and *pl. Obs.* or *arch.* ME. **3.** Violence affecting others; violent injury or harm ME. **b.** with *an* and *pl.* A violent injury or wrong; a gross or wanton offence or indignity. late ME. **c.** *transf.* Said of gross or wanton wrong or injury done to feelings, principles, or the like 1769.

2. I feare some out-rage, and Ile follow her SHAKS. I bore the diminution of my riches without any outrages of sorrow JOHNSON. **3.** Wherever there is war there is misery and o. COWPER. **b.** Phr. *Agrarian o.*: see AGRARIAN *a.* 2. **c.** This unpardonable o. upon private feelings 1808. *Comb.* **o.-monger,** one who trades in outrages for political ends.

Outrage (au·treⁱdʒ), *v.* ME. [f. OUTRAGE *sb.* Cf. (O)Fr. *outrager*. In all the obs. senses, and formerly in 2, stressed on *-ra·ge*.] †**1.** *intr.* To go beyond bounds; to act extravagantly or without self-restraint; to commit excesses, run riot –1718. **2.** *trans.* To do violence to; to wrong grossly, treat with gross indignity or insult 1590. **b.** To infringe flagrantly (law, right, authority, morality, or any principle) 1725. †**3.** (Infl. by RAGE *v.*) To burst out into rage, to be furious, to rage; to rush out in rage –1606.

2. The king stopped, robbed, and outraged by ruffians MACAULAY. **b.** To o. contemporary sentiment 1871.

Outrageous (autrēⁱ·dʒəs), *a.* ME. [– OFr. *outrageus* (mod. *-eux*), f. *outrage*; see OUTRAGE *sb.*, -OUS.] **1.** Exceeding proper limits; excessive, immoderate, extravagant; enormous, extraordinary. **2.** Excessive in action; violent, furious; †excessively bold or fierce. late ME. **3.** Excessive in injuriousness, cruelty, or offensiveness; of the nature of violent or gross injury, wrong, or offence, or of a gross violation of law, humanity, or morality 1456.

1. Violent and outragious Rains 1696. **2.** From an o. lunatic, he sunk afterwards into a quiet, speechless idiot 1751. **3.** Pelted with o. epithet TENNYSON. An o. scandal 1888. Hence **Outra·geous-ly** *adv.*, **-ness.**

Ou·trance. *Obs.* exc. as Fr. (utrāñs). late ME. [– OFr. *oultrance*, (also mod.) *outrance* going beyond bounds, f. *ou(l)trer* pass beyond, f. L. *ultra*, Fr. *oltre*, *outre* beyond. Still occas. in literary use in the form UTTERANCE².] A degree which goes beyond bounds or beyond measure; excess.

Phr. *To* (*unto*) *o.*, beyond all limits, to extremity. *At o.*, at the last extremity. *To fight to* (*the*) or *at o.*, to fight to the death (rendering Fr. *combattre à outrance*, *à toute outrance*).

Outrange (aut,rēⁱ·ndʒ), *v.* 1858. [OUT- C. II. 5, 2, 1.] **1.** *trans. Gunnery.* To have a longer range than. **2.** To surpass in extent of time 1887.

Outray·, *v. Obs.* exc. *dial.* ME. [– AFr. *ultreier*, *outreier*, OFr. *ultreer*, *outreer*, *outrer*, f. L. *ultra* beyond; practically identical with OFr. *ou(l)trer* (see OUTRÉ).] †**1.** *intr.* To go beyond or exceed bounds; to stray; to be or get out of array –1611. **2.** To go beyond bounds; to be extravagant; to go to excess 1440. **3.** *trans.* To go beyond, overcome; to vanquish, crush; to excel. Now *dial.* late ME.

‖**Outré** (utre), *a.* 1722. [Fr., pa. pple. of *outrer* †go beyond due limits, f. *outre* :– L. ULTRA.] Beyond the bounds of what is usual, correct, or proper; eccentric, out-of-the-way; exaggerated. Hence **Ou·tréness.**

Outreach (aut,rī·tʃ), *v.* 1568. [OUT- C. II. 1, 2 c, I. 1, 2.] **1.** *trans.* To exceed in reach; to exceed, surpass. †**2.** To overreach; to outwit –1643. **3.** *trans.* and *intr.* To reach out, extend (*poet.*) 1594.

Outrecuidance (utrəküidāns, ūtəɹkwi·dāns). *arch.* late ME. [– (O)Fr. *outrecuidance*, f. *outrecuider*, f. *outre* beyond (:– L. *ultra*) + *cuider* think (:– L. *cogitare*); see -ANCE.] Excessive self-esteem; over-weening self-confidence or self-conceit; arrogance; presumption.

Ou·t-relie:f. 1892. = *Outdoor relief*; see OUTDOOR *a.* 2.

Outri·de, *v.* 1460. [OUT- C. I. 1, 2. II. 2, 1.] **1.** *intr.* and *trans.* To ride out. *Obs.* or *poet.* **2.** To ride better, faster, or farther than; to outstrip by riding 1530. **3.** Of a ship: To ride out (a storm) 1647.

2. *transf.* Like a Tempest that out-rides the Wind DRYDEN.

Outrider (au·t,rəi:dəɹ). ME. [OUT- A. II. 2.] One who rides out or forth. †**1.** An officer of the sheriff's court who collected dues, delivered summonses, etc. –1607. †**2.** An officer of an abbey or convent, who attended to the external domestic requirements of the community, and looked after the manors belonging to it –1532. †**3. a.** A forager of an army. **b.** A highwayman –1625. **4.** A merchant's travelling agent (*dial.*) 1762. **5.** A mounted attendant who rides in advance of or beside a carriage 1530.

Outrigger (au·t,ri:gəɹ). 1748. [perh. alt., by assoc. with *rig*, of earlier OUTLIGGER.] Something rigged out or projecting. **1.** *Naut.* **a.** A strong beam passed through the portholes of a ship, used to secure the masts and counteract the strain in the act of careening; **b.** A spar to haul out a sheet; **c.** A small spar to thrust out and spread the breast-backstays; **d.** A boom swung out to hang boats clear of a ship; **e.** Any framework rigged up outside the gunwales of a ship 1769. **2.** A contrivance used with canoes in the Indian and Pacific Oceans to prevent capsizing under a press of sail 1748. **3.** An iron bracket, fixed to the side of a rowing-boat, bearing a rowlock at its outer edge, so as to increase the leverage of the oar. **b.** An outrigged boat 1845. **4.** *Building* and *Mech.* Applied to various structures placed so as to project from the face of a wall, a frame, etc. 1835. **5.** An extension of the splinter-bar of a carriage, enabling a second horse to be harnessed outside the shafts; the horse so harnessed 1811. So **Ou·trigged** *ppl. a.* fitted with outriggers.

Outright (aut,rəi·t), *adv.* (*adj.*) ME. [f. OUT *adv.* + -RIGHT.] **1.** Straight out; straight ahead. Now *rare.* †**2.** Of time: Straight, straightway; forthwith, immediately –1714. **3.** So that the act is finished at once; altogether, entirely 1603. **4.** Fully out, entirely, quite; without reservation; openly ME.

3. Phr. *To kill o.*, i.e. so that the victim dies on the spot. *To sell or purchase o.*, i.e. so that the thing disposed of becomes at once the full property of the buyer. **4.** I simper'd sometime,.. But never laugh'd o. BEAUM. & FL.

B. *adj.* **1.** Directed or going straight on (*rare*) 1611. **2.** Direct; downright; thorough, out-and-out 1532. **3.** Complete, entire (*mod.*).

2. The young are seldom tempted to o. wickedness 1851. Hence **Outri·ghtness.**

Outri·ng, *v.* late ME. [OUT- C. I. 1, 2, II. 2.] **1.** *intr.* To ring out. (Prop. two wds.) **2.** *trans.* To outdo in ringing, ring louder than 1635.

Outri·val, *v.* 1622. [OUT- C. II. 2 b.] *trans.* To outdo as a rival; to surpass in any competition.

†**Ou·troad.** 1560. [OUT- A. II. 1.] A riding out; *esp.* a warlike excursion; sally –1865.

That they might make outrodes by the waies of Iudea BIBLE (Genev.) 1 *Macc.* 15:41.

Outroll (aut,rōᵘ·l), *v.* 1585. [OUT- C. I. 2.] *trans.* To roll out or forth; to unroll, unfurl, uncoil.

†**Ou·t-room.** 1602. [OUT- A. I. 1.] An outlying room; an out-building –1668.

Outroot (aut,rū·t), *v.* 1558. [f. OUT *adv.* + ROOT, prob. after L. *eradicare.*] *trans.* To root out, eradicate, exterminate.

Outrun (aut,rʊ·n), *v.* ME. [OUT- C. I. 1, II. 2. 1.] **1.** *intr.* To run out. **2.** *trans.* To outdo in running; to run faster or farther than; hence, to escape or elude. Also *fig.* 1526. **3.** *fig.* To run beyond a fixed point or limit; to go beyond in action 1655.

2. The other disciple did o. Peter, and came first to the Sepulchre *John* 20:4. *fig.* The zeal of the flocks outran that of the pastors MACAULAY. Phr. *To o. the constable*: see CONSTABLE. **3.** Thy tongue outruns thy discretion SCOTT.

Ou·tru:nner. 1598. [OUT- A. II. 2.] One who or that which runs out; *spec.* a horse which runs in traces outside the shaft; *fig.* a fore-runner, an avant-courier.

Ou·trush. 1872. [OUT- A. II. 1.] A rushing out; a violent outflow.

Outsai·l, *v.* 1616. [OUT- C. II. 2, 1.] *trans.* To outdo in sailing; to sail faster or farther than; *transf.* and *fig.* to outstrip.

Ou·tscour. 1883. [OUT- A. II. 1.] The act of scouring out; the action of water in scouring out a channel.

Outsee·, *v.* 1605. [OUT- C. II. 2, 1.] **1.** *trans.* To surpass in length of sight or in mental insight. **2.** To see beyond (a point or limit) 1645.

Outse·ll, *v.* 1611. [OUT- C. II. 2, 2 b.] **1.** *trans.* To sell for more than; *fig.* to exceed in value. **2.** To have or secure a larger sale than 1687.

1. *Cymb.* II. iv. 102.

Ou·t-se:ntry. 1691. [OUT- A. I. 2.] A sentry placed at a distance in advance; an outpost.

Outset (au·tset). 1540. [OUT- A. II. 1.] **1.** An enclosure from the outlying moorland or common. *Sc.* **2.** Ornament or embellishment. *Sc.* 1596. **3.** The act or fact of setting out upon a journey, course of action, business, etc.; start, beginning 1759. **4.** *Mining.* An elevation of the ground, or the like, round the mouth of a sinking pit, to facilitate the disposal of the debris produced in sinking 1881.

3. This is no pleasant prospect at the o. of a political journey BURKE.

Ou·t-se:ttlement. 1747. [OUT- A. I. 1.] An outlying or remote settlement.

Ou·tse:ttler. 1756. [OUT- A. I. 2, II. 2.] **a.** A settler outside of or in the outlying parts of a district. **b.** An emigrant.

Outshi·ne, *v.* 1596. [OUT- C. II. 2, I. 1.] **1.** *trans.* To shine brighter than. Also *fig.* **2.** *intr.* To shine forth (*poet.*) 1865.

1. How changed From him, who in the happy Realms of Light..didst o. Myriads MILT.

Outshoot (aut,ʃū·t), *v.* 1530. [OUT- C. II. 2, 1, I. 2.] **1.** *trans.* To shoot farther or better than. **b.** To shoot beyond as a young branch; also *fig.* 1772. **2.** To shoot beyond (a mark or limit) 1545. **3.** To shoot out or forth 1658.

1. As if they out shot Robin Hood SIDNEY.

Outshow (aut,ʃōᵘ·), *v.* 1558. [OUT- C. I. 2.] *trans.* To show forth, exhibit (*poet.*).

Then high handiwork will I make my life-deed, Truth and light o. T. HARDY.

Outshri·ll, *v.* 1605. [OUT- C. II. 2.] *trans.* To outdo in shrilling; to exceed in shrillness.

Outside (au·tsəi·d, au·tsəid), *sb.*, *adv.*, *prep.*, *a.* 1503. [f. OUT *a.*, OUT- A. I. 3 + SIDE *sb.*; cf. INSIDE.] **A.** *sb.* **1.** That part of anything which is without, or farther from the interior; the external surface 1505. **b.** The outer part or parts of anything 1598. **2.** The outer surface considered as that which is seen; the external person as dist. from the mind or spirit; outward aspect or appearance 1592. **b.** That which is merely external; outward form as opp. to substance 1660. **3.** The position or locality close to the outer side or surface of anything 1503. **4.** The outmost limit; the fullest or highest degree or quantity (*colloq.*). Chiefly in phr. *at the o.* 1707. **5.** Anything situated on or forming the outer side, edge, or border; *spec.* (*pl.*) the outermost sheets, more or less damaged, of a ream of paper 1615. **6.** Shirt for *o. passenger* on a coach, etc. 1804. **7.** In phr. *o. in* (usu. with *turn*): So that the outer side becomes the inner; = inside out 1771.

1. The Duke of Doria's Palace has the best O. of any in Genoa ADDISON. **2.** O what a goodlie o. falsehood hath SHAKS. **3.** Can I open the door from the o., I wonder? DICKENS. **4.** A red light.. distant a quarter of a mile at the o. 1885. **7.** A keeper is only a poacher turned o. in KINGSLEY.

B. *adj.* **1.** That is on, or belongs to, the outer side, surface, edge, or boundary 1634. **2.** Situated, or having its origin or operation, without; that resides without some place or area; that works out of the house, or out of a workshop or factory 1841. **3** Not included in or belonging to the place, establishment, institution, or society in question 1881. †**4.** That has only an outside; having empty show; superficial –1728. **5.** Reaching the utmost limit; greatest, extreme 1857.

1. A Sailor, who was an o. passenger 1815. The o. walls are built hollow 1854. *O. edge* (Skating): (*To cut, do*) *the o. edge*, a particular form of fancy skating on the outer edge of the skate-iron. *O.* (*jaunting*) *car*: see JAUNTING-CAR. **2.** 'Outside' work means work done entirely in the home by an 'outside' worker 1900. An o. porter 1904. **3.** O. opinion has evidently had its influence on the City Fathers 1881. *O. broker*, one not a member of the Stock Exchange. **5.** The very o. prices that are being paid 1893.

C. *adv.* (Short for *on* or *to the o.*) **1.** Of position: On the outside of certain limits; out in the open air; in the open sea beyond a harbour; not within the body or community in question 1813. **2.** To the exterior 1889. **3.** **Outside of,** *prep. phr.* **a.** Not within the walls, limits, or bounds of; exterior to; also, To the exterior of, outward from 1839. **b.** *U.S. colloq.* Beyond the number or body of, with the exception of 1889.

1. They could..see every thing that took place o. 1813. **2.** The men and women were ordered to come o. 1889. *Come o.!* (slang), a challenge to fight or to have it out. **3. a.** *O. of a horse* (*colloq.*), on horseback. *To get o. of* (*slang*), (*a*) to swallow; (*b*) *U.S.* to master or understand. **b.** I do not often see anybody o. of my servants 1890.

D. *prep.* (Shortened from *outside of.*) **1.** Outside of; on the outer side of; external to 1817. **b.** Beyond the limits of (any domain of action or thought, any subject or matter) 1852. **2.** To the outer side of, to the exterior of, to what lies without or beyond 1856.

1. The cause of the tides is to be found o. our earth HUXLEY. **b.** Services, which lie o. the common routine GLADSTONE. **2.** The Court cannot go o. the pleadings 1885.

Outsider (autsəi·dəɹ). 1800. [f. OUTSIDE *sb.* + -ER¹.] **1.** One who is outside any enclosure, barrier, or boundary, material or figurative; *esp.* a person without special knowledge, breeding, etc., or not fit to mix with good society (*colloq.*). **b.** *Horse-racing.* A horse not 'in the running' 1857. **2.** *lit.* One whose position is on the outside of some group or series; an outside man 1857. **3.** An outside jaunting-car 1900. **4.** *pl.* A pair of nippers which can be inserted into a keyhole from the outside so as to grasp and turn the key 1875.

1. He is only an o., and is not in the mysteries DICKENS.

Outsight (au·tsəit). 1605. [OUT- A. II. 1.] Sight of that which is without; faculty of observation or outlook.

Outsi·ng, *v.* 1603. [OUT- C. II. 2, I. 1, 2.] **1.** *trans.* To excel in singing. Also *refl.* **b.** To get the better of by singing 1830. **2.** *intr.* To sing out 1877.

Outsi·t, *v.* 1658. [OUT- C. II. 1, 2.] **1.** *trans.* To sit beyond the time of duration of. **2.** To sit longer than 1885.

Outskirt (au·tskɔ̄ɹt). 1596. [OUT- A. I. 3.] **1.** The outer border. Now only *pl.* **2.** *attrib.* or quasi-*adj.* Situated on the outskirts 1835.

1. One of those barren parishes lying on the outskirts of civilisation GEO. ELIOT. Hence **Outski·rt** *v. rare* and *poet.*, to skirt; to border; to pass along the outskirts of.

Outslee·p, *v.* 1590. [OUT- C. II. 1, 2, I. 3.] **1.** *trans.* To sleep beyond (a specified time, etc.). **2.** To sleep longer than 1690. **3.** To sleep (a period of time) out 1784.

1. I feare we shall out-sleepe the comming morne SHAKS. **3.** He has outslept the winter COWPER.

Ou·tsole. 1884. [OUT- A. I. 3.] The outer sole of a shoe, which comes in contact with the ground.

Ou·tspan, *sb. S. Afr.* 1852. [f. next.] The action of outspanning or unyoking; the time or place of outspanning or encampment.

Outspan (au·tspæn), *v. S. Afr.* 1824. [– Du. *uitspannen*, f. *uit* adv. out + *spannen* span, stretch, put horses to.] To unyoke or unhitch oxen from a wagon; to unharness horses; hence, to encamp. *trans.* and *intr.*

Outspeak (autspī·k), *v.* 1603. [OUT- C. II. 1, 2, I. 2, 1.] †**1.** *trans.* To express more than –1618. **2.** To outdo in speaking 1603. **3.** To speak (something) out; to declare 1635. **4.** *intr.* To speak out 1819.

1. *Hen. VIII*, III. ii. 127. **4.** And now outspake the Corporal LYTTON.

Outspe·nd, *v.* 1586. [OUT- C. II. 1, 2.] **1.** *trans.* To exceed (resources, etc.) in spending. **2.** To spend more than (another) 1840. **3.** In *pa. pple.* **Outspe·nt,** exhausted 1818.

1. We out-spend our means 1811. **2.** He outspent princes 1866. **3.** Outspent with this long course, The Cossack prince rubb'd down his horse BYRON.

Outspi·n, *v.* 1616. [OUT- C. I. 1, 2 b, II. 2.] **1.** *trans.* To spin (a thread) to its full length; said *fig.* of the thread of life, etc. **2.** To outdo in spinning 1742.

Outspo·ken (stress variable), *ppl. a.* orig. *Sc.* 1808. [OUT- B. 2.] **1.** Given to speaking out; candid, frank; direct in speech. **b.** Of things said: Free from reserve, distinct 1869. **2.** Spoken out, uttered 1882.

1. He is not, you know, very o. SCOTT. **b.** Mr. Gladstone's o. observation 1880. Hence **Outspo·ken-ly** *adv.*, **-ness.**

Outspread (au·tspred), *sb.* 1841. [OUT- A. II. 1.] **1.** The action of spreading out; expansion. **2.** *concr.* An expanse or expansion 1856.

Outspread (autspre·d), *v.* ME. [OUT- C. I. 2.] *trans.* To spread out; to expand. Hence **Ou·tspread** *ppl. a.*

Outspri·ng, *v.* ME. [OUT- C. I. 1, II. 2.] **1.** *intr.* To spring out, issue forth. (Now only *poet.*) †**b.** To spring by birth –1596. **2.** *trans.* To spring beyond or farther than 1600.

Outstand (autstæ·nd), *v.* 1571. [OUT- C. I. 2 b, 1, II. 1.] **I.** *trans.* **1.** To stand or hold out against; to resist successfully. Now *dial.* **2.** To stay out or stay beyond (in time). *arch.* 1611.

2. I haue out-stood my time SHAKS.

II. *intr.* **1.** To stand out distinctly or prominently 1755. **2.** Of a ship: To stand out from the land; to sail outwards 1866.

1. Cottages here and there outstanding bare on the mountain CLOUGH.

Ou·tsta·nding (stress variable), *ppl. a.* 1570. [OUT- B. 1.] **1.** That stands out or projects; projecting, prominent, detached. **2.** *fig.* Standing out from the rest; conspicuous, eminent; striking 1830. **3.** That stands over; that remains undetermined, unsettled, or unpaid 1797.

1. O. veins 1870. **2.** The great o. facts, which our Lord has pointed out PUSEY. **3.** An o. debt 1858. Phr. *O. term*: see TERM. Hence **Outsta·ndingly** *adv.* pre-eminently.

Outsta·re, *v.* 1596. [OUT- C. II. 2 b.] *trans.* To outdo in staring; to put out of countenance by staring; to look on (the sun, etc.) without blinking.

I would o. the sternest eyes that look SHAKS.

Outsta·rt, *v.* late ME. [OUT- C. I. 1, II. 1, 2.] **1.** *intr.* To start, spring forth suddenly. (Prop. two wds.) **2.** *trans.* To spring or go beyond; to take or have the start of 1593.

Ou·t-sta:tion. 1844. [OUT- A. I. 1, 3.] A station at a distance from head-quarters or from the centre of population or business.

Outstay (autstē¹·), *v.* 1600. [OUT- C. II. 1, 2.] **1.** *trans.* To stay beyond the limit of; to overstay. **2.** To stay longer than 1689.

1. You are afraid of outstaying your welcome 1893. **2.** Mr. Pepys, and I, outstayed the rest near an hour 1783.

Outste·p, *v.* 1759. [OUT- C. II. 1.] *trans.* To step outside of or beyond; to overstep.

Outstrea·m, *v.* late ME. [OUT- C. I. 1.] *intr.* To stream out or forth.

†**Ou·t-street.** 1585. [OUT- A. I. 1, 3.] A street outside the walls or in the outskirts of a town –1722.

Ou·tstretch, *sb.* 1863. [OUT- A. II. 1.] **1.** The act or fact of stretching out. **2.** An outstretched tract 1864. **3.** The distance to which anything stretches out 1888.

Outstre·tch, *v.* late ME. [OUT- C. I. 2, 2 b, II. 1, 2.] **1.** *trans.* To stretch out or forth. Chiefly *poet.* **2.** To extend in area or content; to expand 1600. **3.** To stretch to its limit, to strain. Now *rare.* 1607. **4.** To stretch beyond (a limit, etc.) 1597.

2. The great city, which lay outstretched before him DICKENS. **3.** Tymon is dead, who hath outstretcht his span SHAKS. Hence **Ou·tstretched** *ppl. a.* (esp. of the arms).

Outstri·de, *v.* 1610. [OUT- C. II. 2.] *trans.* To excel in length of stride; also *fig.*

Outstrip (autstri·p), *v.* 1580. [f. OUT- C. II. 2, 2 c, 1 + STRIP *v.*² 2.] *trans.* To pass in running or swift motion; to outrun, leave behind.

The deer Outstrips the active hound DEKKER. *fig.* They striue one to o. another in giuing most 1607.

Ou·tstroke. 1851. [OUT- A. II. 1.] **1.** A stroke directed outwards 1874. **2.** *Mining.* The act of striking out, i.e. of passing out of a working royalty into another royalty. Also *attrib.*, as *o. rent.*

Outswe·ll, *v.* 1606. [OUT- C. II. 2, 1.] **1.** *trans.* To swell out more than. **2.** To swell beyond (a point or limit) 1658.

†**Out-take, -taken,** *pa. pple., prep., conj.* ME. [pa. pple. of *outtake* vb. = L. *excipere.*] = EXCEPT.

Ou·t-throw, ou·tthrow, *sb.* 1855. [OUT- A. II. 1.] The act of throwing out; ejection, emission; output; matter ejected.

Out-throw, outthrow (autþrōᵘ·), *v.* ME. [OUT- C. I. 2, II. 1,2.] †**1.** *trans.* To throw out, cast out. (Prop. two wds.) –1711. **2.** To throw beyond (a point), or farther than (a person) 1613.

Ou·t-thrust, *sb.* 1842. [OUT- A. II. 1.] The act or fact of thrusting or pushing forcibly outward; an outward thrusting pressure in any structure.

Out-top, outtop (aut,tǫ·p), *v.* 1624. [OUT- C. II. 2 b.] *trans.* = OVERTOP.

Out-tra·vel, *v.* 1619. [OUT- C. II. 1, 2.] *trans.* To exceed in extent or swiftness of travelling.

Outvie (autvəi·), *v.* 1594. [OUT- C. II. 2 b.] *trans.* To vie with and excel.

Outvo·te, *v.* 1647. [OUT- C. II. 2.] *trans.* To outnumber in voting; to defeat by a majority of votes.

Ou·t-vo:ter. 1855. [OUT- A. I. 2.] One who has a parliamentary vote in a constituency in which he does not reside; a non-resident voter qualified by holding property.

Outwalk (aut,wǭ·k), *v.* 1626. [OUT- C. II. 2, 1.] *trans.* To walk faster, farther, or better than; to walk beyond.

Ou·t-wall (-wǭl). 1535. [OUT- A. I. 3.] The outer wall of any building or enclosure. **b.** *fig.* The clothing; the body as enclosing the soul 1605.

Outward (au·t,wǫɹd), *a.* (*sb.*¹) [OE. *ūtweard*, f. *ūt* (see OUT *adv.*) + *-weard* -WARD.] **1.** That is without or on the outer side; out, outer, external, exterior. *Obs.* or *arch.* **b.** Directed or proceeding towards the outside; pertaining to what is so directed 1700. **2.** External; bodily ME. †**3.** External to the country; foreign –1675. **4.** Of or pertaining to outer form as opposed to saner substance or reality 1526. **5.** Applied to things in the external or material world, as opp. to those in the mind or thought 1573. **b.** Applied to things that are external to one's own personality, etc., or that concern one's relations with other persons and external circumstances; extrinsic 1607. **6.** Dissipated, wild or irregular in conduct (*dial.*) 1875.

1. b. The first or O. halves of Return Tickets 1884. **2.** Inward Medicines or o. Applications ADDISON. The vision was not to the o. eye 1867. *O. man* (*Theol.*), the body as opp. to the soul or spirit; *joc.* outward guise, clothing. **4.** An o. and visible sign of an inward and spiritual grace *Bk. Com. Prayer.* **5.** Obstinate questionings Of sense and o. things WORDSW. **b.** The law must define men's o. rights and relations 1869.

B. *sb.* (the adj. used ellipt. or absol.). †**1.** An outer part (of anything) –1545. **2.** Outward appearance; the outside 1606. **3.** in *pl.* Externals. Now *rare* or *arch.* 1627. **4.** That which is outside the mind; the external world 1832.

2. So fair an O., and such stuffe Within SHAKS. Hence **Ou·tward-ly** *adv.*, 1480, †**-most** *a.*

Out-ward (au·t,wǫɹd), *sb.*² 1871. [OUT- A. I. 1.] An outlying ward; a ward outside the original bounds of a borough.

Outward (au·t,wǫ̆rd), *adv.* [OE. *ūtan-*, *ūte-*, *ūtweard.*] **1.** On the outside; without. **b.** From the inside to or towards the outside ME. †**2.** Outside of a specified or understood place; abroad –1673. †**3.** On, or with ref. to, the outside of the body; externally –1543. †**b.** In the body as opp. to the mind or spirit; in outward appearance as opp. to inner reality; outwardly; publicly –1673.

1. Whited tombes which appere beautyfull outwarde TINDALE *Matt.* 23:28. **b.** They myght have their costes owteward & homeward 1497. **3. b.** This o. sainted Deputie..is yet a diuell SHAKS.

Ou·tward-bou·nd, *a.* (*sb.*) 1602. [f. OUTWARD *adv.* + BOUND *ppl. a.*¹] Directing the course outward, esp. going from a home port to a foreign one: of a ship or a person; *transf.* of a voyage. Also *absol.* as *sb.* **b.** *fig.* Dying 1809. **c.** *fig.* Bent on wandering or straying 1742.

Ou·twardness. 1580. [f. OUTWARD *a.* + -NESS.] **1.** The quality or condition of being outward; outward existence; objectivity. **2.** Occupation with or belief in outward things 1835.

Outwards (au·tⁱwǫ̈rdz), *adv.* (*a.*) [OE. *ūtweardes*, f. *ūtweard* OUTWARD *a.* + *-es* (see -s).] **1.** In an outward direction; towards that which is outside. †**2.** In an outward position; outside; externally –1602. **3.** *attrib.* (as *adj.*). For outward goods 1878.

3. The 'Outwards' department of the great goods shed 1878.

Outwatch (autⁱwǫ·tʃ), *v.* 1626. [OUT- C. II. 2, 1.] *trans.* To watch longer than; to watch (an object) till it disappears.

Outwear (autⁱwēᵊ·ɹ), *v.* 1541. [OUT- C. I. 2, 2 b, II. 2.] **1.** *trans.* To wear out, wear away; to consume by wearing. **b.** To exhaust in strength or endurance; chiefly in pa. pple. *outworn* 1610. **2.** *trans.* To wear out, spend, pass (time) 1590. **b.** To outlive, outgrow 1592. **3.** To wear longer than 1579.

1. b. By ceaseless pains outworn WORDSW. **2.** If I the night out-wear POPE. **3.** Teaspoons that have outworn their set 1893.

Outweary (autⁱwīᵊ·ri), *v.* Chiefly *poet.* 1609. [OUT- C. I. 2 b.] *trans.* To weary out; to exhaust in endurance.

Some youthful Troubadour,..Who here out-wearied sank M. ARNOLD.

Outweep (autⁱwī·p), *v.* 1597. [OUT- C. I. 3, II. 2.] **1.** *trans.* To weep out, to expel by weeping (*poet.*). **2.** To outdo in weeping 1631.

Outweigh (autⁱwēⁱ·), *v.* 1530. [OUT- C. II. 2, 2 b.] **1.** *trans.* To exceed in weight; *fig.* to be too heavy for. **2.** To exceed in value, importance, or influence 1632.

Outwell (autⁱwe·l), *v.* 1590. [OUT- C. I. 2, 1.] †**1.** *trans.* To pour forth SPENSER. **2.** *intr.* To well out, to gush forth 1600. Hence **Outwe·lling** *vbl. sb.* and *ppl. a.* 1821.

Outwing (autⁱwi·ŋ), *v.* 1648. [OUT- C. II. 5.] **1.** *trans.* To exceed or surpass in flight; to fly beyond 1717. **2.** *Mil.* Of an army: To outflank (the enemy).

Outwit (autⁱwi·t), *v.* 1652. [OUT- C. II. 5.] **1.** *trans.* To surpass in wit, wisdom, or knowledge (*arch.*) 1659. **2.** To get the better of by superior craft; to prove too clever for 1652.

1. Thou..Shalt outsee seers, and o. Sages EMERSON. **2.** To cheat or, rather (as the Quakers word it) to O. his own Father and Brother 1705.

Ou·tⁱwith, *prep.* and *adv.* Chiefly *north.*; now *Sc.* ME. [f. OUT *adv.* + WITH *prep.*; cf. INWITH and WITHOUT.] Without, outside.

Outwork (au·tⁱwɒɹk), *sb.* 1615. [OUT- A. I. 1, 3.] **1.** Any detached or advanced work forming part of the defence of a place. Also *transf.* and *fig.* **2.** (*out-work.*) Work done outside, i.e. out of doors, out of the house, out of the shop or factory, etc.; in *Cricket* = OUT-FIELDING 1793.

Outwork (autⁱwǒ·ɹk), *v.* 1590. [OUT- C. 1, 2, 2 b, II. 5, 2.] **1.** *trans.* To work out to a conclusion; to complete (*poet.*). †**2.** To excel in work or workmanship –1782. **3.** To outdo in working; to work more or faster than 1611.

Ou·t-wo:rker. 1813. [OUT- A. I. 2.] One who does outwork (see OUTWORK *sb.* 2).

Ou·tⁱwo:rld, out-world, *sb.* 1647. [OUT- A. I. 3.] The outside world; an outlying or outer world.

Outworn, out-worn (autⁱwǭ·ɹn, *attrib.* au·tⁱwǭɹn), *ppl. a.* 1548. [OUT- B. 2, from *wear out.*] **1.** Worn out, as clothes; wasted, consumed, or obliterated by wear or by the action of time; hence *fig.* of beliefs, customs, institutions, etc. **2.** Of living beings, etc.: Exhausted as to physical vigour and vitality, spent 1597.

1. A Pagan suckled in a creed o. WORDSW. **2.** Inglorious, unemployed, with age o. MILT.

Outwrite (autⁱrəi·t), *v.* 1643. [OUT- C. II. 2, 1, I. 2 b.] **1.** *trans.* To surpass or excel in writing. **2.** To get over by writing 1837. **3.** *refl.* To write oneself out 1883.

Outwrought, pa. t. and pple. of OUTWORK *v.*

Ouze, obs. f. OOZE.

Ouzel, ousel (ū·z'l). [OE. *ōsle* (:– **amsle*) = OHG. *amusla, amsala* (G. *amsel*).] **1.** A name of certain birds of the genus *Turdus*. **a.** The blackbird or merle (*T. merula.*) Also attrib. in *o.-cock*. Now *lit.* or *arch.* **b.** Applied to *T. torquatus*, the **Ring-ouzel** 1450. †**c.** *transf.* Used of a person (prob. of dark hair or complexion) –1628. **2.** Applied to other birds, pop. assoc. with the prec. 1622.

1. The Woosell cocke, so blacke of hew, With Orenge-tawny bill SHAKS. **c.** 2 *Hen IV*, III. ii. 9. **2. Brook O.**, the Water Rail (*Rallus aquaticus*). **Water O.**, the DIPPER (*Cinclus aquaticus*); also the American Dipper (*C. mexicanus*).

Ova, pl. of OVUM.

Oval (ōᵘ·văl), *a.* and *sb.* 1570. [– med.L. *ovalis*, f. L. *ovum* egg; see -AL¹. Cf. Fr. *oval* (Rabelais).] **A.** *adj.* **1.** Having the form of an egg; approximately egg-shaped, ellipsoidal 1577. **2.** Having the outline of an egg as projected on a surface; having more or less the form or outline of an elongated circle or ellipse; elliptical 1610. **3.** Of or pertaining to an egg (*rare*) 1646.

1. O. chuck = elliptic chuck; an appendage to a lathe, of such a nature that the work attached to it and cut by the tool in the usual manner becomes of an oval form. **2.** *O. window*, the *fenestra ovalis* of the ear; see WINDOW. **3.** Their ovall conceptions, or egges within their bodies SIR T. BROWNE. Hence **O·val-ly** *adv.*, **-ness.**

B. *sb.* **1.** A plane figure resembling the longitudinal section of an egg; in *mod. Geom.* any closed curve (other than a circle or ellipse) 1570. **2.** Anything having an oval or (usu.) elliptical outline 1650.

1. *Cassinian o.*: see CASSINIAN. **2.** *Kennington O.*, in athletics 'the Oval', an open space at Kennington in South London, where cricket matches, etc., are played.

Ovalbumen, -in (ōᵘvǣlbiū·mėn, -in). 1835. [f. L. *ovi albumen* (Pliny).] *Chem.* The albumen or white of egg; egg albumen.

Ovarian (ovēᵊ·riăn), *a.* 1840. [f. OVARIUM + -AN.] Of, pertaining to, or of the nature of an ovary or ovaries.

Ovario- (ovēᵊ·rio), comb. form of OVARIUM, expressing the participation of the ovary with some other part, as *o.-abdominal*; also with sbs. in sense 'ovarian', as *o.-insanity*.

Ovariole (ovēᵊ·riōᵘl). 1877. [f. OVARIUM + L. dim. suff. *-olum*, after FOLIOLE, PETIOLE.] A small ovary; one of the tubular glands of the compound ovary of some insects.

Ovariotomy (ovēᵊriǫ·tŏmi). 1852. [f. OVARIUM + -TOMY.] *Surg.* The operation of cutting into an ovary to remove an ovarian tumour; also oophorectomy.

Ovarious (ovēᵊ·riəs), *a. rare.* 1730. [f. OVUM; see -ARIOUS.] Of, pertaining to, or of the nature of eggs.

‖**Ovaritis** (ōᵘvărəi·tis). 1857. [f. OVARIUM + -ITIS.] *Path.* Inflammation of the ovaries.

‖**Ovarium** (ovēᵊ·riŏm). *Pl.* **-ia.** 1692. [mod.L. *ovarium* (whence also Fr. *ovaire* masc. 1690); see -ARY¹. Cf. med.L. *ovaria* ovary of a bird (XIII).] = OVARY 1 and 2.

Ovary (ōᵘ·vări), *sb.* 1658. [– mod.L. *ovarium*; see prec.] **1.** *Anat.* and *Zool.* The female organ of reproduction in animals, in which ova or eggs are produced. **2.** *Bot.* The lowest part of the pistil in a flower, consisting of one or more carpels, which ultimately becomes the fruit or seed-vessel; the germen 1751.

Ovate (ǫ·vĕt), *sb.* 1723. [f. an assumed L. pl. *Ovates*, repr. Οὐατεῖς = *vates* soothsayers, prophets, mentioned by Strabo as a third order in the Gaulish hierarchy.] An English equivalent of Welsh *ofydd*, now applied to an Eisteddfodic graduate of a third order, beside 'bard' and 'druid'.

Ovate (ōᵘ·veⁱt), *a.* 1760. [– L. *ovatus* egg-shaped, f. *ovum*; see -ATE² 2.] **1.** Egg-shaped. **2.** In comb. with another adj. with sense 'inclining to ovate', as *o.-lanceolate, -oblong, -rotundate*, etc. 1819. Hence **O·vately** *adv.* = **ovate-, ovato-** 1822.

Ovation (ovēⁱ·ʃən). 1533. [– L. *ovatio*, f. *ovat-*, pa. ppl. stem of *ovare* celebrate a (lesser) triumph; see -ION.] **1.** *Rom. Hist.* A lesser triumph, granted to a commander for achievements insufficient to entitle him to the triumph proper. Also, allusively. †**2.** Exultation –1818. **3.** *transf.* An enthusiastic reception by a concourse of people; a burst of enthusiastic applause 1831.

3. Dr. Stainer received the o. that was his due 1885.

Ovato- (ovēⁱ·to), comb. advb. form of L. *ovatus* OVATE, = 'ovately', 'ovate-', as *o.-acuminate, -oblong, -rotundate*, etc.

Oven (ɒ·v'n), *sb.* [OE. *ofen* = OFris., (M)LG., (M)Du. *oven*, OHG. *ovan* (G. *ofen*), ON. *ofn, ogn*, Goth. **auhns* (acc. sing. *auhn*) :– Gmc. **oχwnaz* :– **ukw(h)nos* (cf. Gr. ἰπνός oven, Skr. *ukhás* cooking-pot).] †**1.** A furnace –1722. **2.** A chamber or receptacle of brick, stonework, or iron, for baking bread and cooking food, by continuous heat radiated from the walls, roof, or floor OE. **3.** A small furnace, kiln, etc., for the heating or drying of substances in chemical, metallurgical, or manufacturing processes 1753.

1. The three Children of Israel cast into the hot fierie O. 1642. **2.** I preached..in a house as warm as an O. WESLEY. *Dutch o.*, (*a*) a large pot heated by surrounding it with fuel, and placing hot coals on the lid; (*b*) a cooking utensil made of sheet-metal, placed in front of a grate and heated by radiation and reflection from the back of the chamber.

attrib. and *Comb.*, as *o. cake, man, mouth, stone, wood*; **o.-coke,** coke obtained by heating coal in a closed retort.

O·ven-bird. 1825. A name for birds which build a domed or oven-shaped nest: applied to the genus *Furnarius* of the neotropical family *Dendrocolaptidæ*, esp. *F. rufus*; also, locally, to the Willow Wren, the Long-tailed or Bottle Titmouse, and the American Golden-crowned Thrush (*Seiurus aurica-pillus*).

O·ver, *sb.* 1584. [OVER *adv.* used absol.] **1.** That which is excessive; an excess, extreme. *Sc.* **2.** An amount in excess, or remaining over; an extra 1882. **3.** *Cricket.* The fixed number of balls bowled from either end of the wicket before a change is made to the other end; the portion of the game comprising a single turn of bowling from one end 1850.

Over (ōᵘ·vəɹ), *a.* [ME. *ouere* (XIII) began as a graphic var. of *uuere* (with *o* for *u* before *u*) :– OE. *ufer(r)a, yfer(r)a, -e* (:– **ubar*, **ubirōzo*), which is directly repr. by dial. *uvver*; superseded in gen. use by the adv. form.] **1.** The upper, the higher in position. (Only *attrib.*, prec. by *the* or an equiv., and used of one of two things.) Now *Obs.* or *dial.* **b.** Upper, outer OE. **2.** Higher in power, authority, or station; upper, superior ME. **3.** That is in excess or in addition; surplus, extra 1494. **4.** Too great, excessive. (Now mostly written in comb.; see OVER- 8.) 1561.

1. b. One pair of o. britches 1598. **3.** O. or spoiled copies 1896. **4.** Without o. care as to which is largest RUSKIN.

Over (ōᵘ·vəɹ), *adv.* [OE. *ofer* = OFris. *over*, OS. *obar* (Du. *over*), OHG. *ubar* prep., *ubiri* adv. (G. *über*, also, from MG., *ober*), ON. *yfir*, Goth. *ufar* :– Gmc. **uberi* :– IE. **uperi*, compar. formation (cf. Skr. *upári*, Gr. ὑπέρ, L. *s|uper*; see HYPER-, SUPER-) on **upó* from under towards (see SUB-).] **I.** In a higher position. **1.** Above, on high. **b.** After *hang, project, jut, lean*, etc.; hence *ellipt.* projecting, leaning, or bent forward and downward 1546. **2.** Above so as to cover the surface, or so as to affect the whole surface. late ME.

1. b. Don't lean o. too far, or you'll fall o. 1904. **2.** *To brush, cover, clothe, daub*, etc., *o.*

II. To or on the other or further side. **1.** Indicating a motion or course that passes or crosses over something, usu. rising on one side and descending on the other OE.; occas. (*b*) esp. with the sense of passing above and beyond, and so *fig.* of going beyond, exaggeration 1599. **2.** Hence = over the edge or brink and down, forward and down. late ME. Also, **b.** of a movement from the erect position, without ref. to any brink 1649; and **c.** in *to bend, double, fold, roll* a thing *o.*, in which the upper surface is turned upside down 1548. **3.** From side to side of an interjacent surface or space OE. **b.** Of measurement: Across; in outside measurement 1585. **c.** *Cricket.* The umpire's call for the players to change ends, on a change of the bowling to the other end, after a fixed number of balls have been bowled from the one end 17... **4.** Expressing transference or transition from one person, side, opinion, etc., to another 1585. **5.** On the other side of something intervening, e.g. a sea, river, street; hence, merely, at some distance ME.

1. *To climb, jump, run, flow, boil o., to look o.*

Toss him o. the bridge MARRYAT. **b.** *fig.* You haue shot ouer SHAKS. Many shot went o., but none struck us 1796. **2.** *To jump, throw* oneself, *push* any one *o.* **b.** *To fall, tumble, topple, knock* a person, a vase, etc. *o.* **c.** He tourned o. the leffe, and began an order of a new life 1548. *To turn* or *roll o. and o.*, i.e. so that each part of the surface in succession rolls forward and downward, and is alternately up and down. **3.** My mother will send o. every day to inquire how Miss McLean is 1894. **4.** And dost thou now fall ouer to my foes? SHAKS. The balance..is brought o. into this [account] 1776. **5.** Over by Dalhem a dome-spire sprang white BROWNING. *O. against* (prep. phr.), opposite to.

III. With the notion of exceeding in quantity, etc. **1.** Above and beyond the quantity named or in question. **a.** Remaining beyond what is taken. **b.** In excess, in addition, more. OE. **2.** Left unpaid, unsettled, or uncompleted; left till a later time or occasion 1647. †**3.** Beyond what has been said; moreover, besides; further –1509. **4.** Too much; excessively; too ME.

1. Their wages..and something ouer SHAKS. Two and two are four, and nothing o. DICKENS. *O. or under*, more or less. **2.** *To remain, lie, stand, hold, leave o.* **4.** O. happy to be proud, O. wealthy in the treasure Of her own exceeding pleasure! WORDSW.

IV. Of duration, repetition, completion, ending. **1.** To the end; from beginning to end. late ME. **2.** Expressing repetition 1550. **3.** Past, gone by, finished, at an end 1611.

1. *To read, repeat, say, tell, count o. To talk, think o.*, i.e. with detailed consideration. **2.** He read it twice o. GOLDSM. *O. and o.*, many times over. **3.** Now the day is o., Night is drawing nigh 1865.

Over (ō^{u}·vəɹ), *prep.* [The same as prec. with object.] **I.** In sense *above.* **1.** Above, higher up than OE. **2.** In (or into) a position in which water, or the like, rises above one's shoes, boots, ears, head, etc. Also *fig.* 1503. **3.** The spatial sense 'above' is **a.** combined with that of purpose or occupation, as in *o. the fire, o. a glass*; **b.** merged in that of having something under treatment, observation, or consideration, as in *to watch* or *talk o., make merry o.* OE.

1. Having his house burnt o. his head BERKELEY. *fig.* A grave doubt hung o. the legitimacy both of Mary and of Elizabeth MACAULAY. Phr. *O.* (one's) *signature, name*, etc., with one's signature, etc., subscribed to what is written. **2.** *O. head and ears*: see HEAD *sb.* **3.** Those hours..which others consume..o. the bottle 1791. We sit down to breakfast, and talk o. it till eleven MRS. CARLYLE.

II. In sense *on, upon.* **1.** On the upper or outer surface of; upon OE. **2.** Upon (with vbs. of motion) OE. **b.** *fig.* Upon, down upon, as an influence OE. **3. a.** (Position) everywhere on; here and there upon. Now esp. *all o.* OE. **b.** (Motion) to and fro upon; all about; throughout. Often *all o.* OE. **c.** Through every part of, all through 1647. **d.** In the above senses often placed after its object. late ME.

1. With his hat low down o. his eyes TROLLOPE. **2.** Let us draw a veil o. this dismal spectacle 1861. **b.** A sudden change came o'er his heart 1834. **3. a.** The People..began to be allarm'd all o. the Town DE FOE. **b.** We may range o. Europe, from shore to shore RUSKIN. **c.** She would have liked to go o. all his notes about his case 1892. **d.** A test which holds good all the world o. 1832.

III. 1. Above in authority, rule, or power OE. **2.** Above or beyond in degree, quality, or action; in preference to; more than OE. †**3.** In addition to, further than; besides, beyond –1772. **4.** In excess of, above, more than (a stated amount or number). late ME.

1. With sbs., as *king, lord o.*; *jurisdiction, rule, triumph o.*; adjs. *victorious o.*; vbs. *to reign, rule, appoint* or *set* any one *o.* Who is Lord ouer vs? *Ps.* 12:4. **2.** The preference given to him o. English captains MACAULAY. **4.** A distance of o. 700 yards 1896.

IV. Across (above, or on a surface). **1.** Indicating motion that passes above (something) on the way to the other side. Occas. expressing only the latter part of this, as in *falling* or *jumping over a precipice*, i.e. over the edge and down. OE. **2.** From side to side of a surface or space; across, to the other side of (a sea, river, boundary, etc.); from end to end of (a line), along OE. †**3.** *fig.* In contravention of, contrary to –1502. **4.** On the other side of; across (of position) OE.

1. O. hedge and ditch 1621. O. the ship's side 1794. The sun is peering o. the roofs 1843. **2.** A free pass o. this company's line of railways 1894. **4.** I have a bed o. the way offered me at three half-crowns a night 1769. *The King o. the water*, Jacobite phr. for the exiled king.

V. Of time. **1.** Beyond in time; after. *Obs.* exc. *dial.* OE. **2.** During, all through OE. †**3.** During the (eve or night) preceding; on the preceding (evening or night). *Obs.* exc. in OVERNIGHT. –1528. **4.** Till the end of; for a period that includes 1806.

2. The repayment..should be spread o. a series of years 1886. **4.** In case you should stay o. Wednesday MRS. CARLYLE.

Over- is used with adverbial, prepositional, and adjectival force, in comb. with sbs.; with adverbial and prepositional force in comb. with vbs.; with adverbial force in comb. with adjs., advbs., and preps. Its combs. are therefore exceedingly numerous. The following are the chief classes. (Cf. SUR-, SUPER-.)

I. In spatial and temporal senses, and in uses directly related to these. **1.** With vbs., or with sbs. forming vbs., etc., in the sense 'over in space, on high, above the top or surface of', as *overcanopy, -hang, -mount, -soar, -spring, -vault*, etc. Also (*b*) in sense of 'rising above', 'overtopping', as OVER-TOP, -TOWER; and (*c*) with the sense of position implying other notions of which it is a condition or element, as OVERJOY, OVERLOOK, etc. **2.** With the senses 'above in power, authority, rank, station'. In vbs., as OVERMASTER, -RULE, etc. **b.** So in sbs. and adjs. derived from or related to vbs., as OVERRULE, -RULER, -SEER, etc.; also in other sbs., in sense of 'higher, superior', as OVER-KING, OVERLORD, etc. **3.** With the sense of inclination to one side so as to lean over the space beneath. In vbs., as *overbias, -lean*, etc.; also in derived sbs. and adjs., as *overbias, overleaning*, etc. **4.** With the sense of passing across overhead, and so 'away, off'. In vbs., as OVERCARRY, *-drive*, etc.; also in derived sbs. and adjs. **5.** With the sense of surmounting, passing over the top, or over the brim or edge. In vbs., as OVERBOIL, -BRIM, *-climb*, -FLOW; occas. (*b*) implying 'passing over without hitting, missing', as OVERLEAP, -LOOK, -SHOOT, *-soar, -spring, -step*; also (*c*) *fig.* of surmounting or getting over an obstacle, an illness, etc., as OVERCOME. **b.** Also in derived or related sbs. or adjs. **6.** With the sense of motion forward and down, and hence of overturning, inversion. In vbs., as OVERBALANCE, -BEAR, -THROW, -TURN, etc.; so in derived sbs. and adjs. **7.** With the sense 'down upon from above'. In vbs., as OVERLEAP, -LOOK, -SEE, etc. **8.** With sense 'upon the surface generally, all over, so as to prevail, or abound over, cover, hide'. In vbs., as OVERCLOUD, *-cover, -crust, -glaze, -gloom*, -GROW, *-heap, -lard, -net, -veil*, etc. **b.** So with ppl. adjs. and vbl. sbs. **c.** With sbs. in the sense of 'overlying, covering, worn over or above', 'upper or outer'; as in OVERCOAT, *-garment*, -SHOE, etc. **9.** With the sense of motion over a surface generally, so as to cover in whole or part; also of motion to and fro upon or all over; as in *overflood, -glide*, -RIDE, -RUN, *-sweep*, etc.; also with derived sbs. and adjs. **10.** With the sense 'across, from side to side, to the other side'; as *overcarve*, etc.; so in derived sbs. and adjs. **11.** With the sense of bringing or gaining over to a party, opinion, etc. In vbs., as *Over-force, -influence*, OVER-PERSUADE, *-talk.* **b.** So also with derived sbs. and adjs. **12.** With (the sense of 'across a boundary'; hence, of trangression; as in OVERGANG, *-lash, -step*, etc. **13.** With the sense 'beyond a point or limit, farther than'; in vbs., as OVERGROW, -REACH, etc.; also in derivs. **14.** As in OVERTAKE. **15.** As in OVERHEAR. **16.** With the sense 'all through' (something extended), 'through the extent of', 'from beginning to end'; in vbs., as OVERLOOK, *-name*, etc. **17.** With the sense 'through', 'to the end of' in time; 'to an end or issue', 'to extinction'; in vbs. as OVERPASS, -RUN 1603. **18.** With the sense 'beyond' in time, 'too long', 'too late'; in vbs., as *overbide*, -LIVE, -STAY. **19.** With the sense 'remaining over', or 'in addition or excess', 'surplus', 'extra'; as in vb. *overleave*; in sbs. as *over-deal*, OVERTIME. **20.** With the notion of repetition, 'over again'; in vbs. as *overact, -hear*, etc.; in sbs., as *overcome*, -WORD. **21.** With the sense of overcoming, putting down, or getting the better of, by the action or thing expressed; in vbs., as OVERAWE, *-brave*, -DARE; so in vbl. derivs.

II. In the sense of 'over or beyond' in degree or quality; hence, of surpassing, excelling, exceeding, excess. **1.** With the notion of doing some action over or beyond another agent, of going beyond, surpassing, or excelling in the action denoted by the simple vb. In vbs., as OVERBID 2, OVERGO 10, OVER-RUN II. 1. **b.** In vbs. formed on sbs., with the sense of 'surpassing in, or in the rôle of', as *over-bulk*; esp. in nonce-phrases, as *over-Macpherson Macpherson*, etc. **2.** In refl. vbs., with the sense of surpassing oneself; often with the sense of exhausting oneself by the action; sometimes merely with the sense of doing too much; as *overbloom itself, Over-drink*, -EAT, -SLEEP *oneself.* **3.** In sense 'more than'; with vbs., as OVERBALANCE, -FILL, -MATCH, etc. **b.** So in derivs.; also in other adjs., as OVERDUE, OVERFULL. **4.** With the sense 'exceedingly, beyond measure, lavishly'. In vbs., often rendering L. *super-*, as OVERABOUND, *-glad, -high*, etc.; in adjs., as OVERDEAR, *-excelling, -glorious.* Now *obs.* or *arch.* **5.** With the sense 'to a greater extent, or at a greater rate, than is usual, natural, or intended; too far'. In vbs., as OVERACT, -BID, *-drive, -esteem*, -ESTIMATE, *-march, -mount*, -RATE, etc.; in adjs., as *overawful*, etc. **6–9.** With the sense 'in or to excess, too much, too'. Now a leading use of *over-* in comb. with vbs., adjs., sbs., and advs. **6.** With vbs. (or with sbs. or adjs. forming vbs.); as *over-affect, -ballast, -burn, -busy, -cloy, -drink, -drive*, -EAT, *-enter, -fatigue, -fire, -fish, -gorge, -leaven*, -LOAD, *-play, -ply, -pot*, -REACH, *-roast, -talk, -use, -water*, etc. **b.** This use is often found with pa. pples., when the other parts of the vb. occur with *over-* rarely, or not at all; as in *over-agitated, -assessed, -coached, -handicapped, -sprung*, etc. **7.** With adjs., as OVERACTIVE, *-bitter*, -BOLD, *-burdensome, -busy, -cold, -costly, -great, -happy, -hardy, -heavy, -high, -kind, -large, -late, -lavish, -loud, -officious, -proud, -rigid, -rigorous, -ripe, -slow, -strict, -subtle, -tedious, -weak*, etc. **b.** With pres. pples., forming ppl. adjs.; as *Over-abounding*, etc. (Unlimited.) **c.** With pa. pples. in *-ed, -en*, etc., forming ppl. adjs., as *overacted, -civilized, -crowded*, OVERDONE, *-fraught*, etc. (Unlimited.) **d.** With adjs. in *-ed* from sbs.; as *over-brained, -garrisoned, -leisured*, etc. (Unlimited.) **8.** With sbs. **a.** Verbal sbs. in *-ing*; as *overabounding, -crowding, -doing, -feeding.* (Unlimited.) **b.** Nouns of action or condition allied to vbs.; as OVERCHARGE, -ISSUE; OVER-ACTION, -EXCITEMENT, *-haste, -love*, -PAYMENT, *-praise, -thought, -trust*, etc. (Unlimited.) **c.** Nouns of quality or state allied to adjs.; as OVERANXIETY, *-bitterness*, -CREDULITY, *-heat, -height, -length*, etc. (Unlimited.) **d.** Various sbs. denoting action, state, quality, etc.; as *over-care*, -CAUTION, *-cunning, -desire*, etc. **9.** With advs., simple or derived from adjs.; as OVERBOLDLY, *late*, -MUCH, *-soon.*

III. Combs. consisting of OVER *prep.* with object. These normally form advs. and adjs.; exceptionally they give rise to sbs. and vbs. The advs. are often written as two words, as *over all* or *overall, over board* or *overboard.*

O:ver-abou·nd, *v.* late ME. [OVER- II. 4, 6.] **1.** *intr.* To abound more, be more plentiful. *arch.* or *Obs.* **2.** To abound too much *with* or *in* something; of things, to be too plentiful 1597. So **O:ver-abu·ndance, -abu·ndant** *a.*, **-ly** *adv.*

Overact (ō^{u}vəræ·kt), *v.* 1611. [OVER- II. 5, 6, 1, I. 13.] **1.** *intr.* To act in excess; to go too far in action. **2.** *trans.* To act (a part) with exaggeration; to overdo in acting 1631. †**3.** To go beyond in acting; to outdo –1661. †**4.** To actuate too powerfully; to overcome –1677.

1. You over-act, when you should under-do B. JONS. So **O:ver-a·ction. O:ver-a·ctive** *a.*, **-acti·vity.**

O·ver-a·ge (stress var.), *adj. phr.* 1886. [OVER *prep.* III. 4 and AGE *sb.* 3.] That is over a certain age or limit of age.

Overall (ōᵘ·vərǭl), *sb.* 1782. [OVER- III; lit. 'over everything'. Partly after Fr. *surtout* SURTOUT.] **1.** (Also *pl.*) A garment worn over the ordinary clothing as a protection against wet, dirt, etc. 1815. **2.** *pl.* Loose-fitting trousers of strong material, canvas, etc., worn as a protective outer garment; also formerly long leather or waterproof leggings 1782. Hence **O·veralled** *ppl. a.* wearing overalls.

†**Overa·ll,** *adv.* OE. [OVER- III.] **1.** Everywhere; in every direction –1596. **b.** In every part; all over, all through –1590. **2.** Beyond everything; pre-eminently; especially –1687.

O·ver-all, *adj. phr.* 1894. [The phr. *over all* used attrib.] Including everything between the extreme points.

A..cruiser, with an 'o.' length of 335 ft. 1894.

Over and above, *phr.* late ME. [Pleonastic, for emphasis.] **A.** as *prep.* **1.** = OVER *prep.* III. 1. *rare.* 1449. **2.** = OVER *prep.* III. 3. 1521.

2. Ouer and aboue all that it had cost him 1585.

B. as *adv.* **1.** In addition, besides 1588. **2.** (Qualifying an adj.) Overmuch, too much, too. *Obs.* exc. *dial.* 1749. **b.** *attrib.* or as *adj.* Overmuch, too great, excessive (*rare*) 1865.

O:ver-a·nxious, *a.* 1741. [OVER- II. 7.] Excessively or unduly anxious, too anxious. So **O·ver-anxi·ety, -a·nxiously** *adv.*

Overarch (ōᵘvərā·ɹtʃ), *v.* 1667. [OVER- I. 1.] **1.** *trans.* To arch over, to bend over in or like an arch. **2.** *intr.* To form an arch overhead; to bend over as an arch 1720.

1. As the heavens over-arch the whole earth SPURGEON. Hence **Overa·rch** *sb.* an arch overhead.

O·ver-arm, *a.* 1864. *Cricket, Tennis.* = OVERHAND *a.* B. 2; also in *Swimming.*

Overawe (ōᵘvərǭ·), *v.* 1579. [OVER- I. 21.] *trans.* To restrain, control, or repress by awe; to keep in awe by superior influence.

Neither over-awed by Force, nor seduced by Faction 1683.

Overbalance (ōᵘvəɹbæ·lăns), *sb.* 1641. [f next.] **1.** Excess of weight, value, or amount; preponderance 1659. †**b.** *Commerce. spec.* Excess in the value of the exports over the imports of a country –1721. **2.** Something that outweighs or overbalances 1658.

Overbalance (ōᵘvəɹbæ·lăns), *v.* 1586. [OVER- II. 3, I. 6.] **1.** *trans.* To do more than balance; to outweigh. Also *absol.* To preponderate. **2.** To destroy the equilibrium of; to capsize; *refl.* and *intr.* To lose one's balance 1834.

1. The expenses overbalanced the profit 1855. **2.** You may o. and bring down the whole concern 1881.

O·verbank, *a.* 1879. [f. OVER *prep.* + BANK *sb.*¹] *Artillery.* Applied to a kind of gun-carriage for muzzle-loading guns, so constructed as to allow of the gun's being fired over the parapet.

Overbear (ōᵘvəɹbēᵊ·ɹ), *v.* late ME. [OVER- I, 4, 6, II. 1.] †**1.** *trans.* To transfer, remove; to put away WYCLIF. **2.** To bear over or down by weight or physical force; to overthrow; to break or crush down 1535. **b.** *fig.* To overcome, put down, or repress, as by power, authority, or influence; to overpower, oppress 1565. **3.** To surpass in weight, importance, etc. 1712.

2. See how force oft ouerbereth ryght 1559. **b.** The barons ouerbear me with their pride MARLOWE. So **Overbea·rance,** overbearing behaviour. **Overbea·ring** *ppl. a.*, **-ly** *adv.*, **-ness.**

Overbe·nd, *v.* 1617. [OVER- I. 3, 1, II. 6.] **1.** (Only in *pple.*) **a.** *trans.* To bend (something) over or to one side. **b.** To bend over (something). **c.** *intr.* To bend or stoop over. **2.** *trans.* To bend too much or to excess 1624.

Overbid (ōᵘvəɹbi·d), *v.* 1616. [OVER- II. 5, 1.] †**1.** *intr.* To bid more than the value BEAUM. & FL. **2.** *trans.* To outbid 1645. **b.** To bid or offer more than the value of (a thing) 1646. **c.** *Bridge.* = OVERCALL *v.* 1909.

Overblow (ōᵘvəɹblōᵘ·), *v.* late ME. [f. OVER- I. 4, 6, 9, II. 6, 5 + BLOW *v.*¹] **1.** *trans.* To blow (a thing) over the top of anything; to blow off or away. **2.** *intr.* Of a storm: To blow over, to pass away overhead; to abate in violence; hence *fig.* of danger, anger, etc. (Perf. tenses often with *be.*) late ME. **3.** *trans.* To blow (a thing) over; to blow down 1562. **4.** To blow over the surface of; to cover by blowing over (as sand or snow does). late ME. †**5.** *intr. Naut.* Of the wind: To blow too hard for topsails to be carried –1823. **6.** *trans. Mus.* To blow or play (a pipe or wind-instrument) with such force as to produce a harmonic or overtone instead of the fundamental note. Also *refl.* (of the pipe, etc.) 1852.

2. The tempest is o'erblown, the skies are clear DRYDEN.

Overboard (ōᵘ·vəɹbōᵊɹd), *adv.* OE. [f. OVER *prep.* IV. 1 + BOARD *sb.* Treated as one word from late XVIII.] **1.** Over the side of a ship or boat, out of or from the ship into the water. **2.** *fig.* esp. in phr. *To throw o.*, to cast aside, discard, renounce 1641.

Overboil (ōᵘvəɹboi·l), *v.* 1584. [OVER- I. 5, II. 6.] **1.** *intr.* To boil over. Chiefly *fig.* 1611. **2.** *trans.* To boil too much 1584.

1. To keep the mind Deep in its fountain, lest it o. BYRON.

O·ver-bo·ld, *a.* 1530. [OVER- II. 7.] Too bold; presumptuous. Hence **O·ver-bo·ldly** *adv.*, **-ness.**

Overbri·m, *v.* 1607. [OVER- I. 5.] **1.** *intr.* To overflow at the brim; to brim over. (Said of the liquid or the vessel.) Mostly *fig.* **2.** *trans.* To flow over the brim of 1818.

1. If the pitcher shall o. with water SCOTT. **2.** The liquor that o'erbrims the cup BROWNING. Hence **Overbri·mmed** *ppl. a.*, **Overbri·mming** *vbl. sb.* and *ppl. a.*

Overbuild (ōᵘvəɹbi·ld), *v.* Pa. t. and pple. **overbuilt.** 1601. [OVER- I. 1, 8, II. 6.] **1.** *trans.* To build over or upon. Chiefly *fig.* 1649. **2.** To build to excess 1642. **3.** To erect more buildings than are required upon (an area) 1601.

Overbu·rden, -bu·rthen, *sb.* 1579. [OVER- II. 8 d, I. 1.] **1.** Excessive burden; excess of burden. **2.** *Mining,* etc. The overlying waste which has to be removed in quarrying or mining, in order to get at the deposit worked 1839.

Overbu·rden, -bu·rthen, *v.* 1532. [OVER- II. 6.] *trans.* To overload, overcharge. Hence **Overbu·rdened, -bu·rthened** *ppl. a.*

Overbuy·, *v.* late ME. [OVER- II. 5, 2.] †**1.** *trans.* To buy at too high a price –1700. **2.** *refl.* and *intr.* To buy beyond one's means 1745.

Overca·ll, *v.* 1909. [OVER- II. 6.] *Bridge.* To bid more on one's hand than it is worth; to bid higher than a previous bid.

Over-ca·pitalize, *v.* 1890. [OVER- II. 6.] *trans.* To fix or estimate the capital of (a joint-stock company, etc.) at too high an amount. So **O:vercapitaliza·tion** 1882.

Overcarry (-kæ·ri), *v.* Now *rare.* late ME. [OVER- I. 10, 13, II. 5.] †**1.** *trans.* To carry over or across; to transport –1513. **b.** To carry beyond the proper point 1897. **2.** To carry too far, overdo; to do more than carry 1606. †**3.** *fig.* To carry (a person) beyond the bounds of moderation, or into error, etc.; to carry away. Also *absol.* –1648.

Overcast (ōᵘ·vəɹkɑst), *sb.* 1569. [f. OVERCAST *v.* or *ppl. a.*] **1.** A person or thing that is cast away; an outcast. *Obs.* exc. *dial.* **2.** Something cast or spread over; a coating; a cloud covering the sky or part of it 1686. **3.** *Mining.* A bridge which carries one subterranean air-passage over another 1867. **4.** *Needlework.* Overcast work 1891.

Overcast (ōᵘvəɹkɑ·st), *v.* ME. [OVER- I. 6, etc.] **1.** *trans.* To overthrow, overturn, cast down, upset (*lit.* and *fig.*). *Obs.* exc. *dial.* [OVER- I. 6.] **2.** To cast or throw (something) over or above something else. Now *rare.* [OVER- I. 1, 8.] ME. **3.** To cover or overspread (*with* something). Now *rare* in general sense. [OVER- I. 8.] late ME. **4.** *spec.* To cover or overspread with clouds, or with something that darkens or dulls the surface. Usu. in *pa. pple.* and of the weather. ME. **b.** *fig.* To overshadow, darken. late ME. **5.** *intr.* To become overspread with clouds; to become dark and gloomy. *Obs.* exc. *dial.* late ME. **6.** *Needlework.* To throw rough stitches over a raw edge or edges of cloth to prevent unravelling; to sew over and over; also, to strengthen or adorn such an edge by buttonhole- or blanket-stitch. [OVER- I. 5.] 1706. †**7.** To over-estimate. [OVER- II. 5] –1765. †**8.** *Bowls.* (? *intr.*) To cast beyond the jack. (Also *pass.* in same sense.) [OVER- I. 13.] –1706. Hence **O·vercast** *ppl. a.* 1569.

4. A dark Cloud..overcasts the Air DE FOE. **b.** Stung to the soul, o'ercast with holy dread POPE.

O:ver-cau·tion. 1714. [OVER- II. 8 d.] Excessive caution.

O·ver-cau·tious, *a.* 1706. [OVER- II. 7.] More cautious than is needful, too cautious. Hence **Over-cau·tious-ly** *adv.*, **-ness.**

Overcharge (ōᵘ·vəɹ,tʃāɹdʒ), *sb.* 1611. [OVER- II. 8 b.] **1.** An excessive charge or load; an excess. **2.** The act of overcharging; an exorbitant charge 1662.

Overcharge (ōᵘvəɹ,tʃā·ɹdʒ), *v.* late ME. [OVER- II. 6; cf. Fr. *surcharger.*] **1.** *trans.* To load, fill, furnish, or supply to excess (*with* something). **b.** *fig.* To exaggerate, overdo. Now *rare* or *arch.* 1711. †**2.** To lay an excessive burden upon; to oppress; to overbear by superior force –1771. †**b.** To accuse too much or extravagantly –1636. **3.** *spec.* To put to too great expense; now, to charge (any one) too much ME. **b.** To charge (so much) more than is justly due 1667.

1. The said Cormucke having..over-charged one of his Pistols 1681. **b.** A little overcharging the likeness ADDISON. **3.** No one likes to be overcharged for what he buys (*mod.*). **b.** The 20 pounds overcharged for the widows 1733.

O·vercheck, *a.* (*sb.*¹) 1875. [f. OVER- I. 5 + CHECK *sb.*¹] In *o. rein,* a rein passing over a horse's head between the ears, so as to pull upward upon the bit; *o. bridle,* a bridle having an overcheck rein.

O·vercheck, *sb.*² 1923. [f. OVER- I. 8 + CHECK *sb.*²] A pattern in which a check is superimposed upon another design.

Overcloud (-klau·d), *v.* 1592. [OVER- I. 8.] **1.** *trans.* To cloud over; to overspread or cover with or as with a cloud or clouds. **2.** *fig.* To cast a shadow over, render gloomy; to obscure 1593. **3.** *intr.* To become overclouded; to cloud over 1862.

Overcoat (ōᵘ·vəɹkōᵘt). 1848. [OVER- I. 8 c.] A large coat worn over the ordinary clothing; a great-coat, top-coat.

Overcolour (-kʌ·ləɹ), *v.* 1823. [OVER- II. 6.] *trans.* To colour too highly (usu. *fig.*); to represent too strongly. So **O:verco·louring** *vbl. sb.*

Overcome (ōᵘvəɹkʌ·m), *v.* [OE. *ofercuman,* f. *ofer-* OVER- + *cuman* COME.] †**1.** *trans.* To come upon, reach, overtake. Only OE. [OVER- I. 7.] **2.** *trans.* To overpower, defeat, get the better of in any contest or struggle. Since 17th c. chiefly with non-material object. [OVER- I. 2, 21.] OE. †**b.** To win (a battle) –1585. **c.** *absol.* or *intr.* To gain the victory ME. **3.** Of some physical or mental force or influence: To overpower; to exhaust, render helpless; to affect excessively with emotion. Chiefly in *pass.*; const. *with,* rarely *by.* In *pa. pple.* occas. (euphem.) = overcome by liquor, intoxicated. [OVER- I. 2, 21.] OE. †**b.** To dominate, possess (the mind, etc.) (*rare*) –1607. †**c.** *fig.* To surpass the capacity of, overflow –1708. **4.** To get over, surmount (a difficulty); to recover from (a blow, etc.) [OVER- I. 5] ME. **5.** To go beyond, exceed, surpass (in quality, measure, etc.). Now *arch.* [OVER- I. 13.] ME. †**6.** To get through; to master, accomplish. [OVER- I. 17.] –1697. **7.** To traverse (a road, etc.) *arch.* ME. **8.** To overrun; to cover. Now *rare.* [OVER- I. 9.] late ME. †**b.** To come over suddenly SHAKS. **9.** *intr.* To 'come to', 'come round' from a swoon. Now *dial.* [OVER- I. 17.] late ME.

2. He..that is slain, is Overcome, but not Conquered HOBBES. **3.** The architect was too much overcome to speak DICKENS. Overcome by sickness 1849. **5.** The idols they had..did even o. the Egyptian idols in number 1643. **6.** I am extremely glad..to find that you have o. your long journey 1652.

O·ver-co·nfident, *a.* 1617. [OVER- II. 7.] Too confident. So **O·ver-co·nfidence,** excess of confidence. **O·ver-co·nfidently** *adv.*

O:ver-corre·ct, *v.* 1867. [OVER- II. 3.] *Optics. trans.* To correct (a lens) for chromatic aberration to such an extent that the focus of the red rays lies beyond that of the violet. Opp. to *under-correct*.

Overcount (-kau·nt), *v.* 1593. [OVER- II. 1, 5.] **1.** *trans.* To outnumber 1606. **2.** To overestimate 1593.

O·ver-cre·dulous, *a.* 1605. [OVER- II. 7.] Too credulous, too ready to believe. So **O·ver-credu·lity,** too great credulity.

Overcrow (ōᵘvəɹkrōᵘ·), *v.* 1562. [OVER- I. 2, 21.] *trans.* To crow over; to exult or triumph over.

Overcrowd (ōᵘvəɹkrau·d), *v.* 1766. [OVER- II. 6.] **1.** *trans.* To crowd to excess. **2.** *intr.* To crowd together in too great a number 1899.

O·ver-cu·rious, *a.* 1561. [OVER- II. 7.] †**a.** Too careful, fastidious, or particular; **b.** Too inquisitive. Hence **O·ver-cu·rious-ly** *adv.*, **-ness.**

Overda·re, *v.* 1586. [OVER- II. 6, 1, I. 21.] **1.** *intr.* To be too daring; to dare too much. †**2.** *trans.* To surpass in or overcome by daring –1611. So **O·verda·ring** *vbl. sb.*

O·ver-dea·r, *a.* 1483. [OVER- II. 4, 6.] Excessively or exceedingly dear (in various senses); too costly.

Overde·ck, *v.* 1509. [OVER- I. 8, II. 6.] †**1.** *trans.* To 'deck' or cover over –1599. **2.** To deck or adorn to excess 1712.

O·ver-de·licate, *a.* 1630. [OVER- II. 7.] Too delicate. So **O·ver-de·licacy,** too great delicacy.

O:ver-deve·lop, *v.* 1869. [OVER- II. 6.] *trans.* To develop too greatly or to excess; *spec.* in *Photogr.*: see DEVELOP *v.* 5. So **O:ver-deve·lopment** 1842.

O:ver-discha·rge, *v.* 1893. [OVER- II. 6.] *trans.* To discharge too greatly; *spec.* in *Electr.*, to discharge an accumulator or storage battery beyond a certain limit, an operation injurious to the battery. So **Over-discha·rge** *sb.* the act of over-discharging or fact of being over-discharged.

Overdo (ōᵘvəɹdū·), *v.* [OE. *oferdōn*, f. *ofer-* OVER- + DO *v.*] **1.** *trans.* To do to excess or too much; to exaggerate. **2.** *intr.* or *absol.* To do too much; to exceed the proper limit. late ME. **3.** *trans.* To carry too far 1623. **4.** To cook (food) too much. (Usu. in pa. pple. *overdone*.) 1683. **5.** To overtax the strength of; to exhaust, overcome 1822. **6.** To outdo, excel. Now *arch.* 1625.

1. Any thing so ouer-done, is from the purpose o Playing SHAKS. 2. Some can not do but they o. 1539. 5. At night ran down too fast, and overdid myself 1858.

Overdone (ōᵘvəɹdʊ·n: stress var.), *ppl. a.* OE. [pa. pple. of prec.] Done too much (in various senses of OVERDO *v.*); exaggerated; overcooked; exhausted; overcome.

Overdose (ōᵘ·vəɹdōᵘs), *sb.* 1690. [OVER- II. 8 b.] An excessive dose, too large a dose.

Overdo·se, *v.* 1727. [OVER- II. 6.] †**1.** *trans.* To administer (medicine) in too large a dose –1777. **2.** To dose (a person) to excess; to give too large a dose to; also *transf.* 1758.

O·verdraft (-drɑft). 1878. [OVER- II. 6.] *Banking.* The action of overdrawing an account; the amount by which a draft exceeds the balance against which it is drawn.

O·verdraught, -draft (-drɑft). 1884. [OVER- I. 1.] A draught passing over or admitted from above a fire, furnace, kiln, etc.

Overdraw (ōᵘvəɹdrǭ·), *v.* late ME. [OVER- I. 10, 4, II. 6.] **I.** †**1.** *trans.* To draw over or across; (Separable comb.) late ME. only. †**b.** To draw off into another vessel –1703. †**2.** *intr.* To draw or move over or across; to pass away. late ME. only.

II. 1. *Banking.* To draw money in excess of the amount which stands to one's credit, or is at one's disposal. Also *absol.*, to make an overdraft. 1734. **2.** To exaggerate or overdo in drawing, depicting, or describing 1844.

1. My finances are not only exhausted, but overdrawn COWPER. Don't o... more than you can help 1890.

Overdre·ss, *v.* 1706. [OVER- II. 6.] **1.** *trans.* To dress to excess. Also *intr.* for *refl.* **2.** To dress or cook too much 1775.

Overdue (ōᵘ·vəɹdiū·; stress var.), *a.* 1845. [OVER- II. 3 b.] More than due; past the time when due. O. bonds for the payment of money 1845. The train is half an hour o. 1904.

O·ver-ea·ger, *a.* 1575. [OVER- II. 7.] Too eager; excessively eager or keen. Hence **O·ver-ea·ger-ly** *adv.*, **-ness.**

O·ver-ea·rnest, *a.* 1586. [OVER- II. 7.] Too earnest. Hence **O·ver-ea·rnest-ly** *adv.*, **-ness.**

Overeat (ōᵘvərī·t), *v.* 1599. [OVER- II. 6.] To eat too much, eat to excess. *intr.* or (usu.) *refl.*

Over-e·stimate, *v.* 1840. [OVER- II. 6.] To estimate too highly; to value at too high a rate. So **O·ver-e·stimate** *sb.* too high an estimate. **O·ver-estima·tion,** the action of over-estimating.

O:ver-exci·te, *v.* 1825. [OVER- II. 6.] *trans.* To excite too much. So **O·ver-excitabi·lity; -exci·table** *a.*; **-exci·tement.**

O:ver-exe·rt, *v.* 1817. [OVER- II. 6.] *trans.* To exert too much; usu. *refl.* So **O·ver-exe·rtion.**

O:ver-expo·se, *v.* 1869. [OVER- II. 6.] *trans.* To expose too much; *spec.* in *Photogr.* to expose (a sensitized plate or film) to the light too long. So **O·ver-expo·sure.**

Overfall (ōᵘ·vəɹfǭl), *sb.* 1542. [OVER- I. 5, 6.] **1.** *Naut.* A turbulent surface of water with short breaking waves, caused by a strong current or tide setting over a submarine ridge or shoal, or by the meeting of contrary currents. **2.** A sudden drop in the sea-bottom 1798. †**3.** A waterfall in a river, a cataract or rapid –1613. **4.** A structure to allow the overflow of water from a canal or a lock on a river, when the water reaches a certain level 1791.

Overfall (ōᵘvəɹfǭ·l), *v. arch. rare.* [OE. *oferfeallan*; see OVER- I. 7, 6.] **1.** *trans.* To fall upon or over ME. **b.** To fall upon, attack OE. **2.** *intr.* To fall over 1530.

Overfault (ōᵘ·vəɹfǭlt). 1883. [OVER- I. 3 + FAULT *sb.* 9.] *Geol.* A fault of which the inclination is towards the upthrow side (hence also called *inverted* or *reverse* fault).

Over-fee·d, *v.* 1609. [OVER- II. 6.] **1.** *trans.* To feed to excess. **2.** *intr.* (for *refl.*) To take too much food 1774. So **O·ver-fe·d** (stress var.) *ppl. a.* fed to excess 1579.

Overfi·ll, *v.* [OE. *oferfyllan*, f. *ofer-* OVER- II. 3 + *fyllan* FILL.] **1.** *trans.* To fill to overflowing. **2.** *intr.* To become full to overflowing 1615.

Over-floa·t, *v.* 1601. [OVER- I. 9, 1.] †**1.** *trans.* To overflow –1697. **2.** To float over (*lit.* and *fig.*) 1658.

Overflou·rish, *v.* 1601. [OVER- II. 6, I. 8.] **1.** *trans.* To cover with blossom or verdure 1601. †**2.** To embellish too greatly –1716.

1. *Twel. N.* III. iv. 404.

Overflow (ōᵘ·vəɹflōᵘ), *sb.* 1589. [OVER- I, 9, 5.] **1.** The act or fact of overflowing; an inundation, a flood. **2.** A flowing over from a vessel that is too full; that which flows over (*lit.* and *fig.*) 1640. **3.** Such a quantity as runs over; excess, superfluity 1589. **4.** Short for *o.-pipe* or *-drain*, a pipe or drain for carrying off excess of water 1895. **5.** *attrib.*, as *o. meeting* (of people that cannot be accommodated at the main place of meeting), *population*; *basin, pipe* 1837.

2. The o. of Teutons came very early thither 1852. 3. Thy ouerflow of good, conuerts to bad SHAKS.

Overflow (ōᵘvəɹflōᵘ·), *v. Pa. pple.* **-flowed,** †**-flown.** [OE. *oferflōwan*; see OVER- I. 9, 5.] **I.** *trans.* **1.** To flow over; to flood, inundate. **2.** *transf.* and *fig.* To pass or spread over like a flood 1533. **3.** To flow over (the brim, banks, or sides) 1548. **b.** To cause to overflow. Chiefly *fig.* 1667. †**4.** To overflow with, pour out (*rare*) –1598.

1. Trinitie Colledge greene..is in the winter time overflowne with water 1585. 2. So they overflowed his house, smoked his cigars, and drank his health R. KIPLING. 4. *Merry W.* II. ii. 157.

II. *intr.* **1.** To flow over the sides or brim by reason of fullness. †Also *transf.* and *fig.* OE. **b.** To remove from one part to another owing to want of room, etc. 1858. **2.** To be so full that the contents run over the brim. late ME.

1. This tyme at Rome the Ryver of Tiber overflowed exceedingly 1560. **b.** The crowd overflowed into the adjoining gardens 1904. **2.** *fig.* To make the comming houre oreflow with ioy SHAKS.

O·verflowing, *ppl. a.* OE. [f. OVERFLOW *v.* + -ING².] That overflows: in the senses of the vb. Hence **Overflow·ing-ly** *adv.*, **-ness.**

Overflu·sh, *v.* 1581. [OVER- II. 6, I. 8.] *trans.* **a.** To flush too much. **b.** To flush over, cover with a flush (*rare*). So **O·verflu·sh** *a.* too flush.

Overfly (ōᵘvəɹfləi·), *v.* 1558. [f. OVER- I. 4, etc. + FLY *v.*¹] **1.** *trans.* To cross or pass over by flying. [OVER- I. 4.] **b.** To fly beyond. Also *refl.* 1854. **2.** To surpass in flight; to fly higher, faster, or farther than. [OVER- II. 1.] 1592. †**3.** To fly (a hawk) too much. [OVER- II. 6.] –1616.

2. Out-stripping crows that strive to over-fly them SHAKS.

Overfold (ōᵘ·vəɹfōᵘld), *sb.* 1883. [f. OVER- I. 3, 6 + FOLD *sb.*², after G. *überfaltung.*] *Geol.* A fold of strata in which the axes of the component anticline and syncline have both been tilted or pushed over beyond the vertical, so that the strata involved in the middle third of the fold are turned upside down. (Also *inclined, overturned, inverted,* or *reflexed fold.*)

Overfold (ōᵘvəɹfōᵘ·ld), *v.* late ME. [OVER- I. 8, 3, 6.] **1.** *trans.* To fold over, or so as to cover. **2.** *Geol.* Of folded strata: In *pass.* To be pushed over beyond the vertical, so as to overhang or overlie the strata on the other side of the axis: see prec. 1883.

O·ver-fo·nd, *a.* 1585. [OVER- II. 7.] Too fond. **1.** Too silly. *Obs.* exc. *dial.* **2.** Too affectionate. Const. *of.* 1611. Hence **O·ver-fo·nd-ly** *adv.*, **-ness.**

O·verfo·rward, *a.* 1631. [OVER- II. 7.] Too forward. So **O·verfo·rward-ly** *adv.*, **-ness** 1593.

O·verfree·, *a.* 1639. [OVER- II. 7.] Too free. So **O·verfree·dom,** too great freedom. **O·verfree·ly** *adv.*

Overfreight (-frē¹·t), *v.* 1530. [OVER- II. 6.] *trans.* To overload. So **O·verfreight** *sb.* an overload.

O·verfu·ll, *a.* [OE. *oferfull*; see OVER- II. 3, 7.] Excessively full, too full. Hence **O:verfu·llness.**

Overga·ng, *v.* Now *Sc.* and *n. dial.* [OE. *ofergangan*; see OVER- I. 1, 21, 9, 13.] **1.** *trans.* To overpower. **2.** To go over, overrun ME. **3.** To go beyond, exceed 1737.

Overget (ōᵘvəɹge·t), *v.* ME. [OVER- I. 14, 5.] **1.** *trans.* To overtake. Now only *dial.* **2.** To get over, recover from the effects of (an illness, etc.) 1803.

Overgild (ōᵘvəɹgi·ld), *v.* [OE. *ofergyldan*; see OVER- I. 8, GILD *v.*] *trans.* To gild over, cover with gilding; *fig.* to tinge with a golden colour. Chiefly in *pa. pple.* **overgi·lt.**

†**Overgi·ve,** *v.* 1444. [f. OVER- (in various senses) + GIVE *v.*] †**1.** *trans.* To give over or up, hand over –1711. †**2.** *intr.* To give over, desist –1592.

†**Overgla·nce,** *v.* 1588. [OVER- I. 16.] *trans.* To glance over.

I will ouerglance the superscript SHAKS.

Overgo (ōᵘvəɹgōᵘ·), *v.* [OE. *ofergān*; see OVER- in various senses.] **I.** *trans.* †**1.** To come upon suddenly; to overtake, catch [OVER- I. 7, 14.] –1581. **2.** To pass over (a wall, river, boundary, etc.); to cross. *Obs.* exc. *dial.* †Also *fig.* [OVER- I. 5, 12.] OE. †**3.** To surmount. [OVER- I. 1.] –1619. **4.** *fig.* To go beyond, exceed, excel. [OVER- I. 13.] ME. **5.** To overpower, oppress, overwhelm. Now *dial.* [OVER- I. 21.] ME. †**6.** To go or spread over so as to cover. [OVER- I. 8, 9.] –1634. **7.** To overrun, overflow. Now *dial.* [OVER- I. 9.] OE. **8.** To travel through, traverse. [OVER- I. 9, 16.] ME. †**9.** To pass, live through (time); also, of time, to pass over (a person). [OVER- I. 17, 4.] –1600. †**10.** To outstrip, overtake. [OVER- II. 1.] –1635. †**11.** To pass over, omit. [OVER- I. 5.] –1622.

4. Abhorring to make the punishment o. the offence SIDNEY. 8. *L. L. L.* v. ii. 196.

II. *intr.* To go or pass by; to pass over or away; to pass (in time). Now *dial.* [OVER- I. 4.] OE.

Overgo·vern, *v.* 1850. [OVER- II. 6.] *trans.* To govern too much. So **Overgo·vernment** 1861.

O·ver-gree·dy, *a.* [OE. *ofergrǣdig*; see OVER- II. 7.] Too greedy, excessively greedy. So **O·ver-gree·dily** *adv.*

O·verground, *a.* 1879. [OVER- III.] Situated over or above ground; opp. to *underground.*

Overgrow (ō^{u}vəɹgrō^u·), *v.* late ME. [OVER- I. 8, etc.] **1.** *trans.* To grow over, to cover with growth; to overrun, overspread. (Now chiefly in *pa. pple.*) Also *transf.* and *fig.* **2.** To grow over so as to choke; to grow more vigorously than. [OVER- I. 21, II. 1.] 1523. **3.** *intr.* To grow too large; to increase unduly. (Perfect tenses often with *be.*) [OVER- II. 5.] 1490. **4.** *trans.* To grow over, above, or beyond; to outgrow (clothes, etc.). [OVER- I. 13.] 1536.

2. The tares ouergrow the wheat 1623. **4.** Phr. *To o. oneself,* to grow beyond one's strength, proper size, etc.

O·vergrowth. 1602. [OVER- II. 8, I. 8.] **1.** Excessive or too rapid growth; the result of this, over-luxuriance or abundance. **2.** A growth over or upon something; an accretion 1883.

Overhair (ō^u·vəɹhē^{ə}ɹ). 1879. [OVER- I. 8.] In fur-bearing quadrupeds, the long straight hair that grows over or beyond the fur.

Overhand, *adv.* and *a.* 1579. [f. OVER *prep.* and *adv.* + HAND *sb.*] **A.** *adv.* (*o:verha·nd*). †**1.** Over, upside down. †**2.** Out of hand, aside –1816. **3.** With the hand over or above the object which it grasps; in *Cricket, Tennis* etc. (with ref. to bowling, etc.), with the hand raised above the shoulder 1861. **4.** *Mining.* From below upwards (in ref. to the working or 'stoping' of a vein). **5.** *Needlework.* In *to sew o.* = OVERSEW.

B. *adj.* (*o·verhand*). †**1.** Characterized by bringing the hand from above downwards –1656. **2.** *Cricket, Tennis,* etc. Of bowling, etc.: Done with the hand raised above the shoulder 1870. **3.** *Mining.* Of the working of a vein: Performed from below upwards. **4.** *O. knot*: a simple knot made by passing the end of a rope, string, etc., over the standing part and through the loop or bight so formed 1840.

O·verhang, *sb.* 1864. [f. next.] The fact or extent of overhanging; a jutting out; also *concr.* an overhanging or projecting part. Chiefly *Naut.* the projection of the upper parts of a ship, fore and aft, beyond the water line.

Overhang (ō^{u}vəɹhæ·ŋ), *v.* Pa. t. and pple. **overhung.** 1599. [OVER- I. 1, 3, 8.] **1.** *trans.* To hang over (something); to be suspended above; to project or jut out above. **b.** *fig.* To impend over; to threaten 1653. **2.** *intr.* To hang over; to project beyond the base; to jut out above 1667. **3.** To support from above 1887.

1. Ascend the hill which overhangs the city JOWETT. **2.** Craggie cliff, that overhung Still as it rose MILT.

O·ver-ha·rd, *a.* and *adv.* 1538. [OVER- II. 7, 9.] Too hard; excessively hard. So **Over-ha·rden** *v.* **O·ver-ha·rd-ly** *adv.*, **-ness.**

O·ver-ha·sty, *a.* 1571. [OVER- II. 7.] Too hasty; rash. So **O·ver-ha·sti-ly** *adv.*, **-ness.**

Overhaul (ō^{u}vəɹhǭ·l), *v.* 1626. [OVER- I. 5, 14. Prob. of LG. origin; the three senses are also repr. in G. *überholen.*] **1.** *Naut. trans.* To slacken (a rope) by pulling in the opposite direction to that in which it is drawn in hoisting; to release and separate the blocks of (a tackle) in this way. **2.** *Naut.* and *gen.* To pull asunder in order to examine in detail; to examine thoroughly (e.g. with a view to repairs, etc.) 1705. **3.** *Naut.* and *gen.* To overtake, come up with, gain upon 1793.

2. His own expressions of 'overhaul', for *investigate,* and 'attackable', are in the lowest style of colloquial slang DE QUINCEY. The drains..are being overhauled 1884. Hence **O·verhaul** *sb.* a thorough examination or scrutiny, esp. with a view to repairs. **Overha·uling** *vbl. sb.*

Overhead, *adv., a.* OE. [*Over head* written as one wd.; see OVER- III.] **A.** *adv.* (*overhea·d*). Above one's head; aloft; up in the air or sky, *esp.* in or near the zenith; on the floor or story above 1532. **b.** So as to be completely submerged or immersed; also *fig.* (See OVER *prep.* 3.) 1653.

b. Her Husband was over-head in Debt 1706.

B. *adj.* (*o·verhead*). **1.** Placed or situated overhead, or at some distance above the ground. (Also applied to driving mechanism placed above the object driven, or to a machine having such mechanism.) 1874. **2.** Applicable to one with another; 'all-round'; general, average 1891.

1. *O. gear,* driving-gear above the object driven. *O. steam-engine,* an engine in which the cylinder is above the crank, the thrust motion being downward. **2. O. charges, costs,** etc. (also **O·verheads** *sb. pl.*), such general expenses of a works, institution, or the like, as rent, lighting, heating, clerical establishment, etc., which cannot be charged up to any particular branch of the work.

Overhear (ō^{u}vəɹhī^ə·ɹ), *v.* [OE. *oferhīeran*; see OVER- I. 15. In sense 2 a new comb. in XVI.] †**1.** *trans.* Not to hearken to; to disregard. OE. only. **2.** To hear (speech, etc.) that is not intended to reach one's ears; to hear (a speaker) without his intention or knowledge 1549.

Overheat (ō^{u}vəɹhī·t), *v.* late ME. [OVER- II. 6.] *trans.* To heat too much, heat to excess, make too hot. Also *intr.* for *pass.* (*mod.*)

Overhouse (ō^u·vəɹhaus), *a.* 1859. [f. OVER *prep.*, OVER- III. + HOUSE *sb.*] Passing over and supported by the roofs of houses (instead of posts); said of telegraph or telephone wires.

Overhung (stress var.), *ppl. a.* 1708. [f. OVERHANG *v.*] **1.** Placed so as to jut out above. **2.** Having something hanging over it 1845. **3.** Suspended or supported from above 1887. **4.** [OVER- I. 18] That has been hung too long, as meat, etc. 1895.

O:ver-indu·lge, *v.* 1741. [OVER- II. 6.] *trans.* To indulge to excess. Also *intr.* for *refl.* So **O:ver-indu·lgence, †-ency** 1631; also **O:ver-indu·lgent** *a.* 1728.

O:ver-info·rm, *v.* 1681. [OVER- II. 6.] *trans.* To inform, animate, or actuate to excess.

Over-i·ssue, *v.* 1837. [OVER- II. 6.] *trans.* To issue in excess; e.g. to issue notes, stocks, shares, etc., beyond the authorized amount or the issuer's ability to pay. So **O·ver-i·ssue** *sb.* an issue in excess.

Overjoy (ō^{u}vəɹdʒoi·), *v.* late ME. [OVER- I. 1 (*c*), II. 4, 6.] †**1.** To rejoice over (tr. L. *supergaudere*) WYCLIF. **2.** *trans.* To transport with joy or gladness. (Now usu. in *pa. pple.*) 1571. **b.** *intr.* To rejoice too much 1720. Hence **Overjoy·ed** *ppl. a.*

Overju·mp, *v.* 1608. [OVER- I. 5, II. 5, 2.] **1.** *trans.* and *intr.* To jump over; *fig.* to pass over; to transcend. **2.** *trans.* To jump too far over. **b.** *refl.* To jump too far for one's strength. 1856.

O·ver-king, o·verking. ME. [OVER- I. 2 b.] *Hist.* A superior king; a king who is the superior of other rulers called kings.

Over-labour (-lē^i·bəɹ), *v.* 1530. **1.** *trans.* To overwork. [OVER- II. 2, 6.] **2.** To labour excessively at; to elaborate to excess. [OVER- II. 6.] 1588.

Overla·de, *v.* late ME. [f. OVER- I. 21, II. 6 + LADE *v.*] *trans.* To load with too heavy a burden, to overload. Hence **Overla·den** *ppl. a.*

O·verland, *sb. local.* 1769. Land held by a particular tenure in the west of England (see O.E.D.).

Overla·nd, over land, *adv.* 1589. [prop. two wds., often hyphened or written as one; f. OVER *prep.* + LAND *sb.*] Over or across land; by land (as opp. to 'by sea').

Overland (ō^u·vəɹlænd), *a.* 1800. [attrib. use of prec.; see OVER- III.] Proceeding or lying over or across land; performed by land; for or connected with a journey over land.

O. route, a route entirely or partly by land; *spec.* (1) the route to India by the Mediterranean; (2) in America, any route westward from the Atlantic to the Pacific across the continent.

O·verlander. *Australia.* 1843. One who journeyed overland from one Australian colony or capital to another (*obs.* exc. *Hist.*); *spec.* one taking cattle from one colony to another or over a long distance. So **Overla·nd** *v.*

Overlap (ō^u·vəɹlæp), *sb.* 1813. [f. next.] A partial superposition or coincidence; the part or place at which one edge or thing overlaps another; *spec.* in *Geol.* (see next, 3). **b.** *attrib. O. joint,* a joint in which one edge overlaps the other.

Overlap (ō^{u}vəɹlæ·p), *v.* 1726. [f. OVER- I. 8 + LAP *v.*[2]] **1.** *trans.* To lap over; to overlie partially. Also *fig.* Also *absol.* or *intr.* **2.** To cover and extend beyond (*lit.* and *fig.*) 1802. **3.** *Geol.* Said of a newer formation which extends beyond the area or edge of the older one on which it mainly rests, and thus partly overlies a still older one below that: *trans.* with either of the lower formations as obj., or *absol.* 1832. **4.** To lap or ripple over (see LAP *v.*[1] 3, 4) 1863.

Overlay (ō^u·vəɹlē^i), *sb.* 1725. [f. next; see OVER- I. 8.] **1.** A cravat, necktie. *Sc.* **2.** *Printing.* A piece of paper cut to the required shape and pasted over the impression-surface of a printing-press in order to make the impression darker in particular places, as in a woodcut 1824. **3.** Something laid as a covering over something else; esp. a coverlet, a small cloth laid upon a table-cloth, etc.; also *fig.* 1794.

Overlay (ō^{u}vəɹlē^i·), *v. Pa. t.* and *pple.* **overlai·d.** ME. [f. OVER- + LAY *v.*] **I.** To lay over. **1.** *trans.* To lay or place over, above, or upon something else (*rare*). [OVER- I. 1, 8.] 1570. **b.** To surmount or span with something extending over (*rare*). [OVER- I. 1.] 1611. **2.** To cover the surface of (a thing) *with* something spread over it. [OVER- I. 8.] **b.** *Printing.* To put an overlay upon (see prec. 2); also *absol.* †**3.** To cover superfluously or excessively; *spec.* to overstock (a pasture *with* cattle, etc.). [OVER- I. 8, II. 6.] –1733.

1. b. To..o. With bridges rivers proud MILT. **2.** The defect..of being overlaid with drapery SIR J. REYNOLDS. **3.** A tree overlaid with blossoms 1633.

II. To lie over. **1.** To lie over (something else); more prop. OVERLIE. [OVER- I. 8.] late ME. **2.** *spec.* = OVERLIE 2 a. 1557. **3.** To affect like or as with a superincumbent weight. [OVER- I. 8, 21.] †**a.** To press severely upon; to distress; to overwhelm, overpower –1769. **b.** To press upon so as to impede the working or activity of; to weigh down; to smother, stifle 1609. **4.** To conceal or obscure as if by covering up 1719. **5.** *Naut.* To cross the cable or anchor of another vessel so as to cause chafing or obstruction. [OVER- I. 10.] 1796.

1. Loose shingle and boulders overlaid the mountain TYNDALL. **2.** Sowes Ouerlaie and squise to death their pigges 1573. **3. a.** We are on euery syde ouerlayed with aduersitee COVERDALE. **b.** I have been overlayd with businesse 1663. **4.** Nor wou'd these scenes in empty words abound Or o. the sentiment with sound 1719. Hence **O·verlayer,** one who or that which overlays or overlies something.

Overlay·ing, *vbl. sb.* late ME. [f. OVERLAY *v.* + -ING[1].] The action of OVERLAY *v.*; *concr.* a covering.

Overleaf (ō^u·vəɹlī·f), *adv.* 1843. [prop. two wds., OVER *prep.* and LEAF *sb.*] On the other side of the leaf (of paper).

Overleap (ō^{u}vəɹlī·p), *v.* [OE. *oferhlēapan.*] **1.** *trans.* To leap over, across, or to the other side of. [OVER- I. 5.] **2.** *trans.* To pass over, omit, skip. (Now only as consciously *fig.* from 1.) OE. †**3.** To surpass in leaping; also *fig.* [OVER- II. 1.] –1603. **b.** *refl.* To leap too far. *Macb.* I. vii. 27.

1. *Macb.* I. iv. 49. **2.** Whatever objection..he finds too heavy to remove, he over-leaps it 1641.

Overleather (ō^u·vəɹle:ðəɹ). late ME. [f. OVER *adj.* + LEATHER.] The upper leather of a shoe.

O·ver-li·beral, *a.* 1601. [OVER- II. 7.] Too liberal. So **O·ver-libera·lity. O·verli·berally** *adv.*

Overlie (ō^{u}vəɹlai·), *v. Pa. t.* **overlay;** *pa. pple.* **overlain.** [Early ME. *oferliggen*; see OVER- I. 8. In XVII–XVIII displaced by OVERLAY; reintroduced in XIX.] **1.** *trans.* To lie over or upon; in *Geol.* said of a stratum resting directly on another. **2.** *spec.* **a.** To smother by lying upon ME. †**b.** To lie with (a woman) –1480. †**3.** *fig.* To oppress –1530.

2. The old idiot wretch Screamed feebly, like a baby overlain E. B. BROWNING.

O·ver-lip. Now *dial.* ME. [orig. two wds., ME. *overe lippe*.] The upper lip.

Overlive (ōᵘvəɹli·v), *v.* Now *rare.* [OE. *oferlibban*, f. *ofer-* OVER- I. 18 + LIVE *v.*] *trans.* = OUTLIVE 1. Also *fig.* of things. **b.** *intr.* To survive OE. **c.** *refl.* To live too long 1861.

All the daies of yᵉ elders that ouerliued Ioshua 1551 *Josh.* 24:31. **b.** MILT. *P.L.* x. 773.

Overload (ōᵘ·vəɹlōᵘd), *sb.* 1645. [OVER- II. 8.] An excessive load or burden; too great a load.

Overload (ōᵘvəɹlōᵘ·d), *v.* 1553. [OVER- II. 6.] *trans.* To put an excessive load on, to overburden; to overcharge (a gun).

O·ver-lo·ng, *adv.* and *adj.* late ME. [f. OVER- II. 9, 7 + LONG *a.*¹, LONG *adv.*] **A.** *adv.* For too long a time. **B.** *adj.* Too long. late ME.

Overlook (ōᵘ·vəɹluk), *sb.* 1584. [OVER- I. 16, 7, 5.] **1.** A glance or survey; inspection or superintendence. **b.** A look down from a height; a place that affords such a view 1861. **c.** The tropical leguminous twining plant, *Canavalia ensiformis* 1837. **2.** An oversight 1887.

Overlook (ōᵘvəɹlu·k), *v.* late ME. [f. OVER- + LOOK *v.*] **1.** *trans.* To look over the top of, so as to see beyond. [OVER- I. 5.] 1559. **b.** *fig.* To overtop. *Obs.* or *rare.* 1567. **2.** To look over and beyond and thus not see; to fail to see or observe; to pass over without notice; to ignore. (The chief current sense.) [OVER- I. 5.] **3.** To look (a thing) over or through; to examine, inspect, survey; to peruse. Now *rare* or *arch.* [OVER- I. 16.] late ME. **4.** To look down upon; to survey from a higher position. [OVER- I. 7.] late ME. **b.** Of a place: To afford or command a view of 1632. †**5.** *fig.* To 'look down upon'; to despise; to slight –1794. **6.** To superintend, oversee. [OVER- I. 7.] late ME. **7.** To look upon with the 'evil eye'; to bewitch. (The popular word for this.) 1596.

1. The wall was just too high to be overlooked HAWTHORNE. **b.** The laughing Nectar overlook'd the Lid DRYDEN. **2.** The French..found it prudent to o. this insult HUME. **3.** *Two Gent.* I. ii. 50. **4.** Have you no more manners than to o. a man when he's a writing? DRYDEN. **b.** The brow of the hill overlooking the Nairn valley 1895. **6.** To..o. the other servants 1830. **7.** Vilde worme, thou wast ore-look'd euen in thy birth SHAKS. Hence **O·verlooker,** one who overlooks; a spy; an overseer.

Overlord (ōᵘ·vəɹlǫɹd), *sb.* ME. [OVER- I. 2 b.] A lord superior; one who is the lord of other lords or rulers. Hence **Overlo·rd** *v. rare*, to lord it over; to rule as an o. **O·ver-lo:rdship,** the position or authority of an o.

Overly (ōᵘ·vəɹli), *a. Obs.* exc. *dial.* ME. [f. OVER *adv.* + -LY¹.] †**1.** Supreme. ME. only. †**2.** Superficial; cursory –1769. **3.** Supercilious, overbearing, haughty. Now only *dial.* 1627.

Overly (ōᵘ·vəɹli), *adv.* OE. [f. OVER *adv.* + -LY².] **1.** = OVER *adv.* III. 4. In OE., *Sc.*, and *U.S.* †**2.** Superficially, carelessly –1853. †**3.** On the surface –1573. †**4.** Haughtily, superciliously, slightingly –1650.

Overman (ōᵘ·vəɹmæ̆n), *sb.* ME. [OVER- I. 2 b.] †**1.** A superior, leader, ruler, chief –1625. **2.** An arbiter, arbitrator, umpire 1470. **3.** A foreman, overseer, esp. in a colliery 1708. **4.** [tr. G. *Uebermensch*] = SUPERMAN 1896.

Overman (ōᵘvəɹmæ·n), *v.* 1636. [OVER- II. 6.] *trans.* To furnish with too many men.

Overmantel (ōᵘ·vəɹmæntʼl). 1882. [OVER- III.] A piece of ornamental cabinet work, often including a mirror, placed over a mantelpiece.

Overma·ntle, *v.* 1827. [OVER- I. 8.] *trans.* To cover over like a mantle.

Overmaster (ōᵘvəɹmɑ·stəɹ), *v.* ME. [OVER- I. 21.] **1.** *trans.* To master completely; to get the better of, overcome, conquer. (Chiefly *fig.*) †**2.** To be master over; to hold in one's power or possession –1648. Hence **Overma·steringly** *adv.*

Overmatch (ōᵘ·vəɹmætʃ), *sb.* 1542. [OVER- II. 3.] †**1.** The condition of being overmatched –1590. **2.** A person or thing that is more than a match for some other. Const. genitive or *for*. Now *rare.* 1589.

Overma·tch, *v.* ME. [OVER- II. 3.] *trans.* To be more than a match for; to defeat by superior strength or skill; to surpass, excel.

Over-measure (ōᵘ·vəɹme·ʒ¹ŭɹ), *sb.* 1641. [OVER- I. 19, II. 8 d.] Measure above what is ordinary or sufficient: excess, surplus.

O·ver-mea·sure, *advb. phr.* late ME. [prop. two wds., OVER *prep.* and MEASURE *sb.*] Above the proper measure or amount; in excess.

O·ver-mo·dest, *a.* 1614. [OVER- II. 7.] Too modest. So **O·ver-mo·destly** *adv.* **O·ver-mo·desty.**

Overmuch (ōᵘ·vəɹmʊ·tʃ; stress var.), *a.* and *adv.* ME. [OVER- II. 7, 9.] **A.** *adj.* Too much. Also *absol.* (rarely as *sb.*) **B.** *adv.* To too great an extent or degree; excessively. late ME. Hence **Overmu·chness,** excess, superabundance.

O·ver-ni·ce, *a.* ME. [OVER- II. 7.] Too nice; too fastidious, scrupulous, or particular. So **O·ver-ni·ce-ly** *adv.*, **-ness.**

Overnight, over night (ōᵘvəɹnəi·t), *advb. phr.* (*sb.*, *a.*) late ME. [f. OVER *prep.* V. 3 + NIGHT *sb.*] **1.** Before the night (as considered in relation to the following day); on the preceding evening; the night before (with implication that the result of the action continues till the following morning). **2.** During the night (till the following morning) 1535.

1. His Head ached every Morning with reading of Men o. ADDISON. **2.** He preferred to stay o. with the family 1894.

B. *sb.* The preceding evening. (Now chiefly *U.S.*) 1581.

C. *attrib.* or *adj.* (*o·vernight*) Of or belonging to the previous evening; done, happening, etc., overnight 1824.

The limit of my o. journey 1870.

Overpaint (-pē¹·nt), *v.* 1611. [OVER- I. 8, II. 6.] †**1.** *trans.* To paint over with another colour –1614. **2.** To colour too highly 1750.

Overparted (ōᵘvəɹpā·ɹtėd), *a.* 1588. [f. OVER- II. 5 + PART *sb.* + -ED².] Having too difficult a part, or too many parts, to play.

Overpass (ōᵘvəɹpɑ·s), *v.* Now somewhat *rare.* ME. [f. OVER- + PASS *v.*] **I.** Transitive senses, in which *over-* is prepositional. **1.** To pass over, travel over, move across or along. **2.** To cross ME. **3.** *fig.* To pass through (a period, an experience, etc.); often including the notion 'to get over, surmount'; more rarely, to pass, spend (time). [OVER- I. 16, 17.] ME. **4.** *fig.* To go (or be) beyond in amount, rate, value, excellence, etc.; to lie beyond the range or scope of; to exceed, excel, surpass ME. †**b.** To transgress –1597. **5.** *fig.* To pass over, leave out, omit. Now *rare.* late ME.

3. Having overpassed many rubs and difficulties 1645. **5.** Some lesser errors..we o. 1831.

II. Intransitive senses, in which *over-* is adverbial. **1.** To pass over, across, or overhead ME. **2.** Of time, actions, experiences, etc.: To pass away, come to an end; to pass. Freq. in *pa. pple.* = At an end, past, over. ME. †**3.** To pass or remain unnoticed, to be let alone or omitted –1575.

2. Now that this storm is overpast MARLOWE.

Overpay (ōᵘvəɹpē¹·), *v.* 1601. [OVER- II. 5.] *trans.* To pay too highly, pay more than is due. So **O·verpay** *sb.* **Over-pay·ment.**

Overpeer (ōᵘvəɹpīᵊ·ɹ), *v.* 1565. [OVER- I. 7, 1 (*b*).] **1.** *trans.* To peer over, look across from above, look down on 1589. †**b.** To 'look down upon', domineer over –1590. **2.** To rise or appear above; to tower over; to excel, outpeer 1565.

Over-peo·ple, *v.* 1683. [OVER- II. 6.] *trans.* To people too much, overstock with people. (Chiefly in *pa. pple.*)

O:ver-persua·de, *v.* 1624. [OVER- I. 11.] *trans.* To bring over by persuasion; *esp.* to persuade against one's own judgement or inclination. So **Over-persua·sion.**

Overpitch (ōᵘvəɹpi·tʃ), *v.* 1859. [OVER- II. 5.] **1.** *Cricket. trans.* To pitch (a ball) too far in bowling. **2.** *fig.* To pitch too high; to exaggerate 1886.

Over-plea·se, *v.* 1611. [OVER- II. 6.] *trans.* To please too much. So **O·ver-plea·sed, O·verplea·sing** *ppl. adjs.*

Overplus (ōᵘ·vəɹplʊs), *sb.* (*adv.*, *a.*) late ME. [Partial tr. of (O)Fr. *surplus* SURPLUS, or med.L. *superplus* (XI), *surplus* (XIII), the latter = OFr.] That which is over in addition to the main amount; an extra quantity; an amount left over, a surplus. **b.** *loosely.* Excess 1850. †**B.** *adv.* or predicatively: In addition, in excess, besides, over –1655. **C.** *adj.* Remaining over, extra, surplus 1640.

A. The landlord is paid out of the proceeds. The o. is returned to the tenant 1875. **B.** *Ant. & Cl.* IV. vi. 22.

Overpoise (ōᵘvəɹpoi·z), *v.* 1555. [f. OVER- I. 3 + POISE *v.*] *trans.* To weigh more than; mostly *fig.* Also *intr.* or *absol.* Hence **O·verpoise** *sb.* the act or fact of outweighing, that which outweighs.

Over-po·pulate, *v.* 1870. [OVER- II. 1.] *trans.* To over-people. (Chiefly in *pa. pple.*) So **O·ver-popula·tion. O·ver-po·pulous** *a.*, **-ness.**

Overpower (ōᵘvəɹpauᵊ·ɹ), *v.* 1593. [OVER- II. 1 b.] **1.** *trans.* To overcome with superior power; to vanquish, master. **2.** To render (a thing) ineffective or imperceptible, by excess of force or intensity 1646. **3.** To overcome by intensity; to be too much for; to crush, overwhelm 1667.

1. Those officers..were overpowered and disarmed MACAULAY. **2.** Strong sauces that o. the natural flavour of the fish 1806. **3.** We might be overpowered with the grandeur of the house 1881. Hence **Overpow·ering** *ppl. a.*, **-ly** *adv.*

Overpraise (ōᵘvəɹprē¹·z), *v.* late ME. [OVER- II. 6.] *trans.* To praise excessively; to praise more than one deserves.

Overpress (ōᵘvəɹpre·s), *v.* Now somewhat *rare.* late ME. [app. orig. a var. of OPPRESS, repr. L. *opprimere*; later assoc. w. literal senses of PRESS *v.*; see OVER-.] **I. 1.** *trans.* To oppress; to oppress beyond endurance. †**2.** To press upon with physical force, so as to overwhelm –1666. †**3.** To overburden, overload –1713.

1. My mind is overpressed with grief MILT.

II. 1. To overcome by entreaty. *rare.* 1818. **2.** To press or insist upon (a matter) unduly 1865. **3.** To put too much pressure on (a person) 1886.

2. He sometimes overpresses his point (*mod.*). So **O·ver-pre·ssure,** excessive pressure; pressing or being pressed too hard (esp. with study, etc.).

O·verprint, *sb.* 1907. [f. next.] **1.** An offprint or reprint 1911. **2.** An addition to the design or inscription of a postage stamp printed over it 1907.

Over-pri·nt, *v.* 1853. [OVER- II. 5.] **1.** *Photogr. trans.* To print (a positive) darker than it is meant to be. **2.** To impress (a printed surface) with additional print 1911. **3.** To put through the press again with added matter; also, to print too many copies of 1911.

Overprize (-prəi·z), *v.* 1589. [OVER- II. 5, 1.] **1.** *trans.* To prize too highly; to overestimate, overrate. **2.** To exceed or surpass in value. *Obs.* or *arch.* 1593.

1. Overprizing what they have already acquired, they make no further search 1663.

Over-produ·ce, *v.* 1894. [OVER- II. 6.] *trans.* To produce (a commodity) in excess of the demand or of a defined amount. So **O·ver-produ·ction,** production in excess of the demand 1822.

O·ver-proof, *a.* (*sb.*) 1807. [OVER- III.] That is 'above proof'; containing a larger proportion of alcohol than is contained in proof-spirit; see PROOF *sb.* Also *ellipt.* as *sb.* = over-proof spirit.

O·ver-propo·rtion, *sb.* 1666. [OVER- II. 8 c.] Excessive proportion; excess *of* one thing in proportion to another. So **O:ver-propo·rtion** *v. trans.* to make or estimate in excess of the true proportion.

Overrate (ōᵘvəɹrē¹·t), *v.* 1611. [OVER- II. 5, 6.] *trans.* To rate too highly or above the real value or amount. **b.** To assess too highly for rating purposes 1884.

Overreach (ōᵘ·vəɹrītʃ), *sb.* 1556. [f. next.] **1.** A reaching over some thing or person. **b.** Too great a reach, stretch, or strain. **2.** In ref. to a horse: The act of striking one of the fore feet with the corresponding hind foot;

the injury so caused 1607. **3.** An act of overreaching in dealing 1615.

Overreach (ō^{u}vəɹī·tʃ), *v.* ME. [OVER- I. 5, 14, 9, 13, 21, II. 2, 5.] **1.** *trans.* To reach or extend over or beyond; to rise above; to stretch beyond in space or time. **2.** To overtake, come up with, attain to. Now *Sc.* ME. †**b.** To overpower –1638. **3.** *trans.* To extend or spread over (something) so as to cover it. Also *absol.* or *intr.* late ME. **4.** *intr.* Of a horse, etc.: To bring a hind foot against the corresponding fore foot in walking or running; *esp.* to strike and injure the heel of the fore foot with the hind foot. **b.** Also, generally, to bring a hind foot in front of or alongside a fore foot. 1523. **5.** *trans.* To gain an advantage over, get the better of, outdo; now always in a bad sense 1577. **6.** *refl.* To reach, stretch, strain oneself beyond one's strength, beyond one's aim, etc. 1568. Also *refl.* and *intr.* with admixture of sense 5. **7.** *intr.* To reach too far (*lit.* and *fig.*).

2. Certaine Players We ore-wrought on the way SHAKS. **5.** He never made any bargain without over-reaching (or, in the vulgar phrase, cheating) the person with whom he dealt FIELDING. Hence **Overrea·cher,** one who or that which overreaches.

Over-read (-rī·d), *v.* [OE. *oferrǣdan*; see OVER- I. 16, 20, II. 2.] †**1.** *trans.* To read over, read through –1648. †**2.** To re-read –1636. **3.** *refl.* and *intr.* To read too much 1805.

Over-re·ckon, *v.* 1615. [OVER- II. 6, 1.] **1.** *trans.* To overestimate. Also *absol.* 1646. †**2.** To overcharge in a reckoning –1680.

O:ver-refine (-rĭfəi·n), *v.* 1832. [OVER- II. 6.] *trans.* To refine too much; *absol.* to make over-fine distinctions. So **O:ver-refi·ned** *ppl. a.* **O:ver-refi·nement,** too subtle refinement.

Over-re·nt, *v.* 1589. [OVER- II. 6.] *trans.* To rent (land, etc.) too highly; to charge (a tenant) too high a rent.

Override (ō^{u}vəɹəi·d), *v.* [OE. *oferrīdan* ride across; see OVER- I. 5, 9, 14, II. 1, 6.] **1.** *trans.* To ride over or across; to cross by riding (*lit.* and *fig.*). **b.** To ride all over (a country), esp. with an armed force, so as to harry, etc. ME. **2.** To ride over or upon (the fallen); to trample down by riding ME. **3.** *fig.* To trample under foot (an ordinance, right, etc.); to set at nought; to assume or have authority superior to 1827. †**4.** To overtake by or in riding; to outride –1642. **5.** To ride (a horse) too much 1596. **6.** To extend or pass over; to slip or lie over; *Surg.* to overlap, as when a bone is fractured and one piece slips over the other 1852.

2. Syr Palomydes cam vpon sir Tristram as he was vpon foot to haue ouer ryden hym MALORY. **3.** Phr. *To o. one's commission*, to go beyond one's commission, discharge one's office in a high-handed and arbitrary manner. **6.** A northern ice-sheet which overrode Canada GEIKIE.

O·ver-rule, *sb.* 1893. [OVER- I. 2 b.] The rule of a higher or supreme power.

Overrule (ō^{u}vəɹrū·l), *v.* 1576. [OVER- I. 2.] †**1.** *trans.* To rule over, have authority over –1640. **2.** To govern or control the rule of (a person, a law, etc.) by superior power or authority 1576. **3.** To prevail over (a person) so as to change or set aside his opinion. Also *absol.* 1591. **4.** Of a thing: To prevail over, overcome 1586. **5.** To rule against, set aside, as by higher authority; *spec.* in *Law*: **a.** To set aside (a previous action or decision) as a precedent; to annul. **b.** To rule against (an argument, plea, etc.); to disallow (an action). 1593. **c.** To rule against (a person), to disallow the arguments or pleas of 1660.

2. To o. them in their prices, so as the same be not sold at any dearer rates 1596. **3.** I found myself led and influenced by another's will, unpersuaded, quietly overruled C. BRONTË. **4.** The general causes that o. personal aims 1877. **5. b.** The chancellor overruled the objections 1875. **c.** Sir John Ernley..insisted..but he was overruled MACAULAY. Hence **Overru·ler,** one who overrules, controls, or directs.

Overrun (ō^{u}vəɹrɒ·n), *v.* OE. [OVER- I. 4, 5, 9, 10, 13, 16, II. 1, 2.] **I.** To run over (something). †**1.** *trans.* To run over or across (a line or surface); to pass over quickly –1649. **b.** To overflow ME. †**2.** To run through (a book, etc.); to glance through rapidly (sometimes implying omission) –1656. †**3.** To overwhelm (as waves); to run over (as a horse or vehicle), run down, trample down, crush. Also *fig.* –1667. **4.** To ride or rove over (a country) as a hostile force and so to harry and destroy; †to harass (a people) thus, to spoil (a city, etc.) late ME. **5.** Of vermin, weeds, etc.: To spread injuriously over; also of ivy, etc.: To grow over rapidly. Chiefly in *pa. pple.*, const. *with.* 1669. **6.** In various *fig.* and *transf.* senses (from 4 and 5). Now chiefly in *pa. pple.*, const. *with.* 1538. **7.** *intr.* To run over (said of a liquid or the containing vessel); to be superabundant or excessive ME.

4. The Northern parts were overrun and harried by the Scots 1631. **5.** The mouldering ruin of an abbey overrun with ivy W. IRVING. A small cell overrun with mice 1887. **6.** The Wife is over-run with Affectation ADDISON.

II. To surpass in running, etc. **1.** *trans.* = OUTRUN 2; hence, to overtake or leave behind by or in running; also *fig.* to surpass. Now *rare.* late ME. **b.** To escape from by running faster than, to run away from; also *fig.* to run away from (duty, etc.); to desert, leave undone. Now only *dial.* 1583. **2.** To run farther than or beyond (a certain point, etc.); *fig.* to exceed 1633. **b.** To extend or project so as to overlie 1850. **c.** *intr.* To extend beyond the due length, or beyond any prescribed or desired limit 1864. **3.** *Printing.* (*trans.* or *absol.*) To carry over words or lines of type into another line or page to provide for the addition of new matter or the removal of matter already composed; to cause to run over 1683.

1. To o. one's age in growth, strength [etc.] SIDNEY. **b.** Phr. *To o. one's creditors, the* CONSTABLE. **2.** Phr. *To o. the scent*, (of hounds) to continue running past a point where the hare or fox turned off, and thus to lose the scent. *To o. oneself*, to run too far; to exhaust or injure oneself with running; also *fig.* Hence **Overru·nner,** one who or that which overruns.

O·versale. 1889. [OVER- II. 8 d.] Speculative sale for future delivery to a greater amount than can be supplied; *pl.* sales beyond the available supply.

Oversco·re, *v.* 1849. [OVER- I. 8.] *trans.* **a.** To score over; to cover with scores, cuts, or deleting lines. **b.** To obliterate by scoring across.

O·ver-scru·pulous, *a.* 1597. [OVER- II. 7.] Too scrupulous. So **O·ver-scrupulo·sity, -scru·pulousness.**

Oversea (ō^{u}vəɹsī), *a.* and *adv.* late ME. [f. OVER *prep.* + SEA.] **A.** *adv.* (*o:ver sea·*). Across or beyond the sea; abroad. **B.** *adj.* (*o·versea*). **1.** Of or pertaining to movement or transport over the sea; transmarine 1552. †**2.** Of foreign make –1651. **3.** Foreign 1553.

Overseas (ō^{u}·vəɹsī·z), *adv.* 1583. [f. OVER *prep.* + *seas* (app.) sb. pl.] = OVERSEA. **b.** quasi-*sb.* (with prep.). Foreign parts 1919.

Oversee (ō^{u}vəɹsī·), *v.* [OE. *ofersēon*, f. *ofer-* OVER- + SEE *v.*] **I. 1.** *trans.* To look down upon, overlook; to survey; to keep watch over. [OVER- I. 7.] **2.** To look over, look through; to inspect, examine; to peruse, esp. by way of revision for the printing-press. *Obs.* or *arch.* [OVER- I. 16.] late ME. **3.** To superintend, supervise; to see after the doing or working of 1449. **b.** *absol.* To act as overseer 1548. **4.** To catch sight of without the knowledge of the person seen 1742. **II. 1.** = OVERLOOK *v.* 2. *Obs.* exc. *dial.* OE. **2.** *refl.* To forget oneself, act unbecomingly; to err, blunder, act imprudently. Also *intr. Obs.* exc. *dial.* late ME.

Overseen (ō^{u}vəɹsī·n), *ppl. a.* late ME. [pa. pple. of prec.] **1.** That has 'overseen himself' (see OVERSEE II. 2); deceived, deluded, in error; acting imprudently, rash in action. Now *arch.* or *dial.* †**2.** Versed, skilled, 'well seen' *in* some subject (cf. OVERSEE I. 2) –1610.

1. However Mr. Adye might have been o. in his Opinion as to the right of Seizure NELSON. Phr. *O. with* (or *in*) *drink*, also simply *o.*, intoxicated. *Obs.* exc. *dial.*

Overseer (ō^{u}·vəɹsī^{ə}ɹ), *sb.* late ME. [f. OVERSEE + -ER[1].] **1.** One who oversees or superintends, a supervisor 1523. †**b.** A person (formerly) appointed by a testator to supervise the executor of the will –1667. **c.** (In full, *O. of the poor.*) An officer (appointed annually) to perform various administrative duties mainly connected with the relief of the poor 1601. †**2.** One who 'oversees' a book, e.g., as critic, censor, reviser, or editor –1685. Hence **O·verseership.**

Over-se·ll, *v.* 1580. [OVER- II. 5, 6.] †**1.** *trans.* To sell at more than the value –1768. **2.** To sell more of (a stock, etc.) than one can deliver, or than exists. Also *refl.* 1879.

Overset (ō^{u}vəɹse·t), *v.* ME. [OVER- I. 7, etc.] †**1.** To oppress; to press hard –1572. †**2.** To overcome, discomfit –1698. **3.** To upset, overturn, capsize; to turn upside down. Now *rare.* [OVER- I. 6.] 1592. **b.** *intr.* To capsize; to be upset. Now *rare.* 1641. **4.** *trans. fig.* To upset (an institution, state, or the like); to cause to fall into confusion. Now *rare.* 1679. **b.** To discompose (a person); to disorder, upset (the stomach, etc.) 1533. **c.** *intr.* To be upset, fall into disorder 1749. **5.** To set up (type) in excess 1897.

3. The postilion..overset the carriage MISS BURNEY. **4. b.** The news is sure to o. him DICKENS. **c.** While kingdoms o., Or lapse from hand to hand TENNYSON. Hence **O·verset** *sb.* the act or fact of oversetting.

Oversew (ō^{u}·vəɹsō^{u}), *v.* 1864. [OVER- I. 5.] *trans.* To sew overhand; to sew together two pieces of stuff, so that the thread between the stitches lies over the edges.

Overshade (ō^{u}vəɹʃē^{i}·d), *v.* OE. [OVER- I. 8.] **1.** *trans.* = OVERSHADOW *v.* 2. **2.** To cast a shade over; to render gloomy or dark; to overshadow. Also *absol.* 1588.

Overshadow (ō^{u}vəɹʃæ·do^{u}), *v.* [OE. *ofersceadwian*; see OVER- I. 8.] **1.** *trans.* To cast a shadow over; to cover or obscure with darkness, overcloud; to overshade. **2.** To cover or overspread with some influence, as with a shadow; to shelter, protect OE. **3.** To tower above so as to cast its shadow over; hence, to rise above, 'cast into the shade' 1581.

1. *fig.* Those misfortunes which were soon to o. her FROUDE. **2.** O. me in the day of battle 1578. **3.** It was natural that the Crown, completely overshadowed by the great barons, should turn.. to the Church 1862. Hence **Oversha·dower. Oversha·dowing** *vbl. sb.* and *ppl. a.*

Overshine (-ʃəi·n), *v.* [OE. *oferscīnan*; see OVER- I. 7, 8.] **1.** *trans.* To shine over or upon, to illumine. **2.** To outshine; chiefly *fig.* 1588.

O·vershoe (-ʃū), *sb.* 1851. [OVER- I. 8 c.] A shoe of india-rubber, felt, etc., worn over the ordinary shoe as a protection from wet, dirt, or cold.

Over-shoe, over-shoes (ō^{u}vəɹʃū·z), *advb. phr.* 1579. [orig. two wds.; see OVER *prep.* I. 2.] Of water, mud, etc.: So deep as to cover the shoes, shoe-deep.

A man may go ouer-shooes in the grime of it SHAKS.

Overshoot (ō^{u}vəɹʃū·t), *v.* late ME. [OVER- I. 13, 4, 5, II. 2, 6.] **1.** *trans.* To shoot, dart, run, or pass beyond (a point, limit, etc.). †**b.** *Naut.* To sail past (a port, etc.) –1803. **2.** To shoot a missile, etc., over or above (the mark) and so to miss; to shoot beyond; also, of the missile: To pass over or beyond (the mark). Also *absol.* (*lit.* and *fig.*) 1548. †**3.** *fig.* To shoot too hard, utter (a word) too violently or unguardedly –1621. **4.** To push or drive beyond the proper limit 1668. **5.** To shoot or dart over or above 1774. **b.** To shoot too much over (a moor, etc.) so as to deplete it of game 1884.

1. Dogs, who running fleeter, over-shoot their game 1755. **2.** *fig. To o. the mark*, to go too far, or farther than is intended or proper. *To o. oneself*, to shoot beyond or over one's mark; to miss one's mark by going too far; to exaggerate; to fall into error. †*To be overshot*, to be wide of the mark; to be mistaken or deceived.

Overshot (ō^{u}·vəɹʃǫt), *a.* (*sb.*) 1535. [= next, with change of stress.] **A.** *adj.* Driven by water shot over from above. **B.** *sb.* The stream of water which drives an overshot wheel 1759.

A. *O. wheel*, a water-wheel turned by the force of water falling upon or near the top of the wheel into buckets placed round the circumference. *O. mill*, a mill supplied with power by an o. wheel.

Oversho·t, *ppl. a.* 1605. [pa. pple. of OVERSHOOT *v.*] **1.** In the senses of the vb. 1774. **2.** Said of a partially dislocated fetlock joint, in which the upper bone is driven over or in front of the lower bones 1881. **3.** Having the upper jaw projecting beyond the lower 1885.

Overside, *adv.* and *a.* 1884. [Short for *over the side*; cf. *overboard*.] **A.** *adv.* (ōᵘvəɹsəi·d). Over the side of a ship (into the sea, a lighter, etc.) 1889. **B.** *adj.* (ōᵘ·vəɹsəid). Effected over the side of a ship; discharging over the side 1884.

Oversight (ōᵘ·vəɹsəit). ME. [Over- I. 7, 5.] **1.** Supervision, superintendence; charge, care, management. **2.** Omission or failure to see or notice, inadvertence; also, an instance of this 1477.

2. It is all rather owing to O., than to any ill Intention 1676. It [the omission] may have been an o. 1865.

O·versize, *sb.* 1849. [Over- II. 8 d.] A size in excess of the proper or ordinary size.

Oversi·ze, *v.* 1602. [f. Over- I. 8, II. 6 + Size *v.*²] †**1.** *trans.* To cover over with size. *Haml.* II. ii. 484. **2.** To size too much 1878.

O·ver-si·zed (stress var.), *ppl. a.* 1801. [f. Oversize *sb.* + -ed².] Over or above the normal size, abnormally large.

O·verskirt. *U.S.* 1883. [Over- I. 8 c.] An outer skirt; drapery arranged over the skirt of a dress.

Overslaugh (ōᵘ·vəɹslǭ), *sb.* 1772. [– Du. *overslag*, f. *overslaan* (see next); or (in sense 1) from next.] **1.** *Mil.* The passing over of one's ordinary turn of duty in consideration of being required for a superior duty. **2.** *U.S.* A bar or sand-bank which impedes the navigation of a river; *spec.* that on the Hudson River below Albany 1776.

Overslaugh (ōᵘ·vəɹslǭ), *v.* 1768. [– Du. *overslaan* pass over, f. *over-* Over- I. 5 + *slaan* strike.] **1.** *trans.* To pass over, skip, omit. **a.** *Mil.* To pass over, skip, or remit the ordinary turn of duty of an officer, a company, etc., in consideration of his (or its) being detailed on that day for a higher duty. **b.** *U.S.* To pass over in favour of another, as in nomination to an office; also, generally, to pass over, ignore 1846. **2.** To bar, obstruct, hinder 1864.

Oversleep (ōᵘvəɹslī·p), *v.* late ME. [Over- I. 18, II. 2] **1.** *intr.* and *refl.* To sleep beyond the time at which one ought to awake. **2.** *trans.* To sleep beyond (a particular time) 1526.

1. They were weary, and overslept themselves De Foe. I will not let you over-sleep, be sure 1881.

Oversleeve (ōᵘ·vəɹslīv). 1857. [Over- I. 8 c.] An outer sleeve covering the ordinary sleeve.

Overslide (ōᵘvəɹsləi·d), *v.* ME. [Over- I. 4, 5.] †**1.** *intr.* To slide or slip away; to pass unnoticed. Usu. with *let*. –1560. †**2.** *trans.* = *to let o.* in 1. –1570. **3.** To slide, slip, or glide over (a place or thing). Also *intr.* or *absol.* 1513.

Overslip (ōᵘvəɹsli·p), *v.* Now *rare.* late ME. **1.** *trans.* To slip or pass by (*fig.*), pass over without notice; to omit, miss. [Over- I. 4, 5.] †**b.** *intr.* or *absol.* To make a slip. Also *refl.* –1641. †**2.** *intr.* To slip or pass by; of time, to elapse (usu. implying the missing of an opportunity). [Over- I. 4.] –1607. †**3.** *trans.* To slip away from, escape (a person); usu. *fig.* –1688. **4.** To slip past or beyond (*lit.*). [Over- I. 13.] 1595. †**5.** To slip beyond or outside of (*fig.*); to transgress through inadvertence –1592.

3. Which all this time hath overslipp'd her thought Shaks.

O·ver-soul. 1841. [Over- I. 2.] Emerson's name for the Deity regarded as the supreme spirit which animates the universe.

Oversow (ōᵘvəɹsōᵘ·), *v.* [OE. *ofersāwan*, f. *ofer-* Over- + Sow *v.*; repr. late L. *superseminare* (Vulg.).] **1.** *trans.* To sow (seed) over other seed, or a crop, previously sown. [Over- I. 1, 8.] **2.** To sow (ground) *with* additional seed. [Over- I. 8, 20.] OE. **3.** To scatter seed over, sow *with* seed. Also *fig.* in *pa. pple.* (Fr. *parsemé*.) [Over- I. 8.] 1618. **4.** To sow too much of (seed). [Over- II. 6.] 1890.

1. His enemy came and oversowed cockle among the wheate N. T. (Rhem.) *Matt.* 13:25.

Overspan (ōᵘvəɹspæ·n), *v.* 1513. [Over- I. 10, II. 1.] **1.** *trans.* To extend above and across (something else) from side to side. †**2.** To span (a space) with an arch, etc., to 'throw' (an arch, bridge, etc.) over a space –1817.

Overspend (ōᵘvəɹspe·nd), *v.* 1586. [Over- I. 17, 13, II. 5, 2.] **1.** *trans.* To spend or use till exhausted; to wear out. Usu. in *pa. pple.* **overspent:** worn out, exhausted with fatigue. **2.** To spend more than (a specified amount) 1667; to spend beyond what is necessary 1857. **b.** *refl.* and *intr.* To spend beyond one's means 1890.

1. Harvest Hinds o'erspent with Toil and Heat Dryden.

Overspread (ōᵘvəɹspre·d), *v.* [OE. *ofersprǣdan*; see Over- I. 8, 9.] **1.** *trans.* To spread (something) over or upon something else. **2.** To spread something over (something else); to cover *with* something spread upon the surface. late ME. **b.** in *passive* with *with* ME. **3.** Of a thing: To spread or extend over (something else); to cover completely (*lit.* and *fig.*) ME.

2. With hostile forces he'll o'erspread the land Shaks. 3. A pink flush overspread her face Geo. Eliot.

†**Oversta·nd,** *v.* 1600. [Over- I. 17.] *trans.* To outstay, overstay –1784.

Overstate (ōᵘvəɹstēⁱ·t), *v.* 1803. [f. Over- II. 6, 5 + State *v.*] *trans.* To state too strongly; to exaggerate. So **O·versta·tement.**

Overstay (ōᵘvəɹstēⁱ·), *v.* 1646. [Over- I. 18.] *trans.* To stay over or beyond (in time).

Overstock (ōᵘ·vəɹstǫk), *sb.* 1565. [Over- I. 8 c, II. 8 d.] †**1.** *pl.* Knee-breeches; cf. *nether-stocks* –1580. **2.** A stock or store in excess of demand or requirement 1710.

Overstock (ōᵘvəɹstǫ·k), *v.* 1649. [Over- II. 6.] *trans.* To stock to excess; to glut.

Overstrain (ōᵘ·vəɹstrēⁱn), *sb.* 1754. [Over- II. 8 b.] Excessive strain.

Overstrain (ōᵘvəɹstrēⁱ·n), *v.* 1589. [Over- II. 6.] To subject to excessive strain (*lit.* and *fig.*). Also *absol.* or *intr.*

Neuer will I ouerstraine my strength 1589. *fig.* This argument is greatly overstrained 1863.

Overstream (ōᵘvəɹstrī·m), *v.* 1616. [Over- I. 9.] *trans.* To stream over or across; to flow over in a stream.

Overstre·tch, *v.* ME. [Over- II. 6, I. 10.] **1.** *trans.* To stretch too much (*lit.* and *fig.*). **2.** To stretch or extend across. late ME. So **O·verstretch** *sb.*

Overstrew (-strū·, -strōᵘ·), *v.* 1570. [Over- I. 8.] **1.** *trans.* To strew or sprinkle (something) over something else. **2.** To oversprinkle *with.* (Chiefly in *pa. pple.*) 1578.

Overstride (-strəi·d), *v.* ME. [Over- I. 5, 10, 13, II. 1, 5.] **1.** To stride over or across. **2.** To stride or extend beyond; *fig.* to surpass 1637. **3.** *intr.* To take longer strides than is natural 1899.

Overstri·ng, *v.* 1880. [Over- I. 1, 10.] *Pianoforte-making. trans.* To arrange the strings of (a piano) in two (or three) sets crossing over one another obliquely.

Overstrung (stress var.), *ppl. a.* 1810. [Over- II. 7 c, I. 1, 10.] **1.** Too highly strung; excessively strained. **2.** Of a piano: Having the strings arranged in two (or three) sets crossing one another obliquely 1880.

Overstudy (-stʊ·di), *v.* 1641. [Over- II. 6, 2.] *trans.*, *refl.*, and *intr.* To study too much. So **O·verstu·dy** *sb.*

O:ver-subscri·be, *v.* 1891. [Over- II. 6.] *trans.* To subscribe for (a loan, shares, etc.) in excess of the amount required. So **O·ver-subscri·ption.**

O:ver-supply·, *sb.* 1833. [Over- II. 8 b.] A supply in excess of the demand or requirement. So **O:ver-supply·** *v. trans.* to supply in excess.

Overswarm (-swǭ·ɹm), *v.* 1587. **1.** *intr.* and *refl.* To swarm in excess. [Over- II. 6, 2.] **2.** *trans.* To swarm over (a place or region); to cover with a swarm. Also *absol.* or *intr.* [Over- I. 9.] 1632.

Oversway (ōᵘvəɹswēⁱ·), *v.* Now *rare.* 1577. [Over- I. 2, 21, 11, 3, 6.] †**1.** *trans.* To exercise sway over, govern; to domineer over, overrule, overpower –1680. †**b.** To prevail over by superior authority. Also *absol.* –1878. †**2.** To lead into some course of action; to prevail upon –1710. **3.** *trans.* and *intr.* To sway over; to cause to incline to one side, or so as to be overturned; to swing or incline thus 1622.

Overswe·ll, *v.* 1586. [Over- II. 4, 6, I. 5, 13.] **1.** *trans.* or *intr.* To swell to excess. (Chiefly in *pa. pple.* **overswollen.**). **2.** *trans.* To swell so as to overflow or cover. Also *absol.* or *intr.* 1595.

Overswi·m, *v.* [OE. *oferswimman*; see Over- I. 1, 8, 9.] *trans.* To swim or float over, across, or upon.

Overt (ōᵘ·vəɹt), *a.* ME. [– OFr. *overt* (mod. *ouvert*), pa. pple. of *ovrir* (*ouvrir*) open :– L. *aperire*.] †**1.** Open, not closed; uncovered –1552. **2.** Open to view or knowledge; evident, plain; unconcealed, not secret ME.

2. The General Judgment shall extend, not only to Mens O., but even their most secret Acts 1705. Phr. *O. act* (*Law*), an outward act, such as can be clearly proved to have been done, from which criminal intent is inferred. *Letters o.* = letters Patent. *Market o.*, see Market *sb.* 1. *Pound o.*, open or public Pound. Hence **O·vertly** *adv.* openly.

Overtake (ōᵘvəɹtēⁱ·k), *v.* [Early ME. f. Over- I. 14 + Take *v.*] **1.** *trans.* To come up with; to come up to in pursuit; to catch up. **b.** *fig.* To come up with in any course of action; *esp.* to get through (a task) when hindered by other business, etc.; to work off within the time ME. †**2.** To get at, reach; to reach with a blow –1680. **3.** Of some adverse agency or influence, as a storm, night, misfortune, etc.: To come upon unexpectedly, suddenly, or violently; to surprise, involve. late ME. **4.** To overcome the will, senses, or feelings of; to 'take'; to overpower with excess of emotion. *Obs.* or *dial.* late ME. †**5.** To overcome the judgement of; to 'take in', deceive; in *pa. pple.* deceived, mistaken –1702. **6.** To overcome or overpower with drink, intoxicate. (Chiefly in *pass.*) Now *dial.* 1587.

1. Phrase: *Well overtaken*; Faire sir, you are well ore-tane Shaks. **b.** It's a job you could o. with the other Stevenson. 3. Overtaken by a thunder storm 1794. 4. We were all so overtaken with this good news, that the Duke ran with it to the King Pepys. 6. To be sure the knight is overtaken a little; very near drunk 1770.

Overta·sk, *v.* 1628. [Over- II. 6.] *trans.* To task too heavily.

Overta·x, *v.* 1650. [Over- II. 6.] *trans.* To tax too greatly or heavily; to exact or demand too much of. Hence **Overta·xed** *ppl. a.*; so **O·vertaxa·tion.**

Overtee·m, *v.* 1602. [Over- II. 5, I. 21.] **a.** *intr.* To teem or breed excessively; also *fig.* **b.** *trans.* To exhaust by excessive breeding or production.

Overthrow (ōᵘ·vəɹþrōᵘ), *sb.* 1513.

I. [f. next.] **1.** An act of overthrowing; the fact of being overthrown; discomfiture; ruin. **2.** *Geol.* An overturning or inversion of strata 1891.

1. The dangerous consorted Traitors, That sought at Oxford, thy dire ouerthrow Shaks.

II. [f. Over- I. 13.] In cricket, a return of the ball by a fielder, in which it is not caught or stopped near the wicket, allowing the batsman to make more runs 1749; in baseball, a throwing of the ball over or beyond the player to whom it is thrown.

Overthrow (ōᵘvəɹþrōᵘ·), *v.* ME. [f. Over- I. 6 + Throw *v.*] **1.** *trans.* To throw (anything) over upon its side or upper surface; to upset; to knock (a structure) down, and so demolish it. **2.** *fig.* To cast down from a position of prosperity or power; to bring to ruin, reduce to impotence. late ME. **3.** To subvert, ruin, bring to nought, demolish (an order of things, a theory, plan, institution, government, etc.). late ME. **4.** †To upset in mental state; to overturn the normal sound condition of (the mind). late ME. †**5.** *intr.* To fall over or down, tumble –1587.

1. Then shal Niniue be ouerthrowen Coverdale *Jonah* 3:4. 2. He..was overthrown with Thiers seven days afterwards 1894. 3. Here's Gloster,.. That seekes to ouerthrow Religion Shaks. 4. O what a Noble minde is heere o're-throwne! Shaks. Hence **O·verthrow·n** (stress var.) *ppl. a.* (*sb.*).

Overthrust (ōᵘ·vəɹþrɒst). 1883. [Over- I. 1, 9.] *Geol.* The thrust of the strata or series of rocks on one side of a fault over those on the other side, esp. of lower over higher strata, as in an OVERFAULT or faulted OVERFOLD.

Overthwart (ōᵘvəɹþwǭ·ɹt), *adv.* and *prep.* Now *Obs.* or *rare.* exc. *dial.* [ME. f. OVER *adv.* + *þwert* adv.; see THWART *adv.*] **A.** *adv.* **1.** Over from side to side, or so as to cross something; across; crosswise, transversely. †**2.** *fig.* Adversely; wrongly, amiss; angrily, 'crossly' –1556. **B.** *prep.* **1.** From side to side of; so as to cross; across. late ME. †**2.** Over against, opposite –1630. **3.** On the opposite side of; across, beyond. Now *dial.* 1784.

3. Far beyond, and o. the stream COWPER.

Overthwart (ōᵘ·vəɹþwǭɹt), *a.* and *sb.* *Obs.* exc. *dial.* ME. [f. prec.] **A.** *adj.* **1.** Placed or lying crosswise, or across something else; transverse, cross-. †**b.** *fig.* Indirect –1656. †**2.** Opposite –1692. **3.** *fig.* Inclined to cross or oppose; perverse, froward; captious, testy, 'cross', unfriendly, unfavourable ME.

1. Two crosse or ouerthwart wayes 1623. **2.** Our o'erthwart neighbours DRYDEN. **3.** Of a Spirit averse and over-thwart 1595. Hence **O·verthwart-ly** *adv.*, †**-ness.**

†**B.** *sb.* [The adj. used absol.] **1.** A transverse or cross direction –1562. **b.** A transverse passage, a by-way, a crossing; a transverse line –1631. **2.** An adverse experience; a 'cross', a rebuff –1609; contradiction; a repartee –1595.

1. Phr. *At an o., to o.*, in a transverse direction; cross.

Overthwart (ōᵘvəɹþwǭ·ɹt), *v.* Now *rare* or *Obs.* late ME. [f. prec. adv. or adj.] **1.** *trans.* To pass or lie athwart or across; to transverse, cross. **b.** To obstruct 1654. **2.** *fig.* To act in opposition to; to thwart. Also *absol.* 1529.

Overtime (ōᵘ·vəɹtəim), *sb.*, *adv.* 1858. [OVER- I. 19.] **A.** *sb.* Time worked over and above the regular hours; extra time. Also *attrib.* as in *o. pay.* **B.** *adv.* During extra time 1873.

Overtire (ōᵘvəɹtəiᵊ·ɹ), *v.* 1557. [OVER- I. 21, II. 6.] *trans.* To tire excessively, exhaust with fatigue. Hence **Overti·red** *ppl. a.* 'tired out'.

Overtoil (ōᵘvəɹtoi·l), *v.* 1577. [OVER- I. 21.] *trans.* To wear out by excessive toil; to overwork, fatigue.

Overtone (ōᵘ·vəɹtōᵘn), *sb.* 1867. [– G. *oberton*, contr. of *oberpartialton* upper partial tone.] *Acoustics*, etc. An upper partial tone; a HARMONIC.

Overtone (ōᵘvəɹtōᵘ·n), *v.* 1889. [OVER- II. 6.] *Photogr.* To 'tone' too much, give too deep a tone to.

Overtop (ōᵘvəɹtǫ·p), *v.* 1561. [OVER- I. 1.] **1.** *trans.* To rise over or above the top of; to surmount, tower above, top 1593. **2.** *fig.* To rise above in power or authority; to override 1561. **b.** To go beyond in degree or quality; to excel, surpass 1581.

1. The crabbed mountaines which overtopped it 1622. **2. b.** In them the man somehow overtops the author LOWELL.

Overto·pple, *v.* 1543. [OVER- I. 6, 3.] **1.** *trans.* To overthrow (something unstable). **2.** *intr.* To topple over 1839.

Overtow·er, *v.* 1831. [OVER- I. 1 (*b*).] *trans.* To tower over or above. So **Overtow·ering** *ppl. a.* 1639.

Overtrade (-trēⁱ·d), *v.* 1622. [OVER- II. 5, 2.] *Comm. intr.* and *refl.* To trade in excess of one's capital, or the needs of the market. **b.** *trans.* To do trade beyond (one's capital, stock, etc.). So **Overtra·der. Overtra·ding** *vbl. sb.* trading in excess of one's capital or the needs of the market.

Over-train (-trēⁱ·n), *v.* 1856. [OVER- II. 6.] *trans.* To train too much, to injure by excessive training. **b.** To train (a creeping plant) too much or too high.

†**Overtrea·d,** *v.* [OE. *ofertredan*; see OVER- I. 1, 9, 13.] **a.** To trample under foot; *fig.* to oppress, subdue. **b.** To step beyond –1620.

Over-trou·ble (-trʋ·b'l), *v.* 1582. [OVER- II. 6.] *trans.* To trouble excessively. So **O·vertrou·bled** *ppl. a.*

Overtru·mp, *v.* 1746. [OVER- II. 1.] *trans.* To play a higher trump than one already played; also *absol.* and *fig.*

Over-tru·st, *v.* ME. [OVER- II. 6.] **1.** *intr.* To trust too much; to be over-confident. **2.** *trans.* To trust (a person or thing) too much 1649.

Overtu·mble, *v.* 1600. [OVER- I. 6, 5.] *trans.* To cause to fall over; to overthrow. Now only *poet.*

Overture (ōᵘ·vəɹtiŭɹ, -tʃŭɹ), *sb.* ME. [– OFr. *overture* (now *ouverture*) :– L. *apertura* APERTURE, w. influence from *ouvrir* open.] †**1.** An opening, orifice, hole. Also *fig.* –1749. †**2.** A revelation, disclosure, discovery –1654. **3.** An opening of negotiations; a formal proposal, proposition, or offer. late ME. **4.** In the General Assembly of the Church of Scotland, and in the supreme court of other Presbyterian churches: A formal motion proposing or calling for legislation 1576. †**5.** An opening for proceeding to action –1768. †**6.** An opening, beginning, commencement –1741. **7.** *Mus.* An orchestral piece, of varying form and dimensions, forming the opening or introduction to an opera, oratorio, etc.; also, as an independent piece 1667. **b.** The introductory part of a poem 1870.

1. Diuers ouertures and holes were made vnder the foundacion 1548. **2.** *Lear* III. vii. 89. **3.** There have been overtures of marriage made unto him 1655.

O·verture, *v.* 1637. [f. prec. sb.] **1.** *trans.* To put forward as an overture or proposal; to offer, propose. **2.** In the supreme court of a Presbyterian church: To bring forward as an overture; to introduce as a motion 1671. **b.** To present or transmit an overture to (a church court); to approach with an overture 1864. **3.** To introduce with, or as with, a musical overture; to prelude 1870.

Overturn (ōᵘ·vəɹtɔ̄ɹn), *sb.* 1592. [OVER- I. 6, 10.] **1.** The act of overturning or fact of being overturned; an upsetting; a revolution. **2.** *Geol.* = OVERFOLD *sb.* 1877. **3.** Turnover in the course of trade 1882.

Overturn (ōᵘvəɹtɔ̄·ɹn), *v.* ME. [OVER- I. 6, ?4, 10.] †**1.** *intr.* Of a wheel, and *fig.* of time: To turn round, revolve –1649. **2.** *trans.* To turn (anything) over upon its side or face; to upset, overthrow; to cause to fall over or down ME. **b.** *intr.* To turn over, capsize, upset. late ME. **3.** *trans.* To overthrow, subvert, bring to ruin. late ME. †**4.** To upset, disorder (stomach, etc.) –1704. †**5.** To turn away; to pervert –1587.

2. They ouerturned their Canoa with a great violence 1555. **3.** We shall o're-turne it [the Kingdome] topsie-turuy downe SHAKS. Hence **Overtu·rnable** *a.* **Overtu·rner.**

Over-value (ōᵘ·vəɹvæːliu), *sb.* 1611. [OVER- II. 8 d.] A value or estimate greater than the worth of a thing.

Overvalue (ōᵘvəɹvæ·liu), *v.* 1597. [OVER- II. 5, 1 b.] **1.** *trans.* To value (a thing) above its worth; to overestimate. **b.** To put too high a money valuation upon 1641. †**2.** Of a thing: To surpass in value –1772.

1. b. If the policy be enormously overvalued, that will be evidence of fraud 1847. So **O·vervalua·tion,** the action of overvaluing.

Overwa·lk, *v.* 1533. [OVER- I. 9, 10, II. 2.] **1.** *trans.* To walk over. **2.** *refl.* To walk too much or too far 1662.

O·verwash (-wǫʃ), *sb.* 1889. [f. next.] *Geol.* The material carried by running water from a glacier and deposited over or beyond the marginal moraine.

Overwash (-wǫ·ʃ), *v.* 1577. [OVER- I. 5, 9.] *trans.* To wash or flow over (something); to bathe by flowing over.

Overwatch (ōᵘvəɹwǫ·tʃ), *v.* 1563. [OVER- I. 1 (*c*), 17, 21.] **1.** *trans.* To keep watch over 1618. †**2.** To watch all through (a night) –1590. **3.** To weary or exhaust by keeping awake or by want of sleep. Now chiefly in *pa. pple.* 1563.

Overwear (ōᵘvəɹwēᵊ·ɹ), *v.* 1578. [OVER- I. 21, 17.] **1.** To wear out or exhaust with toil, etc. **2.** To wear out (clothes, etc.), wear threadbare 1630. **3.** To wear (something) away or to an end; to outwear 1581.

Overweary (ōᵘvəɹwiᵊ·ri), *v.* 1576. [OVER- I. 21, II. 6.] *trans.* To overcome with weariness; to tire out.

Overween (ōᵘvəɹwī·n), *v.* Now chiefly in *ppl. a.* ME. [OVER- II. 5, 6.] **1.** *intr.* To have too high expectations or too high an opinion of oneself; to be arrogant or presumptuous. †**2.** To think too highly (*of*) –1621. †**3.** *trans.* (and *refl.* = 1). To over-esteem (usu. oneself, or something of one's own) –1674. †**4.** To cause to overween –1620.

1. Mowbray, you ouer-weene to take it so SHAKS. Hence **Overwee·ning** *vbl. sb.* (now *rare*), arrogance, self-conceit; over-estimation. **Overwee·ning** *ppl. a.* over-confident; conceited, arrogant, presumptuous, self-opinionated; of opinion, etc., exaggerated. **Overwee·ning-ly** *adv.*, **-ness.**

Overweigh (ōᵘvəɹwēⁱ·), *v.* ME. [OVER- II. 1, 5, I. 21.] **1.** *trans.* To exceed in weight (physical or moral); to overbalance, outweigh. **2.** To weigh down, overburden, oppress 1577. **3.** *intr.* To preponderate; to weigh too much 1862.

2. Say what you can; my false ore-weighs your true SHAKS.

Overweight (ōᵘ·vəɹwēⁱt), *sb.* 1511. [OVER- I. 19, II. 8 c.] **1.** Something over the exact or proper weight; extra weight. **2.** Greater weight (than that of something else); preponderance (physical or moral) 1626. **3.** Too great weight; also *fig.* 1577.

Over-weight (ōᵘ·vəɹwēⁱt), *a.* 1638. [OVER *prep.* + WEIGHT *sb.*] Above, or in excess of, the ordinary weight; too heavy.

I was charged a few pounds of o. luggage 1888.

Overwei·ght, *v.* 1603. [OVER- II. 6.] †**1.** *trans.* To give or attach too much weight to FLORIO. **2.** To weight too heavily; to overburden, overload (*lit.* and *fig.*). Chiefly in *pa. pple.* 1753.

†**O·ver-wet,** *sb.* 1626. [OVER- II. 7.] Too great wetness BACON. So **O·ver-we·tness.**

Overwhelm (ōᵘvəɹhwe·lm), *v.* ME. [f. OVER- I. 6, 8 + WHELM *v.* roll.] **1.** *trans.* To overturn, upset; to turn upside down. *Obs.* exc. *dial.* **2.** *trans.* To cover (anything) as with something turned over and cast upon it; to bury or drown beneath this; to submerge completely (and ruin or destroy) 1450. †**b.** To overhang so as to cover more or less SHAKS. **3.** *fig.* To overcome or overpower; to bring to ruin or destruction; to crush 1529. **b.** To overpower utterly with some emotion 1535. **c.** To 'deluge' *with* 1806.

1. The earthquake..overwhelmed a chain of mountains of free stone more than 300 miles long 1796. **2.** Pompeii was overwhelmed by a vast accumulation of dust and ashes HUXLEY. **b.** *Hen. V*, III. i. 11. **3.** We Starve at home, abroad our debts ore-whelm us 1692. **b.** I was overwhelmed with the sense of my condition DE FOE. **c.** The whole party..were overwhelming him with praises 1806. Hence **Overwhe·lming** *ppl. a.*, **-ly** *adv.*, **-ness.**

Overwind (ōᵘvəɹwəi·nd), *v.* 1682. *Pa.t.* and *pa. pple.* **overwound.** [OVER- II. 5.] *trans.* To wind too tight, as in tuning a musical instrument; to wind (a watch, etc., or, in *Mining*, the hoisting rope or chain) too far.

O·ver-wi·se (-wəiz), *a.* 1588. [OVER- II. 7.] Too wise, affectedly wise. *Not over-wise*, rather deficient in wisdom. Hence **O·ver-wi·se-ly** *adv.*, **-ness. O·ver-wi·sdom.**

O·verword, *sb.* Chiefly *Sc.* 1500. [OVER- I. 20.] A word or phrase repeated again and again; *esp.* the refrain of a song.

Overwork, *sb.* [OE. *oferweorc*, f. *ofer-* OVER- I. 1.] **I.** (ōᵘ·vəɹwɔ̄ɹk). †**1.** A superstructure; *spec.* in OE. a sepulchral monument. OE. and ME. **2.** Extra work. [OVER- I. 19.] 1858. **II.** (ōᵘ·vəɹwɔ̄·ɹk). Excessive work, work beyond one's capacity. [OVER- II. 8 b.] 1818.

Overwork (ōᵘvəɹwɔ̄·ɹk), *v.* Pa. t. and pple. **-wrought, -worked.** [OE. *oferwyrcan*, f. OVER- I. 8.] **I. 1.** *trans.* To work all over, decorate the surface of. (Only in *pa. pple.*) [OVER- I. 8.] †**2.** To work upon successfully; to gain over to a certain course. [OVER- I. 11.] –1661. **II. 1.** *trans.* To cause to work too hard; to work (a man, horse, etc.) beyond his strength; to weary or exhaust with work. [OVER- II. 6, I. 21.] 1530. **b.** To fill too full with work 1876. **c.** *intr.* To work too much 1894. **2.** To work too much upon; to elaborate to excess. (Only in *pa. pple.*) [OVER- II. 6.] 1638. **3.** *trans.* and *fig.* To stir up or excite excessively 1645.

1. Overworking my eyes by candlelight PEPYS. **b.** My days with toil are overwrought LONGF. **3.** Till my brain became, In its own eddy boiling and o'er-wrought, A whirling gulf of phantasy and flame BYRON.

Overworn (ōᵘvəɹwǭɹn; stress variable), *ppl. a.* 1565. [f. OVER- I. 21, 17 + WORN *ppl. a.*] **1.** Much worn, the worse for wear; threadbare; faded. †**2.** Obsolete –1610. **3.** Worn out, exhausted, spent, as with age or toil 1592. **4.** Spent in time; passed away 1592.

1. *fig. Twel. N.* III. i. 66. **4.** Musing the morning is so much o'erworn SHAKS.

Overwrite (ōᵘvəɹəi·t), *v.* 1699. [OVER- I. 8, 20, II. 6, 2.] **1. a.** *trans.* To write (something) over other writing, as a palimpsest. **b.** To write over, to cover *with* writing. **2.** To re-write 1874. **3. a.** *intr.* To write too much; **b.** *refl.* To exhaust oneself by excessive writing; **c.** *trans.* To write too much about (a subject) 1837.

Overwrought (ōᵘ·vəɹǭ·t), *ppl. a.* 1670. [pa. pple. of OVERWORK *v.*] **1. a.** Exhausted by overwork. **b.** Worked up to too high a pitch. **2.** Elaborated to excess; overlaboured 1839.

Over-zeal (ōᵘ·vəɹzī·l). 1747. [OVER- II. 8 d.] Too great zeal; excess of zeal. So **O·ver-zealous** (-ze·ləs) *a.* 1635.

Ovi-¹, comb. form of L. *ovum* egg, as in **Ovi·ferous** [-FEROUS], *a. Anat.* and *Zool.* egg-bearing; applied *esp.* to special receptacles in which the ova of some crustaceans are carried. **O·viform** [-FORM], *a.* having the form of an egg, egg-shaped. **Ovigerm** (ōᵘ·vi,dʒəɹm) [GERM], an (unfertilized) ovum. **Ovigerous** (ovi·dʒĕrəs) [-GEROUS], *a. Anat.* and *Zool.* bearing or carrying eggs. **Ovi·vorous** [L. *-vorus* devouring + -OUS], *a.* egg-eating.

Ovi-², comb. form of L. *ovis* sheep, as *ovibovine, oviform, ovivorous* adjs.

Ovicapsule (ōᵘvikæ·psiul). 1853. [f. OVI-¹ + CAPSULE.] *Anat.* and *Zool.* A capsule or sac containing an ovum or ova; an egg-case, an ovisac. Hence **Ovica·psular** *a.*

Ovicell (ōᵘ·visel). 1870. [f. OVI-¹ + CELL.] **1.** A receptacle for the ova in certain Polyzoa; also called *oocyst* or *oœcium.* **2.** A cell which when impregnated becomes a new individual; an egg-cell; a germ-cell; an ovum or ovule 1875.

Ovicide (ōᵘ·visəid), *joc.* 1845. [f. OVI-² + -CIDE 2.] Sheep-killing. So **O·vicidal** *a.*

Ovicyst (ōᵘ·visist). 1877. [f. OVI-¹ + CYST.] *Zool.* A receptacle in which the ova are hatched in some ascidians. Hence **Ovicy·stic** *a.*

Ovidian (ovi·diăn), *a.* 1617. [-IAN.] Belonging to or characteristic of the Latin poet Ovid (Publius Ovidius Naso, B.C. 43–A.D. 17), or his poetry.

Oviduct (ōᵘ·vidɒkt). 1757. [– mod.L. *oviductus*; see OVI-¹, DUCT.] *Anat.* and *Zool.* The duct or canal forming a passage for the ova or eggs from the ovary, esp. in birds; in mammals the corresponding structure is more usu. called the Fallopian tube. So **Oviducal** (ōᵘ·vidiūkăl) *a.* of the nature of an o.

Ovine (ōᵘ·vəin), *a.* 1828. [– late L. *ovinus*, f. *ovis* sheep; see -INE¹.] **1.** Of, pertaining to, or characteristic of, sheep or a sheep; in *Zool.* belonging to the *Ovinæ*, a subfamily of ruminants, comprising the various kinds of sheep. **2.** *fig.* Sheeplike, sheepish 1832.

Oviparous (ovi·părəs), *a.* 1646. [f. L. *oviparus* + -OUS; see OVI-¹, -PAROUS.] *Zool.* Producing ova or eggs; applied to animals that produce young by means of eggs. (Opp. to VIVIPAROUS.) So **Oviparity** (ōᵘvipæ·rĭti), the condition or character of being o.

Oviposit (ōᵘvipǫ·zit), *v.* 1816. [f. OVI-¹ + L. *posit-*, ppl. stem of *ponere* place; cf. *deposit.*] *Zool. intr.* To deposit or lay an egg or eggs; esp. by means of an ovipositor, as an insect. **b.** *trans.* To deposit or lay (an egg) 1847. So **Oviposi·tion.**

Ovipositor (ōᵘvipǫ·zitǫɹ). 1816. [f. as prec.; see -OR 2.] *Entom.* A pointed tubular organ at the end of the abdomen of the female in many insects, by means of which the eggs are deposited, and (in many cases) a hole bored to receive them.

Ovisac (ōᵘ·visæk). 1835. [f. OVI-¹ + SAC.] *Anat.* and *Zool.* A sac, cell, or pouch containing an ovum (as a Graafian follicle), or a number of ova; an egg-case.

Ovism (ōᵘ·viz'm). 1892. [f. L. *ovum* + -ISM; in mod.Fr. *ovisme.*] *Biol.* The old theory that the ovum or female reproductive cell contains the whole of the future organism in an undeveloped state, the male cell or spermatozoon acting merely as a stimulant; opp. to *spermism* or *animalculism.* So **Ovist** (ōᵘ·vist), one who holds the theory of o. 1836. **Ovi·stic** *a.* 1893.

Ovo- (ōᵘvo), used as a var. of comb. form OVI- as in **O:vo-rhomboi·dal,** etc. See -o-.

Ovogenesis (ōᵘvo,dʒe·nĭsis). 1886. [mod. L., f. OVO- + GENESIS; cf. OOGENESIS.] *Biol.* The production or formation of an ovum. So **Ovogene·tic, Ovo·genous** *adjs.* contributing to the formation or growth of an ovum.

Ovoid (ōᵘ·void), *a.* and *sb.* 1828. [– Fr. *ovoïde* (Buffon) – mod.L. *ovoides*, f. L. *ovum* egg; see -OID.] **A.** *adj.* **1.** Resembling an egg, egg-shaped. **2.** *Comb.*: esp. with another adj., denoting modification of the form expressed by the latter, as *o.-oblong* 1870. **B.** *sb.* A body or figure of ovoid form 1831. So **Ovoi·dal** (ovoi·dăl) *a.* 1799.

Ovolo (ōᵘ·vŏlo). *Pl.* **ovoli** (-li). 1663. [– It. *ovolo*, dim. of †*ovo*, *uovo* :– L. *ovum* EGG *sb.*] *Arch.* A convex moulding of which the section is a quarter-circle or (approx.) a quarter-ellipse, receding from the vertical downwards; also called *quarter-round* or *echinus.*

Ovology (ovǫ·lŏdʒi). 1842. [f. OVO- + -LOGY.] That part of biology or embryology which treats of the formation and structure of the ova of animals. So **Ovolo·gical** *a.* **Ovo·logist.**

‖**O:vo-te·stis.** 1877. [mod.L., f. OVO- + TESTIS.] *Zool.* An organ in certain invertebrates producing both ova and spermatozoa; a hermaphrodite gland.

Ovo-viviparous (ōᵘ:vo,vivi·pǎrəs), *a.* 1801. [f. OVO- + VIVIPAROUS.] *Zool.* Combining oviparous and viviparous characters; producing eggs which are hatched within the body of the parent.

Ovular (ōᵘ·viulăɹ), *a.* 1855. [f. OVULE + -AR¹.] *Biol.* Of, pertaining to, or of the nature of an ovule.

Ovulate (ōᵘ·viulĕt), *a.* 1861. [f. mod.L. *ovulum* OVULE + -ATE².] Having or containing an ovule or ovules. Chiefly in comb., as *biovulate*, etc.

Ovulation (ōᵘviulēⁱ·ʃən). 1853. [f. OVULE + -ATION.] *Physiol.* and *Zool.* The formation and development of ovules or ova, and (*esp.*) their discharge from the ovary, as occurring in female mammals. Hence **O·vulate** *v.*

Ovule (ōᵘ·viul). 1830. [– Fr. *ovule* (Mirbel 1808) – mod. (and med.) L. *ovulum*; see next.] **1.** *Bot.* The rudimentary seed in a phanerogamous plant; the body which contains the female germ-cell, and after fertilization becomes a *seed.* **2.** *Zool.* and *Physiol.* The female germ-cell of an animal; *spec.* the unfertilized ovum 1857. So **Ovuli·ferous,** *a.* bearing or producing ovules. **O·vulist** = OVIST.

‖**Ovulum** (ōᵘ·viulŏm). *Pl.* **ovula.** 1822. [(med. and) mod.L. *ovulum*, dim. of L. *ovum* egg; see -ULE.] **1.** *Zool.* and *Physiol.* = OVULE 2. 1822. **2.** *Zool.* A genus of gastropod molluscs, including the Egg-shell (*O. ovum*) with an egg-shaped shell 1837.

‖**Ovum** (ōᵘ·vŏm). *Pl.* **ova** (ōᵘ·vă). 1706. [L. = egg.] **1.** *Zool.* The female germ in animals, capable when fertilized by the male sperm (and in some cases without such fertilization) of developing into a new individual. **2.** *Arch.* An egg-shaped ornament or carving 1727. **3.** *attrib.*, as *o.-product*, etc.; often with pl., as *ova-duct*, etc. 1753.

Owe (ōᵘ), *v.* [OE. *āgan* = OFris. *āga*, OS. *ēgan*, OHG. *eigan*, ON. *eiga*, Goth. *aigan*; Gmc. perfect-pres. vb. (cf. CAN *v.*¹, DARE *v.*¹, MAY *v.*¹); f. **aiʒ-* :– IE. **oik- *ik-*, repr. also by Skr. *-iś* possess, own. Cf. OWN *a.*] **I.** *trans.* To have; to possess; = OWN *v.* 2. *Obs.* exc. *dial.*

The Oxe . . knowes who owes him, and feedes him 1628.

II. To have to pay. **1.** To be under obligation to pay or repay (money, etc.); to be indebted in, or to the amount of; to be under obligation to render (obedience, honour, etc.). Const. with simple dat. or *to.* (The chief current sense.) ME. **b.** *absol.* To be in debt 1460. **2.** *transf.* **a.** To have towards another (a feeling, regarded as something which is yet to be rendered in action); to bear (good or ill will). *Obs.* exc. in *to owe a grudge.* late ME. **b.** To bear *to* some one or something (a relation, as dependence, etc., which has to be acknowledged); to 'own' (*rare*) 1644. **3.** *fig.* To be indebted or beholden for. Const. *to* (or simple dative). 1591. †**b.** Without direct obj.: To be beholden (*to* a person *for* something) –1686.

1. He seide to the firste, Hou moche owist thou to my lord? WYCLIF *Luke* 16:5. **2.** I o. euen for the clothes vpon my backe 1607. **3.** We o. the discovery of the prismatic spectrum to Sir Isaac Newton 1868.

III. †**1.** To have as a duty; to be under obligation (*to do* something). (Followed by inf. with or without *to*). –1537. †**2.** quasi-*impers.* (usu. with inf. clause as subject): (It) behoves, befits, is due (to); e.g. *him owe* (or *oweth*) = it behoves him, he ought; *as him owe*, as befits him, as is due to him –1500. Hence **Ow·er,** †an owner; a debtor (*rare*). **Ow·ing** *vbl. sb.* that which one owes; debt.

Owelty (ōᵘ·ĕlti). 1579. [– AFr. *owelté*, f. OFr. *owel* :– L. *æqualis* EQUAL; see -TY¹.] *Law.* Equality.

Owenian (ōᵘī·niăn), *a.* 1883. [f. surname *Owen* + -IAN.] Of or pertaining to Robert Owen (1771–1858), a social reformer who advocated the reorganization of society on a system of communistic co-operation, which he endeavoured to carry into practice in various industrial communities. So **Ow·enist, Ow·enite,** a follower of Owen.

Owing (ōᵘ·iŋ), *ppl. a.* late ME. [f. OWE *v.* + -ING².] **1.** That owes; under obligation; indebted, bounden, beholden. Now *rare* or *Obs.* **2.** That is yet to be paid or rendered; owed, due. Const. *to* or simple dat. (The usual current sense.) late ME. **3.** *fig.* **Owing to: a.** *pred.* That owes its existence to; attributable to; caused by, 'due to' 1655. **b.** Hence, as prep. phr.: In consequence of, on account of, because of 1814.

1. I am greatly o. to your Lordship for your last favour PEPYS. **2.** All that was o. for the children 1782. **3. b.** O. to his natural disposition to study . . he had been bred with a view to the bar SCOTT.

Owl (aul), *sb.* [OE. *ūle* = OLG. **ūla* (MLG., MDu. *ūle*, Du. *uil*), ON. *ugla* :– **uwwalōn*, parallel with **uwwilōn*, repr. by OHG. *ūwila* (MHG. *iule*, G. *eule*).] **1.** A nocturnal bird of prey, well known by its doleful 'hoot', having a large head, small face, raptorial beak, and large eyes directed forwards, beset by a disc of radiating feathers; feeding on small birds, mice, and the like. **b.** The common British species are the *Barn O.* (White, Silver, Yellow, Church, Hissing, Hobby, Screech O.); the *Tawny O.* (Brown, Grey, Beech, Ferny, Hoot, Hooting, Ivy, Wood O.); the *Long-eared* or *Horned O.*, etc. late ME. **c.** *Ornith.* Any bird of the suborder *Striges.* (The known species are about 200.) 1706. **d.** In provb. sayings. late ME. **2.** *transf.* and *fig.* Applied to a person in allusion to nocturnal habits, to appearance of gravity and wisdom, etc. Hence = wiseacre, solemn dullard. late ME. **3. a.** A name for the Lump Fish, more fully *Sea O.* 1601. **b.** The owl-ray 1862. **4.** A variety of the domestic pigeon; also called *O.-pigeon* 1725.

1. The clamorous Owle that nightly hoots SHAKS. **d.** *To carry* or *send owls to Athens*, after Gr. γλαῦκ' Ἀθήναζε ἄγειν = to take a commodity where it already abounds. As drunk as owls MARRYAT.

attrib. and *Comb.*, as *o.-flight, -eyed* adj., etc.; **o.-train** *U.S. slang*, a train running during the night. **b.** esp. in names of animals, as **o.-monkey,** a S. Amer. monkey of the genus *Nyctipithecus*; **-moth,** a very large Brazilian moth (*Erebus strix*) resembling an owl in its colouring and in the appearance of its hind wings; **-parrot** = KAKAPO; **-pigeon**: see 4; **-ray**: see 3. Hence **Owl** *v. intr.* to behave like an owl; to pry about, prowl, esp. in the dark. Now chiefly *dial.*

Ow·ler. *Obs.* exc. *Hist.* 1690. [app. f. prec.; see -ER¹ 1.] One engaged in the illegal exportation or 'owling' of wool or sheep from England; also, a vessel so employed, an owling boat. So **Ow·ling** *vbl. sb.* the trade of an o.

Owlery (au·ləri). 1817. [f. OWL *sb.* + -ERY.] **1.** A place where owls are kept; a haunt of owls. **2.** Owlishness 1831.

Owlet (au·lĕt). 1542. [dim. f. OWL + -ET. Cf. HOWLET.] An owl; a young owl or little owl.

Comb. **o.-moth,** an American name for any moth of the genus *Noctua* or family *Noctuidæ*.

Ow·l-glass. 1560. [f. OWL *sb.* + GLASS *sb.* II. 5.] = *Eulenspiegel*, name of a German jester of mediæval times; a prototype of roguish fools; hence, A jester, buffoon.

Owlish (au·liʃ), *a.* 1611. [f. OWL *sb.* + -ISH[1].] Owl-like; resembling an owl, or that of an owl. Hence **Ow·lish-ly** *adv.*, **-ness.**

Owl-light. 1599. [f. OWL *sb.* + LIGHT *sb.*] The dim light in which owls go abroad; twilight, dusk; also (in early use) the dark.

Own (ōᵘn), *a.* [OE. *āgen* = OFris. *ēgen*, *ēin*, OS. *ēgan*, OHG. *eigan* (Du., G. *eigen*), ON. *eiginn* :– Gmc. **aiʒanaz*, adj. use of the pa. pple. of OWE, prop. 'possessed', 'owed'.] That is possessed or owned by the person or thing indicated by the preceding sb. or pron.; of or belonging to oneself or itself; proper, peculiar, particular, individual. **1.** Used after a possessive case or adj., to emphasize the possessive meaning. **b.** Expressing tenderness or affection; also (usu. *joc.*) in *superl.* = very own. late ME. **c.** *Own* in the predicate sometimes has the force of *self* in the subject, as in 'I am my own master' = 'I myself (and not some one else) am my master' 1551. **2.** Without possessive preceding. Now *rare*, and usu. with *an* or in *pl.* OE. **3.** *absol.* (mostly with preceding possessive): That which is (one's) own; property, possessions; (one's) own goods, kinsfolk, friends, etc. Somewhat *arch.* OE.

1. And find no spot of all the world my o. GOLDSMITH. The reader who loves history for its o. sake 1895. Phr. *To be one's o. man* (*woman*), to be independent; to have the full control or use of one's faculties. **b.** By me, thine owne true Knight SHAKS. **2.** *An o. brother*, as dist. from a half-brother or brother-in-law, etc.; *o. cousins*, first cousins. **3.** *Wint. T.* V.iii.123. He gave freely of his o. 1839. Phr. *Of* (*one's*) *o.*, that is one's own; belonging to oneself.

Spec. phrases. *To hold one's o.*, to maintain one's position; not to suffer defeat or derogation. †*To tell one his o.*, to tell him the plain truth about himself. *On one's o.* (colloq.), on one's own account, responsibility, resources, etc. *To get one's o. back* (colloq.), to get even with, to revenge oneself *on* someone. Hence **Ownness** (ōᵘ·nnės), the fact or quality of being one's own or peculiar to oneself 1642.

Own (ōᵘn), *v.* [OE. *āgnian*, f. *āgen* OWN *a.* After OE. and early ME. scarcely found till XVII, the usual word in sense 2 in XIV-XVII being OWE.] †**1.** *trans.* To make (a thing) one's own; to seize, win, gain; to adopt as one's own –ME. **2.** To have or hold as own's own, possess OE. †**b.** To have as one's function or business –1714. **3. a.** To acknowledge as one's own 1610. **b.** To recognize as an acquaintance. *Obs.* exc. *dial.* 1650. †**c.** To claim for one's own –1815. **4.** To acknowledge as approved or accepted; to countenance, vindicate. Somewhat *arch.* 1610. **5.** To acknowledge (something) in its relation to oneself; also, to confess to be valid, true, or actual; to admit 1655. **b.** *intr.* To confess (*to* something) 1776. **c.** *To o. up* (colloq.): to confess fully or frankly. (*intr.* with or without *to*, or with *obj. clause*) 1880. **6.** *spec.* To acknowledge as having supremacy, authority, or power over one; to yield obedience or submission to 1695.

2. Gardens owned by the wealthier residents 1858. **b.** *Wint. T.* IV.iv.143. **3. a.** Thy Brat hath been cast out..No Father owning it SHAKS. **b.** My Lord Chaimberlaine..who owned and spoke to me PEPYS. **5.** Her age was about thirty, for she owned six and twenty FIELDING. I readily o. myself at a loss 1758. I o. to you that I have a great fear of the damage that ridicule might do 1873. **b.** He owns to disliking the Doctor 1853. **6.** Till all Thy creatures o. Thy sway 1870.

Owner (ōᵘ·nəɹ). ME. [f. prec. + -ER[1].] One who owns or holds something; one who has the rightful claim or title to a thing. Also *attrib.*, as *owner-driver, -occupier.*

She now lived upon an estate of which she no longer was the o. MISS BURNEY. Hence **Ow·nerless** *a.* **Ow·nership,** the fact or state of being an o.; property, proprietorship 1583.

Ox (ǫks). [OE. *oxa* = OFris. *oxa*, OS., OHG. *ohso* (Du. *os*, G. *ochse*), ON. *uxi, oxi*, Goth. *auhsa* :– Gmc. **oχson* :– IE. **uksin-*, repr. also by Skr. *ukshán* ox, bull, cattle.] **1.** The domestic bovine quadruped (sexually dist. as *bull* and *cow*); in common use, applied to the male castrated and used for draught purposes, or reared to serve as food. **2.** *Zool.* Any beast of the bovine family of ruminants, including the domestic European species, the 'wild oxen' preserved in certain parks in Britain, the buffalo, bison, gaur, yak, musk-ox, etc. OE. **3.** *transf.* An ancient coin bearing a representation of an ox; also *attrib.* as *ox-coin*, etc. 1607. **4.** *fig.* †**a.** A fool –1640. **b.** The *black ox*, misfortune, adversity; old age 1546.

1. A herd of Beeves, faire Oxen and faire Kine MILT. **2.** *American ox*, the bison or buffalo; *Cape ox, Bos caffer*; *Indian, Brahmin*, or *Dwarf ox*, the zebu (*B. indicus*); *Musk ox*, a ruminant of arctic America, *Ovibos moschatus*. **4. a.** *Merry W.* V.V.126. **b.** Provb. *The black o. has trod on* (*his*, etc.) *foot.*

attrib. and *Comb.*: **o.-antelope,** a bovine antelope; in R.V. (*Num.* 23:22) a marginal reading for 'wild ox', identified as *Bos primigenius*; **-bile** = *ox-gall*; **-biter,** a bird: (*a*) = *ox-pecker*; (*b*) *U.S.* the cow-bird, *Molobrus ater* or *M. pecoris*; **-fly, -gad-fly,** the gad-fly or bot-fly, *Œstrus bovis*; **-gall,** the gall of the ox, used for cleansing purposes, also in painting and pharmacy; **-god,** Apis, the sacred bull of the Egyptians; **-heart** *a.*, heart-shaped and large; applied esp. to a variety of cherry; also as *sb.*; **oxland** = OXGANG; also, plough-land; **-pecker,** the genus *Buphaga* of African birds, feeding on the parasitic larvæ that infest the hide of cattle; also called *beef-eater*; **-ray,** a fish, the large horned ray, *Cephaloptera giorna*. See also Main words.

b. In names of plants (in some of which *ox-*, like *horse-*, denotes a coarse or large species, or means 'eaten by' or 'fit for oxen'): **ox-bane,** a plant injurious to cattle; the Poison-bulb of S. Africa, *Buphane toxicaria*; **-daisy** = *Ox-eye daisy*; **-heal** or **-heel,** Bear's-foot or Fetid Hellebore, *Helleborus fœtidus*; **-mushroom,** a name for very large specimens of the common mushroom. Hence **O·x-like** *a.* and *adv.* like, or resembling that of an ox; after the manner of an ox.

Ox-, a formative of chemical terms. **1.** = OXY- from *oxygen*, as in *ox-* or *oxy-acetic*, *oxiodic*, etc. **2.** A shortening of OXAL-, as in OXAMIC, etc.

Oxal-, comb. element in chemical terms, used in the sense 'derived from or related to oxalic acid', or 'containing the radical oxalyl'. **O·xalan** [-AN 2; cf. *alloxan*] = OXALURAMIDE. **Oxale·thyline,** a poisonous oily liquid of composition $C_6H_{10}N_2$; also a general name for the series to which this belongs, as *chloroxalethyline* $C_6H_9ClN_2$. **O·xalite** *Min.*, native ferrous oxalate.

Oxalate (ǫ·ksălėt). 1791. [– Fr. *oxalate* (G. de Morveau and Lavoisier, 1787), f. OXAL- in *oxalique* OXALIC + -ATE[4].] *Chem.* A salt of oxalic acid.

Oxa·ldehyde. [f. OX- 2 + ALDEHYDE; = *oxalic aldehyde.*] *Chem.* = GLYOXAL.

Oxalic (ǫksæ·lik), *a.* 1791. [– Fr. *oxalique* (G. de Morveau and Lavoisier, 1787), f. L. OXALIS; see -IC.] *Chem.* Of, derived from, or characteristic of the *Oxalis* or Wood Sorrel: *spec.* **a.** *Oxalic acid*: a highly poisonous and intensely sour acid ($C_2H_2O_4$ = $C_2O_3.2HO$), the first member of the dibasic series having the general formula $C_nH_{2n-2}O_4$. **b.** *O. ether*, a name for neutral ethyl oxalate ($C_6H_{10}O_4$ = $C_2O_3.2C_2H_5.O_2$); also extended to the oxalates of the alcohol radicals in general.

‖**Oxalis** (ǫ·ksălis). 1706. [L. *oxalis* (Pliny) – Gr. ὀξαλίς wood-sorrel (Dioscorides), f. ὀξύς sour, acid.] *Bot.* A genus of plants, mostly herbs, with delicate five-parted flowers, and leaves usu. of three leaflets; the common British species is *O. acetosella*, Wood Sorrel.

Oxalo-, comb. element = OXAL-, used bef. consonants; as **O:xalo-ni·trate,** a salt of oxalic and nitrate acid.

Oxaluramide (ǫksălyūᵊ·rămәid). 1866. [See next and AMIDE.] *Chem.* The amide of oxaluric acid ($C_3H_5N_3O_3$), obtained as a white crystalline powder by the action of ammonia and hydrocyanic acid on alloxan; also called *oxalan.*

Oxaluric (ǫksălyūᵊ·rik), *a.* 1836. [f. OXAL- + URIC.] *Chem.* In *O. acid*: a monobasic acid ($C_3H_4N_2O_4$), which may be regarded as oxalic acid and urea *minus* water, obtained as a white crystalline powder, of a very acid taste. Hence **Oxalu·rate,** a salt of o. acid.

Oxalyl (ǫ·ksălil). 1859. [f. OXAL- + -YL.] *Chem.* The hypothetical radical (C_2O_2) of oxalic acid.

Oxamic (ǫksæ·mik), *a.* 1838. [f. OX- 2 = OXAL- + AMIC.] *Chem.* In *O. acid*: a monobasic acid, $C_2H_3NO_3$ (= $NH_2.C_2O_2.OH$), produced by the dehydration of acid oxalate of ammonium, and in other ways; its salts are **O·xamates.** *O. ether*: an ether in which one or other of the hydrogen-atoms of oxamic acid is replaced by an alcohol-radical; e.g. *ethylic oxamate* or **Oxame·thane,** $C_4H_7NO_3$.

Oxamide (ǫ·ksămәid). 1838. [f. OX- 2 + AMIDE.] *Chem.* The diamide $C_2O_2.N_2H_4$, representing two molecules of ammonia in which two atoms of hydrogen are replaced by oxalyl, C_2O_2; also called *oxalamide.*

Oxanilic (ǫksăni·lik), *a.* 1866. [f. OX 2 = OXAL- + ANILIC.] *Chem.* In *O. acid* (= phenyl-oxamic acid): a crystalline substance ($C_8H_7NO_3$) obtained by heating aniline with an excess of oxalic acid; its salts are **Oxa·nilates.** So **Oxani·lamide** (= monophenyl-oxamide), a snow-white flaky substance ($C_8H_8N_2O_2$) obtained in the decomposition of cyaniline by hydrochloric acid; **Oxa·nilide** (= diphenyloxamide), a substance ($C_{14}H_{12}N_2O_2$) crystallizing in white scales, obtained by heating aniline oxalate, or in other ways; **Oxa·niline,** a base (C_6H_7NO) obtained by heating amido-salicylic acid.

O·x-bird, o·xbird. 1547. [f. OX + BIRD 2.] A name applied to various British small wild-fowl; esp. the Dunlin (*Tringa variabilis*).

Ox-bow, oxbow (ǫ·ksbōᵘ). late ME. [f. OX + BOW *sb.*[1]] **1.** = BOW *sb.*[1] 5. **2.** *U.S.* A semicircular bend in a river; hence, the land included in this. Also *attrib.*, as *ox-bow bend.* 1797.

Ox-eye, oxeye (ǫ·ksˌәi). late ME. **1.** The eye of an ox; an eye like that of an ox, a large (human) eye 1688. **2.** A popular name of various birds. **a.** *esp.* the Great Titmouse (*Parus major*) 1544. **b.** Also, locally, the Dunlin, *Tringa variabilis*; etc. 1589. **3.** Applied to various plants: **a.** A species of the genus *Buphthalmum* (N.O. *Compositæ*). late ME. **b.** The British wild plants *Chrysanthemum segetum*, the Corn-marigold or Yellow Ox-eye, and *C. Leucanthemum*, the White Ox-eye, Ox-eye daisy, Dog-daisy, or Moon-daisy 1625. **c.** The American composite plant, *Heliopsis lævis*, with large yellow flowers. **4.** Applied to a drinking-cup in use at certain Oxford colleges 1703. **5.** *Naut.* = BULL'S EYE 10. 1598. Hence **O·x-ey·ed** *a.* having large full eyes like those of an ox.

Oxford (ǫ·ksfǒɹd), name of a university town in England [in OE. *Oxena-*, *Oxnaford* 'ford of oxen', ME. *Oxneford, Oxenford*], used attrib. in various expressions.

O. clay (*Geol.*), a deposit of stiff blue clay underlying the 'coral rag' of the Middle Oolite in the midland counties of England, and esp. in Oxfordshire; **O. corners,** in *Printing*, ruled border lines enclosing the print *of* a book, etc., crossing and extending beyond each other at the corners; **O. frame,** a picture-frame the sides of which cross each other and project at the corners; **O. man,** a man who has been educated at the University of Oxford; **O. mixture,** a very dark grey woollen cloth; **O. Movement** (*Ch. Hist.*), the movement for the revival of Catholic doctrine and observance in the Church of England, which began at Oxford about 1833; **O. oolite** (*Geol.*): the middle division of the Oolitic system; **O. School** (*Ch. Hist.*), the school of thought represented by the Oxford Movement; the body of persons belonging to this; **O. shirting,** a kind of striped material for shirts and dresses; **O. shoe,** a style of shoe laced over the instep; **O. Tracts,** the 'Tracts for the Times' issued 1833–41 in advocacy of the Oxford Movement, whence the movement is also known as TRACTARIAN. Hence **Oxfordian** (ǫksfǭ·ɹdiăn) *a.* pertaining to Oxford; in *Geol.* applied to the lower division of the Middle or Oxford Oolite.

Oxgang (ǫ·ksgæŋ). *Obs.* exc. *Hist.* Chiefly *north.* [f. OX + GANG *sb.*] The eighth part of the CARUCATE or ploughland, varying from 10 to 18 acres, or more; a bovate.

O·x-ha:rrow. 1523. A large and powerful harrow used on clay lands; orig. drawn by oxen.

Ox-head (ǫ·kshed). 1595. [f. OX + HEAD.] **1.** The head of an ox, or a representation of one. (Used in SHAKS. *John* II. i. 292 with ref. to cuckoldry.) **2.** *transf.* A stupid person; a dolt; also *attrib.* or quasi-*adj.* stupid 1634.

O·xherd. [f. OX + HERD *sb.*[2]] A keeper of oxen; a cowherd.

Ox-horn (ǫ·kshǭɹn). 1601. [f. OX +

HORN.] A horn of an ox. (Sometimes used as a drinking-vessel.)

Oxi-, earlier spelling of many words now spelt OXY-.

Oxidable (ǫ·ksidăb'l), *a.* Now *rare.* Also **oxy-**. 1790. [– Fr. *oxidable* (Lavoisier, 1789), now *oxydable*, f. *oxider*; see next, -ABLE.] *Chem.* Capable of being oxidated; oxidizable. Hence **O:xidabi·lity.**

Oxidate (ǫ·ksidēˈt), *v.* Now *rare.* Also **oxy-**. 1790. [f. Fr. *oxider* (G. de Morveau and Lavoisier, 1787) + -ATE³.] *Chem.* **1.** *trans.* = OXIDIZE 1. **2.** = OXIDIZE 2. 1807. Hence **Oxida·tion**, combination with oxygen; conversion into an oxide or oxygen-compound. **O·xidative** *a.* having the property of oxidizing. **O·xidator**, an oxidizing agent; an apparatus for directing a stream of oxygen into the flame of a lamp.

Oxide (ǫ·ksəid, ǫ·ksid), *sb.* Also **oxid** (now chiefly *U.S.*), **oxyde, oxyd.** 1790. [– Fr. *oxide* (de Morveau and Lavoisier, 'Nomenclature Chimique', 1787), now *oxyde*, f. *oxygène* OXYGEN + *-ide*, after *acide* ACID.] *Chem.* A compound of oxygen with another element, or with an organic radical.

Oxidize (ǫ·ksidəiz), *v.* Also **oxy-**. 1802. [f. prec. + -IZE.] *Chem.* **1.** *trans.* To cause to combine with oxygen; to convert into an oxide or oxygen-compound. (In the case of a metal, often = to rust, make rusty.) **2.** *intr.* To take up or enter into combination with oxygen; to become converted into an oxide. (Of a metal, often = to rust, become rusty.) 1826.

Oxidized silver, a name erron. given to silver with a dark coating of silver sulphide. Hence **O·xidizable,** also **oxy-**, *a.* **O:xidiza·tion,** also **oxy-**, oxidation. **O·xidizer,** also **oxy-**, an oxidizing agent.

†**Oxi·dulated,** *ppl. a.* Also **oxy-**. 1806. [– Fr. †*oxidulé*, f. *oxydule*, 'lowest degree of oxidation, protoxide', dim. of *oxyde*; after L. *acidus, acidulus.*] *Chem.* Combined with a smaller proportion of oxygen than in another compound; as in *o. iron*, a former name for the magnetic oxide of iron (Fe_3O_4) as dist. from the peroxide (Fe_2O_3) –1882.

Oxime (ǫ·ksəim), **oxim** (ǫ·ksim). 1891. [f. OX- 1 + *-ime*, shortened from IMIDE.] *Chem.* A chemical compound containing the divalent group: N(OH) joined to a carbon atom, esp. in the combination C_nH_{2n}: as *acetoxime* C_3H_6: N(OH), etc. Also called **O·ximide.**

Oxindole (ǫksi·ndoᵘl). Also **-ol.** 1872. [f. OX- 1 + INDOLE.] *Chem.* A colourless crystalline substance (C_8H_7NO), becoming an oil when heated, consisting of indole combined with one equivalent of oxygen. Hence *dioxindole*, containing two equivalents of oxygen ($C_8H_7NO_2$): see DI-² 2.

Oxlip (ǫ·kslip). [OE. *oxanslyppe*, f. *oxan* gen. sing. of *oxa* OX + *slyppe* slimy or viscous dropping; see COWSLIP.] The name of a flowering herb: applied to a plant intermediate between the Cowslip (*Primula veris*) and Primrose (*P. vulgaris*); now ascertained to be a natural hybrid between these. **b.** By recent botanists appropriated to *Primula elatior* (Jacq.), found in Britain only in Essex and its neighbourhood.

Oxonian (ǫksōᵘ·niăn), *a.* and *sb.* 1540. [f. *Oxonia*, latinization of OE. *Ox(e)naford*, ME. *Ox(e)neford* (see OXFORD) + -AN; see -IAN.] **A.** *adj.* Of or belonging to Oxford 1644. **B.** *sb.* A native or inhabitant of Oxford; usu., a member of the University of Oxford 1540. **b.** A kind of shoe, which covers the instep and is buttoned 1848.

Oxo·nic (ǫksǫ·nik), *a.* 1881. [f. OX- 2 + *carb*)*onic*.] *Chem.* In *O. acid*, $C_4H_5N_3O_4$, a substance formed by the gradual oxidation of uric acid in an alkaline solution, and yielding on decomposition glyoxyl-urea and carbon dioxide. Its salts are **O·xonates.**

Ox-stall (ǫ·ksstǭl). late ME. A stall or stable for oxen.

O·x-tail. 1460. The tail of an ox; esp. as an article of food. Also *attrib.* in *ox-tail soup*, etc.

Oxter (ǫ·kstəɹ). *Sc.* and *n. dial.* 1532. [f. OE. *ōxta, ōhsta*, from same stem as OE. *ōxn* :– **ōhsna* = armpit.] The armpit; also, the under side of the upper arm.

Ox-tongue, oxtongue (ǫ·ks,tʊŋ). ME. **1.** The tongue of an ox. **2.** Pop. name of several plants: = LANGUE DE BŒUF 1. †**a.** *orig.* applied to various plants having rough leaves, more or less tongue-shaped; chiefly species of bugloss, borage, or alkanet –1611. **b.** A composite plant, *Helminthia echioides*, also called *Prickly Ox-tongue* 1760.

Oxy- (ǫksi), repr. Gr. ὀξυ-, comb. form of ὀξύς sharp, keen, acute, pungent, acid. **1.** Words of various kinds, in which *oxy-* stands for 'sharp', 'acute' (in *lit.* or *fig.* sense): as **Oxycephalic** (-sĭfæ·lik) *a.*, *Anthropol.* having a skull of pointed or conical shape; so **Oxyce·phaly.** ‖**Oxyo·pia** [mod.L., f. Gr. ὀπ- see], *Phys.* abnormal acuteness of sight. **2.** Chemical words, in which *oxy-* is taken as the comb. form of OXYGEN (cf. HYDRO- d); denoting either simply the presence of oxygen, as in OXYACID, etc., or the addition of oxygen to the substance denoted by the simple word, and thus in effect = *oxygenated* or *oxidized*. See also OXYCHLORIDE, OXYSULPHATE, etc. A looser use is seen in **oxy-alcohol** (or **oxy-spirit**), **oxy-coal gas, oxy-house-gas,** etc., terms applied to the flame produced by mixing the vapour of a spirit lamp, ordinary house-gas, etc., with oxygen; so *oxy-alcohol blow-pipe, lamp*, etc.; **oxy-paraffin** *a.*, applied to a paraffin lamp with arrangement for the complete oxygenation of the flame. But the most frequent use of *oxy-* is as a prefix to names of organic substances, to denote a derivative or related compound in which an atom of hydrogen is displaced by one of hydroxyl (HO); in which sense *hydroxy-* is now often preferred; see OXYACID 2.

O:xy-ace·tylene, *a.* 1909. Consisting of, or involving the use of, a mixture of oxygen and acetylene.

Oxyacid, oxy-acid (ǫksi,æ·sid). Also **oxi-, ox-acid.** 1836. [f. OXY- 2 + ACID.] *Chem.* **1.** An acid containing oxygen (e.g. carbonic acid, CH_2O_3) as dist. from a *hydracid* (e.g. hydrochloric acid, HCl). **2.** *Organic Chem.* In pl., a name given to several series of acids derived from those of the fatty or the aromatic series, by the substitution of one or more hydroxyl for one or more hydrogen atoms; hence called more exactly *hydroxy-acids*.

Oxy-calcium (ǫksikæ·lsiŏm). 1865. [f. OXY- 2 + CALCIUM.] *Chem.* In *oxy-calcium light* = LIMELIGHT.

O·xychlor-, o·xychloro-. 1818. *Chem.* Containing oxygen and chlorine, as *oxychlorether*, a liquid, $CH_2Cl.CH(OH)(OC_2H_5)$, obtained by the action of water at high temperature on bichlor ether. So **Oxychlo·ride,** a combination of oxygen and chlorine with another element, as *Phosphorus oxychloride* $POCl_3$; also, a compound of a metallic chloride with the oxide of the same metal. Also called **Oxychlo·ruret.**

Oxygen (ǫ·ksidʒĕn). Also †**oxi-,** †**-gene.** 1790. [– Fr. *oxygène* (for *principe oxygène*, earlier *oxygine*), intended for 'acidifying (principle)', *principe acidifiant* (Lavoisier); see OXY- and -GEN 1; oxygen being at first held to be the essential principle in the formation of acids.] One of the non-metallic elements, a colourless invisible gas, without taste or smell. Symbol O: atomic weight 16.

It is the most abundant of all the elements, existing, in the free state (mixed with nitrogen), in atmospheric air, and, in combination, in water and most minerals and organic substances. It combines with nearly all other elements (forming *oxides*), the process of combination being in some cases so energetic as to produce sensible light and heat (*combustion*), in others very gradual, as in the rusting or *oxidation* of metals. It is essential, in the free state, to the life of all animals and plants, and is absorbed into the organism in *respiration*; hence it was formerly called *vital air*. Priestley, who isolated it in 1774, holding it to be common air deprived of PHLOGISTON (q.v.), called it *dephlogisticated air*.

attrib. and *Comb.* **a.** *attrib.* or *adj.* in *o. gas*, a name for oxygen in the free or gaseous state. **b.** The sb. in attrib. use or in comb.; as in *o. acid* (= OXY-ACID 1), *-carrier, treatment*, etc. Hence **Oxyge·nic** *a.* (*rare*) of the nature of, consisting of, o.

Oxygenate (ǫ·ksidʒĕnēˈt, ǫksi·dʒĕnēˈt), *v.* Also †**oxi-.** 1790. [– Fr. *oxygéner*, f. *oxygène*; see -ATE³.] *trans.* To supply, treat, or mix with oxygen; to cause oxygen to combine with (a substance); to oxidate, oxidize; *esp.* to charge (the blood) with oxygen by respiration. So **Oxygena·tion,** the action of oxygenating or condition of being oxygenated; oxidation. **O·xygenator,** an oxidator.

Oxygenize (ǫ·ksidʒĕnəiz, ǫksi·dʒĕnəiz), *v.* 1802. [f. OXYGEN + -IZE; cf. *carbonize*.] *trans.* = OXYGENATE *v.* Chiefly in *pa. pple.* (or *ppl. a.*) Hence **O·xygeni:zable** *a.* that can be oxygenized.

Oxygenous (ǫksi·dʒĕnəs), *a.* 1787. [f. OXYGEN + -OUS.] †**a.** Acidifying; *o. gas*, oxygen; *o. principle*, tr. Lavoisier's *principe oxygine* –1794. **b.** Of the nature of, consisting of, or containing oxygen 1822.

Oxyhæmoglobin, -hemoglobin (ǫ:ksihī-moglōᵘ·bin). 1873. [OXY- 2.] *Chem.* The form in which hæmoglobin exists in arterial and capillary blood where it is loosely combined with oxygen.

Oxyhy·drate. 1876. *Chem.* A hydrated oxide or hydrate of a metal, as *o. of iron*.

Oxyhydrogen (ǫksihəi·drŏdʒĕn), *a.* 1827. [f. OXY- 2 + HYDROGEN.] Consisting of, or involving the use of, a mixture of oxygen and hydrogen.

O. blowpipe, a compound blowpipe in which two streams, of oxygen and hydrogen, meet as they issue; used to produce an extremely hot flame by the burning of the hydrogen in the oxygen. *O. light*, the light obtained by directing such a flame upon lime; lime-light. So *o. flame, jet, lamp*, etc. *O. microscope*, etc., one in which the object is illuminated by an o. light.

Oxymel (ǫ·ksimel). *Obs.* or *arch.* Also †**oxi-,** †**-mell.** late ME. [– L. *oxymel* (also *oxymeli*) – Gr. ὀξύμελι, f. ὀξύς sour + μέλι honey.] A drink or syrup compounded of vinegar and honey, sometimes with other ingredients.

‖**Oxymoron** (ǫksimōᵊ·rǫn). 1657. [– Gr. ὀξύμωρον, subst. use of n. sing. of ὀξύμωρος pointedly foolish, f. ὀξύς (see OXY- 1) + μωρός foolish (see MORON).] A rhetorical figure by which contradictory terms are conjoined so as to give point to the statement or expression. (Now often *loosely* = a contradiction in terms.)

Voltaire..we might call, by an o.., an 'Epicurean pessimist' 1890.

†**Oxymuria·tic,** *a.* 1796. [f. OXY- 2 + MURIATIC.] *Chem.* In *o. acid* (also *o. gas*): a former name of chlorine, as a supposed compound of oxygen and 'muriatic' (hydrochloric) acid –1835. Hence **Oxymu·riate,** a salt of 'o. acid'; a chlorate or chloride, as *oxymuriate of tin* = stannic chloride, *oxymuriate of potash* = potassium chlorate –1830.

Oxyni·trate. 1809. [f. OXY- 2 + NITRATE.] *Chem.* A compound of the oxide and nitrate of a metal.

Oxyntic (ǫksi·ntik), *a.* 1884. [– Gr. ὀξυντέος, verbal adj. from ὀξύνειν sharpen, make acid, f. ὀξύς sharp; see -IC.] *Physiol.* Rendering acid, acidifying; applied to certain glands of the stomach, or to cells in them, supposed to produce the hydrochloric acid of the gastric juice.

Oxyphil(e (ǫ·ksifil), *a.* 1896. [f. OXY- 1 + -PHIL(E.] *Biol.* 'Acid-loving': applied to certain white blood-corpuscles or other cells having an affinity for acids.

Oxyrhynch (ǫ·ksiriŋk). 1839. [f. OXY- 1 + Gr. ῥύγχος snout.] **1.** Any crab of the group *Oxyrhyncha*, characterized by a triangular cephalothorax with projecting rostrum. **2.** A fish; = next.

‖**Oxyrhynchus** (ǫksiri·ŋkŏs). 1661. [– Gr. ὀξύρρυγχος sharp-snouted, epithet of a fish.] A fish (*Mormyrus oxyrhynchus*) found in the Nile, esteemed sacred by the Egyptians.

Oxy-salt (ǫ·ksi,sǫlt). Also †**oxi-.** 1833. [f. OXY- 2 + SALT.] *Chem.* A salt containing oxygen; a salt of an oxyacid.

†**Oxysu·lphate.** 1802. Obs. name for a metallic sulphate containing a larger proportion of oxygen, as *o. of iron* = ferric sulphate –1815. So **Oxysu·lphide,** a compound of an element or positive compound radical with oxygen and sulphur.

Oxytocic (ǫksitǫ·sik), *a.* and *sb.* 1853. [f. Gr. ὀξυτοκία sudden delivery + -IC.] *Med.* **A.** *adj.* Accelerating parturition. **B.** *sb.* A medicine having this property.

Oxytone (ǫ·ksitoᵘn), *a.* and *sb.* Also **oxyton.** 1764. [– Gr. ὀξύτονος having the acute accent, f. ὀξύς sharp + τόνος pitch, tone, accent.] *Gr. Gram.* **A.** *adj.* Having an acute accent on the last syllable. **B.** *sb.* A word so accented.

Oy, oe (oi, ōi). *Sc.* 1470. [– Gael. *ogha, odha* (ō·ă) = OIr. *au* descendant, *úa* grandson.] A grandchild.

Oyer (oi·əɹ). late ME. [– AFr. *oyer* (Britton) = OFr. *oïr* (mod. *ouïr*) :– L. *audire*; see next, -ER[4].] *Law.* **1.** Short for *oyer and terminer*; a criminal trial under the writ so called. **2.** In *Common Law*, the hearing of some document read in court; esp. of an instrument in writing, pleaded by one party, when the other 'craved oyer' of it. (Abolished 1852.) 1602.

Oyer and terminer (oi·ər ənd tə̄·minəɹ). *Law.* **a.** In **Commission of o. and t.,** a commission formerly directed to the King's Judges, Serjeants, etc., empowering them to hear and determine indictments on treasons, felonies, etc.; also called *Writ of o. and t.* Now, the most comprehensive of the commissions granted to judges on circuit, directing them to hold courts for the trial of offences. late ME. **b.** In some States of the American Union: A court of higher criminal jurisdiction 1888.

Oyez, oyes (ōu:ye·s), *int.* (*sb.*). late ME. [– AFr., OFr. *oiez, oyez*, hear ye! imper. pl. of *oïr* hear; orig. pron. *oye·ts*, subseq. *oye·s*, and hence often written *O yes!*] **A.** *imper. vb.*, and *int.* 'Hear, hear ye'; a call by the public crier or by a court officer (usu. thrice uttered) to command silence and attention for the reading of a proclamation, etc.

But when the Crier cried, 'O Yes!' the people cried, 'O No!' BARHAM.

B. as *sb.* A call or exclam. of 'Oyez'. Pl. †*oyesses*, also †*oyes*. 1494.

Crier Hob-goblin, make the Fairy Oyes SHAKS.

Oyster (oi·stəɹ), *sb.* [ME. *oistre* – OFr. *oistre, uistre* (mod. *huître*) – L. *ostrea*, also *ostreum* from Gr. ὄστρεον, rel. to ὀστέον bone, ὄστρακον (cf. OSTRACIZE).] **1.** A well-known edible bivalve mollusc of the family *Ostreidæ*; *esp.* the common European species *Ostrea edulis*, and the N. American species, *O. virginica* of the Atlantic, and *O. lurida*, the Californian oyster, of the Pacific coast. **2.** Applied also to other bivalve molluscs resembling the oyster, as the PEARL-OYSTER, *Meleagrina margaritifera*, of the family *Aviculidæ*; also with qualifications, as **Thorny o.** of the genus *Spondylus*, etc. late ME. **3.** The morsel of dark meat in the front hollow of the side bone of a fowl 1883. **4.** *Vegetable o.*: the salsify 1864.

attrib. and *Comb.*, as **o.-bank,** an oyster-bed; **-bed,** (*a*) a layer of oysters covering a tract of the bottom of the sea, a place where oysters breed or are bred; (*b*) a layer or stratum containing fossil oysters; **†-board,** a board or table used for displaying oysters for sale; applied contempt. to the communion-tables introduced by the early Reformers and the Puritans; **-brood,** the spat of oysters in its second year; **-farm,** a tract of seabottom where oysters are bred artificially; **-field** = *o.-bed*; **-fish,** †(*a*) an oyster; (*b*) the toad-fish (*Batrachus tau*); (*c*) the tautog (*Tautoga onitis*); **-green,** the seaweed *Ulva lactuca*, also *U. latissima*; **-knife,** a knife adapted for opening oysters; **-plant,** (*a*) the sea-lungwort (*Mertensia maritima*); (*b*) the salsify (*Tragopogon porrifolius*); **-plover** = OYSTER-CATCHER; **-shell,** the shell of an o.; **tree,** the mangrove; **†-wench, -wife, -woman,** a girl or woman who sells oysters. Hence **Oy·ster** *v.* to fish for or gather oysters. **Oy·stering** *vbl. sb.* **Oy·stery** *a.* abounding in oysters; like an o.

Oy·ster-ca:tcher. 1731. A maritime wading bird of the family *Hæmatopodidæ* with black-and-white or black plumage, and bill and feet of a brilliant red.

The common European species is *Hæmatopus ostralegus* Linn.; the N. American species is *H. palliatus*.

Oz. 1548. [– It. *ōz* or *o̅z*, XV, abbrev. of *onza, onze*.] An abbrev. used for 'ounce', 'ounces', as in 3 lb. 8 oz.

‖**Ozæna, -ena** (ozī·nă). 1591. [L. – Gr. ὄζαινα a fetid polypus in the nose, f. ὄζειν to smell.] *Path.* A fetid muco-purulent discharge from the nose, due to ulcerative disease of the mucous membrane, frequently with necrosis of the bone 1656.

Ozocerite, ozokerit(e (ozǫ·sĕrəit, ozōu·kĕrit, -əit; ōuzosīə·rəit, -kīə·rəit). 1834. [– G. *ozokerit* (Glocker, 1833), f. Gr. ὄζειν smell + κηρός bees-wax; see -ITE[1] 2 a.] *Min.* A wax-like fossil resin, of brownish-yellow colour and aromatic odour; also called *native paraffin, mineral tallow*, or *mineral wax*. Used to make candles, insulate electrical conductors, etc.

Ozone (ōu·zoun). 1840. [– G. *ozon* (C.F. Schönbein, 1840) – Gr. ὄζον, n. pr. pple. of ὄζειν smell.] *Chem.* An allotropic condition of oxygen, existing in a state of condensation (having three atoms to the molecule, O_3), with a peculiarly pungent and refreshing odour.

It is produced in the electrolysis of water, and by the silent discharge of electricity or the passage of electric sparks through the air (whence it is sometimes perceived after a thunderstorm). Hence **Ozonic** (ozǫ·nik) *a.* of the nature of, or containing, ozone. **Ozonify** (ozōu·nifəi) *v. trans.* to convert into ozone; to ozonize.

Ozonize (ōu·zounəiz), *v.* 1850. [f. prec. + -IZE.] **1.** *trans.* To convert (oxygen) into ozone 1858. **2.** To treat or act upon with ozone 1850. Hence **O:zoniza·tion. O·zonizer,** an apparatus for producing ozone.

Ozonometer (ōuzounǫ·mĭtəɹ). 1862. [f. OZONE; see -METER.] An instrument or device for ascertaining the amount of ozone in the air. So **O:zonome·tric** *a.* pertaining to ozonometry. **Ozono·metry,** the measurement of the ozone in the air.

Ozonoscope (ozōu·nŏskoup). 1872. [f. OZONE; see -SCOPE.] An instrument for showing the presence or amount of ozone in the air. So **Ozonosco·pic** *a.*

P

P (pī), the sixteenth letter of the English alphabet, was the fifteenth in the ancient Roman alphabet, corresponding in position and value to the Greek *Pi*, *Π*, *π*, and identical with the Phœnician and general Semitic *Pe*. The letter represents the labial *tenuis*, or lip unvoiced stop, to which the corresponding sonant or voiced stop is B, and the nasal, M. In English, the simple *p* always represents this sound; but it is sometimes silent, as initially in the combinations *pn-, ps-, pt-* (repr. Gr. πν-, ψ-, πτ-), and medially between *m* and another consonant, as in *Hampstead, Hampton*, etc. See also PH.

I. 1. The letter. *Pl.* P's, p's (pīz). OE. **2.** Used to indicate serial order, as in the signatures of the sheets of a book, the batteries of the Horse Artillery, etc. **3. P and Q.** *To mind one's P's and Q's* (*peas and cues*), to be particular as to one's words or behaviour 1779.

II. Abbrevs. P. = various proper names, as Peter, Paul, etc.; P., p. = past, post; P (*Chem.*) = phosphorus; P (*chess*) = pawn; P (*Mechanics*) = pressure; p- (*Chem.*) = para-; p. = page; *p* (*Mus.*) = *piano*, softly; p. (in a ship's log) = passing showers; *Π* (i.e. Gr. *pi*) (*Math.*) continued product; *π* (*Math.*) = *pi*, the ratio of the circumference to the diameter of a circle, the incommensurable quantity 3.14159265...; Pa. (*U.S.*) = Pennsylvania; P. and O. = Peninsular and Oriental Steam Navigation Co.; P.A. = Post Adjutant; Pb (*Chem.*) = *plumbum*, lead; P.C. = Police Constable, Privy Councillor; p.c. = postcard; P.C.C. = Parochial Church Council; Pd (*Chem.*) = Palladium; pd. = paid; P.M. = Peculiar or Particular Metre or Measure, Police Magistrate; p.m. = *post meridiem*, afternoon; P.O. = post office, postal order, petty officer; P.P. = parish priest; p.p. = *per procurationem*, by proxy (see PER 1); *pp* or *ppp* (*Mus.*) = *pianissimo*, very softly; P.P.C. (written on cards, etc.) = *pour prendre congé*, to take leave; p-p.i = policy sufficient proof of interest; P.R. = proportional representation; P.R.A. = President of the Royal Academy; P.R.B. = Pre-Raphaelite Brotherhood; P.R.S. = President of the Royal Society; P.S. = *post scriptum*, postscript; P.S.A. = Pleasant Sunday Afternoon; Pt (*Chem.*) = Platinum; pt. = part, pint; P.T. = pupil teacher, physical training; P.T.O., p.t.o., = please turn over.

Pa[1] (pā). 1811. Short form of PAPA. Now *vulgar*.

‖**Pa**[2]**, pah** (pā). 1769. [Maori *pà*, f. *pà* block up.] A native fort or fortified camp in New Zealand.

Paas, obs. f. PACE, PASCH.

‖**Pabouch** (pābū·ʃ). 1687. [See BABOUCHE, PAPOOSH.] A heelless oriental slipper.

Pabulary (pæ·biŭlări), *a.* 1835. [f. PABULUM + -ARY[1].] Of or pertaining to fodder or aliment.

†**Pa·bulous,** *a. rare.* 1646. [– late L. *pabulosus*, f. as prec.; see -OUS.] Abounding in or affording food –1755.

‖**Pabulum** (pæ·biŭlŏm). 1678. [L., f. stem *pā-* of *pascere* feed.] Anything taken in by an animal or plant to maintain life and growth; food, nutriment. Also *transf.* and *fig.*

Fire...needs a *P.* to prey upon 1678. Tales of love Form the sweet p. our hearts approve CRABBE.

Paca (pæ·kă). 1657. [– Sp., Pg. *paca* – Tupi *paca* (cf. Guarani *paig*).] *Zool.* A genus (*Cœlogenys*) of large dasyproctid rodents, native to Central and South America; the common species (*C. paca*) is called also *spotted cavy* and *water hare*.

Pacable (pēi·kăb'l), *a.* 1834. [f. L. *pacare* (f. *pax, pac-* peace) quiet, pacify, subdue + -ABLE.] Placable.

Pacation (păkēi·ʃən). 1658. [– L. *pacatio*, f. *pacat-*, pa. ppl. stem of *pacare*; see prec., -ION.] The action of pacifying; pacification.

Pacchionian (pækiōu·niăn), *a.* 1811. [f. name of the Italian anatomist *Pacchioni* (1665–1726) + -AN.] *Anat.* Described by Pacchioni; as *P. corpuscle, gland, line*, etc.

Pace (pēis), *sb.* [ME. *pas, paas* – (O)Fr. *pas* – L. *passus* step, pace, lit. 'stretch (of the leg)', f. *pass-*, pa. ppl. stem of *pandere* stretch, extend. For the sp. *pace* (XIV) cf. MACE[1].] **I.** A step, etc. **1.** A single step in walking, running, or dancing. **2.** The space traversed by one step; hence as a vague measure of distance. late ME. **3.** A definite measure of length or distance; sometimes, the distance from where one foot is set down to where the other is set down (about 2½ feet), as the *military p.*; sometimes, that between successive stationary positions of the same foot (about 5 feet), as the *geometrical p.* ME.

1. Pale cowards, marching on with trembling paces SHAKS. **2.** Ten paces huge He back recoild MILT.

II. The action of stepping, etc. **1.** The action, or (usually) manner, of stepping; gait, step, walk ME. **†b.** Course, way (in walking or running) –1727. **†c.** *transf.* Movement, motion –1611. **†2.** A walking pace, walking. ME. only. **3.** Any one of the various gaits of a horse, mule, etc., esp. when trained 1589. **b.** A particular gait of the horse (or other animal); = AMBLE *sb.*, or now occas. = RACK *sb.* 5 1663.

1. The little creature accommodating her p. to mine DICKENS. **3.** *fig. A.Y.L.* III. ii. 327. Phr. *To put through his paces*, to show the various accomplishments or actions of which a person is capable.

III. Rate of stepping; speed in walking or running ME. **b.** *transf.* and *fig.* Rate of movement in general; speed, velocity. late ME.

The Beggar Sings,..and never mends his p. DRYDEN. **b.** What p. is this that thy tongue keepes? SHAKS. Phr. *P. of the table* (Billiards), *of the wicket* (Cricket), the degree of elasticity of the cushions, or of the ground, as affecting the motion of the ball. *To keep p.*, to advance at an equal rate; to keep up *with*; My legs can keepe no p. with my desires SHAKS. *To go the p.*, to go at great speed; *fig.* to proceed with reckless vigour; to indulge in dissipation. *To set the p.*, to fix or regulate the speed.

IV. Special senses. **1.** A step of a stair or the like; a stage, a platform. See also FOOT-PACE, HALPACE. ME. **†2.** A passage, narrow way; a pass; a strait –1617. **†3.** In a church: A passage or aisle between the seats –1828. **†4.** = PASSUS –1621.

3. *Middle p.*, the nave; *of one p.*, of a nave only. *Comb.*: **p.-maker,** a rider, runner, etc., who makes or sets the pace for another in racing or training.

Pace (pēis), *v.* 1513. [f. prec.] **1.** *intr.* To walk with a slow or regular pace; to step along. **b.** *trans.* with cogn. or advb. object 1598. **2.** *trans.* To walk with measured pace along (a path) or about (a place); hence, To measure by pacing 1571. **3.** *intr.* Of a horse, etc.: To move with the gait called a pace 1614. **4.** *trans.* To train (a horse) to pace; to exercise in pacing 1603. **5.** To set the pace for (a rider, boat's crew, etc.) in racing or training 1886.

1. Pacing forth With solemn steps and slow GRAY. **b.** Sentinels paced the rounds day and night MACAULAY. **2.** I paced it, and found it to bee 70 of my Paces in Length 1693. **4.** *fig.* The third oth' world is yours, which with a Snaffle, You may p. easie, but not such a wife SHAKS.

‖**Pace** (pē^i·si). 1883. [L., abl. sing. of *pax* PEACE, as in *pace tua* by your leave.] By leave of, with all deference to.

Paced (pē^ist), *a.* 1583. [f. PACE *sb.* and *v.* + -ED.] **1.** Having a (specified) pace; as *even-p.* **2.** Traversed or measured by pacing 1869. **3.** *Racing.* Having the pace set by a pace-maker 1899.

Pacer (pē^i·səɹ). 1661. [f. PACE *v.* + -ER[1].] **1.** *gen.* One who paces 1835. **2.** A horse whose gait is a pace 1661. **3.** *Racing.* A pace-maker 1893.

Pacha, -lik, var. ff. **Pasha, -lic.**

‖**Pachisi** (patʃi·si). 1800. [– Hindi *pach(ch)īsī*, lit. 'of *pach(ch)is*', i.e. twenty-five, f. *pach* five.] A four-handed game, played in India, with six cowries for dice; so named from the highest throw, which is twenty-five.

Pachy- (pæ·ki, păki·), bef. a vowel also **pach-,** comb. form of Gr. παχύς 'thick, large, massive': **Pachycarpous** (-kā·ɹpəs) [Gr. καρπός], *a. Bot.* having large thick fruit. **Pachydactyl, -yle** (-dæ·ktil) [Gr. δάκτυλος], *a. Zool.* having thick fleshy digits; *sb.* an animal with thick toes. **Pachyda·ctylous,** *a.* = prec. *a.* **Pachyglo·ssal** [Gr. γλῶσσα], *a. Zool.* of or pertaining to the *Pachyglossæ*, lizards with short or thick fleshy tongues, or the *Pachyglossi*, a tribe of parrots; so **Pachyglo·ssate. Pachymeningitis** (-menindʒəi·tis) [MENINGITIS], *Path.* inflammation of the dura mater of the central nervous system, cerebral or spinal. **Pachymeter** (păki·mĭtəɹ) [-METER], an instrument for measuring the thickness of glass, metal plates, paper, etc. **Pachyote** (pæ·ki,ō^ut) [Gr. οὖς, ὠτ-], *a.* having thick leathery ears; *sb.* a thick-eared bat, of the genus *Pachyotus*; so **Pachyo·tous** *a.*

Pachyderm (pæ·kidəɹm). 1838. [– Fr. *pachyderme* (Cuvier, 1797) – Gr. παχύδερμος thick-skinned, f. παχύς thick + δέρμα skin.] *Zool.* A thick-skinned quadruped; spec. one of the *Pachydermata* of Cuvier. Also *fig.* Hence **Pachyde·rmal, -de·rmic** *adjs.*

‖**Pachydermata** (pækidō·ɹmătă), *sb. pl.* 1823. [mod.L., f. Gr. παχύς thick + δέρμα δερματ- skin; see -A 4.] *Zool.* An order of Mammalia in Cuvier's classification (now discarded), consisting of the hoofed or ungulate quadrupeds which do not chew the cud, as the elephant, rhinoceros, hippopotamus, horse.

Pachydermatous (pækidō·ɹmătəs), *a.* 1823. [f. prec. + -OUS.] **1.** Of or belonging to the *Pachydermata*. **2.** *fig.* Thick-skinned; not sensitive to rebuff, ridicule, or abuse 1854.

Pacifiable (pæ·sifəi,ăb'l), *a.* 1618. [f. PACIFY + -ABLE.] Capable of being pacified or appeased.

Pacific (păsi·fik), *a.* and *sb.* 1548. [– (O)Fr. *pacifique* or L. *pacificus*, f. *pax, pac-* PEACE; see -FIC.] **A.** *adj.* **1.** Making, or tending to the making of, peace; conciliatory, appeasing. **2.** Of peaceful disposition, not belligerent 1641. **3.** Characterized by peace; calm, tranquil, quiet 1633. **4.** †*P. letters*, letters to the church in another city or country recommending the bearer as one in peace and communion with the Church; later, esp. letters recommending the bearer to the alms of the faithful –1725.

1. An Olive leafe he brings, p. signe MILT. **2.** The old grave p. Quakers 1774. **3.** *P. Ocean, Sea*, the 'Great Ocean' stretching between America and Asia; so called by Magellan, because found to be relatively free from violent storms.

B. *sb.* †**1. a.** *pl.* Peace-offerings [tr. L. *pacifica*]. **b.** An overture of peace, an Eirenicon. –1687. **2.** The Pacific Ocean. Also *attrib.* 1821.

2. Like stout Cortez, when with eagle eyes He stared at the P. KEATS. So **Paci·fical** *a.* 1485, **-ly** *adv.*

Pacificate (păsi·fike^it), *v.* 15... [– *pacificat-*, pa. ppl. stem of L. *pacificare*; see PACIFY, -ATE[3].] †**1.** *intr.* To make peace (*with*). *rare.* –1646. **2.** *trans.* To give peace to, to pacify 1827.

Pacification (pæ:sifikē^i·ʃən). 1472. [– Fr. *pacification* – L. *pacificatio*, f. as prec.; see -ION.] The action or fact of pacifying; the condition of being pacified; appeasement, conciliation. **b.** A treaty of peace 1560.

His p. of friends [was] better than his execution of enemies 1615. *Edict of P.*, esp. in *French hist.*, one of the royal edicts in the 16th c. granting concessions to the Protestants; e.g. the Edict of Nantes.

Pacificator (păsi·fike^itəɹ). 1539. [– L. *pacificator*, f. as prec.; see -OR 2. Cf. Fr. *pacificateur*.] One who pacifies; a peace-maker. So **Paci·ficatory** *a.* tending to make peace.

Pacificism (păsi·fisiz'm), **Paci·ficist** (-ist). 1907. [f. PACIFIC *a.* + -ISM, -IST, usually in shortened form PACIFISM, -IST; see next.] Variants of next.

Pacifism (pæ·sifiz'm). 1901. [For *pacificism* (see prec.), after Fr. *pacifisme*, f. *pacifier*; see next, -ISM.] The doctrine or belief that it is desirable and possible to settle international disputes by peaceful means. So **Pa·cifist** (also *attrib.*).

Pacify (pæ·sifəi), *v.* 1460. [– (O)Fr. *pacifier* or L. *pacificare*, f. *pax, pac-* PEACE; see -FY.] **1.** *trans.* To calm or appease (a person, passion, etc.): **2.** To bring or reduce to a state of peace; to calm, quiet 1494. **3.** *intr.* To become peaceful, calm down 1509.

1. Pray say something to p. her 1717. How..I can p. resentment JOHNSON. **2.** It would take 100,000 men to p. the islands 1899. Hence **Pa·cifier.**

Pacinian (păsi·niăn), *a.* 1876. [f. name of *Pacini*, an Italian anatomist (1812–1883) + -AN.] Of or described by Pacini.

P. body, corpuscle, one of numerous oval seed-like bodies attached to nerve-endings, esp. of the cutaneous nerves of the hand and foot.

Pack (pæk), *sb.*[1] [ME. *packe* (XIII) – (M)Flem., (M)Du., (M)LG. *pak*, of unkn. origin.] **1.** A bundle of things enclosed in a wrapping or tied together compactly; *spec.* a bundle of goods carried by a pedlar; a soldier's valise containing his kit and carried on the back. **2.** As a measure of various commodities 1488. **3. a.** A company or set of persons; often merely contemptuous; a 'gang', 'lot' ME. **b.** A large collection, or set (of things, esp. abstract); a 'heap', 'lot'. (Usu. depreciative.) 1591. †**4.** Applied to a person of worthless character; almost always with *naughty* –1738. **5.** A number of animals kept or naturally congregating together; *spec.* of hounds for hunting, or of wild beasts (esp. wolves), and of birds (e.g. grouse) 1648. **b.** *Rugby Football.* The forwards of a side, esp. in relation to the scrum 1887. **6.** A complete set of playing cards 1597. **7.** A large area of floating ice in pieces of considerable size 'packed' together 1791. **8.** *Hydropathy.* The swathing of the body in a wet sheet, blanket, etc.; the state of being so packed; the sheet, etc., used for this. Also *dry-pack*. 1849. **9.** The quantity (of fish, fruit, etc.) packed in a season or year 1889.

1. A pedlar's p., that bows the bearer down COWPER. **2.** A p. of flour or Indian-corn meal, flax, etc. weighs 280 lbs.; of wool 240 lbs. net 1858. **3. a.** A p. of drunken servants GOLDSM. **b.** A p. of lies 1763, of nonsense 1880. **5.** He cast off his friends, as a huntsman his p. GOLDSM.

attrib. and *Comb.*, as **p.-drill,** a military punishment, in which the offender is forced to parade or march up and down in full marching order; **-house,** a warehouse; **-ice,** ice forming a p. (sense 7); **-moth,** a species of clothes-moth (*Anacampsis sarcitella*); **-sheet,** (*a*) a sheet for packing goods in; (*b*) *Med.* a wet sheet for packing a patient in; **-train,** a train of pack-beasts with their packs; **-wool,** wool done up in packs.

†**Pack,** *sb.*[2] 1571. [Goes with PACK *v.*[2]] A clandestine pact or compact; a plot, conspiracy, intrigue –1649.

Pack (pæk), *v.*[1] Pa. t. and pple. **packed** (pækt). ME. [– (M)Du., (M)LG. *pakken*; cf. AFr. *paker, enpaker*, AL. *paccare, impaccare* (XIII).] **I. 1.** *trans.* To make into a pack or package; to put together as a bundle, or in a box, bag, etc., esp. for transport or for storing. Also with *up*. **b.** In *Commerce*: To prepare and put up (meat, fish, eggs, fruit, etc.) in tins, glasses, etc., so as to preserve them 1494. **c.** *absol.* To pack clothes, etc., for a journey. Often with *up*. 1684. **2.** To put together closely or compactly; to crowd together 1563. **3.** To form into a 'pack'. **a.** To form (hounds) into a pack; **b.** To place (cards) together into a pack; **c.** To drive (ice) into a pack; usu. *pass.* 1649. **4.** *intr.* for *refl.* **a.** To collect into a body; esp. to form a pack; said of wolves, grouse, etc., also of ice in the polar seas 1828. **b.** In passive sense: To admit of being packed 1846. **5.** *trans.* To cover with something pressed tightly around 1796. **b.** *Med.* To envelop (the body or a part of it) in a wet sheet or cloth 1849. **6.** To fill (a bag, box, etc.) *with* clothes or goods compactly arranged, (a crevice or interstice) *with* something fitting tightly; to cram, stuff. Also with *up*. 1581. **b.** *transf.* and *fig.* To cram, crowd (any space) *with*. Usu. *pass.*; also predicated of that which occupies the space. 1857. **7.** To load (a beast) with a pack 1596. **8.** To carry or convey in a pack or packs 1850.

1. So p. up a few things, and we'll off FOOTE. The contents of the library were all packed and carried away GEO. ELIOT. **2.** Audiences so packed as to be dangerous 1887. Phr. *To p. on all sail*, to put on all possible sail; to crowd sail. Also *absol.* in same sense. **4. b.** It..packs up easily 1867. **6. b.** [A passage] crowded and packed with meaning 1857. **8.** The ore..having been packed a distance of ten miles on mules 1877.

II. 1. *refl.* and *intr.* To take oneself off with one's belongings, be off. †**a.** *refl.* –1865. **b.** *intr.* 1440. **2.** *trans.* To send away, dismiss summarily, get rid of. Now usu. with *off*. 1589.

1. Voltaire..lost no time in packing himself CARLYLE. **b.** Sure as fate, we'll send you packing BROWNING. **2.** He packed her off to bed at once 1894.

Pack, *v.*[2] 1529. [prob. f. †*pact* vb. (XVI–XVII), f. PACT *sb.*, by apprehending the final *-t* as an inflexion; cf. †*compack*, occas. var. of COMPACT *sb.*[1]] **I.** †**1.** *intr.* To agree in a secret or underhand design; to plot, conspire, scheme, intrigue –1602. †**2.** To bring or let (a person) into a plot; in *pass.* to be an accomplice or confederate in a plot –1600. †**3.** *trans.* To plot (something) –1694.

1. *Tit. A.* IV. ii. 155. **2.** *Com. Err.* V. i. 219.

II. 1. To select or make up (a jury, etc.) in such a way as to secure a partial decision 1587. **2.** To arrange or shuffle (playing-cards), so as to secure a fraudulent advantage. *Obs.* or *arch.* 1599.

2. I learned to p. cards and to cog a dye 1753. Phr. *To p. cards with*, to make a cheating arrangement with; *Ant. & Cl.* IV. xiv. 19. Hence **Pa·cking** *vbl. sb.*[2]

Package (pæ·kėdʒ). 1540. [f. PACK *v.*[1] + -AGE. Cf. AL. *paccagium* XIII.] **1.** The packing of goods, etc.; the mode in which goods are packed. †**2.** A cargo –1802. **3.** A bundle of things packed up; esp. a packet, parcel. (The chief current sense.) 1722. **4.** A case, box, etc., in which goods are packed 1801. Hence **Pa·ckage** *v.* **Pa·ckaging** *vbl. sb.*

4. *Original p.*, the package or case in which goods are sent out from the place of manufacture.

Packer[1] (pæ·kəɹ). ME. [f. PACK *v.*[1] + -ER[1].] One who packs; *esp.* one who packs meat, fish, fruit, etc., for future or distant markets.

Packer[2]. 1586. [f. PACK *v.*[2] + -ER[1].] One who 'packs' cards, juries, etc.; a plotter.

Packet (pæ·kėt), *sb.* 1530. [f. PACK *sb.*[1] + -ET, perh. of AFr. formation; cf. AL. *paccettum* (1304).] **1.** A small pack, package, or parcel; in early use, esp. the State parcel or 'mail' of dispatches to and from foreign countries. **b.** *fig.* A small collection (of things or persons) 1589. **2.** Short for PACKET-BOAT 1709.

1. b. *To sell* (one) *a p.* (colloq.), to take him in, 'sell' him.

attrib. and *Comb.*, as *p.-ship, -vessel* = PACKET-BOAT; **-note,** a size of note-paper, 9 by 11 inches the sheet.

Pa·cket. *v.* 1596. [f. PACKET *sb.* Cf. Fr. *paqueter* (Cotgr.).] **1.** *trans.* To make up into, or wrap up in, a packet. †**2.** *trans.* To send by packet-boat –1747. †**b.** *intr.* To ply with a packet-boat –1813.

Pa·cket-boat. 1641. [f. PACKET *sb.* + BOAT.] A boat or vessel plying at regular intervals between two ports for the conveyance of mails, also of goods and passengers; a mail-boat. (Often shortened to *packet*.)

Pa·ck-horse. 1475. [f. PACK *sb.*[1] + HORSE *sb.*] A horse used for carrying packs or bundles of goods. **b.** *fig.* A drudge. Also *attrib.*

Packing (pæ·kiŋ), *vbl. sb.*[1] ME. [f. PACK *v.*[1] + -ING[1].] **1.** The action of PACK *v.*[1] **2.** *concr.* Any material used to fill up a space or interstice closely or tightly; filling, stuffing 1824.

attrib. and *Comb.*, as **p.-box,** a stuffing-box around the piston-rod of a steam-engine; **-case; -needle** = PACK-NEEDLE; **-sheet** (*a*) a sheet for packing goods in; (*b*) *Med.* a wet sheet in which a patient is packed in hydropathic treatment.

Packman (pæ·kmæ̆n). 1582. [f. PACK *sb.*[1] + MAN *sb.*] A man who travels about carrying goods in a pack for sale; a pedlar.

Pa·ck-nee:dle. ME. [f. PACK *sb.*[1] + NEEDLE.] A large strong needle used for sewing up packages in stout cloth.

Pa·ck-sa:ddle. ME. [f. PACK *sb.*[1] + SADDLE *sb.*] A saddle adapted for supporting a pack or packs to be carried by a pack-beast.

P. roof, a SADDLEBACK roof.

Packstaff (pæ·kstɑf). 1542. [f. as prec. + STAFF.] A staff on which a pedlar supports his pack when standing to rest himself. In phr. †*as plain as a p.* (now *pikestaff*).

Packthread (pæ·kþred). ME. [f. as prec. + THREAD *sb.*] Stout thread or twine for sewing or tying up packs or bundles.

Packwax: see PAXWAX.

‖**Paco** (pā·*k*o). Also **pacos.** 1604. [– Sp. *paco* – Quechua *pako* (see ALPACA).] **1.** = ALPACA. **2.** *Min.* An earthy brown oxide of iron, containing minute particles of silver. (From its colour.) 1839.

Pacquet, obs. f. PACKET.

Pact (pækt). ME. [– (O)Fr. *pacte*, †*pact* – L. *pactum*, *-us*, subst. uses of pa. pple. of *pacisci* make a covenant, f. reduced grade of **pāk-*, repr. by *pāx* PEACE.] An agreement between persons or parties, a compact.

The engagement and p. of society, which generally goes by the name of the constitution BURKE. *Nude, bare,* or *naked p.*, an agreement without consideration, which cannot therefore be legally enforced.

Paction (pæ·kʃən). Now chiefly *Sc.* 1471. [– OFr. *paction* – L. *pactio*, f. *pact-*, pa. ppl. stem of *pacisci*; see prec., -ION.] The action of making a bargain or pact; a bargain, agreement, compact, contract. Hence **Pa·ctional** *a.* of, pertaining to, or of the nature of a pact.

Pactolian (pæktōᵘ·liăn), *a.* 1606. [f. L. *Pactolus*, Gr. Πακτωλός + -IAN.] Of, belonging or relating to, the river Pactolus in Lydia, famed for its golden sands; golden.

Pacu (pakū·, pa·kū). 1825. [– Tupi *pacú*.] *Zool.* A freshwater fish, *Myletes pacu*, of Brazil and Guiana.

Pad (pæd), *sb.*[1] *Obs.* exc. *dial.* ME. [Late OE. or early ME. *pad*, prob. – ON. *padda* = OFris., MDu. *padde* (Du. *pad(de)*), MLG. *padde*, *pedde* (*peddenstōl* toadstool). Cf. PADDOCK *sb.*[1]] **1.** †A toad; *mod. dial.* = PADDOCK *sb.*[1] **2.** A star-fish 1613.

Pad (pæd), *sb.*[2] 1567. [– LG., Du. *pad* PATH. A word of vagabonds' cant, like others of the class introduced XVI.] **1.** A path, track; the road, the way. *slang* or *dial.* **2.** Robbery on the highway. *slang.* 1664. **†3.** A highway robber. Cf. FOOTPAD. –1834. **4.** An easy-paced horse; also *p.-nag* 1617.

4. An abbot on an ambling p. TENNYSON.

Pad (pæd), *sb.*[3] 1554. [prob. of LDu. origin (cf. Flem. †*pad*, *patte*, LG. *pad* sole of the foot).] **I. †1.** A bundle of straw, etc. to lie on –1719. **2.** A soft stuffed saddle without a tree; *esp.* that placed on an elephant 1570. **b.** That part of double harness to which the girths are attached 1811. **3.** Something soft, as a cushion, serving esp. to diminish jarring, to fill up hollows, etc. 1700. **b.** A cushion or stuffing placed under a horse's foot to keep the sole moist, or under the harness to prevent galling 1843. **c.** In *Cricket*, etc.: A guard for the leg or shins 1851. **4.** A number of sheets of blotting-, writing-, or drawing-paper fastened together at the edge to make a block; called also *blotting-*, *drawing-*, or *writing-pad* 1865.

II. 1. Any cushion-like part of the animal body 1878. **2.** The fleshy elastic cushion forming the sole of the foot, or part of it, in feline or canine beasts, the camel, etc. Also, analogous parts in a bird's foot, in insects, etc. 1836. **3.** The foot or paw of a fox, hare, otter, wolf, etc.; also the footprint of such 1790.

3. A silver-mounted otter-pad 1891.

III. 1. *Mech.* The socket of a brace; a tool-handle into which tools of various gauges, etc., can be fitted, as in a pad-saw 1688. **2.** *Watch-* and *Clock-making.* A pallet 1696. **3.** *Shipbuilding.* A piece of timber placed on a beam, to fill up the round of the deck 1867. **4.** (Also *lily-pad.*) A broad floating leaf (of the water-lily). *U.S.* 1858.

attrib. and *Comb.*, as **p.-elephant,** an elephant having on its back a p. only (not a howdah), on which to carry burdens, baggage, game, etc.; **-saddle,** a treeless padded saddle; **-saw:** see sense III. I.

Pad, *sb.*[4] 1579. [var. of PED.] An open pannier, usually of osiers; a measure of fish, fruit, etc., a 'basket'. 1858.

Pad, *sb.*[5] 1594. [Mainly imit., but cf. PAD *v.*[1]] The dull firm non-resonant sound of steps, or of a staff, upon the ground; also, the repeated step or footfall producing this sound.

Pad (pæd), *v.*[1] 1553. [f. PAD *sb.*[2], or – LG. *padden* tread, tramp.] **1.** *trans.* To tramp along (a road, etc.) on foot. **b.** *intr.* To travel on foot; to trudge along. Also *to p. it* 1610. **2.** *intr.* **†a.** Of a horse: To pace 1724. **b.** Of other quadrupeds: To walk or run with steady dull-sounding steps 1871. **3.** *trans.* To tread or beat down by frequent walking (*dial.*) 1764. **†4.** *intr.* To rob on the highway –1736.

1. Phr. *To p. the hoof*, to go on foot, tramp (*slang*). Hence **Pa·dded** *ppl. a.*[1], trodden, beaten hard by treading. **Pa·dding** *ppl. a.*, that pads or paces on.

Pad, *v.*[2] 1821. [f. PAD *sb.*[3]] **1.** *trans.* To stuff, fill out (anything) with a pad or padding; to stuff (something) in or about, so as to serve as a pad. Also *absol.* **2.** *trans.* To fill *out* or expand (a sentence, story, etc.) with unnecessary or useless words or matter 1831. **3.** To impregnate (the cloth) with a mordant in calico-printing 1839. **4.** *East Indies.* To place or pack (big game, etc.) on the pad of an elephant 1878. **5.** To track by the pad or footmarks 1861.

Pa·dded, *ppl. a.*[2] 1799. [f. PAD *sb.*[3], *v.*[2] + -ED.] Furnished or filled out with pads or padding.

P. cell or *room*, a room in a lunatic asylum or prison, having the walls padded, to prevent the person confined from injuring himself against them.

Padder (pæ·dəɹ). 1610. [f. PAD *sb.*[2] or *v.*[1] + -ER[1].] A footpad, highwayman.

Pa·dding, *vbl. sb.* 1828. [f. PAD *v.*[2] + -ING[1].] **1.** The action of PAD *v.*[2] Also *attrib.* 1839. **2.** *concr.* **a.** That of which a pad is made; e.g. cotton, felt, hair, used in stuffing or padding anything 1828. **b.** Extraneous or unnecessary matter introduced into a book, speech, etc., to fill up space and make up size; in magazines, the articles of secondary interest 1869.

Paddle (pæ·d'l), *sb.*[1] 1407. [Of unkn. origin; cf. PADLE, PATTLE.] **1.** A small spade-like implement with a long handle, for clearing a ploughshare, etc. **2.** A short oar used without a rowlock, having a broad blade which is dipped more or less vertically into the water 1624. **3.** One of the boards or floats fitted on the circumference of the 'paddle-wheel' of a steamer; a paddle-board; also, **b.** A float of an undershot mill-wheel. **c.** Short for PADDLE-WHEEL. **d.** Short for *paddle-boat* or *-steamer*. **4.** *Zool.* A limb serving the purpose of a fin or flipper; as the foot of a duck; the wing of a penguin, etc. 1835. **5.** A sliding panel or sluice in a weir or lock-gate to regulate the quantity of water allowed to flow through 1795. **6.** A paddle-shaped instrument or tool, used for stirring or mixing 1662.

attrib. and *Comb.*, as *p.-blade*, etc.; 'having, or propelled by, paddles', as *p.-boat*, *-steamer*, etc.; also, **p.-beam** (*Shipbuilding*), one of two large beams lying athwart a ship, between which the paddle-wheels revolve; **-board** = sense 3; **-box,** the casing which encloses the upper part of a steamer's paddle-wheel; **-fish,** a ganoid fish, *Polyodon* or *Spatularia spatula*, having a long flat paddle-shaped snout, found in the Mississippi; **-shaft,** the revolving shaft which carries the paddle-wheels of a steamer; **-staff,** (*a*) = sense 1; (*b*) *Brewing*, a wooden spade-shaped implement used in mashing; **-wood,** the light elastic wood of a S. Amer. tree, *Aspidosperma excelsum*, from which the Indians make canoe-paddles.

Pa·ddle, *sb.*[2] *Sc.* 1591. [Of unkn. origin.] The lump-fish, *Cyclopterus lumpus* = COCK-PADDLE.

Paddle (pæ·d'l), *v.*[1] 1530. [prob. of LDu. origin; cf. LG. *paddeln* tramp about, frequent. of *padden* PAD *v.*[1]; see -LE.]

I. 1. *intr.* To walk or move the feet about in mud or shallow water; to wade about; to dabble in shallow water. **2.** *intr.* To toy with the fingers (*in, on, with,* or *about* something) 1602. **†b.** *trans.* To finger idly, playfully, or fondly –1622. **†3. a.** *trans.* To trifle away, squander. **b.** *intr.* To trifle. –1840.

1. Ducks p. in the pond before the door COWPER. *fig.* Boys and girls who paddled in rhyme SWINBURNE. **2.** *Oth.* II. i. 259. **b.** *Wint. T.* I. ii. 115.

II. *intr.* To walk with steps like those of a child; to toddle 1792. **b.** *trans.* To trample down by treading over (*dial.*) 1805. Hence **Pa·ddler** 1611.

Paddle, *v.*[2] 1677. [f. PADDLE *sb.*[1]] **1.** *intr.* To move on the water by means of paddles, as in a canoe. Also said of the canoe. **b.** *transf.* To row with oars lightly 1697. **c.** Of a paddle-steamer, etc.: To move by means of paddle-wheels 1844. **d.** Of birds, etc.: To move in the water with paddle-like limbs. **2.** *trans.* To propel by means of a paddle or paddles; also, to transport (a person) in a canoe 1784. **3.** *trans.* To beat with a paddle or the like; to 'spank'. *U.S.* 1856.

1. b. Paddled to Barnes Railway Bridge, and rowed hard. . back to Hammersmith 1866. **2.** Phr. *To p. one's own canoe*, to make one's way by one's own exertions. Hence **Pa·ddle** *sb.*[3], the act of paddling or rowing lightly.

Pa·ddle-whee:l. 1685. [See PADDLE *sb.*[1] 3.] **1.** A wheel used for propelling a boat or ship, having floats or paddle-boards fitted more or less radially round the circumference, so as to press backward like a succession of paddles against the water. **2.** In leather manufacture, a wheel fitted with paddles (PADDLE *sb.*[1] 6) used to keep skins in constant motion in water.

Paddock (pæ·dək), *sb.*[1] ME. [f. PAD *sb.*[1] + -OCK.] **1.** A frog. Now *Sc.* and *n. dial.* **b.** A toad. *Obs.* exc. *arch.* ME.

attrib. and *Comb.*, (chiefly *dial.*), as **p.-pipe,** a species of *Equisetum* (Horse-tail), esp. *E. limosum*; also Mare's Tail, *Hippuris vulgaris*; **-stone** = TOADSTONE; **-stool** = TOADSTOOL.

Paddock (pæ·dək), *sb.*[2] 1622. [var. of PARROCK; cf. *poddish* for *porridge*.] **1.** A small field or enclosure; usu. a plot of pasture-land adjoining a stable. **2.** *spec.* **a.** A course in a park, for hounds to run matches 1678. **b.** *Horse-racing.* A turf enclosure near the race-course, where the horses are assembled before the race 1862. **3.** *Mining.* A store-place for ore, etc. (*Colonial*) 1869. Hence **Pa·ddock** *v.* to shut up or enclose in or as in a p.; *Mining*, to store (ore, etc.) in a p.

Paddy[1] (pæ·di). 1623. [– Malay *pādī*, corresp. to Javanese *pārī*, Canarese *bhatta*.] **1.** Rice in the straw, or (in commerce) in the husk. **2.** = PADDY-BIRD; *ellipt.* its feathers 1777. **3.** *attrib.* 1698.

Paddy[2] (pæ·di). 1780. [Ir. pet-form of *Padraig* = *Patrick*; see -Y[6].] **1.** Nickname for an Irishman. **2.** A bricklayer's labourer 1856. **3.** A passion, temper; also PADDYWHACK, *colloq.* 1894. Hence **Pa·ddyism,** Irishism.

Pa·ddy-bird. 1727. [PADDY[1].] **1.** The Java Sparrow, *Padda* (or *Munia*) *oryzivora*. **2.** Anglo-Ind. name for species of white egret, which frequent the paddy-fields 1858. **3.** A species of Sheathbill, *Chionis minor* 1894.

Paddymelon (pæ·dime:lən). 1827. [alt. of native name, the first element of which may be identical with that of Sydney dialect *patagorang* kangaroo.] A small brush kangaroo. Also *attrib.*

Pa·ddywhack. *colloq.* 1881. [f. PADDY[2].] **1.** An Irishman. **2.** A rage, passion 1899.

Padesoy, obs. f. PADUASOY.

‖**Padishah, padshah** (pā·diʃā, pā·dʃā). 1612. [– Pers. *pād(i)šāh*, Pahlavi *pātakšā(h*, f. *pati* lord + *šāh* SHAH.] A Persian title, taken as = 'Great King' or 'Emperor'; applied to the Shah of Persia, the Sultan of Turkey, and by natives to the British sovereign as Emperor of India.

Padle, paidle (pe·d'l). *Sc.* 1568. [app. Sc. form of PADDLE *sb.*[1]; cf. Sc. pronunc. of *daddle*, *saddle* (de·d'l, se·d'l).] A field or garden hoe.

Padlock (pæ·dlǫk), *sb.* 1478. [f. *pad*, of unkn. meaning + LOCK *sb.*[2]] A detachable lock. designed to hang on the object fastened by a pivoted or sliding bow or shackle, which can be opened to pass through a staple or ring, and then locked.

fig. Put golden padlocks on Truth's lips LOWELL. Hence **Pa·dlock** *v.* to fasten with or secure by means of a p.

‖**Padouk** (padu·k). 1858. [Burmese native name.] A Burmese leguminous tree, *Pterocarpus macrocarpus*, yielding a kind of rosewood; the wood itself.

Padre (pā·dre). 1584. [– It., Sp., Pg. *padre* :– L. *pater, patre-* FATHER.] 'Father'; in Italy, Spain, Portugal, and Spanish America, a title of the regular clergy; in India (since c1800), a minister or priest of any Christian Church; hence, applied by English soldiers and sailors to a chaplain.

‖**Padrone** (padrō·ne). 1660. [It.] = Patron, master; applied to **a.** the master of a trading-vessel in the Mediterranean; **b.** an Italian employer of street musicians, begging children, etc.; **c.** the proprietor of an inn in Italy.

Paduasoy (pæ·diu,ăsoi). 1663. [Earliest form *poudesoy* – Fr. *pou-de-soie*, earlier *pout de soie* (XIV), of unkn. origin; altered to the present form by assoc. with earlier †*Padua say* (XVII), kind of serge (see SAY *sb.*[1]) from Padua in Italy.] A strong corded or grosgrain silk fabric, of which POULT-DE-SOIE is the mod. representative. Also *attrib.*, and *ellipt.* a garment of this.

Pæan (pī·ăn). 1592. [– L. *pæan* – Gr. παιάν hymn to Apollo invoked by the name Παιάν, Doric var. of Ionic Παιήων, Attic Παιών, orig. the Homeric name of the physician of the Gods.] **1.** A hymn or chant of thanksgiving for deliverance orig. addressed to Apollo or Artemis; esp. a song of triumph after victory addressed to Apollo; hence, any solemn song or chant. **2.** *transf.* A song of praise or thanksgiving; a song of triumph 1599.

2. I sung the joyful P. clear.. Waiting to strive a happy strife TENNYSON.

Pæderasty, ped- (pī·d-, pe·dĕræsti). 1609. [– mod.L. *pæderastia* – Gr., f. παιδεραστία, f. παιδεραστής, f. παῖς, παιδ- boy + ἐραστής lover.] Sodomy. Hence **Pæ·derast,** a sodomite. **Pædera·stic** *a.* pertaining to or practising sodomy.

Pædeutics (pĭdiū·tiks); rarely sing. **-ic.** Also **paid-.** 1864. [f. Gr. παιδευτικός of or for teaching, ἡ παιδευτική (sc. τέχνη art) education; see -ICS.] The science or art of education.

Pædo-, pedo- (pī·do), occas. **paido-** (pai·do), bef. a vowel **pæd-, ped-,** comb. form of Gr. παῖς, παιδ- boy, child; as in **Pædogenesis** (-dʒe·nĕsis), *Zool.* production of offspring by immature or larval animals; so **Pæ:dogene·tic** *a.* **Pædo·logy,** child study.

Pædobaptism (pīdobæ·ptiz'm). Also **pedo-.** 1640. [f. PÆDO- + BAPTISM.] The baptism of children; infant baptism. So **Pædoba·ptist,** one who practises or advocates infant baptism.

Pæon (pī·ŏn). 1603. [– L. *pæon* – Gr. παιών; see PÆAN.] *Prosody.* A metrical foot of four syllables, one long and three short, named, according to the position of the long syllable, a first, second, third or fourth pæon. Hence **Pæo·nic** *a.* of or pertaining to a p. or pæons; composed of pæons; *sb.* a pæonic verse or foot.

Pæonin (pī·ŏnin). 1866. [f. L. *pæonia* PEONY (in reference to colour) + -IN[1].] *Chem.* = CORALLIN.

Pæony, var. of PEONY.

Pagan (pēi·găn), *sb.* and *a.* late ME. [– L. *paganus*, orig. 'civilian', opp. to *miles* 'soldier'; in Christian L. 'heathen' as opp. to Christian or Jewish; the Christians called themselves *milites* 'enrolled soldiers' of Christ; f. *pagus* (rural) district, the country; see -AN.] **A.** *sb.* **1.** One of a nation or community which does not worship the true God; a heathen. (†In earlier use practically = non-Christian.) **2.** *transf.* and *fig.* A person of heathenish character or habits, or one who holds a position analogous to that of a heathen 1841. †**b.** *spec.* A paramour, prostitute –1632.

1. Adue,..most beautifull P., most sweete Iew SHAKS. **2. b.** 2 *Hen. IV*, II. ii. 168.

B. *adj.* **1.** Not belonging to a nation or community that acknowledges the true God; heathen 1586. **2.** *fig.* Heathenish 1550.

1. The ideal, cheerful, sensuous, p. life M. ARNOLD.

Hence **Pa·gandom,** the pagan world; heathendom. †**Paga·nic,** †**-al** *adjs.* pagan. **Paga·nity,** paganism. **Pa·ganly** *adv.* †**Pa·gany,** pagandom.

Paganish (pēi·gănĭʃ), *a.* 1583. [f. prec. + -ISH[1].] †**1.** Pagan –1759. **2.** Resembling or befitting a pagan; of pagan character or quality; heathenish 1613. Hence **Pa·ganishly** *adv.*

Paganism (pēi·găniz'm). late ME. [– late (eccl.) L. *paganismus* (Augustine); see PAGAN, -ISM. Cf. Fr. *paganisme* XVII.] **1.** Pagan belief and practices; the condition of being a pagan; heathenism. **2.** Pagan character or quality; the moral condition of pagans 1874.

1. The divisions of Christianity suspended the ruin of P. GIBBON.

Paganize (pēi·gănəiz), *v.* 1615. [– Fr. *paganiser* (trans. and intr.) or late and med.L. *paganizare* (intr.); see PAGAN, -IZE.] **1.** *trans.* To make pagan. **2.** *intr.* To become pagan; to act as a pagan; to assume a pagan character 1640. Hence **Pa:ganiza·tion.**

Page (pēidʒ), *sb.*[1] ME. [– (O)Fr. *page*, perh. – It. *paggio* – Gr. παιδίον, dim. of παῖς, παιδ- boy.]

I. †**1.** A boy, youth, lad –1582. †**2.** A male person of the 'lower orders', or of low condition or manners; a term of contempt; cf. KNAVE 2, 3. –1529. **3.** A boy or lad employed as a servant or attendant; hence, a male servant of the lowest grade in his line of service ME. **4.** *Chivalry.* A boy or lad in training for knighthood, and attached to the personal service of a knight, whom he followed on foot. Now only *Hist.* ME. **5.** A youth employed as the personal attendant of a person of rank 1460. **b.** Hence, a title of various officers of a royal or princely household, as *p. of honour, of the chamber*, etc. late ME. **c.** Hence, now, a boy or lad (usu. in 'buttons' or livery), employed to attend to the door, go on errands, and the like; in U.S., an attendant on a legislative body. Also *p.-boy.* **d.** Also applied to little boys fancifully dressed at a wedding ceremony to bear the bride's train. 1781.

1. A child þat was of half yeer age In Cradel it lay and was a propre p. CHAUCER.

II. Transf. use. *Entom.* Collector's name for a black and green S. Amer. hawk-moth of the family *Uraniidæ* 1886. Hence **Page** *v.*[1], to wait on or follow like a p.; *U.S.* to send a page-boy after (a visitor in a hotel); said also of the page. **Pa·gehood,** the state of being a p. †**Pa·gery,** the office or position of a p., service as a p. **Pa·geship.**

Page (pēidʒ), *sb.*[2] 1589. [– (O)Fr. *page* (reduction of *pagene*) – L. *pagina* vine-trellis, column of writing, page or leaf, f. **pāg-* fix, f. *pangere* fasten, fix in or together.] **1.** One side of a leaf of a book, manuscript, letter, etc. **b.** *Printing.* The type set up, or made up from slips or galleys, for printing a page 1727. **c.** *Type-founding.* One of the parcels into which new type is made up by the founders, to be sent out; usu. 8 inches by 4. 1882. **2.** *fig.* **a.** Any page, or the pages collectively, of a writing; hence, rhetorically, writing, book, record. **b.** An episode, such as would fill a page in a written history. 1619.

2. Her ample p. Rich with the spoils of time GRAY. A bright p. in her military history 1885.

Comb.: *p.-proof*, a pull taken from type made up into paged form.

Page (pēidʒ), *v.*[2] 1628. [f. PAGE *sb.*[2]] **1.** *trans.* To paginate. **2.** To make up (composed type) into pages 1890. **b.** *Type-founding.* To pack up (new type) in pages for sending out 1903. Hence **Paged** (pēidʒd) *a.*, having the pages numbered; having pages of a specified kind or number.

Pageant (pæ·dʒănt, pēi·dʒănt), *sb.* [Late ME. *pagyn* (whence AL. *pagina* XV), of unkn. origin. The later forms *pagend(e, pagent* are repr. by AL. *pagenda* stage, pageant (XV), *pagentes* (pl.) pageants (XIV). For the parasitic *d, t* (from XIV) cf. *ancient, peasant, tyrant.*] **1.** A scene acted on the stage; *spec.* one scene or act of a mediæval mystery play. *Obs.* exc. *Hist.* †**b.** *fig.* The part played by any one in an affair, or in life; performance; esp. in *to play one's p.*, to act one's part –1878. †**2.** A stage or platform on which scenes were acted or tableaux represented; *esp.* in early use, the movable structure used in the open-air performances of mystery plays –1739. †**b.** A piece of stage machinery; also, a mechanical contrivance generally –1719. **3.** Any kind of show, device, or temporary structure, exhibited as a feature of a public triumph or celebration. *Obs.* exc. *Hist.* 1511. **4.** *fig.* An empty show without substance or reality 1608. **5.** A spectacle arranged for effect; *esp.* a procession or parade with elaborate spectacular display 1805. Since 1907 applied to celebrations of local history consisting of a series of representations of events and personages connected with the particular place. **6.** *attrib.* or *adj.* Of or acting in a pageant; stage-, puppet-; specious 1659.

1. Of paiauntis that were played in Ioyous Garde SKELTON. **3.** A raree-shew (or p.) as of old, on the lord mayor's day SWIFT. *Dumb p.*, a dumb show. **4.** It was a name, a shadow, an empty p. GIBBON. **5.** The consecration of a King was then not a mere p. FREEMAN. Hence **Pa·geant** *v. trans.*, to carry *about* as a show or in a procession 1641; †to imitate as in a pageant or play SHAKS.

Pageantry (pæ·dʒăntri, pēi·-). 1608. [f. prec. + -RY.] †**1.** Pageants collectively –1714. **2.** Splendid display; pomp. Also in *pl.* 1651. **3.** Empty display, show without substance 1687.

1. *Per.* V. ii. 6. **2.** The p. of war SOUTHEY. **3.** Chivalry had not yet declined to mere formal pomp and p. 1854.

Paginal (pæ·dʒinăl), *a.* 1646. [– late L. *paginalis*, f. *pagina*; see PAGE *sb.*[2], -AL[1].] Consisting of or referring to pages; page for page. A verbal and p. reprint 1811. So **Pa·ginary** *a.*

Paginate (pæ·dʒineit), *v.* 1884. [– Fr. *paginer* (Dict. Acad. 1835), f. L. *pagina* PAGE *sb.*[2]; see -ATE[3].] *trans.* To mark or number the pages of a book; to page. So **Pagina·tion,** the action of marking the numbers of the pages; an instance of this; the sequence of figures with which the pages are numbered.

Paging (pēi·dʒiŋ), *vbl. sb.* 1775. [f. PAGE *v.*[2] + -ING[1].] The action of PAGE *v.*[2]; pagination.

‖**Pagne** (panʸ). 1698. [– Fr. *pagne* – Sp. *paño* :– L. *pannus* cloth.] A cloth; the single piece of cloth variously worn by natives of hot countries; *spec.* a loin-cloth, or a short petticoat.

Pagod (pæ·gǫd). *arch.* 1582. [– Pg. *pagode*; see next. Pope has *pago·d* as well as *pa·god.*] **1.** = next, 1. **2.** An idol or image of a deity (in India, China, etc.). (Often assoc. w. *god.*) 1582. **3.** = next, 3. 1598.

1. Her pagods hung with music of sweet bells TENNYSON. **2.** *fig.* My poor little p., Napoleon BYRON.

Pagoda (păgōᵘ·dă). 1618. [– Pg. *pagode*, with substitution of *-a* for *-e*; prob. to be referred ult. to Pers. *butkada* idol temple, f. *but* idol + *kada* habitation, alt. by assoc. with Prakrit *bhagodī* divine, holy.] **1.** A temple or sacred building (in India, China, etc.); *esp.* a sacred tower, usu. of pyramidal form, built over the relics of Buddha or a saint, or in any place as a work of devotion 1634. **b.** A small structure in imitation of an oriental pagoda 1796. †**2.** = prec. 2 (*rare*) –1665. **3.** A gold (or silver) coin formerly current in southern India, = about 7*s.* 1618. *attrib.* and *Comb.*, as **p.-flower,** the flower of the PAGODA-TREE, q.v.; **-stone** = PAGODITE.

Pago·da-tree. 1836. **1.** Name given to: **a.** *Sophora japonica*, cultivated in China and Japan; **b.** *Plumeria acutifolia*, a native of the W. Indies, cultivated in India; **c.** *Ficus indica*, the Banyan-tree of India. 1876. **2.** *fig.* A mythical tree joc. feigned to produce pagodas (sense 3).

2. Phr. *To shake the pagoda-tree*, to make a fortune rapidly in India.

Pagodite (pæ·gŏdəit). 1837. [– Fr. *pagodite*, f. *pagode* PAGODA; see -ITE[1] 2 b.] *Min.* A soft mineral carved by the Chinese into figures of pagodas, images, etc.; also called *agalmatolite.*

Pagurian (păgiūᵊ·riăn), *a.* and *sb.* 1840. [f. L. *pagurus* – Gr. πάγουρος a kind of crab; see -IAN.] *Zool.* **a.** *adj.* Belonging to the genus

Pagurus or family *Paguridæ* of decapod crustaceans. **b.** *sb.* One of this genus or family, a hermit-crab.

Pah (păh, pā), *int.* 1592. A natural exclam. of disgust.

Fye fie, fie; pah, pah: Giue me an Ounce of Ciuet; good Apothecary sweeten my immagination SHAKS.

Pah, variant of PA.[2]

‖**Pahlavi** (pā·lăvi), *a.* and *sb.* Also **Pehlevi** (pē·lĕvi), **Pehlvi.** 1777. [– Pers. *pahlawī*, f. *pahlav* :– *parthava* Parthia.] The name given by the followers of Zoroaster to the character in which are written the ancient translations of their sacred books, etc.; now used gen. to designate a mode of writing the language, used in Persia under the Sāsānian kings; loosely, Old Persian.

In divine High piping Pehlevi..the Nightingale cries to the Rose FITZGERALD.

Paid (pēid), *ppl. a.* ME. [pa. pple. of PAY *v.*[1]] †**1.** *predicatively.* Pleased, satisfied, content –1880. **2.** Remunerated with money; in receipt of pay 1862. **3.** Given, as money, in discharge of an obligation; discharged, as a debt; for which the money has been given, as a bill, a cheque 1866.

2. The machinery of paid officials 1862. **3.** *Paid-up capital*, that part of the subscribed capital of an undertaking which has been actually paid.

Paid-: see PÆD-.

Paigle, pagle (pēi·g'l). *dial.* 1530. [Of unkn. origin.] The cowslip, *Primula veris*; also, the oxlip, the buttercup, etc.

Paijama: see PYJAMA.

Paik (pek), *sb. Sc.* and *n. dial.* 1508. [Origin unkn.] A firm blow. So **Paik** *v.*

Pail (pēil). [OE. *pægel* (glossing med.L. *gillo* GILL *sb.*[3]) corresp. to (M)Du. *pegel* gauge, scale, mark, LG. *pegel* half a pint, of unkn. origin. ME. forms with final *e* appear to be due to assoc. with OFr. *paielle, paelle* (mod. *poêle*) pan, bath, liquid measure :– L. *patella* pan.] A vessel of wood, or of sheet-metal, usually cylindrical, and provided with a bail or hooped handle; used for carrying milk, water, etc. **b.** A pailful 1600.

Pailful (pēi·lful). 1591. [f. PAIL + -FUL.] As much as fills a pail.

Paillasse: see PALLIASSE.

Paillette (pælye·t). Also **-et.** 1843. [– Fr. *paillette* (paiyę·t), dim. of *paille* straw, chaff.] **1.** A piece of coloured foil or bright metal, used in enamel painting 1878. **2.** A spangle, used to ornament a woman's dress 1843.

Pain (pēin), *sb.* [ME. *peine, paine* – (O)Fr. *peine* :– L. *pœna* penalty, punishment, (later) pain, grief.] **1.** Punishment, penalty; a fine. *Obs.* exc. in phrases (see quots.). **2.** The opposite of *pleasure*; the sensation which one feels when hurt (in body or mind); suffering, distress. Also with *a* and *pl.* ME. †**b.** *spec.* The punishment or sufferings of hell (or of purgatory) –1598. **3.** Bodily suffering; a distressing sensation as of soreness (usu. in a particular part of the body). late ME. **b.** *spec.* (now always *pl.*) The throes of childbirth; labour ME. **4.** Mental suffering, trouble, grief, sorrow. late ME. †**b.** *spec.* Anxiety –1789. **5.** *pl.* Trouble taken in accomplishing or attempting something. Most freq. in phr. *to take pains, to be at* (*the*) *pains.* 1528. **b.** In this sense *pains* pl. has been freq. construed as a *sing.* (Cf. *means, news.*) 1533.

1. Phr. *Pains and penalties. On, upon, under p. of*, followed by the penalty or punishment in case of not fulfilling the command or condition stated, as *on p. of death*; †also, the crime with which one is liable to be charged, as *on p. of felony.* †*Pain forte et dure*: see PEINE. **2.** P. and pleasure are simple ideas incapable of definition BURKE. Phr. *To put out of* (one's) *p.*, etc., to dispatch (a wounded or suffering person or animal). **3.** Loud he yelled for exceeding paine SPENSER. **b.** She bowed her selfe, and traueled, for her paynes cam vpon her BIBLE (Great) 1 *Sam.* 4:19. **4.** A Mighty p. to Love it is, And 'tis a p. that p. to miss COWLEY. **5.** Yet much he praised the pains he took SCOTT. Phr. *For* (one's) *pains*: in return or recompense for one's labour or trouble; now usu. sarcastic or ironical; I had my journey for my pains 1801.

Pain (pēin), *v.* ME. [– *pein-*, tonic stem of OFr. *pener* (mod. *peiner*), f. late L. *pœnare*, f. L. *pœna* PAIN *sb.*] †**1.** *trans.* To punish; to torture by way of punishment; to fine –1601. **2.** To inflict pain upon; to hurt, distress. late ME. †**3.** *intr.* To suffer pain or distress; to suffer –1591. **4.** *refl.* To take pains or trouble; to endeavour, strive. *Obs.* or *arch.* ME.

2. Transports that pain'd and joys that agonized CRABBE. Pained with the toothache HAWTHORNE. **3.** So shalt thou cease to plague, and I to p. DANIEL. **4.** She her paynd with womanish art To hide her wound SPENSER. Hence **Pained** *ppl. a.* ME.

Painful (pēi·nfŭl), *a.* ME. [f. PAIN *sb.* + -FUL.] **1.** Full of or causing pain or suffering; hurting, afflictive, grievous; annoying, vexatious. **2.** Suffering or affected with (physical) pain. (Usu. of a part of the body which has been wounded or hurt.) 1590. **3.** Causing or involving trouble or labour; difficult, irksome, toilsome, laborious. Now *rare* or merged in 1. late ME. **4.** Characterized by painstaking. *Obs.* or *arch.* late ME. **5.** Of persons: Painstaking, laborious, assiduous, careful, diligent. *Obs.* or *arch.* 1549.

1. Salutary pangs may be painfuller than mortal ones LANDOR. **2.** His wound was p. 1794. **3.** Quick and p. Marches DRYDEN. **5.** The women be verie painefull and the men often idle 1612. Hence **Pai·nful-ly** *adv.*, **-ness.**

Painless (pēi·nlės), *a.* 1591. [f. PAIN *sb.* + -LESS.] Causing no pain. Hence **Pai·nless-ly** *adv.*, **-ness.**

Painstaking (pēi·nztēi:kiŋ), *sb.* 1556. [f. *pains*, pl. of PAIN *sb.* + *taking*, gerund of TAKE *v.*] The taking of pains; the bestowal of careful and attentive labour in doing something. So **Pai·nstaker,** now *rare* or *Obs.*

Pai·nsta:king, *a.* 1696. [f. as prec. + *taking*, pr. pple of TAKE *v.*] That takes pains; careful and industrious. **b.** Of actions, productions, etc.: Marked by attentive care 1866.

A most p. judge 1882. Hence **Pai·nsta:kingly** *adv.*

Paint (pēint), *sb.* 1602. [f. next.] **1.** The act of painting or colouring. **2.** That with which anything is painted: **a.** A solid colouring matter dissolved in a liquid vehicle, used to impart colour by being spread over a surface; also, the solid colouring matter alone; a pigment 1712. **b.** Colouring matter laid on the face or body for adornment; rouge, etc. 1659. **c.** *Med.* An external medicament which is put on like paint with a brush 1899. **3.** *fig.* Colour, colouring; adornment; outward show, fair pretence 1647.

attrib. and *Comb.*, as *p.-box, -brush, -pot*, etc. Hence **Pai·ntless** *a.*, destitute or devoid of paint, **Pai·nty** *a.*, of belonging to, or abounding in paint; of a picture: overcharged with paint; hence **Pai·ntiness.**

Paint (pēint), *v.* [prob. first in pa. pple. (*i*)*peint* – (O)Fr. *peint*(*e*, pa. pple. of *peindre* :– L. *pingere* embroider, tattoo, paint, embellish.] **1.** *trans.* To make (a picture, etc.) on a surface in colours; to depict, portray, delineate, by using colours. **b.** To adorn (a wall, window, etc.) *with* a painting or paintings. (Mostly in *pass.*) ME. **c.** *transf.* Said of the effect of coloured light 1831. **d.** *intr.* or *absol.* To practise the art of painting. late ME. **2.** *fig.* **a.** To display vividly as by painting 1561. **b.** To depict in words; to call up a picture of ME. **3.** To colour with a wash or coating of paint; to colour, stain; hence, to adorn with colours ME. **b.** *transf.* To colour by any means ME. **c.** *fig.* To adorn or variegate with or as with colours; to deck, beautify, ornament. late ME. **4.** To put colour on (the face); to rouge; also *refl.*, and *intr.* for *refl.* late ME. †**b.** *intr.* (*fig.*) To change colour; to blush. *To p. white*, etc.: to turn pale. –1623. **5.** *fig.* (*trans.*) To give a false colouring to; to colour highly, esp. with a view to deception. Now *rare* or *Obs.* late ME. †**6.** *intr.* To talk speciously. **b.** *trans.* To flatter or deceive with specious words. –1632. **7.** *trans.* To apply with a brush, as an external medicament; to treat (any part) in this way 1861.

1. Phr. *To p.* (an object) *black, white, red*, etc., to portray as of that colour. **c.** Like the Iris painted upon the cloud RUSKIN. **2. a.** Desire Was painted in my looks CARY. **b.** What words can p. the guilt of such a conduct? 1766. *To p. black*, to represent as evil or wicked; so *not so black as he is painted.* **3. b.** If God..so paints the Flowers SOUTH. **c.** *To p. the town red* (slang, orig. U.S.), to go on a riotous spree. **4.** *intr.* Let her p. an inch thicke, to this fauour she must come SHAKS. **6.** *L.L.L.* IV. i. 16. **7.** The part affected should be painted with iodine 1904. Hence **Pai·ntable** *a.*, suitable for a painting.

Painted (pēi·ntėd), *ppl. a.* ME. [f. prec. + -ED[1].] **1.** Represented in a picture; executed in colours as a picture, likeness, etc. **2.** Coated or brushed over with colour or paint; ornamented with designs, etc., executed in colour; having the face artificially coloured. late ME. **b.** *fig.* Artificial; feigned, disguised, pretended. late ME. **3.** *fig.* Highly coloured, variegated 1470.

1. As idle as a p. Ship Upon a p. Ocean COLERIDGE. **3.** The pecockes paynted fethers 1526.

Comb.: **p. beauty,** a brilliant American butterfly (*Vanessa huntera*); **P. Chamber,** a chamber in the old Palace of Westminster, the walls of which were painted with a series of battle scenes; **p. cup,** †a name for (*a*) the plant *Bartsia viscosa*; (*b*) any species of the American genus *Castilleia*, having bracts more brilliant and showy than the flowers; **p. finch,** one of several species of *Passerina* or *Cyanospiza*, the nonpareil, the indigo-bird, or the lazuli-finch; **p. lady,** (*a*) a species of butterfly (*Vanessa* or *Pyrameis cardui*) of orange-red colour, spotted with black and white; (*b*) a party-coloured variety of Pink or *Dianthus*; **p. tortoise, turtle,** an American mud-turtle (*Chrysemys picta*) marked on the under surface with red and yellow.

Painter[1] (pēi·ntəɹ). [– OFr. *peintour*, regimen case of *peintre* :– Rom. **pinctor*, f. L. *pictor*, f. *pict-*, pa. ppl. stem of *pingere* paint; see -ER[2], -OUR.] **1.** One who paints pictures: *fig.* a pictorial describer. **2.** A workman who coats or colours woodwork, ironwork, etc. with paint. late ME.

Comb., **painter's colic,** a form of colic to which painters who work with preparations of lead are liable, lead-colic. So **Pai·ntress,** a female p.

Painter[2] (pēi·ntəɹ). ME. [app. – OFr. *penteur* rope running from masthead (= mod. *pantoire*; also rope with eye-splice); cf. G. *pentertakel, -talje*, f. *pentern* fish the anchor (= Eng. †*paynt* XV); but the relations are undetermined.] **1.** = SHANK-PAINTER. **2.** A rope attached to the bow of a boat, for making it fast to a ship, a stake, etc. 1711.

2. Phr. *To cut* (or *slip*) *the p.* (*fig.*), to send a person or thing 'adrift' or away; to clear off; to sever a connection.

Painter[3]. 1823. [var. of PANTHER, prob. from Fr. *panthère* (pronounced pantęr).] The American panther or cougar (*Felis concolor*).

Painter-Stainer. 1504. = PAINTER[1] 1 and 2. The name by which the members of the City of London Livery Company of Painters are designated in their charter.

Painting (pēi·ntiŋ), *vbl. sb.* ME. [f. PAINT *v.* + -ING[1].] **1.** The result or product of applying paint; colouring; pictorial decoration. **2.** *concr.* A representation of an object or scene on a surface by means of colours; a picture. late ME. **3.** The representing of objects or figures by means of colours laid on a surface; the art of so depicting objects 1440. **b.** *fig.* Representation in vivid language 1615. **4.** The action of colouring or adorning with paint; the colouring of the face with paint. Also *fig.* 1497. †**5.** *concr.* Pigment, paint –1650.

†**Painture.** [ME. *peinture*, later *painture* – (O)Fr. *peinture* (†*painture*) :– Gallo-Rom. **pinctura* (med.L. *pinctura* XV), for L. *pictura*, f. *pict-*, pa. ppl. stem of *pingere* paint; see -URE.] **1.** The action or art of painting. Also *fig.* –1718. **2.** That which is painted; pictorial work; a painting –1668.

†**Paiocke.** Commonly taken to be a var. of PEACOCK. *Haml.* III. ii. 295.

Pair (pēəɹ), *sb.* ME. [– (O)Fr. *paire* :– L. *paria* equal or like things, n. pl. of *par* equal, whence OFr. *per* (mod. *pair*) PEER *sb.*

Pair is now followed by *of*; but *of* was formerly omitted, as 'a pair gloves'; cf. G. *ein paar handschuhe.* After a numeral *pair* was formerly used in the sing.; 'three pair (of) shoes' = G. *drei paar schuhe*; but the tendency now is to say 'three pairs'.]

I. A set of two. **1.** Two separate things of a kind that are coupled in use; as 'a pair of gloves, shoes, spurs, stirrups, sculls', etc.; also (*colloq.* and somewhat *joc.*) 'a pair of eyes, ears, arms, hands, wings', etc.; also, 'a pair of folding doors, curtains', etc. **2.** In the names of single articles composed of two corresponding parts, which are not used separately; e.g. 'a pair of breeches, trousers, or stays; a pair of scissors, tongs, bellows, spectacles', etc. ME. **3.** Two persons or animals of opposite sexes. **a.** An engaged or married couple. late ME. **b.** Two partners in a dance 1770. **c.** A mated couple of animals ME. **4.** A set of two (persons, animals, or things); a couple, brace, span ME. **b.** Short for *pair of horses*, two horses harnessed together 1727. **c.** Two voters on opposite sides who mutually agree to abstain from voting in order to be absent from a division without affecting the relative position of parties 1845. **d.** Short for 'pair of oars'; see OAR *sb.* 3 a. 1885. **5.** occas. = *two*, or formerly used loosely for a few, two or three. Now usu. superseded by *a couple*. 1599.

1. Phr. *To take* or *show a clean p. of heels*, to escape by superior speed. *P. of lawn sleeves*, a bishop. *P. of oars*: see OAR *sb.* 3 a. *Another* or *a different p. of shoes* or *boots*, a different matter. **3. c.** All pair'd, and each p. built a nest COWPER. **4.** Phr. *P. of cards*, two of the same value (see also II. 1); *p. of colours*, two flags belonging to a regiment, one the royal, the other the regimental flag; hence, the position or commission of an ensign; *p. of dice*, a set of two.

II. A set, not limited to two. **†1.** A set (of gallows, harness, etc.); a suit (of armour); a string (of beads); a pack (of cards); a chest (of drawers), etc. All *Obs.* or only *dial.* late ME. **b.** *P. of stairs*: a flight of stairs. Often used as = *floor* or *storey*. Also *attrib.*, as in *a two p. lodging*, etc. 1530. **c.** *P. of steps*: a flight of steps; also a portable set of steps 1755. **2.** (Also written *pare*). A company of miners working together (Cornwall, America); a team of mules carrying tin 1839.

Comb. **p.-toed** *a. Ornith.*, having the toes in pairs, two before and two behind.

Pair (pēᵊɹ), *v.*[1] 1603. [f. prec.] **1.** *trans.* To make a pair by matching (two persons or things one with another); to provide with a 'fellow' so as to make a pair 1613. **†b.** To match, equal. DRAYTON. **2.** *intr.* To go *with*, so as to match 1611. **3.** *trans.* To arrange (two persons or things) in a pair or couple 1607. **b.** To unite in love or marriage; to mate (animals) 1673. **4.** *intr.* To form a couple; esp. to make an agreement with an opponent that both shall abstain from voting on a given question or for a certain time; also *to p. off* 1711. **b.** To unite *with* one of the opposite sex; to couple or mate 1611.

2. He might have..pair'd with him in features and in shape 1756. **3.** *To p. off* (a number of persons or things), to put two by two in pairs. **b.** Turtles and doves of diff'ring hues unite, And glossy jett is pair'd with shining white POPE. **4.** Several members had paired 1810. **b.** So Turtles paire That neuer meane to part SHAKS.

Phr. *To p. off*, to go off or apart in pairs; also *to p. off with* (colloq.), to marry. Hence **Paired** *ppl. a.*

Pair, *v.*[2] *Obs.* or *dial.* ME. [Aphetic f. *apeyre, apayre* APPAIR.] **†1.** *trans.* = APPAIR 1. –1625. **2.** *intr.* = APPAIR 2. Now *dial.* ME.

1. Euer it mends Some, and paires Other BACON. Hence **†Pai·rer**, one who impairs WYCLIF. **†Pai·ring** *vbl. sb.*[2] –1617. So **Pai·rment**, impairment (now only *dial.*).

Pair-horse (pēᵊ·ɹhǭɹs), *a.* 1854. [From *pair of horse(s* used attrib.] For a pair of horses.

Pai·ring, *vbl. sb.*[1] 1611. [f. PAIR *v.*[1] + -ING[1].] The action of PAIR *v.*[1]

Comb. **p.-season, -time**, the season at which birds pair; the age at which the sexes begin to pair off.

Pair-oar (pēᵊ·rˌōᵊɹ). 1854. [Condensed from *pair of oars*.] A boat rowed by a pair of oars. Also *attrib.*

Pair-royal (pēᵊɹˌroi·ăl). Also **prial** (prəi·ăl). 1592. A set of three of the same kind. **a.** In cribbage, etc.: Three cards of the same denomination; *double pair-royal*, four such cards 1608. **b.** A throw of three dice all turning up the same number of points 1656. **c.** *transf.* A set of three persons or things; three of a kind 1592.

c. That great pair-royal Of adamantine sisters QUARLES.

Paisley (pēⁱ·zli). 1884. Name of a town in Scotland, used *attrib.* in *P. shawl*, a shawl in soft bright colours resembling a Cashmere shawl, orig. made at P.; *P. pattern*, the characteristic pattern of such a shawl; so *P. cotton, velvet*, etc., cotton, velvet, etc. having this pattern.

Pajamahs, -mas: see PYJAMAS.

Pajock, a mod. sp. of PAIOCKE, q.v.

‖**Paktong** (pæ·kˌtǫŋ). Also **paak-, pack-tong.** 1775. [Cantonese var. of Chinese *peh* (white) *t'ung* (copper).] Chinese nickel-silver; an alloy of copper, zinc, and nickel, resembling silver.

Pal (pæl), *sb. slang* or *low colloq.* 1681. [– Eng. Gipsy *pal* brother, mate = Turk. Gipsy *pral, plal* :– Skr. *bhrātr* BROTHER.] A comrade, mate, partner, 'chum'; an accomplice in crime, etc. Hence **Pal** *v. intr.* to become or be a p. of another; to associate *with*. **Pa·llish, Pa·lly** *adjs.*, on terms of fellowship. **Pa·lliness.**

‖**Palabra** (pălā·bră). 1594. [Sp., = word; cf. PALAVER.] A word; speech, talk, palaver. Often in phr. *Pocas palabras* few words.

Palace (pæ·lės, -ĕs), *sb.* [ME. *paleis* – OFr. *paleis*, (also mod.) *palais* – L. *palatium* orig. name of one of the seven hills of Rome (also called *Mons Palatinus*: see PALATINE *a.*[1]), (later) the house of Augustus there situated, the palace of the Cæsars which finally covered the hill.] **1.** The official residence of an emperor, king, pope, or other sovereign ruler. **b.** The official residence of an archbishop or bishop ME. **c.** In extended applications 1526. **2.** A palatial dwelling-place. late ME. **3.** *transf.* A spacious and highly decorated building, intended as a place of amusement, entertainment, or refreshment; cf. GIN-PALACE 1834. **†4.** The 'house' of a planet. CHAUCER.

1. c. In some inchanted castle or fairy p. MISS BURNEY. Occas. applied to a ducal mansion, e.g. *Blenheim P.*; in *p. of justice*, like Fr. *palais de justice*, to the supreme law-court; etc. **3.** *Crystal P.*, the name of the building of the Great Exhibition of 1851, when removed and erected on Sydenham Hill, near London, as a place of entertainment.

Comb. **p. car** *U.S.*, a railway-carriage fitted up in luxurious style; **-hotel**, a hotel of palatial splendour. Hence **Pa·lace** *v. trans.*, to place or lodge in a p. **Pa·laced** *a.*, having a p. or palaces; living in a p. **Pa·laceward, -wards** *adv.*

Palace Court, pa·lace-cou:rt. 1685. [= Court of the or a palace.] **1.** Name of a court formerly held at the Marshalsea and having jurisdiction in personal actions arising within twelve miles of the palace of Whitehall, the city of London excepted. **2.** The courtyard of a palace 1801.

Paladin (pæ·lădin). 1592. [– Fr. *paladin* – It. *paladino* – L. *palatinus* pertaining to the palace; see PALATINE *a.*[1] and *sb.*[1]] One of the Twelve Peers or famous warriors of Charlemagne's court, of whom the Count Palatine was the foremost; also *transf.* a knightly hero, renowned champion, knight errant. Also *attrib.*

Palæo-, *U.S.* **paleo-** (pæ:liˌo, pēⁱ:liˌo), bef. a vowel usu. **palæ-, pale-**, comb. form of Gr. παλαιός ancient (often opp. to NEO-). The spelling *pale-* is common in America. **Palæ(o)ichthyo·logy** [Gr. ἰχθύς fish], that branch of ichthyology which treats of extinct fossil fishes. **Palæobo·tany**, the botany of extinct or fossil plants; hence **Palæobo·tanist. Palæocri·noid** *Zool.*, *sb.* a crinoid of the division *Palæocrinoidea*, comprising the earlier extinct crinoids; *a.* belonging to or characteristic of this division. **Palæocry·stic, -crysta·llic** [Gr. κρύσταλλος ice] *adjs.*, consisting of ancient ice, applied to parts of the polar seas. **Palæo·logy**, the science or study of antiquities (*rare*); **Palæo·logist. Palæonto·graphy**, the decription of fossil remains; so **Palæontogra·phical** *a.* **Palæophyto·logy** [Gr. φυτόν plant] = PALÆOBOTANY. **Palæornitho·logy**, that branch of ornithology or palæontology which treats of extinct or fossil birds; so **Palæornitholo·gical** *a.* **Pa·læosaur**, a fossil saurian of the genus *Palæosaurus*. **Palæotechnic** (-te·knik) [Gr. τέχνη art] *a.*, pertaining to primitive art.

Palæography, paleo- (pæliˌǫ·grăfi, pēⁱli-). 1818. [– Fr. *paléographie* – mod.L. *palæographia* (1708); see PALÆO-, -GRAPHY.] **1.** Ancient writing, or an ancient style or method of writing 1822. **2.** The study of ancient writing and inscriptions; the science or art of deciphering these and determining their date 1818. So **Pa·læograph**, an ancient writing. **Palæo·grapher**, occas. **-ist**, one skilled in p. **Palæogra·phic, -al** *adjs.* of or pertaining to p.; **-ly** *adv.*

Palæolithic, paleo- (pæ:lioli·þik, pēⁱ:li-), *a.* 1865. [f. PALÆO- + Gr. λίθος stone + -IC.] Characterized by the use of primitive stone implements; applied to the earlier part of the prehistoric 'stone age'; also to things belonging to this period: opp. to *neolithic*. So **Pa·læolith**, a primitive stone implement. **Palæoli·thoid** *a.* resembling, or of the nature of, what is p.

Palæontology, pale- (pæ:liˌǫntǫ·lŏdʒi, pēⁱ:li-). 1838. [f. PALÆO- + Gr. ὄντα, pl. of ὄν being + -LOGY.] The study of extinct organized beings, i.e. of fossil animals and plants; often confined to that of extinct animals (palæozoology). So **Palæontolo·gic, -al** *adjs.*, **-ly** *adv.* **Palæonto·logist.**

Palæothere, paleo- (pæ·liˌoþīᵊɹ, pēⁱ·li-). Also in L. form **palæothe·rium.** 1815. [f. PALÆO- + Gr. θηρίον beast.] A perissodactyl mammal of the extinct genus *Palæotherium*, comprising several species of tapir-like form; their fossil remains are found in Eocene and Miocene strata. Hence **Palæothe·rian** *a.* of or pertaining to the p.; characterized by the palæotheres. **Palæothe·rioid -the·roid** *adjs.* akin to the p.

Palæotype, paleo- (pæ·liˌotəip). 1867. [f. PALÆO- + TYPE *sb.*] A system of writing, devised by A. J. Ellis, in which the 'old types' (i.e. existing Roman letters, etc.) are used to form a universal phonetic alphabet. Also *attrib.* or as *adj.* Hence **Palæoty·pic** *a.*

Palæotypography, paleo- (-təipǫ·grăfi). 1872. [f. PALÆO- + TYPOGRAPHY.] Ancient typography, early printing.

Palæozoic, paleo- (pæ:liˌozōᵘ·ik, pēⁱ:li-), *a.* 1838. [f. PALÆO- + Gr. ζωή life, ζωός living + -IC.] *Geol.* **1.** Characterized by, containing, or pertaining to ancient forms of life. Orig. applied to the Cambrian and Silurian strata; extended to all the fossiliferous strata up to the Permian, the higher strata being MESOZOIC and CAINOZOIC. **2.** *fig.* and *transf.* Belonging to the most ancient, or to the lowest, stage 1851. **B.** *sb. ellipt.* (*pl.*) Palæozoic rocks or strata 1855.

Palæozoology, paleo- (-zoˌǫ·lŏdʒi). 1857. [f. PALÆO- + ZOOLOGY.] That department of zoology, or of palæontology, which treats of extinct or fossil animals. Hence **Pa:læozoolo·gical** *a.*

‖**Palæstra, palestra** (pălī·stră, păle·stră). late ME. [– L. *palæstra* – Gr. παλαίστρα, f. παλαίειν wrestle.] Gr. *Antiq.* A place devoted to the public teaching and practice of wrestling and athletics; a wrestling school, gymnasium; *transf.* the practice of wrestling or athletics; also *fig.* **Palæ·stral, pale·stral** *a.* of or pertaining to the p., or to wrestling or athletics; athletic. So **Palæ·stric, -e·stric** *a.* 1774.

Palætiology (pălītiˌǫ·lŏdʒi). *rare.* 1837. [(For **palæ-ætiology*); see PALÆO-, ÆTIOLOGY.] Used by Whewell for the application of existing principles of cause and effect to the explanation of past phenomena. So **Palæ:tiolo·gical** *a.* **Palæ:tio·logist**, one versed in p.

Palagonite (pălæ·gŏnəit). 1863. [– G. *palagonit* (Waltershausen, 1846), f. *Palagonia* in Sicily, one of its localities; see -ITE[1] 2 b.] *Min.* A volcanic rock of vitreous structure allied to basalt.

‖**Palais de danse** (palę də dāṅs). 1919. [Fr.] An elaborate public dance hall.

‖**Palampore** (pæ·lămpōᵊɹ). 1698. [prob. f. *Pālanpur*, name of a town in Gujarat, India, perh. with contamination from Hind., Pers. *palangpōsh* bed-cover.] A kind of chintz bed-cover formerly made in India.

Palander (pæ·lăndəɹ). *Obs.* exc. *Hist.* 1562. [app. – It. *palandra, palandaria*, Sp. *palandre*, Fr. †*palandre, -ie* (XVI), med.L. *palandaria* (XV); of unkn. origin.] **1.** A flat-bottomed transport vessel used esp. (by the Turks) for transporting horses 1572. **†2.** A fire-ship; a bomb-ketch –1693.

‖**Pala·nk, -ka.** 1685. [– Fr. *palanque* (XVII), or its source It. *palanca* 'a defence made of great poles or stakes'.] A kind of permanent entrenched camp, attached to Turkish frontier fortresses.

‖**Palanquin, palankeen** (pælănkī·n). 1588. [– Pg. *palanquim* – an E. Indian word repr. by Pali *pālankī*, Hindi *pālkī* (whence PALKEE, PALKI) :– Skr. *palyanka, paryanka* bed, couch, f. *pari* round about, PERI-. The final nasal seems to have been a Pg. addition, as in *mandarim* MANDARIN; forms without it, *palanke(e*, were in use XVII–XVIII.] A covered litter, usu. for one person, used in India and the East, carried by four or six (rarely two) men by means of poles projecting before and behind. Also *attrib.*

‖**Palas, pulas** (pălā·s). 1799. [Hindi *palāç, palās*, Skr. *palāça.*] The DHAK-tree of India, *Butea frondosa* and *B. superba.*

Palatable (pæ·lătăb'l), *a.* 1669. [f. PALATE *sb.* and *v.* + -ABLE.] Agreeable to the palate; pleasant to the taste; savoury.

fig. Truth..is seldom p. to the ears of kings 1683. Hence **Palatabi·lity, Pa·latableness. Pa·latably** *adv.*

Palatal (pæ·lătăl), *a.* and *sb.* 1828. [– Fr. *palatal*, f. L. *palatum* PALATE; see -AL^1.] **A.** *adj.* **1.** *Anat., Zool.*, etc. Pertaining to the palate; palatine. **2.** *Phonetics.* Of a consonant or vowel sound: Produced by placing the tongue against the palate, esp. the hard palate; now more commonly called *front.* 1828. **B.** *sb.* **1.** *Anat.* Short for *p. bone*: = PALATINE *sb.*^{2} 1. 1886. **2.** *Phonetics.* A palatal sound; usually, a palatal or front consonant 1828. Hence **Pa·latalize** *v. trans.* to render palatal; esp. to change (a sound) by advancing the point of contact between tongue and palate. **Palataliza·tion.**

Palate (pæ·lĕt), *sb.* late ME. [– L. *palatum.*] **1.** The roof of the mouth; the structures, partly bony and partly fleshy, which separate the cavity of the mouth from that of the nose. **2.** Pop. considered as the seat of taste; hence *transf.* the sense of taste 1526. **b.** *fig.* Mental taste or liking. late ME. **3.** *Bot.* A convex projection of the lower lip closing the throat of the corolla of a personate flower, as the snapdragon 1760. **4.** *attrib.* 1611.

1. *Bony* or *hard p.*, the anterior and chief part of the palate, consisting of bone covered with thick mucous membrane. *Soft p.*, the posterior part of the palate, a pendulous fold of musculo-membranous tissue separating the mouth-cavity from the pharynx, and terminating below in the uvula; also called *veil of the p.* = VELUM 2a. †*Falling down of the p.*, etc., relaxation of the uvula. **2. b.** I heard a little too much preaching,..and lost my p. for it GEO. ELIOT.

Palate (pæ·lĕt), *v. rare.* 1606. [f. prec.] *trans.* To perceive or try with the palate, to taste; to relish. Also *fig.*

Palatial (pălē^i·ʃăl), *a.*^{1} 1754. [f. L. *palatium* PALACE + -AL^1.] Of the nature of a palace; pertaining to or befitting a palace; splendid, magnificent (as a building). Hence **Pala·tially** *adv.*

†**Palatial,** *a.*^{2}, *sb.* 1775. Obs. irreg. form for PALATAL –1832.

Palatinate (pălæ·tinĕt, pæ·lătine^{i}t). 1580. [f. PALATINE *sb.*^{1} + -ATE^1; cf. Fr. *palatinat.*] **1.** The territory under the rule of a palatine or count-palatine 1658. **b.** In England and Ireland: A county palatine or palatine earldom: see COUNTY^1 1 and PALATINE *a.*^{1} 2b. 1614. **c.** *The P., Rhine P.*, a state of the old German empire, under the rule of the Pfalzgraf or Count Palatine of the Rhine 1580. **2.** *attrib.* or *adj.* Of or belonging to a palatinate 1672.

2. *P. purple*, in Durham University, a light purple used in some academical robes, etc.; hence as *sb.*, a blazer of this colour awarded as a distinction in sports; the distinction itself (cf. BLUE *sb.* 8).

Palatine (pæ·lătəin, -in), *a.*^{1} and *sb.*^{1} late ME. [– Fr. *palatin, -ine* – L. *palatinus* of or belonging to the *palatium* or PALACE, as sb. 'officer of the palace, chamberlain'.] **A.** *adj.* **1.** Of or belonging to a palace or court; palatial 1598. **2.** Possessing royal privileges; having a jurisdiction (within the territory) such as elsewhere belongs to the sovereign alone. late ME. **b.** Of or belonging to a count or earl palatine, or to a county palatine, or palatinate 1638. **3.** Of or belonging to the German Palatinate 1644.

2. *Count, Earl (Lord) P.*: see COUNT *sb.*^{2} *County P., P. County*: see COUNTY^1 1. *P. earldom* = County P. **b.** The rich p. city of Durham 1824.

B. *sb.* [the adj. used ellipt.] **I.** Short for Palatine Hill, *Mons Palatinus*, at Rome 1656. **II. 1.** An officer of the imperial palace; orig. the chamberlain, the mayor or major of the palace; a chief minister of the empire 1598. **b.** Hence: A lord having sovereign power over a province or dependency of an empire or realm; a great feudatory 1591. **c.** In England and Ireland: An earl palatine 1612. **2.** *pl.* In ref. to the later Roman Empire: The troops of the palace; the prætorians 1630. †**3.** A county palatine or palatinate –1600. **4.** An inhabitant or native of a palatinate 1610.

4. Emigrant Palatines and Saltzburghers from Germany 1773.

†**III.** [– Fr. *palatine*: so called from the Princess Palatine, wife of the Duke of Orleans: see Littré.] A fur tippet worn by women. Also *p. tippet.* –1880.

Palatine (pæ·lătəin, -in), *a.*^{2} and *sb.*^{2} 1656. [– Fr. *palatin*, f. L. *palatum* PALATE; see -INE^1.] **A.** *adj.* **1.** *Anat.*, etc. Of or belonging to the palate; situated in or upon the palate. †**2.** *Phonetics.* = PALATAL A. 2. –1773. **B.** *sb.* **1.** *Anat.* (*pl.*) Short for *p. bones*: The two bones, right and left, which form the hard palate 1854. †**2.** *Phonetics.* = PALATAL B. 2. –1834.

Palative (pæ·lătiv), *a. rare.* 1682. [f. PALATE *sb.* + -IVE.] Appealing to the palate or taste.

Palato- (pălē^i·to, pæ·lăto), comb. form of L. *palatum* PALATE; as in **Palato-de·ntal** (*Phonetics*) *a.*, pertaining to palate and teeth; applied to consonants produced by placing the tongue against the palate immediately behind the teeth; *sb.*, a consonant so produced. **Palato-pte·rygoid** *a.*, belonging to the palatine and pterygoid bones; *sb.*, a bone composed of these united.

Palaver (pălā·vəɹ), *sb.* 1735. [– Pg. *palavra* :– L. *parabola* PARABLE.] **1.** A talk, parley, conference, discussion; orig. between Portuguese traders and West African natives. **2.** Profuse or idle talk; 'jaw' 1748. **b.** Talk intended to wheedle 1809.

Palaver (pălā·vəɹ), *v.* 1733. [f. prec.] **1.** *intr.* To talk profusely or unnecessarily; to 'jaw', 'jabber'; to talk wheedlingly. **2.** *trans.* To treat with palaver; to flatter, wheedle 1785.

2. To write silly odes, and p. the great 1815. Hence **Pala·verer.**

Pale (pē^{i}l), *sb.*^{1} ME. [– (O)Fr. *pal* :– L. *palus* stake.] **1.** *orig.* A stake, esp. driven into the ground with others, to form a fence; now usu., One of the upright bars nailed vertically to a horizontal rail or rails, to form a paling. late ME. **2.** A fence; a paling, palisade. *Obs.* or *arch.* ME. **b.** *transf.* and *fig.* Any enclosing barrier or line. *Obs.* or *arch.* 1564. **c.** *fig.* A limit, boundary; a restriction; a defence, safeguard. *Obs.* exc. in phr. *within* (or *outside*) *the p. of.* late ME. †**3.** An area enclosed by a fence; an enclosure. *Obs.* or *arch.* late ME. **4.** A district within determined bounds, or subject to a particular jurisdiction; *spec.* (now only *Hist.*) **b.** the *English P.* in France, the territory of Calais 1494; **c.** the *English P.* (also simply *the P.*) in Ireland, that part of Ireland over which English jurisdiction was established 1547. **5.** *Her.* An ordinary consisting of a vertical stripe or band in the middle of the shield, usu. occupying one-third of its breadth 1478. †**b.** A vertical stripe on cloth, etc. CHAUCER. †**6.** *Bot.* The 'ray' of florets in composite flowers –1683. **b.** = IMPALER 1676.

1. Inclosynge it with stakes or pales as his owne 1555. **2.** Herds of deer not confined by any wall or p. 1792. **c.** Nothing within the p. or verge of Reason 1671. **5.** *In p.*: said of a charge or row of charges in the position of a p.; formerly also = palewise, vertically. (*Party*) *per p.*: said of the shield when divided by a vertical line through the middle.

†**Pale,** *sb.*^{2} 1547. [f. PALE *a.*] Paleness, pallor –1832.

Pale, *sb.*^{3} 1866. [– L. *palea* chaff.] = PALEA.

Pale (pē^{i}l), *a.* [– OFr. *pale, palle* (mod. *pâle*) – L. *pallidus* PALLID.] **1.** Of persons, their complexion, etc.: Of a whitish or ashen appearance; pallid; wan. **b.** *gen.* Of a shade of colour approaching white; faintly coloured. late ME. **c.** Qualifying adjs. (or sbs.) of colour 1588. **d.** Relatively lighter in colour 1708. **2.** Wanting in brightness or brilliancy; dim. late ME. **3.** *fig.* Dim, faint, feeble; lacking intensity, vigour, or robustness; timorous, etc. 1530.

1. He starte abak and waxed paale MALORY. The p. cast of Thought SHAKS. **b.** The p. Primrose MILT. **2.** The day sterre wexeth paale and leseth hir lyht CHAUCER. **3.** The p. kyngdome of Pluto 1530. Hence **Pa·le-ly** *adv.*, **-ness.**

Pale (pē^{i}l), *v.*^{1} Now *rare.* ME. [– OFr. *paler*, f. *pal* PALE *sb.*^{1}] **1.** *trans.* To enclose with pales or a fence; to surround, fence *in.* **b.** *transf.* and *fig.* To encircle, hem in. Const. *in, up.* 1563. †**2.** To stripe, to mark with vertical stripes. (Almost always in pa. pple.) late ME.

1. b. *Hen. V*, v. Prol. 10. Hence **Paled** (pē^{i}ld) *ppl. a.*^{1}, †(*a*) = PALY; (*b*) enclosed with pales, fenced. †**Pa·ler,** an officer of a park charged with keeping the fences in repair –1800.

Pale (pē^{i}l), *v.*^{2} ME. [– OFr. *palir* (mod. *pâlir*), f. *pal* PALE *a.*] **1.** *intr.* To grow pale or dim; to lose colour or brilliancy. **2.** *trans.* To make, cause to become, pale; to dim. late ME.

1. The Red Rose pal'd, the White was soil'd in red 1637. **2.** The Glow-worme..gins to p. his vneffectuall Fire SHAKS. Hence **Paled** *ppl. a.*^{2}, rendered pale. **Pa·ling** *ppl. a.*, growing pale.

‖**Palea** (pē^i·li,ă). Pl. **-eæ** (-i,ī). 1753. [L., = chaff.] **1.** *Bot.* A chaff-like bract or scale; *esp.* the inner bracts enclosing the stamens and pistil in the flower of grasses (opp. to the *glumes*); also, those at the bases of the individual florets in many *Compositæ*; the scales on the stems of certain ferns. **2.** *Ornith.* A wattle or dewlap 1890. Hence **Palea·ceous** *a.* furnished or covered with paleæ; of the nature or consistence of chaff. So †**Pa·leous** *a.* of the nature of chaff; chaffy. Sir T. BROWNE.

Pale-face (pē^i·lfē^{i}s). 1822. A person who has a pale face; a name for a white man attributed to the N. Amer. Indians or 'red men'.

Pale-faced (pē^i·lfē^{i}st), *a.* 1592. Having a pale face.

Paleo-: see PALÆO-.

Palestra, etc.: see PALÆSTRA, etc.

Palet (pē^i·lĕt). 1880. [f. PALE *sb.*^{3} + -ET.] *Bot.* = PALEA 1.

‖**Paletot** (pæ·lĕtō^u, pæ·ltō^u). 1840. [Fr., of unkn. origin; see PALTOCK.] A loose outer garment for men or women.

Palette (pæ·lĕt). 1622. [– (O)Fr. *palette*; see PALLET^2.] **1.** A flat thin tablet of wood or porcelain, used by an artist to lay and mix his colours on. **b.** *transf.* The set of colours used by a particular artist or for a particular picture 1882. **2.** A small rounded plate formerly used in armour to protect the armpit 1834. **3. a.** *Conch.* = PALLET^2 7. **b.** *Entom.* a flat expansion upon the legs of some insects. 1834.

Comb. **p.-knife,** a thin flexible blade of steel fitted with a handle, used for mixing colours on a palette, for distributing printing-ink on a surface, etc.

Palewise (pē^i·lwəiz), *adv.* 1721. [f. PALE *sb.*^{1} + -WISE.] *Her.* In the direction of a pale; vertically. Also †**Pa·leways** 1610.

Palfrenier (pælfrĕnī^ə·ɹ). *arch.* 1489. [– (O)Fr. *palefrenier* – Pr. *palafrenier*, f. *palafren*, var. of *palafre* PALFREY; see -IER 2.] A man having charge of horses; a groom.

Palfrey (pǭ·lfri, pæ·l-). ME. [– OFr. *palefrei* (mod. *palefroi*) :– med.L. *palefredus*, for late L. *paraveredus* (v), f. Gr. παρά beside, extra (see PARA-^{1}) + L. *veredus* (hunting-horse in Martial, later courier's horse), of Gaulish origin.] A saddle-horse for ordinary riding as dist. from a war-horse; *esp.* a small saddle-horse for ladies. (Now mainly *Hist.*) Also *attrib.*

A damoysel..on a fayr palfroy MALORY. [He] cried, 'My charger and her p.' TENNYSON.

Pali (pā·li), *sb.* and *a.* 1800. [Short for *pāli-bhāsā*, i.e. language of the canonical texts (as opp. to 'commentary'), f. *pāli* line, canon + *bhāsā* language.] The language used in the canonical books of the Buddhists.

Paliform (pē^i·lifǭɹm), *a.* 1890. [f. L. PALUS stake + -FORM.] *Zool.* Resembling, or having the form of, a palus.

‖**Palikar** (pæ·likāɹ). 1812. [– mod. Gr. παλικάρι, παλληκάρι, dim. of Gr. πάλλαξ, πάλληξ youth.] A member of the band of a Greek or Albanian military chief.

Palil(l)ogy (păli·lŏdʒi). Also in Gr.-L. forms. 1657. [– late L. *palilogia* – Gr. παλιλογία, f. πάλιν again + -λογία -LOGY.] *Rhet.* The repetition of a word or phrase for the sake of emphasis.

||**Palimbacchius** (pæ:limbækəi·ŏs). 1586. [– L. *palimpsestus* – Gr. παλίμψηστος (as sb. -ον, βακχεῖος BACCHIUS.] = ANTIBACCHIUS. Also **Palimba·cchic.**

Palimpsest (pæ·limpsest), *sb.* and *a.* 1661. [– L. *palimpsestus* – Gr. παλίμψεστος (as sb. -ον, sc. βιβλίον book), f. πάλιν again + ψεστός, pa. ppl. formation on ψῆν rub smooth. Cf. Fr. *palimpseste* (XVI).] **A.** *sb.* †**1.** Paper, parchment, etc., prepared for writing on and wiping out again, like a slate –1706. **2.** A parchment, etc., which has been written upon twice, the original writing having been rubbed out 1825. Also *fig.* **3.** A monumental brass turned and re-engraved on the reverse side 1876. **B.** *adj.* **1.** Of a manuscript: see A. 2. 1852. **2.** Of a monumental brass: see A. 3. 1843.

Palindrome (pæ·lindrōᵘm), *sb.* and *a.* 1629. [– Gr. παλίνδρομος running back again, f. πάλιν again + δρομ-, δραμεῖν run.] A word, verse, or sentence that reads the same backwards as forwards. Also *adj.* Palindromic.

Subi dura a rudibus: It is P. 1638. Hence **Palindro·mic, -al** *adjs.*, **-ly** *adv.* **Pa·lindromist,** an inventor of palindromes.

Paling (pēⁱ·liŋ), *vbl. sb.* late ME. [f. PALE *v.*[1] + -ING[1].] †**1.** Decoration with 'pales' or vertical stripes. CHAUCER. **2.** The action of constructing a fence with pales; fencing 1469. **3.** *concr.* **a.** Pales collectively; fencing 1788. **b.** A fence made of pales. (With *a* and *pl.*) 1558. **c.** Each of the pales of a fence; usu. in *pl.* = a set of pales, a fence 1834.

3. a. The firs answer for..p. for fences 1788.

||**Palingenesia** (pæ:lindʒenī·siă). 1621. [med.L. – Gr. παλιγγενεσία birth over again, f. πάλιν again + γένεσις birth.] = PALINGENESY.

Palingenesis (pælindʒe·nėsis). 1818. [f. Gr. πάλιν again + γένεσις birth: cf. prec.] **1.** = PALINGENESY. **2.** *Biol.* Haeckel's term for the form of ontogenesis in which ancestral characters are exactly reproduced, without modification 1879. **3.** *Entom.* = METAMORPHOSIS 3a. 1886. Hence **Palingene·tic** *a.* of, belonging to, or of the nature of p. (sense 2).

Palingenesy (pælindʒe·nėsi). 1643. [– Fr. *palingénésie* – med.L. PALINGENESIA; see -Y[3].] Regeneration, birth over again; revival, reanimation, resuscitation.

Palinode (pæ·linōᵘd). 1599. [– Fr. †*palinode* or late L. *palinodia* – Gr. παλινῳδία, f. πάλιν again + ᾠδή song, ODE.] *orig.* An ode or song in which the author retracts something said in a former poem; hence *gen.* a recantation. So **Palino·dial** *a.*, of the nature of a recantation.

Palinodic (pælinǫ·dik), *a.* 1883. [– Gr. παλινῳδικός, f. παλινῳδία; see prec., -IC.] *Gr. Pros.* Applied to verse in which two 'systems' of corresponding form, as a strophe and antistrophe, are separated by two others also of corresponding form but different from the former.

Palinody (pæ·linoᵘdi). Now *rare* or *Obs.* 1589. [– Fr. *palinodie* – L. *palinodia*; see PALINODE, -Y[3].] = PALINODE.

Palisade (pælisēⁱ·d), *sb.* 1600. [– Fr. *palissade* – Pr. *palissada*, f. *palissa* fence made of pales :– Gallo-Rom. **palicea*, f. L. *palus* PALE *sb.*[1]; see -ADE.] **1.** A fence of pales or stakes. †**b.** *Gardening.* An espalier; hence *transf.* a row of trees or shrubs forming a close hedge –1712. **2.** *Mil.* A strong pointed wooden stake, of which a number are fixed deeply in the ground in a close row, as a defence 1697. **3.** *fig.* Anything likened to a fence of stakes (or one of such stakes) 1601. **b.** *pl.* Name for the lofty cliffs along the western bank of the Hudson above New York 1838.

3. A vast p. of blue ice-pinnacles 1871. *Comb.*: **p.-cell,** a cell of the **p.-tissue,** tissue consisting of elongated cells set closely side by side, as the parenchyma immediately below the epidermis of the upper surface in most leaves; **-worm,** name for various parasitic nematode worms, esp. *Strongylus armatus*, infesting the horse, etc.

Hence **Palisa·de** *v. trans.* to furnish with a p. or palisades. **Palisa·ding** *vbl. sb.* a palisade, paling.

Palisa·do, *sb. Obs.* or *arch.* 1589. [– Sp. *palizada*; see -ADO.] = PALISADE. Hence **Palisa·do** *v.*

Palish (pē̆ⁱ·liʃ), *a.* late ME. [f. PALE *a.* + -ISH[1].] Somewhat pale, rather pale.

||**Palissé** (pa·lise), *a.* 1780. [Fr., pa. pple. of *palisser* (XV) fence in, f. (O)Fr. *palis* fence.] *Her.* Said of a dividing line when broken into parallel vertical pointed projections, like a palisade; **b.** said of the field when divided into vertical piles of alternate tinctures.

||**Palkee, palki** (pā·lkī). *East Ind.* 1678. [Hindi *pālkī*; see PALANQUIN.] = PALANQUIN.

Pall (pǫl), *sb.*[1] [OE. *pæll* – L. *pallium* Greek mantle, philosopher's cloak, later in various eccl. uses; see PALLIUM.] **I.** Cloth, a cloth. **1.** Fine or rich cloth; in OE. 'purple'. *Obs.* exc. as poet. *arch.* **2.** A rich cloth spread over or upon something; a coverlet, canopy, etc. *Obs.* or *arch.* ME. **3.** *Eccl.* **a.** An altar-cloth or frontal. *arch.* **b.** The linen cloth or linen-covered square of cardboard with which the chalice is covered. OE. **4.** A cloth, usu. of black, purple, or white velvet, spread over a coffin, hearse, or tomb 1440.

1. If p. and vair no more I wear SCOTT. **4.** Mourning when their leaders fall, Warriors carry the warrior's p. TENNYSON.

II. A garment, a vestment. **1.** A robe, cloak, mantle. *Obs.* or *arch.* OE. **2.** *spec.* **a.** *Eccl.* = PALLIUM 2. Hence *transf.* The office or dignity of metropolitan or archbishop. 1480. **b.** A robe or mantle put upon the sovereign at coronation; now called the 'royal robe' 1643. **3.** *Her.* A bearing repr. the front half of an archbishop's pallium, consisting of three bands in the form of a capital Y, charged with crosses. (Also called *cross-pall.*) 1562.

1. In a long purple p.,..she was arayd SPENSER. **2. a.** Besides his P., the Pope's Chamberlain, brought him from Rome, a Cardinalls hat 1650.

III. *fig.* Something that covers or conceals, a 'mantle', 'cloak'; in mod. use *esp.* something, such as a cloud, that extends over a thing or region and produces an effect of gloom 1450.

Overhead..a murky p. of smoke 1882.

attrib. and *Comb.*, as *p.-like* adj.; **p.-bearer, -holder, -supporter,** one of those attending the coffin at a funeral, to hold up the corners and edges of the p. Hence **Pall** *v.*[2], to cover with or as with a cloth or p. late ME.

Pall (pǫl), *v.*[1] late ME. [Aphetic f. †*appall*, APPAL.] **I.** *intr.* †**1.** To become faint; to faint, fail (in strength, virtue, etc.) –1602. †**2.** Of fermented or aerated liquors: To become flat, stale, or insipid –1703. **3.** *transf.* and *fig.* To become tasteless, vapid, or insipid to the appetite or interest 1704. **4.** To lose relish or interest; to become cloyed *with* 1765.

3. Beauty is a Thing which palls with Possession STEELE. They would satiate us and p. upon our senses RUSKIN.

II. *trans.* †**1.** To make pale, to dim –1612. †**2.** To make faint or feeble; to weaken; to appal –1686. †**3.** To render flat, stale, or insipid –1807. **4.** To satiate, cloy (the appetite, senses, etc.) 1700.

4. And p. the sense with one continu'd show ADDISON. Hence **Pall** *sb.*[2], a feeling of disgust arising from satiety or insipidity (*rare*).

Pall, var. of PAWL.

||**Palla** (pæ·lă). 1706. [rel. to L. PALLIUM.] **1.** *Rom. Antiq.* A loose outer garment or wrap worn out of doors by women. **2.** *Eccl.* = PALL *sb.*[1] I. 3. 1706.

Palladian (pælēⁱ·diăn), *a.*[1] 1562. [f. L. *palladius* + -AN.] Of or pertaining to Pallas, the goddess of wisdom; hence, pertaining to wisdom, knowledge, or study.

Palla·dian, *a.*[2] 1731. [f. *Palladio* + -AN.] *Arch.* Of, belonging to, or according to the school of the Italian architect Andrea Palladio (1518–80), who imitated ancient Roman architecture without regard to classical principles.

Palladic (pălæ·dik), *a.*[1] 1857. [f. PALLADIUM[2] + -IC 1b.] *Chem.* Applied to compounds of palladium containing a smaller proportion of the metal than those called *palladious.*

Palla·dic, *a.*[2] 1896. [Cf. PALLADIUM[1] (in sense 2); see -IC.] Name of a supposed branch of continental Freemasonry. So **Pa·lladism** 1895. **Pa·lladist.**

Palladious (pălēⁱ·diəs), *a.* 1842. [f. PALLADIUM[2] + -OUS.] *Chem.* Applied to compounds of palladium containing a larger proportion of the metal than those called *palladic.*

Palladium[1] (pălēⁱ·diŏm). late ME. [– L. *palladium* – Gr. παλλάδιον, f. Παλλάς, Παλλαδ- epithet of the goddess Athene.] **1.** *Gr. and L. Myth.* The image of the goddess Pallas, in the citadel of Troy, on which the safety of the city was supposed to depend, reputed to have been brought thence to Rome. **2.** *transf.* and *fig.* Anything on which the safety of a nation, institution, etc., is believed to depend 1600.

2. The *Habeas Corpus* Act..the p. of an Englishman's liberty 1845.

Palladium[2] (pălēⁱ·diŏm). 1803. [– mod.L.; so named (1803) by its discoverer Woollaston from the newly discovered asteroid *Pallas*; see prec., -IUM.] *Chem.* A hard white metal of the platinum group resembling silver, occurring in small quantities chiefly with platinum. Symbol Pd; atomic weight 126.

Pallah (pæ·lă). 1806. [– Sechuana *p'hala*, Zulu *im-pala.*] An antelope (*Æpyceros melampus*) inhabiting parts of S. Africa.

Palled (pǫld). *ppl. a.* late ME. [f. PALL *v.*[1] + -ED[1].] †**1.** Enfeebled, impaired –1668. **2.** Of fermented liquor, etc.: Flat, stale, vapid. late ME. **3.** Satiated, cloyed, disgusted 1691.

Pallescent (păle·sĕnt), *a. rare.* 1657. [– *pallescent-*, pr. ppl. stem of L. *pallescere* become pale, f. *pallēre* be or look pale; see -ESCENT.] Growing or becoming pale. So **Palle·scence.**

Pallet[1] (pæ·lėt). [Late ME. *pail(l)et* – AFr. *paillete* straw (cf. Fr. dial. *paillet* bundle of straw), f. *paille* straw :– L. *palea* chaff, straw. For the phonology cf. MALLET.] **1.** A straw bed; a mattress; a small, poor, or mean bed or couch. Also *p.-bed*, etc. †**2.** *Naut.* A small room for ballast in the hold of a ship –1867.

Pallet[2] (pæ·lėt). 1558. [– (O)Fr. *palette*, dim. of *pale* spade, blade (with west.Fr. vocalism, the regular repr. being *pelle*) :– L. *pala* spade, shovel, rel. to *palus* stake; see PALE *sb.*[1], PEEL *sb.*[2], PALETTE.] **1.** A wooden instrument consisting of a flat blade or plate, with a handle attached; *spec.* that used by potters for shaping their work. **2.** = PALETTE 1. †**3.** A flat board, plate, or disc; e.g. the blade of an oar, the float of a paddle-wheel –1808. *spec.* **b.** *Brickmaking.* A board for carrying away a newly moulded brick 1839. **c.** Each of the series of discs in a chain-pump 1875. **4.** A projection on some part of a machine, which engages with the teeth of a wheel, and thus converts a reciprocating into a rotary motion, or *vice versa*; *esp.* a projection upon the pendulum or the arbor of the balance-wheel of a clock or watch, engaging with the escapement-wheel. [So in Fr.] 1704. **5.** In an organ: Any one of the valves in the upper part of the wind-chest 1840. **6.** *Bookbinding.* A tool for impressing letters, etc. on the back of a book, consisting of a metal block mounted on a handle 1875. **7.** *Conch.* An accessory valve in some molluscs.

Pallet[3] (pæ·lėt). 1562. [dim. of PALE *sb.*[1] 5.] *Her.* An ordinary resembling the pale, but of half its breadth.

Pallial (pæ·liăl), *a.* 1836. [f. PALLIUM + -AL[1].] *Zool.* Of or pertaining to the pallium or mantle of a mollusc (or of a brachiopod).

†**Pa·lliament.** *rare.* 1588. [– OFr. *palliement*, f. *pallier* – L. *palliare* to cloak; see PALLIATE *v.*, -MENT.] The white gown of a candidate for the Roman consulship *Tit. A.* I. i. 182.

†**Pa·lliard.** 1484. [– (O)Fr. *paillard* (OFr. also *-art*), f. *paille* straw; see -ARD.] A professional beggar or vagabond (who sleeps on straw in barns, etc.); *transf.* a low knave; a debauchee –1851.

Palliasse (pæ·liæs). Formerly **paillasse.** 1506. [– Fr. *paillasse* – It. *pagliacchio* :– Rom. **paleaceum*, f. L. *palea* straw, chaff.] A straw mattress; now, usu., an under-mattress stuffed with straw, or the like.

Palliate (pæ·li,ět), *ppl. a.* 1548. [– L. *palliatus* cloaked (f. *pallium*); afterwards pa. pple. of late L. *palliare* (see next); see -ATE[2].] †**A.** as *pa. pple.* Cloaked, covered, concealed; mitigated –1650. **B.** as *adj.* †**1.** Cloaked; disguised –1648. †**2.** Of a cure: Superficial or temporary –1679. **3.** *Zool.* Having a PALLIUM (sense 3); tectibranchiate 1890.

Palliate (pæ·li,e^{i}t), *v.* 1548. [– *palliat-*, pa. ppl. stem of late L. *palliare* cover, hide, conceal (Augustine; *palliatus* cloaked, fig. protected, is earlier), f. PALLIUM; see -ATE[3].] †**1.** *trans.* To cover with or as with a cloak –1656. †**2.** *fig.* To hide, conceal, disguise –1812. **3.** To alleviate the symptoms of a disease; to mitigate the sufferings of; to ease 1588. **4.** To represent (an evil) as less than it really is; to extenuate, excuse 1634. †**5.** To moderate, qualify or tone down. Also *absol.* or *intr.* To take up a more moderate position, to compromise. –1796.

2. There was no palliating the fact MAR. EDGEWORTH. **3.** That which cannot be cured must be palliated 1876. **4.** They endeavoured to p. what they could not justify 1777. Hence **Pa·lliator. Pa·lliatory** *a.* palliating.

Palliation (pæli,ē^i·ʃən). 1577. [– (O)Fr. *palliation* – med.L. *palliatio*, f. as prec.; see -ION.] †**1.** The action of palliating; that which serves to conceal or hide –1794. **2.** Extenuation, excuse; often in phr. *in p. of* 1605. **3.** Alleviation, mitigation, relief 1626.

2. The tyrant's plea of necessity in p. of his evil deeds 1867.

Palliative (pæ·li,ătiv), *a.* and *sb.* 1543. [– (O)Fr. *palliatif, -ive* or med.L. *palliativus*, f. as prec.; see -IVE.] **A.** *adj.* †**1.** Serving to cloak or conceal –1656. **2.** Serving to relieve (disease) superficially or temporarily, or to mitigate (pain, etc.) 1543. **3.** Tending to extenuate or excuse 1779. **B.** *sb.* That which palliates; a palliative agent 1748; an extenuating representation 1724. Hence **Pa·lliatively** *adv.*

Pallid (pæ·lid), *a.* 1590. [– L. *pallidus*, rel. to *pallēre* be pale; see -ID[1].] Lacking depth or intensity of colour, wan, pale. Chiefly *poet.* bef. 1800, exc. in *Bot.*

P. death SPENSER. A blush suffused Her p. cheek SOUTHEY. Hence **Pa·llid-ly** *adv.*, **-ness. Palli·dity**, pallor.

Pallio- (pæ:lio), comb. form of PALLIUM, used in zool. terms relating to the pallium or mantle of a mollusc, etc.; as **Pallio-branchiate** (-bræ·ŋkiĕt) *a.*, belonging to the *Palliobranchiata* or *Brachiopoda*, the tubes of the mantle being supposed to be branchia or gills; etc.

‖**Pallium** (pæ·liŏm). *Pl.* **pallia.** 1564. [– L. *pallium*, rel. to PALLA long wide outer garment of Roman ladies, prob. of Gr. origin, but nothing appropriate is known.] **1.** *Antiq.* A large rectangular cloak or mantle worn by men, chiefly among the Greeks; esp. by philosophers, and by early Christian ascetics (= Gr. ἱμάτιον, HIMATION.) **2.** *Eccl.* A vestment of wool worn by patriarchs and metropolitans (in R.C.Ch. conferred by the Pope) now consisting of a narrow ring-like band lying over the shoulders with a piece pendent thereform at the front and the back. Also, a figure of this, as on the arms of the archbishopric of Canterbury. 1670. **3. a.** *Zool.* The MANTLE of a mollusc (or of a brachiopod) 1872. **b.** *Ornith.* The MANTLE of a bird (*rare*). **4.** *Meteorol.* A sheet of cirro-stratus cloud uniformly covering the whole sky 1883.

Pall-mall (pel,mel, pæl,mæl). Also formerly **pell-mell**, etc. 1568. [– Fr. †*pal(le mail(le* – It. *pallamaglio*, f. *palla* ball (collateral var. of *balla* BALL *sb.*[1]) + *maglio* mallet; see MALL[1], MALLET *sb.*[1]] †**1.** A mallet for striking a ball; *spec.* that used in the game described in 2. –1611. **2.** A game in which a boxwood ball was driven through an iron ring suspended at a height in a long alley 1598. †**3.** The alley in which the game was played –1688. **b.** The name of a street developed from one of these alleys in London, now the centre of London club life 1656.

‖**Pallone** (pallō·ne). 1865. [It., augm. of *palla* ball.] An Italian game, played with a large ball struck with a wooden guard, worn over the hand and wrist.

Pallor (pæ·lŏɹ). 1656. [– L. *pallor*, f. *pall-* in *pallēre* be pale; see -OR 1.] Paleness.

Pally, *a.* 1895. [f. PAL + -Y[1].] See s.v. PAL.

Palm (pām), *sb.*[1] [OE. *palm, palma, palme* = OS., OHG. *palma* (Du. *palm*, G. *palme*), ON. *pálmr*; Gmc. – L. *palma* PALM *sb.*[2] (the palm-leaf was likened to the hand with the fingers extended). In ME. the descendant of the OE. words coincided with the repr. of AFr. (mod. Fr.) *palme*, OFr. *paume*.] **1.** Any tree or shrub of the N.O. *Palmæ* or *Palmaceæ*, a large family of monocotyledons, chiefly tropical, and variously useful to man. Also applied *fig.* to a person 1800.

Palms have the stem usually upright and unbranched, a head of very large pinnate or fan-shaped leaves, and fruit of various forms (nut, drupe, or berry). The palm of Scripture is the date-palm.

b. With defining words, denoting various species of the order *Palmæ*, as **Bamboo P.**, DATE-*p.*, etc. **2.** A 'branch' or leaf of the palm-tree, esp. as anciently carried or worn as a symbol of victory or triumph, and still on festival occasions ME. **3.** *fig.* Victory, triumph; supreme excellence, prize. late ME. **4.** A branch or sprig of any of several trees and shrubs substituted in northern countries, esp. in celebrating Palm Sunday, for the true palm; also applied to the plants themselves (e.g. the willow). late ME.

1. She dwelt vnder ye palme of Debbora betwene Rama & Bethel COVERDALE *Judg.* 4:5. *fig.* You shall see him a Palme in Athens againe SHAKS. **2.** Hauyng in her hande the palme of vyctory LYDG. **3.** He disputed the p. of eloquence with Cicero himself GIBBON. Phr. *To bear the p., yield the p.*, etc.

attrib. and *Comb.*: **p.-branch**, a leaf of the palm-tree with its stalk, used as a symbol of victory, as a decoration, etc.; **-butter**, palm-oil in the solid state; **-cat, -civet**, (*a*) a viverrine animal of the genus *Paradoxurus* or sub-family *Paradoxurinæ*, which frequents palm-trees; (*b*) the ocelot; **-crab**, the tree-crab (*Birgus latro*), which climbs palm-trees for the fruit; **-kernel**, the kernel of the drupaceous fruit of the Oil P.; **-sugar**, see JAGGERY; **-swift**, a small Jamaican swift (*Micropus phœnicobia*) which nests in palm-leaves; **-toddy**, the juice of the Oil P., allowed to ferment, and used as a drink; **-weevil**, any one of various weevils whose larvæ bore into palm-trees; **-willow**, any species of willow the sprigs of which are used instead of palm-branches (see 4), esp. *Salix caprea*; **-wine**, wine made from the sap of the palm-tree; **-worm**, (*a*) some large American centipede; (*b*) the larva of a palm-weevil.

Palm (pām), *sb.*[2] [ME. *paume* – (O)Fr. *paume* :– L. *palma* palm of the hand, part of the trunk of a tree from which branches spring, palm-leaf, palm-tree (see prec.); the ME. form was subseq. assim. to the Latin.] **I. 1.** The part of the hand between the wrist and the fingers, esp. its inner surface. **b.** The part of a glove that covers the palm 1852. **2.** The flat expanded part of the horn in some deer, from which finger-like points project. late ME. **3.** A flat widened part at the end of an arm or armlike projection 1526; *spec.* the blade of an oar 1513; the broad triangular part of an anchor, the inner surface of the fluke 1706. **4.** An instrument used by sailmakers instead of a thimble 1769.

1. *fig.* Let me tell you Cassius, you your selfe Are much condemn'd to haue an itching Palme SHAKS. *To grease* or *oil* (one's) *p.*, to bribe.

II. †**1.** A game resembling tennis, in which a ball was struck with the palm of the hand (= Fr. *la paume, jeu de la paume*). **b.** The ball used in this game. –1530. **2.** A measure of length, equivalent either to the breadth of the palm, i.e. about three to four inches, or to the length of the hand, i.e. about seven to nine inches 1485.

attrib. and *Comb.*, as **p.-grease** (*joc.*), money given as a douceur or bribe; so **-greasing**, petty bribery; **-play** = Sense II. 1; **-veined** *a. Bot.*, palmately veined. Hence **Pa·lmful**, as much as the p. will hold.

Palm (pām), *v.* 1673. [f. PALM *sb.*[2]: in most senses, orig. slang or low colloq.] **1.** *trans.* To touch with the palm, or pass the palm across; to handle; to stroke with the hand; to shake hands with. Also *intr.* 1678. **2.** *trans.* To conceal in the palm of the hand, as in cheating at cards or dice, or in juggling 1673. **3.** To impose (a thing) fraudulently (*on* or *upon* a person); to pass *off* by trickery or fraud 1679. **4.** To 'grease the palm' of, bribe, 'tip' 1747.

2. Is't I who cog or p. the dice GAY. **3.** Thinking you cou'd pawme such stuffe on me 1679. **4.** The heads of this particular firm..admit that they 'palmed' right and left 1890. Hence **Palmed** (pāmd) *ppl. a.*, concealed in the palm. **Pa·lmer** *sb.*[2] one who palms or conceals in the hand.

Palmaceous (pælmē^i·ʃəs), *a.* 1730. [f. mod.L. *Palmaceæ* fem. pl. (f. L. *palma* PALM *sb.*[1]) + -OUS.] *Bot.* Of or belonging to the N.O. *Palmaceæ, Palmæ*, or Palms.

Palma Christi (pæ·lmă kri·sti). 1548. [med.L. (= palm or hand of Christ).] **1.** The Castor-oil plant, *Ricinus communis*, having leaves of a hand-like shape. †**2.** A name for species of *Orchis* having palmate tubers, as *O. maculata* and *O. latifolia* –1597.

Palmar (pæ·lmăɹ). 1831. [– L. *palmaris*, f. *palma* PALM *sb.*[2] and -AR[1].] **A.** *adj. Anat.* Pertaining to, situated in, or connected with the palm of the hand (or the analogous part of the fore-foot of a quadruped).

P. arch, the continuation of the radial artery (*deep p. arch*) and that of the ulnar artery (*superficial p. arch*) in the palm.

B. *sb.* **1.** *Anat.* A palmar muscle, nerve, etc. 1890. **2.** *Zool.* Name for certain joints in the 'arms' of a crinoid. (Also in L. form *palmare*, pl. *-ia*.) 1877.

Palmary (pæ·lmări), *a.*[1] 1657. [– L. *palmarius* that carries off the palm of victory, f. *palma* PALM *sb.*[1]; see -ARY[1].] That bears, or is worthy to bear, the palm; holding the first place, pre-eminent. So **Palma·rian** *a.* (*rare*).

Emendations of the kind which in old days would have been called 'palmary' 1888.

Pa·lmary, *a.*[2] 1696. [– L. *palmaris*, f. *palma* PALM *sb.*[2]; see -ARY[2].] Pertaining to the palm of the hand; palmar.

Palmate (pæ·lme^{i}t), *sb.* 1838. [f. PALM(IC + -ATE[4].] *Chem.* A salt of palmic acid.

Palmate (pæ·lmĕt), *a.* 1760. [– L. *palmatus*, f. *palma* PALM *sb.*[2] + -ATE[2] 2.] *Nat. Hist.* **1.** Of a form like that of an open palm or hand; applied to parts of a plant or animal which have narrow or spreading divisions like fingers projecting or radiating as from a palm. **2.** Of the foot of a bird: Having the toes connected by an expanded membrane; webbed 1826. So **Pa·lmated** *a.* **Palma·tion**, formation; *concr.* each of the divisions of a p. structure. Hence **Pa·lmate-ly** *adv.*

Palmati- (pælmē^i·ti, pælmæ·ti), comb. form of L. *palmatus* PALMATE, in botanical adjs. relating to leaves. **Palma·tifid** [L. *-fidus* split] palmately cleft at least half-way to the base. **Palma:tilo·bate, Palma·tilobed**, palmately divided with rounded divisions or lobes. **Palma:tipa·rted, -pa·rtite** [L. *partitus* divided] palmately divided nearly to the base; so **Palma·tisect, Palma:tise·cted** [L. *sectus* cut].

Palmchrist (pā·mkrist). 1611. Anglicized f. PALMA CHRISTI (sense 1).

†**Palmed** (pāmd), *a.* 1486. [f. PALM *sb.*[2] + -ED[2]; repr. L. *palmatus*.] Having a 'palm', as a deer's horn; palmate; carrying palmate horns –1766.

Palmer (pā·məɹ), *sb.*[1] ME. [– AFr. *palmer, -our*, OFr. *palmier* :– med.L. *palmarius* (XII), f. L. *palma* PALM *sb.*[1]; see -ER[2] 2.] **1.** A pilgrim who had returned from the Holy Land, in token of which he carried a palm-branch or palm-leaf; also, an itinerant monk under a perpetual vow of poverty; often simply = *pilgrim*. **2.** A palmer-worm 1538. **b.** *Angling.* An artificial fly resembling this; a hackle 1651.

1. The Pilgrim had some home, or dwelling place, but the P. had none. The Pilgrim travelled to some certain designed place, or places, but the P. to all. The Pilgrim went at his own charges, but the P. profest wilful poverty, and went upon Alms 1674. Hence **Pa·lmer** *v.* (*Sc.* and *north.*), to wander about like a p. or vagrant.

Palmerin (pæ·lmĕrin). 1611. [f. name of a hero of romances, *Palmerin de Oliva*.] Any of the heroes of the Palmerin romances; hence, any hero of the age of chivalry.

Pa·lmer-wo·rm. 1560. [f. PALMER *sb.*[1] + WORM *sb.*] Name for various hairy caterpillars of migratory or wandering habits destructive to vegetation; in N. America, the larva of a tineid moth, *Ypsilophus pometellus*, destructive to apple-leaves.

Palmette (pælme·t). 1850. [– Fr. *palmette*, dim. of *palme*; see PALM *sb.*[1], -ETTE.] *Archæol.* An ornament with narrow divisions or digitations, somewhat resembling a palm-leaf.

Palmetto (pælme·to). 1583. [– Sp. *palmito* dwarf fan-palm, dim. of *palma* PALM *sb.*[1]; later assim. to It. dims. in *-etto*.] Name for several smaller species of palms, esp. the dwarf fan-palm, *Chamærops humilis*, of S. Europe and N. Africa, and the cabbage palmetto, *Sabal palmetto*, of the South-eastern U.S.

Royal P., *Sabal umbraculifera* and *Thrinax parviflora*, of the W. Indies; **Saw P.**, *Chamærops serrulata*; etc.

attrib. and *Comb.*, as *p. hat, leaf, thatch*, etc.; **p. flag**, the flag of the State of South Carolina, which bears a figure of a cabbage p. tree; so **P. State**, a name for South Carolina.

Palmi- (pælmi), comb. form of L. *palma* PALM *sb.*[1] and [2], as in **Pa·lmigrade** *a. Zool.* = PLANTIGRADE; **Pa·lmilobed** *a.*, palmately lobed; etc.

Palmic (pæ·lmik), *a.* 1838. [– Fr. *palmique* (Boudet 1832), f. L. *palma* (in PALMA CHRISTI); see -IC.] *Chem.* Of or pertaining to castor-oil; in *p. acid*, obtained by saponifying palmin and decomposing with hydrochloric acid; now called *ricinelaïdic acid.*

Palmiferous (pælmi·fĕrəs), *a.* 1664. [– L. *palmifer* palm-bearing + -OUS; see -FEROUS.] Carrying 'palms' or palm-branches.

Palmin (pæ·lmin). 1838. [– Fr. *palmine* (Boudet 1832), f. L. *palma* PALM *sb.*[1]; see -IN[1].] *Chem.* A fatty substance obtained by treating castor-oil with nitric peroxide. Now called *ricinelaïdin.*

Palmiped, -pede (pæ·lmiped, -pīd), *a.* and *sb.* 1610. [– L. *palmipes, -ped-*, f. *palma* PALM *sb.*[2] + *pes* foot.] **A.** *adj.* Of a bird: Having palmate feet 1661. **B.** *sb.* A web-footed bird 1610.

Palmist (pā·mist). 1886. [Back-formation f. PALMISTRY.] One who practises palmistry.

Palmister (pā·mistəɹ). Now *rare.* 1500. [Back-formation f. PALMISTRY.] = prec.

Palmistry (pā·mistri). late ME. [(*Pawmestry*, Lydgate), f. PALM *sb.*[2], of obscure formation, alt. to *-istry* XVI, perh. after *sophistry*.] **1.** The art or practice of telling persons' characters or fortunes by inspection of the palm of the hand; chiromancy. **2.** Applied allusively to pocket-picking, bribery, etc.; also used erron. as = sleight of hand 1698.

Palmite (pæ·lməit). 1834. [– Sp. and Pg. *palmito* PALMETTO, S. Afr. Du. *palmiet*.] A S. Afr. aquatic plant, *Prionium palmita* (N.O. *Juncaceæ*), growing in the beds of rivers, and bearing a tuft of large serrated sword-shaped leaves, affording a strong fibre.

Palmitic (pælmi·tik), *a.* 1857. [– Fr. *palmitique* (Frémy 1840), arbitrarily f. *palme* PALM *sb.*[1]; see -IC.] *Chem.* Of or obtained from palm-oil; in *p. acid*: a fatty acid ($C_{16}H_{32}O_2$) contained in palm-oil and in vegetable and animal fats generally. Hence **Palmitate** (pæ·lmitĕt), a salt of this.

Palmitin (pæ·lmitin). 1857. [– Fr. *palmitine* (Frémy 1840), f. as prec.; see -IN[1].] *Chem.* A natural fat contained in palm-oil and many other fats, obtained as a white solid, the tripalmitate of glyceryl; *pl.* applied to the palmitates of glyceryl or glycerides of palmitic acid in general (cf. *tripalmitin*).

Pa·lm-oil. 1627. [In sense 1 f. PALM *sb.*[1] + OIL; in 2 f. PALM *sb.*[2], with joc. allusion to sense 1.] **1.** Oil produced by various species of palm-tree; *esp.* that obtained from the fruit-pulp of the Oil Palm (*Elæis guineensis*) of West Africa; it is used as food by the natives, and elsewhere for making soap and candles, etc. Also *attrib.* 1705. **2.** *joc.* That with which the palm is 'greased'; money given as a bribe; a 'tip' 1627.

2. Palm-oil will always produce temporary blindness in the officials 1896.

Pa·lm Su·nday. [OE. *palm-sunnandæģ*, tr. eccl.L. *Dominica Palmarum*.] The Sunday next before Easter, observed in commemoration of Christ's triumphal entry into Jerusalem by processions in which palms (see PALM *sb.*[1] 4) are carried. Also *attrib.*

Palm-tree (pā·m,trī). OE. = PALM *sb.*[1] 1. **b.** Applied pop. to other trees, e.g. a willow, a yew-tree 1653.

Palmy (pā·mi), *a.* 1602. [f. PALM *sb.*[1] + -Y[1].] **1.** Containing or abounding in palms; of or pertaining to a palm or palms; palm-like. Chiefly *poet.* 1667. **2.** *fig.* Bearing or worthy to 'bear the palm'; triumphant, flourishing; esp. in *p. days.*

2. In the most high and p. state of Rome SHAKS.

Palmyra (pælməi^ə·ră). 1698. [Formerly *palmeira* – Pg. *palmeira* palm-tree. Erron. conformed in spelling to that of *Palmyra*, Gr. Παλμύρα, in Syria.] A species of palm (*Borassus flabelliformis*), with rounded fan-shaped leaves; commonly cultivated in India and Ceylon, and used as timber, for thatch, matting, umbrellas, hats, etc. Also *attrib.*

‖**Palolo** (pălō^u·lo). 1895. [Native name in Samoa and Tonga.] A nereid worm (*Palolo viridis*), abundant in parts of the Pacific, and esteemed as food by the natives.

Palp (pælp), *sb.* 1835. [– Fr. *palpe* or L. *palpus* feeler.] *Zool.* = PALPUS. Hence **Pa·lpless** *a.*, having no palpi.

Palp (pælp), *v. rare.* 1534. [– L. *palpare* touch softly.] *trans.* To touch, feel; to handle gently, pat. Also *fig.* To speak fair, flatter, cajole.

Palpable (pæ·lpăb'l), *a.* late ME. [– late L. *palpabilis*, f. L. *palpare*; see next, -ABLE.] **1.** That can be touched, felt, or handled; tangible, sensible. **b.** *Med.* Perceptible by palpation 1897. **2.** *transf.* Readily perceived by any of the other senses; perceptible; noticeable, patent. late ME. **3.** *fig.* Easily perceived; plain, evident, apparent, obvious 1545.

1. A hit, a very p. hit SHAKS. *P. darkness*, thick, gross, utter darkness. **2.** The venison pasty was p. beef PEPYS. **3.** Opinions of p. idolatrie HOOKER. P. falsehoods COWPER, fables 1867. Hence **Palpabi·lity, Pa·lpableness. Pa·lpably** *adv.*

Palpate (pæ·lpe^it), *v.* 1849. [– *palpat-*, pa. ppl. stem of L. *palpare*; see PALP *v.*, -ATE[3].] *trans.* To examine by the sense of touch; to feel; *spec.* as a method of medical examination. So **Palpa·tion**, touching; gentle handling; *spec.* medical examination by feeling 1483.

‖**Palpebra** (pæ·lpĭbră). *Pl.* **-æ.** 1706. [L.] *Anat.* An eyelid. Hence **Pa·lpebral** *a.* of or pertaining to the eyelids. **Pa·lpebrate** *a.* having eyelids.

Palpi, pl. of PALPUS.

Palpicorn (pæ·lpikǭɹn), *a.* and *sb.* 1882. [f. mod.L. *palpicornes*, pl. of *palpicornis*, f. PALPUS + *cornu* horn. Cf. Fr. *palpicorne* (Cuvier).] **a.** *adj.* Having palpi like horns or antennæ; *spec.* of or pertaining to the *Palpicornes*, a tribe of pentamerous beetles having slender palpi usually longer than the antennæ. **b.** *sb.* A beetle of the tribe *Palpicornes* 1882.

Palpifer (pæ·lpifəɹ). 1841. [f. L. *palpus* PALP *sb.* + *-fer* bearing, bearer; see -FEROUS.] *Entom.* An outer lobe of the maxilla, bearing the maxillary palp. Hence **Palpi·ferous** *a.* bearing palps, esp. maxillary palps.

Palpiform (pæ·lpifǭɹm), *a.* 1819. [f. as prec. + -FORM. Cf. Fr. *palpiforme*.] Having the form of or resembling a palp.

Palpiger (pæ·lpidʒəɹ). 1841. [f. as prec. + *-ger* carrying, carrier; cf. -GEROUS.] *Entom.* That part of the labium of an insect which bears the labial palpi. So **Palpi·gerous** *a.* bearing palpi.

Palpitant (pæ·lpităṅt), *a.* 1837. [– Fr. *palpitant*, pr. pple. of *palpiter*; see next, -ANT.] Palpitating.

Palpitate (pæ·lpite^it), *v.* 1623. [– *palpitat-*, pa. ppl. stem of L. *palpitare*, frequent. of *palpare* touch soothingly; see -ATE[3]. Cf. Fr. *palpiter*.] **1.** *intr.* To pulsate rapidly and strongly, as the result of exercise, strong emotion, or as a symptom of disease; to throb. **b.** *gen.* To move with a vibrating motion 1849. **2.** *trans.* To cause to pulsate rapidly or throb 1790.

1. b. Fountains palpitating in the heat LONGF. Hence **Pa·lpitating** *ppl. a.*, **-ly** *adv.*

Palpitation (pælpitē^i·ʃən). 1604. [– L. *palpitatio*, f. as prec.; see -ION. Cf. Fr. *palpitation*.] **1.** The action of palpitating; *spec.* increased activity of the heart arising from disease of the organ itself or other parts of the body. **2.** *gen.* A trembling or quivering motion; a tremble 1677.

Palpocil (pæ·lpŏsil). Also **palpicil.** 1871. [f. *palpo-*, taken as comb. form of L. *palpus* PALP + *cilium* eyelash.] *Zool.* A fine hairlike palp or palpus; a tactile hair.

Palpon (pæ·lpǫn). 1888. [f. L. *palpus*, after *siphon*.] *Zool.* An individual member of a siphonophoran colony developed as a feeler; a dactylozooid.

‖**Palpus** (pæ·lpŏs). *Pl.* **-pi** (pəi). 1813. [L. *palpus* feeler, f. *palpare* PALP *v.*] *Zool.* A jointed organ attached to the labia, maxillæ, and mandibles of insects, arachnids, etc., and serving as an organ of sense, a feeler. Also, each of the two fleshy lobes at the sides of the mouth of bivalve molluscs. Hence **Pa·lpal** *a.* of the nature of, pertaining to, or serving as a palp or feeler.

Palsgrave (pǭ·lzgrē^iv). *Hist.* 1548. [– early Du. *paltsgrave* (mod. *paltsgraaf*), f. *palts* palatinate + †*grave, graaf* count, GRAVE *sb.*[3]] A count palatine. So **Pa·lsgravine,** a countess palatine.

Palsied (pǭ·lzid), *ppl. a.* 1550. [f. PALSY *sb.* or *v.* + -ED.] Affected with palsy, paralysed; *fig.* tottering, trembling.

Palstave (pǭ·lstē^iv). Also **-staff,** ‖**paalstave, -stab.** 1851. [– Da. *paalstav* :– ON. *pálstavr*, f. *páll* hoe, spade (– L. *palus* PALE *sb.*[1]) + *stafr* STAVE.] *Archæol.* A form of celt of bronze, or other metal, shaped so as to fit into a split handle, instead of having a socket into which the handle fits.

Palsy (pǭ·lzi), *sb.* (*a.*) [ME. *palesi, parlesi* – (O)Fr. *paralisie* (AFr. *parlesie*) – Rom. **paralisia*, for L. *paralysis* – Gr. παράλυσις PARALYSIS.] **1.** = PARALYSIS 1. **2.** *fig.* Any influence which destroys, or seriously impairs, activity or sensibility; a condition of utter powerlessness; an irresistible tremor ME.

1. He seith to the sike man in palasie..ryse vp, take thi bed WYCLIF *Mark* 2:10. **Bell's p.,** paralysis of the facial nerve. **Creeping p.,** gradually growing paralysis. **Scrivener's p.** = *writer's cramp*, see WRITER. **Shaking p.,** tremulous paralysis in the aged. **2.** So thoroughly does the region now lie under the p. of Mohammedanism 1848.

†**B.** *adj.* (always *attrib.*, and app. attrib. use of sb.) Affected with palsy, palsied –1703.

Pa·lsy, *v.* 1582. [f. prec.] **1.** *trans.* To affect with palsy, to paralyse. Chiefly *fig.* 1615. **2.** *intr.* To shake or tremble as if palsied (*nonce-use*); to become palsied (*rare*) 1582. Hence **Pa·lsying** *ppl. a.*

Palter (pǭ·ltəɹ), *v.* 1538. [Of unkn. origin; perh. ult. rel. to PALTRY. Cf. †*pelt* haggle, †*pelter* peddling person.] †**1.** *intr.* and *trans.* To speak indistinctly or idly; to mumble, babble –1575. **2.** *intr.* To shift, shuffle, equivocate, prevaricate; to deal crookedly; to play fast and loose. Usu. const. *with.* 1601. **b.** To haggle in bargaining; to huckster in matters of duty or honour 1611. †**c.** *trans.* To barter; to corrupt. MILT. †**3.** *trans.* To squander –1706.

2. These Iugling Fiends.., That p. with vs in a double sence, That keepe the word of promise to our eare, And breake it to our hope SHAKS. **b.** Only fools and cowards p. about morality 1883. Hence **Pa·lterer,** one who palters, a shuffler, trifler 1589. †**Pa·ltering** *ppl. a.* trifling, worthless, paltry.

†**Pa·lterly,** *a.* 1667. [app. alt. f. PALTRY *a.*, as if f. PALTER *v.* + -LY[1].] Paltry, mean, shabby –1825.

†**Pa·ltock.** [ME. *paltock* (XIV), app. identical with OFr. *paltoke* (XIV) peasant's smock, AL. *paltokkus* (XIV) sleeved doublet, repr. by mod. Fr. PALETOT cloak.] A short coat, sleeved doublet, or 'jack' –1658.

Paltry (pǭ·ltri), *sb.* Now only *dial.* 1556. [app. f. *palt*, var. of PELT *sb.*[3] Cf. next, and PELTRY[2].] Refuse, rubbish, trash; anything worthless.

Paltry (pǭ·ltri), *a.* 1570. [adj. use (cf. *trumpery*) of prec.; cf. MLG. *palter-* in *palterlappen* rags, LG. *paltrig* ragged, torn. Parallel formations are PELT *sb.*[3], PELTING *a.*, PELTRY[2]; perh. of LG. origin.] Rubbishy, trashy, worthless; petty; despicable.

The p. trick was successful 1867. A p. fellow 1874. Hence **Pa·ltriness.**

Paludal (păl^iū·dăl, pæ·l^iudăl), *a.* 1818. [f. L. *palus, palud-* marsh + -AL[1].] Chiefly *Med.* and *Path.* Of or pertaining to or produced by a marsh; malarial.

Paludament (păl¹ū·dăměnt). 1614. [– L. *paludamentum.*] A military cloak worn by Roman generals and chief officers; hence, a royal cloak; a herald's coat.

Paludi- (bef. a vowel **palud-**), a formative element f. L. *palus, palud-* marsh, in **Palu·dic** *a.*, of or pertaining to marshes; **Palu·dicole** *a.*, inhabiting marshes; etc.

‖**Paludina** (pæl¹udəi·nă). 1833. [mod.L., f. L. *palus, palud-* + *-inus, -ina*; see -INA².] *Zool.* A genus of freshwater gastropod molluscs, also called *pond-snails.*

Paludine (pæ·l¹udin, -əin), *a.* 1858. [f. L. *palus, palud-* + -INE¹.] Of or pertaining to a marsh. So **Palu·dinal, Palu·dinous** *adjs.*

Paludism (pæ·l¹udiz'm). 1890. [f. as prec. + -ISM.] *Path.* = MALARIA b.

Paludous (păl¹ū·dəs), *a. rare.* 1803. [– L. *paludosus* marshy; see prec. and -OUS.] Of or belonging to marshes, marshy; inhabiting marshes. So **Paludo·se** *a.*

‖**Palus** (pē¹·lŏs). *Pl.* **-li.** 1872. [L. *palus* stake.] *Biol.* In corals, one of the thin, upright, calcareous laminæ or plates, which extend up from the bottom of a corallite to the calix, and are connected by their outer edges with the septa. Hence the dim. ‖**Pa·lulus**, pl. **paluli.**

Palustral (pălɒ·străl), *a. rare.* 1879. [f. L. *palustris* (f. *palus* marsh) + -AL¹.] Pertaining to or inhabiting marshes. So **Palu·strian** *a.* 1607; **Palu·strine** *a.* 1839.

Paly (pē¹·li), *a.*¹ Chiefly *poet.* 1560. [f. PALE *a.* + -Y¹.] Pale, or somewhat pale. 2 *Hen. VI*, III. ii. 141.

Paly (pē¹·li), *a.*² 1486. [– (O)Fr. *palé*, f. *pal* PALE *sb.*¹; see -Y⁵.] *Her.* Said of the shield (or of a bearing) when divided palewise.

P. bendy, divided both palewise and bendwise.

Pam (pæm). 1685. [app. abbrev. of Fr. *pamphile*, name of the card game and of the knave of clubs in it; according to Littré – Gr. name Πάμφιλος 'beloved of all'.] **1.** The knave of clubs, esp. in five-card loo, in which this card is the highest trump. **2.** Name of a card-game, akin to nap, in which the knave of clubs was the highest trump card 1691. Hence †**Pam-child,** 'knave-child', male child. H. WALPOLE.

‖**Pampa** (pæ·mpă), usu. *pl.* **pampas** (pæ·mpăz, -ăs). 1704. [– Sp. *pampa* – Quechua *pampa* plain.] The name given to the vast treeless plains of S. America south of the Amazon. (The similar plains north of the Amazon are called *llanos.*)

attrib. and *Comb.*, as *P. Indian*; **p.-cat,** a wild cat of the Pampas (*Felis pajeros*); **p. deer,** a small deer of S. America, *Cariacus campestris*; **p. rice,** a variety of the common Millet (*Sorghum vulgare*), with a drooping panicle.

Pa·mpas-gra:ss. 1850. [f. prec.] A gigantic grass, *Gynerium argenteum* or *Cortaderia argentea*, having ample silky panicles of silvery hue borne on stalks rising to the height of twelve of fourteen feet; a native of S. America.

Pampean, pampæan (pæmpī·ăn, pæ·mpĭăn), *a.* 1839. [f. PAMPA, after *Hyblæan*, etc.] Of or pertaining to the Pampas.

Pampelmous(s)e, var. of POMPELMOOSE.

Pamper (pæ·mpəɹ), *v.* late ME. [In ME. also in pa. pple. *forpampred* (Chaucer); frequent. (see -ER⁴) of synon. †*pamp* (XIV), dial. *pomp*; prob. of LDu. origin; cf. G. dial. *pampen, pampfen* cram, gorge, WFlem. *pamperen*, perh. f. nasalized var. of the base of PAP *sb.*²] **1.** *trans.* To cram with food; to over-indulge with rich food. *Obs.* exc. as in b. **b.** To over-indulge (a person) in his tastes and likings generally; to bring up daintily 1530. †**2.** *intr.* To feed luxuriously –1653.

1. After dinner I went to Snowhill; there I was pampered, and had an uneasy night JOHNSON. *P. up*, to feed up. **b.** *fig.* To p. his own vanity at the price of another's shame FIELDING. Hence **Pa·mperer.**

Pampered (pæ·mpəɹd), *ppl. a.* 1529. [f. prec. + -ED¹.] †Over-fed; luxuriously fed; over-indulged, spoiled by luxury. Also *fig.*

Pamper'd metafors MILT. P. children 1890. Hence **Pa·mperedness.**

‖**Pampero** (pămpē·ro). 1818. [Sp., f. PAMPA + *-ero* suffix.] A piercing cold wind which blows from the Andes across the S. American pampas to the Atlantic.

Pamphlet (pæ·mflět), *sb.* ME. [A generalized use of *Pamphilet* or *Panflet*, a familiar name of a 12th c. L. amatory poem or comedy called *Pamphilus, seu de Amore.* For the termination cf. *Catonet* the Distichs of Cato, *Esopet* the Fables of Æsop.] **1.** A small treatise occupying fewer pages than would make a book, composed and issued as a separate work; always unbound, with or without paper covers. **2.** More spec., a treatise of the size and form above described on some subject of current or topical interest 1592. **3.** *attrib.*, as *p. form, war*, etc. 1646.

1. In regard of the smalnesse of it, it [this Sermon] is indeed but as a little P. 1623. **2.** Grattan's incomparable speech..ought to make a little separate p. BURKE.

†**Pa·mphlet,** *v.* 1592. [f. prec.] **a.** *intr.* To write a pamphlet or pamphlets. **b.** *trans.* To report or describe in a pamphlet. Chiefly in **Pa·mphleting** *vbl. sb.* and *ppl. a.* –1716.

Pamphleteer (pæmflĕtī°·ɹ), *sb.* 1642. [f. prec. + -EER¹.] A writer of pamphlets. (Often contemptuous.)

Pamphletee·r, *v.* 1715. [f. prec.] *intr.* To write and issue pamphlets. Chiefly in **Pamphletee·ring** *vbl. sb.* and *ppl. a.*

†**Pampina·tion.** late ME. [– L. *pampinatio*, f. *pampinat-*, pa. ppl. stem of *pampinare*, f. *pampinus* vine-shoot; see -ION.] The pruning or trimming of vines –1846.

Pampiniform (pæmpi·nifǭɹm), *a.* 1668. [f. L. *pampinus* vine-tendril + -FORM.] *Anat.* Curled like a vine-tendril; applied *esp.* to a convoluted plexus of veins proceeding from the testis or ovary.

Pampootie (pæ̇mpū·ti). *local Irish.* 1846. [Of unkn. origin.] A kind of sandal of undressed cowskin sewn together and tied across the instep. Used in the Isles of Aran.

Pamprodactylous (pæmprodæ·ktiləs), *a.* 1899. [f. Gr. παμ- PAN- + πρό before + δάκτυλος finger or toe + -OUS.] *Ornith.* Having all the toes pointing forwards, as the colies, and a few other birds.

Pan (pæn), *sb.*¹ [OE. *panne* = OFris., OS. *panna*, (M)LG., MDu. *panne* (Du. *pan*), OHG. *phanna* (G. *pfanne*) :– WGmc. **panna*, an early (IV–V) adoption, poss. from a pop. var. of L. *patina* (see PATEN).] **1.** A vessel, of metal or earthenware, for domestic purposes, usu. broad and shallow, and often open. (Often in pl. with *pots.*) **b.** Often differentiated, as *bread-p., saucepan*, etc. **c.** As part of any apparatus 1611. **2.** In techn. uses, applied to pan-like vessels in which substances are exposed to heat, or to mechanical processes; e.g. an open vessel used for boiling, evaporating, etc.; also in *Chem.* a closed vessel for evaporation, a vacuum pan 1674. **3.** The contents of a pan, a panful 1762. **4.** A pan-shaped depression of any vessel, or part of any structure 1764. **b.** *spec.* In obs. types of guns and pistols: That part of the lock which holds the priming 1590. **c.** A socket for a hinge, etc. 1598. **5.** A hollow or depression in the ground; *spec.* a SALT-PAN 1493. **b.** *spec.* in *S. Africa*, A dried-up salt-marsh or poolbed 1786. **6.** = BRAIN-PAN. *Obs.* or *dial.* ME. †**b.** The patella or KNEE-PAN –1753. **7.** A hard substratum of soil, usually more or less impervious to moisture: see HARD-PAN 1784. **8.** A small ice-floe 1863.

1. Ful many a panne of bras CHAUCER. **c.** With the weights in the opposite p. of the balance 1842. *To turn the cat in the p.*: see CAT *sb.* **4. b.** *Flash in the p.*: see FLASH *sb.*²

attrib. and *Comb.*, as **p.-mill,** a miner's apparatus used in separating gold from the alloy of earth; **-washing,** the separating of gold from gravel, etc., by stirring it in water in a p.; **-wood,** the small coal used in salt-works.

Pan (pæn), *sb.*² ME. [– L. *Pan*, Gr. Πάν.] Name of a Greek rural deity, represented as having the head, arms, and chest of a man, and the lower parts (and sometimes the horns and ears) of a goat.

He was supposed to preside over shepherds and flocks, and to delight in rural music; he was also regarded as the author of sudden and groundless terror (PANIC *sb.*²); and in later times, from association of his name with τὸ πᾶν the all, everything, as an impersonation of Nature.

Pan, *sb.*³ Also **pane.** 1719. [– Fr. *pan* part (of a wall), etc.; see PANE *sb.*¹] In a timber-framed or half-timbered house, a square or compartment of timber framework, filled in with bricks or plaster 1842.

‖**Pan, pán** (pān), *sb.*⁴ 1616. [– Hind. *pān* betel-leaf :– Skr. *parṇa* feather, leaf.] The betel-leaf; hence, the combination of betel-leaf, areca-nut, lime, etc., used as a masticatory.

Pan (pæn), *v.*¹ 1825. [f. PAN *sb.*¹] **1.** *trans.* To wash (gold-bearing gravel) in a pan, to separate the gold; to separate by washing in a pan. Const. *off, out.* 1872. **b.** *absol.* or *intr.* To search or try for gold with the pan 1872. **2.** *transf.* and *fig.* (*U.S.* and *Colonial.*) To bring forth, yield (with *out*) 1884. **3.** *intr.* (usu. with *out.*) To yield gold, as gravel, etc. when washed in a pan; hence *transf.* of the vein or mine, to yield precious metal 1865. Also *fig.* with ref. to the issue of a project or the like. **4.** *trans.* To cook or dress in a pan 1871. **5.** *Agric.* and *dial. intr.* Of soil: To cake on the surface 1825.

1. They 'panned' the surface dirt for gold 1880. **2.** The department on being searched only panned out a few copper coins 1884. **3.** *fig.* Unfortunately this business did not 'pan out', to use the American phrase 1892. Hence **Pa·nning** *vbl. sb.* the action of washing sand, etc. for gold; the gold so obtained.

Pan (pæn), *v.*² *Sc.* and *north.* 1556. [Of unkn. origin.] *intr.* To fit, tally, agree. **b.** *trans.* To fit or join together 1884.

Pan-, comb. form and formative element, repr. Gr. παν- from πᾶν, neut. of πᾶς all.

1. With national names, etc., with the sense 'Of, pertaining to, or comprising all (those indicated in the second element)'; with sbs. in -ISM and -IST, gen. expressing the notion of or aspiration for the political union of all those indicated. **Pan-A·frican** *a.* of or pertaining to all persons of African birth or descent. **Pan-Ame·rican** *a.* of or pertaining to all the states of North and South America or to all Americans; hence **Pan-Ame·ricanism. Pan-A·nglo-Sa·xon** *a.* of or including all of Anglo-Saxon race. **Pan-Brita·nnic** *a.* of or comprising all the British dominions. **Pan-denomina·tional** *a.* of or embracing all religious denominations. **Pan-Ge·rman** *a.* of or pertaining to all Germans, or to the union of all Germans in one political state; *sb.* an advocate of this union; hence **Pan-Germa·nic** *a.*; **Pan-Ge·rmanism. Pan-Io·nian, -Io·nic** *adjs.* of or comprising all Ionians. **Pani·slam,** all Islam; (the conception of) a union of the Moslem world; so **Panisla·mic** *a.*, **Pani·slamism. Pan-Presbyte·rian** *a.* of or pertaining to all Presbyterians. **Pan-Sla·v, Pan-Sla·vic** *adjs.* of or pertaining to all the Slavic races; of or favouring **Pansla·vism,** the movement or aspiration for the union of all Slavs or Slavonic peoples in one political organization; so **Pansla·vist, Pan-slavi·stic** *a.* = *Pan-Slavic.* **Panslavo·nian** *a.* Pan-Slavic, Panslavistic. **Pan-Teuto·nic** *a.* of or embracing all Teutonic peoples; hence **Pan-Teu·tonism,** the principle of a union of all Teutonic peoples.

2. Other words. **Panco·smism,** *Philos.*, the doctrine that the material universe is all that exists; hence **Panco·smic** *a.* **Pane·ntheism,** the doctrine that God includes the world as part of his being; so **Panenthei·stic** *a.* **Panidiomo·rphic** *a. Min.*, having all its components idiomorphic. **Pa·nlogism** [mod.L. *panlogismus*], *Philos.*, a term formed by J. E. Erdmann on the analogy of *pantheismus*, to describe the philosophy of Hegel, as one which holds that only the rational is truly real; so **Panlo·gical, -logi·stic** *adjs.* ‖**Panmi·xia,** *Biol.*, Weismann's term for a supposed promiscuous reproduction of all manner of ancestral qualities or tendencies, consequent on the cessation of natural selection in relation to organs which have become useless or little used. **Panomphæ·an** [Gr. ὀμφή voice of a god, oracular response], *a.* of or pertaining to Zeus, as sender of all ominous voices. **Panpha·rmacon** [Gr. φάρμακον drug], a universal remedy, a panacea. **Panpheno·menalism,** *Philos.*, a theory that the universe is purely phenomenal. **Panthele·matism. Pa·nthelism** [Gr. θελημάτ- will; θέλειν to will], *Philos.*, the theory of Schopenhauer that the Ultimate and Absolute is Will. **Pantheo·logy,** a synthetic theology comprehending all deities and religions. **Panzo·ism** [Gr. ζωή life], *Biol.*, a name given to a synthesis of all the elements or factors of vitality.

†**Panabase** (pæ·năbē¹s). 1839. [– Fr. *panabase* (Beudant 1832), irreg. f. Gr. πᾶν PAN- + *base* BASE *sb.*¹] *Min.* = TETRAHEDRITE –1896.

Panace (pæ·năsi). 1513. [– L. *panax* and *panaces*, synonyms of *panacea*; see next.] A fabulous herb, said to heal all diseases.

Panacea (pænăsī·ă). 1548. [– L. *panacea* – Gr. πανάκεια, f. πανακής all-healing, f. παν-

PAN- + base of ἄκος remedy; see -A 2.] **1.** A remedy, cure, or medicine reputed to heal all diseases. †**2.** = PANACE –1741. Hence **Panace·an** *a.* of the nature of a p.; all-healing. **Panace·ist,** one who believes in or applies a p.

Panache (pănɑ·ʃ). 1553. [– Fr. *panache* – It. *pennacchio* :– late L. *pinnaculum*, dim. of *pinna* feather.] A tuft or plume of feathers, esp. when used as a head-dress or an ornament for a helmet; †hence, a tassel or the like. **b.** *Astron.* A plume-like solar protuberance 1887.

He had in his cap a pennach of heron EVELYN. Hence **Pana·ched** *a.* diversified with stripes of colour like a plume.

Panada (pănā·dă). 1598. [– Sp. *panada* = Pr. *panada*, It. *panata*, repr. Rom. **panata*, f. *panis* bread; see -ADE.] Bread boiled to a pulp and flavoured with sugar, nutmeg, etc.

†**Panade**[1]. *rare.* ME. only. [app. rel. to OFr. *pan-*, *penard* cutlass, med.L. *penardus*, *pen(n)atum*, *pennatus*, but the variation of the suffixes is unexplained.] A kind of large knife.

Panade[2] (pănēⁱ·d). 1598. [– Fr. *panade* – It. or Pr.; see PANADA.] = PANADA.

Panama (pænămā·). 1833. [Name of a town and state in Central America, and of the isthmus uniting North and South America.] *attrib.* Of or pertaining to Panama; spec. *Panama hat*, a misnomer for a hat made from the undeveloped leaves of the stemless screw-pine (*Carludovica palmata*) of tropical S. America; also *absol.* as *sb.*

Pan-Anglican (pæn,æ·ŋglikăn), *a.* 1867. [PAN- 1.] Of, pertaining to, or embracing the whole Anglican Church and its branches.

†**Pa·nary,** *sb. rare.* 1611 only. [– L. *panarium* bread-basket, f. *panis* bread; see -ARY[1].] A store-house for bread, a pantry.

Panary (pæ·nări), *a.* 1818. [f. L. *panis* bread + -ARY[1].] Of or pertaining to bread; esp. in *p. fermentation.*

‖**Panathenæa** (pænæþinī·ă). Also **-aia.** 1603. [– Gr. παναθήναια adj. neut. pl. (sc. ἱερά solemnities), f. παν- PAN- + Ἀθηναῖος Athenian, f. Ἀθῆναι Athens, or Ἀθήνη Athene, patron goddess of Athens.] The national festival of Athens, held, in a lesser form every year, in a greater every fifth year, to celebrate the union of Attica under Theseus. Hence **Panathenæ·an, Panathena·ic** *adjs.* of or pertaining to this festival.

Panatrope (pæ·nătrōᵘp). 1926. [irreg. f. PAN- 2 + Gr. -τροπος turning.] An electrical apparatus for the reproduction of gramophone records through a loud-speaker.

Pancake (pæ·nkēⁱk), *sb.* late ME. [f. PAN *sb.*[1] 1 + CAKE *sb.*] **1.** A thin flat cake, made of batter fried in a pan. (Often as the type of flatness.) **2.** Applied to various objects thin and flat like a pancake 1843.

1. The country is as flat as a p. 1860.
attrib. and *Comb.*: **p. day, Tuesday,** Shrove Tuesday, from the custom of eating pancakes on that day; **p.-ice,** floating ice in thin flat pieces, forming in the polar seas at the approach of winter. Hence **Pa·ncake** *v. intr.* (of an aeroplane) to descend vertically in a level position (*slang*).

†**Pa·nchart.** 1587. [– med.L. *pancharta*, f. Gr. παν- PAN- + L. *charta* leaf, paper.] A charter, orig. app. one of a general character, or that confirmed all special grants, but later almost any written record –1762.

Pancheon (pæ·nʃən). 1601. [app. derived from PAN *sb.*[1]] A large shallow earthenware bowl or vessel, wider at the top than at the bottom, used for setting milk to stand in, etc.

Panchroma·tic, *a.* 1904. [PAN- 1.] = ORTHOCHROMATIC.

‖**Panchway, pansway** (pæ·ntʃwēⁱ, pæ·nswēⁱ). 1757. [– Hindi *pansoī*, Bengali *pançoī*, *pançī* boat.] A light kind of boat used on the rivers of Bengal.

Panclastite (pænklæ·stəit). 1883. [f. Gr. παν- PAN- + κλαστός broken, -κλαστης breaker + -ITE[1] 4a.] An explosive formed in mixing liquid nitrogen tetroxide with carbon disulphide, nitrotoluene, or other liquid combustible.

Pancratic (pænkræ·tik), *a.* 1660. [(1) f. next + -IC; (2) f. PAN- 2 + Gr. κράτος strength + -IC.] **1.** Of or pertaining to the pancratium; hence, fully disciplined or exercised in mind. So †**-ical** 1581. **2.** Of an eyepiece: Capable of adjustment to many degrees of power 1831.

‖**Pancratium** (pænkrēⁱ·ʃiŏm), **-ion** (-iǫn). 1603. [L. – Gr. παγκράτιον, f. παν- PAN- + κράτος bodily strength; see -IUM.] **1.** *Gr. Antiq.* An athletic contest, combining both wrestling and boxing. **2.** *Bot.* A genus of bulbous plants of the N.O. *Amaryllidaceæ*, bearing an umbel of large white flowers terminating a solid scape 1664. Hence **Pancra·tian** *a.* of or belonging to the p. (sense 1). So **Pancra·tiast, Pa·ncratist,** a combatant or victor in the p. **Pancratia·stic** *a.* of or pertaining to a pancratiast.

Pancreas (pæ·ŋkri,æs). 1578. [– mod.L. *pancreas* – Gr. πάγκρεας, -κρεατ-, f. παν- PAN- + κρέας flesh.] A lobulated racemose gland situated near the stomach, and discharging into the duodenum a digestive secretion, the *pancreatic juice*; called in animals, when used as food, the *sweetbread*. Hence **Pancrea·tic** *a.* of or belonging to the p.

Pancreatin (pæ·ŋkri,ătin). 1873. [f. Gr. stem παγκρεατ- (PANCREAS) + -IN[1].] *Chem.* A proteid compound, one of the active principles of pancreatic juice; also, a preparation extracted from the pancreas and used to aid digestion. So **Pa·ncreatize** *v.* to treat with p. so as to make digestible.

‖**Pancreatitis** (pæŋkri,ătəi·tis). 1842. [f. as prec. + -ITIS.] *Path.* Inflammation of the pancreas.

Pand (pænd). *Sc.* 1561. [– MDu., MFlem. *pand* = (O)Fr. *pan*, also †*pand* PANE *sb.*[1]] A valance.

Panda (pæ·ndă). 1835. [Nepali name.] A racoon-like animal (*Ælurus fulgens*) of the south-eastern Himalayas; the red bear-cat.

‖**Pandal** (pæ·ndăl). *E. Ind.* 1717. [– Tamil *pendal* shed.] A shed, booth, or arbour, esp. for temporary use.

‖**Pandanus** (pændēⁱ·nŏs). 1846. [mod.L. – Malay *pandan.*] *Bot.* A genus of plants, type of the order *Pandanaceæ*, the screw-pines, found chiefly in the E. Indian archipelago. Also *attrib.*

Pandean, -dæan (pændī·ăn), *a.* and *sb.* 1804. [irreg. f. PAN *sb.*[2]] **a.** *adj.* Of or pertaining to Pan 1807. **b.** *sb.* A member of a pandean band 1804.

a. *P. band*, a band consisting mainly of players of the pan-pipe. *P. pipe* = PAN-PIPE. *P. harmonica*, a mouth-organ resembling the pan-pipe.

Pandect (pæ·ndekt). 1531. [– Fr. *pandecte* or L. *pandecta, -tes* – Gr. πανδέκτης (pl. πανδέκται as a title), f. παν- PAN- + δέχεσθαι receive.] **1.** *pl.* (rarely *sing.*) A compendium in fifty books of Roman civil law made by order of the Emperor Justinian in the 6th c., systematizing the opinions of eminent jurists, to which the Emperor gave the force of law. **b.** *transf.* and *fig.* (Also *sing.*) A complete body of the laws of any country or of any system of law 1553. **2.** (*sing.*) A treatise covering the whole of a subject 1591. **3.** A manuscript copy of the whole Bible 1893.

2. That..the commons would please to form a p. of their own power and privileges SWIFT. 3. Complete Bibles ('Pandects', they are called) are very rare 1908.

Pandemian (pændī·miăn), *a.* 1818. [f. Gr. πανδήμιος of all the people + -AN.] = PANDEMIC A. 2.

Pandemic (pænde·mik), *a.* and *sb.* 1666. [f. Gr. πάνδημος, f. παν- PAN- + δῆμος people, populace; in sense 2 repr. Gr. πάνδημος ἔρως, as opp. to οὐράνιος. Cf. Plato *Symp.* 180 E.]
A. *adj.* **1.** General, universal. *esp.* Of a disease: Prevalent over the whole of a country or continent, or over the whole world. Dist. from *epidemic*, which may connote limitation to a smaller area. **2.** Of or pertaining to vulgar or sensual love 1822. **B.** *sb.* A pandemic disease 1853.

Pandemoniac (pændimōᵘ·niæk), *a.* 1849. [f. as next, after *demoniac.*] Of or pertaining to Pandemonium; infernal. So **Pandemoniacal** (-əi·ăkăl) *a.* characteristic of Pandemonium; esp. of din or noise.

Pandemonium (pændimōᵘ·niŏm). Also **-dæmon-.** 1667. [mod.L. (MILT. *P.L.* I. 756), f. Gr. παν- PAN- + δαίμων DEMON; see -IUM.] **1.** The abode of all the demons; in Milton, the capital of Hell, containing the council-chamber of the Evil Spirits; in common use, = hell or the infernal regions. **2.** *transf.* **a.** A centre or headquarters of vice or wickedness. **b.** A place or gathering of wild lawless violence, confusion, and uproar 1779. **c.** A distracting fiendish 'row' 1865.

1. Pandæmonium, the high Capital Of Satan and his Peers MILT. Hence **Pandemo·nian** *a.* pandemoniac; *sb.* an inhabitant of P.

Pander (pæ·ndəɹ), *sb.* late ME. [Earliest form *pandar*; appellative use of *Pandare* – It. *Pandaro* (– L. *Pandarus*, Gr. Πάνδαρος), name used by Boccaccio and thereafter by Chaucer for the man who procured for Troilus the love of Criseyde (Griseida). The sp. *pander* is due to assoc. with -ER[1].] **1.** As proper name. **2.** A go-between in clandestine amours; a male bawd or procurer 1450. **b.** Less usu., a panderess 1585. **c.** *transf.* and *fig.* Said of a thing 1582. **3.** One who ministers to the baser passions or evil designs of others 1603.

1. *Tr. & Cr.* III. ii. 210. 2. He that was the Pandor to procure her NORTH. c. Make virtue a p. to vice BURKE. 3. Pandars to folly and extravagance JOHNSON. So **Pa·nderess** (now *rare*), a female p. **Pa·nderism,** the practice of a p. **Pa·nderly** *a.* of the nature of or befitting a p. (*Obs.* or *arch.*); so †**Pa·nderous** *a.*

Pander (pæ·ndəɹ), *v.* Also **-ar.** 1602. [f. prec.] **1.** *trans.* To act as a pander to; to minister to the gratification of (another's lust). Also *fig.* **2.** *intr.* To play the pander. Const. *to.* 1603.

1. *fig.* Frost..as actiuely doth burne, As Reason panders Will SHAKS.

Pandiculation (pændikiulēⁱ·ʃən). 1649. [f. *pandiculat-*, pa. ppl. stem of L. *pandiculari*, f. *pandus* (with dim. element) bent, crooked, curved, f. *pandare* bend, bow, curve; see -ION.] The extension of the legs, the raising and stretching of the arms, and the throwing back of the head and trunk, accompanied by yawning, as occurring before and after sleeping, in hysteria, etc.

Pandora[1] (pændōᵊ·ră). Also †**Pandore.** 1579. [– Gr. πανδώρα lit. 'all-gifted', f. παν- PAN- + δῶρον gift.] *Gr. Myth.* Name of the first mortal woman, on whom, when made by Vulcan and brought to Epimetheus, all the gods and goddesses bestowed gifts.

Pandora's box, the gift of Jupiter to Pandora, a box containing all human ills, which flew forth when the box was foolishly opened by Epimetheus; according to another version, the box contained all the blessings of the gods, which, on its opening, escaped and were lost, with the exception of hope, which was at the bottom. Hence fig. and in allusive uses.

Pandora[2] (pændōᵊ·ră), **pandore** (pændōᵊ·ɹ). 1597. [Also †*pandure*; – It. †*pandora*, *-iera*, *pandura* (whence Fr. *pandore*) – late L. *pandura* – Gr. πανδοῦρα, -δοῦρα three-stringed lute, prob. of Oriental origin. Cf. BANDORE[1], MANDOLINE.] = BANDORE[1].

Pandour, pandoor (pæ·ndūᵊɹ). 1747. [– Fr. *pandour*, G. *pandur* – Serbo-Croatian *pandur* constable, etc., prob. – med.L. *banderius* guard of cornfields and vineyards, apparitor.] **1.** In *pl.* The name borne by a local force organized in 1741 by Baron Trenck on his own estates in Croatia to clear the country near the Turkish frontier of bands of robbers; subseq. enrolled as a regiment in the Austrian army, where, under Trenck, their rapacity and brutality made *Pandour* synonymous with 'brutal Croatian soldier'. ‖**2.** In local use in Croatia, etc.: A guard; an armed retainer; a member of the local mounted constabulary 1880.

1. His style might have better suited a colonel of pandours than a Christian bishop 1791.

Pandowdy (pændau·di). *U.S.* 1846. [Of unkn. origin.] A kind of apple pudding, usu. seasoned with molasses, and baked in a deep dish with or without a crust.

Pandurate (pæ·ndiŭrĕt), *a.* 1847. [f. late L. *pandura* PANDORA[2] + -ATE[2].] = next.

Panduriform (pændiūᵊ·rifǫɹm), *a.* 1753. [f. as prec. + -FORM.] Fiddle-shaped; chiefly in *Bot.* and *Entom.*

Pane (pēⁱn), *sb.*[1] [ME. *pan*, later *pane* – (O)Fr. *pan* :– L. *pannus* cloth, piece of cloth. Branch I survives in COUNTERPANE.] **I.** †**1.** A cloth; a piece of cloth; any distinct portion of a garment, a lap, a skirt –1580.

†**2.** A piece, width, or strip of cloth, of which several were joined together side by side, so as to make one cloth, curtain, or garment –1694. †**b.** *pl.* Strips made by cutting or slashing a garment longitudinally for ornamental purposes –1653. **II.** A piece, portion, or side of anything. †**1.** A length of a wall or fence –1672. †**2.** A side of a quadrangle, cloister, court, or town –1560. **3.** A flat side, face, or surface of any object having several sides: e.g. a side of a stone or log, of a nut or bolt-head, of the table of a brilliant-cut diamond. late ME. **III.** A division of a window, etc. **1.** One of the lights of a mullioned window (*obs.*), or a subdivision of this; now, One compartment of a window, etc. consisting of one sheet of glass held in place by a frame; the piece of glass itself, or of horn, paper, or the like 1466. **2.** = PANEL *sb.* III. 2. 1582. **3.** A rectangular division of some surface; one of the compartments of a chequered pattern 1555. **b.** Each of the blocks of burr-stone of which a mill-stone is constructed 1839. **4.** A section or plot of ground more or less rectangular in shape; *spec.* in *Irrigation*, a division of ground bounded by a feeder and an outlet drain 1805. Hence **Pa·neless** *a.*, having no panes.

Pane (pēⁱn), *sb.*[2] 1578. [app. – Fr. *panne*, in same sense, – Du. *pen*, MFlem. *penne* peg – L. *pinna* point, pinnacle. Cf. PEEN.] The pointed or edged end of a hammer: = north. dial. *peen*.

Pane (pēⁱn), *v.* 1504. [f. PANE *sb.*[1]] **1.** *trans.* To make up (a piece of cloth, a garment) of strips of different sorts or colours, joined side by side. Chiefly in *pa. pple.* **2.** To fit (a window) with panes 1726.

Paned (pēⁱnd), *ppl. a.* 1546. [f. PANE *v.* and *sb.*[1] + -ED.] **1.** Made of strips of different coloured cloth joined together, or of cloth cut into strips, between which ribs or stripes of other material or colour are inserted. **2.** Of a window or door: Having panes of glass 1756.

Panegyric (pænĭdʒi·rik), *sb.* and *a.* 1603. [– Fr. *panégyrique* – L. *panegyricus* public eulogy, subst. use of adj. – Gr. πανηγυρικός pertaining to public assembly, f. πανήγυρις; see PANEGYRIS, -IC.] **A.** *sb.* **1.** A public speech or writing in praise of some person, thing, or achievement; a formal or elaborate encomium. Const. *on*, *upon*, †*of*. **2.** Eulogy; laudation 1613.

1. I profess to write, not his panegyrick..but his Life BOSWELL.

B. *adj.* = PANEGYRICAL 2. 1605. Hence †**Panegy·ric** *v. intr.* to utter or write a p.; *trans.* to praise in a p.

Panegyrical (pænĭdʒi·rikăl), *a.* 1592. [f. as prec. + -AL[1]; see -ICAL.] †**1.** Of the nature of a general assembly –1679. **2.** Of the nature of a panegyric or eulogy; encomiastic, laudatory 1592.

‖**Panegyris** (pănī·dʒiris). 1647. [– Gr., f. παν- PAN- + ἄγυρις = ἀγορά assembly.] *Gr. Antiq.* A general assembly; *esp.* a festal assembly in honour of a god.

Panegyrize (pæ·nĭdʒirəiz), *v.* 1617. [– Gr. πανηγυρίζειν celebrate πανήγυρις or a public festival; see prec., -IZE.] **1.** *trans.* To pronounce or write a panegyric upon; to eulogize. **2.** *intr.* To compose or utter panegyrics 1827. So **Panegyrist** (pænĭdʒi·rist), an encomiast; one who writes or utters a panegyric 1605.

Panegyry (pæ·nĭdʒĭri). 1641. [f. Gr. πανήγυρις, with change of suffix.] *Gr. Antiq.* = PANEGYRIS 1. Also, A religious festival.

Panel (pæ·nĕl), *sb.* [– OFr. *panel* piece of cloth, saddle-cushion, piece (mod. *panneau*) :– Rom. **pannellus*, dim. of L. *pannus* PANE *sb.*[1]; see -EL.]

I. A piece of cloth, etc. **1.** A piece of cloth placed under the saddle, or, now, the pad or stuffed lining of a saddle, employed to prevent galling. **2.** A kind of saddle; generally applied to a rough treeless pad 1540. **II.** A small piece or slip of parchment, etc. **1.** A slip or roll of parchment, *esp.* the slip on which the sheriff entered the names of jurors and which he affixed to the writ 1440. **2.** A list of jurymen; the jury itself. late ME. **b.** *transf.* A list of men, or of beasts 1575. **3.** *Sc. Law.* In the phr. *on* or *upon the p.* = upon (his, one's) trial. Also, later, *in the p.* 1557. **b.** The person or persons indicted, the accused 1555. **4.** A list of doctors who are prepared to accept as patients persons registered under the National Health Insurance Acts; a doctor's list of such patients 1913. **III.** A distinct portion of some surface, etc., usu. contained in a frame or border. **1.** A section or compartment of a fence or railing; a hurdle 1489. **2.** A distinct compartment of a wainscot, door, shutter, cover of a book, etc., often sunk below or raised above the general level, set in a border or frame 1600. **b.** A piece of stuff of different kind or colour, laid or inserted lengthwise in the skirt of a woman's dress 1889. **3.** A compartment in a stained glass window, containing a separate subject 1873. **4.** *Coal-mining.* **a.** A piece of coal left uncut in a mine. **b.** A compartment of a mine separated from the rest by thick masses or ribs of coal. 1747. **IV.** A thin wooden board used as a surface for oil painting; also, the painting on such a board 1688. **b.** A large size of photograph, much greater in height than width. Chiefly *attrib.* 1888. **V. 1.** *Artillery.* The carriages which carry mortars and their beds upon a march 1853. **2.** *Mining.* A heap of dressed ore 1858.

attrib. and *Comb.*, as *p.-cupboard*, *sleeve*, etc.; (sense II. 4) *p.-doctor*, *-patient*, etc.; **-house**, a brothel in which the walls have sliding panels for the purpose of robbery (*U.S.*); **-strip**, a strip of wood or metal to cover the joint between a post and a p., or between two panels; **-thief**, a thief in a panel-house (*U.S.*); **-work**, (*a*) work in wood, etc., consisting of or containing panels; (*b*) the working of a mine by division into panels. Hence **Panel(l)ed** (pæ·nĕld) *ppl. a.* **Pa·nel(l)ing**, panels collectively; p.-work.

Panel (pæ·nĕl), *v.* 1451. [f. PANEL *sb.*] **1.** *trans.* To empanel (a jury). **2.** *Sc. Law.* To bring to trial; to indict 1576. **3.** To put a panel on (a mule, ass, etc.); to saddle with a panel 1530. **4.** To fit, furnish, or adorn (a room, wall, etc.) with panels 1633. **5.** To fit or place as a panel in its frame 1832. **6.** To ornament (a skirt, etc.) with a panel or panels 1901. **7.** *Telegr.* To arrange wires in parallels 1890.

Panful (pæ·nful). 1874. [f. PAN *sb.*[1] + -FUL.] The quantity that fills a pan.

Pang (pæŋ), *sb.* 1526. [In earliest use *pange(s) of deth*, *panges of child bed*; unexpl. var. of earlier †*pronge* (XV, *prongys of deth*, *wommanys pronge*), †*prange*; but cf. the OE. vars. *pætiġ*, *prættiġ* PRETTY, *spǣć*, *sprǣć* SPEECH. The forms in *pr-* correspond to MLG. *prange* pinching, early Du. *prang(h)e* oppression, constraint, shackle, Du., LG. *prangen* pinch, Goth. *anapraggan* oppress, ME. *prangled* pressed tightly, Sc. *prang* (var. with *pang*) pack tight, cram.] **1.** A brief keen spasm of pain which appears to shoot through the body or any part of it; a shooting pain. **2.** *fig.* A sudden sharp mental pain 1570. †**3.** A sudden transitory fit of keen feeling or emotion –1694.

1. In the pange & distresse of deth 1526. **2.** *Twel. N.* II. iv. 94. Hence **Pa·ngful** *a.* full of pangs, sorrowful (*rare*). **Pa·ngless** *a.* without a p.

Pang (pæŋ), *v.* Now *rare.* 1502. [See PANG *sb.*] *trans.* To afflict with pangs; to pierce or penetrate with acute physical or mental pain. Also *absol.*

Pangenesis (pændʒe·nĕsis). 1868. [f. Gr. παν- PAN- + γένεσις -GENESIS.] *Biol.* Name given by Darwin to his hypothesis, advanced to explain the phenomena of heredity, that every separate unit or cell of an organism reproduces itself by contributing its share to the germ or bud of the future offspring. So **Pangene·tic** *a.* of or pertaining to p. **Pangene·tically** *adv.*

Pangolin (pæŋgōᵘ·lin). 1774. [– Malay *peng-gōling* roller, f. *peng-* (denominative) + *gōling* roll, in ref. to its power of rolling itself up.] A scaly ant-eater.

Panhandle (pæ·nhæ:nd'l). 1887. [f. PAN *sb.*[1] + HANDLE.] The handle of a pan; hence *U.S.* a narrow strip of a State or Territory extending between two others. **Pa·n-ha:ndler** *U.S. slang*, a beggar. So **Pa·n-handle** *v.*

Panharmonic (pænhaɹmǫ·nik), *a.* 1875. [f. PAN- + HARMONIC.] **a.** Adapted to all the 'harmonies' or musical modes. **b.** Universally harmonic, harmonizing with all 1886. So **Panharmo·nicon**, a mechanical musical instrument of the orchestrion type, invented by J. N. Maelzel in 1800.

Panhellenic (pænhelī·nik, -e·nik), *a.* 1847. [f. PAN- 1 + HELLENIC, after Gr. πανελλήνιος, etc.] Of, concerning, or representing all men of Greek race. So **Panhe·llenism**, the idea of a political union of all Greeks; the P. spirit and aims. **Panhe·llenist.**

Panic (pæ·nik), *sb.*[1] OE. [– L. *panicum*, rel. to *panus* thread wound on a bobbin, swelling, ear of millet – Gr. πῆνος web (πηνίον bobbin). See PANICLE.] A grass or graminaceous plant; orig. applied to *Panicum italicum* of Linnæus, otherwise called Italian Millet; also extended to other species of the genus *Panicum* and its sub-genera. **p.-grass**, any grassy species of *Panicum*.

Panic (pæ·nik), *a.* and *sb.*[2] 1603. [– Fr. *panique* – mod.L. *panicus* (in *p. terror* tr. πανικὸν δεῖμα, τάραχος πανικός, θόρυβος ὁ καλούμενος πανικός) – Gr. πανικός (also n. -όν as sb.), f. Πάν name of a deity part man part goat, whose appearance or unseen presence caused terror and to whom woodland noises were attributed; see -IC.] **A.** *adj.* (Now often taken as attrib. use of B.) In *p. fear*, *terror*, etc.: Such as was attributed to the action of the god Pan: = B. 2. **b.** Of the nature of or resulting from a panic 1741.

B. *sb.*[2] [= mod.Fr. *une panique.*] †**1.** Contagious emotion such as was attributed to the influence of Pan –1708. **2.** A sudden and excessive feeling of alarm or fear, usually affecting a body of persons, and leading to extravagant or injudicious efforts to secure safety. (With and without *a* and *pl.*) 1708. **b.** *spec.* A condition of widespread apprehension in relation to financial and commercial matters, leading to hasty and violent measures, the tendency of which is to cause financial disaster 1757.

1. We may..call every Passion Pannick which is rais'd in a Multitude, and convey'd by Aspect, or as it were by Contact or Sympathy SHAFTESB. **2.** The Uncertainty of what they fear'd made their Fear get greater..And this was what in after-times men call'd a Pannick SHAFTESB.

attrib. and *Comb.*: **p.-monger**, one who endeavours to create or foster a p.; an alarmist; hence **-mongering**; **-stricken**, **-struck** *adjs.*, stricken with p. Hence **Pa·nic** *v. trans.* to affect with p.; *intr.* to be affected with p. So **Pa·nical** *a. rare*, = PANIC *a.* A; **-ly** *adv.* **Panicky** (pæ·niki) *a. colloq.* of the nature of, or having a tendency to p.

Panicle (pæ·nik'l). 1597. [– L. *paniculum*, dim. of *panus* thread; see PANIC *sb.*[1], -CLE.] *Bot.* A compound inflorescence, usu. of the racemose type, forming a loose and irregularly spreading cluster, as in oats and many grasses. Hence **Pa·nicled** *a.* paniculate; furnished with a p. or panicles.

Paniculate (pănĭ·kiŭlĕt), *a.* 1727. [– mod.L. *paniculatus*, f. *panicula* PANICLE + -ATE[2].] Arranged in a panicle; panicled. So **Pani·culated** *a. rare.* 1719.

Panification (pænifikēⁱ·ʃən). 1779. [– Fr. *panification*, f. *panifier* make into bread, f. L. *panis* bread; see -FICATION.] The making into bread; conversion into the substance of bread, esp. as a chemical process.

Panjandrum (pændʒæ·ndrɒ̆m). 1755. A nonsense formation, occurring in the string of nonsense composed by S. Foote to test the memory of Macklin, who had asserted that he could repeat anything after once hearing it. Hence, A mock title for a mysterious or exalted personage; a local magnate of great airs; a pompous pretender 1880.

And there were present the Picninnies, and the Joblillies, and the Garyulies, and the Grand P. himself, with the little round button at top FOOTE. The P. of Biblical Science and Scotch Presbyterianism 1892.

‖**Pa·nnag.** 1611. [Heb.] 'Perhaps a kind of confection' (R. V. margin, Ezek. 27:17).

Pannage (pæ·nĕdʒ). late ME. [– OFr. *pannage*, *paan-*, *pasn-* (mod. *panage*) :– med.L. *pastionaticum*, f. *pastio* feeding, pasturing, f. *past-*, pa. ppl. stem of L. *pascere*; see PASTURE, -AGE.] **1.** *Law.* **a.** The feeding of swine, etc. in a forest or wood; pasturage for swine; **b.** The right or privilege of pasturing swine in a forest; **c.** The payment made to the owner of a woodland for this right; the profit thus accruing. 1450. **2.** *concr.* Acorns, beech-mast, etc., on which swine feed. late ME.

‖**Panne** (pæn, ‖pan). 1875. [Fr., of unkn. origin.] A soft kind of cloth with a long nap, resembling velvet. Also *attrib.* as *p. velvet.*

†**Pa·nnicle.** 1590. [– OFr. *pan(n)icle* – L. *panniculus* rag, dim. of *pannus* cloth; see -CLE.] ¶**1.** App. misused as = brain-pan. SPENSER. **2.** *Bot.* A membranous covering in plants, as the scales investing a leaf-bud 1671.

Pannier (pæ·niəɹ), *sb.*[1] ME. [–(O)Fr. *panier*, †*pannier* :– L. *panarium* bread-basket, f. *panis* bread; see -IER 2.] **1.** A basket; *esp.* a large basket for carrying provisions, fish, etc.; in later use, mostly one of those carried by a beast of burden (usu. in pairs), or on the shoulders of a man or woman. **b.** A covered basket for holding surgical instruments and medicines for a military ambulance 1854. †**2.** *Arch.* = CORBEIL 2. **3.** A frame of whalebone, wire, etc., used to distend the skirt of a woman's dress at the hips 1877. Hence **Pa·nniered** *a.* laden with a p. or panniers.

Pannier (pæ·niəɹ), *sb.*[2] *colloq.* 1823. [Of unkn. origin.] The name by which the robed waiters at table are known in the Inner Temple.

Pa·nnierman. 1482. [f. PANNIER *sb.*[1]] A paid officer in the Inns of Court, who brought provisions from market (with a horse and panniers). (Abolished 1900.)

Pannikin (pæ·nikin). 1823. [f. PAN *sb.*[1] + -KIN, after CANNIKIN.] A small metal (usu. tinned iron) drinking vessel; also, the contents of this.

Pa·nning, *vbl. sb.* [f. PAN *v.*[1] + -ING[1].] See PAN *v.*[1]

‖**Pannus** (pæ·nŏs). 1706. [perh. L. *pannus* cloth.] *Path.* A vascular condition of the cornea of the eye, with thickening and opacity.

Panoply (pæ·nŏpli). 1576. [– Fr. *panoplie* or mod.L. *panoplia* – Gr. πανοπλία full armour of a HOPLITE, f. παν- PAN- + ὅπλα arms; see -Y[3].] A complete suit of armour, the 'whole armour' of a soldier of ancient or mediæval times. Also *transf.* and *fig.*, often with ref. to τὴν πανοπλίαν τοῦ Θεοῦ 'the whole armour of God' (Eph. 6:11, 13).

Hee in Celestial Panoplie all armd MILT. *fig.* Patience is the P. or whole Armour of the man of God 1650. *transf.* Both of the Bears, and Orion, in golden p. dight 1887. Hence **Panoplied** (pæ·nŏplid) *a.* clad in complete armour; also *fig.*

Panoptic (pænǫ·ptik), *a.* 1826. [f. Gr. πάνοπτος seen of all, πανόπτης all-seeing + -IC.] **1.** All-seeing. **2.** In which all is seen; cf. PANOPTICON 1845.

Panopticon (pænǫ·ptikǫn). 1768. [f. Gr. παν- PAN- + ὀπτικόν, n. of ὀπτικός OPTIC.] **1.** Bentham's name for a proposed form of prison of circular shape having cells built round a central 'well', whence the warders could at all times see the prisoners. Also *attrib.* or as *adj.* 1791. Also *transf.* and *fig.* **2.** Name given to an optical instrument 1768.

Panorama (pænŏrā·mă, -æ·mă). 1796. [f. Gr. παν- PAN- + ὅραμα view.] **1.** A picture of a landscape, etc., either arranged on the inside of a cylindrical surface round the spectator as a centre (CYCLORAMA), or unrolled or unfolded so as to pass before him in successive portions. **2.** An unbroken view of the whole surrounding region 1828. **b.** *fig.* A comprehensive survey of a subject 1801.

1. *transf.* The endless moving p. of the London streets 1876. **2.** The P. from the top of the Brocken 1836. Hence **Panora·mist,** a painter of panoramas.

Panoramic (pænŏræ·mik), *a.* 1813. [f. prec. + -IC.] Of, pertaining to, or of the nature of a panorama.

P. camera, a photographic camera made to rotate automatically so as to take an extended landscape.

‖**Panorpa** (pănǭ·ɹpă). *Pl.* **-æ.** 1878. [mod.L. (Linnæus 1748); derivation not stated.] *Entom.* A genus of neuropterous insects, the type of a family *Panorpidæ*, the scorpion-flies. Hence **Pano·rpian, Pano·rpine** *adjs.* of or pertaining to the genus *P.* **Pano·rpid,** an insect of the family *Panorpidæ.*

Pan-pipe (pæ·npəip). Also **Pan's pipe, Pan's-pipe.** 1820. [PAN *sb.*[2]] A primitive musical instrument made of a series of reeds graduated in length so as to form a scale, the upper and open ends being level; its invention was ascribed to Pan; a syrinx, mouth-organ.

Pan-se·xualism. 1915. [f. PAN- 2 + SEXUAL + -ISM.] *Psychol.* The view that the sex instinct plays a part in all human thought and activity and is the chief or only source of energy. **Pan-se·xual** *a.*, **-se·xualist, -sexua·lity.**

Pansophy (pæ·nsofi). 1642. [f. Gr. παν- PAN- + σοφία wisdom.] **1.** Universal or cyclopædic knowledge; a scheme or cyclopædic work embracing the whole body of human knowledge. **2.** The claim or pretension to universal knowledge 1792. So **Panso·phic** *a.* of or pertaining to p. **Pa·nsophism** = 2. **Pa·nsophist,** a pretender to universal knowledge.

Panspermy (pænspə̄·ɹmi). Also in mod.L. form **panspe·rmia.** 1842. [– Gr. πανσπερμία the doctrine of Anaxagoras and Democritus that the elements were a mixture of all the seeds of things, f. πάνσπερμος, f. παν- PAN- + σπέρμα SPERM.] The biogenetic theory that the atmosphere is full of minute germs which develop on finding a favourable environment. So **Panspe·rmatism, Panspe·rmism** = PANSPERMY. **Panspe·rmatist, Panspe·rmist,** one who holds the doctrine of p. **Panspe·rmic** *a.*, of or pertaining to p.

Pansy (pæ·nzi). 1500. [Formerly *pensee*, *pensy* – (O)Fr. *pensée* thought, fancifully applied to the plant, f. *penser* think – L. *pensare* weigh, ponder, consider, in Rom. think.] The common name of *Viola tricolor*; the wild plant has small flowers compounded of purple, yellow, and white; the cultivated form has large richly and variously coloured flowers. Also called HEARTSEASE, *love-in-idleness*, etc.

The Pansie freakt with jeat MILT. Hence **Pa·nsied** *a.* adorned with or abounding in pansies.

Pant (pænt), *sb.* 1500. [f. next.] **1.** One of a series of short quick efforts of laboured breathing; a gasp, a catching of the breath. **2.** A throb or heave of the breast in laboured breathing or palpitation of the heart 1581. **3.** *transf.* The regular throb and gasping sound of a steam-engine, as the valves open and shut 1840.

Pant (pænt), *v.* late ME. [– AFr. **panter*, based on OFr. *pantaisier* be agitated, gasp, pant :– Rom. **pantasiare*, for **phantasiare* be oppressed as with a nightmare, gasp with oppression – Gr. φαντασιοῦν cause to imagine, make game of, f. φαντασία PHANTASY.] **1.** *intr.* To breathe hard or spasmodically; to gasp for breath. late ME. **b.** To run or go panting 1713. **c.** *transf.* To emit hot air, vapour, etc. in loud puffs, as a furnace or engine 1743. **2.** To gasp (for air, water, etc.); hence *fig.* To gasp with desire; to yearn (*for, after*, or *to* with *inf.*) 1560. **3.** To throb or heave violently or rapidly; to palpitate, pulsate, beat 1460. **4.** *transf.* Of a plated ship: To have its plating bulge in and out in the struggle with the waves 1869. **5.** *trans.* To utter gaspingly; to gasp *out*, etc. 1605.

1. They blowe, and p. like discomfited souldiers 1576. *fig.* If I were..A wave to p. beneath thy power SHELLEY. **b.** As a hare..Pants to the place from whence at first he flew GOLDSM. **2.** As the Hart panteth after the water brookes, so panteth my soule after thee, O God *Ps.* 42:1. **3.** A breast that panted with alarms COWPER.

Pant- = Gr. παντ-, shortened form of παντο- PANTO- bef. a vowel. **Pantamo·rphic** [Gr. ἄμορφος formless], *a.* generally deformed. **Pa·ntarchy** [Gr. ἀρχή rule], a state in which the rule is vested in the whole people.

Panta- erron. f. PANTO-.

Pantagruelian (pæntăgrue·liăn). 1694. [– Fr. *Pantagruel*, name of a giant in Rabelais' work + -IAN; cf. GARGANTUAN.] **A.** *adj.* Of, pertaining to, characteristic of, or appropriate to, Pantagruel, represented as a coarse and extravagant humorist, dealing satirically with serious subjects. **B.** *sb.* = *Pantagruelist* 1899.

Pantagruelism (pæntăgrū·ĕliz'm). 1835. [– Fr. *pantagruélisme*, f. *Pantagruel*; see prec. and -ISM.] The theory and practice ascribed to Pantagruel, one of the characters of Rabelais; extravagant and coarse humour with a satirical or serious purpose. So **Pantagru·elist,** an imitator, admirer, or student of Pantagruel, or of Rabelais 1611. **Pa:ntagrueli·stic, -al** *adjs.*

Pantalettes, -lets (pæntăle·ts), *sb. pl.* (*rare* in *sing.*) Chiefly *U.S.* 1847. [dim. formation from *pantaloon*; see -ETTE.] Loose drawers with a frill at the bottom of each leg, worn by young girls *c*1825–53; *transf.* euphemistically to drawers, cycling 'knickerbockers', or the like, worn by women.

Pantaloon (pæntălū·n). 1590. [– Fr. *pantalon* – It. *pantalone* 'a kind of mask on the Italian stage, representing the Venetian' (Baretti), of whom *Pantalone* (from *San Pantaleone* or *Pantalone*, formerly a favourite saint of the Venetians) was a nickname.] **1. a.** The Venetian character in Italian comedy, represented as a lean and foolish old man, wearing spectacles, pantaloons (see 3), and slippers. **b.** Hence, in mod. pantomime, a foolish old man who is the butt of the clown's jokes, and his abettor in his tricks 1781. **2.** Hence, a dotard, an old fool. *Obs.* exc. as echo of Shaks. 1596. **3.** Chiefly in *pl.* Applied to garments of different styles for the legs; *esp.* A tight-fitting kind of trousers fastened with ribbons or buttons below the calf, or, later, by straps passing under the boots. **b.** Hence, trousers generally (esp. in U.S.). 1798.

2. *A.Y.L.* II. vii. 158. Hence **Pantaloo·ned** *a.* wearing pantaloons; trousered. **Pantaloo·nery,** the performance of a p. in the pantomime.

Pantechnicon (pænte·knikǫn). 1830. [f. Gr. παν- PAN- + τεχνικόν adj. n. belonging to the arts.] Orig., the name of a bazaar of all kinds of artistic work; now, a large warehouse for storing furniture; also, *colloq.* short for *p. van*, a furniture-removing van. Also *attrib.*

†**Pa·nter**[1]. *Obs.* (exc. *Hist.*) [ME. *paneter* – AFr. *paneter* = (O)Fr. *panetier* :– Rom. **panatarius* (in med.L. *pane-*, *panitarius*), for *panarius* (in late L.) bread-seller, f. *panis* bread; see -ER[2] 2.] Orig., a baker, but in ME. usu. the officer of a household who had charge of the pantry –1580.

Pa·nter[2]. *Obs.* exc. *dial.* [– OFr. *panter* 'tendicula, lacum' (mod. *pantière*), in med.L. *panthera*; L. *panthera* 'rete aucupale' (Gloss.), 'rete quoddam' (Varro), Gr. πανθήρα bird-catcher's entire capture.] A fowling net, a fowler's snare; a net, trap, noose. Also *fig.*

Panter[3] (pæ·ntəɹ). 1700. [f. PANT *v.* + -ER[1].] **1.** One who or that which pants 1729. **2.** *slang.* The heart. (Partly a pun upon 'hart'.) 1700.

Panterer (pæ·ntərəɹ). Now only *Hist.* late ME. [Expanded form of PANTER[1]; cf. *adulterer, upholsterer*; see -ER[1] 3.] = PANTER[1].

Pantheism (pæ·nþiˌiz'm). 1732. [f. PANTHEIST; see -ISM.] **1.** The belief or theory that God and the universe are identical (implying a denial of the personality and transcendence of God); the doctrine that God is everything and everything is God. **2.** The heathen worship of all the gods 1837.

Pantheist (pæ·nþiˌist). 1705. [First used by John Toland (1670–1722); f. Gr. πᾶν all + θεός god; see PAN-, THEIST.] One who holds the doctrine of pantheism. Hence **Panthei·stic, -al** *adjs.* of or pertaining to pantheists, or pantheism; **-ly** *adv.*

Pantheon (pæ·nþiˌǫn, pænþī·ǫn). [ME. *panteon* – med.L. *pant(h)eon*; adopted afresh XVI – L. *pantheon* – Gr. πάνθειον, f. παν- PAN- + θεῖος divine, θεός god (see THEISM).] **1.** A temple or sacred building dedicated to all the gods; *spec.* that at Rome, orig. built by Agrippa *c*25 B.C. and also called the *Rotunda.* **b.** *fig.* 'Temple' or 'shrine of all the gods' 1596. **c.** *transf.* A building in which the illustrious dead of a nation are buried, or have memorials erected to them 1713. **2.** A habitation of all the gods; the deities of a people collectively 1550. **b.** Name for a treatise on all the gods 1698. **3.** Name of a large building in London opened as a place of entertainment in 1772; also *gen.*

Panther (pæ·nþəɹ). [ME. *panter(e* – OFr.

pantere (mod. *panthère*) – L. *panthera* – Gr. πάνθηρ.] **1.** The leopard, *Panthera pardus*; pop. applied to large leopards. **2.** Applied in America to the puma or cougar, *Felis concolor*; and, sometimes, to the jaguar, *F. onca* 1730.

attrib. and *Comb.*, as **p.-cat,** the ocelot; **-cowry,** a spotted cowry, *Cypræa pantherina* of the East Indies; **-lily,** *U.S.*, the Californian lily, *Lilium pardatinum*. Hence **Pa·ntheress,** a female p. **Pa·ntherine** (-rəin, -rin) *a.* spotted, etc., like a p.; of, belonging to, or characteristic of, a p.

Panties (pæ·ntiz). 1846. [f. PANTS; see -Y[6].] **a.** *U.S.* Drawers. **b.** In British use, women's and children's drawers 1905.

Pantile (pæ·n₁təil). 1640. [f. PAN *sb.*[1] + TILE *sb.*, prob. after Du. *dakpan* 'roof pan' (cf. G. *dachpfanne, pfannenziegel* 'pantile'.)] **1.** A roofing tile transversely curved to an ogee shape, one curve being much larger than the other. **b.** Erron. applied to flat Dutch or Flemish paving tiles, and so to the Parade at Tunbridge Wells which was paved with these 1774. **2.** *joc.* Hard sea biscuit, etc. 1873.

Pantisocracy (pæntisǫ·krăsi, -əis-). 1794. [f. PANT- + ISOCRACY.] A Utopian community in which all are equal and all rule. So **Pantisocrat** (pæntəi·sŏkræt), one who advocates p. **Pantisocra·tic, -al** *adjs.* pertaining to, involving, or upholding p. **Pantiso·cratist** = *pantisocrat*.

Pantler (pæ·ntləɹ). Now only *Hist.* ME. [app. altered f. PANTER[1], PANTERER, perh. after *butler*.] = PANTER[1].

Panto (pæ·nto), abbrev. f. PANTOMIME.

Panto- (pænto, pæntǫ), bef. a vowel PANT-, repr. Gr. παντο- (παντ-), comb. f. πᾶς, πᾶν (stem παντ-) all; as in **Pa·ntograph** [Gr. -γράφος writing, writer], an instrument for the mechanical copying of a plan, etc., on the same or an enlarged or reduced scale; hence **Panto·grapher; Pantogra·phic, -al,** *adjs.*; **-ly,** *adv.* **Panto·graphy,** complete description (*rare*). †**Pa·ntomancer,** a diviner upon all kinds of things. **Panto·meter** [Gr. μέτρον measure], an instrument for measuring angles and distances, and taking elevations. **Panto·metry,** †universal measurement; the use of a pantometer; hence **Pantome·tric, -al,** *adjs.* **Pa·ntomorph** (erron. **panta-**) [Gr. παντόμορφος], that which takes any or all shapes; so **Pantomo·rphic** *a.* (**panta-**), assuming any or all forms. **Panto·phagist** [Gr. παντοφάγος all-devouring], a man or animal that devours things of all kinds; so **Panto·phagous** *a.*; **Panto·phagy. Pa:ntopragma·tic** *a.* (*joc.*) universally meddling, occupied with everything; *sb.* a pantopragmatic person.

Pantofle (pæ·ntǫ̆f'l, -tuf'l), 1494. [Earliest in Sc. (XV) *pantufle* – Fr. *pantoufle* – It. *pantofola*, †*pantufola*, of obscure origin. In Sc. use from XV, in common Eng. use from *c*1570 to *c*1650–60; after that chiefly an alien or historical word.] A slipper; formerly applied esp. to the high-heeled cork-soled chopines; also to out-door overshoes or goloshes, sandals, and the like.

Pantology (pæntǫ·lŏdʒi). Also *erron.* **panta-.** 1819. [f. Gr. παντο- PANTO- + -λογια -LOGY.] A systematic view of all branches of knowledge; universal knowledge; also, a compendium of universal information. So **Pantolo·gic, -al** *adjs.* of or pertaining to p. Hence **Panto·logist,** one versed in all knowledge. (All joc. or sarcastic.)

Pantomime (pæ·ntŏməim), *sb.* (*a.*) Also †**Pantomimus.** 1589. [– Fr. *pantomime* (XVI) or L. *pantomimus* – Gr. παντόμιμος adj. and sb.; see PANTO-, MIME *sb.*] **1.** A Roman actor, who performed in dumb show; hence, gen., a mimic actor; one who expresses his meaning by gestures and actions without words. Now only *Hist.* **2.** 'A kind of dramatic entertainment in which the performers express themselves by gestures to the accompaniment of music' (Grove *Dict. Mus.*) 1735. **3.** An English dramatic performance, orig. consisting of action without speech, but now of a dramatized tale, the dénouement of which is often a transformation scene followed by the broad comedy of clown and pantaloon and the dancing of harlequin and columbine 1739. **4.** Dumb show 1791. **5.** *attrib.* or *adj.* Of the nature of pantomime (sense 2); of, belonging to, or characteristic of the pantomime (sense 3) 1746.

3. The p. has gradually interwoven itself into our recognized Christmas festivities, so as to become an essential part of them 1892. **4.** As..he could not speak a word of French..he was obliged to convey this sentiment into p. 1871. Hence **Pa·ntomime** *v. intr.* to express oneself by p.; *trans.* to represent by p. **Pantomi·mist** = sense 1.

Pantomimic (pæntŏmi·mik), *a.* and *sb.* 1617. [– L. *pantomimicus*, f. *pantomimus*; see prec., -IC.] **A.** *adj.* **1.** Of the nature of pantomime; expressed by dumb show 1680. **2.** Of or belonging to the pantomime 1805. **b.** Like a pantomime, in its sudden transformations 1895. †**B.** *sb.* = PANTOMIME *sb.* 1. –1689. So **Pantomi·mical** *a.*, **-ly** *adv.*

Pantopod (pæ·ntŏpǫd). 1887. [f. PANTO- + Gr. πούς, ποδ- foot.] *Zool.* One of the *Pantopoda*, a name for the *Pycnogonidæ* or Sea-spiders, when treated as a sub-order; a sea-spider.

Pantoscope (pæ·ntŏskoᵘp). Also *erron.* **panta-.** 1875. [f. PANTO- + -SCOPE.] **1.** A form of photographic lens having a very wide angle. **2.** A pantoscopic camera 1890.

Pantosco·pic, *a.* 1875. [f. as prec. + -IC.] Having a wide range of vision.

P. camera, a panoramic camera. *P. spectacles*, those so constructed as to have different focal lengths in the upper and lower parts, the upper being for long distance vision, and the lower for short; bi-focal spectacles.

Pantry (pæ·ntri). ME. [– AFr. *panetrie*, OFr. *paneterie*, f. *panetier*; see PANTER[1], -RY.] A room or apartment in a house, etc., in which bread and other provisions are kept; also (*butler's* or *housemaid's p.*), one in which the plate, linen, etc. for the table are kept.

attrib. and *Comb.*: **p.-boy,** an assistant in the commissariat department on board a passenger-ship; **-man,** a man in charge of or employed in the p. (or in the commissariat department of a passenger-ship).

Pants (pænts), *sb. pl.* 1841. [Short for *pantaloons* (PANTALOON 3).] **a.** *U.S.* Trousers. **b.** In British use, men's drawers 1874.

Panurgic (pænǭ·ɹdʒik), *a. rare.* 1873. [– late Gr. πανουργικός knavish, f. πανοῦργος ready to do anything, f. παν- PAN- + ἔργον work; reminiscent of *Panurge*, a character in *Pantagruel* (Rabelais).] Able or ready to do anything.

‖**Paolo** (pā·olo, pau·lo). 1617. [It., :– L. *Paulus* Paul.] An obs. Italian silver coin, worth about fivepence sterling, so called from Pope Paul.

Pap (pæp), *sb.*[1] [ME. *pappe*, prob. immed. from Scand. (cf. Sw. and Norw. dial. *pappe*), ult. f. an imit. base *pap- expressing blowing out the cheeks and the noise of sucking; cf. L. *papilla*, late L. *papula* nipple.] **1.** A teat or nipple; a mamilla (chiefly *north. dial.* or *arch.*). **2.** *transf.* Something resembling a pap in form. **a.** A small round tumour or swelling; a pimple 1552. **b.** *pl.* Formerly, a name for two (or more) conical hill summits rising side by side; still used locally 1572.

1. The pappes which gave the sucke TINDALE *Luke* 11:27. **2. b.** The great 'Paps of Jura' were hidden in the mists 1873.

Pap (pæp), *sb.*[2] late ME. [prob. – (M)LG. *pappe*, corresp. to MG. *pap* (G. *pappe*), MDu. *pappe*, Du. *pap*, prob. – med.L. **pappa*, *papare* – L. *pappare* eat, *pap(p)a* used by infants in calling for food (Varro).] **1.** Soft or semi-liquid food for infants or invalids, made of bread, meal, etc., moistened with water or milk. Also *fig.* **2.** Any soft semi-liquid substance; a mash, paste, pulp. late ME. †**b.** The pulp of an apple, esp. when roasted –1761.

1. †*P. with a hatchet*, an ironical phr. for doing a kind thing in an unkind manner, or giving punishment in the guise of a kindness.

Comb.: **p.-boat,** (*a*) a boat-shaped vessel for holding p. for feeding infants; (*b*) a shell of the family *Turbinellidæ* used on the Malabar coast to hold anointing oil. Hence **Pap** *v.* to feed with p.; to feed *up*.

Papa[1] (păpā·). 1670. [– Fr. *papa* – late L. *papa* – Gr. πάππας, πάπας child's word for father. At first only in courtly use; now largely abandoned even by children. In early use the form varied between *papā·* and *pa·ppa*; from the latter the U.S. *po·ppa*.] A word used as the equivalent of *father*; chiefly in the voc., or preceded by a possess. pron. (as 'my papa'); also without any article; less usu. with *a* or in *pl.*

‖**Papa**[2] (pā·pă). 1559. [– eccl.L. *papa* bishop (Tertullian), later (V) applied spec. to the Bishop of Rome; see POPE[1].] †**1.** The pope (of Rome) –1861. **2.** A parish priest or any of the lower clergy in the Orthodox Eastern Church. Also in Gr. form *papas*. 1591.

Papable (pēⁱ·păb'l), *a. rare.* 1592. [– Fr. *papable*, after It. *papabile*; cf. AL. *papabilis*; see PAPA[2], -BLE.] Qualified for the office of pope.

Papacy (pēⁱ·păsi). late ME. [– med.L. *papatia*, f. *papa* POPE[1]; see PAPA[2], -ACY.] **1.** The office or position of pope (of Rome); tenure of office of a pope. **2.** The papal system, ecclesiastically or politically; esp. *Hist.* the papal government as one of the states of Europe 1550.

Papagay, obs. f. POPINJAY.

Papain (păpēⁱ·in). 1890. [f. *papay*(*a* PAPAW + -IN[1].] *Chem.* A proteolytic ferment obtained from the half-ripe fruit of the papaw (*Carica papaya*).

Papal (pēⁱ·păl), *a.* ME. [– (O)Fr. *papal* – med.L. *papalis*, f. eccl.L. *papa* POPE[1]; see PAPA[2], -AL[1].] **1.** Of or pertaining to a pope, or to the pope, his dignity or office. **b.** That is a pope 1802. †**2.** Adhering to or supporting the pope; belonging to the Church of Rome; popish –1814.

1. The P. benediction 1687. *P. cross*, one with three transoms; a triple cross. *P. crown*, or *tiara*, a mitre of cloth of gold, encircled with three coronets or circles of gold. **2.** P. darkness SOUTHEY. Hence **Pa·palism,** the p. system. **Pa·palist,** an adherent of the p. system. **Pa·pally** *adv.* in a p. manner.

†**Papa·lity.** 1456. [– Fr. †*papalité* (mod. *papauté*), med.L. *papalitas*; see PAPAL, -ITY.] The papal office, dignity, or authority; the papal see –1824.

Papalize (pēⁱ·păləiz), *v.* 1624. [f. PAPAL + -IZE.] **1.** *intr.* To become papal or popish. **2.** *trans.* To render papal; to imbue with papist principles or doctrines 1839.

†**Pa·palty.** 1577. [– OFr. *papalté* (mod. *papauté*), f. *papal* PAPAL after *royalté*, *royauté*; see -TY[1].] = PAPALITY –1859.

Paparchy (pēⁱ·păɹki). *rare.* 1839. [f. eccl.L. *papa* POPE[1]; see -ARCHY.] Papal rule.

Papaveraceous (păpēⁱvərēⁱ·ʃəs), *a.* 1846. [f. mod.L. *Papaveraceæ* (f. L. *papaver* poppy) + -OUS; see -ACEOUS.] *Bot.* Of or belonging to the N.O. *Papaveraceæ*, the poppy family.

Papaverine (păpēⁱ·vərəin). 1848. [f. L. *papaver* poppy + -INE[5].] *Chem.* An alkaloid ($C_{20}H_{21}NO_4$) contained in opium, obtained in colourless needles.

Papaverous (păpēⁱ·vərəs), *a.* 1646. [f. as prec. + -OUS.] Pertaining to, resembling, or allied to the poppy; papaveraceous; *fig.* soporific.

Papaw (păpǭ·, pǭpǭ·). 1598. [Formerly *papaya, papay* – Sp. and Pg. *papaya*, *papayo* (the tree), adopted from a Carib dialect. The change to *papaw* (XVII) is unexplained.] **1. a.** The fruit of *Carica papaya* (see b), usu. oblong and about 10 inches long, of a dull orange colour, with a thick fleshy rind, and containing numerous black seeds embedded in pulp; used in tropical countries as food. **b.** The tree *Carica papaya* (N.O. *Papayaceæ*), a native of S. America, somewhat resembling a palm. The stem, leaves, and fruit contain an acrid milky juice which has the property of rendering meat tender (see PAPAIN.) 1613. **2.** (Only in forms *papaw*, *pawpaw*.) U.S. name for a small N. American tree, *Asimina triloba* (N.O. *Anonaceæ*), with dull purple flowers and ovate leaves (*p.-tree*); or for its edible fruit 1760. **3.** *attrib.*, as *p.-bush* (= 2), etc. 1704.

Papayaceous (pæpăyēⁱ·ʃəs), *a.* 1846. [f. mod.L. *Papayaceæ* (f. *Papaya*; see prec.) + -OUS; see -ACEOUS.] *Bot.* Belonging to the N.O. *Papayaceæ* (sometimes reckoned as a sub-order of *Passifloraceæ*), of which the Papaw-tree, *Carica papaya*, is the type.

Papegay, -jay, -joy, obs. ff. POPINJAY.

Paper (pēⁱ·pəɹ), *sb.* [Late ME. *papir* – AFr. *papir*, (O)Fr. *papier* – L. *papyrus* – Gr.

πάπυρος PAPYRUS.] **I.** Without *a* or *pl.* (exc. as denoting a particular kind). **1.** A substance composed of fibres interlaced into a compact web, made from linen and cotton rags, straw, wood, certain grasses, etc., which are macerated into a pulp, dried, and pressed; it is used for writing, printing, or drawing on, for wrapping things in, for covering the interior of walls, etc. **b.** Also applied to other substances used for writing upon, as the PAPYRUS of the ancients; or to substances of similar texture, as that made by wasps for their nests. late ME. **c.** Applied familiarly to substances made from paper-pulp, as mill-board, papier mâché, etc. 1670. **2.** *Comm.* **a.** Negotiable documents, bills of exchange, etc. collectively. **b.** Paper money or currency as opp. to coin, bank-notes, etc. 1674. **3.** *slang.* Free passes of admission to a theatre, etc.; *transf.* persons admitted by these 1873.

1. Phr. *To commit to p.*, to write down. *To put pen to p.*, to commence writing, to write. *On p.*, in writing, in print; said esp. of a sketch or plan, in contrast to the reality; hence = in theory, theoretically. **2. a.** The bankers will not look at his p. (*mod.*).

II. Individual singular with *a* and *pl.* **1.** A piece, sheet, or leaf of paper 1628. **b.** A piece of paper serving as a wrapper or receptacle; often including the contents; a paperful; a sheet or card of paper containing pins or needles stuck in it 1511. **c.** A curl-paper. (Usu. in *pl.*) 1876. **2.** A sheet, leaf, or piece of paper, bearing writing; a note, bill, or other legal instrument; in *pl.* written notes, memoranda, letters, official documents, etc. late ME. **†b.** A note, fastened on the back of a criminal undergoing punishment, specifying his offence –1688. **†c.** *pl.* = STATE-PAPERS, as in *Office of His* (*Her*) *Majesty's Papers*, etc. –1799. **d.** *pl.* The collection of documents establishing a person's identity, standing, etc.; the certificates which accompany an officer's application for permission to resign 1685. **e.** A set of questions in an examination; also, the written answers to these 1838. **3.** = NEWSPAPER 1642. **4.** A written or printed essay, dissertation, or article on some particular topic; now *esp.* a communication read or sent to a learned society. 1669.

1. But, in truth, the mind can never resemble a blank p. J. H. NEWMAN. **b.** A p. of sandwiches DICKENS. **2. b.** 2 *Hen. VI*, II. iv. 31. **d.** *To send in one's papers*, to resign. *Ship's papers*, the set of papers carried by a ship for the manifestation of her ownership, nationality, destination, etc. **3.** The office of the local p. STEVENSON.

III. *attrib.*, passing into *adj.* **a.** Of paper; made or consisting of paper 1596. **b.** *fig.* Like paper; slight, thin, flimsy, frail, feeble (as if made of paper) 1615. **c.** *fig.* Consisting of, pertaining to, or carried on by means of letters to journals, pamphlets, or books; literary 1592. **d.** Written on paper, in written form; *esp.* theoretical, hypothetical 1638.

a. Money of credit, which they commonly call p. currency BURKE. A *large-paper* copy of a book; see LARGE A. II. **b.** *P. ship*, a ship built of inferior material and badly put together 1891. **d.** P. profits were divided as if they were real 1893.

attrib. and *Comb.* **1.** General: as *p.-case*, *-circulation*, *-factory*, *-fibre*, *-pulp*, *trade*, etc.; *p.-saving* adj.; *p.-fastener*, *-holder*, *-maker*, etc.; *p.-bound*, *-covered*, *-panelled* adjs. **2.** Special: **p.-back,** a book with a p. back or cover; **p. birch** (see BIRCH *sb.* 1b); **p. boards** (*Bookbinding*), a style of binding with paper covering the usual board stiffening; **†-book,** (*a*) a book of blank p. to write in; (*b*) *Law*, a copy of the demurrer book which contains the pleadings in an action, when the issue is one of law; **-boy,** a boy employed to sell newspapers; **-chase,** the game of hare and hounds when paper is used for the 'scent'; **-cutter,** (*a*) a paper-knife; (*b*) a machine for cutting the edges of p.; **-faced,** (*a*) having a face like p., i.e. thin or pale; (*b*) faced with p.; **-folder,** an instrument for folding p., as the folding-stick used in bookbinding; **-knife,** a knife of ivory, wood, etc., used *esp.* to cut open the leaves of an uncut book; **-marl,** a kind of marl occurring in thin layers; **-mill,** a mill in which p. is made; **-mulberry,** a small tree (*Broussonetia papyrifera*) allied to the mulberry, from the bark of which p. is made in China and Japan; **p. nautilus** = NAUTILUS a; **†P. Office** = Office of His Majesty's Papers (II. 2c.), the STATE PAPER Office; **-rush,** the papyrus; **p. sailor,** the p. nautilus; **-tree,** name for trees or shrubs from which paper is made; **-wasp,** a wasp that constructs its nest of a papery substance made from dry wood moistened into a paste; **-weight,** a small heavy object intended to be laid upon loose papers to prevent their being disarranged; **-work,** the written work of a student in a class or examination.

Paper (pēⁱ·pəɹ), *v.* 1594. [f. prec.] **1.** *trans.* To set down on paper; to describe in writing. Now *rare.* **2.** To enclose in, put *up* in, paper; to stick (pins, etc.) in a sheet or card of paper 1599. **3.** To stick paper upon (a wall, etc.); to decorate (a room) with paper-hangings 1774. **b.** *Bookbinding.* To paste the end-papers and fly-leaves at the beginning and end of (a volume) before putting on the cover 1875. **4.** To supply with paper 1883. **b.** *slang.* To fill (a theatre, etc.) by means of free passes; see PAPER *sb.* I. 3. 1866. Hence **Pa·perer,** one who papers; *spec.* a paper-hanger 1844.

Pa·per-ha:nger. 1809. A man whose business it is to cover the walls of rooms, etc. with paper-hangings.

Pa·per-ha:nging. 1693. **1.** *pl.* Paper, usually printed in ornamental designs, used for covering the walls of a room, etc. (so called as taking the place of the cloth hangings formerly used); wall-paper. **2.** The decorating of a room with wall-paper; the occupation of a paper-hanger 1904.

Pa·per mo:ney. 1691. [PAPER *sb.* I. 1, 2.] Negotiable documents used instead of money, esp. bank-notes; more strictly, a paper currency, which by the law of the country represents money and is a legal tender. Also *attrib.*

Pa·per-stai:ner. 1596. **1.** One who stains or colours paper; *joc.* an (inferior) author. **2.** A maker of paper-hangings 1756.

Papery (pēⁱ·pəri), *a.* 1602. [f. PAPER *sb.* + -Y¹.] Of the consistence of paper; like paper; thin or flimsy in texture.

Papess (pēⁱ·pės). 1620. [– Fr. *papesse* (XVI), It. *papessa* – med.L. *papissa*, f. eccl.L. *papa* POPE¹; see PAPA², -ESS¹.] A female pope. (*Hist.* of the alleged Pope Joan, A.D. 853–5.)

‖**Papeterie** (pæpėtrī·). 1847. [Fr., = paper-manufacture, stationer's shop, writing case, f. *papetier* paper-maker.] A case or box for paper and other writing materials; a stationery-case.

Paphian (pēⁱ·fiăn), *a.* and *sb.* 1614. [f. L. *Paphius* adj. (f. *Paphos*) + -AN.] **A.** *adj.* **1.** Of or belonging to Paphos, a city of Cyprus sacred to Aphrodite or Venus (*the P. Goddess*). **2.** *transf.* Pertaining to love; *esp.* to unlawful sexual indulgence; belonging to the class of prostitutes 1650. **B.** *sb.* **1.** An inhabitant or native of Paphos. **2.** A devotee of the Paphian Venus; a prostitute 1811.

‖**Papier mâché** (pa·pye mɑ·ʃe). 1753. [– Fr. *papier* paper, *mâché* chewed, pa. pple. of *mâcher* :– L. *masticare* chew. Not of French origin.] A substance consisting of paper-pulp or paper reduced to a pulp and shaped by moulding; used for boxes, jars, trays, fancy articles, etc. Also *attrib.* (usu. = made of papier mâché).

Papilionaceous (păpi:liŏnēⁱ·ʃəs), *a.* 1668. [– mod.L. *papilionaceus*, f. L. *papilio* butterfly; see PAVILION, -ACEOUS.] **1.** Of or pertaining to a butterfly or butterflies; of the nature of a butterfly; belonging to the butterfly tribe. Now *rare* or *Obs.* Also *fig.* **2.** *Bot.* Applied, from its fancied likeness to a butterfly, to that form of flower found in most leguminous plants, having an irregular corolla consisting of a large upper petal (the *vexillum* or standard), two lateral petals (the *alæ* or wings), and two narrow lower petals between these (forming the *carina* or keel). Also said of the plant. 1668.

‖**Papilla** (păpi·lă). *Pl.* **-æ.** 1693. [L., = nipple, dim. of PAPULA.] **1.** *Zool.* and *Anat.* **a.** The nipple of the breast; the mamilla. (*rare* in Eng. use.) **b.** Any minute nipple-like protuberance, usu. soft and fleshy, in a part or organ of the body: e.g. the papillæ on the tongue 1713. **c.** *Path.* A small papule or pimple 1797. **2.** *Bot.* A small fleshy projection upon any part of a plant 1848. So **Papillar** (pæ·pilăɹ, păpi·lăɹ), **Papillary** (pæ·pilări, păpi·lări) *adjs.* of the form or nature of a p.; containing, furnished with, or consisting of papillæ; of, pertaining to, or affecting papillæ. **Pa·pillate(d** *a.* furnished or covered with papillæ; formed into a p., papillary. **Papilli·ferous** *a.* bearing papillæ. **Papi·lliform** *a.* of the form of a p.; nipple-shaped. **Pa·pillose** *a.* full of or beset with papillæ. **Papi·llous** *a.* (now *rare* or *Obs.*), papillose.

‖**Papillitis** (pæpiləi·tis). 1892. [f. PAPILLA + -ITIS.] *Path.* Inflammation of the optic papilla.

‖**Papilloma** (pæpilōᵘ·mă). *Pl.* **-ata.** 1866. [f. PAPILLA + -OMA.] *Path.* A tumour of the skin or of a mucous membrane, consisting of an overgrown papilla or group of papillæ, usu. covered with a layer of thickened epidermis or epithelium; e.g. a wart, corn, condyloma, etc. Hence **Papillo·matous** *a.* of, pertaining to, or of the nature of a p.

†Papillote (pæ·piloᵘt, -ǫt). 1748. [– Fr. *papillote* (XVII) in same sense.] A curl-paper –1845.

Papillule (pæ·pilⁱul). 1826. Also in L. form. [– mod.L. *papillula*, dim. of PAPILLA; see -ULE.] A minute papilla; esp. a small elevation or depression with a minute papilla in the centre. Hence **Papi·llulate** *a.* beset with papillules.

Papish (pēⁱ·piʃ), *a.* and *sb.* Now *dial.* 1546. [By suffix-alteration f. PAPIST.] **A.** *adj.* Papistical, popish. (A hostile epithet.) **B.** *sb.* = PAPIST. Now *dial.* 1604. So **†Pa·pisher** = B.

Papism (pēⁱ·piz'm). 1550. [– Fr. *papisme* or mod.L. *papismus*; see next, -ISM.] The papal system; popery; Roman Catholicism.

Papist (pēⁱ·pist). 1534. [– Fr. *papiste* or mod.L. (also AL., XV) *papista*, f. eccl.L. *papa*; see PAPA², -IST.] **1.** An adherent of the pope; esp. an advocate of papal supremacy; also, more gen., a member of the Roman Catholic Church. (Usu. hostile or opprobrious.) **2.** *attrib.* or quasi-*adj.* = PAPAL 1819.

Papistic (păpi·stik), *a.* 1545. [– Fr. *papistique* or med.L. *papisticus*; see prec., -IC.] Of, pertaining to, or of the nature of a papist or papists; adhering to the pope; of, pertaining or adhering to, the Church of Rome and its doctrines; popish. (Usu. hostile or opprobrious). So **Papi·stical** *a.* 1537, **-ly** *adv.* 1572.

Papistry (pēⁱ·pistri). 15.. [f. PAPIST + -RY.] The doctrine or system of papists; popery; the Roman Catholic religion or faith. (A hostile term.)

†Pa·pize, *v.* 1612. [f. PAPIST + -IZE, on the anal. of similar pairs.] **a.** *intr.* To play the pope; to act on the side of the pope or papal system; **b.** *trans.* To render papal or popish. Hence **†Pa·pized** *ppl. a.* imbued with popery. **†Pa·pizing** *vbl. sb.* and *ppl. a.* –1843.

‖**Papoose** (păpū·s). 1634. [Algonquin.] A North-American Indian young child.

Papoosh, papouch(e (păpū·ʃ). 1682. [– Pers. *pāpūš* BABOUCHE; the Turk. *pabuc* is repr. by PABOUCH.] A Turkish or Oriental slipper.

Pappescent (pæpe·sĕnt), *a.* Also *erron.* **papesc-.** 1720. [f. L. PAPPUS; see -ESCENT.] *Bot.* Producing a pappus, as composite plants.

Pappose (pæpōᵘ·s), *a.* 1691. [f. next + -OSE¹.] *Bot.* Furnished with or of the nature of a pappus, downy. So **Pa·ppous** *a.*

‖**Pappus** (pæ·pŭs). 1704. [L. – Gr. πάππος (i) grandfather, (ii) down on plants.] *Bot.* The downy or feathery appendage on certain fruits, esp. on the achenes or 'seeds' of many *Compositæ*, as thistles, dandelions, etc.; hence extended to the reduced calyx of *Compositæ* generally, whether downy, bristly, scaly, toothed, or membranous.

Pa·ppy, *a.* 1670. [f. PAP *sb.*² + -Y¹.] Of the nature or consistence of pap; soft and wet.

‖**Paprika** (pæ·prikă, pæprī·kă). 1898. [Magyar.] A condiment prepared from the fruit of the *Capsicum annuum*; Hungarian red pepper.

‖**Papula** (pæ·piŭlă). *Pl.* **-æ.** 1706. [L., = pustule, pimple; see PAP *sb.*¹] = PAPULE. Hence **Pa·pular** *a.*

Papulation (pæpiulēⁱ·ʃən). 1877. [f. PAPULE, PAPULA + -ATION, on the anal. of similar pairs, as *granule*, *granulation*.] The formation of papules.

Papule (pæ·piul). 1864. [– L. *papula*; cf. Fr. *papule*.] **1.** *Path.* A small, solid, somewhat pointed swelling of the skin, usu. inflammatory, without suppuration; a pimple. **2.** *Zool.* and *Bot.* = PAPILLA 1 b, 2. 1872.

Papulo- (pæ·piulo), used as comb. form of PAPULA, PAPULE; as in **Pa:pulo-erythe·ma,** erythema accompanied by papules; etc.

Papulose (pæ·piulōᵘs), *a.* 1776. [– mod.L. *papulosus*; see PAPULA and -OSE¹.] Covered with papules or papillæ; papillose.

Papulous (pæ·piuləs), *a.* 1818. [f. PAPULE, PAPULA + -OUS.] Covered with papules, papulose; of the nature of a papule.

Papyraceous (pæpirēⁱ·ʃəs), *a.* 1752. [f. L. *papyrus* (see PAPER) + -ACEOUS. Cf. mod.L. *papyraceus* (XVI).] *Nat. Hist.* Of the thinness or nature of paper; papery.

Papyrian (păpi·riăn), *a.* Also **-ean.** 1754. [f. late and med.L. *papyrius* + -AN; see -IAN.] Pertaining to or composed of papyrus.

Papyrin (pæ·pirin). Also **-ine.** 1860. [f. L. PAPYRUS + -IN¹.] = PARCHMENT *paper.*

Papyrine (păpəi·rin), *a.* 1816. [– L. *papyrinus* of papyrus; see -INE².] Made of papyrus.

Papyro-, comb. form of Gr. πάπυρος PAPYRUS (also in sense 'paper'); as in **Papy·rotype,** name given to a modification of photolithography, in which the picture is first printed on a sensitized gelatin film supported on paper, and afterwards transferred to a lithographic stone or to zinc.

Papyrograph (păpəiᵊ·rǒgrɑf), *sb.* 1877. [f. PAPYRO- + -GRAPH.] Name of an apparatus for copying documents by chemical agents acting through a porous paper-stencil. Hence **Papy·rograph** *v. trans.* to copy with a p. **Papyrogra·phic** *a.* pertaining to or produced by a p. or papyrography.

Papyrography (pæpirǫ·grăfi). 1848. [f. PAPYRO- + -GRAPHY.] A process of writing or drawing on paper and transferring the design to a zinc plate whence it is printed. **b.** The process of copying with a papyrograph.

Papyrology (pæpirǫ·lǒdʒi). 1898. [f. PAPYRO- + -LOGY.] The study of papyri. Hence **Papyro·logist.**

‖**Papyrus** (păpəiᵊ·rǒs). *Pl.* **papyri** (-əiᵊ·rəi). late ME. [– L. *papyrus* – Gr. πάπυρος paper-rush, of unkn. (prob. Oriental) origin; cf. PAPER.] **1.** An aquatic plant of the sedge family, the Paper Reed or Paper Rush (*Cyperus papyrus* or *Papyrus antiquorum*); formerly abundant in Egypt. **2.** A substance prepared, in the form of thin sheets, from the stem of the papyrus plant, by laying thin slices or strips of it side by side, with another layer crossing them, and usually a third layer again parallel to the first, the whole being then soaked in water pressed together, and dried; used by the ancient Egyptians, Greeks, Romans, etc., as a writing material 1727. **3.** (With pl. *papyri.*) An ancient manuscript or document written on papyrus 1824. **4.** *attrib.* 1837.

2. The few rolls of p. which the ancients deemed a notable collection of books LYTTON. **3.** Those Biblical codices which most resemble the Herculanean papyri 1875.

Par (pāɹ), *sb.*¹ 1622. [– L. *par* equal, equality.] **1.** Equality of value or standing; an equal footing, a level. Now chiefly in *on* or *upon a p.* 1662. **2.** *Comm.* **a.** The recognized value of the currency of one country in terms of that of another; in full, *p. of exchange*: see EXCHANGE *sb.* 4. 1622. **b.** Equality between the market value of stocks, shares, etc., and the nominal or face value 1726. **c.** *attrib. P. value* = value at par 1861. **3.** An average or normal amount, quality, degree, or condition 1778. **4.** *Golf.* The number of strokes a scratch player should require for a hole or the course, calculated according to a formula, and usu. less than BOGEY 1898.

2. b. Phr. *At p.*, at the face value; *above p.*, at a price above the face value, at a premium; *below p.*, at a discount. **3.** *On a p.*, on an average. *Above* or *below* (*under*) *p.*, above or below the average, normal, or usual amount, degree, condition, or quality; I think he caught a chill, and being below p. he succumbed 1886. So *up to p.*; I am about up to p., and not without hope [etc.] 1899.

Par (pāɹ), *sb.*² *colloq.* 1879. Abbrev. of *paragraph.*

‖**Par** (par, pāɹ), *prep.* ME. [– (O)Fr. *par* :– Rom. **pra*, **per ad* (L. *per* PER-, *ad* AD-).] **1.** Occurring in ME. in certain asseverations (mostly obs.), as *par charite* (where it was sometimes confused with OFr. *pur*, Fr. *pour* :– L. *pro* for). **b.** See PERADVENTURE (*par aunter*), PARAMOUNT, PARAVAIL, PARAVANT, PERCASE, etc., which have coalesced into single words. **2.** In mod. Eng., in advb. phrases from mod. Fr., often hardly naturalized. Such are PARBLEU; *par exemple*, for instance; *par force* = PERFORCE *adv.* 1597. ‖**b. Par excellence** [L. *per excellentiam*], by virtue of manifest superiority; pre-eminently; above all others that may be so called 1695.

Par-, *prefix*, repr. Fr. *par-*, L. *per-* 'through, thoroughly', occurring in words from Fr., as PARBOIL, PARDON, PARVENU; esp. common in ME. in words now obs., or in which *par-* has now become PER- after L., as *parfit* PERFECT, etc.

Par, var. PARR.

‖**Para**¹ (pā·ră). 1687. [– Turk. – Pers. *pārah* piece, portion, coin so called.] A small Turkish coin, the fortieth part of a piastre, formerly of silver, but now of copper, and of the value of about one-twentieth of a penny.

‖**Para**² (pā·ră). Also **parra, parah.** 1698. [Hindi.] An East Indian measure of capacity; also a weight of North Borneo.

‖**Pará**³ (parā·, pā·ră). 1848. Name of a seaport on the south estuary of the Amazon, in Brazil. Used *attrib.*, esp. in **P. grass,** a Brazilian forage-grass, *Panicum barbinode*, now cultivated in the Southern U.S. **P. nut** = Brazil-nut: see BRAZIL 4. **P. rubber,** an india-rubber obtained from the coagulated milky juice of *Hevea brasiliensis* (N.O. *Euphorbiaceæ*), a tree growing on the banks of the Amazon.

Para-¹ (pærā), bef. a vowel or *h* usually **par-,** repr. Gr. παρα-, παρ-, comb. form of παρά *prep.* As a prep., Gr. παρά had the sense 'by the side of, beside', whence 'alongside of, by, past, beyond', etc. In composition it had the same senses, with such cognate advb. ones as 'to one side, amiss, faulty, irregular, disordered, improper, wrong'; also expressing subsidiary relation, alteration, perversion, simulation, etc. These senses also occur in Eng. derivs.; see below and PARABLE, PARADOX, PARASITE; PARALLEL; PARENTHESIS; PARHELION; PARISH; PAROCHIAL, PARODY, PAROXYSM, etc.

1. Terms (sbs. or adjs.) chiefly *Anat.*, *Nat. Hist.*, and *Path.*, as **Paraba·sal** *a. Zool.* in crinoids, situated next to and articulated with a basal plate; also as *sb.* **Pa·rablast** [Gr. βλαστός sprout, germ], *Embryol.* the nutritive yolk of a meroblastic ovum, as dist. from the formative yolk or archiblast; hence **Parabla·stic** *a.* ‖**Parabra·nchia,** the modified osphradium of certain gastropod molluscs, considered as a secondary branchia or gill; hence **Parabra·nchial, Parabra·nchiate** *adjs.* **Parace·ntral** *a.* situated beside a centre; in *Anat.* applied to parts of the brain lying alongside the central fissure. **Paracho·rdal** *a. Embryol.* situated beside the notochord: applied to two plates of cartilage, forming the foundation of the skull in the embryo; also as *sb.* **Pa·racyst** *Bot.* one of a pair of sexual organs in certain fungi. ‖**Paræsthe·sia** *Path.* disordered or perverted sensation; a hallucination of any of the senses. **Pa·ragaster** [Gr. γαστήρ belly, stomach] *Zool.* the central or gastric cavity of a simple sponge. **Paraga·stric** *a. Zool.* (*a*) situated alongside the stomach or gastric cavity, as certain canals in *Ctenophora*; (*b*) pertaining to the paragaster of a sponge. ‖**Paraglo·ssa** [Gr. γλῶσσα tongue] *Entom.* each of two lateral appendages of the ligula in various insects; hence **Paraglo·ssal, Paraglo·ssate** *adjs.* **Para·gnathous** [Gr. γνάθος jaw] *a. Ornith.* having the mandibles of equal length. **Pa:raheliotro·pic** [Gr. ἥλιος sun, -τροπος turning] *a. Bot.* of leaves: turning their edges in the direction of incident light. **Pa:rahelio·tropism** *Bot.* a tendency in plants when exposed to brilliant light to turn their leaves parallel to the incidence of the light-rays. **Parama·stoid** *a. Anat.* situated near the mastoid process: applied to certain processes of the occipital bone, also called *paroccipital*; also as *sb.* **Paranu·cleus** *Biol.* a small subsidiary nucleus in certain *Protozoa*; hence **Paranu·clear, Paranu·cleate** *adjs.* ‖**Paraphimo·sis** *Path.* permanent retraction of the prepuce. ‖**Paraphra·sia** *Path.* incoherent or disordered speech. ‖**Para·physis** [Gr. φύσις growth], a sterile filament accompanying the reproductive organs in certain cryptogams. **Pa·raplasm** *Biol.* (*a*) Kupffer's name for the more fluid part of a cell-substance; (*b*) a neoplasm; hence **Parapla·smic, Parapla·stic** *adjs.* ‖**Parapo·dium** [Gr. ποδ- foot] *Zool.* one of the jointless lateral processes or rudimentary limbs of annelids, which serve as organs of locomotion, and sometimes of sensation or respiration; hence **Parapo·dial** *a.* ‖**Parapo·physis** [APOPHYSIS] *Anat.* an interior or ventral transverse process of a vertebra, in some animals serving as articulation for the head of a rib. **Parasphe·noid** *a. Zool.* and *Comp. Anat.* lying alongside the sphenoid bone; applied to a bone extending in the median line along the base of the skull in birds, reptiles, amphibians, and fishes; also as *sb.* **Paraste·rnal** [STERNUM] *a.* lying alongside the sternum or breastbone; in *p. line*, a line drawn vertically down the surface of the chest from a point in the collar-bone one-third of its length from its inner end. **Para·stichy** [Gr. στίχος row, rank] *Bot.* a secondary spiral or oblique rank of lateral members around the stem or axis, in a phyllotaxis in which the leaves, scales, etc. are close together, as in certain leaf-rosettes, pine-cones, etc. **Parathe·rmic** [Gr. θερμός warm, hot] *a.* name given by Sir J. Herschel to invisible rays accompanying the orange and red rays in the spectrum, so called in ref. to the neighbouring thermic or heat rays. **Parathy·roid,** one of several bodies adjacent to the thyroid gland. **Parato·nic** *a. Bot.* pertaining to the effect of light or other external stimuli in causing movements or influencing growth in plants. **Paratri·ptic** [Gr. τριπτ-, f. τρίβειν rub] *a.* having the property of preventing waste of bodily tissue; also as *sb.* **Para·xial** *a. Anat.* and *Zool.* lying alongside, or on each side of, the axis of the body. ‖**Parazo·a** [Gr. ζῷον animal] *sb. pl. Zool.* in some classifications, a name for the Sponges considered as a division co-ordinate with *Protozoa* and *Metazoa*; hence **Parazo·an** *a.* and *sb.* **Parelectro·nomy** *Physiol.* a condition marked by weakening of the electrical current of muscle; hence **Parelectrono·mic** *a.* ‖**Parepidi·dymis** [EPIDIDYMIS] *Anat.* the organ of Giraldes, a mass of convoluted tubules just above the epididymis. **Parocci·pital** *a. Anat.* situated at the side of the occiput, or beside the occipital bone; applied *spec.* to certain bones, or processes of bone (also called *paramastoid*), as the jugular process of the occipital bone; also as *sb.* ‖**Paroophoron** (pæroₒǫ·fŏrǫn) [mod.L. *oophoron* ovary] *Anat.* (*a*) = *parovarium*; (*b*) a small remnant of the Wolffian body in the female, corresp. to the parepididymis. **Paro·rchid** [Gr. ὄρχις testicle] *Anat.* the epididymis. ‖**Parova·rium** *Anat.* a remnant of the Wolffian body in the female, corresp. to the epididymis in the male. **Parumbi·lical** [L. *umbilicus* navel] *a. Anat.* situated around or near the navel.

2. *Chem.* **a.** Names of substances that are (or have been supposed to be) modifications of those to the names of which *para-* is prefixed, or that have been produced along with or instead of these, or, sometimes, that merely occur with them, as **Parabe·nzene,** a hydrocarbon isomeric with benzene, occurring along with it in light coal oil. **Parachlo·ralide,** an isomer of chloral produced by the action of chloral on wood spirit. **Paracya·nogen,** an isomer or polymer of cyanogen, formed in small quantity when cyanogen is prepared from cyanide of mercury. **Paraglo·bulin,** a name given to distinguish the particular form of GLOBULIN found in blood-serum. **Parala·ctic** *a.* in *p. acid*, an isomeric modification of lactic acid, one of the two constituents of sarcolactic acid. **Para·ldehyde,** a polymer of ALDEHYDE, used as a narcotic and as a remedy against insomnia.

b. (More systematically) Names of isomeric benzene di-derivatives in which the two hydrogen-atoms replaced by another element or radical are symmetrically disposed in the benzene ring, being separated on each side by two other atoms; as 1 and 4 in the ring $1^{23}_{65}4$; e.g. *paradichlorobenzene*, $C_6ClHHClHH$. These are unlimited in number.

3. Other terms, often – Gr. words, as **Pa·rachrose** [as if f. Gr. χρῶσις colouring] *a. Min.* that changes colour by exposure to weather. ‖**Paradiastole** (-dəi,æ·stŏli) [L. – Gr. παραδιαστολή] *Rhet.* a figure in which a favourable turn is given to something unfavourable by the use of an expression that conveys only part of the truth. **Paradiploma·tic** *a.* aside or apart from what is strictly diplomatic or concerned with the evidence of the manuscript texts. **Paradro·mic** [f. Gr. παράδρομος] *a.* running side by side; *p. winding*, winding in courses that run side by side. **Pa·ramorph** [Gr. μορφή form] *Min.* a pseudomorph formed by a change of physical characters without a change in chemical composition; hence **Paramo·rphic** *a.*, **Paramo·rphism. Paranate·llon** [Gr. ἀνατέλλων rising] *Astrol.* a star that rises at the same time as another star or other stars. **Pa·rascene** [Gr. παρασκήνιον] *Gr.* and *Rom. Antiq.* the part of an ancient theatre on either side of the stage, comprising rooms to which the actors retired. **Paraschema·tic** *a.* (*rare*) formed by a slight change of an existing element. ‖**Parasy·nesis** [Gr. παρασύνεσις] *Philol.* misunderstanding or misconception of a word, resulting in an alteration or corruption of it; hence **Parasyne·tic** *a.* ‖**Parata·xis** [Gr. παράταξις] *Gram.* the placing of propositions or clauses one after another, without indicating by connecting words the relation between them; opp. to *hypotaxis*; hence **Parata·ctic, -al** *adjs.* ‖**Parembole** (-e·mbŏli) [Gr. παρεμβολή] *Rhet.* a kind of parenthesis. ‖**Parempto·sis** [Gr. παρέμπτωσις] = *parembole*.

Para-[2], – Fr. – It. *para-*, imperative of vb. *parare* to defend, cover from, shield, etc., orig. 'to prepare' :– L. *parare* PARE *v.*; used with a sb. object, in phrases which have themselves become sbs., as *para-sole* lit. 'defend or shelter from sun', hence 'a sunshade', etc.; on the analogy of these were formed Fr. *parapluie, parachute*, etc. Thence English has PARAPET, PARACHUTE, PARASOL, etc., with occasional unnaturalized formations, as **parapluie** [Fr. *pluie* rain], umbrella; **paratonnerre** [Fr. *tonnerre* thunder], a lightning conductor.

Parabanic (pærăbæ·nik), *a.* 1838. [f. PARA-[1], prob. in sense 'instead of' + (*allox*)*anic*, with euphonic *b.*] *Chem.* In *p. acid*, a dibasic acid, $CO_2(NH.CO)$, produced by the action of nitric acid on uric acid or alloxan. Hence **Pa·rabanate**, a salt of p. acid.

‖**Parabasis** (pără·bāsis). *Pl.* **-bases** (-bāsīz). 1820. [– Gr. παράβασις, f. παραβαίνειν go aside, step forward; see PARA-[1].] In ancien Gr. comedy, a part sung by the chorus, addressed to the audience in the poet's name, and unconnected with the action of the drama.

Parable (pæ·răb'l), *sb.* ME. [– (O)Fr. *parabole* – L. *parabola* comparison, in Chr. L. allegory, proverb, discourse, speech – Gr. παραβολή comparison, analogy, proverb, f. παραβάλλειν put alongside, compare, f. παρά PARA-[1] + βάλλειν cast, throw.] A comparison, a similitude; any saying or narration in which something is expressed in terms of something else; an allegory, an apologue. Also, any kind of enigmatical or dark saying. *arch.* (exc. as in b). **b.** *spec.* A fictitious narrative (usually of something that might naturally occur), by which moral or spiritual relations are typically set forth, as the parables of the New Testament. late ME. **c.** *dial.* An example or illustration (to follow or avoid) 1800.

Doubtless ye will say unto me this p., Physician, heal thyself N.T. (R.V.) *Luke* 4:23. Phr. *To take up one's p.*, to begin to discourse (arch.). †*Parables of Solomon*, the book of Proverbs. **b.** Heare ye therefore the p. of the sower *Matt.* 13:18. Hence **Pa·rable** *v.* (*rare*) *intr.* to speak or discourse in parables; *trans.* to represent or express by means of a p.

†**Pa·rable,** *a.* 1581. [– L. *parabilis*, f. *parare* procure; see -BLE.] That can be readily prepared or procured –1741.

Parabola (păræ·bŏlă). 1579. [– mod.L. *parabola* – Gr. παραβολή application, spec. in geom. of a given area to a given straight line, f. παραβάλλειν (see PARABLE).] *Geom.* One of the conic sections; the plane curve formed by the intersection of a cone with a plane parallel to a side of the cone; also definable as the locus of a point whose distance from a given point (the focus) is equal to its distance from a given straight line (the directrix). **b.** Extended to curves of higher degrees resembling a parabola in running off to infinity without approaching to an asymptote, or having the line at infinity as a tangent 1664.

Cubic or *cubical p.*, a p. of the third degree. *Double p.*, a p. having the line at infinity for a double tangent. Hence **Parabo·liform** *a.* of the form of a p.

‖**Parabole** (păræ·bŏli). 1589. [– Gr. παραβολή PARABLE.] *Rhet.* A comparison, a metaphor (in the widest sense).

Parabolic (pærăbǫ·lik), *a.* and *sb.* 1449. [– late L. *parabolicus* – late Gr. παραβολικός figurative, f. παραβολή PARABLE, PARABOLA; see -IC.] **A.** *adj.* **1.** Of, pertaining to, or of the nature of a parable. **b.** Of or pertaining to parabole; metaphorical 1696. **2.** *Geom.* Of the form of, or resembling, a parabola; of which the section is a parabola: also, having relation to the parabola 1702.

1. The P. Teaching of Christ 1882. **2.** *P. reflector*, a reflector, usu. of polished metal, made in the form of a paraboloid of circular section, so as to reflect parallel rays to a focus, or reflect in parallel lines the rays of a lamp placed at the focus. *P. spindle*, a figure formed by the revolution of an arc of a parabola about its (double) ordinate. *P. spiral* = HELICOID parabola.

B. *sb. Geom.* A parabolic figure; a parabola or paraboloid (*rare*) –1807.

Parabolical (pærăbǫ·likăl), *a.* 1554. [f. as prec. + -AL[1]; see -ICAL.] **1.** Of or pertaining to parable; involving, or constituting parable; having a figurative existence or value. **2.** *Geom.* = prec. A. 2. Now *rare*. 1571. Hence **Parabo·lically** *adv.*

Parabolist (păræ·bŏlist). 1651. [f. Gr. παραβολή PARABLE, PARABOLA + -IST.] **1.** One who deals in any way with parables or parabole. **2.** One who deals with the parabola 1831.

Parabolize (păræ·bŏlaiz), *v.* 1600. [orig. – med.L. *parabolizare* speak in parables (XIV); in mod. use, f. as prec. + -IZE.] **1.** *trans.* To express in a parable. Also *absol.* **2.** To make parabolic or paraboloidal in shape 1890. Hence **Para·bolizer.**

Paraboloid (păræ·bŏloid), *sb.* (*a.*) 1656. [f. PARABOLA + -OID.] **A.** †**1.** = PARABOLA b. –1710. **2.** A solid or surface of the second degree, some of whose plane sections are parabolas; formerly restricted to that of circular section, generated by the revolution of a parabola about its axis, now called *p. of revolution* 1702. **B.** *adj.* Paraboloidal (*rare*) 1857. So **Paraboloi·dal** *a.* of the form of a p. 1825.

Paracelsian (pæræse·lsiăn). 1574. [f. proper name *Paracelsus* + -IAN.] **A.** *sb.* A follower of the Swiss physician, chemist, and natural philosopher Philippus Aureolus Paracelsus, i.e. Theophrastus Bombast von Hohenheim (1490–1541), or of his medical or philosophical principles; in the former sense opp. to GALENIST. **B.** *adj.* Of, pertaining to, or characteristic of Paracelsus 1617. Hence **Parace·lsianism,** the medical principles of Paracelsus. So **Parace·lsist** *sb.*

‖**Paracentesis** (pærăsentī·sis). 1597. [L. – Gr. παρακέντησις, f. παρακεντεῖν, f. παρα- PARA-[1] 1 + κεντεῖν prick, stab.] *Surg.* The perforation of some cavity of the body, esp. for the removal of fluid or gas; tapping.

Paracentric (pæræse·ntrik), *a.* 1704. [– mod.L. *paracentricus* (Leibnitz, 1689); see PARA-[1], CENTRIC.] Lying unevenly about a centre. **b.** Applied to the key or keyhole of a type of lock with longitudinal ribs and grooves.

P. motion (Kinetics), rendering *motus paracentricus* of Leibnitz, used by him to express that motion which, compounded with harmonic circulation, he supposed to make up the actual motion of a planet. So **Parace·ntrical** *a.*

Parachronism (păræ·krŏniz'm). 1641. [f. Gr. παρα- PARA-[1] + χρόνος time + -ISM, or as a var., by prefix-substitution, of contemp. ANACHRONISM.] An error in chronology by which an event is referred to a later date than the true one. (Cf. ANACHRONISM.)

Parachute (pæră∫ū·t, pæ·ră∫ūt), *sb.* 1785. [– Fr. *parachute*, f. PARA-[2] + *chute* fall. See CHUTE.] **1.** An apparatus like a large umbrella used for descending safely from a great height in the air, esp. from a balloon or aeroplane. **2.** *gen.* Any contrivance, natural or artificial, serving to check a fall through the air, or to support something in the air; e.g. the expansible fold of skin or *patagium* of the flying squirrel 1833. **3.** *Mining.* A contrivance, such as a safety-catch, to prevent a too rapid descent of a cage in a shaft, or of the boring-rod in a boring 1881. Hence **Parachu·te** *v. trans.* to convey by means of a p.; *intr.* to descend by or as if by a p. **Parachu·tist.**

Paraclete (pæ·răklīt). 1450. [– (O)Fr. *paraclet* – Chr.L. *paracletus*, also *-clitus* (Tertullian) – Gr. παράκλητος advocate, intercessor, f. παρακαλεῖν call to one's aid, f. παρά PARA-[1] + καλεῖν call. Παράκλητος was assoc. by the Greek Fathers with the Hellenistic sense 'console, comfort'.] **1.** A title of the Holy Spirit (repr. Gr. παράκλητος in John 14:16, 26, etc.); prop. 'an advocate, an intercessor', but often taken as = 'comforter'. Also (rarely) repr. Gr. παράκλητος 'advocate' as applied to Christ (1 John 2:1). †**2.** *gen.* An advocate or intercessor –1701.

1. The P., the Holy Ghost, whom the Father will send in my name N.T. (Rhem.) *John* 14:26.

‖**Paracme** (păræ·kmi). 1706. [– Gr. παρακμή, f. παρα- past + ἀκμή ACME.] A point or period at which the prime is past; the point when the crisis of a fever is past. So **Paracma·stic** *a.* past the culmination or crisis.

†**Para·da, -a·do.** 1621. [Altered form (see -ADO 2) of Fr. *parade.*] = PARADE *sb.* –1690.

Parade (părē^{i}·d), *sb.* 1656. [– Fr. *parade* – Sp. *parada* and It. *parata* (i) display, (ii) parry, (iii) pulling-up of a horse – Rom. **parata*, subst. use of fem. pa.pple. of L. *parare* prepare, which in Rom. acquired specific applications repr. in the Fr., Sp., and It. words given above; see -ADE.] **1.** Show, display, ostentation. **2.** A muster of troops for inspection or display; esp. one which takes place regularly at set hours or for any special purpose 1656. **3.** A march or procession; esp. in *U.S.* one organized on a grand scale, for some political purpose 1673. **b.** A crowd of promenaders 1722. **4.** A parade-ground 1704. **5.** A public square or promenade. Also as the name of a street. 1697. **6.** *Fencing.* = PARRY. [Fr. *parade.*] 1692.

1. *To make a p. of*, to display ostentatiously; Making an empty p. of knowledge which we do not really possess 1789. **3.** The Rites perform'd, the Parson paid, In State return'd the grand P. SWIFT. **6.** *fig.* Marks, which serve best to shew, what they [men] are. . especially when they are not in P. and upon their Guard LOCKE. *Comb.* **p.-ground,** the place where troops assemble for p.

Parade (părē^{i}·d), *v.* 1686. [f. prec.] **1.** *trans.* To assemble (troops, etc.) for inspection or review. **2.** *intr.* To march in procession or with great display; to promenade in a public place, esp. for the sake of 'showing off' 1748. **3.** *trans.* To march through (a place of public resort) in procession or with great display; to promenade (some place), esp. for the sake of 'showing off' 1809. **4.** To march (a person) about either for show or to expose him to contempt 1807. **5.** *intr.* To make a parade; to 'show off'. *rare* or *Obs.* 1754. **6.** *trans.* To make a parade of, to 'show off' 1818.

1. The troops were paraded WELLINGTON. **4.** They set him on a camel and paraded him about the city BURTON. **6.** The very last. . to p. his feelings 1865. Hence **Para·der,** one who parades 1748.

Paradigm (pæ·rădəim, -dim). 1483. [– late L. *paradigma* – Gr. παράδειγμα example, f. παραδεικνύναι show side by side, f. παρά PARA-[1] + δεικνύναι show. Cf. Fr. *paradigme* (XVI).] **1.** A pattern, exemplar, example. **2.** An example or pattern of the inflexion of a noun, verb, or other part of speech 1599.

1. The Universe. . was made exactly conformable to its Paradigme, or universal Exemplar 1669. Hence **Paradigmatic** (pæ:rădigmæ·tik) *a.* exemplary; †*sb.* one who writes lives of religious persons to serve as examples of Christian holiness (*rare*). †**Pa:radigma·tical** *a.*, **-ly** *adv.* So †**Paradi·gmatize** *v. trans.* to set forth as a model, to make an example of.

Paradisaic (pærădisē^{i}·ik), *a.* 1754. [f. PARADISE, after *Judaic*, *Mosaic*.] Paradisiacal. So **Paradisa·ical** *a.* 1623, **-ly** *adv.*

Paradisal (pærădəi·săl), *a.* 1560. [f. PARADISE + -AL[1].] Of or pertaining to Paradise.

Paradise (pæ·rădəis), *sb.* [ME. *paradis*, also *parais* (XII–XV) – (O)Fr. *paradis*, also in semi-pop. form *paraïs* – Chr. L. *paradisus* – Gr. παράδεισος, first used by Xenophon of the parks of Persian kings and nobles, (hence) garden, orchard, in LXX and N.T. Eden, abode of the blessed – Av. *pairidaēza* enclosure, f. *pairi* around, PERI- + *diz* mould, form. Cf. PARVIS.] **1.** The garden of Eden. Also called *earthly p.*, to distinguish it from the *heavenly p.* **2.** Heaven, the abode of God and his angels and the final abode of the righteous. (Now chiefly *poet.*) ME. **b.** The Moslem heaven. late ME. **c.** An intermediate place or state where the departed souls of the righteous await resurrection and the last judgement (Luke 23:43) 1690. **3.** A place like Paradise; a region of surpassing beauty, or of supreme bliss ME. **b.** *fig.* A state of supreme felicity. late ME. **4.** An oriental park or pleasure-ground, *esp.* one enclosing wild beasts for the chase. **b.** Hence, an English park in which foreign animals are kept. 1613. †**5.** A pleasure-garden; *spec.* the garden of a convent –1875. **6.** *slang.* The gallery of a theatre, where the 'gods' are 1873.

1. Bytwene the grete Inde & erthly paradyse CAXTON. *Apples of p.*, the fruit of the plantain, *Musa paradisiaca*. *Bird of p.*, see BIRD *sb.*[1] *Grains of p.*, see GRAIN *sb.*[1] I. 4. **3.** [Australia] is a rather overdone P. of the working man 1891. **b.** Comfort..seems to many Englishmen the only real p. 1902.

attrib. and *Comb.*: **p. apple,** (*a*) a variety of apple; (*b*) the Forbidden Fruit or Pomello; †**p.-bird** = bird-of-paradise; see BIRD *sb.*; **-fish,** (*a*) a species of *Polynemus*, esteemed as food in India; (*b*) a brilliantly coloured E. Indian fish (*Macropodus viridiauratus*) sometimes kept in aquariums; **-flycatcher,** a bird of the genus *Terpsiphone*, remarkable for the length of its middle tail-feathers; **p. stock,** a hardy slow-growing apple-tree used as a stock by nurserymen for dwarfing other varieties. Hence **Pa·radise** *v. trans.* to make into P.; to make supremely blessed or beautiful.

Paradisiac (pærădi·siæk, -di·ziæk), *a.* 1632. [– Chr. L. *paradisiacus* – Gr. παραδεισιακός, f. παράδεισος PARADISE.] Of, pertaining to, or belonging to Paradise; supremely blest; peacefully beautiful; celestial. So **Paradisiacal** (pærădisəi·ăkăl, -zəi·ăkăl) 1649, **Paradi·sial, Paradi·sian, Paradi·sic, -al** (*rare*), *adjs.* in same sense.

Parados (pæ·rădǫs, ‖parado). 1834. [– Fr. *parados*, f. PARA-[2] + *dos* back (:– L. *dorsum*).] *Fortif.* An elevation of earth behind fortified places, to secure them from any sudden attack from the rear.

Paradox (pæ·rădǫks), *sb.* 1540. [– late L. *paradoxum*, *-doxon*, subst. use of n. of *paradoxus* – Gr. παράδοξος, f. παρά PARA-[1] + δόξα opinion. Cf. Fr. *paradoxe* (Montaigne, 1580).] **1.** A statement or tenet contrary to received opinion or belief; sometimes with favourable, sometimes with unfavourable connotation. (In actual use rare since 17th c.) **2.** A statement seemingly self-contradictory or absurd, though possibly well-founded or essentially true 1569. **b.** Often applied to a proposition that is actually self-contradictory, and so essentially absurd or false 1570. **3.** (Without *a* or *pl.*) = PARADOXY 2. 1589. **4.** *transf.* A phenomenon that exhibits some conflict with preconceived notions of what is reasonable or possible; a person of perplexingly inconsistent life or behaviour 1625.

1. *Ham.* III. i. 115. That pleasant and true P. of the Annual Motion of the Earth 1653. **2.** The legal p., that a libel may be the more a libel for being true COLERIDGE. **b.** It is therefore no p. to say that in some case the strength of a kingdom doth consist in the weakness of it FULLER. **3.** The love of p. GIBBON. **4.** *Hydrostatic p.*: see HYDROSTATIC 1. Hence **Pa·radox** *v. rare,* to utter paradoxes. **Parado·xal** *a,* = PARADOXICAL *a.* **Pa·radoxer, Pa·radoxist,** a propounder of paradoxes.

Paradoxical (pærădǫ·ksikăl), *a.* 1581. [f. prec.; see -ICAL.] **1.** Of the nature of a paradox, exhibiting or involving paradox. **2.** Fond of or given to paradox 1613. **3.** Of a phenomenon, circumstance, etc.: Exhibiting some contradiction with known laws or with itself 1646.

1. Comedians, p. as it may seem, may be too natural LAMB. Hence **Pa:radoxica·lity,** p. character or quality. **Parado·xical-ly** *adv.*, **-ness.**

Paradoxi·dian, *a.* 1882. [f. mod.L. *Paradoxides* (see -ID[3]), f. Gr. παράδοξος; see PARADOX and -IAN.] *Palæont.* Of or pertaining to the *Paradoxides*, a genus of large trilobites of the Middle Cambrian age.

Paradoxology (pærădǫksǫ·lŏdʒi). 1646. [– Gr. παραδοξολογία, f. παραδοξολόγος telling of paradoxes; see -LOGY.] A putting forward of paradoxical opinions, a speaking by paradox.

Paradoxure (pærădǫ·ksiuᵊɹ). 1843. [– mod.L. *paradoxurus*, f. Gr. παράδοξος (see PARADOX) + οὐρά tail.] *Zool.* An animal of the genus *Paradoxurus*, family *Viverridæ*, or of an allied genus, so called because of its remarkably long curving tail; a palm-cat, -marten, or -civet.

So **Paradoxurine** (pærădǫ·ksiurəin) *a.* and *sb.* [mod.L. *Paradoxurinæ*] of or pertaining to (a member of) the sub-family *Paradoxurinæ*, of which *Paradoxurus* is the typical genus.

Paradoxy (pæ·rădǫksi). 1646. [– Gr. παραδοξία, f. παράδοξος; see PARADOX, -Y[3].] †**1.** A paradox. SIR T. BROWNE. **2.** Paradoxical quality or character 1796.

‖**Parænesis, paren-** (pări·nĭsis, -e·nĭsis). 1604. [Late L. – Gr. παραίνεσις exhortation, f. παραινεῖν, f. παρα- PARA-[1] + αἰνεῖν speak of, praise.] Exhortation, advice; a hortatory composition. Hence **Paræne·tic, -ene·tic, -al** *adjs.* hortatory, advisory.

Paraffin (pæ·răfin), *sb.* Also **-ine.** 1835. [– G. *paraffin* (Reichenbach, 1830), f. L. *parum* too little, barely + *affinis* related; so named with ref. to its neutral quality and the small affinity it possesses for other bodies.] **1.** A colourless (or white), tasteless, inodorous, crystalline, fatty substance, solid at ordinary temperatures (chemically a mixture of hydrocarbons of the series C_nH_{2n+2}), discovered by Reichenbach in 1830; obtained by dry distillation from wood, coal, peat, petroleum, wax, etc., and also occurring native in coal and other bituminous strata; used for making candles, for electrical insulators, etc. **2.** Short for *p. oil* 1861. **3.** *Chem.* A general name for the saturated hydrocarbons of the series C_nH_{2n+2}, of which the first four members, methane, ethane, propane, quartane (see -ANE), are at ordinary temperatures gaseous, those higher in the series, oily liquids, and those higher still, solids; all are remarkable for their chemical indifference, the hydrogen being combined in the highest proportion possible with the carbon 1872.

attrib. and *Comb.*, as *p. candle, lamp.*; **p. oil,** any one of several oils obtained by distillation of coal, petroleum, etc., used as illuminants and lubricants; also called simply *paraffin, kerosene*, or *petroleum*; **p. wax,** solid p. (= sense 1). Hence **Pa·raffin** *v. trans.* to cover, impregnate, or treat with p.

†**Pa·rage.** ME. [– (O)Fr. *parage*, f. *per* (mod. *pair*); see PEER *sb.*, -AGE.] **1.** Lineage, descent, rank; *esp.* noble lineage –1652. **2.** Equality of birth or station –1670. **3.** (See quot.)

3. When a fief is divided among brothers;..the younger hold their part of the elder by P., i.e. without any homage or service...This P. being an equality of duty, or service among brothers or sisters CHAMBERS *Cycl.*

Paragenesis (pærădʒe·nĕsis). 1855. [f. PARA-[1] + -GENESIS.] **1.** *Biol.* **a.** The production in an organism of characters belonging to two different species, as in hybridism 1890. **b.** *spec.* Hybridism in which the offspring is partially sterile 1892. **c.** A name for unusual or subsidiary modes of reproduction 1891. **2.** *Min.* The formation of minerals in close contact, whereby the development of the individual crystals is interfered with, and the whole locked together in a crystalline mass; the structure so formed as in granite or marble 1855. Hence **Paragene·sic** *a.* pertaining to or of the nature of p. (sense 1). **Paragene·tic** *a.* **a.** pertaining to or originating by p.; **b.** *Min.* originating side by side, as in *p. twin* (crystal); so **Parage·nic** *a.*

Paragoge (pærăgōᵘ·dʒi). 1656. [– late L. *paragoge* – Gr. παραγωγή derivation, addition to the end of a syllable, f. παρα- PARA-[1] + ἀγωγή carrying, leading.] *Gram.* The addition of a letter or syllable to a word, either inorganically as in *peasan-t*, or, as in Hebrew, to give emphasis or modify the meaning. Hence **Parago·gic, -al** *adjs.* of, pertaining to, or of the nature of p.; (of a letter) added to a word by p.

Paragon (pæ·răgǫn), *sb.* (*a.*) 1548. [– Fr. †*paragon* (now *parangon*) – It. *paragone* (also *parangone*) touchstone, comparison – med. Gr. παρακόνη whetstone.] **I. 1.** A pattern of excellence; a person or thing of supreme excellence. †**2.** A match; a mate, companion; a consort in marriage; a competitor. (Also of a thing.) –1824. †**3.** Comparison; competition, emulation, rivalry –1664.

1. A p. of a wife 1833. The p. of easy-chairs 1861. **3.** Of both their beauties to make paragone SPENS.

II. *spec.* and *techn.* **1.** A perfect diamond; now applied to those weighing more than a hundred carats 1616. †Also *p.-stone* –1698. †**2.** A kind of double camlet –1739. †**3.** A kind of black marble –1839. **4.** *Printing.* A large size of type intermediate between great primer and double pica, about 3⅞ lines to the inch. Also called 'two-line long primer' 1706.

B. *adj.* (*attrib.* use of sb.) Of surpassing excellence 1601.

Those jewels were p., without flaw, hair, ice, or cloud SIR T. BROWNE.

Paragon (pæ·răgǫn), *v.* 1586. [f. prec.] **1.** *trans.* To place side by side; to parallel, compare. (Now *arch.* or *poet.*) **2.** To match, mate. (Now *poet.*, etc.) 1615. †**3.** To surpass SHAKS. †**4.** To set forth as a paragon or perfect model SHAKS. †**5.** *intr.* To compare, compete, vie *with* –1620.

1. Lucifer, so by allusion calld, Of that bright Starr to Satan paragond MILT. **3.** A Maid That paragons description SHAKS. **5.** Few or none could for Feature p. with her SHELTON.

Paragonite (pæ·răgŏnəit). 1849. [f. Gr. παράγων pr. pple., leading aside, misleading + -ITE[1] 2b.] *Min.* A hydrous mica containing sodium, and so dist. from common or potash mica (muscovite).

P.-schist, a mica-schist in which p. takes the place of muscovite. Hence **Paragoni·tic** *a.*

Pa·ragram. 1679. [f. Gr. phr. τὰ παρὰ γράμμα σκώμματα, lit. 'jokes by the letter'.] A kind of play upon words, consisting in the alteration of one letter or group of letters of a word. So **Paragra·mmatist,** a maker of paragrams.

Paragraph (pæ·răgrɑf), *sb.* 1490. [–(O)Fr. *paragraphe* or med.L. *paragraphus*, *-um* – Gr. παράγραφος short horizontal stroke written below the beginning of a line in which a break of sense occurs, passage so marked, f. παρά (PARA-[1]) + -γραφος written (-GRAPH).] **1.** A symbol or character (now usually ¶ or ⁋) formerly used to mark the commencement of a new section; now sometimes to introduce an editorial *obiter dictum*, or as a ref. to a marginal note or footnote 1538. **2.** A distinct passage or section of a discourse, chapter, or book, dealing with a particular point, the words of a particular speaker, etc. This was at first usu. indicated by the mark described above; but subseq., as now, by beginning on a new line, which is indented, and ending without running on to the next passage. 1490. **b.** A distinct article or section of a law or legal document, usu. numbered 1552. **3.** A short passage, notice, or article in a newspaper or journal; an item of news 1769. **4.** *attrib.* 1769.

2. b. I beg your Lordship's particular attention ..to the 13th p. of the instructions WELLINGTON. **3.** Fresh and sparkling paragraphs of Court and fashionable gossip 1882. Hence **Paragra·phic, -al** *adjs.* of, pertaining to, or of the nature of a p. or paragraphs; **-ly** *adv.*

Paragraph (pæ·răgrɑf), *v.* 1601. [f. prec.] †**1.** *trans.* = PARAPH *v.* –1652. **2.** To mention in a paragraph; to write a short notice about. Also *absol.* 1764. **3.** To divide into or arrange in paragraphs. (Chiefly in *pass.*) 1799.

2. No one was more paragraphed and puffed 1880. Hence **Pa·ragrapher, Pa·ragraphist,** a professional writer of newspaper paragraphs.

Paraguay (pæ·răgwēⁱ). 1727. [Name of a river and Republic of S. America.] The S. American shrub *Ilex paraguayensis*, commonly called MATÉ, the leaves of which are dried and roasted, and infused as a beverage in the same way as tea. Hence *P.-tea*.

Parakeet (pæ·răkīt, pærăkī·t). Also **paroquet,** †**-quito,** †**-keeto,** etc. 1581. [Three types are repr.: (i) *parroket*, *-quet*, *perroquet* XVI, (ii) *paraquito*, *-quetto* XVI, (iii) *par(r)akeet* XVII, the last being anglicized forms of the former, which are – OFr. *paroquet* (mod. *perroquet* parrot), It. *parrocchetto*, *perrochetto*, Sp. *periquito*, the interrelation of which is uncertain. The coexistence of west.Fr. *perrot* (see PARROT), Fr. *perruche* parakeet (XVII), Guernsey *perrounet* parrot, Sp. *perico* parakeet, suggests that all the forms may be ult. based on a dim. of the name 'Peter' (Fr. *Pierrot*, Sp. *Perico*).] A bird of the parrot kind; now *spec.* applied to the smaller birds included in the order, esp. those having long tails. **b.** Applied allusively to persons, i.e. in reference to the chattering of the birds, or to their gay plumage 1596.

‖**Paralipomena** (pærăləipǫ·mĕnă), *sb. pl.* Now rarely in sing. **paralipomenon (-leip-).**

ME. [eccl.L. *paralipomena*, gen. pl. *-on* (Cyprian) – Gr. παραλειπομενα (things) left out, f. παραλείπειν leave on one side, omit.] †**1.** (usu. *Paralipomenon*, repr. genit. pl. Παραλειπομένων (sc. βιβλία), the title in LXX and hence in the Vulgate.) The Books of Chronicles in the O.T.; so called as containing particulars omitted in the Books of Kings –1706. **2.** Things omitted in the body of a work, and appended as a supplement. (Rarely in sing. *-on.*) 1662.

‖**Paralipsis** (pærăli·psis). Also **-leipsis;** *erron.* **-lepsis, -lepsy.** 1586. [– late L. *paralipsis* (Aquila) – Gr. παράλειψις passing by, omission, f. παραλείπειν (see prec.).] *Rhet.* A figure in which the speaker emphasizes something by affecting to pass it by without notice, usu. by such phrases as 'not to mention', 'to say nothing of'.

Parallax (pæ·rălæks). 1594. [– Fr. *parallaxe* – mod.L. *parallaxis* – Gr. παράλλαξις change, alternation, mutual inclination of two lines meeting in an angle.] *Astron.* Apparent displacement, or difference in the apparent position, of an object, caused by actual change (or difference) of position of the point of observation; *spec.* the angular amount of such displacement or difference of position, being the angle contained between the two straight lines drawn to the object from the two different points of view, and constituting a measure of the distance of the object 1612. **b.** *fig.* 1594.

There are two kinds of p., viz. *diurnal* and *annual*, the former when a celestial object is observed from opposite points on the earth's *surface*, the latter when observed from opposite points of the earth's *orbit*. As the mean or proper position of the body is that which it would have if viewed in the one case from the earth's centre (or a point in line with it), in the other case from the centre of its orbit, the p. is actually calculated and stated from these central points, and called *geocentric* and *heliocentric* respectively. *Horizontal p.*, the diurnal p. of a heavenly body seen on the horizon. **b.** The sort of p. which exhibits Whitman's fame at so different an angle in his own country and in England 1892. Hence **Paralla·ctic, †-al** *adjs.* pertaining, relating, or due to p.

Parallel (pæ·rălel), *a.* and *sb.* 1549. [– Fr. *parallèle* – L. *parallelus* – Gr. παράλληλος, f. παρά alongside + ἄλληλος one another.] **A.** *adj.* **1.** Lying or extending alongside of one another and always at the same distance apart; also of one line, etc. Extending alongside another at a continuously equal distance (const. *to*, *with*). **b.** *transf.* Applied esp. to mechanical contrivances of which some essential parts are parallel, or which are used to produce parallelism of movement, etc. 1594. **2.** *fig.* Having the same or a like course, tendency, or purport; precisely similar, analogous, or corresponding 1604. **b.** Side by side in time; contemporary in duration 1746. **3.** *Mus.* **a.** Applied to parts which move so that the interval between them remains the same; also to the movement of such parts (*p. motion*), and to the interval between such parts (usu. called *consecutive*) 1864.

1. *P. lines* (Geom.), straight lines in the same plane, which never meet however far produced in any direction, or (in mod. geometry) which intersect at infinity. *P. bars*, a pair of bars supported on posts about 4 to 6 feet above the ground, used for gymnastic exercises. **b.** *P. circuit* (Electr.), a term loosely applied to a circuit connecting the same two points as are connected by another circuit; so *p. connection*, etc. *P. motion*, (*a*) the motion of anything which always remains p. to itself, i.e. in the same direction; (*b*) a mechanical device by which alternating rectilinear is converted into circular motion, and *vice versa*. *P. perspective*, perspective in which the plane of the drawing is p. to a principal surface of the object delineated. *P. rod*, the rod which connects the cranks of the driving-wheels on the same side of a locomotive; the coupling-rod. *P. ruler* (or *rulers*), an instrument for drawing p. lines, consisting of two or more straight rulers connected by jointed cross-pieces so as to be always p., at whatever distance they are set. *P. sphere*, the celestial or terrestrial sphere in that position or aspect in which the equator is p. to the horizon, i.e. at either of the poles; dist. from *oblique* and *right sphere*. **2.** Having observed it to happen before in a p. Case 1758. The p. passage in the ninth book 1875.

B. *sb.* **I. 1.** *pl.* Parallel lines (see A. 1); rarely in *sing.* a line parallel to another 1551. **b.** *pl.* Things running parallel 1589. **2.** *Geog.* Each of the parallel circles imagined as traced upon the earth's surface, or actually drawn upon a map, in planes perpendicular to the axis, and marking the degrees of latitude; in full, *p. of latitude*. Also *Astron.* each of the corresponding circles on the celestial sphere (*parallels of declination*), or of smaller circles parallel to the ecliptic (*parallels of latitude*), or to the horizon (*parallels of altitude*). 1555. **3.** *Mil.* In a siege: A trench (usu. one of three) parallel to the general face of the works attacked, serving as a way of communication between the different parts of the siege-works 1591. **4.** *Printing.* A reference-mark consisting of two parallel vertical lines (‖) 1771. **5.** *fig.* A thing or person agreeing with another in essential particulars (see A. 2); a counterpart, equal, match 1599.

1. Who made the spider parallels design, Sure as Demoivre, without rule or line? POPE. **2.** *attrib. P. sailing* (Naut.), sailing along a p. of latitude, i.e. directly east or west. **5.** Why, this is without p., this B. JONS.

II. 1. Parallel position; parallelism 1654. **2.** *fig.* Agreement in all essential particulars; analogy, parallelism 1617. **3.** Comparison, or a comparison; a statement of parallelism, a simile 1599.

1. Lines that from their P. decline 1699. **2.** The two republics stand in continual p. HALLAM. *In p.* (Electr.), said of two or more circuit-wires connecting the same points. **3.** You are drawing Parallels between the greatest Actors of the Age STEELE. Hence **Pa·rallelist,** one who draws a p. or comparison. So **Paralleli·stic** *a.* relating to or characterized by parallelism. **Pa·rallelly** *adv.*

Pa·rallel, *v.* 1598. [f. prec.] **1.** *trans.* To place (one thing) beside another (const. *with*, *to*), or (two or more things) side by side mentally, so as to exhibit a likeness between them; to compare as being like. †**2.** To make parallel, equalize –1669. **3.** To bring forward something parallel to; to match 1606. **4.** To be parallel or equal to; to match 1601. †**5.** *intr.* To be parallel; to correspond; to 'compare' (*with*) –1657. **6.** To run parallel with, run alongside of. (Chiefly *U.S.*) 1885.

1. [He] parallels to-day's outcry against Ritualism with yesterday's against Methodism 1881. **2.** His life is paralel'd Euen with the stroke and line of his great Iustice SHAKS. **3.** Well may we fight for her, whom..The world's large spaces cannot paralell SHAKS. **6.** He had then..crossed over a ridge that paralleled their rear KIPLING.

Parallelepiped (pæ:rălele·piped); earlier in Gr. form **parallelepipedon** (pæ:rălelĭpi·pédǫn), pl. **-a.** Often *erron.* **parallelo-.** 1570. [– Gr. παραλληλεπίπεδον, f. παράλληλος PARALLEL + ἐπίπεδον plane surface, adj. n. used sb. (f. ἐπί upon + πέδον ground).] A solid figure contained by six parallelograms, of which every two opposite ones are parallel; a prism whose base is a parallelogram. Hence **Parallelepi·pedal** *a.* having the form of a p.

Parallelism (pæ·răleliz'm). 1610. [– Gr. παραλληλισμός comparison of parallels, f. παραλληλίζειν to PARALLEL.] **1.** The state or position of being parallel; direction parallel *to* or *with* something. **b.** The state or fact of remaining parallel to itself, *i.e.* of maintaining the same direction; constancy of direction 1666. **2.** *fig.* The quality of being parallel (see PARALLEL *a.* A. 2) 1638. **b.** An instance of this; a parallel case, passage, etc. (Usu. in *pl.*) 1664. **3.** *spec.* Correspondence, in sense or construction, of successive clauses or passages, esp. in Hebrew poetry; a passage exemplifying this 1778. †**4.** = PARALLEL *a.* B. II. 3. –1660.

2. This p. between the ancient or genuine Platonick and the Christian Trinity CUDWORTH. **3.** The very laws of Hebrew composition which make the second phrase in a p. repeat the first in other words M. ARNOLD.

Parallelize (pæ·ralelǝiz), *v.* 1610. [– Gr. παραλληλίζειν, f. παράλληλος PARALLEL; see -IZE.] **1.** *trans.* = PARALLEL *v.* 1. 1610. **2.** = PARALLEL *v.* 3, 4. *rare.* 1634.

Parallelogram (pærăle·lǒgræm). 1570. [– Fr. *parallélogramme* – late L. *parallelogrammum* – Gr. παραλληλόγραμμον, f. παράλληλος PARALLEL + γραμμή line.] **1.** *Geom.* A four-sided rectilineal figure whose opposite sides are parallel; occas. *spec.* applied to a rectangle. **2.** Anything of the form of this figure, as a block of buildings, a space of ground (cf. *square*), a brick, card, domino, etc. 1820. †**b.** = PANTOGRAPH –1741.

1. *P. of forces* (Dynamics), a figure illustrating the theorem that if two forces acting at one point be represented in magnitude and direction by two sides of a p., their resultant will be similarly represented by the diagonal drawn from that point; hence, the theorem itself. Hence **Paralle:logramma·tic, Pa:rallelogra·mmic, -al** *adjs.* pertaining to, or of the form of, a p.

Paralogism (pǎræ·lǒdʒiz'm). 1565. [– Fr. *paralogisme* or late L. *paralogismus* – Gr. παραλογισμός, f. παραλογίζεσθαι reason falsely, f. παράλογος; see PARA-[1], LOGOS, -ISM.] A piece of false reasoning; a faulty syllogism; a fallacy, *esp.* (as dist. from a *sophism*) one of which the reasoner is himself unconscious. So **Para·logist,** one who commits a p. **Paralogi·stic** *a.* fallacious.

Paralogize (pǎræ·lǒdʒǝiz), *v.* 1599. [– Fr. *paralogiser* or med.L. *paralogizare* – Gr. παραλογίζεσθαι; see prec., -IZE.] *intr.* To commit a paralogism; to reason falsely or illogically. So †**Para·logy,** faulty reasoning. **Paralo·gical** *a.* fallacious, illogical.

Paralyse, -ze (pæ·rălǝiz), *v.* 1804. [– Fr. *paralyser*, f. *paralysie* (see PALSY). Cf. ANALYSE.] **1.** *trans.* To affect with paralysis; to palsy. **2.** *fig.* To deprive of power of action; to render helpless or ineffective; to cripple, deaden 1805.

2. His pride paralysed his love 1866. Hence **Pa:ralysa·tion. Pa·ralysed, Pa·ralysing** *ppl. adjs.*

Paralysis (pǎræ·lĭsis). 1525. [– L. *paralysis* – Gr. παράλυσις, f. παραλύεσθαι be 'loosened' or disabled at the side, pass. of παραλύειν, f. παρά PARA- + λύειν loosen. This form superseded †*paralysie* (XIV); see PALSY.] **1.** *Path.* An affection of the nervous system characterized by impairment or loss of the motor or sensory function of the nerves, esp. of those belonging to a particular part or organ, thus producing functional inactivity in such part. **2.** *fig.* A condition of utter powerlessness, incapacity of action, or suspension of activity; the state of being 'crippled', helpless, or impotent 1813.

1. *Bell's p.*, etc.: see PALSY *sb. General p.* (*of the insane*), a disease characterized by a stage of mental excitement with exalted delusions, followed by dementia.

Paralytic (pærăli·tik), *a.* and *sb.* ME. [– (O)Fr. *paralytique* – L. *paralyticus* – Gr. παραλυτικός, f. παραλύειν; see prec., -IC.] **A.** *adj.* **1.** Affected with or subject to paralysis; palsied. **2.** *fig.* Deprived of power of action; ineffective, characterized by impotency 1642. **3.** Of the nature of or pertaining to paralysis 1818.

1. His shabby clothes and p. limb DICKENS. **3.** A second p. attack 1818.

B. *sb.* A sufferer from paralysis, a palsied person. late ME.

General p., a sufferer from general paralysis. So †**Paraly·tical** *a.* –1788.

Param (pæ·ræm). 1866. [f. PARA-[1] 2 + AM(IDE.] *Chem.* A synonym of dicyanodiamide, a polymer of cyanamide.

Paramagnetic (pæ:rămægne·tik), *a.* 1851. [f. Gr. παρα- PARA-[1] + MAGNETIC.] Having the property of being attracted by the pole of a magnet, and hence, when suspended or placed freely in a magnetic field, of taking a position parallel to the lines of force; opp. to DIAMAGNETIC. Hence **Pa:ramagne·tically** *adv.* So **Parama·gnetism,** the quality of being p.; the phenomena exhibited by p. bodies.

Paramatta (pærămæ·tă). 1834. [f. *Paramatta* (prop. *Parramatta*) in New South Wales.] A light dress fabric having a weft of combed merino wool and a warp formerly of silk, but now usu. of cotton.

†**Pa·rament.** late ME. [– OFr. *parament*, *parement* – late L. *paramentum*, f. L. *parare* prepare, adorn; see -MENT.] An ornament, a decoration –1706. **b.** A decorated robe, a robe of state –1656.

b. Lordes in paramentz on hir courseres CHAUCER. So ‖**Parame·nto** = b.

Paramere (pæ·rămĭǝɹ). 1883. [f. Gr. παρα- PARA-[1] + μέρος part.] *Biol.* **1.** One of a series of radiating parts or organs, as a ray of a star-fish; an actinomere. **2.** Each of the halves of a bilaterally symmetrical animal, or of a segment or somite of such 1884. Hence

Parameric (-me·rik) *a.*

Parameter (pǎræ·mǐtəɹ). 1656. [– mod.L. *parameter, -metrum* (C. Mydorge, 1631), f. Gr. παρά beside, subsidiary to + μέτρον measure; see PARA-[1], -METER.] *Math.* **1.** In conic sections: The third proportional to any given diameter and its conjugate (or, in the parabola, to any abscissa on a given diameter and the corresponding ordinate); this is the *p. of the given diameter. spec.* The parameter of the transverse axis (*principal p.* or *p. of the curve*), i.e. the latus rectum, or focal chord perpendicular to the axis. **2.** *gen.* A quantity which is constant (as distinct from the ordinary variables) in a particular case considered, but which varies in different cases; *esp.* a constant occurring in the equation of a curve or surface, by the variation of which the equation is made to represent a family of such curves or surfaces 1852. **†b.** *Astron.* pl. The data necessary to determine the orbit of a heavenly body –1841. **c.** *Cryst.* Each of the intercepts made upon the axes in a crystal by the plane which is chosen for a face of the unit or primary pyramid 1839. Hence **Para·metral, Parame·tric, -al** *adjs.* of or pertaining to a p.

‖**Paramo** (pa·ramo). 1760. [– Sp., Pg. *paramo* – L. *paramus.*] A high plateau in the tropical parts of S. America, bare of trees, and exposed to wind and thick cold fogs.

Paramount (pæ·rǎmaunt), *a.* (*sb.*) 1531. [– AFr. (Law Fr.) *paramont, peramont*, adj. use of adv. *paramont* above, f. (O)Fr. *par* by + *amont* above; see PAR *prep.*, AMOUNT.] **1.** Above in a scale of rank or authority; superior 1579. **b.** *gen.* Above all others in rank, order or jurisdiction; supreme 1531. **2.** Superior *to* all others in influence, power, etc.; pre-eminent 1625. **b.** With ellipsis of *to* (now *rare* or *Obs.*) 1596.

1. *Lord p.*, lord superior, overlord; *spec.* the supreme lord of a fee; hence *transf.* one who exercises supreme power. So *lady p.*, a woman in supreme authority; also *transf.* the woman who has made the highest score in an archery tournament. **b.** To make Britain the p. power in India MACAULAY. **2.** Their first duty..is p. to all subsequent engagements 1769. Matters of p. importance 1877. **b.** A Generall Councell is p. the Pope 1643.

B. *sb.* A lord paramount, overlord, supreme ruler or proprietor 1645. Hence **Pa·ramountly** *adv.* pre-eminently, above all. **Pa·ramoun(t)cy,** the condition or status of being p.

Paramour (pæ·rǎmūᵊɹ), *adv. phr.* and *sb.* [– OFr. *par amour(s* by or through love; see PAR *prep.*, AMOUR.] **A.** *adv. phr.* **†1.** Through or by way of love; out of (your) love, for love's sake; *occas.*, Of your kindness, as a favour, if you please –1611. **†2.** For or by way of sexual love –1848. **B.** *sb.* **†1.** Love; *esp.* sexual love; an amour –1586. **2.** A 'love', lover, sweetheart; also of animals and *fig.* (*arch.* and *poet.*) ME. **†b.** The lady-love of a knight, for whose love he did battle; hence, the object of chivalrous attachment (*poet.*) –1630. **3.** An illicit lover or mistress taking the place, but without the rights, of a husband or wife. Now, the illicit partner of a man or woman. late ME.

B. 2. To wanton with the Sun her lusty P. MILT. **b.** Chloris, the queen of flowers:..The top of paramours B. JONS.

‖**Parang** (pā·ræŋ). 1852. [Malay.] A large heavy sheath-knife used by the Malays as a weapon, etc.

‖**Paranoia** (pærǎnoi·ǎ), **paranœa** (-nī·ǎ). 1857. [mod.L. – Gr. παράνοια, f. παράνοος distracted, f. παρα- PARA-[1] + νόος, νοῦς mind.] *Path.* Mental derangement; *spec.* chronic mental unsoundness characterized by delusions and hallucinations. Hence **Paranoi·ac** *a.* afflicted with p.; also as *sb.*

Paranymph (pæ·rǎnimf). 1593. [– late L. *paranymphus*, fem. *-nympha* – Gr. παράνυμφος masc. and fem.; see PARA-[1], NYMPH.] **1.** *Gr. Antiq.* The 'friend of the bridegroom', who accompanied him when he went to fetch home the bride; also, the bridesmaid who escorted the bride to the bridegroom; hence, a modern 'best man', or a bridesmaid 1600. **2.** *transf.* and *fig.* A person or thing that woos or solicits for another; an advocate, spokesman, or orator, who speaks in behalf of another 1593.

Parapegm (pæ·rǎpem). Now usu. in Gr.-L. form **parapegma** (pærǎpe·gmǎ). 1641. [– L. *parapegma*, pl. *-pegmata* – Gr. παράπηγμα, -πήγματα a thing fixed beside or near, f. παρα- PARA-[1] + πῆγμα anything fastened.] *Gr. Antiq.* A tablet set up with some public information or announcement, as a law, a proclamation, or a calendar of annals or astronomical observations; a canon, rule, or precept; a fixed date or epoch.

Parapet (pæ·rǎpėt). 1590. [– Fr. *parapet* (Rabelais) or its source It. *parapetto* wall breast-high, f. *para-* PARA-[2] + *petto* (:– L. *pectus*) breast.] *lit.* A defence breast-high, a breastwork. **1.** *Mil.* A defence of earth or stone to cover troops from the enemy's observation and fire. **2.** A low wall or barrier, placed at the edge of a platform, balcony, roof, etc., or along the sides of a bridge, pier, quay, etc., to prevent people from falling over 1598. **b.** *transf.* Anything resembling a parapet 1636.

Comb.: **p. line,** the line or level of the bottom o the p., esp. on a roof; **p. wall,** a low wall serving as a p. Hence **Pa·rapet** *v.* chiefly in **Pa·rapeted** *ppl. a.* furnished with or defended by a p.

Paraph (pæ·ræf), *sb.* late ME. [– Fr. *paraphe, -afe* – med.L. *paraphus*, syncopated form of *paragraphus* PARAGRAPH.] **†1.** A paragraph –1483. **2.** *Diplomatics.* A flourish made after a signature, orig. as a precaution against forgery 1584. Hence **Pa·raph** *v.* to affix a p. to; hence to sign, esp. with initials, to initial 1667.

‖**Parapherna** (pærǎfɔ̄·ɹnǎ), *sb. pl.* 1706. [– late L. *parapherna* – Gr. παράφερνα n. pl. articles of property held by a wife besides her dowry, f. παρά beside, PARA-[1] + φερνή dowry.] **1.** *Rom. Law.* Those articles of property held by a wife over and above the dowry she brought to her husband, and which remained under her own control. **2.** = PARAPHERNALIA 2. 1876. Hence **Paraphe·rnal** *a.* of, belonging to, or of the nature of p.; also as *sb.* (serving as sing. to next).

Paraphernalia (pærǎfəɹnēⁱ·liǎ), *sb. pl.* 1651. [– med.L. *paraphernalia*; subst. use (sc. *bona* goods) of n. pl. of *paraphernalis*, f. late L. *parapherna*; see prec., -AL[1].] **1.** *Law.* Those articles of personal property which the law allowed a married woman to keep and, to a certain extent, to deal with as her own. **2.** Personal belongings, *esp.* articles of adornment or attire, trappings; appointments or appurtenances in general. Also as collect. sing. 1736.

2. The p. of justice,—the judge, and the jury, and the lawyers TROLLOPE.

‖**Paraphonia** (pærǎfōᵘ·niǎ). 1776. [– Gr. παραφονία harmony; see PARA-[1], -PHONY.] **1.** *Gr. Mus.* The harmony or concord of fourths and fifths. **2.** Alteration of the voice from physiological or pathological causes 1799.

Paraphragm (pæ·rǎfræm). 1877. [– Gr. παράφραγμα parapet.] *Zool.* One of the outer divisions of an endosternite in Crustacea. Hence **Paraphragmal** (pærǎfræ·gmǎl) *a.*

Paraphrase (pæ·rǎfrēⁱz), *sb.* 1548. [– Fr. *paraphrase* or L. *paraphrasis* – Gr. παράφρασις, f. παραφράζειν, tell in other words; see PARA-[1], PHRASE.] **1.** An expression in other words of the sense of any passage or text; a free rendering or amplification of a passage. (Sometimes, by extension, of a musical passage.) **b.** Without *a* and *pl.*, as a process or mode of literary treatment 1656. **†c.** *fig.* A practical exemplification of or commentary upon some principle, maxim, etc. –1670. **2.** In the Ch. of Scotland, etc.: Each of the hymns contained in the 'Translations and Paraphrases, in verse, of several passages of Sacred Scripture' usu. appended to the Metrical Psalter in Scottish editions of the Bible or New Testament 1745.

1. Not a literal Translation, but a kind of P. DRYDEN. *Chaldee Paraphrases*, the TARGUM. **b.** P., or translation with latitude, where the author is kept in view.., but his words are not so strictly followed as his sense DRYDEN. **c.** A glittering prelate without inward ornaments was but the p. of a painted wall 1670.

Paraphrase (pæ·rǎfrēⁱz), *v.* 1606. [f. prec.; cf. Fr. *paraphraser.*] **1.** *trans.* To express the meaning of (a word, phrase, etc.) in other words; to render or translate with latitude. Also *fig.* **2.** *intr.* To make a paraphrase 1633. **†3.** To comment *on*, to enlarge *upon*, a subject –1683.

1. Dr. Whately..paraphrases Hume, though he forgets to cite him HUXLEY. So **Pa·raphraser** 1548.

‖**Paraphrasis** (pǎræ·frǎsis). 1538. [L.; see PARAPHRASE.] = PARAPHRASE *sb.* 1, 1 b.

Paraphrast (pæ·rǎfræst). 1549. [– med.L. *paraphrastes* – Gr. παραφραστής, f. παραφράζειν; see PARAPHRASE *sb.* Cf. Fr. *paraphraste* (XVII).] One who paraphrases; a paraphraser.

Paraphrastic (pærǎfræ·stik), *a.* 1623. [– med.L. *paraphrasticus* – Gr. παραφραστικός, f. παραφραστής PARAPHRAST; see -IC.] Of, pertaining to, or of the nature of paraphrase; addicted to the use of paraphrase. So **Paraphra·stical** *a.* (now *rare* or *Obs.*) 1549, **-ly** *adv.* 1557.

‖**Paraphronesis** (pærǎfronī·sis). 1857. [mod.L. – Gr. παραφρόνησις wandering of mind.] = next.

‖**Paraphrosyne** (pærǎfrǫ·zinī). 1693. [mod.L. – Gr. παραφροσύνη, f. παράφρων out of one's wits, f. παρα- PARA-[1] + φρήν mind.] A mild form of delirium or temporary mental derangement.

‖**Paraplegia** (pærǎplī·dʒiǎ). 1657. [mod.L. – Gr. παραπληγία = παραπληξία a stroke on one side, hemiplegia, f. παραπλήσσειν strike at the side, f. παρα- + πλήσσειν; see -IA[1].] *Path.* Paralysis of the lower limbs and a part or the whole of the trunk, resulting from an affection of some part of the spinal cord. So **Paraple·gic** *a.* marked by or characteristic of p.; affected with p.; *sb.* a person affected with p.

Paraquet, var. f. PARAKEET.

Parasang (pæ·rǎsæŋ). 1594. [– L. *parasanga* – Gr. παρασάγγης, of Persian origin (cf. FARSANG).] A Persian measure of length, usu. reckoned as between 3 and 3½ English miles. Also *fig.*

Parasceve (pæ·rǎsīv, ‖pærǎsī·vi). 1548. [– Chr. L. *parasceve* – Gr. παρασκευή preparation, in N.T. day of preparation for the Sabbath, in later use, Good Friday, sb. of παρασκευάζειν prepare, f. παρά PARA-[1] + σκευάζειν make ready, f. σκεῦος instrument, pl. equipment.] **1.** The day of preparation for the Jewish sabbath, the eve of the sabbath, Friday; *spec.* Good Friday (from Mark 15:42, etc.). *Obs.* in vernacular use. **†2.** *gen.* Preparation –1654.

‖**Paraselene** (pærǎsǐlī·ni). *Pl.* **-næ** (-nī). 1653. [mod.L., f. Gr. παρα- PARA-[1] + σελήνη moon (after PARHELION).] A bright spot on a lunar halo, somewhat resembling the moon itself; a mock moon. Hence **Pa:rasele·nic** *a.*

Parasite (pæ·rǎsəit), *sb.* 1539. [– L. *parasitus* – Gr. παράσιτος lit. one who eats at the table of another; orig. an adj. = feeding beside; f. παρα- PARA-[1] + σῖτος food. Cf. Fr. *parasite* (Rabelais).] **1.** One who eats at the table or at the expense of another (always opprobrious); a hanger-on from interested motives; a 'toady'. **b.** *Gr. Antiq.* One admitted to the table kept up for a public officer, or to the feast after a sacrifice 1697. **2.** *Biol.* An animal or plant which lives in or upon another organism (its *host*) and draws its nutriment directly from it. Also extended to animals or plants that live as tenants of others, but not at their expense (strictly called *commensal* or *symbiotic*); also to those which depend on others in various ways for sustenance, as the skua-gull, cuckoo, etc.; and (inaccurately) to plants which grow upon others, deriving support but not nourishment from them (*epiphytes*), or which live on decaying organic matter (*saprophytes*) 1727. **b.** Applied, loosely or *poet.* to a plant that creeps or climbs about another plant, or a wall, trellis-work, etc. 1813. **c.** *fig.* A person whose part or action resembles that of an animal parasite 1883. **d.** *Philol.* A parasitic vowel or consonant; see PARASITIC 3 b. 1888. **3.** *Min.* A mineral developed upon or within another; *spec.* [– G. *parasit*] a plumose variety of BORACITE, the result of alteration 1868.

1. You knot of Mouth-Friends:..Most smiling,

smooth, detested Parasites SHAKS. *fig.* Hath made his pen an hired p. BP. HALL. **2. b.** Like tendrils of the p. Around a marble column SHELLEY.

Comb. **p.-diphthong,** a diphthong formed by the development of a p. beside the original vowel. Hence **Pa·rasite,** *v.* (*rare*) (*a*) *trans.* to infest as a p.; (*b*) *intr.* (*Philol.*) to develop a parasitic sound SWEET. **Pa·rasital** *a.* parasitic.

Parasitic (pærăsi·tik), *a.* 1627. [– L. *parasiticus* – Gr. παρασιτικός, f. παράσιτος; see prec., -IC.] **1.** Of, pertaining to, or characteristic of a parasite, sycophantic. **2.** *Biol.* Of, belonging to, or having the nature of a plant or animal parasite 1731. **3.** *transf.* (from 2.) Applied to something subsidiary growing upon or attached to something else 1811. **b.** *Philol.* Applied to a non-original vowel, consonant, or other element, attached to an original phonetic element, out of which it has been developed, or to which it has been added; e.g. the sounds denoted by the *d* in *thunder*, the *e* in *flower*, etc. 1870.

1. Some parasitick Preachers 1648. So **Parasi·tical** *a.*, **-ly** *adv.*, **-ness.**

Parasiticide (pærăsi·tisəid). 1864. [f. L. *parasitus* + -CIDE 1.] *Med.* An agent that destroys parasites, e.g. such as infest the skin.

Parasitism (pæ·răsəiti:z'm). 1611. [f. PARASITE *sb.* + -ISM.] **1.** Sycophancy, servile complaisance. **2.** *Biol.* The condition of being a (plant or animal) parasite; parasitical quality or habits 1853. **3.** *Path.* Parasitical infestation; disease caused by this 1884.

Parasitize (pæ·răsitəi:z), *v.* 1890. [f. PARASITE *sb.* + -IZE.] *trans.* To infest as a parasite. Chiefly in *pa. pple.*, infested with parasites.

Parasitology (pærăsəitǫ·lŏdʒi). 1882. [f. PARASITE *sb.* + -LOGY.] That branch of biology, and of medical science, which treats of parasites and parasitism. Hence **Pa:rasitolo·gical** *a.* **Parasito·logist.**

Parasol (pærăsǫ·l, pæ·răsǫl), *sb.* 1616. [– Fr. *parasol* – It. *parasole*, f. *para-* PARA-[2] + *sole* sun. Cf. AL. *parasol* sunshade (XIII).] **1.** A small light umbrella carried by women as a defence against the sun; a sunshade 1660. †**2.** *transf.* Anything serving as a defence from the rays of the sun –1801.

attrib. and *Comb.*: **p. ant,** a leaf-carrying ant, esp. *Œcodoma cephalotes* of S. America; **p. pine,** the stone-pine (*Pinus pinea*), from the form of its head of branches. Hence **Paraso·l** *v. trans.* to serve as a p. for, to shade from the sun. **Parasole·tte,** a small p.

‖**Parasynthesis** (pærăsi·nþĭsis). 1862. [– Gr. παρασύνθεσις; see PARA-[1], SYNTHESIS.] *Philol.* Derivation from a compound; conjoint combination and derivation, as a process of word-formation.

Parasynthetic (pærăsinþe·tik), *a.* (*sb.*) 1862. [f. Gr. παρασύνθετος (f. παρα- PARA-[1] + σύνθετος put together) + -IC.] *Philol.* Formed from a compound; formed by a conjoint process of combination and derivation. **b.** *sb.* A parasynthetic formation or derivative.

‖**Parathesis** (pǎræ·þĭsis). 1657. [mod.L. – Gr. παράθεσις a putting beside, etc., f. παρατιθέναι, f. παρα- PARA-[1] + τιθέναι to place.] †**1.** *Gram.* = APPOSITION[2] 4. –1678. **b.** In Gr. and L. grammar: Simple composition of two words without change, as in Διόσκυροι, *res-publica*; opp. to *synthesis* and *parasynthesis* 1862. †**2.** *Rhet.*, etc. A parenthetical word, clause, sentence, or remark –1711. **3.** *Gr. Ch.* A commendatory prayer 1864. So **Parathe·tic** *a.* pertaining to or characterized by p.

Paratyphoid (pærătəi·foid), *a.* and *sb.* 1903. [PARA-[1].] *Path.* Applied to a fever resembling typhoid but taking a milder course.

Paraunter, obs. f. PERADVENTURE.

Paravai·l, *adv* (*a.*) *Obs.* exc. *Hist.* 1579. [– OFr. *par aval* down, f. *par* through, by + *aval*, *à val* adv. and prep., down :– L. *ad vallem* to the valley, as opp. to *amont*, *ad montem*.] Down below or beneath; below one in position; as *tenant paravail*, one who holds under another who is himself a tenant; *spec.* the lowest tenant, he who actually worked or occupied the land, etc. Opp. to PARAMOUNT.

Paravane (pæ·răvē̆ⁱn). 1919. [f. PARA-[1] + VANE.] An apparatus for cutting the moorings of submerged mines, towed by warships, etc., during the war of 1914–18, at a depth regulated by its vanes or planes.

†**Paravant, -aunt,** *adv.* 1590. [– OFr. *paravant* adv. and prep., 'before', f. *par* through, by + *avant* :– pop.L. *abante* from before.] Before; in front; before the rest, preeminently SPENSER.

‖**Parbleu** (parblö), *int.* 1709. [Fr., perversion of *pardieu* by God.] A minced oath.

Parboil (pā·ɹboil), *v.* late ME. [– OFr. *parboillir, parbouillir* :– late L. *perbullire* boil thoroughly, f. *per* PAR- + *bullire* BOIL. *Par-* has been erron. identified with *part*, whence sense 2.] †**1.** *trans.* To boil thoroughly –1655. **2.** To boil partially, half boil 1440. **3.** *fig.* usu. in ref. to overheating 1566.

†**Parbreak** (paɹbrēⁱ·k), *v.* late ME. [A compound of BRAKE *v.*[5], subseq. referred to BREAK *v.*] **1.** *trans.* and *intr.* To vomit = BRAKE *v.*[5] –1610. **2.** *fig.* (*trans.*) To utter recklessly or offensively; to vomit forth –1629. Hence †**Pa·rbreak** *sb.* (*rare*).

Parbuckle (pā·ɹbʌk'l), *sb.* 1626. [orig. *parbunkle, -buncle*, alt. XVIII by assoc. w. BUCKLE; of unkn. origin.] **a.** A sling formed by passing the two ends of a rope round a heavy object and through a bight of the rope, and tightening, the weight of the object serving to keep it tight. **b.** A rope having a bight looped round a post, etc., at the level to or from which an object is to be raised or lowered, and the two ends passed round the object, and hauled in or paid out to raise or lower it, the object acting as a movable pulley; used in hoisting casks or other cylindrical bodies. Hence **Pa·rbuckle** *v. trans.* to raise or lower (a cask, gun, etc.) by means of p.

‖**Parcae** (pā·ɹsī), *sb. pl.* late ME. [L.] The (three) Fates of Roman mythology; identified with the Gr. Μοῖραι.

Parcel (pā·ɹsĕl, pā·ɹs'l), *sb.* [ME. *parcelle* – (O)Fr. *parcelle* :– Rom. **particella*, f. L. *particula* PARTICLE.] **A.** *sb.* **1.** *gen.* A part *of* anything, considered separately, as a unit; a small portion, a particle (*arch.*). late ME. **b.** A component part (*of* something), something included in a whole. (Often without article.) *arch.* exc. in phr. *part and p.* (see PART *sb.* I. 1 c.). late ME. **2.** *spec.* **a.** A piece of land; *esp.* as part of a manor or estate. (Often without article.) 1449. **b.** A small portion or instalment *of* a sum of money (now *rare* or *Obs.*) 1491; †a small portion of a book, e.g. the Bible or the Koran –1655. †**3.** Each of the units which make up a complex whole; an item, detail, particular, point; *esp.* an item of an account –1641. †**4.** A small piece, particle; a (small or moderate) quantity or amount; a lot –1830. †**5.** A fragment, piece. Also *fig.* –1783. **6.** A small party, company, or collection (of persons, animals, or things); a detachment; a group, lot, set; a drove, flock, herd. *Obs.* exc. *dial.* or as in b. 1588. **b.** A 'lot', 'set', 'pack' (contemptuous) 1607. **7.** A quantity of anything or a number of things (esp. goods) wrapped up in a single (small) package; an item of goods in carriage or postage; a package: now chiefly used of packages wrapped in brown paper. Also *transf.* and *fig.* 1692. **b.** *Comm.* A quantity (sometimes definite) of a commodity dealt with in one transaction; *esp.* in the wholesale market, a 'lot' 1832. **8.** *Law.* (*pl.*) That part of a conveyance, etc., which follows the operative words, and describes the property dealt with 1766.

1. A certein parcelle of the body of a man CHAUCER. The p. of truth any..individual can seize M. ARNOLD. **b.** Being p. of the common mass COWPER. Phr. *Of a p. with*, consonant with. **2. a.** Owners of certain parcels of Land 1720. **3.** 1 *Hen. IV*, III. ii. 159. **5.** *fig.* What p. of man hast thou lighted on for a Master? B. JONS. **6.** Sheep are kept in small parcels 1780. **b.** I think the English a p. of brutes MISS BURNEY. **7.** His brown-paper p. DICKENS. *fig.* A p. of half-forgotten observations HAZLITT. Phr. *Bill of parcels*: see BILL *sb.*[3] 6. **b.** Cocoa.—At public sale to-day the parcels offered went off freely at dearer prices 1897.

attrib. and *Comb.*, as *p. boy, office, van*, etc.; **parcel(s) delivery,** the action of, or an agency for, delivering parcels (also *attrib.*); **p. paper,** stout paper, usually brown and unsized, made or used for wrapping parcels; **p. post,** that branch of the postal service which undertakes the carriage and distribution of parcels.

B. *adv.* or quasi-*adv.*, or *adj.* In part, partly. late ME.

Parcell for pride, p. for gladnesse 1430. P. lawyer, p. devil, all knave 1611. Hawkins, Frobisher and Drake, parcel-soldiers all of them 1867. *P. blind, deaf, drunk*, etc. (often hyphened, but improperly exc. when the adj. is used *attrib.*). *P. ass, poet, Protestant*, etc. (often hyphened, but properly so only when it has an adj. force).

Parcel (pā·ɹsĕl, pā·ɹs'l), *v.* 1584. [f. prec.] **1.** *trans.* To divide into 'parcels' or (small) portions. (Usu. with *out*.) **b.** To distribute in parcels 1699. **2.** To make into a parcel or parcels 1775. **3.** *Naut.* **a.** To cover (a caulked seam, etc.) with canvas strips and daub with pitch. **b.** To wrap (a rope) round with canvas strips or *parcelling* (to be then bound with spun yarn) 1627.

1. The empire..was parcelled into twelve grand divisions 1796. **2.** The mechanical art of weighing and parcelling up the tea 1887. Hence **Parcelled, parceled** (pā·ɹsĕld) *ppl. a.*

Pa·rcel-gilt, *a.* (*sb.*) 1465. [f. PARCEL *sb.* B. + GILT *ppl. a.*] Partly gilded; *esp.* of silver ware, as bowls, cups, etc., having the inner surface gilt. **b.** quasi-*sb.* Parcel-gilt ware. Also *fig.* 1610.

b. Or changing His parcell guilt to massie gold B. JONS.

Pa·rcelling, pa·rceling, *vbl. sb.* 1584. [f. PARCEL *v.* + -ING[1].] **1.** The action of PARCEL *v.* **2.** *concr.* (*Naut.*) A strip of canvas (usually tarred) for binding round a rope, to keep the interstices water-tight 1750.

Parcenary (pā·ɹsĕnări). 1544. [– AFr. *parcenarie* = OFr. *parçonerie*, f. *parçonier*; see next, -ARY[1].] *Law.* = COPARCENARY 1.

Parcener (pā·ɹsĕnəɹ). ME. [– AFr. *parcener* = OFr. *parçonier*, Rom. **partionarius* for **partitionarius*, f. L. *partitio* PARTITION; see -ER[2] 2. Cf. COMPARCIONER.] †**1.** One who shares, or has a part in, something with another or others; a partner; a sharer, partaker –1621. **2.** *Law.* = COPARCENER ME.

Parch (pāɹtʃ), *v.* late ME. [Of unkn. origin.] **1.** *trans.* To dry by exposure to great heat; to roast or toast slightly (corn, pease, and the like). **2.** To make hot and dry; to scorch; said of the action of the sun's heat, or of fever or thirst 1555. **b.** *transf.* To dry, shrivel, or wither with cold 1573. **3.** *intr.* To become very dry and hot; to shrivel up with heat 1530.

2. Parch'd are the Plains, and frying is the Field DRYDEN. **b.** The parching Air Burns frore, and cold performs th' effect of fire MILT. **3.** We were better p. in Affricke Sunne SHAKS. Hence **Parch** *sb.* (*rare*), the action of parching or being parched. **Parched** (pāɹtʃt, pā·ɹtʃĕd) *ppl. a.*, **-ly** *adv.*, **-ness.** **Pa·rching** *vbl. sb.* **Pa·rching** *ppl. a.* that parches; drying to excess; scorching; that becomes parched.

Parchment (pā·ɹtʃmĕnt). Also †**parchemin.** [ME. *parchemin* – (O)Fr. *parchemin*, earlier *parcamin* :– Rom. **particaminum*, which resulted from a blending of L. *pergamina* with *Parthica pellis* 'Parthian skin', leather dyed scarlet (whence OFr. *parche* parchment, Pr. *pargue* kind of leather). *Pergamina* (sc. *charta* paper) writing-material prepared from skins, invented at *Pergamum* (now Bergama) is repr. by Pr. *pargami*, Sp. *pergamino*, OIt. *pergamina*.] **1.** The skin of the sheep or goat, etc., dressed and prepared for writing, painting, engraving, etc. **2.** A skin, piece, scroll, or roll of parchment; a manuscript or document on parchment ME. **3.** A skin or membrane resembling parchment; *spec.* the husk of the coffee-bean 1677.

1. *Cotton p.*, a parchment-like material made by soaking cotton fibre in a solution of sulphuric acid, glycerin, and water, and then rolling it into sheets. *Vegetable p.* = p.-paper (see *Comb.*). **2.** I am a scribled forme drawne with a pen Vpon a P. SHAKS.

Comb.: **p.-coffee,** the coffee-bean while still in its husk; **-paper,** a tough, transparent, glossy kind of paper resembling p., made by soaking ordinary unsized paper in dilute sulphuric acid; **-skin,** a piece of p.; also *fig.*; also, a disease of the skin in which it resembles p. Hence **Pa·rchmenty** *a.* of the nature of p.

Parclose (pā·ɹklōᵘz), **perclose** (pɔ̄·ɹklōᵘz), *sb.* [ME. *parclos, parclose* – OFr. *parclos* m., *parclose* fem., pa. pple. of *parclore* (see next) used subst.] †1. Close, conclusion –1671. **2.** A partition, screen, or railing, serving to shut off a space in a building; now only, a screen or railing in a church enclosing an altar, a tomb, etc., or separating a chapel, etc. from the main body of the church ME.

1. Let the Perclose of her thoughts be this, To study what Man was, and what Man is QUARLES.

Parclo·se, perclose, *v.* 1577. [– OFr. *parclore*, pa. pple. *parclos, -close*, f. *par-* PAR- + *clore* :– L. *claudere* CLOSE.] †**1.** To close, conclude –1667. **2.** *trans.* To enclose; to shut off with a parclose. *rare.* 1577.

Pard[1] (pāɹd). ME. (Now only *arch.* or *poet.*) [OE. *pard*; in ME. – OFr. *pard* – L. *pardus* – Gr. πάρδος (f. πάρδαλις PARDAL), of Indo-Iranian origin. See LEOPARD.] A panther or leopard.

A Soldier, Full of strange oaths, and bearded like the P. SHAKS.

Pard[2] (pāɹd). *slang*, chiefly *U.S.* 1872. [For *pardner* PARTNER.] A partner, mate.

†**Pa·rdal.** 1553. [– L. *pardalis* a female panther – Gr. πάρδαλις fem.; see PARD[1].] A name for the panther or leopard –1661.

†‖**Parda·o.** *E. Ind.* 1582. [Pg. – XV W. Indian form *partāb*, ult. :– Skr. *prātāp* splendour, majesty.] A coin of Goa, worth orig. about 4*s.* 6*d.*, but later only 10½*d.*; used also as a money of account –1858.

Parde(e, var. f. PARDIE.

Pardie (paɹdī·). **perdie** (pəɹdī·), *int.* or *adv. arch.* ME. [– OFr. *par dé* (mod. *pardieu*, colloq. *pardi*) 'by God' :– L. *per deum*; see PAR- *prefix*.] A form of oath; = 'By God!'; hence as an asseveration: Verily, assuredly, indeed.

The hous is myne, pardie 1475. *Ham.* III. ii. 305.

Pardon (pā·ɹdən, pā·ɹd'n), *sb.* ME. [– OFr. *pardun, perdun* (mod. *pardon*), f. *pardoner*; see next. Cf. med.L. *perdonum* XII.] †**1.** Remission of something due, as of a debt, tax, etc. –1536. **2.** The passing over of an offence without punishment; forgiveness (but often coloured by sense 4) ME. **b.** *Theol.* Forgiveness of sins ME. **3.** *Eccl.* = INDULGENCE II. 1. ME. **b.** A church festival at which indulgence is granted; the festival of the patron saint 1477. **4.** *Law.* A remission, either free or conditional, of the legal consequences of crime 1447. **5.** The document conveying a pardon (senses 3, 4). late ME. **6.** (from 2.) The excusing of a fault or what the speaker politely treats as one; courteous forbearance or indulgence; excuse; acquittance of blame. Often in phrases of polite apology. 1548. †**b.** Leave, permission –1606. †**c.** Allowance for defect, toleration –1639.

2. Let me ask my sister p. SHAKS. **4.** I hope it is some p., or repreeue For the most gentle Claudio SHAKS. *General p.*, a pardon for offences generally, or for those committed by a number of persons not named individually. **5.** Their pardons, and other of their tromperye, hath bene bought and solde in Lombard strete 1542. *Meas. for M.* II. iv. 152. **6.** Phr. *I beg your p.*, besides being used in its natural sense, is used also as a courteous expression of dissent or contradiction, = 'Excuse me'; e.g. 'I beg your p., it was not so'; and interrogatively = 'I do not catch what you say', or 'what you mean'. Often shortened to *Pardon.* **b.** *Haml.* IV. vii. 46.

Pardon (pā·ɹdən, pā·ɹd'n), *v.* late ME. [– OFr. *pardoner, perduner* (mod. *pardonner*) :– med.L. *perdonare* (IX), f. L. *per* PAR- *pref.* + *donare* give.] †**1.** *trans.* To remit (something due, a duty, debt, fine, penalty, forfeit) –1643. **2.** To remit the penalty of (an offence); to pass over (an offence or offender) without punishment or blame; to forgive. (A more formal term than *forgive.*) late ME. **3.** To make courteous allowance for; to excuse 1509.

1. I p. thee thy life before thou aske it SHAKS. **2.** He will not p. your transgressions *Exod.* 23:21. In this thing the Lord p. thy seruant 2 *Kings* 5:18. *absol.* Hee will abundantly p. *Isa.* 55:7. **3.** P. my impatience 1648. Hence **Pa·rdoner**[2], one who pardons or forgives 1581. **Pardonee·.**

Pardonable (pā·ɹdənăb'l), *a.* 1548. [– (O)Fr. *pardonnable*, f. *pardonner*; see prec., -ABLE.] That can be pardoned or forgiven; excusable. **a.** Said of an offence. **b.** Of an offender (or his condition). Now *rare.* 1638.

a. A p. Inadvertency ADDISON. **b.** I dare say your daughter is p. 1803. Hence **Pa·rdonableness. Pa·rdonably** *adv.*

Pardoner[1] (pā·ɹdənəɹ). Now only *Hist.* late ME. [– AFr. *pardoner*; see PARDON *sb.*, -ER[2] 2. Cf. AL. *perdonarius* (XIV).] A person licensed to sell papal pardons or indulgences.

Pare (pē³ɹ), *v.* ME. [– (O)Fr. *parer* adorn, arrange, peel (fruit) :– L. *parare* PREPARE, which in Rom. acquired specialized uses.] †**1.** *trans.* To get ready, to prepare; to deck out –1617. **2.** To trim by cutting off irregular or superficial parts; to cut away the outer edge or outside of (something), *e.g.* the skin or rind of (a fruit), in thin layers, slices, or flakes ME. **b.** †To prune by cutting off superfluous shoots; to reduce the thickness of (a hedge, etc.). late ME. **3.** To slice off the turf or other vegetation covering the surface of the ground 1530. **4.** To reduce (a thing) by cutting or shaving *away*; hence, to reduce little by little; to bring *down* in size or amount. Also *absol.* 1530. **5.** To cut, shave, or shear *off* or away (an outer border, surface, rind, etc.). late ME. **b.** *fig.* To cut off or remove 1549. **c.** To make or form by paring or cutting away 1708.

2. What a cursed wretch was I to p. my nails today! a Friday MIDDLETON. Take some pippins, p., core, and boil them 1769. Phr. *To p. to the quick*, to cut away the epidermis, etc., so deep as to reach the sensitive parts; to p. so as to hurt. Also *fig.* **3.** Phr. *To p. and burn*, to cut the turf to the depth of two or three inches, and burn it, in order to use the ashes as manure. **4.** To p. down the..redundance of rhetorical expression 1864. **5.** To pass a halfcrown, after paring a pennyworth of silver from it MACAULAY. **b.** Nor haue ye a little piece onlye of the carnall man pared awaye COVERDALE. Hence **Pared** (pē³ɹd, *poet.* pē³rĕd) *ppl. a.*

†**Paregal, peregal,** *a.* and *sb.* ME. [– OFr. *parigal, paregal*, etc., f. *par* PAR- *pref.* + *egal* EQUAL.] **A.** *adj.* Fully equal; equal (esp. in power, rank, value, etc.) –1636. **B.** *sb.* An equal, peer, match –1602.

Paregoric (pærĭgǫ·rik). 1684. [– late L. *paregoricus* – Gr. παρηγορικός encouraging, soothing (Galen), f. παρηγορεῖν console, soothe.] **A.** *adj.* Of medicines: Assuaging pain, soothing. **B.** *sb.* A medicine to assuage pain, an anodyne 1704; *spec.*, in the British Pharmacopœia = *p. elixir.*

P. elixir, a camphorated tincture of opium, flavoured with aniseed and benzoic acid.

†**Pareil,** *a.* and *sb.* late ME. [– (O)Fr. *pareil* :– pop.L. *pariculus* (Salic Law), dim. of L. *par* PAR *sb.*[1]] **A.** *adj.* Equal –1610. **B.** *sb.* Equality; a mate, fellow; an equal, a match –1638.

Pareira (părē³·ră). 1715. [– Pg. *parreira* vine trained against a wall.] A drug made of the root of a Brazilian plant, used in disorders of the urinary passages.

Parellic (păre·lik), *a.* 1866. [f. mod.L. *parella* – (O)Fr. *parelle*, repr. med.L. *paratella*; see -IC.] *Chem.* In *p. acid* ($C_9H_6O_4$), obtained from a crustaceous lichen, *Lecanora parella*; also called **Pare·llin.** Hence **Pare·llate,** a salt of p. acid.

Parenchyma (păre·ŋkimă). *Pl.* **parenchy·mata.** Also **pare·nchym, -me.** 1651. [– Gr. παρέγχυμα, -ματ- 'something poured in besides', f. παρά PARA-[1] + ἔγχυμα infusion; cf. ENCHYMA.] **1.** *Anat.* and *Zool.* The special or proper substance of a gland or other organ of the body, as dist. from the connective tissue or *stroma*, and from *flesh* proper 1657. **b.** The soft tissue composing the substance of the body in sponges, certain worms, etc. 1665. **2.** *Bot.* Tissue consisting of cells of about equal length and breadth placed side by side, usually soft and succulent; found esp. in the softer parts of leaves, the pulp of fruits, etc. (Dist. from PROSENCHYMA.) **Pare·nchymal, -ma·tic** *adjs.* of, pertaining to, or consisting of p.

Parenchymatous (pæreŋki·mătəs), *a.* 1667. [f. as prec. + -OUS.] **1.** *Anat.* and *Zool.* **a.** Consisting of or having the nature of parenchyma (sense 1). **b.** Of or belonging to the parenchyma of an organ; occurring in or affecting the parenchyma 1822. **2.** *Bot.* Consisting of or having the nature of parenchyma (sense 2); of or belonging to the parenchyma 1791. So **Pare·nchymous** *a.* (now *rare*) 1666.

Parent (pē³·rĕnt), *sb.* late ME. [– (O)Fr. *parent* :– L. *parens, -ent-* father or mother, pl. *parentes* parents, progenitors, kinsfolk, pr. pple. of *parere* bring forth; see -ENT.] **1.** A person who has begotten or borne a child; a father or mother 1450. **b.** By extension: A progenitor, a forefather; esp. in *our first parents*, Adam and Eve. late ME. **c.** *transf.* A person who holds the position of a parent; a protector, guardian, etc. 1526. †**2.** A relative; a kinsman or kinswoman. [So in Fr., etc.] *Obs.* or *alien.* –1771. **3.** Any organism (animal or plant) considered in relation to its offspring 1774. **4.** *fig.* That from which another thing springs or is derived; a source, cause, origin 1590.

1. No man can select his own parents 1883. The crusty old parent-in-law 1899. **c.** *Spiritual p.*, a sponsor, god-parent; also, a person to whom one owes one's conversion. **4.** P. of sweet and solemn-breathing airs GRAY.

attrib. and *Comb.*: **p.-cell** (*Biol.*), a cell from which other cells are derived; a cytula; **-kernel,** the nucleus of the fertilized egg-cell; a cytococcus. Hence **Pa·rent** *v. rare. trans.* to be the p. of, beget, produce; to be or act as a p. to. **Pa·renthood,** the state or position of a p. **Pa·rentless** *a.* without parents, orphaned; having no (known) parents, author, or source.

Parentage (pē³·rĕntėdʒ). 1489. [– (O)Fr. *parentage*, f. *parent* PARENT; see -AGE.] **1.** Exercise of the functions of a parent (*rare*). †**2.** Parents collectively (*rare*) –1590. **3.** Derivation from parents; 'birth', lineage 1565. **b.** *fig.* Origin 1581. **4.** *spec.* Hereditary degree or quality; 'family', 'birth'; *absol.* good birth 1490. †**5.** Relationship; *concr.* relations collectively –1768. **6.** Parenthood. Also *fig.* 1876.

3. The alleged p. of her son Harold was generally doubted 1870. **4.** He askt me of what p. I was; I told him of as good as he SHAKS. Born of humble p. 1838.

Parental (păre·ntăl), *a.* 1623. [– L. *parentalis*; see PARENT, -AL[1].] **1.** Of, pertaining to, or characteristic of a parent or parents; fatherly or motherly. **2.** Of the nature of a parent; *fig.* that is the source or origin from which something springs 1647.

2. The principal, and (so to speak) p. agent in that scheme 1877. Hence **Parenta·lity,** parenthood. **Pare·ntally** *adv.*

†**Pare·ntate,** *v.* 1620. [– *parentat-*, pa. ppl. stem of L. *parentare* in same sense, f. *parens, -ent-*; see PARENT, -ATE[3].] *intr.* To offer funeral obsequies, esp. those of parents or relations. So **Parenta·tion,** the performance of the funeral rites of parents or relations; hence, any memorial service for the dead.

†**Parente·le.** ME. [– Fr. *parentèle* – late L. *parentela.*] **1.** Kinship; kindred –1541. **2.** = PARENTAGE 3, 4. –1734.

Parenthesis (păre·nþĭsis). *Pl.* **-theses** (-sīz). 1564. [– late L. *parenthesis* – Gr. παρένθεσις, f. παρεντιθέναι place in besides; see PARA-[1], EN-[2], THESIS.] **1.** An explanatory or qualifying word, clause, or sentence inserted into a passage with which it has not necessarily any grammatical connection, and usu. marked off from it by round or square brackets, dashes, or commas. **2.** *transf.* An interval; an interlude; a hiatus 1599. **3.** The upright curves ( ) collectively, used to include words inserted parenthetically; now usu. in pl. *parentheses*; 'round brackets'. Also *transf.* 1715.

1. You see the inconveniency of a long p.; we have forgot the sense that went before 1659. **2.** I ne're knew tabacco taken as a p., before B. JONS. **3.** *transf.* Those ingenious parentheses called cat-cradles LAMB.

Parenthesize (păre·nþĭsəiz), *v.* 1837. [f. prec. + -IZE.] **1.** *trans.* To insert as a parenthesis; to state in parenthesis (usu. with obj. cl.). **2.** To put between marks of parenthesis 1866.

Parenthetic (pærĕnþe·tik), *a.* 1776. [f. PARENTHESIS, after *synthesis, synthetic*, etc.] **1.** Of, pertaining to, or of the nature of a parenthesis; inserted as a parenthesis. **b.** *fig.* Interposed 1876. **2.** Addicted to parenthesis (*rare*) 1782.

1. They speak of him with many p. qualifications 1883. So **Parenthe·tical** *a.* 1624, **-ly** *adv.*

Parer (pē³·rəɹ). 1573. [f. PARE *v.* + -ER[1].] An instrument for paring; a person that pares 1862.

‖**Parergon** (pǣrə̄·ɹgǫn). *Pl.* **parerga.** 1601. [L., extra ornament in art – Gr. πάρεργον subordinate or secondary business, f. παρά PARA-[1] + ἔργον work.] †**1.** In Painting: Something subordinate to the main subject; hence, *gen.* and *fig.*, ornamental accessory, grace, embellishment. **2.** By-work; work apart from one's main business or ordinary employment 1618. Hence **Pare·rgal** *a.* subsidiary, supplemental.

†**Pare·rgy.** 1646. [f. prec. with altered suffix.] A thing beside the main purpose –1656.

‖**Paresis** (pæ·rĭsis). 1693. [mod.L. – Gr. πάρεσις letting go, paralysis, f. παριέναι, f. παρα- PARA-[1] + ἱέναι let go.] *Path.* Incomplete paralysis, affecting muscular motion but not sensation. So **Pare·tic** *a.* of or pertaining to p.; affected with or characterized by p.

Par excellence: see PAR *prep.* 2 b.

Pargasite (pā·ɹgăsəit). 1818. [– G. *pargasit* (Steinheil, 1814), f. *Pargas* in Finland, where found; see -ITE[1] 2 b.] *Min.* A green or greenish variety of HORNBLENDE.

Parge (pāɹdʒ), *v.* 1701. [app. short for PARGET *v.*] = PARGET *v.* 1; hence **p.-work** = PARGET *sb.* 2.

Parget (pā·ɹdʒĕt), *sb.* late ME. [app. f. PARGET *v.*] **1.** Plaster spread upon a wall, ceiling, etc.; whitewash; roughcast. **2.** *spec.* Ornamental work in plaster; a facing of plaster with ornamental designs in relief or indented, used for decoration of walls; also called *pargeting. Obs.* or *Hist.* 1569. †**3.** *transf.* Paint (for the face) DRAYTON.

Parget (pā·ɹdʒĕt), *v.* late ME. [– OFr. *pargeter, parjeter* (now dial. fill up joints in masonry), f. *par* through, all over (PAR- *prefix*) + *jeter* cast :– med.L. *jectare*, for L. *jactare* throw (see JET *v.*[2]); cf. the use of *cast* as in *rough-cast*.] **1.** *trans.* To cover or daub with parget or plaster, to plaster (a wall, etc.); to adorn with pargeting. †**b.** To daub or plaster over *with* (anything) –1698. †**c.** To cover or decorate (a surface) with ornamental work of any kind, as gilding, precious stones, etc. –1886. †**2.** *transf.* To daub or plaster (the face or body) with paint; to paint. Also *intr.* –1660. †**3.** *fig.* To 'whitewash', smooth or gloss over –1824.

1. The walles to be parieted without, and within, and diuersly paincted 1555. **2.** She's aboue fiftie too, and pargets! B. JONS. **3.** Thus they did..p., or rough-cast their vices 1640. So †**Pa·rgeter,** a plasterer; a whitewasher.

Pargeting (pā·ɹdʒĕtiŋ), *vbl. sb.* late ME. [-ING[1].] **1.** The action of PARGET *v.* **2.** *concr.* = PARGET *sb.* 1, 2. late ME.

Parhelion (paɹhī·liŏn). *Pl.* **parhelia** (-iă). 1648. [– L. *parelion* – Gr. παρήλιον, also παρήλιος, f. παρα- PARA-[1] + ἥλιος sun.] A spot on a solar halo at which the light is intensified (usu. at the intersection of two halos), often prismatically coloured; a mock sun.

fig. The sky was full of parhelions of delusive glory 1867. Hence **Parheliacal** (pāɹhĭlɔi·ăkăl), **Parhelic** (paɹhī·lik or -he·lik) *adjs.* pertaining to or resembling a p.

Pariah (pē·riă, pā·riă, pæ·riă). 1613. [– Tamil *paṛaiyar*, pl. of *paṛaiyan* lit. 'hereditary drummer', f. *paṛai* 'the large drum beaten at certain festivals' (Yule & Burnell).] **1.** *prop.* One of a low caste in Southern India, especially numerous at Madras, where its members supply most of the domestics in European service. **2.** Hence, A member of any low Hindoo caste, or of no caste 1711. **3.** *fig.* A social outcast 1819. **b.** = *Pariah dog* 1816. **4.** *attrib.* 1711.

Comb.: **p.-dog,** a vagabond dog of low breed which frequents towns and villages in India and the East; **-kite,** the Scavenger-kite of India (*Milvus govinda*). Hence **Pa·riahdom, Pa·riahship,** the condition of a p.

Parian (pē·riăn), *a.* (*sb.*) 1638. [f. L. *Parius* of Paros + -AN.] **1.** Belonging to the island of Paros, one of the Cyclades, famed for a white statuary marble. **2.** Applied to a fine white kind of porcelain: usu. as *sb.* 1850.

Paridigitate (pæridi·dʒitĕt), *a.* 1864. [f. *pari-*, stem of L. *par* equal + DIGITATE.] *Zool.* Having an even number of toes on each foot; artiodactyl.

‖**Paries** (pē·riˌīz). *Pl.* **parietes** (părəi·ĭtīz). 1727. [L. *paries, pariet-* wall, partition-wall.] *Anat.*, etc. A part or structure enclosing a cavity in an animal or plant body or other natural formation; a wall (of a hollow bodily organ, an abscess or wound, a capsule of a plant, a cell of a honeycomb, etc.) Chiefly in *pl.*

Parietal (părəi·ĭtăl), *a.* (*sb.*) 1506. [– Fr. *pariétal* or late L. *parietalis*, f. prec. + -AL[1].] **1. a.** *Anat.* and *Zool.* Belonging to or connected with the wall of the body or of any of its cavities. **b.** *Bot.* Belonging to, connected with, or attached to the wall of a hollow organ or structure, esp. of the ovary, or of a cell 1830. **2.** In U.S., Pertaining to residents and order within the walls of a college, as in *P. Board, P. Committee*, at Harvard College 1837. **3.** *gen.* Of or belonging to a wall (*rare*) 1845. **B.** *sb.* = Parietal bone 1706.

1. *P. bones*, a pair of bones, right and left, forming part of the sides and top of the skull, between the frontal and occipital bones.

†**Pa·rietary.** ME. [– AFr. *paritarie* = OFr. *paritaire* (mod. *pariétaire*) – late L. *parietaria* (sc. *herba*), subst. use of fem. of adj. *parietarius*, f. *pariet-*; see PARIES, -ARY[1].] The herb Pellitory (*Parietaria officinalis*) –1696.

Parieto- (părəi:ĭto), used as comb. form of PARIES or PARIETAL, denoting **a.** Belonging to or connected both with the parietal bone, and (the structure indicated by the second element); as **Pari:eto-ma·stoid** *a.*, etc. **b.** Belonging to or connected with the wall of (a cavity), or of the body and (some structure); as **Pari:eto-spla·nchnic** *a.* belonging to the walls of the viscera, viscero-pleural; etc.

Parillin (păr·i·lin). Also **pariglin** (pări·lɪ'in). 1831. [f. Sp. *parilla* (see SARSAPARILLA) + -IN[1].] *Chem.* A white or colourless, odorous, crystalline substance ($C_{40}H_{70}O_{18}$) obtained from sarsaparilla-root; also called **Pari·llic acid,** *salsaparin, sarsaparillin, sarsaparilla-saponin,* or *smilacin.*

‖**Pari mutuel** (pari mütüẹl). 1881. [Fr., = mutual wager.] A form of betting in which those who have backed the winning horse divide among themselves the total of the stakes on the other horses (less a percentage for management).

Paring (pēᵊ·riŋ), *vbl. sb.* ME. [f. PARE *v.* + -ING[1].] **1.** The action of pruning, or cutting off the edge or surface, or anything superficial (*lit.* and *fig.*) late ME. **2.** *concr.* A thin portion pared off the surface of anything; a shaving ME.

‖**Pari passu** (pēᵊ·rəi pæ·siū), *advb. phr.* 1567. [L., = 'with equal step'.] Side by side at an equal rate of progress; simultaneously and equally. In *Law*, On an equality, without preference.

Paripinnate (pæripi·nĕt), *a.* 1857. [f. L. *par, pari-* equal + PINNATE.] *Bot.* Pinnate with an even number of leaflets, i.e. without a terminal leaflet.

Paris (pæ·ris), name of the capital of France, in various collocations.

†**P. ball,** a tennis ball; **P. blue,** (*a*) a bright shade of Prussian blue; (*b*) a bright blue colouring matter obtained from aniline; **P. green,** a vivid light green pigment composed of aceto-arsenite of copper; **P. white,** a fine kind of whiting used in polishing.

Parish (pæ·riʃ). [ME. *pa·roche, -osse, -issche* – AFr., OFr. *paroche* and (O)Fr. *paroisse* – eccl.L. *parochia*, alt. (after *parochus* – Gr. πάροχος public purveyor) of *parœchia* – Gr. παροικία sojourning, f. πάροικος dwelling near, sojourner, stranger, f. παρά beside, PARA-[1] + οἶκος dwelling, house.] **1.** In the United Kingdom, the name of a sub-division of a county. **a.** *orig.* A township or cluster of townships having its own church and clergyman, to whom its tithes and eccl. dues are (or were) paid. **b.** A later division of such a parish for eccl. purposes only, having its own church and clergyman. **c.** A corresponding eccl. area in ancient times or in foreign countries 1839. †**d.** A parishful SHAKS. **2.** A district, often identical with an original parish, constituted for purposes of civil government, and thus designated a *civil p.*; primarily, such an area constituted for the administration of the Poor-Law, and sometimes distinguished as a *poor-law p.* 1634. **3.** The inhabitants of a parish collectively ME. **b.** *U.S.* The body of people associated for Christian worship and work in connection with a particular church; a congregation; hence, a denomination 1851. **4.** *U.S.* In Louisiana, a territorial division corresponding to the county of other states 1839. **5.** A diocese, or district under the spiritual charge of a bishop (usu. *Hist.*, in sense of Gr. παροικία) 1587.

2. *On the p.*, in receipt of parochial relief.

attrib. and *Comb.*: often = 'parochial', as *p. bell, bounds, constable*, etc.; *p. doctor, magazine, nurse, school*; *p.-boy, poor, relief, workhouse*, etc.; also **p. lands,** landed property belonging to a p., and administered by the churchwardens; **p. priest,** the priest having the cure of souls in a p.; **p.-pump,** used allusively to denote politics or other matters of local interest and importance only; **p.-register** (cf. REGISTER *sb.*[1] 3 a); †**-top,** a whipping top kept for the use of the parishioners.

Pa·rish chu·rch. ME. The church of a parish.

Pa·rish cle·rk. late ME. An official appointed by the incumbent of a parish to assist in various duties connected with the church and its services; esp. formerly, to say the responses.

Pa·rish Cou·ncil. 1772. A council of a parish; *spec.* the local administrative body created in rural civil parishes of more than 300 inhabitants by the Act of 1894. Hence **Pa·rish Cou·ncillor,** a member of this body.

†**Pari·shional,** *a.* 1604. [f. PARISHION(ER + -AL[1].] Of or pertaining to a parish; parochial; of parishioners –1803. Hence †**Pari·shionally** *adv.*

Parishioner (pări·ʃənəɹ). 1471. [Superseded earlier †*parishion*, †*parishen* (XIV), alt., after PARISH, of †*paroschian, -ien* (XIII), *parochian* – OFr. *parochien, -ossien* (mod. *paroissien*), f. *paroche*, etc.; -ER[1] was added to suggest more clearly a personal designation.] One of the inhabitants or community of a parish.

Parisian (pări·ziăn, -i·ʒ'ăn), *sb.* and *a.* 1530. [– Fr. *parisien*, f. *Paris* Paris; see -IAN.] **A.** *sb.* A native or inhabitant of Paris. **B.** *adj.* Of or pertaining to Paris; resembling Paris or that of Paris. Hence **Pari·sianism. Pari·sianize** *v. trans.* to make P.

‖**Parisienne** (parizyẹn). 1886. [Fr. fem. of *Parisien.*] A female Parisian.

Parisite (pæ·risəit). 1846. [Named 1845 after J. J. *Paris*, its discoverer; see -ITE[1] 2 b.] *Min.* A fluo-carbonate of the metals of the cerium group, found in the emerald mines of California.

‖**Parison**[1] (pæ·risǫn). *Pl.* **parisa.** 1586. [– Gr. πάρισον n. of πάρισος exactly balanced, f. παρ(α- PARA-[1] + ἴσος equal.] *Rhet.* An even balance in the members of a sentence. Hence †**Pari·sonal, Pariso·nic** *adjs.* characterized by p.

Parison[2] (pæ·risən). 1832. [– Fr. *paraison* f. *parer* prepare.] *Glass-blowing.* The rounded mass into which the molten glass is first gathered and rolled when taken from the furnace.

Parisyllabic (pæ:risilæ·bik), *a.* and *sb.* 1656. [f. L. *par, pari-* equal + *syllaba* syllable + -IC; cf. *syllabic.*] *Gram.* **A.** *adj.* Of Gr. and L. nouns: Having the same number of syllables in the nominative as in the oblique cases of the singular. **B.** *sb.* A p. noun 1893. So †**Parisylla·bical** *a.*

†**Paritor** (pæ·ritəɹ). 1530. [Aphetic f. APPARITOR.] An apparitor of an ecclesiastical court –1825.

Parity[1] (pæ·rĭti). 1572. [– (O)Fr. *parité* or late L. *paritas*, f. *par* equal, PAR *sb.*[1]; see -ITY.] **1.** The state or condition of being equal, or on a level; equality 1613. **2.** Equality of rank or status; *esp.* equality among the members, or among the ministers, of a church 1572. **3.** Likeness, analogy; parallelism; as in *p. of reason* or *reasoning*. (Cf. L. *pari ratione*) 1620. †**4.** Of numbers: Evenness –1646. **5.** *Comm.* A standard of price expressed in another currency 1886. **b.** = PAR *sb.*[1] 2 b. 1900. **6.** Equality, as legal tender or money, between coins of one metal and coins of another 1895.

3. There is..no p. of case between Spirit and Matter BERKELEY.

Parity[2] (pæ·rĭti). 1878. [f. PAROUS *a.* + -ITY.] *Obstet. Med.* The condition of being parous; the fact of having borne children.

Park (pāɹk), *sb.* ME. [– (O)Fr. *parc* :– med.L. *parricus* ('Lex Ripuaria' VIII) – Gmc. base repr. by OHG. *pfarrih, pferrih* (G. *pferch*) pen, fold, corresp. to OE. *pearruc* (see PADDOCK *sb.*², PARROCK). In sense 5 and 6 from later uses of Fr. *parc*, and occas. so spelt.] **1.** *Law.* An enclosed tract of land held by royal grant or prescription for keeping beasts of the chase. (Dist. from a *forest* or *chase* by being enclosed, and from a *forest* also by having no special laws or officers.) **b.** Hence, a large ornamental piece of ground, usu. comprising woodland and pasture, attached to a country house or mansion, and used for recreation, and often for keeping deer, cattle, etc. 1715. **c.** *fig.* 1579. **2.** An enclosed piece of ground, within or near a city or town, ornamentally laid out and devoted to public recreation, a 'public park' 1661. **b.** An extensive area of land set apart as national property to be kept in its natural state for the public benefit, as the *Yellowstone P.* in the U.S. 1871. **3.** In Ireland, Scotland, etc.: An enclosed piece of ground for pasture or tillage; a field; a paddock 1581. **4.** In Colorado, Wyoming etc.: A high plateau-like valley among the mountains 1808. **5.** *Mil.*, etc. The space occupied by the artillery, wagons, beasts, stores, etc., in an encampment; these objects themselves collectively; a complete set of artillery, of tools, etc. 1683; also, a place where motor (and other) vehicles may be left 1925. **6.** An enclosed area, overflowed at every high tide, in which oysters are bred 1867.

1. b. Hungerford Castle—a fine old place in a beautiful p. 1813. **c.** [Christ Church, Oxford], Learning's receptacle, Religion's parke 1606. **2.** *The P.* (in London), in 17th c. St. James's Park, now esp. Hyde Park. **3.** *Town parks* (Ireland), small plots of ground lying round a town or village, usu. let for tillage or pasture to the townsmen or villagers.

Comb.: **p.-hack,** a horse for riding in the p.; **-keeper,** the keeper of a park; **†-leaves,** the shrub Tutsan (*Hypericum androsæmum*).

Park (pāɹk), *v.* 1526. [f. PARK *sb.*] **1.** *trans.* To enclose in, or as in, a park. **2.** *Mil.*, etc. To arrange (artillery, waggons, etc.) in a park 1812; to leave (a vehicle) in a car-park or other reserved space 1911. **b.** *transf.* To leave in a suitable place until required 1908.

1. How are we park'd and bounded in a pale! SHAKS. Hence **Pa·rking** *vbl. sb.* the action of the vb. (also *attrib.* as in *p.-place* for vehicles); *concr.* ground laid out like a park; in U.S., a strip of turf in the centre of a street.

Parker (pā·ɹkəɹ). ME. [– AFr. *parker* = med.L. *parcarius*, f. *parc* PARK *sb.*; see -ER² 2.] **1.** A park-keeper. *Obs.* exc. *Hist.* **2.** A rabbit that lives in a park 1846.

Parkin (pā·ɹkin). *n. dial.* 1828. [Of local origin; perh. f. proper name *Parkin, Perkin*, dim. of *Per*, Peter.] A kind of gingerbread made of oatmeal and treacle.

Parky (pā·ɹki), *a. colloq.* 1898. [Of unkn. origin.] Nippingly cold.

Parlance (pā·ɹlăns). 1579. [– OFr. *parlance*, f. *parler* speak; see PARLE *v.*, -ANCE.] **1.** Speaking, speech, *esp.* debate, parleying, parley (*arch.*). **2.** Way of speaking, language, idiom; as *in common, legal, ordinary, vulgar p.*, etc. 1787.

1. Battel and not P. should determine his right, and title 1611.

Pa·rlatory. 1651. [– med.L. *parlatorium*, f. *parlare* PARLE *v.*; see -ORY¹, -ORIUM.] A convent parlour.

Parle (pāɹl), *sb. arch.* and *dial.* 1575. [f. PARLE *v.*] **1.** Speech; talk; conversation 1587. **2.** A conference, discussion, debate; *spec.* = PARLEY *sb.* 2. 1575.

2. When in an angry p. He smot the sledded Pollax on the Ice SHAKS.

Parle (pāɹl), *v. Obs.* or *arch.* and *dial.* late ME. [– (O)Fr. *parler* :– Rom. **paraulare*, f. **paraula* (see PAROLE) :– L. *parabola* PARABLE.] **1.** *intr.* To speak; to talk in conference. **2.** *intr.* To parley (*with* an opponent); to hold a parley 1558.

2. The Jacobite and the presbyterian. . parled together DE FOE.

Parley (pā·ɹli), *sb.* 1581. [perh. – OFr. *parlee*, subst. use of fem. pa. pple. of *parler* speak; see PARLE *v.*, -Y⁵.] **1.** Speech, speaking, talk; conference; debate, argument. (Now usu. coloured by 2.) 1582. **2.** A conference for the debating of points in dispute; esp. *Mil.*, an informal conference with an enemy, under a truce, for the discussion of terms, etc. 1580.

2. Phr. *To beat* or *sound a p.*, to call for a p. by sounding a drum or trumpet; The Herald soundes a parlee, and none answers DEKKER.

Parley (pā·ɹli), *v.*¹ 1570. [f. PARLEY *sb.*] **1.** *intr.* To speak, talk; to confer (*with*). Now *arch.* 1591. **b.** *trans.* To speak; *esp.* to speak a foreign language 1570. **2.** *intr.* To treat, discuss terms; *esp.* to hold a parley (*with* an enemy, etc.). Also *fig.* 1600. **b.** *trans.* To grant a parley to (a person); to hold discussion with, speak to 1611.

2. We. . offered a truce to p. DE FOE.

Parley, *v.*² *U.S.* 1895. = PAROLI *v.*

Parleyvoo (pāɹlivū·), *sb. joc.* 1754. [f. Fr. *parlez-vous* (parlevu) in *parlez-vous français?* do you speak French?] **1.** The French language, French; French lessons. **2.** A Frenchman 1815. So **Parleyvoo·** *v. slang* or *joc. intr.* to speak French, or a foreign tongue; to palaver.

Parliament (pā·ɹlĭmĕnt), *sb.* [ME. *parlement* – (O)Fr. *parlement*, f. *parler*; see PARLE *v.*, -MENT. The present form follows AL. *parliamentum* (XIII), which is prob. based on Eng. *parli-*; it appears in XV, when four main forms were current, *parle-, -la-, -li-, -lia-*.] **†1.** The action of speaking; a 'bout' of speaking; a speech; a colloquy; a discussion or debate –1542. **†b.** = PARLEY *sb.* 2. –1610. **2.** A formal conference or council for the discussion of some matter or matters of general importance; *spec.* applied to great councils of the early Plantagenet Kings. (Now only *Hist.*) ME. **3.** The Great Council of the nation, which forms, with the Sovereign, the supreme legislature of the United Kingdom, consisting of the three estates, viz. the Lords Spiritual and Temporal (forming together the House of Lords), and the representatives of the counties, cities, etc. (forming the House of Commons) ME. **4.** Name of corresponding legislative bodies in the colonies, and in other countries. late ME. **5.** Applied to various consultative assemblies; (*a*) one formerly held by tinners in the Stannaries 1574; (*b*) one of the members of the Middle or the Inner Temple 1533. **b.** *fig.* and *transf.* late ME. **6.** In France (before the Revolution of 1789), the name given to a certain number of supreme courts of justice 1560. **7.** Short for *p.-cake* 1812.

1. Thus ended the parlement betwene the fader and the sone 1450. **2.** They made request that it might be lawfull for them to sommon a Parlament of Gallia at a certain day 1563. **3.** The privileges of p. BLACKSTONE. Phr. *Act of P.*, a statute passed by both Houses of P. and ratified by the royal assent. *Clerk of the Parliaments* (*†Parliament*), the chief official of the House of Lords, who reads the royal assent to bills before P. assembled as a corporate body in the House of Lords. *High Court of P.*, a name formerly applied collectively (as in Bk. of Com. Prayer) to the two houses of P. in session; now mostly said of P. in its judicial capacity. *To open P.* **5. b.** The P. of Bees 1640, of man TENNYSON. The Cricket P. at Lord's 1903. **7.** Gorging the boy with apples and p. THACKERAY.

Phrases. **Barebone's P.,** the *Little P.*, so called from Praise-God Barbon, one of the members for London. **Little P.,** the assembly of 120 members, nominated by Cromwell and his Council of Officers, which sat from 4 July to 12 Dec. 1653. **Long P.,** that which met on 3 Nov. 1640, and was finally dissolved in 1660. **Rump P.,** the remnant of the Long P., in its later history. **Short P.,** that which sat from 13 April to 5 May 1640, before the Long P.

attrib. and *Comb.*, as *p. army, buildings, news*, etc.; also **P. Act,** *spec.* the Act of Parliament passed in 1911 by which the powers of the House of Lords were restricted; **p.-cake, -gingerbread,** a thin crisp rectangular cake of gingerbread; **-chamber,** the room in which a p. meets, *spec.* that in the Old Palace of Westminster; **p. ordinance:** see ORDINANCE 6; **P. Roll:** see ROLL *of p.* Hence **†Parliame·ntal** *a.* parliamentary –1775. **Parliamentee·r** (*Hist.*) = PARLIAMENTARIAN A. 1.

Pa·rliament, *v. rare.* 1491. [Late ME. *parlement* – OFr. *parlementer*, f. *parlement*; see prec. Cf. med.L. *parlamentare* parley, hold a Parliament (XIII, XIV).] **†1.** *intr.* To talk, converse; to parley –1610. **2.** *intr.* To attend Parliament. Also with *it.* 1642.

Parliamentarian (pā:ɹlimentēᵊ·riăn). 1644. [f. PARLIAMENT + -ARIAN.] **A.** *sb.* **1.** *Hist.* One who took the side or was in the service of the Parliament during the Civil War of the 17th c. **2.** One versed in parliamentary usages and tactics; a skilful parliamentary debater 1834. **B.** *adj.* = PARLIAMENTARY *a.* Hence **Pa:rliamenta·rianism,** the parliamentary principle or system.

Parliamentary (pāɹlĭme·ntări), *a.* (*sb.*) 1616. [f. as prec. + -ARY¹.] **1.** Of, belonging to or relating to a parliament, or parliament as an institution; of the nature of a parliament 1626. **b.** Of, belonging or adhering to, the Parliament in the Civil War of the 17th c. 1761. **2.** Enacted, ratified, or established by Parliament 1616. **3.** Consonant with the usages or agreeable to the practice of Parliament 1625. **b.** Of language: Such as is permitted to be used in Parliament; hence *allusively*, civil, courteous 1818.

1. An old P. hand GLADSTONE. *P. agent*, a person professionally employed to take charge of the interests of a party concerned in or affected by any private legislation of P. **2.** Cheerfully pay all p. taxes PRIESTLEY. Phr. *P. train*, a train carrying passengers at a rate not exceeding one penny a mile, which, by Act of Parliament, every railway company was formerly obliged to run daily each way over its system. So *p. carriage, fare, ticket*, etc. **3. b.** Two gentlemen politely and in strictly P. language calling one another incompetent administrators 1885.

B. *sb.* **I. 1.** A member of Parliament 1626. **2.** Short for *parliamentary train*; see 2 above 1864. **II.** A person sent to parley with the enemy 1865. Hence **Parliame·ntarily** *adv.*

Parliament house. late ME. The building in which a parliament meets. (Still used of the building in Edinburgh in which the Scottish Parliament met.)

Parliament man. Now *Hist.* or *dial.* 1605. **1.** A member of the Parliament, orig. of England, also of Scotland and Ireland, later of the United Kingdom; usu. applied, like 'Member of Parliament' now, to a member of the House of Commons. **2.** = PARLIAMENTARIAN A. 1. (*rare*) 1853.

Parlour, parlor (pā·ɹləɹ). ME. [– AFr. *parlur*, OFr. *parleor, parleur* (mod. *parloir*), f. Rom. **paraulare* PARLE *v.* The ending is assim. to -OUR, -OR 2.] **1.** An apartment in a monastery or convent for conversation with persons from outside, or among the inmates. **2.** In a mansion, dwelling-house, town-hall, etc., *orig.* A smaller room apart from the great hall, for private conversation (e.g. a banker's parlour, the mayor's parlour in a town-hall). Hence, in a private house, the ordinary sitting-room of the family. †Formerly often simply = 'room' or 'chamber'. late ME. **†b.** Used as a dining or supper room. –c1850. **3.** A room in an inn more private than the tap-room where people may converse apart 1870. **4.** *orig. U.S.* An elegantly or showily fitted apartment, for some special business or trade use, as *beauty p., cinema p., ice-cream p.* 1890.

2. b. To the Parler where they used to sup SIDNEY. *attrib.* and *Comb.*: **p.-boarder,** a boarding-school pupil who lives in the family of the principal; **-car** (*U.S.*), a luxuriously fitted railway carriage, a 'drawing-room' car; **-maid,** a female domestic servant who waits at table; **-organ,** a reed-organ suitable for a private room; **p. tricks** *slang*, society arts or accomplishments.

Parlous (pā·ɹləs), *a.* (*adv.*) *arch.* and *dial.* [ME. *perlous, parlous*, syncopated form of *perelous, parelous* PERILOUS.] **A. 1.** Perilous, dangerous, hazardous. **b.** Risky to deal with; ticklish, awkward, precarious 1658. **2.** Dangerously cunning, clever, etc.; keen, shrewd; mischievous; very bad, 'shocking'; surprising, 'terrible', 'awful'. (In later use *colloq.* and *dial.*) late ME. **B.** *adv.* Excessively, 'terribly', 'awfully', 'desperately' 1599.

1. A perlous tyme 1535. **b.** A p. liquor 1658. **2.** A p. Boy: go too, you are too shrew'd SHAKS. Hence **Pa·rlous-ly** *adv.*, **-ness.**

†Parmace·ty. 1545. **1.** A pop. corruption of SPERMACETI –1828. **2.** In full *p. whale*: The Cachalot or Sperm whale –1851.

Parmesan (pāɹmĭzæ·n), *a.* and *sb.* 1519. [– Fr. *parmesan* – It. *parmegiano*, f. *Parma.*] **A.** *adj.* Of or belonging to Parma in Northern Italy, *esp.* applied to a cheese made there and elsewhere in North Italy. **B.** *sb.* Parmesan cheese. (Now usu. with capital *P.*) 1556.

Parnassian (paɹnæ·siăn), *a.* and *sb.* 1644.

[f. L. *Parnas(s)ius, -eus* (f. *Parnasus* PARNASSUS) + -AN.] **A.** *adj.* **1.** Of or belonging to Parnassus; of or belonging to poetry, poetic. **b.** *spec.* Epithet of a school of French poetry, from the title *Parnasse contemporain* of a collection of their poems published in 1866; also *transf.* **2.** *Entom.* Belonging to the genus *Parnassius* of butterflies, found in mountainous regions of the northern hemisphere. **B.** *sb.* **1.** A poet 1659. **b.** *spec.* A poet of the Parnassian school 1882. **2.** *Entom.* A butterfly of the genus *Parnassius* or subfamily *Parnassiinæ*. Hence **Parna·ssianism,** the principles or practice of the P. school of poets (see A. 1 b).

Parnassus (pa.ɹnæ·sǒs). late ME. [– L. *Parnas(s)us* – Gr. Παρνασός, later Παρνασσός.] A mountain in central Greece, anciently sacred to Apollo and the Muses; hence used allusively in ref. to literature, esp. poetry. **b.** As the title of a collection of poems 1600.

Parnellism (pā·ɹněliz'm). 1885. [See -ISM.] The principles or policy of the Irish Home Rule party in the House of Commons led by Charles Stewart Parnell from 1880 to 1891. So **Pa·rnellite,** a member of this party.

Paroccipital: see PARA-¹.

Parochial (pǎrōᵘ·kiǎl), *a.* (*sb.*) late ME. [– AFr. *parochiel,* OFr. *parochial* – eccl.L. *parochialis,* f. *parochia*; see PARISH, -AL¹.] **A.** *adj.* **1.** Of, belonging, or pertaining to a parish, or parishes in general. **2.** *fig.* Pertaining or confined to a narrow area or domain; narrow, provincial 1856. **B.** *sb.* (*rare*). **a.** A parish church 1637. **b.** A parish clergyman 1853.

P. church council, a parochial governing body in the Church of England, consisting of the incumbent, the churchwardens, and elected parishioners. Hence **Paro·chial-ly** *adv.*, **-ness.**

Parochialism (pǎrōᵘ·kiǎliz'm). 1847. [f. PAROCHIAL + -ISM.] **1.** Parochial character or tendency; local narrowness of view; petty provincialism. **2.** Absorption in parish duties 1884.

Parochiality (pǎrōᵘkiæ·lǐti). 1769. [f. PAROCHIAL + -ITY.] The quality or state of being parochial (*lit.* and *fig.*). In *pl.* Affairs of the parish; narrow or restricted interests or affairs.

Parochialize (pǎrōᵘ·kiǎləiz), *v.* 1846. [f. PAROCHIAL + -IZE.] **1.** *trans.* To make parochial. **2.** *intr.* To do parish work 1871. Hence **Paro:chializa·tion.**

†**Paro·chian,** *sb.* and *a.* ME. [– OFr. *parochien* – med.L. *parochianus,* f. eccl.L. *parochia*; see PARISH, -AN.] **A.** *sb.* **1.** An inhabitant of a parish, a parishioner –1765. **2.** A parish clergyman (*rare*) –1715. **B.** *adj.* Parochial –1644.

A. 1. I gyue and bequeth to the poure parochians ..xˡⁱ T. CROMWELL. **B.** The P. Pope, or independent Soveraigne in every Parish 1644.

†**Pa·rochin(e.** *Sc.* 1500. [f. ME. *paroche* PARISH; the suffix is unexplained; cf. *parishing,* also north. Eng. XV–XVI.] = PARISH –1824 (*Hist.*).

Parode (pæ·roᵘd). 1861. [– Gr. πάροδος entrance from the side, f. παρ(α- PARA-¹ + ὁδός way.] In ancient Gr. drama, the first ode sung by the chorus after its entrance.

†**Paro·dic,** *a.*¹ *rare.* 1684. [– Gr. παροδικός passing, f. πάροδος passing, passage; cf. prec., see -IC.] *Math.* Applied to any one of the series of degrees or powers of the unknown or variable below the highest that occurs in an equation –1775.

Parodist (pæ·rǒdist). 1742. [– Fr. *parodiste,* f. *parodie* PARODY.] The author of a parody. So **Pa·rodize** *v.* to parody 1658.

Parody (pæ·rǒdi), *sb.* 1598. [– late L. *parodia* or Gr. παρῳδία burlesque poem or song, f. παρά beside, subsidiary, mock- + ᾠδή song, poem; see PARA-¹, ODE, -Y³.] **1.** A composition in which the characteristic turns of thought and phrase of an author are mimicked and made to appear ridiculous, especially by applying them to ludicrously inappropriate subjects. Also applied to a burlesque of a musical work. **2.** *transf.* and *fig.* A poor or feeble imitation, a travesty 1830.

2. The Brussels riot..is a wretched p. on the last French revolution COLERIDGE. A p. of justice 1900. So **Paro·dic** *a.*², **-al** *adjs.* of the nature of a p., burlesque.

Parody (pæ·rǒdi), *v.* 1745. [f. prec.. prob. after Fr. *parodier.*] **1.** *trans.* To compose a parody on (a work or an author); to ridicule (a composition) by mimicking it. **b.** *intr.* To compose a parody 1875. **2.** *trans.* To imitate in a way that is no better than a parody 1801.

2. After his death, his [Pitt's] finance was parodied by incapable successors 1869.

‖**Parœmia** (pǎrī·miǎ). 1586. [L. – Gr. παροιμία by-word, proverb, f. πάροιμος by the way, f. -παρ(α- PARA-¹ + οἶμος way.] *Rhet.* A proverb, adage. So **Parœmio·grapher,** a writer of proverbs. **Parœmio·logy,** the study of proverbs.

Parœmiac (pǎrī·miæk), *a.* (*sb.*) 1699. [– Gr. παροιμιακός, f. παροιμία PARŒMIA.] **1.** *prop.* Of the nature of a proverb, proverbial 1820. **2.** *Gr. Pros.* (also *sb.*) (Applied to) the short line (anapæstic dimeter catalectic) with which an anapæstic system usually ends 1699.

Parol (pæ·rǫl), *sb.* and *a.* 1474. [– (O)Fr. *parole,* in Law Fr. *parol*; see next.] **A.** *sb.* **1.** Something said or spoken; an oral statement; an utterance; a word. Chiefly in *Law*; now only in phr. *by p.*, by word of mouth. **2.** *Law.* The pleadings filed in an action (formerly presented by word of mouth) 1625.

1. A tenancy at will may be created by p., or by deed 1844.

B. *adj.* [the sb. used attrib.] **1.** Expressed or given orally; verbal. Now only in *Law*, in *p. evidence,* etc. 1601. **2.** *Law.* Made (as a contract or lease) by word of mouth or in a writing not sealed 1590.

Parole (pǎrōᵘ·l), *sb.* 1616. [– (O)Fr. *parole* word, in the sense 'formal promise, engagement' (as in phr. *parole d'honneur*) :– Rom. **paraula* :– L. *parabola* PARABLE. Cf. PARLE *v.*] **1.** In full, *p. of honour*: Word of honour given or pledged; esp. *Mil.* the undertaking given by a prisoner of war that he will not try to escape, or that, if liberated, he will return to custody under stated conditions, or will refrain from taking up arms against his captors for a stated period. A person so liberated is said to be *on p.* **b.** *ellipt.* The condition of being on parole 1667. †**2.** *Mil.* The password used only by the officers or inspectors of the guard; dist. from the *counter-sign* given to all the men on guard –1844. **3.** *attrib.* 1812.

1. They had broken their p. and fled 1880. **b.** This man had..forfeited his military p. MACAULAY.

Parole (pǎrōᵘ·l), *v.* 1716. [f. prec.] †**1.** *intr.* To pledge one's word –1716. **2.** *trans.* To liberate (a prisoner) on parole 1863. **b.** *U.S.* To liberate (a prisoner) on his own recognizances 1888.

Paroli (pā·rǒli), *sb.* 1701. [– Fr. *paroli* – It. *paroli,* f. *paro* like :– L. *par* PAR *sb.*¹] In faro, etc., the leaving of the money staked and the money won as a further stake; the staking of double the sum before staked. Hence as vb.

My friendship goes to sleep like a p. at Pharoah, and does not wake again till their deal is over H. WALPOLE.

Paromology (pæromǫ·lǒdʒi). Chiefly in L. form. 1586. [– L. *paromologia,* Gr. παρομολογία partial admission, f. παρ(α- PARA-¹ + ὁμολογία HOMOLOGY.] *Rhet.* A figure in which something is conceded to an adversary in order to strengthen one's own position.

‖**Paronomasia** (pǎrǫnomēⁱ·ziǎ, -siǎ). Also †**parono·masy.** 1579. [L. – Gr. παρονομασία, f. παρ(α- PARA-¹ + ὀνομασία naming.] A playing on words which sound alike; a word-play; a pun. Hence **Paronoma·sial, Paronoma·sian** *adjs.* of or pertaining to p. So **Parono·ma·stic, -al** *adjs.*, **-ly** *adv.*

You catch the paronomasia, play 'po' words CALVERLEY.

‖**Paronychia** (pæroni·kiǎ). 1597. [L. – Gr. παρωνυχία a whitlow, f. παρ(α- PARA-¹ + ὄνυξ, ὀνυχ- nail.] **1.** *Path.* An inflammation about the finger-nail; a whitlow. **2.** *Bot.* A genus of herbaceous plants (N.O. *Illecebraceæ*); whitlow-wort 1666.

Paronym (pæ·rǒnim). 1846. [– Gr. παρώνυμον subst. use of n. of adj. παρώνυμος, f. παρά PARA-¹ + ὄνυμα, var. of ὄνομα name.] A word which is derived from another, or from the same root; a derivative or cognate.

Paronymous (pǎrǫ·nimǝs), *a.* 1661. [f. Gr. παρώνυμος (see prec.) + -OUS.] **1.** Of words: Derived from the same root; radically connected, cognate. **2.** Having the same sound, but different orthography and meaning 1836.

Paronymy (pǎrǫ·nimi). 1885. [f. Gr. παρώνυμος PARONYM + -Y³.] Formation from a word in another language with but slight change.

Paroophoron, Parorchid: see PARA-¹ 1.

Paroquet (pæ·rǒkėt). var. of PARAKEET.

Comb. **p.** (**perroquet**) **auk,** a small auk, *Ombria psittacula* (*Cyclorhynchus psittaculus*), inhabiting the coasts and islands of the northern Pacific.

Parosteal (pǎrǫ·stiˌǎl), *a.* 1854. [f. PARA-¹ + Gr. ὀστέον bone + -AL¹.] *Anat.*, etc. = PAROSTOTIC.

‖**Parostosis** (pærǫstōᵘ·sis). 1893. [f. as prec. + -OSIS.] *Anat.*, etc. The formation of bone outside the periosteum, as in the sheaths of blood-vessels, etc. So **Parosto·tic** *a.* of or formed by p. 1870.

Parotic (pǎrǫ·tik), *a.* 1857. [f. PARA-¹ + Gr. οὖς, ὠτ- ear, ὠτικός of the ear.] *Anat.*, etc. Situated beside or near the ear; parotid.

Parotid (pǎrǫ·tid), *a.* and *sb.* 1687. [– Fr. *parotide* – L. *parotis, parotid-* PAROTIS.] *Anat.*, etc. **A.** *adj.* Situated beside or near the ear; applied esp. to a lobulated racemose gland just in front of the ear, and having a duct (*p. duct* or *Stenson's duct*) opening into the mouth opposite the second upper molar tooth. **B.** *sb.* The parotid gland 1770.

‖**Parotis** (pǎrōᵘ·tis); usu. in *pl.* **parotides** (-tidīz). 1615. [L. – Gr. παρωτίς, παρωτιδ-, f. παρα- PARA-¹ + οὖς, ὠτ- ear; see -ID².] **1.** The parotid gland. †**2.** A parotid tumour –1893. Hence ‖**Parotidi·tis** [see -ITIS] = next.

Parotitis (pærotǝi·tis). 1822. [irreg. for *parotiditis,* f. prec.; see -ITIS.] *Path.* Inflammation of the parotid gland, or of neighbouring structures; usu. constituting the disease called *mumps.* Hence **Paroti·tic** *a.* affected with p.

Parotoid (pǎrōᵘ·toid), *a.* (*sb.*) 1873. [irreg. f. PAROTIS + -OID.] *Zool.* Applied to certain glands of the skin forming warty excrescences near the ears in some batrachians, as toads. Also as *sb.*

Parous (pæ·rǝs), *a.* 1896. [f. as next.] Having borne children.

-parous, *suffix,* f. L. *-parus* bearing (*parĕre* bring forth) + -OUS, as in *multiparous, oviparous, viviparous,* etc. adjs.

‖**Parousia** (pǎrū·siǎ). 1875. [– Gr. παρουσία presence (of persons), in eccl. Gr. the Advent (Matt. 24:27, 1 Cor. 15:23), f. παρεῖναι be present.] *Theol.* The second coming or advent of Christ.

Parovarium: see PARA-¹ 1.

Paroxysm (pæ·rǒksiz'm). 1604. [– Fr. *paroxysme* – med.L. *paroxysmus* irritation, exasperation – Gr. παροξυσμός, f. παροξύνειν, f. παρά in addition, PARA-¹ + ὀξύνειν sharpen, f. ὀξύς sharp.] **1.** *Path.* An increase of the acuteness or severity of a disease, usu. recurring periodically in its course; a fit. **2.** A violent access of action or emotion; a fit, convulsion 1641. **b.** (Without *pl.*) The acute stage (of any action, etc.). Now *rare.* 1650. †**3.** An open quarrel –1702.

2. He was cast into paroxysms of rage and despair 1839.

Paroxysmal (pærǒksi·zmǎl), *a.* 1651. [f. prec. + -AL¹.] Pertaining to or of the nature of a paroxysm; marked by paroxysms; violent, convulsive. **b.** *spec.* in *Geol.* Of or pertaining to a violent natural convulsion; occas. = CATASTROPHIC, CATACLYSMIC 1830.

In a paroxismal frenzy of contending passions SHELLEY. Hence **Paroxy·smalist,** also **Pa·roxysmist** (*Geol.*), a catastrophist. **Paroxy·smally** *adv.* **Paroxy·smic** *a. rare.*

Paroxytone (pǎrǫ·ksitoᵘn), *a.* and *sb.* 1764. [– mod.L. *paroxytonus* – Gr. παροξύτονος, f. παρα- PARA-¹ + ὀξύτονος OXYTONE.] **A.** *adj.* Having an acute accent on the last syllable but one. **B.** *sb.* A word so accented.

Parpen(t (pā·ɹpěn(t). late ME. [XV (*perpend,* etc.) – OFr. *parpain, per-* (mod. *parpaing*), in med.L. *perpanus, parpanus, perpent' achillar'* 'parpeyn ashlar' (XV); prob. :– Rom. **perpannius,* f. L. *per* through + *pannus* in Rom. use, section of a wall; see PER-, PANE *sb.*¹] **1.** A stone which passes through a wall from side to side. **2.** Short for *p.-wall*, a thin wall built of p. stones, as in interior partition walls.

Parquet (pā·ɹke, paɹke·t), *sb.* 1816. [– (O)Fr. *parquet* small marked-off space, etc., dim. of *parc* PARK; see -ET.] **1.** A flooring; *spec.* a flooring composed of pieces of wood, often of different kinds, arranged in a pattern; a flooring of parquetry. **2.** (Also erron. *parquette.*) Part of the auditorium of a theatre, the front part of the ground-floor nearest the orchestra. (Chiefly *U.S.*) 1848. ‖**3.** In France, etc.: The branch of the administration of law concerned with the prevention, investigation, and punishment of crime 1892. **4.** *attrib.*, as *p.-flooring*, etc. 1874. So **Pa·rquet** *v. trans.* to floor (a room) with parquet-work; to make of inlaid woodwork 1678. **Pa·rquetage** = next.

Parquetry (pā·ɹkėtri). Also ‖**parqueterie** (parkẹtri). 1842. [– Fr. *parqueterie*, f. *parquet*; see prec., -ERY.] Inlaid work of wood, in which a pattern is formed of different kinds of wood; esp. in flooring. Also *attrib.*

Parr, par (pāɹ). 1715. [Of unkn. origin.] **1.** A young salmon before it becomes a smolt; distinguished by the parallel transverse bands on its side. **2.** A young coal-fish or black cod, less than a year old; a sillock (*local*) 1769.

Comb. **p.-tail**, an artificial fly used in salmon fishing.

Parrel, parral (pæ·rĕl), *sb.* late ME. [Earliest in *truss parrel* 1409–11, *mast parrel* 1419–22 (Sandahl), var. of †*parel* equipment, apparatus, tackle (cf. OFr. *parail* rigging XIV), aphetic form of APPAREL.] *Naut.* A band of rope, a chain, or iron collar by which the middle of a yard is fastened to the mast. Hence **Pa·rrel, parral** *v.* to fasten by means of a p.

‖**Parrhesia** (părī·ziă, -rī·siă). 1577. [med.L. *parrhesia* – Gr. παρρησία free-spokenness, f. παρα- PARA-[1] + ῥῆσις speech.] *Rhet.* Frankness or freedom of speech.

Parricidal (pærisəidăl), *a.* 1627. [– L. *parricidalis*, f. *parricida* PARRICIDE[1]; see -AL[1].] Of, pertaining to, or of the nature of a parricide; guilty of parricide. Hence **Parrici·dally** *adv.*

Parricide[1] (pæ·risəid). 1554. [– (O)Fr. *parricide* or L. *par(r)icida* of uncert. origin, but assoc. by the Romans with *pater* FATHER and *parens* PARENT; see -CIDE 1.] One who murders his father or either parent or other near relative; also, the murderer of any one whose person is held sacred; *transf.* one who is guilty of treason against his country. **b.** *attrib.* = prec. 1686.

Pa·rricide[2]. 1559. [– Fr. *parricide* or L. *par(r)icidium*; see prec., -CIDE 2.] The murder of a father, parent, near relative, ruler, etc.; the crime of a parricide; *transf.* the crime of treason against one's country. **b.** *attrib.* = PARRICIDAL 1806. Hence **†Parrici·dial, †Parrici·dious** *adjs.* parricidal.

Parrock (pæ·rək), *sb.* Now chiefly *dial.* [OE. *pearruc*; see PARK *sb.*] **1.** An enclosed space of ground; a small field, a paddock. **2.** A small apartment or narrow cell in a building; a stall, coop, or pen for animals 1440. Hence **Pa·rrock** *v. trans.* to enclose, shut up, confine within narrow limits.

Parrot (pæ·rət), *sb.* 1525. [prob. appellative use of Fr. †*Perrot* (cf. PIERROT), dim. of *Pierre* Peter; *pérot* is given by Littré as a familiar name in mod. Fr. for the bird, and *pierrot* for house-sparrow; cf. PARAKEET.] **1.** A bird of the order *Psittaci*, or family *Psittacidæ*, and spec. of the genus *Psittacus*; these are scansorial and zygodactyl, and have a short hooked bill and naked cere; many of the species have beautiful plumage, and some are excellent mimics and learn to enunciate words and phrases; hence, much valued as cage-birds, esp. the Grey Parrot (*Psittacus erithacus*) of West Africa. **2.** Applied contemptuously to a person who mechanically repeats the words or imitates the action of others 1581. **3. Sea-parrot. a.** The coulterneb or puffin, so called from the shape of its bill 1668. **b.** Some kind of fish: see PARROT-FISH 1666.

1. A very little wit is valued in a woman, as we are pleased with a few words spoken plain by a p. POPE.

attrib. and *Comb.*, as *p. cage, species*, etc.; *p.-cry, -echo, -faculty, teacher, etc.*; **-green**, a yellowish green like the colouring of some parrots; **p. tongue**, a tongue like that of a p.; *spec.* a dry shrivelled condition of the human tongue in typhus, etc.; **-weed**, the Tree Celandine, *Bocconia frutescens*, a tropical American plant; **-work**, merely imitative repetition; **-wrasse** = PARROT-FISH a. Hence **Pa·rrotism**, mechanical repetition or imitation (*rare*). **Pa·rrotize** *v.* to parrot (*rare*). **Pa·rrotry**, the mechanical or servile repetition of the sayings, etc., of others.

Parrot (pæ·rət), *v.* 1596. [f. prec.] **1.** *intr.* To chatter like a parrot; to repeat words and phrases mechanically like a parrot. Now only as *absol.* use of next. **2.** *trans.* To repeat (words) mechanically like a parrot; to iterate to weariness; to repeat or imitate without understanding or sense 1649. **3.** *trans.* To teach to repeat in a parrot-like manner; to drill like a parrot 1775.

2. To p. the *ipsissima verba* of Kant DE QUINCEY. Hence **Pa·rroter**, one who repeats something learned by rote.

Pa·rrot-coal. *Sc.* and *n. dial.* 1789. [Origin of *parrot* unkn.] Cannel coal.

Pa·rrot-fish. 1712. A name given to some fishes from their brilliant colouring, or as having a strong hard mouth resembling the bill of a parrot. *spec.* **a.** A fish of the family *Scaridæ* found in tropical seas and having a very strong jaw. **b.** A fish of the Australian labroid genus *Labrichthys*, esp. *L. psittacula*. **c.** One of the gymnodonts.

Parry (pæ·ri), *sb.* 1705. [f. PARRY *v.* Substituted for PARADE 6.] **1.** The action of parrying. **2.** *gen.* The warding off of any attack 1709.

Parry (pæ·ri), *v.* 1672. [prob. repr. Fr. *parez* (used as a word of command in fencing), imper. of *parer* – It. *parare* ward off (see PARA-[2]), specialized use of the sense 'prepare' (cf. PARADE).] **1.** *intr.* To ward off or turn aside a weapon or blow by opposing to it one's own weapon, etc. Also *fig.* **2.** *trans.* To stop, ward off, or turn aside (a weapon, a blow, etc.) in this way 1692. **b.** *gen.* and *fig.* To turn aside (anything threatened, an awkward question, etc.); to avoid, evade 1718.

1. The Spaniards p. with the poniard. The ancients parried with their bucklers 1727. **2.** To p. a cudgel with a small sword 1824. **b.** I parried her questions by the best excuses I could offer 1859.

Parse (pāɹz, *Sc.* and *U.S.* pāɹs), *v.* 1553. [Of doubtful origin; perh. orig. f. ME. *pars* (XIII–XV) parts of speech (– OFr. *pars*, pl. of *part* PART), and later infl. by L. *pars*, as in the question *Quæ pars orationis?* What part of speech?; but the (XVI–XVII) forms *peirse, pearse, pearce* are in any case difficult of explanation.] *trans.* To describe (a word in a sentence) grammatically, by stating the part of speech, inflexion, and relation to the rest of the sentence; to resolve (a sentence, etc.) into its component parts of speech and describe them grammatically. Also *intr.* or *absol.* **b.** *intr.* for *pass.* To admit of being parsed 1880.

Let the childe, by and by, both construe and p. it ouer againe ASCHAM. **b.** Anxious..whether his sentences will p. 1880. Hence **Pa·rser**, one who parses; a book on parsing.

Parsec (pāɹse·k). 1913. [f. PAR(ALLAX + SEC(OND.] A unit of measure used for interstellar distances.

Parsee (pāɹsī·). 1615. [– Pers. *Pārsī* Persian, f. *Pārs* Persia.] **1.** One of the descendants of those Persians who fled to India in the 7th and 8th centuries to escape Moslem persecution, and who still retain their religion (ZOROASTRIANISM); a Guebre. Also *attrib.* **2.** The language of Persia under the Sassanian kings 1840. **Parsee·ism**, Zoroastrianism.

Parseval (pā·ɹsėvăl). 1909. Also **Parsefal.** [f. the name of the inventor, August von *Parseval.*] Type of non-rigid German airship.

Parsimonious (pāɹsimōᵘ·niəs), *a.* 1598. [f. PARSIMONY + -OUS.] Characterized by parsimony; careful in the use or disposal of money or resources; sparing, saving, 'close'. Also *fig.* **b.** Of things: Yielding sparely; meagre, scanty; poor, mean 1713.

Hence **Parsimo·nious-ly** *adv.*, **-ness.**

Parsimony (pā·ɹsiməni). late ME. [– L. *parsi-, parcimonia, -monium*, f. *pars-*, pa. ppl. stem of *parcere* refrain, spare; see -MONY. Cf. Fr. *parcimonie*, †*parsi-*.] Carefulness in the employment of money or resources; saving or economic disposition. Also in bad sense 1561.

The misplaced parcimony of the Treasury 1896. Phr. *Law of p.*, the logical principle that no more causes or forces should be assumed than are necessary to account for the facts.

Parsley (pā·ɹsli). OE. [app. repr. a blend of (i) OE. *petersilie*, corresp. to MDu. *petersilie* (mod. *-selie*), OHG. *petersilia* (G. *petersilie*) – Rom. **petrosilium*, for L. *petroselinum* – Gr. πετροσέλινον, f. πέτρα rock, πέτρος stone + σέλινον parsley, with (ii) ME. *percil, per(e)sil* (surviving dial. *parsel*) – OFr. *peresil* (mod. *persil*), of the same origin.] A biennial umbelliferous plant (*Petroselinum sativum*, sometimes classed as *Apium* or *Carum petroselinum*), having white flowers and aromatic leaves, which are finely divided, and are used for seasoning and garnishing various dishes; in another variety (*Hamburg p.*) the large spindle-shaped root is dressed and eaten. Hence, the leaves of this plant, or the plants collectively. (Not with *a* or in *pl.*, exc. as = kind of parsley.)

Hamburg P. (see above); **Milk, Milky P.**, a name for species of *Peucedanum* and *Selinum* with milky juice; **Wild P.**, name for various wild umbellifers with finely-divided leaves. See also COW-*p.*, HEDGE-*p.*, STONE-PARSLEY, etc.

attrib. and *Comb.*, as *p. sauce*; **p.-bed**, a bed of p.; **-fern**, name for the Rock Brake (*Allosorus crispus* or *Cryptogramme crispa*), aslo applied to a variety of the Lady Fern (*Athyrium filix-femina*).

Parsley-piert (-piᵊɹt). Also **-pert.** 1597. [app. pop. corruption of Fr. *perce-pierre*, lit. 'pierce-stone'; cf. BREAKSTONE.] A dwarf annual herb (*Alchemilla arvensis*), allied to the Lady's Mantle, growing on dry barren ground, hedge-banks, etc.

Parsnip (pā·ɹsnip). [XVI *pars(e)nep* alt. of earlier *pas(se)nep* – (with assim. to ME. *nep* NEEP) OFr. *pasnaie* (mod. *panais*) :– L. *pastinaca*. Cf. TURNIP.] A biennial umbelliferous plant (*Pastinaca sativa*), having pinnate leaves, yellow flowers, and a pale yellow root, used in the cultivated state as a culinary vegetable. Hence, the root or edible part of this plant. Also extended to the genus *Pastinaca*. Also *attrib.*

Prov. *Fine* (*fair, soft*) *words butter no parsnips.* **Meadow P.**, (*a*) Cow-parsnip, *Heracleum sphondylium*; (*b*) the N. American genus *Thaspium*; **Wild P.**, the wild form of *Pastinaca sativa* (see above). See also COW-*parsnip*, WATER-*parsnip*.

Parson (pā·ɹsən, pā·ɹs'n). [ME. *person*, later *parso(u)n* – OFr. *persone*, (law Fr.) *parsone* :– L. *persona* PERSON, used in the eccl. sense XI.] **1.** *Eccl.* A holder of a parochial benefice in full possession of its rights and dues; a rector. **2.** Extended, in pop. use, so as to include a vicar, or any beneficed clergyman; a chaplain, a curate, any clergyman; a nonconformist minister or preacher. In the extended sense only *colloq.*, and often dyslogistic. 1588. **3.** *transf.* Applied to animals with black fur or markings, or to birds with black feathers. See also PARSON-BIRD. 1806. **4.** *fig.* A finger-post. Chiefly *dial.* 1785.

1. *P. imparsonee*: see IMPARSONEE. **2.** 'Mr. C.! He ain't a parson. He's a Man' 1899. **3.** *Isle of Wight p.*, the cormorant.

attrib. and *Comb.*: **p.-gull**, the great black-backed gull (*Larus marinus*); **p.-in-the-pulpit**, a pop. name of two plants, cuckoo-pint and monkshood; **parson's nose**, the rump of a fowl, etc.; **parson's week**, the time taken as a holiday by a clergyman who has a Sunday off, lasting usu. from Monday to the Saturday week following. Hence **Pa·rsondom**, the quality of a p.; parsons collectively. **Pa·rsoned** *ppl. a.* furnished with a p.; married in church or chapel (*colloq.*). **Pa·rsoness** (*joc.*), the wife of a p. **Parso·nic, -al** *adjs.* of or pertaining to a p.; characteristic of parsons; **-ly** *adv.*

Parsonage (pā·ɹsənėdʒ). late ME. [– AFr., OFr. *personage* eccl. benefice, etc. (whence med.L. *personagium* XII) – med.L. *personaticum* (XI); see PARSON, -AGE.] **1.** The benefice or living of a parson; a rectory. *Obs.* exc. in *Law.* **2.** (= *P.-house.*) The house attached to a parson's living, the rector's house. Sometimes applied to the residence provided for any minister of religion. late ME. †3. The parson's tithe. *Sc.* –1818. 4. *attrib.*, as *p.-house*, etc. 1566.

3. What have I been paying stipend and teind, p. and vicarage for, ever sin' the [year] aughty-nine? SCOTT.

Pa·rson-bird. 1857. [See PARSON 3.] 1. A New Zealand bird (*Prosthemadera novæ-zelandiæ*), so called from its dark plumage and white neck-feathers; also called *poe-bird* or *tui*. 2. The Rook 1902.

Part (pāɹt), *sb.* (*adv.*) [OE., repl. by ð (O)Fr. *part* :– L. *pars, part-* share, part of a whole, side, direction, perh. rel. to *portio* PORTION, and *parere* produce (see PARENT).] **A.** *sb.* **I.** Portion of a whole. **1.** That which with another or others makes up a whole; a certain amount, but not all, of any thing or number of things; a portion, division, section, element, constituent, piece. (When denoting a number of persons or things, often taken as a noun of multitude with pl. verb.) ME. **b.** Often used without article. late ME. **c.** *spec.* An essential or integral portion; a constituent, element. (Also without article.) 1732. **2.** *spec.* †**a.** = *part of speech.* (The earliest use.) –1637. **b.** A division of a book, play, poem, etc.; also *spec.* Each of the portions of a work issued at intervals, a fascicule 1450. †**c.** An element or constituent *of* some quality or action (with no stress on its being merely a part); a point, particular. Hence *absol.* Point; matter; affair; respect. –1719. **3.** A portion of an animal body. Usu. *pl.*; also *absol.* (*euphem.*) = private parts. late ME. †**4.** A minute portion of matter; a particle –1800. **5.** *spec.* (with a numeral): Each of the equal portions of a whole; an aliquot part, exact divisor, submultiple ME. †**b.** Used by confusion as if = 'times' as in (*by*) *a thousand parts*, etc. –1625. **c.** In expressing the proportions of the ingredients of a mixture: One of a number of equal portions of indeterminate amount 1615.

1. The greatest p. of the Indian cavalry were cut to pieces 1774. Whatever is the p. of a p., is a p. of the whole 1836. **b.** He burneth p. thereof in the fire *Isa.* 44:16. Great p. perished before they could reach the wall SOUTHEY. **c.** The rider sate as if he had been a p. of the horse SCOTT. *P. and parcel* (emphatic). **5.** Possession..being nine parts of the law 1813. **c.** Take of pure sulphate of copper, two parts; subcarbonate of ammonia, three parts 1811.

II. Portion allotted, share. **1.** A portion of something allotted to a particular person; a share. Also, Sharing, participation; interest, concern ME. **b.** Allotted portion; possession; one's lot in life. *Obs.* or *arch.* late ME. **2.** What one has to do; function, office, business, duty. late ME. **3.** *Theatr.* The character assigned to an actor in a dramatic performance; a rôle. Also, the words spoken by an actor in such a rôle; hence, a copy of these. 1495. **b.** *fig.* late ME. **4.** *Mus.* The melody assigned to a particular voice or instrument in concerted music, or a copy of this; each of the constituent melodies or successions of notes which make up a harmony. Hence *transf.* Each of the voices or instruments which join in a concerted piece. 1526. †**5.** A piece of conduct, an act –1632. **6.** A personal quality or attribute; almost always in *pl.* Abilities, capacities, talents. Also *absol.* = high intellectual ability, cleverness. Now *arch.* or *literary.* 1561.

1. Phr. *To have p.*, to share, partake (*in*, †*of*). *To have neither p. nor lot in*, to have no share or concern in. **2.** Accuse not Nature, she hath don her p. MILT. **3.** All the world's a stage..And one man in his time playes many parts SHAKS. **b.** Phr. *To play* (*act*) *the p. of*, to act as or like. *To play* (*act*) *a p.*, to perform a function, or pursue a course of action; also, to sustain a feigned character, act deceitfully; He was unskilled to act a p. and speak half the truth 1886. **6.** A gentleman.. of very excellent good partes B. JONS. A man of Parts, but a most vile, stinking Whigg HEARNE.

III. Region; side. **1.** A portion of a country, etc., or of the world; a region, quarter. (Usu. in *pl.*; often with a vague collective sense.) late ME. †**2.** Side (*lit.*); hence, direction in space –1774. **b.** = HAND *sb.* (see *On hand* e.) Now *rare.* 1485. **3.** Side in a contest, dispute, contract, etc.; party; cause. late ME. **b.** *concr.* A party; a body of partisans; a faction. Now *rare* or *Obs.* ME.

1. To propagate the Gospel in foreign parts BERKELEY. **2.** *Luke* 17:24. **b.** On the other p., I judged that I might lose nearly as much STEVENSON. **3.** An agreement made..Between—..(the vendor) of the one p., and—..(the purchaser) of the other p. 1884.

IV. [f. PART *v.*] The parting of the hair. *U.S.* 1890.

Phrases. **P. of speech** (*Gram.*) [L. *pars orationis*], formerly also *p. of reason*, or simply *part*, each of the classes of words as determined by the kind of notion or relation which they express in the sentence. **Most p.,** the greatest p., most; as *adv.* mostly; †*the more p.*, the majority. **Take p.:** **a.** To share, partake *of* or *in* (cf. II. 1); **b.** To participate *in* (some action), to assist, co-operate (cf. II. 2). **For my p.,** as regards my share in the matter, as far as I am concerned; so *for his, our, your p.*, etc. **In p.,** partly. **In good p.,** favourably or without offence; *in ill p.*, unfavourably. Chiefly with *take* or the like. **On the p. of** (any one, *on his p.*, etc.), on the side of; as regards (his, etc.) share in the action; as far as (he, etc.) is concerned; also, proceeding from (the person or party mentioned) as agent; made or performed by; by.

Comb.: **p.-music,** music in parts (esp. vocal); **-singing,** singing in parts; **-writing,** composition of music in parts, combination of parts in musical composition (see II. 4).

B. *adv.* or quasi-*adv.* or *adj.* In part, partly, to some extent. Usu. hyphened when qualifying a sb. or an adj. used *attrib.* 1513.

This wretch hath p. confest his Villany SHAKS. A part-heard case of alleged dealing in bogus cheques 1891. *P.-payment*, payment in p., action of partly paying. *P.-time*, applied to a person employed for part of his or her time, or to such an employment.

Part (pāɹt), *v.* ME. [– (O)Fr. *partir* :– L. (Rom.) *partire, partiri* divide, distribute, part, f. *pars, part-* (see prec.).] **I. 1.** *trans.* To divide into parts; to divide, break, sever. Now somewhat *rare.* **b.** To separate (the hair), as with a comb, on each side of a dividing line or *parting* 1615. **c.** *Naut.* To break, or suffer the breaking of (a rope) so as to get loose from an anchor, a mooring, etc. 1793. **2.** *intr.* To suffer division, break, cleave, come in two or in pieces 1579. **3.** *trans.* To dissolve (a connection, etc.) by separation of the persons or parties concerned. late ME. **4.** To put asunder, sunder (two or more persons or things, or one *from* another); to separate (combatants, companions, lovers, etc.). Also *fig.* to separate in thought, to distinguish ME. **b.** To keep asunder or separate; to separate as a boundary 1575. **c.** *spec.* in techn. uses; esp. (*Metall.*), to separate (gold and silver) from each other by an acid 1487. **d.** *intr.* or *absol.* To make or cause separation or division 1611.

1. Thou shalt p. it in pieces, and powr oyle thereon *Lev.* 2:6. *To p. the hoof*, to have cloven hoofs; Every beast that parteth the hoofe *Deut.* 14:6. **c.** In the attempt, it parted the grappling rope 1793. **2.** The frigate parted amidships MARRYAT. **3.** Phr. *To p. company* (= sense II. 2). *To p. a fight, fray*, to put an end to a fight by separating the combatants. †*To p. beds*, to cease to live together in wedlock. **4.** The Lord doe so to me, and more also, if ought but death p. thee and me *Ruth* 1:17. While he blessed them, hee was parted from them, and caried vp into heauen *Luke* 24:51. **b.** Where seas or deserts p. them from the rest COWPER.

II. 1. *intr.* To become or be separated (*from* something); to be liberated or detached; to emanate; to come off (*rare*) ME. **2.** In reciprocal sense: To go or come apart, to separate. Of persons: To quit one another's company. ME. **b.** *absol.* To part with something, esp. money; to give or pay money. *slang* or *colloq.* 1873. **3.** *intr.* To take one's leave or departure; to go away; to set out (*arch.*) ME. **b.** *To p.* (*hence, out of this life*, etc.): to die ME. †**4.** *trans.* = DEPART *v.* II. 4. –1812.

2. But dearest friends, alas! must p. GAY. Here our roads parted (*mod.*). *P. from*, (*a*) to go away from, leave; *b.* = sense II. 3 b (now *rare*). *P. with* (*a*) = sense II. 2 (now *rare*); (*b*) to let go, give up; to send away, dismiss; of a body or substance: to lose, give off (heat, etc.); Oh, that I should p. with so much gold! MARLOWE. **3.** But now he parted hence SHAKS. **b.** A [= he] parted eu'n iust betweene Twelue and One SHAKS. **4.** *Rich. II*, III. i. 3.

III. 1. *trans.* To divide to or among a number of recipients; to distribute in shares. Somewhat *arch.* ME. **2.** To share with another or others; (of one person) to give a share of to another; (of several) to divide among themselves. Now *rare* or *Obs.* exc. *dial.* ME. †**3.** *intr.* To make division into shares; to give, take, or have a share; to 'go shares' (*with* a person; *of* or *in*, rarely *with*, a thing) –1670.

1. To p. her time 'twixt reading and bohea POPE. **3.** They shall p. alike 1 *Sam.* 30:24. So †**Pa·rtable** *a.* = PARTIBLE –1632. **Pa·rter,** one who or that which parts (now *rare*).

‖**Partage** (partā·ʒ). 1456. [Fr., f. *partir* to PART; see -AGE. Formerly naturalized; now treated as Fr.] **1.** Division; esp. division into shares 1598. **2.** A part, share, lot 1456.

Partake (paɹtē^i·k), *v.* 1561. [Back-formation from PARTAKER, PARTAKING.] **I.** *trans.* **1.** To take a part in, to share in 1589. **b.** To share (a meal); hence, To eat or drink of, to 'take'. Now *rare* or *Obs.* 1611. †**c.** To be made acquainted with (news, etc.) –1667. †**2.** To impart, communicate (*to* or *with*); *esp.* to make known –1611. †**3.** To inform (a person) *of* (news, etc.) –1590.

1. The old man Partook that feeling SOUTHEY. **c.** Let her with thee p. what thou hast heard MILT. **2.** *Wint. T.* v. iii. 132.

II. *intr.* **1.** To participate in some action or condition. Const. *in*, *of* (†*with*) the thing; *with* the person sharing. 1585. **b.** *esp.* (with *of*) To get, have a share or portion of. Often = to take some of, take of, take 1601. **c.** To have something *of* (a quality or attribute) 1615. †**2.** To take sides *with* a person –1627.

1. Bred in a luxurious court, without partaking in its effeminacy GOLDSM. **b.** Her solitary meals she partook of in the apartment next the eating room 1805. **2.** When I against my selfe with thee pertake SHAKS. *Sonn.* cxlix. Hence **Parta·kable, -takeable** *a.* capable of †partaking, or of being partaken.

Partaker (paɹtē^i·kəɹ). late ME. [f. PART *sb.* + TAKER, after L. *particeps.*] **1.** One who takes a part or share, a partner, participator. (Now viewed as = one who partakes.) †**2.** One who takes another's part; a supporter, partisan –1700.

1. All the other are part-takers therof more or lesse 1561. Alike p. of my joys or grief 1774. **2.** To the..long unquieting of kyng Henry and his partakers 1548.

Partaking (paɹtē^i·kiŋ), *vbl. sb.* late ME. [f. PART *sb.* + TAKING *vbl. sb.*, after late L. *participatio* PARTICIPATION.] **1.** The taking of a part or share; participation. †**2.** The taking the part of some one; taking sides (in a dispute, etc.) –1657.

Partan (pā·ɹtăn). *Sc.* and *n. dial.* late ME. [app. Celtic; in Gael. *partan*; ult. history unkn.] A crab; *esp.* the common crab, *Cancer pagurus*; *fig.* an ill-natured person.

Parted (pā·ɹtėd), *ppl. a.* late ME. **I.** [*pa. pple.* of PART *v.*; see -ED[1].] **1.** Divided into parts; severed, cloven; divided, as the hair, by a parting 1590. **b.** *Bot.* Cleft nearly to the base, as a corolla or calyx, as 3-*parted*, tripartite 1880. **c.** *Her.* = PARTY *a.* 3; hence of cloth, trappings, etc. 1478. **2.** Separated, sundered 1611. **3.** Departed, dead (*arch.*) 1593. **II.** [f. PART *sb.* + -ED[2].] †**1.** Furnished with or having (good, mean, etc.) parts; gifted, talented –1668. **2.** Charged with a dramatic part 1612.

1. A Man well p., a sufficient Scholler B. JONS.

Parterre (paɹtē^ə·ɹ). 1639. [– Fr. *parterre*, subst. use of phr. *par terre* on or along the ground.] **1.** A level space in a garden occupied by flower-beds ornamentally arranged. Also *fig.* **2.** The part of the ground-floor of the auditorium of a theatre behind the orchestra; also, its occupants 1711.

Parthenic (paɹþe·nik), *a.*[1] *rare.* 1834. [– Gr. παρθενικός, f. παρθένος virgin; see -IC.] Of or belonging to, or of the nature of, a virgin; *fig.* unviolated. So **Parthe·nian** *a.* 1656.

Parthenic (paɹþe·nik), *a.*[2] 1877. [f. L. *parthenium*, a name of several plants (– Gr. παρθένιον feverfew); in the herbalists a species of camomile; see -IC.] In *p. acid*, an acid obtained from some species of *Parthenium*; so **Pa·rthenine,** an alkaloid obtained from *P. hysterophorus* and used as a remedy for fever and neuralgia.

Parthenogenesis (pā:ɹþĕnodʒe·nėsis). 1849. [mod.L., f. Gr. παρθένος virgin; see -GENESIS.] *Biol.* Reproduction without concourse of opposite sexes or union of sexual elements. So **Pa:rthenogene·tic** *a.*

pertaining to, of the nature of, or characterized by p.; reproducing by p. **Pa:rthenogene·tically** *adv.*

‖**Parthenogonidium** (pā:ɹþĕnogoni·diŏm). 1895. [mod.L., f. Gr. παρθένος virgin + GONIDIUM.] *Bot.* A gonidium in certain algæ, as *Volvox*, by which they are reproduced asexually.

Parthenospore (pā·ɹþĕnospōᵊːɹ). 1889. [f. Gr. παρθένος virgin + SPORE.] *Bot.* A reproductive cell in certain algæ, resembling a zygospore, but produced without conjugation.

Parthian (pā·ɹþiăn), *a.* and *sb.* 1526. [See -AN, -IAN.] **A.** *adj.* Of or pertaining to Parthia, an ancient kingdom of western Asia 1590.

The Parthian horsemen were accustomed to discharge their missiles backwards while in real or pretended flight; hence used allusively in *P. shaft, shot, glance*, etc.

B. *sb.* A native or inhabitant of Parthia.

Or like the P. I shall flying fight SHAKS.

‖**Parti** (parti). 1814. [Fr., = party; side, match, resolution taken for oneself.] **1.** A marriageable person considered in reference to means, etc., or as a 'match'. **2.** *Parti pris*, side taken, mind made up, bias 1871.

Parti-[1], extended use of *parti-* in PARTI-COLOURED, as in †**pa·rtie-coated,** having a parti-coloured or motley coat (SHAKS.). So in †**pa·rti-me·mbered,** having members or limbs of two kinds (MILTON); etc.

Parti-[2], comb. form of L. *pars, part-* PART; as in **parti-pa·rtial** *a.* (*Logic*), applied by Sir W. Hamilton to a proposition in which both terms are partial or particular; **parti-to·tal,** in which one is particular and one universal.

Partial (pā·ɹʃăl), *a.* (*sb.*) ME. [– OFr. *parcial* (mod. *partial* in sense I, *partiel* in II) – late L. *partialis*, f. L. *pars, part-* PART *sb.*; see -AL[1], -IAL.] **A.** *adj.* **I.** Inclined antecedently to favour one party in a cause, or one side of the question more than the other; biased; interested; unfair. (Opp. to *impartial.*) **b.** Prejudiced or biased in some one's favour; hence: Favourably disposed, kindly, sympathetic. Const. *to*. Now *rare.* 1585. **c.** With *to*: Having a liking for, fond of (*colloq.*) 1696.

1. I perseaue, that God is not parciall TINDALE *Acts* 10:34. **b.** So obliging, so p. to our Sophist BENTLEY. **c.** I am not more p. to my arm chair.. than of yore 1827.

II. 1. Pertaining to or involving a part only; constituting a part only; incomplete 1641. **b.** *spec.* That is one of the parts that make up a whole; constituent, component 1481. **2.** In techn. senses. **a.** *Astron.* Applied to an eclipse in which part only of the disc of the luminary is covered or darkened 1704. **b.** *Math.* (*a*) Applied to differentials, differentiation, etc. relative to one only of the variables involved, the rest being for the time supposed constant. (*b*) *P. determinant* = MINOR *determinant* 1816. **c.** *Bot.* Forming one of the parts of a compound structure; secondary, subordinate; as *p. umbel*, each of the smaller umbels of a compound umbel; etc. 1760. **d.** *Acoustics* and *Mus.* Applied to any one of the simple tones which together form a complex tone. *Upper p. tones* (or *upper partials*): those higher in pitch than the fundamental tone; also called *harmonics* or *overtones.* 1879. **e.** *R. C. Ch.* Of an indulgence: Remitting part only of the temporal punishment of sin 1885.

1. Or p. Ill is universal Good POPE. P. damage to merchandise 1886.

B. *sb. Acoustics* and *Mus.* Short for *p. tone*; see 2 d above. Hence **Pa·rtialness.**

Partialism (pā·ɹʃăliz'm). 1864. [f. PARTIAL *a.* + -ISM.] **1.** A partial theory or view, which does not take into account all the facts 1872. **2.** *Theol.* = PARTICULARISM 1. 1864.

Partialist (pā·ɹʃălist). 1597. [f. as prec. + -IST.] **1.** *gen.* A partial, prejudiced, or biased person; a partisan. **2.** One whose knowledge or outlook is limited 1841. **3.** *Theol.* = PARTICULARIST 1864.

Partiality (pāɹʃiæ·lĭti). late ME. [– (O)Fr. *parcialté, -alité* – med.L. *partialitas*, f. late L. *partialis*; see PARTIAL, -ITY.] **1.** The quality or character of being partial (see PARTIAL I); prejudice, bias, unfairness; an instance of this. **b.** Prepossession in favour of a particular person or thing; hence, Favourable disposition, predilection, fondness for some one or something. Const. *to, for, towards* 1581. †**2.** Party-spirit, rivalry; factiousness –1752.

1. Gyue trew iugement without ony fauoure or parsealyte LD. BERNERS.

Partialize (pā·ɹʃăləiz), *v.* 1592. [– Fr. *partialiser*, f. *partial* PARTIAL; see -IZE.] †**1.** *intr.* To be partial –1656. **2.** *trans.* To render partial; to bias 1593.

Partially (pā·ɹʃăli), *adv.* 1460. [f. PARTIAL + -LY[2].] **I.** (= Fr. *partialement.*) In a biased manner, with partiality; unfairly, unjustly. Now *rare.* 1495. **b.** With special favour or affection. Now *rare.* 1633.

Their own transgressions p. they smother SHAKS.

II. (= Fr. *partiellement.*) In a partial way or degree; incompletely; partly 1460.

Which was but p. true SIR T. BROWNE.

Partible (pā·ɹtĭb'l), *a.* 1540. [– late L. *partibilis*, f. L. *partire, -iri* divide, PART; see -IBLE.] Capable of being parted or separated; subject to partition; divisible; separable. **b.** That involves partition of inheritance 1653.

A father's land was p. among all his children 1863. Hence **Partibi·lity,** p. quality.

Participable (paɹti·sipăb'l), *a.* 1450. [– OFr. *participable* (in sense 1) and med.L. *participabilis* (in sense 2), f. *participer, participare*; see PARTICIPATE *v.*, -ABLE.] †**1.** Liable to participate. **2.** Capable of being participated or shared 1610.

Participant (paɹti·sipănt), *a.* and *sb.* 1549. [– (O)Fr. *participant*, pr. pple. of *participer*; see PARTICIPATE *v.*, -ANT.] **A.** *adj.* Participating, partaking, sharing. **B.** *sb.* One who participates in anything; a sharer, partaker 1562.

The chief participants in the recent massacre 1891.

Participate (paɹti·sipĕt), *ppl. a.* Now *rare* or *Obs.* 1450. [– L. *participatus*, pa. pple. of *participare*; see next, -ATE[2].] †**1.** = prec. A. –1657. **2.** as *pa. pple.* Shared, participated 1850.

Participate (paɹti·sipeⁱt), *v.* 1531. [– *participat-*, pa. ppl. stem of L. *participare*, f. *particeps, particip-* taking part, f. *pars, part-* PART *sb.* + *cip-*, weakened form of *cap-* of *capere* take; see -ATE[3].] **I.** *trans.* **1.** = PARTAKE I. 1. †**2.** = PARTAKE I. 2. –1707.

1. The one [the soul] we p. with goddes, the other [the body] with bestes ELYOT.

II. *intr.* = PARTAKE II. 1 (but not now said of sharing in material things). Const. *with* a person, *in* (†*of*, †*with*) a thing. 1565. **b.** = PARTAKE II. 1 c. 1578.

Millie and I..participated very little in the general conversation 1873. **b.** Both members p. of harmony JOHNSON. Hence **Parti·cipating** *vbl. sb.* and *ppl. a.* (*spec.* profit-sharing). **Parti·cipatingly** *adv.*

Participation (paɹtisipeⁱ·ʃən). late ME. [– (O)Fr. *participation* – late L. *participatio*, f. as prec.; see -ION.] **1.** The action or fact of partaking, having or forming part *of*; †the partaking of the substance, quality, or nature *of*. **2.** The fact or condition of sharing in common (*with* others, or with each other); partnership, fellowship; profit-sharing. late ME. **b.** A taking part (with others) in some action or matter 1667.

1. As for the other Sacrament, make conscience of a frequent p. thereof 1631. **2.** For thou hast lost thy Princely Priuiledge, With vile p. SHAKS. Sharing in whatever surplus profits are realised by the more efficient labour which p. calls forth 1881.

Participative (paɹti·sipeⁱtiv), *a.* 1651. [– med.L. *parcipitativus*, f. as prec.; see -IVE.] Having the quality of participating.

Participator (paɹti·sipeⁱtəɹ). 1796. [f. PARTICIPATE *v.* + -OR 2.] One who participates; a partaker, sharer. So **Parti·cipatory** *a.* characterized by participation or profit-sharing.

Participial (pāɹtisi·piăl), *a.* and *sb.* 1570. [– L. *participialis*, f. *participium*; see PARTICIPLE, -AL[1].] **A.** *adj.* Of the nature of a participle; of, pertaining to, or involving a participle 1591. **B.** *sb.* A verbal derivative of the nature of, or akin to, a participle 1570.

A. *P. adjective*, an adjective that is a participle in origin and form. Hence **Partici·pialize** *v.* to make p., turn into a participle. **Partici·pially** *adv.* as a participle.

Participle (pā·ɹtisip'l), *sb.* late ME. [– OFr. *participle*, by-form of *participe* – L. *participium*, f. *particeps* (see PARTICIPATE *v.*), after Gr. μετοχή, f. μετέχειν partake. For the parasitic *l* cf. *manciple, principle, treacle.*] †**1.** A person, animal, or thing that partakes of the nature of two or more different classes –1694. **2.** *Gram.* A word that partakes of the nature of a verb and an adjective; a deriv. of a verb which has the function and construction of an adjective (qualifying a noun), while retaining some of those of the verb (*e.g.* tense, government of an object); a verbal adjective. Formerly often reckoned a separate part of speech.

2. *To whom coming as unto a living stone*: the p. notes a continued motion 1681.

Particle (pā·ɹtik'l), *sb.* late ME. [– L. *particula*, dim. of *pars, part-* PART; see -CLE.] **1.** A small part or portion of a whole. Now *rare* or *Obs.*, or merged in 2. **b.** A very small part of any proposition, writing, etc.; a clause; an article of a formula 1526. **2.** A very minute portion of matter; formerly often = atom or molecule; in *Dynamics*, a minute mass of matter, which while still having inertia and attraction is treated as a point, i.e. as having no magnitude. late ME. **b.** The smallest conceivable portion of something immaterial 1620. **c.** *Liturg.* A fragment of the Host or consecrated bread 1727. **3.** *Gram.* A minor part of speech, esp. one that is short and indeclinable, a relation-word; also, a prefix or suffix having a distinct meaning, as *un-, -ly, -ness* 1533.

1. Ane p. of beif 1567. **2.** Every p. of matter attracts every other p. 1871. **b.** They had never entertained a p. of doubt PALEY.

Parti-coloured, particoloured (pā·ɹtikɒ·ləɹd; stress var.), *a.* Also **party-.** 1535. [In early use *partie* or *party coloured* beside *particoloured*; amplification of PARTY *a.* by combination with *coloured.*] Partly of one colour and partly of another; diversi-coloured. **b.** *fig.* Varied, chequered 1622.

The Pope's parti-coloured body guard 1879. **b.** Life party-colour'd, half pleasure, half care PRIOR. Hence †**Parti-colour** *a.*; also as *sb.* –1662. †**Parti-colour** *v.* to make parti-coloured, colour variously (*rare*).

Particular (păɹti·kiŭlăɹ), *a.* and *sb.* [ME. *particuler* – OFr. *particuler* (mod. *-ier*) – L. *particularis* (opp. to *universalis*, Apuleius), f. *particula* PARTICLE; see -AR[1]; in XVI conformed to L.] **A.** *adj.* **I.** †**1.** Partial; not universal –1643. **2.** Relating to a single definite thing or person, a set of things or persons, as dist. from others; of one's (its, etc.) own; special; not general. late ME. †**b.** Proper, peculiar, restricted (*to*) –1725. **c.** *Logic.* Applied to a proposition in which something is predicated of some, not all, of a class; opp. to *universal* 1551. †**3.** Private, personal, not public –1768. **4.** That is a unit or definite one among a number; taken or considered by itself; individual, single, separate 1529. **5.** Distinguished among others of the kind; marked; special 1485. †**b.** Noteworthy; peculiar, singular –1791. †**c.** Singular, strange, odd –1817. **d.** Used in the names of certain modifications of ordinary iambic metres common in hymns, as *Common P. Metre* (8.8.6.8.8.6.), *Long P. Metre* (8.8.8.8.8.8.), etc. Chiefly *U.S.* **6.** Relating to or dealing with the separate parts, elements, or details of a whole; detailed, minute, circumstantial 1450. †**7.** Specially attentive to a person; bestowing marked attentions; familiar in manner –1771. **b.** Closely acquainted, intimate. (Now assoc. w. 5) 1706. **8.** Attentive to or scrupulous concerning details of action; hence exacting as to details, nice in taste, fastidious 1814.

1. The Three yeares Drought, in the time of Elias, was but P., and left People Aliue BACON. **2.** These are not my p. Sentiments BURKE. *P. average*: see AVERAGE *sb.*[2] 4. *P. Baptists*, a body of Baptists holding the Calvinistic doctrines of *p. election* and *p. redemption*, i.e. the Divine election etc., of some, not all, of the human race. **c.** 'Some lakes have an outlet' is a p. judgment 1860. **4.** Make..each p. haire to stand an end SHAKS. **b.** Johnson's mode of penmanship, which at all times was very p. BOSWELL. **6.** The p. Description of the several

Instruments 1669. I am thus p. in the relation of every incident 1803. 7. Never suffer this Fellow to be p. with you again FIELDING. b. These are p. friends of mine SHERIDAN. 8. People who have to work for their living must not be too p. 1879. Phr. *P. estate* (Law), 'that interest which is granted..out of a larger estate, which then becomes an expectancy either in reversion or remainder' (Wharton). So *p. tenant*, the tenant of a p. estate.

II. Absol. uses. 1 **The p.** That which is particular 1551. **2. In p.** †**a.** (Each) by itself, individually, severally; in detail –1737. **b.** In distinction from others; particularly, especially 1502. †**c.** In private –1702. †**3. In the p.** In the particular or special case; opp. to *in the general* –1827.

1. This argument is from the p., to the vniuersall 1551.

B. *sb.* †**1.** A part of a whole; *spec.* a division or 'head' of a discourse or argument –1859. **2.** A detail, item, point, circumstance 1533. **b.** *pl.* Items or details of statement or information; information as to details; a detailed account 1606. †**3.** A minute account, description, or enumeration; a minute –1846. †**4. a.** Each one of a number or group of things; an individual thing or article –1743. **b.** An individual person; occas. *spec.* a private person, one not holding a public position –1766. **5.** More vaguely: A particular case or instance. (Usu. in *pl.*; opp. to *generals* or *universals.*) 1600. **b.** *Logic.* = *particular proposition* (see A. I. 2 c) 1551. †**6.** (One's) individual case; personal interest or concern; part. Chiefly in phr. *for, in, as to,* etc. (*one's*) *p.* –1790. †**b.** Personal or private interest, profit, or advantage –1653. †**c.** Personal relation, intimacy; personal interest, regard, or favour (*rare*) –1631. **7.** *colloq.* or *slang.* **a.** Something specially belonging to, or characteristic of, a place or person, as *London p.*, a London fog 1807. **b.** A special friend 1828.

1. Let us devide the discourse..into foure particulars 1601. **2.** Examine mee vpon the particulars of my Life SHAKS. **b.** But how, but how, giue me particulars SHAKS. **5.** Deliberation for the most part is of Particulars HOBBES. **6.** We have all admired it..and for my own p., I return you my sincerest thanks COWPER. **c.** *Cor.* v. i. 3. Hence **Parti·cularly** *adv.* in a p. manner, or with a p. reference.

Particularism (păɹti·kiŭlăriz'm). 1824. [*Theol.*, after Fr. *particularisme* (Bossuet) or mod.L. *particularismus*; *Polit.*, after G. *partikularismus*; see prec., -ISM.] **1.** *Theol.* The doctrine of particular election or particular redemption (see PARTICULAR A. I. 2) 1828. **2.** Exclusive devotion to one's particular party, sect, nation, etc.; exclusiveness 1824. **3.** *Politics.* The principle of leaving each state in an empire or federation free to retain its own government, laws, and rights; esp. in German politics after *c*1850. 1853. So **Parti·cularist,** an advocate of p.; also as *adj.*

Particularity (păɹtikiŭlæ·rĭti). 1528. [– (O)Fr. *particularité* or late L. *particularitas* (Boethius), f. *particularis*; see PARTICULAR, -ITY.] **1.** The quality of being particular as opp. to general or universal 1587. †**b.** A particular case or instance –1598. **2.** The quality of being special or of a special kind; the fact of being noteworthy (now *rare*) 1570. †**b.** Singularity, oddity –1791. **3.** An attribute belonging particularly to the thing in question; a peculiarity (now *rare*) 1588. †**4.** A particular point or circumstance, a detail –1796. **5.** Minuteness or detailedness of description, statement, etc. 1638. †**6.** Special attentiveness *to* a person; familiarity –1815. **7.** Attentive to details; scrupulous preciseness 1671.

1. b. 2 *Hen. VI*, v. ii. 44. **4.** And so..entered into the particularities of the matter 1528. **6.** Objectionable p. to another woman JANE AUSTEN. **7.** A p. as to the saving of string 1882.

Particularize (păɹti·kiŭlărəiz), *v.* 1588. [– Fr. *particulariser*; see -IZE.] **1.** *trans.* To render particular (as opp. to general); to restrict to a particular thing or class (*rare*). **2.** To name or state specially, or one by one; to speak or treat of individually, or in detail; to specify. (The usual sense.) 1593. **b.** *intr.* To go into particulars or detail 1601. **3.** *trans.* To render distinct or separate; to individualize, distinguish, differentiate (*rare*) 1643.

2. In mentioning your friends, I must p. Mr. Pope 1741. **b.** In our hasty narrative..we have not paused to p. 1834. Hence **Parti:culariza·tion.**

Particulate (păɹti·kiŭlĕt), *a.* Only in scientific use. 1874. [f. L. *particula* PARTICLE + -ATE².] Existing in the condition of minute separate particles. **b.** Of or relating to minute separate particles 1881.

Pa·rticule. *Obs.* exc. in sense 2, as Fr. (partikü·l). 1540. [– Fr. *particule* – L. *particula* PARTICLE.] †**1.** A particle –1647. ‖**2.** *spec.* Applied to the French preposition *de* used as a prefix of nobility in personal names 1889.

‖**Partie** (parti·). 1678. [Fr.] **a.** A match in a game, a game. **b.** *P. carrée*, a party of four 1739.

Partile (pā·ɹtəil, -til), *a.* 1576. [– late L. *partilis* divisible, f. *partire, -iri* divide; see -ILE.] †**1.** = PARTIAL *a.* II. –1697. **2.** *Astrol.* Of an aspect: Exact to the same degree and minute, or, at least, within a degree. Opp. to PLATIC. 1610.

2. *P. conjunction*, exact conjunction; so *p. opposition*; *p. trine*, positions exactly 120° apart.

Parting (pā·ɹtiŋ), *vbl. sb.* ME. [f. PART *v.* + -ING¹.] The action of PART *v.*, partition; the result, or place, of this action; something that parts. **1.** Division, breaking, cleaving 1530. **b.** The division or dividing line of the hair when combed 1698. **2.** Separation; *spec.* in techn. uses (cf. PART *v.* I. 4 c) ME. **b.** The place at which two or more things separate; as the *p. of the ways* (often *fig.*); *water-p.*, a WATERSHED. late ME. **c.** *concr.* Something that parts or separates two things; *esp.* in techn. uses, as (*a*) *Mining* and *Geol.* A layer of rock, clay, etc. lying between two beds of different formations; (*b*) *Founding.* Fine sand (*p.-sand*) or other powdery substance used to prevent adhesion of the surfaces of the parts of a mould 1708. **3.** Mutual separation of two or more persons; leave-taking ME. **4.** Departure; also *fig.* (*euphem.*) decease, death (*arch.*) ME.

1. There being great danger of the ship's p. 1748. **3.** P. is such sweete sorrow, That I shall say good night, till it be morrow SHAKS. The p. with a beloved Child 1705.

attrib. and *Comb.* **a.** *attrib.* Of or pertaining to parting; *esp.* (in adjectival construction) Given, taken, performed, etc. at parting; 'farewell', concluding, final. **p. cup,** (*a*) a drinking-cup with two handles, used by two persons in taking a draught of liquor at parting; (*b*) a kind of 'cup' or compound beverage made with ale and sherry. **b.** Of or pertaining to separation, as *parting-point*; *esp.* in names of technical appliances used for separating something, etc., as **p.-bead** = *p.-strip*; **-sand** (see 2 c); **-strip,** a strip of material used for separating two parts, e.g. the vertical strip of wood inserted at the side of the frame of a sash window to keep the sashes apart when raised or lowered; **-tool,** name of various tools used for separating pieces of material, for trimming, cutting fine outlines and markings, etc.

Pa·rting, *ppl. a.* late ME. [f. as prec. + -ING².] That parts. **1.** Separating, dividing; forming a boundary between two things 1699. **2.** Dividing, breaking, going to pieces 1719. **3.** Going away, departing; *fig.* dying 1577. †**4.** Sharing, participating; *p. fellow*, sharer, partner –1514.

3. The curfew tolls the knell of p. day GRAY.

Partisan, partizan (pā·ɹtizæ̆n, pāɹtizæ·n), *sb.*¹ (*a.*) 1555. [– Fr. *partisan* – It. dial. *partisano, partežan*, Tuscan *partigiano*, f. *parte* PART.] **A.** *sb.* **1.** One who takes part or sides with another; *esp.* a zealous supporter of a party, person, or cause; often in bad sense: a blind, prejudiced, unreasoning or fanatical adherent. **2.** *Mil.* A member of a party of light or irregular troops employed in scouring the country, making forays, etc.; a member of a volunteer force similarly employed, a guerrilla 1692. **b.** A leader of a body of such troops; a guerrilla chief 1706.

1. The clergyman must never be a p. 1866.

B. *attrib.* or as *adj.* **1.** Of, pertaining to, or characteristic of a partisan; biased, prejudiced, one-sided 1842. **2.** *Mil.* Of or pertaining to military partisans; pertaining to irregular or petty warfare 1708.

1. P. malice 1842, politics 1882. **2.** The system of guerilla or partizan warfare [in Spain] SCOTT. *P. ranger* = RANGER 3. Hence **Partisanship,** the state, condition, or practice of a p.; zealous or blind support of one's party.

Partisan, partizan (pā·ɹtizæ̆n), *sb.*² *Obs.* from *c*1700 until revived by Scott. 1556. [– Fr. †*partizane* (now *pertuisane*, after *pertuiser* bore through) – It. †*partesana*, dial. var. of *partigiana*, subst. use (sc. *arma* arm, weapon) of fem. of *partigiano* (see prec.), so called as being used by some faction.] **1.** A weapon used by infantry in the 16th–17th centuries, consisting of a long-handled spear, the blade having one or more lateral cutting projections. **b.** Used as a 'leading-staff' and borne as a halberd by civic and other guards 1611. **2.** *transf.* A soldier, etc. armed with a partisan 1693.

1. I had as liue haue a Reede that will doe me no seruice, as a Partizan I could not heaue SHAKS.

Partite (pā·ɹtəit), *a.* 1570. [– L. *partitus* parted, divided. Cf. BIPARTITE, etc.] **a.** Divided into parts or portions. **b.** *Bot.* and *Entom.* Divided to the base, or nearly so, as a leaf, corolla, or insect's wing 1760.

The leaves are..palmate, five-p. 1880.

Partition (păɹti·ʃən), *sb.* late ME. [– (O)Fr. *partition* – L. *partitio*, f. *partit-*, pa. ppl. stem of *partiri* divide, share; see -ION.] **1.** The action of parting or dividing into parts; the fact of being so divided; division 1509. **b.** Division into shares or portions; distribution. late ME. **2.** The action of parting or separating two or more persons or things; the fact or condition of being separated; separation, division 1530. **3.** Something that separates; *esp.* that which separates one part of a space from another; *e.g.* a structure separating rooms or parts of a room (*esp.* when slighter than a wall proper); a septum or dissepiment in a plant or animal body; etc. 1545. **4.** Each of the parts into which a whole is divided, as by boundaries or lines; a portion, part, division, section; a compartment; a pane, a panel; a pocket (of a bag); an apartment, chamber, room 1561. **5.** *Law.* A division of real property, esp. of lands, between joint tenants, tenants in common, or coparceners, by which their co-tenancy or co-ownership is abolished and their individual interests are separated 1474. **6.** *Logic.* Analysis by systematic separation of the integrant parts of a thing; enumeration of parts. (Dist. from *division.*) 1551. **7.** *Math.* †**a.** = DIVISION 5. –1729. **b.** Any one of the ways of expressing a number as a sum of positive integers (*e.g.* the partitions of 4 are 1+1+1+1, 1+1+2, 1+3, 2+2) 1855. **8.** *Mus.* A score. Now *rare* or *Obs.* 1597. **9.** *Her.* **a.** The division of a shield into two parts of different tinctures by one of the dividing lines (see PARTED, PARTY *a.*) ?*Obs.* †**b.** An ordinary which lies between common charges on a shield. **c.** Each of the divisions of a parted or quartered shield. 1486.

1. The p. of the Empire 1741. **b.** The first p. of Poland in 1773 W. TOOKE. **2.** Can we not P. make..Twixt faire, and foule? SHAKS. **3.** Great wits are sure to madness near allied, And thin partitions do their bounds divide DRYDEN. Did I not overhear your scheme..through the p.? 1763. **4.** The Hold was divided in many small Partitions 1697.

attrib. and *Comb.*, as *p.-line*, etc.; **P. Treaty,** name of each of the two treaties (of 11 Oct. 1698 and 11 Oct. 1700) attempting to settle the question of the Spanish Succession after the death of Charles II; **-wall,** a wall forming a p.; *esp.* an internal wall.

Partition (păɹti·ʃən), *v.* 1741. [f. prec.] **1.** *trans.* To divide into parts or portions; to dismember and deal *out.* **b.** *spec.* To divide (land) into severalty 1880. **2.** To separate by a partition; to divide *off* 1832. Hence **Parti·tionment,** the action or fact of partitioning; *concr.* a partition, a compartment.

Partitioned (păɹti·ʃənd), *ppl. a.* 1625. [f. PARTITION *sb.* and *v.* + -ED.] Having partitions; divided or separated by partitions. (Also with *off.*)

Partitive (pā·ɹtitiv), *a.* and *sb.* 1520. [– Fr. *partitif* or med.L. *partitivus*, f. *partit-*; see PARTITION *sb.*, -IVE.] **A.** *adj.* Having the quality or function of dividing into parts; characterized by or indicating partition; *spec.* in *Gram.* Denoting or indicating that only a part of a collective whole is spoken of: esp. applied to a noun, etc. denoting such a part; also to the genitive used with such words in Greek, Latin, etc. (repr. in Eng. by *of* with the sb.). **B.** *sb. Gram.* A partitive word; a word denoting a part of a whole 1530. Hence **Pa·rtitively** *adv.* in a p. way; *Gram.* in a p. sense.

Partlet[1] (pā·ɹtlėt). late ME. [– OFr. *Pertelote*, of unkn. origin.] Used as the proper name of any hen, often *Dame P.*; also applied, like 'hen', to a woman.

Partlet[2]. *Obs.* exc. *Hist.* 1519. [Earlier Sc. and north. †*patelet* (XV) – OFr. *patelette*, dim. of *patte* paw, band or belt of stuff; see -LET.] An article of apparel worn about the neck and upper part of the chest, chiefly by women: orig. a neckerchief; a collar or ruff. Also *attrib.*

Partly (pā·ɹtli), *adv.* 1523. [f. PART *sb.* + -LY[2].] With respect to a part; in part; in some measure or degree; not wholly. **b.** Usu. hyphened to a ppl. adj. which precedes its sb. 1888.

Reflexions, which were p. private, and p. political ADDISON. **b.** A partly-heard conversation 1888.

Partner (pā·ɹtnəɹ), *sb.* ME. [alt. of PARCENER by assoc. with PART *sb.*] **1.** One who has a share or part with another or others; a partaker, sharer. Const. *with*, rarely *of* (a person); *of, in*, †*to* (a thing). **2.** One who is associated in any function, act, or course of action; an associate, colleague (occas. merely = companion). Formerly often: An accomplice. ME. †**b.** One who takes part in some action –1565. **3.** *spec.* **a.** *Comm.* One who is associated with another or others in some business, the expenses, profits, and losses of which he proportionately shares 1523. **b.** A husband or wife 1749. **c.** One's companion in a dance 1613. **d.** A player associated on the same side with another in whist, tennis, etc. 1680. **4.** *Naut.* (in *pl.*) A framework of timber fitted round any hole or scuttle in a ship's deck, through which a mast, capstan, pump, etc. passes, and serving to strengthen the deck and to relieve strain 1608. **5.** *attrib.*: formerly quasi-*adj.* = associated 1639.

1. A wife worthy to be the p. of his Empire 1870. **2.** A p. in conspiracie 1602. **3.** Phr. *Sleeping* (or *dormant*) *p.*, a p. who has capital in a business and shares in its profits without taking any part in the management. *Predomindnt p.*: see PREDOMINANT. **b.** So forth I set. . And took the p. of my life with me SOUTHEY. Hence **Pa·rtnerless**, without a p.

Partner (pā·ɹtnəɹ), *v.* 1611. [f. prec. sb.] **1.** *trans.* To make a partner, to join or associate. **2.** To be or act as the partner of; to associate oneself with as a partner 1882.

Partnership (pā·ɹtnəɹʃip). 1576. [-SHIP.] **1.** The fact or condition of being a partner. **2.** *Comm.* An association of two or more persons for the carrying on of a business, of which they share the expenses, profit, and loss 1700. **b.** The persons so associated collectively 1802. **3.** *Arith.* = FELLOWSHIP *sb.* 9. 1704. **4.** *attrib.* 1770.

1. A scandal which charged Emma herself with a p. in the deed 1877. **2.** His brother took him into p. MAR. EDGEWORTH.

Pa·rt-ow:ner. 1562. [f. PART *sb.* + OWNER; = owner in part.] One who owns something in common with another or others; each of two or more joint owners or tenants in common.

Partridge (pā·ɹtridʒ). [ME. *partrich*, north. and Sc. *partrick*, also *per-* – OFr. *perdriz*, *-triz* (mod. *perdrix*), alt. of *perdiz* – L. *perdix*, *-ic-*. For the development of the final consonant cf. CABBAGE *sb.*[1]] **1.** The name of certain well-known game-birds; esp. *Perdix cinerea*, the *Common* or *Grey P.* More widely, used to include all species of the genus *Perdix*, and some allied genera. **b.** In British Colonies and U.S., pop. applied to several birds of the *Tetraonidæ* or Grouse Family and *Phasianidæ* or Pheasant Family, esp. in New England, the Ruffed Grouse (*Bonasa* or *Tetrao umbellus*), in Pennsylvania, etc. the Virginian Quail, Colin, or Bob-white (*Ortyx virginianus*) 1634. **c.** The bird, or its flesh, as used for food ME. **2.** *Ornith.* With defining words, applied to particular species of the genus *Perdix*, or of the sub-families *Perdicinæ*, *Odontophorinæ*, and *Caccabineæ*, of family *Phasianidæ*, also to some species of *Tetraonidæ*, all of order *Gallinæ*; in S. Africa, to some of order *Pterocletes* (Sand-grouse) 1611. †**3.** *Mil.* A charge for cannons consisting of a number of missiles fired together, similar to langrage or case-shot; also *p.-shot* –1867. **4.** **Sea p.** †**a.** The sole. [Cf. Fr. *perdrix de mer.*] **b.** A local name of the Golden Wrasse or Gilt-head, *Crenilabrus melops* 1633.

1. A fat partrich CHAUCER. Plump as any p. was each Miss Mould DICKENS. **2. Bamboo P.**, of North China, *Bambusicola thoracica*; **Greek P.**, of Southern Europe (the original Gr.-L. πέρδιξ, *perdix*), *Caccabis saxatilis*; **Painted P.** (or Francolin), of S. Africa, *Francolinus pictus*; **Red-legged P.** of Europe, *Caccabis rufa*; **Snow P.**, *Lerwa nivicola* also *Tetraogallus himalayensis*. Also **Night P.**, U.S. name for the American woodcock, *Philohela minor*.

attrib. and *Comb.*, as *p.-drive, wing*, etc.; *p.-shooting*, etc.; also, **p.-cane** (see PARTRIDGE-WOOD 1); **-dove**, a ground-dove of Jamaica (*Geotrygon cristata*), also called mountain-witch (ground-dove); **p. pea**, (*a*) a speckled or mottled variety of field pea; (*b*) a yellow-flowered leguminous plant (*Cassia chamæcrista*) of U.S.; also called *sensitive pea*; (*b*) a plant (*Heisteria coccinea*, N.O. *Olacineæ*) having red fruits enclosed in an enlarged fleshy calyx; **-shell**, a large univalve shell (*Dolium perdix*) with partridge-like mottlings; **-vine** = PARTRIDGE-BERRY a. Hence **Pa·rtridging** *vbl. sb.* shooting partridges.

Pa·rtridge-be:rry. 1714. Name of two N. American plants and their fruit: **a.** *Mitchella repens* (N.O. *Cinchonaceæ*), a trailing evergreen herb with edible but insipid scarlet berries; also called *partridge-vine*. **b.** *Gaultheria procumbens* (N.O. *Ericaceæ*), the CHECKER-BERRY or WINTER-GREEN, whose red berries furnish food for partridges.

Pa·rtridge-wood. 1830. **1.** A hard red wood, having darker parallel stripes, much prized for cabinet work, also used for walking-sticks, etc., from the W. Indies, supposed to be (at least in part) obtained from the leguminous tree *Andira inermis*; called also *pheasant-wood*. **2.** A name for the appearance of wood when attacked by the saprophytic fungus *Stereum frustulosum*, on account of its speckled colour 1894.

Pa·rt-song. 1850. [f. PART *sb.* II. 4 + SONG.] A song for three or more voice-parts, usu. without accompaniment, and in simple harmony (dist. from *glee* and *madrigal*).

Parturiate (paɹtiū̆ᵊ·rie¹t), *v. rare.* 1660. [irreg. f. L. *parturire* + -ATE[3].] **a.** *intr.* To bring forth young; to bear fruit. **b.** *trans.* To bring forth.

Parturiency (paɹtiū̆ᵊ·riĕnsi). 1652. [f. next; see -ENCY.] Parturient condition or quality: usu. *fig.*

Parturient (paɹtiū̆ᵊ·riĕnt), *a.* 1592. [– *parturient-*, pr. ppl. stem of L. *parturire* be in labour, inceptive f. *part-*, pa. ppl. stem of *parere* bring forth; see PARENT, -ENT.] **1.** About to bring forth; travailing; *transf.* bearing fruit. **2.** *fig.* 'Big' or 'in travail' with (a discovery, idea, etc.) 1599. **3.** Of or pertaining to parturition 1748.

1. Allen's p. mountaines produced a. . ridiculous Mouse 1657.

Parturifacient (paɹtiū̆ᵊrifē¹·ʃ¹ĕnt), *a.* and *sb.* 1853. [f. L. *parturire* (see prec.) + -FACIENT.] = OXYTOCIC *a.* and *sb.*

Parturition (pāɹtiŭri·ʃən). 1646. [– late L. *parturitio*, f. as prec.; see -ITION.] The action of bringing forth or of being delivered of young; childbirth. (Chiefly *techn.*; also *fig.*)

Party (pā·ɹti), *sb.* [ME. *parti(e* – (O)Fr. *partie* part, share, side in a contest, contract, etc., litigant :– Rom. **partita*, subst. use of fem. pa. pple. of L. *partire, -iri* PART *v.*] **I.** Part, portion, side. [= Fr. *partie.*] †**1.** A division of a whole; a part or portion; an aliquot part: a part or member of the body –1654. †**2.** = PART *sb.* III. 1, 2. –1588. †**3.** = PART *sb.* III. 3. –1854.

3. I cannot tell on whose partie first to commence UDALL.

II. A company or body of persons. **1.** *concr.* A number of persons united in maintaining a cause, policy, opinion, etc., in opposition to others who maintain a different one ME. **b.** *abstr.* The system of taking sides on public questions; party feeling or spirit; partisanship 1701. **2.** *Mil.* A small body of troops selected for a particular service or duty 1645. **3.** A company of persons travelling together or engaged in any common pursuit; a number of persons met together for amusement, study, etc. 1773. **4.** A social gathering or entertainment, esp. of invited guests at a private house; also with qualification, as *garden-p.* 1696. †**5.** A game or match, esp. at piquet –1796.

1. My end is mirth, And pleasing, if I can, all parties 1625. **b.** [Burke] to p. gave up what was meant for mankind GOLDSM. **3.** A reading p., a house p. 1904. **4.** I determined to give parties of my own 1809.

III. A single person considered in some relation. **1.** Each of two or more persons (or bodies of people) that constitute the two sides in an action at law, a contract, etc. ME. **2.** A participator; an accessory. Const. *to.* †*in.* late ME. **3.** The individual concerned or in question; more vaguely, the person (defined by some adj., etc.). (Formerly in serious use; now shoppy, vulgar, or joc., the proper word being *person.*) 1460. **b.** With *a.*: A person. Now *low colloq.* or *slang.* 1686.

1. It appears to be a narrative written by a third p. 1853. Phr. *Party-and-party* (attrib.), as between the two parties in an action at law. **2.** He was a p. to all their proceedings DICKENS. **3.** 'Tis the p., madame. What p.? Has he no name? B. JONS. 'Do you know, my Lord', (said the old p. solemnly) 1888. **b.** I should say he was a go-ahead p. 1855.

IV. Senses mostly repr. Fr. *parti.* †**1.** A decision on one side or the other, determination; *esp.* in *to take a p.* (cf. Fr. *prendre son parti*) –1760. †**2.** A person to marry; a (good or bad) match or offer –1855. †**3.** A proposal, an offer –1765.

2. A girl in our society accepts the best p. wnich offers itself THACKERAY.

Comb. **p.-verdict**, one person's share in a joint verdict (*Rich. II*, I. iii. 234). Hence †**Pa·rty** *v.* (*Sc. rare*) *trans.* to take the side of, side with; *intr.* to side (*with*). **Pa·rtyism**, the system of parties; party-spirit.

Party (pā·ɹti), *a.* late ME. [– (O)Fr. *parti* :– L. *partitus*, pa. pple. of *partire, -iri* divide, PART *v.*] †**1.** Parted, divided, separate; *fig.* different. ME. only. †**2.** Parti-coloured, variegated –1707. **3.** *Her.* Said of a shield divided into parts of different tinctures, usually into two such parts by a line in the direction of an ordinary (indicated by *per*) 1486.

2. She gadereth floures p. white & rede CHAUCER. **3.** Phr. *P. per pale*, divided by a vertical line through the middle; *p. per fess*, by a horizontal line through the middle; so *p. per bend, p. per chevron*: see PALE, FESS. etc. †*P. per pale* (fig.), having two different, esp. contrasted, qualities; of mixed character; half-and-half.

Pa·rty-man. 1693. [f. PARTY *sb.* + MAN.] †**1.** *Mil.* A soldier belonging to, or officer commanding, a party (PARTY *sb.* II. 2) –1724. **2.** = PARTISAN *sb.*[1] 1. 1701.

Pa·rty-wall. 1667. [f. PARTY *sb.* (used *attrib.*) + WALL *sb.*] A wall between two buildings or pieces of land intended for distinct occupation, in the use of which each of the occupiers has a partial right. Also *fig.*

Parumbilical: see PARA-[1] 1.

‖**Parure.** *Obs.* or *alien.* late ME. [– (O)Fr. *parure*, f. *parer* adorn; see PARE *v.*, -URE.] †**1.** An apparel for an alb or amice –1552. ‖**2.** A set of jewels or other ornaments intended to be worn together; a set of decorative trimmings for a dress 1818.

Parvanimity (pāɹvăni·mĭti). 1691. [f. L. *parvus* small, after MAGNANIMITY; cf. PARVITUDE.] Littleness of mind, meanness; also, an instance of this, or *transf.* a person characterized by it.

‖**Parvenu** (pā·ɹvĕniu, ‖parvənü), *sb.* and *a.* Also fem. **parvenue.** 1802. [Fr., subst. use of pa. pple. of *parvenir* arrive, reach a position :– L. *pervenire*, f. *per* PER- *pref.*[1] + *venire* come.] **A.** *sb.* A person of obscure origin who has gained wealth or position; an upstart. **B.** *adj.* That has but recently risen to wealth or position; like or characteristic of a parvenu 1839.

A. The ladies their wives, who could not bear the parvenue [Rebecca] THACKERAY.

Parvi- (pāɹvi), comb. form of L. *parvus* small, as in **Parvi·potent** *a.*, having little power; **Parvi·scient** *a.*, knowing little; etc.

Parvis (pā·ɹvis). Also *erron.* **parvise.** late ME. [– (O)Fr. *parvis*, †*parevis* (beside *pareïs*) :– Rom. **paravisus*, for late L. *paradisus* PARADISE (applied in the Middle Ages to the atrium in front of St. Peter's, Rome).] **1.** The enclosed area or court in front of a building, esp. of a cathedral or church; sometimes applied to a single portico or colonnade in front of a church, and (in dictionaries) explained as a church-porch. ¶**b.** Erron. applied to 'a room over a church-porch' 1836. †**2.** A public or academic conference or disputation. (So called from being originally held in the court or portico of a church.) –1706.

Parvitude (pā·ɹvitiud). *rare.* 1653. [f. L. *parvus* small, after MAGNITUDE.] Smallness 1657. †**b.** An extremely small thing, atom –1709.

Parvoline (pā·ɹvŏləin). 1855. [f. L. *parvus* small + *-oline*, after *quinoline*.] *Chem.* A ptomaine dimethylethylpyridine, obtained as an oily liquid with a disagreeable odour, from decaying mackerel and horse-flesh, and also from certain shales and bituminous coals.

‖**Pas** (pa). 1704. [Fr., = step, precedency, etc.] **1.** The right of going first; precedence. Also *fig.* 1707. **2.** A step in dancing; a kind of dance 1775. **3.** *Pas-de-souris* [Fr. lit. 'mouse-steps'], *Fortif.* a staircase from the ravelin to the ditch 1704.

1. Phr. *To dispute, give, take, yield, the p.* **2.** *P. de deux*, a dance or figure for two persons. *P. seul*, a dance or figure for one.

Pasan, pasang (pā·zăn, -ăŋ). 1774. [– Pers. †*pāzan* the mountain goat.] A species of wild goat (*Capra ægagrus*), found in western Asia and Crete; the bezoar-goat. ¶Erron. identified by Buffon with the gemsbok.

Pasch (pɑsk). Now *arch.* or *Hist.* [ME. *pasch(e*, *pask(e*, also pl. *pasches*, *paskes* (esp. Eastertide). – OFr. *pasches*, *paskes* (mod. *Pâques*) – eccl.L. *pascha* – Gr. πάσχα – Aram. *pasḥa*, rel. to Heb. *pesaḥ* PASSOVER.] **1.** The Jewish feast of the Passover. **2.** The Christian festival of Easter (*arch.* or *local*) ME. **3.** *attrib.* ME.

Paschal (pɑ·skăl), *a.* and *sb.* late ME. [– (O)Fr. *pascal* – eccl. L. *paschalis*, f. *pascha*; see prec., -AL[1].] **A.** *adj.* **1.** Of or pertaining to the Jewish Passover. **2.** Of or pertaining to Easter; used in Easter celebrations. late ME.

1. *P. lamb*, the lamb slain and eaten at the Passover; applied to Christ; hence, = AGNUS DEI b and c. **2.** *P. candle*, a large candle blessed and lighted in the service of Holy Saturday, and remaining on the gospel side of the altar till Ascension day.

B. *sb.* **1.** A Paschal candle. **b.** A candlestick to hold this. late ME. **2.** The Passover celebration, Passover supper, or Passover lamb 1579.

Pasch-egg (pɑ·skˌeg). Also **paste-egg.** *Sc.* and *n. dial.* 1579. An Easter egg; an egg dyed of various colours and boiled hard.

Pash (pæʃ), *sb.*[1] *Obs.* exc. *dial.* 1611. [Of unkn. origin.] A head.

Pash (pæʃ), *v.* Now chiefly *dial.* late ME. [prob. imit.; cf. *bash*, *dash*, *smash*.] **1.** *trans.* To throw (something) violently, so as either to break it against something, or to break something with it. *Obs.* exc. *dial.* **2.** To dash (a thing) in pieces; to smash by blows. late ME. **3.** To strike violently, usu. so as to bruise or smash. Also *absol.* 1440. **4.** *intr.* Said of the dashing action of heavy rain (now *dial.*); also of that of a wave upon a rock 1589. Hence **Pash** *sb.*[2] a crash, heavy fall; also, debris, medley.

‖**Pasha, pacha** (pɑ·ʃa, păʃā·). 1646. [Turkish *paşa*, prob. = earlier *başa*, from *baş* head, chief.] A title in Turkey of officers of high rank, as military commanders, and governors of provinces. Formerly, esp. of military commanders, written BASHAW.

There are three grades of pashas, formerly distinguished by the number of horse-tails (three, two, or one) displayed as a symbol in war; a pasha of three tails being the highest in rank.

Pashalic, pachalic (pɑ·ʃalik, păʃā·lik), *sb.* (*a.*) 1745. [Turkish *paşalık*, from *-lık*, suffix of quality or condition.] The jurisdiction of a pasha; the district governed by a pasha. **B.** *adj.* Of or pertaining to a pasha 1863.

‖**Pashm** (pæ·ʃ'm). 1880. [Pers. *pašm* wool.] The under-fur of hairy quadrupeds inhabiting Tibet, etc., esp. that of the goat, of which Cashmere shawls are made. So ‖**Pashmina** (pæʃmī·nă) [Pers. *pašmīn* adj., woollen].

Pashto: see PUSHTU.

Pasigraphy (păsi·grăfi). 1796. [irreg. f. Gr. πᾶσι for all + -GRAPHY.] A system of writing proposed for universal use, with characters representing ideas instead of words, so as to be (like the numerals, 1, 2, 3, etc.) intelligible to persons of all languages. Hence **Pa·sigraph** *v.* to represent in p. **Pasigra·phic, -al** *adjs.* of or pertaining to p.

Pasilaly (pæ·silăli). *rare.* 1805. [irreg. f. Gr. πᾶσι for all + -λαλια speaking.] A spoken language for universal use.

†**Pask, Pasque**, var. ff. PASCH.

Pasque-flower (pɑ·skflauᵊɹ). 1578. [orig. *passeflower* – Fr. *passe-fleur* 'a variety of anemone'; changed by Gerarde to *pasque-flower*, after *pasque* PASCH.] A species of Anemone (*A. pulsatilla*) blossoming in April, with bell-shaped usu. purple or white flowers clothed with silky hairs. Called also *pasque-anemone*.

Pasquil (pæ·skwil), *sb.* 1533. [– med.L. *Pasquillus* – It. *Pasquillo*, dim. of *Pasquino*; in Fr. *Pasquille*; see next.] †**1.** = PASQUIN 1. –1651. **2.** A pasquinade 1542. Hence †**Pa·squil** *v. intr.* to compose pasquils; *trans.* to lampoon. **Pa·squillant** *sb.* the writer of a p.; *adj.* lampooning. **Pa·squiller,** the composer of a p. or pasquils.

Pasquin (pæ·skwin), *sb.* 1566. [ult. – It. *Pasquino*, in L. *Pasquinus*, Fr. *Pasquin*. *Pasquino* or *Pasquillo* was the name given to a mutilated statue disinterred at Rome in 1501, and set up by Cardinal Caraffa at the corner of his palace near the Piazza Navona. On this satirical Latin verses were annually posted on St. Mark's Day, and the anonymous authors of these often sheltered themselves under the name 'Pasquin'.] **1.** The Roman Pasquino (man or statue), upon whom pasquinades were fathered; hence, the imaginary personage to whom anonymous lampoons were ascribed. †**2.** = PASQUINADE –1745.

1. The Grecian wits, who Satire first began, Were pleasant Pasquins on the life of man DRYDEN. **2.** I hope you will not think this a pasquine SWIFT. Hence **Pa·squin** *v.* to lampoon.

Pasquinade (pæskwinēⁱ·d), *sb.* 1658. [– It. *pasquinata* (whence also Fr. *pasquinade* (XVII), which may have infl. the Eng. form); see PASQUIN, -ADE.] A lampoon affixed to some public place; a squib, libel, or piece of satire generally. Hence **Pasquina·de** *v.* to satirize or libel in a p. **Pasquina·der.**

Pass (pɑs), *sb.*[1] [ME. *pas*, *paas* (XIII), var. of PACE *sb.* which became restricted to the sense 'passage' (as between mountains, across a river), prob. through contact with Fr. *pas* (*d'une montagne, d'une rivière*); the sp. was infl. by PASS *v.*] **I.** †**1.** Occasional spelling of *pas*, PACE *sb.* –1615. †**2.** = PASSUS –1647.

II. 1. A way or opening by which one passes through an otherwise impassable region, or through any barrier: *esp.* **a.** A passage through a mountainous region or over a mountain range, or (less usually) through a forest, marsh, bog, etc. ME. **b.** Chiefly *Mil.* Such a passage viewed as commanding the entrance into a country or place; hence, any place which holds the key to such entrance. Also *fig.* 1683. **c.** *gen.* A way through; a passage, road, route. Also *fig.* 1608. **d.** A place at which a river can be crossed by ford, ferry, or *rarely* a bridge. Now *rare.* 1649. **e.** A navigable channel, esp. at a river's mouth 1698. **f.** Applied to other narrow passages, e.g. in a road or street 1710. **g.** A passage for fish over or past a weir 1861. **2.** *Mining.* A wooden frame through which the ore slides down into the coffer of the stamping-mill 1671.

1. a. The height of the p. is 6890 feet 1833. **b.** When Philip reached Thermophylæ, he found the p. strongly guarded 1838. Phr. *To gain, hold, keep, the p.*; *to sell the pass*, often fig. to betray one's allies or one's cause.

Pass (pɑs), *sb.*[2] 1481. [Partly – Fr. *passe*, f. *passer* to pass; partly f. PASS *v.*] **I. 1.** An act or the fact of passing; passage 1599. **b.** Departure from life, death. Also *fig.* 1645. †**2.** Demeanour, course of action –1603. †**3.** The fact of passing as approved; reputation; currency –1601. **4.** The passing of an examination; *esp.* in a university, the attainment of a standard that satisfies the examiners without entitling the candidate to honours. Often *attrib.* 1838.

1. Charming the narrow seas To giue you gentle Passe SHAKS. **2.** *Meas. for M.* V. i. 375. **3.** *All's Well* II. v. 58.

II. The condition to or through which anything passes. †**1.** Event, issue; completion, accomplishment –1649. **2.** A position or situation; *esp.* a position qualified in some way; a critical position, a juncture, a predicament 1560.

1. To no other passe my verses tend Then of your graces and your gifts to tell SHAKS. Phr. (now somewhat arch.). *To bring to p.* (rarely †*unto p.*), to bring to accomplishment; to carry out; to bring about. *To come to p.*, to come to the event or issue; to be carried out, accomplished, or realized; to turn out in the event; to come about. Also, quasi-*impers.*, with *it*, and subord. cl. To come to be the fact, to come about (esp. in Scriptural lang.); It came to passe after these things, that God did tempt Abraham *Gen.* 22:1. **2.** Where is the patriotism of bringing things to this p.? 1833.

III. Permission to pass. **a.** Permission to go or come anywhere; *esp.* a written permission to pass into, out of, or through a place; a passport; also, authorization to pass, *e.g.* through the lines of an army 1591. **b.** *Mil.* A certificate of leave of absence to a soldier for a short time 1617. †**c.** An order passing a pauper to his or her parish –1786. **d.** A document authorizing the holder to travel free on a railway, etc. Usu. *free p.* **e.** An order, etc., giving free admission to a theatre or the like. 1858.

a. The Dutch have ordered a passe to be sent for our Commissioners PEPYS.

IV. The causing of something to pass. **1.** *Fencing.* A lunge, a thrust; a bout of fencing 1598. †**b.** *fig.* A sally of wit; a witty thrust or stroke –1822. **2.** The manipulation of a juggler; the changing of the position of anything by sleight of hand; a trick 1599. **3.** A passing of the hands over or along anything; manipulation; esp. in mesmerism 1848. **4.** *Football, Hockey*, etc. A transference of the ball by one of the players to another on his own side 1891.

1. In a dozen passes between yourself and him, he shall not exceed you three hits SHAKS. **b.** *Temp.* IV. i. 244. **2.** Phr. *To make the p.* (in card tricks), to alter the position of the cards in the pack, e.g. by dexterously shifting the top or bottom card.

V. More fully *p.-hemp*, the third quality of Russian hemp 1744.

attrib. and *Comb.*, as (sense I. 4) *p.-degree*, *examination*, *schools*, etc.; (sense III) *p.-inspector*, etc.; also, **p.-boat**, a broad flat-bottomed boat; a punt, or the like; **-box**, a box for transferring cartridges from the magazine to the guns on the field; **-check**, a ticket of admission to a place of entertainment allowing the holder to go out and re-enter; **-hemp**: see sense V.

Pass (pɑs), *v.* *Pa.t.* and *pple.* **passed; past** (now rare as pa. t.). ME. [– (O)Fr. *passer* :– Rom. **passare* (med.L. *passare* trans. and intr.), f. L. *passus* step, PACE *sb.*] **A.** Intransitive uses. **I. 1.** To go on, move onward, proceed; to make one's way. Now usu. with some prep., adv., etc. **b.** Of something inanimate or involuntary: To move on under any force, to be moved, carried onward; to flow, as water, a stream, etc. ME. **c.** Of a line, string, path, etc.: To extend, 'run' 1703. **d.** To proceed in narration, consideration, or action. Now usu. only in *pass on.* late ME. **2.** With ref. to place or object of destination. Chiefly with *to* (*unto*, *into*). ME.

1. I was imploy'd in passing to and fro, About relieuing of the Centinels SHAKS. She once had past that way TENNYSON. **c.** The path passes round a bay 1813. **d.** Er That I ferther in this tale pace CHAUCER. **2.** Passing through Nature, to Eternity SHAKS. This riuer. .passeth southward 1600.

II. †**1.** To go about, to travel; to move about, be astir –1585. **2.** To be handed about; to circulate, be current 1589.

2. Our money they thought would not p. BURNET. *To p. current* (†*for current*): see CURRENT *a.* *To p. for, as*, to be accepted as (often with the implication of being something else). *To p. by*, to be currently known by (a name, etc.). †*To p. on, upon*, to impose upon; to gain credit with.

III. 1. To go or be transported from one place or set of circumstances to another. (Usu. with prep.) ME. **2.** To be changed from one form or state to another; to undergo chemical, structural, or other gradual conversion *into*. late ME. **3.** *Law*. Of property: To go by conveyance, or come by inheritance *to*, *into the hands of*. late ME. **4.** To be uttered between two (or more) persons mutually; to be interchanged or transacted 1568.

1. To p., in descending a mountain, from snow to rain 1860. **2.** The hatred of theologians has passed into a proverb 1855. **4.** I know what has past between you GOLDSM.

IV. With reference to place left. **1.** To go away; to depart *from* (†*of*, *off*) a place, thing, or person. Of a thing: To be taken away (*from*). ME. **b.** *fig*. To depart, diverge *from* a course, practice, principle. late ME. **2.** To depart from this life, die. Now *arch*. or *dial*. when used *simply*. ME.

1. If it be possible, let this cup passe from me *Matt*. 26:39. **2.** Vex not his ghost, O let him passe *Lear* v. iii. 314.

V. 1. To go by. (Now the leading intr. sense of the simple verb.) ME. **b.** Of things: To be moved or impelled past; to flow past. Also *fig*. ME. **2. a.** Of time: To glide by, come to an end ME. **b.** Of things in time ME.

1. Allow me to p., please 1904. **b.** My Lord stand backe, and let the Coffin passe SHAKS. It is done every day, and passes unregarded 1766. **c.** With compl. adjs., as *to p. unheeded*, *unnoticed*. late ME. **2. a.** The first day passed without any thing doyng LD. BERNERS. **b.** Not to let th' occasion p. MILT.

VI. 1. To go or get through; to have, obtain, or force passage, to make one's way. Also of things, ME. **b.** Of things: e.g. to be admitted through a customs barrier 1637. **c.** To go through a duct; to be voided 1731. **2.** To go uncensured; to go without check or challenge; to pass muster; to 'do' ME. **3.** To be allowed and approved by a court, legislature, or deliberative body; to 'get through'; to be ratified 1568. **4.** To get through any trial successfully; *spec*. in an examination, to reach or satisfy the required standard 1600.

1. My Lord you passe not heere SHAKS. **2.** Indeed and indeed, the trick will not p., Jonas WYCHERLEY. I never suffer a line to p. till I have made it as good as I can COWPER. **3.** The bill passed without substantial alteration 1880. **4.** If I p., which I trust I shall be able to do MARRYAT. *To p. master*, etc. to graduate as master, etc. (in some faculty); cf. PASSED-, PAST-MASTER.

†**VII.** To excel, to surpass; to go to excess –1611. †**b.** quasi-*impers*. *It passes*: it passes description, 'beats everything' –1689.

VIII. Of events: To go on in the course of things; to take place, occur, happen 1542.

I am attentive to all that passes BERKELEY.

IX. Used in ref. to process of law. **1.** Of a jury (assize, inquest): To sit in inquest *on* or *upon*; to decide or adjudicate *between* parties; to give a verdict *for* or *against* (*arch*.) ME. **b.** To serve *on* (*upon*, †*in*) a jury, assize, or trial 1574. **c.** Of a court, a judge, the law: To adjudicate, pass sentence *on*, *upon*. Also *transf*. 1532. **2.** Of a verdict, sentence, or judgement: To be given or pronounced; of justice: To be executed. late ME.

2. A similar sentence passed against some of his adherents GOLDSM.

†**X.** To care, to reck (usu. with neg.) –1671.

XI. Elliptical or absol. uses of B or C. **1.** *Fencing*. To make a pass (PASS *sb*.[2] IV. 1). Const. *on*, *upon*. 1595. **2.** *Cards* and *Dice*. **a.** In primero, poker, etc.: To throw up one's hand, retire from the game 1599. **b.** In euchre, napoleon, etc.: To decline one's opportunity (as of making the trump): see EUCHRE *sb*. 1. 1884. **3.** To pass the ball at Football, etc. (See C. III. 1 b.) 1888.

B. Transitive uses. (From A. V, VI, VII.)

I. 1. To go by, proceed past; to leave behind or on one side as one goes on ME. †**2.** *fig*. To go by without attending to; to neglect, disregard, omit –1719. **b.** To leave unmentioned 1585. **c.** orig. *U.S.* To omit payment of (a dividend, etc.) 1890. †**d.** *To p. one's flag* (Naval), to decline promotion to flag rank, and become a retired captain NELSON.

1. So p. I hostel, hall, and grange TENNYSON. **2.** *John* II. i. 258.

II. To go through, across, or over (something). **1.** To go from side to side of, or across; to cross (a sea, barrier, frontier, etc.); also (less frequently) to go through, traverse, (a forest, way, etc.) ME. **b.** Of a book, etc.: To go through (the printing-press, or successive editions) 1665. †**2.** To pierce, to penetrate: said of a spear, etc., also of the person driving it –1720. **3.** *fig*. To experience, undergo, endure, put up with, suffer. Now usu. *pass through*. ME. **4.** To go through the process of being considered, examined, and approved by; to come up to the standard required by. late ME.

1. The waies are dangerous to passe SHAKS. **3.** The Battaile, Sieges, Fortune, That I haue past SHAKS. **4.** My Bill hath passed the Lords House and was this day read in the House of Commons 1670. You'll p. your exams with distinction 1901. *To p. muster*: see MUSTER *sb*.[1] 3. *To p. the seals*, to receive royal (or other) ratification by sealing.

III. To go beyond, surpass, exceed. **1.** To go beyond (a point or place); to overshoot (a mark); to outrun; to surmount. late ME. **2.** To overstep (bounds or limits); to transgress. *fig*. To go beyond (one's province, warrant, knowledge, etc.). ME. **3.** To be too great for, transcend (any faculty or expression). late ME. **4.** To surpass in some quality; to exceed in degree (*arch*.) ME. **b.** To exceed in number, measurement, or amount. Now *rare*. ME. †**5.** To get beyond (a stage or condition of life or existence) –1685.

1. Mount Athos is so high, that it passeth the skies 1585. **2.** Let not the cobler passe his pantofle 1604. He pass'd the flaming bounds of Place and Time GRAY. **3.** That grief which passes show 1820. **4.** Thy loue to me was wonderfull, passyng the loue of wemen BIBLE (Great) 2 *Sam*. 1:26.

IV. *To p. the lips*, †*the mouth of*: to come out of the mouth of, to be spoken or uttered by 1526.

C. Causative uses. **I. 1.** To cause or enable (a person or thing) to go, proceed, or make his way anywhere; to carry, convey, send; *esp*. to convey across a river, a ferry, etc., to transport. late ME. **2.** To make (a thing) go in any specific manner or direction; to move, draw, push (a thing) 1705. **3.** To cause to pass or go by 1852. **4.** To cause or allow (a person or thing) to go past or through some barrier or obstruction 1611. **5.** To cause or allow to pass or go by, to spend (time, one's life, a season, etc.) ME.

1. Every vagrant Person may..be..pass'd back to their last legal Settlement DE FOE. **2.** *To p. one's hand over*, *to p. one's eye over* (to glance rapidly over), *to p. a wet sponge over* (often *fig*. to obliterate the memory of), *to pass the sweeper over* a floor, *to p. a rope* or *string round* anything, etc. **3.** *To p. in review*, (orig.) *Mil*. To cause (troops) to march by for inspection; hence *fig*. **5.** *To p. the winter at a place*, *p. one's time in sleep*, *p. a pleasant evening*, etc.

II. †**a.** To carry through its stages; to execute (a matter, a business); to complete (a voyage) –1748. **b.** To carry or get carried (a measure in Parliament, a resolution); to agree to, confirm, sanction, endorse 1529. **c.** To allow or enable (a person) to pass an examination 1833. †**d.** To overlook, excuse, pass over (something) –1802.

a. *Tam. Shr*. IV. iv. 57. **b.** Their majority will p. the bill 1799. **c.** I'll p. you..I can conscientiously report you a healthy subject DICKENS.

III. 1. To cause to go from one to another; to hand over, hand round, hand, transfer 1596. **b.** *Football*. To transfer (the ball) to another player on the same side. Also *absol*. (sense A. XI. 3.) 1865. **c.** To put into circulation (coin, esp. base coin, or the like). Also *fig*. 1589. **2.** *Law*. To convey, make over, with legal effect 1587. **3.** To give in pledge (one's word, promise, oath); †to pledge (one's faith, etc.) 1469.

1. P. the word to reduce the cartridges MARRYAT. They passed buckets of water from hand to hand 1901. **c.** Utterers of base coin have a trick of passing a bad shilling between two good ones 1864. **2.** The delivery of the key of the trunk was held to p. the trunk and its contents 1891. **3.** He wil not passe his word..that you are no Foole SHAKS.

IV. 1. To discharge from the body by excretion 1698. **2.** To utter, pronounce (speech, criticism, censure); rarely, to put (a question); occas., to exchange (words). 1615. **b.** To pronounce judicially 1590.

2. How to p. Complements upon Almighty God 1698. Phr. *To p. the time of day* (dial. or colloq.), to exchange salutations or gossip in passing. **b.** Sentence of death was passed upon him 1820.

V. †**1.** *Fencing*. To make or execute (a thrust) SHAKS. **2.** To perform the pass on a pack of cards; see PASS *sb*.[2] IV. 2. 1884.

With preps and advs. **I.** With preps. **Pass beyond** —. **a.** See simple senses and BEYOND *prep*. **b.** To pass the limits of, exceed, transcend. **P. by** —. †**a.** To go through or by way of. **b.** To go past; to pass. **c.** To take no notice of, disregard, omit. **P. over** —. **a.** To cross, to traverse (a sea, river, or expanse). Also *fig*. **b.** To pass the hand over. †**c.** *trans*. To spend (time). **d.** To pass a thing without dwelling on it, or without notice or remark, to omit. **P. through** —. **a.** To go from side to side of, to cross, traverse. **b.** In ref. to times, stages, states, processes, actions, experiences, etc. **c.** To make or force a passage through; to penetrate; to pierce through; to send a shot through. Also *fig*. **d.** *causal*. To cause (a thing) to pass or go through; to put, thrust, or impel through.

II. With adverbs. **Pass away. a.** See simple senses and AWAY *adv*. **b.** *intr*. Of persons: To depart; also, to get or break away (as from restraint). **c.** *intr*. To die, expire. **d.** *intr*. Of time: To come to an end. **e.** *intr*. Of things: To come to an end, cease to be, be dissolved, perish. **f.** *trans*. To spend (time, etc.); to while away, to pass. †**g.** To transfer away (rights, etc.); to convey away (property). **P. by. a.** *intr*. To go past; to move on without stopping; to flow past. Also *fig*. and in ref. to time. **b.** *trans*. To go past (a thing or person) without stopping, or without taking notice; to overlook; to omit; to disregard, ignore; = *pass over* d, e. **P. forth. a.** *intr*. To go out or away (*arch*.). †**b.** To go forward, go on, continue. **P. in.** *trans*. To hand in (e.g. a cheque to a bank). **P. off. a.** *intr*. To go off or disappear gradually, as sensations, moisture, etc. **b.** *intr*. To go or be carried through (with more or less success). **c.** *trans*. To put into circulation, or dispose of (esp. deceptively); to palm off; to impose. **d.** To cause (a person) to be accepted in some false character; *esp*. *refl*. (with *for* or *as*) to give oneself out as what one is not, to pretend to be. **P. on. a.** *intr*. See simple senses and ON *adv*. **b.** *trans*. To send or hand (anything) on to the next member of a series. **P. out.** *intr*. See simple senses and OUT *adv*.; chiefly, to go out through a passage. *To p. out of*, to issue from, leave; *to p. out of sight*, to go beyond the reach of sight. **P. over. a.** *intr*. To go across; to cross to the other side. In *Chem*., said of the volatilized substances which pass from the retort in distillation, and are condensed in the receiver. **b.** *intr*. Of a period of time: To go by, come to an end. **c.** *trans*. To hand over *to* another; to transfer. **d.** To pass (a thing) without touching it, or without remark or notice, esp. in narration; to omit, skip, disregard; to ignore the claims of (a person) for promotion, etc., to pass by in selection for a post, etc. **e.** To let go unpunished, to overlook (an offence). **P. through**: emphatic of sense A. VI. 1.

Pass-, vb.-stem or imper. of PASS *v*., used in a few combs., as **pa·ss-out** *a*. (of a ticket) that enables the holder to pass out of and return to a place of entertainment.

Passable (pɑ·săb'l), *a*. late ME. [– (O)Fr. *passable*, f. *passer*; see PASS *v*., -ABLE.] **1.** That may be passed, crossed, or traversed. †**2.** Able to pass or have passage –1762. **3.** Of money: That has valid currency, current; of a book: fit for circulation. Also *fig*. 1590. **4.** That can pass muster; tolerable; sufficient, presentable 1489. **5.** quasi-*adv*. = Passably 1581.

1. The ford was not p. DE FOE. **3.** The vertue of your name, Is not heere p. SHAKS. The coin may cease to be of value as a p. thing, as money 1888. **4.** A p. knowledge of living languages SOUTHEY. **5.** P. good Christians 1706. Hence **Pa·ssableness. Pa·ssably** *adv*. tolerably; fairly well, moderately.

‖**Passacaglia** (passăkā·lyă). 1659. [It. – Sp. *pasacalle* (pasăka·lye), f. *pasar* pass + *calle* street; because often played in the streets.] An early kind of dance tune (of Spanish origin) having a movement slower than the CHACONNE, generally constructed on a ground bass and written in triple time; also the dance to this.

Passade (păsē[i]·d). *rare*. 1656. [– Fr. *passade* (XV) – It. *passata* or Pr. *passada*, f. *passare* PASS *v*.; see -ADE.] *Horsemanship*. A turn or course of a horse backwards and forwards on the same plot of ground. †**2.** = next, 1. –1741.

†‖**Passa·do.** 1588. [alt. of Sp. *pasada* (cf. Pr. *passada*, It. *passata*, Fr. *passade*); see -ADO.] **1.** *Fencing*. A forward thrust with the sword, one foot being advanced –1830. **2.** = PASSAGE *sb*. III. 1 b. –1656.

Passage (pæ·sėdʒ), *sb*. ME. [– OFr. *passage*, f. *passer* PASS *v*.; see -AGE.] **I.** The action of passing. **1.** A going or moving onward, across, or past; transition, transit. **b.** The passing of people; hence nearly = people passing (*rare*) 1590. **c.** The migratory flight of birds 1774. **2.** *fig*. Transition from one state or condition to another (*spec.* from this life to the next, by death); the passing of time; the course of events, etc.; a passing in thought or speech from one point, idea, or subject, to another. late ME. †**b.** *absol.* Departure, death –1837. **3.** Possibility, power, or opportunity of passing; liberty, leave, or right to pass (*lit.* and *fig.*) ME. **4.** A journey; a voyage across the sea from one port to another, a crossing ME. **b.** Right of transit or conveyance as a passenger, esp. by sea; accommodation as a passenger 1632. †**5.** A charge or custom levied upon passengers –1883. †**6.** The fact of being generally accepted, as coins, customs, etc.; currency –1644. **7.** The passing into law of a legislative measure 1587. **8.** *Horsemanship.* A slow trot, in which the horse brings the diagonally opposite legs to the ground at the same moment 1727. **9.** *Med.* An evacuation of the bowels, a 'motion'; also *concr.* 1778. **10.** The action of causing something to pass; transmission, transference, etc. (*rare*) 1860.

1. The p. of the chyldren of Israel from Egypte 1526. **b.** *Oth.* V. i. 37. **c.** *Bird of p.*, a bird that migrates from one region to another at a particular season and returns at another, a migratory bird (also *fig.*). **2.** Wyth good p. out of thys lyf 1430. **b.** *Haml.* III. iii. 86. **3.** To..guard all p. to the Tree of Life MILT. **4.** A rough p. 1877. **b.** Free p. home 1864.

II. a. That by which a person or thing passes or may pass; a way, road, path, route, channel, esp. when serving as an entrance or exit ME. **b.** *spec.* A crossing; a ford, ferry, or bridge. *arch.* ME. **c.** A corridor or alley leading to or giving access to an apartment, garden, etc. 1611.

a. A new attempt upon the North-West or North-East passages DE FOE. The liver and its bile passages 1897.

III. 1. Something that 'passes', goes on, takes place, occurs, or is done; an incident, event; an act, transaction, or proceeding. *Obs.* or *arch.* (exc. as in b and c.) 1568. **b.** A negotiation between two persons; an interchange of communications, confidences, or amorous relations 1612. **c.** (Now usu. *p. of* (or *at*) *arms.*) An exchange of blows between two persons, a fight; also *fig.* 1599. **2.** An indefinite portion of a discourse or writing, taken by itself 1549. †**b.** A digression –1663. †**c.** A remark, observation (in speech or writing); a phrase, expression –1660. **d.** *Mus.* In early use, a figure or phrase; now, a portion of a composition, of no great length, forming more or less of a unity 1727. **e.** *gen.* An indefinite portion of a course of action; an episode (*rare*) 1848.

1. *Twel. N.* III. ii. 77. **b.** Certain passages..between Will Stephen and this simple country maid 1901. **c.** Luther..had not forgotten his early p. at arms with the English Defender of the Faith 1856. **2.** To look for the p. in the original author 1802. **e.** Despite such passages of gloom he worked on 1897.

†**IV.** [The *passing* or exceeding of ten = It. *passa-dieci*, Fr. *passe-dix*, i.e. pass-ten.] An obsolete game at dice, played with three dice, in which the thrower *passes* or wins when he throws above ten –1755.

attrib. and *Comb.*: **p.-bed** (*Geol.*), a stratum showing transition from one formation to another; **-hawk**, a falcon taken when full-grown, during its 'passage' or migration, for the purpose of training (opp. to *eyas*); **-money**, money charged for p., fare; **-way**, a way affording passage; a passage esp. in a building (chiefly *U.S.*). Hence **Pa·ssage** *v.*[1] (*a*) to make a p., as in a ship or boat; to move across, pass; (*b*) to carry on a p. of arms; *fig.* to fence with words.

Passage (pæ·sėdʒ), *v.* Chiefly in vbl. sb. **passaging.** 1796. [– Fr. *passager*, altered from *passéger* – It. *passeggiare* walk, pace, f. L. *passus* PASS *sb.*[1]] **a.** *intr.* To move sideways in riding, by pressure of the rein on the horse's neck and of the rider's leg on the opposite side; said of the horse, or of the rider. **b.** *trans.* To cause (a horse) to 'passage'.

Pa·ssage-boa:t. 1598. A boat for the conveyance of passengers, plying regularly between two places.

Passant (pæ·sănt), *a.* ME. [– (O)Fr. *passant*, pr. pple. of *passer* PASS *v.*; see -ANT.] †**1.** Surpassing; excelling –1485. †**2.** Passing, transitory, fugitive –1715. †**3.** Passing, going on; proceeding –1710. **4.** *Her.* Of a beast: Walking, and looking towards the dexter side, with the dexter fore-paw raised 1506. †**5.** Current, in general use, in vogue –1844. †**6.** Cursory, done in passing –1693.

2. Our p. words, and our secret thoughts 1677. **5.** Many opinions are p. concerning the Basilisk SIR T. BROWNE. **6.** On a P. review of what..I wrote to the Bp. 1693.

Pa·ss-book. 1828. [app. = book passing between bank, etc., and customer.] **1.** = BANK-BOOK. **2.** *U.S.* A book in which a merchant or trader makes an entry of goods sold to a customer, for the customer's information 1839.

‖**Passé** (pase), *a.* Also (fem.) **passée.** 1775. [Fr., pa. pple. of *passer* PASS *v.*, used as adj.] Past, past the prime; *esp.* of a woman: past the period of greatest beauty; also, behind the times, superseded.

Pa·ssed-ma:ster. 1563. [f. phr. *pass master*: see PASS *v.* A. VI. 4.] One who has passed as a master; a qualified or accomplished master; cf. PAST-MASTER.

†**Passemea·sure.** 1568. [Alteration of It. *passe-*, *passa-mezzo.*] A slow dance of Italian origin, app. a variety of the pavan; the music for this, in common time. Also called *passe-measures paven*, etc., *passy measures* = It. *passe-mezzo pavana.* –1726.

Then he's a Rogue, and a passy measures Pauyn: I hate a drunken rogue *Twel. N.* V. i. 205.

Passement (pæ·smĕnt), *sb. Obs.* exc. *Hist.* 1535. [– Fr. *passement* (XVI), f. *passer* PASS *v.*; see -MENT.] = LACE *sb.* 4. †**b.** *attrib.*, as *p. lace*, *silk* –1613. Hence **Pa·ssement** *v.* to adorn with p. or lace; to edge (a garment) with decorative braiding 1539. So ‖**Passementerie** (pasmӑ̃ntri), trimming of gold or silver lace, or, later, of gimp, braid, or the like, or of jet or metal beads.

Passenger (pæ·sėndʒəɹ). [ME. *passager* – (O)Fr. *passager*, subst. use of adj. passing, f. *passage* PASSAGE; see -ER[2]. For the intrusive *n* cf. *harbinger*, *messenger*, etc.] **1. a.** A passer by or through. **b.** A traveller (usu. on foot). Now unusual, exc. in *foot-passenger*. **2.** One who travels in some vessel or vehicle, esp. on board ship or in a ferry- or passage-boat; later applied also to travellers by any public conveyance entered by fare or contract. (The prevailing sense.) 1511. †**3.** A passenger-boat; a ferry-boat –1630. †**4.** A bird of passage. Also *attrib.* –1672. †**b.** *spec.* A passage-hawk; also, a name for the Peregrine falcon; in full, *p. falcon* –1694. **5.** *slang.* An ineffective member of the crew of a racing-boat, a football team, etc. 1885. **6.** *attrib.*, as *p. boat*, *depot*, *fare*, *ship*, *traffic*, etc. 1836.

Pa·ssenger-pi:geon. 1802. [See PASSENGER 4.] The 'Wild Pigeon' of N. America (*Ectopistes migratorius*), noted for its exceptional powers of long and sustained flight.

‖**Passe-partout, passepartout** (pas,partu·). 1675. [Fr.; f. *passer* PASS *v.* + *partout* everywhere.] **1.** That which passes, or permits to pass, everywhere; *spec.* a master-key; also *fig.* and *attrib.* **2.** An ornamental mat or plate of cardboard, etc., with the centre cut out, serving as a mount or border to a photograph, drawing, etc. when framed. Hence *p. frame*, a frame ready made with such a mount 1867.

Passer (pɑ·səɹ). late ME. [f. PASS *v.* + -ER[1].] **1.** One who passes, travels, or goes by. **2.** One who causes to pass. (See PASS *v.* C.) 1832.

Pa:sser-by·. 1568. [f. *pass by*; see PASS *v.*] One who passes by, *esp.* a casual passer.

‖**Passeres** (pæ·sĕrīz), *sb. pl.* 1872. [L., pl. of *passer* sparrow.] *Ornith.* An order of birds typified by the genus *Passer*, including the perchers generally, and comprehending more than half of existing birds. So **Pa·sseriform** *a.* sparrow-like; *spec.* of or pertaining to the *Passeriformes* or oscinine group of *Passeres*.

Passerine (pæ·sĕrəin), *a.* (*sb.*) 1776. [f. as prec. + -INE[1].] **1.** Of or belonging to the PASSERES. **2.** Of about the size of a sparrow, as the Passerine Parrot (*Psittacula passerina*), etc. 1883. **B.** *sb.* A passerine bird 1842.

Pa·ss-guard. *Obs.* exc. *Hist.* 1548. [app. f. PASS *sb.*[2] IV. 1 + GUARD *sb.*] An item of ancient tilt armour; said to be a separate piece provided to accompany the grand guard, being screwed upon the left elbow; also *elbow-shield*.

Passible (pæ·sib'l), *a.* ME. [– (O)Fr. *passible* or Chr. L. *passibilis*, f. *pass-*, pa. ppl. stem of *pati* suffer; see -IBLE.] **1.** Capable of suffering, liable to suffer; susceptible of sensation or emotion. †**2.** Liable to suffer change or decay –1655. †**3.** Capable of being suffered or felt –1621.

1. The Paradise Saints have bodies of flesh, p., and such as must have food 1691. So **Passibi·lity**, the quality of being p. **Pa·ssibleness.**

Passiflora (pæsiflōᵊ·ră). 1763. [mod.L., f. L. *pass-* as stem of *passio* PASSION + *-florus* flowering. Formed by Linnæus, 1737, on the earlier mod.L. name *flos passionis* PASSION-FLOWER.] *Bot.* The genus of plants containing the Passion-flower. Hence **Passiflo·rine** *Chem.*, an alkaloid substance obtained from the root of the Passion-flower.

‖**Passim** (pæ·sim), *adv.* 1803. [L., = 'scatteredly', f. *passus* scattered, pa. pple. of *pandere* spread out.] Used chiefly after the name of a book or author cited, to indicate that something occurs here and there throughout the book or writings.

Passimeter (pæsi·mĭtəɹ). 1923. [f. PASS *v.* or PASS(ENGER + -METER.] An automatic railway ticket-booking machine.

Passing (pɑ·siŋ), *vbl. sb.* ME. [f. PASS *v.* + -ING[1].] **1.** The action of PASS *v.* in various senses. **b.** A passing-place; a ford; a railway siding 1825. **2.** *concr.* A gold or silver thread made by winding a thin strip or ribbon of the metal about a core of silk 1882.

attrib. and *Comb.*: **p.-bell** = DEATH-BELL; *fig.* the 'knell'; †**-penny**, the obolus placed by the ancient Greeks on the tongue of the dead to pay their fare over the Styx; hence, a passport to the future world; **-place**, (*a*) a ford; (*b*) a railway siding.

Pa·ssing, *ppl. a.* (*adv.* and *prep.*) ME. [-ING[2].] That passes, in various senses; *esp.* transient, fleeting; ephemeral; done, given, etc. in passing; cursory.

A p. remark 1862. Some p. traveller from distant lands 1874. The confounding of the P. with the Permanent 1899.

B. *adv.* In a passing or surpassing degree; exceedingly. Now somewhat *arch.* ME.

A man he was..p. rich with forty pounds a year GOLDSM.

†**C.** quasi-*prep.* Beyond, more than (usu. with neg.); more or better than; rather than –1830.

Men paste feare, and hardie p. measure 1561. Hence **Pa·ssing-ly** *adv.*, **-ness.**

Pa·ssing-note. 1730. *Mus.* A note not belonging to the harmony, interposed between two notes essential to it, for the sake of smooth transition.

Passion (pæ·ʃən), *sb.* ME. [– (O)Fr. *passion* – Chr. L. *passio*, *-on-* suffering, affection, f. *pass-*, pa. ppl. stem of L. *pati* suffer; see -ION.] **I.** The suffering of pain. **1.** (Now usu. with capital.) The sufferings of Jesus Christ on the Cross (also often including the Agony in Gethsemane). Formerly also in *pl.* **b.** The narrative of the sufferings of Christ from the Gospels; also, a musical setting of this ME. **2.** The sufferings of a martyr, martyrdom (*arch.*) ME. †**3.** Suffering or affliction generally –1656. **4.** A painful disorder of the body or of some part of it. *Obs.* exc. in certain phrases. late ME.

1. By thy crosse and p.,..Good lorde deliuer us *Bk. Com. Prayer. Instruments of the P.*, the cross, the crown of thorns, the nails, scourge, etc. **b.** [Bach's] 'Passion according to S. Matthew' is..the finest work of the kind 1880. **3.** *Ant. & Cl.* V. i. 63. **4.** *Colic, iliac, sciatic p.*: see the adjs.

II. The being passive. [Late L. *passio*, as tr. Gr. πάθος.] **a.** The being affected from without. Now *rare* or *Obs.* late ME. †**b.** A passive quality, property, or attribute –1707.

a. The work of p. rather than of action 1846. **b.** What's the proper p. of mettalls? B. JONS.

III. An affection of the mind. [L. *passio* = Gr. πάθος.] **1.** Any vehement, commanding, or overpowering emotion; in psychology or art, any mode in which the mind is affected or acted upon, as ambition, avarice, desire, hope, fear, love, hatred, joy, grief, anger, revenge. Occas. personified. late ME. **b.** Without article or *pl.*: Commanding, vehement, or overpowering feeling or emotion 1590. **c.** A fit or mood of excited feeling; an outburst of feeling 1590. **d.** A passionate speech or outburst. *Obs.* or *arch.* 1582. **2.** *spec.* An outburst of anger or bad temper 1530. **b.** Without *a*: Angry feeling 1524. **3.** Amorous feeling; love; †also in *pl.*, amorous desires 1588. **b.** *transf.* A beloved person 1783. **4.** Sexual desire or impulse 1641. **5.** An overmastering zeal or enthusiasm for some object 1638. **b.** *transf.* An aim or object pursued with zeal 1732.

1. We also are men of like passions with you *Acts* 14:15. The ruling P. conquers Reason still POPE. **b.** Is this the Nature Whom P. could not shake? SHAKS. **c.** She burst into an hysterical p. of weeping 1856. **d.** *Mids. N.* v. i. 321. **2.** Folks who put me in a p. BROWNING. **b.** P. made his dark face turn white SOUTHEY. **3.** P. lends them Power, time, meanes to meete SHAKS. The most wretched of all martyrs to this tender p. FIELDING. **5.** The growing p. for the possession of land 1874. **b.** Golf has become a p. with him 1904.

attrib. and *Comb.*: **p.-music,** music to which the narrative of the P. is set (cf. I. 1 b); **-play,** a mystery-play representing the P. of Christ. Hence **Pa·ssional** *a.* of or pertaining to p. or the passions; characterized by p.

Passion (pæ·ʃən), *v.* 1468. [– (O)Fr. *passionner*, f. *passion* PASSION *sb.*] **1.** *trans.* To affect or imbue with passion. †**2.** To affect with suffering, afflict –1626. **3.** *intr.* To show, express, or be affected by passion or deep feeling; formerly *esp.* to sorrow 1588.

1. For whose soul-soothing quiet, turtles P. their voices cooingly KEATS. **3.** 'Twas Adriadne, passioning For Theseus periury, and vniust flight SHAKS. Hence **Pa·ssioned** *ppl. a.* = PASSIONATE *a.* 2.

Passional (pæ·ʃənăl), *sb.* 1650. [– med.L. *passionale*, subst. use of n. of late L. adj. *passionalis* (Tertullian), f. *passio*; see PASSION *sb.*, -AL[1].] A book containing accounts of the sufferings of saints and martyrs, for reading on their festival days. So **Pa·ssionary** 1475.

Passionate (pæ·ʃənĕt), *a.* (*sb.*) 1450. [– med.L. *passionatus* (cf. Fr. *passionné*), f. *passio* PASSION *sb.*; see -ATE[2].] **1.** Easily moved to angry passion; hot-tempered; irascible. †**b.** Enraged, angry –1817. **c.** Of language, etc.: Angry, wrathful 1590. **2.** Of persons: Affected with passion or vehement emotion; enthusiastic, ardently desirous; †zealously devoted 1526. **b.** Of language, etc.: Expressive of strong emotion, impassioned 1581. **c.** Of an emotion: Vehement 1567. **3.** Subject to passion; easily moved to strong feeling; impressible, susceptible; of changeful mood 1589. †**4.** *spec.* Affected with the passion of love –1704. †**5.** Moved with sorrow; sorrowful –1665. **b.** Compassionate. Now *dial.* 1594. †**c.** That moves to compassion –1595. **B.** *sb.* One who is influenced by passion, †*esp.* one who is in love 1651.

A. 1. Homer made Achilles p., Wrathfull, revengefull 1613. **c.** This p. expletive 1693. **2.** He.. swept with p. hand the ringing harp SOUTHEY. **b.** Forgive this p. language '*Junius' Lett.* **5.** She is sad and p. at your highness Tent SHAKS. **b.** *Rich. III*, I. iv. 121. Hence **Pa·ssionate-ly** *adv.*, **-ness.**

†**Pa·ssionate,** *v.* 1566. [f. Fr. *passionner*, f. *passion* PASSION *sb.*; see -ATE[3].] **1.** *trans.* To excite or imbue with passion, or with a passion, as love, fear, etc. –1658. **2.** To express or perform with passion –1615.

Pa·ssion-flower. 1633. [f. PASSION *sb.* I. 1 + FLOWER *sb.*; in XVI L. *flos passionis*; see PASSIFLORA.] The name of plants of the genus *Passiflora*; so called because of the fancied resemblance of parts of the flower to the instruments of the Passion.

Passionist (pæ·ʃənist), *sb.* (*a.*) 1833. [= Fr. *passioniste*, f. PASSION *sb.*; see -IST.] *R.C.Ch.* A member of 'The Congregation of the Discalced Clerks of the most Holy Cross and Passion of our Lord Jesus Christ' founded in Italy by Paolo della Croce in 1720. **b.** *attrib.* or as *adj.* 1844.

Passionless (pæ·ʃənlĕs), *a.* 1612. [-LESS.] Void of passion; unimpassioned.

Hopeless grief is p. 1844. Hence **Pa·ssionless-ly** *adv.*, **-ness.**

Passion Sunday. late ME. [tr. med.L. *Dominica in Passione.*] The fifth Sunday in Lent; reckoned as the beginning of Passiontide.

Pa·ssion(-)ti:de. 1861. The season immediately before Easter, in which Christ's Passion is commemorated; see prec.

Pa·ssion Wee:k. 1449. [f. PASSION *sb.* I. 1 + WEEK; cf. med.L. *hebdomada passionis.*] The week immediately before Easter, in which the Passion of Christ is commemorated; Holy Week. **b.** In recent use applied by some to the fifth week of Lent, beginning with Passion Sunday 1852.

Passive (pæ·siv), *a.* and *sb.* late ME. [– (O)Fr. *passif, -ive* or L. *passivus, -iva* (*Gram.* tr. Gr. ὕπτιος), f. *pass-*; see PASSION, -IVE.] **A.** *adj.* †**1.** Suffering, liable to suffer –1655. **2.** Suffering action from without; that is the object, as dist. from the subject, of action; acted upon by external force; produced by external agency. late ME. **3.** *Gram.* An epithet of voice in verbs used transitively; opp. to ACTIVE 3. Applied to that form of, or that mode of using, the verb, in which the action denoted by it is treated as an attribute of the thing towards which the action is directed. late ME. **4.** *Sc. Law.* Involved by acceptance of the property of an ancestor 1576. **5.** Suffering or receiving something without resistance or opposition; readily yielding to external force or influence, or to the will of another; submissive 1626. **6.** Not active; quiescent, inactive, inert 1477. **7. a.** *Path.* Of an inflammation, congestion, or the like: Characterized by sluggish or diminished flow of blood 1813. **b.** *Chem.* Not readily entering into chemical combination; inert, inactive 1849. **c.** *Law* and *Comm.* Of a bond, debt, or share: On which no interest is paid. Of a trust: On which the trustees have no duties to perform; nominal 1837.

2. The mind is to be considered as merely p., receiving like wax the impressions of external objects 1773. **5.** P. she, all the while, mere clay in the hands of the potter CARLYLE. *P. obedience, prayer, resistance, righteousness*: see the sbs. **b.** I am p. in their disputes 1710.

B. *sb.* [The adj. used ellipt.] **1.** A passive thing, quality, or property. Now usu. in *pl.* late ME. **2.** *Gram.* The passive voice; a passive verb 1530. **3.** An unresisting or submissive person or creature. Now *rare.* 1626.

1. A due conjunction of actives and passives SIR T. BROWNE. Hence **Pa·ssive-ly** *adv.*, **-ness.**

Passivity (pæsi·vĭti). 1659. [f. PASSIVE + -ITY.] †**1.** Passibility –1680. **2.** The quality, condition, or state of being passive. Also, with *a* and *pl.*, an instance of this 1659. **3.** Submissiveness 1681. **4.** Want of activity, inertness, †inertia 1667.

2. The liability of matter to be shaped, and the liability of the mind to have perceptions and ideas, are pure passivities 1885.

Pass-key (pɑ·s,kī). 1817. [f. PASS *v.* or *sb.* + KEY *sb.*[1]] A key (other than the ordinary key) of a door or gate, *spec.* **a.** A master-key; also *fig.*; **b.** a private key to a gate, etc.; **c.** a latch-key.

Passless (pɑ·slĕs), *a.* 1656. [f. PASS *sb.* + -LESS.] Impassable. *poet.*

Pass-man (pɑ·s,mæ̆n). 1860. [f. PASS *sb.*[2] I. 4 + MAN.] A student who takes a 'pass' degree at a university; opp. to *class-man, honours man.*

Passover (pɑ·sōᵘvəɹ). 1530. [f. phr. *pass over* pass without touching (PASS *v.*, OVER *prep.*), rendering Heb. *pesaḥ*; see PASCH.] **1.** The name of a Jewish feast, held on the evening of the fourteenth day of the (first) month Nisan, commemorative of the 'passing over' of the houses of the Israelites when the Egyptians were smitten with the loss of their firstborn. †**2.** *contextually*, The Paschal Lamb. **b.** *fig.* Applied to Christ (1 *Cor.* 5:7). –1680. **3.** *attrib.* 1545.

1. *Passover*..also called the feast of unleavened bread 1840.

Passport (pɑ·s,pōɹt), *sb.* 1500. [– Fr. *passeport* (cf. It. *passaporto*), f. *passer* PASS *v.* + *port* PORT *sb.*[1]] †**1.** Authorization to pass from a port, to leave a country, or to enter or pass through a country –1606. **2.** A document issued by competent authority, granting permission to the person specified in it to travel, and authenticating his right to protection 1536. †**b.** A permit for discharged inmates of a hospital, soldiers, etc. to proceed to a specified destination –1608. **3.** *Naval.* A document granted to a neutral merchant-vessel, esp. in time of war, by a power at peace with the state to which it belongs, authorizing it to proceed without molestation in certain waters; a sea-letter 1581. †**4.** A licence to import or export dutiable goods duty-free, or contraband goods on payment of the duties –1741. **5.** *fig.* **a.** An authorization to pass or go anywhere 15.. **b.** A warrant of admission into some society, state, or sphere of action 1581. **c.** A voucher 1578.

1. *Letters of p.* = sense 2. **2.** *transf.* Formal passports, signed and sealed for heaven 1717. **5. a.** Goe lyttle Calender, thou hast a free passeporte SPENSER. **b.** His p. is his innocence and grace DRYDEN. **c.** Looke on his Letter Madam, here's my Pasport SHAKS. Hence **Pa·ssport** *v.* to furnish with a p. **Pa·ssportless** *a.*

‖**Passus** (pæ·sŏs). 1575. [L., = step, pace, etc.] A section, division, or canto of a story or poem.

Password (pɑ·s,wɒɹd). 1817. [f. PASS *sb.*[2] + WORD *sb.*] A word authorizing the utterer to pass; *esp. Mil.* a parole, a watchword. **b.** *fig.* = Watchword; secret of admittance 1836.

Passy-measures: see PASSEMEASURE.

Past (pɑst), *ppl. a.* and *sb.* ME. [pa. pple. of PASS *v.*; cf. Fr. *passé*, L. *præteritus.*] **A.** *ppl. a.* **I.** Predicatively after *be*: Gone by in time; elapsed; over.

Surely the bitteresse of death is p. 1 *Sam.* 15:32.

II. *attrib.* **1.** That is passed away, bygone; elapsed (of time); belonging to former days ME. **2.** Gone by immediately before the present time; just past. Often strengthened by *last* (see LAST *adv.* B. 2). ME. **3.** Of or relating to bygone time; in *Gram.*, Expressing past action or state, preterite; as in *p. tense, p. participle* 1530. **4.** In the use of various societies: Having served one's term of office. Cf. PAST-MASTER.

1. A narration of events, either p., present, or to come JOWETT. **2.** About forty years p. (= ago) WALTON. For several months p., I have enjoyed such liberty BERKELEY. *ellipt.* I have yours of the 28th p. (= last month, *ultimo*) to acknowledge WARBURTON.

B. *sb.* [ellipt. uses of A.] **1.** *The p.*: All time before the present; bygone days collectively, past time 1590. **b.** That which happened in the past 1665. **2.** A past life, career, or history; a stage that one has passed through; *esp.* a past life over which a veil is drawn 1836. **3.** *Gram.* (*ellipt.*) = *Past tense*: see A. 3. 1783.

1. The storied P. TENNYSON. **2.** A woman..who has had a p. 1876.

Past (pɑst), *prep.* and *adv.* ME. [Developed from pa. pple. of PASS *v.* (conjugated with the vb. *to be*) in uses such as 'Now is (= has) the king *passed* (*past*) the sea'.] **A.** *prep.* **1.** Beyond in time (as the result of passing); after; beyond the age or time for. **b.** *ellipt.* Beyond the age of (so many years) 1560. **2.** Beyond in place (as the result of passing); further on than ME. **b.** Of motion: By (in passing) 1542. **3.** Beyond the reach, range, or compass of; incapable of. Occas. = No longer capable of or within the scope of. late ME. **b.** Beyond the ability or power of (*colloq.*) 1611. **c.** Beyond the limits of; without (now *dial.*) 1470. †**4.** More than, above –1668. **b.** Beyond in manner or degree. Now *rare.* 1611.

1. It was passed 8 of the clokke CHAUCER. After he was p. the Age of one hundred Years 1709. **b.** Augustus..injoin'd Marriage to all p. 25 Years 1718. **2.** Until we be [*R.V.* have] p. thy borders *Num.* 21:22. **b.** Phr. *To go p.*, to pass; so *to flow, ride, run, hurry*, etc. *p.* (a person or place). **3.** Phr. *P. belief, comprehension, cure, finding out*, etc.; also, *p. praying for* (colloq.): hopeless. **c.** *P. himself*, beside himself (now *dial.*).

B. *adv.* (absol. use of the prep.; = past the speaker or what is spoken of.) **1.** So as to pass; by 1805. **2.** On one side, aside. *Sc.* and *north Irel.* 1830.

1. The alarum of drums swept p. LONGF. **2.** Phr. *To lay p.*, to put by or save up.

Paste (pēⁱst), *sb.* late ME. [– OFr. *paste* (mod. *pâte*) :– late L. *pasta* small square piece of a medicinal preparation, Marcellus Empiricus *c* 400; (cf. med.L. *pasta* dough) – Gr. πάστη, also pl. παστά, πασταί barley porridge, subst. uses of παστός sprinkled, f. πάσσειν sprinkle.] **1.** *Cookery.* Flour moistened and kneaded, dough; now only, with addition of butter, lard, suet, or the like. **b.** Applied to compositions of this consistence used as baits in angling 1653. **c.** A relish of some fish, crustacean, or meat, cooked, pounded or minced, and seasoned; as *anchovy-p.*, *shrimp-p.* 1817. **2.** A cement made of flour and water (sometimes with starch) boiled together; used for sticking paper, etc. 1530. **3.** *gen.* Any soft and plastic composition or mixture 1604. **4.** *fig.* The material of which a person is figuratively said to be made (in ref. to quality) 1645. **5.** A hard vitreous composition (of fused silica, potash, white oxide of lead, borax, etc.), used in making imitations of precious stones; a gem made of this. Also called STRASS. Also *attrib.* 1662. **6.** *Min.* A mineral substance in which other minerals are embedded 1828. †**7.** A head-dress (app. with a foundation of pasteboard) worn by women –1592.

4. The Inhabitants of that Town, methinks, are made of another p. 1645.

Comb.: **p.-cutter,** an instrument for cutting p. into shapes for pastry; **-eel,** a small nematoid worm (*Anguillula glutinis*) found in sour p.: **p. grain,** split sheep-skin with p. put on the back to harden it and give it a better grain.

Paste (pēⁱst), *v.* 1561. [f. prec.] **1.** *trans.* To fasten with paste. Also *transf.* and *fig.* **2.** To cover by (or as by) pasting over 1609. **3.** *slang.* To beat, thrash: cf. BASTE *v.*³ 1851.

1. *To p. up*, to stick up (on a wall, etc.) with paste **2.** Pasting a screen..all over with prints 1849.

Comb.: **p.-down,** an outer blank leaf of a book pasted on the cover; **-in** *a.*, pasted in, inserted by pasting.

Pasteboard (pēⁱ·stbōᵊɹd), *sb.* (*a.*) 1548. [f. PASTE *sb.* or *v.* + BOARD *sb.*] **A. I.** †**1.** A substitute for a thin wooden board made by pasting sheets of paper together; *esp.* a board of a book so made (cf. BOARD *sb.*) –1796. **2.** A stiff firm substance made by pasting together, compressing, and rolling three or more sheets of paper; a piece of this 1562. **b.** *fig.* As the type of anything flimsy, unsubstantial, or counterfeit 1829. **3.** *slang.* A card. **a.** A visiting-card 1837. **b.** A playing-card; also playing-cards collectively 1859. **c.** A railway-ticket 1901. **II.** *Cookery.* (Usu. with hyphen.) A board on which paste or dough is rolled out for making pastry, etc. 1858. **B.** *attrib.* (or as *adj.*) Made of pasteboard 1599. **b.** *fig.* Unsubstantial; unreal, counterfeit, sham 1659.

b. The p. triumph and the cavalcade GOLDSM.

Paste-egg: see PASCH-EGG.

Pastel¹ (pæ·stĕl). 1578. [– Fr. *pastel* – Pr. *pastel*, dim. of *pasta* PASTE *sb.*; see -EL.] The plant Woad, *Isatis tinctoria*; also, the blue dye obtained from it.

Pastel² (pæ·stĕl). 1662. [– Fr. *pastel*, or its source It. *pastello*; see prec.] **1.** A kind of dry paste made by compounding ground pigments with gum-water, used as a crayon or for making crayons. **2.** A drawing in pastel; also, the art of drawing with pastels 1855. **3.** Applied to certain soft tints of dress-material; usu. *attrib.* 1899.

2. Two charming portraits,..two pastels 1893. Hence **Pa·stellist, pastelist,** an artist who works with pastels.

Paster (pēⁱ·stəɹ). 1737. [f. PASTE *v.* + -ER¹.] **1.** One who pastes. **2.** *U.S.* A small slip of gummed paper, which a voter pastes over any name he objects to on the ballot paper 1888.

Pastern (pæ·stəɹn). [ME. *pastron* – OFr. *pasturon* (mod. *pâturon*), f. *pasture* (dial. *pâture*) hobble, alt. by change of suffix of **pastoire* – med.L. *pastoria*, *-orium*, subst. uses of fem. and n. of L. *pastorius*, pertaining to a shepherd, f. *pastor* PASTOR. Cf. AL. *pastro*, *pastronus* (XIII, XIV).] †**1.** A shackle fixed on the foot of a horse, or other beast; a hobble –1625. **2.** That part of a horse's foot between the fetlock and the hoof 1530. **b.** The corresponding part in other animals; also *transf.* the human ankle 1555. **3.** = Pastern-bone 1656.

attrib. and Comb.: **p.-joint,** the joint or articulation between the cannon-bone and the great pastern-bone; **p.-bone,** each of the two bones (*upper* or *great*, and *lower* or *small p.*) between the cannon-bone and the coffin-bone, being the first and second phalanges of the foot of a horse.

Pasteurism (pɑ·störiz'm). 1883. [f. name of Louis *Pasteur*, a Fr. scientist (1822–95) + -ISM.] Pasteur's method of treating certain diseases, esp. hydrophobia, by successive inoculations with attenuated virus gradually increasing in amount.

Pasteurize (pɑ·störəiz), *v.* 1881. [f. as prec. + -IZE.] **1.** *trans.* To sterilize by Pasteur's method; to prevent or arrest fermentation in (milk, wine, etc.) by exposure to a high temperature so as to destroy microbes or germs. **2.** To treat by the method of PASTEURISM 1886. Hence **Pa:steuriza·tion. Pa·steurizer,** an apparatus for pasteurizing milk.

‖**Pasticcio** (pasti·ttʃo). 1752. [– It. *pasticcio* pie, pasty, etc. :– Rom. **pasticius*, f. late L. *pasta* PASTE *sb.*] A medley; a hotchpotch, farrago, jumble; *spec.* **a.** A musical composition made up of pieces from different sources, a pot-pourri; **b.** A picture or design made up of fragments pieced together, or in professed imitation of the style of another artist; also the style of such a picture, etc.

‖**Pastiche** (pasti·ʃ). 1878. [Fr. – It. *pasticcio*; see prec.] = prec.

Pastil, pastille (pæ·stil, pæstī·l), *sb.* 1648. [– Fr. *pastille* – L. *pastillus* little loaf or roll, lozenge, dim. of **pasnis*, *panis* loaf.] **1.** A small roll of aromatic paste for burning as a perfume, now esp. as a fumigator, deodorizer, or disinfectant 1658. **2.** A sugared confection of a rounded flat shape (often medicated); a troche, lozenge 1648. **3.** = PASTEL² 1. 1662. **4.** *attrib.* 1833.

Pastime (pɑ·stəim), *sb.* 1489. [f. PASS *v.* + TIME; in sense 1 tr. Fr. *passe-temps.*] **1.** *gen.* That which serves to pass the time agreeably; diversion, entertainment, amusement, sport; occas. †occupation. (No *pl.*) 1490. **b.** With *a* and *pl.* A recreation; a sport, a game 1489. †**2.** A passing or elapsing of time; a space of time; an interval between two points of time –1529.

1. b. The Wood-Nymphs deckt with Daisies trim, Their merry wakes and pastimes keep MILT. Hence **Pa·stime** *v.* (now *rare*) *intr.* to pass one's time pleasantly, to entertain or amuse oneself; *trans.* to divert, amuse.

Past-master, past master (pɑ·st mɑ:stəɹ). 1762. [In sense 1 f. PAST *ppl. a.*; in sense 2 later sp. of PASSED-MASTER.] **1.** One who has filled the office of 'master' in a guild, civic company, freemasons' lodge, etc. **2.** A thorough master (of a subject). Const. *in*, *of*. 1868. So **Pa·st-mi:stress** (in sense 2).

Pastor (pɑ·stəɹ), *sb.* late ME. [– AFr., OFr. *pastour* (mod. *pasteur*), acc. of *pastre* (mod. *pâtre* shepherd) :– L. *pastor*, *pastōr-*, f. *past-*, pa. ppl. stem of *pascere* feed, graze; see -OR 2.] **1.** A herdsman or shepherd. Now *rare.* **2.** A shepherd of souls; *spec.* the minister in charge of a church or congregation, with particular ref. to the spiritual care of his 'flock'. late ME. **3.** One who protects or guides a number of people. late ME. **4.** *Ornith.* A genus of starlings, of which the species *Pastor roseus* is an occasional visitor to the British islands 1825. **5.** A small tropical fish (*Nomeus gronovii*); called also *Portuguese man-of-war fish* 1902.

3. A Moses or a David, pastors of their people BACON. Hence **Pa·stor** *v.*, to take charge of (a spiritual flock) as a p. **Pa·storage** (*rare*), †the function of a p.; also, a parsonage.

Pastoral (pɑ·stŏrăl), *a.* and *sb.* late ME. [– L. *pastoralis*, f. *pastor* PASTOR. Cf. (O)Fr. *pastoral.*] **A.** *adj.* **I. 1.** Of or pertaining to shepherds or their occupation; of the nature of a shepherd. **2.** Of land: Used for pasture. Hence of scenery, etc.: Having the simplicity or natural charm associated with such country. 1790. **3.** Of literature, music, etc.: Portraying country life; expressed in pastorals 1581.

1. Or sound of p. reed with oaten stops MILT.

II. Of or pertaining to a pastor or shepherd of souls; having relation to the spiritual care to a 'flock' of Christians 1526.

P. epistles, the epistles of Paul to Timothy and Titus, which deal largely with the work of a pastor. *P. staff* = CROSIER 3.

B. *sb.* (The adj. used ellipt.) **I.** †**1.** *pl.* Pastoral games SIDNEY. **2.** A poem, play, etc., in which the life of shepherds is portrayed, often in a conventional manner; also extended to works dealing with country life generally 1584. **b.** A pastoral picture 1819. **c.** *Mus.* = PASTORALE 1851. **3.** Pastoral poetry as a mode of literary composition 1598.

3. The Golden Age is not to be regilt; P. is gone out, and Pan extinct HOOD.

II. 1. a. 'A book relating to the cure of souls' (J.). late ME. **b.** A letter from a spiritual pastor to his flock; *esp.* a letter from a bishop to the clergy or people of his diocese 1865. **c.** *pl.* The pastoral epistles; see A. II. 1901. **2.** A pastoral staff, a crosier 1658. Hence **Pa·storally** *adv.* **Pa·storalism,** p. quality or character; the p. style in literature. **Pa·storalist,** a writer of pastorals; also, one who lives by keeping flocks of sheep or cattle; *spec.* (*Australia*) a sheep-farmer, a squatter.

‖**Pastorale** (pastorā·le, *-i*). *Pl.* **-ali** (-ā·li), **-ales.** 1724. [It., sb. use of *pastorale* adj. PASTORAL.] *Mus.* **a.** An instrumental composition in pastoral style, or representing pastoral sounds and scenes; usu. a simple melody in 6–8 time. **b.** An opera, cantata, etc., the subject of which is pastoral.

Pastorality (pɑstŏræ·lĭti). 1506. [f. PASTORAL + -ITY.] Pastoral quality or character.

Pa·storalize, *v.* 1825. [f. as prec. + -IZE.] **1.** *trans.* To make pastoral or rural. **2.** To put into or celebrate in a pastoral 1839.

Pastorate (pɑ·stŏrĕt). 1795. [f. PASTOR + -ATE¹.] **1.** The office or position of a pastor; the tenure of such office. **2.** Pastors collectively 1846.

Pastorly (pɑ·stəɹli), *a.* 1616. [f. PASTOR + -LY¹.] Of, pertaining to, or befitting a pastor; pastor-like.

Pastorship (pɑ·stəɹʃip). 1563. [f. PASTOR + -SHIP.] = PASTORATE.

Pastry (pēⁱ·stri). 1539. [f. PASTE *sb.*, after OFr. *pastaierie*, f. *pastaier* pastry-cook; see -RY.] **1.** Articles of food made of or with paste (see PASTE *sb.* 1); now only, such articles when baked, as pies, tarts, etc. **2.** A place where pastry is made. *Obs.* exc. *Hist.* 1570. †**3.** The art and business of a pastry-cook –1752.

Comb. **p.-cook,** one who makes p., *esp.* for public sale.

Pasturable (pɑ·stiŭrăb'l, -tʃər-). *a.* 1577. [– Fr. †*pasturable* (now *pâturable*) in same sense; see PASTURE, -ABLE.] That may be pastured; fit for pasture.

Pasturage (pɑ·stiŭrĕdʒ, -tʃər-). 1533. [– OFr. *pasturage* (mod. *pâturage*); see PASTURE, -AGE.] **1.** The action or occupation of pasturing; grazing 1579. **2.** = PASTURE *sb.* 3. 1540. **3.** = PASTURE *sb.* 4. 1533.

Pasture (pɑ·stiŭɹ, -tʃəɹ), *sb.* ME. [– OFr. *pasture* (mod. *pâture*) :– late L. *pastura*, f. *past-*, pa. ppl. stem of L. *pascere* feed, pasture; see -URE.] **1.** The action of feeding (said of animals); *spec.* the grazing of cattle (*rare*). late ME. †**2.** Food, sustenance (*lit.* and *fig.*) –1786. **3.** The growing herbage eaten by cattle ME. **4.** A piece of land covered with this; grass-land. ME.

3. Twenty acres..For p. ten, and ten for plough PRIOR. *Common p.*, the use of p. by the cattle of a number of owners.' *Common of p.*: see COMMON *sb.* 4. **4.** *fig.* The Lord my P. shall prepare ADDISON. So **Pa·stural** *a.* of or pertaining to p.

Pasture (pɑ·stiŭɹ, -tʃəɹ), *v.* late ME. [– OFr. *pasturer* (mod. *pâturer*), f. *pasture* (*pâture*); see prec.] †**1.** *intr.* Of cattle, sheep, etc.: To graze. Also *fig.* **2.** *trans.* To lead or put (cattle) to pasture. late ME. **3.** (Of sheep or cattle) To graze upon (herbage, grass-land), to eat down; (of persons) to put sheep or cattle on (grass-land, etc.) to graze 1533.

2. Here Uzziah pastured his cattel FULLER. Hence **Pa·sturer** (*rare*), one who pastures cattle, a herdsman or grazier.

Pasty (pæ·sti, pēⁱ·sti), *sb.* ME. [– OFr. *pastée*, *paste* (mod. *pâtée*, *pâté*) :– med.L. **pastata*, *-latum*, f. late L. *pasta* PASTE; cf. MDu. *pastei(d)e*, (M)HG. *pastete*, see -Y⁵.] A pie, consisting usu. of seasoned venison or other meat, but sometimes of apples, jam, etc., enclosed in a crust of pastry, and baked without a dish.

The venison p. was palpable beef, which was not handsome PEPYS.

Pasty (pēⁱ·sti), *a.* 1607. [f. PASTE *sb.* + -Y¹.] Like paste in consi tence, appearance, or colour; *esp.* of the complexion: pale and dull. **b.** Of or pertaining to paste jewellery 1865. Hence **Pa·stiness,** p. quality.

Pat (pæt), *sb.*[1] [Late ME. *pat, patte*; prob. imit. App. formed anew in XVII f. the verb.] **I.** The action. **1.** A stroke or blow with a flat or blunt surface. *Obs.* exc. *dial.* **2. a.** A stroke or tap with a flat surface, so as to flatten or smooth. **b.** *spec.* A gentle tap with the hand or fingers, esp. as a caress or in approbation. Also *fig.* 1804.

2. b. A word of approbation — a little p. on the back, as I may say 1898.

II. a. A small mass of some soft substance (*e.g.* butter) formed or shaped by patting 1754. **b.** Something of the shape and size, or appearance, of a pat of butter, etc. 1852. **III.** The sound. **a.** The sound made by striking lightly with something flat; *esp.* with the foot in walking or running 1697. **b.** Reduplicated to express repetition 1876.

Pat (pæt), *sb.*[2] 1825. [abbrev. of *Patrick.*] A nickname for an Irishman; cf. PADDY[2].

Pat (pæt), *v.* 1567. [f. or related to PAT *sb.*[1]] †**1.** *trans.* To cause (something) to strike or hit *upon* any surface GOLDING. **2.** To hit, to strike, prop. with a flat or blunt instrument; also, to drive by so striking, as a ball with the hand. *Obs.* exc. *dial.* 1591. **3.** *intr.* To tap or beat lightly (*upon* any surface) 1601. **4.** *trans.* To strike (something) gently with a flat surface, so as to flatten or smooth; to flatten down by such action 1607. **5.** *esp.* To strike or clap gently with the fingers or hand, by way of approbation, encouragement, sympathy, etc.; hence *fig.* to express such feeling to (any one), esp. in *to p. on the back* 1714. **6.** *intr.* To tap or strike lightly so as to produce a characteristic sound. Also reduplicated, *pat-pat.* 1760. **7.** The vb.-stem as adv. or int. 1681.

5. The child patted Caroline's cheek 1813. We.. p. every man on the back who has the courage of his convictions 1884. **6.** A short quick step she hears Come patting close behind 1801. **7.** Still on, p., p., the Goblin went 1801.

Comb.: **p.-ball,** the game of rounders; also, poor or feeble lawn tennis.

Pat (pæt). *adv.* and *a.* 1578. [app. closely related to PAT *sb.*[1], *v.*; perh. from the vb.-stem.] **1.** *adv.* In a way that hits its object or aim; appositely; opportunely; so as to be ready for any occasion, readily, promptly. **2.** *predic.* as *adv.* or *adj.* 1638. **3.** *attrib.* or as *adj.* That comes or lies exactly to the purpose; apposite, apt; opportune. (Said esp. of things spoken.) 1646. **b.** *P. hand* (Poker), a hand so good when first dealt that it is not likely to be improved by drawing other cards. *Stand p.*: see STAND *v.* I. 10. 1889.

1. I came just p. to be a godfather PEPYS. **2.** A passage..very p. to his purpose 1656. **3.** A story so p., you may think it is coined COWPER. Hence **Pa·tly** *adv.* = 1. **Pa·tness,** the quality or condition of being p. or to the point; aptness.

Pa·t-a-cake. First words of a nursery rhyme, said or chanted to accompany the action of patting or clapping together a child's hands; also a game played in doing this.

‖**Pata·che.** 1589. [– Fr. *patache* (XVI) or Sp. *patache* – Arab. *baṭāš* large two-masted ship.] A small boat, used for communications between the vessels of a fleet. *Obs.* exc. *Hist.*

†**Patacoo·n.** 1584. [– Sp. *patacon,* also *patacchina* – Pg. *patacão,* augm. of *pataca* piece of eight, dollar.] A Pg. and Sp. silver coin, worth, in the 17th c., about 4*s.* 8*d.* English –1749.

‖**Patagium** (pætădʒəi·ŏm). *Pl.* **-ia.** 1826. [med.L., from ancient L. *patagium* gold edging on a tunic = Gr. παταγεῖον.] **a.** A fold of skin or membrane extending along the side of the body of certain flying mammals and reptiles; the wing-membrane of a bat, etc. **b.** *Ornith.* The fold or integument occupying the angle between the upper arm and the forearm of birds. **c.** *Entom.* Name for each of a pair of processes or appendages on the pronotum or thorax of certain Lepidoptera. Hence **Patagial** (pătē[i]·dʒiăl), **Pata·giate** *adjs.*

†**Pa·tagon.** 1579. [– Sp. *patagon* large clumsy foot.] A member of a tribe of S. American Indians, whence Patagonia received its name –1773.

Patagonian (pætăgō[u]·niăn), *a.* and *sb.* 1767. [f. *Patagonia*; see prec. and -AN.] **A.** *adj.* Of or pertaining to Patagonia or its inhabitants; hence †Gigantic, huge, immense. **B.** *sb.* A S. American Indian of a race inhabiting southern Patagonia, said to be the tallest known people; hence, *fig.* †a giant, a gigantic specimen 1767.

‖**Patas** (patā·). 1745. [Fr., from a dialect of Senegal.] The red monkey (*Cercopithecus patas*) of W. Africa.

Patavinity (pætăvi·nĭti). 1607. [– L. *patavinitas,* f. *Patavinus* of *Patavium,* now Padua, the birthplace of Livy; see -INE[1], -ITY.] The dialectal characteristics of Patavium or Padua, as shown in Livy's writings; hence *gen.* Provincialism in style; also, an instance of this.

Patch (pætʃ), *sb.*[1] [Late ME. *pacche, patche* perh. var. of *peche* (Ancren Riwle) – AFr. **peche,* OFr. *pieche,* dial. var. of *piece* PIECE; for the vocalism cf. CRATCH *sb.*[1], MATCH *sb.*[2]] **1.** A piece of cloth, leather, metal, etc., put on to mend a hole or rent, or to strengthen a weak place. **b.** A piece of court-plaster or the like put over a wound 1591. **c.** A pad worn to protect an injured eye 1598. **2.** A small piece of black silk or court-plaster worn on the face, esp. in 17th and 18th centuries, either to hide a fault or to show off the complexion by contrast 1592. Also *attrib.*, esp. in *p.-box.* **3.** A large or irregular spot on any surface 1573. **b.** A small piece or area of ground, or of anything lying or growing on it 1577. **c.** An area of floating pieces of ice, overlapping one another, of a circular or polygonal form 1817. **d.** *Anat.* and *Path.* A small well-defined area of the skin, etc. distinct in colour or appearance 1797. **4.** A piece of cloth sewed together with others to form patchwork or to adorn a garment 1529. **5.** A small scrap, piece, or remnant of anything 1529. **6.** Anything suggesting a patch (sense 1) in the way it is fastened, or in shape or size, or otherwise 1835.

1. A foul coat full of patches HOBBES. *Phr. Not a p. on* (colloq.), not comparable to, nowhere near. **2.** Your black patches you wear variously, Some cut like stars, some in half moons 1625. **3. b.** A p. of April snow WORDSW. Here and there a p. of potatoes or beans 1894. **5.** A King of shreds and patches SHAKS.

attrib. and *Comb.*: **p. head** (*U.S.* local), the surf-scoter, *Œdemia perspicillata*; **-ice,** pieces of ice overlapping so as to form a p.; **-leather,** leather used in patching; **-polled** *a.*, having a p. of colour on the head, esp. in *patch-polled coot* = *p. head.*

Patch (pætʃ), *sb.*[2] 1549. [perh. anglicized f. It. *pazzo* fool.] A domestic fool; a clown, dolt, booby. Now only *dial.* or *colloq.* applied to an ill-natured person, esp. a child, etc. Hence †**Pa·tchery**[2], the conduct of a p.; roguery, knavery –1607.

Patch (pætʃ), *v.* 1500. [f. PATCH *sb.*[1]] **1.** *trans.* To put a patch or patches on; of a thing, to serve as a patch to 1516. **b.** In pa. pple., said of a person in reference to his clothing, etc. 1500. **2.** To mend, repair, or make whole, in various *fig.* applications. (Usu. with *up,* and implying a hasty, clumsy, or temporary manner.) 1573. **3.** To make by joining pieces together as in patchwork; hence, to botch *up* 1529. **4.** To put on or in as a patch. Also *fig.*; often depreciatory. 1549. **b.** To piece together 1630. **5.** To diversify or variegate with patches. (Chiefly in pass.) 1595. **6.** To adorn (a person, the face) with patches. Also *intr.* for *refl.* 1674.

1. Windows patched with rags and paper DICKENS. *P. up,* to mend by putting patches on. **2.** Sin that amends, is but patcht with vertue SHAKS. You'll have to..p. up your quarrel 1875. **3.** Out of what booke patched you out Cicero's Oration? LODGE. **4. b.** It is just possible to p. the two narratives together 1867. **5.** Grey rocks patched with moss 1774. **6.** But alas, Madam, who patch'd you today? STEELE. Hence **Patched** *ppl. a.* **Pa·tcher;** also *patcher-up.* **Pa·tchery**[1], the action of patching; a patchwork (usu. *fig.*). **Pa·tching** *vbl. sb.*, the action of the vb.; also the condition of being patched.

Pa·tch-box. 1674. [f. PATCH *sb.*[1] 2 + BOX *sb.*[2]] A box for holding patches for the face.

Patchouli (pæ·tʃuli, pătʃū·li). 1845. [Vernacular name in Madras.] **1.** An odoriferous plant (*Pogostemon patchouli,* N.O. *Labiatæ*), native to Silhat, Penang, and the Malay Peninsula; it yields an essential oil, from which the scent (sense 2) is derived 1851. **2.** A penetrating perfume made from this plant 1845. **3.** *attrib.*, as *p. oil* 1881.

Patchwork (pæ·tʃ,wɒɹk). 1692. [f. PATCH *v.* or *sb.*[1] + WORK *sb.*] **1.** Work made up of pieces or fragments put together, esp. in an incongruous manner; a thing patched up; a medley, a jumble. Now often viewed as *fig.* from 2. **b.** Work of patching up SWIFT. **2.** Work consisting of small pieces of cloth of different kinds and colours sewn together by the edges, so as to make a counterpane, cushion, tea-cosy, etc. 1726. **b.** Any surface divided like such a counterpane 1865. **3.** *attrib.*, as *p. quilt* 1713.

2. *Crazy p.*, that in which the pieces are quite irregular in shape and size. **3.** Second-hand minds and p. intellects 1814.

Patchy (pæ·tʃi), *a.* 1798. [f. PATCH *sb.*[1] + -Y[1].] Abounding in or consisting of patches; resembling patchwork in appearance or structure. Hence **Pa·tchily** *adv.* **Pa·tchiness.**

Pate (pē[i]t). ME. [Of unkn. origin.] **1.** The head, the skull; esp. the crown of the head. (Not now in serious or dignified use.) **2.** The head as the seat of intellect; hence, skill, cleverness, 'brains', and formerly occas. for a person having these (*arch.* or *poet.*) 1610. **3.** The skin of a calf's head 1687.

1. His vnhappynes shall come vpon his owne heade, and his wickednes shall fall vpon his owne p. COVERDALE *Ps.* 7:16. **2.** An excellent passe of p. SHAKS.

‖**Pâté** (pate). 1704. [Fr. (OFr. *pasté*; see PASTY *sb.*)] **1.** A pie, pasty, or patty. **2.** *Fortif.* (Erron. written *pate.*) A kind of oval platform, with a parapet, usu. erected in marshy grounds to cover a gate of a town 1704.

1. *P. de foie gras,* pasty of fatted goose liver, Strasburg pie.

Pated (pē[i]·tėd), *a.* 1580. [f. PATE + -ED[2].] Having a pate (of a specified kind); as *empty-p.*

†**Patefa·ction.** 1553. [– L. *patefactio,* f. *patefact-,* pa. ppl. stem of *patefacere*; see next, -ION.] The action of making open, visible, or known; a disclosing, revelation, declaration –1872.

†**Pa·tefy,** *v.* 1533. [– L. *patefacere* disclose, f. *patere* be open + *facere* make; see -FY.] *trans.* To make open; to disclose, manifest –1788.

‖**Patella** (păte·lă). 1671. [L., = pan, knee-pan, dim. of *patina* PATEN.] **1.** *Anat.* The knee-pan or knee-cap. Also *transf.* **2.** *Archæol.* A small pan or shallow vessel; the vessel so called by the Romans 1851. **3.** A natural formation in plants or animals in the form of a shallow pan 1671. **4.** *Zool.* A genus of Mollusca, containing the common limpet 1753. Hence **Patellar** (pæ·tĕlăɹ, pătĕ·lăɹ) *a.* of or pertaining to the p. or knee-pan. **Pa·tellate** *a.* furnished with, or formed into or like, a p. **Pate·lliform** *a.* having the form of a p., knee-pan, or limpet-shell.

‖**Patellula** (păte·liŭlă). 1890. [mod.L. dim. of *patella*; see -ULE.] A small patella; one of the sucking discs or cups on the tarsus of water-beetles.

Paten (pæ·tĕn). [ME. *pateyne, patyn* – AFr. **pateine,* (O)Fr. *patène* or L. *patina, -ena* shallow dish or cooking-pan – Gr. πατάνη plate, dish.] **1.** The shallow dish, usu. circular and of silver, on which the bread is laid at the celebration of the Eucharist. **2.** *gen.* A shallow dish or plate. *arch.* or *Hist.* late ME. **3.** A thin circular plate of metal; anything resembling or suggesting this 1596.

3. Looke how the floore of heauen Is thicke inlayed with pattens of bright gold SHAKS.

Patency (pē[i]·tĕnsi). 1656. [f. PATENT; see -ENCY.] **1.** The state or condition of being open or exposed to view. **2.** The condition of being open, expanded, or unobstructed, as a passage 1843.

Patent (pē[i]·tĕnt, pæ·t-), *sb.* late ME. [Ellipsis of *letter(s* in *letter(s) patent* (see next). So AFr. *patente,* AL. *patens.*] **1.** = *letters patent*: see next I. 1. †**b.** = INDULGENCE II. 1. ME. only. †**c.** An official certificate or licence; *esp.* a health certificate –1666. **2.** A licence to manufacture, sell, or deal in an article, to the exclusion of other persons; now, a grant from a government to a person or persons conferring for a certain definite time the exclusive privilege of making, using, or selling some new invention 1588. **3.** A process which has been patented 1862. **4.** A territory, district, or piece of land conferred by letters patent. *U.S.* 1632. **5.** *fig.* A sign or token that one is entitled to something; authority to do something; title to possess something 1590.

1. I..was examined..and gott my p. of Doctor ther 1695. **2.** Abuses practised by Monopolies and Patents of priviledge 1597. **4.** It is not my intent to wander far from our P. 1634. **5.** Giue her pattent to offend, for if it touch not you, it comes neere no body SHAKS.

attrib. and *Comb.*, as *p. law*; **p. office,** an office where patents are issued and where the claims to patents are examined; **p.-right,** the exclusive right conferred by letters patent; **-roll,** a parchment roll containing the letters patent issued in Great Britain in any one year. Hence **Pa·tentor** (*a*) one who grants a p.; (*b*) a patentee.

Patent (pēⁱ·tĕnt, pæ·tĕnt), *a.* late ME. [In I – (O)Fr. *patent, -ente* – L. *patens, patent-*, pr. pple. of *patēre* lie open; orig. – (O)Fr. *lettres patentes*, med.L. *litteræ patentes*; in II directly – L.] **I. 1.** In *letters p.* (L. *litteræ patentes*, Fr. *lettres patentes*): An open letter or document, usu. from a sovereign or person in authority, issued for various purposes; now esp. to grant for a statutory term to a person or persons the sole right to make, use, or sell some invention. Also *fig.* **2.** Conferred by letters patent; endowed with a patent. Of a person: Appointed by letters patent. 1597. **3.** Of an invention: Protected or covered by letters patent. Also in the names of inventions of which the patent has expired, as *p. leather*: see LEATHER *sb.* 1. 1707. **b.** *fig.* and *transf.* To which one has a proprietary claim; also, special for its purpose; sovereign, superlative 1797.

1. Richard II was the first to confer the peerage by letters-p. 1863. The Letters P. were..written upon open sheets of parchment, with the Great Seal pendent at the bottom 1891. **3.** The venders of p. or quack medicines 1799. **b.** That p. Christianity which has been for some time manufacturing at Clapham SYD. SMITH.

II. 1. Open as a door, gate, etc. 1513. **2.** Open as to situation; unenclosed; freely accessible. Now *rare*. late ME. **3.** Spreading, expanded; *spec.* in *Bot.* opening wide, as petals; diverging widely from the axis, as branches or leaves; *Zool.* patulous; having a wide aperture, or a shallow cavity 1753. **4.** = OPEN *a.* I. 5, II. 1. 1508. **5.** Open to general knowledge or use; public 1566.

2. A circular temple, p. to the sun 1839. **4.** A p. fact, as certain as anything in mathematics 1874. Hence **Pa·tently** *adv.* in a p. manner; openly, evidently, clearly.

Patent (pēⁱ·tĕnt, pæ·t-), *v.* 1822. [f. PATENT *sb.* and *a.*] **1.** *trans.* To grant a patent to; to admit to some privilege or rank by letters patent (*rare*) 1828. **2.** To take out or obtain a patent for 1822. **3.** To obtain a patent right to land. *U.S.* 1874.

2. *fig.* A tendency..to fall into a style patented by Ouida 1900. Hence **Pa·tentable** *a.* capable of being patented.

Patentee (pēⁱtĕntī·, pæt-). late ME. [f. PATENT *sb.* + -EE¹.] One to whom letters patent have been granted; now *esp.* one who has patented an invention. Also *fig.*

‖**Pater.** ME. [L., = father.] **1.** (pæ·təɹ) = PATERNOSTER 1. **2.** (pēⁱ·təɹ) Schoolboys' slang for *father* 1728.

‖**Patera** (pæ·tĕră). *Pl.* **-æ.** 1658. [L., f. *patēre* be open.] **1.** *Rom. Antiq.* A broad flat saucer or dish, used esp. in pouring out libations as sacrifices. **2.** *Arch.* An ornament resembling a shallow dish; any flat round ornament in bas-relief 1776.

‖**Paterfamilias** (pēⁱ:təɹ-, pæ:təɹfămi·liæs). late ME. [L., f. *pater* father + arch. gen. of *familia* FAMILY.] **1.** *Rom. Law.* The head of a family or household; also, a person of either sex and any age who is *sui juris* and free from parental control 1850. **2.** The (male) head of a family or household. late ME. Now chiefly *joc.*

Paternal (pătə̄·ɹnăl), *a.* 1605. [– late L. *paternalis*, f. L. *paternus*, f. *pater* father; see -AL¹. Cf. Fr. *paternel.*] **1.** Of or belonging to a father or to fathers; fatherly. **b.** Of or belonging to one's father 1667. **c.** That is a father 1667. **2.** Inherited or derived from a father; related on the father's side 1611.

1. *P. government*, government as by a father, paternalism. **c.** P. God in Filial shines, And in our Bliss with Filial joyns KEN. **2.** My p. grandmother ..ran away with my p. grandfather RUSKIN. So **Pate·rnally** *adv.* 1603.

Paternalism (pătə̄·ɹnăliz'm). 1881. [-ISM.] **1.** The principle and practice of paternal administration; government as by a father. **2.** The principle of acting in a way like that of a father towards his children 1893. So **Paternali·stic** *a.* of, pertaining to, or of the nature of p.

Paternity (pătə̄·ɹnĭti). late ME. [– (O)Fr. *paternité* or late L. *paternitas*, f. *paternus*; see -ITY.] **1.** The quality of being a father; the relation of a father; fatherhood 1582. †**b.** Patriarchal rule –1711. **2.** The quality or personality of an eccl. father: used as a title, *Your, His P.*; †also, a monk or priest. late ME. **3.** Paternal origin or descent. Also *fig.* 1868.

1. Having been spared the cares..of p. 1786. **3.** The secret of the baby's p. 1882. *fig.* Many of the historical proverbs have a doubtful p. EMERSON.

Paternoster (pæ·təɹnǫ·stəɹ), *sb.* OE. [– L. *pater noster* 'our Father', the first two words of the Lord's Prayer in Latin.] **1.** The Lord's Prayer, esp. in Latin. **b.** A repetition of this as an act of worship ME. **2.** *transf.* **a.** Any form of words repeated by way of a prayer, imprecation, or charm. late ME. **b.** A long nonsensical or tedious recital or utterance 1663. **3.** A special bead in a rosary indicating that a paternoster is to be said; also, the whole rosary ME. **4.** Anything resembling a rosary: in *Fishing*, = *p.-line* 1839.

2. a. *Black P., White P.*, names of specific charms. *Devil's P.*, a murmured or muttered imprecation. *Ape's P.*, a 'dithering' or chattering with the teeth.

attrib. and *Comb.*: **p.-line,** a line used in fishing, with hooks attached at intervals, and weights to sink it; **-pump,** a chain-pump; **-wheel,** a device for raising water, having a number of buckets on a chain; **-while,** the time it takes to say a p. Hence **Pa:terno·ster** *v. intr.* to fish with a paternoster-line.

Path (pɑþ), *sb. Pl.* **paths** (pāðz). [OE. *pæþ* = OFris. *path, pad*, OLG. (Du.) *pad*, (O)HG. *pfad* :– WGmc. *pap-, of unkn. origin.] **1.** A way beaten or trodden by the feet of men or beasts, not expressly planned and constructed; a footway or footpath; hence also a walk made for foot-passengers. **b.** A track specially laid for foot or cycle racing. **c.** A track constructed for some part of machinery to run upon. 1883. **2.** The way, course, or line along which a person or thing moves, passes, or travels OE. **3.** *fig.* A course of action or procedure, line of conduct, etc.; less commonly, a line of thought, argument, etc. OE.

1. The perplex't paths of this drear Wood MILT. **2.** Thy waye was in the see, and thy pathes in the greate waters COVERDALE *Ps.* 76[7]:19. **3.** The paths of glory lead but to the grave GRAY.

Comb.: **p.-finder,** one who discovers a p. or way; an explorer; **-racer,** a bicycle made for racing upon a prepared p. or track; so **p.-racing.** Hence **Pa·thless** *a.*, **-ness.**

†**Path,** *v.* [OE. *pæþþan*, f. *pæþ* PATH *sb.*; later prob. formed anew f. the *sb.*] **1.** *trans.* To go upon or along, to 'tread' (a way, etc.). *lit.* and *fig.* –1807. **2.** To tread, beat down by treading, as a path; usu. *fig.* –1765. **3.** *intr.* To go in or as in a path; to pursue one's course. Also *refl.* –1601.

1. Pathing young Henries unadvised wayes 1598.

Pathan (paþā·n, -thā·n). 1665. [Hind. *Pathān.*] One of a race inhabiting Afghanistan and noted for courage and fierceness in war.

Pathematic (pæþĭmæ·tik), *a. rare.* 1822. [– Gr. παθηματικός liable to passions, f. πάθημα, f. stem παθ-; see next.] Pertaining to the passions or emotions; caused or characterized by emotion. So **Pathema·tically** *adv.* **Pathe:mato·logy,** the doctrine of passions or emotions.

Pathetic (păþe·tik), *a.* (*sb.*) 1598. [– Fr. *pathétique* – late L. *patheticus* – Gr. παθητικός sensitive, f. παθητός liable to suffer, f. παθε- of πάθος; see PATHOS, -IC.] **1.** Producing an effect upon the emotions; moving, stirring, affecting. *Obs.* in gen. sense. **b.** In mod. use: Exciting pity, sympathy, or sadness; full of pathos 1737. †**2.** Arising from strong emotion, passionate, earnest –1755. **3.** Pertaining or relating to the passions or emotions of the mind 1649. **4.** *Anat.* A name for the fourth pair of cranial nerves, also called *trochlear*. So *p. muscle*, the superior oblique muscle of the eyeball, connected with the trochlear nerve. 1681.

1. b. Our parting with our uncle was quite p. LYTTON. **3.** All violent feelings..produce..a falseness in..impressions of external things, which I would generally characterize as the 'P. fallacy' RUSKIN.

B. *absol.* or as *sb.* **1.** *absol. The p.*: that which is pathetic; pathetic quality, expression, or feeling 1712. **2.** †**a.** *sing.* Pathos, or the expression of pathos –1849. **b.** *pl.* Pathetic expressions or sentiments; cf. *heroics* 1748. **3.** *pl.* The study of the passions or emotions 1896. **4.** *Anat.* Short for *p. nerve*: see A. 4. So **Pathe·tical** *a.* (now *rare*), pathetic 1573; **-ly** *adv.*; **-ness** (now *rare* or *Obs.*).

Pathic (pæ·þik), *sb.* and *a.* Now *rare* or *Obs.* 1603. [– L. *pathicus* – Gr. παθικός, f. παθ-; see PATHOS, -IC.] **A.** *sb.* **1.** A man or boy upon whom sodomy is practised; a catamite. **2.** One who suffers or undergoes something 1636.

2. A mere p. to Thy devilish art MASSINGER.

B. *adj.* **1.** Being, or pertaining to, a catamite 1657. **2.** Undergoing something, passive (*rare*) 1857. **3.** Pertaining to suffering or disease; morbid 1853.

Patho- (pæ·þo, păþǫ·), repr. Gr. παθο-, comb. form of πάθος suffering, feeling, disease, etc., as in **Pa·thogen** [-GEN], a micrococcus or bacterium that produces disease. ‖**Pathopœ·ia** [Gr. -ποιία a making] (*a*) *Rhet.* a speech or figure of speech designed to arouse passion or emotion; (*b*) *Path.* production of disease.

Pathogenesis (pæþodʒe·nėsis). 1876. [f. PATHO- + -GENESIS.] *Med.* and *Path.* Production or development of a disease. Also **Pathoge·nesy, Patho·geny,** in same sense. So **Pathogene·tic, Pathoge·nic** *adjs.* producing, or relating to the production of, disease or bodily affection.

Pathognomonic (păþǫgnomǫ·nik), *a.* (*sb.*) 1625. [– Gr. παθογνωμονικός (Galen), skilled in judging of symptoms or diseases, f. παθο- PATHO- + γνωμονικός, f. γνώμων judge.] *Med.* and *Path.* **A.** *adj.* Specifically characteristic or indicative of a particular disease. **B.** *sb.* A pathognomonic sign or symptom 1704.

Pathognomy (păþǫ·gnŏmi). 1793. [f. as prec., after *physiognomy*.] **1.** The knowledge or study of the passions or emotions, or of the signs or expressions of them. **2.** The knowledge of the signs or symptoms by which diseases may be distinguished (*rare*) 1822. So **Pathogno·mic** *a.* of or pertaining to p. 1681. **Pathogno·mical** *a.* 1643.

Pathologic (pæþolǫ·dʒik), *a.* 1656. [– Gr. παθολογικός, f. παθο- PATHO-; see -LOGIC. Cf. Fr. *pathologique.*] Of or belonging to pathology.

Patholo·gical, *a.* 1688. [f. as prec. + -AL¹; see -ICAL.] **1.** Pertaining to or dealing with pathology. **b.** That is or may be the subject of pathology; morbid 1845. **2.** Pertaining to the passions or emotions (*rare*) 1800. Hence **Patholo·gically** *adv.* in relation to pathology.

Pathologist (păþǫ·lŏdʒist). 1650. [f. PATHOLOGY + -IST.] One versed in pathology; a student of or writer upon diseases.

Pathology (păþǫ·lŏdʒi). 1611. [– Fr. *pathologie* or mod.L. *pathologia*; see PATHO-, -LOGY.] **1.** The science or study of disease; that department of medical science, or of physiology, which treats of the causes and nature of diseases, or abnormal bodily affections or conditions. **b.** *transf.* The sum of morbid processes or conditions 1672. **c.** Extended to the study of morbid or abnormal mental or moral conditions 1842. **2.** The study of the passions or emotions (*rare*) 1681.

Pathos (pēⁱ·þǫs). 1579. [– Gr. πάθος suffering, feeling, rel. to πάσχειν suffer, πένθος grief.] **1.** That quality in speech, writing, music, or artistic representation (or *transf.* in events, persons, etc.) which excites a feeling of pity or sadness; power of stirring tender or melancholy emotion 1668. **b.** A pathetic expression or utterance (*rare*) 1579. **2.** Suffering (bodily or mental). *rare.* 1693. **3.** In reference to art, esp. ancient Greek art: The quality of the transient or emotional, as opp. to the permanent or ideal 1881.

1. The tale of Protestant sufferings was told with a wonderful p...by John Foxe 1874.

Pathway (pɑ·pwēⁱ). 1536. A way that constitutes or serves as a path; a path, track, way. (Often *fig.*)

A playne pathwaye to Christ and hys kyngedome BALE. High in his p. hung the Sun SCOTT.

-pathy, repr. Gr. -πάθεια, lit. 'suffering, feeling', the second element of HOMŒOPATHY, extended to ALLOPATHY, and applied, with the sense 'method of cure, curative treatment', to other compounds, as *hydropathy*, etc.

†**Pa·tible,** *sb.* ME. [– L. *patibulum* a fork-shaped yoke, gibbet, etc., f. *patēre* lie open + *-bulum*, forming names of instruments, etc.] A gibbet, a cross; the horizontal bar of a cross –1745.

†**Pa·tible,** *a.* 1600. [– L. *patibilis*, f. *pati* suffer; see -IBLE.] **1.** Capable of suffering or subject to something –1834. **b.** Capable of or liable to suffering; passible –1691. **2.** Capable of being suffered, endurable (Dicts.) –1755.

Patibulary (pǎti·biŭlări), *a. rare.* 1646. [f. L. *patibulum* PATIBLE *sb.* + -ARY[1].] Of or pertaining to the gallows; resembling the gallows; suggesting the gallows or hanging. Chiefly *joc.*

I never saw a more p. phyz 1697. So **Pati·bulate** *v. trans.* to hang.

Patience (pēⁱ·ʃĕns). ME. [– (O)Fr. *patience*, †*pacience* – L. *patientia*, f. *patient-*, pr. ppl. stem of *pati* suffer; see -ENCE.] **I.** The practice or quality of being patient. **1.** The suffering or enduring (of pain, trouble, or evil) with calmness and composure; the quality or capacity of so suffering or enduring. **b.** Forbearance under provocation of any kind; esp. bearing with others, their faults, limitations, etc. late ME. **c.** The calm abiding of the issue of time, processes, etc. late ME. **d.** Constancy in labour, exertion, or effort 1517. **e.** personified. late ME. **2.** With *of*: The fact or capacity of enduring; patient endurance *of* (*rare*) 1530. †**3.** Sufferance; leave –1610.

1. That..We may with p. bear our moderate ills COWPER. **b.** I doe intreat your p. To heare me speake SHAKS. **c.** In your p. possess ye your souls *Luke* 21:19. He had not the p. to expect a present, but demanded one 1615. **d.** He learnt with p., and with meekness taught 1774. **e.** She sate, like P. on a Monument, Smiling at greefe SHAKS. Phrases. *To have p. with* (†*in, toward*), to show forbearance toward; so, *to have no p. with* (colloq.), to be unable to bear patiently. *Out of p.*, advb. phr. (sometimes adj.), provoked so as no longer to have p. with. **2.** P. of hunger 1772. **3.** I can goe no further, Sir,..by your p., I needes must rest me SHAKS.

II. Special senses. **1.** A species of Dock (*Rumex patientia*), formerly used instead of spinach, in salads, etc. *Wild P.*, *Rumex obtusifolius.* 1440. **2.** A game of cards, of which there are many varieties; usu. for one player 1816.

Patience-dock. 1776. [f. PATIENCE II. 1 + DOCK *sb.*[1]] **1.** = prec. II. 1. 1884. **2.** In the north of England, the Bistort (*Polygonum bistorta*), there also called *Passions*, *Passion-dock*, of which the leaves are eaten as greens 1776.

Patient (pēⁱ·ʃĕnt), *a.* and *sb.* ME. [– (O)Fr. *patient* – L. *patiens, patient-*; see PATIENCE, -ENT.] **A.** *adj.* **1.** Bearing or enduring (evil of any kind) with composure; exercising or possessing patience. **b.** Long-suffering, forbearing (*to, towards*). late ME. **c.** Quietly awaiting the course or issue of events, etc. late ME. **d.** Persistent, constant, unwearied in the face of difficulties and hindrances 1590. **e.** *fig.* of things 1820. **2.** Const. *of*: Enduring or able to endure (evil, etc.). 1440. **b.** Of words, etc.: Capable of bearing (a particular interpretation) 1638. **3.** Passive. (Correl. to *agent.*) *rare.* 1611.

1. Job the patientest of men MILT. **b.** Be ȝe pacient to alle men WYCLIF 1 *Thess.* 5: 14. **c.** I know twenty persevering girls for one p. one RUSKIN. **d.** P. continuance in well doing *Rom.* 2: 7. **e.** The same bright, p. stars KEATS. **2.** Neither are they so p. of hunger as of thirst 1600.

B. *sb.* †**1.** A sufferer; one who suffers patiently –1795. **2.** One who is under medical treatment. late ME. **3.** A person or thing that undergoes some action, or to whom or which something is done, as correl. to *agent*, and dist. from *instrument*; a recipient 1580.

2. He brings his Physicke After his Patients death SHAKS. **3.** He that is not free is not an Agent, but a P. WESLEY. Hence †**Pa·tient** *v. trans.* to make p.; esp. *refl.* to calm oneself; *intr.* to be p. **Pa·tient-ly** *adv.*, **-ness** (now *rare*).

Patina (pæ·tină). 1748. [In sense 1 – L. *patina*, *-ena* broad shallow dish or pan; in sense 2 – It. *patina* (whence Fr. *patine*) – L. *patina.* Cf. PATEN.] †**1. a.** *Archæol.* The ancient Roman vessel so called. **b.** *Eccl.* = PATEN 1. –1868. **2.** A film or incrustation produced by oxidation on old bronze, usu. of a green colour. Hence extended to a similar alteration of the surface of other substances. 1748.

2. The vase is of bronze, covered by a *p.* of very fine green 1797. Hence **Pa·tinated, Pa·tinous** *adjs.* covered with a p. (sense 2). **Patina·tion,** formation of a p. So ‖**Patine** (patī·n) = 2.

‖**Patio** (pā·tiₒo). 1828. [Sp., = court of a house.] **1.** An inner court, open to the sky, in a Spanish, or Spanish-American house. **2.** *Mining.* A yard where ores are cleaned and sorted; also, the Spanish process of amalgamating silver ores on an open floor 1877.

‖**Patisserie** (pati·səri). 1784. [Fr. *pâtisserie*, f. (ult.) med.L. *pasticium* pastry (f. *pasta* PASTE) + *-erie* -ERY.] Articles of food made by a pastry-cook; pastry.

‖**Patois** (pæ·twa). 1643. [– (O)Fr. *patois* 'rough speech', perh. f. OFr. *patoier* handle roughly, trample, f. *patte* paw, of unkn. origin.] A provincial form of a language spoken in a restricted area and having no literary status. Also *gen.* any dialect or subdialect. **b.** *transf.* 1790. **c.** *attrib.* or as *adj.* Of, pertaining to, or of the nature of a patois 1789.

The Dutch p. spoken in South Africa 1893. **b.** Their language is in the *patois* of fraud BURKE.

Patonce (pǎtǫ·ns), *a.* 1562. [perh. alt. of POTENCÉ.] *Her.* In *cross p.*, a cross with its arms usu. expanding in a curved form from the centre, having ends somewhat like those of the cross fleury.

Patrial (pēⁱ·triăl), *a.* (*sb.*) *rare.* 1629. [– Fr. †*patrial* or med.L. *patrialis*, f. L. *patria* fatherland; see -AL[1].] **1.** Of or belonging to one's native country. **2.** *Gram.* Applied to a word denoting a native or inhabitant of the country or place from the name of which it is derived; also to a suffix forming such words. Also as *sb.* A word of this class. 1854.

2. P. *isc*..connotes origin from a place or stock: ..*Engl-isc*, English 1870.

Patriarch (pēⁱ·triāɹk). [– (O)Fr. *patriarche* – eccl. L. *patriarcha* – Gr. πατριάρχης head of a family, f. πατρία family, clan + -αρχης -ARCH.] **1.** The father and ruler of a family or tribe; *spec.* (*pl.*) in N.T., etc., the twelve sons of Jacob, from whom the tribes of Israel were descended; also, the fathers of the race, Abraham, Isaac, and Jacob, and their forefathers. **2.** In later Jewish history, applied (as repr. Heb. *nāsī* prince, chief) to the Chief or President of the Sanhedrim in Palestine (*c*180 B.C.–A.D. 429) 1795. **3.** *Eccl.* **a.** In ref. to the primitive Church: in earliest use, an honorific designation of bishops generally, becoming at length the official title of the bishops of Antioch, Alexandria, and Rome, also, later, of Constantinople, and of Jerusalem. **b.** Hence, in the *Orthodox Eastern Ch.*, the title of the bishops of the four patriarchates of Constantinople, Alexandria, Antioch, and Jerusalem, the Patriarch of Constantinople being the *Œcumenical P.* Also the title of the heads of the other Eastern Churches. **c.** *R.C.Ch.* (*a*) A bishop second only to the Pope in episcopal, and to the Pope and Cardinals in hierarchical, rank. (*b*) The title of the Latin bishops of Constantinople, Alexandria, Antioch, and Jerusalem ME. **d.** *transf.* Applied unofficially to the chief dignitaries of other Churches 1477. **4.** The father or founder of an order, institution, etc., or of a science, school of thought, or the like 1566. **5.** A venerable old man; *esp.* the oldest man, the 'father' of a village, class, profession, etc. 1817. **b.** *transf.* The head of a flock or herd: the most venerable object of a group 1700.

4. The p. of political economy, Adam Smith 1866. **5.** Mr. George Bancroft, now the p. of American literature 1888. **b.** The monarch oak, the p. of the trees DRYDEN. A goat, the p. of the flock SCOTT. Hence **Pa·triarchdom, Pa·triarchship** (*rare*) the state or office of a p.; the position or authority of an ancient p.

Patria·rchal (pēⁱtriā·ɹkăl), *a.* 1570. [– late L. *patriarchalis*, f. *patriarcha*; see prec., -AL[1].] **1.** Of or belonging to a patriarch; of or characteristic of the patriarchs or their times 1656. **2.** *Eccl.* Of or belonging to a hierarchical patriarch; ruled by a patriarch; of the nature or rank of a patriarch 1570. **3.** Of, pertaining to, or of the nature of a patriarchy 1828. **4.** Venerable, aged; like that of a patriarch 1837. **b.** *transf.* 1837.

1. Who could to P. years live on 1687. **2.** *P. church*, any one of the five great Roman basilicas, viz. St. John Lateran, St. Peter's, St. Paul's, St. Mary the greater, and St. Lawrence extra muros. *P. cross* (Her.), one with two transverse pieces, the upper being the shorter (an emblem of the patriarchs of the Gr. Church). **3.** The P. theory of society is..the theory of its origin in separate families, held together by the authority and protection of the eldest valid male ascendant 1883. **4. b.** Along the spoor of the p. old black buck 1850. Hence **Patria·rchally** *adv.* **Patria·rchalism,** a p. system of society or government.

Patriarchate (pēⁱ·triāɹkĕt). 1617. [– med. L. *patriarchatus*, f. as prec.; see -ATE[1].] **1.** The office, see, or residence of an ecclesiastical patriarch. **2.** = PATRIARCHY 2. 1651.

†**Patria·rchical,** *a.* 1606. [f. PATRIARCH + -ICAL.] **1.** = PATRIARCHAL 2. –1670. **2.** Of, pertaining to, or of the nature of the ancient patriarchs, or of the patriarchal system of government; like a patriarch, venerable –1698. Hence **Patria·rchically** *adv.* 1887.

Patriarchism (pēⁱ·triaɹkiz'm). 1666. [f. as prec. + -ISM.] The patriarchal system of organization, government, etc.

Patriarchy (pēⁱ·triāɹki). 1561. [– med.L. *patriarchia* – Gr. πατριαρχία, f. πατριάρχης; see PATRIARCH, -Y[3].] †**1.** = PATRIARCHATE 1. **b.** The government of the Church by a patriarch or patriarchs. **2.** A patriarchal system of society or government; a family, tribe, or society so organized 1632.

Patrician (pătri·ʃən), *sb.*[1] and *a.*[1] late ME. [– (O)Fr. *patricien*, f. L. *patricius*, subst. use of the adj. 'of a noble father', f. *pater, patr-* father; see -ICIAN.] **A.** *sb.* **1.** A person belonging to one of the original citizen families or *gentes*, of which the ancient Roman *populus* consisted; a Roman noble 1533. **b.** In the later Roman Empire, A member of a new noble order nominated by the Emperor of Byzantium; also, an officer, orig. a member of this order, sent as representative of the Emperor to administer the western provinces of Italy and Africa. late ME. **c.** Applied to the hereditary noble citizens of some of the mediæval Italian republics, and to the higher order of the Free Cities of the German Empire 1611. **d.** *gen.* A nobleman, aristocrat 1631. **2.** One versed in the writings of the Fathers (*rare*) 1810.

1. c. The sentence pass'd on Michel Steno, born P. BYRON. **2.** Luther was no great P. COLERIDGE.

B. *adj.* Of, belonging to, or composed of the patricians of ancient Rome; see A. 1. 1620. **b.** *gen.* Of or belonging to the patricians in Italian or German cities; noble, aristocratic 1615. **c.** Applied to aristocratic or non-popular parties in later times 1812.

He had a p. disdain of mobs 1879. **b.** You have strange thoughts for a p. dame BYRON. Hence **Patri·cianism,** p. quality, style, or spirit; also, patricians collectively. **Patri·cianly** *adv.*

Patri·cian, *sb.*[2] 1659. [– L. (pl.) *Patriciani*, f. the name of their founder, *Patricius.*] *Ch. Hist.* A member of a 4th c. heretical sect, which held that the substance of the flesh was the work of the devil, not of God.

Patri·cian, *a.*[2] *rare.* 1882. [f. L. *Patricius* + -AN.] Pertaining to, or founded by, St. Patrick.

Patriciate (pătri·ʃiĕt). 1656. [– L. *patriciatus*, f. *patricius*; see PATRICIAN *sb.*[1], -ATE[1].] **1.** The position or rank of a patrician. **2.** A patrician order or class; the aristocracy 1795.

Patricidal (pætrisəi·dăl), *a.* 1821. [f. next

+ -AL[1].] Of, pertaining to, or resembling a patricide.

Patricide[1] (pæ·trisəid). *rare.* 1593. [Late and med.L. *patricida*, alt. (after *pater* and *fratricida*) of L. *parricida* PARRICIDE[1].] = PARRICIDE[1].

Pa·tricide[2]. *rare.* 1625. [Late and med.L. alt. of L. *patricidium* PARRICIDE[2]; see prec.] = PARRICIDE[2]. Also *attrib.*

Patrico (pæ·triko). *Vagabonds' Cant.* 1550. [prob. reduced form of earlier *patryng cove*, i.e. *pattering*, ppl. a. of PATTER *v.*[1], COVE *sb.*[2], quasi 'praying fellow' (cf. †*co* lad, youth XVI–XVII).] A priest or parson; *esp.* a hedge-priest.

Patrimony (pæ·trimәni). ME. [– (O)Fr. *patrimoine* – L. *patrimonium*, f. *pater, patr-* father; see -MONY. Later conformed to L.] Property inherited from one's father or ancestors; heritage, inheritance. late ME. **b.** *transf.* The ancient estate or endowment of an institution, corporation, etc.; *esp.* that of a church or religious body ME. **c.** *fig.* 1581.

To reaue the Orphan of his Patrimonie SHAKS. **b.** *P. of St. Peter*, the Papal States or territory formerly held by the Pope in Italy. **c.** The p. of a poor man lies in the strength and dexterity of his hands ADAM SMITH. Hence **Patrimo·nial** *a.* pertaining to or constituting a p. **Patrimo·nially** *adv.*

Patriot (pē^{i}·triǫt, pæ·t-), *sb.* (*a.*) 1596. [– Fr. *patriote* – late L. *patriota* fellow-countryman – Gr. πατριώτης, f. πάτριος of one's fathers, πατρίς fatherland; see -OT[2].] †**1.** A compatriot (*rare*) –1629. **2.** One who exerts himself to promote the well-being of his country; one who maintains and defends his country's freedom or rights 1605. **b.** Assumed at various times by persons or parties whose claim to it has been denied or ridiculed by others. Hence, in 18th c. used for 'a factious disturber of the government' (J.). So sometimes, 'Irish Patriot'. 1644. ¶**c.** Erron. (with *of* or possessive) as if = lover, devotee –1641. **B.** *attrib.* or *adj.* That is, or has the character of, a patriot; characteristic of a patriot; patriotic 1732.

A. 2. Such as were known patriots, Sound lovers of their country B. JONS. **b.** Gull'd with a Patriots name, whose Modern sense Is one that wou'd by Law supplant his Prince DRYDEN. So **Pa·triotess** (*rare*), a female p.

Patriotic (pē^{i}triǫ·tik, pæt-), *a.* 1653. [– late L. *patrioticus* – Gr. πατριωτικός, f. πατριώτης PATRIOT; see -IC.] †**1.** Of or belonging to one's country –1653. **2.** Having the character of a patriot; characteristic of a patriot; marked by devotion to the wellbeing or interests of one's country 1757.

2. The threatened invasion..roused the p. feeling of all classes 1867. So **Patrio·tical** *a.* (*rare*). **Patrio·tically** *adv.*

Patriotism (pē^{i}·triǫtiz'm, pæ·t-). 1726. [f. PATRIOT + -ISM. Cf. Fr. *patriotisme.*] The character or passion of a patriot; love of or zealous devotion to one's country. Sometimes ironical (cf. PATRIOT 2 b).

P. must be founded in great principles, and supported by great virtues 1738. P. is the last refuge of a scoundrel JOHNSON.

Patripassian (pætripæ·siăn), *sb.* and *a.* 1574. [– eccl. L. *patripassianus* (Filastrius IV), f. L. *pater, patr-* + *passus* having suffered; see PASSION, -IAN. Cf. Fr. *patripassien.*] **A.** *sb.* One who held, as certain early heretics, that God the Father suffered with or in the person of the Son for the redemption of man. **B.** *adj.* Belonging to, or involving the doctrine of, the Patripassians 1727. Hence **Patripa·ssianism.**

Patristic (pătri·stik), *a.* and *sb.* 1837. [– G. *patristisch*, f. L. *pater, patr-*; see -ISTIC.] **A.** *adj.* **a.** Of or pertaining to the study of the writings of the Fathers of the Church, as in *p. learning*; **b.** hence, loosely, of or pertaining to the Fathers themselves, or their writings, as in *p. works, doctrines* 1874. **B.** *sb.* **1.** A student or adherent of the doctrines or opinions of the Fathers 1842. **2.** *pl.* The study of the lives, writings, or doctrines of the Fathers 1847. So **Pa·trist** (*rare*), one versed in the lives or writings of the Fathers. **Patri·stical** *a.* 1831, **-ly** *adv.* **Patri·sticism,** prop., a system founded upon the study of the Fathers; loosely, the doctrine or mode of thought of the Fathers themselves.

Patrix (pē^{i}·triks). Also **patrice.** *Pl.* **patrices.** 1883. [f. L. *pater, patr-* father, as a correlative term to *matrix.*] A die, punch, or pattern used to form matrices in type-founding, etc.

†**Patro·cinate,** *v.* 1611. [f. *patrocinat-*, pa. ppl. stem of L. *patrocinari* patronize, defend, rel. to *patronus* PATRON; see -ATE[3].] *trans.* To champion, maintain, patronize (a cause, etc.) –1822. So †**Patrocina·tion,** †**Patro·ciny,** patronage, protection 1450.

Patrol (pătrō^{u}·l), *sb.* 1664. [– G. *patrolle*, *-ouille* – Fr. *patrouille*, f. *patrouiller*; see next.] **1.** The action of going the rounds of a garrison, camp, etc. for the purpose of watching, guarding, and checking disorder; the perambulation of a town or district by a police constable or detachment of police for the protection of life and property. Also *fig.* and *transf.* **2.** A detachment of the guard, a police constable, or a detachment of police, told off for these purposes 1670. **3.** A detachment of troops sent out in advance of a column, regiment, etc., to reconnoitre 1702. **4.** One of the smaller units of a troop of Boy Scouts, consisting of six scouts, commanded by a *p. leader* 1908.

3. The French pushed their patroles of cavalry near the town SOUTHEY.

attrib. and *Comb.* as *p. duty*, etc.: **p.-wagon** (*U.S.*), a prison-van. Hence **Patro·lman** (chiefly *U.S.*), a man who is on p.; *spec.* a police constable attached to a particular beat or district.

Patrol (pătrō^{u}·l), *v.* Infl. **patrolled, patrolling.** 1691. [– Fr. *patrouiller* paddle about in mud (cf. OFr. *patoier*), f. *patte* paw, foot, with ending from dial. *gadrouille* mud, dirty water.] **1.** *intr.* To act as patrol; to reconnoitre as a patrol. **b.** To traverse a beat or district as constable or patrolman. **2.** *trans.* To go over or round (a camp, garrison, town, etc.) for the purpose of watching, guarding, etc.; to traverse (a beat or district) as constable, etc.; to traverse leisurely in all directions 1765.

Patron (pē^{i}·trәn), *sb.* ME. [– (O)Fr. *patron* – L. *patronus* protector of clients, advocate, defender, f. *pater, patr-* father.] **I.** Senses conn. w. ancient L. *patronus.* **1.** One who stands to another or others in relations analogous to those of a father; a lord or master; a protector; †a lord superior; †a founder of a religious order. **2.** *Rom. Antiq.* The former master of a manumitted slave, who retained certain legal claims upon him. **b.** A person of distinction who protected a client (see CLIENT 1) in return for certain services. Hence allusively. 1560. **c.** *Rom. Antiq.* An advocate, a pleader; hence *fig.* late ME. **3.** One who lends his influential support to advance the interests of a person, cause, art, etc.; *spec.* in 17th and 18th c. the person who accepted the dedication of a book. late ME. **b.** An advocate or champion of a theory or doctrine. Now *rare.* 1573. **c.** One who supports a practice, a form of sport, an institution, etc. Also (in tradesmen's language), a regular customer. 1605.

3. Books..ought to have no patrons but truth and reason BACON. A p. of some thirty charities TENNYSON. **c.** The patrons of the public-house (*mod.*).

II. Senses arising in med. Latin. **1.** One who holds the right of presentation to an eccl. benefice. (The earliest sense in Eng. use.) ME. **2.** The special tutelary saint of a person, place, craft, etc.; often *p. saint.* late ME. †**b.** A tutelary pagan divinity –1697.

2. Saint Nicholas is the great P. of Mariners 1718.

III. Senses repr. mod. Romanic uses. **1.** The captain or master of a galley, or of a coasting vessel in the Mediterranean (now *rare*). late ME. †**2.** A master or owner of slaves or captives (in the Levant, etc.) –1719. ‖**3.** The host or landlord of an inn (in Spain) 1878.

IV. Applied to things. **a.** A case for holding pistol-cartridges. (Fr. *patron, patronne.*) **b.** A cartridge (G. *patrone*). *Obs.* exc. *Hist.* 1683.

attrib. and *Comb.*, as *p. deity, god, martyr*, etc.: **p. saint** = sense II. 2. So **Pa·tron** *v.* (*rare*) to act as p. to, to champion as a p.; to patronize. **Patronal** (pătrō^{u}·năl, pæ·t-, pē^{i}·trŏnăl) *a.* of or pertaining to a p. or p. saint (e.g. the *p. festival* of a church); of the nature of a p. 1611. **Pa·tronate,** the position, right, or duty of a p.; the jurisdiction or possession of a p. **Pa·tronless** *a.* **Pa·tronship.**

Patron, obs. variant of PATTERN.

Patronage (pæ·trŏnėdʒ), *sb.* late ME. [– (O)Fr. *patronage*, f. *patron*; see PATRON, -AGE. Cf. med.L. *patronaticum, patronagium.*] The office or action of a PATRON. **1.** *Eccl.* The right of presentation to an eccl. benefice; advowson. **2.** Guardianship, tutelary care, as of a divinity or saint. *arch.* or *Obs.* 1582. **3.** The action of a patron in supporting, encouraging, or countenancing a person, institution, work, art, etc. Orig. implying the action of a superior. 1553. †**b.** *spec.* Protection, defence; protectorship –1844. **c.** The action of patronizing or condescending to a person 1829. **d.** In commercial or colloq. use: The financial support given by customers in making use of a line of steamers, a hotel, store, shop, etc. 1804. **4.** The control of appointments to offices, privileges, etc., in the public service 1769.

3. Henry's p. of letters was highly commendable 1839. **c.** There was a little savor of p. in the generous hospitality she exercised among her simple neighbors 1883.

attrib.: **P. Secretary** (in Great Brtitain), the Secretary of the Treasury through whom the p. of that department is administered and appointments to departments under its control made. Hence †**Pa·tronage** *v. trans.* to PATRONIZE.

Patroness (pē^{i}·trәnės, pæ·t-), *sb.* late ME. [– med.L. *patronissa*, fem. of L. *patronus*; see PATRON, -ESS[1].] A female patron, patron saint, or tutelary deity; also *fig.*

P. of a ball BYRON. *fig.* Befriend me Night best P. of grief MILT.

Patronize (pæ·trŏnəiz), *v.* 1589. [– Fr. †*patroniser* or med.L. *patronizare*; see PATRON, -IZE.] **1.** *trans.* To act as a patron (or †patron saint) towards; to protect, support, countenance, encourage. Also *absol.* †**b.** To defend, support, stand by; to countenance –1785. †**c.** Said of things –1710. **2.** To treat with a manner or air of condescending notice 1797. **3.** In commercial or colloq. use: To frequent as a customer or visitor; to favour with one's presence, resort to 1801.

1. He patronizes the Orphan and Widow, assists the Friendless, and guides the Ignorant ADDISON. **2.** The aristocracy..patronized him with condescending dexterity DISRAELI. Hence **Patroniza·tion,** the action or fact of patronizing. **Pa·tronizer. Pa·tronizingly** *adv.* with the manner or air of a patron.

Patronym (pæ·trŏnim). *rare.* 1834. [– Gr. πατρώνυμος, f. πατήρ, πατρ- father + ὄνομα, Doric ὄνυμα name.] = next, B.

Patronymic (pætrŏni·mik), *a.* and *sb.* 1612. [– late L. *patronymicus* – Gr. πατρωνυμικός, f. πατρώνυμος; see prec. and -IC.] **A.** *adj.* Of a name: Derived from the name of a father or ancestor, esp. by addition of a suffix or prefix indicating descent. Also said of such a suffix or prefix. 1669. **B.** *sb.* A patronymic name; a name derived from that of a father or ancestor; a family name.

A. The English p. suffix corresponding to the Danish *-son* is *-ing* 1894. **B.** Their original p. is MacAlpine SCOTT. So **Patrony·mical** *a.* 1656; **-ly** *adv.* by a p.

Patroon (pătrū·n). 1662. [var. of PATRON in some Fr. applications. In sense 4 – Du. *patroon*; see -OON.] †**1.** = PATRON I. 3. –1697. †**2.** = PATRON III. 2. –1704. **3.** = PATRON III. 1. Now *rare.* 1743. **4.** In *U.S.* A possessor of a landed estate and certain manorial privileges, granted under the old Dutch governments of New York and New Jersey, to members of the (Dutch) W. India Company 1758. Hence **Patroo·nship,** the position, or estate, of a p.

‖**Pat(t)amar** (pæ·tămāɹ). *E. Ind.* 1598. [– Pg. *patamar* – Marathi *pattamāri*, f. *patta* tidings + *-māri* carrier.] †**1.** A courier –1782. **2.** An Indian advice-boat or dispatch-boat; *spec.* a lateen-rigged sailing-vessel used on the west coast of India 1704.

Pat(t)ée (pate, pæ·ti), *a.* 1486. [– Fr. *patté(e*, f. *patte* paw, of unkn. origin. In early form *paty*; see -Y[5].] *Her.* Applied to a cross the arms of which are nearly triangular, being very narrow where they meet and widening out towards the extremities, so that the whole composes nearly a square.

Patten (pæ·t'n), *sb.* late ME. [– (O)Fr. *patin*, f. *patte* paw, foot (see prec.) + *-in* (repr. L. *-inus* -INE[1]).] **1.** A name applied at different periods to various kinds of footgear, e.g. to wooden shoes or clogs, 'chopins', etc. Now only in sense b. **b.** *spec.* A kind of overshoe worn to raise the ordinary shoes out of the mud or wet; consisting of a wooden sole mounted on an iron oval ring, or the like, by which the wearer is raised an inch or two from the ground 1575. **2.** A skate (*local* or *alien*). [= Fr. *patin*.] 1617. **3.** *Arch.* A base or foot: the base of a column; the sole for the foundation of a wall, etc. 1643.

1. b. Good housewives. . Safe thro' the Wet on clinking Pattens tread GAY. Phr. *To run on pattens* (said *fig.* of the tongue), to make a great clatter.

Comb., as **p.-maker** (now esp. as the name of one of the London City Companies). Hence **Pa·tten** *v. intr.* to go about on pattens; also, to skate (*local*). **Pa·ttened** *a.* wearing pattens.

Patter (pæ·təɹ), *sb.*[1] 1758. [f. PATTER *v.*[1], sense 3.] **1.** The cant or peculiar lingo of any profession or class; any language not generally understood. **b.** Name for the oratory of a Cheap Jack, a conjurer, or the like; also for 'jaw' 178. . **c.** *colloq.* Mere talk; chatter, gabble 1858. **2.** Rapid speech introduced into a song; also, *familiarly*, the words of a song, comedy, etc. 1876.

1. 'That's my name in your p.', said the gipsy 1875.

attrib. and *Comb.*, as *p.-speech*; **p.-song,** a humorous song in which many words are fitted to a few notes and sung rapidly.

Patter (pæ·təɹ), *sb.*[2] 1844. [f. PATTER *v.*[2]] The action or fact of pattering; a quick succession of pats, taps, etc.

Patter (pæ·təɹ), *v.*[1] late ME. [f. PATER 1 = Paternoster: from the rapid recitation of the *paternoster*, etc. as in saying the rosary.] †**1.** *intr.* To repeat the Paternoster, esp. in a rapid, mechanical, or indistinct way; to mumble one's prayers –1642. **2.** *trans.* To say over (prayers, charms, etc.) in a rapid mechanical manner. late ME. **3.** *intr.* To talk rapidly, without much regard to sense or matter; to jabber; to prattle. **b.** *In Pedlars' slang*, To talk, to speak; to 'speechify', like a Cheap Jack, or a conjurer. **c.** To talk the slang or 'patter' of thieves, beggars, etc. late ME. **4.** *trans.* (*slang.*) To talk (some language) 1812.

2. For mass or prayer can I rarely tarry, Save to p. an Ave Mary SCOTT. **4.** You all p. French more or less 1857. *To p. flash*, to speak slang. Hence **Pa·tterer,** one who patters or speaks patter.

Patter (pæ·təɹ), *v.*[2] 1611. [dim. and frequent. of PAT *v.*; see -ER[5].] **1.** *intr.* To make a rapid succession of pats, taps, or the like, as raindrops on a window-pane. **2.** To run with a rapid succession of short quick sounding steps 1806. **3.** *trans.* (*causal*) To cause to come or fall with a rapid succession of slight sounding strokes 1819.

1. The rain pattered dismally against the panes 1818. **2.** Away she pattered full speed 1824.

Pattern (pæ·təɹn), *sb.* [ME. *patron* – Fr.; a doublet of PATRON. The pron. (pa·tr'n, pa·təɹn) began to be used in XVI, and by 1700 *patron* and *pattern* had been differentiated.] **1.** An example or model deserving imitation; a model of a particular excellence. late ME. **2.** A model, design, plan, etc., from which something is to be made. Also *fig.* ME. **3.** *spec.* In *Founding.* †**a.** A matrix, a mould. **b.** A figure in wood or metal from which a mould is made for a casting. 1508. †**4.** A copy; a likeness, similitude (*rare*) –1714. **5.** A sample. Also *fig.* 1644. **6.** An example, an instance; *esp.* a typical instance, a signal example 1555. †**7.** A precedent –1672. **8.** A decorative or artistic design, as for china, etc.; this design carried out in the manufactured article; style, type, or class of design. Also *transf.* 1582. **9.** A specimen model of a proposed coin, not subsequently adopted. Dist. from a *proof.* 1837. **10.** A dress-length. *U.S.* 1847. **11.** *Gun-making.* The marks made by the shot from a gun on a target, in respect of their closeness together and even distribution within a given radius from the central point 1881. **12.** In Ireland, A patron saint's day; hence *transf.* the festivities of the day 1745. **13.** *attrib.* or *adj.* Serving as a model; typical, archetypal; ideal, model. Occas. hyphened to the sb. 1809.

1. For all an example, for no one a p. SWIFT. A p. of the domestic virtues 1870. **2.** *fig.* By th' patterne of mine owne thoughts, I cut out The puritie of his SHAKS. **5.** A tailor, with his books of patterns just imported from Paris 1829. **6.** The only p. of consistent gallantry I have met with LAMB. **7.** *Tit. A.* V. iii. 44. **8.** *transf.* The broken frames. . cast patterns on the ground DICKENS. **13.** Two p. young ladies, . . with p. deportment C. BRONTË.

attrib. and *Comb.*: **p.-book,** (*a*) a book of patterns or designs; (*b*) a blank book of cardboards to hold patterns; **-box** (*Weaving*), a box containing several shuttles, any one of which may be sent along the 'shed' as required by the pattern in colour-pattern weaving; **-card,** (*a*) a sample-card (of cloth, etc.); also, a book of such cards; (*b*) *Weaving* = CARD *sb.*[2] 6; also *attrib.*, as *pattern-card cutter*, etc.; **-chain** (*Weaving*), a device for bringing the shuttles automatically from the p.-box to the picker in the required sequence; **-designer, -drawer; -maker,** one who makes patterns; *spec.* one who arranges textile patterns for weaving.

Pa·ttern, *v.* 1581. [f. prec.] **I.** †**1.** *trans.* **a.** To design, sketch, plan. SIDNEY. †**b.** To be a pattern for; to prefigure –1654. **2.** To make (something) after a pattern or model; to model, fashion. Const. *after, on, upon*; †also *by, from, to* 1608. **3.** To match, to parallel, to equal; to compare (a person or thing *to* or *with* another). *Obs.* or *arch.* 1586. **4.** To take as a pattern; to imitate, copy (*rare*) 1601.

1. b. *Meas. for M.* II. i. 30. **2.** To patterne our obedience to the holy Angels 1608. †*P. out*, to work out according to some p. **3.** *Wint. T.* III. ii. 37.

II. 1. *trans.* To work or decorate with a pattern; also *transf.* to adorn with light and shade, or with variegated colouring 1857. **2.** *intr.* Of a gun: To distribute the shot in a pattern: see PATTERN *sb.* 11.

1. The walls. . that Giotto patterned RUSKIN. Hence **Pa·tterning** *vbl. sb.* the production or arrangement of patterns; *concr.* work done according to a pattern. **Pa·tterner,** one who draws or composes patterns.

Pattinsonize (pæ·tinsənəiz), *v.* 1859. [f. name of H. L. *Pattinson*, inventor of the process; see -IZE.] *trans.* To extract silver from (argentiferous lead-ore) by the Pattinson process. So **Pattinsoniza·tion** 1881.

Pattle, pettle (pa·t'l, pe·t'l). *Sc.* and *n. dial.* late ME. [Cf. PADDLE *sb.*[1], with which it partly coincides in meaning.] A tool like a small spade with a long handle, used chiefly to remove the earth adhering to a plough.

Patty (pæ·ti). 1710. [alt. of PÂTÉ by assoc. with PASTY.] A little pie or pasty. Hence **Pa·tty-cake;** ¶also erron. for PAT-A-CAKE.

Pattypan (pæ·tipæn). 1660. [f. prec. + PAN *sb.*[1]] †**1.** = PATTY –1700. **2.** A small tin pan or shape in which patties are baked 1694.

Patulous (pæ·tiŭləs), *a.* 1616. [f. L. *patulus* spreading, f. *patēre* be open; see -OUS.] **1.** Open; expanded; wide open. **2.** Spreading; said esp. of the boughs of a tree 1682. **3.** *Bot.* Spreading outwards 1756.

2. His hands and feet are large and p. 1875. Hence **Pa·tulous-ly** *adv.*, **-ness.**

Pauci- (pǭ·si), comb. form of L. *paucus* few, little, as in **Pauci·loquent,** uttering few words; whence **Pauci·loquently** *adv.* **Pauci·loquy,** sparingness of speech. **Paucispi·ral** *a.* having few whorls, as a shell; so **Paucispi·rated** *a.*

Paucity (pǭ·sĭti). late ME. [– (O)Fr. *paucité* or L. *paucitas*, f. *paucus* few; see -ITY.] **1.** Fewness; a small number. **2.** Smallness of quantity; scantiness 1650.

1. Having to capitulate owing to. . the p. of its defenders JOWETT. **2.** P. of evidence 1858.

Paughty (pǭ·ti, *Sc.* pāχti), *a.* *Sc.* and *n. dial.* 1572. [Of unkn. origin.] Haughty; insolent.

Paul (pǭl). late ME. [– OFr. *Pol* (mod. *Paul*) :– L. *Paulus*.] **1.** English form of L. *Paulus*, the 'Apostle of the Gentiles' (Acts 13:9). **2.** [repr. It. *Paolo* Paul.] = PAOLO 1767. **3.** **Paul Pry:** a very inquisitive person (name of a character in a comedy by John Poole, 1825); also *attrib.* 1829. **b.** Hence **Paul-Pry** *v. intr.* to be impertinently prying 1839. †**4.** **Paul's:** pop. name of St. Paul's Cathedral in London; formerly a resort of loungers and gossips. (Now always *St. Paul's.*) Hence *attrib.* in *Paul's Alley, Cross*, etc. late ME.

1. For proverbial phr. cf. PETER. **3.** *attrib.* It will cure her of her Paul-Pry tricks 1870. **4.** This oyly Rascall is knowne as well as Poules SHAKS.

Comb. with *Paul's*: **Paul's betony,** a species of *Veronica*, the Wood Speedwell (*V. officinalis*).

Pauldron. 1594. Var. of POULDRON.

Paulian (pǭ·liăn). 1449. [– eccl. L. *Paulianus* (Ambrosiaster), f. *Paulus*; see -IAN.] *Ch. Hist.* One of a sect who rejected the personality of the Logos and the Holy Spirit, and denied the pre-existence of Christ as 'the eternal Son of God'; founded by Paul of Samosata in the 3rd c. So **Pau·lianist, Pau·lianite.**

Paulician (pǭli·ʃ'ăn), *sb.* and *a.* 1574. [– med.L. *Pauliciani*, Gr. Παυλικιανοί, f. (most prob.) Paul of Samosata (see prec.), with whom they had affinities; see -ICIAN.] *Ch. Hist.* **A.** *sb.* A member of a sect which arose in Armenia in the 7th c., holding modified Manichæan opinions. **B.** *adj.* Of or belonging to this sect.

Pauline (pǭ·ləin), *a.* and *sb.* late ME. [– med.L. *Paulinus*, f. *Paulus* PAUL; see -INE[1].] **A.** *adj.* Of, pertaining to, or characteristic of St. Paul, his writings, or his doctrines 1817.

The P. Epistles 1876.

B. *sb.* **1.** A member of certain religious orders so named. late ME. **2.** A scholar of St. Paul's School, London 1867.

1. Some be Paulines, some be Antonynes 1550. **2.** The Paulines were especially famous for calligraphy 1867. Hence **Pau·linism,** P. theology. **Pau·linist,** an adherent of St. Paul or his doctrine. **Paulini·stic** *a.* of or pertaining to a Paulinist or Paulinism.

Paulism (pǭ·liz'm). 1823. [f. PAUL + -ISM.] The doctrine of St. Paul; Paulinism.

Paulist (pǭ·list). 1678. [f. as prec. + -IST.] **1.** In India, a name for a Jesuit, from their church of St. Paul in Goa. **2.** A member of a Roman Catholic association, the Congregation of the Missionary Priests of St. Paul the Apostle, founded at New York in 1858.

Paulite (pǭ·ləit). 1839. [f. name of St. *Paul*, L. *Paulus* + -ITE[1] 1.] One of an order of monks, also called Hermits of St. Paul, founded in 1215, at Budapest. Also *attrib.*

Paulo-post-future (pǭ:lo,pōᵘst,fiū·tiŭɹ, -tʃəɹ), *a.* and *sb.* 1824. [– mod.L. *paulo post futurum*, tr. Gr. ὁ μετ' ὀλίγον μέλλων the future after a little. In XIX grammars called also 'third future', 'futurum exactum', 'futurum perfectum', 'future perfect'.] **1.** A name of a tense of the passive voice of Greek verbs, used chiefly to state that an event will take place immediately. **2.** *allusively.* A future which is a little after the present; a by-and-by; (belonging to) an immediate or proximate future 1848.

2. Shelley's. . anticipated profits were in the paulo-post-future 1887. So **Pau:lo-po·st** *a.* [L. *paulo post*], a little subsequent; also **Pau:lo-pa·st** *a.* relating to something lately finished. (*nonce-wds.*)

‖**Paulownia** (pǭlǭ·vniă, pǭlōᵘ·niă). 1847. [After Anna *Paulowna*, daughter of the Tsar Paul I; see -IA[1].] *Bot.* A genus of *Scrophulariaceæ*, comprising the single species *P. imperialis*, a Japanese ornamental tree with purplish trumpet-shaped flowers blossoming in early spring.

Paunch (pǭnʃ), *sb.*[1] late ME. [– AFr. *pa(u)nche*, ONFr. *panche*, var. of OFr. *pance* (mod. *panse*) :– Rom. **pantice*, L. *pantex*, *pantic-* (esp. pl.) bowels, intestines.] **1.** = BELLY *sb.* 5. Now usu. dyslogistic, implying prominence, gluttony, etc. **2.** The first and largest stomach of a ruminant; the rumen. late ME. **b.** esp. as used for food; tripe. late ME.

Paunch, panch (pǭnʃ), *sb.*[2] 1626. [prob. identical with prec. through use of OFr. *pance* for belly armour.] *Naut.* **a.** A thick strong mat, made of interlaced spun yarn or strands of rope, used on a ship to prevent chafing. **b.** A wooden covering or shield on the fore side of a mast (*rubbing p.*), to preserve it from chafing when the masts or spars are lowered.

Paunch (pǭnʃ), *v.* Now *rare* or *dial.* 1530. [f. PAUNCH *sb.*[1]] **1.** *trans.* To stab in the paunch; also *loosely*, to stab. **2.** To cut open the paunch of (an animal); to disembowel, eviscerate 1570. †**3.** To fill the belly, to glut. (Also *intr.* for *refl.*) –1635.

1. Batter his skull, or p. him with a stake SHAKS.

Paunchy (pǭ·nʃi), *a.* 1598. [f. PAUNCH *sb.*[1] + -Y[1].] Having a large paunch; big-bellied. Hence **Pau·nchiness.**

Pauper (pǭ·pəɹ). 1516. [– L. *pauper* poor.]

1. A poor person. **a.** In Law: One allowed, on account of poverty, to sue or defend in a court of law, without paying costs (*in forma pauperis*) 1631. **b.** *gen.* A person destitute of means of livelihood; a beggar. (Now assoc. with c.) 1516. **c.** *spec.* A person in receipt of poor-law relief 1775. **2. a.** *attrib.* (in apposition) or as *adj.* That is a pauper; destitute 1809. **b.** *attrib.* Of, belonging or relating to, or intended for a pauper or paupers, as *p.-asylum, -grave, -rate, -system* 1823.

1. c. The p. lives better than the free labourer; the thief better than the p. EMERSON. **2. a.** Educating p. children 1846. Hence **Pau·perdom,** the condition of a p., destitution; paupers collectively. **Pau·perism,** the condition of paupers; the existence of a p. class; poverty, with dependence on public relief; *concr.* paupers collectively.

Pauperize (pǭ·pərəiz), *v.* 1834. [f. prec. + -IZE.] *trans.* To reduce to the condition of a pauper; *esp.* to make dependent on public relief. Also *absol.*

The charity that pauperizes 1902. Hence **Pau:periza·tion.**

Pausal (pǭ·zăl), *a.* (*sb.*) 1877. [f. PAUSE *sb.* + -AL[1].] Of or pertaining to a pause or the pause in a sentence; in *Heb. Gram.* applied to the form which a word receives in the pause.

Pause (pǭz), *sb.* 1440. [– (O)Fr. *pause* or L. *pausa* – Gr. παῦσις, f. παύειν stop, cease. In the mus. sense – It. *pausa.*] **1.** A short interval of inaction or silence; occas. *spec.* an intermission arising from uncertainty, a hesitation. **b.** (Without article.) Intermission, waiting, hesitation, suspense 1593. **2.** *spec.* An intermission, stop, or break made, according to the sense, in speaking or reading; in *Prosody*, a cæsura; also, a break of definite length in a verse, occupying the time of a syllable or a number of syllables. Also *transf.* in a piece of music. 1440. **3.** *Mus.* †**a.** A character denoting an interval of silence; a rest –1674. **b.** The character 𝄐 or 𝄑 placed over or under a note or rest to indicate that it is to be lengthened indefinitely. (Also placed over a double bar at the conclusion of a piece, and rarely over a single bar in the course of it.) 1806.

1. There was a p. before the preacher spoke again GEO. ELIOT. **b.** Sad p. and deep regard beseem the sage SHAKS. Phr. *To give p. to, to put to a p.*, to cause to stop or hesitate; to 'pull up'. *At p.*, pausing, not proceeding; in suspense; You stand there at p., and silent RUSKIN. Hence **Pau·seful** *a.*, **-ly** *adv.* **Pau·seless** *a.*, **-ly** *adv.*

Pause (pǭz), *v.* 1526. [f. PAUSE *sb.* or Fr. *pauser* or L. *pausare.*] **1.** *intr.* To make a pause; to stop (temporarily), to wait; to stop for deliberation or on account of uncertainty; to hesitate, hold back. †**b.** *refl.* in same sense 2 *Hen. IV*, IV. iv. 9. **2.** To dwell, linger *upon*, some particular word or thing 1530.

1. Why doth the Iew p.? take thy forfeiture SHAKS. I p. for a Reply SHAKS. **2.** Other Offenders we will p. vpon SHAKS. Hence **Pau·ser** (*rare*), one who pauses. **Pau·singly** *adv.*

‖**Pauxi** (pǭ·ksi). 1753. [– Sp. *pauxi*, now *pauji* (pau·χi) – Mexican *pauxi* (pau·ʃi).] The Galeated Curassow (*Pauxis galeata*).

Pavage (pēⁱ·vėdʒ). ME. [– (O)Fr. *pavage* (in med.L. *pavagium* XII), f. *paver*; see PAVE *v.*, -AGE.] **1.** A tax or toll towards the paving of highways or streets; also, the right to levy this. **2.** The action of paving, the laying of a pavement. Also *attrib.* 1553.

Pavan (pæ·văn). 1535. [– Fr. *pavane* – Sp. *pavana*, poss. f. *pavon* :– L. *pavo, -on-* PEACOCK.] A grave and stately dance, in which the dancers were elaborately dressed; introduced into England in the 16th c. **b.** Music for this dance or in its rhythm, which is duple and very slow 1545.

Pave (pēⁱv), *v.* ME. [– (O)Fr. *paver*, prob. back-formation from †*pavement* PAVEMENT.] **1.** *trans.* To lay or cover with a pavement (a road, street, yard, etc.; hence, a town, house, etc.); see PAVEMENT 1. **b.** To overlie as a pavement 1600. **2.** *fig.* To cover or overlay as with a pavement. late ME.

1. The court is pavid with Mosaique stone 1585. **b.** They had more Rubies than wold paue Cheapside 1600. **2.** Hell is paved with good intentions 1771. Phr. *To p. the way*, to prepare the way (*for* something to come); to lead on to an object in view.

‖**Pavé** (pave). 1764. [Fr., subst. use of pa. pple. of *paver* PAVE *v.*] **1.** A paved street, road, or path. **2.** A setting of diamonds, etc., placed close together like the stones of a pavement, so that no metal is visible. Also *attrib.*, as *p.-effect* 1871.

1. *On the pavé*: see *on the* PAVEMENT.

Paved (pēⁱvd), *ppl. a.* late ME. [f. PAVE *v.* + -ED[1].] Laid with a pavement; having a pavement; †set or laid together as a pavement.

There was vnder his feet, as it were a paued worke of a Saphire stone *Exod.* 24:10.

Pavement (pēⁱ·vmĕnt), *sb.* ME. [– OFr. *pavement* – L. *pavimentum* beaten or rammed floor, f. *pavire* beat down, ram; see -MENT.] **1.** A piece of paved work, a paved surface; the superficial covering of a floor, yard, street, etc., formed of stones, bricks, tiles, or, in later times, blocks of wood, fitted closely together; also, an undivided surface of cement, concrete, asphalt, etc. **b.** The paved part of a public thoroughfare; now only *spec.* the paved footway by the side of a street, as dist. from the roadway ME. **c.** *U.S.* = ROADWAY 2. **d.** The floor of a mine 1839. **e.** A seam of fire-clay underlying a seam of coal. **2.** *Anat.* and *Zool.* A level hard surface formed by close-set teeth, bony plates, or the like 1847.

1. b. *On the p.* (after Fr. *sur le pavé*), walking the streets, without lodging, abandoned; I was left completely on the p. 1818. *fig.* Or like a gallant Horse falne in first ranke, Lye there for pauement to the abiect reere SHAKS.

attrib. and *Comb.*, as *p.-stone*, etc.; **p.-artist,** one who draws figures or scenes on the flagged p. in coloured chalks in order to get money from passers-by; **-tooth,** a broad flat tooth forming with others a p. in sense 2, as in the Port Jackson shark. Hence **Pa·vement** *v. trans.* to lay with a pavement; to pave (chiefly in *pa. pple.*) 1634.

Paven (pēⁱ·vĕn), *ppl. a.* Chiefly *poet.* 1634. [irreg. f. PAVE *v.*, after *shaven*, etc.] = PAVED.

Paver (pēⁱ·vəɹ). ME. [f. PAVE *v.* + -ER[1].] **1.** One who paves, a paviour. **2.** A paving-stone or tile 1696.

‖**Pavia** (pēⁱ·viă). 1753. [mod.L.; named after Peter Paaw (Pavius), Professor of Botany at Leiden 1589–1617; see -IA[1].] *Bot.* A genus of trees and shrubs (N.O. *Sapindaceæ*) closely allied to the Horse-chestnut, but distinguished by having a smooth, not prickly, capsule; hence called Buck-eye, or Smooth-fruited Horse-chestnut. Hence **Paviin** (pēⁱ·viˌin), *Chem.* a fluorescent substance, $C_{16}H_{18}O_{10}$, existing in the bark of *P.* and other trees; also called FRAXIN.

Pavid (pæ·vid), *a. rare.* 1656. [– L. *pavidus*, f. *pavēre* quake with fear; see -ID[1].] Fearful, timid.

Pavilion (păvi·lyən), *sb.* ME. [– (O)Fr. *pavillon* tent, canopy :– L. *papilio, -on-* butterfly, tent.] **I. 1.** A tent, esp. a large one, rising to a peak above. **b.** *Her.* A tent as a heraldic bearing 1725. †**c.** A canopied litter –1703. **2.** *fig.* Anything likened to a tent 1535.

1. This mountaine..resembling perfectly the fashion of a p., or of a sugar loafe 1604. **2.** He made darknes his pauylion rounde aboute him COVERDALE 2 *Sam.* 22:12.

II. In transf. and techn. uses, chiefly from French. **1.** A French gold coin struck by Philip VI of Valois in 1329, the obverse of which represented the king seated under a canopy or *pavillon*. Also applied to the *royal d'or* struck by the Black Prince for use in Guienne, etc. 1755. **2.** A light ornamental building or pleasure-house; also, a building attached to a cricket or other ground, for the convenience of spectators and players 1687. **3.** A projecting subdivision of a building or façade, often elaborately decorated, forming an angle, or the central feature of a large pile 1676. **b.** A detached or semi-detached subdivision of a hospital 1858. †**4.** A flag or ensign –1778. †**5.** *Bot.* The spreading part of the corolla of a flower; the *vexillum* or standard in a papilionaceous flower –1796. **6.** The part of a brilliant-cut diamond between the girdle and the collet 1751. **7.** *Anat.* **a.** The pinna or auricle of the ear 1842. **b.** The fimbriated extremity of a Fallopian tube 1857.

2. The handsome p. which was recently built [at Lord's] 1891.

attrib. and *Comb.*: **p.-facet,** any one of the four largest facets in the p. of a brilliant-cut diamond.

Pavilion (păvi·lyən), *v.* ME. [f. prec.] **1.** *trans.* To set, place, or enclose in or as in a pavilion; to canopy. **2.** To furnish or set (a field, etc.) with pavilions 1667.

2. The field Pavilion'd with his Guardians bright MILT.

Paving (pēⁱ·viŋ), *vbl. sb.* late ME. [-ING[1].] The action of PAVE *v.*; *concr.* a pavement; the material of which a pavement is composed. Also *attrib.*, as *p.-stone, -tile*, etc.

Paviour, -ior (pēⁱ·viəɹ). late ME. [Earlier *pavier*, alt. (see -IER 2) – (O)Fr. *paveur*, f. *paver* PAVE *v.* + *-eur* -ER[2] 3; see -OUR.] **1.** One who paves or lays pavements. Also *fig.* **b.** A rammer for driving paving-stones 1875. **2.** = PAVER 2. 1611.

Pavis, pavise (pæ·vis), *sb.* Now *Hist.* [Late ME. *paveis* – OFr. **paveis, pavais* (now *pavois*) – It. *pavese* – med.L. *pavense* (sc. *scutum* shield), f. *Pavia* name of a town in Italy where such shields were orig. made.] **1.** A convex shield, large enough to cover the whole body, used as a defence against archery, and esp. in sieges; hence, any large shield. †**b.** As used on board a ship (ranged along the sides as a defence against archery) –1562. †**2.** A screen of pavises; a pavisade; any screen or shelter used in fighting –1582. †**3.** *fig.* A defence, protection –1534.

3. He was their bulwark, their paues, and their wall 1529. Hence **Pavis, pavise** (pæ·vis) *v.* to cover, shelter, or defend with a p. (*Obs.* or *Hist.*) **Pavisa·de, pavesa·de,** †**Pavisa·do, pavesa·do,** a defence or screen made of pavises or shields joined together in a continuous line; hence, a screen of canvas run round the sides of a ship for protection against missiles, etc. **Pa·viser, -or,** a man armed with or bearing a p.

†**Pavo·ne.** *rare.* [– It. *pavone* :– L. *pavo, pavon-* peacock.] A peacock. SPENSER.

Pavonian (păvōᵘ·niăn), *a.* 1793. [f. L. *pavo, pavon-* peacock + -IAN.] Of or pertaining to a peacock; pavonine.

Pavonine (pæ·vŏnəin), *a.* and *sb.* 1656. [– L. *pavoninus*, f. *pavo, pavon-* peacock; see -INE[1].] **A.** *adj.* **1.** Of or pertaining to, resembling or characteristic of a peacock. **b.** *Zool.* Of or pertaining to the genus *Pavo* or sub-family *Pavoninæ*, including the peafowl 1895. **2.** Resembling the neck or the tail of the peacock in colouring 1688. **B.** *sb.* **1.** An iridescent lustre found on some ores or metals; peacock-tail tarnish 1805. **2.** *Zool.* A bird of the sub-family *Pavoninæ* 1895.

Pavy (pēⁱ·vi). 1675. [– Fr. *pavie*, f. *Pavie* Pavia.] A hard clingstone peach or nectarine.

Paw (pǭ), *sb.* [ME. *powe, pawe* – OFr. *powe, poue, poe* :– Rom. **pauta* – Frankish **pauta* (MDu. *pōte*, Du. *poot*).] **1.** The foot of a beast having claws or nails. (Dist. from *hoof.*) **b.** The foot of any animal; *esp.* the claw of a bird (*rare*). late ME. **2.** *joc.* The hand, esp. when clumsy or awkwardly used (*colloq.*) 1593. **b.** Handwriting; 'fist'; signature 1702. **3.** [f. PAW *v.*] The action, or an act, of pawing 1611.

1. Whatsoeuer goeth vpon his pawes, among all maner of beasts *Lev.* 11:27.

†**Paw** (pǭ), *a. slang* or *colloq.* 1668. [app. a var. of *pah*, adj. use of PAH *int.*] Improper, naughty, obscene –1730.

Paw (pǭ), *v.* 1604. [f. PAW *sb.* Cf. *to claw.*] **1.** *trans.* and *intr.* To touch or strike with the paw 1611. **2.** To strike or scrape the ground with the hoofs; said of a horse, etc. 1611. **3. a.** *trans.* To pass the hand over, handle, *esp.* awkwardly, coarsely, or rudely (*colloq.*) 1604. **b.** *intr.* To pass the hand clumsily, etc. 1848.

2. He paweth in the valley, and reioyceth in his strength *Job* 39:21. **3. a.** Our great court-Galen..paw'd his beard, and mutter'd 'catalepsy' TENNYSON.

Pawk, pauk (pǭk). *Sc.* and *n. dial.* 1513. [Of unkn. origin.] Trick, artifice, cunning device. Hence **Paw·ky** *a.* tricky, artful, sly, cunning, shrewd; esp. dryly humorous. **Paw·kily** *adv.* **Paw·kiness.**

Pawl (pǭl), *sb.* 1626. [perh. – LG., Du. *pal* rel. to adj. *pal* immobile, fixed, of unkn. origin.] **1.** *Naut.* Each of the short stout bars made to engage with the whelps, and prevent a capstan, windlass, etc. from recoiling. **2.** A bar pivoted at one end to a support, and engaging at the other with the teeth of a ratchet-wheel or ratchet-bar, so as to hold it in a required position 1729.

Comb., as **p.-bitt, -post** (*Naut.*), a strong vertical post in which the pawls of a windlass are fixed; **-head** (*Naut.*), the part of the capstan to which the pawls are attached; **-rim** (*Naut.*), a notched cast-iron ring for the pawls to catch in.

Pawl, *v.* Chiefly *Naut.* 1704. [f. prec.] **1.** *trans.* To stop or secure (a capstan, ratchet-wheel, etc.) by means of a pawl or pawls. **2.** *fig.* (*colloq.* or *slang.*) **a.** *trans.* To bring to a standstill, stop, check, 'pull up'. **b.** *intr.* To stop, cease, *esp.* to stop talking. 1825.

Pawn (pǭn), *sb.*[1] [Late ME. *poun* – AFr. *poun*, OFr. *poön*, *peon* pawn :– med.L. *pedo*, *pedon-* foot-soldier, f. L. *pes*, *ped-* foot. Cf. PEON.] One of the pieces of smallest size and value in the game of chess. Also *fig.* (usu. of a person).

Councillors of State..playing their high chess-game, whereof the pawns are Men CARLYLE.

Pawn (pǭn), *sb.*[2] 1496. [– OFr. *pan*, also *pand*, *pant* pledge, security, plunder :– WGmc. **panda*, repr. by OFris. *pand*, OS., MDu. *pant* (Du. *pand*), OHG. *pfant* (G. *pfand*).] **1.** A thing (or person) given, deposited, or left in another's keeping, as security for a debt, or for the performance of some action; a pledge, surety, gage. (Now *rare.*) **b.** *fig.* 1573. †**c.** = GAGE *sb.*[1] 2. SHAKS. **d.** A person held as security for a debt, and used as a slave 1837. **2.** The state of being pledged, or held as a pledge (*lit.* and *fig.*). Usu. in phr. *in p.*, *at p.*, †*to p.* (The usual sense.) 1554. **b.** The action of pawning 1824.

1. He must leave behind, for pawns, His mother, wife, and son DRYDEN. **c.** *Rich. II*, I. i. 74. **2.** Her plate and jewels are at pawne for money PEPYS. **b.** The Contract of P. as it exists at Common Law 1883.

Comb. **p.-ticket**, a ticket issued by a pawnbroker in exchange for a pledge deposited with him, and bearing particulars of the loan.

†**Pawn**, *sb.*[3] 1548. [= Du. *pand*; a Du. development of Fr. *pan*; see PANE *sb.*[1] II. 1, 2.] A gallery or colonnade, a covered walk or passage, esp. one in a bazaar, exchange, etc. alongside which wares are exposed for sale –1888.

Pawn (pǭn), *v.* 1567. [f. PAWN *sb.*[2]] *trans.* To give or deposit as security for the payment of a sum of money, or for the performance of some action (something to be forfeited in case of non-payment or non-performance); to pledge; to stake, wager; to risk. **a.** *lit.* 1570. **b.** *fig.* (e.g. one's life, honour, word, etc.) 1567.

a. He is over head and ears in debt, and has pawned several things SWIFT. **b.** I will p. my life for her, she will never be pert RICHARDSON. Hence **Paw·nable** *a.* that can be pawned.

Pawnbroker (pǭ·nbrōᵘːkəɹ). 1678. [f. PAWN *sb.*[2] + BROKER 2.] One engaged in the business of lending money upon interest on the security of articles of personal property pawned or pledged. Hence **Paw·nbroːking** *vbl. sb.* the action or business of a p.

Pawnee (pǭnī·). 1683. [f. PAWN *v.* + -EE[1].] The person with whom something is deposited as a pawn or pledge. (Correl. to next.)

Pawner (pǭ·nəɹ). Also (in legal use) **-or.** 1745. [f. PAWN *v.* + -ER[1] or -OR 2d.] One who pawns; one who deposits something as a pledge, esp. with a pawnbroker.

Pawnshop (pǭ·nʃǫp). 1849. [f. PAWN *sb.*[2] + SHOP.] A pawnbroker's shop or place of business.

Paw-paw (pǭ·pǭː), *a. slang* or *colloq.* ?*Obs.* 1720. [redupl. of PAW *a.*] Nursery term for 'nasty, improper, naughty', used euphem. for 'indecent, obscene, immoral'.

Pawpaw, var. of PAPAW.

Pax[1] (pæks). late ME. [– L. *pax* peace.] ‖**1.** The L. word meaning 'peace' 1485. **b.** *Eccl.* In L. salutations, etc., as *P. vobis* peace be with you 1593. **c.** quasi-*int.* (in schoolboy slang). 'Keep quiet!' 'Truce!' 1852. **2.** *Eccl.* The kiss of peace: see PEACE *sb.* 4; the ceremony of kissing the pax: see sense 3. *rare.* 1440. **3.** *Eccl.* A tablet with a projecting handle behind, bearing a representation of the Crucifixion, etc., which was kissed by the officiating priests and congregation at Mass; an osculatory. late ME. **4.** *transf.* (Public school slang.) A friend; good friends 1781.

1. *P. Dei*, *Ecclesiæ*, *Regis*, the peace of God, the Church, the king's peace. *P. Romana*, the peace within the Roman empire; so *p. Britannica*, the peace imposed by British rule. **4.** *To be good p.*, to be good friends.

†**Pax**[2]. 1641. Corrupt f. POX –1716.

‖**Paxilla** (pæksi·lă). *Pl.* **-æ.** 1870. [mod. L., f. cl.L. *paxillus* small stake, peg.] *Zool.* A pillar-like pedicel in echinoderms, surmounted by a tuft of minute calcified spinelets attached to the integument. Hence **Paxi·llar** *a.* **Paxi·llate** *a.* having paxillæ. **Paxi·lliform** *a.*

Paxillose (pæ·ksilōᵘs), *a.* 1882. [f. L. *paxillus* (see above) + -OSE[1].] **a.** *Geol.* Resembling a small stake. **b.** Of or pertaining to the *Paxillosæ*, a group of echinoderms bearing paxillæ 1895.

Paxwax (pæ·ksˌwæ·ks). Now *dial.* and *colloq.* late ME. [alt. of earlier *fax wax*, *fex wex* (XIV), also *fix-fax* (XV), which survived in dial. *fic-fac*, *fig-fag*; presumably f. FAX *sb.* + **weaxe* growth (see WAX *v.*[1]).] The stout elastic tendon extending from the dorsal vertebræ to the occiput, and serving to support the head; the nuchal ligament.

Pay (pēⁱ), *sb.* ME. [– (O)Fr. *paie*, f. *payer*; see next.] †**1.** Satisfaction, liking –1602. **2.** The action of paying, payment (esp. of wages or hire) 1440. **b.** The condition of being paid, or receiving wages or hire 1596. **3.** *concr.* Money paid for labour or service; wages, hire, salary, stipend ME. **4.** *fig.* Retaliation or punishment inflicted; penalty or retribution suffered; recompense, etc. bestowed. Now *rare* or *Obs.* ME. **5.** *Mining.* A remunerative yield of metal in a bed of ore 1877.

2. Rather to score it up against the future, than require present p. 1647. **3.** I take the Queen's P. in Quin's Regiment THACKERAY. Phr. †*Dead p.*: see DEAD PAY. **5.** It is in this stratum..where the rich p. will be found RAYMOND.

Phr. *To be good* (etc.) *p.*, to be sure to pay one's debts (colloq.); *fig.* to afford profit.

Pay (pēⁱ), *v.*[1] Pa. t. and pple. **paid** (pēⁱd). ME. [– (O)Fr. *payer* :– L. *pacare* appease, pacify, med.L. pay, f. *pax*, *pac-* PEACE; the sense 'pay' was developed through that of pacifying a creditor.] †**1.** *trans.* = APAY *v.* 1. Chiefly in *pa. pple.* Satisfied, content, pleased –1501. **2.** *trans.* To give to (a person) what is due in discharge of a debt, or as a return for services done, or goods received, etc.; to remunerate, recompense ME. **3.** *fig.* or *gen.* To reward, recompense, requite, give what is due or deserved to (a person). late ME. **b.** To give (one) his deserts, punish 1450. **c.** *spec.* To beat, flog. Now *dial.* or *slang.* 1581. **4.** To recompense, reward (a service, work, etc.); in good or bad sense. Also, of a thing, To yield or recompense for. late ME. **5.** To hand over (money, etc.) in return for goods or services, or in discharge of an obligation; to render (a sum or amount owed). Also *transf.*; cf. 6 b. ME. **6.** To give money in discharge of (a debt, dues, tribute, tithes, ransom, hire, etc.). late ME. **b.** *transf.* Of a thing: To furnish (money, etc.) for the discharge of (a debt, etc.) 1656. **7.** *fig.* To give or render (anything, owed, due, or deserved); to discharge (an obligation). In good or bad sense. ME. **b.** *Arith.* In subtraction, to compensate for 'borrowing' (see BORROW *v.*[1] 1 c) by mentally adding a unit to the subtrahend of the next higher denomination. Usu. *to p. back.* 1897. **8.** (With the notion of debt weakened or lost.) To render, bestow, (attention, respect, a compliment, a visit, etc.). 1590. **9.** *absol.* or *intr.* To give money, etc., in return for something or in discharge of an obligation; also *fig.* ME. **10.** *absol.* or *intr.* Of a thing or action: To yield an adequate return; to be profitable or advantageous 1812. **b.** *trans.* To be profitable to (a person) 1883. **11.** *P. for*: To give money or other equivalent value for. Also *transf.* of a thing, sum of money, etc.: To furnish an equivalent for; to be sufficient to defray the cost of. late ME. **b.** *fig.* To atone for; more usu., To suffer or be punished for. late ME. †**12.** *trans.* = *pay for*: see 11. –1842. †**b.** *fig.* To make up for –1790. **13.** *Naut.* To let out (a rope or chain) by slackening it. (Also in ref. to something let out by the rope.) Now always with *out* or *away*. 1627. **14.** *Naut.* (*trans.*) To cause (a ship) to fall to leeward, or fall away from the wind. Now always with *off*. 1627. **b.** *intr.* for *pass.* To fall to leeward 1625.

2. He had been..paid by the job 1813. Phr. *To p. off* (rarely *up*), to pay in full and discharge; *spec.* to pay and discharge the crew of (a ship) upon completion of a commission. Also *intr.* for *pass.* *To p. out*, to get rid of by paying; The Man in Possession had been paid out 1887. **3. b.** They, in return, (as the vulgar phrase has it,) 'p. him out' 1863. **c.** Thence home, and find the boy out of the house and office..I did p. his coat for him PEPYS. **4.** Haste still paies haste SHAKS. It will more than p. the trouble I have taken to write it CHESTERF. **5.** Have pacience with me, and I will paye the all TINDALE *Matt.* 18:29. Phr. *To p. away*, *in*, *over*, *out*, etc. *P. down*, to lay down (money) in payment; to pay on the spot (also *fig.*). **6.** Phr. *P. off*, to p. in full; to clear off (a debt) by payment. *P. up*, to make up arrears of payment. **b.** That this estate should be liable to p. these debts 1818. **7.** Yᵉ traytours were payed ther desertes LD. BERNERS. Made mee p. the price of pillage with my bloud 1587. Praise, everlasting praise, be paid To him that earth's foundation laid WATTS. To forget the pain he paid for his discoveries 1890. Phr. *To p. one's debt to nature*, or *nature's debt*, (*spec.*) to die; see DEBT *sb.* **8.** They paid little heed to the sermon 1882. **9.** The vngodly borroweth and paieth not agayne COVERDALE *Ps.* 36(7):21. **10.** You won't find it p. in the long run 1885. **11.** [He] shal paye for al þat by the wey is spent CHAUCER. **b.** Lot payes deare for his rashnesse BP. HALL.

Phr. *The* DEVIL *to p.*, *to p. through the* NOSE, *to p. the* PIPER, *to p. one's* WAY: see these sbs. Hence **Pay·ing** *vbl. sb.*; also with advs., as *paying-in*, etc. **Pay·ing** *ppl. a.* that pays, remunerative.

Pay (pēⁱ), *v.*[2] Chiefly *Naut.* Pa. t. and pple. **payed (paid).** 1594. [– OFr. *peier* :– L. *picare*, f. *pix*, *pic-* PITCH *sb.*[1]] *trans.* To smear or cover with pitch, tar, resin, tallow, or the like, as a defence against wet, etc.

Pay- in comb. [PAY *sb.* or stem of PAY *v.*[1]]

1. In sbs. denoting persons or things connected with the payment of money, esp. wages; as *p.-clerk*, *-inspector*; PAYMASTER, PAYMISTRESS; *p.-bill*, *-book*, *-list*, *-roll*, *-sheet*; *p.-envelope*; *p.-office*, *-room*, *-train*; PAY-DAY, *p.-night*, *-week*.

2. *Mining.* Containing mineral in sufficient quantity to be profitably worked; as *p.-channel*, *-dirt* (also contemptuous for 'money'), *-gravel*, *-ore*, *-rock*, *-vein*.

3. The vb.-stem in comb. with object; as **p.-all**, he who or that which pays all, or bears the whole charge; **-rent** *a.*, furnishing money to p. the rent.

Payable (pēⁱ·ăb'l), *a.* 1447. [f. PAY *v.*[1] + -ABLE. Cf. (O)Fr. *payable.*] **1.** *Comm.* Of a sum of money, a bill, etc.: That is to be paid; due; falling due (usu. *at* or *on* a specified date, or *to* a specified person). **b.** Of a person: That is to be paid 1617. **2.** *Mining.* (In active sense.) Of a mine, a bed of ore, etc.: That can be made to pay; capable of being profitably worked. Hence *transf.* Commercially profitable; paying 1859.

1. A bill..p. here at the shortest sight 1725. **2.** Never again did we hit upon p. gold 1879. Hence **Payabi·lity** (*rare*), capability of being profitably worked (as a mine). **Pay·ably** *adv.*

Pay·-day. 1529. [PAY- 1.] The day on which payment is, or is to be, made; *esp.* a periodically recurring day for the payment of wages; on the *Stock Exchange*, the day on which a transfer of stock has to be paid for.

Payee (pēⁱˌī·). 1758. [f. PAY *v.*[1] + -EE[1].] The person to whom a sum of money is, or is to be, paid; *esp.* the person to whom a bill or cheque is made payable.

†**Pay·en.** ME. [– OFr. *paien* (mod. *païen*) :– L. *paganus* PAGAN.] = PAGAN –1550.

Payer (pēⁱ·əɹ). late ME. [f. PAY *v.*[1] + -ER[1].] One who pays; *esp.* one who pays a sum of money. (As correl. to *payee* occas. spelt *payor*.)

Paymaster (pēⁱ·mɑːstəɹ). 1550. [f. PAY- 1 + MASTER.] An official (*esp.* an officer in the army or navy) whose duty it is to pay troops, workmen, or other persons. Also *fig.*

P.-general, the officer at the head of the department of the Treasury through which payments are made. Hence **Pay·maːstership, Pay·master-ge·neralship.**

Payment (pēⁱ·mĕnt). ME. [– (O)Fr. *paiement*, f. *payer* PAY *v.*[1]; see -MENT.] **1.** The action, or an act, of paying. **2.** A sum of money (or other thing) paid; pay, wages; price 1449. **3.** *fig.* The action, or an act, of rendering to a person anything due, deserved, or befitting, or of discharging an obligation; the thing so rendered ME. **4.** *attrib.* 1581.

1. The great principle of p. by results 1892. When goods are offered in exchange for goods, it is popularly distinguished as 'payment in kind' 1893.

Paymistress (pēⁱ·mi:strės). 1583. [f. PAY-1 + MISTRESS, after *paymaster*.] A woman who superintends the payment of persons or services; also *fig.*

Paynim (pēⁱ·nim), *sb.* (*a.*) *arch.* [ME. *painim(e* – OFr. *pai(e)nime* :– eccl. L. *paganismus* heathenism, f. L. *paganus* PAGAN; see -ISM.] **A.** *sb.* A pagan, a heathen; a non-Christian; *esp.* a Moslem, a Saracen. *arch.* and *poet.* late ME. **B.** *adj.* (orig. *attrib.* use of sb.) Of pagans; pagan, heathen; non-Christian; chiefly = Moslem or Saracen. In mod. writers *poet.* or *Hist.* ME.

Champions bold Defi'd the best of Panim chivalry To mortal combat MILT. Hence **Pay·nimry,** paynims collectively, heathenry.

Paynize (pēⁱ·nəiz), *v.* 1844. [f. *Payne*, inventor's name; see -IZE.] *trans.* To impregnate (wood) with a solution of calcium (or barium) sulphide followed by one of calcium sulphate, to harden and preserve it.

‖**Paysage.** *Obs.* exc. as Fr. (peizā·ʒ). 1611. [Fr., f. *pays* country; see -AGE.] **a.** A representation of rural scenery. **b.** A rural scene, landscape. Hence **Paysagist** (pēⁱ·zădʒist), a landscape-painter.

‖**Paysanne** (peiza·n). 1748. [Fr., fem. of *paysan* PEASANT.] A peasant-woman; a countrywoman.

Paytamine (pēⁱ·tāmə̄in). 1879. [f. *Payta* + AMINE.] *Chem.* An amorphous alkaloid, obtained from *Payta-bark*, a pale variety of cinchona bark, shipped from Payta in Peru. So **Paytine** (pēⁱ·təin), a crystallizable alkaloid obtained with p. 1875.

Pea[1] (pī). 1666. [New sing. f. the earlier sing. and pl. PEASE, sometimes written *peas*, where *s* was regarded as a pl. inflexion.] **I.** The seed or plant. **1.** The round seed of *Pisum sativum* (see 2), used for food. **2.** The plant *Pisum sativum*, a hardy climbing leguminous annual, with large papilionaceous flowers succeeded by long pods each containing a row of round seeds. Usu. dist. as *p.-plant*. 1699. **3.** Applied with defining words to leguminous plants allied to the common pea 1783.

1. To find the p., which I put under one of my thimbles BORROW. *Green peas*, peas gathered for food while still green and unripe. Provb. *As like as two peas.* **3. Angola P.** = *Congo Pea*; **Beach-p.** = *Sea-pea*; **Butterfly-p.,** *Clitoria mariana* of S. America and India; **Congo P.,** a variety (*bicolor*) of *Cajanus indicus*, with yellow flowers marked with crimson; **Egyptian P.,** the CHICK-PEA; **Everlasting P.** (see EVERLASTING A. 4. b.); **Hoary P.,** the genus *Tephrosia*, which has leaves covered with a grey down; **Milk-p.,** the N. American genus *Galactia*; **Sea-p., Sea-side P.,** *Lathyrus maritimus* (*Pisum maritimum*), a sea-coast species rare in England; also SWEET PEA.

II. Something small and round like the seed; the eggs, roe, or spawn of certain fishes 1758.

attrib. and *Comb.*, as *p.-bloom, -blossom*, etc.; **p.-bean** (see BEAN 3); **-beetle, -bug,** a small coleopterous insect (*Bruchus pisi*), a native of S. America, which infests peas; **-comb,** a triple comb occurring in some varieties of domestic fowl; **-crab,** a small crab of the genus *Pinnotheres*, commensally inhabiting the shell of a bivalve mollusc, as a mussel or oyster; **-dove,** a species of pigeon, *Zenaida amabilis*, found in W. Indies and Florida; **-flour,** flour made of peas, pease-meal; **-green** *a.* and *sb.*, (of) a colour like that of fresh green peas, a nearly pure but not deep green; **-grit,** a coarse pisolitic limestone; **-maggot,** a caterpillar which infests peas, the larva of the *pea-moth*; **-moth,** a small moth (*Tortrix pisi*) which lays its eggs on pea-pods; **-rifle,** a rifle with a thick barrel and a small round bullet like a p.; **-shooter,** a toy weapon, consisting of a tube from which peas are shot by the breath; **-time** (*U.S.*), phr. *the last of p.-t.*; the last stage of anything; **-vine** (*U.S.*), the 'vine', or climbing stem of any p.-plant; *esp.* (*a*) the Hog-peanut; (*b*) an American vetch, *Vicia americana*; **-weevil** = *p.-bug*.

Pea[2] (pī). Also **pee.** 1833. [perh. shortened from *peak*.] = PEAK *sb.*[2] 3 c.

Pea.[3] *local.* 1761. [prob. f. *pease* PEISE, weight, taken as a pl.] The sliding weight used on a steelyard, safety-valve, etc.

Peaberry (pī·beri). 1879. [f. PEA[1] + BERRY *sb.*[1]] A single round seed of the coffee-plant, occurring towards the end of the branches, through abortion of one of the usual two seeds in the fruit.

Peace (pīs), *sb.* [ME. *pais, pes* – AFr. *pes*, OFr. *pais* (mod. *paix*) :– L. *pax, pac-* peace.] **1.** Freedom from, or cessation of, war or hostilities; that condition of a nation or community in which it is not at war with another. **b.** (With article.) A ratification or treaty of peace between two powers previously at war. (†Also, formerly, a truce.) late ME. †**c.** With *possessive* or *of*. A state of peace, concord, and amity with a person –1576. **2.** Freedom from civil commotion; public order and security ME. **3.** Freedom from disturbance or perturbation (esp. as a condition in which an individual is); quiet, tranquillity. Also emphasized as *p. and quiet(ness.* ME. **b.** In or after Biblical use, in expressions of salutation, etc. ME. **4.** Freedom from quarrels or dissension between individuals; concord, amity ME. †**b.** *transf.* An author or maintainer of concord –1560. **5.** Freedom from mental or spiritual disturbance or conflict arising from passion, sense of guilt, etc.; e.g. *p. of mind, soul*, or *conscience* ME. **6.** Absence of noise, movement, or activity; stillness, quiet ME. **b.** *ellipt.* as exclam. after L. *pax*, Fr. *paix*, etc. (Cf. PEACE *v.* 1.) **7.** In generalized sense. late ME.

1. In this weake piping time of P. SHAKS. P. hath her victories No less renowned then warr MILT. **b.** The P. of Amiens CANNING. **3.** Let him sleep in p. GRAY. *Bill of p.*, a bill brought by a person to establish a right, with the object of securing freedom from perpetual litigation. **b.** P., p., be unto thee, and p. be to thine helpers 1 *Chron.* 12:18. **4.** *Kiss of p.*, a kiss given in sign of friendliness; *spec.* a kiss of greeting given in token of Christian love (see PAX) at religious services in early times; now, in the Western Ch., usu. only at High Mass. **b.** And he shalbe our p. BIBLE (Genev.) *Micah* 5: 5. **6.** Calm and deep p. on this high wold TENNYSON. **7.** Every thing that is sincerely good..With Truth, and P., and Love shall ever shine MILT.

Phrases. **a.** Belonging to 1. *P. at any price. P. with honour.* **b.** Belonging to 2. *The king's p.*, orig. the protection secured to certain persons by the king, as those travelling on the king's highway, etc.; hence, the general peace of the kingdom under the king's authority. *The p.* = the king's peace, in its wider sense; as in *to keep the p., breach of the p.*; *to swear the p. against* (any one), to swear that one is in bodily fear of another, so that he may be bound over to keep the peace; also, *commission, justice, officer, of the p.*, etc. *God's p.*, God's requirement of peace and good order. The *Roman p.* = *pax Romana*, the British *p.* = *pax Britannica*; see PAX[1] 1. *To keep the p.*, to refrain, or prevent others, from disturbing the public peace. **c.** In various senses. *At p.*, not at strife or variance; quiet, peaceful. *To hold* (occas. *keep*) *one's p.*, to keep silence (*arch.*). *To make p.*, (*a*) to effect a reconciliation between parties at variance; to conclude peace with a nation at the close of a war; (*b*) to enter into friendly relations with a person; (*c*) to enforce public order. *To make* one's, or a person's, *p.*, to come, or bring some one, into friendly relations (*with* another).

Comb.: **p.-breaker,** one who breaks or violates p.; one who commits a breach of the p.; **p. establishment,** the reduced troops under arms and military supplies maintained in a standing army in time of p.; **-monger,** hostile term for one who advocates p.; **officer,** a civil officer appointed to preserve the public p., as a constable; **-warrant,** a warrant for arrest, issued by a Justice of the Peace. Hence **Pea·celess** *a.* devoid of p., unquiet; **-ness.**

Peace (pīs), *v.* late ME. [f. prec. At first in the imper.; prob. interjectional use of prec.] **1.** *intr.* imper., as exclam.: Be silent, keep silence (*arch.*). †**2.** *intr.* To be or become still or silent; to keep silence –1633.

1. He..sayde vnto the see: p. and be still TINDALE *Mark* 4:39. **2.** When the Thunder would not p. at my bidding SHAKS.

Peaceable (pī·săb'l), *a.* [ME. *peisible, pesible* – OFr. *peisible* (mod. *paisible*), var. †*plaisible* :– late L. *placibilis* pleasing, f. L. *placēre* please; see -IBLE.] **1.** Disposed to, or making for, peace; not quarrelsome or pugnacious. †**b.** Not talkative, taciturn, calm; quiet in behaviour –1826. **2.** = PEACEFUL 2 (now the usual word) ME. Hence **Pea·ceableness. Pea·ceably** *adv.*

Peaceful (pī·sfŭl), *a.* ME. [f. PEACE *sb.* + -FUL.] **1.** Disposed to or making for peace; friendly, pacific. (Now usu. *peaceable.*) **2.** Full of or characterized by peace; free from strife; untroubled, tranquil, quiet. (Now the usual sense.) ME. **3.** Belonging to a time or state of peace 1586.

1. And smooth the frownes of War, with peacefull lookes SHAKS. **2.** The p. hermitage MILT. **3.** Peacefull plenty 1586. Hence **Pea·ceful-ly** *adv.*, **-ness.**

Peacemaker (pī·s,mēⁱ:kəɹ). late ME. [f. PEACE *sb.* + MAKER; tr. L. *pacificus*.] One who makes or brings about peace; one who reconciles opponents. **b.** *joc.* A revolver, warship, etc. 1841.

Blessed are the peacemakers TINDALE *Matt.* 5: 9. So **Pea·cema:king** *sb.* and *a.*

Pea·ce-o:ffering. 1535. [f. PEACE *sb.* + OFFERING.] **1.** An offering or sacrifice presented as a thanksgiving to God, under the Levitical law. **2.** An offering made to make peace; a propitiatory sacrifice or gift 1661.

Peach (pītʃ), *sb.*[1] [ME. *peche* – OFr. *peche*, earlier *pesche* (mod. *pêche*) :– med.L. *persica* (*pessica*), for L. *persicum*, for *Persicum malum* 'Persian apple'.] **1.** The fruit of the tree *Amygdalus persica* (see 2), a large drupe, usually round, of a whitish or yellow colour, flushed with red, with downy skin, highly flavoured sweet pulp, and rough furrowed stone. **2.** The tree *Amygdalus* (*Prunus*) *persica*, N.O. *Rosaceæ*, a native of Asia; the peach-tree. late ME. **3.** Applied to other edible fruits resembling the peach, or to the plants producing them; esp. *Sarcocephalus esculentus*, a climbing shrub of West Africa (*Guinea, Negro*, or *Sierra Leone P.*), bearing a large juicy berry 1760. **4.** Short for *p.-brandy* (U.S.) 1853. **5.** = *P.-colour*; also *attrib.* or as *adj.* 1848. **6.** *slang.* (orig. *U.S.*) Applied to anything particularly good of its kind, as in *she's a p.* 187..

attrib. and *Comb.*, as *p.-stone*, etc.; also **p.-bloom,** (*a*) the delicate powdery deposit on the surface of a ripe peach; hence in ref. to complexion; (*b*) = PEACH-BLOSSOM 1; **-borer,** any insect whose larva bores through the bark of the peach-tree; *spec.* a moth, *Ægeria exitiosa*, and a beetle, *Dicerca divaricata*; **-brandy,** a spirituous liquor made from the fermented juice of peaches; **-colour,** (*a*) the colour of a ripe p., a soft pale red; (*b*) the colour of PEACH-BLOSSOM, a delicate rose or pink; also *attrib.* or as *adj.*; so **-coloured** *a.*; **p. Melba** = PÊCHE MELBA; **-tree** = 2.

Peach, *sb.*[2] 1778. [f. prec.] *Min.* Cornish miners' term for chlorite slate. Hence **Pea·chy** *a.*[2] containing a large proportion of p. 1814.

Peach (pītʃ), *v.* 1460. [Aphetic f. *apeche* APPEACH.] †**1.** *trans.* To accuse (a person) formally; to impeach –1727. **b.** To inform against (an accomplice or associate); to 'round upon'. Now *rare.* 1570. **c.** *transf.* To blab, divulge (*colloq.*) 1852. **2.** *intr.* or *absol.* To turn informer. Const. *upon, against.* Now chiefly *slang* or *colloq.* 1596.

2. If I be tane, Ile p. for this SHAKS. Save my life, and I'll p. 1717. Hence **Pea·cher,** an informer.

Pea·ch-blo:ssom. 1664. **1.** The blossom of the peach-tree. **2.** *attrib.*, *esp.* Of the colour of a peach-blossom, a delicate purplish pink 1702. **3.** A species of moth (*Thyatira batis*), from the colour of the spots on its wings 1819.

Pea·ch-blow. 1861. [See BLOW *sb.*[3]] A delicate purplish-pink colour; cf. prec. 2. **b.** A glaze of this colour on some oriental porcelain. Also *attrib.* 1886. **c.** A variety of potato of this colour 1868.

Pea·-chick. 1542. [f. *pea* (see PEACOCK) + CHICK.] The young of the peafowl. **b.** A young and vain person 1746.

Peachy (pī·tʃi), *a.*[1] 1599. [f. PEACH *sb.*[1] + -Y[1].] Of the nature or appearance of a peach; chiefly of the cheeks: Round, soft, and having a delicate pink flush. Hence **Pea·chiness.**

Pea·-coat. 1845. [f. after *pea-jacket*.] = PEA-JACKET.

Peacock (pī·kǫk), *sb.* [ME. *pecock*, f. *pē (OE. *pēa* :– **pau*) + COCK *sb.*[1] The ME. var. *pocock*, north. *pacock*, is based on ME. *pō, pā* :– OE. *pāwa*; both OE. forms are – L. *pāvō*, whence also MLG. *pāwe* (Du. *pauw*), OHG. *pfāwo* (G. *pfau*).] **1.** The male bird of any species of the genus *Pavo* or peafowl, esp. of the common species *P. cristatus*, a native of India, well known as the most imposing and magnificent of birds; often treated as a type of ostentatious display and vain-glory. **b.**

transf. and *fig.* late ME. **c.** The bird or its flesh as an article of food 1460. **2.** A southern constellation (*Pavo*) 1674. **3.** Short for *p.-butterfly, p.-moth* 1827.

1. The self-applauding bird, the p. COWPER. **b.** Phr. *To play the p.*, to comport oneself vaingloriously.

attrib. and *Comb.*: **p.-blue,** the lustrous blue of a peacock's neck; **-butterfly,** a European butterfly (*Vanessa io*) with ocellated wings; **-coal,** iridescent coal; **-eye,** the ocellus on a peacock's feather; also *attrib.*; **-moth,** *Macaria notata* and *M. alternata*, of family *Geometridæ*; **-throne,** the former throne of the kings of Delhi; adorned with the representation of a peacock's tail fully expanded, composed of precious stones. Hence **Pea·co:ckery, Pea·cockism,** foppery. **Pea·cockish** *a.* like a p. or that of a p.; **-ly** *adv.*; **-ness. Pea·cocklike** *a.* peacockish; *adv.* after the manner of a p. **Pea·cocky** *a.* suggesting a p. in walk, bearing, self-display, or showiness.

Peacock (pī·kǫk), *v.* 1586. [f. prec.] **1.** *trans.* To make like a peacock; to puff up with vanity; *esp. refl.* to strut about or pose like a peacock. **2.** *intr.* To strut about ostentatiously; to make a vainglorious display, pose 1818.

2. People of various nationalities..p. about in fine feathers 1890.

Pea·cock-fi:sh. 1661. A European labroid fish, the blue-striped wrasse (*Crenilabrus pavo*); from its green, blue, red, and white colouring.

Peacock's feather, peacock feather. late ME. A feather of the peacock; *spec.* one of the long tail-feathers, adorned with iridescent ocelli or 'eyes'. Hence taken as a symbol of vainglory, or a decoration of rank, etc.

Peacock's tail. 1570. The tail-coverts of the peacock collectively, which the bird is able to erect in a resplendent vertical circle behind its body. **b.** Hence *transf.*; esp. in *peacock's tail (peacock-tail) tarnish* = PAVONINE B. 1.

Pea·-flower. 1825. The flower of the pea, or any flower resembling this.

Peafowl (pī·faul). 1804. A bird of the genus *Pavo*; a peacock or peahen.

†**Pe·age.** 1456. [– OFr. *paage*, (also mod.) *péage* (whence med.L. *peagium, paagium*) :- med.L. *pedaticum*, f. L. *pes, ped-* foot; see -AGE. Cf. PEDAGE.] Toll paid for passing through a place –1846.

Peahen (pī·hen). [Late ME. *pehen(ne*, f. *pe-*, OE. *pēa* + *henne* HEN. Cf. PEACOCK.] A female peafowl, the female of the peacock.

‖**Peai** (pī,ai·), *sb.* 1613. [– Carib *piai.*] A medicine-man or witch-doctor, among the Indians of S. America; cf. PIACHE.

Pea·-ja:cket. 1725. [prob. (with assim. to JACKET) – Du. *pijjakker*, f. *pij* (MDu. *pīe*; see PEE *sb.*[1]) + *jekker* jacket.] A short stout overcoat of coarse woollen cloth, now commonly worn by sailors.

Peak (pīk), *sb.*[1] [OE. *Pēac* (only in *Pēaclond*) of unkn. origin.] Name of the hilly district in the north-west of Derbyshire, England; the High Peak and the Low or Lower Peak.

Peak (pīk), *sb.*[2] 1530. [prob. back-formation from *peaked*, var. of (dial.) *picked* pointed, f. PICK *sb.*[1] + -ED[2].] **I. 1.** A projecting point; a pointed or tapering extremity; †a beak or bill. Now *rare.* 1578. **b.** *spec.* †The projecting front of a widow's hood –1719. †any pointed part of a garment, etc. –1818; the point of a beard 1592; the projecting part of the brim of a man's cap 1660; a point formed by the hair on the forehead, a 'widow's peak' 1833. **2.** A headland. Now *local.* 1548. **3.** *Naut.* **a.** The narrowed end of a ship's hold at the bow, the FOREPEAK; also the corresponding part at the stern, the *after-peak* 1693. **b.** 'The upper outer corner of those sails which are extended by a gaff' (Smyth); also, the upper end of a gaff. Hence *gaff p., mizzen p.* 1711. **c.** The point at the end of the fluke of an anchor 1793.

1. The moon put forth a little diamond p. KEATS.

II. Later form of PIKE *sb.*[2] and [3]. **a.** The pointed top of a mountain; a mountain or hill having a pointed summit, or of conical form 1634. **b.** *fig.* Highest point, summit 1784. **c.** *transf.* The pointed top of anything 1840. **d.** *Electr.*, etc. The highest point of a load curve, as of the load-time curve of a power station; the maximum value of an alternating quantity during a cycle; *transf.* the (time of) greatest frequency or maximum of other varying quantities, as traffic, trade, prices, etc. 1902.

a. The top of the high Peake of Damoan..like a Sugar-loafe SIR T. HERBERT. **b.** Also *attrib.*, as in *p. month, year*, in which the allusion is now often to the high points of a graph record. **c.** A conical roof going up into a p. DICKENS. **d.** P. load.

†**Peak,** *sb.*[3] 1529. [Of unkn. origin.] A dolt, noodle. See HODDYPEAK. –1580.

Peak (pīk), *v.*[1] 1550. [Of unkn. origin.] †**1.** *intr.* To shrink, to slink –1642. †**2.** To move about dejectedly or silently –1603. **3.** To droop in health and spirits, waste away; to look sickly or emaciated. Chiefly in *p. and pine.* 1605.

2. Yet I..peake Like John a-dreames..And can say nothing SHAKS. **3.** Wearie Seu'nights, nine times nine, Shall he dwindle, peake, and pine SHAKS.

Peak (pīk), *v.*[2] 1577. [f. PEAK *sb.*[2]] **1.** *intr.* To project or rise in a peak. **2.** *trans.* To bring to a head; *fig.* to accentuate 1887.

Peak, *v.*[3] 1626. [prob. aphetic of APEAK *adv.*; cf. Fr. *apiquer* in same sense (1751), f. *à pic* (whence APEAK).] *Naut.* (*trans.*) To place, put, or raise a-peak or vertically. **a.** To tilt up a yard vertically, or nearly so, by the mast; to top a yard; esp. *to p. the mizzen.* **b.** *To p. the oars*: to raise the oar blades out of the water to an almost vertical position 1875. **c.** Of a whale: To raise (his tail or flukes) straight up in diving vertically. Also *intr.* 1839.

Peaked (pīkt, pī·kėd), *a.* 1450. [f. PEAK *sb.*[2] + -ED[2].] **1.** Having a peak; pointed; brought to a peak or point. **b.** *spec.* Of a mountain: Having, or rising into, a peak. Also in comb., as *twin-p.*, etc. So of a roof. 1670. **2.** Sharp-featured, thin, pinched, as from illness or want; sickly-looking. Chiefly *colloq.* 1835.

1. [Charles the first] his Vandyke dress,..and his p. beard MACAULAY. **2.** As pale and p. as a charity-school-girl 1883. Hence **Pea·kedness.**

Peaking (pī·kiŋ), *ppl. a.* Now *dial.* 1598. [f. PEAK *v.*[1] + -ING[2].] **1.** Sneaking, skulking; mean-spirited. **2.** Emaciated, sickly, pining, peaky 1700.

Peakish (pī·kiʃ), *a.*[1] 1519. [f. PEAK *sb.*[3]; sense 2 goes with prec.; see -ISH[1].] †**1.** Slothful, spiritless; stupid; ignorant –1603. **2.** Somewhat 'peaky' (PEAKY *a.*[2]) 1836. Hence †**Pea·kishness.**

†**Pea·kish,** *a.*[2] 1567. [f. PEAK *sb.*[1] + -ISH[1].] Of, pertaining to, or resembling that of the district of the Peak in Derbyshire –1646.

That p. caue HOLLAND. His p. dialect BP. HALL.

Peaky (pī·ki), *a.*[1] 1832. [Connected with PEAK *v.*[1], PEAKED *a.*, PEAKING *ppl. a.*, PEAKISH *a.*[1]; see -Y[1].] **1.** Abounding in, or characterized by having, peaks. **2.** Peaked, pointed; peak-like 1869.

1. Hills with p. tops engrail'd TENNYSON. **2.** A p. nose 1887.

Pea·ky, pee·ky, *a.*[2] *colloq.* and *dial.* 1853. = PEAKING *ppl. a.* 2.

Peal (pīl), *sb.*[1] [Late ME. *pele*, aphetic f. *apele* APPEAL *sb.*] †**I.** = APPEAL *sb.* –1471. **II.** †**1.** The ringing of a bell as a call or summons –1675. **2.** The ringing of a bell, or of a set of bells; *spec.* a series of changes rung on a set of bells. Also *transf.* and *fig.* 1511. **3.** A set of bells tuned to one another; a ring of bells 1789. **4.** A discharge of guns or cannon so as to produce a loud sound; esp. as an expression of joy, a salute, etc. *Obs.* exc. *Hist.* 1515. **5.** A loud outburst or volley of sound 1535.

2. The bells ring..a joyous p. 1812. *transf.* My pockets ring A golden p. MASSINGER. **4.** The Castle discharged a peale of ordinaunce 1577. **5.** Still gazing in a doubt Whether those peales of praise be his or no SHAKS. A rattling p. of thunder DRYDEN.

Peal, peel (pīl), *sb.*[2] 1533. [First in *salmon pele*, of unkn. origin.] **a.** A grilse or young salmon; **b.** A smaller species of salmon, *Salmo cambricus* (or *S. trutta*).

Peal (pīl), *v.*[1] Now *dial.* late ME. Aphetic f. *apele* APPEAL *v.*

Peal (pīl), *v.*[2] 1632. [f. PEAL *sb.*[1]] **1.** *intr.* To sound forth in a peal, to resound. †**2.** *trans.* To storm, din, or assail (the ears, or a person) *with* (loud noise, etc.) –1719. **3.** To give forth in a peal or peals 1714.

1. There let the pealing Organ blow, To the full voic'd Quire below MILT. **3.** Loud thunder is pealed from the skies 1887.

Pean (pīn). 1562. [Of unkn. origin.] *Her.* One of the furs, represented as sable powdered with 'spots' of or.

Peanut (pī·nɒt). 1835. [f. PEA[1] + NUT *sb.* I. 1.] The fruit or seed of *Arachis hypogæa*, or the plant itself, much cultivated in warm climates; the fruit is a pod ripening underground, containing two seeds like peas, valued as food and for their oil. (Also called *ground-nut* or *ground-pea.*) **b.** *attrib.* 1875.

b. *P. politics* (U.S. slang), underhand and secret tactics; so **p. politician.**

Pear (pēᵊɹ). [OE. *pere, peru*, corresp. to MLG., MDu. *pere* (Du. *peer*) – pop. L. **pira*, whence (O)Fr. *poire*, fem. sing. repl. L. *pirum.*] **1.** The fleshy fruit of the pear-tree (see 2), a pome of a characteristic shape, tapering towards the stalk. **2.** The tree *Pyrus communis* (N.O. *Rosaceæ*), or other species with similar fruit; widely grown in many varieties for the fruit (sense 1). More usually *p.-tree.* late ME. **3.** Applied, with defining words, to various other fruits or plants in some way resembling the pear; as ALLIGATOR *p.*, PRICKLY P., etc. **4.** *transf.* Applied to things resembling a pear in shape; *e.g.* the fruit or hip of the rose; a pear-shaped pearl, etc. 1576.

1. Appeles and peres that semen very gode, Ful ofte tyme are roten by the core LYDG.

attrib. and *Comb.*, as *p.-shaped*, etc.; **p.-blight,** (*a*) a destructive disease of pear-trees, caused by a bacterium (*Micrococcus amylovorus*) which turns the leaves rapidly brown; (*b*) a disease of pear-trees caused by a beetle (*Xyleborus*) which bores into the bark (*pear-blight beetle*, also called *pin-borer*); **-drop,** (*a*) a p.-shaped sweetmeat, usu. flavoured with jargonelle-p. essence; (*b*) a p.-shaped jewel used as a pendant; **-gauge,** a gauge invented by Smeaton, consisting of a pear-shaped glass vessel and a hermetically closed tube, for measuring the degree of exhaustion of air in an air-pump; **-slug,** the slug-like larva of a saw-fly, *Selandria cerasi* (*Eriocampa limacina*), which infests the leaves of the pear and other fruit-trees; also called *plum-slug, slug-worm*, etc.; **-tree** = 2; also the wood of this tree.

Pearl (pɔ̄ɹl), *sb.*[1] [ME. *perle* – (O)Fr. *perle* :- Rom. **perla*, prob. for **pernula*, dim. of L. *perna* leg, ham, leg-of-mutton shaped bivalve (cf. It. *perna* pearl, *pernocchia* pearl-oyster).] **I. 1.** A nacreous concretion formed within the shell of various bivalve molluscs around some foreign body (e.g. a grain of sand), composed of filmy layers of carbonate of lime interstratified with animal membrane; it is of hard smooth texture, of globular, pear-shaped, oval, or irregular form, and of various colours, usually white or bluish-grey; often having a beautiful lustre, and hence prized as a gem; formerly also used in medicine. (The chief source is the PEARL-OYSTER.) **b.** (without *a* or *pl.*) As name of the substance ME. **c.** = MOTHER-OF-PEARL. Chiefly *attrib.* **2.** *Her.* In blazoning by precious stones, the tincture argent or white 1500. **3.** *fig.* Something especially precious, noble, or choice ME.

1. b. Like the wounded oyster, he mends his shell with p. EMERSON. **3.** He is the very p. Of curtesie SHIRLEY. Provb. *To cast pearls before swine*, to offer a good thing to one who is incapable of appreciating it. (From Matt. 7: 6.)

II. In transf. senses. **1.** A thin white film or opacity growing over the eye; a kind of cataract. *Obs.* or *dial.* late ME. **2.** A small and round pearl-like drop or globule; e.g. a dew-drop, a tear 1460. **3.** Applied rhet. to teeth. Cf. 'ivory'. 1586. **4.** One of the bony tubercles encircling the bur or base of a deer's antler 1575. **5.** One of several small white or silver balls set on a coronet; a similar ball as a heraldic bearing 1688. **6.** *Printing.* Name of a size of type intermediate between agate and diamond, equal to 5-point 1656.

This line is printed in pearl type.

7. A small fragment or size of various substances, e.g. of molten metal; a small piece of clean coal; a small pill or pilule 1873. **8.** One of the stages in sugar-boiling 1883. **9.** The colour of a pearl, a clear pale bluish-grey. Also *attrib.* or as *adj.* = *p.-coloured.* 1688.

2. Now hung with pearls the dropping trees appear POPE. 3. A girle, Rubie-lipt and tooth'd with p. HERRICK.

attrib. and *Comb.*, as *p.-fisher, -fishery*, etc., **p.-button,** a button made of a p., or of mother-of-pearl or an imitation of it; **-diver,** one who dives for pearl-oysters; **-eye,** †(*a*) = II. 1; (*b*) an eye of a pigeon, etc., resembling a p.; so **-eyed** *a.*; **-fish,** †(*a*) a shell-fish producing pearls; (*b*) a fish (*e.g.* the bleak) from the scales of which artificial p. is made; **-grain,** the grain or unit of weight by which the value of pearls is estimated; a carat-grain, one fourth of a carat; **-grass,** the large quaking-grass (*Briza maxima*), from the shape of its spicules; **-hen,** the guinea-fowl; **-moss,** carrageen (*Chondrus crispus*); **-moth,** a pyralid moth of the genus *Botys* or *Margaritia*, so called from its shining appearance; **-mussel,** a species of mussel bearing pearls; **-nautilus,** the pearly nautilus; **-powder,** a cosmetic used to impart whiteness to the skin; = *p.-white*; **-sago,** sago in small hard rounded grains; **-stone** = PERLITE; **-white** *a.*, pearly-white; *sb.* white oxide of bismuth; = *p.-powder.*

Pearl (pɔ̄ɹl), *sb.*[2] 1824. [var. spelling of PURL *sb.*[1]] One of a row of fine loops forming a decorative edging on pillow-lace, braid, ribbon, gold-lace, etc. Chiefly in Comb., as *p.-edge, -loop*, etc.

Pearl (pɔ̄ɹl), *v.* late ME. [Earliest in Eng. (and in Fr.) as pa. pple. PERLED (*perlé*), which may have been formed directly from the sb.] **1.** *trans.* To adorn, set, or stud with or as with pearls, or with mother-of-pearl. (Only in *pa. pple.*) **2.** To sprinkle with pearly drops 1595. **3.** To make pearly in colour or lustre 18.. **4.** To reduce (barley, sago, etc.) to the shape of small round pearls 1600. **5.** To cover with a coating of 'pearl' sugar (PEARL *sb.*[1] II. 8) 1883. **6.** *intr.* To form pearl-like drops or beads 1595. **7.** To seek or fish for pearls 1639.

2. The evening dew had pearl'd their tresses KEATS. 7. We've pearled on half-shares in the Bay KIPLING. Hence **Pea·rling** *vbl. sb.* seeking or fishing for pearls; coating of comfits with 'pearl' sugar; formation into pearl-like grains.

Pea·rl-ash. 1726. The potassium carbonate of commerce, so called from its pearly hue. Orig. only in pl.

Pea·rl-ba·rley. 1710. [Cf. PEARL *v.* 4.] Barley reduced by attrition to small rounded grains.

Pearled (pɔ̄ɹld), *ppl. a.* late ME. [f. PEARL *sb.*[1] and *v.* + -ED, after Fr. *perlé*; cf. PEARL *v.*] **1.** Furnished, set, or adorned with pearls or mother-of-pearl. **2.** Formed into pearly drops; dew-besprinkled 1586. **3.** Formed into small rounded grains 1600. **4.** Of sugar: Boiled to the degree called 'pearl' (PEARL *sb.*[1] II. 8) 1706.

Pearler (pɔ̄·ɹləɹ). 1887. [f. PEARL *v.* and *sb.* + -ER[1].] A trader engaged in pearl-fishing; also, a small vessel employed in this trade.

Pearling (pɔ̄·ɹliŋ). *Sc.* and *n. dial.* 1621. [Goes with PEARL *sb.*[2]; see -ING[1].] A kind of lace of thread or silk for trimming the edges of garments; also called *p.-lace.* In *pl.*, edgings of this lace; also *transf.* clothes trimmed with it.

Pearlite (pɔ̄·ɹləit). 1833. [f. PEARL *sb.*[1] + -ITE[1] 2 b.] **1.** = PERLITE. **2.** *Metall.* One of the forms in which carbon and iron are combined in cast steel 1889.

Pea·rl-oy:ster. 1668. A pearl-bearing bivalve mollusc of the family *Aviculidæ*; spec. *Meleagrina margaritifera* of the Indian seas.

Pea·rl-shell. 1614. **1.** A shell having a nacreous coating; mother-of-pearl. Also *rhet.* something resembling such a shell. **2.** Any shell producing pearls; a pearl-mussel 1788. **3.** *attrib.* Of or resembling a pearly shell 1618.

Pea·rlwort. 1660. A book-name for the genus *Sagina* of caryophyllaceous plants. Also **Pea·rlweed.**

Pearly (pɔ̄·ɹli), *a.* (*adv.*, *sb.*) late ME. [f. PEARL *sb.*[1] + -Y[1].] **1.** Round and lustrous like a pearl, as a dewdrop, etc. **b.** Like pearl in appearance or lustre 1603. **2.** Abounding in, having, or bearing pearls 1619. **b.** Nacreous 1667. **3.** Made of, set with, adorned with pearls or pearl 1742. **4.** Of the colour of pearl 1790. **5.** *fig.* Exceedingly precious; of supreme (spiritual) purity or lustre 1760. **B.** *adv.* After the manner of, or in respect of, pearl or pearls 1818. **C.** *sb.* in *pl.* Pearl-buttons; clothes adorned with these, as worn by costermongers. 1886.

A. 1. b. Her teeth were of a p. whiteness GIBBON. **2.** A diver in the p. seas KEATS. **b.** Pearlie shells MILT. Hence **Pea·rliness,** p. quality or character.

Pearmain (pēə·ɹmēⁱn). [Late ME. *par-*, *permayn* – OFr. *par-*, *permaine* kind of pear (in AL. *permanus* XII, *pirum parmennorum* 1285), prob. :– Rom. **Parmanus* (repl. L. *Parmensis*) of *Parma*, It. town and province (cf. PARMESAN).] †**1.** A variety of pear; app. the same as the WARDEN –1611. **2.** A variety of apple 1597. **3.** *attrib.* late ME.

Peart (pīəɹt), *a.* Variant of PERT *a.* (q.v.) from XV; still dial. or arch.; *esp.* **a.** Lively, brisk, active; **b.** Clever, intelligent, sharp.

Peasant (pe·zănt), *sb.* 1475. [– AFr. *paisant*, OFr. *païsant*, *païsent* (mod. *paysan*), refash. (with *-ant*) of earlier *païsenc*, f. *païs* (mod. *pays*) country (:– Rom. **pagensis*, f. L. *pagus* country district; cf. PAGAN) + Gmc. *-iŋȝ-*, denoting origin (cf. -ING[3]).] **1.** One who lives in the country and works on the land; a countryman, a rustic. (In early use, prop. only of foreign countries; often connoting the lowest rank, antithetical to *noble.*) †**b.** Serf, villein; also boor, clown –1613. †**c.** A low fellow –1601. **2.** *attrib.* **a.** That is a peasant, as *p.-proprietor*; †formerly, of peasant nature, base 1550. **b.** Of or pertaining to a peasant or peasants 1597.

1. Heaven lies no more open to a Noble mans performances and merits, then a pezants 1642. **2. a.** Oh what a Rogue and Pesant slaue am I SHAKS. **b.** The Tuscan peasant-plays 1878. Hence **Pea·santly** *a.* (*rare* or *Obs.*) of, pertaining to, or characteristic of a p. or peasants.

Peasantry (pe·zăntri). 1553. [f. as prec. + -RY.] **1.** Peasants collectively; a body of peasants. **2.** The condition of being a peasant; the legal position or rank of a peasant; rusticity 1596.

1. A bold p., their country's pride, When once destroy'd, can never be supplied GOLDSM. **2.** Colours so borne, shew Bastardy, peasantry, or dishonor 1622.

Peascod: see PEASECOD.

Pease (pīz), *sb.* [OE. *pise*, pl. *pisan* – late L. *pisa*, pl. *pisæ*, for earlier *pisum*, pl. *pisa* – Gr. πίσον, pl. πίσα. ME. *pese*, pl. *pesen*, survive as arch. and dial. *pease*, *peason*; see also PEA[1].] **1.** The plant, PEA[1] 2. **2.** A single seed, a pea (PEA[1] 1). *Obs.* or *arch.* OE. Also *collect.* esp. in *green p.*, †*peasen* = *green peas*; see PEA[1] 1440.

Comb., as *p.-porridge, pudding*, etc.; **p.-meal,** meal made by grinding peas; also *fig.* a medley, 'mess'.

†**Pease,** *v.* [ME. *paisen* – OFr. *pais(i)er*, f. *pais* PEACE *sb.* Also partly aphetic f. APPEASE.] **1.** *trans.* To make peace between, reconcile (two persons, or one *with* another). Also *intr.* –1652. **2.** *trans.* To quell the hostility of, to appease (a person); to satisfy, content. Also, to quiet, pacify. –1561. **3.** To reduce to peace, still, appease (strife, wrath, etc.). Also, to quiet, pacify (sorrow, violent feeling). –1541. **4.** To pacify (a country or community) –1548. **5.** To reduce to stillness or silence –1526.

Peasecod, peascod (pī·zkǫd). Now *arch.* or *dial.* late ME. [f. PEASE *sb.* + COD *sb.*[1] 2.] The pod or legume of the pea-plant; a pea-pod.

Peason, -en (pī·zən). *arch.* and *dial.* pl. of PEASE, q.v.

Pea·-sou·p. Also **pease-soup.** 1711. [f. PEASE *sb.*, PEA[1] + SOUP.] A soup made from peas. Also *attrib.* (in ref. to its colour and consistency). Hence **Pea·-sou:py** *a. colloq.*, resembling pea-soup (said esp. of a thick yellow fog).

Peastone (pī·stōᵘn). 1821. [f. PEA[1] + STONE *sb.*] A variety of limestone consisting of large rounded grains like peas; PISOLITE.

Peat[1] (pīt). ME. [– AL. *peta* (XII), also in *petamora* 'peat-moor', *petaria*, *-er(i)a* peat-bog, perh. f. the Celtic base **pett-*, which is prob. the ult. source of PIECE *sb.*] **1.** (With *a* and *pl.*) A piece of the substance described in sense 2, usually roughly brick-shaped, for use as fuel. (Chiefly *Sc.* and *n. dial.*) **2.** Vegetable matter decomposed by water and partly carbonized by chemical change, often forming bogs or mosses of large extent, whence it is dug or cut out and 'made' into peats (in sense 1). late ME.

Comb.: **p.-bog,** a bog composed of p.; **-coal,** a soft earthy lignite; **-hag,** broken ground whence peats have been dug; **-moss,** a peat-bog (the regular name in the North); the substance p.; also, the bog-moss (*Sphagnum*); *pl.* the family of mosses that grow in peat-bogs; **-reek,** the smoke of a peat-fire; also *attrib.*; hence, a cant name for whisky distilled over a peat-fire and so flavoured with peat-smoke; also, loosely, Highland whisky generally. Hence **Pea·ty** *a.*

Peat[2] (pīt). *Obs.* or *arch.* 1568. [Reintroduced by Scott. Origin unkn.] †**1.** As a term of endearment = pet of a woman; hence = girl simply, light or merry girl, spoilt girl, etc. –1632. **2.** As a term of obloquy for a woman; esp. in *proud p.* 1599. **b.** As a term of dislike for a man 1818. †**3.** 'Formerly, a lawyer, supposed to be under the peculiar patronage of any particular judge, was invidiously termed his peat or pet' (Scott *Redgauntlet* Let. xiii, note) –1824.

Pea·-tree. 1822. Name for several leguminous trees or shrubs with flowers resembling those of the pea; esp. the genus *Caragana*, of Siberia, China, etc., and the tropical *Sesbania*.

Peav(e)y (pī·vi). *U.S.* 1878. [Inventor's name.] *Lumbering.* A cant-hook having a spike at the end of the lever.

‖**Peba** (pī·ba). 1834. [Shortened from Tupi *tatu-peba* = *tatu* armadillo and *peba* low.] An American armadillo, *Tatusia* (*Dasypus*) *peba*; the seven- or nine-banded armadillo.

Pebble (pe·b'l), *sb.* ME. [Late OE. (i) *papel*, *popel* (found only in comb. with *stān* STONE); (ii) *pyppel* in *pyppelrīpiġ* pebble-stream, surviving in w.midl. *pipple*; a var. of the latter with *b*, **pybbel*, is repr. by s.w. †*puble* (XIII–XIV), midl. †*pibbil* (XIV), later †*pible*, *pibble*, of which *pebble* may be a variant.] **1.** A small stone (less than a *boulder* or *cobble*) worn and rounded by the action of water. Also, a stone rounded by attrition of ice or sand. **2.** Applied to: **a.** A colourless transparent kind of rock-crystal, used instead of glass in spectacles; a lens made of this. **b.** Various kinds of agates, etc., as *Scotch, Egyptian, Mocha p.* **c.** *rhet.* The loadstone. 1600. **d.** A kind of earthenware invented by Wedgwood 1768. **3. a.** Short for *p.-leather.* Also, the grain produced on leather by pebbling 1875. **b.** Short for *p. powder* 1880. **4.** *attrib.* Of or pertaining to a pebble or pebbles; made or consisting of pebbles, or of agate or 'Scotch pebble' 1725.

1. A pibble out of the brook BP. HALL. **2. c.** More than the diamond Koh-i-noor,..they prize that dull p...whose poles turn themselves to the poles of the world EMERSON.

Comb.: **p.-dashed** *a.*, treated with **p.-dash** or **-dashing,** i.e. mortar with pebbles in it; **-leather,** pebbled leather (see next 2); **p. powder,** a slow-burning gunpowder in the form of cubes or prisms of the size of pebbles; **-ware,** a kind of Wedgwood ware in which clays of different colours are incorporated in the paste. Hence **Pe·bbly** *a.*

Pebble (pe·b'l), *v.* 1605. [f. prec. sb.] **1.** *trans.* To pelt with (or as with) pebbles. **2.** *Leather Manuf.* To produce a rough surface, such as might be produced by the pressure of pebbles, upon (leather), by means of a roller having a pattern upon it.

Pebbled (pe·b'ld), *a.* 1600. **1.** [f. PEBBLE *sb.* + -ED[2].] Covered, strewn, or heaped with pebbles; pebbly. (Chiefly *poet.*) **2.** [f. PEBBLE *v.* + -ED[1].] Of leather: Treated by the pebbling process (see prec. 2).

1. Like as the waues make towards the pibled shore SHAKS.

Pe·bble-stone. OE. = PEBBLE *sb.* 1.

‖**Pébrine** (pebrī·n). 1870. [mod. Fr. – Pr. *pebrino*, f. *pebre* pepper, in ref. to the black spots.] A destructive epidemic disease of silk-worms, marked by black spots and stunted growth.

Pecan (pĭkæ·n). 1773. [In XVIII *paccan* = Fr. *pacane*, from the native name in Algonquian dialects.] The nut or fruit, olive-shaped and finely flavoured, of a species of hickory (*Carya olivæformis*) common in the Ohio and Mississippi valleys, often attaining a very great height; also, the tree itself, the pecan-tree. **b.** *Bitter p.*, bitter-seeded hickory (*Carya aquatica*); also called *water-* or *swamp-hickory*.

Peccable (pe·kăb'l), *a.* 1604. [– (O)Fr. *peccable* – med.L. *peccabilis*, f. L. *peccare* sin; see -ABLE.] Capable of sinning, liable to sin.
We hold all mankind to be p. and errable, even the Pope himself BERKELEY. Hence **Peccabi·lity**, liability to sin.

Peccadillo (pekădi·lo). 1591. [– Sp. *pecadillo* (-dīl'o), dim. of *pecado* sin.] A small or venial fault or sin; a trifling offence. So †**Peccadill.**

Peccancy (pe·kănsi). 1611. [– late L. *peccantia* (Tertullian), f. as next; see -ANCY.] **1.** The quality or condition of being peccant; sinfulness 1656. **b.** A sin, offence 1648. †**2.** Faultiness, incorrectness CHAPMAN.

Peccant (pe·kănt), *a.* 1604. [– *peccant-*, pr. ppl. stem of L. *peccare* sin; in sense 3 – (O)Fr. *peccant*, see -ANT.] **1.** Sinning, offending. Also said of things. †**2.** Faulty, incorrect –1841. **3.** Causing disorder of the system; morbid, unhealthy, corrupt; also, inducing disease 1604.
1. The p. Officials..fell on their knees CARLYLE. **3.** The patient..pointing to the p. tooth as the source of his woe 1899. Hence **Pe·ccant-ly** *adv.*, **-ness.**

Peccary (pe·kări). 1613. [– Carib (of Guiana and Venezuela) *pakira.*] An American gregarious quadruped, allied to the swine.

‖**Peccavi** (pekē^i·vəi). 1553. [L., pa. t. of *peccare* sin.] 'I have sinned' in phr. 'to cry *p.*'; hence, an acknowledgement of guilt.
So *pecca·vimus* 'we have sinned'; *pecca·vit* 'he has sinned'.

‖**Pêche Melba** (pę·ʃ me·lbă). [Fr.; *pêche* PEACH + name of Dame Nellie *Melba*, Australian soprano.] A confection of ice-cream and peaches flavoured with liqueurs, etc.

Peck (pek), *sb.*[1] [ME. *pek* – AFr. *pek* (whence AL. *pecca, peccum* XIII), of unkn. origin.] **1.** A measure of capacity for dry goods; the fourth part of a bushel; or two gallons. **2.** A vessel used as a peck measure. late ME. **3.** *loosely.* A large quantity or number, a great deal, a 'heap', 'lot'. Chiefly *fig.* in phr. *a p. of trouble.* 1535.
1. O, Willie brew'd a peck o' maut BURNS. Prov. Every man must eat a p. of dirt in his life 1710. *Comb.* **p. loaf,** a loaf made from a p. of flour.

Peck (pek), *sb.*[2] 1567. [f. PECK *v.*[1]] **1.** An act of pecking; a stroke with the beak or bill; *joc.* a perfunctory kiss 1611. **2.** The mark made by pecking; a prick, hole, or dint; a dot 1591. **3.** *slang.* orig. *Thieves' Cant.* Food, 'grub'; provender 1567.
3. *P. -alley*, the throat.

Peck (pek), *v.*[1] late ME. [prob. – MLG. *pekken* peck with the beak; ult. source unknown.] **I. 1.** *trans.* To strike with the beak, as a bird; to indent or pierce by thus striking. **b.** To make (a hole, etc.) by pecking 1768. **2.** *intr.* To strike with or use the beak, as a bird. late ME. **3.** *trans.* Of birds: To take (food) with the beak; esp. in small bits at a time. Often with *up.* late ME. **4.** *trans.* and *intr.* Of persons: **a.** To eat, to feed. *colloq.* (orig. *Thieves' Cant*). **b.** To bite, to eat daintily or in a nibbling fashion. 1550.
1. These parrots p. the fairest fruit DRYDEN. **2.** They p. and combat with their claws GOLDSM. *P. at*, to aim at with the beak, to try to p.; also *transf.*; 'Tis not long after But I will weare my heart vpon my sleeue For Dawes to pecke at SHAKS. *P. at* (fig.), to try to pick holes in; to carp or nag at; The Scripture hee pecks at 1641. **3.** Little birds..Light on the floor, and p. the table-crumbs 1804.

II. *trans.* To strike (something) with a pick, etc., so as to indent, pit, pierce. †Also *intr.* 1530. Hence **Pecked** (pekt) *ppl. a. Pecked line*, a line formed by short strokes thus - - - - - -.

Peck, *v.*[2] Now chiefly *dial.* 1611. [var. of PICK *v.*[2] = PITCH *v.*[1]] **1.** *trans.* To pitch, cast, fling, throw; to jerk. *Obs.* exc. *dial.* **2.** *intr.* To pitch forward; *esp.* of a horse: to stumble through striking the ground with his toe (*dial.* and *colloq.*) 1770.
1. *Hen. VIII*, v. iii. 94. **2.** The horse pecked and stumbled, and I fell forward on his neck 1898.

Pecker (pe·kəɹ). 1587. [f. PECK *v.*[1] + -ER[1].] **1.** One who, or that which, pecks; a bird that pecks, as FIG-*p.*, FLOWER-*p.*, etc.; also short for WOODPECKER 1697. **2.** An implement for pecking; a kind of hoe 1587. **3.** *slang.* Courage, resolution. Chiefly in phr. *to keep one's p. up.* 1848.

Peckish (pe·kiʃ), *a. colloq.* 1785. [f. PECK *v.*[1] + -ISH[1].] Disposed to 'peck' or eat; somewhat hungry.

Pecksniff (pe·ksnif). 1844. Name of a character in Dickens's 'Martin Chuzzlewit', represented as an unctuous hypocrite, always prating of benevolence, etc., used allusively. Hence **Pecksni·ffery, Pe·cksniffism. Pecksni·ffian** *a.*

Pectase (pe·ktē^is). 1866. [f. PECT(IN or PECT(OSE, after *diastase.*] *Chem.* A ferment having the property of converting pectin into pectic and other related acids.

Pectate (pe·ktĕt). 1831. [f. PECT(IC + -ATE[4].] *Chem.* A salt of pectic acid.

Pecten (pe·kten). *Pl.* **pectines** (pe·ktinīz), **pectens.** late ME. [– L. *pecten, -in-* comb, wool-card, pubic hair, rel. to *pectere*, Gr. πεκτεῖν, πέκειν comb.] *Anat.* and *Zool.* †**1.** The metacarpus –1541. **2.** The pubes; also, the pubic bone or share-bone. ?*Obs.* 1661. **3.** Applied to various comb-like structures in animal bodies. **a.** A pigmented vascular process with projects from the choroid coat of the eye into the vitreous humour in birds, and in certain reptiles and fishes; also called *marsupium* 1713. **b.** Each of two comb-like appendages behind the posterior legs in scorpions 1826. **c.** The pectinated structure on the claws of certain birds. **d.** = CTENOPHORE 1. **4.** A genus of bivalve molluscs, having a rounded shell with radiating ribs suggesting the teeth of a comb; an animal of this genus, a scallop 1682.

Pectic (pe·ktik), *a.* 1831. [– Gr. πηκτικός, f. πηκτός congealed, curdled, f. stem πηγ- in πηγνύειν make firm or solid.] *Chem.* In *p. acid*, a transparent gelatinous substance formed by chemical action from PECTIN, and forming an important constituent of fruit-jellies.

Pectin (pe·ktin). 1838. [f. PECT(IC + -IN[1].] *Chem.* A white neutral substance, soluble in water, formed from PECTOSE by heating with acids, or naturally in the ripening of fruits, and constituting the gelatinizing agent in vegetable juices.

†**Pectinal** (pe·ktinăl), *a.* 1541. [f. L. *pecten, -in-* (see PECTEN) + -AL[1].] **1.** *Anat.* Belonging to the 'pecten' or pubes; *p. bone*, the pubic bone –1541. **2.** *Nat. Hist.* Of the nature of or resembling a comb –1705.

Pectinate (pe·ktinĕt), *a.* 1793. [– L. *pectinatus*, pa. pple. of *pectinare*; see next, -ATE[2].] = PECTINATED. Hence **Pe·ctinately** *adv.* like the teeth of a comb.

Pectinate (pe·ktine^it), *v.* 1646. [– *pectinat-*, pa. ppl. stem of L. *pectinare*, f. *pecten, -in-*; see PECTEN, -ATE[3].] *trans.* and *intr.* To fit together in alternation like the teeth of two combs; to interlock.

Pectinated (pe·ktine^itėd), *ppl. a.* 1671. [f. as PECTINATE *a.* + -ED[1].] Chiefly *Nat. Hist.* Formed like a comb; having straight narrow closely-set projections or divisions like the teeth of a comb.

Pectination (pektinē^i·ʃən). 1646. [f. PECTIN(ATE *v.* + -ATION.] **1.** The action of interlocking or condition of being interlocked like the teeth of two combs. ?*Obs.* **2.** The condition or character of being pectinated; *concr.* a comb-like structure 1819.

Pectineal (pekti·ni,ăl), *a.* 1840. [f. mod.L. *pectineus* (see next) + -AL[1].] *Anat.* Pertaining to the pecten or pubic bone; applied to certain parts of this bone and connected structures.

‖**Pectineus** (pekti·ni,ŏs). 1704. [mod.L., f. L. *pecten, -in-* PECTEN.] *Anat.* For *p. musculus*, a flat muscle arising from the pectineal eminence of the pubic bone and inserted into the thigh-bone just behind the small trochanter.

Pectini-, bef. a vowel **pectin-**, comb. form of L. *pecten* comb.
Pe·ctinibranch (-bræŋk), **-bra·nchian, -bra·nchiate** [BRANCHIA], *adjs.* belonging to the *Pectinibranchia* (or *-branchiata*), a family of gastropod molluscs having comb-like gills (also called *Ctenobranchia*); also as *sb.*, a mollusc of this family. **Pe·ctinicorn** [L. *cornu* horn] *a.* having pectinated antennæ, as the division *Pectinicornia* of lamellicorn beetles; *sb.* a beetle of this division. **Pe·ctiniform** *a.*, (*a*) comb-shaped; (*b*) of the form of a scallop (PECTEN 4).

Pectinite (pe·ktinəit). 1677. [f. L. *pecten, -in-*; see PECTEN 4, -ITE[1] 2 a.] *Palæont.* A fossil pecten or scallop.

Pectize (pe·ktəiz), *v.* 1882. [f. Gr. πηκτός fixed, congealed (cf. PECTIC) + -IZE.] *trans.* and *intr.* To change into a gelatinous mass; to congeal.

Pectolite (pe·ktŏləit). 1828. [– G. *pectolith* (Von Kobell, 1828), f. Gr. πηκτός congealed; see -LITE.] *Min.* A whitish or greyish hydrous silicate of calcium and sodium, found in close aggregations of acicular crystals, usually fibrous and radiated in structure.

Pectoral (pe·ktŏrăl), *sb.* and *a.* 1440. [– (O)Fr. *pectoral* – L. *pectoralis* (*-ale* breastplate), f. *pectus, -tor-* breast, chest; see -AL[1].] **A.** *sb.* **1.** Something worn on the breast. **a.** An ornamental breast-plate; *spec.* that worn by the Jewish High Priest (= BREAST-PLATE 2) 1440. **b.** = BREAST-PLATE 1. 1590. †**c.** An ornamental cloth for the breast of a horse –1662. **2.** A medicine, food, or drink, good for affections of the chest, i.e. the lungs, etc. 1601. **3.** *Anat.* Short for *p. muscle, p. fin* 1758. **B.** *adj.* **1.** Of, pertaining to, situated or occurring in or upon, the breast or chest; thoracic. Chiefly *Anat.* 1578. **2.** *Med.* Of a medicine, food, or drink: Good for diseases or affections of the chest (or, loosely, the internal organs generally) 1576. **3.** Worn, or to be worn, on the breast: as the *p. cross* of a bishop. 1616. **4.** *fig.* Proceeding from the 'breast' or 'heart' 1630.
1. *P. arch* or *girdle*, the shoulder-girdle (see GIRDLE *sb.*[1] 4. a.). *P. fins*, the pair of lateral fins attached to the pectoral arch in fishes. *P. muscles*, the muscles of the chest, esp. the *pectoralis major* and the *pectoralis minor*. **2.** Some p. physick to ease his cough 1637. **4.** His words are then so pithy and so pectorall 1633. Hence **Pe·ctorally** *adv.* (*rare*), in a p. manner or position.

Pectoriloquy (pektŏri·lŏkwi). 1834. [– Fr. *pectoriloquie*, f. L. *pectus, pector-* breast + *-loquium* speaking.] *Path.* The transmission of the sound of the voice through the wall of the chest to the ear in auscultation; usu. a sign of a cavity or some other affection in the lung. So **Pectorilo·quial, Pectori·loquous** *adjs.* of, or of the nature of, p. 1824. **Pectori·loquism,** pectoriloquy 1820.

Pectose (pe·ktō^us). 1857. [f. PECT(IC + -OSE[2].] *Chem.* An insoluble substance related to cellulose and occurring with it in vegetable tissues, esp. in unripe fruits; by the action of acids, etc. it is converted into PECTIN. Hence **Pectosic** (pektǫ·sik) *a.*, in *pectosic acid*, an acid formed immediately from pectin by the action of alkalis, etc., and converted by further action of the same into pectic acid.

Pectous (pe·ktəs), *a.* 1861. [f. as PECTIZE + -OUS.] *Chem.* **a.** Congealed, solidified; said of substances normally fluid. **b.** Related to pectin. *P. acid*, an acid related to pectic acid.

‖**Pectus** (pe·ktŏs). *Pl.* **pectora** (pe·ktŏră). 1693. [L.] *Anat.* and *Zool.* **a.** The breast or chest. **b.** *Entom.* The lower surface of the thorax or prothorax of an insect.

Peculate (pe·kiŭle^it), *v.* 1749. [– *peculat-*, pa. ppl. stem of L. *peculari*, rel. to *peculium*; see PECULIAR, -ATE[3].] †**1.** *trans.* To rob (the state or country) by peculation –1749. **2.** To embezzle or pilfer (money) 1802. Also *intr.* So **Pe·culator,** an embezzler, esp. of public money or property 1656.

Peculation (pekiŭlē^i·ʃən). 1658. [f. as prec. + -ION (for L. *peculatus, -tūs*).] The appropriation of public money or property by one in an official position; the embezzlement of money or goods entrusted to his care.

Peculiar (pĭkiū·liăɹ), *a.* and *sb.* 1460. [– L. *peculiaris* not held in common with others, f. *peculium* property in cattle, private property, f. *pecu* cattle, money. Cf. PECULATE, PECUNIARY.] **A.** *adj.* **1.** That is one's own private property; that belongs exclusively to an individual person, place, thing, or group. Const. with preceding possessive, or with *to.* †**2.** Of separate constitution or existence; independent, particular, individual; single –1799. **3.** Particular, special 1590. **4.** Unlike others, singular, strange, odd, queer 1608.

1. All other goods by fortune's hand are giv'n, A Wife is the p. gift of heav'n POPE. A timidity p. to your sex 1766. †*P. institution*, a cant phrase in U.S. for negro slavery. 2. The single and p. life is bound..To keepe it selfe from noyance SHAKS. 3. A more proper subject of p. taxation ADAM SMITH. 4. Mr. Weller's knowledge of London was extensive and p. DICKENS. A girl of p. temper 1888.

Phrases. *P. jurisdiction* (*authority*, etc.), in *Canon Law*, a jurisdiction proper to itself, exempt from the jurisdiction of the bishop of the diocese. *P. measure* (in hymns, etc.), any metre other than Common, Long, or Short. *P. People*, (*a*) the Jews, as God's own chosen people; hence *transf.*; (*b*) A religious denomination founded in 1838, holding the plenary inspiration of Scripture and practising baptism of believers and divine healing. †*In p.*, as a peculiarity.

B. *sb.* (the adj. used absol.) **I.** *gen.* **1. a.** A property or privilege exclusively one's own 1650. †**b.** = *P. people*: said of the Jews, and of Christian believers –1659. †**2.** A peculiarity –1750. **II.** Spec. and techn. **1.** *Eccl.* A parish or church exempt from the jurisdiction of the ordinary or bishop in whose diocese it lies 1562. **b.** *transf.* and *fig.* A place, district, office, etc. exempt from ordinary jurisdiction 1591. **2. a.** A nick-name in Oxford (*c*1837–8) for members of the Evangelical party 1837. **b.** One of the Peculiar People 1876.

1. *Court of Peculiars*, a branch of the Court of Arches having jurisdiction over the peculiars of the archbishop of Canterbury. 2. a. 'Puseyites and Peculiars' stood shoulder to shoulder 1895. Hence **Pecu·liar-ly** *adv.*, **-ness** (now *rare*).

Peculiarity (pĭkiūli,æ·rĭti). 1610. [f. prec. + -ITY.] †**1.** Exclusive possession; private ownership BP. HALL. **2.** The quality of being peculiar to a single person or thing; also, that which is peculiar to a single person or thing 1646. †**3.** A particular liking; a partiality –1847. †**b.** Special attentiveness to a person RICHARDSON. **4.** The quality of being *sui generis*; singularity, oddity; an odd trait or characteristic 1751. †**5.** The doctrine or pratices of 'Peculiars' (see PECULIAR B. II. 2. a.) *rare.* –1838.

2. We shall speak first of those things wherein they agree; and of their peculiarities afterwards 1726. 4. There is another..p. about Mr. Talfourd; he can't spell 1817.

Peculiarize (pĭkiū·liărəiz), *v.* 1624. [f. as prec. + -IZE.] *trans.* To make peculiar; †to appropriate exclusively *to* –1704.

‖**Peculium** (pĭkiū·liŏm). 1681. [L.; see PECULIAR.] **1.** *Rom. Law.* The property which a father allowed his child, or a master his slave, to hold as his own 1706. **2.** A private or exclusive possession, property, or appurtenance.

2. This is the p. of blame, which your lordship has portioned out to me, and separated from the common stock BURKE.

†**Pecu·nial,** *a.* late ME. [– late and med.L. *pecunialis*, f. L. *pecunia* money; see -AL¹. Cf. OFr. *pecuniel.*] **1.** = PECUNIARY *a.* 1. **b.** Having to do with pecuniary penalties. –1726. **2.** = PECUNIARY *a.* 2. –1530.

Pecuniarily (pĭkiū·niărili), *adv.* 1614. [f. next + -LY².] In a pecuniary manner; in respect of money; †by exaction of money.

Pecuniary (pĭkiū·niări), *a.* (*sb.*) 1502. [– L. *pecuniarius*, f. L. *pecunia* money, orig. 'riches in cattle', f. *pecu* cattle; see PECULIAR, -ARY¹.] **1.** Consisting of money; exacted in money. **b.** Of an offence or law: Having a money penalty 1610. **2.** Of, belonging to, or having relation to money 1623. **3.** Of which money is the object 1672. †**B.** *sb.* Money; *pl.* resources in money; money matters –1767.

A. 1. P. aids STUBBS. 2. Paltry p. difficulties EMERSON. 3. P. Matches SIR T. BROWNE.

Pecunious (pĭkiū·niəs), *a.* Now *rare.* late ME. [– L. *pecuniosus*, f. *pecunia*; see prec., -OUS. Cf. (O)Fr. *pécunieux.*] Well provided with money. So **Pecunio·sity**, the state of being p. 1883.

Ped. late ME. [Of unkn. origin. See PEDLAR.] A wicker pannier; a hamper with a lid.

Pedage (pe·dĕdʒ). *Obs.* exc. *Hist.* late ME. [– med.L. *pedagium* (XI), earlier *pedaticum*; see PEAGE.] = PEAGE.

Pedagogic (pedăgǫ·dʒik), *a.* and *sb.* 1781. [– Fr. *pédagogique* – Gr. παιδαγωγικός (or f. *pédagogie*); see next, -IC.] **A.** *adj.* Of, pertaining to, or characteristic of a pedagogue or pedagogy; having the office or character of a pedagogue. **B.** *sb.* (usu. *pl.* **Pedagogics.**) The science, art, or principles of pedagogy 1864. So **Pedago·gical** *a.* 1619, **-ly** *adv.*

Pedagogue (pe·dăgǫg), *sb.* late ME. [– L. *pædagogus* – Gr. παιδαγωγός slave who took a boy to and from school, f. παῖς, παιδ- boy (cf. PÆDO-) + ἀγωγός leading, guide.] **1.** A man having the oversight of a child or youth; an attendant who led a boy to school. *Obs.* exc. in ref. to ancient times. 1483. †Also *fig.* –1653. **2.** A schoolmaster, teacher, preceptor. (Now usu. hostile, with implication of pedantry, dogmatism, or severity.) late ME.

1. *fig.* S. Paul teaching that the whole law was a p. guiding men to Christ 1609. 2. A Welsh schoolmaster, a good scholar but a very p. PEPYS. Hence **Pe·dagogue** *v.* to instruct as a p.

Pedagoguism, pedagogism (pe·dăgǫg-i:z'm, -gǫdʒi:z'm). 1642. [f. prec. + -ISM.] The character, spirit, or office of a pegagogue: the system of pedagogy.

This tetter of Pedagoguisme MILT.

Pedagogy (pe·dăgǫgi, -goᵘdʒi, -gǫdʒi). Also **pædagogy.** 1583. [– Fr. *pédagogie* (Calvin XVI) – Gr. παιδαγωγία office of a παιδαγωγός; see PEDAGOGUE, -Y³.] **1.** The function, profession, or practice of a pedagogue; pedagogics 1623. **2.** *fig.* Instruction, discipline, training; a means or system of introductory training. (Cf. *Gal.* 3:24.) 1583. **3.** A place of instruction; a school or college. (Also *fig.*) *Obs.* exc. *Hist.* 1625.

Pedal (pe·dăl), *sb.* 1611. [– Fr. *pédale* – It. *pedale* foot-stalk, tree-trunk (*pedale d'organo* organ pedal) :– L. *pedalis*, f. *pes, ped-* foot; see -AL¹.] **1.** A lever worked by the foot, in various musical instruments, and with various functions.

a. In the organ: (*a*) Each of the (wooden) keys played upon by the feet, together constituting the *p. keyboard* or *p.-board*, and usu. operating upon a separate set of pipes of bass tone (*p.-pipes*) forming the *p. organ* (see ORGAN *sb.* 2 d). (*b*) A foot-lever for drawing a number of stops out or in at once, or for other purposes. (*c*) Short for *p. organ* or *keyboard*. b. In the pianoforte, etc.: (*a*) A foot-lever for raising the dampers from the strings, thus rendering the tone fuller (*damper p.*, also loosely called *loud* or *forte p.*). (*b*) One for softening the tone (*soft* or *piano p.*). (*c*) Any one of various others occasionally used for sustaining or otherwise modifying the tone, or for special effects.

2. A lever worked by the foot in various machines; a treadle; *esp.* in a bicycle or tricycle 1789. **3.** *Mus.* A note sustained (or reiterated) in one part, usu. in the bass, through a succession of harmonies some of which are independent of it; in organ-music usu. sustained by holding down a pedal 1854. **4.** *Geom.* A curve or surface which is the locus of the feet of the perpendiculars let fall from a fixed point (the *p. origin* or *pole*) upon the tangents to a given curve or surface 1863.

attrib. and *Comb.* Of, belonging to, connected with, worked by, having, or constituting a p. or pedals (in sense 1 or 2), as *p. action, harp, key, keyboard, mechanism*, etc.; played upon the pedals of an organ, or constituting or involving a p. (in sense 3), as *p. bass, note, passage*; in *Geom.* relating to a p. curve or surface; **p.-board** (see 1 a); **-piano,** a pianoforte fitted with a pedal-board like that of an organ; **-point** = sense 3.

Pedal (pe·dăl, pī·dăl), *a.*¹ 1625. [– L. *pedalis*, f. *pes, ped-* foot; see -AL¹. (Pronounced pī·dăl only in senses 1, 1 b.)] **1.** Of, pertaining to, or connected with the foot or feet (*rare* in *gen.* sense). **b.** *Anat.* and *Zool.*: usu. in reference to the foot or *podium* of a mollusc 1851. **2.** *Geom.* Relating to the feet of perpendiculars; of or pertaining to the pedal of a curve or surface 1863. **3.** *Mus.* That is, or relates to, a pedal or pedals; see PEDAL *sb.* 1, 3.

2. *P. curve* or *surface* = PEDAL *sb.* 4. *P. origin, pole*: see PEDAL *sb.* 4.

Pedal (pe·dăl), *a.*² 1887. [– It. *pedale*; see PEDAL *sb.*] Applied to the lower and thicker part of a kind of straw grown in Italy for plaiting; *ellipt.* a plait made with this straw.

Pedal (pe·dăl), *v.* 1866. [f. PEDAL *sb.*] *intr.* **a.** To play upon the pedals of an organ. **b.** To work the pedals of a bicycle 1888.

Pedalier (pedălīᵊ·ɹ). 1881. [– Fr. *pédalier*, f. *pédale* PEDAL *sb.*] The pedal keyboard of an organ; similar pedals attached to a pianoforte.

Pedant (pe·dănt), *sb.* (*a.*) 1588. [– Fr. *pédant* – It. *pedante*, of obscure origin; the first element is presumably that of PEDAGOGUE, to which has been added the pr. ppl. ending *-ante*, -ANT. In XVI–XVII also †*pedanti(e, -ee*, direct f. It.] †**1.** A schoolmaster, teacher, or tutor –1704. **2.** A person who overrates book-learning or technical knowledge, or parades it; one who has mere learning without practical judgement; one who lays excessive stress upon details or upon strict adherence to formal rules; occas., one who is possessed by a theory, a doctrinaire 1596. **3.** *attrib.* or *adj.* That is a pedant; of or pertaining to a pedant; pedantic 1616.

1. Like a P. that keepes a Schoole i'th Church SHAKS. 2. A Man who has been brought up among Books, and is able to talk of nothing else, is..what we call a P. ADDISON.

†**Peda·nte, -a·ntie, -a·nty.** 1593. [See prec.] **1.** = PEDANT –1630. **2.** A company of pedants MILT.

Pedantic (pĭdæ·ntik), *a.* 1600. [f. PEDANT or †PEDANTE + -IC.] Having the character of, or characteristic of, a pedant; characterized by or exhibiting pedantry.

He does not..sacrifice sense and spirit to p. refinements MACAULAY. So **Peda·ntical** *a.* (now *rare*) 1588, **-ly** *adv.* **Peda·nticism,** a p. expression or notion; a piece of pedantry. **Peda·nticly** *adv.* (now *rare*).

Pedantism (pe·dăntiz'm). Now *rare.* 1593. [f. PEDANT + -ISM.] †**1.** The office or authority of a schoolmaster; the state of being under a schoolmaster, pupillage. Also *fig.* –1658. **2.** Pedantic phraseology, treatment, or method; pedantry 1593. **3.** With *a* and *pl.* A piece of pedantry 1656.

3. History-Books, opulent in nugatory pedantisms CARLYLE.

Pedantize (pe·dăntəiz), *v.* 1611. [f. as prec. + -IZE.] **1.** *intr.* To play the pedant; to speak or write pedantically. Also *to p. it.* **2.** *trans.* To turn into a pedant; to make pedants 1734.

Pedantocracy (pedăntǫ·krăsi). 1859. [f. PEDANT + -CRACY. App. first used in Fr. form *pédantocratie* by J. S. Mill writing to Comte.] A system of government by pedants; a governing body of pedants. So **Peda·ntocrat. Pedantocra·tic** *a.*

Pedantry (pe·dăntri). 1612. [f. PEDANT + -RY, after Fr. *pédanterie* or It. *pedanteria* (used by Sidney).] **1.** The character, habit of mind, or mode of proceeding, characteristic of a pedant; mere learning without judgement; unseasonable display of learning or technical knowledge. **b.** with *pl.* A piece of pedantry 1656. **2.** Undue insistence on forms or details; slavish adherence to rule, theory, or precedent 1845.

1. P. proceeds from much Reading and little Understanding STEELE. That men are frighted at Female p. is very certain 1766.

Pedarian (pĭdēᵊ·riăn), *a.* and *sb.* 1753. [f. L. *pedarius* of or belonging to a foot, of a foot long, f. *pes, ped-* foot; see -ARY¹ and -AN.] *Rom. Antiq.* **A.** *adj.* Applied to Roman senators of an inferior grade, who had no vote of their own, but could merely signify their assent to that of another. **B.** *sb.* A pedarian senator.

Pedate (pe·dĕt), *a.* 1760. [– L. *pedatus* having feet, f. *pes, ped-* foot; see -ATE².] *Nat. Hist.* **1.** Having divisions like toes, or like the claws of a bird's foot; *spec.* in *Bot.* applied to a compound or lobed leaf having a slender midrib passing through the central leaflet or lobe, and two thicker lateral ribs which branch at successive points to form the midribs of the lateral leaflets. Applied also to the venation of a simple leaf when thus arranged. So †**Pedated.** **2.** *Zool.* Furnished with feet 1816. **3.** *Anat.* Expanded (at the end) like a foot 1870. **Pe·dately** *adv.*

Pedati-, comb. form of L. *pedatus* PEDATE, in adjs. relating to leaves: **Pedatifid** (pĭdæ·tifid) [L. *-fidus* split], pedately cleft or divided at least half-way to the base; **Pedatipa·rtite** (pĭdēⁱti-) [PARTITE], pedately divided nearly to the base; so **Peda·tisect, Pedatise·cted** (pĭdēⁱti-) [L. *sectus* cut]; etc.

Peddle (pe·d'l), *v.* 1532. [In I back-formation from PEDLAR; in II prob. var. of PIDDLE *v.* by assoc. in form and sense with I.] **I. 1.** *intr.* To follow the occupation of a pedlar; to go about carrying small wares for sale. **2.** *trans.* To trade or deal in as a pedlar; to carry about and offer for sale. Chiefly *U.S.*

1837. **b.** *fig.* To deal out in small quantities; to 'retail' 1837.

2. **b.** Going around peddling his griefs in private ears 1864.

II. *intr.* To busy oneself with trifles; to trifle, dally. (Cf. PIDDLE *v.*) 1597. **b.** *trans.* with *away*: To fritter away on trifles 1880. So **Pe·ddling** *vbl. sb.* the occupation of a pedlar; also, dealing in trifles or in a trifling manner.

Peddling (pe·dliŋ), *ppl. a.* 1532. [See PEDDLE *v.* and -ING².] **1.** Plying the trade of a pedlar; going about with small goods for sale. **2. a.** Of persons: Busying oneself with trifles, or in a trifling way. **b.** Of things: Trifling, contemptible, petty, trashy 1597.

2. Poor p. Dilettantism CARLYLE. Hence **Pe·ddlingly** *adv.*

Pederast, etc.: see PÆDERAST, etc.

‖**Pedesis** (pĭdī·sis). 1878. [– Gr. πήδησις leaping.] A name given to the *Brownian movement* of minute particles; see BROWNIAN *a.*

Pedestal (pe·dĕstăl), *sb.* 1563. [– Fr. *piédestal* (†*pied d'estal*) – It. *piedestallo*, i.e. *piè* foot, *di* of, *stallo* STALL *sb.*¹; the first syll. was conformed to L. *pes, ped-* foot.] **1.** The base supporting a column or pillar in construction; the base of an obelisk, statue, vase, or the like; also, each of the two supports of a knee-hole writing-table. **2.** A base, support, foundation 1591. **3.** *techn.* †**a.** On a railway, the 'chair' used to support the rails, or a base to support the chair; **b.** an axle-guard or horn-plate; **c.** the standard or each of the standards or supports of various machines or pieces of mechanism; e.g. the standard of a pillow-block, etc. 1774.

2. Self-denial and Mortification, which are the P. of the Crosse JER. TAYLOR. Fain would he make the world his p. YOUNG.

attrib. and *Comb.*: **p.-coil, -coiler,** an upright coil of steam-pipe for use as a radiator; **-cover,** the cap of a pillow-block; **-table,** one with a massive central support or foot. Hence **Pe·destal** *v. trans.* to set or support upon a p.; to furnish with a p. (*lit.* and *fig.*). **Pe·destalled, -aled** *a.* provided with, set upon, or having a p.

Pedestrial (pĭde·striăl), *a.* 1611. [f. L. *pedester* (see next) + -IAL¹.] †**1.** = PEDESTRIAN –1634. **2.** Fitted for walking, as the *p. legs* of a crab 1890. Hence **Pede·strially** *adv.*

Pedestrian (pĭde·striăn), *a.* and *sb.* 1716. [f. Fr. *pédestre* or its source L. *pedester, -tr-* going on foot (after Gr. πεζός), written in prose, f. *pes, ped-*; see -IAN.] **A.** *adj.* **1.** On foot, going on foot; performed on foot; of or pertaining to walking 1791. **b.** Of a statue: Representing a person on foot 1822. **2.** [After L. *pedester*, Gr. πεζός] Applied to plain prose as opposed to verse; prosaic, commonplace 1716.

1. A p. tour WORDSW. **2.** P. Muses BYRON. Verse of a very p. order 1888.

B. *sb.* One who goes or travels on foot; a walker 1793. Hence **Pede·strianism,** the practice of a p., walking; prosaic or commonplace quality or style. **Pede·strianize** *v. intr.* (also with *it*) to act the pedestrian; to go or travel on foot; to walk 1811.

†**Pede·strious,** *a.* 1646. [f. L. *pedester* (see prec.) + -IOUS.] Going on foot –1822.

Pedetentous (pedĭte·ntəs), *a. rare.* 1837. [f. L. *pedetentim* step by step + -OUS.] Proceeding step by step; advancing cautiously.

Pedetic (pĭde·tik), *a.* 1878. [– Gr. πηδητικός, f. πηδητής leaper; cf. PEDESIS.] Of or pertaining to pedesis.

Pedi-, comb. form of L. *pes, ped-* foot, as in L. *pedisequus*, Eng. *pedicure*, etc.

Pe·diform, *a.* having the form of a foot; said chiefly of the organs of insects. **Pedigerous** (pĭdi·dʒĕrəs), *a.* bearing feet or legs.

Pediad (pe·diæd), *a.* 1899. [– Gr. πεδιάς, -αδ- adj. flat, level, f. πεδίον PEDION.] *Cryst.* Of, pertaining to, or consisting of pedia.

Pedicel (pe·disĕl). 1676. [– mod.L. *pedicellus*, dim. of *pediculus* PEDICLE.] **1.** *Bot.* A small stalk or stalk-like structure in a plant; *esp.* each of the subordinate stalks which immediately bear the flowers in a branched inflorescence (the main stalk being the *peduncle*); also, a small peduncle. **2.** *Zool.* and *Anat.* Applied to various small stalk-like structures in animals (mostly also called PEDUNCLE) 1826.

a. In insects, the third joint of an antenna; also, the basal joint of the abdomen when long and slender. **b.** The eye-stalk in some Crustacea, etc. **c.** The stalk by which a brachiopod, etc., is attached. **d.** Each of the ambulacral feet of an echinoderm. **e.** The PEDICLE of a vertebra.

3. *attrib.*, as *p.-cell*, a cell forming a p. 1882. Hence **Pedice·llar** *a.* pertaining to, or of the nature of, a p. **Pe·dicelled, -eled** *a.* pedicellate.

‖**Pedicellaria** (pe:disĕlēᵊ·riă). *Pl.* **-æ.** 1872. [mod.L., f. *pedicellus* PEDICEL.] *Zool.* In echinoderms, Each of a number of small, pincer-like organs, with two, three, or four valves, on the outside of the body, usually among and around the spines.

Pedicellate (pe·disĕleᶦt), *a.* 1824. [f. mod. L. *pedicellus* PEDICEL + -ATE².] *Bot.* and *Zool.* Having a pedicel or pedicels; *spec.* in *Zool.* belonging to the division *Pedicellata* of echinoderms. So **Pe·dicellated** *a.* 1821. **Pedicella·tion,** the condition of being p.

Pedicle (pe·dik'l). 1626. [– L. *pediculus* footstalk, dim. of *pes, ped-* foot; see -CULE.] *Nat. Hist.*, etc. **1.** *Bot.* A small stalk, footstalk, pedicel; formerly, the stalk of a leaf (= *petiole*), or of a flower or fruit (= *peduncle*); now usu., a minute stalk-like support, as those of seeds, glands, etc. **2.** *Zool.*, etc. A small stalk; a pedicel or peduncle.

spec. **a.** *Path.* A stalk by which a tumour, etc., is attached to a part of the body. **b.** *Anat.* Each of the two narrow thickened parts of a vertebra connecting the centrum with the lamina. **c.** *Zool.* The process of bone supporting the horn of a deer, etc. 1753. Hence **Pe·dicled** *a.* having a p., pediculated.

Pedicular (pĭdi·kiŭlăɹ), *a.* 1660. [– L. *pedicularis*, f. *pediculus* louse. Cf. Fr. *pédiculaire*. See -AR¹.] Of or pertaining to a louse or lice; lousy.

Pediculate (pĭdi·kiŭlĕt), *a.* (*sb.*) 1857. [f. L. *pediculus* footstalk + -ATE².] *Nat. Hist.* **1.** = next. **2.** Belonging to the group *Pediculati* of teleost fishes, characterized by the elongated basis of the pectoral fins, resembling an arm. Also as *sb.* A member of this group. 1880.

Pediculated (pĭdi·kiŭleᶦtĕd), *a.* 1822. [f. as prec. + -ATE³ + -ED¹.] Having, or borne upon, a pedicle; stalked. (Chiefly in *Path.* of morbid growths.)

Pedicula·tion. 1719. [– L. *pediculatio*, f. *pediculat-*, pa. ppl. stem of *pediculare*, f. *pediculus* louse (cf. *formicare, formicatio* (Pliny) FORMICATION); see -ION.] *Path.* = PEDICULOSIS.

‖**Pediculo·sis.** 1890. [f. L. *pediculus* louse + -OSIS.] *Path.* Phthiriasis.

Pediculous (pĭdi·kiŭləs), *a.* 1550. [– L. *pediculosus*, f. *pediculus* louse; see -OUS.] Infested with lice, lousy; also, of or pertaining to a louse, or characterized by lice.

Pedicure (pe·dikiuᵊɹ), *sb.* 1842. [– Fr. *pédicure*, f. L. *pes, ped-* foot + *curare* CURE *v.*] **1.** One whose business is the surgical care and treatment of the feet. **2.** The surgical treatment of the feet, esp. in the removal or cure of corns, bunions, etc. 1863. So **Pe·dicure** *v.* to cure or treat (the feet) by the removal of corns, etc. **Pe·dicurism,** the art of a p. **Pe·dicurist** = sense 1.

Pedigree (pe·digrī). late ME. [XV *pedegru*, (*-gre, petegreu, -gree*) – AFr. **pe de gru* = OFr. **pie de grue* crane's foot, i.e. *pie* (mod. *pied*), *de* of, *gru* crane; so called from the mark /|\ used to denote succession in a genealogical tree. Later forms show assim. to *degree*.] **1.** A genealogical stemma or table; a genealogy drawn up in tabular form. **2.** One's line of ancestors; ancestry; descent 1440. **b.** Of animals 1608. **c.** *transf.* Origin, line of succession; etymological descent 1566. **3.** (Without article.) Descent in the abstract; esp. ancient descent; 'birth' 1460. **4.** A line of succession; *loosely*, a long series or 'string' of people 1532. **5.** *attrib.* and *Comb.* Of, pertaining to, or having a recorded line of descent, as *p. cattle*, etc. 1863.

1. I wish. .you would make a p. for me 1711. **2.** Who had no better cover for his sordid extraction than a Welch pedegrew SIDNEY. **c.** The origin and p. of our moral judgments 1833. **3.** Vertue lieth not in P. HOBBES. **5.** Pedigree-mongers nowadays invent pedigrees 1871. Hence **Pe·digreed** *a.* having a recorded p., as cattle.

‖**Pediluvium** (pedilᶦŭ·viŏm). *Pl.* **-ia.** 1693. [med. or mod.L., f. *pes, ped-* foot + *-luvium* washing, f. *luere* wash.] A foot-bath; a washing of feet. Also *attrib.* Hence **Pedilu·vial** *a.*; also *sb. pl.* ceremonies connected with the washing of feet (as a religious act).

Pedimane (pe·dimēᶦn). 1835. [– Fr. *pédimane* (Cuvier, 1797), f. L. *pes, ped-* foot + *manus* hand.] *Zool.* A pedimanous quadruped (see next).

Pedimanous (pĭdi·mănəs), *a.* 1839. [f. as prec. + -OUS.] *Zool.* Having feet like hands; applied to the lemurs and opossums in ref. to their hind feet.

Pediment (pe·dimĕnt). 1592. [Earlier *pedament* (Evelyn), *pedement* (Randle Holme), refash. of *periment* (XVI), explained as 'corrupt English' for *perimeter* in R. Dallington's 'Hypnerotomachia' 1592, but prob. a workman's or rustic's deformation of PYRAMID.] **1.** The triangular part, resembling a low gable, crowning the front of a building in the Grecian style of architecture, esp. over a portico. Also, a similarly-placed member in the Roman and Renaissance styles. Hence, in *Decorative art*, Any member of similar form and position, as one placed over the opening in an ironwork screen, etc. **2.** Referred to L. *pes* (*ped-*) 'foot', and used for: A base, foundation; a pavement 1726. Hence **Pe·dimented** *a.* having a p.; formed with or made like a p.

Pedime·ntal, *a.* 1851. [f. prec. + -AL¹.] **1.** Of or pertaining to a pediment, of the nature of a pediment. **b.** Shaped like a pediment, rising to a vertical angle 1890. **2.** Of or pertaining to a pedestal (see PEDIMENT 2). G. MEREDITH.

Pedion (pe·diǫn). *Pl.* **pedia.** 1899. [– Gr. πέδιον a plane, a flat surface.] *Cryst.* A term for any face of an anorthic crystal, each face being bounded by a set of faces of which no two are necessarily parallel, and which are connected only by a law of rational indices.

Pedipalp (pe·dipælp). Also in L. form **pedipalpus,** pl. **-i.** 1826. [– mod.L. *Pedipalpi* (Latreille, 1806), sb. pl., f. L. *pes, ped-* foot + *palpus* PALP.] *Zool.* **1.** An arachnid of the group *Pedipalpi*, distinguished by large pincer-like palps; formerly including the true scorpions, now only the *Phrynidæ* and *Thelyphonidæ*, or whip-scorpions 1835. **2.** Each of a pair of palps or feelers attached to the head just in front of the ambulatory limbs in most Arachnids; in some cases large and pincer-like or chelate 1826. Hence **Pedipa·lpal** *a.* **Pedipa·lpate** *a.* provided with pedipalps. **Pedipa·lpous** *a.* belonging to the group *Pedipalpi* (see 1); having large pedipalps.

Pedlar (pe·dləɹ), *sb.* Also *U.S.* **ped(d)ler.** late ME. [XIV *pedlere* (Langl.), alt. of †*pedder* (XIII), f. (dial.) PED wicker pannier (XIV), of unkn. origin, + -ER; for the ending *-ler* cf. (dial.) TINKLER (XII), beside TINKER.] **1.** One who goes about carrying small goods for sale (usu. in a bundle or *pack*); a travelling chapman. (Cf. HAWKER.) Also *fig.* **2.** One who peddles, or works in a petty, incompetent, or ineffective way 1585. **3.** *attrib.* 1553.

1. All as a poore pedler he did wend, Bearing a trusse of tryfles at hys backe SPENSER.

Comb. **Pedlar's French,** rogues' and thieves' cant; hence, unintelligible jargon, gibberish.

Pedlary (pe·dləri), *sb.* (*a.*) 1530. [f. prec. + -Y³; cf. BEGGARY.] **A.** *sb.* **1.** The business or practice of a pedlar. Also *fig.* 1604. **b.** Pedlars' wares 1593. **2.** Trifling practices or things; trumpery, trash, rubbish 1530. **B.** *attrib.* or as *adj.* Pedlar's 1550. *fig.* Peddling, trashy –1674.

A. 2. Ear-confession and pardons, with like p. 1530.

Pedo-: see PÆDO-.

Pedology (pĭdǫ·lŏdʒi). 1925. [– Russ. *pedológiya*, f. Gr. πέδον ground + -LOGY.] The science of soils.

Pedometer (pĭdǫ·mĭtəɹ). 1723. [– Fr. *pédomètre* (Bion, 1723), f. L. *pes, ped-* foot (see -O-) + *-mètre* -METER.] An instrument for recording the number of steps taken, and thus approximately measuring the distance travelled on foot; usu. resembling a watch, having a dial-plate marked with numbers, round which a pointer or index-hand travels.

Hence **Pedome·tric, -al** *adjs.* of, pertaining to, or of the nature of, a p.; **-ly** *adv.*

Pedomotive (pe·dŏmōᵘtiv), *a.* and *sb.* 1824. [f. *pedo-* for PEDI- (see -O-) + MOTIVE, prob. after *locomotive.*] (A vehicle) actuated by the foot or feet.

Pedrail (pe·drēⁱl). 1902. [f. L. *pes, ped-* foot + RAIL *sb.*²] A device for facilitating progress of heavy vehicles over rough ground by attachment of broad foot-like supporting surfaces to the wheel-rims.

‖**Pedregal** (pedrega·l, pe·dregăl). Also *erron.* **pedra-.** 1839. [Sp. *pedregal* a stony place, f. *piedra* stone :- L. *petra.*] In Mexico and s.w. U.S., a rough and rocky tract; an old lava-field. Also *transf.* an ice-field.

Pedrero (pedrē·ro). Now *Hist.* 1440. [- Sp. *pedrero* = OFr. *perrier* (whence PERRIER), now *pierrier* :- L. **petrarius* (cf. med.L. *petraria* catapult), f. *petra* stone.] A piece of ordnance orig. for discharging stones, formerly also broken iron, etc., and for firing salutes.

Peduncle (pĭdʌ·ŋk'l). 1753. [- mod.L. *pedunculus* (Linnæus, 1750), f. L. *pes, ped-* + dim. suff. *-unculus.*] **1.** *Bot.* The stalk of a flower or fruit, or of a cluster of flowers or fruits; the primary stalk, or one of the general stalks of an inflorescence, which bears either a solitary flower, a number of sessile flowers, or a number of subordinate stalks (*pedicels*) directly bearing the flowers. (Dist. from a leaf-stalk or *petiole.*) **2.** *Zool.*, etc. A stalk or stalk-like process in an animal body, either normal or morbid; = PEDICEL 2 a, b, c, PEDICLE 2 a; also, applied to several bundles of nerve-fibres in the brain, connecting one part of it with another 1797. So **Pedu·ncled** *a.* pedunculate. **Pedu·ncular** *a.* (*Nat. Hist.*) of, pertaining to, or of the nature of a p.

Pedunculate (pĭdʌ·ŋkiŭlĕt), *a.* 1760. [- mod.L. *pedunculatus*, f. *pedunculus*; see prec. and -ATE².] *Nat. Hist.* Having a peduncle or peduncles; supported by a peduncle; stalked. So **Pedu·nculated** *a.* 1752.

†**Pee,** *sb.*¹ 1483. [= late MDu. *pīe* (now *pij*) coat of coarse woollen stuff; found from XIV in COURTEPY = Du. *korte pīe* short coat of this kind; history obsc. Now only in PEA-COAT, PEA-JACKET.] A coat of coarse cloth worn by men, esp. in the 16th c. -1635.

Pee (pī), *sb.*² 1653. [Of unkn. origin.] *Mining.* The portion common to two veins which intersect.

Pee, *sb.*³ 1747. [Cf. PEA³.] *Mining.* A small piece of ore.

Pee (pī), *v.* 1788. [euphem. or nursery substitute for PISS; cf. Fr. *faire pipi.*] To urinate. Also *sb.*

Peek (pīk), *v.* [Early mod. *pe(e)ke* (Skelton), preceded by rare ME. *pike* (Chaucer); parallel to *kike, keek* (XIV, now Sc. and dial.), which has LG. cogns. Cf. next.] *intr.* To look through a crevice, or out of or into a recess, etc.; to peer, peep, pry, look *in* or *out.* Hence **Peek** *sb.* a peep, a glance 1844.

Peek-bo, peek-a-boo. Now chiefly *U.S.* 1599. [See prec.] = BO-PEEP, PEEP-BO.

Peel (pīl), *sb.*¹ [ME. *pel, pele* - AFr., OFr. *pel* (mod. *pieu*) stake :- L. *palus, palum* PALE *sb.*¹] †**1.** A stake (*rare*). ME. only. †**2.** A palisade formed of stakes; a stockade; a stockaded or palisaded (and moated) enclosure -1596. †**3.** A castle; esp. a small castle or tower -1679. **4.** The general name, in modern writers, for the massive square towers or fortified dwellings built in the 16th c. in the border counties of England and Scotland, for defence against forays 1726. **5.** Hence, the proper name of a place in the Isle of Man 1718. **6.** *attrib.*, as **p.-house, -tower** = sense 4. 1505.

Peel (pīl), *sb.*² [Late ME. *pele* - OFr. *pele* (mod. *pelle*) :- L. *pala* (:- **pagsla*), f. base of *pangere* fix, plant.] **1.** A shovel or shovel-shaped instrument. **2.** *spec.* A baker's shovel for thrusting loaves, pies, etc. into the oven and withdrawing them from it. late ME. **3.** *Printing.* A T-shaped instrument used to hang up damp freshly printed sheets to dry 1683. **4.** The blade or wash of an oar. *U.S.* 1875.

Peel (pīl), *sb.*³ 1583. [repl. earlier PILL *sb.*¹; see PEEL *v.*] The rind or outer coating of any fruit; esp. in *orange-, lemon-, citron-p.*; **candied p.,** the candied rind of species of *Citrus*, esp. the citron.

Peel (pīl), *v.* ME. [Varies with PILL *v.* in early mod. Eng. and dial. The differentiation in literary Eng. between *peel* and *pill* may have been assisted by (O)Fr. *peler* peel, *piller* pillage.] †**I.** To pillage. *trans.* = PILL *v.*¹ 1. -1732. **II.** To decorticate, strip. **1.** To strip anything of its outer layer, as an orange, potato, etc., of its skin or rind, a tree of its bark; also usu. with *off*, to strip off (skin, bark, etc.). late ME. **b.** To make by peeling 1885. **2.** *intr.* Of trees, animal bodies, etc.: To become bare of bark, skin, etc.; to cast the epidermis as after a fever. Of skin or bark: To become detached, scale off. Also **b.** To admit of being peeled or barked. 1599. **3.** *absol.* or *intr.* To strip, as for exercise, etc. (Now *slang* or *colloq.*) 1785.

1. b. And Jacob took him rods of fresh poplar.. and peeled [A. V. pilled] white strakes in them *Gen.* 30:37 (R. V.). **2. b.** A meanes to make them peele better 1641. **3.** He began to p., as the boxers call it MARRYAT.

Peeled (pīld), *ppl. a.* 1470. [f. prec. + -ED¹. See also PILLED.] **1.** Stripped of possessions, plundered 1508. **2.** = PILLED *ppl. a.* 2. 1470. **3.** Worn, threadbare, as a garment; bare of herbage, as ground. **b.** *transf.* Beggarly, mean, wretched. 1510. **4.** Stripped of skin, bark, rind, etc. 1725. **5.** Phr. *Scattered and peeled* (Isa. 18:2), prob. a mistranslation; but *peeled* has been vaguely associated with one or more of the senses above 1611.

1. Is thy land p., thy realm marauded? EMERSON. **4.** Phr. *To keep (one's) eyes p.*, i.e. open, on the alert, *U.S. colloq.* **5.** A people scattered and peeled and trodden under foot WESLEY. Hence **Pee·ling** *vbl. sb.* the action of the vb.; *concr.* that which is peeled or peels off.

Peeler¹ (pī·ləɹ). ME. [f. as prec. + -ER¹. See also PILLER.] †**1.** = PILLER 1. -1608. **b.** A plant that robs or impoverishes the soil 1573. **2.** One who or that which peels 1597.

Peeler² (pī·ləɹ). 1817. [-ER¹.] A nickname for members of the Irish constabulary, founded (1812-1818) by Mr. (later Sir) Robert *Peel*; hence, for a policeman in England. See BOBBY 2.

Peelite (pī·ləit). 1853. [See -ITE¹.] A name given to those Conservatives who sided with Sir Robert Peel when he introduced his measure for the repeal of the Corn Laws in 1846. So **Pee·lism.**

Peen (pīn). *dial., techn.*, and *U.S.* 1683. [XVII *pen*; app. rel. to PANE *sb.*²] The sharp or thin end of a hammer-head, opposite to the face; = PANE *sb.*²

Peenge (pindʒ), *v. Sc.* and *n. dial.* Also **pinge.** 15.. [perh. after *whinge* whine, infl. by *peek, peevish*, etc.] *intr.* To whine, complain in a whining voice.

Peep (pīp), *sb.*¹ late ME. [f. PEEP *v.*¹] **1.** An imitation of the feeble shrill sound made by young birds, mice, etc.; the sound itself; a cheep or faint squeak. Now *arch.* or *local.* 1470. **2.** A pop. name of certain birds, e.g. species of sandpiper, the meadow-pipit, etc. 1794.

Peep (pīp), *sb.*² 1530. [f. PEEP *v.*²] An act of peeping; a surreptitious, furtive, or peering glance 1730. **b.** *fig.* Said esp. of the first appearance of daylight, as in *p. of dawn*, P. OF DAY, etc. Also, a tiny speck of light. 1530. **c.** = PEEP-BO. *Obs.* exc. *dial.* 1677.

Hence that wild suspicious p., Like a rogue that steals a sheep SWIFT. **b.** Oft have we seen him at the p. of dawn GRAY.

attrib. and *Comb.*; **p. hawk** (*dial.*), a kestrel; **-sight,** a backsight for rifles with a slit for bringing the foresight into line with the object aimed at.

Peep (pīp), *v.*¹ [imit.; cf. CHEEP *v.*] **1.** *intr.* To utter the weak shrill sound proper to young birds, mice, and some frogs; to cheep, chirp, squeak. **2.** *transf.* Of persons: To squeak; to 'sing small'. (Chiefly contemptuous.) 1550.

1. There was none that moved the wing, or opened the mouth, or peeped [R. V. chirped] *Isa.* 10:14. **2.** Wizards that peepe and that mutter *Isa.* 8:19.

Peep (pīp), *v.*² 1460. [For the expressive combination of initial *p* with *ee* cf. PEEK *v.*, PEER *v.*², and dial. *pee, pie* (XVII).] **1.** *intr.* To look through a narrow aperture as through the half-shut eyelids or through a crevice, chink, etc. into a larger space; hence, to look furtively, slyly, or pryingly. **2.** *fig.* To emerge into view; to begin to appear or show itself; said of daylight, flowers, distant eminences, etc.; freq. with the suggestion of looking out or over something. 1535. **b.** Of a plant, seed, etc.: To sprout 1593. **c.** Of a characteristic: To come slightly into view unconsciously 1579. **3.** *trans.* To cause to appear slightly; often with *out* 1573. **b.** To cause or allow (the eye) to peep. *rare.* 1818.

1. Some that will euermore peepe through their eyes, And laugh like Parrats at a bag-piper SHAKS. **2.** Sweet as the primrose peeps beneath the thorn GOLDSM. **c.** The way the retired statesman peeps out in his essays LAMB. **3.** This love..Peeps out his coward head to dare my age DRYDEN.

Peep-bo (pī·pbōᵘ:). *colloq.* 1837. [See PEEK-BO.] = BO-PEEP.

Peeper¹ (pī·pəɹ). 1591. [f. PEEP *v.*¹ + -ER¹.] **1.** One who or that which peeps or cheeps 1611. **2.** *spec.* **a.** A young chicken or pigeon 1591. **b.** *U.S.* One of various tree-frogs, esp. the Hylodes 1884.

Peeper² (pī·pəɹ). 1652. [f. PEEP *v.*² + -ER¹.] **1.** One who peeps or peers; *esp.* a 'Paul Pry'. **2.** *slang.* An eye. Chiefly *pl.* 1700. **3.** *Cant.* A looking-glass; also, a spy-glass; *pl.* a pair of spectacles 1694.

1. What would not I give for a peeper's place at the meeting 1663.

Peep-hole (pī·phōᵘl). 1681. A small hole through which one can peep.

Pee·ping, *ppl. a.* 1592. [f. PEEP *v.*² + -ING².] That peeps or peers; that peeps forth. *P. Tom* (see quot.); hence allusively.

The story [of Godiva] is embellished with the incident of P. Tom, a prying inquisitive tailor, who was struck blind for popping out his head as the lady passed 1837.

Peep of day. 1577. [See PEEP *sb.*² b. Cf. DAY-PEEP (1530).] The first appearance of daylight.

Peep-of-day boys, a Protestant organization in the North of Ireland (*c*1784-95), whose members visited the houses of their Roman Catholic opponents at daybreak in search of arms.

Peep-show (pī·pʃōᵘ). 1861. [f. PEEP *v.*² or *sb.*² + SHOW *sb.*] A small exhibition of pictures, etc., viewed through a magnifying lens inserted in a small orifice. Also *fig.*

‖**Peepul, pípal** (pī·pʌl). 1788. [Hindi *pīpal* :- Skr. *pippala.*] = BO-TREE. Also *p.-tree.*

Peer (pīᵊɹ), *sb.* (*a.*) ME. [- AFr., OFr. *per, peer* (mod. *pair*) :- L. *par, par-* equal; cf. PAIR.] **1.** An equal in standing or rank; one's equal before the law. **2.** An equal in any respect ME. **3.** One matched with another; a companion, mate; a rival. *Obs.* or *arch.* ME. **4.** A member of one of the degrees of nobility in the United Kingdom; a duke, marquis, earl, viscount, or baron. Also *transf.* and †*gen.* ME. **5.** *attrib.* That is a peer 1693. **6.** *adj.* or quasi-*adj.* Equal (*to*) 1567.

1. Nor must Strafford suffer by an ordinary way of judicature by his peers,..he must die by Act of Parliament 1660. **2.** Ulysses..Jove's p. in wisdom COWPER. **3.** To stray away into these forests drear, Alone, without a p. KEATS. **4.** *Peers of the United Kingdom* or *of the realm* (up to 1707 called *peers of England*, from 1707 to 1801 *peers of Great Britain*), all of whom may sit in the House of Lords. *Peers of Scotland*, of whom sixteen are elected to each Parliament as representative members to sit in the House of Lords. *Peers of Ireland*, of whom twenty-eight representatives are elected for life to the House of Lords. *Peers of France*, (*a*) = DOUZEPERS; (*b*) those who possessed a territory which had been erected into a lordship and who had a right to sit in the Parliament of Paris; (*c*) members of the Upper Legislative Chamber, 1814-1848. **6.** More than one artist whose hand has not been p. to his feeling 1881. Hence **Pee·rship** = PEERAGE 2, PEERDOM 3.

Peer (pīᵊɹ), *v.*¹ late ME. [- OFr. *perer*, var. of *pairier, parer* :- late L. *pariare* make or be equal (Tertullian), f. L. *par* equal; see PAR *sb.*¹] †**1.** *trans.* To make, or class, as equal; to rank *with* -1662. **2.** To equal, to rank with 1440. **3.** *intr.* To be equal, to rank on an equality. late ME. **4.** [f. prec. sb.] *trans.* To make (a man) a peer. *colloq.* 1753.

2. O, that's the queen o' womankind, And ne'er a ane to p. her BURNS.

Peer (pīᵊɹ), *v.*² 1450. [var. of *pire* (XIV), corresp. to LG. *pīren*; perh. partly aphetic f. APPEAR.] **1.** *intr.* To look narrowly, esp. in order to make something out. **2.** *fig.* Said of inanimate things: To 'peep out' so as just to be seen; to appear slightly 1592. **3.** *transf.* To show (itself); to appear 1592. †**4.** *trans.* To make to peep out SHAKS.

1. Peering in Maps for ports, and peers, and rodes SHAKS. Deep into that darkness peering, long I stood POE. **2.** Already streaks of blue p. through our clouds CARLYLE. **3.** No Shepherdesse, but Flora Peering in Aprils front SHAKS. Hence **Pee·ring** *ppl. a.* that peers 1629.

Peerage (pīə·rėdʒ). 1454. [f. PEER *sb.* + -AGE.] **1.** The body of peers. **b.** *gen.* Nobility, aristocracy 1725. **2.** The rank or dignity of a peer 1671. †**b.** The territory of a peer –1759. **3.** A book containing a list of the peers, with their geneaology, connections, etc. 1766. **4.** *attrib.* as *p.-book*, etc. 1727.

1. When Charlemain with all his P. fell By Fontarabbia MILT. **3.** His name was in the P. 1856.

Peerdom (pīə·ɹdəm). 1603. [f. PEER *sb.* + -DOM.] **1.** = PEERAGE 2. †**2.** The territory of a French peer –1762. **3.** Equality 1891.

Peeress (pīə·rės). 1689. [f. PEER *sb.* + -ESS[1].] The wife of a peer.

P. in her own right, a woman having the rank of a peer by creation or descent.

Peerless (pīə·ɹlės), *a.* ME. [f. PEER *sb.* + -LESS.] Without peer; unequalled, matchless.

The moon..Apparent Queen unvaild her p. light MILT. Hence **Pee·rless-ly** *adv.*, **-ness.**

Peery (pīə·ri), *a.* 1700. [f. PEER *v.*[2] + -Y[1].] Inclined to peer; hence, prying, inquisitive. **b.** *Rogues' Cant.* Knowing, sly 1757.

Two p. gray eyes, which had a droll obliquity of vision SCOTT.

Peesweep (pī·zwīp). *Sc.* and *dial.* 1796. [imit. of the bird's cry.] The lapwing.

Peetweet (pī·twīt). *U.S.* 1844. [imit.; cf. PEWIT.] The spotted sand-piper or sand-lark of N. America (*Tringoides macularius*).

Peeved (pīvd), *ppl. a.* Orig. *U.S.* 1918. [f. PEEV(ISH + -ED[1].] Annoyed, vexed.

Peevish (pī·viʃ), *a.* late ME. [Of unkn. origin.] †**1.** Silly, senseless –1676. †**b.** Beside oneself; mad –1591. †**2.** Spiteful, malignant, mischievous, harmful –1601. †**3.** An epithet of dislike, hostility, etc., expressing rather the speaker's feeling than any quality of the object referred to –1548. †**4.** Perverse; headstrong, obstinate; skittish, capricious, coy –1671. **5.** Morose, querulous, ill-tempered, childishly fretful 1530. **b.** Of personal qualities, actions, etc.: Characterized by petty vexation 1577. **6.** In advb. constr. = *peevishly* 1529.

1. P. chattering FORD. **2.** Peeuishe and mocking rymes GRAFTON. **3.** Sirs, howe is it thus..that this peuysshe douehouse holdeth agaynst vs so longe? 1523. **4.** *Two Gent.* v. ii. 49. **5.** Some men fast to mortifie their lust: and their fasting makes them p. JER. TAYLOR. **b.** With a p. whine in his voice HAZLITT. Hence **Pee·vish-ly** *adv.*, **-ness.**

Peewit: see PEWIT.

Peg (peg), *sb.*[1] 1440. [XV *pegge*, prob. of LDu. origin (cf. MDu. *pegge*, Du. dial. *peg* plug, peg, LG. *pigge* peg; also MLG., MDu. *pegel* peg, pin, bolt).] **1.** A pin or bolt, orig. of wood, also of metal, etc., used to hold together parts of a framework, of machinery, etc., for stopping up a hole, as the vent of a cask, for hanging up hats, clothes, etc., for holding the ropes of a tent, etc., or for marking boundaries, levels, the score in cribbage, etc. Also short for *clothes-p.* **b.** A cricket stump. *colloq.* 1909. **2.** *spec.* **a.** In stringed musical instruments, A pin of wood or metal to which the strings are fastened at one end, and which is turned to adjust the tension in tuning; a tuning-peg. Often in fig. expressions. 1589. **b.** One of a set of pins fixed in a drinking-vessel to measure the quantity each person was to drink 1617. **c.** *Shoemaking.* A pin of wood, etc., used to fasten the uppers to the sole, or the lifts to each other 1765. **d.** The metal pin on which a peg-top spins 1740. **3.** *fig.* ? The interval between two pegs; a step, degree 1589. **4.** A drink; esp. of brandy and soda-water. Chiefly in Anglo-Indian slang. (Cf. 2 b.) 1864. **5.** An implement furnished with a pin, claw, or hook, used for tearing, harpooning, etc. 1731.

1. Phr. *A round p. in a square hole* (or *vice versa*), a man placed in a position unsuited or uncongenial to him. *A p. to hang* (a discourse, opinion, etc.) *on*, an occasion, pretext, excuse for. *To move, start, stir a p.*, to move a limb, make a move. **2. a.** *Oth.* II. i. 202. **b.** Come, old fellow, drink down to your p. LONGF. **3.** Phr. *To take, bring, let* (a person) *down a p.*(*or two*), *a p. lower*, etc., to lower him a degree in his own or the general estimation. Also, *to come down a p.*

attrib. and *Comb.*, as *p.-hole*, etc.; **p.-board**, a board with holes and pegs, used in some games; **-ladder**, a ladder with a single standard having rungs fixed through it, or to one side; **p. leg**, a wooden leg; **-tankard**, one with pegs inserted at intervals to mark the quantity each person is to drink; **-tooth**, a peg-shaped tooth, a canine tooth.

Peg (peg), *sb.*[2] 1694. [Altered from *Meg* = MARGARET; cf. *Poll* = *Moll, Mary*.] **1.** A pet form of *Margaret*. **2.** *Old Peg* (dial.): Skim-milk cheese 1785.

Peg (peg), *v.* 1543. [f. PEG *sb.*[1]] **I. 1.** *trans.* To fix with a peg; to fasten with or as with a peg or pegs. Also with *down, in, out, up*. 1598. **b.** *fig.* To confine; to tie or bind *down* 1824. **c.** *fig.* To fix the market price by buying or selling freely at a given price. *Stock Exchange slang.* 1882. **2.** To insert a peg into. †**a.** To thrust a peg into the nose of (a swine, etc.) to prevent it from routing –1631. †**b.** To plug; to spike (a cannon) –1747. **3.** To strike or pierce with a peg; to strike with a turtle-peg; to harpoon. **b.** *intr.* To aim *at* with a peg or peg-top. 1740. **4.** *Cribbage.* To mark (the score) with pegs on a cribbage-board (also *absol.*); hence *transf.* to score (so many) 1821. **5.** To mark with pegs; *esp.* to mark the boundaries of (a piece of ground, a claim, etc.) with pegs placed at the corners; usu. *p. out* 1852.

3. Silas pegged at him with his wooden leg DICKENS. **5.** Several other claims have been pegged out 1890.

II. †**1.** To drive *in* as a peg by repeated blows –1647. **2.** *intr.* To make one's way with vigour or haste. *dial.* and *colloq.* 1808. **3.** To work on persistently; to 'hammer' away 1805. (Senses 2 and 3 esp. with *away*, etc.)

2. Down the street I pegged like a madman 1884. **3.** It is no good pegging away at one little point 1867.

Peg out. a. *Croquet.* To put (a ball) out by making it hit the winning-peg. **b.** *intr. Cribbage.* To win the game by reaching the last holes before the show of hands. **c.** *intr.* To peg or pitch one's tent. **d.** To die; to be ruined (*slang*). Hence **Pe·gger,** one who pegs; also, a pegging-machine.

Pegamoid (pe·gămoid). 1895. Trade name of a waterproof cloth or imitation leather.

Pegasus (pe·găsə̆s). late ME. [L. – Gr. Πήγασος, f. πηγή spring, fount; named from the πηγαί or springs of Ocean, near which Medusa was said to have been killed. Formerly also, **Pe·gase,** in late ME. **Pegasee.**] **1.** *Gr.* and *L. Myth.* The winged horse fabled to have sprung from the blood of Medusa, and with a stroke of his hoof to have caused the fountain HIPPOCRENE to well forth on Mount Helicon. Hence, represented as the favourite steed of the Muses, and said allusively to bear poets in their poetic 'flights'. Also *attrib.* **b.** *Her.* A winged horse as a bearing, etc. 1562. **c.** *Astron.* A northern constellation, figured as a winged horse, containing three stars of the 2nd magnitude forming with one star of Andromeda a large square (the *square of P.*) 1696. **2.** *Zool.* A genus of fishes, typical of the family *Pegasidæ*, with body somewhat like a horse's head, and one dorsal and one anal fin, suggesting wings; also called *flying sea-horses* 1835.

1. Each spurs his jaded P. apace BYRON. Hence **Pega·sean, -a·sian** *adjs.* pertaining to, connected with, or resembling P.; swift; poetic.

Pegging (pe·giŋ), *vbl. sb.* 1611. [f. PEG *v.* + -ING[1].] **1.** The action of the vb. PEG. **2.** *concr.* Pegs collectively, material for pegs.

attrib. and *Comb.*: **p.-awl**, an awl for drilling holes for the pegs of shoes; **-machine,** a machine for driving in the pegs of shoes.

Peggy (pe·gi). [Alteration of *Meggy, Maggie* = MARGARET. Cf. *Polly*.] **1.** A local name for various warblers (*Sylvia*) and allied genera; also of the Pied Wagtail 1836. **2.** = DOLLY *sb.*[1] 4 a. Also **p.-tub.** 1823. **3.** *P.-with-(her-) lantern* = JACK-O'-LANTERN 1855.

†**Pe·gma, pegme.** 1603. [– L. *pegma* – Gr. πῆγμα framework fixed together, etc., f. πηγνύειν fasten.] A kind of framework or stage used in theatrical pageants, sometimes bearing an inscription; hence *transf.* the inscription itself –1647.

Pegmatite (pe·gmătəit). 1832. [f. Gr. πῆγμα, πηγματ- thing joined together + -ITE[1] 2 b.] *Min.* A coarsely crystallized kind of granite, containing little mica. Hence **Pegmati·tic, Pe·gmatoid** *adjs.*

Pe·g-top, pe·gtop. 1801. [f. PEG *sb.*[1] + TOP *sb.*[2]] **1.** A pear-shaped wooden spinning-top, with a metal peg forming the point, spun by the rapid uncoiling of a string wound about it. **b.** A game of spinning peg-tops 1828. **2.** *pl.* = *p. trousers* 1859. **3.** *attrib.* Having the shape of a peg-top, as *p. whiskers*; **p. trousers,** trousers very wide in the hips and narrow at the ankles 1858.

Pehlevi, Pehlvi: see PAHLAVI.

‖**Peignoir** (pęnʸwar). 1835. [Fr., f. *peigner* to comb.] A loose dressing-gown worn by women while their hair is being combed, or on coming out of a bath; misapplied to a woman's morning gown.

‖**Peine** (pēⁱn, ‖pen). 1554. [Fr. = PAIN.] Pain, punishment. In phr. *p. forte et dure*: 'severe and hard punishment', formerly inflicted on persons arraigned for felony who refused to plead; pressing to death. Also used allusively.

Peirastic (pəiræ·stik), *a. rare.* Also **pir-.** 1656. [– Gr. πειραστικός tentative, f. πειρᾶν try.] Involving, or performing, an attempt; experimental, tentative. So **Peira·stically** *adv.*

†**Pei·sage, pesage.** 1455. [– OFr. *pesage* (whence AL. *pesagium*), f. *peser* weigh; see -AGE. The form *peisage* is assim. to PEISE *v.*] A duty paid for the weighing of goods –1706.

Peise (pēⁱz, pīz), *sb. Obs.* exc. *dial.* [ME. *peis* – AFr., OFr. *peis*, later *pois*; see POISE *sb.*] †**1.** The quality of being heavy; heaviness, weight. Also in semi-*concr.* sense; cf. *load, burden.* –1624. †**b.** Gravity, importance; burden (of blame, etc.); 'ballast' –1602. †**2.** Definite or specified weight; the amount that a thing weighs –1610. **3.** *concr.* A weight; *spec.* (*a*) a standard weight for goods; (*b*) one of the weights of a clock. Now *dial.* ME. †**4.** Forcible impact, as of a heavy body; momentum; a heavy blow or fall –1602. **5.** Balance, poise, equilibrium; suspense; the act of holding poised. Now *dial.* late ME.

Peise (pēⁱz, pīz), *v. Obs.* exc. *dial.* [ME. *peise* – tonic stem of OFr. *peser* :– L. *pensare*; see POISE *v.*] †**1.** *trans.* To weigh, as in a balance. Also *absol.* –1609. **b.** To estimate the weight of, as by poising in the hand. Now *dial.* late ME. †**2.** *fig.* To weigh in the mind; to ponder; to estimate –1633. †**3.** To keep or place in equilibrium; to balance, poise –1633. †**b.** To balance (two things), or (one thing) against another; to make equal in weight. Usu. *fig.* –1622. †**c.** To be of equal weight with, balance, counterbalance –1607. †**4.** To put a weight upon; to load, burden; to weigh down; to oppress (*lit.* and *fig.*) –1627. **5.** *intr.* To weigh (so much). Now *dial.* late ME.

4. Lest leaden slumber peize me down SHAKS. Hence †**Pei·ser,** one who weighs; *spec.* an officer appointed to weigh the tin from the Cornish mines.

†**Pei·trel, pey·trel, pe·trel.** [ME. *peitrel(le, -al* – OFr. *peitrel, -al* :– L. *pectorale* breast-plate; see PECTORAL.] = POITREL –1687.

Pejorate (pī·dʒŏreⁱt), *v.* 1644. [– *pejorat-*, pa. ppl. stem of late L. *pejorare* make worse, f. *pejor* worse; see -ATE[3].] *trans.* To make worse, deteriorate, worsen. Hence **Pejora·tion.**

Pejorative (pī·dʒŏreⁱtiv, pīdʒǫ·rătiv), *a.* and *sb.* 1882. [– Fr. *péjoratif, -ive*, f. as prec.; see -IVE, -ATIVE.] **A.** *adj.* Tending to make worse; depreciatory; applied esp. to a derivative word in which the meaning of a root word is lowered by the addition of a suffix, etc. **B.** *sb.* A word of this character, as *poetaster*, etc. Hence **Pe·joratively** *adv.* in a deteriorated sense.

Pekan (pe·kăn). 1796. [Canadian Fr. *pekan* – Abnaki *pékané*.] A carnivorous beast (*Mustela pennanti*) of the weasel family, valuable for its fur; also, its fur.

Peke (pīk), **Pekie** (pī·ki). 1920. Abbrev. of PEKIN(G)ESE *dog.*

Pekin, -king (pī·ki·n, -ki·ŋ). 1783. [– Fr. *pékin*, f. Chinese place-name (so spelt by Jesuit missionaries) *Pēking* 'northern capital', opp. to *Nānkīng* 'southern capital'; see NANKEEN.] **1.** A kind of silk stuff. ‖**2.** Fr.

pékin, péquin (pekæ̃): A name orig. given by the soldiers under Napoleon I to any civilian; occasional in Eng. use 1827.

Pekin(g)ese (pīkiŋī·z, pīkinī·z), *a.* 1907. [f. PEKIN + -ESE.] Of or belonging to Pekin: *spec.* in *P. dog* or *spaniel*, a small long-haired dog, of the pug type, orig. brought from the Imperial Palace at Pekin; also as *sb.*

Pekoe (pe·ko, pī·ko). 1712. [– Chinese (Amoy dial.) *pek-ho*, f. *pek* white + *ho* down, hair.] A superior kind of black tea, so called from the leaves being picked young with the down still on them.

Pelage (pe·lėdʒ). 1828. [– Fr. *pelage*, f. *poil*, OFr. *peil*, *pel* hair (:– L. *pilus*), after OFr. *pilain* (:– **pilamen*); see -AGE.] A general and collective term for the fur, hair, wool, etc., of a quadruped. (Cf. *plumage*.)

Pelagian (pĭlēⁱ·dʒiăn), *a.*[1] and *sb.*[1] 1449. [– eccl. L. *Pelagianus* (Jerome), f. *Pelagius*, latinized form of the name of a British monk of the 4th and 5th centuries.] **A.** *adj.* Of or pertaining to Pelagius or his doctrines. (He denied the Catholic doctrine of original sin.) 1565. **B.** *sb.* A follower of the doctrine of Pelagius 1449.

The sect of Pelagianys, which helden that a man bi his fre wil mai deserue heuen withoute grace 1449. Hence **Pela·gianism.** **Pela·gianize** *v. intr.* to hold or express P. views.

Pelagian (pĭlēⁱ·dʒiăn), *a.*[2] and *sb.*[2] 1601. [f. L. *pelagius* – Gr. πελάγιος of the sea + -AN.] **A.** *adj.* †**1.** Of or pertaining to the *pelagiæ conchæ* or sea shells whence purple dye was obtained HOLLAND. **2.** = PELAGIC 1746. **B.** *sb.* An inhabitant of the open sea or ocean 1854.

A. 2. Some [shell-fish] are p., or inhabit only the deeps of the sea 1776.

Pelagic (pĭlæ·dʒik), *a.* 1656. [– L. *pelagicus* – Gr. πελαγικός, f. πέλαγος prop. level surface of the sea; see -IC. In XVII perh. f. contemp. PELAGIOUS by substitution of suffix.] Of or pertaining to the open or high sea, as dist. from the shallow water near the coast; oceanic; now *spec.* living on or near the surface of the open sea or ocean, as dist. from its depths. **b.** Of sealing: Carried on or performed on the high seas. So *p. sealer.* 1891. So †**Pela·gious** *a.*

Pelamyd, -mid (pe·lămid). Also in L. form. 1598. [– L. *pelamys, -myd-, pelamis*, – Gr. πηλαμύς, -υδ-.] **1.** A small Mediterranean fish; a young tunny. **2.** Applied to the genus *Pelamys* of scombroid fishes 1863.

Pelargonic (pelaɹgǫ·nik), *a.* 1848. [f. PELARGONIUM; see -IC.] *Chem.* Of or derived from the genus *Pelargonium*; esp. in *P. acid*, a fatty acid, $C_9H_{18}O_2$, prepared from the volatile oil of plants of this genus; nonylic acid.

‖**Pelargonium** (pelăɹgōᵘ·niŏm). 1819. [mod.L. (L'Héritier 1787), f. Gr. πελαργός stork, app. after earlier γεράνιον geranium; see -IUM.] *Bot.* A large genus of plants of the N.O. *Geraniaceæ*, having showy flowers and fragrant leaves, commonly cultivated under the name of *geranium*.

Pelasgian (pĭlæ·zdʒiăn), *a.* and *sb.* 1585. [– Fr. *pélasgien*, later f. L. *Pelasgus*, Gr. Πελασγός, Πελάσγιος, of the Πελασγοί; see -AN, -IAN.] **A.** *adj.* = next. **B.** *sb.* One of the *Pelasgi*, an ancient race widely spread over the coasts and islands of the Eastern Mediterranean and Ægean, and believed to have occupied Greece before the Hellenes.

Pelasgic (pĭlæ·zdʒik), *a.* 1785. [– Gr. Πελασγικός; see prec., -IC.] Of, pertaining to, or characteristic of the Pelasgi or Pelasgians. *P. architecture, building*, the oldest form of masonry found in Greece, constructed of rough or unhewn stones piled up without cement.

Pelecoid (pe·lĭkoid), *a.* and *sb.* 1727. [– Gr. πελεκοειδής, f. πέλεκυς axe; see -OID.] **A.** *adj.* Hatchet-shaped. **B.** *sb.* A figure bounded by a semicircle and two concave quadrants meeting in a point, and so resembling the blade of a battle-axe.

Pelecypod (pĭle·sipǫd), *a.* and *sb.* 1857. [f. Gr. πέλεκυς hatchet + -ποδος footed.] *Zool.* **A.** *adj.* Having a hatchet-shaped foot, as a bivalve mollusc; pertaining to such a mollusc. **B.** *sb.* A p. mollusc. Hence **Pelecy·podous** *a.*

Pelerine (pe·lĕrin, -ī·n). 1744. [– Fr. *pèlerine*, transf. use of fem. of *pèlerin* PILGRIM = pilgrim's mantle or cape.] A name for various kinds of mantles or capes worn by women; in recent use, a long narrow cape or tippet, with ends coming down to a point in front.

Pelf (pelf). ME. [– ONFr. **pelfe*, recorded as *peuffe* (mod. Norman Fr. *peufe*), var. of OFr. *pelfre, peufre* spoil (in AL. *pelfra, pelfrum*), rel. to *pelf(r)er* pillage, rob (in AL. *pelfare, pelfrare* XIII), and **pelferie* PELFRY; of unkn. origin; cf. PILFER.] †**1.** Spoil, booty –1470. †**2.** Property, goods, gear –1847. **3.** Money, wealth, riches; now 'filthy lucre' 1500. †**4.** Trash, frippery –1632. **b.** Refuse; now *dial.*, vegetable refuse 1589.

3. Ye rich men cannot think to carry your pelfe with you into Heaven BP. HALL. So †**Pe·lfry** (*a*) = sense 1. –1565; (*b*) = sense 4. –1551.

Pelham (pe·lăm). 1849. [From the surname.] In full, *P. bit*, a form of bit combining the snaffle and the curb in one. So *P. bridle.*

Pelican (pe·likăn). [OE. *pellican*, reinforced in ME. by (O)Fr. *pélican* – late L. *pelicanus* (Jerome) – Gr. πελεκάν, prob. f. πέλεκυς axe, πελεκᾶν hew with an axe, perh. with ref. to the appearance or action of the bill; cf. πελεκᾶς woodpecker.] **I.** The bird. **1.** One of a genus, *Pelecanus*, of large gregarious fish-eating water-fowls, having an enormously distensible membranous pouch depending from the lower mandible of the long hooked bill, which is used for the storing of fish when caught. **b.** In ref. to the fable that the pelican feeds her young with her own blood. late ME. †**c.** Hence applied symbolically to Christ –1814. **2.** A representation of the pelican. late ME.

1. b. What, would'st thou have me turn P. and feed thee out of my own Vitals? CONGREVE. **c.** [St. John] who lay Upon the bosom of our p. CARY. **2.** *P. in her piety* (*Her.*), a pelican represented as vulning (*i.e.* wounding) her breast in order to feed her young with her blood.

II. *transf.* **1.** An alembic having a tubulated head, from opposite sides of which two curved tubes pass out and re-enter at the body of the vessel; used in distilling liquors by fermentation 1559. **2.** An instrument having a strong curved beak, formerly used for extracting teeth 1597. **3.** An ancient piece of artillery; also, the shot from it 1727.

attrib. and *Comb.*, as *p.-brood*, etc.; **p.-fish**, an eel-like fish (*Eurypharynx pelecanoides*), dredged from a great depth near the Canary Islands; so called from its enormously developed jaws and gular pouch; **-flower**, a W. Indian climbing plant (*Aristolochia grandiflora*), Poisonous Hogweed; **p. ibis**, an Asiatic wood-ibis (*Tantalus leucocephalus*); **pelican's foot**, a gastropod shell (*Aporrhais pespelecani*), so called from its digitate outer lip. Hence **Pe·licanry**, a place where pelicans breed.

Pelisse (pĕlī·s). 1718. [– (O)Fr. *pelisse* – med.L. *pellicia*, see PILCH.] **1.** †**a.** A garment of fur. **b.** A long mantle or cloak lined with fur. **2.** A long mantle of silk, velvet, cloth, etc., worn by women, reaching to the ankles, and having arm-holes or sleeves 1755. **b.** A garment worn out of doors by young children over their other clothes 1852.

Pell (pel). *Obs.* exc. *Hist.* ME. [– AFr. *pell, peal*, OFr. *pel* (mod. *peau*) :– *pellis* skin, leather, parchment.] †**1.** A skin or hide; *esp.* a furred skin used as the lining of a cloak; a cloak so lined, a fur –1596. **2.** A skin or roll of parchment, a parchment; *spec.* each of the two pells, of receipt (*pellis receptorum*) and disbursement (*pellis exituum*), kept at the Exchequer. **b.** In *pl.* The Office of the Exchequer in which these were kept. *Obs.* exc. *Hist.* 1454.

2. *Clerk of the Pells*, an officer formerly charged with the entry of receipts and disbursements on the parchment rolls in the Exchequer. So *Master of the Pells. Obs.* exc. *Hist.*

†**Pellage.** ME. [– AFr. *pellage*, f. *pell*; see prec., -AGE.] An impost formerly levied on exported skins –1691.

‖**Pellagra** (pelēⁱ·gră, -æ·gră). 1811. [– It. *pellagra*, f. *pelle* skin (:– L. *pellis* PELL) + *-agra*, after PODAGRA.] *Path.* An endemic disease often ending in insanity (frequent among the peasantry of Lombardy, etc.), in which the skin reddens, dries, and cracks, and the epidermis peels off. Hence **Pella·grin**, a person afflicted with p. **Pella·gric, Pella·grous** *adjs.* of the nature of or pertaining to p.; affected with p.

Pellet (pe·lėt), *sb.* [Late ME. *pelote, pelet* – (O)Fr. *pelote* :– Rom. **pilotta*, dim. of L. *pila* ball.] **1.** Any (small) globe, ball, or spherical body; a bolus, a pill, etc. **2.** *spec.* A ball, usu. of stone, used as a missile during the 14th and 15th centuries, and shot from mortars, etc.; later, a bullet; now applied to small shot. Also *fig.* late ME. **b.** A toy bullet of clay, wood, paper, etc. 1553. **3.** *Her.* A roundel sable 1572. **4.** A circular boss, rounded or flat, in coins or decorative work 1842.

2. As swifte as pelet out of gonne CHAUCER.

Comb. **p. moulding** *Arch.*, a moulding consisting of a flat band on which are circular flat disks (Gwilt). Hence **Pe·llet** *v. trans.* †(*a*) to form or shape into pellets; to send as a pellet; (*b*) to hit with (paper) pellets, small shot, etc. **Pe·lleted** *ppl. a.* marked or charged with (heraldic) pellets.

Pelletierine (peletiᵊ·rəin). 1881. [f. name of Fr. chemist, Bertrand *Pelletier* (1761–97) + -INE[5].] *Chem.* A colourless alkaloid ($C_8H_{15}NO$) obtained from the bark of a pomegranate.

Pe·llety, *a.* 1572. [f. PELLET *sb.* 3 + -Y[5].] *Her.* Charged with pellets; pelleted.

Pellicle (pe·lik'l). 1541. [– Fr. *pellicule* – L. *pellicula*, dim. of *pellis* skin; see -CULE.] A small or thin skin; a membrane, cuticle, film. Chiefly in scientific use, and applied to natural formations, as a thin membrane in an animal or plant body, etc. So **Pe·llicule** (*rare*). late ME. **Pelli·cular** *a.* of, pertaining to, or of the nature of a p.

Pellitory (pe·litəri). 1533. [In sense 1 alt. of late ME. *peletre* – OFr. *peletre*, alt. of *peretre* – L. PYRETHRUM. In sense 2 alt. of †*peritorie*, †*paretorie* – AFr. *paritarie*, OFr. *paritaire* (mod. *pariétaire*) – late L. *parietaria*, subst. use (sc. *herba* plant) of fem. of *parietarius*, f. *paries, pariet-* wall. For change of ending cf. FUMITORY.] **1.** A composite plant, *Anacyclus pyrethrum*, called distinctively *P. of Spain*, a native of Barbary, the root of which has a pungent flavour, and is used as a local irritant and salivant and as a remedy for toothache. Also, the root (*radix pyrethri*) as thus used. †**b.** Applied to other plants resembling this; *esp.* (*a*) Masterwort, *Peucedanum ostruthium* (also *Great* or *False P. of Spain*); (*b*) Sneezewort, *Achillea ptarmica* (also *Wild* or *Bastard P.*) –1760. **2.** A low bushy plant (*Parietaria officinalis*, N.O. *Urticaceæ*) with small ovate leaves and greenish flowers, growing upon or at the foot of walls; commonly distinguished as *P. of the wall.* Also extended to the whole genus *Parietaria.* 1548. **3.** *attrib.*, as *p. root* 1713.

Pell-mell (pe·lme·l), *adv.* (*a.*, *sb.*) 1579. [– Fr. *pêle-mêle*, OFr. *pesle mesle*, of which there were early vars. *mesle mesle, mesle pesle*, all jingling redupl. on *mesle*, stem of *mesler* (mod. *mêler*) mix, MEDDLE.] **1.** With disorderly or confused mingling; promiscuously 1596. **b.** Of combatants: Without keeping ranks; hence, hand to hand; in a mêlée 1579. †**2.** Indiscriminately; in the mass –1659. **3.** In disorder and hurry; headlong, recklessly 1594.

1. [They] were so closely followed, that our Soldiers entred with them p. into the City 1677. **3.** I went to work p., blotted several sheets of paper with choice floating thoughts W. IRVING.

B. *adj.* (pe·lmel) Tumultuous; confused, indiscriminate 1585. **C.** *sb.* Promiscuous mingling; a hand-to-hand fight, a mêlée 1590.

High deeds Haunt not the fringy edges of the fight But the p. of men CLOUGH.

Pell mell, obs. f. PALL-MALL.

Pellock, -ack, -och (pe·lək, -ǫx). *Sc.* ME. [Of unkn. origin.] The porpoise.

Pellucid (pĕlⁱū·sid), *a.* 1619. [– L. *pellucidus*, f. *pellucēre, per-* shine through; see PER-[1], LUCID.] **1.** Translucent, transparent; clear. **2.** *fig.* †**a.** Easy to 'see through'; 'transparent' –1661. **b.** Clear in style or expression. **c.** Mentally clear. 1822.

1. I will..send the rays..through this slab of p. ice TYNDALL. **2. a.** Their craft was p. 1644. Hence **Pelluci·dity**, p. quality or condition. **Pellu·cid-ly** *adv.*, **-ness.**

Pelmanism (pe·lmăniz'm). 1918. [f. *Pelman* (1899), proprietary name of an educational institute + -ISM.] The memory-training system of the Pelman Institute.

Pelmatozoan (pe:lmătozōᵘ·ăn), *a.* and *sb.* 1891. [f. mod.L. *Pelmatozoa*, neut. pl. (f. Gr. πελματο- sole of the foot + ζῷον animal) + -AN.] (An echinoderm) of the division *Pelmatozoa*, characterized by a stalk by which it is fixed. So **Pe:lmatozo·ic** *a.*

Pelmet (pe·lmėt). 1821. [prob. alt. – Fr. *palmette* palm-leaf design on a cornice, f. *palme* PALM *sb.*[1]; cf. PALMETTE.] A horizontal curtain or valance fixed over a door, window, etc. to hide the fittings of hanging curtains, etc.

Pelo-, comb. form of Gr. πηλός clay, mud; as in **Peloli·thic** [Gr. λίθος stone] *a.*, *Geol.* applied to rock-strata consisting of clay; etc.

‖**Peloria** (pĭlōᵊ·riă). 1859. [mod.L., f. Gr. πέλωρος monstrous, f. πέλωρ monster; see -IA[1].] *Bot.* Regularity or symmetry of structure occurring abnormally in flowers normally irregular or unsymmetrical. **Pelo·rian, -o·riate, -o·ric** *adjs.*

‖**Pelota** (pĭlōᵘ·tă). 1895. [Sp. *pelota* ball, augment. of *pella* :– L. *pila* ball.] A Basque game somewhat resembling tennis or rackets, played in a large court with a ball and a racket of wicker-work fastened on the hand.

Pelt (pelt), *sb.*[1] ME. [Either (i) var. (by a rare kind of syncope) of †*pellet* – OFr. *pel(l)ete*, dim. (see -ET) of *pel* (see PELL); or (ii) back-formation from PELTRY, perh. after *paste, pastry*.] **1.** The skin of a sheep or goat with short wool on; also, the undressed skin of a fur-bearing animal; a fell. **2.** *spec.* A raw skin of a sheep, goat, etc., stripped of its wool or fur 1562. **3.** The human skin (*joc.* or *dial.*) 1605. **4.** †**a.** A garment made of a skin or fell –1649. **b.** Untanned sheepskin used to form a printer's inking-pad; a pelt-ball 1683. **5.** The dead quarry of a hawk, esp. when mangled 1615.

1. Some others of them [Saints] went about in peltes and goates skinnes FOXE.

attrib. and *Comb.*, as **p.-ball** = sense 4 b; **-monger,** one who deals in skins; **-rot,** a skin-disease in sheep.

Pelt, *sb.*[2] 1513. [f. PELT *v.*] **1.** An act of pelting; the act of pelting with missiles or (*fig.*) with obloquy. **b.** The beating of rain or snow 1862. **2.** An outburst of temper, a rage. *Obs.* exc. *dial.* 1573. **3.** The action of pelting (PELT *v.* 6) esp. in *full p.*, (at) full speed 1819.

3. Just fancy a horse that comes full p. HOOD.

Pelt, *sb.*[3] Now only *dial.* 1567. [app. var. of dial. *palt*, whence PALTRY *sb.*] †Trash or rubbish; rags; also *mod. dial.* Refuse, waste.

Pelt (pelt), *v.* 1500. [perh. contr. of PELLET, as if primarily 'throw stones at'. Cf. colloq. Fr. *peloter* beat.] **1.** *trans.* To strike with many or repeated blows (now, with something thrown); to assail with missiles. **b.** *fig.* To assail with reproaches or obloquy 1658. **2.** *intr.* To go on striking vigorously. Also *fig.* 1535. **3.** To strike *at* vigorously with missiles; to go on firing. Also *fig.* 1565. **4.** *trans.* To go on throwing (missiles) with intent to strike. Also *fig.* 1683. †**5.** *intr.* To throw out angry words –1706. **6.** To move at a vigorous and rapid pace 1831.

1. A crowd..pelting one another with Cudgels 1687. Make snowballs and p. each other 1835. **2.** The smith..pelting away at his hot iron HOOD. The rain began to p. 1879. **6.** I saw the rhinoceros pelting away 1872. Hence **Pe·lter,** one who pelts; a pelting shower; (*dial.*) a rage, 'temper'. **Pe·lting** *ppl. a.* that pelts; (*dial.*) violent, passionate.

‖**Pelta** (pe·ltă). *Pl.* **-tæ** (-tī). 1600. [L. – Gr. πέλτη a small light shield of leather.] **1.** *Antiq.* A small light shield used by the ancient Greeks, Romans, etc. **2.** *Bot.* The apothecium of a lichen when without a rim; also, a bract or scale attached by the middle like a peltate leaf 1760.

Peltast (pe·ltæst). 1623. [– L. *peltasta* – Gr. πελταστής, f. πέλτη PELTA.] *Gr. Hist.* A kind of foot-soldier, armed with a pelta and short spear or javelin.

Peltate (pe·lteᵉⁱt), *a.* 1760. [f. PELTA (*Bot.*) + -ATE[2].] *Bot.* and *Zool.* Shield-shaped; usu. of a leaf: Having the petiole joined to the under-surface of the blade at or near the middle (instead of at the base or end); hence, said of other stalked parts similarly attached. So †**Pe·ltated** *a.* 1753. **Pe·ltately** *adv.* in the manner of a p. leaf. **Pelta·tion,** p. condition, or a p. formation.

Pelti-, comb. form of PELTA, in some rarely used scientific terms; as **Pe·ltiform** *a.*, shield-shaped; of a peltate form; etc.

Pe·lting, *a. arch.* 1540. [app. rel. to PELTRY[2] and PALTRY *sb.*] Paltry, mean, insignificant, trumpery; worthless.

Like to a Tenement or pelting Farme SHAKS.

Peltry[1] (pe·ltri). late ME. [– AFr. *pelterie* (Gower), OFr. *peleterie* (mod. *pelleterie*), f. *peletier* furrier, f. *pel* (mod. *peau*); see PELL, -RY.] **1.** Undressed skins; esp. fur-skins; pelts collectively. **b.** *pl.* Kinds of peltry 1809. **2.** *attrib.*, as *p.-man*; †**p.-ware** = sense 1. late ME.

†**Pe·ltry**[2]. Chiefly *Sc.* 1550. [app. var. of PALTRY *sb.*; cf. PELT *sb.*[3], PELTING *a.*] Refuse, rubbish, trash; a piece of rubbish –1808.

‖**Peludo** (pĭlū·do). 1845. [Sp., subst. use of *peludo* hairy, f. *pelo* :– L. *pilus* hair.] The hairy armadillo (*Dasypus villosus*) of S. America.

Pelvi-, comb. form of L. *pelvis* (see below); as in **Pe·lviform** *a.* basin-shaped. **Pelvi·meter** [-METER] an instrument for measuring the diameters of the pelvis; so **Pelvi·metry**; etc.

Pelvic (pe·lvik), *a.* 1830. [f. PELVIS + -IC.] **1.** Of, pertaining to, contained in, or connected with the pelvis (PELVIS 1). **2.** Of or pertaining to the pelvis of a crinoid 1849.

1. *P. arch*, *p. girdle*, the girdle formed by the bones of the pelvis, the hip-girdle. *P. limbs*, the limbs supported by the pelvic arch; as the legs of a man.

‖**Pelvis** (pe·lvis). *Pl.* **pelves** (pe·lvīz). 1615. [L. *pelvis* basin, laver.] **1.** The basin-shaped cavity formed (in most vertebrates) by the haunch bones or *ossa innominata* together with the *sacrum* and other vertebræ. **2.** The basin-like cavity of the kidney, into which the uriniferous tubules open 1678. **3.** The basal part of the calyx of a crinoid 1839.

1. *True p.*, that part of the (human) pelvis below the ilio-pectineal line; *false p.*, the space above this between the iliac fossæ.

Pembroke (pe·mbrŏk). 1778. Name of a town and shire in Wales and of an earldom in the British peerage. Hence **P. table,** or *ellipt.* **Pembroke,** a table supported on four fixed legs, having two flaps, which can be spread out horizontally and supported on legs connected with the central part by joints.

Pemmican (pe·mikăn). Also **pemican.** 1801. [– Cree *pimecan*, *pimekan*, f. *pime* fat.] A preparation made by certain N. American Indians, consisting of lean meat, dried, pounded, and mixed with melted fat, so as to form a paste, and pressed into cakes; hence, beef similarly treated, and usu. flavoured with currants, etc., for the use of arctic explorers, soldiers, etc., as containing much nutriment in little bulk, and keeping for a long time. **b.** Extremely condensed thought or matter 1870.

b. *attrib.* A certain tendency to..the p. style 1900.

‖**Pemphigus** (pe·mfigŏs). 1779. [mod.L. (M. de Sauvages, 1763) f. Gr. πέμφιξ, πεμφιγ- bubble.] *Path.* An affection of the skin characterized by the formation of watery vesicles or eruptions (*bullæ*) on various parts of the body. Hence **Pe·mphigoid, Pe·mphigous** *adjs.*

Pen (pen), *sb.*[1] [ME. *penne* (XIV), presumably repr. OE. *penn*, implied in *onpennad* 'unpenned'; of unkn. origin.] **1.** A small enclosure, for cows, sheep, swine, poultry, etc.; a fold, sty, coop, etc. **b.** *transf.* A number of animals in a pen, or sufficient to fill a pen 1873. **2.** Applied to various enclosures resembling these 1620. **3.** A contrivance for penning the water in a river or canal, so as to form a head of water; a weir, dam, etc. ? *Obs.* 1585.

1. Tel..how my Father stole two Geese out of a P. SHAKS. **b.** A p. of Plymouth Rocks 1904. **2.** The place where visitors were allowed to go was a little p. at the left of the entrance 18...

Pen (pen), *sb.*[2] [ME. *penne* – (O)Fr. *penne* – L. *penna* feather, pl. pinions, wings, in late L. pen.] **I.** A feather, a quill, etc. **1.** A feather of a bird, a plume. *Obs.* or *dial.* late ME. **b.** In *pl.* the flight-feathers (*remiges*) of birds regarded as the organs of flight; hence put for 'wings'. Now a poetic archaism. late ME. **2.** *spec.* The quill or barrel of a feather; the quill of a porcupine. *Obs.* or *dial.* late ME. **3.** *transf.* The internal, somewhat feather-shaped shell of certain cuttle-fishes, as the squids 1872.

1. b. On mighty pens uplifted soars the eagle aloft 1800.

II. A writing tool, etc. **1.** A quill feather or part of one, with the quill pointed and split into two nibs at its lower end, for writing with ink; a quill-pen. Hence, a small instrument made of steel or other metal, pointed and split like the end of a quill-pen; a pen-nib; such a nib with the pen-holder into which it is fitted. Also, any instrument adapted for writing with fluid ink. ME. **b.** Viewed as the instrument of authorship; hence, the practice of writing or literature; †literary ability; manner, style, or quality of writing 1447. **c.** Hence, a writer or author. Now *rare.* 1563. **2.** Anything having the function of a writing pen. †**a.** A stylus; a graver –1650. **b.** A black-lead or other pencil. Now *dial.* 1644.

1. The penne of a ready writer *Ps.* 45:1. DRAWING-*p.*, MUSIC-*p.*; FOUNTAIN-*p.*, STYLOGRAPHIC *p.*, see these words. Phr. *P.-and-pencil* (attrib.), using both pen and drawing-pencil or brush; *p.-and-wash*, using both pen and brush; also PEN-AND-INK. **b.** Tyranny has no enemy so formidable as the p. COBBETT. **c.** [A book] wherein a second P. had a good share JONSON. **2.** *Electric p.*, *pneumatic p.*, modern inventions which perforate the lines of writing in fine dots, whence copies are made in ink by stencilling.

Comb.: **p.-case,** a case or receptacle for a p. or pens; **-name** tr. NOM-DE-PLUME, q.v.; **-picture,** a picture drawn with the p.; usu. *fig.* a picturesque description; **-plume** = PEN-FEATHER; **-point,** (*a*) the point of a p.; (*b*) *dial.* a steel p. or nib; **-portrait** (cf. *p.-picture*); **-tray,** a tray for pens.

Pen, *sb.*[3] 1550. [Of unkn. origin.] A female swan.

Pen, *sb.*[4] *local.* [– Brythonic *pen* head.] A word orig. meaning 'head', frequent in place-names in Cornwall, Wales, etc., as Penzance, Penmaenmawr, etc.; in the south of Scotland, etc., used as a separate word in names of hills, e.g. Ettrick Pen, Lee Pen, etc.; rarely as common noun, 'the pen'.

Pen, *v.*[1] Pa. t. and pple. **penned** (pend); also †**pend.** [OE. **pennian*, as in *onpennad* (see PEN *sb.*[1]); also ME. *bipennen* (XIII).] **1.** *trans.* To fasten, make fast. Now *dial.* **2.** To shut in, shut up, confine. Often with *up*; also *in.* ME. **3.** *spec.* **a.** To dam up (the water) in a river or canal. Now *rare.* 1576. **b.** To confine or shut up (cattle, poultry, etc.) in a pen; to put or keep in a pen 1610.

2. Sonne-bright honour pend in shamefull coupe SPENSER. **3.** Where Shepherds p. thir Flocks at eeve In hurdl'd Cotes MILT. Hence **Penned** (pend) *ppl. a.*[1] shut up in a pen; confined, as water, by a weir or lock; also with *in, up.*

Pen, *v.*[2] Pa. t. and pple. **penned** (pend). 1490. [f. PEN *sb.*[2] II. 1.] *trans.* To write *down* with a pen; to write; to draw up (a document); to compose and write, to indite. †**b.** To set forth in writing –1659.

Panegyrick upon Folly, penn'd in Latin by Erasmus 1683. Penning a letter to the *Times* 1880. Hence **Penned** (pend), *ppl. a.*[2] written (with a pen); set down in writing; also with adv., as *well-penned*.

Penacute (pīnăkiū·t), *a.* 1751. [f. L. *pene* almost + ACUTE, after *penultimate*.] *Heb.* and *Gr. Gram.* Having an acute accent on the penultimate; also as *sb.*

Penal (pī·năl), *a.* late ME. [– (O)Fr. *pénal* or L. *pœnalis*, f. *pœna* PAIN; see -AL[1].] **1.** Of, pertaining to, or relating to punishment. **a.** Punitive; prescribing or enacting the punishment of an offence or transgression. **b.** Of an act or offence: Punishable, esp. by law 1472. **c.** Constituting punishment; inflicted as, or in the way of, punishment 1600. **d.** That is payable or forfeitable as a penalty 1623. **e.** Used or appointed as a place of punishment 1843. **f.** Involving, connected with, or characterized by, a penalty or legal punishment. **g.** Of, pertaining to, or subject to the penal law, penal servitude, etc. 1647. †**2.** Painful; severe, esp. in the way of punishment –1709.

1. a. *P. Laws*, laws which impose a penalty for the commission of any act; *spec.* the laws inflicting penalties upon Nonconformists and Papists. *P. Code* (in Ireland), a name applied to the successive penal statutes passed in 17th and 18th centuries against Papists. **b.** A second edict made it p. to pay more 1872. **c.** *P. servitude*, imprisonment with hard labour at any p. establishment in Great Britain or its dominions; substituted for transportation in 1853. **d.** Let another hand.. exact Thy p. forfeit MILT. **e.** P. settlements 1843. Cayenne is..the p. colony of France 1876. Hence **Pe·nally** *adv.* in the way of punishment.

Penality (pīnæ·lĭti). Now *rare.* 1495. [– Fr. *pénalité* – med.L. *penalitas* (XII), f. L. *pœnalis*; see prec., -ITY.] †**1.** = PENALTY 1. –1513. †**2.** = PENALTY 2. –1548. **3.** The character or fact of being penal 1650.

Penalize (pī·nălǝiz), *v.* 1868. [f. PENAL + -IZE.] **1.** *trans.* To make (an action) penal 1879. **2.** *Sport.* To subject to a penalty; hence *gen.*, to handicap 1868. Hence **Penaliza·tion.**

Penalty (pe·nălti). 1512. [– legal AFr. **penalte* (cf. *severalty, specialty*), for Fr. *pénalité* PENALITY.] †**1.** Pain, suffering (*rare*) –1642. **2.** A punishment imposed for breach of law, rule, or contract; a loss, disability, or disadvantage of some kind, either fixed by law for some offence, or agreed upon in case of violation of a contract; occas. *spec.* the payment of a sum of money imposed in such a case, or the sum of money itself; a fine, mulct. **b.** *fig.* Suffering, disadvantage, or loss, esp. that resulting from an error or fault, or incident to some position or state 1664. **c.** *Sport.* A disadvantage imposed on a competitor or side as punishment for a breach of rules; also, a handicap 1885. **3.** *attrib.*, esp. in *p. goal, kick*, etc. 1889.

2. In the day thou eat'st, thou di'st; Death is the penaltie impos'd MILT. Phr. *On, upon, under p.*, with the liability of incurring p. in case of not fulfilling the command or condition stated. **3. p. envelope** *U.S.* an envelope for the unauthorized use of which a penalty is imposed.

Penance (pe·năns), *sb.* ME. [– OFr. *penance* :– L. *pœnitentia* PENITENCE; see -ANCE.] †**1.** Repentance, penitence –1699. **2.** *Theol.* The sacramental ordinance in which remission of sins is received by a penitent through the absolution of a priest, the necessary parts being contrition, confession, satisfaction, and absolution ME. **3.** The performance of some act of self-mortification or submission to some penalty, as an expression of penitence; penitential discipline or observance; *spec.* in *Eccl.* use, such discipline or observance officially imposed by a priest after confession ME. **b.** Temporal punishment for sin. late ME. **4.** *transf.* ME. †**5.** Punishment –1769.

1. Phr. *To do p.* [L. *agere pœnitentiam*], to repent. **3.** Phr. *To do p.*, to perform acts of self-mortification or undergo penitential discipline. **b.** Trentals, seyde he, delieuren fro penaunce Hir freendes soules CHAUCER. **4.** We..made our horses do p. for that little rest they had DE FOE. **5.** He.. shall, for his obstinacy, receive the terrible sentence of *p.*, or *peine forte de dure* BLACKSTONE. Hence **Pe·nance** *v. trans.* to subject to penance; to discipline, chastise.

Pen and ink, pen-and-ink, *phr.* 1463. **A.** as *sb.* **1.** *lit.* The instruments of writing. **2.** Short for *pen-and-ink drawing* 1890. **B.** as *adj.* (prop. hyphened.) **1.** Using pen and ink; clerkly. Now *rare* or *Obs.* 1676. **2.** Done, made, or executed with pen and ink, as a drawing; also, done or described in writing 1842.

B. 1. The Duke of Bedford..says he is tired of being a pen and ink man H. WALPOLE. So †**Pen and inkhorn,** as writing instruments, carried by clerks, etc.; usu. *attrib.* or as *adj.* (with hyphens): Engaged in writing, clerkly; learned, pedantic.

Penang lawyer: see LAWYER 4.

Penannular (pīnæ·niŭlăɹ), *a.* 1851. [f. L. *pæne* PENE- + ANNULAR.] Nearly annular; of the form of an almost complete ring.

‖**Penates** (pĭnē·tīz), *sb. pl.* 1513. [– L. *Penates* pl., f. *penus* provision of food, rel. to *penes* within.] *Roman Myth.* The guardian deities of the household and of the state, who were worshipped in the interior of every house; often coupled with *Lares* (see LAR); household gods. Also *transf.* and *fig.*

Pence (pens), collect. pl. of PENNY, q.v.

Pencel, pensel, -il (pe·nsĕl). Now only *Hist.* or *arch.* ME. [– AFr. *pencel*, reduced form of PENNONCEL. Cf. AL. *pencellus* (XIII), *pensellus* (XIV).] A small pennon or streamer. †**b.** A lady's token worn or carried by a knight –1485.

‖**Penchant** (paṅʃaṅ). 1672. [Fr. *penchant*, subst. use of pr. pple. of *pencher* incline.] A (strong or habitual) inclination; a favourable bias, bent.

She had a *p.* for brown MISS MITFORD.

Pencil (pe·nsĭl, pe·ns'l), *sb.* [Late ME. *pensel, -cel* – OFr. *pincel* (mod. *pinceau*) :– Gallo-Rom. **penicellum*, for L. *penicillum* paint brush, dim. of *peniculus* brush, dim. of *penis* tail.] **I. 1.** An artist's paint-brush of camel's hair, fitch, sable, etc., gathered into a quill; esp. a small and fine one. Now *arch.* **b.** Put for the painter's art, skill, or style; and transferred to word-painting. late ME. **c.** *fig.* 1581. **2.** An instrument for marking, drawing, or writing; formed of black lead, white or coloured chalk, charcoal, soft slate, aniline, etc., and having a tapering point; *spec.* a thin strip of such substance (usu., when not otherwise described, of plumbago or graphite), enclosed in a cylinder of soft wood, or in a metal case with a tapering end. (Now the prevailing sense.) 1612.

1. b. Truth needs no colour, with his colour fix'd; Beauty no p. SHAKS. **c.** Tinted by the golden p. of autumn DISRAELI.

II. 1. A small tuft of hairs, bristles, feathers, or the like, springing from or close to a point on a surface. Now only in *Nat. Hist.* 1599. **2.** *Optics.* A set of rays converging to or diverging from a single point, or such number of them as may fall upon any surface or be considered collectively 1673. **3.** *Geom.* The figure formed by a set of straight lines meeting in a point 1840. **4.** Anything pencil-shaped 1837.

2. *Optic p.*, the rays that pass from any point through the crystalline lens, and are again brought to a focus on the retina, thus forming a double cone with the crystalline as common base.

Comb.: **p. cedar,** any of several species of juniper the wood of which is used for the casing of lead-pencils; **p. diamond** (see sense II. 4); **p. flower,** a name for the genus *Stylosanthes* of leguminous plants; **p.-lead,** black-lead or graphite as used for making pencils; a slender stick of this for fitting into a pencil-case, etc.; **-sharpener,** an instrument for sharpening a black-lead or slate p. by pushing or rotating it against a cutting edge.

Pencil (pe·nsĭl, -s'l), *v.* 1532. [f. prec.] **1.** *trans.* To paint with a pencil or brush (*obs.* or *arch.*); now, usu., to colour, tint, or mark with or as with a black-lead pencil. Also *fig.* **b.** To depict or represent with the pencil or brush; †*transf.* to depict in words; also (in later use) to outline, sketch, or delineate in pencil. Also *fig.* 1610. **2.** To write or jot down with a pencil 1760. †**3.** *intr.* To form into pencils (of light) –1774. **4.** *trans.* To treat or 'paint' (a wound, etc.) *with* something applied with a fine brush 1822.

1. Time enough to pencill it over with all the curious touches of art MILT.

Pe·ncil-ca:se. 1552. A holder for the reception of a pencil or pencil-lead, etc., usually of metal; also, a case of wood, leather, etc., for keeping pencils in.

Pencilled, -iled (pe·nsĭld, -s'ld), *ppl. a.* 1592. [f. PENCIL *sb.* and *v.* + -ED.] **1.** Having a pencil 1593. **2.** Painted with a 'pencil' or fine brush; depicted with or as with a 'pencil'; now, usu., drawn or sketched in pencil 1593. **3.** Marked with or as with a lead pencil 1592. **4.** Written with a pencil 1794. **5.** Having pencils of rays; radiate 1853. **6.** *Zool.* and *Bot.* Tufted; brushy; penicillate 1846.

3. Small pensild eye browes KYD.

Pencilling (pe·nsĭliŋ, -s'liŋ), *vbl. sb.* 1706. [-ING¹.] **1.** The action of PENCIL *v.*; *esp.* fine colouring or drawing; also *transf.* **2.** *concr.* A drawing or sketch with a pencil; a jotting or note, made in pencil; *fig.* a literary sketch or portrait 1830. **3.** Drawing a line of white paint along a mortar-joint in a brick wall 1875.

1. Whether they are..made by the pencilings of art or nature HOGARTH.

†**Pe·n-clerk.** late ME. [f. PEN *sb.*² + CLERK.] A 'clerk' whose scholarship extended only to the use of the pen (as dist. from *clerk* = clergyman or scholar); a clerk, a secretary; also *fig.* –1634.

Pencraft (pe·nkrɑft). *rare.* 1600. [f. PEN *sb.*² + CRAFT *sb.*] The craft or art of writing; penmanship, authorship.

Pend, *v.* 1480. [app. – Fr. *pendre* :– late L. *pendere* for L. *pendēre* hang. But occas. aphetic f. *apend* APPEND *v.*², or of *depend.*] †**1.** *trans.* To hang; to append –1660. **2.** *intr.* To hang; to depend (*lit.* and *fig.*) 1480.

Pendant (pe·ndănt), *sb.* ME. [– (O)Fr. *pendant*, subst. use of pr. pple. of *pendre* hang; see PENDENT.] †**I.** = Fr. *pendant* = *pente.* Slope, declivity, inclination (of a hill, etc.) –1641. **II.** Something that hangs or is suspended. **1.** A loose hanging ornament; now chiefly, an ornament of some precious metal or stone, attached to a bracelet, necklace, etc.; rarely, an ornamental fringe ME. †**b.** *spec.* The end of a belt or girdle which remained hanging down after passing through the buckle –1577. **c.** *spec.* The pendant part of an ear-ring 1555. **d.** *transf.* 1586. †**2.** A natural hanging part; as *Bot.* an anther –1790. **3.** Applied to mechanical constructions; as †a pendulum –1653; a hanging chandelier, etc. 1858; †a hanging shield –1727. **4.** *Arch.* **a.** In the Decorated and Perpendicular styles: A knop or other terminal together with the stem suspending it, hanging from a vault or from the framing of an open timber roof. **b.** In *Carpentry*, A similar object on the lower end of the newel at the angle of a staircase when this projects below the string. **c.** A representation of fruit, flowers, etc., in a hanging position, as a decorative feature. ME. **5.** *Arch.* In open timber roofs: **a.** A wooden post placed against the wall, usu. resting on a corbel, its upper end secured to the hammer-beam or to the lower end of the principal rafter; also called *p. post.* **b.** A spandrel formed by the side-post, the curved brace, and the tie-beam or the hammer-beam. **c.** In stone-work: A shaft worked on the masonry of the wall, supporting the ribs of a vault or an arch or the pendant-post of an open timber roof, and resting on a corbel or terminating in a decorated boss. ME. **6.** *Naut.* (*Rigging p.*) A short rope hanging from the head of a (main or fore) mast, yard-arm, or clew of a sail, and having at its lower end a block or a thimble spliced to an eye for receiving the hooks of the fore and main tackles. Also a similar device used in other parts of the ship. late ME. **7.** *Naut.* A tapering flag, very long in the fly and short in the hoist; *spec.* that flown at the masthead of a vessel in commission, unless distinguished by a flag or broad pendant. The official form is PENNANT. 1485. **b.** *Broad p.*: a short swallow-tailed pendant flown as the distinctive mark of a commodore's ship in a squadron 1716.

1. b. The buckles and pendentes were all of fyne golde 1548. **d.** Man, ordinarily a p. to events, only half attached EMERSON. **6.** I hoisted my P. on the Irresistible NELSON.

III. 1. That by which something is hung or suspended; now *spec.* the pendant-shank or stem and the pendant-ring or bow of a watch 1580. **2.** A thing, esp. a picture, forming a parallel, match, or companion to another. Also said of a person. Often pron. as Fr. (paṅdaṅ). 1788. **b.** A complementary statement, consideration, etc.; a counterpart 1841.

2. When St. Catharine is grouped with other saints, her usual p. is St. Barbara 1848.

Comb.: **p.-bow,** the ring or 'bow' of a watch-stem; **-fittings,** hanging fittings for electric light; **-post** *Arch.* = sense II. 5 a; **-tackle,** a tackle rigged from the masthead p.

Pendency (pe·ndĕnsi). 1637. [f. PENDENT; see -ENCY.] **1.** The state or condition of being pendent, or awaiting settlement. **2.** Pendent position; droopingness, droop (*rare*) 1770.

Pendent, -ant (pe·ndĕnt, -ănt), *a.* (*prep.*) [Late ME. *penda(u)nt* – (O)Fr. *pendant*; see PENDANT *sb.* About 1600 refash. after L. *pendens, -ent-*; but *pendant* is still frequently used.] **1.** Hanging; dependent. Of a tree: having down-hanging branches. **2.** Overhanging; jutting or leaning over; also, slanting; placed or hanging on a steep slope. late ME. Also *fig.* **3.** Hanging unsupported in the air or in space; supported above the ground on arches, columns, etc. Now *rare* or *Obs.* 1600. **4.** Hanging in the balance, undecided, pending 1633. **5.** *Gram.* Of which the grammatical construction is left incomplete 1849.

1. The p. woodbine WORDSW. **2.** Another pendant towre like that at Pisa EVELYN. **3.** To be.. blowne with restlesse violence about The pendant world SHAKS. Hence **Pe·ndently, -antly,** *adv.*

||**Pendente lite** (pende·nti ləi·ti). 1736. [L., lit. 'with the lawsuit pending'.] *Law.* While a suit is pending; during litigation.

Pendentive (pende·ntiv), *sb.* (*a.*) 1727. [– Fr. *pendentif* (Delorme), f. L. *pendens, -ent-*, pr. pple. of *pendēre* hang; see PENDENT *a.*, -IVE.] **1.** *Arch.* Each of the spherical triangles formed by the intersection of a hemispherical dome by two pairs of opposite arches springing from the four supporting columns; *orig.* supporting an independent dome, cupola, or the like. Also (as in Gothic architecture) extended to each of the similar segments constituting that part of a groined vault resting on a single impost. ¶**2.** Incorrect uses: = PENDANT II. 4, 5. 1845. **B.** *adj.* Of or belonging to pendentives; of the form of or having pendentives 1790.

Pendicle (pe·ndik'l). Chiefly *Sc.* 1488. [– med.L. *pendiculum* anything pendant, appurtenance, f. L. *pendēre* hang + *-culum* -CULE.] **1.** A hanging ornament, a pendant. Now *rare.* **2.** Something dependent on something else; an appurtenance, appendage, dependency; *spec.* a small piece of property, esp. when separately sublet 1530. Hence **Pe·ndicler,** the holder of a p.; an inferior tenant.

Pending (pe·ndiŋ), *ppl. a.* and *prep.* 1642. [Anglicization of (O)Fr. *pendant* (see PENDENT *a.*) in suspense, not concluded or settled, as in OFr. *le plet pendant* the suit being in process, modelled on L. *lite pendente, pendente lite*; for the development of the prep. cf. DURING, NOTWITHSTANDING.] **A.** *ppl. a.* **1.** Remaining undecided, awaiting settlement; orig. of a lawsuit. 1797. **2.** Impending, imminent (*rare*) 1806.

1. The p. negotiations 1838. **2.** These p. ills 1833.

B. *prep.* or quasi-*prep.* During, throughout the continuance of, in the process of. (Orig. used in a construction corresp. to the abl. absol.; thus L. *pendente lite*, Fr. *pendant le procès* (= *le procès pendant*). The pple. when it stood before the sb. came to be viewed as a prep.) 1642. **b.** While awaiting, until 1838.

b. P. his return, Kate and her mother were shown into a dining-room DICKENS.

Pendle (pe·nd'l). *local.* 1808. [Of unkn. origin.] A term for various kinds or beds of stone as occurring in quarries. Also *p.-rock, -stone.*

Pendragon (pen,dræ·gən). 1470. [Welsh = chief leader in war, f. *pen* head + *dragon* dragon, f. L. *draco, dracon-* dragon, the standard of a cohort.] A title given to an ancient British or Welsh prince holding or claiming supreme power; chief leader or ruler.

Hit befel in the dayes of Vther p. when he was kynge of all Englond MALORY. Hence **Pendra·gonship,** the rank of p.

Pendulant (pe·ndiŭlănt), *a.* Also **-ent.** 1650. [f. PENDULUM + -ANT.] Pendulous, pendent.

Pendular (pe·ndiŭlăɹ), *a.* 1878. [f. PENDULUM + -AR[1].] Of or pertaining to a pendulum; resembling that of a pendulum, as a simple vibration.

Pendulate (pe·ndiŭleⁱt), *v.* 1698. [f. PENDULUM + -ATE[3].] *intr.* **a.** To swing like a pendulum. **b.** *fig.* To oscillate between two opposite conditions, be in suspense or undecided.

Pe·ndule. Now *rare.* 1578. [In sense 1 app. – L. *pendulus* PENDULOUS; in senses 2, 3 – Fr. *pendule.*] **1.** Something pendulous or suspended. †**2.** A pendulum. [Fr. *pendule* masc.] –1798. **3.** A time-piece having a pendulum. Now only as Fr. *pendule* (pañdül) fem. 1661. †**4.** *attrib.*, as *p. clock* –1677.

Penduline (pe·ndiŭləin), *a.* (*sb.*) 1802. [– Fr. *penduline* (Buffon), mod.L. *pendulinus*, f. L. *pendulus* PENDULOUS; see -INE[1].] **1.** Applied to a bird that builds a pendulous nest, esp. the *p. titmouse* of Southern and Eastern Europe (*Ægithalus pendulinus*). **2.** Pendulous, as a bird's nest 1885. **B.** *sb.* A titmouse of the genus *Pendulinus*, or allied to this 1890.

Pendulous (pe·ndiŭləs), *a.* 1605. [f. L. *pendulus* pendent (f. *pendēre* hang) + -OUS; see -ULOUS.] **1.** Suspended; hanging down, pendent, drooping. Freq. in *Nat. Hist.* 1656. †**b.** Suspended overhead; overhanging. Also *fig.* Impending. –1800. **c.** Hanging or floating in air or space. Now *rare* or *Obs.* 1638. **2.** *spec.* Suspended so as to swing; oscillating; hence, of movement: Oscillatory, undulating; consisting of simple vibrations 1706. **3.** *fig.* Wavering between two opinions, purposes, or tendencies; vacillating, undecided, doubtful. Now *rare.* 1624.

1. Ears long, broad, and p. 1782. **b.** Lear III. iv. 69. **c.** The p. round Earth MILT. **3.** The Kings mind was wholy p. (or doubtfull) PRYNNE. So **Pendulo·sity** (*rare*) the quality or condition of being p. **Pe·ndulous-ly** *adv.*, **-ness.**

Pendulum (pe·ndiŭlŏm). *Pl.* **-ums,** formerly (*rare*) **-a.** 1660. [mod.L., = med.L. *pendulum* anything pendent, also spec. a balance (XIV), whence the later sense 'pendulum', perh. after It. *pendolo* (Galileo, 1637); subst. use of n. of L. *pendulus* PENDULOUS.] **1.** A body suspended so as to be free to swing or oscillate; usu., an instrument consisting of a rod, with a weight or *bob* at the end, so suspended as to swing to and fro by the action of gravity; esp. as an essential part of a clock, serving (by the isochronism of its vibrations) to regulate and control the movement of the works. **2.** *fig.* In ref. to oscillation between two opposites 1769. †**3.** A pendulum-clock, a pendulum-watch –1706. **4.** *attrib.* 1664.

1. Compound p., (*a*) a p. consisting of a number of weights at fixed distances; an actual material p. regarded theoretically, as opp. to a *simple p.*; (*b*) a compensation p. whose rod consists of bars of different metals. **Conical p.,** a p. so contrived that the bob revolves in a circle, the rod thus describing a cone. **Mercurial** (or †**Quicksilver**) **p.,** a compensation p. with a cylindrical bob containing mercury, whose upward expansion by heat counteracts the lengthening of the rod. **Simple p.,** (*a*) a theoretical p. consisting of a particle having weight but no magnitude, suspended by a weightless inextensible rod, and moving without friction; (*b*) a p. consisting simply of a bob suspended by a cord or wire; (*c*) a p. unconnected with any mechanism. **Spherical p.,** = *conical p.* See also BALLISTIC *p.*, COMPENSATION *p.*, GRIDIRON *p.*, etc. **2.** Man! Thou p. betwixt a smile and tear BYRON.

Comb.: **p.-ball, -bob,** the heavy ball or bob forming the lower end of a p.; **-clock,** a clock that goes by means of a p.; **-level,** a plumb-level; †**-watch,** a watch of the modern type, with a balance-wheel provided with a spring and oscillating regularly, thus having the function of the p. of a clock; **-wheel,** (*a*) the escapement wheel of a clock; †(*b*) the balance-wheel of a watch.

Pene- (pīni), *prefix*, repr. L. *pæne* nearly, almost, all but, bef. a vowel *pæn-, pen-*, in a few words of rare occurrence, as **Pe:necontempora·neous** *a.*; **Pe·neplai:n** (also **-plane**), a tract of land almost a plain; etc.

||**Penelope** (pĭne·lŏpi). 1581. [– Gr. Πηνελόπη.] **1.** Name of the wife of Ulysses in ancient Greek legend, who, during her husband's long absence, nightly unravelled the web she had woven during the day, and thus put off the suitors whose offers were to wait till the web should be finished; hence, allusively, for 'chaste wife'. **2.** *Zool.* A genus of gallinaceous birds of Central and South America, typical of the subfamily *Penelopinæ* or guans 1605.

1. Our absent Penelopes were, doubtless, dreaming 1835. Hence **Penelope·an** *a.* of or pertaining to, or resembling the web or weaving, or time-gaining policy of P. **Pene·lopine** *a. Zool.* belonging to the subfamily *Penelopinæ* of gallinaceous birds.

Penetrability (pe:nĭtrăbi·lĭti). 1609. [– med.L. *penetrabilitas*, f. L. *penetrabilis*; see next, -ITY.] †**1.** Capacity of penetrating –1687. **2.** Capability of being penetrated; *spec.* in *Nat. Phil.* the capacity of simultaneously occupying the same space as something else 1648.

Penetrable (pe·nĭtrăb'l), *a.* late ME. [– (O)Fr. *pénétrable* – L. *penetrabilis*, f. *penetrare*; see PENETRATE *v.*, -BLE.] †**1.** Having the quality or capacity of penetrating; penetrative, penetrating –1668. **2.** Capable of being penetrated or pierced; into or through which access may be gained 1538.

2. It is not p. by the eye of man TOPSELL. *fig.* I am..p. to your kinde entreaties SHAKS. Hence **Pe·netrableness,** penetrability. **Pe·netrably** *adv.* †**a.** penetratingly; **b.** so as to be p.

Penetral (pe·nĭtrăl). Now *rare.* 1589. [– L. *penetral(e* (usu. in pl. *penetralia*; see next), f. *penetralis* interior, innermost, f. stem of *penetrare* PENETRATE.] The innermost part; of a temple, the sanctuary; usu. in *pl.* = next.

||**Penetralia** (penĭtrēⁱ·liă), *sb. pl.* 1668. [L., pl. of *penetral(e*; see prec.] The innermost parts of a building; *esp.* of a temple, the sanctuary or inmost shrine; hence *gen.* Innermost parts.

The p. of the harams of the East 1779. Hence **Penetra·lian** *a. rare.*

†**Pe·netrancy.** 1578. [f. PENETRANT *a.*; see -ANCY.] Penetrating quality; penetrativeness (*lit.* and *fig.*) –1692.

Penetrant (pe·nĭtrănt), *a.* 1543. [– *penetrant-*, pr. ppl. stem of L. *penetrare*; see next, -ANT. Cf. (O)Fr. *pénétrant.*] **1.** *lit.* Having the property of penetrating, piercing, or making its way into anything. **2.** *fig.* Of the mind, intellect, etc.: Acute, subtle 1599.

Penetrate (pe·nĭtreⁱt), *v.* 1530. [– (after (O)Fr. *pénétrer*) *penetrat-*, pa. ppl. stem of L. *penetrare* place within, enter within, f. *penitus* (cf. *intus*/*intrare*) inner, inmost, rel. to *penes* within, in the power of.] **1.** *trans.* To make or find its (or one's) way into or right through (something); usu. implying force or effort; to gain access within; to pierce. **b.** To permeate. Also with personal subj.: To cause to be permeated; to imbue (*with* something). 1680. **2.** *intr.* To make its (or one's) way *into* or *through* something, or *to* some point or place (implying remoteness or difficulty of access); to gain entrance or access 1530. **3.** *fig.* (*trans.*) To pierce the ear, heart, or feelings of; to 'touch' 1591. **b.** *intr.* To touch the heart SHAKS. **4.** *trans.* To gain intellectual access into the inner content or meaning of; to see into or through; to find out, discover, discern 1560. **b.** *intr.* To see *into* or *through* 1589.

1. A cloud which it was almost impossible to p. 1860. **b.** The reader..should have penetrated himself..with the atmosphere of the times 1887. **2.** Born where Heav'n's influence scarce can p. POPE. **3.** A Man penetrated with..Grief 1720. **b.** *Cymb.* II. iii. 14. **4.** Clive penetrated and disappointed his designs 1818. Hence **Pe·netrating** *ppl. a.*, **-ly** *adv.*, **-ness.**

Penetration (penĭtrēⁱ·ʃən). 1623. [– L. *penetratio*, f. as prec.; see -ION. Cf. (O)Fr. *pénétration.*] **1.** The action, or an act, of penetrating; also, mutual permeation as of two fluids. **b.** *Nat. Phil.* The occupation of the same space by two bodies at the same time; formerly *p. of dimensions* 1661. **2.** Power of penetrating, as a measurable quantity or quality. **a.** *Gunnery.* The depth to which a bullet, etc. will penetrate any material against which it is fired 1807. **b.** *Optics.* The power of an optical instrument to enable an observer to see into space, or into an object 1799. **3.** *fig.* Insight, acuteness, discernment 1605.

1. His Magnetic beam,..to each inward part With gentle p.,..Shoots invisible vertue even to the deep MILT. **2. a.** The more p. shells have the better 1901. **3.** You can pretend to be a Man of P. STEELE.

Penetrative (pe·nĭtreⁱtiv), *a.* 1477. [– med. L. *penetrativus*, f. as prec.; see -IVE. Cf. (O)Fr. *pénétratif.*] **1.** Having the quality of penetrating; *spec.* Having the quality of entering through the senses, or of keenly affecting the sense organs; sharp, pungent. Also said of the eye or sight. **2.** *fig.* That penetrates to the seat of the feelings SHAKS. **3.** *fig.* Having the power of mental penetration; intellectually acute 1727.

1. The p. character of temptations TRENCH. **2.** *Ant. & Cl.* IV. xiv. 75. **3.** So..minutely p. was the quality of his understanding MORLEY. Hence **Penetrative-ly** *adv.*, **-ness.**

Pen-feather (pe·n,fe:ðəɹ). 1602. [f. PEN *sb.*[2] + FEATHER.] **1.** A quill-feather of a bird's wing. **2.** = PIN-FEATHER 1877. So **Pe·n-fea:thered** *a.* = PIN-FEATHERED. Also said of a horse or his hair when rough or bristly.

Pen-fish. 1763. [f. PEN *sb.*^{2} + FISH *sb.*^{1}] **1.** A squid 1835. **2.** The sparoid fish *Calamus penna* of the Caribbean Sea 1763.

Penfold (pe·n,fōᵘld), *sb.* and *v.* 1575. [f. PEN *sb.*^{1} + FOLD *sb.*^{1}] = PINFOLD *sb.* and *v.*

Penguin (pe·ŋgwin, pe·ngwin). 1578. [Of unkn. origin.] †**1.** The Great Auk or Gare-fowl (*Alca impennis*) –1792. **2.** Any bird of the family *Spheniscidæ*, including several genera of sea-fowl inhabiting the southern hemisphere, distinguished by having the wings represented by scaly 'flippers' or paddles with which they swim under water 1588.

Comb.: **p. duck**, a variety of the common duck having the feet placed so far back as to induce a nearly erect attitude like that of a p.; **p. grass**, the tussock-grass of the Falkland Islands, *Poa flabellata*. Hence **Pe·nguinery**, a colony of penguins; a place where penguins congregate and breed.

Penholder (pe·nhōᵘ:ldəɹ). 1815. [f. PEN *sb.*^{2} + HOLDER^1.] A holder for a (steel or other) pen; the pen and penholder, together forming a writing instrument or 'pen' of which the pen-holder forms the handle.

Penial (pī·niăl), *a.* 1877. [f. PENIS + -AL^1.] *Anat.* Belonging to or connected with the penis.

Pe·nible, *a.* late ME. [– (O)Fr. *pénible*, f. *peine*; see PAIN, -IBLE.] †**1.** Painstaking; hard-working –1481. **2.** Causing or involving pain or trouble; painful. *Obs.* or *rare arch.*

Penicil (pe·nisil). 1826. [– L. *penicillus* PENCIL.] *Nat. Hist.* A small bundle or tuft of slightly diverging hairs, resembling a paint-brush.

Penicillate (pe·nisilĕt), *a.* 1819. [f. L. *penicillus* PENCIL + -ATE^2.] *Nat. Hist.* **a.** Furnished with a penicil or penicils; having a small tuft or tufts of hairs, scales, etc. **b.** Formed into or forming a small tuft or brush. **c.** Streaked, pencilled.

Penicilliform (penisi·lifǭɹm), *a.* 1811. [– mod.L. *penicilliformis*, f. *penicillus* PENCIL; see -FORM.] Of the form of, or resembling, a hair-pencil.

Peninsula (pĭni·nsiŭlă). *Pl.* **-as** (-ăz), formerly **-æ.** 1538. [– L. *pæninsula*, f. *pæne-* PENE- + *insula* island.] A piece of land that is almost an island, being nearly surrounded by water; hence, any piece of land projecting into the sea so that its boundary is mainly coast-line. **b.** (*spec.*) *The P.*: Spain and Portugal.

Peninsular (pĭni·nsiŭlăɹ), *a.* (*sb.*) 1612. [f. prec. + -AR^1, after Fr. *péninsulaire.*] Of, belonging to, or of the nature of a peninsula. **b.** *spec.* (usu. with capital.) Of or pertaining to the peninsula of Spain and Portugal, or (*esp.*) the war carried on there in 1808–14. 1812. **B.** *sb.* **a.** An inhabitant of a peninsula. **b.** A soldier of the P. war 1888.

Peninsulate (pĭni·nsiŭleᵗt), *v.* 1538. [f. as prec. + -ATE^3; after *insulate.*] *trans.* To make into a peninsula; to divide into peninsulas.

A detached tract peninsulated by sea, lake, or river 1774.

‖**Penis** (pī·nis). *Pl.* **penes** (-īz). 1693. [L., orig. = *cauda* tail.] The intromittent or copulatory organ of any male animal.

Penistone (pe·nistŏn). 1551. [Name of a small town in Yorkshire, where the cloth was made.] †**1.** A kind of coarse woollen cloth formerly used for garments, linings, etc. Also *attrib.* –1834. **2.** *P. flags*, sandstone flags from the coal measures around Penistone, used for paving-stones 1688.

Penitence (pe·nitĕns). ME. [– (O)Fr. *pénitence* – L. *pænitentia*, f. *pænitent-*, pr. ppl. stem of *pænitet* cause want or discontent to, make sorry; see -ENCE.] **1.** = PENANCE *sb.* 3. Now *rare*, and usu. including sense 2. **2.** The fact or state of being penitent; contrition, with desire and intention of amendment; repentance 1591.

2. By P. th' Eternalls wrath's appeas'd SHAKS.

†**Pe·nitencer.** ME. [– AFr. *penitencer* – med.L. *penitentiarius* (XII), whence also OFr. *peneancier*, whence ME. *penancer*; see -ER^2 2.] In the mediæval Church, a priest appointed to hear confession, assign penance, and give absolution in extraordinary cases; a penitentiary.

Penitency (pe·nitĕnsi). Now *rare.* 1450. [– L. *pænitentia*; see PENITENCE and -ENCY.] **1.** Penitence as a state; repentance. †**2.** A penitential practice or discipline (*rare*) –1676.

Penitent (pe·nitĕnt), *a.* and *sb.* late ME. [– (O)Fr. *pénitent* – L. *pænitent-*; see PENITENCE, -ENT.] **A.** *adj.* **1.** That repents, with intention to amend the sin or wrongdoing; contrite. **b.** *transf.* of things: Expressive of repentance 1723. †**2.** Regretful, grieved; relenting, sorry, vexed. Const. *of*, *upon*. *rare.* –1609. **3.** Undergoing penance 1590.

1. A p. prodigal 1840. **b.** Several p. letters DE FOE. **3.** *Com. Err.* I. ii. 52.

B. *sb.* **1.** One who repents; a repentant sinner. late ME. **2.** A person performing (ecclesiastical) penance; one under the direction of a confessor. late ME. **3.** *pl.* A name designating various R.C. congregations or orders, associated for mutual discipline and charitable works. Rarely in *sing.*, a member of one of these. 1693.

attrib. **p.-form**, a form or bench for penitents. Hence **Pe·nitently** *adv.*

Penitential (penite·nʃăl), *a.* and *sb.* 1508. [– (O)Fr. *pénitencial*, also mod. *-ciel* – late L. *pænitentialis* sb. (Cassiodorus), med.L. adj. and sb. (IX), f. L. *pænitentia*; see PENITENCE, -IAL.] **A.** *adj.* **1.** Of, pertaining to, or expressive of penitence or repentance. **2.** Pertaining to, expressive of, or constituting ecclesiastical penance; of the nature of a penance 1535. Also *fig.*

1. *P. Psalms*, seven psalms (6, 33, 37, 51, 102, 130, 143) which are used as penitential devotions. **2.** *P. robe*, a robe worn by a public penitent.

B. *sb.* **1.** A penitent. †Also *joc.* a prisoner. 1627. **2.** A book containing in codified form the canons of the Church relating to penance, its imposition, etc. 1618. **3.** *pl.* Short for *P. Psalms*: see A. 1. 1641. **4.** *pl.* †**a.** The demeanour, appearance, or behaviour of a penitent. **b.** Mourning garments; black clothes (*colloq.*). 1748. Hence **Penite·ntially** *adv.*

Penitentiary (penite·nʃări), *a.* and *sb.* late ME. [– med.L. *pænitentiarius* adj. and sb., f. *pænitentia* PENITENCE; see -ARY^1.] **A.** *adj.* **1.** Of or pertaining to penance; administering or undergoing penance 1577. **2.** Pertaining to, or expressive of, penitence; repentant (*rare*) 1634. **3.** Intended for or relating to the penal and reformatory treatment of criminals 1776. **4.** Of an offence: Punishable by imprisonment in a penitentiary (*U.S.*) 1856.

1. The p. books and canons 1678. **2.** A p. letter 1806. **3.** *P. House* = B. III. 3. *P. Act*, the Act 19 Geo. III, c. 74. **4.** It had been a p. offence to teach a black to read and write 1896.

B. *sb.* **I.** = med.L. *pœnitentiarius.* **1.** A person appointed to deal with penitents or penances; *spec.* in R.C.Ch., an officer vested with power to deal with extraordinary cases 1475. †**2.** = PENITENT *sb.* 1 and 2. –1654. **3.** A member of a religious order so called 1631.

1. *Grand, High* (*Chief, Great*) *P.*, a cardinal who presides over the office called 'penitentiary' (see II), and has the granting of absolution in cases reserved for the papal authority.

II. = med.L. *pœnitentiaria. R. C. Ch.* The office or dignity of a penitentiary; an office or congregation in the Papal Court, presided over by the Grand Penitentiary, and forming a tribunal for deciding upon questions relating to penance, dispensations, etc. 1658. **III.** = OFr. *pen(e)ancerie.* †**1.** A place of penitential discipline or punishment for ecclesiastical offences –1644. **2.** An asylum for penitent prostitutes 1806. **3.** A reformatory prison; a house of correction 1816. **4.** *U.S.* A prison 1898. **IV.** = PENITENTIAL *sb.* 2 (*rare*) 1853. Hence †**Penite·ntiaryship**, the office of p. (see B. I. 1).

Penknife (pe·n,nəif). late ME. [f. PEN *sb.*^{2} + KNIFE.] A small knife, usu. carried in the pocket, used orig. for making and mending quill pens. (Formerly provided with a sheath; now made with a jointed blade or blades which fit inside the handle when closed.)

Penman (pe·nmĕn). *Pl.* **penmen** (pe·nmen). 1591. [f. PEN *sb.*^{2} + MAN *sb.*] **1.** A man employed to write or copy documents, etc.; a clerk, secretary, notary, scrivener. Now *rare.* 1612. **2.** A man skilled in penmanship; a calligrapher. (Qualified as *good*, *expert*, *swift*, etc.) 1591. **3.** An author, a writer 1592. **b.** Const. *of* (that which is written). Now *rare.* 1610.

1. *Penmen of God* or *of the Holy Ghost*, applied to the writers of Scripture regarded as writing from divine dictation or command; St. Paul, one of the first Pen-men of the Holy Ghost 1656. Hence **Pe·nmanship**, the action or performance of a p.

Pennaceous (penēⁱ·ʃəs), *a. rare.* 1819. [f. mod.L. *pennaceus* (f. *penna* feather) + -OUS; see -ACEOUS.] **a.** *Ornith.* Having the structure of a pen-feather or quill-feather. **b.** *Entom.* and *Bot.* Applied to markings resembling feathers, or to surfaces or structures having such markings.

†**Pe·nnage.** *rare.* 1601. [– Fr. *pennage*, f. *penne* plume; see -AGE.] = PLUMAGE –1857.

Pennant^1 (pe·năṅt). 1611. [Blending in form of PENDANT with PENNON.] **1.** = PENDANT *sb.* II. 6. **2.** = PENDANT *sb.* II. 7, PENNON 3. 1698. **b.** = PENNON 1. 1815. **c.** *U.S.* A flag awarded as a distinction 1888.

Pennant^2 (pe·nănt). 1756. [– Welsh *pennant*, lit. 'dale-head', f. *pen(n* head + *nant* valley; also, a common Welsh place-name.] Now usu. *P. grit*: the name of an unproductive series of gritty strata lying between the Upper and Lower Coal-measures, in South Wales, etc. Also *P. flag, rock, stone.*

Pennate (pe·nĕt), *a. rare.* 1857. [– L. *pennatus* winged, f. *penna* feather; see -ATE^2.] **1.** *Nat. Hist.* = PINNATE. **2.** = PENNIFORM 1877. So **Pe·nnated** *a.* (in senses 1, 2); also, feathered 1727.

Pennati-, comb. form of L. *pennatus* PENNATE, as in **Pennatifid** *a.*, etc. = PINNATIFID, etc. (see PINNATI-).

Pennatulacean (penætiŭlēⁱ·ʃⁱăn), *a.* and *sb.* 1857. [f. mod.L. *Pennatulacea* n. pl., f. *Pennatula*, the typical genus; see -ACEAN.] **A.** *adj.* Belonging to the order *Pennatulacea* of alcyonarian polyps. **B.** *sb.* A polyp of this order. So **Pennatula·ceous** *a.* **Penna·tulid**, a polyp of the family *Pennatulidæ*, of which *Pennatula*, the sea-pen, is the typical genus.

Penner^1 (pe·nəɹ). *Obs.* or *dial.* late ME. [– med.L. *pennarium*, f. *penna* pen; see -ARIUM, -ER^2 2.] A case or sheath for pens; a pen-case; in later use, occas., a writing-case.

Penner^2 (pe·nəɹ). 1570. [f. PEN *v.*^{2} + -ER^1.] One who pens or words a writing, document, etc.; a writer *of* something.

Penni-, comb. form of L. *penna* feather, PEN *sb.*^{2}, as in **Penni·ferous** [L. *pennifer*] *a. Nat. Hist.* bearing or producing feathers; feathered. **Pe·nniform** [mod.L. *penniformis*] *a. Nat. Hist.* having the form or appearance of a feather; *spec.* applied to a muscle whose fibres are obliquely arranged on each side of a central tendon. **Pennigerous** (peni·dʒĕrəs) [L. *penniger*] *a.* feather-bearing, feathered. **Pe·nninerved** [NERVE] *a. Bot.* (of a leaf) having nerves or veins diverging on each side of a midrib; feather-veined, pinnately veined; also **Pennine·rvate** *a.* **Pe·nniveined** [VEIN] *a. Bot.* = prec.

Penniless (pe·nilės), *a.* ME. [f. PENNY + -LESS.] Not having a penny; having no money; poor, destitute.

†*P. bench*, name of a covered bench which formerly stood beside Carfax Church, Oxford; and app. of similar open-air seats elsewhere; prob. as being the resort of destitute wayfarers; hence allusively. Hence **Pe·nniless-ly** *adv.*, **-ness.**

‖**Pennill** (pe·nilʰ), usu. in *pl.* **pennillion** (peni·lʰiŏn). 1784. [Welsh *pennill* verse, stanza, f. *penn* head.] A form of improvised verse adapted to an air played on the harp, sung at the Eisteddfod, etc.; a stanza of such verse.

Pennon (pe·nən). late ME. [– (O)Fr. *pennon* :– Rom. deriv. of L. *penna* PEN *sb.*^{2}; cf. -OON.] **1.** A long narrow flag or streamer, triangular and pointed, or swallow-tailed, formerly borne as a distinction by a knight under the rank of banneret; now a military ensign of the lancer regiments. **b.** Any flag or banner. late ME. **c.** *fig.* Applied to things of the shape of a pennon 1618. †**2.** **a.** A knight-bachelor. **b.** An ensign-bearer. –1661. **3.** The long pointed streamer of a ship; also called PENDANT and PENNANT 1627. **4.** *poet.* Used by Milton, and others after him, for: A wing, pinion 1667.

1. c. A pillar of dark smoke, which..spread its long dusky p. through the clear ether SCOTT. **3.** Yachts with pennons flying 1884. **4.** Fluttring his pennons vain plumb down he drops MILT. Hence **Pe·nnoned** (pe·nənd) *a.* having, bearing, or furnished with a p.

Pennoncel (pe·nənsel). *Obs.* exc. *Hist.* late ME. [– OFr. *penoncel*, in med.L. *penuncellus*, dim. of *penon* PENNON; see -EL.] A small pennon borne upon a helmet or lance, a PENCEL; a pennon or pendant of a ship.

Penny (pe·ni). *Pl.* **pennies** (pe·niz), **pence** (pens). [OE. *peniġ*, *pæniġ*, earlier *pen(n)ing*, *pending* = OFris. *penning*, *panning*, OS. (Du.) *penning*, OHG. *pfenning* (G. *pfennig*), ON. *penningr* :– Gmc. **panniŋʒaz*, **pandiŋʒaz* (not in Gothic, and the ON. word may be from Eng.), which has been referred to **pand-* PAWN *sb.*², with suffix *-iŋʒ* as in *shilling*.] **I.** Original senses. **1.** An English coin of the value of $\frac{1}{12}$ of a shilling or $\frac{1}{240}$ of a pound; orig. of silver, later of copper, now of bronze. Denoted (after a numeral) by *d.* (for *denarius*, *denarii*); thus 5*d.*, fivepence. **b.** The pl. *pennies* is now used only of the individual coins (exc. in U.S.); *pence* is usu. collective, and is especially used after numerals, where from *twopence* to *elevenpence* (rarely *twelvepence*) and in *twentypence*, it is stressless (tɒ·pĕns, etc.) and now written in comb. With other numbers *pence* is written separately (or hyphened) and has a separate stress, as *eighteen pence* (ē̆i·tīn,pe·ns). OE. **2.** Rendering L. *denarius* (see DENARIUS); also occas. *argenteus* ('piece of silver'), and *nummus* (= *nummus sestertius*, SESTERCE). Now only in Biblical use. OE. **b.** In U.S. *colloq.* a cent 1889.

1. *Scots p.*, a coin equal in 17th c. to one-twelfth of the English penny. **2.** Shew me a p. Whose image and superscription hath it? And they said, Cæsar's. *Luke* 20:24 (R.V.)

II. From the fact that the (silver) penny was for long the chief or only coin in circulation, the name came to be used in the following senses: **1.** A coin: applied to coins of distinct origin from the ordinary penny. Now *Hist.* 1483. **2.** Used vaguely for a piece of money; hence, a sum of money, money. Now chiefly in phr. *a pretty p.* ME. **b.** In *pl.* = money; orig. as consisting of (silver) pennies; in later use, often depreciative, 'small money', 'coppers', 'small earnings' ME. **†c.** (*Sing.*) With ordinal numeral, expressing an aliquot part of a sum of money, as *the fifth p.*, *i.e.* every fifth penny in any number of pennies = one-fifth of the whole amount –1844. **d.** The particular amount of some tax, impost, or customary payment. With defining word, as EARNEST-P., GOD'S P., PETER-P. (*pence*), etc. ME. **3.** As the type of a coin of small value, or of a small amount of money. Often in contrast with *pound*. ME.

1. *P. of twopence*, a silver coin of the value of twopence, a half-groat. *Gold p.*, a gold coin of the value of 20 shillings. **2.** They may..there be lodged..without paying of any pennie 1585. *†First p.*, prime cost, cost price. **b.** Dispensers of treasure..without price to them that have no pence MILT. **3.** A peny yn seson spent wille safe a pounde 1457.

III. Transf. uses; chiefly ellipt. **†1.** = PENNYWEIGHT –1590. **†2.** The amount bought for a penny –1591.

Phr. and Prov. *A p. for your thoughts*, I would give something to know what you are thinking about (addressed to one in a 'brown study'). *A p. saved is a p. gained* (*got*, *earned*). *A pretty* (*fine*, etc.) *p.*, a considerable sum (in the way of gain or cost). *In for a p., in for a pound*, having entered upon a matter one must carry it through at any cost. *No paternoster, no p.*, no work, no pay. *Take care of the pence and the pounds will take care of themselves. To turn* (*wind*) *the* (*a*) *p.*, to employ one's money profitably; or, to gain money. *Obs.* exc. in *to turn an honest p.* (see HONEST *a.* 4 b).

attrib. and *Comb.* **1.** *attrib.* or as *adj.* Of the price or value of a penny, costing a penny, as *p. bun*, *newspaper*, etc.; *p. dreadful* (see DREADFUL C); so with prefixed numeral, as *fivepenny nail*, a size of nail (orig. a nail which cost 5*d.* a hundred), *tenpenny nail*, etc.; for the use of or admission to which the charge is a penny, as *p. boat*, *bus*, *gaff* (GAFF *sb.*³), etc.; (of a game) at which the stake is a penny, as *p.-nap*, etc.; (of a person) selling something or doing some work for a penny or cheaply; hence, engaged in inferior work, as *p.-barber*, *poet*, *wit*. **2.** *Comb.*: **p.-bank**, a savings bank at which as little as a p. may be deposited; **-cress**, the plant *Thlaspi arvense*, or some other cruciferous plant with flat round pods; **-dog**, a kind of dogfish, also called *miller's dog* or *tope*; **†-farm** (**-ferme**), a money rent, instead of services; **-farthing** *colloq.*, an old fashioned high bicycle having a large and a small wheel; **-father**, one who is too careful of his pence; a niggard, skinflint; **-fee** *Sc.*, a payment of a p.; 'wages paid in money' (Jam.); **-fish**, the John Dory, so called as having a round spot upon either side; **-in-the-slot** *a.* [from the direction 'Put a penny in the slot'], (of mechanical devices for the automatic supply of commodities) actuated by the fall of a p. inserted through a slot; also *fig.*; **-land**, land valued at a p. a year (*Obs.* or *dial.*); **-piece**, a piece of money of the value of a p., a p.; **†-rent**, rent paid in money; periodical payment in cash; **-trumpet**, a toy trumpet costing a p.; also *fig.* in reference to petty boasting; **p. wedding**, a wedding at which each of the guests contributes money to the expenses of the entertainment and to the setting up of the newly-married couple.

Pe·nny-a-li·ne, *a.* 1833. [The phr. (*a*) *penny a line* used attrib.] Of writing or a writer: Paid at the rate of a penny a line; of cheap and superficial literary quality. So **Pe:nny-a-li·ner**, a writer who is paid at a penny a line, or at a low rate (usu. implying one who writes in an inflated style so as to fill as much space as possible); a hack-writer for the press.

Pe·nny-grass. late ME. [f. PENNY + GRASS.] Pop. name of: **a.** Navelwort or Wall Pennywort, *Cotyledon umbilicus*; **b.** Marsh Pennywort, *Hydrocotyle vulgaris* (in both cases from the round leaves); **c.** Yellow-rattle, *Rhinanthus crista-galli* (from the flat roundish pods).

Penny post, penny-post. 1680. [See POST *sb.*¹] An organization for the conveyance of letters or packets at an ordinary charge of a penny each; *esp.* that established in the United Kingdom on 10 Jan. 1840 on the initiative of Rowland Hill. Also *attrib.* So **Pe·nny-po·stage**, the postage of letters, etc. at a charge of a penny each.

Pennyroyal (peniroi·ăl). 1530. [alt. of *puliol*(*e reall* (*ryall*) XV – AFr. *puliol real*, i.e. OFr. *pouliol* (mod. *pouliot*) and *real* ROYAL; *pouliol* :– Rom. **pulegeolum*, f. L. *pule(g)ium*, thyme. The change of *puliol* to *penny* is unexpl.; no intermediate forms are known.] A species of mint (*Mentha pulegium*), with small leaves and prostrate habit; formerly cultivated for its supposed medicinal virtues. Also applied, usu. with qualifying words, to other aromatic labiates, or other plants. Also *attrib.*

Bastard or *False P.*, names of two N. American labiates, *Trichostemma dichotomum* and *Isanthus cæruleus*.

attrib.: **p.-water**, a liquor distilled from the leaves of p., formerly used in medicine.

Pennyweight (pe·niwē̆ⁱt). late ME. [f. PENNY + WEIGHT *sb.*] A measure of weight, = 24 grains, $\frac{1}{20}$ of an ounce Troy, or $\frac{1}{240}$ of a pound Troy. (Formerly = $\frac{1}{240}$ of a Tower pound, i.e. $22\frac{1}{2}$ grains, the actual weight of a silver penny.) Abbrev. *dwt.* **b.** A proportional measure of one-twelfth used in stating the fineness of silver (thus, pure silver is 12 pennyweights fine) 1758.

Pe·nny-wi·se, *adj. phr.*, or *a.* 1607. [Cf. PENNY II. 3.] Wise or prudent in regard to pence, *i.e.* careful (*esp.* over-careful) in small expenditures; usu. in phr. *penny-wise* (*and*) *pound-foolish*, thrifty in small matters while wasteful in large ones. Hence **Penny-wisdom**, the quality of being penny-wise.

Pennywort (pe·niwɒɹt). late ME. [f. PENNY + WORT¹.] **1.** (In full, *Wall P.*) *Cotyledon umbilicus* (N.O. *Crassulaceæ*), having peltate leaves of a rounded concave form, and growing in the crevices of rocks and walls; navelwort. **2.** (*Marsh P.* or *Water P.*) *Hydrocotyle vulgaris*, a small umbelliferous plant with rounded peltate leaves, growing in marshy places. Also extended to other species. 1578.

Pennyworth (pe·niwɒɹþ), contr. **pen-n'orth** (pe·nəþ). OE. [f. PENNY + WORTH *sb.*¹] **1.** The amount which may be bought for a penny; as much as is worth a penny. **b.** *fig.* Amount, sum; *esp.* a very small, or the least, amount; often with neg. = not the least bit; *ironically*, 'a deal', 'a lot'. late ME. **†2.** That which is or may be bought for a given sum, in contrast to the money itself. (Often in *pl.*) –1656. **3.** Money's worth, value for one's money; a bargain; †profit, advantage obtained. Usu. qualified as *bad*, *cheap*, *dear*, *good*, etc.; also *absol.* A good bargain. Also *fig.* ME. **†b.** Price in proportion to value; (cheap, etc.) rate –1729.

1. She..will never buy anything by single penny-worths JOHNSON. **2.** You take your peniworths now. Sleepe for a weeke SHAKS. You will not find it a dear p. 1868. **b.** *At a* (*good*, etc.) *p.*; This tract of land he bought at a very great penny-worth SWIFT.

Penology (pinǫ·lŏdʒi). 1838. [f. L. *pœna* penalty + -LOGY.] The scientific study of the prevention and punishment of crime; the science of prison and reformatory management. Hence **Penolo·gical** *a.* of, pertaining or relating to, p. **Peno·logist**, one versed in p.

Pens, obs. f. PENCE, pl. of PENNY.

‖**Pensée.** ME. [In sense 1 – (O)Fr. *pensée*; in 2, only as Fr.] **†1.** Thoughtfulness, a thought –1477. ‖**2.** (panse) A thought or reflection put in literary form 1886.

‖**Penseroso** (pensĕrōᵘ·so), *a.* and *sb.* 1765. [– It. †*penseroso* (now *pensieroso*), f. †*pensiere* thought – Pr. *pensier*, f. Rom. **pensare*; see POISE *v.*] **A.** *adj.* Meditative, brooding, melancholy. **B.** *sb.* A brooding or melancholy person or personality.

Pensile (pe·nsəil, -sil), *a.* 1603. [– L. *pensilis*, f. *pens-*, pa. ppl. stem of *pendēre* hang; see -ILE.] **1.** Hanging down, pendulous. **b.** 'Hanging' or situated on a declivity 1750. **2.** Hanging in the air or in space; suspended on arches, with void space beneath; vaulted 1613. **3.** That constructs a pensile nest 1802.

1. The p. nests of the weaver bird 1854. **b.** His azure stream, with p. woods enclos'd SHENSTONE. **2.** Babylon..was then the wonder of the world for its walls and p. gardens 1703. **3.** The P. Warbler 1802. Hence **Pe·nsileness, Pensi·lity** (*rare*).

Pension (pe·nʃən), *sb.* late ME. [– (O)Fr. *pension* – L. *pensio* payment, rent, f. *pens-*, pa. ppl. stem of *pendere* weigh, pay, rel. to *pendēre* (prec.); see -ION.] **†1.** A payment; a tribute, tax, charge, imposition; a contribution; a price paid or received; an expenditure. Also *fig.* –1638. **2.** *Eccl.* A fixed payment out of the revenues of a benefice, upon which it forms a charge. late ME. **†3.** Stipend, salary, wages; fee –1776. **b.** A payment made to one who is not a professed servant or employee, to retain his good will, secret service, etc.; a subvention, a fixed allowance. **c.** A regular payment to persons of rank, royal favourites, etc., to enable them to maintain their state; also to men of learning or science, artists, etc., to enable them to carry on work of public interest or value. 1500. **4.** An annuity or other periodical payment made, esp. by a government, a company, or an employer of labour, in consideration of past services or of the relinquishment of rights, claims, or emoluments 1529. **†5.** The annual (or other periodical) payment made by each member of a gild, college, or society, towards its general expenses; *esp.* that levied upon each member of an Inn of Court to defray its standing charges –1838. **†6.** Payment for board and lodging, or for the board and education of a child, etc. –1803. **b.** A boarding-house, a lodging-house at a fixed rate; occas. a boarding-school; †also formerly a tavern. Now only as Fr. (paṅsyoṅ). 1644. **7.** [from 5] A consultative assembly of the members of Gray's Inn, one of the Inns of Court in London 1570.

3. He commanded to giue to all that kept the city, pensions and wages 1 *Esdras* 4:56. **b.** *Pension*, an allowance made to any one without an equivalent. In England it is generally understood to mean pay given to a state hireling for treason to his country JOHNSON. **4.** *Old age p.*, a payment of so much per week or month paid to a workman or poor person (or to every one) on reaching a specified age.

Pension (pe·nʃən), *v.* 1642. [f. prec.] **1.** *intr.* To live or stay in a pension or boarding-house; to board and lodge. **2.** *trans.* To grant a pension to; also (contextually) to buy over with a pension. *To p. off*, to dismiss with a pension. 1702. Hence **Pe·nsionable** *a.* entitled to a pension; of service, etc.: entitling to a pension.

Pensionary (pe·nʃənări), *sb.*[1] 1536. [– med.L. *pensionarius* receiver or payer of a pension, f. *pensio*; see PENSION, -ARY[1].] **1.** = PENSIONER 1. 1548. **2.** [= Du. *pensionaris.*] Formerly, the chief municipal magistrate of a Dutch city, with the function of a legal adviser or speaker. *Hist.* 1587. **b.** *esp.* (prop. *Grand P.* = Du. *Groot Pensionaris*): The first minister of the province of Holland and Zealand in the Seven United Provinces of the Netherlands (1619–1794) 1655. **c.** *transf.* Satirical nickname for English statesmen 1771.

1. The Nabob sank into a p. 1874. **2. c.** The grand p. [Pitt], that weathercock of patriotism SMOLLETT.

Pensionary (pe·nʃənări), *sb.*[2] 1582. [– med.L. **pensionaria* (sc. *domus*), or **pensionarium*, subst. use of the adj., identical with prec.] A place of residence for pensioners; formerly, at Cambridge, a residence for undergraduates not on the foundation of a college.

Pensionary (pe·nʃənări), *a.* 1584. [– med. L. *pensionarius*, f. *pensio*; see PENSION, -ARY[1].] **1.** That is in receipt of a pension; hence, mercenary, hireling, venal. **2.** Consisting, or of the nature, of a pension 1631.

1. An extensive p. clergy 1825. **2.** P. favours 1771.

Pensioner (pe·nʃənəɹ). late ME. [– AFr. *pensioner*, OFr. *-ier* – med.L. *pensionarius*, f. *pensio*; see PENSION, -ER[2] 2.] **I.** One who receives a pension. **1.** One who is in receipt of a pension or regular pay; one who is in the pay of another; in early use, a mercenary; in 17th–18th c. often, a hireling, tool, creature 1487. **b.** *spec.* One who is in receipt of a pension in consideration of past services or on account of injuries received in service; esp. one of the inmates of Chelsea and Greenwich Hospitals 1706. †**2.** *spec.* = *Gentleman p.*; see GENTLEMAN 2. –1737. †**b.** A member of a bodyguard, a retainer. Also *fig.* –1632. **3.** The officer of the Inns of Court who collected the pensions, kept the pension-book or pension-roll, etc. *Obs.* exc. *Hist.* late ME. †**4.** = PENSIONARY *sb.*[1] 2, 2 b. –1756.

1. Charles [II.] became the p. of the French king 1863. **2. b.** *fig.* I serue the Fairy Queene,..The Cowslips tall, her pensioners bee SHAKS.

II. One who makes a stated periodical payment. **1.** At Cambridge University: An undergraduate who is not a scholar on the foundation of a college, or a sizar; one who pays for his own commons, etc.; = *Commoner* at Oxford 1450. †**2.** A boarder; *esp.* a girl or woman living *en pension* in a convent or school in France, Belgium, etc.; = Fr. *pensionnaire* –1827. **3.** *attrib.*, as *p. messenger*, etc. 1678.

Pensionnaire (pańsyonē·r). 1598. [– Fr. *pensionnaire* – med.L. *pensionarius*; see prec., PENSIONARY *sb.*[1]] **a.** One in receipt of a pension; a pensioner, a paid retainer (*rare*). **b.** One who boards in a French lodging-house, institution, or family. **c.** A junior member of the *Comédie Française*.

†**Pe·nsionry.** [f. PENSIONER; see -RY.] A body of pensioners or paid retainers MILTON.

Pensive (pe·nsiv), *a.* (*sb.*) late ME. [– (O)Fr. *pensif, -ive*, f. *penser* think – L. *pensare* weigh, balance, consider; see POISE *v.*, -IVE.] **1.** Plunged in thought; meditative; reflective; often with some tinge of melancholy. †**2.** Full of anxious thought or foreboding; anxious, apprehensive –1654. **3.** 'Sorrowfully thoughtful, sorrowful; mournfully serious; melancholy' (J.); gloomy, sad. late ME. **4.** *transf.* Of things: Associated with thought, anxiety, or melancholy 1548. **5.** *absol.* as *sb.* Pensive manner or mood 1775.

1. He had a greater feare of those who were p. as Brutus 1639. **3.** The heavie burthen of my p. brest DRAYTON. **4.** P. Twilight in her dusky car S. ROGERS. Hence †**Pe·nsived** *a.*? rendered p. or sad. SHAKS. **Pe·nsive-ly** *adv.*, **-ness.**

Penstock (pe·n,stǫk). 1607. [f. PEN *sb.*[1] + STOCK *sb.*[1]] **1.** A sluice for restraining or regulating the flow from a head of water formed by a pen (PEN *sb.*[1] 3), as in a water-mill. Also *attrib.* **2.** = PENTROUGH. (*U.S.*) **b.** A tube by which water is conveyed from a head of water into a turbine. **c.** Also applied to the barrel of a pump. 1828.

‖**Pensum** (pe·nsǒm). *rare.* 1705. [L., weight, charge, duty, f. *pendere* weigh.] A school-task or lesson to be prepared; also, a school 'imposition'.

Pent (pent), *sb.* 1754. [Short for PENTHOUSE, or assumed as the first element of it.] A sloping roof or covering, a PENTHOUSE.

Pent (pent), *pa. pple.* and *ppl. a.* 1550. [In form, pa. pple. of *pend*, obs. var. of PEN *v.*[1]] **1.** Shut up or confined within narrow limits. Often with *in, up.* **2.** Of a place, room, etc.: Shut *up*, confined 1594. †**3.** Having something pent within it; distended or strained by being overfull of something –1728.

1. Long in populous City p. MILT. In vain our p. wills fret M. ARNOLD. Pent-up emotion 1879.

Penta- (pentă), bef. a vowel **pent-**, – Gr. πεντα-, comb. form of πέντε five. In *Chem.* it indicates the presence of five atoms of some element, as in *pentacarbon, pentachloride, pentasulphide, pentoxide*, etc.

Pentabasic (-bē[i]·sik) *a. Chem.* having five atoms of a base, or of replaceable hydrogen. **Pentaca·psular** *a.* having five capsules. **Pentachromic** (-krō[u]·mik) *a.* of five colours, capable of distinguishing (only) five colours in the spectrum. **Pentada·ctyl(e** [Gr. δάκτυλος finger] *a.* having five toes or fingers; *sb.* a person or animal with five digits on each limb. So **Pentada·ctylous** *a.* **Pentadelphous** (-ăde·lfəs) [Gr. ἀδελφός brother] *a. Bot.* (of stamens) united by the filaments in five bundles; (of a plant) having the stamens so united. **Pe·ntafid** [L. *-fidus* split] *a. Bot.* cleft into five. ‖**Pentagy·nia** [Gr. γυνή woman, in sense 'pistil'], an order of plants in the Linnæan system, comprising those having five pistils. Hence **Pentagy·nian, Penta·gynous** *adjs.* **Pentaha·loid** *a. Chem.* containing five atoms of a halogen in the molecule. **Penta·ndria** [Gr. ἀνήρ, ἀνδρ- man, in sense 'stamen'] *Bot.* the fifth class in the Linnæan system, comprising plants having five stamens not cohering. So **Penta·ndrian, Penta·ndrous** *adjs.* **Pentape·talous** *a. Bot.* having five petals. **Pentaphyllous** (-fi·ləs) [Gr. φύλλον leaf] *a.* five-leaved. **Pe·ntaptote** [– Gr. πεντάπτωτος adj.] *Gram.* a noun having five cases. **Pe·ntaptych** (-ptik) [Gr. πτυχή fold, after DIPTYCH, etc.], an altar-piece or the like consisting of five leaves, i.e. a central piece and two folding pieces on each side. **Penta·rsic** [ARSIS] *a. Pros.* having five stresses. **Pentase·palous** *a. Bot.* having five sepals. **Pentaspe·rmous** [Gr. σπέρμα seed] *a. Bot.* having five seeds. **Pe·ntastyle** [Gr. στῦλος pillar] *a. Arch.* having five columns in front or at the end; *sb.* a pentastyle building or portico.

Pentachord (pe·ntăkǭɹd). 1721. [f. PENTA- + CHORD *sb.*[1]] *Mus.* **1.** A musical instrument with five strings. **2.** A system or series of five notes 1811.

Pentacle (pe·ntăk'l). 1594. [– med.L. *pentaculum*, f. Gr. πεντα- PENTA- + *-culum* -CLE.] A certain figure used as a symbol, esp. in magic; app. prop. the same as PENTAGRAM; but also used for the *hexagram* or six-pointed star formed by two interlaced triangles, etc. Hence **Penta·cular** *a.*

Pentacrinite (pentæ·krinəit). 1818. [f. mod.L. *Pentacrinus* sea-lily (f. Gr. πεντα- five + κρίνον lily) + -ITE[1] 2 a.] *Palæont.* An encrinite or fossil crinoid of the genus *Pentacrinus* or family *Pentacrinidæ*. So **Penta·crinoid** *a.* allied to or resembling the genus *Pentacrinus* or family *Pentacrinidæ*; *sb.* a pentacrinoid crinoid.

Pentad (pe·ntæd). 1653. [– Gr. πεντάς, -αδ-, f. πέντε five; see -AD[1].] **1.** The number five (in the Pythagorean system); a group of five. **2.** A period of five years 1880. **3.** *Chem.* An element or radical that has the combining power of five units, i.e. of five atoms of hydrogen. Also *attrib.* or *adj.* 1877. Hence **Penta·dic** *a.* of the nature of a p. (sense 3), pentavalent; whence **Pentadi·city**, the fact of being a p.

Pentadecane (pe·ntădĭkē[i]n). 1872. [f. late Gr. πενταδεκα- for πεντεκαίδεκα fifteen + -ANE 2 b.] *Chem.* The paraffin of the 15-carbon series, $C_{15}H_{32}$. So **Pe·ntadecine** (-dīsəin), the corresponding hydrocarbon of the ethine series, $C_{15}H_{28}$; **Pentade·cyl**, the radical $C_{15}H_{31}$.

Pentagon (pe·ntăgǫn), *a.* and *sb.* 1570. [In A – late L. *pentagonus* (Boethius) – Gr. πεντάγωνος; in B – Fr. *pentagone* or late L. *pentagonum* – Gr. πεντάγωνον, subst. use of n. of the adj.; see PENTA-, -GON.] †**A.** *adj.* Having five angles; pentagonal –1669. **B.** *sb.* A figure, usu. a plane rectilineal figure, having five angles and five sides. In *Fortif.* A fort with five bastions. 1571.

Pentagonal (pentæ·gŏnăl), *a.* (*sb.*) 1570. [– Fr. *pentagonal* or med.L. *pentagonalis*, f. *pentagonum* (prec.); see -AL[1].] **1.** *Geom.*, etc. Of or pertaining to a pentagon; of the form of a pentagon, five-cornered or five-sided 1571. **b.** Applied to a solid figure or body of which the base or section is a pentagon 1570. **c.** Contained by pentagons, as a solid figure 1851. **2.** *P. numbers*: the series of POLYGONAL numbers 1, 5, 12, 22, 35, 51, etc. formed by continuous summation of the arithmetical series 1, 4, 7, 10, 13, 16, etc. **b.** as *sb.* A pentagonal number 1795. Hence **Penta·gonally** *adv.* in a p. form. var. †**Penta·gonous** *a.*

Pentagram (pe·ntăgræm). 1833. [– Gr. πεντάγραμμον, subst. use of n. of πεντάγραμμος of five lines; see PENTA-, -GRAM.] A five-pointed figure formed by producing the sides of a pentagon both ways to their points of intersection, so as to form a five-pointed star; the 'five straight lines' of which the figure consists form one continuous line or 'endless knot'. Formerly a mystical symbol credited with magical virtues. (Also called *pentacle*, †*pentagonon, pentalpha, pentangle.*)

Pentahedral (pentăhī·drăl, -he·drăl), *a.* Also **pentaedral.** 1804. [f. PENTAHEDRON + -AL[1].] Of a solid figure or body: Having five faces; *esp.* having five lateral faces, five-sided (as a prism of pentagonal section). So †**Pentahe·drical, Pentahe·drous** *adjs.* **Pentahe·dron**, a solid having five faces.

‖**Pentalpha** (pentæ·lfă). 1818. [– Gr. πένταλφα, a synonym of πεντάγραμμον PENTAGRAM, f. πέντε five + ἄλφα the letter A; from its presenting the form of an A in five different positions.] = PENTAGRAM.

Pentamerous (pentæ·mĕrəs), *a.* 1826. [f. PENTA- + -MEROUS.] Having, consisting of, or characterized by, five parts or divisions. **1.** *Bot.* Having the parts of the flower-whorl five in number. (Often written 5-*merous.*) 1835. **2.** *Zool.* **a.** Consisting of five joints, as the tarsi of certain insects; also applied to such insects themselves, as the beetles of the group *Pentamera*. **b.** Having five radiating parts or organs, as a star-fish, etc. 1826. So **Penta·meral** *a.* **Penta·meran**, a p. beetle. **Penta·merism**, the condition of being p.

Pentameter (pentæ·mĭtəɹ), *sb.* and *a.* 1546. [– L. *pentameter* – Gr. πεντάμετρος, -ον, subst. uses of masc. and n. of adj. f. πέντε + μέτρον; see PENTA-, -METER.] **A.** *sb.* A verse or line consisting of five feet. **1.** *Gr.* and *L. Pros.* A form of dactylic verse composed of two similar halves (penthemimers), each consisting of two feet and a long syllable; in the first penthemimer each of the two feet may be either dactyl or spondee; in the second they must both be dactyls. Most commonly used in *elegiac* verse; see ELEGIAC A. 1. (The verse was erroneously analysed as two dactyls (or spondees), a spondee, and two anapæsts; hence the name.) 1589. **2.** Applied to lines of verse consisting of five feet in other languages; e.g. the English heroic verse of ten syllables 1706.

1. In the hexameter rises the fountain's silvery column, In the p. aye falling in melody back COLERIDGE.

B. *adj.* (Now attrib. use of sb.) Consisting of five metrical feet; having the form of a pentameter 1546.

Pentane (pe·ntē[i]n). 1877. [f. Gr. πέντε five + -ANE 2 b.] *Chem.* The general name of the paraffins of the pentacarbon series, C_5H_{12}; also called *quintane* and *pentyl hydride.* Three such hydrocarbons are known, all colourless mobile fluids, occurring in petroleum, etc.

attrib., as *p. lamp, vapour*, etc. So **Pentene** (pe·ntīn), an olefine of the pentacarbon series, C_5H_{10}; comprising four known forms, one of which is AMYLENE; **Pentine** (pe·ntəin), also **Pe·ntinine, Pe·ntylene**, the hydrocarbon C_5H_8, of the same series, homologous with acetylene or ethine; **Pento·ic** *a.* applied to fatty acids, aldehydes, etc. of the same series, as *Pentoic* or Valeric acid; **Pe·ntone, Pe·ntonene,** a hydrocarbon of the formula C_5H_6; **Pe·ntyl,** the radical C_5H_{11}, of which one form is AMYL; hence **Penty·lic** *a.*

Pentangle (pe·ntæŋg'l). †Also **pentagle.** ME. [In sense 1 perh. – med.L. **pentangulum*, alt. of *pentaculum* PENTACLE after L. *angulus* ANGLE *sb.*²; in sense 2 f. PENTA- + ANGLE *sb.*²] **1.** = PENTACLE, PENTAGRAM. **2.** = PENTAGON (*rare*) 1658.

Pentangular (pentæ·ŋgiŭlăɹ), *a.* 1661. [f. prec. (sense 2) + -AR¹.] Having five angles or angular points; pentagonal.

Pentapody (pentæ·pŏdi). 1864. [f. Gr. πεντάπους of five feet, f. πεντα- PENTA- + πούς, ποδ- foot; cf. DIPODY.] *Pros.* A verse or line consisting of five feet, or a sequence of five feet in a verse.

‖**Pentapolis** (pentæ·pŏlis). 1838. [L. – Gr. πεντάπολις, f. πεντα- PENTA- + πόλις city.] A confederacy or group of five towns; applied in ancient times to several such groups. So **Pentapo·litan** *a.* of or pertaining to a p., spec. to that of Cyrene in Lybia 1727.

Pentarch (pe·ntaɹk), *sb.* 1793. [– late Gr. πένταρχος, f. πέντα- PENTA- + -αρχος -ARCH.] **a.** The ruler of one of a group of five districts or kingdoms. **b.** One of a governing body of five persons.

Pentarch (pe·ntaɹk), *a.* 1884. [f. Gr. πέντε five + ἀρχή beginning.] *Bot.* Arising from five distinct points of origin, as the woody tissue of a root.

Pentarchy (pe·ntaɹki). 1587. [– Gr. πενταρχία a rule of five, f. πέντε five + -αρχία rule; see -ARCHY.] **1.** A government by five rulers; a group of five districts or kingdoms each under its own ruler. **2.** Government by a body of five persons; a governing body of five. Also *fig.* 1633.

2. *fig.* The P. of sences 1651.

Pentastich (pe·ntăstik). 1658. [– mod.L. *pentastichus* – Gr. πεντάστιχος, f. PENTA- + στίχος row, line.] *Pros.* A group of five lines.

Pentastichous (pentæ·stikəs), *a.* 1857. [f. as prec. + -OUS.] *Bot.* Arranged in five rows, five-ranked; *esp.* of a stem; having five leaves in the spiral row, and thus five vertical rows in the phyllotaxis.

Pentastom(e (pe·ntăstǫm, -oᵘm). 1857. [– mod.L. *Pentastomum*, f. PENTA- + Gr. -στομος adj. formative f. στόμα mouth; so called from the appearance of the mouth and the two pairs of chitinoid hooks adjacent to it.] *Zool.* An animal of the genus *Pentastomum* or *Pentastoma*, comprising internal parasites infesting man and other animals; an aberrant group of *Arachnida*, formerly classed as trematode worms. So **Penta·stomous** *a.* having five mouths or openings.

Pentasyllabic (pe:ntăsilæ·bik), *a.* 1771. [– late L. *pentasyllabus* – Gr. πεντασύλλαβος + -IC, after SYLLABIC.] Of five syllables. So **Pentasy·llable,** a word of five syllables.

Pentateuch (pe·ntătiŭk). 1530. [– eccl. L. *pentateuchus* – eccl. Gr. πεντάτευχος, subst. use of adj. f. πεντα- PENTA- + τεῦχος implement, vessel, (later) book.] **1.** Name for the first five books of the Old Testament taken as a connected group, traditionally ascribed to Moses (hence called 'the five books of Moses'). **2.** *transf.* A volume composed of five books, etc. (*rare*) 1656.

2. The Hebrew Psalter came together not as a book but as a P. 1891. Hence **Pentateu·chal** *a.*

Pentathionic (pe:ntăþəi,ǫ·nik), *a.* 1848. [f. PENTA- + THIONIC.] *Chem.* In *p. acid*, an acid containing five atoms of sulphur in the molecule, $H_2S_5O_6$, colourless, inodorous, and of bitter taste. Hence **Pentathi·onate,** a salt of p. acid.

Pentathlete (pentæ·þlīt). 1828. [– Gr. πενταθλητής, f. πένταθλον; see next.] An athlete who contended in the pentathlon.

‖**Pentathlon** (pentæ·þlǫn). Also in L. form **pentathlum.** *Pl.* **-a.** 1706. [– Gr. πένταθλον, f. πέντε five + ἆθλον contest.] *Gr.* and *Rom. Antiq.* An athletic contest consisting of five exercises (leaping, running, throwing the discus, throwing the spear, and wrestling) performed on the same day by the same athletes.

Pentatomic (pentătǫ·mik), *a.* 1872. [f. PENTA- + ATOM + -IC.] *Chem.* Containing five atoms of some substance in the molecule; *spec.* containing five replaceable hydrogen atoms; also = PENTAVALENT.

Pentatonic (pentătǫ·nik), *a.* 1864. [f. PENTA- + TONE *sb.* + -IC.] *Mus.* Consisting of five notes or sounds; *esp.* applied to a form of scale without semitones.

Pentavalent (pentæ·vălĕnt), *a.* 1871. [f. PENTA- + -VALENT.] *Chem.* Having the combining power of five atoms of a univalent element; quinquivalent.

Penteconta- (pentĭkǫntă), bef. a vowel **-cont-,** comb. form of Gr. πεντήκοντα fifty; as in †**Penteco·ntarch** [– Gr. πεντηκόνταρχος], a commander of fifty men; etc.

‖**Penteco·nter**¹. 1623. [– Gr. πεντηκοντήρ.] *Gr. Antiq.* A commander of a troop of fifty men.

‖**Penteco·nter**². 1790. [– Gr. πεντηκοντήρης.] *Gr. Antiq.* A fifty-oared ship of burden.

Pentecost (pe·ntĭkǫst). [OE. *pentecosten* – acc. of eccl. L. *Pentecoste* – Gr. Πεντηκοστή, subst. use (sc. ἑορτή feast or ἡμέρα day) of fem. ordinal adj. of πεντήκοντα fifty, f. πέντε five + -κοντα; re-adopted in ME. from OFr. *pentecoste* (mod. *-côte*).] **1.** A name of Hellenistic origin for the Jewish harvest festival (in O.T. the Feast of Weeks) observed on the fiftieth day of the OMER (q.v. sense 2). **2.** A Christian festival observed on the seventh Sunday after Easter, in commemoration of the descent of the Holy Ghost upon the disciples on the day of Pentecost (Acts 2); Whit Sunday OE. **3.** *fig.* in allusion to the gift of the Holy Spirit, or the circumstances recorded in Acts 2. 176..

2. Come Pentycost as quickely as it will SHAKS. **3.** Ever the fiery P. Girds with one flame the countless host EMERSON. Hence **Penteco·stal** *sb.* (usu. pl.) offerings formerly made in the Church of England at Whitsuntide to the priest, or to the mother-church; *a.* of or pertaining to P.; like that of the Day of P. in Acts 2.

‖**Pentecostys** (pentĭkǫ·stis). Also irreg. anglicized **pe·ntekosty.** 1808. [– Gr. πεντεκοστύς, f. πεντηκοστός fiftieth.] *Gr. Antiq.* A body of fifty men, as a division of the Spartan army.

Pentelic (pente·lik), *a.* 1579. [– L. *Pentelicus* – Gr. Πεντελικός, f. Πεντελή name of a deme of Attica; see -IC.] Of or from Mount Pentelicus, near Athens; esp. applied to the white marble there quarried. So †**Penteli·cian, Pente·lican** *adjs.*

Penthemimer (penþĭmi·məɹ). 1586. [– late L. *penthemimeres* – Gr. πενθημιμερής, f. πέντε five + ἡμιμερής halved, f. ἡμι- HEMI- + μέρος part.] *Anc. Pros.* A group or catalectic colon of five half-feet; esp. as constituting each half of a pentameter, or the first part of a hexameter when the cæsura occurs in the middle of the third foot. Hence **Penthemi·meral** *a.* applied to a cæsura in the middle of the third foot.

Penthouse (pe·nthaus), **pentice** (pe·ntis), *sb.* [ME. *pentis*, rarely *pendis* – AFr. **pentis*, aphetic of OFr. *apentis, apendis* – med. use of late L. *appendicium* appendage, f. L. *appendere* hang on, attach in a dependent state, f. *ad* AP- + *pendere* hang; refash. (late XIV) by assoc. with *house*, as if 'sloping house'.] **1.** A subsidiary structure attached to the wall of a main building. **a.** Such a structure having a sloping roof, formerly sometimes forming a covered walk, arcade, or colonnade, in front of a row of buildings; a sloping roof or ledge placed against the wall of a building, etc., for shelter from the weather; *occas.*, the eaves of a roof when projecting considerably. †**b.** Any small building attached to a main one, an annex –1886. **c.** A shed with a sloping roof, as a separate structure 1816. **2.** Anything of the nature of or akin to a sloping roof; an awning; a canopy, etc. 1530. **3.** *fig.* Applied to things likened to a penthouse (*e.g.* the eyebrows) 1589.

attrib. SHAKS. *Macb.* I. iii. 2.

Hence **Pe·nthouse** *v.* (usu. in pa. pple.) to furnish with or as with a p.; to cause to project like a p.

Pentode (pe·ntoᵘd), *a.* 1919. [f. Gr. πέντε five + ὁδός way; see -ODE.] Applied to a five-electrode wireless valve. Also as sb.

Pentoxide (pentǫ·ksəid). 1863. [PENTA-.] *Chem.* A binary compound containing five equivalents of oxygen.

Pent-roof (pe·nt,rūf). 1835. [f. *pent-* in PENTHOUSE + ROOF *sb.*] A shed-roof.

Pentrough (pe·n,trǫf). 1793. [f. PEN *sb.*¹ 3 + TROUGH.] A trough, channel, or conduit constructed to convey the water formed by a pen to the wheels of a water-mill, etc.

Pen(t)stemon (pen(t)stī·mən). 1760. [mod. L. *Pentstemon* (Mitchell, 1748), irreg. f. Gr. πέντε five + στήμων, taken as = stamen.] *Bot.* A genus of herbaceous plants of the N.O. *Scrophulariaceæ*, natives of America, having showy clustered flowers, usu. tubular and two-lipped, and of various colours.

Penult (pĭnɒ·lt), *a.* and *sb.* 1539. [orig. abbrev. of PENULTIMA, PENULTIMATE.] **A.** *adj.* Last but one, penultimate. (Now chiefly scientific.) **B.** *sb.* †**1.** The last day but one of a month. *Sc.* –1678. **2.** *Gram.* The last syllable but one 1650.

A. The p. joint of the eight posterior legs DANA.

Penu·ltim(e, *a.* and *sb.* 1532. [– L. *pænultimus*; see next.] = PENULTIMATE.

‖**Penultima** (pĭnɒ·ltimă). 1589. [L. *pænultima* (sc. *syllaba* syllable) subst. use of adj. fem. of *pænultimus*; see next.] The last syllable but one (of a word or verse).

Penultimate (pĭnɒ·ltimĕt), *a.* and *sb.* 1677. [f. L. *pænultimus* (f. *pæne* almost + *ultimus* last), after ULTIMATE.] **A.** *adj.* Last but one. (Chiefly scientific and techn.) Also, occurring on the last syllable but one. **B.** *sb.* The last member but one of a series; *spec.* in *Gram.* the last syllable but one of a word 1727.

‖**Penumbra** (pĭnɒ·mbră). 1661. [mod.L. (Kepler, 1604), f. L. *pæne* almost + *umbra* shadow.] **1.** The partially shaded region around the shadow of an opaque body; the partial shadow, as dist. from the total shadow or umbra; *esp.* that surrounding the total shadow of the moon, or of the earth, in an eclipse. **b.** The lighter outer part of a sun-spot, surrounding the darker central nucleus or umbra 1834. **2.** *fig.* A partial shade or shadow, esp. as bordering upon a fuller or darker one 1801.

2. It is but a p., a twilight of virtue and happiness 1836. Hence **Penu·mbral, Penu·mbrous** (*rare*), *adjs.* of, pertaining to, or characterized by a p. or partial shadow; also *fig.*

Penurious (pĭniūᵊ·riəs), *a.* 1596. [– med. L. *penuriosus*, f. L. *penuria*; see PENURY and -OUS.] **1.** In want; needy, poverty-stricken (also *fig.*); †with *of*, wanting in. †**b.** Of things, circumstances, etc.: Of, pertaining to, or associated with want; poor, exiguous; barren, unfertile –1789. **2.** Niggardly, parsimonious, grudging; *transf.* meagre, slight, 'shabby', mean 1634. †**3.** Fastidious, dainty (*rare*) –1730.

1. Dives, rich in this world, became exceeding p. in the other 1614. **b.** Seven most scant and p. yeares of great famine 1639. **2.** As a p. niggard of his wealth MILT. Hence **Penu·rious-ly** *adv.*, **-ness.**

Penury (pe·niŭri). late ME. [– L. *penuria*, *pænuria*, perh. rel. to *pæne* almost; see -Y³.] **1.** Destitution, indigence; poverty. **2.** Lack, scarcity, want (*of* something material or immaterial) 1447. **3.** Penuriousness, miserliness. Now *rare.* 1651.

1. Chill P. repress'd their noble rage GRAY. **2.** You owe..to your stars your p. of sense 1699. **3.** God sometimes punishes..p. with oppression JER. TAYLOR.

Penwiper (pe·nwəi:pəɹ). 1848. [f. PEN *sb.*² II. 1 + WIPER.] A contrivance, usu. consisting of one or more pieces of cloth folded or fastened together, for cleaning a pen by wiping the ink from it.

Penwoman (pe·nwu:măn). 1748. [f. as prec. + WOMAN, after *penman*.] A woman skilled in the use of the pen. (Usu. qualified as *good, fine*, etc.)

Peon (pī·ǫ̆n). 1609. [– Pg. *peão* and Sp. *peon* = OFr. *peon* (mod. *pion*) :– med.L. *pedo, pedon-* one who goes on foot (in cl.L. broad-footed man), f. *pes, ped-* foot. Cf. PAWN *sb.*¹] **1.** In India: **a.** A foot-soldier. **b.** A native constable. **c.** An attendant or orderly; a footman or messenger. **2.** In Spanish America: A day-labourer; in S. America, a man or boy leading a horse or mule; in Mexico *spec.* a debtor held in servitude by his creditor till his debts are worked off. Also *attrib.* 1828. Hence **Pe·onage, Pe·onism,** the work or service of a p.; the system of having or using peons; in Mexico *spec.* the condition of a p. serf.

Peony (pī·ŏni). Also **pæony.** [OE. *peonie* – L. *peonia, pæonia* – Gr. *παιωνία*, f. *Παιών* physician (orig. of the gods).] **1.** A plant or flower of the genus *Pæonia* (N.O. *Ranunculaceæ*), comprising stout herbs, or rarely shrubs, with large handsome red or white globular flowers, often double under cultivation; esp. *P. officinalis.* **2.** *attrib.* or as *adj.* Dark red; esp. of the cheeks, plump and rosy 1548.

People (pī·p'l), *sb.* [ME. *peple, poeple, people* – AFr. *poeple, people*, OFr. *pople*, (also mod.) *peuple* :– L. *populus.* For the sp. cf. *jeopardy, leopard.*] **1.** = FOLK 1. **a.** In sing., as a collective of unity. **b.** In sing. form, construed as pl. ME. **c.** *pl.* Nations, races (= L. *populi, gentes*). late ME. †**d.** Used in sing. in the sense 'nations' –1793. **e.** *transf.* of animals. late ME. **2.** The persons belonging to a place, constituting a particular concourse, congregation, company, or class. Construed as *pl.* ME. †**b.** As *collect. sing.* A company, a multitude. Also with *pl.* –1662. **3.** Persons in relation to a superior, or to some one to whom they belong. Chiefly with possessive. **a.** The subjects of a king or other ruler; the servants of God, or of Christ; the congregation or flock of a pastor, etc. Const. as *pl.* ME. **b.** The body of attendants, armed followers, retinue, work-people, servants, etc. Const. as *pl.* ME. **c.** Those to whom any one belongs, one's tribe, clan, etc. collectively: *esp.* (colloq.) one's parents, brothers and sisters, and other relatives at home. Const. as *pl.* late ME. **4.** The commonalty, as dist. from the nobility and ruling or official classes. Const. as *pl.* ME. **5.** *Politics.* The whole body of enfranchised or qualified citizens, considered as the source of power; esp. in a democratic state, the electorate 1646. **6.** Men or women indefinitely; persons, folk. Const. as *pl.* ME. **b.** *emphatically* = Human beings 1450. **c.** *transf.* Living creatures. *poet.* or *rhet.* 1667. **7.** Unemphatically, *people* = Fr. *on*, G. *man*; in colloq. use repl. *men* ('men say', etc.) ME.

1. a. A people's voice! we are a p. yet TENNYSON. **b.** Should not a p. seeke vnto their God? *Isa.* 8:19. **c.** All our English-speaking peoples MORLEY. **d.** Hee shall iudge among the nations, and shall rebuke many p. [WYCLIF puples, *R.V.* peoples] *Isa.* 2:4. **e.** The Ants are a p. not strong *Prov.* 30:25. **2.** The p. here want sadly to know what I am 1711. **b.** He..gaderyd a grete peple of menne 1482. **3.** The p. of the Prince that shall come *Dan.* 9:26. **b.** The Douglas p. are in motion on both sides of the river SCOTT. **c.** Mrs. Sterling.. had lived..with his Father's p. CARLYLE. **4.** I speak to the p. as one of the p. '*Junius' Lett.* **5.** The will of the p. MILL. **6.** I have bought Golden Opinions from all sorts of p. SHAKS. *Good p.*, formerly a courteous way of addressing an assemblage; cf. GOOD *a.* 2. **b.** *Raskall* is properly the hunters terme giuen to young deere.., and not to p. PUTTENHAM. **c.** *The little p., the good p.*, the fairies. **7.** P. cannot understand a man being in a state of doubt J. H. NEWMAN. Hence **Peo·pleless,** having no p. or population 1621.

People (pī·p'l), *v.* 1489. [– (O)Fr. *peupler*, f. *peuple*; see prec.] **1.** *trans.* To furnish with people or inhabitants; to populate 1500. **b.** *transf.* To fill or stock (with animals, inanimate objects, etc.) 1533. **c.** *fig.* To imagine or represent as peopled 1817. **2.** To fill or occupy as inhabitants; to constitute the population of (a country, etc.) 1489. **b.** *transf.* and *fig.* of animals, inanimate objects, etc. 1593. †**c.** *absol.* To form a settlement –1604. **3.** *intr.* (for *refl.*) To grow populous 1659.

1. The nearest Regions must have been first and most fully peopled 1696. **c.** This silent spot tradition old Had peopled with the spectral dead SHELLEY. **2.** What vary'd Being peoples every star POPE. **b.** The gay motes that p. the Sun Beams MILT. Hence **Peopled** (pī·p'ld) *ppl. a.* occupied by people; full of inhabitants; inhabited; also *fig.* **Peo·pler,** one who peoples or causes the peopling of a country; a colonizer; an inhabitant.

†**Peoplish,** *a.* [f. PEOPLE *sb.* + -ISH[1].] Clownish, vulgar. CHAUCER.

Pep (pep). 1912. orig. *U.S.* [abbrev. of PEPPER *sb.*] *slang.* Vigour, energy, 'go'.

‖**Peperino** (pepĕrī·no). Also **pip-.** 1777. [It., f. *pepere* pepper; so called from its consisting of small grains.] *Geol.* A light porous volcanic rock or tuff, formed of sand, cinders, etc. cemented together; a name first given to the tufas of Monte Albano near Rome. Hence **Pe·perine** *a. rare*, consisting or composed of p.

‖**Peplos, peplus** (pe·plǫs, -ʊs). 1776. [– Gr. *πέπλος*, in pl. *πέπλα*, whence L. *peplus, peplum.*] An outer robe or shawl worn by women in ancient Greece; *spec.* that woven yearly for the statue of the goddess Athene at Athens, carried in procession to her temple at the greater Panathenæa.

‖**Peplum** (pe·plŏm). 1678. [L.; see prec.] **1.** = PEPLOS. **2.** A kind of overskirt, supposed to resemble the ancient peplum 1893.

‖**Pepo** (pī·po). 1861. [L. *pepo* pumpkin – Gr. *πέπων*, short for *πέπων σίκυος*, a gourd eaten when ripe, f. *πέπων* ripe.] *Bot.* Any fleshy fruit, with numerous seeds attached to parietal placentæ, and a firm rind; as the gourd, melon, cucumber, etc.

Pepper (pe·pəɹ), *sb.* [OE. *piper, -or* = OFris. *piper*, OS. *pipari, pepar* (Du. *peper*), OHG. *pfeffar* (G. *pfeffer*); WGmc. (ON. *piparr* being from Eng.) – L. *piper* – Gr. *πέπερι* – Skr. *pippalī-* berry, peppercorn. In ME. *piper, peper*, the latter type prevailing in later Eng.; cf. *lemon, level.*] **1.** A pungent aromatic condiment, derived from species of *Piper* and allied genera, used for flavouring, and acting as a digestive stimulant and carminative; *esp.* the dried berries of *Piper nigrum*, either whole (PEPPERCORNS) or ground into powder. **b.** Also, the pungent condiments yielded by other plants; see 3. 1838. **2.** The plant *Piper nigrum*, an E. and W. Indian climbing shrub, having alternate stalked leaves, with pendulous green flower-spikes opposite the leaves, succeeded by small berries turning red when ripe. Also, any plant of the genus *Piper* (including *Chavica*), or (by extension) of the N.O. *Piperaceæ.* late ME. **3.** With qualifying words, applied to other plants furnishing pungent condiments; sometimes to plants having leaves of a pungent flavour 1538. **4.** In allusive or proverbial expressions. late ME.

1. P. was a favourite ingredient of the most expensive Roman cookery GIBBON. *Black p.*, that form of the condiment which is prepared from the berries dried when not quite ripe. *White p.*, a less pungent form, from the same berries when fully ripe, or from the black by removing the husk. *Long p.*, a similar condiment prepared from the immature fruit-spikes of the allied plants *Piper* (*Chavica*) *officinarum* and *P. longum*, formerly supposed to be the flowers or unripe fruit of *P. nigrum.* **3. African p.,** (*a*) *Habzelia* (*Xylopia*) *æthiopica* or other species (N.O. *Anonaceæ*); (*b*) *Capsicum fastigiatum.* **Chili p.** (*a*) = PEPPER-TREE a; (*b*) erron. = CHILLI. **Chinese p.** = *Japanese pepper.* **Guinea p.,** (*a*) see GUINEA P.; (*b*) = *African p.* **Japanese p.,** *Xanthoxylon piperitum* of Japan and China. **Melegueta p.** = *grains of Paradise*: see GRAIN *sb.*[1] 4. See also CAYENNE P., CUBEB P., JAMAICA P., RED P. etc. **4.** Heere's the Challenge, reade it: I warrant there's vinegar and p. in 't SHAKS. †*To take p. in the nose*, to take offence. So †*to snuff p.*

attrib. and *Comb.*, as **P. Alley,** name of an alley in London, hence allusively in pugilistic slang; **p.-cake,** local name for gingerbread; **-elder,** name for plants of the genera *Peperomia, Enckea*, and *Artanthe*, allied to the common p.; **-grass,** (*a*) any species of *Lepidium* (as *L. sativum*, garden-cress), from the pungent taste; (*b*) = PILLWORT; **-mill,** a small handmill for grinding p.; **-moth** = PEPPERED *moth*; **-plant,** the plant *Piper nigrum* or any plant producing pepper; **-pod,** the pod of any species of *Capsicum*; **-root,** any species of *Dentaria*, esp. *D. diphylla*, so called from the pungent root; **-sauce,** a pungent sauce or condiment made by steeping 'red peppers' (capsicum pods) in vinegar.

Pepper (pe·pəɹ), *v.* 1581. [f. PEPPER *sb.* Cf. OE. (*ge*)*pip*(*o*)*rian.*] **1.** *trans.* To sprinkle with pepper; to flavour or season with pepper. Also *absol.* **2.** To sprinkle (a surface) as with pepper; to besprinkle, dot, stud. Also *fig.* (Mostly in *pa. pple.*) 1612. **3.** To sprinkle like pepper. Also *fig.* 1821. **4.** To pelt with shot or missiles. Also *fig.* 1644. **b.** *intr.* To discharge shot, etc. (*at* something) 1767. **5.** *trans.* To 'give it (a person) hot'; to beat severely, trounce. Hence †**b.** To give one his death-blow (*lit.* and *fig.*), to 'do for', ruin. 1500. **6.** To give pungency, spice, or flavour to (speech or writing) 1835. †**b.** To dose with flattery –1784. †**7.** To infect with venereal disease. (Fr. *poivrer.*) –1723.

2. Every page was peppered with italic 1896. **4.** You may p. the bishops a little GEO. ELIOT. **b.** Peppering away at the pheasants 1890. **5.** I am pepper'd I warrant, for this world SHAKS. **6. b.** Who pepper'd the highest, was surest to please GOLDSM. Hence **Pe·ppering** *vbl. sb.* the action of the vb.; pelting with shot, missiles, etc. **Pe·ppering** *ppl. a.* that peppers; pungent; falling heavily (as rain).

Pe·pper-and-sa·lt. 1774. Name for a kind of cloth made of dark- and light-coloured wools woven together, showing small dots of dark and light closely intermingled; also, a garment made of this. Usu. *attrib.* or *adj.*

Pe·pper-box. 1546. **1.** A small box, usu. cylindrical, with a perforated lid, for sprinkling powdered pepper. **2.** *transf.* Applied contemptuously to a small cylindrical turret or cupola 1821. **3.** The irregular buttress sticking into the fives-court at Eton 1865. **4.** *fig.* A hot-tempered person 1867. **5.** *attrib.* 1825.

1. Hee cannot creepe into a halfe-penny purse, nor into a Pepper-Boxe SHAKS.

Pe·pper-ca:stor, -ca:ster. 1676. [See CASTOR[2].] **1.** A small vessel with a perforated top, usu. one of the castors of a cruet-stand, for sprinkling pepper at table. **2.** *transf.* **a.** = prec. 2. 1859. **b.** *slang.* A revolver 1889.

Peppercorn (pe·pəɹkǭɹn). OE. [f. PEPPER *sb.* + CORN *sb.*[1] 2.] **1.** The dried berry of black pepper. **b.** Stipulated for as a quit-rent or nominal rent 1607. **2.** *attrib.* Of or consisting in a peppercorn, as *p. rent*; also *fig.* very small, insignificant 1791.

1. b. In modern times building leases sometimes reserve a pepper-corn as rent 1898.

Peppered (pe·pəɹd), *ppl. a.* 1581. [f. PEPPER *v.* + -ED[1].] Sprinkled or seasoned with pepper; sprinkled with small dots like grains of pepper; pelted with shot, etc.

P. moth, collector's name of the Geometrid moth *Amphydasis* (*Biston*) *betularia.*

Pepperer (pe·pərəɹ). ME. [In 1 f. PEPPER *sb.* + -ER[2]; in 2 f. PEPPER *v.* + -ER[1].] **1.** A dealer in pepper and spices; a grocer. (The original name of the Grocers' Company of London.) *Obs.* exc. *Hist.* **2.** One who or that which peppers; *fig.* a hot-tempered person; something pungent 1711.

Pepperidge (pe·peridʒ). Also **-age.** 1823. **1.** Var. of PIPPERIDGE. **2.** *U.S.* The Black Gum, Sour Gum, or Tupelo, a N. Amer. tree of the genus *Nyssa*, having very tough wood 1826.

Peppermint (pe·pəɹmint). 1696. [f. PEPPER *sb.* + MINT *sb.*[2], app. after Bot. L.] **1.** A species or subspecies of mint (*Mentha piperita*), cultivated for its essential oil (*oil of p.*). **2.** The essential oil of peppermint, or some preparation of it 1836. **b.** A lozenge flavoured with peppermint, a peppermint-drop 1884. **3.** (In full *p.-tree.*) Name for several Australian species of *Eucalyptus* (*E. amygdalina, piperita*, etc.) yielding an aromatic essential oil resembling that of peppermint 1790.

Comb.: **P.-camphor** = MENTHOL; **p.-drop, -lozenge,** a lozenge made of sugar, flavoured with p.; **-tree** (see 3).

Pe·pper-pot. 1679. **1.** = PEPPER-BOX 1. Also in allusive and fig. uses. **2.** A W. Indian dish composed of meat (or fish, game, etc.) and vegetables stewed with cassareep and red pepper or other hot spices 1704. **3.** *attrib.* 1883.

Pe·pper-tree. 1691. **a.** An evergreen tree or shrub of S. America, *Schinus molle* (N.O. *Anacardiaceæ*), having a pungent red fruit; **b.** A tree of Australia and Tasmania, *Drimys* or *Tasmannia aromatica*, or other species (N.O. *Magnoliaceæ*), having small pungent fruit used as pepper.

Pepperwort (pe·pəɹwɒɹt). 1562. [See WORT[1].] **1.** A species of cress (*Lepidium latifolium*), formerly also called dittander or dittany; also the genus *Lepidium* in general. **2.** *pl.* A name for the N.O. *Marsileaceæ*, consisting of small aquatic plants allied to the ferns 1846. **b.** Lindley's name for N.O. *Piperaceæ* 1846.

Peppery (pe·pəri), *a.* 1699. [f. PEPPER *sb.* + -Y[1].] **1.** Abounding in pepper; of the nature of or resembling pepper; pungent, 'hot'. **2.** *fig.* **a.** Of speech or writing: Sharp, stinging, pungent. **b.** Of a person, etc.: Hot-tempered, irascible, testy. 1826.

2. a. Some good, strong, p. doctrine DICKENS. Hence **Pe·pperi-ly** *adv.*, **-ness.**

Pepsin (pe·psin). Also formerly **-ine.** 1844. [– G. *pepsin* (Schwann, 1836), f. Gr. πέψις digestion, f. *πεπ- cook, digest; see -IN[1].] A ferment contained in the gastric juice, having the property of converting proteids into peptones in the presence of a weak acid; also used medicinally in cases of indigestion, etc. Hence **Pe·psinate** *v.* to mix or treat with p.

Peptic (pe·ptik), *a.* and *sb.* 1651. [– Gr. πεπτικός able to digest, f. πεπτός cooked, digestive. Cf. DYSPEPTIC.] **A.** *adj.* **1.** = DIGESTIVE A. 1; used *spec.* in relation to the digestion in which pepsin is concerned. **2.** = DIGESTIVE A. 2. 1661. **3.** = EUPEPTIC A. 2. CARLYLE.

1. *P. digestion*, stomachic or gastric digestion. *P. glands*, the glands which secrete the gastric juice.

B. *sb.* **1.** A substance which promotes digestion 1842. **2.** *pl.* The digestive organs (*joc.*) 1842. Hence **Pe·ptical** *a.* = A. **Pepti·cian,** a person who has good digestion. CARLYLE. **Pepti·city,** good p. condition.

Peptogen (pe·ptŏdʒen). 1875. [f. Gr. πεπτός (see prec.) + -GEN.] A general name for substances which stimulate the formation of pepsin in the gastric juice. So **Peptoge·nic, Pepto·genous** *adjs.* having the quality of forming, or stimulating the formation of, pepsin; also, of converting proteids into peptones.

Peptone (pe·ptoᵘn). 1860. [– G. *pepton* (C. G. Lehmann, 1849) – Gr. πεπτόν, n. of πεπτός PEPTIC.] The general name for a class of albuminoid substances into which proteids (the nitrogenous constituents of food) are converted by the action of pepsin or trypsin; differing from proteids in not being coagulable by heat, and in being easily soluble and diffusible through membranes, and thus capable of absorption into the system. Also *attrib.* Hence **Pe·ptonize** *v. trans.* to convert (a proteid) into a p.; *esp.* to subject (food) to an artificial process of predigestion by means of pepsin or pancreatic extract; also *fig.* **Pe:ptoniza·tion. Pe·ptonizer.**

‖**Peptonuria** (peptoniūᵊ·riă). 1891. [mod. L., f. as prec. + Gr. οὖρον urine; see -URIA.] *Path.* The presence of peptones in the urine.

Peptotoxin (pepto,tǫ·ksin). 1890. [f. Gr. πεπτός (see PEPTIC) + TOXIN.] A poisonous alkaloid formed from peptones during digestion.

Per (pəɹ), *prep.* A Latin prep. (whence It., OFr. *per*, Fr. *par*) meaning 'through, by, by means of'; in med.L. also = 'for every.., for each..': used in English in various L. and OFr. phrases, and ult. becoming practically an Eng. prep. used freely with sbs.

I. In Latin (med.L. and It.) phrases. **1. per accidens** [= Gr. κατὰ συμβεβηκός] by accident, by virtue of some non-essential circumstance, contingently, indirectly. (Opp. to *per se.*) 1528. **b.** In *Logic* applied to conversion in which the quantity of the proposition is changed from universal to particular 1677. **2. per annum,** (so much) by the year, every year, yearly 1601. **3. per consequens,** by consequence, consequently. late ME. **4. per contra** [It.], on the opposite side (of an account, etc.); on the other hand; as a set-off 1554. **b.** as *sb.* The opposite side (of an account, etc.) 1804. **5. per diem,** (so much) by the day, every day, daily 1520. **b.** as *sb.* An amount of so much every day (*U.S.*) 1888. **6. per mensem,** (so much) every month 1647. **7. per procurationem** (abbrev. *per proc.*, *per pro.*, *p.p.*; sometimes *per procuration*), by proxy or deputy (often used in signatures to documents on behalf of a firm, etc.) 1819. **8. per saltum,** by a leap, at one bound, all at once 1600. **9. per se,** by or in itself (himself, herself, themselves); intrinsically, essentially; without reference to anything (or any one) else 1572. †**b.** Formerly used in naming a letter which by itself forms a word (*A per se*), or as a symbol which by itself stands for a word (*and per se* = &, AMPERSAND); hence allus. 1475. **10.** In various phr., as *per arsin*, etc. (see ARSIS, etc.); **per capita** (*Law*), 'by heads', applied to succession when divided among a number of individuals in equal shares (opp. to *per stirpes*); **per fas et (aut) nefas,** by right and (or) wrong, by means fair or foul; **per pares,** by (his) peers; **per stirpes** (*Law*), by 'stocks' or 'families'; applied to succession when divided in equal shares among the branches of a family, the share of each branch being then subdivided equally among the representatives of that branch (opp. to *per capita*). late ME.

II. 1. In OFr. phrases, some of which occur with PAR, q.v., as *per charite*, etc.; also †**per maistrie,** by conquest; **per my et per tout** (*Law*), 'by half and by all', by joint-tenancy; **per pais, per pays** (*Law*), 'by the country'. See also PERADVENTURE, PERCHANCE, PERFORCE, etc. ME. **2.** *Her.* In phr. denoting partition of the shield in the direction of any of the principal ordinaries (*per* BEND, *per* CHEVRON, etc.).

III. As an Eng. preposition. **1.** By, by means of, by the instrumentality of; esp. in phrases relating to conveyance, as *per bearer, per carrier, per post*, etc. Also = according to, as stated or indicated by, as (*as*) *per invoice*, (*as*) *per margin*; as laid down by (a judge) 1588. So in joc. slang use, (*as*) *per usual* = as usual. **2.** In distrib. sense, following words of number or quantity, in expressions denoting rate or proportion: For each.., for every... See also PER CENT. 1598.

Per-, *prefix*[1]. The L. prep. *per* (see prec.) used in composition with vbs., adjs., and their derivatives.

I. In senses: **1.** Through, in space or time; throughout, all over; with the verbs (and derivs.), as PERAMBULATE, PERFORATE, PERVADE. **2.** Through and through, thoroughly, completely, to completion, to the end; with verbs (and their derivs.), as PERFECT, PERMUTE, PERPETRATE, PERTURB, etc. **3.** Away entirely, to destruction, 'to the bad'; with verbs (and their derivs.), as PERDITION, PERISH, PERVERT, etc. **4.** Thoroughly, perfectly, extremely, very; with adjs. and advbs., as PERFERVID, etc. Formerly also with derived sbs. (or their analogues), in sense 'very great', 'extreme', as *perdiligence*, etc.

II. *Chem.* (from I. 4). Forming sbs. and adjs. denoting the maximum (or supposed maximum) of some element in a chemical combination; esp. **a.** With names of binary compounds in -IDE (formerly *-uret*), designating that in which the element or radical combines in the largest proportion with another element, e.g. PEROXIDE, PERCHLORIDE 1804. **b.** With adjs. in -IC, naming oxides, acids, etc., designating that compound which contains the greatest proportion of oxygen (and, consequently, the least of the element named), as PERCHLORIC, -MANGANIC, etc. Also in names of salts of these acids, and analogous bodies, as PERCHLORATE, -MANGANATE, etc. Formerly *per-* was also prefixed to adjs. in *-ous*, where *hypo-* is now used, as *persulphurous* = HYPOSULPHUROUS; etc.

Per-, *prefix*[2], repr. OFr. *per* or Fr. *par* (see PAR *prep.*, PER *prep.* II), in phr. which have coalesced into single words, as PERADVENTURE, PERCHANCE, etc.; so also PERHAPS, q.v.

Peract (peræ·kt), *v.* Now *rare.* 1621. [– *peract-*, pa. ppl. stem of L. *peragere* perform, accomplish, f. *per* PER-[1] 2 + *agere* drive, do.] *trans.* To practise, perform; to accomplish.

Peracute (pərăkiū·t), *a.* Now *rare.* late ME. [– L. *peracutus*; see PER-[1] 4 and ACUTE.] *Path.* Of diseases: Very acute or severe; attended with much inflammation.

Peradve·nture, *sb.* 1450. [subst. use of next.] The possibility of a thing being so or not; uncertainty, doubt; a contingency; a conjecture, chance.

Some to be saved infallibly, and others to be left to a p. COWPER. Phr. *Out of, past, beyond, without* (*all*) *p.*, beyond question, without doubt. †*By, at* (*a*) *p.*, by haphazard; at random, randomly.

Peradventure (perădve·ntiŭɹ, -tʃəɹ), *adv. arch.* [ME. *per* or *par auenture* – OFr. *per* or *par auenture* (see PAR *prep.* 1 b, PER *prep.* II, ADVENTURE); reduced at an early date to †*peraunter*, in late XV assim. to L. spelling.] †**1.** In a statement of fact: By chance; as it happened –1624. **2.** In a dependent clause expressing hypothesis or purpose (with *if, unless, that, lest*): By chance or accident, perchance; *if p.*, if it chance that ME. **3.** In a hypothetical or contingent statement: Perchance, haply; maybe, perhaps; not improbably, belike ME. **b.** Qualifying a word or phr., usu. by ellipsis ME.

2. Unless, p., their wives were comely and young LYTTON. **3.** Peraduenture there be fifty righteous within the citie *Gen.* 18:24. **b.** Lo, where he commeth towards, peraduenture to his paine 1575.

Peragrate (pe·răgreⁱt), *v.* Now *rare.* 1542. [– *peragrat-*, pa. ppl. stem of L. *peragrare*, f. *per* through + *ager* field, country; see -ATE[3].] *trans.* To travel or pass through (a country, etc.). Also *fig.* Hence **Peragra·tion** (now *rare*), a travelling through or traversing; as †*month of p.*, the period of the moon's revolution; a sidereal (or tropical) month 1561.

Perai (pīrai·), **piraya** (pirā·yă). 1753. [– Tupi *piraya* (in Brazil *piranʼa*, whence Pg. *piranha* XIX), lit. 'scissors'.] A voracious fresh-water fish, *Serrasalmo piraya*, of the Orinoco, etc.

Perambulate (pěræ·mbiŭleⁱt), *v.* 1568. [– *perambulat-*, pa. ppl. stem of L. *perambulare*, f. *per* through + *ambulare* walk; see -ATE[3].] **1.** *trans.* To walk through, over, or about (a place); formerly to travel through. Also *fig.* **b.** *intr.* To walk about; to move about 1607. **2.** *spec.* **a.** *trans.* To travel through and inspect (a territory). **b.** To walk officially round the boundaries of (a forest, manor, parish, etc.) for the purpose of formally determining or preserving them 1612.

1. There is a great deal of Spain that has not been perambulated JOHNSON. So **Pera·mbulant** *a.* (*rare*) perambulating, itinerant.

Perambulation (pěræmbiŭlēⁱ·ʃən). 1472. [– AFr. *perambulation* or med.L. *perambulatio*, f. as prec.; see -ION.] **1.** The action of walking through; a walk, a journey on foot; formerly, the action of travelling through or about 1485. **2.** The action of travelling through and inspecting a territory or region; a survey. **b.** *transf.* A written account of a survey. 1576. **3.** The ceremony of walking officially round (a forest, manor, parish, or holding) for the purpose of asserting and recording its boundaries; beating the bounds 1472. **b.** *transf.* A record of a perambulation 1610. **4.** The boundary traced, or the space enclosed, by a perambulation; bounds; extent (*lit.* and *fig.*) 1601. †**5.** *fig.* Comprehensive relation or description; also, circumlocution –1652. **6.** *attrib.* 1670.

1. His daily perambulations at Lasswade 1877. **2.** Discrete persons..to make parambulacions & to appoint..wher the boundes..shal extend 1540.

Perambulator (pěræ·mbiŭleⁱtəɹ). 1611. [f. PERAMBULATE *v.* + -OR 2.] **1.** One who perambulates (see the vb.). Now *rare* or *Obs.* †**2.** A machine for measuring distances; a hodometer, waywiser –1828. **3.** A hand-carriage for young children, pushed from behind. (Often colloq. shortened to *pram.*) 1857.

‖**Perameles** (perămī·liz). 1886. [mod.L., f. Gr. πήρα bag, pouch + L. *meles, melis* marten or badger.] *Zool.* A genus of small marsupials of Australia and New Guinea, typical of the family *Peramelidæ*, or true bandicoots.

Percale (pəɹkēⁱ·l, ‖perkā·l). 1618. [In **a.** of uncertain origin; cf. Pers. *pargāla* rag. In **b.** – Fr. *percale* (XVIII) = Sp. *percal*, It. *percallo.*] **a.** A fabric imported from the East Indies in the 17th and 18th centuries. **b.** A closely woven cotton fabric, like muslin, but without gloss 1840.

Percaline (pə̄ɹkălī·n, pə̄·ɹkălin). 1858. [– Fr. *percaline*, dim. of *percale* (prec.).] A glossy kind of French cotton cloth, usually dyed of one colour.

Percarbide (pəɹkā·ɹbəid). 1826. [f. PER-[1] II. a + CARBIDE.] *Chem.* A compound containing the maximum proportion of carbon with another element. Also †**Perca·rburet.** So **Perca·rburetted** *a.* containing a maximum of carbon, as *percarburetted iron.*

Perca·se, *adv. Obs.* (exc. *dial.*) [ME. – AFr. *per cas, par cas*, OFr. *par cas*; see PER and CASE *sb.*[1]] †**1.** = PERADVENTURE *adv.* 1, PERCHANCE 1. –1513. †**2.** *If* (*except, lest*, etc.) *p.*, if (lest, etc.) by chance –1575. **3.** In a hypothetical or contingent statement: It may (might) chance or be the case that..; maybe, perchance ME. †**b.** = PERADVENTURE *adv.* 3 b. –1600.

Perceant (pə̄·ɹsănt), *a. poet. arch.* or *Obs.* late ME. [– (O)Fr. *perçant*, pr. pple. of *percer* PIERCE.] Penetrative, keen, piercing.

The sophist's eye,..Keen, cruel, p., stinging KEATS.

Perceivable (pəɹsī·văb'l), *a.* Now *rare.* 1450. [orig. – (O)Fr. *percevable*; later referred to PERCEIVE *v.*] Perceptible; sensible;

intelligible, appreciable. Hence **Percei·vably** *adv.*

Percei·vance. *Obs.* exc. *dial.* 1534. [orig. – OFr. *percevance*; see PERCEIVE, -ANCE; later assim. to the Eng. verb.] The capacity of perceiving, discernment, wisdom; perception (mental or physical).

Perceive (pəɹsī·v), *v.* ME. [– AFr. **perceiver*, OFr. **perceivre*, *par-*, var. of *perçoivre* (now repl. by *percevoir*) :– L. *percipere* (i) seize, obtain, collect, (ii) understand, apprehend, f. *per* PER-¹ I. 2 + *capere* lay hold of.] **I.** To take in with the mind or senses. **1.** *trans.* To apprehend with the mind; to become aware of; to observe, understand. Also *absol.* †**b.** Of an inanimate object: To be affected by –1626. **2.** To become aware of by sight, hearing, or other sense; to observe ME. †**3.** To apprehend what is not present to observation; to see through, see into –1660.

1. Doe you perceiue the iest? SHAKS. **b.** The Vpper Regions of the Aire perceiue the collection of the matter of Tempest and Winds, before the Aire here below BACON. **2.** They went awaye by nyght so pryvely, that the enemy perceived it not 1560. **3.** They think their designes are too subtile to be perceived HOBBES.

†**II.** To take into possession. **a.** *trans.* To receive (rents, profits, dues, etc.) –1625. **b.** *gen.* To receive, get, obtain –1748.

b. *Two Gent.* I. i. 144. Hence **Perceivedly** (pəɹsī·vėdli) *adv.* **Percei·ver.**

Per cent (pəɹ se·nt), *phr.* (*sb.*) 1568. [See PER III. 2 and CENT¹. Also written with full stop (*per cent.*), as if an abbrev. of **per centum.**] **A.** *phr.* By the hundred; for, in, or to every hundred; expressing a proportion, *esp.* of interest to principal. **b.** Used *attrib.* ('four per cent loan') or as *sb.* in *pl.* ('three per cents') 1720. **B.** *Per cents* as *sb. pl.* Percentages; *spec.* in U.S. schools 1850.

Percentage (pəɹse·ntėdʒ). 1789. [f. prec. + -AGE.] A rate or proportion per cent; a quantity or amount reckoned as so much in the hundred; *loosely*, a proportion (*of* something).

A serious p. of books are not worth reading at all 1886.

Percentile (pəɹse·ntəil, -il), *a.* and *sb.* 1885. [f. *per cent*(*um* (see above), app. after *bissextile*, etc.] **A.** *adj.* Pertaining to percentage; reckoned as a percentage 1890. **B.** *sb.* Each of a series of values obtained by dividing a large number of quantities into a hundred equal groups in order of magnitude 1885.

Percept (pə̄·ɹsept). 1837. [– L. *perceptum* (a thing) perceived, n. of pa. pple. of *percipere* PERCEIVE, after *concept*.] *Philos.* **1.** An object of PERCEPTION. **2.** The mental product of perceiving 1876.

2. A p. is the abstract of sensations 1876. So **Perce·ptual** *a.* of or pertaining to perception; of the nature of percepts.

Perceptible (pəɹse·ptĭb'l), *a.* 1551. [– OFr. *perceptible* or late L. *perceptibilis*, f. *percept-*, pa. ppl. stem of L. *percipere* PERCEIVE; see -IBLE.] †**1.** Percipient, perceptive *of* –1772. **2.** Capable of being perceived, cognizable, apprehensible; observable 1603.

2. The soule is not p. by any sense HOLLAND. Hence **Perce:ptibi·lity,** †perceptivity; capability of being perceived. **Perce·ptibly** *adv.* in or to a p. degree.

Perception (pəɹse·pʃən). 1475. [In I. – (O)Fr. *perception* – L.; in II. – L. *perceptio*, f. as prec.; see -ION.] **I.** From L. *percipere*, to take, receive. **1.** The collection or receiving of rents, etc. Now only in legal use. 1475. †**2.** The partaking of the Eucharist –1674. **II.** From L. *percipere*, to be or become cognizant of. **1.** The taking cognizance of objects in general; occas. practically = consciousness. In Locke esp. as dist. from *volition*. 1611. †**b.** The being affected by an object without contact, though consciousness is absent BACON. **2.** The taking cognizance of a sensible or quasi-sensible object 1704. **3.** The intuitive recognition of a moral or æsthetic quality, e.g. the truth of a remark, the beautiful in objects 1827. **4.** *Philos.* The action of the mind by which it refers its sensations to an external object as their cause. (Dist. from *sensation*, *conception* or *imagination*, and *judgement* or inference.) 1762. **5.** The (or a) faculty of perceiving (in any of these senses) 1712. **6.** = PERCEPT 2. 1690.

1. The two..principal Actions of the Mind..are these two: P., or Thinking, and Volition, or Willing LOCKE. **2.** The whole apparatus of vision, or of p. by any other of our senses 1736. **4.** External things and their attributes are objects of p.: relations among things are objects of conception 1762. **5.** He is a new man, with new perceptions EMERSON. Hence **Perce·ptional** *a.* of, pertaining to, or of the nature of p.

Perceptive (pəɹse·ptiv), *a.* (*sb.*) 1656. [– med.L. *perceptivus*, f. as prec.; see -IVE.] **1.** Characterized by or capable of perceiving; pertaining to or having perception; instrumental to perception. **b.** Of ready perception. Also with *of*. 1860. †**2.** Perceptible –1813. **B.** *sb. pl.* The perceptive faculties or organs 1858.

1. Your mother's p. faculties are extraordinary 1897. Hence **Perce·ptive-ly** *adv.*, **-ness. Percepti·vity,** p. quality.

Perch (pə̄ɹtʃ), *sb.*¹ ME. [– (O)Fr. *perche* :– L. *perca* – Gr. πέρκη.] **1.** A common spiny-finned freshwater fish (*Perca fluviatilis*) of Europe and the British Isles. Also, the common yellow perch of N. America (*P. americana* or *flavescens*), or species of the family *Percidæ* in general. (Now rare in pl., the collect. sing. being used instead.) **b.** Applied on the Pacific coast to any fish of the viviparous family *Embiotocidæ* or surf-fishes, and locally to various other fishes 1882. **2.** With qualifying word, applied to various fishes of the family *Percidæ*, and of other families, resembling the common perch or taking its place as food 1611.

2. Black p., a name for dark-coloured species of *Centropristis*, also called *black bass*; also for other dark-coloured fishes allied to the common p.; **Blue p.,** the BURGALL or CUNNER; **Red p.,** the rose-fish, *Sebastes marinus*; **White p.,** (*a*) *Morone americana*, family *Labracidæ*; (*b*) various species of the *Embiotocidæ*; **Yellow p.** (see 1).

Perch (pə̄ɹtʃ), *sb.*² ME. [– (O)Fr. *perche* :– L. *pertica* pole, measuring-rod.] **I.** A pole, rod, stick, or stake, used *e.g.* for a weapon, a prop, etc. *Obs.* or *dial.* in gen. sense. **b.** A pole set up in the sea, a river, etc., to serve as a mark for navigation 1465. **c.** The centre pole connecting the hinder to the fore-carriage in some four-wheeled vehicles 1668. **II. 1.** A bar fixed horizontally to hang something upon; a peg. *Obs.* or *Hist.* †**b.** A bar to support a candle or candles –1565. **2.** A bar fixed horizontally for a hawk or tame bird to rest upon. late ME. **b.** Anything serving for a bird to alight or rest upon; also *transf.* 1470. **c.** *fig.* An elevated or secure position or station 1526. **d.** *colloq.* An elevated seat on a vehicle for the driver 1841. **3.** A wooden bar, or frame of two parallel bars, used in examining and dressing cloth, blankets, etc. *Obs.* or *dial.* 1553.

2. As Chauntecleer among hise wyues alle Sat on his perche CHAUCER. **b.** *To take one's p.*, to perch, to alight. Phr. *To knock off one's p.*, to upset, vanquish, 'do for', be the death of. So *hop the p.*, to die.

III. A rod of a definite length for measuring land, etc.; hence **a.** A measure of length, esp. for land, etc.; in Standard Measure = $5\frac{1}{2}$ yards, but varying locally. Also called POLE or ROD. late ME. **b.** A superficial measure of land; a square perch or pole (normally $\frac{1}{160}$ of an acre) 1442. **c.** A solid measure used for stone, containing a lineal perch (see a) in length, and usually $1\frac{1}{2}$ feet in breadth and 1 foot in thickness; but varying locally 1823.

Perch (pə̄ɹtʃ), *v.* ME. [– (O)Fr. *percher*, f. *perche* PERCH *sb.*²] **I. 1.** *intr.* To alight or rest as a bird upon a perch. Hence *transf.* of persons or things: To alight or settle, or to stand, sit, or rest, upon something. 1486. **2.** *trans.* To set or place upon a perch; to set up on a height, or as on a perch. Also *refl.* 1575. **3.** *pa. pple.* Standing, seated, or settled upon a perch; set up on an eminence. late ME.

1. Birds of dazzling plume P. on the loaded boughs 1804. **3.** The heights on which the old town is perched 1884.

II. To stretch (cloth from the loom) upon a perch (PERCH *sb.*² II. 3), for the purpose of examining it, etc. 1552.

Percha (pə̄·ɹtʃă). Short for GUTTA-PERCHA.

Perchance (pəɹtʃɑ·ns), *adv. arch.* ME. [– AFr. *par chance*, i.e. (O)Fr. *par* by (PER-²), *chance* CHANCE; with later assim. to PER-. Cf. PERCASE.] **1.** = PERADVENTURE *adv.* 1. *Obs.* exc. *arch.* **2.** = PERADVENTURE *adv.* 2. late ME. **3.** = PERADVENTURE *adv.* 3. late ME. **b.** Qualifying a word or phr., by ellipsis. late ME.

3. b. To sleepe, p. to Dreame: I, there's the rub SHAKS.

Perched (pə̄ɹtʃt, *poet.* pə̄·ɹtʃėd), *ppl. a.* late ME. [f. PERCH *v.*, *sb.*² + -ED¹ and ².] **1.** Seated as a bird upon a perch; set up on a high point; *spec.* in *Geol.* applied to a block or boulder left resting upon a pinnacle or the like by the melting of the ice which carried it. **2.** Furnished with a perch or perches 1671.

Percher¹ (pə̄·ɹtʃəɹ). 1775. [f. PERCH *v.* + -ER¹.] **1.** A person or animal that perches. **2.** *spec.* One of the *Insessores* or perching birds 1835. **3.** A workman employed in perching cloth (see PERCH *v.* II) 1882.

†**Percher**². ME. [f. PERCH *sb.*² II. 1 b.] A tall candle –1706.

‖**Percheron** (pęrʃəroṅ). 1875. [Fr. adj. from *le Perche*, a district of France.] A horse of a noted breed raised in le Perche, combining strength with lightness and speed.

Perchlor-, perchloro-. 1857. Comb. form of *perchloric*, *perchloride*, *perchlorinated*; chiefly indicating a compound in which there is the maximum replacement of hydrogen by chlorine, as in *perchlo:race·tic*, *perchlo:roqui·none*, etc.

Perchlorate (pəɹklō·ᵊrėt). 1826. [f. PER-¹ II. b + CHLORATE.] *Chem.* A salt of perchloric acid. Hence **Perchlo·rated** *ppl. a.*

Perchloric (pəɹklō·ᵊrik), *a.* 1818. [f. PER-¹ II. b + CHLORIC.] *Chem.* In *P. acid*, hydrogen perchlorate, $HClO_4$, the oxygen acid of chlorine, containing more oxygen than CHLORIC acid ($HClO_3$).

Perchloride (pəɹklō·ᵊrəid). 1818. [PER-¹ II. a.] *Chem.* A compound of chlorine with another element or radical, containing the maximum proportion of chlorine. So **Perchlo·rinated,** combined with the maximum proportion of chlorine; hence **Perchlorina·tion.**

Perciform (pə̄·ɹsifǭɹm), *a.* 1880. [– mod. L. *perciformis*, f. L. *perca* PERCH *sb.*¹; see -FORM.] *Ichthyol.* Of the form of, or resembling, a perch; *spec.* belonging to the division *Perciformes* comprising the *Percidæ* and several allied families.

Percipience (pəɹsi·piĕns). 1768. [f. next; see -ENCE.] The action or condition of perceiving; perception. So **Perci·piency,** the quality of being percipient.

Percipient (pəɹsi·piĕnt), *a.* and *sb.* 1662. [– *percipient-*, pr. ppl. stem of L. *percipere*; see PERCEIVE, -ENT.] **A.** *adj.* That perceives or is capable of perceiving; conscious 1692. **B.** *sb.* One who or that which perceives; *spec.* in *Telepathy*, etc., one who perceives something outside the range of the senses 1885.

Percoid (pə̄·ɹkoid), *a.* and *sb.* 1840. [f. L. *perca* PERCH *sb.*¹ + -OID; first in Fr., in pl. *Percoïdes*, the perch family of acanthopterygious fishes (*Percidæ*).] *Ichthyol.* **A.** *adj.* Resembling or akin to a perch; belonging to the family *Percidæ*. **B.** *sb.* A fish of the perch family. So **Percoi·dean** *a.* and *sb.* **Percoi·deous** *a.*

Percolate (pə̄·ɹkŏlĕt), *sb.* 1885. [f. PERCOLATE *v.*, after *filtrate* sb.] A product of percolation.

Percolate (pə̄·ɹkŏleᶦt), *v.* 1626. [– *percolat-*, pa. ppl. stem of L. *percolare*, f. *per* PER-¹ I. 1 + *colare* strain, f. *colum* sieve, strainer; see -ATE³.] **1.** *trans.* To cause (a liquid) to pass through the interstices of a medium; to strain or filter. Also *fig.* **2.** *intr.* Of a liquid: To filter, ooze, or trickle through a porous substance or medium 1684. **b.** *fig.* 1867. **3.** *trans.* Of a liquid: To permeate (a porous body or medium). Also *fig.* 1794.

2. The water which has percolated through the sandy beds HUXLEY. **b.** The worship of Isis had percolated..into the Greek Peninsula GLADSTONE.

Percolation (pəɹkolēᶦ·ʃən). 1613. [f. PERCOLATE *v.* + -ION; see -ATION.] The action or process of percolating; filtration; *spec.* in *Pharmacy*, the process of obtaining an extract by passing a dissolving liquid through a pulverized substance until all the soluble matters are extracted. **b.** An oozing through 1646.

Percolator (pə̄ɹkǒleitəɹ). 1830. [f. PERCOLATE *v.* + -OR 2.] One who or that which percolates. **b.** An apparatus for percolating or straining a liquid (e.g. coffee).

Percomorph (pə̄ɹkǒmǭɹf), *a.* and *sb.* 1885. [f. mod.L. *Percomorphi* pl., f. L. *perca* PERCH *sb.*[1] + Gr. μορφή form.] *Ichthyol.* **A.** *adj.* Belonging to the order *Percomorphi*, comprising most of the spiny-finned fishes. **B.** *sb.* A fish of this order.

Percur (pəɹkɒ̄·ɹ), *v. rare.* 1657. [– L. *percurrere* run through, f. PER-[1] I. 1 + *currere* run.] *trans.* To run through, traverse. So **Percu·rrent** *a. rare*, running through; *spec.* in *Bot.* said of a midrib, etc., extending from the base to the apex of a leaf.

Percursory (pəɹkɒ̄·ɹsŏri), *a. rare.* 1837. [An expressive extension of CURSORY; see PER-[1] I. 1.] Characterized by running through something rapidly or hastily.

Percuss (pəɹkɒ·s), *v.* 1560. [– *percuss-*, pa. ppl. stem of L. *percutere*, strike or thrust through, f. *per* PER-[1] I. 1 + *quatere* shake, strike, dash.] †**1.** *trans.* To strike so as to shake; hence *gen.* to strike, hit, knock. Also *fig.* –1694. **2.** *Med.* To tap or strike gently (some part of the body), for purposes of diagnosis, or of therapeutics. Also *absol.* or *intr.* 1834.

1. Solid Bodies, if..softly percussed, give no Sound BACON.

Percussion (pəɹkɒ·ʃən), *sb.* 1544. [– (O)Fr. *percussion* or L. *percussio*, f. as prec.; see -ION.] **1.** The striking of one body with or against another with some degree of force; impact; a stroke, knock. Usu. in reference to solid bodies. **b.** *transf.* and *fig.* 1607. **2.** *spec.* **a.** The striking of a fulminating powder, or *p. cap*, so as to produce a spark and explode the charge in a fire-arm 1810. **b.** *Med.* The action of striking or tapping with the finger, or with a small hammer, upon a part of the body, either to ascertain the condition of some organ by the sound produced, or for therapeutic purposes. 1834. **c.** *Instrument of p.*: a musical instrument played by percussion 1776. **d.** Instruments of percussion, collectively.

1. *Centre of p.* see CENTRE *sb.* **b.** With..The Thunder-like p. of thy sounds Thou mad'st thine enemies shake SHAKS.

attrib. and *Comb.*, as *p. bullet, fuse, gun, match*, etc. (made so as to be ignited or exploded by p.); *p. massage*, etc.; **p. cap**, a small copper cap or cylinder containing fulminating powder, exploded by the p. of a hammer so as to fire the charge of a fire-arm; **-drill**, a drill worked by p.; **-lock**, a form of lock for a fire-arm in which a charge is fired by a *p. cap*; **p.-powder**, the powder used in p. caps, consisting, since *c* 1823, of mercury fulminate; **-sieve**, an apparatus for sorting ores according to size by means of two inclined sieves agitated by levers; **-table**, an apparatus for sorting ores according to weight, consisting of a slightly inclined table which is shaken by a mechanical appliance. Hence **Percu·ssion** *v.* to fit (a fire-arm) for being fired by p.; to treat with p. massage.

Percussive (pəɹkɒ·siv), *a.* 1793. [f. PERCUSSION (or as prec.) + -IVE.] Having the property of striking; of, pertaining to, or connected with percussion.

Percutient (pəɹkiū·ʃiĕnt), *a.* and *sb.* ? *Obs.* 1626. [– *percutient-*, pr. ppl. stem of L. *percutere*; see PERCUSS, -ENT.] **A.** *adj.* Striking, percussive. **B.** *sb.* Something that strikes; a striking agent or body.

Perdie, var. of PARDIE.

†**Pe·rdifoil, pe·rdifol.** *rare.* 1657. [Anglicized from mod.L. *perdifolius*, f. *perdere* lose + *folium* leaf.] A plant which annually loses its leaves –1803.

Perdition (pəɹdi·ʃən). ME. [– OFr. *perdiciun* (mod. *-tion*) or eccl. L. *perditio*, f. *perdit-*, pa. ppl. stem of L. *perdere* destroy; see -ION.] **1.** Utter destruction, complete ruin. Now *rare.* †**b.** Loss, diminution (*rhet.*) SHAKS. **c.** That wherein ruin lies. *Obs.* or *arch.* 1625. **2.** *Theol.* The condition of final damnation; the fate of those in hell, eternal death. late ME. **b.** In imprecations 1604. †**c.** The place of destruction –1627.

1. A Man may be cheaply vitious, to the p. of himself SIR T. BROWNE. **b.** *Ham.* V. ii. 117. **2.** Children of p. and inheritors of hell fire 1563. **b.** *Oth.* III. iii. 90. **c.** Down To bottomless p. MILT. Hence **Perdi·tionable** *a.* deserving p.

‖**Perdix** (pə̄·ɹdiks). 1609. The L. word for 'partridge', retained in the Douay Bible and used in Ornithology as a generic name.

Perdu, perdue (pə̄ɹdiu, pəɹdiū·, ‖pęrdü), *a.* and *sb.* 1591. [– (O)Fr. *perdu* lost; app. orig. introduced in the Fr. mil. phrase *sentinelle perdue*, and so spelt *perdue*; now usu. treated as alien, and written *perdu* or *perdue* according to gender.] **A.** *adj.* (or *pa. pple.*) †**1.** In *sentinel perdue*: **a.** The post of a sentinel in a very dangerous position. **b.** A sentinel posted in such a position. –1688. **2.** †**a.** Placed in an extremely hazardous position; hence, in a desperate case, lost –1656. **b.** Lying hidden; disguised. Now chiefly as Fr. 1734. **3.** In phrase *to lie perdu.* **a.** *Mil.* Placed as an outpost, scout, etc., in a hazardous position; (lying) in ambush, in wait. Often *transf.* or *fig.* 1607. **b.** Hidden; out of sight 1701.

2. b. A Huguenot perdue in the Louvre 1837. **3. a.** It is unfitting he should lie Perdue, who is to walk the round FULLER. **b.** [It] had lain perdu in my head all that time 1893.

†**B.** *sb.* [Partly short for *sentinel perdue* or Fr. *enfants perdus*, partly ellipt. uses of A. 3.] **1.** A soldier placed in a position of special danger, or ordered on a forlorn hope –1706. **b.** *collect.* The watch, guard –1654. **c.** *pl.* = FORLORN HOPE [Fr. *enfants perdus*] –1656. **d.** *transf.* One who acts as a watcher, scout, or spy –1734. **2.** A desperado; a roué. CHAPMAN.

1. Shepheards lying constant Perdues in defence of their flocks FULLER.

Perduellion (pə̄ɹdiuˌe·liŏn). 1533. [– L. *perduellio, -ion-*, f. *perduellis* public enemy, f. *per* through + *duellis* warrior.] *Rom.* and *Sc. Law.* Hostility against the state or government; treason.

Perdurable (pəɹdiūᵊ·răb'l, pə̄·ɹdiŭrăb'l), *a.* ME. [– OFr. *per-, pardurable* – late L. *perdurabilis* (Boethius), f. L. *perdurare*; see PERDURE, -ABLE.] Enduring continuously, lasting, permanent. **b.** *esp.* (in theol. lang.) Everlasting, eternal. late ME. **c.** Of material things: Imperishable; lasting indefinitely. late ME.

Leaving a name p. on earth SOUTHEY. Hence **Perdurabi·lity, Perdurableness,** the quality of being p. **Perdurably** *adv.*

Perdure (pəɹdiūᵊ·ɹ), *v.* Now *rare.* 1450. [– OFr. *per-, pardurer* – L. *perdurare*, f. *per* PER-[1] 2 + *durare* harden, endure, f. *durus* hard.] *intr.* To continue, endure, last on. So **Perdu·rance**, permanence, duration. **Perdura·tion** (*arch.*), continuous duration.

Peregrinate (pe·rĕgrineit), *v.* 1593. [– *peregrinat-*, pa. ppl. stem of L. *peregrinari* sojourn or travel abroad, f. *peregrinus* foreign; see PEREGRINE, -ATE[3].] *intr.* To travel, journey. **b.** To sojourn in a foreign country 1755. **c.** *trans.* To travel along or across 1835. So **Pe·regrinator** (now only *affected*) one who peregrinates; a traveller; a pilgrim.

Pe·regrinate, *a. rare.* 1588. [f. L. *peregrinatus*, pa. pple. of *peregrinari*; see prec., -ATE[2].] Foreign-fashioned; having the air of one who has travelled abroad.

Peregrination (pe:rĕgrinēi·ʃən). 1523. [– (O)Fr. *pérégrination* or L. *peregrinatio*, f. *peregrinat-*; see PEREGRINATE *v.*, -ION.] **1.** The action of travelling in foreign lands, or from land to land; hence, from place to place 1548. **b.** With *a* and *pl.* A course of travel; a journey, esp. on foot; in *pl.* = travels 1548. **c.** *fig.* A systematic going through a subject, course of study, etc. **d.** The 'journey' of life. 1615. †**2.** A sojourning in a foreign land –1697. †**b.** *fig.* Man's life on earth viewed as a 'sojourn in the flesh' –1733.

1. b. My peregrinations about this great metropolis 1820. **2. b.** In the eighty third year of his p. 1702.

Peregrine (pe·rĕgrin), *a.* and *sb.* late ME. [– L. *peregrinus* coming from foreign parts, foreign, f. *pereger* that is abroad or on a journey, *peregre* adv. abroad, f. *per* through + *ager* field; see -INE[1].] **A.** *adj.* **1.** Foreign; outlandish, strange; imported from abroad; also, †foreign to the matter in hand 1530. **2.** *Astrol.* Of a planet: Situated in a part of the zodiac where it has none of its essential dignities 1588. †**3.** Upon a pilgrimage; travelling abroad –1768. **4. P. falcon:** a typical species of falcon (*Falco peregrinus*), formerly esteemed for hawking. (So named because caught on their passage or 'pilgrimage' from their breeding-place; cf. *passage-hawk.*) late ME.

1. *P. tone* (med.L. *tonus peregrinus*), name of one of the Gregorian 'tones' or chants. **4.** A Faucon peregryn thanne semed she Of fremde Land CHAUCER.

B. *sb.* **1.** A sojourner in a foreign land; now only in *Rom. Antiq.* An alien denizen in ancient Rome 1593. †**2.** A pilgrim; a traveller in a foreign land –1654. **3.** = *P. falcon* 1555.

Peregrinity (perĕgri·nĭti). 1591. [– L. *peregrinitas*, f. *peregrinus* foreigner; see prec., -ITY. Cf. Fr. *pérégrinité* (XVI).] The condition of being a foreigner or alien; †the quality of being foreign; outlandishness. **b.** A journeying abroad CARLYLE.

Peremptory (pe·rĕmptəri), *a.* (*adv.*, *sb.*) 1513. [– AFr. *peremptorie* = (O)Fr. *péremptoire* – L. *peremptorius* deadly, mortal, decisive, f. *perempt-*, pa. ppl. stem of *perimere* take away entirely, destroy, f. *per* PER-[1] 3 + *emere* buy, orig. take; see -ORY[2].] **A.** *adj.* **1.** In Rom. Law, used in the sense 'that puts an end to, or precludes all debate, question, or delay', hence 'decisive, final'; hence, in Eng. Law in same sense (see quots.) 1530. **b.** †(*a*) Of a conclusion, statement, etc.: Incontrovertible; conclusive, final (now merged in 4) –1718. (*b*) Of a command, etc.: Admitting no refusal; imperative 1576. **2.** *Law.* Said of a day or time decreed for the performance of some act. ? *Obs.* 1513. **b.** Hence, Positively fixed; absolutely requisite, essential 1596. †**c.** *colloq.* 'Absolute', utter B. JONS. †**3.** Resolute; resolved, determined (*to do* something, or *that*, etc.); also, obstinate, self-willed –1759. **4.** Of persons, their actions, etc.: Positive in opinion or action; *esp.* in bad sense, intolerant of debate or contradiction; over-confident, dogmatic 1586. **5.** Intolerant of refusal or opposition; imperious, dictatorial. (Now the most usual sense.) 1591. †**6.** Deadly, destructive –1614.

1. *P. challenge* or *exception* (*Law*), an objection without showing any cause allowed to a prisoner, against a certain number of jurymen. *P. mandamus*, a mandamus in which the command is absolute. *P. writ*, an original writ directing the sheriff to enforce the defendant's appearance in court without option; so *p. citation*, etc. **b.** The orders of the Senate were p. 1878. **2. b.** It is a p. point of virtue that a man's independence be secured EMERSON. **4.** His humour is lofty, his discourse peremptorie SHAKS. **5.** The p. tone in which he sent forth his sublime commands GOLDSM.

†**B.** as *adv.* **a.** *colloq.* Absolutely, entirely. **b.** By a peremptory order; without fail. –1709.

†**C.** *ellipt.* as *sb.* Short for *p. challenge, writ*, etc. –1753. Hence **Pe·remptori-ly** *adv.*, **-ness.**

Perennial (pĕre·niăl), *a.* and *sb.* 1672. [f. L. *perennis* lasting through the year or years (f. *per* through + *annus* year) + -AL[1].] **A.** *adj.* **1.** Lasting or continuing throughout the year; said esp. of a spring or stream which flows through all seasons of the year 1703. **2.** Lasting through a long, indefinite, or infinite time; enduring, never-failing; everlasting, eternal 1750. **b.** Of plants, their roots, etc.: Remaining alive through a number of years; opp. to *annual* and *biennial* 1672.

2. A constant and p. softness of manner JOHNSON. **b.** P. herbs and shrubs 1880.

B. *sb.* **1.** A perennial plant; see A. 2 b. 1763. **2.** Something that lasts through a succession of years. (With conscious allusion to sense 1.) 1771. Hence **Pere·nnially** *adv.*

Perennibranch (pĕre·nibræŋk), *a.* and *sb.* 1835. [f. mod.L. *Perennibranchia* n. pl., f. *perennis* PERENNIAL + BRANCHIA.] **A.** *adj.* Having permanent gills; belonging to the division *Perennibranchia* (or *Perennibranchiata*) of Amphibians. **B.** *sb.* An amphibian of this division. Also **Perennibra·nchiate** *a.* and *sb.*

Perennity (pĕre·nĭti). 1597. [– L. *peren-*

nitas, f. *perennis* PERENNIAL; see -ITY.] The quality of being perennial; perpetuity.

†**Pererra·tion.** 1608. [f. *pererrat-*, pa. ppl. stem of L. *pererrare*; see -ION, -ATION.] A wandering or travelling about –1658.

Perfay (pəɹfēⁱ·), *int. arch.* ME. [– OFr. *per* or *par fei*; see PAR *prep.* 1, FAY *sb.*¹] By (my) faith; verily, truly.

Perfect (pɔ̄·ɹfėkt), *a.* (*adv.*, *sb.*) [ME. *parfit(e* – OFr. *parfit(e* – L. *perfectus*, pa. pple. of *perficere* accomplish, f. *per* PER-¹ 2 + *facere* make. Later forms infl. by OFr. *parfet*, *-fait*, and finally assim. to L. *perfectus*.] **A.** *adj.* **I.** *gen.* †**1.** Thoroughly made, formed, done, performed, carried out, accomplished; of full age –1773. **2.** Fully accomplished, versed, trained, conversant. Const. *in*, *with*, †*of*, *arch.* ME. †**b.** Made ready –1568. **c.** Thoroughly learned or acquired. Also of a person: Having learnt one's lesson, etc. thoroughly. 1581. **3.** Complete; not deficient in any particular ME. †**b.** Sound; of sound mind, sane –1619. **4.** Free from any imperfection; faultless. But often used of a near approach to such a state, and hence capable of comparison. ME. **b.** *spec.* Of supreme moral excellence ME. **5.** Completely corresponding to a definition, pattern, or description. late ME. **b.** Of a copy, representation, etc.: Exact, correct 1540. **c.** Entire, unqualified; pure, unalloyed 1590. **d.** Sheer; unmitigated, utter. Chiefly *colloq.* 1611. †**6.** Completely assured, certain; of a statement or speaker (*rare*). †**7.** Satisfied, contented SHAKS.

1. Sonnes at p. age SHAKS. **2.** The Hawke that is most p. for the flight GREENE. **c.** Mrs. Grimley.. undertook to prompt, as the performers were not all very p. 1844. **3.** Perfecte God, and perfecte man *Athan. Creed* 1548. A man of..p. sincerity 1841. **b.** *Lear* IV. vii. 63. **4.** Good and perfit English 1590. **b.** Marke the p. man, and behold the vpright *Ps.* 37:37. Guide me in thy p. way WESLEY. **5.** The p. octahedron 1823. **b.** A more p. copy procured at Aleppo PALEY. **c.** You talk.. like a p. stranger 1699. **d.** A man whose chin terminated in a point..would be a p. horror 1804. **6.** *Cymb.* III. i. 73. **7.** *Macb.* III. iv. 21.

II. *techn.* **1.** *Arith.* Applied to a number which is equal to the sum of its aliquot parts. late ME. **2.** *Gram.* Applied to the tense which denotes a completed event or action viewed in relation to the present; hence (with qualification) to any tense expressing action completed at the time indicated 1530. **3.** *Mus.* (Opp. to IMPERFECT *a.* II. 3.) 1597. **4.** *Physiol.*, *Anat.*, etc. Having its proper characteristics developed to the fullest degree; typical 1693. **5.** *Bot.* Having all four whorls of the flower (calyx, corolla, stamens, and pistils) 1706. **6.** *Entom.* In the most completely developed form or phase, as *p. insect*, *state*, etc. 1834. **7.** *Physics.* Conceived as existing in a state of ideal perfection, as *p. elasticity*, *gas*. 1849.

1. The partes of 6 are 1, 2, 3..wherefore 6 is a p. number 1570. **3.** *P. concords* or *consonances*, a name including the concords of a unison, fifth, and octave, and sometimes a fourth. Hence, applied to the intervals of a fourth, fifth, and octave, in their normal form (opp. to *augmented* and *diminished*). So *p. chord* or *triad*, a name for the common chord in its direct position (involving a perfect fifth). *P. cadence*: a cadence consisting of the direct chord of the tonic preceded by a dominant or subdominant chord (authentic or plagal cadence), and forming a full close.

B. as *adv.* = Perfectly. Obs. exc. *dial.* or *poet.* 1470. **C.** quasi-*sb.* **1.** That which is perfect, perfection (*rare*). *poet.* 1842. **2.** *Gram.* ellipt. for *p. tense*; see A. II. 2. 1841. Hence **Pe·rfect-ly** *adv.*, **-ness.**

Perfect (pɔ̄·ɹfėkt, pəɹfe·kt), *v.* late ME. [f. PERFECT *a.*] **1.** *trans.* To complete; to carry through, accomplish 1494. **b.** *Printing.* To complete the printing of a sheet by printing the second side 1824. †**2.** To bring to full development –1607. **3.** To make perfect or faultless; *loosely*, To bring nearer to perfection; to improve 1449. **4.** To make (a person) perfect *in* some art, etc.; †to inform completely 1603.

1. Labour perfected, with the evening ends QUARLES. Then urg'd, she perfects her illustrious toils POPE. **3.** George especially perfected his accent so as to be able to pass for a Frenchman THACKERAY. **4.** *Meas. for M.* IV. iii. 146. Hence **Perfecter,** one who perfects, completes, or finishes.

Perfectibility (pəɹfektibi·lĭti). 1794. [f. next; see -ILITY.] **1.** Capability of being perfected or becoming perfect; *spec.* the capacity of man to progress indefinitely towards perfection, the doctrine of this capacity. **2.** *loosely.* A state of perfection (*rare*) 1809. Hence **Perfe·ctibilita·rian,** an upholder of human p.

Perfectible (pəɹfe·ktĭb'l, pɔ̄·ɹfėktĭb'l). 1635. [– med.L. *perfectibilis*, f. L. *perfectus*; see PERFECT *a.*, -IBLE. In later use referred to PERFECT *v.*] Capable of being perfected or brought to perfection. So **Perfectibi·lian, Perfecti·bilist,** one who holds the doctrine of **Perfecti·bilism,** the theory of the perfectibility of man.

Perfecting (pɔ̄·ɹfėktiŋ, pəɹfe·ktiŋ), *vbl. sb.* 1494. [f. PERFECT *v.* + -ING¹.] The action of PERFECT *v.*

attrib. **P. machine** or (U.S.) **press,** a printing machine on which the sheet, as it passes through, is printed first on one side and then on the other before leaving the machine.

Perfection (pəɹfe·kʃən), *sb.* ME. [– (O)Fr. *perfection* – L. *perfectio*, f. as prec.; see -ION.] **1.** The action, process, or fact of making perfect; completing, accomplishing. late ME. †**2.** Completed state, completeness –1679. **b.** The full growth or development of anything 1500. †**c.** *Mus.* The condition of being 'perfect' (see PERFECT *a.* II. 3) –1880. **3.** Flawlessness, faultlessness. Also often, Comparative excellence. ME. **b.** *concr.* A perfect person, place, etc. 1594. **4.** The condition of being morally perfect; holiness; †in ME. *spec.* Monastic discipline ME. **5.** The most perfect degree, the highest pitch (*of* a quality, faculty, etc.); the extreme or height (*of* anything good or evil) ME. **6.** (With *a* and *pl.*) A quality, feature, accomplishment, etc. of a high order or great excellence 1572.

1. To study your own p. LAW. **2. b.** They..bring no fruite to p. *Luke* 8:14. **3.** In different glaciers, ..these veins display various degrees of p. TYNDALL. **b.** Is this the citie that men call the p. of beauty? *Lam.* 2:15. **4.** A p. like Buddha's 1882. *Counsel of p.*, see COUNSEL *sb.* 2. **5.** The p. of goodness 1729. **6.** [He] hathe many perfections in him 1572.

Phr. *To p.*, completely, perfectly. Hence **Perfe·ction** *v. trans.* (*rare*) to perfect. **Perfe·ctional** *a.* of, pertaining to, or of the nature of p. So **Perfe·ctionate** *v. trans.* (now *rare*) To make perfect or complete; **Perfectiona·tion,** the action or fact of being made perfect. **Perfe·ctionize** *v. trans.* (*rare*) to bring to p. **Perfe·ctionment,** the action of perfecting.

Perfectionism (pəɹfe·kʃəniz'm). 1846. [f. after next; see -ISM.] A system or doctrine of perfection; *esp.* the theory of the moral perfectibility of man.

Perfectionist (pəɹfe·kʃənist). 1657. [f. PERFECTION *sb.* + -IST.] One who holds any theory or follows any practice for the attainment of religious, moral, social, or political perfection; *esp.* one who holds that religious or moral perfection may be attained; *spec.* (with cap.) a member of the communistic community of Oneida Creek, N.Y. Also *attrib.*

Perfectist (pɔ̄·ɹfėktist). *Obs.* exc. *Hist.* 1618. [f. PERFECT *a.* + -IST.] = PERFECTIONIST.

Perfective (pəɹfe·ktiv), *a.* 1596. [– med.L. *perfectivus*, f. *perfect-*; see PERFECT *v.*, -IVE.] **1.** Tending to make perfect or complete; usu. with *of*. Now *rare*. **2.** In process of being perfected. *rare.* 1848. **3.** *Gram.* Expressing completion of action; opp. to IMPERFECTIVE 1844.

1. That which is..perfectiue of his kind 1620. **2.** Dugès was..able to see..the eight legs in a p. state 1848. Hence **Perfe·ctively** *adv.* in a way tending to completeness.

Perfervid (pəɹfɔ̄·ɹvid), *a.* 1856. [– mod. L. *perfervidus*, f. PER-¹ 4 + *fervidus* FERVID; chiefly in the phr. *perfervidum ingenium Scotorum*, founded on Buchanan's *Scotorum præfervida ingenia*.] Very fervid, glowing, or ardent.

Perficient (pəɹfi·ʃĕnt), *a.* (*sb.*) *rare.* 1641. [– *perficient-*, pr. ppl. stem of L. *perficere* complete; see -ENT.] **A.** *adj.* That accomplishes something; effectual, actual 1659. †**B.** *sb.* One who perfects or completes –1662.

Perfidious (pəɹfi·diəs), *a.* 1598. [– L. *perfidiosus*, f. *perfidia* PERFIDY; see -OUS.] Characterized by perfidy; guilty of breaking faith or violating confidence; treacherous.

P. dealing 1759. The victim of a p. woman LYTTON. Hence **Perfi·dious-ly** *adv.*, **-ness.**

Perfidy (pɔ̄·ɹfidi). 1592. [– L. *perfidia*, f. *perfidus* treacherous, f. *per* PER-¹ 3 + *fides* FAITH; see -Y³.] The deceitful violation of faith or promise; base breach of faith or betrayal of trust; often, the profession of friendship in order to betray.

Many other things he reporteth of the p. of the French nation 1607. The name of Judas has become a byword of covetousness and p. 1885.

†**Perfla·ble,** *a.* late ME. [– L. *perflabilis*, f. *perflare* PERFLATE; see -ABLE.] That may be blown through; allowing of ventilation –1620.

Perflate (pəɹflēⁱ·t), *v.* Now *rare.* 1540. [– *perflat-*, pa. ppl. stem of L. *perflare*, f. *per* PER-¹ 1 + *flare* blow; see -ATE³.] *trans.* To blow through, ventilate. So †**Perfla·tile** *a.* exposed to wind; airy. **Perfla·tion,** free passage of wind or air; ventilation.

Perfluent (pɔ̄·ɹfluĕnt), *a.* 1673. [– *perfluent-*, pr. ppl. stem of L. *perfluere*, f. *per* PER-¹ 1 + *fluere* flow; see -ENT.] Flowing through.

P. battery, a kind of galvanic battery actuated by a liquid flowing through.

Perfoliate (pəɹfōᵘ·liĕt), *a.* 1687. [– mod.L. *perfoliatus* (see *per* PER-¹ 1, FOLIATE *a.*), used in XVI in *perfoliata* THOROUGHWAX.] **1.** *Bot.* Having the stalk apparently passing through the leaf, the edges of the basal lobes uniting round the stem. Said orig. of a plant and its stalk; later *transf.* of the leaf. **2.** *Entom.* Of antennæ: Having the joints dilated or expanded laterally all round. Also **Perfo·liated.** 1752. Hence **Perfolia·tion.**

Perforate (pɔ̄·ɹfŏrĕt), *ppl. a.* 1540. [– L. *perforatus*, pa. pple. of *perforare*; see next, -ATE².] = PERFORATED.

Perforate (pɔ̄·ɹfŏreⁱt), *v.* 1538. [– *perforat-*, pa. ppl. stem of L. *perforare*, f. *per* PER-¹ 1 + *forare* bore, pierce; see -ATE³.] **1.** *trans.* To make a hole or holes right through; to pierce with a pointed instrument or projectile; *spec.* to make rows of small holes separating coupons, stamps, etc., in a sheet. **b.** To bore into (a thing) 1712. **c.** To 'pass through' in position; to extend or be continued through 1820. **2.** To form (a hole, etc.) by boring 1876. **3.** To make or suffer perforation 1775.

Perforated (pɔ̄·ɹfŏreⁱtėd), *ppl. a.* 1486. [f. prec. + -ED¹.] **1.** Pierced with one or more holes. **b.** *Nat. Hist.* Cribrose 1678. **2.** Made or outlined by perforations (*rare*) 1790.

2. P. Initials on Stamps 1891.

Perforation (pɔ̄ɹfŏrēⁱ·ʃən). ME. [– (O)Fr. *perforation* – med.L. *perforatio*, f. as PERFORATE *v.*; see -ION.] **1.** The action of perforating, boring through, or piercing; the fact or condition of being perforated 1440. **b.** *Surg.* The formation, through accident or disease, of a hole through the thickness of any structure, as through the wall of the intestine, etc. 1666. **2.** A hole made by boring, punching, or piercing; an aperture passing through or into anything 1543. **3.** The natural orifice of an organ or part of the body –1797.

2. [Stamps] with pin-pricked perforations 1870.

Perforative (pɔ̄·ɹfŏretiv), *a.* 1597. [– Fr. *perforatif*, *-ive* or med.L. *perforativus*, f. as prec.; see -IVE.] Having the character of perforating; tending to perforate.

Perforator (pɔ̄·ɹfŏreⁱtəɹ). 1739. [f. PERFORATE *v.* + -OR 2.] One who or that which perforates; *esp.* (*Surg.*) an instrument for penetrating the fœtal skull.

Perforce (pəɹfōᵊ·ɹs), *adv.*, *sb.* ME. [– OFr. phr. *par force* by force, with assim. to PER-² as in PERCASE, PERCHANCE.] **A.** *adv.* †**a.** By violence; forcibly –1670. **b.** By moral constraint; compulsorily, of necessity 1542. **c.** quasi-*adj.* 1580.

Patience p., see PATIENCE *sb.* 1. *P. of*, prop. 'per force of', by force of, by dint of.

B. quasi-*sb.* In phrases *by p.*, by compulsion; *of p.*, of necessity 1525.

†**Perfo·rce,** *v.* 1509. [– OFr. *parforcier*, *-forcer*, f. *par* through (see PAR *prep.*) +

forcer to FORCE.] *trans.* To force, constrain –1610.

Perform (pəɹfǭ·ɹm), *v.* ME. [– AFr. *par-*, *perfourmer* (in AL. *performare*), alt. (after *forme* FORM) of OFr. *parfournir* (in med.L. *perfurnire*), f. *par* PER-¹ 2, 4 + *fournir* FURNISH.] †**1.** *trans.* To carry through to completion (an action, process, work, etc.) –1620. †**b.** To complete by adding what is wanting. Also with *up*. –1537. †**2.** To make, construct (a material object); to execute (a piece of work, literary or artistic) –1774. †**3.** To bring about, produce (a result) –1715. **4.** To carry out in action, execute (a command, promise, undertaking, etc.) ME. **5.** To carry out, achieve (any undertaking); to go through and finish, do, make ME. †**b.** *loosely.* To grant, pay, etc. that which is promised –1661. **c.** *absol.* or *intr.* To discharge one's function, do one's part; to do, act (well, ill, etc.). late ME. **6.** *spec.* To do, go through, execute (a duty, public function; a piece of music, play, etc.) 1613. **b.** To play (a part or character) 1610. **c.** *absol.* or *intr.* To act in a play; to play or sing 1836.

2. A garland..of Mosaic, or inlaid work, and not ill performed 1774. **3.** *Temp.* I. ii. 194. **4.** Yᵗ I maye daylie perfourme my vowes COVERDALE *Ps.* 60[1]:8. **5.** Murthers haue bene perform'd Too terrible for the eare SHAKS. **b.** Performing Life to those to whom he promised it FULLER. **c.** *Cor.* I. i. 271. **6.** The Opera..was performed with great Applause STEELE. **b.** In Acting, barely to p. the Part is not commendable STEELE. **c.** He.. performed skilfully on the flute MACAULAY. Hence **Perfo·rmable** *a.* that may be performed or done. **Perfo·rmer,** one who (or that which) performs. **Perfo·rming** *ppl. a.* that performs; applied *spec.* to animals trained to execute feats or tricks at a public entertainment.

Performance (pəɹfǭ·ɹmăns). 1494. [f. prec. + -ANCE; perh. formed in AFr.] **1.** The carrying out of a command, duty, etc. (Often antithetical to *promise.*) 1531. **2.** The accomplishment, carrying out, doing of any action or work; working, action 1494. **b.** An action, act, deed. Often emphatic: A notable deed. 1599. **c.** A piece of work; a composition. Now *rare.* 1665. **3.** *spec.* The action of performing a ceremony, play, part, piece of music, etc. 1611. **b.** A public exhibition or entertainment 1709.

1. Promises are not binding, where the p. is unlawful PALEY. **2.** The p. of some experiment 1879. **b.** Besides her walking, and other actuall performances, what..haue you heard her say? SHAKS. **c.** His performances in prose are bad enough 1875.

†**Pe·rfricate,** *v.* 1597. [– *perfricat-*, pa. ppl. stem of L. *perfricare* rub all over, f. *per* PER-¹ 2 + *fricare* rub; see -ATE³.] *trans.* To rub thoroughly or all over –1755. Hence **Perfrica·tion** 1607.

Perfume (pǭ·ɹfiūm, pəɹfiū·m), *sb.* 1533. [In early use also *par-*, but regularly assim. to PER-¹. – Fr. *parfum*, f. *par-*, †*perfumer*; see next.] **1. a.** *orig.* The odorous fumes given off by the burning of any substance, e.g. of incense. **b.** Hence, The volatile particles, scent, or odour emitted by any sweet-smelling substance; fragrance. **c.** *fig.* Fragrance, savour; repute 1586. **2.** A substance, natural or prepared, which emits an agreeable odour; scent 1542.

1. b. Three April perfumes in three hot Junes burn'd SHAKS. **2.** Cinamome,..Spekenarde, Cassia, sweete perfumes EDEN.

Perfume (pəɹfiū·m), *v.* 1538. [– Fr. *parfumer*, †*perfumer* – It. †*parfumare*, †*per-* (now *pro-*), lit. smoke through (*fumare*); see PER-¹ 1, FUME *v.*] **1.** *trans.* To fill or impregnate with the smoke or vapour of some burning substance; esp. of incense or the like. **2.** To impart a sweet scent to. (Now the ordinary sense.) Also *fig.* 1539.

1. They p. their temples with frankensence EDEN. Hence **Perfu·mer,** one who perfumes; one engaged in making or selling perfumes 1573.

Perfumery (pəɹfiū·məri). 1788. [f. PERFUMER; see -ERY.] **a.** The preparation of perfumes; the business of a perfumer. **b.** Perfumes as a class of substances. **c.** A perfumer's place of business.

Perfunctory (pəɹfʊ·ŋktəri), *a.* 1581. [– late L. *perfunctorius* careless, negligent, f. *perfunct-*, pa. ppl. stem of *perfungi* perform, discharge, get rid of, f. *per* PER-¹ + *fungi*; see FUNCTION, -ORY².] **1.** Of a thing: Done merely for the sake of getting rid of the duty; done as a piece of routine or for form's sake only, and so without interest; formal, mechanical; superficial, trivial. **b.** Of a person: Acting merely by way of duty; official; formal; lacking interest or zeal 1600. †**2.** Stated in formal terms CLARENDON.

1. [He] glanced at the two documents in a p. manner 1885. **b.** The presumptuous rashnesse of a p. licencer MILT. Hence **Perfu·nctorily** *adv.* **Perfu·nctoriness.** So †**Perfuncto·rious** *a.*, †**-ly** *adv.*

Perfuse (pəɹfiū·z), *v.* 1526. [– *perfus-*, pa. ppl. stem of L. *perfundere*, f. *per* PER-¹ 1 + *fundere* pour out.] **1.** *trans.* To overspread with any moisture; to besprinkle (*with* water, etc.); to cover or suffuse (*with* radiance, colour, grace, etc.) **2.** To pour (something) through; to diffuse through or over. Also *fig.* 1666. So **Perfu·sive** *a.* having the character of being shed all over, or diffused all through.

Perfusion (pəɹfiū·ʒən). 1574. [– L. *perfusio*, f. as prec.; see -ION; the spec. (eccl.) sense in Lactantius.] The action of perfusing; *spec.* the pouring over of water in baptism, as opp. to immersion.

Pergameneous (pəɹgămī·niəs), *a.* 1826. [f. L. *pergamena* PARCHMENT + -EOUS.] Of the nature or texture of parchment. So **Pergamenta·ceous** *a.*

‖**Pergola** (pǭ·ɹgŏlă). 1654. [– It. *pergola* :– L. *pergula* projecting roof, vine arbour, f. *pergere* come or go forward.] **1.** An arbour or covered walk formed of growing plants trained over trellis-work 1675. †**2.** An elevated balcony –1656.

‖**Pergunnah, pergana** (pəɹgʊ·nă). 1765. [– Urdu *pargana* district.] A division of territory in India, comprising a group of villages.

Perhaps (pəɹhæ·ps), *adv.* (*sb.*) Also (*colloq.*) **p'raps.** 1528. [f. PER *prep.* II. 1 + pl. of HAP *sb.*¹, repl. ME. phr. *by hap(s* by a single word modelled on PERCASE, PERCHANCE.] **1.** A word qualifying a statement so as to express possibility with uncertainty; = PERCHANCE 3. **2.** = PERCHANCE 2. 1576. **B.** *sb.* **a.** A statement qualified by 'perhaps'. **b.** A mere possibility. 1534.

A. 1. P. I may give farther answer to this query JOHNSON. There are three, or p. four, courses open to us 1883. **2.** Pray God, if p. the thought of thine heart may be forgiven thee *Acts* 8:22.

Peri (pīᵊ·ri). 1777. [– Pers. *pări.*] In Persian mythology, one of a race of superhuman beings, orig. represented as of malevolent character, but subsequently as good genii, endowed with grace and beauty. Hence *transf.* 'a fair one'.

Peri-, *prefix*, repr. Gr. περί prep. and adv., 'round, around, round about, about'.

In numerous scientific terms, chiefly anatomical and pathological, in which *peri-* has a prepositional relation to the implied sb. **a.** In adjs. = situated or occurring about or around, surrounding or enclosing (the part, organ, etc. denoted by the second element); occas. also = pertaining to the part, or thing, denoted by a corresponding sb.; as in: **Peribra·nchial,** around the branchiæ or gills. **Peribro·nchial,** around the bronchial tubes. **Perice·llular,** around a cell or cells. **Pericho·rdal** (-kǭ·ɹdăl), around the notochord or spinal chord. **Perio·tic** [Gr. ὠτικός of the ear], *Anat.* surrounding the ear; applied to those bones of the skull which constitute a protective case for the internal ear; also as *sb.* **Pe:ristoma·tic,** *Bot.* surrounding a stoma of a leaf.

b. In sbs. (mostly in L. form) denoting a part, organ, etc., surrounding or enclosing that denoted by the second element; as PERIANTH, etc.; **Pe·riblem** [Gr. περίβλημα anything thrown round], *Bot.* the embryonic cells of the growing-point of phanerogams from which the primary cortex is developed. ‖**Perica·mbium** = *pericycle.* ‖**Perichæ·tium** [Gr. χαίτη long hair], *Bot.* a whorl or cluster of modified leaves at the base of a group of reproductive organs, or of the fructification, in mosses and some liverworts. ‖**Pericho·ndrium** [Gr. χόνδρος cartilage], *Anat.* a membrane consisting of fibrous connective tissue, enveloping the cartilages except at the joints. **Pe·richord,** the sheath or investment of the notochord. ‖**Pericli·nium** [Gr. κλίνη couch], *Bot.* the involucre of *Compositæ.* **Pe·ricycle** [Gr. περίκυκλος all round], *Bot.* the outer portion of the vascular cylinder, lying between the vascular bundles internally, and the endodermis or innermost layer of the cortex externally. ‖**Perie·nteron** [Gr. ἔντερον intestine], *Embryol.* and *Zool.* a space between the outer and inner layers of a gastrula, the remnant of the blastocœle persisting after gastrulation. **Pe·rilymph,** *Anat.* the clear fluid contained within the osseous labyrinth of the internal ear, and surrounding the membranous labyrinth. **Pe·rimorph** [Gr. μορφή form], *Min.* a mineral enclosing another. ‖**Perimy·sium** [Gr. μῦς muscle], *Anat.* the sheath of connective tissue enveloping a muscle. ‖**Perine·phrium** [Gr. νεφρός kidney], the connective tissue which envelops the kidneys. ‖**Perio·stracum** [Gr. ὄστρακον shell of a mussel], *Zool.* the outer horny covering of the shell of a mollusc or brachiopod. **Pe·riproct** [Gr. πρωκτός anus], *Zool.* that part of the body-wall of an echinoderm which surrounds the anus. **Pe·risarc** [Gr. σάρξ, σαρκ- flesh], *Zool.* the horny or chitinous case investing the cœnosarc in some Hydrozoa. **Pe·risome** [Gr. σῶμα body], *Zool.* the integument or body-wall of an echinoderm, upon which the external calcareous skeleton is developed. **Pe·risperm** [Gr. σπέρμα seed], *Bot.* the mass of nutritive tissue outside the embryo-sac in some seeds; also, the tissue of the nucellus, which sometimes persists in the ripe seed. **Pe·rispore** [Gr. σπόρος seed], *Bot.* the skin or integument of a spore. **Pe·ritreme** [Gr. τρῆμα hole], *Zool.* (*a*) a small chitinous ring surrounding a breathing-hole in an insect; (*b*) = PERISTOME 2 a.

c. *Path.* In sbs. in -ITIS (-əi·tis), denoting inflammation in the parts around or about that denoted by the second element, or in the part denoted by a corresponding sb. (see b); with corresponding adjs. in *-itic* (-i·tik); as PERICARDITIS, etc. **Pe·riadeni·tis** [Gr. ἀδήν gland], inflammation of the connective tissue round a gland. **Pe:richondri·tis,** of the *perichondrium* (see b). **Pe·rinephri·tis,** of the *perinephrium* (see b). **Pe:riprocti·tis** [Gr. πρωκτός the anus], of the connective tissue about the anus. **Pe:rityphli·tis** [Gr. τυφλόν cæcum], of some part around or adjacent to the cæcum (when seated in the *appendix vermiformis*, now called *appendicitis*).

Perianth (pe·riˌænþ). Formerly in L. form **perianthium.** 1706. [– Fr. *périanthe* (Rousseau 1771–7) – mod.L. *perianthium*, f. Gr. περί about, PERI- + ἄνθος flower, after *pericarpium* PERICARP; see -IUM.] *Bot.* A floral envelope; formerly, a synonym of CALYX; now, the outer part of a flower, which encloses the essential organs (stamens and pistils); either *double*, i.e. the calyx and corolla collectively; or *single*, when there is only one. **b.** In liverworts, a leafy or membranous covering surrounding the archegonium; in mosses, the cluster of leaves surrounding the sexual organs in the 'flower' 1857. Also *attrib.*

Periapt (pe·riˌæpt). Also formerly in Gr. form **periapton,** pl. **-a.** 1584. [– Fr. *périapte* – Gr. περίαπτον, f. περί + ἅπτος fastened, f. ἅπτειν fasten.] Something worn about the person as a charm; an amulet.

Helpe ye charming Spelles and Periapts SHAKS.

Periaster, periastron (periˌæ·stəɹ, -æ·strǫn). Also **periastre.** 1851. [f. Gr. περί PERI- + ἄστρον star, after PERIHELION, etc.] *Astron.* That point in the orbit of a heavenly body revolving round a star at which it is nearest to the star. Also *attrib.* Hence **Peria·stral** *a.* of or pertaining to the p.

Periblast (pe·riblæst). 1857. [f. Gr. περί PERI- + -BLAST.] *Biol.* **a.** = PERIPLAST b. **b.** The outer layer of protoplasm in the egg of a teleostean fish, surrounding the central yolk. Hence **Peribla·stic** *a.* (*a*) in Haeckel's nomenclature, applied to one stage in the development of a meroblastic ovum which germinates by segmentation of the superficial part; (*b*) of or pertaining to the p. (sense b).

‖**Peribolus** (pĕri·bŏlŏs), **-os** (-ǫs). 1706. [– Gr. περίβολος circuit, enclosure; f. περί PERI- + βολ-, from βάλλειν throw.] *Gr. Antiq.* An enclosure or court around a temple; the wall bounding this.

Pericardiac (perikā·ɹdiæk), *a.* 1822. [f. PERICARDIUM, after CARDIAC.] = next.

Pericardial (perikā·ɹdiăl), *a.* 1654. [f. as prec. + -AL¹.] Of, pertaining to, occurring in, or connected with the pericardium. So **Perica·rdian, Perica·rdic** *adjs.* 1656.

‖**Pericarditis** (pe:rikaɹdəi·tis). 1799. [f. as prec. + -ITIS.] *Path.* Inflammation of the pericardium.

‖**Pericardium** (perikā·ɹdiŏm). 1576 (**-ion**), 1615 (**-ium**). [– mod.L. – Gr. περικάρδιον (Galen), f. περί PERI- + καρδία heart; see -IUM.] *Anat.* The membranous sac, consisting of an outer fibrous and an inner serous layer, which encloses the heart.

Pericarp (pe·rikāɹp). 1759. [– Fr. *péri-*

carpe or mod.L. *pericarpium* – Gr. περικάρπιον pod, husk, shell, f. περί PERI- + καρπός fruit; see -IUM.] *Bot.* A seed-vessel; the wall of the ripened ovary or fruit of a flowering plant. Hence †**Perica·rpial, Perica·rpic** *adjs.* of or pertaining to a p.

||**Pericarpium** (perikā·ɹpiŏm). Now *rare.* 1691. [mod.L.; see prec.] = prec.

Pericentral (pe·risentrăl), *a.* 1889. [f. PERI- + CENTRE + -AL[1].] *Bot.* Arranged round a centre or central body.

Pericentre (pe·risentəɹ). 1902. [f. PERI- + CENTRE, after *perihelion.*] That point in the (eccentric) orbit of a body revolving round a centre, at which it is nearest to that centre.

Perichætous (perikī·təs), *a.* 1870. [f. mod. L. *Perichæta* (f. PERI- + Gr. χαίτη long hair, 'bristle') + -OUS.] *Zool.* Surrounded by bristles; having segments so surrounded, as earthworms of the genus *Perichæta.*

||**Perichoresis** (pe:rikorī·sis). 1858. [– Gr. περιχώρησις going round, rotation.] *Theol.* = CIRCUMINCESSION.

Periclase (pe·riklēˡs). 1844. [– mod.L. *periclasia* (Scacchi, 1840), erron. f. Gr. περί exceedingly + κλάσις breaking, fracture: intended to refer to its perfect cleavage. (But Gr. περίκλασις means twisting or wheeling round.)] *Min.* A mineral consisting of magnesia and a little protoxide of iron, found in greenish crystals or grains, at Vesuvius and elsewhere. Also called **Peri·clasite.**

Periclean (periklī·ăn), *a.* 1822. [f. *Pericles* + -AN.] Of or pertaining to Pericles (*c*495–429 B.C.) and his age in Athenian history; the period of the intellectual and material pre-eminence of Athens. Also *transf.*

Periclinal (periklǝi·năl), *a.* 1876. [f. Gr. περικλινής sloping on all sides + -AL[1].] **1.** *Geol.* = QUAQUAVERSAL. **2.** *Bot.* [= G. *periklinel*]. Applied to those cell-walls at a growing-point which run in the same direction as the circumference of the shoot. Also as *sb.* = p. wall or plain. 1882.

†**Peri·clitate,** *v.* 1623. [– *periclitat-,* pa. ppl. stem of L. *periclitari,* f. *periculum, periclum* danger; see -ATE[3].] *trans.* To expose to peril; to endanger, risk –1765.

They would p. their lives 1657. So †**Periclita·tion,** the action of exposing or condition of being exposed to peril; also, an experiment; a venture –1897.

||**Pericope** (pĕri·kŏpi). 1658. [– late L. *pericope* – Gr. περικοπή section, f. περί PERI- + κοπή cutting, f. κόπτειν cut.] A short passage, section, or paragraph in a writing; esp. (*Eccl.*) a portion of Scripture appointed for reading in public worship.

||**Pericranium** (perikrēˡ·niŏm). 1541. [– mod.L. *pericranium* – Gr. περικράνιον, subst. use of n. of περικράνιος round the skull; see PERI-, CRANIUM.] **1.** *Anat.* The membrane enveloping the skull, being the external periosteum of the cranial bones. **2.** *loosely* (usu. *affected* or *joc.*): **a.** The skull; **b.** The brain, esp. as the seat of mind. Now *rare.* 1590. So †**Pe·ricrane** (chiefly in sense 2); †**Pe·ricrany.** Hence **Pericra·nial** *a.* of or pertaining to the p., **-ly** *adv.*

†**Peri·culous,** *a.* 1547. [– L. *periculosus,* f. *periculum* danger; see -OUS.] Perilous –1835.

Periderm (pe·ridəɹm). 1849. [mod. f. Gr. περί PERI- + δέρμα skin.] **1.** *Zool.* A hard or tough covering investing the body in certain Hydrozoa 1870. **2.** *Bot.* orig., applied to the corky layers of plant-stems; later, the whole of the tissues formed from the cork-cambium. Hence **Peride·rmal** *a.*

||**Peridiastole** (pe:ridəi,æ·stŏli). 1842. [f. Gr. περί over, beyond + DIASTOLE.] *Physiol.* The interval between the diastole of the heart and the following systole. Hence **Peridiasto·lic** *a.*

||**Peridium** (pĭri·diŏm). *Pl.* **-ia.** 1823. [– Gr. πηρίδιον, dim. of πήρα wallet.] *Bot.* The outer coat or envelope of certain fungi, which encloses the spores. Hence **Peri·dial** *a.*

Peridot (pe·ridǫt). [Late ME. *peritot* – OFr. *peritot* (mod. *-dot*); of unkn. origin.] †**a.** In ME. The chrysolite –1460. **b.** A jeweller's term for OLIVINE 1706. Hence **Perido·tic** *a.* **Pe·ridotite** *Min.* [-ITE[1] 2 b], a mineral consisting of p. (olivine) and various other minerals.

||**Periegesis** (pe:ri,idʒī·sis). 1627. [– Gr. περιήγησις, f. περί PERI- + ἥγησις leading.] A description of a place or region.

Perigee (pe·ridʒī). 1594. Also in L. forms. [– Fr. *périgée* – mod.L. *perigēum, -æum* – late Gr. περίγειον (Ptolemy), subst. use of n. of περίγειος 'close round the earth', f. περί PERI- + γέη, γαῖα, γῆ earth.] **1.** That point in the orbit of a planet (now usu., the moon) at which it is nearest to the earth. (Opp. to APOGEE 1.) †**2.** The point of the heaven at which the sun has the least altitude at noon; i.e. at the winter solstice. (Opp. to APOGEE 2.) –1646. †**3.** *fig.* (cf. APOGEE 3) –1670. So **Perige·al, Perige·an** *adjs.* of or pertaining to p.

Perigone (pe·rigoᵘn). Also in L. form 1819. [– Fr. *périgone* – mod.L. *perigonium,* f. Gr. περί PERI- + γόνος offspring, seed.] **1.** *Bot.* **a.** = PERIANTH. **b.** The male perianth in mosses (PERIANTH b) 1863. **2.** *Zool.* A sac formed by the outer parts of the gonophore of a hydroid 1871. Hence **Peri·gonal, Perigo·nial** *adjs.* pertaining to a p.

||**Périgord** (perigor). 1752. A district in the south-west of France, famous for its truffles. Hence **P. pie,** a meat pie flavoured with truffles.

||**Perigynium** (peridʒi·niŏm). Rarely **perigyn** (pe·ridʒin). 1821. [mod.L., f. Gr. περί PERI- b + γυνή, in Bot. 'pistil'; see -IUM.] *Bot.* **a.** A membranous sac, investing the ovary in the Sedges (*Carex*). **b.** A part of the leafy investment of the female organs of mosses. **c.** In liverworts: = PERIANTH b.

Perigynous (pĕri·dʒinəs), *a.* 1807. [f. mod.L. *perigynus* (f. as prec.) + -OUS.] *Bot.* Situated around the pistil or ovary; said of the stamens when growing upon a part surrounding the ovary; also of a flower in which the stamens are so placed. So **Peri·gyny,** p. condition.

||**Perihelion** (perihī·liǫn). †Also **-ium.** *Pl.* **-ia.** 1666. [Græcized form of mod.L. *perihelium* (Kepler 1596), f. Gr. περί PERI- + ἥλιος sun.] *Astr.* That point in the orbit of a planet, comet, etc., at which it is nearest to the sun. Opp. to APHELION. **2.** *fig.* Highest point, 'zenith' 1804. Hence **Perihe·lial, Perihe·lian** *adjs.*

Perijove (pe·ridʒōᵘv). 1837. [– Fr. *périjove* (Bailly 1766), in mod.L. *perijovium,* f. PERI- + *Jovem* Jupiter, after *perigee, perihelion.*] *Astr.* That point in the orbit of any of Jupiter's satellites at which it is nearest to Jupiter.

Peril (pe·ril), *sb.* ME. [– (O)Fr. *péril* :– L. *peric(u)lum* experiment, risk, f. **per-* in *experiri* try + *-culum* -CLE.] **1.** Risk, jeopardy, danger. **2.** (with *a* and *pl.*) A case or cause of peril; *pl.* dangers, risks ME. †**3.** A matter of danger. Const. *it is p.,* it is dangerous (to do something). –1540.

1. Glory Is the fair child of p. SMOLLETT. At the p. of his life PALEY. A vessel in p. of wreck GEO. ELIOT. Phr. *At* (†*on, to*) *your* (*his,* etc.) *p.,* you (etc.) taking the risk. *Yellow p.*: see YELLOW *a.* **2.** *P. of the sea* (Marine Insurance), strictly, the natural accidents peculiar to the sea, but in law extended to include capture by pirates, losses by collision, etc.

Peril (pe·ril), *v.* 1567. [f. prec.] **1.** *trans.* To expose to danger; to imperil, risk. †**2.** *intr.* To be in danger (*rare*) –1647.

1. Jonathan perilled his life..for..David 1647.

||**Perilla** (pĕri·lă). 1788. [mod.L. (Linnæus); origin unknown.] *Bot.* A small genus of Labiates; esp. *P. ocimoides,* grown on account of its deep-purple leaves.

Perilous (pe·riləs), *a.* (*adv.*) ME. [– OFr. *perillous, -eus* (mod. *périlleux*) :– L. *periculosus,* f. *periculum*; see PERIL *sb.,* -OUS.] **1.** Fraught with peril; full of risk; dangerous; hazardous. †**2.** = PARLOUS A. 2. –1606. †**B.** *adv.* = PARLOUS B. –1849.

1. In a p. predicament 1836. **2.** A p. clymbyng whan beggers up arise To hye estate LYDG. Hence **Pe·rilous-ly** *adv.,* **-ness.**

Perimeter (pĕri·mĭtəɹ). 1592. [– Fr. *périmètre* or L. *perimetros* – Gr. περίμετρος, f. περί PERI- + μέτρον METER.] **1.** The outer boundary of a closed geometrical figure (curved or rectilineal), or of any area or surface; circumference; also, the length of this. **2.** An instrument for measuring the field of vision, and determining the visual powers of different parts of the retina 1875. Hence **Perime·tric** *a.* pertaining to a p. or circumference; pertaining to or obtained by a p. (sense 2) of perimetry. **Perime·trical** *a.,* **-ly** *adv.*

Perimetry (pĕri·mĕtri). 1570. [f. as prec. + -Y[3].] **1.** Measurement round; perimeter. Now *rare.* **2.** Measurement of the field of vision by means of the perimeter (sense 2) 1893.

Perineal (perinī·ăl), *a.* 1767. [f. PERINEUM + -AL[1].] Of, pertaining to, or situated in the perineum.

P. body, the mass of tissue of which the surface of the perineum forms the base.

Perineo-, comb. form of PERINEUM, in a few terms of pathology, etc.; **Perine·o-pla:sty,** a plastic operation on the perineum; **Perineorrhaphy** (-ǫ·răfi) [Gr. ῥαφή sewing], suture of the perineum when ruptured; etc.

||**Perineum, -æum** (perinī·ŏm). 1632. [– late L. *perinæon, -eon* – Gr. περίναιον, περίνεος (or πηριν-).] *Anat.* The region of the body between the anus and the scrotum or vulva; denoting either the surface of this or the perineal body.

||**Perineuritis** (pe:ri,niurəi·tis). 1878. [mod. L., f. next + -ITIS.] *Path.* Inflammation of the perineurium.

||**Perineurium** (peri,niūᵊ·riŏm). 1842. [mod.L., f. Gr. περί PERI- + νεῦρον nerve; see -IUM.] *Anat.* The sheath of connective tissue enveloping a bundle of nerve-fibres. Hence **Perineu·rial** *a.* of or pertaining to the p.

Period (pīᵊ·riǒd), *sb.* late ME. [– (O)Fr. *période* – L. *periodus* cycle, sentence – Gr. περίοδος circuit, revolution, recurrence, course, orbit, rounded sentence, f. περί PERI- + ὁδός way, course.] **I.** A course or extent of time. †**1.** Time of duration –1672. **2.** *Chronol.* A round of time marked by the recurrence of astronomical coincidences, used as a unit in chronology; e.g. the *Dionysian, Julian,* etc., *p.* (Cf. CYCLE *sb.* 2) 1613. **b.** *Astron.* The time in which a planet or satellite performs its revolution 1727. **c.** *Physics.* The interval between the recurrence of phases in a vibration, etc. 1865. **d.** Any round or portion of time occupied by a recurring process or action 1850. **3.** *Path.* The time during which a disease runs its course; also, each of its marked phases 1543. **b.** *pl.* (in full *monthly periods*), the menses 1822. **4.** An indefinite portion of time, of history, or of some continuous process, as life. 1712. **b.** *Geol.* One of the larger divisions of geological time 1833.

1. Many Temples early gray have out-lived the Psalmist's p. SIR T. BROWNE. **d.** The heart beats by periods TYNDALL. **4.** A former p. of language 1870. *The p.,* the time in question; *esp.* the present day; The girl of the p. is a creature who dyes her hair and paints her face 1868. Also *attrib.* = belonging to a particular period, e.g. *p. costume.*

II. Completion, end of any course. **1.** The point of completion; consummation, conclusion, end. late ME. †**b.** The final stage; the concluding sentence, peroration; the finish, issue, outcome –1769. †**c.** Death –1682. †**2.** The highest point reached; the acme –1608. †**3.** A point or stage of advance; a moment, occasion –1841. †**4.** Appointed end (of a journey, etc.) –1789. †**5.** *fig.* The goal –1674.

1. The p. of thy Tyranny approacheth SHAKS. Phr. *To put a p. to*: to put an end to. **5.** There's his p. To sheath his knife in vs SHAKS.

III. In Grammar, Rhetoric, etc. **1.** A complete sentence; esp. one of several clauses, grammatically connected, and rhetorically constructed 1579. **b.** In *Ancient Pros.* A group of two or more cola (COLON[2] 1) 1837. **2.** A full pause such as is properly made at the end of a sentence 1587. **b.** The point that marks the end of a complete sentence; a full stop (.) 1609. **3.** *Mus.* 'A complete musical sentence' (Stainer) 1866. **4.** *Arith.* A set of figures in a large number marked off by commas placed between or dots placed over, as in numeration, circulating decimals, and the extraction of the square or cube root 1674. **5.** *Math.* The interval between any two successive equal values of a periodic function 1879.

1. Not a p. Shall be unsaid for me MILT. 2. Make periods in the midst of sentences SHAKS. Hence †**Pe·riod** *v. trans.* to put a period to; to end; to dissolve; *intr.* to come to a conclusion.

Periodate, per·iodate (pərəi·ŏdeit). 1836. [See PER-¹ II.] *Chem.* A salt of periodic acid. So **Periodic, per·iodic** (pərəi,ǫ·dik), *a.*, as in *Periodic acid*, H_5IO_6, an acid containing a larger proportion of oxygen than iodic acid. **Peri·odide** or †**Perio·duret,** a combination of iodine with another element or radical in a larger proportion than in a simple iodide.

Periodic (pīəriǫ·dik), *a.*¹ 1642. [– Fr. *périodique* or L. *periodicus* – Gr. περιοδικός coming round at certain intervals; see PERIOD, -IC.] **1.** Of, pertaining, or proper to the revolution of a heavenly body in its orbit, as *p. motion*. **2.** = PERIODICAL *a.* 2; *spec.* in *Path.* having regularly recurring symptoms, as *p. fever* 1661. **3.** Pertaining to a rhetorical or grammatical period; expressed in periods 1701.

1. A direct method of ascertaining the p. time of each planet HERSCHEL. 2. *P. function* (*Math.*), one whose values recur in the same order while that of the variable increases or decreases continually. *P. inequality* (*Astron.*), see INEQUALITY. *P. law* (*Chem.*), the statement of the fact that the properties of the chemical elements are p. functions of their atomic weights; i.e. that when arranged in the order of these weights, the elements fall into recurring groups or series, so that those having similar chemical and physical properties recur at regular intervals. 2. Anaxagoras never attained to a connected or p. style JOWETT.

Periodic, *a.*²; see under PERIODATE.

Periodical (pīəriǫ·dikăl), *a.* (*sb.*) 1601. [f. PERIODIC *a.*¹ + -AL¹; see -ICAL.] **1.** = PERIODIC *a.*¹ 1. 1603. **2.** Recurring at regular periods or intervals; *loosely*, reappearing at intervals, intermittent 1601. **3.** *Arith.* Of, pertaining to, or expressed in, periods (sense III. 4). *rare.* 1674. †**4.** = PERIODIC *a.*¹ 3. –1780. **5.** Of magazines, etc.: Published at regular intervals longer than a day, as monthly, etc. **b.** Written in or characteristic of such publications; writing for magazines, etc. 1716. **B.** *sb.* A magazine or miscellany published at regular intervals 1798.

A. 5. b. He..knows good from bad, which is not very often the case with p. critics SOUTHEY. Hence **Perio·dical-ly** *adv.* at regularly recurring intervals; also *loosely*, every now and then; **-ness** (*rare*).

Periodicity (pīə:riŏdi·sĭti). 1833. [– Fr. *périodicité*, f. L. *periodicus*; see PERIODIC, -ITY.] **1.** The quality or character of being periodic, or regularly recurrent. **2.** *Physiol.* Menstruation; cf. PERIOD *sb.* I. 3 b. 1848.

‖**Periœci** (peri,ī·səi), *sb. pl.* 1594. [– Gr. περίοικοι, pl. of περίοικος, lit. dwelling round, neighbouring; XVI *perieces* is from Fr.] **1.** Dwellers under the same parallel of latitude, but opposite meridians. (Cf. ANTŒCI.) **2.** *Gr. Hist.* The dwellers in the country round a city, or in the surrounding country towns and villages 1846.

Periosteal (peri,ǫ·stiăl), *a.* 1830. [f. PERIOSTEUM + -AL¹.] Surrounding or occurring round a bone; of, pertaining to, or connected with the periosteum.

‖**Periosteum** (peri,ǫ·stiŏm). 1597. [mod. L. – Gr. περιόστεον (whence late L. *periosteon* in Cæl. Aur.), f. περί round + ὀστέον bone.] *Anat.* The dense fibro-vascular membrane which envelops the bones (except where they are covered by cartilage). Hence **Periosteo-,** comb. form. ‖**Periosti·tis** *Path.* inflammation of the p.; **Periosti·tic** *a.*

†**Peripate·tian.** 1533. [For *peripatetician – Fr. *péripatéticien*; see next, -IAN.] A peripatetic –1753.

Peripatetic (peripăte·tik), *a.* and *sb.* late ME. [– (O)Fr. *péripatétique* or L. *peripateticus* (Cicero, of the philosophy) – Gr. περιπατητικός, f. περιπατεῖν walk up and down, f. περί PERI- + πατεῖν tread; see -IC.] **A.** *adj.* **1.** Of or belonging to the school of Aristotle; Aristotelian; held or believed by this sect of philosophers. (With capital P.) 1566. **2.** Walking about in connection with one's calling; itinerant 1642.

1. The old peripatetick principle, that Nature abhors a Vacuum 1751.

B. *sb.* **1.** A disciple of Aristotle; an Aristotelian. late ME. **2.** One who walks about; a traveller; an itinerant dealer. (Mostly *joc.*) 1617. So **Peripate·tical** *a.* (now *rare*), **-ly,** *adv.* **Pe·ripate·ticism,** the system of philosophy; (*joc.*) the practice of walking about.

‖**Peripatus**¹, **-os** (pĕri·pătŏs, -ǫs). 1660. [– late L. *peripatus* (Cassiodorus) – Gr. περίπατος, f. περί about + πάτος way, path.] The walk in the Lyceum where Aristotle taught; hence *transf.* the school of Aristotle.

‖**Peripatus**² (pĕri·pătŏs). 1840. [mod.L., – Gr. περίπατος (one) walking about; see prec.] *Zool.* A remarkable genus of Arthropods, constituting the family *Peripatidæ*. The species are worm-like creatures, inhabiting damp places among decaying wood and the like, in tropical America, S. Africa, Australasia.

‖**Peripeteia, -tia** (pe:ripétəi·ă, -tī·ă). Also **peripety** (pĕri·pĭti). 1591. [– Gr. περιπέτεια sudden change, f. (ult.) περί PERI- + stem πετ- of πίπτειν to fall.] A sudden change of fortune or reverse of circumstances (in a tragedy, etc., or in life).

Peripheral (pĕri·fĕrăl), *a.* 1808. [f. PERIPHERY + -AL¹.] Of, pertaining to, or situated in, the periphery; constituting the external surface; esp. in *Anat.*, etc., of the surface or outward part of an organic body. Hence **Peri·pherally** *adv.* in a p. way or position; at the periphery. So **Periphe·ric, -al** *adjs.*, **-ly** *adv.* in same senses.

Periphery (pĕri·fĕri, pe·riféri). 1571. [– late L. *peripheria* – Gr. περιφέρεια, f. περιφερής revolving round, f. περί PERI- + φέρειν BEAR *v.*¹; see -Y³.] The line that forms the boundary, esp. of any round or rounded surface. **b.** *spec.* in *Geom.* The circumference of any closed curvilinear figure; also, the sum of the sides of a polygonal figure; a perimeter. Also *fig.* **c.** The external boundary or surface of any space or body 1666. **d.** *loosely*, A surrounding area 1759.

Periphractic (perifræ·ktik), *a.* 1881. [f. Gr. περίφρακτος fenced around (φράσσειν to fence) + -IC.] *Geom.* Said of a region having one or more internal bounding surfaces (or curves, when the region is plane) unconnected with the external boundary.

Periphrase (pe·rifrēiz), *sb.* 1589. [– Fr. *périphrase* – L. *periphrasis*.] = PERIPHRASIS.

Periphrase (pe·rifrēiz), *v.* 1624. [– Fr. *périphraser*; see prec.] **1.** *trans.* To express by periphrasis. **2.** *intr.* To use circumlocution 1652.

Periphrasis (pĕri·frăsis). *Pl.* **-ses** (sīz). 1533. [– L. *periphrasis* (Quintilian) – Gr. περίφρασις, f. περιφράζειν, f. περί round about + φράζειν declare.] **1.** That figure of speech which consists in expressing the meaning of a word or phrase, etc., by many or several words instead of by few or one; a wordy or roundabout way of speaking; circumlocution. **2.** An instance of this 1579. †**b.** *fig.* An amplification –1658.

1. The loose clumsiness of perpetual p. 1864.

Periphrastic (perifræ·stik), *a.* 1805. [– Gr. περιφραστικός, f. περιφράζειν; see prec., -IC. Cf. Fr. *périphrastique*.] Of the nature of, characterized by, or involving periphrasis; circumlocutory, roundabout.

P. conjugation (in Grammar), a conjugation formed by the combination of a simple verb and an auxiliary. *P. genitive*, a genitive formed with *of* in Eng., *de* in Fr., etc. So **Periphra·stical** *a.*, **-ly** *adv.*

Periphraxy (pe·rifræksi). 1881. [f. late Gr. περίφραξις a fencing round.] *Geom.* The condition of being PERIPHRACTIC (q.v.).

Periplast (pe·riplæst). 1853. [f. PERI- + -PLAST.] *Biol.* †**a.** The intercellular substance in which the organized structures of a tissue are embedded. **b.** The main substance or body of a cell, as dist. from the cell-wall and the internal nucleus. **c.** A cell-wall or cell-envelope. Hence **Peripla·stic** *a.*

‖**Periplus** (pe·riplŏs). 1776. [L. – Gr. περίπλους, f. περί PERI- + πλοῦς voyage.] Circumnavigation; a voyage round a coast-line, etc. **b.** *transf.* A narrative of such a voyage.

Peripneumony (peripniū·mŏni), ‖**peripneumonia** (-pniumōu·niă). Now *rare* or *Obs.* 1550. [– Fr. *péripneumonie* (Paré) – late and med.L. *peripneumonia* – Gr. περιπνευμονία; see PERI-, PNEUMONIA.] *Path.* = PNEUMONIA. Hence **Peripneumonic** (-mǫ·nik) *a.* pertaining to or having pneumonia; *sb.* one so affected.

Peri·pter, -ere. *rare.* 1696. [– Fr. *périptère* – L. *peripteros, -on* (Vitruvius) – Gr. περίπτερος adj., f. περί PERI- + πτερόν wing.] *Arch.* A peripteral building. So **Peri·pteral** *a.* having a single peristyle or row of pillars surrounding it, as a Greek temple.

Perique (pĕrī·k). 1895. [Fr. of unkn. origin.] Dark or black tobacco from Louisiana.

Periscian (peri·siăn, -ʃiăn), *a.* and *sb.* 1594. [f. L. *Periscii* (see next) + -AN. Cf. Fr. *periscien* (XVI).] **A.** *adj.* Of or pertaining to the Periscii. **B.** *sb.* (in *pl.*) = PERISCII.

‖**Periscii** (pĕri·si,əi, -i·ʃi,əi), *sb. pl.* 1625. [Latinized form of Gr. περίσκιοι, pl. of περίσκιος throwing a shadow all round, f. περί around + σκιά shadow.] Those who dwell within the polar circles, whose shadows revolve around them on a summer day.

Periscope (pe·riskoup). 1865. [f. PERI- + -SCOPE.] **1.** A variety of photographic object-glass. **2.** An apparatus used in a submarine or trench, for obtaining a view of objects above the surface by a system of mirrors 1899. Hence **Perisco·pic** *a.* enabling one to see distinctly for some distance around the axis of vision. **Pe·riscopism,** the faculty of periscopic vision.

Perish (pe·riʃ), *v.* ME. [f. *periss-*, extended stem of (O)Fr. *périr* :– L. *perire* pass away, come to nothing, lose one's life, f. *per* PER-¹ 3 + *ire* go.] **1.** *intr.* To come to an untimely end; to suffer destruction; to lose its life. (Chiefly of living beings.) **b.** To incur spiritual death; to suffer moral ruin ME. **c.** Of material things: *spec.* as opposed to things spiritual or eternal, or as the effect of decay or exposure to destructive conditions. late ME. **d.** Of immaterial things: To come to an end, pass away ME. **e.** In imprecations 1526. **2.** In *pa. pple.* with *be*, expressing the resulting state ME. **3.** *trans.* To bring to destruction; to put to death, kill (a person, etc.), wreck (a ship, etc.) *Obs.* or *arch.* late ME. †**b.** To destroy spiritually; to ruin morally –1750. **c.** Said of the effect of cold, hunger, or privation, in shrivelling up, or reducing to a moribund condition. Now chiefly *dial.* 1719.

1. The common rout, That..Grow up and p. as the summer flie MILT. **b.** Knowledge is good..yet man perished in seeking knowledge RUSKIN. **c.** The joints are apt to 'perish' by the action of the acids 1885. **d.** Bards..whose Songs have perished in the Wreck of Time 1763. **e.** P. the man, whose mind is backward now SHAKS. **2.** We were all perished with cold 1845. Hence †**Pe·rishment,** destruction, damage, loss.

Perishable (pe·riʃăb'l), *a.* (*sb.*) 1611. [f. PERISH + -ABLE. Cf. Fr. *périssable*.] **1.** Liable to perish; *esp.* naturally subject to speedy decay. **2. a.** *absol.* quasi-*sb.* *The p.*, that which is transitory 1821. **b.** *sb. pl.* Things liable to decay; said chiefly of foodstuffs in transit 1742.

1. Thou p. flesh and form of clay COWPER. **b.** Perishables like fish and flowers 1895. Hence **Perishabi·lity** (*rare*), **Pe·rishableness,** p. quality. **Pe·rishably** *adv.*

Perisher (pe·riʃəɹ). 1888. [f. as prec. + -ER¹.] *slang.* An extreme (of any course of action); also applied contemptuously to persons.

Those perishers in the gallery didn't know anything about Shakespeare 1896. So **Pe·rishing** *a.* *slang*, 'blighted', 'blinking'; also *adv.* (e.g. *p. cold*).

Perispome (pe·rispōum), *a.* and *sb.* 1818. [abbrev. of **perispo·menon** (also used) = Gr. περισπώμενον, n. of pr. pple. pass. of περισπᾶν draw around, mark with the circumflex.] **A.** *adj.* Having a circumflex accent on the last syllable. **B.** *sb.* A word so accented.

Perissad (pĕri·sæd), *sb.* (*a.*) 1870. [f. Gr. περισσός uneven, odd (f. περί 'over, beyond') + -AD.] *Chem.* An element or radical whose quantivalency is represented by an odd number, as a monad, triad, etc.; opp. to ARTIAD. Also as *adj.*

Perissodactyl, -yle (pĕrisodæ·ktil), *a.* and

sb. 1849. [– mod.L. *perissodactylus*, f. Gr. περισσός uneven + δάκτυλος digit.] *Zool.* **A.** *adj.* Having an odd number of toes on each foot, as an ungulate mammal; belonging to the division *Perissodactyla* of *Ungulata*. **B.** *sb.* A perissodactyl ungulate or hoofed animal; *pl.* in *-s* or *-a*. Opp. to ARTIODACTYL. 1854.

†**Perisso·logy.** 1583. [– late L. *perissologia* – Gr. περισσολογία, f. περισσός redundant + λόγος speech.] *Rhet.* Redundance of speech; use of more words than are necessary; pleonasm –1776. Hence **Perissolo·gical** *a.* (*rare*), redundant in words.

‖**Peristalsis** (peristæ·lsis). 1859. [mod.L., f. (on Gr. analogies) περιστέλλειν; see next.] *Physiol.* Peristaltic movement.

Peristaltic (peristæ·ltik), *a.* 1655. [– Gr. περισταλτικός (Galen) clasping and compressing, f. περιστέλλειν wrap up or round, f. περί round + στέλλειν place; see -IC.] *Physiol.* Applied to the automatic muscular (vermicular) movement, consisting of rhythmic wave-like contractions in successive circles, by which the contents of the alimentary canal or other tubular organ are propelled along it. Hence **Perista·ltically** *adv.*

Peristerite (pĕri·stĕrəit). 1843. [f. Gr. περιστερά pigeon + -ITE[1] 2 b.] *Min.* A variety of ALBITE exhibiting a slight iridescence like that on a pigeon's neck.

Peristeronic (pĕristĕrǫ·nik), *a.* 1868. [– Gr. περιστερών dove-cot, f. περιστερά dove, pigeon (cf. prec.) + -IC.] Pertaining to or concerned with pigeons.

Peristome (pe·ristoᵘm). Also **peri·stoma** (pl. **-ata**), **peristo·mium** (pl. **-ia**). 1796. [– mod.L. *peristoma*, f. Gr. περί PERI- + στόμα mouth; altered to *peristomium* after *pericarpium*, etc.] **1.** *Bot.* The fringe of small teeth around the mouth of the capsule in mosses. **2.** *Zool.* **a.** The margin of the aperture of the shell of a mollusc 1828. **b.** Any special structure or set of parts around the mouth of invertebrates 1875. Hence **Peristo·mal, Peristo·mial** *adjs.*

Peristrephic (peri,stre·fik), *a.* 1827. [irreg. f. Gr. περιστρέφειν turn round + -IC.] Turning round, revolving, rotatory (as a panorama).

Peristyle (pe·ristəil). 1612. [– Fr. *péristyle* – L. *peristylum* – Gr. περίστυλον, subst. use of n. of περίστυλος having pillars all round, f. περί round + στῦλος pillar.] *Arch.* A row of columns surrounding a temple, etc., or a court, cloister, etc.; less properly, the space so surrounded. ¶**b.** Applied to the columned porch of a church, to a pillared verandah, etc. 1694.

‖**Perisystole** (perisi·stŏli). 1664. [mod.L. *perisystole* (Bartholine 1651), f. Gr. περί round + συστολή; see SYSTOLE. Cf. Fr. *périsystole* (1762).] *Physiol.* The interval between the systole and the following diastole of the heart, inappreciable except when the heart's action is failing. Hence **Perisysto·lic** *a.*

†**Perite**, *a.* 1524. [– Fr. †*perit*, *-ite* or its source L. *peritus*.] Experienced, skilled –1820.

‖**Perithecium** (periþī·siŏm -ʃiŏm). Pl. **-ia.** Also **perithece** (pe·ripīs). 1832. [mod.L. (Persoon 1796), f. Gr. περί PERI- + θήκη case; cf. *pericarpium*.] *Bot.* A cup-shaped or flask-shaped receptacle, inclosing the fructification in certain fungi, etc. Hence **Perithe·cial** *a.*

‖**Peritoneum, -æum** (pe:ritŏnī·ŏm). 1541. [– late L. *peritonæum*, *-eum* – Gr. περιτόναιον, -ειον, subst. use of n. of περιτόναιος, f. περίτονος stretched around, f. περί PERI- + -τονος stretched.] *Anat.* The double serous membrane which lines the cavity of the abdomen. In vertebrates below mammals, which have no diaphragm, the membrane lining the whole body-cavity, corresponding to the mammalian p. and pleura combined. Hence **Peritone·al, -æ·al** *a.* of, pertaining to, situated in, or affecting the p. **Peritonitis** (pe:ritŏnəi·tis), inflammation of the p., or of some part of it 1776.

Peritrichan (pĕri·trikăn), *a.* and *sb.* 1875. [f. mod.L. *Peritricha*, f. Gr. περί PERI- + θρίξ, τριχ- hair; see -A 4, -AN.] *Zool.* **A.** *adj.* Belonging to the division *Peritricha* of *Infusoria*, having a band of cilia round the body. **B.** *sb.* An infusorian of this division. So **Peri·trichous** *a.*

‖**Peritrochium** (peritrōᵘ·kiŏm). 1704. [mod.L. – Gr. περιτρόχιον wheel, f. περίτροχος circular; see -IUM.] *Mech.* A wheel, as constituting part of the mechanical power called the wheel-and-axle.

Peritropal (pĕri·trŏpăl), *a. rare.* 1819. [f. mod.L. *peritropus* (Jussieu), f. Gr. περί PERI- + -τροπος turning; see -AL[1]. Cf. Fr. *péritrope* (Richard 1808).] *Bot.* Of an embryo or ovule: = AMPHITROPAL, HEMITROPOUS 2. Also **Peri·tropous** *a.*

Periwig (pe·riwig), *sb.* Now only *Hist.* 1529. [alt., through the stages *perewike*, *-wig*, of *perwike*, *-wick*, vars. of PERUKE (orig. stressed *pe·ruke*), in which *-wi-* repr. an attempt to render (ü) of the Fr. word.] **1.** An artificial imitation of a head of hair (or part of one); a WIG. †**2.** An alleged kind of marine animal –1674. Hence **Pe·riwig** *v. arch.*, to dress or conceal with, or as with, a p. **Pe·riwigged** *ppl. a.* wearing or having a p.

Periwinkle[1] (pe·riwiŋk'l). [ME. *pervenke*, *-vinke* – AFr. *pervenke*, var. of (O)Fr. *pervenche* :– late L. *pervinca*, earlier *vi(n)ca pervi(n)ca* (Pliny). Not continuous with OE. *peruince* – L. The mod. form appears XVI as *per(i)wyncle*, prob. by assim. to next.] The common name of plants of the genus *Vinca* (N.O. *Apocynaceæ*), esp. *V. minor* and *V. major*, the Lesser and Greater Periwinkle, evergreen trailing sub-shrubs with light blue starry flowers, varying in *V. minor* with pure white. Also *attrib.*

Periwinkle[2] (pe·riwiŋk'l). 1530. [XVI *purwincle*, *pere-*, *periwinkle*. Of unkn. origin; OE. *winewinclan* pl., also read as *pinewinclan*, may perh. be repr. by dial. forms in *penny-*; in any case the second element is the same. Shortened to WINKLE from XVI.] A gastropod mollusc of the genus *Littorina*, esp. *L. littorea* the common European coast species, much used for food.

Perjink (pəɹdʒi·ŋk), *a. Sc.* 1808. [Of unkn. origin.] Exact, precise; prim.

†**Pe·rjure**, *sb.* (*a.*) late ME. [– AFr. *perjur* (Gower) = (O)Fr. *parjur(e*, or L. *perjurus* (adj.), f. *perjurare*; see next.] A perjurer –1615. **b.** as *adj.* Perjured –1600.

Perjure (pō·ɹdʒŭɹ), *v.* 1477. [– (O)Fr. *parjurer*, †*per-* – L. *perjurare*, refash. of *pe(r)ierare* swear falsely, f. *per* PER[1] 3 + *jurare* swear.] †**1.** *intr.* To commit perjury; to be false to an oath, promise, etc. –1789. **b.** *refl. To p. oneself*: to forswear oneself. Now the usual const. 1755. **c.** quasi-*pass. To be perjured*; to be guilty of perjury 1477. †**2.** *trans.* To prove false to or break (an oath, vow, etc.) –1809. †**3.** To cause to commit perjury SHAKS. †**4.** To prove false to (a person) to whom one has sworn faith –1610.

1. b. A person who has..perjured himself [is] the bane of society 1772. **4.** She..did pray For me that perjur'd her FLETCHER.

Perjured (pō·ɹdʒŭɹd), *ppl. a.* (*sb.*) 1453. [pa. pple. of prec. vb., after AFr. *perjuré*, OFr. *parjuré* pa. pple. of the intr. vb., lit. (one) that has committed perjury. (Viewed in Eng. as passive; whence prec. 1 c.)] **1.** That has committed perjury; forsworn. Also *absol.* †**2.** Characterized by perjury; perjurious –1814. †**3.** Falsely sworn –1697.

1. P. traitors 1859. **3.** Their periured oth SPENSER.

Perjurer (pō·ɹdʒŭrəɹ). 1533. [app. – AFr. *par-*, *perjurour*, f. *parjurer* PERJURE *v.*; see -OUR, -ER[2] 3.] One who commits perjury, *spec.* in the legal sense; one who is forsworn.

Perjurious (pəɹdʒūᵊ·riəs), *a.* 1540. [f. PERJURY + -OUS; see -IOUS. Cf. contemp. PERJUROUS.] †**1.** Of persons: Guilty of perjury –1829. **2.** Of actions, etc.: Characterized by perjury 1602.

2. P. suits for nullification of marriage 1872. Hence **Perju·rious-ly** *adv.*, **-ness** (*rare*). So †**Pe·rjurous** *a.*

Perjury (pō·ɹdʒŭri). late ME. [– AFr. *perjurie*, OFr. *parjurie* (mod. *parjure*) – L. *perjurium* false oath, oath-breaking, f. *perjurare* PERJURE *v.*; see -Y[3].] The action of swearing to a statement known to be false; *spec.* in *Law*, the crime of wilfully uttering false evidence while on oath. **b.** Applied also to the violation of a promise made on oath 1532. **c.** with *a* and *pl.* 1440.

c. At Louers periuries They say Ioue laught SHAKS.

Perk (pōɹk), *a.* 1579. [Goes with PERK *v.*] Self-assertive, pert, 'cocky'; brisk; smart.

Perk (pōɹk), *v.* late ME. [The earliest instances refer to the action of birds and suggest deriv. from *perk* sb., var. of PERCH *sb.*[2] (now obs. or dial.) – dial Fr. **perque*, **perquer*, vars. of *perche*, *percher*.] **I.** *intr.* To carry oneself smartly, briskly, or jauntily. **b.** To lift one's head, thrust oneself forward briskly, boldly, or impudently. Also with *up*. Also *fig.* 1529. **c.** With *up*: To recover liveliness, as after depression or sickness (*colloq.*) 1656.

b. The old woman perk'd up as brisk as a bee BARHAM. *fig.* He knew that Hagar would quickly p. up, and domineer over Sarah 1703. High garret gable-windows perking into the roofs DICKENS.

II. *trans.* **1.** To make spruce or smart; to prank or trim, as a bird its plumage. Also with *up*, *out*. 1485. **2.** To prick up; to hold *up* briskly or self-assertively 1591.

2. [The blackbird] perks his tail up, and challenges the world with the call already mentioned JEFFERIES.

Perkinism (pō·ɹkiniz'm). *Hist.* 1798. [-ISM.] *Med.* A method of treatment introduced by Elisha *Perkins*, an American physician, for the cure of rheumatic diseases; it consisted in drawing two small pointed rods, one of steel and one of brass, called 'metallic tractors', over the affected region; tractoration. So **Perkine·an, Perkini·stic** *adjs.* **Pe·rkinize** *v.* to practise P.

Perky (pō·ɹki), *a.* 1855. [f. PERK *v.* or *a.* + -Y[1].] Inclined to be self-assertive or to thrust oneself forward; also, smart, brisk.

transf. Amid p. larches and pine TENNYSON. Hence **Pe·rkily** *adv.* **Pe·rkiness.**

Perla·ceous, *a.* 1777. [f. PEARL + -ACEOUS, after *herbaceous*, etc.] Nacreous.

Perlite (pō·ɹləit). Also **pearlite.** 1833. [= Fr. *perlite*, f. *perle* PEARL; see -ITE[1] 2 b.] *Min.* Obsidian or other vitreous rock in form of enamel-like globules; pearlstone. **Perli·tic** *a.*

Perlustrate (pəɹlɒ·streᶦt), *v. Obs.* exc. in techn. use. 1535. [– *perlustrat-*, pa. ppl. stem of L. *perlustrare*, f. *per* PER-[1] 1, 2 + *lustrare* wander through, f. *lustrum*; see LUSTRATE.] *trans.* To travel through and survey thoroughly. Also *absol.* Hence **Perlustra·tion**, the action of perlustrating 1640.

Perm (pōɹm). 1928. Colloq. abbrev. of PERMANENT *wave*. So **Permed** (pēɹmd) *ppl. a.*

Permalloy (pō·ɹmăloi). 1924. [f. PERM(EABLE + ALLOY.] Trade name for an alloy of nickel and iron very sensitive to magnetic forces.

Permanence (pō·ɹmănĕns). ME. [– (O)Fr. *permanence* or med.L. *permanentia*; see PERMANENT, -ENCE.] The fact or quality of being permanent; continuance; abidingness.

Permanency (pō·ɹmănĕnsi). 1555. [f. as prec.; see -ENCY.] **1.** = prec. **2.** A (concrete) example of something permanent; a permanent person, thing, position, etc. 1841.

2. A temporary engagement, not a p. 1905.

Permanent (pō·ɹmănĕnt), *a.* late ME. [– (O)Fr. *permanent* or L. *permanens*, *-ent-*, pr. pple. of *permanēre* remain to the end, f. *per* PER-[1] 1, 2 + *manēre* stay; see -ENT.] **1.** Lasting or designed to last indefinitely without change; enduring; persistent: opp. to *temporary*. †**2.** Of persons: Continuing steadfast *in* a course –1548. **3.** *absol. The p.*, that which endures or persists 1826.

1. Human institutions perish, but nature is p. 1780. *P. gas*, a name formerly given to gases supposed to be incapable of liquefaction, as oxygen, hydrogen. *P. magnet*, a magnet whose property continues after the magnetizing current has ceased to pass through it. *P. wave*, applied to a method of waving the hair supposed to be p. *P. way* (*road*), the finished road-bed of a railway, as dist. from a contractor's temporary way. Hence **Pe·rmanently** *adv.*

Permanganate (pəɹmæ·ŋgănĕt). 1841. [f. next; see -ATE[4].] *Chem.* A salt of permanganic acid, as *potassium p.* or *p. of potash*,

KMnO$_4$, which dissolves in water with a fine purple red, and is used as a disinfectant.

Permanganic (pə̄ɹmæŋgæ·nik), *a.* 1836. [f. PER-[1] II. b + MANGANIC.] *Chem.* In *p. acid*, the acid HMnO$_4$, obtained from manganese.

†**Perma·nsion.** 1646. [– L. *permansio*, f. *permans-*, pa. ppl. stem of *permanēre*; see PERMANENT, -ION.] = PERMANENCE 1. –1659.

Permeability (pə̄:ɹmiˌăbi·lĭti). 1759. [f. next + -ITY.] The quality or condition of being permeable; perviousness.

Magnetic p., conducting power for lines of magnetic force.

Permeable (pə̄·ɹmiˌăb'l), *a.* ME. [– late L. *permeabilis*, f. L. *permeare* PERMEATE; see -ABLE.] **1.** Capable of being permeated or passed through; penetrable, pervious. Const. *by*, *to*. †**2.** Penetrative –1752.

1. Cast steel is..p. to ether 1893. Hence **Pe·rmeably** *adv.*

Permeant (pə̄·ɹmiˌănt), *a.* 1646. [– L. *permeans*, *-ant-*, pr. pple. of *permeare*; see next, -ANT.] Permeating. So **Pe·rmeance.**

Permeate (pə̄·ɹmiˌeⁱt), *v.* 1656. [– *permeat-*, pa. ppl. stem of L. *permeare*, f. *per* PER-[1] 1 + *meare* go, pass; see -ATE[3].] **1.** *trans.* To pass, spread, or diffuse itself through; to penetrate, pervade, saturate 1660. **2.** *intr.* with *through*, *into*, *among*, etc. 1656. Hence **Permea·tion,** penetration; pervasion 1623. **Pe·rmeative** *a.* penetrative; pervasive.

Permian (pə̄·ɹmiăn), *a.* (*sb.*) 1841. [f. *Perm* in Eastern Russia, where these strata are extensively developed; see -IAN.] *Geol.* Name of the uppermost division of the Palæozoic series of strata, lying below the Trias and above the Carboniferous formation, and consisting chiefly of red sandstone and magnesian limestone. Also *ellipt.* as *sb.* The Permian system, or a formation belonging to it; *pl.* = P. strata.

Permissible (pəɹmi·sĭb'l), *a.* late ME. [– Fr. †*permissible* or med.L. *permissibilis*, f. as next; see -IBLE.] That can be or ought to be permitted; allowable. Hence **Permissibi·lity, Permi·ssibleness,** the quality of being p. **Permi·ssibly** *adv.*

Permission (pəɹmi·ʃən). late ME. [– (O)Fr. *permission* or L. *permissio*, f. *permiss-*, pa. ppl. stem of *permittere* PERMIT *v.*; see -ION.] The action of permitting or giving leave; liberty or licence granted to do something; leave.

Do as thou find'st P. from above MILT.

Permissive (pəɹmi·siv), *a.* late ME. [– Fr. †*permissif*, *-ive* or med.L. *permissivus*, f. as prec.; see -IVE.] **1.** Having the quality of permitting or giving permission; not forbidding or hindering 1603. **2.** Permitted, allowed; done, or acting, under permission; optional.

1. Not a Positive but a P. command HY. MORE. **2.** *P. waste* (Law), waste that is allowed to happen by neglect of repairs. Hence **Permi·ssive-ly** *adv.*, **-ness.**

†**Permi·stion.** 1612. [– L. *permistio* (whence Fr. †*permistion*, Paré), var. of *permixtio* PERMIXTION. Cf. contemp. MISTION.] = PERMIXTION –1674.

Permit (pə̄·ɹmit), *sb.* 1714. [f. PERMIT *v.*] **1.** A written order giving permission, a warrant, a licence; esp. a licence for the landing or removal of dutiable or excisable goods. **2.** Permission, leave (esp. formally given). (Formerly stressed *permi·t.*) 1730.

Permit (pəɹmi·t), *v.* 1489. [– L. *permittere* surrender, allow, f. *per* PER-[1] 1, 3 + *mittere* let go.] **I. 1.** *trans.* To admit or allow the doing or occurrence of; to give leave or opportunity for. **2.** To allow (a person or thing) to do (or undergo) something 1514. **b.** *refl.* with *in*: To allow oneself to indulge in or commit 1678. **3.** *absol.* or *intr.* To allow 1553. **b.** *intr.* with *of*: To allow of, admit of 1860.

1. Pitt..would by no means p. the introduction of Sunday papers into his household THACKERAY. **2.** P. me to recommend him to your Grace's protection *'Junius' Lett.* **3.** To examine over all the noted words, as time permits 1612.

II. †**1.** *trans.* To commit, submit, hand over; to give up, leave; to refer (*to* the will of). Const. *to* (*unto*). –1802. †**2.** To leave undone, unused, etc.; to pretermit, omit –1692.

1. What thou livst Live well, how long or short p. to Heav'n MILT. Hence **Permittee·, Permi·tter.**

Permittance (pəɹmi·tăns). *Obs.* or *arch.* 1580. [f. PERMIT *v.* + -ANCE.] Permission.

†**Permi·x,** *v.* 1678. [Back-formation from next; cf. COMMIX, MIX.] *trans.* To mix thoroughly, intermingle –1683.

†**Permi·xed, permi·xt,** *ppl. a.* late ME. [orig. – L. *permixtus*, pa. pple. of *permiscēre* mix thoroughly, f. *per* PER-[1] 2 + *miscēre* MIX. Cf. COMMIXED, MIXED.] Thoroughly mixed, intermixed, intermingled –1660.

†**Permi·xtion.** late ME. [– L. *permixtio*, f. *permixt-*; see prec., -ION. Cf. Fr. *permixtion.*] A thorough mixture or mingling; intermingling –1685.

Permutable (pəɹmiū·tăb'l), *a.* 1662. [– late L. *permutabilis*, f. *permutare*; see PERMUTE, -ABLE.] **1.** Capable of being exchanged; interchangeable 1776. **2.** Liable to change 1662. Hence **Permutabi·lity,** the quality or condition of being p. **Permu·tableness. Permu·tably** *adv.*

Permutation (pə̄ɹmiutēⁱ·ʃən). late ME. [– (O)Fr. *permutation* or L. *permutatio*, f. *permutat-*, pa. ppl. stem of *permutare*; see next, -ION.] †**1.** Exchange of one thing for another; commutation; barter –1754. **2.** Alteration; transmutation. Now *rare.* ME. **3.** *Math.* The action of changing the order of a set of things lineally arranged; each of the different arrangements of which such a set is capable. Hence *gen.*, in *pl.* (usu. in phr. *permutations and combinations*): Variations of order or arrangement. 1710. **4.** *Philol.* The interchange of consonants occurring regularly in cognate words belonging to related languages, as in L. and Gr. *duo*, Eng. *two*, G. *zwei*; L. and Gr. *tria*, Eng. *three*, G. *drei* 1843.

2. The violent convulsions and permutations that have been made in property BURKE. *Comb.* **p.-lock,** a lock in which the parts can be transposed or shifted, so that it is necessary to arrange them in some particular way in order to shoot or withdraw the bolt.

Permute (pəɹmiū·t), *v.* late ME. [– L. *permutare*, f. *per* PER-[1] 2 + *mutare* change. Cf. (O)Fr. *permuter*, perh. partly the source.] †**1.** *trans.* To change one for another; to exchange, interchange –1657. **2.** To change thoroughly; to transmute. Now *rare* or *Obs.* 1440. **3.** *Math.* To subject to permutation (see prec. 3) 1878. **4.** *Philol.* (in *pass.*). To undergo permutation (see prec. 4) 1846. Hence **Permu·ter,** one who permutes.

Pern (pə̄ɹn). 1840. [– mod.L. *pernis* (Cuvier 1817), erron. – Gr. πτέρνις a kind of hawk.] A bird of the genus *Pernis*; the HONEY-BUZZARD.

Pernancy (pə̄·ɹnănsi). 1642. [f. AFr. *pernance* (with subst. of suffix -ANCY, after *tenancy*) = OFr. *prenance* action of taking into possession, f. *pren-*, stem of *prendre* take; see -ANCE. Cf. PERNOR.] The taking or receiving of anything; taking into possession; receipt, as of rents, tithes, etc.

†**Pe·rnel.** late ME. [– OFr. *Per(o)nele* :– med.L. *Petronilla* a woman's name, a saint so named; popularly viewed as a fem. deriv. of *Petrus*, Peter.] A priest's concubine; a wanton young woman; an effeminate man –1581.

†**Perni·cion.** 1530. [– late and med.L. *pernicio*, var. of L. *pernicies*; see next, -ION.] Total destruction –1736.

Pernicious (pəɹni·ʃəs), *a.*[1] 1521. [– L. *perniciosus*, f. *pernicies* destruction, f. *per* PER-[1] 2 + *nex*, *nec-* death, destruction; see -IOUS. Cf. (O)Fr. *pernicieux.*] Having the quality of destroying; destructive, ruinous; fatal. **b.** Wicked; villainous. Now *rare* or *Obs.* 1555.

Men of p. principles 1704. P. anæmia 1898. **b.** Victims of a p. woman's crime COWPER. Hence **Perni·cious-ly** *adv.*, **-ness.**

Perni·cious, *a.*[2] *rare.* 1656. [f. L. *pernix*, *pernic-* fleet + -OUS.] Rapid, swift. So †**Perni·city,** swiftness, celerity 1592.

Pernickety (pəɹni·kĕti), *a.* 1808. [orig. Sc., of unkn. origin.] Of persons, etc.: Particular about trifles; precise; fastidious. Of things: Requiring precise handling or care; ticklish.

Pernoctate (pəɹnǫ·kteⁱt), *v.* 1623. [– *pernoctat-*, pa. ppl. stem of L. *pernoctare*, f. *per* PER-[1] 1 + *nox*, *noct-* night; see -ATE[3].] *intr.* To pass the night; see next.

Pernoctation (pə̄ɹnǫktēⁱ·ʃən). 1633. [– late L. *pernoctatio* (Ambrose), f. as prec.; see -ION.] The action of spending the night; esp. in *Eccl.* use, spending the night in prayer; in University use, passing the night within the bounds of the university in order to keep residence.

†**Pernor.** ME. [– AFr. *pernour* = OFr. *preneor*, *-eur* taker, f. *pren-*, stem of (O)Fr. *prendre* take; see -OUR, -OR 2, and cf. PERNANCY.] *Law.* A taker or receiver, esp. of rents or profits of land –1642.

Perofskite (pĕrǫ·fskəit). Also **perov-, perow-.** 1844. [f. name *Perovski*; see -ITE[1] 2 b. Named 1839.] *Min.* Titanate of calcium, occurring in crystals varying in colour from yellow to black.

‖**Peroné** (pe·rǭnī). 1693. [mod.L. – Gr. περόνη a pin, etc.] *Anat.* = FIBULA 2.

Peroneal (peronī·ăl), *a.* 1831. [f. mod.L. *peronæus* PERONEUS + -AL[1].] *Anat.* Pertaining to or connected with the *perone* or fibula. Hence **Perone·o-,** comb. form.

‖**Peroneus** (peronī·ǒs). 1704. [mod.L. (sc. *musculus* muscle), f. PERONE.] *Anat.* Name for various muscles connected with the fibula.

‖**Peronospora** (peronǫ·spǒră). 1884. [mod. L., f. Gr. περόνη pin + σπόρος seed.] *Bot.* A genus of minute parasitic fungi (moulds or mildews) of which several species cause diseases in plants.

Perorate (pe·rǒrēⁱt), *v.* 1603. [– *perorat-*, pa. ppl. stem of L. *perorare* speak at length, or to the close, f. *per* PER-[1] 1 + *orare* speak; see -ATE[3].] **1.** *intr.* To speak at length. **b.** *trans.* To declaim 1681. **2.** *intr.* To sum up or conclude a speech 1808.

1. Now hauing perorated (as he thinkes) sufficiently, he beginnes to growe to a conclusion 1603.

Peroration (perǒrēⁱ·ʃən). 1440. [– Fr. *péroration* or L. *peroratio*, f. as prec.; see -ION.] **1.** The concluding part of an oration, speech, or written discourse, in which the speaker or writer sums up; any rhetorical conclusion to a speech. **2.** A discourse; a rhetorical passage 1593.

Peroxide (pərǫ·ksəid). 1804. [f. PER-[1] II. a + OXIDE.] *Chem.* That compound of oxygen with another element which contains the greatest possible proportion of oxygen.

Used colloq. for *p. of hydrogen*, which is used to bleach the hair, etc. Hence **Pero·xided,** treated or dyed with hydrogen p. †**Pero·xidate, Pero·xidize** *vbs. trans.* and *intr.*, to convert, or become converted, into a p.; whence **Peroxida·tion, Pero·xidizement,** conversion into a p.

Perpend (pəɹpe·nd), *v. arch.* 1527. [– L. *perpendere* weigh exactly, consider, f. *per* PER-[1] 2 + *pendere* weigh.] *trans.* To weigh mentally, ponder, consider. Also *absol.* or *intr.*

P. my words O Signieur Dewe, and marke SHAKS.

Perpend, obs. var. of PARPEN(T.

†**Perpe·ndicle.** *rare.* late ME. [– OFr. *perpendicle* – L. *perpendiculum*; see next, -CULE.] A plumb-line –1867.

Perpendicular (pə̄ɹpĕndi·kiŭlăɹ), *a.*, *adv.*, and *sb.* late ME. [– L. *perpendicularis*, f. *perpendiculum* plummet, plumb-line, f. *per* PER-[1] I. 2 + *pendēre* hang; see -CULE, -AR[1].] **A.** *adj.* **1.** Situated at right angles to the plane of the horizon, or directly up and down; vertical. **b.** Of an ascent, etc.: Very steep, precipitous 1596. **c.** Of persons: Of erect figure or attitude; also, upright; (*joc.*) in a standing position 1768. †**d.** *fig.* Directly leading *to* –1651. **2.** *Geom.* Of a line or plane: Having a direction at right angles to a given line, plane, or surface. Const. *to* (†*with*). 1570. **3.** *Arch.* Applied to the third or florid style of English pointed architecture, which prevailed from the end of the 14th to the beginning of the 16th century, characterized by the vertical lines of its tracery 1812.

1. In the Sunnes p. glances, wee found it hot 1638. **d.** Causes p. to their effects SIR T. BROWNE.

†**B.** *adv.* Perpendicularly, vertically –1792.

C. *sb.* **1.** An appliance for indicating the vertical line from any point; e.g. a mason's plumb-level, etc. 1603. **2.** A line at right angles to the plane of the horizon, a vertical line; also, a vertical plane or face; *loosely*, a steep. *The p.* (sc. line, direction). 1632. **b.** Upright position; also *fig.* 1859. **c.** *slang.* A meal, party, etc., at which most of the guests stand 1871. **3.** *Geom.* A straight line at right angles to a given line, plane, or surface 1571. Hence **Pe:rpendicula·rity,** verticality; p. position or direction. **Perpendi·cularly** *adv.*

†**Perpe·nsion.** 1646. [– late L. *perpensio* consideration, lit. 'exact weighing', f. *perpens-*, pa. ppl. stem of L. *perpendere*; see PERPEND, -ION.] Mental weighing; thorough consideration –1674.

†**Perpe·nsity.** [f. L. *perpensus* deliberate; see prec., -ITY.] Attention. SWIFT.

†**Perpe·ssion.** 1603. [– L. *perpessio*, f. *per* PER-[1] I. 2 + *passio* PASSION; see -ION.] Endurance of suffering –1659.

Perpetrable (pə̄·ɹpĕtrăb'l), *a.* [f. PERPETRATE *v.* + -ABLE.] Capable of being perpetrated.

Perpetrate (pə̄·ɹpĕtreᶦt), *v.* 1547. [– *perpetrat-*, pa. ppl. stem of L. *perpetrare* perform (in neutral sense), f. *per* PER-[1] 1 + *patrare* bring about; see -ATE[3].] *trans.* To perform, execute, or commit (a crime or evil deed; also (*colloq.*) a pun, or anything treated as shocking).

Sir Philip induced two of his sisters to p. a duet C. BRONTË. All the usual atrocities were perpetrated by the brutal soldiery 1855. Hence **Perpetra·tion,** the action of perpetrating (an evil deed); the action perpetrated; an atrocity. **Pe·rpetrator.**

Perpetuable (pəɹpe·tiu,ăb'l), *a. rare.* 1885. [f. PERPETUATE *v.* + -ABLE.] Capable of being perpetuated.

Perpetual (pəɹpe·tiu,ăl), *a.* (*adv.*) ME. [– (O)Fr. *perpétuel* – L. *perpetualis* (Quintilian, who uses it, with *universalis*, to render Gr. καθολικός), f. *perpetuus*, f. *perpes*, *-pet-* continuous, uninterrupted, f. *per* PER-[1] I. 2 + *petere* be directed towards; assim. to L. form XVI; see -AL[1].] **1.** Lasting for ever; eternal; permanent (during life). **b.** That is applicable, or remains valid for ever, or for an unlimited time 1450. **2.** Continuing or continued without intermission; continuous. late ME. **B.** *adv.* = Perpetually. late ME.

A. 1. [Mountains] enveloped in p. snow HUXLEY. *P. curate*, see CURATE 1; so *p. curacy, cure. P. motion*, motion that goes on for ever; *spec.* that of a hypothetical machine, which being once set in motion should go on for ever, or until stopped by external force or worn out. **b.** Phr. *P. injunction, settlement. P. calendar*, one that may be adjusted so as to supply information for any year or for many years. **2.** [It] will keep her spirits in a p. flutter 1755. Hence **Perpe·tually** *adv.* eternally; for the rest of one's life (*arch.*); incessantly; persistently. **Perpe·tualness.** †**Perpe·tualty,** = PERPETUITY 1.

Perpetuance (pəɹpe·tiu,ăns). 1558. [– OFr. *perpétuance*, f. *perpétuer* perpetuate; see -ANCE.] Perpetuation.

Perpe·tuate, *ppl. a.* 1503. [– L. *perpetuatus*, pa. pple. of *perpetuare*; see next, -ATE[2].] Made perpetual; perpetually continued.

Perpetuate (pəɹpe·tiu,eᶦt), *v.* 1530. [– *perpetuat-*, pa. ppl. stem of L. *perpetuare*, f. *perpetuus*; see PERPETUAL, -ATE[3].] *trans.* To make perpetual; to continue indefinitely; to preserve from extinction or oblivion.

Each courts its Mate, And in their Young themselves p. KEN. Hence **Perpetua·tion,** the action of perpetuating; permanent continuation. **Perpe·tuator.**

Perpetuity (pə̄ɹpĕtiū·ĭti). late ME. [– (O)Fr. *perpétuité* – L. *perpetuitas*, f. *perpetuus*; see PERPETUAL, -ITY.] **1.** The quality or state of being perpetual. **2.** A perpetual possession, tenure, or position. late ME. **b.** *Law.* Of an estate: The quality or condition of being inalienable perpetually, or for a period beyond certain limits fixed by the general law; an estate so restricted or perpetuated 1596. **3.** A perpetual annuity. Hence, The amount or number of years' purchase required to buy a perpetual annuity. 1806.

1. A third attribute of the king's majesty is his p...The king never dies BLACKSTONE. Phr. *In, to, for p.*, for ever, for an unlimited period. **2. b.** The Perpetual Advouson of Staplehurst,..is to be disposed of, either the P., or the next Presentation 1702.

†**Perplex,** *sb. rare.* 1652. [f. PERPLEX *v.*] Perplexity; entanglement –1762.

†**Perple·x,** *a.* late ME. [– (O)Fr. *perplexe* or L. *perplexus* involved, intricate, f. *per* PER-[1] 2 + *plexus*, pa. pple. of *plectere* plait, interweave, involve.] **1.** Perplexed, puzzled –1546. **2.** Of things: Intricate; involved, tangled –1684. Hence †**Perple·xly** *adv.* MILT.

Perplex (pəɹple·ks), *v.* 1595. [Back-formation from PERPLEXED.] **1.** *trans.* To fill (a person) with uncertainty as to the nature or treatment of a thing by reason of its involved or intricate character; to bewilder, puzzle. **2.** To make (a thing) uncertain through intricacy; to complicate, confuse 1619. **3.** To cause to become tangled; to entangle, intertwine; to intermingle 1620.

1. We are perplexed, but not in despaire 2 *Cor.* 4:8. Their contradictory accounts..serve only to p...the student 1855. **2.** It is possible by a cloud of unmeaning words to p. the question GROTE. **3.** Now to p. the ravell'd noose GOLDSM.

Perplexed (pəɹple·kst), *ppl. a.* 1477. [Extension of PERPLEX *a.* + -ED[1].] **1.** Involved in doubt and anxiety about a matter on account of its intricate character; bewildered, puzzled. Formerly: Troubled. **2.** Of things: Intricate, involved, complicated 1529. **3.** Of material objects: Intricate, entangled 1605. Hence **Perple·xed-ly** *adv.*, **-ness.**

Perplexing (pəɹple·ksiŋ), *ppl. a.* 1631. [f. PERPLEX *v.* + -ING[2].] That perplexes; causing perplexity.

With p. thoughts To interrupt the sweet of Life MILT.

Perplexity (pəɹple·ksĭti). ME. [– (O)Fr. *perplexité* or late L. *perplexitas*, f. *perplexus*; see PERPLEX *a.*, -ITY.] **1.** Puzzled condition, bewilderment, distraction. †**b.** Trouble, distress –1658. **2.** With *a* and *pl.* **a.** An instance of this condition 1451. **b.** Something that causes perplexity 1598. **3.** An entangled or confused state *of* anything 1664.

2. a. Accidents which produce perplexities, terrors, and surprises JOHNSON. **b.** The perplexities of Loue 1598.

Per pro.: see PER *prep.* I. 7.

Perquisite (pə̄·ɹkwizit). 1450. [– med.L. *perquisitum* acquisition, subst. use of n. of pa. pple. of L. *perquirere* search diligently for, f. *per* PER-[1] 2 + *quærere* seek.] †**1.** *Law.* Property acquired otherwise than by inheritance –1704. **2.** *Law.* Casual profits that come to the lord of a manor in addition to his regular revenue 1552. **3.** *gen.* Any casual emolument in addition to salary or wages 1565. **b.** Any article that has served its primary purpose, which subordinates or servants claim a customary right to take for their own use 1709. **c.** A customary 'tip' 1721. **d.** The emoluments of any office 1712. †**4.** *concr.* An adjunct of anything –1686. **5.** *fig.* A thing to which one has the sole right 1793.

3. The queen..is intitled to an antient p. called queen-gold, or *aurum reginæ* BLACKSTONE. *fig.* The best Perquisites of a Place are the Advantages it gives a Man of doing Good ADDISON. **4.** My wife very fine to-day, in her new suit of laced cuffs and perquisites PEPYS. **5.** The government kept a most jealous eye upon what it regarded as its own peculiar perquisites 1838.

Perquisition (pə̄ɹkwizi·ʃən). 1461. [– Fr. *perquisition* (XV) or late L. *perquisitio* investigation, research, f. *perquisit-*, pa. ppl. stem of L. *perquirere*; see prec., -ION.] †**1.** The gaining of something otherwise than by inheritance (*rare*). **2.** A thorough or diligent search; *spec.* (after Fr. use) a domiciliary or other search ordered by law for the discovery of a person, incriminating documents, etc. 1611.

Perradial (pəɹrēᶦ·diăl), *a.* 1880. [f. PERRADIUS + -AL[1].] *Zool.* Pertaining to the *perradii* of a cœlenterate; primarily radial. Also *sb.* a p. tentacle.

‖**Perradius** (pəɹrē·diŏs). *Pl.* **-ii** (-i,əi). 1880. [mod.L., f. PER-[1] 4 + RADIUS.] *Zool.* Each of the primary rays or radiating parts of certain cœlenterates.

†**Pe·rrie, -y.** Chiefly *poet.* ME. [– AFr. **perrie*, OFr. *pierrie*, for *p(i)errerie*, f. *pierre* stone; see -ERY 1.] Precious stones collectively; jewellery –1560.

†**Perrier.** late ME. [– OFr. *perrier*, *perrière* (mod. *pierrier*) :– med.L. *petrarium*, *petraria* in same sense, f. L. *petra* stone. Cf. PEDRERO, PETRARY.] A ballistic engine or cannon for discharging stones; later, = PEDRERO –1696.

Perron (pe·rǫn, ‖pęroṅ). late ME. [– (O)Fr. *perron* :– Rom. **petro*, *petron-*, augm. of L. *petra* stone; see -OON.] **1.** A large block or solid erection of stone, used as a platform, the base of a market-cross, etc. **2.** *Arch.* A platform, ascended by steps, in front of a church, mansion, etc., and upon which the door or doors open; sometimes applied to a double flight of steps ascending to such a front door 1723.

Perroquet, p. auk: see PARAKEET, PAROQUET.

Perruque: see PERUKE.

‖**Perruquier** (pęrükye). 1753. [Fr., f. *perruque* PERUKE; see -IER.] One who makes, dresses, or deals in perukes; a wig-maker.

†**Perry**[1], **pery, pirie.** [OE. *pir(i)ġe*, *pirie*, unexpl. var. of *pere*, *peru* PEAR. For the phonology, cf. MERRY.] A pear-tree. Also *attrib.* –1603.

Perry[2] (pe·ri). [ME. *pereye*, *perre(e*, *perrye* – OFr. *peré* :– Rom. **piratum*, f. L. *pirum* PEAR; see -Y[5].] A beverage resembling cider made from the juice of pears. Also *attrib.*

Persalt, per-salt (pə̄·ɹsǫlt). 1820. [f. PER-[1] II. + SALT.] *Chem.* A salt formed by combination of an acid with the peroxide of a metal.

Perscrutation (pə̄ɹskrutēᶦ·ʃən). 1603. [– Fr. †*perscrutation* – L. *perscrutatio*, f. *perscrut-*, pa. ppl. stem of *perscrutare*, f. *per* PER-[1] 2 + *scrutare* search closely; see -ION.] A thorough searching; careful scrutiny, examination.

Perse (pə̄ɹs), *a.* and *sb. arch.* [ME. *pers* – (O)Fr. *pers* :– med.L. *persus* fuscous (Reichenau Glosses), later also *perseus*, *persum*, *persicum*; of unkn. origin.] In early writers, Blue, bluish, bluish-grey; later, often taken (after Italian) as purplish black; also *sb.* the colour, or a stuff of the colour.

A long surcote of pers vp on he hade CHAUCER.

‖**Persea** (pə̄·ɹsiă). 1601. [L. – Gr. περσέα.] **a.** *Ancient Mythol.* A sacred fruit-bearing tree in Egypt and Persia. **b.** *Bot.* A genus of trees and shrubs, N.O. *Lauraceæ*, common in tropical America and the West Indies.

Persecute (pə̄·ɹsĭkiūt), *v.* 1477. [– (O)Fr. *persécuter*, back-formation from *persécuteur* PERSECUTOR.] †**1.** *trans.* To pursue, hunt, drive (with missiles, or with attempts to catch, kill, or injure) –1697. **2.** To pursue with malignancy or injurious action; *esp.* to oppress for holding a heretical opinion or belief 1482. **3.** To harass, worry; to importune 1585.

2. Blessed are ye when men shall revyle you, and p. you,..ffor my sake TINDALE *Matt.* 5:11. **3.** He may..p. with Rhyme POPE.

Persecution (pə̄ɹsĭkiū·ʃən). ME. [– (O)Fr. *persécution* – L. *persecutio*, f. as prec.; see -ION.] **1.** The action of persecuting, *esp.* the infliction of death, torture, or penalties for adherence to a particular religious belief or opinion; the fact of being persecuted; an instance of this. **b.** A particular course or period of systematic infliction of punishment directed against those holding a particular (religious) belief. late ME. **c.** *transf.* Persistent injury or annoyance from any source 1585. †**2.** The action of pursuing; prosecution (of an aim, etc.); quest –1647.

1. P. is a bad and indirect way to plant Religion SIR T. BROWNE. **c.** The..persecutions of the skie SHAKS.

Persecutive (pə̄·ɹsĭkiūtiv), *a. rare.* 1659. [f. PERSECUTE *v.* + -IVE.] Tending or addicted to persecution.

Persecutor (pə̄·ɹsĭkiūtəɹ). 1484. [– (O)Fr. *persécuteur* or late L. *persecutor*, f. *persecut-*, pa. ppl. stem of L. *persequi*, f. PER-[1] 1, 2 + *sequi* follow; see -OR 2. For the var. *persecuter*, see -ER[2] 3.] One who persecutes; *esp.* one who harasses others on account of opinions or beliefs. So **Pe·rsecutress, Pe·rsecutrix** (*rare*), a female p.

Perseid (pə̄·ɹsi,id). 1876. [– mod.L. *Perseis*, pl. *Perseides* – Gr. Περσηΐς, pl. -ιδες, daughter of Perseus; see -ID³.] *Astron. pl.* A group of meteors which appear to radiate from the constellation Perseus. Also *attrib.*

Perseity (pəɹsī·iti). 1694. [– med.L. *perseitas* (Duns Scotus), f. *per se* by itself, tr. Aristotle's καθ' αὑτό; see -ITY.] The quality or condition of existing independently, or of being predicated essentially of a subject.

Perseverance (pə̄ɹsīvī°·răns). ME. [– (O)Fr. *persévérance* – L. *perseverantia*, f. *perseverant-*, pr. ppl. stem of *perseverare*; see PERSEVERE, -ANCE.] **1.** The fact, process, condition, or quality of persevering; constant persistence in an undertaking; steadfast pursuit of an aim. **2.** *Theol.* Continuance in a state of grace leading finally to a state of glory 1555.

1. Job, Whose constant p. overcame Whate're his cruel malice could invent MILT. **2.** *Final p.*, *p. of the saints*, the doctrine that those who are elected to eternal life will never permanently lapse from grace or be finally lost: one of the 'Five points of Calvinism'.

Perseverant (pə̄ɹsīvī°·rănt), *a.* Now *rare.* ME. [– (O)Fr. *persévérant*, pr. pple. of *persévérer*; see next, -ANT.] Steadfast, persistent, persevering. Hence **Perseve·rantly** *adv.* (now *rare*).

Persevere (pə̄ɹsīvī°·ɹ), *v.* Also †**persever.** late ME. [– (O)Fr. *persévérer* – L. *perseverare* abide by strictly, persist, f. *perseverus* very strict; see PER-¹ 4, SEVERE.] **1.** *intr.* To continue steadfastly in a course of action (formerly, also, in a condition, state, or purpose), esp. in the face of difficulty; to continue constant. Const. *in*, *with.* †**b.** Const. *to* with *infin.* –1796. †**2. a.** To continue in a place, state or condition –1784. †**b.** Of things: To continue, last, endure –1696. †**3.** *trans.* To cause to continue; to keep constant, preserve –1655.

1. I will perseuer in my course of Loyalty SHAKS. Thrice happie if they know Thir happiness, and p. upright MILT. Hence **Perseve·ringly** *adv.*

Persian (pə·ɹʃăn). [Late ME. *persien*, *percien* (Chaucer, Gower) – OFr. *persien* – med.L. **Persianus* (repl. L. *Persicus*), f. (after *Asianus*) *Persia*, f. Gr. Περσίς – OPers. *pārsa* (mod. *pārs*, Arab. *fārs*); assim. to -IAN XVI.] **A.** *adj.* **1.** Of or pertaining to Persia, its inhabitants, or language. **2.** In specific names of productions found in or imported from Persia; e.g. *P. carpet*, etc. 1632. **3.** *Arch.* Applied to figures of men serving instead of columns to support entablatures 1727.

1. I do not like the fashion of your garments. You will say they are P. SHAKS. **2. P. berries,** the unripe fruit of *Rhamnus infectorius*, coming from Persia; **P. blinds** = PERSIENNES; **P. cat,** the Angora cat, with long silky hair, and thick bushy tail; **P. drill,** a hand drill operated by the movement of a nut backward and forward on the thread of a revolving screw, which carries the drill; **P. earth** = *Indian red*; **P. fire,** *Path.* = ANTHRAX 1; **P. insect-powder,** an insecticide made of the flowers of *Pyrethrum roseum*; **P. lily,** a fritillary (*Fritillaria persica*); **P. morocco,** a kind of morocco leather made from the skin of a hairy sheep called the Persian goat.

B. *sb.* **1.** A native or inhabitant of Persia. late ME. Also short for *P. cat*, *P. morocco.* **2.** The native language of Persia 1634. **3.** *Arch.* A male figure dressed in the ancient Persian manner serving instead of a column or pilaster to support an entablature 1823. †**4.** A thin soft silk, used for linings. Also called *Persia* or *P. silk.* –1838. **5.** = PERSIENNES 1786.

Persic (pə̄·ɹsik), *a.* and *sb.* 1606. [– L. *Persicus*, f. *Persæ* Persians; see -IC.] **A.** *adj.* = PERSIAN *a.* **B.** *sb.* The Persian tongue 1753.

‖**Persicaria** (pə̄ɹsikē°·riă). 1597. [– med. L. *persicaria* peachwort, water-pepper, f. L. *persicum* (*malum*) peach + *-aria* -ARY¹ 3.] The plant *Polygonum persicaria*, or Peachwort.

Persico(t (pə̄·ɹsiko, -kōᵘ, -kǫt). 1709. [– Fr. *persicot* (XVII), dim. of Savoy dial. *perse* peach – L. *persicum* (*malum*).] A cordial made by macerating the kernels of peaches, apricots, etc. in spirit.

‖**Persiennes** (pə̄ɹʃie·nz, ‖pęrsyęn), *sb. pl.* 1842. [Fr., fem. pl. used subst. of †*persien*; see PERSIAN.] Outside window-shutters, or blinds, made of light laths horizontally fastened to a frame, so as to be movable, like those of Venetian blinds.

‖**Persiflage** (pə̄·ɹsiflāʒ, ‖pęrsiflāʒ). 1757. [Fr., f. *persifler* banter, f. *per-* for *par-* + *siffler* whistle; see -AGE.] Light banter or raillery; a frivolous manner of treating any subject. So ‖**Persifleur** (pęrsiflör), a person addicted to p.

Persimmon (pəɹsi·mən). 1612. [Early forms *putchamin*, *pessemmin*, *posimon* – Algonquian word repr. by Cree *pasiminan*, Lenape *pasimenan.*] **1.** The plum-like fruit of the tree *Diospyros virginiana*; the American Date-plum; it is very astringent until softened by frost, when it becomes sweet and edible. Also, The large red fruit of the Japanese species *D. kaki.* **2.** (More fully *p.-tree.*) The tree *Diospyros virginiana* (N.O. *Ebenaceæ*). Also applied to Japanese P., *D. kaki*, and other species. 1737.

Persist (pəɹsi·st), *v.* 1538. [– L. *persistere*, f. *per* PER-¹ 2 + *sistere* stand.] **1.** *intr.* To continue firmly or obstinately *in* a state, opinion, purpose, or course of action, esp. against opposition. **b.** To persist in saying or asserting 1698. **2.** To remain in existence; to last 1760.

1. Thus to p. In doing wrong, extenuates not wrong SHAKS. **b.** [Callisthenes] persisted in his innocence to the last GOLDSM. **2.** The Calyx.. Persisting, till the Fruit is come to Maturity 1760. Hence **Persi·ster** (*rare*) one who persists.

Persistence (pəɹsi·stĕns). 1546. [In XVI – Fr. *persistance*, f. *persister* PERSIST; subseq. refash. after late and med.L. *persistentia*; see -ANCE, -ENCE.] **1.** The action or fact of persisting; obstinate continuance in a particular course. Also = PERSISTENCY 1. **2.** Continued existence in time or (*rarely*) in space; endurance; continuous occurrence 1621.

2. *P. of an impression*, the continuance of a sensible (esp. of a visual) impression after the exciting cause is removed. *P. of force* or *energy*, *p. of matter*, names for the two principles of the conservation of energy and the permanence of matter.

Persistency (pəɹsi·stĕnsi). 1597. [f. PERSISTENCE: see -ENCY; in XVI perh. – med. L. *persistentia.*] **1.** The quality of persisting or being persistent; also = PERSISTENCE 1. **2.** = PERSISTENCE 2. 1833.

Persistent (pəɹsi·stĕnt), *a.* 1826. [f. PERSISTENCE, or PERSIST, after *insist*/*insistence*/*insistent*; see -ENT.] **1.** Persisting in some action, course, etc., esp. against opposition, or in spite of failure 1830. **2.** Existing continuously in time; enduring 1853. **b.** Of an action or condition: Continuous; constantly repeated 1857. **3.** *spec.* **a.** *Zool.* and *Bot.* Of parts of animals and plants (as the horns, hair, calyces, etc.): Remaining after the period at which such parts in other cases fall off or wither; permanent; continuing; opp. to *deciduous* or *caducous* 1826. **b.** *Geol.* Of a stratum: Extending continuously over the whole area occupied by the formation 1833. Hence **Persi·stently** *adv.* So **Persi·sting** *ppl. a.* (in sense 3). **Persi·stingly** *adv.*

Persi·stive, *a.* 1606. [f. PERSIST *v.* + -IVE.] Persisting, tending to persist.

Person (pə̄·ɹsən, pə̄·ɹs'n), *sb.* ME. [– OFr. *persone* (mod. *personne*) :– L. *persona* mask used by a player, one who plays a part, character acted ('dramatis persona'), character or capacity in which one acts, person as having legal rights, human being, in Christian use of the Trinity (for Gr. ὑπόστασις). See PARSON.] **I.** A part played in a drama, or in life; hence, function, office, capacity; guise, semblance; character in a play or story. (Now chiefly in the phr. *in the p. of* = as representing.)

He comes to disfigure, or to present the p. of Moone-shine SHAKS.

II. An individual human being; a man, woman, or child ME. **b.** (Now only with qualification) A man or woman of distinction or importance; a personage. late ME.

Ninety and nine iust persons *Luke* 15:7. A p. in trade MISS BURNEY. *Young p.*, a young man or young woman; now esp. the latter, when the speaker does not desire to specify her position as 'woman' or 'lady'; They are not young ladies, they are young persons W. S. GILBERT. **b.** A man of my parts and talents..is a p. DRYDEN.

III. 1. The living body of a human being; either (*a*) the actual body, as distinct from clothing, etc., or from the mind or soul, or (*b*) the body with its clothing, etc. Usu. with *of* or possessive. ME. †**b.** (With qualifying adj.) A man or woman of (such and such) a figure –1805. **2.** The actual self of a man or woman, individual personality. With *of* or poss. late ME.

1. For her owne P., It beggerd all description SHAKS. One of his advantages was a fine p. GEO. ELIOT. **b.** A fair persone he was and fortunat CHAUCER. A pale thin p. of a man STERNE. **2.** Phr. *His* (*own*) *p.* = himself; *your p.* = yourself, you personally.

IV. *Law.* A human being (*natural p.*) or body corporate or corporation (*artificial p.*), having rights or duties recognized by law 1444.

V. *Theol.* **a.** Applied to the three modes of the divine being in the Godhead (Father, Son, and Holy Spirit) which together constitute the Trinity ME. **b.** The personality of Christ, esp. as uniting the two natures, divine and human 1562.

a. Þe trinite þat is o god and persones þre ME.

VI. *Gram.* Each of the three classes of pronouns, and corresponding distinctions in verbs, denoting respectively the person speaking (*first p.*), the person spoken to (*second p.*), and the person or thing spoken of (*third p.*); each of the different forms or inflexions expressing these distinctions 1520.

VII. *Zool.* Each individual of a compound or colonial organism; a zooid 1878.

Phr. *In one's* (*own*) *p.*, formerly also *in* (one's) *proper p.*: †**a.** = in person; **b.** In one's own character (not as representing another). *In p.*: personally; oneself. *In the p. of* (*in his* or *her p.*): **a.** as the representative of; **b.** embodied in; impersonated in; (as) personally represented by. *To accept, respect persons*, or *the p. of* any one, to look upon with favour (see *Ps.* 82:2, *Luke* 20:21, *Rom.* 2:11, etc.).

†**Pe·rson,** *v.* [f. prec.] = PERSONATE *v.* 4. MILT.

‖**Persona** (pəɹsōᵘ·nă). [L.; see PERSON *sb.*] **1. P. grata** (grēⁱ·tă), an acceptable person or personage: orig. applied to a diplomatic representative who is personally acceptable to the personage to whom he is accredited. **2.** *In propria persona*: see IN *Lat. prep.*

Personable (pə̄·ɹsənăb'l), *a.* late ME. [f. PERSON *sb.* (see III, IV) + -ABLE.] **1.** Having a well-formed person; handsome; presentable. (Now chiefly in literary use.) †**2.** *Law.* Having the status of a legal person (PERSON *sb.* IV), and as such competent to maintain a plea in court, or to take anything granted or given –1660.

1. Certainly, he was a p. young man 1890. Hence **Pe·rsonableness,** personal handsomeness.

Personage (pə̄·ɹsənėdʒ). 1461. [f. PERSON + -AGE; partly – med.L. *personagium* effigy, eccl. benefice (see PARSONAGE), partly – mod. Fr. (senses 3–5).] †**1.** A representation or figure of a person –1711. †**2.** = PERSON *sb.* III. 1. –1785. †**b.** = PERSON *sb.* III. 1 b. –1807. **3.** A person of high rank, distinction, or importance; a person of note. (Orig. always with *great* or the like.) 1503. **b.** A person; a man or woman (of unspecified status) 1555. †**4.** The sort of person any one is –1598. **5.** One of the characters of a drama, dramatic poem, story, etc. 1573. **b.** Hence, the acting of such a character, the part acted 1559.

2. The Armenians are..of comely P. 1680. **3.** He was fast becoming a p. DISRAELI. **b.** That ready-witted and helpful p. 1890. **5.** Only three speaking personages should appear at once upon the stage JOHNSON. **b.** Phr. *To take upon oneself, put on, play, assume the p. of*; also *fig.* and *transf.* in *to represent the p. of.*

Personal (pə̄·ɹsənăl), *a.* (*sb.*) late ME. [– OFr. *personal*, *-el* (mod. *personnel*) – L. *personalis*, f. *persona*; see PERSON, -AL¹.] **1.** Of, pertaining to, concerning or affecting the individual person or self; individual; private; one's own. **2.** Done, made, performed, held, etc. in person. late ME. †**b.** Present or engaged in person –1617. **3.** Of or pertaining to one's person, body, or figure; bodily. late ME. **4.** Directed to, aimed at, or referring to some particular person or to oneself personally, *spec.* in a hostile sense or manner 1614. **b.** *transf.* Making, or addicted to, personal remarks or reflections 1607. **5.** Of, pertaining to, or having the nature of a person, as opposed to a thing or abstraction 1651. **6.** *Law.* Opp. to *real*: †**a.** orig. in *p. action* (or *plea*), an action wherein the claim was the recovery of damages from the *person*; dist. from a *real* action, for the restitution of the thing itself, and from a *mixed* action in which both restitution and damages were demanded –1888. Hence **b.** *p. property* (*estate*, etc.), things recoverable in the personalty or by a personal action, i.e. chattels and chattel interests in land, or generally all property except land and those interests in land which pass on the owner's death to his heir (cf. REAL) 1544. **7.** *Gram.* Of or pertaining to the three persons; denoting one of these; esp. in *p. pronoun* 1481.

1. I know no personall cause, to spurne at him, But for the generall SHAKS. This is p. to himself 1874. *P.* EQUATION, *p.* IDENTITY; see these words. **2.** Bound by law to p. service in the cavalry 1844. Any p. interview 1880. **b.** When hee was personall in the Irish Warre SHAKS. **3.** He shall have no p. ill-usage SCOTT. The p. ornaments of the Bronze age 1865. **4.** P. invectives 1614, abuse 1801. The strong p. vanity of the man 1830. **b.** Where have I been particular? where p.? B. JONS. **5.** Grief is certainly a p. affection, of which a quality is not capable 1659. **6.** *P. contract*, one which depends upon the existence, or the personal qualities, skill, or services of one of the parties; e.g. a contract of marriage. *P. representative*, an executor or administrator. **7.** *P. verb*, a verb that has inflexions for all three persons (opp. to *impersonal*; now *rare*).

B. *sb. pl.* Personal matters or things; †*spec.* personal property, personalty. 1497. **b.** *pl.* Short for *p. remarks* (now rare), *p. paragraphs* (U.S.), *p. pronouns* (rare).

Personalism (pɔ̄·ɹsənăliz'm). 1846. [f. prec. + -ISM.] The quality or character of being personal; variously used to denote some personal theory, method, characteristic, etc.

Personality (pɔ̄ɹsənæ·lĭti). late ME. [– OFr. *personalité* (mod. *-onn-*) – late L. *personalitas*, f. L. *personalis*; see PERSONAL, -ITY.] **1.** The quality or fact of being a person; that quality which makes a being personal. **b.** The property ascribed to the Deity of consisting of distinct persons (see PERSON *sb.* V.) 1492. **c.** Personal existence; personal identity 1835. **2.** Distinctive individual character, esp. when of a marked kind 1795. **3.** A personal being, a person 1678. **4.** The fact of relating to an individual person, or to particular persons; *spec.* the quality of being aimed at an individual, esp. in a hostile way 1772. **b.** (Usu. in *pl.*) A statement or remark aimed at or referring to an individual person 1769. **5.** *Law.* = PERSONALTY (*rare*) 1658.

1. These capacities constitute p., for they imply consciousness and thought PALEY. **c.** The age of Homer is surrounded with darkness, his very p. with doubt RUSKIN. **4.** He had attacked Wolsey himself with somewhat vulgar p. 1856. **b.** The Senator resorted to personalities 1850.

Personalize (pɔ̄·ɹsənăləiz), *v.* 1727. [f. PERSONAL *a.* + -IZE.] *trans.* To render personal; to personify; to impersonate. Hence **Pe:rsonaliza·tion.**

Personally (pɔ̄·ɹsənăli), *adv.* late ME. [f. PERSONAL *a.* + -LY².] In a personal manner, capacity, etc. **1.** In person: = (by) himself, themselves, etc. **b.** In objective sense, expressing the relation of an action, feeling, etc. to the actual person mentioned 1483. **2.** As a person 1597. **3.** In one's personal capacity; as regards oneself; *esp.* 'for myself' 1849.

1. He..must..answer the damage p. 1765. Phr. *P. conducted*, conducted by some one in person. **b.** The amended writ ought to have been served on them p. 1891. **2.** God the Word, when He took human nature, came into it p. PUSEY. **3.** P. I don't despair 1902.

Personalty (pɔ̄·ɹsŏnălti). 1481. [– law AFr. *personalté*, f. *personal*; see PERSONAL, -TY¹, -Y⁵.] †**a.** (See quot.) **b.** Personal goods, personal estate; also *gen.* personal belongings.

a. Actions were said to be or to sound *in the realty* or *in the p.*, according to the nature of the relief afforded therein. Next the terms, *the realty, the p.* were applied to the things recoverable in real or personal actions 1888.

Personate (pɔ̄·ɹsŏnĕt), *a.* 1597. [– L. *personatus* masked, feigned, f. *persona* mask; see PERSON, -ATE².] †**1.** Personated, counterfeit –1822. †**2.** Personal; impersonated –1689. **3.** *Bot.* Mask-like; applied to a two-lipped corolla having the opening between the lips closed by an upward projection of the lower lip, as in the snapdragon. (Dist. from *ringent*). 1760.

Personate (pɔ̄·ɹsŏneᶦt), *v.* 1591. [– *personat-*, pa. ppl. stem of late L. *personare* (Boethius), f. *persona*; see PERSON, -ATE³.] **1.** *trans.* To act or play the part of (a character in a drama, etc.); to act (a drama, etc.); to represent dramatically 1598. **b.** To assume the character of 1704. **c.** *absol.* To play or act a part 1642. **2.** To pretend to be (another), usually for purposes of fraud 1613. †**3.** To counterfeit (a quality) –1633. †**4.** To represent (a person, etc.) in writing (*esp.* as saying so and so); occas., to symbolize –1693. **5.** To stand for, represent, symbolize, signify; to stand in the place of; to impersonate. Now *rare* or *Obs.* 1611. †**6.** To represent as a person (*rare*) –1823.

1. They [i.e. Stage-players] can act to the life those whom they p. 1647. **c.** The actor's first duty ..is..to p. SIR H. IRVING. **2.** A yong woman.. that personated a man 1694. **3.** His sorrow is not personated 1633. **5.** *Cymb.* v. v. 454. Hence **Pe·rsonated** *ppl. a.* acted, feigned; also = prec. 3. **Persona·tion,** the action of personating (in various senses). **Pe·rsonator.**

Personeity (pɔ̄ɹsŏnī·ĭti). *rare.* 1822. [irreg. f. PERSON, after *corporeity*.] **a.** That which constitutes a person. **b.** *concr.* A personal being. COLERIDGE.

Personification (pəɹsǫ:nifikēᶦ·ʃən). 1755. [f. next; see -FICATION.] **1.** The act of personifying; esp. as a rhetorical figure or species of metaphor. **b.** An imaginary person conceived as representing a thing or abstraction 1850. **2.** A person or thing viewed as embodying a quality, etc., or as exemplifying it in a striking manner; an 'incarnation' (*of* something) 1807. **3.** A dramatic representation, or literary description, of a person or thing 1814.

1. The personifications of church and country as females 1875. **2.** He was popularly regarded as the p. of the Latitudinarian spirit MACAULAY.

Personify (pəɹsǫ·nifəi), *v.* 1727. [– Fr. *personnifier* (Boileau), f. *personne*; see PERSON, -FY.] **1.** *trans.* To figure or represent (a thing or abstraction) as a person, esp. in speech or writing; in art, to symbolize by a figure in human form. **2.** To embody (a quality, etc.) in one's person or self; to exemplify in a typical manner. Chiefly in *pa. pple.* 1803.

1. Greek philosophy has a tendency to p. ideas JOWETT. **2.** The natives of this country are rashness personified 1803. Hence **Perso·nifier,** one who personifies.

†**Personize** (pɔ̄·ɹsənəiz), *v.* 1593. [f. PERSON + -IZE.] **1.** *intr.* To act a part –1593. **2.** *trans.* To personify –1762.

2. Milton has Personiz'd them 1734.

‖**Personnel** (pəɹsŏne·l). 1857. [Fr., subst. use of *personnel* adj., as contrasted with *matériel*.] The body of persons engaged in any service or employment, esp. in a public institution, as an army, navy, hospital, etc.; the human equipment (*of* an institution, etc.).

†**Perspe·ction.** 1549. [– late L. *perspectio*, f. as next; see -ION.] A looking through, into, or at something; contemplation; outlook. *lit.* and *fig.* –1682.

Eye-gate was the place of p. BUNYAN.

Perspective (pəɹspe·ktiv), *sb.* late ME. [– med.L. *perspectiva* (sc. *ars*), subst. use of fem. of late L. *perspectivus* (Boethius), f. *perspect-*, pa. ppl. stem of *perspicere* look at closely, f. *per* PER-¹ 1 + *specere* look.] **I.** †**1.** The science of sight; optics –1658. †**2.** An optical instrument for viewing objects with –1789.

2. Phr. *To look through the wrong end of the p.*, to look upon something as of less importance than it is.

II. 1. The art of delineating solid objects upon a plane surface so as to produce the same impression of relative positions and magnitudes, or of distance, as the actual objects do when viewed from a particular point. (Formerly also *pl.* in same sense.) 1583. **b.** *transf.* The appearance presented by visible objects, in regard to relative position, apparent distance, etc. **c.** *Mod. Geom.* = HOMOLOGY 4. 1857. **d.** *fig.* The proportion in which the parts of a subject are viewed by the mind 1605. **2.** *concr.* A drawing or picture in perspective; a 'view' 1644. †**b.** A picture or figure constructed so as to produce some fantastic effect –1610. **3.** A visible scene, view, or prospect; *esp.* a vista 1620.

1. AERIAL *p.*, ISOMETRIC *p.*, LINEAR *p.*: see these words. *Angular* or *oblique p.*, that in which neither side of the principal object is parallel to the plane of delineation. **d.** Evolution..has thrown the universe into a fresh p. 1894. **2.** Hogarth's lively p. of Cheapside THACKERAY. **b.** *Rich II*, II. ii. 18. **3.** The lofty towers and long perspectives of the church GRAY. *fig.* I saw a long p. of felicity before me GOLDSM.

Phr. *In p.*, **a.** in mental view; in prospect; **b.** drawn or viewed in accordance with the principles of p.; also *fig.*

†**III.** Close inspection; insight –1649.

Perspective (pəɹspe·ktiv), *a.* late ME. [– late L. *perspectivus*; see prec., -IVE.] **I.** †**1.** Relating to sight; optical –1592. †**2.** Useful for looking or viewing; applied to various instruments, etc. Usu. in phr. *p. glass* = prec. I. 2. Also *fig.* –1729.

II. Of or pertaining to, or drawn according to, perspective 1606. Hence **Perspe·ctively** *adv.* †optically; †clearly; in perspective.

†**Pe·rspicable,** *a.* 1660. [– late L. *perspicabilis* (after *conspicabilis*), or f. contemp. Eng. *conspicable* by substitution of prefix. Cf. med.L. *perspicari* see clearly.] Capable of being beheld; visible –1665.

Perspicacious (pɔ̄ɹspikēᶦ·ʃəs), *a.* 1616. [f. L. *perspicax, -ac-*, f. *perspicere*; see PERSPECTIVE *sb.*, -ACIOUS.] **1.** Of clear and penetrating sight; clear-sighted. *arch.* **2.** Of penetrating mental vision or discernment 1640. Hence **Perspica·cious-ly** *adv.*, **-ness.**

Perspicacity (pɔ̄ɹspikæ·sĭti). 1548. [– Fr. *perspicacité* or late L. *perspicacitas*, f. L. *perspicax*; see prec., -ITY.] **1.** Keenness of sight. *Obs.* or *arch.* 1607. **2.** Clearness of understanding; penetration, discernment. So †**Pe·rspicacy.**

†**Pe·rspicil.** 1611. [– mod.L. *perspicillum*, f. L. *perspicere* see through + *-illum* dim. and instr. suffix. Cf. med.L. *perspicilia* 'lunettes.'] An optic glass; a lens; a telescope or microscope. Also *fig.* –1680.

Perspicuity (pɔ̄ɹspikiū·ĭti). 1477. [– L. *perspicuitas*, f. *perspicuus*, f. *perspicere*; see PERSPECTIVE *sb.*, -ITY.] †**1.** Transparency, translucency –1750. **2.** Clearness of statement or exposition; lucidity 1546. †**3.** Conspicuousness (*rare*) –1634. ¶**4.** *improp.* Perspicacity 1662.

Perspicuous (pəɹspi·kiu,əs), *a.* 1477. [f. as prec. + -OUS.] †**1.** Transparent, translucent –1750. **2.** Clear; clearly expressed, lucid; evident 1586. **b.** Of persons: Clear in statement or expression 1593. †**3.** Conspicuous –1805. ¶**4.** *improp.* Perspicacious (*rare*) 1584.

2. The most p. and energetick language BOSWELL. **b.** Prethee.., be plaine and p. with mee DEKKER. Hence **Perspi·cuous-ly** *adv.*, **-ness.**

Perspirable (pəɹspəiᵊ·răb'l), *a.* 1604. [f. PERSPIRE + -ABLE, partly through Fr. *perspirable* (Paré).] **1.** Capable of perspiring; liable to perspire. **b.** Of, pertaining to, or attended with perspiration 1805. †**2.** Liable to be blown through; airy –1669. **3.** Capable of being thrown off in perspiration 1646.

1. b. *P. point*, point of perspiration. Hence **Perspirabi·lity,** liability to perspire.

Perspiration (pɔ̄ɹspĭrēᶦ·ʃən). 1611. [– Fr. *perspiration* (Paré), f. *perspirer*, f. L. *perspirare*; see PERSPIRE, -ATION.] †**1.** Breathing out or through –1710. †**2.** Evaporation, exhalation –1707. **3.** The excretion of moisture through the pores of the skin; sweating 1626. **4.** *concr.* That which is perspired; sweat 1725.

Perspirative (pəɹspəiᵊ·rătiv, pɔ̄·ɹspireᶦtiv), *a. rare.* 1730. [f. PERSPIRE *v.* + -ATIVE, after *purgative*.] = next.

Perspiratory (pəɹspəiᵊ·rătəri), *a.* 1725. [f. PERSPIRAT(ION + -ORY².] **1.** Promoting or subservient to perspiration. **2.** Of, pertaining to, or of the nature of perspiration 1805.

Perspire (pəɹspəiᵊ·ɹ), *v.* 1646. [– Fr. †*perspirer* (Paré) – L. *perspirare* breathe everywhere, f. *per* PER-¹ 1 + *spirare* breathe.] †**1.** *intr.* Of the wind: To breathe gently through. HERRICK. †**2.** *intr.* Of any volatile matter: To pass out or escape through pores; to evaporate; to exhale –1799. **3.** *intr.* To give out watery fluid through the pores of the skin. (Now the ordinary sense.) 1725. **4.** *trans.* To give off (liquid) through pores, either insensibly as vapour, or sensibly as moisture; said of organic bodies. Also *fig.* 1707.

2. The cork being..porous, part of the spirits..p. 1676. **4.** After the blossom unfolds it perspires a sweet honey-like fluid 1837.

Perstringe (pəɹstri·ndʒ), *v.* 1549. [– L. *perstringere*, f. PER-¹ 2 + *stringere* tie, bind.] **1.** To censure; to criticize adversely. †**2.** To touch on; to glance at –1797. †**3.** To dull (the eyes, or light); to dazzle; to dim –1664. Hence †**Perstri·ction** (*rare*), stricture.

Persuadable (pəɹswēⁱ·dăb'l), *a.* 1530. [f. PERSUADE *v.* + -ABLE.] †**1.** Persuasive –1530. **2.** = PERSUASIBLE 2. 1598. Hence **Persuadabi·lity, Persua·dableness; Persua·dably** *adv.*

Persuade (pəɹswēⁱ·d), *v.* 1513. [– L. *persuadēre*, f. *per* PER-¹ 1 + *suadēre* advise, recommend. Cf. (O)Fr. *persuader*.] **I.** To persuade *a person.* **1.** *trans.* To induce (a person) to believe something. Const. *that* (a thing is so); *of* (a fact, etc.), rarely *into, out of* (a belief, etc.). Somewhat *arch.* Also *refl.* Also *absol.* **b.** *pa. pple.* Led to believe; assured, sure 1553. **2.** To prevail upon (a person) to do something. Const. *to* with *inf.*; *to, unto, into* (an action); also *from, out of.* Also *absol.* 1513. †**3.** To seek to induce (a person) to (or from) a belief, a course of action, etc.; eo assure (one) *that*; to counsel strongly –1801.

1. These..perswade women that they can foretell them their fortune 1600. *refl.* Yet can I not perswade me thou art dead MILT. **2.** To p. the lady into a private marriage 1771. The man was persuaded to open the door 1875.

II. To persuade *a thing.* †**1.** To induce belief of (a fact, statement, etc.); to prove –1685. **2.** To lead one to do or practise; to urge successfully upon one (*arch.*) 1538. †**3.** To urge (a statement, opinion, etc.) as credible or true; to go to prove, make probable –1687. †**4.** To commend to adoption, advise, advocate, recommend (an act, course, etc.) –1781.

2. Your King..Sends me a Paper to perswade me Patience SHAKS. **3.** Disputing and perswading the things concerning the Kingdom of God *Acts* 19:8.

III. *intr.* To use persuasion; to succeed in bringing over or inducing 1526.

How I perswaded, how I praid, and kneel'd SHAKS. Phr. †*To p. with*, to use persuasion with, plead with; occas., to prevail with; †*fig.* to prevail or avail with. Hence **Persua·ded** *ppl. a.* prevailed upon; convinced; induced by persuasion; †proved. **Persua·ded-ly** *adv.*, **-ness.**

Persuader (pəɹswēⁱ·dəɹ). 1538. [f. prec. + -ER¹.] One who or that which persuades; esp. (*slang*) a weapon, spurs, etc.

Persuasible (pəɹswēⁱ·sĭb'l, -zĭb'l), *a.* late ME. [– L. *persuasibilis*, f. as next; see -IBLE.] †**1.** Persuasive –1647. **2.** Capable of being persuaded; open to persuasion 1502. †**3.** Credible, plausible –1643. Hence **Persuasibi·lity, Persua·sibleness,** the quality of being p. **Persua·sibly** *adv.*

Persuasion (pəɹswēⁱ·ʒən). late ME. [– L. *persuasio*, f. *persuas-*, pa. ppl. stem of *persuadēre*; see PERSUADE, -ION. Cf. (O)Fr. *persuasion*.] **1.** The action, or an act, of persuading or seeking to persuade; the presenting of inducements or winning arguments to a person to induce him to do or believe something. †**b.** An argument or inducement –1624. **c.** Persuasiveness 1601. **2. a.** The fact or condition of being persuaded; conviction, assurance 1534. **b.** with *pl.* A belief, conviction 1510. **3.** *spec.* Religious belief or opinion; a creed 1623. Hence **b.** A sect holding a particular belief, a denomination 1727. **c.** *slang.* Nationality; sex; kind; sort; description 1864.

1. The English Lords By his perswasion, are againe falne off SHAKS. **c.** Ist possible that my deserts to you Can lacke perswasion? SHAKS. **2. a.** My doubts were..converted into a full p. 1777. **3.** All his Subjects of what perswasion soever *Bk. Com. Prayer*. Pref. The Roman Catholic p. 1813. **b.** The Essenes, a p. that reject pleasure as a positive evil 1863. **c.** A dark little man..of French p. 1903.

Persuasive (pəɹswēⁱ·siv, -ziv), *a.* and *sb.* 1589. [– Fr. *persuasif, -ive*, or med.L. *persuasivus*, f. as prec.; see -IVE.] **A.** *adj.* Having the power of persuading; winning. **B.** *sb.* Something adapted to persuade; a motive or inducement presented 1641.

A. A most p. Preacher 1639. Hence **Persua·sive-ly** *adv.*, **-ness.** So **Persua·sory** *a.* = PERSUASIVE *a.* (now *rare* or *Obs.*).

†**Pe·rsue.** Also **parcy,** etc. 1530. [app. orig. *parcee, *percee – Fr. *percée* act of piercing. Later confused with *pursue*.] *Venery.* The track of blood left by a stricken deer or other wounded beast of the chase –1661.

Persulphate (pəɹsʌ·lfĕt). 1813. [PER-¹ II. b.] *Chem.* That sulphate which contains the greatest proportion of oxygen, or of the sulphuric acid radical SO_4; as *p. of iron*, now named *ferric sulphate*, $Fe_2(SO_4)_3$; etc.

Persulphide (pəɹsʌ·lfəid). 1856. [PER-¹ II.] *Chem.* That sulphide of any element or basic radical which contains the greatest proportion of sulphur; orig. called *persulphuret.*

Pert (pɔ̄ɹt), *a.* (*sb., adv.*) ME. [– OFr. *apert* – L. *apertus* open, pa. pple. of *aperire*; partly blended with OFr. *aspert, espert* :– L. *expertus* expert.] **I.** †**1.** Open, unconcealed; manifest –1579. †**2.** Of personal appearance. **a.** (in early use) Beautiful. **b.** (later) Smart, dapper. –1684. **II.** †**a.** Expert, skilled; ready –1500. **b.** Sharp, intelligent; adroit, clever. late ME. **III. 1.** Forward in speech and behaviour; saucy, 'cheeky', malapert. Now the ordinary sense. late ME. †**b.** As a vague expression of disfavour –1752. **2.** Bold (esp. in a bad sense); forward; audacious. *Obs.* (exc. as merged in prec.) 1535. **3.** Lively; brisk, sprightly; in good spirits, 'jolly'. Often used of the state of an invalid: 'bright', 'chirpy' (esp. in form *peart*). Now *dial.* and *U.S.* 1581.

1. The p. talk of children 1702. As p. a genius as the applause of a common-room ever..spoiled DISRAELI. **b.** A p. bad apartment H. WALPOLE. **3.** The p. Fairies and the dapper Elves MILT. Quick she had always been and 'peart', as we say on Exmoor BLACKMORE.

B. *sb.* (the adj. used *absol.*) A pert person or thing. late ME.

C. *adv.* or quasi-*adv.*: in various senses of the adj. late ME. Hence **Pe·rt-ly** *adv.*, **-ness.**

Pertain (pəɹtēⁱ·n), *v.* [Late ME. *partene, -teine* repr. tonic stem of OFr. *partenir* – L. *pertinēre* extend, tend or belong (to), f. *per* PER-¹ 1 + *tenēre* hold; cf. CONTAIN.] **1.** *intr.* To belong; e.g. as a native, as part of a whole, as an accessory, as dependent, etc. Const. *to.* **b.** To belong as one's care or concern. *To p. to*: to concern. *Obs.* or *arch.* late ME. **c.** To be appropriate *to.* late ME. **2.** To have reference, relate *to.* late ME. †**3.** Phr. *As pertains to* (used impersonally), *as pertaining to* = as regards, in relation to. –1568.

1. If she pertaine to life, let her speake too SHAKS. **b.** The cares of war P. to all men born in Troy 1870. **c.** The things which perteine to peace 1577. **2.** This law pertains, first to vows made to God himself 1770.

Pertinacious (pɔ̄ɹtinēⁱ·ʃəs), *a.* 1626. [f. L. *pertinax, -ac-* (f. *per* PER-¹ 4 + *tenax* tenacious) + -OUS.] Persistent or stubborn in holding to one's own opinion or design; resolute; obstinate. Chiefly as a bad quality. **b.** Obstinately or persistently continuing 1646.

P. importunity 1626. As p. as ivy climbing a wall 1805. Hence **Pertina·cious-ly** *adv.*, **-ness.**

Pertinacity (pɔ̄ɹtinæ·sĭti). 1504. [– Fr. *pertinacité* or med.L. *pertinacitas*, f. as prec.; see -ITY.] The quality of being pertinacious; persistency; usu. in a bad sense: perverse obstinacy or stubbornness. So †**Pe·rtinacy.** late ME.

†**Pe·rtinate,** *a.* 1534. [irreg. formation, perh. after *intimate, intimacy*, etc.] = PERTINACIOUS –1552. So †**Pe·rtinately** *adv.* late ME.

Pertinence (pɔ̄·ɹtinĕns). late ME. [In sense 1 – OFr. *partenance, pertinence*, f. *partenant*, pr. pple. of *partenir* (see PERTAIN); in 2 f. PERTINENT; see -ENCE.] †**1.** = PURTENANCE, APPURTENANCE 1, 2. –1552. **2.** The fact of being pertinent 1659.

Pertinency (pɔ̄·ɹtinĕnsi). 1598. [f. as PERTINENCE; see -ENCY.] **1.** The quality of being pertinent; relevancy, appositeness. †**2.** = APPURTENANCE 1. 1651.

1. Loving p., and by consequence brevitie FLORIO.

Pertinent (pɔ̄·ɹtinĕnt), *a.* and *sb.* late ME. [– (O)Fr. *pertinent* or L. *pertinens, -ent-*, pr. pple. of *pertinēre*; see PERTAIN, -ENT.] **A.** *adj.* †**1.** Pertaining or belonging (*to*) –1635. †**2.** Appropriate, suitable in nature or character –1697. **3.** Pertaining to the matter in hand; relevant; apposite. Const. *to.* late ME.

3. Judges who make p. remarks on the case JOWETT.

B. *sb.* (Chiefly *Sc.*) A minor property, appurtenance. Usu. in *pl.* late ME. Hence **Pe·rtinent-ly** *adv.*, **-ness** (*rare*).

Perturb (pəɹtɔ̄·ɹb), *v.* late ME. [– OFr. *pertourber* – L. *perturbare*, f. *per* PER-¹ 2 + *turbare* disturb, confuse.] **1.** *trans.* To disturb greatly (physically); to unsettle, derange, throw into confusion. **2.** To disturb greatly (mentally); to agitate, discompose ME.

2. His childish imagination was perturbed at a phenomenon for which he could not account SCOTT. Hence †**Pertu·rbance,** great disturbance; molestation; perturbation. **Pertu·rbed** *ppl. a.* disquieted, agitated; confused, deranged. **Pertu·rbedly** *adv.* **Pertu·rber,** a disturber, troubler.

Perturbate (pɔ̄·ɹtʌɹbeⁱt, pəɹtɔ̄·ɹbeⁱt), *a.* 1570. [– L. *perturbatus*, pa. pple. of *perturbare*; see next, -ATE².] Disturbed, put out of order.

Perturbate (pɔ̄·ɹtʌɹbeⁱt, pəɹtɔ̄·ɹbeⁱt), *v. rare.* 1547. [– *perturbat-*, pa. ppl. stem of L. *perturbare*; see PERTURB, -ATE³.] *trans.* = PERTURB. Hence **Pe·rturbator** (now *rare*) = PERTURBER.

Perturbation (pɔ̄ɹtʌɹbēⁱ·ʃən). late ME. [– (O)Fr. *perturbation* – L. *perturbatio*, f. as prec.; see -ION.] **1.** The action of perturbing; the fact or condition of being perturbed; disorder; mental agitation; trouble. Also occas. cause of disturbance. **2.** Disturbance of the regular order or course 1567. **b.** *Astron.* The deviation of a heavenly body from its theoretically regular orbit, caused by the attraction of bodies other than its primary, or by the imperfectly spherical form of the latter 1812.

1. *Rich. III*, V. iii. 161, 2 *Hen. IV*, IV. v. 23. These various perturbations of mind, which are characteristic of a bad conscience NEWMAN. Hence **Perturba·tional** *a.* of, pertaining to, of the nature of p.

Perturbative (pəɹtɔ̄·ɹbătiv, pɔ̄·ɹtʌɹbeⁱtiv), *a.* 1638. [– late and med.L. *perturbativus*, f. as prec.; see -IVE.] Causing or apt to cause perturbation or disturbance.

Pertuse (pəɹtiū·s), *a. rare.* 1721. [– L. *pertusus*, pa. pple. of *pertundere* punch or bore into a hole, f. *per* PER-¹ 1 + *tundere* beat.] Bored through, pierced with holes; spec. in *Bot.*, applied to a leaf. So **Pertu·sed** *a.* †**Pertu·sion,** the action of punching or boring; a hole punched or bored 1626.

‖**Pertussis** (pəɹtʌ·sis). 1799. [mod.L., f. PER-¹ 4 + *tussis* cough.] *Path.* = WHOOPING-COUGH. Hence **Pertu·ssal** *a.*

Peruke (pĕrū·k), *sb.* 1547. [– Fr. *perruque* (XV, †head of hair) – It. *perrucca, parrucca*, of unkn. origin. See PERIWIG.] †**1.** A natural head of hair –1590. **2.** A periwig or wig 1565. **3.** *attrib.*, as *p.- block*, etc. 1547. Hence **Peru·ke** *v. trans. rare*, to furnish with a p.

Perule (pe·rŭl). 1825. [– Fr. *pérule* – mod.L. *perula*, dim. of *pera* – Gr. πήρα purse, wallet.] *Bot.* †**a.** The covering of a seed. **b.** The scaly covering of a leaf-bud. **c.** A kind of sac formed by the adherent bases of the two lateral sepals in certain orchids.

Perusal (pĕrū·zăl). 1600. [f. next + -AL¹.]

1. Survey, examination, scrutiny. *Obs.* or *arch.* 1602. **2.** A reading through or over.

1. He fals to such perusall of my face, As he would draw it SHAKS.

Peruse (pĕrū·z), *v.* 1479. [prob. based on AL. **perusare, perusitare* use up (XIV), f. L. *per* PER-¹ 4 + Rom. **usare* (see USE *v.*), L. *usitari* use often, frequent. f. *us-* USE *sb.*] †**1.** *trans.* To use up –1570. †**2.** *trans.* To go through, deal with, describe, examine (a number of things) one by one –1716. **b.** To consider in detail (*arch.*) 1533. **c.** To travel through scrutinizingly. *Obs.* exc. *dial.* 1523. **3.** *intr.* †To go from one to another of a series, to continue; to travel (*joc.*) 1523. †**4.** *trans.* To go over (a writing, etc.) again; to revise –1632. †**b.** To go through (a book) critically; to criticize; to set forth or expound critically –1551. **5.** To read through or over; hence (loosely) to read 1532.

2. b. My self I then perus'd, and Limb by Limb Survey'd MILT. **5.** I will show what to turn over unread and what to p. STEELE. Hence **Peru·se** *sb.* †perusal; *sailors' colloq.* a 'look round' ashore. **Peru·ser.**

Peruvian (pĕrū·viăn), *a.* (*sb.*) 1663. [f. mod.L. *Peruvia,* latinized name of the country, + -AN.] Of, pertaining to, or native to Peru, in South America.

P. bark, the bark of the Cinchona tree; see BARK *sb.*¹ 6, CINCHONA.

B. *sb.* A native or inhabitant of Peru. **b.** *pl.* Peruvian stocks, bonds, etc. 1656.

Pervade (pəɹvēⁱ·d), *v.* 1653. [– L. *pervadere,* f. *per* PER-¹ 1 + *vadere* go, walk.] **1.** *trans.* To pass through; to flow or extend through. Now *rare* 1656. **2.** To diffuse itself throughout; to permeate, saturate 1659. **b.** *intr.* To diffuse itself. Now *rare.* 1653.

1. I pervaded Westminster Hall and looked into most of the Courts 1892. **2.** An ardent spirit of enquiry pervaded. .Europe 1791. Hence **Perva·ding-ly** *adv.*, **-ness. Perva·sion,** the action of pervading; the condition of being pervaded. **Perva·sive** *a.* having the quality or power of pervading; **-ly** *adv.*; **-ness.**

Perverse (pəɹvə̄·ɹs), *a.* late ME. [– (O)Fr. *pervers, -e* – L. *perversus, -a,* pa. pple. of *pervertere* PERVERT *v.*] **1.** Turned away from what is right; perverted; wicked. **b.** Incorrect; wrong 1568. **c.** *spec.* Of a verdict: against the weight of evidence or the direction of the judge on a point of law 1854. **2.** Obstinate or persistent in what is wrong; self-willed or stubborn (in error) 1579. **3.** Disposed to be obstinately contrary to what is true or good or to go counter to what is reasonable or required. late ME. †**b.** Of things or events: Adverse, unpropitious –1713.

1. O faithless and p. generation, how long shall I be with you *Matt.* 17:17. **2.** P. neglect of the most salutary precepts JOHNSON. **3.** I married the most p. woman in the world 1660. Hence †**Perve·rsed** *ppl. a.* (chiefly *Sc.*) = sense 1; †**-ly** *adv.*; †**-ness. Perve·rse-ly** *adv.*, **-ness.**

Perversion (pəɹvə̄·ɹʃən). late ME. [– L. *perversio,* f. *pervers-,* pa. ppl. stem of *pervertere*; see PERVERT *v.*, -ION. Cf. Fr. *perversion.*] The action of perverting or condition of being perverted; turning aside from truth or right; diversion to an improper use; corruption, distortion; *spec.* change to error in religious belief (opp. to CONVERSION II. 1); *transf.* a perverted form *of* something.

Women to govern men,. .slaves freemen,. .being total violations and perversions of the laws of nature and nations BACON.

Perversity (pəɹvə̄·ɹsĭti). 1528. [– (O)Fr. *perversité* or L. *perversitas,* f. *perversus*; see PERVERSE, -ITY.] Perverseness.

Perversive (pəɹvə̄·ɹsiv), *a.* 1817. [f. PERVERT *v.*, after *subvert/subversive*; see -IVE.] Having the character or quality of perverting in nature, character, or use.

Pervert (pəɹvə̄·ɹt), *v.* late ME. [– (O)Fr. *pervertir,* or its source L. *pervertere* turn round or the wrong way, overturn, ruin, corrupt, f. *per* PER-¹ 2, 3 + *vertere* turn.] †**1.** To turn upside down; to upset; to subvert –1656. **2.** To turn aside from its right course, aim, meaning, etc. late ME. †**b.** To divert SHAKS. **3.** *trans.* To turn (a person, the mind, etc.) away from right opinion or action; to lead astray; to corrupt. late ME. **b.** *spec.* To turn (any one) aside from a right religious belief or system. late ME. **c.** *intr.* To become a pervert. late ME.

2. They perverted the course of justice 1868. **3.** How He [Satan] in the Serpent had perverted Eve, Her Husband shee MILT. Hence †**Perve·rt** *a.* perverted. **Pervert** (pə̄·ɹvəɹt) *sb.* one who has been perverted or corrupted; an apostate. **Perve·rter,** one who perverts (a person or thing). **Perve·rtible** *a.* capable of being perverted.

†**Perve·stigate,** *v.* 1610. [– *pervestigat-,* pa. ppl. stem of L. *pervestigare,* f. *per* PER-¹ 2 + *vestigare* track. Cf. INVESTIGATE *v.*] *trans.* To investigate diligently; to find out by research –1688. Hence †**Pervestiga·tion,** diligent investigation –1715.

†**Pe·rvial,** *a. rare.* 1595. [f. L. *pervius* PERVIOUS + -AL¹.] Pervious. CHAPMAN. Hence †**Pe·rvially** *adv.* clearly.

Pervicacious (pə̄ɹvikēⁱ·ʃəs), *a.* Now *rare.* 1633. [f. L. *pervicax, -cac-* stubborn (f. root *pervic-* of *pervincere,* f. PER-¹ 1 + *vincere* to conquer, prevail against) + -IOUS.] Very obstinate; headstrong, wilful; refractory. Hence **Pervica·cious-ly** *adv.*, **-ness.**

Pervicacity (pə̄ɹvikæ·sĭti). Now *rare.* 1604. [f. as prec. + -ITY. Cf. late and med.L. *pervicacitas.*] The quality or state of being pervicacious. So †**Pe·rvicacy** 1537–1748.

Pervious (pə̄·ɹviəs), *a.* 1614. [f. L. *pervius* (f. PER-¹ 1 + *via* way) + -OUS.] **1.** Allowing of passage through; lying open *to* 1631. **b.** *esp.* Permeable 1627. **c.** *fig.* (*a*) Fully intelligible, 'transparent'; (*b*) Of a person or the mind: Accessible to influence or argument 1614. **d.** *Zool.* and *Bot.* Open, patent, patulous 1806. **2.** Having the quality of passing through; pervasive. Now *rare* or *Obs.* 1684.

1. Every Country is p. to a wise Man 1659. **b.** A coarse argillaceous gravel, p. to water 1807. Hence **Pe·rviousness.**

‖**Pes** (pīz). *Pl.* **pedes** (pe·dīz). 1842. [L., = foot.] **1.** *Comp. Anat.* The terminal segment of the hind limb of a vertebrate animal. **2.** *Bot.* A foot-like part or organ; a peduncle.

‖**Peseta** (pĕsē·tă). 1811. [Sp., dim. of *pesa* weight :– L. *pensa,* pl. of *pensum* (see POISE). Cf. PESO.] A modern Spanish silver coin, equivalent to the French franc; now the unit of value in Spain.

‖**Peshito** (pĕʃī·to), **Peshitta** (pĕʃī·tˌta), *a.* and *sb.* 1793. [Syriac *p'šīṭtā* 'the Simple' or 'Plain'.] The principal version of the Old and New Testaments in ancient Syriac, sometimes styled the Syriac Vulgate.

‖**Peshwa** (pē·ʃwā). 1698. [Pers. *pīšwā* chief.] The chief minister of the Maratha princes (from *c*1660), who made himself in 1749 the hereditary sovereign of the Maratha state.

Pesky (pe·ski), *a. U.S. colloq.* 1775. [poss. alt. of **pesty,* f. PEST + -Y¹.] 'Plaguy', 'confounded'; annoying, disagreeable; hateful, abominable.

‖**Peso** (pē·so). 1555. [Sp., = 'weight' :– L. *pensum*; see PESETA.] A coin, either of gold or silver, formerly current in Spain and its colonies; now, a standard silver coin used in most of the S. American republics.

Pessary (pe·sări). late ME. [– late L. *pessarium,* repl. *pessulum,* f. late L. *pessum, -us* – Gr. πεσσός, -όν draughtboard, oval stone used in a game, medicated plug; see -ARY¹.] **1.** *Med.* A medicated plug of wool, lint, etc., to be inserted in the neck of the womb, etc., for the cure of various ailments; a suppository. **2.** *Surg.* An instrument worn in the vagina to prevent or remedy various uterine displacements 1754.

Pessimism (pe·simiz'm). 1794. [f. L. *pessimus* worst + -ISM, after *optimism.*] †**1.** The worst condition possible; cf. OPTIMISM 2. –1812. **2.** The tendency to look at the worst aspect of things; cf. OPTIMISM 3. 1815. **3.** The doctrine that this world is the worst possible, or that everthing naturally tends to evil; opp. to OPTIMISM 1. 1878.

Pessimist (pe·simist), *sb.* (*a.*) 1836. [f. as prec. + -IST; cf. Fr. *pessimiste.*] **1. a.** One who habitually takes the worst view of things. **b.** One who holds the metaphysical doctrine of pessimism. **B.** *adj.* (the sb. used *attrib.*) Characterized by pessimism 1861.

A p. view of the situation 1868. Hence **Pessimi·stic, -al** *adjs.* pertaining to, of the nature of, or characterized by pessimism; disposed to take the worst view of things; **-ly** *adv.*

‖**Pessulus** (pe·siŭlŏs). 1890. [L., a bolt.] *Anat.* In some birds, the cartilaginous or bony bar extending vertically across the lower end of the windpipe, and forming part of the syrinx.

Pest (pest). 1568. [– Fr. *peste* or L. *pestis* plague, contagious disease.] **1.** Any deadly epidemic disease; pestilence; *spec.* the bubonic plague. Now *rare.* **2.** Any thing or person that is noxious, destructive, or troublesome; a bane, curse, plague 1609.

1. The p. came to Edinburgh 1637. **2.** Philippe IV, the p. of France 1852. *Comb.* **p.-cart** (now *Hist.*), the cart used to carry away the bodies of the dead during a plague or pestilence. Hence †**Pe·stful** *a.* pestiferous, pestilential.

Pestalozzian (pestălǫ·tsiăn), *a.* (*sb.*) 1826. [f. surname *Pestalozzi* + -AN.] **A.** *adj.* Of or pertaining to the system of education introduced by Jean Henri *Pestalozzi* (1746–1827), a Swiss teacher, which aimed at the development of the faculties in a natural order, beginning with the perceptive powers. **B.** *sb.* An adherent of the system of Pestalozzi 1868. Hence **Pestalo·zzianism,** Pestalozzi's system of education.

Pester (pe·stəɹ), *v.* 1524. [app. short for IMPESTER, EMPESTER, or OFr. *empestrer* (mod. *empêtrer*), with which it is synon. in sense 1. In later use infl. by PEST, whence the sense 'plague'.] †**1.** *trans.* To clog, embarrass, obstruct the movements of; to encumber (*lit.* and *fig.*) –1676. †**2.** To obstruct (a place) by crowding; to overcrowd –1748. †**3.** To crowd (persons or things *in* or *into*) –1686. **4.** To annoy, trouble persistently, plague. (The current sense.) 1562.

4. I pestered him with questions 1795. [Malabar] is. .pestered with green adders 1796. Hence **Pe·ster** *sb.* †obstruction; bother; nuisance. Hence **Pe·sterer. Pe·sterment** (*Obs.* exc. *dial.*), pestering or being pestered; †overcrowding; annoyance, worry. **Pe·sterous** *a. rare,* having the quality of pestering; cumbersome; troublesome.

Pe·st-house. 1611. [f. PEST + HOUSE *sb.*] A hospital for persons suffering from any infectious disease, esp. the plague; a lazaretto.

†**Pe·stiduct.** 1624. [f. L. *pestis* plague + *ductus* DUCT.] A channel of the plague, or of any infectious epidemic –1672.

Pestiferous (pesti·fĕrəs), *a.* 1458. [f. L. *pestifer, -ferus,* f. *pestis* PEST; see -FEROUS. Cf. Fr. *pestifère.*] **I. 1.** Bringing pest or plague; noxious, deadly; of the nature of a pest, pestilential 1542. **2.** *fig.* Bearing moral contagion; mischievious, pernicious 1458.

1. These women are a p. kinde of animals 1600. Regions almost desolated by p. exhalations HERSCHEL. **2.** P. hordes of gamblers 1824.

II. [= Fr. *pestiféré.*] Plague-stricken 1665. Multitudes of poore p. creatures begging almes EVELYN. Hence **Pesti·ferous-ly** *adv.*, **-ness.**

Pestilence (pe·stilĕns). ME. [– (O)Fr. *pestilence* – L. *pestilentia,* f. *pestilens, -ent-,* also *pestilentus*; see next, -ENCE.] **1.** Any fatal epidemic disease, affecting man or beast, and destroying many victims. **b.** *spec.* The bubonic plague, the plague *par excellence.* late ME. **2.** *fig.* That which is morally pestilent; that which is fatal to the public peace or well-being. Now *rare.* ME. †**3.** That which plagues in any way –1555. †**4.** As an imprecation –1612.

1. The p. that walketh in darkness *Ps.* 91:6. **b.** This yere was the iij. great pestelens 1556. **2.** O flaterie! o lurkyng p. HOCCLEVE. **4.** A verray p. vpon yow falle CHAUCER. *Comb.* **p.-weed, -wort,** the Butterbur, *Petasites vulgaris* (from its repute against the plague).

Pestilent (pe·stilĕnt), *a.* (*adv.*) late ME. [– L. *pestilens, -ent-,* also *pestilentus,* f. *pestis* PEST; see -ENT.] **1.** Destructive to life; deadly; poisonous. **2.** Infectious as a disease or epidemic; pestilential. Now *rare.* 1613. **3.** *fig.* Injurious to religion, morals, or public peace; noxious, pernicious 1513. **4.** That pesters or annoys; plaguy. Often *joc.* 1592. †**B.** *adv.* Confoundedly; 'plaguy' –1700.

A. 1. The influence of a p. planet 1564. P. opium 1880. **2.** Vapour, and Mist, and Exhalation hot, Corrupt and P. MILT. **3.** P. books 1758. **4.** What a p. knaue is this same SHAKS. **B.** *Oth.* II. i. 251. Hence **Pe·stilent-ly** *adv.*, **-ness.**

Pestilential (pestile·nʃăl), *a.* late ME. [– med.L. *pestilentialis*, f. L. *pestilentia* PESTILENCE; see -AL¹.] **1.** Producing or tending to produce pestilence; noxious to life or health; pestiferous. **2.** Of the nature of or pertaining to pestilence, *esp.* bubonic plague 1530. **3.** Morally baneful or pernicious 1531.

1. A p. malignancy in the air, occasioned by the comet SWIFT. **2.** A p. disease GIBBON. **3.** So p., so infectious a thing is sin JER. TAYLOR. Hence **Pestile·ntially** *adv.* So †**Pestilentious** *a.*

Pestle (pe·s'l, pe·st'l), *sb.* ME. [– OFr. *pestel* – L. *pistillum*, dim. of **pistrum*, f. *pist-*, pa. ppl. stem of *pinsare* pound; see -EL.] **1.** An instrument, (usu. club-shaped) for bruising or pounding substances in a mortar. Also *fig.* **2.** Applied to various appliances for pounding, stamping, pressing, etc.; e.g., a stamp, etc. 1604. **3.** The leg of certain animals, used for food, *esp.* the haunch of a pig. Now *dial.* ME. †**4.** A constable's truncheon or club CHAPMAN. †**5.** *Bot.* Early form of PISTIL, q.v.

1. *P. and mortar*, esp. those used by an apothecary in compounding drugs; hence taken as the symbol of the profession. **3.** Phr. †*The p. of a lark*, *fig.* a trifle, something very small.

Pe·stle, *v.* late ME. [– OFr. *pesteler*, f. *pestel*; see prec.] **1.** *trans.* To beat, pound, or triturate, with or as with a pestle. **2.** *intr.* To use or work with a pestle 1866.

Pestology (pestǫ·lŏdʒi). 1921. [f. PEST + -LOGY.] The study of pests, *esp.* of insect pests.

Pet (pet), *sb.*¹ 1508. [orig. Sc. and north. dial.; of unkn. origin; formally distinct from PEAT².] **1.** Any animal that is domesticated or tamed and kept as a favourite, or treated with fondness; esp. applied to a lamb reared by hand. **2. a.** An indulged (and, usu., spoiled) child 1508. **b.** Any person who is specially indulged; a darling, favourite. Also *transf.* of a thing. 1825. **3.** *attrib.* **a.** Of an animal; kept as pet 1584. **b.** Specially cherished; favourite. Also (*joc.* or ironically) *p. aversion*, that which one specially dislikes. 1832. **c.** Expressing fondness, endearing; chiefly in **p. name** (often hyphened), a hypocoristic name 1829.

1. The other has transferred the amorous Passions of her first Years to the Love of Cronies, Petts and Favourities STEELE. **2. b.** The p. of society 1902. **3. a.** The P. Lamb WORDSW. (*title*). **b.** My own particular p. scrubbing brush has been used for blackleading 1898. Hence **Pet** *v.*¹ to make a p. of; to indulge; to fondle; often in **Pe·tting** *vbl. sb.*

Pet (pet), *sb.*² 1590. [orig. in phr. †*take the pet*; of unkn. origin.] Offence at being (or feeling) slighted or not made enough of; a fit of ill humour from this cause.

To take (the) p., to take offence and become sulky. Hence †**Pet** *v.*² *intr.* to be in a p.; to take offence at one's treatment; to sulk –1837.

Petal (pe·tăl). 1726. [– mod.L. *petalum* (Fabio Colonna, 1649), in late L. metal plate – Gr. πέταλον lamina, leaf, subst. use of n. of adj. πέταλος outspread, f. base πετ-, as in πετάννυσθαι unfold.] *Bot.* Each of the divisions (modified leaves) of the corolla of a flower (see COROLLA 2), esp. when separate. Hence **Petali·ferous** *a.* bearing petals. **Pe·taliform** *a.* petaloid. **Pe·taline** *a.* pertaining to a p.; situated on a p.; consisting of petals; petaloid. **Pe·talled, petaled** *a.* having petals; also in parasynthetic compounds, as *crimson-petalled*, *six-petalled*.

Petalism (pe·tăliz'm). 1612. [– Gr. πεταλισμός, f. πέταλον leaf; see -ISM, PETAL.] *Anc. Hist.* A method of temporary banishment (for five years) practised in ancient Syracuse, similar to the OSTRACISM of Athens, but effected by writing the name of the person on an olive leaf.

Petalite (pe·tăləit). 1808. [f. Gr. πέταλον leaf + -ITE¹ 2 b.] *Min.* A silicate of aluminium and lithium, occurring in whitish or greyish masses having leaf-like cleavage.

Petalody (pe·tăloᵘdi). 1869. [f. Gr. πεταλώδης leaf-like, f. πέταλον leaf, PETAL; see -ODE.] *Bot.* The condition of having other organs or parts of the flower modified into the form of petals; e.g., the stamens in most 'double' flowers.

Petaloid (pe·tăloid), *a.* 1730. [– mod.L. *petaloideus*, f. L. *petalum* PETAL; see -OID.] **1.** *Bot.* Of the form of, or resembling, a petal. **b.** Belonging to the *Petaloideæ*, a division of monocotyledons having normally flowers with ordinary coloured petals or p. parts, as lilies, orchids, etc. 1836. **2.** *Zool.* Applied to the ambulacra of certain echinoids, which have a dilated portion and a tapering extremity, suggesting the petals of a flower 1862. So **Petaloi·dal** *a.*

‖**Petalon** (pe·tălǫn). 1678. [– Gr. πέταλον; see PETAL.] The plate of gold worn on the linen mitre of the Jewish high priest.

Petalostichous (petălǫ·stikəs), *a.* [f. mod. L. *Petalosticha* (f. Gr. πέταλον leaf + στίχος row) + -OUS.] *Zool.* Having petaloid ambulacra; belonging to the division *Petalosticha* of Echinoids.

Petalous (pe·tăləs), *a. rare.* 1730. [f. PETAL + -OUS.] Having petals: opp. to *apetalous*.

Petard (pĭtă·ɹd, pĭtă·ɹ), *sb.* 1598. [– Fr. *pétard*, f. *péter* break wind; see -ARD.] **1.** A small engine of war used to blow in a door or gate, or to make a breach in a wall, etc.; orig. of metal and bell-shaped, later a cubical wooden box, charged with powder, and fired by a fuse. Also *fig.* **2.** A kind of firework; a cracker 1634.

1. To haue the enginer Hoist with his owne petar SHAKS. Hence †**Peta·rd** *v.* to blow open, or breach, with a p. †**Petardee·r, -ier,** a soldier who manages a p.

‖**Petasus** (pe·tăsŏs). 1599. [L. – Gr. πέτασος, f. root πετ- spread out; see PETAL.] A low-crowned broad-brimmed hat worn by the ancient Greeks; also, the winged hat of Hermes.

Petaurist (pĭtǭ·rist). 1656. [– Gr. πεταυριστής a performer on the πέταυρον or spring-board; see -IST.] †**1.** An acrobat, tumbler, rope-dancer (*rare*) –1658. **2.** *Zool.* Any marsupial of the genus *Petaurista* or subfamily *Petaurinæ*, most of which have a parachute enabling them to take flying leaps; a flying phalanger, etc.

Pet-cock. 1848. [app. f. PET *sb.*¹ + COCK *sb.*¹] A small plug-cock fastened in a pipe or cylinder, as in a pump or a steam-engine, for purposes of draining or testing.

‖**Petechia** (pĭtī·kiă); usu. in pl. **petechiæ** (-ki,ī). 1794. [mod.L. – It. *petecchie* pl. skin eruption (whence Fr. *pétéchie* XVIII) :– pop.L. **peticula*, dim. of L. *petigo* scab, eruption.] *Path.* A small red or purple spot in the skin caused by extravasation of blood, occurring in certain fevers, etc. So **Pete·chial** *a.* of the nature of, pertaining to, or characterized by petechiæ 1710.

Peter (pī·təɹ), *sb.* [In XII *Peter* – eccl.L. *Petrus* – eccl. Gr. Πέτρος, lit. 'stone', translating Palestinian Aramaic *kēp̱â* (græcized *Cephas*) the rock, the surname conferred by Christ upon Simon Bar-jona (Matt. 16:17), historically known as St. Peter.] A male Christian name; hence in many transf. uses, mostly referring directly or indirectly to St. Peter.

1. Used in proverbial phrases in conjunction with *Paul*; esp. in *to rob P. to pay Paul*, to take away from one person, cause, etc. in order to pay another; to discharge one debt by incurring another. late ME. **2.** *Thieves' Cant.* A portmanteau or trunk; a bundle or parcel 1668. **3. Blue Peter,** see BLUE *a.* (also simply *Peter*).

Comb. **(St.) Peter's bark, boat,** the (Roman) Catholic Church; **(St.) Peter's fish,** the haddock, or other fish, having marks affirmed in legend to have been made by St. Peter's thumb and finger when he caught the fish for the tribute-money (Matt. 17:27); **Peter's penny:** see PETER-PENNY. **St. Peter's wort** (also **(St.) Peterwort**), (*a*) the Cowslip (= Herb Peter); (*b*) certain species of *Hypericum*; also *Ascyrum*; (*c*) Feverfew, *Pyrethrum parthenium*.

Peter (pī·tə), *v. slang* or *colloq.* 1812. [Of unkn. origin.] **1.** *trans.* To stop, leave off (*slang*). **2.** *intr. To p. out* (orig. *U.S. Mining colloq.*): to run out and disappear (as a stream, a vein of ore); to die out, fail 1865.

Pe·ter-boat. 1540. [app. f. PETER *sb.* + BOAT; cf. PETERMAN.] Local name (on the Thames, etc.) for a decked fishing-boat smaller than a smack or yawl; also a dredger-man's double-ended boat.

Peterman (pī·təɹmæ̆n). late ME. [app. f. PETER *sb.* (in allusion to the occupation of Simon Peter); cf. prec.] A fisherman.

Pe·ter-pe:nny, Peter's penny. Usu. in pl. **Peter's pence.** ME. [f. PETER *sb.* (in ref. to the claim of the see of Rome to the patrimony of St. Peter) + PENNY.] **1.** *Hist.* An annual tax or tribute of a penny from each householder having land of a certain value paid before the Reformation to the papal see. **2.** Applied to voluntary contributions of Roman Catholics to the papal treasury since 1860.

Petersham (pī·təɹʃăm). 1812. [f. Viscount *Petersham*, *c*1812.] (*attrib.*, or *ellipt.* as *sb.*) **a.** Name for a heavy overcoat or breeches formerly fashionable; also for the cloth of which such overcoats are made. **b.** A thick kind of ribbon of ribbed or corded silk, used for hatbands, etc.

Petiole (pe·tioᵘl). 1753. [– Fr. *pétiole* – L. *petiolus* little foot, fruit-stalk, specialized by Linnæus.] **1.** *Bot.* The footstalk of a leaf, by which it is attached to the stem; a leaf-stalk. **2.** *Zool.* A slender stalk-like structure supporting some part, as the eye-stalk in certain Crustacea, etc. 1782. Hence **Pe·tiolar** *a.* of, pertaining to, or of the nature of a p. **Pe·tiolate(d)** *adjs.* having a p.; stalked; borne upon a p. **Pe·tioled** *a.* petiolate.

Petiolule (pe·tiŏliul). 1832. [– mod.L. *petiolulus*, dim. of *petiolus*; see prec., -ULE.] *Bot.* A partial or secondary petiole; the footstalk of a leaflet in a compound leaf. Hence **Petio·lulate** *a.* having, or borne upon, a p.

Petit (†pe·tit), *a.* (*sb.*) ME. [– Fr. *petit*, fem. *petite*. See PETTY.] †**1.** Of small size, small –1675. †**2.** = PETTY *a.* 2. –1759. †**3.** = PETTY *a.* 3. –1641. **4.** In special collocations (rarely hyphened) as a var. of *petty*: **Petit Bag, Officer:** see PETTY BAG, PETTY OFFICER; also **petit** SESSIONS, TREASON, etc. **5. P. point** = TENT-STITCH. ‖**6.** (pəti) In mod.Fr. **petit verre,** a glass of liqueur [*lit.* small glass] 1858. †**B.** *sb.* A junior schoolboy. Also *transf.* –1691.

‖**Petite** (pəti·t, pĕtī·t), *a.* 1712. [Fr., fem. of *petit*; see prec.] †**1.** A var. of PETIT (without ref. to gender or sex). **2.** Of a woman or girl: Little, of small stature or size, tiny 1784. **3.** In Fr. **petite morale,** minor morals; **petite pièce,** a minor performance; in *pl.* the minor writings of an author (formerly as Eng. *petite pieces*) 1712.

‖**Petitio** (pĭti·ʃio). 1706. [L.; see next.] The L. word for 'asking, begging, petitioning, petition', in some phrases: esp. ‖**P. induciarum** (indiūʃiēᵊ·rŏm). *Law* = IMPARLANCE 2. 1706; ‖**P. principii** (pĭti·ʃio prinsi·pi,əi). *Logic* [lit. taking the beginning or a principle for granted], the fallacy of taking for granted a premiss which is either equivalent to, or itself depends on, the conclusion; an instance of this 1531.

Petition (pĭti·ʃən), *sb.* ME. [– (O)Fr. *pétition* – L. *petitio*, f. *petit-* pa. ppl. stem of *petere* aim at, lay claim to, ask, seek; see -ION.] **1.** The action of formally asking, begging, supplicating, or humbly requesting. late ME. **2.** A supplication or prayer; an entreaty; *esp.* a solemn and humble prayer to the Deity, or to a sovereign or superior; also, one of the clauses of a prayer ME. **b.** *transf.* The thing asked or entreated 1440. **3.** A formally drawn up request or supplication; *esp.* a written supplication addressed to a superior, or to a person or body in authority (as a sovereign or legislature), soliciting some favour, right, or mercy, or the redress of some wrong or grievance 1450. **4.** *Law.* A formal application in writing made to a court (*a*) for judicial action concerning the matter of a suit then pending before it; (*b*) for something which lies in the jurisdiction of the court without an action, as a writ of *habeas corpus*, etc.; (*c*) in some forms of procedure initiating a suit or its equivalent 1737. †**5.** *Math.* A postulate; an axiom –1795.

1. P., peaceable p., is the course COBBETT. **2.** Our p. in the Litany, against sudden death RUSKIN. **b.** *Jul. C.* II. i. 58. **3.** Phr. *P. and Advice* (*Eng. Hist.*), the Remonstrance presented by Parliament to Cromwell on 4 Apr. 1657. *P. of Right*, the parliamentary declaration of the rights and liberties of the people, assented to by King Charles I in 1628. **4.** *P. of right* (*Law*), an ancient

Common Law remedy against the Crown for obtaining possession or restitution of real or personal property 1467.

Petition (pǐti·ʃən), *v.* 1607. [f. prec.] **1.** *trans.* To address a petition to; to make a humble request or supplication to; *spec.* to address a formal written petition to (a sovereign, legislature, court, etc.) **b.** To beg for (a thing) 1631. **2.** *absol.* or *intr.* To address or present a petition; to ask humbly (*for* something) 1634.

1. You haue, I know, petition'd All the Gods for my prosperitie SHAKS. **b.** All that I hope, p., or expect CRABBE. Hence **Peti·tioning** *vbl. sb.* the action of making or presenting a petition; *ppl. a.* that petitions; *petitioning creditor*, one who asks for a declaration of bankruptcy against his debtor.

Petitionary (pǐti·ʃənări), *a.* 1579. [f. PETITION + -ARY[1].] **1.** Of the nature of, containing or characteristic of a petition. **2.** Of persons: Suppliant. *Obs.* or *arch.* 1607. †**3.** Containing a *petitio principii* SIR T. BROWNE.

2. To say no to a poor p. rogue LAMB. Hence **Peti·tionarily** *adv.* in a p. manner.

Petitionee (pǐtiʃənī·). 1764. [f. PETITION *v.* + -EE[1].] *U.S. Law.* The person or party against whom a petition is filed.

Petitioner (pǐti·ʃənəɹ). late ME. [f. PETITION *sb.* + -ER[2]; in AL. *petitionarius*. Cf. *pensioner*, *commissioner*.] **1.** One who presents a petition. **b.** *Hist.* One of those who signed the address to Charles II in 1680, petitioning for the summoning of Parliament 1757. **2.** *Law.* **a.** A plaintiff in an action commenced by petition. **b.** A petitioning creditor 1503.

‖ **Petit-maître** (pəti,mɛ̄·tr). 1711. [Fr., = little master.] An effeminate man; a dandy, coxcomb. Also *attrib.*

‖**Petit mal** (pəti mal). 1891. [Fr. 'little evil'; cf. *haut mal* epilepsy.] The milder form of epilepsy.

†**Peti·tor.** *rare.* 1613. [– L. *petitor*, f. *petit-* (see PETITION) + -OR 2.] A seeker, applicant, candidate –1655.

Petitory (pe·titəri), *a.* 1579. [– late L. *petitorius*; see prec. and -ORY[2].] **1.** Petitionary, supplicatory. Now *rare.* **2.** *Law.* Characterized by laying claim to something; in *p. action*, etc., an action claiming title or right of ownership, as distinct from mere possession, in anything 1602.

‖**Petit souper** (pəti supe). 1765. [Fr.] A little supper; an unceremonious supper for a few intimates.

Petralogy: see PETROLOGY.

Petrarchal (pǐtrā·ɹkăl), *a.* 1818. [f. *Petrarch*, It. *Petrarca*, surname + -AL[1].] Of, pertaining to, or in the style of the Italian poet Petrarch (1304–74). So **Petra·rchan** *a.* (also *sb.* = *Petrarchist*) 1827. **Petra·rchian** *a.* 1801. **Pe·trarchist,** an imitator of Petrarch 1823.

Petrary (pe·trări). Now *Hist.* 1610. [– med.L. *petraria* fem., f. L. *petra* stone. Cf. PEDRERO, PERRIER; see -ARY[1].] A mediæval military engine for discharging stones.

Petre (pī·təɹ). 1594. [In sense 1 abbrev. of SALTPETRE; in 2 – L. *petra*, Gr. πέτρα rock.] **1.** = SALTPETRE. (Now only *technical colloq.*) †**2.** *Oil of p.*: rock-oil, petroleum –1741.

Petrean (pǐtrī·ăn), *a. rare* 1632. [f. L. *petræus* (– Gr. πετραῖος rocky, f. πέτρα rock) + -AN.] Rocky; of or pertaining to rocks or stones; of Arabia Petræa.

Petrel (pe·trĕl). 1676. [Early vars. *pitteral*, *pittrel*; in 1703 spelt *petrel* by Dampier, who derives the name from that of St. *Peter* in allusion to his 'walking upon the Lake of Gennesareth' (cf. Matt. 14:30). The Norw. *Soren Peders*, *Pedersfugl*, G. *Petersvogel* are later than the Eng. For the ending cf. *cockerel*, *dotterel*, *hoggerel*, *pickerel*, which may have supplied the analogy.] A small sea-bird, *Procellaria pelagica*, with black and white plumage and long wings; hence extended to any species of the genus *Procellaria* (Storm-Petrels or Stormy Petrels), or of the family *Procellaridæ*, or order *Tubinares*.

†**Petrescent** (pǐtre·sĕnt), *a.* 1663. [f. L. *petra* stone + -ESCENT.] prop. Becoming petrified; but usu., petrifactive. So †**Petre·scence, †-ency,** the process of petrifaction; formation of calculus.

Petrifaction (petrifæ·kʃən). 1646. [f. PETRIFY after *stupefy*, *stupefaction*; superseded PETRIFICATION; see -FACTION.] **1.** The action of petrifying, or condition of being petrified; conversion into stone or stony substance; in *Path.* formation of 'stone' or calculus. **2.** *concr.* Something petrified, or formed by conversion into stone; a stony concretion, as in fossils, stalactites and stalagmites 1686.

1. *fig.* This is making a p. both of love and poetry HAZLITT. **2.** *fig.* He gives you the p. of a sigh HAZLITT. So **Petrifa·ctive** *a.* causing p.

Petrific (pǐtri·fik), *a.* Now *rare.* 1667. [– med.L. *petrificus*, f. L. *petra* rock; see PETRIFY, -FIC.] **1.** Having the quality of petrifying; petrifactive; in *Path.* causing the formation of 'stone' or calculus. **2.** *loosely.* Petrified, stony 1804.

1. Death with his Mace p. MILT. *fig.* A look meant to be nothing less than p. MISS BURNEY.

Petrification (pe:trifikē[i]·ʃən). Now *rare.* 1611. [– Fr. *pétrification* or med.L. *petrificatio*, f. *petrificat-*, pa. ppl. stem of *petrificare*; see next, -ION.] = PETRIFACTION.

Petrify (pe·trifəi), *v.* 1594. [– Fr. *pétrifier* – med.L. *petrificare*, f. L. *petra* – Gr. πέτρα rock, stone; see -FY.] **1.** *trans.* To convert into stone or stony substance; *spec.* to turn (an organic body) into a stony concretion by replacing its original substance by a calcareous or other mineral deposit; also, *loosely*, to encrust with such a deposit. Also *absol.* **2.** *fig.* To change as if into stone. **a.** To harden, benumb, deaden, stiffen 1626. **b.** To make motionless or rigid, e.g. with fear, etc. (Chiefly *passive.*) 1771. **3.** *intr.* (for *pass.*) To become converted into stone or stony substance 1646.

1. Albertus gives an account of a tree..with a nest and birds petrified 1750. **2. a.** To p. a doctrine into an outward formula 1892. **b.** I was almost petrified with horror at the intelligence 1786. **3.** *fig.* Like Niobe we marble grow, And p. with grief DRYDEN. Hence **Pe·trified** *ppl. a.* changed into stone or stony substance; represented or embodied in stone; stupefied, 'paralysed' with surprise, etc.

Petrine (pī·trəin), *a.* 1846. [f. eccl. L. *Petrus* PETER + -INE[1].] Of, pertaining to, or characteristic of the Apostle Peter.

P. claims, the claims of the popes as successors of St. Peter.

Petro- (petro), properly comb. form of Gr. πέτρος stone or πέτρα rock, as in PETROGLYPH, etc. In *Anat.* used to form adjs. descriptive of parts connected with the petrous portion of the temporal bone and some other part: as **Petrohy·oid, Petroma·stoid,** etc.

Petrobrusian (petrobrū·siăn). 1559. [– L. *Petrobrusiani* pl., f. name of Pierre de Bruys (*Petrus Brusianus*).] *Ch. Hist.* A member of a sect founded by Peter or Pierre de Bruys in the South of France in the 12th c., who rejected infant baptism, transubstantiation, etc.

Petroglyph (pe·trŏglif). 1870. [– Fr. *pétroglyphe*, f. Gr. πέτρα rock + γλυφή carving.] A rock-carving (usu. prehistoric). So **Petrogly·phic** *a.* belonging to or of the nature of a p. **Petro·glyphy,** rock-carving.

Petrography (pǐtrǫ·grăfi). 1651. [f. PETRO- + -GRAPHY.] The scientific description of the composition and formation of rocks; descriptive petrology. So **Petrogra·phic, -al** *adjs.* of or pertaining to p.; dealing with p.

Petrol (pe·trǫl). 1585. [– Fr. *pétrole* – med.L. *petroleum*; see PETROLEUM.] †**1.** = PETROLEUM –1811. **2.** *Chem.* A hydrocarbon (C_8H_{10}) occurring in petroleum 1866. **3.** [Reintroduced from Fr.] A name for refined petroleum as used in motor-cars, etc. Also *attrib.*, as *p. engine, pipe, pump.* 1895.

‖**Petrolatum** (petrŏlē[i]·tǒm). 1887. [mod. L., f. PETROL + *-atum* in *acetatum*, etc.; see -ATE[1] c.] The official name in the U.S. Pharmacopœia for pure petroleum jelly, called in the British Pharmacopœia *paraffinum molle*.

Petroleum (pǐtrō[u]·liǒm). 1526. [– med.L. *petroleum* (XII), f. L. *petra* rock + *oleum* OIL.] A mineral oil, varying from light yellow to dark brown or black, occurring in rocks or on the surface of water in various parts of the world, used esp. as a source of oils for illumination and mechanical power; rock-oil.

attrib. and *Comb.*, as *p.-car, -filter, -lamp*, etc.; **p.-ether,** a volatile oil obtained from p., also called *naphthalic ether*; **-oil** = petroleum; in mod. use dist. from **p.-spirit,** whose vapour flashes at lower temperatures. Hence **Petro·leous** *a.* abounding in or containing p.

‖**Pétroleur** (petrolör). 1871. [Fr., f. *pétrole* + *-eur*, ending of masc. agent-nouns.] A (male) incendiary who uses petroleum. Also ‖**Pétroleuse** (petrolǿz) [fem. of prec.], a female who does the same.

Petrolic (pǐtrǫ·lik), *a.* 1899. [f. PETROL + -IC.] Of or pertaining to petrol or petroleum.

Petrolin (pe·trolin). 1831. [f. PETROLEUM or PETROL + -IN[1].] A substance obtained from Rangoon petroleum, identical with *paraffin*. **b.** Trade name for an oil obtained from petroleum.

Petrology (pǐtrǫ·lŏdʒi). 1811. [f. PETRO- + -LOGY; orig. erron. *petralogy*.] That branch of geology which deals with the origin, structure, and composition of rocks. So **Petrolo·gic, -al** *adjs.*, **-ly** *adv.* **Petro·logist,** one versed in p.

Petronel (pe·trŏnĕl). Now *Hist.* or *arch.* 1577. [– Fr. *petrinal*, var. of *poitrinal*, subst. use of adj. 'pertaining to breast or chest', f. *poitrine* :– Rom. **pectorina*, f. L. *pectus*, *pector-* breast; so called because in firing it the butt end rested against the chest.] A kind of large pistol or carbine, used in the 16th and early 17th c., esp. by horse-soldiers.

Petrosal (pǐtrō[u]·săl), *a.* (*sb.*) 1741. [f. L. *petrosus* rocky + -AL[1].] *Anat.* Applied to the petrous portion of the temporal bone (med.L. *os petrosum*), and parts connected with it. **b.** *absol.* as *sb.* = Petrosal bone 1848.

Petrosilex (petro,səi·leks). 1770. [mod. L., f. *petrus* stone + *silex* flint.] *Min.* A hard rock; an early name for felsite. Hence **Pe:trosili·ceous** *a.* consisting of or containing p.

Petrous (pe·trəs), *a.* 1541. [f. L. *petrosus* stony, rocky; see -OUS.] Of the nature of, or as hard as, stone or rock; stony, rocky; in *Anat.* applied to the hard part of the temporal bone protecting the internal ear.

Petted (pe·tĕd), *ppl. a.* 1724. [f. PET *v.*[1] + -ED[1].] Treat as a pet or favourite; spoiled by petting or indulgence.

Pettichaps (pe·ti,tʃæps). 1674. [f. PETTY *a.* + (app.) CHAP *sb.*[2] or [3].] The Garden Warbler (*Sylvia hortensis*). Also applied to other species of warblers; *dial.* the long-tailed titmouse.

Petticoat (pe·tiko[u]t), *sb.* (*a.*) late ME. [orig. two words, *petty coat*, lit. little or small coat.] **1.** †A small coat worn by men beneath the doublet –1542. **2.** *gen.* A garment worn by women, girls, and young children 1464. *spec.* **a.** A skirt as dist. from a bodice, worn either externally, or beneath the gown or frock 1602. **b.** An underskirt 1596. †**c.** The skirt of a woman's riding-habit –1824. **d.** The rudimentary garment worn by women among primitive or uncivilized peoples 1698. **3.** *pl.* Skirts collectively; also, skirts worn by young children; chiefly in phr. (said of a boy) *in petticoats* 1600. **4.** (Chiefly *pl.*) As the typical feminine garment; hence as the symbol of the female sex or character 1593. **b.** (*sing.*) A female; the female sex 1600. **5.** Applied joc. or contemptuously to the skirts of a clergyman's dress; also descriptively to the kilt of the Highlander, the fustanella of the Greek, etc. 1730. **6.** Anything resembling a petticoat; e.g. a toilet-table cover reaching down to the floor 1864; the inverted cup of a p. insulator (see below); also = *p. insulator* 1906.

2. a. A winning wave (deserving note) In the tempestuous petticote HERRICK. She was in her new suit of black sarcenet and yellow petticoate very pretty PEPYS. **b.** A good flannel p. ought to be little the worse for one year's wear 1844. **3.** I have known him ever since he was in petticoats 1877. **4.** Beatrice Cenci is really none other than Percy Bysshe Shelley himself in petticoats KINGSLEY. **b.** Can't do business with a p. in the room 1864.

II. *attrib.* (often = adj.) **a.** In petticoats; female; womanish. (Often hyphened.) Now *rare.* 1625. **b.** Executed, performed, wielded by a woman; feminine 1660.

a. To ridicule the p. pedant 1797. **b.** P. influence 1850.

Comb.: **p. government,** (undue) predominance of women in the home or in politics; **p. insulator,** an inverted cup-shaped insulator of porcelain or the like that supports a telegraph wire; **p.-pipe,** a bell-mouthed pipe in the chimney of a locomotive into which the exhaust-steam enters and which serves to equalize the draught. Hence **Pe·tticoated** *a.* having or wearing petticoats; also *transf.*

Pettifog (pe·tifǫg), *v.* 1611. [Back-formation from PETTIFOGGER.] *intr.* To act as a pettifogger; to conduct a petty case in a minor court of law; to practise legal chicanery; also *transf.* to quibble about very small points.

Pettifogger (pe·tifǫgəɹ). 1564. [f. PETTY + FOGGER[1].] **1.** A legal practitioner of inferior status, who gets up or conducts petty cases; *esp.* one who employs mean, cavilling practices. **2.** *transf.* A petty practitioner in any department; an empiric, pretender 1602. Hence **Pe·ttifoggery,** pettifogging practice; legal chicanery.

Pettifogging (pe·tifǫgiŋ), *vbl. sb.* 1580. [Back-formation from prec.; see -ING[1].] The action of a pettifogger; chicanery, pettifoggery; quibbling.

Pettifogging (pe·tifǫgiŋ), *ppl. a.* 1603. [f. as prec.; see -ING[2].] Acting as a pettifogger; mean, shifty, quibbling; also, pertaining to or characteristic of pettifoggers.

Pettish (pe·tiʃ), *a.* 1591. [f. PET *sb.*[2] + -ISH[1].] Subject to fits of offended ill humour; in a pet; pertaining to, or of the nature of a pet; peevish, petulant; easily put out.

I checked her, which made her mighty p. PEPYS. Hence **Pe·ttish-ly** *adv.*, **-ness.**

Pettitoes (pe·titōᵘz), *sb. pl.* Rarely in *sing.* 1555. [In form and sense corresp. to Fr. *petite oie* 'little goose', defined by Cotgrave 1611 as 'the giblets of a goose; also, the bellie, and inwards or intralls, of other edible creatures'; assim. to PETTY and pl. of TOE took place early.] **1.** Pig's trotters, esp. as used for food; in earlier use the word included the heart, liver, lungs, etc. of pigs, calves, sheep, and other animals. †Also *fig.* in expressions of contempt. **2.** The feet of a human being, esp. of a child 1589.

Pettle (pe·t'l), *v. Sc.* and *n. dial.* 1719. [frequent. of PET *v.*[1]; see -LE.] *trans.* To pet, fondle, indulge.

‖**Petto** (pe·tˌto). 1674. [It. :- L. *pectus.*] The breast.

In p. (It.), in one's own breast; in contemplation; undisclosed.

Petty (pe·ti), *a.* (*sb.*) [Late ME. *pety*, var. of *petit* (Langl.) – (O)Fr. *petit* :- Rom. **pittittus*, f. **pit-*, repr. in late L. *pitinnus, pitulus* very small, and regarded as a symbolic word of child speech. In some technical phr. *petit* is still retained, e.g. *p. constable, p. jury, p. larceny*; see PETIT.] †**1.** Small (in size or stature) –1688. **2.** Of small importance, trivial 1581. **b.** Little-minded, mean 1713. **3.** Minor, inferior; subordinate; on a small scale 1523.

2. Those p. evils, which make prosperous men miserable 1824. **b.** Our p. animosities STEELE. **3.** I fly from p. tyrants to the throne GOLDSM. P. shopkeepers 1831.

Special collocations: **p. average:** see AVERAGE *sb.*[2] 2; **p. cash,** small cash items of receipt or expenditure; whence petty-cash-book; **p. dancers,** the Northern Lights. See also PETTY BAG, P. OFFICER, etc.; and *petty* JURY, LARCENY, SESSION, TREASON, etc. Hence **Pe·ttily** *adv.* **Pe·ttiness.**

†**B.** *sb.* **1.** A little boy at school; a boy in a lower form –1855. **2.** A privy or latrine.

Petty Bag, petty-bag. *Obs.* exc. *Hist.* 1631. [From the small leather bag in which records were put.] An office formerly belonging to the Common Law jurisdiction of the Court of Chancery, for suits for and against solicitors and officers of that court, and for process and proceedings by extents on statutes, recognizances, *scire facias*, to repeal letters patent, etc.

†**Pe·tty ca·non, pe:ttica·non.** 1530. [PETTY *a.* 3.] A minor canon –1769.

†**Pe·tty ca·ptain, pe:ttica·ptain.** late ME. [PETTY *a.* 3.] An officer below the rank of captain; a lieutenant; a centurion. –1633.

Petty officer. 1577. [PETTY *a.* 3.] **1.** *gen.* A minor officer. **2.** *spec.* An officer in the navy corresponding in rank to a non-commissioned officer in the army 1760.

Petulance (pe·tiŭlăns). 1610. [– Fr. *pétulance* – L. *petulantia* (see next).] The fact or quality of being petulant. **1.** Wanton, pert, or insolent behaviour or speech. Now *rare* or *Obs.* **b.** A petulant or saucy expression 1741. **2.** Peevish impatience of opposition or restraint 1784.

1. With the p. of youth she pursued her triumph over her prudent elder sister SCOTT.

Petulancy (pe·tiŭlănsi). 1559. [– L. *petulantia*; see PETULANT, -ANCY.] †**1.** = PETULANCE 1. –1748. **2.** = PETULANCE 2 (*rare*) 1712.

Petulant (pe·tiŭlănt), *a.* (*sb.*) 1599. [– (O)Fr. *pétulant* – L. *petulans, -ant-*, pr. pple. of **petulare*, f. *petere* direct oneself to, attack (with formative as in *postulare* POSTULATE); see -ANT.] **1.** Forward; wanton, lascivious (now *rare*). **2.** Pert; insolent; rude (now *rare*) 1605. **3.** Displaying peevish impatience and irritation, esp. on slight occasion 1755. **B.** *sb.* A petulant person 1682.

A. 2. The p. scribblers of this age DRYDEN. **3.** Laud was p., passionate, and impatient of contradiction 1830. Hence **Pe·tulantly** *adv.*

†**Petum, -un.** 1577. [– Fr. *petun* – Guarani *petȳ.*] Native S. Amer. name of Tobacco –1763.

Petunia (pĭtiū·niă). 1825. [– mod.L. *petunia* (Jussieu, 1789), f. Fr. *petun*; see prec., -IA[1].] *Bot.* **1.** A genus of ornamental herbaceous plants (N.O. *Solanaceæ* or *Atropaceæ*) nearly allied to tobacco, natives of S. America; they bear white, violet or purple, and variegated funnel-shaped flowers. Also, a plant or flower of this. **2.** The dark violet colour of the petunia. Also *attrib.* 1891.

‖**Petuntse** (petu·ntsĕ, pĭtɒ·ntsĕ). 1727. [Chinese (Mandarin) *pai-tun-tzə*, f. *pai* white, *tun* mound, stone + *-tzə* formative ending.] A white earth, consisting of pulverized granite; used in combination with kaolin in the manufacture of Chinese porcelain. Also *attrib.*

Petzite (pe·tsəit). 1849. [f. name of W. *Petz*, a chemist, who analysed it; see -ITE[1] 2b.] *Min.* Telluride of silver, containing a variable amount of gold.

Peucedanin ((piuse·dănin). 1836. [f. mod.L. *Peucedanum* – Gr. πευκέδανον the herb hog's fennel (f. πεύκη pine + ἔδανον eatable, food) + -IN[1].] *Chem.* A neutral substance ($C_{12}H_{12}O_3$) contained in the root of masterwort, *Peucedanum* (*Imperatoria*) *ostruthium*, and other umbelliferous plants; also called *imperatorin.*

Peucyl (piū·sil). 1857. [f. Gr. πεύκη pine + -YL.] *Chem.* An oily hydrocarbon obtained from turpentine-oil; also called *terebilene.*

‖**Peulvan, -ven** (pölvaṅ). 1841. [Fr. – Breton *peûlvan.* f. *peûl* stake, pillar + *van*, mutate of *man* appearance.] *Archæol.* An upright long stone, an undressed stone pillar of prehistoric age; prop. applied to those in Brittany.

Pew (piū), *sb.* [Late ME. *pywe, puwe* – OFr. *puye, puie* – L. *podia*, pl. of *podium* elevated place, parapet, balcony – Gr. πόδιον base, pedestal, dim. of πούς, ποδ- foot.] †**1.** A raised standing-place, stall, or desk in a church; often differentiated, as *minister's p.*, a pulpit, *reader's p.*, the desk at which the service is read, etc. 1479. **2.** A place (often enclosed), usu. raised on a footpace, seated for and appropriated to certain of the worshippers, e.g. for a great personage, a family, etc. late ME. **b.** Now applied to the fixed benches with backs in a church or chapel, each seating a number of worshippers 1631. **3.** A raised seat or bench, for judges, lawyers, etc.; a rostrum used by public speakers, etc.; a 'box' in a theatre, etc. Now only as transf. from 2. 1558.

Comb. †**p.-fellow,** one who sits in the same pew; one of the same communion or persuasion; an associate; **p.-rent,** the rent paid for a p., or for sittings in a church. Hence **Pew** *v. trans.* to fit up with pews; to shut up in or as in a p. **Pew·age,** the provision of pews; rent paid for pews.

Pewee (pĭ·wī). *U.S.* and *Canada.* 1810. [imit.] A name for some small olivaceous fly-catchers of the family *Tyrannidæ*, and so identified with PEWIT 3; by others restricted to the genus *Contopus*, as *C. virens*, the *Wood-p.* of the U.S. and Canada.

Pewit, peewit (pĭ·wit, piū·it). 1529. [imit., from the cry of the bird.] **1.** The Lapwing (*Vanellus vulgaris* or *cristatus*). **b.** The wailing cry of this bird 1812. **2.** (In full **p. gull.**) The black-headed Gull (*Larus ridibundus*); from its cry 1661. **3.** In *U.S.* A name of species of Tyrant Flycatchers, as the Common P., *Sayornis fusca* or *S. phœbe* 1817.

Pewter (piū·təɹ). late ME. [– OFr. *peutre, peaultre* = Pr. *peltre*, It. *peltro* :- Rom. **peltrum* (med.L. *peltrum*), of unkn. origin.] **1.** A grey alloy of tin and lead, or (sometimes) other metals. **b.** Pewter ware 1573. **2.** A pewter pot. Also *fig.* 1839. **3.** A polishing medium used by marble-workers, made by the calcination of tin 1875.

Comb.: **p.-solder,** soft solder, of similar composition to p., but containing a greater proportion of lead. So **Pew·terer,** a worker in p. ME. **Pew·tery** *a.* of the nature of, or characteristic of, p.

Pewterwort (piū·təɹwɒɹt). 1597. [f. prec. + WORT[1].] *Herb.* The plant *Equisetum hyemale*, so named on account of its use in polishing pewter utensils.

Peyerian (pəiˌīᵊ·riăn), *a.* 1799. [f. proper name *Peyer* + -IAN.] *Anat.* Of, pertaining to, or named after the Swiss anatomist J. K. Peyer (1653–1712); as the *P.* (or *Peyer's*) *glands* or *patches*, groups of follicles in the wall of the small intestine.

‖**Peziza** (pĭzəi·ză). 1833. [mod.L. (Dillenius); cf. L. *pezica* or *pezita*, f. Gr. πέζις a stalkless mushroom.] *Bot.* A large genus of discomycetous fungi, of cup-like shape, and often of brilliant colour. Hence **Pezi·ziform, Pezi·zoid** *adjs.* of the form of a P.

‖**Pfennig, -ing** (pfe·nig, -iŋ). 1547. [G. *pfennig*; see PENNY.] A small copper coin of Germany, now the hundredth part of a mark.

Ph, a consonantal digraph, usu. having the phonetic value of F. It was the combination used by the Romans to represent the Gr. letter Φ, φ named Φῖ, *Phī.* In late pop. and med. Latin, and in the Romanic languages, *f* was often substituted for *ph*, as now regularly in Italian and Spanish, and in some French words, whence the spelling of English *fancy* (cf. *phantasy*), *fantastic.* In *phantom* and *pheasant* (Fr. *fantôme, faisan*), there has been etymological reversion to *ph.*

Phacochœre (fæ·kŏkīᵊɹ). Also **-chere.** 1842. [– mod.L. *phacochœrus*, f. Gr. φακός wart + χοῖρος pig.] *Zool.* A wart-hog.

Phacolite (fæ·kŏləit). Also **phako-.** 1843. [– G. *phakolit* (Breithaupt), f. Gr. φακός lentil + λίθος stone; see -LITE.] *Min.* A colourless variety of CHABAZITE, occurring in crystals of lenticular form.

Phæacian (fiˌēⁱ·ʃăn). 1788. [f. L. *Phæacia*, Gr. Φαιακία Scheria + -AN.] One of the inhabitants of Scheria (Corcyra), noted for their luxury; hence, a gourmand.

Phænogam, phe- (fī·nŏgæm). 1846. [f. mod.L. *phænogama* (Willdenow 1804), or *-gamæ*, f. Gr. φαινο- showing + γάμος marriage.] = PHANEROGAM. So **Phænoga·mian, Phænoga·mic, Phæno·gamous** *adjs.*

Phaeton (fēⁱ·tən). 1593. [– Fr. *phaéton* – L. *Phaethon* – Gr. Φαέθων (myth.) son of Helios (sun) and Clymene, famous for his unlucky driving of the sun-chariot, subst. use of pr. pple. φαέθων shining.] †**1.** A rash charioteer like Phaethon; any charioteer; something that, like Phaethon, sets the world on fire –1747. **2.** A species of light four-wheeled open carriage; usu. drawn by a pair of horses, and with one or two seats facing forward 1742.

‖**Phagedæna, -ena** (fædʒidī·nă, fægi-). 1657. [L. – Gr. φαγέδαινα, f. φαγεῖν eat.] *Path.* An eating ulcer; spreading erosion occurring in an ulcer or sore. So **Phagedænic, -enic** (fædʒidī·nik, -e·nik, fægi-) **Phagedæ·nous,** *adjs. Path.* of the nature of, characterized by, or affected with P.

Phagocyte (fæ·gŏsəit). 1884. [f. Gr. φαγο- eating + -CYTE.] *Physiol.* A leucocyte which has the power of guarding the system against infection by absorbing and destroying pathogenic microbes. Hence **Pha·go-cytism, Pha:gocyto·sis,** the destruction of micro-organisms by phagocytes.

-phagous, *suffix*, f. L. *-phagus*, Gr. -φαγος eating + -OUS; as *anthropophagous* man-eating, etc. Also **-phagy,** – Gr. -φαγία eating (*sb.*); as *ichthyophagy*.

Phako-: see PHACO-.

Phalangal (fălæ·ŋgăl), *a. rare.* 1848. [f. L. *phalanx, phalang-* + -AL[1].] = PHALANGEAL. Also **Phala·ngar** *a.*

Phalange (fæ·lændʒ). 1560. [– Fr. *phalange* – L. *phalang-*; see PHALANX.] †**1.** = PHALANX 1. –1689. **2.** = PHALANX 3, 4. 1864.

Phalangeal (fălæ·ndʒiăl), *a.* 1831. [f. PHALANGE + AL[1].] *Anat.* and *Zool.* Pertaining to, or of the nature of, a phalanx or phalanges (PHALANX 3). Also *sb.*

Phalanger (fæ·ləndʒəɹ). 1774. [– Fr. *phalanger* (Buffon, quasi *phalangier*, after *tarsier* TARSIER) f. Gr. φαλάγγιον spider's web, in ref. to the webbed toes of the hind feet.] *Zool.* A quadruped of the genus *Phalangista*, or of the subfamily *Phalangistinæ*, Australian marsupials of arboreal habits; the typical genera (Australian opossums) have prehensile tails; the *flying phalangers* have non-prehensile tails and a flying membrane or parachute.

Phalangid (fălæ·ndʒid). 1835. [– mod.L. *Phalangidæ*, f. L. *phalangium* – Gr. φαλάγγιον venomous spider; see -ID[3].] *Zool.* An arachnid of the family *Phalangidæ* or order *Phalangidea* (typical genus *Phalangium*), related to the mites, but more resembling spiders, without spinnerets or poison-glands, and usu. with very long and slender legs; the common species are known as *harvest-spiders* or *harvestmen*.

Phalangist (fălæ·ndʒist, fæ·lăndʒist). 1835. [– mod.L. *Phalangista*, Cuvier's substitute for PHALANGER.] *Zool.* = PHALANGER. So **Phala·ngistine** *a.* belonging to the subfamily *Phalangistinæ*; *sb.* a marsupial of this subfamily.

Phalangite (fæ·lændʒəit). *Hist.* 1839. [– L. *phalangita* or *-ites* – Gr., f. φάλαγξ; see -ITE[1]1.] A soldier belonging to a phalanx.

Phalanstery (fæ·lænstĕri). 1850. (Earlier in Fr. form.) [Anglicization of Fr. *phalanstère*.] In Fourier's scheme for the reorganization of society, A building or set of buildings occupied by a *phalanx* or socialistic community; hence, such a community numbering about 1800 persons. So **Phalansterian** (fælænstī^ə·riăn) *a.* and *sb.* of, pertaining or relating to a p.; a member of a p. 1843.

Phalanx (fæ·læŋks). *Pl.* **pha·lanxes,** ‖**phalanges** (fălæ·ndʒīz). 1553. [– L. *phalanx, -ang-* – Gr. φάλαγξ.] **1.** *Gr. Antiq.* A line or array of battle; *spec.* a body of heavy-armed infantry drawn up in close order, with shields joined and spears overlapping. Hence **b.** any compact body of troops 1814. **2.** *transf.* A compact body of persons or animals massed or ranged in order, as for attack, defence, etc. 1733. **b.** *fig.* A number or set of persons banded together for a common purpose; a 'united front'; the combination of such (in phr. *in p.*) 1600. **c.** A community of persons living together in a PHALANSTERY, q.v. 1843. **3.** *Anat.* and *Zool.* Each bone of the digits (fingers and toes, or homologous parts). Usu. in pl. *phalanges*. 1693. **4.** *Bot.* A bundle of stamens united by their filaments 1770.

1. The square (whiche the Macedons call p.) 1553. *attrib.* The p. order of battle 1838. **2. a.** The sheep..All huddling into p., stood and gaz'd COWPER. **b.** The crown lawyers opposed in p. 1817. Hence **Pha·lanxed** *a.* drawn up in a p.

Phalarope (fæ·lăro^u p). 1776. [– Fr. *phalarope* (Brisson 1760) – mod.L. *Phalaropus*, irreg. f. Gr. φαλαρίς coot + πούς, ποδ- foot.] *Ornith.* A name applied to several small wading and swimming birds of the family *Phalaropodidæ*, order *Limicolæ*, related to the snipes.

Phaleucian (fălʼū·siăn), *a.* 1571. [f. L. *Phaleucius* (for *Phalæcius*) + -AN.] Pertaining to Phalæcus, an ancient Greek poet; applied to a metre consisting of a spondee, a dactyl, and three trochees.

Phallic (fæ·lik), *a.* 1789. [– Gr. φαλλικός, f. φαλλός; see next, -IC.] Of or relating to the phallus or phallism; symbolical of the generative power in nature. Hence **Pha·llicism, Pha·llism,** the worship of the phallus, or of the organs of sex, as symbols of the generative power in nature.

‖**Phallus** (fæ·lŏs). *Pl.* **-i.** 1613. [– late L. *phallus* – Gr. φαλλός penis.] **1.** An image of the male generative organ, symbolizing the generative power in nature, venerated in various religious systems; *spec.* that carried in procession in the Dionysiac festivals in ancient Greece. **2.** *Bot.* A genus of gasteromycetous fungi, so called from their shape, including the common stinkhorn, *P. impudicus* 1857.

Phane, obs. var. FANE *sb.*[1] 2 = VANE.

Phanero- (fæ·nĕro), bef. a vowel **phaner-,** comb. form of Gr. φανερός visible, evident (opp. to CRYPTO-); used in: **Pha:nerocodo·nic** [Gr. κώδων a bell] *a.*, bell-shaped: said of the gonophores of hydrozoans when possessing a developed umbrella; **Pha:nerocry·stalline** *a.*, of evident crystalline structure; **Pha:nero-glo·ssal, -glo·ssate, -glo·ssous** [Gr. γλῶσσα] *adjs.* having a distinct tongue, as certain frogs.

Phanerogam (fæ·nĕrogæ:m). 1861. [– Fr. *phanérogame*, in mod.L. *phanerogamus* adj.; see PHANERO-, + γάμος marriage.] *Bot.* A phanerogamic or flowering plant. (Opp. to CRYPTOGAM. Chiefly in pl. So **Phanerogamous** (fænĕrǫ·gămǝs) *a.* flowering 1816.

‖**Phanerogamia** (fæ:nĕrogæ·miă). 1821. [mod.L., sing. fem. abstr. f. *phanerogamus*; see prec., -IA[1].] *Bot.* A primary division of the vegetable kingdom, comprising plants having obvious reproductive organs, i.e. stamens and pistils; the sub-kingdom of flowering plants. Hence **Phanerogaˑmic** *a.* phanerogamous 1830.

Phantascope (fæ·ntăsko^u p). 1866. [irreg. var. of PHANTOSCOPE.] **1.** A contrivance for exhibiting phenomena of binocular vision. **2.** = PHENAKISTOSCOPE 1876.

Phantasia, var. form of FANTASIA.

Phantasiast (fæntē^i·ziæst). 1680. [– eccl. Gr. φαντασιαστής, f. φαντασία appearance; see FANTASY.] One of those Docetæ who held that the body of Jesus Christ was a mere phantasm.

Phantasm (fæ·ntæz'm). ME. [– (O)Fr. *fantasme*, †*-esme* – L. *phantasma*; see next, PHANTOM.] **I. 1. a.** Illusion, deceptive appearance. *Obs.* or *arch.* **b.** With *a* and *pl.* An illusion; a deception; a phantom. late ME. **c.** An illusive likeness (*of* something), a 'ghost' or 'shadow'; a counterfeit 1638. †**d.** A counterfeit, an impostor –1641. **2.** An apparition, a ghost. Now only *poet.* or *rhet.* late ME. **b.** *Psychics.* The supposed vision or perception of an absent person, living or dead, presented to the senses or mind of another 1884.

1. b. A fantasm bred by the feaver which had then seis'd him MILT. **2.** That those phantasms.. do frequent Cemeteries, Charnel-houses, and Churches, it is because these are the dormitories of the dead SIR T. BROWNE.

II. 1. *Philos.* A mental image, appearance, or representation, considered as the immediate object of sense-perception 1594. †**2.** Imagination, fancy –1689. **b.** An imagination, a fancy (now always with emphasis on its unreality) 1672.

1. When they are objects of memory and of imagination, they get the name of phantasms 1785. Hence **Phanta·smal,** †**Phantasma·tical, Phanta·smic,** *adjs.* of the nature of a p.; spectral; imaginary, unreal. **Phanta·smally** *adv.*

Phantasma (fæntæ·zmă). †Also **fantasma.** *Pl.* **-as** (ăz), **-ata** (ătă). 1598. [– It. *fantasma* = L. *phantasma* – Gr. φάντασμα, f. φαντάζειν present to (or as to) the eye, f. φαντός visible, f. stem φαν- of φαίνειν show; see prec., PHANTOM.] **a.** An illusion, vision, dream; **b.** An apparition, a spectre.

Phantasmagoria (fæntæzmăgō^ə·riă) Also **Phanta·smagory.** 1802. [prob. – Fr. *fantasmagorie* (1801), f. *fantasme* with fanciful termination.] **1.** An exhibition of optical illusions produced chiefly by means of the magic lantern, first given in London in 1802. Also *transf.* **2.** A shifting series of phantasms or imaginary figures as seen in a dream or fevered condition or as called up by the imagination 1828. **3.** *transf.* A shifting and changing external scene consisting of many elements 1822.

2. Milton's genius has filled the atmosphere with a brilliant p. of contending angels 1875. Hence **Phantasmago·rial, Phantasmago·ric, -al** *adjs.*

Phantasmascope (fæntæ·zmăsko^u p). 1835. [irreg. f. PHANTASMA + -SCOPE.] = PHENAKISTOSCOPE.

Phantast, -asy: see FANTAST, -ASY.

Phantom (fæ·ntəm). [ME. *fantome, -um,* also *-osme* – OFr. *fantosme, -ome* (mod. *fantôme*) :– pop. L. **fantauma* – Gr. φάντασμα PHANTASMA.] †**1.** Illusion, unreality; vain imagination; delusion, falsity –1692. †**b.** With *a* and *pl.* An instance of this; a deception; a lie –1686. **2.** Something that has only an apparent existence; an apparition, a spectre; a spirit, a ghost. late ME. **b.** A (material or optical) image *of* something 1707. **c.** *fig.* A 'vain show'; a person, institution, etc., having the show but not the substance of power; a cipher 1661. **3.** A mental illusion; an image which appears in a dream or which is formed or cherished in the mind; also, a haunting thought 1590. **4.** *attrib.* or *adj.* That is a phantom; merely apparent, illusive. late ME.

2. The pale phantoms of the slain Glide nightly o'er the silent plain SMOLLETT. **c.** The caprice of the Barbarians..once more seated this Imperial p. [Maximus] on the throne GIBBON. **3.** She was a P. of delight When first she gleamed upon my sight WORDSW. **4.** The Phantome-nations of the dead POPE. *Comb.* **p.-tumour,** a temporary abdominal swelling resembling an actual tumour. Hence **Phantoma·tic** *a.* phantom-like, unreal. **Phanto·mic, Phanto·mical** *adjs.* of the nature of, resembling a p.

Phantoscope (fæ·ntŏsko^u p). 1894. [f. Gr. φαντός visible + -SCOPE.] A modification of the kaleidoscope.

-phany, repr. Gr. -φανία, -φάνεια appearance, manifestation, f. stem φαν- of φαίνειν show, appear; as in EPIPHANY, etc.

Pharaoh (fē^ə·ro). OE. [– eccl. L. *Pharaō*, *Pharaōn-* (whence Fr. *Pharaon*) – Gr. Φαραώ – Heb. *par'ōh* – Egypt. *pr-'o* great house. The Eng. final *h* is from Heb.] **1.** The generic appellation of the ancient Egyptian kings; an Egyptian king. **b.** *fig.* A tyrant or taskmaster 1630. †**2.** = FARO –1843.

1. P.'s chicken, the Egyptian vulture (*Neophron percnopterus*); **P.'s mouse** or **rat,** the ichneumon; **P.'s serpent,** a chemical toy composed of sulphocyanide of mercury, which fuses in a serpentine form. Hence **Pharao·nic,** †**-al** *adjs.* of, pertaining to, or like P.

Phare (fē^ə ɹ). 1615. [– Fr. *phare* – L. *pharus* – Gr. φάρος. See PHAROS.] **1.** A lighthouse. †**2.** A strait or channel lighted by a pharos; the Strait of Messina –1723.

†**Pha·rian,** *a.* 1591. [f. L. *Pharius* of PHAROS + -AN.] Of or pertaining to the island of Pharos; *poet.* Egyptian, Nilotic. **b.** *sb.* An Egyptian. 1729.

And past from P. fields to Canaan land MILT.

Pharisaic (færisē^i·ik), *a.* 1618. [– eccl. L. *pharisaicus* – Gr. φαρισαϊκός; see PHARISEE, -IC.] **1.** Of or belonging to the Pharisees. Also **Pharisæ·an, -e·an.** 1643. **2.** Resembling the Pharisees in being strict in doctrine and ritual, without the spirit of piety; laying stress upon the outward show of religion and morality, and assuming superiority on that account; hypocritical; formal; self-righteous.

1. The Pharisaick Sect amongst the Jews CUDWORTH. **2.** Wee are so Punctual and Precise In Doctrine (Pharisaik-wise) 1618. So **Pharisa·ical** *a.*, **-ly** *adv.*, **-ness** 1599.

Pharisaism (fæ·risе,iz'm). 1601. [– Fr. *pharisaïsme*, f. *pharisaïque* (both in Calvin); see prec., -ISM.] **1.** The doctrine and practice of the Pharisees; the fact of being a Pharisee 1610. **2.** The character and spirit of the Pharisees; hypocrisy; formalism; self-righteousness.

2. Of all the Pharisaisms of the day, our Church-going seems to me the masterpiece PUSEY.

Pharisee (fæ·risī). [OE. *fariseus*, early ME. *farisew* – eccl. L. *pharisæus, -ēus* – Gr. φαρισαῖος – Aram. *p'rīšayyā*, emphatic pl. of *p'rīš* = Heb. *pārūš* separated, separatist. The present form is from ME. *f-*, *pharise(e*

– OFr. *pharise* – L.] **1.** One of an ancient Jewish sect distinguished by their strict observance of the traditional and written law, and by their pretensions to superior sanctity. **2.** A person of this disposition; a self-righteous person; a formalist; a hypocrite 1589.

1. Oon a Pharise and the tothir a pupplican WYCLIF *Luke* 18:10. **2.** Not the nation, but the affection makes a P. 1599. Hence **Pha·riseeism,** Pharisaism.

Pharmaceutic (fāɹmăsiū·tik, -kiū·tik), *a.* and *sb.* 1541. [– late L. *pharmaceuticus* – Gr. φαρμακευτικός, f. φαρμακευτής = φαρμακεύς; see PHARMACY, -IC.] **A.** *adj.* Pertaining or relating to pharmacy; pharmaceutical. Now *rare.* 1656. **B.** *sb.* (Usu. in pl. **pharmaceutics.**) The science of pharmacy, or of the use of medicinal drugs 1541. So **Pharmaceu·tical** *a.* pertaining to or engaged in pharmacy; relating to the preparation, use, or sale of medicinal drugs 1648; **-ly** *adv.* **Pharmaceu·tist,** a pharmacist, druggist.

Pharmacist (fā·ɹmăsist). 1834. [f. PHARMACY + -IST.] A person skilled in pharmacy; a druggist or pharmaceutical chemist.

Pharmaco-, repr. Gr. φαρμακο-, comb. form of φάρμακον drug, medicine, poison, as in:

Pha:rmacodyna·mic, *a.* relating to the powers or effects of drugs; so **Pha:rmacodyna·mics** *sb. pl.* the science or subject of the powers or effects of drugs. **Pharmacognosy** (fāɹmăkǫ·gnŏsi) (also **-gno·sia,** and less correctly **-gno·sis**), the knowledge of drugs, *esp.* in their natural or unprepared state.

Pharmacolite (fā·ɹmăkoləi:t). 1805. [f. Gr. φάρμακον poison + -LITE. Named by Karsten 1800.] *Min.* Hydrous arsenate of calcium, occurring in silky fibres.

Pharmacology (fāɹmăkǫ·lŏdʒi). 1721. [– mod.L. *pharmacologia* (W. Harris 1683); see PHARMACO- and -LOGY.] That branch of medical science which relates to drugs, their preparation, uses, and effects, the science of pharmacy. Hence **Pha:rmacolo·gical** *a.*, **-ly** *adv.* **Pharmaco·logist.**

Pharmacopœia (fā:ɹmăkopī·ă). 1621. [mod.L. – Gr. φαρμακοποιΐα the art of a φαρμακοποιός preparer of drugs, f. φαρμακο- PHARMACO- + -ποιος making, maker.] **1.** A book containing a list of drugs and other medicinal substances or preparations, with directions for their preparation and identification; *spec.* one officially published and revised from time to time. **2.** A stock of drugs 1721. Hence **Pharmacopœ·ial** *a.* pertaining to a p.; *spec.* recognized in, or prepared according to the directions of, the official Pharmacopœia.

Pharmacosiderite (fā:ɹmăkosəi·dĕrəit). 1835. [Named by Hausmann, 1813; see PHARMACO-, SIDERITE.] *Min.* Hydrous arsenate of iron, occurring in minute greenish or brownish crystals of cubic form; also called *cube-ore.*

Pharmacy (fā·ɹmăsi). late ME. [– OFr. *farmacie* (mod. *pharmacie*) – med.L. *pharmacia* – Gr. φαρμακεία practice of a φαρμακεύς druggist, f. φάρμακον drug, medicine; see -Y[3].] **1.** The use or administration of drugs or medicines. (Now chiefly *poet.* or *rhet.*). **2.** The art or practice of collecting, preparing, and dispensing drugs, esp. medicinally; the compounding of medicines; the occupation of a druggist or pharmaceutical chemist. (The chief current sense.) 1651. **3.** A drug-store or dispensary 1833.

Pharo: see PHARAOH 2.

Pharos (fēə·rǫs). 1552. [Appellative use of L. *Pharos* – Gr. Φάρος name of an island off Alexandria.] **1.** Name of an island off Alexandria, on which King Ptolemy Philadelphus built a famous tower lighthouse; hence the lighthouse itself 1575. **2.** Any lighthouse or beacon to direct mariners 1552. **3.** *transf.* Any conspicuous light; a lamp, etc. 1759.

1. A most high Tower, like to the Pharo of Alexandria 1617. **2.** *fig.* Their eyes sweet splendor seems a P. bright SYLVESTER.

Pharyngal (fări·ŋgăl), *a.* (*sb.*) 1835. [f. mod.L. *pharynx, pharyng-* + -AL[1].] = next.

Pharyngeal (fări·ndʒiăl), *a.* (*sb.*) 1828. [f. as prec. + *-eal* for -AL[1]; cf. *phalangeal*, etc.] Of, pertaining to, or connected with the pharynx. **b.** *sb.* Short for *p. artery, bone,* etc.; esp. applied to the pharyngeal bones in fishes 1834.

‖**Pharyngitis** (færindʒəi·tis). 1844. [mod. L., f. Gr. φάρυγξ, φαρυγγ- PHARYNX + -ITIS.] *Path.* Inflammation of the pharynx. Hence **Pharyngi·tic** (-i·tik), *a.*

Pharyngo- (fări·ŋgo), comb. form of PHARYNX; as in:

Phary·ngobranch (-bræŋk), *a.*, belonging to the *Pharyngobranchii*, the lowest group of vertebrates, characterized by the pharynx being perforated by the branchial slits; *sb.* an animal of this group, an *Amphioxus* or lancelet; so **Pharyngobra·nchial, Pharyngobra·nchiate** *adjs.* = prec. adj. **Phary·ngognath** [Gr. γνάθος jaw] *a.* belonging to the order *Pharyngognathi* of fishes, having the inferior pharyngeal bones ankylosed; *sb.* a fish of this order. **Pharyngo-laryngeal** (-lări·ndʒiăl) *a.* pertaining to the pharnyx and larynx; applied to the lower cavity of the pharynx. **Phary·ngotome** [Gr. -τομος cutting], an instrument for making an incision into the pharynx; so **Pharyngo·tomy,** incision into the pharynx.

Pharynx (fæ·riŋks). 1693. [– mod.L. *pharynx* – Gr. φάρυγξ throat.] *Anat.* The cavity, with its enclosing muscles and mucous membrane, situated behind, and communicating with the nose, mouth, and larynx, and continuous below with the œsophagus. **b.** A more or less corresponding cavity in many invertebrates 1826.

Phascolome (fæ·skoloᵘm). 1838. [– mod.L. *Phascolomys*, f. Gr. φάσκωλος purse + μῦς mouse.] *Zool.* An animal of the marsupial genus *Phascolomys*, containing the three species of the WOMBAT.

Phase (fēⁱz). 1812. [Partly – Fr. *phase*, partly new sing. deduced from pl. *phases* of PHASIS, q.v.] **1.** Each of the aspects presented by the moon or any planetary body, according to the extent of its illumination. **2.** Aspect; appearance; *esp.* any one aspect of a thing of varying appearances; a state or stage of change or development. **3.** *Physics.* A particular change or point in a recurring sequence of movements or changes, e.g. a vibration or undulation 1864.

2. The most attractive p. of her character LYTTON.

‖**Phasis** (fēⁱ·zis, fēⁱ·sis). *Pl.* **phases** (fēⁱ·zīz, fēⁱ·sīz). 1660. [mod.L. – Gr. φάσις, f. root φα-, φαν- of φαίνειν show, appear.] **1.** = PHASE 1. **b.** The first appearance of the new moon 1880. **2.** = PHASE 2. 1665.

2. It is..only a new p. of an old thing 1886. Hence **Pha·sic** *a.* 1890.

†**Phasm.** 1656. [– L. *phasma* – Gr. φάσμα apparition, f. φάω I shine, or φαίνειν show, appear. (See next.)] **1.** An extraordinary appearance; *esp.* a meteor –1686. **2.** Anything visionary; a phantom, apparition –1822.

‖**Phasma** (fæ·zmă). 1635. [See prec.] †**1.** Earlier form of PHASM, q.v. **2.** *Zool.* A genus of cursorial orthopterous insects, typical of the family *Phasmidæ*, known as spectre-insects or walking-sticks. Hence **Pha·smid** 1872.

Pheasant (fe·zănt). ME. [– AFr. *fesaunt*, for (O)Fr. *faisan* :– L. *phasianus* – Gr. φασιανός (sc. ὄρνις bird) of Phasis, a river in Colchis, whence the bird is said to have spread westwards. As in *phantom*, there has been etymol. reversion to *ph-*. For parasitic *-t* cf. *tyrant.*] **1.** Name of a well-known game-bird, *Phasianus colchicus*, naturalized in Britain and other parts of Europe; hence, applied to all the species of *Phasianus*, and to some related genera. **b.** Locally applied to birds of other families, as the Ruffed Grouse (*Bonasa umbellata*) of the U.S., etc. 1637. **c.** The bird or its flesh as food. late ME. **2.** *Ornith.* With defining words, applied to particular species of the genus *Phasianus* and allied *Phasianinæ*, and *Pavoninæ*; also to other birds in some way resembling the pheasant 1743. **b.** *Sea p.*, the Pintail Duck, *Dafila acuta* 1633.

2. Firebacked P., of the Malay archipelago, etc., *Euplocamus ignitus*; **Gold** or **Golden P.,** of China and Tibet, *Thaumalea picta* or *Chrysolophus pictus*; **Lyre-** or **Lyre-tailed P.,** of Australia = LYREBIRD; **Ring-necked P.,** of China, *Phasianus torquatus*; **Silver P.,** of China, *Euplocamus nycthemerus*; **Water P.,** the pheasant-tailed Jacana, *Hydrophasianus chirurgus.*

attrib. and *Comb.*, as *p.-driving*, etc.; **p.-cock,** the male p.; **-coucal, cuckoo,** *Centropus phasianus*, of New South Wales; **-duck** = *Sea pheasant*; **-hen,** the female p.; **-Malay,** a variety of the domestic fowl; **-wood** = PARTRIDGE-WOOD 1. Hence **Phea·santry,** a place where pheasants are reared or kept.

Pheasant's eye. 1731. **1.** Any plant of the genus *Adonis*, esp. *A. autumnalis.* **2.** The common white Narcissus (*N. poeticus*) 1872. **3.** (also **pheasant-eye, pheasant's eye pink**): The ring-flowered variety of the Garden Pink (*Dianthus plumarius* var. *annulatus*) 1753. So **Phea·sant-e·yed,** *a.* marked like the eye of a pheasant; applied to the flowers of these plants.

Pheasant-shell. A shell of the gastropod genus *Phasianella*, of the Australian seas; named from the brilliantly coloured and polished surface.

Phello- (felo), comb. form of Gr. φελλός cork. **Phe·lloderm** [Gr. δέρμα skin], *Bot.* a layer of parenchymatous cells containing chlorophyll, formed in the stems of some plants from the inner cells of the phellogen. **Phe·llogen** [see -GEN], *Bot.* the layer of meristematic cells from which the cork-cells are formed, the cork-cambium. **Phello-pla·stic,** a cork model or figure; the art of cutting figures or models in cork (also **Phellopla·stics**).

Phen- : see PHÆN-.

Phen-, pheno-, formative element in *Chem.* (for *phæn(o-)* f. Gr. φαινο- shining, φαίνειν show, φαίνεσθαι appear. First used by Laurent, 1841, in 'hydrate de phényle', and 'acide phénique', names for the substance subseq. called PHENOL. These names indicated that the substance was coal-tar product, arising from the manufacture of *illuminating* gas. Hence *phen-, pheno-* was gradually used as the basis of the names of all the bodies derived from benzene. **Phenacetin** (fĭnæ·sĭtin), the acetyl deriv. of phenetidin, the ethylic ether of paramido-phenol $C_6H_4.OC_2H_5.NH(CH_3CO)$, used as an antipyretic 1889. **Phena·nthrene,** a solid hydrocarbon, $(C_6H_4.CH)_2$, prepared from crude anthracene (with which it is isomeric), crystallizing in colourless shining laminæ. **Phene·tidin,** the ethyl deriv. of amidophenol. **Phe·netol,** ethyl phenyl ether, or phenate of ethyl, $C_2H_5.OC_6H_5$, a volatile aromatic-smelling liquid.

Phenacite (fe·năsəit), **-kite** (-kəit). 1834. [f. Gr. φέναξ, φενακ- cheat (as having been mistaken for quartz) + -ITE[1] 2b.] *Min.* A silicate of glucinum, occurring in quartz-like transparent or translucent crystals.

Phenakistoscope (fenăki·stŏskoᵘp). 1834. [f. Gr. φενακιστής cheat, f. φενακίζειν to cheat + -SCOPE.] A disc with figures upon it arranged radially, representing a moving object in successive positions; on turning it round rapidly, and viewing the figures through a fixed slit (or their reflexions in a mirror through radial slits in the disc itself), the persistence of the successive visual images produces the impression of actual motion.

†**Phene** (fīn). 1857. [– Fr. *phène*; see PHEN-.] *Chem.* An early name proposed for BENZENE. Hence **Phenic** (fī·nik, fe·nik) *a.* = PHENYLIC. *P. acid*, PHENOL or carbolic acid. Its salts are **Phe·nates.**

Phenicine, -in (fe·nisəin, -in). 1826. [Etymologically *phœnicin(e*, f. Gr. φοῖνιξ a purple-red, lit. a Phœnician (in ref. to Tyrian purple) + -IN[1], -INE[5].] *Chem.* A colouring matter produced by the action of nitro-sulphuric acid on phenylic alcohol; indigo carmine.

Phenol (fī·nǫl). 1852. [– Fr. *phénole*, f. *phène, phénique*; see PHEN-, PHENE, -OL.] *Chem.* A hydroxyl derivative of benzene, $C_6H_5(OH)$, commonly known as CARBOLIC *acid*, q.v. (also *phenic* or *phenylic acid, phenyl hydrate*). **b.** In pl. **phenols,** the hydroxyl derivatives of the aromatic or benzene series of hydrocarbons 1857. Hence **Pheno·lic** *a.* carbolic.

Phenology (fīnǫ·lŏdʒi). Also **phæn-.** 1884. [f. *pheno-* (in *phenomenon*) + -LOGY.] The study of the times of recurring natural phenomena. So **Phenolo·gical** *a.* 1875.

Phenomenal (fīnǫ·menăl), *a.* (*sb.*) Also

phæn-. 1825. [f. PHENOMENON + -AL[1].] **1.** Of the nature of a phenomenon; consisting of phenomena; apparent, sensible, perceptible. (Opp. to *real*, *absolute*, etc., and in Philosophy to *noumenal*.) Also *absol.*, *the p.*, that which is cognizable by the senses. **b.** Of, relating to, or concerned with phenomena, esp. with the phenomena of any science 1840. **2.** Of the nature of a remarkable phenomenon; extraordinary, exceptional; 'prodigious' 1850. Hence **Pheno·menali:sm, a.** that manner of thinking which considers things from the point of view of phenomena only; **b.** the doctrine that phenomena are the only objects of knowledge, or the only realities. So **Pheno·menalist.** 1856. **Pheno·menalize** *v. trans.* to render p.; to conceive or represent as p.

Phenomenology (fĭnǫmėnǫ·lŏdʒi). 1797. [f. next + -LOGY.] **a.** The science of phenomena as distinct from that of being (ontology). **b.** That division of any science which describes and classifies its phenomena.

Phenomenon (fĭnǫ·mėnǫ̆n). *Pl.* **-a.** 1576. [Also, in early use, *phaino-*, *phæno-*; – late L. *phænomenon*, pl. *-mena* – Gr. φαινόμενον, -α, subst. use of pr. pple. pass. of φαίνειν show, pass. be seen, appear, f. *φαν-, as in φανερός visible, clear.] **1.** A thing that appears, or is perceived or observed; applied chiefly to a fact or occurrence, the cause of which is in question. **2.** *Philos.* That of which the senses or the mind directly takes note; an immediate object of perception. (Opp. to NOUMENON.) 1788. **3.** A highly exceptional or unaccountable fact or occurrence; *colloq.* a prodigy 1771.

1. The common p. of a piece of metal being eaten away by rust 1878. Phr. †*To save* (or *salve*) *the phenomena* (tr. Gr. σώζειν τὰ φαινόμενα): to reconcile the admitted facts with some theory with which they appear to disagree. **3.** This, Sir,..this is the infant p.—Miss Ninetta Crummles DICKENS. Hence **Pheno·menism** = PHENOMENALISM b. **Pheno·menist** = PHENOMENALIST 1830.

Phenose (fī·nōᵘs). 1878. [f. PHEN- + -OSE[2].] *Chem.* A sweetish amorphous deliquescent compound formed by the action of hypochlorous acid on benzene, and having the general formula $C_6H_{12}O_6$ of the carbohydrates.

Phenyl (fī·nil, fe·nil). 1850. [f. PHEN- + -YL, lit. 'radical of benzene (*phene*)'.] *Chem.* The monovalent organic radical C_6H_5 (also symbolized Ph), which exists in the free state as DIPHENYL, $H_5C_6.C_6H_5$, and enters as a radical into benzene (*phenyl hydride*), phenol (*phenyl hydroxyl*), aniline (*phenylamine*), and a very extensive series of organic compounds. Also *attrib.* and *Comb.*, as *p. acetate*; **p.-ace·tamide** = ACETANILIDE; **p.-hy·drazine,** $C_6H_5.NH.NH_2$; etc. Hence **Phe·nylami:ne,** the systematic name of ANILINE (*monophenylamine*), $NH_2.C_6H_5$, and of many other 'organic bases derived from ammonia by the substitution of one or more atoms of phenyl for an equivalent quantity of hydrogen' (Watts). **Phe·nylene,** the hydrocarbon C_6H_4. **Phenylic** (fĭni·lik) *a.* of or derived from phenyl; *phenylic acid*, *alcohol*, other names for phenol or carbolic acid.

Pheon (fī·ǫn). 1486. [Of unkn. origin.] *Her.* 'A charge representing a broad barbed arrow, or head of a javelin' (Fairholt). Either identical with the 'broad arrow', or differing only in being engrailed on the inner edge.

Phew (fiū, fiu), *int.* 1604. [Representing the action of puffing or blowing away with the lips.] A vocal gesture expressing impatience, disgust, or weariness.

Phi (fəi). The Greek letter (Φ, φ) = ph.

Phial (fəi·ăl), *sb.* [Late ME. *fyole* – (O)Fr. *fiole* – L. *phiola*, *phiala* saucer, censer – Gr. φιάλη broad flat vessel.] A vessel for holding liquids, esp. drinks; now usu. a small glass bottle, esp. for liquid medicine. Hence **Phi·al** *v. trans.* to store or keep in a p.

Phil-, form of PHILO- used bef. a vowel or *h.*

-phil (fil), **-phile** (fəil), comb. element repr. Gr. φίλος loving, dear. In Gr., found only in personal names, with the sense 'dear, beloved', as Θεόφιλος Theophilus (dear to God). In med. and mod.L. often used in form *-philus*, *-phila* with sense 'lover, loving'. Hence in French words *-phile*, in Eng. *-phile* or *-phil*, as *Anglophil(e*, etc., for which forms with the prefix PHILO- are etymologically more correct.

Philabeg, erron. f. FILIBEG, a kilt.

Philadelphian (filăde·lfiăn), *a.* and *sb.* 1615. [In sense A. 1 f. Gr. φιλαδελφία brotherly love + -AN; in sense A. 2 in part, and in B., f. Gr. Φιλαδέλφεια *Philadelphia* (i.e. the city of Ptolemy Philadelphus).] **A.** *adj.* **1.** Brother-loving; loving the brethren. **2.** Of or pertaining to the Philadelphians; see B. and cf. Rev. 3:7–13. 1693. **3.** Of or pertaining to any city of the name of Philadelphia, esp. that in Pennsylvania, U.S.A. **4.** Of or pertaining to Ptolemy Philadelphus. **B.** *sb.* (*pl.*) A religious society (the *Philadelphian Society*) organized in England towards the end of the 17th c. 1693. **b.** A native or inhabitant of Philadelphia (cf. A. 3) 1792.

Philander (filæ·ndəɹ), *sb.* 1737. [– Gr. φίλανδρος adj., fond of men, (of a woman) loving her husband, f. φιλο- PHILO- + ἀνήρ, ἀνδρ-; in later use, a proper name for a lover.] †**1.** A lover, one given to making love –1813. **2.** A name for certain marsupial animals: **a.** A small wallaby (*Macropus brunnii*) first described by Philander de Bruyn. **b.** A S. Amer. opossum (*Didelphys philander*). **c.** An Australian bandicoot (*Perameles lagotis*). 1737. Hence **Phila·nder** *v. intr.* to make love, esp. in a trifling manner; to dangle after a woman. Whence **Phila·nderer,** one who philanders; a male flirt 1841.

Philanthrope (fi·læ̆nþrōᵘp). 1734. [– Gr. φιλάνθρωπος adj., f. φιλο- PHILO- + ἄνθρωπος man.] = PHILANTROPIST.

Philanthropic, -al (filæ̆nþrǫ·pik, -ăl), *adjs.* 1789. [– Fr. *philanthropique*, f. Gr. φιλάνθρωπος (see prec.) + -IC + -AL[1].] Characterized by philanthropy; benevolent, humane. So **Philanthro·pically** *adv.* 1787.

Philanthropine (filæ·nþrŏpin). 1802. [– G. *Philanthropin* – Gr. φιλανθρώπινον adj. neut. (formed after ἀνθρώπινον).] Name for the school founded in 1774 by Basedow or Bassedau at Dessau, in Germany, for the education of children by his 'natural system', in the principles of philanthropy, natural religion, etc.; also any similar institution. Hence **Philanthro·pinist,** an advocate of Basedow's system; also, a pupil at a p.

Philanthropism (filæ·nþrŏpiz'm). 1835. [f. PHILANTHROPY + -ISM.] The profession or practice of philanthropy; a philanthropic theory or system.

Philanthropist (filæ·nþrŏpist). 1730. [f. as prec. + -IST.] One who practises philanthropy; one who loves his fellow-men and exerts himself for their well-being. Formerly with the wider sense of 'friend or lover of man'.

Philanthropize (filæ·nþrŏpəiz), *v.* 1826. [f. as prec. + -IZE.] **1.** *intr.* To practise philanthropy. **2.** *trans.* To make (persons) objects of philanthropy 1830.

Philanthropy (filæ·nþrŏpi). 1608. [– late L. *philanthropia* – Gr. φιλανθρωπία, f. φιλάνθρωπος; see PHILANTHROPE, -Y[3].] Love towards mankind; practical benevolence towards men in general; the disposition to promote the well-being of one's fellow-men. †**b.** *spec.* (cf. *Titus* 3:4). The love of God to man –1711.

Philately (filæ·tĭli). 1865. [– Fr. *philatélie* (Herpin, 1864), f. Gr. φιλ(ο- PHILO- + ἀτελής free from charge, ἀτέλεια exemption from payment (ἐξ ἀτελείας *franco*). Gr. ἀτελής = *free* or *franco*, has been taken as = 'postage-stamp', the substitute for the original impressed receipt stamp for the amount prepaid.] Stamp-collecting. Hence **Philate·lic** (-ăte·lik) *a.* relating to or engaged in p. **Phila·telist,** a stamp-collector.

-phile: see -PHIL.

Philharmonic (filhaɹmǫ·nik), *a.* and *sb.* 1762. [– Fr. *philharmonique* – It. *filarmonico*; see PHIL-, HARMONIC.] **A.** *adj.* Loving harmony; devoted to music 1813. **B.** *sb.* A lover of harmony; a person devoted to music.

A. *P. Society*, name of various musical societies, *esp.* that founded in London in 1813 for the promotion of instrumental music; hence *P. concert*, one given by the P. society.

Philhellene (fi·lhelīn), *a.* and *sb.* 1825. [– Gr. φιλέλλην adj. loving the Greeks; see PHIL-, HELLENE.] **A.** *adj.* = next. **B.** *sb.* = PHILHELLENIST.

Philhellenic (filhelī·nik, -e·nik), *a.* 1830. [f. prec. + -IC; see HELLENIC.] Friendly to Greece or the Greeks (esp. in relation to national independence). So **Philhellenism** (filhe·lĭniz·m), the principle of supporting the Greeks. **Philhellenist** (filhelī·nist), a friend or supporter of Greece.

Philibeg, var. of FILIBEG.

Philip (fi·lip). late ME. [– Gr. Φίλιππος, lit. lover of horses.] **1.** A man's name; e.g. that of the king of Macedon, in the expression 'to appeal from Philip drunk to Philip sober' 1531. †**2.** Name of old French, Spanish, and Burgundian coins, issued by kings or dukes of this name –1769. **3.** A former name for a sparrow; contracted to *Phip. Obs.* exc. *dial.*; also applied to the hedge-sparrow. late ME.

Philippic (fili·pik), *sb.* (*a.*) 1592. [– L. *philippicus* (in *orationes Philippicæ*) – Gr. φιλιππικός (in Φιλιππικοὶ λόγοι), f. Φίλιππος; see prec., -IC.] **A.** *sb.* Epithet of the orations of Demosthenes against Philip king of Macedon; hence applied to Cicero's orations against Antony, and *gen.* to any discourse of the nature of a bitter invective. **B.** *adj.* **a.** Of or pertaining to any person called Philip; **b.** of Philippi; **c.** of the nature of a philippic or invective 1614.

Philippina (filipī·nă), **philippine, philopœna.** 1848. [repr. (like Fr. *philippine*, Du. *filippine*, etc.) G. *vielliebchen*, dim. of *viellieb* very dear (cf. *liebchen* darling), altered into *Philippchen* = little or darling Philip).] An amusement in which, at a dinner party, a person finding an almond or other nut with two kernels eats one kernel, and gives the other to a person of the opposite sex; when the parties next meet, the one who first says 'Good morning, Philippine!' is entitled to a present from the other. Also applied to the double nut or kernel, and to the present claimed or given.

Philippize (fi·lipəiz), *v.* 1607. [– Gr. φιλιππίζειν, f. Φίλιππος Philip; see -IZE.] *intr.* To favour, or take the side of, Philip of Macedon; also *gen.* to speak or write as one is corruptly inspired or influenced.

The oracles will P., as long as Philip is the master 1875.

‖**Philister** (fili·stəɹ). 1828. [G. *Philister*, orig. Luther's rendering of Vulg. *Philistæi* or Heb. *pᵉlištîm*; cf. PHILISTINE.] = PHILISTINE *sb.* 3, 4.

Philistia (fili·stiă). 1535. [– med.L. *Philistia* = late L. *Philistæa* (*-thæa*) in Jerome = Gr. φιλιστία.] **1.** The country of the Philistines, in south-west Palestine; also, the people. **2.** The class of 'Philistines' (sense A. 4) 1857. Hence **Phili·stian** *a.* of or pertaining to Philistia or the Philistines.

Philistine (fi·listəin, -tin), *sb.* and *a.* late ME. [– Fr. *Philistin* or Vulg. L. *Philistinus*, also *Palæstinus*, usually pl. – late Gr. Φιλιστῖνοι, Παλαιστῖνοι – Heb. *pᵉlištîm*, rel. to *pᵉlešeṯ* Philistia, Palestine.] **A.** *sb.* **1.** One of an alien warlike people who occupied the southern sea-coast of Palestine, and constantly harassed the Israelites. **2.** *fig.* Applied (humorously or otherwise) to 'the enemy', into whose hands one may fall, e.g. bailiffs, literary critics, etc.; formerly, also, to the debauched or drunken 1600. **3.** = PHILISTER, applied by German students to one not a student at a university 1824. **4.** A person deficient in liberal culture; one whose interests are material and commonplace 1827.

2. That bloodthirsty P., Sir Lucius O'Trigger SHERIDAN. **4.** The people who believe most that our greatness and welfare are proved by our being very rich,..are just the very people whom we call the Philistines M. ARNOLD.

B. *adj.* **1.** Of or pertaining to the people of Philistia 1842. **2.** Like the modern 'Philistine'; uncultured; commonplace; prosaic. (Of persons and things.) 1831.

2. Byron..had in him a cross of the true P. breed SWINBURNE.

Philistinism (fi·listiniz'm, -əiniz'm). 1831.

[f. prec. + -ISM.] The opinions, aims, and habits of social Philistines (see prec. A. 4); the condition of being a Philistine.

Philistinism! we have not the expression in English. Perhaps we have not the word because we have so much of the thing M. ARNOLD.

Phillipsite (fi·lipsəit). 1825. [f. J. W. *Phillips*, Eng. mineralogist; see -ITE[1] 2 b.] *Min.* A hydrous silicate of aluminium, calcium, and potassium, found in cruciform twin crystals of a white colour.

Phillis (fi·lis). Also **Phyllis.** 1632. [– L. *Phyllis* girl's name in Virgil's and Horace's poetry – Gr. Φυλλίς female name (prop. 'foliage'), f. φύλλον leaf; the sp. with *i* instead of *y* may be due to assoc. with Gr. φίλος dear, beloved.] A generic proper name in pastoral poetry for a rustic maiden, or for a sweetheart; also applied (after Milton) to a 'neat-handed' table-maid or waitress.

‖**Phillyrea** (fili·rĭă, filirī·ă). 1664. [mod.L. (Tournefort, Linnæus) for L. *philyrea* – Gr. φιλυρέα, app. f. φιλύρα linden tree.] *Bot.* A genus of ornamental evergreen shrubs (N.O. *Oleaceæ*), natives of the Mediterranean region and the East; also called *jasmine-box* or *mock privet*.

Phillyrin (fi·lirin). 1838. [f. prec. + -IN[1].] *Chem.* A white crystallizable bitter substance obtained from the bark of *Phillyrea latifolia*.

Philo- (filo), bef. a vowel (or *h*) usu. **phil-** (fil), repr. Gr. φιλο-, φιλ-, comb. form from root of φιλεῖν to love, φίλος dear, friend. Employed in English to form new compounds, after the Gr. model, the second element of which is properly Greek, but often Latin, and even English; esp. frequent with national names, as *p.-German*, *p.-Turk*, and the like.

Philobi·blic [Gr. βίβλος book], *a.* fond of books; devoted to literature. **Philogynist** (filǫ·dʒinist) [Gr. γυνή woman], a lover or admirer of women. **Phi·lomath** [Gr. μαθ-, root of μανθάνειν learn], a lover of learning; a student, esp. of mathematics; formerly applied to an astrologer; so **Philoma·thic** *a.*, **Philo·mathy.** (All now *rare.*) **Philote·chnic** [Gr. τέχνη art], *a.* fond of or devoted to the arts, esp. the industrial arts.

Philologer (filǫ·lŏdʒəɹ). 1588. [f. PHILOLOGY + -ER[1] 4; see -LOGER.] = PHILOLOGIST. Now *rare.*

Philologist (filǫ·lŏdʒist). 1648. [f. next + -IST.] **1.** One devoted to learning or literature; a scholar, *esp.* a classical scholar. Now *rare.* **2.** A person versed in the science of language; a student of language 1716.

Philology (filǫ·lŏdʒi). 1614. [– Fr. *philologie* – L. *philologia* – Gr. φιλολογία devotion to dialectic, love of learning and literature, love of language, f. φιλόλογος fond of talking, learning, studious of words, whence L. *philologus*; see PHILO-, LOGOS.] **1.** Love of learning and literature; the study of literature, in a wide sense; literary and classical scholarship; polite learning. Now *rare.* **2.** The science of language; linguistics. (See also COMPARATIVE.) 1716. Hence **Philolo·gic, -al,** *adjs.* of, pertaining to, concerned with, or devoted to the study of p. **Philolo·gically** *adv.*

Philomel (fi·lŏmel), **Philomela** (filŏmī·lă). *poet.* late ME. Also early and erron. **philomene.** [Early *philomene* (XV–XVI), occas. used as a common noun – med.L. *philomena* (XII), alt., presumably by assoc. with Μελπομένη 'the singing muse', of L. *philomela* – Gr. φιλομήλα nightingale.] A poetic name for the nightingale. (Now always with capital P, usu. with ref. to the myth of Philomela metamorphosed into a nightingale.)

And Philomele her song with teares doth steepe SPENSER.

Philonian (fəilōᵘ·niăn), *a.* 1874. [– L. *Philonianus*, f. *Philo*, *-on-* – Gr. Φίλων; see -AN.] Of or pertaining to the Jewish philosopher Philo, who flourished at Alexandria about the beginning of the Christian era. So **Philo·nic** *a.* **Phi·lonism,** the system of Philo.

Philoprogenitive (fi:lo,prodʒe·nitiv), *a.* 1865. [f. PHILO- + *progenit-*, pa. ppl. stem of L. *progignere* beget + -IVE.] **1.** Inclined to production of offspring; prolific. **2.** *Phrenol.* Loving one's offspring; of or pertaining to love of offspring 1876. So **Phi:loproge·nitiveness** 1815.

†**Philosoph, -ophe.** [OE. – L. *philosophus*; ME. – OFr. *filosofe, philosophe* – L.; see PHILOSOPHER.] = PHILOSOPHER 1; now also PHILOSOPHIST 2.

Philosophaster (filǫ·sŏfæstəɹ, filǫsofæ·stəɹ). 1611. [– late L. *philosophaster*, f. L. *philosophus*; see PHILOSOPHER, -ASTER.] A shallow or peusdo-philosopher.

Philosopheme (filǫ·sŏfīm). 1678. [– late L. *philosophema* – Gr. φιλοσόφημα, f. φιλοσοφεῖν philosophize.] A philosophic conclusion or demonstration; a philosophical statement, theorem, or axiom.

Philosopher (filǫ·sŏfəɹ). [– AFr. *philo-, filosofre*, var. of (O)Fr. *philosophe* – L. *philosophus* (Cicero) – Gr. φιλόσοφος 'lover of wisdom', f. φιλο- PHILO- + σοφ- (see SOPHIST); orig. stressed *philoso·fre*; *philo·sopher* (assim. to -ER[1]) has prevailed since XVI. See PHILOSOPH.] **1.** A lover of wisdom; one versed in philosophy or engaged in its study; formerly embracing men learned in physical science as well as those versed in the metaphysical and moral sciences, but now, when unqualified, restricted to the latter. Also differentiated, as *moral p.*, *political p.*; *natural p.* (= physicist). †**2.** An adept in occult science, as an alchemist, diviner, weather-prophet, etc. –1485. **3.** One who regulates his life by the light of philosophy; one who speaks or behaves philosophically 1599.

1. I feare hee will proue the weeping Phylosopher [Heraclitus] when he growes old SHAKS. Pythagoras..is said to have first named himself p. or lover of wisdom COLERIDGE. **3.** For there was neuer yet P. That could endure the tooth-ake patiently SHAKS. Phr. *Oil of philosophers*, an old drug compounded of powdered brick and linseed oil.

Philosopher's stone. late ME. [tr. med. L. *lapis philosophorum* (see prec. 2).] A reputed solid substance or preparation supposed by the alchemists to possess the property of changing other metals into gold or silver, the discovery of which was the supreme object of alchemy. Also *transf.* and *fig.*

Philosophic (filŏsǫ·fik), *a.* (*sb.*) 1644. [– late L. *philosophicus* (cf. adv. *philosophicē*, corresp. to Gr. φιλοσοφικῶς), f. L. *philosophia*; see -IC. Cf. Fr. *philosophique.*] **A.** *adj.* = next. **B.** *sb.* (*pl.*) Studies, works, or arguments pertaining to philosophy 1734.

Philosophical (filŏsǫ·fikăl), *a.* (*sb.*) late ME. [f. as prec.; see -ICAL.] **1.** Of or pertaining to a philosopher or philosophy; of the nature of, consonant with, or proceeding from philosophy or learning; in earlier use including 'scientific' 1500. **b.** Physical, scientific. Now *Obs.* or *arch.* 1471. **2.** Of persons, etc.: Skilled in or devoted to philosophy or learning (formerly including physical science); learned. late ME. **3.** Characterized by practical philosophy or wisdom; befitting a philosopher in respect of wisdom or temperance 1638. †**B.** *sb.* (*pl.*) The subjects of study in a course of philosophy –1716.

1. The cuddy is a fish of which I know not the p. name JOHNSON. My mind is in a state of p. doubt as to animal magnetism COLERIDGE. **b.** Young Watt..exhibited a box of p. toys 1843. **2.** The P. Transactions (of the Royal Society) (*title*). A p. chemist would probably make a very unprofitable business of farming SIR H. DAVY. **3.** His patience was more Philosophicall than his Intellect 1638. Hence **Philoso·phically** *adv.*

Philoso·phico-, comb. form of PHILOSOPHIC: = philosophically-, philosophical and..as in *p.-historic*, etc. 1743.

Philosophism (filǫ·sŏfiz'm). 1792. [– Fr. *philosophisme*, f. *philosophe* philosopher, after *sophisme* sophism; see -ISM.] Philosophizing, or a philosophizing system; usu., in a hostile sense, affectation of philosophy.

The Dryasdust Philosophisms and enlightened Scepticisms CARLYLE.

Philosophist (filǫ·sŏfist). Now *rare.* 1589. [In sense 1 app. from L. *philosophia* + -IST. In sense 2 = Fr. *philosophiste.*] †**1.** = PHILOSOPHER 1. Puttenham. **2.** One who philosophizes erroneously; applied polemically to the French Encyclopædists, and hence to rationalists generally 1798. Hence **Philosophi·stic, -al** *adjs.* rationalistic, sceptical.

Philosophize (filǫ·sŏfəiz), *v.* 1594. [app. after Fr. *philosopher* (XVI) + -IZE; cf. L. *philosophari.*] **1.** *intr.* To play the philosopher; to think, reason, or argue philosophically; to speculate, theorize. Also *trans.* with *into.* **2.** *trans.* To render philosophic; to explain, treat, or construct philosophically 1658.

1. Man philosophises as he lives. He may philosophise well or ill, but philosophise he must 1836. Hence **Philo·sophizer.**

Philosophy (filǫ·sŏfi). [ME. *filosofie, philo-* – OFr. *filosofie*, (now) *philosophie* – L. *philosophia* (Cicero) – Gr. φιλοσοφία, f. φιλόσοφος; see PHILOSOPHER, -Y[3].] **1.** (In the original and widest sense.) The love, study, or pursuit of wisdom, or of knowledge of things and their causes, whether theoretical or practical. †**b.** Occas. used esp. of practical wisdom –1750. **2.** That more advanced study, to which, in the mediæval universities, the seven liberal arts were introductory; it included the three branches of *natural*, *moral*, and *metaphysical philosophy*, commonly called *the three philosophies*. Hence the degree of *Doctor of Philosophy*. late ME. **3.** (= *natural p.*) The knowledge or study of natural objects and phenomena; now usu. called 'science'. Now *rare* or *Obs.* ME. **4.** (= *moral p.*) The knowledge or study of the principles of human action or conduct; ethics. late ME. **5.** (= *metaphysical p.*) That department of knowledge or study which deals with ultimate reality, or with the most general causes and principles of things. (Now the most usual sense.) 1794. **6.** Occas. used esp. of knowledge obtained by natural reason, in contrast with revealed knowledge. late ME. **7.** With *of*: The study of the general principles *of* some particular branch of knowledge, experience, or activity; also, less properly, *of* any subject or phenomenon 1713. **8.** A philosophical system or theory. (With *a* and *pl.*) late ME. **9. a.** The system which a person forms for the conduct of life. **b.** The mental attitude or habit of a philosopher; serenity; resignation; calmness of temper 1771.

1. Depth in Philosophie bringeth Men about to Religion BACON. **b.** The chiefe of all p. consisteth to serve God, and not to offend men 1557. **4.** History is P. teaching by example BOLINGBROKE. **5.** I regard P. then..as the study which 'takes all knowledge for its province' 1902. **6.** Let Phylosophy not be asham'd to be confuted 1640. **7.** The great professor..of the p. of vanity [Rousseau] BURKE. **8.** *Ham.* I. v. 167. **9.** My own infirmities..and the public news coming altogether have put my utmost p. to the trial 1774.

-philous, terminal element in modern formations = 'lover', 'loving', f. med.L. *-philus*, Gr. -φιλος -PHIL (q.v.) + -OUS, as in *ammophilous, dendrophilous, hygrophilous*; hence **-philism, -phily** (Gr. -φιλία), expressing the state or quality of being what is denoted by *-philous*, and occas. *-philist* = lover (of), as *œnophilist.*

Philtre, philter (fi·ltəɹ), *sb.* 1587. [– Fr. *philtre* – L. *philtrum* (also formerly used) – Gr. φίλτρον love-potion, f. φιλ-, stem of φιλεῖν to love, φίλος loving + -τρον suffix of instrument.] A love-potion or love-charm. Sometimes *loosely*, a magic potion. Hence **Phi·ltre, phi·lter** *v. trans.* to charm with a love-potion; *fig.* to bewitch.

‖**Phimosis** (fəimōᵘ·sis). 1674. [mod.L. – Gr. φίμωσις muzzling.] *Path.* Contraction of the orifice of the prepuce, so that it cannot be retracted.

Phit (fit), imitation of a sound like that made by a rifle-bullet 1894.

Phiz (fiz). *joc. colloq.* 1688. [abbrev. of *phiznomy* PHYSIOGNOMY.] Face, countenance; expression of face.

Phleb-, bef. a cons. **phlebo-,** comb. form of Gr. φλέψ, φλεβ- vein, an element in terms of physiology, pathology, etc.

‖**Phlebitis** (flĭbəi·tis). 1822. [mod.L., f. Gr. φλέψ, φλεβ-; see -ITIS.] *Path.* Inflammation of the walls of a vein. Hence **Phlebi·tic** *a.*

Phlebo-, comb. element: see PHLEB-.

Phlebograph (fle·bŏgrɑf) [-GRAPH], an instrument (sphygmograph) for recording diagrammatically the pulsations of a vein. **Phlebolite** (fle·bŏləit), **Phle·bolith** [Gr. λίθος; see -LITE], a morbid calcareous concretion in a vein, a vein-stone. **Phlebology** (flĭbǫ·lŏdʒi) [-LOGY], that part of physiology or anatomy which treats of the veins, etc.

Phlebotomize (flĭbǫ·tŏməiz), *v.* 1596. [– Fr. *phlébotomiser* (in med.L. *flebotomizare* (Du Cange), for the regular *phlebotomare*), f. *phlébotomie*; see next, -IZE.] **a.** *intr.* To practise phlebotomy; to let blood by opening a vein. **b.** *trans.* To bleed (a person, etc.); also *transf.* and *fig.* **c.** *intr.* for *pass.* To be bled. Hence **Phlebo:tomiza·tion**, blood-letting.

Phlebotomy (flĭbǫ·tŏmi). ME. [(Earliest form with *fl-*) – OFr. *flebothomi* (mod. *phlébotomie*) – late L. *phlebotomia* – Gr. φλεβοτομία, f. φλεβότομος opening a vein; see PHLEB-, -TOMY.] **1.** The action or practice of cutting open a vein so as to let blood flow, as a therapeutical operation; venesection, bleeding. **2.** *transf.* and *fig.* The drawing of blood in any way (*lit.* or *fig.*); *esp.* bloodshed; 'bleeding' in purse or pocket 1589.

2. Warre is the P. of the Body Politique 1646. Fiscal P. 1827. Hence **Phlebo·tomist**, one who practises p.; a blood-letter.

||**Phlegethon** (fle·gĭþǫn, fle·dʒ-). late ME. [– Gr. Φλεγέθων, -οντ- = lit. 'blazing'.] *Gr.* and *Lat. Myth.* Name of a fabled river of fire, one of the five rivers of Hades.

Phlegm (flem). ME. [Earlier *fleume*, *fleme*, *fleam(e* – OFr. *fleume* (mod. *flegme*) – late L. *phlegma* clammy moisture of the body – Gr. φλέγμα inflammation, morbid humour as the result of heat, f. φλέγειν burn, blaze. In XVI assim. to Gr.-L. original.] **1.** The thick viscous semifluid substance secreted by the mucous membranes, esp. of the respiratory passages; mucus. **a.** In old physiology, regarded as one of the four bodily 'humours', described as cold and moist. late ME. **b.** In mod. use; esp. when morbid, and discharged by cough, etc. (Not now applied to the mucus of the nasal passages.) 1486. †**c.** With *a* and *pl.* A mass of phlegm or mucus –1727. †**2.** *Old Chem.* One of the five 'principles' of bodies, also called *water*; any watery inodorous tasteless substance obtained by distillation –1812. **3.** The character supposed to result from predominance of phlegm (sense 1a) in the bodily constitution; phlegmatic temperament; coldness or dullness of character; coolness or evenness of temper 1578.

3. The patience of the people was creditable to their p. MEREDITH. Hence **Phlegma·tic** (flegmæ·tik) *a.* of the nature of or abounding in p.; cold, sluggish, apathetic; cool, self-possessed. **Phlegma·tically** *adv.*

||**Phlegmasia** (flegmē¹·siă, -ziă). *Pl.* **-æ.** 1706. [mod.L. – Gr. φλεγμασία.] *Path.* Inflammation, *esp.* inflammation accompanied by fever.

P. dolens, or *p. alba dolens*, milk-leg or white-leg.

Phlegmon (fle·gmǫn). [ME. – L. *phlegmon* or *phlegmona* – Gr. φλεγμονή inflammation, etc., f. φλέγειν burn.] *Path.* An inflammatory tumour, a boil or carbuncle; inflammation, esp. of the cellular tissue, tending to suppuration. Hence **Phlegmo·nic, Phle·gmonous** *adjs.* pertaining to or of the nature of a p. **Phle·gmonoid** *a.* resembling a p.

Phlegmy (fle·mi), *a.* 1550. [f. PHLEGM + -Y¹.] **1.** Mucous; containing or characterized by phlegm. **2.** = PHLEGMATIC 1607.

Phloem (flōᵘ·em). 1875. [(Nägeli in G.) f. Gr. φλόος = φλοιός bark + -ημα passive suffix.] *Bot.* The softer portion of the fibrovascular tissue, as dist. from the xylem or woody portion; the bast with its associated tissues.

Phlogistic (flodʒi·stik, -gi·stik), *a.* 1733. [In sense 1 f. PHLOGISTON + -IC; in 2 and 3 immed. – Gr. φλογιστός inflammable.] **1.** *Chem.* Of the nature of or consisting of phlogiston; connected with or related to phlogiston. **2.** *Path.* Inflammatory 1754. †**3.** Fiery, heated, inflamed (*lit.* and *fig.*) –1855.

Phlogi·sticate, *v. Obs.* exc. *Hist.* 1774. [f. prec. + -ATE³. Cf. Fr. *phlogistiquer*.] *trans.* To render phlogistic; to combine with phlogiston. Chiefly in *pa. pple.*

†*Phlogisticated air* or *gas*, names for nitrogen in the phlogistic theory. (Cf. DEPHLOGISTICATED.) So †**Phlogistica·tion**, combination with phlogiston; now called *deoxidation*.

Phlogiston (flodʒi·stǫn, -gi·stǫn). 1733. [mod.L. – Gr. φλογιστόν, f. φλογίζειν set on fire, f. φλόξ, φλογ- flame, ablaut deriv. of φλεγ-, root of φλέγειν burn.] *Chem.* A hypothetical substance or principle, formerly supposed to exist in combination in all other combustible bodies, and to be disengaged in the process of combustion; the 'principle of inflammability'; the matter of fire, conceived as fixed in inflammable substances. Hence **Phlogi·stian, Phlogi·stonist**, a believer in the existence or theory of p.

Phlogogenetic (flǫ:godʒĭne·tik), *a.* 1893. [f. Gr. φλογο-, comb. f. φλόξ flame + -GENETIC.] *Path.* Producing inflammation. Also **Phlogoge·nic, Phlogo·genous** *adjs.* in same sense.

Phlogopite (flǫ·gŏpəit). 1850. [f. Gr. φλογωπός fiery (f. φλογ- flame + ὤψ, ὠπ- face) + -ITE¹ 2b.] *Min.* A magnesia mica, found in crystalline limestone and serpentine.

||**Phlogosis** (flogōᵘ·sis). *Pl.* **-es** (-īz). 1693. [mod.L. – Gr. φλόγωσις inflammation, f. φλόξ, φλογ- flame; see -OSIS.] *Path.* Inflammation. Hence **Phlogosed** (-ōᵘzd) *ppl. a.* inflamed. **Phlogosin** (-ōᵘ·sin) *Chem.* a product of cultures of certain bacteria, which produces acute local inflammation. **Phlogotic** (-ǫ·tik) *a.* inflammatory.

Phlorizin (florəi·zin, flǫ·rizin). Also formerly called †**phloridzite.** 1835. [f. Gr. φλόος, φλοιός bark + ῥίζα root + -IN¹.] *Chem.* A bitter substance ($C_{21}H_{24}O_{10}$), crystallizing in silky needles, obtained from the bark of the root of the apple, pear, plum, and cherry trees.

Phloro-, bef. a vowel **phlor-**, used in *Chem.*, to form names of substances connected with PHLORIZIN, as

Phloramine (flǫ·răməin) [AMINE], the amine ($C_6H_7NO_2 = C_6H_5O_2.NH_2$) obtained in thin shining films by the action of ammonia on phloroglucin. **Phloretin** (flōᵊ·rĭtin), a sweet crystalline substance ($C_{15}H_{14}O_5$) produced by the action of dilute acids on phlorizin; hence **Phloretic** (flore·tik) *a.*, applied to an *acid* ($C_9H_{10}O_3$) obtained from phloretin by the action of potash; also to *ethers* (*phloretic ethers*) in which an organic radical takes the place of 1 atom of hydrogen in phloretic acid (Watts). **Phloroglucin** (flǫroglū·sin) [Gr. γλυκύς sweet + -IN¹], a colourless or yellowish crystalline, intensely sweet substance ($C_6H_6O_3$), obtained from phloretin, and occurring widely distributed in plants. **Phlorol** (flǫ·rǫl), a phenol, an oily substance ($C_8H_{10}O$) obtained from salts of phloretic acid, or from creosote. **Phlorone** (flǫ·rōᵘn), a yellow crystalline substance ($C_8H_8O_2$), homologous with quinone, obtained by distillation of beech-wood and coal-tar.

Phlox (flǫks). 1706. [– L. *phlox* (Pliny) – Gr. φλόξ a plant (prob. *Silene*), lit. flame. Taken into Bot. as a generic name by Dillenius.] *Bot.* A N. American genus of herbaceous (rarely shrubby) plants (N.O. *Polemoniaceæ*), with clusters of salver-shaped flowers of various colours. **b.** *attrib.* **p.-worm**, the larva of an American moth, *Heliothis phlogophagus*, which feeds upon phloxes.

||**Phlyctæna, -ena** (fliktī·nă). 1693. [mod. L. – Gr. φλύκταινα a blister, f. φλύειν, φλύζειν swell.] *Path.* An inflammatory vesicle, pimple, or blister upon the cuticle or the eye-ball. Hence ||**Phlycte·nula** (-æn-), pl. **-æ** [mod.L. dim. of *phlyctena*], a small p., esp. upon the conjunctiva or cornea of the eye; whence **Phlycte·nular** (-æn-) *a.*

-phobe, – Fr. *-phobe* – L. *-phobus* – Gr. -φόβος -fearing, adj. ending, f. φόβος fear; as in *hydrophobe*, *Anglophobe*, etc.

Phobia (fōᵘ·biă). 1801. [Next used as a separate word.] Fear, horror, or aversion, esp. of a morbid character.

-phobia, – L. *-phobia* – Gr. -φοβία, forming abstr. sbs. from the adjs. in -φόβος (see -PHOBE) with sense 'dread, horror'; as in *hydrophobia*, *Russophobia*, etc. Hence **-pho·bic** forming adjs., **-pho·biac, -phobist** forming sbs.

||**Phoca** (fōᵘ·kă). *Pl.* **phocæ** (fōᵘ·sī), **phocas.** 1599. [L. – Gr. φώκη seal.] *Zool.* A seal; in mod. zoology, restricted to the genus typified by the Common Seal, *P. vitulina.* Hence **Phoca·cean** *a.* of or pertaining to the *Phocidæ* or seal family; *sb.* a member of this family. **Pho·cal** *a.* of or pertaining to a seal. **Pho·cine** (fōᵘ·səin) *a.* pertaining to the sub-family *Phocinæ*, containing the seals proper; *sb.* a member of this family.

Phocenic (fosī·nik, -se·nik), *a.* 1836. [For *phocænic, f. Zool. L. *Phocæna* (– Gr. φώκαινα porpoise, f. φώκη seal) + -IC.] *Chem.* Applied to an acid obtained from porpoise- or dolphin-oil, orig. called DELPHINIC, and subseq. identified with VALERIC acid ($(CH_3)_2.C_2H_3.CO_2H$). So **Pho·cenil, Pho·cenin,** glyceryl valerate, or trivalerin, = DELPHIN *sb.* 2.

Phocodont (fōᵘ·kŏdǫnt), *a.* (*sb.*) [f. Gr. φώκη seal + ὀδούς, ὀδοντ- tooth.] *Zool.* Of or pertaining to the *Phocodontia*, an extinct sub-order of *Cetacea*, furnishing connecting links with the *Phocidæ* or seals. **b.** *sb.* Any member of the *Phocodontia.*

||**Phœbe**¹ (fī·bi). *poet.* 1590. [– L. *Phoebe* – Gr. φοίβη, fem. of φοῖβος bright; cf. PHŒBUS.] Name of Artemis or Diana as goddess of the moon; the moon personified.

To morrow night, when P. doth behold Her siluer visage, in the watry glasse SHAKS.

Phœbe² (fī·bi). 1700. [imit., but spelt after prec.] = PEWIT 3, PEWEE.

||**Phœbus** (fī·bǒs). late ME. [– L. *Phœbus* = Gr. Φοῖβος lit. bright, shining.] A name of Apollo as the Sun-god; the sun personified. Chiefly *poet.* **b.** Apollo as the god of poetry and music, presiding over the Muses; hence, the genius of poetry 1809. So **Phœbe·an** *a.*

Phœnician (fĭni·ʃ¹ăn), *sb.* and *a.* ME. [– (O)Fr. *phénicien*, f. L. *Phœnice*, (sc. *terra* land), synon. with L. *Phœnice*, Gr. Φοινίκη the country, f. Φοῖνιξ, Φοινικ- *sb.* and *a.* Phœnician; see -AN.] **A.** *sb.* **1.** A native or inhabitant of Phœnicia, an ancient country on the coast of Syria, which contained the cities of Tyre and Sidon; also of any Phœnician colony. **2.** The language spoken by this people 1836.

1. Astoreth, whom the Phœnicians call'd Astarte, Queen of Heav'n MILT.

B. *adj.* Of or pertaining to ancient Phœnicia, or its inhabitants or colonists; hence, Punic, Carthaginian 1601.

Phœnicopter (fī·nikǫptəɹ). 1570. [– L. *phœnicopterus* – Gr. φοινικόπτερος flamingo (as adj. 'red-feathered'), f. φοῖνιξ, φοινικ- crimson + πτερόν feather.] *Ornith.* Adopted form of the Gr. and L. name of the flamingo of Southern Europe (*Phœnicopterus roseus* or *antiquorum*).

Phœnix¹, **phenix** (fī·niks). [OE., ME. *fenix* – L. *phœnix* and OFr. *fenix* (mod. *phénix*), the L. being – Gr. φοῖνιξ the bird, also date-palm, etc., identical with φοῖνιξ Phoenician, purple. Assim. to L. sp. in XIV.] **1.** A mythical bird, of gorgeous plumage, fabled to be the only one of its kind, and to live five or six hundred years in the Arabian desert, after which it burnt itself to ashes on a funeral pile, and emerged from its ashes with renewed youth, to live through another cycle of years. **2.** *transf.* and *fig.* **a.** A paragon ME. **b.** That which rises from the ashes of its predecessor 1591. **3.** *Astr.* One of the southern constellations 1674.

1. But from himself the P. only springs: Self-born, begotten by the Parent Flame In which he burn'd, Another and the Same DRYDEN.

||**Phœnix**² (fī·niks). 1601. [mod.L. (Linn.) – Gr. φοῖνιξ date palm, date.] A genus of palms, distinguished by their pinnate leaves. (*P. dactylifera* is the Date Palm.)

||**Pholas** (fōᵘ·læs). *Pl.* **pholades** (fōᵘ·lădīz). 1661. [mod.L. – Gr. φωλάς, φωλαδ- adj. lurking in a hole (φωλεός).] *Zool.* A genus of boring bivalve molluscs (family *Pholadidæ*); an animal of this genus, a piddock. So **Pho·lad, -a·dean, Pho·ladid.**

Phonate (fōᵘ·ne¹t), *v.* 1876. [f. Gr. φωνή voice + -ATE³.] *Physiol. intr.* To utter vocal sound; *trans.* to sound vocally. Hence **Pho·natory** *a.* pertaining or relating to phonation.

Phonation (fonē¹·ʃən). 1842. [f. Gr. φωνή voice + -ATION. Cf. Fr. *phonation.*] *Physiol.* The production or utterance of vocal sound; usu. as dist. from *articulation*; occas. *gen.* vocal utterance, voice-production.

Phonautograph (fonǭ·tŏgraf). 1859. [– Fr. *phonautographe* (Leon Scott 1855), f. Gr. φωνή voice + αὐτο- AUTO- + *-graphe* -GRAPH.]

An apparatus for automatically recording the vibrations of sound by means of a membrane set in vibration by the sound-waves, and having a point attached which makes a tracing upon a revolving cylinder.

Phone (fōᵘn), *sb.*[1] 1890. [– Gr. φωνή voice.] *Phonetics.* An elementary sound of spoken language; a simple vowel or consonant sound. Also, any of the variants of a phoneme.

Phone, *sb.*[2] and *v.* 1884. Colloq. abbrev. of TELEPHONE; also of *ear-* or *head-phone.*

-phone (fōᵘn), terminal element, repr. Gr. φωνή voice, sound, used in the names of instruments for producing, reproducing, transmitting or amplifying sound, as *dictaphone, dyphone* (XVII), *gramophone, megaphone, microphone* (XVII), *photophone, radiophone, telephone.*

Phoneidoscope (fonəi·dǫskōᵘp). 1878. [f. Gr. φωνή voice + εἶδος form + -SCOPE.] An instrument for exhibiting the colour-figures produced by the action of sound-vibrations upon a thin film, e.g. of soap-solution.

Phoneme (fōᵘ·nīm). 1923. [– Fr. *phonème* – Gr. φώνημα sound, speech, f. φωνεῖν speak.] *Philol.* A speech-sound considered in respect of its functional relations in a linguistic system.

Phonetic (fǒne·tik), *a.* 1826. [– mod.L. *phoneticus* (Zoega, 1797, of notation opp. to *ideographic*) – Gr. φωνητικός, f. φωνητός, pa. ppl. formation on φωνεῖν speak, f. φωνή voice; see -IC.] **1.** Representing vocal sounds; applied to signs which represent the (elementary) sounds of speech, or which express the pronunciation of words. **b.** Applied to systems of spelling in which each letter represents invariably the same spoken sound 1848. **2.** Of, pertaining or relating to the sounds of spoken language; consisting of vocal sounds 1861. **b.** Involving vibration of the vocal chords (as opp. to mere breath or whisper) 1880. Hence **Phone·tical** *a.* (*rare*), phonetic; **-ly** *adv.* **Phonetician** (fōᵘnīti·ʃăn) = PHONETIST 1. 1848. **Phone·ticism,** p. quality, or the p. system, of writing or spelling. **Phone·ticist,** an advocate of p. spelling. **Phone·ticize** *v. trans.* to render p., to write phonetically.

Phonetics (fǒne·tiks), *sb. pl.* 1841. [See prec. and -ICS.] That section of linguistic science which treats of the production of the sounds of speech and their representation; the phonetic phenomena (of a language or dialect).

Phonetism (fōᵘ·nītiz'm). 1879. [contr. form of PHONETICISM, f. PHONETIC(S + -ISM.] Phonetic representation; reduction to a phonetic system of writing or spelling.

Phonetist (fōᵘ·nītist). 1864. [contr. form of PHONETICIST, f. PHONETIC(S + -IST.] **1.** A person versed in phonetics; one who studies the sounds of speech. **2.** A phoneticist 1875.

Phoney (fōᵘ·ni), *a. U.S. slang.* 1902. [Of unkn. origin.] Counterfeit, sham.

Phonic (fōᵘ·nik), *a.* 1823. [f. Gr. φωνή voice + -IC. Cf. Fr. *phonique.*] **1.** Acoustic. **2.** = PHONETIC 2, 2 b. 1843. Also *sb. pl.* (1683), †acoustics –1842; phonetics (*rare*) 1844.

Phono- (fōᵘno), bef. a vowel **phon-,** comb. form of Gr. φωνή voice, sound, used extensively in modern technical terms, as PHONOGRAPH, PHONOLOGY, etc. and also in **Phonoca·mptic** [Gr. καμπτός, -ικός, f. κάμπτειν bend] *a.* (*rare*) having the property of reflecting sound, or producing an echo; cataphonic; hence **Phonoca·mptics,** cataphonics, catacoustics. **Pho·nofilm,** a trade name for a cinema film in which the characters speak. **Phono·meter** [Gr. μέτρον measure], an instrument for measuring or recording the number or force of sound-waves. **Pho·noscope** [-SCOPE], (*a*) name for various instruments by means of which sound-vibrations are represented in a visible form; (*b*) = MICROPHONE.

Phonogram (fōᵘ·nǒgræm). 1860. [f. PHONO- + -GRAM; in sense 2 after *telegram.*] **1.** A character representing a spoken sound; *spec.* a letter of (Pitman's) phonography. **2.** The sound-record made by a phonograph; a phonographic record or message 1884.

Phonograph (fōᵘ·nǒgraf), *sb.* 1835. [f. Gr. φωνή voice + (in sense 1) -(ό)γραφος written, (in sense 2) -γράφος writing, writer; see -GRAPH.] †**1.** = prec. 1 (*rare*) –1857. †**2.** = PHONAUTOGRAPH 1863. **3.** (spec. *talking p.*) An instrument, invented by Thomas A. Edison, by which sounds are automatically recorded and reproduced 1877. Hence **Pho·nograph** *v. trans.* **a.** to report in (Pitman's) phonography; **b.** to record or reproduce by or as by a p.

Phonography (fǒnǫ·grăfi). 1701. [f. Gr. φωνή voice (see PHONO-) + -GRAPHY.] †**1.** The art or practice of writing according to sound; phonetic spelling –1851. **2.** *spec.* Pitman's system of phonetic shorthand 1840. **3.** The automatic recording of sounds, as by the PHONAUTOGRAPH, or the recording and reproduction of them by the PHONOGRAPH; the construction and use of phonographs 1861. Hence **Phono·grapher,** a phonetist; one who uses p. (sense 2), or the phonograph. **Phonogra·phic** *a.* phonetic; of, pertaining to, or using p. (sense 2); of, pertaining to, or produced by the phonograph; **-ally** *adv.*

Phonolite (fōᵘ·nǒləit). 1828. [f. PHONO- + -LITE. Cf. Fr. *phonolithe.*] *Min.* Name for various volcanic rocks which ring when struck; clinkstone. Hence **Phonoli·tic** *a.*

Phonology (fǒnǫ·lŏdʒi). 1799. [f. Gr. φωνή (see PHONO-) + -LOGY.] The science of vocal sounds (= PHONETICS), esp. of those of a particular language; also, the system of sounds and phonetic features or conditions of a language. Hence **Phonolo·gic, -al** *adjs.* phonetic; **-ly** *adv.* **Phono·logist,** a phonetist.

Phonopore (fōᵘ·nǒpoᵊɹ). 1886. [f. PHONO- + Gr. πόρος passage.] An apparatus by means of which electrical impulses produced by induction, as in a telephone, may be used to transmit messages along a telegraph wire, without interfering with the current by which ordinary messages are simultaneously transmitted. **Phonopo·ric** *a.* Also **Pho·nophore.**

Phonotype (fōᵘ·nǒtəip), *sb.* 1844. [f. PHONO- + TYPE.] A character of a phonetic alphabet adapted for printing; (without *a* and *pl.*) phonetic print or type. Hence **Pho·notype** *v. trans.* to print in p. **Phonoty·pic, -al,** *adjs.,* **-ly** *adv.* **Pho·notypist** (-təipist), an advocate or user of p. **Pho·notypy** (-təipi), a method or system of phonetic printing.

-phore (fōᵊɹ), mod.L. *-phorus, -phorum* – Gr. -φόρος, -ον bearing, bearer, f. φέρειν bear, used to form various technical words, as *semaphore, gonophore, phonophore.* Hence -PHOROUS.

‖**Phorminx** (fǭ·ɹmiŋks.) 1776. [Gr. φόρμιγξ.] A kind of cithara or lyre used by the ancient Greeks to accompany the voice.

‖**Phormium** (fǭ·ɹmiŏm). 1852. [mod.L. – Gr. φορμίον a species of plant; see -IUM.] *Bot.* A genus of liliaceous plants (suborder *Hemerocalleæ*), comprising a single variable species, *P. tenax,* the New Zealand flax; any of these.

Phorone (forōᵘ·n). 1859. [Shortened from *camphorone* (f. CAMPHOR + -ONE).] †**a.** A substance, $C_9H_{14}O$, now called *camphorphorone*; **b.** An isomer of this substance, *diisopropylidene acetone,* a colourless oil with aromatic odour.

Phoronomy (forǫ·nŏmi). 1877. [– mod.L. *phoronomia* (Hermann 1716) = G., Fr. *phoronomie,* f. Gr. φορά motion (f. φέρειν bear, carry); see -NOMY.] The purely geometrical theory of motion; kinematics. Hence **Phorono·mic** *a.* kinematic. **Phorono·mics** *sb.* = *phoronomy.*

-phorous (fŏrəs), comb. element, f. mod.L. *-phorus,* Gr. -φόρος + -OUS, forming adjs.; synonymous with -FEROUS, but properly used only in words derived from Gr., e.g. *carpophorous, oophorous, phonophorous,* etc.

Phosgene (fǫ·sdʒīn). Also **-gen** (-dʒen). 1812. [f. Gr. φῶς light + *-gene* -GEN. Cf. Fr. *phosgène.*] *Chem.* A name for the gas carbon oxychloride, $COCl_2$, orig. obtained by exposing equal volumes of chlorine and carbonic oxide to the sun's rays. Also called *p. gas.*

Phosgenite (fǫ·sdʒĭnəit). 1849. [Named 1820; f. prec. + -ITE[1] 2 b.] *Min.* A mineral consisting of nearly equal parts of carbonate and chloride of lead, occurring in tetragonal crystals.

Phosph- = PHOSPHO-, comb. form of PHOSPHORUS.

Phospham (fǫ·sfæm). 1866. [f. PHOSPH- + AM(MONIA.] *Chem.* The nitril of phosphoric acid (PHN_2), a white, reddish, or yellowish-red powder.

Phosphate (fǫ·sfēt). 1795. [– Fr. *phosphat* (de Morveau, 1787), f. *phosphore* PHOSPHORUS + *-at* -ATE[4].] *Chem.* A salt of phosphoric acid. **b.** In *pl.,* esp. the phosphates of lime or iron and alumina, as constituents of cereals, etc. 1858. Hence **Pho·sphated** *a.* converted into a p.; combined with or containing phosphoric acid. **Phospha·tic** *a.* of the nature of, characterized by the presence of, or containing a p.

Phosphaturia (fǫsfătiūᵊ·riă). 1876. [f. prec. + -URIA.] *Path.* A morbid state evidenced by the excess of phosphates in the urine. Hence **Phosphatu·ric** *a.*

Phosphene (fǫ·sfīn). 1872. [irreg. f. Gr. φῶς light + φαίνειν to show. Cf. Fr. *phosphène.*] An appearance of rings of light produced by pressure on the eyeball, due to irritation of the retina.

Phosphide (fǫ·sfəid). 1849. [f. PHOSPH- + -IDE.] *Chem.* A combination of phosphorus with another element or a radical. (Earlier name *phosphuret.*)

Phosphine (fǫ·sfəin). 1871. [f. PHOSPH- + -INE[5]; cf. AMINE.] *Chem.* **1.** A name for phosphuretted hydrogen gas, PH_3 (as an analogue of ammonia, NH_3) 1873. **2.** A phosphorus ammonia; a compound having the structure of an *amine,* with phosphorus in place of nitrogen; e.g. *monoethyl p.,* $C_2H_5 . P . H_2$. 1871. Hence **Phosphi·nic** *a.* of, pertaining to, or derived from p.; in *phosphinic acid,* any one of various acids formed from the primary and secondary phosphines by fixation of 3 and 2 atoms of oxygen respectively.

Phosphite (fǫ·sfəit). 1799. [– Fr. *phosphite* (G. de Morveau, 1787); see PHOSPH-, -ITE[1] 4 b.] *Chem.* A salt of phosphorous acid.

Phospho- (fǫ·sfo), bef. a vowel **Phosph-,** comb. form, shortened from PHOSPHORUS.

Phosphonium (fǫsfōᵘ·niŏm). 1866. [f. PHOSPH(ORUS + ending of AMMONIUM.] *Chem.* A combination of hydrogen and phosphorus, PH_4, analogous to ammonium, entering as a monovalent radical into many compounds, as *p. iodide,* PH_4I, etc. Hence **Phospho·nic** *a.,* in *p. acid,* any one of several compounds derived from phosphoric acid by the replacement of hydroxyl (OH) by a hydrocarbon group. Occas. called *phosphinic,* or *phosphenilic acid.*

Phosphor (fǫ·sfǫɹ), *sb.* (*a.*) 1635. [– L. *phosphorus* PHOSPHORUS.] **1.** (With capital P.) The morning star; the planet Venus when appearing before sunrise; Lucifer. Now only *poet.* †**2.** = PHOSPHORUS 2. –1819. **3.** = PHOSPHORUS 3; esp. in *p.-bronze, -copper, -tin, -zinc,* alloys of phosphorus with these metals; see BRONZE, etc. †**B.** *adj.* Light-giving; phosphorescent –1820.

1. Bright P., fresher for the night TENNYSON.

Phosphorate (fǫ·sfŏreᵢt), *v.* 1789. [f. PHOSPHORUS + -ATE[3].] Orig. and chiefly in *ppl. a.* **Pho·sphorated.** *trans.* To combine or impregnate with phosphorus.

Phosphoreal (fǫsfōᵊ·riăl), *a.* 1745. [f. PHOSPHORUS, after *corporeal,* etc.] Of or pertaining to phosphorus; resembling that of phosphorus.

Phosphoresce (fǫsfŏre·s), *v.* 1794. [f. PHOSPHORUS + -ESCE.] *intr.* To emit luminosity without combustion (or by gentle combustion without sensible heat); to shine in the dark.

Phosphorescent (fǫsfŏre·sĕnt), *a.* (*sb.*) 1766. [f. as prec.; see -ESCENT.] Having the property of shining in the dark; luminous without combustion or without sensible heat; self-luminous. **B.** *sb.* A phosphorescent substance 1863. Hence **Phosphore·scence,** the condition or quality of being p.

Phosphoric (fǫsfǫ·rik), *a.* 1784. [– Fr.

phosphorique; see PHOSPHOR and -IC.] **1.** Pertaining to or of the nature of a phosphorus (sense 2); phosphorescent. **2.** *Chem.* Of or pertaining to the element phosphorus; *spec.* applied to compounds in which phosphorus has its higher valency (pentavalent) as opp. to PHOSPHOROUS; esp. in *p. acid* = trihydrogen phosphate, H_3PO_4 = $P(OH)_3O$, a colourless, inodorous, intensely bitter acid 1791.

Phosphorite (fǫ·sfŏrəit). 1796. [f. PHOSPHORUS + -ITE[1] 2 b.] *Min.* A name orig. applied to APATITE, or native phosphate of lime; now only to a non-crystallized variety from Estremadura, Spain, and elsewhere.

Phosphorize (fǫ·sfŏrəiz), *v.* 1799. [– Fr. *phosphoriser* (Lavoisier); see PHOSPHORUS, -IZE.] = PHOSPHORATE. Orig. and chiefly in *ppl. a.* **Pho·sphorized.**

Phosphoro-, comb. form of PHOSPHORUS, used to form chemical and other terms; as **Phosphorogenic** (-dʒe·nik) *a.*, causing phosphorescence; *spec.* applied to those rays of the spectrum which excite phosphorescence in certain objects.

Phosphoroscope (fǫ·sfŏrŏskōᵘp). 1860. [-SCOPE.] **a.** An apparatus for observing and measuring the duration of phosphorescence in such substances as emit light for a very short period; **b.** A scientific toy consisting of an arrangement of glass tubes containing various phosphorescent substances, each glowing with a different coloured light.

Phosphorous (fǫ·sfŏrəs), *a.* 1777. [f. next + -OUS.] **1.** = PHOSPHORESCENT *a.* **2.** *Chem.* Abounding in phosphorus; *spec.* applied to compounds into which phosphorus enters in its lower valency (trivalent), as opp. to *phosphoric*; esp. in *p. acid* = $P(OH)_3$. 1794.

Phosphorus (fǫ·sfŏrǒs). 1629. [– L. *phosphorus* – Gr. φωσφόρος light-bringing, sb. (sc. ἀστήρ star) morning star, f. φῶς light + -φόρος -PHORE.] **1.** (with capital P): The morning star: = PHOSPHOR 1. Now *rare.* **2.** Any substance or organism that phosphoresces; *esp.* (in later use) a substance that absorbs sunlight, and shines in the dark. *Pl.* **†phosphoruses, †'-s, phosphori.** Now *rare.* **3.** *Chem.* One of the non-metallic elements, a yellowish translucent substance resembling wax, widely distributed in nature in combination with other elements; it is extremely inflammable, undergoing slow combustion at ordinary temperatures, and hence appearing luminous in the dark. (Symbol P.) 1680.

attrib. and *Comb.*, as *p. matches, poisoning*; in Chem. = of p., as *p. oxychloride*, etc.; **p. necrosis,** gangrene of some part of the jaw-bone, due to the fumes of p., a disease affecting persons engaged in the manufacture of matches; **p. paste,** a paste containing p., used to kill vermin.

†Phosphuret (fǫ·sfiūret). Also **-oret.** 1799. [– mod.L. *phosphoretum*, after Fr. *phosphure* phosphide; see -URET.] *Chem.* = PHOSPHIDE –1868. Hence **Pho·sphuretted** *a.* (also **phosphor-**), combined chemically with phosphorus, as *phosphuretted hydrogen* = PHOSPHINE.

Phossy (fǫ·si), *a. colloq.* Also **fossy.** 1889. [f. *phos*, colloq. abbrev. of PHOSPHORUS + -Y[1].] In **p. jaw,** pop. name for phosphorus necrosis of the jaw.

Photic (fōᵘ·tik), *a. rare.* 1843. [f. Gr. φῶς, φωτ- light + -IC.] Pertaining or relating to light. So **Pho·tics** *sb. pl.*, (*a*) the science of light and its intrinsic properties (occas. used instead of *optics*); (*b*) applied in U.S. to that class of mechanical inventions embracing illuminating apparatus generally.

Photo (fōᵘ·to). 1870. Colloq. abbrev. of PHOTOGRAPH.

Photo- (fōᵘtŏ), bef. a vowel properly **phot-** (but also in full form *photo-*), repr. Gr. φωτο-, comb. form of φῶς, φωτ- light. **1.** Words in which *photo-* simply denotes 'light'.

‖**Pho:tobacte·rium,** a phosphorescent bacterium. **Photoche·mical** *a.* of or pertaining to the chemical action of light; so **Photoche·mistry. Pho:todyna·mic, -al** *adjs.* [see DYNAMIC], pertaining or relating to the energy of light; so **Pho:todyna·mics,** that part of physics which deals with the energy of light, esp. in relation to growth or movement in plants. **Pho:to-magne·tic** *a.*, applied to certain rays of the spectrum having, or supposed to have, a magnetic influence; so **Photoma·gnetism,** photomagnetic property or character; that branch of physics which deals with the relations between light and magnetism. **Photopho·bia** [-PHOBIA], dread of or shrinking from light, esp. as a symptom of disease of the eyes. **Pho·tophore** [-PHORE], an apparatus with an electric light, used for examination of internal organs of the body, etc. **Photo-the·rapy,** a system of treatment of certain skin diseases by exposure to particular light-rays, introduced by N. R. Finsen of Copenhagen.

2. Words in which *photo-* indicates connection with photography, or some photographic process; being sometimes practically equivalent to PHOTOGRAPHIC, as in *p.-process, -radiogram, -telegram, -tracing, -transfer, -zincograph*, vb., etc.

Pho:to-ele·ctrotype, a process in which a photographic picture is produced in relief, so as to afford, by electro-deposition, a matrix for a cast, from which impressions in ink may be obtained. **Photogra·mmeter** [f. PHOTOGRAM + -METER], a photographic camera combined with a theodolite, for use in surveying, or for taking pictures for use in map-making. **Pho:to-mecha·nical** *a.* combining a photographic and a mechanical process. **Pho:to-relie·f,** an image in relief produced by a photographic process. **Photo-scu·lpture,** a process in which the subject is photographed simultaneously from a number of different points of view all round, and the photographs are used to trace successive outlines on a block of modelling clay which is afterwards finished by hand. **Photo-te·lescope,** a telescope with photographic apparatus, used for photographing stars or other heavenly bodies. **Pho:totypo·graphy** [TYPOGRAPHY], printing from an engraving in relief produced by a photo-mechanical process. **Pho:to-xylography** (-zəilǫ·grăfi) [XYLOGRAPHY], a process of employing photography in the preparation of wood blocks for printing from.

3. Prefixed to the names of chemical salts, etc., and of chemical processes to express the effect of light in changing the molecular constitution of the salt, etc. (by virtue of which it can be employed in photography.) Thus **Pho·to-sa·lt,** a general term for any salt so modified by light; so **photo-bro·mide, -su·lphate,** etc.

Photochromatic (fōᵘ:tŏkromæ·tik), *a.* 1888. [f. PHOTO- + CHROMATIC.] Of or pertaining to the chromatic or colouring action of light; pertaining to or produced by photochromy. So **Pho·tochrome,** name for a coloured photograph. **Photo-chro·motype,** a picture in colours printed from plates prepared by a photo-relief process. **Pho·to-chromy,** (*a*) the art or process of colouring photographs; (*b*) colour-photography.

Pho:to-ele·ctric, *a.* Also **photelectric.** 1863. [f. PHOTO- + ELECTRIC.] **a.** Pertaining to, furnishing, or employing electric light 1863. **b.** Of or pertaining to photo-electricity; producing an electric effect by means of light 1880. **c.** Used for taking photographs by electric light. So **Pho:to-electri·city,** electricity generated or affected by light.

Photoelectrotype: see PHOTO- 2.

Pho:to-engra·ving. 1872. [f. PHOTO- 2 + ENGRAVING.] Any process in which, by the action of photography, a matrix is obtained from which prints in ink can be taken. (Usu. restricted to those cases in which the matrix is in relief, as dist. from PHOTOGRAVURE.)

Pho:to-galvano·graphy. 1855. [f. PHOTO- 2 + GALVANOGRAPHY.] A process of obtaining from a positive photograph, by means of a gutta-percha impression from a relief negative in bichromated gelatine, an electrotype plate capable of being used as in copper-plate printing. So **Pho:to-galva·no-graph,** a print thus formed. **Pho:to-galvanogra·phic** *a.*

Photogen (fōᵘ·tŏdʒen). 1864. [f. Gr. φῶς, φωτ- (PHOTO- 1) + -GEN.] A kind of paraffin oil; kerosene.

Photogene (fōᵘ·tŏdʒīn). 1864. [See PHOTO- 1 and -GEN 2.] *Physiol.* A visual impression (usu. negative) continuing after the withdrawal of the object which produced it; an after-image.

Photogenic (-dʒe·nik), *a.* 1839. [See PHOTO-, -GEN, -IC.] **1.** Produced by light; †photographic (–1867). **2.** Producing or emitting light 1863. **3.** That is an apt subject for artistic photography.

Photoglyph (fōᵘ·tŏglif). 1852. [f. PHOTO- 2 + γλυφή GLYPH.] An engraved plate, such as can be printed from, produced by the action of light. So **Photogly·phic, Photo-gly·ptic** *adjs.* **Pho·toglyphy,** the art or process of engraving by means of the action of light and certain chemical processes; the production of photoglyphic plates and photoglyphs or photogravures.

†Photogram (fōᵘ·tŏgræm). 1859. [f. PHOTO- 2 + -GRAM as in *telegram.*] = PHOTOGRAPH.

Photograph (fōᵘ·tŏgrɑf), *sb.* 1839. [Used for the first time, together with *photographic*, PHOTOGRAPHY, by Sir John Herschel (1839); see PHOTO-, -GRAPH.] A picture, likeness, or facsimile obtained by photography.

Photograph (fōᵘ·tŏgrɑf), *v.* 1839. [f. prec. sb.] **1.** *trans.* To take a photograph of. **b.** *absol.* or *intr.* To take photographs 1861. **c.** *intr.* (for *pass.*) To 'take' (well or badly) 1893. **2.** *trans. fig.* To portray vividly in words; to fix on the mind or memory 1862.

1. When a distant landscape is photographed, a large number of rays of light are concentrated upon the film 1883. **c.** I do not p. at all well 1893. **2.** Indelibly photographed on a memory from which few things. .have been effaced 1862.

Photographer (fŏtǫ·grăfəɹ). 1847. [f. prec. + -ER[1].] One who practises photography, *esp.* as a business. So **†Photo·graphist** 1843.

Photographometer (fōᵘ:tŏgrăfǫ·mĭtəɹ). 1849. [f. as prec. + -METER.] An instrument for ascertaining the degree of sensitiveness of photographic films to the chemical action of light.

Photography (fŏtǫ·grăfi). 1839. [See PHOTOGRAPH, -GRAPHY.] The process or art of producing pictures by means of the chemical action of light on a sensitive film on a basis of paper, glass, metal, etc.; the business of producing and printing such pictures. So **Photogra·phic, -al** *adjs.* of, pertaining to, used in or produced by p.; engaged or skilled in p.; **-ly** *adv.*

Photogravure (fōᵘ:tŏ,grăviūᵊ·ɹ), *sb.* 1879. [– Fr. *photogravure*, f. PHOTO- + *gravure* engraving; see GRAVURE.] Photo-engraving; *esp.* the process of preparing a matrix by transferring a photographic negative to a metal plate, and then etching it in; a picture produced by this process. Hence **Photo-gravu·re** *v. trans.* to reproduce by p.

Photoheliograph (fōᵘtohī·liogrɑf). 1861. [f. PHOTO- + HELIOGRAPH 2.] = HELIOGRAPH 2.

Photolithography (fōᵘ:to,liþǫ·grăfi). 1856. [f. PHOTO- 2 + LITHOGRAPHY.] The art or process of producing, by photography, designs upon lithographic stone, etc., from which prints may be taken as in ordinary lithography. So **Photoli·thograph,** a print produced by p. 1855. **Pho:tolitho·grapher,** one who practises p. **Pho:tolithogra·phic** *a.*

Photology (fotǫ·lŏdʒi). *rare.* 1828. [f. PHOTO- 1 + -LOGY.] The science of light; optics. Hence **Photolo·gic, -al** *adjs.* optical. **Photo·logist,** one versed in p.

Photometer (fotǫ·mĭtəɹ). 1760. [– mod.L. *photometrum* (Lambert, 1760); see PHOTO-, -METER.] An instrument for measuring the intensity of light or comparing the intensity of light from various sources.

Photometry (fotǫ·mėtri). 1824. [– mod.L. *photometria* (Lambert, 1760); see PHOTO-, -METRY.] Measurement of light; comparison of the intensity of light from various sources; the use of a photometer. Hence **Photo-me·tric, -al** *adjs.*; **-ly** *adv.* **Photo-metrician** (-i·ʃăn).

Photomicrograph (fōᵘto,məi·krŏgrɑf). 1858. [f. PHOTO- 2 + *micrograph.*] A photograph of a microscopic object on a magnified scale. So **-micro·graphy.**

Photon (fōᵘ·tǫn). 1926. [f. Gr. φῶς, φωτ- light, after *electron.*] *Physics.* A corpuscle or unit particle of light.

Photophone (fōᵘ·tŏfōᵘn). 1880. [f. PHOTO- 1 + -PHONE.] An apparatus in which sounds are transmitted by light; *esp.* that invented by A. Graham Bell and Sumner Tainter in 1880. See RADIOPHONE. Hence **Photophonic** *a.* **Photo·phony,** the use of the p.; the conveyance of sound-vibrations by means of light.

Photoscope (fōu·tŏskoup). 1872. [f. PHOTO- 1 + -SCOPE.] **a.** A means of examining light, e.g. for purposes of analysis. **b.** [with *photo-* taken as = *photograph.*] A lens or apparatus with lenses, through which photographs are viewed. Hence **Photosco·pic** *a.* pertaining to the examination of light; belonging to a p.

Photosphere (fōu·tŏsfiəɹ). 1664. [f. PHOTO- 1 + SPHERE.] **1.** A sphere or orb of light. **2.** *Astron.* The luminous envelope of the sun (or a star), from which its light and heat radiate 1848. Hence **Photosphe·ric** *a.*

Photostat (fōu·tŏstæt). 1912. [f. PHOTO- 2 + -STAT.] A trade name for a photographic apparatus designed for taking a copy of a flat original on sensitized paper, and giving a negative image; a copy so made. Hence as vb. and **Photosta·tic** *a.*

Photosynthesis (fōutosi·nþĭsis). 1904. [f. PHOTO- 1 + SYNTHESIS.] Chemical combination caused by the action of light; *spec.* in plants the conversion of the carbon dioxide and water of the air into carbohydrates brought about by exposure to light. Hence **Photosy·nthesize** *v. trans.* to convert (carbon dioxide and water into carbohydrates) by p. **Pho:tosynthe·tic** *a.* of or belonging to p.; **-the·tically** *adv.*

‖**Phototonus** (fotǫ·tŏnŏs). 1875. [mod.L. *phototonus* (Sachs), f. Gr. φῶς, φωτο- PHOTO- + τόνος tension.] *Bot.* The normal condition of sensitiveness to light in leaves and other organs, maintained by continued exposure to light. Hence **Phototo·nic** *a.*

Phototropic (fōutotrǫ·pik), *a.* 1899. [f. PHOTO- 1, after HELIOTROPIC.] *Bot.* Bending or turning under the influence of light; a more accurate substitute for HELIOTROPIC.

Phototype (fōu·tŏtəip), *sb.* 1859. [f. PHOTO- + TYPE.] A plate or block for printing from, produced by a photographic process; also, the process by which such a plate is produced, or a picture, etc., printed from it. Hence **Pho·totype** *v. trans.* to reproduce by means of phototypy. **Phototy·pic** *a.* **Pho·totypy,** the art or process of making phototypes.

Photozincography (fōu:tozinkǫ·grăfi). 1860. [f. PHOTO- 2 + ZINCOGRAPHY.] The art or process of producing by photographic methods a design on a zinc plate from which prints can be taken. Hence **Photozi·ncograph** *sb.* a plate, or a picture or facsimile, produced by p. **Photozi·ncograph** *v. trans.* to produce or copy by p. **Pho:tozincogra·phic, -al** *adjs.*

Phra·gmocone. Also *erron.* **phragma-.** 1847. [f. Gr. φραγμός fence + κῶνος CONE.] *Zool.* The conical chambered internal skeleton of a fossil belemnite; also, by extension, the corresponding part in other fossil cephalopods.

Phrase (frēiz), *sb.* 1530. [In earliest use also *phrasis*, from the pl. of which (*phrases*) a sing. *phrase* appears to have been evolved (cf. PHASE). – L. *phrasis* (Seneca the rhetorician, Quintilian) – Gr. φράσις speech, manner of speaking, f. φράζειν indicate, declare, tell. Cf. Fr. *phrase* (1548).] **1.** Manner or style of expression; diction, phraseology, language. **2.** A small group of words expressing a single notion, or entering with some degree of unity into the structure of a sentence; an expression; esp. a characteristic or idiomatic expression 1530. †**b.** Applied to a single word –1699. **c.** *Gram.* A group of words equivalent to a noun, adjective, or adverb, and having no finite verb of its own 1852. **3.** A short, pithy, or telling expression; sometimes, a meaningless, trite, or high-sounding form of words 1579. **4.** *Mus.* Any (comparatively) short passage, forming a more or less independent member of a longer passage, or of a whole movement 1789.

1. Conforme the stile thereof with the P. of our Englishe 1540. **2.** 'If I were you' is a p. often on our lips 1875. **b.** 2 *Hen. IV*, III. ii. 79. **3.** A man.. That hath a mint of phrases in his braine SHAKS. The p. was tossed about till it bore no certain meaning 1841.

Comb.: **p.-book,** a book containing a collection of idiomatic phrases; **-mark,** a sign in musical notation to indicate the proper phrasing; **-monger,** one who deals in fine-sounding phrases; so *p.-maker*. Hence **Phra·sal** *a.* of the nature of or consisting of a p.

Phrase, *v.* 1550. [f. prec. sb.] **1.** *intr.* To employ a phrase or phrases. **2.** *trans.* To put into words; to express in words or a phrase; to express 1570. **3.** To call, designate; †to signify. Now *rare* or *arch.* 1585. **4.** *Mus.* To divide or mark off into phrases, esp. in execution. Also *absol.* 1796.

2. *To p. it*, to express the thing, to 'put it'; He has had, as he phrased it, 'a matter of four wives' JOHNSON. **3.** The papists..p. the preachers to be uncircumcised Philistines 1585.

Phraseogram (frēi·ziŏgræm). 1847. [f. PHRASE + -GRAM, after PHRASEOLOGY.] A written character or symbol representing a phrase, *esp.* in systems of shorthand. So **Phra·seograph** [-GRAPH], (*Shorthand*) a phrase for which there is a phraseogram 1845.

Phraseological (frēiziolǫ·dʒikăl), *a.* 1664. [f. next + -ICAL.] **1.** Using phrases or peculiar expressions; expressed in a special phrase or phrases. **2.** Of or pertaining to phraseology; dealing with phrases or phraseology 1664.

2. A p. peculiarity of these tracts 1899. Hence **Phraseolo·gically** *adv.*

Phraseology (frēiziǫ·lŏdʒi). 1664. [– mod.L. *phraseologia*, spurious Gr. φρασεολογία, irreg. formed by M. Neander in the title of his book of locutions collected from Isocrates, 1558 *Phraseologia Isocratis Græcolatina*, id est, Phraseon sive locutionum (etc.), from Gr. φράσεων, gen. pl. of φράσις PHRASE; see -LOGY.] †**1.** A phrase-book –1776. **2.** Manner or style of expression; the particular form of speech or diction which characterizes a writer, language, etc. 1664.

2. Men, according to their habits and professions, have a p. of their own BURKE. Hence **Phraseo·logist,** one who treats of p.; a phrase-monger.

Phrasing (frēi·ziŋ), *vbl. sb.* 1611. [f. PHRASE *v.* + -ING[1].] **1.** The action of PHRASE *v.*; manner or style of verbal expression; phraseology, wording. **2.** *Mus.* The rendering of musical phrases 1880.

Phratry (frēi·tri). 1833. [– Gr. φρατρία clan, f. φράτηρ clansman, cogn. with BROTHER.] **1.** *Ancient Gr. Hist.* A politico-religious division of the people; in Athens, each of the three subdivisions into which the phyle was divided; a clan. **2.** *transf.* Applied to tribal or kinship divisions existing among primitive races 1876.

‖**Phrenesis** (frĭnī·sis). 1547. [– L. *phrenesis* madness – late Gr. φρένησις, f. φρήν, φρεν-; see next, and FRENZY.] *Path.* = PHRENITIS.

Phrenetic (frĭne·tik), *a.* (*sb.*) late ME. [– (O)Fr. *frénétique* – L. *phreneticus* – late Gr. φρενητικός, for φρενιτικός, f. φρενῖτις delirium, f. φρήν, φρεν- heart, mind; see -ITIS, -IC. Formerly stressed *phre·netic*. See FRANTIC.] †**1.** Of persons: = FRANTIC *a.* 1. –1778. **2.** *transf.* Fanatic, *esp.* in religious matters 1540. **3.** = FRANTIC *a.* 2. 1529. **B.** *sb.* A madman 1612. So †**Phrene·tical** *a.*, **-ly** *adv.*

Phrenic (fre·nik), *a.* (*sb.*) 1704. [– Fr. *phrénique* (= sense 1), f. Gr. φρήν, φρεν- diaphragm, mind; see -IC.] **1.** *Anat.* and *Path.* Of, pertaining to, or affecting the diaphragm. †**2.** Mental –1847. **B.** *sb.* **1.** *Anat.* Short for *p. nerve* 1776. **2.** *pl.* **Phrenics:** That branch of science which relates to the mind; psychology 1841.

‖**Phrenitis** (frĭnəi·tis). 1621. [– Gr. φρενῖτις delirium, f. as prec.; see -ITIS.] *Path.* Inflammation of the brain or of its membranes, attended with delirium and fever; brain-fever. Hence **Phreni·tic** *a.* affected with p.

Phreno-, bef. a vowel **phren-,** – Gr. φρενο- (comb. of φρήν, stem φρεν- midriff, mind), usu. in sense of 'the mind, mental faculties'; as in

Phre·nogram, the curve or tracing made by the phrenograph. **Phren·ograph,** (*a*) an instrument for recording the movements of the diaphragm in respiration; (*b*) a phrenological 'chart' of a person's mental characteristics. **Phreno-ma·gnetism,** the excitation of the phrenological organs by magnetic influence; hence **Phreno-magne·tic** *a.*

Phrenology (frĭnǫ·lŏdʒi). 1815. [f. PHRENO- + -LOGY; designed to cover G. *gehirn- und schädellehre* (1804) encephalology and cranilology.] The scientific study or theory of the mental faculties; *spec.* (and in ordinary use), the theory originated by Gall and Spurzheim, that the mental powers of the individual consist of separate faculties, each having its organ and location in a definite region of the surface of the brain; hence, the study of the external conformation of the cranium as an index to the development and position of these organs, and thus of the degree of development of the various faculties. Hence **Phrenolo·gic, -al,** *adjs.* of or belonging to p.; **-ly** *adv.* **Phreno·logist,** one skilled in p. **Phreno·logize** *v. trans.* to examine or analyse phrenologically.

Phre·nosin. 1878. [f. Gr. φρήν, φρεν- mind + -OSE[2] + -IN[1] (after *myosin*).] *Chem.* A substance ($C_{34}H_{67}NO_8$) obtained from the brain.

Phrensy, -zy, etc., var. of FRENZY.

Phrontistery (frǫ·ntistĕri). Often in Gr. or Latinized forms **phrontiste·rion, phrontiste·rium.** 1614. [– Gr. φροντιστήριον, f. φροντιστής a deep thinker, f. φροντίζειν, f. φροντίς thought.] A place for thinking; a 'thinking shop': a term applied in ridicule to the school of Socrates; hence applied to modern educational institutions.

Phrygian (fri·dʒiăn), *a.* (*sb.*) 1579. [– L. *Phrygianus*, f. *Phrygia*; see -AN.] Of or pertaining to Phrygia, an ancient country of Asia Minor, or its inhabitants.

P. cap, a conical cap or bonnet with the peak turned over in front, now identified with the cap of liberty. *P. mode* (*mus.*): (*a*) an ancient Greek mode of a warlike character, derived from the ancient Phrygians; (*b*) the second of the 'authentic' ecclesiastical modes, having its 'final' on E and 'dominant' on C.

B. *sb.* **a.** A native or inhabitant of Phrygia. **b.** A CATAPHRYGIAN. 1585.

Phthalic (fþæ·lik), *a.* 1857. [abbrev. from NAPHTHALIC.] *Chem.* Of, pertaining to, or obtained from naphthaline, as *p. anhyride*, etc. *P. acid*, a white crystalline compound ($C_8H_6O_4$) produced by the action of nitric acid on naphthaline, alizarin, purpurin, etc. Also called ALIZARIC *acid*.

So **Phtha·late,** a salt of p. acid. **Phthalein** (fþæ·li,in) [-IN[1]], one of a series of organic dyes produced by combining p. anhydride with the phenols, with elimination of water. **Phthalide** (fþæ·ləid) [-IDE, here short for *anhydride*], the anhydrous form of p. acid, a white crystalline substance, $C_8H_4O_3$ = $C_6H_4(CO)_2O$, obtained by distilling the acid. **Phtha·limide** [see IMIDE], a derivative of ammonia in which two atoms of hydrogen are replaced by phthalyl; a colourless crystalline inodorous and tasteless body, $C_8H_4O_2$. NH. **Phthalin** (fþæ·lin) [-IN[1]], a colourless crystalline substance obtained from phthalein. **Phthalyl** (fþæ·lil) [-YL], the radical of p. acid ($C_8H_4O_2$).

‖**Phthiriasis** (þəirəi·ăsis, þəiərĭ,ēi·sis, fþ-). Also **phtheir-.** 1598. [L. – Gr. φθειρίασις, f. φθειριᾶν be lousy; see -ASIS.] *Path.* A morbid condition of the body in which lice multiply excessively, causing extreme irritation; pediculosis.

Phthisic (ti·zik), *sb.* and *a.* Now *rare.* [ME. *tisik*, later *ptisike*, *phthisick* – OFr. *tisike*, *-ique*, later *ptisique*, *thisique* (repl. by mod. *phtisie*) :– Rom. *(*ph*)*thisica*, subst. use of fem. of L. *phthisicus* – Gr. φθισικός consumptive, f. φθίσις; see next, -IC.] **1.** A wasting disease of the lungs; pulmonary consumption. †**2.** *loosely.* A severe cough; asthma –1741. **B.** *adj.* = PHTHISICAL *a.* late ME. Hence **Phthi·sical** (ti·zikăl), *a.* of, pertaining to, characterized by, or affected with phthisis. **Phthi·sicky** (ti·ziki), *a.* phthisical, consumptive; asthmatic, wheezy.

‖**Phthisis** (þəi·sis, təi·sis, fþi·sis). 1543. [– L. *phthisis* (Celsus) – Gr. φθίσις wasting, consumption, f. φθίνειν waste away. Cf. prec.] A progressive wasting disease; *spec.* pulmonary consumption. Hence **Phthisiology** (fþ-, þiziǫ·lŏdʒi), the science or study of p., or a treatise on p.

Phut (fɒt). *slang.* 1892. [f. Hind. *phaṭnā* burst.] *To go p.*: to be a failure, fizzle out.

Phycic (fəi·sik), *a.* 1864. [f. Gr. φῦκος fucus, seaweed + -IC.] In *p. acid*, a crystalline substance extracted from *Protococcus vulgaris* by alcohol.

Phycite (fəi·səit). 1864. [f. as prec. + -ITE[1] 4.] *Chem.* A sweet-smelling crystalline substance ($C_4H_{10}O_4$) extracted from *Protococcus vulgaris*; also called *erythromannite*.

Phyco- (fəi·ko), comb. form of Gr. φῦκος (L. *fucus*) seaweed; used in the formation of mod. scientific terms relating to seaweeds or algæ, as

Phycochrome (fəi·kŏkrōᵘm), the bluish-green colouring matter of some algæ, being chlorophyll modified by an admixture of phycocyanin. **Phycocyan** (fəi:ko,səi·ăn), **Phycocy·anin, Phycocya·nogen,** the blue colouring matter which is combined with chlorophyll in certain algæ. **Phy:co-e·rythrin,** the red colouring matter found similarly in *Florideæ*. **Phyco·logy** [-LOGY], the branch of botany treating of seaweeds; algology. **Phycomycetous** (fəi:koməisī·təs), *a.*, of or pertaining to the *Phycomyceteæ*, a division of Fungi, of which the genus *Phycomyces* is the type. **Phycophæ·in** [Gr. φαιός dusky], a reddish-brown pigment found in the olive-brown seaweeds, as the *Fucaceæ*, etc. **Phycoxa·nthin,** = DIATOMIN.

Phylactery (filæ·ktĕri). late ME. [Early forms *fil-, philaterie* – OFr. **filaterie, -atiere* – Vulg. L. *fyl-, phylacterium* safeguard, amulet, f. φυλακτήρ guard, f. φυλακ-, stem of vb. φυλάσσειν.] **1.** A small leathern box containing four texts of Scripture, Deut. 6:4–9, 11:13–21, Exod. 13:1–10, 11–16, written in Hebrew letters on vellum, and worn by Jews during morning prayer on all days except the sabbath, as a reminder of the obligation to keep the law. Cf. Deut. 11:18. **b.** *fig.* A reminder; a religious observance or profession of faith; an ostentatious display of piety or rectitude, a mark of Pharisaism 1645. **2.** An amulet worn as a preservative against disease, etc.; also *fig.* a charm, safeguard 1809. **3.** A vessel or case containing a holy relic. late ME. **4.** In mediæval art, The inscribed scroll proceeding from a person's mouth or held by him, to indicate his words; *fig.* a record, a roll. Also, the infula of a mitre. 1855.

1. b. Happy are they who. .make their Phylacteries speak in their Lives SIR T. BROWNE. Phr. *To make broad the p.* (from Matt. 23:5), to vaunt one's righteousness.

Phyla·ctocarp (fəil-). 1883. [f. Gr. φυλακτός, vbl. adj., f. φυλάσσειν to guard + καρπός fruit.] *Zool.* A 'fruit-case'; a receptacle in certain hydroids protecting the gonothecæ.

Phylactolæ·matous (fəil-), *a.* 1877. [f. mod.L. *Phylactolæmata*, f. Gr. φυλακτο-, f. φυλάσσειν to guard + λαιμός throat + L. *-ata* (pa. pple.); see -OUS.] *Zool.* Belonging to the *Phylactolæmata*, an order of Polyzoa, having the lophophore bilateral, and the mouth overhung by a small ciliated mobile lobe, the epistome.

Phylarch (fəi·lāɹk). 1551. [– L. *phylarchus* – Gr. φύλαρχος chief of a tribe, f. φυλή tribe; see -ARCH.] **1.** The chief of a phyle or tribe in ancient Greece; hence, any tribal chief 1656. **2.** In ancient Attica, An officer elected to command the cavalry of each of the ten phylæ 1830. **3.** The title of certain magistrates in the ideal commonwealths of Plato, More, etc. 1551. Hence **Phy·larchy,** the office of a p., tribal government.

‖**Phyle** (fəi·lī). *Pl.* **-æ.** 1863. [– Gr. φυλή tribe.] In ancient Greece, a clan or tribe, based on supposed kinship; in Attica, a political, administrative, and military unit; also the cavalry brigade furnished by an Attic tribe.

Phyletic (fəile·tik), *a.* 1881. [– Gr. φυλετικός, f. φυλέτης tribesman, f. φυλή tribe.] *Biol.* Of or pertaining to a phylum or race; racial.

Phyllis: see PHILLIS.

Phyllite (fi·ləit). 1828. [f. Gr. φύλλον leaf + -ITE[1] 2 b.] *Min.* **a.** A species of magnesia-mica, occurring in small scales in argillaceous schist or slate. **b.** A rock consisting of an argillaceous schist or slate containing scales or flakes of mica.

Phyllo- (filo), repr. Gr. φυλλο-, comb. form of φύλλον leaf.

Phyllobranchia (-bræ·ŋkiă), pl. **-æ,** [Gr. βράγχια gills], *Zool.* each of the leaf-like foliaceous, or lamellar gills of certain crustaceans. **Phyllocyanin** (-səi·ănin) [see CYANIN], *Chem.* a blue or bluish-green substance supposed to be a constituent of chlorophyll. **Phy·llocyst** (-sist), *Zool.* a cyst or cavity in the hydrophyllium of certain Hydrozoa. **Phyllomorphic** (-mǫ·ɹfik) [Gr. μορφή form] *a.* leaf-shaped; so **Phyllomo·rphous** *a.*; **Phy·llomorphy** = PHYLLODY *a.* **Phy·llophore** (-foᵊɹ) [Gr. φυλλοφόρος leaf-bearing], *Bot.* the growing-point or terminal bud from which the leaves arise, esp. in palms; so **Phyllo·phorous** *a.*, leaf-bearing; in *Zool.*, bearing parts resembling leaves, as the nose-leaf of certain bats. **Phy·llosome** [Gr. σῶμα body], *Zool.* the larval form of certain macrurous crustaceans; a glass-crab. **Phyllǫxanthin** (filǫksæ·nþin) [– Fr. *phylloxanthine*, f. Gr. ξανθός yellow], *Chem.* a yellow constituent of chlorophyll, also called XANTHOPHYLL.

Phylloclade (fi·loklēⁱd). 1858. [– mod.L. **phyllocladium** (filoklēⁱ·diŏm), f. Gr. φύλλον leaf + κλάδος branch.] *Bot.* A branch of an enlarged or flattened form, resembling or performing the functions of a leaf, as in the *Cactaceæ*.

Phyllode (fi·lōᵘd). 1848. [– mod.L. *phyllodium*, also in Eng. use, f. Gr. φυλλώδης leaf-like, f. φύλλον leaf; see -IUM, -ODE. Cf. Fr. *phyllode*.] *Bot.* A petiole or leaf-stalk of an expanded and (usu.) flattened form, resembling and having the functions of a leaf, as in many Acacias.

Phyllody (fi·lodi). 1888. [f. prec. + -Y[3].] *Bot.* **a.** The condition in which certain organs, esp. parts of the flower, are metamorphosed into ordinary leaves. **b.** The condition in which the leaf-stalk is metamorphosed into a phyllode.

Phylloid (fi·loid), *a.* and *sb.* 1858. [– mod. L. *phylloides*, f. Gr. φύλλον leaf; see -OID.] **A.** *adj.* Resembling a leaf; foliaceous. **B.** *sb.* A part in lower plants analogous to a leaf.

Phyllome (fi·lōᵘm). 1875. [– mod.L. *phylloma*, f. Gr. φύλλωμα foliage, f. φυλλοῦν clothe with leaves, f. φύλλον leaf; see -OME, -OMA.] The general name for a leaf or any organ homologous with a leaf (as a sepal, petal, stamen, carpel, etc.)

Phyllophagan (filǫ·făgăn). 1842. [f. mod. L. *phyllophaga* pl., f. φύλλον leaf + -φάγος eating; see -AN.] *Zool.* A member of the *Phyllophaga*, a name applied to various groups of animals which feed on leaves. So **Phyllo·phagous** *a.* leaf-eating; belonging to the *Phyllophaga*.

Phyllopod (fi·lŏpǫd), *sb.* and *a.* 1863. [– mod.L. *Phyllopoda* pl., f. Gr. φύλλον leaf + πούς, ποδ- foot; see -POD.] *Zool.* **A.** *sb.* A member of the *Phyllopoda*, a group of entomostracous crustaceans, having lamellate or foliaceous swimming feet; a leaf-footed crustacean. **B.** *adj.* Belonging to the *Phyllopoda*; leaf-footed. So **Phyllo·podous** *a.* = prec. B. 1835.

Phyllorhine (fi·lŏrəin), *a.* and *sb.* [– mod.L. *Phyllorhinus*, f. Gr. φύλλον leaf + ῥίς, ῥιν- nose.] *Zool.* **A.** *adj.* Of a bat: Having a nose-leaf; leaf-nosed; *spec.* belonging to the *Phyllorhininæ*, a subfamily of the horseshoe-bats. **B.** *sb.* A leaf-nosed bat; *spec.* one of the *Phyllorhininæ*.

Phyllostome (fi·lostoᵘm). 1858. [– mod.L. *Phyllostoma*, f. Gr. φύλλον leaf + στόμα, στοματ- mouth.] *Zool.* A bat of the genus *Phyllostoma* or family *Phyllostomatidæ*, having a nose-leaf or other appendage of the snout. Also **Phyllo·stomid.**

‖**Phyllotaxis** (filotæ·ksis). 1857. [mod.L., f. Gr. φύλλον leaf + τάξις arrangement.] *Bot.* The arrangement of leaves (or other lateral members) upon an axis or stem; the geometrical principles of such arrangement. Also **Phy·llotaxy.** So **Phyllota·ctic, -al** *adjs.*

‖**Phylloxera** (filǫksiᵊ·ră). 1868. [mod.L., f. Gr. φύλλον leaf + ξηρός dry.] *Entom.* A genus of *Aphididæ* or plant-lice; esp. *P. vastatrix*, also called *vine-pest*, which is very destructive to the European grape-vine. Hence **Phylloxeral** (-īᵊ·răl), **Phylloxeric** (-e·rik) *adjs.* pertaining or relating to the p. **Phyllo·xerated, Phyllo·xerized** *ppl. adjs.* infested with the p.

Phylo-, bef. a vowel **phyl-,** comb. form of Gr. φῦλον, φυλή a tribe, used mostly in biological terms.

Phylogenesis (fəilodʒe·nĭsis). 1875. [f. PHYLO- + -GENESIS.] *Biol.* The evolution of the tribe or race, or of any organ or feature in the race. So **Phy:logene·tic** *a.* of, pertaining to, or characteristic of p. or phylogeny; relating to the race history of an organism or organisms; so **Phy:logene·tical** *a.*, **-ly,** *adv.*

Phylogeny (fəilǫ·dʒĭni). 1870. [– G. *phylogenie* (Haeckel 1866); see PHYLO-, -GENY.] *Biol.* **1.** = prec. 1872. **2.** The race history of an animal or vegetable type; tribal history 1875. **3.** A pedigree showing the racial evolution of a type of organisms 1870. Hence **Phyloge·nic** *a.* phylogenetic. **Phylo·genist,** one versed or skilled in p.

‖**Phylum** (fəi·lŏm). *Pl.* **-la.** 1876. [mod.L. – Gr. φῦλον race.] *Biol.* A tribe or race of organisms, related by descent from a common ancestral form; a primary division or sub-kingdom of animals or plants supposed to be so related.

‖**Phyma** (fəi·mă). *Pl.* **-ata.** 1693. [L. *phyma* (Celsius) – Gr. φῦμα, φυματ- swelling, tumour.] *Path.* An inflamed swelling; an external tubercle.

‖**Physa** (fəi·să). 1842. [mod.L. – Gr. φῦσα bellows.] *Zool.* A small freshwater gastropod.

‖**Physalia** (fəisēⁱ·liă). 1842. [mod.L., f. Gr. φυσαλέος inflated with wind, φυσαλλίς bladder, bubble; see -IA[2].] *Zool.* A genus of oceanic hydrozoa; the Portuguese man-of-war; see MAN-OF-WAR. Hence **Physa·lian** *a.* belonging to this genus; *sb.* a species of P.

Physeter (fəisī·təɹ). 1591. [– L. *physeter* – Gr. φυσητήρ, f. φυσᾶν blow.] †**1.** A large blowing whale –1786. **2.** *Zool.* Generic name of the cachalots or larger sperm-whales 1753. **3.** A filter acting by air-pressure 1842.

Physic (fi·zik), *sb.* [ME. *fisike* – OFr. *fisique* medicine (mod. *physique* natural science, now physics) – L. *physica, -ē* (Cicero) – Gr. φυσική, subst. use (sc. ἐπιστήμη knowledge) of fem. of φυσικός, f. φύσις nature; see -IC.] **1.** = PHYSICS 1. Now *rare.* **2.** The theory of diseases and their treatment; medical science, medicine. *Obs.* or *arch.* late ME. **3.** The art or practice of healing; the medical profession ME. **b.** The medical faculty personified; physicians. late ME. †**c.** Medical treatment –1700. **4.** = MEDICINE *sb.*[1] 2. (Now *colloq.*) 1591. **b.** *spec.* A cathartic or purge 1617. †**5.** *fig.* Wholesome regimen or habit –1699. †**b.** Mental, moral, or spiritual remedy –1703.

1. Physike, which is the studie of naturall things: metaphysike, which is of supernaturall things 1586. **2.** A. .good learned company, many Doctors of Phisique PEPYS. **3. c.** Farewel Phisik; go ber the man to chirche CHAUCER. **4.** Throw Physicke to the Dogs, Ile none of it SHAKS. **5. b.** He is a madman. It is good p. to whip him 1656. *Comb.*: **p.-ball,** medicine in the form of a ball or bolus for a horse, dog, etc.; †**p. garden,** a garden for the cultivation of medicinal plants; hence, a botanic garden. Hence **Phy·sicky** *a.* having the taste, smell, or other qualities of p. or medicine.

Physic (fi·zik), *a.* Now *rare.* ME. [– (O)Fr. *physique* or L. *physicus* – Gr. φυσικός natural; see prec.] **1.** Physical, natural 1563. †**2.** Medical; medicinal. (= prec., *attrib.*) –1736.

Physic (fi·zik), *v.* Infl. **physicked, physicking.** late ME. [f. PHYSIC *sb.* 3–5.] *trans.* To dose with physic, esp. with a purgative. Now *colloq.* **b.** *fig.* To treat with remedies, relieve 1589.

b. The labour we delight in, Physicks paine SHAKS.

Physical (fi·zikăl), *a.* late ME. [– med.L. *physicalis*, f. L. *physica*; see PHYSIC *sb.*, -AL[1].] **I. 1.** Of or pertaining to material nature; pertaining to or connected with matter; material; opp. to *psychical, mental, spiritual* 1597. **b.** Belonging or relating to Natural Philosophy or Natural Science; relating to or in accordance with the regular processes or laws of nature 1580. **c.** Of persons: Dealing with or devoted to natural science 1678. **2.** Belonging to the science of physics; see PHYSICS 2. 1734. **3.** Of the body; bodily, corporeal 1780.

1. Phr. *P. cause, energy, power; p. possibility, impossibility*, etc. **b.** The law of gravitation is a p. axiom HERSCHEL. **2.** The p. properties of matter may be altered without affecting its deeper chemical constitution HUXLEY. **3.** The man gave me the impression of p. strength 1860. The lads. . went through a course of p. drill 1899. *P. exercises, jerks, training,* muscular exercises designed to strengthen or keep the body healthy. So *p. culture.*

II. 1. Of or belonging to medicine; medical. Now *rare.* 1450. †**b.** Of persons: Practising medicine; medical –1796. †**2.** Used in medicine, medicinal –1828; curative, remedial; good (*for* one's health) –1633. **3.** In special phrases 1817.

1. The Medical and P. Journal (*title*) 1799. **3. P. astronomy,** that branch of astronomy which treats of the motions, masses, positions, light, heat, etc. of the heavenly bodies. **P. chemistry,** that branch of chemistry which deals with the structure of molecules. **P. force,** material as opp. to moral force; in politics, the use of armed power, to effect or repress political changes. **P. geography,** that branch of geography which deals with the natural features of the earth's surface. **P. geology,** the study of the formation and history of strata and eruptive rocks apart from palæontology. **P. optics,** that branch of optics which deals with the properties of light itself (as dist. from the function of sight). **P. point,** a point conceived as infinitely small, and yet a portion of matter. **P. science** = PHYSICS. **P. sciences,** the sciences that treat of inanimate matter, and of energy apart from vitality. **P. sign,** a symptom of health or disease ascertainable by bodily examination. Hence **Phy·sically** *adv.* according to nature, or the material laws of nature; according to natural philosophy or science; corporeally; †by medical rules.

Physician (fizi·ʃăn), *sb.* [ME. *fisicien* – OFr. *fisicien* (mod. *physicien* physicist), f. *fisique*; see PHYSIC *sb.*, -IAN, -ICIAN.] †**1.** A student of physics –1833. **2.** One who practises the healing art, including medicine and surgery ME. **b.** One legally qualified to practise the healing art as above; *esp.* as dist. from one qualified as a surgeon only. late ME. **3.** *transf.* and *fig.* A healer; one who cures moral, spiritual, or political maladies. late ME.

2. More needs she the Diuine, then the Physitian SHAKS. **b.** O lord, whi is it so greet difference bitwixte a cirurgian & a phisician 1400. **3.** Time must be her p. 1805. Hence **Physi·cian** *v. trans.* (*a*) to make into a p.; (*b*) to put under the care of a p. **Physi·cianer** *dial.* = PHYSICIAN 2. **Physi·cianship,** the office or position of p.

Physicism (fi·zisiz'm). 1869. [f. PHYSIC *sb.* + -ISM.] A doctrine of physical phenomena; *esp.* one which refers all the phenomena of the universe, including life itself, to physical or material forces; materialism.

In the progress of the species. . anthropomorphism grows into theology, and p. (if I may so call it) developes into Science HUXLEY.

Physicist (fi·zisist). 1840. [f. PHYSIC *sb.* + -IST.] **1.** A student of physics (PHYSICS 2). **b.** A student of nature or natural science in general (cf. PHYSICS 1) 1858. **2.** A believer in physicism; opp. to *vitalist* 1871.

Phy·sic-nut. 1657. [f. PHYSIC *sb.* 4 + NUT.] The fruit of the euphorbiaceous shrub *Jatropha curcas* (*Curcas purgans*), of tropical America, used as a purgative; the Barbadoes- or purging-nut; also the plant itself.

Physico- (fi·ziko), comb. form of Gr. φυσικός natural, physical, usu. an advb. or adj. qualification of the second element, 'physically', 'physical' (see -O- 1); also, sometimes expressing any relation, as simple combination or contact (see -O- 2); as in **Phy:sico-che·mical** *a.* of or belonging to physical chemistry; of or pertaining to physics and chemistry. **Phy:sico-mathema·tical** *a.* of or pertaining to the application of mathematics to physics or mixed mathematics. **Phy:sico-mecha·nical** *a.* of or pertaining to the dynamics of natural forces, or the mechanical branch of natural philosophy. **Phy:sico-me·ntal** *a.* pertaining to both body and mind. So **Phy:sico-mo·ral** *a.*

Phy:sico-theo·logy. 1712. [See prec.] A theology founded upon the facts of nature, and the evidences of design there found; natural theology. So **Phy:sico-theolo·gical** *a.* **Phy:sico-theo·logist.**

Physics (fi·ziks). 1589. [pl. of PHYSIC *a.* used subst., rendering L. *physica* neut. pl. – Gr. τὰ φυσικά lit. 'natural things', the collective title of Aristotle's physical treatises: in Engl., pl. in origin and form, but now constr. as a sing.: cf. *metaphysics*, etc.] **1.** Natural science in general; in the older writers *esp.* the Aristotelian system; hence, natural philosophy in the wider sense. Also, a treatise on this, as *Aristotle's Physics*. **2.** In current usage, restricted to The science, or sciences, treating of the properties of matter and energy, or of the action of the different forms of energy on matter in general (excluding Chemistry and Biology) 1715.

2. P. is divided into *general p.*, dealing with the general phenomena of inorganic nature (dynamics, molecular physics, physics of the ether, etc.), and *applied p.*, dealing with special phenomena (astronomy, meteorology, terrestrial magnetism, etc.). There is a tendency now to restrict the word to the former group. O.E.D.

Physio- (fi·zio), comb. element, repr. Gr. φυσιο-, f. φύσις nature; used as a formative with the sense 'nature' or 'natural', as in PHYSIOGNOMY, PHYSIOLOGY, etc. **Phy:sio-philo·sophy,** a name for the philosophic system of nature of Oken, who 'aimed at constructing all knowledge *a priori*, and thus setting forth the system of nature in its universal relations' 1847.

Physiocrat (fi·zioˌkræt). Also in Fr. form **-crate.** 1798. [– Fr. *physiocrate*, f. *physiocratie*; see PHYSIO- and -CRAT.] One of a school founded by F. Quesnay in France in the 18th c., who maintained that society should be governed according to an inherent natural order, that the soil is the only source of wealth and the only proper object of taxation, and that security of property and freedom of industry and exchange are essential. So **Physio·cracy,** government according to natural order; *spec.* the doctrine of the physiocrats. **Phy:siocra·tic,** †**-al** *adjs.*

Physiogeny (fiziǫ·dʒĭni). 1858. [– mod.L. *physiogenia*; see PHYSIO-, -GENY.] *Biol.* The genesis of vital functions; the development of the functions of living organisms, which are the province of physiology; the science or history of this.

Physiognomic (fi:zionǫ·mik, fi:ziognǫ·mik), *a.* 1704. [f. PHYSIOGNOMY + -IC.] **1.** Of the nature of physiognomy; characteristic. **2.** Of, pertaining to, or skilled in physiognomy 1755.

Physiogno·mical, *a.* 1588. [f. as prec.; see -ICAL.] **1.** Pertaining to, dealing with, or skilled in physiognomy. **2.** Of or pertaining to the face or form (prop.) as an index of character, but often used simply in ref. to personal appearance 1811. Hence **Physiogno·mically** *adv.*

Physiognomist (fiziǫ·nŏmist, -ǫ·gnŏmist). 1570. [– Fr. *physiognomiste* (XVI), f. *physiognomie*; see -IST.] One skilled in physiognomy; formerly, one who professed to tell destiny from the face.

Physiognomonic (fiziǫgnomǫ·nik), *a.* (*sb.*) *rare.* 1755. [– Fr. *physiognomonique* (Dict. Trévoux 1732) – Gr. φυσιογνωμονικός adj., f. φυσιογνωμονία; see next, -IC.] The etymological form for PHYSIOGNOMIC. So †**Physio:gnomo·nical** *a.* –1814.

Physiognomy (fiziǫ·nŏmi, -ǫ·gnŏmi). Vulgarly abbrev. *physiog.*, *phizog.*, and PHIZ. [Late ME. *fisnamye*, *fis-*, *phisonomie*, later *phisnomy* (XV–XVII), *phisognomie* (XVI–XVII), *physiognomy* (XVI) – OFr. *phisonomie*, *-anomie* (mod. *physionomie*) – med.L. *phisonomia*, *physionomia*, also late L. *physiognomia* (Script. Physiog. ?IV) – late Gr. φυσιογνωμία (recorded once as a miswriting), contr. of Gr. φυσιογνωμονία, f. φύσις nature + γνώμων, γνωμον- interpreter, f. *γνω- (see KNOW).] **I. 1.** The art of judging character and disposition from the features of the face or the form and lineaments of the body generally. †**2.** The foretelling of destiny from the features and lines of the face, etc.; the fortune so foretold; *loosely*, fortune foretold (or character divined) by astrology –1651.

1. We know your skill in p. . . Read that countenance C. BRONTË. **2.** According to my little skill in P., I hope he may live yet many a yeer 1651.

II. 1. The face, esp. viewed as an index to the mind and character; expression of face; also, the general cast of features, type of face (of a race); vulgarly, the face or countenance. late ME. †**b.** A portrait –1603. **2.** *transf.* The external features of anything material; e.g. the contour of a country 1567. **3.** *fig.* The ideal, mental, moral, or political aspect of anything as an indication of its character 1680.

1. She did abhorre her husbands phisnomy BURTON. **3.** There is a Kind of P. in the Titles of Books, no less than in the Faces of Men 1680. Hence **Physio·gnomize** *v. trans.* to study physiognomically; to deduce the character from the face.

Physiogony (fiziǫ·gŏni). 1834. [f. PHYSIO- + Gr. -γονία begetting.] The generation or production of nature.

Physiography (fiziǫ·grăfi). 1828. [– Fr. *physiographie*; see PHYSIO-, -GRAPHY.] **1.** A description of nature, or of natural phenomena or productions generally. **2.** A description of the nature of a particular class of objects (e.g. minerals) 1888. **3.** Physical geography 1873. So **Physio·grapher,** one versed in p. **Phy:siogra·phic, -al** *adjs.* 1796, **-ly** *adv.*

Physiolater (fiziǫ·lătəɹ). 1860. [f. PHYSIO- + -LATER.] A worshipper of nature. So **Physio·latry,** nature-worship.

Physiologer (fiziǫ·lŏdʒəɹ). Now *rare* or *Obs.* 1598. [f. late L. *physiologus* – Gr. φυσιολόγος one who discourses on nature; see PHYSIO-, -ER[1] 4, -LOGER.] **1.** A student or teacher of natural science; *spec.* a philosopher of the Ionic sect. **2.** = PHYSIOLOGIST 2. 1680.

Physiologist (fiziǫ·lŏdʒist). 1664. [f. PHYSIOLOGY + -IST.] †**1.** = PHYSIOLOGER 1. 1827. **2.** One versed in animal (or vegetable) physiology; a student or teacher of the science of the functions and properties of organic bodies 1778.

Physiology (fiziǫ·lŏdʒi). 1564. [– Fr. *physiologie* or L. *physiologia* (Cicero) – Gr. φυσιολογία (Aristotle) natural philosophy, natural science; see PHYSIO-, -LOGY.] †**1.** The study and description of natural objects; natural science; also, a particular system or doctrine of natural science –1797. **2.** The science of the normal functions and phenomena of living things 1615.

It comprises *animal* and *vegetable p.*; that part of the former which refers specially to the vital functions in man is called *human p.* O.E.D. So **Phy:siolo·gic, -al** *adjs.* †of or belonging to natural science; pertaining or relating to p.; **-ly** *adv.* †**Physio·logize** *v.* †*intr.* to speculate or reason on nature; †*trans.* to explain in accordance with natural science.

Physique (fizī·k). 1826. [– Fr. *physique* masc., subst. use of *physique* physical.] The physical or bodily structure, organization, and development; the characteristic appearance or physical powers (of an individual or a race).

Physnomy, obs. f. PHYSIOGNOMY.

Physo- (fəiso), repr. Gr. φυσο-, comb. form of Gr. φῦσα bellows, bladder, bubble; used in **Phy·sograde** [– mod.L. *Physograda*, f. *-gradus*], *Zool.* **a.** *adj.* moving by means of a hollow vesicular float or buoy; of or pertaining to the *Physograda*, a group of oceanic hydrozoa furnished with such floating organs; **b.** *sb.* a member of this group. ‖**Physometra** (-mī·tră) [Gr. μήτρα womb], *Path.* the presence of gas in the uterus. **Physopod** (fəi·sopǫd) [Gr. πούς, ποδ- foot], a mollusc of the division *Physopoda* or *Thysanoptera*, rhipidoglossate gastropods, with a sort of sucker on the foot.

Physoclist (fəi·soklist), *a.* and *sb.* 1887. [f. mod.L. *Physoclisti* (pl.), f. Gr. φῦσα bladder + -κλειστος shut, closed.] *Ichthyol.* **A.** *adj.* Belonging to the *Physoclisti*, a group of teleost fishes having the duct between the air-bladder and the intestine closed. **B.** *sb.* A member of this group. So **Physocli·stic, Physocli·stous** *adjs.*

‖**Physophora** (fəisǫ·fŏră). 1869. [mod.L., f. Gr. φῦσα bladder + -φορος bearing, borne; see -PHORE, -A 4.] *Zool.* A genus of oceanic hydrozoa, the species of which float by means of numerous vesicular organs. So ‖**Physo·phoræ** *pl.* (occas. **Physophora**), a suborder or division of *Siphonophora* (an order of *Hydrozoa craspedota*) having the proximal end modified into a pneumatophore or float. **Physo·phoran** *a.* of or pertaining to the *Physophoræ*; *sb.* a member of this division.

‖**Physostigma** (fəisosti·gmă). 1864. [mod. L., f. Gr. φῦσα bladder + στίγμα STIGMA.] *Bot.* A genus of leguminous plants, the flower of which has a spiral keel, and a bent style continued into an oblique hood above the stigma; the only species, *P. venenosum*, produces the highly poisonous Calabar bean. Hence, the Calabar bean, or its extract as a drug. Hence **Physosti·gmine** the alkaloid $C_{15}H_{21}N_3O_2$, constituting the active principle of the Calabar bean.

Physostome (fəi·sǫ̆stoᵘm), *a.* and *sb.* 1880. [f. mod.L. *Physostomi*, f. Gr. φῦσα bladder + στόμα mouth, -στομος -mouthed.] *Ichthyol.* **A.** *adj.* Belonging to the *Physostomi*, a group of teleost fishes, in which the air-bladder is connected with the alimentary canal by an air-duct. **B.** *sb.* A member of this group. So **Physosto·matous, Physo·stomous** *adjs.*

Phyt- (fəit), comb. form used bef. a vowel for PHYTO-, as in **Phyta·lbumin,** vegetable albumin. **Phyta·lbumose,** a form of albumen occurring in plants.

-phyte, a terminal element repr. comb. form of Gr. φυτόν plant, f. φύειν (see BE), and denoting a vegetable organism, as in *saprophyte, zoophyte.*

Phyto- (fəito), comb. form of Gr. φυτόν a plant, lit. that which has grown, f. φύειν to grow; used chiefly to form botanical words. **Phytoche·mistry,** the chemistry of plants; so **Phytoche·mical** *a.* **Phy:togeo·graphy,** the geographical distribution of plants; so **Phy:togeo-gra·phic, -al** *adjs.* **Phytoglyphy** (fəitǫ·glifi, fit-) [see GLYPH], nature-printing, as orig. used for plants; hence **Phytogly·phic** *a.* †**Phyto·gnomy,** [after *physiognomy*; see GNOMIC], vegetable physiognomy. **Phyto·nomy** [see -NOMY], the science of the laws of plant-growth. **Phy:topatho·logy,** (*a*) the study of the pathology or diseases of plants; (*b*) the pathology of diseases due to vegetable organisms, as fungi; mycology; hence **Phy:topatholo·gical** *a.*; **Phytopatho·logist,** one versed in phytopathology (*a*). **Phy:tophysio·logy,** vegetable physiology. **Phytopla·nkton,** floating plant organisms collectively.

Phytogenesis (fəitodʒe·nĭsis). 1858. [f. prec. + -GENESIS.] The generation or evolution of plants. Also **Phyto·geny,** in same sense. So **Phytogene·tic, -al** *adjs.*

Phytography (fəitǫ·grăfi). 1696. [– mod.L. *phytographia*; see PHYTO- and -GRAPHY.] **1.** Description of plants; descriptive botany. **2.** = PHYTOGLYPHY. Hence **Phytogra·phic, -al** *adjs.*

‖**Phytolacca** (fəitolæ·kă). 1753. [mod.L. (Tournefort, 1700), f. Gr. φυτόν plant + mod. L. *lacca* crimson lake.] *Bot.* The genus of plants including the Pocan, Virginian Poke, Pokeweed, or Red-ink plant (*P. decandra*); also various preparations of the plant used medicinally.

Phytology (fəitǫ·lŏdʒi). 1658. [– mod.L. *phytologia*, f. Gr. φυτόν plant + -λογία; see -LOGY.] The science of plants; botany. So **Phýtolo·gical** *a.* relating to the study of plants; botanical 1654; **-ly** *adv.* **Phyto·logist,** one versed in p. (All now *rare.*)

Phytomer (fəi·toməɹ). 1880. [– mod.L. *phytomeron*, pl. *-a*, f. Gr. φυτόν plant + μέρος part.] = next.

Phyton (fəi·tǫn). 1848. [– Fr. *phyton* – Gr. φυτόν plant, f. φύειν produce.] *Bot.* A plant-unit; the smallest part of root, stem, or leaf which will grow when severed from the parent.

Phytophagic (fəitofæ·dʒik), *a.* 1866. [Later var. of next; see -IC.] *Zool.* Of or pertaining to, caused by, the habit of feeding on plants or vegetable matter; said of variation of the colouring of insect larvæ.

Phytophagous (fəitǫ·făgəs), *a.* 1826. [f. PHYTO- + -PHAGOUS.] *Zool.* **a.** Feeding on plants or vegetable substances, as insects, molluscs, etc. **b.** Belonging to the *Phytophaga* = (*a*) leaf-beetles and their allies, (*b*) sawflies and horn-tails, (*c*) certain cyprinoid fishes, (*d*) the plant-eating edentates, (*e*) the plant-eating placental mammals.

Phytotomy (fəitǫ·tŏmi). 1844. [f. PHYTO- + -TOMY.] The dissection of plants; vegetable anatomy. Hence **Phyto·tomist,** one versed in p.

‖**Phytozoon** (fəitozōᵘ·ǫ̆n). Also **-zo·um.** *Pl.* **-zo·a.** 1842. [f. Gr. φυτόν plant + ζῷον animal; lit. 'plant-animal'; cf. *zoophyte.*] **1.** *Zool.* A plant-like animal or zoophyte; a single polyp in a zoophyte. **2.** *Bot.* A male generative cell, a spermatozoid 1861.

Pi (pəi), *sb.* Name of the Greek letter π (in Gr. πῖ, pī); used in *Math.* to express the ratio of the circumference or periphery (περιφέρεια) of a circle to its diameter; see P (the letter).

Pi (pəi), *a. School* and *university slang.* 1870. [abbrev. of PIOUS.] Pious, sanctimonious. **Pi jaw** [JAW *sb.* 6], religious or moral exhortation.

Pia (pəi·ă). *Anat.* Short for PIA MATER.

Piaçaba: see PIASSABA.

‖**Piache** (pia·tʃe). 1555. [Tamanac *piache* = Carib *piai* PEAI; in Sp. *piache.*] A medicine-man or witch-doctor among the Indians of Central and Southern America; a PEAI.

Piacle (pəi·ăk'l). Now *rare.* 1490. [– OFr. *piacle* or – L. *piaculum*, f. *piare* appease; see -CULE.] †**1.** Expiation; expiatory offering –1711. **2.** A wicked action which calls for expiation 1644.

Piacular (pəi,æ·kiŭlăɹ), *a.* 1610. [– L. *piacularis*, f. *piaculum*; see prec., -AR¹. With sense 2 cf. med.L. 'sinful'.] **1.** Making expiation or atonement; expiatory 1647. **2.** Calling for expiation; sinful, wicked, culpable 1610.

2. They held it p. to eat with sinners 1657. Hence **Piacula·rity,** the quality of being p.: (*a*) expiatory character, (*b*) criminality.

Piaffe (pi,æ·f), *v.* 1761. [– Fr. *piaffer* (XVI) strut, make a show.] *Horsemanship* (*intr.*) To move with the same step as in the trot, but more slowly. So **Pia·ffer** *sb.* the action of piaffing 1862.

‖**Pia mater** (pəi·ă mēⁱ·təɹ). late ME. [med. L. rendering of Arab. *al-'umm al-raḳīḳa* the thin or tender mother; cf. DURA MATER.] *Anat.* A delicate fibrous and very vascular membrane which forms the innermost of the three *meninges* enveloping the brain and spinal cord. Hence **Pi·al** *a.* of or pertaining to the pia mater.

Pian (pi,æ·n, ‖ pyaṅ). Also **epian,** and in pl. **pians.** 1803. [= Sp., Pg. *epian* and *pian*, – Galibi (Rio de Janeiro) *pian.* Cf. Fr. *pian* (XVI).] = YAWS.

‖**Pianissimo** (pĭăni·simo), *a.* (*adv.*) *sb.* 1724. [It., superl. of *piano* PIANO *a.*] *Mus.* **A.** *adj.* Very soft. **B.** *adv.* Very softly. **C.** *sb.* A very soft passage. Abbrev. *pp.* or *ppp.*

Pianist (pī·ănist). 1839. [– Fr. *pianiste*; see PIANO² and -IST.] A player on the pianoforte. So ‖ **Piani·ste** [Fr.] = prec.; but often used in Eng. as the feminine form.

‖**Piano** (pi,ā·no), *adv., a., sb.*¹ 1683. [It. :– L. *planus* flat, later of sound, soft, low.] **A.** *Mus.* (abbrev. *p*) *adv.* and *a.* Soft(ly); also *fig.* subdued(ly). **B.** *sb.* A flat or floor in an Italian dwelling-house, hotel, etc. 1860.

Piano (pi,æ·no), *sb.*² 1803. [– It., shortened from next or FORTEPIANO.] **1.** = next. **2.** A keyboard machine for perforating cards for a Jacquard apparatus 1881.

Comb. **p.-player** = PIANOLA 1907.

Pianoforte (pi,æ:no,fǭ·ɹte, pi,æ·nofǫɹt). 1767. [– It., earlier *piano e forte* (*pian e forte*) 'soft and loud', also †*fortepiano* (see FORTEPIANO), used by Cristofori, its inventor, to express the gradation of tone of which it is capable. Now usually PIANO *sb.*²] A musical instrument producing tones by means of hammers, operated by levers from a keyboard, which strike metal strings, the vibrations being stopped by dampers; it is commonly furnished with pedals for regulating the volume of sound. It is essentially a dulcimer provided with keys and dampers, but in other respects imitates the harpsichord and clavichord.

Grand p. or *piano*, a large p., harp-shaped like the harpsichord, and having the strings horizontal and at right angles to the keyboard. *Square p.*, rectangular like the clavichord, having the strings horizontal, but parallel to the keyboard. *Upright* or *cabinet p.*, rectangular upon edge, having the strings vertical. *Oblique* or *cottage p.*, upright but lower, having the strings ascending obliquely or diagonally.

Pianola (pĭănōᵘ·lă). 1901. [app. intended as a dim. of PIANO.] Trade name for a mechanical attachment for playing the piano; also, a piano equipped with this.

Pia·no-o:rgan. 1844. A mechanical piano constructed like a barrel-organ.

Piarist (pəi·ărist). 1842. [– It. *Piaristi* m.pl., f. mod.L. title *patres scholarum piarum* fathers of the religious schools, the Piarists being the regular clerks of the *Scuole Pie* or religious schools.] A member of a Roman Catholic secular order, founded at Rome shortly before 1600. They devote themselves without pay to the instruction of the young.

‖**Piassaba** (pĭăsā·bă). Also **piassava, piaçaba.** 1857. [– Pg. – Tupi *piaçába.*] A stout woody fibre obtained from the leaf-stalks of two Brazilian palm-trees, *Attalea funifera* and *Leopoldinia piassaba*, and imported for the manufacture of brooms, brushes, etc. (Also *p. fibre.*)

Piastre, piaster (pi,æ·stəɹ). 1611. [– Fr. *piastre* – It. *piastra*, short for *piastra d'argento* 'plate of silver'; *piastra* metal plate, coin repr. L. *emplastra* (Gellius), var. of *emplastrum* PLASTER.] **1.** A name for the Spanish *peso duro*, piece of eight, or dollar, and its representatives in Spanish America and other countries 1630. **2.** Name of a small Turkish coin called *ghūrūsh*, $\frac{1}{100}$ of a Turkish pound.

Piazza (pi,æ·ză). 1583. [– It. *piazza* = Fr. *place* PLACE.] **1.** A public square or market-place, usu. one in an Italian town; but in 16th to 18th c. often applied to any open space surrounded by buildings. **2.** Erron. applied to a colonnade or covered gallery surrounding an open square, and hence to a single colonnade in front of a building. Now *rare.* 1617. **b.** (Chiefly U.S.) The verandah of a house 1787.

2. They live in one of the Piazzas in Covent Garden 1605.

Pibroch (pī·brǫχ). 1719. [– Gael. *piobaireachd* the art of playing the bagpipe, f. *piobair* piper (f. *piob* pipe – Eng. *pipe*) + *-achd*, suffix of function.] In the Scottish Highlands, a series of variations for the bagpipe, chiefly martial, but including dirges. ¶Erron. used as if = bagpipe.

Some pipe of war Sends the bold p. from afar SCOTT.

‖**Pic, pike** (pīk). 1599. [= Fr. *pic* – Turk. *pik* – Gr. πῆχυς ell, cubit.] A Turkish measure of length, used for cloth, etc., and varying from 18 to 28 inches, there being a long and a short standard.

Pica¹ (pəi·kă). 1497. [transf. use of AL. *pica* PIE *sb.*³ (but no edition of the 'pie' printed in 'pica' type appears to be known); cf. BREVIER, PRIMER. Sense 2 is prob. f. sense 1.] †**1.** = PIE *sb.*³ 1. (Only Anglo-L.) **2.** *Typogr.* A size of type, next below English, of about 6 lines to the inch, equal to 12 point. Used also as a standard of measurement for large type, leads, borders, etc. *Small p.*, a size between long primer and pica, equal to 11 point 1588.

This is Pica type.

This is Small Pica type.

Two-line p., the size of type having a body equal to two lines of p. *Double p.* (prop. *double small p.*), a size of type equal to two lines of small p.

‖**Pica**² (pəi·kă). 1563. [mod. or med.L., = magpie, prob. tr. Gr. κίσσα, κίττα magpie, also false appetite. So Fr. *pica* (Paré).] *Path.* A perverted craving for substances unfit for food, as chalk, etc.

‖**Picador** (pi·kădǫɹ). 1797. [Sp., lit. 'pricker', f. *picar* prick.] In a bull-fight, A mounted man, who opens the game by provoking the bull with a lance.

Picamar (pi·kămāɹ). 1835. [(Discovered by Reichenbach); f. L. *pix, pic-* pitch + *amarus* bitter.] *Chem.* An intensely bitter, thick transparent oil, obtained in the distillation of wood-tar.

Picaresque (pikăre·sk), *a.* 1810. [– Fr. *picaresque* – Sp. *picaresco*, f. *picaro* roguish, knavish, sb. rogue; see -ESQUE. Cf. next.] Belonging or relating to rogues or knaves; applied esp. to a style of fiction dealing with the adventures of rogues, chiefly of Spanish origin.

Picaroon (pikărū·n), *sb.* 1624. [– Sp. *picarón*, augm. of *picaro*; see prec., -OON.] **1.** A rogue; a knave; a thief; a brigand 1629. **2.** A pirate, sea-robber, corsair 1624. **3.** A privateer or corsair 1625.

1. I see in thy countenance something of the

pedlar—something of the p. SCOTT. Hence **Picaroo·n** *v. intr.* to play the pirate or brigand.

Picayune (pikăyū·n), *sb.* and *a.* *U.S.* 1852. [– Fr. *picaillon* old copper coin of Piedmont, halfpence, cash – mod. Pr. *picaioun*, of unkn. origin.] **A.** *sb.* The U.S. 5-cent piece or other coin of small value; hence *colloq.* an insignificant person or thing. **B.** *adj.* Mean, contemptible 1856. Hence **Picayu·nish** *a.*

†**Pi·ccadill, pi·ckadill.** 1607. [– Fr. *pica-*, *piccadilles* 'the seuerall diuisions or peeces fastened together about the brimme of the collar of a doublet' (Cotgr.), app. repr. a Sp. **picadillo*, dim. of *picado* pricked, pierced, slashed. Hence the name of the street called Piccadilly.] **1. a.** A border of cut work or vandyking inserted on a collar or ruff, etc. **b.** *transf.* An expansive collar, usu. with a broad laced or perforated border, fashionable early in the 17th c. –1821. **2.** A stiff band of linen-covered pasteboard or wire, worn in the 17th c. to support the wide collar or ruff –1688. **3.** *transf.* A halter (*joc.*) –1678.

Piccalilli (pi·kălili). 1769. [prob. fancifully f. PICKLE *sb.*, with reminiscence of CHILLI.] A pickle composed of a mixture of chopped vegetables and hot spices.

Piccaninny, pickaninny (pi·kănini), *sb.* (*a.*) 1657. [A West Indian Negro deriv. of Sp. *pequeño* or Pg. *pequeno* little, small; perh. directly based on Pg. dim. *pequenino*.] A little one, a child: applied esp. to the children of Negroes, or of South African or Australian natives. **b.** *joc.* A child, in general 1785. **B.** *adj.* Very small; tiny, baby 1876.

Piccolo (pi·kŏlo). 1856. [– It., = small; hence absol., a small flute.] **1.** (orig. *p. flute.*) A small flute, an octave higher in pitch than the ordinary flute; also called the *octave flute*. **2.** An organ stop having the tone of the piccolo 1875. **3.** (for *p. piano.*) A small upright pianoforte 1858.

‖**Pice** (pəis). 1615. [– Hindi *paisā*.] A small E. Indian copper coin equal to one fourth of an anna.

Piceous (pi·si,əs), *a.* 1646. [f. L. *piceus* (f. *pix*, *pic-* PITCH *sb.*[1]) + -OUS; see -EOUS.] Of, pertaining to, or resembling pitch: **a.** Inflammable, combustible; **b.** Pitch-black, brownish or reddish-black.

‖**Pichey** (pi·tʃi). 1827. [app. Guarani.] The Little Armadillo, *Dasypus minutus*, of La Plata.

‖**Pichiciago** (pitʃi,syē·go). 1825. [– Sp. *pichiciego*, f. (?) Guarani *pichey* (see prec.) + Sp. *ciego* (:– L. *cæcus*) blind.] A small burrowing edentate animal of Chile, *Chlamyphorus truncatus*, allied to the Armadillos; its back and head are covered with a hard leather-like shell attached only along the spine.

‖**Pichurim** (pi·tʃŭrim). 1842. [Tupi.] A lauraceous S. Amer. tree, *Nectandra puchury*. *P. bean*, the aromatic cotyledon of the seed of this tree, used in cookery and medicinally. Hence **Pichu·ric** *a.* *Chem.* of, pertaining to, or derived from p. beans; *pichuric acid* = LAURIC *acid.*

Piciform (pəi·sifǭɹm), *a.* 1872. [– mod. L. *piciformis*, f. *picus* woodpecker; see -FORM.] Having the form of, or resembling, a woodpecker; of or pertaining to the *Piciformes*, a group of birds of the order *Picariæ*.

Pick (pik), *sb.*[1] ME. [app. a collateral form, with short vowel, of PIKE *sb.*[1]] **I. 1.** A tool consisting of an iron bar, usu. curved, steel-tipped, tapering squarely to a point at one end, and a chisel-edge or point at the other, attached through an eye in the centre to a wooden handle placed perpendicularly to its concave side; a pickaxe, mandril, mattock, 'slitter'; used for breaking up stiff ground or gravel, etc. **b.** A pointed hammer used for dressing mill-stones, etc., 1483.

II. †**1.** = PIKE *sb.*[1] II. 1. –1688. **2.** The name of various pointed or pronged instruments; esp. (*Fishing*) a kind of gaff; an eel-spear (*dial.*) 1875. **3.** An instrument for picking: chiefly in *Comb.*, as TOOTHPICK, etc. 1619.

1. Take down my Buckler, and sweep the Cobwebs off: and grind the p. ont BEAUM. & FL.

III. The diamond in playing-cards. Also *transf.* Now *n. dial.* 1598.

Comb.: **p.-dressing,** in masonry, a pitted facing produced by a pointed tool, broached hewn-work; **-hammer,** a pick with one blunt end, like a hammer.

Pick, *sb.*[2] 1513. [f. PICK *v.*[1]] **1.** An act of picking; a stroke with something pointed. **2.** An act of choosing or selecting; *transf.* that which is selected; the choicest portion or example; the choicest product or contents 1760. **3.** The quantity or portion of any crop picked or gathered at one time; a gathering 1887. **4.** *Printing.* **a.** A speck of hardened ink or dirt that gets into the hollows of types in forme and causes a blot on the printed page. **b.** An intrusive bit of metal on an electrotype or stereotype plate. 1683.

2. Mamma—I wish you would not say 'the pick of them'. .it is rather a vulgar expression GEO. ELIOT.

Pick, *sb.*[3] *n. dial.* 1627. [f. PICK *v.*[2]] **1.** = PITCH *sb.*[2] **2.** *Weaving.* A cast or throw of the shuttle; the stroke that drives the shuttle; taken as a unit of measurement in reckoning the speed of the loom 1851. **b.** *transf.* In textiles, A single thread of the weft (produced by one pick of the shuttle); esp. used in ref. to the number of threads in the inch, as determining the fineness of the fabric 1860.

Pick (pik), *v.*[1] ME. [Succeeded to *pike* XIV (surviving dial.), prob. through the infl. of Fr. *piquer* or MLG., MDu. *picken* (Du. *pikken*).] **I. 1.** *trans.* To pierce, indent, dig into, or break the surface of (anything) by striking it with something sharp and pointed, as to break up (ground, etc.) with a pick. Also *absol.*, to ply the pick, mattock, etc. ME. †**b.** Of a bird: To pierce with the bill, to peck; of an insect: to puncture –1645. **c.** To make by picking; in phr. *to p. a hole* or *holes in* something 1648. **2.** To probe or penetrate with a pointed instrument or the like, so as to remove any extraneous matter; e.g. *to p. the teeth.* late ME. **b.** Applied to a similar use of the finger-nails to remove a pimple, etc. 1676.

1. b. Isopes frogges to whom. .Iupiter sent a hearon to picke them in the hedes 1555. 2. He picked his Nose, which you know is neither graceful or royal 1768.

II. 1. To clear or cleanse (a thing), with the fingers or the like, of any extraneous or refuse substance, as to pick a fowl (of its feathers), fruit, as currants, etc. (of their stalks, etc.). ME. †**2.** To cleanse, trick out, prank; to adorn; of a bird: to preen (its feathers) –1631.

1. Phr. *A crow to p.* (prop. *pluck*): see CROW *sb.*[1] *To p. a bone*, to clear it of all adherent flesh; so *to p. a carcass*, etc. *To have a bone to p. with any one*; see BONE *sb.*

III. 1. To pluck, gather, cull (fruit, growing flowers, etc.); said also of a bird ME. †**b.** *fig.* To 'gather' with the mind; to infer, make out –1621. **2.** Of birds and some beasts: To take up (grains or small bits of food) with bill or teeth; also, of persons, to bite or eat in small bits; *colloq.* to eat. (Cf. PECK *v.*[1]) late ME. **b.** *intr.* To eat with pecking or small bites; of a person, to eat fastidiously; *slang* or *colloq.* to eat 1584.

1. b. Trust me sweete, Out of this silence yet, I pickt a welcome SHAKS. 2. I think. .that I could p. a little bit of pickled salmon DICKENS. b. I could never do mair than pyke at food STEVENSON.

IV. 1. To choose out, select carefully, cull. Now chiefly in *to p. one's men, one's words*, etc. late ME. **2.** To seek and find an occasion of; as *to p. a quarrel with* a person 1449. †*To p. a thank* (*thanks*) *of* (*with*): to curry favour with.

1. Phr. *To p. one's way, steps*, to choose a way carefully through dirty or dangerous ground. *To p. and choose*, to select fastidiously. 2. Phr. †*To p. occasion to do* (something).

V. 1. To rob, plunder (a person or place); to rifle the contents of (anything); †to steal (goods, etc.). Now only in phr. *to p.* a person's *pocket* or *purse*, also *fig.* his *brains*. ME. **b.** *intr.* or *absol.* In later use as a kind of euphemism for: To practise petty theft; to pilfer, filch. Chiefly in phr. *p. and steal.* late ME. **2.** To open (a lock) with a pointed instrument, a skeleton key, or the like; to open clandestinely (esp. in order to rob) 1546.

1. He hath as fine a hand at picking a pocket as a woman GAY. b. To kepe my handes from picking and stealing *Bk. Com. Prayer.* 2. She mynded. . To picke the. .locke 1546.

VI. 1. To separate by picking, to pull or comb asunder 1536. **b.** *intr.* for *pass.* To admit of being picked 1794. **2.** To pluck the strings of a banjo, etc. *U.S.* 1860.

1. They'll p. you to pieces a little among themselves TROLLOPE. Picking oakum in penal servitude 1874. b. The yarn. .will p. into oakum 1794.

VII. Intr. uses with preps. **1.** *To p. at* —: **a.** To make a motion to pick (in various senses) 1525. **b.** *fig.* To gird at, nag at; to carp at. Now only *dial.* and *U.S.* 1670. **2.** *To p. on, upon* —: = prec. b. Now *U.S. dial.* late ME.

Combs. with adverbs. **P. away:** see senses I. 1 and III. 1 and AWAY. **P. in.** To work in or fill in, in a painting or drawing. **P. off. a.** See sense III. 1 and OFF. **b.** To shoot with deliberate selection and aim. **P. out, a.** To extract by picking; to dig out, peck out. **b.** To choose out with deliberation; said also of natural agents, as diseases. **c.** To distinguish from surrounding objects, etc. with the senses. **d.** To make out or gather (sense or meaning); to piece out and ascertain (facts) by combining separate items of information. **e.** To identify the notes of (a tune) and so play it by ear. **f.** To deck out, to adorn; now *spec.* to lighten or relieve the ground colour (of anything) by lines or spots of a contrasted colour following the outlines, mouldings, etc. **P. up. a.** To break up (ground) with a pick; to take up. **b.** To take up with the fingers or beak; to lay hold of and take up from the ground or any low position; in *Knitting*, to take up (stitches) with a knitting-needle. *To p. oneself up*, to recover oneself smartly from a fall, etc. **c.** To acquire, gain, collect as chance offers; to make (a livelihood) by occasional opportunity. **d.** To seize, snap up, capture (a vessel); to capture in detail. Now *rare.* **e.** To take (a person or thing overtaken) along with one, or into a vessel or vehicle; also said of a vehicle, a ship, etc. **f.** To come upon, find (a path, etc., wireless station, wave-length, etc.), *esp.* to recover (a trail, etc.). *To p. up a wind*, to run from one prevalent wind into another with as little intervening calm as possible. *To p. up the range* (of a rifle or gun). **g.** Phrases. *To p. up flesh*, to put on flesh again. *To p. up* (*one's*) *spirit, courage*, etc. **h.** *intr.* To recover, improve, 'look up' after an illness, or any check or depression. **i.** To enter into conversation, make acquaintance *with* (some one casually met). **j.** *colloq.* To take (a person) up sharply.

Pick (pik), *v.*[2] Now only *dial.* or *techn.* ME. [Collateral form of PITCH *v.*[1]] †**1.** *trans.* To fix, stick, plant (something pointed) in the ground, etc.; to pitch (a tent or the like) –1602. **2.** To thrust, drive; to pitch, hurl; to throw. Now *dial.* 1525.

2. As high As I could picke my Lance SHAKS.

Pick- in *Comb.* Mostly the stem or imperative of PICK *v.*[1] with an object, forming sbs. **Pick-cheese** *dial.*, the great and blue tits; the fruit or cheese of the mallow. †**Pick-fault,** a fault-finder. See also Main words.

Pi·ck-a-back, *adv. phr.* (*a.*, *sb.*) Also **a pick back, pickback, pick-pack, piggy-back,** etc. 1565. [Earlier (†*a*) *pick-back*, †*on* or *a pick-pack* (still dial.); of unkn. origin.] On the shoulders or back like a pack or bundle; said in ref. to a person (or animal) carried in this way. **b.** quasi-*adj.* and *sb.* 1590.

b. A p. ride through the surf in a dirty fellow's grasp 1864.

Pickaninny, var. of PICCANINNY.

Pickaxe (pi·k,æks), *sb.* Also **-ax.** [alt., by assim. of the final syll. to AXE, of ME. *pikois*, *-eis* (surviving in s.w. dial. as *peckis*, *pickis*) – OFr. *picois*. Cf. PIKE *sb.*[1]] A miner's, quarryman's, or digger's pick; = PICK *sb.*[1] I. Hence **Pi·ckax(e** *v. trans.* to break with a p.; *intr.* to use a p.

Pickback, var. of PICK-A-BACK.

Picked (pi·kėd), *a.* late ME. [f. PICK *sb.*[1] II. 1 + -ED[2].] **1.** Acuminated, pointed, spiked. Now *arch.* or *dial.* **b.** In names of animals, etc.: Having prickles, spiny 1758. †**2.** Peaked, tapering to a thin end –1771.

1. The shield to be made p. at both ends 1660. b. The p. dog-fish (*Spinax acanthius*). 2. The head of a man, with a hat and p. beard H. WALPOLE.

Picked (pikt, *poet.* pi·kėd), *ppl. a.* late ME. [f. PICK *v.*[1] + -ED[1].] **1.** In senses of PICK *v.*[1] †**2.** Adorned, ornate; spruce, nice, finical, fastidious –1636. **3.** Chosen out, esp. for excellence or efficiency, or for a definite purpose 1548.

1. A gill of p. shrimps 1806. 2. *Ham.* V. i. 151

3. Only a few p. craftsmen can manage it M. ARNOLD. Hence †**Pi·cked-ly** *adv.*, †**-ness.**

†**Picke-devant, pique devant.** 1587. [app. either for Fr. *pique* (or *pic*) *devant*, meant for 'peak in front', or for *piqué devant*, 'peaked in front'.] A peaked or Vandyke beard –1638.

†**Picked-hatch.** 1598. [f. PICKED *a.* + HATCH *sb.*[1]] A hatch or half door, surmounted by a row of pikes or spikes, to prevent climbing over; *spec.* a brothel.

Goe..to your Mannor of Pickt-hatch SHAKS.

Pickeer (pikīə·ɹ), *v.* 1645. [app. – Du. *pickeren* prick, spur (– Fr. *piquer*), with a strange sense-development.] †**1.** *intr.* To maraud, pillage, plunder; to practise piracy –1718. **2.** *trans.* To skirmish, reconnoitre, scout (in war), to bicker (*with* the enemy) 1645. **3.** *fig.* **a.** To scout 1649. †**b.** To dally, flirt –1709. †**c.** To wrangle –1717.

‖**Pickelhaube** (pi·kəlhɑu:bə). 1890. [G.] The spiked helmet of the German army.

Picker[1] (pi·kəɹ). 1526. [f. PICK *v.*[1] + -ER[1].] **1.** *gen.* A person who picks, in any sense. Also a second element in many combinations, as *fruit-*, *hop-*, *potato-*, *rag-p.*, etc. **2.** A tool or instrument for picking. **a.** In agriculture: (*a*) A sort of mattock or pickaxe; (*b*) a part of a picking-machine which separates the potatoes from the soil. Often in comb. as *potato-p.* 1707. **b.** In the textile industries: (*a*) A machine for separating and cleansing the fibres of cotton, wool, and the like; (*b*) an implement for burling cloth 1795. **c.** In *Mining* and *Metallurgy*: in Cornwall, a miner's hand-chisel; a miner's needle for picking out the tamping of an unexploded charge. In *Founding*, a light pointed steel rod, used for lifting small patterns from the sand into which they have been rammed; a tool for piercing a mould. 1874.

1. They are pickers and choosers of God's word 1870. *Pickers and stealers* (see PICK *v.*[1] V. 1), *colloq.* hands. *A p. of quarrels*, one who seeks occasion for quarrels. *Comb.* with *adv.*, as **picker-up**; A mere picker-up of trifles 1874.

Picker[2] (pi·kəɹ). 1841. [f. PICK *v.*[2] + -ER[1].] *Weaving.* In a loom, the small instrument which travels backwards and forwards in the shuttle-box and drives the shuttle to and fro through the warp.

Pickerel (pi·kĕrĕl). ME. [dim. of PIKE *sb.*[4]; see -REL. In AL. *pikerellus* (XIII).] A young pike. **b.** In U.S. and Canada, any of several species of *Esox*, esp. the smaller species; about the Great Lakes, the true pike; also the pike-perch, wall-eye, or glass-eye (*Stizostedion vitreum*).

Pi·ckerel-wee·d. 1653. [f. prec. + WEED *sb.*[1]] **1.** A name locally applied to certain weeds, found in still waters, amongst which pike breed; *esp.* species of *Potamogeton* or Pondweed. **2.** In N. America, Any species of *Pontederia*, lacustrine plants, with sagittate leaves, and spikes of blue flowers 1836.

Pickery (pi·kəri). 1508. [f. PICKER[1]; see -ERY.] Petty theft. *Sc. Law.*

Picket (pi·kėt), *sb.* 1690. [– (O)Fr. *piquet*, f. *piquer* prick, pierce, f. *pic* PICK *sb.*[1]; see -ET.] **I. 1.** A pointed stake, post, or peg, driven into the ground; used e.g. in the construction of a stockade or fence; to mark positions in surveying, etc.; to fasten a rope or string to, esp. in order to tether a horse, or to secure a tent 1702. **2.** A stake with pointed top, used in a military punishment in vogue in the 17th and 18th c. Hence, a name for this punishment. 1690.

II. 1. *Mil.* A small detached body of troops, sent out to watch for the approach of the enemy or his scouts (*outlying p.*), or held in quarters in readiness for such service (*inlying p.*); also applied to a single soldier so employed. In the Army Regulations spelt *piquet.* 1761. **b.** A camp-guard, sent out to bring in men who have exceeded their leave 1787. **c.** *transf.* and *fig.* A party of sentinels; an outlying post 1847. **2.** (usu. *pl.*) Applied to men stationed by a trade-union or the like, to watch men going to work during a strike, and to endeavour to dissuade or deter them 1867.

III. An elongated rifle bullet, with a conoidal front; a cylindro-conoidal bullet. (Said to have been made for Col. Pickett.) *Hist.* 1858.

attrib. and *Comb.*, as *p.-fence*, *rope*, etc.; **p.-guard**, an inlying p., also a p. protecting a position; **-line**, (*a*) a tether; (*b*) a line held by pickets.

Picket (pi·kėt), *v.* 1745. [f. prec. sb.] **1.** *trans.* To enclose or secure with stakes; to palisade. **b.** To tether (a horse, etc.) to a peg fixed in the ground 1814. **2.** To punish or torture with the picket. *Obs.* exc. *Hist.* 1746. **3.** *Mil.* To post as a picket. **b.** *intr.* (for *refl.*) To act on picket duty. 1775. **4.** In strikes, etc.: **a.** *intr.* To act as a picket; **b.** *trans.* To beset with pickets. 1838. Hence **Pi·cketing** *vbl. sb.* the action of the vb.; *spec.* in a labour dispute, the posting of men to intercept non-strikers on their way to work and prevail upon them to desist.

Picking (pi·kiŋ), *vbl. sb.* ME. [f. PICK *v.*[1] + -ING[1].] **1.** The action of PICK *v.*[1] **2.** *spec.* **a.** Stealing, theft; in later use, petty theft, pilfering; esp. in *p. and stealing*. late ME. **b.** *Weaving.* A finishing process of cloth-making 1875. **c.** *Metall.* Rough sorting of ores 1839. **3.** *concr.* That which is or may be picked or picked up; the amount picked; a scrap; *pl.* portions of anything worth picking up 1642. **b.** Chiefly *pl.* Perquisites dishonestly come by; pilfering 1765.

Picking (pi·kiŋ), *ppl. a.* 1535. [f. PICK *v.*[1] + -ING[2].] **1.** That picks (see PICK *v.*[1]); *spec.* thievish. †**2.** Dainty; fastidious –1678.

1. Little p. thievish hands KIPLING.

Pickle (pi·k'l), *sb.*[1] [XV. *pekille*, *pykyl* – MLG., MDu. *pekel* (whence also G. *pökel*), of unkn. origin.] **1.** Brine, vinegar, or other salt or acid liquor, in which flesh, vegetables, etc., are preserved 1440. **2.** Some article of food preserved in pickle; usu. (*pl.*) Vegetables pickled and eaten as a relish 1707. **3.** An acid solution used for cleansing metal or wood, or for other purposes 1776. **4.** *fig.* A condition or situation, usu. disagreeable; a sorry plight. Now *colloq.* 1562. **5.** A troublesome or mischievous child. *colloq.* 1779.

1. Phr. *In p.* (*fig.*), kept in preparation for use; esp. in *a rod in p.*, a punishment in reserve, ready to be inflicted on occasion. **2.** Received a present of pickles from Miss Pilcocks JOHNSON. **4.** I could see no way out of the p. I was in STEVENSON. **5.** Young Sam Tyler,..a thorough P. 1837.

Pickle (pi·k'l), *sb.*[2] *Sc.* and *north.* 1552. [Of unkn. origin.] **1.** A single grain or corn of wheat, barley, or oats. **2.** A small quantity or amount; a little. (Followed by sb. without *of.*) 1724.

Pickle (pi·k'l), *v.* 1552. [f. PICKLE *sb.*[1]] **1.** *trans.* To put into pickle; to preserve in pickle. (Sometimes, to salt, as butter.) **2.** *Naut.* To rub salt, or salt and vinegar, on the back after flogging or whipping; formerly practised as a punishment. *Obs.* exc. *Hist.* 1706. **3.** To treat with some acid or the like, for cleansing or other purposes 1844.

1. *fig.* You are pickling a rod for your own back 1904. So **Pickled** (pi·k'ld) *ppl. a.* preserved in pickle; steeped in acid, etc.; *pickled herring*: see next.

Pi·ckle-he·rring. Now *rare.* 1552. [orig. *pickled herring*; later *pickle-herring*, after MDu. *peeckel-harinck.*] †**1.** *lit.* A pickled herring –1607. **2.** A clown, a buffoon, a merry-andrew. [Of German origin.] 1716.

Pi·ckler. 1683. [f. PICKLE *v.* + -ER[1].] **1.** A cucumber, onion, etc., grown for pickling. **2.** A person or thing that pickles (*lit.* and *fig.*). Also, a pickling-jar. 1862.

Picklock (pi·k,lǫk), *sb.* and *a.* 1553. [f. PICK *v.*[1] + LOCK *sb.*[2]] **1.** A person who picks a lock; *spec.* a thief who does this. **2.** An instrument for picking locks 1581. **B.** *adj.* Used for picking a lock; *esp.* in *p. key* = sense 2. 1607.

1. *fig.* Some crafty fellow, some picklocke o' the Law! B. JONS.

Pi·ck-me-up. *colloq.* 1867. [phr. used as sb.] *orig.* A stimulating alcoholic drink; extended to beverages, medicinal preparations, etc., supposed to have tonic qualities. **b.** *fig.* Anything having a bracing effect 1876.

Pickpocket (pi·kpǫkėt). 1591. [f. PICK *v.*[1] + POCKET; see PICK-.] One who steals from or 'picks' pockets.

†**Pi·ckpurse.** late ME. [See PICK-.] One who steals purses or from purses –1727.

fig. I am no pick-purse of anothers wit SIDNEY. Phr. *Purgatory p.*, *p. purgatory*, a term used orig. app. by Latimer in ref. to the use made of the doctrine of purgatory to obtain payments for masses for departed souls, etc.

Pickthank (pi·kþæŋk), *sb.* and *a.* *arch.* and *dial.* 1500. [See PICK *v.*[1] IV. 2 and PICK-.] **A.** *sb.* One who 'picks a thank', i.e. curries favour with another; a flatterer, sycophant; a tell-tale. **B.** *adj.* (*sb.* used attrib.) Flattering, sycophantic, tale-bearing 1561.

1. 1 *Hen. IV*, III. ii. 25.

Picktooth (pi·ktūþ), *sb.* and *a.* pl. **picktooths.** Now *rare* or *arch.* 1542. [f. PICK *v.*[1] I. 2 + TOOTH.] **A.** *sb.* A toothpick. **B.** *adj.* Idle, easy, leisurely 1728.

Pick-up. *sb.* (*a.*) 1859. [f. phr. *to pick up*; see PICK *v.*[1]] The act of picking up; *spec.* of picking up sides in a game; in *Cricket*, the picking up of the ball. Also, one who or that which is picked up. 1860. **b.** An electrical device fitted to a gramophone in place of the sound-box, for converting the sound into electric current 1926. **c.** *Wireless.* An electrical arrangement for connecting to a studio, etc. a programme produced outside 1925. **B.** *attrib.* or as *adj.* **a.** = that picks up, as in *pick-up apparatus*, *water-trough*, etc. **b.** = picked up for the nonce, as in *pick-up crew*, *dinner*, etc. 1859.

Pickwickian (pikwi·kiăn), *a.* (*sb.*) 1837. [f. *Pickwick*, surname in Dickens's *Pickwick Papers* (1837) + -IAN.] Of or pertaining to Mr. Pickwick, or the Pickwick Club; chiefly *joc.*, said of words used in a technical, constructive, or esoteric sense, or of language 'unparliamentary' in its natural sense. **B.** *sb.* A member of the Pickwick Club 1837.

Picnic (pi·knik), *sb.* Also earlier **pick-nick, pic-nic.** 1748. [– Fr. *pique-nique* (XVII, said by Ménage, 1692, to be of recent introduction); unexplained.] **1.** *orig.* A fashionable social entertainment in which each party present contributed a share of the provisions; now, A pleasure party in which all partake of a repast out of doors. Also *transf.* and *fig.* **2.** *attrib.* Pertaining to or of the nature of a picnic 1802.

1. They held impromptu pic-nics on breezy heights 1866. Phr. *No* or *not a p.*, not an easy job. Hence **Pi·cnic** *v.* (inflected **picnicked, -nicking**) *intr.* to hold or take part in a p., to eat in p. fashion. **Picnicker** (pi·knikəɹ), one who takes part in a p.

Picoid (pəi·koid), *a.* 1809. [f. L. *picus* woodpecker + -OID.] Like the woodpeckers.

Picoline (pi·kŏləin). 1853. [f. L. *pix*, *pic-* pitch + *oleum* oil + -INE[5].] *Chem.* A colourless liquid compound (C_6H_7N) obtained from bone-oil, coal-naphtha, tar, peat, etc.

‖**Picot** (pīko). 1869. [Fr., dim. of *pic* peak, point, prick; see -OT[1].] A small loop of twisted thread, one of a series forming an edging to lace, etc. Also *attrib.*, as *p.-edge.* Also as vb.

Picotee (pikŏtī·). 1727. [– Fr. *picoté*, *-ée*, pa. pple. of *picoter* mark with pricks or points; see PICOT.] A variety of the carnation (*Dianthus caryophyllus*), the flowers of which have a light ground, the petals being edged with a darker colour.

Picquet: see PIQUET.

‖**Picra,** short for HIERA PICRA.

Picric (pi·krik), *a.* 1838. [f. Gr. πικρός bitter + -IC.] *Chem.* In *p. acid*, also called *trinitro-carbolic* or *carbazotic acid*, *artificial indigo-bitter*, a yellow intensely bitter substance ($C_6H_3N_3O_7$), crystallizing in yellow shining prisms or laminæ, used in dyeing, medicine, and in the manufacture of explosives. So **Pi·crate**, a salt of p. acid. **Pi·cryl**, a synonym of trinitrophenyl, the radical of p. acid.

Picrite (pi·krəit). 1814. [f. as prec. + -ITE[1] 2 b.] *Min.* A dark grey-green rock consisting mainly of chrysolite.

Picro- (pi·kro), bef. a vowel sometimes **picr-**, comb. form of Gr. πικρός bitter, (*a*) in the sense 'having a bitter taste or smell', esp. in the names of magnesium minerals, because magnesium salts have a bitter taste; (*b*) in names of derivs. of PICRIC acid, as *picramic acid*, *picramine*, etc.

Among these are **Pi·crolite** [Gr. λίθος stone], *Min.* a fibrous dark-green variety of serpentine. **Pi·cromel** [Gr. μέλι honey], a bitter-sweet substance obtained from bile. **Picroto·xin** [cf.

TOXIN], formerly **picrotoxia,** *Chem.* the bitter poisonous principle ($C_{12}H_{14}O_5$) of the seeds of the *Cocculus indicus.*

Pict (pikt). late ME. [– late L. *Picti*, identical in form with L. *picti* painted or tattooed people (pa. pple. of *pingere* paint), adopted in OE. as *Pihtas*, var. *Peohtas*, whence ME. *Peght*, Sc. *Pecht*.] One of an ancient people of disputed origin, who formerly inhabited parts of north Britain.

Picts' houses, underground structures attributed to the Picts, found in Orkney, etc. Hence **Pi·ctish** *a.*

Pictograph (pi·ktŏgraf). 1851. [f. L. *pictus* painted + -GRAPH.] A pictorial symbol or sign; a writing or record consisting of pictorial symbols. Hence **Pictogra·phic** *a.*

Pictorial (piktōə·riăl), *a.* (*sb.*) 1646. [f. late L. *pictorius* (f. *pictor* painter) + -AL¹.] **1.** Of, belonging to, or produced by the painter; of or pertaining to painting or drawing. Now *rare.* **2.** Consisting of, expressed in, or of the nature of, a picture or pictures 1807. **3.** Containing a picture or pictures; illustrated 1826. **4.** *fig.* Like a picture; picturesque, graphic 1829. **B.** *sb.* A journal of which pictures are the main feature 1880.

1. Far be it from me to say that the p. calling is not honourable THACKERAY. **2.** The hieroglyphs or p. forms were used..above one thousand years after they ceased to represent the vernacular..language of Egypt 1876. **3.** P. Dutch tiles HOOD. **4.** Of all poets Spenser excelled in the p. faculty 1841. Hence **Picto·rially** *adv.*

Pi·ctural, *a. rare.* 1656. [f. L. *pictura* PICTURE + -AL¹.] Of or pertaining to pictures; pictorial.

Picture (pi·ktiŭɹ, pi·ktʃəɹ), *sb.* late ME. [– L. *pictura*, f. *pict-*, pa. ppl. stem of *pingere* paint.] †**1.** The action or process of painting or drawing; the fact of being painted or pictorially represented; the art of painting; pictorial representation –1844. **2.** The concrete result of this process. †**a.** Painting –1580. **b.** An individual painting, drawing, or representation on a surface, of an object or objects; *esp.* as a work of art. (Now the prevailing sense.) 1484. **c.** *spec.* The portrait or likeness of a person. Now *colloq.* or *affected.* 1505. †**d.** A likeness in the solid, esp. a statue or monumental effigy –1771. **e.** A person so strongly resembling another as to seem a likeness of him. Const. *of* 1712. **f.** A tableau; *spec.* at the end of an act or play. Also *living p.* (Fr. *tableau vivant*). 1865. **g.** In full *cinematograph, cinema*, or *moving p.*, a cinematograph film; *the p-s*, the cinema (*colloq.*) 1912. **h.** *fig. colloq.* A very picturesque object. **i.** *Into the p.*, so as to be obvious. *In the p.*, in evidence 1919. **3.** *transf.* A scene; the total visual impression produced by something; hence = IDEA III. 1. 1547. **4.** *fig.* A graphic description, written or spoken, of an object, capable of suggesting a mental image 1588. **5.** A symbol, type, figure; an illustration 1656.

1. P. took her feigning from Poetry B. JONS. **2. b.** Every noble p. is a manuscript book, of which only one copy exists RUSKIN. **c.** *Twel. N.* III. iv. 228. **e.** The sons are the very p. of their father DE FOE. **g.** I saw it done in the pictures, Sir 1916. **h.** The little girl is a p. 1906. **3.** *Clinical p.*, the total impression of a diseased condition, formed by the physician. **5.** He looks the p. of health 1871.

attrib. and *Comb.* **a.** General: as *p.-dealer, -shop*, etc.; *p.-language, -puzzle*, etc.; *p.-cover, -paper*; *p.-cleaner, cleaning, -restorer*, etc.

b. Special: as **p.-book; -card,** a court-card in a pack of cards; **-frame; -frock,** a frock designed in imitation of the style of an earlier period, esp. such a frock copied from a portrait; **p. gallery,** a hall or building containing a collection of pictures; the collection itself; **p. hat,** orig. a lady's wide-brimmed hat, usually black and adorned with ostrich feathers, as in the paintings of Reynolds and Gainsborough; hence, any wide-brimmed hat, usu. of straw and with a curving brim; **p.-house,** a cinema; **p.-moulding,** a horizontal wooden moulding, parallel to the ceiling of a room, for hanging pictures; **p. palace,** a cinema; **p. play,** a cinematograph film; **p. postcard,** a postcard having on the back of it a p.; **-rail, -rod,** a rod occupying the place of a *picture-moulding*; **-theatre,** a cinema.

Picture (pi·ktiŭɹ, -tʃəɹ), *v.* 1489. [f. prec. sb.] **1.** *trans.* To represent in a picture; to draw, paint, depict; *transf.* to reflect as in a mirror. Also with *out.* **b.** To figure, to represent symbolically 1526. **2.** To describe graphically. Also with *out, forth.* 1586. **3.** To form a mental picture of, to imagine. Often *to p. to one's self.* 1738.

1. A cunning painter thus..would p. Justice MASSINGER. **b.** The anxiety of his mind was strongly pictured upon his face 1782. **3.** We must not..p. the early Puritan as a gloomy fanatic 1874. Hence **Pi·cturable** *a.* capable of being painted or pictured. **Pi·ctured** *ppl. a.* represented in or as in a picture; illustrated with a picture or pictures, or *fig.* with word-painting.

Picturesque (piktiŭre·sk, -tʃər-), *a.* 1703. [– (with assim. to *picture*, to express 'in the style of a picture') Fr. *pittoresque* – It. *pittoresco* (F. Redi 1664) 'in the style of a painter', f. *pittore* :– L. *pictor* painter.] **1.** Like a picture; fit to be the subject of an effective picture; possessing pleasing and interesting qualities of form and colour. **2.** Of language, etc.: Strikingly graphic or vivid; sometimes implying disregard of fact 1734. **3.** Having a perception of the picturesque. Now *rare.* 1795. **4.** *absol.* as *sb. The p.*, that which is picturesque; picturesqueness 1794.

1. Susceptible observers..say of a scene 'How picturesque'—meaning by this a quality distinct from that of beauty, or sublimity, or grandeur; meaning to speak..of its fitness for imitation by art BAGEHOT. *P. gardening*, the romantic style of gardening, aiming at irregular and rugged beauty; so *p. gardener.* **2.** P. history is seldom to be trusted 1868. Hence **Picture·sque-ly** *adv.*, **-ness.**

Pi·cture-wri:ting. 1741. The method of recording events or expressing ideas by pictures which literally or figuratively represent the things and actions; *concr.* a writing or inscription consisting of pictorial symbols.

‖**Picul** (pi·kɒl). 1588. [Malay-Javanese *pikul* a man's load.] A measure of weight used in China and the East generally, equal to 100 catties, i.e. about 133⅓ lbs. avoirdupois.

Piculet (pi·kiulėt). 1849. [app. double dim. of L. *picus* woodpecker + -ULE, -ET.] *Ornith.* A bird of the subfamily *Picumninæ*; a small soft-tailed woodpecker.

Piddle (pi·d'l), *v.* 1545. [In sense 1 perh. alt. of PEDDLE *v.* by assoc. with LG. *piddeln*; in sense 2 presumably based on PISS *v.* or PEE *v.*, after PUDDLE.] **1.** *intr.* = PEDDLE *v.* II. (Always depreciatory.) Now *rare.* **b.** To trifle with one's food; to pick at one's food instead of eating heartily 1620. **2.** To make water. Now *vulgar* 1796. Hence **Pi·ddler. Pi·ddling** *ppl. a.* trifling, insignificant, paltry.

Piddock (pi·dǫk). 1730. [Of unkn. origin.] A bivalve mollusc of the genus *Pholas* or family *Pholadidæ.*

Pidgin, pigeon (pi·dʒin, -ən). Also **pidjin.** 1850. A Chinese perversion of Eng. *business.* Hence **Pidgin-English,** the jargon, consisting chiefly of English words, often corrupted in pronunciation, and arranged according to Chinese idiom, used for intercommunication between Chinese and Europeans at seaports, etc.

Pie (pəi), *sb.*¹ ME. [– (O)Fr. *pie* :– L. *pica* magpie, rel. to *picus* green woodpecker.] **1.** The bird now called the MAGPIE. **2.** *fig.* Applied to †**a.** a cunning or wily person; **b.** a chattering or saucy person 1542. **3.** Applied locally to other birds, usu. having black-and-white ('pied') plumage. (See also SEA-PIE.) 1883. **b.** *French p., rain-p., wood-p.*: applied to various species of woodpecker 1677. **4.** *attrib.* In compounds denoting 'particoloured', as *p.-coated* adj. See PIEBALD. 1630.

Pie (pəi), *sb.*² ME. [prob. identical with PIE *sb.*¹ (in AL. *pia* XIII, *pica* XIV); it has been conjectured that the reason for this application is that the magpie collects miscellaneous objects, and CHEWET¹ and HAGGIS have been compared.] **1.** A dish composed of meat, fowl, fish, fruit, or vegetables, enclosed in or covered with a layer of paste and baked. **b.** With defining word, as APPLE-PIE, *venison-pie*, etc.; also PÉRIGORD *p.* 1602. **2.** Any object resembling a pie 1842. **3.** *fig.* A prize, a treat; a bribe. *U.S. slang.* 1895.

1. He koude..wel bake a pye CHAUCER. Phr. *To have a finger in the p.*, to have a share (often officious) in the doing of something. See also HUMBLE PIE. The term is extended to other dishes (as *potato p.*) which have a crust when baked. The use of *pie* as distinguished from *tart* varies locally. **2.** *Bran p.*, a tub full of bran with toys, etc. hidden in it, to be drawn out at random, at Christmas festivities, etc. DIRT-PIE, MUD-PIE.

Comb.: **p.-dish,** the deep dish in which a p. is made (and cooked).

Pie, pye, *sb.*³ Now only *Hist.* 1477. [Rendering of AL. *pica* (identical with PIE *sb.*¹); cf. PICA¹, PIE *sb.*²] **1.** A collection of rules, adopted in the pre-Reformation Church of England, to show how to deal with the concurrence of more than one office on the same day. **b.** Hence app. COCK AND PIE, q.v. †**2.** (Usu. **pye book.**) An alphabetical index to rolls and records –1788.

Pie (pəi), *sb.*⁴ 1659. Also †**pye,** (*U.S.*) **pi.** 1659. [perh. tr. Fr. *pâté* (PIE *sb.*²), as in *caractères tombés en pâté.* Cf. the synon. G. *zwiebelfische.*] A mass of type mingled indiscriminately, such as results from the breaking down of a forme of type. **b.** *transf.* A jumble, medley, confusion, chaos; a 'mess' 1837.

‖**Pie** (pəi), *sb.*⁵ Also **pai, pi.** 1859. [– Hindi, etc. *pā'ī* :– Skr. *pad, padī* quarter; cf. PICE.] The smallest Anglo-Indian copper coin, the twelfth part of an anna; before the depreciation of the rupee, about one-eighth of a penny.

Pie, *v.* 1870. [f. PIE *sb.*⁴] *Printing. trans.* To make (type) into 'pie'; to mix up indiscriminately.

Piebald (pəi·bǫld), *a.* (*sb.*) 1589. [f. PIE *sb.*¹ + BALD *a.* 4.] Of two different colours, esp. white and black (like the plumage of a magpie), usu. arranged irregularly; pied; usu. of animals, esp. horses. Loosely, particoloured 1594. **b.** *fig.* Of mixed characters or qualities (always in bad sense); motley, mongrel 1589. **B.** *sb.* A piebald animal, esp. horse. *fig.* A person or thing of mixed character, a 'mongrel' 1765.

Dusky woods, p. with snow DARWIN. **b.** Shall hurl his p. Latin at thy head 1763. **B.** Three pyebalds and a roan TENNYSON. Hence **Pie·baldness, -ly** *adv.*

Piece (pīs), *sb.* [ME. *pece*, later *piece* – AFr. *pece*, OFr. *piece* (mod. *pièce*) :– Rom. **pettia* (cf. med.L. *petia, pecia, pet(t)ium*), prob. of Gaulish origin; cf. PEAT¹.] **I.** In general sense; or followed by *of.* **1.** A separate portion, part, bit, or fragment of anything; one of the distinct portions of which anything is composed. †**2.** A part *of* a whole, considered as distinct; a portion *of* an immaterial thing. (Now repl. by *part, portion.*) –1755. **b.** A limited portion *of* land, enclosed, marked off by bounds, or viewed as distinct 1450. **3.** A portion or quantity *of* any substance or kind of thing forming a single (usu. small) body or mass; a bit. late ME. **b.** Of something non-material, as *a p. of prose, of music*, etc. 1601. **4.** A length (varying according to the material) in which cloth, etc., is woven; also, a length *of* wall-paper as made (in England, usually 12 yards) 1523. **5.** A cask *of* wine or brandy, usually equivalent to the butt, or to two hogsheads. [Fr. *pièce.*] 1490. **6.** A single object or individual forming a unit of a class or collective group, as *a p. of furniture, of plate, of ordnance*, etc. late ME. **7.** *P. of work*: **a.** A product of work, a (concrete) work 1540. **b.** A task, difficult business; *fig.* a commotion (*colloq.*) 1594. **8.** An individual instance, or example, *of* any form of action or activity, function, abstract quality, etc. 1568.

1. *In pieces*, broken, in fragments; *fig.* at variance. *To pieces*, into fragments, asunder. *To go* or *come to pieces*, to break up. *To take to pieces*, to separate into its parts. **2.** After waiting a day and p. in Winchester WASHINGTON. Phr. *A p. of one's mind*, something of what one thinks; one's candid opinion; a rebuke. **b.** I haue bought a p. of ground *Luke* 14:18. **3.** A hard peece of wood 1657. *P. of water*, a small detached sheet of water, a small lake. *P. of money, of gold, of silver*, a coin. *P. of flesh*, a human being; *p. of goods*, a woman or child (*joc.*) Now *dial.* **b.** Here doth lye Ben Ionson his best p. of poetrie B. JONS. **4.** A *p.* of muslin is 10 yards; of calico, 28 yards; of Irish linen, 25 yards 1858. **5.** Pieces of Conyack Brandy in 32 Lotts 1687. **7. a.** What a p. of worke is a man! how Noble in Reason! [etc.] SHAKS. **8.** A.. delicate P. of Architecture 1686. A rare p. of luck 1876.

II. Absolute uses, without *of* and specification of the substance, etc. **1.** A person, a personage, an individual. *arch.* and *dial.* ME. **2. a.** A piece of armour. late ME. †**b.** A fortified place, stronghold –1721. **3.** A weapon for shooting, fire-arm 1550. **4.** Each of the pieces of wood, ivory, etc., also called 'men', with which chess, draughts, backgammon, etc., are played 1562. **5.** A piece of money; a coin. Often defined as *crown p.*, *penny p.*, etc. 1575. †**b.** *spec.* Popularly applied to the sovereign, and guinea, as either was the current coin –1741. **6.** A portion of time or space. Now *dial.* ME. **7.** A (small) portion of some specific substance. late ME. **b.** Short for 'piece of bread' (with or without butter); *spec.* such a piece eaten by itself, not as part of a meal. *Sc.* and *dial.* 1787. **c.** pl. *pieces.* An inferior quality of crystallized sugar 1867. **8.** A production, specimen of handicraft, work of art; a contrivance. *Obs.* in general sense. See also MASTERPIECE. 1604. **b.** A painting, a picture 1574. **c.** A literary composition, usu. short 1533. **d.** A drama, a play 1643. **e.** A musical composition, usu. short 1825.

1. Hee is another manner of peece then you think for B. JONS. Xanthus having a kind of Nice froward P. to his wife 1694. **3.** The stocke of his p. is ..made..somewhat like a fowling p. 1591. So from a p. two chained bullets flie 1600. **4.** In order to begin the game, the pawns must be moved before the pieces 1797. **5.** *P. of eight*, the Spanish dollar, or *peso*, of the value of 8 *reals*, or about 4*s.* 6*d.*, marked with the figure 8. **8. b.** The walls were thickly covered, chiefly with family pictures: ..now and then some..battle-piece LYTTON. **d.** On the first night of a new p. they always fill the house with orders to support it SHERIDAN.

Phr. *A p.*, *the p.*, *each* or *every p.*, each piece of a number of pieces; each unit of a number, set, or company; each of them or these; esp. in stating the share or price of each unit or individual member. Hence, *advb.*, APIECE, q.v., *the p.*, *per p.* *By the p.*, at a rate of so much for a definite amount or quantity. *On the p.*, at piece-work. *In* or *of one p.*, consisting of a single or undivided p. or mass. *Of a p.* (*with*), of one p., in one mass; often *fig.* of one and the same kind or quality; uniform; in agreement, in keeping. *P. by p.*, one p. or part after another in succession; a p. at a time, gradually.

Comb.: **p.-goods** *sb. pl.*, textile fabrics, woven in recognized lengths for sale; now esp. Lancashire cotton goods exported to the East; **-market**, the market for goods sold by the p.; **-rate**, rate of payment for piece-work; **-work**, work done and paid for by the p.; **-worker.**

Piece (pīs), *v.* late ME. [f. prec. sb.] **1.** *trans.* To mend, make whole, or complete by adding a piece or pieces; to patch. **2.** To put together so as to form one piece; to mend (something broken) by joining the pieces; *absol.* in spinning, to join or piece up threads 1483. **b.** *fig.* To join, unite; *refl.* to join oneself *to*, unite *with* 1579. †**3.** *intr.* To unite, come together; to agree; to join on –1692.

1. *fig. Ant. & Cl.* I. v. 45. **2.** I cannot p. the leg as the doctor can MRS. GASKELL. **b.** Piecing fragments of empty signification MEREDITH. **3.** New Things peece not so well BACON.

Comb. with adverbs. **P. on.** *trans.* and *intr.* To fit on (as the corresponding piece). **P. out.** *trans.* To complete, eke out, or enlarge by the addition of a piece. **P. together.** *trans.* To join together (pieces or fragments) into a whole; to make up of pieces so combined. **P. up.** *trans.* To make up (esp. that which is broken); to patch up.

‖**Pièce** (pyęs). 1789. The French for 'piece'; occurring in French phrases in Eng. use. **a.** A document used as evidence; esp. in *p. justificative*, a document serving as proof of an allegation. **b.** *P. de résistance* (pyęs də rezistāṅs): the most substantial dish in a repast; also *fig.* the chief item in a collection, group, or series.

Piecemeal (pī·smīl), *adv.* (*sb.*, *a.*) [ME. f. PIECE *sb.* + -MEAL.] **1.** One part at a time; piece by piece, by degrees; separately. Also with *by* (rarely *in*). **2.** Piece from piece; into or in pieces; with *break*, *tear*, *cut*, etc. 1570. †**B.** quasi-*sb.* (with *pl.*) A small piece, portion, or fragment; chiefly in phr. *by piecemeals* –1762. **C.** *adj.* (the adv. used *attrib.*) Consisting in pieces; done bit by bit 1600.

1. The business will be done covertly and p. BURKE. **2.** Bruse Thou shalt and peecemeale breake These men like potshards weake SIDNEY. **C.** Giving no opinion on p. reform 1831. Hence **Pie·cemeal** *v.* (now *rare*) to divide p.; to dismember.

Piecen (pī·s'n), *v. local* or *techn.* 1835. [f. PIECE *sb.* + -EN[5] 2.] *trans.* To join, to piece; chiefly, to join broken threads in spinning.

Piecener (pī·s'nəɹ). 1835. [f. prec. + -ER[1].] One who pieces or piecens; a piecer; *spec.* a young person employed in a spinning-mill to keep the frames filled with rovings, and to join together the ends of threads which break; formerly also, to join the cardings or slivers for the slubber, a work now done by machinery.

Piecer (pī·səɹ). 1825. [f. PIECE *v.* + -ER[1].] **1.** *gen.* One who pieces; a patcher 1836. **2.** *spec.* In a spinning-mill: see PIECENER 1825.

Piecrust (pəi·krʊst). 1582. [PIE *sb.*[2]] The baked paste forming the crust of a pie.

Prov. Promises are like pie-crust, made to be broken.

Pied (pəid), *ppl. a.* late ME. [First in *pyed freres* (XIV) friars wearing a parti-coloured habit, repr. OFr. *freres agachies* (Fr. *agace* magpie); f. PIE *sb.*[1] + -ED[1].] Parti-coloured; orig. black and white like a magpie. Also, wearing a parti-coloured dress, e.g. *pied piper.* **b.** Construed as *pa. pple.* = variegated 1632. **c.** In the specific names of many birds and animals 1837.

To weare the p. coate off a foole 1575. **b.** Meadows trim with Daisies pide MILT. **c.** **P. antelope** = BONTEBOK; **p. blackbird,** any Asiatic thrush of the genus *Turdulus*; **p. finch,** the chaffinch, *Fringilla cœlebs*; **p. flycatcher** (*Muscicapa atricapilla*). Hence **Pie·dness.**

‖**Pied-à-terre** (pyęta̦tę̄r). 1839. [Fr. 'foot to earth'.] A place to rest or stay at.

Piedmontite (pī·dmǫntəit). 1854. [f. *Piedmont* (It. *Piemonte*), its locality + -ITE[1] 2 b.] *Min.* A brownish-red or reddish-black silicate of aluminium, iron, manganese, and calcium, resembling epidote; manganese epidote.

Pieman (pəi·mæ̆n). 1820. A man who makes pies for sale; a vendor of pies. So **Pie·-wo:man** 1817.

Piepowder (pəi·paudəɹ), *a.* and *sb.* ME. [– AFr. *piepuldrus* – AL. *pedepulverosus* dusty-footed (XIV), i.e. abl. sing. of L. *pes* foot, and adj. f. L. *pulvis*, *pulver-* dust (see POWDER).] †**A.** (*piepoudrous*, etc.) *adj.* Wayfaring, itinerant; *absol.* as *sb. sing.* and *pl.* = B. –1609. **B.** (*piepowder*) *sb.* †**A** travelling man, a wayfarer, *esp.* an itinerant merchant or trader. Chiefly used in *Court of Piepowders*, a summary court formerly held at fairs and markets to administer justice among itinerant dealers, etc. –1735. **b.** *attrib.* and *sb. sing.*, *P. Court*, *Court of P.* = *Court of Piepowders* 1574.

Pier (piᵊɹ). [ME. *per* – AL. *pera* (XII), of unkn. origin.] **1.** One of the supports of the spans of a bridge, whether arched or otherwise formed. **2.** A solid structure of stone, or of earth faced with piles, extending into the sea or a tidal river, to protect or enclose a harbour and form a landing-stage; also, one of iron or wood, open beneath, forming a pleasure promenade, and often a landing-place; also, a projecting landing-stage or jetty on the bank of a river or lake 1453. †**b.** *transf.* A haven –1721. **3.** *Arch.* and *Building.* A solid support of masonry or the like designed to sustain vertical pressure: **a.** A square pillar or pilaster; **b.** The solid masonry between doors, windows, etc.; **c.** Each of the pillars from which an arch springs 1663.

attrib. and *Comb.*, as **p.-glass,** a tall mirror; orig. one fitted to fill up the p. between two windows, or over a chimney-piece; **-table,** a low table occupying the space between two windows. Hence **Pie·rage,** the toll paid for the use of a pier or wharf.

Pierce (piᵊɹs), *v.* [ME. *perce* (later *pierce* XVI) – (O)Fr. *percer* :– Rom. **pertusiare*, f. L. *pertusus*, pa. pple. of *pertundere* bore through, f. *per* PER- + *tundere* thrust.] **1.** *trans.* To penetrate (a substance), as a sharp-pointed instrument does; of an agent: to stab, prick, puncture (anything) *with* such an instrument. **b.** *transf.* and *fig.*; *spec.* said of the penetrating action of cold. late ME. **2.** To make a hole, opening, or tunnel into or through (something); to bore through; to broach (a cask, etc.) ME. **b.** To make (a hole, etc.) by piercing. late ME. **3.** To force one's way through or into; to break (an enemy's line) ME. **4.** To reach or penetrate with the sight or mind; to discern. late ME. **5.** To penetrate with pain, grief, or other emotion; to wound; to move deeply. late ME. **6.** *intr.* To enter, penetrate, or pass *into* or *through*; *transf.* to project or jut sharply. late ME. **b.** *transf.* and *fig.* To see *into* (anything) 1549.

1. They shall loke on hym, whom they pearsed TINDALE *John* 19:37. His only son..was pierced through the heart by a javelin GIBBON. **2.** Le Ceres, French ship privateer, pierced for 14 guns 1798. **4.** He pierced the mysteries of nature 1850. **5.** Can no prayers p. thee? SHAKS. **6.** Narrow promontories, piercing out into the water 1872. Hence **Pierce** *sb.* the act or process of piercing.

Pierced (piᵊɹst, *poet.* piᵊ·ɹsėd), *ppl. a.* late ME. [f. prec. + -ED[1].] In the senses of PIERCE *v.* **b.** *spec.* in *Her.* (*a*) Said of a charge represented as perforated with a hole, so that the tincture of the field appears through. (*b*) Said of an animal used as a charge, represented as having an arrow, spear, etc., fixed in its body, but not passing through it. 1572.

Piercer (piᵊ·ɹsəɹ). late ME. [XV *persour* – AFr. *persour* (= OFr. *persëoir*, mod. *perçoir*), f. (O)Fr. *percer*; see PIERCE, -ER[2].] **1.** *gen.* One who or that which pierces. **2.** An instrument or tool for piercing or boring holes, as an auger, awl, gimlet, stiletto, etc. late ME. **b.** The sting or the ovipositor of an insect 1691. **3.** A person employed in perforating metal or wood work 1736.

Piercing (piᵊ·ɹsiŋ), *ppl. a.* late ME. [f. PIERCE *v.* + -ING[2].] **1.** Perforating, penetrating, as a sharp-pointed instrument. **2.** Able to 'see into' a thing; having penetration ME.

1. Sorrow's p. dart GRAY. A p. shriek rang through the..air 1884. *fig.* A state of the most p. inquietude 1791. **2.** The most p. eyes I ever beheld are those of Voltaire 1779. Hence **Pie·rcing-ly** *adv.*, **-ness.**

Pier-head. 1682. [f. PIER + HEAD *sb.*] The outward or seaward end of a pier.

Pierian (pəi,iᵊ·riăn), *a.* 1591. [f. L. *Pierius* adj. + -AN.] Belonging to Pieria, a district in N. Thessaly, the reputed home of the Muses; *spec.* an epithet of the Muses; hence in ref. to poetry or learning.

A little learning is a dang'rous thing; Drink deep, or taste not the P. spring POPE.

Pieridine (pəi,e·ridəin), *a.* [– mod.L. *Pieridinæ*, f. *Pieris*, the typical genus; see -ID[3], -INE[1].] *Entom.* Belonging to the family *Pieridæ*, or subfamily *Pieridinæ* of *Papilionidæ*, containing the cabbage butterflies.

Pierrette (piĕre·t, ‖pyęręt). 1888. [Fr. fem. dim. of *Pierre* Peter, corresp. to PIERROT.] A female member of a company of pierrots.

Pierrot (pī·ĕro, ‖pyęro). 1741. [– Fr. *pierrot*, appellative use of pet-form of *Pierre* PETER; see -OT[1].] A typical character in French pantomime; applied in English use to a singer or instrumentalist having usu. a whitened face and wearing loose white fancy dress.

Piet, pyet, pyot (pəi·ət). Now only *Sc.* and *n. dial.* [In ME. *piot*, f. PIE *sb.*[1] + -OT[1], written later -ET.] **1.** The magpie. **b.** The dipper or water-ouzel. Also *water-piet.* 1839. **2.** *fig.* Applied to a talkative or saucy person 1574. **3.** *attrib.* Pied, piebald 1508.

‖**Pietà** (pyeta·). 1644. [It. :– L. *pietatem* PIETY.] A representation, in painting or sculpture, of the Virgin Mary (and other holy women) mourning over the dead Christ.

Pietism (pəi·ėtiz'm). 1697. [– G. (mod.L.) *pietismus*, f. after PIETIST; see -ISM.] **1.** *Ch. Hist.* The movement for the revival and advancement of piety in the Lutheran church (see next 1); the principles or practices of the German Pietists. **2.** Pious sentiment; often implying an affectation or exaggeration of piety 1829.

1. Say what you will of P., no one can deny the real worth of the characters which it formed 1877.

Pietist (pəi·ėtist). 1697. [– G., f. L. *pietas* PIETY + -IST. Applied in derision to the followers of Spener, in ref. to the *collegia pietatis* formed by them *c*1690.] **1.** *Ch. Hist.* One of the party of reformers in the Lutheran church who followed Philipp Jakob Spener in the movement begun by him at Frankfort about 1670 for the deepening of piety and the reform of religious education. **2.** A person characterized by or professing special piety; one who cultivates, or lays stress on, depth of religious feeling or strictness of religious practice, esp. as dist. from intellectual belief. 1767. **3.** *attrib.* That is a pietist; pietistic 1705. Hence **Pieti·stic** *a.*; **-ical** *a.*; **-ly** *adv.*

Piety (pəi·ěti). ME. [– OFr. *piete* (mod. *piété*) – L. *pietas* dutifulness, f. *pius* PIOUS; see PITY, from which *piety* was not fully differentiated till late XVI.] †**I.** An early form of PITY, in various senses –1606.

Thou art a mercifull God..and of a great pietie *Bk. Com. Prayer, Commination*, 1548–1549.

II. The quality or character of being pious. **1.** Habitual reverence and obedience to God (or the gods); godliness, devoutness, religiousness 1604. **2.** Faithfulness to the duties naturally owed to parents and relatives, superiors, etc.; dutifulness, esp. to parents 1579. **3.** With *a* and *pl.* A pious act, observance, or characteristic 1652.

1. True p. is cheerful as the day COWPER. **2.** Let them learne first to shew pietie at home, and to requite their parents 1 *Tim.* 5:4. Phr. *Mount, Mountain of p.*: see MOUNT *sb.*[1] II. 1. *Pelican in her p.*: see PELICAN I. 2.

Piezometer (pəiˌĕzǫ·mĭtəɹ). 1820. [mod. (J. Perkins) f. Gr. πιέζειν press + -METER.] An instrument for measuring pressure (or something connected with pressure); e.g. for measuring the compressibility of liquids, measuring the pressure of water at any point in a water-main, etc.

‖**Piffero** (pi·fero). 1724. [It. *piffero* = Sp. *pifaro*, Fr. *fifre*; see PIPE, FIFE.] A small flute; also, a primitive kind of oboe, or a bagpipe with an inflated sheepskin for reservoir.

Piffle (pi·f'l), *v. dial.* and *slang.* 1847. [Of symbolic origin (cf. -LE 3); so Sc. *piffer*.] *intr.* To talk or act in a feeble or ineffective way. Hence **Pi·ffle** *sb.* foolish nonsense; twaddle. **Pi·ffler,** a trifler, a twaddler. **Pi·ffling** *a.* twaddling, foolish, trivial.

Pig (pig), *sb.*[1] [ME. *pigge* :– OE. **picga*, **pigga* (of similar formation to *docga* DOG), prob. repr. in OE. *picbrēd* 'swine-food', acorn.] **I. 1.** The young of swine; 'a young sow or boar' (J.). **2.** By extension: A swine of any age; a hog 1663. **b.** The figure of the animal used as an ornament, etc. *Sussex p.*, a drinking vessel in this form. 1884. **3.** The animal or its flesh as food (*joc.*, exc. with ref. to a young or sucking pig) late ME. **4.** Any of various species of the family *Suidæ*, as *bush-p.*, *wood-p.*; also extended to animals resembling the pig, as *sea-pig*, (*a*) the porpoise, (*b*) the tunny. See also GUINEA-PIG. 1664. **5.** Applied opprobriously to a person etc. (Cf. Fr. *cochon*.) 1546.

3. A Dissertation upon Roast P. LAMB.

II. Technical uses. **1.** An oblong mass of metal, as obtained from the smelting-furnace; esp. of iron. Also, in mod. use (without *a* or *pl.*), short for *pig-iron*. *P. of ballast*, a pig of iron (rarely of lead) used as ballast. 1589. **b.** Applied to the moulds or channels in the pig-bed 1805. **2.** In various techn. and local uses: e.g. a block or cube of salt; a segment of an orange or apple; etc. 1825. **3.** *Pigs in clover*, a game which consists in rolling a number of marbles into a recess or pocket in a board by tilting the board 1900.

Phrases. *To buy a p. in a poke* (or *bag*), to buy a thing without seeing it or knowing its value. *Please the pigs*, if all's well. *To carry pigs to market*, to try to do business or attain to results. *To drive* (or *bring*) *one's pigs to a fine, pretty*, etc. *market*, (usu. ironical) to be unsuccessful in a venture. *Prov.* Pigs might fly: an expression of incredulity.

Comb.: **p·-fish,** a pop. name in America and Australia of several fishes; **-market,** *a* a market for the sale of swine; (*b*) a name for the proscholium or antechamber of the Divinity School at Oxford; **-mould,** one of the channels in a pig-bed; **-ring,** a ring fixed in the snout of a hog to prevent it from grubbing; **-yoke,** a sextant or quadrant (*slang*).

Pig (pig), *sb.*[2] Now *Sc.* and *Northumb.* late ME. [Of unkn. origin; cf. PIGGIN.] An earthenware pot, pitcher, jar, or other vessel; a crock.

Pigs and whistles, fragments; trivialities; *to go to pigs and whistles*, to be ruined.

Pig, *v.* 1532. [f. PIG *sb.*[1]] **1.** Of a sow: To bring forth pigs; to farrow. Also *transf.* and *fig.* **2.** *intr.* To huddle or herd together like pigs; to sleep in a place like a pigsty. Also *to p. it* (mod. colloq.). 1675. **b.** *trans.* To crowd (persons) together like pigs 1745.

Pi·g-bed. 1821. [f. PIG *sb.*[1] + BED *sb.*] **1.** A pigsty, a pig's lair. **2.** The bed of sand in which pigs of iron are cast 1884.

Pigeon (pi·dʒin, -ən), *sb.* [Late ME. *peion, pyion, pegeon* – OFr. *pijon* young bird, esp. young dove (mod. *pigeon*) :– Rom. **pibio, -on-*, for late L. *pipio, -on-*, f. imit. base **pip-*.] †**1.** A young dove –1601. **2.** A bird of the family *Columbidæ*, a dove, either wild or domesticated 1494. **3.** *fig.* †**a.** A young woman, a girl; a sweetheart; also, a coward –1682. **b.** One who lets himself be swindled, esp. in gaming; a dupe, gull 1593. **4.** A flying target, used as a substitute for a real pigeon.

2. At Modena..pigeons are taught to carry letters to a place appointed, and bring back answers 1756. CARRIER-PIGEON, *homing p.*, *nun p.*, *pouter p.*, *tumbler p.*, etc.; **fruit p., ground p.,** PASSENGER-P., **rock p., wild p., wood-p.:** for the more important of these see the qualifying word. **3. b.** He was a famous p. for the playmen; they lived upon him THACKERAY. Phr. *To pluck a p.*, to 'fleece' a person. **4.** *Clay p.*, a saucer of baked clay thrown into the air from a trap, as a mark at shooting-matches. Phr. *To fly the blue p.* (Naut. slang): to heave the deep-sea lead.

Combs.: **p.-express** = *pigeon-post*; **-fancier:** see FANCIER 3; **-flyer,** one who lets homing pigeons fly, or takes part in pigeon-races; **-hearted** *a.*, faint-hearted, timid; †**-livered** *a.*, gentle, meek; **-match,** a match at shooting pigeons released from traps; **-post,** the conveyance of letters, etc. by homing pigeons; **-poult,** the young of a p.; **-woodpecker** (*U.S.*) = FLICKER *sb.*[2]

b. Combs. with *pigeon's*: **pigeon's blood,** *attrib.* (of a ruby) dark red, rather lighter than beef's blood; **pigeon's egg,** a bead of Venetian glass, of the shape and size of the egg of a p.; **pigeon's-foot** (= Fr. *pied de pigeon*), dove's-foot (*Geranium columbinum*).

Pigeon, *v. arch.* 1675. [f. prec.] *trans.* To make a pigeon of; to gull, cheat, delude, swindle, esp. at cards or any kind of gaming.

Pigeon (English): see PIDGIN.

Pi·geon-be:rry. 1775. [f. PIGEON *sb.* + BERRY *sb.*[1]] In N. America, the Poke-weed, *Phytolacca decandra*; also its berry; in Bermuda *Duranta plumieri*.

Pi·geon-breast. 1849. *Path.* A deformity of the human chest, in which it is laterally constricted so that the sternum is thrust forward, as in a pigeon. So **Pi·geon-brea:sted** *a.* 1815; also **Pi·geon-che:sted** *a.*

Pi·geongram. 1885. [f. PIGEON *sb.*, after *telegram*.] A message transmitted by a homing pigeon.

Pi·geon-hawk. 1807. A hawk that preys on pigeons; in England a name for the sparrow-hawk, and sometimes the goshawk; in U.S. the American merlin (*Falco columbarius*) and related species; also sometimes, the sharp-shinned hawk (*Accipiter velox*).

Pi·geon-hole, *sb.* 1592. [f. PIGEON *sb.* + HOLE *sb.*] **1.** A hole (usu. one of several) in a wall or door for the passage of pigeons; hence *transf.* 1683. **2.** A small recess or hole (usu. one of a series) for domestic pigeons to nest in; hence, any small hole, recess, or room for sitting or staying in 1622. †**3.** A cant name for the stocks –1694. **4.** *Printing.* An excessively wide space between two words. Not now common. 1683. **5.** One of a series of compartments, in a cabinet, writing-table, or range of shelves, open in front, and used for the keeping of documents, etc., also of wares in a shop 1789.

5. Abbé Sieyes has whole nests of pigeon-holes full of constitutions ready made, ticketed, sorted, and numbered BURKE. *fig.* Incapable of arranging his thoughts in orderly symmetrical pigeon-holes 1902.

Pi·geon-hole, *v.* 1848. [f. prec. sb.] **1.** *trans.* To deposit in a pigeon-hole (5); hence, to put aside (a matter) for future consideration, shelve for the present 1861. **2.** To place or label mentally; to classify or analyse exhaustively 1870. **3.** To furnish with or divide into a set of pigeon-holes 1848.

1. Lord Lyveden, by duly pigeon-holing the complaint, added another to the long list of his public services in that line 1861.

Pi·geon-house. 1537. A columbarium, dovecot.

Pi·geon-pea. 1716. [= Fr. *pois-pigeon*.] The seed of a leguminous shrub, *Cajanus indicus*, native of the E. Indies; also, the plant.

Pi·geon-plum. 1747. **1.** A tree of the W. Indies and Florida, *Coccoloba floridana*, N.O. *Polygonaceæ*, the wood of which is used in cabinet-making; also, its edible grape-like fruit. **2.** A W. African tree of the genus *Chrysobalanus*, N.O. *Rosaceæ*; also, its succulent edible fruit 1884.

Pi·geonry. 1840. [-RY.] A pigeon-house.

Pigeon's milk. 1777. **1.** The partly digested food with which pigeons feed their young 1888. **2.** An imaginary article for which children are sent on a fool's errand.

Pi·geon-toe:d, *a.* 1801. **1.** *Ornith.* Having the toes arranged on a level, as in pigeons; peristeropod 1890. **2.** Of persons or horses: In-toed.

Pigeon-wood (pi·dʒənwud). 1745. A name given to the wood of various tropical or sub-tropical trees or shrubs, mostly used in cabinet-work, so called from the marking or colouring.

Piggery (pi·gəri). 1804. [f. PIG *sb.*[1] + -ERY.] **1.** A place where pigs are kept. **2.** Piggish condition; piggishness 1867.

Piggin (pi·gin). Chiefly *dial.* 1554. [perh. f. PIG *sb.*[2]] A small pail, esp. a wooden one with one stave longer than the rest serving as a handle; a milking pail; a vessel to drink out of.

Piggish (pi·giʃ), *a.* 1792. [f. PIG *sb.*[1] + -ISH[1].] Pertaining to a pig, piglike; stubborn; selfish, mean; unclean, vile. Hence **Pi·ggish-ly** *adv.*, **-ness.**

Pigheaded (stress var.), *a.* 1620. [Parasynthetic deriv. of PIG *sb.*[1] + HEAD *sb.* + -ED[2].] Having a head like that of a pig; usu. *fig.*, having the mental qualities ascribed to a pig, obstinate, stupid, perverse. Hence **Pi·ghea·ded-ly** *adv.*, **-ness.**

Pight, arch. pa. t. and pa. pple. of PITCH *v.*[1]

Pightle (pəi·t'l). *local.* ME. [Of unkn. origin. In AL. *pitellum*, etc., XIII.] A small field or enclosure; a close or croft.

Pig-iron. 1665. [f. PIG *sb.*[1] II. 1.] Cast iron in pigs or ingots, as first reduced from the ore.

Pigment (pi·gmĕnt). late ME. [– L. *pigmentum*, f. **pig-*, base of *pingere* PAINT; see -MENT.] A colouring matter or substance. **a.** A paint, dye, 'colour'; in techn. use, a dry substance, usu. in the form of a powder, which, when mixed with a vehicle, constitutes a 'paint'. **b.** *Nat. Hist.* Any organic substance occurring in and colouring any part of an animal or plant; the natural colouring-matter of a tissue 1842. Hence **Pigme·ntal** *a.* pigmentary; **-ly** *adv.* **Pi·gmented** *a.* charged or coloured with p.

Pigmentary (pi·gmĕntări), *sb.* and *a.* late ME. [– L. *pigmentarius* adj., of or belonging to paints or unguents; sb., a dealer in these, f. *pigmentum*; see prec. and -ARY[1].] †**A.** *sb.* An apothecary. late ME. only. **B.** *adj.* †**1.** Pertaining to an apothecary or maker of aromatic confections. late ME. only. **2.** Of, pertaining or belonging to, or consisting of pigment; producing or containing colouring-matter; in *Path.* characterized by the formation or presence of pigment 1851.

Pigmentation (pigmĕntēⁱ·ʃən). 1866. [f. PIGMENT + -ATION, after *fragmentation*.] *Biol.*, *Nat. Hist.*, etc. Coloration or discoloration by formation or deposition of pigment in the tissues.

Pi·g-me:tal. 1731. [f. PIG *sb.*[1] II. 1. + METAL; cf. SOW-METAL.] Metal, usu. iron, in the form of pigs.

Pigmy, var. of PYGMY.

Pignorate (pi·gnŏreⁱt), *v.* Also **pignerate.** 1623. [– *pignerat-*, pa. ppl. stem of L. *pignerare, -ari* give, take as a pledge (in med.L. *pignor-*), f. *pignus, pigner-, pignor-* pledge; see -ATE[3].] *trans.* To give or take as a pledge; to pledge, pawn. Hence **Pignora·tion,**

the action of pledging or pawning. **Pi·g-norative** *a.* pledging, pawning.

Pi·g-nut. 1610. [f. PIG *sb.*^{1} + NUT.] **1.** = EARTH-NUT 1. **2.** = HOG-NUT 2. 1760.

Pi·gskin. 1855. [f. PIG *sb.*^{1} + SKIN.] The skin of the pig or hog; leather made of this. Hence in *Sporting slang*, a saddle.

Pi·gsney, -ny. *arch.* and *dial.* [ME. f. *pigges* pig's + *neyȝe* = *eye* with prosthetic *n*, app. derived from *an eye, min eye*.] **1.** A darling, pet; an endearing form of address, chiefly to a girl or woman. †**2.** An eye; a 'dear little eye' –1774.

1. And the little pigsny has mamma's mouth FARQUHAR.

Pigsticking (pi·gˌsti:kiŋ). 1848. [f. PIG *sb.*^{1} + STICKING *vbl. sb.*] The hunting of the wild boar with a spear. **Pi·gstick** *v. intr.* to hunt the wild boar. **Pi·gsticker,** (*a*) one who follows this sport; (*b*) a horse trained to this sport; (*c*) *colloq.* a long-bladed pocket-knife.

Pigsty (pi·gˌstəi). 1591. A sty or pen for pigs, including a shed. **b.** *transf.* A miserable dirty hovel.

Pi·g's wash, pi·gwash. 1630. The swill of a brewery or kitchen given to pigs; = HOGWASH. Also *transf.*

Pi·gtail. 1688. [From resemblance to the tail of a pig.] **1.** Tobacco twisted into a thin rope. **2.** A plait or queue of hair hanging down from the back of the head, applied *spec.* to that worn formerly by soldiers and sailors, and still occasionally by young girls, and now *esp.* to that customary among the Chinese 1753. **b.** *transf.* A Chinese 1886. **3.** *attrib.*, esp. in sense 'characteristic of the period when pigtails were worn', old-fashioned, pedantic, formal 1746. Hence **Pi·gtailed** *a.* having a tail like a pig's; having a p.; tied up into a p.

Pi·gweed. 1844. Various herbs devoured by swine, as the Goosefoots, Cow-parsnip, etc.

Pi-jaw: see PI *a.*

‖**Pika** (pəi·kă). 1827. [– *piika*, native name among the Tungus of Siberia.] A small rodent quadruped, *Lagomys alpinus*, allied to the guinea-pig, inhabiting boreal and alpine regions of Europe and Asia.

Pike (pəik), *sb.*^{1} [OE. *pic* point, prick, in ME. *pīk, pīke*, of which the var. *pik* with short vowel is repr. by PICK *sb.*^{1} In III superseded by PEAK *sb.*^{2}] **I.** A pickaxe; a pick used in digging, breaking up ground, etc. Now only as *dial.* form of PICK *sb.*^{1} **II. 1.** A sharp point, a spike, as the pointed end of a staff, or of an arrow or spear, the spike in the centre of a buckler ME. **b.** A prickle, a thorn; a hedgehog's prickle or spine. Chiefly *Sc. Obs.* or *dial.* ME. **3.** A staff having an iron point or spike, a pike-staff. Now *dial.* ME. **b.** A pitchfork, a hay-fork. Now *dial.* late ME. **III. 1.** = PEAK. **a.** The long peak of a shoe; a poulaine. *Obs.* exc. *Hist.* late ME. **b.** The 'beak' of an anvil. *Obs.* or *dial.* 1677. **2.** *dial.* A narrow pointed piece of land at the side of a field of irregular shape 1585.

attrib. and *Comb.*, as **p.-pole** *U.S*, a pole with a spike and a hook, used by lumbermen in driving logs, also as a boat-hook; **piketail** *U.S.*, the pintail duck.

Pike (pəik), *sb.*^{2} *north. Eng.* ME. [app. either a local application of PIKE *sb.*^{1} or of Norse origin; cf. West Norw. dial. *pīk* pointed mountain, *pīktind* peaked summit.] **1.** A name for a pointed or peaked summit, or a mountain or hill with a pointed summit; used extensively in the English Lake district. **b.** A cairn, also, a beacon, tower, or pile, on an eminence 1751. **2.** A pointed or peaked stack of hay, made up temporarily in the hayfield; also, a stack of corn, circular in form, pointed, and of no great size 1641.

1. Then there came down from Langdale P. A cloud SHELLEY.

†**Pike** (pəik), *sb.*^{3} 1555. [– Sp. *pico* beak, bill, peak, Pg. *pico* summit, top. Distinct from prec., as being of general use; its later form is PEAK *sb.*^{2} II.] **1.** The earlier form of PEAK *sb.*^{2}, the conical summit of a mountain. (Used first in the name *Pike* (*Picke*) of *Teneriffe*.) –1776. **b.** Hence, Any mountain peak; *esp.* a volcanic cone –1796. **2.** *Naut.* Phr. *On* (*the*) *p.*, vertically, straight up and down –1628.

Pike (pəik), *sb.*^{4} [ME. *pik*, identical with OE. *pīc* point, pick (see PIKE *sb.*^{1}, PICK *sb.*^{1}, PEAK *sb.*^{2}), the fish being so named from its pointed jaw; cf. GED, and Fr. *brochet* pike, f. *broche* spit.] **1.** A large, voracious freshwater fish of the northern temperate zone, *Esox lucius*, with a long slender snout; a jack, luce. Hence, any fish of the genus *Esox* or of the family *Esocidæ*. **2.** Applied in the colonies, etc., to various fishes resembling the pikes proper: e.g. two cyprinoid fishes, *Ptychochilus lucius* and *Gila grandis*, of California, and species of *Sphyræna* of Australia 1871. **b.** Also with distinctive epithets 1810.

1. He..Saw the p., the Maskenozha LONGF. **2. b. Glass-eyed, Goggle-eyed, Wall-eyed P.,** the pike-perch, *Stizostedion americanum* (or *S. vitreum*); **Sand-p.,** the lizard-fish, *Synodus fœtens*; **Sea P.,** the common garfish or gar-pike, *Belone vulgaris*; see also GAR-PIKE.

attrib. and *Comb.*, as **p.-perch,** a percoid fish of the genus *Stizostedion*; esp. *S. americanum* and *S. vitreum*; **-whale** = *piked whale*: see PIKED *a.*

Pike (pəik), *sb.*^{5} Also †**pique,** †**pyke.** 1511. [– (O)Fr. *pique*, back-formation from *piquer* pierce, puncture, f. *pic* PIKE *sb.*^{1}] **1.** A weapon consisting of a long wooden shaft with a pointed head of iron or steel; in the 18th c. superseded by the bayonet. †**2.** *transf.* = PIKEMAN^1 –1649.

1. Phr. *To trail a p.*: see TRAIL *v.* †*To run* (*push, cast oneself*, etc.) *upon the pikes*, (*fig.*) to rush to destruction.

Pike, *sb.*^{6} *dial.* or *local colloq.* and *U.S.* 1837. [Short for TURNPIKE.] **1.** A toll-bar or toll-gate. **b.** *transf.* The toll paid at a turn-pike-gate 1837. **2.** A turnpike road 1852.

Piked (pəikt, pəi·kėd), *a.* ME. [f. PIKE *sb.*^{1} + -ED^2.] **1.** = PICKED *a.* 1, 1 b. **2.** Tapering to a point or peak; pointed, peaked 1538.

2. P. horn, a tall conical head-dress worn by ladies in the 14th and 15th c. **P. shoe,** a shoe with a long peak at the toes; a poulaine. **P. whale,** the lesser rorqual, or pike-headed whale, *Balænoptera rostrata*.

Pikelet (pəi·klėt). 1790. [Shortened from *barapicklet* (W. *bara pyglyd*).] A local name for a crumpet.

Pikeman^1 (pəi·kmæ̆n). *Obs.* exc. *Hist.* ME. [f. PIKE *sb.*^{5} + MAN.] A soldier armed with a pike.

Pikeman^2 (pəi·kmæ̆n). 1845. [f. PIKE *sb.*^{1} + MAN *sb.*] A pickman; a miner; one who hews the coal with a pickaxe.

Pi·keman^3. 1857. [f. PIKE *sb.*^{6} + MAN *sb.*] The keeper of a turnpike.

Pikestaff (pəi·kˌstɑf). ME. [In sense 1 prob. – ON. *pikstafr* (see PICK *sb.*^{1}); in sense 2 f. PIKE *sb.*^{5}.] **1.** A walking stick with a metal point at the lower end like an alpen-stock. **2.** The wooden shaft of a pike (the weapon) 1580.

Phr. *As plain as a p.*, earlier *as plain as a* PACK-STAFF (in ref. to its plain surface).

Pilage (pəi·lėdʒ). 1825. [f. PILE *sb.*^{4} + -AGE.] = PELAGE.

Pilaster (pilæ·stəɹ). 1575. [– Fr. *pilastre* – It. *pilastro*, med.L. *pilastrum*, f. L. *pila* pillar, PILE *sb.*^{2}; see -ASTER.] *Arch.* **1.** A square or rectangular column or pillar; *spec.* such a pillar engaged in a wall, from which it projects a third, fourth, or other portion of its breadth; an anta; formerly also, the square pier of an arch, abutment of a bridge, etc. Hence **Pila·stered** *a.* furnished with or supported on pilasters.

Pilate (pəi·lĕt). late ME. [– Fr. *Pilate*, L. *Pilatus*.] The name (Pontius Pilate) of the Roman procurator of Judæa concerned in the trial of Jesus Christ; hence allus. as a term of reproach.

‖**Pilau, pilaw** (pilau·, pilǭ·, pilō̆u·), **pilaff** (pila·f). 1612. [Turk. *pilâv* = Pers. *palāw* boiled rice and meat.] An oriental dish, rice boiled with fowl, meat, or fish, and spices, raisins, etc.

Pilch (piltʃ), *sb.* [OE. **pileće*, (late) *pyl(e)će* = OHG. *pelliz* (G. *pelz* fur, furred coat) – late L. *pellicia* cloak, for L. *pellicea*, fem. of *pelliceus*, f. *pellis* skin, FELL *sb.*^{1} Cf. PELISSE.] **1.** An outer garment made of skin dressed with the hair; later, a leathern or coarse woollen outer garment. *Obs.* exc. *Hist.* **2.** A light frameless saddle for children 1552. **3.** A triangular flannel wrapper for an infant, worn over the diaper or napkin 1674.

Pilchard (pi·ltʃăɹd). 1530. [Early forms *pilcher, -erd, -ard*. Of unkn. origin; the ending was assim. to -ARD, as in *gurnard*.] A small sea fish, *Clupea pilchardus*, closely allied to the herring; it is taken in large numbers on the coasts of Cornwall and Devon.

Fooles are as like husbands, as Pilchers are to Herrings SHAKS.

Pi·lcorn. ME. [For *pildcorn*, f. PILLED *ppl. a.* + CORN.] A kind of oat, in which the glumes or husks do not adhere to the grain, but leave it bare. Also called *pilled oats*.

Pilcrow (pi·lˌkrōᵘ). *arch.* 1440. [unexpl. alt. of *pylcrafte* (Medulla Gram.), var. of *pargrafte* (Ortus Vocab.), for **pargraf* (cf. AL. *pergraphum*), contr. of *paragraf* PARAGRAPH. Cf. PARAPH.] A paragraph mark.

Pile (pəil), *sb.*^{1} [OE. *pīl* = MLG., MDu. *pīl* (Du. *pijl*), OHG. *pfīl* (G. *pfeil*) – L. *pilum* javelin.] †**1.** A dart; a shaft. –1400. †**b.** The pointed metal head of a dart, lance, or arrow –1700. **c.** Used to render L. *pilum*, the heavy javelin of the Roman foot-soldier 1620. **2.** A (pointed) blade (of grass) 1513. **3.** A pointed stake or post; *spec.* in later use, a large and heavy beam of timber, usu. sharpened at the lower end, of which a number are driven into the bed of a river, or into marshy or uncertain ground, for the support of a bridge, pier, quay, wall, etc. Also extended to cylindrical or other hollow iron pillars used for the same purposes. OE. **4.** *Her.* A charge, one of the ordinaries or sub-ordinaries, having the form of a wedge, usu. issuing from the chief or top of the escutcheon, with the point downwards. *In p.*: arranged in the form of a pile. *Party per p.*: divided by lines in the form of a pile. 1486.

2. Every p. of the grass that springs so sweetly in the meadows 1895. **3.** The houses of Amsterdam, which are reported to stand upon piles driven deep into the quagmire 1768.

attrib. and *Comb.*, as *p.-breakwater*; *p.-village*, etc.; also **p.-building,** a building erected on piles, esp. a prehistoric dwelling; **-cap,** a cap or plate for the head of a pile; also, a beam connecting the heads of piles; **-dwelling,** a dwelling built on piles, esp. in a lake, but sometimes on dry ground; hence **-dweller; -house,** a pile-dwelling; **-worm,** the teredo.

Pile (pəil), *sb.*^{2} late ME. [– (O)Fr. *pile* heap, pyramid, mass of masonry :– L. *pila* pillar, pier, mole.] †**1.** A pillar; a pier, esp. of a bridge –1730. †**2.** A mole or pier in the sea –1652. **3.** A heap of things lying one upon another; also *fig.* 1440. **b.** A series of weights fitting one within or upon another, so as to form a solid cone or other figure. (So Fr. *pile*.) 1440. **c.** *spec.* A heap of combustibles on which a dead body is burnt (*funeral pile*) 1615. **d.** *Metall.* A rectangular mass of cut lengths of puddled iron bars, laid upon each other in rows, for the purpose of being rolled after being raised to a welding temperature 1839. **e.** *ellipt.* (for *p. of wealth, money*, etc.) A heap of money, a fortune. Chiefly in colloq. phr. *to make one's p.* 1731. **4.** A lofty mass of buildings; a large building 1607. **5.** A series of plates of two dissimilar metals, such as copper and zinc, laid one above the other alternately, with cloth or paper moistened with an acid solution placed between each pair, for producing an electric current (*galvanic* or *electric p.*). Also extended to other arrangements of such plates: cf. BATTERY. 1800.

3. A large p. of letters and packages 1891. **e.** On the old Californian principle of 'making a "pile" and vamosing the ranché' 1852. **4.** The magnificent p. of the Escorial 1855. **5.** *Dry p.*, a voltaic p. in which no liquid is used, and which generates a feeble but very permanent current.

Pile (pəil), *sb.*^{3} *arch.* late ME. [– (O)Fr. *pile*, in med.L. *pila*. In Fr. opp. to *croix*, as in Eng. to 'cross'.] †**1.** The under iron of the minting apparatus with which money was struck; its surface bore the die of which the impression was made on the reverse side of the piece; opp. to *trussell* –1876. **2.** Hence, The side of a coin opposite to the 'cross' or face; the reverse (*arch.*) late ME.

2. *Cross and* (*or*) *p.*, in phrases: see CROSS *sb.* 15.

Pile (pəil), *sb.*^{4} ME. [prob. – AFr. *pyle*,

var. of *peile* (Liber Albus) kind of cloth, (O)Fr. *poil* :- L. *pilus* hair.] **1.** Hair, *esp.* fine soft hair, down; *rarely*, a single hair of this kind; the wool of sheep, etc. **2.** A nap upon cloth; now *esp.* the downy nap of velvet, plush, etc.; also, loops in a carpet forming a nap 1568. **b.** Each of the fine hair-like fibres of velvet, flannel, etc. 1787. **c.** *transf.* The burr on a plate in etching 1885.

2. *Double p., p. upon p., two-p., three-p.*, attrib. phr.: having the pile of double or treble closeness.

Comb.: **p.-beam,** a separate warp-beam, upon which the pile-warp is wound and carried; **-warp,** the secondary warp, which furnishes the substance of the p., also called *nap-warp*; it may consist of one, two, or three threads in the loop, producing *single-*, *double-*, or *three-pile velvet.* Hence **Piled** *ppl. a.*[2] covered with p.; having a p. or long nap.

Pile (pəil), *sb.*[5] Usu. *pl.* **piles.** late ME. [prob. – L. *pila* ball, with ref. to the globular form of an external pile. Cf. AL. *pili* (pl.) piles (XIII).] *Path.* A disease characterized by tumours of the veins of the lower rectum; hæmorrhoids.

Pile (pəil), *v.*[1] 1440. [f. PILE *sb.*[1] sense 3.] **1.** *trans.* To furnish or strengthen with piles (esp. of timber); to drive piles into. †**2.** To fix, drive in (as a stake or pile) –1613.

Pile, *v.*[2] 1576. [f. PILE *sb.*[2]] **1.** *trans.* To form into a pile; to heap up. Often with *up*, *on.* **b.** *Metall.* = FAGGOT *v.* 2. 1839. **2.** *transf.* and *fig.* To amass, accumulate 1844. **3.** *intr.* for *refl.* or *pass.* 1613. **4.** *trans.* To cover or load *with* things heaped on 1667. Hence **Piled** *ppl. a.*[1] laid or reared in a pile or piles, heaped. **Pi·ler,** one who piles.

1. *To p. arms* (*Mil.*), to place muskets or rifles (usu. three) in a position in which their butts rest on the ground and their muzzles come together, so as to form a pyramidal figure. **2.** Phr. *To p. up* (or *on*) *the agony* (*colloq.*), to add fresh elements or details to anything already painful. So *to p. it on.* **3.** Money..continues to p. up and up at the bankers 1897. **4.** Its floor Piled with provender for cattle BROWNING.

Pileate (pəi·li,ĕt), *a.* 1828. [– L. *pileatus* capped, f. *pileus*; see PILEUS, -ATE[2].] *Nat. Hist.* Having a pileus or cap.

Pileated (pəi·li,eⁱtėd), *a.* 1728. [f. prec. + -ED[1].] **1.** *Nat. Hist.* = prec.; *spec.* applied to certain Echini or sea-urchins; also, to certain birds, as the *P. Woodpecker* (*Picus pileatus*) of N. America. **2.** Wearing the *pileus* (see PILEUS 1) 1856.

Pi·le-dri:ver. 1772. A machine for driving piles (PILE *sb.*[1] 3) into the ground, usu. consisting of a heavy block of iron, suspended in a frame between two vertical guide-posts, and alternately let fall upon the pile-head, and raised by steam, manual, or other power.

‖**Pileorhiza** (pəili,orəi·ză). Also **-rrh-, -rhize.** 1857. [mod.L., f. *pileus* cap + Gr. ῥίζα root. Cf. COLEORHIZA.] *Bot.* The mass of tissue which covers and protects the growing-point of a root; the root-cap.

Pileous (pəi·li,əs), *a. rare.* 1842. [f. L. *pilus* hair + -OUS, on the anal. of *carneous, osseous*; see -EOUS.] Pertaining to or consisting of hair, hairy.

Piles, hæmorrhoids; see PILE *sb.*[5]

‖**Pileum** (pəi·li,ŏm). 1874. [L., collateral form of *pileus*; see next.] *Ornith.* The whole of the top of the head of a bird, comprising the *frons, corona,* and *occiput.*

‖**Pileus** (pəi·li,ŏs). *Pl.* **pilei** (pəi·li,əi). 1760. [L. *pileus* (better *pilleus*) felt cap. Cf. Gr. πῖλος in same sense.] **1.** *Antiq.* A felt cap without a brim, worn by the ancient Greeks and Romans 1776. **2.** *Bot.* A cap-like formation in various Fungi, esp. in the *Hymenomycetes* (mushrooms, etc.) 1760. **3.** *Ornith.* = PILEUM.

Pilewort (pəi·lwɒɹt). 1578. [f. PILE *sb.*[5] + WORT[1], from its reputed efficacy against piles; cf. FIGWORT.] The Lesser Celandine or Figwort (*Ranunculus ficaria* or *Ficaria verna*). Also used for the whole genus *Ficaria.*

†**Pilfer** (pi·lfəɹ), *sb.* [Late ME. *pylfre, pelfyr* – AFr., OFr. *pelfre* (cf. AL. *pelfra* XIII), f. *pelfrer*; see next, PELF.] That which is pilfered; spoil, plunder, booty –1791.

Pilfer (pi·lfəɹ), *v.* 1548. [– AFr., OFr. *pelfrer* pillage, rob, in AL. *pelfrare*; of unkn. origin. The form was early affected by assoc. with PILL *v.*[1]] **1.** *trans.* To plunder, steal; esp. in small quantities 1550. **b.** To plunder (a person or place). *rare.* 1838. **2.** *intr.* or *absol.* To pillage, plunder; *spec.* to commit petty theft 1548.

1. *fig.* And not a year but pilfers as he goes Some youthful grace that age would gladly keep COWPER. Hence **Pi·lferer. Pi·lfering** *vbl. sb.* petty theft. **Pi·lferingly** *adv.*

Pilgarlic (pilgā·ɹlik). 1529. [For earlier *pilled* (i.e. peeled) *garlic* XVI, a bald head being likened to a peeled head of garlic; see PILL *v.*[1]] A 'pilled' or a bald head; a bald-headed man; from 17th c. applied in a ludicrously contemptuous way: 'poor creature'. Now *dial.* **b.** (usu. *poor P.*) = poor I, poor me. *dial.* and *U.S. colloq.* or *slang.* 1694.

Pilgrim (pi·lgrim), *sb.* [ME. *pilegrim* – Pr. *pelegrin* (= It. *pellegrino*, (O)Fr. *pèlerin*) – L. *peregrinus* foreign; see PEREGRINE. For final *m* from *n* cf. *buckram, grogram, megrim, vellum.*] **1.** One who travels from place to place; a wanderer; a sojourner. (Now *poet.* or *rhet.* in gen. sense.) **2.** *spec.* One who journeys (usu. a long distance) to some sacred place, as an act of religious devotion. (The prevailing sense.) ME. **3.** *Amer. Hist.* Name given to those English Puritans who founded the colony of Plymouth, Massachusetts, in 1620. Now usu. **Pilgrim Fathers.** 1798. **4.** *U.S.* and *Colonial.* An original settler; a recent immigrant (also said of animals) 1851.

1. Any man may be called a p. who leaveth the place of his birth ROSSETTI. **2.** Pilgrimes were they alle That toward Caunterbury wolden ryde CHAUCER. *fig.* The Pilgrim's Progress from this World to That which is to come BUNYAN (*title*). **3.** The Feast of the 'Sons of the Pilgrims' 1798.

attrib. and *Comb.* **a.** *attrib.* That is a pilgrim; going on pilgrimage; consisting of pilgrims; of, pertaining or relating to, a pilgrim or pilgrims; as *p. chief, city, foot, garland, train,* etc. **b.** *spec.* (often with *pilgrim's*): **p.-bottle, pilgrim's bottle** = COSTREL; **P. Fathers** (*Amer. Hist.*): see sense 3; **pilgrim's shell,** a cockle- or scallop-shell carried by a pilgrim as a sign of having visited some sacred place; **pilgrim's sign,** a medal, etc., presented to a pilgrim at a shrine as a sign of his having visited it. Hence **Pi·lgrim** *v. intr.* to make a pilgrimage; to travel or wander like a p. **Pi·lgrimer** (*rare*), a p.

Pilgrimage (pi·lgrimėdʒ), *sb.* [ME. *pelrim-, pilegrimage* – Pr. *pilgrinatge* = (O)Fr. *pèlerinage*; see prec., -AGE.] **1.** A journey made by a pilgrim; the action of taking such a journey. **b.** *transf.* and *gen.* A journey; peregrination; sojourning ME. **c.** *fig.* The course of mortal life figured as a journey ME. **2.** *transf.* A place to which a pilgrimage is made 1517.

1. b. A p. of pleasure 1797. **c.** Se that ye passe the tyme off your pilgremage in feare TINDALE 1 *Pet.* 1:17. Hence **Pi·lgrimage** *v. intr.* †to live among strangers; to make a p.; to go on p.

Pilgrimize (pi·lgrimәiz), *v.* 1598. [See -IZE.] *intr.* To play the pilgrim, go on pilgrimage. Also *to p. it.*

‖**Pilidium** (pəili·diŏm). 1842. [mod.L. – Gr. πιλίδιον, dim. of πῖλος a felt cap; see -IUM.] *Zool.* A name of the cap-shaped larvæ of some species of Nemertean worms, formerly considered as a distinct genus 1877.

Piliferous (pəili·fĕrəs), *a.* 1846. [f. L. *pilus* hair + -FEROUS.] Bearing or having hair; *spec.* in *Bot.* bearing hairs or tipped with a hair.

Piliform (pəi·lifǭɹm), *a.* 1826. [f. L. *pilus* hair + -FORM.] Having the form of a hair; hairlike.

Piligerous (pəili·dʒĕrəs), *a.* 1835. [f. L. *pilus* hair + -GEROUS.] Bearing hair, clothed with hair.

Piling (pəi·liŋ), *vbl. sb.*[1] 1440. [f. PILE *v.*[1] + -ING[1].] **1.** The action of PILE *v.*[1] **2.** A mass of piles; pilework; wood for piles 1488.

Piling (pəi·liŋ), *vbl. sb.*[2] ME. [f. PILE *v.*[2] + -ING[1].] The action of heaping up. **b.** *Leather-making.* The putting of hides in a pile or heap in order to sweat them and cause the hair to come off. *U.S.* 1875.

Pill (pil), *sb.*[1] Now *dial.* late ME. [app. rel. to PILL *v.*[1] as the collateral form PEEL *sb.*[3] is to PEEL *v.*] = PEEL *sb.*[3]

Pill (pil), *sb.*[2] 1484. [– MLG., MDu. *pille*, Du. *pil*, presumably – reduced form of L. *pilula* PILULE.] **1.** A small ball of medicinal substance, of a size convenient to be swallowed whole. **b.** *fig.* Something disagreeable that has to be 'swallowed' or endured 1548. **2.** Any small pill-like body; a pellet 1575. **b.** A cannon-ball; a bullet (*joc.*) 1626. **c.** in *pl.* = BILLIARDS (*slang*) 1896. **d.** A ball (*slang*). **3.** An objectionable person; a bore (*slang*) 1897. **4.** (Also *Pills.*) Nickname for a physician (*slang*) 1860.

1. The cannon-shot, and doctor's p. With equal aim are sure to kill 1763. **b.** It was a bitter p. for the King..to swallow H. WALPOLE.

attrib. and *Comb.*: **p.-beetle,** a small beetle of the genus *Byrrhus*, which, when it feigns death, contracts itself into a ball; **-crab** = *pea-crab.*

Pill (pil), *sb.*[3] Also **pyll.** [In XVI *pille, pill*, app. :- OE. *pyll*, var. of *pull, pul* pool, creek.] A local name on both sides of the Bristol Channel, in Cornwall, etc., for a tidal creek on the coast, or a pool in a creek, etc.

Pill (pil), *v.*[1] OE. [ME. forms *pile, pyle* point to OE. **pilian, pylan* (in infl. form *pyleð* (intr.) peels XII) – L. *pilare* deprive of hair, pillage, f. *pilus* hair. Later superseded by *pill, pille* – Fr. *piller* plunder. See PEEL *v.*] **I.** To pillage, rob: = PEEL *v.* I. **1.** *trans.* To plunder, pillage; to despoil (a person or country) *of* (anything). Now *arch.* ME. †**b.** To exhaust, impoverish (soil) –1610. †**2.** *absol.* To rob, plunder –1678. †**3.** *trans.* To take by violence; to make a prey of –1618. †**4.** To pluck, pull, tear –1605.

1. The Commons hath he pil'd with greeuous taxes SHAKS. **2.** Large-handed Robbers your graue Masters are, And p. by Law SHAKS. **3.** *Rich. III,* I. iii. 159.

II. To decorticate: = PEEL *v.* II. **1.** *trans.* = PEEL *v.* II. 1, 1b. Now *arch.* and *dial.* late ME. **2.** *intr.* Of skin, bark, etc.: To become detached, come off, scale or peel off. **b.** Of animal bodies, trees, etc. = PEEL *v.* II. 2. Now *dial.* OE. †**3.** *trans.* To make bare of hair, remove the hair from; to remove (hair) –1648. †**b.** *intr.* To become bald –1614. **4.** To bare (land) by eating or shaving off, or cutting down crops, etc., close to the ground 1555.

1. The skilfull shepheard pil'd me certaine wands SHAKS. **2.** The whitenesse pilled away from..his eyes *Tobit* 11:13. **3.** Doe they first p. thee, next pluck off thy skin? HERRICK. Phr. *P. and poll,* to ruin by depredations or extortions; to rifle, pillage. Hence †**Pi·ller,** a robber, plunderer; a thief –1674.

Pill, *v.*[2] 1736. [f. PILL *sb.*[2]] **1.** *trans.* To dose with pills. **2.** To blackball (*slang*) 1855. **b.** To fail (a candidate) in an examination (*slang*) 1908.

Pillage (pi·lėdʒ), *sb.* late ME. [– (O)Fr. *pillage*, f. *piller* plunder; see PILL *v.*[1], -AGE.] **1.** The action of plundering; spoliation, plunder; chiefly that practised in war; also, wholesale robbery or extortion. †**2.** Goods forcibly taken, esp. from an enemy in war; booty, spoil, plunder –1750.

Pillage (pi·lėdʒ), *v.* 1592. [f. prec.] **1.** *trans.* To rob, plunder, sack (a person, place, etc.), esp. as practised in war. **2.** To carry off as booty; to make a spoil of; to appropriate wrongfully 1600. **3.** *absol.* or *intr.* To plunder; to rob with open violence 1593.

1. He pillaged many Spanish towns, and took rich prizes FULLER. **3.** They were suffered to p. wherever they went MACAULAY. Hence **Pi·llager.**

Pillar (pi·lăɹ), *sb.* [ME. *piler(e* – AFr. *piler*, (O)Fr. *pilier* :- Rom. **pilare*, f. L. *pila* pillar, pier, PILE *sb.*[2]; assim. to words in -AR[1] from XIV.] **1.** *Arch.* A detached vertical structure of stone, brick, wood, metal, etc., slender in proportion to its height, and of any shape in section, used either as a support for some superstructure, or standing alone as a monument, etc. Cf. COLUMN. **b.** = PILLAR-BOX 1865. **2.** A post, a pedestal; e.g. one of the four posts of a bedstead; the single central support of a table, a machine, etc.; also *attrib.* as *p.* (*and claw*) *table, stand,* etc. ME. **3.** *fig.* **a.** An imaginary prop on which the heavens or the earth is represented as resting ME. **b.** A person who is a main supporter of an institution, principle, etc. ME. **c.** A fact or principle which is a main support of something 1578. **4.** *transf.* An upright pillar-like mass or 'column' of air, vapour, water, sand, etc. ME. †**5.** A portable pillar borne as an ensign of dignity or office.

Obs. exc. *Hist.* 1518. **6.** *Mining.* A solid mass of coal or other mineral, of rectangular section, left to support the roof of the working 1708. **7.** *Anat.* and *Phys.* Applied to certain bodily structures in ref. to their form and function 1807.

1. All good architecture adapted to vertical support is made up of pillars RUSKIN. **2.** A round table is generally described as having 'pillars and claws' 1881. **3.** The pileris of heuene togidere quaken WYCLIF *Job* 26:11. **b.** The p. of the orthodox faith GIBBON. **4.** Blood, and fire, and pillars of smoke *Joel* 2:30. **5.** *Hen. VIII*, II. iv. (*Stage direct.*). **7.** *Pillars of fauces*, two arching folds of mucous membrane containing muscular fibres, which pass from the base of the uvula outwards and downwards on either side.

Phr. *From p. to post*, orig. *from post to p.*: from one party or place of appeal or resource to another; hither and thither; implying repulse and harassment. Orig. a figure drawn from the tennis-court.

attrib. and *Comb.*: **p. apostle,** a chief apostle, as Peter, James, or John (see Gal. 2:9); **p. plate,** the plate of a watch movement next behind the dial; **-post** = *pillar-box*; **-saint** = PILLARIST.

Pillar (pi·lăɹ), *v.* 1607. [f. prec. sb.] **1.** *trans.* To support or strengthen with or as with pillars. **2.** To embody in the form of a pillar; to display in the figure of a pillar (*rare*) 1812.

Pi·llar-box. 1858. A hollow pillar about five feet high, erected in a public place, containing a receptacle for posting letters.

Pillared (pi·lăɹd), *ppl. a.* ME. [f. PILLAR *sb.* or *v.* + -ED.] **1.** Having, supported on or by, or furnished with a pillar or pillars. **2.** Fashioned into or like a pillar or pillars 1698.

1. *fig.* The pillar'd firmament MILT. **2.** P. basalt 1887.

Pillarist (pi·lărist). 1638. [f. PILLAR *sb.* + -IST.] A pillar-saint, a stylite.

Pill-box (pi·lbǫks). 1737. [f. PILL *sb.*[2] + BOX *sb.*[2]] **1.** A shallow cylindrical box of cardboard for holding pills. **b.** Jocularly applied to various boxes, closed vehicles, etc. 1835, a small round concrete emplacement 1918. **c.** *attrib.* and *Comb.* Like a pill-box in shape, or size, as *pill-box hat, house* 1836.

Pilled (pild), *ppl. a. arch.* and *dial.* late ME. [f. PILL *v.*[1] + -ED[1].] **1.** Stripped of skin, bark, rind, etc. *Obs.* or *dial.* **2.** Bereft of hair, feathers, etc.; bald, shaven, tonsured. *Obs.* or *dial.* late ME. †**3.** Bare, threadbare, bare of pasture; poor. Also *fig.* –1613. **4.** Plundered, pillaged. *arch.* or *dial.* 1514.

2. As piled as an Ape was his skulle CHAUCER.

Pillion (pi·lyən). 1503. [– Gael. *pillean, pillin*, Ir. *pillin*, dim. of *pell* (gen. sing. and nom. pl. *pill*) couch, pallet, cushion – L. *pellis* skin.] A kind of saddle, *esp.* a woman's light saddle. Also, a pad or cushion attached to the hinder part of an ordinary saddle for a second person (usu. a woman). *Obs.* exc. *Hist.* **b.** A pad or spring seat for a second person on the back of a motor-bicycle 1911.

The straps of my wife's p. broke down GOLDSM. *Comb.* (sense b), as *p.-rider, -riding, -seat*, etc.

Pilliwinks (pi·liwiŋks). Also **pilnie-.** *Hist.* late ME. [In Eng. use *pyrwykes, pyrewinkes* (XIV–XV), in Sc. use from late XVI *pilli-, pinniwinkes*; of unkn. origin.] An instrument of torture for squeezing the fingers.

Pillory (pi·lŏri), *sb.* [ME. *pillori* – AL. *pillorium* (XII) – (O)Fr. *pilori*, †*pillorie*, †*pellorie* (XII), prob. – Pr. *espilori*, of obscure origin.] A wooden framework erected on a post or pillar, having holes through which the head and hands of an offender were thrust, in which state he was exposed to public ridicule and molestation. In other forms, the culprit was fastened to a stake by a ring round his neck and wrists. Hence **Pi·llorize** *v. trans.* = next.

Pi·llory, *v.* 1600. [f. prec., after Fr. *pilorier.*] *trans.* To set in the pillory; to punish by exposure in the pillory. **b.** *fig.* To expose to public ridicule or abuse 1699.

b. He has Pillouried himself for't in Print, as long as that Book shall last 1699.

Pillow (pi·lo[u]), *sb.* [Late ME. *pilwe* :– OE. **pylw-*, obl. stem of *pyle*, later *pylu*, corresp. to MLG. *pöle*, MDu. *pēluwe, pöluwe* (Du. *peluw*), OHG. *pfuliwi, pfulwo* (G. *pfühl*), repr. WGmc. **pulwī(n* (II–III) – L. *pulvinus* cushion, bolster.] **1.** A support for the head in sleeping or reclining; *spec.* a case made of linen, etc., stuffed with feathers, down, etc.; esp. as forming part of a bed. Also applied to any object improvised for the same purpose. **b.** In various fig. uses. **2.** A pad 1667; a padded support upon which bone lace is made 1781. **3.** In techn. applications; esp. *Naut.* the block of timber on which the inner end of a bowsprit rests 1626. **4.** A kind of plain fustian 1839.

1. Coleridge..slept with the *Observations on Man* under his p. J. MARTINEAU. Phr. *To take counsel of one's p.*, etc.: to 'sleep upon' a matter of importance. **b.** As we..smoothed down his lonely p. WOLFE. **2.** Yon cottager, who weaves at her own door, P. and bobbins all her little store COWPER.

attrib. and *Comb.*: **p.-block,** a cradle or bearing to hold the boxes or brasses forming the journal-bearing of a shaft or roller; **-fight,** a fight with pillows; **-lace,** lace worked on a p. (sense 2); **-slip, -tie** = PILLOW-CASE.

Pi·llow, *v.* 1629. [f. prec. sb.] **1.** *trans.* To rest or place (the head, etc.) on or as on a pillow. **b.** Of a thing: To serve as a pillow for 1801. **c.** In *pa. pple.* Laid on, or as on, a pillow 1794. **2.** *trans.* To support or prop *up* with pillows 1839.

1. When the Sun in bed,..Pillows his chin upon an Orient wave MILT. Hence **Pi·llowed** (-o[u]d) *ppl. a.*

Pi·llow-case. 1745. The washable case of a pillow, usu. of white linen or cotton cloth.

Pillowy (pi·lo[u]i), *a.* 1798. [f. PILLOW *sb.* + -Y[1].] Having the quality or appearance of a pillow; soft; yielding.

Pillwort (pi·lwɒɹt). 1861. [f. PILL *sb.*[2] + WORT[1]; so called from its small globular involucres.] Any plant of the cryptogamous genus *Pilularia*, esp. *P. globulifera.*

Pilo- (pəi·lo), comb. form of L. *pilus* hair, as in **Pilomo·tor** *a.* applied to those nerves which produce movement of the hairs; **Pi:lo-seba·ceous** *a.* applied to sebaceous glands that open into hair-follicles.

Pilocarpine (pəilokā·ɹpəin). 1875. [f. mod. L. *Pilocarpus*, generic name in Bot. (f. Gr. πῖλος wool, felt + καρπός fruit) + -INE[5].] *Chem.* A white crystalline or amorphous alkaloid, $C_{11}H_{16}N_2O_2$, obtained from the leaves of jaborandi, *Pilocarpus pinnatifolius* (or other species), used in pharmacy.

Pilose (pəi·lō[u]s), *a.* 1753. [– L. *pilosus*, f. *pilus* hair; see PILE *sb.*[4], -OSE[1].] Covered with hair, esp. with soft flexible hair; hairy, pilous. So **Pilo·sity,** the quality or state of being p.; hairiness 1605.

Pilot (pəi·lət), *sb.* 1530. [– Fr. *pilote* – med.L. *pilotus* (XV), varying with *pedota, pedotta* – MGr. *πηδώτης, f. Gr. πηδόν oar, pl. rudder, f. *πεδ-, *πηδ- foot; cf. -OT[2].] **1.** One who directs the course of a ship; a steersman; *spec.* a person duly qualified to steer ships into and out of a harbour or wherever local knowledge is required. **b.** One who navigates an aeroplane, etc. 1848. **c.** *transf.* and *fig.* A guide through some unknown place or through difficulties and dangers; a leader in the hunting-field 1593. **d.** Short for *p. boat, engine* 1896. **2.** = *pilot-cloth* 1844. **3.** = COW-*catcher. U.S.* 1864. **4.** = PILOT-FISH 1. 1835.

1. I was like a ship without a p., that could only run before the wind DE FOE. Phr. *To drop the p.* (after his duties on board are finished); hence freq. in allusive and fig. use. **c.** I hope to see my P. face to face When I have crost the bar TENNYSON.

attrib. and *Comb.*, Of or pertaining to a p. or pilots, as *p.-brig, -coble*, etc.; that acts as a p. or in any way as a guide, as *p.-balloon, -engine, -train*, etc.; **p.-bread,** name in the W. Indies for hard or ship biscuit; **-cloth,** an indigo-blue woollen cloth, used for greatcoats, etc.; **-coat** = PEA-JACKET; **-jack,** the 'jack' surrounded by a white border, a signal for a p.; **-jacket** = PEA-JACKET; **-light,** a small permanent light used to ignite gas at a burner; **-snake,** (*a*) a large N. Amer. snake, *Coluber obsoletus*; (*b*) the pine-snake, *Pituophis melanoleucus*; (*c*) the copper-head; **-water** (also **pilot's water**), a piece of water in which a pilot must be employed; **-whale,** the round-headed porpoise or ca'ing whale. Hence **Pi·lotism,** the practice of a p.; pilotage. **Pi·lotless** *a.* (of an aeroplane), not having a p.

Pi·lot, *v.* 1649. [f. prec., after Fr. *piloter.*] **1.** *trans.* To conduct as a pilot; to steer, guide 1693. **2.** *transf.* and *fig.* To guide through unknown or dangerous paths or places, or through a difficult course of affairs; to conduct as a 'pilot' in the hunting-field 1649. **3.** To act as pilot on, in, or over (a course, etc.) 1725.

3. Morn and eve, night and day, Have I piloted your bay BROWNING.

Pilotage (pəi·lətėdʒ). 1618. [– Fr. *pilotage* (XVI), f. *piloter*; see prec., -AGE.] **1.** The action or practice of piloting; the function or office of a pilot; pilotship. Also *transf.* and *fig.* **2.** The charge for piloting; pilotage dues 1622. **3.** *attrib.*, as *p. certificate*, etc. 1830.

Pi·lot-bird. 1678. [f. PILOT *sb.* + BIRD.] A name for: †**a.** A sea-bird of the W. Indies; **b.** An Australian bird, *Pycnoptilus floccosus.*

a. The *P. Bird*, a certain Bird about the Caribe Islands, which gives notice to Ships that sail that way, when they come near any of those Islands 1678.

Pi·lot-boat. 1588. A boat in which pilots cruise off shore in order to meet incoming vessels.

Pi·lot-fish. 1634. [f. PILOT *sb.* + FISH *sb.*[1]] **1.** A small carangoid fish of warm seas, *Naucrates ductor*, reputed to act as a guide to the shark. **2.** A general term for the *Carangidæ*, as the rudder-fish (*Seriola zonata*) 1792.

Pilous (pəi·ləs), *a.* 1658. [f. L. *pilosus*, f. *pilus* hair; see PILE *sb.*[4], -OUS.] Characterized by or abounding in hair; consisting of hair; hairy, pilose.

Pilular (pi·liŭlăɹ), *a.* 1802. [f. PILULE + -AR[1].] Of or pertaining to pills; of the nature of a pill or pills.

Pilule (pi·liul). late ME. [– Fr. *pilule* – L. *pilula*, dim. of *pila* ball; see PILL *sb.*[2], -ULE.] A pill; a small pill.

Pilulous (pi·liŭləs), *a.* 1872. [f. PILULE + -OUS.] Resembling a pill; pill-like, minute.

Pily (pəi·li), *a.*[1] 1638. [f. PILE *sb.*[1] + -Y[5].] *Her.* Divided into a number of piles, the number and direction usu. being indicated.

Pily (pəi·li), *a.*[2] 1533. [f. PILE *sb.*[4] + -Y[1].] Having a pile or nap; of the nature of a pile.

Pimaric (pimæ·rik, pəi-), *a.* 1857. [mod. f. *Pi*(*nus mar*(*itima* + -IC; in Fr. *pimarique.*] *Chem.* In *p. acid*, an acid resin ($C_{20}H_{30}O_2$) occurring in the turpentine of *Pinus maritima.*

Pimelic (pime·lik), *a.* 1838. [f. Gr. πιμελή fat + -IC.] *Chem.* In *P. acid*, an acid ($C_7H_{12}O_4$) obtained in small crystalline grains by the action of nitric acid on various fatty substances.

Pimelite (pi·mĕləit). 1808. [Named by Karsten, 1800; f. as prec. + -ITE[1] 2 b.] *Min.* A hydrous silicate of aluminium, iron, nickel, and magnesium, of apple-green colour, greasy in appearance and to the touch.

Pimento (pime·nto). 1690. [– Sp. *pimiento* – L. *pigmentum* PIGMENT, in med.L. spice, spiced drink.] †**1.** Formerly, Cayenne or Guinea pepper –1697. **2.** Now, The dried aromatic berries of the tree *Eugenia pimenta* (see 3); also called *Jamaica pepper* or *allspice* 1690. **3.** The tree which yields this spice, *Eugenia pimenta* or *Pimenta officinalis* (N.O. *Myrtaceæ*), an evergreen, much cultivated in Jamaica; also, its wood 1756.

Pimlico (pi·mliko). 1848. [imit., from the cry of the bird.] The Australian friar-bird.

Pimp (pimp), *sb.* 1607. [Of unkn. origin.] A pander, procurer. Hence **Pimp** *v. intr.* to act as p.; to pander.

Pimpernel (pi·mpəɹnĕl). late ME. [– OFr. *pimpernelle* (mod. *pimprenelle*), earlier *piprenelle* – Rom. **piperinella*, f. **piperinus* pepper-like, f. L. *piper* PEPPER, the fruit of the burnet resembling a peppercorn.] †**1.** The Great Burnet, *Sanguisorba officinalis*, and Salad Burnet, *Poterium sanguisorba* –1578. **2.** The common name of *Anagallis arvensis* (N.O. *Primulaceæ*), a small annual with smooth ovate opposite leaves, and scarlet (also blue, or, occas., white) flowers, which close in rainy or cloudy weather; distinctively called *Scarlet Pimpernel.* Hence extended to the whole genus. late ME.

2. Water P., (*a*) the greater and lesser Brooklime, *Veronica beccabunga* and *V. anagallis*; (*b*) Brookweed, *Samolus valerandi* or other species.

Pi·mping, *a.* 1687. [Of unkn. origin.] Small, petty, mean; in poor health or condition, sickly.

Pimple (pi·mp'l), *sb.* late ME. [Nasalized

form corresp. to late OE. *piplian* (in pr. pple.) break out into pustules; parallel to obs. and dial. var. *pumple* (XVI; cf. Fr. †*pompette* 'a pumple, or pimple on the nose, or chinne', Cotgr.); similar forms are L. *papula* pustule, Lith. *papās* nipple.] **1.** A small solid rounded tumour of the skin, usu. inflammatory; a papule or pustule. **2.** *fig.* A small rounded swelling, as a bud, etc. 1582. **3.** *attrib.*, as *p.-faced*, etc. 1607.

1. The distilled water..is good against the freckles, spottes, and pimpels of the face 1578. **2.** He pinches from the second stalk A p., that portends a future sprout COWPER. Hence **Pi·mple** *v.* (now *rare*), to make or become pimply. **Pimpled** (pi·mp'ld), *a.* having, or characterized by, pimples. **Pi·mply** *a.* full of pimples; covered or spotted with pimples.

Pin (pin), *sb.* [Late OE. *pinn*, corresp. to MLG. *pin*, (M)LG., (M)Du. *pinne* (Du. *pin*), OHG. *pfinn* (MHG. *pfinne*), Icel. *pinni* – L. *pinna* applied to various objects likened to a wing or feather, but assoc. in use with *penna* PEN *sb.*[2]] **I.** Primary sense: = *peg*. **1.** A small piece of wood, metal, etc., usu. cylindrical, used to fasten or hold together parts of a structure, to hang something upon, to stop up a hole, etc.; a peg, bolt. **b.** An indicator of a long or pointed shape; as †the index of a balance, etc. 1440. †**c.** A peg fixed in the centre of a target –1642. **d.** = PEG *sb.*[1] 2 a. 1587. **e.** = PEG *sb.*[1] 2 b. 1592. **f.** *Naut.* (*a*) A thole-pin. (*b*) Applied to various pegs or bolts used in a ship, e.g. to make fast the rigging (BELAYING-*pins*), etc. 1832. **g.** *Carpentry.* The tenon of a dovetail joint 1847. **h.** *Quoits.* The peg at which the quoit is aimed 1857. **i.** *Golf.* An iron rod bearing a small flag, to mark the position of a hole 1901. †**2.** *fig.* That on which something hangs or depends. late ME.

1. Oak is excellent for..pinns and peggs for tyling, &c. EVELYN. **e.** No jovial din Of drinking Wassail to the p. LONGF.

II. = ME. and Sc. *preen*, Fr. *épingle*. **1.** A slender piece of wire (now usu. of brass or iron, tinned), with a sharp tapered point and a flattened round head, used for fastening together parts of dress, loose papers, etc., and for various purposes. Also applied to larger articles of the same kind made of steel, gold, silver, etc. See also DRAWING-*pin*, HAIRPIN, HAT-*pin*, SAFETY PIN, etc. (The most frequent use.) late ME. **b.** *allusively.* Something very small, or of little value ME. **2.** *transf.* The incipient bur or blossom of the hop 1900.

1. He that will not stoop for a p. will never be worth a pound PEPYS. Phr. *Pins and needles* (colloq.): the pricking or tingling sensation felt in a limb after numbness. *On pins and needles*: in a state of excessive uneasiness. **b.** Phr. *Not worth a p., not to care a p.*, etc. So *Pin's head, pin's point.*

III. (Cf. med.L. *pinna*, Du. *pinne* pinnacle.) **1.** A point, peak, apex. *Obs.* exc. *dial.* 1450. **2.** The projecting bone of the hip, esp. in horses or cattle. Now *dial.* 1703.

IV. Transf. uses. **1.** A leg; usu. in *pl. colloq.* or *dial.* 1530. **2.** A skittle; in *pl.* the game of skittles 1580. †**3.** A knot in wood –1585. **4.** A small cask or keg holding half a firkin, or 4½ gallons 1570. †**5.** A piece at chess, etc. –1784. **6.** Short for ROLLING-*pin*, KNITTING-*pin*, etc. 1894.

1. I never saw a fellow better set upon his pins 1781. **5.** The Queene is the next p. in height to the King 1688.

V. Phraseological uses. **1.** In the phrase *in a merry p.*, in a merry humour or frame of mind. *arch.* or *dial.* late ME. †**2.** Pitch; degree; step; esp. with *higher, lower, utmost, raise, take down.* (Orig. taken from a musical tuning-peg; see I. 1 d.) –1776. **3.** Phr. To *put in the p.* (*colloq.* or *slang*): to call a halt; *esp.* to give up drinking. So *to let loose a p.* 1832.

1. Right glad to find His friend in merry p. COWPER.

attrib. and *Comb.*, as **p.-buttock**, a narrow or sharp buttock; **p. connection**, a connection of the parts of an iron or steel bridge by pins (instead of rivets, etc.; cf. *pin-joint*); **p.-drill**, a drill with a projecting central pin surrounded by a cutting face, used for countersinking, etc.; **-dust**, dust formed of filings of brass or other metal produced in the manufacture of pins; **-joint**, a form of joint in which two parts are connected by a pin passing through an eye in each; **-spot**, each of a number of round spots like pins' heads forming a pattern upon a textile fabric; **-stripe**, a narrow ornamental stripe of the thickness of a pin; hence **p.-striped** *a.*; **p. switch** (*Telegr.*), a switch in which electric connection is made by pins passing through holes in metal plates; **-worm**, a small thread-worm, *Oxyuris vermicularis*, which infests the rectum, esp. in children.

Pin (pin), *v.* ME. [In branch I. f. prec. In branch II. perh. worn down from PIND *v.*] **I.** To transfix, etc., with a pin. **1.** *trans.* To fasten (things *together*) with one or more pins, pegs, or bolts. **2.** To fasten with a pin, or with a brooch, hairpin, or hat-pin; to transfix with a pin; also with a lance or the like. late ME. **3.** *fig.* To attach firmly *to* a person, or ostentatiously *to* or *on* his SLEEVE; to make absolutely dependent or contingent *on* a person or thing; to append, fix, tack on. Now *rare.* 1579. **4.** *transf.* To hold (a man or animal) *down* or *against* something by force; to seize and hold fast 1814. **5.** *fig.* To hold or bind (a person) strictly *to* a promise, etc.; often with *down* 1710.

1. Great peeces of tymber pinned together 1579. **2.** The wardrobe woman was pinning up the Queen's hair MME. D'ARBLAY. The first object is to p. the insect 1852. **3.** Phr. *To p. one's faith upon, on* (a thing, or person, or his SLEEVE), to place entire or openly professed trust or belief in. **4.** While I pinned his arms from behind, Mr. Taylor seized his whip 1859. **5.** One of those pestilent fellows that p. a man down to facts W. IRVING.

II. Cf. PIND *v.* **1.** To enclose by or as by means of bolts or bars; to hem in, shut *up*; *spec.* to put in a pinfold, impound (a beast). late ME. †**2.** To confine, restrict –1638.

1. Pinn'd like a flock, and fleeced too in their fold BYRON.

‖**Piña** (pī·nʸă). 1577. [S. Amer. Sp., (formerly *pinna*), Pg. *pinha* pineapple, orig. pine-cone (– L. *pinea*).] †**1.** (Spelt *pina, pinna, pinia.*) The pineapple –1622. **2.** Pineapple leaf fibres; a fine fabric made of these, also called **p.-cloth, p.-muslin** 1858.

Pinacoid, pinakoid (pi·năkoid), *a.* and *sb.* 1876. [f. Gr. πίναξ, πινακ- slab; see -OID.] **A.** *adj.* Applied to any plane, in a crystallographic system, intersecting one of the axes of co-ordinates and parallel to the other two 1895. **B.** *sb.* A pinacoid plane, or a group of such planes constituting a 'form'.

Pinacolin (pinæ·kŏlin). 1866. [f. next + -OL + -IN[1].] *Chem.* A colourless oily liquid ($C_6H_{12}O$), having an odour of peppermint, variously produced from pinacone.

Pinacone (pi·năkoᵘn). 1866. [f. Gr. πίναξ, πινακ- tablet + -ONE.] *Chem.* A white crystalline substance ($C_6H_{14}O_2$), crystallizing in large tablets, produced by the action of sodium or sodium-amalgam on aqueous acetone.

‖**Pinacotheca** (pi:năkoþī·kă). Also **pi·nacothe:k** (-þek). 1624. [L. – Gr. πινακοθήκη, f. πίναξ, πινακ- tablet, picture + θήκη repository.] A place for the keeping and exhibition of works of art.

Pinafore (pi·năfoᵊɹ), *sb.* 1782. [f. PIN *v.* + AFORE, because orig. pinned upon the dress in front.] A covering of washable material worn by children or others over the frock or gown, to protect it from being soiled. Hence **Pi·nafored** *a.* attired in a p.

Pinaster (pəinæ·stəɹ). 1562. [– L. *pinaster*, f. *pinus* PINE *sb.*[2]; see -ASTER.] *Bot.* A species of pine indigenous to south-western Europe.

‖**Pinax** (pi·næks). *Pl.* **pinaces** (pi·năsīz); also **pinakes.** 1682. [Late L. – Gr. πίναξ tablet, etc.] †**1.** A tablet; hence a list, register, etc. inscribed on a tablet; a catalogue, index –1785. **2.** *Antiq.* A plate, platter, or dish; *esp.* one with anything painted or engraved on it 1857.

‖**Pince-nez** (pęns,ne). 1880. [Fr., f. *pincer* PINCH + *nez* nose.] A pair of eye-glasses with a spring which clips the nose.

Pincers (pi·nsəɹz), *sb. pl.* [ME. pl. *pinsers, -ours* – AFr. **pincers, -ours*, f. OFr. *pincier*; see PINCH *v.*, -ER[2].] **1.** A tool for grasping or nipping anything, consisting of two limbs pivoted together, forming a pair of jaws with a pair of handles or levers by which they can be pressed tightly together. (Usu. *a pair of pincers*; rarely *a pincers.*) **2.** An organ (or pair of organs), in various animals, resembling pincers, and used for grasping or tearing; as the chelæ of crustaceans, etc. 1658. Hence **Pi·ncer** *v. trans.* to compress with or as with pincers; to torture with or as with pincers.

Pinch (pinʃ), *sb.* 1489. [f. next.] **I. 1.** An act of pinching; a firm compression between the finger and thumb or two surfaces; a nip, a squeeze; †a bite 1591. **2.** *fig.* Pressure (usu. of want, etc.); difficulty, hardship 1605. †**3.** The pang of death, or of remorse, shame, etc. –1681. **4.** A strait, exigency, extremity. Now usu. in phr. *at* (*on*) *a p.* 1489. **b.** The crucial point of a matter. Now *rare.* 1639.

1. The stroke of death is as a Louers p. SHAKS. **2.** Necessities sharpe p. SHAKS. **3.** *Temp.* V. i. 77. **4.** But that Apprehension appeared Groundless when it came to the p. 1681. **b.** The very P. of the Argument 1720.

II. A place or part at which something is pinched. †**1.** A pleat or gather, in a skirt, etc. **b.** A bend or fold in the brim of a hat. –1860. **2.** A steep or difficult part of a road. Now *dial.* 1754. **III.** As much of something (esp. snuff) as may be taken with the tips of the finger and thumb; hence *fig.* a very small quantity 1583. **IV.** A crow-bar 1816.

Pinch (pinʃ), *v.* ME. [– AFr., ONFr. **pinchier*, var. of OFr. *pincier* (mod. *pincer*) :– Rom. **pinctiare*, alt. of **punctiare* (see PUNCHEON[1]).] **I. 1.** *trans.* To compress between the tips of the finger and thumb, with the teeth, an instrument, etc.; to nip, squeeze. (The principal literal sense.) Also *absol.* or *intr.* **b.** Said of a tight shoe, etc. which presses painfully upon the part which it covers. (Usu. *absol.* or *intr.*) late ME. **c.** *pass.* To be jammed between two solid objects so as to be crushed 1896. **2.** With *adv.* or *compl.* To bring or get into some state or position by pinching ME. **b.** *Hort.* To nip off part of (a shoot). With *out, back, down.* 1693. **c.** To force out by compression, squeeze out; *fig.* to extort, 'squeeze' (money) *from* or *out of* a person 1770. †**3.** To seize, compress, or snap with the teeth. Often *absol.* –1700. †**4.** Said of actions causing a painful bodily sensation: To pain, torture, torment –1607. **5.** Said of the action of cold, hunger, exhaustion, or wasting disease: including the painful physical sensations and often the mental affliction. In ref. to plants: To nip, to cause to shrivel up. 1548.

1. b. Phr. *To know where the shoes pinches*, i.e. to know (by direct experience) the cause of a trouble or difficulty. (Usu. *absol.* or *intr.*) **c.** He was pinched between the train and the platform 1899. **3.** *3 Hen. VI*, II. i. 16. **5.** Pinched with pouertie & aduersitie 1581. The polyanthuses were a little pinched by the easterly winds 1772.

II. In non-physical and fig. senses. **1.** To straiten; to afflict, harass. *Obs.* exc. as *fig.* from I. 1 or 5. 1548. Also *intr.* or *absol.* †**2.** *intr.* **a.** To encroach *on*; **b.** to put stress *upon* –1734. **3.** †**a.** To be close-fisted, meanly parsimonious, or miserly; to drive hard bargains –1617. **b.** *trans.* To stint; to give barely, or with short measure or weight; to give grudgingly. Now *dial.* 1530. Also *intr.* in refl. or pass. sense. 1549. **4.** *trans.* To restrict narrowly. Now *rare* or *Obs.* 1570. **b.** To reduce to straits (in argument, etc.); to 'put in a tight place'. Now *rare.* 1692.

3. b. I am..pinched for time COWPER. *intr.* I'm forc'd to p., for the Times are hard SWIFT. **4.** That doctrine which pincheth our liberty within so narrow bounds 1677.

III. Technical and slang. **1. a.** *Racing.* To press (a horse); to exhaust by urging 1737. **b.** *Naut.* To sail (a vessel) close-hauled 1895. **2.** *intr. Mining.* Of a vein, etc.: To become narrow or thin; with *out*, to come to an end 1872. **3.** *trans.* **a.** To purloin (a thing); to rob (a person). *slang.* 1673. **b.** To take into custody. *slang.* 1860.

Pinch- in Comb. [chiefly the imperative or vb.-stem; sometimes the sb.]: **P.-bar** = PINCH *sb.* IV.; **-cock** *Mech.*, a clamp used to compress a flexible or elastic tube so as to regulate the flow of liquid, etc.,; **-fist**, a niggard, miser; †**-gut**, one who stints himself or others of food; also *attrib.*

Pinchbeck (pi·nʃbek), *sb.* (*a.*) 1734. [f. Christopher *Pinchbeck*, the inventor, a watchmaker (died 1732).] **1.** An alloy of about five parts of copper with one of zinc, resembling

gold: used in clock-making, cheap jewellery, etc. **2.** *fig.* As a type of what is counterfeit or spurious 1859. **3.** *attrib.* or *adj.* **a.** Made of pinchbeck 1746. **b.** Spurious; sham 1850.
2. Those golden locks were only p. THACKERAY.

Pinched (pinʃt), *ppl. a.* 1530. [f. PINCH *v.* + -ED[1].] **1.** Compressed between the finger and thumb, or two opposing bodies; nipped, squeezed; shaped as if compressed. **2.** Said in ref. to the physical effects of cold, hunger, pain, or old age 1614. **3.** Straitened in extent 1649; straitened in circumstances 1716.

Pincher (pi·nʃəɹ). 1440. [f. PINCH *v.* + -ER[1].] **1.** One who or that which pinches; *fig.* a miser; a haggler. **2.** An instrument for pinching or grasping; in pl. *pinchers* often = PINCERS 1575.

Pinching (pi·nʃiŋ), *vbl. sb.* 1440. [f. PINCH *v.* + -ING[1].] The action of PINCH *v.*, in various senses. **1.** Nipping, squeezing, pressure 1693. **2.** The sensation caused by pinching or gripping; the pressure of pain. Also *fig.* 1495. **3.** Parsimony 1440.
Comb.: **p.-bar** = *pinch-bar* (PINCH-); **-nut** = *jam-nut* (JAM *sb.*[1]).

Pinc-pinc (pi·ŋkpiŋk). 1868. [imit.] A South-African warbler, *Drymœca* or *Cisticola textrix*.

Pincushion (pi·nku:ʃən). 1632. A small cushion used for sticking pins in, to keep them ready for use.

Pind, *v. Obs.* exc. *dial.* [OE. (*ġe*)*pyndan*, f. **pund* POUND *sb.*[2] See also PINFOLD *sb.*, POND, POIND *v.*] *trans.* To shut up, enclose; to dam up (water) –1483. **b.** *spec.* To put (beasts) in a pound, to impound ME.

‖**Pi·nda, pi·ndar.** 1707. [– Pg. *pinda* – Congo *mpinda*, Mpongwe *mbenda*; carried by Negroes to America.] W. Indian and Southern U.S. for the ground-nut or pea-nut (*Arachis hypogæa*).

‖**Pindari** (pindā·ri), *sb.* (*a.*) 1788. [– Hindustani *pinḍārī*, *pinḍārā*, for Marathi *penḍhārī*; perh. from a place-name *Panḍhār*.] **1.** One of a body of mounted marauders who arose in Central India in the 17th c. Also as *adj.* **2.** The dialect of these and their descendants 1901.

Pindaric (pindæ·rik), *a.* and *sb.* 1640. [– L. *Pindaricus* – Gr. Πινδαρικός, f. Πίνδαρος Pindar.] **A.** *adj.* Of or pertaining to the poet Pindar; written, writing, etc., in the style of Pindar. **B.** *sb.* An ode, poem, metre, or form of verse, in imitation of Pindar. Chiefly in *pl.* 1685.
A. Those admirable English Authors who call themselves Pindarick Writers ADDISON. **B.** A Pindarick on the Death of Our Late Sovereign 1685. So †**Pinda·rical** *a.* Pindaric. **Pi·ndarism,** imitation of Pindar. **Pi·ndarist,** a writer of P. verses.

Pinder (pi·ndəɹ). ME. [f. PIND *v.* + -ER[1].] An officer of a manor who impounds stray beasts.

Pine (pəin), *sb.*[1] *Obs.* or *arch.* [Early ME. *pīne* :- OE. **pīne* = OS., OHG. *pīna* (Du. *pijne*, *pijn*, G. *pein*), ON. *pína*, Gmc. – med. L. *pena*, L. *pœna*.] †**1.** Punishment; torment, torture; *spec.* the penal sufferings of hell or purgatory. †**2.** = PAIN *sb.*[1] 3. –1600. **b.** = PAIN *sb.*[1] 4. *Obs.* or *arch.* ME. †**3.** The condition of pining for food; famine; want; starvation –1725.
1. Of Proserpyne That quene ys of the derke pyne CHAUCER.

Pine (pəin), *sb.*[2] [OE. *pīn* – L. *pinus*, coalescing in ME. with adoption of (O)Fr. *pin* from the same source.] **1.** A tree of the genus *Pinus*, or of various allied coniferous genera, having evergreen needle-shaped leaves, of which many species afford valuable timber, and some have edible seeds. **b.** The wood of these trees. late ME. **2.** With qualifying words, applied to various species of *Pinus* or other coniferous genera (or to their wood) 1731. **b.** Also applied to plants of other orders, resembling the true pine in some respect: e.g. certain species of *Lycopodium* or Club Moss (Festoon Pine, *L. rupestre*; Moonfruit Pine, *L. lucidulum*; etc.) 1760. **3.** *transf.* Something made of pine-wood: e.g. a torch, a ship, a mast. Chiefly *poet.* 1586. **4.** = PINEAPPLE 2. 1661. **5.** A figure of a pineapple or pine-cone 1790.
1. His Spear, to equal which the tallest P., Hewn on Norwegian hills,..were but a wand MILT. **2. Norfolk Island P.,** *Araucaria excelsa*; **Norway P.,** (*a*) the Spruce Fir, *Abies* (*Picea*) *excelsa*; (*b*) (in U.S.) the N. American Red Pine, *Pinus resinosa*; (*c*) a variety of the timber of *Pinus sylvestris*; **Nut-pine** (see NUT); **Red P.,** (*a*) *Pinus resinosa* of N. America; (*b*) (of Australia) *Frenela endlicheri*; (*c*) (of New Zealand) *Dacrydium cupressinum*; also the timber = *Riga pine*; **Riga P.,** a variety of the timber of *Pinus sylvestris*; **Scotch P.,** *Pinus sylvestris*, commonly called *Scotch* FIR; **Sugar P.,** *Pinus lambertiana* of California, which yields a sweet resin used for sugar; **White P.,** various species with light-coloured wood, esp. the Norway pine or Spruce, *Pinus strobus* of N. America, and species of *Frenela* and *Podocarpus* of Australia, etc.
attrib. and *Comb.*, as *p.-bark*, *-plantation*, etc.; **p.-beetle,** any one of various small beetles destructive to the bark or wood of pines; **-cone,** the cone or fruit of the pine-tree; **-drops,** the N. Amer. plant *Pterospora andromedea*, parasitic on the roots of pine-trees; **-finch,** (*a*) = *pine grosbeak*; (*b*) = *pine-siskin*; **p. grosbeak,** a large finch, *Pinicola enucleator*, inhabiting pine-woods in Europe and N. America; **p. gum,** a resin resembling sandarach, obtained from Australian trees of the genus *Callitris* or *Frenela*; **p. hawk-moth,** a species of hawk-moth, *Sphinx pinastri*, whose larva feeds on the pine-tree; **-lizard,** the common brown lizard of N. America, *Sceloporos undulatus*; **-marten** (see MARTEN); **-needle,** the needle-shaped leaf of the p.; **-oil,** name for various oils obtained from the leaves, twigs, wood, or resin of pine-trees; **-sap,** a reddish fleshy plant, *Monotropa hypopitys*, formerly supposed to be parasitic on the roots of pine-trees; **-siskin,** a small N. American siskin or finch, *Chrysomitris pinus*, found in pine-woods; **-snake,** a large harmless snake of the N. Amer. genus *Pityophis*, found in pine-woods.

Pine (pəin), *v.* [OE. *pīnian*, corresp. to MLG., MDu. *pīnen* (Du. *pijnen*), OHG. *pīnōn* (G. *peinen*), ON. *pína*; rel. to PINE *sb.*[1]] †**1.** *trans.* To afflict with pain or suffering; to torment, trouble, distress. Also *absol.* –1724. **2.** To exhaust or consume (a person, animal, etc.) by suffering of body or mind; to cause to languish; to wear out, emaciate; to deprive or stint of food, to starve. Also with *away*, *to death*, etc. Now *rare* exc. *dial.* ME. **3.** *intr.* To languish, waste away, esp. from intense grief, etc., wasting disease, or want of sustenance 1440. **b.** *transf.* Of things: To lose bulk, vigour, or intensity; to languish 1727. **c.** *trans.* with *away* or *out*: To spend (life, health, etc.) in pining 1725. **4.** *intr.* To long eagerly; to languish with intense desire. Const. *for*, *after*, or *inf.* 1592. **5.** To repine, fret 1687. **b.** *trans.* To mourn (*arch.*) 1667. **6.** *Sc.* To cause (fish) to shrink in the process of curing 1560.
1. O tell him..how my soule is pin'd 1635. **3.** He ten times pines, that pines beholding food SHAKS. They generally p. away..and die in a short time GOLDSM. **c.** Barristers pining a hungry life out in chambers THACKERAY. **4.** Who died there pining for their native home 1748. **5. b.** We..see, and p. our loss SWINBURNE.

Pineal (pi·niăl, pəi·niăl), *a.* 1681. [– Fr. *pinéal*, f. L. *pinea* pine-cone; see -AL[1].] *Anat.* Resembling a pine-cone in shape: applied to a small somewhat conical body (the *p. body* or *p. gland*), situated behind the third ventricle of the brain, and containing sand-like particles. **b.** Pertaining to or connected with the pineal body, as *p. eye*, *ventricle* 1888.

Pineapple, pine-apple (pəi·nˌæ:p'l). late ME. [f. PINE *sb.*[2] + APPLE.] **1.** The fruit of the pine-tree; a pine-cone. *Obs.* exc. *dial.* **b.** A figure or image of a pine-cone 1483. **2.** The large collective fruit of the ananas, *Ananassa sativa*; so called from its resemblance to a pine-cone. **b.** The plant which bears this, a native of tropical South America. 1664.

Pi·ne-ba:rren. *U.S.* 1737. [f. PINE *sb.*[2] + BARREN *sb.* 2 a.] A level sandy tract of land, scantily covered with pinetrees, chiefly in the Southern States.

Pinery (pəi·nəri). 1758. [f. PINE *sb.*[2] + -ERY.] **1.** A place in which pineapples are grown. **2.** A plantation of pine-trees 1831.

Pine-tree. OE. = PINE *sb.*[2] 1.
attrib. **Pine-tree State,** Maine, U.S., so called from its extensive pine-forests.

‖**Pinetum** (pəinī·tŏm). *Pl.* **-a, -ums.** 1842. [L., 'pine-grove', f. *pinus* PINE *sb.*[2]] A plantation or collection of pine-trees of various species, for scientific or ornamental purposes.

Pi·ne-wood. 1813. [f. PINE *sb.*[2] + WOOD *sb.*] **1.** The wood of the pine-tree 1815. **2.** A wood or forest of pines.

Piney (pəi·ni), **pinnay** (pi·neⁱ). Also **piny.** 1857. [– Tamil *pinnai* or *punnai*, in Skr. *punnāga*.] Name of two E. Indian resinous trees, *Calophyllum inophyllum* (N.O. *Clusiaceæ*), called also **piney-tree,** and *Vateria indica* (N.O. *Dipteraceæ*), used *attrib.*, as in **piney dammar, resin, varnish,** the resin obtained from *Vateria indica*, also called *white dammar*, *Indian* or *Malabar copal*, or *gum animé*; **piney oil, piney tallow,** a fatty or waxy substance from the fruit of the same tree, used in making candles.

Pin-eyed (pi·nˌəi:d), *a.* 1810. [f. PIN *sb.* + EYED *ppl. a.*] Applied to the long-styled form of a flower (esp. *Primula*), which shows the stigma resembling a pin's head, at the top of the corolla-tube.

Pin-feather (pi·nfe:ðəɹ), *sb.* 1775. [f. PIN *sb.* + FEATHER *sb.*] Any young feather from the time that it first pierces the skin, much in the form of a peg, until it bursts its confining sheath and expands its vanes. Hence **Pi·n-fea:thered** *a.* having immature feathers; also *fig.*

Pi·n-fire, *a.* (*sb.*) 1870. [f. PIN *sb.* + FIRE *v.* Cf. NEEDLE-GUN.] Applied to a form of cartridge for breech-loading guns fitted with a pin which, on being struck by the hammer of the lock, is thrust into the fulminate and explodes it. Also applied to a gun in which this is used.

Pinfold (pi·nfōᵘld), *sb.* [Late OE. *pundfald*, f. **pund* POUND *sb.*[2] + *fald* FOLD *sb.*[1] From *c*1400 assoc. with PIND *v.* and PIN *v.* II.] A place for confining stray or distrained cattle, etc.; a pound; later, occas., a fold for sheep, cattle, etc.
fig. Confin'd, and pester'd in this pin-fold here MILT. Hence **Pi·nfold** *v. trans.* to shut up in a p.; hence *fig.* to confine within narrow limits.

Ping (piŋ), *sb.* 1856. [imit.] An abrupt ringing sound, such as that made by a rifle bullet in flying through the air, by a mosquito, etc. So **Ping** *v. intr.* to make such a sound.

Pingle (pi·ŋg'l). *Obs.* exc. *dial.* 1523. [Of unkn. origin. Cf. PIGHTLE.] A small enclosed piece of land; a paddock, a close.

Ping-pong (pi·ŋpǫŋ). 1900. [imit.] A parlour game resembling lawn-tennis, played on a table with bats and celluloid balls; so called from the 'ping' of the bat when striking.

Pinguedinous (piŋgwe·dinəs), *a.* 1599. [f. L. *pinguedo*, *-din-* fatness (f. *pinguis* fat) + -OUS.] Fatty.

Pinguefy (pi·ŋgwĭfəi), *v.* Now *rare.* 1597. [– L. *pinguefacere*, f. *pinguis* fat; see -FY.] **1.** *trans.* To cause to become fat or greasy; also to make (soil) rich or fertile 1599. †**2.** *intr.* To become fat –1825.

Pinguescent (piŋgwe·sĕnt), *a.* 1797. [– *pinguescent-*, pr. ppl. stem of L *pinguescere* become fat, f. *pinguis* fat; see -ESCENT.] Becoming or growing fat, fattening. So **Pingue·scence** (*rare*).

‖**Pinguicula** (piŋgwi·kiŭlă). 1597. [L. fem. (sc. *planta*) of *pinguiculus*, dim. of *pinguis* fat; see -CULE.] **1.** *Bot.* = BUTTERWORT. **2.** *Path.* A small blotch or growth of the conjunctiva, usu. near the edge of the cornea 1858.

Pinguid (pi·ŋgwid), *a.* Now usu. *joc.* or *affected.* 1635. [f. L. *pinguis* fat; see -ID[1]. Cf. GRAVID.] Of the nature of, resembling, or abounding in fat; unctuous, greasy, oily; (of soil) rich, fertile. Also *transf.* and *fig.* Hence **Pingui·dity,** fatness, fatty matter.

Pinguin (pi·ŋgwin). 1696. [Of unkn. origin.] A W. Indian plant (*Bromelia pinguin*) or its fruit; used in fevers and as an anthelmintic.

Pin-head (pi·nhed). 1662. [f. PIN *sb.* + HEAD *sb.*] The head of a pin. Used as a type of something of very small size or value, etc. **b.** *attrib.* Resembling a pin's head; very small and of rounded form 1835.
b. His sharp-nose and pin-head eyes O. W. HOLMES.

Pin-hole (pi·nhōᵘl). 1676. **1.** A hole into

which a pin or peg fits 1677. **2.** A hole made by a pin; any very small aperture or perforation 1676. **3.** *attrib.* (in sense 2). Of the nature of a p. or very small aperture; of the size of a pin-prick 1853.

P. camera, one with a minute hole instead of a lens.

Pinic (pəi·nik), *a.* 1831. [– Fr. *pinique*, f. L. *pinus* PINE *sb.*[2]; see -IC.] *Chem.* Of, pertaining to, or derived from the pine-tree; spec. in *p. acid*, an acid ($C_{20}H_{30}O_2$) obtained from pine resin.

Pinion (pi·nyən), *sb.*[1] ME. [– OFr. *pignon* pl. wing-feathers, wings (now only, gable) :– Rom. **pinnio*, *-on-*, augm. of L. *pinna* PIN *sb.* See PENNON.] **1.** The distal or terminal segment of a bird's wing; hence (chiefly *poet.* or *rhet.*) a wing (always with ref. to its use for flight) 1440. **b.** *Carving.* The part of a wing corresponding to the fore-arm; formerly applied to the whole wing 1655. **2.** *fig.* (In ref. to things poetically represented as having wings.) 1602. **3.** The outermost feather, or any flight-feather, of a bird's wing 1545. **4.** The anterior border of an insect's wing 1720.

1. First a speck, and then a vulture, Till the air is dark with pinions LONGF. **2.** Hope humbly then; with trembling pinions soar POPE. Hence **Pi·nioned** *a.* having pinions or wings; winged.

Pinion (pi·nyən), *sb.*[2] 1659. [– (O)Fr. *pignon*, alt. of †*pignol* :– Rom. **pineolus*, f. L. *pinea* pine-cone, f. *pinus* PINE *sb.*[2]] *Mech.* A small cog-wheel the teeth of which engage with those of a larger one; also a spindle, arbor, or axle, having cogs or teeth which engage with the teeth of a wheel.

P. and rack, also *rack and p.*: see RACK *sb.*[2]

Pinion (pi·nyən), *v.* 1558. [f. PINION *sb.*[1]] **1.** *trans.* To cut off the pinion of one wing, or otherwise disable the wings, in order to prevent a bird from flying. (With the bird, or the wing, as obj.) 1577. **2.** To bind the arms of any one; to disable by so binding; to shackle. (With the person, or the arms, as obj.) 1558. **b.** To bind fast *to* something, or together 1652.

2. *transf.* Yon ancient prude . . Her elbows pinioned close upon her hips COWPER.

Pinite[1] (pi·n-, pəi·nəit). 1805. [– G. *pinit* (Karsten, 1800), from its locality, the Pini mine, Schneeberg, Saxony: see -ITE[1] 2 b.] *Min.* A hydrous silicate of aluminium and potassium, occurring in various crystalline forms.

Pinite[2] (pəi·nəit). 1857. [– Fr. *pinite*, f. L. *pinus* PINE *sb.*[2]; see -ITE[1] 4 a.] *Chem.* A crystallizable saccharine substance ($C_6H_{12}O_{10}$) obtained from the sap of two species of pine-tree, *Pinus lambertiana* and *P. sabiniana*.

Pink (piŋk), *sb.*[1] Now chiefly *Hist.* 1471. [– MDu. *pin(c)ke*, small sea-going vessel, fishing-boat (whence also Fr. *pinque*, Sp. *pinque*, It. *pinco*), of unkn. origin.] A sailing-vessel: orig. one of small size, flat-bottomed and having bulging sides; later, applied to warships, etc. *Comb.* **p.-stern**, a stern like that of a p.; hence, a small vessel having a narrow stern.

Pink (piŋk), *sb.*[2], **penk** (peŋk). 1490. [Of unkn. origin.] **1.** A minnow. Now *dial.* **2.** A young salmon before it becomes a smolt; a samlet, parr 1533.

Pink (piŋk), *sb.*[3] 1512. [f. PINK *v.*[1]] †**1.** A hole or eyelet punched in a garment for decorative purposes; also, scalloping done for the same purpose –1632. †**2.** A stab with a poniard, etc. –1638. **b.** A shot-wound 1885.

Pink, *sb.*[4] and *a.* 1573. [perh. short for *pink-eye* (see PINK-EYED *a.*[1]); cf. synon. Fr. *œillet*, dim. of *œil* eye.] **A.** *sb.* **I. 1.** General name of various species of *Dianthus* (N.O. *Caryophyllaceæ*), esp. of *D. plumarius*, a garden plant with very numerous varieties, having pure white, pink, crimson, or variegated sweet-smelling flowers. **b.** Applied with qualifying words to other species of *Dianthus*, and to other plants allied to or resembling the pink 1573. **2.** *fig.* The 'flower' of excellence; the embodied perfection (*of* some good quality) 1592. **b.** The most perfect condition or degree *of* something; the height, extreme 1767. †**c.** A beauty; an exquisite –1827.

1. b. China or **Chinese P.**, *Dianthus chinensis*; see CHINA *sb.*; **Clove P.**, *D. caryophyllus*; see CLOVE *sb.*[2]; **Maiden, Maidenly,** or **Meadow P.**, *Dianthus deltoides*; **Pheasant's eye P.** = PHEASANT'S EYE 3; **Sea P.**, Thrift, *Statice armeria*; **Wild P.**, any wild species of *Dianthus*. **2.** Nay, I am the very pinck of curtesie SHAKS. **b.** In the very p. of the mode THACKERAY. Phr. *In the p.*, in perfect health (*colloq.* or *slang*).

II. sb. use of B. **1.** A light or pale red colour with a slight purple tinge 1846. **2.** Scarlet when worn by fox-hunters; a scarlet hunting-coat, or the cloth of which it is made 1834. **b.** *transf.* A fox-hunter 1828.

2. Although not in p., [I] was the best mounted man in the field DISRAELI.

B. *adj.* [orig. attrib. use of sense I. 1 of the sb.] **1.** Of the colour of the pink (sense I. 1) in its single natural state; of a pale or light red colour, slightly inclining towards purple; of a pale rose-colour 1720. **2.** Applied to the colour of a hunting-coat 1857.

Comb.: **p. salt,** the ammonium salt of tetrachloride of tin, $2\,NH_4Cl.SnCl_4$, used in calico-printing; **p. saucer,** a saucer containing a pigment used to give a pink tint to the skin, or to garments; *transf.* the pigment itself. Hence **Pi·nkish** *a.* somewhat p. **Pi·nkness,** the quality or state of being p.

Pink, *sb.*[5] 1634. [Of unkn. origin.] A yellowish or greenish-yellow pigment or 'lake' obtained by the combination of a vegetable colouring matter with some white base, as a metallic oxide; as *Brown p.*, *French p.*, *Dutch*, *English*, *Italian p.*

Pink, *a.*: see PINK *sb.*[4] B.

Pink (piŋk), *v.*[1] ME. [perh. of LDu. origin (cf. LG. *pinken* strike, peck).] **1.** *intr.* To make holes; to prick, thrust, stab. Now *rare.* **2.** *trans.* To pierce, prick, or stab with any pointed weapon or instrument 1598. **3.** To ornament (cloth, leather, etc.) by cutting or punching eyelet-holes, figures, etc.; to perforate; also, now, to decorate the raw edge of silk, etc., by scalloping and punching out a pattern on it. Also *to p. out.* 1503. **4.** To adorn, deck 1558.

2. One of them pink'd the other in a duel ADDISON.

Pink (piŋk), *v.*[2] 1540. [= Du. *pinken* shut the eyes, wink, leer. History unkn.] **1.** *intr.* **a.** Of the eyes: To be half shut, to blink; to peer, peep. Now *dial.* **b.** Of a person: To blink or wink; to look slyly. Now *dial.* 1587. **2.** *P. in* (of daylight, etc.): to diminish, 'draw in'. *dial.* 1886.

Pink (piŋk), *v.*[3] 1920. [imit.] *intr.* Of a motor-engine: To 'knock'.

Pinked (piŋkt), *ppl. a.* 1598. [f. PINK *v.*[1] + -ED[1].] **1.** Pierced, pricked, wounded; tattooed 1608. **2.** Of cloth, leather, etc.: Ornamented with perforations, or (later) cut edges; slashed, scalloped 1598. **b.** Of flounces, frills, ribbons, etc.: Having the raw edge stamped or cut into scallops, jags, or narrow points. Often *p. out.* 1884.

Pi·nk-eye. 1795. [f. PINK *a.* + EYE *sb.*[1]] **1.** (Also *pink-eye potato.*) A variety of potato having pink eyes or buds. **2.** A contagious form of influenza in the horse, so called from the colour of the inflamed conjunctiva. **b.** A contagious form of ophthalmia in man, marked by redness of the eyeball 1882.

Pink-eyed (pi·ŋk,əid), *a.*[1] *Obs.* exc. *dial.* 1519. [f. *pink eyes* – early Du. *pinck oogen*, i.e. *pinck* small (cf. Du. *pink* the little finger, etc.), *ooghen*, pl. of *ooghe* EYE *sb.*[1]; see -ED[2].] Having small, narrow, or half-closed eyes; also, squint-eyed.

Pink-eyed, *a.*[2] [f. PINK *a.* + EYE *sb.*[1] + -ED[2].] Having a pink or light red eye or eyes.

Pinkie, -y (pi·ŋki). 1874. Dim. of PINK *sb.*[1]

Pinking (pi·ŋkiŋ), *vbl. sb.* 1503. [f. PINK *v.*[1] + -ING[1].] The action of PINK *v.*[1]; decorating cloth, leather, etc., with holes, or (later) scalloped edges; *concr.* work so treated.

Comb., as **p.-iron,** a sharp instrument for cutting out pinked borders; also *joc.*, a sword.

Pinkroot (pi·ŋk,rūt). 1763. [f. PINK *sb.*[4] + ROOT.] **a.** The root of *Spigelia marilandica*, or of *S. anthelmia*, used as vermifuges and purgatives. **b.** The herb *Spigelia marilandica* (N.O. *Loganiaceæ*), a native of the Southern U.S., called *Carolina Pink*, *Indian Pink*, or *Worm-grass*; also, *S. anthelmia*, of the W. Indies and S. America (*Demerara P.*).

‖**Pinkster** (pi·ŋkstəɹ). *U.S.* (N.Y.) Also **pingster, pinxter.** 1821. [Du. *pinkster*, now *pinksteren* dat. pl.] Whitsuntide; usu. *attrib.*

Pinxter-flower, U.S. name for *Azalea nudiflora*.

Pinky (pi·ŋki), *a.* 1776. [f. PINK *sb.*[4] or *a.* + -Y[1].] Tinged with or inclining to pink.

Pin-money (pi·nmɒ:ni). 1697. [f. PIN *sb.* II. 1 + MONEY.] A sum of money allotted by a man to his wife for personal expenses, *esp.* such a sum provided by a settlement.

‖**Pinna**[1] (pi·nă). 1520. [L., var. of *pīna* – Gr. πῖνα, πίννα, in same sense.] *Zool.* A genus of bivalve molluscs, having a large silky byssus or 'beard'.

‖**Pinna**[2] (pi·nă). *Pl.* **-æ** (formerly also **-as**). 1785. [mod.L. uses of L. *pinna* = *penna* feather, wing, fin.] **1.** *Anat.* The broad upper part of the external ear; also, the whole external ear 1840. **2.** *Bot.* Each primary division (leaflet, petiole with leaflets, or lobe) of a pinnate or pinnatifid leaf, esp. in ferns 1785. **3.** *Zool.* **a.** The fin of a fish; any fin-like structure, as the flipper of a seal, etc. **b.** A wing-like expansion or branch in certain polyps or other invertebrates. 1846.

Pinnace (pi·nĕs). 1546. [– Fr. *pinace*, †*pinasse* (cf. med.L. (Gascon) *pinacia* XIII, *pinassa* XIV) = It. *pinaccia* or Sp. *pinaza*, which have been referred to Rom. **pinacea* (sc. *navis* ship), f. L. *pinus* PINE *sb.*[2]; but this does not account for earlier OFr. *spinace*, AFr. *espynasse* (XIV), late ME. *spinace*, AL. *spinacium* (XIV).] **1.** A small light vessel, usually two-masted and schooner-rigged; often employed as a tender, scout, etc. Since *c*1700 only *Hist.* and *poet.* **2.** A double-banked boat (usu. eight-oared) forming part of the equipment of a man-of-war; also applied to other small boats 1685. †**3.** *fig.* A woman; also *spec.* a mistress; a prostitute –1693.

1. Full of flats and shoulds that our Pinnasse could not passe CAPT. SMITH.

Pinnacle (pi·năk'l), *sb.* [ME. *pinacle* – OFr. *pin(n)acle*, (mod. *pinacle*) – late L. *pinnaculum*, dim. of L. *pinna* feather, wing, pinnacle; see PIN *sb.*, -CULE.] **1.** A small ornamental turret, usu. terminating in a pyramid or cone, crowning a buttress or rising above the roof or coping of a building. †**b.** *transf.* A vertical pointed structure resembling the above; a pyramid –1703. **2.** Any natural peaked formation; *esp.* a peak ME. **3.** *fig.* The highest point or pitch; the culmination; the acme, climax. late ME.

1. They fancied these to be cities adorned with towers and pinnacles 1777. **2.** The pure-white p. of the . . Weisshorn 1878. **3.** The highest P. of my Ambition 1659. Hence **Pi·nnacled** *ppl. a.* having a p. or pinnacles; elevated on or as on a p.

Pi·nnacle, *v.* 1656. [f. prec. sb.] **1.** *trans.* To set on or as on a pinnacle; to rear as a pinnacle. **2.** To form the pinnacle of 1818.

Pinnate (pi·nĕt), *a.* 1727. [– L. *pinnatus*, f. *pinna* feather, wing; see PINNA[2], -ATE[2].] Resembling a feather; having lateral parts or branches on each side of a common axis. **a.** *Bot.* Applied to a compound leaf having a series of leaflets arranged on each side of a common petiole, the leaflets being usu. opposite, sometimes alternate (*alterni-pinnate*). **b.** *Zool.* Having branches, tentacles, or other lateral parts arranged on each side of an axis 1846. Hence **Pi·nnately** *adv.*

Pinnated (pi·neᶦtėd), *a.* 1753. [f. as prec. + -ED[1].] **1.** = prec. Chiefly *Bot.* and *Zool.* **2.** *Zool.* Having parts like wings, or like fins 1776.

P. Grouse, any bird of the genus *Cupidonia*, having wing-like tufts of feathers on the neck, as the prairie-hen of N. America, *C. cupido.*

Pinnati- (pinēᶦ·ti, pinæ·ti), comb. form of L. *pinnatus* PINNATE; chiefly in botanical terms relating to leaves: **Pinna·tifid** (-æti-) *a.*, (of a leaf) pinnately cleft or divided at least half-way to the middle; **Pinna:tilo·bate, Pinna·tilobed** (-ēᶦti-) *adjs.*, pinnately divided with rounded divisions or lobes; **Pinna:tipa·rtite** (-ēᶦti-) *a.*, pinnately divided nearly to the midrib.

Pinnatiped (pinæ·tiped), *a.* and *sb.* 1828. [f. mod.L. *Pinnatipes*, f. PINNATI- + L. *pes, ped-* foot.] *Ornith.* **A.** *adj.* Having the toes furnished with lobes; lobiped, fin-footed.

B. *sb.* A pinnatiped bird; a bird of the group *Pinnatipedes*, having this character.

Pinner[1]. Now *local.* 1495. [var. of PINDER, f. PIN *v.* II. 1 = PIND *v.*] An officer who impounds stray beasts.

Pinner[2]. 1652. [f. PIN *v.* + -ER[1].] One who or that which pins. **1.** A coif with two long flaps, one on each side, pinned on and hanging down; worn by women, esp. of rank, in the 17th and 18th centuries. Now only *Hist.* 1652. **2.** *dial.* A pinafore or apron with a bib 1846.

Pinni- (pi·ni), comb. form of L. *pinna, penna* wing, as **Pi·nnigrade** [L. *-gradus* walking] *a.*, *Zool.* walking by means of fin-like organs or flippers, as the pinniped Carnivora; also as *sb.* a p. animal.

Pinniform (pi·nifǭɹm), *a.* 1752. [f. PINNI- + -FORM.] **a.** Having the form of, or resembling, a fin. **b.** = PENNIFORM. **c.** Of a pinnate form. **d.** Resembling the mollusc called *Pinna* (PINNA[1]).

Pinniped (pi·niped), *a.* and *sb.* 1842. [– mod.L. *Pinnipes* (neut. pl. *Pinnipedia*), L. *pinnapes, pennipes* wing-footed, used in Zool. in sense 'fin-footed'; f. L. *pinna* + *pes, ped-* foot.] **A.** *adj.* Having feet resembling fins, fin-footed; *spec.* belonging to a sub-order (*Pinnipedia*) of *Carnivora*, which have fin-like limbs or flippers. **B.** *sb.* A pinniped mammal; a seal or walrus.

Pinnothere (pi·noþīᵊɹ), **pinnotere** (pi·notīᵊɹ). 1601. [– L. *pinno-, pinoteres (-theres)*, – Gr. πιννοτήρης, f. πῖνα, πίννα PINNA[1] + τηρεῖν to guard.] Any of the small crabs of the genus *Pinnotheres*, which commensally inhabit the shells of various bivalves, as oysters and mussels; a pea-crab. So **Pinnothe·rian** *a.* and *sb.*

Pinnule (pi·niul). Also (in sense 1) **pinule**, (in senses 2 and 3) **pinnula** (pl. **-æ**). 1594. [– L. *pinnula*, dim. of *pinna* plume, wing; see PINNA[2], -ULE.] **1.** Each of the two sights at the ends of the 'alidade' or index of an astrolabe, quadrant, etc. **2.** *Bot.* Each of the secondary or ultimate divisions of a pinnate leaf; a subdivision of a pinna; esp. in ferns 1776. **3.** *Zool.* A part or organ resembling a small wing or fin, or a barb of a feather; *spec.* each of the lateral branches of the arms in crinoids 1748. Hence **Pi·nnulate, Pi·nnulated** *adjs.* having pinnules.

Pinny (pi·ni). Nursery and colloq. abbrev. of PINAFORE.

Pinnywinkles, var. PILLIWINKS.

Pinocle (pi·nok'l) *U.S.* Also **-chle.** 1890. [Of unkn. origin.] A game of cards resembling bezique; also, the occurrence of the queen of spades and knave of diamonds together in this game.

‖**Pinole** (pinō·le). *U.S.* Also **pino·la, pinol** (pinōᵘ·l). 1853. [Amer. Sp. – Aztec *pinolli*.] A meal made from parched cornflour mixed with sweet flour of mesquit-beans, or with sugar and spice.

Pinoleum (pinōᵘ·liŏm). 1878. [f. L. *pinus* PINE *sb.*[2] + *oleum* OIL *sb.*] A material for sun-blinds, composed of slender slips or rods of pine-wood coated with oil-paint and threaded close to each other so as to form a sheet which can be rolled up.

‖**Piñon** (pinyǫ·n, pi·nyən). Also **pinion.** 1851. [Sp. (pinʸo·n), f. L. *pinea* pine-cone; see -OON.] The American nut-pine, *Pinus edulis*, also the species *P. monophylla, P. parryana*; the fruit or nut of these.

Pi·n-prick. 1862. [f. PIN *sb.* II. + PRICK *sb.*] **1.** The prick of a pin; a minute puncture. **2.** *fig.* A petty annoyance, a minute irritation 1885.

2. *Policy of pin-pricks*, a course of petty hostile acts maintained as a national or a party policy.

Pint (pəint). ME. [– (O)Fr. *pinte*, of unkn. origin.] A measure of capacity for liquids (also for corn and other dry substances), equal to half a quart or ⅛ of a gallon. **b.** A vessel containing a pint; a pint-pot 1483. **c.** *ellipt.* A pint of ale, beer, etc. 1767.

Pintado (pintā·do). 1602. [– Pg. (Sp.) *pintado* guinea-fowl, subst. use of pa. pple. ('spotted') of *pintar* :– Rom. **pinctare*, f. **pinctus* for L. *pictus*, pa. pple. of *pingere* paint.] †**1.** A kind of Eastern chintz –1727. **2.** A species of petrel, *Daption capensis*, also called Cape Pigeon. Now *p. bird, petrel.* 1611. **3.** The Guinea-fowl 1666.

Pintail (pi·nˌtēᵊl). 1768. [f. PIN *sb.* I. + TAIL *sb.*[1]] **1.** (In full *p. duck.*) A species of duck (*Dafila acuta*), of which the male has the tail of a pointed shape, the two middle feathers being longer than the rest. **2.** A species of grouse having a pointed tail, as the pintailed sand-grouse (*Pterocles setarius*) of the Old World, and the pintailed or sharp-tailed grouse (*Pediœcetes phasianellus*) of N. America (also called *p. chicken*) 1879. Hence **Pi·ntailed** *a.*

Pintle (pi·nt'l). [OE. *pintel*, dim. of a base repr. by OFris., LG., Du., G. *pint*; cf. *cuckoo-pint* (XVI), *-pintle* (XV), *priest's pintle* wild arum, and see -LE.] **1.** The penis. Now *dial.* or *vulgar.* **2.** A pin or bolt; esp. one on which some other part turns, as in a hinge, etc. 1486.

Pint-pot. 1563. A (pewter) pot containing a pint 1622. †**b.** *joc.* A seller of beer –1596.

‖**Pinto** (pi·nto). *U.S.* 1867. [Sp. *pinto* pointed, mottled :– Rom. **pinctus*; see PINTADO.] Piebald (horse).

Pi·n-wheel. 1696. [f. PIN *sb.* I. + WHEEL.] **1. a.** 'A wheel in the striking train of a clock in which pins are fixed to lift the hammer' (F. J. Britten). **b.** 'A contrate wheel in which the cogs are pins set into the disk' (Knight). **2.** A fire-work, a small catherine-wheel 1869.

Piny (pəi·ni), *a.* 1627. [f. PINE *sb.*[2] + -Y[1].] Abounding in, covered with, or consisting of pine-trees; of or pertaining to a pine-tree.

The long low lines of p. hills RUSKIN.

‖**Piolet** (pyolę). 1868. [Fr., prop. Savoy dial., dim. of *piolo*, app. cogn. w. Fr. *pioche*, *pic.*] An ice-axe used by Alpine climbers.

Pioneer (pəiˌŏnīᵊ·ɹ), *sb.* 1523. [orig. *pion(n)er* – Fr. *pionnier*, OFr. *paonier*, *peon(n)ier*, f. *paon, peon*; see PAWN *sb.*[1], PEON. Orig. stressed *pi·oner*, the suffix being later assim. to -EER.] **1.** *Mil.* One of a body of foot-soldiers who march with or in advance of an army or regiment, having spades, pickaxes, etc., to dig trenches, and clear and prepare the way for the main body. †**2.** *gen.* A digger, excavator; a miner –1640. **3.** *fig.* One who goes before to prepare the way; one who begins some enterprise, course of action, etc.; an original investigator, explorer, or worker; an initiator (*of*) 1605.

3. The great p. of Arctic travel, Sir Edward Parry 1856.

Pionee·r, *v.* 1780. [f. prec. sb.] **1.** *intr.* To act as pioneer; to prepare the way as a pioneer. **2.** *trans.* To prepare, clear, open (a way, road, etc.) as a pioneer (*lit.* and *fig.*) 1794. **3.** To act as a pioneer to, be the pioneer of; to prepare the way for 1819.

Pious (pəi·əs), *a.* 1602. [f. L. *pius* dutiful, pious + -OUS. Cf. Fr. *pieux* (XVI), which may have been the immediate source.] **1.** 'Careful of the duties owed by created beings to God' (J.); devout, godly, religious. **b.** Of fraud and the like: Practised for the sake of religion or for a good object, or 'under the appearance of religion' (J.); see also FRAUD *sb.* 1637. **2.** Faithful to the duties naturally owed to parents, friends, superiors, etc.; dutiful, duteous. Of persons (also of birds), or actions, etc. Now *rare* or *arch.* 1626.

1. Campbell is a good man, a p. man he never passes a church without pulling off his hat JOHNSON. Old p. tracts, and Bibles bound in wood CRABBE. *P. founder*, the founder of a college or other endowment for the glory of God and the good of men. **b.** He sought the presence of his deare brother Benjamin by a p. kind of fraud 1637. **2.** With..p. care She..the aged gossip led KEATS. Hence **Pi·ous-ly** *adv.*

Pip (pip), *sb.*[1] late ME. [– MLG. *pip*, MDu. *pippe* (*pipse*, whence G. *pips*), reduced form corresp. to OHG. *pfiffiz* :– WGmc. **pipit* – med.L. **pip(p)īta*, presumably alt. of L. *pituita* (see PITUITARY).] A disease of poultry and other birds, characterized by the secretion of a thick mucus in the mouth and throat, often with a white scale on the tip of the tongue (often applied to this scale itself). **b.** Applied (usu. *joc.*) to various diseases in human beings; also to any depressed state of mind. late ME.

b. The children ill with the p., or some confounded thing THACKERAY. Phr. *To give* (or *have*) *the p.*

Pip, *sb.*[2] 1596. [orig. *peep*, still used dial.; cf. dial. *ship* for *sheep*. Of unkn. origin.] **1.** Each of the spots on playing-cards, dice, or dominoes. **2.** A spot or speck; *spec.* a spot on a spotted dress fabric; *pl.* specks appearing to dance before the eye. Now *dial.* 1676. **3.** *Gardening.* Each single blossom of a clustered inflorescence, esp. in the cowslip and polyanthus 1753. **4.** Each of the rhomboidal segments of the surface of a pine-apple 1833. **5.** *colloq.* A star on an army officer's uniform, indicating his rank 1919.

Pip, *sb.*[3] 1598. [Shortening of PIPPIN.] †**1.** = PIPPIN 2. –1601. **2.** = PIPPIN 1. 1797.

Pip, *sb.*[4] 1920. Signallers' name for the letter P, used in abbrev., as *pip emma*, P.M.

Pip, *v.*[1] 1659. [In sense 1 app. var. of PEEP *v.*[1] (cf. dial. *ship* for sheep, *kip* for keep). Sense 2 is perh. a distinct word of imit. origin; cf. CHIP *v.*[1]] **1.** *intr.* To chirp, as a young bird. **2.** *trans.* To crack (the shell of the egg), as a young bird.

Pip, *v.*[2] *colloq.* or *slang.* 1880. [f. PIP *sb.*[2] (or [3]) taken *fig.*; cf. PILL *v.*[2]] *trans.* To blackball; to defeat, beat; to hit with a shot.

‖**Pipa** (pipā·, pəi·pă). Also **pipal.** 1718. [– Surinam Negro *pipál* masc., *pipá* fem.] The Surinam toad (noted for its manner of hatching its young; see quot.); hence in *Zool.* the genus of tailless batrachians of which this is the only species.

The male *Pipa*,..as soon as the eggs are laid, places them on the back of the female, and fecundates them...The skin of her back..forms cellules, in which the eggs are hatched, and where the young pass their tadpole state 1838.

Pipage (pəi·pėdʒ). Also **pipeage.** 1612. [f. PIPE *sb.*[1] + -AGE.] The conveyance of water, gas, petroleum, etc. by means of pipes; the laying down of pipes for this purpose; such pipes collectively.

Pipe (pəip), *sb.*[1] [OE. *pīpe* = OFris., MLG., MDu. *pipe* (Du. *pijp*), OHG. *pfīfa* (G. *pfeife*), ON. *pipa* :– Gmc. **pīpa* – Rom. **pīpa*, f. L. *pipare* (Varro) peep, chirp, of imit. origin; reinforced in ME. by (O)Fr. *pipe.*] **I.** A musical tube. **1.** A musical wind-instrument consisting of a single tube of reed, straw, or (now usu.) wood, blown by the mouth. **b.** Each of the tubes (of wood or metal) by which the sounds are produced in an organ; see ORGAN-PIPE 1440. **c.** *Naut.* The boatswain's whistle; the sounding of this as a call to the crew 1638. **d.** *pl.* = *Bagpipes.* Also *poet.* in *sing.* 1706. **2.** *transf.* The voice, esp. in singing; the song or note of a bird, etc. 1580.

1. Their scrannel Pipes of wretched straw MILT. **2.** Thy small p. Is as the maidens organ, shrill, and sound SHAKS. The earliest p. of half-awaken'd birds TENNYSON.

II. A cylindrical tube or stick for other purposes. **1.** A hollow cylinder of wood, metal, etc., for the conveyance of gas, water, vapour, etc., or for other purposes; a tube OE. **2.** †**a.** The account of a sheriff or other minister of the Crown, as sent in and enrolled at the Exchequer. [AFr.] **b.** The department of the Exchequer that drew up the 'pipes', or enrolled accounts, of sheriffs and others (= *pipe-office*) 1455. **3.** A tubular organ, passage, canal, or vessel in an animal body; applied now *esp.* to the respiratory passages. Usu. in *pl.* late ME. **4.** *Mining* and *Geol.* (*a*) A vein of ore of a more or less cylindrical form; also called *pipe vein, pipe-work.* (*b*) A vertical cylindrical hollow filled with sand or gravel, occurring in a stratum of chalk; also called *sand-pipe* or *sand-gall.* (*c*) The vertical eruptive channel which opens into the crater of a volcano. (*d*) Each of the vertical cylindrical masses of blue rock in which diamonds are found embedded in S. Africa (see KIMBERLITE). 1667. **5.** Each of the channels of a decoy for wild fowl 1634.

2. b. The Office of the Clerk of the Pipe 1455. **3.** He loves to clear his Pipes in good Air (to make use of his own phrase) ADDISON.

III. A narrow tube of clay, wood, etc., with a bowl at one end, for drawing in the smoke of tobacco (or other narcotic or medicinal substance); also, a quantity of tobacco which fills the bowl; a pipeful. (See TOBACCO-PIPE.) 1594.

Happy mortal! he who knows Pleasure which a P. bestows 1736. *P. of peace*, the CALUMET of the American Indians. Also allusively *Queen's (King's) P.*, joc. name for a furnace at the London Docks, used formerly for burning contraband tobacco, now for burning tobacco-sweepings, etc. *To put* a person's *p. out*, to take the 'shine' out of, extinguish. *Put that in your p. and smoke it*, put up with that if you can.

attrib. and *Comb.*: **p.-dream** *U.S.*, a fantastic notion likened to a dream produced by opium-smoking; **-light,** a strip of paper folded or twisted for lighting a p., a spill; **-major,** the chief player of a band of bagpipe-players; **-metal,** an alloy of tin and lead, with or without zinc, used for organ-pipes; **-office,** the office of the Clerk of the P. in the Exchequer (see II. 2); **-ore,** iron ore (limonite) in vertical pillars, imbedded in clay; **-organ,** an organ with pipes, esp. as dist. from a *reed-organ*; **-rack,** (*a*) in an organ, a wooden shelf with perforations by which the pipes are supported; (*b*) a rack for tobacco-pipes; **-stopper,** a small plug for compressing the tobacco in the bowl of a p.; **p. vein** (*Mining*): see II. 4 a; **-vine,** a name for the N. American plant *Aristolochia sipho*, from the shape of the flowers and the twining growth (also called *Dutchman's pipe*); **-work** (*Mining*), a p. vein of ore; **-wrench,** a tool with one jaw fixed on a shank and the other movable on a pivot, for gripping a p. when turned in one direction round it.

Pipe, *sb.*[2] late ME. [– AFr. *pipe*, AL. *pipa* (XIII); spec. use of prec. in the sense 'tubular or cylindrical vessel'.] A large cask with its contents (wine, beer, cider, beef, fish, etc.), or as a measure of capacity, equivalent to half a tun, or 2 hogsheads, or 4 barrels, i.e. usu. containing 105 imperial gallons. Sometimes identified with BUTT *sb.*[2] 1.

Pipe (pəip), *v.*[1] [In branch I OE. *pīpian* – L. *pipare* in med.L. sense 'blow a pipe', f. *pipa* PIPE *sb.*[1] In branch II ME. *pipe* – OFr. *piper* :– L. *pipare*; see PIPE *sb.*[1]] **I. 1.** *intr.* To blow or play on a pipe. **b.** To whistle, as the wind, a man, a bird: see II. **2.** *trans.* To play (a tune, music) upon a pipe. late ME. **b.** *transf.* To lead by the sound of a pipe; to entice or decoy, as wild fowl 1546. **3.** *Naut.* To summon, as a boatswain the crew, to some duty, or to a meal, by sounding the pipe or whistle. (*trans.* and *intr.*) 1706.

1. We have pyped vnto you, and ye have nott daunsed TINDALE *Luke* 7:32. **2.** Piping down the valleys wild, Piping songs of pleasant glee BLAKE. **3.** The hands had just been piped to breakfast 1884. *To p. away, down*, to dismiss by sounding the p.

II. †**1.** *intr.* To utter a shrill and weak sound; to cheep, squeak, peep. Repl. by PEEP *v.*[1] –1483. **2.** Variations of sense II. 1, infl. by sense I. 1. **a.** To whistle: said of the wind, a man, a marmot; also to hum or buzz shrilly; to whistle or whizz as a bullet 1513. **b.** To whistle or sing as a bird 1591. **c.** To talk loud and shrilly 1784. **d.** To weep, to cry. *colloq.* or *slang.* 1797. **3.** *trans.* To utter **a.** in a cheeping voice, as a mouse; **b.** in a loud shrill or clear voice, as a bird, a singer, or speaker. late ME. **4.** *To p. one's eye* or *eyes* (orig. *Naut. slang*): to shed tears, weep, cry 1789.

2. a. While rocking Winds are Piping loud MILT. **b.** The thrush piped from the hawthorn 1822. **3.** The boys piped out an hurrah THACKERAY.

III. *Pugilistic slang.* (*intr.*) To pant from violent exertion or exhaustion 1814. **IV.** *P. up.* **a.** *trans.* To begin to play or sing, strike up. late ME. **b.** *intr.* To speak up in a piping voice; to rise, as the wind 1889.

Pipe (pəip), *v.*[2] 1788. [f. PIPE *sb.*[1]] **I.** *trans. Gardening.* To propagate (pinks, etc.) by cuttings taken off at a joint of the stem. **II.** To trim or ornament (a dress, etc.), to ornament (a cake, etc.), with piping 1841. **III. 1.** *trans.* To furnish or supply with pipes 1884. **2.** To convey (water, gas, oil, etc.) through or by means of pipes 1889. **3.** *Mining.* To direct a jet of water from a pipe upon (gravel, etc.): see HYDRAULIC *a.* 1; to supply with water for this purpose 1882.

Pi·pe-clay, *sb.* 1779. A fine white kind of clay, which forms a ductile paste with water; used for making tobacco-pipes, and (esp. by soldiers) for cleaning white trousers, etc. Hence *allus.*, excessive attention to the minutiæ of dress and appearance in the management of regiments. Hence **Pi·pe-clay** *v. trans.* to whiten with pipe-clay; *fig.* to put into spick-and-span order.

Piped (pəipt), *ppl. a.* 1520. [f. PIPE *sb.*[1] and *v.*[2] + -ED.] **1.** Furnished with a pipe or pipes; having the form of a pipe, tubular. **2.** Formed into, or ornamented with, piping 1884. **3.** Conveyed by pipes 1883.

Pi·pe-fish. 1769. [PIPE *sb.*[1]] A fish of the genus *Syngnathus* or family *Syngnathidæ*, having a long slender body and a long snout.

Pipeful (pəi·pful). 1605. [f. PIPE *sb.*[1] and [2] + -FUL.] **1.** [f. PIPE *sb.*[2]] A quantity (of liquor, etc.) sufficient to fill a pipe or large cask. *rare.* **2.** [f. PIPE *sb.*[1]] A quantity (of tobacco, etc.) sufficient to fill the bowl of a pipe 1613.

Pipe-layer (pəi·p,lēⁱ:əɹ). 1851. [f. PIPE *sb.*[1] + LAYER *sb.*] **a.** A workman who lays pipes for the conveyance of water, gas, etc. **b.** *U.S. political slang.* One who schemes to procure corrupt votes. So **Pi·pe-lay:ing** 1848.

Pi·pe-line. 1883. A conduit of iron pipes for conveying petroleum from the oil-wells to the market or refinery, or for supplying water to a town or district.

Pipemouth (pəi·pmauþ). [Cf. PIPE-FISH.] A fish of the genus *Fistularia* or family *Fistulariidæ*, characterized by a long pipe-like snout.

Piper (pəi·pəɹ). [OE. *pīpere*, f. *pīpe* PIPE *sb.*[1]; see -ER[1].] **1.** One who plays on a pipe (*esp.* a strolling musician), in Scotland *spec.* a bagpiper. **2.** Pop. name for several kinds of fish; *esp.* a species of gurnard, *Trigla lyra*, so called from the sound it makes when caught; in New Zealand, the garfish 1601. **3.** A broken-winded horse; cf. *roarer* 1831.

1. Let's haue a dance... Strike vp Pipers SHAKS. Phr. *To pay the p.*, i.e. for piping to lead the dance; hence, to defray the cost, or bear the loss, incident to some proceeding; Londoners had paid the p., and should choose the tune 1895.

Piperaceous (pipĕrēⁱ·ʃəs), *a.* 1674. [f. L. *piper* PEPPER + -ACEOUS.] †**a.** Of the nature of pepper; pungent. **b.** *Bot.* Belonging to the N.O. *Piperaceæ*, the pepper tribe (typical genus *Piper*; see PEPPER).

Piperazine (pi·pĕrăzəin). 1891. [f. L. *piper* PEPPER + AZ(OTE + -INE[5].] *Pharm.* A compound allied to spermin, chemically *diethylenediamine*.

Piperic (pipe·rik), *a.* 1866. [f. L. *piper* PEPPER + -IC.] *Chem.* Pertaining to or derived from pepper; in *p. acid*, an acid obtained by boiling piperine with potash.

Piperidine (pipe·ridəin). 1857. [f. L. *piper* PEPPER + -IDE + -INE[5].] *Chem.* 'A volatile base ($C_5H_{11}N$) produced by the action of alkalis on piperine' (Watts).

Piperine (pi·pĕrəin). 1820. [f. as prec. + -INE[5].] *Chem.* An alkaloid obtained from species of pepper (*Piper nigrum* and *P. longum*), crystallizing in colourless prisms.

Pi·pe-roll. 1612. [f. PIPE *sb.*[1] II. 2 + ROLL *sb.*] The Great Roll of the Exchequer, comprising the various 'pipes', or enrolled accounts, of sheriffs and others for a financial year.

Pi·pe-stone. 1809. [f. PIPE *sb.*[1] + STONE.] = CATLINITE.

Pipette (pipe·t) 1839. [– Fr. *pipette*, dim. of *pipe* PIPE *sb.*[1]; see -ETTE.] A small pipe or tube, used (esp. in chemistry, etc.) to transfer or measure small quantities of a liquid or gas.

Pipewort (pəi·pwɒɹt). 1806. [f. PIPE *sb.*[1] + WORT[1].] Any plant of the genus *Eriocaulon* of aquatic or marsh herbs allied to grasses, with a membranous tube surrounding the ovary.

Piping (pəi·piŋ), *vbl. sb.*[1] ME. [f. PIPE *v.*[1] + -ING[1].] The action of PIPE *v.*[1] **1.** Playing on a pipe; the music of pipes or wind-instruments. **2.** The utterance of a shrill sound, or the sound itself (see PIPE *v.*[1] II.) ME. **3.** Weeping, crying. *slang* or *colloq.* 1779.

Pi·ping, *vbl. sb.*[2] 1660. [f. PIPE *v.*[2] and *sb.*[1] + -ING[1].] **1.** The action of PIPE *v.*[2], q.v. **2.** *Dressmaking.* The trimming or ornamentation of the edge of stuff or the seams of a garment, by means of a fine cord enclosed in a pipe-like fold; *concr.*, the tubular kind of trimming thus formed 1858. **3.** *Confectionery.* The action or art of ornamenting cakes, etc. with cord-like lines of sugar; *concr.* the lines so used 1883.

Pi·ping, *ppl. a.* late ME. [f. PIPE *v.*[1] + -ING[2].] **1.** Playing on a pipe 1638. **b.** Characterized by piping, i.e. the music of the pastoral pipe (as dist. from martial music): in the Shakespearian phr. *p. time(s) of peace* 1594. **2.** Sounding shrilly; whistling 1602. **3.** quasi-*adv.* in phr. **p. hot,** so hot as to make a piping or hissing sound as a dish freshly cooked; hissing hot; hence *gen.* very hot. late ME. **b.** *fig.* Fresh, just come out 1607.

2. P. bullfinch, a bullfinch trained to whistle a tune; **p. crow,** the Australian genus *Gymnorhina*; **p. hare,** the pika or calling hare, *Lagomys*; **p. plover,** *Ægialites melodus*, of N. America.

Pipistrelle, -el (pipistre·l). 1771. [– Fr. *pipistrelle* – It. *pipistrello*, alt. of *vipistrello*, repr. L. *vespertilio* bat, f. *vesper* evening.] A small species of bat, *Vesperugo pipistrellus*, common in Europe.

Pipit (pi·pit). 1768. [prob. imitative of the bird's note.] Any bird of the genus *Anthus* or several allied genera of the family *Motacillidæ*, having a general resemblance to larks.

Pipkin (pi·pkin). 1565. [Of unkn. origin.] A small earthenware pot or pan, used chiefly in cookery. (Formerly including metal pots. Now local.) Hence **Pi·pkinet,** a small p.

Pipperidge (pi·pəridʒ). 1538. [Of unkn. origin.] **1.** A local name of the Barberry, fruit or shrub. **2.** = PEPPERIDGE 2. 1828.

Pippin (pi·pin). [ME. *pepin*, *pipin* (whence AL. *pipina* XV) – OFr. *pepin* (mod. *pepin*, *pépin*), rel. to synon. Sp. *pepita*, It. *pippolo*, *pipporo*, based on obscure Rom. **pipp*-.] **1.** The seed of certain fruits, including those now called *pips*, and others. *Obs.* exc. *n. dial.* **2.** The name of numerous varieties of apple. late ME. **3.** Applied to a person (*slang*) 1664. **4.** *attrib.*, as **p. face,** a round red face 1598.

‖**Pipsissewa** (pipsi·sĭwă). 1818. [Algonquian (Cree *pipipissekweu*).] A low creeping evergreen with whitish flowers, *Chimaphila umbellata* (N.O. *Ericaceæ* or *Pyrolaceæ*), also called Prince's pine. Also, the leaves of this used as a diuretic and tonic.

Pi·p-squeak. *slang.* 1910. [Symbolic and imit.] **1.** An insignificant or contemptible person or thing. **2.** A shell distinguished by its sound in flight 1916.

Pipy (pəi·pi), *a.* 1724. [f. PIPE *sb.*[1] + -Y[1].] Containing pipes; of the form of a pipe.

Piquancy (pī·kănsi). 1664. [f. next; see -ANCY.] The quality of being piquant, in various senses; sharpness; appetizing flavour; etc.

Piquant (pī·kănt), *a.* (*sb.*) 1521. [– Fr. *piquant*, pr. pple. of *piquer*; see PIQUE *v.*[1]] **1.** That pierces or stings; keen, trenchant; severe, bitter. Chiefly *fig. Obs.* or *arch.* **2.** Agreeably pungent of taste; sharp, stinging, biting; appetizing 1645. **3.** *fig.* That stimulates or excites keen interest or curiosity; pleasantly stimulating or disquieting 1695. **B.** *sb. rare.* That which is piquant. **a.** A hedgehog's prickle; **b.** A piquant dish; a whet. 1835.

2. As p. to the Tongue as Salt it self ADDISON. **3.** She disapproved entirely of the p. neatness of Caroline's costume C. BRONTË. That picquante letter-writer, Madame de Sévigné 1873. Hence **Pi·quantly** *adv.*

Pique (pīk), *sb.*[1] 1532. [– Fr. *pique*, f. *piquer*; see PIQUE *v.*[1]] **1.** A personal quarrel between two or more persons; ill-feeling, animosity, enmity. **2.** A feeling of anger, resentment, or ill-will, resulting from some slight or injury; offence taken 1592.

2. A Bishop who had turned monk in a momentary fit of p. FREEMAN.

Pique (pīk), *sb.*[2] 1668. [– Fr. *pic*, in same sense, of unkn. origin.] In piquet, the winning of thirty points on cards and play, before one's opponent begins to count, entitling the player to begin his score at sixty.

Pique (pī·ke, pīk), *sb.*[3] 1748. [– Sp. Amer. – Quichua *piqui*, *piki*.] = CHIGOE.

Pique, *sb.*[4] 1826. Erron. f. PEAK *sb.*[2]

Pique (pīk), *v.*[1] 1664. [– Fr. *piquer* prick,

sting, irritate, *se piquer* take offence :– Rom. **piccare*. See PICK *v.*[1]] **1.** *trans.* To irritate; to offend by wounding pride or vanity 1671. **2.** *trans.* To excite to action by arousing envy, rivalry, jealousy, etc.; to arouse, awake (curiosity, interest). †**b.** *refl.* To put oneself on one's mettle. 1698. †**3.** *absol.* or *intr.* To arouse a feeling of pique; to stimulate –1710. **4.** *refl.* (rarely *intr.*). To take pride *in*, plume oneself *on*. Const. *on, upon*, rarely *at, in* (= Fr. *se piquer de.*) 1705.

1. A little picqued by the excess of his mirth 1796. **2.** You have piqued my curiosity 1870. **3.** Every Verse hath something in it that piques ADDISON. **4.** Men who are thought to p. themselves upon their wit POPE.

Pique, *v.*[2] 1659. [f. PIQUE *sb.*[2]] In *Piquet*: **a.** *trans.* To score a pique against (one's opponent). **b.** *intr.* To score a pique.

‖**Piqué** (pī·ke), *sb.* (*a.*) 1852. [Fr., subst. use ('quilted work, quilting') of pa. pple. of *piquer* prick, pierce, back-stitch.] A rather stiff cotton fabric woven in a strongly ribbed or raised pattern; quilting. **b.** The raised pattern of such a fabric 1890. **B.** *ppl. a.* Inlaid (with little points of gold, etc.). Also as sb. = *p. work* (*a*) decorative needlework in which a pattern is formed by stitching; (*b*) ornamental work in tortoise-shell, etc., formed by means of minute inlaid designs traced in points of gold, etc.

Piquet (pike·t, pi·kėt). Also **picket, picquet,** etc. 1646. [– Fr. *piquet*, †*picquet* (XVI), of unkn. origin.] A card-game played by two persons with a pack of 32 cards (the low cards from the two to the six being excluded).

‖**Pir** (pīᵊɹ). 1672. [Pers., = old man.] A Moslem saint; also, a holy place.

Piracy (pəiᵊ·răsi). 1552. [– AL. *piratia*, f. *pirata* PIRATE + *-ia* -Y[3]; see -ACY.] The action or practice of a pirate. **1.** Robbery and depredation on the sea or navigable rivers, or by descent from the sea upon the coast, by persons not holding a commission from a civilized state; with *a* and *pl.*, an instance of this. **2.** *fig.* Infringement of rights conferred by a patent or copyright 1771.

Piragua (piræ·gwă). Also (*arch.*) **peria·gua.** 1609. [– Sp. *piragua* – Carib *piragua* dug-out; alt. by assoc. of the first syll. with *peri-* and *petty* (e.g. †*pettiagua* XVII, etc.).] **1.** A long narrow canoe hollowed from the trunk of a single tree. **2.** An open flat-bottomed schooner-rigged vessel; a sort of two-masted sailing-barge 1667.

‖**Piranha** (pirā·nʸă). 1869. [Pg.] Now the more usual form of PERAI.

Pirate (pəiᵊ·rĕt), *sb.* ME. [– L. *pirata* – Gr. πειρατής, f. πειρᾶν attempt, attack, πεῖρα attempt, trial.] **1.** One who robs and plunders on the sea, etc.; a sea-robber. **2.** *transf.* A vessel employed in piracy or manned by pirates; a pirate-ship 1600. **3.** Any one who roves about in quest of plunder; one who robs with violence; a marauder, despoiler 1526. **4.** *fig.* One who appropriates or reproduces without leave, for his own benefit, a composition, idea, or invention that he has no right to; esp. one who infringes on the copyright of another 1701. **5.** An omnibus which infringes on the recognized routes; now often applied to any omnibus owned by a private firm or person. Also *transf.* The driver of such an omnibus. 1889. **b.** *attrib.* and *Comb.*, as *p.-ship*, etc. **P. bus, omnibus** (see 5).

1. Notable Pyrate, thou salt-water Theefe SHAKS. **3.** Pirates of the desert 1850. **4.** In 1599 two of them [Shakespeare's Sonnets] were printed by the p. Jaggard 1887.

Pirate (pəiᵊ·rĕt), *v.* 1574. [f. prec. sb.] **1.** *trans.* To practise piracy upon; to rob, plunder. **2.** *intr.* To play the pirate, practise piracy 1685. **3.** *fig. trans.* To appropriate or reproduce (the work or invention of another) without authority, for one's own profit 1706.

3. He had no right to p. a peculiar trade mark 1850.

Piratic (pəiræ·tik), *a.* 1640. [– L. *piraticus* – Gr. πειρατικός, f. πειρατής pirate; see -IC.] Of or pertaining to a pirate or pirates; like a pirate. *P. war*, that waged by Pompey against the pirates in the Mediterranean.

Piratical (pəiræ·tikăl), *a.* 1565. [f. as prec.; see -ICAL.] **1.** Of or pertaining to a pirate or piracy; of the nature of, characterized by, given to, or engaged in piracy; pirate-like 1579. **b.** *fig.* Given to literary piracy, etc. 1736. **2.** Obtained by piracy; pirated 1565.

1. The Moors established the p. states of Algiers and Tunis 1872. **b.** P. publishers 1877. **2.** Two legal editions—two p. ones 1838. So **Pira·tically** *adv.* 1549.

Pirl (pɔ̄ɹl, *Sc.* pi·r'l), *v. arch., Sc.* and *dial.* 1500. [Of unkn. origin. See PURL *sb.*[1], *v.*[3]] **1.** *trans.* To twist, wind, or spin (threads, etc.) into a cord; now esp. *dial.* to twist (horsehair) into fishing-lines, etc. **2.** To cause to revolve, to spin. Also *intr.* To spin. 1791.

Pirn (pɔ̄ɹn, *Sc.* pirn). Now *Sc.* and *dial.* late ME. [Of unkn. origin.] **1.** A weaver's bobbin, spool, or reel 1440. **b.** A reel of sewing cotton 1820. **2.** Any device like a reel, or used for winding; *esp.* a fishing-reel 1782.

Pirogue (pirōᵘ·g). Also **per(i)oque, periogue, piroque.** 1666. [– Fr. *pirogue*, prob. – Galibi, the Carib dialect of Cayenne.] Another form of PIRAGUA; extended to local kinds of open boats, with or without sails.

Pirouette (piru,e·t), *sb.* 1706. [– Fr. *pirouette*, (cf. †*pirouet* teetotum, etc.), of unkn. origin.] **1.** The act of spinning round on one foot, or on the point of the toe, as performed by ballet-dancers. **2.** In the manège: 'A turn or circumvolution which a horse makes, without changing his ground' (Chambers) 1727. So **Piroue·tte** *v. intr.* to dance a p., spin or whirl on the point of the toe; to move with a whirling motion.

Pirrie, -y (pi·ri). Now only *dial.* late ME. [app. imit.] A blast of wind; a squall; a sudden storm of wind, 'half a gale'.

‖**Pis aller** (pizale). 1676. [Fr., f. *pis* worse + *aller* go; based on phr. *au pis aller* 'at the worst procedure'.] The worst that can be, or can happen; what one accepts when one can do no better; a last resource.

Piscary (pi·skări). 1474. [– med.L. *piscaria* fishing rights, n. pl. used subst. of L. *piscarius* pertaining to fishing, f. *piscis* fish; see -ARY[1].] **1.** The right of fishing (as a thing owned). Now usu. in *common of p.* **2.** A place where fish may be caught; a fishing-ground 1625.

1. Common of p. is a liberty of fishing in another man's water, in common with the owner of the soil, and perhaps also with others 1880.

Piscation (piskēⁱ·ʃən). *rare.* 1624. [– late L. *piscatio*, f. *piscat-*, pa. ppl. stem of L. *piscari* fish, f. *piscis* fish; see -ION.] Fishing.

‖**Piscator** (piskēⁱ·tǫɹ, -əɹ). 1653. [L., f. as prec.; see -OR 2.] A fisherman; an angler.

Piscatory (pi·skătəri), *a.* 1633. [– L. *piscatorius* adj., f. *piscator*; see prec., -ORY[2].] **1.** Of or pertaining to fishers or to fishing. So **Piscato·rial** *a.* **2.** Employed in or addicted to fishing 1661.

1. *P. ring*, the signet ring worn by the pope as successor of St. Peter (cf. Matt. 4:19, etc.).

‖**Pisces** (pi·sīz). late ME. [L., pl. of *piscis* fish.] **1.** *Astron.* The twelfth zodiacal constellation, the Fishes; also the twelfth sign of the Zodiac (orig. coincident with the constellation), which the sun enters about Feb. 20. **2.** *Zool.* Fishes, as a class of Vertebrata 1841.

Pisciculture (pi·sikɒltiŭɹ, -tʃəɹ). 1859. [f. L. *piscis* fish, after *agriculture*, etc. Cf. Fr. *pisciculture*, possibly the source.] The breeding, rearing, and preserving of (living) fish by artificial means. Hence **Piscicu·ltural** *a.*; **-ly** *adv.* **Piscicu·lturist**, a person engaged or interested in p.

Pisciform (pi·sifǭɹm), *a.* 1828. [f. L. *piscis* fish + -FORM.] Having the form of a fish.

Piscina (pisī·nă, pisəi·nă). *Pl.* **-æ, -as.** 1599. [– L. *piscina* fishpond, in med.L. in sense 2, f. *piscis* fish.] **1.** A fishpond; a pond, basin, or pool; among the ancient Romans, a bathing-pond. **2.** *Eccl.* A perforated stone basin for carrying away the ablutions, generally placed in a niche on the south side of the altar 1793.

Piscine (pi·sin, pisī·n), *sb.* ME. [– (O)Fr. *piscine* – L. *piscina*; see prec.] = PISCINA 1, 2.

Piscine (pi·səin), *a.* 1799. [f. L. *piscis* fish; see -INE[1].] Of, pertaining to, of the nature of, or characteristic of a fish or fishes.

Piscivorous (pisi·vŏrəs), *a.* 1668. [f. L. *piscis* fish + -VOROUS.] Fish-eating; ichthyophagous.

‖**Pisé** (pī·ze). 1797. [Fr., subst. use of pa. pple. of *piser* beat, pound (earth) :– L. *pinsare.*] Stiff clay or earth kneaded, or mixed with gravel, used for building cottages, walls, etc., by being rammed between boards which are removed as it hardens; also, this mode of building. Also *attrib.*

Pisgah (pi·zgă). 1650. [– Heb. *pisgāh* 'cleft'.] The name of a mountain east of Jordan, whence Moses was allowed to view the Promised Land (Deut. 3:27); hence allusively, esp. *attrib.*, as *P. glance, prospect, view.*

Pish (piʃ), *int.* and *sb.* 1592. [A natural exclamation. Cf. PSHAW.] **A.** *int.* An exclam. expressing contempt, impatience, or disgust. **B.** *sb.* The utterance of this exclam. 1594. Hence **Pish** *v. intr.* to say 'pish' (often with *at*); *trans.* to say 'pish' to.

Pisiform (pəi·sifǭɹm, pi·zi-), *a.* (*sb.*) 1767. [– mod.L. *pisiformis*, f. *pisum* PEA[1]; see -FORM.] **A.** *adj.* Pea-shaped; of small globular form. **B.** *sb.* Short for *p. bone.* (Also in L. form **pisiforme.**) 1808.

A. *P. bone* (Anat.), a small pea-shaped bone of the upper row of the carpus. *P. iron-ore*, iron-ore occurring in small concretions like peas.

Pismire (pi·sməiᵊɹ). *Obs.* exc. *dial.* [ME. *pissemyre*, f. PISS + *mire* ant (prob. of Scand. origin; cf. Da. *myre*, and L. *formica*, Gr. μύρμηξ); so called from the urinous smell of an ant-hill.] An ant. **b.** *fig.* Applied contempt. to a person 1569.

Pisolite (pi·zŏləit, pəi·sŏ-). 1708. [– mod.L. *pisolithus*, f. Gr. πίσος, -ον pea + -LITE.] = PEASTONE. Hence **Pisoli·tic** *a.* of the nature of, consisting of, or resembling p.

Piss (pis), *sb.* Not now in polite use. late ME. [f. next.] Urine, 'water'.

Piss (pis), *v.* Not now in polite use. [– (O)Fr. *pisser* :– Rom. **pišare*, of imit. origin.] **1.** *intr.* To urinate, make water. Also *transf.* **2.** *trans.* To discharge as or with the urine. Also *transf.* and *fig.* ME. **3.** To wet with urine; to put *out* (fire) in this way ME.

Pissabed (pi·săbed). *Obs.* exc. *dial.* 1565. [f. PISS *v.* + ABED, from its diuretic property. After Fr. *pissenlit.*] The dandelion.

Pissasphalt (pi·sæsfælt). Also in alien forms. 1601. [– L. *pissasphaltus* (Pliny) – Gr. πισσάσφαλτος, f. πίσσα pitch + ἄσφαλτος ASPHALT.] A semi-liquid variety of bitumen, mentioned by ancient writers.

Pist, var. PST.

Pistachio (pistā·ʃio, -ă·tʃⁱo, -ēⁱ·ʃio). late ME. [XV *pistace* – OFr. *pistace* (mod. *pistache*), superseded (XVI) by Sp. *pistacho*, It. *pistaccio*. All – L. *pistacium* – Gr. πιστάκιον, πιστάκη (nut and tree) – Pers. *pistah.*] **1.** (Also *p. nut.*) The 'nut' or dry drupe of *Pistacia vera* (see b), or its edible kernel, of a greenish colour. 1533. **b.** (Also *p. tree*) The tree *Pistacia vera* (N.O. *Anacardiaceæ*), a native of Western Asia. late ME. **2.** (Also *p. green.*) A green colour like that of the pistachio nut. Also *attrib.* or as *adj.* 1791. **3.** *attrib.*, as *p. green* (sb. and adj.), *nut, tree*, etc. 1598.

‖**Pistacia** (pistēⁱ·ʃⁱă). late ME. [Late L., = pistachio tree, f. Gr. πιστάκη; see prec.] The pistachio tree = prec. 1 b; in *Bot.* the name of the genus, including also the mastic-tree and the terebinth; the species are collectively called *turpentine-trees.* †**b.** = prec. 1 a –1583.

Pistacite (pi·stăsəit). 1828. [– G. *pistazit* (A. G. Werner, 1803), f. prec. + -ITE[1] 2 b; so named from its colour.] *Min.* = EPIDOTE, or a variety of it.

Pistareen (pistărī·n). 1774. [app. f. PESETA.] An Amer. or W. Ind. name for a small coin formerly current there. **b.** *attrib.* or as *adj.* Petty, paltry (cf. PICAYUNE).

Pistic (pi·stik), *a.* 1646. [– L. *pisticus* (Vulg.) – Gr. πιστικός, of disputed meaning and origin.] In *nard p., p. nard* = Gr. νάρδος πιστική in Mark 14:3, John 12:3 (in Bible versions translated *spikenard*).

Pistil (pi·stil). 1578. [In sense 1 the same word as PESTLE. In sense 2 – Fr. *pistile* (Tournefort, 1694) or L. *pistillum* PESTLE; somewhat earlier the L. form was in use, also after Tournefort.] *Bot.* †**1.** In early use (in form *pestle, pestill*), the thick pestle-like spadix of araceous plants –1672. **2.** The female organ of a flower, comprising (in its complete form) the ovary, style, and stigma 1749. So **Pi·stillary** *a.* of, pertaining to, or of the nature of a p. **Pi·stillate** *a.* having a p. or pistils (and no stamens); female: opp. to *staminate.* **Pistilli·ferous** *a.* pistillate: opp. to *staminiferous.* **Pi·stilline** *a.* pistillate; pistillary.

‖**Pistillidium** (pistili·diŏm). *Pl.* **-ia.** 1854. [mod.L., f. *pistillum* PISTIL + *-idium* = Gr. -ιδιον, dim. suffix.] *Bot.* The female organ in the higher Cryptogams, the ARCHEGONIUM.

†**Pistle.** [OE. *pistol*, aphet. f. *epistol* – L. *epistola* EPISTLE.] **1.** = EPISTLE *sb.* 1–3. –1787. **2.** A (spoken) story or discourse –1550.

Pistol (pi·stəl), *sb.* 1570. [– Fr. †*pistole* – G. *pistole* (XV in documents relating to the Hussite wars) – Czech *pištal.* Cf. the contemp. *howitzer.*] A small fire-arm with a more or less curved stock, adapted to be held in, and fired with, one hand.

Volta's p., a metallic tubular vessel, closed with a cork, in which an explosive mixture of gases may be ignited by an electric spark.

attrib. and *Comb.*: **p.-arm,** the arm with which the p. is held when fired; **-carbine,** a p. with a detachable butt-piece, which can be fired either as a p. or as a carbine; **-pipe** (*Metallurgy*), the blast-pipe of a hot-blast furnace; **-shot,** a shot from a p.; the distance to which a shot can be fired from a p. Hence **Pis·tol,** *v. trans.* to shoot with a p.

Pistole (pistōᵘ·l). 1592. [– Fr. *pistole*, shortening of PISTOLET².] A name formerly applied to certain foreign gold coins; occas. = PISTOLET²; *spec.* from 1600 applied to a Spanish gold coin worth 16*s.* 6*d.* to 18*s.*

Pistoleer (-īᵊ·ɹ). 1832. [See -EER.] A soldier armed with a pistol.

†**Pi·stolet¹.** 1550. [– Fr. *pistolet* (a) small dagger, (b) small fire-arm, pistol, in It. *pistoletto* (XVI), app. dim. from stem of *pistolese* 'great dagger', subst. use of *Pistolese* adj., f. *Pistoia* town in Tuscany.] A small fire-arm; the earlier name of the PISTOL –1650.

†**Pistolet².** 1553. [– Fr. *pistolet* (XVI), of obscure history.] A name given to certain foreign gold coins; in the 16th c. usu. ranging in value from 5*s.* 10*d.* to 6*s.* 8*d.*; in later times = PISTOLE –1659.

Piston (pi·stən). 1704. [– Fr. *piston* (Pascal) – It. *pistone*, var. of *pestone* pestle, rammer, augm. f. *pest-* in *pestello* PESTLE.] **1.** A disc or short cylinder of wood, iron, etc., which fits closely within a hollow cylinder or tube, and can be driven with a reciprocating motion up and down the tube, or backwards and forwards in it; on one side it is attached to a rod (*piston-rod*) by which it imparts motion to machinery (e.g. in a steam-engine), or by which motion is imparted to it (e.g. in a pump). **2.** In the cornet, etc., a sliding valve which moves in a cylinder like a piston, used for increasing the length of the air-passage and thus lowering the pitch of the note 1876.

attrib. and *Comb.*: **p.-head,** the disc of a p., which slides in the tube, as dist. from the *piston-rod*; **-rod** (see 1); **-valve,** (*a*) a valve in a p., as that in a pump; (*b*) a valve formed by a p. sliding backwards and forwards in a tube, for admitting steam into, or exhausting it from, the cylinder of a steam-engine.

Pit (pit), *sb.* [OE. *pytt* = OFris. *pett*, OS. *putti* (MDu. *putte*, Du. *put*), OHG. *pfuzzi* (G. *pfütze* pool, puddle) :– WGmc. **putti*, **putja* (ON. *pyttr* is from OE.) – L. *puteus* well, pit, shaft.] **1.** A hole or cavity in the ground, either natural or formed by digging. **b.** An open deep hole made in digging for some mineral deposit, as CHALK-, CLAY-, GRAVEL-*pit* OE. **c.** A hole made for a special purpose in various industries, as sawing, tanning, etc. OE. **d.** *Agric.* and *Gardening.* A hole made for storing and protecting edible roots, etc. through the winter; or one (usu. with a glazed frame) for protecting young or tender plants 1500. **e.** A dungeon. *Obs.* exc. *Hist.* 1500. **f.** A covered hole to serve as a trap for wild beasts (or enemies); a pitfall 1611. **2.** A well, a water-hole; a pond, pool. *Obs.* or merged in 1. OE. **3.** A grave. *Obs.* or *dial.* (exc. as in *plague-pit*, etc.) ME. **4.** The abode of evil spirits and lost souls; hell, or some part of it. Often in phr. *pit of hell.* ME. **5.** An enclosure in which animals were or are set to fight for sport; *esp.* = COCKPIT 1. 1568. **b.** = COCKPIT 2. **6.** The shaft of a coal-mine; also, the mine as a whole 1447. **7.** *Pit and gallows*, in *Sc. Law*, the privilege, formerly conferred on barons, of executing thieves or other felons by hanging the men on a gallows and drowning the women in a pit (see sense 2) ME.

1. There in the ghastly p...a body was found TENNYSON. **e.** Then took they Jeremiah, and cast him into the dungeon [*marg.* or pit] of Malchiah R. V. *Jer.* 38:6. **f.** He [a young lion] was taken in their p. *Ezek.* 19:4. *fig.* He fals himselfe that digs anothers p. DEKKER. **3.** O Lord..thou hast kept me alive, that I should not go down to the p. *Ps.* 30:3. **5.** Phr. *To fly* or *shoot the p.*, to turn and fly out of the p., as a craven cock; hence *fig.*

II. 1. A hollow or indentation in an animal or plant body, or in any surface: *spec.* A natural hollow or depression in the body, as the ARMPIT ME. **b.** A depressed scar, such as those left on the skin after small-pox 1677. **c.** *Bot.* A minute depression on the inner side of the wall of a cell or vessel, as in the wood-cells of conifers; also, a minute depression on the surface of a seed 1857. **2.** That part of the auditorium of a theatre which is on the floor of the house; now usu. only the part of this which is behind the stalls. Also *transf.* the people occupying this. 1649. **3.** *U.S.* A part of the floor of an Exchange appropriated to a special branch of business, e.g. *grain p.*, *wheat p.* 1886. **b.** Hence, the name of a card game, which mimics a corn exchange 1904.

1. a. *P. of the stomach*, the slight depression in the region of the stomach between the cartilages of the false ribs. **2.** Speak more to the p...—the soliloquy always to the p., that's a rule SHERIDAN. **3.** The world's food should not be at the mercy of the Chicago wheat p. 1903.

Comb.: **p.-bank,** the bank at a pit-head where the coal is sorted and screened; **-brow,** the brow or edge of a p. **-frame,** a framework at the top of a p. or shaft, supporting the pulley; **-head,** the top of a p. or shaft, or the ground immediately around it; **-kiln,** an oven for making coke from coal; **-saw,** a large saw for cutting timber, worked in a sawpit, with handles at the top and bottom; **-sawyer,** the man who stands in a sawpit and works the lower handle of a pit-saw (opp. to *top-sawyer*); **-stall,** a seat situated between the stalls and the pit; **-viper,** a venomous serpent of the family *Crotalidæ*, characterized by a p. or depression in front of each eye; **-work,** the system of pumps and machinery connected with them in a p. or shaft.

Pit, *v.* 1456. [f. prec.] **I. 1.** *trans.* To put or cast into a pit; *esp.* to put (roots, vegetables, etc.) into a pit for storage. **2.** To set (cocks, dogs, pugilists, etc.) to fight for sport, prop. in a 'pit' or enclosure 1760. **3.** *fig.* To match, oppose (persons or things). Const. *against.* Often in passive. 1754.

1. They..liued like beasts, and were pitted like beasts, tumbled into the graue 1621. **2.** Two of the gamest little men ever pitted for twenty-five guineas 1814.

II. 1. To make pits in. **a.** To make hollows or depressions in or upon; to mark with small scars or spots, as those left on the skin after small-pox. Usu. in *pass.* Also *absol.* or *intr.* 1487. **b.** To furnish with pits or holes; to dig pits in 1764. **2.** *intr.* for *pass.* To sink in or contract so as to form a pit or hollow. Also, to become marked with pits. 1737.

1. a. A Gentlewoman, whose Nose was pitted with the Small Pox 1661. Great drops of rain began to p. the white dusty roads 1891.

‖**Pita** (pī·ta). 1698. [Sp. – Peruvian (Quichua) *pita* fine thread from bast.] **a.** Name for the 'American aloe' (*Agave americana*) and allied species. **b.** The tough fibre obtained from these, used for cordage, etc.; also called *p.-fibre, -flax, -hemp, -thread.* **c.** *P.-wood*, the pith-like wood of *Fourcroya gigantea.*

‖**Pitahaya** (pitahā·ya). 1783. [Sp. – Haytian.] Name (in Mexico and South-western U.S.) for the giant cactus (*Cereus giganteus*) or other tall species bearing edible fruit.

Pit-a-pat (pi·tăpæ:t), **pit-pat** (pi·tpæt), *adv.*, *adj.*, *sb.* 1522. [imit. of rapidly alternating sounds; cf. PITTER-PATTER.] An imitation of the alternated sound made by the strong beating of the heart in excitement or emotion; also of that of light and rapid footsteps, etc. **A.** *adv.* With such a sound or sounds; palpitatingly; patteringly: usu. in phr. *to go pit-a-pat.* **B.** *adj.* Palpitating, pattering 1637. **C.** *sb.* The sound itself, or the action producing it 1582.

A. Her feet went pit-a-pat with joy 1760. **C.** 'Tis but the pit-a-pat of two young hearts DRYDEN. Hence **Pit-a-pat** *v. intr.* to go pit-a-pat, to palpitate, to patter.

Pitch (pitʃ), *sb.*¹ [OE. *pić*, corresp. to OS. *pik* (Du. *pek*), OHG. *peh* (G. *pech*), ON. *bik*, Gmc. – L. *pix, pic-*.] **1.** A tenacious, resinous substance, of a black or dark-brown colour, hard when cold, a thick viscid semi-liquid when heated; obtained as a residuum from the boiling of tar, also from the distillation of turpentine; used to stop the seams of ships after caulking, to protect wood from moisture, etc. **2.** Applied to various bituminous substances (*mineral p.*); esp. (*Jew's p.*) = ASPHALT 1, BITUMEN 1. late ME. **3.** Improp. applied to the resin or crude turpentine which exudes from pines and firs. late ME.

2. A Vessel of huge bulk,..Smeard round with P. MILT. **3.** *Burgundy* or *white p.*: see BURGUNDY. *Greek p.* = COLOPHONY.

Phrases. *Black* or *dark as p.*; *He that toucheth p. shall be defiled therewith* (Ecclus. 13:1), etc.

Comb., **p.-black** *a.*, of the brownish-black colour of p.; also, intensely black; **-dark** *a.* (two words when predicative), 'as dark as p.', intensely dark; hence **-darkness**; **-ore,** (*a*) a dark-brown ore of copper, containing bitumen; (*b*) = PITTICITE; (*c*) = PITCH-BLENDE.

Pitch (pitʃ), *sb.*² 1500. [f. next, but the sense-development is obsc.] **I.** Act or manner of pitching. †**1.** An act of setting, laying, or paying down; *concr.* that which is laid or thrown down (*rare*). **b.** An act of pitching upon a thing or place 1791. **2.** An act of plunging head-foremost; *spec.* *Naut.* The downward plunge of a ship's head in a seaway 1762. **3.** The act of pitching or throwing underhand. **a.** *Cricket.* The act or manner of delivering the ball in bowling, or the way in which it alights. **b.** *Baseball.* The act of serving the ball to the batter; the right or turn to do this. **c.** *Golf.* The action of 'lofting' the ball. 1833. **II.** Something that is pitched, or used for pitching. **a.** The quantity of hay, etc. thrown up by a pitchfork 1778. **b.** The quantity of some particular commodity pitched or placed in a market for sale 1866. **III.** Place of pitching. **1.** A place at which one stations oneself or is stationed; *esp.* a spot at which a street performer, a bookmaker, a crossing-sweeper, etc., stations himself 1765. **2.** *Agric.* and *Mining* (Cornw.). A definite portion of a field or of a mine, allotted to a particular workman 1805. **3.** *Cricket.* The piece of ground between and about the wickets 1886.

IV. Highest point, height, etc. †**1.** The highest (or extreme) point, top, apex, vertex –1667. †**2.** A projecting point of some part of the body, as the shoulder, the hip –1611. **3.** The extreme point of a cape or headland 1677. **4.** The height to which a falcon, etc., soars before swooping down on its prey. Often in phr. *to fly a p.* 1591. †**b.** Altitude, elevation –1774. **5.** *fig.* Highest or supreme point or degree; acme, climax. Now *rare* exc. in *at the p. of one's voice.* 1624. †**6.** Height, stature –1807. **7.** Height of an arched roof, or of any roof or ceiling, above the floor, or of the vertex of an arch above the springing line 1615.

4. And beares his thoughts aboue his Faulcons P. SHAKS. *fig.* Rabelais flew to a higher p., too, than Sterne 1798. **5.** When the general hilarity was at its p. 1873.

V. Height in a fig. sense, degree. **1.** Comparative height or intensity of any quality or attribute; degree, elevation, stage, status, level. Almost always used of a high or intense degree. 1568. **2.** *Mus.* That quality of a musical sound which depends on the comparative rapidity of the vibrations producing it; degree of acuteness or graveness of tone. (Sometimes also in ref. to the tone of the voice in speaking.) Also a particular standard of pitch for voices or instruments, as *concert p.* (also *transf.* and *fig.*) 1797. **b.** *transf.* Applied to light, etc., as being analogous to sound 1871.

1. To lowest p. of abject fortune thou art fall'n MILT. **2.** Screaming out..in every conceivable key and p. of shrillness 1867. **b.** The p. of the light..heightens 1871.

VI. Inclination, slope, declivity. Degree of inclination to the horizon, slope; a sloping part or place. *spec.* **a.** A steep place, declivity, a descent, usu. sloping, sometimes perpendicular 1542. **b.** *Mining.* The inclination of a vein of ore or seam of coal from the horizontal 1719. **c.** *Arch.* The inclination of a sloping roof, or of the rafters, to the horizontal; the proportion of the height of a roof to its span 1703. **d.** The slope of a flight of steps: *concr.* a flight of steps 1703. **e.** The setting of a ploughshare for a required depth of penetration. **f.** The rake or inclination of the teeth of a saw. **g.** The inclination of the bit of a plane to the surface that is being planed. 1707. **VII.** *Mech.* The fixed distance between successive points or lines. **a.** The distance between the centres of any two successive teeth of a cog-wheel or pinion, or links of a gear-chain, measured along the *pitch-line* or *pitch-circle* (see *Combs.*); the distance between the successive paddles of a paddle-wheel, measured on the circle passing through their centres. **b.** The distance between the successive convolutions of the thread of a screw, measured in a direction parallel to the axis. **c.** The distance between the centres of successive rivets or stays. 1815.

Comb.: **p.-chain,** a chain consisting of links riveted or bolted together so as to work in the teeth of a toothed wheel; **-circle,** a circular *pitch-like*; **-line,** the imaginary line, usu. a circle, passing through the teeth of a cog-wheel, pinion, rack, etc. so as to touch the corresponding line in another cog-wheel, etc., when the two are geared together; **-point,** the point of contact of the pitch-lines of two cog-wheels, etc. which engage with each other; **-wheel,** a toothed wheel engaging with another.

Pitch (pitʃ), *v.*[1] ME. [The ME. conjugation *pic(c)he, pihte, (i)piht* suggests the existence of an OE. **piċċ(e)an*, rel. to *piċung* 'stigmata', of unkn. origin; pa. t. and pa. pple. *pight* were in full use till XVII, but the new form *pitched* appears XIV.] **I.** To thrust in, fix in; make fast, settle; set, place. †**1.** *trans.* To plant, implant; to fix, stick, fasten. Later, approaching the sense 'to place'. –1775. **2.** To place and make fast with stakes, poles, pegs, etc., as a net or the like. Now *rare.* 1545. **3.** *spec.* To fix and erect (a tent, pavilion, etc.) as a place of lodgement ME. **b.** *absol.* or *intr.* To encamp 1440. **4.** *trans.* To set, plant, place (anything) in a fixed or definite position; to found or set up (a building, pillar, etc.) ME. **b.** *spec.* To set (a stone, etc.) upon end; to set a stone on edge for paving 1623. †**5.** *fig.* To place, implant, plant, set, fix (one's trust, hope, desire, thought, sight, etc.) *in* or *on* some object, or *in* some state –1820. **6.** To place or lay out (wares) in a fixed place for sale; hence, to expose for sale in the market, etc. 1530. **7.** *intr.* (or *refl.*) To place or locate oneself; to take up one's position, settle, alight. Now *rare* or *arch.* 1609. **8.** *trans.* To set, plant, fill, furnish (something) *with* things or persons stuck or placed in or on it; *esp.* to pave (a road, path, etc.) with stones set on end. Also, to form a foundation for a macadamized road with larger stones placed on edge. 1550.

1. Phr. *To p. the wickets* (Cricket), to stick or fix the stumps in the ground and place the bails. **2.** The dext'rous Huntsman . . pitches Toils to stop the Flight DRYDEN. **3.** The tents were pitched where I chose to rest JOHNSON. Phr. *To p. a camp, a caravan*, etc. **b.** To choose a commodious place to p. in HOBBES. **4.** Their mightier Empire there, the middle English pight DRAYTON. **6.** †*P. and pay* (absol. or intr.), ? to pay down at once; The word is, P. and pay: trust none SHAKS. **8.** He wore a gown of purple velvet, pight with pieces of gold FULLER. Paved with bricks or pitched with pebble 1811.

II. To set in order, arrange; to fix the order, position, rate, price, or pitch of. **1.** *trans.* To set in order for fighting, to arrange (a battle, field of battle); to set in array. *Obs.* exc. in PITCHED *ppl. a.* (q.v.). 1470. **2.** To pit (one person) *against* another (*rare*) 1801. †**3.** To determine (something that is to be); to fix, settle –1649. †**4.** To fix, settle, or place in thought; to determine (an existing fact); to ascertain; to come to a conclusion about –1687. **5.** To set at a particular pitch or degree (high, low, etc.). In mod. use mostly *fig.* To set in a particular 'key', or style of expression, feeling, etc. 1633. **b.** *Mus.* To determine the pitch of (a tune, the voice, an instrument) 1674. **6.** *intr.* with *on* or *upon*: To fix upon, decide upon; to select, choose; in mod. use, to select more or less casually; to let one's choice fall *upon* 1628.

1. Our battle, then, in martial manner pitch'd MARLOWE. **4.** First they p. their conclusion, and then hunt about for premises to make it good 1640. **5.** His conversation was pitched in a minor key 1874. **6.** The place which he pitched upon for his trading post 1836.

III. To cast or throw in particular ways. **1.** *trans.* To cast, throw, or fling forward; to hurl; to throw (a thing) underhand so that it may fall and rest on a particular spot. Also *absol.* late ME. **b.** To throw (sheaves, hay, etc.) with a pitchfork. Often *absol.* late ME. **c.** In *Baseball*, etc.: To deliver or serve (the ball) to the batter. In various games, to throw a flat object towards a mark. Also *absol.* 1773. **d.** *slang.* To utter, tell 1867. **2.** *intr.* for *pass.* To fall headlong heavily, or strike forcibly against something, by being thrown ME. **3.** *intr.* Of a ship: To plunge with the head into the trough of the sea; hence, to rise and fall alternately at bow and stern; to plunge in a longitudinal direction (as dist. from *rolling*) 1687. **b.** *trans.* To cast (*away*, *overboard*, etc.) by this movement 1727. **c.** *intr.* Of a person or animal: To plunge forward like a pitching ship 1849.

1. Mrs Villiers, in galloping to cover the other day . . was pitched off 1836. **d.** If he had had the sense to . . p. them a tale, he might have got off 1867. **2.** On his head unhappily he pight SPENSER.

IV. *intr.* To incline forwards and downwards; to dip. Now only in *Mining*, said of a vein of ore or other stratum. 1519. **b.** *intr.* To settle down, as a swelling or loose soil; *fig.* to lose flesh (*dial.*) 1794. **V.** with *adv.* or *prep.* **a.** *P. in*: to set to work vigorously. *colloq.* (chiefly *U.S.*) 1847. **b.** *P. into*: to attack forcibly (with blows, etc., or with words); to reprimand (*colloq.*) 1843. **VI.** The verb-stem in comb. forming *sbs.*, in names of games, in which coins, etc., are thrown at a mark, or into a hole or vessel; as PITCH-AND-TOSS, PITCH-FARTHING, etc.

Pitch (pitʃ), *v.*[2] [OE. (*ġe*)*piċian*, f. *piċ* PITCH *sb.*[1]] *trans.* To cover, coat, or smear with pitch; to brand (a sheep, etc.) with pitch; to stain with pitch.

Pi·tch-and-to·ss. 1810. [From name of the two actions.] A game of combined skill and chance.

Each player pitches a coin at a mark; the one whose coin lies nearest to the mark then tosses all the coins and keeps those that turn up 'head'; the one whose coin lay next in order does the same with the remaining ones, and so on, till none are left.

Pitch-blende (pi·tʃblend). 1770. [– G. *pechblende*, f. *pech* PITCH *sb.*[1]; see BLENDE.] *Min.* Native oxide of uranium, found in blackish pitch-like masses, more rarely crystalline; URANINITE.

Pi·tch-brand. 1631. [f. PITCH *sb.*[1] + BRAND *sb.*] A mark of ownership made upon a sheep, etc.; also *fig.* a distinctive evil mark or characteristic.

Pitched (pitʃt), †**pight** (pəit), *ppl. a.* ME. [pa. pple. of PITCH *v.*[1]] †**1.** Fixed in the ground, staked; set in anything; set with jewels –1615. **2.** Set in orderly array for fighting; said of a battle of which the plans and ground have been chosen and fixed beforehand; a regular battle as dist. from a skirmish, etc.; also *pitched field* 1549. **3.** In other senses of PITCH *v.*[1] 1605. **4.** [Partly f. PITCH *sb.*[2]] Having a (high, low, etc.) pitch, as a roof, building, plough 1615. **b.** Having a specified musical pitch 1622.

Pitcher[1] (pi·tʃəɹ). [ME. *picher, pecher* – OFr. *pichier, pechier* pot (mod. *pichet*) – Frank. **bikari* BEAKER.] **1.** A large vessel usu. of earthenware, with a handle (or two ears) and usu. a lip, for holding liquids. **2.** *Bot.* A leaf, or part of one, modified into the form of a pitcher (see PITCHER-PLANT): = ASCIDIUM 2. 1797.

1. Prov. *Pitchers have ears* (with pun on EAR): used as a warning that one may be overheard; in *little pitchers have long* or *wide ears* (etc.) said in ref. to children. *The p. goes often to the well, but is broken at last* (etc.): said of long-continued success (or impunity), ending at length in failure (or punishment). Hence **Pi·tcherful**, the quantity that fills a p.

Pitcher[2] (pi·tʃəɹ). 1707. [f. PITCH *v.*[1] + -ER[1].] **1.** One who pitches anything; e.g. in *Harvesting*, one who pitches the hay or sheaves to the loader on a cart or rick 1722. **b.** A street vendor who pitches a stall at a definite place or occupies a 'pitch' 1896. **2.** A player who pitches or delivers a ball, *esp.* in *Baseball* 1870. **3.** Something pitched, or used for pitching; *esp.* a stone used for paving; the brick-shaped granite 'setts' used for crossings, etc. 1707.

Pi·tcher-plant. 1835. [f. PITCHER[1] + PLANT *sb.*[1]] Name for several plants, which have the leaves, or some of them, modified into the form of a pitcher, often containing a liquid secretion by means of which insects are captured and assimilated by the plant; *esp.* the E. Indian genus *Nepenthes*, and the N. American genus *Sarracenia*.

Pi·tch-fa:rthing. 1742. [PITCH *v.*[1] III. 1.] = *chuck-farthing* (CHUCK *v.*[2]) q.v.

Pitchfork (pi·tʃfǭɹk), *sb.*[1] 1452. [Also, earlier, *pickfork*, dial. *pikefork*; app. orig. f. PICK *sb.*[1], PIKE *sb.*[1], and subseq. assoc. with PITCH *v.*[1]] A long-handled fork with two sharp prongs for lifting and pitching hay, straw, or sheaves.

Pi·tchfork, *sb.*[2] 1881. [f. PITCH *sb.*[2] V. 2 + FORK *sb.*, after PITCH-PIPE.] A tuning-fork for setting the pitch of a tune or instrument.

Pi·tchfork, *v.* 1837. [f. PITCHFORK *sb.*[1]] **1.** *trans.* To cast with, or as with, a pitchfork; to pitch forcibly or roughly. **b.** *fig.*; *esp.* to thrust (a person) forcibly or unsuitably into some position or office 1844. **2.** To stab or attack with a pitchfork 1854.

1. b. Whether he was pitchforked into the service or rose meritoriously is now a matter of indifference 1863.

Pitching (pi·tʃiŋ), *vbl. sb.* late ME. [f. PITCH *v.*[1] + -ING[1].] **1.** The action of PITCH *v.*[1] **2.** *spec.* The action of setting stones in paving; also, the facing of a bank or slope with stones set on edge close together, as a protection against waves or currents 1703. **b.** *concr.* Pavement composed of cobbles or granite 'setts' firmly set up; also, a facing of stone on a bank or slope 1693. **c.** The foundation of a macadamized road made of stones 6 or 8 inches deep, laid on edge so as to form an arched support for the broken metalling 1830. **3.** The action of throwing, hurling, or lofting something; *esp.* a ball in baseball, golf, etc. 1652.

Comb. **p.-piece,** a piece of timber at the top of a wooden staircase, supporting the 'carriage' or framework (correlative to the *apron-piece* at the bottom).

Pitch-ore: see PITCH *sb.*[1]

Pitch-pine. 1754. [f. PITCH *sb.*[1] + PINE *sb.*[2]] Name of several species of pine with specially resinous wood, or from which pitch or turpentine is obtained; esp. *Pinus rigida* of N. America.

Pi·tch-pipe. 1711. [f. PITCH *sb.*[2] V. 2 + PIPE *sb.*[1]] A small musical pipe, blown by the mouth (either a flue-pipe or a reed-pipe), used to set the pitch for singing or tuning an instrument.

Pitchstone (pi·tʃstōᵘn). 1784. [f. PITCH *sb.*[1] + STONE *sb.*, tr. G. *pechstein* (Werner, 1780).] An old volcanic rock; obsidian or other rock looking like hardened pitch.

Pitchwork (pi·tʃwɒɹk). 1858. [f. PITCH *sb.*[2]] Mining work in which the workmen are paid by receiving a fixed proportion of the output.

Pitchy (pi·tʃi), *a.* (*adv.*) 1513. [f. PITCH *sb.*[1] + -Y[1].] **1.** Full of pitch; bituminous, resinous; coated, smeared, or soiled with pitch; *fig.* sticky like pitch, thievish. **2.** Like pitch; tenacious, viscid; bituminous 1552. **3.** *Nat. Hist.*, etc. Of the colour of pitch; dark-brown inclining to black. Hence *pitchy-black*. 1828. **4.** *fig.* 'As black as pitch'; pitch-dark; of darkness, Intense, thick 1586. **b.** Morally 'black'; grossly wicked 1612.

4. The pitchie night had bereft vs of the conduct of our eyes 1615. **b.** The p. taint of general vice CRABBE. Hence **Pi·tchiness**, intense darkness or blackness.

Pit-coal. Now *rare* or *arch.* 1483. [f. PIT *sb.* + COAL.] Coal obtained from pits or mines (as dist. from *charcoal*), now called simply *coal* (COAL *sb.* 4).

Piteous (pi·tiəs), *a.* [ME. *pito(u)s, pituo(u)s*, later *piteo(u)s* – AFr. *pitous*, OFr. *pitos, piteus* :– Rom. **pietosus*, f. L. *pietas* PIETY, PITY; see -EOUS.] †**1.** Full of piety; godly, devout –1570. **2.** = PITIFUL 2. ME. **3.** = PITIFUL 3. ME. **b.** as *adv.* Piteously. late ME.

1. The Lord knew for to delyuere pitouse men of temptacioun WYCLIF 2 *Pet.* 2:9. **2.** He hath with a p. eye Beheld us in our misery MILT. **3.** A p. thinge was it to se COVERDALE 2 *Macc.* 6:9. Hence **Pi·teous-ly** *adv.*, **-ness.**

Pitfall (pi·tfǭl). late ME. [app. f. PIT *sb.* + FALL *sb.*^{2}, OE. *fealle* a falling trap-door, a trap. Now usu. taken as a 'pit into which one may fall'.] †**1.** A trap for birds in which a trap-door or the like falls over a cavity or hollow –1706. **2.** A concealed pit into which animals or men may fall and be captured. late ME. **3.** *fig.* A 'trap' for the unsuspecting or unwary; any hidden danger or error into which a person may fall unawares 1586.

3. The snares and pitfalls of the law 1827.

Pith (piþ), *sb.* [OE. *piþa*, corresp. to MLG., MDu. *pitte, pit* :– WGmc. **piþ(þ)on*, repr. only in the LG. group, of unkn. origin.] **1.** The central column of spongy cellular tissue in the stems and branches of dicotyledonous plants; the medulla; applied also to the internal tissue of other stems, and to that lining the rind in certain fruits (e.g. the orange). **2.** The spinal cord 1594. **3.** Applied to other substances analogous to the pith of a tree; e.g. the core of various epidermal appendages, as feathers, horn, and hair. late ME. **4.** *fig.* The central or inward part; hence, the essential or vital part (*of* anything); spirit, essence. So *p. and marrow.* OE. **5.** Physical strength or force; vigour; mettle, 'backbone' ME. **b.** Force, energy (of words, speech, etc.) 1526. †**6.** Substance, substantial quality (of words, writings, etc.) –1590. **7.** Importance, gravity, weight 1602.

4. The very p. and marrow of Mr. Wesley's views 1831. **5.** A man of Sampsons p. 1601. **b.** Cool vigour and laconic p. CARLYLE. **6.** It hath in it some p. 1529. **7.** Enterprizes of great p. and moment SHAKS.

attrib. and *Comb.*, as **p. hat, helmet,** a helmet-shaped sun-hat made of dried p. of the Indian Solah or Spongewood of Bengal (*Æschynomene aspera*); **-paper,** a paper made from the p. of various plants; **-plant,** the Chinese rice-paper tree (*Aralia* or *Fatsia papyrifera*). Hence **Pi·thless** *a.* having no p.

Pith (piþ), *v.* 1805. [f. prec. sb.] *trans.* To pierce or sever the pith or spinal cord of (an animal), so as to kill it or render it insensible; *spec.* to slaughter (cattle) in this way.

Pithecanthrope (piþikæ·nþrōup). Also **Pithecanthropos, -us.** 1876. [f. Gr. πίθηκος ape + ἄνθρωπος man.] An ape-man or man-like ape; Haeckel's name (1868) for a hypothetical link between the Apes and Man.

Pithecian (piþī·siăn), *a.* 1890. [– Fr. *pithécien*, f. Gr. πίθηκος ape: see -IAN.] *Zool.* Of or pertaining to *Pithecia*, the typical genus of the *Pitheciinæ*, a subfamily of the *Cabidæ*, S. Amer. monkeys commonly called Sakis.

Pithecoid (piþī·koid), *a.* (*sb.*) 1861. [– Fr. *pithécoïde*, f. Gr. πίθηκος ape; see -OID.] Resembling in form or pertaining to the apes, esp. the higher or anthropoid apes; simian, ape-like. Also *sb.*

Pi·t-hole. 1601. A hole forming a pit; a pit-like hollow or cavity; *spec.* a grave.

Pithy (pi·þi), *a.* ME. [f. PITH *sb.* + -Y^1.] **1.** Consisting or of the nature of pith; abounding in pith 1562. **2.** *fig.* Full of strength; vigorous; of liquor, containing much alcohol. Now *dial.* or *Obs.* ME. **3.** Full of substance or significance; solid; *esp.* of speech, etc.: Containing much matter in few words; condensed; sententious; terse. (Now the prevailing sense.) 1529. **b.** *transf.* of a speaker or writer 1548.

1. The p. bunch of unripe nuts 1821. **3.** Very piththie is this pronown I 1571. He preached. . a plain, short, p. sermon 1893. **b.** In all these particulars [he] was very short but p. ADDISON. Hence **Pi·thily** *adv.* **Pi·thiness.**

Pitiable (pi·tiăb'l), *a.* 1456. [XV *piteable, pytoyable* – OFr. *piteable, pitoi-* (mod. *pitoyable*), f. *piteer, pitier, pitoyer*; see PITY *v.*, -ABLE.] **1.** = PITIFUL 3. 1456. **2.** = PITIFUL 4. 1789.

1. Theese pytoyable thynges thus y-happed CAXTON. **2.** The p. display of short-sighted greed over the Factory Bill 1891. Hence **Pi·tiableness. Pi·tiably** *adv.*

Pitiful (pi·tiful), *a.* 1449. [f. PITY *sb.* + -FUL.] †**1.** Pious (*rare*) –1570. **2.** Full of or characterized by pity; compassionate, tender 1491. **3.** Exciting or apt to excite pity; deplorable, lamentable 1450. †**b.** as *adv.* Pitifully –1599. **4.** To be pitied for its littleness or meanness; despicable, contemptible 1582.

2. The lorde is very pitifull and mercifull TINDALE *Jas.* 5:11. **3.** The p. fate of his friend 1871. **4.** A p. copy of verses PEPYS. Hence **Pi·tiful-ly** *adv.*, **-ness.**

Pitiless (pi·tilės), *a.* late ME. [f. PITY *sb.* + -LESS.] Without pity or compassion; merciless.

The pelting of this pittilesse storme SHAKS. Hence **Pi·tiless-ly** *adv.*, **-ness.**

Pitman (pi·tmæ̆n). 1609. [f. PIT *sb.* + MAN *sb.*] †**1.** The digger of a common grave. J. DAVIES. **2.** A man who works in a pit or mine; *esp.* a collier 1761. **3.** A pit-sawyer 1703. **4.** (*transf.* from 3.) In machinery, a connecting-rod. Chiefly *U.S.* 1846.

Piton (pī·tǫn, piton). 1920. [Fr.] *Mountaineering.* A peg or cramp stuck into a rock-face.

Pitpan (pi·tpæn). 1798. [Mosquito.] = DUG-OUT *sb.* 1, used in Central America.

Pit-pat: see PIT-A-PAT.

‖**Pitta** (pi·tă). 1840. [mod.L. – Telugu *piṭṭa* anything small, a pet.] *Ornith.* A family of passerine birds, type of the family *Pittidæ*, the Ant-thrushes of the Old World, species of which inhabit China, India, and Australia, and one, *P. angolensis*, the W. Coast of Africa.

Pittacal (pi·tăkæl). 1835. [– G. *pittacal* (Reichenbach, 1835), f. Gr. πίττα pitch + καλός beautiful, κάλλος beauty.] *Chem.* A dark-blue solid substance obtained from the high-boiling portions of wood-tar.

Pittance (pi·tăns). [ME. *pita(u)nce* – OFr. *pi(e)tance* – med.L. *pitantia* (XII), *pietantia*, f. L. *pietas* PITY *sb.*; see -ANCE.] **1.** A pious donation or bequest to a religious house or order, to provide extra food, etc., on particular occasions; hence, the allowance or dole itself. Now only *Hist.* **b.** An alms, dole. late ME. **2.** A small allowance of food and drink; scanty rations or diet. Now *rare.* late ME. **b.** A (bare) allowance, remuneration, or stipend, by way of livelihood 1714. **3.** A (small or sparing) allowance, share, or allotment (*of* anything) 1616. **b.** A small proportion of a whole 1561.

1. b. Their usual requests for pittances of food and clothing 1838. **2. b.** Yon cottager, . . Just earns a scanty p. COWPER. **3.** Her small p. of wages FIELDING. **b.** A small p. of Reason and Truth LOCKE.

Pitted (pi·tėd), *ppl. a.* OE. [f. PIT *v.* + -ED^1; and partly f. PIT *sb.* + -ED^2.] **1.** Marked or spotted with pits; *spec.* in *Bot.* of cells, vessels, etc. (see PIT *sb.*). Also, marked *with* small-pox. **2.** Placed or planted in a pit 1799.

Pitter (pi·təɹ), *v. dial.* 1592. [imit.] *intr.* To make a rapid repetition of a sound in quality approaching short *i*, as in the sound made by the grasshopper, or by a thin stream of water running over stones.

Pi·tter-pa·tter, *sb.* (*adv.*) late ME. [redupl. from PATTER *v.*^{1} and ^{2}. Cf. PIT-A-PAT.] †**1.** Pattering repetition –1561. **2.** An imitation of a rapid alternation of light beating sounds, as those made by rain, light footfalls, etc. **a.** orig. as *adv.* 1679. **b.** as *sb.* A designation of such a sound 1863.

Pitticite (pi·tisəit). 1826. [– G. *pittizit* (Hausmann, 1813), f. Gr. πίττα pitch + -IC + -ITE^1 2b.] *Min.* Hydrous sulpharsenate of iron having a vitreous or greasy lustre, occurring in yellowish or reddish-brown, red, and white reniform masses. Also called *pitchy iron ore.*

Pittite^1 (pi·təit). 1808. [See -ITE^1 1.] An adherent of the English statesman William Pitt (1759–1806), or of his policy. So **Pi·ttism,** Pitt's policy.

Pittite^2 (pi·təit). 1807. [f. PIT *sb.* + -ITE^1.] *colloq.* One who occupies a seat in the pit of a theatre.

‖**Pituita** (pitiu,əi·tă). 1699. [L.] *Physiol.* The secretion of the mucous membrane; phlegm, mucus. Also *attrib.* = next.

Pituitary (pitiū·itări), *a.* 1615. [– L. *pituitarius*, f. *pituita* gum, slime, rheum; see -ARY^1.] *Physiol.*, etc. Of, pertaining to, or secreting pituita or phlegm; mucous. **b.** *absol.* or as *sb.* (*a*) = p. membrane; (*b*) = p. gland 1845.

P. body, gland, a small bilobed ductless gland attached to the infundibulum at the base of the brain.

Pituitous (pitiū·itəs), *a.* 1607. [– L. *pituitosus*, f. as prec.; see -OUS.] Of, pertaining to, consisting of, or of the nature of pituita or mucus; of diseases, etc.: Characterized or caused by excess of mucus. **b.** = PHLEGMATIC 1658.

‖**Pituri** (pi·tiŭri). 1863. Native name of an Australian shrub, *Duboisia hopwoodii*, the leaves, etc. of which are used as a narcotic.

Pity (pi·ti), *sb.* [ME. *pite* – OFr. *pité* (mod. *pitié*) :– L. *pietas, -tat-* PIETY. In ME. both *pite* and *piete* are found first in the sense 'compassion', later both are found also in the sense 'piety'; they were not completely differentiated before 1600.] †**1.** The quality of being pitiful; clemency, mercy, mildness, tenderness –1613. **2.** A feeling of tenderness aroused by the suffering or misfortune of another, and prompting a desire for its relief; compassion, sympathy ME. **3.** *transf.* A ground or cause for pity; a regrettable fact or circumstance; a thing to be sorry for. In early use without *a*. late ME. **b.** Idiomatically with *of* (= in respect of). *Obs.* or *arch.* 1450. †**4.** Remorse. *To have p.*, to repent. –1591.

2. Griefe, for the Calamity of another, is Pitty HOBBES. *To have* or *take p.*, prop. to conceive or feel p.; usu. to exercise p., to be compassionate. Const. *on, upon. For pity's sake*, exclam. of entreaty. **3.** Phr. *It is, was, would be* (*a*) *p.*, *the more* (*is*) *the p.*, *a thousand pities, a great p.*, etc. What a p. it is I was not born in the golden age of Louis the Fourteenth H. WALPOLE. It would be a p. to alter it 1880. **b.** But yet the pitty of it, Iago! SHAKS.

Pity (pi·ti), *v.* 1515. [f. prec. sb., perh. after OFr. *piteer, pitier* (mod. *pitoyer*).] **1.** *trans.* To feel pity for; to be sorry for. (Sometimes implying slight contempt.) 1529. †**2.** To move to pity; to grieve. Usu. impersonal. –1835. †**3.** *intr.* (or *trans.* with *inf.* or *obj. cl.*) To be moved to pity; to grieve –1670.

1. Like as a father pitieth his children, so the Lord pitieth them that feare him *Ps.* 103:13. **2.** Thy seruantes haue a loue to hir stones, and it pitieth them to se her in the dust COVERDALE *Ps.* 101[2]:14. **3.** I pitie to see you go from suche good beginnygnes COVERDALE. Hence **Pi·tier,** one who pities. **Pi·tying** *ppl. a.* that pities; compassionate. (In mod. use occas., Feeling slight contempt.) **Pi·tyingly** *adv.*

‖**Pityriasis** (pitirəi·ăsis). 1693. [mod.L. – Gr. πιτυρίασις scurf, f. πίτυρον bran; see -ASIS.] *Path.* A condition of the skin characterized by the formation and falling off of irregular patches of small bran-like scales, without inflammation; the (diseased) formation of dandruff or scurf.

Pivot (pi·vət), *sb.* 1611. [– (O)Fr. *pivot*, prob. f. Rom. base repr. by Fr. dial. *pue* tooth of a comb, harrow, etc., Pr. *pua* (mod. *pivo*), Sp. *pu(y)a* point, of unkn. origin.] **1.** A short shaft or pin, forming the fulcrum and centre on which something turns or oscillates; a pintle, gudgeon. **2.** *Mil.* The officer or man on whom a body of troops wheels; also that flank by which the alignment is corrected 1796. **3.** *fig.* That on which anything turns; a cardinal or central point 1813. **4.** *attrib.* or *adj.* That is the pivot; cardinal; pivotal 1861.

3. The paper-money is the p., on which their all turns COBBETT.

Comb.: **p.-bridge,** a swing-bridge pivoted on a central pier; **-broach, -drill,** watchmakers' tools; **-gun,** a gun which may be turned freely on a p., to alter the directions.

Pi·vot, *v.* 1841. [f. prec. sb., partly after Fr. *pivoter*.] **1.** *trans.* To furnish with, mount on, or attach by means of, a pivot or pivots. (Chiefly in *pass.*) Also *fig.* 1851. **2.** *intr.* To turn as on a pivot; to hinge; in *Mil.* to swing round a point as centre. Chiefly *fig.* 1841.

Pivotal (pi·vətăl), *a.* 1844. [f. PIVOT *sb.* + -AL^1.] Of, pertaining to, of the nature of, or constituting a pivot; central, cardinal, vital.

To have for p. motive nothing but the fear of

death from hunger 1844. Hence **Pi·votally** *adv.* as on a pivot.

Pix: see PYX.

Pixy, pixie (pi·ksi). Also *w. dial.* **pisky.** 1630. [Of unkn. origin.] A supposed supernatural being akin to a fairy.

attrib. and *Comb.*: **p.-ring** = FAIRY-RING; **p. stool,** a toadstool or mushroom.

Pixy-led, *a.* 1659. Led astray by pixies; bewildered.

‖**Pizzicato** (pittsikā·to), *a., adv., sb.* 1845. [It., pa. pple. of *pizzicare* pinch, twitch, f. *pizzare*, f. (O)It. *pizza* point, edge.] *Mus.* **A.** *adj.* and *adv.* Said of a note or passage played on a violin, etc. by plucking the string with the finger instead of using the bow. (Abbrev. *pizz.*) 1880. **B.** *sb.* A note or passage so played.

Pizzle (pi·z'l). Now *dial.* or *vulgar.* 1523. [– LG. *pēsel*, Flem. *pēzel*, dim. of MLG. *pēse*, MDu. *pēze* (Du. *pees* sinew, string, penis), whence also synon. MLG., MDu. *pēserik* (Du. *pezerik*); cf. -LE.] The penis of an animal; often that of a bull, used as a flogging instrument.

Placable (plæ·kab'l, plēi·kăb'l), *a.* 1450. [– OFr. *placable* or L. *placabilis*, f. *placare*; see PLACATE, -ABLE.] †**1.** Pleasing, agreeable –1542. **2.** Capable of being, or easy to be, pacified; gentle, forgiving 1586. ¶**3.** Peaceable, quiet. (*Catachrestic.*) 1611.

2. Methought I saw him p. and mild MILT. Hence **Pla·cableness. Pla·cably** *adv.*

Placard (plæ·kāɹd), *sb.* 1481. [XV *placquart*, etc. – Fr. †*placquart*, *-ard* (mod. *placard*), f. OFr. *plaquier* (mod. *plaquer*) lay flat, plaster – MDu. *placken*.] **1.** An official or public document. **1.** A formal document (orig.) authenticated by a thin seal affixed to its surface; an edict, ordinance, proclamation, official announcement. *Obs.* exc. *Hist.* 1482. **b.** esp. in 17th c., A decree or ordinance of the States General or other competent authority in the Netherlands. In this sense often spelt *placaert, placaet, placaat*, after Du. *Hist.* 1589. **2.** A notice, or other document, written or printed on one side of a single sheet, to be posted up, or otherwise publicly displayed; a bill, a poster 1560.

1. All Placarts or Edicts are publish'd in his name 1645.

II. †**a.** A piece of armour; a breast- or back-plate; esp. an additional plate of steel, iron, etc., worn over or under the cuirass –1826. †**b.** An article of dress, sometimes richly embroidered, app. worn by both sexes in the 15th and 16th c., beneath a coat or gown –1548.

Placard (plæ·kāɹd), *v.* 1813. [f. prec. sb.] **1.** *trans.* To affix or set up placards on or in (a wall, window, town, etc.). **2.** To make public, advertise (something) by means of placards; to display (a poster, notice, etc.) as a placard 1818.

2. Bills..were placarded on all the walls DICKENS.

Placate (plăkēi·t, pleikēi·t), *v.* 1678. [– *placat-*, pa. ppl. stem of L. *placare* appease; see -ATE[3].] *trans.* To render friendly; to pacify, conciliate; to propitiate.

A victory so complete..failed to p. the indignant young actress 1894. Hence **Placa·tion,** the action of placating; conciliation, propitiation. **Placatory** (plæ·kătəri, plēi·k-) *a.* propitiatory.

Pla·ccate. *Obs.* exc. *Hist.* 1588. [app. a var. of PLACARD (in sense II. a.). See also PLACKET and cf. AL. *placatum* (XIV).] = PLACARD *sb.* II. a. Also, a leather doublet lined with strips of steel, worn under the outer armour 1632.

Place (plēis), *sb.* ME. [– (O)Fr. *place* :– Rom. **plattja* (after **plattus* flat), for L. *platea* broad way, open space – Gr. πλατεῖα (sc. ὁδός) broad way, fem. of πλατύς broad; superseded in gen. use native STEAD and STOW *sb.*[1]] **I.** An open space in a city; a square, a market-place. †**a.** Used in OE. as tr. L. *platea* (Vulg.). **b.** In mod. use, forming the second element in the name of a group of houses in a town or city, now or formerly possessing some of the characters of a square, chiefly that of not being properly a street 1585. **II.** A material space. **1.** Space; extension in two (or three) directions; 'room' (*arch.*) ME. **b.** *gen.* Space, extension. (Chiefly *rhet.*, and opp. to *time.*) 1631. **2.** A particular part of space, of definite situation. (= L. *locus.*) Sometimes applied to a part of the earth's surface. ME. **b.** The portion of space actually occupied by a person or thing; locality; situation 1570. †**c.** Short for 'place of battle', 'field' –1705. **3. a.** A general designation for a city, town, village, hamlet, etc. ME. **b.** A residence, dwelling, house; a seat, mansion; *spec.* a manor-house; a country-house with its surroundings ME. †**c.** A fortress, citadel, 'strong place' –1819. **d.** A building, apartment, or spot devoted to a specified purpose; as *a place of amusement*, etc. 1530. **4.** A particular part or spot in a body or surface. late ME. **5.** A particular part, page, etc. in a book or writing ME. †**b.** A text, extract –1743. †**c.** A subject, a topic; esp. in *Logic* and *Rhet.* = LOCUS *sb.* 2. –1697. **6.** In techn. uses: **a.** *Astron.* The apparent position of a heavenly body on the celestial sphere 1669. **b.** *Falconry.* The point or pitch attained by a falcon, etc., before swooping down on its quarry. *Obs.* (or *arch.* after Shaks.) 1605. **c.** *Mining.* A drift or level driven from side to side of a wide lode as a beginning of a slide.

II. 1. Men..calling 'Place! Place!' to clear the way for their master 1852. Phr. *Give p.*: see Phrases. **b.** He pass'd the flaming bounds of P. and Time GRAY. **2.** I haue no p. to fle vnto COVERDALE. *Ps.* 141:4. **b.** We say it hath kept the same P.:..it hath changed its P. LOCKE. **3.** Schools at Tours and other places in France 1843. **b.** Mr. Rodney's p. in Hampshire 1902. **d.** The Coffee-houses have ever since been my chief Places of Resort ADDISON. *Another p.*, in House of Commons phraseology, the other house, the House of Lords. *P. of worship*: see Phrases. **4.** Who..would..Kiss the p. to make it well? 1804. **5.** They shut up her lesson-books and lost her p. 1861. **6. b.** A Faulcon towring in her pride of p. SHAKS.

III. Position in some scale, order, or series. **1.** Position or standing in the social or any scale; rank, station, whether high or low. **b.** *absol.* High rank or position; dignity ME. **c.** *Racing.* A position among the placed competitors; see PLACE *v.* 5 b. 1885. **2.** *Arith.* The position of a figure in a series, in decimal or similar notation, as indicating its value or denomination; in *pl.* with numeral, used to express the number of figures, esp. after the decimal point in a decimal fraction 1542. **3.** A step or point in the order of progression; as *in the first (next, last) p.*, etc. 1639.

1. As an English critic of English literature, his p. is in the front rank 1893. **2.** He also calculated the ratio to 55 decimal places 1841.

IV. Position or situation with ref. to its occupation or occupant. **1.** A proper, appropriate, or natural place (for the person or thing in question to be in or occupy). late ME. **b.** *fig.* A fitting time; occasion, opportunity. late ME. **c.** *fig.* 'Room'; reasonable ground 1638. **d.** = PLACE-KICK. **2.** The space which one person occupies by usage, allotment, or right; a seat or accommodation in a public building, conveyance, or the like, a seat at table. late ME. **b.** With *possessive* or *of*: The space previously or customarily occupied by some other person or thing; room; stead 1450. **3.** An office, employment, situation; occas. *spec.* a government appointment 1558. **b.** Without *a* or *pl.*: Official position, esp. of a minister of state 1568. **c.** The duties of any office or position; (one's) duty or business 1652.

1. Heere's no p. for you maids SHAKS. **c.** In the Sacred Writings there's no p. for Conjectures or Emendations 1721. **2.** After having fee'd very high for places at Mrs. Siddons's benefit 1806. **b.** O God, that Somerset..were in Talbots p. SHAKS. Phr. *In the p. of*, instead of, in substitution for. *To take the p. of*, to be substituted for. **3.** Couldn't let you do it, sir. Much as my place's worth 1871. **b.** P. shows the man 1702.

Phrases. *With other sbs. **Place of arms** [– Fr. *place d'armes*]. **a.** An open space for the assembling of troops. **b.** A strongly fortified city or a fortress, used as an arsenal or magazine, or as a place of retreat. **P. of worship.** A place where religious worship is performed; *spec.* a building (or part of one) appropriated to assemblies or meetings for religious worship 1689. **With preps. **From p. to p.** From one p. to another, and so on in succession. **In p.** †**a.** On the spot. So *upon the p.* **b.** In its original or proper position; in position; *in situ*; *spec.* in *Geol.*; in *Mining*, applied to a vein or lode situated between fixed rocks. **c.** *fig.* In his or its proper or fitting position; in one's element, at home; timely. **d.** *In* (some one's) *p.*: situated as (he) is. **Out of p.** Not situated in the natural or appropriate position; misplaced; *fig.* unsuitable, unseasonable. ***With verbs. **Find p.** To find room to dwell or exist, to have being (*in* something). **Give p.** To make room get out of the way; to give way *to*; to be succeeded by. *arch.* exc. *fig.* **Have p.** To have room to exist; to exist; to be situated. **Take p. a.** To take effect; to be accomplished or realized. *Obs.* or *arch.* †**b.** To find acceptance. †**c.** To take precedence *of.* †**d.** To be present. **e.** To come into existence, happen; to occur (in place or time).

attrib. and *Comb.*, as *p.-name*; *p.-monger*; **p. act,** the Act of Parliament excluding persons holding office under the Crown from sitting in the House of Commons; **p. betting,** backing a horse, etc. for a pl.; **p. horse,** one which comes in among those placed; see PLACE *v.* 5 b. See also Main words.

Place (plēis), *v. Pa. t.* and *pple.* **placed** (plēist). 1548. [f. prec. Cf. Fr. *placer*.] **1.** *trans.* To put or set in a particular place, position, or situation; *fig.* to set in some condition or relation to other things. Often a mere synonym of *put, set.* 1551. **b.** To put or set (a number of things) in their proper places; to arrange 1548. **2.** To appoint (a person) to a place; *spec.* to induct to a pastorate 1550. **b.** To find a place or situation for; to settle 1596. **3.** *spec.* **a.** To put out (money, funds) at interest. Often with *out.* **b.** To put (an order for goods) into the hands of a (selected) person or firm. **c.** To dispose of to a customer. **d.** To arrange for the performance or publication of (a play, book, etc.). 1700. **4.** *fig.* To fix, repose (faith, confidence, etc.) *in* or *on* a particular person or thing 1621. **5.** To assign a place to; to locate; to rank, class; to date 1597. **b.** *Racing.* To state the position of (a horse, etc., usu. the first three only) among the competitors when passing the winning post; *to be placed*, to obtain a place among the first three 1831. **c.** To identify fully; to determine who (or what) a particular person (or thing) is; to assign to a class (orig. *U.S.*) 1855. **6.** To ascribe; to hold (a quality, etc.) to reside or consist *in* something; †to 'put down' *to* 1608. **7.** *Rugby Football.* To get (a goal) from a place-kick 1890.

1. He used to p. the patient under a pump 1800. **b.** (Stage direction) Places chairs SHERIDAN. **3. b.** Many large orders have already been placed for next season 1889. **4.** No confidence could be placed in any of the twelve Judges MACAULAY. **6.** They did not p. honour or honesty simply in victory 1631.

‖**Placebo** (plăsī·bo). *Pl.* **-os, oes.** ME. [– L. (I shall be pleasing or acceptable), 1st sing. fut. ind. of *placēre* please.] **1.** *Eccl.* In the Latin rite: Vespers for the Dead, the first antiphon of which is *Placebo Domino* [etc.], Ps. 114:9. Vulg. †**2.** A flatterer, sycophant –1651. **3.** *Med.* A medicine given more to please than to benefit the patient 1811.

1. Phr. *To sing (a) p.*, etc., to be servile or time-serving.

Pla·ce-brick. 1703. *orig.* A brick made of soft clay, and laid on a prepared 'place' to harden before being burnt; now, a brick which has been imperfectly burnt, through being on the windward side of the kiln or clamp.

Pla·ce-ho:lder. 1818. One who holds office under the government.

Pla·ce-hu:nter. 1713. One who seeks persistently for a post in the public service. (With unfavourable connotation.) So **Pla·ce-hunting** *sb.* and *a.*

Pla·ce-kick, *sb.* 1845. [f. PLACE *sb.* + KICK *sb.*[1]] *Rugby Football.* A kick made by a player when the ball is previously placed on the ground for that purpose by another player. So **Pla·ce-kick** *v.*

Placeless (plēi·slės), *a.* 1598. [f. PLACE *sb.* + -LESS.] **1.** Not confined to place; not bounded or defined. **2.** Having no stated place or locality 1644. **3.** Out of office or employment 1831.

Placeman (plēi·smæ̆n). 1741. [f. PLACE *sb.* + MAN *sb.*] One who holds an appointment in the service of the sovereign or state; usu. in hostile sense: One who is appointed to (or seeks) such a position from motives of interest, without regard to fitness.

Placement (plēi·smĕnt). 1844. [f. PLACE *v.* + -MENT. Cf. Fr. *placement*.] The action of placing, or fact of being placed; placing, arrangement.

‖**Placenta** (plăse·ntă). 1677. [L., cake – Gr. πλακοῦντα, acc. of πλακοῦς flat cake, f. root πλακ- of πλάξ flat plate.] **1.** *Zool.* and *Anat.* (orig. *p. uterina* uterine cake.) The spongy vascular organ, of flattened circular form, to which the fœtus is attached by the umbilical cord, and by means of which it is nourished in the womb, in all the higher mammals, and which is expelled in parturition; the afterbirth 1691. **2.** *Bot.* That part of the carpel to which the ovules are attached. So **Placenti·ferous** *a.* bearing or having a p. 1667.

Placental (plăse·ntăl), *a.* (*sb.*) 1808. [– mod.L. *placentalis*; see next, -AL[1].] **1.** *Zool.*, etc. Of or pertaining to the placenta. **b.** Furnished with a placenta 1840. **2.** *Bot.* Pertaining to the placenta of a plant 1857. **B.** *sb.* A placental mammal 1847.

‖**Placentalia** (plæsĕntē[i]·liă), *sb. pl.* 1842. [mod.L. (L. Bonaparte, 1837), n. pl. of *placentalis* adj., f. L. PLACENTA + -AL[1].] *Zool.* Placental mammals; a primary division of Mammalia, comprising those provided with a placenta; contrasted with *Marsupialia* and *Monotremata*.

Placentary (plæ·sĕntări, plăse·ntări), *a.* (*sb.*) 1843. [f. PLACENTA + -ARY[1].] Of, pertaining or relating to the placenta; placental (*Zool.* and *Bot.*). **b.** *Zool.* Of or pertaining to the *Placentalia*. **B.** *sb.* *Zool.* A placental mammal 1890.

Placentation (plæsĕntē[i]·ʃən). 1760. [– Fr. *placentation*, f. PLACENTA; see -ATION.] **1.** *Zool.* The formation and disposition of the placenta in the uterus 1880. **2.** *Bot.* The disposition of the placenta or placentas in the ovary.

Place·ntiform, *a.* 1858. [f. PLACENTA + -FORM.] *Zool.* and *Bot.* Having the form of a placenta; discoid; cake-shaped.

Placer[1] (plē[i]·səɹ). 1579. [f. PLACE *v.* + -ER[1].] One who places, puts, or sets; often *techn.*, e.g. in *Bookbinding*, a workman who arranges the sheets.

Placer[2] (plē[i]·səɹ). (Chiefly *U.S.*) 1848. [– Amer. Sp. *placer* (plasē·r) deposit, shoal, rel. to *placel* sandbank, f. *plaza* place.] A deposit of sand, gravel, or earth, in the bed of a stream, or any alluvial or diluvial detritus, containing valuable minerals in particles; a place where this is washed for gold, etc.

Placet (plē[i]·set). 1572. [– L. *placet* it pleases, 3rd. sing. pres. ind. of *placēre* PLEASE.] ‖**1.** The Latin for 'it pleases (me or us)'; part of the formula used in the old universities in voting for or against a measure 1592. **2.** as *sb.* **a.** The expression of assent or sanction (by this word) 1589. **b.** A vote of assent in a council, or in the congregation or convocation of a university 1883.

Placid (plæ·sid), *a.* 1626. [– Fr. *placide* or L. *placidus* pleasing, favourable, gentle, f. *placēre* please; see -ID[1].] Of peaceful or tranquil appearance, character, or disposition.

That p. aspect and meek regard MILT. The male population is distinctly of a p. temperament 1871. Hence **Placidity** (plăsi·dĭti), the quality of being p. 1619. **Pla·cid-ly** *adv.*, **-ness.**

‖**Placitum** (plæ·sitŏm). *Obs.* exc. *Hist. Pl.* **placita.** 1668. [L., n. pa. pple. of *placēre* please; in med.L. the sentence of a court, a fine, a trial, a plea.] The decree of a judge, the decision or determination of a public assembly, a court of justice, or the like. Also, in *pl.* the proceedings at such assemblies or courts, trials at law, pleadings or pleas.

Plack (plæk). *Sc.* and *n. dial. Obs.* exc. *Hist.* 1473. [prob. – Flem. *placke, plecke* a small coin of Brabant and Flanders, current in XV; hence Fr. *plaque, plecque,* med.L. *plac(c)a, plaka* (XV). Orig. 'flat disc, tablet'; so Flem. *plak*, Fr. *plaque* PLAQUE.] †**a.** A coin of the Netherlands of the 15th and 16th centuries –1526. **b.** A small copper coin current in Scotland in the 15th and 16th centuries, worth 4 pennies Scots 1473. **c.** The type of something of very small value; a farthing; a bit 1550. **d.** *attrib.* Worth or costing a plack 1560.

c. Phr. *Not worth a p.*, utterly worthless. *P. and bawbee, p. and boddle*, in full, every penny. *Two and a p.*, a trifle.

Placket (plæ·kĕt). 1546. [alt. (by assoc. with -ET) of *plackerd* (XVI), PLACARD.] **1.** An apron or petticoat; hence *transf.* a woman. *Obs.* or *arch.* 1606. **2.** The slit at the top of a skirt or petticoat, for convenience in putting on and off 1546. **3.** A pocket, esp. that in a woman's skirt 1663. *Comb.* **p.-hole,** an opening in the outer skirt to give access to the pocket within; also = sense 2.

Placo- (plæ·ko), bef. a vowel **plac-**, comb. form of Gr. πλάξ, πλακ- a flat plate, tablet. **Pla·coderm** [Gr. δέρμα] *a.*, having the skin encased in broad flat bony plates, as certain fossil fishes; of or belonging to the *Placodermata* or *Placodermi*, an order of Palæozoic fishes having the head and pectoral region thus protected; *sb.* one of the *Placodermata*. **Placoga·noid** [GANOID] *a.*, of or pertaining to the *Placoganoidei*, a division of fossil Devonian fishes, having the head and part of the body protected by large ganoid plates; *sb.* a fish of this division; also **Placoganoi·dean** *a.* and *sb.*

Placoid (plæ·koid), *a.* and *sb.* 1842. [f. Gr. πλάξ, πλακ- flat plate, tablet; see -OID.] *Zool.* **A.** *adj.* **1.** Having the form of a plate; applied to the horny scales and tubercles of the *Placoidei*; see B. **2.** Having placoid scales; of or pertaining to the *Placoidei* 1847. **B.** *sb.* A fish of the division *Placoidei*, containing the sharks and rays, distinguished by having the skin protected by irregularly disposed bony scales, sometimes bearing spines 1852. Hence **Placoi·dean** *a.* and *sb.* 1836.

‖**Plafond** (plafoṅ). 1664. [Fr., f. *plat* flat + *fond* bottom.] *Arch.* A ceiling; hence, a painting executed on a ceiling.

Plagal (plē[i]·găl), *a.* 1597. [– med.L. *plagalis*, f. *plaga* plagal mode, f. L. *plagius* – med. Gr. πλάγιος (πλάγιος ἦχος plagal mode), in ancient Gr. oblique, f. πλάγος side; see -AL[1].] **a.** In *Gregorian Music*, applied to those eccl. modes which have their sounds comprised between the dominant and its octave, the final being near the middle of the compass. Cf. AUTHENTIC *a.* 8. **b.** *P. cadence*: that in which the chord of the subdominant immediately precedes that of the tonic.

Plage (plāʒ). late ME. [– OFr. *plage* region (mod. beach – It. *piaggia*) :– med.L. *plaga* (late L. *plagia*, Gregory) open space.] †**1.** A region, district, clime; occas., a zone –1613. †**2.** Any one of the four principal quarters of the compass; direction, side –1652. ‖**3.** A seashore, seaside resort 1920.

1. From the frozen p. of Heaven MARLOWE.

Plagiarism (plē[i]·dʒiăriz'm). 1621. [f. as PLAGIARY + -ISM.] **1.** The action or practice of plagiarizing; the taking and using as one's own of the thoughts, writings, or inventions of another. **2.** A purloined idea, design, passage, or work 1797. Hence **Pla·giarist,** one who is guilty of plagiarism 1674. **Plagiari·stic** *a.*, **-ally** *adv.*

1. If an author is once detected in borrowing, he will be suspected of p. ever after HAZLITT. **2.** They are full of plagiarisms, inappropriately borrowed 1875.

Plagiarize (plē[i]·dʒiărəiz), *v.* 1716. [f. next + -IZE.] **1.** *trans.* To practise plagiarism upon (a thing, rarely a person). **2.** *intr.* To practise or commit plagiarism 1832.

Plagiary (plē[i]·dʒiări), *sb.* and *a.* 1597. [– L. *plagiarius* kidnapper, literary thief (Martial), f. *plagium* man-stealing, kidnapping – Gr. πλάγιον; see -ARY[1]. Cf. Fr. *plagiaire*.] **A.** *sb.* †**1.** A kidnapper, a manstealer –1697. **2.** = PLAGIARIST 1601. **3.** = PLAGIARISM 1; literary theft 1646. **b.** = PLAGIARISM 2. 1677.

2. Why? the ditt' is all borrowed; 'tis Horaces: hang him p. B. JONS.

B. *adj.* †**1.** That plagiarizes; plagiarizing –1662. †**2.** Obtained by plagiarism; plagiarized –1820.

Plagihedral (plē[i]dʒihī·drăl, -he·drăl), *a.* 1805. [f. PLAGI(O- + Gr. ἕδρα seat, base.] *Cryst.* Having certain faces obliquely situated; also said of such faces.

Plagio- (plē[i]·dʒio-, plæ·gio-), bef. a vowel or *h* **plagi-**, comb. form, repr. Gr. πλάγιος oblique, slanting, f. πλάγος side.

Plagiocephalic (plē[i]·dʒio,sĭfæ·lik) *a.* [Gr. κεφαλή head + -IC] characterized by plagiocephaly; so **Plagioce·phalous** *a.* in same sense. **Plagioce·phaly,** oblique deformity of the skull, consisting in the greater development of the anterior part on one side and of the posterior part on the other. **Pla·gioclase** [Gr. κλάσις cleavage] *Min.* name for the group of triclinic feldspars, the two prominent cleavage directions in which are oblique to one another; so **Plagiocla·stic** *a.* having oblique cleavage; opp. to ORTHOCLASTIC. **Pla·giostome** [Fr.; Gr. στόμα mouth] *sb.* (*a.*) a member of the *Plagiostomi*, cartilaginous fishes, including the sharks and rays, which have the mouth placed transversely beneath the snout; so **Plagio·stomous** *a.* of or pertaining to the plagiostomes; having the mouth placed transversely beneath the snout. **Plagiotro·pic** [Gr. τροπικός inclined, f. τρόπος turning] *a. Bot.* said of members or organs of plants, the two halves of which react differently to the influences of light, gravitation, and other external forces, and which therefore take up an oblique position; opp. to ORTHOTROPIC; hence **Plagio·tropism,** p. character.

Plagionite (plē[i]·dʒiŏnəit). [– G. *plagionit* (G. Rosé, 1833), f. Gr. πλάγιος oblique + -ITE[1] 2 b.] *Min.* A sulphide of lead and antimony occurring in monoclinic thick tubular crystals of a blackish grey colour.

‖**Plagium** (plē[i]·dʒiŏm). 1577. [L.; see PLAGIARY.] *Civil Law.* Kidnapping, man-stealing.

Plague (plē[i]g), *sb.* [XIV *plage* – L. *plaga* stroke, wound, (Vulg.) pestilence, infection, prob. – Gr. (Doric) πλαγά, (Attic) πληγή, f. *πλᾰγ- strike, rel. to L. *plangere*.] †**1.** A blow, a stroke; a wound –1538. **2.** An affliction, calamity, evil, 'scourge'; *esp.* a visitation of divine anger or justice. late ME. **b.** In weakened sense: A nuisance; *colloq.* trouble 1604. **c.** Applied to a person or animal 1551. **3.** A general name for any malignant disease with which men or beasts are stricken. †**a.** An individual affliction, e.g. leprosy –1672. **b.** *esp.* An epidemic attended with great mortality; a pestilence 1548. **c.** *spec. The p.*: the oriental or bubonic plague 1601.

2. Egipte was smyten with x. plages and diseases 1432. This p. of rayne and waters *Bk. Com. Prayer.* **b.** She disliked stiles, she found it such a p. to get over them 1825. **c.** What a P. to Society is a Man who has written a Book 1707. **3. b.** The famous 'plagues', which ravaged Europe, were forms of typhus fever 1871. **c.** His servant died—a bubo on his right groine, and two spots on his right thigh, which is the p. PEPYS.

attrib. and *Comb.*, as **p.-bill,** an official return of the deaths caused by the p. in any district; **-mark** = PLAGUE-SPOT 1; **p. pit,** a deep pit for the common burial of plague victims.

Plague (plē[i]g), *v.* 1481. [f. prec.] **1.** *trans.* To afflict with plague or calamity (esp. in ref. to divine punishment). Now *rare* or *arch.* **2.** In weakened sense: To torment, tease, trouble, bother, annoy 1594.

1. Christians were too intent on plaguing Jews 1787. **2.** Husbands and wives..plaguing one another GAY. Hence **Pla·guer,** one who plagues or harasses. **Pla·guesome** *a.* troublesome, vexatious, plaguy.

Pla·gue-spot. 1711. **1.** A spot on the skin characteristic of the plague, or of some disease so called. **2.** A locality infested with plague. Often *fig.* 1895.

Plaguy (plē[i]·gi), *a.* (*adv.*) 1574. [f. PLAGUE *sb.* + -Y[1].] **1.** Pestiferous, pestilential, pernicious. Now *rare* or *arch.* **b.** Plague-stricken. Now *rare* or *Obs.* 1604. **2.** That is a plague; that causes severe affliction 1598. **b.** In weakened sense: Vexatious, troublesome, annoying, disagreeable; hence *colloq.* = 'pestilent', 'confounded', excessive 1615. **B.** as *adv.* = Plaguily (*colloq.*) 1584.

2. They make charming mistresses but p. wives GAY. **b.** A p. rise in the price of everything 1879. B. You've been a p. long time in coming 1884. Hence **Pla·guily** *adv.* in a p. manner; confoundedly.

Plaice (plē[i]s). [ME. *plais, plaice* – OFr. *plaïz, plaïs,* later *plaise, pleisse* – late L. *platessa* – unrecorded deriv. of Gr. πλατύς broad.] A European flat-fish, *Pleuronectes platessa*, much used as food; in America extended to various allied species of this genus or of the family *Pleuronectidæ*. (Pl. now rare; the collect. sing. *plaice* being used instead.) **2.** *dial.* = FLUKE *sb.*[1] 2. 1722.

attrib. and *Comb.*, as **p.-mouth,** a small puckered or wry mouth; also *attrib.*; so **-mouthed** *a.*

Plaid (plæd, *Sc.* plēd). 1512. [– Gael. *plaide* = Ir. *ploid* blanket, of unkn. origin.] **1.** A long piece of twilled woollen cloth, usu. having a chequered or tartan pattern, forming the outer article of the Highland costume. The Lowland 'shepherd's plaid', of a black chequer pattern on white, is commonly called a MAUD. **2.** The cloth of which plaids are made 1634. **3.** *transf.* A man wearing a plaid; a Highlander. SCOTT.

Comb. **p.-nook (-neuk)** *Sc.*, one end of the folded p. sewn up so as to form a large pocket.

Plaided (plæ·dėd, *Sc.* plē·dėd), *a.* 1802. [f. PLAID + -ED².] **1.** Dressed in or wearing a plaid. **2.** Made of plaid; having a plaid pattern 1814.

Plaidie, -y (plæ·di, *Sc.* plē·di). *Sc.* 1719. [f. PLAID + -IE, -Y⁶.] A small plaid; also, a childish, sentimental, or poetic name for a plaid.

Plaiding (plæ·diŋ, plē·diŋ). 1566. [f. PLAID + -ING¹.] **1.** Material for plaids; a twilled woollen cloth; a cloth of tartan pattern. **2.** A plaid or checkered pattern 1889.

Plain (plē¹n), *sb.* ME. [– OFr. *plain* (superseded by *plaine* :– L. collect. n. pl.) :– L. *planum*, subst. use of n. of adj. See also PLANE *sb.*³] **1.** A flat tract of country; an extent of level ground or flat meadow land; applied *spec.* in *Salisbury Plain*, etc. **b.** Chiefly *pl.* In colonial and U.S. use, any treeless level tract of country; prairie 1779. **c.** *transf.* The level expanse of sea or sky 1567. **2.** An open space as the scene of battle or contest; the field. Now *poet.* late ME. †**3.** A level or flat surface (ideal or material). Now spelt *plane*. = PLANE *sb.*³ 1. –1863. **4.** The floor of the hall in which the French National Convention met at the time of the Revolution; hence applied to the more moderate party who had seats there. (Cf. MOUNTAIN I. 5.) 1827.

1. *Cities of the P.* (sc. *of the Jordan*), Sodom, Gomorrah, etc., before their destruction; Lot dwelled in the cities of the plaine, and pitched his tent toward Sodome *Gen.* 13:12. **c.** The sick'ning stars fade off th'æthereal p. POPE. **2.** I will leade forth my Soldiers to the plaine SHAKS.

attrib. and *Comb.*, as *p.-station*; *plain-like* adj.; also with *plains-*, as *plains-people*, etc.

Plain (plē¹n), *a.*¹ and *adv.* ME. [– OFr. *plain*, fem. *plaine* (surviving in phr. *de plein-pied*, *plain-chant*, etc.) :– L. *planus, -a*, f. base **plā-* flat, of obscure connection. See also PLANE *a.*] **A.** *adj.* **I. 1.** Flat, level, even; free from elevations and depressions. †**b.** *gen.* Flat –1650. †**c.** *Geom.* Now PLANE *a.* 1. –1727. **2.** Smooth, even. *Obs.* exc. in comb. or phrases. ME. **3.** Free from obstructions or interruptions; clear, open; public. *Obs.* exc. *dial.* ME. **b.** *transf.* Unobstructed, clear (*view, sight*) 1613.

1. Follow me then to plainer ground SHAKS. **3.** Able to give him battell in the plaine sea 1579.

II. 1. Open, clear; evident, obvious ME. **2.** That is clearly what the name expresses; manifest; downright, mere, 'flat', absolute ME. **3.** Simple, readily understood. Also *transf.* of a speaker or writer. late ME. **4.** Not complicated; simple 1659.

1. Practical Christianity..is a p. and obvious thing BUTLER. **2.** He reaped p. unequivocal hatred LAMB. **3.** Tell her distinctly what you want.. in few p. words 1861. **4.** P. sewing 1895.

III. 1. Unembellished, not ornate; (of the hair) worn straight, not curled; (of drawings, etc.) not coloured. Also *fig.* ME. **b.** *Cards.* (*a*) Applied to the common as opp. to the picture cards. (*b*) Not trumps. 1844. **2.** Of simple composition; not elaborate. Of food: Not rich or highly seasoned 1655.

1. A young Man..with long p. Hair 1655. Picture-postcards, p. or coloured 1907. **2.** [As a] school-boy counts the currants in an unusually p. cake 1879. *P. bread and butter*, i.e. without preserves, etc. *A p. tea*, tea with p. bread and butter. *P. water*, water without any addition.

IV. 1. Open in behaviour; free from duplicity or reserve; candid, frank. *Obs.* exc. in sense: Plain-spoken. late ME. **2.** Free from evasion or subterfuge, straightforward, direct 1500.

1. I wil sing a Song if any body wil sing another; else, to be p. with you, I wil sing none WALTON. **2.** If you do not give a p. answer to a p. question, you will be committed 1776. Phr. *P. truth* (often with the notion 'uncoloured'). *P. English*: see *Comb.*

V. 1. Ordinary, simple, unsophisticated; such as characterizes ordinary people 1586. **2.** Not distinguished by rank or position; ordinary 1580. **3.** Homely, unaffected 1601. **4.** Simple in dress or habits; frugal 1613. **5.** Of homely appearance; often euphemistically for: Ill-favoured, ugly 1749.

1. I pray thee vnderstand a plaine man in his plaine meaning SHAKS. **2.** I preached to several hundred of p. people WESLEY. **3.** They spoke of.. their Queen..'She is a p. woman, a very p. woman like ourselves' 1904. **4.** His habits of life were remarkably p. and frugal 1871. **5.** Handsome young men must have something to live on, as well as the p. JANE AUSTEN.

Phrases. *P. as a pikestaff* (earlier *packstaff*). *P. as the sun at noonday, as Salisbury* (pun on Salisbury Plain). See also DUNSTABLE.

B. *adv.* (Advb. uses of the adj.) **1.** With clearness of expression; clearly, intelligibly, candidly. late ME. **2.** With clearness of perception or utterance; clearly, manifestly 1590.

1. Sir to tell you plaine, I'le finde a fairer face not washt to day SHAKS. **2.** Did not Torquato Tasso speak p. at six months old? 1784.

Comb.: **p. clothes**, ordinary citizen dress, mufti; opp. to UNIFORM; also *attrib.*, as *plain-clothes constable*; **p. cook** *sb.*, a person, usu. a woman, capable of preparing simple dishes; **p.-cook** *v. intr.*, to do plain cooking; **p. English,** plain straightforward language, plain terms; also, a plain or clear statement; **p. language,** *spec.* the manner of speech used by Quakers; **p.-sail** *Naut.*, sail ordinarily carried; **p. service,** divine service said without music; **-singing** = PLAINSONG. Hence **Plai·n-ly** *adv.*, **-ness.**

†**Plain,** *a.*² [ME. *plein, playn* – (O)Fr. *plein* :– L. *plenus* full.] **1.** Full, plenary, entire, perfect –1653. **2.** Full or complete in number, extent, etc.; esp. of a council, assembly, or court –1677. **3.** In phr. *in p. battle* (*combat, war*), in regular open battle, etc. –1718.

Plain (plē¹n), *v. arch.* or *dial.* [ME. *plei(g)ne, playne* – *plaign-*, pr. stem of (O)Fr. *plaindre* :– L. *plangere*; see COMPLAIN.] = COMPLAIN *v.* in various senses.

I did many times p. my ill hap 1617. Small Cause, I ween, has lusty Youth to p. 1710.

Plai·n chant. 1727. [– Fr. *plain chant*, repr. med.L. *cantus planus*.] = PLAINSONG, CANTO FERMO.

Plain dealer, plain-dealer. Now *rare.* 1571. [f. PLAIN *a.*¹ + DEALER; cf. next.] One who is straightforward and candid in his dealings with others.

Plain dealing, plain-dealing, *sb.* 1573. [f. PLAIN *a.*¹ + DEALING *vbl. sb.*; cf. DOUBLE-DEALING.] Openness of conduct; candour, straightforwardness.

Plai·n-dea:ling, *a.* 1566. [f. PLAIN *adv.* + *dealing* pr. pple.] That deals plainly; straightforward in conduct.

Plain-hearted, *a.* Now *rare.* 1608. [f. *plain heart* (PLAIN *a.*¹) + -ED².] Having a sincere and open heart; without guile; ingenuous, innocent. Hence **Plai:n-hea·rted-ly** *adv.*, **-ness.**

Plaining (plē¹·niŋ), *vbl. sb. arch.* ME. [f. PLAIN *v.* + -ING¹.] The action of PLAIN *v.*; lamentation; complaint.

Plai·n-sai·ling, *sb.* 1827. [pop. use (assoc. with PLAIN *a.*¹ I. 3) of PLANE SAILING, i.e. navigation by a *plane chart* (PLANE *a.*).] Sailing or going on in a plain course, in which there is no difficulty or obstruction; simple or easy course of action.

Plainsman (plē¹·nzmæ̆n). 1881. [f. PLAIN *sb.* + MAN *sb.*] A man of the plain or plains; an inhabitant of a flat country, or of wide open plains.

Plainsong (plē¹·nsǫŋ). 1447. [tr. med.L. *cantus planus* PLAIN CHANT.] **1.** A form of vocal music believed to have been used in the Christian Church from the earliest times, consisting of melodies composed in the mediæval modes (see MODE I. 1 b) and in free rhythm depending on the accentuation of the words, and sung in unison. See AMBROSIAN, GREGORIAN. **2.** A simple melody or theme; often accompanied by a running melody or 'descant' (see DESCANT *sb.*); hence in *fig.* applications. *Obs.* or *Hist.* 1566.

2. *attrib.* The plainsong Cuckow gray SHAKS.

Plain-speaking, *sb.* and *a.* 1852. **A.** *sb.* Plainness of speech, candour, frankness. **B.** *adj.* = next 1884.

Plain-spoken, †**plain-spoke,** *a.* 1678. [f. PLAIN *adv.*; cf. OUTSPOKEN.] **1.** Given to speaking plainly; outspoken. **2.** Plainly spoken; clearly expressed; candid, frank 1703.

2. A rough, bluff, hearty, plain-spoken way of eulogising them to their faces 1836. Hence **Plain-spo·kenness.**

Plaint (plē¹nt), *sb.* [ME. *pleint(e* – (O)Fr. *plainte*, subst. use of pa. pple. fem. of *plaindre*, and OFr. *plaint, pleint* :– L. *planctus*, f. *plangere* PLAIN *v.*] **1.** The action or an act of plaining; lamentation, grieving. (Now chiefly *poet.*). **2.** A statement or representation of wrong, injury, or injustice; a complaint. (Now *rare.*) ME. **3.** *spec.* An oral or written statement of grievance made to a court of law, for the purpose of obtaining redress; an accusation, charge, complaint. late ME.

1. The hapless Paire Sate in their sad discourse, and various p. MILT. **2.** Shee with teares made vnto him her p. 1605.

Plaintiff (plē¹·ntif). late ME. [– law-Fr. *plaintif*, subst. use of (O)Fr. *plaintif*; see PLAINTIVE.] *Law.* The party who brings a suit into a court of law; a complainant, prosecutor; opp. to *defendant*.

Plaintive (plē¹·ntiv), *a.* late ME. [–(O)Fr. *plaintif, -ive*, f. *plaint(e* PLAINT; see -IVE.] **1.** Complaining, lamenting; †suffering. Now *rare.* †**2.** Being or pertaining to the plaintiff in a suit –1596. **3.** Expressive of sorrow; mournful, sad 1579.

3. The fiddle screams P. and piteous COWPER. Hence **Plai·ntive-ly** *adv.*, **-ness.**

Plai·n-work, plain work. 1715. **1.** Work of a simple kind, as dist. from ornamental or 'fancy' work; *spec.* plain needlework or sewing. **2.** *Masonry.* The even surface produced on stone by the chisel, without taking away more than the mere inequalities 1823.

Plaisance, obs. var. of PLEASANCE.

Plaister, obs. f. PLASTER.

Plait (plæt, *Sc.*, *U.S.* plē¹t), *sb.* late ME. [– OFr. *pleit* fold, manner of folding :– Rom. **plic(i)tum*, subst. use of n. of *plicitus*, pa. pple. of L. *plicare* fold (see PLY *v.*¹).] **1.** (Now superseded in gen. use by *pleat.*) A fold, crease, or wrinkle; esp. a flattened fold of cloth made by doubling the material upon itself. **b.** A fold, wrinkle, or crease in any natural structure, e.g. in the lip, brow, or ear 1592. **c.** *fig.* A sinuosity or twist of nature or character; a hidden recess; usu. implying artifice or deceit. *Obs.* or *arch.* 1589. **2.** A contexture of three or more interlaced strands of hair, ribbon, straw, etc.; *esp.* a braided tress of hair, a queue, a pigtail 1530.

1. Then smoothed down the plaits of her apron 1850. **b.** I should fear Some p. between the brows E. B. BROWNING. **2.** Wearing their hair in long plaits down their backs 1880.

Plait (plæt, *Sc. U.S.* plē¹t), *v.* ME. [f. prec.] **1.** *trans.* = PLEAT *v.* 1 (by which it is superseded). **2.** To braid or intertwine (hair, straw, rushes, narrow ribbons, etc.) so as to form a plait, band, or rope.

1. [He] wore his shirt frill plaited and puffed out W. IRVING. **2.** Little Margery..who plaited straw DICKENS. Hence **Plai·ter,** one who or that which plaits.

Plaited (plæ·tėd, *Sc.*, *U.S.* plē¹·tėd), *ppl. a.* late ME. [f. prec. + -ED¹.] **1.** Folded, doubled; furnished with pleats. In this sense superseded by *pleated*. 1440. **b.** Wrinkled, corrugated, fluted, striated 1519. **2.** Braided, formed into a plait; interlaced, interwoven 1594.

2. P. alleys of the trailing rose TENNYSON.

Plan (plæn), *sb.* 1678. [– Fr. *plan* (XVI) ground-plan, alt. (after *plan* adj.; see PLANE *a.*) of †*plant*, f. *planter*, after It. *pianta* plan of an edifice; see PLANT *sb.* This word and PLANE *sb.*³ cover between them the senses of Fr. *plan*.] **I. 1.** A drawing, sketch, etc. of any object, made by projection upon a flat surface (opp. to ELEVATION II. 3); *spec.* (*a*) A drawing showing the relative positions of the parts of a building, or of any one floor of a building on a horizontal plane. (*b*) A large-scale, detailed map of a town or district. See also GROUND-PLAN. **b.** A table or programme indicating the relations of some set of objects, or the times, places, etc. of some intended proceedings 1780. **2.** A scheme of arrangement; *transf.* disposition of parts; a type of structure (viewed as designed); configuration (of a surface) 1732. **3.** A scheme of action, project, design; the way in which it is proposed to carry out some proceeding. Also in weakened sense: Method, way of proceeding. 1706.

2. A mighty maze! but not without a p. POPE. I have not yet drawn out a p. for my stories, but certain germs thereof are budding in my mind THACKERAY. **3.** The good old rule . . the simple p., That they should take, who have the power, And they should keep who can WORDSW. Change your whole p. of campaign 1837.

II. After Fr. *plan*. **a.** *Perspective.* Any one of a number of ideal planes perpendicular to the line of vision passing through the objects represented in a picture 1678. **b.** *Sculpture.* The plane on which the figures in a bas-relief are raised above the ground, *esp.* one of several such planes giving more or less relief to different figures in the design 1780.

Plan (plæn), *v.* 1728. [f. prec. sb.] **1.** *trans.* To make a plan of (a piece of ground, a building, etc.); to plot down, lay down. Also to construct (a plan or diagram). 1748. **2.** To make a plan of (a building, etc., to be constructed); hence to devise, contrive, design (a building, etc., to be constructed) 1728. **3.** To devise, design (something to be done, or some action, etc., to be carried out); to arrange beforehand. Also with clause or *absol.* 1737.

2. The gardens were planned by the best landscape gardeners of the day 1893. **3.** We had planned an ascent of Monte Rosa together TYNDALL.

Planar (plēⁱ·năɹ), *a.* 1850. [f. PLANE *sb.*[3] + -AR[1], after *linear*.] *Math.* Belonging to, situated in, or related in some way to, a plane.

‖**Planaria** (plănēᵊ·riă). 1819. [mod.L. generic name (Müller, 1776), subst. use of fem. of L. *planarius* adj. (used as = 'flat').] *Zool.* A genus of the sub-order *Planarida* of turbellarian worms. Hence **Plana·rian** *a.* belonging or related to the genus *Planaria*; *sb.* a planarian worm, a flat-worm. **Plana·ridan** *a.* belonging to the sub-order *Planarida*; *sb.* a planaridan worm. **Planariform** (-ēᵊ·rifǫɹm) *a.*, **Planarioid** (-ēᵊ·ri,oid) *a.*, of the form of or resembling a planarian.

Planch (plɑnʃ). late ME. [– (O)Fr. *planche* plank, slab; see PLANK *sb.*] **1.** A plank; *dial.* a floor. *Obs.* exc. *dial.* **2.** A slab of metal, stone, baked clay, etc.; *spec.* in *Enamelling*, a slab of baked fire-clay used to support the work during the process of baking 1578.

Plancher (plɑ·nʃəɹ). *Obs.* exc. *dial.* ME. [XV *plauncher*, etc. – Fr. *plancher* (OFr. *-ier*) planking, etc., f. *planche*; see prec., -ER[2]; cf. PLANCIER.] †**1.** A plank, a board; planking, boarding –1720. **2.** A floor (*dial.*) or †platform of planks or boards 1449. †**3.** = PLANCIER –1728.

Planchet (plɑ·nʃėt). 1611. [dim. of PLANCH; see -ET.] The plain disc of metal of which a coin is made; a coin-blank.

Planchette (plănʃe·t, ‖plāṅʃęt). 1860. [– Fr. dim. of *planche* PLANK *sb.*] A small board, supported by two castors and a vertical pencil, which, when one or more persons rest their fingers lightly on the board, is said to trace lines or letters, and even to write sentences, without conscious direction or effort.

Plancier (plænsīᵊ·ɹ). 1664. [– (O)Fr. †*plancier*, collateral form of *planchier*; see PLANCHER.] The under side of the corona of a cornice.

Plane (plēⁱn), *sb.*[1] late ME. [– (O)Fr. *plane* :– L. *platanus* – Gr. πλάτανος f. stem of πλατύς broad.] **1.** A tree of the genus *Platanus*, comprising lofty spreading trees, with broad angular palmately-lobed leaves, and bark which scales off in irregular patches; orig. and esp. *P. orientalis*, the Oriental Plane, a native of Persia and the Levant; also *P. occidentalis*, the Occidental or Virginian Plane or Button-wood. **2.** In Scotland and the North of England applied to the species of maple commonly called 'sycamore' (*Acer pseudoplatanus*), the leaves of which resemble those of *Platanus*; also called False, Mock, or Scotch Plane 1778.

Plane (plēⁱn), *sb.*[2] ME. [– (O)Fr. *plane*, var. (infl. by *planer* vb.) of †*plaine* :– late L. *plana* planing instrument, f. *planare*; see PLANE *v.*[1]] **1.** A tool resembling a plasterer's trowel, used by plumbers, bricklayers, etc., for smoothing the surface of sand, clay in a mould, etc. **2.** A tool used by carpenters and others, for levelling down and smoothing the surface of woodwork by paring shavings from it.

It consists of a *stock* of wood or metal, with a smooth base or *sole* which slides over the surface of the wood, and a steel blade set in it at an angle so that its edge projects slightly through a slit or *mouth* in the sole. BENCH-*p.*, JACK-P., TRYING-*p.*, etc.: see these words.

Plane (plēⁱn), *sb.*[3] 1646. [– L. *planum* flat surface, subst. use of n. of *planus* PLAIN *a.*[1] (for which *plane* was introduced to express the geometrical and allied uses; cf. the supersession of Fr. *plain* by *plan* because of the homophony of *plein* full).] **1. a.** A plane superficies; in *Geom.*, a surface such that every straight line joining any two points in it lies wholly in it, or such that the intersection of two such surfaces is always a straight line; the simplest kind of geometrical surface. Hence *gen.*, An imaginary superficies of this kind in which points or lines in material bodies lie. **b.** A flat or level surface of a material body 1715. **c.** *Cryst.* and *Min.* Each of the natural faces of a crystal; also, an imaginary plane surface related to these in some way 1800. **d.** *Anat.* Any one of certain imaginary plane surfaces used as standards of ref. for the positions of bodily organs, or (in *Craniometry*) of parts of the skull 1830. **e.** (*a*) = AEROPLANE 1. 1824. (*b*) = AEROPLANE 2. 1909. **2.** *Mining.* Any main road in a mine, along which coal, etc., is conveyed in cars or trucks 1877. **3.** *fig.* in ref. to thought, knowledge, moral qualities, social rank, etc.: Higher or lower level, grade, degree 1850.

1. *P. of projection*, a plane upon which points, lines, or figures are projected. *Objective p.* (Perspective), any plane situated in the object itself. *Perspective p.*, a transparent plane, usu. perpendicular to the horizon, supposed to be interposed between the object and the eye, and intersected by straight lines passing from one to the other, which determine the points of the drawing; also called *p. of delineation* or *p. of the picture*. *P. of polarization* (Optics), in polarized light, the plane which passes through the incident ray and the polarized ray, and is perpendicular to the plane of vibration of the ether in the polarized ray. **b.** *Inclined p.*: see INCLINED *ppl. a.* 1. **3.** The superstitious man is on the same p. as the savage 1885.

Plane (plēⁱn), *a.* 1570. [refash. of PLAIN *a.*[1] after Fr. *plan*, fem. *plane*, which was similarly substituted for *plain*, *plaine* in techn. senses; cf. prec.] **1.** *Geom.* Of a surface: Perfectly flat or level, so that every straight line joining any two points in it lies wholly in it (see prec. 1 a). Hence applied to an angle, figure, or curve which lies wholly in such a surface. **b.** *transf.* Relating to or involving plane surfaces or magnitudes 1704. **2.** Of a material surface, etc.: Flat, level; not convex or concave 1666.

p. chart (†*plain chart*), a chart on which the meridians and parallels of latitude are represented by equidistant straight lines (cf. PLANE SAILING); **p. scale** (†*plain scale*), a scale or ruler marked with lines denoting chords, rhumbs, sines, tangents, secants, etc., formerly used, esp. in navigation.

Plane (plēⁱn), *v.*[1] ME. [– (O)Fr. *planer* :– late L. *planare* plane, make smooth, f. L. *planus* PLAIN *a.*[1]] **I.** In gen. sense. **1.** *trans.* To make (a surface) plane, even, or smooth; to level, to smooth. Also *fig.* (Now chiefly in arch. phr. *to p. the way*, or as *fig.* of sense II. 1.) †**2.** *fig.* To make plain or intelligible; to explain, display, show –1659.

1. You planed her path To Lady Psyche TENNYSON.

II. 1. *trans.* To dress with a plane or planing-machine; to smooth down (wood, metal, etc.) with or as with a plane. late ME. **2.** *intr.* To use or work with a plane 1703.

1. Phr. *To p. away, off*: to remove by or as by planing.

Plane (plēⁱn), *v.*[2] 1611. [– Fr. *planer*, f. *plan* plane, because a bird when soaring extends its wings in a plane.] *intr.* Of a bird: To be poised on outspread motionless wings. **b.** [f. PLANE *sb.*[3] 1 e.] To travel in an aeroplane; *esp.* to glide *down* 1909.

Planer (plēⁱ·nəɹ). 1560. [f. PLANE *v.*[1] + -ER[1].] **1.** One who makes level or levels down. **2.** One who planes 1598. **3.** Formerly, a plane; now, a planing-machine 1596. **4.** *Printing.* A block of wood used in beating down projecting types in a form 1858.

Plane sailing. Also formerly **plain s.** 1699. [f. PLANE *a.* in *plane chart.*] In *Navigation*, The art of determining a ship's place on the theory that she is moving on a plane, or that the surface of the earth is plane instead of spherical; navigation by a *plane chart*: see PLANE *a.* **b.** *fig.* A course so simple as to leave no room for mistakes. Now usu. PLAIN SAILING, q.v. 1858.

Planeshear (plēⁱ·nʃīᵊɹ), **planksheer** (plæ·ŋkʃīᵊɹ). 1711. [Perversion of PLANCHER.] A continuous planking covering the timber-heads of a wooden ship, in men-of-war forming a shelf below the gunwale; also loosely applied to the gunwale.

Planet[1] (plæ·nėt). ME. [– (O)Fr. *planète* – late L. *planeta*, *planetes* (only in pl. *planetæ*, for older L. *stellæ errantes*) – Gr. πλανήτης wanderer (pl. ἀστέρες πλανῆται wandering stars), f. πλανᾶν lead astray, wander, rel. to πλάζειν cause to wander.] †**1.** *Old Astr.* A heavenly body distinguished from the fixed stars by having an apparent motion of its own among them. (The seven planets, in the order of their accepted distance from the Earth, were the Moon, Mercury, Venus, the Sun, Mars, Jupiter, and Saturn.) **b.** *esp.* in *Astrol.*, said with ref. to the supposed 'influence' of any one of these bodies in affecting persons and events; in later use said vaguely of an occult controlling fateful power ME. **2.** *Mod. Astron.* The name given to each of the heavenly bodies that revolve in approximately circular orbits round the sun (*primary planets*), and to those that revolve round these (*secondary planets* or SATELLITES) 1640.

The primary planets comprise the *major planets*, viz., in order of distance from the sun, Mercury, Venus, the Earth, Mars, Jupiter, Saturn, Uranus, Neptune, and Pluto, and the *minor planets* or ASTEROIDS, the orbits of which lie between those of Mars and Jupiter.

1. b. I was born under a Threepenny P., never to be worth a Groat SWIFT. **2.** *fig.* Two such political planets 1790.

Comb.: **p.-gear, -gearing**, a system of gearing in which planet-wheels are introduced; a mechanical combination for converting power into speed; **-wheel**, the exterior wheel which revolves round the central or sun-wheel, in the sun-and-planet motion.

Planet[2] (plæ·nėt), ‖**planeta** (plănī·tă). 1602. [– med.L. *planeta* chasuble, perh. shortened f. late L. *planetica* (sc. *vestis*) 'traveller's cloak', subst. use of fem. of *planeticus* wandering; see prec., -IC.] A chasuble.

Pla·ne-ta:ble, *sb.* Also †**plaintable.** 1607. [f. PLANE *a.* + TABLE *sb.*] A surveying instrument used for measuring angles in mapping, consisting of a circular drawing-table mounted horizontally on a tripod, and having an alidade pivoted over its centre. Hence **Pla·ne-ta:ble** *v. trans.* to survey with the plane-table.

‖**Planetarium** (plænėtēᵊ·riŏm). 1774. [mod. L., f. *planetarius*; see next, -ARIUM.] An ORRERY. **b.** A model representing the planetary system 1860.

Planetary (plæ·nėtări), *a.* and *sb.* 1593. [– late L. *planetarius*, prop. adj., but only occurring as sb., an astrologer; see PLANET[1], -ARY[1].] **A.** *adj.* **1.** Belonging to or connected with a planet or planets; of the nature of or resembling a planet; having some attribute of a planet 1602. **b.** esp. in *Astrol.* with ref. to the supposed 'influence' of a planet 1607. **c.** *P. hour*, the twelfth part of the natural day or night. (In *Astrol.* supposed each to be ruled by a planet.) 1593. **2.** Belonging to this planet; terrestrial, mundane 1831. **3.** *fig.* Wandering; erratic 1607.

1. *P. nebula*, one resembling a planet from its disc being round or slightly oval. *P. system*, the system comprising the sun and planets, the solar system; also *fig.* a system of correlated parts. *P. year*: see YEAR. **c.** I was born in the P. hour of Saturn SIR T. BROWNE. **3.** His . . erratical and p. life FULLER. Hence **Pla·netarily** *adv.*

B. *sb.* †**1.** An astrologer, star-gazer –1716. **2.** A planetary body 1819.

Planetesimal (plænėte·simăl), *a.* and *sb.* 1906. [f. PLANET *sb.*[1] + *-esimal*, after *infinitesimal*.] **A.** *adj.* Pertaining to the minute bodies of space. **B.** *sb.* A minute planetary body.

Planetoid (plæ·nėtoid), *sb.* (*a.*) 1803. [f. PLANET *sb.*[1] + -OID.] A body resembling a planet; a minor planet or asteroid. **b.** *adj.* (or *attrib.*) Of or belonging to the asteroids 1862.

Plane-tree (plēⁱ·nˌtrī). late ME. [f. PLANE *sb.*[1] + TREE.] = PLANE *sb.*[1]

Pla·net-stri:cken, *a.* 1600. = next.

Pla·net-struck, *a.* 1600. [f. PLANET *sb.*[1] 1 b + pa. pple. of STRIKE *v.* Cf. *moon-struck.*] Stricken by the supposed malign influence of an adverse planet; blasted.

They being affrighted (as it were Planet-struck) and confounded with shame 1658.

Plangent (plæ·ndʒĕnt), *a.* 1822. [– L. *plangens, -ent-*, pr. pple. of L. *plangere* beat (spec. the breast), strike noisily; see -ENT.] **1.** Making the noise of waves beating on the shore, etc. **2.** Loud-sounding; applied sometimes to a metallic, sometimes to a loud thrilling or plaintive sound 1858.

1. With pulse of p. water like a knell SWINBURNE. **2.** This rugged young King, with his p. metallic voice CARLYLE. Hence **Pla·ngency,** the quality of being p. **Pla·ngently** *adv.*

Plani-, (plēⁱni), comb. form of L. *planus* level, flat, smooth.

Planiform (plēⁱ·nifǭɹm) *a.*, having a flattened shape; *spec.* in *Anat.* = ARTHRODIAL. **Planipennate** (plēⁱnipe·nĕt) [L. *pennatus* winged] *a.*, *Zool.* having flat wings; (*b*) *spec.* in *Entom.* belonging to the suborder *Planipennia* of neuropterous insects, characterized by flat wings not folded when at rest. **Planipe·talous** *a.*, *Bot.* having flat petals.

Planimeter (plăni·mĭtəɹ). Also **-metre.** 1858. [– Fr. *planimètre*, f. PLANI-; see -METER.] An instrument for mechanically measuring the area of an irregular plane figure. So **Planime·tric, -al** *adjs.* **Plani·metry,** the measurement of plane surfaces; plane geometry.

Planing (plēⁱ·niŋ), *vbl. sb.* late ME. [-ING[1].] The action of PLANE *v.*[1] *Comb.*: **p.-machine,** a machine (of various kinds) for planing wood or metal; **-mill,** = planing-machine; also, a workshop where planing is done.

Planish (plæ·niʃ), *v.* late ME. [f. *planiss-*, lengthened stem of OFr. *planir* smooth (now in *aplanir*), f. *plain* PLAIN[1] *a.*, PLANE *a.*; see -ISH[2].] *trans.* To make level or smooth; to level. **b.** *spec.* To flatten (sheet-metal or metal-ware) on an anvil by blows of a smooth-faced hammer, etc.; to flatten and reduce in thickness; to reduce (coining-metal) to the required thickness by passing between rollers; to polish (paper, etc.) by means of a roller 1688. Hence **Pla·nisher,** a person who planishes; a tool or instrument used for planishing. **Pla·nishing** *vbl. sb.*, chiefly *attrib.* and *Comb.*, as **p. hammer,** a hammer with polished slightly convex faces, used for planishing sheet-metal; **-roller,** a roller used in planishing; *esp.* in *pl.*, the second pair of rollers, of hardened and polished iron, between which coining-metal is passed to reduce it to the proper thickness.

Planisphere (plæ·nisfīᵊɹ). [In ME. form *planisperie* – med.L. *planisphærium*, f. L. *planus* PLANE *a.* + *sphæra*, Gr. σφαῖρα SPHERE; in form *planisphere* – Fr. *planisphère.*] A map or chart formed by the projection of a sphere, or part of one, on a plane; now *esp.* a polar projection of half (or more of) the celestial sphere, as in one form of the astrolabe.

Revolving p., a device consisting of a polar projection of the whole of the heavens visible in a particular latitude, covered by a card with an elliptical opening, which can be adjusted so as to show the part of the heavens visible at a given time. Hence **Planisphe·ral, -sphe·ric, -al** *adjs.*

Plank (plæŋk), *sb.* [ME. *planke* – ONFr. *planke* (mod. dial. *planque*) = (O)Fr. *planche* :– late L. *planca* plank, slab, subst. use of fem. of *plancus* flat, flat-footed, used as a cognomen, *Plancus, Plancius, Plancianus.*] **1.** A long flat piece of smoothed timber, thicker than a BOARD; *spec.* a length of timber sawn to a thickness of from two to six inches, a width of nine inches or more, and eight feet or upwards in length. **b.** Without *a* and *pl.* Timber cut into planks; planking 1559. **c.** *fig.* esp. in ref. to the use of a plank to save a shipwrecked man from drowning. **2.** Applied to various things consisting or formed of a flat slab of wood, as a narrow foot-bridge, a table or board, etc. late ME. **3.** *fig.* An item of a political or other programme. (Cf. PLATFORM III. 5 b.) Orig. and chiefly *U.S.* 1848.

1. c. This is indeed the only p. we have to trust to, that can save us from shipwreck 1690. **3.** Another 'plank' is the restriction of Chinese immigration 1884.

Phrases. *P.-over-p.*, with the outside planks overlapping as in a clinker-built vessel. *To walk the p.*, to walk blindfold along a p. laid over the side of a ship until one falls into the sea (as pirates are said to have made their captives do).

attrib. and *Comb.*, as **p.-bed,** a bed of boards resting on low trestles, without a mattress, used as part of the discipline of convents, prisons, etc.; **-road,** a road made of a flooring of planks laid transversely on longitudinal bearing timbers (*U.S.*); **-way,** the narrow portion of deck between the side and the frame of the hatch in a wherry, etc.

Plank (plæŋk), *v.* late ME. [f. prec. sb.] **1.** *trans.* To furnish, lay, floor, or cover with planks. Also with *over.* **b.** To fasten *together* or *down* with planks 1864. **2. a.** To put down; to deposit, plant. *colloq.* 1859. **b.** To table or lay down money; to pay on the spot. Const. *down, out, up. U.S. colloq.* 1824. **3.** *techn.* **a.** To splice together (slivers of wool) into rovings. **b.** To harden (a hat) by felting. 1874. **4.** *U.S.* To fix on a board (a fish that has been split open, or meat) and cook at a hot fire 1855. **5.** *intr.* (also with *it*). To sleep on a plank or a hard surface 1829.

1. The Sides were planck'd with Pine DRYDEN. **b.** Boats planked together two and two CARLYLE.

Planked (plæŋkt), *ppl. a.* 1608. [f. prec. + -ED[1].] **1.** Furnished, laid, etc. with planks. **2.** Of fish, etc.: see sense 4 above.

Planking (plæ·ŋkiŋ), *vbl. sb.* 1495. [f. PLANK *sb.* and *v.* + -ING[1].] **1.** The action of PLANK *v.* **2.** *concr.* Planks in the mass; plank-work; the planks of a structure; *spec.* those forming the outer shell and inner lining of a ship 1751.

Plankton (plæ·ŋktǫn). 1892. [– G. *plankton* (V. Hensen, 1887) – Gr. πλαγκτόν, n. of πλαγκτός wandering, drifting, f. base of πλάζειν strike, cause to wander.] *Biol.* A collective name for all the forms of floating or drifting organic life found at various depths in the ocean, or in bodies of fresh water: opp. to *benthos* and *nekton.* Hence **Plankto·nic** *a.*

Planner (plæ·nəɹ). 1716. [f. PLAN *v.* + -ER[1].] One who plans or makes a plan; *spec.* in *Sc.*, a landscape gardener.

Plano-[1] (plēⁱno), used as comb. form of L. *planus* flat, smooth, level; denoting (*a*) flatly, in a flattened manner, with modification of a specified form in the direction of a plane, as *p.-conical, -orbicular*; (*b*) a combination of a plane with another surface, esp. plane on one side, and of another surface on the other, as PLANO-CONCAVE, -CONVEX, etc. Also **p.-horizontal,** having a plane horizontal surface or position; **-subulate,** of a flat, awl-shaped form.

Plano-[2] (plæno), bef. a vowel or *h* **plan-,** comb. form of Gr. πλάνος wandering, as in **Pla·noblast** [Gr. βλαστός sprout, shoot], *Zool.* the free-swimming generative bud or gonophore of certain Hydrozoa, usu. a craspedote medusa or medusoid.

Pla:no-co·ncave, *a.* 1693. [f. PLANO-[1] + CONCAVE.] Having one surface plane and the opposite one concave, as a lens.

Pla:no-co·nvex, *a.* 1665. [f. as prec. + CONVEX.] **1.** Having one surface plane and the opposite one convex; chiefly of lenses. **b.** Of a crystal: Having some faces plain and others convex 1805. **2.** Having a flattened convex form 1843.

‖**Planorbis** (plănǭ·ɹbis). 1833. [mod.L., f. *planus* PLANE *a.* + *orbis* ORB.] *Zool.* A genus of fresh-water snails (pond-snails), characterized by a flat rounded spiral shell.

Plant (plɑnt), *sb.* [In sense 1 OE. *plante* fem. – L. *planta* sprout, slip, cutting. Later senses are affected by med. or mod. uses of L. *planta*, and by Fr. *plante*, or are derivs. of PLANT *v.*] **I. 1.** A young tree, shrub, or herb for planting; a set, cutting, slip; a sapling. *Obs.* or *dial.* (In local use the name for seedling vegetables at this stage, as 'healthy cabbage plants', etc.) **b.** A young sapling used as a pole, staff, or cudgel. Now chiefly *dial.* late ME. **c.** *fig.* Anything planted; a scion, offshoot, nursling; a young person; a novice. Now *rare.* late ME. **2.** A member of the vegetable kingdom; a vegetable; generally distinguished from an animal by the absence of locomotion and of special organs of sensation and digestion, and by the power of feeding wholly on inorganic substances. Often restricted to the smaller, esp. herbaceous plants, to the exclusion of trees and shrubs 1551.

1. b. Take a p. of stubborn oak And labour him with many a sturdy stroke DRYDEN. **2.** *fig.* Government has been a fossil; it should be a p. EMERSON.

II. Chiefly from PLANT *v.* **1.** *collect.* A crop 1832. **b.** *abstr.* Growth 1844. **2.** The way in which one plants himself; footing, pose 1817. **3.** A deposit of fish-spawn, fry, or oysters; *ellipt.* an oyster which has been bedded or is intended for bedding, as dist. from a native. *U.S.* 1868. **4.** The fixtures, implements, machinery, and apparatus used in carrying on any industrial process. (In Great Britain rarely with *a* or *pl.*) 1789. **b.** *fig.* with ref. to spiritual or intellectual work 1861. **5.** [f. PLANT *v.* III. 2.] A hoard of stolen goods; also the place where they are hidden. *Thieves' slang.* 1796. **6.** A swindle; an elaborately planned burglary or other form of theft or robbery (*slang* or *colloq.*) 1825. **7.** [f. PLANT *v.* I. 2 c.] A spy, a detective; a picket of detectives (*slang*) 1812.

1. b. *In p.*, growing, in leaf; *to lose p.*, to die off; *to fail in* or *miss p.*, to fail to spring from seed. **6.** 'It's a conspiracy', said Ben Allen. 'A regular p.', added Mr. Bob Sawyer DICKENS.

Comb.: **p.-beetle,** a beetle of the family *Chrysomelidæ*, feeding on plants, a leaf-beetle; **-bug,** any one of various hemipterous insects (esp. of the family *Capsidæ*) that infest, and feed upon the juices of, plants; **-cane,** a sugar-cane of one year's growth; **-cutter,** a passerine bird of the S. American genus *Phytotoma*, having the habit of biting off the shoots of plants; **-louse,** any small hemipterous insect that infests plants; *esp.* an aphis.

Plant (plɑnt), *v.* [OE. *plantian* – L. *plantare*, reinforced in ME. from (O)Fr. *planter* :– L. *plantare.*] **I.** To plant a thing in or on a place. **1.** *trans.* To set in the ground so that it may take root and grow (a tree or herb, a shoot, cutting, root, bulb, or tuber; occas., a seed; hence, a crop, a garden, forest, etc.). **b.** To introduce (a breed of animals) into a country; to deposit (young fish, spawn, oysters) in a river, tidal water, etc.; to naturalize 1899. **2.** To place firmly, to fix *in* or *on* the ground, etc.; to set *down* or *up* in a firm position; to fix in position; to post, station. late ME. **b.** To place (artillery) in position for firing 1560. **c.** To station (a person); *esp.* (in slang or vulgar use) to post as a spy or detective 1693. **d.** *refl.* To place, station, post oneself; to take up one's position 1703. **3.** To found, establish, institute (a community, etc., esp. a colony, city, or church). Now *rare.* OE. **b.** To settle (a person) in a place as a colonist, etc. ME. **c.** *refl.* To establish oneself, settle 1560. **4.** To place *in* some local position; to locate, situate; in *pa. pple.* situated 1558. **5.** *fig.* from prec. senses. **a.** To implant, cause (an idea, etc.) to take root in the mind. late ME. **b.** To settle, establish firmly, as a principle, religion, practice, etc. 1529. **c.** To set up (a person or thing) in some position or state 1562.

1. Plaunt þou a vine WYCLIF. Phr. *P. out*, to transfer from a pot or frame to the open ground; to set out (seedlings) at intervals, so as to give room for growth. **2.** He planted the British Colours on the Castle 1714. **b.** Four swivel guns.. were planted at the mouth of each funnel 1748. **c.** He was planted (to use a vulgar phrase) upon me by his party COBDEN. **d.** One grisly old wolf-dog..had planted himself close by the chair SCOTT. **3.** Planting.. schools for the education of youth 1656. **b.** My being planted so well in Brazil DE FOE. **4.** A Town..finely built, but foolishly planted 1624. **5. a.** That noble Thirst of Fame and Reputation which is planted in the Hearts of all Men STEELE. **c.** A man in all the worlds new fashion planted SHAKS.

II. With the place as object. **a.** To furnish (a piece of land) with growing plants 1585. **b.** To furnish *with* a number of things disposed over the surface. late ME. **c.** To furnish a district *with* settlers or colonists; to stock *with* inhabitants, cattle, etc. 1608.

a. With wild Thyme and Sav'ry, p. the Plain DRYDEN. **b.** A vast Ocean planted with innumerable Islands ADDISON.

III. Colloquial uses, orig. slang or vulgar. **1.** To deliver (a blow, etc.) with definite aim. *Pugilistic slang.* 1808. **2.** To hide, conceal; esp. stolen goods. Orig. *Thieves' slang.* 1610. **3.** To 'salt' a mining claim. *Gold-digging slang.* 1850. **b.** To devise as a 'plant' or fraudulent scheme 1892. **4.** To abandon. [Cf. Fr. *planter là.*] *rare.* 1821.

1. I planted a stomacher in his fifth button MARRYAT. **4.** He makes her a most exemplary husband; and then, all at once, he plants her; plants her at once and for ever 1858. Hence **Pla·ntable** *a.* capable of being planted; fit for planting or cultivation.

†**Pla·ntage.** 1606. [– Fr. *plantage*, f. *planter*; see prec., -AGE.] **1.** The cultivation of plants; planting –1688. **2.** Plants in the mass; vegetation, herbage –1825.

2. As true as steele, as p. to the Moone SHAKS.

Plantain[1] (plæ·ntein, -tėn). ME. [– (O)Fr. *plantain*, †*-ein* :– L. *plantago*, *-agin-*, f. *planta* sole of the foot, so called from its broad prostrate leaves.] **1.** A plant of the genus *Plantago*, esp. the Greater Plantain, *P. major*, a low herb with broad flat leaves spread close to the ground, and close spikes of inconspicuous flowers, followed by dense cylindrical spikes of seeds. **2.** Applied with defining words to other plants resembling the plantain 1538.

1. Plantayne or weybrede..is called also..grete plantayne, and groweth in moyst places & playne feldes 1516. Long, Narrow-leaved, or Ribwort P., *Plantago lanceolata.* **2. Bastard P.,** *Limosella aquatica.* **Water P.,** *Alisma plantago.*

Plantain[2] (plæ·ntein, -tėn). Now *Obs.* or *rare.* 1535. [– Fr. †*plantain* (XVI), *plantoine*, used beside *platane* – L. *platanus* PLANE *sb.*[1]] The Plane (*Platanus orientalis.*)

Plantain[3] (plæ·ntein, -tėn). 1555. [In early use also *platan* – Sp. *plátano*, *plántano*, identical with the forms meaning 'plane-tree', to which it is prob. that some native words were assimilated (e.g. Galibi *palatana*, Carib *balatana*, Arawak *pratane*).] **1.** A tree-like tropical herbaceous plant (*Musa paradisiaca*) closely allied to the Banana (*M. sapientum*), having immense undivided oblong leaves, and bearing its fruit in long densely-clustered spikes 1604. **2.** The fruit of this plant, a long, somewhat pod-shaped, or cucumber-like, fleshy fruit (botanically a berry); it forms a staple food in most countries within the tropics.

attrib. and *Comb.*, as **p.-cutter, -eater,** a bird of the genus *Musophaga* or of the family *Musophagidæ*, a TOURACO; **-meal,** the powdered substance of the dried fruit of the p.

Plantal (plæ·ntăl), *a.* Now *rare.* 1642. [f. PLANT + -AL[1], after *animal.*] Pertaining or relating to a plant; vegetable; used by Henry More as tr. Gr. φυτικός.

Pla·nt-a:nimal. Now *rare.* 1621. [– mod. L. *plantanimal* (Budé, 1508), tr. Gr. ζωόφυτον ZOOPHYTE.] A zoophyte or 'animal plant'.

Plantar (plæ·ntăɹ), *a.* 1706. [– L. *plantaris*, f. *planta* sole of the foot; see -AR[1].] *Anat.* Pertaining or relating to the sole of the foot.

Plantation (planteⁱ·ʃən). 1450. [– Fr. *plantation* or L. *plantatio*, f. *plantat-*, pa. ppl. stem of *plantare*; see PLANT *v.*, -ION.] **1.** The action of planting, the placing of plants in the soil so that they may grow. Now *rare.* **b.** The settlement of persons in some locality; *esp.* colonization 1586. **2.** An assemblage of growing plants of any kind which have been planted 1569. **b.** Now *esp.*, a wood of planted trees 1669. †**3.** *fig.* That which has been planted, founded, or settled, as an institution, a mission station –1704. **4.** A settlement in a new or conquered country; a colony. Also *transf. Obs.* exc. *Hist.* 1614. †**b.** A company of settlers or colonists –1715. **5.** An estate or farm, esp. in a tropical country, on which cotton, tobacco, sugar-cane, coffee, or other crops are cultivated, formerly chiefly by servile labour 1706.

1. *fig.* The p. of churches and the propagation of the gospel 1795. **b.** The first p. of Inhabitants, immediately after the Deluge 1625. **2. b.** A plain.. covered with corn, grass, or plantations 1806. **4.** Ireland and the Plantations in America..are a Burthen to England PETTY. Phr. *To send* (prisoners, etc.) *to the plantations*, i.e. to penal servitude or indentured labour in the colonies, a method of punishment in the 17th and 18th c. *Comb.* †**P. Office,** early name of the Colonial Office.

Planted (pla·ntėd), *ppl. a.* ME. [f. PLANT *v.* + -ED[1].] **1.** Set in the ground, as a plant; fixed in the ground, set up, established, etc. (see PLANT *v.*). **2.** Furnished with plants, trees, etc. late ME.

Planter (pla·ntəɹ). ME. [f. PLANT *v.* + -ER[1].] **I.** Of persons. **1.** One who plants or sows; hence, a cultivator of the soil, a farmer, an agriculturist. Also *fig.* **2.** An early settler; a pioneer; a colonist; in Ireland, one of the English or Scotch settlers planted on forfeited lands in the 17th c. *Hist.* 1620. **b.** In Ireland, A person settled in the holding of an evicted tenant 1890. **3.** The proprietor or occupier of a plantation or cultivated estate, *esp.*, now, in tropical and sub-tropical countries. Often in comb., as *cotton-*, *sugar-*, *tobacco-p.* 1647.

II. Of things and beasts. **1.** A machine for planting or sowing seeds, as *potato-p.*, etc. 1856. **2.** *U.S.* A snag formed by a tree-trunk embedded in a more or less erect position in a river 1802. **3.** *colloq.* A horse that has the habit of refusing to move 1864. Hence **Pla·ntership,** the office or condition of a p.

Plantigrade (plæ·ntigrēⁱd), *a.* (*sb.*) 1831. [– Fr. *plantigrade* (Geoffroy and Cuvier, 1795) – mod.L. *plantigradus*, f. *planta* sole + *-gradus* going, walking.] Walking upon the soles of the feet (opp. to DIGITIGRADE); also said of the feet, or of the walk, of an animal. Commonly restricted to the former tribe *Plantigrada* of carnivorous mammals; comprising the bear, wolverene, badger, racoon, etc. **b.** In ref. to human beings: Placing the whole sole of the foot upon the ground at once in walking 1837. **c.** *transf.* Of or belonging to a plantigrade animal, as a bear 1853. **B.** *sb.* A plantigrade animal; *esp.* one of the order *Plantigrada* 1835.

Pla·nting, *vbl. sb.* OE. [f. PLANT *v.* + -ING[1].] **1.** The action of PLANT *v.*, q.v. **2.** A clump or bed of things planted; *esp.* a clump or wood of planted trees; a plantation. Chiefly *Sc.* and *n. dial.* 1632.

Pla·ntlet. 1816. [f. PLANT *sb.* + -LET.] An embryo plant; a diminutive plant.

Planto·cracy. 1846. [irreg. f. PLANT(ER; see -CRACY.] A dominant class or caste consisting of planters (in the W. Indies, etc.).

Plantule (plæ·ntiul). 1733. [– mod.L. *plantula*, dim. of *planta* a shoot; see -ULE.] *Bot.* An embryonic or rudimentary plant.

‖**Planula** (plæ·niŭlă). *Pl.* **-æ.** 1870. [mod. L., a little plane, dim. of *planus* PLANE *a.*] *Zool.* The flat-shaped ciliated free-swimming embryo of certain Hydrozoa; hence extended to a similar embryo in Cœlenterates generally.

Planxty (plæ·ŋksti). 1790. [Of unkn. origin.] *Irish Music.* 'A harp tune of a sportive and animated character, moving in triplets' (Stainer and Barrett).

Plap (plæp), *v.* 1846. [imit.; cf. *flap*, *slap.*] *intr.* To come down or fall with a flat impact, and with the sound that this makes. Also as *sb.* or *adv.*

‖**Plaque** (plak). 1848. [– Fr. *plaque* – Du. *plak* tablet, f. *plakken* stick; cf. PLACARD.] **1.** An ornamental tablet of metal or porcelain, either plain or decorated, intended to be hung up on a wall, inserted in a piece of furniture, etc. 1875. **b.** A small tablet worn as a badge of high rank in an honorary order 1848. **2.** *Path.* A patch of eruption or the like 1876. So ‖**Plaque·tte,** a small p.

Plash (plæʃ), *sb.*[1] [OE. *plæsc*, corresp. to MDu. *plasch* pool, of imit. origin. Cf. PLASH *v.*[2]] A shallow piece of standing water; a marshy pool; a puddle.

Two frogs..consulted when their p. was drie whither they should go BACON.

Plash, *sb.*[2] (*adv.* or *int.*) 1513. [Goes with PLASH *v.*[2]] **1.** The noise made when a body strikes the surface of water so as to break it up, or plunges into or through it; an act accompanied by this noise; a plunge, a splash. **b.** The like noise produced when water, etc., falls upon a body, or when masses of water dash against each other; an act producing this noise 1808. **2.** *advb.* or *int.* With a plash 1842.

2. We go p., p., p., in the lawn-like glade LIVINGSTONE.

Plash, *sb.*[3] *Obs.* or *dial.* 1638. [f. next.] A plashed bough or bush; a plashed thicket.

Plash (plæʃ), *v.*[1] late ME. [– OFr. *plassier*, *plaissier* :– Rom. **plectiare*, f. L. *plectere* weave, plait. Cf. PLEACH.] **1.** *trans.* To bend down and interweave (stems half cut through, branches, and twigs) so as to form them into a hedge or fence 1495. †**b.** To bend down, break down (trees, bushes, etc.) for other purposes –1727. †**c.** To interlace (a fruit-tree in trellis-work); to train against a trellis or a wall –1676. †**d.** To intertwine, like plants in a thicket –1735. **2. a.** To make, dress, or renew (a hedge) by cutting the stems half through, and interlacing stems, branches, and twigs, so as to form a close low fence; to 'lay' (a hedge) 1523. †**b.** To treat (a wood, etc.) in the same way, in order to obstruct a pass or entrance, or defend a fastness; to form hurdles, weirs, etc. by such interweaving –1796.

Plash (plæʃ), *v.*[2] 1582. [Goes with PLASH *sb.*[2], of imit. origin; cf. (M)LG. *plaschen*, (M)Du. *plassen*; app. closely rel. to PLASH *sb.*[1]] **1.** *trans.* To strike the surface of (water) so as to break it up; to plunge into (water, etc.) or drive it against a body or against itself with commotion and noise; to splash. **b.** To dash with breaking water, etc., so as to wet; to splash. Also *absol.* 1602. **c.** To splash (a wall) with wet colouring matter 1864. **2.** *intr.* **a.** To splash through, or dash about in water with commotion and noise 1650. **b.** Of water, etc.: To dash against or upon a body; to tumble about in agitation, with the noise of breaking water 1665.

1. b. The floor all plashed with blood 1856. **2. a.** The fish were jumping and plashing THACKERAY. **b.** Far below him plashed the waters LONGF.

Pla·shing, *vbl. sb.* 1495. [f. PLASH *v.*[1] + -ING[1].] The action of PLASH *v.*[1] Also *concr.* A piece of plashed hedge or thicket.

Plashy (plæ·ʃi), *a.*[1] 1552. [f. PLASH *sb.*[1] + -Y[1].] Abounding in puddles; marshy, swampy, boggy; wet and sloppy; full of plashes of rain.

Those slymie plashie fieldes 1599.

Pla·shy, *a.*[2] 1582. [f. PLASH *sb.*[2] + -Y[1].] That plashes; that dashes or falls with a plash, as water; that splashes the water.

Plasm (plæ·z'm). 1620. [– late L. *plasma*; see next.] †**1.** A mould or matrix in which something is cast or formed; the cast of a fossil. Also *fig.* –1764. **2.** *Phys.* = PLASMA 3. 1876. **3.** *Biol.* The living matter of a cell, protoplasm; occas. *spec.* the general body of protoplasm as dist. from the nucleus 1864.

‖**Plasma** (plæ·zmă). 1712. [Late L., mould, image – Gr. πλάσμα, f. πλάσσειν fashion, form.] †**1.** Form, mould, shape (*rare*) –1829. **2.** A subtranslucent green variety of quartz, allied to chalcedony and heliotrope, anciently used for ornaments 1772. **3.** *Phys.* The colourless coagulable liquid part of blood, lymph, or milk, in which the corpuscles (or, in milk, oil-globules) float; also, the similar liquid obtained from fresh muscle 1845. **4.** *Biol.* = PLASM 3. 1864. So **Plasma·tic** *a.*, relating to the p., esp. of the blood.

Plasmic (plæ·zmik), *a.* 1875. [f. PLASM or PLASMA + -IC.] Pertaining to or consisting of plasm; protoplasmic.

Plasmin (plæ·zmin). 1866. [– Fr. *plasmine*, f. PLASMA + *-ine* -IN[1].] *Chem.* A proteid substance obtained from the plasma of the blood, soluble in water, the solution coagulating into fibrin.

Plasmo-, bef. a vowel **plasm-,** shortened comb. form of Gr. πλάσμα, πλασματ- plasm. (The fuller form is *plasmato-*.)

‖**Plasmodium** (plæzmōᵘ·diŏm). *Pl.* **-ia.** 1875. [mod.L., f. PLASMA + *-odium*; see -ODE.] *Biol.* **1.** A mass or sheet of naked protoplasm, formed by the fusion, or by the aggregation, of a number of amœboid bodies, and having an amœboid creeping movement. **2.** Name given to certain parasitic organisms found in the blood of patients with recent malaria, and quartan and tertian ague 1895. Hence **Plasmo·dial, Plasmodic** (-ǫ·dik) *adjs.* pertaining to, of the nature of, or arising from a p.

Plasmogen (plæ·zmŏdʒėn). 1888. [f. PLASMO- + -GEN.] *Biol.* The chemically highest or most elaborate form, stage, or part of protoplasm, which by its vital activity forms the tissues or other organic products; true or formative protoplasm; bioplasm.

Plasmogeny (plæzmǫ·dʒěni), **-gony** (-gǒni). 1876. [f. PLASMO- + -GENY. The var. *plasmogony* is – G. *plasmogonie* (Haeckel) with suffix repr. Gr. -γονία begetting; cf. *cosmogony*.] *Biol.* A mode of spontaneous generation.

Plasmology (plæzmǫ·lǒdʒi). 1888. [f. PLASMO- + -LOGY.] The study of the ultimate corpuscles of living matter.

‖**Plasmolysis** (plæzmǫ·lisis). 1885. [mod. L. (De Vries, 1877) f. PLASMO- + -LYSIS.] *Biol.* Contraction of the protoplasm of a vegetable cell with separation or freeing of the lining layer from the cell-wall, due to the withdrawal of liquid by exosmosis when the cell is placed in a liquid of greater density than the cell-sap. Hence **Pla·smolyse** *v.* to subject to p. **Plasmoly·tic** *a.* pertaining to, showing, or causing p.

Plasson (plæ·sǒn). 1879. [– G. *plasson* (Haeckel) – Gr. πλάσσων, -ον, pr. pple. of πλάσσειν mould.] *Biol.* The homogeneous protoplasm of hypothetical primitive organisms, not yet differentiated into nucleus and general cell-substance, or that of non-nucleated cells or cytodes.

-plast, comb. element repr. Gr. πλαστός formed, moulded, in *bioplast, endoplast*, etc.

Plaster (plɑ·stəɹ), *sb.* Also *Sc.* and *north. dial.* **plaister** (plē·stəɹ). [OE. *plaster*, corresp. to OS. *plāstar*, OHG. *pflastar* (G. *pflaster*), ON. *plástr* – med.L. *plastrum*, for L. *emplastrum* (prob. through the infl. of *plasticus* PLASTIC) – Gr. ἔμπλαστρον (Galen), f. ἐμπλαστός daubed, plastered, f. ἐμπλάσσειν (cf. PLASTIC); in ME. reinforced in Branch II from OFr. *plastre* (mod. *plâtre*).] **I.** An external curative application, consisting of a more or less solid substance spread upon a piece of muslin, skin, etc., and of such nature as to be adhesive at the temperature of the body; used for the local application of a medicament, or for closing a wound, etc. See also COURT-P., STICKING-P. **b.** *fig.* A healing or soothing means or measure ME.

b. The breath of the people being but a sorry plaister for a wounded conscience 1625.

II. 1. A composition which may be spread or daubed upon a surface, as of a wall, in a plastic state, to harden; *spec.* a mixture of lime, sand, and (usu.) hair, used for covering walls, ceilings, etc. ME. **2.** Sulphate of lime, gypsum: †(*a*) in its natural state; (*b*) powdered, but not calcined; used as a ground for painting and gilding, or for work in relief; (*c*) calcined; = PLASTER OF PARIS. late ME.

attrib. and *Comb.*, as **p.-bronze**, a plaster cast covered with bronze dust, to resemble a bronze; **-jacket**, in orthopædic surgery, a body casing or bandage stiffened with p. of Paris, for correcting curvature of the spine, etc.; **-rock, -stone**, raw gypsum.

Pla·ster, *v.* ME. Also **plaister** (see prec.). [f. prec. sb., or – Fr. *plastrer*, now *plâtrer*, plaster (a wall).] **1.** *trans.* To overlay, or cover with builder's plaster or the like. **b.** *transf.* To bedaub, cover with any adhesive substance; to overlay with excess of (vulgar) ornament. late ME. **c.** *fig.* To cover, load to excess, e.g. with praise; also, to gloze over; to botch, mend, or restore superficially. Also with *over, up*. 1546. **2.** To treat medically with a plaster. Also *absol.* late ME. **b.** *fig.* To soothe, alleviate; hence, *joc.* to give compensation for. late ME. **3.** To apply (something) like plaster (or a plaster) upon a surface 1864. **4. a.** To treat (wine) with gypsum or sulphate of potash to neutralize acidity. **b.** To dust (vines) with gypsum to prevent rot or mildew of the berries. **c.** To treat (land) with plaster of Paris. 1819.

1. Why could he not plaster the chinks? RUSKIN. **b.** The Great Duke (the breast of whose ..coat was plastered with some half-hundred decorations) THACKERAY. **c.** To p. his friends with praise 1865. **2. b.** Clare..gave the man five shillings to p. the blow T. HARDY. Hence **Pla·sterer**, †**plai·sterer**, one who plasters buildings; one who moulds or casts figures in plaster. **Pla·stery** *a.* of the nature of or like plaster; viscid, tenacious.

Pla·stering, *vbl. sb.* 1440. Also **plaistering.** [f. PLASTER *v.* and *sb.* + -ING[1].] **1.** The action of PLASTER *v.* **2.** *concr.* Plastered work; a coating of plaster, or of anything plastered or daubed on 1538.

Plaster of Paris (plɑ:stərǝvpæ·ris). ME. [PLASTER *sb.* II. 2.] A fine white plaster, consisting of gypsum rendered anhydrous by calcination, which swells and rapidly sets when mixed with water; used for making moulds and casts, as a cement, etc.; so called because prepared from the gypsums of Montmartre, Paris.

Plastic (plæ·stik), *a.* 1632. [– Fr. *plastique* or L. *plasticus* (Vitruvius) – Gr. πλαστικός, f. πλαστός, pa. pple. of πλάσσειν mould, form; see PLASMA, -IC.] **I.** In active sense. **1.** Characterized by moulding, or giving form to clay, wax, etc.; capable of shaping or moulding formless matter. **b.** In surgery: Concerned with remedying a deficiency of structure; reparative of tissue; as *p. surgery, a p. operation* 1879. **2.** Causing the growth or production of natural forms, esp. of living organisms; formerly as an attribute of an alleged principle, virtue, or force in nature; formative, procreative; creative 1646. **3.** *fig.* in ref. to immaterial things, conditions, or forms, literary productions, etc. 1662.

1. *P. art*, the art of shaping or modelling; any art in which this is done, as sculpture or ceramics. So *p. artist*; God, the great p. Artist 1741. **2.** In what diminutives the plastick principle lodgeth is exemplified in seeds SIR T. BROWNE. **3.** The p. energy of the imagination 1877.

II. In neuter and passive sense. **1.** Pertaining to moulding or modelling; produced by moulding, modelling, or sculpture, as dist. from that which is drawn on a surface 1726. **2.** Susceptible of being moulded; readily assuming a new shape 1791. **3.** Of immaterial things and conditions: Impressionable, pliable; susceptible to influence; pliant, supple, flexible 1711. **4.** *Biol.* and *Path.* Capable of forming, or being organized into, living tissue, as *p. lymph*, etc.; pertaining to or accompanied by such a process, as *p. bronchitis* 1834.

2. *P. sulphur*, an allotropic form of sulphur; see O.E.D. *P. clay* (*Geol.*), a name given (after Fr. *argile plastique*) to the middle group of the Eocene beds, immediately underlying the London clay, now called the Woolwich and Reading series. **3.** While his mind's ductile and p., I'll place him at Dotheboys Hall 1842.

III. *absol. The p.*: †**a.** The plastic principle or virtue; **b.** plastic art, plastic beauty 1661. Hence **Pla·stically** *adv.* **Plasti·city**, the quality of being p.

Plasticine (plæ·stisīn). 1897. [f. prec. + -INE[4].] Proprietary name of a plastic composition, used in schools, etc. as a substitute for modelling clay.

Plastid (plæ·stid). 1876. [– G. (Haeckel), f. Gr. πλαστός (see -PLAST) + *-id*, after Gr. -ιδιον, dim. suffix.] **1.** *Biol.* An individual mass or unit of protoplasm, as a cell or unicellular organism. **2.** *Bot.* A differentiated corpuscle or granule occurring in the protoplasm of a vegetable cell; e.g. a chlorophyll-granule, a chromoplastid, or a leucoplastid 1885.

Plastidule (plæ·stidiul). 1877. [– G. *plastidul* (Haeckel), dim. of *plastid*; see -ULE.] *Biol.* A hypothetical molecule or ultimate particle of protoplasm, constituting a vital unit, and forming an element or constituent of a plastid or cell.

Plastin (plæ·stin). 1889. [f. Gr. πλαστός (see -PLAST) + -IN[1], after *chromatin*.] *Biol.* A viscous substance found in the nucleus of a cell.

Plastogamy (plæstǫ·gămi). 1891. [f. Gr. πλαστός moulded + -γαμία marriage.] *Biol.* The fusion of the protoplasm of two or more cells or unicellular organisms, as in the formation of a plasmodium. Hence **Plastoga·mic** *a.*

Plastron (plæ·strǫ̆n). 1506. [– Fr. *plastron* – It. *piastrone*, augm. of *piastra* breast-plate (spec. application of the sense 'metal plate', 'lamina') – L. *emplastrum* PLASTER. See also PIASTRE.] **1.** A steel breast-plate formerly worn beneath the hauberk. *Obs.* exc. *Hist.* **b.** A leather-covered wadded shield or pad, worn by fencers over the breast 1693. **2.** In women's dress, A kind of ornamental front to a bodice; also, a loose front of lace, etc. 1876. **b.** In men's dress, a starched shirt-front 1890. **3.** *Zool.* (After Cuvier.) The ventral part of the shell of a tortoise or turtle 1831. **b.** Applied to the corresponding part in various other animals, as in certain echinoderms, etc. 1854.

-plasty, comb. element, repr. Gr. -πλαστία, f. πλαστός formed, used in sense 'moulding, formation', as in *dermatoplasty, osteoplasty*, etc.

Plat (plæt), *sb.*[1] *arch.* or *dial.* ME. [–(O)Fr. *plat* flat surface or thing, (in mod. Fr. dish), subst. use of the adj. *plat*; see PLAT *a.*] **I.** A flat thing, part, or surface. †**1.** A flat piece, a plate (of metal); a sheet, slice –1593. **2.** The flat part or side of anything; †**a.** The flat of a sword; **b.** The mould-board of a plough (*dial.*) late ME. **3.** A flat country, a plateau or table-land. *U.S.* 1812. **4.** *Mining.* A widened space in a level, near the shaft, where trucks may cross, or ore is collected for hoisting, etc. 1874. **II.** A surface or place generally. †**1.** A surface in general (whether plane or not) –1593. **2.** A place, spot, point of space; a locality or situation. *Obs.* exc. *dial.* 1558.

Plat (plæt), *sb.*[2] 1511. [Collateral f. PLOT *sb.*, infl. by prec.] **I.** = PLOT *sb.* I. 2 (which is found earlier). A piece of ground (usually) of small extent; a patch; as *grass-p.*, etc. 1517.

On a P. of rising ground, I hear the far-off Curfeu sound MILT.

II. = PLOT *sb.* II. 1. Now only *U.S.*

Plat (plæt), *sb.*[3] *Obs.* or *dial.* 1503. [Collateral f. PLAIT *sb.*, going with PLAT *v.*[1]] **1.** = PLAIT *sb.* 2. 1535. **2.** *Naut. pl.* Flat ropes made of rope-yarn, and plaited one over another.

1. Her haire nor loose nor ti'd in formall p. SHAKS.

‖**Plat** (pla), *sb.*[4] 1763. [Fr., dish; see PLAT *sb.*[1]] A dish.

Olives..a favourite 'plat' of mine BYRON.

Plat (plæt), *a.* and *adv. Obs.* exc. *dial.* ME. [–(O)Fr. *plat* :– pop. L. **plattus* – Gr. πλατύς broad, flat.] **A.** *adj.* †**1.** Flat, level; plane; plain –1584. †**2.** *fig.* 'Flat', plain, blunt, straightforward, downright, unqualified; esp. in phr. *p. and plain* –1560. **B.** *adv.* †**1.** Of position: In or into a flat position, flatly, flat; level with the ground or any surface –1598. **2.** Of manner: Flatly, bluntly, straightforwardly. Often *p. and plain*. Now *Sc.* and *n. dial.* late ME.

Plat (plæt), *v.*[1] *Pa. t.* and *pple.* **platted.** late ME. [Parallel form of PLAIT *v.*, going with PLAT *sb.*[3]] *trans.* To intertwine, intertwist; to plait (hair, straw, etc.); to form (hats, etc.) by plaiting; = PLAIT *v.* 2. Now a less usual spelling than PLAIT (which, however, in this sense, is usu. pronounced *plat*).

Plat, *v.*[2] 1556. [In origin, collateral form of PLOT *v.*] †**1.** *trans.* To plan; to sketch –1609. **2.** = PLOT *v.* 3. Now only *U.S.* 1751.

Platan (plæ·tăn). Also **-ane.** late ME. [– L. PLATANUS.] The Oriental Plane-tree (*Platanus orientalis*): = PLANE *sb.*[1] 1.

‖**Platanus** (plæ·tănǒs). late ME. [L. – Gr. πλάτανος PLANE *sb.*[1]] **1.** = prec. Also *p.-tree*. Now *rare*. **2.** *Bot.* The name of a genus of trees constituting the N.O. *Platanaceæ*.

Platband (plæ·tbænd). 1696. [– Fr. *platebande*, f. *plate*, fem. of *plat* (see PLAT *a.*) + *bande* BAND *sb.*[1]] **1.** *Arch.* **a.** A flat rectangular moulding or fascia, the projection of which is less than its breadth. **b.** The list or fillet between the flutings of a column. **2.** *Hort.* A narrow bed of flowers or strip of turf forming a border 1727.

Plate (plēⁱt), *sb.* ME. [– OFr. *plate* thin sheet of metal – med.L. *plata* ('plate-armour' in Niermeyer XIII), subst. use of *platus* adj. ('planus' in Chart. Edw. III 1334), app. a var. of pop. L. **plattus* (see PLAT *a.*).] **I.** A flat sheet of metal, etc. **1.** A flat, thin, usu. rigid sheet, slice, leaf, or lamina of metal or other substance, of more or less uniform thickness and even surface. **b.** *Anat., Zool.*, and *Bot.* A thin flat organic structure or formation 1658. **2.** As a material: Metal beaten, rolled, or cast into sheets. late ME. **3. a.** One of the thin pieces of iron or steel composing plate-armour. **b.** (without *a* and *pl.*) Plate-armour; often *attrib.* Cf. BREAST-PLATE, etc. Now *Hist.* or *arch.* ME. **4.** A flat piece or slab of metal, wood, etc., forming or adapted to form part of a piece of mechanism, etc.; e.g. **a.** each of the parallel sheets of metal forming the back and front walls of a lock, or of a watch or clock; **b.** one of the sheets of which ship's armour, steam-boilers, etc. are composed; **c.** (*Dentistry*) the portion of a denture which fits to the mouth and holds the teeth; **d.** a CENTRE-BOARD. late ME.; **e.** (*Wireless*) the anode of a thermionic tube, orig. a flat plate, now a cylinder surrounding the cathode or filament 1918. **5.** A smooth or polished plate of metal, etc. for writing or engraving on. late ME. **b.** Such a plate of metal, etc., bearing a name or inscription, for affixing to anything, as BRASS *p.*, DOOR-*p.*, NAME-*p.* 1668. **c.** *Photogr.* A thin sheet of metal, porcelain, or (now usu.) glass, coated with a film sensitive to light, on which photographs are taken 1840. **6.** A polished sheet of copper or steel engraved to print from; hence **b.** an impression from this, an engraving. Also short for BOOK-PLATE. **c.** A stereotype or electrotype cast of a page of composed movable types, from which the sheets are printed 1824. **7.** *Arch.* A horizontal timber at the top or bottom of a framing, as *ground, roof, wall, window p.* 1449. **8.** A wheel-track consisting of a flat strip of iron or steel with a projecting flange to retain the wheels, on which colliery trams are run; an early form of rail-road; also *p.-rail.* Locally retained for a railway rail; cf. PLATE-LAYER. 1825. **9.** *Mining.* Shale, thin slaty rock 1794.

1. Plates of glass 1665. **b.** *Blood-p.* = HÆMATOBLAST a. **3.** In mail and p. of Milan steel SCOTT. **5.** **c.** A *whole-plate* measures $8\frac{1}{2} \times 6\frac{1}{2}$ inches; *half-plate* (English) $6\frac{1}{2} \times 4\frac{1}{4}$ inches; (*U.S.*) $5\frac{1}{2} \times 4\frac{1}{4}$ inches; *quarter-plate*, $4\frac{1}{4} \times 3\frac{1}{4}$ inches. *Dry p.*: see DRY *a.*

II. A thin piece of silver or gold; silver or gold utensils. †**1.** A silver coin; usu. in full *p. of silver, silvern p.*; *spec.* from 16th c. the Spanish coin *real de plata*, the eighth part of a piastre –1606. **2.** Precious metal; bullion; from 16th c. usu. silver, after Sp. *plata.* Now only *Hist.* late ME. **3.** *collect. sing.* Utensils for table and domestic use, ornaments, etc., **a.** orig. of silver or gold. late ME. **b.** Extended to plated ware, and to other kinds of metal, as *pewter p., electro-p.*, etc. 1545. **4.** *Her.* A roundel argent 1562. **5.** Orig., in *Horse-racing*, a prize consisting of a gold or silver cup or the like given to the winner of a race; now, also, a prize in other contests; loosely, a contest in which the prize is a plate 1675.

1. Realms & Islands were As plates dropt from his pocket SHAKS. **3.** A salt-cellar of silver..one of the neatest pieces of p. that ever I saw PEPYS. **b.** Spoons and forks of real silver, not trumpery p. 1889. **5.** *Selling-p.*, a horse-race the condition of entry to which is that the winner must be sold at a price previously fixed.

III. A shallow, usu. circular vessel, orig. of metal or wood, now commonly of earthenware or china, from which food is eaten; as *dessert, dinner, fruit, soup p.* 1450. **b.** *transf.* That which is placed on a plate; *spec.* †(*a*) a supply of food; eating and drinking; †(*b*) a dish or course 1577. **c.** A similar vessel of metal or wood used for taking the collection at places of worship, etc.; hence *colloq.*, the amount taken up. 1779.

attrib. and *Comb.*: **p.-basket.** (*a*) a baize-lined basket in which silver spoons, forks, etc. are kept; (*b*) a metal-lined basket for removing plates, etc. which have been used at table; **-bolt,** (*a*) a bolt which slides on a flat plate; (*b*) a bolt having a wide flat head; **-bone,** the shoulder-blade; **-cultivation, -culture,** the culture of micro-organisms on glass plates; **-day,** the day of the race for a p.; **-horse** = PLATER 3; **-lock,** a lock having the outer case of wood; also, a lock in which the works are pivoted on an iron plate; **-man,** a man who has charge of silver plate; **-matter,** stereotype matter for newspapers such as is sometimes supplied from a central establishment to local journals; **-paper,** paper of fine quality on which engravings are printed; **-powder,** a polishing powder for silver ware; **-rack,** a frame in which plates are placed to drain, or in which they are usu. kept; also, a grooved frame for draining photographic plates; **p. tracery,** *Arch.* that kind of solid tracery which appears as if formed by piercing a flat surface with ornamental patterns; **-wheel,** a wheel in which the hub is connected with the rim by a p., instead of by spokes.

Plate (plēit), *v.* late ME. [f. prec.] **1.** *trans.* To cover, or overlay with plates of metal, for ornament, protection, or strength; to cover (ships, locomotives, etc.) with armour-plates. **2.** To cover articles made of the baser metals with a coating of gold or silver; also iron with tin 1704. **b.** with *on, upon*, and construction reversed 1790. **3.** To make a stereotype or electrotype plate of for printing 1907. **4.** *Philately.* To assign (a stamp, etc.) to its place as originally printed on a sheet; to reconstruct (a sheet of stamps) thus 1896.

Plateau (plæ·tou, plætō·). *Pl.* **plateaux, -eaus** (-ōuz). 1791. [– Fr. *plateau*, OFr. *platel*, f. *plat*; see PLAT *a.*, -EL².] **1.** *Geog.* An elevated tract of comparatively flat or level land; a table-land 1796. **2.** *Hist.* **a.** An ornamented tray or dish for table-service. **b.** A decorative plaque 1791.

Plateful (plēi·tful). 1766. [f. PLATE *sb.* + -FUL.] The quantity with which a plate is filled.

Pla·te-gla·ss. 1727. [f. PLATE *sb.* + GLASS *sb.*] A fine quality of thick glass, cast in plates, used for mirrors, shop-windows, etc.

Plate-layer (plēi·tˌlēi:əɹ). 1836. *orig.* One who lays, keeps in order, and renews the plates (see PLATE *sb.* I. 8) on a tramway or railway; hence, a man employed in fixing and keeping in order the permanent way of a railway. So **Pla·te-lay:ing.**

Pla·te-mark. 1858. [f. PLATE *sb.* + MARK *sb.*¹] **1.** A name for the various marks legally impressed on gold and silver plate for the purpose of indicating maker, degree of purity, hall or place of assay, date, etc.; = HALL-MARK. **2.** The impression left on the margin of an engraving by the pressure of the plate 1889. Hence **Pla·te-marked** *a.* having a plate-mark.

Platen, platten (plæ·tĕn, -'n). [XV *plateyne* – (O)Fr. *platine*, f. *plat* flat; see PLAT *a.*, -INE⁴.] †**1.** A flat plate of metal for various purposes –1813. †**2.** = PATEN 1. –1624. **3.** *Printing.* An iron (formerly wooden) plate in a printing-press, which presses the paper against the inked type so as to secure an impression. Also applied to similar parts in other machines. 1594.

Comb. **p.-machine, p. printing machine,** a press having a p., as opp. to a rotary or cylinder-press.

Plater (plēi·təɹ). 1771. [f. PLATE *v.* and *sb.* + -ER¹.] **1.** One who plates articles with a film of gold, silver, etc., as *electro-p.*, etc. **2.** A man who manufactures or applies metal plates, esp. in shipbuilding 1864. **3.** *Horse-racing.* A horse that competes chiefly in plate or prize races; an inferior race-horse 1859.

Plateresque (plætəre·sk), *a.* 1842. [– Sp. *plateresco*, f. *platero* a silversmith, etc. (f. *plata* silver) + *-esco*; see -ESQUE.] Resembling silver work; applied to a rich grotesque style of decoration, etc.

Platform (plæ·tfǫɹm), *sb.* 1550. [– Fr. *plateforme* plan, f. *plate*, fem. of *plat* (see PLAT *a.*) + *forme* FORM *sb.*] **I.** A plane surface; a plane on the flat. †**1.** *Geom.* A plane figure (as a triangle, etc.); also, a plane surface, a plane; any surface –1674. †**2.** A plan or representation on the flat (*of* any structure existing or projected); a ground-plan; a chart, map; a draught to build by 1551. **II.** Fig. uses derived from sense I. 2. †**1.** A plan, design; a model –1827. †**b.** A written outline or sketch; a scheme; a description –1727. **2.** †**a.** A plan of action; a scheme, design –1815. **b.** *spec.* A plan or draught of church government and discipline. Now *Hist.* 1573. †**c.** A plan of government or administration; a plan of political action –1757.

II. 1. You will..follow the p. of the London petition BURKE. **2. b.** No existing Church can find any pattern or p. of its government in those early days 1881.

III. The surface or area on which anything stands. †**1.** The site of a group of buildings, a fort, a camp, or any structure –1796. †**b.** *fig.* The ground, or basis *of* an action, event, calculation, condition, etc. –1832. **c.** *fig.* A plane or level *of* action, thought, etc. *rare.* 1870. **2.** A raised level surface or area: **a.** A level place for mounting guns in a battery 1560. **b.** A natural or artificial terrace; a table-land, a plateau 1580. †**3.** A division of the orlop of a man-of-war, between the cockpit and the mainmast –1741. **4.** A raised level surface formed with planks, boards, or the like 1727. **b.** A horizontal piece of flooring resting on wheels, as in a railway carriage, truck, or tram-car 1832. **c.** A raised floor along the side of the line at a railway station, for convenience in entering and alighting from the trains 1838. **5.** *spec.* A piece of raised flooring in a hall, or in the open air, from which a speaker addresses his audience, and on which the promoters of a meeting sit; hence *transf.* or allusively in ref. to discussion on a platform, platform oratory, etc. 1820. **b.** *fig.* A basis on which persons unitedly take their stand and make their public appeal; *spec.* in U.S. politics, a public declaration of principles and policy issued by the representatives of the party assembled to nominate candidates for an election 1844.

1. c. Conversation in society is found to be on a p. so low as to exclude science, the saint, and the poet EMERSON. **2. b.** The station chosen..was on a grassy p. 1860. **4. c.** Subway to platforms 1, 2, 3, and 4. 1907. **5.** He lamented the growth of the p. He ignored the Press 1901. **b.** I care nothing for names. All I ask for is a p. and an issue 1847.

attrib. and *Comb.*, as **p.-car** (*U.S.*), **-carriage,** a low four-wheeled wagon or truck without sides, for transporting mortars and other heavy articles; **-crane,** a crane mounted on a railway-truck; **-scale,** a weighing-machine with a p. on which the object to be weighed is placed.

Pla·tform, *v.* 1592. [f. prec.] †**1.** *trans.* To plan, outline, sketch, draw up a scheme of (*lit.* and *fig.*) –1641. †**2.** To furnish (a building) with a platform –1796. **3.** To place on or as on a platform 1793. **4.** *intr.* To speak on a platform 1859.

1. To grant that church discipline is platformed in the Bible MILT. Hence **Pla·tformer.**

Plathelminth: see PLATYHELMINTH.

Platic (plæ·tik), *a.* 1625. [– late L. *platicus* (Firmicus) broad, general – Gr. πλατικός broad, diffuse, f. πλατύς broad; see -IC.] *Astrol.* Of an aspect: Not exact or within a degree, but within half the sum of the 'orbs' of two other planets.

Platin- (plæ·tin), comb. f. PLATINUM bef. a vowel, as in *platinamine*, an amine of platinum.

Platina (plæ·tină, plătī·nă). Now *rare* or *Obs.* 1750. [– Sp. *platina*, dim. of *plata* silver; see -INE⁴.] The earlier name of PLATINUM.

Plating (plēi·tiŋ), *vbl. sb.* 1543. [f. PLATE *v.* + -ING¹.] **1.** The action of PLATE *v.*; *esp.* **a.** The process of coating with a thin layer of precious metal 1825. **b.** Plate-racing 1865. **2.** *concr.* The result or product of this action; *esp.* an external layer or sheath of plates 1843; the surface of precious metal with which copper, etc. is plated 1833. **3.** *attrib.* = 'occupied or used in plating', as **p. hammer,** (*a*) a heavy hammer for clinching; (*b*) a steam-hammer for working on armour-plate, etc. 1543.

Platinic (plăti·nik), *a.* 1842. [f. PLATINUM + -IC.] *Chem.* Applied to those compounds of platinum in which it exists in its higher degree of valency, i.e. as a tetrad; as *p. chloride* $PtCl_4$; opp. to PLATINOUS.

Platiniferous (plætini·fĕrəs), *a.* 1828. [f. PLATINUM + -FEROUS.] Bearing or yielding platinum.

Platinize (plæ·tinəiz), *v.* 1825. [f. PLATINUM + -IZE.] *trans.* To coat with platinum. Hence **Platiniza·tion.**

Platino- (plæ·tino), comb. form of PLATINUM; *spec.* in *Chem.* denoting compounds in which it is divalent.

Platinode (plæ·tinōud). 1839. [f. PLATINUM + Gr. ὁδός path, as in *anode*, etc.] *Electr.* The negative plate or pole (cathode) of a voltaic cell (often of platinum); opp. to ZINCODE.

Platinoid (plæ·tinoid), *a.* and *sb.* 1864. [f. PLATINUM + -OID.] **A.** *adj.* Resembling platinum. **B.** *sb.* Name for an alloy of nickel, zinc, copper, and tungsten, of a silvery white colour, and resembling platinum in non-liability to tarnish, etc. 1885.

Platino·so-, comb. form of mod.L. *platinosus* PLATINOUS.

Platinotype (plæ·tinŏtəip). 1880. [f. PLATINO- + -TYPE.] *Photogr.* A process of photographic printing by which prints in platinum-black are produced; a print produced by this process 1884.

Platinous (plæ·tinəs), *a.* 1842. [f. next + -OUS c.] *Chem.* Applied to those compounds of platinum in which it exists in its lower degree of valency, i.e. as a dyad. Cf. PLATINIC.

Platinum (plæ·tinŏm). 1812. [mod.L., altered from PLATINA, after the names of other metals in *-um.*] **1.** A somewhat rare metal (orig. named PLATINA), of a white colour like silver, but less bright, very heavy, ductile, and malleable, unaffected by all simple acids, and fusible only at an extremely high temperature; used chiefly in chemical and other scientific processes, and in setting precious stones. Symbol Pt. **2.** *attrib.* **a.** Made or consisting of platinum 1840. **b.** Of, related to, containing, or combined with platinum; as *p. ore, p. salts*; with names of other metals denoting alloys, as *p.-iridium, -steel* 1849.

Comb.: **p.-black**, a black powder resembling lamp-black, consisting of p. in a finely-divided state; **-lamp**, an incandescent lamp having the filament made of p.; **-metals**, name for the class of metals comprising p. and certain others, viz. iridium, osmium, palladium, rhodium, and ruthenium, associated with it; **-zinc** *a.* formed of plates alternately of p. and zinc, as a voltaic cell.

Platitude (plæ·titiūd). 1812. [– Fr. *platitude*, f. *plat* flat (see PLAT *a.*), after *certitude, exactitude*, etc.; see -TUDE.] **1.** Flatness, dullness, insipidity, commonplaceness (in speech or writing). **2.** A flat, dull, or commonplace remark or statement; esp. one uttered with an air of importance 1815.

1. A repartee..which has all the profound p. of mediæval wit ROSSETTI. Hence **Platitu·dinize** *v.* to utter platitudes.

Platitudinarian (plæ:titiūdinēᵊ·riăn), *sb.* and *a.* 1854. [f. PLATITUDE, after *latitudinarian*; see -ARIAN.] **A.** *sb.* One who utters or deals in platitudes. **B.** *adj.* Characterized by platitude; addicted to the use of platitudes 1866.

A. A political p. as insensible as an ox to everything he can't turn into political capital GEO. ELIOT. Hence **Platitudina·rianism.**

Platitudinous (plætitiū·dinəs), *a.* 1862. [f. as prec. + -OUS; cf. *multitudinous.*] Characterized by or of the nature of a platitude; full of platitudes; uttering or writing platitudes. Hence **Platitu·dinous-ly** *adv.*, **-ness.**

Platonic (plătǫ·nik), *a.* and *sb.* 1533. [– L. *Platonicus* – Gr. *Πλατωνικός*, f. *Πλάτων* Plato; see -IC.] **A.** *adj.* **1.** Of or pertaining to Plato (B.C. 429–c347), or his doctrines; conceived or composed after the manner of Plato. **b.** Of a person: That is a follower of Plato 1654. **2.** Applied to love that is purely spiritual for one of the opposite sex. (As orig. used, *amor platonicus* was a synonym of *amor socraticus*, which denoted the kind of interest in young men with which Socrates was credited, and had no ref. to women.) 1636. **b.** Feeling or professing Platonic love 1650.

†*P. bodies* (Geom.), a former name for the five regular solids (tetrahedron, cube, octahedron, dodecahedron, icosahedron). *P. year*, a cycle in which the heavenly bodies were supposed to go through all their possible movements and return to their original relative positions; sometimes identified with the period of revolution of the equinoxes (about 25800 years; see PRECESSION).

B. *sb.* †**1.** A follower of Plato; a Platonist –1840. †**2.** A Platonic lover –1757. **3.** (Usu. *pl.*) Platonic love; the acts or doings of a Platonic lover 1796. So **Plato·nical** *a.* = above adj. in all senses; **-ly** *adv.*, **-ness.**

Platonism (plēⁱ·tŏniz'm). 1570. [– mod. L. *platonismus*, f. Gr. *Πλάτων* Plato; see -ISM.] **1.** The philosophy of Plato, or of his followers. **2.** (with *pl.*) A doctrine or tenet of Platonic philosophy; a saying of, or like those of, Plato 1610. **3.** The doctrine or practice of Platonic love 1782.

Platonist (plēⁱ·tŏnist). 1549. [– med.L. *platonista*, f. as prec. + -IST.] A follower of Plato; one who holds the doctrines or philosophy of Plato. **b.** A Platonic lover 1756.

Platonize (plēⁱ·tŏnəiz), *v.* 1608. [– Gr. *πλατωνίζειν*, f. *Πλάτων* Plato; see -IZE.] **1.** *intr.* To follow the doctrine of Plato; to philosophize after the manner of Plato; to be a Platonist. **2.** *trans.* To give a Platonic character to; to render Platonic 1850.

Platoon (plătū·n), *sb.* 1637. [– Fr. *peloton* little ball, platoon, dim. of *pelote*; see PELLET *sb.*, -OON.] **1.** *Mil.* A small body of foot-soldiers, operating as an organized unit; a squad detached for purposes of drill or firing a volley, etc.; disused from c1850 to 1913, since when it has denoted: A quarter of a company. †**b.** *transf.* A volley fired by a platoon –1889. **2.** *fig.* A squad; a company or set of people 1711.

2. If you speak of the age, you mean your own p. of people EMERSON.

Platter (plæ·təɹ). Now chiefly *arch.* or *U.S.* [XIV *plater* – AFr. *plater*, f. *plat* dish, subst. use of (O)Fr. *plat* flat; see PLAT *a.*, PLATE.] A flat dish or plate for food; later, often a wooden plate.

Comb. †**p.-faced** *a.* having a broad, round, flat face.

Pla·tting, *vbl. sb.* 1483. [f. PLAT *v.*[1] + -ING[1].] **1.** Plaiting. **2.** Plaited straw, grass, palmetto, or the like, in ribbon-like strips, for making hats, etc. 1725.

Platy (plēⁱ·ti), *a.* 1533. [f. PLATE *sb.* + -Y[1].] †**1.** Consisting or formed of plates; plate-like –1612. **2.** *Geol.* Consisting of or easily separating into plates; flaky 1806.

Platy- (plæti), = Gr. *πλατυ-*, comb. form of *πλατύς* broad, flat.

Platycephalic (-sĭfæ·lik), **-cephalous** (-se·fāləs) [Gr. *κεφαλή* head] *adjs.*, having a flat or broad head; *spec.* in *Craniom.* applied to a skull of flattened form, having a vertical index of less than 70. **Platycnemic** (-knī·mik) [Gr. *κνήμη* tibia] *a.*, *Anat.* of the tibia, broad and flat; also, of a person, having such tibiæ; so ‖**Platycne·mia** [mod.L.], **-cne·mism, -cne·my,** platycnemic condition. **Platymeter** (plăti·mĭtəɹ) [-METER], *Electr.* an apparatus for measuring the inductive capacity of different dielectrics in the form of plates or discs.

Platyhelminth (plætihe·lminþ). Also **plathelminth.** 1890. [f. mod.L. pl. *Platyhelmintha, -thes*, f. PLATY- + Gr. *ἕλμινς* (*ἑλμινθ-*) worm; see HELMINTH.] *Zool.* An animal of the group *Platyhelmintha* or *Platyhelminthes*, comprising the nemertean, trematode, cestode, and turbellarian worms; a flat-worm.

Platypod (plæ·tipǫd), *a.* and *sb.* 1846. [f. Gr. *πλατύπους, πλατυποδ-* flat-footed; cf. next.] *Zool.* Having broad or flat feet; *spec.* belonging to the group *Platypoda* of monotrematous mammals (typical genus *Platypus*), or to the group *Platypoda* of gastropod molluscs, having a broad flat foot adapted for crawling; also in *Ornith.* syndactyl. Also *sb.*, an animal of this group.

‖**Platypus** (plæ·tipŏs). 1799. [mod.L. – Gr. *πλατύπους* flat-footed, f. *πλατύς* flat + *πούς* foot.] *Zool.* A name of the ORNITHORHYNCHUS or duck-mole of Australia.

Platyrrhine, platyrhine (plæ·tirəin), *a.* (*sb.*) 1842. [– mod.L. *platyrrhinus*, f. Gr. *πλατύς* PLATY- + *ῥίς, ῥιν-* nose.] **1.** *Zool.* Belonging to the division *Platyrrhini* of the order *Quadrumana*, including all the apes of the New World and comprising those apes or monkeys which have the nostrils considerably apart and directed forwards or sideways, and the thumbs nearly or quite non-opposable. **b.** *sb.* A platyrrhine monkey. **2.** *Anthropol.* Having the nose, or the nasal bones, flat or broad; having a nasal index of from 51 to 58. **b.** *sb.* A platyrrhine person or skull 1886.

Plaud, *v.* Now *rare* or *Obs.* 1598. [– L. *plaudere* applaud, clap the hands.] *trans.* To applaud; to praise. Hence **Plaud** *sb.* applause, praise.

Plaudit (plǭ·dit). 1624. [Shortened from next.] An act of applauding; a round of applause; any emphatic expression of approval.

The noisy plaudits of the pit and gallery 1883.

‖**Plaudite** (plǭ·ditī). 1567. [L., 2 pl. imper. of *plaudere* applaud; the customary appeal for applause made by Roman actors at the end of a play. The final *-e* ult. became mute, whence PLAUDIT.] An appeal for applause at the end of a performance.

Plau·ditor. [irreg. f. PLAUDIT + -OR 2, after *auditor.*] One who applauds. COLERIDGE. So **Plau·ditory** *a.* applauding, applausive.

Plausibility (plǭzĭbi·lĭti). 1596. [f. L. *plausibilis* (see PLAUSIBLE) + -ITY.] The quality of being plausible. †**1.** Readiness to applaud –1644. †**2.** The quality of deserving applause or approval; agreeableness of manner or behaviour, affability; with *pl.* an instance of this –1681. **3.** Of an argument, statement, etc.: Appearance of reasonableness; speciousness 1649. **b.** (with *pl.*) A plausible argument, statement, or the like 1660. **c.** Of a person: Fair-spokenness 1754.

3. The last excuse..was allowed..to have more p., but less truth SWIFT. **b.** Political plausibilities will reconcile men to everything, save the deprivation of their property 1881.

Plausible (plǭ·zĭb'l), *a.* (*sb.*) 1541. [– L. *plausibilis*, f. *plaus-*, pa. ppl. stem of *plaudere*; see PLAUDITE, -IBLE.] †**1.** Deserving of applause; praiseworthy, commendable –1711. †**2.** Acceptable, agreeable, pleasing; generally acceptable, popular –1828. †**b.** Of persons, etc.: Agreeable, ingratiating, winning –1841. **3.** Having a show of truth, reasonableness, or worth; apparently acceptable; fair-seeming, specious. (Chiefly of arguments or statements.) 1565. **b.** Of persons: Fair-spoken (with implication of deceit) 1846. **B.** *absol.* or as *sb.* That which is plausible; a plausible statement, etc. 1654.

3. Little aided by conjecture, however p. 1876. **b.** A p., cunning kind of fellow 1875. Hence **Plau·sibleness** (now *rare*), plausibility. **Plau·sibly** *adv.*

Plausive (plǭ·siv), *a.* Now *rare.* 1598. [f. as prec. + -IVE; in sense 1 perh. aphetic of contemp. APPLAUSIVE.] **1.** Having the quality of applauding; applausive. †**2.** = PLAUSIBLE 1, 2, 3. SHAKS.

2. *Ham.* I. iv. 30; *All's Well* IV. i. 29.

Plautine (plǭ·təin), *a.* 1881. [– L. *Plautinus*, f. *Plautus*; see -INE[1].] Pertaining to, characteristic of, or in the style of the Roman comic poet Plautus (died B.C. 184).

Play (plēⁱ), *sb.* [OE. *pleġa, plæġa* rapid movement, exercise, sport, f. the verb.] **I.** Exercise, free movement or action. †**1.** Of living beings: Active bodily exercise; brisk and vigorous action of the body or limbs, as in dancing, leaping, etc. –ME. **b.** The action of lightly and briskly wielding and plying (a weapon, etc.). Also in comb., as *sword-p.* OE. **2.** Of physical things: Rapid, brisk, or light movement; elusive change or transition (of light or colour); light motion about or impact upon something 1628. **3.** *fig.* and *gen.* Action, activity, operation, working; often implying the ideas of rapid change, variety, etc. (Now usu. of feeling, fancy, thought, etc.; formerly of persons.) 1599. **4.** Free or unimpeded movement (usu. from or about a fixed point); the proper motion of a piece of mechanism, or a part of the living body 1653. **b.** Freedom or room for movement; the space in or through which anything can or does move 1659. **c.** *fig.* and *gen.* Free action; scope for activity 1641.

2. Iridescent p. of colours 1875. **3.** Euen p. of Battaile SHAKS. The lively p. of fancy 1875. Phr. *In full p.*: acting with its full force. *To hold* or *keep* (a person, etc.) *in p.*: to keep exercised, occupied, or engaged; to give (a person) something to do (usu. in the way of self-defence or delay). *To come into p.*: to come into action or operation. *To bring* or *call into p.*: to bring into action, make active. *To make p.*: in *Racing* and *Hunting*, to exercise pursuers or followers; in *Pugilism*, to deliver blows actively; hence *gen.* to act effectively; to hasten or hurry on. *To make p. with*: to exercise or display freely. **4.** Give him [the chub] p. enough before you offer to take him out of the water WALTON. The girl was an arch, ogling person, with..a great p. of shoulders 1897.

II. Exercise or action for amusement, etc. **1.** Exercise or action by way of recreation; amusement, sport. *At p.*, engaged in playing. ME. †**b.** Amorous disport; dalliance. –1667. **2.** Jest, fun, sport (as opp. to *earnest*); trifling. Often in phr. *in p.* ME. **3.** (with *pl.*) A particular diversion; a game, a sport. Now *rare* or *Obs.* OE. †**4.** A trick, dodge, 'game' (*Obs.* exc. as in 7) –1746. **5.** The playing of a game 1450. **b.** Manner or style of playing; skill in playing 1531. **c.** A point in playing, a special device in a game 1778. **6.** *spec.* Gaming, gambling ME. **7.** In phrases *fair p., foul p.*: rarely *lit.*; usu. *fig.* action, conduct, dealing; see FAIR *a.*, FOUL *a.* 1440. **8.** [from the notion of recreation, sense II. 1] Cessation or abstinence from work; the condition of being idle, or not at work 1601.

1. All work and no p. makes Jack a dull boy *Provb.* **2.** The king..made her answer part in ernest, part in p. merely 1513. Phr. †*P. of words*: a playing or trifling with words so as to produce a rhetorical or fantastic effect. *P. on* or *upon words*: a pun. 3. She was fond of all boy's plays JANE AUSTEN. 5. P. was very slow,..twenty minutes being consumed in getting ten runs 1882. Phr. *In p.*: said of a ball, etc. = being played with. So *out of p.* Hence *p.*, transf. (in *Cricket* and *Football*), that part of the ground within definite boundaries, in which the game is carried on. *Child's p.*, a very easy or trifling matter. 6. A young nobleman,..ruined by p. 1769. 7. It was hardly fair p.—it was almost swindling LYTTON. 8. When miners and colliers strike they term it going to p. DISRAELI.

III. Mimic action. **1.** A dramatic or theatrical performance OE. **b.** *transf.* A performance, proceeding, piece of action (in real life) 1581. **2.** A dramatic piece, a drama 1440.

1. Wee had a p. called Twelve Night 1601. Phr. *at* or *to the p.* **b.** This little p. being achieved, the Marquis of Steyne made..two profound bows.. and passed on THACKERAY.

†**IV.** Performance on a musical instrument. *rare.* –1755.

attrib. and *Comb.*, as **p.-acting,** the performance of a play or plays; now usu. *joc.* playing a part, posing; **-actor,** an actor of plays, a dramatic performer; **-actress,** a female actor of plays; †**-club** (*Golf*), a driver; **-right,** the author's proprietary right of performance of a musical or dramatic composition; **-room,** a room in which children may play; **-table,** a gaming table.

Play (plēⁱ), *v.* [OE. *pleġ(i)an, plæġian* = MDu. *pleien* dance, leap for joy, rejoice; doubtfully rel. to OFris. *plega* be wont, OS. *plegan* (Du. *plegen*), OHG. *pflegan* (G. *pflegen*) have charge of, attend to, be in the habit of.] **I.** To exercise oneself, act or move energetically; to actuate, exercise (a craft etc.). †**1.** *intr.* To exercise or occupy oneself; to act, operate, work –1677. **b.** To strut, dance, or otherwise display itself, as a cock bird before the hens. Also *p. up.* 1765. **2.** Of living beings: To move about swiftly, with a lively or capricious motion; to fly, dart to and fro; to frisk; to flit, flutter OE. **3.** Of things; To move briskly or lightly, esp. with irregular motion, as lightning, flame, etc.; to change rapidly, as colours in iridescence; to strike lightly upon something, as waves, wind, light, etc. 1590. **4.** To bubble and roll about as a boiling liquid; to boil. *Obs.* exc. *dial.* late ME. **5.** To move, revolve, or oscillate freely (usu. within a definite space); to have its proper unimpeded movement, as a piece of mechanism, a limb, etc.; to have free play 1595. **6.** *trans.* To cause to play, to ply. **a.** To wield (something) lightly and freely; to keep in motion or exercise 1589. **b.** To discharge, fire, let *off* (artillery, etc.) *on* or *upon* persons or things; to cause (a fountain, etc.) to play 1595. **c.** *Angling.* To give play to (a fish); to allow (it) to exhaust itself by pulling against the line 1741. **d.** To cause to move or pass lightly, flutter, glitter, etc.; to exhibit with brilliant effect; to draw lightly upon a surface 1716. **7.** *intr.* To operate artillery, to fire (*on* or *upon* persons or things); also said of the artillery, or of a mine, etc.: To be discharged or fired 1601. **8.** Of a fire-engine, fountain, etc.: To emit a jet of water, to spout. Also said of the water, or of a fireman, etc. 1666. **9.** *trans.* To practise, perform, do (some action); to execute (a movement); usu. to practise in the way of sport, deceit, etc. (a trick, joke, etc.: const. *on* or *upon*, or with simple dative). In mod. use also with *off* (implying successful action; see OFF A). late ME.

1. There is an invisible Agent,..who plays in the dark upon us SIR T. BROWNE. 2. Bats..as they p. over pools and streams 1767. 3. A splendid silk.. Where like a shoaling sea the lovely blue Play'd into green TENNYSON. *fig.* Alfred allows his fancy to p. round the idea 1869. 5. Warme life playes in that infants veines SHAKS. The Tiller playeth in the Gunroome 1627. 6. a. †*To p. (a good) knife and fork*, to eat (well or heartily); so *to p. a good stick*, to fence well. 7. The Cannon on each Side began to p. STEELE. 8. The fountains played in his honour MACAULAY. 9. Man..Plaies such phantastique tricks before high heauen, As makes the Angels weepe SHAKS.

II. To exercise oneself in the way of diversion or amusement. **1.** *intr.* To amuse or divert oneself in any way; to sport, frolic OE. **b.** To sport amorously; *euphem.* to have sexual intercourse. Now *rare* or *Obs.* OE. **2.** *P. with*: to amuse oneself with; to treat (anything) lightly or frivolously; to dally, trifle, or toy with ME. **3.** To trifle *with.* late ME. **4.** To make sport or jest at another's expense; to mock. Now *rare.* OE. **5.** To abstain from work; to take a holiday. [From sense II. 1.] Now *dial.* (esp. of men on strike or out of work). late ME.

1. To playe with fooles, oh, what a foole was I 1576. 2. As children, we p. with our meat when we should eat it BAXTER. 3. I'd recommend you not to p. with 'post captains' MARRYAT. *P. on* or *upon a word* or *words*, to pun. 4. *P. with*, to make sport of, ridicule, mock at; to befool. 5. Master Slender is let the Boyes leaue to play SHAKS. Of the 70,000 men 'playing', 40,000 are non-unionists 1894.

III. To engage in a game, etc. **1.** *trans.* To exercise oneself in, engage in, practise (a definite game) OE. **b.** To represent or imitate in sport; to practise or deal with in a trifling way. Also with *obj. cl.* to pretend (*that..*) for sport. late ME. **2.** *intr.* To take part in a game. In *Cricket* said esp. of the batsman. ME. **b.** *spec.* To play for stakes; to game, gamble 1511. **c.** imper. *Play!* In *Cricket*, said by the bowler immediately before the delivery of the ball, or by the umpire at the beginning of a match or innings; also in *Lawn Tennis* by the server at the beginning of each service 1787. **d.** *transf.* In *Cricket*, said of the 'wicket' in ref. to the effect of its condition upon the play 1866. **3.** *fig.* or *gen.* To act, behave, conduct oneself (in some specified way) 1440. **4.** *P. at*: **a.** To take part in (a specified game); also *fig.* ME. **b.** To represent in sport 1840. **5.** *trans.* with personal object. **a.** To play against. late ME. **b.** *Cricket*, etc. To employ in a match; to include in a team 1887. **6.** To stake in a game; to hazard at play 1483. **b.** To play for, or in order to gain (something); to gain by playing; in phr. *to p.* BOOTY, *to p. a* PRIZE. **7. a.** *Chess*, etc. To move (a man) to another square on the board 1562. **b.** *Cards.* To take (a card) from one's 'hand' and lay it face upwards on the table, in one's turn 1680. **c.** In cricket, and other ball-games: To strike (the ball) with the bat, racket, stick, cue, etc., or to deliver it with the hand, so as to send or place it in a particular direction or position 1850. **d.** *P. on* (*Cricket*): of a batsman, to play the ball on to his own wicket, putting himself 'out' 1882. **8.** To bring into some condition by playing, e.g. *to p. oneself in*, to get into form for play 1869. **9.** *fig.* **a.** To use or treat as a counter or plaything. COWLEY. **b.** To pit (one person, thing, or party *against* another), esp. for one's own advantage. Now usu. *p. off.* 1643. **c.** *P. off*: to cause (a person) to exhibit himself disadvantageously 1712. **d.** To palm off 1768.

1. To p. BO-PEEP, DUCK AND DRAKE, FAST AND LOOSE (see these words). *To p. the game*: i.e. according to the rules, fairly; hence to 'play fair', act honourably (*colloq.*). **b.** We played that we were gypsies 1890. 2. Well played, sir! 1884. **b.** Playing for his last stake 1809. 3. *To p. fair*: to play according to the rules, without cheating; hence, to act justly or honourably. *To p. false, foul, foully*; also *to p.* a person *false*: to cheat in a game or contest; to deceive, betray. *To p. into the hands of*: to act so as to give an advantage to (another, either partner or opponent). *To p. it on*: to p. a trick upon, take in, cheat; so *to p. (low) down on*, to take a mean or unfair advantage of (slang or colloq.). *To p. on* or *upon the square* (see SQUARE). 4. a. The kyng & the Emperor playd at tennice 1548. There, two can p. at that game LYTTON. **b.** To p. at holding courts and receiving petitions MACAULAY. 5. a. 'I'll p. you for a hundred pounds, Doctor!' 1832. **b.** Bowlers who are played for their bowling only 1892. 6. *Twel. N.* II. v. 207. *P. away*: to lose in gambling; *fig.* to waste, squander. 7. **b.** *fig. To p. one's cards well* (fig.), to make good use of one's resources or chances. 8. *To p. time out*, to extend the play until the appointed time. 9. **b.** The Sultan likes to p. off one Power against another 1885.

IV. To perform instrumental music. **1.** *intr.* To perform upon a musical instrument. Const. *on, upon.* OE. **b.** Said of the instrument or the music itself 1588. **2.** *trans.* To perform (music, a piece of music) on an instrument 1509. **3.** To perform on (a musical instrument); to cause (it) to sound 1727. **4.** With *in, out, off, down, up*, etc.: To lead, dismiss, or accompany (persons) with instrumental music 1844. **5.** *fig.* **a.** *P. on* or *upon*: to practise upon 1602. **b.** *To p. first*, etc., *fiddle*: see FIDDLE *sb.* So *to p. second*; to take a subordinate part. 1809.

1. Ther herd I pleyen vpon an harpe..Orpheus ful craftely CHAUCER. 2. When thou, my music, music play'st, Upon that blessed wood SHAKS. 5. You would p. vpon mee; you would seem to know my stops SHAKS.

VI. To perform dramatically, etc. **1.** *trans.* To perform as a spectacle upon the stage, etc. to act (a drama, etc.). late ME. **2.** *P. out*: to perform to the end; *fig.* to bring to an end; *refl.* to become obsolete or effete 1596. **b.** *intr.* for *refl.* or *pass.* 1835. **c.** pa. pple. *Played out*: performed to the end, over and done with; also, exhausted, effete, worn out 1863. **3.** *trans.* To act the part of. late ME. **4.** Hence *fig.* in real life: To sustain the character of. (Almost always with *the* before the object.) late ME. **5.** To act (*a part, the part of*). *lit.* or *fig.* 1470. **6.** *intr.* To act a drama, or a part in a drama; to perform 1580. **7.** *P. up to* (*Theatr. slang*): to act in a drama so as to assist another actor; hence, to back up; to flatter, toady 1809.

1. The whil'st this Play is Playing SHAKS. 2. He was decidedly of opinion that Mr. Gladstone was played out 1887. 3. I could p. Ercles rarely SHAKS. 4. Phr. *To p. the* DEVIL, *the* FOOL, *the* MAN, *the* MISCHIEF, POSSUM, TRUANT, etc.: see the sbs. 5. In the final struggle..England played her part well 1881. Hence **Play·able** *a.* capable of being played; (of a cricket or football ground) fit for playing on.

Play-bill (plēⁱ·bil). 1673. A bill or placard announcing a play and giving the names of the performers.

Play-book (plēⁱ·buk). (Also as one word or two.) 1535. A book of plays.

Play-day (plēⁱ·dēⁱ). 1601. A day given up to play; *esp.* a school holiday. *Obs.* or *arch.* **b.** A week-day on which miners, etc. do not work 1892.

Player (plēⁱ·əɹ). [OE. *pleġere*, f. *pleġ(i)an*; see PLAY *v.*, -ER[1].] **1.** One who plays; one who is practised or skilful at some game, usu. specified in the context. late ME. **b.** A gambler 1483. **c.** A professional player (at a game or sport) 1861. **2.** A dramatic performer; an actor 1453. **3.** One who plays on a musical instrument 1463. **4.** *Billiards* (*Pool*), *Croquet.* The ball which, after the person playing has finished his break, will play on his ball 1866.

1. The by standers (whiche commonlye see more then the plaiers) 1562. 2. *A. Y. L.* II. vii. 140. 3. *Comb.* **P.-piano,** a piano fitted with an apparatus enabling it to be played automatically.

Pla·yfe:llow. 1513. [f. PLAY *sb.* + FELLOW.] A companion in play; usu. said of children or young people.

Playful (plēⁱ·fŭl), *a.* ME. [f. PLAY *sb.* + -FUL.] Full of play, frolicsome, sportive; also, pleasantly humorous or jocular, merry. Hence **Play·ful-ly** *adv.*, **-ness.**

Playgoer (plēⁱ·gōᵘəɹ). 1822. [f. PLAY *sb.* + GOER; cf. *church-goer.*] One who (habitually) goes to the theatre. So **Play·-go:ing** *sb.* and *a.*

Play·ground. 1794. A piece of ground used for playing on, esp. one attached to a school; hence, any place of recreation.

fig. Switzerland, the p. of Europe (*mod.*).

Play·house. 1599. A building in which plays are acted; a theatre.

Playing (plēⁱ·iŋ), *vbl. sb.* ME. [f. PLAY *v.* + -ING[1].] The action of PLAY *v.*

attrib. and *Comb.*, as **p.-card** = CARD *sb.*[2] 1; **-field,** a field or piece of ground for playing in; orig. applied esp. to the playgrounds at Eton, now to any school fields used for games.

Play·let. 1911. [f. PLAY *sb.* + -LET.] A short play.

Playmate (plēⁱ·mēⁱt). 1642. [f. PLAY *sb.* + MATE *sb.*[2]] A companion in play, a playfellow.

Play·-off. 1906. [f. PLAY *v.* + OFF *adv.*] An additional match to decide a draw or tie; a replay.

Playsome (plēⁱ·sŏm), *a.* Now chiefly *dial.* 1612. [f. PLAY *sb.* + -SOME[1].] Inclined to play; playful. Hence **Play·some-ly** *adv.*, **-ness.**

Plaything (plēⁱ·þiŋ). 1675. [f. PLAY *sb.* + THING.] A toy to play with. **b.** *fig.* A man, animal, or thing, treated as a toy 1680.

Playtime (plēⁱ·təim). 1661. [f. PLAY *sb.* + TIME *sb.*] A time for play or recreation.

Play·wright. 1687. [f. PLAY *sb.* + WRIGHT.] A maker or author of plays; a dramatist.

‖**Plaza** (plā·þa, plā·sa). 1683. [Sp.; see PLACE *sb.*] In Spain, etc., A market-place, square.

Plea (plī). [ME. *ple*, also *plai, plait, plaid* – AFr. *ple, plai*, OFr. *plait*, earlier *plaid* agreement, talk, lawsuit, discussion – L. *placitum* decision, decree, subst. use of pa. pple. n. of *placēre* PLEASE. Cf. PLEAD *v.*] **I.** In Law. **1.** A suit or action at law; the presentation of an action in court. Now *Hist.* and *Sc.* **2. a.** A pleading; an allegation formally made by a party to the court, in support of his case. late ME. **b.** A formal statement, written or oral, made by or on behalf of a prisoner or defendant, alleging facts either in answer to the indictment, or to the plaintiff's declaration, bill, or statement of claim, or showing cause why the prisoner or defendant should not be compelled to answer 1449. **c.** *Special plea*: in civil or criminal law, a plea either in abatement or in bar of an action or prosecution, alleging some new fact; opp. to *the general issue* 1699.

1. A p. between two country squires about a barren acre upon a common 1735. Phr. *To hold pleas*, to try actions at law, to have jurisdiction; *to hold a p.*, to try an action. *Common pleas*: orig., legal proceedings on matters over which the Crown did not claim exclusive jurisdiction; later, actions at law brought by one subject against another, identified with *civil actions*. *Pleas of the Crown* (*placita Coronæ*): orig., legal proceedings on matters over which the Crown claimed an exclusive jurisdiction, as being breaches of the king's peace; later, in England, including all criminal proceedings, as opp. to common pleas or civil proceedings. **2. b.** *Declinatory, dilatory*, etc. *p.*: see the adjs.

II. 1. Controversy, quarrel, strife. Now only *Sc.* ME. **2.** That which is pleaded in justification or excuse; a pleading; an apology, pretext, excuse 1550. †**3.** That which is demanded by pleading; a claim. SHAKS.

2. So spoke the Fiend, and with necessity, The tyrant's p., excused his devilish deeds MILT. **3.** *Merch. V.* IV. i. 198, 203.

Pleach (plītʃ), *v.* [XIV *pleche* – OFr. **plechier* (mod. dial. *plêcher*), var. of *ple(i)ssier, pla(i)ssier* PLASH *v.*^{1}] **1.** *trans.* = PLASH *v.*^{1} 1. **2.** = PLASH *v.*^{1} 2. 1523. **3.** *gen.* To entwine, interlace, tangle, plait 1830.

3. Poppied hair of gold Persephone Sad-tressed and pleached low down about her brows SWINBURNE.

Pleached (plītʃt, *poet.* plī·tʃėd), *ppl. a.* 1599. [f. prec. + -ED^{1}.] **1.** Of boughs: Interlaced, tangled; *transf.* of the arms, folded together 1606. **2.** Fenced or overarched with pleached boughs, as an arbour. Now as a Shakespearian expression revived by Scott.

2. Walking in a thick p. alley in my orchard SHAKS.

Plead (plīd), *v. Pa. t.* and *pple.* **pleaded;** also **pled** (now *Sc., dial.*, and *U.S.*), †**plead.** [ME. *plaide, plede* – AFr. *pleder*, OFr. *plaidier* (mod. *plaider*), f. *plaid* PLEA.] **I.** Intransitive uses. †**1.** To litigate –1550. **b.** *fig.* To wrangle, argue *with, against* –1593. **2.** To address the court as an advocate on behalf of either party ME. **b.** Hence *fig.* To urge a suit or prayer; to make an earnest supplication; to beg, implore. Const. *with* the person appealed to; *for* the thing desired, or the person for whom one speaks; also *against*. late ME. **3.** To put forward a plea. Cf. PLEADING *vbl. sb.* 3. 1444. **b.** *esp.* To put forward an answer or objection to the plaintiff's bill. late ME.

2. b. All Roger's services could not p. against this ill-timed tenderness to a foe 1869. **3. a.** *P. over*, to follow up an opponent's pleading by replying, etc., so overlooking some defect to which exception might have been taken WHARTON.

II. Transitive uses. †**1.** To go to law with, sue (a person) –1500. **2.** To maintain (a plea or cause) by argument in a court of law. Also *transf.* 1482. **3.** To sue for in a court of law. Also *transf.* To beg, entreat for. ME. **4. a.** To allege formally in the course of the pleadings. (Cf. PLEA *sb.* I. 2 a.) 1460. **b.** To allege formally as a plea (PLEA *sb.* I. 2 b.) *P. specially*, to allege as a special plea (PLEA *sb.* I. 2 c) 1531. **c.** Hence *fig.* To allege as a plea, esp. in defence, apology, or excuse, or as extenuating an offence 1454.

2. P. the widow's cause 1777. **4. b.** It would be vain to p...the king's command to do an unlawful act 1863. **c.** I can only p. my inexperience in this branch of literature W. IRVING. Phr. *To p. not guilty* (in civil and criminal law), to deny liability or guilt; in Law-French, *plaider de rien coupable*. So *to p. guilty*; also *fig.* to confess to an accusation or imputation. *Guilty* is technically not a *plea*, but a confession.

Pleadable (plī·dăb'l), *a.* [ME. – AFr. *pledable* = OFr. *plaidable*, f. *plaidier* PLEAD; see -ABLE.] That may be pleaded. **b.** *gen.* That may be claimed, urged or alleged in behalf of a cause 1565.

Pleader (plī·dəɹ). [ME. *playdour, -ur* – OFr. *plaideor* (mod. *plaideur*), f. *plaidier* PLEAD *v.*; see -OUR, -ER^{2} 3.] **1.** One who pleads in a law-court; an advocate. **2.** *gen.* One who pleads, entreats, or intercedes 1607. **3.** See SPECIAL PLEADER.

2. But sure if you Would be your Countries P., your good tongue..Might stop our Countryman SHAKS.

Pleading (plī·diŋ), *vbl. sb.* ME. [f. PLEAD *v.* + -ING^{1}.] The action of PLEAD *v.* †**1.** Litigation; hence, a lawsuit, action; a controversy –1556. **2.** The advocating of a cause in a court of law; the art of drawing pleadings; the body of rules, etc. constituting this art. late ME. **3.** A formal allegation now usually in writing, setting forth the cause of action or the defence; in pl. *pleadings*, the formal statements on both sides; in strict use, excluding the count or declaration 1531. **4.** *gen.* Intercession, advocacy, earnest entreaty. late ME. **5.** See SPECIAL PLEADING.

Plea·ding, *ppl. a.* 1818. [f. PLEAD *v.* + -ING^{2}.] That pleads. Hence **Plea·ding-ly** *adv.*, **-ness.**

Pleasance (ple·zăns). late ME. [– (O)Fr. *plaisance*, f. *plaisant*, pr. pple. of †*plaisir* PLEASE *v.*; see -ANCE.] **1.** The condition or feeling of being pleased; delight, pleasure, joy. *arch.* and *poet.* †**2.** The disposition to please; complaisance; courtesy –1599. **b.** A pleasantry. *Obs.* exc. *poet.* 1681. **3.** Pleasure-giving quality; pleasantness. *Obs.* exc. *poet.* late ME. **b.** That in which one delights. *Obs.* exc. *poet.* 1485. **4.** A pleasure-ground, usu. attached to a mansion. (Now sometimes surviving as the name of a street or 'place'.) 1585.

1. Thus is this quyen in plesaunce & in Ioye CHAUCER. **3.** With pleasaunce of the breathing fields yfed SPENSER. **4.** A charming old pleasaunce with bowling-green and long grass walks 1888.

Pleasant (ple·zănt), *a.* (*adv.*) late ME. [– (O)Fr. *plaisant*, pr. pple. of †*plaisir* (mod. *plaire*); see PLEASE *v.*, -ANT.] **1.** *orig.*, = PLEASING; now, more vaguely: Agreeable to the mind, feelings, or senses; such as one likes. **2.** Having pleasing manners, demeanour, or aspect; agreeable, good-humoured 1560. †**3.** Humorous, facetious; merry, gay –1782. **b.** Hilarious from drink (*rare* or *arch.*) 1596. †**4.** Amusing, ridiculous, funny –1760.

1. The pleasantest time of all the twenty-four hours KINGSLEY. *Pleasant Sunday Afternoon* (abbrev. *P.S.A.*): a kind of service, usu. held in a place of worship on a Sunday afternoon, diversified with music and addresses. **2.** Content and even p. under Hardships 1705. A clever woman is always a pleasanter companion than a clever man 1873. **4.** With such other like p. iestes 1583. Hence **Plea·sant-ly** *adv.* **-ness.**

Pleasantry (ple·zăntri). 1655. [– OFr. *plesanterie* (mod. *plais-*), f. *plaisant*; see prec., -RY.] **1.** A pleasant and sprightly humour in conversation; jocularity; raillery. **b.** With *a* and *pl.* A humorous passage, action, or (now esp.) speech; a joke 1701. †**2.** Pleasure, pleasantness, enjoyment –1790.

1. Pumping his brain for p., and labouring for wit to entertain the sneering crowd around him 1763. **b.** With their Censorious Plaisanteries upon the greatest of Authors and Worthies 1716.

Please (plīz), *v.* [ME. *plaise, plese* – OFr. *plaisir* (repl. by *plaire*) :– L. *placēre* be pleasing.] **I.** †**1.** *intr.* To be agreeable; to give pleasure. Const. *to, with.* ME. only. **2.** *trans.* To be agreeable to; to gratify, satisfy, delight. Also *absol.* ME. **b.** *refl.* To gratify oneself. Also *colloq.* to do as one likes. 1586. **3.** *Impersonally*, with formal subject *it*: To seem good to one; to be one's will or pleasure. (Equiv. to 'will', 'choose', 'think proper', etc., with the person as subject.) ME. **b.** With omission of *it*: in *p. your honour, p. God*, etc. 1440. **4.** *Passive.* *To be pleased*: to be gratified or delighted. Const. *with*. late ME. **b.** with *inf.* (or *clause*) expressing the subject of satisfaction. Also (*b*) To have the will or desire; to be moved; (*c*) To think proper, vouchsafe, choose; to be so obliging as; (*sarcastically*) to have the humour. late ME. **5.** *trans.* To appease, pacify, satisfy. *Obs.* or *dial.* late ME.

2. The thing pleased the king, and he did so *Esther* 2:4. *absol.* For we that live to p., must p. to live JOHNSON. **b.** *A.Y.L.* V. iv. 78. **3.** It pleased Silas to abide there still *Acts* 15:34. **4.** Nor can God be pleased with the perverted adoration 1850. **b.** Be pleased then To pay that dutie which you truly owe SHAKS. My dear Sir! you are pleased to be amusing this morning DISRAELI.

II. *intr.* To be pleased, to like; to have the will or desire; to have the humour; to think proper. (Partly from the impersonal use (sense I. 3); cf. LIKE *v.*) 1500.

You may make what use of it you p. ADDISON. Phrases. *If* (†*and, an*) *you p.*: if it please you, if you like, if it is your will or pleasure; a courteous qualification to a request, etc.; also (parenthetically) a sarcastic way of emphasizing any surprising statement, as if asking leave to make it. *Please!* (imper. or optative) was app. short for *p. you* (I. 3 b) = 'may it (or let it) please you'; but is now taken as = 'Be pleased' (imper. of II), or as short for 'if you please'. *Come here, p.* (= if you p.); *P.* (= be pleased) *not to lose the book.* Hence **Plea·ser,** one who or that which pleases or aims at pleasing.

Pleased (plīzd), *ppl. a.* late ME. [f. prec. + -ED^{1}.] Affected by feelings of satisfaction or pleasure; contented, gratified. Hence **Plea·sed-ly** *adv.*, **-ness.**

Pleasing (plī·ziŋ), *vbl. sb.* late ME. [f. PLEASE *v.* + -ING^{1}.] **1.** The action of PLEASE *v.* †**2.** = PLEASINGNESS –1594.

Plea·sing, *ppl. a.* late ME. [f. PLEASE *v.* + -ING^{2}.] That pleases. Hence **Plea·sing-ly** *adv.*, **-ness.**

Pleasurable (ple·ʒ'ŭrăb'l), *a.* 1579. [f. next + -ABLE, after *comfortable*.] **1.** Affording, or capable of affording, pleasure; agreeable. †**2.** Pleasure-seeking, pleasure-loving –1709. Hence **Plea·surableness, Plea·surably** *adv.*

Pleasure (ple·ʒ'ŭɹ), *sb.* [XIV *plesir* – OFr. *plesir*, (also mod.) *plaisir* :– Rom. subst. use of the infin. (see PLEASE *v.*); the final syll. was assim. XV to -URE.] **1.** The condition of consciousness induced by the enjoyment or anticipation of what is felt or viewed as good or desirable; enjoyment, delight, gratification. The opposite of *pain*. **b.** In bad sense: Sensuous enjoyment as a chief object of life or end in itself 1526. **c.** In strictly physical sense: Sensual gratification 1450. **2.** One's will, desire, choice. late ME. **3.** A source or object of pleasure or delight 1495. **4.** The quality which gives pleasure; pleasureableness 1530. **5.** *attrib.* as *p.-boat, -garden, -ground, -house, -resort*, etc. 1712.

1. Pain and p. are simple ideas, incapable of definition BURKE. P. is what all creatures desire 1894. **b.** Men, some to Bus'ness, some to P. take; But every Woman is at heart a Rake POPE. But pleasures are like poppies spread, You seize the flower, the bloom is shed BURNS. **2.** I will wait vpon his p. SHAKS. They were determined not to submit..to her will and p. HUME. **3.** Your..love of truth renders this a duty as well as a p. 1858. **4.** The p. of pale colours 1869.

Phrases. *At* (*one's*) *p.*, *at p.*: as or when one pleases; at will, at discretion. *During* (*one's*) *p.*: while one pleases. *To do* (*one*) *a p.*: to do a favour; to please, gratify. *Man* (*woman*) *of p.*: one who is devoted to the pursuit of sensual pleasure. *To take* (*a*) *p.*: to be pleased, to delight (*in, to do* something, etc.). Hence **Plea·sureful** *a.* full of or fraught with p. **Plea·sureless,** devoid of p., joyless.

Pleasure (ple·ʒ'ŭɹ), *v.* 1538. [f. prec. sb.] **1.** *trans.* To give pleasure to; to gratify (now *rare*) 1559. **2.** *intr.* To take pleasure, to delight. Const. *in* or *to* with *inf.* 1538.

Plea·surer. 1833. [f. PLEASURE *sb.* or *v.* + -ER^{1}.] A pleasure-seeker: a holiday-maker.

Plea·sure-see:ker. 1852. One who seeks pleasure; *spec.* a holiday-maker.

Plea·surist. 1682. [f. PLEASURE *sb.* + -IST.] **a.** A devotee of pleasure, a voluptuary. **b.** A pleasure-seeker.

Pleat (plīt), *sb.* 1581. [By-form of PLAIT *sb.*] = PLAIT *sb.* 1. *Box-p.*: see BOX *sb.*^{2}

Pleat (plīt), *v.* late ME. [By-form of PLAIT *v.*, going with prec. sb.] **1.** *trans.* To fold (cloth, etc.); now *esp.* to gather (loose or flowing drapery) into pleats or regular folds fixed in position at the edge. **2.** = PLAT *v.*[1] *dial.* 1483.

Accordion-pleated, pleated (by machinery) with very fine equal single pleats; *knife-pleated*, pleated by hand with the blade of a knife (or by a machine producing the same result).

Plebe (plīb). 1612. [In sense 1 app. – (O)Fr. *plèbe* – L. *plebs, pleb-* (see PLEBS). In sense 2 app. shortened from PLEBEIAN.] †**1.** The Roman plebs; hence, the commonalty of any nation –1635. **2.** *U.S. colloq.* A member of the lowest class at a military or naval academy; a freshman. Also *pleb.* 1884.

Plebeian (plĭbī·ăn). 1533. [f. L. *plebeius*, f. *plebs, pleb-* commonalty of ancient Rome, + -AN. Cf. (O)Fr. *plébéien*. In Shaks. occas. stressed *ple·bean.*] **A.** *sb.* **a.** A member of the Roman plebs; a Roman commoner, as opp. to the patricians, etc. **b.** *gen.* One of the common people, a commoner 1586.

a. The dull Tribunes, That with the fustie Plebeans, hate thine Honors SHAKS. **b.** A Yeoman, or Plebeyan;..any lay man that is no Gentleman 1611. *fig.* To the brave, there is but one sort of p., and that is the coward LYTTON.

B. *adj.* **a.** Of or belonging to the Roman plebs; that was a plebeian 1566. **b.** Of low birth or rank; pertaining to or connected with the common people; popular 1600. **c.** Having qualities attributed to the lower classes; commonplace, undistinguished; vulgar or vulgar-looking 1615.

c. An important gentleman..of rather p. countenance DICKENS. Hence **Plebei·anism**, p. character or style. **Plebei·anize** *v. trans.* to reduce to p. rank; to make common. **Plebei·an-ly** *adv.*, **-ness.**

Plebiscite, -it (ple·bisəit, -it). Also **plébiscite.** 1533. [– (O)Fr. *plébiscite* – L. *plebiscitum*, f. *plebs, pleb-* PLEBS + *scitum* ordinance, subst. use of n. pa. pple. of *sciscere* approve, vote for.] **1.** *Rom. Hist.* = PLEBISCITUM 1. **2.** In mod. politics. A direct vote of the whole of the electors of a state to decide a question of public importance; also by extension, a public expression, with or without binding force, of the wishes or opinion of a community 1860.

2. He [Louis Napoleon] knew how to strangle a nation in the night-time with a thing he called a 'P.' KINGLAKE. Hence **Plebi·scitary** *a.* relating to, based on, favouring, or of the nature of a p.

‖**Plebiscitum** (plĭbisəi·tŏm). *Pl.* **-a.** 1577. [L.; see prec.] **1.** *Rom. Hist.* A law enacted by the plebs assembled in the *comitia tributa.* **2.** = PLEBISCITE 2. 1859.

Plebs (plebz). 1647. [L. (earlier *plebes*).] *Rom. Hist.* The commonalty, orig. comprising all citizens that did not belong to one of the patrician *gentes*, to which privileged order were afterwards added the *equites* or knights 1835. **b.** *transf.* The common people; the mob 1647.

Plectognath (ple·ktŏgnæþ), *a.* and *sb.* 1835. [f. mod.L. *Plectognathi*, f. Gr. πλεκτός plaited, twisted + γνάθος jaw.] *Ichthyol.* **A.** *adj.* Of or pertaining to the *Plectognathi*, a suborder of teleostean fishes, having the upper jaw attached to the cranium, and the skeleton imperfectly ossified. **B.** *sb.* A fish of this suborder. So **Plectognathian** (-gnē¹·þiăn) *a.* and *sb.* **Plectognathik** (-gnæ·þik), **Plectognathous** (-ǫ·gnăþəs) *adjs.* = A.

Plectospondyl (plektoˌspǫ·ndil), *a.* and *sb.* [f. mod.L. *Plectospondyli*, f. Gr. πλεκτός (see prec.) + σπόνδυλος vertebra.] *Ichthyol.* **A.** *adj.* Belonging to or having the characters of the *Plectospondyli*, teleostean fishes having some of the vertebræ co-ossified. **B.** *sb.* A fish of this order. So **Plectospo·ndylous** *a.*

‖**Plectrum** (ple·ktrŏm). Pl. **-a.** 1626. Also anglicized **plectre** (1603). [L. – Gr. πλῆκτρον anything to strike with, f. πλήσσειν strike.] A small instrument of ivory, horn, quill, or metal, with which the strings of the cithara or lyre were plucked; now used for playing the zither, mandolin, etc.

Pled: see PLEAD *v.*

Pledge (pledʒ), *sb.* [XIV *plege* – OFr. *plege* (mod. *pleige*) :– Frank. L. *plebium* (VI), corresp. to *plebire* warrant, assure, engage, perh. f. Gmc. base **pleʒ-* of PLIGHT *sb.*[1], crossed with L. *præbēre* furnish, supply.] **1.** *Law* and *gen.* A person who becomes surety for another; a bail; a member of a frank-pledge or frithborh (mod.L. *plegius*). *Obs.* exc. *Hist.* †**b.** A hostage –1633. **2.** Anything put in the possession of another, as security for the performance of a contract or payment of a debt, or as a guarantee of good faith, etc., and liable to forfeiture in case of failure (med.L. *plegium*) 1489. **b.** *spec.* A thing put in pawn 1800. **c.** A gage of battle 1590. **d.** *fig.* Applied to a child, as a token of mutual love and duty between parents, or as a hostage given to fortune 1590. **3.** Something given or taken as a sign of favour or the like, or as an earnest of something to come 1526. **4.** An assurance of allegiance or goodwill; e.g. the drinking of a health to a person, party, etc.; a toast 1635. **5.** A solemn engagement; a promise, vow 1814. **6.** The condition of being given or held as a pledge; the state of being pledged. late ME.

1. Petruchio patience, I am Grumio's p. SHAKS. **2.** What P. haue we of thy firme Loyalty? SHAKS. **b.** Any time during which the said p. shall remain in pawn 1800. **d.** The first p. of their union, a fine little girl 1856. **5.** He obtained them..under the p. of secrecy 1855. *The (temperance, total abstinence) p.*: a solemn engagement to abstain from intoxicating drink. *To take, sign, keep the p.* **6.** Phr. *To be, lay, put in p., to give, have, lay, put to p., to take out of p.*, etc.

Pledge (pledʒ), *v.* 1450. [f. prec. sb.; cf. OFr. *plegier* (mod. *pleiger*).] †**1.** *trans.* To make oneself responsible for (a person, thing, or statement) –1474. **2.** To deliver, deposit, or assign as security for the repayment of a loan or the performance of some action; to pawn 1515. **b.** *fig.* as in *to p. the future*; also, to plight or stake (one's life, honour etc.) 1775. **3.** To bind by or as by a pledge 1571. **4. a.** To guarantee the performance of. **b.** To promise solemnly. 1593. **5.** To give assurance of friendship or fidelity to (any one) by or in the act of drinking. Also *absol.*, or with the drink as obj. †**a.** To drink in response to another; to drink to a health which has been proposed. **b.** To drink to the health of; to toast. 1546.

1. †*To p. out*: to redeem (a thing) from pawn; to ransom or bail (a person) from prison. **2. b.** My vows are pledged to her SHERIDAN. **3.** I p. myself, before God and my country..to make good my charge against you *'Junius' Lett.* **4. a.** And heere to p. my Vow, I giue my hand SHAKS. **5. a.** Drink to me, only with thine eyes, And I will p. with mine B. JONS. **b.** P. him in a bumper of port 1802. Hence **Ple·dgeable** *a.*

Pledgee (pledʒī·). 1766. [f. prec. + -EE[1].] One with whom a pledge is deposited.

Pledger (ple·dʒəɹ). Also (in legal use) **pledgor** (pledʒǭ·ɹ). 1576. [f. PLEDGE *v.* + -ER[1], -OR 2.] **1.** One who deposits something as a pledge. **2.** One who drinks in response to, or to the health of, another.

Pledget (ple·dʒĕt). 1540. [Early forms *plaget, pleggat, pleget*, of unkn. origin.] A small compress or flattened mass of lint, etc. (often steeped in some medicament), for applying over a wound, sore, etc.

Pleiad (pləi·ăd). *Pl.* **Pleiads;** more commonly ‖**Pleiades** (pləi·ădīz). late ME. [– L. *Plēïas*, pl. *Plēïades* – Gr. πλειάς, pl. -άδες; see -AD.] *Astron.* In *pl.*, A close group of small stars in the constellation Taurus, commonly spoken of as seven, though only six are visible to the average naked eye.

According to Greek Mythology, the Pleiades were the seven daughters of Atlas and Pleione, the eldest of whom, Electra, was 'the lost Pleiad', and not represented by a star.

b. *fig.* (*sing.*) A brilliant cluster of persons or things, esp. of seven, as the group of poets of the French Renaissance, called in French *La Pléiade* 1822.

Plein-air (also **plain-air**), from the Fr. phr. *en plein air* (aṅplęnę̄ɹ) 'in the open air' used attrib. to denominate certain impressionist schools and styles of painting, which arose in France about 1870, and aimed at the representation of effects of atmosphere and light that cannot be observed in the studio 1894.

Pleio-, plio- (pləiˌo), **pleo-** (plīˌo), comb. forms of Gr. πλείων (poet. πλέων), πλεῖον more, compar. of πολύς, -ύ much; see POLY-. *Plio-*, which follows L. spelling, is chiefly used in generic names and their derivs., as *Pliosaurus, Pliosaurian.*

Pleiocene, Pleiohippus: see PLIO-.

Pleistocene (pləi·stŏsīn), *a.* (*sb.*) 1839. [f. Gr. πλεῖστος most + καινός new, recent.] *Geol.* Epithet applied at first to the newest division of the Pliocene or Upper Tertiary formation (as containing the greatest number of fossils of still existing species), also called Newer Pliocene; afterwards to the older division of the Post-tertiary or Quaternary, also called Post-Pliocene. Also applied to the animals, etc., of either of these periods. **B.** *ellipt.* as *sb.* = pleistocene division or formation.

Plenarty (plī·năɹti). [Late ME. – AFr. *plenerte*, OFr. *plenierete* fullness, f. *plenier, plener* complete; see -TY.] *Eccl. Law.* Of a benefice: The state of being full or occupied.

Plenary (plī·nări), *a.* 1450. [– late L. *plenarius*, f. *plenus* full; see -ARY[1].] **1.** Of full scope or extent; complete or absolute in force or effect; as *p. indulgence, power, remission.* **2.** Of an assembly, etc.: Composed of all the members; fully constituted, fully attended 1532. Hence **Ple·narily** *adv.*

Plenilune (plī·nilˈūn, ple·ni-). Chiefly *poet.* late ME. [– L. *plenilunium* full moon, prop. adj. of the full moon (sc. *tempus* time), f. *plenus* full + *luna* moon.] **a.** The time of full moon. **b.** A full moon. Hence **Plenilu·nal, -lu·nar, -lu·nary** *adjs.* belonging to or resembling the full moon.

Plenipo (ple·nipo). 1687. Colloq. shortening of PLENIPOTENTIARY.

Pleni·potency. *rare.* 1624. [app. f. next; see -ENCY. Cf. contemp. *plenipotence* (Milton perh. after It. *plenipotenza*).] The quality of being plenipotent; full authority. So **Pleni·potence**, *rare*, full power or authority.

Plenipotent (plĭni·pŏtĕnt), *a. rare.* 1658. [– late (Priscian) and med.L. *plenipotens, -ent-*, f. as next after *omnipotens*; see OMNIPOTENT.] Invested with or possessing full power or authority. So **Plenipote·ntial** *a. rare*, possessed of full authority; of or belonging to a plenipotentiary.

Plenipotentiary (ple:nipŏte·nʃări). 1645. [– med.L. *plenipotentiarius*, f. L. *plenus* full, complete + *potentia* power; see -ARY[1].] **A.** *adj.* Invested with full power, esp. as the representative of a sovereign ruler; exercising absolute power or authority. **b.** Of or belonging to a plenipotentiary (see B); absolute, full 1648. **B.** *sb.* A person invested with full or discretionary powers, *esp.* in regard to a particular transaction; an envoy or ambassador deputed by his sovereign to act at his own discretion 1656.

I know not why the Character of P. may not agree with that of Envoy Extraordinary on all Hands 1668.

Plenish (ple·niʃ), *v.* Chiefly *Sc.* 1470. [f. *pleniss-* (see -ISH[1]), lengthened stem of OFr. *plenir* fill, f. *plein* full :– L. *plenus.*] *trans.* To fill up, furnish, stock; to replenish. Orig. *Sc.* and *n. dial.* **b.** *spec.* To furnish (a house, etc.) *Sc.* and *n. dial.* 1578. Hence **Ple·nishing** *vbl. sb.* the action of filling up or furnishing; stock, furniture; the outfit of a bride.

Plenist (plī·nist). 1660. *Hist.* [f. L. PLENUM + -IST.] An adherent of the theory that all space is full of matter, and that no vacuum exists.

Plenitude (ple·nitiud). late ME. [– OFr. *plenitude* – late L. *plenitudo*, f. *plenus* full; see -TUDE.] **1.** The condition of being absolutely full or complete; fullness, completeness, perfection. **b.** *Her.* Fullness (of the moon) 1864. **c.** Comparative fullness, abundance, amplitude 1653. **2.** The condition of being filled or full 1662. †**3.** *Med.* Repletion; plethora –1802.

1. Pawle sayth the plenytude of the lawe is loue and charyte CAXTON. **c.** P. of incident without confusion 1794.

Plenteous (ple·ntĭəs), *a.* Now chiefly *poet.* [ME. *plentivous, -ifous*, later *plentevous, plentuous, plentious, -eous* (cf. BOUNTEOUS) – OFr. *plentivous, -evous*, f. *plentif, -ive*, f. *plenté* + *-if, -ive* = -IVE.] **1.** Present or existing in plenty; abundant, plentiful, copious. **2.** Bearing or yielding abundantly; fertile, productive. Const. *in, of.* ME. †**3.** Possessing abundance; rich –1643. †**4.** Giving abundantly; bountiful –1700.

1. A p. crop of such philosophers COLERIDGE. **2.**

The seasons had been p. in corn GEO. ELIOT. **4.** P. of Grace, descend from high, Rich in thy Sevenfold Energy DRYDEN. Hence **Ple·nteous-ly** *adv.*, **-ness.**

Plentiful (ple·ntifŭl), *a.* 1470. [f. next + -FUL.] **1.** Full of plenty; furnished with or yielding abundance; opulent. Now *rare.* **2.** Present or existing in plenty; abundant, ample 1510. †**3.** Generous, lavish –1625.

1. If it be a long winter, it is commonly a more p. year BACON. **2.** They haue a plentifull lacke of Wit SHAKS. **3.** He that is Plentifull in Expences of all Kindes, will hardly be preserved from Decay BACON. Hence **Ple·ntiful-ly** *adv.*, **-ness.**

Plenty (ple·nti), *sb.* (*a.*, *adv.*) [ME. *plenteth* (surviving as *plentith* XVII), later *plente*, *-ee*, *-ie* – OFr. *plentet* (= *-ep*), mod. dial. *plenté* :– L. *plenitas*, *-tat-*; see -TY[1]. With the adj. use cf. *choice*, *dainty*.] **A.** *sb.* **1.** The state of abounding or being in abundance; plentifulness, abundance. **2.** A full supply; as much as one could desire; abundance *of* something ME. **b.** with *a*: an abundance (*of*). Now chiefly *U.S.* 1627. **3.** Abundance of the necessaries and comforts of life; a condition of general abundance. late ME. †**b.** *concr.* in *pl.* Things that constitute 'plenty'; provisions, possessions –1723.

1. *In p.*: plentiful; plentifully, abundantly; Compliments passed in p. 1852. **2.** We were in p. of time 1885. **3.** To scatter p. o'er a smiling land GRAY. *Horn of p.* = CORNUCOPIA. **b.** *Hen. V*, V. ii. 35.

B. *adj.* or quasi-*adj.* Existing or present in abundance; abundant, plentiful, numerous. Now chiefly *colloq.*, *arch.*, or *U.S.* ME.

Gold and syluer plente to spend MALORY. Where money is p., and land scarce 1656.

C. quasi-*adv.* Abundantly (*colloq.*) 1842.

They're p. large enough 1884.

‖**Plenum** (plī·nŏm). 1678. [L., neut. of *plenus* adj. full (sc. *spatium* space); cf. *vacuum*.] **1.** *Physics.* A space completely filled with matter; *spec.* the whole of space regarded as being so filled; opp. to VACUUM. **b.** *transf.* A condition of fullness; a full place 1795. **2.** A full assembly; one at which all the members are expected to be present 1772.

attrib. P. method, system, a system of artificial ventilation in which fresh air, forced into the building to be ventilated, drives out the vitiated air.

Pleochroic (plīˌokrōᵘ·ik), *a.* 1864. [f. *pleo-* PLEIO- + Gr. χρώς colour, -χροος coloured + -IC; cf. DICHROIC.] *Cryst.* Showing different colours when viewed in two or in three different directions (*dichroic* or *trichroic*), as certain double-refracting crystals. So **Pleochroism** (pliˌǫ·kroˌiz'm), the quality of thus exhibiting different colours; **Ple:ochroma·tic** *a.* = *pleochroic*; **Pleochro·matism** = *pleochroism*; **Pleochroous** (plīˌǫ·kroˌəs) *a.* = *pleochroic.*

Pleomorphic (plīˌomǭ·ɹfik), *a.* 1886. [f. as prec. + Gr. μορφή form + -IC.] Having more than one form: (*a*) *Biol.* exhibiting different forms at different stages of the life-history, as certain bacteria and parasitic fungi; (*b*) *Chem.* and *Min.* crystallizing in two or more fundamentally different forms. So **Pleomo·rphism**, the fact or condition of exhibiting a plurality of forms. **Pleomo·rphous** *a.* = *pleomorphic.*

Pleon (plī·ǫn). 1855. [Arbitrarily – Gr. πλέων, pr. pple. of πλεῖν swim, sail.] *Zool.* The abdomen in Crustacea, which bears the swimming limbs (see PLEOPOD).

Pleonasm (plī·ŏnæz'm). 1586. [– late L. *pleonasmus* – Gr. πλεονασμός, f. πλεονάζειν be superfluous, f. πλέον more.] **1.** *Gram.* and *Rhet.* The use of more words in a sentence than are necessary to express the meaning; redundancy of expression; with *a* and *pl.*, an instance of this, or the superfluous words or phrase itself. **2.** *gen.* Superfluity, redundancy; something superfluous or redundant. Now only *fig.* from 1. 1617.

1. What the energetic p. of our ancestors denominated 'a false lie' 1860. Hence **Pleona·stic**, †**-al** *adjs.*; **-ly** *adv.*

Pleonaste (plī·ŏnæst). Also **pleonast.** 1804. [– Fr. *pléonaste* (Haüy, 1801) – Gr. πλεοναστός abundant, f. πλεονάζειν; see prec.] *Min.* = CEYLONITE.

Pleopod (plī·ŏpǫd). 1855. [f. as PLEON + Gr. πούς, ποδ- foot.] *Zool.* One of the swimming limbs attached to the pleon in Crustacea.

‖**Pleroma** (pliᵊrōᵘ·mă). 1765. [– Gr. πλήρωμα that which fills, f. πληροῦν, f. πλήρης full.] Fullness, plenitude; in Gnostic theology, the spiritual universe as the abode of God and of the totality of the Divine powers and emanations. **b.** Used in ref. to Colossians 2:9, where the Eng. versions from 1388 have 'fullness'.

Plerome (pliᵊ·roᵘm). 1875. [– G. *plerom* (Hanstein, 1868) – Gr. πλήρωμα; see prec.] *Bot.* The innermost layer of the primary tissue or meristem at a growing-point, which develops into the fibrovascular tissue, or into this and the pith.

Plerophory (pliᵊrǫ·fŏri). Now *rare.* 1605. [– Gr. πληροφορία (Heb. 6:11, 10:22, etc.) fullness of assurance, f. (ult.) πλήρης full + -φόρος bearing.] Full assurance or certainty.

A P. or full Assurance that I am forgiven WESLEY.

Plesance, -aunce, obs. ff. PLEASANCE.

Plesio-, comb. form from Gr. πλησίος near.

Plesiomorphous (plī:siomǭ·ɹfəs), *a.* 1837. [f. PLESIO- + Gr. μορφή form + -OUS.] *Cryst.* Very near in form; crystallizing in forms closely resembling, but not identical with each other. So **Ple:siomo·rphic** *a.* **Ple:siomo·rphism,** the fact or condition of being p.

‖**Plesiosaurus** (plī:siosǭ·rŏs). *Pl.* **-i.** 1825. [mod.L. (W. D. Conybeare), f. PLESIO- + Gr. σαῦρος lizard.] *Palæont.* A genus of extinct marine reptiles, having a long neck, a small head, a short tail, and four large paddles, found in the Lias and neighbouring formations. Hence **Ple·siosaur**, a reptile of the extinct genus *Plesiosaurus* or order *Plesiosauria.* **Ple:siosau·rian** *a.* belonging to the order *Plesiosauria*; *sb.* a reptile of this order.

Plessimeter (plesi·mĭtəɹ). 1857. [– Fr. *plessimètre.*] = PLEXIMETER.

Plethora (ple·þŏră, plĭþō·ră). See next. 1541. [– late L. *plethora* (Oribasius) – Gr. πληθώρη fullness, repletion, f. πλήθειν be full.] **1.** *Path.* A morbid condition, characterized, according to older writers, by over-fullness of blood or of any other humour (or of juices in a plant), according to later writers, by an excess of red corpuscles in the blood. **2.** *fig.* Any unhealthy repletion or excess 1700.

2. We are . . suffering under a p. of capital 1835. So **Plethoric** (plĭþǫ·rik, ple·þǫrik) *a.* *Path.* characterized by p.; *fig.* full to excess; inflated, turgid. late ME. †**Pletho·rical** *a.*, **-ly** *adv.*

Plethory (ple·þŏri). Now *rare.* 1624. [prob. f. *plethoric* (see prec.), after *allegoric*, *-ory.*] = PLETHORA.

‖**Plethron** (ple·þrǫn). *Pl.* **-a.** 1623. [– Gr. πλέθρον.] An ancient Greek measure of length, = 100 Greek, or about 101 English feet; also a square measure, in extent somewhat less than an imperial rood.

Plethysmograph (plĭþi·zmŏgraf). 1872. [f. Gr. πληθυσμός enlargement (ult. f. πληθύς fullness) + -GRAPH.] *Physiol.* An instrument for recording and measuring the variation in the volume of a part of the body, esp. as due to the changes in the circulation of the blood produced by emotion, etc. Hence **Plethysmogra·phic** *a.* **Plethysmo·graphy,** the use of the p.

‖**Pleura** (plūᵊ·ră). *Pl.* **-æ.** 1664. [med.L., – Gr. πλευρά side, rib.] *Anat.* and *Zool.* **1.** One of the two serous membranes which line the thorax and envelop the lungs in mammals; each forms a closed sac, one side of which (*pulmonary p.*) invests the lung, while the other (*costal* or *parietal p.*) is attached to the inner wall of the chest. **2.** In invertebrates: Name for a part of the body-wall on each side in arthropods 1826. **b.** In molluscs: The region on each side of the rachis of the lingual ribbon of the odontophore 1851. **Pleu·ral** *a.*[1] of or pertaining to the p.

Pleu·ral, *a.*[2] 1887. [f. PLEURON + -AL[1].] Of or pertaining to the pleuron; costal, lateral.

‖**Pleuralgia** (pluræ·ldʒiă). 1822. [mod.L., f. PLEURA + Gr. ἄλγος pain; see -IA[1].] *Path.* Pleurodynia. Hence **Pleura·lgic** *a.*

‖**Pleurapophysis** (plūᵊrăpǫ·fisis). *Pl.* **-yses** (-isīz). 1854. [mod.L., f. PLEURA + APOPHYSIS.] *Compar. Anat.* Each of the lateral processes of a typical vertebra, forming part of the hæmal arch. Hence **Pleu:rapophy·sial** *a.*

‖**Pleurenchyma** (plure·ŋkimă). Also **pleure·nchym.** 1842. [mod.L.; see PLEURA, ENCHYMA.] *Bot.* The woody tissue, of which the woody parts of plants are mainly formed. Hence **Pleurenchy·matous** *a.*

Pleurisy (plūᵊ·rĭsi). late ME. [– OFr. *pleurisie* (mod. *pleurésie*) – late L. *pleurisis* (Prudentius), in mod.L. *pleuresis*, for earlier *pleuritis* (Vitruvius) – Gr. πλευρῖτις (Hippocrates), f. πλευρά; see PLEURA-, -ITIS.] *Path.* Inflammation of the pleura, with or without effusion of fluid into the pleural cavity, and usu. characterized by pain in the chest or side. Formerly often with *a* and *pl.*

attrib. **P.-root,** name for *Asclepias tuberosa*, also called Butterfly-weed, a popular remedy for p.

Pleuritic (pluri·tik), *a.* 1570. [– (O)Fr. *pleurétique* – L. *pleuriticus* (Pliny) – Gr. πλευριτικός (Hippocrates); see prec., -IC.] **1.** Affected with or suffering from pleurisy. **2.** Of or pertaining to pleurisy; symptomatic of pleurisy 1652.

‖**Pleuritis** (plurəi·tis). *rare.* 1693. [L. – Gr. πλευρῖτις; see PLEURISY.] *Path.* = PLEURISY.

Pleuro- (plūᵊro), bef. a vowel **pleur-,** comb. form of Gr. πλευρά side, PLEURA, πλευρόν rib; used chiefly in senses 'side' and 'pleura', occas. in that of 'rib'.

‖**Pleurobranchia** (-bræ·ŋkiă), also **pleurobranch** (-bræŋk), *Zool.* a pleural branchia or gill, i.e. one attached to the epimeron of a thoracic somite, in Crustacea. **Pleurobra·nchial** *a.*, of or pertaining to a pleurobranchia. **Pleurobra·nchiate** *a.*, having pleurobranchiæ, as a crustacean; having gills along the sides, as a gastropod mollusc of the order *Pleurobranchiata.* **Pleuroca·rpous** [Gr. καρπός fruit] *a.*, *Bot.* lateral-fruited. ‖**Pleuroce·ntrum** (*pl.* **-a**), *Anat.* each lateral half of the centrum of a vertebra, a hemicentrum; hence **Pleuroce·ntral** *a.* **Pleurodiran** (-dəiᵊ·răn) [Gr. δειρή neck] *a.*, *Zool.* applied to those tortoises which bend the neck sideways in the shell (opp. to *cryptodirous*); *sb.* a p. tortoise. **Pleu·rodont** [Gr. ὀδούς, ὀδοντ-, tooth], *Zool.* a lizard having teeth fixed to the side of the jawbone; *a.* belonging to the *Pleurodontes*, a group of lizards having this character. **Pleu:ro-perica·rdial** *a.*, belonging to the pleura and the pericardium; applied to a friction-sound heard in auscultation in cases of pleurisy. **Pleu:ro-pericardi·tis** *Path.*, inflammation involving the pleura and pericardium. ‖**Pleuro·steon** (pl. **-ea**) [Gr. ὀστέον bone], *Zool.* a lateral part on each side of the sternum in birds, to which the ribs are attached; hence **Pleuro·steal** *a.* See also Main words.

‖**Pleurodynia** (plūᵊrodi·niă). Also †**pleurodyne** (-ǫ·dinī), **pleurodyny** (-ǫ·dini). 1802. [f. PLEURO- + Gr. -οδυνία in comb., f. ὀδύνη pain; see -IA[1].] *Path.* Pain in the side caused by rheumatism in the muscles of the chest.

‖**Pleuron** (plūᵊ·rǫn). *Pl.* **pleura.** 1706. [– Gr. πλευρόν rib, side.] *Anat.* and *Zool.* The lateral part of the body-wall, the side; *spec.* in Arthropoda, the lateral part of each somite or section of the body (in insects, of each thoracic somite).

Pleuronect (plūᵊ·rŏnekt). 1849. [– mod. L. *Pleuronectes*, f. Gr. πλευρά side + νήκτης swimmer.] *Ichthyol.* A fish of the genus *Pleuronectes* or family *Pleuronectidæ*; a flat-fish. So **Pleurone·ctid, -ne·ctoid** *sb.* a fish of the family *Pleuronectidæ*; *a.* belonging to this family.

‖**Pleu:ro-peritone·um, -æ·um.** 1875. [mod.L., f. PLEURO- + PERITONEUM.] *Anat.* The serous membrane lining the body-cavity and enveloping the viscera in vertebrates below mammals; corresponding to the pleuræ and peritoneum in mammals. Also called simply PERITONEUM. So **Pleu:ro-peritone·al, -æ·al** *a.* of or belonging at once to the pleuræ and the peritoneum, or the pleuro-peritoneum 1872.

‖**Pleuro-pneumonia** (plūᵊ:roˌniumōᵘ·niă). 1725. [mod.L., f. PLEURO- + PNEUMONIA. Cf. Fr. *pleuropneumonie* (XVI).] *Path.* Inflammation involving the pleura and the lung; pneumonia complicated with pleurisy; *esp.* a contagious febrile disease peculiar to horned cattle.

‖**Pleurothotonos** (plūᵊroþǫ·tŏnǫs), **-us** (-ŏs). 1822. [mod.L., f. Gr. πλευρόθεν from the side (f. πλευρά side) + -τονος stretched, stretching.] *Path.* Tetanic bending of the body to one side.

Pleurotomid (plurǫ·tŏmid). [– mod.L. *Pleurotomidæ* pl., f. *Pleurotoma* name of the typical genus, f. Gr. πλευρά side + τομή cutting; see -ID³.] *Zool.* A gastropod mollusc of the family *Pleurotomidæ*.

Plexiform (ple·ksifǭɹm), *a.* 1828. [f. PLEXUS + -FORM.] *Anat.* Of the form of a plexus; forming a plexus or plexuses.

Pleximeter (pleksi·mĭtəɹ). Also (irreg.) **plexometer.** 1842. [f. Gr. πλῆξις percussion (f. πλήσσειν strike) + -METER (with the sense of 'estimating').] *Med.* A small thin plate of ivory, etc. which is placed firmly upon some part of the body and struck with a PLEXOR in medical percussion.

Plexor (ple·ksǭɹ). 1844. [irreg. f. Gr. πλῆξις or πλήσσειν (see prec.) + -OR 2, after *flexor*, etc.] *Med.* A small hammer, etc. used (with a PLEXIMETER) in medical percussion; a percussion-hammer.

Plexure (ple·ksiŭɹ). *rare.* 1671. [f. *plex-*, pa. ppl. stem of L. *plectere* plait, etc. + -URE, after FLEXURE (– L. *flexura*).] A plaiting or interweaving; something plaited or interwoven.

‖**Plexus** (ple·ksŏs). *Pl.* **plexuses,** rarely **plexus.** 1682. [L., f. *plectere, plex-*; see prec.] **1.** *Anat.* A structure in the animal body consisting of a network of fibres or vessels closely interwoven and intercommunicating; as *gastric p., solar p.*, etc. **2.** *gen.* A network, complication 1769.

Pliable (plɔi·ăb'l), *a.* 1483. [– Fr. *pliable*, f. *plier* bend; see PLY *v.*¹, -ABLE.] **1.** Easy to be bent; flexible, supple; †plastic. **2.** *fig.* Flexible in disposition or character; yielding, docile; adaptable. Sometimes in bad sense. 1494.

1. A plyable flexure of joynts SIR T. BROWNE. 2. P. judges were previously chosen 1863. Hence **Pliabi·lity, Pli·ableness,** p. quality or property. **Pli·ably** *adv.*

Pliancy (plɔi·ănsi). 1711. [f. next; see -ANCY.] The quality of being pliant; flexibility.

P. of mind 1810. The agile p. of youth 1835.

Pliant (plɔi·ănt), *a.* ME. [– (O)Fr. *pliant*, pr. pple. of *plier* bend; see PLY *v.*¹, -ANT.] **1.** Bending; supple, flexible; †plastic. **2.** *fig.* Readily influenced for good or evil; compliant, complaisant. late ME. **b.** = FLEXIBLE 3. 1835.

1. The fisher, with his p. wand 1880. 2. A committee thus instructed was likely to be sufficiently p. 1860. Hence **Pli·ant-ly** *adv.*, **-ness** (now *rare*).

‖**Plica** (pli·kă, plɔi·kă). *Pl.* **plicæ.** 1684. [mod.L. (whence Fr. *plica, plique* XVIII) – med.L. *plica* fold, f. L. *plicare*; see PLY *v.*¹] **1.** *Path.* (More fully *pli·ca polo·nica.*) A matted filthy condition of the hair due to disease; Polish plait. **2.** A fold or folding of any part, as of the skin or a membrane 1706.

Plicate (plɔi·kĕt), *a.* 1760. [– L. *plicatus*, pa. pple. of *plicare* fold; see -ATE².] Folded, pleated. So **Pli·cated** *ppl. a.* 1753. **Pli·cately** *adv.*

Plication (pli-, plɔikē̆ⁱ·ʃən). late ME. [orig. – med.L. *plicatio*, f. L. *plicare* fold; in mod. use f. L. *plicare* after *complicate/complication.*] **1.** The action of folding; folded condition. **2.** *concr.* A folding, a fold 1748. **3.** *Geol.* The folding of strata; a fold in a stratum 1859.

Plicato- (pli-, plɔikē̆ⁱ·to), comb. adv. form from L. *plicatus* plicate, prefixed to other adjs. in the sense 'plicately —', 'plicate and —', as *p.-contorted* (plicately contorted), *p.-papillose* (papillose with plications or wrinkles), etc.

Plicature (pli·kătiŭɹ). 1578. [– L. *plicatura* folding, f. *plicat-*, pa. ppl. stem of *plicare* fold; see -URE.] = PLICATION.

Plicidentine (pliside·ntin). 1849. [f. *plici-*, used as comb. form of L. *plicare* fold, + DENTINE.] A form of dentine in which it is folded on a series of vertical plates, causing the surface of the tooth to be fluted.

Plier (plɔi·əɹ). 1490. [In sense 1 f. PLY *v.*¹ and ²; in sense 2 f. PLY *v.*¹; see -ER¹.] **1.** One who plies (see PLY *v.*) 1673. **2.** *pl.* Pincers, usu. small, having long jaws mostly with parallel surfaces, sometimes toothed, for bending wire, handling small objects, etc.

Plight (plɔit), *sb.*¹ [OE. *pliht* = OFris., (M)Du. *plicht*, OHG. *pfliht* (G. *plicht* duty), f. Gmc. *plex-, whence OE. *pleoh* peril, risk. In sense 3 prob. deduced from *trothplight*, which was orig. *troth plight* 'plighted troth'.] †**1.** Peril, danger, risk. –late ME. †**2.** Sin, offence; guilt, blame. ME. only. **3.** Undertaking (of a risk or obligation); pledge (under risk of forfeiture); engagement, plighting ME.

3. *Lear* I. i. 103.

Plight (plɔit), *sb.*² [XIV *plit, plyt* – AFr. *plit*, var. of OFr. *ploit, pleit* fold, PLAIT *sb.* In II perh. infl. by prec.] **I.** Fold, manner of folding; plait. †**1.** = PLAIT *sb.* 1, 1 b. –1697. †**2.** = PLAIT *sb.* 2. –1800. †**3.** A recognized length or 'piece' of lawn –1535. **II.** Manner of being; condition, state. (Cf. *complexion.*) **1.** Condition, state, trim. (Orig. neutral or good; now usually evil.) ME. **2.** State as to health; now esp. of cattle. late ME. **b.** *absol.* Health 1460. †**3.** Mood. esp. *to do* something –1726. **4.** State or position from a legal point of view 1540. **5.** Attire, dress (*rare*) 1590.

1. Being in so excellent a p. DRAYTON. He was now in a woful p. GOLDSM. 3. 'Less Philomel will daign a Song, In her sweetest, saddest p. MILT.

Plight (plɔit), *v.*¹ Now chiefly *poet.* or *rhet.* ME. [f. PLIGHT *sb.*¹ Cf. OE. *plihtan* endanger, OHG. *pflihten* engage oneself, MDu. *plichten* guarantee.] †**1.** *trans.* To put (something) in danger or risk of forfeiture; to pledge or engage (one's faith, oath, etc.), esp. in ref. to betrothal or marriage ME. †**2.** To pledge oneself to do or give (something); to promise –1587. **3.** To engage or bind (oneself); *pass.* to be engaged or bound *to* some one. late ME.

1. To p. faith to William, rightful and lawful King 1855. Hence **Pli·ghter** *rare*, one who or that which plights or pledges.

†**Plight,** *v.*² [XIV *plite*, etc., collateral form of PLAIT *v.*; later *plight*, going with PLIGHT *sb.*²] **1.** *trans.* = PLAIT *v.* 1; also to contract into folds or wrinkles –1658. **2.** = PLAIT *v.* 2; to knit, to tie in a knot –1633.

Plim (plim), *v.* Chiefly *dial.* 1654. [Of unkn. origin.] **a.** *intr.* To swell, fill *out.* **b.** *trans.* To swell, inflate 1881.

Pli·msoll. 1881. [Name of S. *Plimsoll*, M.P. for Derby, to whom the Merchant Shipping Act of 1876 was largely due.] In *P. line*, (also *Plimsoll's*) *mark*: see MARK *sb.*¹ III. 3. **b.** *sb. pl.* A kind of rubber-soled canvas shoes 1927.

Plinth (plinþ). 1611. [– Fr. *plinthe* or L. *plinthus* (Vitruvius) – Gr. πλίνθος tile, brick, stone squared for building.] **1. a.** 'The lower square member of the base of a column or pedestal' (Gwilt). **b.** The projecting part of a wall immediately above the ground. Also *attrib.*, as *p.-stone.* 1823. **c.** *fig.* A plinth-like base 1803. **2.** The uppermost projecting part of a cornice or wall. Now *rare.* 1613.

Pliocene (plɔi·ŏsīn), *a.* (*sb.*) Also **pleio-** 1833. [f. Gr. πλείων, -ον more (see PLEIO-) + καινός new.] *Geol.* Epithet applied to the newest division of the Tertiary formation; called also Upper Tertiary. Also applied to animals, etc. of this period. **b.** *absol.* as *sb.* = Pliocene division or formation.

‖**Pliosaurus** (plɔi,osǭ·rŏs). Also **pleio-.** 1841. [f. Gr. πλείον more, PLEIO- + σαῦρος lizard; so called because more near to the saurian type than the ICHTHYOSAURUS.] *Palæont.* A genus of fossil marine reptiles, resembling *Plesiosaurus*; their remains are found in the Upper Oolite. Also **Pli·osaur.**

Pliotron (plɔi·ŏtrǫn). *Wireless Telegr.* 1918. [irreg. f. *plio* PLEIO- + *-tron* of ELECTRON.] A three-electrode valve the bulb of which is as highly evacuated of air as possible.

‖**Ploce** (plǫ·sī). 1577. [Late L. – Gr. πλοκή plaiting, f. πλέκειν to plait.] *Rhet.* The repetition of a word in an altered or pregnant sense, or for the sake of emphasis.

Ploce,..as, In that great victory Cæsar was Cæsar 1678.

Plod (plǫd), *v.* 1562. [Of unkn. origin, but prob. symbolic.] **1.** *intr.* To walk heavily; to move laboriously, to trudge. Also *p. on. lit.* and *fig.* 1566. **b.** *trans.* To trudge along, over, or through (a road, etc.) 1750. **2.** *intr.* To work with steady laborious perseverance; to toil in a laborious, stolid, monotonous fashion. Const. *at, on, upon.* 1562.

1. Bare-foot p. I the cold ground vpon SHAKS. **b.** The plowman homeward plods his weary way GRAY. 2. The secret of good work—to p. on and still keep the passion fresh MEREDITH. Hence **Plod** *sb.*, an act or spell of plodding; a heavy tiring walk. **Plo·dder,** one who plods. **Plo·dding** *ppl. a.*; hence **Plo·dding-ly** *adv.*, **-ness.**

Plop (plǫp), *sb.* and *adv.* 1833. [imit.] **A.** *sb.* The sound made by a smooth object dropping into water without splashing, or the like; the act of falling with this sound **B.** *adv.* or *int.* With a plop. So **Plop** *v.* to fall with or as with a plop. Also *trans.* in causative sense.

Plosion (plō̆ᵘ·ʒən). 1899. [Extracted from EXPLOSION and IMPLOSION.] *Phonetics.* The percussive shutting off or release of the breath, as in the pronunciation of stops such as (p), (b). Hence **Plo·sive** *a.* and *sb.* (a speech sound) characterized by this.

Plot (plǫt), *sb.* [In I, late OE. *plot*, of unkn. origin (see PLAT *sb.*²). In II, alt. of *plat* (early XVI, now U.S.), orig. a var. of *plot* in Branch I, now dial., or (as in *grass plat*, etc.), partly assoc. with late ME. *plat* flat place or space (PLAT *sb.*¹). In III superseding earlier COMPLOT.] **I.** †**1.** A small portion of any surface differing in character or aspect from the rest; a patch, spot –1834. **2.** A piece (of small or moderate size) of ground, or of what grows or lies upon it; a patch, spot. Cf. PLAT *sb.*² 1. OE. †**b.** The site, situation, of a building, town, city, etc. –1603.

2. The grass p. before the door W. IRVING.

II. In these senses *plat* occurs earlier. **1.** A ground plan of a building, field, farm, etc.; a map, a chart. *Obs.* or *arch.* exc. in *U.S.* 1551. †**2.** A sketch or outline of a literary work –1626. **3.** The plan or scheme of a play, poem, work of fiction, etc. 1649.

1. The ruins of the cathedral of Elgin..Its whole p. is easily traced JOHNSON. 3. In every narrative, there is a certain connexion of events..which, in a work of fiction, is called a p. 1852.

III. Perh. infl. by COMPLOT. A plan or project, secretly contrived, to accomplish some wicked, criminal, or illegal purpose; a conspiracy; also later, *joc.*, a sly plan, an innocent scheme 1594.

The Powder-plot. Inuented by hellish Malice. 1617.

Plot (plǫt), *v.* 1588. [f. prec. sb.] **1.** *trans.* To make a plan, map, or diagram of (an existing object, as a building, etc.); to lay down on a map (as a ship's course, etc.); to represent by a plan or diagram (the course or result of any action or process). Also with *down.* 1590. **2.** To make a plan of (something to be laid out, constructed, or made.) Also with *out.* 1588. **3.** To plan, contrive, or devise (something to be carried out or accomplished). Now always in evil sense. 1589. **4.** *intr.* To scheme, lay plans, contrive, conspire 1607.

1. This treatise plotteth downe Cornwall, as it now standeth 1602. 3. They..plotted the..merciless, devilish, and damnable gunpowder-treason 1631. Had he plotted to dethrone a princess H. WALPOLE. 4. The wicked plotteth against the iust *Ps.* 37:12. Hence **Plo·tter,** one who plans or devises anything (now *rare*); *spec.* a conspirator.

Plotinian (ploti·niăn), *a.* 1678. [f. L. *Plotinus* – Gr. Πλωτῖνος, proper name, + -AN.] Of or pertaining to Plotinus (A.D. 204–270), the most noted philosopher of the Neo-Platonic school. So **Ploti·nic, -al** *a.* **Plo·tinist,** a follower of Plotinus.

Plough (plau), *sb.*¹ Also *U.S.* **plow.** [Late OE. *plōh* ploughland (pl. *plōges* XII) – ON. *plógr* = OFris. *plōch*, OS. *plōg* (Du. *ploeg*), OHG. *pfluoc* (G. *pflug*) :- Gmc. *plōʒaz – north. Italic *plōg-, repr. by Lombardic L. *plovus* and Rhætian *plaumatorum* (Pliny), and prob. L. *plaustrum, plōstrum, plōxenum, -inum.* The native OE. word was *sulh* (rel. to L. *sulcus* furrow).] **1.** An agricultural implement, used to prepare the soil for sowing or planting, by cutting furrows in it and turning it up. It consists essentially of a cutting blade, fixed in a frame, drawn by oxen or horses (or, now, by steam, etc.), and guided by a man. Often used as the symbol of agriculture. ME. **2.** Chiefly *s.w. dial.* A team of draught beasts harnessed to a wagon 1505. **3.** †**a.** = PLOUGH-LAND 1. –1791. **b.** Ploughed land. (Chiefly *hunting slang.*) 1861. **4.** *transf.* The group of seven stars, also called Charles's Wain, in the constellation *Ursa Major*; also, that constellation as a whole 1513. **5.** Applied to various instruments, etc., resembling a plough in shape or action; *esp.* **a.** An instrument for cutting or trimming the edges of books 1688; **b.** A plane for cutting rabbets or grooves 1678. **6.** An antler or branch on the horn of a caribou 1892.

1. I think that whosoever doth not maintain the P., destroys this Kingdom 1601. ICE-, SNOW-P., etc.: see those words. Phrases. *To be at the p., to follow* or *hold the p. To put (lay, set) one's hand to the p.* (after Luke 9:62): to undertake a task. *Under the p.*: (of land) in cultivation. **2.** The driver of a p.,..laden with tin, for Penzance coinage 1762.

attrib. and *Comb.*: **p.-beam,** the central longitudinal beam in a plough, to which the other principal parts are attached; **-cutter** = *plough-press*; **-iron,** any iron of a p., *esp.* in *pl.*, the coulter and share; **-knife,** the knife of a bookbinder's plough-cutter; **-plane** = sense 5 b; **-point,** the point of a plough-share; **-press,** in bookbinding, a press in which a book is held while the edges are cut or 'ploughed'; **-tree,** a plough-handle; **-wright,** a maker of ploughs. See also Main words. Hence **Plou·gher,** one who ploughs; a ploughman.

Plough, *sb.*² *slang.* 1863. [f. PLOUGH *v.* 8.] The act or fact of rejecting a candidate in an examination.

Plough (plau), *v.* late ME. Also *U.S.* **plow.** [f. PLOUGH *sb.*¹] **1. a.** *trans.* To make furrows in and turn up (the earth) with a plough, esp. as a preparation for sowing; also *absol.* to use a plough. **b.** To make (a furrow, ridge, line) by ploughing 1589. **2.** *intr.* (or *absol.*) To use the plough, work as a ploughman, till the ground 1535. **b.** *intr.* in pass. sense (of land): To stand ploughing (well, etc.); to prove (tough, etc.) in the ploughing 1762. **3.** *trans.* By extension: To furrow as by ploughing; to gash, tear up, scratch (any surface). Often *p. up.* 1588. **b.** *intr.* To move through soft ground, snow, etc., furrowing it 1847. **4.** *fig.* Of a ship, boat, swimming animal, etc.: To cleave the surface of the water. Chiefly *poet. trans.* and *intr.* 1607. **5.** *trans. fig.* To furrow (the face, brow, etc.) deeply with wrinkles; also with resultant object 1725. **6.** In various fig. applications 1535. **7. a.** *Bookbinding.* To cut with a 'plough' or plough-press 1873. **b.** *Carpentry.* To cut or plane (a groove, rabbet) with a 'plough'. Also *intr.* 1805. **8.** *Univ. slang.* To reject (a candidate) in an examination 1853.

1. As much land as a yoke of oxen could p. in one day 1796. **2.** That hee that ploweth, should plow in hope 1 *Cor.* 9:10. **3.** [He] Fell prone and plough'd the Dust 1740. The course which the river had ploughed for itself down the valley SCOTT. **4.** *trans.* He and his eight hundred Shall p. the wave no more COWPER. **5.** Italia!..On thy sweet brow is sorrow plough'd by shame BYRON. **6.** Cromwell..who through a cloud..To peace and truth thy glorious way hast plough'd MILT.

With advbs. *P. around*: *lit.* in ref. to stumps left in cultivated land; *fig.* to feel one's way. *P. in, p. into the land*: to embed or bury in the soil (manure, vegetation, etc.) by ploughing. *P. up*: to break up (ground) by ploughing; to throw or cast up (roots, weeds) with the plough; to cut up roughly, furrow or scratch deeply by any similar action.

Phrases. *To p. with any one's heifer* (*ox*, †*calf*) after *Judg.* 14:18. *To p. the sands*: a type of fruitless labour. Also *to p. the air.* Hence **Plou·ghable** *a.* that can be ploughed; arable.

Plou·gh-boy. 1569. A boy who leads the team that draws a plough; hence, a young rustic.

Plough-head, 1453. [f. PLOUGH *sb.*¹ + HEAD *sb.*] †**1.** The share-beam of a plough; a wooden frame to which the share was fixed –1613. **2.** The front part of a plough 1733.

Plough-land (plau·lænd). ME. [f. PLOUGH *sb.*¹ + LAND *sb.*] **1.** *Hist.* The unit of assessment of land in the N. and E. counties of England, after the Norman Conquest, based upon the area capable of being tilled by one plough-team of eight oxen in the year; cf. HIDE *sb.* **2.** Arable land 1530.

Ploughman (plau·mæn). ME. A man who follows and guides the plough; hence, a farm-labourer or rustic.

Comb. **Ploughman's Spikenard:** see SPIKENARD.

Plough-Monday (plau:mɒ·ndeⁱ, mɒ·ndi). 1542. The first Monday after Epiphany, on which, esp. in the N. and E. of England, the commencement of the ploughing season was celebrated by a procession of disguised ploughmen and boys drawing a plough from door to door.

Ploughshare (plau·ʃēᵊɹ). late ME. [See SHARE *sb.*¹] **1.** The large pointed blade of a plough, which, following the coulter, cuts a slice of earth, and passes it on to the mould-board. **2.** *Anat.* The vomer.

attrib. and *Comb.* **p.-bone** *Anat.*, (*a*) the vomer; (*b*) the pygostyle of a bird.

Plou·gh-staff. ME. A staff, ending in a small spade or shovel, used to clear the coulter and mould-board from earth, roots, weeds, etc.

Plou·gh-tail. 1523. The rear or handles of a plough. Symbolically, farm-labour; as *at, from the plough-tail.*

Plover (plɒ·vəɹ). ME. [– AFr. *plover*, OFr. *plovier, plouvier* (mod. *pluvier*, alt. after *pluie* rain) :– Rom. **ploviarius*, **pluviarius*, f. L. *pluvia* rain.] **1.** The common name of several gregarious grallatorial (limicoline) birds of the family *Charadriidæ*, esp. those of the genera *Charadrius* and *Squatarola*; also popularly given to the Lap-wing, the eggs of which are sold as 'Plovers' eggs'. **2.** With defining words, applied to species of the family *Charadriidæ*, and extended to some of the allied *Thinocoridæ* and *Scolopacidæ* or Snipe family, and to the isolated genus *Dromas* (Crab Plover) 1538.

Plover-page, plover's page. *Sc.* 1837. [f. prec. + PAGE *sb.*¹] The dunlin (*Tringa alpina*), which is said to attend or follow the golden plover; applied also to other species of *Tringa*, and to the Jack Snipe.

Ploy (ploi). *Sc.* and *north.* 1722. [Of unkn. origin.] Anything in which one personally engages; a hobby; a game, pastime, or sport; an escapade; a trick.

Pluck (plɒk), *sb.* late ME. [f. next.] **I. 1.** An act of plucking; a tug, a jerk, a snatch. †**b.** *fig.* A bout; an attempt; a 'go' –1762. **2.** In examinations: The act of plucking or rejecting a candidate; the fact of being plucked 1852.

1. b. They being come to By path Stile, have a mind to have a p. with Gyant Dispair BUNYAN.

II. 1. The heart, liver, and lungs (sometimes with other viscera) of a beast, as used for food 1611. **b.** In ref. to human beings 1710. **2.** *colloq.* (orig. app. *pugilistic slang.*) The heart as the seat of courage; courage, spirit; determination not to yield but to keep up the fight in the face of danger or difficulty 1785.

1. b. It vexes me to the p. that I should lose walking this delicious day SWIFT. **2.** The one thing the English value is p. EMERSON. Hence **Plucked** (plɒkt) *a.* having p. or courage; as in *good-p., rare-p.*, etc. (*colloq.* 1848.) **Plu·ckless** *a.* without p., courage, or spirit.

Pluck (plɒk), *v.* [Late OE. *ploccian, pluccian*, corresp. to MLG. *plucken*, MDu. *plocken* (Flem. *plokken*), ON. *plokka, plukka* :– Gmc. **plukkōn*, **-ōjan*, a parallel form with mutation **plukkjan* being repr. by OE. **plyććan* (ME. *plicchen*); prob. all to be referred to Rom. **piluccare.* whence OFr. *peluchier, espeluchier* (mod. *éplucher* pluck).] **1.** *trans.* To pull off (a flower, fruit, hair, feather, etc.) from where it grows; to pick off or out; to cull, gather. **2.** To drag; to snatch. With *away, in, out, off, on, up*, etc. *arch.* (Now usu. expressed by *pull.*) late ME. **b.** *absol.* or *intr.* To draw or drag; to snatch or take by force; to steal ME. **3.** *trans. fig.* To pull, draw, or snatch something intangible, or something from or into a state or condition; to snatch *from* danger. Now *rare.* late ME. †**b.** With *down*, etc. To bring down, bring low –1672. **4.** To give a pull at; to pull with a jerk; to sound (the strings of a musical instrument) by doing this, to twang. Also, to pull (a person, etc.) *by* some part of the body or dress. late ME. **b.** *intr.* To pull sharply or forcibly, to tug (*at* something). Also, to snatch *at.* late ME. **5.** To strip or make bare; *esp.* to strip (a bird) of feathers by pulling them off. late ME. **6.** *fig.* To rob; to plunder; to swindle, fleece. late ME. **7.** To reject (a candidate) as below the required standard in an examination; usu. in pass. *To be plucked*, to fail to pass 1713.

1. Let him..From off this Bryer p. a white Rose with me SHAKS. **2.** Yf thy right eye offende the plucke hym out and caste him from the TINDALE *Matt.* 5:29. They plucke downe townes; and leaue nothing stondynge 1551. **4.** 'Tis most ignobly done To plucke me by the Beard SHAKS. Phr. *To p. the Proctor's gown*, the means formerly used (and still usable) for objecting to the granting of a degree to a person who has passed the requisite examinations. **5.** Since I pluckt Geese, plaide Trewant, and whipt Top SHAKS. Phr. *A crow to p.*: see CROW *sb.*¹ **6.** I did p. those Ganders, did rob them DEKKER. Phr. *To p. a pigeon*: see PIGEON *sb.* 3 b.

Pluck up. a. *To p. up (one's) heart, spirits, courage*, etc.: to summon up courage, rouse one's spirits, cheer up. **b.** To pull up; to uproot, eradicate; to raze, demolish. Now *rare* or *arch.* Hence **Plu·cker,** one who or that which plucks.

Plucky (plɒ·ki), *a. colloq.* 1826. [f. PLUCK *sb.* + -Y¹.] Characterized by pluck; showing determination to fight. **b.** *Photogr.* Of a print or negative: Bold, decided, clear 1885.

The pluckiest charge of all that hard fought day 1857. Hence **Plu·ckily** *adv.* **Plu·ckiness.**

Pluff (plɒf), *sb.* (*int.*) *Sc.* 1663. [imit.] **1.** A strong puff or explosive emission of air, gas, or smoke (as in the firing of gunpowder), or of dust; hence, *colloq.* a shot of a musket, etc. **2.** as *int.* or *adv. colloq.* 1860.

Plug (plɒg), *sb.* 1618. [– MLG., MDu. *plugge* (Du. *plug*), of which there are by-forms, MLG. *plügge* (LG. *plüg*); (M)LG. *plock, pluck*, MHG. *pfloc, pflocke* (G. *pflock*). Ult. origin unkn.] **1.** A piece of wood or other material, driven into or used to stop up a hole, to fill a gap, or act as a wedge; also *transf.* a natural or morbid concretion having a similar action. **2.** *spec.* in technical applications; *esp.* **a.** A tapering block of wood driven into a wall between the stones or bricks so as to bear a nail. **b.** In railways, A wedge-pin driven between a rail and its chair. **c.** *Dentistry.* The filling of a hollow tooth. 1766. **d.** The release-mechanism of a water-closet flushing apparatus. **3.** The cock on a public water-pipe; a fire-plug 1727. **4. a.** Tobacco pressed into a flat oblong cake or stick. **b.** A piece of cake or twist tobacco cut off for chewing, etc. 1728. **5.** Applied variously to inferior or defective persons, animals, or objects. *U.S.* and *Colonial.* 1872. **6.** Short for *plug-hat* (see below). *U.S. slang.* 1864.

Comb.: **-basin,** a wash-hand basin having a plug-hole for letting the water out; **-hat** (*U.S. slang*), a silk, 'top', or 'chimney-pot' hat [perh. because the head fits in it like a p.]; **-hole,** an aperture fitted with a p. by which it can be closed; **-rod,** a contrivance attached to the beam of a steam-engine, for opening and closing the valves of the cylinder; **-switch** (*Electr.*), a switch in which connection is made by inserting a metal p.; **-tobacco** = sense 4.

Plug (plɒg), *v.* 1630. [f. prec. sb.] **1.** *trans.* To stop, close tightly, or fill (a hole) with or as with a plug; to drive a plug into. Chiefly with *up.* **b.** *intr.* with *in* (*Electr.*): To complete a circuit by inserting a key or plug between metal plates 1903. **2.** *trans.* To put a bullet into, to shoot (*slang*) 1888. **3.** To strike with the fist (*slang*) 1875. **4.** *intr.* **a.** To 'stick to it' 1865. **b.** To labour with piston-like strokes against resistance (*slang*) 1898.

4. a. We plugged for all we were worth 1865. Hence **Plu·gger,** one who or that which plugs.

Plugging (plɒ·giŋ), *vbl. sb.* 1708. [-ING¹.] **1.** The action of PLUG *v.* **2.** *concr.* Plugs 1875.

Plug-ugly (plɒg,ɒ·gli). *U.S. slang.* 1860. [Of unkn. origin.] A city ruffian or rowdy.

Plum (plɒm), *sb.* [OE. *plūme*, corresp. to MLG. *plūme*, MHG. *pflūme* (G. *pflaume*; in OHG. *pflūmo* plum-tree), ON. *plóma* (perh. – OE.), with by-forms (M)LG., MDu. *prūme* (Du. *pruim*), OHG. *pfrūma* – med.L. *prūna* (see PRUNE *sb.*), orig. pl. of *prunum* plum (cf. *prunus* plum-tree), parallel to Gr. προῦμνον plum.] **1.** The fruit of the tree *Prunus domestica*, a roundish fleshy drupe, covered with a glaucous mealy bloom, and having a somewhat flat pointed stone and sweet pulp. **2.** The tree bearing this fruit. *Prunus domestica* (N.O. *Rosaceæ*) OE. **3.** With qualifying words. Applied to many species (and varieties) of the genus *Prunus.* **4.** A dried grape or raisin as used for puddings, cakes, etc. 1660. **b.** *fig.* A 'good thing', a tit-bit; also, the pick or best of a collection of things, animals, etc. 1780. **5.** The sum of £100,000. *slang*, now *rare.* 1689. †**b.** *transf.* One who is possessed of this sum –1774.

1. Damascene, †**Damasco,** or **Damson P:** see

DAMASK, DAMSON; **Wild P.**, in Britain, *P. insititia* or *spinosa*; in N. America. *P. americana* and *P. subcordata*. Also applied to trees resembling the p., esp. in fruit: **Australian P.** or **Black P. of Illawarra,** *Cargillia australis*, N.O. *Ebenaceæ*; **Blood P.** of Sierra Leone, *Hæmatostaphis barteri*; N.O. *Anacardiaceæ*; **Cocoa P.** of tropical America and Africa, *Chrysobalanus icaco*; **Grey P.** or **Guinea P.**, of Sierra Leone, *Parinarium exelsum*, N.O. *Chrysobalanaceæ*. See also DATE-*p.*, GINGERBREAD-*p.*, etc. 1626. **4. b.** The reviewer who picks all the 'plums' out of a book 1889. The posts named are justly regarded as plums of the Indian Civil Service 1901.

Comb. **p.-colour,** a shade of purple; so **-coloured** *a.*; **-gouger,** a weevil (*Coccotorus scutellaris*).

Plumage (plū·médʒ). 1481. [– (O)Fr. *plumage*, f. *plume* PLUME *sb.*; see -AGE.] **1.** Feathers collectively; the covering of a bird. **2.** A bunch or tuft of feathers used as an ornament; a plume. Now *rare*. 1656.

1. *fig.* All the strength and p. of thy youth WORDSW. Hence **Plu·maged** *a.* feathered; having p.

Plumassier (plūmăsīᵊ·ɹ). 1598. [– Fr. *plumassier*, f. †*plumasse* great plume; see -IER.] One who works or trades in ornamental feathers or plumes.

Plumb (plʊm), *sb.* [ME. *plumbe*, prob. – OFr. **plombe* (repr. by OFr. *plomme* sounding-lead) :– Rom. **plumba*; later assim. to (O)Fr. *plomb* lead.] A mass or ball of lead; *esp.* the weight attached to a mason's plumb-line, to secure its perpendicularity. **b.** A sounding lead, a mariner's plummet 1440.

Plumb, plum (plʊm), *a.* and *adv.* late ME. [f. prec. sb.] **A.** *adj.* **1.** Vertical, perpendicular 1460. **2.** Downright; sheer (Now *U.S.*) 1748; in *Cricket*, (of the wicket) level, true 1902. **B.** *adv.* **1.** Of motion or position: Vertically, perpendicularly; straight *down*; rarely, straight *up*. late ME. **2.** *transf.* and *fig.* **a.** Exactly, directly, precisely 1601. **b.** As an intensive: Completely, absolutely, quite. Chiefly *U.S. slang*. 1587.

1. Fluttring his pennons vain p. down he drops MILT.

Plumb (plʊm), *v.* late ME. [f. PLUMB *sb.* and *a.*; perh. partly after Fr. *plomber*.] **I.** †**1.** *intr.* To sink or fall like a plummet; to fall or plump straight down. WYCLIF. **II. a.** *trans.* To sound (the sea, etc.) with a plummet; to measure (the depth) by sounding 1568. **b.** *fig.* To sound the depths of; to fathom 1599.

a. The depth having been carefully plumbed 1867.

III. 1. To render vertical, to adjust or test by a plumb-line 1711. **2.** To place vertically above or below 1838. **b.** *intr.* To hang vertically 1867. **IV. 1.** *trans.* To weight with lead 1450. **2.** To seal (luggage) with a leaden seal 1756. **V.** [Back-formation from *plumber*.] *intr.* To work in lead as a plumber. Also *trans.* 1889.

Plumbagin (plʊmbēⁱ·dʒin). 1830. [– Fr. *plombagine*, f. L. *plumbago* (see next) + *-ine* -IN¹.] *Chem.* The acrid principle of the root of *Plumbago europæa*.

Plumbago (plʊmbēⁱ·go). 1612. [– L. *plumbago* (i) lead ore, (ii) leadwort, fleawort, f. *plumbum* lead; used in both senses by Pliny, tr. Gr. μολύβδαινα (Dioscorides), deriv. of μόλυβδος lead.] †**1.** Applied to the yellow oxide of lead (litharge); also sometimes to the sulphide (galena) –1669. **2.** *Min.* Black lead or graphite; one of the allotropic forms of carbon; used for pencils, etc., also, mixed with clay, for making crucibles 1712. **3.** *Bot.* A genus of herbaceous plants, having spikes of subsessile flowers, with a tubular five-parted calyx; lead-wort; so called from the colour of the flowers 1747. Hence **Plumba·ginous** *a.* of the nature of or pertaining to p. or graphite.

Plumb-bob (plʊ·m,bǫ:b). 1835. [BOB *sb.*¹] The leaden bob, usu. conoidal, forming the weight of a plumb-line.

Plumbeous (plʊ·mbiəs), *a.* 1578. [f. L. *plumbeus* leaden (f. *plumbum* lead) + -OUS.] Made of or resembling lead, leaden; lead-coloured. Chiefly in *Zool.* **b.** *Ceramics.* Lead-glazed 1875.

Plumber (plʊ·məɹ). ME. [– OFr. *plommier* (mod. *plombier*) :– L. *plumbarius*, f. *plumbum* lead; see -ER² 2.] An artisan who works in lead, zinc, and tin, fitting in, soldering, and repairing water and gas pipes, cisterns, boilers, and the like in buildings; orig., a man who dealt and worked in lead.

Plumber-block: see PLUMMER-BLOCK.

Plumbery (plʊ·məri). [XV *plomerye* – OFr. *plommerie*, (also mod.) *plomberie* lead-work, plumber's workshop, f. *plommier*; see prec., -ERY.] **1.** A plumber's workshop. **2.** Plumber's work; plumbing 1464.

Plumbic (plʊ·mbik), *a.* 1799. [f. L. *plumbum* lead + -IC.] Of or pertaining to lead. **a.** *Chem.* Combined with lead; applied to compounds in which lead has its higher valency (divalent), as *p. acid*, dioxide of lead, PbO_2. **b.** *Path.* Due to the presence of lead 1875.

Plumbi·ferous, *a.* 1796. [f. L. *plumbum* lead + -FEROUS.] Containing lead.

Plumbing (plʊ·miŋ), *vbl. sb.* 1666. [-ING¹.] The action of PLUMB *v.*; now *esp.* the work of a plumber. **b.** *concr.* That which is made by this action; plumber's work 1756. **c.** *attrib.*, as **p.-line, -rope,** a lead-line, sound-line.

Plumbism (plʊ·mbiz'm). 1876. [f. L. *plumbum* lead + -ISM.] *Path.* Lead poisoning.

Plumb-line (plʊ·mləin). 1538. **1.** A line or cord having at one end a metal bob or plummet, for testing or determining vertical direction; occas. = PLUMB-RULE. †**2.** *Geom.* A vertical or perpendicular line; a straight line at right angles to another –1704. **3.** A mariner's sounding-line; also *fig.* 1648.

Plumbo-, bef. a vowel **plumb-**, comb. form of L. *plumbum* lead, forming chemical and mineralogical terms.

Plumbous (plʊ·mbəs), *a.* 1685. [– L. *plumbosus* full of lead; see -OUS.] †**1.** Leaden; *fig.* dull –1737. **2.** *Chem.* Applied to compounds in which lead has its lower valency. Cf. PLUMBIC a. 1895.

Plumb-rule (plʊ·m,rūl). late ME. [f. PLUMB *sb.* + RULE *sb.*] A plummet and line attached to and swinging freely on the surface of a narrow straight-edged board, marked with a longitudinal line which, when its position is vertical, coincides with the string. Used by builders, masons, carpenters, etc. for ensuring or testing the verticality of an erection.

Plum-cake. 1635. A cake containing raisins, currants, and other preserved fruits.

Plum-duff. Also **-dough.** 1840. [f. PLUM *sb.* 4 + DUFF *sb.*¹] Plain flour pudding with raisins or currants in it, boiled in a cloth or bag.

Plume (plūm), *sb.* late ME. [– (O)Fr. *plume* :– L. *pluma* a small soft feather, down.] **1.** A feather; now chiefly *poet.* and *rhet.*; also, a large or conspicuous ornamental feather, as a plume of an ostrich, etc.; in *Ornith.* a contour-feather, as dist. from a plumule. **b.** *fig.* with ref. to the feathers of birds as used in flight, displayed in pride, etc. 1591. **2.** Downy plumage, down; plumage generally 1552. **3.** An ornament, usu. symbolizing dignity or rank, consisting of a large feather or bunch of feathers, or a waving feather-like tuft or bunch of hair, etc.; esp. when attached to a helmet or hat, or worn in the hair, as the *court p.* of ostrich feathers; also used at funerals 1530. **b.** *fig.* (Cf. *a feather in one's cap.*) 1605. **4.** *transf.* Anything resembling the down of feathers or a feather, in form or lightness 1601. **b.** *Bot.* A plumose pappus or other appendage of a seed, by which it floats away 1578. **c.** *Zool.* A plumose or feather-like part or formation 1834.

1. With ruffled plumes and flagging wing GRAY. **b.** Our plumes fall, and we begin to be humble 1642. He is stripped of his borrowed plumes 1802. **3.** These nodding plumes and dragging trains BYRON. **b.** Ambitious to win From me som P. MILT. **4.** The long p. of smoke over the plain STEVENSON.

attrib. and *Comb.*, such as **p.-bird,** a bird with conspicuous plumes, such as are used for ornament; *spec.* a bird of paradise of the subfamily *Epimachinæ*; **-grass,** a grass of the genus *Erianthus*, having a plume-like inflorescence, a Woolly Beard-grass; **-moth,** any species of the family *Pterophoridæ* (*Alucitidæ*), small moths whose wings are divided into feathery lobes. Hence **Plu·meless** *a.*

Plume (plūm), *v.* late ME. [In branch I – (O)Fr. *plumer*, f. *plume* (prec.); in branch II f. PLUME *sb.* or – L. *plumare* cover with feathers.] **I.** †**1.** *intr. Falconry.* To pluck the feathers of its prey, as a hawk; const. *upon, on*. Also *fig.* –1667. **2.** *trans.* To pluck (a bird); hence, to strip, bare. Now *rare*. 1599. †**b.** To pluck (feathers) from a bird –1681. †**c.** *fig.* To pluck, despoil, plunder –1760.

2. I will so pluck him as never hawk plumed a partridge SCOTT.

II. 1. *trans.* To furnish or cover with plumes, feathers, or plumage; to fledge, feather. late ME. **2.** *refl.* **a.** Of a bird: To dress its feathers. **b.** To dress oneself with borrowed plumes. Chiefly *fig.* 1702. **c.** *fig.* Usu. with *on, upon*: To pride oneself, show self-satisfaction, esp. regarding something trivial, ridiculous, or unworthy, or to which one has no just claim 1643. **3.** *trans.* To preen or dress (the feathers or wings); to prepare for flight 1821.

1. The Swan . . is a Bird excellently plumed 1627. **2. c.** Pluming and praising himself, and telling fulsome stories in his own commendation 1715. **3.** *fig.* And calumny plumed her wings for a fresh attack MOTLEY. Hence **Plumed** *ppl. a.*, feathered 1526.

Plumelet (plū·mlėt). 1850. [f. PLUME *sb.* + -LET.] A minute plume.

Plu·me-like, *a.* 1847. [f. PLUME *sb.* + -LIKE.] Resembling a plume; feathery.

Plumet (plū·mėt). 1585. [– Fr. *plumet*, f. *plume*: see PLUME *sb.*, -ET.] A small plume.

Plu·micorn. 1884. [f. L. *pluma* plume + *cornu* horn.] *Ornith.* One of the pair of horn-like or ear-like feathers on the head of several species of owls, often called horns or ears.

Plumiform (plū·mifǭɹm), *a.* [f. as prec. + -FORM.] Feather-shaped.

Plummer-block (plʊ·məɹ,blǫk). Also **plumber-.** 1814. [perh. from a surname + BLOCK *sb.* 5.] = *pillow-block* (PILLOW *sb.*).

Plummet (plʊ·mėt). [XIV *plomet* – OFr. *plommet, plombet*, dim. of *plomb*; see PLUMB *sb.*, -ET.] **1.** A ball of lead, or other weight, attached to a line, and used for determining the vertical; esp. the bob of a plumb-line used by masons, builders, carpenters, etc.; also, the whole instrument, bob, line, and board. late ME. **2.** A piece of lead, etc. attached to a line and used for sounding; a sounding-lead. late ME. †**3.** A ball or lump of lead used for various purposes –1612. **b.** *fig.* That which weighs down, like a dead weight 1625. **4.** *spec.* †**a.** A weight enclosed in a cestus –1661. †**b.** The weight of a clock; also *fig.* a spring of action –1697. **c.** In angling, a small piece of lead attached to a line, for various purposes 1616. †**5.** A pencil of lead, formerly used to rule lines –1828.

2. My Sonne i'th Ooze is bedded; and I'le seeke him deeper then ere p. sounded SHAKS. **3. b.** Hang early Plummets upon the Heels of Pride SIR T. BROWNE. *Comb.*, as *p.-line*, etc.

Plummy (plʊ·mi), *a.* 1759. [f. PLUM *sb.* + -Y¹.] **1.** Consisting of, abounding in, or like plums. **2.** *fig.* Of the nature of a 'plum'; rich, good, desirable. *slang* or *colloq.* 1812.

2. Signing one's self over to wickedness for the sake of getting something p. GEO. ELIOT.

Plumose (plūmōᵘ·s), *a.* 1697. [– L *plumosus*, f. *pluma* PLUME *sb.*; see -OSE¹.] Furnished with feathers or plumes; feathery; resembling a feather or plume in having two series of fine filaments on opposite sides; *esp.* in *Zool.*, *Bot.*, and *Min.*

Plumosite (plū·mŏsəit). 1864. [– G. *plumosit* (Haidinger, 1845), f. L. *plumosus*; see prec., -ITE¹ 2 b.] *Min.* = JAMESONITE.

Plump (plʊmp), *sb.*¹ Now *arch.* and *dial.* late ME. [Of unkn. origin; perh. symbolic.] A compact body of persons, animals, or things; a band, troop, company; a flock; a cluster, clump.

A p. of spears (arch.), a band of spearmen (revived by Scott).

Plump (plʊmp), *sb.*² 1450. [f. PLUMP *v.*¹] **1.** An act of plumping (see PLUMP *v.*¹ 1); an abrupt plunge or heavy fall. *familiar*. **2.** A sudden heavy fall of rain. *Sc.* 1822.

Plump (plʊmp), *a.*¹ 1481. [XV *plompe* – (M)Du. *plomp*, MLG. *plomp, plump* blunt, obtuse, unshapen, blockish (whence G. *plump*), perh. identical with PLUMP *v.*¹ With branch II cf. MLG. *plumpich* 'corpulentus'.] **I.** †**1.** Blunt (in manners); not 'sharp' in intellect; dull, clownish, rude –1620. †**2.** Of an arrow-head: Blunt and broad. ASCHAM. **II.** Of full and rounded form; chubby; having the skin well filled or elastically distended 1545. **b.** Of coins: Of full size and weight, not clipped 1867. **c.** *fig.* 'Fat', rich, abundant; well-supplied; full and round in tone; great, big; complete, round. Now *rare.* 1635.

The p. convivial parson COWPER. He..looked as p. as a pincushion MRS. CARLYLE. Hence **Plu·mp-ly** *adv.*, **-ness. Plu·mpy** *a.* plump.

Plump, *a.*²: see PLUMP *adv.*

Plump (plʌmp), *v.*¹ late ME. [– (M)LG. *plumpen* = (M)Du. *plompen* fall into water (whence G. *plumpen*); of imit. origin.] **1.** *intr.* To fall, drop, plunge, or come down (or against something) flatly or abruptly (usu. implying 'with full or direct impact'). **b.** *transf.* and *fig.* To come plump, i.e. all at once (into some place or condition); to plunge, burst (*in* or *out*). *familiar.* 1829. **2.** *trans.* To drop, throw down, plunge abruptly (into water, etc., or upon a flat surface); to pay *down* at once and in one lot; *refl.* to drop down abruptly and heavily. late ME. **3.** *transf.* and *fig.*: *esp.* To utter abruptly, to blurt out. *familiar.* 1579. **4.** *intr.* [Short for *to vote plump*, or *give a plumper*.] To vote at an election for one candidate alone (when one could vote for two or more). Also *loosely*, to 'vote for' (something). 1806.

1. It will give you a Notion how Dulcissa plumps into a Chair STEELE. **b.** With a convulsive gurgle, out plumped the words 1874. **2.** She plumped down the money and walked out 1892. **4.** We'll p. for Tarleton, to prove we are free 1806.

Plump, *v.*² 1533. [f. PLUMP *a.*¹ II.] **1.** *trans.* To make plump; to fill *out*, distend; to fatten *up*. **2.** *intr.* To swell *out* or *up* 1602.

1. Fowls..plumped for sale by the poulterers of London JOHNSON. **2.** Her cheeks had plumped out 1882.

Plump (plʌmp), *int.*, *adv.*, and *a.*² 1594. [f. PLUMP *v.*¹] **A.** †*int.* Imitative of the sound of a heavy body falling into water 1597. **B.** *adv.* (Mostly *familiar.*) **1.** With a sudden drop or fall into water 1610. **2.** With a sudden or abrupt fall or sinking down; with sudden direct impact, flat upon or against something; with a sudden encounter 1594. **3.** Directly, at once, straight; *esp.* With ref. to a statement, etc.: In plain terms, bluntly, flatly 1734.

2. Sitting p. on an unsuspected cat in your chair 1806. **3.** Hayes first said no, p. THACKERAY.

C. *adj.* Now *rare.* **1. a.** Descending directly, vertical. **b.** Directly facing in position. 1611. **2.** *fig.* Of statements, etc.: Direct, blunt, straightforward, unqualified, 'flat'. 1789. **3.** Plumped down; paid down at once 1865.

2. P. assertion or p. denial for me MAR. EDGEWORTH.

Plumper¹ (plʌ·mpəɹ). 1690. [f. PLUMP *v.*² + -ER¹.] That which plumps or makes plump; as a small ball or disc sometimes carried in the mouth, to fill out hollow cheeks.

Plumper² (plʌ·mpəɹ). 1761. [f. PLUMP *v.*¹ or *adv.* See -ER¹.] **1. a.** An act of plumping, as into water, or to the ground 1810. †**b.** *slang.* A heavy blow –1796. **2.** A vote given solely to one candidate at an election (when one has the right to vote for two or more). Also attrib. *p. vote.* 1761. **b.** A voter who 'plumps'. *rare.* 1818. **3.** A downright lie. *vulgar.* 1812.

Plum-pie. 1660. [f. PLUM *sb.* + PIE.] †**1.** A pie containing raisins and currants; esp. a mince-pie. **2.** A pie containing plums or prunes 1830.

†**Plu·m-po·rridge.** 1591. Porridge containing prunes, raisins, currants, etc.; formerly in favour as a Christmas dish –1808. So †**Plu·m-po·ttage,** app. in same sense.

Plum pudding, plum-pudding (plʌ·m,pu·diŋ). 1711. A pudding containing plums. **a.** (= *Christmas p.*) *spec.* A boiled pudding now composed of flour, bread-crumbs, suet, raisins, currants, etc., with eggs, spices, etc., eaten at Christmas; also, an ordinary suet pudding with raisins. **b.** A pudding of fresh plums contained in a crust 1813.

attrib. and *Comb.*, as **plum-pudding breed, -dog,** the Dalmatian or Spotted Coach breed of dog; **plum-pudding stone** (*Geol.*), orig. a conglomerate of flint pebbles embedded in a siliceo-calcareous matrix; now, *loosely*, any conglomerate.

Plum-tree (plʌ·m,trī). OE. = PLUM *sb.* 2.

‖**Plumula** (plū·miŭlă). 1760. [L., dim. of *pluma* PLUME.] *Bot.* = PLUMULE 1.

Plumularia (plūmiulēᵊ·riă). 1859. [mod. L., f. *plumula* (see prec.) + *-aria*; see -ARY¹ 3.] *Zool.* A genus of hydroids having a plume-like form. Hence **Plumula·rian** *a.* of or pertaining to *P.*, or the family of which it is the type; *sb.* a member of this family.

Plumule (plū·miŭl). 1727. [– Fr. *plumule* or L. *plumula*, dim. of *pluma* PLUME *sb.*; see -ULE.] **1.** *Bot.* The rudimentary shoot, bud, or bunch of undeveloped leaves in a seed; the stem of the embryo plant. **2.** A little feather; *spec.* in *Ornith.*, a down-feather 1847.

Plumy (plū·mi), *a.* 1582. [f. PLUME *sb.* + -Y¹.] †**1.** Composed of down, downy –1700. **2.** Abounding in plumes; feathery, feathered 1597. **3.** Adorned with a plume or plumes 1700. **4.** Plume-like 1611.

1. Her head did on a p. pillow rest DRYDEN. **4.** When the first sheaf its p. top uprears 1798.

Plunder (plʌ·ndəɹ), *sb.* 1643. [f. next.] **1.** The action of plundering or taking as spoil; *spec.* as practised in war; pillage, spoliation, depredation. Now *rare* or *Obs.* **b.** *transf.* The acquisition of property by violent or questionable means; spoliation 1672. **2.** Goods taken from an enemy by force; spoil, booty, loot 1647. **b.** *transf.* Property acquired by illegal or questionable means; also (*slang*), profit, gain 1790.

1. I abhorre all violence, p., rapine, and disorders in Souldiers 1643. **2.** The instigator of the depredations sharing in the p. 1844. **b.** A love of p. and of place 1865.

Plunder (plʌ·ndəɹ), *v.* 1632. [– (M)LG. *plündern* – (M)LG. *plünderen* pillage, sack, lit. rob of household effects, f. MHG. *plunder* bed-clothes, clothing, household stuff (mod. G. lumber, trash); cf. MLG., MDu. *plunde*, *plunne* (LG. *plünde*, *plünn* (pl.) rags, old clothes), Du. *plunje* clothes, baggage.] **1.** *trans.* To rob (a place or person) of goods, etc., by forcible means, or as an enemy; esp. as done in war; to pillage, spoil; to rob systematically. **2.** To take (goods, valuables, etc.) with illegal force, or as an enemy; to embezzle; to take by robbery, steal 1645. **3.** *absol.* or *intr.* To commit depredations 1638.

1. Many Townes and Villages he [Prince Rupert] plundered, which is to say robb'd, for at that time first was the word p. used in England, being borne in Germany 1647. **2.** If they neither steal men or p. their goods 1869. Hence **Plu·nderer. Plu·nderous** *a. rare*, given to plundering.

Plunderage (plʌ·ndərėdʒ). 1796. [f. prec. + -AGE.] The action of plundering; pillage, spoliation; *spec.* in *Maritime Law*, embezzling goods on shipboard; *concr.* spoil obtained by such means.

Plunge (plʌndʒ), *sb.* late ME. [f. next.] **I. 1.** A place where one can plunge; a deep pool (*dial.*); a plunge-bath. **2.** An act of plunging; a dive, dip; also *fig.* 1711. **3.** *transf.* A sudden and heavy or violent pitching forward of the body 1496. **4.** The fall or breaking of a wave; a heavy downpour of rain (*rare*) 1781.

2. After his first P. into the Sea ADDISON. **3.** By directing the animal's plunges judiciously I got him also on *terra firma* 1889.

II. The point of being plunged or overwhelmed in trouble, difficulty, or danger; a crisis, strait; a dilemma; esp. in phr. *at (in) a p.*, *to put to* or *into the p.* or *plunges*. *Obs.* exc. *dial.* 1535.

When I was in the greatest p. for money 1656.

attrib. and *Comb.*: **p.-bath,** a bath in which a plunge is taken, e.g. after exercise.

Plunge (plʌndʒ), *v.* [XIV *plunge*, *plonge* – OFr. *plungier*, *plongier* (mod. *plonger*) :– Rom. **plumbicare*, f. L. *plumbum* lead; see PLUMB *sb.*] **1.** *trans.* To put violently, thrust, or cast *into* a liquid, a penetrable substance, or a cavity; to immerse, submerge. **2.** *fig.* To thrust, force, or drive *into* some thing, condition, state, or sphere of action. late ME. †**3.** *fig.* To overwhelm, esp. *with* trouble or difficulty; to put to straits –1681. **4.** *Gardening.* To sink (a pot containing a plant, less usu., a plant itself) in the ground 1664. **5.** *intr.* To throw or hurl oneself *into* water or the like; to dive head-foremost; to fall or sink (involuntarily) *into* a deep place (as a pit or abyss); also, to penetrate impetuously *into* any thing or place in which one is submerged or lost to view. late ME. **b.** *transf.* To enter impetuously or abruptly *into* (a place). Also with *upon.* 1834. **c.** *transf.* To descend abruptly and steeply; to dip suddenly (as a road or stratum) 1854. **6.** To enter impetuously or determinedly *into* some state, condition, or affair; to involve oneself deeply 1694. **7.** *transf.* To fling oneself violently forward, esp. with a diving action; of the chest: to expand with falling of the diaphragm 1530. **8.** To spend money or bet recklessly; to speculate deeply; to run into debt. *colloq.* 1876.

1. The holy Man bid him p. his Head into the Water ADDISON. You have only to p. a lighted taper into it HUXLEY. **2.** The Councels themselves ..plung'd into worldly ambition MILT. **5.** I plunged in, And bad him follow SHAKS. He plunged into the thickest portion of the little wood DICKENS. **6.** The character of their party is to be very ready to p. into difficult business BURKE. **7.** Wounded, he rears aloft, And plunging, from his Back the Rider hurls Precipitant 1735.

Plunger (plʌ·ndʒəɹ). 1611. [f. prec. + -ER¹.] **I. 1.** One who plunges; a diver. **2.** In techn. applications; an instrument or part which works with a plunging or thrusting motion; *esp.* **a.** Any solid piston, as that of a force-pump, *esp.* the piston of a Cornish pump. **b.** The firing pin in some breech-loading firearms. **c.** *Pottery.* A vessel in which clay is beaten to paste or slip. 1777. **II. 1.** *Mil. slang.* A cavalry man 1854. **2.** *slang.* One who bets, gambles, or speculates wildly 1876.

attrib. and *Comb.*, as **p.-bucket, -lift,** in a pump, a bucket having no valve; also = next (*b*); **-piston,** (*a*) a solid cylindrical piston used in a plunger-pump; (*b*) a similar piston used in a pressure-gauge, steam-indicator, etc.; **-pump,** one with a solid piston, as a force-pump.

Plunging (plʌ·ndʒiŋ), *vbl. sb.* 1450. [-ING¹.] The action of PLUNGE *v.*; *spec.* †immersion in baptism.

attrib. and *Comb.*, as *p.-bath*, etc.; **p.-battery;** (*Electr.*), a battery in which the plates may be plunged into or withdrawn from the fluid at pleasure. **Plu·nging,** *ppl. a.* [-ING².] In senses of the verb PLUNGE. **p. fire** (= Fr. *feu plongeant*), direct fire upon an enemy from a superior position. Hence **Plu·ngingly** *adv.*

Plunk (plʌŋk), *int.*, *sb.*, *v.* 1805. orig. *dial.* Imitative of the sound of the forcible plucking of the strings of a musical instrument, a heavy blow or plunge, the drawing of a cork, or the like.

Pluperfect (plupə̄·ɹfėkt, plū·pə̄ɹfėkt), *a* (*sb.*) Also †**plus-.** 1530. [– mod.L. *plusperfectum*, for L. (*tempus præteritum*) *plus quam perfectum* '(past tense) more than perfect', tr. Gr. (χρόνος) ὑπερσυντελικός; cf. Fr. *plus-que-parfait*.] **1.** *Gram.* Applied to that tense of the verb which expresses a time or action completed prior to some past point of time, specified or implied. Also *absol.* or as *sb.*, *ellipt.* for *p. tense*, **2.** *gen.* More than perfect; *spec.* in *Mus.* (rarely) applied to an augmented (as dist. from a perfect) fourth or fifth 1802.

Plural (plūᵊ·răl), *a.* (*sb.*) [XIV *plurel* – OFr. *plurel* (mod. *pluriel*) – L. *pluralis* (Quintilian) adj. with *numerus*, *genitivus*, also sb. (sc. *numerus* number), f. *plus*, *plur-* more; see PLUS, -AL¹.] **1.** *Gram.* Applied to the form of a word which denotes more than one (or, in languages having a dual form, more than two); opp. to *singular*. **2.** More than one in number; consisting of, containing, pertaining to, or equivalent to, more than one 1591. **B.** *sb.* **a.** *Gram.* The plural number. **b.** The fact or condition of there being more than one. ME.

2. Better haue none Then plurall faith, which is too much by one SHAKS. *P. livings*: see PLURALITY. *P. vote*, the right of giving more than one vote, or of voting in more than one constituency; hence *p. voter*, *voting*. **3.** *P. of excellence* or *majesty*, *p. intensive*, terms applied in Heb. Grammar to a p. sb. used as the name of a single person: as 'ᵉlōhīm, lit. gods, used as the name of (the one) God. Hence **Plu·rally** *adv.*

Pluralism (plūᵊ·răliz'm). 1818. [f. prec. + -ISM, after next.] **1. a.** *Eccl.* The holding of more than one benefice at the same time by one person. **b.** The holding of two or more offices of any kind together. **2.** *Philos.* A system of thought which recognizes more than one ultimate principle; opp. to MONISM 1887.

Pluralist (plūᵊ·rălist). 1626. [f. PLURAL + -IST. Cf. contemp. DUALIST.] *Eccl.* One who holds two or more benefices at the same time. **b.** *gen.* One who combines two or more offices, professions, or conditions.

The odious Names of Pluralists and Non-residents 1692. Hence **Plurali·stic** *a.* of or belonging to a p. or to pluralism, in any sense; **Plurali·stically** *adv.*

Plurality (pluræ·lĭti). late ME. [– (O)Fr. *pluralité* – late L. *pluralitas* (in med.L. in sense I. 2); see PLURAL, -ITY. In II treated as an immed. deriv. of L. *plus, plur-* more.] **I.** Related in sense to *plural.* **1.** The state of being plural, or denoting, comprising, or consisting of more than one. **b.** The fact of there being many; numerousness; hence, a large number or quantity; a multitude. late ME. **2.** *Eccl.* **a.** The holding of two or more benefices concurrently by one person. **b.** A benefice held concurrently with another or others; *pl.* two or more benefices held together. late ME. **c.** *transf.* and *gen.* 1678.

1. The p. of wives was by a special prerogative suffered to the fathers of the Old Testament 1563. **b.** Doe you count it lawfull to haue such pluralitie of seruants? B. JONS. **2.** I do not reckon the holding poor livings that lie continguous, a p. 1715.

II. Related in sense to L. *plus* more. **1.** = MAJORITY 3. 1578. **2.** *U.S. Politics.* An excess of votes polled by the leading candidate in an election above those polled by the one next to him, in cases where there are three or more candidates; as dist. from *majority*, which in such cases is applied to an absolute majority of all the votes given 1828.

Pluralize (plūᵊ·răləiz), *v.* 1803. [f. PLURAL + -IZE. Cf. Fr. *pluraliser.*] **1.** *trans.* To make plural; to attribute plurality to; to express in the plural. **2.** *intr.* To hold more than one benefice (or office) at one time; to be or become a pluralist 1842. Hence **Pluraliza·tion,** the act of pluralizing. **Plu·ralizer,** *spec.* = PLURALIST.

Pluri- (plūᵊri), comb. form of L. *plus, plur-* more, pl. *plures* several; as in: **Plurili·teral** *Heb. Gram.* [L. *littera* letter] *a.* containing more than three letters in the root; *sb.* a root consisting of more than three letters. **Pluri-se·rial** *a.* consisting of several series or rows; hence **Plurise·rially** *adv.* **Plurise·riate** *a.* arranged in several series.

‖**Pluries** (plūᵊ·riˌīz), in full **P. capias.** 1444. [L. = '(thou mayest take) several times'.] *Law.* A third writ of attachment, issued when the CAPIAS and ALIAS prove ineffectual.

Pluripresence (plūᵊripre·zĕns). 1773. [f. PLURI- + PRESENCE, after *omnipresence.*] Presence in more than one place at the same time.

Plus (plɒs). 1615. [– L. *plus* more.] **1.** quasi-*prep.* In mathematical use as the oral rendering of the symbol +. Hence *gen.* With the addition of; with...besides. (Opp. to MINUS 1.) 1668. **b.** *predicatively.* Having (something) in addition, having gained (opp. to MINUS 1 b) 1856. **2.** As the oral rendering of the sign + in its algebraical use to denote a positive quantity, as + *x*, read *plus x.* Hence *attrib.* or *adj.* in *p. quantity*, a quantity having the sign + prefixed (or not having the sign −), a positive quantity. (Only as opp. to MINUS 2, 2 b.) 1579. **b.** *Electr.* (*a*) *adv.* Positively. (*b*) *adj.* Positive; positively electrified. (Opp. to MINUS 2 d.) 1747. **c.** *adv.* And an indefinite quantity more, as £100,000 *plus.* (*colloq.*) **3.** *adj.* Additional, extra 1756. **4.** Applied to golfers whose handicap is denoted by 'plus 1', etc. 1909. **5.** *sb.* **a.** The mathematical symbol +; also *plus sign.* **b.** A quantity added; an addition, a gain. **c.** A positive quantity (also *fig.*). Opp. to MINUS 3. 1654.

1. Plus fours, long wide knickerbockers, or a suit having such; so named because, to produce the overhang, the length was originally increased by four inches. **c.** *ellipt.*, indicating a fractional amount more (e.g. raising the school age to 15 plus), also indicating a slightly higher grade (*Beta plus*, β+).

Plush (plɒʃ). 1594. [– Fr. †*pluche*, contr. of *peluche*, f. OFr. *peluchier* (see PLUCK *v.*) – It. *peluzzo*, dim. of *pelo* :– L. *pilus* PILE *sb.*[4]] **1.** A kind of cloth, of silk, cotton, wool, etc., having a nap softer and longer than that of velvet, used for upholstery, etc. **b.** *pl.* Plush breeches (as worn by footmen) 1844. **2.** *transf.* A natural substance likened to these 1619. **3.** *attrib.*, usu. in sense Made or consisting of plush; also, of or pertaining to plush 1629. **Plu·shy** *a.* soft and shaggy, like p.

Plushette (plɒʃe·t). 1910. [f. prec. + -ETTE.] An imitation plush.

Plutarchy (plū·tāɹki). 1643. [f. Gr. πλοῦτος wealth + -αρχία; see -ARCH.] The rule or dominion of wealth, or of the wealthy; plutocracy.

‖**Pluteus** (plū·tiˌɒs). *Pl.* **-ei** (-iˌəi). 1832. [L.; see sense 1.] **1.** *Rom. Antiq.*, etc. **a.** *Arch.* A barrier or light wall placed between columns. **b.** *Mil.* A kind of shed or penthouse for protection of the soldiers, sometimes running on wheels. **c.** A shelf for books, small statues, busts, etc. **2.** *Zool.* The larva of an echinoid or ophiuroid; known from its shape as the 'painter's easel larva' 1877. Hence **Plu·teal** *a.*

Plutocracy (plutǫ·krăsi). Also **plout-.** 1652. [– Gr. πλουτοκρατία, f. πλοῦτος wealth; see -CRACY.] **1.** The rule or sovereignty of wealth or of the wealthy. **2.** A ruling or influential class of wealthy persons 1832. So **Plu·tocrat,** a member of a p.; a person possessing power or influence over others in virtue of his wealth. **Plutocra·tic** *a.* of or pertaining to plutocrats; characterized by p.

Plutolatry (plutǫ·lătri). 1889. [f. Gr. πλοῦτος wealth; see -LATRY.] Worship of mere wealth.

Plutonian (plutōᵘ·niăn), *a.* (*sb.*) 1667. [f. L. *Plutonius* (– Gr. Πλουτώνιος, f. Πλούτων Pluto, god of the infernal regions) + -AN.] **1.** Of or pertaining to Pluto; belonging to or suggestive of the infernal regions; infernal. **2.** *Geol.* = PLUTONIC 1. 1828. **B.** *sb. Geol.* = PLUTONIST 1828.

Plutonic (plutǫ·nik), *a.* (*sb.*) 1796. [f. Gr. Πλούτων Pluto; see prec. and -IC.] **1.** *Geol.* **a.** Pertaining to or involving the action of intense heat at great depths upon the rocks forming the earth's crust; igneous. Applied *spec.* to the theory that attributes most geological phenomena to the action of internal heat. 1796. **b.** *spec.* Applied to that class of igneous rocks, such as granite and syenite, which are supposed to have been formed by fusion and subsequent slow crystallization at great depths below the surface, as dist. from *volcanic* rocks 1833. **2.** Belonging to or resembling Pluto; Plutonian 1819. **B.** *sb. Geol.(pl.)* Plutonic rocks 1856. So **Plutonism** (plū·tŏniz'm), the Plutonic theory. **Plu·tonist,** one who holds the P. theory (see 1a).

Plutonomy (plutǫ·nŏmi). 1851. [f. Gr. πλοῦτος wealth, after *economy.*] The science of the production and distribution of wealth; political economy. So **Plutono·mic** *a.* **Pluto·nomist,** a political economist.

Pluvial (plū·viăl), *sb. Obs.* exc. *Hist.* 1669. [– med.L. *pluviale* rain-cloak, subst. use of n. of L. *pluvialis*; see next.] *Eccl.* A long cloak worn by ecclesiastics as a ceremonial vestment; = COPE *sb.*[1] 2; also, a similar garment worn by monarchs as a robe of state.

Pluvial (plū·viăl), *a.* 1656. [– L. *pluvialis* pertaining to rain, f. *pluvia*, f. *pluere* rain; see -AL[1].] Of or pertaining to rain; rainy; characterized by much rain. **b.** *Geol.* Caused by rain 1859.

Pluviometer (plūviǫ·mĭtəɹ). 1791. [f. L. *pluvia* rain + -METER.] An instrument for measuring the rain; a rain-gauge. Hence **Pluvoime·tric, -al** *adjs.*; **-ly** *adv.* **Pluvio·metry.**

Pluvious (plū·viəs), *a.* late ME. [– OFr. *pluvieus* (mod. *-eux*) or L. *pluviosus*; see PLUVIAL *a.*, -OUS.] Of, pertaining to, or characterized by rain; bearing rain or moisture; rainy.

Ply (pləi), *sb.* 1470. [– (O)Fr. *pli*, f. *plier*, †*pleier*; see next.] **I. 1.** A fold; each of the layers or thicknesses produced by folding cloth, etc.; a strand or twist of rope, yarn, or thread 1532. **2.** A bend, crook, or curvature; *spec.* in *Falconry*, of a hawk's wing. Now *rare* or *Obs.* 1575. **3.** The condition of being bent or turned to one side; a twist, turn; a bent, bias, inclination; esp. in phr. *to take a* (*the*, one's) *p.* Chiefly *fig.* 1605.

1. *Two-p., three-p., four-ply*: a fold of two, three, etc., layers; used *attrib.* to designate woollen yarns, and carpets made of two or more interwoven webs; also of wood (cf. PLYWOOD). **3.** It is true that late learners cannot so well take the plie BACON.

II. Plight, condition; esp. in phrases *in p.*, *in good p.*; so *out of p. Sc.* 1470..

Ply (pləi), *v.*[1] Now *rare* or *dial.* Pa. t. and pple. **plied** (pləid). ME. [– (O)Fr. *plier*, alt. f. OFr. *pleier* (mod. *ployer*) :– L. *plicare* fold.] **1.** *trans.* To bend, bow; to fold or double (cloth or the like); to mould or shape (anything plastic). Now chiefly *dial.* †**b.** *fig.* To bend in will or disposition; to bend the sense of (words); to adapt, accommodate –1657. †**2.** *intr.* To bend or be bent; to yield, give (*to* pressure, etc.) –1753. **3.** *fig.* To yield, give way *to*; to incline, tend; to submit, comply, consent; to be pliant. Now *rare* or *Obs.* ME.

1. Right as men may warm wex with handes plye CHAUCER. **3.** With kindly indulgence plied into the daughter's will CARLYLE.

Ply (pləi), *v.*[2] Pa. t. and pple. **plied** [ME. *plye*, aphet. f. APPLY *v.*] **I.** To apply, employ, work busily at. **1.** *intr.* To employ or occupy oneself busily or steadily; to work *at* something; to apply closely *to.* Now *rare.* **2.** *trans.* To use or wield vigorously (a tool, etc.); to exert (a faculty) ME. **3. a.** To keep at work at; to attack or assail vigorously or repeatedly (*with* some instrument or process). **b.** To press (one) to take; to continue to supply *with* food, gifts, etc. 1548. **4.** To importune, urge; to keep on at (a person) *with* questions, petitions, etc. 1587.

1. Ere half these Authors be read (which will soon be with plying hard and daily) MILT. **2.** The town in which they plied their trade 1867. Together their oars they p. 1887. **3. b.** To p. them more pressingly with food than with arguments 1856. **4.** In vain did he p. Christ with questions 1883.

II. *Naut.*, etc. **1.** *intr.* To beat up against the wind; to tack, work to windward 1556. **b.** *gen.* To direct one's course, steer. Now only *poet.* 1595. **2.** *intr.* Of a vessel or its master: To sail or go periodically to and fro *between* certain places; also said of land-carriage 1803. **3.** *intr.* Of a boatman, porter, cabman, omnibus, taxi, etc.: To attend regularly, to have one's stand *at* a certain place for hire or custom 1700.

1. Neither might wee plie up unto the iland, the winde was soe contrarie for our course 1595. Phr. *To p. about, off and on, to and again, up and down,* etc. **b.** Wee plied for Plimworth 1595. **3.** He was ..forced to think of plying in the Streets as a Porter ADDISON.

Plyer: see PLIER.

Plymouth Brethren. 1842. [See *Brethren* in BROTHER *sb.* 3.] A religious body calling themselves 'the Brethren', recognizing no official order of ministers, and having no formal creed, which arose at Plymouth *c*1830. **Plymouth brother** (also **Plymouth sister**), a member of this body. So **Ply·mouthism,** the system or doctrine of the Plymouth Brethren 1876.

†**Plymouth cloak.** *slang.* 1608. A cudgel or staff, carried by one who walked *in cuerpo*, and thus joc. assumed to serve as a cloak –1855.

Plymouth Rock (pli:məþˌrǫ·k). 1873. [The spot at which the passengers of the Mayflower landed in New England in 1620.] Name of a breed of domestic fowls of American origin, characterized by large size, ashen or grey plumage barred with blackish stripes, and yellow beak, legs and feet.

Plywood (pləi·wud). orig. *U.S.* 1917. [f. PLY *sb.* 1 + WOOD.] A compound wood made of three (five, etc.) thin layers glued or cemented together under pressure, and arranged so that the grain of one layer runs at right angles to the grain of any adjacent layer.

P.M., abbrev. of POST MERIDIEM.

Pn-, an initial comb. occurring only in words from Greek; the *p* is usually mute in English.

Pneo- (pnīˌo, nīˌo), comb. element from Gr. πνέειν, πνεῖν to blow; as in **Pneo·meter** [-METER], an instrument for measuring the amount of air inspired and expired, a pneumatometer, spirometer; **Pneo·metry;** etc.

Pneum(e (pniūm, niūm). 1879. [– Gr. πνεῦμα; see next.] *Mus.* = NEUME 2.

‖**Pneuma** (pniū·mă, niū·mă). 1880. [– Gr. πνεῦμα wind, breath, spirit, prop. that which is blown or breathed, f. πνέειν, πνεῖν blow, breathe.] **1.** The Greek word for 'spirit' or 'soul' 1884. **2.** *Mediæval Mus.* **a.** = NEUME 1. **b.** = NEUME 2. 1880.

Pneumatic (niumæ·tik), *a.* (*sb.*) 1659. [– Fr. *pneumatique* or L. *pneumaticus* – Gr. πνευματικός, f. πνεῦμα, -ματ-; see prec., -IC.] **1.** Pertaining to, or acting by means of, wind or air. **b.** Belonging to or transmitted by pneumatic dispatch 1903. **2.** Of, or relating or belonging to, gases. Now *rare*, exc. in *p. trough.* 1793. **3.** *Zool.*, *Anat.*, and *Phys.* **a.** Pertaining to breath or breathing; respiratory (*rare*) 1681. **b.** Containing or connected with air-cavities, as those in the bones of birds, etc. 1831. **4.** Belonging or relating to spirit or spiritual existence; spiritual. (Usu. with direct ref. to Gr. πνευματικός.) 1797.

1. Phr. *P. dispatch*, a system by which parcels, etc. are conveyed along tubes by compression or exhaustion of air. *P. engine*, formerly applied spec. to the air-pump. *P. tyres*, tyres filled with compressed air 1890. **2.** *P. trough*, a trough by means of which gases may be collected in jars over a surface of water or mercury. **4.** †*P. philosophy*: = PNEUMATOLOGY 1.

B. *sb.* **1.** = PNEUMATOLOGY 1a. (*rare*) 1836. **2.** Name in Gnostic theology for a spiritual being of a high order 1876. **3.** A pneumatic tyre, or a cycle having such tyres 1890. So **Pneuma·tical** *a.* in senses 1, 2, 4; †*sb.* a gaseous substance. **Pneuma·tically** *adv.*

Pneumaticity (niūmăti·sĭti). 1858. [f. PNEUMATIC + -ITY.] The quality or condition of being pneumatic.

Pneumatico-, comb. form from L. *pneumaticus* or Gr. πνευματικός PNEUMATIC.

Pneumatics (niumæ·tiks). 1660. [In form, pl. of PNEUMATIC *a.* = pneumatic treatises or matters; see -IC.] **1.** That branch of physics which deals with the mechanical properties (as density, elasticity, pressure, etc.) of air, or other elastic fluids or gases. **2.** = PNEUMATOLOGY 1 a, b. *Obs.* exc. *Hist.* 1695.

Pneumato- (niū·măto, pniū·-), bef. a vowel **pneumat-**, – Gr. πνευματο-, comb. form of πνεῦμα air, breath, spirit.

Pneu·matocele [Gr. κήλη tumour], *Path.* a tumour or hernia containing air or gas. **Pneu·matocyst** *Zool.* (*a*) an air-sac serving as a float in certain 'colonial' or compound Hydrozoa; the pneumatophore, or the cavity contained in this; (*b*) an air-sac in the body of a bird. **Pneu·matogram,** a diagram or tracing of the movements of the chest in respiration, obtained by a pneumograph. **Pneumato·meter,** an instrument for measuring the amount of air breathed in or out at each inspiration or expiration, or for measuring the force of inspiration or expiration; so **Pneumato·metry.** **Pneu·matophore** [Gr. -φορος bearing], (*a*) *Zool.* in certain 'colonial' Hydrozoa of the order *Siphonophora*, a specialized part or individual of the 'colony', containing an air-cavity, and serving as a float; (*b*) *Bot.* a structure having numerous lenticels, and supposed to serve as a channel for air, arising from the roots of various tropical trees which grow in swampy places. **Pneu·matotho·rax** = PNEUMOTHORAX.

Pneumatology (niūmătǫ·lŏdʒi, pniū-). 1678. [– mod.L. *pneumatologia* (J. Prideaux, *a*1650); see PNEUMATO-, -LOGY.] **1. a.** The science, doctrine, or theory of spirits or spiritual beings; considered as comprehending the doctrine of God as known by natural reason, of angels and demons, and of the human soul. **b.** Later, The science of the nature and functions of the human soul or mind, now called PSYCHOLOGY 1785. **2.** *Theol.* The, or a, doctrine of the Holy Spirit 1881. **3.** The science or theory of air or gases; pneumatics 1767. Hence **Pneu:matolo·gical** *a.* of or relating to p. **Pneumato·logist.**

Pneumatomachian (-mēⁱ·kiăn), *sb.* and *a.* 1707. [– eccl. Gr. πνευματομάχος (Athanasius), f. πνεῦμα spirit + -μάχος fighting, fighter; see -MACHY, -IAN.] **A.** *sb.* Name of a 4th c. sect who denied the divinity or personality of the Holy Spirit. **B.** *adj.* Belonging to such a sect or holding such a doctrine. Also **-o·machist** 1654.

Pneumo- (niūmo-, pniū-), comb. form and verbal element. **a.** Gr. πνεῦμα wind, etc. (see PNEUMA), = PNEUMATO- in some scientific terms. **b.** Short for PNEUMONO-, f. Gr. πνεύμων, -μον- lung; chiefly in terms of pathology.

‖**Pneumococcus** [Gr. κόκκος berry], name for two different micro-organisms of oval form which have been found in the rusty sputum of pneumonia, and supposed to be the cause of the disease; hence **Pneumoco·ccal, -co·ccic, -co·ccous** *adjs.* **Pneu·mograph,** an instrument for automatically recording the movements of the chest in respiration. **Pneumo·graphy,** (*a*) a description of the lungs; (*b*) the recording of the respiratory movements, as by a pneumograph. **Pneumo·logy** (*rare*), a treatise on, or the scientific description or knowledge of, the lungs. **Pneumo·meter** = PNEUMATOMETER; so **Pneumo·metry. Pneu:motho·rax** (also *pneumatothorax*) *Path.* the presence of air or gas in the cavity of the thorax, i.e. of the pleura, usu. caused by a wound or by perforation of the lung.

Pneumogastric (niūmogæ·strik, pniū-), *a.* (*sb.*) 1831. [f. PNEUMO- b + GASTRIC.] *Anat.* **a.** Pertaining to the lungs and the stomach or abdomen. **b.** *ellipt.* as *sb.* The p. nerve 1874.

a. *P. nerve*, name for the tenth pair of cerebral nerves, which, with their branches, supply the lungs and other respiratory and vocal organs, stomach, œsophagus, spleen, liver, intestines, heart, etc.

Pneumonia (niumōᵘ·niă). 1603. [– mod. L. *pneumonia* – Gr. πνευμονία, f. πνεύμων, πνευμον- lung; see -IA¹.] *Path.* Inflammation of the substance of the lungs.

Called *single* or *double p.*, according as one or both lungs are affected. *attrib.*: **p. bacillus, coccus, microbe** = PNEUMOCOCCUS.

Pneumonic (niumǫ·nik), *a.* (*sb.*) 1675. [– Fr. *pneumonique* or mod.L. *pneumonicus* – Gr. πνευμονικός of the lungs, affected with lung-disease.] †**1.** Pertaining to the lungs; pulmonary. *rare.* **2.** Pertaining to, of the nature of, characterized by, or affected with pneumonia 1783. **B.** *sb.* †**a.** A person affected with lung-disease –1681. **b.** A remedy for lung-disease. *rare.* 1727.

‖**Pneumonitis** (niūmŏnəi·tis, pniū). 1822. [mod.L., f. Gr. πνεύμων lung + -ITIS.] *Path.* = PNEUMONIA. Hence **Pneumoni·tic** *a.* = PNEUMONIC 2.

Pneumono- (niūmŏno, pniū-), bef. a vowel **pneumon-**, comb. form of Gr. πνεύμων, πνευμον- lung. (Often contracted to PNEUMO-.) **Pneumono·meter** [-METER] = PNEUMATOMETER. **Pneumonophorous** (-ǫ·fŏrəs) [Gr. -φόρος bearing] *a.*, bearing or having lungs.

‖**Pnyx** (pniks). 1822. [– Gr. Πνύξ.] The public place of assembly in Ancient Athens, a semicircular level cut out of the side of a little hill west of the Acropolis.

Po (pōᵘ). *colloq.* = POT *sb.*¹ 1 e.

‖**Poa** (pōᵘ·ă). 1753. [mod.L. – Gr. πόα grass.] *Bot.* A large genus of grasses widely distributed in temperate and cold regions; meadow-grass.

Poach (pōᵘtʃ), *v.*¹ 1450. [– OFr. *pochier* (mod. *pocher*), orig. enclose in a bag, f. *poche* bag, pocket; see POKE *sb.*¹] *trans.* To cook (an egg) by dropping it, without the shell, into boiling water. Hence **Poached** *ppl. a.*

Poach (pōᵘtʃ), *v.*² 1528. [In XVI *poche*; perh. – (O)Fr. *pocher* in spec. use of 'pocket'; see prec. and cf. slang use of BAG *v.*¹] **I. 1.** *trans.* = POKE *v.*¹ 1; also, to stir *up* by poking; to ram or roughly push (things) together; *fig.* to instigate. Now *dial.* **2.** To thrust or push (a stick, a finger, a foot, etc.) into any hole or thing. Now chiefly *dial.* 1673. †**3.** To stab, pierce –1644. †**b.** To make a thrust *at* as in fencing (*rare*). Also *fig.* –1624.

1. He bid him beat abroad, and not p. up the Game in his Warren FIELDING. **3. b.** *Cor.* I. x. 15. They have rather poached and offered at a number of enterprizes, than maintained any constantly BACON.

II. 1. *trans.* To thrust or stamp down with the feet; to trample (soft or sodden ground) into muddy holes; to cut *up* (turf, etc.) with hoofs 1677. **2.** *intr.* To sink (into wet heavy ground) in walking; to tramp heavily or plungingly 1600. **3.** Of land; To become sodden, miry, and full of holes by being trampled 1707. **4.** *trans.* To make sodden 1881. **5.** To mix with water and reduce to a uniform consistency. (Also *potch.*) 1873.

1. The cattle of the villagers had poached into black mud the verdant turf SCOTT.

III. 1. *intr.* To encroach or trespass (*on* the land or rights of another) esp. in order to steal game; hence, to take game, etc. illegally, or by unsportsmanlike devices 1611. **2.** *trans.* **a.** To trespass on (land or water), esp. in order to kill or catch game 1715. **b.** To catch and carry off (game or fish) illegally, or by unsportsmanlike methods. Also *fig.* 1862. **c.** *Sporting slang.* To filch (an advantage, e.g., at the start in a race) by unfair means; in tennis, to return a ball that should normally be dealt with by one's partner 1891.

1. The politician feels that he is poaching on the preserves of the geographer 1868. **2. b.** You were always 'poaching' our best men 1895.

Poacher (pōᵘ·tʃəɹ). 1667. [f. prec. + -ER¹.] **1.** One who poaches; one who takes or kills game unlawfully. **2. a.** *U.S.* The widgeon, *Mareca americana.* **b.** The sea-poacher, a fish of the family *Agonidæ.* **3.** (Also **potcher.**) *Paper-making.* One of the series of engines by which rags, etc. are comminuted, washed, bleached, and reduced to pulp 1877.

Poachy (pōᵘ·tʃi), *a.* 1707. [f. as prec. + -Y¹.] Of land: Spongy, retentive of moisture, and so liable to be trampled into muddy holes; sodden, swampy. Hence **Poa·chiness.**

Pob (pǫb). *Sc.* 1747. [Of unkn. origin.] The refuse of flax or jute.

Pocan (pōᵘ·kăn). 1858. [app. native Amer. Indian name.] = POKE *sb.*⁴ 2 a.

‖**Pochade** (poʃa·d). 1872. [Fr., f. *pocher* sketch in the rough, also to blur; see -ADE.] A rough, smudgy, or blurred sketch. BROWNING.

Po'chaise, -'chay, pochay. 1827. Colloq. contractions of POST-CHAISE.

Pochard (pōᵘ·tʃ-, pōᵘ·kăɹd, pǫ·kăɹd). 1552. [Of unkn. origin; for the ending cf. *mallard.*] A European diving-bird, *Fuligula* or *Æthyia ferina*, of the family *Anatidæ*, characterized by the bright reddish-brown colour of the head and neck; also called *red-headed p.*, *poker*, *widgeon*, DUN-BIRD. Also applied to other species as the Red-crested P., *F.* or *Nyroca rufina*, of India; the Tufted P., *F. cristata*, of Europe and Asia; and in U.S. to the RED-HEAD, *Anas americana.*

Pochette (pǫʃe·t). 1923. [– Fr. *pochette*, lit. 'little pocket'.] A lady's handbag in the shape of a flat pouch or envelope.

Pock (pǫk), *sb.* [Late OE. *poc*, *pocc-* pustule, ulcer = MLG., MDu. *pocke* (Du. *pok*, LG. *pocke*, whence G. *pocke*) :- Gmc. **pukno-*, f. **puk-* (repr. also by OE. *pohha*, *pocca* bag, MHG. *pfoch*).] **1.** A pustule in any eruptive disease, esp. (since 1700) in small-pox. **2.** A disease characterized by such pustules; *esp.* (*a*) small-pox; (*b*) 'great (French or Spanish) pox', syphilis. In *pl.* now written POX; in *sing.* now *dial.* and *vulgar.* ME. †Also *fig.* (*sing.*) –1607.

1. And it is hool anon, and forthermoor Of pokkes, and of scabbe, and euery soor CHAUCER. *attrib.* and *Comb.*, as **p.-hole, -mark,** a scar, mark, or 'pit' left by a pustule, esp. of small-pox; **-broken, -frecken, -fret, -fretted (-fretten), -marked, -pitted (-pitten)** *adjs.*, scarred, marked, or 'pitted' with pustules, esp. of small-pox; **-lymph,** the lymph of cow-pox, as used in vaccination. Hence **Pock** *v. trans.* to mark with pocks, or with disfiguring spots.

Pocket (pǫ·kėt), *sb.* late ME. [– AFr. *poket(e*, dim. of *poke* POKE *sb.*¹, var. of OFr. *pochet*, (O)Fr. *pochette.* In AL. *poketta*, *pochettus* XIII/XIV pouch; see -ET.] **1.** A bag or sack. Sometimes used as a measure of quantity; now chiefly for hops (= half a sack), or wool (= about 168 lbs.). **2.** A small bag or pouch worn on the person; spec. one inserted in a garment, for carrying a purse, etc. late ME. **b.** *esp.* That in which money is carried; hence = one's purse or stock of cash; private means 1717. **3.** *Billiards.* One of the open-mouthed pouches placed at the corners and on each side of the table, into which the balls are played 1753. **4.** *Zool.* and *Anat.* A sac-shaped or pocket-like cavity in the body of an animal; as the abdominal pouch of a marsupial, etc. 1773. **5. a.** *Mining.* A cavity in the earth filled with gold or other ore; also, an accumulation of alluvial gold 1850. **b.** A small cavity in a rock; esp. (*Geol.*) one filled up with foreign material 1850. **c.** A subterranean cavity containing water 1852. **d.** A hollow in the ground, or among hills, as a glen, etc. 1869. **e.** (More fully *air-p.*) a patch of rarefied air, or a downward eddy, which causes an aeroplane to lose altitude 1914. **6.** A recess or cavity resembling a pocket in use or position; e.g. a receptacle in the cover of a book for a folded map, etc.; a small cabin or coal bunker on board ship; etc. 1881. **7.** *Racing.* The position in which a competitor is hemmed in by others and so has no chance of winning 1890. **8.** *attrib.* and *Comb.* **a.** Adapted or intended to be carried in the pocket, as *p.-comb, -lens,* etc. 1612. **b.** Small enough to be so carried; tiny, diminutive 1621. **c.** (from 2.) Having reference to money 1705.

2. A Prodigal is a P. with a Hole in the Bottom 1680. Phr. *To put in one's p.*, to put away, conceal, suppress; I put my pride in my p. 1885. *In (some one's) p.*, (*a*) in close attendance on (some one); (*b*) under the personal control of (some one). **b.** A gentleman can't consider his p. R. BRIDGES. *In p.*, (*a*) having money available; (*b*) having (so much) money left over or to profit, as 'to be ten shillings in p. by the transaction'. *Out of p.*, †out of funds; *to be out of p.*, to be a loser (by some transaction). Hence *attrib.* as *out-of-p. expenses,* (an allowance or payment for) expenses by which one would otherwise be out of p. **8. b.** A p. Switzerland EMERSON.

Comb.: **p.-borough,** a borough of which the parliamentary representation was under the control of one person or family; **†-expenses,** small personal outlays; **-mouse,** a rodent of the family *Saccomyidæ*, a pouched mouse; **-piece,** a piece of money kept in the p. as a charm; often one which is damaged or spurious; **-pistol** (*a*) a small pistol to be carried in the p.; (*b*) *joc.* a pocket spirit-flask; **-sheriff,** a sheriff nominated by the sole authority of the crown; **-veto** *sb.* and *v. U.S.* (cf. next, 3 b).

Pocket (pǫ·kėt), *v.* 1589. [f. prec.] **1.** *trans.* To put into one's pocket. Also with *up.* **b.** To confine or enclose as in a pocket. (Chiefly in *pass.*) 1681. **c.** *Racing.* To hem in (a competitor) in front and at the sides, so as to prevent him from winning 1890. **2.** To appropriate; sometimes with implication of dishonesty 1637. **3.** *fig.* **a.** To take or accept (an affront, etc.) without showing resentment; to submit to, 'swallow' 1589. **b.** To conceal, give no indication of (pride, anger, etc.); to refrain from publishing (a report, letter, etc); in U.S. politics (of the President or the Governor of a State): To retain (a bill) unsigned, so as to prevent it from becoming law 1610. **4.** *Billiards.* To play (a ball) into one of the pockets 1780. **5.** To hold under private control; *esp.* the representation of a constituency 1882. **6.** To furnish with pockets (Chiefly in *pass.*) 1896. **7.** *Path.* and *Surg.* To convert or form into a pouch, cavity, or depression 1885. **8.** *intr.* To form pockets or bag-like recesses. **b.** *U.S.* To pucker or become bagged (*rare*). 1614.

2. These sums were pocketed by Edward VI, or rather by his advisers 1879. **3. a.** I must p. vp these wrongs SHAKS. The United States must p. the rebuff with a pleasant diplomatic smile 1891. Hence **Po·cketable** *a.* that may be put or carried in the p.

Pocket-book (pǫ·kėtˌbuk). 1617. **1.** A small book, to be carried in the pocket. Now usu. two words. **2.** A note-book, to be carried in the pocket; also, a book-like case for papers, bank-notes, bills, etc. 1685. **3.** *attrib.* 1819.

Pocketful (pǫ·kėtˌful). 1611. [f. POCKET *sb.* + -FUL.] As much as fills a pocket.

A whole p. of money THACKERAY.

Pocket-handkerchief (pǫ·kėtˌhæ·ŋkəɹtʃif). 1781. A handkerchief to be carried in the pocket.

Pocket-knife (pǫ·kėtˌnəif). 1727. A knife with one or more blades which fold into the handle, for carrying in the pocket.

Po·cket-mo:ney. 1632. Money carried in the pocket for occasional expenses; *esp.* that allowed to schoolboys or schoolgirls.

Pockety (pǫ·kėti), *a.* 1874. [f. POCKET *sb.* + -Y¹.] Of a mine or mineral deposit: Characterized by pockets; having the ore unevenly distributed.

†Po·ckwood. 1590. [f. POCK *sb.* + WOOD *sb.*] The wood of a tree of the genus *Guaiacum*, formerly used for the cure of syphilis; = GUAIACUM 2. –1764.

Pocky (pǫ·ki), *a.* Now *rare.* ME. [f. POCK *sb.* + -Y¹.] **1.** Full of or marked with pocks or pustules; *spec.* infected with the pox (i.e., usu. syphilis). **†b.** As a coarse expression of dislike, or an intensive. (Cf. *mangy.*) –1663. **2.** Pertaining to, or of the nature of, a pock or pustule, or the pox; syphilitic or variolous 1555.

1. b. These French villains have p. wits B. JONS. Hence **Po·ckiness.**

‖**Poco-curante** (pōːkoˌkura·nte), *a.* and *sb.* 1762. [It., f. *poco* little + *curante* caring.] Caring little; indifferent, nonchalant. Also *sb.* Hence **Po:cocura·nt(e)ism,** indifference; indifferentism.

‖**Pocosin, poquosin** (pǒkōᵘ·sĭn). *U.S.* 1709. [Algonquin *poquosin.*] In Southern U.S., A tract of low swampy ground, usually wooded: a marsh, a swamp.

Poculiform (pǫ·kiŭlifǭɹm), *a.* 1832. [f. L. *poculum* cup + -FORM.] *Nat. Hist.* Of the form of a cup or drinking-vessel.

Pod (pǫd), *sb.*¹ 1573. [Of unkn. origin.] Earlier form of PAD *sb.*³ III.; the socket of a brace in which the end of a bit is inserted.

Comb. **p.-bit,** a boring-tool adapted to be used in a brace.

Pod (pǫd), *sb.*² 1688. [Back-formation from dial. *podware, podder* (XVI), of unkn. origin, which succeeded to †*codware* (see COD *sb.*¹, WARE *sb.*¹).] **1.** A seed-vessel of a long form, usually dry and dehiscent; prop. of leguminous and cruciferous plants; a legume or siliqua. **2.** *transf.* **a.** The cocoon of the silk-worm. **b.** The case of the eggs of a locust. 1753. **3.** A purse net with a narrow neck for catching eels. Also *p.-net.* 1882. **†4.** The blade of a cricket-bat –1862.

Comb. **p.-pepper,** a common name for capsicum.

Pod, *sb.*³ orig. *U.S.* 1827. [Of unkn. origin.] A small herd or school of seals or whales, etc.; a small flock of birds.

Pod (pǫd), *v.*¹ 1734. [f. POD *sb.*²] **1.** *intr.* To bear or produce pods. **2.** *trans.* To hull or empty peas out of pods 1902.

Pod, *v.*² 1887. [f. POD *sb.*³] *trans.* To drive (seals, etc.) into a pod or bunch for the purpose of clubbing them.

‖**Podagra** (pǫ·dăgră, podæ·gră). late ME. [L. – Gr. ποδάγρα, f. πούς, ποδ- foot + ἄγρα seizure, trap, f. a base meaning 'chase', 'catch'.] *Med.* Gout in the feet; hence, gout generally. Hence **Po·dagral** *a.* of or pertaining to gout; gouty. **Poda·gric** *a.* podagral; *sb.* a sufferer from gout. **†Poda·grical** *a.* **Po·dagrous** *a.* gouty.

‖**Podalgia** (podæ·ldʒiă). 1842. [mod.L., f. Gr. πούς, ποδ- foot + ἄλγος pain; see -IA¹.] Pain in the foot, as from gout, rheumatism, etc.

Podded (pǫ·dėd), *a.* 1753. [f. POD *sb.*² + -ED².] **1.** Bearing pods; leguminous; growing (as a seed) in pods. **2.** *fig.* (transl. Fr. *cossu.*) Well-off, comfortable 1889.

Podder (pǫ·dəɹ). 1681. [f. POD *sb.*² or *v.*¹ + -ER¹.] A person employed in gathering peas in the pod.

‖**Podestà** (podesta·). 1548. [It., :– L. *potestas, -tat-* power, authority, magistrate.] **a.** A governor appointed by the Emperor Frederick I (Barbarossa) over one or more cities of Lombardy. **b.** A chief magistrate elected annually in mediæval Italian towns. Also *transf.* **c.** A subordinate judge or magistrate in modern Italian municipalities.

‖**Podetium** (podī·ʃiŏm). *Pl.* **-ia.** 1857. [mod.L., arbitrary f. Gr. πούς, ποδ- foot; see -IUM.] *Bot.* In some lichens, a stalk-like or shrubby outgrowth of the thallus, bearing the apothecium or fruit; also, any stalk-like elevation.

‖**Podex** (pōᵘ·deks). Now only *Zool.* 1598. [L.] The fundament, the rump; also, the last dorsal segment of the abdomen of insects, the pygidium. Hence **Po·dical** *a.* *Zool.* pertaining to the p.; anal; *p. plates,* two or more small plates surrounding the p. in some insects.

Podge (pǫdʒ). *dial.* or *colloq.* 1833. [A parallel form of PUDGE *sb.*] Anything podgy; *spec.* a short fat man or woman; a short stout thick-set animal. Hence **Po·dgy** *a.* short, thick, and fat; squat. **Po·dgily** *adv.*

Podite (pǫ·dəit). 1875. [f. Gr. πούς, ποδ- foot + -ITE¹ 3.] *Zool.* A leg or ambulatory limb of an arthropod, esp. of a crustacean. Usu. in comb. Hence **Podi·tic** *a.*

‖**Podium** (pōᵘ·diŏm). *Pl.* **podia.** 1789. [L., elevated place, balcony – Gr. πόδιον, dim. of πούς, ποδ- foot; see -IUM.] **1.** *Arch.* **a.** A continuous projecting base or pedestal, a stylobate. **b.** A raised platform surrounding the arena in an ancient amphitheatre. **c.** A continuous seat or bench round a room. **2.** *Anat.* and *Zool.* The fore or hind foot of a vertebrate; in birds, the junction of the toes, or the toes collectively. Also in compounds, as EPIPODIUM, etc. 1858.

Podley: see POLLACK.

Podo- (pǫdo), bef. a vowel **pod-,** – Gr. ποδο-, comb. form of πούς, ποδ- foot, as in:

‖**Podarthri·tis,** *Med.* inflammation of joints of the foot. **Po·dobranch** (-bræŋk) [Gr. βράγχια gills], *Zool.* a breathing organ of crustaceans attached to the legs; a foot-gill; so **Podobra·nchial** *a.* of or pertaining to foot-gills. **Po·docarp** [Gr. καρπός fruit], *Bot.* a footstalk bearing the fruit of a plant. **Podoce·phalous** [Gr. κεφαλή head], *a.* *Bot.* bearing a head of flowers on a long footstalk. ‖**Podogynium** (-dʒi·niŏm) [mod.L., f. Gr. γυνή female], *Bot.* = BASIGYNIUM. **Podophy·llous** [Gr. φύλλον leaf], *a.* (*a*) *Entom.* having, as some insects, compressed leaf-like locomotive organs or feet; (*b*) *Zool.* in *p. tissue,* the layer of tissue composed of leaf-like vascular lamellæ beneath the coronary cushion of a horse's hoof. **Po·doscaph** [Gr. σκάφος ship], a canoe-shaped float attached to the foot for moving on water; also a water-velocipede. **Po·dosperm** [Gr. σπέρμα seed], *Bot.* the stalk of a seed. **Podosto·matous** [Gr. στόμα mouth], *a.* *Zool.* belonging to the *Podostomata*, a group of *Arthropoda* characterized by having a foot-like mouth. ‖**Podothe·ca** [mod. L., f. Gr. θήκη sheath], *Zool.* the scaly leg-covering of a bird or reptile; also, the sheath covering the leg of an insect in the pupa; hence **Podothe·cal** *a.*

Podophthalmate (pǫdǫfþæ·lmĕt), *a.* 1835. [f. PODO- + ὀφθαλμός eye + -ATE².] *Zool.* Having the eye at the end of a movable stalk, stalk-eyed; of or pertaining to the stalk-eyed crustaceans. So ‖**Podophtha·lmia,** an order of Crustacea, including those with eyes set on movable footstalks, as crabs and lobsters. **Podophtha·lmian** *a.*, pertaining to the *Podophthalmia*; *sb.* a member of the *Podophthalmia*. **Podophtha·lmic, Podophtha·lmous** *adjs.*

‖**Podophyllum** (pǫdofi·lŏm). 1760. [mod. L., f. Gr. ποδο- PODO- + φύλλον leaf.] **a.** *Bot.* A genus of *Ranunculaceæ* with two known species, *P. peltatum* of eastern N. America, and *P. emodi* of the Himalayas, having long thick creeping rhizomes, large long-stalked palmately lobed leaves, and a solitary white flower. **b.** *Pharm.* The dried rootstock of *P. peltatum.* Also *attrib.* Hence **Podophy·llin** *Chem.*, a yellow bitter resin having cathartic properties, obtained from the dried rhizome of *P. peltatum*; = *resin of p.*

‖**Podura** (podiūᵊ·ră). 1797. [mod.L. (Linn., 1748), f. Gr. πούς, ποδ- foot + οὐρά tail.] *Entom.* A genus of apterous insects, having a terminal forked springing organ; hence known as springtails. Hence **Podu·ran** *a.* of or pertaining to the genus *P.*; *sb.* an insect of this genus or of the family *Poduridæ*; so **Podu·rid** *a.* and *sb.*

Poë-bird (pōᵘ·iˌbəɹd). 1777. [From the Otaheitan word for ear-rings; so named from the little tufts of curled hair under the throat.] A New Zealand bird, *Prosthemadera novæ-zelandiæ*, now called PARSON-BIRD.

‖**Pœcile** (pī·sili). 1819. [– Gr. (ἡ) ποικίλη (στόα) the painted porch.] Name of a portico in the market-place of ancient Athens, adorned with a variety of paintings.

†Pœcilite (pī·siləit). 1832. [f. Gr. ποικίλος variegated + -ITE¹ 2b.] *Geol.* A name proposed for the Upper New Red Sandstone. Hence **Pœcilitic** (pīsili·tik) *a.* = POIKILITIC.

Pœcilo- (pī·silo), bef. a vowel **pœcil-** from Gr. ποικίλος many-coloured, various, a formative element in scientific terms; as in **Pœ·cilopod** [Gr. πούς, ποδ- foot], *Zool.* a member of the *Pœcilopoda*, a division, now abandoned, of *Crustacea*, distinguished by limbs of various forms and functions; hence **Pœcilo·podous** *a.*

Poem (pōᵘ·ėm). 1548. [– (O)Fr. *poème* or L. *poema* (Plautus) – Gr. πόημα, early var. of ποίημα work, fiction, poetical work, f. ποεῖν, ποιεῖν make, create.] **1.** 'The work of a poet, a metrical composition' (J.); a composition of words, expressing facts, thoughts, or feelings in poetical form; a piece of poetry. **b.** *transf.* Applied to a composition which, without the form, has some quality or qualities in common with poetry 1581. **2.** *fig.* Something (other than a composition of words) of a nature or quality akin or likened to that of poetry 1642. **3.** *attrib.* 1806.

1. And may not I..say that the holy Dauids Psalmes are a diuine P. SIDNEY. **2.** The Celts..gave to the seas and mountains names which are poems EMERSON.

Poephagous (po,e·făgəs), *a. rare.* 1839. [f. mod.L. *Poephaga*, neut. pl. (– Gr. ποηφάγος herbivorous, f. πόα grass + -φάγος eating) + -OUS.] *Zool.* Eating grass or herbs; *spec.* belonging to the division *Poephaga* of marsupials.

Poesy (pōᵘ·ėsi), *sb. arch.* ME. [– (O)Fr. *poésie* – Rom. **poēsia*, f. L. *poēsis* – Gr. πόησις, ποίησις creation, poetry, poem; see POEM, -Y^{3}.] **1.** = POETRY. **a.** Poetical work or composition; poems collectively or generally; poetry in the concrete, or as a form of literature. Now an arch. or poet. synonym of *poetry*. **b.** Poetry in the abstract, or as an art. **c.** Faculty or skill of poetical composition. 1579. †**2.** (with *a* and *pl.*) A poetical (or, earlier, imaginative) composition; a poem –1843. †**3.** = POSY 1. –1602. †**4.** = POSY 2. –1688.

1. It is not ryming and versing, that maketh Poesie SIDNEY. **b.** The high-water mark of English P. 1879. **3.** Is this a Prologue, or the Poesie of a Ring? SHAKS. Hence **Po·esy** *v. intr.* to speak or write poetically KEATS.

Poet (pōᵘ·ėt). ME. [– (O)Fr. *poète* – L. *poeta* (Plautus) – Gr. ποητής, ποιητής maker, author, poet; see prec.] One who composes poetry; a writer in verse. (The ordinary current use.) †**b.** Formerly (after Gr. and L. use): An author, writer –1678. **c.** In emphatic sense: A writer in verse (or sometimes in elevated prose) distinguished by imaginative power, insight, sensibility, and faculty of expression 1530.

Fumbling baronets and poets small GRAY. *P.-laureate*: see LAUREATE *a.* **c.** The Poets eye in a fine frenzy rolling, Doth glance from heauen to earth, from earth to heauen SHAKS.

Comb. **Poets' Corner,** (*a*) a part of the south transept of Westminster Abbey, which contains the graves and monuments of many distinguished poets; (*b*) applied joc. to a part of a newspaper, etc., containing short poetical contributions. Hence **Po·etship,** the position or function of a p.; also with *poss. adj.* as a mock title for a p.

Poetaster (pōᵘ·ėtæstəɹ, pōᵘėtæ·stəɹ). 1599. [– mod.L. *poetaster* (Erasmus, 1521), f. L. *poeta*; see prec., -ASTER.] A paltry poet; a writer of trashy verse; a rhymester.

There are always poetasters enough 1883. Hence **Poetastery, -try,** the work of a p.

Poetess (pōᵘ·ėtės). 1530. [f. POET + -ESS^{1}. Cf. late.L. *poetissa* (VI).] A female poet.

Poetic (po,e·tik). 1530. [– (O)Fr. *poétique* – L. *poeticus* – Gr. πο(ι)ητικός, f. πο(ι)ητής POET; see -IC.] **A.** *adj.* **1.** Belonging or proper to poets or poetry. **2. a.** That is a poet 1640. **b.** Of a poet or poets 1712. **3.** = POETICAL 3. 1656. **b.** Having the style or character proper to poetry as a fine art 1826. **4.** = POETICAL 4. 1704. **5.** Celebrated in poetry; affording a subject for poetry 1742. **6.** In sense of Gr. ποιητικός: Making, creative; relating to artistic creation (*rare*) 1872.

1. Poetique Fires DRYDEN. *P.* JUSTICE, LICENCE: see the sbs. **2. a.** The p. Earl of Surrey D'ISRAELI. **b.** The p. tribe COWPER. **3.** P. Prose 1749.

B. *sb.* **1.** *sing.* and *pl.* That part of literary criticism which treats of poetry; also, a treatise on poetry; *esp.* that of Aristole 1727. **2.** *pl.* Poetic composition 1851.

Poetical (po,e·tikăl), *a.* late ME. [f. as prec.; see -ICAL.] **1.** = POETIC *a.* 1. **2.** Characteristic of a poet or poets 1585. **b.** Having the character of a poet 1581. †**c.** That is a poet; composing in verse –1720. **3.** Composed in poetry; written in verse 1549. **b.** Of the style or character proper to poetry as a fine art 1447. **4.** Relating to or dealing with poetry; occupied with or fond of poetry 1779.

1. *P.* JUSTICE, LICENCE: see the sbs. **2. b.** Truly, I would the Gods hadde made thee poeticall SHAKS. **4.** A new p. philosophy 1851. Hence **Poe·tically** *adv.*

Poe·ticize (-səiz), *v.* 1804. [f. POETIC + -IZE.] **1.** *trans.* To make poetic; to treat poetically; to put into poetry. **2.** *intr.* To write or speak poetically or as a poet 1850.

Poetico- (po,e·tiko), comb. form of L. *poeticus* POETIC, to denote a combination of the poetic with another quality, as *p.-antiquarian.*

Poeticule (po,e·tikiul). 1872. [f. POET + -CULE, on L. analogies.] A petty or insignificant poet.

Poetize (pōᵘ·ėtəiz), *v.* 1581. [– (O)Fr. *poétiser*, f. *poète*; see POET, -IZE.] **1.** *intr.* To play the poet; to compose poetry. †**b.** To deal in poetical fiction; to romance –1639. **2.** *trans.* **a.** To make poetical; to turn into poetry 1762. **b.** To celebrate in poetry 1837.

1. Not onely to read others Poesies, but to poetise for others reading SIDNEY. **b.** I versifie the troth, not p. DANIEL. **2. b.** To p. the moon 1884.

Poetry (pōᵘ·ėtri). late ME. [– med.L. *poetria* (VII), f. L. *poeta* POET, prob. after L. *geometria* GEOMETRY.] **I.** In obsolete senses. †**1.** = med.L. *poetria* in sense of an *ars poetica* –1447. †**2.** Fable, fiction –1601.

2. Their profession of Poëtry, that is to say, of faining and deuising fables HOLLAND.

II. In existing use. **1.** The art or work of the poet. **a.** Composition in verse or metrical language. late ME. **b.** The product of this art as a form of literature; the writings of a poet or poets; poems collectively or generally; verse. (Opp. to *prose*.) 1586. **c.** The expression of beautiful or elevated thought, imagination, or feeling, in appropriate language, such language containing a rhythmical element and having usu. a metrical form 1581. **d.** Extended to creative art in general (*rare*) RUSKIN. **2.** *pl.* Pieces of poetry; poems collectively (*rare*). late ME. **3.** *fig.* Something compared to poetry; poetical quality, spirit, or feeling 1816. **4.** A class in Roman Catholic schools and colleges intermediate between *Syntax* and *Rhetoric* 1629. **5.** *attrib.* 1798.

1. b. The end of p... is to please 1807. **c.** I will proue those Verses to be very vnlearned, neither sauouring of Poetrie, Wit, nor Inuention SHAKS. *Prose-p.*, expression in non-metrical language having the harmonic and emotional qualities of p. **3.** To live p., indeed, is always better than to write it 1874.

Poggy (pǫ·gi). 1874. [Of unkn. origin.] A small arctic whale; supposed to be the young of the common whale, *Balæna mysticetus.*

Pogo (pōᵘ·go). 1922. [Of unkn. origin.] In full *p.-stick*, a toy resembling a stilt with a spring on which the player jumps about.

‖**Pogrom** (pŏgro·m). 1905. [Russ. = devastation, destruction, f. *gromit'* destroy.] An organized massacre in Russia for the annihilation of any body or class; *esp.* one directed against the Jews.

Pogy (pōᵘ·gi). local *U.S.* Also **-ie.** 1888. [Contraction of *pauhaugen.*] The menhaden.

Poh (po), *int.* 1679. An exclam. of contemptuous rejection. (Cf. POOH.)

‖**Poi** (poi). Also **poe.** 1840. [Hawaiian name.] A dish made in Hawaii from the root of the taro or kalo plant, by grinding, mixing, and allowing it to ferment; also, a dish made from the banana and pandanus fruit. Also *attrib.*

Poietic (poi,e·tik), *a. rare.* 1905. [– Gr. ποιητικός active, effective, f. ποιεῖν do, make.] Creative, formative, productive, active.

Poignancy (poi·nʸănsi). 1688. [f. POIGNANT; see -ANCY.] The quality or fact of being poignant.

A..p. of grief 1787. The p. of their wit 1838.

Poignant (poi·nʸănt), *a.* [XIV *poyna(u)nt* – (O)Fr. *poignant*, pr. pple. of *poindre* :– L. *pungere* prick; see -ANT.] †**1.** Of weapons, etc.; Sharp-pointed, piercing –1695. **b.** *fig.* Of the eye or look: Piercing, keen 1787. **2.** Sharp, pungent, piquant to the taste or smell. late ME. **3.** Painfully sharp to the physical or mental feelings. late ME. **b.** Stimulating; piquant 1649. **4.** Of words or expressions: Sharp, stinging; also, piquant 1542.

2. Poynaunt sauce CHAUCER. The rich, p. perfume 1864. **3.** This pang is made more p. by exile 1887. **b.** A..p. felicity HAWTHORNE. **4.** P. sarcasm DISRAELI. Hence **Poi·gnantly** *adv.*

Poikilitic (poikili·tik), *a.* 1836. [var. of PŒCILITIC.] *Geol.* A term formerly applied to the Triassic and Permian systems, as being mainly composed of variegated rocks.

Poi·kilo-, var. of PŒCILO-.

‖**Poilu** (pwalü). 1916. [Fr. = hairy.] French slang for: A private soldier.

Poind (pünd, pind), *sb. Sc.* 1563. [f. next.] **a.** An act of poinding, a distraint. **b.** A beast or chattel poinded.

Poind (pünd, pind), *v. Sc.* late ME. [Sc. repr. of OE. *pyndan* shut in, impound, = PIND.] **1.** *trans.* To distrain upon (a person or his goods). **b.** *absol.* To distrain 1500. **2.** *trans.* To impound 1450. Hence **Poi·nder,** a person who distrains goods or impounds cattle.

‖**Poinsettia** (poinse·tiă). 1867. [mod.L.; after J. R. *Poinsett*, American Minister to Mexico; see -IA^{1}.] A Mexican species of Euphorbia, *E.* (*Poinsettia*) *pulcherrima*, having large scarlet floral leaves surrounding small greenish-yellow flowers.

Point (point), *sb.*^{1} ME. [In A – (O)Fr. *point*, in B – (O)Fr. *pointe*, repr. respectively L. *punctum*, subst. use of n. pa. pple. of *pungere* pierce, prick, and Rom. (med.L.) *puncta*, corresp. use of fem. pa. pple. In C, app. – Fr. *pointe* or f. POINT *v.*^{1}] **A.** = Fr. *point.* **1.** A prick, a dot. **1.** A dot, a minute spot or speck, on a surface; also, anything appearing like a speck. late ME. **2.** A dot or other small mark used in writing or printing. **a.** A punctuation-mark; *esp.* the *full p.* or full stop. late ME. **b.** In Semitic alphabets, any one of the dots, minute strokes, or groups of these used to indicate the vowels; in Hebrew also to indicate variation or doubling of the consonant, stress accent, punctuation, in Arabic and Persian to distinguish consonants otherwise identical in form 1614. **c.** A dot used in writing numbers: (*a*) in decimals, separating the integral from the fractional part; also, placed over a repeating decimal, or over the first and last figures of a circulating decimal. (*b*) A dot or stroke used to separate a line of figures into groups. 1794. **3.** A dot or mark used in mediæval musical notation. **a.** A mark indicating a tone or sound; corresp. to the modern 'notes' 1674. **b.** = DOT *sb.*^{1} 5 d. 1597.

1. As the fix'd Stars..appear but as so many points LAW. **2. a.** The p. of Interrogation,? The p. of Exclamation, ! 1824.

II. A separate or single article, item, or clause in an extended whole; a detail, a particular; †an instance (of some quality, etc.) ME.

This is the p. upon which the whole reasoning turns 1701. The 'six points' of modern Ritualism 1897. Phr. †*To stand (up)on (one's) points*, to be punctilious or scrupulous. *To strain* or *stretch a p.*; see the vbs.

III. A minute part or particle of anything; the smallest unit of measurement. †**1.** A jot, whit, particle of something –1477. †**2.** A moment, instant, of time –1533. †**3.** *Sensible p.*: the least discernible portion of matter or space (*rare*) –1704. **4.** *Mus.* A short strain or snatch of melody ME. **b.** An important phrase or subject, usu. in a contrapuntal composition, esp. in relation to its entry in a particular part; the entry of such a phrase or subject 1597. †**5.** The twelfth part of the side or radius of a quadrant, etc.; *spec.* in *Astron.* One of the 24 (or, according to some, 12) equal divisions of the diameter of the sun or moon, by which the degree of obscuration in an eclipse was measured –1594. **6.** *Nine* or *eleven points*, usu. in the saying 'Possession is nine (or eleven) points of the law', i.e. out of a supposed ten or twelve points (= a vast majority of the points) that may be raised in a legal action 1670. **7.** A unit of count in the score of a game 1746. **b.** *spec.* in *Piquet*: The number of cards of the most numerous suit in one's hand after discarding; the number scored by the player who holds the highest number of one suit 1719. **8.** A unit in appraising the qualities of a competitor, or of an exhibit in a competitive show. Also *fig.* 1777. **9.** A recognized unit in quoting variations in the price of stocks, shares, commodities, etc. **10.** *Printing.* A unit of measurement for type bodies; in the French or Didot system the seventy-second part of a French inch; in the U.S. system, ·0138 of an inch 1890.

1. †*No p.* (cf. Fr. *ne point*), not a bit, not at all. **4.** Phr. *P. of war*, etc., a short phrase sounded on an instrument as a signal; To perform the beautiful and wild p. of war SCOTT. **7.** Cumberland scored 14 points [at Football] 1895. Phr. *To give points to*, to allow (a rival) to count so many points at starting, to give odds to; *colloq.* to have the advantage of, be superior to; so *to gain a p., get points*, to gain an advantage. **8.** All these were points against him 1886.

IV. Something having definite position, without extension. **1.** *Geom.* That which has position, but not magnitude (as the extremity of a line). late ME. **2.** A place having definite spatial position, but no extent, or of which the position alone is considered; a spot ME. **b.** *spec.* The spot at which a policeman is stationed 1888. **c.** *Hunting. colloq.* A spot to which a straight run is made; hence, a cross-country run 1875. **3.** *Her.* Any of nine particular spots or places upon a shield, which serve to determine accurately the position a charge is to occupy. late ME. **4.** A definite position in a scale of any kind; a step, stage, or degree in progress or development, or in increase or decrease, as of temperature (e.g. *boiling-p., freezing-p.*, etc.). late ME. **b.** A critical position in the course of affairs; a juncture; the precise moment for action. late ME. **5.** In time, that which has position, but not duration; an instant, moment, as the moment of death. late ME. †**6.** Condition, plight –1732.

1. If a P. be supposed to be moved any way, it will by its Motion describe a Line 1704. CARDINAL, EQUINOCTIAL, SOLSTITIAL, VERTICAL *p.*: see those words. **2. c.** Phr. *To make his p.* (of a fox), to run straight to a p. aimed at. **d.** (*colloq.*) A stopping-place on a tramway, omnibus, or other route, from which fare-stages are reckoned 1885.

V. fig. and transf. senses. †**1.** The highest part or degree; the height, summit, zenith, acme –1728. **2.** A distinguishing mark or quality; a characteristic 1470. **b.** *spec.* A physical feature in an animal; *esp.* one by which excellence or purity of breed is judged. Hence *transf.* in ref. to a person or thing. 1546. **3.** *The p.*: the precise matter in discussion; the important thing. late ME. **4.** That at which one aims, or for which one contends; aim, object, end. Often in phr. *to carry one's p.* ME. †**5.** A conclusion, culmination, 'period'. Also *full p.* –1833. †**6.** Decision, resolution –1738.

2. It is become. . a p. of good fellowship. . to take a pipe of Tobacco JAMES I. Description was not Lettice's strong p. 1889. **b.** Versed in the points of a horse 1841. **3.** Phr. *To come to the p., to keep to the p.*, etc. *To make a p. of* (= Fr. *faire un point de*), to treat (something) as indispensable; to make (it) a special object. **4.** *To make a p.*, to establish a proposition, to prove a contention; also *gen.* to attain something aimed at. **6.** I begin to come to a p.; I intend to go along with this good man BUNYAN.

VI. (From 16th c. Fr. *point* = 15–16th c. It. *punto*; derived from the sense 'prick', through that of 'stitch', 'work done with stitches' with the needle.) Thread lace made wholly with the needle (more fully *p. lace, needle-p. lace, needle-p.*); also improp. applied to pillow lace imitating that done with the needle, and occas. to lace generally 1662. †**b.** A piece of lace used as a kerchief or the like –1756.

B. = Fr. *pointe*. **I. 1.** A sharp end to which anything tapers; as of a weapon, tool, pin, pen, pointer ME. **b.** Short for *p. of the sword* (or other weapon) 1596. **2.** The (or a) salient or projecting part of anything; a tip, apex; a sharp prominence. late ME. **b.** *spec.* A tapering promontory, or cape; often in names, as Start P., P. of Ardnamurchan. Also, a peak of a mountain or hill. 1553. **c.** *Mil.* The small leading party of an advanced guard 1589. **d.** *pl.* The extremities of a horse 1855. **3.** An object or instrument consisting of or characterized by a point (in sense 1), or which pricks or pierces. †**a.** A dagger, pointed sword, or the like; also, a bodkin –1719. **b.** An etching-needle; a small punch or chisel used by stoneworkers; etc. 1727. **c.** A tine of a deer's horn 1856. **d.** *Electr.* A metallic point at which electricity is discharged or collected; also, each of the carbon points or pencils in an electric light (see also below) 1836. **e.** On a railway: A tapering movable rail by which vehicles are directed from one line of rails to another. Usu. in *pl.* See also DIAMOND POINT 2. 1838. **f.** One of the twelve tapered divisions on each 'table' of a backgammon board 1588. **g.** In other applications, e.g. one of the pointed legs of a pair of compasses, an angular fragment of diamond adapted for glass-cutting 1545. **4.** *Printing.* One of the short sharp pins fixed on the tympan of a press so as to perforate the sheet and serve to make register 1683. **b.** Short for *p.-plate* 1683.

1. *fig. To put too fine a p. upon*, to express with unnecessary delicacy. **b.** Phr. *To come to points*, to begin fighting (with swords). **2. d.** A little bay with black points 1872. **3. d.** Also, a socket connected by wiring to a source of electricity from which current can be obtained 1927.

II. 1. A tagged lace or cord, for attaching the hose to the doublet, lacing a bodice, etc.; often used as a type of something of small value (esp. *blue p.*) Now *arch.* or *Hist.* late ME. **2.** *Naut.* One of the short pieces of flat braided cord attached near the lower edge of a sail for tying up a reef 1769. **3.** A short buckling strap 1875. **III.** Each of the equidistant points on the circumference of the mariner's compass, indicated by one of the thirty-two rays drawn from the centre; also *transf.* the angular interval between two successive points (one-eighth of a right angle, or 11° 15′). Hence, any (corresponding) point of the horizon. (In ordinary use, usu. *p. of the compass.*) 1500. **IV. a.** The salient feature of a story, discourse, epigram, joke, etc.; effective or telling part. Also, a witty or ingenious turn of thought. 1728. **b.** That quality in speech or writing which arrests attention 1643.

IV.a. The p. and cream of the joke DICKENS.

V. *Cricket.* The position of the fieldsman who is stationed more or less in a line with the popping-crease, a short distance on the off-side of the batsman (orig. close to the point of the bat); *transf.* the fieldsman himself 1833. **b.** In *Lacrosse*, The position of the player who stands a short distance in front of the goalkeeper, or the player himself; in *Baseball*, The positions occupied by the pitcher and catcher 1868.

C. Noun of action of French or English origin. †**1.** A feat; *esp.* a feat of arms, a deed of valour, an exploit; also, an encounter, skirmish. [OFr. *pointe*.] –1602. **2.** *Falconry.* Of a hawk: The action of rising vertically in the air; esp. in phr. *to make* (*her*) *p.* 1651. **3.** Of a pointer or setter: The act of pointing (see POINT *v.*^{1} IV. 3). Usu. in phr. *to make, come to a p.* Also *fig.* 1771. **4.** The act of pointing 1831. **5.** An indication; a hint, suggestion, direction 1882. **6.** *Arch.* An amount or degree of pointedness; in phr. *of the third* (or *fourth*) *p.*, tr. It. *di terzo* (or *quarto*) *acuto* 1703.

1. †*Points of war*, warlike exercises. **4.** Phr. *Bread* or *potatoes and p.* (joc.), bread or potatoes only to eat, and the relish, such as bacon, fish, etc., merely to p. or look at. **5.** Supposing that he could have given Solomon points about women 1892.

Phrases and Combs. (chiefly from A.). *With preps. **At p.** [= Fr. *à point*.] †**a.** Aptly, conveniently. †**b.** (Also *at a p.*) In readiness. **c.** *At* (*the*) *p. to* (with inf.), ready to, just about to (*arch.*). †**d.** *At a p.*, agreed; decided, resolved. **e.** *At all points*, in every part, in every respect. (Usu. with *armed*.) **f.** *At the p. of*, on the verge of, just about to do something. †*At the p. of day* [Fr. *au point du jour*], at daybreak. **From p. to p.** [OFr. *de point en point*.] From one p. or detail to another, in every particular, in detail (*Obs.* or *arch.*). **In p.** †**a.** In order. **b.** *predic.* (Cf. Fr. *à point* = *à propos*.) Apposite; appropriate. **c.** *In p. of*, in the matter of; as regards. *In p. of fact*, see FACT 5. **On** or **upon the p. of.** [Fr. *sur le point de*.] On the very verge of, just about to do something. Formerly in reference to a specified time or number: Very near, close upon. **To p. a.** To the smallest detail; exactly, completely (*arch.*). **b.** *To the p.*, apposite, apt, pertinent. **With other sbs. **P. of honour** [Fr. *point d'honneur*]. A matter regarded as vitally affecting one's honour. Hence, the obligation to demand satisfaction (esp. by a duel) for a wrong or insult. **Point-to-point,** *a.* (Made, reckoned, etc.) from one point or place to another in a direct line; chiefly of a cross-country race; hence *ellipt.* as *sb.* a cross-country race, a steeple-chase. **P. of view** [Fr. *point de vue*]. The position from which anything is viewed or seen, or from which a picture is taken; also, the position or aspect in which anything is seen or regarded.

attrib. and *Comb.* **1.** General: as *p.-hole* (Printing), *-system*, etc. In Phonetics, used to describe a consonant articulated with the point of the tongue, as *t, d*; also in comb. as *p.-side* (as *l*), *p.-teeth* (as *þ*) adjs.

2. Special: **p.-bar,** in the Jacquard apparatus, one of the needles governing the warp-threads, by the motion of which the pattern is produced; **-constable,** a constable on point-duty; **-handle, -lever,** the lever by which a p. or railway-switch is moved; **-net,** simple p. lace; **-paper,** pricked paper for making, copying, or transferring designs; **-plate** (*Printing*), the adjustable plate carrying the points; **-policeman** = *p.-constable*.

‖**Point** (pwæ̃n), *sb.*^{2} 1645. The French for POINT *sb.*^{1} A., occurring in phrases used in English, as *p. d'appui*, point of support, fulcrum; *p. d'arrêt, p. saillant* (Geom.): see quots. **b.** *esp.* In names of kinds of lace, as (from the real or supposed place of manufacture) *p. d'Alençon, p. d'Espagne, p. de Venise*; also of various stitches in lace and embroidery.

A *p. d'arrêt* is a point at which a single branch of a curve suddenly stops. A *p. saillant* is a point at which two branches of a curve meet and stop without having a common tangent 1871.

Point (point), *v.*^{1} ME. [Partly – (O)Fr. *pointer*, f. *point, pointe* POINT *sb.*^{1}, partly – POINT *sb.*^{1}] **I.** †**1.** *trans.* To prick; to pierce, puncture –1570. †**2.** To mark with, or indicate by, pricks or dots; to jot down, note, write, describe –1669. **3.** To insert the proper points or stops in (writing); to make the proper pauses in (something read or spoken); to punctuate. Also *absol.* Now *rare.* late ME. **b.** To mark (the Psalms, etc.) for chanting, by means of points 1604. **c.** To insert the vowel (and other) points in the writing of Hebrew, etc.; also, in shorthand 1631. **d.** To mark *off* (figures) into groups by dots or points; *esp.* to mark *off* the decimal fraction from the integral part 1706.

3. When sentences be euill pointed, and the sence thereby depraued 1551.

II. 1. To furnish with a point or points; to work to a point, to sharpen. Also *fig.* ME. **2.** *fig.* To give point to (words, action, etc.) 1704. †**3.** To fasten or lace with tagged points or laces; to adorn with such points –1598.

1. Phr. *To p. a cable* or *rope*, to taper off the ends, and finish them neatly and securely. **2.** To p. a morale, or adorn a tale JOHNSON.

III. 1. †To work or deepen with a point or graving-tool 1662. **2. a.** *Building.* To fill in the lines of joints of (brickwork) with mortar or cement, smoothed with the point of the trowel. late ME. **b.** *Gardening.* To prick *in* (manure, etc.) to a slight depth with the point of the spade; also, to turn *over* (the surface of the soil) in this way; to prick *over* 1828. **c.** *Naut.* To insert the point of (a mast or spar) through an eye or ring which secures its foot; to thread 1882. **IV. 1.** *intr.* To indicate position or direction by or as by extending the finger; to direct attention *to* or *at* something in this way 1470. **b.** *fig.* To direct the mind or thought in a certain direction; to indicate, hint *at*, allude *to*. late ME. **2.** *trans.* To indicate the place or direction of (something); to direct attention to, show. Now almost always *p. out* 1489. **3.** Of a dog: To indicate the presence and position of (game) by standing rigidly looking towards it. *trans.* and *intr.* 1717. **4.** *trans.* To direct (the finger, a weapon, etc.) *at*; to direct (a person, his attention, or his course) *to*; to turn (the eyes or mind) *to* or *upon* 1547. **5.** *intr.* Of a line, etc.: To lie or be situated with its point or length directed *to* or *towards* something; to have a specified direction; also, of a house, etc., to look or face 1678. **b.** To aim *at*, have a motion or tendency *towards* or *to* (also with *inf.*) 1771. †**6.** To project or stick *out* in a point –1703. **7.** Of an abscess: To form a point or head; to come to a head 1876. **8.** *trans.* To place (a man) in Backgammon, etc., on a point 1680.

1. He shewed hym, pointyng with his finger, a man with a bottle Nose 1553. **b.** Everything pointed to the probability of a French protectorate being proclaimed 1886. **2.** He pointed out that there were certain formalities to be observed 1907. **3.** Young pointers will p. birds' nests in hedges or trees JEFFERIES. **4.** The fixed Figure for the time of Scorne To p. his slow, and mouing finger at SHAKS. **5. b.** Our ships endeavouring to form a junction, the Enemy pointing to separate us NELSON.

†**Point**, *v.*[2] 1440. [Aphetic f. APPOINT *v.*] **1.** *trans.* To fix (a time or place); to prescribe, ordain, decree; to nominate (a person) *to* an office –1711. **2.** To equip, furnish, fit up –1514.

Point-blank (poi·nt blæ·ŋk), *a.*, *sb.*, and *adv.* 1571. [app. f. POINT *v.*[1] + BLANK the white spot in the centre of a target, = Fr. *blanc.*] **A.** *adj.* **1.** That points or aims straight at the mark, esp. in shooting horizontally; hence, aimed or fired horizontally; level, direct, straight 1591. **2.** Straightforward, direct, plain, 'flat', blunt 1656.

1. Phr. *P. shot, fire, firing, trajectory. P. distance, range, reach,* the distance within which a gun may be fired horizontally at a mark; the distance the shot is carried before it drops appreciably below the horizontal plane of the bore. **2.** A p. refusal to go into the division lobbies 1901.

B. *sb.* **1.** = *P. range* or *distance*: see A. 1. †Also *fig.* 1571. †**2.** A p. shooting or shot –1781.

1. *fig.* Within point-blanke of our Iurisdiction Regall SHAKS.

C. *adv.* **1.** With a direct aim; esp. in a horizontal line 1594. **2.** Directly, straight (in space) 1607. **b.** *fig.* Directly, exactly (in purport or effect). Now *rare* or *Obs.* 1621. **3.** *fig.* Of a statement, question etc.: **a.** Without qualification or circumlocution; directly, flatly 1627. **b.** Straight away, offhand 1679.

2. b. So p. against the common sentiment 1704. **3. a.** Origen point blanck denies the charge 1672. **b.** Called upon to deliver his judgement point-blank 1887.

Poi·nt-devi·ce, *phr.*, *a.*, *adv.* [orig. in late ME. phrase *at point devis*, app. repr. an OFr. or AFr. phrase **à point devis* arranged properly or to perfection.] **A.** *phr.* †*At point device*, at or to the point of perfection, perfectly; precisely. late ME. only. **B.** *adj.* Perfectly correct; neat or nice in the extreme; extremely precise or scrupulous. *Obs.* or *arch.* 1526.

You are rather point deuice in your accoustrements SHAKS. Thus he grew up, in Logic p. LONGF.

C. *adv.* Completely, perfectly, to perfection; in every point; = A. *arch.* 1500.

Poi·nt-du·ty. 1888. The duty of a police constable stationed at a particular point in a thoroughfare, to regulate traffic.

Pointed (poi·ntėd), *ppl. a.* ME. [f. POINT *v.*[1] and *sb.*[1] + -ED.] In various senses of the verb; *spec.* **1.** Having a point or points; tapering to or ending in a point. **b.** *Arch.* In *p. arch*, an arch with a pointed crown; hence applied to the style of architecture having this feature; cf. GOTHIC A. 3 b. 1750. **2.** *fig.* Piercing, cutting, stinging, pungent, 'sharp'; having point 1665. **3.** Directed, aimed; *fig.* marked, emphasized, clearly defined, made evident 1578. **b.** Exact to a point; precise 1727.

1. I saw a row of p. rocks at some distance below me TYNDALL. **2.** The most p. thing to say about a person is that he 'means well' 1897. **3.** His attention. . is so p., that it always confuses me 1778. Hence **Poi·nted-ly** *adv.*, **-ness.**

Pointel (poi·ntĕl). Now *rare.* ME. [– OFr. *pointel* point of a spear, dim. of *pointe*; see POINT *sb.*[1], -EL.] **1.** A small pointed instrument; a stylus, a pencil. *Obs.* exc. *Hist.* **2.** The pistil or style of a flower; formerly also applied to a stamen. Now *rare* or *Obs.* 1597. †**3.** A slender style-like organ on the body of an animal, as the 'horn' of a snail, etc. –1713.

2. White flowers with yellow pointels in the middle 1597.

Pointer (poi·ntəɹ). 1621. [f. POINT *v.*[1] + -ER[1].] One who or that which points; *spec.* **1.** A rod used to point to what is delineated or written on a map, blackboard, etc. 1658. **b.** The index-hand of a clock, balance, etc. 1667. **2.** A dog of a breed nearly allied to the true hounds, used by sportsmen to point at game, esp. birds; on scenting which the dog stands rigidly, with muzzle stretched towards the game, and usu. one foot raised 1717. **3.** *pl.* The two stars α and γ in the Great Bear, a straight line through which points nearly to the pole star 1574. **4.** *Naut.* (*pl.*) Timbers sometimes fixed diagonally across the hold, to support the beams 1769. **5.** *colloq.* A hint 1890.

Pointillism (pwæṅ·tiliz'm). Also ‖**-isme.** 1901. [– Fr. *pointillisme*, f. *pointiller* mark with dots, f. *pointille* – It. *puntiglio*, dim. of *punto* point; see PUNCTILIO, -ISM.] A method invented by French impressionist painters, of producing luminous effects by crowding a surface with small spots of various colours, which are blended by the eye. So **Poi·ntillist,** an artist who follows this style; also *attrib.* 1893.

Pointing (poi·ntiŋ), *vbl. sb.* late ME. [f. POINT *v.*[1] + -ING[1].] The action of POINT *v.*[1], or its result. *spec.* **1.** The insertion of stops; punctuation 1440. **b.** In Semitic langs., the insertion of vowel points 1659. **2.** The removal of points from grain in preparing it for the mill 1879. **3.** The filling up with special strong mortar of the exterior face of the joints in brickwork; *concr.* the protective facing thus given to the joints 1483. **4.** The action of indicating or directing, as with the finger or the point of anything; also *fig.* a prompting; a hint in words 1553. **b.** Of a yacht, etc.: The action of sailing with its prow close to the wind 1899. **5.** The disposition of the points on a railway 1902.

Comb. †**p.-stock,** a person pointed at; an object of scorn, derision, or ridicule.

Poi·nt-la·ce. 1672. [f. POINT *sb.*[1] A. VI. + LACE *sb.* 5.] Lace made with the needle on a parchment pattern, as dist. from that made with bones or bobbins on a pillow. Also *attrib.*

Pointless (poi·ntlės), *a.* ME. [f. POINT *sb.*[1] + -LESS.] **1.** Without a point; blunt. **2.** Without point; ineffective, meaningless 1726. **3.** Of a competitor, side: Not having scored a point. Of a game, etc.: In which no point is scored. 1876.

1. A pointeless sword 1548. **2.** P. wit POPE. **3.** A p. draw 1892. Hence **Poi·ntless-ly** *adv.*, **-ness.**

Pointlet (poi·ntlėt). 1866. [f. as prec. + -LET.] A small point. So **Poi·ntleted** *a. Bot.* terminating in a small point; apiculate 1839.

Pointrel (poi·ntrĕl). *rare.* 1688. [dim. of POINT *sb.*[1] B; see -REL.] **a.** = POINTEL 1. **b.** The pointed extremity of the lobe of a leaf.

Pointsman (poi·ntsmæ̆n). 1849. [f. POINT *sb.*[1] + MAN *sb.*] **1.** A man who has charge of the points on a railway. **2.** A police-constable stationed on point-duty 1883.

Poise (poiz), *sb.* late ME. [– OFr. *pois* (mod. *poids*), earlier *peis* (whence PEISE *sb.*) :– Rom. **pesum*, for L. *pensum* weight, subst. use of n. of pa. pple. of *pendere* weigh, rel. to *pendēre* (see PENDENT).] **I.** Weight. †**1.** The quality of being heavy; weight. Also in semi-concr. sense. –1665. †**b.** *fig.* Gravity; burden; burdensomeness –1752. †**2.** Definite weight; the amount that a thing weighs –1706. †**b.** A standard of weight –1614. †**3.** A weight; e.g. a weight of a clock –1688. **b.** *fig.* Something that acts like a weight; a bias; one of the *halteres* of a fly. Now *rare* or *Obs.* 1615. †**4.** Forcible impact, as of a heavy body; momentum; a heavy blow or fall –1606.

3. b. Such a hint was likely enough to give an adverse p. to Gwendolen's own thought GEO. ELIOT. **4.** *Tr. & Cr.* I. iii. 207.

II. Equality of weight, balance. **1.** *Equal* or *even p.*: The condition of being equally weighted on both sides; balance, equilibrium. *lit.* and *fig.* 1555. **2.** Hence *absol.*: Balance, equilibrium, stability 1711. **b.** Carriage (of the body, head, etc.) 1770. **c.** A balanced condition; a pause between two periods of motion or change 1867. **d.** Balanced condition; state of indecision; suspense 1713.

1. And that demands a mind in equal poize YOUNG. **2. d.** The event was long on the p. 1787.

Poise (poiz), *v.* late ME. [– OFr. *pois-* (earlier *peis-*, whence PEISE *v.*), tonic stem of (O)Fr. *peser* :– Rom. **pesare*, for L. *pensare*, frequent. of *pendere* (see prec.).] †**1.** *trans.* (or *intr.* with *compl.*) = PEISE *v.* 5. –1587. †**2.** = PEISE *v.* 1, 1 b. –1695. **3.** *fig.* = PEISE *v.* 2. Now *rare.* 1483. †**4.** To add weight to; to load, burden; to weigh *down*, oppress; to incline or sway as by weight. *lit.* and *fig.* –1711. †**b.** To steady or render stable, as by adding weight; to ballast –1710. **5.** To place or keep in equilibrium; to balance. *lit.* and *fig.* 1639. **b.** To weigh or balance (one thing *with* or *against* another, or two things against each other); to bring into mutual equilibrium; to equalize. Usu. *fig.* Now *rare.* 1592. †**c.** To be of equal weight with (usu. *fig.*); to counterbalance; to match –1742. **6.** To hold or carry in equilibrium; to carry steadily or evenly 1598. **7.** *intr.* for *refl.* To be balanced; to hang supported or suspended 1847.

3. A thousand resolutions. . weighed, poised, and perpended STERNE. **4.** When a man is biassed and poised by his heart to a thing 1677. **b.** That Sobriety of Thought which poises the Heart STEELE. **5.** Where Earth now rests Upon her center pois'd MILT. **6.** Their favourite mode of carrying things is to p. them on the top of the head 1870. **7.** A butterfly. . Poising in sunshine GEO. ELIOT. Hence **Poi·ser,** that which poises or balances; an organ used for balancing; *spec.* in *Entom.*, each of the pair of appendages which replace the hind wings in dipterous insects; see HALTERES 2.

Poison (poi·z'n), *sb.* (*a.*) [ME. *puison, poison* – OFr. *puison*, (also mod.) *poison* (in OFr. magic potion) :– L. *potio, potion-* POTION.] †**1.** A potion –1579. **2.** Any substance which, when introduced into or absorbed by a living organism, destroys life or injures health; pop. applied to a substance which destroys life by rapid action, and when taken in a small quantity. late ME. **3.** *fig.* Any baneful principle, doctrine, or influence; any baneful element taken in from without 1470.

2. They hate each other like p. 1907. *Slow p.*, a drug or agent having a cumulative deleterious effect when taken for a length of time. **3.** The poyson of seditious doctrines HOBBES.

attrib. and *Comb.*, as *p.-fang, -gland, -sac*; **p.-cup,** (*a*) a cup containing p.; (*b*) a cup, etc., reputed to break on p. being poured into it; **-gas,** gas liberated from cylinders, a burst shell, etc., for the purpose of poisoning or asphyxiating enemy forces; **-ring,** a ring by which p. was communicated in the grasp of the hand. **b.** *esp.* in names of plants having poisonous qualities: **p.-ash, -dogwood, -elder** = *p.-sumac*; **-hemlock,** *U.S.* the common hemlock, *Conium maculatum*; **-ivy,** a trailing or climbing species of sumac, *Rhus toxicodendron*, of N. America, having trifoliolate leaves, and producing poisonous effects when touched; **-nut,** (*a*) the violently poisonous seed of *Tanghinia venenifera* (N.O. *Apocynaceæ*), used by the natives of Madagascar in trial by ordeal, also the tree; (*b*) = NUX VOMICA; **-oak,** the low-growing variety of *Rhus toxicodendron* (see *poison-ivy*); also the allied *R. diversiloba* of Pacific N. America; **-sumac,** *Rhus venenata*, a tall N. American shrub with pinnate leaves, also called *p.-ash* and *p.-elder*, and having properties resembling those of the allied *p.-ivy*; **-tree,** applied to various trees having poisonous properties.

†**B.** *adj.* Poisonous, poisoned –1822.

With what p., deadly, and venomous hate hateth a man his enemy TINDALE. Hence †**Poi·sonsome** *a.* poisonous –1688.

Poison (poi·z'n), *v.* ME. [– OFr. *poisonner* give to drink, f. *poison*; see prec.] **1.** *trans.* To administer poison to; to kill or injure by means of poison, poisonous gases, etc. **b.** To produce morbid effects in (the blood, a wound, etc.) by impregnation or infusion of poison, ptomaine, etc. 1605. **2.** To infect (air, water, etc.) with poison; to charge or smear (a weapon) with poison. late ME. **3.** *fig.* To corrupt, pervert morally, to influence perversely. late ME. **b.** To prove destructive or fatal to (an action, state, etc.) 1605. **4.** *transf.* To render (a thing) foul and unfit for its purpose by some noxious addition or application 1500.

1. The Pope hireth men to poyson other 1560. **b.** Tooth that poysons if it bite SHAKS. The bite of some insects may p. the blood 1907. **2.** Poisoning the points of their arrows 1851. **3.** Another voice. . ever ready to p. the royal mind 1868. **b.** A word of bitterness to p. the pleasure 1894. **4.** The land will be poisoned with noxious roots and plants 1816. Hence **Poi·sonable** *a.* poisonous;

capable of being poisoned. **Poi·soner,** one who or that which poisons (*lit.* and *fig.*).

Poisoning (poi·z'niŋ), *vbl. sb.* late ME. [-ING[1].] The action of the verb POISON. **b.** As the second element in combs. with words denoting (*a*) the agent or medium, as *beer-, food-, phosphorus-p.*, (*b*) the object, as **blood-poisoning,** applied to diseases caused by the introduction into the blood of decomposing organic matter; toxæmia.

Poisonous (poi·z'nəs), *a.* 1565. [f. POISON *sb.* + -OUS.] **1.** Containing or of the nature of, having the properties of, a poison; venomous. **2.** *fig.* Morally destructive or corrupting; malevolent, malignant. Also with *of.* 1586.

2. The falsehood of their p. lips SHELLEY. **Poi·sonous-ly** *adv.*, **-ness.**

Poi·sonwood. 1716. **a.** Name for certain poisonous species of *Rhus*, as *R. venenata*, and *R. metopium*. **b.** *Sebastiana lucida* (N. O. *Euphorbiaceæ*), of the W. Indies.

‖**Poissarde** (pwasard). 1790. [Fr., fem. of †*poissard* pickpocket, rogue, f. *poix* pitch + -ARD (because things 'stick to his fingers'); also a fishwife (by association with *poisson*).] A Frenchwoman of the lowest class, *esp.* one of the Parisian market-women, who led riots during the first revolution. **b.** A French fishwife 1818.

Poitrel (poi·trěl). Now *Hist.* and *arch.* 1489. [– OFr. *poitral*, earlier *peitral* (whence PEITREL) :– L. *pectorale* PECTORAL.] A piece of armour to protect the breast of a horse. **b.** A breast-plate; a stiff stomacher 1607.

‖**Poivrade** (pwavrad). 1699. [Fr., f. *poivre* pepper; see -ADE.] Pepper-sauce.

Poke (pōᵘk), *sb.*[1] Now chiefly *dial.* ME. [– ONFr. *poque, poke* (cf. AL. *poca* XIII), var. of (O)Fr. *poche*; see POUCH, POACH *v.*[1]] **1.** A bag; a small sack; applied usu. to a bag smaller than a *sack*. Now chiefly *dial.* **b.** A pocket worn on the person. *Obs.* or *arch.* 1600. **2.** A morbid bag-like swelling on the neck. †**a.** Goitre, also called *Bavarian p.* –1673. **b.** In sheep, a bag growing under the jaws, symptomatic of the rot; hence, the disease marked by this 1798. **3.** The stomach of a fish. *colloq.* or *dial.* 1773.

1. Phr. *To buy a pig in a p.*: see PIG *sb.*[1] **b.** Then he drew a diall from his poake SHAKS.

Poke, *sb.*[2] 1770. [prob. f. POKE *v.*[1]] **1.** A projecting brim or front of a woman's bonnet or hat. **2.** Short for POKE-BONNET 1815.

Poke, *sb.*[3] 1796. [f. POKE *v.*[1]] **1.** An act of poking; a thrust, push, nudge. **2.** A contrivance fastened upon cattle, pigs, etc., to prevent them from breaking through fences 1828. **3.** *U.S. colloq.* A lazy person; a dawdler 1860.

Poke, *sb.*[4] [N. Amer. Indian; in sense 1 app. = Narraganset *puck* smoke; in sense 2 app. shortened f. POCAN.] †**1.** Some plant smoked by the N. Amer. Indians, hence called *Indian tobacco* –1865. **2. a.** A name for American species of *Phytolacca*, esp. *P. decandra*, Virginian Poke, Poke-berry, Poke-weed. **b. Indian P.,** the Green Hellebore or Poke-root, *Veratrum viride*. 1731.

Comb.: **p.-berry,** the black berry of *Phytolacca decandra*, also the plant (2 a); **-root,** (*a*) the white hellebore of N. America, *Veratrum viride* (2 b), also its root; (*b*) the root of **poke-weed,** *Phytolacca* (2 a).

Poke (pōik), *v.*[1] late ME. [– (M)LG., (M)Du. *poken* (whence perh. OFr. *poquer* thrust out), of unkn. origin.] **1.** *trans.* To thrust or push (anything) with one's hand or arm, the point of a stick, or the like. **b.** To shut *up* or confine in a poky place (*colloq.*) 1860. **c.** To make, find *out*, stir *up*, by poking 1646. **2.** *fig.* To urge, incite, stir up, excite, irritate. Now *rare* or *Obs.* late ME. †**3.** To crimp (a ruff) with a poking-stick. Also *absol.* –1636. **4.** *intr.* or *absol.* To make a thrust or thrusts with a stick, the nose, etc. 1608. **5.** *trans.* To thrust forward (the finger, head, nose, etc.); *esp.* to thrust obtrusively 1700. **6.** *intr.* **a.** To poke one's nose, go prying into corners or looking about one; *fig.* to make curious investigation 1715. **b.** To potter 1796. **7.** trans. *To p. the head*, and absol. *to p.*; to carry the head thrust forward; to stoop 1811.

1. Aleyn the clerk. .He poked John and seyde slepestow CHAUCER. *To p. through*, to thrust through (*with* a weapon). **b.** To be poked up in a town 1864. **c.** Children who p. a hole in a drum 1823. **4.** To go and p. at the fire 1784. **5.** *To p. fun* (*at*), to assail with jest, banter, or ridicule, esp. in a sly or indirect manner. **6. a.** Having a lawyer to p. and pry into his accounts 1888. **b.** I should enjoy poking about a bit 1877. **7.** 'A quarter's dancing' would be well bestowed on the young lady, as she certainly poked most terribly 1811.

Poke, *v.*[2] 1828. [f. POKE *sb.*[3] 2.] *trans.* To put a poke on (an ox, etc.).

Po·ke-bo·nnet. 1820. [f. POKE *sb.*[2] + BONNET.] A bonnet with a projecting brim; *spec.* one of this shape worn in the early 19th c. **b.** Applied to the form of bonnet worn by Quakeresses, and later to that of Salvation Army women, etc.; hence, to the wearers of such 1848.

Po·ke-pu:dding. Also (*Sc.*) **pock-.** 1552. [f. POKE *sb.*[1] + PUDDING.] **1.** A pudding made in a bag. Now *Sc.* and *dial.* **2.** *Sc.* Applied contempt. to a corpulent or gluttonous person; a designation in Scotland for an Englishman. Now *joc.* 1730. **3.** A local name for the Long-tailed Titmouse 1856.

Poker (pōᵘ·kəɹ), *sb.*[1] 1534. [f. POKE *v.*[1] + -ER[1].] **1.** A stiff metal rod with a handle; used for poking or stirring a fire. **b.** *fig.* A person with a rigid stiff carriage or manner 1812. †**2.** = *Poking-stick*; see POKING *vbl. sb.* 2. –1606. **3.** *transf.* **a.** *joc.* The staff carried by a verger, bedel, etc. 1844. **b.** *Univ. slang.* One of the bedels at Oxford and Cambridge, who carry staves or maces ('pokers') before the Vice-Chancellor 1841. **4.** *Red-hot p.*, pop. name of a species of S. African liliaceous plants, bearing spikes of scarlet or yellow flowers; called also FLAME-*flower* 1884. **5.** The implement with which poker-work is done; hence, short for POKER-WORK. Also *attrib.* 1827. **6.** A person who pokes 1608.

Phr. *By the holy p.*, a humorous asseveration, of Irish origin and uncertain meaning.

Comb.: **p.-bearer,** a (University) bedel; **-drawing, -painting** = POKER-WORK; **-picture,** a picture made by poker-work. Hence **Po·kerish** *a.*[1] inclined to be 'stiff as a p.', esp. in manner.

Poker (pōᵘ·kəɹ), *sb.*[2] Now *U.S. colloq.* 1598. [perh. from Norse; corresp. to Da. *pokker*, Swed. *pocker* the devil. Cf. also PUCK.] A hobgoblin, bugbear, demon. *Old P.*, the devil.

As if old p. was coming to take them away H. WALPOLE. Hence **Po·kerish** *a.*[2] (*U.S. colloq.*) ghostly, uncanny.

Poker (pōᵘ·kəɹ), *sb.*[3] Chiefly *U.S.* 1848. [orig. U.S., of doubtful origin, but cf. G. *poch(spiel)* 'bragging game', f. *pochen* brag, perh. cogn. with POKE *v.*[1]] An American card game, a variety of BRAG, played by two or more persons, each of whom, if not bluffed into declaring his hand, bets on the value of it, the player with the highest combination of cards winning the pool.

Comb.: **p.-face,** an inscrutable face, not easily betraying emotion; hence applied *colloq.* to a person with such a face; **p.-faced,** *a.*

Poker, *sb.*[4], a kind of duck; see POCHARD.

Poker (pōᵘ·kəɹ), *v.* 1787. [f. POKER *sb.*[1]] **1.** *trans.* **a.** To poke, stir, or strike with a poker. **b.** *P. up*: to make as stiff as a poker. *nonce-uses.* **2.** To draw in or adorn with pokerwork 1897.

Po·ker-work. 1813. [f. POKER *sb.*[1] + WORK *sb.*] Ornamental work produced by burning a design on the surface of white wood, leather, etc. with a heated pointed implement.

Poking (pōᵘ·kiŋ), *vbl. sb.* 1582. [f. POKE *v.*[1] + -ING[1].] **1.** The action of POKE *v.* Also *attrib.* **2. Po·king-stick (-iron).** A rod used for stiffening the plaits of ruffs; orig. of wood or bone, later of steel so as to be applied hot. *Hist.* 1592.

2. Pins, and poaking-stickes of steele SHAKS.

Poking (pōᵘ·kiŋ), *ppl. a.* 1769. [f. POKE *v.*[1] + -ING[2].] **1.** Projecting, thrust forward; esp. of the head 1799. **2.** = POKY *a.*[1] 1 a, b. 1769.

2. Some p. little country-curacy KINGSLEY.

Poky (pōᵘ·ki), *a.*[1] 1849. [f. POKE *v.*[1] + -Y[1].] **1. a.** Of a person or his work: Pottering, peddling; hence petty, mean 1856. **b.** Of a place: Petty in size or accommodation; confined, mean, shabby 1849. **c.** Of dress, etc.: Shabby, dowdy 1854. **2.** *Cricket.* Inclined to 'poke' in batting 1891.

Poky, *a.*[2] and *sb. rare.* 1861. [f. POKE *sb.*[2] + -Y[1].] In full *p. bonnet* = POKE-BONNET.

‖**Polacca**[1] (polæ·kă, ‖pola·kka). 1813. [It., subst. use of fem. of *polacco* Polish, f. G. *Polack*; see next.] A Polish dance, a polonaise; also, the music for it.

Polack (pōᵘ·lăk), *sb.* (*a.*) 1599. [– Fr. *Polaque*, G. *Polack* – Pol. *Polak.*] A Pole. **B.** *adj.* Polish. CARLYLE.

Polacre (polā·kəɹ), **polacca**[2] (polæ·kă). 1625. [– Fr. *polacre, polaque*, It. *polacra, polacca* = Sp., Pg.. *polacra* (whence Du. *polaak*, G. *polack(e, polacker*); see prec.] A three-masted merchant vessel of the Mediterranean, usu. without either top-mast or top-gallant-mast. Also *attrib.*

Poland (pōᵘ·lănd). 1564. [f. POLE *sb.*[4] + LAND *sb.*] A country of E. Europe; hence short for *P. oats* or *wheat*, *P. fowl*.

Comb.: **P. fowl,** one of a breed of domestic fowls, having black plumage and a white topknot; **P. wheat,** white cone wheat (*Triticum polonicum*). Hence **Po·lander,** a Pole (*obs.*); also a Poland fowl.

Polar (pōᵘ·lăɹ), *a.* (*sb.*) 1551. [– Fr. *polaire* or mod.L. *polaris* (in med. L. = heavenly); see POLE *sb.*[2], -AR[1].] **1.** *Astron.* and *Geog.* Of or pertaining to the poles of the celestial sphere or of the earth; situated near or connected with either pole. **2.** *Magn.* Having polarity; of or pertaining to a magnetic pole or poles (see POLE *sb.*[2] 5); magnetic 1692. **3.** *Electr.* Pertaining to the poles of a voltaic battery; having positive and negative electricity 1836. **4.** *Physics.* **a.** Of forces: Acting in two opposite directions. (Also in *fig.* uses.) 1809. **b.** Of molecules: Regularly or symmetrically arranged in a definite direction (as though under the action of a magnetic force) 1850. **5.** *Biol.* Of or pertaining to the poles of a nerve-cell, an ovum, etc. (See POLE *sb.*[2] 7.) 1878. **6.** *Geom.* Relating or referred to a pole (see POLE *sb.*[2] 8); *spec.* Reciprocal to a pole; of the nature of a polar (see B.) 1816. **7.** *fig.* **a.** Analogous to the pole of the earth, or to the pole-star; of or pertaining to a central or directive principle 1799. **b.** Directly opposite in character, action, or tendency 1832.

1. P. Winds MILT. Cold as P. Ice 1711. *P. bear*, the white bear, *Ursus maritimus*. *P. circle*, each of the circles parallel to the equator at the distance of 23° 28′ from either pole, bounding the Arctic and Antarctic zones. *P. dial*, a dial having its gnomon in the plane of the earth's axis. *P. distance*, the angular distance of any point on a sphere from the nearer pole; the complement of declination or latitude. *P. hare*, the white hare, *Lepus arcticus*. *P. lights*, the aurora borealis or australis. *P. projection*: see PROJECTION. *P. star*, the POLE-STAR; also *fig.* = guiding-star, guide, cynosure. **6.** *P. co-ordinates*: see CO-ORDINATE *sb.* 2. *P. equation*, an equation in p. co-ordinates. **7. a.** A king over men; whose movements were p., and carried. .those of the world along with them CARLYLE.

B. *sb. Geom.* A curve related in a particular way to a given curve and a fixed point called the pole; in conic sections, the straight line joining the points at which tangents from the fixed point touch the curve 1848.

Polari- (polæ·ri), comb. form. of mod.L. *polaris* polar.

†**Po·larily,** *adv.* [f. POLARY *a.* + -LY[2].] Magnetically. SIR T. BROWNE.

Polarimeter (pōᵘlări·mǐtəɹ). 1864. [f. POLARI- + -METER.] A form of polariscope for measuring the amount of rotation of the plane of polarization, or the amount of polarized light in a beam. Hence **Polarime·tric** *a.* **Polari·metry,** the art or process of measuring or analysing the polarization of light.

‖**Polaris** (polēᵊ·ris). 1907. *Astron.* Short for mod.L. *stella polaris* = Polar star, POLE-STAR.

Polariscope (polæ·riskoᵘp). 1842. [f. POLARI- + -SCOPE.] An instrument for showing the polarization of light, or viewing objects in polarized light. Also *attrib.* Hence **Polarisco·pic** *a.* of or pertaining to, made, obtained, or viewed by, a p. **Polari·scopy,** the art of using a p.

Polarity (polæ·rīti). 1646. [f. POLAR + -ITY, repl. *polity* (1613) – AL. *politas* (XVII).] **1.** *Magnetism.* The quality or property possessed by certain bodies, as a lodestone or magnetized bar, of turning (when free to move) so as to point with their two extremities to the two (magnetic) poles of the earth; the quality of being polar, or possessing magnetic poles. **2.** Hence *gen.* A property of matter or force, analogous or compared to that of a magnet or magnetism. **a.** The disposition of a body or an elementary molecule to place its mathematical axis in a particular direction 1674. **b.** The possession of two points called poles having contrary qualities or tendencies 1818. **c.** Tendency to develop in two opposite directions in space, time, serial arrangement, etc. 1848. **3.** *Electr.* The relation of a body to the poles or electrodes of an electric circuit; the electrical condition of a body as positive or negative 1849. **4.** *Optics.* The quality of light which admits of its polarization; hence, the condition of being polarized. (An inaccurate use.) 1861. **5.** *fig.* **a.** (from 1.) Direction (of thought, feeling) towards a single point; tendency or trend in a certain direction 1767. **b.** (from 2 b.) Possession or exhibition of two opposite or contrasted aspects, principles, or tendencies 1862.

2. b. P., or action and reaction, we meet in every part of nature EMERSON. **5. a.** This p. of mind, this intellectual magnetism towards universal truth, has always been a characteristic of the greatest minds 1834.

Polarization (pōᵘlărəizēⁱ·ʃən). 1812. [In sense 1 – Fr. *polarisation*. In later uses n. of action from the vb.] **I.** A modification of the condition of light or radiant heat, whereby the ray exhibits different properties on different sides, so that opposite sides are alike, while the maximum difference is between two sides at right angles to each other; the production of this condition, the action of polarizing.

Angle of p. = *polarizing angle* (POLARIZING *vbl. sb.*). *Plane of p.*, the plane which contains the incident ray and the reflected or refracted ray which is polarized.

II. 1. *Electr.* and *Magn.* **a.** See POLARIZE *v.* 2. 1866. **b.** In voltaic electricity, the production of an electromotive force at the electrodes, due to the presence of the products of electrolytic decomposition of the fluid between them, and acting in an opposite direction to the original current, thus producing an apparent increase of the resistance 1839. **2.** The arrangement of molecules, etc., in a definite direction 1846.

Polarize (pōᵘ·lărəiz), *v.* 1811. [In sense 1 – Fr. *polariser* (Malus, 1811), f. Fr. *pôle* POLE *sb.*[2] In other senses f. POLAR + -IZE.] **1.** *Optics.* (*trans.*) To cause the vibrations of light (radiant heat, etc.) to be modified in a particular way, so that the ray exhibits different properties on different sides, opposite sides being alike, and those at right angles to each other showing the maximum of difference. **2.** *Magn.* and *Electr.* To give polarity to; to give opposite magnetic properties to opposite ends of (a bar, coil, etc. of iron, etc.). Also *intr.* To acquire polarity. 1838. **b.** In voltaic electricity: see POLARIZATION 2 b. 1856. **3.** *fig.* To give an arbitrary direction, or a special meaning or application, to 1860. **b.** To give unity of direction to 1868. Hence **Po·larizable** *a.* capable of being polarized.

Polarizer (pōᵘ·lărəizəɹ). 1854. [f. prec. + -ER[1].] One who or that which polarizes; *spec.* that plate or prism in a polariscope which polarizes the incident ray of light (opp. to *analyser*).

Polarizing (pōᵘ·lărəiziŋ), *vbl. sb.* 1812. [f. as prec. + -ING[1].] The action of POLARIZE *v.*

attrib. In *p. angle* (Optics), that angle of incidence (differing for different substances) at which the maximum polarization of the incident light takes place.

Polarly (pōᵘ·lăɹli), *adv.* 1830. [f. POLAR *a.* + -LY[2].] In a polar direction, manner, or degree; with reference to poles.

†**Po·lary,** *a.* 1559. [– mod.L. *polaris*, f. L. *polus* POLE *sb.*[2]; see -ARY[2].] **1.** = POLAR *a.* 1. –1658. **2.** = POLAR *a.* 2. –1665.

‖**Polatouche** (pǫlătūʃ). 1827. [Fr. – Russ. *poletukha*.] *Zool.* The small flying squirrel of Europe and N. Asia, *Sciuropterus volans.*

Poldavy (pǫldēⁱ·vi), **poldavis** (pǫldēⁱ·vis). Now *rare.* 1481. [prob. orig. collect. pl. *poldavis*, for **poldavides*, f. *Poldavide* town in Brittany, whence the art of making the stuff was introduced.] A coarse canvas or sacking, orig. woven in Brittany, and formerly much used for sailcloth. Also *attrib.*

Polder (pōᵘ·ldəɹ). 1604. [prob. – MDu. *polre*, (mod.) *polder*.] A piece of low-lying land reclaimed from the sea, a lake, or a river, from which it is protected by dikes. Also *attrib.*

Pole (pōᵘl), *sb.*[1] [Late OE. *pāl*, corresp. to OFris., (M)LG. *pāl*, MDu. *pael* (Du. *paal*), OHG. *pfāl* (G. *pfahl*), ON. *páll*; Gmc. – L. *pālus* stake, prop.] **1.** orig., A stake, without ref. to length or thickness; now, a long, slender, and more or less cylindrical piece of wood (rarely metal); used as a support for a tent, hops or other climbing plants, telegraph or telephone wires, etc., for scaffolding, and for other purposes. **2.** *spec.* **a.** A long tapering wooden shaft fitted to the fore-carriage of a vehicle and attached to the yokes or collars of the draught-animals 1619. **b.** Used as a tradesman's sign 1566. **c.** *Naut.* A ship's mast. Also, the upper end of a mast, rising above the rigging. 1669. **3.** A pole (in sense 1) of definite length used as a measure; hence, a lineal measure; in statutory measure, = 5½ yards; a PERCH, a ROD 1502. **b.** As a measure of area: A square rod or perch; 30¼ square yards 1637.

1. Slang phr. *Up the p.*, in great difficulties; crazy, 'dotty'; under the influence of drink. **2. b.** By a statute still in force, the barbers and surgeons were each to use a p. 1797. **c.** Phr. *With* or *under* (*bare*) *poles*, with no sail set; with furled sails.

attrib. and *Comb.*: **p.-bean,** any climbing bean; **-cap,** the insulating cap of a telegraph pole; †**-clipt** *a.*, hedged in by poles; **-hedge** = ESPALIER 1; **-horse,** a horse harnessed alongside of the p., a wheeler; **-lathe,** a lathe in which the work is turned by a cord passing round it, and fastened at one end to the end of an elastic p., and at the other to a treadle; **-mast,** a mast formed of a single spar; so **-masted** *a.*: **-torpedo,** a torpedo carried on the end of a p., projecting from the bows of a vessel, a spar-torpedo; **-trap,** a circular steel trap set on the top of a post.

Pole, *sb.*[2] late ME. [– L. *polus* end of an axis – Gr. πόλος pivot, axis. Cf. (O)Fr. *pôle*, in part the source.] **1.** Each of the two points in the celestial sphere (*north p.* and *south p.*) about which as fixed points the stars seem to revolve; being the points at which the earth's axis produced meets the celestial sphere. Sometimes also = POLE-STAR. **2.** Each of the extremities (north and south) of the axis of the earth; also of any rotating spherical or spheroidal body (*p. of revolution*) 1551. **3.** Geom. *P. of a circle of the sphere*: each of the two points on the surface of the sphere, in which the axis of that circle cuts the surface; as the poles of the ecliptic on the celestial sphere. late ME. **b.** Hence in *Cryst.*, the point at which a straight line perpendicular to a face or plane of a crystal meets the (ideal) sphere of projection 1878. **4.** *poet.* The sky, the heavens. Also *pl. arch.* or *Obs.* 1572. **5.** *Magn.* Each of the two opposite points or regions on the surface of a magnet at which the magnetic forces are manifested 1574. **6.** *Electr.* Each of the two terminal points (positive and negative) of an electric cell, battery, or machine 1802. **7.** *Biol.* Each extremity of the main axis of any organ of more or less spherical or oval form 1834. **8.** *Geom.* **a.** A fixed point to which other points, lines, etc., are referred; as, the origin of polar co-ordinates; the point of which a curve is a polar. **b.** The point from which a pencil of lines diverges. 1849. **9.** *fig.* Each of two opposed or complementary principles to which the parts of a system or group of phenomena, ideas, etc., are referable 1471.

2. Oh sleep! it is a gentle thing, Beloved from p. to p. COLERIDGE. We're as far apart as the Poles 1880. **4.** Stars unnumber'd gild the glowing p. POPE. **5.** *Magnetic p.*, each of the two points in the polar regions of the earth where the dipping needle takes a vertical position. **9.** The..Nominalists and Realists..each maintained opposite poles of the same truth COLERIDGE.

attrib. and *Comb.*, as **p.-cell** (sense 6); **-changer,** a switch or key for reversing the direction of an electric current; **-piece,** a mass of iron forming the end of an electromagnet, through which the lines of magnetic force are concentrated and directed. Hence **Po·leward** *adv.* towards or in the direction of the (north or south) p.; *adj.* directed or tending towards the p. **Po·lewards** *adv.*

Pole (pōᵘl), *sb.*[3] *rare.* 1668. [– Fr. †*pole* kind of flat fish.] A species of deep-water flounder, *Pleuronectes* (*Glyptocephalus*) *cynoglossus*. Also *p.-dab, -flounder, -fluke.*

Pole, *sb.*[4] 1533. [– G. *Pole*, sing. of *Polen*, in MHG. *Polān*, pl. *-āne* – Polish *Poljane* 'field-dwellers', f. *pole* field.] †**1.** Poland –1671. **2.** A native of Poland 1656. **b.** A Poland fowl 1885.

Pole, *v.* 1573. [f. POLE *sb.*[1]] **1.** *trans.* To furnish with poles. **2.** To attach (a horse) to the carriage-pole 1861. **3.** To push, poke, or strike with a pole; to stir *up*, push *off*, with a pole 1753. **b.** To strike or pierce with a carriage pole 1728. **4.** To propel (a boat or raft) with a pole. Also *intr.* or *absol.* 1774. **5.** To stir (molten metal or glass) with a pole of green wood, to reduce the proportion of oxygen in the mass 1842.

4. *intr.* We poled and paddled up the river 1895.

-pole, comb. element from Gr. -πώλης a seller, dealer, f. πωλεῖν to sell, used rarely to designate a merchant, as in BIBLIOPOLE, etc.

Pole-axe, poleaxe (pōᵘ·l,æks), *sb.* [ME. *pol(l)ax, -ex* – MDu. *pol(l)aex*, MLG. *pol(l)exe*, f. *pol, polle* POLL *sb.*[1] + *æx* AXE; later assoc. with POLE *sb.*[1]] **1.** A kind of axe formerly used as a weapon of war, a battle-axe; also, a short-handled form of this used later in naval warfare for boarding, resisting boarders, cutting ropes, etc. **2.** A halbert or the like carried by the bodyguard of a king or great personage 1562. **3.** An axe with a hammer at the back, used to fell or stun animals; a butcher's axe 1719. Hence **Po·leaxe** *v. trans.* to fell with a p.

Polecat, pole-cat (pōᵘ·lkæt). [The first element is of unkn. origin (OFr. *pole, poule* chicken, fowl, has been suggested; see PULLET), the second is CAT *sb.*[1]] **1.** A small dark-brown carnivorous quadruped, *Putorius fœtidus*, of the *Mustelidæ* or Weasel family, a native of Europe. Called also *fitchet, fitchew, foumart.* **b.** Applied to other species of *Putorius*; also to other *Mustelidæ*, esp. in *U.S.* the skunks 1688. **2.** *fig.* Applied contempt. to a vile person; a courtesan, a prostitute 1598. **3.** *attrib.* 1596.

Poleman (pōᵘ·lmæn). 1838. [f. POLE *sb.*[1] + MAN.] A man who uses, carries, or fights with a pole. **b.** At the Montem at Eton, a name for lower boys, who followed the Oppidans of the fifth form with long white poles 1844.

Polemarch (pǫ·lĭmāɹk). 1656. [– Gr. πολέμαρχος, f. πόλεμος war; see -ARCH.] *Anc. Hist.* An officer in ancient Greece, orig., a military commander-in-chief, but having also civil functions varying according to date and locality.

Polemic (pǫle·mik), *a.* and *sb.* 1638. [– med. L. *polemicus* – Gr. πολεμικός, f. πόλεμος war; see -IC.] **A.** *adj.* Of or pertaining to controversy; controversial, disputatious 1641.

Senseless questions of p. theology 1866.

B. *sb.* **1.** A controversial argument or discussion; aggressive controversy; in *pl.* the practice of this, esp. as a method of conducting theological controversy; opp. to *irenics* 1638. **2.** A controversialist: esp. in theology 1680.

1. Religious polemics..have seldom formed a part of my studies 1800. **2.** The divines of James I.'s court were all casuists and polemics 1886. So **Pole·mical** *a.* warlike, military; also = POLEMIC *a.*; *sb.* a polemical discussion, a controversy (*rare*); **-ly** *adv.* **Pole·micist** (-sist) a writer of polemics.

Polemist (pǫ·lĭmist). 1825. [– Gr. πολεμιστής warrior, f. πόλεμος war; see -IST.] = POLEMIC *sb.* 2.

Po·lemize, *v.* 1828. [– Gr. πολεμίζειν wage war, f. πόλεμος war; see -IZE.] *intr.* To argue polemically; to carry on a controversy.

‖**Polenta** (pole·ntă). OE. [L.; in later use, repr. It. *polenta*.] †**a.** Pearl-barley. †**b.** A kind of barley meal. **c.** Porridge made from steeped and parched barley, or, later, of meal of chestnuts, maize flour, etc.; much used in Italy.

Poler (pō^u·ləɹ). 1688. [f. POLE *sb.*[1] or *v.* + -ER[1].] †**1.** A stirring pole; used in tanning –1775. **2.** One who sets up hop-poles 1848. **3.** The horse harnessed alongside the pole; a wheeler 1881. **4.** One who propels a barge, boat, or canoe by means of a pole 1895.

Pole star (pō^u·lstāːɹ). 1555. [f. POLE *sb.*[2] + STAR *sb.*] **1.** The star α *Ursæ Minoris*, at present about 1° distant from the north pole of the heavens; also called *Polar star* and *Polaris*. **2.** *fig.* A guide or director, a lodestar, a governing principle; a cynosure 1604.

Polewig (pō^u·lwig). *local.* 1880. [See POLLIWOG.] **1.** A tadpole 1882. **2.** A small Thames fish, the Spotted or Freckled Goby 1880.

Poley, polley (pō^u·li), *a. Eng. dial.* and *Austral.* 1844. [f. POLL *sb.*[4] + -Y[1].] Hornless, polled.

Police (pŏlī·s), *sb.* 1530. [– Fr. *police* – med.L. *polītia* for L. *politia*; see POLICY *sb.*[1], POLITY, -ICE. Formerly pronounced (pǫ·lis), as it is still in Scotland and Ireland.] †**I.** = POLICY *sb.*[1] I. 3, 4, 4b. –1768. **II.** †**1.** Civil organization; civilization –1845. **2.** The regulation, discipline, and control of a community; civil administration; enforcement of law; public order 1716. See O.E.D. for historical details. †**b.** In commercial legislation, Public regulation or control of a trade; an economic policy –1866. **c.** The keeping clean of a camp or garrison; the condition of a camp or garrison in respect of cleanliness. *U.S.* 1893. **3.** The department of government which is concerned with the maintenance of public order and safety and the enforcement of the law 1730. **4.** The civil force to which is entrusted the duty of maintaining public order, enforcing regulations for the prevention and punishment of breaches of the law, and detecting crime; construed as *pl.* the members of a police force; the constabulary of a locality 1800. **b.** *transf.* Any body of men, officially employed to keep order, enforce regulations, or maintain a political or ecclesiastical system 1837.

1. A barbarous nation [the Turks], with a barbarous neglect of p., fatal to the human race BURKE. **2.** The p. of the seas was imperfectly kept 1850. **3.** The p. of Glasgow consists of three bodies; the magistrates with the town council, the merchants house, and the trades house 1774. **4.** The entire success of the P. in London. It is impossible to see anything more respectable than they are. WELLINGTON. *Marine P.*, the force instituted *c*1798 to protect the merchant shipping on the Thames in the Port of London. **b.** The railway p. 1837.

attrib. and *Comb.*: **p. captain,** a subordinate officer in the police force in large cities of U.S.; **p. magistrate,** a stipendiary magistrate who presides in a p. court; **p. officer,** a member of a p. force, a constable; †**-runner,** a p. officer of the lowest rank.

Police (pŏlī·s), *v.* 1589. [Partly – Fr. *policer*, f. *police*; partly f. POLICE *sb.*] †**1.** *trans.* To keep in (civil) order, organize, regulate (a state or country). Chiefly in *pass.* –1791. **b.** To make or keep clean (a camp). *U.S.* 1862. **2.** To control, regulate, or keep in order by means of the police, or a similar force 1841. **b.** To furnish, provide, or guard with a police force, or some similar force 1858. **c.** *fig.* To keep in order, administer, control 1886.

2. The navy which polices the seas 1891. **b.** They are building gunboats to p. their coasts 1868.

Poli·ce cou:rt. 1823. A court of summary jurisdiction for the trial or investigation of charges preferred by the police. (At first called POLICE OFFICE.) Also *attrib.*

Policed (pŏlī·st), *ppl. a.* 1591. [f. POLICE *v.* or *sb.* + -ED; orig. (pǫ·list).] †**1.** Politically organized, regulated, or ordered; governed, disciplined –1858. **2.** Provided with or guarded by a police force 1897.

Policeman (pŏlī·smĕn). 1829. A member of the police force; a paid constable. Also *fig.* **b.** A soldier-ant 1877. So **Poli·ce-wo:man,** a woman member of the police force.

Poli·ce O·ffice. 1798. The head-quarters of the police force in a city or town, at which the police business is transacted.

These formerly included a court-room in which offenders were tried, and a place of detention; hence the name was formerly regularly applied to what is now called a POLICE COURT.

Poli·ce sta·tion. 1858. The office or headquarters of a local police force, or of a police district.

Policy (pǫ·lĭsi), *sb.*[1] [In Branch I, XIV *policie* – OFr. *policie* – L. *politia* – Gr. πολιτεία citizenship, government, etc., f. πολίτης, f. πόλις city, state. (See POLICE *sb.*) Branch II is due to the association of this Græco-L. word with L. *politus* polished, refined.] **I. 1.** A constitution, polity. Now *rare* or *Obs.* †**b.** An organized state, a commonwealth –1558. †**2.** Government, administration; political science –1796. **3.** Political sagacity; statecraft; diplomacy; in bad sense, political cunning. late ME. **4.** In ref. to conduct or action generally: Prudent, expedient, or advantageous procedure; prudent or politic course of action; as a quality of the agent: sagacity, shrewdness, artfulness; in bad sense, cunning, craftiness. late ME. †**b.** A device, expedient, contrivance; a crafty device, stratagem, trick –1849. **5.** A course of action adopted and pursued by a government, party, ruler, statesman, etc.; any course of action adopted as advantageous or expedient. (The chief living sense.) late ME.

2. Turne him to any Cause of Pollicy The Gordian Knot of it he will vnloose SHAKS. *Court of P.*, the Legislative Council in British Guiana. **3.** In this..he was actuated by p. rather than sentiment FREEMAN. **4.** Our grosse conceipts, who think honestie the best policie 1599. **5.** Thys was the crafty polycye of the clergye 1544. Edward's foreign p. 1861.

II. Sc. senses influenced by L. *politus* polished, etc. †**a.** The improvement or embellishment of an estate, building, town, etc. –1555. †**b.** The improvements, etc., so made; property created by human skill and labour –1594. **c.** The (enclosed, planted, and partly embellished) park or demesne land lying around a country seat or gentleman's house 1775.

Policy (pǫ·lisi), *sb.*[2] 1565. [Earliest form *police* – Fr. *police* – Pr. *polissa, -issia*, Cat. *-ice*, prob. :– med.L. *apódissa, -ixa*, alt. of L. *apodixis* – Gr. ἀπόδειξις demonstration, proof, f. ἀποδεικνύναι (see APODICTIC).] **1.** More fully *p. of assurance* or *insurance p.*: A document containing an undertaking, in consideration of a *premium* or *premiums*, to pay a specified amount or part thereof in the event of a specified contingency. **b.** A conditional promissory note, depending on the result of a wager 1623. **c.** A form of gambling in which bets are made on numbers to be drawn in a lottery. *U.S.* 1890. †**2.** [= It. *polizza* ticket.] A voting-paper; a voucher, warrant –1675.

1. *Floating p.*, a p. in which there is no limitation of the risk to a particular ship, as where goods 'on ship or ships' are insured for the same voyage. *Open p.*, one in which the value of the subject insured is left to be estimated in case of loss. *Wager* or *wagering p.*, a p. of insurance taken out where the insured has no real interest in the thing insured: now declared illegal as a species of gambling.

Comb.: **p.-shop,** *U.S.* a place for gambling by betting on the drawing of certain numbers in a lottery.

†**Po·licy,** *v.* 1565. [– Fr. †*policier* administer, f. †*policie*; see POLICY *sb.*[1], POLICE *v.*] = POLICE *v.* 1. –1824. Hence †**Po·licied** *ppl. a.* civilly organized.

Poling (pō^u·liŋ), *vbl. sb.* 1573. [f. POLE *v.* + -ING[1].] **1.** The action of POLE *v.*, in various senses. **2.** *concr.* Poles collectively, as used for poling hops, or for lining the sides of a tunnel 1842.

‖**Poliomyelitis** (pǫːlio,mai,ĕlai·tis). 1880. [mod.L., f. Gr. πολιός grey + μυελός marrow + -ITIS.] *Path.* Inflammation of the grey matter of the spinal cord.

-polis, repr. Gr. πόλις city, as in METROPOLIS, etc.; occas. used (in the form *-opolis*) to form nicknames of cities or towns, e.g. COTTONOPOLIS (Manchester), *Porkopolis* (Chicago).

Polish (pǫ·liʃ), *sb.* 1597. [f. POLISH *v.*] **1.** The act of polishing or condition of being polished; smoothness and usu. glossiness of surface produced by friction 1704. **2.** *fig.* Refinement 1597. **3.** A substance used to produce smoothness or glossiness on any surface, as FRENCH P., etc. 1819.

1. Another Prism of clearer Glass and better P. NEWTON. **2.** This Roman p., and this smooth behaviour ADDISON.

Polish (pō^u·liʃ), *a.* 1704. [f. POLE *sb.*[4] + -ISH[1].] Of or pertaining to Poland or its inhabitants.

Polish (pǫ·liʃ), *v.* [ME. *polis(s* – *poliss-*, lengthened stem of (O)Fr. *polir* – L. *polire*; see -ISH[2], POLITE.] **1.** *trans.* To make smooth and (usu.) glossy by friction. **b.** *intr.* for *pass.* †(*a*) To become bright. (*b*) To become smooth, take a smooth and (usu.) glossy surface. late ME. **2.** *fig. trans.* To free from roughness, rudeness, or coarseness; to make more elegant or cultured; to refine ME. **b.** *intr.* for *pass.* To become refined 1727. **3.** *trans.* To bring to a finished or complete state; to deck out, adorn. Const. *out, up.* 1581. **4.** *To p. off*: to finish off quickly; to do for or get rid of summarily. *colloq.* (orig. *Pugilistic slang*). 1829.

1. Hard Wood they p. with Bees-wax 1703. **b.** A kind of steel..which would p. almost as..bright as silver BACON. **2.** Arts that p. Life MILT. Hence **Po·lishable** *a.* capable of being polished. **Po·lished-ly** *adv.*, **-ness.**

Polisher (pǫ·liʃəɹ). ME. [f. prec. + -ER[1].] One who, or that which, polishes, *lit.* or *fig.*

Polishing (pǫ·liʃiŋ), *vbl. sb.* 1530. [f. as prec. + -ING[1].] The action of POLISH *v.*; the fact of being polished.

attrib. in names of tools, appliances, etc., used in producing a polish; as *p.-block, -iron, -paste, -powder, -stick, -wheel*; **p.-mill,** a lap of metal or other material used by lapidaries in polishing gems (Knight); **-slate,** (*a*) a grey or yellow slate found in the coal-measures of Bohemia, etc., used for polishing; (*b*) a kind of whetstone; **-snake,** a kind of serpentine formerly used for polishing lithographic stones.

Polite (pŏlai·t), *a.* 1450. [– L. *politus*, pa. pple. of *polire* smooth, polish.] †**1.** *lit.* Smoothed, polished, burnished –1737. †**b.** Cleansed, trim, orderly –1703. **2.** *transf.* **a.** Of the arts, literature, etc.: Polished, refined, elegant; correct, scholarly. (Now only in certain collocations.) 1501. **b.** Of persons: Polished, refined, cultivated, well-bred, modish 1629. **c.** Of refined manners; courteous, mannerly, urbane. (The chief current use.) 1762.

1. P. Bodies, as Looking-Glasses 1678. **2. a.** P. Learning BENTLEY. A p. education 1786. **b.** Whatever the p. and learned may think MACAULAY. **c.** The French are the politest enemies in the world 1772. Hence **Poli·te-ly** *adv.*, **-ness.**

‖**Politesse** (politęs). 1717. [Fr. – It. *politezza, pulitezza*, f. *pulito* POLITE *a.*] Politeness; now usu. *depreciatory.*

Politic (pǫ·litik), *a.* and *sb.* late ME. [– (O)Fr. *politique* sb. and adj. – L. *politicus* – Gr. πολιτικός civic, civil, political (as sb., politician), f. πολίτης citizen, f. πόλις city, state; see -IC.] **A.** *adj.* †**1.** = POLITICAL *a.* 1 (by which it is now superseded) –1756. **b.** Pertaining to a constitutional state, as dist. from a despotism; constitutional (*rare*) 1449. **2.** Characterized by policy; (of persons) sagacious, prudent, shrewd; (of actions or things) judicious, expedient, skilfully contrived. late ME. **b.** In a sinister sense: Scheming, crafty, cunning; diplomatic, artfully contriving or contrived 1580.

1. †*P. body* = *body p.*: see BODY *sb.* IV. 1. **2.** Enrich'd With politike graue Counsell SHAKS. A prudent and Politick Captain 1686. To learn of an enemy has always been accounted politick JOHNSON. **b.** These being the craftiest and politiquest sort of knaves 1667.

B. *sb.* †**1.** A politician –1738. †**b.** An indifferentist in matters of religion, a worldly-wise man; see POLITIQUE –1633. †**2.** Policy; politics –1715. **3.** *pl. Politics.* The science and art of government; the science dealing with the form, organization, and administration of a state or part of one, and with the regulation of its relations with other states (hence *imperial, national,* *domestic, municipal, parochial, foreign politics*, etc.). Also †*the politics*, that branch of moral philosophy dealing with the state or social organism as a whole. 1529. **b.** *The Politics*: name of Aristotle's treatise on political science, τὰ πολιτικά 1651. †**c.** Political actions or practice; policy –1741. **d.** Political affairs or business; political life 1693. **e.** The political principles, opinions, or sympathies *of* a person or party 1769. **f.** *fig.* Conduct of private affairs; politic management, scheming, planning 1693.

1. Amongst states men and politikes BACON. **b.** Worldlings, and Depraued Politickes, who are apt to contemne Holy Things BACON. **2.** This did not suit with Popish P. BENTLEY. **3.** Machiavelli.. founded the science of politics for the modern world 1883. **c.** Confound their politicks, Frustrate their knavish tricks *God save the King*. **d.** She now agrees with me, that Politicks is not the Business of a Woman 1714. **e.** Most men's politics sit much too loosely about them '*Junius' Lett.* **f.** A lecture on prudence, and matrimonial politics FIELDING. Phr., *Not practical politics*; Hence **Po·liticly** *adv.*, in a politic manner. with policy; shrewdly; artfully 1477.

Political (pŏli·tikăl), *a.* (*sb.*) 1551. [f. L. *politicus* (see prec.) + -AL[1]; see -ICAL.] **A.** *adj.* **1.** Of, belonging or pertaining to, the state, its government and policy; public, civil; of or pertaining to the science or art of politics. **b.** Of persons: Engaged in civil administration; *spec.* in India, having, as a government official, the function of advising the ruler of a native state on political matters, as *p. agent, resident*. 1849. **2.** Having an organized government or polity. †Said also of bees, ants, etc. 1657. **3.** Concerned or dealing with politics or the science of government 1646. **4.** Belonging to or taking a side in politics; in a bad sense, partisan, factious 1769. †**5.** = POLITIC A. 2. –1817.

1. The true p. spirit; the faculty of nation-making GLADSTONE. **3.** The highest positions in p. life 1885. **4.** The malice of p. writers '*Junius' Lett.*

Phrases. *P. economy*: see ECONOMY 2. *P. geography*, that part of geography which deals with the boundaries, divisions, and possessions of states. *P. prisoner*, a person imprisoned for a p. offence. *P. verse* [Gr. πολιτικός popular], in Byzantine and mod. Gr. literature, verse composed by accent, not quantity, with an accent on the last syllable but one.

B. *sb.* (the adj. used ellipt.) **1. a.** = Political agent, officer, resident; see above, 1 b. 1848. **b.** = *political prisoner*; see above 1888. †**2.** *pl.* Political matters, politics –1734. Hence **Poli·tically** *adv.* 1588.

Politicaster (poli·tikæstəɹ). *rare.* 1641. [– It. (or Sp.) *politicastro*; see POLITIC B., -ASTER.] A petty, feeble, or contemptible politician.

Politician (pǫliti·ʃăn). 1588. [f. as POLITIC + -IAN.] †**1.** A politic person; *esp.* a crafty intriguer –1764. **2.** One versed in the theory of government or the art of governing; one practically engaged in conducting the business of the state; a statesman 1589. **b.** One interested in politics; one who engages in party politics, esp. as a profession; also (esp. in *U.S.*) in a sinister sense, one who lives by politics as a trade 1628. †**3.** = POLITIQUE –1681. **4.** *attrib.* 1638.

1. 1 *Hen. IV*, I. iii. 241. **2.** That felicity Politisians search after, as being the end of civil life 1634. **b.** That insidious and crafty animal, vulgarly called a statesman or p. ADAM SMITH.

Politicize (poli·tisəiz), *v.* 1758. [f. as POLITIC + -IZE.] **1.** *intr.* To act the politician; to engage in or talk politics. **2.** *trans.* To give a political character to 1846.

Poli·tico-, comb. form of Gr. πολιτικός civil, political, denoting **a.** 'politically, as applied to politics', as *p.-ethical, -geographical*, etc.; **p.-economical,** pertaining to political economy; **b.** 'political and...' as *p.-commercial, -military, -theological*, etc.; **p.-religious,** pertaining to politics as influenced by or dependent on religion; at once political and religious; also used to form sbs., as **poli:ticopho·bia,** a horror of politics.

‖**Politique** (politīk). 1609. [Fr., prop. adj. 'political'.] One of an opportunist and moderate party, which arose in France c1573, during the Huguenot wars, and regarded peace and political reform as more urgent than the decision by arms of the religious quarrel; also, a sympathizer with this party elsewhere, and opprobriously, an indifferentist, a temporizer.

Politize (pǫ·litəiz), *v. rare.* 1598. [f. POLITY + -IZE.] †**1. a.** *trans.* To deal with or treat (a matter) politicly, diplomatically, or craftily. **b.** *intr.* To deal politicly or diplomatically. –1641. **2.** †**a.** To have political relations. **b.** To deal in politics (*rare*). 1623.

†**Po·liture.** 1592. [– Fr. †*politure* – L. *politura*, f. *polit-*, pa. ppl. stem of *polire*; see POLISH *sb.*, -URE.] Polishing; polish, smoothness –1776. **b.** Elegance of form; polish of style, manners, or habits; refinement –1720.

Polity (pǫ·lĭti). 1538. [– L. *politia* – Gr. πολιτεία; see POLICY *sb.*[1]] **1.** Civil order. **b.** Administration of a state; civil government 1715. **2. a.** A particular form of political organization 1597. **b.** An organized society; a state 1650. †**3.** = POLICY *sb.*[1] I. 2–4. –1843.

1. Nor is it possible that any form of politie, much lesse politie ecclesiasticall should be good, vnlesse God himselfe bee authour of it HOOKER. **2. b.** The soul of man is intended to be a well-ordered p. 1840.

Politzerize (poli·tsĕrəiz), *v.* 1879. [f. Adam *Politzer*, a physician of Vienna, who introduced the method; see -IZE.] *trans.* To inflate the tympanic cavity of (a patient) through the Eustachian tube. Hence **Poli:tzeriza·tion.**

†**Polk,** *v.* 1845. [– Fr. *polker*, f. *polka*; see next.] *intr.* To dance the polka –1876.

Polka (pǫ·lkă, pōᵘ·lkă), *sb.*[1] 1844. [– G., Fr. *polka* – Czech *půlka* half-step, f. *půl* half. Cf. MAZURKA.] **1.** A lively dance of Bohemian origin, the music for which is in duple time. **2.** A piece of music for this, or in its time or rhythm 1844. Hence **Po·lka** *v. intr.* to dance the p.

†**Po·lka,** *sb.*[2] 1844. [f. prec.] A woman's tight-fitting jacket, usu. knitted; more fully *p.-jacket* –1859.

Poll (pōᵘl), *sb.*[1] ME. [perh. of L.Du. origin (cf. obs. Du., LG. *polle*); but OE. *poll* in place-names, possibly meaning 'hill', may orig. have meant 'head'.] **I. 1.** The human head. (Not now in serious literary use.) **2.** *spec.* **a.** The part of the head on which the hair grows; the head as characterized by the colour or state of the hair 1602. **b.** The crown or top of the head. late ME. **c.** The nape of the neck 1671. **3.** = HEAD *sb.* I. 7, 7 b. *Obs.* exc. in legal phr. CHALLENGE *to the polls*. ME. **4.** Short for *p.-tax*. *Obs.* or *Hist.* 1684.

2. a. All Flaxen was his Pole SHAKS. **c.** The arrow pierced his neck from throat to p. HOBBES. **3.** Twenty poule of pultrey 1544. *P. by p.*, one by one; Take them p. by p. PRYNNE.

II. From I. 3, app. infl. by POLL *v.* †**1. a.** Muster –1613. **b.** Counting of heads; census –1697. **2.** The counting of voters; the entering of votes, in order to their being counted; esp. at the election of parliamentary or other representatives 1625. **b.** The voting at an election 1832. **c.** The number of votes recorded 1853.

1. a. *Cor.* III. i. 134. **2.** It is not a question to be decided by a p. 1857. **b.** The recent reverses at the p. 1877. **c.** He stood at the head of the p. 1853.

III. Transf. uses. **a.** The top or crown of a hat or cap 1704. **b.** The blunt end of the head of a miner's pick or hammer 1603.

attrib. and *Comb.*: **p.-book,** an official register, previous to the Ballot Act, of the votes given; now, of those qualified to vote; **-clerk,** a clerk who records the votes polled; **-evil,** an inflamed or ulcerous sore between the ligament and the first bone of the neck of a horse; **-pick,** a miner's pick with a p.; †**-money,** capitation, poll-tax; **-tax,** a capitation or head-tax.

Poll (pǫl), *sb.*[2] 1630. [alt. f. MOLL; var. of and contemp. with POLLY.] Used as the conventional proper name of any parrot; hence = parrot. So **Poll-pa·rrot** (also used *fig.* and *attrib.*), whence **Poll-pa·rrot** *v. trans.* and *intr.* = PARROT *v.*

Poll (pǫl), *sb.*[3] *Camb. Univ. slang.* Also **pol.** 1831. [Explained as – Gr. οἱ πολλοί the many.] *The P.*: the passmen. *To go out in the P.*: to come out in the list of those who take a pass degree. Also *attrib.*

Poll (pōᵘl), *a.* and *sb.*[4] late ME. [Short for *pold* POLLED *ppl. a.*] **A.** *adj.* **1.** Polled or cut even at the edge (see POLL *v.* II. 2); as in DEED POLL, POLL DEED 1523. **2.** In *Comb.* **a.** In names of animals without horns, as *poll-sheep* 1773. †**b.** (Usu. *pol-*.) In names of beardless cereals, as *polbarley, polbere, polwheat* –1601. **B.** *sb.* Short for *p.-beast, -ox, -cow* (see A. 2 a); *esp.* one of a breed of hornless oxen 1789.

Poll (pōᵘl), *v.* ME. [f. POLL *sb.*[1]] **I.** *trans.* To cut short the hair of (a person or animal); to crop, clip, shear; also with the head, hair, etc. as object. *Obs.* or *arch.* **II. 1.** To cut off the top of (a tree or plant); *esp.* to pollard; also, to lop the branches of. Also *transf.* and *fig.* 1577. †**b.** To behead –1661. **2.** To cut even the edge of (a sheet, as in a deed executed by one person) 1628. **3.** To cut off the horns of (cattle) 1607.

2. A deed made by one party only is not indented, but polled or shaved quite even BLACKSTONE.

III. *fig.* To plunder by or as by excessive taxation; to pillage, rob, fleece; to despoil (a person or place) of (anything). *arch.* †Also *absol.* or *intr.* 1489. **IV.** †**1.** To count heads –1711. **2.** To take the votes of; in *pass.* to have one's vote taken, to record a vote 1625. **b.** Of a candidate: To bring to the poll as voters; to receive (so many votes) 1846. **3.** *intr.* To vote at a poll 1678. **b.** *trans.* To give or record (a vote) 1717.

2. That more excellent way of polling by the Ballot BRIGHT. **b.** Birney polled just enough votes to defeat Clay 1892.

Pollack, pollock (pǫ·lək). Also †**podlok, podley.** 1602. [Earlier Sc. *podlock* (XVI), later *podley*; of unkn. origin.] A sea-fish of the genus *Pollachius*, allied to the cod, but having the lower jaw protruding; *esp.* the true or whiting p., *Pollachius pollachius*, of European seas, also called *green-fish, lythe*, etc.; and the green p. or COAL-FISH, *Pollachius virens* or *carbonarius*, of the North Atlantic generally.

Pollan (pǫ·lăn). 1713. [perh. f. Ir. *poll* inland lake + *-an*, Celt. deriv. formative.] A species of freshwater fish, *Coregonus pollan*, found in the inland loughs of Ireland.

Po·llard, *sb.*[1] *Obs.* exc. *Hist.* ME. [app. f. POLL *sb.*[1] + -ARD (in ref. to its device, a head); cf. TESTER[3], TESTON.] A base coin of foreign origin, current in England in the 13th c., as an equivalent of the penny; in 1299 declared illegal.

Pollard (pǫ·lăɹd), *sb.*[2] (*a.*) 1523. [f. POLL *v.* + -ARD.] **I. 1.** An animal that has cast or lost its horns, as a stag; also, an ox, sheep, or goat of a hornless variety 1546. **2.** A tree which has been polled or cut back, so as to produce a thick close growth of young branches, forming a rounded head or mass 1662. †**3.** Short for *pollard wheat* –1688. **II.** Bran sifted from flour; *techn.* a finer grade of bran containing some flour; also, flour or meal containing the finer bran. (Cf. TOPPINGS.) 1577. **B.** *attrib.* or *adj.* †**1.** Of wheat: Beardless, awnless –1765. **2.** That is a pollard (tree); polled, lopped 1669.

Pollard (pǫ·lăɹd), *v.* 1670. [f. prec.] *trans.* To cut off the branches of (a tree), leaving only the main trunk; to make a pollard of.

I hate to see trees pollarded—or nations 1836.

Po·ll deed. Now *rare.* 1523. [f. POLL *a.* + DEED.] = DEED POLL.

Polled (pōᵘld), *ppl. a.* ME. [f. POLL *v.* + -ED[1].] †**1.** Having the hair cut short; shorn, shaven; also of the hair: clipped –1650. **2.** Hornless 1607. **3.** Of trees: Pollarded 1611. †**4.** *P. deed* = POLL DEED –1706.

1. With pollid heed WYCLIF. P. lockes SIDNEY. **2.** A herd of Red P. Cattle 1902.

Pollen (pǫ·lĕn), *sb.* 1523. [– L. *pollen* flour, fine powder, rel. to POLENTA, *pulvis* powder, *puls* PULSE *sb.*[2]] †**1.** Fine flour or meal; fine powder –1736. **2.** *Bot.* The fine powdery substance, produced by and discharged from the anther of a flower, constituting the male element that fecundates the ovules 1760.

Comb.: **p.-cell,** (*a*) a cell which develops into a pollen-grain, or forms part of one; (*b*) = *p.-sac*;

(*c*) a cell in a honeycomb in which p. is stored; **-grain,** each of the grains of which p. consists; **-granule,** each of the ultimate granules contained in a pollen-grain; also = *p.-grain*; **-sac,** each of the (usu. four) cavities or loculi of an anther, in which the p. is contained; **-tube,** a tube formed by protrusion of the intine of a pollen-grain when deposited upon the stigma, which penetrates the style so as to convey the fecundating substance to the ovule. Hence **Po·llen** *v. trans.* to convey p. to, to pollinate.

†**Po·llenin.** 1816. [– Fr. *pollénine*, f. POLLEN; see -IN[1].] *Chem.* A supposed peculiar substance obtained from pollen, and from the spores of *Lycopodium* –1895.

Poller (pōᵘ·ləɹ). 1513. [f. POLL *v.* + -ER[1].] †**1.** A barber or hair-cutter –1688. **b.** One who polls trees 1828. †**2.** A plunderer, extortioner, despoiler –1674. **3. a.** A voter 1776. **b.** One who registers voters 1828.

‖**Pollex** (pǫ·leks). *Pl.* **pollices** (-isīz). 1835. [L., = thumb, great toe.] *Anat.* The innermost digit of the fore limb in air-breathing vertebrates; in man, etc. the thumb. Occas. including the corresponding digit of the hind limb (the great toe), distinctively called HALLUX.

Pollicitation (pǫlisitēⁱ·ʃən). 1528. [– Fr. *pollicitation* or L. *pollicitatio*, f. *pollicitari* bid at auction, f. *pollicēri* promise; see -ATION.] The action of promising; a promise; a document containing a promise; *Civil Law*, a promise not formally accepted, and therefore in certain cases revocable.

Pollinate (pǫ·lineⁱt), *v.* 1875. [f. L. *pollen, pollin-*; see POLLEN, -ATE[3].] *trans.* To besprinkle with pollen or shed pollen upon (the stigma, etc.) in order to fertilization. So **Pollina·tion,** the action of pollinating. **Po·llinator,** an insect which assists pollination.

†**Polli·nctor.** 1646. [– L. *pollinctor*, f. *pollingere* wash (a corpse) and prepare it for the funeral pile.] One who prepared a dead body for burning or embalming, by washing, etc. –1705.

Polling (pōᵘ·liŋ), *vbl. sb.* late ME. [f. POLL *v.* + -ING[1].] The action of POLL *v. spec.* **1.** The cutting off of the top of a tree 1626. †**2.** Plundering, extortion, robbery –1665. **3.** The registering or casting of votes 1625.

attrib., as *p.-agent, -booth, -clerk*, etc.; †**p.-penny, -pence,** money exacted as poll-tax; hence, esp. in *pl.*, a poll-tax.

Polliniferous (pǫlini·fĕrəs), *a.* Also erron. **pollen-.** 1830. [f. L. *pollen, -in-*; see POLLEN, -FEROUS.] *Bot.* Bearing or producing pollen.

Pollinigerous (pǫlini·dʒĕrəs), *a.* 1819. [f. as prec. + -GEROUS.] *Entom.* Carrying, or adapted for carrying, pollen.

‖**Pollinium** (pǒli·niǒm). *Pl.* **-ia.** 1862. [mod. L., f. *pollen, pollin-* POLLEN 2 + *-ium* as in *antheridium*; see -IUM.] *Bot.* A coherent mass of pollen grains in each cavity of the anther, characteristic of the *Orchidaceæ* and *Asclepiadaceæ.*

‖**Pollinodium** (pǫlinōᵘ·diǒm). 1875. [mod. L., f. as prec. + *-odium*; see -ODE, -IUM.] *Bot.* The antheridium or male reproductive organ in ascomycetous fungi. Hence **Pollino·dial** *a.* pertaining to or of the nature of a p.

Polliwog, pollywog (pǫ·liwǫg). *dial.* and *U.S.* [XV *polwygle*, later *polwigge* (XVI), f. POLL *sb.*[1] + WIGGLE and synon. dial. *wig*, alt. by assim. of the vowels of initial and final syllables.] A tadpole.

Pollucite (pǫ·liusəit). 1868. [orig. named *Pollux* (Breithaupt, 1846), being assoc. with *Castor* or CASTORITE.] *Min.* Silicate of aluminium and cæsium, found in brilliant transparent colourless crystals.

Pollute (pǒlⁱū·t), *ppl. a. Obs.* exc. *poet.* late ME. [– L. *pollutus*, pa. pple. of *polluere*; see next, -ATE[2].] = POLLUTED *ppl. a.*

Pollute (pǒlⁱū·t), *v.* late ME. [– *pollut-*, pa. ppl. stem of L. *polluere*, f. **por-* PRO-*pref.*[1] + base of *lutum* mud.] **1.** *trans.* To render ceremonially or morally impure; to profane, desecrate, to sully, corrupt. **2.** To make physically impure, foul, or filthy; to dirty, stain, taint, befoul 1548.

1. Churches and altars were polluted by atrocious murders GIBBON. **2.** Thei..with their proper bloud, embrued and polluted their awne handes HALL. Hence **Pollu·ted** *ppl. a.* defiled, rendered impure or unclean. **Pollu·ted-ly** *adv.*, **-ness. Pollu·ter,** one who pollutes.

Pollution (pǒlⁱū·ʃən). ME. [– (O)Fr. *pollution* or L. *pollutio*, f. as prec.; see -ION.] **1.** The action of polluting, or condition of being polluted; defilement; uncleanness or impurity. late ME. **2.** Ceremonial impurity or defilement; profanation. late ME. **3.** Seminal emission apart from coition ME.

2. Thir strife p. brings Upon the Temple MILT.

Pollux (pǫ·lǒks). 1526. [– L. *Pollux*, earlier *Polluces* – Gr. Πολυδεύκης.] *Gr. Myth.* Name of one of the twin sons of Tyndarus and Leda; hence in *Astron.* the second star in the constellation Gemini; see CASTOR[3].

Polly (pǫ·li). 1616. Dim. (see -Y[6]) of POLL *sb.*[2]; as female name, and name for a parrot.

Polo (pōᵘ·lo). 1872. [– Balti (Indus valley) *polo* ball, = Tibetan *pulu.*] **1.** A game of Eastern origin resembling hockey, played on horseback with long-handled clubs and a wooden ball. **2.** A ball-game with goals played by swimmers (*water p.*); †hockey played on skates (*rink p.*) 1884. **3.** *attrib.* as *p.-match, pony*, etc.

Polonaise (pǫlŏnēⁱ·z, pōᵘl-), *sb.* 1773. [– Fr. *polonaise* (sc. *robe* dress, *danse* dance), subst. use of fem. of *polonais* Polish, f. med. L. *Polonia* Poland.] **1.** A dress or over-dress consisting of a bodice, with a skirt open from the waist downwards; orig. suggested by the dress of Polish women. **2.** A slow dance of Polish origin, consisting chiefly of an intricate march, procession, or promenade of the dancers in couples; also, the music for this, or any music written in its peculiar triple rhythm 1797. Hence **Polonai·se** *v. intr.* to dance a p.; to move in a slow and stately manner.

†**Polone·se,** *sb.* and *a.* 1755. [– Fr. *polonais* Polish, It. *Polonese*; see prec., -ESE.] **A.** *sb.* **1.** = POLONAISE 1, or the material for this –1774. **2.** A Pole –1810. **B.** *adj.* = POLISH *a.* –1744.

Polonian (pǒlōᵘ·niăn), *a.* and *sb. Obs.* or *arch.* 1555. [f. med.L. *Polonia* Poland + -AN.] Polish; a Pole.

Polonium (pǒlōᵘ·niǒm). 1898. [– Fr. (mod.L.) *polonium*, f. med.L. *Polonia* Poland; see -IUM. Named from the Polish nationality of Madame Curie.] *Chem.* A highly radio-active metallic element, discovered in 1898 by Prof. and Madame Curie in pitchblende.

Polony (pǒlōᵘ·ni). 1764. [Earliest as *pullony sausage*; prob. for *Bolognian, Bologna, sausage*; see BOLOGNA.] A sausage made of partly cooked pork.

Polt (pōᵘlt). *Obs.* exc. *dial.* 1610. [Of unkn. origin.] **1.** A blow, a hard knock. Now *dial.* †**2.** A pestle or club –1612.

‖**Poltergeist** (pǫ·ltəɹ,gəist). 1838. [G., f. *poltern* make a noise, create a disturbance + *geist* GHOST.] A spirit which makes its presence known by noises; a noisy spirit.

Po·lt-foot. *arch.* 1579. [app. f. POLT 2 + FOOT *sb.*] **1.** A club-foot. **2.** *attrib.* (often **poltfoot**) = *polt-footed* 1589. Hence **Po·lt-footed** *a.* club-footed.

Poltroon (pǫltrū·n). 1529. [– Fr. *poltron*, †*poultron* – It. *poltrone* sluggard, coward (cf. med.L. *pultro* XIII St. Francis), perh. f. †*poltro* bed (as if 'lie-abed').] A spiritless coward; a mean-spirited, worthless wretch; a craven. Also *attrib.* So **Poltroo·nery,** the behaviour of a p.; †laziness; pusillanimity, cowardice. **Poltroo·nish** *a.*

Poly, poley (pōᵘ·li). 1578. [– L. *polium*, *polion* (Plin.) – Gr. πόλιον an aromatic plant, perh. f. πολιός hoary.] †A species of Germander, *Teucrium polium*, an aromatic herb of Southern Europe; also extended to other species of *Teucrium*, as Golden P. (*T. aureum*), Yellow P. (*T. flavescens*) –1608. **b. Poly-mountain,** also **poly of the mountain, mountain poly** [– L. *polium montanum*], name of an aromatic herb, variously identified 1578.

Poly- (pǫli), repr. Gr. πολυ-, comb. form of πολύς, πολύ much, in pl. πολλοί, -αί, -ά many, forming the first element in compounds, the second element of which is prop. of Greek origin, often of Latin, and occas. English.

1. General words. **Po·lyarch** [Gr. ἀρχή beginning], *a. Bot.* proceeding from many points of origin; said of the primary xylem or woody tissue of a stem or root. **Po·lyarchy** [Gr. -αρχία rule], the government of a state or city by many; *Bot.* the condition of being polyarch. †**Poly-auto·graphy,** early name for LITHOGRAPHY, as applied to the production of numerous copies of autographs, etc. **Polyca·rpellary,** *a. Bot.* having or consisting of several carpels. **Poly-ca·rpic** (*rare*), **-ca·rpous** [Gr. καρπός fruit], *adjs. Bot.* †(*a*) bearing fruit many times, as a perennial plant; (*b*) = *polycarpellary*. **Poly-chro·ic** [Gr. χρόα colour], *a. Cryst.* = PLEOCHROIC. **Polycli·nic,** (*a*) an institution giving clinical instruction in all kinds of diseases; (*b*) a hospital for the treatment of all kinds of disease. **Poly-cotyle·don,** *Bot.* a plant of which the seed contains more than two cotyledons. **Po·lycrase** [Gr. κρᾶσις mixture], *Min.* a shining black mineral, consisting of columbate and titanate of uranium, zirconium, yttrium, etc. **Polyda·ctyl,** *a. Zool.* having more than the normal number of fingers or toes; *sb.* a polydactyl animal. **Polydi·psia,** morbid or abnormal thirst. **Polydyna·mic** [Gr. δύναμις power], *a.* relating to or possessing many forces or powers. **Polye·mbryonate,** *a. Bot.* containing more than one embryo, as a seed; so **Polyembryo·nic** *a.*; **Polye·mbryony,** the formation or presence of more than one embryo in a seed. **Polyga·stric,** *a.* having many stomachs or digestive cavities; belonging to certain infusorians formerly called *Polygastrica*; also as *sb.* **Polygoneu·tic** [Gr. γονεύειν beget], *a. Zool.* producing several broods in a year. **Po·lygram** [Gr. γραμμή line], a figure consisting of many lines, with their points of intersection. ‖**Polyhæ·mia** [Gr. αἷμα blood], *Path.* fullness or excess of blood; plethora. **Polylogy** (pǒli·lŏdʒi) [-LOGY], much speaking, loquacity (*rare*). **Polymeni·scous** [MENISCUS], *a.* composed of many lenses, as the eye of an insect. ‖**Poly-o·ptron** [Gr. -οπτρον, naming instruments of sight], an optical instrument through which objects appear multiplied. **Po·lypetal** (*rare*), **-pe·talous,** *adjs. Bot.* having many petals; usu. = having the petals distinct or separate, not coherent or united. ‖**Polypha·gia,** *Phys.* and *Path.* excessive eating; voracious or ravenous appetite; *Zool.* the habit of feeding on various kinds of food. **Poly·phagous** [Gr. -φάγος eating], *a.* eating much, voracious; *Zool.* feeding upon various kinds of food. **Polypha·rmacy,** *Med.* the use of many drugs or medicines in the treatment of disease. **Polyphyle·tic** [PHYLETIC], *a.* belonging to several tribes or families; polygenetic. **Polyphy·llous,** *a. Bot.* having many leaves; usu., having the (perianth-) leaves separate, not united. **Polypragma·tic,** *a.* busying oneself about many affairs; meddlesome, officious; †also as *sb.*; so †**Polypragma·tical** *a.*; **Polypra·gmatism. Polypro·todont** [Gr. πρῶτος first + ὀδούς, ὀδοντ- tooth], *a. Zool.* having more than two front or incisor teeth in the lower jaw; *sb.* a polyprotodont marsupial. **Polypsychical** (-psəi·kikăl) [Gr. ψυχή soul], *a.* having many souls, many-souled; so **Polypsy·chic** *a.*, **Polypsy·chism. Polyptych** (pǫ·liptik) [Gr. πτυχή fold], anything consisting of more than three leaves or panels folded together. ‖**Polysarcia** (-sā·ɹsiă) [Gr. σάρξ, σαρκ- flesh], *Path.* excessive growth of flesh (or, loosely, of fat); corpulence, obesity. **Polyse·palous** [mod.L. *sepalum* SEPAL], *a. Bot.* prop., having numerous sepals; but used for, having the sepals distinct or separate, not coherent or united. **Po·lysperm** [Gr. σπέρμα seed], *a. Bot.* having or producing many seeds (*rare*). **Po·lyspermy,** *Phys.* impregnation of an ovum by more than one spermatozoon. **Po·lyspore,** *Bot.* (*a*) a spore-case containing numerous spores; (*b*) a compound spore, as in certain algæ; so **Polyspo·rous,** *a.* having or producing numerous spores. **Polysto·matous** [Gr. στόμα, στοματ- mouth], having many or several mouths or suckers; *spec.* belonging to the *Polystomata*, a name for the Sponges, etc. **Po·lystome,** *a.* having many mouths; *sb.* an animal having many mouths or suckers, as a sponge, etc. **Polytha·lamous** [Gr. θάλαμος bed-chamber], *a. Nat. Hist.* having or consisting of several chambers or cells; many-chambered. **Poly·tocous,** *a. Zool.* producing several young at a birth; *Bot.* bearing fruit many times. **Polytro·pic** [Gr. τρόπος turn], *a.* capable of turning to various courses or expedients; *Math.* turning several times round a pole; also applied to a function which has several different values for one of the variable. **Poly·valent,** *a. Chem.* = MULTIVALENT; *Med.* having the property of counteracting many zymotic poisons. **Polyzo·nal,** *a.* applied to a form of lens composed of a number of annular segments or zones; chiefly used in lighthouses.

2. In *Chem.*, a prefix indicating generally the higher members of a series of *mono-*, *di-*, *tri-*, etc. compounds; sometimes including all except the *mono-* member.

a. Prefixed to sbs., forming sbs. used as the names of compounds formed by the combination of two or more atoms, molecules, or radicals (sometimes with elimination of hydrogen atoms, water molecules, etc.) as *polye·thylene* = $(C_2H_4)_n$ (e.g. hexethylene alchohol $(C_2H_4)_6\ H_2O_7$); *poly-o·xide*, a binary compound containing several oxygen atoms, as a pentoxide; so *polysu·lphide*, etc. **b.** Prefixed to adjs. or sbs., forming adjs., meaning 'containing or derived from two or more molecules of the substance expressed by the second element'; e.g. *polya·cid, polyca·rbic*, etc.

‖**Polyadelphia** (pǫli,ăde·lfiă). 1828. [mod. L., f. Gr. πολυ- POLY- + ἀδελφός brother + -IA¹.] *Bot.* The eighteenth class in the Linnæan Sexual System, comprising plants whose flowers have the stamens united in three or more bundles. Hence **Polyade·lphian, -ade·lphous** *adjs.* belonging to this class; having the stamens so united; also said of such stamens.

Polyandria (pǫli,æ·ndriă). 1753. [mod.L. – Gr. πολυανδρία, f. πολύανδρος (f. πολυ- POLY- + ἀνδρ- man, male), employed by Linnæus in the sense 'having many stamens or male organs'.] **1.** *Bot.* The thirteenth class in the Linnæan Sexual System, comprising plants having twenty or more stamens inserted on the receptacle. Also the name of one of the orders in certain classes, as the *Monadelphia, Gynandria, Monœcia*, in which the number of stamens is used to subdivide them into orders. **2.** *Zool.* and *Anthropol.* = POLYANDRY 1876. So **Polya·ndrian, Polya·ndric** *adjs.* = POLYANDROUS.

Polyandrous (pǫli,æ·ndrəs), *a.* 1830. [f. Gr. πολύανδρος (see POLYANDRIA) + -OUS.] **1.** *Bot.* Having numerous stamens; *spec.* belonging to the class *Polyandria.* **2.** Having more than one, or several, husbands; practising, pertaining to, or involving polyandry. (Corresp. to POLYGYNOUS 2.) 1865.

Polyandry (pǫ·li,ændri). 1780. [f. POLY- + Gr. ἀνήρ man + -Y³. Cf. POLYGYNY.] That form of polygamy in which one woman has two or more husbands at the same time; plurality of husbands. (Corresp. to POLYGYNY.) **b.** *Zool.* The fact of a female animal having more than one mate 1871.

Polyanthus (pǫli,æ·nþǫs). 1727. [– mod.L. *polyanthus*, f. Gr. πολυ- POLY- + ἄνθος flower.] **1.** A cultivated form of *Primula*, having flowers of various shades, chiefly brown or crimson with yellow eye and border, in an umbel on a common peduncle. **2.** *attrib.* or *adj. P. narcissus*: any one of a group of species of Narcissus, as *N. tazetta*, which have the flowers in an umbellate cluster on a common peduncle. So *P. Primrose* = sense 1. 1866.

Polyatomic (pǫli,ătǫ·mik), *a.* 1857. [f. POLY- + ATOMIC.] *Chem.* Containing or consisting of many atoms of some substance; *esp.* having many replaceable hydrogen atoms; also = multivalent.

Polybasic (pǫlibēⁱ·sik), *a.* 1842. [f. POLY- + BASIC.] *Chem.* Having more than two bases, or atoms of a base.

P. acid, an acid containing three or more atoms of replaceable hydrogen.

Polybasite (pǫli·băsəit). 1830. [– G. *polybasit* (H. Rosé, 1829), f. Gr. πολυ- POLY- + βάσις; see -ITE¹ 2 b. According to Chester, alluding to the large amount of the base, sulphide of silver.] *Min.* A sulpharseno-antimonite of silver and copper, of an iron-black colour, and metallic lustre, occurring in short tabular hexagonal prisms, also massive and disseminated.

Polycephalic (pǫ:lisĭfæ·lik), *a. rare.* 1850. [f. Gr. πολυκέφαλος (f. πολυ- POLY- + κεφαλή head) + -IC.] Many-headed. So **Polyce·phalous** *a.*

Polychæte, -chete (pǫ·likīt), *a.* and *sb.* 1886. [– mod.L. *Polychæta*, f. Gr. πολυχαίτης, f. πολυ- much + χαίτη mane (here 'bristle'; cf. OLIGOCHÆTE).] *Zool.* **A.** *adj.* Belonging to the *Polychæta*, one of the two divisions of the *Chætopoda*, a class of worms characterized by numerous bristles on the footstumps. **B.** *sb.* A worm of this division.

Polychord (pǫ·likǭd), *a.* and *sb.* 1674. [– Gr. πολύχορδος, f. πολυ- POLY- + χορδή CHORD.] **A.** *adj.* Having many strings, as a musical instrument. **B.** *sb.* **1.** An instrument having ten gut strings, resembling a double-bass without a neck, played with a bow or with the fingers 1838. **2.** Trade-name for a kind of octave-coupler 1858.

†**Polychrest** (pǫ·likrest). 1656. [– late L. *polychrestus* (Vegetius) – Gr. πολύχρηστος, f. πολυ- POLY- + χρηστός useful.] Something adapted to several different uses; *esp.* a drug or medicine serving to cure various diseases –1812.

attrib. †*P. salt* (also *salt p.*), neutral sulphate of potassium; also, sodio-potassic tartrate. So **Poly-chre·stic** *adj.* serving for various uses.

Polychroite (pǫ·likro,əit). 1815. [– Fr. *polychroïte*, f. Gr. πολύχροος many-coloured; see -ITE¹ 4 a.] *Chem.* Name for the colouring matter of saffron (also called SAFRANIN), which exhibits various colours under different reagents.

Polychromatic (pǫ:likromæ·tik), *a.* 1849. [f. POLY- + CHROMATIC.] Having or characterized by various colours; many-coloured. *P. acid* (Chem.) = POLYCHROMIC *acid.*

Polychrome (pǫ·likrōᵘm), *a.* and *sb.* 1801. [– Fr. *polychrome* – Gr. πολύχρωμος many-coloured, f. πολυ- POLY- + χρῶμα colour.] **A.** *adj.* Polychromatic; *esp.* painted, decorated, or printed in many colours 1837. **B.** *sb.* **1.** A work of art in several colours; *spec.* a coloured statue 1801. **2.** Varied colouring 1882. **3.** *Chem.* A name for ÆSCULIN, from the fluorescence of its solution and infusion 1838.

Polychromic (pǫlikrōᵘ·mik), *a.* 1825. [f. as prec. + -IC.] **1.** = prec. A. **2.** *Chem.* In *p. acid*, a name for aloetic acid, from the various colours it exhibits in powder, in solution, and in combination 1863. So **Po·lychro:mous** *a.*

Polychromy (pǫ·likrōᵘmi). 1854. [– Fr. *polychromie*, f. as POLYCHROME; see -Y³.] The art of painting or decorating in several colours, esp. as used in pottery, architecture, etc.

†‖**Polychro·nicon.** 1570. [med.L., f. Gr. πολυ- POLY- + χρονικόν, in pl. (sc. βιβλία books) annals.] A chronicle of many events or periods –1815.

Polyconic (pǫlikǫ·nik), *a.* 1864. [f. POLY- + CONIC.] Involving or based upon a number of cones; applied to a system of map-projection in which each parallel of latitude is represented by the development of a cone touching the earth's surface along that parallel. Also *sb.* a polyconic projection.

Polydæmonism, -demonism (pǫlidī·-mŏniz'm). 1711. [f. Gr. πολυ- POLY- + δαίμων, divinity, demon + -ISM, after *polytheism.*] A belief in many divinities (i.e. simply, supernatural powers, or *spec.* evil spirits).

Polyedral, etc.: see POLYHEDRAL, etc.

‖**Polygamia** (pǫligēⁱ·miă). 1753. [Linnæan use of late L. or Gr.; see POLYGAMY.] *Bot.* The twenty-third class in the Linnæan Sexual System, comprising species which bear both hermaphrodite and unisexual (male or female) flowers, on the same or different plants. Hence **Polyga·mian** *a.* belonging to the class *P.*; *sb.* a plant of this class. **Polyga·mious** *a.*

Polygamic (pǫligæ·mik), *a.* 1819. [f. POLYGAMY + -IC.] Of or pertaining to polygamy; (less correctly) polygamous.

Polygamist (pǒli·gămist). 1637. [f. as prec. + -IST.] One who practises or favours polygamy; usu., a man who has several wives. **b.** *attrib.* Practising polygamy, polygamous 1875. Hence **Polygami·stic** *a.*

Poly·gamize, *v. rare.* 1598. [f. as prec. + -IZE.] *intr.* To practise polygamy.

Polygamous (pǒli·gămәs), *a.* 1613. [f. as prec. + -OUS.] **1.** Practising or addicted to polygamy; of, pertaining to, or involving polygamy. **2.** *Zool.* Having more than one, or several, mates of the opposite sex, as an animal; characterized by polygamy, as a species. Usu. = *polygynous.* 1834. **3.** *Bot.* Belonging to the Linnæan class *Polygamia* 1760.

2. The war is, perhaps, severest between the males of p. animals DARWIN. Hence **Poly·gamously** *adv.*

Polygamy (pǒli·gămi). 1591. [– Fr. *polygamie* (Calvin) – late L. *polygamia* – eccl. Gr. πολυγαμία, f. πολύγαμος often married, polygamous; see POLY-, -GAMY.] **1.** Marriage with several, or more than one, at once; plurality of spouses; usu. the practice or custom according to which one man has several wives. **b.** *fig.*: esp. applied to plurality of benefices 1638. **2.** *Zool.* The habit of mating with more than one, or several, of the opposite sex; usu., one male with several females (*polygyny*), as in gallinaceous birds 1890.

Polygenesis (pǫli,dʒe·nĭsis). 1862. [f. POLY- + GENESIS.] *Biol.* (Theoretical) origination of a race or species from several independent ancestors or germs; in ref. to man usu. called POLYGENY.

Polygenetic (pǫ:li,dʒĭne·tik), *a.* 1861. [f. prec., after GENETIC.] **1.** *Biol.* Of or pertaining to polygenesis. **2.** *Geol.* Having more than one origin; formed in several different ways 1873. Hence **Polygene·tically** *adv.*

Polygenic (pǫli,dʒe·nik), *a.* 1858. [f. Gr. πολυγενής of many kinds (f. πολυ- POLY- + γένος kind) + -IC; in sense 2 f. POLY- + -GEN 1 + -IC.] **1.** *Geol.* = POLYGENOUS 1. **2.** *Chem.* Forming more than one compound with hydrogen or other monovalent element 1873.

Polygenism (pǒli·dʒĭniz'm). 1878. [f. POLYGENY + -ISM.] The doctrine of polygeny; the theory that mankind are descended from several independent pairs of ancestors, or that the human race consists of several independent species. So **Poly·genist**, an adherent of the theory of polygeny; also *attrib.* 1857.

Polygenous (pǒli·dʒĭnəs), *a.* 1799. [f. Gr. πολυγενής of many kinds (f. πολυ- POLY- + γένος kind) + -OUS.] **1.** Composed of constituents of different kinds; *spec.* in *Geol.* composed of various kinds of rocks. **2.** *Chem.* = POLYGENIC 2. 1870. **3.** Of or pertaining to, or involving polygeny 1860.

Polygeny (pǒli·dʒĭni). 1865. [f. POLY- + -GENY.] The (theoretical) origination of mankind (or of any species) from several independent pairs of ancestors; *loosely*, the theory of such origination, polygenism.

Polyglot (pǫ·liglǫt), *a.* and *sb.* 1645. [– Fr. *polyglotte* – Gr. πολύγλωττος, f. πολυ- POLY- + γλῶττα tongue.] **A.** *adj.* **1.** Of a person: That speaks or writes several languages 1656. **2.** Of or relating to many languages: *esp.* of a book or writing: In many or several languages 1673.

1. P. waiters who can tell us when the train starts in four or five languages 1873. **2.** The Polyglott Bible, a Polyglott Dictionary 1706.

B. *sb.* **1.** One who speaks or writes several languages 1645. †**b.** A bird that imitates the notes of other birds –1776. **2.** A book or writing (*esp.* a Bible) in several languages 1666. **b.** A mixture of several languages (*rare*) 1715.

1. A p. or good linguist 1645. **b.** It [sedge warbler] is a most entertaining p., or mocking bird PENNANT. **2. b.** His wrath aired itself in a polyglott 1830. So **Polyglo·ttic, Polyglo·ttous** *adjs.* = *polyglot* A.

Polygon (pǫ·ligǒn), *sb.* and *a.* 1570. [– late L. *polygonum* – Gr. πολύγωνον, subst. use of n. of adj. πολύγωνος, f. πολυ- POLY- + -γωνος, from stem of γωνία angle; see -GON. Used first in L. forms **polygo·num, polygo·nium.**] **A.** *sb.* **1.** *Geom.* A figure (usu. a plane rectilineal figure), having many, i.e. (usu.) more than four, angles (and sides); a many-sided figure 1571. **b.** *Arith.* A polygonal number: see POLYGONAL 2. Hence extended to higher orders of figurate numbers, as the PYRAMIDAL numbers, etc. 1842. **2.** A material object of the form of a polygon 1669.

1. *P. of forces*, a polygonal figure illustrating a theorem relating to a number of forces acting at one point, each of which is represented in magnitude and direction by one of the sides of the figure, analogous to the *parallelogram of forces*; hence, the theorem itself. So *p. of velocities*, etc. **2.** *Funicular p.*: see FUNICULAR 2.

B. *adj.* Having many angles; polygonal. ? *Obs.* 1570.

Polygonaceous (pǫ:ligǒnēⁱ·ʃəs), *a.* 1874. [f. mod.L. *Polygonaceæ* (f. POLYGONUM; see -ACIÆ) + -OUS; see -ACEOUS.] *Bot.* Belonging to the N.O. *Polygonaceæ*, of which the typical genus is POLYGONUM.

Polygonal (pǒli·gǒnăl), *a.* (*sb.*) 1704. [f.

POLYGON + -AL[1].] **1.** Having the form of a polygon; many-sided. As applied to a solid body, denoting a prismatic or similar form whose base or section is a polygon. 1727. **2.** *Arith.* Applied to the first order of figurate numbers (see FIGURATE *ppl. a.* 3 b.) So called because each of these numbers, represented (e.g.) by dots, can be arranged according to a certain rule in the form of the corresponding regular polygon. 1704. **b.** as *sb.* A polygonal number (*rare*) 1795.

Polygonometry (pǫ:ligonǫ·mĕtri). *rare* 1811. [f. as POLYGON + -METRY.] *Math.* A branch of mathematics dealing with the measurement and properties of polygons, as trigonometry with those of triangles.

Polygonous (pǒli·gŏnəs), *a.* Now *rare* or *Obs.* 1660. [f. POLYGON + -OUS.] = POLYGONAL *a.*

‖**Polygonum** (pǒli·gŏnǒm). 1706. [mod.L. – Gr. πολύγονον knotgrass, etc., f. πολυ- POLY- + γόνυ knee, joint.] *Bot.* A large and widely distributed genus of plants, type of the N.O. *Polygonaceæ*, with swollen stem-joints, sheathed by the stipules, including knotgrass, snakeweed, persicaria, etc. Also *attrib.*

†**Poly·gony.** 1450. [– L. *polygonium*, f. Gr. πολύγονον.] A plant of the genus *Polygonum*; esp. Snakeweed, *P. bistorta* –1706.

Polygraph (pǫ·ligrɑf). 1794. [In I app. f. POLY- + -GRAPH; in II f. subst. use of Gr. πολυγράφος adj. writing much; cf. Fr. *polygraphe* (XVI).] **I. 1. a.** An apparatus for producing two or more identical drawings or writings simultaneously. **b.** A copying-machine; *esp.* a gelatine copying-pad. 1805. †**2.** *fig.* A person who imitates, or is a copy of, another; an imitator or imitation –1797. **3.** A myograph 1876. **II.** A writer of many works; a voluminous author 1883.

Polygraphic (pǫligræ·fik), *a.* (*sb.*) 1735. [f. POLYGRAPHY + -IC.] **1.** Writing much; treating of many subjects (*rare*). **2.** Applied to a method of mechanically copying pictures; see POLYGRAPHY III a. 1788. †**3.** *fig.* That is an exact copy or imitation of another –1824. **4.** Of or pertaining to a POLYGRAPH (sense I); used for multiplying copies of a drawing or writing; produced by a polygraph 1828.

2. P. transparencies..to be had for next to nothing LANDOR. **4.** A sheet of damped p. paper 1883. So **Polygra·phical** *a.* 1588.

Polygraphy (pǒli·grăfi). 1593. [– Gr. πολυγραφία a writing much; see POLY-, -GRAPHY. Cf. Fr. *polygraphie* (XVI).] †**I.** A kind of cipher or secret writing; also applied to a particular system of shorthand –1855. **II.** Much writing; copious or various literary work 1661. **III. a.** A method of producing copies of paintings, invented by Joseph Booth *c*1788. **b.** The use of a POLYGRAPH (sense I a) 1828.

‖**Polygynia** (pǫli͵dʒi·niă). 1760. [f. mod.L. *polygynus*, f. Gr. πολυ- POLY- + γυνή woman, wife (here 'pistil'); see -IA[1].] **1.** *Bot.* An order in some classes of the Linnæan Sexual System, comprising plants having flowers with more than 12 styles. **2.** = POLYGYNY (*rare*) 1865. Hence **Polygy·nian** *a. rare* = POLYGYNOUS 1.

Polygynist (pǒli·dʒinist). 1876. [f. POLYGYNY + -IST.] One who practises or favours polygyny.

Polygynous (pǒli·dʒinəs), *a.* 1841. [f. mod.L. *polygynus* (see POLYGYNIA) + -OUS.] **1.** *Bot.* Having many pistils, styles, or stigmas; *spec.* belonging to the order *Polygynia*. **2.** Having more than one, or several, wives (or concubines); practising, pertaining to, or involving polygyny 1874. **b.** *Zool.* Of a male animal: Having several mates; characterized by polygyny, as a species.

Polygyny (pǒli·dʒini). 1780. [f. POLY- + Gr. γυνή woman, wife + -Y[3]; cf. POLYANDRY.] That form of polygamy in which one man has several wives (or concubines). **b.** *Zool.* Of a male animal: The having more than one female mate.

Polyhalite (pǫlihæ·ləit). 1818. [– G. *polyhalit* (Stromeyer, 1818), f. Gr. πολυ- POLY- + ἅλς salt; see -ITE[1] 2 b.] *Min.* Hydrous sulphate of calcium, potassium, and magnesium, usu. occurring in fibrous masses of a red or yellowish colour.

Polyhedral (pǫlihī·drăl, -he·drăl), *a.* Also **polyedral.** 1811. [f. POLYHEDRON + -AL[1].] **1.** Of the form of a polyhedron; having many faces or sides, as a solid figure or body. **2.** Pertaining or relating to a polyhedron; in *Algebra* applied to a class of functions 1880. **3.** Of an angle: Formed by three or more planes meeting at a point. (Usu. called a *solid angle.*) 1864. So **Polyhe·dric, -al** *adjs.* = sense 1; also *fig.* many-sided. **Polyhe·drous** *a.* polyhedral.

Polyhedron (pǫlihī·drǫn, -he·drǫn). Also **polyedron.** *Pl.* **-a** (rarely **-ons**). 1570. [– Gr. πολύεδρον, subst use of n. of πολύεδρος adj. f. πολυ- POLY- + ἕδρα base.] *Geom.* A solid figure contained by many (i.e. usu. more than six) plane faces; a many-sided solid. Hence, a material body having such a form. **b.** *spec.* A lens having many facets, multiplying the image of an object; a multiplying-glass 1727.

Polyhistor (pǫlihi·stǭɹ). 1588. [– Gr. πολυΐστωρ very learned, f. πολυ- POLY- + ἵστωρ (see HISTORY).] A man of much or varied learning; a great scholar. So **Polyhisto·rian,** polyhistor. **Polyhisto·ric** *a.* **Polyhi·story.**

Polymath (pǫ·limæþ), *sb.* (*a.*) 1621. [– Gr. πολυμαθής having learnt much, f. πολυ- POLY- + μαθ-, stem of μανθάνειν learn.] A person of much or varied learning; one acquainted with various subjects of study. Also *attrib.* So **Polyma·thic** *a.* pertaining to a p., characterized by varied learning. †**Poly·mathist** = *polymath.* **Poly·mathy** [– Gr. πολυμαθία], much or varied learning.

Polymer (pǫ·limər). 1866. [– G. *polymer* (Berzelius, 1830) – Gr. πολυμερής having many parts, f. πολυ- POLY- + μέρος part, share. See ISOMER.] *Chem.* A substance polymeric with another; any one of a series of polymeric compounds. So **Poly·meride** = *polymer.*

Polymeric (pǫlime·rik), *a.* 1847. [f. prec. + -IC, after G. *polymerisch.*] *Chem.* Of two or more compounds, or of one compound in relation to another (const. *with*): Composed of the same elements in the same proportions, but so that the numbers of atoms of the several elements in the molecule in one substance are some multiple of those in another, and thus the molecular weight of the one is the same multiple of that of the other. (Dist. from ISOMERIC.)

Polymerism (pǫli·mĕriz'm). 1847. [f. as prec. + -ISM.] **1.** *Chem.* The condition of being polymeric. **2.** *Biol.* The condition of being polymerous 1849.

Polymerize (pǫ·limĕrəiz), *v.* 1865. [f. POLYMER + -IZE.] **1.** *Chem.* **a.** *trans.* To render polymeric; to form a polymer of. **b.** *intr.* To become polymeric; to be converted into a polymer. **2.** *Biol.* (*trans.*) To render polymerous 1879. Hence **Poly:meriza·tion,** the action or process of polymerizing; formation of polymers.

Polymerous (pǒli·mĕrəs), *a.* 1858. [f. as prec. + -OUS.] *Nat. Hist.* Composed of many parts, members, or segments.

Polymorph (pǫ·limǫɹf). 1828. [– Gr. πολύμορφος, f. πολυ- POLY- + μορφή form.] **1.** *Nat. Hist.* A polymorphous organism, or an individual of a polymorphous species. **2.** *Chem.* and *Min.* A substance that crystallizes in two or more different forms 1890. So **Polymo·rphic** *a.* = POLYMORPHOUS 1, 2.

Polymorphism (pǫlimǭ·ɹfiz'm). 1839. [f. POLYMORPH(OUS + -ISM.] The condition or character of being polymorphous; the occurrence of something in several different forms.

Polymorpho-, comb. form repr. Gr. πολύμορφος multiform; as in **P.-nu·clear, -nu·cleate** *adjs.*, having several nuclei of various shapes.

Polymorphous (pǫlimǫ·ɹfəs), *a.* 1785. [f. Gr. πολύμορφος multiform + -OUS.] Having, assuming, or occurring in, many or various forms; multiform. **1.** *gen.* 1823. **2.** *Nat. Hist., Biol., Path.* **a.** Having many varieties; as a species of animal or plant, an eruptive disease, etc. **b.** Assuming various forms successively; as an amœba, infusorian, etc. **c.** Having several definitely marked metamorphoses. 1785. **3.** *Chem.* and *Min.* Crystallizing in two or more forms, esp. in forms belonging to different systems; dimorphous or trimorphous 1866.

Polymorphy (pǫ·limǭɹfi). 1846. [– Gr. πολυμορφία multiformity; see prec., -Y[3].] = POLYMORPHISM.

Poly-mountain: see POLY b.

Polynesia (pǫlinī·ʃ'ă, -siă). 1766. [mod.L. form of Fr. *Polynésie* (De Brosses, 1756), f. Gr. πολυ- POLY- + νῆσος island; see -IA[1].] Collective name for the numerous small islands in the Pacific Ocean, east of Australia and the Malay archipelago. Hence **Polyne·sian** *a.* belonging to P.; *sb.* a native or inhabitant of P., a South Sea islander.

‖**Polyn̈ia** (poli·niă). 1853. [Russ. *polȳn'yá*, f. root of *pole* field.] A space of open water in the midst of ice, esp. in the arctic seas.

Polynomial (pǫlinō[u]·miăl), *a.* and *sb.* 1674. [var. of earlier MULTINOMIAL by substitution of prefix POLY-.] **A.** *adj.* **1.** *Alg.* Consisting of many terms; multinomial 1704. **2.** Characteristic of a nomenclature in which the genus, species, sub-species, variety, etc. are indicated by more than two terms 1889.

1. *P. theorem* (also called *multinomial theorem*), an extension of the binomial theorem, for the expansion of any power of a polynomial expression.

B. *sb.* **1.** *Alg.* An expression consisting of many terms; a multinomial 1674. **2.** A scientific name consisting of many terms (see A. 2) 1885. Hence **Po·lynome** = B. 1.; *adj.* having many names.

Polyonymous (pǫli͵ǫ·niməs), *a.* 1678. [f. Gr. πολυώνυμος (f. πολυ- POLY- + ὄνομα, Æol. ὄνυμα) + -OUS; cf. *anonymous.*] Having many names or titles; called or known by several different names. So **Po·lyonym** (*a*) = SYNONYM (*rare*); (*b*) used by Buck for a technical term consisting of two or more words, as *pia mater*, etc. **Polyony·mic** *a.* of the nature of a polyonym.

Polyonymy (pǫli͵ǫ·nimi). 1678. [– Gr. πολυωνυμία, f. πολυώνυμος; see prec. and -Y[3].] **1.** The use of several different names for the same person or thing. **2.** Polynomial nomenclature 1889.

Polyp, polype (pǫ·lip). Late ME. [– Fr. *polype* – L. *polypus*; see POLYPUS.] **1.** *Zool.* Prop., an animal having many feet or foot-like processes. †**a.** *orig.* A cephalopod having eight or ten arms, as an octopus or a cuttle-fish –1752. **b.** In later use, applied to various animals of low organization; chiefly to cœlenterates of different classes, esp. a hydra or other hydrozoan, a 'coral-insect' or other anthozoan; also to the polyzoa, to certain echinoderms, and loosely to rotifers, infusorians, etc. **c.** Many of these being 'colonial' organisms, the term is hence used *spec.* for a single individual, 'person', or zooid of the colony. 1742. **2.** *Path.* = POLYPUS 2 (*rare*). late ME.

Comb. **p.-stem, -stock,** = POLYPARY, POLYPIDOM. So **Poly·pean** *a. rare* pertaining to, or resembling that of, a p.

Polypary (pǫ·lipări). 1750. [– mod.L. *polyparium* (also used), f. *polypus* POLYP + -ARIUM.] The common stem, stock, or supporting structure of a colony of polyps, to which the individual zooids are attached, usu. each in a cell or cavity of its own; = POLYPIDOM.

Polypheme (pǫ·lifīm). 1641. [– Fr. *Polyphème* – L. POLYPHEMUS.] A one-eyed giant in Homer's *Odyssey* ix; hence *allusively*.

‖**Polyphemus** (pǫlifī·mǒs). 1829. [L. – Gr. Πολύφημος, lit. many-voiced, also much spoken of.] **1.** = prec.; a Cyclops, a one-eyed giant. **2.** *Zool.* **a.** A one-eyed animal. **b.** A very large American silkworm-moth, *Telea polyphemus.* 1890.

Polyphone (pǫ·lifō[u]n). 1655. [– Gr. πολύφωνος having many tones, etc., f. πολυ- POLY- + φωνή voice, sound.] †**1.** A musical instrument, somewhat resembling a lute, but having a large number of wire strings –1789. **2.** *Philol.* A written character used to represent different sounds 1872.

Polyphonic (pǫlifǫ·nik), *a.* 1782. [f. Gr. πολύφωνος (see prec.) + -IC.] **1.** *Mus.* Composed or arranged for several voices or parts, each having a melody of its own; consisting of a numer of melodies combined; contrapuntal; of or pertaining to polyphonic music. **2.** Producing many sounds; many-voiced 1864. **3.** *Philol.* Of a letter or other symbol: Having more than one phonetic value (as *c, g, s*) 1891.

2. A grand organ..called a p. organ 1890. So **Poly·phonous** *a.* = *polyphonic* 1677.

Polyphonism (pǫ·lifoniz'm). *rare.* 1713. [In sense 1 f. as POLYPHONE + -ISM; in sense 2 f. POLYPHONY + -ISM.] **1.** Multiplication of sound, as by echo. **2.** *Mus.* The use of polyphony; polyphonic style or composition 1864.

Polyphonist (pǫ·lifonist). *rare.* 1829. [f. as prec.; see -IST.] **1.** A ventriloquist. **2.** *Mus.* One versed in polyphony; a contrapuntist 1864.

Polyphony (pǫ̆li·fǫ̆ni, pǫ·lifoᵘni). 1828. [– Gr. πολυφωνία, f. πολύφωνος; see POLYPHONE.] **1.** = POLYPHONISM 1. **2.** *Mus.* The simultaneous combination of a number of parts, each forming an individual melody, and harmonizing with the others; polyphonic composition; counterpoint 1864. **3.** *Philol.* The symbolization of different vocal sounds by the same letter or character; the fact or quality of being polyphonic 1880.

Polypide (pǫ·lipəid). 1850. [f. POLYP + *-ide*; cf. -ID[3].] *Zool.* An individual or zooid of a compound polyzoan.

Polypidom (pǫ̆li·pidǫ̆m, pǫ·lip-). 1824. [f. L. *polypus* POLYP + *domus*, Gr. δόμος house.] = POLYPARY.

Polypier (pǫ·lipiᵊɹ). 1828. [– Fr. *polypier* (Réaumur, *a* 1757), f. *polype* POLYP + *-ier*, as in *poirier* pear-tree, etc.] *Zool.* = POLYPARY; sometimes, a distinct part of this to which an individual zooid is attached.

Polypifer (pǫ̆li·pifəɹ). 1822. [Anglicization of mod.L. *Polypifer(a*; see next.] *Zool.* A polypary or polypidom; also, the whole compound organism; usu. in pl. as an Eng. equivalent of L. *Polypifera*.

Polypiferous (pǫlipi·fĕrəs), *a.* 1775. [f. mod.L. *Polypifera*, a former division of Invertebrates; see POLYP, -FEROUS.] *Zool.* Bearing polyps, as a polyp-stock or polypary.

Polypite (pǫ·lipəit). 1828. [f. L. *polypus* POLYP + (in sense 1) -ITE[1] 2 and (in sense 2) -ITE[1] 3.] **1.** *Palæont.* A fossil polyp. **2.** *Zool.* An individual or zooid of a compound polyp, esp. of a cœlenterate. Also sometimes applied to a free polyp, as a *Hydra*. 1867.

Polypod (pǫ·lipǫd), *sb.*[1] Now *rare.* late ME. [– OFr. *polipode* (mod. *polypode*) – L. POLYPODIUM.] = POLYPODY.

Po·lypod, *a.* and *sb.*[2] 1753. [– Fr. *polypode* adj., f. Gr. πολυποδ-, stem of πολύπους many-footed; see POLYP.] **A.** *adj.* Having many feet or foot-like organs 1826. **B.** *sb.* An animal having many feet, e.g. a millepede 1753.

‖**Polypodium** (pǫlipōᵘ·diǒm). 1525. [L. – Gr. πολυπόδιον, f. πολυ- many + πούς, ποδ- foot, with dim. suffix -ιον; from the many branches of the root-stock; see -IUM.] *Bot.* A large and widely distributed genus of ferns, of various forms.

Polypody (pǫ·lipǒdi). late ME. [– L. *polypodium*; see prec.] A fern of the genus *Polypodium*; esp. *P. vulgare*, the Common Polypody (formerly known as *p. of the oak* or *of the wall*).

Polypoid (pǫ·lipoid), *a.* 1842. [f. POLYP + -OID.] **1.** *Zool.* Resembling or of the nature of a polyp 1850. **2.** *Path.* Resembling or of the nature of a polypus 1842.

Polypous (pǫ·lipəs), *a.* 1748. [f. POLYP or POLYPUS + -OUS.] **1.** *Zool.* Pertaining to, or of the nature of, a polyp; also *fig.* like that of a polyp. **2.** *Path.* Pertaining to, or of the nature of, a polypus; characterized by polypi 1758. So **Po·lipose** *a.* 1731.

Polypterid (pǫ̆li·ptĕrid). 1849. [f. mod.L. *Polypterus* (Geoffroy, 1802), generic name, – Gr. πολύπτερος many-winged, f. πολυ- POLY- + πτερόν feather, wing; see -ID[3].] *Ichthyol.* A fish of the family *Polypteridæ* of crossopterygian ganoids, having the dorsal fin replaced by a series of spines with finlets attached; now represented only by the genus **Poly·pterus** of tropical African rivers. So **Poly·pteroid** *a.* akin in form to *Polypterus*, belonging to the sub-order *Polypteroidei*; *sb.* a polypteroid fish.

‖**Polyptoton** (pǫliptōᵘ·tǫn). 1586. [Late L. – Gr. πολύπτωτον, subst. use of n. of adj. (sc. σχῆμα rhetorical figure), f. πολυ- POLY- + πτωτός falling (πτῶσις case).] *Rhet.* A figure consisting in the repetition of a word in different cases or inflexions in the same sentence.

Polypus (pǫ·lipǒs). *Pl.* **-pi** (-pəi). late ME. [– L. *polypus* – Doric, Æolic πώλυπος, var. of Attic πολύπους cuttle-fish, polypus in the nose, etc., f. πολυ- POLY- + πούς foot.] **1. a.** = POLYP 1 a. (*Obs.* exc. in allusion to L. or Gr.) 1520. **b.** = POLYP 1 b, c. Now *rare* or *Obs.* 1742. **2.** *Path.* A general term for tumours of various kinds, arising from a mucous or serous surface, usu. pedunculated, and having ramifications like the tentacles of a polyp. Also formerly applied to a fibrinous blood-clot in the heart or blood-vessels. late ME. **3.** *attrib.* 1607.

Polyscope (pǫ·liskoᵘp). 1704. [f. POLY- + -SCOPE.] **1.** An optical instrument through which objects appear multiplied; a multiplying-glass. **2.** An apparatus for examining cavities of the body 1881.

Polysyllabic (pǫ:li,silæ·bik), *a.* 1782. [f. med.L. *polysyllabus*, Gr. πολυσύλλαβος (f. πολυ- POLY- + συλλαβή syllable) + -IC. Cf. Fr. *polysyllabique* (XVI).] **a.** Of a word: Consisting of many (i.e., usu., more than three) syllables. **b.** Of language, etc.: Characterized by polysyllables. So **Polysylla·bical** *a.* 1656, **-ly**, *adv.*

Polysyllable (pǫlisi·lăb'l), *sb.* and *a.* 1570. [f. med.L. *polysyllaba*, fem. (sc. *vox* word) of *polysyllabus* (see prec.), after SYLLABLE.] **A.** *sb.* A word of many (i.e., usu., more than three) syllables. **B.** *adj.* = POLYSYLLABIC. Now *rare.* 1589.

‖**Polysyndeton** (pǫlisi·ndĭtǫ̆n). 1589. [mod. L., f. POLY- after ASYNDETON.] *Rhet.* A figure consisting in the use of several conjunctions close together; usu., the repetition of the same conjunction (as *and, or, nor*).

Polysynthesis (pǫlisi·nþĭsis). 1869. [f. POLY- + SYNTHESIS.] Synthesis or composition of many elements; complex or multiple synthesis; *spec.* in *Philol.* = INCORPORATION 1 b.

Polysynthetic (pǫ:li,sinþe·tik), *a.* 1805. [f. Gr. πολυσύνθετος much compounded; see POLY- and SYNTHETIC.] Of the nature of or characterized by polysynthesis; combining numerous elements; complex. *spec.* **1.** *Cryst.* Applied to a compound crystal consisting of a series of twin crystals united so as to form a laminated structure. **2.** *Philol.* Characterized by combining several words of a sentence into one word 1821.

2. The Isolating, P., Agglutinative, Inflectional and Analytic forms of language 1889. Hence **Polysynthe·tical** *a.*, **-ly** *adv.* **Polysynthe·ticism, Polysy·nthetism**, p. character or condition.

Polytechnic (pǫli,te·knik), *a.* and *sb.* 1805. [– Fr. *polytechnique* (*école polytechnique*, 1795), f. Gr. πολύτεχνος skilled in many arts + *-ique* -IC; see POLY-, TECHNIC.] **A.** *adj.* Pertaining to, dealing with, or devoted to, various arts; esp. in *p. school*, an institution for giving instruction in various technical subjects.

P. Institution, an institution in London, opened in 1838, for the exhibition of objects connected with the industrial arts; now, a technical and recreative school. (After the *école polytechnique*, an engineering school in Paris, founded 1794.)

B. *sb.* Short for *P. Institution* (rarely for *p. school*); see A. Hence *gen.* 1881. So **Polyte·chnical** *a.* = A.

Polytheism (pǫ·liþi,iz'm), 1613. [– Fr. *polythéisme* (XVI), f. Gr. πολύθεος, f. πολυ- POLY- + θεός god; see -ISM.] Belief in, or worship of, many gods (or more than one god).

Some Temples..furnish with wooden gods for politheisme 1638.

Polytheist (pǫ·liþi,ist), *sb.* (*a.*) 1619. [f. as prec. + -IST.] One who believes in or worships many gods (or more than one); an adherent of polytheism. Also *attrib.* or as *adj.* Hence **Po:lythei·stic** *a.* of, pertaining to, holding, or characterized by polytheism 1770. **Polythei·stical** *a.* = polytheistic; having a polytheistic character or tendency 1678; **-ly** *adv.*

Polytomous (pǫ̆li·tǒməs), *a.* 1858. [f. mod.L. *polytomus*, f. Gr. πολυ- POLY- + -τομος cut; cf. next, and see -OUS.] Divided, or involving division, into many parts. **1.** *Bot.* **a.** *spec.* Applied to a leaf having several divisions, but not articulated with the midrib so as to form leaflets. **b.** Applied to branching in which the axis divides into more than two secondary axes at the same point. **2.** *Logic.* Involving polytomy; see next, 2.

Polytomy (pǫ̆li·tǒmi). 1864. [f. POLY- + -TOMY, after *dichotomy, trichotomy*.] **1.** *Bot.* Division into several (more than two) branches at the same spot 1875. **2.** *Logic.* Division into several (usu. more than three) members 1864.

Polytype (pǫ·litəip). 1802. [– Fr. *polytype*; see POLY- and TYPE.] A cast, or form of stereotype, made from an intaglio matrix obtained by pressing a woodcut or other plate into semi-fluid metal; a copy of an engraving, of printed matter, etc. made from such a cast. Also *attrib.* So **Po·lytype** *v. trans.* to produce a p. of.

‖**Polyzoa** (pǫlizōᵘ·ă), *sb. pl.* Sing. **polyzoon** (-zōᵘ·ǫn). 1842. [mod.L., f. Gr. πολυ- POLY- + ζῷον animal; see -A 4.] *Zool.* = BRYOZOA.

Polyzoan (pǫlizōᵘ·ăn), *a.* and *sb.* 1864. [f. prec. + -AN.] **A.** *adj.* Belonging to or having the character of the *Polyzoa*. **B.** *sb.* A polyzoon; an individual of a polyzoan colony.

Polyzoary (pǫlizōᵘ·ări). Also in L. form **polyzoarium** (pǫ:lizo,ēᵊ·riǒm), pl. **-ia.** 1856. [– mod.L. *polyzoarium*, f. POLYZOA + *-arium* -ARY[1].] *Zool.* The polypary or polypidom of a colony of *Polyzoa*, or the colony as a whole.

Polyzoic (pǫlizōᵘ·ik), *a.* 1855. [f. POLYZOA + -IC.] *Zool.* Pertaining to or of the nature of the *Polyzoa*; compound, colonial. **b.** In *Sporozoa*, Applied to a spore which produces many germs or sporozoites 1901.

Polyzoon, sing. of POLYZOA.

Pom (pǫm), abbrev. f. POMERANIAN *sb.* b.

Pomace (pɒ·mĕs). late ME. [– med.L. *pomacium* cider (f. L. *pomum* apple), with transference of sense.] **1.** The mass of crushed apples in the process of making cider after or before the juice is pressed out. **2.** *transf.* **a.** Anything crushed or pounded to a pulp 1555. **b.** Any solid refuse whence oil has been expressed or extracted 1861.

Pomaceous (pomēⁱ·ʃəs), *a.* 1706. [f. L. *pomum* apple; see -ACEOUS.] **1.** Of, pertaining to, or consisting of apples. **2.** *Bot.* Of the nature of a pome or apple; of or pertaining to the *Pomeæ*, a division of rosaceous trees bearing pomes or pome-like fruits 1858.

Pomade (pǒmā·d, pǒmēⁱ·d), *sb.* 1562. [– Fr. *pommade* (in same sense) – It. *pomata* :– med.L. **pomata*, (cf. Du Cange *pomata* cider), fem. corresp. to mod.L. POMATUM, f. L. *pomum* apple; see -ADE.] A scented ointment (in which apples were perh. orig. an ingredient) for application to the skin; now used esp. for the skin of the head and the hair. Hence **Poma·de** *v. trans.* to anoint or dress with p.

Pomander (pōᵘ·-, pǫ·măndəɹ, pomæ·ndəɹ). Now *Hist.* 1492. [orig. *pom(e)amber* (XVI) – AFr. **pome ambre*, for OFr. *pome d'embre* – med.L. *pomum ambræ, pomum de ambra* (XIII) 'apple of AMBER'.] **1.** A mixture of aromatic substances, usu. made into a ball, to be carried about with one, esp. as a safeguard against infection. **b.** *transf.* and *fig.* Something scented, or having a sweet odour 1599. **2.** The case in which the perfume was carried, usu. a hollow ball of gold, silver, ivory, etc. 1518. **3.** *attrib.*, as *p. box*, etc. 1599.

‖**Pom(m)ard** (pomā·ɹ). 1833. [Name of a

village in the department of Côte d'Or, France.] A red Burgundy wine.

Pomarine (pǫ·mărəin), *a.* 1831. [– Fr. *pomarin*, arbitrary repr. of mod.L. *pomatorhinus*, f. Gr. πῶμα, -ατ- lid, cover + ῥίς, ῥιν- nose.] *Ornith.* Having the nostrils partly covered with a scale; applied to a species of Skua.

Pomatum (pŏmēⁱ·tŏm), *sb.* 1562. [– mod. L. *pomatum*; see POMADE.] = POMADE *sb.* Also *attrib.* Hence **Poma·tum** *v. trans.* = POMADE *v.*

Pome (pōᵘm), *sb.* late ME. [– OFr. *pome* (mod. *pomme*) :– Rom. **poma* apple, orig. pl. of L. *pōmum* 'fruit', (later) 'apple'.] **1.** A fruit resembling an apple; now only *poet.* an apple. **b.** *Bot.* A succulent inferior fruit, consisting of a firm fleshy body formed of the enlarged calyx, enclosing two or more few-seeded carpels of cartilaginous or bony texture, forming the core; as an apple, quince, pear, haw, etc. 1816. **†2.** The heart or head of a cabbage, cauliflower, or broccoli –1664. **3.** *transf.* A ball or globe, esp. of metal; the royal globe or ball of dominion = *golden apple* (APPLE 5). late ME.

†Pome, *v.* 1658. [– Fr. *pommer*, f. *pomme*; see prec.] *intr.* To form a close compact head or heart, as a cabbage, lettuce, etc. –1727.

†Pome-ci·tron. 1555. [f. POME *sb.* + CITRON. Cf. AL. *pomum cedrinum* (XIII), *p. citrinum* (XIV).] = CITRON 1. –1802.

Pomegranate (pǫ·m-, pɒ·mgrænėt, pǫm-, pɒmgræ·nėt). ME. [– OFr. *pome grenate*, *p. garnate*, etc., i.e. *pome* (see POME *sb.*) apple, *grenate* (mod. *grenade*) pomegranate :– Rom. **granata* for L. (*malum*) *granatum* 'apple having many seeds'; corresp. to med.L. *pomum granatum, poma granata.*] **1.** The fruit of the tree *Punica granatum*, N.O. *Myrtaceæ*, a large roundish many-celled berry, with many seeds, each enveloped in a pleasantly acid juicy reddish pulp, enclosed in a tough rind of a golden colour tinged with red. **b.** The tree *Punica granatum*, a native of northern Africa and western Asia. late ME. **c.** The flower of the pomegranate; usu. scarlet 1873. **2.** A representation of a pomegranate as an ornament or decoration. late ME. **3.** *attrib.*, as *p. apple*, etc.; **p.-tree** = 1 b. late ME.

Pomelo (pǫ·mĕlo, pɒ·mĕlo). 1858. [Of unkn. origin.] **a.** In the E. Indies, a synonym of POMPELMOOSE or SHADDOCK. **b.** In America, a variety of *Citrus*, also called 'grape-fruit'.

Pomeranian (pǫmĕrēⁱ·niăn). *a.* (*sb.*) 1760. [f. *Pomerania*, name of the province, + -AN.] Of or pertaining to Pomerania, a district on the south coast of the Baltic Sea, now a province of Prussia. **B.** *sb.* **a.** An inhabitant of Pomerania. **b.** Short for *P. dog*, a small (black, white, or brown) breed of dog characterized by long silky hair forming a frill round the neck, bushy tail, sharp muzzle, and pointed ears.

Pomeridian (pōᵘmĕri·diăn), *a.* 1560. [– L. *pomeridianus*, f. *post* after + *meridianus* MERIDIAN.] **†a.** = POSTMERIDIAN *a.* –1653. **b.** *Entom.* Flying in the afternoon, as some lepidopterous insects. **c.** *Bot.* Opening or closing in the afternoon, as a flower. 1866.

Po·mewa:ter. *Obs.* exc. *dial.* late ME. [app. f. POME + WATER *sb.*] A large juicy kind of apple.

Pomeys, pomeis (pōᵘ·mis), *sb. pl.* 1562. [perh. old spelling of *pommes*, pl. of POME *sb.*] *Her.* The name given to roundels when of a green colour.

Pomfret (pǫ·mfrėt). 1727. [app. f. Pg. *pampo*, Fr. *pample.*] A fish of the genus *Stromateoides*, inhabiting the Indian and Pacific Oceans, much esteemed for food, esp. *S. niger*, the *black p.*, and *S. sinensis*, the *white p.*, known when young as *silver p.* **b.** A species of sea-bream, *Brama rayi*, found near Bermuda 1890.

Pomfret-cake (pǫ·mfrėt kēⁱk). 1838. [f. *Pomfret* (now spelt *Pontefract*), a town in Yorkshire.] A liquorice cake made at Pontefract.

Pomiculture (pōᵘ·mikɒltʃəɹ). 1876. [f. L. *pomum* fruit + CULTURE.] The art or practice of fruit-growing.

Pomiferous (pomi·fĕrəs), *a.* 1656. [f. L. *pomifer* + -OUS; see -FEROUS.] Producing fruit, or specifically apples; *spec.* in *Bot.*, bearing pomes or pome-like fruits (formerly including cucumbers, melons, etc.).

Pommage (pǫ·mėdʒ). 1570. [Cf. Fr. *pommage* cider harvest or production, f. *pomme* apple + -AGE. In sense 2 perh. a var. of POMACE.] **†1.** Cider (*rare*) –1577. **2.** = POMACE 1. 1789.

‖**Pommé, -ee** (pome), *a.* 1727. [Fr. *pommé*, pa. pple. of *pommer* POME *v.*] *Her.* = POMMETTY.

Pommel (pɒ·mĕl), *sb.*[1] ME. [– OFr. *pomel* (mod. *pommeau*) :– Rom. **pomellum*, dim. of L. *pomum* fruit, apple.] **†1.** A globular body or prominence; a ball; a round boss, knob, or button –1688. **†2.** A ball or spherical ornament forming a finial, or the like –1720. **3. a.** The knob terminating the hilt of a sword, dagger, or the like ME. **†b.** = CASCABEL 1. –1692. **†4.** A rounded or semi-globular projecting part; as the rounded top of the head, etc.; also, a bastion –1687. **5.** The upward projecting front part of a saddle; the saddle-bow 1450.

4. He pighte hym on the pomel of his heed CHAUCER. *Comb.* **p.-foot**, a club-foot.

Pommel (pɒ·mĕl), *sb.*[2] 1839. [perh. f. next.] A wooden block with a convex ribbed face for making leather supple.

Pommel (pɒ·mĕl), *v.* 1530. [f. POMMEL *sb.*[1] 3 a.] *trans.* To beat or strike repeatedly with or as with a pommel; to beat or pound with the fists; to bruise. See also PUMMEL.

†Pomme·lion. 1796. [Extension of POMMEL *sb.*[1] 3 b, perh. infl. by *trunnion.*] = CASCABEL 1. –1867.

Pommery (pǫ·mĕri). 1892. A brand of champagne.

Pommetty (pǫ·mĕti), *a.* 1611. [– Fr. *pommetté*, f. *pommette*, dim. of *pomme* apple; see -Y[5].] *Her.* Terminating in a knob or knobs, as the arms of a cross.

Pommy (pǫ·mi). *Australian.* 1916. [Of unkn. origin.] A newcomer from 'the old country'.

‖**Pomœrium** (pomiᵊ·riŏm). 1598. [L., f. *post* + *mœrus, murus* wall.] *Rom. Antiq.* The open space running inside and outside the walls of a city, which was consecrated by the pontifex and ordained to be left free from buildings. Hence *transf.*

Pomology (pomǫ·lŏdʒi). 1818. [f. L. *pomum* fruit, (later) apple + -LOGY. Cf. Fr. *pomologie.*] The science and practice of fruit-culture; also, a treatise on this. Hence **Pomolo·gical** *a.* **Pomo·logist.**

Pomona (pŏmōᵘ·nă). 1584. [L.] *Rom. Myth.* The goddess of fruits and fruit-trees; hence, the fruit-trees of a country, or a treatise on them (cf. *flora*).

P. green, green in which yellow predominates.

Pomp (pǫmp), *sb.* ME. [– (O)Fr. *pompe* – L. *pompa* – Gr. πομπή sending, solemn procession, train, parade, display, f. πέμπειν send.] **1.** Splendid display or celebration; splendour, magnificence. Also with *a* and *pl.* **†2.** A triumphal or ceremonial procession or train; a pageant –1807. **†b.** *fig.* –1712. **†3.** Ostentatious display; parade; vain-glory; esp. in phr. *p. and pride* –1772. **b.** *pl.* ME.

1. The boast of heraldry, the p. of pow'r GRAY. *fig.* I saw the p. of day depart LONGF. **2.** Here, while the proud their long-drawn pomps display GOLDSM. **3. b.** The pomps and vanities of the wicked world *Bk. Comm. Prayer* (1603) *Catechism.* Hence **†Pomp** *v. intr.* to exhibit p. or splendour; to conduct oneself pompously. **Po·mpal** *a. rare*, splendid, showy.

Pompadour (pǫ·mpădūᵊɹ). 1752. Name of the Marquise de Pompadour, mistress of Louis XV (1721–64), used as sb. and attrib. to designate fashions, a colour, etc. **1.** Designating fashions of dress, hair-dressing, furniture, etc. **2.** A shade of crimson or pink; also, a fabric of this colour. Also *attrib.* 1756. **3.** Designating a pattern consisting of sprigs of flowers in pink, blue, and sometimes gold, scattered on a white ground 1807. **4.** A tropical S. Amer. bird (*Xipholena pompadora*), having brilliant crimson-purple plumage. Also *attrib.* 1759. **5.** A style of arranging women's hair, in which it is turned back off the forehead in a roll. Also *attrib.* 1899.

Pompano (pǫ·mpăno). Also **pompono.** 1863. [– Sp. *pámpano.*] **1.** One of various W. Indian and N. American fishes, highly esteemed for the table; as **a.** In the W. Indies, *Trachynotus carolinus.* **b.** In California, *Stromateus simillimus.* **c.** In Florida, *Gerres olisthostoma*, known as the *Irish p.* **2. P.-shell.** A bivalve shell of the genus *Donax*; found on the coast of Florida 1890.

†Pompa·tic, *a.* 1535. [– late L. *pompaticus*, f. *pompare* to do (a thing) with pomp, f. *pompa* POMP *sb.*; see -ATIC.] Pompous, splendid, ostentatious –1677.

Pompeian (pǫmpī·ăn), *a.* †Also **Pompeiian.** 1834. [– L. *Pompeianus*, f. *Pompeii*; see -AN.] Of or pertaining to Pompeii, an Italian town, buried by an eruption of Mount Vesuvius in A.D. 79.

P. red, a shade of red resembling that found on the walls of houses in Pompeii.

Pompelmoose, pampelmous(**s**)**e** (pǫ·mp-, pæ·mp'lˌmūs). 1696. [– Du. *pompelmoes*, perh. repr. Du. *pompoen* pumpkin + Old Javanese *limoes*, borrowed from Pg. *limoes* pl. of *limão*, lemon; i.e. 'pumpkin-like citron'.] The large fruit of *Citrus decumana*, called also SHADDOCK; esp. the larger variety. Also the plant itself.

Pompey (pǫ·mpi), *v.* 1860. [Extended f. dial. *pomp* to pamper; a word of Dickens.] *trans.* To pamper.

‖**Pompholyx** (pǫ·mfŏliks). 1541. [– Gr. πομφόλυξ bubble, slag of ore.] **†1.** *Chem.* Crude zinc oxide –1725. **2.** *Path.* A vesicle on the skin; also, an eruption of vesicles, without inflammation or fever, appearing chiefly on the palms of the hands and the soles of the feet 1818. Hence **Pompho·lygous** *a.* affected with p.

‖**Pompier** (pǫ·mpiəɹ). 1893. [Fr., f. *pompe* PUMP *sb.*; see -IER.] A fireman.

P. ladder, a fireman's scaling ladder, with a hook at the top to attach it to a building.

Pompion, pumpion (pɒ·mpiən). Now *rare.* 1545. [XVI *pompon*(*e* – Fr. †*pompon*, nasalized form of †*popon*, var. of **pepon* – L. *pepo, pepon-* – Gr. πέπων large melon, subst. use of πέπων ripe.] **1.** The large fruit of *Cucurbita pepo*; a pumpkin; also the plant itself. **†2.** Occas. applied to the POMPELMOOSE –1704. **†3.** Applied in contempt to a (big) man –1625.

3. This vnwholsome humidity, this grossewatry Pumpion SHAKS.

Pompoleon (pǫmpōᵘ·liǫn). 1837. [– Fr. *pompoléon*; app. conn. w. *pompelmoose.*] The SHADDOCK or POMPELMOOSE (*Citrus decumana*).

Pom-pom (pǫ·mpǫm). 1899. [From the sound of the discharge.] Name given to the Maxim automatic quick-firing gun; see MAXIM[2]. Also *fig.*, and *attrib.* as *p. gun* 1900.

Pompon (pǫ·mpǫn, ‖poṅpoṅ). Also **pom-pom.** 1748. [– Fr. *pompon* tuft, top-knot; of unkn. origin.] **1.** A jewel or ornament attached to a long pin; a tuft or bunch of ribbon, velvet, threads of silk, etc., formerly worn in the hair, or on the cap or dress; now worn on women's and children's hats and shoes, etc., and used to ornament the edge of curtains, etc.; also, the round tuft on a soldier's or sailor's cap, the front of a shako, etc. **2.** A variety of Chrysanthemum, and of Dahlia, bearing small globular flowers. Also *attrib.* 1861.

Pomposity (pǫmpǫ·sĭti). late ME. [– late L. *pompositas*, f. *pomposus*; see next, -ITY.] The quality of being pompous; †pomp, solemnity; ostentatiousness in deportment or language.

Pompous (pǫ·mpəs), *a.* late ME. [– (O)Fr. *pompeux* – late L. *pomposus*, f. *pompa* POMP; see -OUS.] **1.** Characterized by pomp; magnificent, splendid; †processional. **2.** Characterized by an exaggerated display of self-importance or dignity; consequential, pretentious, ceremonious; of language: inflated, turgid. late ME.

1. Many processions and other p. shows 1841. **2.** A well-meaning, civil, prosing, p. woman, who thought nothing of consequence, but as it related to her own..concerns JANE AUSTEN. Hence **Po·mpous-ly** *adv.*, **-ness.**

‖**Ponceau** (poṅso). 1835. [Fr.] The bright red colour of the corn poppy. Also, a coal-tar dye of red colour.

Poncho (pǫ·ntʃo, pǫ·nʃo). 1748. [– S. Amer. Sp. – Araucanian *poncho.*] A S. Amer. cloak, consisting of an oblong piece of cloth with a slit in the middle for the head.

Pond (pǫnd), *sb.* [ME. *ponde, poonde, pounde,* identical with POUND *sb.*[2]] **1.** A small body of still water of artificial formation. Often distinguished as a *duck-p., fish-p., mill-p., village p.,* etc. Formerly often *spec.* = fish-pond. **b.** Locally applied to a natural pool, tarn, mere, or small lake 1480. **2.** Applied *fig.* or *joc.* to the sea, esp. the Atlantic Ocean; cf. HERRING-POND 1641. **3.** In a canal: = POUND *sb.*[2] II. 1 b.

attrib. and *Comb.*: **p.-fish,** (*a*) a fish usu. reared in a pond, as a carp; (*b*) *spec.* in *U.S.*, a fish of the genus *Pomotis* or *Lepomis*, a sunfish; **-life,** the animals, esp. the invertebrata, that live in ponds or stagnant water; **-lily,** a water-lily, as the yellow *Nuphar lutea*, or the white *Nymphæa alba*; **-snail,** any freshwater snail inhabiting ponds; **-spice,** a N. Amer. shrub (*Tetranthera geniculata*) growing in sandy swamps; **-tortoise, -turtle** (*U.S.*), any freshwater tortoise of the family *Emydidæ*; a terrapin or mud-turtle.

Pond (pǫnd), *v.* 1673. [f. prec.; cf. POUND *v.*[2] 3.] **1.** *trans.* To hold *back* or dam *up* (a stream) into or as into a pond; to pound. **2.** *intr.* Of water, etc.: To form a pool or pond; to collect by being held back 1857.

Pondage (pǫ·ndėdʒ). 1877. [f. POND *sb.* + -AGE.] Storage or ponding of water; the capacity of a pond or dam for holding water.

Ponder (pǫ·ndəɹ), *v.* ME. [– (O)Fr. *pondérer* consider (mod. balance, moderate) – L. *ponderare* weigh, reflect upon, f. *pondus, ponder-* weight, rel. to *pendere* weigh.] †**1.** *trans.* To weigh. Also *fig.* –1645. †**2.** To estimate the worth, value, or amount of; to appraise –1566. **3.** To weigh (a matter, words, etc.) mentally; to give due weight to; to think over, meditate upon. late ME. **4.** *intr.* To consider, meditate, reflect; to think deeply or seriously *on*, muse *over* 1605.

3. Consydre thys mater and p. my cause LYDG. Pondering only how he might save that monarch's crown 1848. **4.** Pondering on his unhappy lot DICKENS. Hence †**Po·nder,** an act of pondering. **Po·nderable** *a.* capable of being weighed; having appreciable weight. **Ponderabi·lity, Po·nderableness,** weight, heaviness. **Po·nderer. Po·nderingly** *adv.*

Ponderal (pǫ·ndərăl), *a.* 1674. [f. L. *pondus, ponder-* + -AL[1]; in XVII/XVIII f. AL. (*pecunia, libra*) *ponderalis* by weight.] Of or pertaining to weight; determined or estimated by weight.

Ponderance (pǫ·ndərăns). 1812. [app. extracted f. PREPONDERANCE.] Weight; gravity, importance. So **Po·nderary** *a.* = PONDERAL 1845.

Ponderate (pǫ·ndəreɪt), *v.* 1513. [– *ponderat-*, pa. ppl. stem of L. *ponderare* weigh; see PONDER, -ATE[3].] **1.** *intr.* To have weight; to be heavy, to weigh 1659. †**2.** *trans.* To weigh down; to influence, bias –1709. †**3.** To weigh in the mind, ponder –1753. **4.** To estimate the importance or value of; to appraise (*rare*) 1649. So **Ponderation,** weighing; balancing; also *fig.*

Ponderosity (pǫndərǫ·sĭti). 1450. [– OFr. *ponderosité* or med.L. *ponderositas*, f. L. *ponderosus*; see next, -ITY.] **1.** The quality of being ponderous; weightiness, weight. **2.** *fig.* Weightiness, importance; heaviness, dullness 1589.

Ponderous (pǫ·ndərəs), *a.* late ME. [– L. *ponderosus*, f. *pondus, ponder-* weight; see -OUS.] **1.** Having great weight; heavy; massive; clumsy, unwieldy. Also *fig.* †**b.** Having some weight; ponderable SIR T. BROWNE. †**2.** Of great weight in proportion to bulk –1800. †**3.** *fig.* Of grave import; weighty, important, profound –1794. †**4.** Given to weighing or pondering matters; deliberate –1647. **5.** Of a task, etc.: Heavy, laborious. Of style: Laboured; grandiloquent; tedious. 1704.

1. Why the Sepulcher..Hath op'd his p. and Marble iawes SHAKS. **2.** *P. earth, spar* = HEAVY SPAR. **5.** Sir John Hawkins's p. labours BOSWELL. Hence **Po·nderous-ly** *adv.*, **-ness.**

Po·ndweed. 1578. [f. POND *sb.* + WEED *sb.*[1]] An aquatic weed that grows in ponds and still waters; *spec.* in Great Britain, the species of *Potamogeton.*

American, Canadian, or Choke P., *Elodea canadensis* (*Anacharis alsinastrum*); Horned or Triple-headed P., *Zannichellia palustris.*

†‖**Pone**[1] (pōᵘ·ni). ME. [AL. (XII), legal AFr. *ponc* (XIII), = sing. imper. of L. *ponere* place.] *Law.* **a.** A writ by which a suit was removed from an inferior court to the Court of Common Pleas. **b.** A writ requiring the sheriff to secure the appearance of the defendant by attaching his goods or by causing him to find sureties for his appearance. –1768.

Pone[2] (pōᵘ·ni). 1890. [f. as prec.] The leader, or the leader's partner, in some card games. Also written *pony.*

Pone[3] (pōᵘn). 1634. [– Algonquian *pone, apone, oppone* bread, perh. orig. pa. pple. = 'baked'.] Any bread made of maize; orig. that of the N. Amer. Indians, made in thin cakes, and cooked in hot ashes; also, very fine light bread, enriched with milk, eggs, and the like, and made in flat cakes. Also *attrib.* **b.** A cake or loaf of such bread 1796.

Ponent (pōᵘ·nĕnt), *a.* (*sb.*) 1538. [– It. *ponente* (= Fr. †*ponent, -ant*), repr. L. *ponens, -ent-*, pr. pple. of *ponere* place. Cf. LEVANT *sb.*[1]] †**1.** Situated in the west; occidental. Also as *sb.* The west; the occident. –1819. **2.** *Geol.* Name for a subdivision of the Palæozoic strata of the Appalachian chain 1858. **3.** *Logic.* That posits 1837.

1. Forth rush the Levant and the P. Windes MILT.

Pongee (pǫndʒī·). 1711. [– N. Chinese *pun-chī* = Mandarin *pun-kī* 'own loom' or *pun-cheh* 'own weaving', i.e. home-made.] A soft unbleached kind of Chinese silk; known in the East as Chefoo silk; also *attrib.*

‖**Pongo** (pǫ·ŋgo). 1625. [Congolese *mpongo, mpongi, impungu.*] In early writers, a large anthropoid African ape; variously identified with the Chimpanzee, and the Gorilla. **b.** Transferred (erron.) to the Orang-outang 1834.

Poniard (pǫ·nyăɹd). 1588. [– Fr. *poignard*, repl. OFr. *poignal* – med.L. *pugnalis*, n. *-ale*, f. L. *pugnus* fist; cf. -ARD.] A short stabbing weapon; a dagger.

fig. Shee speakes poynyards, and euery word stabbes SHAKS. Hence **Po·niard** *v. trans.* to stab or pierce (esp. to stab to death) with a p. 1601.

‖**Pons** (pǫnz). The L. word for 'bridge', used in certain phrases. **1. Pons asinorum** (= bridge of asses): a joc. name for the fifth proposition of the first book of Euclid, which beginners, etc., find difficulty in 'getting over'. Hence allusively. 1751. **2. Pons Varolii** (= bridge of Varolius or Varoli, an Italian anatomist of the 16th c.), also **pons cerebri** or **cerebelli,** and often simply **pons:** a band of nerve fibres in the brain, just above the medulla oblongata, consisting of transverse fibres connecting the two hemispheres of the cerebellum, and longitudinal fibres connecting the medulla with the cerebrum 1693.

Pontage (pǫ·ntėdʒ). Now *Hist.* or *local.* 1447. [– law AFr. (whence AL. *pontagium* XII), OFr. *pontage* – med.L. *pontaticum, pontaticus*, f. L. *pons, pont-* bridge; see -AGE.] A toll paid for the use of a bridge; a tax paid for the maintenance and repair of a bridge or bridges; bridge-toll.

Pontic (pǫ·ntik), *a.* 1477. [– L. *Ponticus* – Gr. ποντικός, f. πόντος sea, spec. the Black Sea, hence the country of Pontus.] **1.** Of, belonging to, found in, or obtained from the district of Pontus 1551. †**2.** Having a somewhat sour and astringent taste [? like Pontic rhubarb] –1684.

1. P. nut, the hazel nut. **P. rhubarb,** *Rheum rhaponticum.* **P. wormwood,** *Artemisia pontica.* **P. sea,** the Black Sea.

‖**Pontifex** (pǫ·ntifeks). *Pl.* **pontifices** (pǫnti·fisīz). 1579. [L. *pontifex, -fic-*, f. *pons, pont-* bridge + *-fic-*, *facere* make.] **1.** *Rom. Antiq.* A member of the principal college of priests in ancient Rome, the head of which was the *P. Maximus* or chief priest. **2.** *Eccl.* = PONTIFF 2. 1651. **3.** With allusion to the reputed etymological meaning = Bridge-maker 1831.

Pontiff (pǫ·ntif). 1610. [– Fr. *pontife* – L. *pontifex*; see prec.] **1.** *Rom. Antiq.* = prec. 1. 1626. **2.** A bishop; *spec.* and usu., the bishop of Rome, the pope (in full, *sovereign p.*) 1677. **3.** *gen.* A chief or high priest. Also *fig.* 1610.

Pontific (pǫnti·fik), *a.* Now *rare* or *Obs.* 1644. [Extracted from earlier PONTIFICAL; see -ICAL. Cf. Fr. †*pontifique* adj. and sb.] **1.** *Rom. Antiq.* = PONTIFICAL *a.* II. **2.** = PONTIFICAL *a.* I. 1–3. 1716. ¶**3.** *catachr.* Pertaining to a bridge (*joc.*) STERNE.

Pontifical (pǫnti·fikăl), *a.* and *sb.* ME. [– Fr. *pontifical* adj. and sb. or L. *pontificalis*; see PONTIFEX, -AL[1], -ICAL.] **A.** *adj.* **I. 1.** Pertaining or proper to a bishop or prelate; episcopal 1440. **2.** *spec.* Of or pertaining to the pope; papal 1447. **3.** *gen.* Of or pertaining to a chief or high priest; high-priestly 1440. **4.** Characterized by the pomp, state, authority, or dogmatic character of a pontiff 1589.

4. Comte's arrogance, his p. airs, and his hatred of liberty 1892.

II. *Rom. Antiq.* Of or belonging to the *pontifices* of ancient Rome; see PONTIFEX 1. 1579. **III.** Bridge-making, bridge-building 1667.

B. *sb.* †**1. a.** *pl.* The offices or duties of a pontifex or pontiff. **b.** An office celebrated with pontifical ceremony. –1691. **2.** (Now always *pl.*) = PONTIFICALIA ME. **3.** An office-book in the Western Church, containing the forms for rites and ceremonies to be performed by bishops 1584. †**4. a.** A pontiff, a church dignitary. **b.** An adherent of the pontiffs or prelates. –1590. Hence **Ponti·fically** *adv.*

‖**Pontificalia** (pǫntifikēɪ·liă), *sb. pl.* 1577. [L., subst. use of n. pl. of *pontificalis*; see prec.] The vestments and other insignia of a bishop (or of a priest). Also *transf.* Official robes.

In pontificalibus: see ‖IN 13; hence *pontificalibus* is occas. used as if an ordinary English noun. late ME.

Pontificality (pǫntifikæ·lĭti). 1556. [– Fr. †*pontificalité* pontifical dignity; see PONTIFICAL and -ITY.] **1.** Pontifical office or dignity; esp. that of the pope. **b.** *transf.* or *gen.* Priesthood; high-priesthood 1593. †**2.** (Usu. in *pl.*) Pontifical robes, pontificals –1645. **3.** A pontifical rite, ceremony, or function CARLYLE.

Pontificate (pǫnti·fikėt), *sb.* 1581. [– L. *pontificatus*, f. PONTIFEX; see -ATE[1]. Cf. Fr. *pontificat* (XV).] **a.** The office of an ancient Roman *Pontifex.* **b.** The office, or period of office, of a bishop; usu. of the pope; papacy; popedom 1674. **c.** *gen.* High-priesthood 1727.

Pontificate (pǫnti·fikeɪt), *v.* 1818. [– *pontificat-*, pa. ppl. stem of med.L. *pontificare*, f. L. *pontifex*; see -ATE[3] and cf. EPISCOPATE *v.*] **1.** *intr.* To perform the functions of a pontiff or bishop; to officiate as a bishop, esp. at mass. **2.** To act the pontiff, assume the airs of a pontiff. Also *fig.* to issue dogmatic decrees. 1825.

†**Po·ntifice.** [f. L. *pons, pont-* bridge, after *edifice.*] The edifice of a bridge; a bridge MILT.

†**Pontifi·cial,** *a.* and *sb.* 1591. [f. L. *pontificius* pertaining to a pontifex + -AL[1].] **A.** *adj.* **1.** = PONTIFICAL *a.* I. 1, 2. –1769. **2.** Popish, papistical –1684. **3.** = PONTIFICAL *a.* I. 4. –1709. **B.** *sb.* An adherent of the prelates, or of the pontiff –1838.

A. 1. *P. law,* canon law. **2.** P. Princes and Prelates, the sworn Enemies to the Protestant Religion 1641. Hence †**Pontifi·cially** *adv.* So †**Pontifi·cian** *a.* and *sb.*

Pontil (pǫ·ntil). 1832. [– Fr. *pontil*, app. – It. *pontello, puntello*, dim. of *punto* point, etc.] *Glass-making.* An iron rod used for handling soft glass in the process of formation, esp. in the manufacture of crown-glass. Cf. PUNTY.

Pontine (pǫ·ntəin), *a.* 1899. [f. L. *pons, pont-* bridge + -INE[1].] *Anat.* and *Path.* Pertaining to or occurring in the *pons Varolii*; see PONS.

‖**Pont-levis** (ponləvi, pǫnt,le·vis). 1489. [Fr. *pont-levis* i.e. *pont* bridge, *levis*, OFr. *leveïs* movable up and down.] A drawbridge.

Pontoneer, -ier (pǫntonīᵊ·ɹ). 1830. [– (O)Fr. *pontonnier* :– med.L. *pontonarius* ferryman, f. *ponto*; see next, -EER, -IER 2.] *Mil.* One who has charge of pontoons, or of the construction of a pontoon-bridge.

Pontoon (pǫntū·n), *sb.*[1] 1676. [– (O)Fr. *ponton* :– L. *ponto, ponton-* punt, bridge of boats, f. *pons, pont-* bridge, see -OON.] **1.** A flat-bottomed boat used as a lighter, ferry-boat, or the like; *spec.* in *Mil. Engineering*, such a boat, or other floating vessel (as a hollow metal cylinder), of which a number are used to support a temporary bridge over a river. **2.** *Naut.* A large flat-bottomed barge or lighter furnished with cranes, capstans, and tackle, used for careening ships, raising weights, etc. 1769. **3.** *Hydraulic Engineering* = CAISSON 2 b, c. 1875.

attrib. and *Comb.*: **p.-bridge,** a bridge constructed upon pontoons; **-train,** a train of wagons carrying pontoons. Hence **Pontoo·n** *v. trans.* to cross (a river) by means of pontoons; also *fig.*

Pontoo·n, *sb.*[2] 1900. Alteration (orig. army slang) of the name of the card-game VINGT-UN.

Pony (pōᵘ·ni), *sb.* 1659. [perh. for *poulney – Fr. *poulenet*, dim. of *poulain* foal; see PULLEN.] **1.** A horse of any small breed; *spec.* a horse not more than 13 or (in pop. use) 14 hands high. **2.** *slang.* The sum of twenty-five pounds sterling 1797. **3.** *U.S. slang.* A school or college 'crib' 1832. **4.** *slang.* A small glass of liquor 1884.

attrib. and *Comb.*, as *p.-chaise*, etc.; also, **p. engine,** a small locomotive for shunting; **-truck,** a two-wheeled leading or trailing truck in some forms of locomotive; **-truss,** a truss so low that overhead bracing cannot be used.

‖**Pood** (pūd). 1554. [Russ. *pud* – LG. or ON. *pund* POUND *sb.*[1]] A weight, equal to 40 lb. Russian, or about 36 lb. avoirdupois.

Poodle (pū·d'l), *sb.* 1825. [– G. *pudel*, short for *pudelhund*, f. LG. *pud(d)eln* splash in water, the poodle being a waterdog.] One of a breed of pet dogs with long curling hair, usu. black or white, which is often clipped or shaved in a fantastic manner. Also *attrib.*

Comb. **p.-faker,** one who cultivates female society; also **-faking.** Hence **Poo·dle** *v. trans.* to clip and shave the hair of (a dog).

Poof (puf), *int.* Also **pouf.** 1857. [Cf. Fr. *pouf.*] A sound imitating a short puff of the breath, as in blowing out a candle; hence an expression of contemptuous rejection.

Pooh (pū, puh), *interj.* (*sb.*) 1593. A 'vocal gesture' expressing the action of puffing anything away, and hence impatience or contemptuous disregard. **B.** as *sb.* 1667.

Affection, puh! You speake like a greene Girle SHAKS. Hence **Pooh** *v. intr.* and *trans.*

Pooh Bah (pū bā). 1888. [Name of a character in W. S. Gilbert's *Mikado* (1885), joc. made up of the interjections *pooh* and *bah.*] One who holds many offices at one time.

Pooh pooh (pū·pū·), *int.* (*sb.*, *a.*) 1679. Reduplication of POOH *int.* **B.** *sb.* (*pooh-pooh*). An utterance of this exclam.; one who is addicted to using this exclam. 1798. **C.** *attrib.* or *adj.*, as in *pooh-pooh theory*, the theory that language is a development of natural interjections 1860. Hence **Pooh-pooh** *v. trans.* to express contempt or disdain for; to make light of 1827.

‖**Pookoo, puku** (pū·ku). 1890. [– Zulu *mpuku.*] A red water-buck or antelope (*Cobus vardoni*) of southern Central Africa.

Pool (pūl), *sb.*[1] [OE. *pōl* = OFris., (M)LG., MDu. *pōl* (Du. *poel*), OHG. *pfuol* (G. *pfuhl*), f. WGmc. *pōl-.] **1.** A small body of standing or still water; usu., one of natural formation. **b.** A small shallow collection of any liquid; a puddle 1843. **c.** *transf.* and *fig.* 1587. **2.** A deep and still place in a river or stream OE.

1. The noisy geese that gabbled o'er the p. GOLDSM. **b.** Wallowing in a p. of blood MACAULAY. **c.** On the floor..A little p. of sunlight 1875. **2.** *The P.*, the part of the Thames between London Bridge and Cuckold's Point.

Pool, *sb.*[2] 1693. [– Fr. *poule* stake, prop. hen (see PULLET); cf. Sp. *polla* hen, stake at ombre; assoc. with POOL *sb.*[1] was prob. furthered by the identification of *fish* (in the pool) with Fr. *fiche* counter (see FISH *sb.*[2]).] **1.** In certain card games, etc.: The collective amount of the stakes and fines of the players joining in the game 1711. **b.** The receptacle containing the stakes; the pool-dish 1770. †**2.** A party in a card-game in which there is a pool –1859. **3.** A game played on a billiard-table, in which each player has a ball of a distinctive colour with which he tries to pocket the balls of the other players in a certain order, each player contributing an agreed sum, the whole of which the winner takes; also, a similar game in U.S., played with balls numbered 1 to 15, the number of each ball a player pockets being added to his score 1848. **4. a.** *Rifle-Shooting.* A contest in which each competitor pays a certain sum for every shot he fires, the proceeds being divided among the winners. Also *attrib.* 1861. **b.** *Betting.* The collective stakes in an instance of PARI MUTUEL 1881. **5.** A common fund into or from which all gains or losses of the contributors are paid; hence, a 'combine' 1872. **6.** An arrangement between previously competing parties, by which rates or prices are fixed, and business or receipts divided, in order to do away with mutually injurious competition (orig. *U.S.*) 1881. **7.** *Fencing.* A contest between teams, in which each member of one side opposes each member of the other 1901.

2. Monday, when we played six pools 1801. *To make* (*up*) *a p.*, to form or make up the party. **5.** The fifty-million dollar p. in Union Pacific Preferred Stock 1906.

Pool (pūl), *v.*[1] 1793. [f. POOL *sb.*[1]] *trans.* In quarrying granite: To sink or make (a hole) for the insertion of a wedge. In coal-mining: To undermine (coal) so as to cause it to fall.

Pool (pūl), *v.*[2] 1879. [f. POOL *sb.*[2]] *trans.* To throw into a common stock to be distributed according to agreement; to combine (capital or interests) for the common benefit; *spec.* of competing railway companies, etc.: To share or divide (traffic or receipts).

‖**Poon** (pūn). 1699. [Sinhalese *pūna*, Tamil *punnai.*] Any of several large E. Indian trees of the genus *Calophyllum*, esp. *C. inophyllum*; also, their timber. Chiefly *attrib.*

‖**Poonac** (pū·nĕk). 1890. [Tamil *punnakku*, Sinhalese *punakku.*] The oil-cake or mass left after the oil has been expressed from coco-nut pulp; used as fodder or manure.

Poonah (pū·nă). 1821. Name of a city in the Bombay Presidency.

attrib.: **P. painting,** painting on rice (or other thin) paper, in imitation of oriental work, by the application of thick body-colour, with little or no shading, and without background.

‖**Poonga-oil** (pū·ŋgă,oil). 1866. [f. Tamil *punga.*] A dark-yellow oil expressed from the seeds of *Pongamia glabra*, used in India as lamp-oil and as a remedy in skin-diseases.

Poop (pūp), *sb.* 1489. [– OFr. *pupe, pope* (mod. *poupe*) :– Rom. *puppa for L. *puppis* poop, stern.] **1.** The aftermost part of a ship; the stern; also, the aftermost and highest deck, often forming the roof of the cabin built in the stern. †**2.** *transf.* The dickey or seat at the back of a coach; the hinder part of a man or animal. *colloq.* or *vulgar.*

1. The Poope was beaten Gold SHAKS.

Comb.: **p.-royal,** the deck forming the roof of the poop-cabin.

†**Poop** (pūp), *v.*[1] 1575. [Cf. Du. *poep* clown.] *trans.* To cheat, befool –1663.

Poop (pūp), *v.*[2] 1727. [f. POOP *sb.*] *Naut. trans.* Of a wave: To break over the stern of (a vessel). **b.** *transf.* Of a ship: To receive (a wave) over the stern; to ship (a sea) on the poop 1894.

Pooped (pūpt), *a.* 1879. [f. POOP *sb.* + -ED[2].] Having a poop; chiefly in comb. as *high-p.*

Poor (pūᵊɹ), *a.* (*sb.*) [ME. *povere, pou(e)re, pore* – OFr. *povre*, (also mod. dial.) *poure* (mod. *pauvre*) :– L. *pauper* (Rom. *pauperus). For similar loss of *v* before *r* cf. *curfew, kerchief, lord.*] **I. 1.** Having few, or no, material possessions; wanting means to procure the comforts, or the necessaries, of life; needy, destitute; *spec.* (esp. in legal use), so destitute as to be dependent on gifts or allowances for subsistence. In common use expressing various degrees of poverty. The opposite of *rich* or *wealthy*. **b.** Of, involving, or characterized by poverty ME. **2.** Ill-supplied, lacking (*in* some possession or quality). late ME. **b.** Of soil, ore, etc.: Yielding little, unproductive 1592. **3.** In lean or feeble condition from ill feeding 1539. **4.** Small in amount; less than is wanted or expected; scanty, inadequate ME. **5.** Not worth much; of inferior quality, paltry, sorry; mean, shabby. Usu. of abstract things. ME. **b.** Mentally or morally inferior; mean-spirited; despicable, 'small'; spiritless. late ME. **c.** Slight, insignificant 1603. **d.** In modest or apologetic use: Of little worth or pretension; humble, insignificant. late ME. **6.** Such, or so circumstanced, as to excite one's compassion or pity; unfortunate, hapless. In many parts of England regularly said of the dead whom one knew; = late, deceased. Chiefly *colloq.* ME.

1. If thou be'st as poore for a subiect, as hee's for a King, thou art poore enough SHAKS. *fig.* Blissed be þai þat er pouer in spirit 1400. *P. people*, the poor as a class; often connoting humble rank or station; They are almost like p. people's children! C. BRONTË. **b.** Forced..to take..p. and painful Employments FULLER. **2.** Stratified masses,..p. in mineral substances 1863. **b.** P. and hungry soils SIR H. DAVY. **4.** One poore peny-worth of Sugar-candie SHAKS. The crop of wheat would be thought p. MACAULAY. **5.** They made but p. work of it DE FOE. It was p. consolation to know [etc.] (*mod.*). **b.** A Man of a poore Minde, and not valiant 1627. He is a p. creature and more of a Genoese than an Englishman NELSON. **d.** For mine owne poore part, Looke you, Ile goe pray SHAKS. **6.** Till his book of p. Dr. Johnson's life is finished MME. D'ARBLAY. He looked dreadfully weak still, p. fellow! 1857.

II. *absol.* or as *sb.* (usu. in sense 1). **a.** *absol.* in *pl.* sense (usu. with *the*): poor people as a class; those in necessitous or humble circumstances; *spec.* those dependent upon charitable or parochial relief ME. **b.** possessive *poor's* (in sing. or pl. sense). Now *rare.* exc. *dial.* late ME.

a. The short and simple annals of the p. GRAY. Money left to the p. of the parish 1907.

Combs. and Phrases. **P. child,** a pupil at a charity school (CHILD *sb.* I. 4); **p.-chest** = POOR-BOX; **p. Clares,** the order of nuns of St. Clare; **p. relation,** a relative or kinsman in humble circumstances (also *transf.*); **p. white** (see WHITE *a.* 4). Hence **Poo·rness,** the quality or condition of being p. ME.

Poo·r-box. Also †**poor's box.** 1621. A money-box (esp. in a church) for gifts towards the relief of the poor.

Poorhouse (pūᵊ·ɹhaus). Also **poorshouse** (*Sc.* and *U.S.*). 1781. A house in which poor people in receipt of public charity are lodged.

Poor John, poo·r-john. 1585. [f. POOR *a.* + JOHN.] Hake salted and dried for food; often a type of poor fare. *Obs.* exc. *Hist.*

Poor-Iohn and Apple-pyes are all our fare 1612.

Poor-law (pūᵊ·ɹlǭ). 1752. The law, or system of laws, relating to the support of paupers at the public expense. **b.** *attrib.*, as *p. bill, officer*, etc.; **p. parish:** see PARISH 2.

Poorly (pūᵊ·ɹli), *adv.* and *a.* ME. [f. POOR *a.* + -LY[2].] In a poor manner or condition. **A.** *adv.* **1.** In a state of poverty or indigence; necessitously. Now somewhat *rare.* late ME. **2.** With deficiency of some desirable quality; scantily, defectively; in mean style, humbly; in an inferior way, rather badly: not highly, with low estimation ME. †**3.** Meanly, shabbily –1723. †**4.** Abjectly, humbly; despicably; mean-spiritedly –1811. **B.** *adj.* Chiefly *colloq.* In a poor state of health; unwell, indisposed. (Always *predicative.*) 1750.

A. 1. Poorely content is better then richlye couetous GREENE. **2.** Long lines of poorly-lighted streets DICKENS. **3.** 'Twas p. done, unworthy of your self OTWAY. **4.** He, instead of opposing..did p. go on board himself, to ask what De Ruyter would have PEPYS. **B.** His wife had..been p. MACAULAY. Hence **Poo·rlyish** *a.* somewhat p. (*rare*).

Poor man. ME. **1.** *lit.* A man who is poor (in any sense); *esp.* a man who is indigent or needy, or who belongs to the class of the poor. **2.** *Poor man of mutton* (Sc. colloq.): the remains of a shoulder of mutton, broiled 1818.

2. I think, landlord..I could eat a morsel of a poor man SCOTT.

Combs.: **poor man's mustard**: see MUSTARD 2 b; **poor man's weather-glass,** the pimpernel, *Anagallis arvensis,* from its closing its flowers before rain.

Poo·r-rate. Also †**poor's rate.** 1601. A rate or assessment for the relief or support of the poor.

Poor-spi·rited, *a.* 1648. Having or showing a poor spirit; deficient in spirit, cowardly. Hence **Poo:r-spi·ritedness.**

Poortith (pū°·ɹtiþ). *Sc.* and *n. dial.* 1508. [repr. OFr. *povertet,* with the loss of *v* as in POOR and retention of final *þ* of AFr. as in *dainteth, plenteth*; see DAINTY, PLENTY.] Poverty.

Poo·r-will. *U.S.* 1888. [In imitation of its note.] A bird of the N. American genus *Phalænoptilus,* esp. *P. nuttalli.* Cf. WHIP-POOR-WILL.

Pop (pǫp), *sb.*[1] late ME. [imit.; goes with POP *v.*] **1.** An act of popping; now, a slight rap or tap. *Obs.* exc. *dial.* **2.** A short abrupt sound of explosion 1591. **3.** A shot with a fire-arm 1657. **b.** *slang.* A pistol 1728. **4.** A name for any effervescing beverage, esp. ginger-beer, from the sound made when the cork is drawn (*colloq.*) 1812. **5.** A mark made by a slight rapid touch; a dot; a spot, a speck. Also *fig.* 1718. **6.** *slang.* The act of pawning 1866.

3. *fig.* Prestige, you know, I always like to have a p. at FREEMAN. **6.** *In p.,* in pawn.

Pop (pǫp), *sb.*[2] 1862. Colloq. abbrev. of *popular concert.*

Pop (pǫp), *sb.*[3] 1865. [perh. from L. *popina* or Eng. *lollipop shop,* 'the rooms having orig. been in the house of Mrs. Hatton, who kept such a shop'.] A social club and debating society at Eton College, founded in 1811.

Pop, *sb.*[4] *U.S.* 1840. Shortened f. POPPA.

Pop (pǫp), *v.* late ME. [imit.; goes with POP *sb.*[1], *int., adv.*] **1.** *trans.* To strike with a slight rap or tap (*dial.*). **2.** *intr.* To make a small quick explosive sound; to burst or explode with a pop 1576. **3.** *trans.* To cause to go off with a pop; to fire, let off, as an explosive or fire-arm (also *fig.*) 1595. **4.** *intr.* To shoot, fire a gun (*colloq.*) 1725. **b.** *trans.* To shoot *down*; to pick *off* with a shot 1762. **5.** *trans.* To put promptly, suddenly, or unexpectedly; usu. with *down, in, on, out, up, into* or *out of* (a place), etc. 1529. **6.** To put (a question) abruptly; spec. *to p. the question* (*slang* or *colloq.*), to propose marriage 1593. **7.** *slang.* To put in pledge, to pawn 1731. **8.** *intr.* To pass, move, go or come promptly, suddenly, or unexpectedly (*up, down, in, out, between,* etc.) 1530. **b.** *To p. off* (also *off the hooks*): to die (*slang*) 1764.

2. When the chestnuts popped in the ashes 1859. **3.** *To p. corn,* to parch or roast Indian corn until it 'pops' open. **4.** Popping at pheasants BARHAM. **5.** She..popt it into her mouth, and swallowed it all at once 1662. P. me down among your fashionable visitors DICKENS. **8.** He that hath..Popt in betweene th'election and my hopes SHAKS. **b.** I am afraid I shall p. off just when my mind is able to run alone KEATS. Hence **Po·pping** *vbl. sb.* 1652.

Pop (pǫp), *int., adv.* 1621. [See prec.] With (the action or sound of) a pop; instantaneously, abruptly; unexpectedly.

I heard it go p. 1907. *P. goes the weasel,* name of a country dance in which these words were sung while one of the dancers darted under the arms of the others; also the name of the tune.

Pop-, usu. the verb in comb. with a sb. or adv., meaning something that pops; rarely the sb. or adv.: **p.-eye,** a bulging prominent eye; hence **-eyed** *a.*; **-valve** = PUPPET-VALVE; **-weed,** the Bladderwort; etc.

‖**Popadam** (pǫ·pădăm). 1820. [Tamil *pappaḍam,* contr. from *paruppu-aḍam* 'lentil cake' (Yule).] Small cakes eaten with curries.

Po·p-corn. *U.S.* 1858. [f. POP *v.* 3 + CORN *sb.*[1] 3.] **a.** Maize or Indian corn parched till it bursts open and exposes the white inner part of the grain. **b.** A variety of maize suitable for popping. Also *attrib.*

Pope[1] (pō^u^p). [OE. *pāpa* – eccl. L. *pāpa* bishop (Tertullian), from the time of Leo the Great (V) applied spec. to the Bishop of Rome, – eccl. Gr. *πάπας, παπᾶς* bishop, patriarch, later form of *πάππας* father (see PAPA[1]).] **I. 1.** The Bishop of Rome, as head of the Roman Catholic Church. **2.** An effigy of the pope burnt on the anniversary of the Gunpowder Plot (Nov. 5), or at other times. *Obs.* or *dial.* 1673. **3. a.** *transf.* Applied to the spiritual head of a non-Christian religion. late ME. **b.** *fig.* One who assumes, or is considered to have, a position or authority like that of the pope 1589. †**4.** In early times, A bishop of the Christian Church; *spec.* in the Eastern Church, the title of the Bishop or Patriarch of Alexandria –1850.

3. b. Dr. McMill..the present Low-Church p. of Liverpool 1854.

II. Transf. uses. **1.** A freshwater fish of the Perch family; the Ruff 1653. **2.** A local name for various birds (e.g. the Puffin, the Bullfinch), from their colouring or stout form 1674.

Comb. **pope's nose** = *parson's nose.*

Pope[2] (pō^u^p). 1662. [– Russ. *pop* :– OSl. *popŭ* – WGmc. *papo (cf. OHG. *pfaffo*) – eccl. Gr. *πάπας*; see prec.] A parish priest of the Greek Church in Russia, Serbia, etc.

Popedom (pō^u^·pdəm). [Late OE. *pāpdōm,* f. *pāpa* POPE[1]; see -DOM.] **1.** = PAPACY 1. **b.** *transf.* Applied to a position of supreme authority in any religious system; also *ironically* 1588. **2.** = PAPACY 2. 1641. **b.** An eccl. polity resembling the papacy 1545.

1. b. The p. of Paternoster-Row 1837.

†**Pope-holy** *a.* (*sb.*) late ME. [app. f. POPE[1] + HOLY *a.*, but taken to represent Fr. *papelard* hypocritical.] Pretending to great holiness; characterized by a show or pretence of piety. **B.** *sb.* Hypocrisy. late ME.

Pope Joan. 1590. [After the fabulous female pope Joan.] A card-game played by three or more persons, with a pack from which the eight of diamonds has been removed, the stakes being won by the players of certain cards.

Popeling (pō^u^·pliŋ). 1561. [f. POPE[1] + -LING[1] 1, 2.] †**1.** An adherent of the pope; a papist –1705. **2.** A little or petty pope 1588.

Popery (pō^u^·pəri). 1534. [f. POPE[1] + -ERY.] The doctrines, practices, and ceremonial associated with the pope; the papal system; the Roman Catholic religion, or adherence to it. (A hostile term.)

The cry of 'No P.' is foolish enough in these days CARLYLE.

Pope's eye. 1673. The lymphatic gland surrounded with fat in the middle of a leg of mutton; regarded as a tit-bit.

Pope's head. 1609. [From its appearance.] **1.** A species of Cactus, *Melocactus communis,* producing its flowers on a woolly cushion or head, beset with bristles and spines. **2.** A round brush or broom with a long handle, for sweeping ceilings, etc.; called also *Turk's head* 1824.

Po·p-gun, po·pgun, *sb.* 1662. [f. POP *sb.*[1] or *v.* + GUN *sb.*] **1.** A child's toy; a tube from the mouth of which a tight-fitting pellet is expelled with a pop by compressing the air in the tube with a piston. Also *attrib.* **2.** A small, inefficient, or antiquated fire-arm (*contempt.*) 1849.

Popinjay (pǫ·pinˌdʒē^i^). [ME. *pape(n)iai, pope(n)iay, -gay* – AFr. *papeiaye,* OFr. *papegay, papingay* (mod. *papegai*) – Sp. *papagayo* – Arab. *babaġā*; for intrusive *n* cf. *messenger*; the final syll. is assim. to JAY.] **1.** A parrot. *Obs.* or *arch.* **2.** A representation of a parrot; *esp.* as a heraldic charge or bearing ME. **3.** The figure of a parrot fixed on a pole as a mark to shoot at. *Obs.* exc. *Hist.* 1548. **4.** *fig.* Taken as a type of vanity or empty conceit, and thus applied contemptuously to a person; cf. PARROT 2. 1528. †**5.** The prevailing colour of the green parrot; a shade of green; also *attrib.* –1865. **6.** A local name of the green woodpecker 1833.

4. As pert and as proud as any p. SCOTT.

Popish (pō^u^·piʃ), *a.* 1528. [f. POPE[1] + -ISH[1].] †**1.** Of or pertaining to the pope; papal –1567. **2.** Of or pertaining to popery; of or belonging to the Church of Rome; papistical. (In hostile use.) 1528. Hence **Po·pish-ly** *adv.*, **-ness.**

Poplar (pǫ·plăɹ). [ME. *popler(e* – AFr. *popler,* OFr. *poplier* (mod. *peuplier*), f. *pople* (whence POPPLE *sb.*[1]) :– L. *populus.* With the form *poplar* (XVI) cf. contemp. *briar, cedar, medlar.*] **1.** A tree of the genus *Populus,* comprising large trees of rapid growth, some species remarkable for tremulous leaves; also, the timber of this tree. The Black P., White P., Lombardy P., and Trembling P. or Aspen are the familiar European species. **2.** Applied to other trees resembling the poplar in some respect; *esp.* the Tulip-tree (also **Tulip-P.**) of N. America (*Liriodendron tulipifera*) 1766. **3.** *attrib.* late ME.

Poplin (pǫ·plin). 1710. [– Fr. †*papeline,* dubiously held to be from It. *papalina,* subst. use of fem. of *papalino* papal, and to be so named because orig. manufactured at Avignon, which was a papal town from 1309 to 1791; see -INE[1].] A mixed woven fabric, consisting of a silk warp and worsted weft, and having a corded surface; now made chiefly in Ireland. Hence **Poplinette,** a woollen or linen fabric in imitation of p. 1861.

Popliteal (pǫpli·tiăl), *a.* 1786. [f. mod.L. *popliteus* adj. (f. L. *poples, poplit-* ham, hough) + -AL[1].] *Anat.* Pertaining to, situated in, or connected with the ham, or the hollow at the back of the knee; as *p. artery, tendons* (= hamstrings), etc.

Po·ppa. *U.S. colloq.* 1902. = PAPA[1].

Popper (pǫ·pəɹ), *sb.* 1750. [f. POP *v.* + -ER[1].] **1.** A gun, fire-arm, or the like; *spec.* a pistol (*slang*). **2.** A utensil for popping 'corn' (maize). *U.S.* 1875.

Poppet (pǫ·pėt). [ME. *popet(te,* of obsc. origin; based ult. on L. *pupa, puppa* girl, doll; cf. PUPPET (its later variant) and -ET.] **1.** A small or dainty person; now, usu., a term of endearment; darling, pet. †**2.** A doll –1729. †**3.** = PUPPET *sb.* 3, 3 b. –1745. **4.** One of the upright pieces in a turning-lathe, in which the centres are fixed on which the work turns; a lathe-head 1665. **b.** = PUPPET-VALVE 1875. **5.** *Naut.* Applied to short pieces of wood, used for various purposes; *esp.* **a.** stout vertical squared pieces placed beneath a ship's hull to support her in launching; **b.** pieces on the gunwale of a boat, forming the rowlocks 1792.

Po·ppet-hea·d. 1665. **1.** = prec. 4. **2.** *Mining.* = HEAD-GEAR 3. (Often in *pl.* in same sense.) 1874.

Poppied (pǫ·pid), *a.* 1805. [f. POPPY *sb.* + -ED[2].] **1.** Having, or affected by, the sleep-inducing quality of the poppy; slumberous, drowsy, narcotic. **2.** Filled or adorned with poppies 1818.

1. The p. sleep, the end of all SWINBURNE.

Po·pping-crease. 1774. [f. POPPING *vbl. sb.,* prob. in sense 'striking' + CREASE *sb.*[2] 2.] *Cricket.* A line drawn four feet in front of and parallel to the wicket, within which the batsman must stand.

Popple (pǫ·p'l), *sb.*[1] Now *dial.* and *U.S.* late ME. [– OFr. *pople* (mod. dial. *peuple*); see POPLAR.] = POPLAR.

Popple (pǫ·p'l), *sb.*[2] Now *local.* late ME. [Of unkn. origin.] **1.** = COCKLE *sb.*[1] 1. †**b.** = COCKLE *sb.*[1] 2. –1644. **2.** Extended to the Corn Poppy, Charlock, etc., and their seeds 1855.

1. b. That malicious one did sow p. among the good Wheat 1644.

Popple (pǫ·p'l), *sb.*[3] 1875. [Goes with next.] An act or condition of poppling; a rolling or tossing of water in short tumultuous waves; a strong ripple. Hence **Po·pply** *a.* broken, choppy, ripply.

Popple (pǫ·p'l), *v.* ME. [prob. – (M)Du.

popelen murmur, babble, quiver, throb, of imit. origin.] *intr.* To roll or tumble about; to bubble up; to ripple; to toss to and fro in short waves.

Poppy (pǫ·pi). [OE. *popæġ, papæġ*, later *popiġ* :– **papāg*, **popāg*, for **pāpau* – med. L. **papāuum* (whence OFr. *pavou*, mod. *pavot*), alt. of L. *papāver*.] **I. 1.** A plant (or flower) of the genus *Papaver*, having milky juice with narcotic properties, showy flowers with petals of various colours, and roundish capsules containing numerous small round seeds. **2.** With qualifying words, applied to various species of *Papaver* or other genera of *Papaveraceæ* ME. **3.** The plant or its extract used in pharmacy 1604. **4.** *fig.* With reference to the narcotic qualities of the plant 1591.

1. Sleepy poppies DRYDEN. The blushing p. with a crimson hue PRIOR. **2. Californian P.**, *Platystemon californicus* and the genus *Eschscholtzia*; **Corn, Field P.**, the common wild p. of cornfields, *Papaver rhœas*, with bright scarlet flowers, or any other species growing in corn; **Horn P., Horned P.**, any plant of the genus *Glaucium*, distinguished by its long horn-like capsules; **Iceland P.**, see ICELAND[2]; **Prickly P.**, *Argemone mexicana*, with yellow or white flowers and prickly leaves and capsules.

II. = POPPY-HEAD 2. late ME.

attrib. and *Comb.*: **p.-bee**, a kind of upholsterer-bee (*Anthocopa papaveris*) which lines its cells with the petals of poppies; **-colour**, a bright scarlet; **P. Day**, the anniversary of Armistice Day, 11 Nov. 1918, commemorated by wearing an artificial red poppy (a Flanders poppy) made by disabled ex-service men in aid of Earl Haig's British Legion Appeal Fund.

Poppycock (pǫ·pikǫk). *U.S. slang.* 1863. Nonsense, rubbish.

Po·ppy-hea·d. 1585. **1.** The capsule of the poppy. Also *attrib.* **2.** *Arch.* An ornamental finial, often richly carved, at the top of the end of a seat in a church. Also *attrib.* 1839.

Po·ppy-seed. late ME. **1.** The, or a, seed of the poppy. **†2.** As a measure of length, varying from $\frac{1}{12}$ to $\frac{1}{20}$ of an inch –1729.

Poppywort (pǫ·piwǒɹt). 1846. [f. POPPY *sb.* + WORT[1].] **a.** Lindley's name for plants of the N.O. *Papaveraceæ*. **b.** Satin P., *Meconopsis wallichiana*.

Po·p-shop. *slang.* 1772. [f. POP *v.* 7 + SHOP *sb.*] A pawnbroker's shop. Also *attrib.*

Populace (pǫ·piŭlěs). 1572. [– Fr. *populace* – It. *popolaccio, -azzo*, f. *popolo* PEOPLE.] The mass of the people of a community, as dist. from the titled, wealthy, or educated classes; (*contempt.*) the mob, the rabble.

T'accommodate..the Peeres, and please the Populasse DANIEL. So **†Po·pulacy**, the p.; also, populousness; popular government, democracy.

Popular (pǫ·piŭlăɹ), *a.* (*sb.*) 1490. [– AFr. *populer*, OFr. *populeir* (later and mod. *populaire*) or L. *popularis*, f. *populus* PEOPLE, see -AR[1].] **1.** *Law.* Affecting, concerning, or open to all or any of the people; public; esp. in *action p.* **2.** Of, pertaining to, or consisting of the common people, or the people as a whole; constituted or carried on by the people 1548. **†b.** Plebeian –1691. **†3.** Full of people; populous; crowded –1811. **4.** Adapted to the understanding, taste, or means of ordinary people 1573. **†5.** Studious of, or designed to gain, the favour of the common people; devoted to the cause of the people –1771. **6.** Finding favour with the people, or with many people; favourite, acceptable, pleasing 1608. **7.** Prevalent among, or accepted by, the people generally; common, general; †(of sickness) epidemic 1603.

1. *P. action*, brought by one of the public to recover some penalty given by statute to any one who chooses to sue for it WHARTON. **2.** P. tumults HUME. A completely p. election 1833. **4.** In a p. style which boys and women could comprehend MACAULAY. The foundation of the P. Concerts in 1859. 1902. All seats at p. prices 1907. **5.** The first acts of an usurper are always p. GOLDSM. **6.** The p. Preachers 1812. **7.** Sir, that's a p. error, deceiues many B. JONS.

B. *absol.* or as *sb.* (from sense 2.) **†a.** In collective sense, or *pl.*: the populace; the common people, the commons –1633. **b.** Short for *p. concert* 1885. Hence **Po·pular-ly** *adv.*, **-ness** (*rare*).

Popularity (pǫpiŭlæ·rĭti). 1548. [f. prec. + -ITY, or – Fr. *popularité* – L. *popularitas*, f. *popularis*; see prec., -ITY.] **†1.** Popular or democratic government –1701. **†2.** The principle of popular government; democracy –1689. **†3.** The action or practice of courting popular favour –1715. **4.** The fact or condition of being admired, approved, or beloved by the people, or by many people 1601. **†5.** = POPULOUSNESS (*rare*) –1720.

2. The spirit of p. and republicanisme 1689. **3.** P. is a courting the favour of the people by undue practices 1697. **4.** His popularitie gained him a Consulship 1601.

Popularize (pǫ·piŭlărəiz), *v.* 1797. [f. POPULAR *a.* + -IZE.] *trans.* To make popular. **a.** To cause to be generally known and accepted, liked, or admired. **b.** To render democratic 1831. **c.** To present (a technical subject, etc.) in a popular form 1836.

a. To preserve their power they must popularise themselves 1835. **c.** Engaged in..popularising history or science 1871. Hence **Po:pulariza·tion Po·pularizer.**

Po·pulate, *ppl. a. Obs.* exc. *poet.* 1574. [– med.L. *populatus*, f. *populare*; see next, -ATE[2].] Peopled.

Populate (pǫ·piŭlᵉ't), *v.* 1578. [– *populat-*, pa.ppl. stem of med.L. *populare*, f. L. *populus* people; see -ATE[3].] **1.** *trans.* **a.** To inhabit, form the population of (a country). **b.** To supply (a country) with inhabitants; to people. **2.** *intr.* Of people: To grow in numbers by propagation (*rare*) 1625. **3.** *intr.* (for *refl.*) To become populous *U.S. rare.* 1796. Hence **Po·pulator**, one who or that which populates or peoples.

Population (pǫpiŭlēⁱ·ʃən). 1578. [– late L. *populatio*, f. as prec.; see -ION.] **†1.** *concr.* An inhabited place –1613. **2.** The degree in which a place is populated or inhabited; hence, the total number of its inhabitants. Also *transf.* 1612. **3.** The action or process of peopling a place or region; increase of people 1776.

2. P...increases in a geometrical ratio, subsistence in an arithmetical ratio MALTHUS. **3.** The p. of the province was extremely rapid 1796.

Populin (pǫ·piŭlin). 1838. [– Fr. *populine* (Braconnot, 1831), f. L. *populus* poplar; see -IN[1].] *Chem.* A white crystalline substance, $C_{20}H_{22}O_8$, obtained from the aspen (*Populus tremula*).

Populist (pǫ·piŭlist). 1892. [f. L. *populus* people + -IST.] **1.** An adherent of a political party formed in the U.S. in Feb. 1892, having for its objects the public control of railways, limitation of private ownership of land, free coinage of silver and increased issue of paper-money, a graduated income-tax, etc. **2.** A member of a Russian socio-political party advocating a form of collectivism 1895.

1. A people's party,—Populists as..they are called 1893. So **Po·pulism**, the political doctrine or principle of the Populists 1893.

Populous (pǫ·piŭləs), *a.* 1449. [– late L. *populosus*, f. *populus* people; see -OUS.] **1.** Full of people; thickly inhabited; fully occupied. **b.** Of a time or season: Productive, prolific 1789. **†2.** Of a body of people: Numerous, abundant –1662. **3.** = POPULAR *a.* in various senses. *Obs.* exc. *poet.* 1592.

1. A continuall p. Market PURCHAS. P. districts 1880. **2.** Furnished with a p. army HALL. Hence **Po·pulous-ly** *adv.*, **-ness**. So **†Populo·sity**, populousness.

Porbeagle (pǭ·ɹ,bī:g'l). 1758. [Origin unkn.; orig. Cornish dial.] A shark of the genus *Lamna*, esp. *L. cornubica*, sometimes 10 feet in length, and having a pointed snout; a mackerel-shark.

Porcelain (pǭ·ɹslĕn, pōᵊ·ɹ-). 1530. [– Fr. *porcelaine* – It. *porcellana* (XIII, Marco Polo) Venus shell, cowrie, polished substance of this, (hence) china ware (from its resemblance to this substance), deriv. in fem. adj. form of *porcella*, dim. of *porca* sow :– L. *porca*, fem of *porcus* swine.] **1.** A fine kind of earthenware, having a translucent body and a transparent glaze; = CHINA[1] II. **2.** An article or vessel made of porcelain; a piece of porcelain. Usu. in *pl.* 1604. **3.** The COWRIE (*Cypræa moneta*). Only in *p. shell.* 1601. **4.** *attrib.* or as *adj.* Made of porcelain or china 1598; *fig.* like porcelain; fine, fragile; superfine 1638.

1. *fig.* The precious p. of human clay BYRON. **4.** A maid who had broken a p. cup JOHNSON.

attrib. and *Comb.*, as **p. cement**, a cement for mending china or glass; **-clay**, the clay used in the manufacture of p.; china-clay, kaolin; **-crab**, a crab of the genus *Porcellana*, so called from its smooth and polished shell; **p. jasper** = PORCELLANITE; **p. shell:** see sense 3; **p. tower**, a famous tower at Nankin in China, covered with p. tiles. Hence **Po·rcelainize** *v. trans.* to convert into p. or a substance of the same nature. **Po·rcelainous** *a.* = next.

Porcellaneous (pōᵊɹsĕlēⁱ·nĭəs), *a.* 1799. [f. It. *porcellana* PORCELAIN + -EOUS.] Of the nature of or resembling porcelain. So **Porcellanous** (poɹse·lănəs) *a.*

Porcellanite (poɹse·lănəit). 1796. [– G. *porzellanit* (Peithner, 1794), f. *porzellan* PORCELAIN + *-it* -ITE[1] 2 b.] *Min.* A hard naturally-baked clay, somewhat resembling jasper; also called *porcelain jasper.*

Porch (pōᵊɹtʃ). ME. [– (O)Fr. *porche* :– L. *porticus* colonnade, gallery, porch (rendering Gr. στοά; cf. STOIC), f. *porta* 'passage', PORT *sb.*[3]] **1.** An exterior structure forming a covered approach to the entrance of a building; sometimes applied to an interior space serving as a vestibule. Also *transf.* and *fig.* **†2.** A colonnade, portico, cloister –1687. **b.** *U.S.* A verandah 1840. **3.** spec. *The P.*, the Painted Porch (Gr. στοὰ ποικίλη), a public ambulatory in the agora of ancient Athens, to which Zeno the philosopher and his disciples resorted; hence (οἱ τῆς στοᾶς, those of the porch), the Stoic school, the Stoic philosophy 1670.

1. Of hewen stone the p. was fayrely wrought SPENSER. **2.** They stay for me In Pompeyes P. SHAKS.

Porcine (pǭ·ɹsəin), *a.* 1656. [– Fr. *porcin*, *-ine* or L. *porcinus*, f. *porcus* swine; see -INE[1].] **1.** Of or consisting of swine; related to or resembling the swine. **2.** Like that of a hog; swinish, hoggish 1660.

Porcupine (pǭ·ɹkiŭpəin), *sb.* [XV *porc despyne*, later *porke-*, *porcupine* – OFr. *porc espin* (also *porc d'espine*), mod. *porcépic* – Pr. *porc espi(n* :– Rom. **porcospinus*, f. L. *porcus* pig, PORK + *spinus* SPINE.] **1.** A rodent quadruped of the genus *Hystrix* or family *Hystricidæ*, having the body and tail covered with defensive erectile spines or quills; formerly supposed to shoot or dart its spines at an enemy. **b.** A figure of this animal, esp. as a device 1578. **2.** *fig.* 1594. **3.** Applied to machines having numerous projecting spikes or teeth; *esp.* an apparatus for heckling flax, worsted, or cotton; a kind of masher used in brewing 1869. **4. a.** = *P. ant-eater*; **b.** = *P. fish.* 1875.

1. Like Quilles vpon the fretfull Porpentine SHAKS.

attrib. and *Comb.*, as **p. ant-eater**, an Australian monotremate mammal (*Echidna hystrix*), having spines; **p. crab**, a Japanese crab (*Lithodes hystrix*), having spiny carapace and limbs; **p. fish**, a fish having the skin covered with spines, as *Diodon hystrix*; a sea-porcupine; **p. grass**, (*a*) *Triodia irritans* and other species, of Australia, with stiff sharp-pointed leaves; (*b*) *Stipa spartea*, of the western U.S., with long stiff awns; **p.-wood**, the wood of the coco palm, which when cut across shows variegated markings like those of a porcupine-quill.

Pore (pōᵊɹ), *sb.* late ME. [– (O)Fr. *pore* – L. *porus* – Gr. πόρος passage, pore.] **1.** A minute opening or orifice (usu. one imperceptible to the unaided eye) through which fluids (rarely solids) pass or may pass. **a.** In an animal body esp. applied to those in the skin. **b.** *fig.*, esp. in phr. *at every p.* 1632. **c.** In a plant (or vegetable substance); as the stomata in the epidermis of leaves, etc. late ME. **d.** In inanimate bodies or substances. late ME. **†2.** A passage, channel, canal, duct (*rare*) –1615.

1. b. I see him chafe and fret at every p. DICKENS.

Pore (pōᵊɹ), *v.* [ME. *pure, poure, powre*, perh. :– OE. **pūrian*, f. **pūr-*, a mutated form of which (OE. **pȳran*) may be the source of late ME. *pire*; see PEER *v.*[2]] **1.** *intr.* **a.** To look intently or fixedly (*in, on, upon, at, over*); to search *for* or *into* something by gazing. (Now always with admixture of sense b.) **b.** To look at something (usu. a book) with fixed attention, in the way of study; to be absorbed in reading or study. (Const. *on, upon*, (now chiefly) *over*). late ME. **c.** To meditate, muse, or think intently upon something. Const. *on, upon, over.* late ME. †**2.** To look closely, as a near-sighted person; to peer –1862. **3.** *trans.* To bring into some state by poring 1593.

1. b. Instead of poaring on a booke, you shall holde the plough LYLY. **3.** Phr. †*To p. one's eyes out*, to ruin one's eyes by close reading. Hence **Po·rer. Po·ringly** *adv.*

Po·rgo, pa·rgo. 1557. [– Sp., Pg. *pargo*, app. – L. *pagrus* kind of fish.] The sea bream.

Porgy (pǭ·ɹgi). Also **paugie.** 1725. [Of obsc. and app. various origin. Cf. prec.] *U.S.* Applied to various sea-fishes, chiefly N. Amer. species of *Sparidæ* or Sea Breams, but also locally to fishes of other families.

‖**Porifera** (pori·fĕră), *sb.pl.* 1843. [mod.L., n. pl. of *porifer*, f. L. *porus* PORE *sb.* + *-fer* bearing.] *Zool.* The Sponges, reckoned as a class or main division of *Cœlenterata*, characterized by having the body-wall perforated by numerous inhalant pores. Hence **Pori·feran** *a.* belonging or relating to the *P.*; *sb.* a member of the *P.*

†**Po·riness.** 1653. [f. PORY + -NESS.] Porosity; also *concr.* a porous part –1676.

Porism (pōᵊ·riz'm, pǫ·r-). late ME. [– late L. *porisma* – Gr. πόρισμα deduction, corollary, problem, f. πορίζειν carry, deduce, f. πόρος way, passage; see PORE *sb.*, -ISM. Cf. Fr. *porisme.*] *Math.* A kind of geometrical proposition; app. one arising during the investigation of some other proposition, either by immediate deduction from it (= COROLLARY *sb.* 1), or by consideration of some special case in which it becomes indeterminate. So **Porisma·tic** *a.* pertaining to or of the nature of a p. Also **Poristic** (pori·stik) *a.* 1704.

Porite (pōᵊ·rəit). 1828. [– mod.L. *Porites*, f. Gr. πόρος passage, pore, or πῶρος calcareous stone; see MADREPORE, -ITE¹ 3.] *Zool.* A coral of the genus *Porites* or family *Poritidæ* of perforate sclerodermatous corals.

Pork (pōᵊɹk). ME. [– (O)Fr. *porc* :– L. *porcus* swine.] **1.** A swine, a hog, a pig. Sometimes dist. from a pig or young swine. *Obs.* exc. *Hist.* late ME. **2.** The (fresh) flesh of swine used as food ME. **3.** *U.S. slang.* Money, position, etc. for a district, obtained from the (Federal) government; also *transf.* Cf. *p.-barrel.* 1916.

Comb.: **p.-barrel** *spec.* (*U.S. slang*), the Federal treasury viewed as a source of grants for local purposes; **-butcher**, one who slaughters pigs for sale; **-pie**, a raised pie of chopped pork; (in full, *p.-pie hat*) a hat with a flat crown and a brim turned up all round, worn by women *c*1855–65.

Porker (pōᵊ·ɹkəɹ). 1657. [f. prec. + -ER¹ 1.] A young hog fattened for pork; also, any pig raised for food.

Porket (pōᵊ·ɹkėt). Now *dial.* 1554. [– ONFr. *porket*, OFr. *porchet*, dim. of *porc* PORK.] A small or young pig or hog; *dial.* = prec.

Porkling (pōᵊ·ɹkliŋ). 1542. [f. PORK + -LING¹.] A small or young pig 1570. †**b.** Applied to a person. Also *attrib.* –1602.

Po·rkwood. 1880. [f. PORK + WOOD *sb.*] **a.** A bush or small tree (*Kigellaria capensis*) found in the warmer parts of Africa; **b.** *Pisonia obtusata*, the Pigeon-wood, Beefwood, or Cork-wood of the W. Indies.

Pornocracy (pǫɹnǫ·krăsi). 1860. [f. Gr. πόρνη harlot + -CRACY.] Dominating influence of harlots; *spec.* the government of Rome during the first half of the tenth century.

Pornographer (pǫɹnǫ·grăfəɹ). 1850. [f. Fr. *pornographe* – Gr. πορνογράφος, f. πόρνη prostitute; see -ER¹ 4, -GRAPHER.] One who writes of prostitutes or obscene matters.

Pornographic (pǭɹnŏgræ·fik), *a.* 1880. [f. next + -IC.] Of, pertaining to, or of the nature of pornography; dealing in the obscene.

Pornography (pǫɹnǫ·grăfi). 1864. [f. Gr. πορνογράφος (see PORNOGRAPHER) + -Y³; see -GRAPHY.] Description of the life, manners, etc. of prostitutes and their patrons; hence, the expression or suggestion of obscene or unchaste subjects in literature or art.

Poroplastic (pǫro-, pōᵊroplæ·stik), *a.* 1879. [f. Gr. πόρος PORE + PLASTIC.] Both porous and plastic; applied to a kind of porous felt, plastic when heated, becoming stiff when cold, used for splints and other surgical appliances.

Porosity (porǫ·sĭti). late ME. [– med.L. *porositas*, f. *porosus*; see next, -ITY.] The quality or fact of being porous; porous consistence. **b.** *concr.* A porous part or structure; an interstice or pore 1597.

Porous (pōᵊ·rəs), *a.* late ME. [– (O)Fr. *poreux* – med.L. *porosus*, f. L. *porus* PORE *sb.*; see -OUS.] Full of pores; having minute interstices through which water, air, light, etc. may pass. Also *fig.*

P. plaster, a plaster having numerous small holes pierced through it so as to enable it to lie smoothly. Hence **Po·rous-ly** *adv.*; **-ness,** porosity.

Porpentine, obs. f. PORCUPINE.

Porphyr-, porphyro-, repr. Gr. πορφυρ(ο-, comb. stem of πόρφυρος purple; a formative element in senses 'purple' and 'porphyry' as in **Porphyra·ceous,** *a.* (*rare*) of the nature of or allied to porphyry; porphyritic, etc. **Po:rphyrogene·tic,** *a.* producing or generating porphyry.

Porphyrian (pǫɹfi·riăn), *a.* (*sb.*) 1593. [f. L. *Porphyrius* – Gr. Πορφύριος + -AN.] Of or pertaining to Porphyrius or Porphyry, the neo-Platonic philosopher and antagonist of Christianity (A.D. 233–*c*306), or to his doctrines.

P. scale or *tree*, a definition of *man* in the form of a kind of genealogical table or tree, displaying the series of subaltern genera to which he may be assigned below the summum genus *substance*, and the differentiæ by which each subaltern genus is distinguished within the genus next above it.

B. *sb.* A disciple or follower of Porphyry 1678.

‖**Porphyrio** (pǫɹfi·rio). 1609. [L. – Gr. πορφυρίων the purple coot.] *Ornith.* A name given by the ancients to the purple coot; taken by Brisson as name of the genus of *Rallidæ* including this.

Porphyrite (pǭ·ɹfĭrəit), *sb.* 1577. [– L. *porphyrites* – Gr. πορφυρίτης adj. like purple, π. λίθος stone of this colour, porphyry, f. πόρφυρος purple; see -ITE¹ 2 b.] †**1.** = PORPHYRY 1. –1736. **2.** *Min.* = PORPHYRY 2. 1796.

Porphyritic (pǭɹfĭri·tik), *a.* late ME. [– med.L. *porphyriticus*, for L. *-eticus*, f. *porphyrites*; see PORPHYRY, -IC.] Of or pertaining to the porphyry of the ancients; of the nature or structure of the porphyry of modern mineralogists; *spec.* containing distinct crystals or crystalline particles embedded in a compact ground-mass. So **Porphyri·tical** *a.*, **-ly** *adv.*

Porphyrogenite (-ǫ·dʒėnəit). *Obs.* exc. in L. form. 1614. [– med.L. *porphyrogenitus*, – late Gr. πορφυρογέννητος, f. Gr. πορφυρο- PORPHYR(O- + γεννητός born.] Orig., one born of the imperial family at Constantinople, and (as is said) in a chamber called the *Porphyra* (πορφύρα). Hence, a child born after his father's accession to the throne; and, vaguely, one born 'in the purple'; see PURPLE *sb.*

Hence **Porphyroge·nitism,** the doctrine of succession in a royal family which prefers a son born after his father's accession to one born before. **Porphyroge·niture,** the condition of being born 'in the purple' (see above).

Porphyroid (pǭ·ɹfiroid), *sb.* (*a.*) 1796. [f. PORPHYRY + -OID.] *Geol.*, etc. **A.** *sb.* A rock resembling porphyry or of porphyritic structure. **B.** *adj.* Resembling porphyry 1798.

Porphyry (pǭ·ɹfĭri). [Late ME. *porfurie*, *purfire*, later (XVI) *porphyry*, ult. – med.L. *porphyreum*, for L. *porphyrites* – Gr. πορφυρίτης, f. πόρφυρος PURPLE.] **1.** A beautiful and very hard rock quarried anciently in Egypt, composed of crystals of white or red plagioclase felspar embedded in a fine red groundmass. By modern poets often used vaguely, in the sense of a beautiful red stone taking a high polish. **2.** *Geol.* and *Min.* **a.** A rock consisting of a compact base of felspathic or other unstratified rock containing scattered crystals of felspar of contemporary age 1796. **b.** *gen.* Any unstratified or igneous rock having a homogeneous base in which crystals of one or more minerals are disseminated 1813.

Comb.: **p. chamber,** a room in the palace of the Emperors at Byzantium; **p.-shell,** a shell of the genus *Murex*, esp. that from which the purple dye was obtained.

Porpoise (pǭ·ɹpəs). [ME. *porpays, -poys, -pas* – OFr. *po(u)rpois, -peis, -pais* :– Rom. **porcopiscis* (f. L. *porcus* swine + *piscis* fish), for L. *porcus marinus* 'sea hog'.] A small cetaceous mammal (*Phocæna communis*) about five feet in length, blackish above and paler beneath, having a blunt rounded snout not produced into a 'beak' as the dolphin's. Hence extended to other small cetaceans. (Formerly also, like *fish*, as collect. sing.) Hence **Po·rpoise** *v. intr.* spec. of aircraft: to make a series of plunges when taking off or landing 1920.

Porraceous (pǫrēⁱ·ʃəs), *a.* 1605. [f. L. *porraceus*, f. *porrum* leek; see -ACEOUS.] Of the nature or colour of the leek; leek-green.

Porrect (pŏre·kt), *a.* 1819. [– L. *porrectus*, pa. pple. of *porrigere*; see next.] *Zool.* Stretched out or forth; extended, esp. forward.

Porrect (pŏre·kt), *v.* late ME. [– *porrect-*, pa. ppl. stem of L. *porrigere*, f. *por-* = PRO-¹ + *regere* stretch, direct.] **1.** *trans.* To stretch out, extend (usu., a part of the body). Now only in *Nat. Hist.* **2.** To put forward, tender (a document, etc.); to produce for examination or correction. *Obs.* exc. in eccl. law. 1774. So **Porre·ction,** †extension (*rare*); proffering; presentation (now only *Eccl.*)

Porret (pǫ·rėt). Now only *dial.* [ME. *poret, -ette* – OFr. *poret* leek, f. L. *porrum* leek + dim. suffix *-et* -ET.] A young leek or onion.

Porridge (pǫ·ridʒ), *sb.* 1532. [alt. of POTTAGE, intermediate forms being repr. by *podech* (XVI), *podditch, -idge.* In Sc. and Eng. dial. usu. collect. plural.] †**1.** Pottage made by stewing vegetables, herbs, or meat, often with a thickening of pot-barley, etc. –1805. **2.** A soft food made by stirring oatmeal (or other meal or cereal) into boiling water (or milk); often dist. as *oatmeal p., wheatmeal p., rice p.* 1643. **3.** *fig.* A conglomeration, a hotchpotch; unsubstantial stuff 1642.

Provb. phr. *To keep one's breath to cool one's p.*, to reserve one's advice, etc. for one's own use. *Comb.*: **p.-pan,** a double pan in which p. is made; **-pot,** the pot in which p. is cooked; **-stick,** a stick used for stirring p.

‖**Porrigo** (pŏrəi·go). 1706. [L., = 'scurf'.] *Path.* A name for several diseases of the scalp characterized by scaly eruptions. So **Porri·ginous** *a.* affected with p.

Porringer (pǫ·rindʒəɹ). 1522. [alt.,through the var. †*poddinger* (XV), of (dial.) POTTINGER, †*potinger* (XV), †*poteger* – (O)Fr. *potager*, f. *potage*; see POTTAGE, -ER². For the intrusive *n* cf. *harbinger*, etc.] A small basin or the like, from which soup, porridge, children's food, etc. is eaten. **b.** A hat resembling a porringer (*joc.*) 1613.

Port (pōᵊɹt), *sb.*¹ [OE. *port* – L. *portus*, rel. to *porta* (see PORT *sb.*³). In ME. prob. a new word – (O)Fr. *port* :– L. *portus.*] **1.** A place by the shore where ships may run in for shelter from storms, or to load and unload; a harbour, a haven. **2.** A town possessing a harbour to which vessels resort to load or unload, from which they start or at which they finish their voyages; *spec.* a place where customs officers are stationed to supervise the entry of goods OE. †**3.** *The five ports* = CINQUE PORTS. Also the barons of the Cinque Ports.–1631.

1. To set me safe ashore in the first p. where we arrived SWIFT. *fig.* Doubt was expressed..as to the possibility of the measure reaching p. this year 1879. **2.** *Free P.*,..a p. open and free for merchants of all nations to load and unload their vessels in.. *Free P.* is also used for a total exemption and franchise..for goods imported into a state, or those of the growth of the country exported. CHAMBERS. *Close ports*, those which lie up rivers SMYTH.

Comb.: **p.-bar,** (*a*) a shoal or bank across the entrance to a p.; (*b*) = BOOM *sb.*² 3; **-bound** *a.*, detained in p. by contrary winds, etc.; **-charge, -duty,** harbour-due (see HARBOUR *sb.*¹); **-pay,** wages due for time during which one's ship is detained in p.

Port, *sb.*[2] *Obs.* exc. *Hist.* or in *Comb.* [OE. *port* = MFl., MDu. *port* town, burgh, city; in origin the same word as prec. or as next.] †A town; perh. *spec.* a walled town, or a market town; but identified with *burh* as a rendering of L. *civitas* –ME. **b.** *attrib.* and *Comb.* as PORT-REEVE, etc. OE.

Port (pōᵊɹt), *sb.*[3] [ME. *porte, port* – (O)Fr. *porte* :– L. *porta* door, gate (see PORT *sb.*[1]).] **1.** A gate or gateway; from 14th c., usu. that of a city or walled town. Now chiefly *Sc.* OE. **2.** *Naut.* **a.** An opening in the side of a ship for entrance and exit, and for the loading and discharge of cargo. **b.** Each of the apertures in a ship of war through which cannon were pointed; now, an aperture for the admission of light and air. late ME. **c.** The shutter of a port-hole; a port-lid 1627. **3.** *Mech.* An aperture for the passage of steam, gas, or water; *esp.* in a steam-engine, for the passage of steam into or out of the cylinder, a *steam-p.* 1839. **4.** The curved mouthpiece of some bridle-bits 1587.

1. Him I accuse: The City Ports by this hath enter'd SHAKS. *fig.* O pollish'd Perturbation!.. that keep'st the Ports of Slumber open wide To many a watchfull Night SHAKS.

attrib. and *Comb.*, as **p.-bit** (sense 4), a bridle-bit of which the mouth is curved into an arch; also called **p.-mouth**; **-piece**, an obsolete kind of ship's gun; **-rope**, a rope for raising and lowering a port-lid; **-stopper**, a revolving shutter for closing a p. in a turret-ship; **-way** = sense 3. Hence **Po·rted** *a.* having ports or gates (*rare*).

Port (pōᵊɹt), *sb.*[4] late ME. [– (O)Fr. *port*, f. *porter* PORT *v.*[1] :– L. *portare*, f. *portus* PORT *sb.*[1]] **I. 1.** The manner in which one bears oneself; external deportment; carriage, bearing. **b.** *fig.* Bearing, purport (of a matter) 1568. **2.** Style of living; *esp.* a grand or expensive style; state; hence *transf.* social position, station. Now *rare* or *Obs.* 1523. **†b.** *transf.* A train of attendants; a retinue. Also *fig.* –1621.

1. With them comes a third of Regal p. MILT. **2.** The name and p. of gentlemen SCOTT.

II. †1. The action of carrying; the fee or price of carrying; carriage, postage –1692. **2.** *Mil.* [from phr. *Port arms*.] The position required by the order '*Port arms*'; see PORT *v.*[1] 2. 1833.

Port (pōᵊɹt), *sb.*[5] (*a.*) 1543. [prob. orig. the side turned towards the port (PORT *sb.*[1]) or place of lading (cf. LARBOARD).] **1.** = LARBOARD 1. (Often in phr. *to p.*, A-PORT.) **2.** *attrib.* or as *adj.* = LARBOARD 2. 1857.

Port (pōᵊɹt), *sb.*[6] 1691. [Shortened f. *O Porto* (*wine*), f. *Oporto* (Pg. *O Porto*, lit. 'the Port') a city of Portugal, the chief port of shipment for the wines of the country.] A strong dark-red wine of Portugal, having a sweet and slightly astringent taste. Also *attrib.*

Port (pōᵊɹt), *sb.*[7] *Sc.* 1721. [– Gael. *port* tune.] A lively tune, a catch, an air.

The pipe's shrill p. aroused each clan SCOTT.

Port (pōᵊɹt) *v.*[1] 1566. [– (O)Fr. *porter* :– L. *portare*. See PORT *sb.*[1]] **†1.** *trans.* To carry, bear, convey, bring –1711. **2.** *Mil.* To carry or hold (a pike, etc.) with both hands; *spec.* to carry (a rifle or other weapon) diagonally across and close to the body, so that the barrel or blade is opposite the middle of the left shoulder; esp. in the command *Port arms!* 1625.

1. To p. Books about to sell 1706. **2.** On the approach of any person, the sentry will p. Arms, and call out Halt, who comes there? 1877. Hence **Po·rted** *ppl. a.* held in the position of the port.

Port (pōᵊɹt), *v.*[2] 1580. [f. PORT *sb.*[5]] **1.** *trans.* In *to p. the helm*, to put or turn it to the left side of the ship; also ellipt. *to p.* **2.** *intr.* Of a ship: To turn or go to her port or left side 1890.

‖**Porta** (pōᵊ·ɹtă). late ME. [L., a gate; also applied to a part of the liver. See PORT *sb.*[3]] *Anat.* **a.** The transverse fissure of the liver, at which the portal vein, hepatic artery, etc. enter it; the portal fissure. **b.** The *vena portæ* or portal vein; see PORTAL *a.*

Portable (pōᵊ·ɹtăb'l), *a.* late ME. [– (O)Fr. *portable* or late L. *portabilis*, f. *portare* carry; see PORT *v.*[1], -ABLE.] **1.** Capable of being carried by hand or on the person; capable of being moved from place to place; easily carried or conveyed. **b.** Said of liquid substances congealed, and of gaseous substances liquefied, so as to be more conveniently carried or transported 1753. **†2.** *fig.* Bearable; endurable –1653. **†3.** Capable of carrying ships or boats; navigable –1696.

1. A very convenient p. camera obscura 1831. *fig.* This p. Quality of Good-humour STEELE. *P. derrick, furnace, steam engine*, etc., modified movable forms of these. **b.** P. Soup..P. Milk 1849. **2.** How light and p. my pain seems now SHAKS. Hence **Portabi·lity, Po·rtableness,** the quality or state of being p.

Portage (pōᵊ·ɹtėdʒ), *sb.*[1] late ME. [– Fr. *portage*. f. *porter*; see PORT *v.*[1], -AGE. Cf. med.L. *portagium*.] **I. 1.** The action or work of carrying or transporting; carriage 1440. **†b.** That which is carried or transported; cargo; freight; baggage –1667. **2.** The cost of carriage; porterage; freight-charges; †also, a due levied in connection with the transport of goods. *Obs.* exc. *Hist.* 1472. **†3.** *Naut.* Burden of a vessel; tonnage –1710. **4.** In full, *mariner's p.*: A mariner's venture, in the form of freight or cargo, which he was entitled to put on board, if he took part in the common adventure and did not receive wages; the space allowed to a mariner for his own venture or to be let by him for freight payable to him in lieu of wages; hence, in late use, a mariner's wages. *Obsol.* 1550.

2. The cheapest Letter, that ever I paid p. for DONNE. **4.** *fig. Per.* III. i. 35.

II. The carrying or transporting of boats and goods from one navigable water to another, as between two lakes or rivers. (Orig. *U.S.*) 1698. **b.** A place at or over which such portage is necessary 1698.

†Po·rtage, *sb.*[2] [f. PORT *sb.*[3] + -AGE.] Provision of ports or port-holes SHAKS.

Po·rtage (pōᵊ·ɹtėdʒ), *v.* 1864. [f. PORTAGE *sb.*[1] II.] *trans.* To carry or transport (boats, goods, etc.) overland between navigable waters; to convey over a portage. Also with the place (rapids, etc.) as obj.; also *absol.*

†Portague, -igue. 1532. [app. a false sing. deduced from *porta-*, *porteguse* (PORTUGUESE B. 3), taken as a pl., as if *portagues*.] A Portuguese gold coin, the great 'crusado', current in the 16th c.

Portail (pōᵊ·ɹtēˡl). 1483. [– Fr. *portail* façade of a church, alt. of OFr. *portal* (XIII) – med.L. *portale* (see next, with which *portail* has been confused in Fr. and Eng.).] *Arch.* = next 1.

Portal (pōᵊ·ɹtăl), *sb.* [– OFr. *portal* – med.L. *portale*, subst. use of n. of *portalis* (med.L. = janitor), f. L. *porta* gate; see PORT *sb.*[3], -AL[1].] **1.** A door, gate, doorway, or gateway, of stately or elaborate construction; the entrance, esp. of a large or magnificent building. Hence often poet. for 'door' or 'gate'. **†2.** A space within the door of a room, partitioned off, and containing an inner door; also, such a partition itself –1703. **3.** *attrib.* 1592.

1. The portals of Abbeville..are some of the finest specimens of this style 1862. *fig.* As doth the blushing discontented Sunne, From out the fierie Portall of the East SHAKS.

Portal (pōᵊ·ɹtăl), *a.* 1845. [– mod.L. *portalis*, f. L. *porta* gate; see PORT *sb.*[3], -AL[1].] *Anat.* Pertaining to the *porta* or transverse fissure of the liver.

P. vein, the *vena portæ*, or great vein formed by the union of the veins from the stomach, intestine, and spleen, conveying blood to the liver, where it divides again into branches. *Renal p.* or *reniportal vein*, a vein similarly passing to the kidney and dividing into branches there, in many of the lower vertebrates.

‖**Portame·nto.** 1774. [It., lit. a carrying.] *Mus.* A gliding or passing continuously from one pitch to another, in singing, or in playing a violin or similar instrument. Also *attrib.*

Portance (pōᵊ·ɹtăns). *arch.* 1590. [– Fr. †*portance*, f. *porter*; see PORT *v.*[1], -ANCE.] Carriage, bearing, demeanour; conduct, behaviour.

Cor. II. iii. 232.

Portas, -eous, -es. Now only *Hist.* [ME. *portehors* (XIII), *porthous* (XIV) – OFr. *portehors*, f. *porter* carry (see PORT *v.*[1]) + *hors* out of doors. Cf. med.L. *portiforium* (XIII), *liber portatorius* (XIV).] **1.** A portable breviary in the mediæval church. Also *attrib.* **2.** *Sc. Law.* (In later use *porteous roll.*) A roll of the names of offenders, prepared, by the old custom of the Justiciary court, by the Justice-Clerk. Late ME.

1. Their Seruice bookes, Portesses, and Breuiaries BIBLE *Transl. Pref.*

Portate (pōᵊ·ɹtĕt), *a.* 1562. [– L. *portatus*, pa. pple. of *portare* PORT *v.*[1]] *Her.* In *cross p.*, a cross represented in a sloping position (*in bend*), as if carried on the shoulder.

Portative (pōᵊ·ɹtătiv), *a.* and *sb.* [XIV *portatif* – (O)Fr. *portatif, -ive*, app. alt. of *portatil* – med. L. *portatilis*, f. as prec.; see -ILE, -IVE.] **A.** *adj.* **1.** Portable; *spec.* applied to a kind of small organ. Now chiefly *Hist.* **2.** Having the function of carrying or supporting 1881. **B.** *sb.* (usu. *pl.*) A portative organ. *Obs.* exc. *Hist.* 1450.

Port-crayon (pōᵊɹtˌkrēˡ·ǫn), ‖**porte-crayon** (portˌkreyoṅ). 1720. [– Fr. *porte-crayon*; see PORTE-, CRAYON.] An instrument (e.g. a metal tube split at the end and held by a sliding ring) used to hold a crayon for drawing.

Portcullis (poɹtkɒ·lis), *sb.* [ME. *port colice, -coles* – OFr. *porte coleïce*, i.e. *porte* door, *col(e)ïce, coulice* (see COULISSE), fem. of *couleïs* gliding, sliding :– Rom. **colaticius*, f. L. *colare, colat-* filter.] **1.** A strong and heavy frame or grating, suspended by chains, and made to slide up and down in vertical grooves at the sides of the gateway of a fortress or fortified town, so as to be quickly let down as a defence against assault. Also *fig.* **2.** A figure of a portcullis, as an ornament or a heraldic charge. In *Her.* also applied to a number of vertical and horizontal strips crossing each other over the field. 1485. **3.** *P. coins, money*, numismatists' name for the coins (crown, half-crown, shilling, and sixpence) struck by Queen Elizabeth in 1600–2 for the East India Company, having the figure of a portcullis on the reverse 1784. **4.** Title of one of the English Pursuivants of Arms, from his badge 1491.

1. And.., Forthwith the huge P. high up drew MILT. Hence **Portcu·llis** *v. trans.* to furnish with a p.; to close with or as with a p. **Portcu·llised** *a.* furnished with or having a p.; *Her.* latticed.

Porte (pōᵊɹt). 1609. [– Fr., in full *la Sublime Porte*, transl. Turkish official title of the central office of the Ottoman Government.] (In full, *the Sublime* or *Ottoman P.*) The Ottoman court at Constantinople; hence *transf.* the Turkish Government.

‖**Porte-** (port), stem of Fr. *porter* bear, carry, occas. anglicized as *port*. **Porte-bonheur** (-bonőr) [Fr. *bonheur* good luck], an amulet, or a trinket worn like an amulet. **Porte-bouquet** (-buke), a bouquet-holder. **Porte-feu** (-fö) [Fr. *feu* fire] = PORTFIRE. **Portefeuille** (-fōˡy) [Fr. *feuille* leaf, sheet], = PORTFOLIO. **Porte-monnaie** (-monę) [Fr. *monnaie* MONEY], a flat leather purse or pocket-book.

‖**Porte-cochère** (portˌkoʃę̄r). 1698. [Fr., f. *porte* PORT *sb.*[3] + *cochère* adj. fem. f. *coche* COACH *sb.*] A gateway for carriages, leading into a court-yard; a carriage-entrance.

Portend (poɹte·nd), *v.* late ME. [– L. *portendere*, f. **por-* = *prŏ-* PRO-[1] + *tendere* stretch, TEND *v.*[1]] **1.** *trans.* To presage as an omen; to foreshow, foreshadow. **b.** Hence: To point to beforehand; to give warning of 1592. **2.** Of a person: To foretell, prognosticate (*rare*) 1611. **†3.** To signify, symbolize, indicate –1782.

1. b. What portends thy cheerful countenance? KYD. **2.** Some great misfortune to p., No enemy can match a friend SWIFT. **3.** *Twel. N.* II. v. 130.

Portent (pōᵊ·ɹtent). 1563. [– L. *portentum*, f. *portendere* PORTEND. Orig. stressed *porte·nt*.] **1.** That which portends or foretells something about to happen, esp. of a calamitous nature; an omen, significant sign. **b.** The fact or quality of portending; in phr. *of dire* (etc.) *p.* 1715. **2.** Something considered portentous; a prodigy, wonder, marvel 1741.

1. My Loss by dire Portents the Gods foretold DRYDEN. Lowering with portents of rain HAWTHORNE. 2. What p. can be greater than a pious notary? GEO. ELIOT.

Portentous (poɹte·ntəs), *a.* 1540. [– L. *portentosus*, f. *portentum* PORTENT; see -OUS.] **1.** Of the nature of a portent; ominous, threatening, warning. **2.** Applied to any object exciting wonder, awe, or amazement; marvellous, monstrous, prodigious; hence as an intensive (sometimes *joc.*) = extraordinary 1553.

1. The p. blaze of comets MILT. 2. A p. apple-dumpling 1823. Hence **Porte·ntously** *adv.*

Porter (pōᵊ·ɹtəɹ), *sb.*^{1} ME. [– AFr. *porter*, (O)Fr. *portier* – late L. (Vulg.) *portarius*, f. *porta*; see PORT *sb.*^{3}, -ER^{2} 2.] One who has charge of a door or gate; a gate-keeper, door-keeper, janitor. Also *fig.*

Comb. **porter's lodge,** a lodge for the p. at the gate of a castle, park, etc. (formerly a place of corporal punishment for servants and dependants). Hence **Po·rter** *v.*^{1} *intr.* to be or act as a p.

Porter (pōᵊ·ɹtəɹ), *sb.*^{2} late ME. [– (O)Fr. *port(e)our* (mod. *porteur*) :– med.L. *portator, -or-*, f. *portare* carry; see PORT *v.*^{1}, -ER^{2} 3, -OUR.] **1.** A person employed to carry burdens; now *esp.* a servant of a railway company who carries luggage at a station (in full, *railway p.*). **b.** *gen.* and *fig.* A bearer, carrier 1581. **2.** An iron bar attached to a heavy body to be forged, by which it may, when suspended from a crane, be guided beneath the hammer or into a furnace 1794.

Hence **Po·rter** *v.*^{2} *trans.* to carry as a p. (sense 1).

Porter (pōᵊ·ɹtəɹ), *sb.*^{3} 1727. [Short for *porter's ale, porter's beer,* or *porter beer*, app. because orig. made for porters and other labourers.] A kind of beer, of a dark-brown colour and bitterish taste, brewed from malt partly charred or browned by drying at a high temperature. Also *attrib.*

My electors shall have p. at threepence a pot 1781.

Porterage (pōᵊ·ɹtərėdʒ). late ME. [f. PORTER *sb.*^{2} + -AGE.] The action or work of a porter; carriage or transportation of goods; also, the charge for this. Also *attrib.*

Po·rter-house. Chiefly *U.S.* 1800. [f. PORTER *sb.*^{3} + HOUSE *sb.*] A house at which porter and other malt liquors are retailed; also, one where steaks, chops, etc. are served.

attrib. **porter-house steak** (*U.S.*), a thick juicy beef-steak cut from between the sirloin and the tenderloin, supposed to derive its name from a well-known porter-house in New York.

Portfire (pōᵊ·ɹtfəiᵊɹ). 1647. [After Fr. *porte-feu*, in same sense; see PORTE-.] A device used formerly for firing artillery, and now for firing rockets, etc., and for igniting an explosive in mining, etc.

Portfolio (poɹtfōᵘ·lio). 1722. [orig. *porto folio* – It. *portafogli*, f. *porta*, imper. of *portare* carry + *fogli* leaves, sheets of paper, pl. of *foglio* :– L. *folium*; first element assim. to Fr. *portefeuille*.] **1.** A receptacle or case, usu. in the form of a large book-cover, for keeping loose sheets of paper, prints, drawings, maps, music, etc. **2.** *spec.* Such a receptacle containing the official documents of a state department; *fig.* the office of a minister of state. **3.** orig. *U.S.* A list of the securities owned by a financial institution, a bill-broker, etc. 1934.

2. *Minister without p.* (Fr. *sans portefeuille*), a member of the Cabinet who is not in charge of any department of state.

Comb. **p.-stand,** a piece of furniture for holding portfolios, drawings, music, etc.

Port-hole (pōᵊ·ɹtˌhōᵘl). 1591. [f. PORT *sb.*^{3} + HOLE *sb.*] **1.** *Naut.* = PORT *sb.*^{3} 2 b. **2.** *transf.* **a.** An aperture in a wall for shooting through, etc.; an embrasure; **b.** a similar aperture in other structures, e.g. in the door of a furnace 1644. **3.** A steam port (PORT *sb.*^{3} 3) 1875.

Porthors, early f. PORTAS.

Portico (pōᵊ·ɹtiko). *Pl.* **-os, -oes.** 1605. [– It. *portico* :– L. *porticus* porch.] *Arch.* An ambulatory consisting of a roof supported by columns placed at regular intervals, usu. attached as a porch to a building; a colonnade. Also *transf.* and *fig.* **b.** *spec.* The Painted Porch at Athens; see PORCH 3; hence *fig.* the Stoic philosophy. Also *allus.* 1788.

b. From the p. the Roman civilians learned to live, to reason, and to die GIBBON. Hence **Po·rticoed** *a.* furnished with a p.

‖**Portière** (portyę̄r). 1855. [Fr., f. *porte* door (see PORT *sb.*^{3}) + *-ière* (:– L. *-aria* -ARY^{1}).] A curtain hung over a door or doorway, to prevent draught, to serve as a screen, or for ornament.

Portion (pōᵊ·ɹʃən), *sb.* [ME. *porcion, portion* – OFr. *porcion*, (also mod.) *portion* – L. *portio, -on-*, attested first in phr. *pro portione* in PROPORTION.] **I. 1.** The part (of anything) allotted to one person; a share. Also *fig.* **b.** An allowance of food allotted to, or enough for, one person 1484. **2.** The part or share of an estate given or passing by law to an heir, or to be distributed to him in the settlement of the estate. Also *fig.* ME. **3.** Dowry; a marriage portion 1511. **4.** That which is allotted a person by providence; lot, destiny, fate ME.

1. Giue me the p. of goods that falleth to me *Luke* 15:12. 3. I married Mrs. Mary Burton.. with whom I received four hundred pounds for a p. SWIFT. 4. When Labour was pronounced to be the P. of Man STEELE. Brief life is here our p. 1851.

II. 1. = PART *sb.* I. 1. ME. **2.** A (limited) quantity or amount; some ME.

1. A p. of the pressure was transmitted laterally TYNDALL. 2. But grace, ye the leest porcyon of grace,..is sufficyent 1526. Hence **Po·rtionless** *a.* without a p.; dowerless.

Portion (pōᵊ·ɹʃən), *v.* ME. [– OFr. *portionner* (med.L. *portionare*), f. the sb.] **1.** *trans.* To divide into portions or shares; to share *out.* **b.** = APPORTION *v.* 1. 1871. **2.** To dower, endow 1712.

1. The petty chiefs among whom the country was portioned out 1859. 2. When I marry with their consent they will p. me most handsomely DICKENS.

Portional (pōᵊ·ɹʃənăl), *a. rare.* late ME. [– late L. *portionalis* partial, f. L. *portio*; see PORTION *sb.*, -AL^{1}.] Pertaining to or of the nature of a portion or part. Hence **Po·rtionally** *adv.* by way of a portion or part; partly, in part.

Portioner (pōᵊ·ɹʃənəɹ). 1508. [f. PORTION *sb.* or *v.* + -ER^{1,2}.] **1.** *Scots Law.* The proprietor of a small piece of land forming a portion of an original forty-merk land. **b.** *Heir-* or *heiress-p.*, one of two or more heirs female who succeed to equal portions of a heritage; or the male representative of such an heiress 1576. †**2.** *Eccl.* = PORTIONIST 2. –1848. **3.** *Eng. Law.* One of several persons among whom a settled fund is appointable (*rare*) 1884.

Po·rtionist. 1672. [– med.L. *portionista* (in AL., postmaster at Merton), f. L. *portio*; see PORTION *sb.*, -IST.] **1.** In ref. to Merton College, Oxford: A rendering of the L. term *portionista*, applied to the class of poor scholars usu. called *postmasters*. **2.** *Eccl.* One of two or more incumbents who share the duties and revenues of a benefice 1743.

Portland (pōᵊ·ɹtlǣnd). 1720. A peninsula or 'island' on the coast of Dorsetshire; *attrib.* in names of products of Portland Island, or of objects connected with it; as **P. cement,** a cement resembling *P. stone* in colour; also *attrib.*; **P. oolite,** a limestone of the Upper Oolite formation, especially developed in the Isle of Portland; **P. stone,** a valuable building stone quarried in the Isle of Portland; etc.

Portly (pōᵊ·ɹtli), *a.* 1529. [f. PORT *sb.*^{4} + -LY^{1}.] Characterized by stateliness or dignity of bearing, appearance, and manner; stately, dignified; imposing. **b.** Now usu., connoting 'Large and bulky in person; stout, corpulent' 1598. **c.** Of things: Stately, magnificent, fine 1548.

b. He dwindled. from a p. and even corpulent man to a skeleton MACAULAY. Hence **Po·rtliness.**

Po·rtman. Now *local.* OE. [f. PORT *sb.*^{2} + MAN *sb.*] In OE. use, a citizen of a town, a burgess or burgher; *spec.* (after the Conquest) = *capital* or *head p.*, one of a select number of citizens chosen to administer the affairs of a borough.

Portmanteau (poɹtmæ·nto), *sb.* 1584. [– Fr. *portemanteau* official who carried a prince's mantle, valise, clothes-rack, f. *porter* carry (see PORT *v.*^{1}) + *manteau* MANTLE *sb.*] **1.** A case or bag for carrying clothing and other necessaries when travelling; now, an oblong stiff leather case, which opens like a book, with hinges in the middle of the back. ‖**2.** A clothes-rack, an arrangement of pegs to hang clothes on 1727. **3.** *attrib.*, as in *p. horse*, etc.; **p. word,** a word like those invented by 'Lewis Carroll', made up of the blended sounds and combining the meanings of two distinct words (as *slithy*, meaning 'lithe and slimy').

Po·rtmote. *Obs.* exc. *Hist.* ME. [f. PORT *sb.*^{1,2} + ME. *imote* MOOT *sb.*] **1.** The court of a borough; a borough-mote. **2.** The court of a (legal) sea-port town 1598.

‖**Portolano** (pōᵊɹtolā·no), **portulan** (pōᵊ·ɹtiŭlăn). 1850. [It. *portolano*, f. *porto* PORT *sb.*^{1}; hence Fr. *portulan*.] A book of sailing directions, describing harbours, etc. and illustrated with charts.

Portrait (pōᵊ·ɹtrėt), *sb.* 1570. [– Fr. *portrait*, subst. use of pa. pple. of OFr. *portraire*; see PORTRAY.] **1.** A figure drawn, painted, or carved upon a surface to represent some object; *spec.* (now almost always) a likeness of a person, esp. of the face, made from life by drawing, painting, photography, engraving, etc. †**b.** A solid image, a statue –1638. **2.** *fig.* An image, representation, type; likeness, similitude 1577. **b.** A verbal picture; a graphic description 1596.

1. The..Coines, the portracts whereof I haue here shewed 1610. What's here, the p. of a blinking idiot SHAKS. The gentleman who wanted to take your p. 1858. 2. Poetes terme sleepe an image, or pourtraite of death 1577.

Comb.: **p.-bust,** a bust giving an exact likeness; **-gallery,** a gallery containing a collection of portraits, or the collection itself; also *fig.*; **-lens,** a compound photographic lens adapted for taking portraits; **-painter; -painting.** Hence **Po·rtraitist,** one whose occupation it is to take portraits; esp. a p.-painter.

†**Po·rtrait,** *v.* 1548. [orig. as pa. pple. *portraited*, app. an extended form of the ME. (orig. Fr.) pa. pple. *portrait*; see prec.] **1.** *trans.* = PORTRAY *v.* 1. –1864. **2.** *fig.* = PORTRAY *v.* 4. –1665. **3.** *transf.* = PORTRAY *v.* 1 b. –1669.

Portraiture (pōᵊ·ɹtrėtiŭɹ, -tʃəɹ). [XIV – OFr. *portraiture*, f. pa. pple. *portrait*; see PORTRAIT *sb.*, -URE.] **1.** The action or art of portraying; delineation. Also in concr. or collective sense; esp. in phr. *in p.* = portrayed, delineated. **2.** *concr.* = PORTRAIT *sb.* 1. late ME. †**b.** = PORTRAIT *sb.* 1 b. –1720. **3.** *gen.* and *fig.* An image, representation; a mental image, idea, †a type. late ME. **4.** = PORTRAIT *sb.* 2 b. 1610. †**5.** Figure, likeness, appearance (as an attribute of a thing) –1797.

1. The Portraitures of insignificant People by ordinary Painters STEELE. 4. Shakespeare's p. of John of Gaunt 1863. Hence †**Po·rtraiture** *v. trans.* to make a p. or portrait of, to portray (*lit.* and *fig.*).

Portray (poɹtrēⁱ·), *v.* ME. [– OFr. *portrai-*, stem of *portraire*, f. *por-* (:– L. *pro-* PRO-^{1}) + *traire* draw (:– Rom. ***tragere**, for L. *trahere*).] **1.** *trans.* To make a picture, image, or figure of. †**b.** *transf.* To make (a picture, image, or figure); to draw, paint, or carve; to trace –1604. †**2.** *transf.* To paint or adorn (a surface) *with* a picture or figure 1667. **3.** *fig.* †**a.** To picture to oneself; to fancy. **b.** To represent (e.g. dramatically). ME. **4.** *esp.* To represent in words, describe graphically, set forth. late ME.

2. Shields..with boastful Argument portraid MILT. 4. Well hast thou pourtray'd..The face and personage of a wondrous man MARLOWE. Hence **Po·rtray** *sb.* the act of portraying; portrayal; a portrait. **Portray·al,** *lit.* pictorial representation; *fig.* representation in general; *esp.* verbal picturing. **Portray·er.**

Portreeve (pōᵊ·ɹtˌrīv). [OE. *portġerēfa*, f. PORT *sb.*^{2} + *ġerēfa* REEVE *sb.*^{1}] **1.** *orig.* The ruler or chief officer of a town or borough; after the Norman Conquest often identified with the mayor; in later times, sometimes an officer inferior to the mayor; a bailiff. **2.** Erron. referred to PORT *sb.*^{1} 2, as if the reeve of a sea-port town 1607.

Portress (pōᵊ·ɹtrĕs), **porteress** (pōᵊ·ɹtərĕs). late ME. [f. PORTER *sb.*[1] + -ESS[1].] A female porter; esp. in a nunnery. Also *fig.*

Port-Royal (pōᵊɹtˌroi·ăl). 1692. Name of a convent near Versailles (*Port-Royal des Champs*) which in the 17th c. became the home of a lay community celebrated for its connection with Jansenism and its educational work. Hence **Port-Roy·alist** 1727.

†**Po·rt-sa:le.** 1494. [f. PORT *sb.*[2] or *sb.*[3] + SALE.] Public sale to the highest bidder; sale by auction –1670.

Portsman (pōᵊ·ɹtsmæ̆n). 1626. [f. PORT *sb.*[1] 3 + MAN *sb.*] A citizen or inhabitant of one of the Cinque Ports. (Usu. in pl.)

Portuary (pōᵊ·ɹtiuˌări). *arch.* 1867. [f. *portuas*, or other var. of PORTAS, perh. after *breviary*.] = PORTAS. Also *attrib.*

Portugal (pōᵊ·ɹtiŭgăl). late ME. [– Pg. *portugal*, earlier *Portucal* – med.L. *Portus Cale*, the port of Gaya, Oporto.] **1.** A country in the west of the Iberian peninsula. †**2.** A native or inhabitant of Portugal –1707. †**3.** *attrib.* or as *adj.* = PORTUGUESE A. –1719.

1. A French Shallop which he tooke in the Bay of Portingall RALEGH. **3.** Great P. ships 1691.

Portuguese (pōᵊɹtiŭgī·z), *a.* and *sb.* 1586. [– Pg. *Portuguez*, in med.L. *Portugalensis*; see prec., -ESE.] **A.** *adj.* Pertaining to Portugal or its people 1662.

P. man-of-war: see MAN-OF-WAR.

B. *sb.* **1.** A native of Portugal. [pl. *Portugueses* in 17th c.; now *Portuguese* sing. and pl.] 1622. **2.** The Portuguese language 1617. †**3.** = PORTAGUE –1668.

‖**Portulaca** (pōᵊɹtiŭlē[i]·kă). 1548. [L., purslane (*P. oleracea*) taken by Tournefort, 1700, as a generic name.] *Bot.* A genus of plants, comprising low succulent herbs bearing white, yellow, red, or purple terminal flowers, expanding only once in direct sunshine; esp. a plant of a cultivated species of this. Hence **Portulaceous** (-ē[i]·ʃəs) *a.* *Bot.* of or pertaining to the N.O. *Portulaceæ*, comprising succulent herbs or shrubs, chiefly American.

Po·rt-wi·ne. 1700. = PORT *sb.*[6]; *attrib.* in **p. mark** = NÆVUS.

†**Po·ry,** *a.* 1535. [f. PORE *sb.* + -Y[1].] Full of pores; porous –1826.

‖**Posaune** (pozau·nĕ, pǒzǭ·n). 1724. [G.] †**1.** A trombone –1814. **2.** A reed-stop on an organ 1843.

Pose (pōᵘz), *sb.* 1818. [– Fr. *pose*, f. *poser*; see next.] An act of posing. **1.** An attitude or posture of the body, or of a part of the body, esp. one deliberately assumed, or in which a figure is placed for effect, or for artistic purposes. **2.** *fig.* An attitude of mind, esp. one assumed for effect 1884.

Pose (pōᵘz), *v.*[1] *Pa. t.* and *pple.* **posed.** ME. [– (O)Fr. *poser* :– late L. *pausare* cease, PAUSE; in Rom. this vb. took over the senses of L. *ponere* place, pa. t. *posui*, pa. pple. *positum*, and became its regular repr., the application of *ponere* being specialized in the sense 'lay eggs' (cf. Fr. *pondre*).] †**1.** *trans.* To suppose for argument's sake –1528. **2. a.** To lay down, put forth (an assertion, claim, instance, etc.) ME. **b.** To propose (a question, problem) 1862. **3. a.** To place in an attitude (as an artist's model, etc.). 1859. **b.** *intr.* To assume a certain attitude, esp. for artistic purposes 1850. **c.** *fig.* To set up *as*, give oneself out *as*; to attitudinize 1840.

2. b. Hesiod poses the eternal problems: what is the origin and destiny of mankind? 1873. **3. a.** In studied attitude, like one posėd for a daguerreotype 1868. **b.** It is more easy to p. than to act 1885. **c.** Politicians have of late years begun to p. as the special friends of the working man 1888. Hence **Po·ser**[2], one who poses or attitudinizes.

Pose (pōᵘz), *v.*[2] 1526. [Aphetic f. APPOSE.] †**1.** *trans.* = APPOSE *v.*[1] 1. –1722. **2.** To nonplus with a question or problem 1593.

2. A question wherewith a learned Pharisee thought to p. or puzzle him 1677.

‖**Posé** (poze), *a.* 1725. [Fr., pa. pple. of *poser* place.] *Her.* = STATANT.

Poser[1] (pōᵘ·zəɹ). 1587. [Aphetic f. APPOSER; see POSE *v.*[2]] **1.** One who sets testing questions; an examiner. Now *rare.* **2.** A puzzling question or problem 1793.

‖**Poseur** (pozȫr). 1881. [Fr., f. *poser* POSE *v.*[1]] One who practises an affected mental or social attitude. Also ‖**Poseuse** fem.

Posh (pǫʃ), *a. slang.* 1918. [perh. adjectival use of sl. *posh* (XIX) money, a dandy, of unkn. origin.] Smart, 'swell'; fine, splendid.

Posied (pōᵘ·zid), *a.* 1597. [f. POSY + -ED[2].] **1.** Inscribed with a posy or motto (*arch.*). **2.** Furnished with nosegays; flowery. *dial.* 1797.

1. Many a ring of P. gold SHAKS.

Posit (pǫ·zit), *v.* 1647. [f. L. *posit-*, pa. ppl. stem of *ponere* place.] **1.** *trans.* To put in position; to set, dispose, or situate; to place. (Chiefly in *pa. pple.* or *pass.*) **2.** To put down or assume as a fact; to postulate. Chiefly in *Logic* and *Philos.* 1697.

2. In so far as anything is a cause, it posits something different from itself as an effect 1877.

Position (pǒzi·ʃən), *sb.* late ME. [– (O)Fr. *position* or L. *positio*, f. as prec., rendering Gr. θέσις THESIS, θέμα THEME.] **I. 1.** The action of positing; the statement of a proposition or thesis; affirmation. Chiefly in *Logic* and *Philos.* **2.** Something posited; a statement, assertion, tenet 1451. **3.** *Arith.* A method of finding the value of an unknown quantity by positing one or more values for it, finding the error as indicated by the results, and then adjusting it. Also called *rule of (false) p., rule of trial and error*, etc. 1551. †**4.** The action of positing or placing; disposition –1735. **5.** The manner in which a body, or the several parts of it, are disposed or arranged; disposition, posture, attitude 1703. **b.** *fig.* Mental attitude 1905. **6.** *Mus.* The arrangement of the constituent notes of a chord, with respect to their order, or to the intervals between them 1880.

2. It is a p. in the Mathematiques that there is no proportion betweene somewhat and nothing BACON. **5.** *Eastward p.*, the p. of the officiating priest at the Eucharist, when he stands facing east with his back to the people.

II. 1. The place occupied by a thing, or in which it is put; situation, site, station 1541. **b.** *Mil.* A site chosen for occupation by an army, usu. as having a strategic value 1781. **2.** *Phonology.* The situation of a vowel in an open or closed syllable; *spec.* in *Gr.* and *L. Prosody*, the situation of a short vowel before two consonants or their equivalent, making the syllable metrically long (phr. *in p.* said of such a vowel) 1580. **3.** The situation which one metaphorically occupies in relation to others, to facts, or to circumstances 1827. **b.** Place in the social scale; status, rank 1865. **c.** An official situation, place, or employment 1890.

1. Phr. *In p.*, in its (his, etc.) proper place; so *out of p.* *Angle of p.*, (*a*) the angle between any two points subtended at the eye; (*b*) *Astron.* the angle between the circles of declination and latitude of a celestial body. *Circle of p.*, any one of six great circles of the celestial sphere passing through the north and south points of the horizon. *Gun of p.*, a heavy field gun, not designed for executing quick movements. **3.** We are now in a p. to discuss the air thermometer 1871. **b.** A man of considerable p. 1868. **c.** A p. in a bank 1890.

attrib. and *Comb.*, as **p.-artillery**, heavy field-artillery; so **p.-battery; p. error**, the error of a watch when laid in certain positions; **-finder**, an apparatus by means of which a gunner is enabled to aim a gun at an object not visible to him.

Position (pǒzi·ʃən), *v.* 1817. [f. prec.] *trans.* To place in a particular or appropriate position. **b.** To determine the position of; to locate 1881.

Positional (pǒzi·ʃənăl), *a.* 1571. [f. POSITION *sb.* + -AL[1].] Of, pertaining to, or determined by position.

Positive (pǫ·zitiv), *a.* and *sb.* ME. [– (O)Fr. *positif, -ive* or L. *positivus* (late L. gram., med.L. logic), f. as prec.; see -IVE.] **A.** *adj.* **I. 1.** Formally laid down or imposed; arbitrarily or artificially instituted; conventional; opp. to *natural.* **2.** Explicitly laid down; admitting no question; express, definite, precise; emphatic; †objectively certain 1598. **3.** Of persons: Confident in opinion or assertion; convinced; also, opinionated, cock-sure, dogmatic, dictatorial 1665.

1. Again, of p. laws some are human, some divine; and of human p. laws, some are distributive, some penal HOBBES. **2.** P. orders oblige us to go tomorrow 1709. P. proof 1870. **3.** Nor is Socrates p. of anything but the duty of enquiry JOWETT.

II. Unqualified, unrelated, absolute. **1.** *Gram.* Applied to the primary form of an adjective or adverb, which expresses simple quality, without qualification, comparison, or relation to increase or diminution 1447. **2.** Having no relation to or comparison with other things; absolute, unconditional; opp. to *relative* and *comparative* 1606. **b.** *colloq.* Nothing less than, downright; 'out-and-out' 1802.

2. Patroclus is a foole positiue SHAKS. Beauty is no p. thing, but depends on the different tastes of the people 1727. **b.** You are a p. enigma 1853.

III. 1. Dealing only with matters of fact; practical; not speculative or theoretical 1594. **2.** Actual, real; sensible, concrete (*rare*) 1831.

1. *P. philosophy* = POSITIVISM 1. **2.** *P. image* = real image; see REAL *a.*[2] I. 1 d.

IV. Having real existence; opp. to *negative.* **1.** Characterized by the presence, and not merely by the absence, of features or qualities; of an affirmative nature 1618. **b.** Of a term, etc.: Denoting the presence, as opp. to the absence, of a quality 1725. **2.** *Alg.* Of a quantity: Greater than zero; additive; the opp. of NEGATIVE *a.* II. 2. 1704. **b.** Hence, Reckoned or tending in the direction taken (naturally or arbitrarily) as that of increase, progress, or onward motion 1873. **3.** *Electr.* Applied to that form of electricity which is produced by rubbing glass with silk; vitreous; opp. to NEGATIVE *a.* II. 3. 1755. **b.** Of, pertaining to, or marked by the presence or production of positive electricity; *spec.* denoting that member of a voltaic couple which is most acted upon by the solution, and from which a current of positive electricity proceeds 1808. **4.** *Magnetism.* Applied to the north-seeking pole of a magnet, and the corresponding (south) pole of the earth 1849. **5.** *Optics.* **a.** Of a double-refracting crystal: Having the index of refraction of the extraordinary ray greater than that of the ordinary ray 1831. **6.** *Photogr.* Showing the lights and shades as seen in nature; opp. to NEGATIVE *a.* II. 5. 1840.

1. Ease from misery occasioning for some time the greatest p. enjoyment 1729. **2.** *P. sign*, the sign +, used to mark a p. quantity. **5.** *P. eyepiece*, an eyepiece consisting of two plano-convex lenses, having their convex sides facing each other, in which the object is viewed beyond both lenses.

V. Adapted to be placed or set down. *P. organ*, a small organ, orig. app. portable, but placed upon a stand when played 1727.

B. *sb.* (the adj. used absol. or ellipt.) **1.** *Gram.* The positive degree (see A. II. 1); an adj. or adv. in the positive degree 1530. **2.** That which has an actual existence, or is capable of being affirmed; a reality 1620. **3.** Elliptically or contextually for *p. quantity* (see A. IV. 2); *p. plate, metal*, etc. (see A. IV. 3); *p. organ* (see A. V.); etc. 1706. **4.** *Photogr.* A picture in which the lights and shades are the same as in nature; opp. to NEGATIVE *sb.* 4. 1853. Hence **Po·sitive-ly** *adv.*, **-ness.**

Positivism (pǫ·zitiviz'm). 1854. [– Fr. *positivisme* (Comte) for earlier *philosophie positive* (1830); see prec., -ISM.] **1.** A system of philosophy elaborated by Auguste Comte, which recognizes only positive facts and observable phenomena, with the objective relations of these and the laws which determine them, abandoning all inquiry into causes or ultimate origins; also, a religious system founded upon this philosophy, in which the object of worship is Humanity considered as a single corporate being. **2. a.** Definiteness, peremptoriness; **b.** Certainty, assurance 1854.

Positivist (pǫ·zitivist). 1854. [– Fr. *positiviste*; see prec., -IST.] An adherent or supporter of POSITIVISM; a Comtist. Also *attrib.* or as *adj.* Hence **Positivi·stic** *a.* of or pertaining to positivists; of the nature of positivism.

Positivity (pǫziti·vĭti). 1659. [f. POSITIVE

+ -ITY.] The quality, character, or fact of being POSITIVE; positiveness.

Posnet (pǫ·snėt). Now *arch.* and *dial.* [ME. *possenet* – OFr. *poçonnet*, dim. of *poçon* vase.] A small metal pot or vessel for boiling, having a handle and three feet.

Posology (poso·lŏdʒi). 1811. [– Fr. *posologie*, f. Gr. πόσος how much + -LOGY.] **1.** That part of medicine which relates to the quantities or doses in which drugs should be administered 1823. **2.** Used by Bentham for the science of quantity, i.e. mathematics 1811. Hence **Posolo·gical** *a.* pertaining to p. **Poso·logist,** one who compounds doses SYD. SMITH.

‖**Pospolite** (pǫspǫ·lite). 1697. *Hist.* [Polish *pospolite* adj. n. general, universal; as sb. = *pospolite ruszenie* general levy.] The Polish militia.

Poss (pǫs), *v.* Now only *dial.* late ME. [Of unkn. origin.] **1.** *trans.* To drive or thrust; to dash or toss with a blow; to knock. Also *fig.* **2.** To pound, beat down flat, squash; *spec.* to beat or stamp (clothes, etc.) in water, in the process of washing 1611.

2. Nasty women possing clothes with their feet THORESBY. Hence **Po·sser,** an implement for possing clothes. **Po·ss-tub,** a wash-tub.

Posse (pǫ·si). 1583. [– med.L. subst. use of L. *posse* be able; in 1 for *posse comitatus* (see next); in 2 from scholastic terminology.] **1.** *Law.* = next. Now chiefly *U.S.* 1659. **b.** A force, *esp.* of constables 1697. **c.** *transf.* A company (*of* persons, animals, or things) 1645. ‖**2.** The fact or state of being possible; potentiality (opp. to *esse*); esp. in phr. *in p.* opp. to *in esse* 1583.

‖**Posse comitatus** (pǫ·si kǫmitēⁱ·tŏs). 1626. [med. (Anglo-) L., force of the county; see prec., COUNTY.] The body of men above the age of fifteen in a county (exclusive of peers, clergymen, and infirm persons), whom the sheriff may summon or raise to repress a riot or for other purposes; also, a body of men so raised and commanded by the sheriff. (See also prec. 1.) **b.** *transf.* = POSSE 1 c. 1819.

Possess (pŏze·s), *v.* 1465. [– OFr. *possesser*, f. *possess-*, pa. ppl. stem of L. *possidēre*, f. *potis* (see POTENT) + *sedēre* SIT.] **I.** †**1.** *trans.* To hold, occupy (a place or territory); to reside or be stationed in; to inhabit –1713. †**b.** Of a thing; To occupy (a space or region); to be situated at, on, or in –1755. †**c.** To occupy, engross the attention or thoughts of –1719. **2.** To hold as property; to own 1500. **b.** *Law.* To have possession of, as distinct from ownership 1888. **c.** To have as a faculty, attribute, quality, etc. (Often = the simple *have*.) 1576. **d.** (after Fr. *posséder.*) To have knowledge of; to be master of or conversant with (a language) 1852. **3.** To seize, take; to come into possession of, obtain, win (*arch.*) 1526. **4.** To keep, maintain (oneself, one's mind, soul) *in* a state or condition (of patience, quiet, etc.); often in allusion to Luke 21:19 (the proper sense being misunderstood; see quot. in 3). Also (without *in*) to maintain control over. 1643. **5.** Of a demon or (usu. evil) spirit: To occupy and dominate, control, or actuate 1596. **6.** Of an idea, etc.: To take or have hold of (a person); to affect strongly and persistently. (Formerly also of bodily conditions.) 1591.

1. Dominion giv'n Over all other Creatures that possesse Earth, Aire, and Sea MILT. **2.** He could not give to others what he did not himself p. 1881. **c.** The former may p. many times the intensity of the latter 1860. **3.** With your pacience possesse your soules TINDALE, *Luke* 21:19. **4.** All Christians..are obliged..to p. their souls in patience 1654. **5.** I am possest with the duell and cannot sleepe DEKKER. **6.** What can p. this young lord to be out of his bed at this hour? 1814.

II. Causal uses; = cause to possess. †**1.** To put in possession of (lands, etc.); to settle or establish *in* –1708. **2.** To endow with, put in possession *of*; to give (something) to. Now *rare* or *Obs.* exc. as in b or c. 1549. **b.** *refl.* = sense I. 3. 1593. **c.** *pass.* To be in possession *of*; to possess 1495. **3.** To cause to be possessed by (a feeling, idea, etc.); to imbue, inspire, permeate *with*; to cause to feel or entertain 1597. †**b.** Without const.: To prepossess –1681. **4.** To put in possession *of*, furnish *with* (information, etc.); to instruct *in*; to acquaint *that*. *Obs.* or *arch.* 1596.

2. I will possesse you of that ship and Treasure SHAKS. **b.** All that the plaintiffs did was to p. themselves..of the securities 1885. **c.** *Possessed of* or *with*, having possession of, possessing; Every human being possessed of reason COLERIDGE. **3.** What Devil possesses them with such wicked designs? 1670. **b.** In all causes the first tale possesseth much BACON. **4.** I haue possest your grace of what I purpose SHAKS. Hence **Possessed** (pŏze·st) *ppl. a.* occupied, held as property; inhabited or controlled by a demon or spirit; lunatic, crazy.

Possession (pŏze·ʃən). ME. [– (O)Fr. *possession* or L. *possessio*, f. as prec.; see -ION.] **1.** The action or fact of possessing, or condition of being possessed; the holding something as one's own; actual occupancy, as dist. from ownership. **b.** *Law.* The visible possibility of exercising over a thing such control as attaches to lawful ownership; the detention or enjoyment of a thing by a person himself or by another in his name; the relation of a person to a thing over which he may at his pleasure exercise such control as the character of the thing admits, to the exclusion of other persons; *esp.* the having of such exclusive control over land, in early instances sometimes used in the technical sense of SEISIN 1535. **2.** *concr.* That which is possessed or held as property; (with *a*, etc.) a thing possessed, a piece of property; *pl.* belongings, property, wealth ME. **3.** A territory subject to a soverign ruler or state; now chiefly applied to the foreign dominions of an independent country 1818. **4.** The fact of a demon possessing a person; the fact of being possessed by a demon or spirit 1590. **5.** The action of an idea or feeling possessing a person; *transf.* an idea or impulse that holds one strongly; †a prepossession 1621. **6.** The action of keeping (oneself, one's mind, etc.) under control (*rare* exc. in SELF-POSSESSION) 1703.

1. Philosophy is the p. of knowledge JOWETT. **b.** Phr. *In p.*, said (*a*) of a thing, actually possessed or held; (*b*) of a person, usu. *in p. of*, actually possessing, holding, or occupying something. *Chose in p.*: see CHOSE 1. *Man in p.*, a duly authorized person who is placed in charge of chattels upon which there is a warrant for distress. *To take p. of*, to take for one's own or into one's control, to seize. Provb. *P. is nine points of the law*: see POINT *sb.*¹ III. 6. **2.** The ȝong man..wente awei sorewful, for he hadde many possessiouns WYCLIF *Matt.* 19:22. **3.** Canada became a British p. in 1763. 1850. **4.** How long hath this p. held the man? SHAKS. Hence **Posse·ssional** *a. rare*, pertaining to p.; having possessions or property; propertied. **Posse·ssionary** *a.* constituted by p.; having, pertaining to, or relating to p.

Posse·ssioner. *Hist.* late ME. [– AL. *possessionarius* (for more usual *possessionatus*), f. as prec. = *-arius* -ARY¹.] One who is in possession or holds possession *of* something; a holder, occupier; an owner; an owner of possessions. **b.** *spec.* A member of a religious order having possessions or endowments; an endowed clergyman or ecclesiastic. late ME.

Possessive (pŏze·siv), *a.* (*sb.*) 1530. [– L. *possessivus* (Quintilian), tr. Gr. κτητική (πτῶσις case), f. as prec.; see -IVE.] **1.** *Gram.* Denoting possession; qualifying a thing (or person) as belonging to some other. **2.** Of or pertaining to possession; indicating possession 1560. **b.** Having the quality of being in possession 1838. **B.** *sb. Gram. ellipt.* (*a*) for *p. pronoun* or *adjective*; (*b*) for *p. case* 1591.

1. *P. pronoun* (*p. adjective*), a word derived from a personal or other pronoun, and expressing possession. *P. case*, a name for the genitive case in modern English, ending (in nouns) in *'s, s'*, and expressing possession. Hence **Posse·ssive-ly** *adv.* in a p. sense or relation; in the way of possession; **-ness.**

Possessor (pŏze·səɹ). [Late ME. *possessour* – AFr. *possessour* = (O)Fr. *-eur* – L. *possessor*, f. as prec. + -OR 2. Later *possesser* (XVI–XVIII), then conformed to L.; see -ER² 3, -OR 2.] One who possesses; one who holds something as property or in actual control; one who has something belonging to him; a holder, an owner, proprietor. Const. *of* or with *poss. pron.* **b.** *spec.* (mainly *Law*). One who takes, occupies, or holds something without ownership, or as dist. from the owner 1565.

The most hye God, p. of heauen and earth COVERDALE *Gen.* 14:19. This charm was too dangerous to its p. MRS. RADCLIFFE. **b.** The p. remains liable to the true owner 1800. Hence **Posse·ssorship.**

Possessory (pŏze·sŏri). *a.* late ME. [– late L. *possessorius*, f. *possessor*; see prec., -ORY².] **1.** *Law.* **a.** Pertaining to a possessor; relating to possession. **b.** Arising from possession, as *p. interest, right, title* 1615. **2.** That is a possessor; holding something in possession 1633. **3.** Of, belonging to, or characterizing a possessor 1659.

1. a. *P. action*, an action in which the plaintiff's claim is founded upon his or his predecessor's possession, and not upon his right or title.

Posset (pǫ·sėt), *sb.* [XV *poshote, possot*; of unkn. origin.] A drink composed of hot milk curdled with ale, wine, or other liquor, often with sugar, spices, etc.; formerly much used as a delicacy, and as a remedy for colds, etc. Also *attrib.* Hence **Po·sset** *v.* †*trans.* to curdle like a p.; *intr.* to make a p.

Possibilist (pǫsi·bilist). 1881. [– Fr. *possibiliste* or Sp. *posibilista*; see POSSIBLE, -IST.] A member of a political party whose aims at reform are directed to what is immediately possible.

spec. (*a*) of a party of Republicans in Spain; (*b*) of a party of Socialists in France. Also *attrib.* or as *adj.*

Possibility (pǫsibi·lĭti). late ME. [– (O)Fr. *possibilité* or late L. *possibilitas*, f. L. *possibilis*; see next, -ITY.] **1.** The state, condition, or fact of being possible; capability of being done, happening, or existing. **b.** The quality or character of representing or relating to something that is possible 1638. **2.** A possible thing or circumstance; something that may exist or happen. (Usu. with *a* or *pl.*) late ME. †**3.** Regarded as an attribute of the agent: The fact of something being possible to one, in virtue either of circumstances or of one's own powers; hence, Capacity, power, ability; pecuniary ability, means –1815. †**b.** *sing.* and *pl.* Pecuniary prospects –1637.

1. Science and Revelation come into..collision on the p. of miracles 1884. Phr. *By any p.*, in any possible way, by any existing means, possibly; so *by no p.* *In p.*, (*a*) = *in* POSSE; (*b*) in relation to something possible, but not actual; potentially. *After p.* (Law), ellipt. for *after p. of issue is extinct*, i.e. when there is no longer any p. of issue. **b.** To consult on the p. of certain views DISRAELI. **2.** Her clearer intellect saw possibilities which did not occur to him TROLLOPE. **3.** I haue speeded hither with the very extremest ynch of possibilitie SHAKS. **b.** *Merry W.* I. i. 65.

Possible (pǫ·sĭb'l), *a.* (*sb.*, *adv.*) ME. [– (O)Fr. *possible* or L. *possibilis*, f. *posse* be able; see -IBLE.] **1.** That may be (i.e. is capable of being); that may or can exist, be done, or happen; that is in one's power, that one can do, exert, use, etc. (const. *to* the agent). **b.** That can or may be or become (what is denoted by the sb.); as *a p. object of knowledge* = something that can or may be known 1736. **2.** That may be (i.e. is not known not to be); that is perhaps true or a fact; that perhaps exists. (Sometimes nearly = credible, thinkable.) 1582. **b.** That may be (what is denoted by the sb.); that perhaps is or will be 1882. †**3.** Having the power *to do* something; capable (*rare*) –1667. **4.** *Math.* = REAL *a.*² I. 1 c; opp. to IMPOSSIBLE A. 2. 1874. **5.** With ellipsis of some qualification: Possible to deal with, get on with, understand, etc. (*rare*) 1865.

1. All thynges are possyble to hym that belevith TINDALE *Mark* 9:23. To express ourselves with all p. energy BURKE. Phr. *If p.*, if it be (or were) p., if it can (or could) be. *As much as p.*, as much as may (or might) be, as much as one can (or could). **2.** In such an age, it is p. some great genius may arise, to equal any of the ancients DRYDEN. **3.** Firm we subsist, yet p. to swerve MILT.

B. *absol.* or as *sb.* **1. a.** *absol.* (usu. with *the*): That which is possible 1646. **b.** as *sb.* A possible thing. (Almost always in *pl.*) 1657. ¶ **c.** *To do one's p.* (after Fr. *faire son possible*): to do what is possible to one, to do one's utmost 1797. **2.** *colloq.* (orig. *highest p.*), short for 'highest possible score or number of points' (esp. in rifle practice) 1866. †**C.** as *adv.* = POSSIBLY. (As an intensive qualification of *can* or *could.*) –1799.

Possibly (pǫ·sĭbli), *adv.* late ME. [f. POSSIBLE + -LY[2].] **1.** In a possible manner; according to what may or can be (in the nature of things); by any existing power or means. (Usu., now always, as an intensive qualification of *can* or *could.*) **2.** According to what may be (as far as one knows); perhaps, maybe. (Often as intensive qualification of *may* or *might.*) 1600.

1. He cannot p. live till Five in the Morning ADDISON. How could you p. think so? 1907. **2.** P. I might have some poor low relations C. BRONTË.

Possum (pǫ·sǒm), *sb.* Now *colloq.* 1613. Aphetic form of OPOSSUM.

To play p. (U.S. colloq.), to feign; to pretend illness; in allusion to the opossum's habit of feigning death when threatened or attacked. Hence **Po·ssum** *v. intr.* to play p.; to hunt opossums.

Post (pōust), *sb.*[1] [OE. *post* – L. *postis*, prob. reinforced in ME. from OFr. and MLG., MDu. *post.*] **I. 1.** A stout piece of timber, etc., of considerable length, and usu. cylindrical or square, used in a vertical position, esp. in building as a support for a superstructure. **b.** As a type of lifelessness, stupidity, ignorance, deafness, or hardness. late ME. **2.** A stake, stout pole, or the like, set upright in or on the ground, for various purposes ME. †**b.** Formerly set up by the door of a mayor, sheriff, or other magistrate –1845. **3.** With prefixed words indicating special purpose 1643. **4.** Contextually for various specific kinds of posts: **a.** A door-post or gate-post ME. **b.** *Racing.* A starting-post or winning-post 1642. **c.** *Naut.* The upright timber on which the rudder is hung; the sternpost; †hence *transf.* the stern of a ship 1622. †**5.** The door-post on which the reckoning at a tavern was kept; hence, the score –1604.

1. b. Phr. *Between you and me and the p.* (*bed-p.*, *gate-p.*), as something that no one else is to hear or know; as a secret, in confidence. **2.** Like Posts of direction for Travellers MILT. **b.** *Twel. N.* I. v. 157. **3.** *Draw-p.*, a post used in wire fences, provided with winders for tightening the wires; *kerb-p.*, a post set at the edge of a pavement. See also BED-*p.*, DOOR-*p.*, GATE-P., GOAL-*p.*, KING-P., LAMP-P., SIGN-P. **4. a.** The Gates of Azza, P., and massie Bar MILT. **5.** *Com. Err.* I. ii. 64.

II. Transf. uses. **a.** A vertical mass or stack of stratified rock between two 'joints' or fissures 1712. **b.** Any thick compact stratum of sandstone or limestone 1794. **c.** = PILLAR *sb.* 6.

Phrases. *From p. to pillar*: see PILLAR *sb.* *To run one's head against a p.*: in fig. use. *On the right* or *the wrong side of the p.*, etc. (referring to posts marking the right course); hence *fig.*

Comb.: **p.-hole**, a hole made in the ground to receive the foot of a p.; also *attrib.*; **-mill**, a windmill pivoted on a p., so as to be turned round to catch the wind.

Post (pōust), *sb.*[2] 1506. [– Fr. *poste* – It. *posta* – Rom. **posta*, contr. of *posita*, fem. pa. pple. of L. *ponere* place (see POSITION).] **I.** †**1.** Orig. applied to men with horses stationed or appointed at intervals along the post-roads, the duty of each being to ride with, or forward to the next stage, the king's 'packet', and later the letters of other persons, and to furnish change of horses to messengers riding post –1628. **2.** One who travels express with letters, messages, etc., esp. on a fixed route; *orig.* a courier, a post-rider (now chiefly *Hist.*); a letter-carrier, a postman (now chiefly *dial.*). Also *transf.* and *fig.* 1507. **3.** A vehicle or vessel used in the conveyance of the mails; a mail-coach or cart; †a packet-boat. †Also, in early use, a post-horse. 1597. **4.** A single dispatch of letters, etc. from or to a place; also *concr.*, the letters, etc. collectively, as dispatched or conveyed, with that which carries them; the mail. Also *colloq.* the portion of a mail cleared from a receiving-box, or delivered at one house. 1674. **5.** = POST-OFFICE 1; the official conveyance of letters, books, parcels, etc. 1663. **b.** = POST-OFFICE 2; also the postal letter-box 1808.

1. In the 16th and 17th c., these 'posts' had also usu. the exclusive privilege of furnishing post-horses to ordinary travellers, and of conducting the business of a posting establishment O.E.D. Phr. *To lay posts*, to establish a chain of posts along a route for the speedy forwarding of dispatches. **2.** The Postes come tyring on, And not a man of them brings other newes SHAKS. Now my days are swifter than a p. *Job* 9:25. **3.** I haue fowndred nine score and odde Postes SHAKS. **4.** The state of foreign affairs varied every p. 1715. **5.** *Book-p.*, *parcel-p.*, the departments of the post-office which carry books and parcels.

†**II.** One of a series of stations where post-horses are kept for relays; a posting-house; also, the distance between two successive posting-houses; a stage –1809.

'Twill scarce be ten posts out of my way STERNE.

III. Phrases and senses arising out of them.

a. *By p.*, †*orig.* by posting; by courier; by relays of post-horses; in current use, through the post-office. **b.** *By return of p.* (Fr. *par retour du courrier*), †*orig.* by return of the 'post' or courier who brought the dispatch; now, by the next mail in the opposite direction. †**c.** *In p.* (= Fr. *en poste*), in the manner or capacity of a courier or bearer of dispatches, as a post; hence, at express speed, in haste; whence *post* becomes = haste, full speed. **d.** *To ride p.* = *to ride in p.* (c); see POST *adv.* †**e.** *To take p.*, to start on a journey with post-horses.

IV. Transf. uses. **1.** A frequent title of newspapers 1681. **2.** A parlour game; short for *general post* 1868. **3.** orig. *post-paper*: A size of writing-paper, the half-sheet of which when folded forms the ordinary quarto letter-paper. So-called because its original water-mark was a postman's horn. 1711.

attrib. and *Comb.*, as **p.-bag**, a bag for carrying letters and other postal matter; *transf.* the letters delivered to or sent from any one house or person; **-boat**, a boat or ship engaged in the conveyance of mails; also, a boat which conveys travellers between certain points; **-box**, a box in which letters are posted or deposited for dispatch, a letter-box; **-cart**, a cart in which local mails are carried; **-chariot**, a chariot for travelling post; *spec.* a light four-wheeled carriage, differing from a p.-chaise in having a driver's seat in front **-paid** *a.*, having the carriage prepaid; **-paper**, (see IV. 3); **-rider**, one who rides p.; a mounted letter-carrier; **p.-wagon** [Du., G. *postwagen*], a mail or stage coach in the Netherlands, etc.; **-woman**, a female letter-carrier.

Post (pōust), *sb.*[3] 1598. [– Fr. *poste* (m.) – It. *posto* (whence also Du. *post*, G. *posten*) – Rom. **postum*, contr. of pop. L. *positum*, pa. pple. of *ponere* (cf. prec.).] **1.** *Mil.* The place where a soldier is stationed. **b.** *transf.* and *fig.* The appointed place; the place of duty 1692. **2.** *Mil.* A position taken; a place at which a body of soldiers is stationed, or the force occupying this; *esp.* a strategic position taken by a commander. Cf. OUTPOST. Also *transf.* and *fig.* 1692. **b.** A place where armed men are permanently quartered for defensive or other purposes; a fort 1703. **c.** *transf.* A place occupied for purposes of trade, esp. in an uncivilized or unsettled country 1837. **d.** *attrib.*, as *p.-adjutant*, etc. 1878. **3.** An office or situation to which any one is appointed; position, place; employment 1695. **4.** *Naval.* Position as a full-grade captain, i.e. commission as officer in command of a vessel of 20 guns or more; hence, position or order of seniority in the list of captains 1720.

1. Clive..was awakened by the alarm, and was instantly at his p. MACAULAY. **b.** My daily p. was by the bed of disease and suffering LYTTON. **2.** Phr. *To take p.*, to occupy a position; Richard.. had taken p. at Nottingham HUME. **b.** This P. was Garisoned by 600 Men 1703. **c.** The trading p. of the Hudson's Bay Company 1837. **3.** Those posts in the public service supposed to be posts for gentlemen M. ARNOLD. **4.** Phr. *To give p.*, said of a ship of 20 guns or more, the officer in command of which had the rank of captain; *to take p.*, said of the officer, to receive the commission of captain of such a vessel; also *to be made p.*, to be appointed post captain. Now *arch.* or *Hist.* **Post captain**, a captain who 'takes post'; a designation formerly applied to a naval officer holding a commission to distinguish him from an officer having merely the courtesy title of captain. *Obs.* exc. *Hist.* †**P. ship**, a ship of not less than 20 guns, the commission to command which 'gave post' to a captain.

†**Post** (pōust), *sb.*[4] 1528. [app. – It. *posta* stake laid down, repr. L. *pos(i)ta*, pa. pple. fem. of *ponere* place; cf. med.L. *positare* lay out, spend (XII).] **a.** Name of an obs. card game, app. the same as *p. and pair* –1688. **b.** *P. and pair*, a card game, played with three cards each, in which the players bet on their own hands –1887.

Post, *sb.*[5] 1727. [app. – G. *posten* parcel, lot, batch of ore – It. *posto* :– L. *positum* n. pa. pple. of *ponere* place; cf. AL. *posta* roll of cloth (XIV).] **1.** *Paper-making.* A pile of from four to eight quires of hand-made paper fresh from the mould, laid with alternate sheets of felt ready for pressing. **2.** *Metall.* A batch of ore for smelting at one time 1839.

Post (pōust), *sb.*[6] 1885. [app. from POST *sb.*[3] 1; short for 'call to post', or the like.] A bugle-call giving notice of the hour of retiring for the night. Usu. *first* or *last p.*

It is customary to sound the 'last p.' beside a soldier's grave after the interment.

Post (pōust), *v.*[1] 1533. [f. POST *sb.*[2], or – obs. Fr. *poster.*] **I. 1.** *intr.* To travel with relays of horses (orig. as a bearer of letters). **2.** To travel with speed or haste; to hasten, hurry 1558.

1. We posted from morning till night HAKLUYT. **2.** Gray haires come posting on 1632.

†**II.** *trans.* To cause to post or hasten; to hasten, hurry (a person) –1807. **III.** †**1.** To convey in the manner of a post; to convey swiftly –1682. **2.** †**a.** To send by special messenger –1724. **b.** To send through the post office; to put (a letter, etc.) into a post-office or letter-box for transmission by the post 1837.

1. *Cymb.* II. iv. 27. **2. b.** His letter was posted two days later 1870.

IV. *Book-keeping*, etc. **1.** To carry or transfer (an entry) from an auxiliary book to a more formal one, esp. from the day-book into the ledger; to carry (an item or entry) to the proper account; also, by extension, to enter (an item) in proper form in any of the books 1622. **b.** To complete (the ledger or other book) by transferring to it all the items in the auxiliary books, and entering them in their proper accounts; to make the proper entries in all the books; often *p. up* (i.e. up to date, or to completion) 1707. **2.** *fig.* (orig. *U.S. colloq.*) To supply with full information or latest news on a subject. Often *p. up*. Usu. in *pass.* 1847.

1. To see the crimes of new democracy posted as in a ledger against the crimes of old despotism BURKE. **b.** You have not posted your books these ten years 1712. **2.** To..keep myself 'posted up'..with the literature of the day THACKERAY.

Post (pōust), *v.*[2] 1520. [f. POST *sb.*[1] With I cf. AL. *postare* (XIV) in same sense.] **I.** *trans.* To square (timber) before sawing it, or in order to form it into posts. *Obs.* or *dial.* **II.** To attach or moor (a vessel) to a post 1868. **III. 1.** To affix (a paper, etc.) to a post or in a prominent position; to stick *up* in a public place 1650. **2.** To make known, advertise (some fact, thing, or person) by or as by posting a placard. Also with *up.* 1633. **b.** *spec.* To expose to ignominy, or ridicule, by this means. Now *rare.* 1642. **c.** In some colleges: To place in a list, which is posted up, the names of (students who fail to pass in the college examinations) 1852. **d.** To publish the name of (a ship) as overdue or missing 1886. **3.** To placard (a wall, etc.) with bills 1854.

1. The old bill-stickers went to Trafalgar Square to attempt to p. bills DICKENS. **2. b.** I'll p. you for a swindler and a coward THACKERAY.

Post (pōust), *v.*[3] 1683. [f. POST *sb.*[3] Cf. Fr. *poster* (XVI).] **1.** *trans.* To place, station. **2.** *Mil.* and *Naval.* To appoint to a post or command; *spec.* to appoint to command a ship which 'gave post'; to commission as captain. Chiefly *pass.* 1800.

2. I am posted, and appointed to the *Semiramis* frigate 1833.

Post (pōust), *adv. Obs.* or *arch.* 1549. [Originating in the phr. *ride in post* (POST *sb.*² III. c), abbrev. to *ride post.*] With post-horses; by post; express; with speed or haste.

To speake hastily.., to talke p., as they say 1632. He set out P. for Paris 1716.

‖**Post** (pōᵘst). 1704. The L. prep. meaning 'after', occurring in phrases in Eng. use, as *p. meridiem, p. mortem*; also in **1. Post bellum,** after the war 1883. **2. Post hoc,** after this. *Post hoc, ergo propter hoc,* after this, therefore because of this; expressing the fallacy that a thing which follows another is therefore caused by it 1704. **3. Post partum,** after child-birth 1857. **4. Post terminum** (*Law*): see POST TERM.

Post- (pōᵘst), *prefix*, repr. L. *post*, adv. and prep., after, behind. Widely used, esp. in the prepositional relation, not only in compounds formed on words from L., but also, in techn. terms, from Gr., and sometimes even on Eng. or other words, as *p.-war* a. etc. **A.** Words in which *post-* is adv. or adj. In compounds derived or formed from L., or on L. analogies, as POST-DATE, -PONE, -SCRIPT, etc.; also in nonce-wds.

1. Relating to time or order. **a.** In adverbial relation: = After, afterwards, subsequently; as *p.-determined* (opp. to *predetermined*). **Post-exi·st** *v.* (*rare*) to exist after; to live subsequently; so **Post-exi·stence. Postfi·x** *v.* to affix after, or at the end; to append, as a postfix. **b.** In *quasi*-adjectival relation to a sb. forming, or implied in, the second element: = Occurring or existing after, coming after, subsequent, later; as *p.-act, -legitimation.* †**Post-dissei·sin** *Old Law*, a second or subsequent disseisin; also a writ that lay for one who had a second time been disseised, after a recovery by novel disseisin; so **Post-dissei·sor. Po·st-entry,** a subsequent or late entry; *spec.* an additional or supplemental entry, in the manifest of a vessel, of an item or items of dutiable merchandise; the warrant issued on this is a **Post-warrant. Po·stfix** [after PREFIX *sb.*], a word, syllable, or letter affixed or added to the end of a word, a suffix. **Po·stlude** [after PRELUDE], a concluding piece or movement played at the end of an oratorio or the like. **Po·st-note** *U.S.* (*Obs.* exc. *Hist.*) a note issued by a bank, payable to order at a future specified date.

2. Of local position. **a.** In advb. relation to a vbl. sb.: = Behind, posteriorly; as *postjacent*, etc. **b.** In adjectival relation to a sb. expressed or implied; as **Post-abdo·men,** the posterior part of the abdomen; *esp.* in invertebrates, the portion posterior to the abdominal cavity; hence **Post-abdo·minal** *a.* **Postcava** (-kē·vă), *Anat.* the inferior vena cava; so called as being behind or posterior in animals generally. **Postcla·vicle,** *Anat.* and *Zool.* the posterior bone of the scapular arch of some fishes. ‖**Postfu·rca** [L. *furca* fork], the hindmost of the three apodemes in the thoracic somites of insects. ‖**Postnares** (-nēᵊ·rīz) [L. *naris* nostril] *pl.*, the posterior nostrils, the openings of the nasal chamber into the pharynx. ‖**Postscute·llum,** *Entom.* the fourth sclerite of each of the segments of the thorax in an insect, situated behind the *scutellum*. **Postsphenoid** (-sfī·noid) *a.*, *Anat.* in *p. bone*, the posterior part of the sphenoid bone of the skull; also *ellipt.* as *sb.* **Postzygapophesis** (-zigăpǫ·fisis), each of the two posterior or inferior precesses on the neural arch of a vertebra.

B. Compounds in which *post-* is prepositional.

1. Relating to time or order: = After, subsequent to, following, succeeding, later than. **a.** With sbs., forming adjs. (or attrib. phrases), usu. of obvious meanings; as *p.-Asce·nsion, -Ea·ster, -ele·ction, -war* (esp. after the war of 1914–18), etc. **b.** With adjs., or formed from *post* + a L. or Gr. sb. with an adjectival ending, as *p.-Ada·mic, -bapti·smal, -Carte·sian* (see CARTESIAN), *-Darwi·nian, influe·nzal, na·tal, nu·ptial,* etc. **Post-exilian** (-egzi·liăn), of or pertaining to the period of Jewish history subsequent to the Babylonian exile. **Postmille·nnial,** of or belonging to the period following the millennium; so **Postmille·nialism,** the doctrine that the second Advent will follow the millennium. **c.** Rarely with sbs., forming sbs., as **Po·st-fine,** *Law* (*Obs.* exc. *Hist.*) a duty paid to the Crown for the royal licence to levy a fine. **2.** Relating to locality: = Behind, situated at the back of, posterior to. In many adjs. (rarely sbs.), chiefly *Anat.* and *Zool.*, indicating parts or organs situated behind (more rarely, in the hinder parts of) other parts or organs; as **Post-a·xial,** of, pertaining to, or situated on that side of a limb (in vertebrates) which is posterior to a line drawn at right angles to the body axis through the axis of the limb. **Post-fro·ntal** [L. *frons* forehead], (*a*) situated behind the forehead, or at the back of the frontal bone; (*b*) situated in the hinder part of the frontal lobe of the brain; *sb.* the external angular process of the frontal bone, which is situated at the back part of the brim of the orbit of the eye. **Posto·cular,** situated behind the eye; *sb.* a postocular scale, as in snakes. **Post-o·ral,** situated behind the mouth; applied to certain visceral arches in the embryo of vertebrates. **Postsca·pular,** situated behind or below the spine of the scapula, as in *p. fossa*. **Post-te·mporal,** situated behind the temporal region of the skull. **Post-tympa·nic,** behind the tympanic bone; applied to a bone, and a process of bone, in some Carnivora; also as *sb.* = *post-tympanic bone* or *process*.

Postage (pōᵘ·stėdʒ). 1590. [f. POST *sb.*² + -AGE.] †**1.** The conveyance of letters, etc., by post –1693. †**2.** The postal service; a postal service between particular points –1779. **3.** The amount charged for carrying a letter or postal packet; now usu. prepaid by means of a POSTAGE STAMP or stamps 1654. †**4.** Travelling by means of post-horses; posting; also *transf.* a rapid journey –1808.

Po·stage sta·mp. 1840. [f. prec. + STAMP *sb.*] An official stamp, either a stamp embossed on an envelope or impressed on a card or wrapper, or (now usu.) a small adhesive label having a specified face-value, sold by or on behalf of the Post Office, to be affixed to any letter or packet sent by post, as a means and evidence of prepayment of postage. Also *attrib.*

Postal (pōᵘ·stăl), *a.* (*sb.*) 1843. [– Fr. *postal(e,* f. *poste* POST *sb.*²; see -AL¹.] Of or pertaining to the post; relating to the carriage of mails. **B.** as *sb. U.S.* Short for *p. card, p. note*; also for *p. car, p.* (i.e. mail) *train.*

Comb.: **p. car,** a railway car for the carriage of mails (*U.S.*); **p. card** (*U.S.*) = POSTCARD, when issued by the post office itself; **p. note,** (*U.S.*) an order issued by a post office for any sum of less than five dollars payable at any other post office; **p. order,** a form of money order issued by a post office of the United Kingdom for one of a number of fixed sums, payable at any post office; **p. union,** a union of the governments of various countries for the regulation of international postage.

Po·st-boy. 1588. [f. POST *sb.*² + BOY *sb.*] **1.** A boy or man who rides post; a letter-carrier. **2.** = POSTILION 2. 1707.

2. The post-boys cracked their whips LYTTON.

Post-captain: see POST *sb.*³ 4.

Postcard (pōᵘ·sˌkāɹd). [(1 Oct. 1870), f. POST *sb.*² + CARD *sb.*², after G. *feldpostkarte* (25 June 1870), which was preceded by *postblatt* (1865) and *korrespondenzkarte* (1869).] A pasteboard card of a regulation size, used for correspondence.

Pictorial or *picture p.*, a p. bearing a picture on the reverse side.

Post-chaise (pōᵘ·stˌʃēⁱz), *sb.* Also *colloq.* **postchay, -shay,** PO'CHAISE, etc. 1712. [f. POST *sb.*² + CHAISE.] A travelling carriage, either hired from stage to stage, or drawn by horses so hired. Also *attrib.*

Post-cla·ssical, *a.* 1867. [f. POST- B. 1 + CLASSICAL.] Occurring or existing subsequent to the classical period of any language, literature, or art; *spec.* of the Greek and Latin.

Post-commu·nion, *sb.* (*a.*) 1483. [– med. L. *postcommunio*; see POST- B. 1 c, COMMUNION. Earlier †*post-common* (XIV). Cf. OFr. *pocumenion,* (also mod.) *postcommunion.*] The or a part of the eucharistic office which follows the act of communion. **B.** *adj.* Following the act of communion; used after communion 1890.

Post-date (pōᵘ·stˌdēⁱt), *sb.* 1611. [f. POST- A. 1 b + DATE *sb.*² Cf. Fr. *postdate* (XVI).] A date affixed to a document, or assigned to an event, later than the actual date.

Post-date (pōᵘstˌdēⁱ·t), *v.* 1624. [f. POST- A. 1 a + DATE *v.* Cf. Fr. †*postidater* (XVI), *postdater* (XVIII).] *trans.* To affix or assign a date later than the actual date to (a document, book, event, etc.).

Post-dilu·vial, *a.* 1823. [f. as next + -AL¹.] **a.** *Geol.* Posterior to the diluvial or drift period. **b.** *gen.* = next A.

Post-diluvian (pōᵘstˌdil'ū·viăn), *a.* and *sb.* 1680. [f. POST- B. 1 b + L. *diluvium* deluge + -AN.] **A.** *adj.* Existing or occurring after the Flood or Noachian deluge. **B.** *sb.* One who lived, or lives, after the Flood 1684.

‖**Postea** (pǫᵘ·stiˌă). 1596. [L. = afterwards; being the first word of the usual beginning of the record.] *Law.* That part of the record of a civil process which sets forth the proceedings at the trial and the verdict given.

†**Po·stel.** ME. [– OFr. *postel* (mod. *poteau*), dim. of *post*; see POST *sb.*¹, -EL.] A door- or gate-post –1631.

Poster¹ (pōᵘ·stəɹ). 1605. [f. POST *v.*¹ + -ER¹.] **1.** One who travels 'post', expeditiously, or swiftly. Also *fig.* Now *rare* or *Obs.* **2.** A post-horse 1817.

1. The weyward Sisters,..Posters of the Sea and Land SHAKS.

Poster² (pōᵘ·stəɹ). 1838. [f. POST *v.*² + -ER¹.] **1.** One who posts or sticks up bills; a bill-poster 1864. **2.** A placard posted or displayed in a public place as an announcement or advertisement. Also *attrib.* 1838.

‖**Poste restante** (postˌrẹstā̃nt). 1768. [Fr., = letter(s) remaining (i.e. at the post office).] A direction written upon a letter which is to remain at the post office till called for; in Eng. use, transf. to the department in a post office in which letters for visitors or travellers are kept till applied for.

Posterior (pǫstīᵊ·riəɹ), *a.* and *sb.* (*adv.*) 1534. [– L. *posterior*, compar. of *posterus* following, future, f. *post* prep., after; see -IOR.] **A.** *adj.* **1.** Later, subsequent in time; opp. to *prior*. **2.** Coming after in a series or order 1626. **3.** Hinder; situated behind, or farther back than something else. Opp. to *anterior*. 1632.

1. The precepts of the art of poesy were p. to practise 1756. **3.** The legs are called anterior, p., and intermediate 1868.

B. *sb.* **1.** *pl.* Those who come after; descendants, posterity 1534. **2.** *pl.* The hinder parts of the body; the buttocks 1605. †**3.** *pl.* The later part (*joc.*) SHAKS.

1. Neither he, nor his posteriors from generation to generation SCOTT.

C. *adv.* Subsequently 1826. Hence **Poste·riorly** *adv.*

Posteriority (pǫstīᵊriˌǫ·rīti). late ME. [– med.L. *posterioritas*, f. L. *posterior*, see prec., -ITY. Cf. Fr. *postériorité* (XV).] **1.** The state or quality of being later or subsequent in time. Opp. to *priority*. †**2.** Inferiority in order, rank, or dignity –1704.

Posterity (pǫste·rīti). [XIV *posterite* – (O)Fr. *postérité* – L. *posteritas*, f. *posterus*; see POSTERIOR, -ITY.] **1.** The descendants collectively of any person; all who have proceeded from a common ancestor. **2.** †**a.** A later generation (with *pl.*). **b.** All succeeding generations (collectively). 1535.

1. Thy posterite shalbe as the grasse vpon the earth COVERDALE *Job* 5:25. **2.** The ocean and the sun will last our time, and we may leave p. to shift for themselves JOHNSON.

Postern (pōᵘ·stəɹn), *sb.* (*a.*) ME. [– OFr. *posterne* (mod. *poterne*), alt. of *posterle* :- late L. *posterula* (sc. *janua* gate, *via* way), dim. of *posterus*; see POSTERIOR, -ULE.] **1.** A back door; a private door; any door or gate distinct from the main entrance. **b.** *Fortif.* A tunnel serving as a means of access to the ditch and outworks 1704. **2.** *fig.* A way of escape or refuge. **b.** An entrance other than the usual and honourable one. **c.** An obscure passage. 1579. **3.** *attrib.* or as *adj.* Placed at the back; private, side, inferior, esp. in *p. door* or *gate*; also *fig.* ME.

Postero- (pǫ·stĕro), comb. form of L. *posterus* hind, hinder, prefixed to adjs., in the sense (*a*) hinder and —, as in *postero-external*, etc.; (*b*) on the back part of that which is —, as **postero-lateral,** placed at the posterior end of a lateral margin or part; etc.

Post-free, *a.* 1882. [f. POST *sb.*² + FREE *a.*] Free from charge for postage, either as being officially carried free of charge, or as being prepaid.

Post-glacial (-glēⁱ·ʃ'ăl), *a.* 1855. [f. POST- B. 1 b + GLACIAL *a.*] *Geol.* Existing or occurring subsequent to the glacial period or ice age.

Post-gra·duate, *a.* (*sb.*) orig. *U.S.* 1858. [f. POST- B. 1 b + GRADUATE.] Pertaining or relating to a course of study carried on after graduation. **B.** *sb.* A student who takes a postgraduate course 1890.

Post-haste (pōᵘ:sthēⁱ·st), *sb.*, *adv.*, and *adj.* 1545. [From the old direction on letters 'Haste, post, haste'; taken subseq. as a comb. of POST *sb.*² and HASTE *sb.*] **A.** *sb.* Haste or speed like that of one travelling post; great speed in travelling (*arch.*). **B.** *adv.* With the speed of a post; with all possible expedition 1593. †**C.** *adj.* Done with all possible speed SHAKS.

B. Her Coach is order'd, and Post-haste she flies 1709. **C.** *Oth.* I. ii. 37.

Post-horn (pǫᵘ·sthǭɹn). 1675. [f. POST *sb.*² + HORN *sb.*] A horn formerly used by a postman or the guard of a mail-coach, to announce his arrival.

Post-horse (pōᵘ·sthǭɹs). 1527. A horse kept at a post-house or inn for the use of postriders, or for hire by travellers.

Post-house (pōᵘ·sthaus). *Obs.* exc. *dial.* 1653. [f. POST *sb.*² + HOUSE *sb.*¹] **1.** A post office. *Obs.* or *dial.* †**2.** An inn or other house where horses are kept for the use of travellers; a posting-house –1833.

Posthumous (pǫ·stiŭməs), *a.* 1608. [f. L. *postumus* last, superl. f. *post* after; in late L. referred to *humus* the earth or *humare* bury; see -OUS.] **a.** Of a child: Born after the death of its father 1619. **b.** Of a book or writing: Published after the death of the author 1668. **c.** Of an action, reputation, etc.: Occurring, arising, continuing after death 1608. Hence **Po·sthumously** *adv.*

‖**Posthumus** (pǫ·stiŭmŏs), *a.* and *sb.* 1591. [L. *post(h)umus* POSTHUMOUS.] †**A.** *adj.* = POSTHUMOUS –1660. **B.** *sb.* †**a.** (*pl.* **-i.**) A posthumous child –1677. **b.** *neut. pl.* **posthuma.** Posthumous writings 1655.

†**Po·stic,** *a.* 1638. [– L. *posticus* hinder, f. *post* behind; cf. *anticus* ANTIQUE.] Hinder, posterior, 'back' –1664.

‖**Postiche** (posti·ʃ), *a.* and *sb.* 1854. [Fr. (XVI) – It. *posticcio* counterfeit, feigned.] **A.** *adj.* **a.** Counterfeit, artificial. **b.** Applied to an ornament superadded to a finished work of sculpture or architecture, esp. when inappropriate. **B.** *sb.* **a.** An imitation substituted for the real thing. **b.** Counterfeiting, feigning, pretence. 1876.

Posticous (pǫstəi·kəs), *a.* 1866. [f. L. *posticus* POSTIC + -OUS.] *Bot.* Posterior, hinder; applied variously to parts of a flower or inflorescence.

Postil (pǫ·stil), *sb.* Now only *Hist.* late ME. [– OFr. *postille* :– med.L. *postilla*, conjectured by Du Cange to be L. *post illa* (sc. *verba*) after those words, i.e. of the text, used as a direction to the scribe.] **1.** A marginal note or comment upon a text of Scripture or upon any passage. **2.** A series of such comments; *spec.* an expository discourse or homily upon the Gospel or Epistle for the day, read or intended to be read in the church service 1483. **b.** A book of such homilies 1566. **3.** *attrib.* 1635. So †**Po·stil,** †**Po·stillate** *vbs. trans.* to write comments or marginal notes on. †**Po·stiller.**

Postilion, postillion (posti·lyən). 1565. [– Fr. *postillon* – It. *postiglione* post-boy, f. *posta* POST *sb.*²] †**1.** A post-boy; a swift messenger. Also *fig.* –1708. **2.** One who rides the near horse of the leaders when four or more are used in a carriage or post-chaise; one who rides the near horse when one pair only is used without a driver 1623.

Po:st-impre·ssionism. 1910. Art of a more 'advanced' style than IMPRESSIONISM, in which representation of form is subordinated to the subjective view of the artist.

Posting (pōᵘ·stiŋ), *vbl. sb.* 1559. [f. POST *v.*¹ + -ING¹.] The action of POST *v.*¹ **1.** †**a.** The dispatching of letters, etc., by a messenger riding post. **b.** Travelling by means of relays of horses. **c.** The keeping of post-horses, vehicles, etc., as a business. **2.** The dispatching or conveying of letters and other postal matter through or by the post office 1871. **3.** *Book-keeping.* The carrying of an entry from the journal or other auxiliary book into the ledger; the formal entry of an item in a book of accounts; the bringing of account books up to date 1682.

Postliminary (-li·minări), *a.* 1702. [f. L. *post* after + *limen, limin-* threshold + -ARY¹; but in sense 1 assoc. w. POSTLIMINIUM.] **1.** Pertaining to or involving the right of postliminium. **2.** Subsequent; opp. to *preliminary* 1826.

Postliminious (-limi·niəs), *a.* 1656. [f. L. *postliminium* + -OUS.] **1.** Of or pertaining to postliminium (*rare*). **2.** = POSTLIMINOUS 1684.

‖**Postliminium** (-limi·niŏm). 1638. [L., a return 'behind one's threshold', f. *post* POST- B. 2 + *limen, -in-* threshold.] *Rom. Law.* = POSTLIMINY.

Postliminous (-li·minəs), *a.* 1714. [f. L. *post* after + *limen, -in-* threshold + -OUS.] Subsequent; of the nature of an appendix; opp. to *preliminary*.

Postliminy (-li·mĭni). 1658. [Anglicized f. POSTLIMINIUM.] *Rom. Law.* The right of any person who had been banished or taken captive, to assume his former civic privileges on his return home. Hence, in *Internat. Law*, The restoration to their former state of persons and things taken in war, when they come again into the power of the nation to which they belonged.

Postman¹ (pōᵘ·stmæ̆n). 1529. [f. POST *sb.*² + MAN *sb.*] **1.** A bearer or carrier of letters or other postal matter; a letter-carrier. †**2.** A newsman, a news-writer –1709.

2. You want..some news: therefore let me be your p. PEPYS.

Postman². *Obs.* exc. *Hist.* 1768. [f. POST *sb.*¹ + MAN *sb.*] A barrister in the Court of Exchequer, who had precedence in motions except in Crown business; the name was derived from the post, the measure of length in excise cases, beside which he took his stand.

Po·stmark, *sb.* 1678. [f. POST *sb.*² + MARK *sb.*¹] A mark officially impressed upon letters or other postal packages; now, usu. a mark giving the place, date, and hour of dispatch, or of the arrival of the mail. Hence **Po·stmark** *v. trans.* to mark with the post-office stamp, esp. that showing date and place of posting.

Postmaster¹ (pōᵘ·stmāstəɹ). 1513. [f. POST *sb.*² + MASTER *sb.*¹] **1.** †**a.** *orig.* A master of the posts; the officer who had the charge or direction of the post-messengers –1708. †**b.** In the 17th and 18th c.: The post-office servant at each of the stations or stages of a post-road; orig. called POST (*sb.*² 1). **c.** Now, The person who has official charge of a post office, and the superintendence of all business there transacted. 1603. **2.** The keeper of a posting establishment 1581. Hence **Po·stma:stership**¹.

Postmaster² (pōᵘ·stmāstəɹ). 1593. [Of unkn. origin. Cf. AL. *portionista* (XIV) one who receives a prescribed portion, PORTIONIST.] The name given at Merton College, Oxford, to the class of poor scholars instituted in 1380 by John Wyllyot; now the equivalent in that college of the term 'scholar' in general collegiate use. Hence **Po·stma:stership**².

Po·stmaster ge·neral. 1626. [f. POSTMASTER¹ + GENERAL *a.*] The administrative head of the postal service of a country or state, who is in Great Britain often, and in U.S. always, a member of the cabinet. Hence **Po·stmaster-ge·neralship.**

Postmeridian (-mĕri·diăn), *a.* 1626. [– L. *postmeridianus* in the afternoon, f. *post* after + *meridianus* MERIDIAN *a.* **1.** Occurring after noon or midday; or of pertaining to the afternoon. Also *fig.* **2.** *Geol.* Applied to a subdivision of the Palæozoic strata of the Appalachian chain 1858.

‖**Post meridiem** (pōᵘst mĕri·diĕm), *phr.* 1647. [L., after midday.] After midday; applied to the hours between noon and midnight; abbrev. P.M. or p.m.

Postmistress (pōᵘ·stmi:strĕs). 1697. [f. POST *sb.*² + MISTRESS.] A woman who has charge of a post office. **Po·stmi:stress-ship.**

‖**Post mortem, post-mortem,** *advb. phr.*, *a.*, and *sb.* 1734. [L., after death.] **A.** *advb. phr.* (*post mortem*). After death.

The fistulas are but rarely found post-mortem 1897.

B. *adj.* (*post-mortem*). Taking place, formed, or done after death 1835.

A *post mortem* examination 1837.

C. *sb.* Short for *post-mortem examination.* Also *attrib.* 1850. **b.** *transf.* Discussion of a game or match after it is finished 1922.

Post-mortems show the cause of death 1903.

‖**Postnatus** (-neⁱ·tŏs), pl. **-i.** 1609. [mod. L. *post natus* born after; not continuous with med.L. *postnatus* puisne, younger (XIII).] One born after a particular event; *spec.* in Scotland, one born after the Union of the Crowns.

Post-obit (pōᵘstˌǫ·bit, -ōᵘ·bit). 1751. [Shortened from L. *post obitum* after decease.] **A.** *adj.* **1.** Taking effect after some one's death; esp. in *post-obit bond* 1788. **2.** Post-mortem. *rare.* 1822. **B.** *sb.* (Short for *post-obit bond.*) A bond given by a borrower, securing to the lender a sum of money to be paid on the death of a specified person from whom the borrower has expectations 1751.

Ready gold, to be paid back, post-obit fashion, on a father's coffin-lid 1851.

Post office, post-office (pōᵘ·stˌǫ:fis). 1652. [f. POST *sb.*² + OFFICE; first (1635) called *letter-office.*] **1.** The public department charged with the conveyance of letters, etc. by post. **2.** A house or shop where postal business is carried on, where postage stamps are sold, letters are registered and posted for transmission, etc. 1657.

2. *General Post Office* (abbrev. *G.P.O.*), the central or head post office of a country or state, as that in London; also pop. applied to the head office in a city or town.

attrib. and *Comb.*, as *p. clerk*, etc.; **p. annuity, insurance,** a system whereby annuities can be purchased and lives insured through the post office; **p. car,** *U.S.* a mail-van or coach on a railway; **p. department** = sense 1; **p. order** (abbrev. P.O.O.), a money-order for a specified sum, issued at one post office and payable at another therein named, to a person whose name is officially communicated in a letter of advice; **p. savings-bank,** a bank having branches at local post offices where sums within fixed limits are received on government security, at a small rate of interest; **p. stamp,** a stamp officially imprinted on a letter by the post office; also the instrument used for stamping the postmark.

Postorbital (-ǭ·ɹbităl), *a.* (*sb.*) 1835. [f. POST- B. 2 + ORBITAL.] *Anat.* and *Zool.* Situated behind, or on the hinder part of, the orbit of the eye. Also *ellipt.* as *sb.* **a.** The postorbital bone or process. **b.** A scale behind the eye in snakes.

Post-pliocene (-pləi·ŏsīn), *a.* (*sb.*) 1841. [f. POST- B. 1 b + PLIOCENE.] *Geol.* Applied to the lowest division of the Post-tertiary or Quaternary formation, immediately overlying the Pliocene or Upper Tertiary; also to the whole of the formations later than the Pliocene. Also applied to animals, etc. of this period. Also *ellipt.* as *sb.* = p. division or formation.

Postpone (poᵘˢtpōᵘ·n, pŏs-), *v.* 1500. [– L. *postponere*, f. *post* after = *ponere* place. In XVI, Sc. only.] **1.** *trans.* To put off to a later time; to defer. †**b.** To 'put (a person) off', i.e. to keep him waiting for something expected –1705. **c.** *intr. Path.* Of ague or the like: To recur after a longer interval than is usual or expected 1843. **2.** To place after in serial order or arrangement; to put at, or nearer to, the end 1620. †**3.** To place after in order of precedence, rank, importance, or value; to subordinate –1893.

1. The project had to be postponed W. IRVING. **3.** You have postpon'd the publick interest to your own 1670. Hence **Postpo·nement,** the action or fact of postponing. **Postpo·nence** (*rare*), subordination. **Postpo·ner.**

†**Postpo·se,** *v.* 1598. [– Fr. †*postposer* (XVI), f. *post* POST- A + *poser* POSE *v.*¹] *trans.* = POSTPONE –1656.

Postposit (pōᵘstpǫ·zit), *v. rare.* 1661. [– *postposit-*, pa. ppl. stem of L. *postponere* POSTPONE.] *trans.* = POSTPONE 2, 3. Hence **Postpo·sited** *ppl. a.*

Postposition (pōᵘstpǒzi·ʃən). 1638. [– late and med.L. *postpositio*, f. as prec.; see -ION.] **1.** The action of placing after; the condition or fact of being so placed. **2.** A particle or relational word placed after another word, usu. as an enclitic; esp. a word having the function of a preposition, which follows its object, as L. *versus* 1846. Hence **Postposi·tional** *a.* = next.

Postpositive (poᵘstpǫ·zĭtiv), *a.* (*sb.*) 1786. [– late and med. L. *postpositivus* (gram.), f. as prec.; see -IVE.] Characterized by postposition; having the function of being suffixed; enclitic. **B.** *sb.* A postpositive particle or word 1846.

Postprandial (-præ·ndiăl), *a.* 1820. [f. POST- B. 1 b = L. *prandium* meal + -AL[1]. Cf. PRANDIAL.] Done, made, taken, happening, etc. after dinner; after-dinner. (Chiefly *joc.*)

Men far advanced in post-prandial potations 1890.

Po·st-roa:d. 1657. A road on which a series of post-houses or stations for post-horses is (or was) established; a road on which the mails were carried.

‖**Postscenium** (pōᵘstˌsī·niǒm). 1727. [L. *postscænium*, f. *post* after + *scæna* – Gr. σκηνή stage, scene.] *Class. Antiq.* The back part of a theatre, behind the scenes. Cf. PROSCENIUM.

Postscribe (pōᵘstˌskrəi·b), *v.* 1614. [– L. *postscribere*, f. *post* after + *scribere* write.] *trans.* To write (something) after; to write as a postscript or appendix.

Postscript (pōᵘ·sˢskript), *sb.* Also **postscriptum**, pl. **-ta.** 1523. [– L. *postscriptum*, subst. use of n. pa. pple. of *postscribere*; see prec.] Something written at the end of a letter, after the signature, containing additional matter (often expressing an afterthought). **b.** *transf.* A paragraph written or printed at the end of any composition, containing some appended matter 1638. So **Postscri·ptal** *a.* of the nature of, or relating to, a p.

Post term. 1607. *Law.* A partial rendering of L. phrase **post terminum** after the term, used *advb.*, as *adj.*, and as *sb.* for: The return of a writ after term, and the fee payable for its then being filed.

Po:st-te·rtiary, *a.* (*sb.*) 1854. [f. POST- B. 1 b + TERTIARY.] *Geol.* Applied to the formations, or the period, subsequent to the Tertiary, the most recent of the geological series; quaternary; hence to animals, etc. of this period. Also *ellipt.* as *sb.*

Po·st-town. 1635. [f. POST *sb.*[2] + TOWN.] **1.** A town having a (head) post office, or one that is not merely a sub-office of another. †**2.** A town at which post-horses are kept –1838.

Postulant (pǫ·stiŭlănt). 1753. [– Fr. *postulant* or L. *postulans, -ant-*, pr. pple. of *postulare*; see next, -ANT.] One who asks or petitions for something; a petitioner; a candidate; *esp.* a candidate for admission into a religious order or community. Hence **Po·stulancy,** the condition, or period, of being a p.

Postulate (pǫ·stiŭlĕt), *sb.* 1588. [– L. POSTULATUM, subst. use of n. pa. pple. of *postulare* demand; see -ATE[1].] **I.** A demand, a request; *spec.* a demand of the nature of a stipulation. Now *rare.* **II. 1.** *Logic* and *gen.* A proposition demanded or claimed to be granted; *esp.* something claimed or assumed as a basis of reasoning, discussion, or belief; hence, a fundamental condition or principle 1646. **b.** An unproved assumption, a hypothesis. *rare.* 1646. **c.** A prerequisite of some actual or supposed occurrence or state of things 1841. **3.** *spec.* in *Geom.* (or derived use). A claim to take for granted the possibility of a simple operation, e.g. that a straight line can be drawn between any two points; a simple problem of self-evident nature; dist. from AXIOM (a self-evident theorem) 1660.

1. Christianity is essentially miraculous. This is a p. of Biblical criticism 1860.

Postulate (pǫ·stiŭleˈt), *v.* 1533. [– *postulat-*, pa. ppl. stem of L. *postulare*; see prec., -ATE[3].] **1.** *trans.* To demand; to require; to claim 1593. **b.** *intr.* To make a request; to stipulate 1860. **2.** *trans. Eccl. Law.* To ask authority to admit (a nominee) by dispensation; hence, to nominate or elect to an ecclesiastical dignity, subject to the sanction of the superior authority 1533. **3.** To claim or take for granted the existence, fact, or truth of (something); *esp.* to assume as a basis of reasoning, discussion or action 1646. **b.** To assume the possibility of (some construction or operation) 1817.

1. Logic..postulates to express in words what is already in the thoughts MILL. **2.** The chapter was then allowed to p. the bishop of Bath STUBBS. **3.** Reason postulates God, though it cannot prove him 1885. So **Postula·tion,** the action of postulating; a request, demand, claim; an assumption. **Po·stulator,** one who postulates; *spec.* in *R.C.Ch.* a pleader in favour of a candidate for beatification or canonization.

Postulatory (pǫ·stiŭlătəri), *a.* Now *rare.* 1631. [– L. *postulatorius* adj.; see prec., -ORY[2].] **1.** Making request; supplicatory. **2.** Of the nature of an assumption; hypothetical 1646.

†‖**Postula·tum.** *Pl.* **-a.** 1619. [L.; see POSTULATE *sb.*] = POSTULATE *sb.* 1, 2. –1827.

Posture (pǫ·stiŭɹ, -tʃəɹ), *sb.* 1605. [– Fr. *posture* (Montaigne) – It. *postura* :– L. *positura* position, situation, f. *posit-*, pa. ppl. stem of *ponere* place; see -URE.] **1.** The relative disposition of the various parts of anything; *esp.* the position and carriage of the limbs and the body as a whole; attitude, pose 1606. †**2.** Position, situation –1835. **3.** A state of being; a condition or situation in relation to circumstances 1642. **4.** *fig.* A mental or spiritual attitude or condition 1642.

1. Restlessness, which caused a constant variation of p. 1804. **2.** To give intelligence of the forces, or p. of the enemy GOLDSM. **3.** The present p. of affairs round Paris RUSKIN. **4.** Therewith we broke up, all in a sad p. PEPYS. A certain.. p. of the soul 1866. Hence **Po·stural** *a.* pertaining or relating to p.

Posture (pǫ·stiŭɹ, -tʃəɹ), *v.* 1628. [f. prec.] †**1.** *trans.* To place in position; to set –1677. **2.** To dispose the body or limbs of (a person) in a particular way 1628. **3.** *intr.* To assume a particular posture of body; also, to put the limbs, or body, in an artificial position 1851. **4.** *fig.* **a.** To pose for effect. **b.** To take up an artificial mental position. 1877.

2. And still these two were postured motionless, Like natural sculpture in cathedral cavern KEATS. **4.** Jewell..occasionally postured as a buffoon 1880. Hence **Po·sturer,** one who poses for effect.

Po·sture-ma:ker. 1711. **a.** One who makes postures; a contortionist; an acrobat. **b.** A teacher of postures or callisthenics.

Posy (pōᵘ·zi). Now *arch.* or *dial.* 1533. [Syncopated f. POESY.] **1.** A short motto, orig. a line or verse of poetry, inscribed on a knife, within a ring, as a heraldic motto, etc. **2.** A bunch of flowers; a nosegay, a bouquet. Now somewhat *arch.* or *rustic.* 1573. **b.** A collection of 'flowers' of poetry or rhetoric. Cf. ANTHOLOGY. *arch.* 1569.

1. Let this be your Posie rather,..Manners makes man 1569. **2.** I will make thee beds of roses, And a thousand fragrant posies MARLOWE. *Comb.* **p.-ring,** a finger-ring with a motto inside.

Pot (pǫt), *sb.*[1] [Late OE. *pott*, corresp. to OFris., (M)LG., (M)Du. *pot* – pop.L. **pottus* (whence OFr., Pr. *pot*); cf. late L. *potus* (for *pottus*) drinking-cup (Venantius, VI), AL. *pottus, -um* (XIII). Prob. reinforced in ME from (O)Fr. *pot*; ult. origin unkn.] **1.** A vessel of rounded form, and rather deep than broad, made of earthenware or metal (less commonly glass), used to hold liquids or solids, for various purposes. (Often with defining word as *glue-p., ink-p., jam-p., water-p.*, etc.) **b.** *spec.* Such a vessel used for cooking or boiling. Hence *transf.* the vessel with the food boiling in it; also allus. = cooking, food (as in phr. *for the p.*); also in fig. allusions ME. **c.** Such a vessel used to contain wine, beer, coffee, tea, etc. 1440. **d.** A FLOWER-POT 1615. **e.** A chamber-pot 1705. **f.** Any of various receptacles used in manufactures, etc. 1676. **g.** *slang.* A vessel, usu. of silver, given as a prize in athletic sports. Also applied to any prize so given. 1865. **2.** Such a vessel with its contents; hence, a potful 1450. **b.** *ellipt.* A pot of liquor; *transf.* liquor, drink; drinking, potation (also *pl.*) 1583. **3.** Used as a measure of various commodities 1530. **4.** A steel cap or small helmet, worn esp. by cavalry in the 17th c. *Obs.* exc. *Hist.* 1639. **5.** A wicker basket used as a trap for fish or crustaceans; a fish-pot, lobster-pot, etc. 1669. **6.** = CHIMNEY-*pot* 1845. **7.** A large sum of money (*colloq.*) 1871. **b.** *slang.* A large sum staked or betted 1823. **c.** *Racing.* 'A horse backed for a large amount, a favourite' (Farmer) 1823. **d.** A person of importance. (Usu. *big p.*) 1891. **8.** In full, **pot-paper:** A size of printing or writing paper; orig. bearing the watermark of a pot. Also *attrib.* as **p.-folio, -octavo, -quarto.** (Now usu. spelt **pott.**) 1579. **9.** As the name of a substance: Earthenware, stoneware; *attrib.* made of pot 1825.

1. b. Henry the Fourth [of France] wished that he might live to see a fowl in the p. of every peasant BURKE. Pots and pans 1875. **2.** A p. of ale and a piece of cheese SWIFT. **b.** He carries her into a public-house to give her a p. and a cake DE FOE. **7.** He went to India..and came back..with a p. of money TROLLOPE.

Phrases, etc. *The p. goes so long* (or *often*) *to the well that it is broken at last. The p. calls the kettle black* (etc.), said of a person who blames another for something of which he himself is also guilty. *A little p. is soon hot*, a little person is soon roused to anger. *To boil the p., make the p. boil* (= Fr. *faire bouillir le pot*), to provide one's livelihood. So, *to keep the p. boiling*; also, to keep anything going briskly. *To go to p.* (formerly also *to the p.*), to be cut in pieces like meat for the p.; to be ruined or destroyed (*colloq.*).

attrib. and *Comb.*: **p.-ale,** the completely fermented wash in distillation; **-bank** *dial.*, a pottery; **-clay,** clay used for making earthenware; **p. cultivation, p. culture,** cultivation of plants in pots; **p. hat** (*colloq.*), a low-crowned stiff felt hat, a 'bowler'; **-paper** (see sense 8); **-sleeper,** a metal sleeper for railways, of dish-like form; **-still,** a still to which heat is applied directly as to a p., not by means of a steam-jacket; *attrib.*, applied to whisky distilled in a pot-still.

Pot (pǫt), *sb.*[2] *Sc.* and *dial.* ME. [perh. identical with prec., or of Scand. origin; cf. Sw. dial. *putt, pott* water-hole, abyss. Cf. POT-HOLE[1].] A deep hole; e.g. †the shaft or pit of a mine; a hole out of which peat has been dug.

Pot, *sb.*[3] 1888. Short for POT-SHOT.

Pot (pǫt), *v.* 1562. [f. POT *sb.*[1]] **I.** *intr.* To drink beer, etc. out of a pot; to tipple. *Obs.* or *arch.* 1594. **II. 1.** *trans.* To put up and preserve (flesh, butter, etc., usu. salted or seasoned) in a pot, jar, or other vessel. Also *absol.* Also *fig.* 1616. **b.** *Sugar manuf.* To transfer (crude sugar) from the coolers to perforated 'pots' or hogsheads, for the molasses to drain off 1740. **2.** To set (a plant) in earth in a flower-pot for cultivation; to plant in or transplant into a pot 1664. **3.** *Billiards* = POCKET *v.* 4. 1860. **4.** *colloq.* or *slang.* To shoot or kill (game) for the pot, i.e. for cooking; to 'bag'; *gen.* to bring down by a pot-shot (a man or animal) 1860. **b.** *intr.* To take a pot-shot (*at*) 1854. **c.** *trans.* To win, secure, 'bag' 1900.

4. He'll have to show himself, and if he does I'll p. him 1889. **b.** To be potted at like a woodcock 1861.

III. To outdo, outwit, deceive. Now *slang.* 1562. **IV.** To manufacture, as pottery, etc.; *esp.* to shape and fire, as a preliminary to decoration 1743.

Potable (pōᵘ·tăb'l), *a.* (*sb.*) 1572. [– Fr. *potable* or late L. *potabilis*, f. *potare* drink; see -ABLE.] **A.** *adj.* Drinkable. **B.** *sb pl.* Things potable; drinkables, liquor 1623.

A. Sweet p. liquor 1645. *P. gold*, a preparation of nitro-muriate of gold deoxydized by some volatile oil, formerly esteemed as a cordial medicine; drinkable gold. So *p. Mars* (= iron). Hence **Potabi·lity, Po·tableness,** p. quality.

‖**Potage** (potāʒ). 1567. [– (O)Fr. *potage*; see POTTAGE.] Soup of any kind.

Potamian (potēⁱ·miăn, -æ·miăn), *a.* and *sb.* 1850. [f. Gr. ποταμός river + -IAN.] **A.** *adj.* Of or pertaining to the *Potamites* or *Trionychidæ*, the soft-shelled river tortoises. **B.** *sb.* A tortoise of this group, a mud turtle.

Potamic (potæ·mik), *a.* 1883. [f. as prec.

+ -IC.] Of or pertaining to rivers; fluviatile.

Potamo·logy. 1829. [f. as prec. + -LOGY.] The scientific study of rivers. Hence **Potamolo·gical** *a.* of or pertaining to p. **Potamo·logist,** one who studies or is versed in p.

Potash (pǫ·tæʃ), *sb.* 1648. [– Du. *potasschen* (mod. *potasch*); see POT *sb.*[1], ASH *sb.*[2]] **1.** An alkaline substance obtained orig. by lixiviating the ashes of terrestrial vegetables, and evaporating the solution in large iron pans or pots (whence the name). Chemically, this is a crude form of potassium carbonate. **a.** *orig.* pl., *pot ashes, pot-ashes*: now applied to the crude substance. (When purified by calcination and re-crystallization, known as *pearl-ashes* or *pearl-ash.*) **b.** sing., *pot-ash, potash*: applied esp. to the purified carbonate 1751. **2.** *Chem.* The hydroxide or hydrate of potassium, KOH; a hard white brittle substance, soluble in water and deliquescent in air, having powerful caustic and alkaline properties; *caustic p.* 1800. **b.** Now sometimes applied to POTASSA; in non-chemical works vaguely to any compound of potassium 1843. **c.** In names of compounds = POTASSA, and now in chemical use mostly repl. by POTASSIUM 1791. **3.** Short for *p.-water* 1876.

2. c. *Carbonate of p.* = potassium carbonate; *sulphate of p.* = potassium sulphate.

Comb.: **p.-mica** = MUSCOVITE *sb.*[2]; **-water,** an aerated beverage; water impregnated with carbonic acid gas, to which is added potassium bicarbonate.

Potass (potæ·s, pǫ·tæs). Now *rare.* 1799. [– Fr. *potasse* POTASH.] *Chem.* An anglicized form, variously used for potash, potassa, and (in names of compounds) potassium.

‖**Potassa** (potæ·să). 1812. [mod.L. form of POTASH.] *Chem.* Davy's name for potassium monoxide, K_2O, also called *anhydrous potash*; sometimes also applied to the hydrate or hydroxide, KOH ($=K_2H_2O_2$), also called *potassa fusa* and *caustic potash.*

Liquor potassæ, an aqueous solution of potassium hydrate, containing about 5·84 per cent. of the hydrate.

Potassamide (potæ·sămaid). 1838. [f. POTASS(IUM + AMIDE.] *Chem.* An amide of potassium formed by the substitution of one or more atoms of potassium for those of the hydrogen of ammonia (NH_3).

Potassic (potæ·sik), *a.* 1858. [f. POTASS(IUM + -IC.] *Chem.* Of, pertaining to, or containing potassium or potash; = *potassium* in comb.

Pota·ssio-, comb. form of POTASSIUM, in the names of double salts of potassium and another substance, as *p.-tarta·ric* adj., *p.-ta·rtrate,* etc.

Potassium (pŏtæ·siŏm). 1807. [In form, mod.L. (Davy, 1807), f. POTASS or POTASH, after names of metals in -IUM.] *Chem.* One of the elements, an alkaline monad metal, the basis of POTASH; it is a highly lustrous white metal with a slight tinge of pink, soft at ordinary temperatures, of specific gravity 0·865, being the lightest solid body known except lithium; when exposed to the air it at once tarnishes or oxidizes, and when thrown upon water instantly decomposes it, uniting with the oxygen and causing the liberated hydrogen to burn with a characteristic violet flame. Symbol K (for *Kalium*); atomic weight 39·1. Also *attrib.* in names of chemical compounds, as *p. carbonate, permanganate,* etc.

Potation (potēi·ʃən). late ME. [XV – OFr. *potation* or L. *potatio,* f. *potat-,* pa. ppl. stem of *potare* drink; see -ION.] **1.** Drinking; a drinking, a drink, a draught 1479. †**b.** A drinking party, compotation –1574. **c.** Intemperate drinking 1800. **2.** Liquor for drinking; a drink, a beverage. late ME.

1. Potations, pottle-deepe SHAKS. Indulging in moderate potations 1875.

Potato (pŏtēi·to), *sb.* 1565. [– Sp. *patata* – native name (*batata*) in Haiti; see BATATA.] **1.** = BATATA. Now known as *Sweet* or *Spanish p.* **2.** The plant *Solanum tuberosum,* a native of the Pacific slopes of S. America, now widely cultivated for its farinaceous tubers 1597. **b.** The tuber of this plant, of roundish or oblong shape; now a well-known article of food in most temperate climes 1663. **3.** With distinctive words. **a.** *Carolina, Spanish, Sweet p.* = sense 1. 1599. **b.** *Chilian p., Irish p.* (now U.S.), *White p.* (U.S.) = sense 2. 1664. **4.** Applied to other plants having tubers, mostly edible 1629.

1. Let the skie raine Potatoes SHAKS. **2. b.** As to potatoes, it would be idle to consider them ..as an article of human food, which ninety-nine hundredths of the human species will not touch 1792. Phr. *Potatoes and point*: see POINT *sb.*[1] C. 4. **4. Seaside p.,** *Ipomæa biloba* (*Pes-capræ*), N.O. *Convolvulaceæ,* a tropical creeping shore-plant of both hemispheres; **Wild p.,** (*a*) *Convolvulus panduratus*; (*b*) of Jamaica, *Ipomæa fastigiata.*

Phrases (colloq.). *Small potatoes* (orig. *U.S.*), 'no great things', said also of persons. *The p.,* the (very or real) thing, what is correct or excellent (*slang*).

Comb.: **p.-beetle,** (*a*) the COLORADO Beetle, *Doryphora decemlineata*; (*b*) the Three-lined Leaf Beetle, *Lema trilineata,* or its larva; **p. blight** = *p. disease*; **p. bug** = *p.-beetle*; **p.-chips,** potatoes sliced and fried crisp in fat or oil; **p. disease,** a very destructive disease of potatoes, caused by a parasitic fungus, *Phytophthora infestans,* which attacks the leaves, stems, and tubers; also called *p. blight, murrain, rot*; **-eye,** a bud of the potato tuber; see EYE *sb.*[1] III. 1; **-fly,** one of the various blister beetles of the genus *Lytta,* which are injurious to potato-plants in U.S. and Canada; **p. murrain** = *p. disease*; **p. pit,** a shallow pit, usu. covered with a mound of straw and earth, in which potatoes are stored in winter; **p. rot** = *p. disease*; **-spirit,** alcohol distilled from potatoes; **-stalk weevil, p. weevil,** an American beetle that injures p. crops, *Baridius trinotatus*; **-trap** (*slang*), the mouth. Hence **Pota·to** *v. trans.* to plant or crop with potatoes.

Potator (potēi·təɹ). *rare.* 1660. [– L. *potator,* f. *potat-*; see POTATION, -OR 2.] A drinker, toper.

Potatory (pōu·tătəri), *a.* 1834. [joc. f. POTATION, after pairs in *-ation, -atory*; see -ORY[2].] Of, pertaining to, or given to drinking.

Pot-bellied (pǫ·tˌbe:lid), *a.* 1657. [f. next + -ED[2].] Having a pot-belly. Also *transf.*

Pot-belly (pǫ·tˌbe·li). 1714. [f. POT *sb.*[1] + BELLY *sb.*] **1.** A swollen or protuberant belly. **2.** *transf.* A pot-bellied person 1871.

Po·t-boi:ler. 1803. [f. phr. *to make the pot boil*; see POT *sb.*[1]] **1.** One who boils a pot; *spec.* in *Eng. Politics* = POTWALLER (*rare*) 1824. **2.** *colloq.* Applied depreciatively to a work of literature or art executed for the purpose of 'boiling the pot'; a writing, picture, etc. made to sell 1803. **b.** One who produces 'pot-boilers' 1892. **3.** *Anthropol.* One of the rounded pebbles, with marks of fire upon them, which are supposed to have been heated for the purpose of boiling water 1874.

Po·t-bound, *a.* 1850. [f. POT *sb.*[1] 1 d + BOUND *ppl. a.*] Said of a plant when its roots fill a flower-pot and have no more room to expand. Also *fig.*

Po·t-boy. 1795. [f. POT *sb.*[1] + BOY *sb.*] A boy or young man employed at a public house to serve the customers with liquor; a publican's assistant.

Potch, Potcher, var. ff. POACH *v.*[2], POACHER, esp. in paper-making.

Pot-earth. 1644. [POT *sb.*[1]] Potter's earth; potter's clay; *Geol.* the BRICK-EARTH of the London basin.

Poteen, potheen (pǫti·n, pǫþi·n). 1812. [– Ir. *poitin* (dim. of *pota* POT *sb.*[1]), in full *uisge poitin* 'little-pot whisky'; see -EEN[2].] Whisky distilled in Ireland in small quantities, privately, i.e. the produce of an illicit still. Also *attrib.*

Potence[1] (pōu·tĕns). late ME. [– OFr. *potence* power – L. *potentia,* f. *potent-* (see POTENT *a.*[1]) + *-ia* -IA[1]; see -ENCE.] **1.** Power, ability, strength. **2.** Degree of power or intensity 1817.

Potence[2] (pōu·tĕns). 1500. [– (O)Fr. *potence* †crutch, etc., (mod.) gallows, etc. – L. *potentia* power; see prec.] †**1.** A cross or gibbet –1816. **b.** *Engineering.* A supporting framework formed like a gallows 1853. **2.** *Watchmaking.* A stud screwed to the top plate in which is made the bearing for the lower pivot of the verge; any stud or fixture supporting a bearing 1678. †**3.** A military formation, in which a line is thrown out at right angles to the main body –1865.

Potencé (pōu·tĕnse:), *a.* Also improp. **potence.** 1572. [– Fr. *potencé,* f. *potence*; see prec.] *Her.* = POTENT *a.*[2]

Potency (pōu·tĕnsi). 1539. [– L. *potentia* power; see POTENCE[1], -ENCY.] The quality of being potent. **1.** Power, ability to effect something; inherent capacity; authority. **b.** Power to affect one physically; of liquor, etc., strength 1637. **2.** *transf.* A person or body wielding power; a power 1645. **3.** Capability of active development; potentiality 1644. **4.** Degree of (latent) force 1691.

1. b. The p., vertue, and operation of our English Ale 1637. **3.** Books..doe contain a potencie of life in them to be as active as that soule was whose progeny they are MILTON.

Potent (pōu·tĕnt), *sb.*[1] and *a.*[2] late ME. [As sb., alt. of (O)Fr. *potence* POTENCE[2]; as adj., attrib. use of *sb.* See prec., POTENCE.] **A.** *sb.* †A crutch; a staff with a cross piece to lean upon; also *transf.* a crozier –1480. **b.** *fig.* A support, stay. *Obs.* or *arch.* late ME. **B.** *adj. Her.* Having the limbs terminating in potents or crutch-heads, as *cross p.*; formed by a series of potents 1610.

Potent (pōu·tĕnt), *a.*[1] and *sb.*[2] 1500. [– L. *potens, potent-,* pr. pple. of **potēre, posse* be powerful or able, for *potis esse*; see -ENT.] **1.** Powerful; mighty; used of persons and things, in many shades of meaning, as the power implied is political, military, social, moral, mental, etc. (Usu. a poet. or rhet. word, felt to be stronger than *powerful.*) **b.** Of reasons, motives, etc.: Cogent, effective, convincing 1606. **2.** Having strong physical or chemical properties, as a solvent, drug, etc. 1715. **3.** Possessing sexual power 1899.

1. The Doctor is well monied, and his friends P. at Court SHAKS.

†**B.** *sb.* **1.** Power; a power –1631. **2.** A potent person; a potentate –1642. **3.** A military warrant or order –1690. Hence **Po·tently** *adv.*

Potentate (pōu·tĕnteit). late ME. [– (O)Fr. *potentat* or L. *potentatus* power, dominion, in late L. potentate, f. *potent-*; see prec., -ATE[1].] **1.** A person endowed with independent power; a prince, monarch, ruler. **2.** A powerful city, state, or body 1624.

1. But Kings and mightiest Potentates must die SHAKS.

Potential (pŏte·nʃăl), *a.* and *sb.* [XIV *potencial* – OFr. *potencial* (now *-tiel*) or late L. *potentialis,* f. *potentia*; see POTENCY, -AL[1].] **A.** *adj.* **1.** Possessing potency or power; potent; commanding. Now *rare.* 1485. **2.** Possible as opp. to actual; existing *in posse*; capable of coming into being; latent. late ME. **3.** *Med. P. cautery,* an agent which produces the same effects on the skin as an *actual cautery* or red-hot iron. So *p. corrosive.* late ME. **4.** *Gram.* That expresses potentiality or possibility 1530. **5.** *Physics.* **a.** *P. function*: a mathematical function or quantity by the differentiation of which the force at any point in space arising from any system of bodies, etc. can be expressed 1828. **b.** *P. energy*: energy existing in a positional form, not as motion; *see* ENERGY 6. 1853.

1. *Oth.* I. ii. 13. **4.** *P. mood,* a name sometimes given to the subjunctive mood when used to express possibility. Hence **Pote·ntial-ly** *adv.,* **-ness.**

B. *sb.* That which is possible; a possibility 1817. **2.** *Gram.* Short for *potential mood*; see A. 4. **3.** *Physics.* Short for *potential function*; see A. 5 a. Hence, the amount of energy or quantity of work denoted by this, considered as a quality of the matter, electricity, etc. in question. Also *attrib.* 1828.

Potentiality (pŏtenʃiæ·lĭti). 1625. [– med.L. *potentialitas,* f. late L. *potentialis*; see prec., -ITY.] **1.** The quality of being powerful or having power 1627. **2.** *esp.* The state or quality of possessing latent power or capacity capable of development into activity; possibility of action or active existence; opp. to *actuality* 1625. **b.** With *a* and *pl.*: An instance of this quality; a capacity or possibility, or that in which it is embodied 1668.

2. We are not here to sell a parcel of boilers and vats, but the p. of growing rich beyond the dreams of avarice JOHNSON. **b.** The seed is the p. of the plant 1875.

Potentialize (pŏte·nʃăləiz), *v.* 1856. [f. POTENTIAL + -IZE.] *trans.* To make potential; *spec.* to convert (energy) into a potential condition.

Potentiate (pote·nʃi͵eᶦt), *v.* 1817. [f. POTENCE or POTENCY + -ATE[3], after *substance, substantiate.* In Coleridge after G. *potenzieren.*] **1.** *trans.* To endow with power or potency. **2.** To make possible 1865.

‖**Potentilla** (pōᵘtĕnti·lă). 1548. [med.L., f. L. *potens, -ent-* POTENT *a.*[1] + dim. *-illa.*] *Bot.* An extensive genus of *Rosaceæ*, comprising herbs and undershrubs, of which the Silverweed, Cinquefoil, and Tormentil are common British species.

Potentiometer (potenʃi͵q·mĭtəɹ). 1881. [f. POTENTI(AL *sb.* 3 + -METER.] An instrument for measuring differences of electrical potential.

Po·tentize, *v.* 1857. [f. POTENT *a.*[1] + -IZE, after G. *potenzieren* (Hahnemann).] *trans.* To make potent; *spec.* to develop the power of (a medicine) by trituration or succussion.

‖**Potestas** (potestæs). 1870. [L., power.] *Rom. Law.* The power or authority of the head of a family over those depending on him; *esp.* parental authority.

†**Po·testate.** late ME. [– L. *potestas, potestat-* power. Cf. OFr. *potestat.*] †**1.** A person possessed of power over others; a superior, potentate –1678. **2.** Rendering *potestas* in the Vulgate (Eph. 6:12, 1 Pet. 3:22); cf. POWER II. 3. –1610. **3.** = PODESTA b; *transf.* a chief magistrate in certain Turkish towns –1603.

1. Lawfull for the potestates, the nobilitie, the gentrie 1583.

Potestative (pōᵘ·testeᶦtiv), *a.* 1630. [– Fr. *potestatif, -ive* (sense 2), or late L. *potestativus* (sense 1), f. as prec.; see -IVE.] Befitting a potestate; having power or authority; authoritative.

P. condition, a condition within the power or control of one of the parties concerned.

†**Po·t-gu:n, po·tgun.** 1549. [f. POT *sb.*[1] + GUN *sb.*] **1.** A short piece of ordnance with a large bore, a mortar; so called from its shape –1599. **2.** = POP-GUN 1, 2. –1801. **3.** *fig.* A loud talker, a braggart –1693.

2. How! fright me with your p.? 1619. **3.** That sign of a man there, that p. charged with wind CONGREVE.

Po·thecary. Now only *dial.* late ME. Aphet. f. APOTHECARY, formerly in common use. Also *attrib.*

Pother (pǫ·ðəɹ), *sb.* 1591. [Also *pudder*; rhymes with *other, mother*, and the like point to an orig. stem vowel ō, but no source is known; perh. infl. by *bother.*] **1.** A choking smoke or atmosphere of dust 1627. **2.** Disturbance, commotion; a tumult; a noise, din. Cf. DUST *sb.* 4. 1591. **b.** *transf.* A verbal commotion, fuss 1609. **3.** Mental perturbation; display of sorrow or grief 1641.

1. *To kick up a p.*, to raise a choking dust. **2.** The great Goddes, That keepe this dreadfull pudder o're our heads SHAKS. **b.** All this p. for an apple! MASSINGER. **3.** Well! if all husbands keep so great a p., I'll live unmarried—till I get another 1738.

Pother (pǫ·ðəɹ, pɒ·ðəɹ), *v.* 1692. [app. f. POTHER *sb.*; but occas. assoc. w. BOTHER *v.*] **1.** *trans.* To put into a fuss; to fluster, worry. **2.** *intr.* To make a fuss; to fuss, to worry 1735.

2. I found the old Gentleman..pothering over the Newspaper 1778.

Pot-herb (pǫ·thəɹb). 1538. [f. POT *sb.*[1] + HERB.] A herb grown for boiling in the pot; any of the herbs cultivated in a kitchen-garden.

Po·t-hole. 1839. [f. POT *sb.*[1] + HOLE *sb.*] *Geol.* A deep hole of more or less cylindrical shape; esp. one formed by the wearing away of rock by the rotation of a stone, or gravel, in an eddy of running water, or in the bed of a glacier. **b.** *Archæol.* A hole from which clay for pottery has been taken 1898. **2.** = POT *sb.*[2]; now *esp.* a deep hole in the surface of a road.

Pot-hook (pǫ·thuk). 1467. [f. POT *sb.*[1] + HOOK *sb.*] **1. a.** A hook suspended over a fireplace, for hanging a pot or kettle on; a crook. **b.** An iron rod with a hook at the end, for lifting a heated pot, stove-lid, etc. **2.** A curved or hooked stroke made in writing; now usu. a hooked stroke as made by children in learning to write. (Often with *hanger*; cf. HANGER[2] 4 c.). 1611.

2. She's scrawling pothooks and hangers on a dirty sheet of paper 1887.

Pot-house (pǫ·thaus). 1697. [f. POT *sb.*[1] + HOUSE *sb.*[1]] †**1.** A house where pottery is made (*rare*) –1761. **2.** An ale-house; a small, unpretentious, or low public-house 1724. **b.** *attrib.* Belonging to or characteristic of a pot-house; low, vulgar 1816.

2. b. Reeking yet with p. odours DICKENS.

Po·t-hu:nter. 1592. [f. POT *sb.*[1] + HUNTER.] †**1.** An opprobrious appellation; perh. a sycophant, parasite. **2.** 'A sportsman who shoots anything he comes across, having more regard to filling his bag than to the rules which regulate the sport' 1781. **3.** *slang.* One who takes part in any contest merely for the sake of winning a prize 1873. So **Po·t-hu:nting** *sb.* and *a.*

Potichomania (pǫti:ʃo͵mēᶦ·niă). 1855. [– Fr. *potichomanie* (also used), irreg. f. *potiche* an oriental porcelain vase + *-manie* -MANIA.] The craze for imitating Japanese or other porcelain by covering the inner surface of glass vessels, etc., with designs on paper or sheet gelatine; the process of doing this.

Potion (pōᵘ·ʃən), *sb.* ME. [– (O)Fr. *potion* – L. *potio, -on-* drink, poisonous draught, f. *pot-*, stem of *potare* drink, *potus* having drunk.] A dose of liquid medicine or of poison; a draught.

fig. Your Lordship may minister the P. of imprisonment to me SHAKS. Hence **Po·tion** *v. trans.* to treat or dose with potions; to drug.

Pot-lead (pǫ·tled), *sb.* 1890. [– Du. *potlood*, f. *pot* POT *sb.*[1] + *lood* lead.] Black-lead or graphite. Hence **Po:tlea·d** *v. trans.* to coat with pot-lead.

Pot-lid. late ME. [f. POT *sb.*[1] + LID *sb.*] **1.** The lid of a pot. **2.** *Geol.* Pop. name for a concretion occurring in various sandstones and shales 1827.

Po·t-lu·ck. 1592. [f. POT *sb.*[1] + LUCK *sb.*] One's luck or chance as to what may be in the pot, i.e. cooked for a meal; used in ref. to a person invited to a meal without any special preparation having been made for him; chiefly in phr. *to take p.* (= Fr. *courir la fortune du pot*). Also *transf.* or *gen.*

Potman (pǫ·tmăn). 1589. [f. POT *sb.*[1] + MAN *sb.*] †**1.** A toper –1685. **2.** A man employed at a public-house to attend to the pots and serve the liquor 1846.

Pot-metal (pǫ·tme:tăl). 1693. [f. POT *sb.*[1]] **1.** An alloy of lead and copper of which pots were formerly made. **2.** Stained glass coloured in the melting-pot, so that the colour pervades the whole substance 1832. **3.** A kind of cast iron suitable for making pots 1864.

‖**Potoo** (potū·). 1847. [imit.; from its cry.] Name in Jamaica for one of the Night-jars (*Nyctibius jamaicensis*).

‖**Potoroo** (pǫtŏrū·). 1790. [Native name in New South Wales.] = KANGAROO-RAT.

Pot-pie. Chiefly *U.S.* 1823. [f. POT *sb.*[1] + PIE *sb.*[2]] A meat pie made in a pot.

‖**Pot-pourri** (pōᵘ·pu·ri, ‖*popuri*). 1611. [Fr., 'rotten pot', f. *pot* POT *sb.*[1] + *pourri*, pa. pple. of *pourrir* rot; tr. Sp. OLLA PODRIDA.] †**1.** A stew, a hotch-potch –1725. **2.** A mixture of dried petals of different flowers mixed with spices, kept in a jar for its perfume 1749. **3.** *fig.* A musical or literary medley 1864.

Potsherd (pǫ·t͵ʃəɹd). Now somewhat *arch.* ME. [f. POT *sb.*[1] + SHARD, SHERD, *sb.*[1]] A fragment of a broken earthenware pot; a broken piece of earthenware.

Po·t-sho·t. 1858. [POT *sb.*[1]] A shot taken at game merely for the purpose of filling the pot for a meal. Hence *transf.* A shot aimed at a person or animal that happens to be within easy reach, without giving any chance of self-defence; e.g. at an enemy from ambush.

Potstone (pǫ·t͵stōᵘn). 1771. [f. POT *sb.*[1] + STONE *sb.*; tr. L. *lapis ollaris.*] A granular variety of STEATITE or SOAPSTONE.

Pottage (pǫ·tédʒ). [ME. *potage* – (O)Fr. *potage*, lit. 'what is put in a pot', f. *pot* POT *sb.*[1]; see -AGE. Orig. stressed *pota·ge.*] **1.** A dish composed of vegetables, alone or with meat, boiled to softness in water, and seasoned; soup, *esp.* a thick soup. **b.** *fig.* Often with ref. to Esau's 'mess of pottage' (see MESS *sb.* I. 2 quots.) late ME. †**2.** Oatmeal porridge –1797.

1. Potage is not so moche vsed in al Crystendom as it is vsed in Englande 1542.

Potted (pǫ·téd), *ppl. a.* 1646. [f. POT *v.* + -ED[1].] **1.** Of meat, fish, etc.: Minced or pounded and preserved in a closed pot or other vessel. **2.** Of a plant: Planted or grown in a pot 1849.

1. *fig. P.* learning in the form of popular abridgments 1883.

Potter (pǫ·təɹ), *sb.*[1] [Late OE. *pottere*, f. POT *sb.*[1] + -ER[1].] **1** A maker of pots or of earthenware vessels. **2.** A vendor or hawker of earthenware. *n. dial.* 1500.

1. Thou and all mankind are as clay in the hand of the p. 1720. *attrib.* and *Comb.* (also with *potter's*): **potter's asthma,** a form of fibroid phthisis to which persons exposed to the dust of pottery making are subject; **potter's clay, potter's earth,** any plastic clay free from iron; **potter's field,** a name given (after Matt. 27:7) to a piece of ground used as a burial place for the poor and for strangers; **potter's lead, potter's ore,** lead ore used for glazing pottery, galena; **p. wasp,** a wasp which builds a cell or cells of clay in a cylindrical cavity, as *Eumenes fraterna*; **potter's wheel,** the horizontal revolving disc of the lathe used by potters, on which the prepared clay is moulded into shape.

Potter (pǫ·təɹ), *v.* 1530. [frequent. of (dial.) *pote*, OE. *potian* thrust, push, PUT *v.*[1], = MLG. *poten*; see -ER[5].] **1.** *intr.* To poke again and again. Now only *dial.* **2.** *trans.* To trouble, perplex, bother (*dial.*) 1746. **3.** *intr.* To meddle, interfere; to tamper (*with*). Now *dial.* 1655. **4.** To occupy oneself in an ineffectual or trifling way; to work or act in a feeble or desultory manner; to trifle; to dabble (*in* something) 1740. **5. a.** To move or go about poking or prying into things in an unsystematic way, or doing slight and desultory work 1840. **b.** To saunter, dawdle, loiter 1829.

4. I suppose your husband is pottering on in his old way MANNING. **5. a.** Pottering about in the Bodleian, and fancying I should like to be a great scholar 1861. **b.** The slowest of Sunday trains, pottering up to London 1888. Hence **Potter** *sb.*[2] trifling action or (in Scott) talk. **Po·tterer. Po·ttering** *vbl. sb.* and *ppl. a.*

Pottery (pǫ·təri). 1483. [– (O)Fr. *poterie*, f. *potier* POTTER *sb.*[1] In later use referred to POT *sb.*[1]; see -ERY. Cf. AL. *potaria* (Domesday).] **1.** A potter's workshop or factory. **2.** The potter's art, ceramics; the manufacture of earthen vessels 1727. **3.** Pottery-ware, earthenware 1785. **4.** *attrib.*, as *p. trade*, etc. 1839.

1. *The Potteries*, a district in N. Staffordshire, including Hanley and Stoke-upon-Trent, the chief seat of the English p. industry.

Potting (pǫ·tiŋ), *vbl. sb.* 1594. [f. POT *v.* + -ING[1].] **1.** Drinking (of ale, etc.); tippling (*arch.*). **2.** The making of pottery or earthenware 1743. **3.** The preserving of butter, meat, fish, etc. in pots or other vessels 1615. **4.** Planting in, or transplanting into, a pot 1845.

1. I learn'd it in England; where indeed they are most potent in P. SHAKS.

Comb.: **p.-shed,** a shed in which delicate plants are reared in pots for planting out later.

Pottinger (pǫ·tindʒəɹ). Now *dial.* 1466. [See PORRINGER.] A vessel of metal, earthenware, or wood, for holding soup, broth, etc.; a small basin, porringer.

Pottle (pǫ·t'l). [ME. *potel* – OFr. *potel*, dim. of *pot* POT *sb.*[1]; see -EL[2].] **1.** A measure of capacity for liquids, etc., equal to half a gallon: now abolished. **b.** A pot or vessel of about this capacity 1698. **c.** *ellipt.* A pottle of wine, etc.; hence, drink, liquor 1700. **2.** A small wicker or 'chip' basket, esp. a conical one used for strawberries 1771.

1. b. By his elbow stood a p. of spiced ale 1888. **2.** One never sees a p. of strawberries now 1880. *Comb.*: **p.-pot,** a two-quart pot or tankard; *transf.* a heavy drinker.

Potto (pǫ·to). 1705. [Alleged to be from a Guinea dial.] **1.** A W. African lemur (*Perodicticus potto*), commonly called a 'sloth'. **b.** *Calabar p.*, a species of lemur (*Arctocebus calabarensis*), inhabiting the district of Old Calabar. **2.** The kinkajou 1790.

Potty (pǫ·ti), *a. slang.* 1899. [Of unkn. origin.] Of no importance; petty, trivial, insignificant. Also, silly, crazy.

Po·t-va:liant, *a.* 1641. [f. POT *sb.*[1] + VALIANT.] Valiant or courageous through drink. So **Po·t-va:lour,** courage induced by drink; 'Dutch courage'.

Potwaller (pǫ·twǫ:lǝɹ). 1701. [lit. 'pot-boiler', f. POT *sb.*[1] + *waller*, agent-noun (-ER[1]), f. WALL *v.*[1]] In some English boroughs, before 1832, a man qualified for a parliamentary vote as a householder; the test being his having a separate fire-place, on which food was cooked for himself and his family.

Potwalloper (pǫ·twǫ:lǝpǝɹ). 1725. [pop. alteration of prec. (after WALLOP *v.* boil with agitation).] **1.** = POTWALLER. **b.** Used as a term of reproach 1820. **2.** A scullion; also, a cook, esp. on board a whaler 1860.

Pouch (pautʃ), *sb.* late ME. [– ONFr. *pouche* (cf. AL. *pocha, pucha* XIII), var. of (O)Fr. *poche* bag, pouch, (now) pocket; cf. POKE *sb.*[1]] **1.** A bag, sack, or receptacle of moderate size; a pocket worn outside the dress. **b.** *spec.* A small bag in which money is carried; a purse. Now chiefly *arch.* or *literary.* late ME. **c.** A leathern bag or case used by soldiers for carrying ammunition 1627. **d.** A small flat bag of leather, rubber, etc. for carrying tobacco; a *tobacco-p.* 1687. **2.** *Naut.* One of a number of divisions made by small bulkheads or partitions in a ship's hold, for stowing corn or other loose cargo 1627. **3.** Applied to a natural receptacle resembling a bag or pocket. **a.** *Anat., Zool., Path.* A cavity like a bag; a sac, cyst. *spec.* †(*a*) the stomach of a fish; (*b*) the distensible gular sac beneath the bill in pelicans, cormorants, etc.; (*c*) a cheek-pouch in certain mammals; (*d*) the receptacle in which marsupial mammals carry their undeveloped young; the marsupium. 1450. **b.** *Bot.* A bag-like cavity, sac, or cyst, in a plant; *spec.* a seed-vessel resembling a bag or purse, a pod, a silicle 1577.

Pouch (pautʃ), *v.* 1566. [f. prec.] **1.** *trans.* To put into or enclose in a pouch; usu., to pocket; also *fig.* to 'bag'; to 'pocket', put up with. **2.** To take into the stomach, to swallow: said of fishes, and of certain birds 1653. **3.** To supply the purse or pocket of; to 'tip'. *slang* or *colloq.* 1810. **4.** *Dressmaking.* To make or arrange (a part of dress) so as to hang loosely in a pouch-like form. **b.** *intr.* said of the dress. 1897. **5.** To form a pouch or pouch-like cavity 1698.

3. To p. those venal villains, the reviewers 1810.

Pouched (pautʃt), *a.* 1834. [f. POUCH *sb.* and *v.* + -ED.] **1.** Furnished with or having a pouch or pouches. **2.** Put or enclosed in a pouch 1905.

1. A..p. bodice of mauve and white foulard 1897.

‖**Poudrette** (pudret). 1840. [Fr., dim. of *poudre* POWDER; see -ETTE.] A manure made from night-soil dried and mixed with charcoal, gypsum, etc.

‖**Pouffe** (puf). Also **pouf(f.** 1817. [Fr. (XVIII), ult. of imit. origin.] **1. a.** A kind of elaborate female head-dress fashionable late in the 18th c. **b.** A high roll or pad of hair worn by women. **2.** *Dressmaking.* A part of a dress gathered up in a projection or bunch 1869. **3.** A very soft stuffed ottoman or couch; a large soft cushion used as a low seat 1884.

‖**Poulaine** (pulē·n). 1464. [OFr. *Poulaine* Poland, *souliers à la Poulaine* shoes in Polish fashion, crakows; hence the pointed beak of such shoes.] The long pointed toe of a shoe.

Poulard (pulā·ɹd). 1732. [– Fr. *poularde*, f. *poule* hen + *-arde*; see -ARD.] A young hen fattened for the table; a spayed hen.

Pouldron (pōu·ldrǝn), **pauldron** (pǭ·ldrǝn). *Obs.* exc. *Hist.* 1465. [ult. aphetic f. OFr. *espauleron*, f. *espaule*, mod.Fr. *épaule* shoulder; with parasitic *d.*] A piece of armour covering the shoulder; a shoulder-plate.

‖**Poulet** (pulę). 1848. [Fr. = PULLET, also a love-letter, sometimes folded in the shape of a wing.] A love-letter, a (neatly-folded) note.

Poulp(e (pūlp). 1601. [– Fr. *poulpe* :– L. *polypus* POLYPUS.] An octopus, cuttle-fish, or other cephalopod.

Poult (pōult). [XV *pult*, contr. f. *poulet* PULLET.] The young of the domestic fowl, turkey, pheasant, guinea-fowl, or various game-birds. Also *attrib.* **b.** *transf.* A child; a youth. *colloq.* or *dial.* 1739.

‖**Poult-de-soie** (pudǝswa). 1850. [Fr., of unkn. origin; see PADUASOY.] A fine corded silk; 'a plain silk of rich quality in a soft and bright *grosgrain* make' (see GROGRAM); now usu. applied to coloured goods.

Poulter (pōu·ltǝɹ). *arch.* ME. [– OFr. *pouletier*, f. *poulet* PULLET; see -ER[2] 2.] **1.** = POULTERER. *Obs.* exc. as name of a London City Company. †**2.** An officer in a great household, who attended to the purchase of poultry, etc. –1601.

Poulterer (pōu·ltǝrǝɹ). 1638. [Extended f. prec., prob. after *poultery*, var. of POULTRY; see -ER[1] 3.] One whose business is the sale of poultry (and usu. hares and other game); a dealer in poultry.

Poultice (pōu·ltis), *sb.* 1542. [orig. pl. *pultes*, later taken as sing., – L. *pultes*, pl. of *puls, pult-* pottage, pap. See PULSE *sb.*[2]] A soft mass of bread, meal, bran, linseed, etc., usu. made with boiling water, and spread upon muslin, linen, etc., applied to the skin as an emollient for a sore or inflamed part, or as a counter-irritant (e.g. a mustard-poultice); a cataplasm. Also *attrib.* Hence **Pou·ltice** *v. trans.* to apply a p. to; to treat with a p.

Poultry (pōu·ltri). [XIV *pultrie, poultre* – OFr. *pouletrie*, f. *pouletier* POULTER; see -RY. Cf. AL. *poletria* (XIII).] †**1.** The office of a POULTER (sense 2); the superintendence of the purchase of fowls and other provisions; also, the room in which such provisions were stored –1601. **2.** †**a.** A place where fowls are reared; a poultry-farm. †**b.** A poultry-market. –1570. **c.** Hence, the name of a street at the east end of Cheapside in London, where there was formerly a poultry-market. late ME. **3.** Domestic fowls collectively; those tame birds which are reared for their flesh, eggs, or feathers, as barndoor fowls, ducks, geese, turkeys, guinea-fowls (excluding pigeons, pheasants, etc.); sometimes limited to the barndoor fowl with its varieties; also applied to the birds as dressed for market or prepared for food. (Usu. collect. pl.; formerly also as individual pl. after a numeral.) late ME.

attrib. and *Comb.* as *p.-fancier, -farm*, etc.

Pounce (pauns), *sb.*[1] 1486. [perh. shortening of PUNCHEON[1]. See also PUNCH *sb.*[1]] The claw or talon of a bird of prey; rarely of other animals. **b.** *fig.* in ref. to persons 1641.

In his pounces strong A fawn he bore COWPER. **b.** The King and the Duke (which latter they thought already in their Pounces) 1734.

Pounce (pauns), *sb.*[2] 1706. [– (O)Fr. *ponce* :– pop.L. **pomice*, for L. *pumex, pumic-* PUMICE.] **1.** A fine powder, as pulverized sandarac, etc., used to prevent the ink from spreading in writing over an erasure or on unsized paper, and also to prepare the surface of parchment to receive writing. **2.** A fine powder, as powdered sandarac, pipeclay, or charcoal, dusted over a perforated pattern sheet to transfer the design to the object beneath; stamping-powder 1727.

attrib. and *Comb.* as *p.-box*, etc.; **p.-paper,** a transparent paper for drawing, tracing, etc.

Pounce, *sb.*[3] 1841. [f. POUNCE *v.*[2]] An act of pouncing; a sudden swoop or spring; quick or eager movement to an object. *On the p.*, watching for an opportunity to pounce.

Pounce (pauns), *v.*[1] late ME. [var. of PUNCH *v.* Cf. POUNCE *sb.*[1]] **I. 1.** *trans.* To emboss (metal-work) as a decoration, by raising the surface with blows struck on the under side, as in *repoussé* work. *Obs.* exc. *Hist.* **2.** = PINK *v.*[1] 3. Also *p. out. Obs.* exc. *Hist.* late ME. **b.** To cut the edges of (a garment) into points and scallops; to jag; chiefly pass. of the cloth or garment. *Obs.* exc. *Hist.* 1542. **II.** †**1.** To bruise with blows; *esp.* to bruise, stamp, pound, or beat small –1662. **2.** To beat, thump, thrash (a person) 1827. **III.** †**1.** To prick, puncture, pierce, stab –1678. †**2.** To tattoo –1650.

Pounce (pauns), *v.*[2] 1686. [f. POUNCE *sb.*[1]] **1.** *trans.* To seize, as a bird of prey, with the pounces or talons; to swoop down upon and lay hold of suddenly. **2.** *intr.* To make a pounce; to spring suddenly *upon* or *at* in the way of attack 1744. **3.** To spring or jump unexpectedly; to 'come down' 1836.

1. They cannot p. the quarry on the ground G. WHITE. **2.** *To p. on* or *upon* (transf.) to seize upon suddenly; *fig.* to 'lay hold of' eagerly, suddenly, or promptly. **3.** At a quarter past seven Mr. Smith 'pounced', and the Closure was carried 1890.

Pounce (pauns), *v.*[3] 1580. [– (O)Fr. *poncer*, f. *ponce* POUNCE *sb.*[2]] **1.** *trans.* To smooth down by rubbing with pumice or pounce; *spec.* to smooth or finish (the surface of a hat) with pumice, sand-paper, or the like. **2.** To trace or transfer (a design) on or to a surface by dusting a perforated pattern with pounce; also, to copy a design upon (a surface) by means of pounce 1594. †**3.** To sprinkle with powder; to powder, dust; *esp.* to powder (the face) with a cosmetic. **b.** To sprinkle with specks, spots, or the like. –1685.

3. b. Thy azure robe..pounc't with stars.. Like a celestial canopie HERRICK.

Pou·ncet-box. 1596. [perh. orig. misprint for *pounced-box* = perforated box.] app. A small box with perforated lid for perfumes. (A Shakespearian word revived by Scott.)

Pound (paund), *sb.*[1] [OE. *pund* (pl. *pund*) = OFris., OS. *pund* (MDu. *pont*, Du. *pond*), OHG. *pfunt* (G. *pfund*), ON., Goth. *pund* :– Gmc. **pundo* – L. *pondo* (indeclinable) pound weight.] **I.** A measure of weight derived from the ancient Roman *libra*, but very variously modified in different countries; in the British Empire now = 16 ounces avoirdupois, and 12 ounces troy; fixed for use in trade by a Parliamentary standard. Denoted by *lb.* (L. *libra*). Formerly, and still *dial.* and *colloq.* uninflected in pl.; also in *comb.*, as *a twenty p. shot.* **b.** *One's p. of flesh*: used proverbially, with ref. to Shaks. *Merch. V.*

b. All the other Great Powers want their p. of flesh from Turkey 1887.

II. 1. An English money of account (orig. a pound weight of silver), of the value of 20 shillings or 240 pence, and now represented by the gold sovereign. Denoted by £ before the numeral (occas. by *l.* after it), and dist. by the epithet *sterling.* OE. †**b.** The 'pound Scots', orig. the same as the English, was at the Union of the Crowns equal to one-twelfth of a pound sterling, being divided into 20 shillings each of the value of an English penny –1814. **c.** Applied to the Turkish and Egyptian gold pieces of 100 piastres, the former of 111·36 grains, the latter of 131·18 grains 1883.

Phrases. *In the p.*, reckoned at so much for each p. *Pounds, shillings, and pence*: = money; also *attrib.* = monetary; *fig.* = concerned chiefly with the money value of things; matter-of-fact, realistic; Even in this low, pounds-shillings-and-pence point of view SOUTHEY.

Comb.: **p. note,** a bank-note for one p.; also an English treasury-note of the value of one p.; **-rate,** a rate of so much in the p.; **-velo,** a unit of momentum; the momentum of a body of mass 1 lb. moving with a velocity of 1 foot per second; **-worth, pound'sworth,** as much of anything as is worth or may be bought for a p.

Pound (paund), *sb.*[2] [XIV *poonde* :– OE.

pund*, known only in comb. *pundfald* PINFOLD, and early ME. *pundbreche* POUNDBREACH, of unkn. origin. See POND *sb.*] **I. 1. An enclosure maintained by authority, for the detention of stray or trespassing cattle, and for the keeping of distrained cattle or goods until redeemed; a pinfold. **b.** An enclosure for sheltering or dealing with sheep or cattle in the aggregate. **2.** *transf.* and *fig.* A place of confinement; a pen, a pent-up position; a trap; a spiritual 'fold'; in *Hunting*, a position from which escape is impossible or difficult. late ME.

1. *P. close* or *covert*, a p. to which the owner of impounded animals may not have access; *p. open* or *overt*, one which is not roofed, and to which the owner may have access to feed his beasts.

II. 1. a. = POND *sb.* 1. Now *dial.* **b.** *esp.* A body of water held up or confined by a dam or the like, as the reach of a canal above a lock, etc. late ME. **2.** An enclosure for fish; *spec.* the last compartment of a p. net, in which the fish are finally caught; the bowl or pocket 1809.

Comb.: **p.-fee**, a fee paid for the release of cattle or goods from the p.; **-keeper**, one who has charge of a public p.; a pinder; **-lock**, a lock on a river for pounding up the water; **p. net**, *U.S.*, an enclosure formed by nets in the sea near the shore, consisting of a long straight wall or leader, a first enclosure (the 'heart') into which the fish are conducted by the leader, and a second enclosure (the p., bowl, or pocket) from which they cannot escape.

Pound (pound), *sb.*^{3} 1832. [f. POUND *v.*^{1}] **1.** An apparatus for pounding or crushing apples for cider; a cider-mill. **2.** A heavy beating blow; a thump, also, the sound caused by this, a thud 1890.

Pound (paund), *v.*^{1} [Late OE. *pūnian*, ME. *poune* (till XVII), also *ġepūnian*, f. **pūn-* (whence also Du. *puin*, LG. *pūn* rubbish), of which no further cognates are known. For the final *d* (XVI) cf. ASTOUND *v.*, BOUND *ppl. a.*^{1}, etc.] **1.** *trans.* To break down and crush by beating, as with a pestle; to reduce to pulp or powder; to bray, bruise, pulverize. **2.** To strike or beat with repeated heavy blows; to thump, to pummel 1700. †**3.** With inverted construction: To deliver (heavy blows) *on* some one SPENSER. **4.** *intr.* To deliver heavy blows, fire heavy shot (*at*, *on*) 1815. **b.** Of a ship or boat: To beat the water, rise and fall heavily 1903. **5.** To walk, run, or dance with heavy steps; to ride hard and heavily; *transf.* of a steamer, to paddle or steam along forcibly 1802.

1. The Peasant..who pounds with Rakes The crumbling Clods DRYDEN. *fig.* The Lord Advocate ..pounded it [the Bill] to powder 1884. **2.** I.. pounded a piano, and sang a little 1875. The fortifications might be pounded to pieces 1884. **4.** *To p. away*, to continue delivering blows. **b.** The vessel is lying far inside the reef, and is pounding heavily 1906. **5.** A fat farmer sedulously pounding through the mud KINGSLEY.

Pound (paund), *v.*^{2} 1450. [f. POUND *sb.*^{2} Cf. PIND *v.*, POIND *v.*] **1.** *trans.* To place or shut *up* (trespassing or straying cattle) in a pound; to impound. **2.** To shut up or confine in any enclosure, material or otherwise. Also with *up*. 1589. **b.** *spec.* in *Fox-hunting* (*pass.*), said of a rider who gets into an enclosed place from which he cannot get out. *To p. the field*: see quot. 1827. **3.** To dam (water); to dam *up*. Now chiefly *dial.* 1649.

2. b. In hunting, an impassable barrier is said 'to p. the field'. So also a bold rider who clears a fence which others cannot do is said 'to p. the lot' 1886.

Pound, *v.*^{3} 1890. [f. POUND *sb.*^{1} 1.] *Coining.* To test the weight of coins (or blanks to be minted) by weighing the number of these which ought to make a pound weight (or so many pounds), and ascertaining how much they vary from the standard.

Poundage^1 (pau·ndėdʒ). ME. [f. POUND *sb.*^{1} + -AGE.] **1.** An impost, duty, or tax of so much per pound sterling; *spec.* a subsidy, usu. of 12 pence in the pound, formerly granted by Parliament to the Crown, on all imports and exports except bullion and commodities paying tonnage. Now *Hist.* **2.** A payment of so much per pound sterling upon the amount of any transaction in which money passes 1599. **b.** A percentage of the total earnings of any concern, paid as wages to those engaged in it, sometimes in addition to a fixed wage 1892. **3.** A payment or charge of so much per pound weight; payment by weight 1500. **4.** *Betting.* Extravagant odds 1816. Hence **Pou·ndage** *v.*

Poundage^2 (pau·ndėdʒ). 1554. [f. POUND *v.*^{2}, *sb.*^{2} + -AGE.] †The action or right of pounding stray cattle (*obs.*); the charge levied upon the owner. **b.** The keeping of cattle in a pound or enclosure; also, the enclosure 1866.

Poundal (pau·ndăl). 1879. [f. POUND *sb.*^{1}] The force which, acting on one pound of matter for one second, generates a velocity of one foot per second.

Poundbreach (pau·ndbrītʃ). ME. [f. POUND *sb.*^{2} + BREACH *sb.*] *Law.* The breaking open of a pound; hence, the illegal removal or recovery by the owner of goods lawfully impounded.

Pou·nd-cake. 1841. [f. POUND *sb.*^{1} + CAKE *sb.*] A rich cake so called as containing a pound of each of the principal ingredients, flour, butter, sugar, fruit, etc.

Pounder^1 (pau·ndəɹ). 1533. [f. POUND *v.*^{1} + -ER^1; cf. OE. *pūnere*, f. *pūnian* POUND *v.*^{1}] **1.** An instrument for pounding; a pestle, a crushing beetle; a beater 1564. **b.** A mortar 1891. **2.** A person who pounds 1533.

Pounder^2 (pau·ndəɹ). 1695. [f. POUND *sb.*^{1} + -ER^1.] **I.** Something of a pound weight, e.g. a fish 1834. **II.** In comb. with prefixed numeral. **1.** Something weighing so many pounds; *spec.* a gun carrying a shot of a specified weight; *rarely*, a projectile of a specified weight 1695. **2.** A person possessing, having an income of, or paying (e.g. as rent) so many pounds sterling; a woman having a marriage-portion of so many pounds 1706. **b.** Any article of the value of a specified number of pounds sterling 1755.

1. A battery of twenty-four sixty pounders 1756. **2.** Rich Miss Dripping, the twenty-thousand-p. from London THACKERAY.

Pou·nd-foo·lish, *a.* Foolish in dealing with large sums; antithetical to PENNY-WISE.

Pounding (pau·ndiŋ), *vbl. sb.* 1591. [-ING^1.] The action of POUND *v.*^{1} **1.** Crushing or bruising into pulp or powder; trituration, pulverizing. **b.** *concr.* Pounded substance; the quantity pounded at one time 1872. **2.** Striking or beating with or as with the fist; beating, knocking, thumping; heavy firing; an instance of this 1815. **3.** Heavy riding 1833.

Comb. **p.-match** (*nonce-wd.*), a battle.

Pou·nd-wei·ght, *sb.* 1538. [f. POUND *sb.*^{1} + WEIGHT *sb.*] A weight of one pound; *spec.* a piece of metal of the weight of a pound avoirdupois, and stamped to that effect, used in weighing.

Pour (pō^{ə}ɹ), *sb.* 1790. [f. next.] **1.** A pouring stream (*lit.* and *fig.*). *rare.* **2.** A heavy fall of rain; a downpour 1814. **3.** *Founding.* **a.** The act, process, or operation of pouring melted metal. **b.** The amount of melted metal poured at one time. 1884.

Pour (pō^{ə}ɹ), *v.* ME. [Of unkn. origin. The earlier *pur*, *poure*, *powre*, later *power*, are reflected in mod. dial. pronunc. pau^{ə}ɹ, which is found in rhymes from Pope to Tennyson and Swinburne, though the two latter show also pō^{ə}ɹ; the present standard pronunc. is indicated as early as XV by the sp. *pore*, the development of which is unexplained.] **I.** *trans.* **1.** To emit in a stream; to cause (a liquid or granular substance) to flow out of a vessel or receptacle; to discharge copiously; also, to emit (rays of light). Often with advs., *forth*, *out*, *in*, *down*, *off*, etc. **2.** Said of a river, etc.: To cause the water to flow in a flood; *refl.* to flow with strong current; to fall *into* the sea, etc. 1665. **3.** *transf.* and *fig.* To send forth as in a stream; to discharge copiously or in rapid succession; to bestow profusely 1451.

1. Drynke my wyne, which I haue poured out for you COVERDALE *Prov.* 9:5. Trying to p. oil on the troubled waters KINGSLEY. To p. cold water..upon the zeal of his Irish friends 1893. *absol.* Poure out for the people, that they may eat BIBLE (Genev.) 2 *Kings* 4:41. **3.** How London doth powre out her Citizens SHAKS. He.. poured forth..torrents of frantic abuse MACAULAY.

II. *intr.* (for *refl.*) **1.** Of liquids, etc.: To flow in a stream; of rain: to fall heavily 1538. **b.** *impers.* To rain heavily or copiously 1726. **2.** *transf.* and *fig.* To run or rush in a stream or crowd; to stream, to swarm 1573.

1. *Lear* III. iv. 18. The torrent brooks..From craggy hollows pouring,..Sound all night long TENNYSON. **b.** Prov. *It never rains but it pours*, events (esp. misfortunes) come all together or happen in rapid succession. **2.** Troops poured towards the Rhine MACAULAY. Business prospered, and money came pouring in 1891.

‖**Pourboire** (purbwār). 1836. [Fr., prop. *pour boire* for drinking.] A gratuity to be spent on drinking; hence *gen.* a gratuity, 'tip'.

Pourer (pō^ə·rəɹ). 1594. [f. POUR *v.* + -ER^1.] One who or that which pours; a vessel used in pouring anything.

This..teapot..is not a good p. 1881.

‖**Pourparler** (purparle). 1795. [Fr., subst. use of OFr. *po(u)rparler* discuss, f. *po(u)r-* (intensive), PRO-^{1} + *parler* speak.] An informal discussion preliminary to actual negotiation.

Pourpoint (pū^ə·ɹpoint), **purpoint** (pō·ɹ-point). *Obs.* exc. *Hist.* late ME. [– OFr. *po(u)rpoint*, orig. pa. pple. of *pourpoindre* perforate, quilt, f. *pour* (cf. PRO-^{1}), substituted for *par* (L. *per*), + *poindre* :– L. *pungere* prick.] Something quilted. **a.** A doublet, stuffed and quilted, worn by men in the 14th and 15th centuries, as part both of civil costume and of armour. †**b.** A quilt, as a bed-covering –1459.

Poussette (puse·t), *sb.* 1814. [– Fr. *poussette*, dim. of *pousse* a push; see -ETTE.] An act of poussetting; see next.

Poussette (puse·t), *v.* 1812. [f. prec.] *intr.* To dance round and round with hands joined, as a couple in a country dance.

‖**Pou sto** (pau stō^u). 1847. [Gr. ποῦ στῶ 'where I may stand', from the saying of Archimedes, δός μοι ποῦ στῶ, καὶ κινῶ τὴν γῆν 'give me (a place) where I may stand, and I will move the earth'.] A place to stand on; *fig.* a basis of operation.

Pout (paut), *sb.*^{1} [OE. **pūta* in *ǣle-pūta* EEL-POUT; app. f. stem **pūt-* inflate; see POUT *v.*] A name for several kinds of fish, esp. the BIB or *whiting-p.*

Pout (paut), *sb.*^{2} 1591. [f. POUT *v.*] A protrusion of the lips, expressive of pique or annoyance. Also *transf.*

In the pouts, in a pouting mood, sulky.

Pout, *sb.*^{3} Sc. and dial. f. POULT *sb.*

Pout (paut), *v.* ME. [Of unkn. origin; perh. repr. OE. **pūtian*, f. **pūt-* be inflated, which appears to be the base of Sw. dial. *puta* be inflated, Sw., Norw. *puta* pad, Da. *pude* cushion; cf. POUT *sb.*^{1}] **1.** *intr.* To protrude the lips, esp. in expression of displeasure or sullenness; hence, to show displeasure. **b.** Without implication of displeasure: To swell out, to protrude, as lips 1598. **2.** *trans.* To protrude (esp. the lips) 1784. **b.** To say with a pout 1877.

1. Like a misbehav'd and sullen wench, Thou pout'st upon thy fortune and thy love SHAKS. Hence **Pou·tingly** *adv.*

Pouter (pau·təɹ), *sb.* 1725. [f. POUT *v.* + -ER^1.] **1.** One who pouts 1809. **2.** A breed of the domestic pigeon with a great power of inflating the crop 1725. **3.** The whiting-pout 1889.

attrib.; **p.-fish** = 3; **p.-pigeon** = 2.

Poverty (pǫ·vəɹti). [ME. *poverte* – (i) OFr. *poverte* :– L. *paupe·rtas* nom.; this type survived as *povert* till XVI; (ii) OFr. *poverté* (mod. *pauvreté*) :– L. *paupertat-*, stem of *paupertas*, f. *pauper* poor; see -TY^1, POORTITH.] The quality or condition of being poor. **I.** The condition of having little or no wealth or material possessions; indigence, destitution, want (in various degrees). **b.** *fig.* in allusion to *Matt.* 5:3. ME. **c.** Personified and applied to a person, or persons gen., in whom it is exemplified 1813.

Ther is no warre but it causeth pouerte LD.

BERNERS. **c.** Alike must Wealth and P. Pass heedless and unheeding by BYRON.

II. 1. Deficiency, dearth, scarcity; smallness of amount. late ME. **2.** Deficiency in the proper or desired quality; inferiority, meanness. late ME. **3.** Deficiency *in* some property, quality, or ingredient; (of soil, etc.) unproductiveness. late ME. **4.** Poor condition of body; leanness or feebleness resulting from insufficient nourishment, etc. 1523.

1. The p. of modern literature 1838. **2.** The p. of your understanding WATTS. **3.** The..p. of north and north-eastern Africa in river-producing power 1880.

Comb.: **p.-grass,** (*a*) a N. American grass, *Aristida dichotoma*; (*b*) = **p.-plant,** a small N. American heath-like shrub, *Hudsonia tomentosa* (N.O. *Cistaceæ*); both plants growing in poor soil.

Po·verty-stri:cken, *a.* 1844. Stricken or afflicted with poverty; extremely poor or destitute. Earlier **Po·verty-struck** *a.* (now *rare* or *Obs.*) 1813.

Powan (pōᵘ·wăn, pōᵘ·ăn). 1633. [Sc. form of POLLAN.] A species of freshwater fish, *Coregonus clupeoides*, belonging to the same genus as the vendace and the pollan, with which it was formerly identified, and is still often confused, under the name of *fresh-water herring*.

Powder (pau·dəɹ), *sb.*[1] [ME. *poudre, pouldre* (whence *poulder* XV–XVII) – (O)Fr. *poudre*, earlier *pol(d)re* :– L. *pulvis, pulver-* dust.] **1.** The mass of dry impalpable particles or granules produced by the grinding, crushing or disintegration of any solid substance; dust. **b.** Applied to the pollen of flowers, or the spores of *Lycopodium* 1676. **2.** A preparation in the form of powder, for some special use or purpose, e.g. in medicine, for the face or hair, etc. ME. **3.** = GUNPOWDER 1. late ME.

1. He shall grynd him to p. TINDALE *Matt.* 21:44. **2.** Such an one has great faith in Ward's pill, or James' p. 1768. We wore p. in those days THACKERAY. **3.** Bothwell with pulder blew him in the air 1570. *P. and shot*, the matériel expended in warfare; hence, the cost or effort expended for some result. *Food for p.*: see FOOD *sb.* 1. *The smell of p.*, actual experience of fighting. *To keep one's p. dry*, to be prepared for action in any emergency.

attrib. and *Comb.*: **p.-flag,** the red flag carried by a *p.-hoy*, or hoisted on a ship when taking in or discharging gunpowder; **-house,** a building for storing gunpowder; **-hoy,** an ordnance vessel expressly fitted to convey p. from the land magazine to a ship; **-magazine,** a place where gunpowder is stored in a fort or on board ship; **-mill,** a mill for making gunpowder; **-tax,** a tax upon hair-powder.

Powder (pau·dəɹ), *sb.*[2] *Obs.* exc. *dial.* 1600. [Of unkn. origin.] An impetus, a rush; force, impetuosity. Chiefly in phr. *with* (dial. *at, in*) *a p.*, impetuously, violently.

Jordan..comes down with a p., and at set times overflowes all his bankes 1650.

Powder (pau·dəɹ), *v.*[1] ME. [– (O)Fr. *poudrer*, f. *poudre* POWDER *sb.*[1]; in some senses f. the Eng. sb.] **I. †1.** *trans.* To sprinkle (food) with a condiment of powdery nature; to season, spice –1440. **†b.** *fig.* To mix with some modifying ingredient; to 'season'; to 'alloy' –1790. **2.** To sprinkle (meat) with salt or powdered spice; to salt; to cure. *Obs.* exc. *dial.* late ME. **3.** To sprinkle powder upon; to cover *with* or as *with* some powdery substance ME. **b.** To apply powder to (the hair, etc.) as a cosmetic. Also with the person as obj.; also *absol.* or *intr.* for *refl.* 1599. **4.** To ornament with spots or small devices scattered over the surface; to sprinkle or spangle (a surface) with. Usu. in *pa. pple.* ME.

1. b. Powdering their lives with improbable passages to the great prejudice of truth 1661. **2.** She roasted red veal, and she powder'd lean beef 1715. **3.** That Milky way Which nightly as a circling Zone thou seest Pouderd with Starrs MILT. **b.** 'A red nose..she can always p. it.' 'She would scorn to p. it', says Edwin. DICKENS. **4.** Gold shoes powdered with pearls 1766.

II. To sprinkle or scatter like powder; to disperse here and there upon a surface. Usu. in *pa. pple.* ME.

To p. violets on a silk ground 1890.

III. 1. To reduce to powder; to pulverize 15.. **2.** *intr.* To fall to powder, become pulverized 1846. Hence **Pow·derable** *a. rare.*

Pow·der, *v.*[2] *colloq.* and *dial.* 1632. [f. POWDER *sb.*[2]] *intr.* To rush; to hurry with rushing speed: said esp. of a rider.

Pow:der-blue·. *sb.* and *a.* 1707. [f. POWDER *sb.*[1]] **A.** *sb.* Powdered smalt, esp. for use in the laundry. **B.** *adj.* Having the deep blue colour of smalt. **b.** *sb.* A name for this colour. 1894.

Pow·der-dow:n. 1861. [f. POWDER *sb.*[1] + DOWN *sb.*[2]] Name for peculiar down-feathers or plumules, found in various birds in definite tracts or patches; so called from the bluish-white powdery or scurfy substance into which they disintegrate. Also *attrib.*, as in *p. patch*, etc.

Powdered (pau·dəɹd), *ppl. a.* late ME. [f. POWDER *v.*[1] + -ED[1].] **1.** Preserved; cured; corned. *Obs.* exc. *dial.* **2.** Decorated with a multitude of spots or small figures scattered over the surface. late ME. **b.** *Zool.* Marked as if dusted over with powder. Said esp. of moths. 1832. **3.** Of the hair or skin: Dressed with powder as a cosmetic. Also said of the person. 1655. **4.** Reduced to powder or dust 1591.

3. The powder'd footman GAY. **4.** P. glasse 1646.

Pow·der-fla:sk. 1753. A case for carrying gunpowder, orig. of horn, later of leather or metal.

Pow·der-ho:rn. 1533. A powder-flask made of the horn of an ox or a cow with a wooden or metal bottom at the larger end.

Powdering (pau·dəriŋ), *vbl. sb.* late ME. [f. POWDER *v.*[1] + -ING[1].] The action of POWDER *v.*[1], or the result of this.

Comb. **p.-closet, -room,** a room appropriated to powdering the hair; **-tub,** a tub in which the flesh of animals is powdered, or salted and pickled; †also *joc.*, a sweating-tub used for the cure of venereal disease.

Pow·der-mo:nkey. 1682. Joc. term for a boy employed on board ship to carry powder to the guns.

Pow·der-puff. 1704. A soft pad, usu. of down, for applying powder to the skin. **b.** An instrument like a small bellows formerly used for powdering the hair.

Powdery (pau·dəri), *a.* late ME. [f. POWDER *sb.*[1] + -Y[1].] **1.** Of the nature or consistence of powder; pulverulent; dusty. **b.** Easily disintegrated into powder; friable 1728. **2.** Covered with or full of powder; dusty 1708.

1. The p. snow WORDSW. **b.** A brown, p. Spar 1728. **2.** Auriculas with p. leaves and stems 1874.

Power (pau·əɹ, pauᵊɹ). [ME. *poer, pouer* (po,ē·r, pu,ē·r) – AFr. *poer, po(u)air*, OFr. *poeir*, later *pooir, povoir* (mod. *pouvoir*) :– Rom. **potēre*, superseding L. *posse* be able (see POSSE). By shift of stress (pu,ē·r) became (pū·er), whence (pau·əɹ). The spelling *power* has been the most usual since XIV.] **I.** As a quality or property. **1.** Ability to do something or anything, or to act upon a person or thing. **b.** With *a* and *pl.* A particular faculty of body or mind 1483. **c.** *pl.* Power put forth in various directions or on various occasions 1586. **2.** Ability to act or affect something strongly; physical or mental strength; vigour, energy; force of character; effect 1440. **b.** Political or national strength 1701. **3.** Of things: Active property; capacity of producing some effect 1592. **b.** The sound expressed by a character or symbol; the meaning expressed by a word or phrase in a particular context 1727. **4.** Possession of control or command over others; dominion; government, sway; authority *over* ME. **b.** Liberty or permission to act ME. **c.** Personal or social ascendancy, influence 1535. **d.** Political ascendancy or influence 1833. **5.** Legal ability, capacity, or authority to act; *esp.* delegated authority 1486. **b.** A document, or clause in a document, giving legal authority 1483.

1. Is it not in your p. to open your eyes? 1713. Money is p. 1853. **b.** Memory, reason, & wyll. And these ben the thre powers of the soule. 1526. **c.** His powers of attention 1852. **2.** More p. to your elbow LOWELL. **b.** *Balance of p.*: see BALANCE *sb.* 12. **3.** The P. of Herbs can other Harms remove GRAY. The p. of heat to burn JOWETT. **4.** The p. and jurisdiction of the Parliament COKE. **b.** The bishops,..had no p. to imprison priests 1856. **c.** A man's p. means the readiness of other men to obey him MILL. **d.** The governing party has always come into p. by means of revolution 1878. **5.** The borrowing powers of the company 1891. **b.** *P. of attorney*, a document appointing a person or persons to act as the attorney or attorneys of the appointer.

II. As a person, body, or thing. **1.** An influential or governing person, body, or thing; in early use, one in authority, a ruler, governor. late ME. **b.** In late use, A state or nation from the point of view of its international authority or influence 1726. **2.** A celestial or spiritual being having control or influence; a divinity. Chiefly in pl.; often in exclams., etc., as *by (all) the powers! merciful powers!* 1596. **3.** In med. angelology, the sixth order of angels in the celestial hierarchy; see ORDER *sb.* II. 1. 1667. **4.** A force of armed men; a host, an army; in pl. = *forces*, i.e. distinct hosts, or different kinds of troops composing an army. Orig. less concrete, without *a* or *pl.* Now *rare* or *arch.* ME. **5.** A large number of persons; a large number, quantity, or amount of things; 'a lot'. Now *dial.* or *vulgar colloq.* 1661.

1. The powers that be *Rom.* 13:1. This..banker who was..something of a p. in Greece 1874. **b.** There was no talk then of being a World P. 1901. **3.** Thrones, Dominations, Princedoms, Vertues, Powers MILT. **4.** Brutus and Cassius are leuying Powers; We must straight make head SHAKS. *P. of the county*, POSSE COMITATUS. **5.** It has done a p. of work DICKENS.

III. Techn. uses. **1.** *Math.* The result of taking a quantity (*a*) a given number of times (*x*) as a factor, the number of times being indicated by an exponent (except in the case of 1), thus a^x; *gen.* the result of operating on a quantity by any exponent, positive or negative, integral or fractional 1674. **b.** *P. of a point* with regard to a circle: the square of the distance from that point to the point of contact of the tangent drawn from it 1885. **2.** *Mech.* An instrument by means of which energy may be applied to mechanical purposes 1671. **3.** Any form of energy or force available for application to work. *spec.* **a.** Mechanical energy (as that of running water, wind, steam, electricity, etc.). **b.** Force applied to produce motion or pressure; the acting force in a lever, etc., as opp. to the *weight*. **c.** The mechanical advantage gained by the use of a machine. 1727. **4.** Capacity for exerting mechanical force, as measured by the rate at which it is exerted, or the work done by it (cf. HORSE-POWER); also applied to a measurable capacity for producing some other physical effect 1806. **5.** *Optics.* The capacity of a lens (or combination of lenses) for magnifying the apparent size of an object; also *ellipt.*, the lens itself 1727.

1. 2 is the root, or 1st p. of 2. 4 is the 2d p., or square of 2. 1827. **2.** *Mechanical (†mathematical, †mechanic) powers*, the simple machines by means of which energy may be advantageously applied; now reckoned as six, viz. the lever, wheel and axle, pulley, wedge, inclined plane, and screw. **3.** Plans..for..working the weaving loom by the application of p. 1808.

Phrases. *In p.*, in a position of authority. *In one's p.*, within one's ability, under one's control. *To the best, uttermost*, or *extent of one's p.*, as far as one is able. *P. of pit and gallows*: see PIT *sb.* I. 7.

Comb.: **p.-gas,** coal-gas used for supplying power, not illumination; **p. house, p. station,** a building in which power (esp. electrical or mechanical) is generated; **-load** *Electr.*, the amount of current delivered for use in driving machinery, as dist. from that used for lighting. Hence **Power** *v.*, to supply the power for (an engine, etc.) 1899.

†Pow·erable, *a.* 1584. [f. POWER *sb.* + -ABLE.] **1.** = POWERFUL –1632. **2.** Extreme, excessive (*rare*) –1598.

Powerful (pau·əɹ-, pauᵊ·ɹfŭl), *a.* (*adv.*) late ME. [f. POWER *sb.* + -FUL.] **1.** Having, or capable of exerting, great (moral, physical, or other) power; potent. **2.** Producing great effect. **b.** Having power to influence greatly; impressive, convincing, telling. 1596. **3.** Great in quantity or number. *dial.* or *vulgar.* 1852. **B.** as *adv.* Powerfully, exceedingly. *dial.* or *vulgar.* 1835.

1. The powerfullest King on the Sea-coast of

Malabar 1727. P. stimulants 1802. **2.** There is a p. force in a father's command DE FOE. **B.** He was p. tired W. IRVING. Hence **Pow·erful-ly** *adv.*, **-ness.**

Powerless (pau·əɹ-, pauᵊ·ɹlės), *a.* 1552. [f. POWER *sb.* + -LESS.] Without power; devoid of power or ability; helpless. Hence **Pow·erless-ly** *adv.*, **-ness.**

Pow·er-loo:m. 1808. A weaving loom worked by mechanical power (water, steam, etc.), as dist. from a hand-loom.

Powwow, pow-wow (pau·wau), **pawaw** (pawǭ·), *sb.* 1624. [Earlier *powah, paw(w)aw, powow* – Algonquian (Narragansett) *powah·, powwaw·* he dreams, (hence) magician; the two sylls. were early assimilated.] **1.** A priest, sorcerer, or medicine-man of the N. Amer. Indians. **2.** A ceremony of the N. Amer. Indians, esp. one where magic was practised and feasting indulged in; also, a council of Indians, or conference with them 1663. **3.** *transf.* A political or other meeting, a friendly consultation, or a merrymaking; a 'palaver' of any kind. (Chiefly *U.S.*) 1812.

2. To find the thief the Indians held the Powwow 1887. **3.** I was not at the Cambridge powwow HUXLEY.

Powwow (pau:wau·), *v.* 1642. [f. prec.] **1.** *intr.* Of N. Amer. Indians: To practise medicine or sorcery; to hold a powwow. **b.** *transf.* To confer, deliberate, talk, hold palaver. (Chiefly *U.S.*) 1780. **2.** *trans.* To doctor, to treat with magic 1856.

Pox (pǫks), *sb.* 1476. [Altered spelling of *pocks*, pl. of POCK *sb.*, used collectively (cf. *mumps*, etc.), and at length as a sing.] **1.** Name for different diseases characterized by 'pocks' or eruptive pustules on the skin; see POCK *sb.* 2. **†a.** = SMALL-POX –1819. **b.** With qualifying words: (*a*) See CHICKEN-*p.*, COW-POX, SMALL-POX; (*b*) *Great, French,* or *Spanish p.*, syphilis 1503. **†2.** In imprecations, etc. –1820.

2. A P. of that iest SHAKS. Hence **Pox** *v. trans.* to infect with the p. (usu. syphilis). Also in imprecations. *Obs.* or only in vulgar use.

†Poz (pǫz). *colloq.* 1710. [abbrev. of POSITIVE.] Positive, certain; esp. in phr. *that's p.* Also as *adv.* = positively. –1839.

‖**Pozzolana, pozzuolana** (pottso-, pottswolā·nă). 1706. [It. *pozz(u)olana*, prop. adj. (sc. *terra* earth) 'belonging to Pozzuoli' (L. *Puteoli* little springs), a town near Naples.] A volcanic ash, containing silica, alumina, lime, etc., found near Pozzuoli, etc., much used in the preparation of hydraulic cement. Also, a name for similar artificial preparations.

Prabble: see PRIBBLE.

Practic (præ·ktik), *sb.*¹ *arch.* late ME. [– OFr. *practique* (mod. *pratique*) – med.L. *practica* – Gr. πρακτική, subst. use of fem. of πρακτικός; see next.] The earlier Eng. and esp. Sc. equivalent of PRACTICE. **1.** = PRACTICE 1. **b.** An action, deed; *pl.* doings, practices; practical matters 1641. **†2.** = PRACTICE 2 c. –1653. **3.** Legal usage; case-law; esp. in Scots Law 1533. **†4.** = PRACTICE 3. –1734. **†5.** Artful dealing, contrivance, cunning, policy; also with *a* and *pl.* –1693.

Practic (præ·ktik), *a.* (*sb.*²) *arch.* late ME. [– Fr. †*practique*, var. of *pratique*, or late L. *practicus* – Gr. πρακτικός, f. πράττειν do, act; see -IC. Superseded by PRACTICAL.] **1.** = PRACTICAL 1. 1551. **b.** Opp. to *theoretic, speculative, contemplative. arch.* or *Obs.* late ME. **†2.** = PRACTICAL *a.* 2, 4. –1642. **†3.** Experienced, practised –1639. **†4.** Artful, cunning –1590. **†B.** *sb.*² (absol. use of the adj.) A practical man, as opp. to a theorist; *spec.* a member of the Jewish sect of the Essenes who took part in the active affairs of life –1650.

1. b. The Art and Practique part of Life, Must be the Mistresse to this Theorique SHAKS.

Practicable (præ·ktikăb'l), *a.* 1670. [– Fr. *praticable*, f. *pratiquer* put into practice, use, f. *pratique*; see PRACTIC *sb.*¹, -ABLE.] **1.** Capable of being carried out in action; feasible. **2.** Capable of being used or traversed, as a road, ford, etc. 1710. **b.** *Theatr.* Said of windows, doors, etc., which are capable of actual use in the play. Also (*colloq.*) *ellipt.* as *sb.* 1838.

1. Ascended the glacier as far as p. 1860. **2.** The road to Cadiz is likewise very p. for ladies W. IRVING. Hence **Pra:cticabi·lity, Pra·cticableness,** the quality of being p. **Pra·cticably** *adv.*

Practical (præ·ktikăl), *a.* 1570. [f. PRACTIC *a.* + -AL¹ (see -ICAL).] **1.** Of, pertaining, or relating to practice; exhibited in practice or action. Opp. to *speculative, theoretical*, or *ideal.* 1617. **b.** Applicable in practice; practically useful 1642. **2.** Engaged in practice; practising, working 1604. **3.** Inclined to action (as opp. to speculation, etc.); also, having ability for action 1667. **4.** That is such in practice; that is such in effect, though not nominally or professedly so; virtual 1642. **†5.** Crafty, scheming, artful FOXE.

1. *P. agriculture, chemistry, logic,* etc. *P. joke*: see JOKE *sb.* 1; He said solemnly that he did not approve of p. jokes THACKERAY. **b.** A p. work for p. men 1858. P. politics is to do what you can, and not what you ought 1897. **2.** The p. iron men are much better judges than we theorists 1788. **3.** The p. man, who relies on his own experience 1875. **4.** In a word, if he was not a practicall Atheist, I know not who was FULLER. Hence **Practica·lity,** the quality of being p.; also, a p. matter or affair (chiefly in *pl.*). **Pra·cticalize** *v. trans. rare*, to render p. **Pra·ctical-ly** *adv.*, **-ness.**

Practice (præ·ktis). 1494. [Formerly *practyse, -ize*, f. PRACTISE, after *advice/advise, device/devise*; superseded PRACTIC *sb.*¹] The action, or an action, of practising, etc. **1.** The action *of* doing something; performance; working, operation; method of working. *Obs.* or merged in 2. 1553. **b.** An action, a deed; *pl.* doings. *Obs.* or merged in 2. 1565. **2.** The habitual doing or carrying on *of* something; customary or constant action; action as dist. from profession, theory, knowledge, etc.; conduct 1509. **b.** *Law.* The method of procedure used in the law-courts 1623. **c.** A habit, custom; (with *pl.*) a habitual action 1568. **3.** Exercise in any art, handicraft, etc., for the purpose of attaining proficiency 1525. **†4.** An exercise; a practical treatise –1712. **5.** *spec.* The exercise of a profession or occupation; the professional work or business of a lawyer or medical man 1576. **6.** The action of scheming, esp. (now only) in an underhand way and for an evil purpose; machination, treachery; artifice. *arch.* 1494. **b.** Dealings; *esp.* in evil sense, Conspiracy, intrigue, collusion (*with* a person, *between* persons). *arch.* 1540. **c.** (with *pl.*) A scheme, plot, intrigue, manœuvre, artifice 1539. **7.** The action, or an act, of practising *on* or *upon* a person, etc.: see PRACTISE 11. *rare.* 1614. **8.** *Arith.* A compendious method of performing multiplication by means of aliquot parts, in cases where one or both quantities are expressed in several denominations; e.g. in finding the value of so many articles at so many pounds, shillings, and pence each 1574.

1. *Much Ado.* V. i. 255. **2.** His P. of Religious Severities 1717. To stoop from speculation to p. MACAULAY. **c.** A man of free principles, shewn by practices as free RICHARDSON. **3.** Through practise made perfect 1553. A pleasant bit of mountain p. 1860. **5.** The mysteries of mingled medicines, and the practise of Physicke 1576. He sold this p. and removed into Dunchester 1898. **6.** The Practise of the Deuill 1560. He.. died a martyr's death, through the p. of the Lady Ælfthryth FREEMAN. **c.** Plots and practises of the popish faction 1645. **7.** Another piece of p. on the fears of the assembly 1759.

Phrases. *In practice.* **a.** In the realm of action; practically, as a fact. **b.** In the condition of being exercised so as to maintain skill or ability. **c.** Of a lawyer, doctor, etc.: Engaged in practising his profession. *To put in* (or *into*) *p.*, to exercise, carry out in action. *To make a p. of* (something), to do it habitually and of purpose.

Practician (prækti·ʃăn). 1500. [– Fr. †*practicien* (mod. *praticien*), f. *practique* (mod. *pratique*) + *-ien* -IAN. See PRACTIC *sb.*¹] One who practises any art, profession, or occupation; a practitioner; a practical man.

Practise (præ·ktis), *v.* late ME. [– OFr. *pra(c)tiser* or med.L. *practizare* (AL. *practizans* medical practitioner XII, *practizare in medicina* XIV), alt. of *practicare*, f. *practica* PRACTIC *sb.*¹ The change from the earlier stress *practi·se* to *pra·ctise* involved the change of final z to s.] **1.** *trans.* To perform, execute, carry on, exercise (any action or process). Now *rare*, or merged in 2. 1460. **†b.** To work out (a problem, etc.); to perform, act (a play) –1685. **c.** *intr.* To act, work, proceed, operate 1553. **2.** *trans.* To carry on, or do, habitually or constantly; to make a practice of; to carry out in action 1526. **b.** With *inf.* To be wont (*arch.*) 1674. **c.** *intr.* To act habitually 1681. **3.** *trans.* To exercise, pursue (an occupation, profession, or art) 1560. **b.** *spec. intr.* To exercise the profession of law or of medicine 1538. **†4.** *trans.* To put into practice, execute (a law, command, etc.) –1771. **5.** To exercise oneself in (any art, process, or act) for the purpose of attaining proficiency. Also with *obj. inf.* late ME. **b.** *absol.* or *intr.* To exercise oneself in the performance of music, etc. with the view of acquiring skill 1596. **6.** *trans.* To exercise (any one) *in* some action; to train, drill 1598. **b.** *pa. pple.* Experienced by practice; skilled, versed, proficient (*in*) 1542. **†7.** To put to practical use; to make use of, employ –1740. **†b.** To frequent, haunt [after Fr. *pratiquer*] –1718. **†8.** To bring about, compass, effect –1736. **†b.** To devise means to bring about (a result); to plan, intend (something to be done). With *simple obj.* or *obj. clause.* –1711. **9.** *intr.* To lay schemes or plans, esp. for an evil purpose; to scheme, plot, conspire, intrigue (*with* or *against* a person, *to do* something). Now *rare.* 1537. **†b.** *trans.* To plot, conspire (some evil) –1634. **10.** *intr.* To have dealings, to negotiate or treat *with* a person; *esp.* to deal *with* so as to gain over to some course of action. *Obs.* or *arch.* 1538. **†b.** *trans.* To influence (a person) by underhand dealings, win over, 'get at', corrupt –1715. **11.** *To p. upon*: To practise tricks or artifices upon; to act upon, by artifice, so as to induce to do or believe something; to impose upon, delude; to work upon (a person or his feelings, etc.) 1596. **†12.** To make trial of practically –1802.

1. To thinke, that you haue ought but Talbots shadow, Whereon to p. your seueritie SHAKS. **c.** Being little inclined to p. upon others, and as little that others should p. upon me TEMPLE. **2.** Practice as much of Religion as you Talk 1698. Phr. *To p. religion*, to perform the religious duties which the Church requires of its members; to be a practising and not merely a nominal member (esp. in *R.C.Ch.*); also *absol.* and *intr.* **c.** If he practises as well as he preaches, he must be a paragon 1907. **3.** They admit of no Trade, but p. Piracy 1727. **b.** A counsel practising at the bar 1883. **5.** Ere I learne loue, Ile p. to obey SHAKS. The young people..practised hymns 1863. **b.** She will never play really well unless she practises more JANE AUSTEN. **6.** The captain practises his company in all the phases of war 1888. **9.** Hee will p. against thee by poyson SHAKS. **11.** I..will so p. upon Benedicke, that.. hee shall fall in loue with Beatrice SHAKS.

Practised (præ·ktist), *ppl. a.* 1568. [f. prec. + -ED¹.] **1.** That has had practice; experienced, skilled. **2.** Put into practice; exercised 1590.

1. A companie of..p. souldiours 1568.

Practiser (præ·ktisəɹ). [ME. *practisour*, prob. – AFr. **practisour*, f. OFr. *practiser*; see PRACTISE *v.*, -OUR, -ER² 3.] One who exercises a profession or occupation; a practitioner. **b.** *gen.* One who practises any art, science, manner of life, course of action, etc.; one who carries out a theory, etc., in action 1540.

Practitioner (prækti·ʃənəɹ). 1544. [Extension with -ER¹ of †*practitian* PRACTICIAN; cf. dial. *musicianer*, †*physicianer.*] **1.** One engaged in the practice of any art, profession, or occupation; esp. in medicine, surgery, or law. **†2.** A learner, novice, beginner; a probationer –1801. **3.** One who practises anything; a habitual doer 1548.

1. *General p.*, one who practises both medicine and surgery; also opp. to *specialist* in either branch.

†Pra·ctive, *a.* (*sb.*) late ME. [f. stem *pract-* in PRACTIC + -IVE, after *active*, etc.] **1. a.** Devoted to practice or action –1610. **b.** Adept, skilful, dexterous –1594. **2.** Belonging to practice; practical –1658. **B.** *sb.* Practice; actual doing or working –1523.

Prad (præd). *slang.* 1798. [By metathesis from Du. *paard* horse.] A horse.
He's in the gig, a-minding the p. DICKENS.

Præ- in med.L. also PRE-, a L. prep. and adv., meaning 'before'. In Eng. the L. spelling is now usual only in words that are still regarded as Latin, as *præmunire*, or that belong to Roman antiquities, as *prætor*.

‖**Præcipe** (prī·sipi). 1500. [L., imper. of *præcipere* admonish, enjoin (see PRECEPT). The opening word of the writ, *præcipe quod reddat* enjoin (him) that he render.] *Law.* **1.** A writ requiring something to be done, or demanding a reason for its non-performance. **2.** A note containing particulars of a writ which must be filed with the officer of the Court from which the writ issues, by the party asking for the writ, or by his solicitor 1848.

Præcocial (prīkōᵘ·ʃ'ăl), *a.* 1872. [f. L. *præcoces* (pl. of *præcox* early mature; see PRECOCIOUS) + -AL¹.] *Ornith.* Of or pertaining to the *Præcoces*, applied to those birds whose young are able to leave the nest and to feed themselves as soon as they are hatched.

‖**Præcognitum** (prīkǫ·gnitŏm). *Pl.* **-a.** 1634. [L., pa. pple. n. of *præcognoscere* know beforehand, f. *præ* before + *cognoscere* know.] Something known beforehand; *esp.* something necessary to be known as a basis of reasoning, investigation, or study; a principle.

‖**Præcordia** (prikǭ·ɹdiă). 1681. [L. pl., midriff, diaphragm, entrails, f. *præ* before + *cor, cord-* heart.] *Anat.* The forepart of the thoracic region; the parts or region of the body about the heart.

Præcordial, etc.: see PRECORDIAL, etc.

‖**Præmunientes** (prīmiūniˌe·ntīz). 1700. [med.L., for L. *præmonentes*, pr. pple. pl. of *præmonēre*; see next.] *Law. P. clause*: the clause of the writ of Edw. I, 1295, in which the bishops and abbots summoned to parliament are ordered to summon representatives of the minor clergy to attend with them. So *p. writ.*

‖**Præmunire** (prīmiunəiᵊ·ri), *sb.* late ME. [L., fortify or protect in front, in med.L. (by assoc. with *præmonēre*; see PREMONITION) forewarn, admonish.] **1.** (More fully *p. facias.*) A writ by which the sheriff is charged to summon a person accused, orig., of prosecuting in a foreign court a suit cognizable by the law of England, and later, of asserting or maintaining papal jurisdiction in England; also, the statute of 16 Richard II (*Statute of P.*), on which this writ is based 1449. †**2.** *transf.* **a.** An offence against the statute of præmunire; also, any offence incurring the same penalties –1678. **b.** The penalties incurred by an offender against the statute of præmunire, which was subseq. applied to various offences not connected with its original purpose –1724. †**3.** A difficulty, predicament. (Often *joc.*) –1814.
3. If the law finds you with two wives at once, There's a shrewd premunire 1599. Hence **Præmunire** (-əiᵊ·ɹ) *v. trans.* to issue a writ of p. against; to convict of breach of the statute of p. *Obs.* exc. *Hist.*

‖**Prænomen** (prīnōᵘ·men). Also **pre-.** 1706. [L., a forename, f. *præ* before + *nomen* name.] *Rom. Antiq.* The first name, preceding the nomen and cognomen; the personal name, as Marcus in Marcus Tullius Cicero. Hence, the Christian name.

‖**Præpostor, pre-** (pripǫ·stǭɹ). 1768. [Syncopated f. *præpositor* PREPOSITOR.] In some English public schools, the term for those senior pupils elsewhere called prefects or monitors.

‖**Prætexta** (prite·kstă). Also **pre-.** 1601. [L., short for *toga prætexta* gown bordered in front; pa. pple. fem. of *prætexere* weave before.] *Rom. Antiq.* A long white robe with a purple border, worn orig. by the magistrates and some of the priests, but afterwards by the children of the higher classes, viz. by boys till they were entitled to assume the *toga virilis*, and by girls till marriage.

Prætor (prī·tǭɹ). late ME. Also (*U.S.*) **pretor.** [– Fr. *préteur* or L. *prætor*, dubiously analysed as **præitor* 'one who goes before', f. *præ* before + pa. ppl. stem of *ire* go + *-or* -OR 2.] Orig., The title of a Roman consul as leader of the army; later, that of an annually elected curule magistrate who performed some of the duties of the consuls. Of these magistrates there were at first one, later two (*p. urbanus, p. peregrinus*), and eventually eighteen. **b.** *transf.* One holding high civic office, as a mayor or chief magistrate 1494. Hence **Præto·rial, pre-**, *a.* of or pertaining to a Roman p.; prætorian. **Præ·torship, pre·torship,** the office, or term of office, of a Roman p.

Prætorian (pritōᵊ·riăn), *a.* and *sb.* late ME. Also (*U.S.*) **pre-.** [– L. *prætorianus*; see prec. and -IAN.] **A.** *adj.* **1.** Of, belonging or pertaining to a Roman prætor or to the office or rank of prætor 1598. **2.** Of or belonging to the bodyguard of a Roman military commander or of the emperor. late ME. **b.** Of or pertaining to the prætorian soldiers 1741. **c.** *fig.* Like the prætorian cohort in venality 1907.
2. Augustus set up the P. Guard of 10000 men 1651. **c.** The calling into existence of a Pretorian band of pauper labour through doles for the encouragement of the unemployed 1907.
B. *sb.* **1.** A man of prætorian rank; as an expraetor, etc. 1756. **2.** A soldier of the prætorian guard 1625. **b.** *fig.* One of a company whose function or interest is to defend an established power or system 1647. Hence **Præto·rianism,** military despotism, esp. when venal.

‖**Prætorium** (pritōᵊ·riŏm). 1600. Also (*U.S.*) **pre-.** [L., a general's tent, etc.; subst. use of n. of *prætorius* adj., belonging to a prætor.] **1.** The tent of the commanding general in a Roman camp; the space where this was placed. **2.** The palace or court of the governor of a Roman province 1611. **b.** By extension: The court or palace of an ancient king; also, a town-hall, etc. 1611. **3.** The quarters of the Prætorian Guard in Rome 1670.

Pragmatic (prægmæ·tik), *a.* and *sb.* 1587. [– late L. *pragmaticus* (in *pragmatica sanctio*, Codex Justiniani; earlier 'skilled in affairs', Cicero) – Gr. πραγματικός, f. πρᾶγμα, πραγματ- act, deed, affair, f. πρακ- of πράττειν do.] **A.** *adj.* **1.** Relating to the affairs of a state or community 1643. **2.** Busy, active; *esp.* officiously busy in other people's affairs; interfering, meddling 1616. **3.** Opinionated; dictatorial, dogmatic 1638. **4.** Treating the facts of history in their connection with each other as cause and effect, and with ref. to their practical lessons. [= G. *pragmatisch.*] 1853. **5.** = PRAGMATICAL *a.* 2. 1853. **6.** Belonging or relating to philosophical pragmatism 1902.
1. *P. sanction*, 'an imperial decree relating to the affairs of a community', the technical name given to some imperial and royal ordinances issued as fundamental laws: applied esp. to the edict of Charles VII of France in 1438, which was the basis of the liberties of the Gallican Church; and to the ordinance of the emperor Charles VI, in 1724, settling the succession to the Austrian throne. **2.** Common estimation puts an ill character upon p. medling people 1674. **3.** She is as p. and proud as the Pope 1771. **5.** A strict and p. people, like the mass of the Scotch 1853.
B. *sb.* **1.** = *p. sanction*; see A. 1. 1587. †**2.** One versed in business; an agent –1625. **3.** An officious or meddlesome person; a conceited person 1645.

Pragmatical (prægmæ·tikăl), *a.* 1543. [f. as PRAGMATIC + -AL¹; see -ICAL.] **1.** = PRAGMATIC *a.* 1. Now *rare.* **2.** Of, pertaining to, or dealing with practice; practical. *Obs.* exc. as used after G. *pragmatisch.* 1597. †**3.** Actively engaged; active, busy; methodical; energetic –1661. **b.** Experienced in affairs; expert; shrewd. Now *rare.* 1656. **4.** = PRAGMATIC *a.* 2. Now *rare.* 1611. **b.** Self-important; opinionated, dogmatic; doctrinaire; crotchety 1704. **5.** = PRAGMATIC *a.* 6. 1903.
2. The practical or p. form of Christianity associated with the name of James 1906. **4.** A wise man is not p., for he declines the doing of any thing that is beyond his office 1656. **b.** Which..may perhaps give me the title of p. and overweening SWIFT. Hence **Pragma·tical-ly** *adv.*, **-ness.**

Pragmatism (præ·gmătiz'm). 1863. [f. Gr. πρᾶγμα, πραγματ- deed, act + -ISM. Cf. G. *pragmatismus.*] **1.** Officiousness; pedantry; an instance of this. **2.** Matter-of-fact treatment of things 1872. †**3.** A method of treating history in which the phenomena are considered with special ref. to their causes, antecedent conditions, and results, and to their practical lessons –1884. **4.** *Philos.* The doctrine that the whole meaning of a conception expresses itself in practical consequences 1898.
3. I have drawn attention..to the prophetic p. of Matthew 1865. So **Pra·gmatist**, a pragmatical person; an adherent of the doctrine called p.

Pragmatize (præ·gmătəiz), *v.* 1831. [f. as prec. + -IZE.] *trans.* To represent (what is imaginary or subjective) as real or actual; to materialize or rationalize (a myth). Hence **Pra·gmatizer.**

Prairie (prēᵊ·ri). 1773. [– Fr. *prairie*, OFr. *praerie* :– Rom. **pratari·a*, f. L. *pratum* meadow; see -RY.] A tract of level or undulating grass-land, without trees, and usu. of great extent; applied chiefly to the grassy plains of North America.
The P., or meadow ground on the eastern side, is at least twenty miles wide 1773.
attrib. and *Comb.*: **p.-chicken,** the Pinnated Grouse, *Cupidonia* or *Tympanuchus cupido*, a gallinaceous bird of N. America; **-dog,** a N. Amer. rodent animal, genus *Cynomys*, of the squirrel family; *spec. C. ludovicianus*, the Louisiana Marmot, having a cry like the bark of a dog; **-grouse** = *p.-chicken*; **-hawk,** the American Sparrow-hawk, *Tinnunculus* or *Falco sparverius*; **-hen** = *p.-chicken*; **-marmot** = *p.-dog*; **-mole,** a silvery mole, *Scalops argentatus*, found on the western prairies; **p. rattler** or **rattlesnake,** one of various rattlesnakes of the prairies, as *Sistrurus catenatus*, or *Crotalus confluentus*; **-rent:** see *p. value*; **-squirrel,** a N. Amer. ground-squirrel of the genus *Spermophilus*, inhabiting the prairies; **P. State,** the state of Illinois, U.S.; in pl. more general, including Wisconsin, Iowa, Minnesota, and States to the south of these; **-turnip,** a hairy herbaceous plant (*Psoralea esculenta*) of N. W. America, or its edible farinaceous tuber; **p. value** *Pol. Econ.*, the rental value of p. land, or of any waste land; **-warbler,** a small warbler, *Dendrœca discolor*, of eastern N. America; **-wolf** = COYOTE.

Praisable (prēⁱ·zăb'l), *a.* Now *rare.* ME. [f. PRAISE *v.* + -ABLE.] Praiseworthy, laudable. Hence **Prai·sableness. Prai·sably** *adv.*

Praise (prēⁱz), *sb.* late ME. [f. next. Not common till after 1500; superseding LOSE *sb.*, PRICE *sb.* III. 2.] **1.** The action or fact of praising; commendation of the worth or excellence of a person or thing; eulogy. **b.** The fact or condition of being praised 1533. **2.** The expression of admiration and ascribing of glory, as an act of worship; hence, worship by song. late ME. **3.** *transf.* The ground of praise; praiseworthiness; merit, virtue. *arch.* 1526. †**b.** An object of praise –1787.
1. For they loved the prayse that is geven off men, more then the prayse, that commeth of god TINDALE *John* 12:43. **b.** The p. of politeness and vivacity could now scarcely be obtained except by some violation of decorum MACAULAY. **2.** The pealing anthem swells the note of p. GRAY. **3.** A restless crowd,..Whose highest p. is that they live in vain COWPER. **b.** He is thy prayse, & thy God COVERDALE *Deut.* 10:21. Hence **Prai·seless** *a.* without p. or honour; undeserving of p.

Praise (prēⁱz), *v.* ME. [– OFr. *preisier* price, value, prize, praise :– late L. *pretiare*, f. L. *pretium* PRICE; cf. PRIZE *v.*¹] **I. 1.** *trans.* To set a price or value upon; to value, appraise. *Obs.* or *dial.* †**2.** To value, esteem; to PRIZE –1567.
2. They preysed nothing the thinges that were erthely CAXTON.
II. 1. To commend the worth, excellence, or merits of; to express warm approbation of; to laud, extol. (The leading current sense.) ME. **2.** To extol the glorious attributes of (God, or a deity), esp., to sing the praises of; to glorify, magnify, laud ME.
1. They extolled and praysed him farre above the Starres 1513. P. the sea, but keep on land G. HERBERT. **2.** Let the people prayse the (o God) let all people prayse the COVERDALE *Ps.* 67:5.

Praiseful (prēⁱ·zfŭl), *a.* late ME. [f.

PRAISE *v.* or *sb.* + -FUL.] †**1.** Praiseworthy –1818. **2.** Eulogistic, laudatory 1613. Hence **Prai·seful-ly** *adv.*, **-ness.**

Praiser (prēⁱ·zəɹ). late ME. [f. PRAISE *v.* + -ER¹.] †**1.** One who appraises; a valuer –1707. **2.** One who praises, commends, or extols. late ME.

2. The sweete wordes of flaterynge preiseres CHAUCER.

Praiseworthy (prēⁱ·z,wɒ̄:ɹði), *a.* 1538. [f. PRAISE *sb.* + WORTHY *a.*] Worthy of praise; laudable, commendable.

That right good and praise-worthy man 1610. Hence **Prai·sewo:rthily** *adv.* **Prai·sewo:rthiness.**

Prakrit (prā·krit). 1786. [– Skr. *prākṛta* natural, unrefined, vulgar; opp. to *saṃskṛta* prepared, refined, polished (SANSKRIT).] A general name for those popular langs. or dialects of Northern and Central India which existed alongside of or grew out of Sanskrit. Hence **Prakri·tic** *a.*

Praline (prā·līn), **prawlin** (prǭ·lin). Chiefly *U.S.* 1727. [– Fr. *praline*, f. name of Marshal de Plessis-*Praslin* (1598–1675), whose cook invented the confection.] Almonds or nuts browned in boiling sugar; also *transf.*

‖**Pram**¹, **praam** (prām). 1548. [– MDu. *prame*, *praem* (Du. *praam*), MLG. *prām(e* (whence also G. *prahm*) = OFris. *prām*; – OSl. *pramŭ*.] A flat-bottomed boat or lighter, used esp. in the Baltic or the Netherlands for shipping cargo, etc.

Pram² (præm). *colloq.* 1884. [See sense 1.] **1.** Abbrev. of PERAMBULATOR 3. **2.** A milkman's hand-cart; also *attrib.* as *p.-round* 1897.

Pramnian (præ·mniăn), *a.* 1601. [f. L. *Pramnium* (*vinum*), Gr. Πράμνιος (οἶνος) + -AN.] *Gr.* and *Rom. Antiq.* In *P. wine*, a wine from the neighbourhood of Smyrna.

‖**Prana** (prā·na). 1913. [Skr. = breath of life.] *Theosophy.* The life-principle. Hence **Pra·nic** *a.*

Prance (prɑns), *sb.* 1751. [f. next.] The act of prancing; a prancing movement or walk.

Prance (prɑns), *v.* late ME. [Of unkn. origin.] **1.** *intr.* Of a horse: 'To spring and bound in high mettle' (J.); to rise by springing from the hind legs; to move by a succession of such springs. **b.** *trans.* To cause (a horse) to prance 1530. **2.** *intr.* To ride (or drive) with the horse prancing; to ride ostentatiously; to ride gaily, proudly, or insolently. late ME. **3.** To move or walk in a manner suggestive of a prancing horse, or (more gen.) an elated or arrogant manner; to swagger. late ME.

1. I have a little white favourite [horse]..he prances under me with so much fire 1717. **2.** His Majesty prancing in person at the head of them all THACKERAY. **3.** Rawdon..pranced off to engage lodgings THACKERAY. Hence **Pra·ncer,** one who or that which prances; *esp.* a mettled or prancing horse; *slang*, a cavalry officer.

Prandial (præ·ndiăl), *a. affected* or *joc.* 1820. [f. L. *prandium* late breakfast + -AL¹.] Pertaining or relating to dinner. Hence **Pra·ndially** *adv.* in connection with dinner.

Prank (præŋk), *sb.* 1525. [Of unkn. origin.] A trick, a frolic. †**a.** In early use, a trick of malicious or mischievous nature; sometimes rendering L. *scelus* or *facinus* –1737. †**b.** A trick of magic, conjuring, or the like –1840. **c.** A mad frolic, a practical joke 1576. **d.** Said of capricious or frolicsome movements of animals, and of erratic actions of machines 1692.

a. Infamous..for many lewd pranks (as that he killed his brother, and then his owne sister) 1654. **b.** Like those priests of Bel, whose pranks Daniel found out MILT. **c.** The pranks..of healthy schoolboys 1884. Hence **Pra·nkish** *a.* of the nature of a p.; inclined to pranks. **Pra·nksome** *a.* addicted to pranks; frolicsome.

Prank, *v.*¹ *Obs.* or *dial.* 1519. [Of unkn. origin.] *intr.* = PRANCE *v.* (in various senses); to caper; to dance.

Prank (præŋk), *v.*² 1546. [rel. to MLG. *prank* pomp, display, Du. *pronk* show, finery, G. *prunk* pomp, ostentation; cf. Du. *pronken*, G. *prunken* show off, display.] **1.** *trans.* To dress or deck in a gay, bright, or showy manner; *refl.* to deck oneself *out*, dress oneself *up*. **b.** *fig.* To dress up 1607. **c.** *transf.* To dress, adorn; to set out with colours; to spangle 1591. **2.** *intr.* (for *refl.*) To show oneself off, make display. Also *to p. it.* 1567.

1. She..spends halfe a day in pranking her selfe if she be inuited to any strange place 1592. **c.** Broad flag-flowers, purple prankt with white SHELLEY. **2.** White houses p. where once were huts M. ARNOLD.

Prase (prēⁱz). late ME. [– Fr. *prase* – L. *prasius* sb. – Gr. πράσιος adj. leek-green, f. πράσον leek.] *Min.* A cryptocrystalline or crystalline variety of translucent quartz, of a leek-green colour.

Praseolite (prēⁱ·ziŏləit). 1864. [– Sw. *praseolith* (Erdmann, 1840), irreg. f. Gr. πράσον or πράσιος (see prec.) + -LITE.] *Min.* A form of iolite.

Prasine (prēⁱ·zin), *sb.* and *a.* ME. [– med. L. *prasina* green chalk (Isidore), green gem – L. *prasinus* adj. (Pliny) – Gr. πράσινος leek-green. Cf. Fr. †*prasine* adj.; as sb. green earth.] **A.** *sb.* A green-coloured mineral; now a synonym of pseudo-malachite. **B.** *adj.* Leek-like; leek-green in colour. *rare.* 1528.

Praso-, repr. Gr. πράσον leek; as in **Praso·phagous** [Gr. -φαγος] *a.*, eating leeks.

Prate (prēⁱt), *sb.* 1569. [f. next. Cf. MDu. *praet*, Du., LG. *praat.*] The act or action of prating; talk; now *esp.* idle talk; chatter.

Prate (prēⁱt), *v.* late ME. [– (M)LG., (M)Du. *praten*, prob. of imit. origin. Cf. PRATTLE *v.*] **1.** *intr.* To talk, to chatter: usu. dyslogistic, implying speaking much or long to little purpose; to tell tales, blab. **2.** *trans.* To utter or tell in a prating manner; to repeat to little purpose 1489.

1. Sober wretches, who p. whole evenings over coffee 1713. **2.** What Nonsense wou'd the Fool thy Master p. DRYDEN. **Pra·ter,** one who prates; a chatterer; formerly also, a boaster, an evil-speaker.

Pratincole (præ·tiŋkoᵘl). 1773. [– mod. L. *pratincola* (Kramer, 1756), f. L. *pratum* meadow + *incola* inhabitant.] *Ornith.* One of several species of the genus *Glareola*, grallatorial (limicoline) birds allied to the plovers.

‖**Pratique** (præ·tik, ‖pratīk). 1609. [– (O)Fr. *pratique* practice, intercourse, corresp. to or – It. *pratica* – med.L. *practica*, subst. use (sc. *ars* art) of *practicus* PRACTIC *a.*] Permission or licence granted to a ship to hold intercourse with a port after quarantine, or on showing a clean bill of health. Used esp. in connection with the south of Europe.

attrib. **p. boat, house,** the boat, house, of the quarantine officer.

Prattle (præ·t'l), *sb.* 1555. [f. next.] The act or action of prattling; that which is prattled; idle or childish chatter, small talk.

Let him..keep his babble and p. to himselfe 1600.

Prattle (præ·t'l), *v.* 1532. [– MLG. *pratelen*, f. *praten* PRATE *v.*; see -LE 3.] **1.** *intr.* To chatter in a childish or artless fashion; to be loquacious about trifles; formerly equivalent to PRATE; now chiefly said, without contempt, of the talk of young children. Also *transf.* and *fig.* **2.** *trans.* To utter in an idle, garrulous, or (now usu.) childish way 1560.

1. He had the Mastery of his Parents ever since he could P. 1692. The light leaves prattled to neighbour ears MEREDITH. **2.** Ambling and prattling scandal as he goes COWPER. **Prattlement** (præ·t'lmĕnt), idle talk, prattle, prattling. *rare.* **Pra·ttler,** one who prattles; now *esp.* a prattling child.

Pravity (præ·vĭti). 1550. [– L. *pravitas*, f. *pravus* crooked, perverse; see -ITY. Superseded by DEPRAVITY.] **1.** Moral perversion or corruption; depravity. Now *rare* or *Obs.* **2.** *gen.* Corrupt or evil quality 1620.

1. The natural p. of man 1847. **2.** Scarcity or p. of food 1822.

Prawn (prǭn), *sb.* [XV *prayne, prane*, of unkn. origin.] A small long-tailed decapod marine crustacean (*Palæmon serratus*), larger than a shrimp, common off the coasts of Britain, and used as food.

Praxinoscope (præ·ksino,skōᵘp). 1882. [– Fr. *praxinoscope*, irreg. f. Gr. πρᾶξις action + -SCOPE.] A scientific toy resembling the zoetrope, in which the reflexions of a series of pictures produce the impression of an actually moving object.

‖**Praxis** (præ·ksis). 1581. [– med.L. *praxis* – Gr. πρᾶξις doing, action.] **1.** Action, practice; *esp.* accepted practice, custom. **2.** An example or collection of examples to serve for practice in a subject, esp. in grammar 1612. †**b.** A means or instrument of practice in a subject; a practical specimen or model –1800.

1. For as Aristotle sayth, it is not *Gnosis*, but *P.* must be the fruit SIDNEY.

Pray (prēⁱ), *v.* [ME. *preie* – OFr. *preier* (mod. *prier*) :– late L. *precare*, for L. *precari* entreat.] **I.** *trans.* with personal obj. **1.** To ask earnestly, humbly, or supplicatingly, to beseech; *esp.* in religious use, to make devout and humble supplication to (God, or an object of worship). *arch.* †**2.** To entreat (a person) to come to a feast, or the like; to invite –1603.

1. I will p. the Father, and hee shall giue you another Comforter *John* 14:16. I p. God your friends..stick as well to you 1613. Praying their Lordships to relieve him from the expenses..of a lawsuit NELSON.

II. With the thing asked as object. To ask (something) earnestly in prayer; to ask or beg (a thing) with supplication; to crave. late ME.

They were inforced to p. his aid 1594. He p. a thousand praiers for thy death SHAKS. [They] prayed to be exempted from the operation of the law 1844.

III. *intr.* To make earnest request or petition; *esp.* to present petitions to God, or to an object of worship ME. **b.** In the formal ending of a petition to the Sovereign, to Parliament, a petition in Chancery, etc. The words after 'pray' were at length reduced to 'etc.', which is now usu. omitted. late ME.

How I perswaded, how I praid, and kneel'd SHAKS. That will duly and truly prea for yee 1641. Shall we believe a God, and not p. to him for future benefits? 1732. **b.** The familiar expression 'and your petitioner[s] shall ever p., &c.'..came in about the middle of the fifteenth century 1896.

Phrases, etc. *To p. in aid*, to crave the assistance *of* some one. †*I p. you* (*thee*), used parenthetically to add instance or deference to a question or request; so *p. you*, *p. thee*, etc.; also contracted to *pray*.

Pray, -e, obs. ff. PREY.

Prayer¹ (prēᵊɹ). [ME. *preiere* – OFr. *preiere* (mod. *prière*) :– Gallo-Rom. **precaria*, subst. use of fem. of L. *precarius* obtained by entreaty.] **1.** A solemn and humble request to God, or to an object of worship; a supplication, petition, or thanksgiving, usu. expressed in words. **b.** The action or practice of praying to the Divine Being ME. **c.** *pl.* Petitions to God for His blessing upon some one; hence, earnest good wishes 1597. **2.** A formula used in praying; e.g. *the Lord's P.* (LORD *sb.* I. 7). late ME. **3.** A religious observance, public or private, of which prayer to God forms a principal part; in *pl.* with possessive, one's private devotions ME. **4.** An entreaty made to a person ME. **5.** The thing prayed for or entreated; *spec.* that part of a memorial or petition that specifies this. late ME.

1. And so would I..make my speciall prayour to God 1529. **b.** More things are wrought by p. Than this world dreams of TENNYSON. **c.** He..shall haue my Prayers While I shall haue my life SHAKS. **3.** The Assassinates found him at his prayers 1678. Phr. *Morning* or *Evening P.*, *family prayers*. **4.** I held it in spite of..her prayers, and, at last, her tears 1858. **5.** His p. was granted by the Deity HOBBES.

Comb.: **p.-carpet, -mat, -rug,** a small carpet, mat, or rug used, esp. by a Moslem, when engaged in p.; **-meeting,** a religious meeting for devotion, in which several of those present offer p.; **-tower,** a minaret; **-wheel,** a cylindrical box inscribed with or containing prayers, revolving on a spindle: used esp. by the Buddhists of Tibet.

Prayer² (prēⁱ·əɹ). Also **pray-er.** 1440. [f. PRAY *v.* + -ER¹.] One who prays.

Pray·er-book. 1595. A book of forms of prayer; *spec.* the Book of Common Prayer, containing the public liturgy of the Church of England.

Prayerful (prēᵊ·ɹfŭl), *a.* 1626. [f. PRAYER¹ + -FUL.] **1.** Much given to prayer; devout.

2. Characterized by or expressive of prayer 1652.

2. With p. earnest eyes 1871. Hence **Pray·erfully** *adv.*, **-ness.**

Pray·erless, *a.* 1631. [f. PRAYER[1] + -LESS.] Without prayer; not having the habit of prayer. **b.** *transf.* (Of times, places, states, etc.) 1816.

Untaught, ungoverned p. families 1653. **b.** Scarce a lamp Burnt on the p. shrines 1826. Hence **Pray·erless-ly** *adv.*, **-ness.**

Pray·ing, *vbl. sb.* ME. [f. PRAY *v.* + -ING[1].] The action of PRAY *v.*; prayer, earnest request.

attrib. and *Comb.* = Used for or in prayer, as **p.-carpet, -mat, -rug** = PRAYER-*carpet*; **-cylinder, -drum, -jenny, -machine, -wheel** = PRAYER-*wheel.*

Pray·ing, *ppl. a.* 1483. [-ING[2].] That prays.

p.-insect, the MANTIS (*p. mantis*, or *p. locust*). Hence **Pray·ingly** *adv.* in a p. manner.

Pre- (prī, pri, prĭ) *prefix*, repr. L. *præ* adv. and prep. (of place, rank, and time) before, in front, in advance. In Eng. sometimes written *præ-* after the Revival of Learning, but now regularly *pre-*. See PRÆ-.

In English many Latin verbs and their derivs. in *præ-* have their representatives in *pre-*, which is also sometimes prefixed to words of English or modern origin, as *pre-embody, pre-plot*, etc. The prepositional construction has in English become the second great living use, *pre-* being preferred to *ante-* as the opposite of *post-* in new formations, and often substituted for it, as in *pre-Christian, prehistoric*, etc.

Nonce-words and casual compounds of English formation in *pre-* are usu. hyphened; other compounds, as *precaution, predestination*, are regularly written *indivisim*, except where the hyphen adds clearness, or emphasizes the function of the prefix.

A. Combinations in which *pre-* is adverbial or adjectival.

I. Of time or order of succession. **1.** With vbs., or ppl. adjs. and vbl. sbs. derived from them, in sense 'fore-, before, beforehand, previously, in advance', as *pre-acquaint, -admonish, -act, -cogitate, -condemn, -conform, -elect, -intimate, -limit, -warn*, etc., and in many others of obvious meaning. **2.** With a sb., this being usu. a deriv. from a vb. to which *pre-* is in adverbial relation: = Existing or taking place previously, placed before (something else), previous, preceding, earlier; as *pre-accusation, -adjustment, -connection, -condition*, etc. Also with other sbs.: **Preanti·quity,** previous antiquity; **Pre-bo·ding,** foreboding; **Pre-de·stiny,** preappointed destiny or fate; **Pre-ete·rnity,** previous eternity, eternal previous existence; **Pre-name,** a forename, 'Christian' name. **3.** With an adj.: as *precognizant, pre-essential*, etc.

II. Of local position. (Chiefly *Anat.*) Usu. without hyphen. **a.** In adverbial relation to an adj.: = Before, anteriorly, in front; as **Prede·ntate,** having teeth in the fore part of the upper jaw only, as some cetaceans. Also in adjs. = 'anterior', as **Pre:cerebe·llar** = anterior cerebellar (artery), etc. **b.** In quasi-adjectival relation to a sb.: = 'Situated in front, anterior, fore-', with derivative adjs.; as **Pre-abdo·men,** Latreille's name for the first five segments of the abdomen of Crustacea; etc. **c.** In advb. relation to a vb.; in compounds formed in L., as PRECLUDE, PREFIX.

III. Of order, rank, importance, quality, degree. In sense 'before in order or importance, above, in preference to, superior to, more than, beyond'; as in PRECEDE *v.*, PREDOMINATE *v.*, PREPONDERATE *v.*, etc.

B. Combinations in which *pre-* is prepositional, having as its object the sb. forming, or implied in, the second element.

I. Relating to time or order of succession; in which *pre-* = before; anterior, prior, or previous to; preceding, earlier than. These are properly hyphened. **1.** With adjs. (and their derivative advs. and sbs.), or f. *pre-* + a (Lat.) sb. + adjectival ending, as *pre-reformational*; forming adjs., with derivative advs. and sbs. **a.** Formed on proper nouns (or their adjs.), esp. on names of persons, races, nations, dynasties, and religions, as *pre-Alfredian, -Darwinian, -Messianic; pre-Aryan, -Hellenic, -Islamic, -ite, -Norman*; etc. **b.** In names of geological formations and of prehistoric periods, as *pre-Cambrian* (earlier than the Cambrian); *pre-metallic* (before the knowledge of metals); etc. **c.** In pathological terms, as *pre-albuminuric* (previous to the appearance of albuminuria); so *pre-phthisical*, etc. **d.** Formed on other adjs. (or the L. or other sbs. to which these belong); as *pre-anæsthetic* (before the use of anæsthetics), *pre-artistic* (before the cultivation of art), *-classical, -critical, -lingual, -monarchical, -prophetic, -telegraphic*, etc. **2.** With sbs. or phrases (adj. + sb.) forming *quasi*-adjs., or attrib. phrases of obvious meaning; as *pre-advertisement, -advertising* (belonging to the days before advertising was usual), *-civilization, -Conquest, -marriage, -Mutiny, -war* (e.g. before World War I or II), etc. **b.** with personal names, meaning 'before the time or public work of'; as *pre-Chamberlain, pre-Conqueror, pre-Jenner*, etc.

II. Denoting local position; in which *pre-* = before, in front of, anterior to. These are usu. written without the hyphen. In adjs. (also sometimes used as sbs.), chiefly *Anat.* and *Zool.*, denoting parts or organs situated in front of (or, rarely, in the front part of) other parts or organs; as *pre-aortic, prebronchial*, PREOCULAR, *pre-oral*, etc.

Preace, obs. by-form of PRESS *sb.*[1] and *v.*[1]

Preach (prītʃ), *v.* [ME. *preche* – OFr. *prechier* (mod. *prêcher*), earlier *preëchier* :– L. *prædicare* proclaim, eccl. L. preach.] **1.** *intr.* 'To pronounce a public discourse upon sacred subjects' (J.); to deliver a sermon or religious address. **b.** To utter an earnest exhortation, esp. moral or religious. Now usu. dyslogistic: To give moral or religious advice in an obtrusive or tiresome way. 1523. **2.** *trans.* To proclaim by public discourse (the gospel, something sacred or religious). Also with *obj. cl.* ME. **b.** To set forth or teach (anything) in the way of exhortation; to advocate by discourse or writing; to exhort people to (some act or practice). Also with *obj. cl.* ME. **3.** To utter or speak publicly, deliver (a sermon, a religious or moral discourse). late ME. †**4.** To preach to; to exhort –1709. **5.** To affect in some way by preaching 1609.

1. On Sunday morneing I went to hear on Bayly of Maudlins p. 1674. **b.** Why do you p. to me in that manner? 1875. **2.** Y[e] Lorde hath anoynted me, and sent me, to p. good tydinges vnto the poore COVERDALE *Isa.* 61:1. **b.** My M[r] preaches patience to him SHAKS. *P. up*, to extol by preaching; to discourse in praise of. *P. down*, to decry, oppose, or put down by preaching. **5.** We had a Preacher that would p. folke asleepe still B. JONS.

Hence **Preach** *sb.* (*colloq.*) an act of preaching; preachment. **Prea·chable** *a.* capable of being preached, or preached about or from. **Prea·chy** *a.* (*colloq.*) given to preaching; characterized by a preaching style.

Preacher (prī·tʃəɹ). [ME. *prech(o)ur, precheour* – AFr. *prech(o)ur*, OFr. *prech(e)or*:– eccl. L. *prædicator* preacher, f. *prædicare* PREACH; see -OUR, -ER[2] 3.] One who preaches. **1.** One who proclaims religious doctrine by public discourse; *esp.* a minister of religion; *spec.* one licensed to preach. **b.** One who exhorts earnestly; one who inculcates something by speech or writing. late ME. **c.** With *of*: One who preaches (something specified). late ME. **2.** *spec.* A name for Solomon as supposed speaker in the Book of Ecclesiastes; hence, that book itself 1535.

1. To church, and there being a lazy p. I slept out the sermon PEPYS. *Friars Preachers*: see FRIAR 2. **b.** No p. is listened to but Time SWIFT. **c.** A perpetual p. of his own virtues MILT. **2.** All is but vanite, saicth y[e] p. COVERDALE *Eccles.* 1:2. Hence **Prea·chership,** the office of a p.

Preachify (prī·tʃifəi), *v. colloq.* 1775. [f. PREACH + -FY; cf. *speechify*.] *intr.* To preach in a factitious or tedious way; to make a preachment. Often merely contempt. for *preach.*

Preaching (prī·tʃiŋ), *vbl. sb.* ME. [f. PREACH + -ING[1].] **1.** The action of PREACH *v.* **2.** With *a* and *pl.* The delivering of a sermon, that which is preached, a sermon or discourse 1449.

attrib. and *Comb.*, as **p.-cross,** a kind of cross formerly erected on a highway or in an open place, at which monks and others used to preach.

Prea·ching, *ppl. a.* 1583. [f. PREACH + -ING[2].] That preaches.

P. friar (spec.) a Dominican.

Prea·ching-house. 1760. [f. PREACHING *vbl. sb.* + HOUSE *sb.*] A house devoted to preaching; *spec.* Wesley's name for a Methodist place of worship.

Preachment (prī·tʃmĕnt). ME. [– OFr. *prechement* :– med.L. *predicamentum* preaching, sermon, in late L. that which is predicated; see PREDICAMENT.] **1.** The action or fact of preaching; delivery of a sermon or exhortation, now esp. of a tedious character. **2.** A sermon or hortatory discourse: usu. *contemptuous.* late ME.

Pre-adamite (prī,æ·dăməit), *sb.* and *a.* Also unhyphened, and with capital A. 1662. [– mod.L. *præadamita*; see PRE- B. I. 1 a, ADAM, -ITE[1].] **A.** *sb.* **1.** One who lived (or one of a race held to have existed) before the time of Adam. †**2.** A believer in the existence of men before Adam –1774. **B.** *adj.* **1.** That existed before Adam; prehuman 1786. **2.** Relating to the time, or to a race, previous to Adam; belonging to the Pre-adamites (sense A. 1) 1882.

Hence **Pre-adami·tic, -al** *adjs.* = B. 1. So **Pre-ada·mic** *a.*

Pre,admi·ssion. 1887. [PRE- A. I. 2.] Admission beforehand; *spec.* the admission of a certain amount of steam into the cylinder of a steam-engine before the end of the back stroke.

Preamble (prī·æmb'l, pri,æ·mb'l), *sb.* late ME. [– (O)Fr. *préambule* – med.L. *præambulum* preamble, subst. use of n. sing. of late L. *præambulus* going before, in med.L. preliminary; see PRE- A. I. 1, AMBLE *v.*] **1.** A preliminary statement, in speech or writing; a preface, prologue, introduction. **b.** *spec.* An introductory paragraph or part in a statute, deed, etc., setting forth the grounds and intention of it 1628. **c.** A (musical) prelude (*poet.*) 1667. **2.** *gen.* An introductory fact; a preliminary; *esp.* a presage, prognostic 1548.

1. c. With Præamble sweet Of charming symphonie they introduce Thir sacred Song MILT. **2.** This was the p. of the great troubles that after followed 1663.

Preamble (pri,æ·mb'l), *v.* 1621. [f. prec.] **a.** *trans.* To state by way of preamble. Also, to make a preamble to. **b.** *intr.* To make a preamble or introductory statement 1641.

Preambular (pri,æ·mbiŭlăɹ), *a. rare.* 1645. [f. med.L. *præambulum*; see PREAMBLE *sb.*, -AR[1].] Preambulatory. So **Prea·mbulary** *a.*

Preambulate (pri,æ·mbiŭle[i]t), *v. rare.* 1608. [In sense 1 – *præambulat-*, pa. ppl. stem of late L. *præambulare*; in sense 2 f. med.L. *præambulum*; see PREAMBLE *sb.*, -ATE[3].] †**1.** *intr.* To walk or go before or in front –1660. **2.** = PREAMBLE *v.* b. 1608. So **Preambula·tion,** the making of a preamble. late ME. **Preambulatory** (pri,æ·mbiŭlătəri) *a.* having the character of a preamble; prefatory, preliminary 1608.

Preapprehension (prī:æprĭhe·nʃən). 1633. [PRE- A. I. 2.] **1.** A conception formed beforehand; a preconceived idea 1646. **2.** A preconceived fear of what may happen; foreboding 1633.

Prearrange (prī,ărē[i]·ndʒ), *v.* 1851. [PRE- A. I. 1.] *trans.* To arrange beforehand. Hence **Pre,arra·ngement,** previous arrangement.

Preassurance (prī,ăʃū[ə]·răns). 1635. [PRE- A. I. 2.] **1.** An assurance given or received beforehand. **2.** A previous feeling of certainty in one's own mind; an assured presentiment 1671. So **Preassu·re** *v. trans.* to assure or make certain beforehand.

Preaudience (prī,ǭ·diĕns). 1768. [PRE- A. I. 2.] The right to be heard before another; precedence or relative rank (of lawyers at the Bar).

Pre-a·xial, *a.* 1872. [f. PRE- B. II. + AXIS + -AL[1].] *Anat.* Situated in front of the axis of the body or of a limb. Hence **Pre-a·xially** *adv.*

Prebend (pre·bĕnd). late ME. [– (O)Fr. *prébende* – late L. *præbenda* pension, pittance, church living, lit. 'things to be supplied', n. pl. of gerundive of L. *præbēre*, f. *præ* forth, PRE- + *habēre* hold.] **1.** The portion of the revenues of a cathedral or collegiate church granted to a canon or member of the chapter as his stipend. **2.** The separate portion of land or tithe from which the stipend is gathered (hence known as the *corps of the p.*); the tenure of this as a benefice. late ME. **3.** = PREBENDARY 1. 1556.

Prebendal (prĭbe·ndăl), *a.* 1751. [– med. L. *præbendalis*, f. *præbenda* PREBEND; see -AL[1].] Of or pertaining to a prebend or prebendary.

Prebendary (pre·bĕndări), *sb.* (*a.*) late ME. [– med.L. *præbendarius*, f. *præbenda*;

see PREBEND and -ARY¹.] **1.** The holder of a prebend; a canon of a cathedral or collegiate church who holds a prebend. †**2.** The office of a prebendary; a prebend –1725. **3.** *attrib.* or *adj.* = PREBENDAL 1731. **Pre·bendaryship,** the office or benefice of a p.; a prebend.

Precalculate (prīkæ·lkiŭleit), *v.* 1841. [PRE- A. I. 1.] *trans.* To calculate or reckon beforehand. **Preca·lculable** *a.* **Precalcula·tion.**

Preca·ncel, *v.* 1905. [PRE- A. I. 1.] (orig. and esp. in U.S.) To cancel (postage stamps) in advance of use, usu. with the name of the city (and state), for business firms, etc. sending postal matter in bulk. So **Preca·ncel** *sb.* **Precancella·tion.**

Precarious (prĭkēə·riəs), *a.* 1646. [f. L. *precarius* (f. **prex*, *prec-* entreaty, prayer) + -OUS; see -ARIOUS. Cf. (O)Fr. *précaire.*] **1.** Held by the favour and at the pleasure of another; hence, uncertain. **2.** Question-begging, taken for granted; unfounded, doubtful 1659. **3.** Dependent on circumstances or chance; unstable 1687. **4.** Perilous 1727. †**5.** Suppliant; importunate –1697.

1. *P. tenure,* a tenure held during the pleasure of the superior. **3.** A scanty and p. support 1794. **4.** The p. track through the morass SCOTT. **Pre·ca·rious-ly** *adv.*, **-ness.**

Precative (pre·kătiv), *a.* 1662. [– late L. *precativus,* f. *precat-*, pa. ppl. stem of L. *precari*; see PRAY *v.*, -IVE, -ATIVE.] Expressing entreaty or desire; supplicatory.

In *Gram.* applied to a word, particle, or form, expressing entreaty, or the like.

Precatory (pre·kătəri), *a.* 1636. [– late L. *precatorius,* f. as prec.; see -ORY².] Of, pertaining to, of the nature of, or expressing entreaty or supplication. In *Gram.*, = prec.

P. words, words in a will praying or expressing a desire that a thing be done. When these are deemed to have an imperative force, they constitute a *p. trust.*

Precaution (prĭkǭ·ʃən). 1603. [– Fr. *précaution* – late L. *præcautio, -ion-*, f. *præcaut-*, pa. ppl. stem of L. *præcavēre*; see PRE-, CAUTION *sb.*] **1.** Caution exercised beforehand to provide against mischief or secure good results; prudent foresight. **2.** An instance of this; a measure taken beforehand to ward off an evil or to ensure a good result. (With *a* and *pl.*) 1603.

1. I have used all the care and p. that I could 1782. **2.** The Governor..had taken several precautions to prevent us from forcing our way into the harbour 1748. Hence **Precau·tional, Precau·tionary** *adjs.* suggesting provident caution; of the nature of p.

†**Precau·tion,** *v.* 1654. [– Fr. *précautionner* f. *précaution* (see prec.).] **1.** *trans.* To forewarn (any one) *against* something –1768. **2.** To put (any one) upon his guard *against* something; esp. *refl* to be on one's guard *against* –1805. **3.** To say beforehand by way of caution –1690.

Precautious (prĭkǭ·ʃəs), *a.* 1711. [f. PRECAUTION; see -OUS, CAUTIOUS.] Using precaution; displaying previous caution or care.

‖**Precava, præ-** (prīkēi·vă). 1866. [f. PRE- A. II. b. + CAVA for *vena cava*; cf. *postcava* (POST- A. 2 b).] *Anat.* The superior or anterior vena cava. Hence **Pre-, præca·val** *a.* (*sb.*).

Precede (prĭsī·d), *v.* late ME. [– (O)Fr. *précéder* – L. *præcedere* go before; see PRE- A. III., CEDE.] †**1.** *trans.* To go before or beyond (another) in quality or degree; to surpass; to exceed. **2.** To go before in rank or importance; to take precedence of 1485. **3.** To come or go before in order or arrangement 1494. **4.** To go before; to walk or proceed in advance of 1530. **5.** To come before in time; to happen, occur, or exist before; to be earlier than 1540. **6.** *intr.* or (now only) *absol.* (in senses 2–5) 1540. **7.** *trans.* To cause to be preceded (*by*); to preface (*with, by*) 1718.

2. All the sons of viscounts and barons are allowed to p. baronets 1819. **4.** As harbingers preceding still the fates SHAKS. **5.** He told them of signes which should preceed the day of Judgement 1653. **6.** A statement different from anything that precedes or follows 1907. **7.** The emperor precedes his visit by a royal present 1718.

Precedence (pre·sĭdĕns, prĭsī·dĕns). 1484. [f. PRECEDENT *a.*; see -ENCE.] †**1.** = PRECEDENT *sb.* 2, 3. –1546. †**2.** = PRECEDENT *sb.* 1. –1610. **3.** The fact of preceding another or others in time or succession; priority 1605. **4.** The fact of preceding another or others in order, rank, importance, estimation, or dignity; higher position; pre-eminence, supremacy 1658. **b.** *spec.* The right of preceding others in ceremonies and social formalities. Hence: The order to be ceremonially observed by persons of different ranks. 1598.

2. *Ant. & Cl.* II. v. 51. **3.** The payment of interest..will take p. of other Egyptian obligations 1884. **4.** The Andalucian horse takes p. of all 1845. **b.** Disputes concerning Rank and P. ADDISON.

Precedency (pre·sĭdĕnsi, prĭsī·dĕnsi). 1599. [f. as prec. + -ENCY.] †**1.** The being or serving as a precedent –1657. **2.** = prec. 3. 1612. **b.** *spec.* = prec. 4 b. 1599.

Precedent (pre·sĭdĕnt), *sb.* late ME. [– (O)Fr. *précédent,* subst. use of the adj.; see next.] **1.** A thing or person that precedes or goes before another. †**a.** That which has been mentioned just before. Usu. in *pl.* –1607. †**b.** That which precedes in time; an antecedent –1788. **2.** A previous instance or case taken as an example or rule for subsequent cases or as supporting or justifying some similar act or circumstance. (The prevailing sense.) late ME. **b.** *Law.* A previous judicial decision, method of proceeding, or draft of a document which serves as an authoritative rule or pattern in similar or analogous cases 1523. **c.** *collect.* or *gen.* (without article or *pl.*) *Without p.*, unprecedented. 1622. †**3.** *transf.* A written or printed record of some past proceeding or proceedings, serving as a guide or rule for subsequent cases –1650. †**4.** A pattern, model, exemplar –1709. †**b.** An example, illustration, specimen –1695.

2. The president were to yvel to be admytted CROMWELL. **b.** One p. creates another.—They soon accumulate, and constitute law. 1772. **c.** Each comforts himself that his faults are not without p. JOHNSON.

Precedent (prĭsī·dĕnt), *a.* Now *rare*; largely repl. by PRECEDING. late ME. [– (O)Fr. *précédent,* pr. pple. of *précéder,* and repr. L. *præcedens, -ent-*, pr.pple. of *præcedere*; see PRECEDE, -ENT.] **1.** Existing or occurring before something else; previous, former. **2.** Coming or placed before 1483. **b.** Mentioned or said just before; preceding 1530. **3.** Having or taking precedence 1613.

2. Phr. *The p.*, that coming immediately before, the foregoing. Hence **Prece·dently** *adv.* previously, beforehand.

Precedent (pre·sĭdĕnt), *v.* 1614. [f. PRECEDENT *sb.*] *trans.* To be a precedent for; to support or justify by a precedent. Now only in *pa. pple.*: see next.

Precedented (pre·sĭdentĕd), *ppl. a.* 1653. [f. PRECEDENT *sb.* or *v.* + -ED.] Furnished with or having a precedent; in accordance with precedent; usu. *predic.*

Precedential (presĭde·nʃăl). *a.* Now *rare.* 1641. [f. PRECEDENT *sb.* or PRECEDENCE, after *consequential,* etc.] **1.** Of the nature of, constituting, or furnishing a precedent. **2.** Having precedence, preceding, preliminary 1661.

Preceding (prĭsī·diŋ), *ppl. a.* 1494. [f. PRECEDE + -ING².] That precedes in order, time, or movement; *spec.* in *Astr.* said of a heavenly body, etc. situated to the west of another, and therefore moving in front of it in the apparent diurnal rotation of the heavens.

Precent (prĭse·nt), *v.* 1732. [Back-formation from next.] *intr.* To officiate as precentor. **b.** *trans.* To lead in singing (a psalm, antiphon, etc.).

Precentor (prĭse·ntǫɹ). 1613. [– Fr. *précenteur* or L. *præcentor*, f. *præcent-*, pa.ppl. stem of *præcinere,* f. *præ* PRE- + *canere* sing; see -OR 2.] One who leads or directs the singing of a choir or congregation; *spec.* **a.** in cathedrals of the Old Foundation, a member of the chapter (ranking next to the dean), whose duties as precentor are now commonly discharged by the succentor; **b.** in those of the New Foundation, one of the minor canons or a chaplain, who performs the duties in person; **c.** the leader of the congregational singing in churches which have no choir, and esp. in those in which there is no instrumental accompaniment. **Pre·ce·ntorship.** So **Prece·ntrix,** a female p.

Precept (prī·sept). late ME. [– L. *præceptum* maxim, order, subst. use of n. pa. pple. of *præcipere* take beforehand, warn, instruct, enjoin, f. *præ* PRE- + *capere* take. Cf. Fr. *précepte,* †*précept.*] †**1.** An authoritative command to do some particular act; an order, mandate –1513. **2.** A general command or injunction; *esp.* an injunction as to moral conduct; a maxim. Usu. applied to divine commands. late ME. **b.** One of the practical rules of an art; a direction 1553. †**3.** A written order or mandate authorizing a person to do something; a warrant –1771. **4.** *spec.* **a.** A written or printed order issued by the King, a court, or a judge, to require the attendance of members of parliament, a court, or a jury, to direct the holding of an assize, to procure the appearance, arrest, or imprisonment of a delinquent, etc.; a writ, warrant 1444. **b.** A written order to arrange for and hold an election; usu. that issued by the sheriff to the returning officer 1684. **c.** An order for collection or demand for payment of money due under a rate 1877.

2. Example draws where p. fails 1708. **4. b.** The p. for the election has arrived 1865. **c.** The amount of the p. has been thus reduced 1888.

Preception (prĭse·pʃən). 1619. [– L. *præceptio, -ion-*, f. *præcept-*, pa. ppl. stem of *præcipere*; see prec., -ION. Cf. Fr. *préception.*] †**1.** A previous conception; a preconception, presumption (*rare*) –1640. **2.** *Rom. Law.* The right of receiving beforehand, as a part of an inheritance before partition 1875.

Preceptive (prĭse·ptiv), *a.* 1456. [– L. *præceptivus,* f. as prec.; see -IVE. Cf. OFr. *preceptif, -ive.*] Of the nature of, pertaining to, or conveying a precept; mandatory; didactic, instructive.

The Law hath two parts,..the P. and the Punitive 1672. The didactive or p. Manner 1711.

Preceptor (prĭse·ptəɹ). 1440. [– L. *præceptor* teacher, f. as prec.; see -OR 2. Cf. Fr. *précepteur.*] **1.** One who instructs; a teacher, tutor. **2.** The head of a preceptory of Knights Templars 1710. So **Precepto·rial** *a.* of or pertaining to a p. **Prece·ptress,** a female p.

Preceptory (prĭse·ptəri). 1540. [– med.L. *præceptoria* in same sense, subst. use of fem. of *præceptorius* giving instructions, f. as prec.; see -ORY¹.] A subordinate community of the Knights Templars; the estate or manor supporting this, or its buildings. Cf. COMMANDERY.

‖**Preces** (prī·sīz), *sb. pl.* 1450. [L., pl. of **prex, prec-* prayer.] *Liturg.* The short petitions which are said as verse and response by the minister and the congregation alternately.

Precession (prĭse·ʃən). ME. [– late L. *præcessio, -ion-* (Boethius), f. *præcess-*, pa. ppl. stem of L. *præcedere* PRECEDE; see -ION.] †¶**1.** An error for *procession* –1529. **2.** The action or fact of preceding; precedence 1628. **3.** *Phonetics.* Advance in oral position 1844.

P. of the equinoxes, often ellipt. *precession* (Astr.): the earlier occurrence of the equinoxes in each successive sidereal year, due to the retrograde motion of the equinoctial points along the ecliptic, produced by the slow change of direction in space of the earth's axis, which moves so that the pole of the equator describes a circle (see NUTATION) around the pole of the ecliptic once in about 25,800 years. Hence commonly used to denote this motion of the equinoctial points, of the earth's axis, or of the celestial pole or equator. *Lunisolar p.*, that part of the p. which is caused by the combined attractions of the moon and sun upon the mass of the earth. Hence **Prece·ssional** *a.* (*Astron.*).

Pre-Christian (prīkri·styăn, -tʃən), *a.* 1828. [PRE- B. I. 1.] **1.** Of or pertaining to times prior to the birth of Christ or the Christian era. **2.** Prior to the introduction of Christianity 1861.

‖**Précieuse** (presyǿz), *sb.* (*a.*) 1727. [Fr.,

fem. of *précieux* PRECIOUS (sense 3), used as sb. See Molière's *Les Précieuses ridicules.*] A woman affecting a refined delicacy of language and taste; usu. connoting ridiculous over-fastidiousness. **B.** *adj.* Affected after the style of *les précieuses* 1785.

Precinct (prī·siŋkt), *sb.* late ME. [– med.L. *præcinctum*, subst. use of n. pa. pple. of L. *præcingere* gird about, encircle, f. *præ* PRE- A. II. c + *cingere* gird.] **1.** The space enclosed by the walls or other boundaries of a particular place or building, or by an imaginary line drawn around it; *esp.* the ground immediately surrounding a religious house or place of worship 1547. **b.** *esp.* in *pl.* The environs 1464. **2.** A girding or enclosing line or surface; a boundary, a compass. Also *fig.* 1542. **3.** A district defined for purposes of government or representation; *spec.* in U.S., a subdivision of a county or ward for election and police purposes. late ME.

1. b. Ye citie of York, suburbs, or precinctes of ye same 1485. *fig.* The warm precincts of the chearful day GRAY. **2.** Within the precincts of a petty island 1843. **3.** The smallest P. was that of the Parish 1647.

Precinct (prĭsi·ŋkt), *pa. pple.* and *ppl. a. rare.* 1641. [– L. *præcinctus*, pa. pple. of *præcingere*; see prec.] Girt about; engirdled, encompassed.

Preciosity (preʃiǫ·sĭti). late ME. [– (O)Fr. *préciosité* – L. *pretiositas*, f. *pretiosus*; see PRECIOUS, -ITY.] **1.** The quality of being precious or costly; preciousness. Now *rare* or *Obs.* **2.** Anything very costly. Now *rare* or *Obs.* 1485. **3.** Affectation of refinement or distinction, esp. in the use of language 1866.

3. The circles of Oxford p. 1887.

Precious (pre·ʃəs), *a.* (*sb.*, *adv.*) ME. [– OFr. *precios* (mod. *précieux*) – L. *pretiosus*, f. *pretium* PRICE; see -OUS.] **1.** Of great price; valuable; costly. **b.** Used ironically; cf. FINE *a.* III. 1. 1619. **2.** Of great moral, spiritual, or non-material worth; held in high esteem ME. **3.** Affecting distinction in conduct, manners, language, etc.; fastidious; *esp.* in mod. use (after Fr.), affecting fastidious refinement in language, workmanship, etc.; often with an implication of over-refinement. late ME. **4.** *colloq.* As an intensive: Egregious, out-and-out, arrant; in some uses, a mere emotional intensive. late ME.

1. The Generalls pretious Jewel, or his Treasure HOBBES. *P. metals*: gold and silver; sometimes including platinum, and rarely mercury. *P. stone*, a gem; *p.* GARNET, OPAL, etc.: see those words. **b.** Are not these p. instructers of youth? WESLEY. **2.** Justice, which is a treasure far more p. than gold JOWETT. *P. blood*, the blood of Christ shed for man's redemption. So *p. body*. **3.** Elaborate embroidery of p. language 1887. **4.** It's hard enough to see one's way, a p. sight harder than I thought 1857.

B. *sb.* Precious one, dear 1706. **C.** *adv.* (qualifying adj. or adv.) **a.** = Preciously 1595. **b.** With intensive force: Extremely, very: *p. few*, few indeed. *colloq.* 1837. Hence **Pre·cious-ly** *adv.*, **-ness.**

Precipice (pre·sipis), *sb.* 1598. [– Fr. *précipice* or L. *præcipitium*, f. *præceps, præcip-* headlong, steep, or *præcipitare* PRECIPITATE *v.*] †**1.** A headlong fall or descent, esp. to a great depth –1650. **2.** A vertical or very steep face of rock, etc.; a cliff, crag, or steep mountain side 1632. **b.** *fig.* A perilous situation 1651.

2. A Torrent, rowling down a P. DRYDEN. **b.** The precipices which environ beauty 1651. Hence **Pre·cipiced** (-ist) *ppl. a.* having, furnished, or formed with precipices.

Precipitable (prĭsi·pităb'l), *a.* 1670. [f. PRECIPITATE *v.* + -ABLE.] Capable of being precipitated from solution in a liquid, or from a state of vapour. Hence **Preci:pitabi·lity,** capability of being precipitated.

Precipitancy (prĭsi·pitănsi). 1619. [f. PRECIPITANT *a.*; see -ANCY.] The quality of being precipitant. **1.** Headlong speed, violent hurry 1646. **2.** Great want of deliberation; hastiness, rashness; an instance of this 1619. So **Preci·pitance** 1667.

Precipitant (prĭsi·pitănt), *a.* and *sb.* 1608. [As adj., – Fr. †*précipitant* (XVI), pr. pple. of *précipiter*; see PRECIPITATE *v.*, -ANT; as sb., correl. of PRECIPITATE *sb.* Cf. Fr. *précipitant.*] **A.** *adj.* (Now *rare*; usu. repl. by PRECIPITATE *a.*) **1.** Falling headlong; descending vertically or steeply; headlong; falling to the bottom as a precipitate or sediment 1620. **2.** Rushing headlong; moving hurriedly or very swiftly onwards 1671. **3.** Acting or taking place with great hurry, rapidity, or suddenness; very sudden or unexpected, abrupt 1641. **4.** Hasty, rash, headstrong 1608.

1. He..plunging, from his Back the Rider hurls P. 1735. **2.** That troop so blithe and bold, ..P. in fear, wou'd wing their flight POPE. **3.** It was hard..either to discern the Rise, or apply a Remedy to that p. Rebellion 1641.

B. *sb. Chem.* A substance that causes precipitation. Sometimes const. *of* (the substance precipitated). 1684. Hence **Preci·pitantly** *adv.*

Precipitate (prĭsi·pitĕt), *sb.* 1563. [– mod.L. *præcipitatum*, subst. use of n. pa. pple. of L. *præcipitare*; see PRECIPITATE *v.*] That which is precipitated; the product of precipitation. **a.** *Chem.* A body precipitated from any solution; any substance which, by the action of a chemical reagent, or of heat, etc., is separated from the liquid in which it was previously dissolved, and deposited in the solid state 1594. **b.** *Old Chem.* and *Pharm.*, applied *spec.* to certain preparations of mercury obtained by precipitation 1563. **c.** *Physics*, etc. Moisture condensed from the state of vapour by cooling, and deposited in drops, as rain, dew, etc. 1832.

b. *P. per se*, or *red p.*, mercuric oxide or red oxide of mercury, HgO; *white p.*, mercurammonium chloride, $HgH_6N_2Cl_2$ (*fusible white p.*), or dimercurammonium chloride, $Hg_2H_4N_2Cl_2$ (*infusible white p.*).

Precipitate (prĭsi·pitĕt), *a.* 1607. [– L. *præcipitatus*, pa. pple. of *præcipitare*; see next, -ATE[2].] **1.** Hurled headlong; descending steeply or directly downwards; headlong 1614. †**b.** Of a place, etc.: Very steep, precipitous –1630. **2.** Moving or moved with excessive haste or speed; violently hurried 1654. **3.** Performed, taking place, acting, or passing with very great rapidity; greatly hurried; exceedingly sudden or abrupt 1658. **4. a.** Of persons, their dispositions, etc.: Over-hasty, rash, inconsiderate, headstrong 1607. **b.** Of acts, etc.: Done in sudden haste; hurried, rash, unconsidered 1618.

1. On the Shepherd's Fold He [an Eagle] darts p. 1703. **2.** The general escaped by a p. flight GIBBON. **3.** Their service consisted in p., and very irreverent chattering of certain Prayers and Hymns 1703. **4. a.** If I could perswade these p. young Gentlemen to compose this Restlessness of Mind STEELE. **b.** A p. burning of his papers a few days before his death BOSWELL. Hence **Preci·pitately** *adv.*

Precipitate (prĭsi·piteit), *v.* 1528. [– *præcipitat-*, pa. ppl. stem of L. *præcipitare* throw or drive headlong, f. *præceps, -cipit-* headlong, f. *præ* before + *caput* head; see -ATE[3].] **I. 1.** *trans.* To throw down headlong; to hurl or fling down. (Often *refl.*) 1575. **b.** *fig.* To hurl, fling (*into* some condition, or *upon* an object of attack) 1528. †**2.** *intr.* (for *refl.* or *pass.*) To fall headlong; to fall, gravitate –1785. †**b.** To descend steeply, as a river –1793. †**c.** *fig.* To 'plunge' *into* some condition or act; to fall or come suddenly to ruin or destruction –1758.

1. The garrison had no alternative but to perish by the..sword, or to p. themselves into the ocean 1774. **b.** Precipitated from the height of prosperity, into the depth of adversity 1662. **2.** *Lear* IV. vi. 50.

II. 1. *trans.* To cause to move, pass, act, or proceed very rapidly; to hasten, hurry, urge on 1558. **b.** To bring on quickly, suddenly, or unexpectedly; to hasten the occurrence of 1625. **2.** *intr.* To rush headlong; to hurry; to move, act, or proceed very quickly 1622. †**b.** To be precipitate in action –1670.

1. Men are impatient, and for precipitating things 1736. **b.** They could not p. his departure 1748.

III. 1. *Chem. trans.* To deposit, or cause to be deposited, in a solid form from solution in a liquid, by chemical action; see PRECIPITATE *sb.* Also occas. to produce precipitation in (the solution); †to deposit from suspension or admixture in a liquid, as sediment, etc. 1644. **b.** *Physics*, etc. To condense (moisture) into drops from a state of vapour, and so deposit or cause to fall, as dew, rain, etc. 1863. **c.** *transf.* and *fig.*; *spec.* in *Spiritualism* = MATERIALIZE 2. 1825. **2.** *intr.* (for *refl.*) To be deposited from solution (or from suspension); to settle as a precipitate 1626.

1. b. The mass of ice cools the surrounding air, and thus precipitates its moisture HUXLEY. **c.** The world is mind precipitated EMERSON. **2.** By what strong water every metal will p. BACON.

Precipitation (prĭsipitēi·ʃən). 1502. [– Fr. *précipitation* or L. *præcipitatio*, f. as prec.; see -ION.] **I.** The action of precipitating from a height; the fact of being precipitated; headlong fall or descent 1607. **b.** Precipitousness (*rare*) 1607.

In perill of p. From off the Rocke Tarpeian SHAKS.

II. 1. Violent onward motion 1624. **2.** Sudden and hurried action; hurry 1502. **b.** Unduly hurried action; inconsiderate haste 1629. **3.** Hastening, hurrying; acceleration 1621.

2. The lady having seized it, with great p., they retired DICKENS. **b.** We must not act with p. DISRAELI. **3.** This..gave p. to his own downfall GOLDSM.

III. 1. *Chem.* Separation and deposition of a substance in a solid form from solution in a liquid, by the action of a chemical reagent, or of electricity, heat, etc. 1612. **b.** *concr.* The product of this process; a precipitate 1605. **2.** *Physics* and *Meteorol.* Condensation and deposition of moisture from the state of vapour, as by cooling; *esp.* in the formation of dew, rain, snow, etc. **b.** *concr.* That which is so deposited. 1675. **3.** *fig.*; *spec.* in *Spiritualism* = MATERIALIZATION 1891.

Precipitator (prĭsi·piteitəɹ). 1660. [f. PRECIPITATE *v.* + -OR 2.] **1.** One who precipitates something; a hastener. **2.** *Chem.* and *Physics.* A precipitant 1681. **b.** An apparatus for precipitation; *spec.* a tank for purifying hard water or sewage 1883.

Precipitin (prĭsi·pitin). 1900. [irreg. f. PRECIPIT(ATE + -IN[1]. Cf. Fr. *précipitine.*] *Biol. Chem.* A substance that causes precipitation from a solution.

Precipitous (prĭsi·pitəs), *a.* 1646. [– Fr. †*précipiteux* = Sp., It., Pg. *precipitoso*, f. L. *præcipit-*, stem of *præceps*; see PRECIPITATE *v.*, -OUS.] **I.** †**1.** = PRECIPITATE *a.* 4. –1734. †**2.** = PRECIPITATE *a.* 3. –1666. **3.** = PRECIPITATE *a.* 2. *rare.* 1774. **II.** Of the nature of a precipice; consisting of or characterized by precipices. (The usual sense.) 1806.

Salisbury Craig..is noted chiefly for its steep p. front 1806. Hence **Preci·pitous-ly** *adv.*, **-ness.**

‖**Précis** (prēi·si). 1760. [Fr. (*presi*), sb. use of *précis*; see next.] A concise or abridged statement; a summary; an abstract. **b.** *attrib.*, as *p.-writing*, etc. 1809. Hence **Pré·cis** *v. trans.*

Precise (prĭsəi·s), *a.* 1526. [– Fr. *précis, -ise* – L. *præcisus*, pa. pple. of *præcidere* cut short, abridge, f. *præ* PRE- + *cædere* cut.] **1.** Strictly expressed; exactly defined; (of a person) definite and exact in statement. **b.** Of the voice or tone: Distinctly uttered 1848. **2.** Strict in the observance of rule, form, or usage; correct; punctilious, particular; occas., over-exact, fastidious; (of a practice or action): strictly observed 1530. **b.** *esp.* Strict in religious observance; in 16–17th c., puritanical 1566. **3.** Exact; neither more nor less than; perfect, complete; opp. to *approximate* 1571. **4.** Distinguished with precision from all others; identified, or stated, with exactness; *the p.*, the very, the exact 1628.

1. It is in a sense less strict and p., that we take the word 1775. He is very p. about dates and facts 1875. **2.** Learned without pride, Exact, yet not p. COWPER. **b.** Men are now called 'precise', who will not connive at sin PUSEY. **3.** A definition..should be P., that is, contain nothing unessential, nothing superfluous 1837. **4.** The p. moment at which a traveller is passing 1860. Hence **Preci·se-ly** *adv.*, **-ness.**

Precise (prĭsəi·s), *v.* 1866. [– Fr. *préciser* determine exactly, f. *précis*: see prec.] *trans.* To make precise; to define precisely or exactly; to particularize.

Precisian (prĭsi·ʒăn). 1571. [f. PRECISE *a.* + -IAN.] One who is rigidly precise in the observance of rules or forms. **b.** *spec.* One who is precise in religious observances; in the 16–17th c. synonymous with *Puritan*.
A man may dwell upon words till he becomes.. a mere p. in speech 1834. **b.** A profane person calls a man of piety a p. 1725. Hence **Preci·sianism,** the practice of a p.; orig. applied to Puritanism.

Precision (prĭsi·ʒən). 1640. [– Fr. *précision* or L. *præcisio*, f. pa. ppl. stem of *præcidere*; see PRECISE *a.*, -ION.] **1.** The fact, condition, or quality of being precise; exactness, definiteness; distinctness, accuracy 1740. †**2.** The cutting off of one thing from another; *esp.* the mental separation of a fact or idea; abstraction. (App. used for *prescission*.) –1710.
1. The p. of statement, which..distinguishes science from common information HUXLEY. Hence **Preci·sionist** (also *erron.* (after *precisian*) **-anist**) one who makes a profession or practice of precision in observance or expression; a purist.

Precisive (prĭsəi·siv), *a. rare.* 1679. [f. PRECISION, after *incision/incisive*; see -IVE.] **1.** That cuts off, separates, or defines one (person or thing) from another or others, as in *p. abstraction*. (app. for *prescissive*). **2.** Characterized by precision 1807.

Preclude (prĭklū·d), *v.* 1618. [– L. *præcludere*, f. *præ* PRE- A. II. c + *claudere* shut.] **1.** *trans.* = FORECLOSE 2, 5. 1629. **2.** To close the door against, shut out; to exclude, prevent; to render impracticable by anticipatory action 1618. **3.** = FORECLOSE 3. 1736.
1. Every intellect was precluded by Prejudice JOHNSON. **2.** They hesitated till death precluded the decision JOHNSON. **3.** Employed in staff offices which p. them from the performance of regimental duties 1800. Hence **Preclu·sion** (now *rare*), the action of precluding; prevention by previous action. **Preclu·sive** *a.* that tends to p.; shutting out beforehand; preventive (*of*). **Preclu·sively** *adv.*

Precoce (prĭkōᵘ·s), *a.* (*sb.*) *rare.* 1664. [– Fr. *précoce* – L. *præcox*, *præcoc-*; see next.] **1.** Of plants: Early flowering. **2.** = PRECOCIOUS 2. 1689. **B.** *sb.* An early plant; *spec.* = *p. tulip* 1699.

Precocious (prĭkōᵘ·ʃəs), *a.* 1650. [f. L. *præcox*, *præcoc-*, f. *præcoquere* boil beforehand, ripen fully, f. *præ* PRE- A. I. 1 + *coquere* cook; see -IOUS.] **1.** Of a plant: Flowering or fruiting early; *spec.* having blossoms before the leaves; also said of the blossoms or fruit. **2.** *fig.* Of persons: Prematurely developed in some faculty or proclivity 1678. **b.** Of, pertaining to, or indicating precocity 1672. **c.** Of things: Of early development 1838.
1. Some expressions in Scripture concerning p. Figgs SIR T. BROWNE. **2.** She was somewhat p. in love matters 1868. **b.** Untimely decrepitude was the penalty of p. maturity 1827. Hence **Preco·cious-ly** *adv.*, **-ness.**

Precocity (prĭkǫ·sĭti). 1640. [– Fr. *précocité*, f. *précoce*; see PRECOCE, -ITY.] The quality of being precocious. **1.** Of plants: Early flowering or ripeness 1656. **2.** Early maturity, premature development 1640. **b.** *transf.* A precocious child 1882.
2. Their productions..bear the marks of p. and premature decay HAZLITT.

Precognition (prĭkǫgni·ʃən). 1611. [– late L. *præcognitio* (Boethius), f. *præ* PRE- A. I. 2; see COGNITION. Cf. Fr. †*précognition*.] **1.** Antecedent cognition or knowledge; foreknowledge. **2.** *Scots Law.* The preliminary examination of witnesses likely to know about the facts of a case, in order to obtain, with a view to trial, a general knowledge of the available evidence; a statement taken from such a witness 1661.

Precognosce (prĭkǫgnǫ·s), *v.* 1753. [f. PRE- A. I. 1 + COGNOSCE.] *Sc. Law. trans.* To make a preliminary examination of (witnesses); cf. prec. 2.

Preconceive (prĭkǫ̆nsī·v), *v.* 1580. [PRE- A. I. 1.] *trans.* To conceive or imagine beforehand; to anticipate in thought. Hence **Preconcei·ved** *ppl. a.*

Preconception (prĭkǫ̆nse·pʃən). 1625. [f. PRE- A. I. 2 + CONCEPTION.] The action of preconceiving; usu. (with *a* and *pl.*), a conception or opinion entertained prior to actual knowledge; a prepossession; an anticipation.

Preconce·rt, *v.* 1748. [f. PRE- A. I. 1 + CONCERT *v.*] *trans.* To concert or arrange beforehand. Hence **Preconce·rted** *ppl. a.*; **-ly** *adv.*, **-ness.**

Preconization (prīkǫ̆nəizēⁱ·ʃən). 1644. [– med.L. *præconizatio*, f. *præconizat-*, pa. ppl. stem of *præconizare*; see next, -ION. Cf. (O)Fr. *préconisation*.] **1.** Public proclamation. **2.** *spec.* in *R.C.Ch.* The public confirmation of an appointment (as that of a bishop) by the Pope 1692.

Preconize (prī·kǫ̆nəiz), *v.* Also **præ-.** late ME. [– med.L. *præconizare*, f. L. *præco*, *præcon-* public crier, herald; see -IZE. Cf. (O)Fr. *préconiser*.] **1.** *trans.* To proclaim publicly; to commend or extol publicly, to cry up. **b.** To summon by name 1863. **2.** *spec.* in *R. C. Ch.* Of the Pope: To approve publicly the appointment of (a bishop) 1692.

Pre:-conque·stal, -conque·stual, *a.* 1878. [PRE- B. I. 1.] Existing in, or belonging to, times preceding the (Norman) Conquest. Now **Pre-Co·nquest.**

Preconscious (prīkǫ·nʃəs), *a.* 1870. [PRE- B. I. 1.] Antecedent to consciousness, or to conscious action of some specified kind.

Preconsider (prīkǫnsi·dəɹ), *v.* 1647. [PRE- A. I. 1.] *trans.* To consider beforehand or previously. So **Pre:considera·tion** 1598.

Pre-contract (prīkǫ·ntrækt), *sb.* 1483. [PRE- A. I. 2.] A pre-existing contract; a contract or agreement previously entered into: **a.** of marriage; **b.** *gen.* 1610.
a. He is your husband on a p. SHAKS.

Pre-contract (prīkǫ̆ntræ·kt), *v.* 1579. [PRE- A. I. 1.] *trans.* **a.** To affiance or betroth beforehand. **b.** To establish (an agreement, etc.) by contract in advance. **c.** To acquire (habits, etc.) beforehand.
a. Nor could a contract with Percy have invalidated her marriage with the king..Percy having been pre-contracted to another person FROUDE.

Preco·racoid, *a.* and *sb.* 1870. [PRE- B. II.] **A.** *adj.* Situated anterior to the coracoid 1872. **B.** *sb.* A precoracoid bone or cartilage.

Precordial, præ- (prikǭ·ɹdiăl), *a.* 1562. [f. PRAECORDIA + -AL¹.] Situated in front of or about the heart; of or pertaining to the PRÆCORDIA.

‖**Precuneus, præ-** (prikiū·niŏs). 1890. [f. L. *præ* PRE- B. II. + *cuneus* wedge.] *Anat.* The quadrate lobule of the brain, situated immediately in front of the cuneate.

Precursive (prīkɔ̄·ɹsiv), *a.* 1814. [f. PRECURS(OR + -IVE.] = PRECURSORY.

Precursor (prīkɔ̄·ɹsəɹ). 1504. [– L. *præcursor*, f. *præcurs-*, pa. ppl. stem of *præcurrere*, f. *præ* PRE- + *currere* run; see -OR 2.] **1.** One who or that which runs or goes before; a forerunner; *esp.* a harbinger; *spec.* applied to John the Baptist. **2.** One who precedes in some course or office 1792.
1. Shame, the p. of saving penitence 1856. **2.** Cowper..by his genuine love of nature was a p. of Wordsworth 1879. Hence **Precu·rsorship,** the office or function of a p.; prior occurrence.

Precursory (prīkɔ̄·ɹsəri), *a.* (*sb.*) 1599. [– L. *præcursorius*; see prec., -ORY².] Having the character of a precursor; preceding, esp. as the harbinger or presage of something to follow; preliminary, introductory. **b.** as *sb.* A precursory fact, condition or symptom; an antecedent 1660.
Another symptom which is sometimes p. of exophthalmic goitre 1899.

Predacious (prĭdēⁱ·ʃəs), *a.* 1713. [f. L. *præda* booty, plunder + -ACIOUS, after *herbacious* (f. L. *herbaceus*, f. *herba*).] **1.** Of animals: Naturally preying upon other animals; predatory, raptorial. Also of cells and organisms. **2.** Of or pertaining to predatory animals 1822. Hence **Preda·city.**

Predate (prīdēⁱ·t), *v.* 1864. [f. PRE- A. I. 1 + DATE *v.*] **1.** *trans.* To date before the actual time; to antedate. **2.** To precede in date 1889.

Predatory (pre·dătəri), *a.* 1589. [– L. *prædatorius*, f. *prædator*, f. *prædari* plunder, spoil; see -ORY².] **1.** Of, pertaining to, characterized by, or consisting in plundering, pillaging, or robbery. **2.** Addicted to, or living by, plunder; plundering, marauding, thieving 1781. †**3.** Destructive, wasteful, deleterious –1711. **4.** Of an animal: That preys upon other animals; carnivorous. Also, of its organs of capture. 1668.
1. Prædatory excursions by sea and land GIBBON. **2.** A p. and formidable race, the Mahrattas WELLINGTON. **3.** Exercise..maketh the Spirits more hot and p. BACON. Hence **Pre·datorily** *adv.* **Pre·datoriness.**

Predecease (prīdĭsī·s), *v.* 1593. [f. PRE- A. I. 1 + DECEASE *v.* Cf. Fr. *prédécéder* (XVI).] *trans.* To die before (some person, or, rarely, some event). So **Predecea·se** *sb.* the death of one person before another 1765.

Predecessor (prī·dĭsesəɹ, prīdĭse·səɹ). ME. [– (O)Fr. *prédécesseur* – late L. *prædecessor*, f. L. *præ* PRE- A. I + *decessor* retiring officer, f. *decedere* depart.] **1.** One who has preceded another in any office or position. **b.** A thing to which another has succeeded 1742. **2.** An ancestor, a forefather (now *rare*). late ME.
1. Eadmer's immediate p. in the see of St. Andrews was Turgot 1861. **b.** To-day is Yesterday return'd;..Let it not share its predecessor's fate 1742.

Predefine (prīdĭfəi·n), *v.* 1542. [PRE- A. I. 1.] *trans.* To define, limit, appoint, or settle previously; to predetermine. So **Prede·finite** *a.* predetermined. **Predefini·tion,** predetermination.

Predella (prĭde·lă). 1848. [– It. *predella* kneeling-stool.] **1.** The step or platform upon which an altar is placed, an altar-step, foot-pace; also, a painting or sculpture upon the vertical face of this 1853. **2.** = GRADINO 1848. **b.** *attrib.*, as *p. panel*, *picture* 1884.

Predesignate (prĭde·zignĕt, -de·s-), *a.* 1837. [f. PRE- A. I. 1 + DESIGNATE *ppl. a.*] **a.** Designated or specified beforehand. **b.** *Logic.* Of a proposition or term: Having a sign of quantity prefixed.

Predesignation (prīdezignēⁱ·ʃən, -des-). 1641. [PRE- A. I. 2; see -ATION.] **1.** Previous designation, appointment, or specification. **2.** *Logic.* A sign of quantity prefixed to a term or preposition 1840.

Predestinarian (prīdestinēᵊ·riăn, prī-), *sb.* and *a.* 1638. [f. PREDESTINATION or PREDESTINY + -ARIAN.] **A.** *sb.* One who believes or maintains the theological doctrine of predestination; a fatalist 1667. **B.** *adj.* Of, pertaining to, concerning, or relating to predestination; holding or maintaining the doctrine of predestination.
b. Every Fatalist or P. scheme destroys merit J. MARTINEAU. Hence **Predestina·rianism,** the doctrine of predestinarians.

Predestinate (prĭde·stinĕt), *ppl. a.* and *sb.* late ME. [– eccl. L. *prædestinatus*, pa. pple. of *prædestinare*; see next, -ATE² and ¹.] **A.** *ppl. a.* (as *adj.* or *pple.*) **1.** *Theol.* Foreordained by the eternal purpose of God to eternal life, or to any specified fate or lot. Also of things: Foreordained by divine decree. Const. *to*, or inf. with *to*. **2.** In more general sense: Destined beforehand; fated 1500.
1. Can the p. be lost, or the reprobate saved? 1833. **2.** So some Gentleman or other shall scape a p. scratcht face SHAKS.
B. *sb. Theol.* A person predestinated to eternal life; one of the elect 1529.

Predestinate (prĭde·stineⁱt), *v.* 1450. [– *prædestinat-*, pa. ppl. stem of eccl. L. *prædestinare* appoint beforehand (in Christian use from III, rendering Gr. προορίζειν in Romans 8:29, 30) f. *præ* PRE- A. I. 1 + *destinare* make fast or firm, establish; see DESTINE.] **1.** *Theol.* Of God: To foreordain: **a.** to eternal life; **b.** to any fate or lot; to foreordain everything that comes to pass. **2.** To destine (as by fate); to fix beforehand by human (or animal) determination 1593.
1. a. He that is predestynate is written in the boke of lyfe 1530. **b.** These..taught that certain were by God's foreknowledge so predestinated

to death that neither Christ's passion nor baptism..could help them 1887.

Predestination (prīdestinēⁱ·ʃən, prī-). ME. [– eccl. L. *prædestinatio* (Augustine, Boethius), f. *predestinare*; see prec., -ION. Cf. (O)Fr. *prédestination*.] **1.** *Theol.*, etc. The action by which God is held to have immutably determined all (or some particular) events by an eternal decree or purpose. **a.** The action of God in foreordaining certain of mankind through grace to salvation or eternal life (= *election*, and opp. to *reprobation*). **b.** The action of God in foreordaining whatever comes to pass; *esp.* the lot and fate of all men. late ME. **2.** *gen.* Previous determination or appointment; fate, destiny 1631.

1. a. The most blessed and comfortable doctrine of P. 1579. **b.** P. is as well to the reprobate, as to the Elect. Election pertaineth only to them that be saved. P., in that it respecteth the Reprobate, is called Reprobation: in that it respecteth the saved, is called Election. 1563. **2.** A kind of moral p., or over-ruling principle which cannot be resisted JOHNSON.

Predestine (prīde·stin), *v.* late ME. [– (O)Fr. *prédestiner* or eccl. L. *prædestinare*; see prec.] *trans.* To destine beforehand; to ordain or decree previously. (Usu. *pass.*)

Predetermination (prī:dĭtəɹminēⁱ·ʃən). 1646. [– med. L. *predeterminatio* (XIV), f. late and med. (eccl.) L. *prædeterminare*; see next, -ATION. In some uses f. PRE- A. I. 2 + DETERMINATION.] The action of predetermining; the fact or condition of being predetermined; previous determination.

The Calvinists are fierce in the matters of absolute P. JER. TAYLOR. Hear me, then, I beg of you, with no pre-determination to disregard me MISS BURNEY.

Predetermine (prīdĭtə·ɹmin), *v.* 1625. [– late and med. (eccl.) L. *prædeterminare*, f. *præ* PRE- A. I. 1 + L. *determinare* DETERMINE. Cf. Fr. *prédéterminer* (XVI).] To determine beforehand. **1.** *trans.* To fix beforehand; to decree beforehand, to predestine. Also with *obj. cl.* or *inf.* **2.** To direct or impel beforehand (*to* something) 1667. **3.** *intr.* To determine beforehand or previously (*to do* something) 1823.

1. Every man's end being predetermined, and unalterably..decreed DE FOE. **3.** He had almost predetermined to assent to his brother's prayer LYTTON. Hence **Predete·rminable** *a. rare*, determinable beforehand. **Predete·rminate** *a.* determined beforehand.

Predial (prī·diăl), *a.* (*sb.*) Also **prædial.** 1464. [– med.L. *prædialis*, f. L. *prædium* farm, estate; see -AL¹.] **1.** Consisting of or pertaining to land or farms; 'real', landed; rural; agrarian 1529. **2.** Arising from the occupation of farms or lands: agrarian 1641. **3.** Attached to farms or to the land; owing service as tenanting land 1754. **B.** *sb.* [adj. used ellipt.] †A predial tithe; a predial slave 1531.

2. The p. or rural disorders of Ireland 1833. *P. tithe*: tithe derived from the produce of the soil. **3.** *P. serf, slave, labour, servitude, villeinage*, etc.

Predicable (pre·dikăb'l), *a.* and *sb.* 1551. [– med.L. *prædicabilis* that may be affirmed, predicable, also as n. sb. *prædicabile* (in cl. L. = praiseworthy), f. L. *prædicare*; see PREDICATE *v.*, -ABLE. Cf. Fr. *prédicable* adj. and sb. (XVI).] **A.** *adj.* That may be predicated or affirmed; capable of being asserted 1598.

A people of whom great good is p. CARLYLE. Hence **Pre:dicabi·lity.**

B. *sb. gen.* That which may be predicated 1785. **b.** *spec.* in Aristotelian Logic (in *pl.*, tr. Gr. κατηγορικά): The classes or kinds of predicates viewed relatively to their subjects, to one or other of which classes every predicated thing may be referred; second intentions of predicates in relation to subjects 1551.

Of these relations Aristotle (*Topica* I. iv. v) recognized four, viz. *genus* (γένος), *definition* (ὅρος), *property* (ἴδιον), *accident* (συμβεβηκός). The 'Five Predicables', *genus, species, difference, property, accident*, are due to Porphyry and the Schoolmen, who substituted *species* for *definition*.

Predicament (prĭdi·kămĕnt). late ME. [– late L. *prædicamentum* (Augustine, Isidore; tr. Gr. κατηγορία CATEGORY, of Aristotle), f. L. *prædicare*; see PREDICATE *v.*, -MENT. Cf. (O)Fr. *prédicament*.] **1.** That which is predicated or asserted; *spec.* in *Logic.* (in *pl.*) the ten categories formed by Aristotle; see CATEGORY 1. **2.** A class about which a statement is made 1548. **3.** State of being; condition, situation, position; *esp.* an unpleasant, trying, or dangerous situation 1586.

3. His deep sense of..the cruel p. to which he was reduced SCOTT. Hence **Predicame·ntal** *a.*; **-ly** *adv.*

Predicant (pre·dikănt), *a.* and *sb.* 1590. [– L. *prædicans, -ant-*, pr. pple. of *prædicare*, in eccl. L., preach; see PREDICATE *v.*, -ANT. As sb. (now only in Du. form PREDIKANT) – Fr. *prédicant*.] **A.** *adj.* Given to or characterized by preaching; applied esp. to the Dominicans or Black Friars 1629. **B.** *sb.* A preacher; *spec.* a member of a predicant religious order. Now *rare* or *Obs.* 1590. **b.** = PREDIKANT.

These stipendiary, roving predicants 1590.

Predicate (pre·dikĕt), *sb.* 1532. [– late L. *prædicatum* 'quod dicitur de subjecto' (Boethius), tr. Gr. κατηγορεύμενον, n. pa. pple. of L. *prædicare* proclaim, declare (cf. PREACH), in med.L. predicate, f. *præ* PRE- + *dicare* make known, rel. to *dicere* say; see -ATE¹. Cf. (O)Fr. *prédicat*.] **1.** *Logic.* That which is predicated or said of the subject in a proposition; the second term of a proposition, which is affirmed or denied of the first term by means of the copula. (At first used in L. form, *prædicatum*.) **2.** *Gram.* The statement made about a subject, including the logical copula (which in a verb is expressed by the personal suffix) 1638. **b.** An appellation that asserts something 1882. **c.** A quality, an attribute 1872.

1. Existence is its own p. [i.e. The word *is* when it means *exists* is a p. as well as a copula] COLERIDGE. **2.** Thus in the sentence 'Time flies', *time* is called the subject, and *flies* the p...In using the word *predicate*, we mean the p. and copula combined. 1858.

Predicate (pre·dikeⁱt), *v.* 1552. [– *prædicat-*, pa. ppl. stem of L. *prædicare*; see prec., -ATE³.] **1.** *trans.* To proclaim, declare; to affirm, assert; also, to preach; to preach up, extol (*rare* or *obs.*) **b.** *intr.* or *absol.* To assert, affirm; to make a statement 1827. **2.** *spec. trans.* To assert or affirm as a quality, property, or attribute (*of* something) 1614. **b.** *Logic.* To state or assert (something) about the subject of a proposition 1570. **3.** To affirm (a statement or the like) *on* some given grounds; hence, 'to found a proposition, argument, etc. *on* some basis or data' (Bartlett); and *transf.* to found or base (anything) *on* or *upon* stated facts or conditions. *U.S.* 1766. ¶**4.** *erron.* = PREDICT *v.* 1623.

1. b. To think is mentally to p. 1866. **2. b.** The famous..*Dictum de omni et nullo*, that whatever is predicated..universally of any Class..may be also predicated of any part of that Class 1864. **3.** This..is predicated upon my confidence in his ability 1839.

Predication (predikēⁱ·ʃən). ME. [– (O)Fr. *prédication* or L. *prædicatio* proclamation, praising (in eccl. L. preaching, in med.L. also predication), f. as prec.; see -ION.] **1.** The action of publicly or loudly proclaiming; preaching; an instance of this; a sermon, discourse. *Obs.* or *arch.* **2.** The action of predicating or asserting, or an instance of this; assertion, affirmation 1579. **b.** *spec.* in *Logic*: The assertion of something of or about a subject 1638.

Predicative (prĭdi·kătiv), *a.* 1846. [– L. *prædicativus*, f. as PREDICATE *v.*; see -IVE.] Having the quality of predicating, affirming, or asserting. Hence **Predi·catively** *adv.*

Predicator (pre·dikeⁱtəɹ). Now *rare.* 1483. [– OFr. *predicatour* (mod. *prédicateur*) or L. *prædicator* proclaimer, in eccl. L. preacher; f. as prec.; see -OR 2.] One who or that which predicates; *spec.* a preacher, a preaching friar. So **Predicatory** (pre·-dikĕtəri, -keⁱ:təri) *a.*

Predict (prĭdi·kt), *v.* 1546. [f. pa. ppl. stem of L. *prædicere*, f. *præ* PRE- A. I. 1 + *dicere* say.] †**1.** *trans.* To mention previously –1599. **2.** To foretell, prophesy, announce beforehand (an event, etc.) 1623. **3.** *intr.* To utter prediction; to prophesy 1652.

2. How often an observer can p. a man's actions 1884. **3.** No one can p. as to the length of her life MRS. CARLYLE. Hence **Predi·ctable** *a.* **Predictabi·lity. Predi·ctive** *a.* having the quality of predicting; **-ly** *adv.*; **-ness. Predi·ctor, -er,** one who or that which predicts. **Predi·ctory** *a.* of or pertaining to a predictor; predictive.

Prediction (prĭdi·kʃən), *sb.* 1561. [– L. *prædictio* premising, prediction, f. as prec.; see -ION. Cf. Fr. *prédiction* (XVI).] The action of predicting; also, an instance of this, a prophecy.

Dreames, and Predictions of Astrologie BACON.

Predigest (prīdidʒe·st, -dəi-), *v.* 1663. [f. PRE- A. I. 1 + DIGEST *v.*] *trans.* To digest beforehand; *spec.* to treat (food), before its introduction into the body, by a process similar to digestion.

Predigestion (prīdidʒe·styən, -tʃən, -dəi-). 1607. [f. PRE- A. I. 2 + DIGESTION.] †**1.** Over-hasty digestion –1698. **2.** Digestion by artificial means before introduction into the stomach 1890.

‖**Predikant** (predika·nt). Also **predicant.** 1849. [Du.; see PREDICANT.] A minister of the Dutch Protestant Church, esp. in S. Africa.

Predilection (prīdile·kʃən). 1742. [– Fr. *prédilection* – med.L. **prædilectio, -on-*, f. *prædiligere* prefer, f. *præ* PRE- + L. *diligere*; see -ION.] A mental preference or partiality; a favourable predisposition or prepossession.

Robert had never testified much p. for violent exertion SCOTT.

Predisponent (prīdispōᵘ·nĕnt), *a.* and *sb.* 1649. [f. PRE- A. I. 1, 2 + DISPONENT.] **A.** *adj.* Predisposing. Now *rare.* **B.** *sb.* A predisposing influence or cause 1771.

Predispose (prīdispōᵘ·z), *v.* 1646. [PRE- A. I. 1.] **1.** *trans.* To dispose (a person, etc.) beforehand; to render subject or liable *to* something; to incline or adapt previously. Also *absol.* **2.** To dispose of before 1666.

1. The majority of his judges..came predisposed to condemn him 1871. So **Predispo·sal,** previous disposal. **Predispo·sed** *ppl. a.* disposed or inclined beforehand; previously or already liable or subject.

Predisposition (prī:dispŏzi·ʃən). 1622. [PRE- A. I. 2.] **1.** The condition of being predisposed or inclined beforehand (*to* or *to do* something); a previous inclination or favourable state of mind 1626. **2.** *spec.* A physical condition which renders its possessor liable to the attack of certain diseases 1622.

1. A p. to heresy MACAULAY. **2.** P. to Small-pox 1801.

Predominance (prĭdǫ·minăns). 1602. [– Fr. *prédominance* or AL. *predominantia* (XIII); see next, -ANCE.] The fact or position of being predominant: **a.** *Astrol.* Ascendancy, superior influence 1605. **b.** *gen.* Prevailing or superior influence; prevalence, preponderance 1602.

b. The early p. of intellectual vigour BOSWELL. So **Predo·minancy**, the quality or fact of being predominant.

Predominant (prĭdǫ·minănt), *a.* and *sb.* 1576. [– (O)Fr. *prédominant* or med.L. **prædominant-*, pr. ppl. stem of **prædominari*; see PREDOMINATE *v.*, -ANT.] **A.** *adj.* Having ascendancy, power, influence, or authority over others; superior, ascendant, prevalent. **b.** More vaguely: More abundant; more frequent; prevailing 1601. **c.** *fig.* Superior in position 1797.

The temporary effect of a p. passion JOHNSON. *P. partner*: applied (after Lord Rosebery) to England among the several constituents of the United Kingdom. **b.** The p. winds HUXLEY. **c.** Made the roofs boldly p. 1867.

B. *sb.* That which predominates; a predominating person, influence, power, or authority; a predominating quality, fact, or feature 1589. Hence **Predo·minantly** *adv.*

Predo·minate, *a.* mistaken form for prec.

Predominate (prĭdǫ·mineⁱt), *v.* 1594. [– *prædominat-*, pa. ppl. stem of med.L. **prædominari*; see PRE- A. III, DOMINATE *v.* Cf. Fr. *prédominer* (XVI).] †**1.** *intr. Astrol.* To have ascendancy, to exert controlling influence –1633. **2.** *gen.* **a.** To have or exert controlling power, to lord it *over*; to be superior 1618. **b.** To be the stronger, main, or leading element; to preponderate 1594. **c.** To tower *over* 1814. **3.** *trans.* To dominate over, control. Now *rare.* 1607.

1. *Merry W.* II. ii. 294. **2. a.** The women in those parts never p. 1638. **b.** The desires that p. in our hearts JOHNSON. **3.** *Timon* IV. iii. 142. So **Predomina·tion**, the action, fact, or condition of predominating; predominance; ascendancy 1586.

Predoom (prīdū·m), *v.* 1618. [PRE- A. I. 1.] *trans.* **a.** To pronounce the doom of beforehand. **b.** To foreordain (some doom) *to*.

Pre-election (prī,ĭle·kʃən), *sb.* Also **præ-.** 1589. [PRE- A. I. 1.] †**1.** Selection, preference –1629. **2.** Previous choice; an anticipatory election 1611.

Pre-election (prī,ĭle·kʃən), *adj. phr.* 1893. [f. PRE- B. I. 1 + ELECTION.] Occurring or given before a parliamentary (or other) election.

Pre-eminence (pri,e·minĕns). Also †**preh-** (*h* inserted to avoid hiatus). ME. [– late L. *præeminentia*, f. L. *præeminens, -ent-*; see next, -ENCE. Cf. (O)Fr. *prééminence* (XIV).] Surpassing eminence. **1.** Higher rank or distinction; precedence; superiority. **2.** Superiority in any quality; the possession or existence of a quality or attribute in a pre-eminent degree. late ME. **3.** With *a* and *pl.* An individual case or instance of pre-eminence. Now *rare.* ME.

1. They allowed p. to their Magistrates rather than Supremacy 1647. **2.** Shakspere's p. consists chiefly in this, that he did supremely well what all were doing 1883. **3.** The office, the powers and preheminences annexed to it, differ very widely BURKE. So **Pre-e·minency** (now *rare*).

Pre-eminent (pri,e·minĕnt), *a.* Also †**preh-.** late ME. [– *præeminent-*, pr. ppl. stem of L. *præeminēre* project forwards, rise above, excel, f. *præ* PRE- A. III. Cf. Fr. *prééminent* (XV).] Eminent before or above others; excelling others; distinguished beyond others.

MILT. *P. L.* VIII. 279. Hence **Pre-e·minently** *adv.*

Pre-empt (pri,e·mᵖt), *v.* Chiefly *U.S.* 1857. [Back-formation from next.] *trans.* To obtain by pre-emption; hence (*U.S.*), to occupy (public land) so as to establish a pre-emptive title. Also *absol.* **b.** *fig.* To appropriate beforehand, pre-engage. Also *intr.* 1872. **c.** *Bridge.* To make a pre-emptive bid 1914. So **Pre-e·mptive** *a.* relating or belonging to, or of the nature of pre-emption. **Pre-e·mptor** (*U.S.*), one who acquires land by pre-emption.

Pre-emptive bid (Bridge): a bid intended to be high enough to prevent further bidding.

Pre-emption (pri,e·mᵖʃən). 1602. [– med.L. *præemptio*, f. *præempt-*, pa. ppl. stem of *præemere*, f. *præ* PRE- A. I. 2 + *emere* buy; see -ION.] Purchase by one person or corporation before an opportunity is offered to others; also, the right to make such purchase; *spec.*

a. Formerly in England, the prerogative of the sovereign of buying household provisions in preference to other persons, and at special rates. **b.** In U.S., Australia, etc., the purchase, or right of purchase, in preference and at a nominal price, of public land by an actual occupant, on condition of his improving it.

Preen (prīn), *sb.* Now *Sc.* and *n. dial.* [OE. *prēon*, corresp. to MLG. *prēme*, (M)Du. *priem(e* bodkin, dagger, MHG. *pfrieme* (G. *pfriem*) awl, ON. *prjónn* pin, peg.] **a.** A pin, a brooch. **b.** As type of a thing of small value 1470.

Preen (prīn), *v.*[1] Now *Sc.* and *n. dial.* ME. [f. prec. sb.; cf. Du. *priemen* stab, pierce, MLG. *prünen, prunen*, LG. *prünen, prienen* stitch together roughly.] †**1.** *trans.* To sew; to stitch up –1513. †**2.** To pierce; to transfix –1460. **3.** To fasten with a pin; to pin 1572.

Preen (prīn), *v.*[2] [Late ME. *preyne, prayne*, varying with *proyne* (see PRUNE *v.*[2]), of which it may be an alt. by assim. to PREEN *sb.*, with ref. to the boring or pricking action of the bird's beak.] **1.** *trans.* Of a bird: To trim (the feathers) with the beak 1486. **2.** *refl.* Of a person: To trim oneself up; to smooth and adorn oneself. Also, to pride oneself. late ME.

Pre-engage (prī:ėngē¹·dʒ), *v.* 1646. [PRE- A. I. 1.] **1.** *trans.* To bind in advance by a pledge or promise; to put under obligation beforehand 1649. **b.** *spec.* To betroth beforehand. Usu. *pass.* or *refl.* 1673. **c.** *intr.* To guarantee or engage beforehand. (With *inf.* or *subord. cl.*) 1654. **2.** *trans.* **a.** To win over beforehand, to prepossess 1646. **b.** To bespeak for oneself beforehand 1683. **3.** To preoccupy. Now *rare.* 1656.

1. She pressed me to stay dinner, but..I informed her that I was pre-engaged 1785. **2. b.** To preingage his Vote 1712.

Pre-engagement (prī:ėngē¹·dʒmĕnt). 1647. [PRE- A. I. 2; or f. prec. vb. + -MENT.] **1.** The act of pre-engaging, or fact of being already engaged. **2.** An engagement previously given or made 1647. **b.** *spec.* A prior marriage engagement 1684.

1. Two chairs had been tilted up in token of pre-ĕngagement 1896.

Pre-establish (prī,ėstæ·bliʃ), *v.* 1643. [PRE- A. I. 1.] *trans.* To establish beforehand.

Pre-established harmony (after Fr. *harmonie préétablie* Leibnitz): see HARMONY 1.

Pre-exilian (prī,ėgzi·liăn, -ėks-), *a.* 1863. [f. PRE- B. I. 1 + L. *exilium* EXILE *sb.* + -IAN.] Before exile; *spec.* of or belonging to the period of Jewish history before the Babylonian exile. So **Pre-exi·lic, Pre-e·xile** *adjs.*

Pre-exist (prī,ėgzi·st), *v.* 1599. [– Fr. *préexister* (XV) – late and med.L. *præexistere*; in later use f. PRE- A. I. 1 + EXIST.] **1.** *intr.* To exist before. **b.** To exist before the present life 1647. **c.** To exist ideally, before material embodiment 1775. **2.** *trans.* To exist before (something) 1778.

Pre-exi·stence. 1652. [– Fr. *préexistence* or late and med.L. *præexistentia* (XIV); in later use f. PRE- A. I. 2 + EXISTENCE.] Previous existence; *esp.* of the soul before its union with the body.

Pre-existent (prī,ėgzi·stĕnt), *a.* 1624. [– Fr. *préexistent* (XV) or late and med.L. *præexistens, -ent-*; in mod. use f. PRE- A. I. 2 + EXISTENT.] Existing beforehand, or before some person, thing, or event.

Preface (pre·fĕs), *sb.* late ME. [– (O)Fr. *préface* – med.L. *præfatia*, for L. *præfatio*, f. *præfari, -fat-*, f. *præ* PRE- + *fari* speak.] **I.** In the liturgies of Christian Churches: The introduction or prelude to the central part of the Eucharistic service (the consecration, etc.) concluding with the Sanctus.

Proper P., a variation of the Common P., to be used at certain seasons, including a special part proper to the particular occasion.

II. 1. The introduction to a literary work, usu. explaining its subject, purpose, scope, and method. late ME. **2.** The introductory part of a speech; an introduction 1530. **3.** *fig.* Something preliminary or introductory 1594.

1. I have run into a p., while I professed to write a dedication FIELDING. **2.** This superficiall tale, Is but a p. of her worthy praise SHAKS.

Preface (pre·fĕs), *v.* 1616. [f. prec. sb.] **1.** *intr.* To make introductory remarks 1619. **2.** *trans.* To write or say (something) as a preface; to state beforehand. Now *rare* or *Obs.* 1628. †**3.** *fig.* To introduce, precede, herald –1807. **4.** To furnish (a book, etc.) with a preface; to commence (a writing or speech) with a preface or introduction 1691. **5.** *fig.* To place in front of; to face (*with* something) 1658. **6.** To come before as an introduction 1843.

1. I will p. no longer, but proceed WALTON. **4.** I must p. this letter with an honest declaration SWIFT. **5.** Not prefacing old Rags with Plush 1658. **6.** A depressing..passage has prefaced every new page I have turned in life C. BRONTË. Hence **Pre·facer**, one who makes or writes a p.

Prefatorial (prefătōᵊ·riăl), *a.* 1799. [f. as next + -AL¹.] Of or pertaining to a prefacer or a preface; prefatory. Hence **Prefato·rially** *adv.*

Prefatory (pre·fătəri), *a.* 1671. [f. L. *præfatio* preface + -ORY².] Of the nature of a preface; introductory, preliminary.

The P. Note which precedes the volume 1860. Hence **Pre·fatorily** *adv.*

Prefect, præfect (prī·fekt). ME. [– OFr. *prefect*, mod. *préfet*, – L. *præfectus* subst. use of pa. pple. of *præficere* set over, f. *præ* PRE- A. III + *facere* make, constitute.] **1.** A person appointed to a position of command. Applied as a title to various officers in ancient or modern times. **a.** Repr. L. *præfectus*, In ancient Rome and the Roman empire, the title of various officers civil and military, e.g. the prefect or chief magistrate of the city, *præfectus urbi*, the civil governor of a province, a colony, or provincial city, the commander of the pretorian troops, *præfectus prætorio*, etc. ME. **b.** *esp.* (repr. Fr. *préfet.*) The chief administrative officer of a department of France. *P. of Police*, the head of the police administration in Paris and the department of the Seine. 1827. **2.** *transf.* In some English Schools, one of the body of senior pupils to whom authority is delegated for the maintenance of order and discipline 1629. So **Prefe·ctoral, Prefecto·rial** *adjs.* of or pertaining to a p. or prefects; *esp.* in the English Public School system. **Pre·fectship** = next 1.

Prefecture (prī·fektiŭɹ). 1577. [– (O)Fr. *préfecture* or L. *præfectura*, f. *præfectus*; see prec., -URE.] **1.** The office or position of prefect, ancient or modern; the period during which such office is held 1608. **2.** A district under the government of a prefect 1577. **b.** = Chinese *fu*, an administrative district of a province; also a corresponding district in Japan 1885. **3.** The official residence of a prefect or French *préfet* 1848. Hence **Prefe·ctural** *a.* So **Prefe·ctureship** 1559.

Prefer (prĭfɜ̄·ɹ), *v.* late ME. [– (O)Fr. *préférer* – L. *præferre*, f. *præ* PRE- A. III + *ferre* bear.] **I. 1.** *trans.* To put forward, in status, rank, or fortune; to promote (*to* a position or office). **b.** *transf.* To promote (in various uses) 1533. †**2.** To forward, advance, promote (a result); to assist in bringing about –1647.

1. Happy..that he never preferred a Man who has not proved remarkably serviceable to his Country STEELE. **b.** All Grasiers preferre their Cattell from meaner Pastures to better BACON. **2.** Thus fingring money to preferre the case 1600.

II. †**1.** *trans.* To put or set in front or before –1575. **2.** To put (something) before any one for acceptance; to hold out, offer; to introduce or recommend. *Obs.* or *arch.* 1573. **3.** To lay (a matter) before any one formally for consideration, approval, or sanction; to bring forward (a statement, bill, indictment, etc.) 1559.

2. He spake, and to her hand preferr'd the bowl POPE. **3.** Preferring an indictment against her for stealing his goods 1884.

III. To set or hold (one thing) before another in favour or esteem; to choose rather; to like better. Now the chief sense. late ME. **b.** *Law.* To give preference to as a creditor. late ME.

Afore all worldly thynges prefarre thou the honour & medytacion of god 1502. Hence **Pre·ferable** *a.* worthy to be preferred; more desirable; whence **Pre:ferabi·lity, Pre·ferableness**, the quality of being preferable. **Pre·ferably** *adv.* **Prefe·rred** *ppl. a.* in senses of the vb.; *Preferred share, stock* = PREFERENCE *share, stock.*

Preference (pre·fĕrĕns). 1603. [– (O)Fr. *préférence* – med.L. *preferentia*, f. *præferent-*, pr. ppl. stem of L. *præferre*; see prec., -ENCE.] **1.** The action of preferring or the fact of being preferred; liking for one thing before another; prior favour or choice 1656. †**2.** Precedence, superiority –1793. **3.** That which one prefers; the favourite 1864. **4.** Preferment; promotion. Now *rare.* 1656. **5.** A prior claim to something; *spec.* priority of payment given to a certain debt or class of debts; a prior right to payment 1665. **b.** Short for *p. share* 1890. **6.** *Pol. Econ.* The practical favouring of one customer before others in business relations; *spec.* the favouring of one country by admitting its products at a lower import duty than that levied on those of others or of foreigners generally, or by levying a duty on the latter while admitting the former free 1887.

1. [It] can't be that the mind is indifferent before it comes to have a choice, or till it has a P. 1754. **3.** Of the two, this is my p. (*mod.*

colloq.). 5. *Fraudulent p.*, prior payment made by a bankrupt with the object of preventing the equal distribution of his assets among all his creditors. 6. Still less am I afraid to preach to you p. with our Colonies J. CHAMBERLAIN. *attrib.* and *Comb.*, as **p. bond, share, stock,** i.e. on which dividend or interest is payable before any is paid on ordinary stock.

Pre·ferent, *a.* 1883. [f. PREFERENCE, after *difference, different*; see prec., -ENT.] Having preference or precedence; having a right to priority of payment or consideration.

Preferential (prefĕre·nʃăl), *a.* 1849. [f. as prec., after *difference, differential*; see -IAL.] Of, pertaining to, or of the nature of preference; showing or giving, receiving or enjoying, a preference. **b.** *Pol. Econ.* Of the nature of or characterized by import duties favouring particular countries, *spec.* in favour of trade between Great Britain and her colonies 1903.

The king was allowed a 'p.' claim on the public revenue STUBBS. **b.** A p. treatment of 12½ per cent. 1903. Hence **Prefere·ntialism,** the system of giving preference in the fixing of a tariff. **Prefere·ntialist,** an advocate of preference in tariff relations. **Prefere·ntially** *adv.*

Preferment (prǐfə̄·ɹmĕnt). 1451. [f. PREFER + -MENT.] **I.** †**1.** Furtherance, promotion –1581. **2.** Advancement in condition, status, or position in life; in early use, also, that which is done or given towards the advancement of the children of a family 1478. **3.** A post which gives social or pecuniary advancement; usu. an eccl. appointment 1536.

2. Vpon hope of p. to the diuinitie lecture in Oxforde 1553.

II. †**a.** The action or fact of preferring as more desirable; the giving of preference; preference, advantage –1754. **b.** *spec.* Priority of right, claim, or privilege; *esp.* prior right to receive payment, or to purchase or offer for anything to be sold or let. *arch.* 1451.

Prefigurate (prǐfi·giŭreit), *v.* Now *rare.* 1530. [– *præfigurat-*, pa. ppl. stem of eccl. L. *præfigurare* PREFIGURE; see -ATE³.] = PREFIGURE. So **Prefi·gurate** *ppl. a.* prefigured.

Prefiguration (prǐfigiŭrēi·ʃən). late ME. [– eccl. L. *præfiguratio* (Cyprian), f. as prec.; see -ION.] **1.** The action of prefiguring; representation beforehand by a figure or type. **2.** That in which something is prefigured; a prototype 1600.

Prefigurative (prǐfi·giŭrĕtiv), *a.* 1504. [– med.L. *præfigurativus*, f. as prec.; see -IVE.] Prefiguring, foreshadowing by a figure or type.

Prefigure (prǐfi·gəɹ, -iŭɹ), *v.* 1450. [– eccl. L. *præfigurare*; see PRE- A. I. 1, FIGURE *v.* Cf. (O)Fr. *préfigurer*.] **1.** *trans.* To represent beforehand by a figure or type. **2.** To figure or picture to oneself beforehand 1626.

1. The Jews Baptisme prefigured our spiritual washing 1651. Hence **Prefi·gurement,** the action or fact of prefiguring; the embodiment of this.

Prefix (prī·fiks), *sb.* 1646. [– mod.L. *præfixum*, subst. use of n. of *præfixus*, pa. pple. of L. *præfigere* fix in front; see PRE- A. II. c, FIX *v.*] **1.** *Gram.* A verbal element placed before and joined to a word or stem to add to or qualify its meaning, or (in some languages) as an inflexional formative. **2.** A title prefixed to a person's name, as *Mr., Dr.*, etc. 1836. **3.** The act of prefixing (*rare*) 1793.

Prefix (prǐfi·ks, *in* I. 1 *also* prī·fi·ks), *v.* late ME. [– (O)Fr. *préfixer*; see PRE- A. I. 1, II. c, and FIX *v.*] **I.** In ref. to time. **1.** *trans.* To fix beforehand (esp. a time). Now *rare.* †**2.** To fix or determine in one's mind beforehand; to resolve on; to make up (the mind) beforehand –1652. **II.** In ref. to order or place. **1.** To place at the beginning of a book or writing, esp. as an introduction or title 1538. **2.** *Gram.* To place (a word or particle) before a word, esp. in combination with it; cf. PREFIX *sb.* 1. Const. *before* (rare), *to*. 1605.

1. The legislator..will p. preambles to his principal laws 1875. **2.** In English, we generally p. the relative Article to the names of our rivers 1845.

Prefixion (prǐfi·kʃən). 1526. [– (O)Fr. *préfixion* or med.L. *præfixio* preappointment, f. *præfix-*, pa. ppl. stem of L. *præfigere*; see PREFIX *sb.*, -ION.] †**1.** Preappointment –1754. **2.** *Gram.* Employment of a prefix 1811.

Prefixture (prǐfi·kstiŭɹ). Also **præ-.** 1821. [f. PREFIX *v.* after FIXTURE.] **1.** The action of prefixing, esp. in grammar 1824. **2.** A word prefixed; a prefix 1821.

Prefloration (prǐflorēi·ʃən). 1832. [– Fr. *préfloraison*, f. *pré-* PRE- B + *floraison* flowering.] = ÆSTIVATION 3.

Prefoliation (prǐfōᵘli,ēi·ʃən). Also **præ-.** 1856. [– Fr. *préfoliation*; see PRE- B., FOLIATION. Cf. prec.] = VERNATION.

Preform (prǐ-, prifǭ·ɹm), *v.* 1601. [f. PRE- A. I. 1 + FORM *v.*¹ Cf. Fr. *préformer* (XVIII).] *trans.* To form or shape beforehand. Hence **Preformed** (prǐ·fǭ·ɹmd) *ppl. a.* formed beforehand, previously formed.

Preformation (prǐfǫɹmēi·ʃən). Also **præ-.** 1732. [f. PRE- A. I. 2 + FORMATION. Cf. Fr. *préformation* (XVIII).] The action or process of forming or shaping beforehand; previous formation.

Theory of p. (Biol.): the theory, formerly prevalent, that all the parts of the perfect organism exist previously formed in the germ, and are merely 'developed' in the process of reproduction; opp. to *theory of* EPIGENESIS.

Preformative (prǐfǭ·ɹmătiv), *a.* (*sb.*) Also **præ-.** 1821. [PRE- A. I. 3, II.] **1.** Having the quality or capacity of forming beforehand 1841. **2.** *Philol.* Prefixed as a formative element; said of a letter, syllable, etc. 1821. **B.** *sb. Philol.* A preformative particle; a prefix (esp. in Semitic langs.) 1821.

Prefrontal (prǐfrǫ·ntăl), *a.* (*sb.*) Also **præ-.** 1854. [f. PRE- A. II. a + FRONTAL.] *Anat.*, etc. **a.** Situated in front of the frontal bone of the skull. **b.** Situated in the fore part of the frontal lobe of the brain. **B.** *sb.* (*ellipt.* for *p. bone.*) A portion of the ethmoid, which forms a distinct bone in some reptiles, batrachians, and fishes 1854.

Pre-glacial (prǐglēi·ʃiăl), *a.* 1855. [PRE- B. I. 1 b.] Existing or occurring previous to the glacial period.

Pregnable (pre·gnăb'l), *a.* [XV *prenable* – (O)Fr. *prenable* takable, (OFr. also *pregnable*), f. *pren-*, stem of *prendre* take :– L. *prehendere*; see -ABLE. For the *g*, see IMPREGNABLE.] Of a fortress: Capable of being taken by assault. Also *transf.* **b.** *fig.* Open to attack; vulnerable 1836.

A strong hold kept by a coward is p. HOLLAND. **b.** A hard-headed English infidel, p. to neither religion nor common-sense 1837.

Pregnancy¹ (pre·gnănsi). 1529. [f. PREGNANT *a.*²; see -ANCY.] **1.** The condition of being pregnant, or with child or young; gestation. **2.** *transf.* Of the soil, etc.: Fertility, fruitfulness; abundance 1615. **3.** *fig.* In ref. to the mind: Fertility, productiveness, inventiveness, imaginative power; quickness of wit 1550. **4.** In ref. to speech words, actions, etc.: Latent capacity to produce results, potentiality 1818.

3. Pregnancie is made a Tapster, and hath his quicke wit wasted in giuing Recknings SHAKS. **4.** The political p. of certain words in these had excited my interest 1884.

†**Pre·gnancy**². 1649. [f. next; see -ANCY.] Cogency, force of an argument; clearness of evidence or proof; a weighty reason –1677.

†**Pre·gnant,** *a.*¹ late ME. [– Fr. *preignant* (XVI; perh. earlier in AFr.), pr. pple. of *preindre*, earlier *priembre* :– L. *premere* PRESS *v.*¹; see -ANT.] Of an argument, proof, etc.: Pressing, weighty; cogent, convincing; hence, clear, obvious –1766.

The Proofs were so P. and the Crime so black 1718. Hence †**Pre·gnantly** *adv.*¹

Pregnant (pre·gnănt), *a.*² late ME. [– Fr. *prégnant* or L. *prægnans, -ant-*, alt., by assim. to *-ans* -ANT, of *prægnas*, prob. f. *præ* PRE- + base of (*g*)*nasci* be born.] **I. 1.** With child or with young. Const. *with, of* (the offspring), *by* (the male parent). 1545. †**2.** *transf.* **a.** Of a plant or seed: Fertilized; fruitful –1769. **b.** Of the soil, etc.: Fertile, fruitful; prolific, teeming. Const. *with.* –1796.

1. *fig.* The p. quarry teem'd with human form GOLDSM. **2. b.** An Isle..call'd Marmora, very p. with Metals 1715.

II. In non-physical uses. **1. a.** Of a person or his mind: Teeming with ideas, imaginative, resourceful, ready. Const. *of, in,* or *to* with *inf. arch.* or *Obs.* late ME. †**b.** *esp.* of young persons, or their faculties: Apt to conceive or apprehend, quick-witted, promising –1707. †**c.** Apt to be influenced; receptive; ready. (Chiefly in Shaks.) –1628. **2.** Of words, symbolic acts, etc.: Full of meaning; suggesting more than is expressed; also, †full *of*, replete *with* (something significant) 1450. **3.** Fertile or fruitful in results; big *with* consequences 1591.

1. That Oxford scholar poor Of p. parts and quick inventive brain M. ARNOLD. **b.** She was a very p. Lady above her age, and died..when not full four years old FULLER. **c.** *Twel. N.* III. i. 100. **2.** The style is what was called p., leaving much to be filled up by the reader's reflection 1838. *P. construction*, in *Gram.* or *Rhet.*, a construction in which more is implied than the words express. *Negative p.*, in *Law*, a negative implying or involving an affirmative. **3.** They hold a p. lie well told, Is worth at least its weight in gold 1820. Hence **Pre·gnantly** *adv.*²

‖**Prehallux, præ-** (prǐhæ·lǫks). 1888. [mod. L. (Bardeleben, 1885), f. *præ* PRE- B. II. + HALLUX.] *Anat.* etc. A rudimentary structure, found on the inner side of the tarsus of some Mammalia, Reptilia, and Batrachia, and supposed to represent an additional digit.

Prehensile (prǐhe·nsəil, -sil), *a.* 1781. [– Fr. *préhensile* (Buffon), f. *prehens-*, pa. ppl. stem of L. *prehendere* seize; see -ILE.] Chiefly *Zool.* Capable of prehension; having the capacity of laying hold of anything.

Not any of the limbs of fishes are p. 1854. Hence **Prehensi·lity,** p. quality.

Prehension (prǐhe·nʃən). 1534. [– L. *prehensio* seizing, f. as prec.; see -ION.] **1.** The action of taking hold (physically); grasping, seizing. Chiefly *Zool.* 1828. †**2.** Seizure or arrest in the name of justice or authority; apprehension –1802. **3.** Mental apprehension 1836.

Prehistoric (prǐhistǫ·rik), *a.* 1851. [– Fr. *préhistorique*; see PRE- B. I. 1, HISTORIC.] Of, belonging to, or existing in the period antecedent to history, or to the first historical accounts of a people.

Homer and Troy lie far back in the p. period GLADSTONE. So **Prehisto·rical** *a.*, **-ly** *adv.*

Prehistory (prǐhi·stŏri). 1871. [f. PRE- + HISTORY, after prec.] The account of events or conditions prior to written or recorded history.

Prehnite (prēi·nəit). 1795. [– G. *prehnit*, f. Colonel von *Prehn*, who brought it from the Cape of Good Hope; see -ITE¹ 2 b.] *Min.* A hydrous silicate of aluminium and calcium, found in more or less globular masses of a pale green colour and vitreous lustre. Hence **Prehni·tic** *a. Chem.*, in *Prehnitic acid*, $C_{10}H_6O_8$, crystallizing in large prisms resembling the mineral p.

Prejacent (prǐ,dʒēi·sĕnt), *a.* (*sb.*) 1546. [– OFr. *préjacent* placed in front, pre-existent, or med.L. *præjacens, -ent-* pre-existent, prior to modification (in cl. L. lying in front), f. *præ* PRE- + *jacere* lie; see -ENT.] †**1.** Pre-existent –1703. **2.** *Logic.* Laid down previously; constituting the original proposition from which another is inferred. Hence *ellipt.* as *sb.* 1840.

Prejudge (prǐ,dʒɒ·dʒ), *v.* 1579. [f. PRE- A. I. 1 + JUDGE *v.*, after Fr. *préjuger* or L. *præjudicare*.] **1.** *trans.* To pass judgement, or pronounce sentence on, before trial, or without proper inquiry; hence, to judge (a person, cause, opinion, action, etc.) prematurely and without due consideration. †**b.** To judge unfavourably in advance BACON. †**2.** To anticipate (another) in judging –1719.

1. An unauthorised attempt to p. the very question to be inquired into 1845. So **Preju·dg(e)ment,** the action of prejudging; a conclusion formed before examination of the facts; prejudice.

†**Preju·dicate,** *ppl. a.* 1570. [– L. *præjudicatus*, pa. pple. of *præjudicare*; see next, -ATE².] **1.** Judged, or decided beforehand (*rare*) –1677. **2.** Formed (as an opinion)

prior to knowledge of the case; preconceived –1725. **3.** Affected by a preconceived opinion; prejudiced, biased –1716.

1. Neither were ignorant..how yᵉ cause was preiudicate before 1570. **2.** A..preiudicate opinion 1583. **3.** Their reasons enforce beliefe even from p. Readers SIR T. BROWNE.

†**Preju·dicate**, *v.* 1553. [– *præjudicat-*, pa. ppl. stem of L. *præjudicare* judge before, prejudice, etc., f. *præ* PRE- A. I. 1 + *judicare* judge; see -ATE³.] **1.** *trans.* = PREJUDICE *v.* I. –1670. **2.** = PREJUDGE 1. –1734. Also *intr.* or *absol.* **3.** = PREJUDICE *v.* II. 2. –1698.

1. It is euident, that the fault of the father may preiudicate the sonnes 1594. **2.** If that Vote had not prejudicated the Matter 1734.

Prejudication (prīˌdʒūdikēⁱ·ʃən). 1616. [f. prec; see -ATION.] The action of prejudicating; a judging beforehand; a previously formed decision or opinion.

Prejudice (pre·dʒŭdis), *sb.* ME. [– (O)Fr. *préjudice* – L. *præjudicium*, f. *præ* PRE- A. I. 2 + *judicium* judgement.] **I.** Injury, detriment, or damage, caused to a person by judgement or action in which his rights are disregarded; hence, injury to a person or thing likely to be the consequence of some action. †**b.** *gen.* Injury, damage, loss –1790.

Phr. *In p. of*, to the (intended or consequent) detriment or injury of. *To the p. of*, to the (resulting) injury of. *Without p.*, without detriment to any existing right or claim; *esp.* in *Law*, without detracting from one's own rights or claims.

II. †**1.** A previous judgement; *esp.* a premature or hasty judgement –1835. **2.** Preconceived opinion; bias favourable or unfavourable; prepossession; when used *absol.*, usu. with unfavourable connotation 1643. **b.** With *a* and *pl.*: An instance of this; a prepossession; an unreasoning predilection or objection 1654. †**3.** A preliminary or anticipatory judgement; an anticipation –1771.

2. P. renders a man's virtue his habit BURKE. Ignorance is the mother of p., whether among nations or individuals 1861. **b.** A historian dares not have a p., but he cannot escape a purpose 1894.

Prejudice (pre·dʒŭdis), *v.* 1472. [– (O)Fr. *préjudicier* to prejudice, f. *préjudice*; see prec.] **I.** *trans.* To affect injuriously or unfavourably; to injure or impair the validity of (a right, claim, statement, etc.). **b.** To injure materially; to damage. Now *rare*. 1591.

Yet no prescription of time could p. the title of the King of Heaven 1639. **b.** A wicket very much prejudiced by the rain 1884.

II. †**1.** To prejudge, *esp.* unfavourably (*rare*) –1642. **2.** To affect or fill with a prejudice; to give a bias or bent to, influence the mind or judgement of beforehand (often, unfairly). Const. *against*, *in favour of*, †*to*. 1610.

2. I wished..to p. my readers' minds in their favour rather than against them KINGSLEY.

Prejudicial (predʒŭdi·ʃăl), *a.*¹ late ME. [XV also *-el* – (O)Fr. *préjudiciel* †causing prejudice (in mod. Fr. = next).] **1.** Causing prejudice; detrimental, damaging (to rights, interests, etc.). †**2.** Of the nature of prejudice; prejudiced (*to* = against), unfavourably prepossessed –1643.

1. The existing system..was p. both to commerce and to learning MACAULAY. **2.** It was no time then to contend with their slow and prejudiciall belief MILT. Hence **Prejudi·cial-ly** *adv.*, **-ness.** So **Prejudi·cious** *a.* (now *rare*), in sense 1.

Pre-judicial (prīˌdʒudi·ʃăl), *a.*² 1651. [– late L. *præjudicialis*, f. *præjudicium* a judicial examination previous to trial (see PREJUDICE *sb.*) + -AL¹.] *Rom. Law.* Applied to a class of actions, whereby questions of right or fact, esp. as regards status, were determined, usu. with a view to further proceedings.

Prelacy (pre·lăsi). ME. [– AFr. *prelacie* – med.L. *prelatia*, f. *prælatus* PRELATE; see -ACY.] **1.** The office, position, or dignity of a prelate; a prelatic benefice or see. **2.** The order or rank of prelates; the body of prelates or of bishops collectively ME. †**3.** The authority of a prelate; ecclesiastical power –1577. **4.** The system of church government by prelates or bishops of lordly rank; a term, chiefly hostile, for EPISCOPACY 2. late ME.

1. Nominated by the king to titular bishoprics and other prelacies 1827. **4.** The Cleere Antithesis..betweene Presbytery and P. 1644. Others..began to associate p. with popery 1850.

Prelate (pre·lĕt), *sb.* ME. [– (O)Fr. *prélat* – med.L. *prælatus* subst. use of pa. pple. corresp. to L. *præferre* PREFER; see -ATE¹.] **1.** An eccl. dignitary of exalted rank, as a bishop, archbishop, metropolitan, or patriarch. †**b.** Applied to a chief priest of a non-Christian religion –1601. †**2.** A person having superiority, a chief, head, principal, superior –1780.

1. The curates are ill-paid, and the prelates are overpaid 1856. **b.** The kepers..shewed vnto the prelattes all thinges whych had hapened TINDALE *Matt.* 28:11. **2.** The humble subieccyon of the subiecte to the p. 1502. Hence **Pre·lateship**, the office, or tenure of office, of a p. **Pre·latess**, a female p.; an abbess or prioress; also, the wife of a p. (*joc.*). **Prela·tial** *a.* *rare*, of, pertaining to, or proper to a p. or prelacy. **Prela·tic, -al** *a.* of, pertaining to, or like a p.; governed by or adhering to prelates or prelacy; episcopal; episcopalian; **-ly** *adv.* **Pre·latism**, prelacy, lordly episcopacy; adherence to this; so **Pre·latist.**

†**Pre·late**, *v.* 1548. [f. prec. sb.] *intr.* To act the prelate; to perform the office of a prelate –1656.

Prelation (prĭlēⁱ·ʃən). Now *rare* or *Obs.* [ME. *prelacioune* – OFr. *prelacion* (mod. *prélation*) – L. *prælatio, -on-*, f. *prælat-*; see PRELATE *sb.*, -ION.] †**1.** Uttering, pronunciation (*rare*) –1659. **2.** The action of preferring or condition of being preferred; preferment; pre-eminence, superiority, dignity; preference. late ME.

Prelatize (pre·lătəiz), *v.* 1641. [f. PRELATE *sb.* + -IZE.] †**1.** *intr.* To be or become prelatical MILT. **2.** *trans.* To make prelatical; to bring under prelatic government 1864.

Prelatry (pre·lătri). 1641. [f. as prec. + -RY.] Prelacy.

Prelature (pre·lătiŭɹ). 1607. [– (O)Fr. *prélature* – med.L. *prælatura*; see PRELATE *sb.*, -URE.] = PRELACY 1, 2.

†**Pre·laty.** *rare.* 1641. [– med.L. *prælatia*; see PRELACY.] **1.** = PRELACY 4. –1644. **2.** The office or superiority of a prelate –1642.

Prelect, præ- (prĭle·kt), *v.* 1620. [– *prælect-*, pa. ppl. stem of L. *prælegere* read to others, lecture upon, f. *præ* PRE- + *legere* choose, read.] †**1.** *trans.* To choose in preference to others –1656. **2.** *intr.* To lecture or discourse (*to* an audience, *on* or *upon* a subject); to deliver a lecture 1785.

Prelection, præ- (prĭle·kʃən). 1587. [– L. *prælectio*, f. as prec.; see -ION.] **1.** A public lecture or discourse; *esp.* a lecture by a teacher to students at a college or university. **2.** A previous reading 1655.

Prelector, præ- (prĭle·ktəɹ). 1586. [– L. *prælector*, f. *prælegere*; see PRELECT, -OR 2.] A public reader or lecturer, esp. in a college or university. Hence **Prele·ctorship.**

Prelibation (prīləibēⁱ·ʃən). 1526. [– late L. *prælibatio*, f. *prælibare* taste beforehand; see PRE- A. I., LIBATION. Infl. (esp. in sense 2) by LIBATION.] **1.** A foretaste. Chiefly *fig.* **2.** An offering of first-fruits, or of the first taste, of anything. Now *rare*. 1635.

1. The wicked have a p. of that darkness they shall go unto hereafter 1633.

Prelim., abbrev. f. PRELIMINARY (examination, etc.).

Preliminary (prĭli·minări), *sb.* and *a.* 1656. [– Fr. *préliminaire* or mod.L. *præliminaris*, f. *præ* PRE- + L. *limen, limin-* threshold; see -ARY¹ and ².] **A.** *sb.* A preparatory step, measure or arrangement. Chiefly in *pl.* **b.** *ellipt.* Preliminary examination. (In student slang, often *prelim.*) 1882. **B.** *adj.* Preceding and leading up to the main subject or business; introductory; preparatory 1667.

A. The preliminaries for the lord Mohuns tryall 1693. **B.** It is for want of this p. knowledge 1890. Hence **Preli·minarily** *adv.*

Prelude (pre·lⁱūd), *sb.* 1561. [– Fr. *prélude* (Rabelais) or med.L. PRÆLUDIUM, f. *præludere*; see next.] **1.** An introductory performance, action, event, or condition, coming before one of more importance; an introduction, preface. **2.** *Mus.* A movement or piece forming the introduction to a musical work; *esp.* one preceding a fugue or forming the first piece of a suite 1658.

1. A sort of p. to the still greater work which he had to do 1869. **2.** *attrib.* So the hoarse thunder Growl'd long—but low—a p. note of death HOOD.

Prelude (pre·lⁱūd), *v.* 1640. [– L. *præludere* play beforehand, preface, f. *præ* PRE- A. I. 1 + *ludere* play, f. *ludus* play. Till *c*1830 (prĭlⁱū·d).] **1.** *trans.* To serve as a prelude to; to prepare the way for, introduce; to foreshadow 1655. **b.** Of an agent: To introduce with a prelude or preliminary action 1697. **2.** *intr.* To give a prelude or introductory performance *to* some later action 1640. **b.** To be introductory (*to*) 1838. **3.** *Mus.* **a.** *intr.* To play a prelude before the main composition 1678. **b.** *trans.* (*a*) To play as a prelude; (*b*) to introduce with a prelude 1795.

1. When the gray Of morn preludes the splendour of the day DRYDEN. **2.** He..was even in his Youth preluding to his Georgics, and his Æneis DRYDEN. **3. b.** And I—my harp would p. woe—I cannot all command the strings TENNYSON. Hence **Pre·luder**, one who plays or performs a prelude.

Preludial (prĭlⁱū·diăl), *a.* 1649. [f. med.L. *præludium* (see next) + -AL¹.] Pertaining to, or of the nature of, a prelude; serving to introduce. So **Prelu·dious** *a.*

‖**Preludium, præ-** (prĭliū·diŏm). Now *rare*. 1570. [med.L.; see PRELUDE *sb.*] A prelude or introduction; a preliminary.

Prelusion (prĭlⁱū·ʒən). 1597. [– L. *prælusio*, f. *prælus-*, pa. ppl. stem of *præludere*; see PRELUDE *v.*, -ION.] The performance of a prelude; an introduction.

Prelusive (prĭlⁱū·siv), *a.* 1605. [f. as prec. + -IVE.] Of the nature of or serving as a prelude; introductory to what is to follow. Hence **Prelu·sively** *adv.*

Prelusory (prĭlⁱū·səri), *a.* 1640. [– late L. *prælusorius* (Ambrose), f. as prec.; see -ORY².] = prec.

Premature (prī·-, pre·mătiŭɹ, prī:mătiūᵊ·ɹ), *a.* 1529. [– L. *præmaturus* very early, f. *præ* PRE- A. + *maturus* MATURE *a.*] Occurring, existing, or done before the proper time; too early; over-hasty.

His birth was p. 1838. The advance of p. age 1874. Hence **Premature-ly** *adv.*, **-ness.**

Prematurity (prī-, premătiūᵊ·rĭti). 1611. [– Fr. *prématurité*; see PRE- A. I. 2 and MATURITY.] †**1.** Of plants: Early ripening or flowering –1707. **2.** = PRECOCITY 2. 1778. **3.** Undue earliness or haste (of any action or event); precipitancy 1706.

2. P. of thought and feeling has often an early grave 1907.

‖**Premaxi·lla, præ-.** 1866. [mod.L., f. PRE- B. + MAXILLA, after next.] *Zool.* The premaxillary bone.

Premaxillary (prīmæksi·lări), *a.* and *sb.* 1854. [f. PRE- B. II. + MAXILLARY.] *Anat.* **A.** *adj.* Situated in front of the maxilla or upper jaw. **B.** *sb.* The premaxillary bone.

Premeditate (prĭme·diteⁱt), *v.* 1548. [– *præmeditat-*, pa. ppl. stem of L. *præmeditari*; see PRE- A. I. 1, MEDITATE *v.*] To meditate beforehand. **1.** *trans.* To study with a view to subsequent action, to think out beforehand; now *esp.* to plan or contrive previously. **2.** *intr.* To think deliberately beforehand or in advance (*on* or *of* something) 1586.

1. I began now to p. the Destruction of the next that I saw there DE FOE. **2.** I never p., dear lady 1849. Hence **Preme·ditated** *ppl. a.* previously contrived or planned. **Preme·ditatedly** *adv.* with premeditation.

Premeditation (prī-, prĭmeditēⁱ·ʃən). Also †**præ-.** late ME. [– (O)Fr. *préméditation* or L. *præmeditatio*, f. as prec.; see -ION.] The action of premeditating; previous thinking out of something to be done; now *esp.* designing, planning, or contrivance to do something.

Premiate (prī·mieⁱt), *v.* *rare.* 1537. [– *præmiat-*, pa. ppl. stem of L. *præmiari* stipulate for a reward, f. *præmium* reward; see -ATE³.] *trans.* To reward; to award a prize to. Hence **Pre·miated** *ppl. a.*

Premier (pre·miəɹ, prī·miəɹ), *a.* and *sb.*[1] 1470. [– (O)Fr. *premier* :– L. *primarius* PRIMARY *a.*] **A.** *adj.* **1.** First in position, importance, or rank; chief, leading, foremost. **2.** First in time; earliest 1652.

1. One of the p. knights of the order of the garter 1630. †*P. minister, Minister p.* [cf. Fr. *premier ministre*], = B. **2.** The p. advertisement of opera in England 1882.

B. *sb.* [Short for *p. minister.*] **a.** *gen.* The first or chief minister of any ruler; the chief officer of an institution 1711. **b.** The first minister of the Crown, the PRIME MINISTER of Great Britain or one of its colonies 1726. **c.** *U.S.* The Secretary of State 1905. **Pre·miership.**

‖**Premier** (prəmye), *sb.*[2] 1865. [Fr., short for *premier étage.*] The first floor, in a hotel, etc.

‖**Première** (prəmyę̄r). 1895. [Fr., short for *première représentation.*] A first performance of a play; a 'first night'.

Premillennial (prī:mile·niăl), *a.* 1846. [f. PRE- B. I. 1 + MILLENNIAL *a.*] Occurring before the millenium; said particularly of the Second Advent of Christ; also, pertaining to the world as it now is before the millennium. So **Premille·nnian** *a.*

Premise, premiss (pre·mis), *sb.* late ME. [– (O)Fr. *prémisse* – med.L. *præmissa*, subst. use (sc. *propositio*) of fem. sing. and n. pl. pa. pple. of L. *præmittere* send or set before, f. *præ* PRE- A + *mittere* put, send.] **I.** in *Logic.* (Often *premiss.*) A previous proposition from which another follows as a conclusion; *spec.* in *pl.* the two propositions from which the conclusion is derived in a syllogism.

Her foe's conclusions were not sound, From premisses erroneous brought SWIFT.

II. in *Law* and *gen.* (Now always *premise(s.)* **1.** *pl.* The matters or things stated or mentioned previously; the aforesaid, the foregoing. Rarely in *sing.* Now *rare* or *Obs.* exc. in techn. use. late ME. **2.** *Law.* (*pl.*) That part in the beginning of a deed or conveyance which sets forth the names of the grantor, grantee, and things granted, together with the consideration or reason of the grant 1641. **3.** *Law.* (*pl.*) (*spec.* use of 1.) The subject of a conveyance or bequest, specified in the premises of the deed; = the houses, lands, or tenements beforementioned 1480. **4.** (*pl.*) A house or building with its grounds or other appurtenances 1730. †**5.** Previous circumstances or events –1759.

1. To discuss questions conformably to the premises thus agreed on 1830. **3.** Alice Higgins devised the premises, being a term for 999 years, to trustees 1818. **4.** Nor shall any coroner's inquest be held on such licensed premises 1902.

Premise (prĭmai·z), *v.* 1526. [f. prec. sb.; cf. PREMIT.] **1.** *trans.* To state before something else; to say or write by way of introduction. (With *simple obj.* or, now usu., *obj. cl.*) **b.** *Logic.* To state in the premises. Also *absol.* 1684. †**2.** To make, do, perform, or use beforehand –1836. **3.** *transf.* To preface or introduce (*with, by* something else) 1823.

1. b. For if only *some* is premised, we cannot conclude *all* 1864. **2.** In the first case, of ulcers, I premised a seton in the arm 1836.

†**Premi·t,** *v.* 1540. [– L. *præmittere*; see PREMISE *sb.*] **1.** *trans.* = PREMISE *v.* 1. –1784. **2.** = PREMISE *v.* 2. –1670.

Premium (prī·miŭm). *Pl.* **-iums,** formerly **-ia.** 1601. [– L. *præmium* booty, profit, reward, f. *præ* PRE- A. I. 1 + *emere* buy, orig. take.] **1.** A reward given for some specific act or as an incentive; a prize. **2.** The amount agreed on, in an insurance policy, to be paid at one time or from time to time in consideration of a contract of insurance 1661. **3.** A bonus; a bounty on the production or exportation of goods 1695. **4.** A fee paid for instruction in a profession or trade 1765. **5.** The charge made for changing one currency into another of greater value; agio; hence, the excess value of one currency over another 1717.

1. He knew the p. set upon his head 1765. **2.** The conditions of insurance are 2s. per cent. premium 1766. **3.** If no p. were allowed for the hire of money, few persons would care to lend it 1766. **5.** *At a p.*: at more than the nominal or usual value; above par; *fig.* in high esteem; When the exchange is unfavourable, and bills at a p., this p. . . varies from day to day 1863.

Comb.: **p. bonus system, p. system,** a system by which a bonus is paid in addition to wages in proportion to the amount or value of work done.

Premolar (prīmōᵘ·lăɹ), *sb.* (*a.*) 1842. [f. PRE- B. II. + MOLAR.] One of the set of molar teeth in front of the true molars, replacing the molars or grinders of the milk dentition; a false molar, in man called 'bicuspid'. **B.** *adj.* That is a premolar 1880.

Premonish (prĭmǫ·niʃ), *v.* Now *rare.* 1526. [f. L. *præmonēre* forewarn, after MONISH, ADMONISH.] *trans.* To forewarn; to admonish beforehand. **b.** *intr.* or *absol.* 1550.

Premonition (prīmoni·ʃən). 1456. [– Fr. *prémonition* or late L. *præmonitio*, f. pa. ppl. stem of L. *præmonēre*; see prec., -ION. Cf. PREMUNITION.] The action of premonishing; a previous notification or warning of subsequent events; a forewarning.

Premonitor (prĭmǫ·nitəɹ). 1656. [– L. *præmonitor*, f. as prec.; see -OR 2.] One who or that which forewarns. So **Premo·nitory** *a.* giving or conveying premonition. **Premo·nitorily** *adv.*

Premonstrant (prĭmǫ·nstrănt), *sb.* and *a.* 1700. [– OFr. *premonstrant*, pr. pple. of *premonstrer* foreshow, used to repr. med.L. PREMONSTRATENSIS.] *Eccl. Hist.* **A.** *sb.* = next A. **B.** *adj.* = next B. 1872.

Premonstratensian (prĭmǫnstrăte·nsiăn), *sb.* and *a.* Also †**præ-.** 1695. [f. med.L. *Præmonstratensis* (see next) + -AN.] **A.** *sb.* A member of the order of regular canons founded by St. Norbert at Prémontré, near Laon, in 1119. Also, a member of a corresponding order of nuns. **B.** *adj.* Belonging to this order 1695.

‖**Premonstrate·nsis, præ-,** *a.* and *sb.* late ME. [med.L. = belonging to Prémontré, (*locus*) *Præmonstratus* lit. the place foreshown, so called because prophetically pointed out by St. Norbert.] = prec. *a.* and *sb.*

†**Premonstra·tion.** 1450. [– late (eccl.) L. *præmonstratio*, f. pa. ppl. stem of L. *præmonstrare* show beforehand.] The action of making known beforehand; a showing forth beforehand –1623. So **Pre·monstrator** 1660.

Premorse (prĭmǭ·ɹs), *a.* Also **præ-.** 1753. [– L. *præmorsus*, pa. pple. of *præmordēre* bite (off), f. *præ* PRE- A. II. c. + *mordēre* bite.] *Bot.* and *Entom.* Having the end abruptly truncate, as if bitten or broken off.

Premotion (prīmōᵘ·ʃən). 1643. [– med. L. *præmotio*, f. late L. *præmovēre* move (anything) beforehand; see PRE- A. I. 2, MOTION.] Motion or impulse given beforehand; *esp.* applied to divine action held to determine the will of the creature. So **Premove** *v. trans.* 1598.

Premunire: see PRÆMUNIRE.

Premunition (prīmiuni·ʃən). Now *rare.* 1456. [– L. *præmunitio* (in rhet. 'preparation'), f. L. *præmunire* fortify or protect in front, f. *præ* PRE- A. II. c. + *munire* fortify, defend. Cf. PRÆMUNIRE.] **1.** The action of fortifying or guarding beforehand; a forearming 1607. **2.** By confusion, = PREMONITION. (The earlier use.) *Obs.* exc. as referring to PRÆMUNIENTES. So **Premu·nitory** *a.* = PREMONITORY *a.*

Prenatal (prīnēⁱ·tăl), *a.* 1826. [f. PRE- B. I. 1 d + NATAL *a.*] Existing or occurring before birth; antenatal.

Prender (pre·ndəɹ). 1597. [subst. use of AFr. *prender* = (O)Fr. *prendre* take; see -ER[4].] *Law.* The power or right of taking a thing without its being offered.

Prenominal (prĭnǫ·minăl), *a.* 1646. [f. L. *prænomin-*, stem of PRÆNOMEN + -AL[1].] Pertaining to the *prænomen* or personal name; also, to the first word in binominal specific names.

Prenotion (prīnōᵘ·ʃən). Now *rare.* 1588. [– L. *prænotio*, tr. Gr. πρόληψις of the Epicureans; see PRE- A. I. 2, NOTION. Cf. Fr. *prénotion.*] **1.** A mental perception of something before it exists or happens. Also, prescience. **2.** A previous notion; a preconceived idea 1605.

Prentice (pre·ntis), *sb.* Now *arch.* or *dial.* ME. [aphet. f. APPRENTICE.] **1.** = APPRENTICE *sb.* 1. †**2.** *Law.* = APPRENTICE *sb.* 2. –1530. †**3.** *fig.* = APPRENTICE *sb.* 3 –1586. **4.** *attrib.*, as *p.-boy, ear, hand,* etc. 1594. Hence **Pre·ntice** *v. trans.* (*arch.* or *dial.*) = APPRENTICE *v.* †**Pre·nticehood** = APPRENTICESHIP 1. **Pre·nticeship** = APPRENTICESHIP 1–3.

†**Prenu·nciate, -tiate,** *v.* 1623. [– *prænuntiat-*, pa.ppl. stem of L. *prænuntiare* foretell, f. *præ* PRE- A. I. 1 + *nuntiare* announce; see -ATE[3].] *trans.* To announce beforehand; to foretell, predict –1652. So †**Prenuncia·tion,** announcement beforehand, prediction.

Preoccupancy (prĭ,ǫ·kiŭpănsi). 1755. [f. PRE- A. I. 2 + OCCUPANCY.] **1.** = PREOCCUPATION 3. **2.** The state of being preoccupied or engaged 1893.

†**Preo·ccupate,** *v.* 1582. [– *præoccupat-*, pa. ppl. stem of L. *præoccupare*; see PREOCCUPY, -ATE[3].] **1.** *trans.* To take possession of beforehand or before another; to usurp –1727. **2.** To take at unawares, surprise, overtake –1654. **3.** To prepossess; to influence, bias, prejudice –1681. **4.** To anticipate, forestall –1678.

4. Revenge triumphes over death,..greif flyeth to it, feare preoccupateth it BACON.

Preoccupation (prī,ǫkiŭpēⁱ·ʃən). 1552. [– Fr. *préoccupation* or L. *præoccupatio*, f. as prec.] The action of preoccupying. †**1.** The meeting of objections beforehand. In *Rhet.* A figure of speech in which objections are anticipated and prevented; prolepsis. –1683. **2.** Prepossession; bias; prejudice 1603. **3.** Actual occupation (of a place) beforehand 1658. **4.** Occupation that takes precedence of all other 1873. **5.** Mental absorption 1854.

4. Marrying and giving in marriage is now and always has been the great p. of man and womankind 1885. **5.** The p. of men's minds with this absorbing subject 1854.

Preoccupied (prĭ,ǫ·kiŭpəid), *ppl. a.* 1849. [f. next + -ED[1].] Occupied previously. **a.** Absorbed in thought. **b.** *Zool.* and *Bot.* Of a name: already used for something else. Hence **Preo·ccupiedly** *adv.*

Preoccupy (prĭ,ǫ·kiŭpəi), *v.* 1567. [f. PRE- A. I. 1 + OCCUPY, after L. *præoccupare* seize beforehand.] **1.** *trans.* To occupy or engage beforehand; to engross; †to prepossess, to bias. **2.** To take possession of before another; to appropriate for use in advance 1622.

1. *Cor.* II. iii. 240. **2.** The name of Antoninus being preoccupied by Antoninus Pius M. ARNOLD.

Preocular (prĭ,ǫ·kiŭlăɹ), *a.* (*sb.*) 1826. [PRE- B. II. + L. *oculus* + -AR[1].] Situated in front of the eye; *spec.* applied to certain plates in the head of a reptile.

Pre-operculum, præ- (prī,opə̄·ɹkiŭlŏm). 1828. [f. PRE- A. II. + OPERCULUM.] **1.** *Ichthyol.* The foremost of the four bones forming the operculum in fishes. **2.** *Bot.* = OPERCULUM 2. 1864. So **Pre-ope·rcular** *a.* of or pertaining to the p.; also *absol.* or as *sb.*, the p.

Pre-option (prĭ,ǫ·pʃən). 1666. [PRE- A. I. 2.] An option before any one else; right of first choice.

Pre-orbital (prĭ,ǭ·ɹbităl), *a.* (*sb.*) Also **præ-.** 1852. [f. PRE- B. II. + ORBIT + -AL[1].] *Zool.* Situated in front of the orbit or eye-socket. **B.** *sb.* The pre-orbital bone or process 1897.

Pre-ordain (prī,ǫɹdēⁱ·n), *v.* 1533. [f. PRE- A. I. 1 + ORDAIN, repr. late L. (Vulg.) *præordinare* predestine; so Fr. †*préordiner* (mod. *préordonner*).] *trans.* To ordain or appoint beforehand; in *Theol.* to foreordain. So **Pre-ordina·tion** (*rare*).

Pre-o·rdinate, *ppl. a. arch.* late ME. [– late L. (Vulg.) *præordinatus* foreordained, pa. pple. of *præordinare*; see prec., -ATE[3].] Foreordained, predestined.

Prep (prep). 1862. *School slang.* **1.** Short for PREPARATION (sense 1 c). **2.** Short for PREPARATORY *a.* (sense 2) 1905.

Preparation (prepărēⁱ·ʃən). late ME. [– (O)Fr. *préparation* – L. *præparatio*, f. *præparat-*, pa. ppl. stem of *præparare*; see PREPARE *v.*, -ION.] **1.** The action of preparing, or condition of being prepared; making or getting ready; fitting out, equipment. **b.** A preparatory act or proceeding; usu. in *pl.* Things done to make ready *for* something 1560. **c.** *spec.* The preparing of lessons, as a part of the routine of school work (abbrev. *prep*) 1862. **2.** The action or special process of putting something into proper condition for use; dressing and serving up (*of* food); composition, manufacture (*of* a chemical, medicinal, or other substance); drawing up (*of* a document) 1495. †**3.** *concr.* That which is prepared, esp. for warfare; an equipment; an armament –1781. **4.** *concr.* A substance specially prepared, e.g. as food or medicine, or in the arts or sciences. late ME. **b.** A specimen of a natural object specially prepared for some scientific purpose; *esp.* an animal body or part of one prepared for dissection, or preserved for examination 1753. **5.** The observances preliminary to the celebration of the Jewish sabbath or other festival; hence *transf.* (= *day of p.*) the day before the sabbath, etc. 1557. **6.** In devotional use: The action of preparing for Holy Communion; a set of prayers used before a celebration by the officiant and his ministers, or by a person intending to communicate; also, the first part of the Communion Office 1650. **7.** *Mus.* The preparing of a discord (see PREPARE *v.* 8 a); opp. to *percussion* and *resolution* 1727.

1. Be yare in thy p., for thy assaylant is quick, skilfull, and deadly SHAKS. **b.** The preparations for the marriage were commenced 1856. **2.** A new edition is in active p. 1895. **3.** The Turke with a most mighty P. makes for Cyprus SHAKS. **4.** The most commonly used preparations of opium 1836. **5.** And it was the p. of the Passeouer *John* 19:14.

attrib. and *Comb.* **p. day**: see 5.

Preparative (pri̇pæ·rătiv), *a.* and *sb.* late ME. [– (O)Fr. *préparatif*, *-ive* or med.L. *præparativus*, f. as prec.; see -IVE.] **A.** *adj.* **1.** Having the function or quality of preparing; serving as a preparation; preliminary; preparatory 1530. †**b.** *spec.* Of medicine: Serving to prepare the system for a course of treatment –1747. **c.** quasi-*adv.* In preparation 1632. **2.** Used in or for preparing (*rare*) 1745.

1. c. Such notes as she had taken p. to her trial GOLDSM.

B. *sb.* **1.** Something that prepares the way for something else; a preliminary; a preparation 1440. †**b.** *Med.* Something to prepare the system for medicine, or for a course of treatment. Often *fig.* –1778. **2.** A military or nautical signal sounded on a drum, bugle, etc., as an order to make ready 1635.

1. The preparatives against France are so terrible in Italy 1707. Hence **Prepa·ratively** *adv.*

Preparator (pre·pārēⁱtəɹ). *rare.* 1762. [– late L. *præparator*, f. as prec.; see -OR 2.] One who makes a preparation; a preparer (of medicine, etc.).

Preparatory (pri̇pæ·rătəri), *a.* and *sb.* late ME. [– late L. *præparatorius*, f. as prec.; see -ORY¹ and ².] **A.** *adj.* **1.** That prepares for something following; preliminary, introductory. **b.** quasi-*adv.* = Preparatorily. Const. *to.* 1649. **2.** Applied to a junior school in which pupils are prepared for a higher school 1828; or in U.S. in which older boys are prepared for college.

1. b. They were weighing it p. to sending it to town 1877. **2.** The children of the rich are sent to p. schools 1828.

B. *sb.* **1.** = PREPARATIVE *sb.* 1. Now *rare* or *Obs.* 1620. **2.** Short for *p. school* 1907. Hence **Prepa·ratorily** *adv.* in a p. manner.

Prepa·re, *sb.* 1535. [f. next.] **1.** The act of preparing; preparation. *Obs.* or *dial.* **2.** A substance used to prepare stuff for a dye 1874.

Prepare (pri̇pēᵊ·ɹ), *v.* 1466. [– Fr. *préparer* or L. *præparare*, f. *præ* PRE- A. I. 1 + *parare* make ready.] **1.** *trans.* To get ready, make ready, to fit or put in order beforehand for something. **2.** *intr.* for *refl.* To put oneself, or things, in readiness; to get ready, make preparation 1509. †**3.** *refl.* and *intr.* To make preparation for a journey; to get ready to go (*to*, *into*, etc. a place); hence, to go, repair –1784. **4.** *trans.* To get or have in readiness beforehand; to provide. Now *arch.* or merged in 1. 1535. **5.** To make ready (food, a meal) for eating 1490. **6.** To bring into proper state for use by some special or technical process; to work up; to dress 1722. **7.** To manufacture, to make or compound (a chemical product, a 'preparation', etc.) 1535. **b.** To draw up (a writing or document) 1797. **8.** *Mus.* **a.** To lead up to (a discord) by sounding the dissonant note in it as a consonant note in the preceding chord. **b.** To lead up to (a shake or other grace) by a preliminary note, turn, etc. 1727.

1. P. my Horses SHAKS. And now p. thee for another sight MILT. In this manner I prepared almost all my sermons that summer 1866. For ten years he has 'prepared'..pupils for Army and other examinations 1900. Phr. *To be prepared*: to be ready, inclined, disposed (*for*, *to do* something). **2.** P. to meete thy God, O Israel *Amos* 4:12. **5.** Goo and p. vs the ester lambe, that we maye eate TINDALE *Luke* 22:8. **6.** Sheep-skins are sometimes prepared to imitate morocco 1879. **7.** Writing Ink may be..prepared in many different ways 1875. **b.** A code is preparing for the regulation of commerce 1854. Hence **Pre·parable** *a. rare*, capable of being prepared. **Prepa·red-ly** *adv.*, **-ness. Prepa·rer**, one who or that which prepares.

Prepay (prīpēⁱ·), *v.* 1839. [f. PRE- A. I. 1 + PAY *v.*¹] *trans.* To pay (a charge) beforehand; *esp.* to pay (the postage of a letter or parcel) before dispatching it (as by affixing a postage stamp). Also *transf.* with the letter, etc. as obj.

Pre-paying a letter..used to be thought little short of an insult 1858. Hence **Prepay·able** *a.* that may or must be prepaid. **Prepay·ment**, payment in advance; also *attrib.*

Prepense (pri̇pe·ns), *a.* 1702. [For earlier PREPENSED.] Considered and planned beforehand; premeditated; intentional. **a.** in *Malice p.* (Law): malice premeditated or planned beforehand; wrong or injury purposely done. Also *joc.* **b.** *gen.* 1770.

a. He..plunges into slang, not irreverently..but of malice p. L. STEPHEN. Hence **Prepe·nsely** *adv.*

†**Prepe·nse**, *v.* 1509. [alt. from earlier *purpense* – AFr., OFr. *purpenser*; see next.] **1.** *trans.* To plan or contrive beforehand –1633. **2.** To consider beforehand –1656.

Prepe·nsed, *ppl. a.* 1529. [alt. from †*purpensed* (XV) – AFr., OFr. *purpensé*, pa. pple. of *purpenser*, f. *pur-*, *pour-* PRO-¹ + *penser* think.] **a.** esp. in legal phr. *malice p.*, *p. malice*: see PREPENSE *a.* –1704. **b.** = PREPENSE *a.* b. –1670.

Pre:perce·ption. 1871. [PRE- A. I. 2.] Previous perception; a condition preceding perception.

Prepollent (pri̇pǫ·lĕnt), *a.* Now *rare.* Also **præ-.** 1657. [– *præpollent-*, pr. ppl. stem of L. *præpollēre* exceed in power or strength, f. *præ* PRE- A. III. + *pollēre* be strong; see -ENT.] Having superior power, weight, or influence; predominating, prevailing.

‖**Prepo·llex, præ-.** 1889. [mod.L., f. *præ* PRE- B. II. + POLLEX.] *Anat.*, etc. A rudimentary structure found in certain animals on the radial border of the hand or fore-foot, and supposed to represent an additional digit.

Preponder (pri̇pǫ·ndəɹ), *v.* Now *rare.* 1624. [– Fr. *prépondérer* or L. *præponderare*; see PREPONDERATE *v.*¹] **1.** *trans.* To outweigh in importance. **2.** *intr.* = PREPONDERATE *v.*¹ 1. 1676.

Preponderance (pri̇pǫ·ndərăns). 1681. [f. next; see -ANCE.] **1.** The fact of exceeding in weight; greater heaviness. **b.** *Gunnery.* The excess of weight of that part of a gun which is to the rear of the trunnions over that in front of them 1864. **2.** Superiority or excess in moral weight, power, influence, or importance 1780. **3.** Superiority in number or amount 1845.

2. The good would have an incontestible p. over the evil 1780. **3.** Their immense p. in point of numbers 1845. So **Prepo·nderancy** (now *rare*), the quality or fact of being preponderant 1646.

Preponderant (pri̇pǫ·ndərănt), *a.* 1660. [– *præponderant-*, pr. ppl. stem of L. *præponderare*; see next, -ANT.] **1.** Surpassing in weight; heavier 1664. **2.** Surpassing in influence, power, or importance, predominant 1660.

2. The Roundhead party was now decidedly p. MACAULAY. Hence **Prepo·nderantly** *adv.*

Preponderate (pri̇pǫ·ndərēⁱt), *v.*¹ 1611. [– *præponderat-*, pa. ppl. stem of L. *præponderare* outweigh, f. *præ* PRE- A. III. + *ponderare*; see PONDER *v.*, -ATE³.] **I.** *intr.* **1.** To weigh more; to be heavier; to turn the scale 1623. **b.** *fig.* To have the greater moral or intellectual weight 1659. **c.** To exceed in power, force, or influence; to exceed in amount, number, etc.; to predominate 1799. **2.** To incline downwards, as one scale of a balance, on account of greater weight; to weigh or be weighed down; to show a preponderance 1678.

1. Where neither side doth p., the balance should hang even 1672. **b.** These last reasons did p. with me FULLER. **c.** The good in this state of existence preponderates over the bad DICKENS.

II. *trans.* †**1.** To weigh more than; to turn the scale when weighed against (something else); to outweigh –1774. †**2.** To cause to descend, as one scale of a balance, by reason of greater weight; to weigh down. Also *fig.* –1796. Hence **Prepo·nderatingly** *adv.*

†**Pre-po·nderate**, *v.*² 1599. [f. PRE- A. I. 1 + PONDERATE *v.*] *trans.* and *intr.* To ponder previously; to weigh mentally or consider beforehand –1838.

Prepondera·tion. Now *rare* or *Obs.* 1653. [– late L. *præponderatio*; see PREPONDERATE *v.*¹, -ION.] **1.** The action or fact of preponderating; preponderance. **2.** The adding of weight to one side; greater inclination or bias 1653.

†**Prepo·se**, *v.* 1491. [– Fr. *préposer*, after L. *præponere* put before; see PRE- A. and POSE *v.*¹] **1.** *trans.* To set over; to appoint as chief or superior –1655. **2.** To preface, prefix –1850. **3.** To propose, purpose, or intend –1635.

Preposition (prepŏzi·ʃən). late ME. [– L. *præpositio* putting before, (tr. Gr. πρόθεσις) preposition, f. *præponere*; see PRE-, POSITION. Cf. Fr. *préposition* (XV).] **1.** *Gram.* One of the parts of speech; an indeclinable word or particle serving to mark the relation between two notional words, the latter of which is usu. a sb. or a pronoun; as, sow *in* hope, good *for* food, etc. The following sb. or pron. is said to be 'governed' by the preposition. †**2.** More widely: Any word or particle prefixed to another word; a prefix –1661. **3.** The action of placing before; position before or in front (*rare*) 1586.

1. *Inseparable p.*: a p. when combined as prefix with a verb or other part of speech. Hence **Prepositi·onal** *a.* of, pertaining to, or expressed by a p. **Preposi·tionally** *adv.*

Prepositive (pri̇pǫ·zitiv), *a.* (*sb.*) 1583. [– late L. *præpositivus*, f. as prec.; see PRE- A. I. 3, POSITIVE. Cf. (O)Fr. *prépositif.*] Proper to be placed before or prefixed. **B.** *sb.* A prepositive word or particle 1693.

Prepositor, præ- (pri̇pǫ·zitǫɹ). 1518. [alt. of L. *præpositus* president, head, subst. use of pa. pple. of *præponere* set over, f. *præ* PRE- + *ponere* place.] = PRÆPOSTOR.

Prepossess (prīpŏze·s), *v.* 1614. [f. PRE- A. I. 1 + POSSESS, prob. after med.L. *præpossidēre* (in *prepossessus* seized beforehand, XIV).] **1.** *trans.* To take or get possession of beforehand, or before another; to have prior possession of. Now *rare.* **2.** To possess (a person) beforehand *with* or *by* a feeling, notion, etc.; to imbue, inspire, or affect strongly beforehand. Chiefly in *pass.* 1639. **3.** *spec.* To bias, prejudice (a person) against or in favour of a person or thing; now chiefly, To impress favourably beforehand 1647.

1. Hope is that which antedates and prepossesses a future good 1716. **2.** They were..prepossest with an ill opinion of him 1657. **3.** His talk prepossessed me still more in his favour 1866.

Preposse·ssing, *ppl. a.* 1642. [f. prec. + -ING².] **1.** Biasing; causing prejudice. **2.**

spec. That predisposes favourably; causing an agreeable first impression; pleasing 1805.

1. This awkward p. visage of mine GOLDSM. **2.** Its expression was eminently gentle and prepossessing LYTTON. Hence **Preposse·ssing-ly** *adv.*, **-ness.**

Prepossession (prīpǒze·ʃən). 1648. [f. PREPOSSESS *v.*, after POSSESSION.] **1.** The having or taking of possession beforehand; prior possession or occupancy. Now *rare.* **2.** The condition of being mentally prepossessed; a preconceived opinion which tends to bias the mind; unfavourable or favourable antecedent opinion; prejudice, predisposition 1649.

2. The prepossessions of the Vulgar for men in power and authority are blind 1702.

Preposterous (prīpǫ·stərəs), *a.* 1542. [f. L. *præposterus* reversed (f. *præ* before and *posterus* coming after) + -OUS.] **1.** Having last that which should be first; inverted in order. Now *rare.* 1552. **2.** Contrary to nature, or to reason or common sense; monstrous; perverse, nonsensical; in later use, utterly absurd 1542.

1. The fatal effects of this p...procedure 1856. **2.** The muff and fur are p. in June 1713. The p. idea of convincing the mind by tormenting the body 1809. Hence **Prepo·sterous-ly** *adv.*, **-ness.**

Prepostor, var. of PRÆPOSTOR.

Prepotency (prīpōᵘ·tĕnsi). 1646. [– L. *præpotentia* superior power; see next, -ENCY.] **1.** The quality of being prepotent; predominance, prevalence. **2.** *Biol.* The prepotent power of a parent organism to transmit special characteristics to offspring 1859. So **Prepo·tence** (in sense 1).

Prepotent (prīpōᵘ·tĕnt), *a.* 1450. [– *præpotent-*, pr. ppl. stem of L. *præposse* be more or very powerful; see PRE- A. 3, POTENT *a.*[1]] **1.** Having great power, force, influence, or authority; pre-eminent in power. **b.** Predominant 1641. **2.** *Biol.* Having a greater power of transmitting hereditary features or qualities; having a stronger fertilizing influence 1859.

2. When two species are crossed, one has sometimes a p. power of impressing its likeness on the hybrid DARWIN.

Preprandial (prīpræ·ndiăl), *a.* 1822. [f. PRE- B. I. 1 + L. *prandium* luncheon + -AL[1].] Done or happening before dinner.

Pre-pre·ference, *a.* 1882. [PRE- B. I. 2.] Ranking before preference bonds, shares, claims, etc., in security, payment of dividend or interest. So **Pre-preferential** *a.*

‖**Prepubis, præ-** (prī·piū·bis). Also **-es.** 1888. [PRE- A. II.] *Anat.* The pre-acetabular portion of the pubis, esp. in Dinosaurs. So **Prepu·bic** *a.* pertaining to the p.; situated in front of the pubis.

Prepuce (prī·piūs). late ME. [– L. *præputium*, whence Fr. *prépuce.*] The loose fold of integument which covers the glans penis (or the glans clitoridis); the foreskin. †**b.** *transf.* The state of the uncircumcised, uncircumcision –1582. So **Prepu·tial** *a.*

Pre-Raphael (prīræ·fĕ,ĕl), *a.* (*sb.*) 1850. [PRE- B. I. 2.] Previous to Raphael; a painter (or painting) before the time of Raphael. **b.** = Pre-Raphaelite. So **Pre-Ra·phaelism, pre-ra·ph-, præ-,** = PRE-RAPHAELITISM; by Ruskin and others applied to the art of the painters who preceded Raphael.

Pre-Raphaelite, preraphaelite, præ- (prīræ·fĕ,ĕləit), *sb.* and *a.* Also **-Raffael-.** 1849. [f. PRE- B. I. 1 + RAPHAEL (It. *Raffaelo, Raffaele*) + -ITE[1].] **A.** *sb.* **1.** An artist who aims at producing work in the spirit which generally imbued art before the time of Raphael; *spec.* one of the group of English artists, including Holman Hunt, Millais, and D. G. Rossetti, who called themselves the 'Pre-Raphaelite Brotherhood' (P.R.B.). **2.** One of the painters who preceded Raphael 1850.

1. The Pre-Raphaelites imitate no pictures: they paint from nature only RUSKIN.

B. *adj.* (or attrib. use of sb.) **1.** Of, belonging to, or characteristic of the Pre-Raphaelites, or their principles and style 1849. **2.** Existing before Raphael 1855.

1. The P. movement 1873. **2.** In these p. productions Florence is very rich 1855.

Pre-Ra·phaelitism, preraph-, præ-. 1851. [f. prec. + -ISM.] The principles, methods, or style of painting adopted by the Pre-Raphaelite Brotherhood and their followers; sometimes applied to a similar tendency in poetry and other arts.

Prerequisite (prīre·kwizit), *a.* and *sb.* 1633. [f. PRE- A. I. 3 + REQUISITE *a.* and *sb.*] **A.** *adj.* Required beforehand; requisite as a previous condition 1651. **B.** *sb.* That which is required beforehand; a condition previously necessary 1633.

Prerogative (prīrǫ·gătiv), *sb.* late ME. [– (O)Fr. *prérogative* or L. *prærogativa* tribe or century to which it fell by lot to vote first in the comitia, previous choice, prognostic, privilege, subst. use (orig. sc. *tribus* or *centuria*) of *prærogativus*; see next.] **1.** A prior, exclusive, or peculiar right or privilege. **a.** *esp.* in *Constitutional Hist.* That special pre-eminence which the sovereign, by right of regal dignity, has over all other persons and out of the course of the common law, the *royal p.*, a sovereign right (in theory) subject to no restriction or interference. **b.** *gen.* The peculiar right or privilege of any person, class, or body of persons. late ME. **2.** *fig.* A natural or divinely-given advantage or privilege. late ME. †**b.** Precedence, superiority –1671. **3.** The right of giving the first vote and thus of serving as a guide or precedent to the votes that follow. (Only an etym. use in English.) 1600.

1. The parliament by perseverance, and by taking advantage of foreign wars, disputed successions and other circumstances, gradually set limits to p. 1839. **b.** Freedom, an English subjects sole p. DRYDEN. **2.** Rare Qualities may sometimes be Prerogatives, without being Advantages 1665.

attrib. and *Comb.*: **p. court,** the court of an archbishop for the probate of wills and trial of testamentary causes in which effects to the value of five pounds had been left in each of two (or more) dioceses within his province; its jurisdiction was transferred in 1857 to the Court of Probate; **p. lawyer,** a lawyer retained in behalf of the royal p.; **p. writ,** a writ issued on extraordinary occasions in the exercise of the royal p. Hence **Prero·gatived** *ppl. a.* endowed with or possessed of a p.

Prerogative (prīrǫ·gătiv), *a.* late ME. [– L. *prærogativus*, f. *prærogat-*, pa. ppl. stem of *prærogare* ask before (others), f. *præ* PRE- A. I. 1 + *rogare* ask; see -IVE.] **1.** *Rom. Hist.* Characterized by having the right to vote first. Of a vote: Given first and serving as a precedent for those that follow. 1600. **2.** Of, pertaining to, or arising from prerogative; enjoyed by exclusive privilege; privileged. late ME. **3.** Having precedence or priority; pre-eminent (*rare*) 1646.

2. Such p. modes of process, as are peculiarly confined to the crown 1768. Hence **Prero·gatively** *adv.* as a prerogative.

Prerupt (prīrv·pt), *a. rare.* 1603. [– L. *præruptus*, pa. pple. of *prærumpere* break off before (the point), f. *præ* PRE- A. I. 3 + *rumpere* break.] = ABRUPT *a.* 4.

Presage (pre·sĕdʒ, formerly prīsēⁱ·dʒ), *sb.* late ME. [Chiefly – Fr. *présage*, but in Gower immed. – L. *præsagium*, f. *præsagire* forebode; see next.] **1.** An indication of a future event; an omen, sign, portent. **b.** Without *pl.* Indication of the future; chiefly in phr. *of evil* (etc.) *p.* 1671. **2.** A prediction, prognostication. Now *rare.* 1595. **3.** A presentiment, a foreboding; an intuition of the future 1593.

1. A very euil signe and p. for him, to enter into Rome with such bloudshed 1579. **b.** If there be aught of p. in the mind, This day will be remarkable in my life By some great act MILT. **3.** He had a strong p. upon his mind that he had only a very short time to live 1812.

Presage (pre·sĕdʒ, prīsēⁱ·dʒ), *v.* 1562. [– Fr. *présager* or L. *præsagire* forebode, f. *præ* PRE- A. I. 3 + *sagire* perceive keenly.] **1.** *trans.* To signify beforehand (supernaturally); to portend. **b.** *transf.* To give warning of (by natural means) 1591. **2.** Of a person: To augur, predict, forecast. †In Spenser: To make known. 1578. **b.** *intr.* To form or utter a presage or prediction 1592. **3.** *trans.* To have a presentiment or prevision of 1594. **b.** *intr.* To have a presentiment 1586.

1. Have not eclipses been esteemed as omens presaging some direful calamity? 1816. **b.** The rising of the mercury presages, in general, fair weather 1822. **2.** Lands he could measure, terms and tides p. GOLDSM. Hence **Presager,** one who or that which presages or portends. **Presa·gingly** *adv.*

Presageful (stress var.), *a.* 1591. [f. PRESAGE *sb.* + -FUL.] **1.** Full of presage; ominous. **2.** Full of presentiment 1729.

2. Dark remembrance and p. fear COLERIDGE.

†**Presa·gement.** 1595. [f. PRESAGE *v.* + -MENT.] The action or fact of presaging. **a.** Prognostication; an omen, a portent –1646. **b.** Presentiment; foretelling power –1646.

a. The falling of Salt is an authenticke p. of ill lucke SIR T. BROWNE.

Presanctified (prīsæ·ŋktifəid), *ppl. a.* 1839. [PRE- A. I. 1.] *Liturg.* In *mass* or *liturgy of the p.* [tr. med.L. *missa præsanctificatorum*], a celebration of the Eucharist at which the elements used have been consecrated at a previous celebration, used in the Eastern Church during Lent and in the Western Church on Good Friday.

‖**Presbyopia** (prezbi,ōᵘ·piă). Rarely **pre·sbyopy.** 1793. [mod.L., f. Gr. πρέσβυς an old man + -ωπία, f. ὤψ, ὠπ- eye; see -IA[1].] An affection of the eyes incident to advancing age, in which the power of accommodation to near objects is lost, and only distant objects are seen distinctly; a form of long-sightedness. So **Presby,opic** (-ǫ·pik) *a.* pertaining to or affected with p.

Presbyter (pre·zbitəɹ, *Sc.* and *U.S.* pres-). 1597. [– eccl. L. *presbyter* (Tertullian) – Gr. πρεσβύτερος, in N.T. 'elder' of the Jewish sanhedrim, 'elder' of the apostolic church, subst. use of compar. (older, elder, senior) of πρέσβυς old (chiefly sb. old man). Cf. PRIEST.] **1.** An elder in the Christian church. **a.** In the early church: One of a number of officers who had the oversight and management of the affairs of a local church or congregation, some of them having also the function of teaching. **b.** In Episcopal churches: A minister of the second order; a priest 1597. **c.** In Presbyterian churches: Occasional name for an elder; *esp.* one who is a member of a PRESBYTERY 1615. †**2.** A Presbyterian –1827.

1. b. In truth the word P. doth seeme more.. agreeable than Priest with the drift of the whole Gospell of Iesus Christ HOOKER. **c.** New P. is but Old Priest writ large MILT.

Presbyteral (prezbi·tərăl), *a.* 1611. [– (O)Fr. *presbytéral* or late (eccl.) L. *presbyteralis*, f. *presbyter*; see prec., -AL[1].] **1.** Of or pertaining to a presbyter or priest; consisting of presbyters. **2.** = PRESBYTERIAN *a.* 1651.

Presbyterate (prezbi·tərĕt), *sb.* 1641. [– eccl. L. *presbyteratus*, f. *presbyter*; see PRESBYTER, -ATE[1].] **1.** The office of presbyter; presbytership, eldership 1642. **2.** A body of presbyters; the order of presbyters 1641.

†**Pre·sbyteress.** 1546. [– med.L. *presbyterissa* (= late L. *presbytera*) in both senses, f. as prec. + *-issa* -ESS[1].] **1.** The wife of a presbyter or priest –1675. **2.** A female presbyter; one of an order of women in the early church, having some of the functions of presbyters –1682.

Presbyterial (prezbitiᵊ·riăl), *a.* (*sb.*) 1592. [– med.L. *presbyterialis*, f. *presbyterium* (see PRESBYTERY) + *-alis* -AL[1]; see -IAL.] **1.** Of or pertaining to a presbytery or body of elders 1600. **2.** = PRESBYTERIAN *a.* 1592.

Presbyterian (prezbitiᵊ·riăn, *Sc.* and *U.S.* pres-), *a.* and *sb.* Now usu. w. capital *P.* 1641. [f. eccl. L. *presbyterium* + -AN; in AL. *presbyterianus* (XVII).] **A.** *adj.* Pertaining to or characterized by government by presbyters or presbyteries; applied to a system of church polity; belonging to or maintaining this system; see next.

1. *Reformed P.*, of or pertaining to those Presbyterians who protested against the constitution of Church and State in Scotland at the Revolution Settlement in 1689; also pop. called CAMERONIAN. *United P.*, of or pertaining to the united church or denomination formed in Scotland in 1847 by the union of the United Secession and Relief churches. (Abbrev. U.P.) In 1900 this body united with the Free Church of Scotland, to form the denomination then named the United Free Church of Scotland.

B. *sb.* One who maintains the Presbyterian

system of church government; a member or adherent of a Presbyterian church 1641.

Presbyterianism (prezbiti°·riăniz'm, *Sc.* and *U.S.* pres-). 1644. [f. prec. + -ISM.] The Presbyterian system of church government, in which no higher order than that of presbyter or elder is recognized, the 'bishop' and 'elder' of the N.T. being held to be identical and all elders being ecclesiastically of equal rank.

Presbyte·rianize, *v.* 1843. [f. as prec. + -IZE.] **a.** *trans.* To make Presbyterian; to organize on Presbyterian lines. **b.** *intr.* To act as a Presbyterian or in a way tending towards Presbyterianism.

‖**Presbyte·rium, -ion.** 1565. [eccl. L.; see PRESBYTERY.] **1.** = PRESBYTERY 1. **2.** = PRESBYTERY 3. 1886.

Pre·sbytership. 1597. [f. PRESBYTER + -SHIP.] = PRESBYTERATE 1.

Presbytery (pre·zbitəri, *Sc.* and *U.S.* pres-). late ME. [– OFr. *presbiterie* – eccl. L. *presbyterium* – eccl. Gr. πρεσβυτέριον, f. πρεσβύτερος; see PRESBYTER, -Y⁴.] **1.** A part of a church reserved for the clergy; the eastern part of the chancel beyond the choir, in which the altar is placed; the sanctuary. †**2.** = PRESBYTERATE 1. –1704. **3.** A body of presbyters or elders 1611. **4.** In the Presbyterian system: A body or assembly of presbyters or elders, consisting of all the ministers, and one ruling elder (or sometimes two) from each parish or congregation within a particular local area, constituting the eccl. court next above the kirk-session and below the synod 1578. **b.** *transf.* The district comprising the parishes or congregations represented by a presbytery 1581. **5.** The Presbyterian polity or system; Presbyterianism. (Contrasted with *episcopacy* or *prelacy*, and with *independency*.) Now *rare.* 1590. **6.** A presbyter's or priest's house; a parsonage. (Now only in *R.C.Ch.*) 1825.

‖**Prescapula** (pri̦skæ·piŭlă). 1890. [PRE- A. II. b.] *Anat.* That part of the scapula or shoulder-blade above (or in quadrupeds, anterior to) its spine or median axis. Hence **Presca·pular** *a.* anterior to the spine or long axis of the shoulder-blade.

Prescience (pre·ʃiĕns, -s-). late ME. [– (O)Fr. *prescience* – eccl. L. *præscientia* (Tertullian) – *præscient-*; see next, -ENCE.] Knowledge of events before they happen; foreknowledge; esp. as a divine attribute. **b.** as a human quality: Foresight. late ME.

Predestination..cannot be avoided, if we hold an universal p. in the Deity BOSWELL **b.** Statesmen of a more judicious p., look for the fortunate moment too BURKE.

Prescient (pre·ʃiĕnt, -s-), *a.* 1626. [– *præscient-*, pr. ppl. stem of L. *præscire* know before, f. *præ* PRE- A. I. 1 + *scire* know; see -ENT.] Having foreknowledge or foresight; foreseeing.

James Harrington, one of the most p. minds of that great age 1888. Hence **Pre·sciently** *adv.*

Prescientific (prīsəi̦ĕnti·fik), *a.* 1858. [f. PRE- B. I. 1 + SCIENTIFIC.] Of or pertaining to times prior to the rise of modern science, or to the application of the scientific method.

Prescind (prĭsi·nd), *v.* 1636. [– L. *præscindere* cut off in front, f. *præ* PRE- A. + *scindere* cut.] **1.** *trans.* To cut off prematurely or abruptly; to cut away at once. **2.** To cut off *from*; to abstract 1660. **3.** *intr.* (for *refl.*): To withdraw the attention *from*; to leave out of consideration 1890.

2. An abstract idea of happiness, prescinded from all particular pleasure 1710.

Prescribe (prĭskrəi·b), *v.* 1531. [– L. *præscribere* write before, etc., f. *præ* PRE- A. + *scribere* write.] **I.** †**1.** *trans.* To write first or beforehand; also, to describe beforehand –1653. **2.** To write or lay down as a rule or direction to be followed; to appoint, ordain, direct, enjoin. Const. *to* or dative. 1535. †**b.** *absol.* or *intr.* To lay down a rule; to dictate, appoint, direct. Of a law or custom: To be of force. –1716. **3.** *Med. trans.* To advise or order the use of (a medicine, etc.) with directions for the manner of using it 1581. **b.** *absol.* or *intr.* Also *fig.* 1598. †**4.** *trans.* To limit; to confine within bounds –1726.

2. Wood prescribes to the news mongers in London what they are to write SWIFT. And ten were prescribed the whip BROWNING. **3.** To leech his head and p. tartar emetic 1843. **b.** His motto was that no statesman should p. until he was called in 1899.

II. *Law.* **1.** *intr.* To make a claim by prescription; to assert a prescriptive right or claim (to or *for* something; also with *inf.* or *clause*) 1531. †**2.** To plead prescription of time (PRESCRIPTION II. 1) *against* an action, statute, or penalty; to cease to be liable on account of the lapse of the prescribed time –1672.

1. A man might..p. that he and his ancestors had from time immemorial exercised a certain right in gross 1844.

Prescript (prī·skript, †prĭskri·pt), *sb.* 1540. [– L. *præscriptum*, subst. use of n. pa. pple. of *præscribere* PRESCRIBE. Cf. Fr. †*prescript*.] **1.** That which is prescribed or laid down as a rule; an ordinance, law, command; a regulation, direction. **2.** Medicine prescribed; also *transf.* a medical prescription. Now *rare.* 1603.

Prescript (prĭskri·pt), *a.* 1460. [– L. *præscriptus*, pa. pple. of *præscribere*; see prec.] Prescribed or laid down beforehand as a rule; ordained, appointed. Now *rare.*

Prescription (prĭskri·pʃən). late ME. [– (O)Fr. *prescription* – L. *præscriptio*, f. *præscript-*; see prec., -ION.] **I. 1.** The action of prescribing or appointing beforehand; that which is prescribed; written or explicit direction or injunction 1549. **2.** A direction or formula (usu.) written by a physician for the composition and use of a medicine; *transf.* the medicine prescribed. In early use, more widely, 'doctor's orders'. 1579. †**3.** Restriction, limitation –1718.

1. In the recognition of conduct as 'right' is involved an authoritative p. to do it 1874. **2.** This P. the Sub-prior faithfully made up, and put into Phials for use 1679.

II. *Law.* **1.** Limitation of the time within which an action or claim can be raised. Now commonly called *negative p.* 1474. **b.** Uninterrupted use or possession from time immemorial, or for a period fixed by law as giving a title or right; hence, title or right acquired by such use or possession; sometimes called *positive p.* late ME. **c.** *transf.* and *fig.* (*a*) Ancient or continued custom, esp. when viewed as authoritative 1589. (*b*) Claim founded upon long use 1625. †**2.** The action of prescribing or claiming by prescription –1818.

1. There's no p. to inthrall a King 1605. **b.** 'Tis said in our Law Books, that the Publick acquires a Right by Custom, but only private Persons acquire it by P. 1726. **c.** (*b*) Narrow selfended Souls make p. of good [illegible]fices SIR T. BROWNE.

Prescriptive (prĭskri·ptiv), *a.* 1748. [– late L. *præscriptivus* pertaining to a legal exception or demurrer, f. as prec.; see -IVE.] **1.** That prescribes or directs; †appointed by prescription. **2.** Derived from or founded on prescription or lapse of time, as *p. right* or *title* 1766. **3.** Arising from or recognized by long-standing custom or usage; prescribed by custom 1775. **4.** Giving or recognizing prescription or prescriptive right. BURKE.

1. P. rules for the preservation of health 1788. **3.** To have his regular score at the bar..and his p. corner at the winter's fireside 1837. **Prescri·ptive-ly** *adv.*, **-ness.**

Presence (pre·zĕns). ME. [– (O)Fr. *présence* – L. *præsentia*, f. *præsens, -ent-*; see PRESENT, -ENCE.] **1.** The fact or condition of being present; the state of being before, in front of, or in the same place with a person or thing; being there. **b.** In ref. to the manner in which Christ is held to be present in the Eucharist (see REAL *a.* I. 2) 1552. **2.** In certain connections, used with a vague sense of the place or space in front of a person, or which immediately surrounds him ME. **b.** Without *of* or possessive; usu. preceded by prep., as *in (the) p., to (the) p.*, etc.; *spec.* (now only) in ref. to ceremonial attendance upon a person of superior, esp. royal, rank; formerly also = 'company', 'polite society'. late ME. †**c.** Hence, a presence-chamber –1735. †**3.** *concr.* Those who are present; an assembly, a company –1788. **4.** With possessive, denoting the actual person (or thing) that is present; hence occas. = embodied self, objective personality. Chiefly *poet.* late ME. **b.** Hence, a person who is corporally present; usu. with implication of impressive appearance or aspect 1826. **5.** Demeanour, carriage, or aspect of a person, esp. when stately or impressive 1579. **6.** Something present; a present being; a divine, spiritual, or incorporeal being or influence felt or conceived as present 1667. **7** *P. of mind*: the state or quality of having one's wits about one; calmness in exacting circumstances; freedom from embarrassment, agitation, or panic 1665.

1. Our Law forbids at thir Religious Rites My p. MILT. **b.** The doctrine of the objective p. in, under, or with, the consecrated elements 1901. **2.** He was always very collected in the p. of danger 1908. *In his p.* = before or with him, where he is, in his company; *from his p.* = from being with him, from where he is, out of his company, etc.; also *poet.* and *rhet.* with demonstrative or other adjs.; e.g. *in this (august) p.* = in the presence of this (august) personage. **b.** 'Tis very true: You were in p. (= present) then, And you can witnesse with me, this is true SHAKS. **c.** *Hen. VIII*, III. i. 17. **4.** As in a fiery column charioting His Godlike p. MILT. **b.** And over him who stood but Herakles? There smiled the mighty p., all one smile BROWNING. **5.** More was a man of stately and handsome p. H. WALPOLE. **6.** And I have felt A p. that disturbs me with the joy Of elevated thoughts WORDSW.

attrib. and *Comb.*: **p.-lobby,** the lobby or ante-room of a presence-chamber; **-room** = next.

Pre·sence-cha:mber. 1575. [Cf. prec. 2 c.] The chamber in which a sovereign or other great personage receives guests, or persons entitled to appear before him; a reception-room in a palace or great house.

Presensation (prī̦sensē¹·ʃən). 1653. [PRE- A. I. 2.] = next.

Presension (prise·nʃən). Now *rare* or *Obs.* 1597. [– L. *præsensio* foreboding, presentiment, f. *præsens-*, pr. ppl. stem of *præsentire*, f. *præ* PRE- + *sentire* feel; see -ION.] Feeling or perception of something before it exists, occurs, or manifests itself; foreknowledge, foresight; presentiment.

Present (pre·zĕnt), *sb.*¹ ME. [Elliptical or absol. use of PRESENT *a.*; in most senses already so used in OFr. (see next). In ME. orig. *prese·nt.*] †**1.** = PRESENCE 1, 2, 2 b. –1470. †**2.** The thing or person that is present; affair in hand; present occasion; *pl.* things present, circumstances –1764. **b.** *This p.*, more commonly *these presents*: the present document or writing; these words or statements. Chiefly, now only, in legal use. late ME. **3.** The present time, the time that now is 1600. †**b.** With ellipsis of *month* (usu. *this p.*) –1661. **c.** *Gram.* Short for *present tense*: see PRESENT *a.* II. 2. *P. stem*, the stem of the present tense. 1530.

2. Shall I be charg'd no further then this p.? Must all determine heere? SHAKS. **b.** Know all men by these presents, that I [etc.] 1752. **3.** Better this p. than a past like that BROWNING.

Phrases with preps. †**In present,** (*a*) now; (*b*) immediately; (*c*) at that time, then. So *in this p.* = (*a*). **At p.,** at the present time, now. **For the p.,** for the time; †for that time, just then; in mod. use, for this time, just now. **Until the p., up to the p.,** until now, up to now.

Present (pre·zĕnt), *sb.*² [ME. *present* – (O)Fr. *présent* offering, gift, also *in, to present*, repr. OFr. phr. (*mettre une chose*) *en présent* (*à quelqu'un*), put a thing before any one, in which *en présent* was in effect = *en don* as a gift.] **a.** = GIFT *sb.* II. 1. (The ordinary current sense.) **b.** = GIFT *sb.* I. 1. Usu. in phr. *to make a p. of* = to present, give, bestow. ME. †**c.** An offering to God or a deity –1707.

c. Were the whole realm of nature mine, That were a p. far too small WATTS.

Present (prĭze·nt), *sb.*³ 1833. [f. PRESENT *v.*] The act of presenting or aiming a weapon, esp. a fire-arm; the position of the weapon when presented; *esp.* the position from which a rifle is fired.

Bring the carbine down to the 'P.' 1833.

Present (pre·zĕnt), *a.* (*adv.*) ME. [– (O)Fr. *présent* – L. *præsens, præsent-*, pr. pple. of *præesse*, f. *præ* PRE- + *-sens*, pr. pple. of *sum* I am.] An adj. of relation; expressing a local or temporary relation to a person or thing which is the point of reference. **I.** Senses relating to place, etc. **1.** Being in the place considered or mentioned; that is here (or there). Chiefly in predicate. Opp. to ABSENT *a.* 1. **b.** Existing in the thing, class, or case mentioned or under consideration; not wanting; 'found'. Opp. to ABSENT *a.* 1. 1809. **2.** That is actually being dealt with, written, discussed, or considered; often used in a writing to denote the writer himself. late ME. **3.** Of which one is conscious; directly thought of, remembered, or imagined. Usu. const. *to*. 1500. **4.** Attentive (opp. to ABSENT *a.* 2); having presence of mind, collected, self-possessed (in this sense usu. *p. to oneself*); prompt to perceive or act, ready, quick. Now *rare* or *Obs.* 1451. **5.** Ready at hand; *esp.* ready with assistance, 'favourably attentive, not neglectful, propitious' (J.). *arch.* 1539.

1. A p. deity, they shout around DRYDEN. P. at his burial 1839. **b.** In the Hemiptera..wings may be p. or absent HUXLEY. **2.** The said parties to these p. Indentures 1592. The entire subject ..cannot be fully considered in such a paper as the p. 1895. **3.** The legends of the place are p. to the imagination throughout the discourse 1875. **5.** God is our hope & strength: a very p. helpe in trouble BIBLE (Great) *Ps.* 46:1.

II. Senses relating to *time*. **1.** That is, or that is so, at this time or now; current, contemporary; modern. Opp. to *past* and *future*. ME. **b.** Actually existing, actual 1774. **2.** *Gram.* Applied to that tense of a verb which denotes an action now going on or a condition now existing (or one considered generally). Opp. to *past* (or *preterite*) and *future*. late ME. **3.** That was, or that was so, at that time. Now *rare*. 1450. **†4.** Without delay; immediate, instant –1836. **†b.** Of a remedy or poison: Taking immediate effect, acting speedily –1694.

1. All things past, p., and to come, are p. before God PUSEY. **b.** In the p. state of nature, the means of safety are rather superior to those of offence GOLDSM. *P. value* or *worth* of a sum due at a definite future date (*Comm.*): that sum which, together with compound interest upon it from now until that date, will amount to the sum then due. **2.** The..P. Perfect ONIONS. **3.** The p. business was to attend to p. needs 1908. **4.** Peter stroke Ananias ..with p. death BACON.

†B. as *adv.* **1.** = PRESENTLY *adv.* 2. –1654. **2.** In or into the presence of some one; in the (or this) very place, there (or here) –1554.

1. Or let me deye p. in this place CHAUCER.

Present (prĭze·nt), *v.* ME. [– (O)Fr. *présenter* – L. *præsentare* place before, etc., in med.L. present to a person as a gift; see prec., and PRESENT *sb.*[2]] **I.** To make present *to*, bring into the presence of. **1.** *trans.* To bring or place (a person) before, into the presence of, or under the notice of, another; to introduce; *spec.* to introduce at court, or before a sovereign, etc. **b.** To bring before or into the presence of God; to dedicate by so bringing ME. **†c.** To give greeting from, to 'remember' (any one) *to* –1792. **2.** *refl. To p. oneself*: to appear, attend. late ME. **3.** *trans.* **a.** To name and recommend (a clergyman) to the bishop for institution to a benefice. Often *absol.* ME. **b.** To nominate to the benefits of any foundation 1820. **4.** To show, exhibit, display; also (in recent use), to exhibit, be characterized by (some quality or attribute) 1500. **b.** *P. arms* (Mil.), to hold a fire-arm, etc. in a position expressing honour or deference, in saluting a person of superior rank 1759. **5.** To make present or suggest to the mind; to set forth or describe; to represent (*as* or *to be*); to set forth 1579. **6.** *refl.* (from 4, 5) To show itself, appear; to suggest itself, come into one's mind; to occur 1590. Also *intr.* (now *rare*). **7.** *trans.* To symbolize; to represent; to stand for, denote; to be a picture of (*arch.*) late ME. **b.** To represent (a character) on the stage; to act; to personate (*arch.*) 1588. **†c.** To act (a play, or scene in a play) –1637. **8.** *Law.* To make presentment of. **a.** To make a formal statement of; to submit (a fact, or a request, etc.). Also *absol.* late ME. **b.** To bring (an offence, etc.) formally under the notice of the proper authority, for inquiry or action. late ME. **c.** To charge (a person) formally; to report or bring up for trial 1526. **9.** To place (a thing) in, or give to (it), a particular direction or position. **a.** To point (a fire-arm, etc.) at something; to hold (it) out in the position of taking aim. Also *absol.* (esp. as word of command). 1579. **b.** *Obstetrics.* Of the fœtus: To direct (a particular part) towards the *os uteri* during labour; usu. *intr.* for *refl.* said of the part so directed 1597. **c.** To point, direct, or turn (a thing) to face something, or in a specified direction. Also *intr.* 1793. **10.** To bring (a substance) into the presence of or into close contact with another 1758.

1. The Dutchesse..presented mee to kisse the Queene's hand 1670. A candidate is said to present himself for examination; one who has qualified for, or is honoured with a degree, is presented for the degree; a theatrical manager is said (in recent use) to present an actor, etc. O.E.D. **b.** They brought hym to hierusalem, to p. hym to the lorde TINDALE *Luke* 2:22. **c.** P. me cordially to Mrs. Champion BURKE. **2.** Now there was a day, when the sons of God came to p. themselues before the Lord *Job* 1:6. **3.** A lunatic cannot p. to a church, nor his committee 1818. **4.** The few points which p. any difficulty 1885. **5.** Hear what to my mind first thoughts p. MILT. **6.** A remedie presents it selfe SHAKS. **7. b.** He presents Hector of Troy SHAKS. **c.** A Maske presented at Ludlow Castle MILT. (*title*). **9. a.** He sees me cock and p. DE FOE. **10.** If a pure Alkali be presented to a pure Acid, they rush together with violence 1758.

II. To offer, deliver, give. **1.** *trans.* To bring or place (a thing) before or into the presence of a person, or to put (it) into his hands, for acceptance; to offer, hand over, bestow, give (usu. in a formal or ceremonious manner) ME. **b.** To deliver, convey, give (a message, greeting, etc.); to offer (compliments, regards, etc.) ME. **c.** To deliver (a document, as a written address, petition, bill, etc.) to the proper quarter, for acceptance, or to be dealt with according to its tenor 1509. **d.** Of things: To offer, furnish, afford, supply 1604. **†2.** To make presentation of (a benefice) *to* a clergyman –1796. **3. a.** *To p.* a person *with* a thing = *to present* a thing *to* a person (sense II. 1). Also *fig.* to furnish or supply *with* something. ME. **†b.** With personal obj. only; rarely *absol.* –1712.

1. I beseech you therefore, brethren,..that ye p. your bodies a liuing sacrifice, holy, acceptable vnto God *Rom.* 12:1. [They] presented vnto him a mulet 1585. To p. to the world..a full and clear Narration CLARENDON. **b.** To p. you my complements 1638. **c.** My Soul more bent To serve therewith my Maker, and p. My true account MILTON. **3. a.** Yesterday week Mrs. Morse presented me with a fine daughter 1803.

Presentable (prĭze·ntăb'l), *a.* 1540. [orig. – med.L. *præsentabilis*; later f. prec. + -ABLE.] **1.** Capable of, or suitable for, presentation 1626. **2.** *Law.* That may or should be formally brought up or charged; as an offence, an offender, etc. 1540. **3.** *Eccl.* Of a benefice: = PRESENTATIVE 1. 1636. **4.** Suitable, by attire and appearance, to be introduced into society or company; of decent appearance, fit to be seen. (Properly of persons; often also of things.) The usual current sense. 1827.

1. A p. claim 1868. **4.** Is he a p. sort of a person? THACKERAY. This table looks very fine.., but only the ends are of mahogany and have p. legs 1898. Hence **Presentabi·lity. Prese·ntably** *adv.*

Presentation (prezĕntēⁱ·ʃən). late ME. [– (O)Fr. *présentation* – late L. *præsentatio*, f. *præsentat-*, pa. ppl. stem of L. *præsentare*; see PRESENT *v.*, -ION.] **I. 1.** The action of presenting or introducing a person: see PRESENT *v.* I. 1. **2.** *Eccl.* The action, or the right, of presenting a clergyman to a benefice, or to the bishop for institution; see PRESENT *v.* I. 3. late ME. **†3.** *Law.* = PRESENTMENT 2. –1610.

1. His p. at St. James's JANE AUSTEN. The P. for Doctor's Degrees 1883. *The P. of Christ in the Temple*: see Luke 2:22–39. *The P. of the Virgin Mary* as a child, as narrated in the Apocryphal Gospels. Also in *Art*, a representation of either of these incidents. **2.** Locke..was made Secretary of Presentations—that is, of the Chancellor's church patronage 1880.

II. The action of offering for acceptance; handing over, delivery; bestowal, gift, offering. late ME. **b.** Something offered for acceptance; a present, gift, donation; an address 1619.

Prayers..are..sometimes a p. of mere desires HOOKER.

III. 1. Theatrical, pictorial, or symbolic representation; a display, show, exhibition 1600. **b.** An image, likeness, semblance; a representation, a symbol 1594. **2.** A setting forth, a statement 1597. **3.** *Metaph.* and *Psychol.* (tr. G. *Vorstellung*). All the modification of consciousness directly involved in the knowing or being aware of an object in a single moment of thought 1842. **4.** The action of placing, or condition of being placed, in a particular direction or position with respect to something else or to an observer; the mode in which a thing is presented or presents itself; *spec.* in *Obstetrics* (see PRESENT *v.* I. 9. b) 1754.

1. He vses his folly like a stalking-horse, and vnder the p. of that he shoots his wit SHAKS. **b.** *Rich. III*, IV. iv. 84. **2.** I have not further to trouble yr Excell[cy] then w[t] the p. of my reall desires to serve you 1674.

attrib. in sense II., as *p. copy, clock*, etc. Hence **Presenta·tional** *a.* of or pertaining to p. (sense III. 3). **Presenta·tionalism, Presenta·tionism,** the doctrine that in perception the mind has an immediate cognition of the object; **Presenta·tionalist, Presenta·tionist,** one who holds this doctrine.

Presentative (prĭze·ntătiv), *a.* late ME. [prob. orig. – med. L. **præsentativus* (cf. *præsentabilis* PRESENTABLE), f. as prec.; see -IVE.] **1.** *Eccl.* Of a benefice: To or for which a patron has the right of presentation. Also said of the advowson, the tithes, etc. connected with such a benefice. Opp. to APPROPRIATE, COLLATIVE, DONATIVE, IMPROPRIATE. 1559. **†2.** = REPRESENTATIVE *a.* 1, 2. –1653. **3.** Having the function or power of presenting an idea or notion to the mind 1855. **4.** *Metaph.* and *Psychol.* Of pertaining or relating to, or of the nature, of presentation (sense III. 3) 1842.

Presentee (prezĕntī·). 1498. [– AFr. *presentee* = Fr. *présenté*, pa. pple. of *présenter*; see PRESENT *v.*, -EE[1].] **1.** A person presented; *spec.* a clergyman presented (for institution) to a benefice. **2.** One to whom something is presented 1854.

Presenter (prĭze·ntəɹ). 1544. [f. PRESENT *v.* + -ER[1]. See also PRESENTOR.] One who presents (in various senses).

Presential (prĭze·nʃăl), *a.* Now *rare.* Also **præ-**. 1635. [– med.L. *præsentialis* present, f. L. *præsentia* PRESENCE; see -AL[1].] **1.** Of or pertaining to presence; having or implying actual presence with a person or in a place; present. **2.** = PRESENT *a.* I. 4. 1649. **3.** Pertaining to present time 1846. **b.** *Gram.* Applied to those tenses formed on the present stem 1898.

1. To see the presentiall countenance of God 1635. So **Presentia·lity** (now *rare*), presentness (in time): the being present in place, presence.

Presentiate (prĭze·nʃiˌeⁱt), *v.* Now *rare.* 1659. [perh. f. PRESENT *a.* + -ATE[3], after *different/differentiate*.] *trans.* To make present in time or place.

Presentient (prĭse·nʃⁱĕnt), *a.* 1814. [– L. *præsentiens, -ent-*, pr. pple. of *præsentire* feel or perceive beforehand; see PRE- A. I. 3, SENTIENT.] Feeling or perceiving beforehand; having a presentiment; scenting beforehand.

Presentiment (prize·ntimĕnt, pris-). 1714. [– Fr. †*présentiment* (mod. *press-*), f. *pré-* PRE- + *sentiment* SENTIMENT.] **1.** A mental impression or feeling of some future event; a vague expectation, seeming like a direct perception of something about to happen; an anticipation, foreboding (usu. of something evil). **2.** A previously conceived sentiment or opinion; a prepossession (*rare*) 1751. Hence **Presentime·ntal** *a.*

Presentive (prĭze·ntiv), *a.* (*sb.*) 1871. [irreg. f. PRESENT *v.* + -IVE; used in distinction from *presentative*.] Presenting an object or conception directly to the mind (opp. to *symbolic*); also *sb.*, a presentive word. Hence **Prese·ntive-ly** *adv.*, **-ness.**

Presently (pre·zĕntli), *adv.* late ME. [f. PRESENT *a.* + -LY[2]; orig. after med.L. *præsentialiter*.] **†1.** So as to be, or as being, present; on the spot; in person, personally

–1579. **2.** At the present time; now. *Obs.* or *dial.* 1485. †**b.** At the time referred to; just then –1740. **3.** At the very time; at once; immediately, instantly, quickly, promptly. *Obs.* or *arch.* late ME. **4.** In blunted sense (from 3): In the space of time that immediately follows, in a little while, before long, soon, shortly. Now the ordinary use. 1566. †**5.** Immediately (in space or relation); directly, closely –1661. **6.** As a direct result or conclusion; consequently, thereupon; necessarily, *ipso facto. Obs.* or *arch.* 1634.

2. A reward to be rendred hereafter, not p. 1637. **3.** Go p., and take this Ring with thee SHAKS. **4.** Toys..which are p. put out of order 1699. The struggle, as we shall p. see, lasted two generations 1857. I cannot attend to it at once; I will do so p. 1908. **6.** We do not infer, nor doth it p. follow, that the present reading is corrupt and false 1659.

Presentment (prize·ntmĕnt). ME. [– OFr. *presentement*; see PRESENT *v.*, -MENT.] The act of presenting or fact of being presented, presentation; an instance or embodiment of this; chiefly in techn. or spec. uses. **1.** The act of presenting a person to or for any office, esp. a clergyman for institution to a benefice. *Obs.* exc. *Hist.* **2.** *Law.* The act of presenting or laying before a court or person in authority a formal statement of some matter to be legally dealt with. **a.** A statement on oath by a jury of a fact within their knowledge. late ME. †**b.** A similar statement (formerly) made by a magistrate or justice of the peace, or by a constable –1875. **c.** *Eccl.* A formal complaint or report of some offence or fault, made by the churchwardens, etc., to the bishop or archdeacon at his visitation 1576. **3.** = PRESENTATION II, I. 1. Now *rare.* 1607. **4.** = PRESENTATION III. 1. 1605. **b.** Delineation; usu. quasi-*concr.* a picture, portrait, image, likeness 1602. **c.** The appearance, aspect, form, or mode in which anything is presented; exhibition, display 1634. **5.** Statement, setting forth, description; the form or mode of so stating 1611. **6.** The act of presenting to consciousness, or to the imagination; suggestion; the conception thus given 1633. **b.** *Metaph.* and *Psychol.* = PRESENTATION III. 3. 1842.

4. An honored guest at the p. of a burlesque masque 1834. **b.** The counterfet p. of two Brothers SHAKS. **c.** To cheat the eye with blear illusion, And give it false presentments MILT. **5.** A scientific and exact p. of religious things M. ARNOLD.

Presentness (pre·zĕntnės). 1530. [f. PRESENT *a.* + -NESS.] The quality or condition of being present in place, time, or thought.

Presentor (prize·ntǫɹ). 1532. [– AFr. *presentour*, f. *presenter*; see PRESENT *v.*, -OR 2. Cf. PRESENTER.] One who makes a presentment. **b.** One who presents to a benefice 1865.

Preservation (prezəɹvēi·ʃən). 1472. [– (O)Fr. *préservation* – med.L. *præservatio*, f. *præservat-*, pa. ppl. stem of late L. *præservare*; see PRESERVE *v.*, -ION.] **1.** The action of preserving or keeping from injury or destruction; the fact of being preserved. **2.** The state of being (well or ill) preserved; state of keeping 1751. †**3.** A preservative –1617.

1. We bless thee for our creation, p., and all the blessings of this life *Bk. Com. Prayer.* **2.** The foxtails are still in great p. 1816.

Preservative (prizə·ɹvătiv), *a.* and *sb.* late ME. [– (O)Fr. *préservatif* – med.L. *præservativus, -um*, f. as prec.; see -IVE.] **A.** *adj.* Having the quality of preserving; tending to preserve; protective. **B.** *sb.* (absol. use of adj.) **1. a.** A medicine that preserves health, protecting from or preventing disease; a safeguard against poison or infection; a prophylactic. Now *rare.* 1466. **b.** *gen.* A safeguard *from* (or *against*) any danger or injury 1526. **2.** That which preserves, or tends to preserve or protect from decay, loss, or destruction 1503. **3.** *spec.* A chemical substance or preparation used to preserve perishable food-stuffs, etc. 1875.

1. a. To swallow a Vipers head was a most certain P. and Remedy against the biting of a Viper 1672. **3.** The introduction of preservatives into articles of food 1898.

Preservatory (prizə·ɹvătəri), *a.* and *sb.* *rare.* 1649. [f. prec. by substitution of suffix; see -ORY[1] and [2].] **A.** *adj.* Tending to preserve; preservative. **B.** *sb.* (absol. use of *adj.*) **1.** A preservative 1654. **2.** = PRESERVE *sb.* 3. 1823. **3.** *U.S.* An apparatus for preserving substances for food 1875.

Preserve (prizə·ɹv), *sb.* 1552. [f. next.] †**1.** A preserving agent; a preservative –1677. **b.** *pl.* Goggles used to protect the eyes from dust, excess of light, etc. 1887. **2.** A confectionery preparation of fruit, etc., preserved with sugar; jam; often in *pl.* 1600. **3.** A wood or other ground set apart for the protection and rearing of game; a piece of water for fish; a vivarium 1807. **b.** *transf.* and *fig.* (often *pl.*) A thing over which one claims special rights 1829.

3. b. In the Colonies..we have not so much neutral markets, as preserves 1897.

Preserve (prizə·ɹv), *v.* late ME. [– (O)Fr. *préserver* – late L. *præservare*, f. *præ* PRE- + *servare* keep, protect.] **1.** *trans.* To keep safe from harm or injury; to take care of, guard. Const. *from* (†*of, out of*). **2.** To keep alive (*arch.*); to keep from decay, make lasting (a material thing, a name, a memory) 1560. **b.** To maintain (a state of things) 1676. **c.** To keep in one's possession; to retain (a possession, acquisition, quality, etc.) 1617. **3. a.** To prepare (fruit, meat, etc.) by boiling with sugar, salting, or pickling, so as to prevent its decomposition or fermentation. Also *absol.* 1579. **b.** To keep (organic bodies) from decomposition, by chemical treatment, freezing, etc. 1613. **4.** To keep (game) undisturbed for personal use in hunting, shooting, or fishing; to keep (game runs, fishing rivers, etc.) for private use 1807.

1. Forto kepe and to p. The bodi fro siknesses alle GOWER. Oh, the Lord preserue thy good Grace SHAKS. See also WELL-PRESERVED. **2.** A tiny little village preserves the name of the Percy 1874. **b.** Means..effectual in preserving discipline 1810. **c.** In politics they often yield the name while they p. the thing 1828. **3. a.** Hast thou not learn'd me how To make Perfumes? Distill? Preserue? SHAKS. **4.** A man who preserves is always respected by the poachers TROLLOPE. Hence **Prese·rvable** *a.* **Prese·rval**, preservation. **Prese·rver**, one who or that which preserves; *esp.* one who keeps safe from destruction or injury; a saviour.

Preside (prizəi·d), *v.* 1611. [– Fr. *présider* – L. *præsidēre*, f. *præ* PRE- + *sedēre* sit.] **1.** *intr.* To occupy the chair or seat of authority in any assembly, or at the ordinary meetings of a society or company; to act as chairman or president. **b.** To sit at the head of the table 1871. **2.** To exercise superintendence, direction, or control. Also *fig.* to sit or reign supreme. 1656. **3.** *trans.* To control, direct (*rare*) 1665. **4.** *intr. To p. at the organ*, or *piano*, etc. *orig.* To conduct the band on the instrument in question; now, in pop. use, To be (or act as) organist or pianist during any social, religious, or musical assembly 1799.

1. By his place, he presided in all Publick Councils CLARENDON. **2.** In none of their meetings have they [Quakers] a President; as they believe Divine Wisdom alone ought to p. 1796. Hence **Presi·der**, one who presides.

Presidence (pre·zidĕns). 1595. [– (O)Fr. *présidence* – med.L. *præsidentia*; see next, -ENCE.] **1.** The action or fact of presiding; superintendence, direction. **2.** = next 1. Now *rare.* 1606.

Presidency (pre·zidĕnsi). 1591. [– Sp., Pg. *presidencia*, It. *presidenza* – med.L. *præsidentia*, f. *præsident-*; see next, -ENCY.] **1.** The office or function of president; presidentship, chairmanship; superintendence, direction; also, the term during which a president holds office. **2.** A district under the administration of a president; *spec.* in India, Each of the three divisions of the East India Company's territory, which were orig. governed by the Presidents of the Company's three factories. Loosely, the seat of government of each of these. *Obs.* in official use. 1698.

1. In the days of the p. of Washington CANNING. **2.** The term 'P.'..applied to the Provinces or Governments of Bengal, Madras, and Bombay, is no longer applicable to the present condition of things, and in the case of Bengal is positively misleading 1872.

President (pre·zidĕnt), *sb.* late ME. [– (O)Fr. *président* – L. *præsidens, -ent-*, subst. use of pr. pple. of *præsidēre*; see PRESIDE, -ENT.] **1.** The appointed governor or lieutenant of a province, or division of a country, a dependency, colony, city, etc. Now chiefly *Hist.* **b.** *fig.* A presiding deity, patron, or guardian 1611. **2.** The head of a temporary or permanent body of persons, who presides over their meetings and proceedings. **a.** *gen.* late ME. **b.** The title often borne by the head of a college in a university, or in U.S. of a university consisting of a single college 1464. **c.** The person elected to preside over the meetings and proceedings of an academy, society, or institution, literary, scientific, artistic, or the like 1660. **d.** In U.S. the title of one who presides over the proceedings of a financial, commercial, or industrial company, as a bank, railway, mining company, etc. 1781. **3.** The head of an advisory council, or administrative board or department of government, as, in Great Britain, the (Lord) P. of the Council, the P. of the Board of Agriculture, of Education, of Trade, etc.; also of certain courts of justice, as the Court of Session in Scotland, the Court of Probate in England, etc. 1530. †**b.** Formerly the title of the chief magistrate in some of the British North American colonies, and in the States to which they gave rise –1817. **4.** The officer in whom the executive power is vested in a modern republic, the elected head of the government 1783.

2. a. He receiv'd publick thanks from the Convocation, of which he was P. 1663. **b.** He..was ons ellect presydent of Maudlen Colledge 1530. **3.** *Lord P. of the Council*: an officer of the English crown whose duty is to preside at the meetings of the Privy Council, and to report to the King the business transacted there. **4.** Four Presidents (Harrison, Taylor, Lincoln, Garfield) have died in office, and been succeeded by Vice-Presidents 1889.

President (pre·zidĕnt), *a.* Now *rare.* late ME. [– L. *præsidens, -ent-*; see prec.] That presides or occupies the chief place; superintending.

Pre·sidentess. 1782. [f. PRESIDENT *sb.* + -ESS[1].] **a.** A female president. **b.** The wife of a president.

Presidential (prezide·nʃăl), 1603. [– med.L. *præsidentialis*, f. *præsidentia* PRESIDENCY; see -AL[1].] **1.** Of or pertaining to a president or his office. **2.** Of the nature of a president; presiding 1650.

2. The next P. Election looms always in advance 1860. Hence **Preside·ntially** *adv.*

Pre·sidentship. 1525. [-SHIP.] The office or function of a president; the period of this.

Presidial (prisi·diăl), *a.* and *sb.* 1598. [– Fr. *présidial* sb. and adj. – late L. *præsidialis*, f. *præses, -id-* the governor of a province; see -AL[1]. In sense 4 f. L. *præsidium* garrison, fort.] **A.** *adj.* **1.** *French Hist.* Of or pertaining to a province, provincial 1611. †**2.** Of a Roman province: Under a *præses* or president –1771. **3.** Of or pertaining to a president or the action or function of presiding (*rare*) 1598. **4.** †**a.** = PRESIDIARY *a.* **b.** Of or pertaining to a presidio. 1598. **B.** *sb. French Hist.* A presidial court of justice in France 1683.

Presidiary (prisi·diări), *a.* and *sb.* 1599. [– L. *præsidiarius* that serves for defence, f. *præsidium* garrison, f. *praesidēre* PRESIDE; see -ARY[1].] **A.** *adj.* Of, pertaining to, or serving as a garrison; garrisoned. **B.** *sb.* A guard, a protection 1623.

Presi·ding, *ppl. a.* 1667. [f. PRESIDE + -ING[2].] That presides. *P. officer*, an official appointed to superintend the counting of votes at an election.

‖**Presidio** (prisi·dio). 1808. [Sp., garrison, fort :– L. *præsidium.*] In Spain and the s.w. U.S., etc.: A fort, a fortified settlement, a military station, a garrison town. Also a Sp. penal settlement in a foreign country.

Presignification (prisi:gnifikēi·ʃən). Now *rare.* 1603. [f. PRE- A. I. 1 + SIGNIFICATION; cf. late (eccl.) L. *præsignificatio.*] The action of signifying or indicating beforehand; an indication or sign (of what is coming).

Presignify (prīsi·gnifəi), *v.* 1586. [– Fr. †*présignifier* or L. *præsignificare*; see A. I. 1, SIGNIFY.] *trans.* To signify or intimate beforehand.

Presphenoid (-sfī·noid). 1854. [f. PRE- A. II. + SPHENOID.] *Anat.* The anterior part of the sphenoid bone of the skull, which forms a separate bone in (human) infancy. Hence **Presphenoidal** (prī:sfīnoi·dăl) *a.*

Press (pres), *sb.*[1] [ME. *presse* – (O)Fr. *presse*, f. *presser*, see PRESS *v.*[1] Also ME. *prēs*, in XVI–XVII *prese*, *preas(e*, *preace*, only in early senses.] **I. 1.** The condition of being crowded or thronged; a crowd, a throng, a multitude (*arch.*). **b.** A throng or crush in battle; the thick of the fight; a mêlée. late ME. **2.** A crowding or thronging together ME. **†3.** The condition of being hard pressed; a critical situation; straits, distress –1677. **4.** Pressure of affairs; urgency, hurry. late ME.

1. Who is it in the presse, that calles on me? SHAKS. **b.** He..fought, sword in hand, in the thickest p. MACAULAY. **2.** Give gently way, when there's too great a p. BYRON. **4.** Amid the flame and armes ran I in preasse 1547. The eager p. of our modern life 1883.

II. 1. The act of pressing (something); pressure 1513. **2.** A mark made by pressing; a crease; *fig.* an impression 1601. **3.** The action of pressing (forward) 1893. **4.** Naut. *P. of sail, canvas* (formerly *p. sail, prest sail, pressing sail*): 'as much sail as the state of the wind, etc., will permit a ship to carry' (Smyth) 1592.

4. He bore away with a p. of sail for Malta 1806.

III. An instrument or machine by which pressure is communicated. **1.** An instrument used to compress a substance into smaller compass, denser consistency, a flatter shape, or a required form; as *coining, copying p.*, etc.; *cheese, clothes p.*, etc.; *cam, hydraulic, screw, toggle p.*; etc. late ME. **b.** The apparatus for inflicting the torture of *peine forte et dure*. *Obs.* exc. *Hist.* 1734. **2.** An apparatus for expressing or extracting the juice, or the like, out of anything; as *wine, oil, cider, sugar p.*, etc. late ME. **3.** A machine for printing, a printing-press 1535. **b.** A printing-house or printing-office. Often used in the names of printing establishments, e.g. the Clarendon P., Oxford, the Pitt P., Cambridge, etc. Hence, contextually, for the *personnel* of such an establishment. 1579. **c.** The printing-press in operation, the work or function of the press; the art or practice of printing 1579. **d.** (Also *periodical* or *public p.*, *daily p.*, etc.) The newspapers, journals, and periodical literature generally; the newspapers and journals of a country, district, party, etc., as the French P., the London P., the Conservative P., the religious p., etc. Hence sometimes the title of a newspaper. 1797.

3. b. The Presses swelld with the most virulent Invectives against them CLARENDON. **c.** These are the new dark ages, you see, of the popular p. TENNYSON. **d.** I seldom..read..the ordinary animadversions of the p. RUSKIN.

Phrases. *At, in,* †*under* (*the*) *p.*, in the process of printing, being printed. *Off the p.*, finally printed, issued. †*Out of p.*, = prec., also out of print. *To pass the p.*, etc. *To correct the p.*, i.e. the printing, or the errors in composing the type. Now *rare*. *Freedom* or *liberty of the p.*, free use of the printing-press; the right to print and publish anything without submitting it to previous official censorship. So in *free p.*, *unfettered p.*, etc. *A good* or *bad press*, favourable or unfavourable reception by the newspapers.

IV. A large (usu. shelved) cupboard, esp. one placed in a recess in the wall, for holding clothes, books, etc.; in Scotland, also for victuals, plates, dishes, and other table requisites. Cf. CLOTHES-*p.* late ME.

attrib. and *Comb.* **a. p.-copy** *sb.*, a copy of a writing made by transfer in a copying-press; hence **-copy** *v.*; **-pack** *v.*, to pack or compress (something) into small compass by means of a p.; **-printing,** printing by a p.; a method of printing porcelain. **b.** (connected with printing and journalism): **p. agent,** a man employed in connection with a theatre or the like to attend to the advertising, and the reporting of the performances; **-box,** a shelter for newspaper reporters in the open air, as at a cricket or football match; **p. cutting,** a paragraph, article, or notice, cut from a newspaper; also *attrib.* as *p.-cutting agency*; **-gallery,** a gallery or part of the house at any public meeting, set apart for reporters; esp. that in the House of Commons; **-proof, -revise,** the last proof examined before printed matter goes to p.

Press (pres), *sb.*[2] Now *rare*. 1596. [alt., under influence of prec., of PREST *sb.* 5.] **1.** The impressing of men for service in the navy or (less frequently) the army. Now *Hist.* 1599. **b.** A warrant giving authority to impress recruits. *Obs.* exc. *Hist.* 1596. **2.** *transf.* and *fig.* Impressment into service of any kind; a requisition 1667. **3.** *attrib.*, as PRESS-GANG, PRESS-MONEY, etc. 1688.

1. b. I haue mis-vs'd the King's Presse SHAKS.

Press (pres), *v.*[1] [ME. *presse* – (O)Fr. *presser* – L. *pressare*, frequent. f. *press-*, pa. ppl. stem of *premere* press. Also, chiefly in Branch III, ME. *prēse*, *prēce* with lengthened vowel; cf. PRESS *sb.*[1]] **I.** Literal and directly connected senses. **1.** *trans.* To exert a steady force against (something in contact), e.g. by weight (downwards), or by other physical agency (in any direction); to subject to pressure. **b.** *To p.* (*to death*): to execute the punishment of *peine forte et dure* upon (a person arraigned for felony who stood mute and would not plead); see PEINE. *Obs.* exc. *Hist.* 1544. **c.** As a sign of affection or courtesy (with a person, the hand, etc., as object) 1700. **d.** *intr.* To exert pressure; to bear with weight or force *on, upon, against* 1815. **2.** *trans.* To cause to move by pressure; to push, drive, thrust. (With advbs. and preps.) late ME. **b.** *fig.* (usu. with *down*) ME. **3.** To extract by pressure; to express; to squeeze (juice, etc.) *out of* or *from* something. late ME. **4.** To subject to pressure so as to reduce to a particular shape, consistence, smoothness, thinness, or bulk, or so as to extract juice, etc., from ; to compress, squeeze. late ME. **5.** To print. *Obs.* or *arch.* 1579.

1. Her step seemed to pity the grass it prest SHELLEY. *To p. the button* (fig.): to set things in motion. **c.** The Minstrel's hand he kindly pressed SCOTT. **d.** Since air possesses weight, it necessarily presses upon any object exposed to its influence HUXLEY. **2.** Good measure, pressed doune..and runnynge ouer TINDALE *Luke* 6:38. **3.** Wine is pressed from the grape 1744. **4.** P. them as long as there is any milk in the almonds 1796.

II. Figurative senses. **1.** *trans.* (fig. of I. 1.) Of an enemy, etc.: To bear heavily on; to reduce to straits; to beset, harass. Now chiefly in *hard pressed*. late ME. **†b.** Of a tyrant, circumstances, etc.: To oppress; to crush; to distress, afflict –1793. **c.** To weigh down, burden, oppress (the feelings, mind, spirits, etc.) 1604. **d.** To put to straits, as by want of time, means, etc.; in passive, usu. with *for* 1678. **2.** *intr.* To produce a strong mental or moral impression *upon*; now usu., to bear heavily, weigh *upon*; (the mind, etc.) 1561. **3.** *trans.* To urge on; to constrain, compel, force. late ME. **b.** Said of danger, business, etc., or of time. Now only *absol.* or *intr.* To compel dispatch; to be pressing; to demand immediate action. 1440. **c.** To urge on, drive quickly (*rare*) 1611. **d.** With the movement as obj. 1742. **4.** To urge on by words or arguments; to importune, beg, entreat (a person *to do* something or *for* something) 1593. **b.** *intr.* or *absol.* To ask or seek importunately. Const. *for* or *inf.* late ME. **5.** *trans.* To urge, insist on the doing of (something); to solicit, request (a thing) earnestly. Const. *on, upon* (a person). 1625. **6.** To urge, insist on the belief, admission, or mental acceptance (of something); to impress (a thing) on the mind; to plead with insistence (a claim, etc.). Const. *on, upon* (a person, his attention, etc.) 1625. **7.** To urge, thrust (something to be taken or accepted) *upon* a person 1797. **8.** To push forward (arguments, views, positions, etc.) 1665.

1. Although hard pressed at first, the force eventually gained a..victory 1893. **c.** I haue this while with leaden thoughts beene prest SHAKS. **d.** In writing the last Number I was pressed for time 1817. **3.** Why should hee stay whom Loue doth presse to go? SHAKS. **b.** Let it be done with Dispatch, for the time presses 1746. **d.** Fast as they prest their flight 1742. **4.** To avoid being pressed..to stay another day DE QUINCEY. **b.** Don't p. for an answer yet 1833. **6.** Remember, if you mean to please, To p. your point with modesty and ease COWPER. **8.** Stephen pressed his advantage 1874.

III. Senses connected with the notion of a throng, or of pushing one's way as in a throng. Primarily *intr.* **1.** *intr.* To crowd, throng about a person or place ME. **b.** *trans.* To crowd upon, throng. *Obs.* or *arch.* 1549. **2.** *intr.* To push or strain forward; to hasten onward, urge one's way ME. **3.** To push one's way into a person's presence, or into a place, boldly, presumptuously, or insistently; to venture; to obtrude oneself, intrude. late ME. **†4.** To strive, try hard, attempt *to do* something (usu. with eagerness or haste); to aim at, endeavour after something. Also in weaker sense: To essay, undertake. –1642. **5.** To strive, contend, make resistance (*rare*). late ME.

1. No humble suters prease to speake for right SHAKS. The enemy presseth harde upon us 1648. **2.** I..preace vnto the marke apoynted TINDALE *Phil.* 3:14. Pressing forward like the wind SCOTT. **3.** Prease not into yᵉ place of greate men COVERDALE *Prov.* 25:6.

IV. *Comb.*: **p.-stud,** a stud which is fastened by pressing.

Hence **Pressed** (prest) *ppl. a.*, subjected to pressure; compacted or moulded by pressure; often qualifying articles in the preparation of which pressure is specially used, as *p. beef, brick, glass*, etc.

Press (pres), *v.*[2] *Pa. t.* and *pple.* **pressed**; **†prest.** 1543. [Altered from PREST *v.*[2], by assoc. with PRESS *v.*[1]; see PRESS-MONEY.] *trans.* To force (a man) to serve in the army or navy; cf. IMPRESS *v.*[2], PREST *v.*[2] **b.** *intr.* or *absol.* 1625. **c.** *trans.* To take authoritatively for royal or public use 1633. **d.** *transf.* To seize and force into some service 1598.

The peaceful Peasant to the Wars is prest DRYDEN. **b.** The King is fain to p. now MARVELL.

Press-bed. *Obs.* exc. *dial.* 1660. A bed constructed to fold up, when not in use, into a press (PRESS *sb.*[1] IV) closed by a door or doors; sometimes less correctly applied to a box-bed shut in by folding doors.

The Judge and I..lay in one press bed PEPYS.

Presser (pre·səɹ). 1545. [f. PRESS *v.*[1] + -ER[1].] **1.** One who presses, or works a press of any kind. **2.** An instrument, machine, etc., which applies pressure 1725.

Comb.: **p.-bar,** (*a*) the presser in a knitting-machine, which drives the barb of the needle into the groove of the shank; (*b*) the vertical bar in a sewing-machine which bears the presser-foot; **-foot,** the foot-plate of a sewing-machine which hold the cloth down to the feed-plate.

Pre·ss-gang, *sb.* 1693. [f. PRESS *sb.*[2] or *v.*[2] + GANG *sb.*] A body of men employed, under the command of an officer, to press men for service in the army or navy. Hence **Pre·ss-gang** *v. trans.* and *intr.* = PRESS *v.*[2]

Pre·ssing, *ppl. a.* 1591. [f. PRESS *v.*[1] + -ING[2].] That presses, in the senses of the verb; *esp.* calling for immediate attention, urgent. **b.** Of a request, etc., expressed with an earnest desire for compliance; also of the person, persistent, importunate 1705.

Discharging the most p. and crying debts 1616. **b.** My Mother..is very p. with me to marry STEELE. A p. summons 1855. Hence **Pre·ssingly** *adv.*, **-ness.**

Pression (pre·ʃən). Now *rare*. 1661. [– Fr. *pression* – L. *pressio*, f. *press-*; see PRESS *v.*[1], -ION.] **1.** The action of pressing; pressure. Sometimes applied *spec.* to a particular pressure used in massage. **†2.** In the Cartesian physics: Pressure or impulse communicated to and propagated through a fluid medium –1756.

Pressiroster (presirǫ·stəɹ). 1842. [– Fr. *pressirostre* (Cuvier) – mod.L. *pressirostris* adj., f. L. *pressus* pressed + *rostrum* beak, bill.] *Ornith.* A bird of the *Pressirostres* of Cuvier, now included in the *Charadriomorphæ* or plover-snipe group. So **Pressiro·stral** *a.* having the characteristics of the *Pressirostres.*

Pressive (pre·siv), *a.* 1619. [– Fr. †*pressif*, *-ive*, f. *presser*; see PRESS *v.*[1], -IVE.] **†1.**

Pressing, oppressive. *rare.* –1623. **2.** Characterized by pressure 1822.

Pre·ssman. 1598. [f. PRESS *sb.*[1] + MAN *sb.*] **1.** A man who operates a printing-press; *esp.* a hand-press printer. **2.** One who writes or reports for the press; a reporter, journalist 1859. **3.** In shoemaking: A workman who stamps out the sole-leather for boots or shoes with a press 1895.

Pre·ss-mark. 1802. [PRESS *sb.*[1] IV.] In libraries, a mark or number written or stamped in or on each book, and also given in the library catalogue, specifying the room, shelf, etc., where the book is kept. Hence as vb.

Pre·ss-mo:ney, †pre·st-mo:ney. Now only *Hist.* late ME. [orig. *prest-money*, f. PREST *sb.* + MONEY.] = PREST *sb.* 1, 3, 4.

Pressor (pre·sǫɹ), *a.* 1890. [Agent-n. in L. form from *premere* to press, used attrib.] *Phys.* That presses; stimulating, exciting.

P. nerves, nerves whose stimulation increases activity of vaso-motor centres 1890.

Pre·ss-room. 1683. [f. PRESS *sb.*[1] + ROOM *sb.*] **1.** The room in a printing-office in which the presses stand, and where the printing is done. **2.** A room in which a press of any kind is kept 1696.

Pressure (pre·ʃ[i]ŭɹ, pre·ʃəɹ). late ME. [– L. *pressura*, f. *press-*; see PRESS *v.*[1], -URE. Cf. OFr. *pressure.*] **I. 1.** The action or fact of pressing; the fact or condition of being pressed (see PRESS *v.*[1]); compression, squeezing, crushing, etc. 1601. **2.** *Physics.* The force exerted by one body on another by its weight, or by the continued application of power, viewed as a measurable quantity, the amount being expressed by the weight upon a unit area 1660. **b.** *Electr.* 'That which causes or tends to cause an electric current' (Trotter) 1889. **†3.** The mark, form, or character impressed; impression, stamp, image –1809.

1. The soft p. of a melting kisse 1602. **2.** *Absolute p.*, the total p. (of steam, etc.), found by adding the amount of the atmospheric p. to that indicated by the ordinary steam-gauge (which shows the *relative p.*, or p. above that of the atmosphere). *Centre of p.*: see CENTRE. *P. of the atmosphere*; The weight or p. of the atmosphere is about 15 lbs. in every square inch HUXLEY. **3.** *Haml.* I. v. 100, III. ii. 27.

II. 1. The condition of being painfully oppressed in body or mind; affliction, oppression. late ME. **†2.** The action of political or economic burdens; a heavy charge; the condition of being weighed down by these –1719. **b.** A state of trouble or embarrassment; *pl.* straits 1648. **c.** Urgency of affairs 1845. **3.** The action of anything that influences the mind or will; constraining influence 1625.

1. In presure and in paine My joyes thy preceptes give 1586. The p. of grief 1794. **2. b.** A period of financial p. 1868. **c.** Writing hastily and under p. 1885. **3.** His virtue, such as it was, could not stand the p. of occasion 1791.

Phrases. **High p.** *orig.* A p. higher than that of the atmosphere, but now only a relative term without any absolute limits; esp. in ref. to compound engines in which the steam is used at different pressures in the different cylinders; mostly *attrib.*, as in *high-p. engine, steam*, etc. **b.** *transf.* of speed, work, business, etc., and in *Path.*, as a *high-p. pulse.* **c.** In *Meteorol.* said of a dense condition of the atmosphere over a certain region, as in *high-pressure area, system* (of winds). So **low p.**

Comb. **p.-button,** a 'button' or stud, by pressing which a spring is liberated or an electric bell rung; **-gauge, -gage,** an instrument for showing the p. of an elastic agent, as steam or gas; also, one for showing the p. in a cannon or fire-arm at the instant of explosion of the charge; **-paralysis,** paralysis caused by p. on part of the brain; **-pipe,** the pipe of the p.-gauge of a steam-engine.

Pre·ss-wa:rrant. Now *Hist.* 1688. [f. PRESS *sb.*[2] + WARRANT *sb.*] A warrant giving authority to impress men for the service of the army or navy.

Pre·ss-work. 1771. [f. PRESS *sb.*[1] + WORK *sb.*] **1.** The work and management of a printing-press; the printing off on paper, etc., of what has been 'composed' or set up in type; the work so turned out, esp. from the point of view of its quality. **2.** Literary work done for the press 1888. **3.** *Pottery.* The making of ware by pressing the clay into moulds 1839.

Pre·ss-yard. *Obs.* exc. *Hist.* 1654. [f. PRESS *v.*[1] I. 1 b + YARD.] Name of a yard or court of old Newgate Prison, in which the torture of *peine forte et dure* (PEINE) is supposed to have orig. been carried out; and from which, later, prisoners started for the place of execution.

†Prest, *sb.* late ME. [– OFr. *prest* loan, advance pay for soldiers (mod. *prêt*), f. *prester*; see PREST *v.*[1]] **1.** An advance of money, a loan; *esp.* one made to the sovereign in an emergency; a forced loan; a grant, gift, bequest –1643. **2.** A charge, duty, or impost; a deduction made from or in connection with any payment –1548. **3.** A payment or wages in advance –1657. **4.** *esp.* Earnest-money paid to a sailor or soldier on enlistment –1588. **5.** An enlistment of soldiers or sailors –1602. **6.** *In p.*: as a prest or loan; in advance; on account; as earnest-money –1603.

Comb. **p.-warrant,** a warrant for paying prest money.

†Prest, *a.* and *adv.* ME. [– OFr. *prest* (mod. *prêt*) :– late or pop. L. *præstus* ready, for L. *præsto* at hand.] **A.** *adj.* **1.** Ready; at hand; prepared –1697. **2.** Ready in mind, disposition, or will; willing; prompt, eager, keen –1697. **b.** Alert, sprightly, brisk –1573. **3.** Close at hand –1589. **B.** *adv.* Readily, quickly 1558. Hence **†Pre·st-ly** *adv.*

A. 1. A huge Nauy p. at all Essayes 1635. **2.** Every Knight is..P. for their Country's Honour DRYDEN.

†Prest, *v.*[1] 1539. [– OFr. *prester* (mod, *prêter*) afford, lend :– L. *præstare* furnish. med. L. lend, rel. to *præsto* at hand, within reach.] **1.** *trans.* To lend (money); to advance on loan –1561. **2.** To advance (money) on account of work to be done or not yet completed –1586.

†Prest, *v.*[2] 1513. [f. PREST *sb.*] **1.** *trans.* To hire the services of (a person) or the use of (a ship, etc.) by part-payment in advance –1545. **2.** *esp.* To engage (men) for military service on land or sea by giving part-payment or earnest-money in advance; to enlist, levy (generally); to press –1600.

Pre·stable, *a.* *Sc.* Now *rare.* 1650. [– Fr. †*prestable* (mod. *prêtable*) or med.L. *prestabilis*, f. *prester* (*prestare*); see PREST *v.*[1], -ABLE.] Capable of being paid or advanced; capable of being performed or discharged.

To offer my fortune so far as it was p..., to make good all claims upon Ballantyne & Co. SCOTT.

Prestate (pre·ste[i]t), *v.* 1880. [– *præstat-*, pa. ppl. stem of L. *præstare* vouch for, answer for; see PREST *v.*[1], -ATE[3].] *Rom. Law. trans.* To undertake, take upon oneself, become responsible for; to furnish, manifest.

Prestation (prestē[i]·ʃən). 1473. [– OFr. *prestation* action of lending, tendering, etc. (also mod. in other senses) or late and med.L. *præstatio* payment, etc., in cl.L. 'warranty', f. as prec.; see -ION.] The action of paying, in money or service, what is due by law or custom, or feudally; a payment or the performance of a service so imposed or exacted; also, the performance of something promised.

†Pre·ster. late ME. [– L. *prester* – Gr. πρηστήρ fiery (or scorching) whirlwind, also a kind of venomous serpent.] **1.** A serpent, the bite of which was fabled to cause death by swelling –1847. **2.** A burning or scorching whirlwind –1797.

Pre·ster Jo·hn. [ME. *Prestre Johan* – OFr. *prestre Jehan* (mod. *prêtre-Jean*), med.L. *presbyter Iohannes* 'Priest John'.] The name given in the Middle Ages to an alleged Christian priest and king, orig. supposed to reign in the extreme Orient, but generally identified later with the king of Ethiopia or Abyssinia.

‖**Pre-ste·rnum, præste·rnum.** 1828. [PRE- A. II. b.] **1.** *Entom.* = PROSTERNUM. **2.** *Comp. Anat.* The front part of the sternum; the part corresponding to the first segment of the human sternum 1872. Hence **Preste·rnal** *a.* of or pertaining to the presternum, as *pre-sternal bone, region*, etc.

Prestidigitator (pre:sti₍di·dʒitē[i]təɹ). Also in Fr. form ‖**prestidigitateur** (prẹstidiʒitatǒr). 1843. [– Fr. (Jules de Rovère, *a*1830), f. *preste* nimble, PREST *a.* + L. *digitus* finger + *-ateur* :– L. *-ator*; perh. suggested by Fr. †*prestigiateur* PRESTIGIATOR, or due to a perverted derivation of it.] One who practises sleight of hand or legerdemain; a juggler, a conjurer; hence *fig.* a juggler with words, a trickster. So **Prestidigitation** (pre:sti₍didʒitē[i]·ʃən), sleight of hand, legerdemain.

Prestige (presti·ʒ). 1656. [– Fr. *prestige* – late L. *præstigium* illusion, in cl.L. *præstigiæ* fem. pl. juggler's tricks.] **†1.** An illusion; a conjuring trick; a deception, an imposture. Usu. *pl.* –1881. **2.** *transf.* Blinding or dazzling influence; 'magic', glamour; influence or reputation derived from previous character, achievements, or success 1829.

2. Such is the p. of broad cloth 1845.

Prestigia·tion. Now *rare.* 1540. [In form, agent-n. f. late L. *præstigiare, -ari*, f. *præstigium, -iæ*; see prec., -ATION.] The practice of juggling, sorcery, or magic; conjuring.

Prestigiator (presti·dʒi₍ē[i]təɹ). 1614. [– L. *præstigiator* (Plautus); see prec.] A juggler; a conjurer; †a cheat.

Prestigious (presti·dʒəs), *a.* Now *rare.* 1546. [– L. *præstigiosus* (Gellius), f. as prec.; see PRESTIGE, -OUS.] Practising juggling or legerdemain; cheating; deceptive, illusory. Hence **Presti·gious-ly** *adv.*, **-ness.**

‖**Prestissimo** (presti·ssimo), *a., adv., sb.* 1724. [It., superl. of *presto* adj. and adv.; see PRESTO.] *Mus.* A direction: Very quick; very fast; as *sb.* a very quick piece or movement.

Prest-money, earlier form of PRESS-MONEY.

‖**Presto** (pre·sto), *a.*[1], *adv.*[1], *sb.*[1] 1683. [It. = quick, quickly (*tempo presto* quick time) :– late L. *præstus*; see PREST *a.*] *Mus.* **A.** *adj.* or *adv.* A direction: In quick time, fast. **B.** *sb.* A movement or piece in quick time 1869.

Presto (pre·sto), *adv.*[2], *a.*[2], *sb.*[2] 1598. [– It.; the same word as prec.] **A.** *adv.* (interj.) Quickly, immediately, at once; used by conjurers and jugglers in various phrases of command, esp. *P., be gone, Hey p., pass*, etc.; hence, = immediately, instanter. Also interjectionally. **B.** *sb.* An exclam. of 'presto!' 1622. **C.** *adj.* or *attrib.* At hand, in readiness; active, ready, quick, instantaneous; of the nature of a magical transformation; juggling 1644.

A. Put in your money..; P. be gone—'Tis here agen SWIFT. Hence **Pre·sto** *v. trans.* to conjure.

Presume (prĭziū·m), *v.* late ME. [– (O)Fr. *présumer* – L. *præsumere* anticipate, (later) assume, venture, f. *præ* PRE- A. I. 1 + *sumere* take.] **†1.** *trans.* To take possession of without right; to usurp. late ME. only. **2.** To take upon oneself, undertake without adequate authority or permission; to venture upon. late ME. **b.** with *inf.* To take the liberty; to venture, dare (*to do* something). late ME. **†3.** *trans.* (with *inf.* or *cl.*) To profess, pretend –1652. **4.** To assume or take for granted; to presuppose; to count upon. *spec.* in *Law*: To take as proved until evidence to the contrary is forthcoming. late ME. **5.** *intr.* To act on the assumption of right or permission; to be presumptuous, take liberties. Often *p. on, upon* (†*of*): to act presumptuously on the strength of; also in neutral sense, to take advantage of. late ME. **6.** To press forward presumptuously; to aspire presumptuously; to presume to go. Now *rare* or *Obs.* late ME. **7.** *P. on, upon* (†*of*): to rely upon, count upon, take for granted; to look for. Now *rare* or *Obs.* 1586.

2. Hopes of excellence which I once presumed, and never have attained JOHNSON. **b.** Know then thyself, p. not God to scan POPE. **4.** At any time beyond the first seven years they might fairly p. him dead 1805. **5.** To take no care, is to p. upon providence 1708. **6.** Up led by thee, Into the Heav'n of Heavens I have presumed, An earthly guest MILT. **7.** How uncertain our lives are, and how little to be presumed of PEPYS. Hence **Presu·mable** *a.* probable, likely; to be counted on beforehand; **Pre-**

su·mably *adv.* **Presu·medly** *adv.* **Presu·mer,** a presumptuous person; one who assumes something without proof. **Presu·mingly** *adv.* presumptuously.

Presumption (prĭzɒ·mᵖʃən). ME. [– OFr. *presumpcion, presompcion* (mod. *présomption*) – L. *præsumptio, -on-*, f. *præsumpt-*, pa. ppl. stem of *præsumere*; see prec., -ION.] †**1.** Seizure and occupation without right; usurpation (*of* an office). *rare.* –1810. **2.** The taking upon oneself of more than is warranted; forward or over-confident opinion or conduct; arrogance, pride, effrontery, assurance ME. **3.** The taking of something for granted; also, that which is presumed; assumption, assumed probability, supposition, expectation ME. **b.** *spec.* in *Law*. (See quots.) 1596. **4.** A ground for presuming or believing; presumptive evidence 1586.

2. God smote him there because of his presumpcion, so that he dyed there besyde the Arke of God COVERDALE 2 *Sam.* 6:7. **3.** The..p. that a relatively late text is likely to be a relatively corrupt text 1881. **b.** *P. of fact* (Law), the inference of a fact not certainly known, from known facts. *P. of law*, (*a*) the assumption of the truth of anything until the contrary is proved; (*b*) an inference established by the law as universally applicable to certain circumstances. **4.** There seems strong internal p. against the authenticity of these epistles 1838.

Presumptive (prĭzɒ·mᵖtiv), *a.* 1561. [– Fr. *présomptif, -ive* – late L. *præsumptivus*, f. as prec.; see -IVE.] **1.** = next 1. Now *rare* or *Obs.* 1609. **2.** Giving reasonable grounds for presumption or belief 1561. **3.** Based on presumption; presumed, inferred 1628.

2. This is strong p. evidence, but we have positive proof—the evidence of our own senses DICKENS. **3.** *Heir p.*: see HEIR *sb.* 1. Hence **Presu·mptively** *adv.*

Presumptuous (prĭzɒ·mᵖtiuəs), *a.* ME. [– OFr. *presumptueux* (mod. *présomptueux*) – late L. *præsumptuosus*, var. of *-tiosus*, f. as prec.; see -OUS, -UOUS.] **1.** Characterized by presumption; unduly confident; arrogant, presuming; forward, impertinent. †**2.** = PRESUMPTIVE 2. *rare.* –1653.

1. A mouth speakynge p. thinges COVERDALE *Dan.* 7:20. That glorious, that p. thing, call'd man 1635. No less brave in action than p. in conduct 1777. Hence **Presu·mptuous-ly** *adv.* **-ness.**

Presupposal (prīsŏpōᵘ·zăl). Now *rare.* 1589. [f. next + -AL¹. Cf. SUPPOSAL.] A presupposition.

Presuppose (prīsŏpōᵘ·z), *v.* late ME. [– (O)Fr. *présupposer*, after med.L. *præsupponere*; see PRE- A. I. 1, SUPPOSE *v.*] **1.** *trans.* Of a person: To suppose, lay down, or postulate beforehand; hence, to assume to start with; to presume. **2.** To suppose beforehand or *a priori* 1530. **3.** Of a thing: To involve or imply as an antecedent 1526. **4.** *pass.* (from 1 or 3). To be implied or involved as something previously or already present or in existence. Formerly with *to*. 1526.

1. Pre-supposing such a desire to please 1809. **2.** Men of corrupted minds p. that honesty groweth out of simplicity of manners BACON. **3.** An effect presupposes a cause 1877.

Presupposition (prīsɒpŏzi·ʃən). 1533. [– med.L. *præsuppositio, -on-*, f. *præsupponere*; see prec., POSITION. Cf. (O)Fr. *présupposition*.] **1.** The action or an act of presupposing; a supposition antecedent to knowledge. **2.** That which is presupposed; a supposition, notion, or idea assumed as a basis of argument, action, etc.; a preliminary assumption 1579.

‖**Presystole** (prīsi·stŏli). 1884. [mod.L., f. PRE- B. I. 1 + SYSTOLE.] *Physiol.* The interval immediately preceding the systole. So **Presysto·lic** *a.*

Pretaxation (prītæksēⁱ·ʃən). *Hist.* Also **præ-.** 1769. [– med.L. *prætaxatio, -on-*, f. med.L. *prætaxare* count beforehand; see PRE- A. I. 2, TAXATION.] The action of giving a vote before others; prior election.

Prete·mporal (prī-), *a.* (*sb.*) 1866. [– mod.L. *prætemporalis*; see PRE- B. II. and TEMPORAL.] Situated in front of the temporal region of the skull: applied to a muscle. Also *ellipt.* as *sb.*

Pretence (prĭte·ns). late ME. Also (now U.S.) **pretense.** [– AFr. *pretense* – AL. **pretensa*, subst. use of fem. sing. or n. pl. of med.L. *pretensus* pretended, alleged, for cl.L. *prætentus*, pa. pple. of *prætendere* PRETEND.] **1.** The putting forth of a claim; a claim. Now *rare.* **b.** *Her. In p.*, borne on an inescutcheon to indicate a pretension or claim, e.g. that of a husband to the estates of his wife. *Escutcheon of p.*, such an inescutcheon. 1562. **2.** The putting forth of a claim to merit, dignity, etc.; pretension, profession; ostentation, display 1526. †**3.** An expressed intention, purpose, or design; an intending or purposing; the end purposed –1783. **b.** *esp.* A false or hypocritical profession or pretension 1545. **4.** A profession of purpose; *esp.* a pretext, a cloak 1538. **5.** A (false or misleading) assertion, allegation, or statement as to fact 1608. **b.** Make-believe, as in children's play 1863. **6.** The assertion of a ground, cause, or reason for any action; an alleged ground or reason, a plea; now usu., a trivial, groundless, or fallacious plea or reason, a pretext 1560.

1. Spirits that in our just pretenses arm'd Fell with us from on high MILT. **2.** Persons..who yet make great pretences to religion 1729. **3. b.** How often do we see p. cultivated in proportion as virtue is neglected 1763. **4.** He had some other object—this is all a p. 1845. **5.** The p. is that the noble is of unbroken descent from the Norman...But the fact is otherwise. EMERSON. **b.** This is a fairy tale and all fun and p. KINGSLEY. **6.** And ring for the servants on the smallest pretense 1880.

Pretenced, pretensed (-e·nst), *ppl. a.* late ME. [orig. *pretensed*, f. med.L. *pretensus* (see prec.) + -ED¹ 2.] **1.** = PRETENDED 1. *arch.* †**2.** Intended, purposed, designed –1596. Hence **Prete·ncedly, prete·nsedly** *adv. rare.*

Pretend (prĭte·nd), *v.* late ME. [– Fr. *prétendre* or L. *prætendere* stretch forth, put forward, allege, claim, f. *præ* PRE- A. + *tendere* stretch, TEND *v.*²] **I.** †**1.** *trans.* To stretch, or hold (something) before, in front of, or over a person or thing (e.g. as a covering or defence) –1670. †**2.** To proffer, present; to bring (a charge, an action at law) –1690. **3.** †**a.** *refl.* To put oneself forward in some character; to profess or claim (with *inf.* or *compl.*) –1680. **b.** Without refl. pron., in same sense as a; whence: To put forth an assertion or statement (expressed by an *inf.*) about oneself; now usu., to feign *to be* or *do* something. (A leading mod. sense.) late ME. **c.** To feign in play; to make believe 1865. **4.** *trans.* To give oneself out as having (something); now always, To profess falsely, to feign (some quality). Now *rare.* late ME. †**b.** *esp.* To claim to have (a right, title, power, etc.); to claim –1784. †**5.** To put forth or lay a claim to (a thing); to claim –1761. †**6.** To put forward as a reason or excuse; to use as a pretext –1776. **7.** To allege; now *esp.* to allege or declare with intent to deceive. (A leading current sense.) 1610. †**8.** To intend, purpose, design, plan –1728. **9.** To aspire to; to take upon one; to venture, presume; to attempt, endeavour, try. Const. with *inf.* 1482. †**10.** To portend, presage, foreshow –1634. †**11.** To indicate, signify, import, mean –1639.

3. a. Poor, petty, pitiful persons, who pretended themselves princes 1660. **b.** He was ignorant, or at least pretended to be so FIELDING. **4.** The enchantress then related..how she pretended illness 1850. **5.** As both the archbishops pretended to sit on his right hand, this question of precedency begat a controversy between them HUME. **7.** Pretending that he was sickly 1610. To p. difficulties and inconsistencies BERKELEY. **8.** Women when they be most pleasaunt, p. most mischiefe 1579. **9.** The people offered to fire at them, if they pretended to go forward DE FOE.

II. *intr.* (from prec. senses.) †**1.** To stretch forward; to move or go forward; to extend, tend; to make *for* –1650. **2.** *To p. to.* †**a.** To aspire to, aim at; to be a suitor or candidate for –1672. **b.** *spec.* [= Fr. *prétendre à.*] To make suit for, try to win in marriage. Now *rare.* 1650. **c.** To lay claim to 1647. **d.** To claim or profess to have; to affect 1659. †**e.** To make pretensions on behalf of –1670. **3.** To make pretence; to make believe; to feign 1526. **b.** In imagination or play: *absol.* of I. 3 c.

1. Who pretendith to god, God attendeth to hym CAXTON. **2. a.** When that my friend pretendeth to a place, I quit my interest, and leave it free G. HERBERT. **b.** He might p. surely to his kinswoman's hand THACKERAY. **c.** Yet they pretended to no Share of the Spoil 1683. **d.** People who p. to supernatural wisdom 1868. **3.** Weak to perform, though mighty to p. COWPER. **b.** *Let's p.*, a child's game of 'make-believe'. Hence **Prete·ndingly** *adv.*

Pretendant, -ent (prĭte·ndănt, -ĕnt), *sb.* and *a.* 1594. [– Fr. *prétendant*, pr. pple. of *prétendre*; see prec., -ANT.] **A.** *sb.* A claimant; esp. to a throne. Now *rare.* 1600. **b.** A mere pretender 1826. **2.** A suitor: **a.** at law: **b.** a wooer 1652. †**B.** *adj.* That claims to be (somebody); of or pertaining to a claimant –1620.

Prete·nded, *ppl. a.* 1461. [f. PRETEND *v.* + -ED¹.] **1.** Alleged, asserted; claimed to be such. **a.** Reputed, so-called 1461. **b.** Applied to things of which the speaker does not admit the existence, reality, or validity 1500. **c.** Professed falsely or insincerely 1643. **2.** Hence, Fictitious, counterfeit, feigned 1727. †**3.** Intended, designed, purposed, proposed –1703.

1. a. One Isaac Bickerstaff, a P. Esquire STEELE. **2.** An open foe may prove a curse, But a p. friend is worse GAY. Hence **Prete·ndedly** *adv.*

Pretender (prĭte·ndəɹ). 1612. [f. PRETEND *v.* + -ER¹.] **1.** One who puts forth a claim, or who aims at something; a claimant, candidate, aspirant; now, one who makes baseless pretensions 1622. †**b.** A suitor, wooer –1728. **c.** A claimant to a throne or the office of a ruler; *orig.* in a neutral sense, but now always applied to a claimant who is held to have no just title 1697. **2.** One who makes a profession, show, or assertion, esp. on inadequate grounds, or with intent to deceive; a deceiver, charlatan 1631.

1. c. *The Old* and *the Young P.* (Eng. Hist.), the designation of the son and grandson of James II of England, who successively asserted their claim to the British throne against the house of Hanover. **2.** To distinguish the p. in medicine from the true physician 1871. Hence **Prete·ndership,** the position or character of a p.

Pretension (prĭte·nʃən). Also †**-tion.** 1600. [– med.L. *prætensio, -on-*, also *-tio*, f. pa. ppl. stem of L. *prætendere*; see PRETEND, -ION. Cf. Fr. *prétention*, †*prétension*.] The action of pretending. **1.** An allegation or assertion the truth of which is not proved or admitted; hence, a pretext, pretence 1609. **2.** The assertion of a claim as of right; a claim put forth, a demand 1600. **b.** A rightful claim, a title 1710. **3.** The claim that one is or has something; profession. Also of things. Const. *to*. 1662. **b.** Pretentiousness, ostentation 1727. †**4.** An intention, a design; aim, aspiration –1782.

1. Miss Bird..declares all the viands of Japan to be uneatable—a staggering p. 1894. **2.** Ecclesiastical pretensions were still formidable under the Tudors FROUDE. **3.** I..have little or no Pretensions to Beauty 1718. **b.** Good without noise, without p. great POPE.

Pretentious (prĭte·nʃəs), *a.* 1845. [– Fr. *prétentieux*, f. *prétention*; see prec., -IOUS.] Full of pretension; making claim to great merit or importance, esp. when unwarranted; showy, ostentatious. Hence **Prete·ntious-ly** *adv.*, **-ness.**

†**Pre·ter,** *a.* (*sb.*) 1530. [The contraction *præter* for *præteritum* preterite, in *preterperfect*, etc., prefixed in the same way to *tense*, and at length treated as a separate word.] **A.** *adj. Gram.* = PRETERITE, past –1747. **B.** *sb.* **a.** *ellipt.* for *p. tense*. **b.** Past time, the past. –1675.

Preter-, præter- (prī·təɹ), *prefix*. The L. adv. and prep. *præter* past, by, beyond, above, more than; in addition to, besides; comparative of *præ* before, = further forward.

1. In Latin *præter* adv. was prefixed only to verbs and their derivative sbs. and adjs., as *præterire* to go or pass by, etc., whence *preterite*, *preterition*, etc. **2.** In Scholastic Latin, adjs. began to be formed from L. phrases with *præter* prep. + sb., e.g. *præternaturalis*, from *præter naturam* beyond or outside nature. From these adjs. advs. and nouns of quality, as *preternaturally*, *preternaturalism*, are always possible.

Preterhuman (prītəɹhiū·măn), *a.* 1811.

[f. PRETER- + HUMAN.] Beyond or outside of what is human; often = *superhuman.*

Pre:terimpe·rfect, *a.* (*sb.*) Now *rare.* 1530. [– L. *præteritum imperfectum* 'uncompleted past'; see PRETER, IMPERFECT.] *Gram.* = IMPERFECT II. 1. Also *absol.* as *sb.*

Preterist (pre·tĕrist), *sb.* (*a.*) Also **præ-.** 1843. [f. PRETER + -IST.] *Theol.* One who holds that the prophecies of the Apocalypse have been already fulfilled.

Preterite, -it (pre·tĕrit), *a.* (*sb.*) ME. [– (O)Fr. *prétérite* or L. *præteritus* gone by, pa. pple. of *præterire*, f. *præter* PRETER- + *ire* go (cf. *ambit, exit, transit*).] **A.** *adj.* **1.** = PAST *a.* II. 1. **2.** *Gram.* Expressing past action or state; past; as *p. tense, p. participle.*

1. Things and persons as thoroughly p. as Romulus or Numa LOWELL.

B. *sb.* [the *adj.* used ellipt.] †**1.** Past time, the past; also *pl.* past times or events. *rare.* late ME. only. **2.** *Gram.* = Preterite tense 1530. Hence **Pre·teriteness,** the state or condition of being past.

Pre·terite-pre·sent, *a.* (*sb.*) 1874. [– mod.L. *præterito-præsens*, neut. pl. *-præsentia*, f. *præteritus* PRETERITE + *præsens* PRESENT *a.*] *Gram.* Applied to verbs of which the tense now used as present was orig. a preterite (or to this tense); e.g. *can, may, must, shall, will.*

Preterition (prītəri·ʃən). Also **præ-.** 1609. [– late L. *præteritio, -on-*, f. *præterit-*, pa. ppl. stem of L. *præterire*; see PRETERITE, -ION. Cf. Fr. *prétérition* (XVII).] †**1.** Passing by, passage (of time) –1647. **2.** The action of passing over or fact of being passed by or over, without notice; omission, neglect; with *a* and *pl.* an instance of this 1609. **3.** *Rhet.* A figure by which summary mention is made of a thing, in professing to omit it 1612. **4.** *Theol.* The passing over of the non-elect; non-election to salvation 1621. **5.** *Rom. Law.* The omission by a testator to mention in his will one of his children or natural heirs 1722.

Preteritive (prīte·ritiv), *a. rare.* 1885. [f. as prec.; see -IVE.] *Gram.* Used only in the preterite forms 1847; *p. present* = next 1885.

Preterito-present (prīte·rito,pre·zĕnt), *a.* = PRETERITE-PRESENT.

Preterlabent (prītəɹlēⁱ·bĕnt), *a. rare.* Also **præter-.** 1670. [– *præterlabent-*, pr. ppl. stem of L. *præterlabi* glide or flow by; see -ENT.] Gliding or flowing past.

Pretermission (prītəɹmi·ʃən). Also **præter-.** 1583. [– L. *prætermissio, -on-*, f. *prætermittere*; see PRETER-, MISSION. Cf. Fr. *prétermission* (XVI).] **1.** The passing over, overlooking, or disregarding of anything; omission of anything. **2.** Ceasing to do something (for a time); leaving off the practice of anything 1677. **3.** *Rhet.* = PRETERITION 3. 1727. **4.** *Rom. Law.* = PRETERITION 5. 1795.

Pretermit (prītəɹmi·t), *v.* Also **præter-.** 1513. [– L. *prætermittere*, f. *præter* PRETER- + *mittere* let go, send.] **1.** *trans.* To leave out of a narrative; to omit 1538. **b.** *Rom. Law.* To omit mention of (a descendant or natural heir) in a will 1875. **2.** To allow to pass without notice; to overlook intentionally 1542. **3.** To fail to do; to leave undone, neglect, omit 1513. **4.** To neglect to avail oneself of (time or opportunity); to miss, lose. Now *rare.* 1538. **5.** To leave off for the time or for a time; *erron.*, to leave off, cease 1828.

1. The recitall whereof I p. for breuitie 1598. **5.** Some customs..have been fortunately pretermitted STEVENSON. Hence **Pretermi·ttently** *adv.*, erron. for INTERMITTENTLY.

Preternatural (prītəɹnæ·tiŭrăl, -tʃərăl), *a.* Also **præter-.** 1580. [– med.L. *præternaturalis*, f. L. phr. *præter naturam*; see PRETER-.] That is out of the ordinary course of nature; beyond, surpassing, or differing from what is natural; non-natural; formerly = abnormal, exceptional, unusual; sometimes = UNNATURAL. **b.** Used as = SUPERNATURAL 1774.

A preternaturall, or supernaturall ominous worke of God 1580. Mrs Transome..seemed to hear and see what they said and did with p. acuteness GEO. ELIOT. **b.** P. impressions are sometimes communicated to us for wise purposes 1829. Hence **Preterna·turalness,** p. quality. **Preterna·turally** *adv.*

Preterna·turalism. 1834. [f. prec. + -ISM.] **1.** The character of being preternatural; that which is preternatural; with *a* and *pl.* a preternatural occurrence. **2.** A recognition of the preternatural; a system or doctrine of the preternatural 1864.

2. A religion of p. is doomed M. ARNOLD.

Preterperfect (prītəɹpə̄·ɹfĕkt), *a.* (*sb.*) 1534. [– late L. *præteritum perfectum* 'complete past', with contraction; see PRETER, PERFECT.] *Gram.* Past perfect; applied to a tense which indicates a past or completed state or action. Also as *sb.* Now *rare* or *Obs.*

Pre:terplupe·rfect, *a.* (*sb.*) 1530. [– late L. *præteritum plusquamperfectum* (Priscian); see PRETER, PLUPERFECT.] **1.** *Gram.* = PLUPERFECT *a.* 1. Also *ellip.* as *sb.* Now *rare* or *Obs.* **2.** *gen.* or *allusively.* More than pluperfect; superlatively perfect. (Chiefly *joc.*) 1599.

Pretext (prī·tekst), *sb.* 1513. [– L. *prætextus* outward display, f. *prætext-*, pa. pple. stem of *prætexere* weave in front, border, disguise, f. *præ-* PRE- + *texere* weave. Cf. Fr. *prétexte* (XVI). Formerly stressed *prete·xt.*] That which is put forward to cover the real purpose or object; the ostensible reason or motive of action; an excuse, specious plea.

Publick benefit would soon become the p., and perfidy and murder the end BURKE.

Pretext (prīte·kst), *v.* 1606. [– Fr. *prétexter* take as a pretext, f. *prétexte* PRETEXT *sb.*] *trans.* To use or assign as a pretext; to allege as an excuse; to pretend. Also *absol.*

Pretone (prī·tōᵘn). 1864. [f. PRE- B. + TONE.] *Phonology.* The syllable or vowel preceding the stressed or tonic syllable. So **Preto·nic** *a.* coming immediately before the stressed or tonic syllable.

Prettify (pri·tifəi), *v. colloq.* 1850. [f. PRETTY *a.* + -FY.] *trans.* To make pretty; to represent prettily in a painting or writing.

Prettily (pri·tili), *adv.* late ME. [f. PRETTY *a.* + -LY².] In a pretty manner. †**1.** Cleverly, ingeniously; aptly –1776. **2.** In a way that pleases the eye, ear, or æsthetic sense; 'nicely'. late ME. †**3.** Considerably, fairly –1826.

1. I find how p. this cunning Lord can be partial and dissemble it in this case PEPYS. **2.** *Eat, ask, behave p.* (nursery language). **3.** I.. had an ear that served me p. BYRON.

Prettiness (pri·tinės). 1530. [f. next + -NESS.] The quality of being pretty. **1.** Beauty of a slight, diminutive, dainty, or childish kind, without stateliness. †**2.** Pleasantness, agreeableness –1658. **3.** With *a* and *pl.* That which is pretty; a pretty act, thing, feature, etc. 1649. **4.** Affected or trivial beauty of expression, style, or execution in literature or art. Also, an instance of this. 1660.

1. The feeble p. of Worcester Chapel 1874. **2.** *Haml.* IV. v. 189. **4.** He..uttered a thousand prettinesses in the way of compliment SMOLLETT.

Pretty (pri·ti), *a.* (*sb.*) [OE. *prættiġ*, corresp. to MLG. *prattich* capricious, overbearing, MDu. (*ghe*)*pertich* brisk, clever, roguish, Du. †*prettig* sportive, humorous; f. WGmc. **pratt-* trick (whence OE. *præt*), of unkn. origin.] †**I.** In OE. Cunning, crafty, artful, astute. **II.** From 15th c. **1. a.** Of persons: Clever, skilful; apt. *Obs.* or *arch.* late ME. **b.** Of things: Ingenious, artful, clever. *Obs.* or *arch.* 1440. **2.** A general epithet of admiration or appreciation. **a.** Of persons: Having the proper appearance, manners, or qualities of a man, etc.; conventionally applied to soldiers: Brave, gallant, stout (chiefly *Sc.*). *P. fellow*, a fine fellow, a 'swell', a fop: common in 18th c. Now *arch.* late ME. **b.** Of things: Fine, nice; proper 1566. **c.** Used ironically: cf. FINE *a.* III. 1. 1538. **3.** Beautiful in a slight, dainty, or diminutive way, as opp. to *handsome*; usu. of women or children 1440. **b.** Of things: Pleasing to the eye, the ear, or the æsthetic sense 1472. **c.** Often conjoined with *little*; see LITTLE A. I. 3. late ME. **4.** Considerable in number, quantity, or extent, as in *a p. deal, while, way*, etc. Now *arch.* or *dial.* 1485. †**b.** *P. and* (with another adj.) = PRETTY *adv.* 1. –1633.

1. a. 'There goes the prettiest fellow in the world..for managing a jury' 1712. **2. a.** A p. fellow—that is a fine dress'd man with little sense and a great deal of assurance GAY. He gaed out with other p. men in the Forty-five SCOTT. **b.** He has a p. wit SHERIDAN. **c.** A p. pass things are come to, when hussies like this are to be..bepitied THACKERAY. **3.** She was a very p. Woman, and is so still, only too fat 1722. While my little one, While my p. one, sleeps TENNYSON. **b.** She can have a prettier room at the Hook 1888. **4.** The transfer of his commission, which brought a p. sum into his pocket THACKERAY. Phr. *A p. penny*, a considerable sum. **b.** The weather..was p. and warme 1633.

B. *sb.* (The adj. used absol.) **a.** A pretty man, woman, or child; a pretty one; in phr. *my p.! my pretties!* 1599. **b.** A pretty thing; an ornament 1882. **c.** The fluted or ornamented part of a glass or tumbler 1890. **d.** The fairway of a golf course 1907.

Pretty (pri·ti), *adv.* 1565. [The adj. in advb. use.] **1.** To a considerable extent; fairly, moderately, tolerably; rather. (Qualifying an adj. or adv.). **2.** = PRETTILY. Now *rare* and *illiterate.* 1667.

1. It is p. like a young Willow 1727. The other men..lived p. much as they did 1861. *Comb.*: **p.-behaved** = prettily-behaved; **-spoken** = speaking prettily. *colloq.*

Prettyish (pri·ti,iʃ), *a. colloq.* 1741. [-ISH¹.] Somewhat pretty, rather pretty.

Prettyism (pri·ti,iz'm). 1806. [-ISM.] Studied prettiness of style or manner; an instance of this.

Pre·tty-pre·tty, *a.* and *sb.* 1875. [redupl. of PRETTY *a.*] **A.** *adj.* That overdoes the pretty; in which the aim at prettiness is overdone 1897. **B.** *sb.* (*pl.*) Pretty things; ornaments, knick-knacks 1875.

‖**Pretzel** (pre·tsĕl), **bretzel** (bre·tsĕl). *U.S.* 1879. [G.] A crisp biscuit baked in the form of a knot and flavoured with salt; used by Germans as a relish with beer.

‖**Preux** (prö), *a.* 1771. [Fr.; see PROUD, PROW *a.*] Brave, valiant, gallant; chiefly in *p. chevalier*, gallant knight.

Prevail (prīvēⁱ·l), *v.* [XIV *prevayle* – L. *prævalēre* have greater power (see PRE-, VAIL *v.*), with assim. to AVAIL.] †**1.** *intr.* To become very strong; to increase in vigour or force (*rare*) –1755. **2.** To be superior in strength or influence; to have or gain the superiority or advantage; to gain the mastery or ascendancy; to be victorious. Const. *against, over,* †*of,* †*upon.* 1450. **3.** To be effectual or efficacious; to succeed. late ME. †**b.** *trans.* To persuade, induce –1834. †**4.** *intr.* = AVAIL *v.* 2. –1584. †**b.** *trans.* = AVAIL *v.* 3. –1593. †**c.** = AVAIL *v.* 5. Usu. *refl.* –1681. **5.** *intr.* To be or become the stronger, more wide-spread, or more frequent usage or feature; to predominate. (A weakening of sense 2.) 1628. **b.** Hence, To be in general use or practice; to be prevalent or current 1776.

2. Hell gates shall not prevayle ageinste them 1529. Great is truth, and it shall prevaile 1650. **3.** But why Prevailed not thy pure prayers? TENNYSON. Phr. †*To p. to* (a thing) or *to do* (something), to succeed in doing, attaining, etc. (*rare*). *To p. on, upon,* †*with*, to succeed in persuading, inducing, or influencing. **4. c.** P. yourself of what occasion gives DRYDEN. **5.** Soon as the Evening Shades p., The Moon takes up the wondrous Tale ADDISON. **b.** Their way of thinking is far better than any other which now prevails in the world JOWETT. Hence **Prevai·ling** *ppl. a.* **Prevai·lingly** *adv.* in a prevailing manner or degree.

Prevalence (pre·vălĕns). 1592. [– Fr. †*prévalence* – late and med. L. *prævalentia* superior force, predominance, f. L. *prævalēre*; see prec., -ENCE. In XVI–XVII also *prevailance*, f. PREVAIL.] **1.** The fact or action of prevailing; the having or obtaining of predominance or mastery. Now *rare.* **2.** Effective force or power; influence, weight; efficacy; prevailingness. Now *rare.* 1631. **3.** The condition of being prevalent, or of general occurrence or existence; common practice or acceptance. (The ordinary current sense.) 1713.

1. The final p. of the good over the evil 1833. **2.**

Example has great p., whether good or bad 1802. **3.** The p. of ambition STEELE. The steady p. of winds in the westerly quarter BURKE. So **Pre·valency** (now *rare*), in all senses.

Prevalent (pre·vălĕnt), *a.* 1576. [– *prævalent-*, pr. ppl. stem of L. *prævalēre*; see PREVAIL, -ENT.] **1.** Having great power or force; effective; efficacious, potent. Now *rare.* **2.** Having the superiority or ascendancy; predominant, victorious. Now *rare.* 1614. **3.** Most extensively used or practised; generally accepted; of frequent occurrence; extensively existing; in general use 1658.

1. Ill-affected persons, who are so p. with His Majestie 1642. Cider..is also p. against the stone 1676. **2.** The Puritans, though then p., did not think proper to dispute this great constitutional point HUME. **3.** The cholera was p. in that year 1870. Hence **Pre·valently** *adv.*

Prevaricate (prĭvæ·rike^{i}t), *v.* 1582. [– *prævaricat-*, pa. ppl. stem of L. *prævaricari* go crookedly, deviate from the right path, (of an advocate) practise collusion, (Vulg.) transgress, f. *præ* PRE- + *varicare* spread the legs apart, straddle, f. *varus* knock-kneed; see -ATE[3].] **I.** *intr.* †**1.** To go aside from the right course, method, or mode of action; to deviate, go astray, transgress –1681. **2.** To deviate from straightforwardness; to act or speak evasively; to quibble, shuffle, equivocate 1631. †**3.** *Law.* **a.** To betray the cause of a client by collusion with an opponent. **b.** To undertake a matter falsely and deceitfully in order to defeat the object professed to be promoted. –1716.

2. Do not hesitate nor p.; but answer faithfully and truly to every question I ask FIELDING.

II. *trans.* †**1.** To deviate from, transgress (a 'law', etc.) –1604. †**2.** To turn (anything) from the straight course, application, or meaning; to pervert –1705.

2. He may not p. this duty of a judge JER. TAYLOR.

Prevarication (prĭværikē^i·ʃən). late ME. [– L. *prævaricatio, -on-*, f. as prec.; see -ION. So (O)Fr. *prévarication.*] †**1.** Divergence from the right course, method, or mode of action –1701. †**2.** Deviation from duty; violation of trust; corrupt action, esp. in a court of law –1741. †**b.** *Law.* See PREVARICATE *v.* 3. –1710. **3.** Avoidance of plain dealing; evasion, quibbling, equivocation, double-dealing, deception 1655.

1. That all Men do not die through the Death and P. of Adam 1701. **2.** *P.* is also used for a secret abuse committed in the exercise of a public office, or of a commission given by a private person 1727. **3.** Hume..was a man..utterly incapable of falsehood, or of p. of any kind 1862.

Prevaricator (prĭvæ·rike^{i}təɹ). 1542. [– L. *prævaricator* one who violates his duty, (eccl. L.) trangressor, f. as prec.; see -OR 2.] †**1.** One who prevaricates; a transgressor –1755. †**b.** One who betrays a cause or violates a trust –1637. †**2.** One who diverts something from its proper use; a perverter –1907. **3.** A quibbler, shuffler, equivocator 1650. **4.** At Cambridge University: An orator who made a jocose or satirical speech at Commencement; called also *varier. Obs.* exc. *Hist.* 1614. †**5.** *Law.* (See PREVARICATE *v.* 3.) –1793. So **Preva·ricatory** *a.* (*rare*), prevaricating; evasive.

Preve, obs. f. PROOF, PROVE.

Prevenance (pre·vĭnăns). 1823. [– Fr. *prévenance* (prevənɑ̃s), which is also in Eng. use, f. *prévenir* anticipate, prepossess; see PREVENE, -ANCE.] Courteous anticipation of the desires or needs of others; an obliging manner; complaisance.

She did everything he asked carefully and well, but the sweet p. was gone 1876.

†**Preve·ne**, *v.* Chiefly *Sc.* 1456. [– L. *prævenire*, f. *præ* PRE- A. + *venire* come.] *trans.* To take action before or in anticipation of (a person or thing) –1708.

Prevenient (prĭvī·niĕnt), *a.* 1607. [– *prevenient-*, pr. ppl. stem of L. *prævenire* come before, anticipate; see prec., -ENT.] **1.** Coming before, preceding, previous 1656. **b.** Hence, Anticipatory, expectant. Const. *of.* 1814. **2.** Antecedent to human action 1607.

2. *P. grace* (Theol.), the grace of God which precedes repentance and conversion, predisposing the heart to seek God, previously to any desire or motion on the part of the recipient. Hence **Preve·niently** *adv*, previously (*rare*).

Prevent (prĭve·nt), *v.* late ME. [– *prævent-*, pa. ppl. stem of L. *prævenire* precede, anticipate, hinder; see PREVENE.] **I.** †**1.** *trans.* To act in anticipation of or in preparation for (a future event, or a point of time); to act as if the event or time had already come –1813. **b.** To meet beforehand (an objection, question, command, desire, want, etc.). *arch.* 1533. †**c.** *intr.* or *absol.* To come, appear, or act before the time –1626. **2.** *trans.* To act before or more quickly than (another person or agent); to anticipate in action. Now *rare* and *arch.* 1523. **3.** To come, arrive, or appear before, to precede; to outrun, outstrip. Now *rare* and *arch.* 1523. **4.** *Theol.* To go before with spiritual guidance and help; said of God, or of his grace anticipating human action or need. *arch.* 1531. **b.** Said of the action of God's grace; see PREVENIENT 2. *arch.* 1548. †**c.** To come in front of; to meet –1611.

1. Thus we p. the last great day, And judge our selves 1633. **b.** Your goodness still prevents my wishes DRYDEN. **3.** I went..to Geneva, where I found..my fame had prevented my coming 1648. **4.** That thy grace maye alwayes preuente and folowe us *Bk. Com. Prayer.* **c.** The euill shall not ouertake nor preuent vs *Amos* 9:10.

II. †**1.** To forestall, balk, or baffle by previous measures –1737. **2.** To cut off beforehand, debar, preclude *from*, deprive *of* a purpose, expectation, etc. Now *rare.* 1549. **3.** To stop, keep, or hinder *from* doing something. Often with const. omitted. 1663. **4.** To provide beforehand against the occurrence of (something); to preclude, stop, hinder 1548. †**5.** To keep (something) from befalling oneself; to escape by timely action –1710. †**6.** To frustrate, defeat, bring to nought (an expectation, plan, etc). –1652. †**7.** *intr.* or *absol.* To use preventive measures –1723.

2. A wall prevents me from this sight L. HUNT. **3.** To..p. the enemy from erecting their magazines SWIFT. To p. this becoming a serious affair MORLEY. **4.** Should any thing occur..to p. his return W. IRVING. I shall not p. your going 1847. **7.** *Jul. C.* II. i. 28.

†**III. 1.** *causative.* To bring about or put before the time or prematurely; to anticipate –1683. **2.** To preoccupy, prejudice (a person's mind) –1718.

2. Endeavouring to p. your Lordship in Favour of my Author 1718. Hence **Preve·ntable** 1640, **-ible** 1850, *adjs.* that may be prevented. **Preventabi·lity, -ibi·lity.**

Preventative (prĭve·ntătiv), *a.* and *sb.* 1654. [f. PREVENT *v.* + -ATIVE.] = PREVENTIVE *a.* 2, 2 b, 2 c, and *sb.*

Preventer (prĭve·ntəɹ). 1587. [f. as prec. + -ER[1].] †**1.** One who goes or acts before another; an anticipator BACON. **2.** A person or thing that hinders, restrains, or keeps something from occurring or being done 1587. **3.** *Naut.* orig. *p.-rope*, an auxiliary rope to support spars, etc., during a strong gale; later, applied to any additional rope, etc. used to strengthen or take the place of another 1711.

attrib. and *Comb.*, as *p.-backstay, -brace, -rope, -stay*, etc.; also, denoting other secondary or additional parts serving to strengthen or take the place of the main ones, as *p.-bolt, -plate*, etc.

Prevention (prĭve·nʃən). 1528. [– (O)Fr. *prévention* or late L. *præventio, -on-*, f. *prevent-*; see PREVENT, -ION.] †**1.** Previous occurrence, anticipation; in *Theol.* the action of prevenient grace –1705. **2.** *Canon Law.* The privilege claimed by an ecclesiastical superior of forestalling an inferior in the execution of an official act regularly pertaining to the latter 1528. †**3.** Action or occurrence before the expected, appointed, or normal time; anticipation –1711. **4.** †**a.** The action of forestalling –1667. †**b.** Precaution; a precaution, a defensive measure –1774. **c.** The action of keeping from happening or of rendering impossible an anticipated event or an intended act 1661. †**d.** A means of preventing; a safeguard; an obstacle, obstruction –1821. †**5.** A mental anticipation; a presentiment –1801. †**6.** Prepossession, bias, prejudice –1829.

4. a. Caska be sodaine, for we feare preuention SHAKS. **c.** Lord Erskine's Bill for the P. of Cruelty towards Animals 1813. *Prov.* P. is better than cure.

Preventive (prĭve·ntiv), *a.* and *sb.* 1639. [f. PREVENT + -IVE. Cf. PREVENTATIVE.] **A.** *adj.* †**1.** That comes or goes before something else; antecedent, anticipatory –1698. **2.** That anticipates in order to ward against; that acts as a hindrance or obstacle 1639. **b.** *Med.* Having the quality of keeping off disease; prophylactic 1646. **c.** Belonging to that department of the Customs which is concerned with the prevention of smuggling; *spec.* of or belonging to the Coast Guard 1827.

2. A p. war, grounded on a just fear of an invasion FULLER. Statutes p. of blasphemy and profaneness 1822. **b.** Physicke is either curative or p. SIR T. BROWNE.

B. *sb.* A preventive agent or measure; a hindrance, obstacle, obstruction 1639. **b.** *Med.* A prophylactic 1674. Hence **Preve·ntively** *adv.*

Previous (prī·viəs), *a.* (*adv.*) 1625. [f. L. *prævius* going before, leading the way (f. *præ* PRE- A. + *via* way) + -OUS.] †**1.** Going before or in front; leading the way. Also *fig.* –1678. **2.** Coming or going before (in time or order); preceding, prior. Also with *to* (now *rare*). 1625. **3.** *slang* or *colloq.* (orig. *U.S.*) Coming too soon, hasty, premature. (Usu. with *too.*) 1885.

2. A p. blast foretels the rising storm YOUNG. Phr. *P. question* (in parliamentary procedure), the question whether a vote shall be taken on the main question or issue, moved before the main question is put. *P. Examination* (Cambridge Univ.), the first examination for the B.A. degree; colloq. called *Littlego.* (Also ellipt. as *sb.*)

B. as *adv.* Previously; usu. *p. to* = before, prior to 1719.

P. to Ordination, they may be subjected to some literary ordeal 1849. Hence **Pre·vious-ly** *adv.*, **-ness.**

Previse (prĭvəi·z), *v.* 1597. [– *prævis-*, pa. ppl. stem of L. *prævidēre* foresee, anticipate, f. *præ* PRE- A. I. 1 + *vidēre* see.] **1.** *trans.* To foresee; to forecast. Also *absol.* **2.** To inform beforehand. LYTTON.

Prevision (prĭvi·ʒən), *sb.* 1612. [– late and med.L. *prævisio* foresight, f. as prec.; see -ION. Cf. (O)Fr. *prévision.*] The action or faculty of foreseeing; knowledge of or insight into the future; an instance of this. Hence **Previ·sion** *v. trans.*, (*a*) to endow with p.; (*b*) to have p. of, to foresee. **Previ·sional** *a.* relating to, depending on, characterized by, or exhibiting p.; **-ly** *adv.*

Prey (prē^i), *sb.* [ME. *praie, preie* – OFr. *preie* (mod. *proie*) :– L. *præda* booty.] **1.** That which is taken in war, or by pillage or violence; booty, spoil, plunder. Formerly, often with *pl. arch. rare.* **b.** *fig.* (In Scriptural use.) That which one brings away or saves from any contest, etc. late ME. **2.** An animal hunted or killed by carnivorous animals for food; quarry. Now only *collect.* ME. **3.** One who or that which falls or is given into the power of a hostile person or an injurious influence; a victim; esp. in const. *to be* or *become a p. to* ME. **4.** The action of preying; seizing or taking by force or violence, or (of an animal) in order to devour; depredation, pillage, capture. Now *rare.* 1523.

1. b. He shall have his life for a p., and shall live *Jer.* 38:2. **2.** As the Tigre his time awaiteth In hope forto cacche his preie GOWER. **3.** Jerusalem fell an easy p. to his arms BURKE. To dumb Forgetfulness a p. GRAY. **4.** The whole little wood..is a world of plunder and p. TENNYSON. *Beast, bird, fish*, etc., *of p.*, one that kills and devours other animals. Hence †**Prey·ful** *a.* (*rare*), killing much p., prone to prey.

Prey (prē^i), *v.* ME. [– OFr. *preier, preer* :– late L. *prædare*, for earlier *prædari*, f. *præda* PREY *sb.*] †**1.** *trans.* To plunder, pillage, spoil; to rob, ravage (a place, person, etc.) –1654. **2.** *intr.* To take booty; to pillage, plunder; *to p. on, upon* = sense 1. ME. **3.** To seek for or take prey, as an animal; esp. with *on, upon*: To seize and kill as prey; to kill and devour, to feed on ME. **4.** To exert a baneful, wasting, or destructive influence *on, upon*; to destroy gradually 1713.

2. The buccaneers preying upon Spanish commerce 1872. **3.** *fig.* Brokers I meane and Vsurers, that like vultures p. vpon the simple 1610. **4.** The secret which preyed upon his mind 1798. Hence **Prey·er,** one who or that which preys.

Prial: see PAIR-ROYAL.

Priapean (prəiˌăpī·ăn), *a.* 1693. [– Fr. *priapéen*, f. L. *Priapeius* (– Gr. Πριάπειος adj., f. Πρίαπος) + *-en* -AN.] **1.** Priapic. **2.** *Anc. Pros.* Applied to a logacœdic metre consisting of a catalectic Glyconic and a Pherecratean, associated with poems to Priapus.

Priapic (prəiˌæ·pik), *a.* 1786. [f. PRIAPUS + -IC.] Of or relating to Priapus or his cult.

Priapism (prəi·ăpiz'm). 1598. [– Fr. *priapisme* – late L. *priapismus* – Gr. πριαπισμός (Galen), f. πριαπίζειν act Priapus, be lewd, f. Πρίαπος; see next and -ISM.] **1.** *Path.* Persistent erection of the penis. **2.** = PRIAPUS 3. 1662. **3.** Licentiousness; intentional indecency. Also *fig.* 1758.

Priapus (prəiˌē·pŏs). late ME. [– L. *Priapus* – Gr. Πρίαπος.] **1.** The Greek and Roman god of procreation, (and so) of gardens, vineyards, etc. **2.** A statue or image of the god Priapus; often placed in gardens to protect them from depredators or as a scarecrow 1632. **3.** A phallus. **b.** A drinking vessel of phallic shape. 1613.

Pri·bble. 1598. Weakened echo of PRABBLE, dial. var. of BRABBLE.

P. and prabble (SHAKS.), *p.-prabble*, petty disputation, vain chatter.

Price (prəis), *sb.* [ME. *pris(e* – OFr. *pris* (mod. *prix*) :– L. *pretium* price, value, wages, reward. See PRAISE, PRIZE, which superseded this word in some of its meanings, but *prize* was repl. by PRICE *v.* assign a price to XV.] **I.** Money, or the like, paid for something. **1.** The money (or other equivalent) for which anything is bought or sold; the rate at which this is done or proposed; also, less usu., wages; rate of wages. **b.** Payment of money in purchase of something. *Obs.* exc. in phr. *without p.* = without payment, gratis (*arch.*). late ME. **c.** Estimation of value 1582. **2.** A sum of money offered for the capture, apprehension, or death of a person 1766. **3.** *Betting.* = ODDS 5. 1882. **4.** The amount of money, or other consideration, by which a man's support or interest may be purchased 1780. **5.** *fig.* What it costs to obtain some advantage. late ME.

1. To haue vytaylles at resonable prys CAXTON. Labour was the first p., the original purchase-money that was paid for all things ADAM SMITH. Slang phr. *What price..?*, a taunting questioning of the vaunted value of something. **b.** Come, buy wine and milke without money, and without p. *Isa.* 55:1. **c.** *Above, beyond, without p.* = PRICELESS 1. **2.** *To set (put) a p. on (the head of*, etc.). **3.** The starting p. of Mr. Perkin's horse was 5 to 1. 1882. **4.** Every man has his p. BENTHAM. **5.** *At any p.*, whatever it may cost, whatever loss or disadvantage is or may be entailed; He determined to bring his design to pass at any p. whatsoever 1653.

II. Value, worth. *Obs.* or *arch.* **1.** Preciousness, value, worth. Usu. qualified as *great, dear, little, no*, etc. *arch.* ME. **2.** *Of p.*, of great value, worth, or excellence. *arch.* ME. †**3.** Esteem, estimation, regard –1662. †**b.** Valuation, appraisement SHAKS.

2. Faire pillars of marble..and other stones of p. 1615. **3.** Wel biloued and holden in greet prys CHAUCER. Phr. *To have* or *hold in p.*, to value highly. **b.** Cæsars no Merchant, to make prize with you Of things that Merchants sold SHAKS.

†**III. 1.** Honour, glory, renown –1600. **2.** = PRAISE *sb.* 1. –1567. †**IV. 1.** The position of excelling others; first or highest place; pre-eminence. Usu. in phr. *to bear* or *have the p.*, to have the pre-eminence. –1573. †**2.** The position of excelling in a match or struggle; superiority, victory –1542. †**3.** = PRIZE *sb.*[1] ME.

2. If yᵉ flemynges had achyued the prise ouer them 1523. *attrib.* and *Comb.*: **p.-current,** a list of current prices of commodities; a price-list; **-cutting,** the action of 'cutting down' or lowering prices, esp. in or by way of competition; also *attrib.*; **-list,** (*a*) a list of the prices of commodities offered for sale; (*b*) a list of the 'prices' or odds in betting.

Price (prəis), *v.* 1490. [var., assimilated to prec. sb., of the earlier *prise*, now PRIZE *v.*[1]] **1.** *trans.* To fix the price of (a thing for sale); to state the price of. †**2.** To pay the price for, pay for –1590. **3.** To enquire the price of, bargain for 1845. †**4.** = PRIZE *v.*[1] 3. –1643.

1. London ale was priced 5*s.* a barrel more than that of Kent 1845. **2.** So that thi confessioun ma thi synnes pryce DUNBAR. **4.** Men p. the thing ungained more then it is SHAKS.

Priced (prəist), *ppl. a.* 1552. [f. PRICE *sb.* or *v.* + -ED.] **1.** Having the price fixed or stated; containing a statement of prices. **2.** Having a (specified or indicated) price; in parasynthetic combs., as *high-, low-p.*

Priceite (prəi·səit). 1873. [f. name of Thomas *Price*, an American metallurgist; see -ITE[1] 2b.] *Min.* Hydrous borate of calcium.

Priceless (prəi·slės), *a.* 1593. [f. PRICE *sb.* + -LESS.] **1.** Having a value beyond all price or equivalent; invaluable. **b.** Having no market price; that cannot be obtained for money 1884. **2.** Having no value; worthless 1771. **3.** Incredibly amusing or absurd (*slang*) 1907.

Prick (prik), *sb.* [OE. *prica*, also *pricca*, *price* = MLG. *pricke* (LG., Du. *prik*). Cf. next.] **I. 1.** A minute hole or impression made by pricking; a puncture. **b.** *spec.* in *Farriery.* A puncture or wound in the quick or sole of the foot of a horse 1607. **c.** The track of a hare 1598. **2.** A minute mark made by slightly pricking or indenting a surface with a pointed tool; a dot, tick, point. OE. †**b.** Each of the marks dividing the circumference of a dial, or any scale –1593. †**3.** = POINT *sb.*[1] I. 2, 3. –1749.

1. The less credulous tooke the pricke of a pinne for a Saintes marke 1638. **2.** Set ther a prikke of ynke CHAUCER. **b.** *Rom. & Jul.* II. iv. 119.

†**II.** A minute particle. **1.** A point of space (or particle of matter), in ref. to its minuteness, a mere point –1616. **2.** = POINT *sb.*[1] III. 1. –1645. **3.** = POINT *sb.*[1] III. 2. –1579.

1. This little pricke of the world (for surely the earth is nothing else in comparison of the whole) HOLLAND. **2.** Not one jot or p. of the Law shall perish 1645.

†**III.** A point in ref. to position. **1.** A point in space, a geometrical point –1619. **2.** A point marking a stage in progression; degree, pitch –1606. †**IV.** In archery. The mark aimed at in shooting; the spot in the centre of a target; hence, a target –1845. **V.** Anything that pricks or pierces. **1.** A small sharp projecting organ or part; a thorn or prickle; a spine on the skin of an animal, or the like. Also †*fig.* Now *rare* or *Obs.* ME. **2.** A goad for oxen ME. †**3.** A slender piece of wood or metal tapering to a sharp point; a skewer; a pin for fastening one's clothes; a thatcher's broach –1721. **4.** A pointed weapon or implement; e.g. †a dagger; a chisel; etc. 1552. **5.** The penis. (Not now in polite use.) 1592. **6.** A small roll (of tobacco). 1666.

1. As pricks be hidden under Roses 1579. *fig.* Forsoth the pricke of deeth is synne WYCLIF 1 *Cor.* 15:55. **2.** *To kick against the pricks*, said of oxen; now *arch.* and usu. *fig.* (after *Acts* 9:5).

VI. The act of pricking, or the fact of being pricked; a puncture. Also *fig.*, esp. in *p. of conscience* (med.L. *stimulus conscientiæ*), stinging compunction, remorse; in earlier use, that which pricks the conscience or causes remorse. ME.

Gentlewomen that liue honestly by the pricke of their Needles SHAKS. A p. with a Catfishes Fin 1699.

attrib. and *Comb.*: **p.-hedge,** a thorn hedge; **-line,** a dotted line; **-spur,** a spur having a single point; **-tobacco,** tobacco made up into a small roll; see V. 6; **-wheel,** a toothed wheel mounted on a handle, used by saddlers for marking places for stitches at regular intervals. Hence **Pri·cky** *a. dial.* prickly.

Prick (prik), *v.* [OE. *prician* = (M)LG., (M)Du. *prikken*; cf. OE. *āpriċċan* (WGmc. **prikkjan*), whence ME. and dial. *pritch*. Ult. origin unkn.] **I.** To pierce, or indent with a sharp point. **1.** *trans.* To pierce slightly, make a minute hole in (a surface or body) with a fine or sharp point; to puncture; hence, to wound (or hurt) with or as with a pointed instrument. Said also of the instrument. **b.** To make (a hole or mark) by pricking 1680. **c.** *Farriery.* To pierce the foot of (a horse) to the quick in shoeing, causing lameness 1591. **d.** To affect with a sensation as of pricking. late ME. **2.** *fig.* To cause sharp mental pain to; to sting with sorrow or remorse; to grieve, pain, vex. Also *absol.* OE. **3.** *intr.* To perform the action of pricking or piercing; to cause a pricking sensation; also, to have the quality of pricking, to be sharp OE. **4.** To thrust *at* something as if to pierce it; to make a thrust or stab *at* 1470. †**b.** *Archery.* To shoot at a 'prick' or target; hence *fig.* to aim *at* –1622. **5.** *intr.* or *absol.* Of a hare: To make a track in running. late ME. **b.** *trans.* To look for or find the 'pricks' of (a hare); to trace or track (a hare) by its footprints. Also *absol.* or *intr.* late ME. **6.** *intr.* To have a sensation of being pricked; to tingle 1850. **7.** Of wine, beer, etc.: To become or begin to be sour; to be touched or tained with acetous fermentation; = Fr. *se piquer* 1594.

1. I could perceive her to take pins out of her pocket to p. me PEPYS. Phr. *To prick a* or *the bladder* or *bubble*, to show the emptiness of a person or thing that has passed for important or formidable. **2.** His conscience pricks him so much that he cannot rest 1874. **3.** The Thorn, or Bryar, which p., and scratch BACON. Phr. *To p. for*, to try, choose, or decide for something by pricking; also *fig. To p. (in) the belt, garter, loop*, to play at FAST-AND-LOOSE. **5. b.** You have been pricking up and down here upon a cold scent DRYDEN. **6.** When the blood creeps, and the nerves p. and tingle TENNYSON.

II. 1. *trans.* †To urge forward (a beast) with a goad; to spur (a horse) (*arch.*) ME. **2.** *fig.* To drive or urge as with a spur; to incite, stimulate, provoke ME. **3.** *intr.* To spur or urge a horse on; to ride fast; hence, to ride ME.

2. So priketh hem nature in hir corages CHAUCER. **3.** A gentle Knight was pricking on the plaine SPENSER.

III. To mark by or with pricks or dots. †**1.** *trans.* To write or set down (music) by means of 'pricks' or notes –1826. **2.** To mark or indicate by a 'prick'; *esp.* to mark (a name, or an item) in a list by making a 'prick' through or against it; hence, to mark off or tick off in this way; *spec.* (of the sovereign) to select (persons) for the office of sheriff from a list by this means; also, to appoint, choose, pick *out*. Also *p. down, off*, etc. 1557. **3.** To mark or trace something on (a surface) by pricks or dots; also, to mark or trace (a position, direction, design, etc.) on a surface by pricks or dots. Also *p. off, out*. 1598.

1. To my chamber, to p. out my song 'It is Decreed' PEPYS. **2.** My friend was pricked as High Sheriff of the county 1853. **3.** To p. the Chart..at Sea, signifies to make a Point in their Chart whereabout the Ship is now 1704.

IV. To put into some position or condition by piercing or transfixing. †**1.** To secure or fasten with a pin or skewer, or the like –1819. **2.** To attire (a person) elaborately with the aid of pins, bodkins, etc.; to dress *up*. Now *dial.* ME. †**3.** To remove, or bring into some position, by pricking –1683. **4.** To plant (seedlings) in small holes made by piercing the ground at suitable intervals. Const. *in, out, off*. Also, *to p. in* (manure). 1608. **5.** *To p. up* (in plastering on laths): to scratch or score the surface of the first coat so as to afford a hold for the next; hence, to lay on the first coat 1778.

1. *Tam. Shr.* III. ii. 70. **3.** *Rom. & Jul.* I. iv. 66. **4.** Cabbage plants are pricked in in March 1854.

V. To insert or stick as a point. †**1.** To thrust or stick (a pointed object) *into* something; to set, fix, or insert by the point; to stick *in, on* –1669. †**2.** To stick (something) *full of*, or set (it) *with* pointed objects or points; hence, to stud, mark, or dot *with* something. 1530. **VI.** To stick up as or in a point. **1.** To raise or erect, as the ears of an animal when listening; hence, of a person, *to p. up one's ears*, to become attentive 1587. **2.** *intr. P. up*, to rise or stand erect with the point directed upward; to point or stick up 1610.

1. At this the town of Mansoul began to p. up its ears BUNYAN. **2.** His ears..p. up at the sound of a fiddle 1887.

Pri·ck-ea:r, prick ear. 1634. [app. back-formation from next.] **1.** *pl.* The erect pointed ears of some beasts, *spec.* of dogs; ears that are pricked up or stand erect; hence *fig.* those of a person on the alert to hear. **b.** Applied to the ears of a 'Roundhead'; cf. next 2. 1641. †**2.** A person having prick-ears; one whose ears are conspicuous; a nickname for a Puritan –1642.

Prick-eared (pri·kˌiᵊ·ɹd), *a.* late ME. [app. f. PRICK *sb.* (branch V) + EARED.] **1.** Having erect ears; *spec.* of dogs. **b.** *fig.* Having the ears pricked or erected in attention; hence, attentive, alert 1550. **2.** Of a man: Having the hair cut short and close, so that the ears are prominent; applied to Puritans or 'Roundheads'; whence opprobriously, priggish 1641.

1. b. Jealousy is p., and will hear the wagging of a hair MIDDLETON. **2.** These Prickear'd, starch, sanctify'd Fellows 1707.

Pricker (pri·kəɹ). late ME. [f. PRICK *v.* + -ER¹.] One who or that which pricks. **1.** One who pricks or goads. Also *fig.* **2.** One who spurs or rides a horse; a horseman; hence, a mounted soldier, *esp.* a light horseman employed as a skirmisher or scout. *arch.* and *Hist.* late ME. **3.** *spec.* A mounted attendant at a hunt, a huntsman. Now chiefly in YEOMAN *p.* 1575. **4.** An instrument or tool for pricking or piercing. late ME.

Pricket (pri·kėt). late ME. [– AL. *prikettus, -um*, dim. f. PRICK *sb.*; see -ET.] **1.** A buck in its second year, having straight unbranched horns 1440. **2.** A spike on which to stick a candle; hence, *p. candlestick*, a candlestick having one or more of these. late ME.

Pricking (pri·kiŋ), *vbl. sb.* ME. [f. PRICK *v.* + -ING¹.] The action of PRICK *v. esp.* **1.** Piercing, puncturing, wounding. With *a* and *pl.*, an instance of this. late ME. **b.** The sensation of, or as of, being pricked; smarting, tingling ME. **2.** The footprint or track of a hare (rarely of other beasts). Hence, the tracking of a hare by its pricks. late ME. **3.** *P. up* (Plastering): see PRICK *v.* IV. 5. 1778.

1. b. By the p. of my Thumbes, Something wicked this way comes SHAKS.

Prickle (pri·k'l), *sb.*¹ [OE. *pricel*, later form of *pricels*, f. base of PRICK *sb.* (see -ELS, -LE); corresp. to MLG., MDu. *prickel, prēkel* (Du. *prikkel*).] †**1.** A thing to prick with; a goad –1609. **2.** A rigid sharp-pointed process developed from the bark or any part of the epidermis of a plant, consisting of a compound hair 1580. **3.** A hard-pointed spine or outgrowth of the epidermis of an animal, as in the hedgehog, etc. 1567. **4.** *fig.* Something that pricks the mind or feelings. (Chiefly in *pl.*) 1638.

4. The Rose has prickles, so has Love, Though these a little sharper prove 1705.

Prickle (pri·k'l), *sb.*² 1609. *Obs.* or *local.* [Of unkn. origin.] A wicker basket, esp. for fruit or flowers. **b.** *spec.* As a measure 1674.

Prickle (pri·k'l), *v.* 1513. [Partly from PRICKLE *sb.*¹; partly dim. of PRICK *v.* Cf. MDu. *prickelen*, Du. *prikkelen*, LG. *prikkeln.*] **1.** *trans.* (or *absol.*) To prick, as with a goad, etc.; hence, to goad, instigate. **b.** *transf.* To affect with a prickling sensation 1855. **2.** *intr.* To tingle as if pricked 1634.

Pri·ckle-back. 1711. [f. PRICKLE *sb.*¹ + BACK *sb.*¹] The three-spined stickleback.

Pricklouse (pri·kˌlaus). Now *dial.* 1500. A derisive name for a tailor.

Prickly (pri·kli), *a.* 1578. [f. PRICKLE *sb.*¹ + -Y¹.] **1.** Having, armed with, or full of prickles; aculeate. Also *fig.* **2.** Having a sensation as of many pricking points; smarting; tingling 1836.

Special collocations: **p. ash,** an aromatic N. Amer. shrub, *Xanthoxylum americanum*; **p. palm, pole,** a West Indian palm, *Bactris plumierana*; **p. rat,** any one of the species of *Ctenomys* and allied genera of S. Amer. burrowing rodents, the hair of which is usu. intermingled with sharp spines. Hence **Pri·ckliness.**

Prickly heat. 1736. A common name for *Lichen tropicus*, an inflammatory disorder of the sweat glands, prevalent in hot countries, characterized by eruption of small papules or vesicles, accompanied by a sense of pricking or burning.

Prickly pear. 1760. Any species of the cactaceous genus *Opuntia*, prickly plants with pear-shaped fleshy edible fruit; also the fruit.

†**Pri·ck-ma:dam.** 1545. [Altered from Fr. *trique-madame* (XVI).] *Herb.* An old name of the Stone-crops, esp. *Sedum acre*; also *S. album* and *S. reflexum* –1883.

Pri·ck-seam. 1632. [f. PRICK *sb.* or *v.* + SEAM.] A particular stitch used in glove-sewing. Also *attrib.*

Prick-song (pri·kˌsoŋ). *Obs.* exc. *Hist.* 1463. [Shortened from *pricked song, prickt song*; cf. PRICK *v.* III. 1. Cf. AL. *cantus precatus* (XVI).] *Mus.* **1.** Music sung from notes written or 'pricked'; written vocal music. **2.** *esp.* A written descant; hence, *gen.* descant or 'counterpoint' accompanying a simple melody (also *fig.*) 1501.

Pri·ckwood. 1661. [PRICK *sb.* V. 3.] **a.** The Spindle-tree. **b.** The Wild Cornel 1869.

Pride (prəid), *sb.*¹ [Late OE. *prȳde*, secondary form (prob. after *prūd* PROUD or ON. *prýði*) of *prȳte, prȳtu*, abstr. sb. f. *prūd*, presumably on the model of such pairs as *hlūd* loud/*hlȳd* sound, noise, *fūl* foul/*fȳlþ* filth.] The quality of being proud. **I. 1.** A high or overweening opinion of one's own qualities, attainments, or estate; inordinate self-esteem. **b.** in pl. *rare.* OE. **c.** Personified, esp. as the first of the seven deadly sins. late ME. **2.** The exhibition of this quality in attitude, bearing, conduct, etc.; arrogance, haughtiness ME. **3.** A consciousness of what is befitting or due to oneself or one's position; as a good quality, 'honest' or 'proper pride'; also as a misapplied feeling, 'false pride' ME. **4.** A feeling of elation or high satisfaction derived from some action or possession; esp. in *to take a p. in* 1597. **5.** That of which any person or body of persons is proud; hence, the flower, the best, of a class, country, etc. late ME. **b.** In names of plants 1629.

1. P. goeth before destruction *Prov.* 16:18. Spiritual p. JER. TAYLOR. P. must have a fall JOHNSON. P. of birth 1797. **2.** P. in their port, defiance in their eye, I see the lords of human kind pass by GOLDSM. **3.** Chatterton, the marvellous Boy, The sleepless Soul that perished in his p. WORDSW. **4.** My Grauitie Wherein..I take p. SHAKS. **5.** A bold peasantry, their country's p. GOLDSM. **b. P. of China, p. of India,** a tree, the AZEDARAC; **p. of London** = LONDON PRIDE.

II. 1. Magnificence, splendour; pomp, display. *poet.* and *rhet.* ME. †**b.** Love of display or ostentation –1680. **2.** Magnificent, splendid, or ostentatious adornment or ornamentation (*arch.*) ME. †**3.** Honour, glory –1591. **4.** The best, highest, most excellent or flourishing state or condition; the prime; the flower. late ME. **5.** Mettle or spirit in a horse 1592. †**6.** Sexual desire, 'heat'; esp. in female animals –1604. **7.** *Falconry. P. of place*: see PLACE *sb.* I. 6 b. **8.** A 'company' of lions in the wild state c1452 (taken up latterly by writers on big game).

1. Oh farewell..all Qualitie, Pride, Pompe, and Circumstance of glorious Warre SHAKS. *P. of life, p. of the world*, worldly p. or ostentation, vainglory (*arch.*). *In his p.* (Her.), applied to a peacock represented with the tail expanded and the wings drooping. **2.** Loftie trees, yclad with sommers p. SPENSER. **3.** 1 *Hen. VI*, IV. vi. 57. **4.** Since we have seen the p. of Nature's works..Let us depart MARLOWE. Hence **Pri·deful** *a.* full of p., arrogant. (Chiefly *Sc.*) **Pri·deless** *a.* devoid of p.

Pride (prəid), *sb.*² *local.* 1490. [perh. abbrev. from †*lamprid* = med.L. *lampreda, lamprida* LAMPREY.] The fresh-water or river lamprey; also called *sand-pride.*

Pride (prəid), *v.* [f. PRIDE *sb.*¹] †**1.** *intr.* To be or become proud –1802. **2.** *trans.* To make proud. Chiefly in *pass.* ME. **3.** *refl.* To make or show oneself proud; to plume oneself. Const. *on, upon, in, that*, etc. ME. **b.** *intr.* in same sense. Now *rare.* 1470.

3. He prided himself on his punctuality 1882.

Pridian (pri·diăn), *a. rare.* 1656. [– L. *pridianus*, f. *pridie* adv., on the day before; see -AN.] Of or pertaining to the previous day.

‖**Prie-dieu** (prīdyö). 1760. [Fr., lit. 'pray God'.] **a.** A praying-desk, kneeling-desk. **b.** A chair with tall sloping back for use in praying; also, a chair of this form for ordinary use. Also *p. chair.*

Priest (prīst), *sb.* [OE. *prēost* (with unexpl. *ēo*), corresp. to OHG. *priast, prēst*, ON. *prestr* (perh. from OE. or OLG.); shortening of the form repr. by OFris. *prēstere*, OS., OHG. *prēster* (MDu., Du., MHG., G. *priester*) – eccl. L. *presbyter* PRESBYTER, through pop. **prēster* (whence OFr. *prestre*, Fr. *prêtre*), repr. in Eng. PRESTER JOHN.] †**1.** A PRESBYTER or elder of the early church (*rare*) –1582. **2.** In hierarchical Christian churches: A clergyman in the second of the holy orders (above a deacon and below a bishop) having authority to administer the sacraments and pronounce absolution. **3.** *gen.* A clergyman, a member of the clerical profession, a minister of religion OE. **b.** *fig.* as in *a p. of nature, of science*, etc. 1697. **4.** A sacrificing priest, a minister of the altar. **a.** In the Jewish Church, and other pre-Christian systems ME. **b.** In specific Christian use, The officiant at the Eucharist and other sacerdotal offices OE. **c.** Applied (*a*) to Christ in his sacrificial or mediatorial character. (After Heb. 5:6, 7:15–21.) ME.; (*b*) to all believers (after Rev. 1:6), and to the Christian Church. late ME. **5.** An official minister of a pagan or non-Christian religion ME. †**b.** Applied to a priestess (*rare*) –1614. †**6.** Allus., *To be* (a person's) *p.*: to kill him. (In allusion to the function of a priest in performing the last offices to the dying.) –1800.

2. The Priests and Deacons (whom we usually class together under the common name of Clergymen) 1833. In every Catholic parish the p. is at the very heart of things 1901. **3. b.** Ye sacred Muses..Whose P. I am DRYDEN. **5.** Mathan.. the prest of Baal, thei slewen before the auter WYCLIF 2 *Kings* 11:18. Orthodox Islam has never had real priests 1885. **b.** *Per.* V. i. 243. **6.** 2 *Hen. VI*, III. i. 272.

attrib. and *Comb.*: **p.-cap, priest's cap,** (*a*) *lit.* a cap worn by a p.; (*b*) *Fortif.* an outwork with three salient and two re-entrant angles; **priest's hole,** a hiding-place for a (R.C.) p. (in times of the penal laws); **priest's hood,** the wild Arum (*A. maculatum*), from the form of the spathe; **-vicar,** in some cathedrals, a vicar choral who is a priest; a minor canon. Hence **Prie·stdom,** †the office of p.; the rule or dominion of priests. †**Prie·stery,** a body or company of priests (*contempt.*) MILT. **Prie·stism,** the system, spirit, methods, or practices of priests (in hostile use). **Prie·stless** *a.* not having, or not attended by, a p. **Prie·stling,** a little, young, or insignificant p. (usu. *contempt.*).

Priest (prīst), *v.* late ME. [f. prec.] †**1.** *intr.* To exercise the ministry or functions of a priest –1642. **2.** *trans.* usu. *pass.* To make a priest; to ordain to the priesthood 1504.

Priestcraft (prī·stkraft). 1681. Priestly craft or policy; the arts used by ambitious and worldly priests to impose upon the multitude or further their own interests.

Priestess (prī·stės). 1693. [f. PRIEST *sb.* + -ESS¹.] **1.** A female priest; a woman who holds the office and performs the functions of a priest, or (loosely) of a minister of religion. Also *fig.* and *transf.* **2.** A priest's wife (*colloq.*) 1709.

Priesthood (prī·stˌhud). [OE. *prēosthād*; see PRIEST *sb.*, -HOOD.] **1.** The office or function of a priest; the condition of being a priest; the order of priest. **b.** The priestly office of Christ, of his Church, or of believers OE. **2.** The system of priests; the or a body of priests. Also *transf.* and *fig.* late ME.

Priestlike (prī·stləik), *a.* (*adv.*) 1470. [f. PRIEST *sb.* + -LIKE.] Like, or like that of, a priest; characteristic of or befitting a priest; priestly, sacerdotal. **B.** *adv.* Like a priest; in the character or manner of a priest 1565.

A. The moving waters at their p. task Of pure ablution round earth's human shores KEATS.

Priestly (prī·stli), *a.* OE. [f. PRIEST *sb.* + -LY¹; in OE. *prēostlić.*] **1.** Of or pertaining to a priest or priests; sacerdotal. **2.** = PRIESTLIKE *a.* 1465. **3.** That is a priest 1817.

2. A prystly man and vertusly dysposyd 1465. *Per.* III. i. 70. Hence **Prie·stliness,** p. quality or character.

Priest-ridden (prī·stˌri:d'n), *ppl. a.* Also **-rid** (*obs.* or *arch.*). 1653. [f. PRIEST *sb.* + RIDDEN *ppl. a.*] 'Ridden', i.e. managed or controlled by a priest or priests; held in subjection by priestly authority.

I..know better than to be p. SCOTT.

Prig (prig), *sb.* 1567. [Of unkn. origin. Cf. next.] **I.** †**1.** *Rogues' Cant.* A tinker. **2.** *slang.* A (petty) thief 1610.

2. *Wint. T.* IV. iii. 108.

II. *slang* and *colloq.* †**1.** A spruce fellow, a

fop; a coxcomb –1835. †2. A vague term of dislike or disrespect –1749. †3. In late 17th and early 18th c.: Applied to a precisian in religion, *esp.* a nonconformist minister –1752. **4.** A precisian in speech or manners; one who cultivates or affects a propriety of culture, learning, or morals, which offends or bores others; a conceited or didactic person. (Only in later use including women.) 1753.

1. A Cane is Part of the Dress of a P., and always worn upon a Button STEELE. **2.** What does the old p. threaten then? CHESTERF. **4.** A p. is a fellow who is always making you a present of his opinions GEO. ELIOT. Hence **Pri·ggery**, the action or conduct of a p. **Pri·ggism**, †professional thievery or roguery; priggishness.

Prig (prig), *v.* 1513. [Goes w. prec.] **I.** *trans.* To steal. (*Thieves' Cant.*) Now usu. said of petty theft. 1561. **II. 1.** *intr.* To chaffer, to haggle about the price of anything. *Sc.* and *n. dial.* 1513. **b.** *fig.* To try to drive a hard bargain 1632. **2.** To beg, importune 1714. Hence **Pri·gger** (*slang*), a thief.

Priggish (pri·giʃ), *a.* 1700. [f. PRIG *sb.* + -ISH[1].] Having the character of a prig; †thievish; †coxcombical –1835; conceited, pragmatical 1752. Hence **Pri·ggish-ly** *adv.*, **-ness.**

Prill[1] (pril). Now *local.* 1603. [Phonetic var. of *pirle* PURL *sb.*[2]] A small stream of running water; a rill.

Prill[2]. 1778. [Local term in Cornwall.] *Mining.* **1.** In Cornish copper-mining: The rich copper ore which remains after cobbing and separating the inferior pieces. **2.** Hence, A button or globule of metal obtained by assaying a specimen of ore in the cupel. *U.S.* and *Colonies.* 1864.

Prim, *a.* 1709. [rel. to next, and prob. to †*prim* sb. pretty young woman (XVI); perh. all originating in cant or sl. use and ult. – OFr. *prin*, fem. *prime* = Pr. *prim* excellent, fine, delicate :– L. *primus* PRIME *a.*] Of persons, their manner, speech, etc.: Consciously or affectedly strict or precise; formal, stiff, demure. **b.** Of things: Formal, regular, stiff 1771.

A p. Quakeress 1838. **b.** A square prim garden, arranged in parallelograms TROLLOPE. Hence **Pri·m-ly** *adv.*, **-ness.**

Prim, *v.* 1684. [See prec.] **1.** *intr.* To assume a formal, precise, or demure air. **2.** *trans.* To form (the face or mouth) into an expression of preciseness or demureness; to close (the lips) primly 1706. **b.** 'To deck up precisely' (J.); chiefly with *up, out.* In later use, to make prim. 1721.

1. They mince and p. and pout, and are sigh-away and dying-ducky G. MEREDITH. *To p. up*, to bridle up, set the face or mouth firmly, as if to repel familiarities; Tell dear Kitty not to p. up as if we had never met before MME. D'ARBLAY.

‖**Prima**[1] (prəi·mă). 1880. [L. *prima* (*pagina*) first (page); see PRIME *a.*] *Typogr.* The page of printer's copy on which a new sheet begins and on which the first word of the sheet is marked.

‖**Prima**[2] (prī·mă). It. fem. of *primo* first, used in PRIMA DONNA, and other phrases (chiefly musical).

Primacy (prəi·măsi). late ME. [– (O)Fr. *primatie* or med.L. *primatia*; see PRIMATE, -Y[3], -ACY.] **1.** The state or position of being 'prime' or first in order, rank, importance, or authority; the first or chief place; preeminence, superiority. **2.** *Eccl.* The first place or leadership in spiritual matters; the office, dignity, or authority of a primate; *spec.* the chief dignity in an eccl. province 1470.

2. They yeild a Primacie to the Pope, if he be Orthodox, but no Supremacie 1635.

‖**Prima donna** (prī·mă, prəi·mă dǫ·nă). *Pl.* **prime donne, prima donnas.** 1812. [It., 'first lady'.] The first or principal female singer in an opera.

‖**Prima facie** (prəi·mă fēi·ʃi,i), *adv.* and *adj. phr.* late ME. [L. *prīmā faciē*, i.e. abl. of fem. of *prīmus* first, PRIME *a.*, and of *faciēs* FACE *sb.*] **A.** *adv.* At first sight; on the face of it. **B.** *adj.* Arising at first sight; based on the first impression 1800.

A. And indeed, *prima facie* they haue reason 1624. **B.** *Prima facie case* (Law), a case resting on *prima facie* evidence. So ‖**Prima fronte** (prəi·mă frǫ·nti) *adv. phr.*. at first appearance, on the face of it 1790.

Primage[1] (prəi·mĕdʒ). 1540. [– AL. *primagium*, f. L. *primus* first, PRIME *a.*; cf. synon. Sc. †*primegilt* (XVI–XVII) – MLG. *primgelt*, and med.L. *primator* stevedore; see -AGE.] A customary allowance formerly made by the shipper to the master and crew of a vessel for the loading and care of the cargo; now, a percentage addition to the freight, paid to the owners or freighters of the vessel.

Pri·mage[2]. 1881. [f. PRIME *v.*[1] 5.] *Engineering.* The amount of water carried off suspended in the steam from a boiler.

Primal (prəi·măl), *a.* 1602. [– med.L. *primalis*, f. L. *primus* PRIME *a.*; see -AL[1].] **1.** Belonging to the first age or earliest stage; original; primitive, primeval. **2.** Of first rank, standing, or importance 1812. **3.** *Geol.* Applied to the earliest or lowest member of the palæozoic strata of the Appalachian chain, and to the period at which this was deposited 1858.

1. My offence..hath the primall eldest curse vpon't, A Brothers murther SHAKS. Hence **Prima·lity** (*rare*), p. quality or condition. **Pri·mally** *adv.*

Primary (prəi·mări), *a.* and *sb.* 1471. [– L. *primarius* chief, f. *primus*; see PRIME *a.*, -ARY[1].] **A.** *adj.* **1.** Of the first order in time or temporal sequence; earliest, primitive, original. **b.** *Geol.* Of the first or earliest formation; formerly applied to crystalline rocks, as having been formed before the appearance of life on the earth; now = PALÆOZOIC 1. 1813. **c.** *Biol.* Belonging to or directly derived from the first stage of development or growth 1848. **2.** Of the first importance; principal, chief 1565. **3.** Of the first order in any sequence or process, esp. of derivation or causation 1621. **b.** *Cryst.* = PRIMITIVE *a.* II. 2 b. 1823.

1. *P. amputation* (Surg.), amputation performed at the earliest possible stage, before inflammation supervenes. *P. education* or *instruction*, that which begins with the rudiments or elements of knowledge; *P. school*, one at which such instruction is given; so *p. scholar* 1802. *P. assembly* or *meeting*, a gathering at which a preliminary selection of candidates, or of delegates, is effected; *spec.* in *U.S.*, a meeting of the voters belonging to a party in an election district, for this purpose. **2.** Every apostle..assigns to faith a p. importance 1850. *P. feather*, one of the large flight-feathers of a bird's wing, growing from the manus. †*P. humours*, the 'cardinal humours'; see HUMOUR *sb.* 2 b. **3.** The large p. branches of the carotid artery ABERNETHY. The Sun..gives us the p. division of time into day and night 1868. Poverty, due to absolute deficiency of money income, is called 'p.' 1901. *P. colours*: see COLOUR *sb.* 2. *P. qualities* (Philos.), the extension, the figure, and the solidity of external objects. *P. planets*, those planets which revolve directly around the sun as centre. *P. rainbow*, the rainbow produced by the simplest series of refractions and reflexions; the inner and usu. brighter when two are seen. *P. battery* (Electr.), a battery in which a current is produced. *P. coil, wire*, that which conveys the current from the battery, and induces a current in the secondary coil or wire.

B. *sb.* [ellipt. use of adj. Mostly in *pl.*] **1.** That which (or one who) is first in order, rank, or importance; anything from which something else arises or is derived. Usu. *pl.* = Primary things; first principles. 1760. **2.** Short for *p. planet*: see A. 3. 1721. **3.** A primary feather: see A. 2. 1776. **4.** *U.S.* Short for *p. meeting* or *assembly*, a caucus: see A. 1.; so *p. election a*1861. Hence **Pri·marily** *adv.* 1617.

Primate (prəi·mĕt). [ME. *primat*, later *-ate* – (O)Fr. *primat* – L. *primas, -at-* orig. sb., later adj. 'of the first rank' (Apuleius), in med.L. (a) magnate, (b) primate; f. L. *primus* PRIME *a.*] **1.** One who is first in rank or importance; a chief, superior, leader. Now *rare.* **2.** *Eccl.* An archbishop, or †sometimes a bishop, holding the first place among the bishops of a province; also applied to a patriarch or exarch of the Eastern Church ME. **3.** *Zool.* Anglicized sing. of next.

‖**Primates** (prəimēi·tīz, prəi·meits), *sb. pl. Sing.* **primas** (prəi·mæs), also anglicized **primate.** 1774. [mod. L. use (Linnæus) of pl. of *primas*; see prec.] *Zool.* The highest order of the *Mammalia*, including man, monkeys, and lemurs, and, in the Linnæan order, bats.

Pri·mateship. 1631. [f. PRIMATE + -SHIP.] The office or position of primate.

Primatial (prəimēi·ʃăl), *a.* 1623. [– Fr. *primatial* – med.L. *primatialis*, f. *primatia* (for earlier *primatus*); see PRIMARY, -AL[1].] **1.** Of, pertaining to, or having ecclesiastical primacy; pertaining to a primate. **2.** *Zool.* Of or pertaining to the mammalian order *Primates* 1864.

Primatic (prəimæ·tik), *a.* 1687. [– med.L. *primaticus*, f. *primas, -at-* PRIMATE; see -IC. Cf. Fr. †*primatique* (XV).] †**1.** = PRIMATIAL *a.* 1. –1826. **2.** = PRIMATIAL 2. 1890. So **Prima·tical** *a.*, in sense 1. 1677.

‖**Prima vista** (prī·ma vi·sta). 1591. [It., = first sight.] †**1.** An old game at cards –1652. **2.** *Mus.* At sight; as, to play or sing *prima vista.*

Prime (prəim), *sb.*[1] [OE. *prīm* – L. *prima* (sc. *hora*) first (hour), reinforced from (O)Fr. *prime*, from which or independently from L. the non-eccl. senses were derived; see PRIME *a.*] **I.** In eccl. and connected senses. **1.** One of the day hours of the Western Church: a canonical hour of the Divine Office, appointed for the first hour of the day, i.e. 6 A.M. (or, sometimes, sunrise); also, the hour or time of this office. **2.** Hence *gen.*, The first hour of the day, beginning either at six o'clock throughout the year, or at sunrise; also sometimes used for the period between the first hour and terce ME.

2. *High p.* or *p. large*, perh. the end of the period between p. and terce; Then to Westmynster-Gate I presently went, When the sonn was at hyghe pryme LYDG. *Comb.* **p.-song** *Hist.* [repr. OE. *primsang*], the office or service of prime (= sense 1).

II. The beginning of a period or cycle. **1.** The Golden Number: see GOLDEN 5 (*arch.*) ME. †**2.** The beginning or first appearance of the new moon –1704. **3.** *fig.* The beginning or first age of anything. late ME. **b.** The beginning or first age of the world 1616. **4.** The first season of the year (when this began at the vernal equinox); spring 1541. **5.** The 'springtime' of human life; the time of early manhood or womanhood, from about 21 to 28 years of age. Now *rare.* 1592.

3. b. Thou, thou art not a Child of Time, But Daughter of the Eternal P. WORDSW. **4.** The teeming Autumne big with ritch increase, Bearing the wanton burthen of the p. SHAKS. **5.** Lady that in the p. of earliest youth, Wisely hath shun'd the broad way and the green MILT.

III. That which is first in quality or character. **1.** Of human life: The period of greatest perfection or vigour 1615. **b.** Of things, material or immaterial: The best stage or state; the state of full perfection 1536. **2.** The chief or best one of a group 1579. **b.** The best part of anything 1635.

1. He was still in the p. of life, not more than four-and-forty GEO. ELIOT. **b.** Where the summer's p. Never fades away BLAKE. **2. b.** [He] always chused to have the p. of everything MISS BURNEY.

Prime (prəim), *sb.*[2] 1594. [absol. use of PRIME *a.*, or of its L. or Fr. equivalent.] **I. 1.** *Arith.* A prime number; see PRIME *a.* 7. **2.** A subdivision of any standard measure or dimension, which is itself subdivided in the same ratio into seconds, and so on; e.g. $\frac{1}{60}$ of a degree, a minute ($\frac{1}{60}$ of which is in its turn a *second*); the twelfth part of a foot, an inch 1604. **b.** *Printing.* The symbol ′ or [1], written above and to the right of a letter or figure, to denote primes, or merely to distinguish it from another not so marked 1875. **3.** *Fencing.* The first of the chief guards 1710. **4.** *Mus.* **a.** A tone represented by the same staff degree as a given tone; the pitch relation between two such tones. **b.** The tonic, or first tone, of a scale. **c.** Short for *p. tone* (see next). 1788. †**II.** Related to PRIMA VISTA, PRIMERO. *Cards.* A hand in primero consisting of a card from each of the four suits. Also, an old game of cards. –1816.

Prime (prəim), *a.* (*adv.*) late ME. [– (O)Fr. *prime* (now only in some phr.) – L. *primus* first, f. **prī-*, rel. to *præ-* PRE-, *prŏ-* PRO-[1], PRO-[2].] **1.** First in order of time or occurrence; early, youthful; primitive, primary. **2.** Of persons: First in rank, authority, or dignity; highest in degree; principal, chief

1610. **3.** First in importance, excellence, or value; principal, chief, main 1610. **4.** 'First-class', 'first-rate'; of the best quality; now esp. of cattle and provisions 1628. †**5.** Ruttish SHAKS. **6.** Primary, original, fundamental; from which others are derived, or on which they depend 1639. **7.** *Arith.* Of a number: Having no integral factors except itself and unity. So *p. divisor, factor, quotient,* etc. **b.** Of two or more numbers in relation to each other: Having no common measure except unity. 1570. **8.** First in numerical order, as in *p. meridian,* the first meridian (of any system of reckoning) 1878.

1. It befell in the p. time of the world 1587. **2.** The nobility and p. gentry of the nation HUME. **3.** That p. ill, a talking wife PRIOR. **4.** *P. fish,* the more valuable kinds of fish caught for food; opp. to OFFAL 3. **6.** *P. feathers,* primary feathers; see PRIMARY *a.* 2.

Spec. collocations: **p. entry,** an entry of two-thirds of a ship's cargo liable to duty, made before discharge (on which an estimate of the duty is paid); **p. ratio,** the initial limiting ratio between two variable quantities which simultaneously recede from definite fixed values or limits; **p. tone** (*Mus.*), the fundamental note of a compound tone; **p. vertical,** (*a*) in full *p. vertical circle,* a great circle of the heavens passing through the east and west points of the horizon, and through the zenith; (*b*) short for *p. vertical dial,* a dial the plane of which lies in that of the prime vertical circle, a north and south dial. Also *p.* CONDUCTOR, COST, MOVER, etc.: see the sbs.

B. as *adv.* In prime order, excellently (*dial.*) 1648. Hence **Pri·me-ly** *adv.*, **-ness.**

Prime (prəim), *v.*[1] 1513. [Connected with PRIMAGE[1], Sc. †*primegilt,* but the basic meaning is not clear.] **1.** *trans.* To fill, charge, load. Now chiefly *dial.* **2.** To supply (a fire-arm of old-fashioned type, or more strictly its pan) with gunpowder for firing a charge. Also *intr.* or *absol.* 1598. **3.** *fig.* and *transf.* **a.** To charge, fill, or fully furnish (a person) beforehand *with* information, etc. 1791. **b.** To fill with liquor 1823. **4.** To cover (a surface) with a ground or first colour or coat of paint, or with size, oil, etc. to prevent the paint from being absorbed 1609. †**b.** *transf.* To 'make up' (the face, etc.) with cosmetics –1782. **5.** *intr. Engineering.* Of an engine boiler: To let water pass to the cylinder in the form of spray along with the steam 1832.

3. a. Every man present..is primed with a speech 1884. **b.** A fat little man, primed with port 1854.

Prime (prəim), *v.*[2] 1756. [f. PRIME *a.* or *sb.*[1]] †**1.** To be first; to domineer; to lord it –1821. **2.** Of a tide: To come at a shorter interval. (So Fr. *primer.*) 1890.

Prime (prəim), *v.*[3] Now only *dial.* 1565. [Of unkn. origin.] *trans.* To prune or trim (trees).

Prime (prəim), *v.*[4] 1787. [Of unkn. origin.] *intr.* Of a fish: To leap or 'rise'.

Pri·me Mi·nister. 1646. [PRIME *a.* 2.] †**1.** *gen.* A principal or chief minister, servant, or agent. Often in *pl.* –1713. **2.** The first or principal minister or servant of any sovereign, ruler, or state, or more vaguely of any person of rank or position 1655. **3.** In Great Britain (orig. *prime minister of state*): A descriptive designation which is now the official title of the First Minister of State or leader of the administration 1694. **b.** Also used in some of the self-governing British colonies 1901.

Primer (pri·məɹ, prəi·məɹ), *sb.*[1] late ME. [– AFr. *primer* – med.L. *primarius* (sc. *liber* book), *primarium* (sc. *manuale* manual), subst. uses of masc. and n. of L. *primarius* PRIMARY. See -ER[2] 2.] **1.** A prayer-book or devotional manual for the use of the laity, before, and for some time after, the Reformation. **2.** An elementary school-book for teaching children to read. late ME. **b.** Hence, a small introductory book on any subject 1807. **c.** *fig.* That which serves as a first means of instruction 1640. **3.** *Typogr.* **a.** *Great P.*, a size of type between Paragon and English, of 51 ems to a foot.

Great Primer type.

b. *Long P.*, a size between Small Pica and Bourgeois, of 89 ems to a foot. *Two-line long p.* = PARAGON II. 4. 1598.

Long Primer type.

2. Horne bookes and primers to be giuen to poore children of the said parish 1639. **c.** Spell in lovers' primers sweetly 1871.

Primer (prəi·məɹ), *sb.*[2] 1497. [f. PRIME *v.*[1] + -ER[1].] **1.** A priming-wire; see PRIMING *vbl. sb.*[1] **2.** A cap, wafer, cylinder, etc., containing fulminating powder or other compound, for igniting a charge of gunpowder when exploded 1819. **3.** A person who primes 1890.

Primer (pri·məɹ, prəi·məɹ), *a.* 1448. [– AFr. *primer* = OFr. *primier,* var. of (O)Fr. *premier* :– L. *primarius*; cf. PRIMER *sb.*[1]] †**1.** First in time; early; primitive –1622. †**2.** First in position or rank; chief, premier –1747. **3. a. P. fine,** in *Feudal Law,* the sum paid to the crown by a plaintiff who sued for the recovery of lands by a writ of covenant. Now only *Hist.* 1634. **b. P. seisin,** in *Feudal Law,* a right of the English Crown to receive from the heir of a tenant *in capite* who died seised of a knight's fee the profits of his estate for the first year. Now only *Hist.* 1488.

‖**Primero** (primēᵊ·ro). *Hist.* 1533. [alt. (cf. -ADO) of Sp. *primera,* fem. of *primero* first :– L. *primarius* PRIMARY.] A gambling card-game, in which four cards were dealt to each player, each card having thrice its ordinary value.

Primeval, primæval (prəimī·văl), *a.* 1662. [f. L. *primævus,* f. *primus* PRIME *a.* + *ævum* age; see -AL[1].] Of or pertaining to the first age of the world or of anything ancient; primitive.

With Night primæval, and with Chaos old POPE. This is the forest primeval LONGF. Hence **Prime·vally** *adv.* in the first age of the world; also, in a p. manner or degree. So †**Prime·vous, -æ·vous** *a.* 1656.

Primigenial (prəimi,dʒī·niăl), *a.* Now *rare.* 1602. [f. L. *primigenius* first of its kind (f. *primi-*, comb. f. *primus* first + *genus* kind, or *gen-*, stem of *gignere* beget) + -AL[1].] †**1.** First generated or produced; earliest formed; original, primitive, primary –1822. **2.** *Zool.* Applied to species belonging to a primitive type (rendering the specific name *primigenius,* as in *Bos primigenius,* etc.) 1851. So **Pri·migene** (*rare*), **Primige·nian** (*rare*), †**Primige·nious** *adjs.*

Primine (prəi·min). 1832. [– Fr. *primine* (Mirbel, 1828), f. L. *primus* + -INE[1].] *Bot.* The first of the two coats or integuments of an ovule; i.e. **a.** (orig.) the outer one; but subseq. **b.** the inner, as being formed first 1875.

Priming (prəi·miŋ), *vbl. sb.*[1] 1598. [f. PRIME *v.*[1] + -ING[1].] The action of PRIME *v.*[1] **1.** The putting of gunpowder in the pan of an old-fashioned fire-arm. **2.** *concr.* The gunpowder so placed; also, the train of powder connecting a fuse with a charge in blasting, etc. 1625. **3.** The preparing of (a surface) for painting, by coating it with a body colour, etc. Also *transf.* 1609. **4.** *concr.* **a.** The mixture used by painters for the preparatory coat. **b.** A coat or layer of the substance. 1625. **5.** The hasty imparting of knowledge; cramming 1859. **6.** *Engineering.* (See PRIME *v.*[1] 5.) 1841.

attrib. and *Comb.*: **p.-horn,** (*a*) a horn containing priming-powder formerly carried by gunners; (*b*) the powder-horn carried by miners and quarry-men; **-iron, -wire,** a sharp pointed wire used in gunnery and blasting to ascertain whether the touch-hole or vent is free and to pierce the cartridge.

Priming (prəi·miŋ), *vbl. sb.*[2] 1833. [f. PRIME *v.*[2] 2 + -ING[1].] *P. of the tides*: the acceleration of the tides, taking place from the neap to the spring tides; opp. to *lagging.*

‖**Primipara** (prəimi·pără). 1842. [L., f. *primus* first + *-parus,* from *parere* bring forth.] A female that brings forth for the first time. Hence **Primi·parous** *a.* bearing a child (or young) for the first time.

Primipilar (prəimipəi·lăɹ), *a.* 1600. [– L. *primipilaris,* f. *primipilus* chief centurion of the *triarii* in a legion, f. *primus* first, *pilus* a body of pikemen, f. *pilum* javelin.] *Rom. Antiq.* Belonging to, or that is, a *primipilus.*

Primitive (pri·mĭtiv), *a.* and *sb.* late ME. [– (O)Fr. *primitif, -ive* or L. *primitivus* first or earliest of its kind, f. *primitus* in the first place, f. *primus* PRIME *a.*; see -IVE.] **A.** *adj.* **I.** *gen.* **1.** Of or belonging to the first age, period, or stage; original; early, ancient 1486. **2.** Having the quality or style of that which is early or ancient; simple, rude, or rough like that of early times; old-fashioned 1685. **3.** Original as opp. to derivative; primary; radical. late ME.

1. The p. pastoral ages LONGF. *P. Church,* the Christian Church in its earliest times. **2.** A poor good p. creature H. WALPOLE. Her very p. wardrobe 1838. **3.** God is the p...cause 1628.

II. *spec.* and *techn.* **1.** *Gram.* and *Philol.* Of a word or language: Original, radical: opp., or correl. to *derivative* 1530. **2.** *Math.,* etc. Applied to a line or figure from which some construction or reckoning begins; or to a curve, surface, magnitude, equation, operation, etc., which is not derived from another 1690. **b.** *Cryst.* Applied to a fundamental crystalline form from which all the other forms may be derived by geometrical processes 1805. **3.** Of colours: see PRIMARY *a.* 3. 1759. **4.** *Geol.* Belonging to the earliest geological period; primary 1777. **5.** *Biol., Anat.,* etc. **a.** Applied to a part or structure in the first or a very early stage of formation; rudimentary, primordial. **b.** Applied to the minute or ultimate elements of a structure, or to some part connected with these; as the *p. fibrillæ* of a nerve; the *p. sheath* investing each of these. 1857. **6.** *P. Methodist Connection*: a society of Methodists founded by Hugh Bourne in 1810 by secession from the main body; so called as adhering to the original methods of preaching, etc., practised by the Wesleys and Whitefield 1812.

2. *P. circle* or *plane,* the circle or plane upon which projection is made. **5. a.** *P. streak* or *trace,* the faint streak which constitutes the earliest trace of the embryo in the fertilized ovum; *p. groove,* (*a*) = *p. streak*; (*b*) a groove or furrow which appears (in vertebrates) in the upper surface of the p. streak, and marks the beginning of the vertebral column. **6.** *P. Methodist,* a member or adherent of the P. Methodist Connection. *P. Methodism,* the principles of this society, or adherence to it.

B. *sb.* **I. 1.** †**a.** A primitive Christian; a member of the early Church –1686. **b.** An aboriginal; a man of primitive (esp. prehistoric) times 1779. **2.** Short for *P. Methodist* (see A. II. 6). **3.** In art criticism: **a.** A painter of the period before the Renaissance; also *transf.* a modern who imitates the style of these. **b.** A picture painted by any of these. 1892. **II. 1.** *Gram.* A word from which another or others are derived; a root-word. Opp. to *derivative.* 1565. **2.** *Math.* Any algebraical or geometrical form in relation to another derived from it. (Short for *p. expression, equation, curve,* etc.: see A. II. 2.) Hence **Pri·mitive-ly** *adv.*, **-ness. Primiti·vity,** p. quality, character, or condition.

Primogenital (prəimo,dʒe·nităl), *a.* 1657. [– late L. *primogenitalis,* f. *primogenitus* (taken as sb.); see -AL[1].] Of or pertaining to the first-born or to primogeniture. So **Primoge·nitary** *a.* **Primoge·nitive** *a.*; †also as *sb.* = PRIMOGENITURE 2. SHAKS.

Primogenitor (prəimodʒe·nitǫɹ). 1654. [var. of PROGENITOR by substitution of *primo-*; cf. next.] First parent, earliest ancestor; *loosely,* ancestor, progenitor.

Primogeniture (prəimodʒe·nitiŭɹ, -tʃəɹ). 1602. [– med.L. *primogenitura,* f. L. *primo* adv. first + *genitura* GENITURE; after L. *primogenitus.* Cf. (O)Fr. *primogéniture.*] **1.** The fact or condition of being the first-born of the children of the same parents. **2.** The right of succession or inheritance belonging to the first-born; the principle, custom, or law by which the property or title descends to the eldest son (or eldest child); *spec.* the feudal rule of inheritance by which the whole of the real estate of an intestate passes to the eldest son 1631.

1. *Right of p.*, the right (of succession, etc.) of the first-born; In the division of personal estates,..no right of p. is allowed BLACKSTONE. Hence **Primoge·nitureship** (now *rare*) = sense 2.

Primordial (prəimǭ·ɹdiăl), *a.* (*sb.*) late ME. [– late L. *primordialis* that is first of all, f. PRIMORDIUM; see -AL[1].] **1.** Of, pertaining to, or existing at (or from) the very beginning; first in time, original, primitive, primeval. **2.** Constituting the beginning or starting-point; original, not derivative; fundamental; elementary 1529. **3.** *Anat.* and *Zool.* = PRIMITIVE *a.* II. 5 a. 1786. **4.** *Bot.* **a.** Earliest formed in the course of growth; said of leaves, fruit, etc. 1785. **b.** Applied to tissues, etc., in their rudimentary stage or condition 1849. **5.** *Geol.* and *Palæont.* †**a.** = PRIMITIVE *a.* II. 4. –1802. **b.** Applied to a series of strata in Bohemia, containing the earliest fossil remains there found; hence to corresponding strata elsewhere, forming part of the Cambrian system; also applied to fossils found in these strata 1885.

1. The p. tenets of the Tory party DISRAELI. **4. b.** *P. cell*, a cell in its simplest form, consisting merely of a mass of protoplasm, without cell-wall, cell-sap, etc. *P. utricle*, the layer of denser protoplasm lining the wall of a vacuolate cell.

B. *sb.* Something primordial; beginning, origin; a first principle, an element (*rare*) 1522. Hence **Primo·rdialism,** p. nature or condition. **Primo·rdially** *adv.* in a p. way.

‖**Primordium** (prəimǭ·ɹdiǒm). *Pl.* **-ia.** 1671. [L., subst. use of n. of adj. *primordius* original, f. *primus* PRIME *a.* + base of *ordiri* begin; see -IAL.] The very beginning, the earliest stage; introduction, opening part; primitive source, origin. **b.** *Biol.* The first rudiment of an organ or structure 1890.

Primrose (pri·mrōᵘz), *sb.* (*a.*) [XV *primerose* corresp. to OFr. *primerose* (now, hollyhock), med.L. *prima rosa* 'first' or 'earliest' rose; the reason for the name is not known. Superseded †*primerole* (XIV).] **1.** A plant (*Primula vulgaris*) bearing pale yellowish flowers in early spring, growing wild in woods and hedges, and on banks. Also, the flower of this plant. Occas. extended to include other species of the genus PRIMULA. **2.** Applied to some other plants having flowers resembling those of the common p.; as **Evening** (**Night,** †**Nightly**) **P.,** the genus *Œnothera*; **Peerless P.** = P. PEERLESS 1760. †**3.** *fig.* The first or best; the finest, or a fine, example; the 'flower', 'pearl' –1664. **4.** Ellipt. for *p. colour*: A pale greenish yellow or lemon colour 1882.

1. The rathe P. that forsaken dies MILT.

Comb.: **P. day,** the anniversary of the death (19th April, 1881) of Benjamin Disraeli, Earl of Beaconsfield, with whose memory the p. is associated; **P. League,** a political association formed in 1883 in support of the principles of Conservatism as represented by Lord Beaconsfield; **p. path, way,** a path abounding in primroses; *fig.* the path of pleasure (*Ham.* I. iii. 50, *Macb.* II. iii. 21). Hence **Pri·mrosy** *a.*

Pri·mrose pee·rless. 1578. A name formerly given to the species of Narcissus, including the wild daffodil; now spec. to *Narcissus biflorus*, the two-flowered narcissus.

Primula (pri·miŭlă). 1753. [– med.L. *primula*, fem. of *primulus*, dim. of *primus* first; orig. in *primula veris*, applied first app. to the cowslip, and at an early date also to the field daisy.] *Bot.* A genus of herbaceous perennial plants, of low-growing habit, having radical leaves, and yellow, white, pink, or purple flowers mostly borne in umbels. Hence **Primula·ceous** *a.* belonging to the natural order *Primulaceæ*, of which *P.* is the typical genus.

‖**Primum mobile** (prəi·mǒm mōᵘ·bili). 1460. [med.L., lit. 'first moving thing', f. L. *primus* first, *mobilis* movable; see PRIME *a.* and MOBILE *sb.*¹ Tr. Arab. *al-muḥarrik al-awwal* the first mover (Avicenna).] **1.** The supposed outermost sphere, added in the Middle Ages to the Ptolemaic system of astronomy, and supposed to revolve round the earth from east to west in 24 hours, carrying with it the (eight or nine) contained spheres. **2.** *transf.* and *fig.* A prime source of motion or action; a prime mover, mainspring 1612.

‖**Primus** (prəi·mǒs), *a.* and *sb.* 1592. [L., 'first'; see PRIME *a.*] **A.** *adj.* **1.** In L. phrases, as *primus inter pares*, first among equals; *primus motor*, prime mover. **2.** In some boys' schools, used to distinguish the oldest (or senior) of those having the same surname 1796. **B.** *sb.* **1.** In the Scottish Episcopal Church: The presiding bishop, who has certain ceremonial privileges, but no metropolitan authority 1860. **2.** (In full *primus stove*.) Trade name of a stove burning vaporized paraffin oil 1907.

Primy (prei·mi), *a. rare.* 1602. [f. PRIME *sb.* + -Y¹.] That is in its prime.

A Violet in the youth of P. Nature SHAKS.

Prince (prins), *sb.* ME. [– (O)Fr. *prince* – L. *princeps, princip-* chief, leader, sovereign, f. *primus* PRIME *a.* + *-cip-*, comb. form of *capere* take.] **I. 1.** A sovereign ruler; a monarch, king. Now *arch.* or *rhet.* †**b.** Applied to a female sovereign –1650. †**2.** One who has the chief authority; a ruler, commander, governor –1611. **3.** One who or that which is first or pre-eminent in a specified class or sphere; the chief, the greatest ME. **4. a.** Applied to Christ, *esp.* in *p. of peace*. **b.** = PRINCIPALITY 5. **c.** Applied to Satan in the phrases *p. of the air, darkness, evil, this world*, etc. ME.

1. Phr. *To live like a p.*; The iolly fellowes that once in England liued like Princes in their Abbeies GREENE. **4. c.** WYCLIF *John* 12:31.

II. Spec. uses. **1.** The ruler of a principality, actually, nominally, or orig. a feudatory of a king or emperor ME. **2.** A male member of a royal family; *esp.* in Great Britain, a son or grandson of a king or queen. Also called *p. of the blood* (*royal*). **3.** The English rendering of a title of nobility in some foreign countries 1727. **b.** Applied as a title of courtesy in certain connections to a duke, marquis, or earl 1707. **c.** *P. of the* (*Holy Roman*) *Church*, a title applied to a Cardinal 1674.

2. *P. Albert* (*coat*) [f. *Prince Albert* Edward, afterwards Edward VII] (*U.S. colloq.*), a frock-coat. *P. Consort*, the husband of a reigning female sovereign being himself a p. *P. Rupert's drops*: see DROP *sb.* I. 8. *P. of Wales's feathers*: see FEATHER *sb.* II. 3.

Comb. with *prince's*: **prince's metal,** also **Prince Rupert's metal,** an alloy of about three parts of copper and one of zinc, in colour resembling gold; **prince's pine,** (*a*) the Grey Pine, *Pinus banksiana*; (*b*) = PIPSISSEWA. Hence **Prince** *v. intr.* with *it*, to play the p., carry oneself as a p. **Pri·ncehood** (now *rare*). **Pri·ncekin** (*joc.*), a little, young, or diminutive p. **Pri·ncelet, -ling,** a little or petty p.; the ruler of a small principality. **Pri·ncelike** *a.* and †*adv.*

Pri·nce-bi·shop. 1849. A bishop who is also a prince (sense II. 1); also, one who enjoyed the temporal possessions and authority of a bishopric, with princely rank.

Princedom (pri·nsdəm). 1560. [f. PRINCE *sb.* + -DOM.] = PRINCIPALITY 2, 4, 5.

Thrones, Princedoms, Powers, Dominions MILT.

Pri·nce-ele·ctor. 1560. (= G. *Kurfürst*.) One of the princes who elected the Holy Roman (German) Emperor.

Princely (pri·nsli), *a.* 1500. [f. PRINCE *sb.* + -LY¹.] **1.** Of, pertaining, or belonging to a prince or princes; held or exercised by a prince; royal, regal, kingly 1503. **2.** That is a prince; royal, kingly 1582. **3.** Princelike; dignified, stately, noble 1500. **4.** Like that of a prince; sumptuous, magnificent, munificent 1539.

1. The p. houses of Western Europe 1869. **3.** I see him yet, the p. boy! SCOTT. **4.** Sir E— G—'s gift..is 'p.' 1889. Hence **Pri·nceliness,** the quality of being p. **Pri·ncely** *adv.* (now *rare*) in a p. manner.

‖**Princeps** (pri·nseps), *a.* and *sb.* Pl. **pri·ncipes** (-sipīz). 1809. [L.; see PRINCE.] **A.** *adj.* First, original; *spec.* of a book, from L. phrase *editio princeps* original edition. **b.** Also frequent in L. phr. *facile princeps*, easily the first or chief. **B.** *sb.* **1.** The title under which Augustus Cæsar and his successors exercised supreme authority in the Roman Empire; now gen. used by historians to describe the constitutional position of the head of the state 1837. **2.** *ellipt.* for *editio princeps*; see A.

Pri·nce Re·gent. 1789. A prince who is regent of a country, during a minority, or in the absence or disability of the sovereign; *spec.* the title commonly given to George Prince of Wales (afterwards George IV) during the mental incapacity of George III, 1811–1820.

Prince royal. 1702. [– Fr. *prince royal*.] The eldest son of a reigning monarch; *spec.* of the king of Prussia.

Prince's feather. 1629. **a.** London Pride (*Saxifraga umbrosa*). Now *dial.* **b.** A garden plant, *Amaranthus hypochondriacus*, bearing feathery spikes of small red flowers; also *A. speciosus*, a larger species 1721.

Princess (prinse·s, pri·nses). [XIV *princesse* – (O)Fr. *princesse*, fem of *prince*; see -ESS¹. In med.L. *principissa* (XV).] **1.** A female sovereign or ruler; a queen (*arch.*). **2.** The wife of a prince. late ME. **3.** The daughter or grand-daughter of a sovereign; a female member of a royal or princely family. 1508. **4.** Applied to a female, or anything personified as feminine, that is likened to a princess in pre-eminence or authority; formerly often to the Virgin Mary. late ME.

1. So excellent a p., as the present queen SWIFT. **2.** *P. dowager*: see DOWAGER. **3.** *P. of the blood*: see BLOOD *sb.* III. 2. *P. royal*, the eldest daughter of the sovereign in Great Britain; also formerly in Prussia.

Comb. **p. dress,** a lady's dress of which the lengths of the bodice and skirt are cut in one piece; also applied to modifications of this shape; so *p.-shape, p. frock, petticoat*, etc.; also *p.-shaped* adj., and *p.* adj. or ellipt. = p.-shaped.

Pri·nce-wood. Also **prince's wood.** 1686. A dark-coloured and light-veined timber produced by two W. Indian trees, *Cordia gerascanthoides* and *Hamelia ventricosa*; also called *Spanish elm*.

Principal (pri·nsĭpăl), *a.* and *sb.* ME. [– (O)Fr. *principal* – L. *principalis* first, chief, original, f. *princeps, princip-* PRINCE; see -AL¹.] **A.** *adj.* **I.** *gen.* **1.** First in rank or importance. **2.** Less definitely: Belonging to the first or highest group in rank or importance; prominent, leading. ME. **3.** Specially great; of high degree or importance; special, eminent. Now *rare* or *Obs.* late ME. †**4.** Princely, royal –1591.

1. He was the p. projector of the fund for decayed musicians 1795. Their p. food is flour and meal JOWETT. *P. boy*, the principal male character in a pantomime (usu. played by a woman); so *p. girl*. **2.** Certaine of the Principallest Gentlemen of the citie 1598. Character is..a p. source of interest.. employed by the drama 1874. **3.** A principall portion of Gods spirit 1611.

II. *spec.* and *techn.* **1.** Of money: Constituting the original sum; that is the capital sum invested or lent, and yielding interest; capital, capitalized ME. **2.** *Law.* **a.** That is the chief person concerned in some action or proceeding; *esp.* that is the actual perpetrator of, or directly responsible for, a crime. **b.** *P. challenge*: a challenge against a jury, or against a particular juror, alleging a fact such as, if proved, would disqualify such jury or juror as a matter of law. 1448. **3.** *Gram.* Said of a sentence or clause, or of a word, in relation to another which is auxiliary to or dependent upon it; opp. to *subordinate* or *dependent*. *P. parts* (of a verb), those from which the other parts can be derived, or which contain the different stems in the simplest forms. 1590. **4.** *Building.* Applied to the main rafters, posts, or braces in the wooden framework of a building, which support the chief strain 1594. **5.** *Math.*, etc. 1704.

5. *P. axis*, (*a*) of a conic, that axis which passes through the foci, the transverse axis (opp. to *conjugate axis*); (*b*) each of three lines in a body or system used as the chief lines of reference in relation to forces operating upon it. *P. plane*, of a symmetrical body, an imaginary plane of symmetry, as, in an oblate or prolate spheroid, the plane passing through the centre at right angles to the axis of revolution. *P. point*, in *Perspective*, the point where the *p. ray* meets the plane of delineation. *P. ray*, in *Perspective*, the straight line from the point of sight perpendicular to the plane of delineation. *P. section* of a crystal, any section passing through the optical axis.

B. *sb.* **I. 1.** A head man or woman; a chief, ruler, superior; a governor, a presiding officer, as the head of a religious or educational institution, the manager of a house of business, etc.; †the master or mistress of a household. late ME. **b.** In Great Britain, outside Oxford and Cambridge, the most usual designation of a head of a college or hall 1438. **2.** A chief actor or doer; the person for whom and by whose authority another acts 1625. **b.** A person directly responsible for a crime, either as the actual perpetrator (*p. in the first degree*), or as present, aiding and abetting, at the commission of it (*p. in the sec-*

ond degree) 1594. **c.** A person for whom another is surety 1576. **d.** Each of the combatants in a duel, as dist. from their *seconds* 1709.

2. We were not principals, but auxiliaries in the war SWIFT.

II. †**1.** The chief, main, or most important thing, part, point, or element –1845. †**2.** The original document, drawing, painting, etc., from which a copy is made –1660. **3.** A principal rafter or post; any one of the rafters upon which rest the purlins which support the common rafters. Also applied to a main iron girder. 1448. †**4.** An upright pillar or stem having branches to bear tapers; formerly used on a hearse –1849. **5.** The original sum dealt with in any transaction, as dist. from any later accretions; the capital sum as dist. from the interest; also, capital as dist. from income. late ME. **6.** *Mus.* An organ-stop of the same quality as the Open Diapason, but an octave higher in pitch 1613. Hence **Pri·ncipally** *adv.* in the chief place, mainly, above all; for the most part, in most cases. **Pri·ncipalship,** the office of p. (of a college, etc.).

Principality (prinsĭpæ·lĭti). late ME. [– OFr. *principalité* (mod. 'headship of a college'); varying (XIV–XV) with *principalte* – OFr. *principalté* (mod. *principauté* princedom) – late L. *principalitas*; see PRINCIPAL, -ITY.] **1.** The quality, condition, or fact of being principal; chief place or rank; pre-eminence. Now *rare.* **2.** The position, dignity, or dominion of a prince or chief ruler; sovereignty; supreme authority. late ME. **3.** The sovereignty, rule, or government of the prince of a small or dependent state 1459. **4.** A region or state ruled by a prince. late ME. **5.** A spiritual being (evil or good) of a high order; *spec.* in *pl.*, in mediæval angelology, one of the nine orders of angels (see ORDER *sb.* II. 1) (Repr. L. *principatus*, Gr. ἀρχαί.) 1560. **6.** The office of principal of a college, university, etc.; principalship. Now *rare.* 1641.

4. Samos...A p. of the Ottoman Empire, more or less independent 1905. *The P.*, Wales. **5.** Nisroc, of Principalities the prime MILT.

Principate (pri·nsipĕt). ME. [– (O)Fr. *principat* or L. *principatus* first place, etc., f. *princeps, princip-*; see PRINCE, -ATE[1].] **1.** = PRINCIPALITY 1, 2. Now *rare.* **b.** *Rom. Hist.* The rule of the PRINCEPS; the imperial power of Augustus and his successors, while some of the republican forms were still retained; the period of rule of a princeps 1862. **2.** = PRINCIPALITY 4. 1494.

‖**Principia,** L. pl. of PRINCIPIUM.

†**Princi·pial,** *a.* [f. L. *principium* beginning + -AL[1].] Standing at the beginning; initial BACON.

†**Princi·piant,** *a.* 1615. [– Fr. †*principiant*, pr. pple. of †*principier* (XV) begin – late and med.L. *principiare*, f. L. *principium*; see next, -ANT.] Constituting the beginning of something; originating; primary –1675.

‖**Principium** (prinsi·piŏm). *Pl.* **-ia.** 1600. [L., f. *princeps, princip-* first in time or order.] **1.** = PRINCIPLE *sb.* in various senses. **b.** *pl. Principia*: abbreviated title of a work by Sir Isaac Newton, setting forth the principles of natural philosophy or physics 1727. **2.** *Rom. Antiq.* (*pl.*) The general's quarters in a camp 1581.

Principle (pri·nsĭp'l), *sb.* late ME. [– AFr. **principle*, var. of (O)Fr. *principe* – L. *principium* beginning, source, (pl.) foundations, elements; see prec. For parasitic *l* cf. *manciple, participle.*] Often emphasized by prefixing *first.* **I.** Origin, source; source of action. †**1.** Beginning; fountain-head; original or initial state –1674. †**2.** That from which something takes its rise, originates, or is derived. *Obs.* (exc. as in 3.) –1697. **3.** In gen. sense: a fundamental source; a primary element, force, or law which produces or determines particular results; the ultimate basis of the existence of something; cause. late ME. **4.** An original tendency or faculty; a natural disposition. late ME.

3. Those Idolaters adore two Principles; the P. of Good, and that of Evil SWIFT. **4.** Of verray womanly benignytee That nature in youre principles hath yset CHAUCER. Out of a P. of good will I have to you 1669.

II. Fundamental truth, law, or motive force. **1.** A fundamental truth or proposition, on which many others depend; a fundamental assumption forming the basis of a chain of reasoning. late ME. **b.** *Physics*, etc. A highly general or inclusive theorem or 'law', exemplified in a multitude of cases 1710. **2.** A fundamental quality or attribute; essential characteristic or character; essence 1662. **3.** A general law or rule as a guide to action; a fundamental motive or reason of action, esp. one consciously recognized and followed 1532. **b.** Used *absol.* for *good, right*, or *moral p.* (Also in *pl.*) 1653. **4.** A general fact or law of nature by virtue of which a machine or instrument operates; hence, the general mode of construction or operation of a machine, etc. 1802.

1. Principles of political economy 1825. First principles..should be carefully considered JOWETT. **3.** The barbarian lives without p. and without aim J. H. NEWMAN. **b.** If I were to choose any servant..I would choose a godly man that hath principles CROMWELL. Thus my pride, not my p...kept me honest DE FOE. *On p.*, as a matter of (moral) p.; from a settled (conscientious) motive. **4.** This thermometer is sometimes varied in its form and arrangement, but the p. remains the same 1858.

III. Rudiment, element. †**1. a.** *pl.* The earliest parts of a subject of study; elements, rudiments –1706. †**b.** *concr.* A germ, embryo, bud (of a natural structure) –1732. †**2.** A component part, ingredient, constituent, element –1732. †**b.** *Old Chem.* Chiefly in *pl.*: The five supposed simple substances or elements of which all bodies were believed to be composed –1799. **c.** *Chem.* One of the constituents of a substance as obtained by chemical analysis; usu., one which gives rise to some characteristic quality, or causes some special action or effect, as *active, bitter, neutral p.* 1732.

2. A confluence of buyers, sellers, and lookers-on, which are the three principles of a fair 1655. Hence †**Principle** *v. trans.* to ground (any one) in the principles or elements of a subject, to impress with principles of action; to be the principle, source, or basis of; to originate –1760.

Principled (pri·nsipl'd), *ppl. a.* Now *rare* (exc. in comb.). 1642. [f. PRINCIPLE *sb.* and *v.* + -ED.] **1.** Established in principles; holding or habitually actuated by particular principles; that is so or such on principle. Often in comb., as *high-, well-p.* **2.** Having good or right principles. (Opp. to *unprincipled.*) 1697. **3.** Founded on a principle; instilled into the mind as a principle 1784.

Pri·ncock, -cox. *Obs.* exc. *dial.* 1540. [Of unkn. origin.] A pert, forward, saucy boy or youth; a coxcomb. (*joc.* or *contempt.*) **b.** *attrib.* or as *adj.*, esp. in *p.-boy* 1595.

Prink (priŋk), *v.* 1576. [Related to PRANK *v.*[2]] **1.** *trans.* To make spruce or smart; to dress *up*; esp. *refl.* to dress oneself *up. colloq.* **b.** *intr.* To dress oneself up; make oneself look smart. *colloq.* 1709. **2.** *trans.* Of a bird: To trim (the feathers); to preen. Also *intr.* 1575.

1. To gather king-cups in the yellow mead, And p. their hair with daisies COWPER.

Print (print), *sb.* [ME. *prient(e, preint(e* – OFr. *priente, preinte*, subst. use of fem. pa. pple. of *preindre*, older *priembre* :– L. *premere* PRESS *v.*[1] Cf. (M)LG., (M)Du. *prent.*] **I. 1.** The impress made in a plastic material by a stamp, seal, die, or the like; a distinctive stamped or printed mark or design, as on a coin. **2.** *fig.* **a.** An image or character stamped upon the mind or soul; a mental impression. Now *rare.* ME. **b.** An image or likeness of anything. late ME. **3.** *gen.* Any indentation in a surface preserving the form left by the pressure of some body; also, a mark, spot, or stain produced on any surface by another substance. late ME. **4.** An instrument, etc. which produces a mark or figure by pressing; a stamp or die; a mould. Also *fig.* late ME. **b.** *Founding.* A support for the core of a casting 1864. **5.** A pat of butter, moulded to a shape 1754. **6.** A printed cotton fabric; a piece of printed cotton cloth. Often *attrib.* 1824.

2. b. Y[e] fathers owne figure,..y[e] very prent of his visage MORE. **3.** The prynte of the hors shoo and nayles abode euer in his vysage CAXTON. The recent prints of a bear and two cubs 1853. **6.** He chose the p. stuff for his wife's dresses STEVENSON.

II. Typographical uses. **1.** The state of being printed; printed form 1482. **2.** *concr.* Language embodied in a printed form; typography; esp. with ref. to size, form, or style, as *small p., clear p.* 1623. †**3.** A printing-press (with its accessories). Hence, the work of the press, the process of printing. –1691. **4.** An impression of a work printed at one time; an edition 1535. **5.** A printed publication; *esp.* a printed sheet, news sheet, newspaper (now chiefly *U.S.*) 1570. **6.** A picture or design printed from a block or plate 1662. **7.** *Photogr.* A picture produced from a negative 1851.

1. Rush like a hero into p. PRAED. *In p.*, (*a*) in printed form; (*b*) of a book or edition, not yet sold out. *Out of p.* (of a book or edition), sold out. **2.** *fig.* All the wickedness of the world is P. to him DICKENS. **5.** I have often admired your talents in the daily prints SHERIDAN. **6.** There is a p. of him, painted by John Lyvyus, and engraved by Vosterman H. WALPOLE.

III. Transf. uses, of uncertain origin. *In p.* **a.** In a precise and perfect way or manner; with exactness; to a nicety. Now *dial.* 1576. †**b.** With a sb.: *A man, fool* (etc.) *in p.*, a perfect or thorough man, fool, etc. –1633. †**c.** Applied to the exact crimping of the pleats of a ruff –1641. **d.** Said of the beard or hair. So also *out of p.*, out of proper order. *Obs.* or *dial.* 1605.

attrib. and *Comb.*: **p. hand,** handwriting imitating p.; so **p. letters; -holder,** a small frame for holding a photograph or engraving; **-room,** a room in a museum or the like, containing a collection of prints; **-seller,** one who sells prints or engravings; **-shop,** a p.-seller's shop; **-washer,** an apparatus for washing photographic prints after fixing; **-work(s,** a factory in which cotton fabrics are printed. Hence **Pri·ntless** *a.* making or leaving no p. or trace; that has received, or that retains, no p.

Print (print), *v.* [ME. *prente, printe*, f. prec.] **I. 1.** *trans.* To impress or stamp (a surface) with a seal, die, or the like; to mark with any figure or pattern; to brand. Said also of footsteps upon soft or yielding ground. **2.** To impress or stamp (a form, figure, mark, etc.) in or on a yielding substance; also, by extension, to set or trace (a mark, figure, etc.) on any surface, by carving, writing, or otherwise. late ME. **b.** *fig.* To impress (an image, thought, saying, etc.) upon the heart, mind, or memory; to fix in the mind. late ME. **3.** To press (anything hard) into or upon a yielding substance, so as to leave an indentation or imprint. Also with *in.* late ME. †**4.** To commit (anything) to writing; to express in written words; to inscribe –1588.

1. Little footsteps lightly p. the ground GRAY. **2.** The child prints many a playful kiss Upon their hands 1812. **b.** This sentence is very meet for women to p. in their remembrance 1563. **3.** Horses..Printing their prowd Hoofes i' the receiuing Earth SHAKS. **4.** *Tit. A.* IV. i. 75.

II. Senses relating to typography. **1.** To produce (a book, picture, etc.) by applying to paper, vellum, etc., in a press or machine, inked types, blocks, or plates, bearing characters or designs 1511. **2.** Said of an author or editor: **a.** To cause (a manuscript, book, etc.) to be printed; to give to the press 1530. **b.** To express or publish in print (ideas, etc.) 1638. **3.** *intr.* or *absol.* To exercise the vocation of a printer; to employ the press in printing 1699. **4.** *trans.* To take an impression from (a forme of type, a plate, block, etc.); to use in printing 1727. **5.** To form (letters) in the style of printed letters; also *absol.* 1837.

1. 160 Englishe Bibles were printed at Paris 1560. His Majesty's Picture, printed in natural Colours 1720. **2. a.** Some said, John, p. it; others said, Not so BUNYAN. **4.** The stone is then etched, washed out, and printed 1875.

III. Techn. senses analogous to II. **1.** *trans.* To mark (a textile fabric) by hand or machinery with a pattern or design in colours. Also *absol.* 1588. **2.** *Pottery.* To transfer to the unglazed surface a decorative design in colour from paper, or in oil from a gelatine sheet or bat. With the pottery, or the design, as obj. 1839. **3.** *Photogr.* To produce (a positive picture) by the transmission of light through a negative placed immediately upon the sensitized surface, or, in an enlarging camera, before it. Also with *off, out.* 1851. **b.** *intr.* Of a negative: To produce a photograph (*well, badly,* etc.) 1852. **4.** See NATURE-PRINTING.

Hence **Pri·ntable** *a.* capable of being printed, or printed from.

Printer (pri·ntəɹ). 1504. [f. PRINT *v.* + -ER¹.] **1.** A person who prints, in any sense of the word 1567. **b.** *spec.* One whose business is the printing of books, etc.; the owner of a printing business; a workman in a printing-office 1504. **2.** An instrument or appliance used for printing 1890. **3.** *Trade.* A cotton cloth made to be printed on 1864. **4.** *attrib.*, as *p.-author, -journalist* 1663.

Comb. with *printer's*: **printer's devil:** see DEVIL *sb.* 5; **printer's mark,** a monogram or other device used by a p. as a trade-mark. **b.** With *printers'*, as *printers' ink* (see INK *sb.*¹), *pie* (see PIE *sb.*⁴); **printers' bible,** the Bible which contains the misreading 'Printers have persecuted me without a cause' (Ps. 119:161).

Printery (pri·ntəri). Chiefly *U.S.* 1638. [f. prec.; see -ERY.] **1.** A printing-office. **2.** A cotton-printing factory 1846.

Printing (pri·ntiŋ), *vbl. sb.* late ME. [f. PRINT *v.* + -ING¹.] The action of PRINT *v.*, in various senses; an instance of this.

attrib. and *Comb.*, as **p.-cloth,** cotton cloth made specially for printing; **-frame** (*Photogr.*), a frame in which sensitized paper is placed beneath a negative and exposed to light; **-ink** = *printers' ink*; **-machine,** a printing-press for rapid work on a large scale, usu. one in which mechanical power is employed; **-office,** an establishment in which books, newspapers, etc. are printed; **-paper,** (*a*) paper used for printing on; (*b*) in *Photogr.* sensitized paper on which pictures are printed (also *printing-out paper*, abbrev. P.O.P.).

Pri·nting-house. Now only *Hist.* 1576. A building in which printing is carried on, a printing-office.

Printing House Square, a small square in London, the site of the office of the *Times* newspaper.

Pri·nting-press. 1587. An instrument or machine for printing on paper, etc., from types, blocks, or plates; sometimes restricted to a hand-press, as dist. from a *printing-machine.*

Prior (prəi·əɹ), *sb.* [OE. *prior*, reinforced in ME. by OFr. *priur, priour* (mod. *prieur*) – L. *prior, -ōr-*, subst. use of *prior* former, elder, superior, compar. of OL. *pri* (L. *præ*, PRE-) before. In med.L. as sb. spec. a prior.] **1.** A superior officer of a religious house or order. **2. a.** In foreign countries, the title of the elected head of a guild of merchants or craftsmen. **b.** The title of a chief magistrate in some of the former Italian republics, e.g. Florence. *Obs.* exc. *Hist.* 1604. **3.** *Commerce.* The head of a firm. Now *rare.* 1853.

1. *Grand P.*, the commander of a priory of the knights of St. John of Jerusalem, or of Malta. Hence **Pri·oral** *a.* **Pri·orship,** the office or dignity of p.

Prior (prəi·əɹ), *a.* (*adv.*) 1714. [– L. *prior*; see prec.] Preceding (in time or order); earlier, former, anterior, antecedent. **B.** as *adv.* with *to*: Previously to, before 1736.

The sin is p. to..the action 1714. A p. marriage 1765.

Priorate (prəi·ŏrĕt). late ME. [– late L. *prioratus* (Gregory) office of a prior (etc.), f. *prior*; see PRIOR *sb.*, -ATE¹.] **1.** The office and dignity of a prior; also, the term of office of a prior. **2.** A priory; also, the inmates as a community 1749.

Prioress (prəi·ŏrĕs). ME. [– OFr. *prioresse* = med.L. *priorissa* (XII), f. as prec.; see -ESS¹.] A nun holding a position similar to that of a prior.

Priority (prəi,ǫ·rĭti). [XIV *priorite* – (O)Fr. *priorité* – med.L. *prioritas*, f. L. *prior* PRIOR *a.*; see -ITY.] **1.** The condition or quality of being earlier in time, or of preceding something else. **2.** Precedence in order, rank, or dignity. late ME. **3.** *Law.* A precedence among claims, or a preference in order of payment 1766.

1. The preeminence of prioritie in birth HOOKER. **2.** *Tr. & Cr.* I. iii. 86.

attrib. **p.-bond** = *preference bond.*

Priory (prəi·ŏri). ME. [– AFr. *priorie* = med.L. *prioria*; see PRIOR *sb.*, -Y³.] A monastery or nunnery governed by a prior or prioress; usu. an offshoot of an abbey on which it was dependent; also, a house of Canons Regular.

Alien p.: see ALIEN *a.* 1.

Prisage (prəi·zĕdʒ). Now *Hist.* 1505. [– AFr. *prisage*, f. *prise* PRISE *sb.* + -AGE.] An ancient custom levied upon imported wine; in later times correlated to and often identified with BUTLERAGE 1. (Abolished 1809.) **b.** *attrib.*, as *p. fund, lease, wine* 1586.

Priscian (pri·ʃ'ăn). 1525. [– L. *Priscianus.*] Name of a celebrated Roman grammarian, *c*500–530.

Phr. *To break Priscian's head*, to violate the rules of grammar.

Priscillianist (prisi·liănist), *sb.* and *a.* 1574. [– Fr. *Priscillianiste* or late and med.L. *Priscillianista*, f. *Priscillianus* Priscillian; see -IST.] **A.** *sb.* A disciple of Priscillian, bishop of Avila, in Spain, in the 4th c., who taught doctrines alleged to be Gnostic or Manichæan. **B.** *adj.* Of or pertaining to the Priscillianists or their doctrines 1887.

Prise (prəiz, ‖prīz). *Obs.* or *Hist.* ME. [– (O)Fr. *prise*, subst. use of fem. pa. pple. of *prendre* take, seize; in AL. *prisa.* See PRIZE *sb.*³] **1.** The taking or seizing of anything by a lord for his own use from his feudal tenants or dependants; a thing requisitioned for the king's use, or for the use of the garrisons in his castles; the right of such seizure. *Obs.* exc. *Hist.* **2.** *pl.* (rarely *sing.*) The king's customs; that is, portions taken by him from goods brought into the realm, or duties levied in lieu thereof 1455.

Prism (priz'm). 1570. [– late L. *prisma*, – Gr. πρῖσμα, -ματ- (Euclid), lit. thing sawn, f. πρίζειν saw.] **1.** *Geom.* A solid figure of which the two ends are similar, equal, and parallel rectilineal figures, and the sides parallelograms. **2.** Any body or object of this form 1661. **3.** *Optics.* A transparent body of this form, usu. a triangular geometrical prism, of which the refracting surfaces are at an acute angle with each other 1612. **b.** Loosely used for a spectrum produced by refraction through a prism: *pl.* prismatic colours 1840. **4.** *Cryst.* A 'form' consisting of three or more planes parallel to the vertical axis of the crystal 1878.

3. *Nicol('s) p.* = NICOL. Hence **Pri·smal** *a.* = next.

Prismatic (prizmæ·tik), *a.* 1709. [– Fr. *prismatique* – Gr. πρῖσμα, -ματ-; see prec., -IC.] **1.** Of or pertaining to a prism; prism-like. **2.** Of or pertaining to the optical prism; formed, effected, separated, or distributed by or as by a transparent prism; hence, of varied colours, bright-coloured, brilliant 1728. **3.** *Cryst.* = ORTHORHOMBIC *a.* 1858.

1. *P. powder*, a gunpowder the grains of which are hexagonal prisms. **2.** *P. colours*, the seven colours into which a ray of white light is separated by a prism. *P. compass*, a surveying compass so arranged that by means of a prism the angle of position of the object sighted can be read at the same time as the object itself is seen. So **Prisma·tical** *a.* 1654; **-ly** *adv.*

Prismatoid (pri·zmătoid), *a.* and *sb.* 1858. [f. Gr. πρῖσμα, -ματ- PRISM + -OID. Cf. Fr. *prismatoïde.*] **A.** *adj. Cryst.* Applied to any plane, in a crystallographic system, parallel to one of the three axes of co-ordinates and intersecting the other two; so called because a group of eight such planes would form a prism. **B.** *sb. Geom.* A solid figure having parallel polygonal ends connected by triangular sides 1890. So **Prismatoi·dal** *a.* resembling a prism; also, = PRISMOIDAL.

Prismoid (pri·zmoid). 1704. [f. PRISM + -OID, app. after *rhomboid.* Cf. Fr. *prismoïde.*] A body approaching in form to a prism, with similar but unequal parallel polygonal bases. Hence **Prismoi·dal** *a.* of the form of, or pertaining to, a p.

Prison (pri·z'n), *sb.* [Early ME. *prisun* – OFr. *prisun*, (also mod.) *prison* :– L. *prensio, -on-*, for *præhensio*, f. *præhendere*; see APPREHEND.] *orig.* The condition of being kept in captivity or confinement; imprisonment; hence, a place in which such confinement is ensured; *spec.* a jail. **a.** Without article. **b.** with *a, the*, etc., or in *pl.* ME. **c.** *transf.* and *fig.* ME.

a. Phr. *To break p.* (BREAK *v.* IV. 3); *to cast, put, set in p.*; *to keep, lay, lie in p.* **b.** There are no prisons in al his empire: for..iustice is executed out of hand 1600. Stone Walls doe not a P. make Nor Iron bars a Cage LOVELACE. *State p.*, (*a*) a p. for the confinement of political offenders; (*b*) *U.S.* a p. under the control of the authorities of a State. **c.** The Island was certainly a P. to me DE FOE.

attrib. and *Comb.*, as *p.-accommodation, camp, -industry*, etc.; also **p.-bars,** the iron bars by which a prison, its door, windows, etc., are made fast; bars which imprison; **-crop,** hair cut very short; **p. editor,** an editor (of a newspaper) who takes the legal responsibility for what appears in the newspaper, and serves the terms of imprisonment that conviction for an offence may entail; **-fever** = JAIL-FEVER; **-van,** a close carriage for the conveyance of prisoners.

Prison (pri·z'n), *v.* ME. [f. prec.] *trans.* To put in prison, make a prisoner of; to keep in a place of confinement; to detain in custody. Now *poet.* or *rhet.*, and *n. dial.* **b.** *transf.* and *fig.* To confine. late ME.

b. His true respect will p. false desire SHAKS.

Prisoner (pri·z'nəɹ). [ME. *presoner, prisoner* – AFr. *prisoner* = OFr. *prisonier* (mod. *-nn-*); see PRISON *sb.*, -ER² 2. Superseded earlier *prison* so used.] **1.** One who is kept in prison or in custody; *spec.* one who is in custody as the result of a legal process. **2.** One who has been captured in war; a captive. Now often *p. of war.* ME. **3.** *transf.* and *fig.* One who or that which is confined to a place or position. late ME. **4.** *attrib.* Of or pertaining to a prisoner; that is a prisoner 1846.

1. Phr. *P. at the bar*, a person in custody upon a criminal charge, and on trial in a court of justice. *P. of state, state p.*, one confined for political or state reasons. **2.** *To take* (a person) *p.*, to seize and hold as a p., esp. in war. **3.** An vntimely Ague Staid me a P. in my Chamber SHAKS.

Prisoners' bars, base. 1801. Earlier †**prison-bars** (1611), **-base** (1598). [See PRISONER and BAR *sb.*¹, BASE *sb.*²] = BASE *sb.*²

Pri·son-house. late ME. A house of imprisonment; a building that is or serves as a prison. Often *fig.*

Pristine (pri·stəin, *U.S.* -in), *a.* 1534. [– L. *pristinus* former; see -INE².] Of or pertaining to the earliest period or state; original, former; primitive, ancient.

To restore it to its p. purity 1782. The p. simplicity of our Saxon-English 1841.

Pritchel (pri·tʃ'l). *dial.* late ME. [Southern form of PRICKLE *sb.*¹] A sharp-pointed instrument or tool; esp. for punching the nail-holes in horse-shoes.

Prithee (pri·ði), *int. phr.* 1577. Archaic colloquialism for '(I) pray thee'.

Pr'ythee don't send us up any more Stories of a Cock and a Bull ADDISON.

Prittle-prattle (pri·t'l,præ:t'l). Now *rare.* 1556. [Reduplicated extension of PRATTLE *sb.*] Trivial, worthless, or idle talk; also, small talk; chatter; childish prattle.

‖**Prius** (prəi·ŏs). 1891. [L., n. of *prior* PRIOR.] **a.** That which takes precedence. **b.** That which is prior, *esp.* that which is a necessary prior condition.

Privacy (prəi·văsi, pri·v-). 1450. [f. PRIVATE *a.*; see -CY.] **1.** The state or condition of being withdrawn from the society of others, or from public interest; seclusion. **2.** *pl.* Private or retired places; private apartments; places of retreat. Now *rare.* 1678. **3.** Absence or avoidance of publicity or display 1598. **4.** A private matter, a secret; *pl.* private or personal matters or relations. Now *rare.* 1591. **5.** = PRIVITY 4 (*rare*) 1719.

1. To guard the independence and p. of their homes EMERSON. **3.** A marriage..solemnised with strict p. in the chapel of Leigh Court 1876.

Private (prəi·vĕt), *a.* and *sb.* late ME. [– L. *privatus* withdrawn from public life, peculiar to oneself, sb. man in private life, prop. pa. pple. of *privare* bereave, deprive, f. *privus* single, individual, private; see -ATE².] **A.** *adj.* **1.** Of a person: Not holding public office or official position. **b.** *P. soldier*: a soldier below the rank of a non-commissioned officer 1579. **c.** *P. member*, a member of the House of Commons who is not a member of the Ministry 1863. **2.** Kept or removed from public view or knowledge; not within the cognizance of people generally 1472. **b.** *P. parts*, the pudenda 1885. **3.** Not open to the public; intended only for the use of particular and privileged persons. late ME. **b.** Not open to the public, or not publicly done or performed, dist. from a thing of the same kind that is 'public' 1560. **4.** That belongs to or is the property of a particular individual; belonging to oneself, one's own 1502. **5.** Of or pertaining to a person in a non-official capacity 1613. **6.** Of, pertaining or relating to, or affecting a person, or a small group of persons apart from the general community; individual, personal 1526. **7.** By one's self, alone; without the presence of any one else 1592. **8.** Of a conversation, etc.: Intended only for the person or persons directly concerned 1560. **9.** Retiring; retired; secluded 1494. †**10.** quasi-*adv.* Privately, secretly –1704.

1. A Woman of Quality; married to a p. Gentleman STEELE. **2.** Lady Alethea's privet wedding 1677. **3.** A p. staircase conducted into the gardens LYTTON. News which reached him through p. channels MACAULAY. **b.** He resygned his crowne, & lyued a holy pryuate lyfe 1526. *P. assembly, function, meeting*, etc.; *p. baptism, communion, education, funeral, marriage*, etc.; *p. boarding-house, brougham, carriage, chapel, hotel, theatricals*, etc. *P. view* (e.g. of an exhibition of pictures or the like). **4.** The institution of p. property 1845. *P. house*, the dwelling-house of a p. person, or of a person in his p. capacity. *P. family*, the family occupying a p. house. *P. school*, a school owned and carried on by a person or persons for their own profit. *P. judgement*: see JUDGEMENT 7. **5.** A tribute to p. worth and public usefulness 1864. **6.** For your priuate satisfaction..I will let you know SHAKS. Phr. *P. bill, act*, a parliamentary bill or act affecting the interests of a particular individual or corporation only. **8.** P. Confession is retained in the reformed churches 1650. A letter..marked 'p.' TROLLOPE. **10.** Every body now drink the King's health.. whereas before, it was very p. that a man dare do it PEPYS.

B. *sb.* **I.** Of a person. †**1.** A private person –1671. †**b.** *The p.*: private people, opp. to *the public* –1734. †**2.** An intimate, a favourite. (With play on sense II. 3) SHAKS. **3.** A private soldier 1781. **II.** Of things or affairs. †**1.** A private matter, business, or interest; *pl.* private affairs –1642. †**2.** Retirement, privacy –1653. **b.** *In p.*, privately, not publicly; in private company; in private life 1581. **3.** *pl.* The private parts.

2. Go off, I discard you: let me enjoy my priuate SHAKS. **b.** Laugh and spare not So't be in priuate 1615. Hence **Pri·vate-ly** *adv.*, **-ness** (now *rare*).

Privateer (prəivătīᵊ·ɹ), *sb.* 1664. [f. PRIVATE *a.* + -EER, after *volunteer*; earlier called *private man of war*.] **1.** An armed vessel owned and officered by private persons, and holding a commission from the government, called 'letters of marque', authorizing the owners to use it against a hostile nation, and esp. in the capture of merchant shipping. **2.** The commander, or *pl.* the crew, of such a vessel 1674. **3.** *attrib.*, as *p. brig*, etc. 1675.

2. Privateers were little scrupulous as to what kind of victim they pounced upon 1883. Hence **Privatee·r** *v. rare, intr.* to practise privateering. **Privatee·ring** *vbl. sb.* the occupation of a p.; often *attrib.*; also *fig.* **Privatee·rsman** (*U.S.*), an officer or seaman of a p.

Privation (prəivē¹·ʃən). ME. [– L. *privatio*, f. *privat-*, pa. ppl. stem of *privare*; see PRIVATE, -ION.] **1.** The action of depriving or taking away; the fact or condition of being deprived *of* or †cut off *from* something; deprivation. Now *rare*. **b.** *Law.* = DEPRIVATION 2; in *R. C. Ch.* = SUSPENSION. Now *rare* or *Obs.* late ME. **2.** *Logic.* The condition of being without some attribute formerly or properly possessed; the loss, or (loosely) the mere absence of a quality, a negative quality. late ME. **3.** Want of the usual comforts, or esp. of some of the necessaries of life 1790.

1. All general privations are great because they are all terrible; Vacuity, Darkness, Solitude, and Silence BURKE. **2.** Cold, which is the p. of heat EMERSON. **3.** A needy band of mercenaries, urged by hunger and p. 1845.

Privative (pri·vătiv), *a.* (*sb.*) 1588. [– Fr. *privatif, -ive* or L. *privativus* denoting privation, f. as prec.; see -IVE.] **1.** Having the quality of depriving; tending to take away 1600. **2.** Consisting in or characterized by the taking away or removal of something, or by the loss or (loosely) absence of some quality or attribute normally or presumably present 1598. **3.** Of terms: Denoting or predicating privation, or (loosely) absence of a quality or attribute 1646. **4.** *Gram.* Expressing privation or negation; esp. applied to a particle or affix (e.g. the Greek prefix α-) 1590. **B.** *sb.* A privative attribute, quality, proposition, word, or particle 1588.

1. If the thing should become p. of, or opposite to, the publick good 1650. Hence **Pri·vative-ly** *adv.*, **-ness** (*rare*).

Privet (pri·vėt). 1542. [Obscurely rel. to contemp. synon. *primprint* (Turner, Lyte), abbrev. (dial.) *prim, primp*; of unkn. origin.] **1.** A bushy evergreen shrub, *Ligustrum vulgare* (N.O. *Oleaceæ*), a native of Europe, having elliptic-lanceolate smooth dark-green leaves, and clusters of small white flowers, succeeded by small shining black berries; much used for garden hedges. **2.** Applied to other species of *Ligustrum*, and other shrubs resembling p. 1597.

2. Egyptian p. = HENNA; **Evergreen p.**, any evergreen species of the genus *Rhamnus*; **Mock p.**, the evergreen genus PHILLYREA, N.O. *Oleaceæ*. *Comb.* **p. hawk (-moth)**, a large species of hawk-moth which deposits its eggs on the p.

Privilege (pri·vĭlėdʒ), *sb.* [Early ME. *privilegie, privilege* – AFr. **privilegie*, (O)Fr. *privilège* – L. *privilegium* legal provision affecting an individual, prerogative, f. *privus* (see PRIVATE) + *lex, leg-* law.] **1.** *Rom. Antiq.* A special ordinance having reference to an individual 1483. **2.** A right, advantage, or immunity granted to or enjoyed by a person, or class of persons, beyond the common advantages of others ME. **b.** In extended sense: A special advantage, with ref. to divine dispensations, gifts of fortune, etc. ME. †**c.** Advantage yielded, superiority SHAKS. **3.** A privileged position; the possession of an advantage over others or another. late ME. **4.** The special right or immunity attaching to some office, rank, or station; prerogative ME. **5.** *R. C. Ch.* A special ordinance issued by the Pope, granting exemption from all such acts as are necessary for the purpose for which it is obtained. late ME. **6.** A grant of special rights or immunities to an individual, corporation, community, or place; a franchise, monopoly, patent; †*spec.* the sole right of printing or publishing a book or the like. late ME. †**7.** The right of affording security from arrest, attached to certain places; the right of asylum or sanctuary –1683.

2. A monopoly of privileges is always invidious 1879. **b.** All the greater Prophets claimed..the p. of married life 1862. **3.** Inequalities of legal p. between individuals or classes MILL. **4.** *The p.*, the royal prerogative. *P. of clergy* = *benefit of clergy*: see CLERGY 5. *P. of Parliament*, the immunities enjoyed by either house of parliament, or by individual members, as such. *Bill of p.*, a petition of a peer demanding to be tried by his peers. *Writ of p.*, a writ to deliver a privileged person from custody when arrested in a civil suit.

Privilege (pri·vĭlėdʒ), *v.* ME. [– (O)Fr. *privilégier* – med.L. *privilegiare*, f. *privilegium*; see prec.] **1.** *trans.* To invest with a privilege or privileges; to invest (a thing) with special honourable distinctions. **2.** To authorize, license (what is otherwise forbidden); to justify, excuse 1592. **3.** To exempt *from* a liability or burden to which others are subject 1542.

2. Kings cannot p. what God forbade DANIEL. **3.** Some things are priuiledged from iest BACON.

Privileged (pri·vĭlėdʒd), *ppl. a.* late ME. [f. prec. vb. or sb. + -ED.] Invested with or enjoying certain privileges or immunities.

P. communication, in *Law*, (*a*) a communication which a witness cannot be legally compelled to divulge; (*b*) a communication made between such persons and in such circumstances that it is not actionable, unless made with malice. **P. debt**, a debt having a prior claim to satisfaction. **P. share, stock**, preference stock.

Privity (pri·vĭti). Now chiefly *techn.* (in Law, etc.). [ME. *privete, -ite* – OFr. *priveté, -ité* – med.L. *privitas*, f. *privus*; see PRIVATE, -ITY.] †**1.** A thing that is kept hidden or secret –1625. †**2.** The condition of being private; privacy, seclusion –1661. **3.** The private parts. Chiefly in *pl.* Now *rare*. late ME. **4.** The fact of being privy to something; participation in the knowledge of something private or secret, usu. implying concurrence or consent; private knowledge or cognizance 1560. **5.** *Law.* Any relation between two parties recognized by law, e.g. that of blood, covenant, tenure, service, etc.; mutual interest in any transaction or thing 1523.

1. Yet neither shewed to other their hearts p. SPENSER.

Privy (pri·vi), *a.* and *sb. arch.* or *techn.* (in Law, etc.). [ME. *prive, privey, privy* – (O)Fr. *privé* (as sb. in OFr., familiar friend, private place) :– L. *privatus* PRIVATE; see -Y⁵.] **A.** *adj.* **I.** †**1.** That is of one's own private circle or companionship; intimate, familiar –1645. **2.** = PRIVATE *a.* 4. *Obs.* exc. in P. CHAMBER, COUNCIL, COUNCILLOR, SEAL. ME. **3.** Participating in the knowledge of something secret or private; in the secret; accessory to some secret transaction. late ME.

3. The clergy believed that they alone were p. to the counsels of the Almighty 1862.

II. 1. Withdrawn from public sight, knowledge, or use; kept secret; hidden; secluded. *arch.* ME. **2.** Acting or done in secret or by stealth; clandestine, furtive, surreptitious, sly. *arch.* ME.

1. In at a preuy posterne gate, By night she stale 1440. **2.** From all sedicion and priuye conspiracie..Good lorde deliuer us *Bk. Com. Prayer.* Collocations with sbs. **P. parts** (see PRIVATE *a.* 2 b). **P. purse. a.** The allowance from the public revenue for the private expenses of the monarch. **b.** Short for *Keeper of the P. Purse*, an officer of the royal household charged with the payment of the private expenses of the sovereign. **P. signet:** see SIGNET. **P. verdict**, a verdict given to the judge out of court.

B. *sb.* [The adj. used absol. or ellipt.] **I.** *Law.* One who is a partaker or has any part or interest in any action, matter, or thing 1483. **II. 1.** A private place of ease, a latrine. late ME. †**2.** That which is secret, secrecy; in phr. *in p.*, in secret, covertly –1569. Hence **Pri·vily** *adv.* (now *arch.* or *literary*).

Pri:vy cha·mber. Now *Hist.* late ME. [PRIVY *a.* I. 2.] **1.** *gen.* A private room, in which one is not liable to interruption or disturbance. Also *fig. Obs.* or *arch.* **2.** *spec.* A private apartment in a royal residence 1540.

Pri:vy cou·ncil. [ME. *prive counseil* = OFr. *privé conseil*, med.L. *consilium privatum*; see PRIVY *a.* I. 2, COUNCIL *sb.*] †**1.** *gen.* A private consultation or assembly for consultation –1825. **2.** The private counsellors of the sovereign; *spec.* in Great Britain a body of advisers selected by the sovereign, together with certain persons who are members by usage, as the princes of the blood, the archbishops, and the chief officers of the present and past ministries of state 1450. **b.** Applied to a council of state in a foreign country, etc. 1450. **c.** A similar body formed to assist the Lord Lieutenant of Ireland, and the governors of some British colonies or dominions 1765.

Pri:vy cou·nsellor, cou·ncillor. [ME. *prive counseiller*; see PRIVY *a.* I. 2 and COUNSELLOR; often spelt *councillor* after prec.; but *counsellor* is the official form.] **1.** A private or confidential adviser. **2.** *spec.* in Great Britain: One of the private counsellors of the sovereign; a member of the Privy Council 1647. Hence **Pri:vy-Cou·nsellorship, -Cou·ncillorship.**

Pri:vy sea·l. late ME. [– AFr. *prive seal* = AL. *privatum sigillum*; see PRIVY *a.* I. 2.] **1.** The seal affixed to documents that are afterwards to pass the Great Seal; also to documents of less importance which do not require the Great Seal. **2.** A document to which the privy seal is affixed; *spec.* a warrant, under the privy seal, demanding a loan; hence *transf.* a forced loan, a benevolence. Now only *Hist.* late ME. **3.** The keeper of the privy seal; now *Lord Privy Seal*. late ME.

1. *Keeper of the privy seal*: see KEEPER 1.

Prizable, prizeable (prəi·zăb'l), *a.* Now chiefly *dial.* 1569. [f. PRIZE *v.*¹ + -ABLE.] Worthy to be prized; valuable.

Prize (prəiz), *sb.*¹ ME. [Variant, now differentiated in spelling and pronunciation, of ME. *pris, prise* PRICE *sb.* (The mod. spelling appears *c*1600.)] **1.** A reward, trophy, or symbol of victory or superiority in any contest or competition. **b.** In colleges, schools, etc.: A reward in the form of money, books, or the like, given to the pupil who excels in attainments 1752. **c.** A premium offered to the person who exhibits the best specimens of natural productions, works of art, or manufactures, at a competition, or at an exhibition 1775. **2.** A sum of money or a thing of value, offered for competition by chance or hazard 1567. **3.** *fig.* Anything striven for or worth striving for; a thing of value won by or inspiring effort 1606. †**b.** An advantage, privilege; something prized –1638. **4.** *attrib.* That gains a prize; *fig.* such as would or might gain a prize; first-class 1803.

1. We overvalue the p. for which we contend HUME. *Consolation p.*, a p. won in a consolation match; see CONSOLATION 1. **c.** The first p. for 12 Ranunculuses 1845. **2.** A twenty thousand p. in the lottery 1842. **3.** Place, ritches, and fauour, Prizes of accident as oft as merit SHAKS. **b.** Tis warres prise to take all auantages SHAKS. **4.** A P. Essay 1803. There was a p. ox, a p. pig, and ploughman BYRON.

Comb.: **p.-fellowship,** a fellowship in a college given as a reward for eminence in an examination; hence **-fellow; -list,** a list of the winners of prizes in any competition; **-medal,** a medal offered or gained as a p.

†**Prize,** *sb.*[2] 1565. [perh. transf. use of prec.; cf. Gr. ἄθλον 'prize', also 'contest'.] A contest, match; a public athletic contest; *pl.* the public games of the Greeks and Romans; in late use, a prize-fight. –1715.

Here we saw a p. fought between a soldier and a country fellow PEPYS. Phr. *To play a p.*, to engage in a match, esp. a fencing-match; also (*fig.*) *to play one's p.*, to play one's part.

Prize (prəiz), *sb.*[3] late ME. [– (O)Fr. *prise* capture, booty, captured vessel or cargo; see PRISE. In origin, a special sense of PRISE, which late in XVI began to be phonetically spelt *prize*, and thus to be identified with PRIZE *sb.*[1]] †**1.** The action of taking; capture, seizure –1721. **2.** Anything seized or captured, esp. in war; booty, plunder; a captive of war. *Obs.* exc. as in b. late ME. **b.** *esp.* A ship or property captured at sea in virtue of the rights of war 1512. **c.** without *a* or *pl.* Property seized as in war; esp. in the phr. *to make p.* 1594. **d.** In *good, fair, free, just, lawful p.*, with ref. to the legality of the seizure 1550.

2. b. They took a p. of nine hundred tunnes PURCHAS. **c.** P. or not P., must be determined by Courts of Admiralty 1755.

Comb.: **p. court,** a department of the admiralty court, which adjudicates concerning prizes; **p. crew,** a crew of seamen put on board a prize ship to bring her into port; **-list,** a list of persons entitled to receive prize-money on the capture of a ship; **-money,** money realized by the sale of a p., and distributed among the captors.

Prize, prise (prəiz), *sb.*[4] [XIV *prise* – (O)Fr. *prise* grasp, seizure, PRIZE *sb.*[3] Cf. PRY *sb.*[2], *v.*[2]] **1.** An instrument for prizing; a lever. Now *dial.* **2.** The act of prizing; leverage, purchase 1835.

Prize (prəiz), *v.*[1] [XIV *prise* (earlier Sc. *priss*) – *pris-*, tonic stem of OFr. *preisier* PRAISE *v.*] †**1.** *trans.* To value; to account as worth (so much); to account, reckon –1724. †**2.** To fix the money value of; to appraise; to fix the price of (a thing for sale). Now PRICE –1755. **3.** To value or esteem highly; to think much of. late ME.

3. P. your time now, while you have it 1720. Hence **Pri·zer**[1], one who prizes (now *rare*).

Prize, *v.*[2] 1535. [f. PRIZE *sb.*[3]] *trans.* To seize, take, capture; to seize as forfeited, to confiscate. *Obs.* exc. as in b. **b.** *spec.* To seize (a ship or her cargo) as a prize of war 1568.

Prize, prise (prəiz), *v.*[3] 1686. [f. PRIZE *sb.*[4]] *trans.* To raise or move by force of leverage; *esp.* to force open in this way.

Prize-fight (prəi·zfəi:t). 1824. [Back-formation from next.] A public contest between prize-fighters; a boxing-match for money.

Prize-fighter (prəi·zfəi:təɹ). 1703. [orig. f. PRIZE *sb.*[2] + FIGHTER, from the phr. 'to fight a prize'; now assoc. with PRIZE *sb.*[1]] †**a.** *orig.* One who engaged in a public fighting-match or contest. **b.** A professional pugilist or boxer, who fights publicly for a prize or stake. So **Pri·ze-fi:ghting** *sb.* and *a.*

Prizeman (prəi·zmæ̆n). 1800. [f. PRIZE *sb.*[1] + MAN *sb.*] A man who wins a prize.

Pri·zer[2]. *arch.* 1599. [f. PRIZE *sb.*[2] + -ER[1].] One who engages in a 'prize' or contest; a prize-fighter.

And fought like prizers, not as angry rivals 1679.

Prize-ring (prəi·z,ri:ŋ). 1840. [f. after PRIZE-FIGHT; see RING *sb.*[1]] A ring or enclosed space (now a square area enclosed by poles and ropes) for prize-fighting; hence *transf.* the practice of prize-fighting.

‖**Pro**[1] (prōᵘ). late ME. The L. prep. *pro* before, in front of, for, on behalf of, instead of, in return for, on account of, etc. **A.** as *prep.* in various L. phrases, used in Eng.

1. pro aris et focis (ēᵊ·ris et fōᵘ·sis), for altars and hearths; for the sake of, or on behalf of, religion and home 1621. **2. pro bono publico** (bōᵘ·no pʊ·bliko) for the public good 1726. **3. pro fo·rma,** for form's sake; as a matter of form. Also *attrib.* 1573. **4. pro hac vice** (hæk vəi·si), for this turn or occasion (only) 1653. **4. pro rata** (rēⁱ·tă) [= 'according to the rate': RATE *sb.*[1] 2], in proportion to the value or extent (of his interest); proportionally. Also *attrib.* or as *adj.*, proportional. 1575. **6. pro re nata** (rī nēⁱ·tă), 'for the affair born, i.e. arisen'; for an occasion as it arises. Also *attrib.* 1578. **7. pro tanto** (tæ·nto), 'for so much', so far, to such an extent. Also *attrib.* 1780. **8. pro tempore** (te·mpŏri), for the time, temporarily; *attrib.* or as *adj.* temporary. (Abbreviated *pro tem.*)

B. as *sb.* An argument for or in favour of something, as opp. to one against it. (Now usu. in PRO AND CON.) **b.** A person who sides or votes in favour of some proposal. late ME.

Pro.[2] 1848. Familiar abbrev. of various compounds of PRO- *prefix*[1], esp. *proproctor* and *professional*.

Pro-, *prefix*[1]. The L. adv. and prep. (see above) used in comb. with verbs and their derivs., and occas. with other words not of verbal derivation.

A large number of L. wds. so formed were taken into English through French. In later times words of this kind have been adopted or adapted in Eng. directly from L., or have been formed from L. elements.

I. As an etymological element.

1. a. Forward, to or towards the front, from a position in the rear, forth, out, into a public position; as PROCLAIM, PRODUCE, PROJECT, PROMINENT, etc. **b.** To the front of, down before (the face of), forward and down; as PROCUMBENT, PROFLIGATE, PROSTRATE, etc. **c.** Forth from its place, away; as PRODIGAL, etc. **d.** Forward, onward, in a course or in time; as PROCEED, PROCRASTINATE, PROGRESS, PROPEL, etc. **e.** Out, with outward extension; as PROLIX, PROPAGATE, PROTRACT, etc. **f.** Before in place, in front of; as PROSCRIBE, PROTECT. **g.** Before in time, in anticipation of, in provision for; as PRODIGY, PROVIDE, etc. **h.** For, in preparation for, on behalf of; as PROCURE, PROFIT, etc. **i.** With worn-down or obscure force; as PROFANE, PROFOUND, PROMISCUOUS, PROVERB, PROVINCE, etc.

2. Freq. prefixed in L. to names of relationship, answering to Eng. 'great' or 'grand'; as *avus* grandfather, *pro-avus* great-grandfather; etc. So †**pro·nephew** (*Sc.*), a great-grandson.

II. As a living prefix.

1. In Latin, *pro-*, in the sense 'for', 'instead of', 'in place of', was prefixed to a sb., app. orig. in prepositional construction, as *pro consule* (one acting) for a consul, subseq. combined with the sb., as *proconsul* = deputy-consul; etc.; so in a few names of things, as *pronomen* PRONOUN, etc. English has examples of *pro-* prefixed **a.** to names of persons, 'acting as deputy', as PROCONSUL, PROPROCTOR, etc. **b.** to names of things, as PROCATHEDRAL, etc. **2.** In sense 'for, in favour of, on the side of'. This use has no precedent or analogy in Latin, and appears to have arisen from the use of *pro* in PRO B. b. **a.** Prefixed to a sb., sb. phr., or adj., forming adjs. with sense 'favouring or siding with (what is indicated by the second element)'; as *pro-Boer, -clerical, -tariff reform,* etc. Some of these are also used as sbs., as *pro-Boer* = 'one who is on the side of the Boers'. **b.** In comb. with a sb. (or verb-stem) + -ER or -ITE, forming a nonce-sb., in sense 'one who sides with..'; as *pro-flogger* (one who favours flogging), *pro-liquorite* (one in favour of the unrestricted sale of alcoholic drinks). **c.** In comb. with a sb. or adj. + -ISM, forming abstract sbs. = 'the principle or character of being in favour of..', as *pro-Boerism, -clericalism,* etc.

Pro- (proᵘ), *prefix*[2], repr. Gr. prep. πρό before (of time, position, preference, priority, etc.), forming in Gr. many compounds—vbs., sbs., and adjs. Many of these forms, as latinized, have been adopted or adapted in the modern languages generally, in the nomenclature of modern science and philosophy.

1. In sense 'Before in time': forming (*a*) sbs., chiefly scientific terms denominating the earlier, or (supposed) primitive type of an animal, plant, organ, or structure (with derived adjs.); (*b*) adjs. meaning 'previous to or preceding that which is expressed by the second element'. **Probouleu·tic** *a. Gr. Hist.* that deliberates preliminarily; *spec.* applied to the Athenian senate, which discussed measures before they were submitted to the Assembly. ‖**Proca·mbium** [CAMBIUM], *Bot.* the young tissue of a fibrovascular bundle, before its differentiation into permanent cells of wood, bast, etc. ‖**Proempto·sis** [Gr. ἔμπτωσις] an anticipation or occurrence of a natural event earlier than the time given by a rule; esp. the occurrence of the new moon earlier than the Metonic cycle would make it. **Promorpho·logy,** *Biol.* the morphology of fundamental forms; the branch of morphology that treats of organic forms from a mathematical standpoint. **Pro·-ode,** an introductory ode in a Greek chorus; an overture or prelude. **Proparo·xytone** *a. Gram.* having an acute accent on the antepenult; *sb.* a word so accented. **Pro·plasm** [PLASM], a mould, a matrix (*rare*). **Prosi·phon** [SIPHON], *Zool.* the primitive siphon in an embryonic ammonite, a kind of ligament attached to the protoconch. ‖**Protha·llium, -tha·llus,** *Bot.* in vascular cryptogams, a minute cellular structure or thallus, bearing the sexual organs, forming the first of the two alternate generations, much simpler than the fully-developed (asexual) plant. ‖**Protrachea·ta** *sb. pl., Zool.* a class of arthropodous animals (representing the supposed ancestral form of all the tracheate *Arthropoda*), represented by the single genus *Peripatus*.

2. Of local position; forming sbs. and adjs., chiefly anatomical and zoological terms (often correlated with words in META- and MESO-); (*a*) in adjectival relation to the second element, denoting either 'an anterior or front (thing of the kind)', or 'an anterior or front part (of the thing)'; (*b*) in prepositional relation to the second element = 'lying before or in front of (the thing)'. **Procepha·lic** [Gr. κεφαλή] *a., Zool.* belonging to the fore part of the head; applied to certain lobes or processes in Crustacea and other Arthropoda. **Pro·cerite** [Gr. κέρας horn], *Zool.* the many-jointed terminal segment of the antenna in certain Crustacea, as lobsters. **Procho·rdal** *a., Embryol.* anterior to the notochord. **Procœ·lian** [Gr. κοῖλος hollow] *a.*, having procœlous vertebræ; pertaining to the *Procœlia*, a suborder of *Crocodilia*. **Procœlous** (-sī·ləs) *a.*, concave or cupped in front: applied to vertebræ. ‖**Proglo·ttis** [Gr. προγλωσσίς point of the tongue], a sexually mature segment or joint of a tapeworm. ‖**Prone·phron, -ne·phros** [Gr. νεφρός kidney], the anterior division of the primitive kidney or segmental organ in the embryos of lower vertebrates. ‖**Prono·tum** [NOTUM], *Entom.* the dorsal part of the prothorax of an insect; the anterior division of the notum. ‖**Pro-·ostracum** [Gr. ὄστρακον potsherd], *Palæont.* the anterior prolongation, usu. lamellar, of the guard or rostrum of a fossil cephalopod. **Pro-o·tic** *a.*, that is in front of the ear; applied distinctively to one of the three bones which together form the periotic capsule; *sb.* the pro-otic bone. **Pro·podite** [Gr. ποδ- foot], *Zool.* the penultimate joint of a developed endapodite limb, as of a crustacean. ‖**Propo·dium,** the anterior lobe of the foot in some molluscs; hence **Propo·dial** *a.* ‖**Propterygium,** *Ichthyol.* the anterior cartilaginous portion of the fin in elasmobranch fishes. ‖**Proso·ma** [Gr. σῶμα body], *Zool.* the anterior or cephalic segment of the body in certain animals, as cephalopods, etc. ‖**Prosto·mium,** *Zool.* the part of the body situated in front of the mouth in certain invertebrates.

Proa (prōᵘ·ă), ‖**prahu** (prā·u). 1582. [– Malay *p*(*ă*)*rā*(*h*)*ū* a boat.] A Malay boat propelled by sails or by oars; *spec.* a sailing boat of the type used in the Malay archipelago.

Pro and con. late ME. [Earlier *pro and* or *et contra* for and against; i.e. L. *pro* PRO[1], *et* and, CONTRA.] **A.** *adv. phr.* For and against; on both sides. So *pro or con.*

The matter throughly handled *Pro* and *Con* 1572.

B. *sb. phr.* (now always in pl., *pros and cons.*) Reasons for and against; reasonings, arguments, statements, or votes on both sides of a question 1589.

Stating all the pros and cons of the case 1880.

C. *vb.* To weigh the arguments for and against; to debate both sides of a question 1694.

Wasted a precious minute in pro-and-conning 1835.

Probabiliorism (prŏbăbi·liŏriz'm). 1845. [f. L. *probabilior* more probable + -ISM.] The doctrine of the probabiliorists; according to which it is claimed, in opposition to probabilism, that that side on which the evidence preponderates is more probably right and therefore ought to be followed. So **Probabi·liorist,** one who holds the doctrine of p. 1727.

Probabilism (prǫ·băbiliz'm). 1842. [f. L. *probabilis* PROBABLE + -ISM.] **1.** *R. C. Casuistry.* The doctrine that in matters of conscience on which authorities differ, it is lawful to follow any course in support of which the authority of a recognized doctor of the Church can be cited. **2.** *Philos.* The theory that there is no absolutely certain knowledge, but that there may be grounds of belief sufficient for practical life 1902. So **Pro·babilist,** one who holds the casuistic doctrine of probabilism 1657; one who holds the philosophical theory of probabilism 1847.

Probability (prǫbăbi·lĭti). 1551. [– (O)Fr. *probabilité* or L. *probabilitas*, f. *probabilis*; see PROBABLE, -ITY.] **1.** The quality or fact of being probable; likelihood. **2.** A probable event, circumstance, belief, etc.; something which, judged by present evidence, is likely to be true, to exist, or to happen 1576. **3.** *Math.* As a measurable quantity: The amount of antecedent likelihood of a particular event, as measured by the relative frequency of occurrence of events of the same kind in the whole course of experience 1718.

1. Phr. *In p.*, probably; considering what is probable. (Now always *in all p.*) **2.** Wolsey's return to power was discussed openly as a p. 1856.

Probabilize (prǫ·băbiləiz), *v.* 1802. [f. L. *probabilis* + -IZE.] *trans.* To render probable.

Probable (prǫ·băb'l), *a.* (*sb.*) late ME. [– (O)Fr. *probable* – L. *probabilis* provable, credible, f. *probare*; see PROVE, -ABLE.] **1.** Capable of being proved; demonstrable, provable. Now *rare.* 1485. †**2.** Such as to approve itself to the mind; worthy of acceptance or belief; rarely in bad sense, specious, colourable. (Now merged in 3.) –1872. **3.** Having an appearance of truth; that may reasonably be expected to happen, or to prove true; likely 1606. **B.** as *sb.* †Something p., a probability; a probable (member, candidate, etc.) 1647.

1. Neither proved nor p. GROTE. **2.** He assigns the most p. reasons for that opinion 1780. **3.** This was the more p. solution 1891. Hence **Pro·bably** *adv.*

Probang (prōᵘ·bæŋ). 1657. [The inventor's name was *provang*, of unkn. origin; subseq. altered, prob. after PROBE *sb.*] *Surg.* A long slender strip of whalebone with a sponge, ball, button, etc. at the end, for introducing into the throat to apply a remedy or to remove a foreign body.

Probate (prōᵘ·bĕt), *sb.* late ME. [– L. *probatum* thing proved, subst. use of n. pa. pple. of *probare* PROVE; see -ATE¹.] †**1.** The act of proving or fact of being proved; that which proves; proof; evidence –1842. **2.** *Law.* The official proving of a will; also, the officially verified copy of a will together with the certificate of its having been proved, which are delivered to the executors 1463.

attrib. **P. Act,** an English statute passed in 1857, by which the jurisdiction of p. and administration was removed from eccl. and other courts, and transferred to a new Court of P. **P. court,** a court having jurisdiction of p. and administration. **P. judge,** a judge having jurisdiction in probate and testamentary causes.

Probate (prōᵘ·beᵉt), *v.* 1792. [– *probat-*, pa. ppl. stem of L. *probare*; see prec., -ATE³.] *trans.* To obtain probate of, to prove (a will). Now chiefly *U.S.*

Probation (prŏbēⁱ·ʃən). late ME. [– (O)Fr. *probation* or L. *probatio*, f. as prec.: see -ION.] **I.** †**1.** The action or process of testing or putting to the proof; trial, experiment; investigation, examination. *Obs.* (exc. as in 2). –1865. **2.** The testing or trial of a person's conduct, character, or moral qualifications; a proceeding designed to ascertain these: esp. in ref. to the period or state of trial. **a.** Of a candidate for membership in a religious body, order, or society, for holy orders, for fellowship in a college, etc. late ME. **b.** In theological and religious use: Moral trial or discipline; the divinely appointed testing of character and principle, esp. as taking place in this life in view of a future state of rewards and punishments 1526. **c.** *gen.* 1616. **3.** In criminal jurisdiction: A system of releasing on suspended sentence during good behaviour young persons, and esp. first offenders, and placing them under the supervision of a *p. officer*, who acts as a friend and adviser 1897.

2. b. Of the various views under which human life has been considered, no one seems so reasonable as that which regards it as a state of p. PALEY. **c.** For a yeare of probacion of his manners and good behavior 1616.

II. The action of proving or showing to be true; proof, demonstration; an instance of this. Now *rare* or *Obs.* exc. *Sc.* 1475. †**b.** = PROBATE *sb.* 2. –1590.

attrib. and *Comb.*, as *p. sermon*; *p.-state*; *p. law, officer, system*; etc. Hence **Proba·tionship,** a state or condition of p.; a term or period of p. (*rare*).

Probationary (prŏbēⁱ·ʃənări), *a.* 1664. [f. as prec. + -ARY².] **1.** Of, pertaining or relating to, or serving for probation; made, performed, or observed in the way of probation. **2.** Undergoing probation; that is a probationer; consisting of probationers 1818.

Probationer (prŏbēⁱ·ʃənəɹ). 1603. [f. as prec. + -ER²; cf. AL. *probationarius* (XVI).] A person on probation or trial; a candidate; a novice. **b.** *spec.* (*a*) A candidate for a fellowship in a college, admitted on probation 1609. (*b*) A novice in a religious house or order 1629. (*c*) A candidate for the ministry of a church, etc.; one licensed to preach but not yet ordained 1645. (*d*) In criminal jurisdiction, an offender under probation 1907. **c.** *transf.* and *fig.* 1642. **d.** *attrib.*: chiefly *appositive* = that is a probationer 1649.

He is still a Prentise and a p. FLORIO. **c.** To make my selfe a canting P. of orisons MILT. **d.** A p. nurse at Poplar Hospital 1905. Hence **Proba·tionership,** the position or condition of a p.

Probative (prōᵘ·bătiv), *a.* 1453. [– L. *probativus*, f. *probat-*; see PROBATE *v.*, -IVE.] **1.** Having the quality or function of testing; serving for trial or probation; probationary. Now *rare.* **2.** Having the quality or function of proving or demonstrating; affording proof or evidence 1681.

Probatory (prōᵘ·bătŏri), *a.* 1593. [– med.L. *probatorius*, f. as prec.; see -ORY².] = PROBATIVE. Now *rare.*

Probe (prōᵘb), *sb.* 1580. [– late L. *proba* proof, med.L. examination, f. L. *probare* PROVE *v.*] **1.** A surgical instrument, commonly of silver, with a blunt end, for exploring the direction and depth of wounds and sinuses. **2.** *transf.* **a.** The proboscis of an insect 1664. **b.** *Angling.* A baiting-needle 1681. **3.** [f. PROBE *v.*] An act of probing; a piercing or boring 1890. **b.** *fig.* (*U.S.*) An inquiry, investigation 1921.

attrib. and *Comb.*: **p.-needle,** a needle used in the manner of a p.; **-scissors,** scissors used for opening wounds, having a button on the point of the blade.

Probe (prōᵘb), *v.* 1649. [f. PROBE *sb.*; occas. infl. by L. *probare.*] **1.** *trans.* To explore (a wound or cavity of the body) with a probe. Also with the person as obj. 1687. **2.** *fig.* To search into, so as thoroughly to explore, or to discover or ascertain something; to try, prove, sound; to interrogate closely 1649. **3.** *transf.* To pierce or penetrate with something sharp, esp. in order to test or explore 1789. **4.** *intr.* To perform the action of piercing with or as with a probe; to penetrate, as a probe 1835.

1. I probed him carefully, and found no Stone 1758. **2.** Stand firm, while I p. your prejudices BERKELEY.

Probity (prǫ·bĭti, proᵘ·b-). 1514. [– Fr. *probité* or L. *probitas*, f. *probus* good, honest; see -ITY.] Moral excellence, integrity, rectitude, uprightness; conscientiousness, honesty, sincerity.

Of much reputation for p. and integrity of life CLARENDON.

Problem (prǫ·blĕm, -əm). late ME. [– (O)Fr. *problème* or L. *problema* – Gr. πρόβλημα; f. προβάλλειν put forth, f. πρό PRO-² + βάλλειν throw.] †**1.** A difficult question proposed for solution; a riddle; an enigmatic statement –1602. **2.** A question proposed for academic discussion or scholastic disputation. *Obs.* exc. *Hist.* 1529. **b.** *Logic.* The question involved in a syllogism, and of which the conclusion is the solution or answer 1656. **3.** A doubtful or difficult question; a matter of inquiry, discussion, or thought 1594. **4.** *Geom.* A proposition in which something is required to be done; opp. to *theorem* 1570. **5.** *Physics* and *Math.* A question or inquiry which starting from some given conditions investigates some fact, result, or law 1570. **6.** *Chess.* An arrangement of pieces upon the chessboard, in which the player is challenged to discover the method of accomplishing a specified result 1817. **7.** *attrib.*, as *p. drama, novel, play*, etc.

3. Elizabeth..had hardly mounted the throne.. when she faced the p. of social discontent 1874. Hence **Pro·blemist,** one who devotes himself to, studies, or composes problems 1615.

Problematic (prǫblĕmæ·tik, -bləm-), *a.* 1609. [– Fr. *problématique* or late L. *problematicus* – Gr. προβληματικός, f. πρόβλημα; see prec., -IC.] **1.** Of the nature of a problem; presenting a problem; difficult of solution or decision; doubtful, questionable. **2.** *Logic.* Enunciating or supporting what is possible but not necessarily true 1610. **3.** *Chess.* Of or relating to problems 1890.

Problematical (prǫblĕmæ·tikăl, -bləm-), *a.* 1588. [f. as prec.; see -ICAL.] **1.** = prec. 1. 1611. **2.** = prec. 2. 1588.

1. A very p. assertion 1815. A dialect of peculiar and p. character 1875. **2.** *P. question*, a question put forth merely for discussion, but not of any practical bearing; an academic question. Hence **Problema·tically** *adv.*

Problematist (prǫ·blĕmătist). 1668. [f. Gr. πρόβλημα, -ματ- PROBLEM + -IST.] One who occupies himself with problems.

‖**Proboscidea** (prǫbǫsi·dĭă), *sb. pl.* 1836. [mod.L. n. pl., f. L. *proboscis*, *-id-* PROBOSCIS; see -A 4.] *Zool.* An order of mammalia containing the elephant and its extinct allies; characterized by having a long flexible proboscis and the incisors developed into long tusks.

Proboscidean, -ian (prǫbǫsi·dĭăn, -iăn), *a.* and *sb.* 1835. [f. prec. + -AN, or f. L. *proboscis*, *-id-* + -EAN, -IAN.] **A.** *adj.* **1.** Of or belonging to the *Proboscidea* 1839. **2.** Having a proboscis 1836. **3.** Of, pertaining to, or resembling a proboscis 1875. **B.** *sb.* A mammal of the order *Proboscidea* 1835.

Proboscidiferous (probǫsidi·fĕrəs), *a.* 1828. [f. L. *proboscis*, *-id-* + -FEROUS.] Bearing or having a proboscis; *spec.* in *Conch.*, belonging to a division of pectinibranchiate gastropods (*Proboscidifera*) characterized by a long retractile snout.

Proboscidiform (prǫbǫsi·difǭɹm), *a.* 1837. [f. as prec. + -FORM.] Having the form or shape of a proboscis; proboscis-like. So **Probo·sciformed** *a.*

Proboscis (prŏbǫ·sis). *Pl.* **probo·scides** (-idīz), **probo·scises** (-isĕz). 1609. [– L. *proboscis* (Pliny) – Gr. προβοσκίς lit. 'means of providing food', f. πρό PRO-² + βόσκειν (cause to) feed.] **1.** An elephant's trunk; also applied to the long flexible snout of the tapir, the proboscis-monkey, etc. **2.** *joc.* The human nose 1630. **3.** *Entom.* Applied to various elongated, often tubular and flexible, parts of the mouth of insects 1645. **4.** An extensible tubular structure in other invertebrates, *esp.* a sucking organ in various worms, and the tongue of some molluscs 1796.

Comb. **p.-monkey,** a large semnopithecine ape, *Nasalis larvatus*: = KAHAU.

Procacity (prokæ·sĭti). Now *rare.* 1621. [– Fr. †*procacité* or L. *procacitas*, *-tat-*, f. *procax*, *procac-* bold; see -ITY.] Forwardness, petulance; sauciness, pertness.

‖**Procatalepsis** (prōᵘkætăle·psis). 1586. [Gr. προκατάληψις, f. προκαταλαμβάνειν take up beforehand.] *Rhet.* A figure by which an opponent's objections are anticipated and answered.

Pro-cathedral (prōᵘˌkăþī·drăl), *a.* and *sb.* 1868. [f. PRO-¹ II. 1 + CATHEDRAL *sb.*] **A.** *adj.* Used as the substitute for a cathedral. **B.** *sb.* A church used instead of, or as a substitute for a cathedral church.

‖**Procedendo** (prōᵘside·ndo). 1593. [L. (*de*) *procedendo* (*ad judicium*) 'of proceeding (to judgement)'; see PROCEED *v.*] *Law.* A writ which formerly issued out of the common law jurisdiction of the Court of

Chancery, commanding a subordinate court to proceed to judgement, either when judgement had been wrongfully delayed, or when the action had been removed to a superior court on insufficient grounds.

Procedure (prŏsī·diŭɹ, -dʒəɹ). 1611. [– (O)Fr. *procédure*, f. *procéder* PROCEED; see -URE.] **1.** The fact or manner of proceeding or going on; proceeding, in ref. to its mode or method; conduct, behaviour. **b.** With *a* and *pl.* A particular action or mode of action 1677. **c.** *spec.* Legal action or proceeding; the mode or form of conducting judicial proceedings 1676. **d.** The mode of conducting business in Parliament 1839. †**2.** Progress, course of an action or process –1716.

1. b. This was, indeed, a p. truly Roman COTTON. 2. The hindrance of the P. of the Work 1703.

Proceed (prōu·sīd), *sb.* 1628. [f. next.] †**1.** Procedure; course –1674. **2.** That which proceeds from something; produce, outcome, profit. Now usu. in *pl.* **proceeds.** 1643.

2. The only procede..you can expect is thanks 1645. Handing over the proceeds of sale 1885.

Proceed (prŏsī·d), *v.* [XIV *procede* – (O)Fr. *procéder* – L. *procedere*, f. *pro* PRO-[1] + *cedere* go; see CEDE.] **1.** *intr.* To go, move or travel forward; to make one's way onward; *esp.* to move onward after interruption or stoppage. **2.** To go on with an action, a discourse, an investigation, etc. late ME. **b.** To deal *with*; to treat, act (esp. judicially) with regard to. late ME. **c.** *spec.* To take legal proceedings (*against* a person) 1440. **3.** With stress on the progress or continuance of the action: **a.** To go on with or continue what one has begun; to advance from the point already reached; to go on after interruption. late ME. **b.** To go on *to do* something; to advance *to* another action, subject, etc. late ME. **c.** *absol.* To continue or pursue one's discourse 1509. †**d.** In emphatic sense: To make progress, get on; to prosper –1777. **4.** *intr.* To advance, in one's university course, from graduation as B.A. to some higher degree, as master or doctor. In the Inns of Court, to be admitted a barrister. 1479. **b.** *transf.* and *fig.* To advance to some status or function; to become 1579. **5.** Of an action, process, etc.: **a.** To go on, take place; to take effect 1440. **b.** To go on to a certain point; to continue 1670. **6.** To go or come forth; to issue (*lit.* and *fig.*). late ME. **b.** *spec.* To be the issue or descendant *of*; to spring *from* (a parent, ancestor, or stock). Now *rare* or *Obs.* 1480.

1. Before we procede on our iuorney 1526. 2. The true Philosopher must always p. with a sober Pace 1718. c. In what manner he should p. against such as refused CLARENDON. 3. a. Exhorting him to procede as he hath begonne 1560. b. Then shal the Bisshop procede to the Communion *Bk. Com. Prayer.* c. To p., the land of Egypt is highly renowned 1660. 4. b. As you haue proued learned Philosophers, you will also proceede excellent diuines LYLY. 5. a. He will..tell you What hath proceeded worthy note to day SHAKS. 6. a. Every worde that proceadeth out off the mouth off God TINDALE *Matt.* 4:4. b. We all p. from the loins of Adam 1768. Hence **Procee·der** (now *rare*).

Proceeding (prŏsī·diŋ), *vbl. sb.* 1517. [f. prec. + -ING[1].] The action of PROCEED *v.* **1.** The action of going onward; advance. **2.** = PROCEDURE 1. 1553. **b.** A particular action or course of action; a piece of conduct or behaviour; a transaction. Usu. in *pl.*: Doings, actions, transactions. 1553. **c.** *pl.* A record of the doings of a society; sometimes *spec.* a record of the business done, with abstracts of the less important papers not included in the *Transactions* 1830. **3.** *spec.* The instituting or carrying on of an action at law; a legal action or process; any act done by authority of a court of law; any step taken in a cause by either party 1546.

2. b. The..Dayly Proceedings of Both Houses, in this Great and Happy Parliament 1641. 3. Proceedings were begun against the Papists 1643.

Proceleusmatic (prǫsĕliŭsmæ·tik), *a.* (*sb.*) 1751. [– late L. *proceleusmaticus* – Gr. προκελευσματικός, f. προκέλευσμα, -ματ-, f. προκελεύειν incite.] **1.** Serving for incitement; animating, inspiriting 1773. **2.** *Pros.* **a.** Epithet of a metrical foot of four short syllables; pertaining to or consisting of such feet. **b.** *sb.* A proceleusmatic foot 1751.

Procellarian (prǫselē·riăn), *a.* and *sb.* 1864. [f. mod.L. *Procellaria* (f. *procella* storm) + -AN.] *Ornith.* **A.** *adj.* Belonging to or resembling the genus *Procellaria* or family *Procellariidæ* of sea-birds. **B.** *sb.* A bird of this family, a petrel.

Procerity (prose·rĭti). Now *rare.* 1550. [– Fr. †*procérité* or L. *proceritas*, *-tat-* tallness, f. *procerus* high, tall; see -ITY.] Tallness, loftiness, height; length.

Process (prōu·sés, prǫ·sés), *sb.* [ME. *proces* – (O)Fr. *procès* – L. *processus*, f. pa. ppl. stem of *procedere* PROCEED.] **1.** The fact of going on or being carried on; progress, course. **2.** Course, lapse (of time). Chiefly in *in p. of time.* ME. †**3.** Course (of a narrative, etc.); drift, tenor, gist –1643. †**4.** A narrative; a discourse or treatise; a discussion –1784. **5.** Something that goes on or is carried on; proceeding, procedure ME. **6.** A continuous and regular action or succession of actions, taking place or carried on in a definite manner; a continuous (natural or artificial) operation or series of operations 1627. **b.** A particular method of operation in any manufacture, as *Bessemer p.*, *collodion p.*, etc.; in recent use *spec.* applied to methods other than simple engraving by hand of producing blocks for printing from; *ellipt.* a print from such a block 1839. **7.** *Law.* **a.** The whole of the proceedings in any action at law; the course or method of carrying on an action; an action, suit ME. **b.** *spec.* The formal commencement of any action at law; the mandate, summons, or writ by which a person or thing is brought into court for litigation. late ME. **8.** *fig.* Of action, time, etc.: Progress, advance; development. Now *rare.* 1638. **b.** *Logic.* The act of proceeding from a term in one of the premisses to the corresponding term in the conclusion; only in ILLICIT *p.* 1864. †**9.** A formal command or mandate. SHAKS. **10.** A projection from the main body of something; esp. a natural appendage, extension, or outgrowth 1578.

1. New edifices..are in p. of erection HAWTHORNE. 2. Three beautious springs to yellow Autumne turn'd In processe of the seasons haue I seene SHAKS. 4. *Haml.* I. v. 37. 5. Behinde the Arras I'le conuey my selfe To heare the Processe SHAKS. 6. Such are the different processes for procuring carbonic oxide 1807. 7. b. They..had servid proces upon him 1577.

attrib. and *Comb.*, as **p. block**, a block to print from, produced by some p. other than simple engraving by hand; **p. printing**, a method of printing, from half-tone plates, in three colours, yellow, red, and blue (and, usu., black); **-server**, a sheriff's officer who serves processes or summonses; **-serving.**

Process (prōu·sés, prǫ·sés), *v.*[1] 1532. [In sense 1 – OFr. *processer* prosecute, f. *procès*; in 2 f. prec.] **1.** *trans.* To institute a process or action against; to sue, prosecute; to obtain a summons against (a person); to serve a process on. orig. *Sc.* **2.** To treat by a special process; e.g. to reproduce (a drawing, etc.) by a mechanical or photographic process 1884.

Hence **Pro·cessing** *vbl. sb.*, *attrib.* **p. tax** (*U.S.*), a tax imposed on agricultural commodities while going through the first process after leaving the farmer.

Process (prŏse·s), *v.*[2] *colloq.* or *joc.* 1814. [Back-formation from next, after *progress*, etc.] *intr.* To go, walk, or march in procession.

Procession (prŏse·ʃən), *sb.* [Early ME. – (O)Fr. *procession* – L. *processio*, *-on-*, f. *process-*, pa. ppl. stem of *procedere* PROCEED; see -ION.] The action of proceeding. **1.** The action of a body of persons going or marching along in orderly succession, esp. as a religious ceremony or on a festive occasion. **b.** *transf.* Of boats, barges, etc. 1843. **2.** *concr.* A body of persons marching in this way. late ME. **3.** *transf.* A litany, form of prayer, or office, said or sung in a religious procession. *Obs.* exc. *Hist.* 1543. **4.** The action of proceeding, issuing, or coming forth from a source; emanation. Chiefly *Theol.* in ref. to the Holy Spirit. late ME. **5.** Onward movement, progression, advance (now *rare*). 1585.

1. Phr. *To go, walk* (etc.) *in p.*; The Commons went in p. to Whitehall with their address on the subject of the test MACAULAY. b. From Fawley it was simply a p., the London pair winning anyhow 1902. 4. The Greeks..maintain the p. of the Holy Spirit from the Father alone FULLER.

attrib. and *Comb.*: **p. caterpillar, moth** (PROCESSIONARY *a.* 2); **-day,** a day on which a p. is made; *spec.* (*pl.*) the Rogation days; **-week,** Rogation week, so named for the processions then made. Hence **Proce·ssioner,** a person going in p.; a processionary caterpillar. **Proce·ssionist,** one who goes in a p. **Proce·ssionize** *v. intr.* to go in p.

Procession (prŏse·ʃən), *v.* 1546. [f. prec.] **1.** *trans.* To honour by a procession; to carry in procession. **2.** *intr.* To go in procession 1671. **3.** *trans.* To go round (something) in procession; *spec.* (*local* in *U.S.*), to make a procession around a piece of land in order formally to determine its bounds (with the land, or bounds, as obj.). Also, to walk along (a street, etc.) in procession. 1710.

Processional (prŏse·ʃənăl), *sb.* late ME. [– med.L. *processionale*, subst. use of n. of *processionalis*; see next.] *Eccl.* An office-book containing litanies, hymns, etc., for use in religious processions. **b.** A processional hymn; see the adj. 1884.

Processional (prŏse·ʃənăl), *a.* 1611. [– med.L. *processionalis*; see PROCESSION, -AL[1].] Of, pertaining to, or of the nature of a procession; characterized by processions. Of a hymn, psalm, litany, etc.: sung or recited in procession. **b.** Used or carried in processions 1846. **c.** Walking or going in procession; forming a procession 1855.

The ceremonial of Egyptian worship was essentially p. 1877. c. *P. caterpillar*: see next. Hence **Proce·ssionalist,** a processionist. **Proce·ssionally** *adv.*

Processionary (prŏse·ʃənări), *a.* 1597. [– med.L. *processionarius*; see PROCESSION *sb.* and -ARY[1].] = PROCESSIONAL *a.*; *Entom.* applied to caterpillars which go in procession, esp. those of the moth *Cnethocampa processionea*; hence, *p. moth* 1765.

Processive (prŏse·siv), *a. rare.* 1819. [f. PROCEED, PROCESSION, after *recede*/*recession*, etc., perh. infl. by *progressive*.] Having the quality of proceeding; progressive.

‖**Procès verbal** (prosę vęrbal). *Pl.* **procès verbaux** (-bo). 1635. [Fr.] A detailed written report of proceedings; minutes; in *Fr. Law*, an authenticated written statement of facts in support of a criminal or other charge.

‖**Prochain** (proʃę̃n), *a.* 1473. [Fr., near, neighbouring.] *Law.* In *p. ami* = next friend (see NEXT *a.* 3.).

Prochronism (prōu·krŏniz'm). 1646. [f. PRO-[2] + Gr. χρόνος time + -ISM; cf. ANACHRONISM.] The referring of an event, etc., to an earlier date than the true one.

†**Proci·nct.** 1611. [– L. *procinctus* girding up, (hence) readiness for action, in phr. *in procinctu*, f. *pro* PRO-[1] + *cingere* gird.] *In p.*, in readiness for action, ready, prepared –1839.

Proclaim (prŏ,klēi·m), *v.* [XV *proclame* – L. *proclamare* cry out; see PRO-[1], CLAIM *v.*] **1.** *trans.* To make official announcement of (something) by word of mouth in some public place; also, to cause this to be done. **b.** To publish (the banns of marriage) 1596. **2.** To make official announcement of or concerning (a person or thing) 1494. **b.** Short for 'to proclaim (a person) as a rebel or outlaw'. Also, to denounce (a person or thing). 1500. **c.** To proclaim the accession of (a sovereign) 1714. **d.** To place (a district, country, etc.) under legal restrictions by proclamation 1881. **3.** *transf.* To declare publicly; to publish. late ME. **4.** *fig.* Of things: To make known or manifest; to intimate, prove 1597. **5.** *intr.* To make proclamation or public announcement 1470.

1. He caused it to be proclamed thorow out all his empyre COVERDALE 2 *Chron.* 36:22. Phr. *To p. war*, to make public declaration of war *against* another power; to declare war. 2. When he found himself proclaimed a traitor 1858. b. *Lear* II. iii. 1. 4. The Apparell oft proclaimes the man SHAKS. Hence **Proclai·mer.**

Proclamation (prǫklămēi·ʃən). late ME. [XV – (O)Fr. *proclamation* – L. *proclamatio*, *-on-*, f. *proclamare*; see prec., -ATION.] **1.** The action of proclaiming; the official giving of public notice. **b.** *spec.* The formal announcement of the accession of a king or ruler; the fact of being proclaimed king 1593. **c.** The action of denouncing by a public notice; the fact of being so proclaimed; proscription 1561. **2.** That which is proclaimed, publicly announced, or posted up in public places. late ME. †**3.** *transf.* Open declaration; manifestation; favourable or unfavourable notice –1607.

2. They say the King hath put out a P. to forbid maskerades 1671.

Proclitic (proˌkli·tik), *a.* and *sb.* 1846. [– mod.L. *procliticus* (Hermann, 1801), f. Gr. προκλίνειν lean forward, after late L. *encliticus* ENCLITIC.] **A.** *adj.* In *Gr. Gram.*, used of a monosyllabic word that is so closely attached in pronunciation to the following word as to have no accent of its own; applied gen. to a similar word in any language. **B.** *sb.* A proclitic word 1864.

Proclivity (proˌkli·vĭti). 1591. [– L. *proclivitas*, f. *proclivis* inclined, f. *pro* PRO-[1] + *clivus* slope; see -ITY.] A condition of being inclined to something; an instance of such condition; inclination, tendency, leaning, propensity.

This naturall p. of men, to hurt each other HOBBES. Persons with Jacobite proclivities 1708.

Proconsul (prōᵘkǫ·nsŏl). late ME. [– L. *proconsul*, from earlier *pro consule* '(one acting) for the consul'; see PRO-[1] II. 1, CONSUL.] *Rom. Hist.* An officer who acting as governor or military commander in a Roman province discharged the duties and had most of the authority of a consul. **b.** *transf.* Applied rhet. to a governor of a modern colony, etc. 1827. Hence **Pro·co·nsular** *a.* of or pertaining to a p.; of a province, under the administration of a Roman p. **Proco·nsulship.**

Proconsulate (prokǫ·nsiŭlĕt). 1656. [– L. *proconsulatus*; see prec., -ATE[1].] The office of a proconsul; the district under the government of a proconsul.

Procrastinate (proˌkræ·stineⁱt), *v.* 1588. [– *procrastinat-*, pa. ppl. stem of L. *procrastinare*, f. *pro* PRO-[1] + *crastinus* belonging to tomorrow, f. *cras* tomorrow; see -ATE[3].] **1.** *trans.* To postpone till another day; to put off from day to day; to defer, delay. Now *rare.* **2.** *intr.* To defer action, delay; to be dilatory 1638.

1. Many such deuices they fained to p. the time 1624. Hence **Procra·stinatingly** *adv.* **Procra·stinative** *a.* that tends to p. **Procra·stinator,** one who procrastinates. **Procra·stinatory** *a.* given to or implying procrastination; dilatory.

Procrastination (proˌkræstinēⁱ·ʃən). 1548. [– L. *procrastinatio*, f. as prec.; see -ION.] The action or habit of procrastinating or putting off; delay, dilatoriness. Also with *of.*

P. is the thief of time YOUNG.

Procreant (prōᵘ·kriănt), *a.* (*sb.*) 1588. [– (O)Fr. *procréant* or L. *procreans, -ant-*, pr. pple. of *procreare*; see next, -ANT.] **1.** That procreates or begets; producing young; generating. **2.** Of, pertaining or subservient to procreation 1605. †**B.** *sb.* One who or that which procreates; a generator –1641.

Procreate (prōᵘ·kriˌeⁱt), *v.* Now *rare.* 1536. [– *procreat-*, pa. ppl. stem of L. *procreare*, f. *pro* PRO-[1] + *creare* CREATE, after †*procreate* pa. pple. (XV) and (O)Fr. *procréer*; see -ATE[3].] *trans.* To beget, engender, generate. Also *transf.* and *fig.* **b.** *absol.* or *intr.* To produce offspring 1646.

b. Couples marry and p. on the idea, not the reality, of a maintenance 1792. Hence **Pro·creative** *a.* pertaining to procreation; having the power of producing offspring. **Pro·creativeness. Pro·creator,** a parent.

Procreation (prōᵘˌkriˌē̆ⁱ·ʃən). late ME. [– OFr. *procreacion*, (also mod.) *-tion*, or L. *procreatio*, f. as prec.; see -ION.] The action of procreating or begetting; generation; the fact of being begotten. Also *transf.* and *fig.*

Procrustean (prokrʊ·stiăn), *a.* 1846. [f. PROCRUSTES + -AN.] Of or pertaining to Procrustes; aiming or tending to produce uniformity by violent and arbitrary methods.

Procrustes (prokrʊ·stīz). 1583. [– Gr. Προκρούστης, personal name, lit. 'one that stretches', f. προκρούειν beat or hammer out.] A fabulous robber of Attica who made his victims conform to the length of his bed by stretching or mutilation. Also *attrib.*

Procryptic (prokri·ptik), *a.* 1891. [f. PRO-[1] or [2] + Gr. κρυπτικός fit for concealing, f. κρύπτειν to hide. App. f. after *protective.*] *Zool.* Having the function of protectively concealing; applied to the protective mimicry of colour and form, observed in insects and some other animals. Hence **Procry·ptically** *adv.*

Procto- (prǫ·kto), bef. a vowel **proct-**, comb. form of Gr. πρωκτός anus; used to form modern scientific terms, chiefly medical and surgical. **Procti·tis** [-ITIS], inflammation of the rectum and anus. ‖**Proctodæ·um** [Gr. ὁδαῖος that is on or by the road], *Embryol.* the posterior portion of the digestive tract, beginning as an invagination of the epiblast; hence **Proctodæ·al** *a.* **Proctu·chous** *a.* [Gr. ἔχειν have], having an anus; applied to one division of turbellarians, the *Proctucha*, as dist. from the *Aprocta.*

Proctor (prǫ·ktəɹ), *sb.* late ME. [A syncopated form of *procuratour* PROCURATOR.] **1.** = PROCURATOR 2. *Obs.* or *arch.* exc. in techn. use. 1449. †**b.** A steward –1578. **c.** An agent for the collection of tithes and other church dues; a tithe-farmer. In full *tithe-p.* 1607. **2.** At Oxford and Cambridge, each of two officers (*Senior* and *Junior P.*) appointed annually by the colleges in rotation, and charged with various functions, esp. with the discipline of all persons *in statu pupillari*, and the summary punishment of minor offences 1536. **3.** *Law.* One whose profession is to manage the causes of others in a court administering civil or canon law; corresponding to an attorney or solicitor in courts of equity and common law. (Now retained chiefly in courts of eccl. jurisdiction.) late ME. **4.** A deputy elected to represent the chapter of a cathedral or collegiate church, or the clergy of a diocese or arch-deaconry (*p. of the clergy*), in the Lower House of Convocation of either province 1586. †**5.** One who collected alms on behalf of lepers or others who were debarred from begging for themselves; *esp.* one having a licence to do this for the occupants of a 'spital-house' 1529.

2. *Proctors' dogs* or *bulldogs* (Univ. slang), the sworn constables who accompany the proctors in their nightly perambulation of the streets. **3.** *King's* (*Queen's*) *P.*, an official of the Probate, Divorce, and Admiralty Division of the High Court of Justice, who has the right to intervene in probate, divorce, and nullity cases, when collusion or suppression of material facts is alleged. Hence **Pro·ctorage,** management by a p. **Procto·rial** *a.* of or pertaining to a p. (at the Universities, or in the eccl. courts). **Pro·ctorize** *v. trans.* to exercise the proctorial authority on (an undergraduate, etc.). **Pro·ctorship,** the office, position, or function of a p.

Procumbent (prokʊ·mbĕnt), *a.* 1668. [– L. *procumbens, -ent-*, pr. pple. of *procumbere* fall forwards, f. *pro* PRO-[1] + *-cumbere* lay oneself; see -ENT.] **1.** Lying on the face; prone, prostrate 1721. **2.** *Bot.* Of a plant or stem: Lying flat on the ground without throwing out roots; having a prostrate or trailing stem 1668.

Procurable (prŏkiūᵊ·răb'l), *a.* 1611. [f. PROCURE *v.* + -ABLE.] That can be procured or obtained.

†**Pro·curacy.** late ME. [– med.L. *procuratia*, for cl. L. *procuratio* PROCURATION.] **1.** The office or action of a procurator; management or action for another –1762. **2.** A document empowering a person to act for another; a proxy, a letter of attorney –1607.

1. *Letters of p.* = 2.

Procurance (prokiūᵊ·răns). 1553. [f. PROCURE *v.* + -ANCE.] The action of procuring; the action by which something is attained or brought about; agency.

Procuration (prǫkiŭᵊrēⁱ·ʃən). late ME. [– OFr. *procuracion*, (also mod.) *-tion*, or L. *procuratio, -on-*, f. *procurat-*, pa. ppl. stem of *procurare*; see PROCURE, -ION.] †**1.** The action of taking care of, looking after, or managing –1677. **2.** The appointment of a procurator or attorney; the power thus delegated; also, the authorized action of one's agent; the function of an attorney or representative 1489. **b.** A formal document whereby a person gives legal authority to another to act for him; a letter or power of attorney. Now *rare.* late ME. **3.** *Eccl.* The provision of entertainment for the bishop, archdeacon, or other visitor by the incumbent, parish, etc., visited; later commuted to a payment in money 1450. **4.** The action of procuring; procurement 1533. **b.** *spec.* The negotiating of a loan for a client; also, the fee for this 1678. **c.** The action of a procurer or procuress; pimping 1696.

2. *Letters of p.* = 2 b. *By p.*, by attorney or proxy (cf. p. p. s.v. P II).

attrib. **P. fee, money,** a fee paid for procuring a loan.

Procurator (prǫ·kiūreⁱtəɹ). ME. [– OFr. *procurateur* or L. *procurator* manager, agent, deputy, collector in a province, f. as prec.; see -ATOR.] **1.** *Rom. Hist.* An officer who collected the taxes, paid the troops, and had charge of the interests of the imperial treasury, in an imperial province. **2.** One who manages the affairs of another; an agent, an attorney ME. **3.** *Law.* An agent in a court of law: = PROCTOR 3; *spec.* in Scotland, a law-agent practising before the inferior courts, an attorney. (Now *rare.*) late ME. **4.** (repr. It. *procuratore.*) In some Italian cities, A public administrator or magistrate; also repr. Fr. *procureur* (see PROCUREUR) 1618.

2. *P. general*, an agent-general. **4.** *P. of St. Mark*, a senator, afterwards each of two senators, of the Venetian Republic, charged with high administrative functions. Hence **Procurato·rial** *a.* of or pertaining to a p. or proctor. **Pro·curatorship,** the office, function, or period of office of a p.

Pro·curator-fi·scal. [See FISCAL *a.*] 1583. In Scotland, the public prosecutor of a shire or other local district.

Procuratory (prǫ·kiūrĕtəri), *a.* and *sb.* 1459. [– late L. *procuratorius*, f. *procurator*; see PROCURATOR, -ORY[2]; hence med.L. *-orium* sb., whence B.] **A.** *adj.* Of or pertaining to a procurator or procurators, or to procuration. Now *rare* or *Obs.* **B.** *sb.* *Civil* and *Sc. Law.* Authorization of one person to act for another; an instrument or clause giving such power; esp. in *letters of p.* 1540.

Procuratrix (prǫkiūrēⁱ·triks). 1660. [– med.L. use of L. *procuratrix*, fem. of *procurator* PROCURATOR; see -TRIX.] The inmate who attends to the temporal concerns of a nunnery.

Procure (prŏkiūᵊ·ɹ), *v.* ME. [– (O)Fr. *procurer* – L. *procurare* take care of, attend to, manage, f. *pro* PRO-[1] + *curare* look after; see CURE *v.*] **1.** *trans.* To bring about by care or pains; also (more vaguely) to bring about, cause, effect, produce. *rare* or *arch.* **2.** To obtain by care or effort; to acquire ME. **b.** To obtain (women) for the gratification of lust. Usu. *absol.* or *intr.* To act as a procurer or procuress. 1603. **3.** To prevail upon, induce, persuade (a person) *to do* something. *Obs.* or *arch.* ME. †Also with adv. of place or without const. –1625.

1. A drinke called Coffa..which helpeth.. digestion, and procureth alacrity 1615. An ingenious lover procured his..rival to be arrested for lunacy 1866. **2.** She endeavoured to p. employment as a needle-woman 1776. Books were..impossible to p. 1874. **3. b.** What vnaccustom'd cause procures her hither? SHAKS. Hence **Procu·rement,** the action of procuring; management; contrivance; acquisition, getting, gaining.

Procurer (prŏkiūᵊ·rəɹ). late ME. [– AFr. *procurour*, OFr. *procureur* :– L. *procurator*; see PROCURATOR, -ER[2] 3.] †**1.** = PROCURATOR, in various uses –1658. **2.** One who or that which brings about, effects, or induces something; *esp.* a promotor, prime mover, ultimate author. Now *rare* or *Obs.* 1451. **3.** One who procures or obtains 1538. **4.** A pander; a procuress 1632.

Procuress (prŏkiūᵊ·rĕs). 1712. [Syncopated from OFr. *procureresse*, fem. of Fr. *procureur* PROCURER; cf. *governess.*] A woman who makes it her trade to procure women for the gratification of lust; a bawd.

‖**Procureur** (prokürör). 1598. [Fr.; see PROCURER.] A procurator (esp. in sense 3); an attorney, agent, or legal representative.

Procyon (prōᵘ·siǫn). 1658. [– L. *Procyon* – Gr. Προκύων (in sense 1), f. πρό before + κύων dog; so called as rising before the dog-star Sirius.] **1.** The principal star in the constellation *Canis Minor.* **2.** *Zool.* A genus of plantigrade carnivorous mammals, including the racoons, typical of the family *Procyonidæ* 1843.

Prod (prǫd), *sb.* 1787. [f. next.] **1.** An act of prodding; a thrust with some pointed instrument; a poke, a stab 1802. **2.** A name for various pointed instruments, as a goad, a skewer, a brad, etc. 1787.

Prod (prǫd), *v.* 1535. [perh. of purely symbolic origin, but possibly a blending of POKE *v.*[1] with *brod* vb., f. BROD *sb.*] **1.** *trans.* To thrust or stab; to poke with a pointed instrument, or with the end of a stick. **b.** *fig.* To goad mentally; to stir up; to irritate 1871. **2.** *intr.* To thrust, to poke 1696. **3.** *trans.* To make by prodding 1865.

1. I..have vitality enough to kick..when prodded HUXLEY. Hence **Pro·dder.**

Prodigal (prǫ·digăl), *a.* and *sb.* (*adv.*) 1450. [– late L. *prodigalis* (implied in *prodigalitas, -aliter*), f. L. *prodigus* lavish; see -AL[1].] **A.** *adj.* **1.** Given to extravagant expenditure; recklessly wasteful. **2.** Of things or actions: Wastefully lavish 1500. **3.** Lavish in the bestowal or disposal of things 1595. **b.** with *of*; also with *in* (*rare*) 1588.

1. The nobility is..prodigall in expenses, spending more than their reuenues in diet and apparell 1601. Nature is p. of human life 1864. *P. son, child*, in ref. or allusion to the parable, in Luke 15:11–32. **2.** Our little suppers they traduce as p. 1672. **3.** P. veins of Gold and Silver 1652. **b.** When..May is p. of flowers 1778.

B. *sb.* **1.** One who spends his money extravagantly and wastefully; a spendthrift, waster 1596. **2.** In pregnant sense, with allusion to the career of 'the Prodigal Son' (A. 1). 1596.

1. A bankrout, a prodigall, who dare scarce shew his head on the Ryalto SHAKS. Phr. *To play the p.*, to act prodigally; to act like 'the p. son'.

C. as *adv.* Prodigally, lavishly SHAKS. Hence **Pro·digalize** *v. trans.* to spend profusely or lavishly. **Pro·digally** *adv.* 1530.

Prodigality (prǫdigæ·lĭti). ME. [– (O)Fr. *prodigalité* – late L. *prodigalitas* (Boethius), f. *prodigalis*; see prec., -ITY.] **1.** Reckless extravagance in expenditure, wastefulness; esp. of money. **2.** Lavishness, profuseness; lavish display, profuse supply 1594.

2. *Rich. III*, I. ii. 244.

Prodigious (prŏdi·dʒəs), *a.* (*adv.*) 1552. [– L. *prodigiosus*, f. *prodigium*; see next, -OUS. Cf. Fr. *prodigieux* (Rabelais).] †**1.** Of the nature of a prodigy; ominous, portentous –1705. **2.** Having the appearance of a prodigy; unnatural, abnormal 1579. **3.** Causing wonder; marvellous, amazing; (in bad sense) monstrous 1568. **4.** Of extraordinary size, extent, power, or amount; vast, enormous. (Often hyperbolical.) 1601. **b.** As an exclam. 1730. **B.** quasi-*adv.* Amazingly, exceedingly, 'mightily'. *arch.* 1676.

1. *Mids. N.* V. i. 419. **2.** All p. things..Gorgons and Hydra's, and Chimera's dire MILT. **4.** Five thousand Marks, a p. sum in that age FULLER. Satan, who that day P. power had shewn MILT. At great depths, the pressure must be p. HUXLEY. **B.** The Sea running p. high 1676. Hence **Prodi·gious-ly** *adv.*, **-ness.**

Prodigy (prǫ·dĭdʒi). 1494. [– L. *prodigium*, f. *prod-*, var. of *pro* PRO-[1] + an element variously referred to *aio* (:– **agjo*) I say, and *agere* ACT *v.*; see -Y[4].] **1.** Something extraordinary from which omens are drawn; an omen, portent. Now *rare.* **2.** An amazing or marvellous thing; *esp.* something abnormal or monstrous 1626. **3.** Anything that causes wonder, astonishment, or surprise; a wonder, a marvel 1660. **b.** A wonderful example *of* (some quality) 1646. **c.** A person endowed with some quality which excites wonder; *esp.* a child of precocious genius 1658.

1. Omens and prodigies have lost their terrors JOHNSON. **2.** A climate, where rain is considered as a p. 1748. **3.** Monstrous untruths, and prodigies of lies 1660. **b.** This bird..is a p. of understanding GOLDSM. **c.** This infant p. 1831.

Prodition (prodi·ʃən). Now *rare.* [XV *prodycyon* – OFr. *prodicion* – L. *proditio, -on-*, f. *prodere* betray; see -ITION.] Betrayal, treason, treachery.

†**Pro·ditor.** late ME. [– AFr. *proditour* = OFr. *proditeur* – L. *proditor*, f. as prec.; see -OR 2.] A betrayer; a traitor –1678. Hence **Prodito·rious** *a.* traitorous, perfidious; *fig.* apt to betray what is hidden or in the mind. (*Obs.* or *arch.*) †**Pro·ditory** *a.* traitorous.

Prodrome (prǫ·drǭm). 1822. [– Fr. *prodrome* – mod.L. PRODROMUS.] **1.** A preliminary or introductory treatise or book 1866. **2.** *Path.* A premonitory symptom 1822. So **Pro·dromal, Prodro·mic** *adjs.* forerunning; introductory, preliminary; in *Path.* premonitory (of disease).

‖**Prodromus** (prǫ·dromŏs). *Pl.* **prodromi.** 1645. [mod.L. – Gr. πρόδρομος sb. precursor, f. πρό PRO-[2] + δραμεῖν run, δρόμος running.] **1.** A forerunner, a precursor, a premonitory event. **2.** A book or treatise which is introductory to some larger work 1672. **3.** *Path.* = PRODROME 2. 1693.

Produce (prǫ·diūs), *sb.* 1699. [f. PRODUCE *v.*] **1.** The amount produced, yielded, or derived; the proceeds; the return, yield. Now chiefly in the assay of ore. 1707. **2.** The thing (or things collectively) produced; product, fruit 1699. **b.** Result, effect, consequence 1730. **c.** Offspring, progeny (*rare*) 1845. **3.** Agricultural and natural products collectively, as dist. from manufactured goods. Also *raw p.* 1745. **4.** *techn.* Materials produced from breaking up ordnance or other military or naval stores 1904.

3. Raw p., wool and hides, corn, beer, and cheese 1861. **4.** Phr. *Brought to p.*, broken up, and the material assorted into various kinds or classes.

Produce (prŏdiū·s), *v.* 1499. [– L. *producere*, f. *pro* PRO-[1] + *ducere* lead.] **1.** *trans.* To bring forward, bring forth or out; to offer for inspection or consideration, exhibit. **b.** To introduce; now *spec.* to bring (a performer or performance) before the public; to put (a play) on the stage before the public with the necessary complement of actors and scenic apparatus 1585. †**c.** To bring (to a specified condition) –1741. **2.** *Geom.* To extend (a line) in length; to continue; hence *gen.* to lengthen (anything) out; to extend longitudinally 1570. **3.** To bring forth, bring into being or existence. **a.** *gen.* To bring (a thing) into existence from its raw materials or elements; to give rise to, bring about, effect (an action, condition, etc.) 1513. **b.** Of an animal or plant: To generate, bring forth, yield (offspring, seed, fruit, etc.) 1526. **c.** Of a country, river, mine, process, etc.: To give forth, yield, furnish, supply 1585. **d.** To compose or bring out (a work of literature or art); to work up from raw material, manufacture (material objects); in *Pol. Econ.* often blending with sense c. 1638.

1. P. your cause, saith the Lord, bring foorth your strong reasons *Isa.* 41:21. The books must be produced, as we cannot receive parole evidence of their contents 1776. **3. a.** Art may make a Suit of Clothes. But Nature must p. a Man. HUME. **b.** The goat produces but two at a time GOLDSM. Flowers..capable of producing seeds 1857. **c.** England hath of late produced great philosophers BERKELEY. **d.** Nectar that the bees p. GRAY. Such volumes..were here multiplied as fast as the press could p. them 1856. Hence †**Produ·cement**, production. **Producibi·lity**, the capability of being produced. **Produ·cible, -eable** *a.* capable of being, fit to be, produced.

Producent (prodiū·sĕnt), *a.* and *sb.* Now *rare.* 1604. [– L. *producens, -ent-*, pr. pple of *producere* PRODUCE; see -ENT.] **A.** *adj.* That produces; in *Eccl. Law*, that brings forward a witness or document. **B.** *sb.* One who or that which produces; a producer; the party producing a witness or document 1622.

Producer (prŏdiū·səɹ). 1513. [f. PRODUCE *v.* + -ER[1].] **1.** One who or that which produces; *spec.* one who 'produces' a play; *U.S.* the manager or proprietor of a theatre. **2.** *Pol. Econ.* One who produces (grows, makes) an article of consumption: opp. to *consumer* 1790. **3.** Short for *gas p.*, a furnace in which carbon monoxide gas is produced for use as fuel; hence *p.-gas*, gas so produced 1881.

Product (prǫ·dɒ̆kt), *sb.* late ME. [– L. *productum*, subst. use of n. pa. pple. of *producere* PRODUCE. In sense 1 in Albertus Magnus.] **1.** *Math.* The quantity obtained by multiplying two or more quantities together. **2.** A thing produced by nature or a natural process; also *collect.* = produce, fruit 1653. **3.** That which is produced by any action, operation, or work; a production; the result 1575. **4.** That which results from the operation of a cause 1651. **5.** *Chem.* A compound not previously existing in a body, but formed during its decomposition 1805.

2. These are the p. Of those ill-mated Marriages thou saw'st MILT. The products of distant countries JOHNSON. **3.** The fruit and p. of his labours past DRYDEN.

Produ·ctible, *a. rare.* 1830. [f. †*product* vb. produce + -IBLE, after *conductible, deductible.*] = PRODUCIBLE. Hence **Produ:ctibi·lity**, the quality or fact of being producible.

Production (prŏdɒ·kʃən). [XV – (O)Fr. *production* – L. *productio, -on-*, f. *product-*, pa. ppl. stem of *producere*; see PRODUCE *v.*, -ION.] **I. 1.** The action of producing; the fact or condition of being produced; with *a* and *pl.*, an act of producing 1483. **2.** That which is produced; a thing that results from any action, process, or effort. late ME. **b.** *spec.* A literary or artistic work. Chiefly in *pl.* 1651.

1. The P. and Modulation of the Voice BOYLE. **2. b.** The finest productions of Praxiteles 1879.

II. The action of bringing forward or exhibiting; in *Law*, the exhibiting of a document in court 1562. **III.** Drawing out, extending, or lengthening in †time or space; prolongation, extension 1536.

Productive (prŏdɒ·ktiv), *a.* 1612. [– Fr. *productif, -ive* or late L. *productivus*, f. as prec.; see -IVE.] **1.** Having the quality of producing or bringing forth; tending to produce; creative, generative. Also with *of.* **2.** That causes or brings about; causative. Always with *of.* 1647. **3.** *Pol. Econ.* That produces or increases wealth or value; producing commodities of exchangeable value; esp. in *p. labour, classes* 1776. **4.** That produces abundantly; prolific, fertile 1846.

1. Shakespeare..during his p. period 1870. Oak trees..p. of gall nuts 1870. **2.** It may be p...of incalculable good 1806. Hence **Produ·ctive-ly** *adv.*, **-ness. Producti·vity.**

Productor (prŏdɒ·ktəɹ). 1624. [f. †*product* vb. (cf. PRODUCTIBLE) + -OR 2. Cf. Fr. *producteur.*] One who or that which produces; a producer. So **Produ·ctress,** a female p. or producer. Chiefly *fig.*

Proem (prō^u·ĕm). [XIV *proheme* – OFr. *pro(h)eme* (mod. *proème*) or L. *prooemium* (med.L. *prohemium*) – Gr. προοίμιον prelude, f. πρό PRO-[2] + οἴμη song, lay.] An introductory discourse to a book or other writing; a preface, preamble. **b.** The prefatory part of a speech or discourse; an exordium 1541. **c.** *fig.* A beginning, prelude 1641.

Thus much may serve by way of p.; Proceed we therefore to our poem SWIFT. Hence **Proe·mial** *a.* prefatory, introductory.

†**Profa·ce,** *int.* 1515. [– Fr. †*prou fasse!* (in full, *bon prou vous fasse!* 'may it do you good'), f. *prou* PROW *sb.*[2] + *fasse* 3rd. pers. sing. pres. subj. of *faire* do.] A formula of welcome or good wishes at a meal, = 'may it do you good' –1638.

Master Page, good M. Page, sit: P. SHAKS.

Profanation (prǫfănēⁱ·ʃən). 1552. [– Fr. *profanation* or late L. *profanatio*, f. *profanare*; see PROFANE *v.*, -ATION.] The action of profaning; desecration or violation of that which is sacred; defilement, pollution. **b.** By extension: The degradation or vulgarization of anything worthy of being held in reverence or respect; cheapening by familiarity 1588.

A wall was built round the tomb to protect it from p. 1877. **b.** 'Twere prophanation of our joyes To tell the layitie our love DONNE.

Profane (prŏfēⁱ·n), *a.* (*sb.*) 1483. [XV–XVIII *prophane* – OFr. *prophane* (mod. *profane*) or L. *profanus* (med.L. *prophanus*) not sacred, uninitiated, impious, lit. 'before, i.e. outside, the temple', f. *pro* PRO-[1] + *fanum* temple, FANE.] **1.** Not pertaining or devoted to what is sacred or biblical, esp. in *p. history, literature*: secular, lay, common; civil, as dist. from ecclesiastical. **b.** Of persons: *orig.* Not initiated into the religious rites or sacred mysteries; *transf.* not admitted to some esoteric knowledge; uninitiated 1616. **2.** Unhallowed; ritually unclean or polluted; esp. said of the rites of an alien religion; heathen, pagan 1500. **3.** Characterized by disregard or contempt of sacred things; irreverent, blasphemous; impious, irreligious, wicked 1560. **4.** *absol.* or as *sb.* One who is profane 1529.

1. b. Hence, ye Prophane; I hate ye all; Both the Great Vulgar, and the Small COWLEY. **2.** Nothing

p. can dwell with Thee WESLEY. **3.** The Bill against Atheism and prophane Swearing we have sent up to the Lords MARVELL. Hence **Profa·nely** *adv.*, **-ness.**

Profane (prǒfēi·n), *v.* [XIV–XVIII *prophane* – L. *profanare* (med.L. *proph-*), f. *profanus* PROFANE *a.* Cf. Fr. *profaner.*] *trans.* To treat (what is sacred) with irreverence, contempt, or disregard; to desecrate, violate. **b.** To misuse, abuse (what ought to be reverenced or respected); to violate, defile, pollute 1563.

Neither shalt thou prophane the Name of thy God: I am the Lord *Lev.* 19:12. Guilty of profaning the Lord's day DE FOE. **b.** So idly to prophane the precious time SHAKS. No callous chatter to p. his ear DISRAELI. Hence **Profa·ner,** one who profanes.

Profanity (prǒfæ·nĭti). 1607. [– late L. *profanitas* (Tertullian), f. as prec.; see -ITY.] The quality or condition of being profane; profaneness; profane conduct or speech; in *pl.* profane words or acts.

Profection (profe·kʃən). Now *rare.* 1540. [Partly – Fr. †*profection* progression (*Astrol.*), f. L. *profect-*, pa. ppl. stem of *proficere* go forward; partly – L. *profectio* setting out, departure, f. *proficisci* set out.] **1.** The action or fact of going forward; progression, advance. *Obs.* exc. *Astrol.* 1597. †**b.** The degree of advancement attained; proficiency –1631. †**2.** Advancement in process or rank –1657.

Profecti·tious, *a.* 1656. [f. late L. *profecticius, -itius* that proceeds from some one (f. *profect-*, pa. ppl. stem of *proficisci*) + -OUS.] *Rom. Law.* That proceeds or is derived from a parent or ancestor.

Profe·r, *v. Obs.* or *rare arch.* late ME. [app. – (O)Fr. *proférer* utter, pronounce – L. *proferre* bring forth.] †**1.** To produce, yield –1600. **2.** To bring out (words), utter, pronounce. late ME.

Profert (prōu·fəɹt). *Obs.* exc. *Hist.* 1719. [f. L. *profert* (*in curia*) 'he produces (in court)', f. *proferre*; see prec.] *Law.* The production or exhibition of a deed in court.

Profess (prǒfe·s), *v.* ME. [In earliest use in pa. pple., repl. ME. †*profess* (– (O)Fr. *profès* – L. *professus*); later f. *profess-*, pa. ppl. stem of L. *profiteri* declare aloud or publicly, f. *pro* PRO-[1] + *fateri* CONFESS.] **1.** *trans.* **a.** Orig. in pass. form, *to be professed*, to have made one's profession of religion; to make one's profession, to take the vows of some religious order, *esp.* to become a monk or nun; later app. viewed as passive in sense, whence **b.** in active use, to receive the profession of, to receive into a religious order. **c.** *refl.* and *intr.* To make one's profession (*rare*) 1510. **2.** *trans.* To declare openly, announce, affirm; to avow, acknowledge, confess 1526. **3.** To make profession of, to lay claim to (some quality, feeling, etc.); often implying insincerity; to pretend to 1530. **b.** *refl.* and *intr.* To make a profession or professions; *esp.* to profess friendship or attachment 1601. **4.** *trans.* To affirm or declare one's faith in or allegiance to (a religion, principle; God, a saint, etc.) 1560. **5.** To make profession of (some art or science); to declare oneself expert or proficient in; to make (a thing) one's profession or business. *Obs.* or *arch.* 1577. **6.** To teach (some subject) as a professor 1560. **b.** *intr.* To perform the duties of a professor 1610.

1. c. The young man went back to France, and professed there in some religious order SOUTHEY. **2.** All who p. and call themselves Christians *Bk. Com. Prayer.* They one by one professed their faith in Christ J. H. NEWMAN. **3.** That love of truth which ye eminently professe MILT. **b.** *Wint. T.* I. ii. 456. **4.** The God..whom Israel still professed 1631. **5.** War was the only art which he professed GIBBON.

Professed (prǒfe·st, profe·sĕd), *ppl. a.* late ME. [f. prec. + -ED[1].] **1.** That has taken the vows of a religious order. **b.** *transf.* Of or pertaining to professed persons 1526. **2.** Self-acknowledged; openly declared by oneself; sometimes = Alleged, ostensible, pretended 1569. **3.** That professes to be duly qualified; professional 1675.

1. b. The Profess'd House of the Jesuits 1662. **2.** My Friend profest SHAKS. **3.** I do not pretend to teach p. cooks MRS. GLASSE. Hence **Professedly** (prǒfe·sĕdli) *adv.* avowedly; ostensibly.

Profession (prǒfe·ʃən). ME. [– (O)Fr. *profession* – L. *professio, -on-* public declaration, f. *profiteri*; see PROFESS *v.*, -ION.] The act or fact of professing; that which is professed. **I. 1.** The declaration, promise, or vow made on entering a religious order; hence, the action of entering such an order; the fact of being professed in a religious order. **2.** The action of declaring or avowing (truly or falsely) an opinion, belief, intention, practice, etc. 1526. **b.** with *a* and *pl.* An act of professing; a declaration 1674. **3.** The profession of religion; the declaration of belief in and obedience to religion or a religion; hence, the faith or religion which one professes 1526. **b.** A religious system, communion, or body. Now *rare* or *Obs.* 1600.

1. The novice kneeling before him made her p. 1797. **2.** Here, too, p. was at variance with fact 1817. **b.** Professions of friendship 1755.

II. The occupation which one professes to be skilled in and to follow. **a.** A vocation in which a professed knowledge of some department of learning is used in its application to the affairs of others, or in the practice of an art founded upon it. Applied *spec.* to the three learned professions of divinity, law, and medicine; also to the military profession. 1541. **b.** In wider sense: Any calling or occupation by which a person habitually earns his living 1576. **c.** The body of persons engaged in a calling 1610.

The Captain looks upon himself in the military capacity as a gentleman by p. GAY. **b.** Joseph her Spouse, by P. a Carpenter 1733. **c.** *The p.*, in theatrical use, actors as a body; public performers generally.

Professional (prǒfe·ʃənăl), *a.* (*sb.*) 1747. [f. prec. + -AL[1].] **1.** Pertaining to, proper to, or connected with a or one's profession or calling. **2.** Engaged in one of the learned or skilled professions 1793. **3.** That follows an occupation as his (or her) profession, lifework, or means of livelihood; *spec.* applied to one who follows, by way of profession, what is generally followed as a pastime, as a *p. cricketer*, etc. Disparagingly applied to one who 'makes a trade' of politics, etc. 1805. **b.** Of play, sports, etc.: Engaged in for money; engaged in by professionals (as dist. from amateurs) 1884. **4.** That is skilled in the theoretic or scientific parts of a trade; that raises his trade to the dignity of a learned profession 1860.

1. As perfectly p. as the mourning of an undertaker 1870. **2.** There has been a great upward movement of the p. class 1888. **3.** Ladies raised.. to the..position of 'p. beauty' 1887.

B. *sb.* **1.** One who belongs to one of the learned or skilled professions 1848. **2.** One who makes a profession or business of what is ordinarily followed as a pastime; see A. 3. 1811. Hence **Profe·ssionally** *adv.*

Professionalism (prǒfe·ʃənăliz'm). 1856. [f. prec. + -ISM.] **1.** Professional quality, character, method, or conduct; the stamp of a particular profession. **2.** The position of a professional as dist. from an amateur; the class of professionals 1884. So **Profe·ssionalist,** one who follows an occupation as a profession; a representative of professionalism. **Professionalize** *v.* to render or become professional.

Professor (prǒfe·səɹ). late ME. [– (O)Fr. *professeur* or L. *professor*, f. *profess-*; see PROFESS, -OR 2.] **I.** One who makes open declaration of his sentiments, beliefs, etc.; one who professes (sometimes opp. to one who practises) 1538. **b.** A professing Christian. Now chiefly *Sc.* and *U.S.* 1597.

There is no Error to be named, which has not had its Professors LOCKE. **b.** As he was a p., he would drive a nail for no man on the Sabbath SCOTT.

II. 1. A public teacher of the highest rank in a specific faculty or branch of learning; *spec.* one who holds a 'chair' in a university or one of its colleges. late ME. **b.** Prefixed as title to the name (sometimes abbrev. *Prof.*) 1706. **2.** One who makes a profession of any art or science. Also, in mod. use, a 'professional' as opp. to an 'amateur' in any branch of sport. 1563. **b.** Assumed as a grandiose title by teachers and exponents of dancing, jugglery, phrenology, etc. 1864.

1. Our Regius Professour of Physick BURTON. **2.** Asbolius, a p. of wrestling HOLLAND. Hence **Profe·ssorate,** professorship; a body of professors. **Profe·ssoress,** a female p. **Professo·rial** *a.* of or pertaining to a p.; pedagogic, dogmatic; **-ly** *adv.* **Professoriate** (prǒfesōə·riĕt), a body of professors; the professorial staff of a university; the office of p. **Profe·ssorship,** the office or function of a p.

Proffer (prǫ·fəɹ), *sb.* [ME. *profre* – AFr. *profre* = OFr. **poroffre*, f. *poroffrir*; see next.] **1.** The act of offering something, or of proposing to do something; an offer, a proposal. Now chiefly *literary.* †**2.** An act or movement as in beginning something; a show of intention to do something; an essay, attempt –1703. **3.** *Law.* A provisional payment of estimated dues into the Exchequer by a sheriff or other officer at certain appointed times 1450.

1. Hoping that the enemy..would make a p. of peace BURKE.

Proffer (prǫ·fəɹ), *v.* [ME. *prof(f)re* – AFr. *proffrer, -ir*, OFr. *proffrir*, earlier *poroffrir*, *puroffrir*, f. *por* (:– L. *pro* PRO-[1]) + *offrir* OFFER.] **1.** *trans.* To put before a person for acceptance; to offer, present, tender. Now *literary.* Also *absol.* **2.** with *inf.* To propose or offer (to do something). *Obs.* or *arch.* ME. †**3.** with *inf.* To attempt, essay –1655. †**b.** *absol.* or *intr.* To begin to act or move, and then stop or turn back; *spec.* of a stag –1650.

1. Mr. Winkle seized the wicker bottle which his friend proffered DICKENS. **2.** He proffereth to go for a coach and lets the servant go LAMB. Hence **Pro·fferer.**

Proficiency (prǒfi·ʃĕnsi). 1544. [f. next; see -ENCY.] †**1.** Advance towards completeness or perfection; improvement in skill or knowledge –1855. **2.** The state or degree of improvement attained; the quality or fact of being proficient; adeptness, expertness 1639.

1. We are now in a State of P., not of Perfection 1690. **2.** His P. in the noble Science of Detraction 1699. So †**Profi·cience.**

Proficient (prǒfi·ʃĕnt), *a.* and *sb.* 1590. [– L. *proficiens, -ent-*, pr. pple. of *proficere* advance, f. *pro* PRO-[1] + *facere* do, make; see -ENT.] **A.** *adj.* Advanced in the acquirement of some kind of skill; skilled; expert 1590.

2. To become p. in the use of the gun 1892.

B. *sb.* †**1.** A learner who makes progress in something; opp. to one who is perfect –1742. **2.** One who has made good progress in some art or branch of learning; an advanced pupil; an expert, an adept 1610. Hence **Profi·ciently** *adv.* skilfully.

Profile (prōu·fəil, -fīl -fil), *sb.* 1656. [– It. †*profilo*, now *proffilo* (whence also Fr. *profil*, whence perh. some of the Eng. senses), f. †*profilare*; see next.] **1.** A drawing or other representation of the outline of anything; esp. of the human face, outlined by the median line. **b.** In journalistic use, a biographical sketch 1942. **2.** The actual outline or contour of anything, esp. of the human face 1664. **3.** *Arch.*, *Surveying*, and *Engineering.* A sectional drawing, usu. vertical; *esp.* in *Fortif.*, a transverse vertical section of a fort 1669. **b.** *transf.* The comparative thickness of an earthwork or the like 1810. **4.** In *Pottery* (and *Bell-founding*). A plate in which is cut the exterior or interior outline of one side of the object to be made 1756. **5.** *Theatr.* A flat piece of scenery or property on the stage of a theatre, cut out in outline 1904.

1. *In p.*, as seen from one side. *Comb.* **p. paper,** paper ruled with equidistant vertical and horizontal lines, for convenience in drawing to scale. Hence **Pro·filist,** one who produces silhouettes.

Profile (prōu·fəil, -fīl, -fil), *v.* 1715. [– It. †*profilare* draw in outline, f. *pro* PRO-[1] + *filare* spin, †draw a line – L. *filare*, f. *filum* thread. See also PURFLE *v.*] **1.** *trans.* To represent in profile; to outline. **2.** To furnish with a profile (of a specified nature); also, to cause to form a profile 1823.

Profit (prǫ·fit), *sb.* ME. [– (O)Fr. *profit* :– L. *profectus* progress, profit, f. *profect-*, pa. ppl. stem of *proficere* advance (see PROFICIENT).] **1.** The advantage or benefit (of a person, community, or thing); use, interest; the gain, good, well-being. Formerly sometimes *pl.* **b.** *transf.* Something advantageous or profitable SHAKS. †**2.** The advantage or benefit of or resulting from something –1628.

†3. = PROFICIENCY 1. SHAKS. **4.** That which is derived from or produced by some source of revenue; proceeds, returns. Chiefly *pl.* late ME. **5.** The pecuniary gain in any transaction; the excess of returns over the outlay of capital; in commercial use chiefly in pl. In *Pol. Econ.*, The surplus product of industry after deducting wages, cost of raw material, rent, and charges. 1604.

1. Posts of Honour, Dignity, and P. ADDISON. **b.** *Oth.* III. iii. 379. **5.** Nobody would be an inn-keeper if it were not for the p. 1845. His profits diminished at the rate of 60 per cent 1893.

Phrase. **P. and loss,** an inclusive expression for the gain and loss made in a series of transactions, and the gain or loss made in one transaction; esp. in *p. and loss account*, an account in book-keeping to which all gains are credited and all losses debited, so as to ascertain the net gain or loss at any time. In *Arith.*, a rule by which the gains or losses on commercial transactions are calculated.

Comb.: **p.-rent,** a rent of which the amount is due to a tenant's improvements; **-sharing,** the sharing of profits, *spec.* between employer and employed, or between capital and labour; so *profit-sharer*; **-taking** (*Stock-exchange*), the act of realizing the profit obtainable by the sale of stock, etc., in which a rise in price has taken place. Hence **Pro·fitless** *a.* void of p.; unprofitable, useless.

Profit (prǫ·fit), *v.* ME. [– (O)Fr. *profiter*, f. *profit*; see prec.] †**I.** *intr.* To make progress; to advance; to improve (in some respect) –1612.

My husband saies my sonne profits nothing in the world at his Booke SHAKS.

II. 1. *trans.* Of a thing: To be of advantage, use, or good to; to benefit, further, promote. (Orig. *intr.*, with indirect (dative) obj.) ME. **b.** *intr.* To be of advantage, use, or benefit; avail. Const. *to*. ME. **2.** *intr.* (for *refl.*) To be benefited. late ME. **b.** *esp.* with preps. †*with*, *by*, *of*, *from*: To derive benefit from; to avail oneself of; to take advantage of. late ME.

1. Whatt shall hit proffet a man, yf he shulde wyn all the whoole worlde: so he loose hys owne soule? TINDALE *Matt.* 16:26. **2. b.** Mrs. Burke.. has not profited of the bathing BURKE. All of these..profited by the opportunity to effect their escape 1797.

Profitable (prǫ·fitǎb'l), *a.* ME. [– (O)Fr. *profitable*; see PROFIT *v.*, -ABLE.] **1.** Yielding profit or advantage; beneficial, useful, valuable. (Rarely of persons.) Formerly, also, useful as a remedy. **2.** Yielding pecuniary profit; lucrative, remunerative 1758.

1. Silence or flight were much profitabler for you 1627. **2.** The p. employment of millions upon millions of capital 1825. A p. voyage 1845. Hence **Profitabi·lity, Pro·fitableness,** the quality of being p. **Pro·fitably** *adv.* in a p. manner.

Profiteer (prǫfitī͝ə·ɹ), *sb.* 1797. [f. PROFIT *sb.* + -EER.] One who profits; *spec.* one who makes or attempts to make excessive profit on the sale of necessaries during a period of scarcity, e.g. in war-time. Hence **Profitee·r** *v. intr.* to make excessive profits; to act like a p.

Profligacy (prǫ·fligǎsi). 1738. [f. next; see -ACY 3.] The quality or condition of being profligate.

Profligate (prǫ·fligět), *a.* and *sb.* 1535. [– L. *profligatus* ruined, dissolute, pa. pple. of *profligare* cast down, ruin, f. *pro* PRO-[1] + base *flig-* beat (cf. *afflict*, *conflict*, *inflict*); see -ATE[2].] †**1.** (Const. as *pa. pple.*) Overthrown, overwhelmed, routed –1663. **2.** Abandoned to vice or vicious indulgence; recklessly licentious or debauched; dissolute; shamelessly vicious 1647. **b.** Recklessly prodigal, extravagant, or profuse 1779. **B.** *sb.* A profligate or dissipated person 1709.

2. P. in their lives, and licentious in their compositions JOHNSON. Hence **Pro·fligate-ly** *adv.*, **-ness** (now *rare*).

†**Profligate** (prǫ·fligeⁱt), *v.* 1542. [– *profligat-*, pa. ppl. stem of L. *profligare*; see prec., -ATE[3].] *trans.* To overcome in battle or conflict, to rout; to put to flight; disperse (*lit.* and *fig.*) –1845.

Profluence (prōᵘ·fluěns). Now *rare.* 1568. [– L. *profluentia*, f. *profluent-*; see next, -ENCE.] †A flowing forth or onward; current, stream –1693. **b.** *fig.* The onward flow (of events, etc.). *rare.* 1639.

Profluent (prōᵘ·fluěnt), *a.* late ME. [– L. *profluens, -ent-*, pr. pple. of *profluere*, f. *pro* PRO-[1] + *fluere* flow; see -ENT.] Flowing forth or onward; flowing in a full stream. Also *fig.*

‖**Profluvium** (proflū·viǒm). *Pl.* **-ia.** 1603. [L., f. *profluere*; see prec.] A flowing forth; a copious flow or discharge. (Chiefly *Path.*)

Profound (prǒfau·nd), *a.* (*sb.*) ME. [– AFr., OFr. *profund*, (also mod.) *profond* :– L. *profundus*, f. *pro* PRO-[1] + *fundus* bottom.] **1.** Deep (as a physical or material quality). **a.** Having great or considerable downward (or inward) measurement. late ME. **b.** Deep-seated, deep-reaching. late ME. **c.** Originating in, or coming from, a depth; carried far down (as an inclination of the body) 1550. **2. a.** Of a person: Characterized by intellectual depth; that has penetrated deeply into a subject of knowledge; very learned ME. **b.** Of personal attributes, actions, or works: Showing depth of insight or knowledge; marked by great learning. late ME. **3.** Of non-material things figured as having depth. **a.** Of a subject of thought: Deep in meaning; abstruse, recondite; *occas.*, Difficult to understand; having a meaning that does not lie on the surface. late ME. **b.** Of a condition, state, or quality: Having depth or intensity; in which one may be intensely immersed or engaged; unbroken or undisturbed (as *p. silence, sleep, peace*); deep-seated; deeply-buried, hence, concealed (as a *p. secret*) 1599. **c.** Said of reverence, respect, submission, or the like; often with some ref. to the notion of bowing low 1526.

1. Profoundest Hell MILT. **c.** A sigh, so pittious and p. SHAKS. The three ambassadors..made a p. reverence 1732. **2. a.** Their Abbot..was pious, painfull, and a p. Schollar FULLER. **b.** Their profoundest Speculations 1664. **3. a.** A higher and profounder doctrine 1583. **b.** Profoundest ignorance 1853. **c.** They treat themselves with most p. respect POPE.

B. *sb.* That which is profound; a vast depth; an abyss (chiefly *poet.*) 1640. **b.** *spec.* The depth of the sea or other deep water; 'the deep' (*poet.*) 1621.

b. Expert to try The vast p., and bid the vessel fly POPE. Hence **Profou·nd-ly** *adv.*, **ness.**

Profulgent (profɒ·ldʒěnt), *a. rare.* 1500. [f. PRO-[1] + L. *fulgens, -ent-* FULGENT.] Shining forth, effulgent, radiant.

Profundity (prǒfɒ·ndĭti). late ME. [– OFr. *profundité* (mod. *-fond-*) or late L. *profunditas*, f. L. *profundus*; see PROFOUND, -ITY.] **1.** Depth, in a physical sense. †**a.** *gen.* = DEPTH 1. –1696. **b.** The quality of being (very) deep; deepness; extreme lowness (of a bow) 1604. **c.** *concr.* or quasi-*concr.* A very deep place; the deepest part of something; a (vast) depth, an abyss. Also *fig.* late ME. **2.** Intellectual depth; depth of meaning or content; abstruseness 1450. **b.** *pl.* Depths of thought or meaning; 'deep things' 1582. **3.** Intensity, thoroughness, extremeness of degree 1576.

1. c. Through the vast profunditie obscure MILT. **2.** The profundity of the scripture 1679. **b.** The Spirit searcheth al things, yea the profoundities of God N.T. (Rhem.) 1 *Cor.* 2:10.

Profuse (prǒfiū·s), *a.* late ME. [– L. *profusus*, adj. use of pa. pple. of *profundere* pour forth, f. *pro* PRO-[1] + *fundere* pour.] **1.** Expending, bestowing, or producing abundantly; lavish; wasteful, prodigal. Const. *in*, *of*. **2.** Of actions, conditions, or things: Very abundant; exuberant; copious; excessive 1610.

1. Justinian was so p. that he could not be liberal GIBBON. *fig.* On a green shadie Bank p. of Flours MILT. **2.** The kisses of an enemy are p. R.V. *Prov.* 27:6. Hence **Profu·se-ly** *adv.*, **-ness.**

†**Profu·se,** *v.* 1611. [– *profus-*, pa. ppl. stem of L. *profundere*; see prec.] *trans.* To pour forth; to expend, bestow, or produce freely; to lavish, squander, waste –1771.

Profusion (prǒfiū·ʒən). 1545. [– Fr. *profusion* or L. *profusio, -on-*, f. as prec.; see -ION.] **1.** The action of pouring forth; outpouring (of a liquid); spilling, shedding. Now *rare*. 1604. **2.** Lavish or wasteful expenditure of money, etc. 1545. **3.** The fact, condition, or quality of being profuse; lavishness, wastefulness 1692. **4.** Abundance; lavish or copious supply 1705.

2. A wanton p. of the public wealth D'ISRAELI. **3.** The p...with which he lavished his gold 1838. **4.** Fields, where summer spreads p. round GOLDSM.

Profusive (prǒfiū·siv), *a.* 1638. [f. PROFUSION, after *effusion, effusive*.] Marked by or tending to profusion or lavishness. Hence **Profu·sive-ly** *adv.*, **-ness.**

Prog (prǫg), *sb.*[1] 1615. [Of unkn. origin.] A piercing instrument or weapon; a spike; a skewer; a stiletto.

Prog (prǫg), *sb.*[2] 1655. [perh. f. PROG *v.*[1], = that which is got by progging.] Food, victuals, provender; esp. *colloq.* provisions for a journey or excursion; *slang.* food generally. **b.** *fig.* Food for the mind 1770.

Rings, watch, and so forth, fairly went for p. 1704.

Prog, *sb.*[3] *Undergraduates' slang.* Also **proggins.** 1898. [Perversion of PROCTOR.] A proctor at Oxford or Cambridge. Hence **Prog** *v.*[3] = PROCTORIZE *v.*

Prog (prǫg), *v.*[1] *Obs.* exc. *dial.* 1622. [Of unkn. origin.] **1.** *intr.* To poke about *for* anything that may be laid hold of; to hunt about, *esp.* for food; to forage; also, to beg, to go about begging. †**2.** *trans.* To search or hunt out; to poke out –1656.

Prog, *v.*[2] *dial.* 1811. [f. PROG *sb.*[1]] *trans.* To prick, stab, pierce; to prod.

†**Proge·nerate,** *v. rare.* 1611. [– *progenerat-*, pa. ppl. stem of L. *progenerare* beget, engender; see PRO-[1], GENERATE *v.*] *trans.* To beget, propagate, procreate –1824.

To p. a..far better race LANDOR. So †**Progenera·tion,** procreation, propagation, begetting.

Progenitive (proˌdʒe·nĭtiv), *a.* 1838. [f. *progenit-*, pa. ppl. stem of L. *progignere*; see next, -IVE.] Having the quality of producing offspring; possessed of reproductive power or properties.

Progenitor (proˌdʒe·nitəɹ). late ME. [– OFr. *progeniteur* – L. *progenitor* ancestor, f. *progenit-*, pa. ppl. stem of *progignere*, f. *pro* PRO-[1] + *gignere* beget. See -OR 2.] **1.** An ancestor, a forefather. **b.** *Biol.* An ancestor or ancestral species of animals or plants 1859. **2.** *fig.* A spiritual, political, or intellectual 'ancestor' or predecessor 1577.

1. The most renommed of alle his noble progenytours CAXTON. Hence **Progenito·rial** *a.* of or pertaining to progenitors; ancestral. **Proge·nitorship,** the position or fact of being a p. **Proge·nitress, -trix,** a female p.

Progeniture (proˌdʒe·nitiŭɹ, -tʃəɹ). 1801. [f. L. *progenit-*; see prec., -URE.] **1.** Begetting of offspring; generation. **2.** Offspring, progeny 1893.

Progeny (prǫ·dʒĭni). ME. [– OFr. *progenie* – L. *progenies* descent, family, f. *pro* PRO-[1] + **gen-*, after *progignere* beget; see PROGENITOR.] **1.** The offspring (of a father or mother, or of both); issue, children collectively; descendants. **b.** Of lower animals, and plants 1697. **c.** *fig.* Spiritual or intellectual descendants, followers, disciples 1451. **2.** *fig.* That which originates from something; issue, product, outcome, result. late ME. †**3.** A race, stock, or line descended from a common ancestor –1697. †**4.** Lineage; descent –1775.

1. From this union sprang a vigorous p. HAWTHORNE. **c.** The Lutherans, and all their p. 1616.

Prognathic (prǫgnæ·þik), *a.* 1850. [f. as PROGNATHOUS + -IC.] = PROGNATHOUS *a.*

Prognathism (prǫ·gnǎþiz'm). 1864. [f. as next + -ISM.] The condition of being prognathous. So **Pro·gnathy.**

Prognathous (prǫ·gnǎþəs), *a.* 1836. [f. PRO-[2] + Gr. γνάθος jaw + -OUS.] Having projecting jaws; having a low facial angle; also, of the jaws: prominent, protruding. Opp. to *opisthognathous* and *orthognathous*.

‖**Progne** (prǫ·gnĭ). late ME. [L. *Progne*, var. of *Procne*, Gr. Πρόκνη, name of Philomela's sister, transformed into a swallow.] **1.** A poetic name for the swallow. **2.** *Ornith.* An Amer. genus of *Hirundinidæ* or Swallows, including the common Purple Martin of the United States (*P. purpurea* or *subis*).

‖**Prognosis** (prǫgnōᵘ·sis). *Pl.* **-oses** (-ōᵘ·sīz). 1655. [Late L. – Gr. πρόγνωσις, f. προγιγνώσκειν know beforehand; see PRO-[2], GNOSIS.] **1.** *Med.* A forecast of the probable course of a case of disease; also, the action or art of making such a forecast. **2.** *gen.* Prognostication, anticipation 1706.

Prognostic (prǫgnǫ·stik), *sb.* [XV–XVI *pron-* – OFr. *pronostique* (mod. *-ic*) – L. *prognosticum, -con* – Gr. προγνωστικόν, subst. use of n. of adj. f. προγιγνώσκειν; see prec., -IC.] **1.** That from which the future may be foreknown; a pre-indication, token, omen. **2.** A prediction of the future drawn from such an indication; a forecast, prophecy 1634. **3.** *Med.* A symptom or indication on which prognosis is based 1621.

1. A..comet appeared about the time of her death, and the vulgar esteemed it the p. of that event 1761.

Prognostic (prǫgnǫ·stik), *a.* 1603. [– med.L. *prognosticus* – Gr. προγνωστικός; see prec.] Characterized by prognosticating; foreshowing, predictive. **b.** *Med.* Of or pertaining to prognosis 1648. So **Progno·stically** *adv.*

Prognosticate (prǫgnǫ·stikeit), *v.* 1529. [– *prognosticat-*, pa. ppl. stem of med.L. *prognosticare*, f. L. *prognosticum*; see PROGNOSTIC *sb.*, -ATE[3].] *trans.* To know or tell of (an event, etc.) beforehand; to predict, prophesy, forecast. **b.** Of things: To betoken; to indicate beforehand 1533.

Prudent men prognisticated evil 1842. **b.** Everything seems to p. a hard winter COBBETT. So **Progno·sticative** *a.* characterized by prognosticating; tending to p. **Progno·sticator,** one who or that which prognosticates; †a maker or publisher of almanacs containing forecasts for the ensuing year; also, such an almanac. **Progno·sticatory** *a.* of the nature of a prognostication; serving to p.

Prognostication (prǫgnǫstikē·ʃən). late ME. [– OFr. *prognosticacion, -tion* – med.L. *prognosticatio, -on-*, f. as prec.; see -ION.] **1.** The action or fact of prognosticating; prediction, prophecy 1490. **b.** with *a* and *pl.* A forecast, prediction, prophecy 1440. **c.** A presentiment, foreboding 1760. **†2.** An astrological or astrometeorological forecast for the year, published in (or as) an almanac; hence, an almanac containing this –1643. **3.** An indication of something about to happen; a sign, token, portent, prognostic. Now *rare.* late ME.

3. *Ant. & Cl.* I. ii. 54.

Program, programme (prōu·græm). 1633. [orig., in spelling *program*, – Gr.-L. *programma* (see next); subseq. reintroduced from Fr. *programme*, and now more usu. so spelt.] **†1.** A public notice. *Sc.* –1824. **2.** A descriptive notice, issued beforehand, of any formal series of proceedings, as a festive celebration, a course of study, etc.; a prospectus, syllabus; now *esp.* a list of the items or 'numbers' of a concert, etc., in the order of performance; hence *transf.* the items themselves collectively, the performance as a whole 1805. **b.** *gen.* and *fig.* A definite plan of any intended proceedings 1837. **3.** = PROGRAMMA 2. 1831.

Comb. **p.-music,** music intended to convey the impression of a definite series of objects, scenes, or events; descriptive music.

‖**Programma** (progræ·mă). *Pl.* **-gra·mmata.** 1661. [Late L. – Gr. πρόγραμμα, f. προγράφειν write publicly, f. πρό PRO-[2] + γράφειν write.] **1.** A public notice. (In *Gr.* and *Rom. Antiq.*, and formerly in universities.) –1820. Hence **b.** = PROGRAM 2. –1820. **2.** A written preface or introduction; in *pl.*, = prolegomena 1711.

Progress (prōu·grĕs, prǫ·grĕs), *sb.* late ME. [– L. *progressus*, f. pa. ppl. stem of *progredi* go forward, f. *pro* PRO-[1] + *gradi* step, walk, go, f. *gradus* step.] **1.** The action of stepping or moving forward or onward; travel; a journey, an expedition. Now *rare.* 1475. **2.** *spec.* A state journey made by a royal or noble personage, or by a church dignitary; also, an official tour; a circuit. Now somewhat *arch.* 1461. **3. a.** Onward movement in space; course, way 1595. **b.** *fig.* Going on; course or process (of action, events, narrative, time, etc.) late ME. **4. a.** Forward movement in space; advance 1500. **b.** *fig.* Advance, advancement; growth, development; usu. in good sense, continuous improvement 1603.

1. The Pilgrim's P. from this world, to that which is to come BUNYAN (*title*). **2.** His official tours.. were scarcely inferior in pomp to royal progresses MACAULAY. **3. a.** For see the Morn..begins Her rosie p. smiling MILT. **b.** *In p.*, proceeding, taking place; While these changes were in p. MACAULAY. **4. b.** The p. of manufactures greatly outstrips the p. of agriculture 1862.

Progress (prŏgre·s), *v.* 1590. [f. prec.; earlier stress usu. *pro·gress*; became obs. in England in XVII, but retained or formed afresh in America, whence it was readopted in England *c*1800.] **1.** *intr.* To make a 'progress' or journey; to travel; *spec.* to make a state journey. Now *rare* or *Obs.*, or merged in 2. **†b.** *trans.* To travel through –1641. **2.** *intr.* To go or move forward or onward; to make one's way, advance 1595. **3.** *fig.* Of action or an agent: To go on, proceed, advance; to be carried on as an action; to carry on an action 1607. **4.** *fig.* To make progress; to advance, get on; to develop; usu., to improve continuously 1610. **5.** *trans.* To cause to advance; to push forward. *lit.* and *fig.* 1875.

1. b. Progressing the datelesse and irrevoluble Circle of Eternity MILT. **2.** This honourable dewe, That siluerly doth progresse on thy cheekes SHAKS. **3.** The controversy is progressing 1906. **4.** Our country..is fast progressing in its political importance and social happiness WASHINGTON. Her convalescence had so far progressed HAWTHORNE.

Progression (prŏgre·ʃən). late ME. [– Fr. *progression* or L. *progressio, -on-*, f. *progradi*; see PROGRESS *sb.*, -ION.] **1.** The action of stepping or moving forward or onward. **†a.** = PROGRESS *sb.* 1. –1548. **b.** = PROGRESS *sb.* 3 a, 4 a. 1588. **2.** *fig.* Continuous action conceived as onward movement; going on (of action, life, time, etc.), proceeding, process. Now *rare* or merged in 4. 1474. **3.** *fig.* The action of passing successively from each item or term of a series to the next; succession; a series 1549. **4.** *fig.* = PROGRESS *sb.* 4 b. 1586. **5.** *Math.* The succession of a series of quantities, between every two successive terms of which there is some particular constant relation; such a series itself. late ME. **6.** *Mus.* **a.** The action of passing (in melody) from one note to another, or (in harmony) from one chord to another; a succession of notes or chords. **b.** Sometimes = SEQUENCE. 1609.

2. There is a p.—I cannot call it a progress—in his work toward a more and more strictly prosaic level STEVENSON. **4.** The p. and retrogression of the arts 1877. Hence **Progre·ssional** *a.* of, pertaining to, or involving p.

Progressionist (prŏgre·ʃənist). 1849. [f. prec. + -IST.] **1.** An advocate of progression or progress; a progressive. **2.** One who holds that life on the earth has been marked by gradual progression from lower to higher forms 1859. **3.** *attrib.* or as *adj.* 1871. So **Progre·ssionism,** the theory or principles of a p.

Progressist (prōu·grĕsist, prǫ·g-). 1848. [– Fr. *progressiste*; see PROGRESS *sb.*, -IST.] One who advocates progress, esp. in political or social matters; a reformer, a progressive. **b.** *attrib.* or as *adj.* 1889. So **Pro·gressism,** the principles of a p.

Progressive (prŏgre·siv), *a.* (*sb.*) 1607. [– (O)Fr. *progressif, -ive* or med.L. *progressivus*, f. *progress-*; see PROGRESS *sb.*, -IVE.] **1. a.** Characterized by moving onward, as in the locomotion of men and animals generally 1644. **b.** *gen.* Moving forward (in space); of the nature of onward motion 1667. **2.** Proceeding step by step; occurring one after another, successive 1620. **b.** Applied to certain games at cards, when played by several sets of players simultaneously at different tables, certain players passing after each round to the next table 1890. **3.** Characterized by progress or advance 1607. **b.** *Path.* Of a disease: Continuously increasing in severity or extent 1736. **4.** Advocating progress or reform, esp. in political, municipal, or social matters 1884.

1. b. Thir wandring course..P., retrograde, or standing still MILT. **3.** A people..may be p. for a certain length of time, and then stop MILL. He had to teach that the creation was not merely orderly, but p. 1884. **4.** P. Conservatism is to adopt Liberal principles, and say they were always your own 1897.

B. *sb.* One who advocates or aims at progress or reform 1865. Hence **Progre·ssively** *adv.*, **-ness. Progre·ssivism,** the principles of a p.; advocacy of progress or reform.

Prohibit (prŏhi·bit), *v.* late ME. [– *prohibit-*, pa. ppl. stem of L. *prohibēre* hold back, prevent, forbid, f. *pro* PRO-[1] + *habēre* hold.] **1.** *trans.* To forbid (an action or thing) by or as by a command or statute; to interdict. **2.** To prevent, hinder, or debar (an action or thing) by physical means 1548. **3.** To forbid or prevent (a person) *from* doing something; also with inf. (*arch.*) 1523.

1. They altogether prohibite the use of wine in fevers 1669. **2.** Gates of burning Adamant Barr'd over us p. all egress MILT. **3.** There is no Act.. prohibiting the Secretary of State for Foreign Affairs from being in the pay of continental powers MACAULAY. Hence **Prohi·biter, Prohi·bitor,** one who prohibits.

Prohibition (prōuhibi·ʃən). late ME. [– (O)Fr. *prohibition* or L. *prohibitio, -on-*, f. as prec.; see -ION.] **1.** The action of forbidding by or as by authority; an edict, decree, or order that forbids; a negative command. **2.** *Law.* A writ issuing from a superior court, forbidding some court, and the parties engaged in it, from proceeding in a suit, on the ground that this is beyond the cognizance of the court in question 1548. **3.** The interdiction by law of the importation of some foreign article of commerce 1670. **4.** *spec.* The forbidding by law of the manufacture and sale of alcoholic drinks for common consumption 1851.

3. Manufacturers in want of customers cried out for trade prohibitions 1872.

attrib. **P. party,** a political party in U.S., formed in Sept. 1869 to nominate or support only persons pledged to vote for the p. of the liquor traffic. Hence **Prohibi·tionist,** one who favours p., *spec.* of the manufacture and sale of alcoholic drinks; also *attrib.*

Prohibitive (prŏhi·bitiv), *a.* 1602. [In earliest use – Fr. *prohibitif, -ive* or med.L. *prohibitivus*; later f. PROHIBIT *v.* + -IVE.] **1.** Having the quality of prohibiting; that forbids or restrains from some course of action. **2.** Of taxes, prices, etc.: Such as serve to prevent the use or abuse of something 1886. **3.** *Gram.* That expresses prohibition 1875.

2. The cab-rates are p. M. ARNOLD. A well-nigh p. price 1898. Hence **Prohi·bitive-ly** *adv.*, **-ness.**

Prohibitory (prohi·bitəri), *a.* 1591. [– L. *prohibitorius* restraining; see PROHIBIT *v.*, -ORY[2].] **1.** = prec. 1; esp. with ref. to the liquor traffic, as in *p. law, party*, etc. **2.** = prec. 2. 1849.

Project (prǫ·dʒĕkt, prōu·dʒĕkt), *sb.* late ME. [– L. *projectum*, n. of pa. pple. *projectus* of *proicere*; see next.] **†1.** A plan, draft, scheme, or table of something; a tabulated statement; a design or pattern –1627. **†2.** A mental conception or idea; speculation –1727. **3.** Something projected for execution; a plan, scheme, purpose; a proposal 1601.

2. 2 *Hen. IV*, I. iii. 29. **3.** Projects of draining surrounded grounds 1623. New Projects were every day set on foot for Money, which serv'd only to..incense the People CLARENDON.

Project (prŏdʒe·kt), *v.* 1477. [– *project-*, pa. ppl. stem of L. *proicere* throw forth, expel, f. *pro* PRO-[1] + *jacere* throw.] **I. 1.** *trans.* To plan, contrive, or design (something to be done, or some action to be carried out); to form a project of. Also with *inf.* (now *rare* or *Obs.*). **†2.** To set forth, exhibit; to present to expectation –1697.

1. I projected and drew up a plan for the union FRANKLIN. Sketches projected but abandoned 1865. **2.** I cannot proiect mine owne cause so well To make it cleare SHAKS.

II. Of physical operations. **†1.** *trans.* To throw or cast away (*lit.* and *fig.*) –1603. **2.** To cast, throw, hurl, shoot, impel, or cause to move forward, or onward in any direction. Also *fig.* 1596. **b.** To throw or cast (a substance) *in, into, on, upon* something. (Chiefly in *Alchemy* and *Chem.*) 1599. **3.** To place (a thing) so that it protrudes or juts out. Now *rare.* 1624. **4.** *intr.* To jut out; to protrude beyond the adjacent parts 1718. **5.** *trans.* To throw or cause to fall (light or shadow) upon a surface or into space. Also *fig.* 1664. **b.** To cause (a figure or image) to appear or 'stand out' *on* or *against* a background 1831. **6.** *Geom.* To draw straight lines or 'rays' from a centre through every point of a given figure, so that they fall upon or intersect a surface and produce upon it a new figure of which each point corresponds to a point of the original. (With either the rays, the resulting figure, or the original figure as obj.) Hence, to represent or delineate (a figure) according to any system of correspondence between its points and the points of the surface on which it is delineated. 1679. **b.** *Chartography*. To make a geometrical or other projection or representation on a plane surface of (the earth, sky, etc.) 1855.

2. Before his feet her selfe she did p. SPENSER. *fig.* Can we not p. ourselves..into the future? 1878. **b.** When projected on red-hot nitre, it [plumbago] should detonate 1800. **4.** The booths..projected far into the streets MACAULAY. **5.** The Shade my Body projected, near Noon BOYLE. **b.** He..saw Huxley's form projected against the sky 1860.

Projectile (prǒ₍dʒe·ktəil, -il), *a.* and *sb.* 1665. [– mod.L. *projectilis* adj., *-ile* sb., f. as prec.; see -ILE.] **A.** *adj.* **1.** Of motion or velocity: Caused by impulse or projection. Now *rare* or *Obs.* 1696. **2.** Of force, etc.: Impelling forward or onward; projecting 1715. **3.** Capable of being projected by force, esp. of being thrown as a missile 1865.

3. *P. anchor*, in life-saving apparatus, an anchor adapted to be shot out of a tube towards the place where it is intended to grapple.

B. *sb.* A projectile object; *spec.* a missile adapted to be discharged from a cannon by the force of some explosive 1665.

Comb.: **p. theory,** (*a*) that branch of mechanics which treats of the motion of projectiles, as affected by gravity and the resistance of the air; (*b*) = the emission theory of light: see EMISSION 4.

Projection (prǒ₍dʒe·kʃən). 1557. [– L. *projectio, -on-*, f. as prec.; see -ION. Cf. (O)Fr. *projection*.] **I. 1.** The action of projecting; the fact of being projected; throwing or casting forth or forward 1599. **2.** The casting of some ingredient into a crucible; esp. in *Alchemy*, the casting of the powder of philosopher's stone (*powder of p.*) upon a metal in fusion to transmute it into gold or silver; the transmutation of metals 1594. **b.** *fig.* Change from one thing to another; transmutation 1630. **II. 1.** The forming of mental projects; scheming, planning 1599. †**2.** That which is projected; a project; a proposal –1804.

II. 1. The p. of a canal 1838.

III. The action of placing a thing or part so that it sticks or stands out beyond the general line or surface; the fact or condition of being so placed as to project 1644. **b.** *concr.* Anything which projects; a projecting part 1756.

b. The projections at the corners..are called buttresses 1815.

IV. 1. *Geom.* The drawing of straight lines or 'rays' through every point of a given figure, usu. so as to fall upon a surface and produce upon it a new figure each point of which corresponds to a point of the original figure. Hence, each of such rays, or of such points of the resulting figure, is said to be the p. of a point of the original one; or the whole resulting figure is said to be a p. of the original. 1731. **2.** The drawing according to scale, and on mathematical principles, of a plan, chart, or map of a surface, or a diagram on the flat of a machine or the like; *spec.* the representation of any spherical surface on the flat, e.g. of the whole or any part of the earth, more fully called *map-p.* 1557. **b.** *Chartography*. A representation on a plane surface of the whole or any part of the surface of the earth, or of the celestial sphere; any one of the modes in which this is done 1570. **c.** *Cryst.* The projection of a point in each face of a crystal upon an imaginary containing sphere, called the *sphere of p.* 1878. **3.** The action of projecting, or fact of being optically projected, as a figure or image, against a background 1881. **4.** A mental image visualized and regarded as an objective reality 1836.

2. b. CYLINDRICAL, GNOMONIC, ORTHOGRAPHIC, etc. *p.*: see the adjs. **4.** The youth, intoxicated with his admiration of a hero, fails to see that it is only a p. of his own soul which he admires EMERSON.

Projective (prǒ₍dʒe·ktiv), *a.* 1682. [f. PROJECT *v.* + -IVE.] **1.** *Geom.*, etc. Of, pertaining to, or produced by the projection of lines or figures on a surface. **2.** Jutting out, projecting (*rare*) 1703. **3.** Having the quality of being mentally projected, or the power of projecting 1834.

1. *P. property*, a property (of a figure) which remains unchanged after projection. *P. Geometry*, that branch which deals with p. properties. Hence **Proje·ctively** *adv.*

Projector (prǒ₍dʒe·ktəɹ). 1596. [f. as prec. + -OR 2.] **1.** One who forms a project, who plans or designs some enterprise or undertaking. **b.** A schemer; one who lives by his wits; a promoter of bubble companies; a speculator, a cheat 1616. **2.** One who or that which projects or throws something forward 1674. **3.** An apparatus for projecting rays of light; a parabolic reflector or a combination of lenses 1887. **b.** A camera for throwing an image upon a screen 1884.

1. b. Let not the P. pretend the publike good, when he intends but to robbe the riche and to cheat the poore 1636.

Projecture (prǒ₍dʒe·ktiŭɹ, -tʃəɹ). Now *rare*. 1563. [– L. *projectura* (Vitruvius), f. *project-*; see PROJECT *v.*, -URE.] The fact or state of projecting beyond the general line; in *Arch.*, a projecting architectural member or moulding.

‖**Projet** (proʒę). 1808. [Fr. – L. *projectum* PROJECT *sb.*] A proposition, proposal; the draft of a proposed treaty, etc.

Prolapse (prolæ·ps), *sb.* 1822. [Anglicized f. PROLAPSUS.] *Path.* = PROLAPSUS.

Prolapse (prolæ·ps), *v.* 1736. [– *prolaps-*, pa. ppl. stem of L. *prolabi* slip forward or down; see PRO-¹, LAPSE *v.*] *Path. intr.* To slip forward or down out of place.

‖**Prolapsus** (prolæ·psǒs). 1797. [mod.L., f. late L. *prolapsus* fall, f. as prec.] *Path.* A slipping forward or down of a part or organ, esp. of a part of the viscera, from its normal position into a cavity or through an opening; *spec.* that of the uterus or of the rectum.

Prolate (prōᵘ·leⁱt), *a.* 1694. [– L. *prolatus*, used as pa. pple. of *proferre* bring forward, produce, f. *pro* PRO-¹ + *ferre* BEAR *v.*; see -ATE².] **1.** *Geom.* Lengthened in the direction of the polar diameter: said of a spheroid formed by the revolution of an ellipse about its longer axis. Cf. OBLATE *a.* **2.** Extended or extending in width; *fig.* widely spread 1846.

Prolation (prolēⁱ·ʃən). late ME. [– L. *prolatio*, f. *prolat-*; see prec., -ION.] †**1.** The bringing forth of words; utterance –1734. **2.** In mediæval music, A term used to indicate the relative duration or time-value of the minim to the semibreve in the rhythm of a piece. late ME. †**3.** *Theol.* The 'emission', origination, or procession of the Logos –1721.

Prolative (prolēⁱ·tiv), *a.* 1867. [f. L. *prolatus* in the sense extended, enlarged; see PROLATE *a.*, -IVE.] *Gram.* Having the function of extending or completing the predication.

‖**Prolegomenon** (prōᵘlègǫ·menǫn). *Pl.* **-mena** (-ă). 1652. [L. – Gr. προλεγόμενον, n. of pr. pple. pass. of προλέγειν say beforehand, f. πρό PRO-² + λέγειν say.] A preliminary discourse prefixed to a literary work; esp. a learned preamble; chiefly in *pl.* introductory observations on the subject of a book. Hence **Prolego·menal, Prolego·menary** *adjs.* introductory, preliminary.

‖**Prolepsis** (prole·psis, -lī·psis). *Pl.* **-ses** (-sīz). 1577. [Late L. – Gr. πρόληψις, f. προλαμβάνειν anticipate, f. πρό PRO-² + λαμβάνειν take.] **1.** The taking of something future as already done or existing; also, the assignment of an event, a name, etc. to a too early date; an anachronism, prochronism. **2.** *Rhet.* and *Gram.* **a.** = PROCATALEPSIS 1611. **b.** The anticipatory use of an attribute 1850.

2. b. P. or anticipation..an effect to be produced represented as already produced, by the insertion of an epithet:..'Hang his poison in the sick air' 1875.

Proleptic (prole·ptik, -lī·ptik), *a.* 1656. [– Gr. προληπτικός, f. προλαμβάνειν; see prec. and -IC.] **1.** Of, pertaining to, or characterized by prolepsis; anticipative. **2.** *Gram.* Of, pertaining to, or exemplifying prolepsis; see prec. 2. b. 1866. So **Prole·ptical** *a.* (*rare*) 1627, **-ly** *adv.*

Proletaire (prōᵘlĭtēᵊ·ɹ). Also as Fr. **prolétaire.** 1820. [– Fr. *prolétaire* – L. *proletarius* a Roman citizen of the lowest class who served the state only with his offspring; f. *proles* offspring.] = PROLETARIAN *sb.*

Proletarian (prōᵘlĭtēᵊ·riăn), *a.* and *sb.* 1658. [f. L. *proletarius* PROLETAIRE + -AN.] **A.** *adj.* Of or pertaining to the lowest class of the people. †**a.** In hostile use: Vile, low, vulgar –1734. **b.** Of or pertaining to the proletariate in the modern sense 1851. **B.** *sb.* One of the proletariate 1658. Hence **Proleta·rianism,** the condition of a p.; the political principles and practice of the proletarians.

Proletariate, -at (prōᵘlĭtēᵊ·riět, -ăt). 1853. [– Fr. *prolétariat*, f. L. *proletarius* (see PROLETAIRE) + *-at* -ATE¹.] **1.** *Anc. Hist.* The lowest class of the community in ancient Rome, regarded as contributing nothing to the state but offspring. Also with ref. to other ancient states. 1861. **2.** In ref. to modern society. **a.** Applied to the lowest class of the community. (Often *hostile*.) 1853. **b.** *Pol. Econ.* The class of wage-earners who have no reserve or capital; sometimes extended to include all wage-earners; working men 1858.

2. b. The proletariat or hand-to-mouth wage-earners 1883.

Proletary (prōᵘ·l-, prǫ·lĭtări), *a.* and *sb.* 1579. [– L. *proletarius*; see PROLETAIRE, -ARY¹.] = PROLETARIAN.

Proliferate (proli·fĕreⁱt), *v.* 1873. [Back-formation from next.] **1.** *intr.* To reproduce itself by proliferation; to grow by multiplication of elementary parts. **b.** *Zool.* To produce new individuals, esp. sexual as dist. from nutritive zooids 1878. **2.** *trans.* To produce or form by proliferation 1885. So **Proli·ferative** *a.* characterized by or tending to proliferation. (Chiefly *Path.*)

Proliferation (prolifĕrēⁱ·ʃən). 1858. [– Fr. *prolifération*, f. *prolifère*; see next, -ATION.] **1.** *Path.*, etc. The formation or development of cells by budding or division 1867. **b.** *Zool.* The production of (sexual) zooids, by some hydrozoans 1894. **2.** *Bot.* The condition or fact of being PROLIFEROUS (3 a) 1858.

Proliferous (proli·fĕrəs), *a.* 1654. [f. L. *proles* offspring + -FEROUS.] †**1.** Producing offspring; prolific –1692. **2.** Producing many flowers; prolific (*rare*) 1682. **3.** Of, pertaining to, or characterized by proliferation. **a.** *Bot.* Producing leaf- or flower-buds from a leaf or flower, or other part which is normally terminal; also, Producing new individuals from buds 1702. **b.** *Zool.* Reproducing itself by budding; *spec.* producing sexual or generative (as opp. to nutritive) zooids 1856. **c.** *Path.* Spreading by proliferation 1874. Hence **Proli·ferously** *adv.*

Prolific (prǒli·fik), *a.* 1650. [– med.L. *prolificus*, f. L. *proles* offspring; see -FIC. Cf. Fr. *prolifique*.] **1.** Generating or producing offspring; fertile, not barren. **b.** *Bot.* Producing fertile seed 1828. **2. a.** Producing much offspring or fruit; abundantly productive 1653. **b.** Abundantly productive *of*; abounding *in* 1693. **3.** Causing abundant production; fertilizing 1669. **b.** Characterized by abundant production 1695.

2. a. *fig.* The public lands—that p. source of corruption in the hands of the profligate 1850. **b.** This age being not very prolifique of customers for such a commodity PEPYS. **3.** By Nile's p. torrents delug'd o'er 1738. **b.** A p. year for apples 1908. So **Proli·ficacy,** p. quality or state. †**Proli·fical** *a.* = PROLIFIC *a.* 1, 2. 1608. **Proli·fically** *adv.* **Proli·fic·ly** *adv.*, **-ness.**

Prolificate (proli·fikeⁱt), *v. rare.* 1658. [– *prolificat-*, pa. ppl. stem of med.L. *prolificare*, f. *prolificus*; see prec., -ATE³.] *trans.* To render prolific or fruitful; to fertilize.

Prolification (prolifikēⁱ·ʃən). late ME. [– med.L. *prolificatio*, f. as prec.; see -ION.] **1.** The generation or production of offspring; also, reproductive power; fecundity, fertility. **2. a.** *Bot.* = PROLIFERATION 2. 1760. **b.** *Zool.* = PROLIFERATION 1 b. 1865.

Prolificity (prōᵘlifi·sĭti). 1725. [f. PROLIFIC + -ITY.] The quality of being prolific.

Proligerous (proli·dʒĕrəs), *a.* 1836. [f. L. *proles* offspring + -GEROUS.] **1.** Bearing offspring; generative; germinative. **2.** *Bot.* = PROLIFEROUS *a.* 3 a. 1890.

Prolix (prōᵘ·liks, proli·ks), *a.* late ME. [– (O)Fr. *prolixe* or L. *prolixus* spreading abroad, extended, lit. 'poured forth', f. *pro* PRO-¹ + pa. ppl. formation on base of *liquēre* be LIQUID.] **1.** Of long duration, lengthy; of a speech or writing, wordy, tedious. **2.** Of a person: Given to lengthy tediousness in speech or writing; long-winded 1527. **3.** Long in measurement or extent. Now *rare.* 1650.

1. Prolixe prayers, hindering the preaching of the Word 1651. **2.** Conscious dulness has little right to be p. JOHNSON. **3.** With wig p., down flowing to his waist COWPER. Hence **Prolix-ly** *adv.*, **-ness.**

†**Proli·xious,** *a.* 1527. [irreg. f. L. *prolixus* + -OUS.] **1.** = PROLIX *a.* 1, 2. –1632. **2.** Long in extent or duration –1604.

2. Lay by all nicetie, and p. blushes SHAKS.

Prolixity (proli·ksĭti). late ME. [– (O)Fr. *prolixité* – late L. *prolixitas,* f. L. *prolixus;* see PROLIX, -ITY.] **1.** The quality or state of being prolix; length of discourse; copiousness of detail; *esp.* tedious or tiresome lengthiness. **2.** Material length. Now *joc.* 1543.

1. The..verbose p. of the narrative 1864. **2.** The monkey..with a thick tail curling out into preposterous p. HAWTHORNE.

Prolocution (prǫl-, prōᵘlŏkiū·ʃən). 1597. [Partly – late L. *prolocutio* preamble, f. *proloqui,* here identified with *præloqui* to speak before; partly f. PRO-¹ + LOCUTION.] **1.** A preliminary speech or remark (*rare*). †**2.** The use of ambiguous language so as to mislead –1716. **3.** Acting as spokesman (*rare*) 1826.

Prolocutor (prōᵘ·lŏkiŭtǫɹ, prolǫ·kiŭtəɹ). 1475. [– L. *prolocutor* pleader, advocate, agent-noun of *proloqui* speak out; see PRO-¹, LOCUTION.] One who speaks for another or others; a spokesman. Now *rare* in gen. sense. **b.** The chairman of the Lower House of Convocation of either province of the Church of England; he is spokesman of that body in the Upper House 1560. **c.** The presiding officer of an assembly; a chairman, 'speaker' 1591. Hence **Prolocutorship,** the office of p.

Prologize (prǫ·lŏdʒəiz, prōᵘ·l-), *v.* See also PROLOGUIZE. 1608. [– med.L. *prologizare* – Gr. προλογίζειν speak the prologue; see next, -IZE.] *intr.* To compose or speak a prologue. Hence **Pro·logizer.**

Prologue (prōᵘ·lǫg), *sb.* [ME. *prolog* – (O)Fr. *prologue* – L. *prologus* – Gr. πρόλογος, f. πρό PRO-² + λόγος speech.] **1.** The preface or introduction to a discourse or performance; *esp.* a discourse or poem introducing a dramatic performance. **b.** *transf.* and *fig.* An introductory or preliminary act, proceeding, or event 1593. **2.** One who speaks the prologue to a play 1579.

1. b. My death..is made the P. to their Play SHAKS. Hence **Pro·logue** *v. trans.* to introduce or furnish with a p.; also *fig.*

Prologuize (prōᵘ·lŏgəiz), *v.* 1761. [f. prec. + -IZE.] *intr.* To write or deliver a prologue.

Prolong (prŏlǫ·ŋ), *v.* late ME. [XV *prolonge* – (O)Fr. *prolonger;* later – late L. *prolongare,* f. *pro* PRO-¹ + *longus* LONG. Cf. OFr. *prolonguer.*] **1.** *trans.* To lengthen out in time; to extend in duration; to continue, carry on. †**2.** To delay, postpone –1785. †**b.** To prorogue (parliament) –1649. †**3.** *intr.* To delay, put off. Also with *inf.* –1623. **4.** *trans.* To lengthen the pronunciation of (a word or syllable); to draw out (a sound) 1560. **5.** To extend in spatial length; to make longer 1573.

1. To sing thy Praise, wou'd Heav'n my Breath p. DRYDEN. **2.** But wherto now shold I p. my death? SURREY. **5.** Up to which the fault..had prolonged itself as a crevasse TYNDALL. Hence **Prolo·ngable** *a.* **Prolonger** (-ǫ·ŋgəɹ). **Prolo·ngment** (*rare*), prolongation.

Prolongate (prōᵘ·lǫngeⁱt), *v. rare.* 1597. [– *prolongat-,* pa. ppl. stem of late L. *prolongare;* see prec., -ATE³.] *trans.* To prolong, lengthen.

Prolongation (prōᵘlǫŋgēⁱ·ʃən). late ME. [– (O)Fr. *prolongation* or late L. *prolongatio,* f. as prec.; see -ION.] **1.** Lengthening or extension in time; extension of the duration of anything. †**2.** Delay, postponement –1622. **3.** The lengthening or prolonging of a syllable, note, etc. 1589. **4.** Linear extension in space; with *a* and *pl.*, an instance of this; an addition by which the length is increased 1671.

‖**Prolonge** (prolõnʒ). 1858. [Fr., f. *prolonger* PROLONG.] *Mil.* A rope composed of three pieces joined by two open rings, and having a hook at one end and a toggle at the other, used for moving a gun when unlimbered, and for various other purposes.

Prolusion (prolⁱū·ʒən). 1601. [– L. *prolusio, -on-,* f. *prolus-,* pa. ppl. stem of *proludere,* f. *pro* PRO-¹ + *ludere* play; see -ION.] **1.** A display introductory to a game, performance, or entertainment; a preliminary attempt. **2.** A preliminary essay or article; a slight literary production 1627.

2. My Treatise..was intended but for a p. EVELYN. So **Prolu·sory** *a.* preliminary, introductory.

Prom, colloq. abbrev. of PROMENADE *sb.* 2, b. and PROMENADE *concert.*

Promenade (prǫmĕnā·d, -ən-, -ēⁱ·d), *sb.* 1567. [– Fr. *promenade,* f. *se promener* walk, refl. of *promener* cause to walk; see -ADE.] **1.** A walk taken (usu. at a leisurely pace) for exercise or amusement, or (esp.) to and fro for display, or as part of a social ceremony. Also *transf.* **2.** A place for promenading; *esp.* a paved public walk for social promenades 1648. **b.** *U.S.* A ball or dance at a school or college 1905.

1. To see the exhibition lit up for a p. SCOTT. *attrib.*: *p. deck;* **p. band,** a band that performs at a p. concert; **p. concert,** a concert at which the audience walk about instead of being seated.

Promenade (prǫmĕnā·d, -ən-, ēⁱ·d), *v.* 1588. [f. prec.] **1.** *intr.* To make a promenade; to walk about (or ride, etc.), esp. for amusement or display; to parade. **2.** *trans.* To make a promenade through, to walk about (a place) 1837. **3.** (= Fr. *promener*): To lead (a person, etc.) about a place, esp. in the way of display. Also *fig.* 1850.

1. Promenading gently on horseback CARLYLE. Hence **Promena·der.**

‖**Promerops** (prǫ·mĕrǫps). *Pl.* **promeropes** (-me·ropīz). 1827. [mod.L. (Réaumur) f. Gr. πρό before + μέροψ bee-eater.] *Ornith.* A South African genus of birds, including the Cape Promerops, *P. cafer,* a small bird with a long curved slender bill and a very long tail, and the Natal species, *P. gurneyi.*

Promethean (prŏmī·þiăn), *a.* (*sb.*) 1588. [f. PROMETHEUS + -AN; see -EAN.] **1.** Of, pertaining to, or resembling Prometheus, in his skill, art, or punishment. †**2.** Applied to a contrivance invented in 1828 and used before the introduction of phosphorus or lucifer matches for obtaining a light readily –1889.

1. *L.L.L.* IV. iii. 304.

Prometheus (prŏmī·þiūs). 1588. [L. *Prometheus,* Gr. Προμηθεύς.] *Gr. Myth.* A demigod (son of the Titan Iapetus), who made man out of clay, stole fire from Olympus, and taught men the use of it and various arts, for which he was chained by Zeus to a rock in the Caucasus, where his liver was preyed upon every day by a vulture. Hence allusively.

Prominence (prǫ·minĕns). 1598. [– Fr. †*prominence* – L. *prominentia* jutting out; see next, -ENCE.] **1.** The fact or condition of being physically prominent 1611. **2.** That which is prominent; a projection, protuberance 1598. **3.** The quality or state of being conspicuous or plainly apparent 1828. **4.** Any conspicuous or salient point or matter 1827.

2. *Solar p.*, a projecting cloud of incandescent hydrogen, etc., above the chromosphere of the sun, best seen during an eclipse. Also *attrib.*, as *p.-spectrum.* **3.** Its importance comes into historical p. STUBBS. So **Pro·minency.**

Prominent (prǫ·minĕnt), *a.* (*sb.*) 1545. [– L. *prominens, -ent-,* pr. pple. of *prominēre* jut out, f. *pro* PRO-¹ + base meaning 'jut' (cf. *eminent, imminent, menace*); see -ENT.] **1.** Jutting or standing out; projecting, protuberant. **2.** Conspicuous 1759. **b.** *fig.* Standing out so as to strike the attention; conspicuous; distinguished above others 1849.

1. An orifice with p. tumid lips 1870. **2.** The most p. object was a mountain on the other side of the valley 1883. **b.** Attachment to France had been p. among the crimes imputed by the Commons to Clarendon MACAULAY.

B. *sb.* Any cuspidate moth of the genus *Notodonta* 1819. Hence **Pro·minent-ly** *adv.*, **-ness.**

Promiscuity (prǫmiskiū·ĭti). 1849. [f. next + -ITY. Cf. Fr. *promiscuité.*] **1.** The condition of being promiscuous; indiscriminate mixture; promiscuousness. **2.** Promiscuous sexual union 1865.

Promiscuous (prŏmi·skiu,əs), *a.* 1603. [f. L. *promiscuus,* f. *pro* PRO-¹ + *miscēre* mix; see -UOUS.] **1.** Consisting of members or elements of different kinds massed together without order; of mixed and disorderly composition or character; also, with *pl. sb.*, of various kinds mixed together. **b.** Rarely of a single thing 1663. **2.** That is without discrimination or method; confusedly mingled, indiscriminate 1605. **b.** Of an agent or agency: Making no distinctions; undiscriminating 1633. **3.** Casual, carelessly irregular (*vulgar* or *colloq.*) 1837. **4.** quasi-*adv.* Promiscuously 1671.

1. While the p. croud stood yet aloof MILT. **b.** A wild p. sound POPE. **2.** To forbid the p. Use of Women 1650. Hence **Promi·scuous-ly** *adv.* in a p. manner; **-ness** (*rare*).

Promise (prǫ·mis), *sb.* late ME. [– L. *promissum,* subst. use of n. pa. pple. of *promittere* send or put forth, promise, f. *pro* PRO-¹ + *mittere* send.] **1.** A declaration made to another person with respect to the future, stating that one will do, or refrain from, some specified act, or that one will give some specified thing. (Usu. in good sense.) **2.** In religious use: A Divine assurance of future good or blessing; *spec.* that made to Abraham with respect to his posterity (Gen. 12:2, etc.) 1502. **3.** *transf.* The thing promised; *contextually* (with *claim*) = the fulfilment of a promise 1526. **4.** *fig.* That which affords a ground of expectation of something to come, esp. of future good; a pledge, earnest, pre-indication (*of* something) 1532.

1. Geuyng them faire wordes, and makyng large promises 1548. *Breach of p.* = breach of a p. to marry; also *attrib.* as in *breach-of-p. case.* **2.** *Land of p.* (tr. τὴν γῆν τῆς ἐπαγγελίας, Heb. 11:9): = PROMISED *land;* also *fig. Bow of p.*, the rainbow (see Gen. 9:12–17). **3.** He stood once more before her face, Claiming her p. TENNYSON. **4.** Phr. *To give* (*afford, show,* etc.) *p.*, to afford expectation *of* something, esp. good. *Of great* (*high,* etc.) *p.*, such as leads one to expect future excellence; very promising.

Promise (prǫ·mis), *v.* late ME. [f. prec., after (O)Fr. *promettre* or L. *promittere.*] **1.** *trans.* To make promise of; to undertake or engage, by word or writing addressed to another person, to do or refrain from (some specified act), or to give (some specified thing): usu. to the advantage of the person concerned. Often with dative (with or without *to*) of the promisee. **2.** *absol.* or *intr.* To make a promise; to engage to do or give something 1447. **3.** *spec. trans.* To engage to give (e.g. a daughter) in marriage to another; to betroth 1548. **4.** *To p. oneself* (something): to entertain the (pleasing) expectation of 1617. **5.** *colloq.* With *obj. cl.* or *parenthetically,* and with *dat.* of person: To assert confidently, to declare; chiefly in phr. *I p. you* = I assure you, I tell you plainly 1440. **6.** *fig.* To afford ground of expectation of; to lead one to expect (something good or bad); to give pre-indication of 1594. **b.** *absol.* or *intr.* To encourage expectation, to give tokens; usu. with adv., as *fair, well* 1601.

1. They did p. and vowe three things in my name *Bk. Com. Prayer, Catechism.* He promis'd to meete me two howres since SHAKS. **3.** Her father..will not p. her to any man, Vntill the elder sister first be wed SHAKS. **5.** You wont get a lamb out of our fold, I p. you 1777. Magnificent dandies, I p. you, some of us were THACKERAY. **6.** He..promised to be stout when grown up DE FOE. **b.** The weather promising fair 1687. Hence **Pro:missee·,** the person to whom a promise is made. **Pro·miser, -or,** the person who makes a promise.

Promised (prǫ·mist), *ppl. a.* 1538. [f. prec. + -ED¹.] Undertaken to be done or given; of which promise is made.

P. land, the land of Canaan, as promised to Abraham and his posterity (Gen. 12:7, 13:15, etc.); hence applied to heaven or any place of felicity.

Promising (prǫ·misiŋ), *ppl. a.* 1601. [f. as prec. + -ING².] **1.** *lit.* That makes a promise or promises 1720. **2.** *fig.* Affording expectation of good; showing signs of future excellence or success; likely to turn out well 1601.

Promissive (promi·siv), *a.* Now *rare.* 1635. [– late L. *promissivus* promising, applied to the future tense; see PROMISE, -IVE.] Conveying, implying, or having the character of a promise; promissory.

Promissory (prǫ·misəri), *a.* 1649. [– med.L. *promissorius*, f. L. *promissor*; see -ORY².] Conveying, containing, or implying a promise; of, pertaining to, or of the nature of a promise. Also *fig.*

P. note, a signed document containing a written promise to pay a stated sum to a particular person (or to the bearer), either at a date specified, or on demand. Hence **Pro·missorily** *adv. rare*, in the way of a promise.

Promontory (prǫ·mǫ̆ntəri). 1548. [– med.L. *promontorium*, alt. (after *mons, mont-* MOUNT *sb.*¹) of L. *promunturium*, gen. considered to be f. *pro* PRO-¹ and a deriv. of *mons*; cf. -ORY¹.] **1.** A point of high land which juts out into the sea or other expanse of water; a headland. Also *transf.* and *fig.* **2.** *Anat.* Applied to certain prominences of the body 1831. **3.** *attrib.* (or *adj.*) Resembling a promontory, projecting, outstanding 1579.

1. Monaco stands on a p. of rock which falls in bold cliffs into the sea 1876. **2.** *P. of the sacrum*, an angular prominence formed by the junction of the last lumbar vertebra with the sacrum. *P. of the tympanum*, a protuberance of the inner ear caused by the projection of the cochlea. **3.** Each bold and p. mound CAMPBELL. Hence **Pro·montoried** *a.* formed into or furnished with a p. or projection.

Promote (prǒmōᵘ·t), *v.* late ME. [– *promot-*, pa. ppl. stem of L. *promovēre* move forward; see PRO-¹, MOVE *v.*] **I. 1.** *trans.* To advance (a person) *to* a position of honour, dignity, or emolument; *esp.* to raise to a higher grade or office; to prefer. **b.** *Chess.* To raise (a pawn) to the rank of a piece 1803. **2.** To further the growth, development, progress, or establishment of (anything); to further, advance, encourage 1515. **b.** To support actively the passing of (a law or measure); now *spec.* to take the necessary steps for obtaining the passing of (a local or private act of parliament) 1721.

1. Boniface..was promoted to..the Archbishopric of Canterbury 1874. **2.** The Honᵇˡᵉ Society for Promoting Christian Knowledge 1698.

II. †**1.** To put forth into notice; to publish; to assert, advance (a claim) –1683. **2.** To cause to move forward in space or extent; to extend. *Obs.* exc. *dial.* 1652. **III.** †**1.** To inform against (a person); to lay an information of (a delinquency, etc.); also *intr.* or *absol.* to act as informer –1623. **2.** *Eccl. Law.* To set in motion (the office of the ordinary or judge) in a criminal suit in an ecclesiastical court; to institute (a suit *ex officio promoto*) by permission of the ordinary 1681. Hence **Promo·table** *a.* that may be or is to be promoted.

Promoter (prǒmōᵘ·təɹ). 1450. [AFr. and early mod.E. *promotour* = Fr. *promoteur* – med.L. *promotor*, agent-n. f. *promovēre* PROMOTE. From XVI usu. spelt with *-er*, as if f. PROMOTE *v.* + -ER¹.] **I. 1.** One who or that which promotes or furthers any movement or project. **b.** *Legisl.* One who takes steps for, or actively supports, the passing of a law; now *spec.* of a local or private act of parliament 1741. **c.** *Finance.* One who promotes the formation of a joint-stock company; one who is a party to the preparation or issue of the prospectus; a company-promoter. (Usu. in an opprobrious sense.) 1876. **2.** One who advances another in dignity or position 1425.

1. c. A p., *quoad* p., is not necessarily a bad man 1876.

II. †**a.** One whose business was to prosecute or denounce offenders against the law; a professional accuser, an informer –1670. **b.** *Eccl. Law.* The prosecutor of a suit in an ecclesiastical court 1754.

Promotion (prǒmōᵘ·ʃən). late ME. [– (O)Fr. *promotion* – L. *promotio*, f. *promot-*; see PROMOTE, -ION.] **1.** Advancement in position; preferment. **b.** *Chess.* The elevation of a pawn to the rank of a higher piece 1803. **2.** The action of helping forward; the fact or state of being helped forward; furtherance, advancement 1483. **b.** The getting up of a joint-stock company 1886.

1. Phr. *On p.*, on the way to p., on trial; *to be on one's p.*, to conduct oneself with a view to p. (also *colloq.* to marriage). **2.** Institutions for the p. of learning 1845. Hence **Promo·tional** *a.* of or pertaining to p.

Promotive (prǒmōᵘ·tiv), *a.* 1644. [f. PROMOTE + -IVE, in XVII after AL. *promotivus* (XIII).] Having the quality of promoting; tending to the promotion (*of* a thing). Hence **Promo·tiveness.**

†**Promo·ve**, *v.* late ME. [– L. *promovēre* (see PROMOTE). Cf. OFr. *promovoir* (mod. *promouvoir*), perh. partly the source.] **1.** *trans.* = PROMOTE *v.* 1, 2. –1702. **2.** To move mentally, provoke, incite –1637. **3.** *intr.* To advance, make progress –1655. Hence †**Promo·ver** = PROMOTER 1.

Prompt (prǫmᵖt), *sb.* 1597. [In branch I. f. PROMPT *v.*; in II. f. PROMPT *a.*] **I.** An act of prompting; instigation; something said to incite to action, or to help the memory. **b.** *Theatr.* The act of the prompter 1784.

Comb.: **p.-bell**, the bell used by a prompter to call an actor; **-book**, a copy of a play prepared for the prompter's use; **-box**, the prompter's box on a stage; **-copy** = *prompt-book*; **-side**, the side of the stage on the actors' left (in England), right (in U.S.).

II. *Commerce* (ellipt. for *p. date, day, time*). A limit of time given for payment of the account for produce purchased; the limit being stated on a note of reminder called a *p.-note*; hence = due-date 1755. **b.** ellipt. for *prompt goods*, goods sold under an agreement as to a p. or time-limit.

Prompt (prǫmᵖt), *a.* (*adv.*) late ME. [– (O)Fr. *prompt* or L. *promptus* brought forth, manifest, ready, disposed, pa. pple. of *promere* bring forth, f. *pro* PRO-¹ + *emere* take.] **1.** Ready in action; quick to act when occasion arises; acting with alacrity; ready and willing. †**b.** Ready in mind; inclined, disposed SHAKS. **2.** Of action, speech, etc.: Characterized by readiness or quickness; done, performed, etc. at once, at the moment, or on the spot 1526. **3.** *Commerce.* For immediate delivery (and payment); also, due at once, or at the date fixed 1879. **4.** as *adv.* Promptly; sharp (*mod.*).

1. A man of p. wytte 1555. Tell him, I am p. To lay my Crowne at 's feete, and there to kneele SHAKS. **2.** Such p. eloquence Flowed from their lips, in prose or numerous verse MILT. We deduct 10 per cent for p. cash 1877. **4.** She must be called p. at seven o'clock 1908. Hence **Pro·mpt-ly** *adv.*, **-ness.**

Prompt (prǫmᵖt), *v.* ME. [– med.L. **promptare*, f. L. *promptus* PROMPT *a.*] **1.** *trans.* To incite to action; to move (a person, etc.) *to do* or *to* something. **2.** To assist (a speaker when at a loss) by suggesting something to be said, or (a reciter) by supplying the words that come next. late ME. †**b.** To put (one) in mind SHAKS. **3.** To urge, suggest, or dictate (a thing); to inspire, give rise to (thought, action) 1602.

1. Defer what your passion promts you to do 1673. *absol.* They migrate..as their necessities p. 1856. **3.** Whisp'ring Angels p. her golden dreams POPE.

Prompter (prǫ·mᵖtəɹ). 1440. [f. prec. + -ER¹.] **1.** One who prompts or incites to action. **2.** One who helps a speaker or reciter by prompting him when at a loss 1592. **b.** *spec. Theatr.* A person stationed out of sight of the audience, to prompt any actor at a loss in remembering his part 1604.

Promptitude (prǫ·mᵖtitiūd). 1450. [– Fr. *promptitude* or late L. *promptitudo*, f. L. *promptus*; see PROMPT *a.*, -TUDE.] Quickness or readiness of action; promptness. †**b.** Inclination –1712.

Assurance of address, and p. of reply JOHNSON.

Promptuary (prǫ·mᵖtiu,ări), *sb.* Now *rare.* late ME. [– L. *promptuarium* storehouse; see -ORY¹.] †**1.** A place where supplies, etc. are kept in readiness for use; a storehouse, a repository; the source whence anything is derived –1774. **2.** Applied to a handbook or note-book containing a digest of information, etc. 1577.

Prompture (prǫ·mᵖtiŭɹ). *rare.* 1603. [f. PROMPT *v.* + -URE.] Prompting.

Promulgate (prǫ·mǒlgeⁱt, prōᵘ·-, *formerly* promɒ·lgeⁱt), *v.* 1530. [– *promulgat-*, pa. ppl. stem of L. *promulgare* expose to public view, f. *pro* PRO-¹ + base of *mulgēre* milk, (hence) cause to issue forth, bring to light; see -ATE³.] *trans.* To make known by public declaration; to publish; *esp.* to disseminate (some creed or belief), or to proclaim (some law, decree, or tidings).

The arrogant pedant does not communicate, but promulgates his knowledge CHESTERF. Hence **Pro·mulgator**, one who promulgates or publishes.

Promulgation (prǫmǒlgeⁱ·ʃən, prōᵘ-). 1604. [– (O)Fr. *promulgation* or L. *promulgatio*, f. as prec.; see -ION.] The action of promulgating or fact of being promulgated; publication. **b.** *spec.* The official publication of a new law, ordinance, etc., putting it into effect 1618.

b. The p...of the celebrated Edict of Nantes 1867.

Promulge (promɒ·ldʒ), *v. arch.* 1488. [– L. *promulgare*; see PROMULGATE. Cf. (O)Fr. *promulguer.*] **1.** *trans.* To publish or proclaim formally (a law or decree). Now chiefly an *official archaism.* **2.** To set forth, declare, or teach publicly (a creed, doctrine, opinion, etc.); to bring before the public, to publish (a book, etc.) 1614. Hence **Promu·lger.**

‖**Promuscis** (promɒ·sis). 1576. [Late L., altered f. L. *proboscis.*] †**1.** The proboscis or trunk of an elephant –1709. **2.** *Entom.* The proboscis in certain orders of insects; *spec.* that of the Hymenoptera 1658.

‖**Pronaos** (pronẽⁱ·ǫs). 1613. [L. – Gr. πρόναος (-ον) the hall of a temple, prop. adj.; see PRO-², NAOS.] *Gr.* and *Rom. Antiq.* The space in front of the body of a temple, enclosed by the portico and the projecting side walls; the vestibule. Also, = NARTHEX.

Pronate (prōᵘ·neⁱt), *v.* 1836. [Back-formation from next.] *Physiol. trans.* To render prone; to put (the hand, or the fore limb) into the prone position; to turn the palm downwards: opp. to SUPINATE. So **Pro·nate** *ppl. a.* bent forward and downward (*rare*).

Pronation (prōᵘnẽⁱ·ʃən). 1666. [f. PRONE *a.* (or L. *pronus*) + -ATION; cf. SUPINATION.] *Physiol.* The putting of the hand or fore limb into the prone position, i.e. with the palmar surface downwards (or backwards); the position or condition of being pronated: opp. to SUPINATION.

Pronator (prōᵘnẽⁱ·tǫ̆ɹ). 1727. [– mod.L. *pronator* (see PRONATE *v.*), after *supinator.*] *Anat.* A muscle that effects or assists in pronation; *spec.* one of two muscles of the fore limb, *p.* (*radii*) *teres* and *p.* (*radii*) *quadratus*: opp. to SUPINATOR.

Prone (prōᵘn), *a.* late ME. [– L. *pronus*, f. *pro* forward (PRO-¹), with suffix as in *infernus* INFERNAL.] **1.** Having the front or ventral part downwards; bending forward or downward; situated or lying face downwards, or on the belly. Of the hand: with the palm downwards (or backwards); also, of the fore-arm, or the radius, in the corresponding position. 1578. **2.** *loosely* (as if opp. to *erect*): Lying (or so as to lie) flat; in (or into) a horizontal posture; prostrate. Often predicative or quasi-advb., with *lie, fall*, etc. = flat down. 1697. **3.** Having a downward aspect or direction; having a downward slope. Also *loosely*, steeply descending, headlong. Often predic. or quasi-advb. 1627. **4.** *fig.* Directed 'downwards', or towards what is base; grovelling, abject 1645. **5.** Having a natural inclination or tendency to something; inclined, disposed, apt, liable. Const. *to* with sb. or inf. late ME. **6.** Ready in mind (for some action); eager. *Obs.* or *arch.* 1553.

1. A Creature who not p. And Brute as other Creatures,..might erect His Stature MILT. **2.** The broken column, vast and p. 1835. **3.** From high Olympus p. her flight she bends POPE. **4.** Erect in stature, p. in appetite! YOUNG. **5.** I am not p. to weeping SHAKS. More p. to concord 1665. Not being p. to inflammation ABERNETHY. **6.** *Cymb.* V. iv. 208. Hence **Pro·ne-ly** *adv.*, **-ness.**

Prong (prǫŋ), *sb.* 1492. [In early use also

prang and varying with (dial.) *sprong* (XV); the form suggests connection with MLG. *prange* pinching instrument, Du. *prang* pinching, LG., Du. *prangen* press.] **1.** An instrument with two, three, or more points or tines; a forked instrument, a fork. **b.** Any forked object, appendage, or part 1846. **2.** Each pointed tine or division of a fork 1697. **b.** A projecting spur of any natural object, as a tooth, a deer's horn, a rock, etc. 1802.

Comb.: **p.-hoe,** an agricultural implement with two curving prongs, used like a hoe; hence **-hoe,** *v. trans.*, to break up or dig with a prong-hoe. Hence **Prong** *v. trans.* to pierce with a p.; to turn up the soil with a p.; to fork; to furnish with prongs or prong-like points.

Prongbuck (prǫ·ŋbʊk). 1834. [f. PRONG *sb.* + BUCK *sb.*[1]] = PRONGHORN (strictly, the male).

Pronged (prǫŋd), *a.* 1767. [f. as prec. + -ED[2].] Furnished with or having prongs.

Pronghorn (prǫ·ŋ,hǭɹn). Short for *prong-horn(ed antelope*: see next.

Prong-horned (prǫ·ŋ,hǭɹnd), *a.* 1815. [f. PRONG *sb.* + HORNED *a.*] In *prong-horned antelope*: A North Amer. ruminant (*Antilocapra americana*), resembling a deer, the male of which has hollow deciduous horns with a short 'prong' or snag in front. Also called CABRIE.

Pronominal (prŏnǫ·minăl), *a.* (*sb.*) 1680. [– late L. *pronominalis*, f. L. *pronomen, -min-*; see next, -AL[1].] **A.** *adj.* Of, pertaining to, or of the nature of a pronoun. **B.** *sb.* A pronominal word 1871. Hence **Prono·minalize** *v. trans.* to render p. **Prono·minally** *adv.*

Pronoun (prōᵘ·naun). 1530. [f. PRO-[1] II. 1 + NOUN, after Fr. *pronom* and L. *pronomen* (Varro, Quintilian), tr. Gr. ἀντωνυμία, f. ἀντί ANTI- + ὄνυμα, ὄνομα name.] One of the parts of speech: a word used instead of a noun substantive, to designate an object without naming it, when that which is referred to is known from context or usage, has been already mentioned or indicated, or, being unknown, is the subject or object of inquiry.

Pronounce (prŏnau·ns), *v.* ME. [– OFr. *pronuncier* (mod. *prononcer*) – L. *pronuntiare* proclaim, narrate, f. *pro* PRO-[1] + *nuntiare* ANNOUNCE.] **I. 1.** *trans.* To utter, declare, or deliver (a sentence or statement) formally or solemnly; to proclaim authoritatively or officially. **2.** To declare aloud, make known; to tell, narrate, report. *Obs.* or merged in 1. late ME. **3.** To state definitely; to declare as one's opinion or judgement, or as a known fact. late ME. **4.** *intr.* To make a statement or assertion, now always, an authoritative or definite one; to pass judgement, give one's opinion or decision. Now usu. const. *on* or *upon*; also *for* or *against*. late ME. **b.** *refl.* To declare oneself 1837.

1. The absolucion to be pronounced by the Minister alone *Bk. Com. Prayer*. The pronouncing of Sentence of Death LOCKE. **3.** Pronouncing you a Genteel, Fine, Beautiful Woman 1718. The child was pronounced out of danger 1908. **4.** The majority..pronounced in favour of William's undertaking MACAULAY.

II. 1. *trans.* To utter, speak, articulate. late ME. **b.** With ref. to the mode of pronunciation 1620. **2.** To deliver, declaim, in a certain manner. *Obs.* or passing into I. 1. 1560. (All also *absol.*)

1. Language of Man pronounc't By Tongue Of Brute MILT. **b.** The word is sometimes pronounc'd with a *b* 1686. He pronounces English quite different from other foreigners 1775. **2.** Speake the Speech I pray you, as I pronounc'd it to you trippingly on the Tongue SHAKS. Hence **Pronou·nceable** *a.* that can be pronounced. **Pronou·nced** *ppl. a.* spoken, articulated; *fig.* clearly expressed, strongly marked; decided. **Pronou·ncedly** *adv.* **Pronou·ncement,** the action or an act of pronouncing; a formal statement; a decision or opinion given. **Pronou·ncer.**

Pronou·ncing, *vbl. sb.* late ME. [-ING[1].] The action of the verb PRONOUNCE.

attrib.: **p. dictionary,** a dictionary in which the received pronunciation of the words is indicated.

Pronto (prǫ·nto), *adv. U.S. slang.* 1918. [Sp. :– L. *promptus* PROMPT.] Quickly.

‖**Pronucleus** (proniū·kliŏs). 1880. [mod.L. (E. van Beneden), f. Gr. πρό PRO-[2] + NUCLEUS.] *Biol.* A primitive or prior nucleus; in *Zool.* the nucleus of a spermatozoön or of an ovule, before these unite to form the definitive nucleus of the fertilized ovum; in *Bot.* the nucleus of a gamete, which, by coalescing with another of the opposite sex, forms the germ nucleus.

Pronunciamento (pronɒnsiăme·nto). 1843. [– Sp. *pronunciamiento*, f. *pronunciar* (– L. *pronuntiare* PRONOUNCE) + *-miento* -MENT.] A proclamation, a manifesto; often applied to one issued by insurrectionists, esp. in Spanish-speaking countries.

Pronunciation (prŏnɒnsi,ēⁱ·ʃən). late ME. [– (O)Fr. *prononciation* or L. *pronuntiatio, -on-*, f. *pronuntiat-*, pa. ppl. stem of *pronuntiare*; see PRONOUNCE, -ION.] **1.** The pronouncing of a word or words; the mode in which a word is pronounced. †**2.** Oratorical utterance; elocution; delivery –1748. †**3.** Declaration, promulgation; a pronouncement –1674.

1. They have utterly neglected the frenche mennes manner of pronounciation, and so rede frenche as theyr fantasy..dyde lede them PALSGR. **2.** By P., the Antients understood both Elocution and Action 1748.

Pronunciator (prŏnɒ·nsi,eⁱtəɹ, -nɒ·nʃi,eⁱtəɹ). *rare.* 1846. [– L. *pronunciator* reciter, f. as prec.; see -OR 2.] One who pronounces. So **Pronu·nciatory** *a.* of or pertaining to pronunciation; of the nature of a pronouncement 1806.

‖**Procemium** (pro,ī·miŏm). 1456. [L. – Gr. προοίμιον PROEM.] = PROEM *sb.*

Proof (prūf), *sb. Pl.* **proofs.** ME. [Later ME. *prōf* (obl. form *prōve*), superseding earlier *prēf, preove* – OFr. *preve, proeve, prueve* (mod. *preuve*) :– late L. *proba*, f. *probare* PROVE. Substitution of *prōf* for *prēf* was due to assim. to the verb; the devocalization of *v* to *f* was consequent upon the loss of final *e* (cf. *belief*).] **I. 1.** That which makes good or proves a statement; evidence sufficient (or contributing) to establish a fact or produce belief. **b.** *Law.* (*gen.*) Evidence such as determines the judgement of a tribunal. Also *spec.* (*a*) A written document so attested as to form legal evidence. (*b*) A written statement of what a witness is prepared to swear to. (*c*) The evidence given in a particular case, and entered on the court records. 1481. **2.** The action, process, or fact of proving a statement; the action of evidence in convincing the mind; demonstration ME.

1. As a p. of his esteem and confidence 1832. P. positive that he had thought better of his intention 1883. **b.** Every creditor who has lodged a p. shall be entitled to see and examine the proofs of other creditors 1883. **2.** The burthen of p. was of course thrown on the heresiarch KEBLE. Capable of experimental p. 1860.

II. 1. The action or an act of making trial of anything, or the condition of being tried; test, experiment; examination, probation; assay. late ME. **b.** *Arith.* An operation serving to check the correctness of a calculation. late ME. †**2.** The action of experiencing; also, knowledge derived from this; experience –1613. †**3.** That which anything proves to be; the issue, result, effect, fulfilment; esp. in phr. *to come to p.* –1612. **4.** *esp.* The fact, condition, or quality of turning out well or producing good results; thriving; good condition, good quality; goodness, substance. Now only *dial.* 1616. **5.** The testing of cannon or small fire-arms by firing a heavy charge, or by hydraulic pressure 1669. **b.** A place for testing fire-arms or explosives 1760. **6.** Proved or tested power; *orig.* of armour and arms, whence *transf.* and *fig.*: impenetrability, invulnerability (*arch.*) 1456. **7.** The standard of strength of distilled alcoholic liquors (or of vinegar); now, the strength of a mixture of alcohol and water having a specific gravity of 0·91984, and containing 0·495 of its weight, or 0·5727 of its volume, of absolute alcohol. Also *transf.* Spirit of this strength. 1705.

1. The P. of the Pudding is in eating it 1727. Phr. *To bring, put, set*, etc. (something) *in, on, to p.* **3.** The proofe is best, when Men keepe their authoritye towardes theire Children, but not theire purse BACON. **6.** Phr. *Armour* (etc.) *of p.*; I was cloathed with Armour of p. BUNYAN.

III. 1. A means or instrument for testing. **1.** *Typog.* A trial impression taken from composed type 1563. **2.** *Engraving.* Orig., An impression taken by the engraver from an engraved plate, stone, or block, to examine its state during the progress of his work; now, each of an arbitrary number of careful impressions made from the finished plate before the printing of the ordinary issue, and usu. before the inscription is added (*p. before letter(s)* 1797. **3.** †A coin or medal struck as a test of the die; also, one of a limited number of early impressions of coins struck as specimens 1762. **4.** An instrument or vessel for testing. (*a*) A test-tube. (*b*) An apparatus for testing the strength of gunpowder. 1790. **5.** *Bookbinding.* The rough uncut edges of the shorter or narrower leaves of a book, left in trimming it to show that it has not been cut down 1890.

2. *Artist's* or *engraver's p.*, a p. taken for examination or alteration by the artist or engraver; *signed p.*, an early p. signed by the artist. *Letter* or *lettered p.*, a p. with the signature of the artist and engraver, and the inscription.

Comb.: **p.-gallon,** a gallon of proof-spirit; **-glass,** a deep cylindrical glass for holding liquids while under test; **-mark,** a mark impressed on a fire-arm to show that it has passed the p.; **-plane,** a small flat or disc-shaped conductor fixed on an insulating handle, used in measuring the electrification of any body; **-press,** a press used for taking proofs of type; **-reader,** one whose business is to read through printer's proofs and mark errors for correction; so **-reading; -sheet,** a sheet printed from a forme of type for the purpose of examination and correction; **p. strength** = sense II. 7; **p. vinegar,** vinegar of standard strength. Hence **Proo·fless** *a.* unsupported by p. or evidence.

Proof (prūf), *a.* 1592. [The sb. used as adj., app. by ellipsis of *of*.] **1.** Of tried strength or quality; *esp.* of armour: of tested power of resistance; hence *transf.* and *fig.* strong, impenetrable, invulnerable. Const. *against, to.* **b.** Often as the second element in compounds, as *fire-p., fool-p., water-p.* etc. **2.** Of distilled alcoholic liquors: Of standard strength; cf. PROOF *sb.* II. 7. 1709.

1. Not incorruptible of Faith, not prooff Against temptation MILT.

Proof (prūf), *v.* 1834. [f. PROOF *sb.* or *a.*] **1.** *trans.* To test, prove; to take a proof impression of (an engraved plate, or the like). **2.** To render proof against or impervious to something; *esp.* to render (a fabric) impervious to water, to waterproof 1885.

Proof-spirit. 1790. Spirit of wine, or any distilled alcoholic liquor, of proof strength; see PROOF *sb.* II. 7.

Prop (prǫp), *sb.*[1] 1440. [prob. – MDu. *proppe* vine-prop, support, corresp. in form to MLG. *proppe* plug, stopper (whence G. *propfen* stopper), but the diversity of sense makes difficulties.] A stick, rod, pole, stake, beam, or other rigid support, used to sustain an incumbent weight; esp. when such an appliance is auxiliary, or does not form a structural part of the thing supported. **b.** *spec.* in *Coal-mining*: A piece of timber set upright to support the roof or keep up the strata. (Also *pit-p.*) 1756. **c.** *dial.* or *slang.* The leg; also, the arm extended in boxing; hence, a straight hit (usu. in *pl.*) 1793. **d.** *fig.* Any person or thing that serves as a support or stay; *esp.* one who upholds some institution 1571.

The vine must be set vp with props 1573. **d.** The boy was the verie staffe of my age, my verie p. SHAKS.

Prop (prǫp), *sb.*[2] 1850. [= MDu. *proppe*, Du. *prop* broach, skewer, etc.; cf. prec.] *Thieves' slang.* A scarf-pin.

Prop, *sb.*[3] 1871. *colloq.* or *School slang.* Short for PROPOSITION.

Prop, *sb.*[4] *U.S.* 1833. [Of unkn. origin.] (Usu. in *pl.*) Cowrie shells, used in a gambling game; hence the game itself.

Prop (prǫp), *sb.*[5] 1865. *Theatr. slang.* Short for PROPERTY *sb.* 3. (Usu. *pl.*)

Prop (prǫp), *v.* 1492. [f. PROP *sb.*[1], or – (M)LG., (M)Du. *proppen* 'prop, stay, or bear up'.] **1.** *trans.* To support or keep from falling by or as by means of a prop; to hold up: said both of the prop and of the person who places it. Also with *up.* **2.** *fig.* To support, sustain, esp. a failing cause or institution 1549. **3.** To hit straight; to knock down (*slang*) 1851.

1. To p. the Ruins, lest the Fabrick fall DRYDEN.

Propt on a staff, a beggar old and bare POPE. 2. *Hen. VIII*, I. i. 59.

Propædeutic (prōᵘpidiū·tik), *a.* and *sb.* 1836. [f. PRO-² + PÆDEUTICS, after Gr. προπαιδεύειν teach beforehand.] **A.** *adj.* Pertaining to or of the nature of preliminary instruction; preliminarily educational 1849. **B.** *sb.* **1.** A subject or study which forms an introduction to an art or science, or to more advanced study generally 1836. **2.** *pl.* **Propædeutics.** The body of principles or rules introductory to any art, science, or subject of special study; preliminary learning 1842. Hence **Propædeu·tical** *a.* = A.

Propagable (prǫ·păgăb'l), *a.* 1651. [f. PROPAGATE + -ABLE.] Capable of being propagated. Hence **Pro:pagabi·lity, Pro·pagableness.**

Propagand (prǫpăgæ·nd), *v.* 1901. [Back-formation from next.] *intr.* To carry on a propaganda.

Propaganda (prǫpăgæ·ndă). 1718. [– It. *propaganda*, from the mod.L. title *Congregatio de propaganda fide*; see sense 1.] **1.** (More fully, *Congregation* or *College of the P.*) A committee of Cardinals of the R.C. Church having the care and oversight of foreign missions, founded in 1622. **2.** Any association, systematic scheme, or concerted movement for the propagation of a particular doctrine or practice. Sometimes erroneously treated as a plural. 1842.

Propagandism (prǫpăgæ·ndiz'm). 1818. [f. prec. + -ISM.] The practice of a propaganda; systematic work at propagating any opinion, creed, or practice.

Propagandist (prǫpăgæ·ndist), *sb.* (*a.*) 1829. [f. as prec. + -IST.] **1.** A member or agent of a propaganda; one who devotes himself to the propagation of some creed or doctrine. **2.** *spec.* A missionary or convert of the R. C. Congregation of the Propaganda 1833. **B.** *adj.* Given or inclined to propagandism 1856.

Propagandize (prǫpăgæ·ndəiz), *v.* 1844. [f. as prec. + -IZE.] *trans.* To disseminate (principles) by organized effort; to subject to a propaganda. Also *intr.*

Propagate (prǫ·păgeⁱt), *v.* 1570. [– *propagat-*, pa. ppl. stem of L. *propagare* (prop.) multiply by means of layers or slips, rel. to *propago, propages* set, layer, offspring, f. *pro* PRO-¹ + **pag-* fix; see -ATE³.] **1.** *trans.* To multiply specimens of (a plant, animal, disease, etc.) by any process of natural reproduction from the parent stock; to procreate, reproduce, breed; to cause to breed; *refl.* to reproduce its kind. **b.** *absol.*, or *intr.* for *refl.* To breed, to produce offspring; to reproduce its kind 1601. **c.** *transf.* (*trans.*) To hand down from one generation to another; to reproduce in the offspring 1601. **2. a.** *fig.* To cause to increase or multiply 1592. **b.** To extend (anything material or immaterial) 1647. **c.** *intr.* for *refl.* To increase, multiply itself 1670. **3.** *trans.* To spread from person to person, or from place to place; to disseminate, diffuse (a statement, belief, practice, etc.) 1600. **4.** To extend the action or operation of; to transmit, spread, convey (motion, light, sound, etc.) in some direction, or through some medium 1656.

1. Men..are often content to p. a race of slaves GOLDSM. c. *All's Well* II. i. 200. 2. a. *Rom. & Jul.* I. i. 193. c. As Heresie did p. and increase 1670. 3. To p. the Gospel in foreign parts 1725. Men who made and propagated false rumours 1868. 4. The manner in which the earthquake is propagated from place to place HERSCHEL. Hence **Pro·pagative** *a.* having the quality of propagating; tending to propagation. **Pro·pagator,** one who or that which propagates.

Propagation (prǫpăgēⁱ·ʃən). 1450. [– (O)Fr. *propagation* or L. *propagatio, -on-*, f. as prec.; see -ION.] **1.** The action of propagating; procreation, generation, reproduction. †**2.** *fig.* Increase; enlargement; extension in space or time –1741. **3.** Dissemination, diffusion, esp. of some principle, belief, or practice 1588. **4.** Transmission of some action or form of energy, as motion, light, sound, etc. 1656.

1. Of þe erth & of þe cley we haue owur propagacyon 1450. 2. *Meas. for M.* I. ii. 154. 3. The p. of error MILL. 4. The Nature and P. of Heat 1804.

Propane (prōᵘ·pēⁱn). 1866. [f. PROP(IONIC + -ANE 2.] *Chem.* The paraffin or saturated hydrocarbon C_3H_8, the third member of the series C_nH_{2n+2}; a colourless gas occurring in petroleum.

Propargyl (propā·ɹdʒil). 1866. [f. PROP(IONIC + *arg-* (one of its proportions of hydrogen being characteristically replaceable by silver, *argentum*) + -YL.] *Chem.* A hydrocarbon radical, C_3H_3, = CH ≡ C.CH₂.

Propel (prŏpe·l), *v.* 1658. [– L. *propellere* drive before one, f. *pro* PRO-¹ + *pellere* drive.] *trans.* To drive forward or onward; to impart an onward motion to. **b.** *fig.* To give a forward impulse to 1762.

Treatise on propelling Vessels by Steam 1816.

Propellent (prŏpe·lĕnt), *a.* and *sb.* 1644. Also **-ant.** [f. prec. + -ENT. In XVII f. L. *propellens, -ent-*.] **A.** *adj.* Propelling, driving forward; *spec.* (of an explosive) Adapted for propelling a bullet, etc. from a fire-arm. **B.** *sb.* Something that propels; *fig.* an incentive, a stimulus; *spec.* an explosive for use in fire-arms 1814.

Propeller (prŏpe·ləɹ). 1780. [f. PROPEL + -ER¹.] **1.** *gen.* One who or that which propels. **2.** *spec.* An appliance or mechanism for propelling a ship, aeroplane, or other vessel; most commonly a revolving shaft with blades, often set at an angle and twisted like the thread of a screw 1809. **b.** *transf.* A steamer with a screw propeller 1860.

†**Prope·nd,** *v.* 1545. [– L. *propendēre* hang forward or down, f. *pro* PRO-¹ + *pendēre* hang.] **1.** *intr.* To hang or lean forward or downward; to incline in a particular direction; of a scale, to weigh down, to preponderate –1691. **2.** *fig.* To incline, be disposed, tend (*to* or *towards* something, or *to do* something) –1844.

2. Some sports..more p. to be ill than well used FULLER.

Propendent (prope·ndĕnt), *a.* 1593. [– *propendent-*, pr. ppl. stem of *propendēre*; see prec., -ENT.] Hanging forward, outward, or downward.

Propene (prōᵘ·pīn). 1866. [f. as PROPANE + -ENE.] *Chem.* The olefine C_3H_6, more commonly called PROPYLENE.

Propense (prŏpe·ns), *a.* Now *rare.* 1528. [– L. *propensus* inclining, inclined (towards), pa. pple. of *propendēre*; see PROPEND.] Having an inclination, bias, or propensity to something; disposed, prone; ready, willing. Const. *to* with *sb.* or *inf.* †**b.** Biased in favour of some person, cause, etc.; favourable, partial –1797.

He appears always p. towards the side of mercy JOHNSON. Hence **Prope·nse-ly** *adv.*, **-ness** (now *rare*).

Propension (prŏpe·nʃən). Now *rare.* 1530. [– L. *propensio, -on-*, f. *propens-*; see prec., -ION.] **1.** = PROPENSITY. †**2.** Tendency to move in some direction or to take some position; inclination, as of the scale of a balance –1709.

1. I feele A strong p. in my braine, to court Sleepe 1640. 2. He defines Gravity to be a Natural p. towards the Centre of the Earth HOBBES.

Propensity (prŏpe·nsĭti). 1570. [f. PROPENSE + -ITY.] The quality or character of being 'propense' or inclined to something; inclination, tendency, bent. Const. *to, towards,* (rarely *for, of*) with *sb.*, or *to* with *inf.*

A natural p. in us to do evil DE FOE.

Propenyl (prōᵘ·pĭnil). 1866. [f. PROPENE + -YL.] *Chem.* The hypothetical hydrocarbon radical C_3H_5, the trivalent hydrocarbon radical of the propyl or trityl series.

Proper (prǫ·pəɹ), *a.* (*adv.*, *sb.*) [ME. *propre* – (O)Fr. *propre* – L. *proprius* one's own, special, peculiar.] **A.** *adj.* **I. 1.** Belonging to oneself or itself; (one's or its) own; owned as property; intrinsic, inherent. Usu. preceded by a possessive; sometimes also by *own*. *arch.* exc. in special connections. **2.** Belonging or relating to the person or thing in question distinctively or exclusively; special, particular, distinctive; peculiar, restricted; individual; of its own. Const. *to.* ME. **b.** *Gram.* Applied to a name or noun (written with an initial capital letter) which is used to designate a particular individual object. Opp. to COMMON *a.* III. 2. ME. **3.** *Her.* Represented in the natural colouring, not in any of the conventional tinctures 1572.

1. With his own propre Swerd he was slayn 1400. To judge..with my p. eyes 1877. Phr. *P. motion* (Astron.), that part of the apparent motion of a heavenly body (now usu. of a 'fixed' star) supposed to be due to its actual movement in space. 2. Local Infirmities p. unto certain Regions SIR T. BROWNE. *P. psalms, lessons,* etc., in liturgies, those specially appointed for a particular day or season. b. P. names have strictly no meaning: they are mere marks for individual objects MILL.

II. 1. Strictly belonging or applicable; accurate, exact, correct 1449. **2.** To which the name accurately belongs; strictly so called; genuine, real; normal. In mod. use often following its noun. late ME. **b.** *Arith. P. fraction*, a fraction whose value is less than unity, the numerator being less than the denominator 1656. **3.** Answering fully to the description; thorough, complete, out-and-out. Now *arch.* or *dial.* late ME. **4.** Such as a thing of the kind should be; excellent, admirable, of high quality. Now *arch.* or *vulgar.* late ME. **b.** Of good character or standing; respectable, worthy. *Obs.* or merged in III. 2 b. 1597. **5.** Of goodly appearance or make; 'fine', good-looking, handsome. *arch.* and *dial.* late ME.

1. As I was walking along the common—blown along would be the properer phrase 1828. 2. The earths p. do not unite with oxygen 1807. 3. Old Markham seems in a p. taking 1853. 4. She had a p. wytte & coulde both reade and wryte 1548. b. A p. Gentlewoman SHAKS. 5. These Indians.. were very p., tall and lusty men 1648.

III. 1. Adapted to some purpose or requirement; fit, apt, suitable; fitting, befitting; *esp.* appropriate to the circumstances; right ME. **2.** In conformity with the demands or usages of society; decent, decorous, respectable, 'correct' 1738. **b.** *transf.* of persons. (Somewhat *colloq.*) 1818.

1. Choose not alone a p. mate, But p. time to marry COWPER. 2. b. You hear very p. people.. cry out against some of us 1880.

B. *adv.* Properly. **1.** Excellently; genuinely, thoroughly. Now *dial.*, *vulgar*, or *slang.* 1450. †**2.** Suitably, appropriately –1774.

1. 'Had 'em that time—had 'em p.!' said he 1898.

C. *sb.* or quasi-*sb.* †**1.** That which is one's own; private possession, private property –1550. **2.** *Eccl.* An office, or some part of an office, as a psalm, etc., appointed for a particular occasion or season. Opp. to COMMON *sb.* 5. 1548.

1. How moche thou mayste despende of thyn owyn propyr 1422. †*In p.*, in individual possession; as one's own (opp. to *in common*); They haue their lands and gardens in p. PURCHAS. Hence **Pro·per-ly** *adv.*, **-ness** (now *rare*).

Properispome (prope·rispōᵘm), *a.* and *sb.* 1818. [abbrev. of **properispo·menon** (also in use) = Gr. προπερισπώμενον, neut. pr. pple. pass. of προπερισπᾶν, f. πρό PRO-² + περισπᾶν; see PERISPOME.] *Gr. Gram.* **A.** *adj.* Having a circumflex accent on the penultimate syllable. **B.** *sb.* A word so accented.

Propertied (prǫ·pəɹtid), *a.* 1606. [f. next + -ED².] †**1.** Having a specified property, quality, nature, or disposition –1633. **2.** Possessed of, owning, or holding property 1760.

2. The p. and satisfied classes M. ARNOLD.

Property (prǫ·pəɹti), *sb.* [ME. *proprete* – AFr. **proprete*, (O)Fr. *propriété* – L. *proprietas* PROPRIETY.] **1.** The condition of being owned by or belonging to some person or persons; hence, the fact of owning a thing; the holding of something as one's own; the right (*esp.* the exclusive right) to the possession, use, or disposal of anything; ownership, proprietorship. **2.** That which one owns; a possession or possessions collectively, (one's) wealth or goods ME. **b.** A piece of land owned; a landed estate 1719. **3.** *Theatr.* Any portable article, as an article of costume or furniture, used in acting a play; a stage requisite. Chiefly *pl.* late ME. †**4.** *fig.* A mere means to an end; an instrument, a tool, a cat's-paw –1764. **5.** An attribute or quality belonging to a thing or person ME. **b.** *Logic.* Reckoned as one of the PREDICABLES 1551. †**6.** Usu. with *the*: The characteristic quality of a person or thing; character, nature –1703.

2. They..had no p., but all was in commune 1526. The personal p. of 24 English Bishops 1838. Real p. always falls in value in the vicinity of barracks COBDEN. b. Small properties, much divided 1792. 3. I wil draw a bil of properties, such as our play wants SHAKS. 5. The philosophers had suche ..desyre to knowe the natures & propertees of

thynges 1526. He hath this p. of an honest man, that his word is as good as his hand FULLER. **b.** P...may perhaps be best described as any quality which is common to the whole of a class, but is not necessary to mark out that class from other classes 1870. **6.** It is the p. of error to contradict it self 1651.

Comb.: **p. qualification,** a qualification for office (e.g. of a member of parliament), or for the exercise of a right (e.g. of voting), based on the possession of p. to a certain amount; **p. tax,** a direct tax levied on p. **b.** In sense 3 (*Theatr.*): **p.-man, -master,** a man who furnishes and has the charge of stage-properties at a theatre; **-room,** the room in which the properties are kept.

Pro·perty, *v. Obs.* or *rare.* 1595. [f. prec.] †**1.** *trans.* To make a 'property' or tool of, to use for one's own ends –1758. **2.** To make one's own property, to appropriate 1607.

1. *John* v. ii. 79. **2.** His large Fortune..Subdues and properties to his loue and tendance All sorts of hearts SHAKS.

Prophecy (prǫ·fĭsi). ME. [– OFr. *profecie* (mod. *prophétie*) – late L. *prophetia* – Gr. προφητεία, f. προφήτης prophet; see -CY.] **1.** The action, function, or faculty of a prophet; divinely inspired utterance. **2.** The spoken, or esp., the written utterance of a prophet, or of the prophets ME. **3.** The foretelling of future events; orig. as an inspired action; extended to foretelling by any means; an instance of this ME. **4.** The interpretation and expounding of Scripture or of divine mysteries; applied in the 16th and 17th centuries, and sometimes later to exposition of the Scriptures, esp. in conferences, and to preaching. late ME.

1. P., or the authorized declaration of God's will KEBLE. **2.** The 53rd Chapter of the Prophesie of Isaiah BURNET. **3.** Until the prophesies of Merlin should be fulfilled 1584. Of all forms of error p. is the most gratuitous 1897.

Prophesier (prǫ·fĭsəi,əɹ). 1477. [f. next + -ER¹.] One who or that which prophesies; *esp.* one who predicts or foreshows.

Prophesy (prǫ·fĭsəi), *v.* [XIV *profecy, prophecie* – OFr. *prophecier*, f. *prophecie* PROPHECY; the differentiation between vb. and sb. became established after 1700; for the pronunc. of final *-y* cf. verbs in -FY, and *multiply*.] **1.** *intr.* To speak by (or as by) divine inspiration, or in the name of a deity; to speak as a prophet. **b.** *spec.* To foretell future events. late ME. **c.** In the Apostolic churches, To interpret or expound the Scriptures, to utter divine mysteries (as moved by the Holy Spirit); hence, later, to preach the Gospel. late ME. **2.** *trans.* To utter by (or as by) divine inspiration; *esp.* so to announce (a future event); to predict, to foretell. late ME. †**b.** *fig.* To foreshow SHAKS.

1. Sone of man, prophecy thou, and sey, Thes thingis seith the Lord God WYCLIF *Ezek.* 30:2. **b.** Half-extinguished words, which prophesied of change SHELLEY. **2.** I p. you will not succeed better than I have 1802. **b.** Me thought thy very gate did prophesie A Royall Noblenesse *Lear* V. iii. 177.

Prophet (prǫ·fĕt). [ME. *profete, -phete* – (O)Fr. *prophète* – L. *propheta, -tes* – Gr. προφήτης interpreter, spokesman, esp. of the will of a deity, as in LXX and N.T., f. πρό PRO-² + -φήτης speaker, f. φη-, φάναι speak.] **1.** One who speaks for God or for any deity, as the inspired revealer or interpreter of his will; *loosely*, one who claims to have this function; an inspired or quasi-inspired teacher. †**b.** As tr. L. *vates* or *poeta*, an 'inspired' bard –1840. **c.** Sometimes applied to those who preach or 'hold forth' in a religious meeting 1560. **d.** *fig.* (In non-religious sense.) The accredited spokesman, proclaimer, or preacher of some principle, cause, or movement 1848. **2.** *spec. The P.*: **a.** Mohammed, the founder of Islam 1615. **b.** Applied by (or after) the Mormons to the founder of their system, and his successors 1844. **3.** *pl.* The prophetical writers or writings of the Old Testament. late ME. **4.** One who foretells what is going to happen; a prognosticator ME. **b.** An omen, a portent 1591. **c.** *slang.* One who predicts the result of a race; a tipster 1884.

1. Elisee þe profete WYCLIF. A certayne sorserer, a falce p. which was a iewe TINDALE *Acts* 13:6. **4.** I protest, I know no more than a p. what is to come H. WALPOLE. **b.** 1 *Hen. VI*, III. ii. 32. Hence **Pro·phetess,** a female p.; *spec.* a woman who foretells events. **Pro·phethood. Pro·phetship.**

Prophetic (prŏfe·tik), *a.* 1595. [– Fr. *prophétique* or late L. *propheticus* – Gr. προφητικός; see PROPHET, -IC.] **1.** Of, pertaining or proper to a prophet or prophecy; having the character or function of a prophet 1604. **2.** Characterized by, containing, or of the nature of prophecy; predictive 1595. **3.** Spoken of in prophecy; predicted 1651.

1. Till old experience do attain To something like P. strain MILT. Phr. *P. present, perfect*, the present or perfect tense used to express a certain future. **2.** Now heare me speake with a propheticke spirit SHAKS. So **Prophe·tical** *a.* 1456, **-ly** *adv.*

Prophetism (prǫ·fĕtiz'm). 1701. [f. PROPHET + -ISM.] The action or practice of a prophet or prophets; the system or principles of the Hebrew prophets.

Prophylactic (prǫfilæ·ktik), *a.* and *sb.* 1574. [– Fr. *prophylactique* – Gr. προφυλακτικός, f. προφυλάσσειν keep guard before; see PRO-², PHYLACTERY.] *Med.* **A.** *adj.* That defends from or tends to prevent disease; also *transf.* preservative, precautionary. **B.** *sb.* A p. medicine 1642. So †**Prophyla·ctical** *a.*, **-ly** *adv.*

‖**Prophylaxis** (prǫfilæ·ksis). 1842. [mod. L., f. Gr. πρό PRO-² + φύλαξις a guarding, after prec.] *Med.* The preventive treatment of disease. Also *transf.* So **Prophylaxy** (prǫ·filæksi).

Propine (prōᵘ·pəin), *sb.* 1866. [f. as PROPANE + -INE⁵ 2.] *Chem.* = ALLYLENE.

Propine (propəi·n), *v.* Chiefly *Sc. Obs.* or *arch.* late ME. [– L. *propinare* to pledge; – Gr. προπίνειν, lit. drink before or above, f. πρό PRO-² + πίνειν drink.] **1.** *trans.* To offer or give to drink; to present with (drink). **2.** To offer for acceptance; to present; to put before one, propose 1450. **3.** To present (a person) *with* something 1450.

Propinquity (propi·ŋkwĭti). late ME. [– OFr. *propinquité* or L. *propinquitas*, f. *propinquus* neighbouring, f. *prope* near; see -ITY.] Nearness, closeness, proximity: **a.** in space: Neighbourhood 1460. **b.** in blood or relationship: Near or close kinship. late ME. **c.** in nature, belief, etc.: Similarity, affinity 1586. **d.** in time: Near approach, nearness 1646.

Propio-, propion-. *Chem.* A formative derived from PROPIONIC, entering into the names of compounds related to propionic acid.

Propionic (prōᵘpiǫ·nik), *a.* 1851. [– Fr. *propionique*, f. Gr. πρό PRO-² + πίων fat, in ref. to its being the first in order of the fatty acids.] *Chem.* **P. acid,** the monatomic monobasic acid of the propyl or tri-carbon series, the third acid of the fatty series, $C_3H_6O_2$.

Propitiable (prŏpi·ʃi,ăb'l), *a.* 1557. [– L. *propitiabilis* easy to be appeased; see next, -ABLE. Cf. Fr. *propitiable* (XV).] Capable of being propitiated or made propitious.

Propitiate (prŏpi·ʃi,ēⁱt), *v.* 1645. [– *propitiat-*, pa. ppl. stem of L. *propitiare*, f. *propitius* favourable, gracious; see -ATE³.] *trans.* To render propitious or favourably inclined; to appease, conciliate (one offended).

That they [the Gods] can be propitiated..is not to be allowed or admitted for an instant JOWETT. So **Propi·tiator,** one who propitiates.

Propitiation (prŏpiʃi,ēⁱ·ʃən). late ME. [– late (eccl.) L. *propitiatio, -on-*, f. as prec.; see -ION. Cf. (O)Fr. *propitiation*.] The action or an act of propitiating; appeasement, conciliation; atonement, expiation. **b.** A propitiatory offering or sacrifice (*arch.*) 1552.

b. He is the propiciation for our synnes *Bk. Com. Prayer, Communion.*

Propitiatory (prŏpi·ʃiătəri), *sb.* and *a.* ME. [As sb. – eccl. L. *propitiatorium*, rendering Gr. ἱλαστήριον (LXX and N.T.); subst. use of n. sing. of eccl. L. *propitiatorius* adj. (whence the adj. B.), f. *propitiator*; see PROPITIATE, -ORY.] **A.** *sb.* **1.** The mercy-seat. **b.** *transf.* and *fig.*, esp. applied to Christ 1549. †**2.** *Theol.* A propitiation; an offering of atonement; esp. said of Christ –1726. **B.** *adj.* That propitiates or tends to propitiate; of or pertaining to propitiation; appeasing, atoning, conciliating, expiatory; ingratiating 1551.

Looking about him with a p. smile DICKENS.

Propitious (prŏpi·ʃəs), *a.* 1447. [– OFr. *propicieus*, or f. L. *propitius* favourable, gracious; see -OUS.] **1.** Disposed to be favourable; favourably inclined; gracious. **b.** Indicative of, or characterized by, favour; of favourable import; boding well 1586. **2.** Presenting favourable conditions; favourable, advantageous 1601.

1. Astrology considers some of the Planets in their Influences as p. to Mankind 1681. **b.** The auspices were not p. 1734. **2.** The circumstances were p. to the designs of an usurper GIBBON. Hence **Propi·tious-ly** *adv.*, **-ness.**

‖**Propolis** (prǫ·pŏlis). 1601. [L. (Plin.) – Gr. πρόπολις suburb, also bee-glue, f. πρό PRO-² + πόλις city.] A red, resinous, aromatic substance collected by bees from the viscid buds of trees, as the horse-chestnut; used to stop up crevices, and fix the combs to the hives; bee-glue.

Propone (prŏpōᵘ·n), *v.* Now only *Sc.* late ME. [– L. *proponere* put or set forth, f. *pro* PRO-¹ + *ponere* put, place.] **1.** *trans.* To propound as a question or matter for decision. †**2.** To set before any one as an example or aim; to propose or offer as a reward –1653.

Proponent (prŏpōᵘ·nĕnt), *a.* and *sb.* 1588. [– *proponent-*, pr. ppl. stem of L. *proponere*; see prec., -ENT.] **A.** *adj.* That brings forward or proposes 1687. **B.** *sb.* One who brings forward a proposition or argument; a propounder, a proposer 1588.

‖**Propontis** (propǫ·ntis). 1642. [L. – Gr. προποντίς, lit. 'the fore-sea', f. πρό PRO-² + πόντος a sea, spec. the Euxine.] Ancient name of the Sea of Marmora. Hence **Propo·ntic** *a.* of or pertaining to the P.; *sb.* the Propontic Sea, Sea of Marmora.

Proportion (prŏpōᵊ·ɹʃən), *sb.* late ME. [– (O)Fr. *proportion* or L. *proportio, -on-* (Cicero, tr. Gr. ἀναλογία analogy), derived from phr. *pro portione* (tr. Gr. ἀνὰ λόγον) proportionally, i.e. *pro* PRO-¹ + abl. of *portio* PORTION.] **I.** *gen.* **1.** A portion or part in its relation to the whole; a comparative part, a share; *occas.*, a portion, division, part. **2.** The relation existing between things or magnitudes as to size, quantity, number, etc.; comparative relation, ratio. Also *fig.* late ME. **3.** *transf.* A relation, other than that of quantity, between things; comparison; analogy 1538. **4.** (= *due* or *proper p.*) Due relation of one part to another; such relation of size, etc., between things or parts of a thing as renders the whole harmonious; balance, symmetry, agreement, harmony. late ME. **5.** Size or extent, relatively to some standard; also *fig.* extent, degree. late ME. **b.** Now only in *pl.* Dimensions 1638. †**6.** The action of making proportionate; proportionate estimate, reckoning, or adjustment –1605. **7.** Configuration, form, shape; a figure or image of anything. Now only *poet.* late ME.

1. Therefore let our proportions for these Warres Be soone collected SHAKS. The sea which covers so large a p. of the earth's surface HUXLEY. **2.** The p. of Births to Burials BENTLEY. Phr. *In p.*; The rooms large, but some of them not lofty in p. H. WALPOLE. **4.** Let thy recreations..bear p. with thine age FULLER. *Out of p.*, having no due relation in size, amount, etc. (usu. implying excess). **5. b.** The ice-crags..seemed of gigantic proportions TYNDALL. **6.** *Macb.* I. iv. 19.

II. In techn. senses. **1.** *Math.* An equality of ratios, esp. of geometrical ratios; a relation among quantities such that the quotient of the first divided by the second is equal to that of the third divided by the fourth. late ME. **b.** *Arith.* The rule or process by which, three quantities being given, a fourth may be found which is in the same ratio to the third as the second is to the first 1542. **2.** *Mus.* Ratio (of duration of notes, rates of vibration, lengths of strings, etc.): = sense I. 2, in specific applications 1609. Hence **Propo·rtionless** *a.* that is wanting in p.; disproportionate.

Proportion (prŏpōᵊ·ɹʃən), *v.* late ME. [– OFr. *proporcioner* (mod. *proportionner*) or med.L. *proportionare*, f. L. *proportio*; see prec.] **1.** *trans.* To adjust in proper proportion *to* something else; to make proportionate. Const. *to, with.* 1449. **2.** To adjust the proportions of; to fashion, form, shape. *Obs.* exc. in *ppl. a.* late ME. †**3.** To be in proportion to; to correspond to, to equal –1666. †**4.** To divide into proportionate parts; to mete out –1724. †**5.** To estimate the relative proportions of –1711.

1. The punishment should be proportioned to the

offence MILL. 3. *Hen. V*, III. vi. 134. 4. Proportioning the Glory of a Battle among the whole Army STEELE. Hence **Propo·rtioned** *ppl. a.* adjusted in due proportion, measure, or relation to something else; formed with 'proportions', composed; also in *comb.* as *well-proportioned.* **Propo·rtionment,** the act or fact of proportioning.

Proportionable (prŏpōə·ɹʃənăb'l), *a.* late ME. [– (O)Fr. *proportionable* or late L. *proportionabilis* (Boethius), f. *proportionare*; see prec., -ABLE.] 1. That is in due proportion; corresponding, agreeable, commensurate, proportional. 2. Well-proportioned; symmetrical. *Obs.* or *arch.* 1625.

1. For vs to leuy power P. to th' enemy, is all impossible SHAKS. 2. Nature having done her part in giving him p. lineaments 1625. Hence **Propo·rtionableness. Propo·rtionably** *adv.*

Proportional (prŏpōə·ɹʃənăl), *a.* and *sb.* late ME. [– late L. *proportionalis*; see PROPORTION *sb.*, -AL¹.] **A.** *adj.* 1. Of or pertaining to proportion; relative; also, used in obtaining proportions 1561. 2. That is in proportion, or in due proportion; corresponding, esp. in degree or amount. late ME. 3. *Math.* That is in proportion (sense II. 1); having the same or a constant ratio 1570.

1. *P. compasses*, compasses having two opposite pairs of legs turning on a common pivot, which is adjustable so as to vary the distance apart of the points at each end in any desired ratio. 2. P. Representation finds little favour with the caucuses 1884. 3. The heat is p. to the square of the velocity TYNDALL.

B. *sb.* 1. *Math.* One of the terms of a proportion 1570. †2. *Chem.* A combining equivalent; the proportional weight of an atom or molecule –1855. Hence **Propo·rtionalism,** *Chem.* the system, doctrine, or fact of the combination of elements in definite proportions; the theory or practice of p. representation. **Proportiona·lity,** the quality, character, or fact of being p. **Propo·rtionally** *adv.*

Proportionate (prŏpōə·ɹʃənĕt), *a.* late ME. [– late L. *proportionatus*, f. *proportio*; see PROPORTION *sb.*, -ATE².] Proportioned; that is in due proportion. †**b.** Adequately adapted –1680.

No more is your giuing p. to my liking 1576. Hence **Propo·rtionate-ly** *adv.*, **-ness.**

Proportionate (prŏpōə·ɹʃəneᶦt), *v.* 1570. [f. prec. (see -ATE³), or f. med.L. *proportionare* (see PROPORTION *v.*).] 1. *trans.* = PROPORTION *v.* 1. †2. = PROPORTION *v.* 3. –1666.

Proposal (prŏpōᵘ·zăl). 1653. [f. next + -AL¹.] †1. The action, or an act, of putting before the mind; setting forth, propounding, statement –1678. 2. *spec.* An offer of marriage 1749. 3. The action, or an act, of proposing something to be done; an offer to do something; a scheme or plan proposed 1657. **b.** *U.S.* An offer or tender 1914.

2. Dearest Mamma,—I have had a p.! 1900. 3. Proposals for doing the whole work 1748.

Propose (prŏpōᵘ·z), *v.* ME. [– (O)Fr. *proposer*, repr. L. *proponere*; see PRO-¹, POSE *v.*] 1. *trans.* To put forward for consideration, discussion, solution, etc.; to put before the mind; to state, propound. late ME. †**b.** To set before one's mind as something to be expected; to anticipate –1749. **c.** To put forward as something to be attained 1601. †**d.** To contemplate as a supposition SHAKS. 2. To put forward for acceptance 1586. **b.** *absol.* To make an offer of marriage (*colloq.*) 1764. 3. *trans. spec.* with an action as obj. **a.** To lay before another or others as something which one offers to do or wishes to be done 1647. **b.** To put before one's own mind as something that one is going to do; to design, purpose, intend 1500. **c.** *absol.* To make a proposal or motion; to form a design or purpose ME. †4. *intr.* To carry on a discussion; to confer, converse, discourse SHAKS.

1. Nature herself does not give an answer to the riddles which she proposes 1892. **b.** *Tr. & Cr.* II. ii. 146. **c.** *Ham.* III. ii. 204. 2. P. the Oath my Lord SHAKS. I p. the head boy..for chief 1871. The second part of his duty was to p. the health of the honorary Fellows 1892. 3. **a.** The king proposed the marching to London DE FOE. **b.** He had proposed to conquer Jerusalem 1853. **c.** Prov. *Man proposes, God disposes.* 4. *Much Ado* III. i. 3. Hence **Propo·ser,** one who proposes.

Proposition (prǫpŏzi·ʃən). ME. [– (O)Fr. *proposition* or L. *propositio, -on-*, f. *proposit-*, pa. ppl. stem of *proponere* PROPOUND; see -ION.] 1. The action of setting forth or presenting to view or perception; presentation, exhibition. Now *rare.* late ME. †2. The action of offering for acceptance; an offer –1649. 3. The action of propounding something, or that which is propounded; something proposed for discussion, or as a basis of argument; *spec.* an introductory part of a speech or literary work in which is set forth the subject to be treated. Now *rare* or *Obs.* ME. †**b.** A question proposed for solution; a problem –1600. 4. The making of a statement about something; a statement, an assertion. (*b*) in *Logic*, a form of words in which something (the PREDICATE) is affirmed or denied of something (the SUBJECT), the relation between them being expressed by the COPULA. late ME. **b.** *spec.* Either of the premisses of a syllogism; *esp.* the major premiss (opp. to ASSUMPTION 9). Now *rare* or *Obs.* 1551. 5. *Math.* A formal statement of a truth to be demonstrated (*theorem*) or of an operation to be performed (*problem*); in common use often including the demonstration 1570. 6. The action of proposing something to be done; something put forward as a scheme or plan of action; a proposal. late ME. **b.** A problem, task, or undertaking (*transf.* a person) to be dealt with (orig. *U.S.*) 1893.

2. *Tr. & Cr.* I. iii. 3. 3. The custom of beginning all Poems, with a P. of the whole work COWLEY. **b.** *A.Y.L.* III. ii. 246. 6. When the protector had harde the proposicion, he loked very strangely therat HALL. Hence **Proposi·tional** *a.*, **-ly** *adv.*

Propound (prŏpau·nd), *v.* 1537. [alt. of †*propoune*, for earlier PROPONE. For parasitic *d* cf. *compound, expound.*] 1. *trans.* To set forth, propose, or offer for consideration, discussion, acceptance, or adoption; to put forward as a question for solution. **b.** *Eccl. Law.* To bring forward (an allegation, etc.) in a cause 1685: **c.** *absol.* or *intr.* To make a proposal 1570. 2. *trans.* To propose or nominate for an office or position, as a member of a society, etc. Now *U.S.* 1573. †3. To set before one as an example, reward, aim, etc. –1719. †4. To propose (to do or the doing of something) –1709. †**b.** To purpose (something) –1692. 5. *Law.* To put forth or produce (a will, or other testamentary document) before the proper authority, in order to have its legality established 1753.

1. They propounded Articles of peace and friendship 1634. To answer such questions as they shall p. to you 1720. This theory is formally propounded 1836. 4. After dinner propounds to me my lending him 500 *l.* PEPYS. Hence **Propou·nder,** one who propounds, *esp.* in sense 1.

Propraetor (prōᵘprī·tǫɹ). 1579. [– L. orig. *pro prætore* (one acting) for the prætor.] *Rom. Antiq.* A magistrate who after holding the office of prætor was given the administration of a province not under military control, with the authority of a prætor. Also, one who acted in place of a prætor. Hence **Propræto·rial, Propræto·rian,** *adjs.*

Proprietary (prŏprəi·ĕtări), *sb.* and *a.* 1450. [– late L. *proprietarius* (in med.L. as sb., proprietor), f. *proprietas* PROPERTY; see -ARY¹.] **A.** *sb.* †1. = PROPRIETOR 2. –1790. 2. *Amer. Hist.* The grantee or owner, or one of the grantees or owners, of any one of certain N. American colonies. Also *Lord P.* 1637. 3. A proprietary body; proprietors collectively 1803. 4. Proprietorship 1624. †5. Something held as property; *esp.* a landed property –1846.

3. Certain burdens..borne exclusively by the landed p...of this country 1849. 4. 'Peasant p.' or 'occupying ownership' 1886.

B. *adj.* 1. Belonging to a proprietor or proprietors; owned or held as property; held in private ownership 1589. 2. Holding property; that is a proprietor, or consisting of proprietors 1709. 3. *Amer. Hist.* Pertaining or subject to the proprietor or owner of any one of certain N. American colonies, which were granted by the Crown to particular persons; being such a proprietor; see A. 2. 1704. 4. Of or relating to property or proprietorship 1832.

1. Certain well-known p. tobacco 1900. 2. The p. classes 1844. 4. The p. rights of the Crown 1855. Hence **Propri·etarily** *adv.*

Proprietor (prŏ,prəi·ĕtəɹ). 1639. [f. prec. by substitution of suffix -OR 2.] 1. *Amer. Hist.* = prec. A. 2. Also *Lord P.* 2. One who holds something as property; one who has the exclusive right or title to the use or disposal of a thing; an owner 1645.

2. *Peasant p.*, a man of the peasant class who is the owner of the land he cultivates. Hence **Proprieto·rial** *a.* of or pertaining to a p.; that is a p.; consisting of proprietors; **-ly** *adv.* **Propri·etorship,** the position or condition of a p.; ownership. **Propri·etory** *sb.* = prec. A. 3; *adj.* = prec. B. **Propri·etress,** a female p.

Propriety (prŏ,prəi·ĕti). 1456. [– (O)Fr. *propriété* – L. *proprietas, -tat-* peculiarity, ownership; f. *proprius* proper. Later (XVI) assim. to L.; see -ITY.] †1. = PROPERTY *sb.* 1. –1827. †2. = PROPERTY *sb.* 2. –1711. **b.** = PROPERTY *sb.* 2 b. Now only *Amer. Hist.* 1661. 3. Proper or particular character; own nature, disposition; essence, individuality; *occas.*, proper state or condition. Now *rare.* 1456. †4. = PROPERTY *sb.* 5. –1868. 5. Fitness, suitability; conformity with requirement, rule, or principle; rightness, correctness 1615. 6. Conformity with good manners or polite usage; correctness of behaviour or morals 1782.

1. When men give, they transfer P. to another 1671. 3. Silence that dreadfull Bell, it frights the Isle, From her p. SHAKS. This p., or characteristic in the individual 1876. 4. The several proprieties of the Magnet HOBBES. 5. They..appointed a committee to consider the p., of impeaching Arlington MACAULAY. 6. Propriety's cold cautious rules Warm fervour may o'erlook BURNS. *The proprieties*, the details of conventionally correct or proper conduct.

‖**Proprium** (prōᵘ·priŏm). *Pl.* **-ia.** 1551. [L., neut. sing. of *proprius* PROPER.] **a.** *Logic.* = PROPERTY *sb.* 5 b. **b.** A distinctive characteristic; the essential nature, selfhood 1795.

Pro-proctor (prōᵘ:prǫ·ktəɹ). 1650. [f. PRO-¹ + PROCTOR.] orig. One who acted for the proctor of a university; now, an assistant or deputy proctor in the universities.

‖**Proptosis** (prǫptōᵘ·sis). 1676. [Late L. – Gr. πρόπτωσις, f. προπίπτειν fall forwards.] *Path.* Prolapse or protrusion of some bodily part, esp. of the eye.

†**Propu·gn,** *v.* 1555. [– L. *propugnare* go forth to fight, f. *pro* PRO-¹ + *pugnare* fight.] *trans.* To contend for; to defend, vindicate (an opinion, doctrine, etc.) –1676.

†**Propugna·tion.** 1586. [– L. *propugnatio, -on-*, f. *propugnat-*, pa. ppl. stem of *propugnare*; see prec., -ION.] Defence, protection, vindication –1647.

Propugnator (prōᵘ·pǫgnēᶦtəɹ). 1450. [– L. *propugnator* defender, f. as prec.; see -OR 2.] A defender, champion.

Propulsion (prŏpɒ·lʃən). 1611. [f. †*propulse* v. (XVI–XVII) drive off, repel – L. *propulsare*, frequent. of *propellere* PROPEL; see -ION.] †1. The action of driving forth or away; expulsion, repulsion –1756. 2. The action of driving or pushing forward or onward; the condition of being impelled onward; propulsive force or effort 1799. **b.** *fig.* Impelling influence, impulse 1800.

2. **b.** I set to, with an unconquerable p. to write, with a lamentable want of what to write LAMB.

Propulsive (prŏpɒ·lsiv), *a.* 1758. [f. as prec. + -IVE.] Having the quality of propelling, or the tendency to propel; that drives forward or onward.

The p. movement of the foot in walking 1874. So **Propu·lsory** *a. rare.*

Propyl (prōᵘ·pil). 1859. [f. PROP(IONIC + -YL; so called as being the radical of propionic acid.] *Chem.* The hypothetical alcohol radical of the tricarbon series, C_3H_7; also called *trityl.* Chiefly *attrib.* = PROPYLIC.

‖**Propylæum** (prǫpilī·ŏm). *Pl.* **-æa.** 1706. [L. – Gr. προπύλαιον, subst. use of n. adj. 'before the gate', f. πρό PRO-² + πύλη gate.] The entrance to a temple or other sacred enclosure; *spec.* the entrance to the Acropolis at Athens. Hence, A gateway, porch, or vestibule. **b.** *fig.* An introduction; *pl.* prolegomena 1727.

Propylene (prōᵘ·pilīn). 1850. [f. PROPYL + -ENE.] *Chem.* The olefine of the tricarbon or propyl series, C_3H_6, a colourless gas.

Propylic (propi·lik), *a.* 1850. [f. as prec. + -IC.] *Chem.* Of or belonging to propyl, containing propyl.

Propylite (prǫ·piləit). 1867. [f. Gr. πρόπυλον (see next) + -ITE¹ 2 b. So named as opening the Tertiary volcanic epoch.] A volcanic rock occurring in and considered to be characteristic of various silver-mining regions.

||**Propylon** (prǫ·pilǫn). 1831. [L. – Gr. πρόπυλον, f. πρό PRO-² + πύλη gate.] = PROPYLÆUM. Also *transf.*

Pro-rate (prōᵘ₁rēⁱ·t), *v.* Chiefly *U.S.* 1864. [f. *pro rata* (PRO¹ 5).] *trans.* To divide or assess *pro rata*; to distribute proportionally. **b.** *intr.* To make arrangement or agreement on a basis of proportional distribution 1867.

Prore (prōᵊɹ). Now *poet.* and *rare.* 1489. [– Fr. †*prore* or L. *prora*; see PROW *sb.*] The prow of a ship or boat. **b.** *poet.* A ship 1645.

Pro-rector (prōᵘ:₁re·ktəɹ). 1618. [f. PRO-¹ + RECTOR; also mod.L.] The deputy or substitute of a rector in a university, college, etc.; a vice-rector. Now chiefly in German use. Hence **Prore·ctorate,** the office of a pro-rector.

†||**Pro·-rex.** 1586. [f. L. *pro* PRO-¹ + *rex* king.] A deputy king, a viceroy –1679.

Prorogate (prōᵘ·rŏgeⁱt), *v.* Chiefly *Sc.*: now only *Sc. Law.* late ME. [– *prorogat-*, pa. ppl. stem of L. *prorogare*; see PROROGUE, -ATE³.] †**1.** *trans.* = PROROGUE 1. –1693. **2.** = PROROGUE 2, 3. 1569. **3.** *Sc.* and *Civil Law.* To extend (the jurisdiction of a judge or court) to a cause in which it would otherwise be incompetent 1601.

Prorogation (prōᵘrŏgēⁱ·ʃən, prǫro-). late ME. [– (O)Fr. *prorogation* or L. *prorogatio, -on-*, f. as prec.; see -ION.] **1.** The action of lengthening in duration; extension of time; further continuance. Now *rare* or *Obs.* exc. in *Sc. Law.* **2.** The action of proroguing an assembly, esp. Parliament 1472. **b.** *transf.* The time during which Parliament stands prorogued 1548. **3.** *Sc. Law.* The extension of the jurisdiction of a judge or court to causes which do not properly come within it 1838.

Prorogue (prorōᵘ·g), *v.* [XV *proroge*, later *-rogue* (XVI) – (O)Fr. *proroger*, †*-guer* – L. *prorogare*, f. *pro* PRO-¹ + *rogare* ask.] **1.** *trans.* To prolong, extend (in time or duration); to continue, protract. (*Obs.* exc. as a Latinism.) †**2.** To defer, postpone –1716. **3.** To discontinue the meetings of (a legislative or other assembly) for a time without dissolving it; to dismiss by authority until the next session. Orig. and chiefly in ref. to the British Parliament. 1455. **b.** *intr.* in *pass.* sense: To be prorogued; to discontinue meeting until the next session 1642.

2. The Kinges journey into Scotland must be prorogued untill another yeare 1632. **3. b.** No opportunity was afforded..of discussing the question before Parliament prorogued 1896.

Prosaic (prŏzē·ik), *a.* 1656. [– Fr. *prosaïque* or late L. *prosaicus*, f. L. *prosa*; see -IC.] **1.** Of, pertaining to, or written in prose; (of an author) writing in prose. Now *rare* or *Obs.* **2.** Having the character, style, or diction of prose as opp. to poetry; lacking poetic beauty, feeling, or imagination; plain, matter-of-fact 1746. Hence **b.** *transf.* Unpoetic, unromantic; commonplace, dull, tame 1813.

2. The verses were easy and..p. enough to be intelligible to the meanest capacity 1795. **b.** Marriage settlements are very p. things 1877. So **Prosa·ical** *a.*, **-ly** *adv.*, **-ness. Prosa·icism** = next.

Prosaism (prōᵘ·ze₁iz'm). 1787. [– Fr. *prosaïsme*, f. L. *prosa* PROSE; see -ISM.] **1.** Prosaic character or style. **2.** (with *pl.*) A prosaic expression 1817. So **Pro·saist,** one who writes in prose; a prosaic person.

||**Proscenium** (prosī·niŏm). *Pl.* **-a.** 1606. [L. – Gr. προσκήνιον, f. πρό PRO-² + σκηνή SCENE.] **1. a.** In the ancient theatre, The space between the 'scene' or background and the orchestra, on which the action took place; the stage. **b.** In the modern theatre, The space between the curtain or drop-scene and the orchestra 1807. **2.** *transf.* and *fig.* The front, the foreground 1648.

attrib. as *p. arch, box*, etc.

||**Proscholium, -ion** (proskōᵘ·liŏm, -iǫn). 1676. [mod.L. – Gr. προσχόλιον ante-room of a school, f. πρό PRO-² + σχολή SCHOOL + dim. suffix -ιον (see -IUM). Cf. late Gr. προσκήνιον entrance of a tent, porch of a house.] The 'vaulted walk' fronting the eastern end of the Divinity School at Oxford.

Proscribe (prŏskrəi·b), *v.* 1560. [– L. *proscribere* publish in writing, f. *pro* PRO-¹ + *scribere* write.] **1.** To write up or publish the name of (a person) as condemned to death and confiscation of property; to put out of the protection of the law, to outlaw; to banish, exile. **2.** To denounce (a thing) as useless or dangerous; to interdict; to proclaim (a district or practice) 1622.

1. Ro. Vere, Earle of Oxford, was..banished the realme and proscribed SPENSER. **2.** Before their religion was proscribed and their country confiscated 1850. Hence **Proscri·ber.**

Proscript, *a.* and *sb.* 1576. [– L. *proscriptus*, pa. pple. of *proscribere*; see prec.] †**A.** *adj.* (pro₁skri·pt). Proscribed –1628. **B.** *sb.* (prōᵘ·skript). One who is proscribed 1576.

Proscription (pro₁skri·pʃən). late ME. [– L. *proscriptio, -on-*, f. *proscript-*, pa. ppl. stem of *proscribere*; see PROSCRIBE, -ION.] **1.** The action of proscribing; the condition or fact of being proscribed; decree of condemnation to death or banishment; outlawry. **2.** Denunciation, interdiction, prohibition by authority; exclusion or rejection by public order 1659.

1. This cuntry..was very well quieted by a p. of the O'Connors made by the erle of Kildare 1600.

Proscriptive (pro₁skri·ptiv), *a.* 1757. [f. PROSCRIPTION, after *description/descriptive*, etc.] Characterized by proscribing; tending to proscribe; of the nature or character of proscription. Hence **Proscri·ptive-ly** *adv.*, **-ness.**

Prose (prōᵘz), *sb.* ME. [– (O)Fr. *prose* – L. *prosa* (sc. *oratio*, 'straightforward discourse'), subst. use of fem. of *prosus*, for earlier *prorsus* straightforward, direct.] **1.** The ordinary form of written or spoken language, without metrical structure; esp. as a division of literature. Opp. to *poetry, verse, rhyme*, or *metre.* **b.** with *a* and *pl.* A piece of prose; a prose exercise. Now only in school or college use. 1589. **2.** *Eccl.* A piece of rhythmical prose or rhymed accentual verse, sung or said between the epistle and gospel at certain masses; also called a *sequence* 1449. **3.** *fig.* Plain, simple, matter-of-fact, (and hence) dull or commonplace expression, quality, spirit, etc. 1561. **4. a.** A prosy discourse or piece of writing 1688. **b.** *Old colloq.* Familiar talk, chat; a talk 1805. **5.** *attrib.* (often hyphened). **a.** Consisting of, composed or written in prose 1711. **b.** Composing or writing in prose 1668. **c.** *fig.* = PROSAIC 2. 1818.

1. Things unattempted yet in P. or Rhime MILT. The definition of good p. is—proper words in their proper places COLERIDGE. **b.** When my tutor fond supposes I am writing Latin proses 1901. **3.** A broad embodiment of the p. and commonplace of her class 1900. **4. b.** Long p. with the Duke of Portland till one in the morning 1807. **5. a.** Bunyan..is the Ulysses of his own prose-epic 1875. **b.** Poets and prose-authors in every kind SHAFTESB.

Comb.: **p.-poem,** a p. work having the style or character of a poem; so **-poet, -poetry; -writer,** an author who writes in p.

Prose (prōᵘz), *v.* late ME. [f. prec.] **1.** *trans.* To express in prose; to translate or turn into prose. **b.** *intr.* To compose or write prose 1805. **2.** To talk or write prosily; *old colloq.* and *dial.* to chat, gossip 1797.

1. Al schal passyn þat men p. or ryme CHAUCER. **b.** I've rhymed, I've prosed..In short done everything 1834. **2.** Eternally prosing about the weather 1879.

Prosector (prose·ktəɹ). 1857. [– late L. *prosector* anatomist (Tertullian), perh. through Fr. *prosecteur*; see PRO-¹, SECTOR.] One whose business is to dissect dead bodies in preparation for anatomical research or demonstration, as assistant to a lecturer on anatomy, or the like.

Prosecute (prǫ·sĭkiut), *v.* late ME. [– *prosecut-*, pa. ppl. stem of L. *prosequi* pursue, accompany, f. *pro* PRO-¹ + *sequi* follow.] **1.** *trans.* To follow up, pursue (some action, undertaking, etc.) with a view to completing it. **2.** To carry out, perform; to engage in, practise, exercise, follow 1576. **3.** To follow out in detail; to go into the particulars of, investigate; to deal with in greater detail 1538. †**4.** = PURSUE –1697. **5.** *Law.* **a.** To institute legal proceedings against (a person) for some offence; to arraign before a court of justice for some crime or wrong. Also with the crime or offence as obj. 1579. **b.** *intr.* or *absol.* To institute or carry on a prosecution, to be prosecutor 1611. †**6.** To follow (*fig.*) *with* honour, regard, execration, or other feeling or its expression –1741. †**7.** To persecute –1704.

1. Determined to p. their intended tour 1754. **3.** I do not further p. this subject 1873. **4.** We.. prosecuted them home to Warrington Town CROMWELL. **5. a.** Trespassers will be prosecuted 1909. Phr. *To p. an action, a claim*, †*the law.* Hence **Pro·secutable** *a.* that may be prosecuted.

Prosecution (prǫsĭkiū·ʃən). 1567. [– OFr. *prosecution* or late L. *prosecutio, -on-*, f. as prec.; see -ION.] The action of prosecuting. **1.** The following up, continuing, or carrying out *of* any action, scheme, or purpose, with a view to its accomplishment or attainment. **2.** The carrying on, exercise, performance, or plying *of* a pursuit, occupation, etc. 1631. †**3.** The action of pursuing; a literal pursuit, chase, or hunting –1649. **4.** *Law.* **a.** A proceeding by way either of indictment or of information in the criminal courts, in order to put an offender on his trial; the exhibition of a criminal charge against a person before a court of justice. **b.** *gen.* The institution and carrying on of legal proceedings against a person. **c.** Loosely: The party by whom criminal proceedings are instituted and carried on. Also *attrib.* 1631.

1. Nothing was to be gained by the further p. of the war 1884. **3.** *fig. Ant. & Cl.* IV. xiv. 65. **4.** *Director of public prosecutions*, an English law officer, appointed in 1879, to institute and conduct criminal proceedings in the public interest.

Prosecutor (prǫ·sĭkiutəɹ). 1599. [Partly – med.L. *prosecutor*, f. as prec.; see -OR 2; partly f. PROSECUTE.] **1.** One who follows up or carries out any action, project, or business. **2.** One who institutes and carries on proceedings in a court of law, esp. in a criminal court 1670.

2. *Public p.*, a law officer appointed to conduct criminal prosecutions on behalf of the crown or state or in the public interest; *spec.* in Scotland, the Procurator fiscal in each county, etc. So **Prosecu·trix,** *pl.* **-trices,** a female p.

Proseity (pro₁sī·iti). 1899. [f. L. *pro se* for oneself + -ITY, after *seity*, etc.] *Metaph.* The quality or condition of existing for itself, or of having itself for its own end.

Proselyte (prǫ·sĭləit), *sb.* late ME. [– late (Chr.) L. *proselytus* – Gr. προσήλυθος stranger, sojourner (LXX), convert to Judaism (N.T.), f. 2nd aorist stem (προσηλυθ-) of προσέρχεσθαι come to, approach.] **1.** One who has come over from one opinion, belief, creed, or party to another; a convert. **2.** *spec.* A Gentile convert to the Jewish faith. late ME.

1. *Wint. T.* V. i. 108. **2.** Jewis, and proselitis, men of Crete and Arabye WYCLIF *Acts* 2 : 10. Hence **Pro·selyte** *v. trans.* to make a p. of; to proselytize. Also *absol.*

Proselytism (prǫ·sĭləit-, -litiz'm). 1660. [In sense 1 f. prec. + -ISM; in 2 f. PROSELYTIZE.] **1.** The fact of becoming or being a proselyte; the state or condition of a proselyte. **2.** The practice of proselytizing 1763.

Proselytize (prǫ·sĭlitəiz), *v.* 1679. [f. PROSELYTE *sb.* + -IZE.] **1.** *intr.* To make proselytes. **2.** *trans.* To make a proselyte of 1796.

2. One of these whom they endeavour to p. BURKE. Hence **Pro·selytizer.**

Proseminary (prose·minări). 1774. [f. PRO-¹ + SEMINARY *sb.*] A preparatory seminary or school.

||**Prosencephalon** (prǫs₁ense·fălǫn). *Pl.* **-a.** 1846. [mod.L., f. Gr. πρός toward (used as if = πρό PRO-² 2); see ENCEPHALON.] *Anat.* The anterior part of the brain, consisting of the cerebral hemispheres and other structures; the fore-brain. Hence **Prosencepha·lic** *a.* pertaining to or connected with the p.

Prosenchyma (prǫs₁e·ŋkimă). 1832. [mod. f. Gr. πρός to, toward + ἔγχυμα infusion, after PARENCHYMA.] *Bot.* Tissue consisting of elongated cells closely packed with their ends interpenetrating, and often with the terminal partitions obliterated so as to form ducts or vessels. Also *attrib.* Hence **Prosenchy·matous** *a.* belonging to, consisting of, or having the nature of p.

Proser (prōᵘ·zəɹ). 1627. [f. PROSE *v.* + -ER[1].] **1.** A writer of prose. **2.** One who proses; one who talks or writes in a prosy, dull, or tiresome way 1769.

Prosily (prōᵘ·zili), *adv.* 1849. [f. PROSY *a.* + -LY[2].] In a prosy manner.

Prosiness (prōᵘ·zinės). 1814. [f. PROSY *a.* + -NESS.] Prosy or prosaic quality; commonplaceness; tediousness of writing or speech.

Prosobranch (prǫ·sobræŋk), *sb.* (*a.*) 1851. [– mod.L. *Prosobranchia*, n. pl., f. Gr. πρόσω forwards + βράγχια gills.] *Zool.* A prosobranchiate gastropod. **B.** *adj.* = next.

Prosobranchiate (-bræ·ŋkiĕt), *a.* (*sb.*) 1877. [f. mod.L. *Prosobranchiata* = *Prosobranchia*; see prec. and -ATE[2].] *Zool.* Having the gills in front of the heart, as some aquatic gastropod molluscs. **B.** *sb.* = prec.

Prosodiacal (prǫsodəi·ăkăl), *a.* 1774. [f. late L. *prosodiacus* (= Gr. προσῳδιακός) + -AL[1].] = PROSODIC. Hence **Prosodi·acally** *adv.*

Prosodial (prosōᵘ·diăl), *a.* 1775. [f. L. *prosodia* PROSODY + -AL[1].] = PROSODIC.

Prosodian (prosōᵘ·diăn), *sb.* and *a.* 1623. [f. as prec. + -AN.] **A.** *sb.* = PROSODIST. **B.** *adj.* = next 1817.

Prosodic (prosǫ·dik), *a.* 1774. [f. L. *prosodia* PROSODY + -IC.] Of, pertaining or relating to prosody. So **Proso·dical** *a.*, **-ly** *adv.*

Prosodist (prǫ·sŏdist.). 1779. [f. as prec. + -IST.] One skilled or learned in prosody.

Prosody (prǫ·sŏdi). 1450. [– L. *prosodia* accent of a syllable (Varro, Quintilian) – Gr. προσῳδία song sung to music, tone of a syllable, mark indicating this, f. πρός to + ᾠδή song, ODE; see -Y[3].] **1.** The science of versification; that part of the study of language which deals with the forms of metrical composition; formerly reckoned as a part of grammar, and including also *phonology* or *phonetics*, esp. in relation to versification. Also, a treatise on this. **2.** Correct pronunciation of words; observance of the laws of prosody (*rare*) 1616.

‖**Prosopalgia** (prǫsopæ·ldʒiă). 1831. [mod. L., f. Gr. πρόσωπον a face (f. πρός to + ὤψ, ὠπ- eye, face) + ἄλγος pain.] *Path.* Facial neuralgia; face-ache.

†**Proso·pole:psy.** 1646. [– Gr. προσωποληψία (a Hebraism of the N.T., cf. Rom. 2:11) acceptance of the face of a person, f. προσωπολήπτης, f. πρόσωπον face + λαμβάνειν take, accept.] Acceptance or 'acception' of the person of any one (see ACCEPTION 2); respect of persons; partiality –1849.

‖**Prosopopœia** (prǫsŏpŏpī·ĭă). 1561. [L. (Quintilian) – Gr. προσωποποιία representation in human form, f. πρόσωπον face, person + ποιεῖν make.] **1.** *Rhet.* A figure by which an imaginary or absent person is represented as speaking or acting; the introduction of a pretended speaker. **2.** *Rhet.* = PERSONIFICATION 1. 1578. **b.** *transf.* An impersonation, embodiment *of* some quality or abstraction 1826. Hence **Prosopopœ·ic, -al** *adjs.*

Prospect (prǫ·spekt), *sb.* late ME. [– L. *prospectus* view, f. *prospicere*, f. *pro* PRO-[1] + *specere* look.] **I.** †**1.** The action or fact of looking forth or out; the condition of facing in a specified direction; outlook, aspect, exposure –1845. †**b.** A place which affords an open view; a look-out –1885. **2.** An extensive sight or view; the view of the landscape from any position 1538. **3.** That which is seen from any point of view; a spectacle, a scene; the visible landscape 1633. †**4.** The appearance presented by anything; aspect (*rare*) –1715. †**5.** A picture, a sketch of a scene or the like –1771.

1. [Armenia] hath a p. to the Caspian sea HOLLAND. **b.** Him God beholding from his p. high,.. Thus..spake MILT. **2.** Phr. †*In* (*within*) or *into p.*, in or into sight or view; within view. **3.** A goodly p...of hills, and dales, and woods, and lawns, and spires THOMSON. **4.** *Oth.* III. iii. 398. **5.** I went to Putney..to take prospects in crayon EVELYN.

II. †**1.** A mental view or survey; also, a description –1764. **2.** A scene presented to the mental vision, esp. of something future 1641. **3.** A mental looking forward 1605. **b.** *esp.* Expectation, or reason to look for something to come; that which one has to look forward to. Often *pl.* 1665. **c.** A possible or likely purchaser, subscriber, or customer 1923.

1. The Traveller; or, a P. of Society GOLDSM. **2.** The surmounting of one difficulty is wont still to give us the p. of another 1672. **3.** *Macb.* I. iii. 74. **b.** Seeing no p. of fine weather, I descended to Saas 1860. Phr. *In p.*, expected, or to be expected.

III. *Mining.* **a.** A spot giving prospects of the presence of a mineral deposit 1839. **b.** A sample of ore or 'dirt' for testing; also, the resulting yield of ore 1879.

Comb. **p.-glass,** a 'prospective glass', telescope, field glass. Hence **Pro·spectless** *a.* having no p. or outlook; without prospects for the future.

Prospect (prǫ̆spe·kt, prǫ·spekt), *v.* 1555. [In branch I – L. *prospectare*, frequent. of *prospicere* (see prec.); in II, a new formation from PROSPECT *sb.* III.] †**I. 1.** *intr.* To look forth or out; to face; to afford a prospect in some direction –1613. **2.** *trans.* To look out upon or towards; to look at, view –1698. **II.** *Mining*, etc. Orig. U.S. **1.** *intr.* To explore a region *for* gold or other minerals 1848. **b.** *fig.* To search about (*for* something 1867. **2.** *trans.* **a.** To explore (a region) for gold, etc. **b.** To work (a mine or lode) experimentally so as to test its richness. 1858. **c.** *fig.* To survey as to prospects 1864. **3.** *intr.* Of a mine, reef, or ore: To give (good or bad) indications of future returns; to 'promise' (well or ill). Also to prove (rich or poor) on actual trial. 1868.

1. I've sent my mate to p. for a new claim 1885. **2.** A shaft is being sunk to p. the ground RAYMOND. **3.** Some of it prospects fully 20 ounces to the ton 1897.

Prospecting, *vbl. sb.* 1677. [f. prec. + -ING[1].] The action of PROSPECT *v.*

attrib., as *p. drill, shaft, work*; **p. claim,** the first claim, marked out by the discoverer of the deposit.

Prospection (prŏ̆spe·kʃən). Now *rare.* 1668. [f. PROSPECT *v.* + -ION. Cf. med.L. *prospectio* foresight (XIII).] The action of looking forward; anticipation; regard to the future; foresight.

Prospective (prŏ̆spe·ktiv), *a.* and *sb.* 1588. [As. adj. – Fr. †*prospectif, -ive* or late L. *prospectivus.* As *sb.* – Fr. †*prospective* view, prospect; but in senses 1 and 2 short for next.] **A.** *adj.* **1.** Characterized by looking forward into the future 1590. †**2.** Used or suitable for viewing at a distance (*lit.* and *fig.*) –1652. †**3.** Fitted to afford a fine prospect –1817. **4.** That looks or has regard to the future; operative with regard to the future 1800. **5.** That looks forward or is looked forward to; that is in prospect; future 1829.

4. The language..is entirely p. and not retrospective 1884. **5.** All the pupils above fourteen knew of some p. bridegroom C. BRONTË.

B. *sb.* †**1.** = next 1. –1626. †**2.** = next 2. –1727. **3.** The action of looking out (*lit.* or *fig.*). Now *rare.* 1599. †**4.** A scene, a view –1745. †**5.** The art of drawing in perspective; also, a perspective view –1684.

3. *In p.*, in view; in prospect or anticipation. Hence **Prospe·ctive-ly** *adv.*, **-ness.**

†**Prospe·ctive glass.** 1584. **1.** A magic crystal, in which it was supposed that distant or future events could be seen –1628. **2.** A spy-glass, field-glass, telescope. Also *pl.* spectacles, binocular glasses. –1738.

Prospector (prŏspe·ktəɹ, prǫ·spektəɹ). 1857. [f. PROSPECT *v.* II. + -OR 2.] One who prospects; *esp.* one who explores a region for gold or the like.

Prospectus (prŏspe·ktŏs). *pl.* **-uses.** 1777. [– L. *prospectus* view, prospect, prob. after Fr. use (XVIII).] A description or account of the chief features of a forthcoming work or proposed enterprise, circulated for the purpose of obtaining support.

The plaintiff applied for shares in this company on the faith of the p. 1890.

Prosper (prǫ·spəɹ), *v.* 1460. [– (O)Fr. *prospérer* or L. *prosperare*, f. *prosper, prosperus* doing well or successfully.] **1.** *intr.* To be prosperous, fortunate, or successful; to thrive, succeed, do well. **2.** *trans.* To cause to flourish; to be propitious to 1530.

1. What soeuer he doth, it shal prospere COVERDALE *Ps.* 1:3. Why wicked men have often prospered in this world HOBBES. Where such Plants grow and p. 1682. **2.** O prospere thou oure hondy worke COVERDALE *Ps.* 89[90]:17. If Heaven prospered them, they might seize a Spanish ship 1855.

Prosperity (prǫspe·rĭti). ME. [– (O)Fr. *prospérité* – L. *prosperitas, -tat-*, f. *prosper, prosperus*; see prec., -ITY.] The condition of being prosperous; good-fortune, success, well-being. **b.** *pl.* Instances of prosperity, prosperous circumstances ME.

P. is not apt to receive good lessons, nor always to give them BURKE. **b.** The vitious and bad triumph with so great prosperities 1598.

Prosperous (prǫ·spərəs), *a.* 1445. [– Fr. †*prospereus*, f. as prec.; see -OUS.] **1.** Having continued success or good fortune; flourishing 1472. **2.** Promoting or conducing to success; favourable, propitious 1445.

1. The Churches Prayers made him so p. SHAKS. The causes which make one nation more rich and p. than another 1878. **2.** We sayled euer with p. wynde 1555. Hence **Pro·sperous-ly** *adv.*, **-ness.**

Prosphysis (prǫ·sfisis), *a.* 1693. [mod.L. – Gr. πρόσφυσις, f. πρός to + φύσις growth.] *Path.* An adhesion; morbid adhesion of parts.

Prostate (prǫ·steᶦt), *sb.* (*a.*) 1646. [– Fr. *prostate* (Paré) – mod.L. *prostata* – Gr. προστάτης one that stands before, guardian, f. πρό- PRO-[2] + στατός placed, standing.] *Anat.* A large gland, or each of a number of small glands, accessory to the male generative organs, surrounding the neck of the bladder and the commencement of the urethra, in man and other Mammalia. **b.** *attrib.* or *adj.* esp. in *p. gland* 1754. Hence **Prosta·tic** *a.* pertaining to, produced by, or connected with the p.; *prostatic body, gland*, the p. ‖**Prostati·tis,** inflammation of the p.

‖**Prosternum** (proˌstə̄·ɹnŏm). 1826. [mod. L., f. PRO-[2] 2 + STERNUM.] *Entom.* The sternal, ventral, or under segment of the prothorax of an insect.

‖**Prostheca** (prǫsˌþī·kă). 1826. [mod.L. – Gr. προσθήκη, f. προστιθέναι put to, add.] *Entom.* A process on the mandibles in certain coleopterous insects.

‖**Prosthesis** (prǫ·sþĭsis). 1553. [Late L. – Gr. πρόσθεσις, f. προστιθέναι add, f. πρός to; see THESIS.] **1.** *Gram.* The addition of a letter or syllable at the beginning of a word. **2.** *Surg.* That part of surgery which consists in supplying deficiencies, as by artificial limbs, teeth, etc. 1706.

Prosthetic (prǫsþe·tik), *a.* 1837. [f. prec., after *epenthesis/epenthetic, synthesis/synthetic*, etc.] **1.** *Gram.* Pertaining to, or of the nature of prosthesis; prefixed, as a letter or syllable. **2.** *Surg.* Pertaining to or of the nature of prosthesis 1902.

Prostitute (prǫ·stitiut), *ppl. a.* and *sb.* 1563. [– L. *prostitutus* (fem. *prostituta* as sb.), pa. pple. of *prostituere* expose publicly, offer for sale, prostitute, f. *pro* PRO-[1] + *statuere* set up, place.] **A.** *adj.* **1.** Offered or exposed to lust (as a woman), prostituted; also, licentious. (Sometimes const. as *pa. pple.*) Now *rare* or *Obs.* 1572. **2.** *fig.* Debased or debasing; abandoned; corrupt. Now *rare.* 1563. †**3.** Given over, devoted; exposed, subjected (*to* something, usu. evil) –1708.

1. Made bold by want, and p. for bread PRIOR. **2.** No courtier, even the most p., could go farther than the parliament itself 1754.

B. *sb.* **1.** A woman who is devoted, or (usu.) offers her body to indiscriminate sexual intercourse, esp. for hire; a common harlot 1613. **2.** A person given over to infamous practices; an abandoned person; *esp.* a base hireling, a corrupt and venal politician. Now *rare.* 1647.

1. Your friendship as common as a prostitute's favours GOLDSM. **2.** He [Lord Brougham] is a notorious p., and is setting himself up to sale 1804.

Prostitute (prǫ·stitiut), *v.* 1530. [– *prostitut-*, pa. ppl. stem of L. *prostituere*; see prec.] **1.** *trans.* To offer (oneself, or another) to unlawful, esp. indiscriminate, sexual intercourse, usu. for hire; to devote or expose to lewdness. (Chiefly *refl.* of a woman.) **b.** To seduce, debauch (a woman). *rare.* 1658. **2.** *fig.* To surrender or put to an unworthy or infamous use; to sell for base gain or hire 1593.

1. *Lev.* 19:29. He recovered his liberty by prostituting the honour of his wife GIBBON. **2.** Justice was prostituted in the ordinary courts to the royal will GREEN. So **Pro·stitutor,** one who prostitutes (usu. *fig.*) 1611.

Prostitution (prǫstitiū·ʃən). 1553. [– (O)Fr. *prostitution* or late L. *prostitutio, -on-*, f. as prec.; see -ION.] **1.** Of women: The offering of the body to indiscriminate lewdness for hire (esp. as a practice or institution); whoredom, harlotry. **2.** *fig.* Devotion to an unworthy use; degradation, debasement, corruption 1647.

1. P. seems never to have been recognized at Rome as a legal institution 1878. 2. The p. of their talents to gratify..personal animosities 1874.

Prostrate (prǫ·strĕt, -eⁱt), *a.* late ME. [– L. *prostratus*, pa. pple. of *prosternere* throw in front, cast down, f. *pro* PRO-¹ + *sternere* lay low; see -ATE².] **1.** In strict use, Lying with the face to the ground in token of submission or humility; more loosely, Lying at full length (on the ground or other surface). **b.** Of things usu. erect, as trees, pillars, etc.: Levelled with the ground, overthrown 1677. **2.** *fig.* Laid low in mind or spirit; submissive; overcome, powerless 1591. **b.** In a state of physical exhaustion or complete weakness; unable to rise or exert oneself 1871. **3.** *Bot.* In its habit of growth, lying flat upon the ground; procumbent 1776. **b.** Closely appressed to the surface; lying flat: as, p. hairs or setæ.

1. Whiles we on grassie bed did lie p. 1642. **b.** The mournful waste Of p. altars WORDSW. **2.** The violent reaction which had laid the Whig party p. MACAULAY. Hence **Pro·strately** *adv.*

Prostrate (prǫ·streⁱt), *v. Pa. t.* and *pple.* **prostrated.** late ME. [– *prostrat-*, pa. ppl. stem of L. *prosternere*; see prec., -ATE³.] †**1.** *intr.* To become prostrate; = sense 3. –1755. **2.** *trans.* To lay flat on the ground, etc.; to throw down, level with the ground, overthrow (something erect) 1483. **3.** *refl.* To cast oneself down prostrate; to bow to the ground in reverence or submission 1530. **4.** *trans. fig.* To lay low, overcome; to make submissive or helpless 1562. **b.** To reduce to extreme physical weakness: said of disease, fatigue, and the like 1829.

2. A storme, that all things doth p. SPENSER. **3.** Sethos, upon entring, prostrated himself at his feet 1732. **4.** You are to p. your reason to divine revelation KEN. **b.** He appeared exceedingly low and prostrated 1843.

Prostration (prǫstrēⁱ·ʃən). 1526. [f. PROSTRATE *v.* + -ION; partly – (O)Fr. *prostration.*] **1.** The action of prostrating oneself or one's body, esp. as a sign of humility, adoration, or servility; the condition of being prostrated, or lying prostrate. **2.** *fig.* Veneration; abject submission, adulation; humiliation, abasement 1646. **3.** *fig.* Debasement of any exalted principle or faculty 1647. **4.** Extreme physical weakness or exhaustion; also extreme dejection 1651. **5.** The reduction of a country, party, or organization to a prostrate or powerless condition 1844.

1. The comely prostrations of the body..in time of Divine Service 1645. **2.** The p. of the intellect 1823. **4.** Nervous p. 1887. **5.** The p. of Greece under the Turkish yoke 1844.

Prostrative (prǫ·strĕtiv), *a. rare.* 1817. [f. as prec. + -IVE.] **a.** Having the quality or faculty of prostrating. **b.** Characterized by prostration or abjectness.

Prostyle (prōᵘ·stəil), *sb.* and *a.* 1696. [– L. *prostylos* (Vitruvius) adj. having pillars in front; see PRO-², STYLE *sb.*] *Anc. Arch.* **A.** *sb.* A portico in front of a Greek temple, of which the columns stood in front of the building 1697. **B.** *adj.* Having a prostyle 1696.

Prosy (prōᵘ·zi), *a.* 1821. [f. PROSE *sb.* + -Y¹.] **1.** Resembling, or having the character of, prose. Sometimes = PROSAIC 2; commonplace and tedious; dull and wearisome. **2.** Of persons: Given to talking or writing in a commonplace, dull, or tedious way 1838.

Prosyllogism (pro,si·lŏdʒiz'm). 1584. [– late L. *prosyllogismus* – Gr. προσυλλογισμός; see PRO-², SYLLOGISM.] *Logic.* A syllogism of which the conclusion forms the major or minor premiss of another syllogism.

Protagon (prōᵘ·tăgǫn). 1869. [– G. *protagon*, f. Gr. πρῶτος first + ἄγον, n. pr. pple. of ἄγειν lead.] *Physiol. Chem.* A highly complex crystalline substance, containing nitrogen and phosphorus, found in brain and nerve tissue.

Protagonist (protæ·gŏnist). 1671. [– Gr. πρωταγωνιστής, f. πρῶτος first, PROTO- + ἀγωνιστής combatant, actor, f. ἀγωνίζεσθαι contest, AGONIZE; see -IST.] **1.** The chief personage in a drama; the principal character in the plot of a story, etc. **2.** A leading personage in any contest; a champion of any cause 1839.

1. 'Tis charg'd upon me that I make debauch'd Persons..my protagonists, or the chief persons of the drama DRYDEN.

Protamine (prōᵘ·tăməin). 1895. [f. PROTO-3 c + AMINE.] *Physiol. Chem.* One of the simple proteins, a basic organic substance $C_{16}H_{32}N_9O_2$.

Protandrous (protæ·ndrəs), *a.* 1875. [f. PROT(O- + -ANDROUS.] *Bot.* = PROTERANDROUS. So **Prota·ndric** *a.*

‖**Protasis** (prǫ·tăsis). 1616. [L. (Apuleius, Donatus) – Gr. πρότασις proposition, problem, etc., f. προτείνειν put forward, tender, f. πρό PRO-² + τείνειν stretch.] **1.** That which is put forward; a proposition, a maxim (*rare*) 1656. **2.** In the ancient drama, The first part of a play, in which the characters are introduced, as opp. to the *epitasis* and *catastrophe* 1616. **3.** *Gram.* and *Rhet.* The first or introductory clause in a sentence, *esp.* in a conditional sentence; opp. to the *apodosis* 1638.

Protatic (protæ·tik), *a.* 1668. [– late L. *protaticus* appearing in the protasis, and Gr. πρωτατικός capable of advancing a proposition.] Of or pertaining to the or a protasis; in *p. character, person*, appearing only in the protasis (sense 2).

‖**Protea** (prōᵘ·tiă). 1753. [mod.L., generic name (Linn.), f. PROTEUS, in allusion to the great variety of the species.] *Bot.* A large genus of shrubs or small trees, type of the *Proteaceæ*, chiefly natives of S. Africa, bearing large cone-like heads of flowers; also, a plant of this genus.

Proteaceous (prōᵘti,ēⁱ·ʃəs), *a.* 1835. [f. mod.L. *Proteaceæ*, f. prec.; see -ACEOUS.] Of or pertaining to the *Proteaceæ*, a natural order of trees, shrubs, or (rarely) perennial herbs, mainly S. African and Australian, typified by the genus *Protea*.

Protean (prōᵘ·ti,ăn), *a.* 1598. [f. PROTEUS + -AN.] Of or pertaining to Proteus; like that of Proteus; hence, variable in form; characterized by variability or variation; changing, varying. **b.** *spec. Zool.* Varying in shape; of or pertaining to the proteus-animalcule; amœboid, proteiform 1802. Hence **Pro·teanly** *adv. rare*, with variation of form.

Protect (prŏte·kt), *v.* 1526. [– *protect-*, pa. ppl. stem of L. *protegere* cover in front, f. *pro* PRO-¹ + *tegere* cover.] **1.** *trans.* To defend or guard from injury or danger; to shield; to keep safe, take care of; to extend patronage to. **b.** To act as official or legal protector or guardian of SHAKS. **2.** *Pol. Econ.* To assist or guard (a home industry) against the competition of foreign productions by means of imposts on the latter 1827. **3.** *Comm.* To provide funds to meet (a draft or bill of exchange) 1884. **4. a.** To furnish (*spec.* warships) with a protective covering 1839. **b.** To provide (machinery, etc.) with appliances to prevent injury from it 1900.

1. To every man remaineth..the right of protecting himselfe HOBBES. To p. the eyes from..excessive light 1879. **b.** 2 *Hen. VI*, II. iii. 29. **2.** Their industries were protected and ours were not 1885. Hence **Prote·ctingly** *adv.*

Protectee (prŏtektī·). 1602. [f. PROTECT *v.* + -EE¹.] One who is under protection; *spec.* in 16–17th c., †an Irishman who had accepted the protection of the English government.

Protection (prŏte·kʃən). late ME. [–(O)Fr. *protection* or late L. *protectio, -on-*, f. *protect-*; see PROTECT, -ION.] **1.** The action of protecting; the fact or condition of being protected; defence from harm, danger, or evil; patronage, tutelage. **b.** *euphem.* The keeping of a mistress in a separate establishment 1677. **2.** A thing or person that protects. late ME. **3.** A writing that protects or secures from molestation; a safe-conduct, passport, pass. In U.S. a certificate of American citizenship issued by the customs authorities to seamen. 1450. **4.** *Pol. Econ.* The theory or system of protecting home industries against foreign competition by imposing duties or the like on foreign productions 1828.

1. I leve this castel in your proteccyon & sauff garde CAXTON. Ireland..must be protected, and there is no p. to be found for her, but either from France or England BURKE. **2.** His quiver and his laurel 'Gainst four such eyes were no p. GRAY. **3.** Moved that the speaker sign protections for such persons as are called before the Committee for inspecting Treasury and Revenue 1658. Hence **Prote·ctionism**, the economic doctrine, policy, or system of p. **Prote·ctionist**, an advocate of protectionism; as *adj.* supporting p.

Protective (prŏte·ktiv), *a.* (*sb.*) 1661. [f. PROTECT *v.* + -IVE. Cf. med.L. *protectivus.*] **1.** Protecting; tending to protect; defensive; preservative. **2.** *Pol. Econ.* Of or relating to the economic doctrine or system of protection 1829. **B.** *sb.* Anything employed to protect; e.g. in *Surgery*, carbolized oiled silk used for the protection of wounds 1875.

1. The favour of p. Providence 1661. Examples of p. colouring among insects 1909. Hence **Prote·ctive-ly** *adv.*, **-ness.**

Protector (prŏte·ktəɹ). late ME. [– (O)Fr. *protecteur* – late L. *protector*, f. *protect-*; see PROTECT *v.*, -OR 2.] **1.** One who protects; a defender; a guardian, a patron. **b.** A thing that protects; a guard; *esp.* a device to prevent injury to or from something; e.g. *chest-p., cuff-p.*, etc. 1849. **2.** *Eng. Hist.* **a.** One in charge of the kingdom during the minority, absence, or incapacity of the sovereign; a regent. late ME. **b.** The official title, in full *Lord P. of the Commonwealth*, borne by Oliver Cromwell 1653–1658, and by his son Richard 1658–1659.

1. The wulues kyld the dogges whiche were capytayns and protectours of the sheep CAXTON. **2. a.** The p., Humphry, Duke of Gloucester GRAY. **b.** Saw the superb funerall of the P. EVELYN. Hence **Prote·ctoral** *a.* of or pertaining to a p., *esp. Hist.* to the p. of a kingdom or commonwealth. So **Protecto·rial** *a.* **Prote·ctress**, ‖**Prote·ctrix**, a female p.; a patroness.

Protectorate (prŏte·ktŏrĕt), *sb.* 1692. [f. PROTECTOR + -ATE¹.] **1.** The office, position, or government of the Protector of a kingdom or state; *spec.* the period (1653–9) during which Oliver and Richard Cromwell held the title of Lord Protector. **2.** The office, position, or function of a protector or guardian. *Internat. Law*: **a.** orig. The relation of a strong to a weaker state which it protects. **b.** The relation of a suzerain to a vassal state; suzerainty. **c.** now *spec.* The relation of a European power to a territory inhabited by native tribes, and not ranking as a state. 1836. **3.** A state or territory placed or taken under the protection of a superior power; *esp.* a protected territory inhabited by native tribes 1884.

Protectorship (prŏte·ktəɹʃip). 1460. [f. as prec. + -SHIP,] **1.** = PROTECTORATE 1. **2.** The position, character, or function of a protector; guardianship, patronage 1576.

‖**Protégé** *masc.*, **protégée** *fem.* (prǫ·tēʒeⁱ, ‖proteʒe). 1778. [Fr., pa. pple. of *protéger* – L. *protegere* PROTECT.] One who is under the protection or care of another, esp. of a person of superior position or influence.

Proteid (prōᵘ·ti,id). 1871. [f. PROTE(IN; see -ID⁴.] *Chem.* One of a class of organic compounds previously known as 'protein bodies', and now by preference called 'proteins'; see PROTEIN.

Proteiform (prōᵘ·ti,ifǭɹm), *a.* 1833. [f. PROTEUS + -FORM.] Changeable in form, or assuming many various forms; protean.

Protein (prōᵘ·ti,in). 1868. [– Fr. *protéine*, G. *protein*, f. Gr. πρωτεῖος primary, f. πρῶτος first; see PROTO-, -IN¹.] *Chem.* Any one of a class of organic compounds, consisting of carbon, hydrogen, oxygen, and nitrogen, with a little sulphur, in more or less unstable combination; forming an important part of all living organisms, and the essential nitrogenous constituents of the food of animals. Also called *albuminoids*, and *proteids*.

The name was applied earlier by Mulder to a residual substance obtained from casein, etc. and regarded by him as the essential constituent of organized bodies. Hence **Prote,inaceous** (-ēⁱ·ʃəs), **Prote,inic** (-i·nik), **Proteinous** (protī·inəs) *adjs.* of the nature of, or consisting of, p.

Protend (prote·nd), *v.* Now *rare.* late ME. [– L. *protendere*, stretch forth, extend, f. *pro* PRO-¹ + *tendere* stretch.] **1.** *trans.* To stretch forth; to hold out in front of one. **b.** *intr.* for *refl.* To stick out, protrude 1726. **2.** *trans.* To extend in length, or in one dimension of space; to produce (a line); usu. *pass.* to extend (from one point to another). late ME. **3.** To extend in duration. late ME.

1. [Ajax] Now shakes his spear, now lifts, and now protends POPE.

Protension (prote·nʃən). *rare.* 1681. [– late L. *protensio, -on-*, f. *protens-*, pa. ppl. stem of L. *protendere*; see prec., -ION.] A stretching or reaching forward; length; duration.

Protensive (prote·nsiv), *a. rare.* 1643. [f. after *intensive, extensive*, by substitution of the prefix PRO-¹.] **1.** Continuing, lasting, enduring. **2.** Extending lengthwise 1836. Hence **Prote·nsively** *adv.*

‖**Proteolysis** (prōᵘti,ǫ·lisis). 1880. [mod. L., f. *proteo-*, assumed comb. form of PROTEIN + -LYSIS.] *Phys. Chem.* **a.** The separation of the proteins from a protein-containing mixture; **b.** The splitting up of proteins by ferments. Hence **Pro·teolyse** *v. trans.* to decompose or split up (proteins). **Proteoly·tic** *a.* having the quality of decomposing proteins.

Proteose (prōᵘ·ti,ōᵘs). 1890. [f. PROTE(IN + -OSE².] *Phys. Chem.* One of a class of products of protein-hydrolysis, including albumose, globulose, gelatose, etc.

Proterandrous (prǫtĕræ·ndrəs), *a.* 1875. [f. PROTERO- + -ANDROUS.] **1.** *Bot.* Having the stamens or male organs mature before the pistil or female organ. **2.** *Zool.* Of a hermaphrodite animal or a colony of zooids: Having the male organs, or individuals, sexually mature before the female. Hence **Protera·ndry,** p. quality.

Proteranthous (prǫtĕræ·nþəs), *a.* 1832. [f. as prec. + Gr. ἄνθος flower + -OUS.] *Bot.* Having flowers appearing before the leaves.

Protero- (prǫtĕro), bef. a vowel **proter-** (prǫtĕr), comb. form from Gr. πρότερος fore, former, anterior, in place, time, order, rank; used in a few scientific terms; as **Pro·terosaur** (-sǭr) [Gr. σαῦρος lizard], a saurian of the extinct genus *Proterosaurus* or group *Proterosauria*, comprising some of the oldest reptiles.

Proterogynous (prǫtĕrǫ·dʒinəs), *a.* 1875. [f. PROTERO- + -GYNOUS.] **1.** *Bot.* Having the pistil or female organ mature before the stamens or male organs. **2.** *Zool.* Of a hermaphrodite animal, or a colony of zooids: Having the female organs, or individuals, sexually mature before the male. So **Protero·gyny,** p. quality or state.

Protervity (protə̄·ɹvĭti). Now *rare.* 1500. [– Fr. †*protervité* or L. *protervitas*, f. *protervus* impudent, etc.; see -ITY.] Waywardness, frowardness, stubbornness; pertness, insolence; petulance; an instance of this.

Protest (prōᵘ·test), *sb.* ME. [– Fr. †*protest* (mod. *protêt*), f. *protester*; see next.] An act of protesting. **1.** = PROTESTATION 1. **2.** The action taken to fix the liability for the payment of a dishonoured bill; *spec.* a formal declaration in writing, usu. by a notary-public, that a bill has been duly presented and payment or acceptance refused 1622. **3.** A written declaration made by the master of a ship, attested by a justice of the peace or a consul, stating the circumstances under which injury has happened to the ship or cargo, or under which officers or crew have incurred any liability 1755. **4.** A formal declaration of dissent from, or of consent under certain conditions only to, some action or proceeding; a remonstrance 1751. **b.** A written statement of dissent from any motion carried in the House of Lords, recorded and signed by any Peer of the minority 1712.

4. The husband appeared under p. 1822. Paying under p. 1885.

Protest (prŏte·st), *v.* 1440. [– (O)Fr. *protester* – L. *protestari* declare formally, f. PRO-¹ + *testari* be a witness, assert.] **1.** *trans.* To state formally or solemnly (something about which a doubt is stated or implied). **b.** *intr.* To make protestation or solemn affirmation 1560. **c.** As a mere asseveration 1587. **2.** *trans.* To make a formal written declaration of the non-acceptance or non-payment of (a bill of exchange) when duly presented 1655. †**3.** To assert publicly; to proclaim; to declare, show forth –1644. †**4.** To vow –1660. †**5.** To call to witness; to appeal to –1675. **6.** *intr.* To give formal expression to objection, dissent, or disapproval; to make a formal (often written) declaration *against* some proposal, decision, or action; to remonstrate 1608.

1. I p. to you, the Gentleman has not spoken to me STEELE. She then..solemnly protested her innocence 1839. **b.** The Lady protests to much, me thinkes SHAKS. **c.** I will doe it I p. DEKKER. **2. b.** *U.S.* To protest against 1904. **3.** *Much Ado* v. i. 149. **4.** On Dianaes Altar to p. For aie, austerity, and single life SHAKS. **6.** A minister of religion may fairly p. against being made a politician J. H. NEWMAN.

Protestant (prǫ·tĕstănt), *sb.* and *a.* 1539. [– mod. L. *protestans, -ant-* = pr. pple. of L. *protestari* PROTEST *v.*] **A.** *sb.* **I.** *Eccl.* **1.** *Hist.*, usu. *pl.* Those German princes and free cities who made a declaration of dissent from the decision of the Diet of Spires (1529), which re-affirmed the edict of the Diet of Worms against the Reformation; hence, the adherents of the Reformed doctrines and worship in Germany. **2.** A member or adherent of any Christian church or body severed from the Roman communion in the Reformation of the 16th c.; hence, gen. any member of a Western church outside the Roman communion 1553. **b.** *spec.* In the 17th c., *Protestant* was generally accepted and used by members of the Established Church, and was even so applied to the exclusion of Presbyterians, Quakers, and Separatists 1608. **II.** *General.* Often pron. (prote·stănt). One who protests. **a.** One who protests devotion; a suitor (*rare*) 1648. **b.** One who protests against error 1836. **c.** One who makes a protest *against* any decision, proceeding, practice, custom, or the like; a protester 1853.

a. Bid me to live, and I will live Thy P. to be HERRICK.

B. *adj.* **1.** Of, pertaining to, or of the nature of Protestants or Protestantism 1539. **2.** Also (prote·stănt). Protesting; making a protest 1844.

1. To heare & see the manner of the French P. Churches service EVELYN. **P. Episcopal,** official title of the church in U.S. descended from and in communion with the Church of England. Hence **Pro·testantize** *v. trans.* to render P.; *intr.* to follow P. practices.

Protestantism (prǫ·tĕstănti:z'm). 1649. [f. prec. + -ISM.] **1.** The religion of Protestants, as opp. to Roman Catholicism; the condition of being Protestant; adherence to Protestant principles. **2.** Protestants, or the Protestant churches, collectively 1662. **3.** An attitude of protest (*rare*) 1854.

3. There needs, then, a p. in social usages 1854.

Protestation (prǫtĕstēⁱ·ʃən). ME. [–(O)Fr. *protestation* or late L. *protestatio, -on-*, f. *protestat-*, pa. ppl. stem of L. *protestari*; see PROTEST *v.*, -ION.] The action of protesting; that which is protested. **1.** A solemn affirmation of a fact, opinion, or resolution; a formal public assertion or asseveration. †**2.** *Law.* In pleading, an affirmation or denial, introduced in form of a protest, of some allegation the truth of which the pleader cannot directly affirm or deny without duplicating his plea, and which he cannot pass over lest he should be held to have tacitly waived or admitted it –1797. **3.** = PROTEST *sb.* 4, 4 b. 1624.

1. If there had been any faith in mens vows and protestations COWLEY. *To make p.*, to protest in a solemn or formal manner.

Protester (prŏte·stəɹ). 1601. [f. PROTEST *v.* + -ER¹.] **1.** One who makes a protestation or solemn affirmation. **2.** One who makes a protest or remonstrance 1651. **3.** One who protests a bill or other commercial document 1849. So **Prote·stor** 1550.

‖**Proteus** (prōᵘ·tiŭs, prōᵘ·tiŭs). late ME. [L. – Gr. Πρωτεύς proper name.] **1.** *Gr.* and *Rom. Myth.* A sea-god, the son of Oceanus and Tethys, fabled to assume various shapes. **2.** Hence allus., One who, or that which, assumes various forms, or characters; a changing, varying, or inconstant person or thing 1585. **3.** *Zool.* and *Biol.* **a.** An AMŒBA. (Now disused as a generic name.) Also *p. animalcule.* 1802. **b.** A genus of tailed amphibians with persistent gills, having four short slender legs and a long eel-like body, found in subterranean caves in Austria 1835. **4.** *attrib.* Changeable like Proteus, protean 1687.

4. O P. Conscience, never to be tied! DRYDEN.

‖**Prothalamion** (prōᵘþălēⁱ·miŏn). Also **-ium.** 1597. [Invented by Spenser, after *epithalamion*; see PRO-².] A song sung before a wedding.

‖**Prothesis** (prǫ·þĭsis). 1577. [– Gr. πρόθεσις a placing before or in public, f. PRO-² + θέσις placing.] **1.** *Eccl.* The placing of the elements, etc., in readiness for use in the eucharistic office; hence, a credence-table, or the part of the church where this stands. **2.** *Gram.* = PROSTHESIS 1. 1870. Hence **Prothe·tic** *a.* **Prothe·tically** *adv.*

Prothoracic (prōᵘþoræ·sik), *a.* 1826. [f. mod.L. *prothorax, -ac-* (see next) + -IC.] *Entom.* Of or pertaining to the front of the thorax; pertaining to or situated on the prothorax.

‖**Prothorax** (propō̆ᵊ·ræks). 1826. [mod.L.; see PRO-² 2 and THORAX.] *Entom.* The first of the three thoracic somites, or divisions of the thorax of an insect, which bears the first pair of legs.

‖**Protista** (proti·stă), *sb. pl.* 1878. [mod.L. (= G. *Protisten*, Haeckel 1868) – Gr. πρώτιστα n. pl. of πρώτιστος the very first, superl. of πρῶτος first.] *Biol.* A third kingdom of organized beings, not definitely distinguished as either animals or plants (thus comprising the Protozoa and Protophyta, with those forms indeterminately assigned to either group). Hence **Protist** (prōᵘ·tist), one of the P.; also *attrib.* **Proti·stan** *a.* of or belonging to the P.; *sb.* = *protist.*

Proto- (prōᵘto), bef. a vowel or *h* properly **prot-** (prōᵘt), or with *h* (prōᵘþ), repr. Gr. πρωτο-, comb. form of πρῶτος first.

In modern formations, esp. in group 1 below, the tendency is to leave *proto-* unchanged; e.g. *proto-apostate, proto-hippus.*

1. In words of rare occurrence, often self-explaining; *proto-* (which, when prefixed to a word already in English, is usu. hyphened) denoting (*a*) 'First in time, earliest, original, primitive', as in *proto-historian, -apostate, -chemistry*, etc.; (*b*) 'First in rank or importance, chief, principal', as in *proto-architect, -chemist, -rebel, -traitor*, etc.

2. In many mod. scientific and techn. terms (sbs. and adjs.). **a.** Prefixed to adjs. from names of countries or races, forming adjs. denominating primitive or original tribes, languages, writings, works of art or manufacture, styles of architecture, etc.; as *proto-Arabic, -Babylonian, -Celtic, -Doric*, etc. **b.** In terms, chiefly of Zoology or Biology: usu. designating an (actual or hypothetical) original or primitive form, type, organism, structure, etc. **Pro·toconch** [see CONCH], the embryonic shell in certain cephalopods; hence **Protoco·nchal** *a.* **Pro·tomorph** [Gr. μορφή form], a primitive or original form; so **Protomo·rphic** *a.*, having the primitive or simplest form or structure. ‖**Protone·ma** [Gr. νῆμα thread], in mosses, the confervoid or filamentous thallus which produces the full-grown plant by lateral branching. **Proto·o·rganism,** a primitive or unicellular organism, animal or vegetable; a protozoön or protophyte. **Proto·pathy** [-PATHY], primary pain or suffering; *Path.* a primary disease or affection. **Proto·podite** [see PODITE], in Crustacea, the first or basal joint of a limb, which articulates with its somite; hence **Protopodi·tic** *a.* ‖**Proto·pterus,** a genus of dipnoan fishes, containing only the African mud-fish, having the pectoral and ventral fins reduced to long fringed filaments. **Protoso·mite,** each of the rudimentary somites of the embryo in arthropods and annelids.

3. In Chemistry. **a.** With names of binary compounds in -IDE (formerly *-uret*), designating that in which the element or radical combines in the first or smallest proportion with another element. **Protochlo·ride,** a compound of chlorine with another element or radical, containing the minimum proportion of chlorine; so **Protosu·lphide, Proto·xide. Pro·tosalt,** a salt formed by combination of an acid with the protoxide of a metal. Hence in derived vbs., ppl. adjs., etc. **b.** In ternary compounds *proto-* was formerly used to designate salts produced from protoxides (cf. PROTOSALT), which thus contain the smallest (or smaller) proportion of the acid radical. **c.** In Organic and Physiological Chemistry, *proto-* occurs in senses rather akin to its use in 1 or 2. Thus in *protocatechuic acid* ($C_7H_6O_4$) the name was given because the substance has some resemblance to *catechuic* acid or *catechu*, but has a simpler composition.

Protocanonical (proᵘ:tokănǫ·nikăl), *a.* 1629. [f. mod.L. *protocanonicus*; see PROTO-1, CANON, -ICAL.] Of the books of Scripture: Canonical of the first order. Opp. to DEUTEROCANONICAL.

‖**Protococcus** (prōᵘtokǫ·kŏs). *Pl.* **-cocci** (-kǫ·ksai). 1842. [mod.L.; see PROTO-, COCCUS.] *Bot.* A genus of microscopic unicellular algæ, of spheroidal form.

Protocol (prō^u·tǒkǫl), *sb.* 1541. [orig. *prothocoll* (in earliest use Sc.) – OFr. *prothocole* (mod. *protocole*) – med.L. *protocollum* – Gr. πρωτόκολλον first leaf of a volume, fly-leaf glued to the case and containing an account of the contents, f. πρῶτος first, κόλλα glue.] **1.** The original note or minute of a negotiation, agreement, or the like, drawn up by a notary, etc. and duly attested, which forms the legal authority for any subsequent deed, agreement, or the like based upon it. **2.** *spec.* The original draught, minute, or record of a dispatch, negotiation, treaty or other diplomatic document or instrument; *esp.* a record of the propositions agreed to in a conference, signed by the parties, to be embodied in a formal treaty 1697. **3.** A formal or official statement of a transaction or proceeding 1880. **4.** In France, The formulary of the etiquette to be observed by the Head of the State in official ceremonies, etc.; the etiquette department of the Ministry of Foreign Affairs; the office of the Master of the Ceremonies 1896. **5.** *Diplomatics.* The official formulas used at the beginning and end of a charter, papal bull, etc., as distinct from the *text*, which contains its subject-matter 1908. Hence **Pro·tocolist,** one who draws up a p.

Pro·tocol, *v.* 1832. [f. prec.] *intr.* and *trans.* To draw up, or record in, a protocol.

Protogine (prō^u·tǒdʒin). 1832. [– Fr. *protogine* (Jurine, 1806), irreg. f. Gr. πρῶτος first + γίνεσθαι be born or produced.] *Geol.* A variety of granite occurring in the Alps, in which chlorite often takes the place of biotite, and in which a foliated structure has frequently been produced by dynamic action.

Protogynous (protǫ·dʒinəs), *a.* 1875. [f. PROTO- + -GYNOUS.] *Bot.* = PROTEROGYNOUS. Hence **Proto·gyny** = PROTEROGYNY.

‖**Protohippus** (prō^uto,hi·pŏs). 1876. [mod. L., f. PROTO- + Gr. ἵππος horse.] *Palæont.* An extinct genus of quadrupeds, ancestrally related to the horse.

Protomartyr (prō^u·to,mā:ɹtəɹ). [XV *prothomartir* – med.L. *prot(h)omartyr* – eccl. Gr. πρωτόμαρτυρ; see PROTO-, MARTYR.] The first martyr; the earliest of any series of martyrs; *spec.* applied to St. Stephen.

‖**Proton** (prō^u·tǫn). 1920. [n. of Gr. πρῶτος first.] *Physics.* A unit constituent of matter associated with (or consisting of) an invariable charge of positive electricity.

Protonotary, prothonotary (prō^u:to,-, prō^u:þonō^u·tări; protǫ·n-, proþǫ·nǒtări). 1447. [– med.L. *protonotarius* (also *protho-*) – late Gr. πρωτονοτάριος, f. πρωτο- PROTO- + νοτάριος – L. *notarius* NOTARY *sb.*] **1.** A principal notary, chief clerk, or recorder of a court; orig., the holder of that office in the Byzantine court. **2.** In England, formerly, The chief clerk or registrar in the Courts of Chancery, of Common Pleas, and of the King's Bench 1460. **3.** *R.C.Ch.* A member of the college of twelve (formerly seven) prelates called *Protonotaries Apostolic(al*, whose function is to register the papal acts, to make and keep records of beatifications, to direct the canonization of saints, etc. 1494. **b.** *Gr. Ch.* The principal secretary of the Patriarch of Constantinople 1835. **4.** A chief secretary in some foreign courts; also *transf.* and *fig.* 1502. Hence **Proto-, Prothono·taryship.**

‖**Protopapas** (prō^u·topæ:păs). 1682. [– eccl. Gr. πρωτοπαπᾶς chief priest, f. πρωτο- PROTO- + παπᾶς priest.] = PROTOPOPE.

‖**Protophyta** (protǫ·fită), *sb. pl.* 1855. [mod.L., pl. of *protophytum*, f. Gr. πρῶτος PROTO- + φυτόν plant.] *Bot.* A primary division of the vegetable kingdom, comprising the most simply organized plants (usu. of microscopic size), each individual consisting of a single cell. So **Protophyte** (prō^u·tofəit), a plant belonging to the division *Protophyta*.

Protoplasm (prō^u·tǒ,plæz'm). 1848. [– G. *protoplasma* (H. von Mohl, 1846), f. Gr. πρωτο- PROTO- + πλάσμα PLASM.] *Biol.* A viscid, semifluid, semitransparent, colourless or whitish substance, consisting of oxygen, hydrogen, carbon, and nitrogen (often with a small amount of some other elements) in extremely complex unstable combination, and manifesting 'vital properties'; constituting the physical basis of life in all plants and animals. Hence **Pro:toplasma·tic, Protopla·smic** *adjs.* of, pertaining to, or having the nature of p.; relating to p.; acting upon p.

Protoplast[1] (prō^u·tǒ,plæst). 1532. [– Fr. *protoplaste* or late L. *protoplastus* first created being (i.e. Adam) – Gr. πρωτόπλαστος (LXX); see PROTO-, -PLAST.] **1.** That which is first formed, fashioned, or created; the first-made thing or being of its kind; the original, archetype. **2.** *Biol.* A unit or mass of protoplasm, such as constitutes a single cell; a bioplast. Sometimes applied to a unicellular organism; *spec.* one of the suborder *Protoplasta* of rhizopods. 1884.

1. In Salem citie was Adam our p. created 1600.

Pro·toplast[2]. 1600. [app. f. after prec., with *-plast* taken as repr. Gr. πλάστης former, moulder, for πλαστός.] The first former, fashioner, or creator.

Protoplastic (prō^uto,plæ·stik), *a.* 1652. [f. PROTOPLAST[1] + -IC.] **1.** Of the nature of a protoplast; first formed; original, archetypal. **2.** *Biol.* = PROTOPLASMIC 1855.

Protopope (prō^u·topō^up). 1662. [– Russ. *protopóp* – eccl. Gr. πρωτοπαπᾶς PROTOPAPAS; cf. POPE[2].] A chief priest, or priest of higher rank, in the Greek Church.

‖**Prototheria** (prō^utoþī^ə·riă), *sb. pl.* 1880. [mod.L., f. Gr. πρωτο- PROTO- + θηρία beasts.] *Zool.* The lowest subclass of Mammals, comprising the single order *Monotremata*, with their hypothetical ancestors. Hence **Pro·tothere,** a member of the P. **Protothe·rian** *a.* belonging to the P.; *sb.* a protothere.

Prototype (prō^u·tǒtəip). 1603. [– Fr. *prototype* or late L. *prototypus* – Gr. πρωτότυπος; see PROTO-, -TYPE.] The first or primary type of anything; a pattern, model, standard, exemplar, archetype. Hence **Pro·totypal** *a.* of the nature of, or constituting, a p.; of or pertaining to a p.; archetypal.

‖**Protozoa** (prō^uto,zō^u·ă), *sb. pl.* 1834. [mod.L. (Goldfuss, 1818), f. Gr. πρωτο- PROTO- + ζῷα animals; see -A[4].] *Zool.* One of the two (or three) great divisions of the animal kingdom, comprising animals of the simplest or most primitive type, each consisting of a single cell, usu. of microscopic size: correlated with METAZOA. Also in sing. **Protozoon** (-zō^u·ǫn), a member of the division *P.* Hence **Protozo·al** *a.* of, pertaining to, or connected with protozoa; in *Path.* caused, as a disease, by a parasitic protozoon.

Protozoan (prō^uto,zō^u·ăn), *a.* and *sb.* 1864. [f. prec. + -AN.] **A.** *adj.* Of or belonging to the *Protozoa* or a protozoon; also = PROTOZOAL. **B.** *sb.* A protozoon.

Protozoic (prō^uto,zō^u·ik), *a.* 1838. [In sense 1 f. Gr. πρωτο- PROTO- + ζωή life + -IC; in 2 f. PROTOZOA + -IC.] **1.** *Geol.* and *Palæont.* Applied to those strata which contain the earliest remains or traces of living beings; also to fossils found in such strata. **2.** *Zool.* and *Path.* = PROTOZOAN *a.* 1864.

Protozoology (prō^u:to,zo,ǫ·lǒdʒi). 1904. [f. PROTOZOA + -LOGY.] That department of zoology, or of pathology, which deals with protozoa, esp. with parasitic disease-producing protozoa.

Protract (prǒtræ·kt), *v.* 1548. [– *protract-*, pa. ppl. stem of L. *protrahere* prolong, defer (in med.L. also = Branch III), f. *pro* PRO-[1] + *trahere* draw; cf. PORTRAY.] **I.** †**1.** *trans.* To prolong (time) so as to cause delay; to waste (time) –1769. **2.** To lengthen out (an action); to cause to last longer; to prolong 1563. †**3.** To put off, postpone (an action) –1808. †**4.** *intr.* To make delay, to delay –1677.

1. This they did merely to p. time ROBERTSON. **2.** Ne're could he so long p. his speech SHAKS. Their stay was protracted for some weeks 1838. **3.** He attempted, however, to prevent, or at least to p., his ruin GIBBON.

II. *trans.* To extend in space or position 1658. **III.** To draw, represent by a drawing; *spec.* to draw to scale; to delineate by means of a protractor and scale; to plot out 1563. Hence **Protra·cted-ly** *adv.*, **-ness.**

Protractile (protræ·ktil, -əil), *a.* 1828. [f. prec. + -ILE; cf. CONTRACTILE.] *Zool.* Capable of being lengthened out or extended.

Protraction (prǒtræ·kʃən). 1535. [– Fr. *protraction* or late L. *protractio, -on-*, f. as PROTRACT; see -ION.] The action of protracting. **I. 1.** The lengthening out of time or of the duration of anything; prolongation. **2.** A stretching out or extension; the action of a protractor (muscle) 1890.

1. The long p. of the suit 1868.

II. The drawing to scale or laying down of the figure of any surface, esp. of a piece of land 1607. **b.** A chart or plan drawn or laid down to scale; a survey 1669.

†**Protra·ctive,** *a.* 1606. [f. PROTRACT *v.* + -IVE.] Characterized by protraction; lengthening out, delaying –1819.

Protractor (prǒtræ·ktəɹ). 1611. [f. PROTRACT + -OR 2.] One who or that which protracts. **1.** One who lengthens out time or any action; †one who puts off or delays action. **2.** An instrument, usu. having the form of a graduated semicircle, used in setting off and measuring angles 1658. **3.** *Surg.* An instrument for extracting foreign bodies from wounds 1727. **4.** *Anat.* A muscle which serves to protract or extend a limb or member. Also *p. muscle.* 1861.

Protreptic (protre·ptik), *a.* and *sb.* 1656. [As adj. – Gr. προτρεπτικός, f. πρό PRO-[2] + τρέπειν to turn; as sb. – L. *protrepticon* (*-um*) = Gr. προτρεπτικόν, n. of the adj.] **A.** *adj.* Directive, instructive, didactic 1658. **B.** *sb.* A book, writing, or speech intended to exhort or instruct 1656. So **Protre·ptical** *a.*

Protrude (prǒtrū·d), *v.* 1620. [– L. *protrudere*, f. *pro* PRO-[1] + *trudere* thrust.] †**1.** *trans.* To thrust forward; to push or drive onward –1834. **2.** To push or thrust into any position; to cause to project; to extend 1646. **b.** *fig.* To obtrude 1840. **3.** *intr.* To stick out 1626.

2. When young Spring protrudes the bursting gems THOMSON. **b.** Critics, who..p. their nonsense upon the town THACKERAY. **3.** A pair of feet protruding from under the curtains 1868. Hence **Protru·dable** *a.* capable of being protruded; so **Protru·sible.**

Protrusile (protrū·sil, -əil), *a.* 1847. [f. *extrusile*, by substitution of prefix PRO-[1].] Adapted to be extended or thrust out, as a limb, tentacle, etc.

Protrusion (prǒtrū·ʒən). 1646. [f. PROTRUDE, after *intrude/intrusion, extrude/extrusion.*] **1.** The action of protruding; the fact or condition of being protruded. **2.** *concr.* That which protrudes or juts out; a protruding part, a protuberance, a prominence 1704.

2. The fantastic gables, pinnacles, and protrusions, which intercepted the light 1862.

Protrusive (prǒtrū·siv), *a.* 1676. [f. PROTRUDE, after *intrude/intrusive.*] **1.** Thrusting forward or onward; propulsive. **2.** Obtrusive 1840. **3.** Protruding, projecting, protuberant 1858. Hence **Protru·sive-ly** *adv.*, **-ness.**

Protuberance (prǒtiū·bĕrăns). 1646. [f. PROTUBERANT; see -ANCE.] **1.** The fact or condition of being protuberant; bulging out or projecting in a rounded form 1681. **2.** That which is protuberant; a rounded prominence, projection, or swelling; a knob, a bump 1646.

2. *Solar p.* = solar PROMINENCE. So **Protu·berancy.**

Protuberant (prǒtiū·bĕrănt), *a.* 1646. [– *protuberant-*, pr. ppl. stem of late L. *protuberare*, f. *pro* PRO-[1] + *tuber* bump, swelling; see TUBER, -ANT.] Bulging or swelling out beyond the surrounding surface; prominent.

Eocha III...is remembered for his p. nose 1807. Hence **Protu·berantly** *adv.*

Protuberate (prǒtiū·bĕrē^it), *v. rare.* 1578. [– *protuberat-*, pa. ppl. stem of late L. *protuberare*; see prec., -ATE[3].] *intr.* To bulge out, to form a rounded prominence.

‖**Protyle** (prō^u·təil). Also **prothyl.** 1886. [irreg. f. Gr. πρωτ(ο- PROTO- + ὕλη HYLE.] Proposed name for the hypothetical original undifferentiated matter, of which the chemical substances provisionally regarded as elements may be composed.

Proud (praud), *a.* (*adv.*) [Late OE. *prūd* (also *prūt*) = ON. *prúðr* – OFr. *prud, prod,* nom. *pruz, proz, prouz* (mod. *preux*) valiant, gallant – Rom. **prodis* (late L. *prode*, n. in pre-Vulg.), f. L. *prodesse* be of value, be good, f. *prod*, var. of *pro* PRO-[1] + *esse* be. Cf. PREUX, PROW *a.*, PRIDE.] **I. 1.** Having a high or lofty opinion of oneself; valuing oneself highly on account of one's position, rank, attainments, possessions, etc. Usu. in bad sense, implying arrogance or hauteur. **2.** Highly sensible of, or elated by, some honour done to one; taking pride or having high satisfaction in something; in early use sometimes merely = highly gratified or pleased; *colloq.* feeling highly honoured. Often const. *of*, or inf. ME. **3.** Having a becoming sense of what is due to or worthy of oneself or one's position; feeling or showing a proper pride 1738. **4.** *transf.* Of actions, etc.: Proceeding from or indicating pride; arrogant, presumptuous; arising from lofty self-respect. late ME. **5.** That is a ground or cause of pride; of which one is or may be proud (now usu. in good sense) ME.

1. They are as bragge and as proude as pecockes 1560. Hee was a p. insolent Delegate 1613. Most of our women are extreamly p. Of their faire lookes 1616. They say he's as p. as Lucifer 1782. **2.** The author of the *Plain Dealer*, whom I am p. to call my friend DRYDEN. **4.** There be sixe thinges, which the Lorde hateth..A proude loke [etc.] COVERDALE *Prov.* 6:17. **5.** The p. inheritance of their stainless loyalty 1868.

II. 1. As a poetic or rhetorical epithet. **a.** Of exalted station, of high degree, of lofty dignity; lordly ME. **b.** Of things: Stately, magnificent, 'gallant', splendid ME. **2.** Characterized by great vigour, force, or vitality, such as indicates or suggests pride; in various applications. †**a.** Of warriors (or their acts): Valiant, brave; mighty –1697. **b.** Of animals: Spirited, high-mettled; moving with force and dignity. (Chiefly *poet.*) late ME. **c.** Of the sea or a stream: Swelling, swollen, strong, in flood 1535. **d.** Of organic structures: Overgrown, exuberant; swelling or swollen, tumid. (*b*) Applied to overgrown flesh in a healing wound; see also PROUD FLESH. 1593. †**3.** Sensually excited; 'swelling', lascivious –1641. †**b.** *spec.* Of certain female animals: In a state of sexual excitement –1781.

1. a. High though his titles, p. his name, Boundless his wealth SCOTT. **b.** View..The p. ships sail, and gay clouds move 1794. One of the proudest cities of the ancient world THIRLWALL. **2. b.** Like a p. Steed reind MILT. **c.** Then the p. waters had gone ouer our soule *Ps.* 124:5.

Phr. *To do* (a person) *p.* (colloq.), to make p., gratify highly, do honour to.

B. as *adv.* Proudly, in a proud manner ME. Hence **Prou·dish** *a.* somewhat p. **Prou·d-ly** *adv.*, **-ness.**

Proud flesh. late ME. [See prec. II. 2 d.] Overgrown flesh arising from excessive granulation upon, or around the edges of, a healing wound.

Prou·d-hea·rted, *a.* late ME. Having a proud heart or spirit; proud, haughty.

Proustite (prū·stəit). 1835. [– Fr. *proustite* (1832) after J. L. *Proust*, a French chemist; see -ITE¹ 2 b.] *Min.* Native sulpharsenide of silver, occurring in crystals or granular masses of a cochineal-red colour.

Provand (prǫ·vănd). ME. [– (O)Fr. *provende*; see PROVEND *sb.*] Provisions, provender; *esp.* the food and fodder provided for an army.

Provant (prǫ·vănt), *sb.* (*a.*) 1450. [app. – MLG. *provant*, later form of *provande* PROVAND; perh. sometimes confounded with †*provent* produce, revenue.] **1.** Provand, provender; an allowance of food. **2.** *attrib.* or as *adj.* Of or belonging to the p. or soldier's allowance; hence, of inferior quality. *arch.* 1598.

Prove (prūv), *v.* Infl. **proved, proving;** pa. pple. also (orig. in Sc. legal use) **proven.** ME. [– OFr. *prover* (mod. *prouver*) :– L. *probare* test, approve, demonstrate, f. *probus* good.] **I.** To make trial of, try, test. **1.** *trans.* To make trial of; to try the genuineness or qualities of; to test. *arch.* exc. in techn. uses. **b.** To subject to a testing process (any natural, prepared, or manufactured substance or object) ME. **c.** *Arith.* To test the correctness of (a calculation) 1806. **d.** To take a proof impression of (composed type or an electro- or stereotype plate) 1797. **2.** To find out, learn, or know by experience; to experience, 'go through', suffer; also, to find by experience (a person or thing) to be (something) ME.

1. Proue all things: hold fast that which is good 1 *Thess.* 5:21. **c.** Multiplication is also very naturally proved by Division 1806. **2.** They only shall his Mercy p. WESLEY.

II. To make good, establish. **1.** *trans.* To establish (a thing) as true; to demonstrate the truth of by evidence or argument ME. **2.** To show the existence or reality of; to give proof of by action; to evince ME. **3.** To establish the genuineness or validity of (a thing or person); to show to be such as is asserted or claimed 1517. **b.** *spec.* To establish the genuineness and validity of (a will); to obtain probate of. late ME. **4.** *intr.* for *refl.* To be shown or found by experience or trial to be (so and so); to turn out (to be). late ME. **5.** To come to be, become, grow (*arch.*) 1560.

1. He went about also to proue hym selfe a Germayne 1560. **3.** It is very hard to p. a Witch FULLER. **6. P. up** (*U.S.*): to adduce or complete the proof of right to (something); *spec.* to show that one has fulfilled the requirements for receiving a patent for (government land) 1867. Hence **Pro·v(e)able** *a.* capable of being proved. **Pro·v(e)ableness. Pro·v(e)ably** *adv.*

Provect (prove·kt), *v.* 1652. [f. *provect-*, pa. ppl. stem of L. *provehere*, f. *pro* PRO-¹ + *vehere* carry.] †**1.** *trans.* To carry forward or onward –1776. **2.** *Philol.* To change or 'mutate' a consonant in the direction of the sound-shift formulated for Germanic in Grimm's Law; *esp.* in Celtic, to change a voice consonant into a breath consonant of the same series 1861.

Provection (prove·kʃən). 1652. [– late L. *provectio, -on-*, f. as prec.; see -ION.] †**1.** Advance, proficiency; advancement –1660. **2.** *Philol.* **a.** The sound-shift formulated for Germanic langs. in Grimm's Law; also in Celtic, the mutation of voice consonants to breath consonants 1861. **b.** The carrying on of the final letter of a word to the succeeding one 1868.

Proveditor (prove·ditǫɹ), also in It. form ‖**Proveditore** (provedito̅·re). 1549. [– obs. It. *proved-*, mod. *provveditore* provider, purveyor, f. *provedere* PROVIDE.] **1.** The title of certain officers of the Venetian republic; a governor, overseer, inspector. **2.** A purveyor, caterer, steward 1599.

Provedore (prǫvĭdōᵊ·ɹ). 1578. [– various Rom. forms, all the agent-n. from the vb. repr. L. *providere* PROVIDE; cf. prec.] = prec.

Proven (prū·v'n, *Sc.* prōᵘ·v'n), *ppl. a.* 1653. [pa. pple., orig. Sc. (*provin*, *c*1536) of *preve*, early var. of PROVE *v.*, after str. vbs. like *cleave, cloven.*] **1.** Shown to be true, or to be as stated; demonstrated by evidence. **2.** Tried, tested (pseudo-*arch.*) 1870.

1. A p. falsehood LANDOR. *Not proven*, a form of verdict in criminal trials in Sc. Law, which is admitted beside 'Guilty' and 'Not guilty'.

Provenance (prǫ·vĕnăns). 1861. [– Fr. *provenance*, f. *provenant*, pr. pple. of *provenir* come forth – L. *provenire*, f. *pro* PRO-¹ + *venire* come; see -ANCE.] The fact of coming from some particular source or quarter; derivation.

The date and p. of Jewish apocalypses 1906.

Provençal (provaṅsal), *a.* and *sb.* 1589. [– Fr. *provençal* – L. *provincialis* PROVINCIAL; see next.] **A.** *adj.* Of or pertaining to Provence and its inhabitants.

Dance, and P. song, and sunburnt mirth! KEATS.

B. *sb.* **1.** An inhabitant of Provence 1600. **2.** The Romanic language spoken there 1671.

Provence (‖provā·ṅs, prǫ·vĕns). 1578. [– (O)Fr. *Provence* :– L. *provincia* PROVINCE.] The name of a former province in the south-east of France east of the Rhône; used *attrib.*, as in *P. oil*, olive oil from P.

Provend (prǫ·vĕnd), *sb. Obs.* or *arch.* ME. [– (O)Fr. *provende* :– Rom. **probenda*, alt. of L. *præbenda* PREBEND.] **1.** = PREBEND 1; also, the portion or allowance of food supplied to each inmate of a monastery. **2.** = next. ME.

Provender (prǫ·vĕndəɹ), *sb.* ME. [– OFr. *provendre*, var. of *provende* PROVEND.] Food, provisions; *esp.* dry food, as corn or hay for horses, etc.; fodder, forage. In ref. to human beings, now *joc.*

They must be dyeted like Mules, And haue their Prouender ty'd to their mouthes SHAKS. Hence **Pro·vender** *v. trans.* to provide (horses, etc.) with provender, to fodder.

Provenience (prŏvī·niĕns). 1882. (Common in U.S.) [f. L. *proveniens, -ent-*, pr. pple. of *provenire*; see -ENCE.] = PROVENANCE.

‖**Proventriculus** (prōᵘventri·kiŭlŏs). 1835. [mod.L., f. *pro* PRO-¹ + *ventriculus* VENTRICLE.] **a.** *Ornith.* The glandular or true stomach of birds, which lies between the crop and the gizzard. **b.** In some insects, the crop or ingluvies, an expansion of the œsophagus; in worms, a muscular crop 1877.

Prover (prū·vəɹ). late ME. [In sense 1 f. PROVE + -ER¹; in 2 = AL. *probator*, AFr. *provour, pruvour.*] **1.** One who tries, tests, or puts to the proof. *Obs.* or *arch.* **b.** An instrument or apparatus for testing 1751. **c.** *Engraving.* A skilled workman employed to print proof impressions 1875. †**2.** = APPROVER¹ 1. –1769.

Proverb (prǫ·vəɹb), *sb.* ME. [– (O)Fr. *proverbe* or L. *proverbium*, f. *pro* PRO-¹ + *verbum* word + *-ium*, collective suffix.] **1.** A short pithy saying in common use; a concise sentence, which is held to express some truth ascertained by experience or observation and familiar to all; an adage, a wise saw. **2.** †**a.** = BYWORD 2 –1791. **b.** *transf.* A thing that is proverbial or a matter of common talk 1655. †**3.** An oracular or enigmatical saying that requires interpretation; an allegory, a parable –1841. **4.** A play of which a proverb is taken as the foundation of the plot 1842. **5.** *pl.* Any of various round games played with popular sayings.

1. *The Book of Proverbs*, a book of the O.T., consisting of maxims ascribed to Solomon and others. Phr. *To a p.*, to an extent that has become proverbial; The new chief justice, Sir Robert Wright, was ignorant to a p. MACAULAY. **2. a.** And thou shalt be a wonder, a prouerbe & a commune talke among all people BIBLE (Genev.) *Deut.* 28:37. **3.** To vnderstand a prouerbe, and the interpretation; the wordes of the wise, and their darke sayings *Prov.* 1:6.

Proverb (prǫ·vəɹb), *v.* late ME. [f. prec.] **1.** *trans.* To utter in the form of a proverb; to make a byword of. **2.** To furnish or provide with a proverb SHAKS. **3.** *intr.* To utter or compose proverbs MILT.

1. Am I not sung and proverbd for a Fool In every street? MILT. **2.** I am prouerb'd with a Grandsier Phrase SHAKS.

Proverbial (prŏvə̄·ɹbiăl), *a.* late ME. [– L. *proverbialis*, f. *proverbium*; see prec., -AL¹.] **1.** Like, characteristic of, or of the nature of a proverb; expressed in a proverb or proverbs. **2.** That has passed into a proverb; current as a proverb; notorious 1571.

1. Yet is not all true that is proverbiall SIR T. BROWNE. **2.** The p. London fog HUXLEY. Hence **Prove·rbialism,** a p. saying. **Prove·rbialist,** one who originates, uses, or records p. sayings. **Proverbia·lity,** the quality of being p. **Prove·rbialize** *v. intr.* to make or utter proverbs. **Prove·rbially** *adv.* in a p. manner; to a p. degree.

Proviant (prǫ·viănt). 1637. [– G. *proviant*, Du. *proviand*, in It. *provianda*, app. alt. f. *provenda* PROVEND. Brought into Eng. by soldiers who served in the Thirty Years' War, 1618–1648.] Food supply, esp. for an army; commissariat.

Pro:-vice-cha·ncellor. 1660. [See PRO-¹] One of the deputies appointed by the vice-chancellor of a university on his election.

Provide (prŏvəi·d), *v.* late ME. [– L. *providēre* see before, etc., f. *pro* PRO-¹ + *vidēre.*] **I.** †**1.** *trans.* To foresee –1640. **2.** *intr.* To exercise foresight in taking due measures in view of a possible event. Const. *for, against.* late ME. **b.** To lay it down as a provision; to stipulate *that.* late ME.

2. In tyme of peace, prouide for war GRAFTON. The Mayers wyfe..prouided in her wyll, that she would be buried without any pompe or noyse 1560.

II. 1. *trans.* To prepare, get ready, or arrange (something) beforehand. Now *rare.* late ME. †**2.** *intr.* To make preparation, get ready –1727. †**b.** *trans.* with *vbl. sb.* SHAKS. **3.** *trans.* To supply or furnish for use; to yield, afford 1447. **4.** To furnish or appoint (an incumbent) *to* a vacant benefice; *esp.* of the pope: To appoint (a person as successor) *to* a benefice not yet vacant, thus setting aside the right of the patron. Now only *Hist.* late ME.

1. The wise Ant her wintry Store provides DRYDEN. **2.** Very few men..live at present, but are providing to live another time POPE. **3.** Prouide me ynke and paper, and I will write 1581.

III. 1. To fit out (a person, etc.) with what is necessary for a certain purpose; to furnish or supply with something implied 1465. †b. *refl.* To equip oneself, to make oneself ready, prepare (*to do* something, *for* or *against* something) –1652. 2. To furnish (a person, etc.) with something. Often in indirect passive. late ME. 3. *intr.* To make provision *for* a person, his needs, etc. Often in indirect passive. 1535.

1. b. Neice prouide your selfe SHAKS. 2. Prouided with all complete prouisions of Warre CAMDEN. 3. His wonted Followers Shall all be very well prouided for SHAKS.

Provided (prŏvəi·dėd), *ppl. a.* and quasi-*conj.* 1460. [pa. pple. of PROVIDE *v.*] I. *ppl. a.* In senses of PROVIDE *v.* 1579. II. *pa. pple.* and quasi-*conj.* With the provision or condition (that); it being provided or stipulated (that); used chiefly in legal and formal statements; also, in general use: On the condition, supposition, or understanding (that) 1460. b. without *that*: = if only 1604.

I. *P. school*, a public elementary school provided by the local education authority. II. P. that all is safe, you may go 1879. b. Now or whensoeuer, prouided I be so able as now SHAKS.

Providence (prǫ·vidĕns). ME. [– (O)Fr. *providence* or L. *providentia*, f. *providēre* PROVIDE; see -ENCE.] 1. The action of providing; provision, preparation, arrangement. Now *dial.* late ME. b. That which is provided; a supply, a provision. Now *dial.* 1475. 2. Foresight, prevision; *esp.* anticipation of and preparation for the future; hence, prudent or wise management, government, or guidance. Also, an instance of this. late ME. b. Regard to future needs in the management of resources; thrift 1608. 3. In full, *p. of God* (etc.), *divine p.*: The foreknowing and beneficent care and government of God (or of nature, etc.); divine direction, control, or guidance ME. 4. Hence applied to the Deity as exercising prescient power and direction 1602. b. *transf.* A person who acts or appears in the character of Providence (*colloq.*) 1856. 5. An instance or act of divine intervention; an event or circumstance which indicates divine dispensation 1643.

2. In this matter the p. of king Henry the seventh was in all men's mouths BACON. b. When there should have been p. there has been waste RUSKIN. 3. Almyȝty god, whos prouidence in hys ordinaunce faileþ noȝt 1400. 4. What P. has reserved for me he only knows DE FOE. 5. *Special p.*, a particular act of direct divine intervention.

Provident (prǫ·vidĕnt), *a.* late ME. [– L. *providens, -ent-*, pr. pple. of *providēre* PROVIDE; see -ENT.] 1. Foreseeing; that has foresight of and provides for the future, or for some future event. 2. Economical; frugal, thrifty, saving 1596.

1. By Solomon God sends the Sluggard to school to the Ant, to learn a p. Industry BOYLE. *P. society* = FRIENDLY *society*. 2. He will always be poor, because he never was a p. man 1888. Hence **Pro·vident-ly** *adv.*, **-ness** (*rare*).

Providential (prǫvide·nʃăl), *a.* 1648. [f. PROVIDENCE (and PROVIDENT) + -IAL, after *evidence, evident, evidential*, etc.] †1. Of the nature of providence; provident, prudent –1845. 2. Of, pertaining to, or ordained by divine providence 1648. b. That is, or is thought to be, by special interposition of providence; opportune, lucky, fortunate 1719.

2. A p. disposition of things 1736. b. [It] was by them considered as a p. escape BURKE. Hence **Provide·ntially** *adv.*

Provider (prŏvəi·dəɹ). 1523. [f. PROVIDE *v.* + -ER¹.] One who provides or supplies; a purveyor. *Lion's p.*: see LION 1.

Province (prǫ·vins). ME. [– (O)Fr. *province* – L. *provincia* charge, official duty, administration or region of conquered territory; of unkn. origin.] I. 1. *Rom. Hist.* A country or territory outside Italy, under Roman dominion, and administered by a governor sent from Rome. late ME. 2. An administrative division of a country or state; any principal division of a kingdom or empire. Formerly sometimes applied to the shires of England. late ME. b. Applied to the N. American colonies of Great Britain, now provinces of the Dominion of Canada; also formerly to several of those which afterwards united to form the United States of America 1622. c. *fig.* A main division of any 'realm' 1869. 3. *Eccl.* The district within the jurisdiction of an archbishop or a metropolitan. late ME. b. One of the territorial divisions of the Knights Templars, the Franciscans, the Jesuits, or any similar order 1727. 4. More vaguely, A country, territory, district, or region; a part of the world, or of one of its continents ME. 5. *pl.* A comprehensive designation for all parts of a country outside the capital; e.g. of England apart from London 1804. 6. *Nat. Hist.* A faunal or floral area less extensive than a 'region'; a sub-region 1877.

2. They divided the country into four provinces, viz. Ulster, Leinster, Munster, and Connaught, each of which had its King 1804. c. Our earth is but a p. of a wider realm 1869. 4. Some had long moved to distant provinces JOHNSON. 5. She had ..starred the provinces with great eclat and had come back to London THACKERAY.

II. The sphere of action of a person or body of persons; duty, office, business, function, department 1626.

My p. was..to carry home the goods 1775. How he had secured an entrance..it is not our p. to inquire 1888.

III. *fig.* from I. A department, division, or branch of learning, science, art, government, or any subject 1709.

In the provinces of Æsthetics and Morals 1874.

Provincial (prŏvi·nʃăl), *a* and *sb.* late ME. [– (O)Fr. *provincial* – L. *provincialis*, f. *provincia*; see prec., -AL¹.] A. *adj.* 1. Of or pertaining to a province or provinces. †2. Having the relation of a province to a sovereign state –1708. 3. Of or belonging to a province or provinces as dist. from the nation or state of which they form a part; local; hence, of the 'provinces' as dist. from the capital; situated in 'the provinces' 1638. b. *transf.* Said of foxhunting outside the 'shires' 1861. 4. Having the manners or speech, *esp.* the narrow views, etc., of a province or 'the provinces'; wanting the culture or polish of the capital 1755. †5. Of roses of Provence –1633.

2. The other parts of it..are still as much p. to Italy, as..in the time of the Roman Empire DRYDEN. 3. Those many barbarisms which characterize a p. education 1772. P. or local words 1787. Paris and the great p. towns 1844. 4. *Provincial*,..rude; unpolished JOHNSON. 5. *Haml.* III. ii. 288.

B. *sb.* [the adj. used absol. or ellipt.] 1. *Eccl.* The ecclesiastical head of a province; the chief of a religious order in a district or province. late ME. 2. A native or inhabitant of a province (Roman or modern); in *pl.* auxiliary troops raised in a province; formerly applied to the native Irish 1605. b. An inhabitant of the N. American colonies before the revolution; applied esp. to those engaged in military service 1758. 3. One who dwells in or comes from the 'provinces' as dist. from the capital; hence, a 'countrified' person 1711.

3. Provincials, narrow in thought, in culture, in creed 1865. Hence **Provi·ncialist,** a native or inhabitant of a province or of the provinces, as dist. from the capital. **Provincia·lity,** the quality or condition of being p.; a p. trait. **Provi·ncialize** *v. trans.* and *intr.* to make or become p. **Provi·ncially** *adv.* in a p. manner or capacity.

Provincialism (prŏvi·nʃăliz'm). 1793. [f. prec. + -ISM.] 1. *Politics.* Attachment to one's own province, its institutions, interests, etc., before those of the nation or state; desire for the autonomy of the province or provinces rather than national unity 1820. 2. Provincial manner, fashion, mode of thought, etc. as dist. from that which is (or is held to be) national, or which is the fashion of the capital; hence, narrowness of view, thought, or interests, unpolished speech or manners 1836. b. with *a* and *pl.* A local peculiarity or variety 1845. 3. *esp.* The manner of speech characteristic of a particular province; with *pl.*, A local word, phrase, or peculiarity of pronunciation 1793.

Provinciate (prŏvi·nʃi,ēˈt), *v.* 1629. [f. L. *provincia* PROVINCE + -ATE³.] *trans.* To reduce to the condition of a province or of provincials.

Provine (provəi·n), *v.* 1440. [– OFr. *provaignier, -veign-* (mod. *provigner*), f. *provain* (mod. *provin*) :– L. *propago, -gin-* young shoot, slip, or layer. Cf. PROPAGATE.] *trans.* To propagate (a vine or the like) by layering. Also *absol.*, and *intr.* in *pass.* sense.

Provision (prŏvi·ʒən), *sb.* late ME. [– (O)Fr. *provision* – L. *provisio, -on-*, f. *provis-*, pa. ppl. stem of *providēre* PROVIDE; see -ION.] 1. The action of providing; seeing to things beforehand; the fact or condition of being made ready beforehand 1456. b. *esp.* The providing or supplying of necessaries for a household, an expedition, etc. 1484. 2. *Eccl.* Appointment to a see or benefice not yet vacant; *esp.* such appointment made by the pope in derogation of the right of the regular patron. Now *Hist.* late ME. 3. Something prepared or arranged in advance; a preparation, a previous arrangement; a measure provided to meet a need; a precaution 1494. 4. A supply of necessaries or materials provided; a store of something 1451. 5. *spec.* A supply of food; now chiefly *pl.* supplies of food, victuals, eatables and drinkables 1610. 6. Each of the clauses or divisions of a legal or formal statement, or such a statement itself, providing for some particular matter; also, a clause in such a statement which makes an express stipulation; a proviso 1473.

1. Due p. for education..is..a duty of the state HUXLEY. Phr. *To make p.*, to provide *for*. 3. There was no..p. for a rudder 1832. 4. Here they deposit their p. of nuts and acorns 1796. 5. The English for want of provisions were forced to breake up Siege HOLLAND. The price of provisions is exorbitant 1773. 6. *Provisions of Oxford*, ordinances for checking the king's misrule, drawn up at a meeting of the barons under Simon de Montfort, held at Oxford in 1258.

Provision (prŏvi·ʒən), *v.* 1805. [f. prec.] *trans.* To supply with provisions or stores. b. *intr.* (for *refl.*) To supply oneself with provisions; to lay in provisions.

He raised a regiment of horse and provisioned it 1859.

Provisional (prŏvi·ʒənăl), *a.* 1601. [f. PROVISION *sb.* + -AL¹, after Fr. †*provisionnal* (mod. *-el*), med.L. *provisionalis, -aliter.*] 1. Of, belonging to, or of the nature of a temporary provision or arrangement; provided or adopted for present needs or for the time being; also, accepted or used in default of something better. †2. Provident (*rare*) –1763.

1. To come to a prouisionall agreement 1601. The Church should not be without a p. Pastor 1726. Hence **Provi·sional-ly** *adv.*, **-ness.**

Provisionary (prŏvi·ʒənări), *a.* Now *rare.* 1617. [f. as prec. + -ARY¹; cf. PROVISORY.] 1. = prec. 1. †2. = prec. 2. –1784. 3. Of or pertaining to papal provisions; see PROVISION *sb.* 2. 1736. 4. Of, pertaining to, or of the nature of a proviso, a provision, or provisions (in a law, etc.) 1774.

Proviso (prŏvəi·zo). *Pl.* **-oes.** 1467. [– L. *proviso*, abl. sing. n. of pa. pple. of *providēre* PROVIDE, as used in med.L. phr. *proviso quod* (or *ut*)..it being provided that..(cf. Fr. *pourvu que*..).] A clause inserted in a legal or formal document, making some condition, stipulation, exception, or limitation, or upon the observance of which the operation or validity of the instrument depends; a condition; hence *gen.*, a stipulation, provision.

Provisor (prŏvəi·zəɹ, -ǭɹ). late ME. [– AFr. *provisour* (Fr. *proviseur*) – L. *provisor*, f. as PROVISION; see -OR 2.] I. The holder of a provision or grant (esp. from the pope) giving him the right to be presented to a benefice when next vacant. Now *Hist.*

Statute of Provisors, the Act 25 Edw. III, 1350–1351, enacted to prevent the granting of these provisions by the pope.

II. †1. One who is in charge; a supervisor; an agent, deputy –1533. †2. One who provides for another; a guardian, protector –1730. 3. A purveyor; the steward or treasurer of an establishment. Now *Hist.* 1498. 4. *R.C.Ch.* A vicar-general; a deputy-inquisitor 1560.

3. P. General of Pork for the Army 1683. Hence **Provi·sorship** (*rare*), the office or position of a p.

Provisory (prŏvəi·zəri), *a.* 1611. [– Fr. *provisoire* or med.L. *provisorius*, f. as prec.; see -ORY².] 1. Subject to a provision or proviso; conditional. 2. = PROVISIONAL *a.* 1. 1788. Hence **Provi·sorily** *adv.* in a p. manner; provisionally.

Provocation (prǫvŏkēˈ·ʃən). late ME. [–

(O)Fr. *provocation* or L. *provocatio, -on-*, f. *provocat-*, pa. ppl. stem of *provocare*; see PROVOKE, -ION.] **I.** †**1.** The action of invoking the office of a court or judge; *esp.* an appeal to a higher ecclesiastical court –1726. **2.** The action of calling; invitation, summons 1548. **II. 1.** The action of inciting; impulse; instigation; an incentive, a stimulus. late ME. **2.** The action or an act of exciting anger, resentment, or irritation 1539. **b.** A cause of anger, resentment, or irritation 1716.

2. To the..prouocacion of the terrible wrath of god 1540. You ought not to give way to your temper, under whatever p. 1876.

Provocative (prǒvǫ·kǎtiv), *a.* and *sb.* late ME. [– Fr. †*provocatif, -ive* – late L. *provocativus*, f. as prec.; see -IVE.] **A.** *adj.* **1.** Having the quality of provoking, calling forth, or giving rise to (const. *of*); *spec.* stimulating, irritating 1649. **2.** *spec.* Serving to excite appetite or lust 1621. **B.** *sb.* **1.** That which provokes, excites, or draws forth; an incentive 1638. **2.** *spec.* Anything that excites appetite or lust; *esp.* an aphrodisiac. late ME. Hence **Provo·catively** *adv.*

Provokable (prǒvōᵘ·kǎb'l), *a.* 1678. [f. PROVOKE *v.* + -ABLE.] Capable of being provoked.

Provoke (prǒvōᵘ·k), *v.* late ME. [– (O)Fr. *provoquer* or L. *provocare*, f. *pro* PRO-¹ + *vocare* call.] **I.** †**1.** *trans.* To call forth, invoke; to summon, invite. Also *absol.* –1708. †**2.** *intr.* To call to a judge or court to take up one's cause; to appeal (*from* a lower *to* a higher eccl. tribunal) –1682. †**3.** *trans.* To call out to a fight; to challenge, to defy –1697.

3. Tertullian..provokes all the world to contradict it, if they could EVELYN.

II. 1. To incite or urge (a person or animal) *to* some act or *to do* something; to stimulate to action. Now *arch.* exc. as infl. by next. late ME. **2.** To incite to anger (a person or animal); to enrage, irritate. Also *absol.* late ME. **3.** To excite, stir up (feeling, action, etc.); to give rise to, call forth 1533.

1. Beautie prouoketh theeues sooner then gold SHAKS. **2.** You are really enough to p. a saint 1800. **3.** My Tale prouokes that question SHAKS. Hence **Provo·ked** *ppl. a.* having received provocation; irritated, annoyed. †**Provo·kement,** the action of provoking; a provocation. **Provo·ker,** one who or that which provokes. **Provo·kingly** *adv.*

Provost (prǫ·vəst). [Late OE. *profost*, corresp. to MLG., MDu. *provest*, MDu. *proofst* (Du. *proost*), OHG. *probost* (G. *probst, propst*), ONorw. *prófastr*; in ME. reinforced from AFr. *provost*, also *prevost* (mod. *prévôt*) – med.L. *propositus*, used alongside *præpositus*, subst. use of pa. pple. of L. *præponere*, f. *præ* PRE-, PRO-¹ + *ponere* place.] **I.** In eccl. and scholastic use. **1.** The head or president of a chapter, or of a community of religious persons; in conventual bodies prop. the official next in rank to the abbot. Now chiefly *Hist.* **b.** In mod. use, tr. G. *propst*, Da. *provst*, etc., as the title of the Protestant clergyman in charge of the principal church of a town or district 1560. **2.** The specific title of the heads of certain colleges 1442. **II.** A secular officer, etc. †**1.** One appointed to preside over or superintend something; usu. the representative of the supreme power in a district or sphere of action. Sometimes, without explicit ref. to his delegated or appointed position, = Ruler, chief, head, captain, etc. –1631. **2.** An officer or official in charge of some establishment, undertaking, or body of men; a ruler, manager, steward, overseer, keeper. Now *Hist.* ME. **3.** †The chief magistrate of a town; *spec.* the head of a Scottish municipal corporation or burgh ME. †**4.** An officer charged with the apprehension, custody, and punishment of offenders –1873. **5.** *spec. Mil.* An officer of the military police in a garrison or camp, or in the field: see next. (In this sense usu. pronounced prǒvōᵘ·.) 1692.

4. Here comes Signior Claudio, led by the Prouost to prison SHAKS.

Comb.: **p.-cell,** a cell for confining military prisoners; **-sergeant,** a sergeant of the military police. Hence **Pro·vostship,** the office or position of a p.

Provost-marshal (prǒvōᵘ:mā·ɹʃǎl), 1513. [f. prec. + MARSHAL *sb.*] In the army, An officer appointed to a force in camp or on active service, as the head of the military police. In the navy, the 'Master-at-arms' of the ship in which a court martial is to be held (being the Chief Petty Officer in charge of the ship's police) is appointed by warrant Provost-marshal for the occasion.

Prow (prau), *sb.*¹ Now chiefly *literary.* 1555. [– (O)Fr. *proue* – Pr. *proa* or It. dial. (Genoese, Sicilian) *prua* :– L. *prora* – Gr. πρῷρα, f. base repr. by L. *pro* before, in front.] **1.** The fore-part of a ship or boat; the part about the stem. **2.** A point or pointed part projecting in front, like the prow of a ship; *spec.* in *Zool.* either of the two points of a cymba or C-shaped sponge-spicule 1656. **3.** *transf.* A ship (*poet.*) 1738.

3. Prows, that late in fierce Encounter mett GRAY. Hence **Prowed** (praud) *a.* having a p.

†**Prow,** *sb.*² [ME. *pru, prou* – OFr. *pru, prou*, subst. use of *pru, prou* adj.; see next.] Advantage, profit, benefit, weal, good –1570.

It maye bee for his prowe, To thynke on it *c*1470.

Prow (prau), *a. arch.* late ME. [– OFr. *prou* adj. (earlier *prod*, etc., later *preu*, mod. *preux*) – Rom. **prodis*; see PROUD *a.* Cf. PREUX, PRIDE.] Doughty, valiant.

The prowest knight that ever field did fight SPENSER.

Prowess (prau·ės). Now chiefly *literary.* ME. [– OFr. *proesce* (mod. *prouesse*), f. OFr. *prou*; see prec., -ESS².] Valour, bravery, gallantry, martial daring; manly courage, active fortitude. **b.** An act of bravery; a valiant deed. (Chiefly in *pl.* = deeds of valour.) ME.

His hye prowes was suche that no paynym durst abyde him 1533.

·**Prowl** (praul), *v.* [In XIV *prolle*, of unkn. origin.] **1.** *intr.* Orig., To go or move about, esp. in search of something; hence, to rove, roam, or wander about in search of plunder, prey, etc., or with predatory intent. In mod. use, chiefly of wild beasts or of men acting like them. †**b.** *fig.* To seek for advantage in an underhand way; to 'cadge' –1669. †**2.** *trans.* To obtain (something) in a clandestine way; to pilfer, filch –1677. **3.** To traverse (a place or region) esp. on the look out for prey; to traverse stealthily 1586.

1. [Wolves] Priuely prolling two and froe SPENSER. How the troops of Midian P. and p. around 1850. **b.** An other pretie practise of the pope to proll for monie, was this FOXE. Hence **Prowl** *sb.* an act or the action of prowling; *on* or *upon the prowl*, prowling about. **Prow·ler,** one who prowls; a parasite; †a pilferer, cheat, plunderer. **Prow·lingly** *adv.*

‖**Proxenus** (prǫ·ksėnǒs). Also **proxenos.** *Pl.* **-i** (-əi). 1838. [mod.L. – Gr. πρόξενος, f. πρό PRO-² + ξένος guest, stranger.] *Gr. Antiq.* A resident citizen of a state appointed by another state to represent and protect its interests there. So **Pro·xeny,** the office or function of a p.; the system of *proxeni.*

Proximad (prǫ·ksimǎ̆d), *adv.* 1803. [f. as next + -AD II.] *Anat.* In the direction of its point of attachment: opp. to DISTAD.

Proximal (prǫ·ksimǎl), *a.* 1803. [f. L. *proximus* nearest + -AL¹.] *Anat.* Situated towards the centre of the body, or the point of origin or attachment of a limb, bone, etc.: opp. to DISTAL. Hence **Pro·ximally** *adv.* in a p. position; towards or near the p. end or part.

Proximate (prǫ·ksimět), *a.* 1597. [– L. *proximatus*, pa. pple. of *proximare* approach, f. *proximus* nearest; see -ATE².] **1.** Next, nearest (in space, serial order, quality, etc.); close. **b.** Coming next or very near in time 1845. **2.** Coming next (before or after) in a chain of causation, agency, reasoning, etc.; immediate: opp. to *remote* or *ultimate* 1661. **3.** Approximate 1796.

2. *P. principle, constituent*, or *element* (Chem.), one of those compounds of which a more complex body is directly made up, and which are therefore first arrived at in the process of analysis; so *p. analysis.* **3.** A p. notion of the extent of the carnage KINGLAKE. Hence **Pro·ximately** *adv.* in a p. position or manner; approximately.

‖**Proxime accessit** (prǫ·ksimi ækse·sit). 1878. [L. phr. = 'he has come very near (or next)'.] Phr. indicating that the person in question has come next to the winner of a prize, scholarship, etc.; hence as *sb.* applied to the person himself or his position. Also *colloq.* abbrev. *proxime.*

Proximity (prǫksi·mĭti). 1480. [– (O)Fr. *proximité* or L. *proximitas*, f. *proximus* nearest; see -ITY.] The fact, condition, or position of being near or close by; nearness: **a.** in space 1579; **b.** in kinship, affinity of nature, time, etc. 1480.

b. Marriages in p. of blood are amongst us forbidden FLORIO.

‖**Proximo** (prǫ·ksimo). 1855. [L. *proximo* (sc. *mense*) in the next (month).] In or of next month, as *on the 3rd p.* Abbrev. *prox.*

Proxy (prǫ·ksi). 1440. [contr. from PROCURACY, as *proctor* from *procurator.*] **1.** = PROCURACY 1, PROCURATION 2; chiefly in phr. *by p.* **2.** A letter of attorney. *Obs.* exc. as in b. 1460. **b.** *spec.* A writing authorizing a person to vote instead of another, at a meeting, etc., or formerly in the House of Lords; a vote so given 1587. **3.** A person appointed to act instead of another; an attorney, agent, representative 1614. Also *fig.* of things. †**4.** *Eccl.* Provision or entertainment for a visiting bishop or his representative; an annual payment in commutation of this –1725.

1. Not content to acquire glory by p. H. WALPOLE. **3.** Another privilege is, that every peer.. may make another lord of parliament his p., to vote for him in his absence BLACKSTONE. Hence **Pro·xyhood, Pro·xyship,** the office or function of a p.

Prude (prūd), *a.* and *sb.* 1704. [– Fr. *prude* adj. and sb. (Molière), back-formation from *prudefemme*, misunderstood as adj. + sb. but prop. fem. (f. **preu de femme*) corresp. to *prud' homme* good man and true; see PRUDHOMME.] **A.** *adj.* That maintains or affects extreme propriety of speech and behaviour, esp. in regard to the relations of the sexes; excessively modest, demure, or prim; prudish; usu. applied adversely. Now *rare.* 1709. **B.** *sb.* A woman who is of extreme propriety in conduct or speech; usu. applied adversely with implication of affectation. Hence **Pru·dish** *a.* having the character of or resembling a p.; **-ly** *adv.*, **-ness.**

Prudence (prū·děns). ME. [– (O)Fr. *prudence* – L. *prudentia*, contr. from *providentia* PROVIDENCE.] The quality of being prudent. **1.** Ability to discern the most suitable, politic, or profitable course of action, esp. as regards conduct; practical wisdom, discretion. **b.** An instance of this; a prudent act 1667. †**2.** Wisdom; knowledge of or skill in a matter –1859.

1. Beyond all bounds of p. and discretion HUME. **2.** Harken with your eares, that you may know p. BIBLE (Douay) *Baruch* 3:9. So †**Pru·dency.**

Prudent (prū·děnt), *a.* late ME. [– (O)Fr. *prudent* or L. *prudens, -ent-* foreseeing, sagacious, contr. from *providens* PROVIDENT, with weakening of the notion of 'foreseeing'.] **1.** Of persons, etc.: Sagacious in adapting means to ends; having sound judgement in practical affairs; circumspect, discreet, worldly-wise. †**2.** Wise, discerning –1579. **3.** Of conduct, action, etc.: Characterized by, exhibiting, or proceeding from prudence; politic, judicious. late ME.

1. So stears the p. Crane Her annual Voiage MILT. **2.** Thou hast hyd these thynges from the wyse and p., and hast opened them vnto babes TINDALE *Matt.* 11:25. Hence **Pru·dently** *adv.*

Prudential (prude·nʃǎl), *a.* and *sb.* 1641. [f. PRUDENT, PRUDENCE + -IAL, on the analogy of similar groups, as *evident, evidence, evidential*, etc.] **A.** *adj.* **1.** Of, of the nature of, or involving prudence; characterized by forethought and deliberation. **2.** Of persons: Exercising prudence; (in New England) appointed to conduct the affairs of a town, society, etc. 1642.

1. Cultivating p. habits 1863. More thinking and p. persons SCOTT.

B. *sb.* **1.** *pl.* **a.** Matters that fall within the scope of prudence; *esp.* (in *U.S.*) matters of local government and administration for which there is no need to go to the law courts 1646. **b.** Prudential considerations 1658. †**2.** A prudential maxim or precept –1734. Hence **Prude·ntialism,** a system or theory of life based upon p. considerations. **Prude·ntialist. Prudentia·lity,** p. quality, nature, or character. **Prude·ntial-ly** *adv.*, **-ness.**

Prudery (prū·dəri). 1709. [– Fr. *pruderie* (Molière), f. *prude* PRUDE; see -ERY.] The quality or character of being prudish; excessive regard for the proprieties in speech or behaviour; extreme or affected modesty or demureness.

A lady..has carried her p. so far, as to separate the writings of male and female authors in her library 1813.

Prudho·mme. 1701. [– Fr. *prud'homme* good man and true, earlier *prodome* (f. **pro de ome* 'fine thing of a man'), f. *pro, prod* (see PROW *a.*) + *ome* (mod. *homme*) man. See PRUDE.] **1.** *Hist.* A man of valour and discretion; a knight or freeholder who was summoned to sit on the jury or to serve in the king's council. ‖**2.** A member of a French tribunal appointed to decide labour disputes 1887.

Pruinose (prū·inōᵘs), *a.* 1826. [– L. *pruinosus*, f. *pruina* hoar-frost; see -OSE[1].] *Nat. Hist.* Covered with a fine whitish powdery substance giving the appearance of hoar-frost.

Prune (prūn), *sb.* ME. [– (O)Fr. *prune* :– Rom. **pruna*, fem. sing., for L. *pruna*, n. pl. of *prunum* – Gr. προῦνον, later form of προῦμνον plum.] †**1.** The fruit of the plum-tree; a plum; also the tree, *Prunus domestica* –1698. **b.** *U.S.* A variety of plum suitable for drying 1902. **2.** The dried fruit of several varieties of the common plum-tree, largely used for eating, raw or stewed; a dried plum. Formerly dist. as *dry p.* ME. **3.** *transf.* The dark reddish purple colour of the juice of prunes; also called *p.-purple* 1884. **4.** Phr. *Prunes and prism(s*: see Dickens, *Little Dorrit* II. v. Thence, applied to a prim and mincing manner of speech, and to superficial 'accomplishments'. 1855.

Comb. **p.-tree,** (*a*) a plum-tree; (*b*) *Prunus occidentalis*, a West Indian timber-tree.

Prune (prūn), *v.*[1] *Obsol.* [In XIV *prune, pruyne*, also *proyne*, Sc. *prunȝe* (XV–XVI) – pres. stem *poroign-* of OFr. *poroindre*, f. *por-* (mod. *pour-*) :– L. *pro* PRO-[1] + *oindre* :– L. *ungere* anoint. Cf. PREEN *v.*[2]] **1.** *trans.* and *intr.* for *refl.* Of a bird, etc.: = PREEN *v.*[2] 1. **2.** Of a person: To trim, dress up with minute nicety; to prink, deck out, adorn. late ME. †**3.** *refl. fig.* To plume oneself, pride oneself –1672.

Prune (prūn), *v.*[2] [In XV *prouyne*, XVI *proine*, etc. – OFr. *proignier*, earlier *prooignier* :– Rom. *prorotundiare*, f. *pro* PRO-[1] + **rotundiare* cut round, f. *rotundus* ROUND.] **1.** *trans.* To cut or lop superfluous branches or twigs from (a vine, tree, or shrub) in order to promote fruitfulness, induce regular growth, etc.; to trim. Also *absol.* 1547. **2.** To cut or lop off (branches, boughs, shoots) 1572. **3.** *fig.* To 'cut down', mutilate; *esp.* to cut down or reduce by rejecting superfluities; also to rid *of* what is superfluous or undesirable. late ME. **b.** To remove (superfluities, deformities) 1680.

1. Sixe yeeres thou shalt p. thy Vineyard *Lev.* 25:3. **3.** Some..Authors..began to p. their Words of all superfluous Letters ADDISON. Hence **Pru·ner,** one who prunes trees or shrubs.

Prunella[1] (prune·lă). 1656. [Of unc. origin; †*prunello* and *prunella* may be alterations after Sp. or It. of Fr. *prunelle* (XVIII), derived by some from *prune* plum (PRUNE *sb.*), as if 'plum-coloured stuff'.] **1.** A strong stuff, orig. silk, afterwards worsted, formerly used for graduates', clergymen's, and barristers' gowns; later, for the uppers of women's shoes. **2.** *attrib.* Made or consisting of prunella 1706.

1. *Leather and p.*: see LEATHER *sb.* 1.

‖**Prune·lla**[2]. 1599. [Bot.L., alt. of *Brunella*; cf. BRUNEL.] *Bot.* A genus of herbaceous labiates, including *P. vulgaris*, Self-heal.

†‖**Prune·lla**[3]. 1627. [mod.L., earlier *brunella*, dim. of med.L. *brunus* brown.] **1.** *Path.* The Hungarian or camp-fever which prevailed among the imperial troops in Germany in 1547 and 1566. In later times applied to quinsy, and other disorders of the throat or fauces –1895. **2.** *Pharmacy.* Chiefly in comb. **p. salt, prunelle salt,** a preparation of fused nitre, so called as used for the disorder of the throat –1868.

Prunello (prune·lo). 1616. [Altered from obs. It. *prunella*, dim. of *pruna* plum, prune.] †**a.** A variety of plum or prune. **b.** The finest kind of prunes or dried plums, made from the greengage and other varieties.

Pruni·ferous, *a. rare.* 1668. [f. L. *prunum* PRUNE *sb.* + -FEROUS.] Bearing plums or stone-fruits; drupiferous.

Pru·ning, *vbl. sb.* 1548. [f. PRUNE *v.*[2] + -ING[1].] The action of PRUNE *v.*[2] Also *fig.* **b.** *concr.* (*pl.*) Portions cut off in pruning 1832.

Comb., esp. in the names of tools, etc., used in pruning, as *p.-bill*; **p.-hook,** a curved cutting instrument used in pruning; **-knife.**

Prunt (prɒnt). 1891. [perh. a provincial form of *print*.] A piece of ornamental glass, laid on to a body of glass, as a vase; also the tool with which this ornament is moulded or impressed with its patterns. Hence **Pru·nted** *a.* ornamented with prunts.

‖**Prunus** (prū·nɒ̆s). 1706. [L., = plum-tree – Gr. προῦνος = προύμνη; also, a sloe-bush.] **1.** *Bot.* A genus of trees and shrubs, N.O. *Rosaceæ*, containing the common sloe, bullace, plum, apricot, and other species, bearing drupaceous fruits. **2.** In *Oriental Pottery.* A representation of a Chinese and Japanese species, *P. mume*, on porcelain, etc. Hence *p. decoration.* 1878.

Prurience (prūᵊ·riĕns). 1688. [f. as PRURIENT; see -ENCE.] **1.** The fact or sensation of itching. **2.** *fig.* Mental itching or craving 1829. **3.** = next 3. 1781.

Pruriency (prūᵊ·riĕnsi). 1669. [f. as prec.; see -ENCY.] **1.** The quality of itching; itchingness (*rare*). **2.** *fig.* The quality or condition of mental itching 1711. **3.** Tendency towards lascivious or impure thought; an instance of this 1795.

2. A constant P. of inordinate Desire STEELE.

Prurient (prūᵊ·riĕnt), *a.* 1639. [– L. *pruriens, -ent-*, pr. pple. of *prurire* itch, long, be wanton; see -ENT.] **1.** That itches physically, itching. *rare.* **2.** *fig.* Having an uneasy or morbid desire or curiosity. *rare.* 1653. **3.** Given to the indulgence of lewd ideas; impure-minded 1746. **4.** Unduly forward or excessive in growth 1822. **5.** *Bot.* Applied to plants which cause a slightly stinging sensation (*rare*) 1858.

2. The reading public..in its usual p. longing after anything like personal gossip KINGSLEY. Hence **Pru·riently** *adv.* in a p. manner.

Pruriginous (pruri·dʒinəs), *a.* 1609. [– late L. *pruriginosus*, f. *prurigo, -gin-*; see next, -OUS. Cf. Fr. *prurigineux*.] Affected by or liable to prurigo or itching; pertaining to or of the nature of prurigo; †prurient.

‖**Prurigo** (prurəi·go). 1846. [L., an itching, lasciviousness, f. *prurire* to itch.] An itching; *spec.* in *Path.*, a diseased condition of the skin attended by a violent and chronic itching, and characterized by the presence of flat slightly red papules, and a thickening of the part affected. Also *attrib.*

‖**Pruritus** (prurəi·tɒ̆s). 1653. [L., f. *prurire* to itch.] Itching; *esp.* itching of the skin without visible eruption. Also *fig.*

Prussian (prɒ·ʃăn), *a.* and *sb.* 1677. [f. *Prussi* (or *Borussi*), a people belonging to the Balto-Slavic group whose language (*Old P.*) became obsolete in XVII; see -IAN. Med.L. forms were *Pruscenus* (XIII), *Prucianus* (XIV), *Prucinus* (XV).] **A.** *adj.* Of or pertaining to Prussia or its inhabitants; also designating things actually or reputedly coming from Prussia 1702.

P. carp, a smaller form of the common carp. *P. blue*, a deep blue pigment, consisting essentially of hydrated ferric ferrocyanide, usu. mixed with varying quantities of potassioferrous ferricyanide. (Called *Prussian* from being discovered by a colour-maker in Berlin.) Also, a variety of pea. *P. brown, P. green*, pigments derived from or allied to Prussian blue.

B. *sb.* A native or inhabitant of Prussia (the ethnic territory, the duchy, or the kingdom) 1677. Hence **Pru·ssianize** *v. trans.* to render P. or like Prussia in organization or character.

Prussiate (prɒ·s-, prɒ·ʃiĕt). 1790. [– Fr. *prussiate* (de Morveau, 1787), f. *prussique*; see next, -ATE[4].] *Chem.* A salt of prussic acid; a cyanide. Also, a ferro- or ferri-cyanide.

Prussic (prɒ·sik), *a.* 1790. [– Fr. *prussique* (de Morveau, 1787), f. *Prusse* Prussia; see -IC.] *Chem.* Of, pertaining to, or derived from Prussian blue. Chiefly in *P. acid* = HYDROCYANIC *acid.*

Prut (prɒt), *int.* and *sb.* ME. [imit, repr. a slight explosive sound. Cf. AL. *ptrut, phrut* (XIII), an exclam. of scorn.] **1.** An exclam. of contempt. **2.** The sound of a rifle shot 1898.

†**Prute·nic,** *a.* (*sb.*) 1615. [– med.L. *Prutenicus*, f. *Prut(h)eni* Prussians; see -IC.] Prussian; in *P. tables*, the Copernican planetary tables published in 1551 by Erasmus Reinhold; so named in compliment to Albert, Duke of Prussia. Also as *sb.* in *pl.*, the P. tables. So †**Prute·nical** *a.* 1594.

Pry (prəi), *sb.*[1] 1750. [f. PRY *v.*[1]] **1.** An act or the action of prying. **2.** An inquisitive person. Cf. *Paul Pry* (PAUL 3). 1845.

Pry (prəi), *sb.*[2] *dial.* and *U.S.* 1823. [f. PRIZE *sb.*[4]; see PRY *v.*[2]] A lever or crow-bar for prizing.

Pry (prəi), *v.*[1] ME. [Of unkn. origin.] **1.** *intr.* To look, *esp.* to look closely or curiously; to peer inquisitively or impertinently; to spy. †**2.** *trans.* To look for, look through, or look at closely; to observe narrowly –1632.

1. Thus..glide obscure, and prie In every Bush and Brake MILT. Endeavour to p. into the nature ..of the Almighty 1754. He pries into all the stratagems of Camillus MOTLEY. Hence **Pry·ingly** *adv.*

Pry (prəi), *v.*[2] *dial.* and *U.S.* 1823. [Evolved from PRIZE *v.*[3] through apprehending the final cons. as the ending of the 3rd. sing. pres. ind.; cf. PRY *sb.*[2]] *trans.* To force or prize up, etc.

Pryse, pryce. *arch.* [ME. – OFr. or AFr. *pris* taken, or OFr. *prise* taking, capture. Cf. PRISE, PRIZE *sb.*[3]] *Hunting.* In phr. *to blow the pryse*, to sound a blast on the hunting-horn as a signal that the stag is taken.

‖**Prytaneum** (pritănī·ɒ̆m). 1600. [L. – Gr. πρυτανεῖον, f. πρύτανις; see next.] *Gr. Antiq.* The public hall of a Greek state or city, in which the sacred fire was kept burning; *esp.* in ancient Athens, the hall in which distinguished citizens, foreign ambassadors, and the successive presidents of the senate were entertained at the public charge.

‖**Prytanis** (pri·tănis). *Pl.* **-nes** (-nīz). 1656. [L. – Gr. πρύτανις prince, ruler (at Athens), president.] **1.** In ancient Athens, A member of that division of the Council of Five Hundred which was presiding at the time. **2.** The chief magistrate of a Greek state, as of Rhodes, Lycia, or Miletus 1682. **3.** *transf.* A president 1847. So **Pry·tany,** each of the ten divisions of the Athenian Council of Five Hundred during its presidency; also the period of five weeks during which each division presided.

P.S., abbrev. of L. *post scriptum* POSTSCRIPT, often pronounced (pī·e·s).

Psalm (sām), *sb.* [OE. *psalm, psealm, s(e)alm* (reinforced in ME. from OFr.), corresp. to OHG. *(p)salmo* (G. *psalm*), ON. *psalmr* – late L. *psalmus* – Gr. ψαλμός plucking with the fingers, sounding of the harp, (in LXX and N.T.) song sung to the harp, f. ψάλλειν pluck, twang, play with the fingers, sing to the harp.] **1.** *gen.* Any sacred song sung in religious worship; a hymn; esp. in biblical use. **2.** *spec.* Any one of the sacred songs or hymns which together form the 'Book of Psalms'; a version or paraphrase of any of these, esp. as read or sung in public or private worship OE. **3.** *attrib.* OE.

1. Hymns devout and holy Psalms Singing everlastingly MILT. **2.** *Proper psalms*, see PROPER *a.* 2. *The Psalms, the Book of Psalms*, one of the books of the O.T., forming the hymn-book of the Jewish church, and used also in Christian worship from the earliest times; the Psalter; often called *the Psalms of David*, from the belief that David, king of Israel, composed them or some of them.

Psalm, *v.* [OE. *sealmian*; f. prec.] **1.** †**a.** *intr.* To sing psalms. **b.** *trans.* To sing or celebrate in psalms. **2.** To say or sing a psalm to or over (*rare*) 1800.

Psalmist (sā·mist). 1483. [– late L. *psalmista*, f. *psalmus*; see -IST.] **1.** The author of a psalm or psalms; almost always with def. art. as a title for David considered as the author of the Psalms, or as a designation of the author of any one of them. **2.** *Eccl. Hist.* A member of one of the minor clerical orders, discharging the functions of a chorister or cantor 1565. Hence †**Psa·lmistry,** the office or work of a p.

Psalmodic (sælmǫ·dik), *a.* 1749. [f. PSALMODY + -IC.] Of or pertaining to psalmody; having the style or character of psalmody. So **Psalmo·dial, Psalmo·dical** *adjs.*

Psalmodist (sā·mŏdist, sæ·lm-). 1652. [f. PSALMODY + -IST.] **1.** One who practises or is skilled in psalmody; a singer of psalms 1659. †**b.** = PSALMIST 2. 1726. †**2.** A writer of psalms –1886.

Psalmodize (sā·mŏdəiz, sæ·lm-), *v.* 1513. [– med.L. *psalmodizare*, f. *psalmodia*; see next, -IZE.] *intr.* To practise psalmody; to sing psalms.

Psalmody (sā·mŏdi, sæ·lm-), *sb.* ME. [– late L. *psalmodia* (Jerome) – Gr. ψαλμῳδία, f. ψαλμῳδός psalmist, f. ψαλμός psalm + ᾠδή song; see -Y³.] The action, practice, or art of singing psalms (or sacred vocal music in general), esp. in public worship. **b.** The arrangement of psalms for singing; hence, psalms and hymns so arranged, collectively 1554. Hence **Psa·lmody** *v. trans.* to celebrate as in psalmody; to hymn (*rare*).

†**Psa·lmograph.** 1542. [– late L. *psalmographus* – Gr. ψαλμογράφος, f. ψαλμός psalm + -γραφος -GRAPH.] = PSALMIST 1. –1657.

Psalter (sǫ·ltəɹ). [OE. (*p*)*saltere*, corresp. to OHG. (*p*)*salteri*, ON. (*p*)*saltari* – late L. *psalterium* – Gr. ψαλτήριον stringed instrument, (in Christian L. and Gr. writers) the book of Psalms of the O.T., f. ψάλλειν (see PSALM). ME. *sauter* – AFr. *sauter*, OFr. *sautier* (mod. *psautier*).] **I. 1.** The Book of Psalms. **b.** A translation or particular version of the Book of Psalms: e.g. a Latin, English, metrical P.; the Prayer-book P., etc. OE. **c.** A copy of the Psalms, esp. as arranged for liturgical or devotional use OE. **2.** *transf. Our Lady's p.*, the rosary (because it contains the same number (150) of Aves as there are psalms in the Psalter); also, a book containing this. late ME. **4.** Applied to certain old Irish chronicles in verse (*P. of Cashel*, etc.) 1685. **II.** = PSALTERY 1. *Obs.* or *arch.* OE.

Psalterial (sǫltīᵊ·riăl), *a.* 1865. [f. PSALTERIUM + -AL¹.] *Anat.* and *Zool.* Pertaining to the psalterium.

Psalterian (sǫltīᵊ·riăn), *a.* 1819. [f. L. *psalterium* PSALTERY + -AN.] Of, like, or having a sound like that of, a psaltery.

‖**Psalterion** (sǫltīᵊ·riǫn). [In ME. – OFr. *salterion* – L. *psalterium*; in mod. use a transliteration of Gr. ψαλτήριον.] = PSALTERY 1.

‖**Psalterium** (sǫltīᵊ·riŏm). 1857. [L.; cf. next.] *Anat.* and *Zool.* **a.** = LYRA 3. **b.** The third stomach of a ruminant; the omasum or manyplies.

Psaltery (sǫ·ltəri). [ME. *sautre, sautrie* – OFr. *sautere, -erie* – L. *psalterium* – Gr. ψαλτήριον; both finally superseded by latinized forms in *ps-*, which have been exclusively used since 1600.] **1.** An ancient and mediæval stringed instrument, resembling the dulcimer but played by plucking the strings with the fingers or a plectrum. †**2.** = PSALTER 1. *rare.* –1890.

1. Bothe his harpe and sawtrey 1557.

Psammo- (psæmo, sæmo), bef. a vowel **psamm-**, repr. Gr. ψαμμο-, comb. form of ψάμμος sand, entering into some scientific terms, as **Psammoli·thic** *a.*, *Geol.* consisting of sandstone. **Psammo·philous** *a.*, *Bot.* sand-loving, growing in sandy soil.

Psarolite (psæ·rolǝit). 1859. [f. Gr. ψάρ starling (or ψαρός speckled) + λίθος stone (see -LITE); app. rendering G. *starstein.*] *Palæont.* Name for the silicified stems of tree-ferns found in the Permian or Lower New Red Sandstone, from the speckled markings they exhibit in section.

Psephism (ps-, sī·fiz'm). 1656. [– Gr. ψήφισμα, f. ψηφίζειν to vote, prop. with pebbles, f. ψῆφος pebble.] *Gr. Antiq.* A decree enacted by a vote of a public assembly, esp. of the Athenians.

‖**Pseudepigrapha** (siūdėpi·grăfă, ps-), *sb. pl.* 1692. [– Gr. n. pl. of ψευδεπίγραφος 'with false title', f. ψευδ- PSEUD(O- + ἐπιγράφειν inscribe (see EPIGRAPH).] A collective term for books or writings bearing a false title, or ascribed to another than the true author; *spec.* applied to certain Jewish writings ascribed to various patriarchs and prophets of the O.T. Also *sing.* in anglicized form **Pseude·pigraph.** Hence **Pseudepi·graphal, Pseudepigra·phic, -al, Pseudepi·graphous** *adjs.* pertaining to or having the character of p.; spurious. **Pseudepi·graphy,** false ascription of authorship.

Pseudo (siū·do, ps-), quasi-*adj.*, (*sb.*) late ME. [The comb. element PSEUDO- as a separate word.] False, counterfeit, pretended, spurious. (Now usu. hyphened to the following noun; see PSEUDO- 1.) †**B.** *sb.* (with *pl.*) A false person, a pretender.

Luxuries which, when long gratified, become a sort of p. necessaries SCOTT.

Pseudo- (siūdo, ps-), before a vowel usu. **pseud-**, repr. Gr. comb. element ψευδο-, ψευδ- 'false, falsely', from stem of ψευδής false, ψεῦδος falsehood.

1. Prefixed to any noun or adj., forming combs., mostly nonce-wds., with the sense 'false, pretended, counterfeit, spurious, sham, falsely so called or represented; falsely, spuriously, apparently but not really'; as *pseudo-archaic, -classic(al, -Gothic, -patriotic*; *pseudo-philanthropist, -prophet.* Here *pseudo-* is properly hyphened. **2.** Special combs.: nearly all terms of modern science, (*a*) indicating close or deceptive resemblance to the thing denoted by the second element, without real identity or affinity with it; or sometimes simply denoting an abnormal or erratic form or kind of the thing; (*b*) denoting something which does not correspond with the reality, or to which no reality corresponds, as false perceptions, errors of judgement or statement. ‖**Pseudæsthe·sia** [mod.L.; cf. ANÆSTHESIA], *Path.* false or depraved sensation, as that occurring apparently in an amputated limb. **Pseude·lephant,** *Zool.* an animal resembling an elephant, as a mastodon. **Pseude·mbryo,** *Zool.* a spurious embryo; a term applied to various larval forms in sea-urchins, star-fishes, and sponges; hence **Pseudembryo·nic** *a.* **Pseu·docœle** (-sīl) [Gr. κοῖλος hollow], *Anat.*, (*a*) applied to the body-cavity of certain invertebrates, derived from spaces developed secondarily in the mesoblast, not directly from the blastocœle or original cavity of the embryo; (*b*) applied to the fifth ventricle of the brain. ‖**Pseudofila·ria,** *Zool.* a stage in the development of certain *Gregarinida*, resembling a thread-worm of the genus *Filaria*. **Pseudogale·na,** *Min.* native zinc sulphide, resembling black lead sulphide or galena. **Pseudohype·rtrophy,** *Path.* enlargement of an organ by growth of fat or connective tissue, with atrophy of its proper substance; so **Pseudo-hypertro·phic** *a.*, applied to a form of paralysis caused by pseudo-hypertrophy of the muscles. **Pseudometa·llic** *a.*, resembling, but not of the nature of, a metal; said of lustre which is perceptible only when held towards the light. **Pseu·doscope,** an optical instrument containing two reflecting prisms which can be so adjusted as to produce an apparent reversal of the convexity or concavity of an object. **Pseu·dosphere,** *Geom.*, (*a*) a surface having constant negative curvature (as a sphere has positive); (*b*) a sphere in non-Euclidean geometry; so **Pseudosphe·rical** *a.* ‖**Pseudostoma** [Gr. στόμα mouth], *Anat.* a point on the surface of a serous membrane, regarded by some as the mouth of one of the absorbents or lymphatic vessels which begin in such membranes. **Pseu·dostome,** *Zool.* in a sponge, a false osculum or excurrent opening, the mouth of a secondary canal arising from fusion. **Pseudo·vary,** *Zool.* the ovary or generative gland of certain imperfect female insects which reproduce parthenogenetically.

Pseudo-carp (siū·dokāɹp, ps-). 1835. [f. PSEUDO- + Gr. καρπός fruit.] *Bot.* A fruit formed by the modification and enlargement of other parts of the flower besides the ovary, or of parts not belonging to the flower.

Pseudo-ca·tholic, *a.* and *sb.* 1601. [PSEUDO- 1.] **A.** *adj.* Falsely or erroneously called or claiming to be catholic 1605. **B.** *sb.* A Catholic falsely so called 1601.

Pseudo-Christ (siū·doˌkrəist, ps-). late ME. [– eccl. L. *pseudochristus*, Gr. ψευδόχριστος (Mark 13:22); see PSEUDO-.] A false Christ; one pretending to be the Christ or Messiah. So **Pseudo-Chri·stian** *a.* falsely called or professing to be Christian; also as *sb.* 1579.

Pseudodipteral (siūdoˌdi·ptĕrăl, ps-), *a.* 1696. [f. late Gr. ψευδοδίπτερος + -AL¹; see PSEUDO- and DIPTEROS.] *Anc. Arch.* Having, as a temple, etc., a single peristyle or surrounding row of columns, placed at the same distance from the walls as the outer of the two rows in the dipteros. So ‖**Pseudodi·pteron,** a building of this type.

Pseudodox (siū·dŏdǫks, ps-). 1615. [– Gr. ψευδόδοξος, ψευδοδοξία; f. ψευδο- PSEUDO- + δόξα opinion.] A false or erroneous opinion.

Pseudograph (siū·dograf, ps-). 1828. [– late L. *pseudographus* – Gr. ψευδογράφος; see PSEUDO- and -GRAPH.] A spurious writing; a literary work purporting to be by another than the real author. So **Pseudo·graphy,** the writing of words falsely; false, incorrect, or bad spelling; an instance of this.

Pseudology (siudǫ·lŏdʒi, ps-). 1658. [– Gr. ψευδολογία, ψευδολόγος; see -LOGY.] False speaking; the making of false statements; the 'art of lying'. So **Pseudo·loger, Pseudo·logist,** a maker of false statements, a (systematic) liar.

Pseudomorph (siū·domǭɹf, ps-). 1849. [f. Gr. ψευδο- PSEUDO- + μορφή form.] A false or deceptive form; *spec.* in *Min.* a crystal or other body consisting of one mineral but having the form proper to another. So **Pseudomo·rphic** *a.* **Pseudomo·rphism,** the formation or occurrence of pseudomorphs, or the condition of a p. **Pseudomo·rphous** *a.*

Pseudonym (siū·dŏnim, ps-). 1846. [– Fr. *pseudonyme* – Gr. ψευδώνυμον, n. of ψευδώνυμος (ὄνυμα, ὄνομα name).] A false or fictitious name, *esp.* one assumed by an author.

Pseudonymous (siudǫ·niməs, ps-), *a.* 1706. [– Gr. ψευδώνυμος; see prec., -OUS.] **1.** Bearing or assuming, esp. writing under, a false or fictitious name; belonging to or characterizing one who does this. **2.** Written under an assumed or fictitious name; bearing the name of another than the real author 1727. So **Pseudony·mity,** the condition of being p.; the use of a pseudonym. **Pseudo·nymously** *adv.*

‖**Pseudoperipteros, -on** (psiūdopĕri·ptĕrǫs, -ǫn). 1696. [– late Gr. ψευδοπερίπτερος, f. ψευδο- PSEUDO- + περίπτερος PERIPTER.] *Anc. Arch.* A form of temple or other building with free columns forming a portico in front (and sometimes in rear) as in a peripteral building, but the rest of the columns engaged in the walls instead of standing free. Hence **Pseudoperi·pteral** *a.*

‖**Pseudopodium** (siūdopōᵘ·diŏm, ps-). *Pl.* **-ia.** 1854. [mod.L., f. PSEUDO- + PODIUM.] **1.** *Zool.* In certain Protozoa (esp. Rhizopoda), Each of a number of processes temporarily formed by protrusion of any part of the protoplasm of the body, and serving for locomotion, prehension, or ingestion of food. Also, a similar formation in an amœboid cell, as a leucocyte. **2.** *Bot.* A false pedicel or footstalk; applied to certain elongations of the stem in mosses 1861. **Pseu·dopod, -po·dial** *a.*

Pshaw (ʃǭ, pʃǭ), *int.* and *sb.* 1673. [A natural expression of rejection.] An exclam. expressing contempt, impatience, or disgust.

Pshah, how silly that is SWIFT. *sb.* Pishes and Pshaws, or other well-bred Interjections STEELE. Hence **Pshaw** *v. intr.* to say 'pshaw!'; *trans.* to show contempt for by saying 'pshaw!'

Psilanthropism (psəilæ·nþrŏpiz'm). 1810. [f. eccl. Gr. ψιλάνθρωπος merely human (f. ψιλός bare, mere + ἄνθρωπος man) + -ISM.] The doctrine that Jesus Christ was a mere man. So **Psilanthro·pic** *a.* of, pertaining to, or in accordance with p. **Psila·nthropist,** one who holds this doctrine. **Psila·nthropy.**

Psilo- (psəilo, səilo), bef. a vowel **psil-**, comb. form of Gr. ψιλός bare, smooth, mere, as in : **Psilopædic** (-pī·dik) [Gr. παῖς, παιδ- + -IC] *a.*, *Ornith.* of a bird: hatched naked or without down. **Psilo·sophy** [see -SOPHY], shallow philosophy; so **Psilo·sopher.**

Psilomelane (psəilǫ·mĕleⁱn). 1883. [f. PSILO- + Gr. μέλαν, neut. of μέλας black.] *Min.* A common ore of manganese, occurring in smooth black amorphous masses, or in botryoidal or stalactitic shapes.

‖**Psilosis** (psəilōᵘ·sis). 1904. [Gr. ψίλωσις, f. ψιλοῦν strip bare; see -OSIS.] *Greek Gram.* The substitution of a *tenuis* for an aspirate (as in ῥάπυς for ῥάφυς), or of the *spiritus lenis* for the *spiritus asper*.

Psittaceous (psitē·ʃəs), *a.* 1835. [f. L. *psittacus* (– Gr. ψιττακός parrot) + -EOUS.] *Ornith.* Of or belonging to the parrot family of birds, *Psittacidæ*. So **Psi·ttacid** *a.*

Psittacine (psi·tăsəin), *a.* (*sb.*) 1888. [– L. *psittacinus*, f. *psittacus*; see prec., -INE¹.]

Of parrots; *fig.* parrot-like. **B.** *sb.* A bird of the parrot family.

‖**Psittacosis** (sităkōᵘ·sis). 1897. [mod.L., irreg. f. L. *psittacus* – Gr. ψιττακός parrot; see -OSIS.] A contagious disease of birds, esp. parrots, characterized by diarrhœa and wasting, and causing bronchial pneumonia when communicated to human beings.

Psoas (psōᵘ·æ̆s). 1681. [prop. pl. of *psoa*, – Gr. ψόα, usu. in pl. ψόαι, acc. ψόας, the muscles of the loins.] *Anat.* The name of two muscles of the hip: (*a*) *P. magnus*, a large flexor muscle of the hip-joint which arises from the lumbar vertebræ and sacrum. (*b*) *P. parvus* or *minor*, a muscle which in many animals forms a powerful flexor of the pelvis upon the spine.

‖**Psora** (psōᵊ·ră). 1681. [L. – Gr. ψώρα itch, mange = L. *scabies*. Cf. next.] A contagious skin disease; scabies, the itch.

‖**Psoriasis** (sorəi·ăsis, ps-). 1684. [mod.L. – Gr. ψωρίασις, f. ψωριᾶν have the itch, f. ψώρα.] A disease of the skin, marked by dry reddish patches covered with scales.

Psoric (psōᵊ·rik), *a.* and *sb.* 1822. [– L. *psoricus* adj., *psoricum* sb. – Gr. ψωρικός; see PSORA, -IC.] Of or pertaining to, a remedy for, psora.

‖**Psorophthalmia** (psōᵊrǫfþæ·lmiă). 1656. [mod.L., f. Gr. ψώρα PSORA + OPHTHALMIA.] *Path.* Scurfy inflammation of the eyes.

Psorosperm (psōᵊ·rospɔ̄ɹm). 1866. [f. Gr. ψώρα PSORA + σπέρμα seed.] An individual of a group of Sporozoa (*Psorospermiæ*), parasitic protozoa found in the mucous membranes, muscles, and liver of domestic animals, and occas. in man.

Psychagogue (səi·kăgǫg). 1843. [f. Gr. ψυχή PSYCHE + ἀγωγός leading, leader.] **1.** One who directs or leads the mind (*rare*) 1847. **2.** One who calls up departed spirits; a necromancer 1843. So **Psychagogic** (-ăgǫ·dʒik) *a.* influencing or leading the mind or soul; evoking the spirits of the dead (*rare*).

Psy·chal, *a. rare.* 1844. [f. PSYCHE + -AL¹.] Of or pertaining to the soul; spiritual; psychical.

Psyche (səi·ki, ps-). 1647. [– L. *psyche* – Gr. ψυχή breath, soul, life, rel. to ψύχειν breathe.] **1.** The soul, or spirit, as dist. from the body; the mind 1658. **b.** In later *Gr. Myth.*, personified as the beloved of Eros (Cupid or Love), and represented as having butterfly wings, or as a butterfly. Hence *attrib.* in sense 'like that of Psyche'. 1876. **2. a.** (After Gr.) A butterfly 1878. **b.** *Entom.* A genus of day-flying bombycid moths, typical of the family *Psychidæ* 1832. **3.** A cheval-glass. [mod.Fr.] 1838.

Psychiater (səikəi·ătəɹ, ps-). 1857. [f. Gr. ψυχή PSYCHE + ἰατήρ, ἰατρός healer.] One who treats mental disease; an alienist.

Psychiatric (-iæ·trik), *a.* (*sb.*) 1847. [f. as prec. + -IC.] Of or pertaining to psychiatry. **B.** *sb. pl.* **Psychia·trics.** The theory or practice of psychiatry 1847.

Psychiatry (-əi·ătri). 1846. [f. Gr. ψυχή PSYCHE + ἰατρεία healing, medical treatment, f. ἰατρός healer.] The medical treatment of diseases of the mind. Hence **Psychi·atrist**, a student of p.

Psychic (səi·kik, ps-), *a* (*sb.*) 1858. [– Gr. ψυχικός of the soul or life.] **1.** = PSYCHICAL *a.* 1. 1873. **b.** Characterized by being susceptible to psychic or spiritual influence 1905. **2.** Pertaining to, or characterized by, the 'lower soul' or animal principle, as dist. from the spirit or 'higher soul'; natural, animal. (After St. Paul's use of ψυχικός, 1 Cor. 2:14, etc.) 1858. **3.** = PSYCHICAL *a.* 3. 1887. **B.** *sb.* One who is particularly susceptible to 'psychic' influence (see PSYCHICAL 3); a medium 1871.

1. The varied stimuli, p. and physical 1883. **3.** *P. force*, a supposed force, power, or influence, not physical or mechanical, exhibiting intelligence or volition, and assumed as the cause of certain so-called spiritualistic phenomena. Hence **Psy·chicism**, the theory or study of psychical or spiritistic phenomena.

Psychical (səi·kikăl, ps-), *a.* 1642. [f. as prec. + -AL¹; see -ICAL.] **1.** Of or pertaining to the mind; mental, as dist. from *physical*; *spec.* in *Path.*, due to mental affection or influence. **2.** Repr. Gr. ψυχικός: Of or pertaining to the animal or natural life of man, as opp. to the spiritual (πνευματικός) 1708. **3.** Of or pertaining to phenomena and conditions which appear to lie outside the domain of physical law, and are therefore attributed by some to spiritual or hyperphysical agency. *P. research*, investigation of such phenomena. 1878.

1. *P. blindness, deafness*, inability of the brain to interpret impressions received by the visual or auditory organs. **3.** Why, he asks, call the subject matter of their investigation 'p. research', when it is really, . . only a branch of morbid psychology? 1901. Hence **Psy·chically** *adv.* with reference to the soul or mind; mentally.

Psychics (səi·kiks, ps-). 1811. [f. PSYCHIC *a.*, after sbs. in *-ics* = Gr. -ικά see -IC 2.] The science of psychical or mental phenomena; psychology.

Psychism (səi·kiz'm, ps-). 1871. [f. Gr. ψυχή PSYCHE + -ISM.] **1.** ANIMISM 1890. **2.** The doctrine or theory of the existence of forces unexplainable by physical science in connection with spiritistic phenomena 1871. So **Psy·chist**, a psychologist; also, one who engages in psychical research.

Psycho- (səi·ko, ps-), bef. a vowel regularly **psych-**, repr. Gr. ψυχο-, ψυχ-, comb. form of ψυχή PSYCHE. In mod. use, taken in the sense of 'mind', 'psychic organism', 'mental', 'psychical', mainly in scientific compounds.

Psy:chodyna·mic *a.*, of or pertaining to mental powers or activities; hence **Psy:chodyna·mics,** the science of the laws of mental action. **Psycho·ge·nesis,** (*a*) the genesis or origin of the soul or mind; (*b*) origin or evolution due to the activity of the soul or mind itself. **Psy·chogram,** a 'spirit-writing'; a writing or message supposed to come from a spirit; so **Psy·chograph,** an instrument by means of which psychograms are written; also = *psychogram*. **Psycho·graphy,** the history, description, or delineation of the mind or soul, or of mind in the abstract; also, supposed 'spirit-writing' by the hand or intervention of a medium. **Psy·chomancy,** †(*a*) divination through communication with the spirits of the dead; (*b*) occult intercommunication between souls or with spirits. **Psy·cho-mo:tor** *a.*, inducing movement by psychic or mental action; involving such movement. **Psy:cho-physio·logy,** the department of physiology which deals with mental phenomena; experimental psychology. **Psy·choplasm,** the basis of consciousness conceived as a substance corresponding and correlative to PROTOPLASM. **Psychozo·ic** *a.*, of the geological period of living creatures having souls or minds, i.e., the human period.

Psychoanalysis (səi:ko,ănæ·lisis). 1910. [f. PSYCHO- + ANALYSIS; after G. *psychoanalyse*.] The name given (1896) by Dr. Sigmund Freud of Vienna to the theory and practice of his method of treating psychopathic disorders; analysis of the unconscious mind by the method of 'free association'. So **Psycho·a·nalyst,** one who practises p. **Psychoanaly·tic(al** *a.* of or pertaining to p. **Psycho·a·nalyse** *v. trans.* to treat by p.; to analyse the mind of (a person) by the method of p.

Psychologic (-ǒlǫ·dʒik), *a.* 1787. [f. as PSYCHOLOGY + -IC.] Of or belonging to psychology.

Psychological (səikǒlǫ·dʒikăl, ps-), *a.* 1776. [f. as PSYCHOLOGY + -ICAL.] **1.** Of, pertaining to, or of the nature of psychology; dealing with or relating to psychology 1812. **2.** Loosely used for PSYCHICAL: Of or pertaining to the mind, mental; opp. to *physical* 1776.

P. moment = Fr. *moment psychologique*, applied to 'the moment in which the mind is in actual expectation of something that is to happen'; the psychologically appropriate moment; often misused for 'the critical moment', 'the very nick of time'. (The Fr. use was orig. due to G. *das psychologische Moment* the psychological 'momentum' or factor being mistaken for *der psychologische Moment* the psychological moment of time.) Hence **Psycholo·gically** *adv.*

Psychologism (səikǫ·lǒdʒiz'm, ps-). 1858. [f. PSYCHOLOGY + -ISM.] *Philos.* Idealism as opp. to sensationalism.

Psychologist (səikǫ·lǒdʒist, ps-). 1727. [f. as prec. + -IST.] One who makes a study of or is versed in psychology.

Psychologize (səikǫ·lǒdʒəiz, ps-), *v.* 1836. [f. as prec. + -IZE.] **1.** *intr.* To study or treat of psychology; to theorize or reason psychologically. **2.** *trans.* To analyse or describe psychologically 1856. **3.** To subject to 'psychical' influence 1885.

Psy·chologue (-ǒlǫg). *rare.* 1872. [– Fr. *psychologue*; see PSYCHO-, -LOGUE.] = PSYCHOLOGIST.

Psychology (səikǫ·lǒdʒi, ps-). 1693. [– mod.L. *psychologia* (XVI, Melanchthon, Freigius, Goclenius); see PSYCHO-, -LOGY. Cf. Fr., G. *psychologie*.] The science of the nature, functions, and phenomena of the human soul or mind. **b.** A treatise on, or system of, psychology 1791.

Psychometry (səikǫ·mėtri, ps-). 1854. [f. PSYCHO- + -METRY.] **1.** The (alleged) faculty of divining, from physical contact or proximity only, the qualities or properties of an object, or of persons or things that have been in contact with it. **2.** The measurement of the duration and intensity of mental states or processes 1883. So **Psycho·meter,** one who practises p. **Psychome·tric, -al** *adjs.* of, pertaining to, or of the nature of p.; **-ly** *adv.* **Psycho·metrist.**

Psychopannychy (psəiko,pæ·niki). 1642. [– mod.L. *psychopannychia* (Calvin), f. Gr. ψυχο- + παννύχιος lasting all night.] All-night sleep of the soul; a state in which (according to some) the soul sleeps between death and the day of judgement. So **Psychopa·nnychist,** one holding this doctrine; **-pa·nnychism.**

Psychopath (səi·kopæþ, ps-). 1885. [f. PSYCHO- + Gr. -παθής, f. πάθος suffering.] One affected with psychopathy; a mentally deranged person; also = PSYCHOPATHIST.

Psychopathy (səikǫ·păþi, ps-). 1847. [f. PSYCHO- + -PATHY.] *Path.* **1.** Mental disease or disorder; mental disorder considered apart from cerebral disease. **2.** The treatment of disease by 'psychical' influence, e.g. by hypnotism 1891. Hence **Psychopa·thic** *a.* **Psycho·pathist,** one who studies or treats psychopathy or mental disease. **Psy:chopatho·logy,** the science of mental disease.

Psycho-physic (səi:ko,fi·zik, ps-), *a.* and *sb.* 1879. [f. PSYCHO- + PHYSIC.] **A.** *adj.* = next 1890. **B.** *sb.* Commonly in pl. **Psychophy·sics.** The science of the general relations between mind and body; *spec.* the investigation of the relations between physical stimuli and psychic action in the production of sensations 1879.

Psycho-phy·sical, *a.* 1879. [f. as prec. + -AL¹; see -ICAL.] Of or pertaining to psycho-physics; having to do with psychology and physics, or the connection of the psychical and the physical.

Psychopomp (səi·kopǫmp, ps-). 1863. [– Gr. ψυχοπομπός, f. ψυχή soul + πομπός conductor.] A conductor of souls to the place of the dead.

‖**Psychosis** (səikōᵘ·sis, ps-). *Pl.* **-oses** (-ōᵘ·sīz). 1847. [– late Gr. ψύχωσις animation, principle of life, f. ψυχόω I give soul or life to; but in mod. use taken as = condition of the psyche or mind; see -OSIS.] **1.** *Path.* Any kind of mental affection or derangement; esp. one which cannot be ascribed to organic lesion or neurosis. **2.** *Psychol.* An activity or movement of the psychic organism, as dist. from neurosis (NEUROSIS 2) 1871.

Psychostasy (-ǫ·stăsi). 1850. [– Gr. ψυχοστασία, f. ψυχή soul + στάσις weighing.] A weighing of souls; in *Anc. Myth.* supposed to take place during a combat, the combatant having the lighter soul being slain.

Psycho-therapeutic (səi:koperăpiū·tik, ps-), *a.* and *sb.* 1887. [f. PSYCHO- + THERAPEUTIC.] **A.** *adj.* Of or pertaining to the treatment of mental or psychic disease 1890. **B.** *sb.* in pl. form **Psy:cho-therapeu·tics.** The subject of the treatment of psychic disease 1887.

Psychrometer (-ǫ·mĭtəɹ). 1727. [f. Gr ψυχρός cold + -METER; lit. a measurer of cold.] *Meteorol.* orig., A thermometer; now, an instrument for measuring the relative humidity of the air; a wet-and-dry bulb thermometer. Hence **Psychrome·tric, -al** *adjs.* of or pertaining to the p. or to psychrometry. **Psychro·metry,** the measurement of the humidity of the atmosphere by means of a p.

Ptarmigan (tā·ɹmigăn). 1599. [= Gael. *tàrmachan*; history and origin unkn. The spelling with *pt-* arises from false analogy with Gr. words in *pt-*] A bird of the grouse family (*Lagopus alpinus* or *mutus*) which inhabits high altitudes in Scotland and northern Europe, the Alps and Pyrenees. **b.** Also extended to other species of *Lagopus*, as *L. albus* of Europe and Asia, *L. rupestris* of N. America, etc.

Ptenoglossate (tī:noglǫ·sĕt, pt-), *a.* [f. Gr. πτηνός feathered + γλῶσσα tongue + -ATE².] *Zool.* Of certain molluscs: Having no median teeth of the odontophore, but a large number of lateral teeth resembling the barbs of a feather.

Pterichthys (tĕri·kþis, pt-). 1842. [mod.L., f. Gr. πτερόν wing + ἰχθύς fish.] *Palæont.* A fossil genus of fishes of the Devonian period, having a pair of wing-shaped lateral appendages.

Pterido- (terido, pt-), bef. a vowel **pterid-**, comb. form of Gr. πτερίς, πτεριδ- fern. **Pterido·graphy**, a description of ferns. **Pterido·logy** [-(O)LOGY], that branch of botany which treats of ferns; hence **Pte:ridolo·gical** *a.*, **Pterido·logist.** **Pte·ridophyte** [Gr. φυτόν plant], a member of the *Pteridophyta*, a division of plants including the ferns and their allies; a vascular cryptogam.

Ptero- (tero, pt-), bef. a vowel **pter-**, comb. form of Gr. πτερόν feather, wing.

Pteroglo·ssal [Gr. γλῶσσα tongue] *a.*, having a tongue finely notched or divided like a feather, as a toucan of the genus *Pteroglossus*. ‖**Ptero·poda** *sb. pl.*, a class or division of *Mollusca*, having the mesopodium or middle part of the foot expanded into a pair of lobes, like wings or flippers (the **Pteropo·dium**), with which the animal swims; hence **Pte·ropod**, a mollusc of the class *Pteropoda*. **Pterosti·gma** [Gr. στίγμα spot, mark], *Entom.* a peculiar mark or spot on the wings of some insects, esp. Hymenoptera.

Pterodactyl (terodæ·ktil, pt-). 1830. [– mod.L. *Pterodactylus*, f. Gr. πτερόν wing + δάκτυλος finger.] *Palæont.* A winged reptile or pterosaur of the extinct genus *Pterodactylus*.

‖**Pteropus** (te·rŏpŭs, pt-). *Pl.* **-i.** 1835. [mod.L. – Gr. πτερόπους wing-footed.] *Zool.* A genus of tropical and subtropical bats having membranous wings, known as flying foxes or fruit-bats; an animal of this genus. Hence **Pte·ropid, Pte·ropine** *adjs.* belonging to or having the characteristics of the *Pteropidæ* or flying-fox family.

Pterosaur (te·rosǭɹ, pt-). 1862. [– mod.L. *Pterosaurus*, f. PTERO- + Gr. σαῦρος (= σαύρα) lizard.] *Palæont.* A member of the *Pterosauria*, an extinct order of Mesozoic saurian reptiles, having the fifth digit of each forefoot prolonged for the purpose of supporting a membrane for flight. Hence **Pterosau·rian** *a.* of the nature of a p.; of or belonging to the *Pterosauria*; also *sb.*

Pterotic (tĕrōᵘ·tik, pt-), *a.* (*sb.*) 1870. [f. Gr. πτερόν wing + *-otic* in *periotic*.] *Anat.* Applied to a wing-like expansion of the petrosal bone or periotic capsule, occurring in some vertebrates. **b.** as *sb.* The p. bone or expansion.

‖**Pterygium** (ptĕri·dʒiŏm). 1657. [L. – Gr. πτερύγιον little wing, fin, dim. of πτέρυξ wing.] **1.** *Path.* A diseased condition of the conjunctiva of the eye. **2.** *Bot.* Term applied to petals, etc. when shaped like wings 1895.

Pterygo- (te·rigo, pt-), bef. a vowel **pteryg-**, comb. form of Gr. πτέρυξ, πτερυγ- wing, fin.

1. In general sense of 'wing', 'fin', or 'wing-like appendage'. **Pte·rygobla:st** [Gr. βλαστός germ], *Ichth.* a germinal fin-ray. ‖**Pte:rygopo·dium** [Gr. πούς, ποδ-], *Ichth.* one of the claspers of a shark, etc. **Pte·rygosto:me** [Gr. στόμα mouth], the space between the anterior edges of the carapace in crabs and other crustacea.

2. Used as comb. form of PTERYGOID, denoting attachment or relation to the pterygoid processes of the sphenoid bone. **P.-ma·xillary** [L. *maxilla* jaw] *a.*, belonging to or connected with the pterygoid processes and the superior maxillary bone. **P.-pa·latal, -pa·latine** *adjs.*, of or belonging to the pterygoid and the palatine bones. **P.-quadrate** (-kwǫ·drĕt) *a.*, pertaining to or combining the pterygoid and quadrate bones.

Pterygoid (te·rigoid, pt-), *a.* (*sb.*) 1722. [f. Gr. πτέρυξ, -υγ- wing, fin (cf. prec.) + -OID.] *Anat.* Having the form or appearance of a wing, wing-like, wing-shaped. *P. process*: Each of two processes of bone descending (on each side) from the junction of the body and great wing of the sphenoid bone. **b.** Connected with the pterygoid processes 1746. **B.** *sb.* **a.** The pterygoid bone. **b.** Each of the pterygoid muscles. 1831.

‖**Pteryla** (te·rilă, pt-). *Pl.* **-æ.** 1867. [mod. L. (Nitzsch, 1833), f. Gr. πτερόν feather + ὕλη wood.] *Ornith.* A definite clump, patch, or area of feathers, one of a number on the skin of a bird, separated by *apteria* or featherless spaces. Hence **Pterylo·graphy**, the scientific description of, or a treatise on, pterylosis. **Pterylo·sis**, the arrangement of the pterylæ, or of the feathers of birds.

Ptilo- (tilo, pt-), bef. a vowel **ptil-**. comb. form of Gr. πτίλον a soft feather, a plumelet. **Pti·locerque** (-sǝɹk) [Gr. κέρκος tail], *Zool.* an elephant shrew of the genus *Ptilocercus*, having a long tail with distichous hairs towards the end; the pen-tailed shrew. **Ptilopædic** (-pī·dik) [Gr. παῖς, παιδ- child] *a.*, *Ornith.* of birds: hatched with a complete covering of down.

Ptisan (ti·zăn, tizæ·n). late ME. [In XV *tizanne, tysan*, later *ptisan(e* (XVI) – (O)Fr. *tisane* (XVI †*ptisane*) – L. *ptisana* – Gr. πτισάνη peeled barley, barley-water, f. base of πτίσσειν peel, bray.] A nourishing decoction of slightly medicinal quality; orig. barley-water; now often applied more widely.

Ptochogony (tōᵘkǫ·gŏni, pt-). 1839. [f. Gr. πτωχός poor + -γονία begetting.] The begetting or production of beggars.

Ptolemæan (tǫlĕmī·ăn), *a.* and *sb.* 1647. [f. L. *Ptolemæus* + -AN.] = next *a.* 1 and *sb.*

Ptolemaic (tǫlĕmēⁱ·ik), *a.* and *sb.* 1674. [f. Gr. Πτολεμαῖος (L. *Ptolemæus*) Ptolemy + -IC.] **A.** *adj.* **1.** Of or pertaining to Ptolemy, a celebrated astronomer who lived at Alexandria in the second century A.D. **2.** Of or pertaining to the Ptolemies, the Macedonian Greek rulers of ancient Egypt from the death of Alexander the Great to Cleopatra 1771.

1. *P. system* or *theory*, the astronomical system or theory elaborated by Ptolemy, in which the relative motions of the sun, moon, and planets were explained to take place round the earth, which was supposed to be stationary.

B. *sb.* An adherent of the P. theory; a Ptolemaist 1751. Hence **Ptolema·ist**, one who holds the P. theory.

Ptomaine (tōᵘ·meⁱn, tomēⁱ·n, tōᵘ·meⁱǝin). 1880. [– Fr. *ptomaïne* – It. *ptomaina* (Selmi, 1878), irreg. f. Gr. πτῶμα, πτωματ- corpse; see -INE⁵.] *Chem.* The generic name of certain alkaloid bodies found in putrefying animal and vegetable matter, some of which are very poisonous. Also *attrib.*, as *p. poisoning*.

‖**Ptosis** (ptōᵘ·sis). 1743. [– Gr. πτῶσις falling, fall.] **a.** Drooping of the upper eyelid from paralysis of the elevator muscle. **b.** Prolapsus of any of the viscera (*rare*) 1897.

Ptyalin (tǝi·ălin, pt-). 1845. [f. Gr. πτύαλον spittle + -IN¹.] *Physiol. Chem.* An amylolytic ferment in saliva.

Ptyalism (tǝi·ăliz'm, pt-). 1684. [– Gr. πτυαλισμός, f. πτυαλίζειν expectorate, f. πτύαλον (see prec.).] Excessive secretion or flow of saliva; salivation.

Pub (pɒb). *colloq.* 1865. Shortened f. PUBLIC *sb.* 4. Also *attrib.*, as *p.-crawl*.

Puberal (piū·bĕrăl), *a.* 1836. [– med.L. *puberalis*, f. *puber*; see PUBERTY, -AL¹.] Of or at the age of puberty.

Pubertal (piū·bǝɹtăl), *a.* 1897. [irreg. f. next + -AL¹.] Of or pertaining to puberty.

Puberty (piū·bǝɹti). late ME. [– L. *pubertas* (or the derived Fr. *puberté*), f. *puber*, *pubes, -is* (*-er-*) adult, *pubes* PUBES; see -TY¹.] The state or condition of having become functionally capable of procreating offspring. (In England the legal age of puberty is fourteen in boys and twelve in girls.)

Puberulent (piube·rⁱŭlĕnt), *a.* 1864. [f. L. *puber* downy + -ULENT, after *pulverulent*, etc.] Covered with down; pubescent. So **Pube·rulous** *a.*

‖**Pubes** (piū·bīz). 1570. [L. *pubes, -is.*] **1.** The pubic hair. **2.** The hypogastric region, which in the adult becomes covered with hair 1682. **3.** *Zool.* and *Bot.* = next, 2, 3. 1826.

Pubescence (piube·sĕns). 1646. [– Fr. *pubescence* or med.L. *pubescentia*, f. as next; see -ENCE.] **1.** The fact or condition of arriving at puberty; also = PUBERTY. **2.** *Bot.* The soft down which grows on the leaves and stems of many plants; the character or condition of being pubescent 1760. **3.** *Zool.* The soft down which occurs on certain parts of various animals, esp. insects 1826. So †**Pube·scency**, the quality or state of being pubescent.

Pubescent (piube·sĕnt), *a.* (*sb.*) 1646. [– Fr. *pubescent* or L. *pubescens, -ent-*, pr. pple. of *pubescere* reach the age of puberty, inceptive verb f. *pubes* PUBES; see -ESCENT.] **1.** Arriving or arrived at the age of puberty. **2.** *Bot.* and *Zool.* Having pubescence; covered with short soft hair; downy 1760. **B.** *sb.* A youth at the age of puberty 1894.

Pubic (piū·bik), *a.* 1831. [f. PUBES + -IC.] Of, pertaining to, or connected with the pubes or pubis.

Pubis (piū·bis). 1597. [Short for L. *os pubis* i.e. *os* bone, *pubis* gen. sing. of *pubes* PUBES.] **1.** That portion of the innominate bone which forms the anterior wall of the pelvis. ¶**2.** *erron.* = PUBES 2. 1681.

Public (pɒ·blik), *a.* and *sb.* late ME. [– (O)Fr. *public, -ique* or L. *publicus*, based on *pubes* adult (see PUBERTY) with crossing from *poplicus*, f. *populus* PEOPLE; see -IC.] Usu. opp. to PRIVATE. **A.** *adj.* **I.** Pertaining to the people of a country or locality. **1.** Of or pertaining to the people as a whole; common, national, popular. late ME. **2.** Done or made by or on behalf of the community as a whole; representing the community 1560. **b.** In the old universities: Belonging to, made or authorized by, acting for or on behalf of, the whole university (as dist. from the colleges, etc.) 1550. **3.** That is open to, may be used by, or may or must be shared by, all members of the community; generally accessible or available; generally levied (as a rate or tax). Also (in narrower sense), That may be used, enjoyed, shared, or competed for, by all persons legally or properly qualified. 1542. **4.** Open to general observation; existing, done, or made in public; manifest; not concealed. Also of an agent: Acting in public. 1548. **b.** Of a book, writing, etc.: (chiefly in phr. *made p.*) Made accessible to all, published, in print 1641. **5.** Of, pertaining to, or engaged in the affairs or service of the community 1571. **6.** Of or pertaining to a person in the capacity in which he comes in contact with the community; official 1538. **7.** Devoted or directed to the promotion of the general welfare; public-spirited, patriotic. Now chiefly in phr. *p. spirit*. 1607.

1. Well employed..in the publique service 1570. The event was celebrated by a p. holiday 1909. Phr. *p. good, weal, p. wealth*, the common or national good or well-being. *P. act, bill, statute*, a parliamentary act or bill which affects the community at large. *P. office*, a building used for various departments of civic business, including the judicial, police, and coroner's courts, the meeting place of the local authority, the departments of municipal officials, etc. **2.** *P. utilities*, the services or supplies commonly available in large towns, such as omnibuses, electricity, water, etc. **b.** *P. examination, lecture, schools*; *p. orator, reader*, etc. (In some collocations now apprehended as = 'performed publicly', 'open to the public'.) **3.** *P. baths, library, park*, etc. *P. worship, meeting*. **4.** A publike exemple of infamie N.T. (Genev.) *Matt.* 1:19. **b.** The first of his dispatches has never been made p. 1777. **5.** When I embarked in p. life 1861. *P. notary, notary p.*: see NOTARY 2 b. **7.** The greatest Instances of publick Spirit the Age has produced STEELE.

II. With extended, international, or universal ref. **a.** Of or pertaining to the nations generally, or to the European, Christian, or civilized nations, regarded as a single community; general; international; esp. in *p. law* 1560. **b.** Of, pertaining or common to, the whole human race (*rare*) 1653.

a. The publique Quarrels in Christendome 1665.

B. *sb.* (the adj. used absol. or ellipt.) **1.** †**a.** The nation, the state; the commonwealth; the well-being of the community; = L. *res publica*. Usu. construed as sing. –1783. **b.** The community as an aggregate, but not as organized; hence, the members of the community (now usu. const. as pl.) 1665. **2.** With *a* and *pl.* A particular section, group, or portion of a community, or of mankind 1709. **3.** *In public*: In a situation, condition, or state open to public view or access; openly, publicly: opp. to *in private* 1450. **4.** Short for PUBLIC HOUSE. *colloq.* 1709. **b.** *attrib.* Of the public house 1756.

1. a. Hee's scarce a friend vnto the publike B. JONSON. **b.** The publick is the theatre for mountebanks and imposters BURKE. **2.** There is a separate p. for every picture, and for every book RUSKIN. **4.** He is a statesman, though he keeps a p. SCOTT. **b.** I suppose it was something in the p. line DICKENS. Hence **Pu·blic-ly** *adv.*, **-ness.**

Publican (pɒ·blikăn). ME. [– (O)Fr. *publicain* – L. *publicanus*, f. *publicum* public revenue, subst. use of n. of *publicus* PUBLIC *a.*; see -AN.] **1.** *Rom. Hist.* One who farmed the public taxes; hence, a tax-gatherer. (Chiefly in Scriptural quots. and allusions.) **b.** *transf.* Any collector of toll, tribute, customs, or the like 1644. **2.** One who keeps a public house; a licensed victualler; a keeper of an ale-house or tavern 1728.

1. Whi etiþ your Maistir wiþ puplicans? WYCLIF.

†**Pu·blicate,** *v.* 1540. [– *publicat-*, pa. ppl. stem of L. *publicare*; see PUBLISH, -ATE[3].] *trans.* To publish, make publicly known –1808.

Publication (pɒblikēi·ʃən). late ME. [– (O)Fr. *publication* – L. *publicatio*, f. as prec.; see -ION.] The action of publishing or that which is published. **1.** The action of making publicly known; public notification or announcement; promulgation. **b.** *spec.* in *Law*. Notification or communication to those concerned, or to a limited number regarded as representing the public 1590. **2.** The issuing, or offering to the public, of a book, map, engraving, piece of music, etc.; also the work or business of producing and issuing copies of such works 1576. **3.** A work published; a book or the like printed or otherwise produced and issued for public sale 1656.

1. The P. of the Gospel to us Gentiles 1748. **b.** A man may tell his wife a thing, and that is not p.; or he may tell his next door neighbour, and that is 1897. **b.** The periodical publications of the day 1831.

Public house. (Now often with hyphen.) 1574. **1.** A public building. *Obs.* exc. with allusion to sense 2. **2. a.** An inn or hostelry providing food and lodging, or light refreshments for members of the general public; usu. licensed for the supply of ales, wines, and spirits. Now commonly merged in b. 1669. **b.** A house in which the principal business is the sale of alcoholic liquors to be consumed on the premises; a tavern 1768.

Publicist (pɒ·blisist). 1792. [– Fr. *publiciste*, f. L. (*jus*) *publicum* public law, after *canoniste* (XIV). Cf. CANONIST (XVI).] **1.** One who is learned in 'public' or international law; a writer on the law of nations. **2.** *loosely.* A writer on current public topics; a political journalist 1833. **3.** A publicity agent 1930.

1. Problems which baffle the p. 1868.

Publicity (pɒbli·sĭti). 1791. [– Fr. *publicité*, f. *public*; see PUBLIC, -ITY.] The quality of being public; the condition or fact of being open to public observation or knowledge. **b.** The business of making goods or persons publicly known 1904.

attrib.: **p. agent,** one employed to ensure that an actor, etc. is frequently brought into, or kept prominently in, public notice, by means of newspaper articles or the like.

Public school. 1580. A school which is public. **1.** In England, orig., A grammar-school, endowed for the use or benefit of the public, and carried on under some kind of public management or control; often contrasted with a 'private school'. In modern use, applied esp. to such of these as have developed into large boarding-schools, drawing, from the well-to-do classes, pupils who are prepared mainly for the ancient universities or for the public services, and also to some large modern schools with similar aims. **b.** *attrib.* as *public school boy, system*, etc. 1843. **2.** In Scotland, British colonies, and U.S.: A school provided at the public expense and managed by public authority, as part of a system of public (and usu. free) education 1644.

Public-spirited (stress var.), *a.* 1654. Characterized by public spirit; animated by zeal for the public good; directed to the common welfare. Hence **Pu:blic-spi·rited-ly** *adv.*, **-ness.**

Publish (pɒ·bliʃ), *v.* [ME. *puplise, -ische, publishe*, f. stem of OFr. *puplier*, (also mod.) *publier* – L. *publicare* make public, f. *publicus*; see PUBLIC *a.*, -ISH[2].] **1.** *trans.* To make publicly or generally known; to declare openly or publicly; to tell or noise abroad; also, to propagate (a creed or system). **2.** *esp.* To announce in a formal or official manner; to pronounce (a judicial sentence), to promulgate (a law or edict); to proclaim. late ME. **b.** To ask (the banns of marriage) 1488. †**3.** To proclaim (a person) publicly as something, or in some capacity or connection; also, (without compl.) to denounce, to 'show up' –1733. †**b.** To give public notice of –1710. **4.** *spec.* To issue or cause to be issued for sale to the public (copies of a book, engraving, etc.); said of an author, editor, or *spec.* of a professional publisher 1529. **b.** To make generally accessible or available; to place before or offer to the public. *Obs.* exc. as said of doing this by literary means. 1638.

1. Do not p. Your shame 1896. Phr. *To p. one's will*, to execute it properly before witnesses. *To p. a libel*, to communicate a libel to one or more persons. **3.** *Wint. T.* II. i. 98. **4. b.** The celebrated Leonard Euler had published a somewhat similar theory 1842. Hence **Pu·blishable** *a.* that may be published.

Publisher (pɒ·bliʃəɹ). 1453. [f. prec. + -ER[1].] **1.** One who makes something public. Now *rare*. **2.** One whose business is the issuing of books, periodicals, music, etc., as the agent of the author or owner; one who produces copies of such works, and distributes them to the booksellers and other dealers, or to the public. (Without qualification, usu. a *book-publisher*.) 1740.

1. The Authors and Publishers of these vain Prophesies 1554. **2.** Petty dealers, or venders of small ware, like our publishers 1797. So **Pu·blishing** *vbl. sb. spec.* = PUBLICATION 2.

Publishment (pɒ·bliʃmĕnt). Now *rare*. 1494. [f. PUBLISH + -MENT.] The action of publishing; publication, proclamation, announcement; *esp.* in *U.S.*, publication of the banns of marriage.

Pubo-, assumed comb. form of L. *pubes*, used in the sense 'of or belonging to the pubes or *os pubis* and (some other part)'; as **p.-femoral** *a.*, belonging to the pubes and the femur; etc.

Puccoon (pɒkū·n). 1612. [Algonquian.] The Virginian Indian name of a N. Amer. plant or plants yielding a red dye; orig., of the Red P. or Blood-root, *Sanguinaria canadensis*, and Hoary P., *Lithospermum canescens*.

Puce (piūs), *a.* (*sb.*) 1787. [– (O)Fr. *puce* flea (*couleur puce* 'flea colour' XVII) :– L. *pulex, pulic-* flea.] Of a flea colour; purple brown or brownish purple. **b.** as *sb.* = puce colour 1882.

Pucelle. late ME. [– (O)Fr. *pucelle* :– late L. *pulicella* (Lex Salica), f. pop. L. **puellicella*, also **pullicella*, dim. of L. *puella* girl and *pullus* young animal, foal.] **1.** A girl, a maid. *Obs.* (exc. as Fr.). **b.** *spec.* The Maid of Orleans, Joan of Arc. *Obs.* exc. *Hist.* 1450. †**2.** A drab, a slut, a courtesan –1700.

1. Three prety puzels az bright az a breast of bacon 1575.

‖**Puceron** (püsərŏn, püsrŏn). 1752. [Fr., deriv. of *puce* flea.] A plant-louse or aphis.

Puck (pɒk), **pook** (puk), *sb.*[1] [Late OE. *pūca* (in glosses and place-names) = ON. *púki* mischievous demon; cf. W. *pwca, pwci*, Ir. *púca*; whether the Engl. word is of Gmc. or Celtic origin is uncertain.] An evil or mischievous spirit. **a.** Form the 16th c. (with capital P) the name of a fancied mischievous or tricksy goblin or sprite, called also Robin Goodfellow and Hobgoblin. **b.** with *a* and *pl.* One of a class of such demons, goblins, or sprites OE. **c.** *transf.* One given to mischievous tricks, esp. a mischievous child or youngster 1852. Hence **Pu·ckish** *a.* of the nature of or characteristic of Puck; impish, mischievous. **-ly** *adv.*, **-ness.**

Puck, *sb.*[2] 1834. [Of unkn. origin.] **1.** (Also *p. bird.*) The nightjar or goatsucker 1883. **2.** A disease in cattle attributed to the nightjar 1834.

Puck (pɒk), *sb.*[3] 1891. [Of unkn. origin.] A flat india-rubber disc used for a ball in ice-hockey.

Pucka: see PUKKA.

Pucker (pɒ·kəɹ), *sb.* 1741. [f. next.] **1.** A ridge, wrinkle, or corrugation of the skin or other substance, or a number of small wrinkles running across and into one another 1744. **2.** *fig.* A state of agitation or excitement (*colloq.*) 1741. Hence **Pu·ckery** *a.* given to puckering, marked with puckers; that draws the mouth together, astringent.

Pucker (pɒ·kəɹ), *v.* 1598. [prob. frequent. f. base *pok-* of POKE *sb.*[1], POCKET, as if 'make pockets', 'form into bag-like gatherings'; see -ER[5]. Cf. Fr. *faire des poches* bag, pucker.] **1.** *intr.* To contract or gather into wrinkles, small folds, cockles, or bulges; to cockle. Often with *up*. **2.** *trans.* To draw together or contract into wrinkles, bulges, or fullnesses; to draw (the skin, lips, etc.) into ridges and furrows; to gather one side of (a seam) more fully than the other, either as a fault in sewing, or intentionally for some purpose. Often with *up*. 1616. **b.** *absol.* To make puckers or bulges in sewing 1862.

1. His waistcoat. .had a propensity to p. up over his chest 1847.

Puckfist (pɒ·kfist). 1599. [f. PUCK *sb.*[1] + obs. *fist* puff-ball.] **1.** The puff-ball, *Lycoperdon bovista*. Also abbrev. *puck*. 1601. **2.** An empty braggart 1599.

2. A base besognio, and a p. SCOTT.

Pud (pɒd). 1654. [Of unkn. origin, but poss. a var. of PAD *sb.*[3] II.] A nursery word for the hand of a child or for the fore-foot of some animals.

Pudder (pɒ·dəɹ), *v.* *Obs.* or *dial.* ME. [Of unkn. origin.] **1.** *intr.* To poke or stir about with the hand or a stick; (of an animal) to poke or rout; to dabble in water, mud, or dust. **2.** To go 'poking' *about*; to potter; to meddle and muddle, to dabble (*in*) 1624.

Pudding (pu·diŋ), *sb.* [ME. *poding, pudding* – (O)Fr. *boudin* black pudding :– Gallo-Rom. **botellinus*, f. L. *botellus* pudding, sausage (Martial), small intestine; see BOWEL. For the initial consonant, cf. PURSE (late L. *bursa*, Fr. *bourse*), †*purrele* (Fr. *burelle*).] **I. 1.** The stomach or one of the entrails of a pig, sheep, or other animal, stuffed with minced meat, suet, seasoning, etc., boiled and kept till needed; a kind of sausage. Now chiefly *Sc.* and *dial.* **2.** (Chiefly *pl.*) The bowels, entrails, guts. Now *dial.* and *Sc.* 1444. **3.** *Naut.* **a.** A wreath of plaited cordage placed round the mast and yards of a ship as a support; a dolphin. **b.** A pad to prevent damage to the gunwale of a boat; a fender. **c.** The binding on rings, etc., to prevent the chafing of cables or hawsers. 1625.

1. P. which is called the Haggas. .of whose goodnesse it is vain to boast 1615. He had sent a string of Hogs-puddings. .to every poor Family in the Parish ADDISON.

II. 1. A preparation of food of a soft or moderately firm consistency, in which the ingredients, animal or vegetable, are either mingled in a farinaceous basis, or are enclosed in a farinaceous crust, and cooked by boiling or steaming. Preparations of batter, milk and eggs, rice, sago, and other farinaceous substances, suitably seasoned, and cooked by baking, are now also called puddings. **2.** *fig.* Material reward or advantage; esp. in allit. antithesis to *praise* 1728. **3.** *transf.* Anything of the consistency or appearance of a pudding 1731. †**4.** = JACK-PUDDING –1680.

1. Mr. Carter of Norwich, that used to eat such abundance of pudden 1670. One solid dish his weekday meal affords, An added p. solemniz'd the Lord's POPE. *Prov.* The proof of the p. is in the eating. **2.** He turn'd, preferring p. to *no* praise BYRON.

attrib. and *Comb.*, as *p.-bowl, -cloth*, etc.; **p.-face,** a large fat face; hence **-faced** *a.*; **-head,** a stupid person; hence **-headed** *a.*; †**-sleeve,** a large bulging sleeve drawn in at the wrist or above; hence **-sleeved** *a.*; **-stone,** = CONGLOMERATE *sb.* 1; †**-time,** the time when p. is to be had; hence *fig.*, a time when one is in luck; a favourable time. Hence **Pu·dding** *v. trans.* to supply or treat with pudding or a pudding-like substance; *Naut.* to wrap with tow as a protection against chafing.

Pudding-pie. 1593. A name for various forms of pastry; *esp.* a dough pudding containing meat, baked in a dish. Also *attrib.*

Puddle (pɒ·d'l), *sb.* [ME. *podel*, later *puddel*, dim. of OE. *pudd* ditch, furrow; see -LE. Cf. G. dial. *pudel, pfudel* pool.] **1.** A small body of standing water, foul with mud, etc., or with a muddy bottom; a small dirty pool. †Formerly including a pond, a pit full of water, or even an extensive slough or swamp. **2.** *fig.*, esp. with ref. to moral defilement, or to false doctrine, etc., regarded as polluting 1533. **b.** *fig.* A confused collection or heap; a muddle, mess. Now only *colloq.* or *dial.* 1587. **3.** Foul or muddy water such as is found in puddles. Chiefly *fig.* Now *dial.* 1555. **4.** A preparation of clay, or of clay and sand, mixed with water and tempered, used as a water-tight covering for embankments, lining for canals, etc. Also called *puddling.* 1795. Hence **Pu·ddly** *a.* having the quality of a p.; muddy, turbid; more gen. foul, dirty; also full of puddles.

Puddle (pɒ·d'l), *v.* 1440. [Cf. Du. *poedelen*, LG. *pud(d)eln* dabble or splash in water.] **1.** *intr.* To dabble or poke about, esp. in mud or shallow water; to wallow in mire; *fig.* to 'muddle' or 'mess' about. **2.** *trans.* To bemire; to wet with mud or dirty water 1535. **3.** To make (water) muddy or dirty 1593. **b.** To muddle, confuse; to sully the purity or clearness of 1604. **4.** To reduce the surface of the ground, earth, clay, etc., into mud or puddle; *spec.* to knead and temper a mixture of wet clay and sand so as to form puddle (see prec. 4) 1762. **b.** To cover or line with puddle; to render water-tight by the application of puddle 1810. **5.** *Iron Manuf.* To stir about and turn over (molten iron) in a reverberatory furnace, so as to expel the carbon and convert it into malleable iron 1798.

1. Children..are playing and puddling about in the dirt everywhere THACKERAY. **3. b.** Something sure of State,..Hath pudled his cleare Spirit SHAKS.

Comb.: **p.-ball**, a rounded mass of iron formed in puddling; **-bar**, a flat bar formed by passing a *puddle-ball* between *puddle-rolls*; **-roll**, each of a pair of large heavy rollers with grooved surfaces, between which puddled iron is passed to be flattened into bars; **-steel**, steel made by puddling. Hence **Pu·ddler**, one who puddles, chiefly in techn. senses. **Pu·ddling**, the action of the verb; also *concr.* = prec. 4; also *attrib.* as *puddling-furnace*, etc.

Pudency (piū·dĕnsi). 1611. [– late L. *pudentia*, f. *pudens*, *-ent-*, pr. pple. of *pudēre* be ashamed; see -ENCY.] Susceptibility to the feeling of shame; modesty, bashfulness.

‖**Pudendum** (piude·ndɒ̆m). Usu. in pl. **pudenda.** 1634. [L. *pudenda* (sc. *membra*), subst. use of n. pl. of *pudendus*, gerundive of *pudēre* be ashamed.] The privy parts; the external genital organs. Hence **Pude·ndal** *a.* of or pertaining to the pudenda; pudic.

Pudge (pɒdʒ). *dial.* and *colloq.* 1808. [Parallel form of PODGE.] A short thick-set or fat person or animal; anything short and thick. Hence **Pu·dgy** *a.* short and thick or fat.

Pudic (piū·dik), *a.* (*sb.*) 1490. [– (O)Fr. *pudique* or L. *pudicus* chaste, f. *pudēre* make or be ashamed.] †**1.** Modest, chaste –1610. **2.** *Anat.* = PUDENDAL 1807. **B.** *sb. Anat.* The pudic artery 1827.

Pudicity (piudi·sĭti). Now *rare.* 1567. [orig. – Fr. *pudicité*; see PUDIC, -ITY.] Modesty, chastity.

Pudsy (pɒ·dzi), *a.* 1754. [perh. f. PUD, after contemp. FUBSY; see -SY.] Plump.

‖**Pudu** (pu·du). 1886. [Native Chilean.] The venada, *Pudua humilis* or *Cervus pudu*, a very small species of deer, native to Chile.

‖**Pueblo** (pue·blo, pwe·blo). 1818. [Sp., = people :– L. *populus* PEOPLE.] **1.** A town or village in Spain or Spanish America; esp. a communal village or settlement of Indians. **2.** Short for *P. Indian* 1850.

1. *P. Indians*, partly civilized and self-governing Indians, dwelling in pueblos, in New Mexico and Arizona.

Puerile (piū·ĕrəil), *a.* 1661. [– Fr. *puéril* or L. *puerilis*, f. *puer* boy, child; see -ILE.] **1.** Of, pertaining or proper to a boy or child; youthful, boyish, juvenile. Now *rare* exc. as in 2. **b.** Of respiration: Characterized by the louder pulmonary murmur found in children, which in adults is usu. a sign of disease 1822. **2.** Merely boyish or childish; immature, trivial 1685.

2. Mere p. declamation COLERIDGE. Hence **Pu·erile-ly** *adv.*, **-ness.**

Puerility (piū,ĕri·lĭti). 1450. [– Fr. *puérilité* or L. *puerilitas*, f. *puerilis*; see prec., -ITY.] **1.** The condition of being a child; childhood; in *Civil Law*, the age between seven and fourteen 1512. **2.** The quality of being puerile; (mere) childishness, triviality 1576. **b.** With *a* and *pl.* An instance of childishness 1450.

2. b. Those..Puerilities that are so often to be met with in Ovid ADDISON.

Puerperal (piu,ɔ·ɹpĕrăl), *a.* 1768. [f. L. *puerperus* parturient, f. *puer* child + *-parus* bringing forth; see -AL¹.] Of, pertaining to, accompanying, or ensuing upon parturition.

Pue·rpery. *rare.* 1602. [– L. *puerperium*, f. *puerperus*; see prec.] Childbirth; 'confinement'.

Puff (pɒf), *sb.* ME. [See next.] **1.** An act of puffing; a short impulsive blast of breath or wind; an abrupt emission of air, vapour, or smoke; a whiff. **b.** The sound of such an emission of air or the like 1834. **c.** *concr.* A small quantity of vapour, smoke, etc., emitted at one momentary blast; a whiff 1839. **2.** A swelling caused by inflation or otherwise; a blister, tumour, protuberance, excrescence 1538. **b.** In costume, A rounded soft protuberant mass formed by gathering in the stuff at the edges and leaving it full in the middle as if inflated. Also, a similar mass formed of ribbons or small feathers, or of hair on the head 1601. **3.** †**a.** An instrument like a small bellows, formerly used for blowing powder on the hair. **b.** A small pad of down or the like, for applying powder to the hair or skin; a POWDER-PUFF. 1658. **4.** A name for various kinds of very light pastry or confectionery; now *esp.* a piece of puff-paste enclosing jam or the like. late ME. †**5.** *fig.* An inflated speech or piece of display; vainglory or pride; vain show; bombast; brag, bluff –1821. **6.** Undue or inflated commendation; an extravagantly laudatory advertisement or review of a book, a performer or performance, a tradesman's goods, or the like 1732. **7.** Applied to a person. **a.** A boaster, braggart. *arch.* 1599. †**b.** A writer of puffs –1789. **c.** *slang.* A decoy in a gambling-house 1731.

1. A lityl puffe of wynde..sholde soone caste hym downe 1400. **c.** Puffs of vapour were rising at various points 1869. **2. b.** Mrs. Steward, very fine, with her locks done up with puffes, as my wife calls them PEPYS. P. of muslin, forming a panier 1889. **5.** Any thing like p., or verbal ornament, I cannot bring myself to 1821. **6.** The last puffs written for a morning concert RUSKIN.

Comb.: **p.-box**, a box to hold toilet-powder and a powder-puff; **-breeches**, puffed or inflated breeches; **-leg**, a humming-bird of the genus *Eriocnemis*, having tufts of down upon the legs; **-stone**, local name for the soft porous marlstone of the Middle Lias.

Puff (pɒf), *v.* Pa. t. and pple. **puffed** (pɒft). [In the earliest exx. *puf* sb., *puffe* vb., pa. t. *pufte*, the *u* may denote either u or ü, and may repr. OE. **puf* or *pyf(f* sb., **puffan* or *pyffan* vb., corresp. to (M)Du. *puffen*, Du. *pof*, *poffen*, LG. *pof*, *puf*. Of echoic origin, imit. of the sound of the breath.] **1.** *intr.* To emit a puff of air or breath; to escape as a puff. *To p. out*, *up*, to issue, arise in puffs. **b.** To breathe hard, pant violently; often *to p. and blow*; hence, to run or go with puffing or panting. late ME. **c.** To send forth puffs of vapour or smoke, as a steam-engine, or a person smoking tobacco; to move *away*, *in*, or *out*, with puffing, as a locomotive or steamboat 1781. †**2.** To say 'pooh!' or the like; to speak or behave scornfully or insolently, to swagger. *P. at*, to pooh-pooh. –1677. **3.** *trans.* To drive, impel, or agitate by puffing; to blow *away*, *down*, *up*, etc. with a quick short blast; to emit (smoke, steam, etc.) in puffs ME. **b.** To blow *out* 1547. **c.** To smoke (a pipe or cigar) in puffs 1809. **d.** To apply powder with a powder-puff 1838. **4.** To cause (something) to swell by puffing air into it; to blow *out* or *up*; to inflate; to distend by inflation, or in any way 1539. **b.** *intr.* To swell *up* 1725. **5.** *fig.* (*trans.*) To inflate with vanity, pride, ambition, or the like; to elate; *rarely*, to cause to swell with anger, to enrage. Usu. in pa. pple. with *up*. 1526. **6.** To commend in extravagant terms; *esp.* to advertise with exaggerated or falsified praise 1735. **b.** *intr.* To bid at an auction for the purpose of inflating the price 1760.

1. Like foggy South, puffing with winde and raine SHAKS. **b.** Puffing and blowing as if..very much out of Breath ADDISON. **c.** Sanders..puffed away at his cigar 1861. Where the trains now go puffing in and out of Cannon Street Terminus 1870. **2.** As for all his enemies, he puffeth at them *Ps.* 10:5. **3.** The clearing North will p. the Clouds away DRYDEN. **b.** Yet we go out, Like candles puffed 1879. **5.** Not stain'd with cruelty, nor puft with pride DRYDEN. Hence **Pu·ffer**, one who or that which puffs; *spec.* a person employed by a vendor to bid at an auction for the purpose of running up the price and inciting others to buy; also, a child's name for a railway engine or train. So **Pu·ffery**, the practice of a 'puffer'; inflated laudation, esp. by way of advertisement.

Pu·ff-adder. 1824. [– S. Afr. Du. *pofadder*; see PUFF *v.*] A large and very venomous African viper (*Bitis* or *Clotho arietans*), which puffs out the upper part of its body when excited.

Pu·ff-ball. 1649. [f. PUFF *sb.* or *v.* + BALL *sb.*¹] A fungus of the genus *Lycoperdon* or of some allied genus; so called from the ball-like shape of the ripe spore-case, and its emission of the spores in a cloud of fine powder when broken.

Pu·ff-bird. 1821. Any bird of the family *Bucconidæ* or fissirostral barbets, so called from their habit of puffing out their feathers.

Puffin (pɒ·fin). [ME. *poffin*, *pophyn*, in AL. *puffo*, *poffo*, *puffonus*, *paphinus* (XIII–XIV); of unkn. origin, perh. Cornish.] A sea-bird of the genus *Fratercula*, of the family *Alcidæ* or Auks; *esp.* the common *F. arctica*, found on the coasts of the N. Atlantic, having a very large furrowed and parti-coloured bill. **b.** Erron. applied to a species of Shearwater (*Puffinus anglorum*), found in the Isle of Man and the Scilly Islands 1674. **c.** Applied locally in Ireland to the Razor-bill 1885.

Pu·ff-paste. 1602. [f. PUFF *sb.* or vb.-stem.] *Cookery.* A fine kind of flour paste, made very light and flaky by successive rollings and butterings 1611. **b.** *fig.* Applied to persons or things of a light, flimsy, or unsubstantial character 1602. So **Pu:ff-pa·stry,** fine pastry made with puff-paste.

Pu·ff-puff. 1870. [imit.] An imitation of the puffing of a steam-engine; hence, a nursery name for a locomotive, or a railway train.

Puffy (pɒ·fi), *a.* 1599. [f. PUFF *v.* or *sb.* + -Y¹.] **1. a.** Of wind: Blowing in puffs, gusty; also, characterized by such wind. **b.** Of a person or animal: Easily caused to puff; short-winded. **c.** Of a sound: Dull, muffled. 1616. **2.** Swollen or inclined to swell, by or as by puffing or inflation; turgid, tumid, puffed out; of persons, fat, corpulent and flabby 1664. **3.** *fig.* Puffed up, vain, inflated, bombastic (*rare*) 1599.

1. I am too p. to enjoy hill-climbing 1844. **2.** The [owl's] round p. head 1874. The p. sleeve 1899. **3.** A rather p. and consequential man 1853. Hence **Pu·ffiness**, p. quality or condition.

Pug (pɒg), *sb.*¹ Now only *dial.* 1440. [Of unkn. origin.] The chaff of wheat or oats, the awns of barley, etc.; the refuse corn separated in winnowing.

Pug (pɒg), *sb.*² 1566. [poss. of LDu. origin; cf. WFlem. *Pugge*, substituted for a Christian name, as *Pugge Willems* (De Bo).] **I.** Applied to a person, etc. †**1.** A term of endearment –1611. †**2.** A courtesan, mistress, harlot, punk –1719. †**3.** A bargeman –1611. **4.** In servants' use: An upper servant in a large establishment 1847. **II.** An imp, a dwarf animal, etc. †**1.** A small demon or imp; a sprite; Puck –1678. **2.** A monkey, an ape. Also applied to a child. Now *dial.* 1664. **3.** orig. *pug-dog*: A dwarf breed of dog, resembling a bull-dog in miniature; much kept as a pet 1749. **4.** A *quasi*-proper name for a fox 1809. **5.** Also *p.-moth*: Collectors' name for geometrid moths of the genus *Eupithecia* 1819. **6.** In full *p.-engine*: A small locomotive used chiefly for station or shunting purposes; a contractor's engine 1880.

attrib. and *Comb.*: **p.-face**, a face compared to that of a monkey; a squat flat-nosed face; **-fox**, a small-sized, blunt-nosed variety of fox; **-peal**, a young grilse or salmon; **-trout**, a sea-trout. Hence **Pu·ggish** *a.* resembling or characteristic of a pug or a pug-nose.

Pug (pɒg), *sb.*³ 1872. [See PUG *v.*²] Loam or clay comminuted, thoroughly mixed, kneaded, and prepared for brickmaking, etc. *Comb.*: **p.-cylinder,** the cylinder of a pug-mill; **-mill,** a machine for making clay into pug.

‖**Pug** (pɒg), *sb.*⁴ *Anglo-Ind.* 1865. [Hindi *pag* footprint.] The footprint of a beast.

Pug (pɒg), *v.*¹ Now *dial.* 1575. [perh. symbolic formation with structure resembling that of *lug, plug, slug, tug.*] *trans.* To pull, tug.

Pug (pɒg), *v.*² 1823. [Of unkn. origin. Cf. WFlem. *pug(ge* hard prod, kick, knock.] **1.** *trans.* To temper (clay) for brickmaking, by kneading and working it into a soft and plastic condition, as in a pug-mill 1843. **2.** To pack or fill up (a space) with pug, cement, etc.; *esp.* to pack the space under a floor with earth, old mortar, sawdust, etc. to prevent the passage of sound 1823. Hence **Pu·gging,** the materials used to pug the space under a floor.

Pug (pɒg), *v.*³ *Anglo-Ind.* 1866. [f. PUG *sb.*⁴] *trans.* To track by footprints.

Puggree, puggaree (pɒ·gri, pɒ·gări). 1665. [– Hind. *pagrī.*] **1.** A light turban worn by Indian natives. **2.** A scarf of thin muslin or a silk veil wound round the crown of a sun-helmet and falling down behind as a shade 1859.

Pugil (piū·dʒil). *arch.* 1576. [– L. *pugillus,* f. root *pug-* as in *pugnus* fist.] Strictly, A handful; but now, as much as can be taken up between the thumb and the next two (or sometimes three) fingers; a little handful or big pinch.

Pugilism (piū·dʒiliz'm). 1791. [f. L. *pugil* boxer + -ISM.] The art or practice of fighting with fists; boxing.

Pugilist (piū·dʒilist). 1790. [f. as prec. + -IST.] A boxer, a fighter; *fig.* a vigorous controversialist. Hence **Pugili·stic** *a.* of or pertaining to pugilists or pugilism. **Pugili·stical** *a. rare,* **-ly** *adv.*

Pugnacious (pɒgnēⁱ·ʃəs), *a.* 1642. [f. L. *pugnax, -ac-* (f. *pugnare* to fight, f. *pugnus* fist) + -OUS; see -ACIOUS.] Disposed to fight; given to fighting; quarrelsome; contentious. Hence **Pugna·cious-ly** *adv.*, **-ness.**

Pugnacity (pɒgnæ·sĭti). 1605. [– L. *pugnacitas,* f. *pugnax*; see prec., -ITY.] Tendency or inclination to fight; quarrelsomeness.

Pug nose, pug-nose (pɒ·gnōᵘ·z). 1778. [f. PUG *sb.*² II. 2 or 3 + NOSE *sb.*] A short nose with a wide base sloping upward; a short squat or snub nose.

Pug-nose(d eel, a deep-sea species of eel, *Simenchelys parasiticus,* found off the Newfoundland bank, having a short and blunt nose. Hence **Pu·g-no:sed** *a.*

Puisne (piū·ni), *a.* and *sb.* 1598. [Legal spelling of PUNY.] **A.** *adj.* **1.** Born later, younger; junior (in appointment, etc.). Now only in legal use. 1613. **b.** Applied to an inferior or junior judge in the superior courts of common law 1688. **2.** Later, more recent, of subsequent date. Now only in legal use. 1655. †**3.** Small, insignificant, petty; now spelt PUNY –1782.

2. They were incumbrancers p. to the plaintiffs 1885. **3.** *A.Y.L.* III. iv. 46.

B. *sb.* †**1.** A junior; an inferior or underling; a novice –1663. **2.** *spec.* A puisne judge 1810.

Puissance (piū·isăns, piu,i·săns, pwi·săns). *arch.* late ME. [– (O)Fr. *puissance,* f. *puissant*; see next, -ANCE.] **1.** Power, strength, force, might; influence. †**2.** *concr.* An armed force –1595.

1. To prove his p. in battell brave SPENSER. Our p. is our own, our own right hand Shall teach us highest deeds MILT. **2.** *John* III. i. 339.

Puissant (piū·isănt, piu,i·sănt, pwi·sănt), *a. arch.* 1450. [– (O)Fr. *puissant* :– Gallo-Rom. **possiant-* (f. L. *posse* be able), for L. *potens, potent-* POTENT.] Possessed of or wielding power; having great authority or influence; mighty, potent, powerful.

Or who from France a puisant Armie brings? DRAYTON. And with p. stroke the head to bruize 1642. The p. crowned, the weak laid low M. ARNOLD. Hence **Puissant-ly** *adv.*, **-ness** (*rare*).

†**Puke,** *sb.*¹ 1466. [In XV *pewke, puke* – MDu. *puuc, puyck,* of unkn. origin.] **1.** A superior kind of woollen cloth, of which gowns were made –1612. **2.** A colour formerly used for woollen goods; app. a bluish black or inky colour –1725.

Puke (piūk), *sb.*² 1737. [f. PUKE *v.*] **1.** An act of vomiting, a vomit. **2.** An emetic, a vomit 1743.

Puke (piūk), *v.* 1600. [prob. of imit. origin; cf., for similar expressive elements, LG. (whence G.) *spucken* spit, Flem. *spukken* spew, spit. Cf. SPEW.] **1.** *intr.* To eject food from the stomach; to vomit. **2.** *trans.* To eject by vomiting; to vomit 1601.

1. At first the Infant, Mewling, and puking in the Nurses armes SHAKS. Hence **Pu·ker,** one who vomits; †a medicine causing vomiting.

‖**Pukka** (pɒ·kă), *a.* 1698. [– Hindi *pakkā* cooked, ripe, mature; thorough, substantial.] **a.** Applied to the larger of two weights of the same name: Of full weight, full, good; also, genuine, thorough. **b.** Sure, certain; thorough, out-and-out 1776. **c.** Permanent, as an appointment, a building, etc. 1784.

Pulchritude (pɒ·lkritiūd). late ME. [– L. *pulchritudo,* f. *pulcher* beautiful; see -TUDE.] Beauty.

Pule (piūl), *v.* 1534. [prob. of imit. origin; cf. Fr. *piauler,* dial. *pioular* chirp, whine, and MEWL.] **1.** *intr.* To cry in a thin or weak voice, as a child; to whine, to cry in a querulous tone. **2.** To pipe plaintively, as a chicken, etc.; also said of the cry of the kite 1598. **3.** *trans.* To utter (something) in a whining or querulous tone 1535.

1. Don't come puling to me when it's too late 1877. Hence **Pu·ler,** one who pules or whines; †a fledgeling.

Pulicine (piū·lisəin), *a. rare.* 1656. [f. L. *pulex, pulic-* flea + -INE¹.] Of or relating to fleas.

Pulicous (piū·likəs), *a. rare.* 1658. [– L. *pulicosus,* f. as prec.; see -OUS.] Abounding in fleas. So **Pu·licose** *a.* infested with fleas, flea-bitten; *Path.* resembling flea-bites.

Puling (piū·liŋ), *ppl. a.* 1529. [f. PULE *v.* + -ING².] **1.** Crying as a child, whining, feebly wailing; weakly querulous. †**2.** Pining, weakly –1706.

1. The unmaskuline Rhetorick of any p. Priest MILT. Hence **Pu·lingly** *adv.*

‖**Pulka** (pɒ·lkă). 1796. [– Finn. *pulkka,* Lapp *pulkke.*] A Lapland travelling-sledge in shape like the front half of a boat, drawn by a single reindeer.

Pull (pul), *sb.* ME. [f. next.] **I.** The act, action, or faculty of pulling. **1.** An act of pulling or drawing towards oneself with force 1440. **b.** The force expended in pulling or drawing; pulling power or force; draught, traction, strain; the force of attraction 1833. **c.** The drawing or dragging of a weight; the exertion of carrying one's own weight up an ascent 1841. **2.** *spec.* or *techn.* **a.** *Printing.* A pull of the bar of the hand-press; hence, an impression taken by this; now *spec.* a rough 'proof' 1683. **b.** A pull at the bridle in order to check a horse; *spec.* in *Racing,* a check dishonestly given to a horse to prevent his winning 1737. **c.** A pull at an oar; hence, a short spell at rowing 1793. **d.** The act of pulling the trigger of a fire-arm; also, the force required for this 1888. **e.** *Cricket.* A hit which brings a ball pitched to the off side round to leg. So in *Golf,* a hit which causes the ball to swerve in its flight towards the left (i.e. of a right-handed player). 1892. **f.** *Long p.* (in public-house use): the supply of an amount of beer, etc. exceeding that asked for 1908. †**3.** A trial of strength; a bout, a set-to; often in *to stand* or *wrestle a p.* –1747. **4.** Advantage possessed by one party, course, or method over another; esp. in phr. *to have a* or *the p. of, on, upon,* or *over* some one 1584. **b.** *spec.* Personal or private influence capable of being brought to bear to one's advantage. orig. *U.S. slang.* 1889. **5.** A long or deep draught of liquor 1575.

1. A long p., a strong p., and a p. all together 1883. **b.** The amount of this magnetic p. may be very considerable 1900. **c.** A stiff p...that brought us to the top 1861. **4.** Phr. *The p. of the table,* in gambling games, the advantages possessed by the dealer or banker. **b.** I have got a p., and any one who has got a p. can do a great deal 1894.

II. Concrete senses. **1.** That part of a mechanism with which a pull is exerted; a handle or the like; often in comb. as *beer-p., bell-p.*; also, an instrument or device for pulling 1810. **2.** A part of a road where extra effort is necessary; *esp.* a steep ascent 1798.

Pull (pul), *v.* [OE. *pullian,* also *āpullian,* having ostensible similarity in form and sense to LG. *pūlen* shell, strip, pluck, MDu. *polen* 'decorticare' (Kilian), and (M)LG. *pūle,* Du. *peul* husk, shell, the meaning 'pluck, snatch' being prob. the original (cf. PLUCK *v.*); sense II. 6 is in Du., LG. *pullen.*] **I.** In senses akin to *pluck.* **1.** *trans.* = PLUCK *v.* 1. **a.** To pluck or draw out (feathers, hair, etc.). *Obs.* or *dial.* **b.** To pluck or draw up by the root (plants, e.g. carrots, etc.) ME. **c.** To pluck, gather (fruit, flowers, or leaves) from the trees, etc., on which they grow. Now chiefly *Sc.* ME. **2.** *trans. To p. caps*: to snatch off one another's caps; hence, to scuffle, to quarrel. So *to p. wigs.* 1778. **3.** *intr.* To snatch or tear *at* something; *spec.* of a hawk: To tear or pluck at food 1826. **4.** *trans* = PLUCK *v.* 5. Now *rare* or *dial.* OE.

1. a. Wee'le p. his Plumes SHAKS. **c.** We'll pou the daisies on the green RAMSAY. **2.** A man..for whom half the females of Paris were pulling caps 1823.

II. To draw with force, etc. **1.** *trans.* To exert upon (anything) a force that tends to snatch, draw, or drag it away; to drag or tug at OE. **2.** To draw, drag, or haul with force or effort towards oneself (or into some position so pictured) ME. **3.** *intr.* To perform the action of pulling; to exert drawing, dragging, or tugging force. Often with *at.* late ME. **b.** *spec.* Of a horse: To strain (esp. habitually) against the bit 1791. **c.** To move, go, or proceed by pulling or by some exertion of force 1877. †**4.** *trans.* To take away with difficulty; to tear off, to wrench away –1625. **5.** *fig.* To bring forcibly into or out of some state or condition. *rare* or *Obs.* late ME. **6.** To take a draught of (liquor); to draw or suck (a draught of liquor) into the mouth; †to drink from (a vessel). late ME. **b.** *intr.* To draw or suck *at* (a pipe, cigar, etc.) 1861. †**7.** Implying an adv. = *pull down* –1655.

1. Phr. *To p. by the ear, nose, sleeve,* etc., to gain attention, or to punish or insult, by pulling at these parts. *To p. a bell,* to p. the bell-rope or handle in order to ring the bell. *To p. one's leg*: see LEG *sb.* 1 a. *To p. the strings, wires*: see the sbs. **2.** He placidly pulled his nightcap over his ears THACKERAY. Phr. *To p. in* or *to pieces,* etc., to separate the parts of (anything) forcibly; to demolish; also *fig.* to analyse and criticize unfavourably. **3.** Phr. *P. devil, p. baker* (†*parson*), an incitement to effort in a contest for the possession of something. **6.** To p. the tankards cheerfully 1595. **b.** Joe..pulled hard at his pipe DICKENS. **7.** Let them p. all about mine Eares SHAKS.

III. In techn. senses, with specific objects expressed or understood. **1.** *trans. Printing.* In the old hand-press, To draw (the bar of the press) towards one, so as to press down the platen upon the sheet or forme; also *intr.* or *absol.* Hence, To print upon (a sheet) or from (a forme) in this way; to make or take (an impression, proof, or copy) by printing; to print off 1653. **2.** *intr.* or *absol.* To pull an oar so as to move a boat; to row; to proceed by rowing 1676. **b.** *trans.* To pull (an oar or sculls); hence, to row, to propel (a boat) by rowing; to transport in a boat by rowing 1820. **3.** To arrest in the name of justice (*slang*) 1811. **4.** *Racing.* To hold in or check (a horse), *esp.* so as to cause him to lose a race. Also *absol.* 1800. **5.** *Cricket.* To strike (a ball) from the off to the leg; *Golf,* to drive a ball so that it swerves to the left. Also *absol.* 1884.

1. A few copies were pulled before the disaster occurred 1900. **2. b.** Phr. *To p. one's weight,* to row with effect in proportion to one's weight; also *transf.* to perform one's share of work, etc.

Phrases. *To p. a face, faces,* to draw the countenance into a grimace, to distort the features. *To p. a* (*sanctimonious,* etc.) *face,* to put on a (sanctimonious, etc.) expression. *To p. a long face*: see LONG *a.*¹ 1.

IV. With adverbs. **Pull about.** *trans.* To p. this way and that way; *colloq.* to treat roughly or unceremoniously. **P. back. a.** See simple senses and BACK *adv.* **b.** *trans.* To draw or keep back (in space or progress). **P. down. a.** See simple senses and DOWN *adv.* **b.** *trans.* To demolish (a building). **c.** To seize and bring to the ground; to overcome (a hunted animal). **d.** To lower or depress in health, spirits, size, strength, value, etc.; also, to 'bring low', humble. **e.** To depose (a sovereign) violently; to overthrow (a government) by force. **P. in. a.** See simple senses and IN *adv.* **b.** *trans.* To rein in (one's horse); hence *fig.* Also *intr.* or *absol.* To check oneself in any course. **P. off. a.** See simple senses and OFF *adv.* **b.** *Sporting.*

(*trans.*) To win (a prize or contest); hence to succeed in gaining or effecting (something). **P. out. a.** See simple senses and OUT *adv.* **b.** *absol.* or *intr.* Of a locomotive engine or train: To move out of a station; to draw out; hence, of a person: To go away, take his departure. Also, to 'get out' of an undertaking. Chiefly *U.S.* **P. through. a.** See simple senses and THROUGH *adv.* **b.** *trans.* To get (a person) through a difficult, dangerous, or critical condition or situation; to bring (a thing) to a successful issue. **c.** *intr.* To get through sickness, a trial, etc. with effort or difficulty. **P. together. a.** See senses II. 2 and TOGETHER. **b.** *To p. oneself together*, to rouse or recover oneself; to rally. **c.** *intr.* To work in harmony; also, to 'get on' together. **P. up. a.** See simple senses and UP *adv.* **b.** *trans.* To root out, demolish. **c.** To cause to stop; to stop; to arrest, to apprehend; *esp.* to apprehend and take before a magistrate; hence, to reprimand, reprove. **d.** To tighten (reins) by drawing them towards oneself; to bring (a horse) to a standstill by doing this; also *transf.* to check (a person) in any course of action, esp. a bad course. **e.** *absol.* Of a driver, etc.: To bring a horse or vehicle to a stop; also, of a horse or vehicle: To come to a standstill. **f.** *refl.* and *intr.* for *refl.* To check or stop oneself in any course of action. **g.** *intr.* To advance one's position in a race, etc.

Pull-, the stem of PULL *v.* (or PULL *sb.*) in comb.

1. With advbs., forming sbs. or adjs., in senses (*a*) *sb.* the act of pulling in the direction specified; (*b*) *adj.* that pulls or is pulled in the direction specified. **Pull-on**: see PULL-OVER 3. **Pu·ll-through,** a piece of gimp, etc. with which the tow or rag for cleaning the barrel is pulled through from breech to muzzle of a rifle. **2.** With sbs. used *attrib.* in sense used by, for, or in pulling.

Pu·ll-back. 1591. [f. phr. *to pull back.*] **1.** The action or an act of pulling back 1668. **2.** That which pulls back; a retarding influence; a check. Now *colloq.* and *dial.* 1591. **3.** A contrivance for pulling something back 1703.

Pu·ll-down. 1588. [f. phr. *to pull down.*] **1.** The act of pulling down, or fact of being pulled down. **2.** In the organ, a wire which pulls down a pallet or valve when the key is depressed, thus admitting wind to the pipe 1852.

Pulled (puld), *ppl. a.* late ME. [f. PULL *v.* + -ED[1].] **1.** In the senses of PULL *v. esp.* **2.** Denuded of feathers, plucked; stripped of wool or hair. late ME.

P. bread, the inside of a loaf pulled out and lightly browned. *P. chicken, fowl*, chicken or fowl cooked, skinned, and boned, and the flesh cut up and put into a rich white sauce. *P. figs*, dried figs manipulated so that the eye is in the centre, and packed flat. *P. wool*, inferior wool separated from the skin by the aid of chemicals.

Pullen (pu·lėn). *Obs.* exc. *dial.* ME. [app. – (O)Fr. *poulain* foal, identified in Eng. with *poulaille* poultry.] **1.** Poultry; the flesh of poultry as food. **2.** Chickens collectively; young; rarely, a chicken; *fig.* a child 1631.

Puller (pu·ləɹ). late ME. [f. PULL *v.* + -ER[1].] One who or that which pulls.

Proud setter vp, and p. downe of Kings SHAKS.

Pullet (pu·lėt). ME. [– (O)Fr. *poulet*, *-ette*, dim. of *poule* hen :– Rom. **pulla*, fem. of L. *pullus* young animal, chicken. Cf. POULTRY.] **1.** A young (domestic) fowl; *spec.* and *techn.* a young hen from the time she begins to lay till the first moult. **2.** In full, *P. Carpet-shell*: a bivalve mollusc, *Tapes pullastra* 1890.

Pulley (pu·li), *sb.* [ME. *poley* – OFr. *polie* (mod. *poulie*) :– Rom. **polidia* (n. pl. used as fem. sing.), pl. of **polidium*, prob. – med. Gr. *πολίδιον, dim. of πόλος POLE *sb.*[2], also windlass, capstan.] **1.** One of the simple mechanical powers, consisting of a grooved wheel mounted in a block, so that a cord or the like may pass over it; used for changing the direction of power, esp. for raising weights by pulling downwards. Also, a combination of such wheels in a BLOCK (*sb.* 4), or system of blocks in a TACKLE, by means of which the power is increased. **2.** A wheel or drum fixed on a shaft and turned by a belt or the like for the application or transmission of power; usu. to increase speed or power 1619.

1. *Fixed p.*, a p. the block of which is fixed. *Frame p.*, a p. in which the wheels or sheaves are fixed in a frame.

attrib. and *Comb.*, as *p.-block*, etc.; also **p.-drum,** the block or shell in which the sheave or sheaves are mounted; **-frame,** the gearing above a pit, upon which the pulleys are supported; **-stile,** one of the vertical side-pieces of a window sash-frame, in which the pulleys are pivoted.

Pu·lley, *v.* 1599. [f. prec.] **1.** *trans.* To raise or hoist with or as with a pulley. **2.** To furnish or fit with a pulley; to work by means of a pulley 1767.

†Pu·llicate. 1794. [f. *Pulicat*, a town on the Madras coast.] **a.** A coloured handkerchief, orig. made at Pulicat –1839. **b.** A material made in imitation of these, woven from dyed yarn –1891.

Pullman (pu·lmăn). 1874. [f. name of the designer, George M. Pullman (1831–97), of Chicago, U.S.A.] In full *P. car* (*saloon*): a railway carriage constructed and arranged as a saloon, and (usu.) with special arrangements for use as a sleeping-car.

Pu·ll-on. 1923. [f. phr. *to pull on.*] Used chiefly *attrib.* of garments, boots, and the like, which are pulled on without fastening.

Pu·ll-o:ver. 1883. [f. phr. *to pull over.*] **1.** The action or an act of pulling over or from side to side; also *attrib.* or as *adj.* having the function of pulling over 1894. **2.** A knitted jumper or sweater, made without fastenings, so that it must be pulled over the head 1925.

Pullulant (pɒ·liŭlănt), *a.* 1889. [– Fr. *pullulant*, pr. pple. of *pulluler*; see next.] Budding.

Pullulate (pɒ·liŭleᶦt), *v.* 1619. [– *pullulat-*, pa. ppl. stem of L. *pullulare* spring forth, grow, f. *pullulus*, dim. of *pullus* young of an animal, chick; see -ATE[3]. Cf. (O)Fr. *pulluler* in same senses.] **1.** *intr.* Of a growing part, shoot, or bud: To sprout out, bud. **b.** Of a seed: To sprout, to germinate. Of a plant or animal: To propagate itself by budding; to breed, to multiply; now usu. with the connotation of rapid increase 1621. **2.** *intr. transf.* and *fig.* **a.** To be produced as offspring, to spring up abundantly 1657. **b.** To teem, to swarm 1835.

2. b. As to the beggars, they p. in the place 1883.

Pullulation (pɒliulēᶦ·ʃən). 1641. [f. prec. + -ATION. Cf. Fr. *pullulation.*] The action of pullulating. Also, the product of this; offspring, progeny. **b.** *spec.* in *Biol.* Generation or reproduction by budding 1822.

Pu·ll-up. 1854. [f. phr. *to pull up.*] **1.** The act of pulling up a horse or vehicle; a sudden stop; hence *fig.* **2.** A stopping-place for riders or drivers 1887.

Pulmo- (pɒ·lmo), shortened from PULMONI-, comb. form of L. *pulmo, -on-* lung; as in ‖**Pulmobranchiæ** (-bræ·ŋkiˌī) *sb. pl.*, lung-sacs; hence **Pulmobra·nchial, Pulmobra·nchiate** *adjs.*, having, or breathing by means of pulmobranchiæ. **Pulmoga·steropod, -ga·stropod** *a.*, belonging to the *Pulmogastero·poda*, the pulmonate or air-breathing gastropods; *sb.* one of these.

‖**Pulmonaria** (pɒlmŏnēᵊ·riă). 1578. [med. L. *pulmonaria* (sc. *herba*), subst. use of fem. sing. of L. *pulmonarius* (see next) diseased in the lungs, (later) beneficial to the lungs; so called from its assumed virtue in curing disease of the lungs, as supposed to be indicated by the spotted leaves resembling the lungs.] *Bot.* A genus of boraginaceous plants; lungwort.

Pulmonary (pɒ·lmŏnări), *a.* (*sb.*) 1704. [– L. *pulmonarius* (see prec.), f. *pulmo, -onlung* + *-arius* -ARY[1].] **1.** Of, pertaining to, situated in, or connected with the lungs. (Chiefly *Anat.*) **b.** Constituting a lung or lung-like organ; of the nature of a lung 1834. **c.** Carried on by means of lungs 1826. **2.** Occurring in or affecting the lungs (chiefly *Path.*); of or pertaining to disease of the lungs 1727. **b.** Affected with or subject to lung-disease: consumptive. Also *transf.* 1843. **3.** *Zool.* Having lungs, lung-sacs, or pulmonary organs 1833. **B.** *sb. Zool.* A pulmonary arachnidan, as a spider or a scorpion 1835.

Pulmonate (pɒ·lmŏnĕt), *a.* (*sb.*) 1842. [– mod.L. *pulmonatus*, f. L. *pulmo, -on-* lung; see -ATE[2] 2.] *Zool.* Having lungs, as the higher vertebrates, or lung-like respiratory organs, as the orders *Pulmonata* of gastropod molluscs and *Pulmonaria* of arachnids. **B.** *sb.* A pulmonate mollusc (or, less usu., arachnid). So **Pu·lmonated** *a.*

Pulmoni- (pɒlmōᵘ·ni), comb. form of L. *pulmo, pulmon-*, as in **Pulmonibra·nchiate** *a.* and *sb.*; see *pulmobranchiate* (PULMO-).

Pulmonic (pɒlmǫ·nik), *a.* (*sb.*) 1661. [– Fr. *pulmonique* (Paré) or mod.L. *pulmonicus*, f. L. *pulmo, -on-* lung; see -IC.] **1.** = PULMONARY *a.* 1. 1702. **2.** = PULMONARY *a.* 2. 1661. **B.** *sb.* A person subject to or affected with disease of the lungs 1735. So **†Pulmo·nical** *a.* 1597.

Pulmoniferous (pɒlmŏni·fĕrəs), *a.* 1835. [f. PULMONI- + -FEROUS.] *Zool.* Bearing or having lungs (or lung-like organs); pulmonate; *spec.* belonging to the group *Pulmonifera* (= *Pulmonata*) of gastropod molluscs. So **Pulmo·nifer,** a p. gastropod.

Pulmono-, comb. form of L. *pulmo* lung, occas. used instead of PULMONI- or PULMO-.

Pulp (pɒlp), *sb.* 1563. [– L. *pulpa.*] A soft, moist, homogeneous or formless substance or mass. **1.** The fleshy succulent part of a fruit; the soft pith in the interior of the stem of a plant. **2.** Any soft muscular or fleshy part of an animal body; *esp.* the soft nervous substance which fills the interior cavity of a tooth 1611. **3.** A soft formless mass, esp. of disintegrated organic matter 1676; *spec.* the fibrous material, as linen, wood, etc., reduced to a soft uniform mass, from which paper is made; paper-pulp 1727. **b.** Ore pulverized and mixed with water; slimes. *Dry p.*, dry crushed ore. 1837.

attrib. and *Comb.*, as **p.-canal, -cavity, -chamber,** the space in the interior of a tooth which contains the p.; **-digester,** a machine for reducing paper-stock and obtaining the fibre free from extraneous matter; **-mill,** a mill in which wood is reduced to paper-pulp; also, a factory in which pulping is carried on; **-wood,** wood suitable for making paper-pulp.

Pulp, *v.* 1662. [f. prec.] **1.** *trans.* To reduce to pulp or to a pulpy mass. **2.** To remove the surrounding pulp from (coffee-beans, etc.) 1791. **3.** *intr.* To become pulpy, to swell with juice 1818. Hence **Pu·lper,** a machine for reducing fruit, paper-stock, etc. to pulp; a machine for removing the pulp from the coffee bean.

Pu·lpiness. 1846. [f. PULPY *a.* + -NESS.] The quality or state of being pulpy; softness, flabbiness.

Pulpit (pu·lpit), *sb.* ME. [– L. *pulpitum* scaffold, platform, stage, in late and med.L. pulpit.] **1.** In ref. to ancient times: A scaffold, stage, or platform for public shows, speeches, or disputations. *Obs.* or *arch.* late ME. **2.** A raised structure or enclosed platform, usu. supplied with a desk, seat, etc., from which the preacher in a church or chapel delivers the sermon. **b.** *fig.* The place from which anything of the nature of a sermon, as a moral lecture, is delivered 1616. **3.** *transf.* The occupants of the pulpit; Christian ministers or the Christian ministry as occupied with preaching 1570. **4.** Applied to other places elevated so as to give the occupant a conspicuous position, etc.; e.g. an auctioneer's desk or platform (now *local*). late ME.

1. *Jul. C.* III. i. 229. **2.** Phr. *To occupy the p.*, to preach, or to conduct divine service. **3.** The Bar, the P. and the Press Nefariously combine To cry up an usurped Pow'r And stamp it right divine 1695. **4.** Come, get to your p., Mr. Auctioneer SHERIDAN. Hence **Pu·lpit** *v. trans.* to provide with a pulpit, or place in the pulpit; *intr.* to officiate in the pulpit, to preach. **Pu·lpiter** = PULPITEER. **Pulpi·tic, -al,** *adjs.*, **-ly** *adv.* **Pu·lpitish** *a.*

Pulpiteer (pulpitīᵊ·ɹ), *sb.* 1642. [f. prec. + -EER[1].] A preacher by profession; usu. *contempt.* Hence **Pulpitee·r** *v. intr.* to preach.

Pu·lpitry. 1606. [f. as prec. + -RY.] The work or service of the pulpit; preaching; the conventional talk of the pulpit; sermonizing.

Pulpous (pɒ·lpəs), *a.* 1601. [– L. *pulposus*, f. *pulpa* PULP *sb.*; see -OUS.] Of the nature of or consisting of pulp; resembling pulp; pulpy. Hence **Pu·lpousness** (*rare*).

Pulpy (pɒ·lpi), *a.* 1591. [f. PULP *sb.* + -Y[1].] Of the nature of, consisting of, or resembling pulp; soft, fleshy, succulent; also *fig.* flabby.

‖**Pulque** (pu·lke). 1693. [Sp. Amer.; origin unkn.] A fermented drink made in Mexico from the sap of the agave or maguey (*Agave americana*).

Pulsate (pɒ·lseᶦt, pɒlsēᶦ·t), *v.* 1794. [– *pulsat-*, pa. ppl. stem of L. *pulsare*, frequent. of *pellere, puls-* drive, strike, beat.] **1.** *intr.* To expand and contract rhythmically, as the heart or an artery; to exhibit a pulse; to beat, throb. (Chiefly in scientific use.) **2.** *gen.* To strike upon something with a rhythmical succession of strokes; to move with a regular alternating motion; to exhibit such a movement; to beat, vibrate, quiver, thrill 1861.

1. *fig.* Life pulsates in rock or tree EMERSON. **2.** The air pulsates with the flash of arms 1861.

Pulsatile (pɒ·lsătil, -əil), *a.* 1541. [– med.L. *pulsatilis*, spec. in *vena pulsatilis* (XIV) artery, f. as prec.; see -ILE.] **1.** *Anat.* and *Phys.* Having the capacity or property of pulsating or throbbing, as the heart, etc.; exhibiting pulsation. **b.** Of, or characterized by, pulsation 1684. **2.** Of a musical instrument: Played by percussion; percussive 1769.

‖**Pulsatilla** (pɒlsăti·lă). 1597. [mod.L., dim. of L. *pulsata* beaten, driven about.] *Bot.*, *Pharm.* The Pasque-flower, a species of Anemone (*A. pulsatilla*); earlier, a generic name; now in *Bot.* a subgenus including this and other species; also, the extract or tincture of this plant.

Pulsation (pɒlsēⁱ·ʃən). 1541. [– L. *pulsatio*, f. *pulsat-*; see PULSATE *v.*, -ION.] **1.** The movement of the pulse in a living animal body; rhythmic dilatation and contraction, as of the heart, an artery, etc.; beating, throbbing. **b.** with *pl.* = PULSE *sb.*[1] 1 b. 1645. **2.** *gen.* Rhythmical beating, vibration, or undulation. Also with *a* and *pl.* 1658. **3.** The action of striking, knocking, or beating; with *pl.* A stroke, knock, blow 1656.

2. A dove..Some..message knit below The wild p. of her wings TENNYSON.

Pulsative (pɒ·lsătiv), *a.* Now *rare.* late ME. [– med.L. *pulsativus*, spec. in *vena pulsativa* (XIII) artery, f. as prec.; see -IVE.] = PULSATILE 1.

Pulsator (pɒ·lseⁱtəɹ, pɒlsēⁱ·təɹ). 1656. [f. as prec. + -OR 2; cf. med.L. *pulsator* attacker, plaintiff (XIII). In senses 2, 3, f. PULSATE *v.*] **1.** One who or that which knocks or strikes (*rare*). **2.** A machine, working on the principle of the jigger, for separating diamonds from the earth in which they are found 1890. **3.** = PULSOMETER 1884.

Pulsatory (pɒ·lsătəri), *a.* 1613. [f. PULSATE *v.* + -ORY[2].] Having the quality of pulsating; characterized by or of the nature of pulsation. **b.** = PULSATILE 1. 1802.

Pulse (pɒls), *sb.*[1] [ME. *pous, pouce*, later *puls* – OFr. *pous*, later (latinized) *pouls* :– L. *pulsus* beating (spec. *venarum* of the veins), f. base of *pellere* drive, beat.] **1.** The 'beating', throbbing, or rhythmical dilatation of the arteries as the blood is propelled along them by the contractions of the heart in the living body; esp. as felt in arteries near the surface of the body; usu. in ref. to its rate and character as indicating the person's state of health; often in phr. *to feel one's p.* **b.** Each successive beat or throb of the arteries, or of the heart. Usu. in *pl.* late ME. **2.** *fig.* and *allus.*, denoting life, vitality, energy, feeling, sentiment, tendency, drift, inclination, etc.; with *pl.* a throb or thrill of life, emotion, etc. 1540. **3.** The rhythmical recurrence of strokes, vibrations, or undulations; beating, vibration 1657. **b.** A single vibration or wave; a beat 1673. **c.** *Pros.* and *Mus.* A beat or stress in the rhythm of a verse or piece of music 1885.

1. Giue me your hand, and let mee feele your p. SHAKS. **2.** And now I see with eye serene The very p. of the machine WORDSW. Phr. *To feel the p. of*, fig. to try to discover the sentiments, tendency, drift, etc. of; to 'sound'; With whom my Lord had occasion to talk and to feel his P. 1707. **3. b.** The last faint p. of quivering light KEBLE.

attrib. and *Comb.*: **p.-curve, -tracing,** the curve traced by a sphygmograph, indicating the character of a pulse-wave; **-wave,** any of the component elements of the apparently simple movement of the pulsating artery. Hence **Pu·lseless** *a.* having or exhibiting no pulsation; devoid of life, energy or movement; **-ness.**

Pulse (pɒls), *sb.*[2] [ME. *pols* – OFr. *pols* (mod. dial. *poul(s, pou*) :– L. *puls, pult-* thick pottage of meal or pulse (cf. Gr. πόλτος porridge), rel. to POLLEN. Latinized in form from XV.] **1.** The edible seeds of leguminous plants, as peas, beans, lentils, etc. **a.** *collect. sing.*; sometimes const. as *pl.* **b.** with *a* and *pl.* A kind or sort of such seeds 1555. **2.** *collect. sing.* (sometimes const. as *pl.*) Plants yielding pulse; esculent leguminous plants. late ME.

Pulse (pɒls), *v.* 1549. [– L. *pulsare*, frequent. of *pellere* drive, beat.] **1.** *trans.* To drive, impel; to drive *forth*, expel. *Obs.* (exc. as in 4). **2.** *intr.* = PULSATE 1 (now only literary) 1559. **3.** *gen.* = PULSATE 2. 1851. **4.** *trans.* To drive or send out in or by pulses or rhythmic beats 1819.

Pulsi·fic, *a.* Now *rare.* 1634. [f. L. *pulsus* PULSE *sb.*[1] + -FIC.] Producing or causing the pulsation of the arteries; also, pulsatory, throbbing.

Pulsimeter (pɒlsi·mĭtəɹ). 1842. [f. PULSE *sb.*[1]; see -METER.] An instrument for measuring the rate or force of the pulse. Also *attrib.*, as *p. watch.*

Pulsion (pɒ·lʃən). Now *rare.* 1634. [– late L. *pulsio, -on-*, f. *puls-*, pa. ppl. stem of L. *pellere* drive, beat; see -ION.] The action of driving or pushing.

Pulsive (pɒ·lsiv), *a.* Now *rare.* 1602. [f. L. *puls-* (see prec.) + -IVE.] Having the quality of driving or impelling; compelling; impulsive; propulsive.

Pulsometer (pɒlsǫ·mĭtəɹ). 1875. [f. PULSE *sb.*[1]; see -METER.] A steam-condensing vacuum-pump with two chambers so arranged that the steam is condensed in and the water admitted to each alternately; so called from the pulsatory action of the steam. (Proprietary term.) Also *p. pump.*

Pultaceous (pɒltēⁱ·ʃəs), *a.* 1668. [f. L. *puls, pult-* (see PULSE *sb.*[2]) + -ACEOUS.] **1.** Of the nature or consistency of pap; soft, semi-fluid, pulpy. **2.** Of the nature or class of pulse 1762.

‖**Pulu** (pū·lū). 1858. [Hawaiian.] A fine yellowish silky vegetable wool obtained from the base of the leaf-stalks of the Hawaiian tree-ferns, *Cibotium menziesii*, *C. chamissoi*, and *C. glaucum.*

Pulverable (pɒ·lvĕrăb'l), *a.* 1657. [f. contemp. †*pulver* vb., or its source L. *pulverare* reduce to powder (see next) + -ABLE.] Capable of being reduced to powder; pulverizable.

Pulveration (pɒlvĕrēⁱ·ʃən). 1623. [f. †*pulver* vb. or – L. *pulveratio, -on-*, f. *pulverare*, f. *pulvis, pulver-* dust; see -ATION.] Reduction to powder or dust; pulverization.

Pulverescent (pɒlvĕre·sĕnt), *a.* 1805. [f. L. *pulvis, pulver-* dust + -ESCENT.] Tending to fall to powder or to be powder. So **Pulvere·scence.**

Pulverine (pɒ·lvĕrin). 1836. [Cf. It. *polverina* fine powder.] Ashes of barilla.

Pulverization (pɒ:lvĕrəizēⁱ·ʃən). 1658. [f. next + -ATION. Cf. Fr. *pulvérisation.*] The action of pulverizing; reduction to the state of powder or dust. **b.** *techn.* The separation (of a liquid) into minute particles, as spray 1861.

fig. The complete p. of their case by the Minister whom they approached 1884.

Pulverize (pɒ·lvĕrəiz), *v.* late ME. [– late L. *pulverizare*, f. L. *pulvis, pulver-* dust; see -IZE. Cf. Fr. *pulvériser* (Paré).] **1.** *trans.* To reduce to powder or dust; to comminute, to triturate. **b.** *techn.* To divide (a liquid) into minute particles or spray 1807. **2.** *fig.* To demolish, to break down utterly 1631. **3.** *intr.* To crumble or fall to dust; to become disintegrated 1801. **4.** Of a bird: To roll in the dust (*rare*) 1890.

1. Cultivable land must be pulverised and watered 1868. **2.** We have iron hammers To p. rebellion MASSINGER. **3.** *fig.* The stern old faiths have all pulverized EMERSON. Hence **Pu·lverizable** *a.* capable of being pulverized. **Pu·lverizer,** one who or that which pulverizes; an instrument that reduces to powder; also *techn.* one that reduces a liquid to spray.

Pulverous (pɒ·lvĕrəs), *a.* 1778. [f. L. *pulvis, pulver-* dust + -OUS.] Powdery; dusty.

Pulverulent (pɒlve·rⁱŭlĕnt), *a.* 1656. [– L. *pulverulentus*, f. *pulvis, pulver-* dust; see -ULENT.] **1.** Consisting of or having the form of powder or dust; powdery. **2.** Covered with powder or dust; dusty; spec. in *Entom.* and *Bot.* 1744. **3.** Of very slight cohesion; crumbling to dust 1794. **4.** Of birds: Addicted to lying or rolling in the dust 1828. So **Pulve·rulence,** dustiness, powder.

Pulvil (pɒ·lvil), *sb. arch.* 1691. [– It. *polviglio*; see next.] Cosmetic or perfumed powder for powdering the wig or perfuming the person. Hence †**Pu·lvil** *v. trans.* to powder or perfume with p.

‖**Pulvilio, -villio** (pulvi·lyo). Now *Hist.* 1675. [– It. *polviglio* fine powder, f. *polve, polvere* powder.] = prec.

‖**Pulvillus** (pɒlvi·lŏs). 1706. [L., contr. from *pulvinulus*, dim. of *pulvinus* cushion.] **1.** A little cushion; in *Surg.*, a small mass of lint used for plugging deep wounds. **2.** *Entom.* A cushion-like process on the feet of an insect; a foot-cushion 1826.

‖**Pulvinar** (pɒlvəi·năɹ). 1599. [L. *pulvinar* couch, f. *pulvinus* cushion, pillow.] **1.** *Rom. Antiq.* A couch or cushioned seat of the gods; also, the cushioned seat in the circus 1600. **2.** *Anat.* The posterior inner tubercle of the optic thalamus 1886.

Pulvinate (pɒ·lvinĕt), *a.* 1824. [– L. *pulvinatus*, f. *pulvinus* cushion; see -ATE[2].] Pillowy, cushion-like; in *Bot.* and *Entom.*, cushion-shaped, swelling or bulging like a cushion. Hence **Pu·lvinately** *adv.*

Pulvinated (pɒ·lvineⁱtĕd), *a.* 1773. [f. as prec. + -ED[1].] **1.** *Arch.* Swelling or bulging; esp. applied to a frieze having a convex face. **2.** *Bot.* Having a pulvinus 1880. **3.** *Entom.* = prec. 1858.

‖**Pulvinus** (pɒlvəi·nŏs). 1857. [L., cushion, pillow.] *Bot.* Any cushion-like swelling or expansion of a stem or petiole; *esp.* one forming a special organ for movement of some leaves.

Puma (piū·mă). 1777. [– Sp. *puma* – Quechua *puma.*] A large American feline quadruped, *Felis concolor*, also called COUGAR. **b.** The flesh of this animal 1845.

Pumice (pɒ·mis), *sb.* [In XV *pomys* – OFr. *pomis* – L. dial. *pomic-*, var. of *pumic-*, nom. *pumex*; cf. POUNCE *sb.*[2]; in XVI assim. to L. form.] **1. a.** A light kind of lava, usu. consisting of obsidian made spongy or porous by the escape of steam or gas during the process of cooling. **b.** with *pl.* A piece of this 1483. **c.** As a material used for smoothing or polishing (parchment, etc.), or removing stains; as an absorbent of ink, moisture, etc.; as proverbial for its dryness. late ME. **2.** *attrib.* Consisting of or resembling pumice 1592. Hence **Pu·mice** *v. trans.* to rub, smooth, polish, clean with p. **Pu·miced** *ppl. a.* rubbed smooth with pumice; also, applied to a horse's hoof that has become spongy from disease.

Pumiceous (piumi·ʃəs), *a.* 1676. [f. L. *pumiceus* (f. *pumex, pumic-* pumice) + -OUS.] Consisting of pumice; having the character or texture of pumice.

Pumice-stone (pɒ·mis,stoᵘn, pɒ·mistoᵘn), *sb.* 1550. = PUMICE *sb.* Hence **Pu·mice-stone** *v. trans.* = PUMICE *v.*

Pummel (pɒ·m'l), *v.* 1548. [Alteration of POMMEL *v.*] *trans.* To beat or strike repeatedly, esp. with the fist; to pound, thump. Also *intr.*

Pump (pɒmp), *sb.*[1] late ME. [In earliest use naut.; corresp. to late MDu. *pompe* wood or metal pipe, stone conduit, Du. *pomp* ship's pump, LG. *pump(e*, whence early mod. G. *pumpe* (XVI), Sw. *pump*, Da. *pompe*, Fr. *pompe* (XVI); the evidence is inadequate to decide whether the word was earlier in Eng. or in LG. The coexistence of synon. Eng. †*plump* (XV–XVII), G. dial. *plumpe, plumpfe*, and Cat., Sp., Pg. *bomba*, suggests a series of more or less independent imit. formations.] **I.** A mechanical device, commonly consisting of a tube or cylinder, in which a piston, sucker, or plunger is moved up and down by means of a rod and lever, so as to raise water by lifting, suction, or pressure, the movement of the water being regulated by a suitable arrangement of valves or clacks; now, a generic term for a great variety of machines and mechanical devices for the raising or moving of liquids, compressing or rarefying of gases, etc. **b.** *fig.* or *allus.* 1602. **c.** As employed in medical treatment, esp. at a place where a mineral spring is used; cf. PUMP-ROOM, etc. 1631. **d.** *transf.* Applied to the heart, the sucker or proboscis of an insect, the lachrymal glands 1796.

Pumps are variously qualified according to the principle of action, manner of construction, means of operating, purpose, etc., as *force, suction p.*;

centrifugal, centripetal, chain-, rotary p.; hand-, steam-p.; air-, beer-, bicycle-, feed-, oil-, stomach-p., etc.

II. [from the vb.] **1.** An act of pumping; a stroke of the pump. Also *transf.* 1676. **2. a.** An attempt at extracting information from any one by skilful questioning. **b.** One who is clever at this. 1741.

attrib. and *Comb.* as *p.-gear, -tube, -valve,* etc.; also **p.-brake,** the handle of a (ship's) p., esp. one having a transverse bar for several persons to work at it; **-house,** *(a)* the p.-room of a spa; *(b)* a place in which pumps are made; *(c)* a pumping station; **-rod,** a rod connecting the piston or plunger of a p. with the motive power; in mines a heavy iron or wooden beam or system of beams; **-stock,** the body of a p.

Pump (pɒmp), *sb.*[2] 1555. [Of unkn. origin.] A kind of light shoe; a slipper for indoor wear; now *spec.*, a light, low-heeled shoe, usu. of patent leather and without fastening, worn with evening dress and for dancing.

Pump (pɒmp), *v.* 1508. [f. PUMP *sb.*[1]] **I.** Literal senses. **1.** *intr.* To work a pump (in early use, always a ship's pump); to raise or move water or other fluid by means of a pump. **2.** *trans.* To raise or remove (water or other fluid) by means of a pump. Chiefly with *out, up.* 1530. **3.** To free from water, etc. by means of a pump or pumps. Said simply in ref. to a ship; of other things with *dry, empty,* etc. 1650. †**4.** To put (any one) under a stream of water from a pump –1840. **5.** *To p. up*: to inflate (a pneumatic tyre, or the like) by pumping air into it 1892.

3. They pumped the well dry 1890. 4. P. him soundly, impudent fellow! SHADWELL.

II. Transferred and *fig.* senses. **1.** To draw or force up or out, in a manner likened to the working of a pump; to move up, draw out, pour forth, or eject; said of the shedding of tears, the motion of the blood, the firing of projectiles from a gun (esp. a machine-gun), etc. Also *absol.* or *intr.* 1604. **2.** *trans.* To subject (a person or thing) to a process likened to pumping, with the object of extracting something; to obtain something by persistent effort; also, to drain, exhaust 1610. **b.** *spec.* To subject (a person) to such a process in order to elicit information; to ply with questions in an artful or persistent manner 1656. **3.** To extract, raise, or bring forth by persistent or factitious effort or art 1663. **b.** To elicit (information, etc.) by such means. Const. *out of* a person. 1633. **4.** *intr.* To labour or strive **a.** *for* the obtaining of something 1633; **b.** for the eliciting of information 1669. **5.** *trans.* and *intr.* To work with action like that of the handle or piston of a pump 1803. **6.** *trans.* To put completely out of breath from excessive exertion. Also with *out*. Usu. *pass.* 1858. **7.** *intr.* Of the mercury in a barometer: To rise and fall instantaneously in the tube as the result of sudden local alterations of pressure or of mechanical disturbance 1875.

1. *absol.* Our men were exposed to fearful odds, especially with two quick-firers pumping at them 1899. 2. b. I am going to p. Mr. Bentley for designs H. WALPOLE.

Comb. Pump- is used to qualify names of mechanical contrivances in which an essential part moves out and in, like the plunger of a force-pump, as *p.-cylinder, -screw,* etc. Hence **Pu·mpage,** the work done at pumping, the quantity pumped. **Pu·mper,** one who or that which pumps or works a pump; *U.S.* an oil well from which the oil is pumped, as dist. from a natural spring.

‖**Pumpernickel** (pu·mpəɹnik'l). 1756. [G., transf. use of earlier 'lout', 'stinker' (1628), f. *pumpe(r)n* pedere + *Nickel* Nicholas.] Bread made from coarsely ground unbolted rye; wholemeal rye bread: associated esp. with Westphalia.

Pu·mp-ha:ndle, *sb.* 1794. The handle by which a pump, esp. the ordinary hand- or house-pump, is worked. **b.** *attrib.*, as in *p. movement,* etc. 1820. Hence **Pu·mp-handle** *v. trans.* (*colloq.*), to shake (a person's hand, or a person by the hand) as if working a p.

Pu·mping, *vbl. sb.* 1598. [f. PUMP *v.* + -ING[1].] The action of PUMP *v.*

attrib. and *Comb.*, as *p.-well*; esp. in ref. to the machinery used in raising or moving water in mines and waterworks, air in refrigerators, etc., as *p.-engine, -station,* etc.

Pumpkin (pɒ·mᵖkin). Also (*U.S.*) **punkin.** 1647. [Altered f. *pumpion* (see POMPION), with the ending conformed to the suffix -KIN.] **1.** The large fruit of a cucurbitaceous plant (*Cucurbita pepo*), egg-shaped or nearly globular with flattened ends; cultivated for the fleshy edible layer next the rind, used for pies, and as a food for cattle. **b.** The plant producing this fruit. Also called *p.-vine.* 1698. **2.** *fig.* **a.** A stupid self-important person 1830. **b.** *U.S. slang.* A person or matter of importance; esp. in phr. *some pumpkins* 1848.

2. b. Afore I left the settlements I know'd a white gal, and she was some punkins 1848.

Comb. **p.-pie,** a pie of which the p. is a chief ingredient; in U.S. considered especially appropriate to Thanksgiving day. Hence **Pumpkinifica·tion,** suggested by the travesty (ascribed to Seneca) of the apotheosis of the emperor Claudius, under the title of ἀποκολοκύντωσις transformation into a p.

Pu·mpkin-seed. 1781. **a.** The flattish oval seed of the pumpkin. **b.** A fresh-water fish of N. America, *Lepomis gibbosus*, the sun-fish, pond-perch 1889.

Pu·mp-room. 1742. A room or building where a pump is worked; *spec.* a place at a spa where the medicinal water is dispensed for drinking, etc.

Pu·mp-well. 1769. **a.** The well of a ship, in which the pumps work. **b.** A well having a pump combined with it 1812.

Pun (pɒn), *sb.* 1662. [prob. one of a group of clipped words which became fashionable in Restoration times (cf. CIT, MOB *sb.*[1], PUNCH *sb.*[4]); app. short for †*pundigrion*, which occurs with †*punnet* and *quibble* in 1676, and may be a fanciful alt. of PUNCTILIO.] The use of a word in such a way as to suggest two or more meanings, or the use of two or more words of the same sound with different meaning, so as to produce a humorous effect; a play on words. Also *attrib.*

Laud. . turned out Archy, the King's fool, for a p. [viz. for saying as grace 'Great praise be to God, and little Laud to the devil', or words to that effect] D'ISRAELI. Hence **Punno·logy,** the subject or study of puns.

Pun (pɒn), *v.*[1] 1670. [Goes with PUN *sb.*] **1.** *intr.* To make puns; to play on words. **2.** *trans.* To bring or drive by punning 1711.

1. He that would p. would pick a Pocket 1729. 2. The Sinner was punned into Repentance ADDISON.

Pun, *v.*[2] 1559. [Early and dial. var. of POUND *v.*[1]] **1.** *trans.* = POUND *v.*[1] in various senses. **2.** *spec.* (in techn. use). To consolidate by pounding or ramming down (as earth or rubble, in making a roadway, etc.) 1838. **b.** To work *up* to a proper consistency with a punner 1825.

‖**Puna** (pū·nă). 1613. [Peruv., in sense 1.] **1.** A high bleak plateau in the Peruvian Andes. **2.** Difficulty of breathing arising from a too rarefied atmosphere; mountain sickness 1842.

Punch (pɒnʃ), *sb.*[1] 1462. [Shortening of PUNCHEON[1], if not f. PUNCH *v.*; partly synon. with POUNCE *sb.*[1]] **1.** An instrument or tool for pricking, piercing, or making a hole in anything; also for enlarging a hole already made, driving a bolt, etc. out of a hole (*starting p.*), or forcing a nail beneath the surface after it has been driven (*driving p.*) 1505. **2.** A tool or machine for impressing a design or stamping a die upon or into some material; in *Coining* and *Die-sinking*, a hardened steel cameo for forming a die; in *Type-founding*, a steel die having a letter cut in relief on its face, for making the intaglio impression in the copper matrix from which types are cast; in *Plastic Art*, a rod, handle, or wheel-rim having a figure or pattern upon it in relief for impressing a design on clay, etc. 1628. **3.** A post supporting the roof in a coal-mine 1462. **4.** *Hydraulic Engin.* A lengthening block or extension piece placed on a pile that has been driven too low to be reached by the ram; a dolly 1875.

1. **Bell-p.,** a conductor's or ticket p. having a signal bell which announces the punching of a ticket; **cold-p.,** a p. used for perforating cold metal; **ratchet-p.,** a screw punching machine operated by a lever, pawl, and ratchet-wheel; etc.

Punch (pɒnʃ), *sb.*[2] late ME. [f. PUNCH *v.*] An act of punching; a thrusting blow, now usu. one delivered with the fist; also (*obs.* or *dial.*) a kick. **b.** Force, vigour (orig. *U.S.*) 1911.

Punch (pɒnʃ), *sb.*[3] 1632. [Stated by Fryer ('Account of East India', 1698) to be the Marathi and Hindi *pānch* (Skr. *pañchan* five), so named from the five ingredients of the drink; but the mod. pronunc. descends from earlier (punʃ) which is not a normal repr. of *ā* or *a* of the Indian word *pānch, panch-* (in comps.).] **1.** A beverage now usu. composed of wine or spirits mixed with hot water or milk and flavoured with sugar, lemons, and some spice or cordial. Usu. qualified as *brandy, gin, rum, tea, whisky,* etc. *p.* **2.** With *a* and *pl.* **a.** A bowl or drink of punch. **b.** A party at which punch is drunk. 1682.

Punch (pɒnʃ), *sb.*[4] and *a.* Now chiefly *dial.* 1669. [Shortening of PUNCHINELLO.] **A.** *sb.* †**1.** A short fat man, or anything short and thick –1836. **2.** One of a breed of heavy draught horses (in full *Suffolk Punches*), characterized by a short and very thick-set body and neck, and short legs 1813. **B.** *adj.* Short and thick, stout. Now only *dial.* Said esp. of horses. 1679.

Punch (pɒnʃ), *sb.*[5] 1709. [Shortening of PUNCHINELLO.] **1.** Name of a grotesque hump-backed figure in the puppet-show called Punch and Judy. Also *attrib.* in *P. and Judy show*, etc. **2.** The title of a comic weekly journal published in London, of which 'Mr. P.' is the assumed editor. Also *attrib.* 1841.

1. Phr. *As pleased, as proud as P.*

Punch (pɒnʃ), *v.* late ME. [var. of POUNCE *v.*[1]] **I.** †**1.** *trans.* = POUNCE *v.*[1] III. 1. –1664. **2.** To poke or prod, esp. with a stick or other blunt instrument. Now *U.S.* and *Colonial*: To drive cattle (by prodding them on). late ME. **b.** To put *out* or stir *up* by punching or poking 1863. **3.** To deliver a sharp blow or forward thrust at; *esp.* to strike with the closed fist; to beat, thump 1530. **b.** To strike with the foot; to kick. *n. dial.* 1538. **II. 1.** To pierce or cut (anything) in the manner of a punch, so as to make a hole or holes in or through it; to perforate (a plate of metal, a sheet of cloth or paper, etc.) 1594. **b.** With the hole as obj. 1677. **c.** To take *out* (a piece) by punching 1827. **2.** *intr.* To penetrate, pierce, or cut (as a punch) 1683.

1. My Annointed body By thee was punched full of holes SHAKS. To p. a railway ticket (*mod.*).

Punch-ball: see PUNCHING-*ball*.

Pu·nch-bowl. 1692. [f. PUNCH *sb.*[3] + BOWL *sb.*[1]] **1.** A bowl in which the ingredients of punch are mixed, and from which it is served with a ladle. **2.** *attrib.* Resembling a punch-bowl. Hence *sb.* A round deep hollow between hills or in a hill-side. 1855.

Puncheon[1] (pɒ·nʃən). [In XIV *pons(y)on, ponchon* – OFr. *poinson, po(i)nchon* (mod. *poinçon*) :– Rom. **punctio, -on-*, f. Rom. **punctiare* prick, punch.] **I. 1.** A pointed tool for piercing; a bodkin. †**b.** A graving tool, a burin. late ME. **2.** = PUNCH *sb.*[1] 2. Now *rare* or *Obs.* 1504. **II.** In building and carpentry. **1.** A short, upright piece of timber in a wooden framing which serves to stiffen one or more long timbers or to support or transmit a load; a supporting post; a post supporting the roof in a coal-mine 1466. **2.** A piece of timber with one face roughly dressed, or a split trunk, used for flooring and rough building. *U.S.* 1807.

Puncheon[2] (pɒ·nʃən). Now *rare* exc. *Hist.* 1479. [Identical in form, in both OFr. and Eng., with prec., but if it is the same word the sense-development is obscure.] A large cask for liquids, fish, etc.; *spec.* one of a definite capacity, varying for different liquids and commodities.

Puncher (pɒ·nʃəɹ). 1681. [f. PUNCH *v.*[1] + -ER[1].] One who or that which punches; an instrument for doing this. **b.** *U.S.* Short for Cow-*p.* 1894.

Punchinello (pɒnʃine·lo). Also **polichinello.** 1666. [– Neapolitan dial. *Polecenella* (XVII), in literary It. *Pulcinella*, perh. based on dim. of *pollecena* young of the turkey-cock (to the hooked beak of which the nose of the mask of Punch bears some resemblance), f. *pulcino* chicken :– Rom. **pullicinus*, f. L. *pullus* (see PULLET). The forms in *Pun-* appear to have resulted from assim. of *l* to the following *n.*] **1.** Name of the principal character in a puppet-show of Italian origin, the prototype of Punch; hence applied to the show; sometimes to a living performer. **2.** *transf.* Applied to any person, animal, or thing, thought to resemble the puppet, esp. in being short and stout. (Cf. PUNCH *sb.*[4]) 1669.

2. His gun, which, from the shortness and bigness, they do call P. PEPYS.

Punching, *vbl. sb.* 1440. [-ING[1].] The action of PUNCH *vb.*

Comb.: **P.-ball,** an inflated ball held in position by elastic bands or supported on a flexible rod, which is punched by the fists as an athletic exercise (also *punch-ball*).

Punchy (pʊ·nʃi), *a.* 1791. [f. PUNCH *sb.*[4] + -Y[1].] Short and stout, squat, stumpy.

Punctate (pʊ·ŋkteˡt), *a.* 1760. [f. L. *punctum* POINT *sb.*[1] + -ATE[2].] **1.** *Nat. Hist.* and *Path.* Marked or studded with points, dots, spots, or (esp.) depressions resembling punctures; of the nature of or characterized by such markings. **2.** *Path.* Having or coming to a definite point 1899. So **Pu·nctated** *a.* (in sense 1).

Punctation (pʊŋktēˡ·ʃən). 1617. [In sense 1 – med.L. *punctatio* (XIII), f. *punctare* (*Gram.*); in sense 2 f. prec. + -ION.] **1.** †**a.** = PUNCTUATION 3, 3 b. –1748. **2.** *Nat. Hist.*, etc. The action of marking or fact of being marked with points or dots; the condition of being punctate; also *concr.* one, or a series, of such dots 1852. ‖**3.** [repr. G. *punktation.*] A laying down of points; a stipulation; a contract or agreement 1864.

Punctiform (pʊ·ŋktifǭɹm), *a.* 1822. [f. L. *punctum* point; see -FORM.] *Nat. Hist.*, etc. **1.** Having the form of a puncture, point, or dot. **2.** Punctate: esp. in pathology, of eruptions, etc. 1839.

Punctilio (pʊŋkti·lio). 1596. [– It. *puntiglio*, Sp. *puntillo*, dim. of *punto* POINT *sb.*[1]; with later assim. to L. *punctum*.] †**1.** A small or fine point or mark, esp. one of those on a dial (*rare*) –1599. †**2.** A minute point, detail, or particular; a jot; a trifle –1815. **3.** A minute detail of action or conduct; a nice point of behaviour, ceremony, or honour; a petty formality 1599. **b.** (without *pl.*) Petty formality in behaviour; punctiliousness 1596.

1. He shall finde the Puntilio of his honour blunted 1596. **2.** When one of the parties..will not..abate a single p. BURKE. **3.** The Bishop stood upon his punctilios 1626. **b.** The preliminaries had been conducted with proper p. 1820.

Punctilious (pʊŋkti·liəs), *a.* 1634. [– Fr. *pointilleux*, f. *pointille* – It. *puntiglio*; see prec., -OUS.] Attentive to punctilios; strictly observant of nice points or details of action or behaviour.

The p. honour of a Spanish gentleman has passed into a byeword 1858. Hence **Puncti·liously** *adv.*, **-ness.**

Punctist (pʊ·ŋktist). 1859. [f. L. *punctum* POINT *sb.*[1] + -IST.] One who holds the vowel-points in the Hebrew Scriptures to be authoritative.

Punctual (pʊ·ŋktiuăl, -tʃuăl), *a.* (*sb.*) late ME. [– med.L. *punctualis*, f. L. *punctum* POINT *sb.*[1]; see -AL[1]. Cf. Fr. *ponctuel.*] †**I.** *Surg.* **a.** Of the nature of a point or puncture. **b.** Used for making punctures, sharp-pointed. –1597. **II. 1.** Of, pertaining to, or made by, a point or dot; of or belonging to punctuation (*rare*) 1609. **b.** *Geom.* Of or pertaining to a point: as *p. co-ordinates*, the co-ordinates of a point. †**2.** Like a point or speck; small, minute –1667.

2. This opacous Earth, this p. spot MILT.

III. †Bearing directly on the point; to the point, apposite, apt –1642. **b.** Express, direct; explicit, definite (*arch.*) 1615.

b. A plain and p. testimony BENTLEY.

IV. 1. Exact in every point; precise, accurate. Now *rare* or *arch.* 1620. **b.** Of time or date; Exact. Now *rare* or *arch.* 1639. **c.** Exactly or aptly timed; timely (*rare*) 1611. **d.** Of or belonging to a precise place (*rare*) 1805. †**2.** Dealing with a matter point by point; minute, detailed –1772.

1. The p. accuracy of our statement 1852. **2.** A p. relation of all the circumstances HOWELL.

V. 1. (Of persons, or their actions, etc.) Attentive to, or insisting upon, points or details of conduct; punctilious 1598. **2.** *spec.* Exactly observant of an appointed time; up to time, in good time; not late 1675.

1. So much on p. niceties they stand 1725. His p. discharge of his duties FROUDE. **2.** The undeviating and p. sun COWPER. Hence **Pu·nctual-ly** *adv.*, **-ness** (now *rare*).

†**Pu·nctualist.** 1641. [f. prec. + -IST.] One who discusses or treats of points of conduct or ceremony MILT.

Punctuality (pʊŋktiuˌæ·lĭti, -tʃu-). 1620. [f. PUNCTUAL + -ITY; cf. med.L. *punctualitas*, Fr. *ponctualité.*] **1.** The quality or character of being punctual (in various senses); an instance of this. *esp.* **2.** Exact observance of an appointed time; the fact or habit of being in good time 1777.

Punctuate (pʊ·ŋktiuˌeˡt, -tʃuˌeˡt), *v.* 1818. [– *punctuat-*, pa. ppl. stem of med.L. *punctuare* prick, point, etc., f. L. *punctum* POINT *sb.*[1] Cf. Fr. *ponctuer.*] **1.** *Nat. Hist.* To mark with points or dots, esp. with small depressions resembling punctures (*rare*). **2.** To insert the punctuation-marks in (a sentence, etc.); to mark or divide with points or stops. Also *absol.* 1818. **b.** *fig.* To interrupt at intervals (as a speech) by exclamations, etc. 1882. **3.** To give point to; to emphasize, accentuate 1883.

2. b. Mr. Gladstone's speech was..punctuated by cheers 1892.

Pu·nctuated, *ppl. a.* 1818. [f. prec. + -ED[1].] **1.** = PUNCTATE 1. **2.** Having the punctuation marks inserted 1841.

Punctuation (pʊŋktiuˌēˡ·ʃən, -tʃu-). 1539. [– med.L. *punctuatio, -on-*, f. *punctuare*; see PUNCTUATE *v.*, -ION.] †**1.** The pointing of the psalms; the pause at the mediation –1782. **2.** = POINTING *vbl. sb.* 1 b. 1659. **3.** The practice, art, method, or system of inserting points or 'stops' to aid the sense, in writing or printing; division into sentences, clauses, etc. by means of points or stops 1661. **b.** *transf.* Observance of the pauses, as indicated by the points or stops, in reading or speaking 1807.

3. On the p. of this..verse [Rom. 9:5] a great controversy has arisen FARRAR. *attrib.* as *p. mark*, etc.

Punctuative (pʊ·ŋktiuˌĕtiv), *a.* 1855. [f. PUNCTUATE *v.* + -IVE.] Of, pertaining to, or serving for punctuation.

Punctuator (pʊ·ŋktiuˌēˡtəɹ). 1659. [– med.L. *punctuator*, f. *punctuat-*; see PUNCTUATE *v.*, -OR 2.] **1.** *Heb. Gram.* One who inserts the vowel (and other) points in writing. **2.** One who inserts the stops in writing or printing 1846.

Punctulate (pʊ·ŋktiŭlĕt), *a.* 1847. [f. next + -ATE[2].] *Nat. Hist.* Marked or studded with punctules; minutely punctate. So **Pu·nctulated** *ppl. a.* **Punctula·tion,** the condition of being p.; also *concr.* a number or mass of punctules.

Punctule (pʊ·ŋktiul). 1640. [– L. *punctulum*, dim. of *punctum* point.] A small point. *Nat. Hist.*, etc., a small punctum.

‖**Punctum** (pʊ·ŋktŏm). *Pl.* **-ta.** 1590. [L., orig. neut. of *punctus*, pa. pple. of *pungere* prick.] †**1.** A point, in various fig. senses –1683. **2.** *Nat. Hist.* and *Path.* A minute rounded mark or visible object; a speck, dot; a minute rounded spot of colour, or of elevation or depression (esp. the latter) upon a surface 1665. **3.** In mediæval music: An inflexion used in singing collects, etc.; a grave accent denoting a descending note; a square note 1853.

2. *P. lachrymale* (also *lachrymal p.*, or simply *p.*), the minute orifice of each of the two lachrymal canals at the corner of the eye. *P. saliens* (cf. τοῦτο δὲ τὸ σημεῖον πηδᾷ, Aristotle), the first trace of the heart in an embryo, appearing as a pulsating point or speck.

Puncturation (pʊŋktiŭrēˡ·ʃən). 1733. [f. PUNCTURE *v.* + -ATION.] **1.** The action or operation of puncturing (*rare*). **2.** *Nat. Hist.* = PUNCTUATION 2. 1890.

Puncture (pʊ·ŋktiŭɹ, -tʃəɹ), *sb.* late ME. [– L. *punctura*, f. *punct-*, pa. ppl. stem of *pungere* prick; see -URE.] **1.** An act, or the action, of pricking; a prick; perforation; in recent use *spec.* an accidental perforation of a pneumatic tyre. **2.** A mark, hole, or wound made by pricking 1595.

Pu·ncture, *v.* 1699. [f. prec.] **1.** *trans.* To subject to puncture; to prick; to perforate; esp. in *Surgery*. **b.** *spec.* To mark (the skin) with punctures; to tattoo 1784. **c.** *Nat. Hist.* To mark with spots or dots resembling punctures: chiefly in *pa. pple.* 1847. **2.** To make (a hole, etc.) by pricking 1831. **3.** *pass.* and *intr.* or *absol.* To get a puncture; said of a pneumatic tyre, or *transf.* of the cycle or rider. (*colloq.*) 1893.

1. I punctured the tire within one mile of the start 1896. Hence **Punctured** (pʊ·ŋktiŭɹ'd, -tʃəɹd), *ppl. a.* pricked, pierced, perforated; made by puncturing; composed of punctures.

‖**Pundit** (pʊ·ndit). 1672. [– Hindi *paṇḍit* :– Skr. *paṇḍita* learned, skilled.] A learned Hindu; one versed in Sanskrit and in the philosophy, religion, and jurisprudence of India. **b.** *transf.* A learned expert or teacher (*joc.*) 1816.

Pung (pʊŋ), *sb. U.S.* 1840. [Shortened from *tom-pung*, of Algonquian origin; cf. TOBOGGAN.] A one-horse sleigh or sledge used in New England; also, a toboggan. Hence **Pung** *v. intr.*, to 'coast' on a sleigh, to toboggan.

Pungency (pʊ·ndʒĕnsi). 1649. [f. PUNGENT; see -ENCY.] **1.** The quality or property of pricking; the fact of having a sharp point or points (*rare*) 1656. **2.** The quality of having a pungent smell or taste; such smell or taste itself; a stinging, irritant, or caustic property. Also *fig.* 1649.

2. The air had a perceptible p. upon inspiration 1856.

Pungent (pʊ·ndʒĕnt), *a.* (*sb.*) 1597. [– L. *pungens, -ent-*, pr. pple. of *pungere* prick; see -ENT. Superseded †*poinant*, POIGNANT in several senses.] **1.** Pricking, piercing, sharp-pointed. Now only in *Nat. Hist.* 1601. **2.** *fig.* (of pain or grief). Sharp, keen, acute, poignant; causing or inflicting sharp pain; keenly distressing 1597. **b.** Of appetite or desire: Keen, eager; piercing. Now *rare* or *Obs.* 1710. **3.** Keenly or strongly affecting the mind or feelings (now usu. with allusion to sense 4) 1637. **4.** Affecting the organs of smell or taste (or the skin, etc.) with a sensation resembling that produced by pricking; penetrating and irritant 1668. **5.** as *sb.* (or *absol.*) A pungent substance; an irritant 1822.

1. Terminating in a very sharp-pointed p. leaf 1787. **2.** Intolerably p. grief and sorrow 1684. **3.** A very good and p. sermon PEPYS. A few p. epigrams 1874. **4.** P. radish, biting infant's tongue SHENSTONE. Hence **Pu·ngent-ly** *adv.*, **-ness.**

Punic (piū·nik), *a.* and *sb.* 1533. [– L. *Punicus*, earlier *Pœnicus*, f. *Pœnus*, f. Gr. Φοῖνιξ PHŒNICIAN, Carthaginian; see -IC. Cf. Fr. *punique.*] **A.** *adj.* **1.** Belonging to Carthage; Carthaginian. **b.** †*P. apple* (L. *Punicum malum*), the pomegranate 1601. **c.** Having the character attributed by the Romans to the Carthaginians; treacherous, perfidious 1600. †**2.** Purple 1501–1607.

1. *P. wars*, the three wars between the Romans and Carthaginians waged between B.C. 264 and 146. **c.** *P. faith*: see FAITH *sb.* III. 2; Yes, yes, his faith attesting nations own; 'Tis P. all, and to a proverb known ! 1738.

B. *sb.* †**1.** An inhabitant of Carthage, a Carthaginian –1696. **2.** The Carthaginian tongue, an offshoot of Phœnician and allied to Hebrew 1813.

Puniceous (piuni·ʃiəs), *a.* 1730. [f. L. *puniceus* Punic; also red, purple (f. *Punicus* PUNIC) + -OUS.] Of a bright red, purplish-red, or reddish-yellow colour.

Punish (pʊ·niʃ), *v.* [ME. *punisse, ische* – (O)Fr. *puniss-*, extended stem of *punir* :– L. *punire*, earlier *pœnire*, f. *pœna* PAIN; see -ISH[2].] **1. a.** *trans.* To cause (an offender) to suffer for an offence; to subject to judicial chastisement as retribution or requital, or as a caution against further transgression; to inflict a penalty on. **b.** To inflict a penalty for (something) ME. **c.** *absol.* To inflict punishment. late ME. **2.** *transf.* (*trans.*) To handle severely; to inflict heavy damage, injury, or loss on. Also *absol.* 1812.

1. 'Tis against the Law of Nature, To p. the Innocent HOBBES. **c.** God does not p. that way DE FOE. **2.** We..drank freely—punished his claret 1825. The Oxonian's [bowling] was..severely punished 1883. Hence **Pu·nisher,** one who punishes; *Boxing slang*, a hard hitter; *transf.* a thing that hits one hard, a heavy or severe task.

Punishable (pʊ·niʃăb'l), *a.* 1531. [f. prec. + -ABLE. Cf. (O)Fr. *punissable*, perh. the immediate source.] Liable to punishment;

capable of being punished. **b.** Of an offence: Entailing punishment 1548.

It is a pity these hags are not p. by law FIELDING. **b.** Wherefore emonge the Jewes, onely periury is punyshable 1548. Hence **Punishabi·lity, Pu·nishableness,** the quality of being p. **Pu·nishably** *adv.* in a p. manner or to a p. degree.

Punishment (pɒ·niʃmĕnt). late ME. [– AFr., OFr. *punissement*, f. *punir*; see PUNISH, -MENT.] **1.** The act of punishing or the fact of being punished; also, that which is inflicted as a penalty; a penalty imposed to ensure the application and enforcement of a law. **2.** *slang* and *colloq.* Severe handling; belabouring, mauling; orig. that inflicted by a pugilist upon his opponent; pain, damage, or loss inflicted (without any retributive or judicial character) 1856.

1. We must, wherever we suppose a Law, suppose also some Reward or P. annexed to that Rule LOCKE. **2.** Tom Sayers could not take p. more gaily than they do THACKERAY.

Punition (piuni·ʃən). Now *rare.* late ME. [– (O)Fr. *punition* – L. *punitio, -on-*, f. *punit-*, pa. ppl. stem of *punire* PUNISH; see -ION.] The action of punishing.

Punitive (piū·nitiv), *a.* 1624. [– Fr. *punitif, -ive* or med.L. *punitivus*, f. as prec.; see -IVE.] Awarding, inflicting, or involving punishment; retributive.

A British P. Expedition captured Benin City 1897. Hence **Pu·nitive-ly** *adv.*, **-ness.**

Punitory (piū·nitəri), *a.* 1710. [– med.L. *punitorius*, f. as prec.; see -ORY².] = prec.

Punk[1] (pɒŋk). *Obs.* or *rare arch.* 1596. [Of unkn. origin.] A prostitute, strumpet, harlot.

Punk[2] (pɒŋk). Chiefly *U.S.* 1707. [Of unkn. origin; cf. FUNK *sb.*¹, SPUNK.] **1.** Rotten wood, or a fungus growing on wood, used in a dry state for tinder; touchwood, amadou. **2.** A composition that will smoulder when ignited, used to touch off fireworks 1869. **3.** Chinese incense 1890. Hence **Punk** *a.*, **Pu·nky** *a.* (chiefly *U.S.*), rotten.

‖**Punkah, punka** (pɒ·ŋkă). 1625. [– Hindi *pankhā* fan :– Skr. *pakshaka*, f. *paksha* wing.] **1.** A large fan, usu. made from the leaf of the palmyra. **2.** A large swinging fan made of cloth stretched on a rectangular frame, suspended from the ceiling or rafters, and worked by a cord 1807.

Comb.: **p.-coolie, -wallah,** a native Indian servant who works a p.

Punner[1] (pɒ·nəɹ). Now *rare.* 1689. [f. PUN *v.*¹ + -ER¹.] A punster.

Punner[2] (pɒ·nəɹ). 1611. [f. PUN *v.*² Cf. POUNDER¹.] One who or that which puns or rams earth, etc.; *spec.* a tool for ramming earth about a post, etc. Hence **p.-bar,** a p. and crow-bar combined.

Punnet (pɒ·nĕt). *local.* 1822. [perh. dim. f. *pun*, dial. var. of POUND *sb.*¹; see -ET.] A small round shallow chip basket, used chiefly for fruit or vegetables.

Punster (pɒ·nstəɹ). 1700. [f. PUN *v.*¹ + -STER.] A professed maker of puns; one skilled in punning.

Punt (pɒnt), *sb.*¹ 1500. [In earliest use (E. Anglian) *pontebot, punte boot* – MLG. *punte, punto* (LG. *pünte, pünto*) ferry-boat, mud-boat, corresp. to OE. *punt* (which did not survive), MDu. *ponte* (Du. *pont*) ferry-boat, pontoon – L. *ponto* Gaulish transport vessel (Cæsar), PONTOON.] A flat-bottomed shallow boat, broad and square at both ends; also = PONTOON 2; now *spec.*, a boat of this kind propelled by means of a long pole thrust against the bottom of a river, or shallow water.

attrib. and *Comb.*: **p.-fisher,** one who fishes from a p.; so **-fishing; -gun,** a gun used for shooting water-fowl from a p.; so **-gunner, -gunning; -pole,** the long pole used in propelling a p. Hence **Pu·nter**², one who goes fishing or shooting in a p.; later, one who punts, or manages a p.

Punt, *sb.*² 1845. [Goes w. PUNT *v.*³] *Football* (Rugby). An act of punting; a kick given to the ball dropped from the hands, before it reaches the ground.

Punt, *sb.*³ 1832. [Short for PUNTY, PONTIL, PUNTO¹.] *Glass-making.* = PONTIL.

Punt (pɒnt), *v.*¹ 1706. [– Fr. *ponter*, rel. to *ponte* punt in ombre, player against the bank – Sp. *punto* POINT *sb.*¹] *intr.* At basset, faro, baccarat, etc.: To lay a stake against the bank. **b.** *slang* and *colloq.* To bet upon a horse, etc. 1873.

Punt, *v.*² 1816. [f. PUNT *sb.*¹] **1.** *trans.* To propel (a punt or other boat) by thrusting a pole against the bottom of the river, etc.; to propel or shove off, in the manner of a punt. **b.** *intr.* or *absol.* To propel a punt, or any boat in the manner of a punt 1846. **2.** *trans.* To convey in a punt, or by punting 1853.

Punt, *v.*³ 1845. [prob. spec. use of dial. *punt* push with force, BUNT *v.*² (Northamptonshire, near the border of which Rugby is situated), poss. blending of BUNT *v.*² and PUT *v.*¹] **1.** *Football* (Rugby). *trans.* To kick (the ball), after dropping it from the hands, before it reaches the ground. Also *absol.* **2.** To strike, hit, knock (*rare*) 1886.

Punter[1] (pɒ·ntəɹ). 1706. [f. PUNT *v.*¹ + -ER¹.] **1.** A player who 'punts' or plays against the bank at faro, etc. **2.** *transf.* A small professional backer of horses; also, a gambler in stocks and shares 1873.

Punter[2]: see PUNT *sb.*¹

Punto[1] (pɒ·nto). 1591. [– It. or Sp. *punto* :– L. *punctum* POINT *sb.*¹] †**1.** A small point or detail; a particle, a jot; a moment, instant –1706. †**2.** = PUNCTILIO 3. –1766. †**3.** *Fencing.* A stroke or thrust with the point of the sword or foil –1624. **4.** *Glass-making.* = PONTIL 1839.

3. *P. dritto*, a direct thrust. *P. riverso*, a back-handed thrust; Ah the immortall Passado the P. reuerso, the Hay SHAKS.

Punto[2] (pu·nto). 1728. [– Sp. *punto* point; see prec.] *Card-playing.* The ace of trumps, when the trump suit is diamonds or hearts.

Punty, ponty (pɒ·nti). 1662. [– Fr. *pontil* PONTIL.] **1.** An iron rod used in glass-blowing. **2.** A round hollow made on a glass object to remove the mark made in breaking off the p.-rod; a small circular or oval hollow made as an ornamentation on glass 1884.

Comb., as *p.-mark*; **p.-iron, -rod** = sense 1.

Puny (piū·ni), *a.* and *sb.* 1548. [Phonetic spelling of PUISNE.] **A.** *adj.* †**1.** = PUISNE *a.* 1, 1 b. –1733. †**2.** Raw, inexperienced; that is a novice or tyro –1712. **3.** Of inferior size, force, or importance; minor; petty, weak; diminutive, tiny 1593. **b.** esp. of human beings and animals: Undersized and weakly 1604.

2. 1 *Hen. VI*, IV. vii. 36. **3.** A punie subiect strikes At thy great glory SHAKS. **b.** He was a very P. Man, yet he had often done things beyond the strength of a Giant 1693.

†**B.** *sb.* **1.** A junior pupil or student in a school or university, or in the Inns of Court –1678. **2.** A raw or inexperienced person; a novice, tyro –1688. **3.** A person of small account; a subordinate –1711.

Pup (pɒp), *sb.*¹ 1773. [Back-formation from PUPPY, as if this were a dim. in -Y⁶.] **1.** A young dog, a whelp, a young puppy. **2.** Applied to the young of the fur seal 1858.

1. Phr. *To sell* (any one) *a p.*, to swindle, esp. by selling something on its prospective value.

Pup, *sb.*² 1871. *College slang.* Abbrev. of PUPIL, joc. associated with prec.

Pup, *v.* 1725. [Shortened f. PUPPY *v.*] *trans.* and *intr.* To bring forth pups, to litter.

‖**Pupa** (piū·pă). Pl. **-æ.** 1815. [mod.L. (Linn., 1758), a use of L. *pupa* girl, doll.] **1.** An insect in the third and usu. quiescent state (of complete metamorphosis), preceding that of the imago; a chrysalis. **b.** A stage in the development of some other invertebrates, as cirripeds, holothurians 1877. **2.** *Conch.* Name of a genus of pulmonate molluscs; a chrysalis-shell.

attrib.: **p.-case,** the horny case of a p. or chrysalis. Hence **Pu·pal** *a.* of, pertaining to, or characteristic of a p; nymphal. **Pu·pate** *v. intr.* to become a p. or chrysalis. **Pupa·tion,** the formation of the p.

‖**Puparium** (piupēᵊ·riɒ̆m). 1815. [mod.L., f. prec. + -ARIUM, after *herbarium*, etc.] The coarctate pupa of some Diptera and other insects, the case of which is formed by the last larval skin.

Pupigerous (piupi·dʒĕrəs), *a.* 1884. [f. PUPA; see -GEROUS.] Of a larva: Forming a PUPARIUM; having the pupa enclosed within the last larval skin.

Pupil[1] (piū·pĭl). late ME. [– (O)Fr. *pupille* m. and fem. or its source, L. *pupillus, -illa* orphan, ward, secondary dim. (on *pupulus, -ula*) of *pupus* boy, *pupa* girl.] **1.** An orphan who is a minor and hence a ward; in *Civil* and *Sc. Law*, a person below the age of puberty who is under the care of a guardian. **2.** One who is taught by another; a scholar; a disciple 1563.

2. He took pupils to increase his income 1891. *Comb.*: **p.-room** (at Eton), the room in which a tutor takes his pupils; the work done there by a p.

Pupil[2] (piū·pĭl). 1567. [– (O)Fr. *pupille* or L. *pupilla*, secondary dim. of *pupa* girl, doll, pupil of the eye (see prec.).] **1.** The circular opening (appearing as a black spot) in the centre of the iris of the eye, which expands or contracts in regulating the passage of light through it to the retina; the apple of the eye. **2.** *fig.* and *transf.*; in *Entom.* The dark central spot of an ocellus 1599.

Pupil(l)age (piū·pilĕdʒ). 1590. [f. PUPIL¹ + -AGE.] **1.** The condition of being a minor or ward; the period of this; nonage, minority. **2.** The condition or position of being a pupil or scholar 1658.

1. *fig.* Thus the colonies are kept in a state of perpetual pupillage 1777. **2.** In the days of my medical pupillage 1882.

Pupil age. 1596. [f. PUPIL¹ + AGE *sb.*; app. due to erron. analysis of prec.] The age during which one is a pupil; minority.

His Pupill age Man-entred thus, he waxed like a Sea SHAKS.

Pupil(l)arity (piūpilæ·rĭti). 1583. [– (O)Fr. *pupillarité* – med.L. **pupillaritas*, f. L. *pupillaris*; see next, -ITY.] *Civil* and *Sc. Law.* The state of being below the age of puberty; the period of this.

Pupil(l)ary (piū·pilări), *a.*¹ 1611. [– Fr. *pupillaire* or L. *pupillaris*, f. *pupillus, -illa*; see PUPIL¹, -ARY².] **a.** Of or pertaining to a person in pupillarity. **b.** Belonging to a pupil or scholar 1848.

Pu·pil(l)ary, *a.*² 1793. [f. L. *pupilla* PUPIL² + -ARY².] Of or pertaining to the pupil of the eye.

Pupil teacher (piū·pĭl,tī·tʃəɹ). 1838. A boy or girl preparing to be a teacher, who spent part of the period of preliminary education as a teacher in an elementary school under the supervision of the head teacher, and concurrently received general education either from him or in some place of higher education.

‖**Pupipara** (piupi·pără), *sb. pl.* 1874. [mod.L., n. pl. of *pupiparus* bringing forth pupæ (f. *parere* bring forth).] *Entom.* A division of *Diptera* in which the young are born in, or ready to pass into, the pupal state. Hence **Pupi·parous** *a.* of or pertaining to the *P.*; producing or bringing forth young already advanced to the pupal state.

‖**Pupivora** (piupi·vŏră), *sb. pl.* 1836. [mod.L., n. pl. of *pupivorus* devouring pupæ.] *Entom.* A division of hymenopterous insects containing those, such as the Ichneumon flies, which deposit their eggs in the larvæ of other insects. Hence **Pu·pivore,** one of the *P.* **Pupi·vorous** *a.* of or pertaining to the *P.*; devouring the pupæ of other insects; parasitic on pupæ.

Puppet (pɒ·pĕt), *sb.* 1538. [Later f. POPPET.] **1.** A contemptuous term for a person (usu. a woman) 1586. **2.** A figure (usu. small) representing a human being; a child's doll. *Obs.* or *arch.* 1562. **3.** A human figure, with jointed limbs, moved by means of strings or wires; *esp.* one of the figures in a puppet-show 1538. **b.** *fig.* A person whose acts are suggested and controlled by another 1550. †**c.** A living personator in dramatic action; an actor in a pantomime –1668. **4.** A lathe-head 1680.

3. You look like a p. moved by clockwork! ARBUTHNOT. **b.** Charles remained for some while a p. in the hands of Herbert 1867. **c.** *Lear* II. ii. 39.

attrib., as *p.-stage, -theatre*, etc.; **p.-clack** = P.-VALVE. Hence †**Pu·ppet** *v. intr.* to play the p. **Puppetee·r. Pu·ppetish** *a.* (*rare*) pertaining to or of the nature of a p.

Pu·ppet-play:. 1591. **1.** A play or dramatic performance acted by means, or with the aid, of puppets 1599. **2.** The playing or acting of puppets 1591. So **Pu·ppet-play:er,** †a performer in a pantomime; one who manages or exhibits a p.

Puppetry (pɒ·pėtri). 1528. [f. PUPPET *sb.* + -RY.] **1.** Mimic action or representation as of puppets; masquerade, mummery; make-believe; *spec.* applied to idolatrous or superstitious observances. **2.** Puppet-play; debased dramatic action 1613. †**3.** Appearance or dress as of a puppet –1638. **4.** Something compared to a puppet or a set of puppets; *esp.* an unreal character in fiction; a set of such characters 1610.

1. The pupetry in the Church of the Minerva, representing the Nativity EVELYN. **4.** The stage-properties and p. of a Highland romance 1898.

Pu·ppet-show:. 1650. [f. as prec. + SHOW *sb.*] A show, display, or exhibition of puppets; *esp.* a puppet-play.

Pu·ppet-va:lve. Also **poppet-valve.** 1829. [f. as prec. + VALVE; in allusion to its movement.] A disc valve which is opened by being bodily lifted from its seat, not by turning upon a hinge.

Puppy (pɒ·pi), *sb.* 1486. [In XV *popi(e,* corresp. in form to OFr. *popée,* (also mod.) *poupée* doll, lay figure, (contextually) toy, plaything :– Rom. **puppata,* f. **puppa*; see POPPET, -Y[5].] †**1.** A small dog kept as a lady's pet or plaything –1655. **2.** A young dog, a whelp 1591. **b.** A young seal 1890. **3.** Applied to a person as a term of contempt; esp. a vain, empty-headed, impertinent young man; a fop, a coxcomb 1589. **4.** A white bowl or buoy used in the herring-fishery to mark the position of the net nearest the fishing-boat 1890.

1. A foolish woman may..dote upon a p. more than on her gold 1655. **3.** Has no conceit about him like the puppies of our day 1849. Hence **Pu·ppydom,** puppyhood; puppies collectively. **Pu·ppyhood,** the state or time of being a p. **Pu·ppyish** *a.* of the nature or character of a p. (sense 3). **Pu·ppyism,** the character, style, or manners of a p. (sense 3); impertinent conceit, affectation, 'side'.

Puppy (pɒ·pi), *v.* 1589. [f. prec.] *intr.* and *trans.* To bring forth puppies; to whelp, litter; to pup.

Pur-, *prefix.* The usual AFr. form of OFr. *por-, pur-* :– L. *por-, pro-,* prep. and prefix; as in *purchase, purlieu, purloin,* etc.

‖**Purana** (purā·nă). 1696. [Skr. *purāṇá* belonging to former times, f. *purā* formerly.] One of a class of sacred poetical works in Sanskrit, containing the mythology of the Hindus. Hence **Pura·nic** *a.* of or pertaining to the Puranas; also *absol.* as *sb.* a Puranic work or author; a believer in the Puranas.

Purbeck (pɔ̄·ɹbek). 1691. Name of a peninsula on the Dorset coast; in full, Isle of Purbeck; used *attrib.*

P. beds. *Geol.,* the three strata of the P. series, reckoned as the uppermost members of the Oolite formation, or the lowest of the Wealden. **P. marble,** the finer qualities of P. stone. **P. stone,** a hard limestone obtained from P., and used in building and paving.

Purblind (pɔ̄·ɹbləind), *a.* ME. [orig. *pur(e blind,* i.e., *pur(e,* ME. advb. use of PURE (with assim. to PUR-), and BLIND *a.* For the change of sense from 'utterly' to 'partially' cf. PARBOIL.] †**1.** Quite or totally blind –1615. **2.** Of impaired or defective vision: †**a.** Blind of one eye –1617. **b.** Nearsighted 1523. **c.** Partially blind; almost blind; *gen.* dim-sighted 1531. **3.** *fig.* Stupid, obtuse, dull 1533.

1. *L. L. L.* III. i. 181. **3.** Man is such a pur-blind creature, that he cannot unerringly see a day before him 1660. Hence **Purbli·nd** *v. trans.* to make p.; to impair the sight of. **Pu·rblind-ly** *adv.* (*rare*), **-ness.**

Purchasable (pɔ̄·ɹtʃėsăb'l), *a.* 1611. [f. PURCHASE *v.* + -ABLE.] That may be purchased.

Purchase (pɔ̄·ɹtʃės, -ăs), *sb.* ME. [– AFr. *pur-,* OFr. *porchas,* f. the vb.; see next.] **I.** The act or action of purchasing. †**1.** The action of hunting; the chase; the catching or seizing of prey; hence, seizing forcibly; pillage, plunder, robbery, capture –1725. †**2.** The action or process of procuring, obtaining, or acquiring for oneself in any way; acquisition, gain, attainment –1589. **3.** The action of making one's profit or gaining one's sustenance in any way; esp. irregularly, as by begging, or by shifts of any kind; shifting for oneself. late ME. **4.** *Law.* The acquirement of property by one's personal action, as dist. from inheritance 1460. **5.** *spec.* Acquisition by payment of money or an equivalent; buying 1611. **b.** The action or system of buying commissions in the army; payment made for an appointment or promotion in the commissioned ranks 1796. **6.** *fig.* Acquisition at the cost of something immaterial, as effort or suffering, sacrifice 1651.

1. We were bound now upon traffick, and not for p. DE FOE. **3.** His purchas was wel bettre than his rente CHAUCER. **5.** Miss Black's shop, where I wanted to make a p. 1833. **6.** They that pay thus dear for damnation well deserve to enjoy the purchace 1658.

II. That which is purchased or acquired. †**1.** That which is obtained, gained, or acquired; gains, winnings, acquisitions; in later use, chiefly, a prize, or booty, taken by a privateer –1725. **2.** The annual return or rent from land; in the phr. *at so many years' p.,* used in stating the price of land 1584. **3.** That which is purchased or bought 1587. †**b.** A (good, bad, dear, etc.) bargain –1857. †**4.** The purchase-money –1742.

1. A..distressed Widow,..Made prize and p. of his wanton Eye SHAKS. **2.** *fig.* The life of General Walpole would not have been worth half an hour's p. 1893. **3.** *Ham.* V. i. 117. **b.** This might..be thought a dear p. 1812.

III. [f. PURCHASE *v.* III.] **1.** Hold or position for advantageously exerting or applying power; mechanical advantage, leverage, fulcrum 1711. **2.** Any contrivance for increasing applied power; esp. *Naut.* such a device consisting of a rope, pulley, windlass, or the like 1711. **3.** *fig.* A hold or position of advantage for accomplishing something; a means by which one's power or influence is increased 1790.

1. If I could have calculated on a safe p. for my foot TYNDALL.

Purchase (pɔ̄·ɹtʃės, -ăs), *v.* ME. [– AFr. *purchacer,* OFr. *pourchacier* seek to obtain, procure, f. *pur-, por-, pour-* PUR- + *chacier* (mod. *chasser*) CHASE *v.*] **I.** †**1.** *trans.* To try to procure or bring about; to contrive (esp. something evil) *to* or *for* a person –1549. †**2.** *intr.* To exert oneself for the attainment of some object; to endeavour; to strive –1674. †**3.** *trans.* To bring about, cause, effect, produce; to procure, manage –1678.

2. *Timon* III. ii. 52.

II. †**1.** *trans.* To procure for oneself, acquire, get possession of; to gain –1703. **b.** To obtain from a constituted authority (a brief, a licence, etc.); *spec.* in *Law, To p. a writ,* to sue out, to obtain and issue a writ; hence, to commence an action. Now *Hist.* ME. **2.** *spec. Law.* To acquire (property, esp. land) otherwise than by inheritance or descent; occas., to get by conquest in war. *Obs.* or *arch.* ME. **3.** To acquire by the payment of money or its equivalent; to buy. late ME. **b.** *fig.* To acquire at the cost of toil, suffering, danger, or the like; to earn, win; to bring upon oneself, incur (mischief). late ME.

2. His faults in him..Hereditarie, Rather then purchaste SHAKS. **3.** The field which Abraham purchased of the sonnes of Heth *Gen.* 25:10. **b.** Dearly, indeed, do I p. experience! MISS BURNEY.

III. *Naut.* To haul in, draw in (a rope or cable); *spec.* to haul up (the anchor) by means of the capstan; hence, to haul up, hoist, or raise (anything) by the aid of a mechanical power, as the pulley, lever, etc. 1567.

Pu·rchase-mo:ney. 1763. The sum for which anything is or may be purchased.

Purchaser (pɔ̄·ɹtʃėsəɹ). [– AFr. *purchasour,* OFr. *porchaceor,* f. the verb.; see PURCHASE *v.,* -OUR, -ER[2] 3.] †**1.** One who acquires or aims at acquiring possessions –1591. **2.** *Law.* One who acquires land or property in any way other than by inheritance ME. **3.** One who purchases for money; a buyer 1625.

2. If I give land freely to another, he is in the eye of the law a purchasor BLACKSTONE.

‖**Purdah** (pɔ̄·ɹdă). *E. Ind.* 1800. [– Urdu and Pers. *pardah* veil, curtain.] A curtain; *esp.* one serving to screen women from the sight of men or strangers. **b.** As typical of the seclusion of Indian women of rank; hence, the system of such seclusion 1865.

Pure (piūᵊɹ), *a.* (*sb., adv.*) ME. [– (O)Fr. *pur,* fem. *pure* :– L. *purus.*] **I.** In physical sense. **a.** Unmixed; free from admixture or adulteration. **b.** *esp.* Not mixed with, or not having in or upon it, anything that defiles, corrupts, or impairs; unsullied, untainted, clean. **c.** Visibly or optically clear, spotless, stainless. **d.** Of a sound or voice: Free from discordant quality; clear; *spec.* in *Mus.* and *Acoustics,* said of tones that are perfectly in tune: esp. as opp. to *tempered* 1872.

The morning air p. from the city's smoke 1804. The snow was of the purest white 1860. **d.** A perfectly clear and p. tenor 1873.

II. In non-physical or general sense. **1.** Without foreign or extraneous admixture; simple, homogeneous, unmixed, unalloyed. late ME. **b.** Of unmixed descent, pure-blooded 1475. **c.** *Law.* Having no condition annexed; absolute 1536. **d.** Of a subject of study or practice: Restricted to that which essentially belongs to it. (Often denoting the simply theoretical part of a subject, as in *p. mathematics*; opp. to APPLIED 2, MIXED 4.) Also said of a student who confines himself to one subject or branch of a subject. 1641. **e.** *Logic.* Of a proposition or syllogism; opp. to MODAL *a.* 4. 1697. **f.** *Gram.* (*a*) In Greek (*καθαρός*), of a vowel: Preceded by another vowel. Of the stem of a word: Ending in a vowel. Of a consonant (as *s*): Not accompanied by another consonant. (*b*) In Arabic, etc., of a syllable: Ending in a vowel, open. 1650. **2.** Taken by itself, with nothing added; ..and nothing else; mere, simple. Often in phr. *p. and simple,* following the sb. ME. **b.** Nothing short of.., absolute, sheer, utter, complete ME.

1. An act of P. Thought 1864. *P. naturals*: see NATURAL *sb.* II. 2. **b.** That horse..is very nearly a p. Arab 1866. **d.** He is a p. physicist; he does not know chemistry 1909. **2.** Alas Sir, we did it for p. need SHAKS. P. procrastination and dilatoriness 1861. **b.** A lot of p. nonsense 1902.

III. Free from corruption or defilement. **1.** Unadulterated, uncorrupted, uncontaminated; conforming accurately to a standard of quality or style; faultless, correct ME. **2.** Free from moral defilement or corruption; guiltless, innocent; guileless, sincere. Often absol., *the p.* (*sc.* persons). ME. **3.** Sexually undefiled; chaste. late ME. **4.** Free from ceremonial defilement; fit for sacred service or use 1611.

1. In suche places..as the pureste englyshe is spoken 1540. **2.** Blessed are the p. in herte TINDALE *Matt.* 5:8.

IV. *slang* or *colloq.* A general term of appreciation: Fine, excellent, capital, nice, splendid. Now *rare* or *Obs.* 1675. **b.** In conjunction with another adj.: *P. and..* = nice and.., fine and..; excellently; thoroughly. Now *dial.* 1742.

Is it not p. that we shall meet in a fortnight? 1734.

B. *sb.* (or *absol.*). **1.** That which is pure; purity. *poet.* 1625. **2.** A 'pure' physician or surgeon (see II. 1 d). *Med. colloq.* 1827.

1. Her eies shrowd pitie, pietie, and p. LODGE.

C. *adv.* **1.** Absolutely, entirely, thoroughly, quite. Now *dial.* or *Obs.* ME. **2.** Purely; simply, merely; rightly; chastely. *poet. rare.* 1460. **3.** Qualifying an adj. of colour (chiefly *white*): Purely, with no admixture ME.

2. For his sake, Did I expose my selfe (p. for his loue) Into the danger SHAKS. Hence **Pu·re-ly** *adv.,* **-ness.**

Pure, *v.* ME. [– OFr. *purer* – med.L. *purare* refine (ore, metal), f. L. *purus* PURE *a.*] †*trans.* To make pure; to cleanse, purify, refine (*lit.* and *fig.*) –1635. **b.** *Tanning.* To cleanse (hides) by steeping them in a bate or alkaline lye 1883. Hence †**Pured** *ppl. a.* purified, cleansed; refined; of fur: trimmed or cut down so as to show one colour only.

‖**Purée** (püre). 1824. [(O)Fr., in form fem. pa. pple. of *purer*; see prec.] A broth or soup made of vegetables, meat, or fish, boiled to a pulp and passed through a sieve.

Purfle (pɔ̄·ɹf'l), *sb.* late ME. [– OFr. *porfil,* f. *porfiler*; see next.] A border; *esp.* the embroidered border or edge of a garment.

Purfle (pɔ̄·ɹf'l), *v.* ME. [– OFr. *purfiler* – Rom. **profilare,* f. *pro* PRO-[1] + L. *filum* thread. Cf. PROFILE *v.*] **1.** To border; *esp.* to adorn (a robe) with a border of thread work or embroidery; to trim with gold or silver lace, pearls, fur, etc. *arch.* **b.** *intr.* or *absol.* To do purfling 1890. †**2.** *trans.* To give to (leaves, flowers, etc.) a border or edge of a particular kind; in *pa. pple.*, denoting the outline, contour, or distinctive colouring of the edge –1640. **3. a.** *Arch.* To ornament (the edge or ridge of any structure) *with* crockets, etc. 1849. **b.** To adorn (the back or belly of a violin, etc.) with a border of inlaid work 1848. **4.** To adorn, ornament, beautify 1470.

1. A robe of scarlet, open before, and purfled with minever 1840. Hence **Purfled** (pɒ·ɹfl'd) *ppl. a.* in senses of the vb.; *transf.* of a person: decorated with purfling; *Arch.*, etc. ornamented in a manner resembling drapery, embroidery, or lace-work. **Pu·rfling** *vbl. sb.*, the action of the vb.; (*b*) *Arch.* the ornamentation of an edge or ridge; (*c*) the inlaid bordering of the backs and bellies of violins, etc.

Purgation (pɒɹgēⁱ·ʃən). late ME. [– (O)Fr. *purgation* or L. *purgatio, -on-*, f. *purgat-*, pa. ppl. stem of *purgare* PURGE *v.*; see -ION.] The action of purging. **1.** The clearing away of impurities or extraneous matter; purification. **b.** *spec.* The discharge of waste matter from the body; now only the evacuation of the bowels, esp. by means of a cathartic; the administration of cathartics; purging. †**c.** Menstruation; *pl.* catamenia –1737. **2.** Ceremonial or ritual cleansing from defilement. late ME. **3.** Moral or spiritual cleansing; *spec.* in *R. C. Ch.*, the purification of the soul in purgatory. late ME. **4.** The action of clearing oneself from the accusation or suspicion of crime or guilt. Now *Hist.* late ME.

2. Even the slaughter of enemies required a solemn p. among the Jews BLACKSTONE. **4.** If any man doubt that, let him put mee to my p. SHAKS. *Canonical p.*, the affirmation on oath of his innocence by the accused in a spiritual court, confirmed by the oaths of several of his peers. *Vulgar p.*, a test by the ordeal of fire or water, or by wager of battle.

Purgative (pō·ɹgătiv), *a.* and *sb.* late ME. [– (O)Fr. *purgatif, -ive* or late L. *purgativus*, f. as prec.; see -IVE.] **A.** *adj.* Having the quality of purging; cathartic; cleansing or freeing from defilement. **B.** *sb.* A cathartic; any cleansing or purifying agent or means 1626. Hence **Pu·rgative-ly** *adv.*, **-ness.**

Purgatorial (pōɹgătō̆ᵊ·riăl), *a.* 1450. [f. late L. *purgatorius* cleansing, in med.L. spec. *Theol.*, (f. as prec. + *-orius* -ORY²) + -AL¹.] Of a spiritually purifying quality; also, of, pertaining to, or of the nature of purgatory.

Purgatorian (pōɹgătōᵊ·riăn), *a.* and *sb. rare.* 1550. [In A f. as prec. + -AN; in B f. next + -AN.] **A.** *adj.* Of, pertaining to, or relating to purgatory; purgatorial 1624. **B.** *sb.* A believer in purgatory 1550.

Purgatory (pō̆·ɹgătəri), *sb.* ME. [– AFr. *purgatorie*, (O)Fr. *purgatoire* – med.L. *purgatorium* (St. Bernard XII), subst. use of late L. *purgatorius* cleansing, f. *purgat-*; see prec., -ORY¹.] **1.** A condition or place of spiritual purging and purification; *spec.*, a state in which souls who have departed this life in the grace of God are cleansed by suffering and are thereby prepared for heaven. **2.** *fig.* Any place or state of temporary suffering, expiation, etc. late ME. **3.** *U.S.* **a.** A cavern. **b.** A deep narrow gorge or ravine, with vertical or steep sides; also, a brook flowing through such a gorge. (Usu. as a place-name.) 1766.

Purgatory (pō̆·ɹgătəri), *a.* late ME. [– late L. *purgatorius*; see PURGATORIAL.] Having the quality of cleansing or purifying; of or pertaining to purgation.

Purge (pōɹdʒ), *sb.* 1563. [f. next, or (in sense 2) – (O)Fr. *purge.*] **1.** That which purges; *spec.* an aperient medicine, a purgative. **2.** The act of purging; purgation; ridding of objectionable or hostile elements 1598.

2. *Pride's P.* (Eng. Hist.), the exclusion by Colonel Pride, on the 6th of December, 1648, of those members of the Long Parliament who were suspected of Presbyterian and Royalist learnings.

Purge (pōɹdʒ), *v.* ME. [– OFr. *purgier*, (also mod.) *purger* :– L. *purgare* purify, f. *purus* PURE.] **1.** *trans.* To make physically pure or clean; to rid of anything impure or extraneous; to clear or free *of, from.* **2.** = PURIFY 2, 4. ME. †**b.** = PURIFY 3. –1600. **3.** *transf.* To remove by some cleansing or purifying process (*lit.* or *fig.*); to clear *away, off, out*; to expel or exclude; to void. Also *intr.* for *refl.* ME. **4.** *Med.* To empty (the stomach, bowels, etc.); to deplete or relieve (the bowels) by evacuation. Also *refl.* and *intr.* late ME. **b.** *absol.* To induce purgation; (of a drug) to act as a purge 1606. **5.** *trans.* and *refl.* To clear (oneself or another, one's character, etc.) of a charge or suspicion of guilt; to exculpate; *spec.* in *Law*, by assertion or oath, with the support of compurgators, or by wager of battle ME. **6.** *Law.* To atone for (an offence, etc.) by expiation and submission, with the prospect of relief from penalties; to 'wipe out' (the offence or sentence) 1681. †**7.** *refl.* and *intr.* (also *pass.*) Of a liquid: To clear itself, to be made clear or pure by settlement or defecation –1833.

1. They p. the barley from the bran 1737. **2.** From mental mists to p. a nation's eyes 1798. He insisted that the Senate must be purged of its corrupt members FROUDE. **3.** I shal..purely p. away thy drosse BIBLE (Bishops') *Isa.* 1:25. **5.** He so well purged himself, that he was again restored to his Office CLARENDON. Hence **Pu·rgeable** *a.* capable of being purged. **Pu·rger,** one who or that which purges; †*spec.* a cathartic. **Pu·rging** *vbl. sb.* the action of the vb.: *spec.* = PURGATION 1 b. **Pu·rging** *ppl. a.* that purges; often in names of plants having cathartic qualities as **purging flax,** *Linum catharticum.*

Purgery (pɒ·ɹdʒĕri). 1864. [– Fr. *purgerie*, f. *purger*; see prec., -ERY.] A bleaching or refining room for sugar.

Purification (piūᵊ:rifikēⁱ·ʃən). late ME. [– (O)Fr. *purification* or L. *purificatio, -on-*, f. *purificat-*, pa. ppl. stem of *purificare*; see PURIFY, -ION.] **1.** Freeing from dirt or defilement; cleansing; separation of dross, dregs, refuse, etc. so as to obtain the substance in a pure condition 1598. **2.** Ceremonial or ritual cleansing; *spec.* the observances enjoined upon a woman after child-birth by the Jewish law; hence formerly applied to the churching of women. late ME. **3.** Moral or spiritual cleansing; clearing from taint of guilt 1660. **4.** Freeing from fault or blemish (in ideal or general sense); the action of clearing from debasing or corrupting elements 1753.

2. *The P. of St. Mary* (*of our Lady*, etc.), also simply *the P.*, a name in the Western Church for the festival (Feb. 2) of the Presentation of Christ in the Temple by the Virgin Mary (*Luke* 2:22); also called CANDLEMAS.

Purificator (piūᵊ·rifikeⁱtəɹ). 1853. [In sense 1 mod. var. of next; in sense 2 f. *purification* after similar pairs; see -OR 2.] **1.** *Eccl.* A cloth used at communion for wiping the chalice and paten, and the fingers and lips of the celebrant. **2.** One who or that which purifies (*rare*) 1866.

Purificatory (piūᵊ·rifikeⁱ:təri), *sb.* 1670. [– med.L. *purificatorium*, subst. use of n. of *purificatorius*; see next, -ORY¹.] = prec. 1.

Pu·rificatory, *a.* 1610. [– late (eccl.) L. *purificatorius*, f. *purificat-*, pa. ppl. stem of L. *purificare*; see PURIFY, -ORY².] Having the quality of purifying; tending to purification.

Purifier (piūᵊ·rifəiˌəɹ). 1471. [f. PURIFY + -ER¹.] **1.** One who or that which purifies; a cleanser; a refiner. **2.** An apparatus for purifying. *spec.* **a.** A gas-purifier. **b.** A separator to remove bran scales and flour from grits or middlings. 1834.

Puriform (piū·rifǫɹm), *a.* 1797. [f. L. *pus, pur-* PUS + -FORM.] *Path.* Having the form or character of pus; resembling pus.

Purify (piūᵊ·rifəi), *v.* ME. [– (O)Fr. *purifier* – L. *purificare*, f. *purus* pure; see -FY.] **1.** *trans.* To free from extraneous matter, esp. such as pollutes or deteriorates; to rid of (material) defilement or taint; to cleanse 1440. **2.** To cleanse from moral or spiritual defilement ME. **3.** To make ceremonially clean; to free from ceremonial uncleanness. Formerly *spec.* of the churching of women (mostly in *pass.*). ME. **4.** To free from blemish or corruption (in ideal or general sense); to clear of foreign or alien elements 1548. **5.** *Law.* To make (a contract, etc.) 'pure' by freeing it from conditions; also, to fulfil (a condition) so as to render the obligation 'pure' 1590. **6.** *intr.* for *refl.* To become pure 1668.

1. Fires..to purifie the aire HOBBES. **3.** In the Consecrated stream..to wash off sin, and fit them so Purified to receive him pure MILT. **4.** He saw the French Tongue abundantly purifi'd 1665. **6.** He does not put it in water to p. 1800.

‖**Purim** (piūᵊ·rim, ‖pūrī·m). late ME. [Heb., pl. of *pūr*, a foreign word, explained in Esther 3:7, 9:24, as = Heb. *gôrāl* lot.] A Jewish festival observed in commemoration of the defeat of Haman's plot to massacre the Jews.

Purine (piūᵊ·rəin). 1899. [– G. *purin*, f. L. *purum* pure, and *uricum* URIC; see -INE⁵.] *Chem.* A white crystalline basic substance $C_5H_4N_4$, of very complicated structure which when oxidized forms uric acid ($C_5H_4N_4O_3$).

Purism (piūᵊ·riz'm). 1803. [– Fr. *purisme*, f. *pur* pure; see -ISM.] Scrupulous or exaggerated observance of, or insistence upon, purity or correctness, esp. in language or style 1804. **b.** with *pl.* An instance of this 1803.

Purist (piūᵊ·rist). 1706. [– Fr. *puriste*, f. *pur* PURE + -IST.] **1.** One who aims at, affects, or insists on scrupulous or excessive purity, esp. in language or style; a stickler for correctness. **2.** One who maintained that the New Testament was written in pure Greek 1835. Hence **Puri·stic, -al** *adjs.*

Puritan (piūᵊ·rităn), *sb.* and *a.* 1572. [prob. alt. of contemp. synon. CATHARAN (also earlier †*Catharite*) by substitution of late L. *puritas* for the first element; so mod.L. *Puritani* (Du Cange), Fr. *puritain* (Ronsard). Early evidence points to its being a self-assumed name, the hostile application being later.] **A.** *sb.* **1.** *Hist.* A member of that party of English Protestants who regarded the reformation of the church under Elizabeth as incomplete, and called for its further 'purification' from unscriptural and corrupt forms and ceremonies retained from the unreformed church; subsequently, often applied to those who separated from the established church on points of ritual, polity, or doctrine. **b.** *transf.* A member of any religious sect or party that advocates special purity of doctrine or practice 1577. **c.** A member of any (non-religious) party or school who practises extreme adherence to its principles; a purist 1885. **2.** Applied, chiefly in ridicule, to one who is, affects to be, or is accounted extremely strict, precise, or scrupulous in religion or morals 1592.

1. But one P. amongst them, and he sings Psalmes to horne-pipes SHAKS. Branded with the odious names of Puritanes FULLER. **c.** The Puritans of 'economic principle' 1885. **2.** He that hath not for euery word an oath..they say hee is a p., a precise foole, not fitte to hold a gentleman company RICH.

B. *adj.* **a.** Of, pertaining to, or characteristic of the Puritans; strict and scrupulous in religious matters. **b.** That is a Puritan. 1589.

Puritanic (piūᵊritæ·nik), *a.* 1606. [f. prec. + -IC; after *Satanic*, etc.] = PURITAN *a.* (now *rare*); having the character or manner of a puritan.

Puritanical (piūᵊritæ·nikăl), *a.* 1607. [f. as prec. + -ICAL.] Pertaining to or characteristic of the Puritans, or of puritans generally; having the character or qualities of puritans. (Chiefly *disparaging.*)

I do not want to be thought queer or p. 1878. Hence **Purita·nically** *adv.*

Puritanism (piūᵊ·rităniz'm). 1573. [f. as prec. + -ISM.] **1.** The Puritan system; the doctrines and principles of the Puritans; Puritan opinion or practice. Also *transf.* **2.** Excessive (or affected) strictness or preciseness like that of the Puritans; puritanical behaviour or principles; precisianism 1592.

2. That moderate austerity..which may, without p., be recommended 1832.

Puritanize (piūᵊ·ritănəiz), *v.* 1625. [f. as prec. + -IZE.] **1.** *intr.* (with *it*). To act the puritan; to practise, conform to, or affect puritanism. **2.** *trans.* To make puritan, imbue with puritanism 1648.

2. He has been puritanized till he is good for nothing 1853. Hence **Pu·ritanizer.**

Purity (piūᵊ·rīti). [ME. *purete* – (O)Fr. *pureté*, with later assim. to the late L.

puritas, -tat-, f. L. *purus* PURE *a.*; see -ITY.] The quality or condition of being pure. **1.** The state of being unmixed; freedom from admixture of any foreign substance or matter, *esp.* from matter that corrupts or debases; physical cleanness 1526. **2.** In non-physical or general sense: Freedom from any foreign or extraneous element, esp. from such as corrupt or debase; unalloyed or unadulterated condition; faultlessness, correctness 1561. **3.** Freedom from moral corruption, from ceremonial or sexual uncleanness, or pollution; innocence, chastity, ceremonial cleanness ME.

1. The puritie and whitenesse of my Sheetes SHAKS. Snow of perfect p. TYNDALL. **2.** From Chaucer the p. of the English tongue began DRYDEN. **3.** Clennesse of vertue & purite of lyfe 1526.

Purkinjean (pɒɹki·ndʒiăn), *a.* 1835. [f. name of J. E. *Purkinje*, Bohemian physiologist (1787–1869) + -AN.] *Anat.* and *Phys.* Pertaining to or named after Purkinje.

P. capsules in the cement of a tooth; *P. vesicle*, the nucleus of the ovum. So *Purkinje's cells*, large branching cells in the cortex of the brain; etc.

Purl (pɔ̄ɹl), *sb.*[1] 1535. [orig. *pyrle, pirle* (see PIRL *v.*), of unkn origin. In sense 4 often spelt *pearl* (PEARL *sb.*[2]) and may be a different word.] **1.** Thread or cord made of twisted gold or silver wire, used for bordering and embroidering. **2.** Each of the minute loops or twists used to ornament the edges of lace, braid, ribbon, etc.; hence, collectively, a series or chain of such loops 1611. **3.** †'The pleat or fold of a ruff or band', as worn about 1600; a frill. Also *transf.* 1593. **4.** *Knitting.* (Formerly often *pearl.*) An inversion of the stitches, producing a ribbed appearance of the surface; as in *p. knitting, -stitch* 1825.

Purl (pɔ̄ɹl), *sb.*[2] 1552. [Akin to PURL *v.*[2]] †**1.** A small rill in which the particles of water are in a whirl of agitation –1651. **2.** The action or sound of purling as a rill 1650.

1. Receiving sundry pirles to it and many a running rill HOLLAND. **2.** The p. of waters through the weirs T. HARDY.

Purl (pɔ̄ɹl), *sb.*[3] *Hist.* 1659. [Origin unkn.] orig. A liquor made by infusing wormwood or other bitter herbs in ale or beer; later, a mixture of hot beer with gin (also called *dog's nose*), sometimes also with ginger and sugar; in repute as a morning draught.

Drank a Glass of P. to recover Appetite ADDISON.

Purl, *sb.*[4] *slang* or *colloq.* 1825. [Goes w. PURL *v.*[3] 3.] An act of whirling, hurling, or pitching head-over-heels or head-foremost; a header or cropper; a spill; an upset.

Mr. Tollemarsh got an awful p. over a Gate 1829.

Purl, *v.*[1] 1526. [f. PURL *sb.*[1]] †**1.** *trans.* To embroider with gold or silver thread; to edge embroidered figures with gold or silver thread. Chiefly in *pa. pple.* and *ppl. a.* –1688. **2.** *absol.* To border or edge with or as with purls (PURL *sb.*[1] 2). Chiefly in *pa. pple.* and *ppl. a.* 1766. †**3.** To pleat or frill like a ruff; to frill the edge of; also *transf.* –1653. **4.** *Knitting.* To invert the stitches so as to produce a furrow or 'seam' 1825.

Purl (pɔ̄ɹl), *v.*[2] See also PIRL *v.* 1586. [prob. imit.; cf. Norw. *purla* bubble up, gush out, Sw. dial. *porla* ripple, gurgle.] **1.** *intr.* Of water, a brook; To flow with whirling motion of its particles, or twisting round small obstacles: often with ref. to the murmuring sound of a rill. **2.** *transf.* Said of a stream of air, breath, wind, etc. 1593. **b.** *trans.* To utter with 'purling'. HERRICK.

1. The gravel-paved brook..He often sat to see it p. along CLARE.

Purl, *v.*[3] 1791. [In sense 1 app. a var. of PIRL *v.* (sense 2), perh. rel. to PURL *v*[1].] **1.** *intr.* To whirl round rapidly, as a wheel; to spin round, as a peg-top, etc. **2.** To wheel *round* suddenly, as a horse 1857. **3.** *trans.* and *intr.* To turn upside down, overturn, upset, capsize; to turn head over heels. *dial.* and *colloq.* 1856.

3. He hit the fence, and then purled over 1874.

Purler (pɔ̄·ɹləɹ). *colloq.* 1869. [f. prec. + -ER[1].] A throw or blow that hurls any one head-foremost; a knock-down blow.

Purlieu (pɔ̄·rlᵗū). 1482. [orig. *purlew*, presumably alt. (by assim. to *leu* LIEU) of AFr. *pu·rale(e, -ley* perambulation (in AL. *puralea, porale, purale*), OFr. *pourallee*, f. *po(u)raler* traverse, f. *por-, pour-* PUR- + *aller* go.] **1.** A piece or tract of land on the fringe or border of a forest; orig., one that, after having been included in the forest, was disafforested by a new perambulation, but still remained in some respects subject to provisions of the Forest Laws. **2.** *transf.* and *fig.* A place where one has the right to range at large; a haunt; one's bounds, limits, beat 1643. **3.** *pl. transf.* The parts about the border of any place; the outskirts (*arch.*) 1650. **4.** †A suburb; also, the meaner streets about some main thoroughfare; a mean, squalid, or disreputable street or quarter 1618.

1. Where in the Purlews of this Forrest, stands A sheep-coat? SHAKS. **2.** Wit has its walks and its purlieus, out of which it may not stray the breadth of an hair SWIFT. †*To hunt in p., in the purlieus*, to pursue illicit love. **3.** A wolf..was skulking about the purlieus of the camp 1835. **4.** A wretched shed in the most beggarly p. of Bethnal Green LAMB.

Purlieu-man, purley-man (pɔ̄·ɹlimæ̆n). 1574. [f. prec. + MAN *sb.*] The owner of freehold land within the purlieu of a forest.

Purlin (pɔ̄·ɹlin). 1447. [In AL. *perlio, -ion-* (XV), poss. f. L. *per* through + stem of *ligare* bind; cf. Fr. *lien* tie in carpentry.] A horizontal beam, usu. one of two or more which run along the length of a roof, resting upon the principal rafters, and lending support to the common rafters or boards of the roof.

Purloin (pɒɹloi·n), *v.* 1440. [– AFr. *purloigner*, OFr. *porloigner*, f. *por-, pour-* PUR- + *loign* (mod. *loin*) far.] †**1.** *trans.* To put far away; to remove; to put away; to do away with; to make of no effect –1660. **2.** To make away with; to steal, esp. under circumstances which involve a breach of trust; to pilfer, filch 1548. **3.** *transf.* and *fig.* 1593.

2. I took..an opportunity of purloining his key from his breeches-pocket FIELDING. **3.** Galleries purloined from the first floor of each house PENNANT. Hence **Purloi·ner**, a petty thief, a pilferer.

Puro- (piūᵊ·ro), comb. f. L. *pur-* PUS, used instead of the more usual PYO- of Greek origin.

Purpa·rty. *arch.* ME. [– AFr. *purpartie* (in AL. *purpartia*), f. *pur-* PUR- + *partie* division, part; see PARTY.] *Law.* A proportion, a share, esp. in an inheritance.

Purple (pɔ̄·ɹp'l), *a.* and *sb.* [OE. (late Northumb.) *purple*, reduced and dissimilated form (cf. MARBLE) of *purpuran*, obl. case of *purpure* 'purple' clothing or garment – L. *purpura* (whence also OHG. *purpura* (G. *purpur*), ON. *purpuri*, Goth. *paurpaura*) – Gr. πορφύρα (shellfish that yielded) Tyrian purple dye, cloth dyed therewith. Before 1500 the commoner form was *purpur(e*; see PURPURE.] **A.** *adj.* **1.** Of the distinguishing colour of the dress of emperors, kings, etc.; = L. *purpureus*, Gr. πορφύρεος, in early use meaning crimson; hence, imperial, royal. **b.** Of persons: Clad in purple; of imperial or royal rank. *poet.* or *rhet.* 1704. **2.** Of the colour described in B. 1 b. c. late ME. **b.** Of this colour as being the hue of mourning (esp. royal or eccl. mourning), or of penitence 1466. **c.** Used *poet.* to describe the colour of blood. Hence, Bloody, blood-stained. 1590. **3.** *rhet.* Bright-hued, brilliant, splendid, gaudy, gay; (of sin) deep-dyed, grave, heinous 1598.

1. They did put on hym a p. garment TINDALE *John* 19:2. **b.** P. tyrants vainly groan GRAY. **2.** Heathbell with her p. bloom SCOTT. That lovely dark p. colour of our Welsh and Highland hills RUSKIN. **c.** His p. spear GRAY. When Mathouse-burn to Melrose ran All p. with their blood SCOTT. **3.** All the Glories of the P. Spring DRYDEN. I never said bridge was a p. sin 1905. *P. patch, passage, piece*, an ornate passage in a literary composition (after L. *purpureus pannus*, Horace).

B. *sb.* **1.** The name of a colour. **a.** Anciently, that of the dye obtained from species of molluscs (*Purpura* and *Murex*), commonly called *Tyrian p.*, which was a crimson; **b.** in the Middle Ages applied vaguely to many shades of red; **c.** now applied to mixtures of red and blue in various proportions, usu. containing also some black or white, or both 1440. **d.** The Tyrian dye, or any pigment of the above-mentioned colours 1638. **2.** Purple cloth or clothing; a purple robe 1460. **b.** As the distinguishing dress of emperors, kings, consuls, and chief magistrates; hence *fig.*; spec. *the p.*, imperial, royal, or consular rank, power, or office. Also the colour of imperial and royal mourning. 1440. **c.** *The p.* in ref. to the scarlet colour of the official dress of a cardinal; hence the rank, state, or office of a cardinal; the cardinalate 1685. **d.** In phr. *born, cradled in* (*the*) *p.*: said of a child of an imperial or royal reigning family; hence *transf.* (Commonly assoc. w. sense 2, but see PORPHYROGENITE *a.*) 1790. **3.** Any of the molluscs which yielded the Tyrian purple; now, a mollusc of the genus *Purpura* 1580. **4.** *pl.* **a.** A disease characterized by an eruption of purplish pustules; esp. PURPURA 1533. **b.** Swine fever 1887. **c.** A disease in wheat caused by *Vibrio tritici* 1808. **5.** A purple flower 1840.

2. *P. and pall*, an alliterative collocation in which *pall* has the more general sense of 'rich clothing'. **b.** Diocletian and Maximian had resigned the p. GIBSON. **c.** He was raised to the p. 1898.

Combs. and collocations. **1.** Of the adjective: **p. chamber:** see PORPHYROGENITE; **p. copper (ore),** *Min.* a native sulphide of copper and iron; **p. powder of Cassius** = GOLD-*p.*; named after Andreas Cassius (died 1673). **b.** In names of species or varieties of animals or plants characterized by a purple or purplish coloring, as *p. beech, heron, martin, sandpiper*, etc.; **p-bird, p. coot,** the purple gallinule of Europe (see PORPHYRIO); **p.-shell,** (*a*) = B. 3; (*b*) an ocean snail of the genus *Ianthina.* **2.** Of the sb.; **p.-gland,** the gland in some gastropods which yields the purple dye.

Purple (pɔ̄·ɹp'l), *v.* late ME. [f. PURPLE *a.*] **1.** *trans.* To make purple; to colour or dye with purple. **2.** *intr.* To become purple 1646.

1. When Morn Purples the East MILT. We purpled the seas with our blood 1783.

Pu·rple-re·d, *a.* and *sb.* 1578. Red inclining to or tinged with purple.

Purplish (pɔ̄·ɹpliʃ), *a.* 1562. [f. PURPLE *a.* + -ISH[1].] Somewhat purple; tinged with purple.

Purply (pɔ̄·ɹpli), *a.* 1725. [f. PURPLE *a.* + -Y[1].] Purplish.

Purport (pɔ̄·ɹpɒ̆ɹt), *sb.* 1455. [– AFr., OFr. *pur-, porport* produce, contents, f. *purporter*; see next.] **1.** That which is conveyed or expressed, esp. by a formal document; bearing, tenor, import, effect; meaning, sense. †**b.** Outward bearing. SPENSER. **2.** That which is intended to be done or effected by something; object, purpose, intention. Now *rare.* 1654.

1. And with a looke so pitious in p., As if he had been loosed out of hell SHAKS. **Pu·rportless** *a.*

Purport (pɒɹpōᵊ·ɹt, pɔ̄·ɹpɒ̆ɹt), *v.* 1528. [– AFr., OFr. *purporter* :– med.L. *proportare* (in AL., XII), f. L. *pro* PRO-[1] + *portare* carry, bear; see PUR-.] **1.** *trans.* To have as its purport; to convey to the mind; to mean, imply. **b.** Const. inf.: To profess or claim by its tenor 1790. **2.** To purpose (*rare*) 1803.

1. b. This epistle purports to be written after St. Paul had been at Corinth PALEY.

Purpose (pɔ̄·ɹpəs), *sb.* ME. [– OFr. *porpos, purpos*, (mod. *propos*, after L. *propositum*), f. *por-, purposer*; see next.] **1.** The object which one has in view. **2.** Without *a* or *pl.* The action or fact of intending or meaning to do something; intention, resolution, determination ME. **3.** The object for which anything is done or made, or for which it exists; end, aim. late ME. †**4.** That which one propounds; a proposition, question, or argument; a riddle; *pl.* a game of questions and answers –1611. †**b.** Discourse, conversation; = Fr. *propos* –1599. **5.** That which forms the subject of discourse; the matter in hand; the point at issue. Now only in phr. *to, from, the p.* late ME. **6.** = PURPORT *sb.* 1. 1606.

1. The diuell can cite Scripture for his p. SHAKS. Phr. *To answer* or *serve one's p.*, to be of service in effecting one's object; to do what one wants. **2.** Infirme of p.: Giue me the Daggers SHAKS. **3.** To what p. is this waste? *Matt.* 26:8. *To little, some, no p.*: with such result or effect. *For practical purposes*: in relation to actual performance or achievement. **4. b.** *Much Ado* III. i. 12. **5.** Come; you are a tedious foole: to the p. SHAKS. **6.** Other common topics to the same p. SWIFT.

Phr. **In p.** *To be in p.*, to be minded, to intend (*to do* something). Also occas. *to have in p.* (*arch.*). **Of p.** = *on p.* Now *rare* or *arch.* exc. in *of set p.* **On p. a.** By design; purposely, intentionally. **b.** With *inf.* or *that*: With the express purpose mentioned; in order *to do* something; with the design or aim *that*. Also with *for*, †*to*: Expressly for. Hence **Pu·rpose-like** *a.* having the appearance of being efficient, suitable, or fit for a p. (*Sc.*); having a definite p.

Purpose (pǭ·ɹpəs), *v.* late ME. [– OFr. *por-*, *purposer* design, intend, f. L. *proponere* PROPOSE, after *poser*; see POSE *v.*[1], PUR-.] †**I.** *trans.* = PROPOSE *v.* 1. –1633. †**b.** *absol.* or *intr.* To discourse, talk. Also with *it*. –1598. **II. 1.** *trans.* To place before oneself as a thing to be done or attained; to form a purpose of doing (something); to resolve upon the performance of. Const. chiefly *inf.*; also *that* and *cl.*, *vbl. sb.*, and ordinary *sb.* late ME. **b.** *pass.* To be resolved. late ME. †**2.** *intr.*, *refl.*, and *pass.* ellipt. for *to p. to go*: To be bound *for* a place –1632. †**3.** *absol.* or *intr.* To have a purpose, plan, or design; esp. in *Man purposes* (now *proposes*), *God disposes*. Also, To mean (well or ill) *to* any one. –1656.

1. It is a capitall crime to devise or p. the death of the King SPENSER. My friend purposes to open an office JOHNSON. **b.** I am purposed instantly to return SCOTT. **2.** He purposeth to Athens SHAKS. Hence **Pu·rposer**, †one who states a proposition or propounds a question or argument (*rare*); one who intends or plans anything.

Purposeful (pǭ·ɹpəsfŭl), *a.* 1853. [f. PURPOSE *sb.* + -FUL.] Having a purpose or meaning; indicating purpose; designed, intentional. **b.** Having a definite purpose in view 1865. Hence **Pu·rposeful-ly** *adv.*, **-ness.**

Purposeless (pǭ·ɹpəslės), *a.* 1552. [f. as prec. + -LESS.] **a.** Devoid of purpose or design. **b.** Having no purposes, plans, or aims 1868. Hence **Pu·rposeless-ly** *adv.*, **-ness.**

Purposely (pǭ·ɹpəsli), *adv.* 1495. [f. PURPOSE *sb.* + -LY[2].] **1.** Of set purpose; designedly. **2.** With the particular object specified; on purpose; expressly 1528.

1. If the throng By chance go right, they [the learned] p. go wrong POPE. **2.** The Queen herself came..p. to see him 1787.

Purposive (pǭ·ɹpəsiv), *a.* 1855. [f. PURPOSE *sb.* or *v.* + -IVE.] **1.** Serving or tending to serve some purpose, esp. in the animal or vegetable economy. **2.** Acting or performed with conscious purpose or design 1863. **3.** Of or pertaining to purpose 1899. **4.** Characterized by purpose and resolution 1903.

1. The stings of nettles are p., as stings. They act as protectors. 1894. **2.** We have..p. intelligence distinctly opposed to natural selection 1884. **4.** They are strong in mind and body, truthful and p. 1903. Hence **Pu·rposive-ly** *adv.*, **-ness.**

Purpresture (pɒɹpre·stiŭɹ, -tʃəɹ). late ME. [– OFr. *pur-*, *porpresture*, alt. of *porpresure*, f. *porprendre* occupy, usurp, enclose, f. *por-* PUR- + *prendre* take, seize :– L. *præhendere*.] *Law.* An illegal enclosure of or encroachment upon the land or property of another or (now only) of the public; as by an enclosure or building in royal, manorial, or common lands, or in the royal forests, an encroachment on a highway, public water-way, etc. **b.** A payment or rent paid to a feudal superior for liberty to enclose land or erect any building upon it. late ME.

‖**Purpura** (pǭ·ɹpiŭră). 1753. [L. – Gr. πορφύρα purple shell-fish, purple.] **1.** *Path.* A disease due to a morbid state of the blood or blood-vessels, characterized by purple or livid spots scattered irregularly over the skin. **2.** *Zool.* A genus of gastropods, including some of those from which the ancient purple dye was obtained; a mollusc of this genus 1753.

Purpurate (pǭ·ɹpiŭrĕt), *sb.* 1818. [f. as PURPURIC + -ATE[4].] *Chem.* A salt of purpuric acid.

Purpurate (pǭ·ɹpiŭrĕt), *a.* late ME. [– L. *purpuratus* clad in purple, f. *purpura* PURPLE; see -ATE[2].] **1.** Purple-coloured, purple; also, clothed in purple. *Obs.* or *arch.* **2.** Of or pertaining to the disease purpura 1846.

Purpure (pǭ·ɹpiŭɹ), *sb.* and *a.* *arch.* [OE. *purpure*, ME. *purpre*, *purper*, *-ur*, reinforced from OFr. *purpre* (mod. *pourpre*) :– L. *purpura*; see PURPLE.] **A.** *sb.* †**1.** Purple cloth or clothing; a purple robe or garment; *spec.* as the dress of an emperor or king –1614. †**2.** = PURPLE *sb.* 1. –1496. **b.** *Her.* Purple as a colour or tincture; in engraving represented by diagonal lines from sinister to dexter 1535. **B.** *adj.* †**1.** = PURPLE *a.* 2. –1614. **2.** *Her.* Of the colour called purpure; see A. 2 b. 1562.

Purpureal (pɒɹpiūᵊ·riăl), *a.* Chiefly *poet.* 1712. [f. L. *purpureus* (– Gr. πορφύρεος purple) + -AL[1].] Of purple colour; purple. So **Purpu·rean** *a.* (*rare*) 1615.

Purpureo- (pɒɹpiūᵊ·rio), comb. f. L. *purpureus* adj. purple; as *p.-cobalt*, *-cobaltic* adj.

Purpuric (pɒɹpiūᵊ·rik), *a.* 1818. [f. L. *purpura* PURPLE + -IC.] **1.** *Chem.* Applied to a hypothetical acid ($C_8H_5N_5O_6$), the salts of which are purple or red. **2.** *Path.* Of, pertaining to, or of the nature of purpura or purples; marked by a purple rash 1839.

Purpurin (pǭ·ɹpiŭrin). 1839. [f. L. *purpura* + -IN[1].] *Chem.* A red colouring matter, $C_{14}H_5O_2(OH)_3$, used in dyeing, orig. extracted from madder, hence called *madder-purple*; also prepared artificially by oxidation of alizarin.

Purr (pǭɹ), *sb.* 1601. [Goes w. next.] An act of purring; the soft murmuring sound made by a cat when pleased; also, any similar sound.

Purr (pǭɹ), *v.* 1620. [imit.] **1.** *intr.* Of a cat, etc.: To make a low continuous vibratory sound expressive of satisfaction or pleasure. **2.** *transf.* **a.** Of persons: To show satisfaction by low murmuring sounds, or by one's behaviour or attitude; also, to talk on in a quiet self-satisfied way 1668. **b.** Of things: To make a sound suggestive of the purring of a cat, as that caused by the boiling or bubbling of a liquid, etc. 1657. **3.** *trans.* To utter or express by purring 1740.

1. It is said that the lion, jaguar, and leopard do not p. DARWIN.

Purre (pǭɹ). 1611. [From the voice of the bird.] A local name of the Dunlin (*Tringa variabilis*).

‖**Puree** (pɒ·rī). 1852. [Hindi *peorī*.] A yellow colouring matter, from which INDIAN *yellow* is prepared.

Purse (pǭɹs), *sb.* [OE. *purs* (with *p* after *pung* purse, *pusa* wallet) – late L. *bursa*, var. of *byrsa* – Gr. βύρσα leather.] **I.** A money-bag or -receptacle and its contents. **1.** A small pouch or bag of leather or other flexible material, used for carrying money on the person; orig. a small bag drawn together at the mouth with a throng or strings. **2.** A purse with its contents; hence *transf.* money, funds ME. **3.** A sum of money collected as a present or the like; a sum subscribed as a prize for the winner in a contest 1650. **4.** As tr. Arab., Pers., Turkish *kīsa*, *kīse* 'purse', used in the Turkish empire for a definite sum of money 1686. **5.** A fragment of live coal starting out of the fire with a report: regarded as a prognostic of good fortune 1766.

1. Put Money in thy p. SHAKS. A heavy p. makes a light heart B. JONSON. **2.** Phr. *A common p.*, funds possessed and shared by a number of people in common. *A heavy* or *long p.*, wealth. *A light p.*, poverty. *The public p.*, the national treasury or wealth. *Privy p.*: see PRIVY *a.* **3.** His Friends made a P. for him, when he was to travel to Ægypt BENTLEY. **4.** *The p.* (*of silver*) = 500 piastres. *The p. of gold* = 10,000 piastres.

II. A bag or bag-like receptable. †**1.** A wallet, scrip, pouch –1771. **2.** *transf. Organ-building.* A small leather bag formerly used in connection with the pull-downs which passed through the bottom board of the wind-chest, to prevent the escape of wind 1852. **3.** Applied to various natural receptacles (in animals or plants) resembling a bag; e.g. a marsupium, a cyst 1528. **b.** *spec.* The scrotum 1440.

3. With a naturall p. vnder her belly, wherein she putteth her young PURCHAS.

attrib. and *Comb.*: **p.-crab**, a crab of the genus *Birgus* living in burrows on the E. Indian islands; **-net**, a bag-shaped net, the mouth of which can be drawn together with cords; **-seine**, a fishing-net or seine which may be pursed or drawn into the shape of a bag, used for catching shoal-fish.

Purse (pǭɹs), *v.* ME. [f. prec.] **1.** *trans.* To put into one's purse; to pocket. Also with *up*. Now *rare*. †**2.** *fig.* To pocket (an affront); to withdraw or keep back (a boast); to take possession of, shut up –1691. **3.** *trans.* To draw together (the lips, brow, etc.) in wrinkles or puckers, like the drawn-in mouth of a purse. Often with *up*. 1604. **b.** *intr.* and *absol.* To become wrinkled, to pucker 1709. **4.** *trans.* To close *up* like a purse (*rare*) 1823. †**5.** To steal purses, to rob –1616. **6.** *U.S. trans.* To draw a purse-seine into the shape of a bag so as to close it.

1. I never p. one penny of it 1659. **2.** *Ant. & Cl.* II. ii. 192. **3.** Their Action is only to p. up the Mouth, as in whistling and blowing 1746. **5.** I'll p.; if that raise me not, I'll bet at bowling-alleys BEAUM. & FLETCHER. Hence **Pu·rsing** *vbl. sb.* (also attrib.) and *ppl. a.*, as **pursing-block, -gear, -line, -weight**, the block, etc., used in working a purse-seine.

Pu·rse-bea:rer. ME. **1.** The carrier of a purse; one who has charge of the money of another or of a company; a treasurer, bursar. **2.** *spec.* The official who carries the Great Seal in front of the Lord Chancellor in a receptacle called 'purse' or 'burse' 1688. **3.** A marsupial 1851.

Pu·rse-proud, *a.* 1681. Proud of wealth; puffed up on account of one's wealth. So **Pu·rse-pride** 1606.

Purser (pǭ·ɹsəɹ). ME. [f. PURSE *sb.* + -ER[1].] †**1.** A maker of purses –1638. †**2.** An officer charged with managing money matters and keeping accounts. *Obs.* in gen. sense. –1816. **b.** The officer on board a ship who keeps the accounts, and usu. has charge of the provisions 1458. **c.** In Cornwall, the treasurer of a mine, esp. one worked on the cost-book principle 1832. Hence **Pu·rsership.**

Pu·rse-string. late ME. Usu. in *pl.*: The two threaded strings by drawing which the mouth of a purse is closed; hence *fig.*

Phr. *To hold the purse-strings*, to control the expenditure of money. *To tighten* or *loosen the purse-strings*, to be sparing, or generous, in spending money.

attrib. **purse-string suture** (*Surgical*), a suture running in and out.

Pursiness (pǭ·ɹsinės). late ME. [f. PURSY *a.*[1] + -NESS.] Short-windedness, dyspnœa.

Pursive (pǭ·ɹsiv), *a. arch.* late ME. [– AFr. *porsif*, alt. of OFr. *polsif* (mod. *poussif*), f. *polser* breathe with difficulty, pant :– L. *pulsare* drive or agitate violently (see PUSH *v.*). See PURSY *a.*[1]] Short-winded, broken-winded, asthmatic; orig. said esp. of a horse. **Pu·rsiveness** = prec.

Purslane (pǭ·ɹslĕn). [In XIV *purcelan(e* – OFr. *porcelaine*, identical in form with the Fr. word for PORCELAIN, and prob. assim. to that from L. *porcil(l)aca* (Pliny), more usu. *portulaca*.] **1.** A low succulent herb, *Portulaca oleracea*, used in salads, and sometimes as a pot-herb, or for pickling. Also called *Common* or *Garden P.* **2.** With qualification, denoting other species of *Portulaca* 1578.

2. Crimson-flowered P., *Portulaca thellussoni*. **Red-flowered P.,** *Portulaca splendens*. **Yellow-flowered P.,** *Portulaca aurea*. **Sea-P.,** *Atriplex portulacoides*, and *Arenaria peploides*. **Water-P.,** *Peplis portula*, and *Isnardia palustris*. *Comb.* **p.-tree,** a S. African shrub, *Portulacaria afra*.

Pursual (pŏɹsiū·ăl). *rare.* 1814. [f. PURSUE *v.* + -AL[1].] The action of fact of pursuing; pursuance.

Pursuance (pŏɹsiū·ăns). 1596. [f. as PURSUANT; see -ANCE.] †**1.** = PURSUIT I. 2. –1693. **2.** = PURSUIT II. 1. (Now with *end*, *object*, or the like.) 1640. **3.** The action of following out (a process); continuation, prosecution 1605. **4.** The action of proceeding in accordance with a plan, direction, or order; prosecution, following out, carrying out 1660.

2. To start in p. of that object 1878. **3.** In p. of some train of thought 1859. **4.** When they reached London in p. of their little plan DICKENS.

Pursuant (pŏɹsiū·ănt), *sb.* and *a.* [In XIV *poursuiant* – OFr. *por-*, *poursuiant*, pr. pple. of *por-*, *poursuir*, also *-suivir* (mod. *poursuivre*); see next. Subseq. conformed to AFr. *pursuer* and PURSUE *v.*; see -ANT.]

†A. *sb.* One who prosecutes an action (at law); a suitor; a prosecutor –1657. **B.** *adj.* †**1.** Prosecuting (in a court of law) –1543. **2.** With *to*, rarely *upon*; Following upon, consequent on and conformable to; in accordance with. *Obs.* exc. as in b. 1648. **b.** quasi-*adv.* = PURSUANTLY 1675. **3.** Going in pursuit; following after, pursuing 1691.

2. If..the fine is levied p. to the deed CRUISE. **b.** P. to our method..we have concluded it necessary 1675. Hence **Pursu·antly** *adv.* in a way that is p. or consequent *to*.

Pursue (pɒ̆ɹsiū·), *v.* [ME. *pursiwe, -sewe* – AFr. *pursiwer, -suer* = OFr. *porsivre*, etc. (mod. *poursuivre*) :– Rom. **per-*, **prosequere*, for L. *prosequi* PROSECUTE.] **I.** *trans.* **1.** To follow with hostility or enmity; to seek to injure (a person); to persecute; to harass, worry, torment. Now *rare* or *Obs.* exc. as in 2. †**b.** To follow with punishment –1697. **2.** To follow with intent to capture or kill; to chase, hunt. late ME. **3.** To prosecute in a court of law, to sue (a person). Chiefly *Sc.* 1580. **4.** To follow, as an attendant; to come after in order, or in time. Now *rare* or *Obs.* 1470. **b.** To follow the course of (in description, etc.); to trace. *poet.* 1697. **5.** To sue for, to seek after; to aim at. late ME. †**6.** To seek to attain to, to make one's way to –1681. **7.** To follow (a path, way, course); to proceed along. Now chiefly *fig.* late ME. **8.** To proceed in compliance or accordance with. Now only with *method, plan*, and the like. late ME. **9.** To follow up (a course of action, etc. begun) 1456. **b.** *Law.* To carry on (an action etc. begun) 1456. **b.** *Law.* To carry on (an action); to lay (information); to present (a libel). Chiefly *Sc.* late ME. **10.** To follow as an occupation or profession; to make a pursuit of 1523.

1. Those may justly be pursued as enemies to the community of nature JOHNSON. **b.** *Meas. for M.* v. i. 109. **2.** P. and take him, for there is none to deliuer him BIBLE (Genev.) *Ps.* 71:11. *fig.* The cold still pursued me BORROW. **5.** He pursued Pleasure more than Ambition STEELE. **7.** We too far the pleasing Path p. DRYDEN. **8.** As we were going to p. this advice SMOLLETT. **9.** The subject was pursued no farther JANE AUSTEN. **10.** He persued..his studies..without persecution 1779.

II. *absol.* and *intr.* **1.** To go in chase or pursuit ME. **b.** *To p. after* = sense I. 2. late ME. **2.** To sue in a court of law; to make suit as plaintiff or pursuer. In later use chiefly *Sc.* late ME. **3.** To continue (to do or say something); to go on (speaking). Also with *on*. 1500.

1. The wicked flee when no man pursueth *Prov.* 28:1. Hence **Pursu·ingly** *adv.*

Pursuer (pɒ̆ɹsiū·əɹ). late ME. [f. prec. + -ER[1].] One who pursues; *spec. Civil* and *Sc. Law*, a suitor; a plaintiff, a petitioner; a prosecutor.

Pursuit (pɒ̆ɹsiū·t). late ME. [– (O)Fr. *poursuite*; see PUR-, SUIT *sb.*] **I.** †**1.** Persecution, annoyance –1639. **2.** The action of pursuing a fleeing object, as a hunted animal or an enemy. late ME. †**3.** The action of suing or entreating; a suit, request, petition instance –1701. **4.** *Law.* An action at law; a suit; prosecution. In later use chiefly *Sc.* late ME.

2. Each that passed that way Did join in the p. COWPER. *In p. (of)*, said of the pursuer; *in p.* formerly sometimes of the pursued, = in flight.

II. 1. The action of seeking, or striving to obtain, attain, or accomplish something; search; †endeavour, attempt (*to do* something) 1606. **b.** *transf.* The object aimed at; aim 1592. **2.** The action of following or engaging in something, as a profession, business, recreation, etc.; that which one engages in or follows 1529. †**3.** The pursuing *of* a plan, etc. –1655. †**4.** A continuation, a sequel –1725.

1. You may hear men talk as if the p. of wealth was the business of life J. H. NEWMAN. **b.** Be love my youth's p., and science crown my Age GRAY. **2.** In our daily pursuits 1862. **4.** I return now to the p. of our voyage DE FOE.

Pursuivant (pɒ̄·ɹswivănt), *sb.* late ME. [– OFr. *pursivant*, subst. use of pr. pple. of *pursivre*; see PURSUE, -ANT]. **1.** Formerly, A junior heraldic officer attendant on the heralds; also one attached to a particular nobleman. Now, an officer of the College of Arms, ranking below a Herald. Also *p. at (of) arms.* †**2.** A royal or state messenger with power to execute warrants; a warrant-officer –1823. †**b.** *transf.* and *fig.* = 'messenger' –1631. **3.** A follower; an attendant 1513.

1. Pursevantes and herauldes That crien ryche folkes laudes CHAUCER. **2. b.** That great pursueaunt, Johan Baptist 1530. Hence †**Pu·rsuivant** *v. trans.* to send a p. after; to summon or arrest by a p.

Pursy (pɒ̄·ɹsi), *a.*[1] 1440. [Later form of PURSIVE, prob. assoc. with *purse*; for the ending cf. *hasty, jolly, tardy*.] **1.** = PURSIVE. **2.** Fat, corpulent 1576.

2. *fig. Haml.* III. iv. 153.

Pursy (pɒ̄·ɹsi), *a.*[2] 1552. [f. PURSE *sb.* + -Y[1].] **1.** Of cloth, the skin, etc.: Having puckers, puckered; drawn together like a purse-mouth. **2.** Having a full purse; wealthy; purse-proud 1602.

Purtenance (pɒ̄·ɹtĭnăns). *arch.* ME. [– AFr. **purtinaunce*, with change of prefix, for OFr. *pertinance*; thus an earlier form of PERTINENCE, corresp. in vocalization to APPURTENANCE, of which in later times it may have been taken as an aphetic form.] That which pertains or appertains, or forms an appendage, to that which is the principal thing. †**1.** *Law.* That which pertains or is an appendage to a possession or estate –1525. **2.** The 'inwards' of an animal 1440.

Purulence (piūᵊ·r¹ŭlĕns). 1597. [– Fr. *purulence* or late L. *purulentia*, f. L. *purulentus*; see next, -ENCE.] **a.** The fact of being purulent; the formation of pus; suppuration, festering. **b.** Purulent matter, pus. So **Pu·rulency**, the quality or state of being purulent.

Purulent (piūᵊ·r¹ŭlĕnt), *a.* 1597. [– Fr. *purulent* or L. *purulentus*, f. *pus, pur-* PUS; see -ULENT.] **1.** Consisting of, of the nature of, or resembling pus, or corrupt matter; also *gen.* corrupt, putrid (*rare*). **2.** Full of, forming, or discharging pus; suppurating, festering 1615. **b.** Characterized by or accompanied with the formation of pus 1834. Hence **Pu·rulent-ly** *adv.*, **-ness.**

Purvey (pɒ̆ɹvē¹·), *v.* [ME. *porvaie, -veie* – AFr. *por-, purveier*, OFr. *porveeir* (mod. *pourvoir*) :– L. *providēre* PROVIDE.] **I.** †**1.** *trans.* = PROVIDE *v.* II. 1. –1548. †**2.** *intr.* To take measures, arrange, or prepare beforehand. Const. *inf.* or *that* –1612. †**3.** To make provision for some event or action, or for the supply of something needed. Const. *for, of.* –1658. **II. 1.** *trans.* To provide, furnish, supply (something) ME. **b.** Now in ref. to articles of food, and as the act of a purveyor ME. †**2.** = To furnish or supply (a person) *with* something –1843. **3.** *intr.* To furnish or procure material necessaries or the like; to act as purveyor; *esp.* to make provision *for* a person, his needs, etc. 1440. **b.** Const. *to* (*rare*). late ME.

1. Get thy wounds healed, p. thee a better horse SCOTT. **b.** Purueying victuals for her nourishment 1576. **3.** Purveying for the troops 1872. **b.** Their turpitude purveys to their malice BURKE. Hence **Purvey·able** *a.* (*rare*) provident; procurable.

Purveyance (pɒ̆ɹvē¹·ăns). [ME. *porveance* – OFr. *por-, purvea(u)nce* :– L. *providentia* PROVIDENCE. Subseq. conformed to prec. vb.] †**1.** = PROVIDENCE 1, 2, 3. –1607. **2.** The providing (of some necessary), *esp.* the purveying of victuals. late ME. **3.** *spec.* The requisition and collection of victuals, etc., as a right or prerogative; *esp.* the right formerly appertaining to the crown of buying whatever was needed for the royal household at a price fixed by the PURVEYOR, and of exacting the use of horses and vehicles for the king's journeys ME. †**4.** That which is purveyed; a supply, stock, provision –1599.

Purveyor (pɒ̆ɹvē¹·əɹ). ME. [– AFr. *purveür, -eour*, OFr. *porveour, -eur*, f. *purveier, porveeir*; see PURVEY, -OR 2.] †**1.** One who makes preparation or prearrangement; a manager, director, steward –1448. **2.** One who procures or supplies anything necessary, or something specified, *to* or *for* others. In *commercial use*, One who makes it his business to provide victuals, etc., esp. luncheons, dinners, etc., on a large scale. ME. **b.** An official charged with the supply of requisites or of some necessary to a garrison, army, city, or the like 1475. **3.** A domestic officer who made purveyance of necessaries, transport, and the like for the sovereign (*king's* or *queen's p.*), or for some other great personage. Also *transf.* one who exacts supplies or contributions. Now *Hist.* late ME.

Purview (pɒ̄·ɹviu). 1442. [– AFr. *purveü*, OFr. *porveü* (mod. *pourvu*), pa. pple. of *porveeir* PURVEY; orig. clause introduced by *purveu est* it is provided, or *purveu que* provided that. Cf. PROVISO.] **1.** The body of a statute, following next after the preamble, and beginning with the words 'Be it enacted'; the enacting clauses; hence, the provision, scope, or intention of an act or bill 1461. †**b.** A provisional clause; a proviso –1755. **2.** By extension, The scope or limits of any document, statement, scheme, subject, book, etc.; also, the range, sphere, or field of a person's labour or occupation 1788. **3.** Infl. by VIEW: Range of vision, physical or mental; outlook; contemplation, consideration 1837.

2. The objects of instruction, so far as they lie within the p. of a school-teacher 1881.

Pus (pɒs). 1541. [– L. *pus, pur-*.] *Path.* A yellowish-white, opaque, somewhat viscid matter, produced by suppuration; it consists of a colourless fluid in which white corpuscles are suspended. Also *attrib.*

Puseyism (piū·zi,iz'm). 1838. [f. name of E. B. *Pusey* (1800–82), professor of Hebrew and Canon of Christ Church at Oxford + -ISM.] A hostile term for the theological and ecclesiastical principles and doctrines of Pusey and those with whom he was associated in the 'Oxford Movement' for the revival of Catholic doctrine and observance in the Church of England. Now chiefly *Hist.* So **Pu·seyist** = PUSEYITE; also **Puseyi·stic, -al** *a.* of or pertaining to P. or Puseyites.

Puseyite (piū·zi,əit). 1838. [f. as prec. + -ITE[1].] A follower of Pusey; a supporter or promoter of Puseyism. Also *attrib.* or as *adj.* Hence **Puseyi·tical** *a.*

Push (puʃ), *sb.*[1] 1563. [f. PUSH *v.*] **1.** An act of pushing; a shove, thrust; †a blow, stroke, knock 1582. **b.** *spec.* in *Billiards.* A stroke in which the ball is pushed instead of being struck with the cue, or in which the cue, the cue ball, and the object ball are all in contact at the time the stroke is made; also, in *Cricket* and *Golf*, a push-stroke 1873. **c.** *fig.* An exertion of influence to promote a person's advancement by one who is 'at his back' 1655. **2.** A thrust of a weapon, or of the horn of a beast 1577. †**3.** An attack, a vigorous onset. Also *fig.* –1800. **4.** An effort, a vigorous attempt; a turn, bout, 'go' 1596. **b.** A determined advance; in phr. *to make a p.* Const. *at* or *for.* 1803. **5.** Pressure; *esp.* in *Building*, the thrust of an arch or the like 1715. **6.** *fig.* The pressure of affairs or circumstances; the condition of being 'pushed'; a case or time of stress or urgency; an extremity, a 'pinch' 1570. **7.** Determined effort to get on; enterprise, esp. that which is inconsiderate of the rights of others 1855.

1. c. It is money or 'push' which secured the place that should have been awarded to merit 1889. **4.** Phr. *At one p., at the first p., to make a p.* (*at, for, to do* something). **b.** Making a 'push' of 400 miles 1828. **7.** Like what is called 'push' in a practical man, Sidney Smith's style goes straight to its object 1855.

II. Concrete senses. **1.** A 'press' of people; a crowd, throng. Now *rare* exc. as *slang.* 1718. **2.** *slang.* A 'crowd' or band of thieves; a gang of convicts at penal labour; *esp.* in *Australia*, A gang of larrikins; hence, Any company or party; a 'crowd', 'set', 'lot' 1884. **4.** A contrivance which is pushed or pressed in order to operate a mechanism; as in *bell-p.* 1889.

Push (puʃ), *sb.*[2] *Obs.* exc. *dial.* late ME. [Of unkn. origin.] A pustule, pimple, boil.

Push (puʃ), *v.* ME. [– AFr. **pusser*, (O)Fr. *pousser*, †*pou(l)ser* :– L. *pulsare*, frequent. f. *puls-*, pa. ppl. stem of *pellere* drive, thrust.] **I.** Of physical action. **1.** *trans.* To exert force upon or against (a body) so as to move it away; to move by such exertion of force; to shove, thrust, drive (opp. to *draw* or *pull*). **b.** with an adverb or advb. phr., e.g. *to p. back, down*, etc.

1450. **c.** To drive or repulse by force of arms; to drive in the chase 1634. **d.** To move (a force) against opposition or difficulty 1748. **e.** *absol.* 1735. **f.** *trans.* or *absol.* in *Billiards.* To make a push-stroke 1873. **g.** (*absol.*) *P. off.* Of a person in a boat (and *transf.* of the boat): To push oneself away from the bank or the like; to shove off; hence (*slang*), to go away. 1726. **h.** *intr.* To sit abaft an oar and propel a boat with forward strokes. **2.** To thrust with a pointed weapon, stick, or the like (const. *at*); to tilt, fence; to use a spear, short sword, poniard, etc. *Obs.* or *arch.* 1599. **3.** To thrust or butt with the horns; chiefly biblical. Also *trans.* Now *dial.* 1535. **4.** *trans.* To thrust (a weapon); to thrust (a limb, organ, root, etc.) into some position; to put (anything) out in a projecting manner 1692. **5.** To thrust *out*, stick *out* (an organ or part). Of a plant: To send forth (a shoot, runner, root); also, to put *forth* (fruit). 1614. **b.** *intr.* To stick out, project. Of a plant or stem: To shoot out or grow; to sprout, bud. 1720. **6.** To exert pressure upon something in the way described in 1. 1613. **7.** To make one's way with force or persistence; esp. in *to p. on*, to press forward 1718. **b.** *To p. one's way*, to make one's way by thrusting obstacles or opponents aside 1781.

1. The tram..is sometimes pushed by the boy, and sometimes pulled by a pony 1893. **b.** She turned the key and pushed open the door 1898. **c.** After we had thus pushed the enemy's cavalry DE FOE. **d.** Henry pushed his scouts along the road towards Windsor 1879. **2.** As manhood shal compound: p. home SHAKS. **3.** If the ox shall p. a manservant or a maidservant *Exod.* 21:32. **4.** Some..weeds..p. their roots among the stones 1765. **5.** To encourage the plants to p. fresh roots 1849. **6.** We may as well p. against Powles as stirre 'em SHAKS. **7.** Cæsar, after a short rest, pushed on and came under their walls FROUDE.

II. Of action other than physical. **1.** *intr.* To put forth vigorous effort or endeavour; to press; to aim *at* with endeavour to attain; to press *for*; to seek actively, labour *after*. Now *rare.* 1595. **2.** *trans.* To urge, press, impel (a person, etc.) *to do* something, or *to* some course; to urge or egg *on* 1578. **3.** To impel (a horse, etc.) to greater speed; *spec.* to urge (it) forward beyond its natural speed or endurance; also in ref. to other animals, a steamship, etc. 1727. **b.** To force (a thing) into more intense action. Now *rare.* 1756. **4.** To press forward, press with vigour (some action or operation); to urge, press (a claim, etc.) 1611. **b.** Phr. *To p. one's fortune*, to engage actively in making one's fortune 1657. **c.** To extend operations vigorously forward in space, or to more distant places 1842. **5.** To carry out (a matter, action, principle, etc.) to a farther point, or to the farthest limit 1713. **6.** To advance or try to advance or promote; to press the adoption, use, practice, sale, etc. of (a thing); to exert oneself for the advancement of (a person); also with *forward*, *on* 1714. **b.** To press (something) *on* or *upon* a person for attention, acceptance, or adoption 1723. **7.** To press or bear hard upon (a person) in dealing with him; *esp.* in *passive*, To be hard pressed or put to straits, as by lack of time, means, etc.; often with *for* 1761.

1. The manner in which the manufacturers 'pushed' for orders 1844. **2.** Wild-Beasts.. pushed on to fight 1730. **4.** Since the churchmen pushed on so wicked a business 1720. **c.** They pushed their trade to still more distant parts 1872. **5.** *To p. through*, to press or carry by force to a conclusion. **6.** Pushing the sale of British goods 1888. **b.** Physicians are too apt to p. their prescriptions upon the healthy 1869. **7.** I'm a little pushed for time 1890.

Push-, stem of PUSH *v.*, or PUSH *sb.*[1], in comb.

a. General: in the senses (*a*) moved or actuated by a push, or by pushing, as *p.-pick, -tap*, etc.; (*b*) used for pushing, communicating a push, as *p.-pedal, -rod.* etc. **b.** Special: **p.ball,** a game in which a very large ball is pushed by the hands and bodies of the players towards the opponents' goal; also *attrib.*; **-barred** *a.* (*Billiards*), in which a PUSH is barred or forbidden; **-bike** (*colloq.*), = *push-cycle*; **-car** *U.S.* (*a*) a hand-car; (*b*) a bogie car used to connect an engine with a train which is on a ferry-boat; (*c*) a plate-layers' trolley; **-cart,** a hand-cart or perambulator; **-chair,** a conveyance for a child, of the form of a chair on wheels, propelled by hand; **-cycle** (*colloq.*), a pedal-propelled bicycle as dist. from a motor-cycle; so **-cyclist; -stroke,** in *Billiards, Cricket, Golf*, etc. a stroke in which the ball is pushed instead of being hit.

Pusher (pu·ʃəɹ). 1591. [f. PUSH *v.* + -ER[1].] One who or that which pushes (*lit.* and *fig.*). Also in various techn. uses.

attrib. **p. aeroplane,** one in which the propeller is behind the pilot; called also **p.** 1914.

Pushful (pu·ʃfŭl), *a.* 1896. [f. PUSH *sb.*[1] + -FUL.] Full of 'push' (see PUSH *sb.*[1] I. 7); active and energetic in prosecuting one's affairs; self-assertive; aggressively enterprising. Hence **Pu·shful-ly** *adv.*, **-ness.**

Pu·shing, *ppl. a.* 1692. [f. PUSH *v.* + -ING[2].] **a.** Thrusting, shoving, driving 1693. **b.** *fig.* That pushes forward; enterprising, keen to do business; also, self-assertive, officious 1692. Hence **Pu·shing-ly** *adv.*, **-ness.**

Push-pin (pu·ʃpin). 1588. [f. PUSH- + PIN *sb.*[1]] A child's game, in which each player pushes his pin with the object of crossing that of another player. **b.** *fig.* Child's play 1672. **c.** *U.S.* A drawing-pin.

‖**Pushtu, Pashto** (pɒ·ʃtū, -tō[u]), *sb.* and *a.* 1815. [– Pers. *puštū*, Afghan *păxtō.*] The native name of the language of the Afghans.

Pusillanimity (piŭ:silæni·mĭti). late ME. [– (O)Fr. *pusillanimité* or late (eccl.) L. *pusillanimitas*, f. *pusillanimis* (tr. Gr. ὀλιγόψυχος), f. *pusillus* very small, weak + *animus* mind; see -ITY.] The quality or character of being pusillanimous; pettiness of spirit; cowardliness, timidity.

Pusillanimous (piŭsilæ·nimәs), *a.* 1586. [f. late (eccl.) L. *pusillanimis* (see prec.) + -OUS.] **1.** Lacking in courage and strength of mind; faint-hearted, mean-spirited, cowardly. **2.** Of qualities, actions, etc.: Proceeding from or manifesting a want of courage 1611.

1. Where didst thou learne to be so agueish, so p.? MILT. **2.** Excuses..for a conduct so p. 1797. Hence **Pusilla·nimous-ly** *adv.*, **-ness.**

Puss (pus). 1530. [prob. – MLG. *pūs* (also *pūskatte*), Du. *poes*; cf. Lith. *puž, puiž*, Ir., Gael. *pus*; of unkn. origin.] **1.** A conventional proper name of a cat; usu., a call-name. **b.** A nursery or pet-name for 'cat' 1605. **2.** Quasi-proper name for: **a.** A hare 1668; **b.** A tiger 1837. **3.** Used playfully of a girl or woman, as a term of endearment, often connoting slyness 1610. **4.** Short for PUSS-MOTH 1819.

P. in the corner, a game played by children, of whom one stands in the centre and tries to capture one of the 'dens' or 'bases' as the others change places; also, a sailors' game in the British Navy.

Pu·ss-cat. 1565. = PUSSY-CAT.

Pussley, -ly (pɒ·sli). 1861. A corruption of PURSLANE, common in U.S.

Pu·ss-moth. 1806. [f. PUSS + MOTH, from its downy appearance.] A large European bombycid moth, *Dicranura vinula*, having the fore-wings of a whitish or light grey colour with darker markings and spots.

Pussy (pu·si). 1583. [f. PUSS + -Y[6].] **1.** A cat: used much in the same way as PUSS 1726. **2.** A proper name for the hare 1785. **3.** Applied to a girl or woman 1583. **4.** In nursery use, anything soft and furry, as a fur necklet, a willow or hazel catkin, etc. 1858. Hence **Pu·ssy-cat,** nursery name for a cat.

Comb. **p.-willow,** orig. *U.S.*, any willow having silky catkins, esp. the Amer. *Salix discolor* 1869.

Pu·ssy-foot, *v. U.S.* 1905. [f. prec.] *intr.* To tread softly or lightly; to proceed stealthily. Hence **Pu·ssyfoot** *sb.*, nickname of W. E. Johnson (1862–1945), American prohibition lecturer; hence, an advocate or supporter of prohibition; also *attrib.* and allusively 1919. **Pu·ssy-footer, -footing** *vbl. sb.* and *ppl. a.*

He pussy-footed in and got his things out 1919.

Pustulant (pɒ·stiŭlănt), *a.* and *sb.* 1871. [– *pustulant-*, pr. ppl. stem of late L. *pustulare* blister, f. *pustula*; PUSTULE; see -ANT.] (An irritant) giving rise to the formation of pustules.

Pustular (pɒ·stiŭlăɹ), *a.* 1739. [f. PUSTULE + -AR[1].] **1.** Of, pertaining to, of the nature of pustules; characterized by pustules. **2.** *Bot.* and *Zool.* Having low glandular excrescences like blisters or pustules 1776.

Pustulate (pɒ·stiŭlĕt), *a.* 1607. [– late L. *pustulatus*, pa. pple. of *pustulare*; see PUSTULANT, -ATE[2].] Furnished with, or having pustules; pustulous, pustular.

Pustulate (pɒ·stiŭle[i]t), *v.* 1732. [– *pustulat-*, pa. ppl. stem of late L. *pustulare*; see PUSTULANT, -ATE[3].] **a.** *trans.* To form into pustules. **b.** *intr.* To form pustules. Hence **Pustula·tion,** formation of pustules; occas., also, blistering.

Pustule (pɒ·stiul). late ME. [– (O)Fr. *pustule* or L. *pustula*; see -ULE.] **1.** A small rounded elevation of the cuticle, with erosion of the cutis, inflammatory at the base and containing pus; a pimple; formerly, occas., a blister. **b.** *Maligant p.*, the carbuncular disease produced by the anthrax bacillus 1864. **2.** *Bot.* A small wart or swelling, natural or caused by parasitic influences. **b.** *Zool.* A warty excrescence of the skin, as in the toad; a pimple. 1776. **3.** *transf.* An eruptive swelling of the ground 1849.

Pustulous (pɒ·stiŭləs), *a.* 1543. [– L. *pustulosus*, f. *pustula*; see prec., -OUS.] Abounding in or characterized by pustules.

‖**Puszta** (pu·ʃtă). 1842. [Magyar.] The Hungarian prairie land.

Put (put), *sb.*[1] ME. [f. PUT *v.*[1]] An act of putting. **1.** An act of thrusting or pushing; a push. Now *dial.* late ME. **2.** The act of casting a heavy stone or weight overhand, as a trial of strength ME. **3.** *Stock-jobbing*, etc. The option of delivering a specified amount of a particular stock or produce at a certain price within a specified time: see OPTION 4. 1717.

Put, *sb.*[2]: see PUTT.

Put(t (pɒt), *sb.*[3] *Obs.* or *arch.* 1680. [app. f. PUT *v.*] An old game at cards for two, three, or four players, somewhat resembling nap, three cards being dealt to each player; the score at this game.

Put (pɒt), *sb.*[4] *Obs.* or *arch.* 1688. [Origin unkn.] A stupid man, blockhead, 'duffer'; *country p.*, a lout, a bumpkin (*slang* or *colloq.*).

Put (put), *v.*[1] Pa. t. and pple. **put** (put). [Fully evidenced from XII onwards; infin. *puten*, pa. t. *putte*, pa. pple. *put* (XIV–XV also *putted*), repr. OE. **putian* (*u* of uncertain quantity), repr. only in noun of action *putung* instigation; parallel forms are OE. *potian*, ME. *pote, potte*, mod. dial. *pot*, OE. *pȳtan* (*ūt* out), *āpȳtan* put out, ME. *pitte*, pa. pple. (*i*)*pit*, mod. dial. *pit*; ult. origin unkn.]

I. To thrust, push, and allied senses. †**1.** *trans.* To thrust, push, shove; to knock –1440. **b.** To butt with the head or horns. Now *n. dial.* late ME. †**c.** *absol.* or *intr.* To give a push or knock; to push, knock (*at*, *on*, etc.) –1785. **2.** *trans.* To propel (a stone or weight) mainly by the swing of the body from the right hand raised and placed close to the shoulder: as an athletic exercise. Usu. in phr. *putting the stone* (*shot, weight*). ME. **3.** To thrust or plunge (a weapon) †*home* or *into* a body; to drive or send (a missile) *through* ME. **4.** *Coal-mining.* To propel (a tram or barrow of coal), orig. by pushing behind; now also by means of a pony, a stationary engine, etc. Also *absol.* 1708. †**5.** *Naut.* Of the wind or a storm: To drive or cast (a ship) on or from shore, to sea, etc. –1780. **6.** To launch (persons, a boat, a fleet, etc.). Now chiefly *p. off, out.* 1470. **7.** *Naut. intr.* To set out, set forth, proceed, take one's course (to sea, into harbour, etc.) 1590. **b.** To set out; to start; to pass, make one's way. *Obs.* exc. *U.S. colloq.*, to make off, be off, 'clear out'. late ME. †**c.** Of a stream, etc.: To make its way, to flow (*into* or *out of* a larger piece of water). *U.S.* Also of sap: to flow (in some direction). –1807. **8.** Of a plant: To shoot out or grow; to sprout, bud. Now *dial.* 1615.

3. *To p. a knife into*, to stab; *to p. a bullet through*, to shoot. **5.** One..on her voyage was put ashore at Black Sod 1780. **7.** *Erin*..was among the first vessels to p. down the bay this morning 1899. **8.** The roots of trees do some of them p. downwards deep into the ground BACON.

II. To move (a thing or person) physically into or out of some place or local position. **a.** *trans.* To move (a thing) so as to place it in some situation; to place, lay, set ME. **b.** To remove, send away; to turn away or divert *from*. *Obs.* or *arch.* ME. **c.** To place (a garment, etc.) *on, upon* (also †*off*) the body. late ME. **d.** *spec.* To place upon or affix *to* a writing or document (a title, seal, signature, etc.) 1449. **e.** To harness (a draught animal) *to* a vehicle; to place *in* the shafts of a cart, etc. 1565. **f.** To introduce (a male animal *to* a female, or vice versa) for breeding ME. **g.** To convey (a person, etc.) across a river, etc.; to set down on the other side 1649. **h.** *Stock-jobbing.* To deliver (stock or produce) at a specified price within a specified time 1814. **i.** with abstract obj. late ME.

a. This Figure, that thou heere seest put, It was for gentle Shakespeare cut B. JONS. P. your Hand to your Heart and tell me fairly 1699. P. about an ounce of butter into a frying-pan 1756. *To stay put* (U.S.), to remain in one's or its place. **c.** Bring foorth the best robe, and p. it on him *Luke* 15:22. **d.** To this number..I also put my initials J. H. NEWMAN. **i.** Your Excellencies..conduct..has..put new lives into the Ministers 1707. The thing had been put before her in such vivid reality 1889. Phr. *To p. it across*, to administer chastisement or rebuke to.

III. To place or bring (a thing or person) in or into some condition, state, mode, or form. **1.** To place (a thing or person) *in* or *into* the hands or power of, *in* or *under* the care of a person. late ME. †**b.** To place with (a person); to apprentice *to* –1772. **2.** To place, set, or cause to be in some place or position, in a general or figurative sense, or when the name of a thing or place stands for its purpose, as *to p.* a person *to bed, to school, in prison*, etc. late ME. **3.** To place with or in, by way of addition; to add. Const. *to, in*. late ME. **4.** To place, insert, or enter (a name or an item) in a list, account, or table. Now usu. *p. down*. 1513. **5.** To place (a thing or person) in a scale of estimation or a classification. late ME. **6.** †To convert or change *into* something else; *esp.* to translate or render *into* another language or form of expression. late ME. **b.** To express (something) *in* spoken or written words; to turn *into* speech or writing ME. **c.** To express or state (in a particular way) 1699. **7.** To assign or attribute one thing to another in some relation. **a.** To assign or set (a quality, meaning, value, price) *on, upon, to* a thing. late ME. **b.** To assign or ascribe (a thing) to something else as cause, reason, or basis; to base, found, rest *upon* 1722. **8.** To apply *to* a use or purpose. late ME. **9.** To set mentally or conceptually *in the place of* (something else); to substitute (one thing) *for* another, in thought or expression 1483. **10.** To establish or introduce and bring to bear (a state, condition, relation, or alteration) *in, on,* or *to* an existing thing, action, or state of things. late ME. **b.** To place, repose (trust, confidence, etc.) *in* 1526. **11.** To commit (the fate of something) *to* a risk or hazard; to stake *on, upon* 1611. **b.** To invest or venture (one's money) in 1604. **c.** *To p. oneself on* or *upon*: to entrust or commit oneself to the ruling or verdict of 1660. **12.** To place before a person for consideration or answer; to propound (a question, supposition, etc.) ME. **b.** *spec.* To submit (a point for decision) formally to the vote of an assembly 1683. **c.** *To p. it*: to present a question, statement, etc. *to* a person for consideration or by way of appeal 1747. **13.** To impose (something) *on, upon* a person, etc. late ME. **b.** *absol. To p. upon*: †(*a*) to play a trick upon, befool; (*b*) to oppress, victimize. Chiefly in indirect passive. 1693. **14.** To lay the blame of (something) *on* or *upon*; to tax with; to charge *against*, impute *to*. late ME. **15.** To place *in*, bring *into*, or reduce (a person or thing) *to* some state or condition ME. **b.** With complement: To cause to be or become something; to make, render so-and-so. late ME. **16.** To subject (a person, etc.) *to* the suffering or endurance of something ME. **b.** *spec.* To subject (a piece of ground) to the plough, or to the raising of a particular crop. Const. *to, into, under* the crop, etc. 1845. **17.** To set (a person or animal) to do something, or upon some course of action. late ME. **b.** To set to learn, study, or practise. Const. *to*, †*on*, †*upon* (something). late ME. **c.** To direct or urge (a horse) towards something, esp. an obstacle to be cleared; also, to cause (a horse) to perform a particular pace, a leap, etc.; const. *to, at*, etc. 1589. **d.** To set (cattle) to feed upon; to restrict (a person) to a diet or regimen of. Const. *to, on, upon*. 1620. **18.** To force or drive (a person, etc.) to the performance of some action, e.g. of making a choice, etc. late ME. **b.** Const. *inf.* To oblige, compel, require *to do* something. *Obs.* or *arch.* 1603. **c.** *To p.* (a person) *to it*. (*a*) To force, urge, challenge, or call upon (him) to do what is indicated by the context. Chiefly *pass.* 1581. (*b*) *spec.* To force (one) to do one's utmost; to reduce to straits; to hamper or embarrass. Now always *pass.* 1603. †**19.** To posit, suppose, assume. With obj. cl. or simple obj. –1654. †**20.** To 'lay down'; to state, affirm as a fact –1607.

1. Will ye putte yourselfe nowe wholye into my handes? 1553. A very fine healthy young man put himself under my care 1843. **2.** Having others put over their heads 1698. **3.** P. no rum in thy tea 1849. **4.** You are like to be put in the black List 1692. **5.** *To p. at*, to estimate or price at; A circulation which a competent authority puts at three millions 1890. **6. b.** Fables That..other poetes p. in ryme CHAUCER. **c.** A good story well put 1889. **7. a.** Putting the best construction upon all men's words and actions 1708. **8.** O glorious strength Put to the labour of a Beast MILT. **9.** P. yourself in his place 1870. **10.** *To p. an end, stop, period to*, to bring to an end, stop; so *to p. a stopper, veto on*, etc. **b.** P. not youre trust in prynces COVERDALE *Ps.* 165[6]:3. **11.** *Cymb.* I. iv. 133. A Frenchman who had..put his money on Reluisant 1885. **12.** *To p.* (*the*) *case*, to propound a hypothetical instance or illustration. **b.** The resolution was put and carried 1830. Let us p. it to the vote 1888. **13.** If I p. any trickes vpon em SHAKS. The obligation he had put upon us DE FOE. She put herself upon him for a saint 1752. Putting upon you gifts of no real value 1825. **14.** *Macb.* I. vii. 70. **15.** *To p. at ease, at rest; to p. in doubt, fear, mind; to p. in* (*into*) *action, communication, force, motion, possession, shape; to p. on one's guard, one's honour, on oath, record, to rights, silence, sleep, in the wrong*; see also the sbs. **b.** The least mistake..would p. the calculation all wrong 1892. **16.** *To p. to torture; to p. to death; to p. to ransom; to p. to expense, loss, trouble; to p. to the rack, the sword; to p. to confusion, shame; to p. upon one's trial*; see also the sbs. **17.** 'Tis they haue put him on the old mans death SHAKS. I suppose they'll p. me to herd the swine 1889. **c.** *To p. through*, to cause (a horse) to perform (a particular movement); *transf.* to cause (a person) to go through an exercise, course of study, etc.; Mr. Pumblechook then put me through my pence-table DICKENS. **18.** *To p. to flight*, etc.; see also the sbs. **c.** There is nothing a man of the world can't do when he's put to it 1868. We were hard put to it..to get it done in so short a time DICKENS. **19.** P. that Christ did not dye for them 1626. **20.** As common bruite doth p. it SHAKS.

IV. With adverbs in special senses. **Put about. a.** *Naut. trans.* To lay (a sailing vessel) on the opposite tack. Also *transf.* to cause (a horse, a body of men, etc.) to turn round so as to face in another direction. **b.** *Naut. absol.* or *intr.* To turn on to the other tack; to go about. Also *transf.* **c.** *trans.* To circulate, publish (a statement). **d.** To trouble; to distress. (Chiefly *Sc.* and *n. dial.*) **P. asunder.** *trans.* To separate. **P. away. a.** *trans.* To send away, get rid of; to reject; *spec.* to divorce. Somewhat *arch.* †**b.** To drive away, dispel; to put an end to. **c.** To stow away; also, to lay by for future use (money, etc.); = *put by*. **d.** *slang* or *colloq.* (*a*) To consume as food or drink; (*b*) to put in jail; (*c*) to pawn; (*d*) *dial.* to put in the grave. **P. back.** †**a.** *trans.* To repulse; to refuse, reject. **b.** To reduce to a lower position or condition; to retard, or check the advance of. **c.** To move (the hands of a clock) back; to set back; also *fig.* **d.** To defer; = *put off*. **e.** To restore to its former place or position. **f.** *Naut. intr.* To reverse one's course. **P. by. a.** *trans.* To thrust or set aside; to reject; to neglect. †**b.** To turn aside, avert (a blow, or *fig.* a calamity, etc.) Also *absol.* **c.** To turn aside, evade (a question, argument, etc.); to p. off (a person) with an excuse or evasion. †**d.** To divert *from* something. **e.** To lay aside (something out of use); to stow away; to lay by (money, etc.) for future use. **P. down. a.** *trans.* To suppress by force or authority; †to abolish. **b.** To depose from office, authority, or dignity; to dethrone, degrade. Somewhat *arch.* **c.** To 'take down'; to snub; to refute, put to silence. †**d.** To excel, surpass, 'beat' by comparison. **e.** To cease to keep up (something expensive). **f.** To write down; to enter in a written account, list, etc. **g.** *fig.* To account or reckon; to estimate *as, at*; to take *for*; to count or attribute *to*. **h.** To sink (a shaft, pit, etc.) **i.** *To p. one's foot down*; see FOOT *sb.* **P. forth. a.** *trans.* To stretch forth, extend (the hand or other member of the body, etc.). Now *rare* or *arch.* **b.** To set forth; *fig.* to display, exhibit. **c.** To set forth in words, propound. †**d.** To thrust, push, or send into view or prominence; to put out to service, etc.; *refl.* to come forward; to offer oneself. **e.** To put in operation; to exert (one's strength), lift up (one's voice). **f.** To issue, put in circulation. **g.** Of a plant: To send out (buds or leaves). Also *intr.* or *absol.* (*b*) *intr.* for *refl.* Of buds, leaves, etc.: To sprout out, shoot out, come out. †**h.** To lay out (money) to profit. **i.** *intr.* To start on one's way, esp. to sea; to make one's way forward. *arch.* **P. forward. a.** *trans.* To push into view or prominence. **b.** To advance for consideration or acceptance; to propound, advance, urge; to allege; to represent *as*. †**c.** *intr.* To press forward; to come forward. **P. in. a.** *trans.* To install in or appoint to an office or position; sometimes with mixture of literal sense, as *to p. in a caretaker, a bailiff*; so *to p. in a distress, an execution*. **b.** To present, or formally tender, as in a law court (a document, evidence, a plea, a claim, surety, an APPEARANCE, etc.). **c.** *intr.* To make a claim, plea, or offer: (*a*) to apply *for*; to enter *for*, bid *for*; (*b*) to plead or intercede *for* some one or something. **d.** *trans.* To drive in: (*a*) *Naut.* (a ship) into a port or haven; (*b*) *Falconry*, (the game) into covert. **e.** *intr.* To go in, enter. **f.** *trans.* To interpose (a blow, shot, etc.; a word or remark; also, the actual words); to get in (a word). *To p. in one's oar*: see OAR *sb.* 1. †**g.** *intr.* or *absol.* To intervene. **h.** *trans.* To 'throw in'; to insert as an addition or supplement. **i.** To perform (a piece of work, etc.) as part of a whole, or in the midst of other occupations. **j.** *colloq.* To pass, spend (a portion or period of time), usu. by means of some occupation. **P. off. a.** *trans.* To postpone to a later time; to defer. Also *absol.* **b.** To divest oneself (rarely another) of (clothes, etc.). †**c.** To dismiss, put away: (*a*) from one's mind; (*b*) from one's service or employment. **d.** To get rid of (as an importunate person or demand) by evasion or the like; to baffle by giving something less acceptable (const. *with*); *occas.*, to bid to wait. **e.** To divert *from* one's purpose; to hinder; to dissuade *from* doing something. Now usu. (without const.), to hinder (a person) from performing some act by diverting his attention or exciting his aversion. **f.** To pass, get through (time). *Obs.* or *dial.* **g.** To make to 'go off', to sell. Now *dial.* **h.** To pass off for what it is not; (now *rarely*) to palm off or foist *upon* some one. **i.** (*a*) *Naut. intr.* To leave the land; to start on a voyage; also, to leave a ship, as a boat. (*b*) To depart, make off. Now only *U.S.* (*c*) *trans.* To push off, send off (a boat) from the land, or from a ship. **P. on. a.** *trans.* To impose or inflict as a burden or charge. *To p. it on*, to add to the price, to overcharge. **b.** To don; to clothe oneself (or another) with. Also *fig.* in scriptural language; of a plant, to 'clothe itself' with (leaves or blossoms). †(*b*) *absol.* To put on one's hat, to 'be covered'. **c.** *fig.* To take upon oneself, assume (a character or quality, real or feigned). **d.** In mod. emphatic use: To assume deceptively or falsely; to affect, pretend. *To p. it on*, to pretend to something more than the fact. **e.** To add. (*a*) To develop additional (flesh or weight). (*b*) To add (so much) to the charge or price. (*c*) To add (runs, a goal, etc.) to the score. **f.** To lay, stake, bet (a sum of money). †**g.** To urge onward; to incite, impel; to promote (a state of things). †**h.** *intr.* To go faster; to push on; to go on, proceed. **i.** *trans.* To push forward (the hands of a clock, the time) so as to make it appear later. **j.** To bring into action or operation, as a brake, pressure, etc.; to apply; to exert. **k.** To set or appoint (a person) to do something; in *Cricket*, to set (a person) on to bowl; to set (a train, steamer, etc.) to make regular journeys or voyages; to lay (a hound) on the scent. **P. out.** *trans.* **a.** To thrust, drive, or send out of a place; to eject, turn out. (*b*) To blind (an eye), either by literally gouging it out or otherwise. (*c*) To put out of joint; to dislocate. **b.** To turn out of office, dignity, possession, etc.; to depose, dismiss. Now *rare* or *arch.*, exc. in sense 'to put out of play', in games, etc.; esp. in *Cricket*, to cause (a batsman) to be out. **c.** To extinguish, put an end to, destroy, abolish. **d.** To extinguish (fire light, etc.). **e.** To disconcert, confuse, embarrass; (*b*) to distress, 'upset' (mentally); in mod. use, to put out of temper, annoy, vex; (*c*) to put to inconvenience. **f.** = *put forth* e. **g.** = *put forth* f. Now *rare*. **h.** (*a*) *Naut.* To send or take (a vessel) out to sea (*rare*). (*b*) *intr.* To go out to sea; to set out on a voyage. (*c*) To depart, make off; to set out. (Chiefly *U.S.*). **i.** To stretch forth, extend, protrude (the hand, etc.); to cause to stick out or project; to display, hang out. **j.** = *put forth* g. Now *rare*. **k.** (*a*) To place (a person) away from home under the care of some one, or in some employment; to turn out (a beast) to graze or feed; to plant out (seedlings, etc.). (*b*) To lend (money) at interest, or lay it out to profit. (*c*) To give (work) to be done off the premises, or by some one not in one's regular employment.

P. over. orig. *U.S.* To secure a hearing for (a dramatic production); hence *gen.* to get accepted or favourably received. **P. through. a.** To cause to pass through any process; to carry (successfully) through; to get done with. (Chiefly *U.S.*) **b.** To place a person in telephonic connection with another through one or more exchanges. **P. to.** †**a.** *trans.* To add (actually or mentally). Also *absol.* **b.** To exert, apply, put forth. *To p. one's hand to*: to set to work at something; to render assistance. Now *rare* or *arch.* **c.** To attach (a horse, etc.) to a vehicle; *transf.* (an engine) to a train. **d.** To shut. Now *arch.* and *dial.* **e.** *Naut. intr.* To put in to shore; to take shelter. **f.** *pass.* = *to be put to it*; see III. 18 c. **P. together. a.** To combine, unite (parts) into a whole; to join, e.g. in marriage. **b.** To form (a whole) by combination of parts. **c.** To combine mentally; to add together; often in *pa. pple.* taken together, collectively. *To p. this and that together*, to consider two facts together and draw a conclusion from them. So *to p. two and two together*: see Two. **d.** *Cricket.* To make up, 'compile', as a score. **P. up. a.** *trans.* To raise; to lift; see also the sbs. BACK, HAIR, SHUTTER, etc. (*b*) To set up or mount (a person, esp. a jockey) on horseback, to employ as a jockey. (*c*) To put (a play, etc.) on the stage for performance. **b.** *Hunting.* To cause (game) to rise from cover. **c.** To raise in amount. **d.** *colloq.* To show, exhibit (a game, play); phr. *to p. up a good fight.* **e.** To offer (prayer or worship) to God or a divine being 'on high'; to present a petition to any exalted personage. **f.** To propose for election or adoption. (*b*) *trans.* (with mixture of lit. sense): To bring forward (a person) to stand up and speak. **g.** To hand in (a communication) to be published in a church in the course of the service; also, to publish (banns). **h.** To offer for sale by auction, or for competition. **i.** To place in a receptacle for safe keeping; to stow away; to pack up, do up, make up into a parcel, or place in small vessels, etc., so as to be ready for use. (*b*) To put into the sheath, to sheathe (a sword); also *absol. arch.* (*c*) To shut up, enclose (a beast for fattening, a meadow for hay). (*d*) To settle (any one) to rest or repose; to settle (a patient) in bed (*rare*). (*e*) To deposit, stake (a sum of money); to pay up. Also *absol.* orig. *U.S.* and *Colonial.* **j.** (*a*) To lodge and entertain (man or beast). (*b*) *intr.* for *refl.* or *pass.* To take up one's lodging, to 'stop' (at an inn, etc.). **k.** *fig.* †(*a*) *trans.* To 'pocket', submit to (an affront or injury). Now (*b*) *To p. up with*, to submit to (an injury), to suffer without resentment; in wider sense, To bear, endure, tolerate, do with (anything inconvenient or disagreeable). **l.** *trans. To p.* (a person) *up to* (colloq.): (*a*) To make conversant with or aware of; to inform of, instruct in (something, orig. some artifice or expedient). (*b*) To stir up, instigate (*to* some action, etc., or *to do* something). **m.** To erect, set up (a building, etc.); to construct, build. **n.** To concoct or plan in combination with others; to preconcert (a robbery or underhand piece of work): orig. and chiefly *Thieves' slang.*

Put, *v.*[2]: see PUTT *v.*

‖**Putamen** (piutēⁱ·měn). 1830. [L., what falls off in pruning, f. *putare* prune.] *Bot.* The endocarp of a fruit when hard and woody, as the 'stone' of a plum, etc.; rarely, the shell of a nut. **b.** *Anat.* A structure at the base of the brain 1890.

Putative (piū·tătiv), *a.* late ME. [– (O)Fr. *putatif, -ive* or late L. *putativus* (Tertullian), f. *putat-*, pa. ppl. stem of L. *putare* (1) prune, (2) reckon, think; see -IVE.] That is such by supposition: reputed, supposed.

P. marriage, in *Canon law*, a marriage which though legally invalid was contracted in good faith by at least one of the parties. Hence **Pu·tatively** *adv.*

‖**Putchuk, putchock** (pɒ·tʃɒ̆k). 1617. [Southern Hind. *pachak*; origin doubtful.] The root of the plant *Aplotaxis auriculata*, a native of Kashmir, used as a medicine and for making the Chinese joss-sticks.

Puteal (piū·tiăl). 1850. [– L. *puteal*, orig. neut. of *putealis*, f. *puteus* well.] *Rom. Antiq.* The stone curb surrounding a well.

Putid (piū·tid), *a.* Now *rare.* 1580. [– L. *putidus*, f. *putēre* stink; see -ID[1].] Foul, base; rotten or worthless. Hence **Puti·dity, Pu·tidness**, p. quality. **Pu·tidly** *adv.*

Putlog, putlock (pɒ·tlǫg, -lǫk). 1645. [perh. f. *put*, pa. pple. of PUT *v.*[1]; the form *-lock*, which is much the earlier, is obscure.] One of the short horizontal timbers on which the scaffold-boards rest.

Pu·t-off. Pl. **put-offs.** 1549. [f. the phr. *put off.*] An act of putting off. **1.** An evasion, a shift. **2.** An act of postponing something; a putting a person off to a later time 1623.

Put-on, (stress var.), *ppl. a.* 1621. [pa. pple. of *to put on.*] *fig.* Assumed, affected, feigned, pretended.

Putrefaction (piūtrĭfæ·kʃən). late ME. [– (O)Fr. *putréfaction* or late L. *putrefactio, -on-*, f. *putrefact-*, pa. ppl. stem of L. *putrefacere*; see PUTREFY, -ION.] **1.** The action or process of putrefying; the decomposition of animal and vegetable substances, with its attendant loathsomeness of smell and appearance; rotting; corruption. **b.** Decomposition of tissues or fluids in a living body, as in ulceration, suppuration, or gangrene. late ME. †**2.** *Alchemy* and *Old Chem.* The disintegration of a substance by chemical or other action; also, the oxidation or corrosion of metals, etc. –1671. **3.** *concr.* Decomposed or putrid matter 1605. **4.** *fig.* Moral corruption and decay 1631.

Putrefactive (piūtrĭfæ·ktiv), *a.* late ME. [– (O)Fr. *putréfactif, -ive* or med. L. *putrefactivus*, f. as prec.; see -IVE.] **1.** Causing or inducing putrefaction; putrefying. **2.** Of, pertaining to, or characterized by putrefaction; indicative of putrefaction 1646.

2. *P. fermentation*, putrefaction scientifically viewed as a species of fermentation. Hence **Putrefa·ctiveness.**

Putrefy (piū·trĭfəi), *v.* late ME. [– L. *putrefacere*, f. *puter, putr-* rotten + *facere* make; see -FY. Cf. Fr. *putréfier.*] **1.** *trans.* To render putrid; to cause to rot or decay with a fetid smell. Now *rare.* †**b.** *Alchemy* and *Old Chem.* To decompose chemically; e.g. to oxidize –1651. **2.** *intr.* To become putrid; to decay with an offensive smell; to rot, 'go bad'. late ME. **b.** Of the tissues or fluids in a living body: To become putrid or gangrenous; to fester, suppurate 1500. **c.** *fig.* To become corrupt or decay morally, socially, etc. 1526.

1. They would but stinke, and putrifie the ayre SHAKS. **2. c.** The name of vnrighteous persons shall putrifie HOOKER. Hence **Pu·trefiable** *a.*

Putrescence (piutre·sĕns). 1646. [f. as next; see -ENCE.] The action or process of rotting or becoming putrid; incipient or advancing rottenness. **b.** *concr.* Putrescent matter 1843. **c.** *fig.*; esp. Moral rottenness 1840. So **Putre·scency,** the state of being putrescent.

Putrescent (piutre·sĕnt), *a.* 1732. [– *putrescens, -ent-*, pr. pple. of L. *putrescere*, inceptive of *putrēre* be rotten; see -ESCENT.] **1.** Becoming putrid; in process of putrefaction. **2.** Of, pertaining to, or accompanying putrescence 1775.

1. P. manures 1834. **2.** We find game, in a p. state, eaten as a luxury 1849.

Putrescible (piutre·sĭb'l), *a.* 1797. [f. as prec.; see -IBLE. Cf. (O)Fr. *putrescible.*] Liable to rot; subject to putrefaction. Hence **Putrescibi·lity.**

Putrescine (piutre·səin). 1887. [f. as prec. + -INE[5].] *Physiol. Chem.* One of the ptomaines or cadaveric alkaloids.

Putrid (piū·trid), *a.* 1598. [– L. *putridus*, f. *putrēre* rot, f. *puter* rotten. Cf. (O)Fr. *putride.*] **1.** Of organic bodies: Decomposed, rotten. **2.** Pertaining to, causing, proceeding from, accompanying or infected with putrefaction; foul 1610. **3.** *fig.* (*a*) Morally, socially, or politically corrupt; æsthetically abominable. (*b*) Corrupting, noxious, noisome. 1628. (*c*) Of poor quality, 'rotten' (*slang*) 1902. †**4.** Of soil: Loose, friable –1780.

1. Stagnant sea-water, like fresh, soon grows p. GOLDSM. **2.** *P. fever*, typhus fever. *P. sore throat*, gangrenous pharyngitis; sometimes applied to diphtheria. **3.** In respect to electoral morality, Pontefract is p. 1893. Hence **Pu·trid-ly** *adv.*, **-ness.**

Putridity (piutri·dĭti). 1639. [f. as prec. + -ITY.] **1.** The condition of being putrid; rottenness. **b.** *fig.* Moral or metaphorical rottenness 1823. **2.** *concr.* Putrid matter 1790.

Putrilage (piū·triledʒ). 1657. [– late L. *putrilago*, f. *puter* rotten; see -AGE.] Putrid matter. Hence **Putrila·ginous** *a.*

Putt, put (pɒt), *sb.* 1743. [A differentiated pronunc. of PUT *sb.*[1], of Sc. origin; cf. next.] *Golf.* An act of putting (see next 2); a gentle stroke given to the ball to make it roll along the putting-green, with the purpose of getting it into the hole.

Putt, put (pɒt), *v.* Pa. t. and pa. pple. **putted.** ME. [Formally identical with PUT *v.*[1], with differentiated pronunc., and pa. t. and pa. pple. *putted.*] **1.** *trans.* = PUT *v.* I. 2. *Sc.* **2.** *Golf.* To strike the ball gently and carefully (with the PUTTER), so as to make it roll along the putting-green, with the object of getting it into the hole: orig. *Sc.* 1743.

‖**Puttee** (pɒ·ti). 1886. [Hindi *paṭṭī* band, bandage.] A long strip of cloth wound spirally round the leg from the ankle to the knee, worn as a protection and support to the leg.

Putter (pu·təɹ), *sb.*[1] late ME. [f. PUT *v.*[1] + -ER[1].] **1.** One who or that which puts (in current senses of the vb.). **2.** *Coal-mining.* A man or boy employed in 'putting' or propelling the trams or barrows of coal from the workings; a haulier; see PUT *v.*[1] I. 4. 1708.

Putter (pɒ·təɹ), *sb.*[2] 1743. [f. PUTT *v.* + -ER[1].] **1.** One who 'puts' or throws a heavy stone or other weight; see PUTT *v.* Chiefly *Sc.* 1820. **2.** *Golf.* **a.** A club used in 'putting' 1743. **b.** A player who 'puts' 1857.

Putting (pu·tiŋ), *vbl. sb.*[1] [Late OE. *putung*; see PUT *v.*[1], -ING[1].] The action of PUT *v.*[1] in various senses; *esp.* the exercise of throwing a heavy stone or weight from the shoulder.

Putting (pɒ·tiŋ), *vbl. sb.*[2] 1805. [f. PUTT *v.* + -ING[1].] *Golf.* The action of striking the ball with the putter in order to get it into the hole.

Comb.: **p. cleek**, a cleek used in p.; **-green,** the part of the ground around each **p.-hole,** where the ball is 'putted'; **-iron,** an iron putter.

Putting-stone (pu·tiŋ-, *Sc.* pɒ·tiŋ,stōⁿn). 17.. [f. PUTTING *vbl. sb.*[1]] A heavy stone used in the athletic exercise of putting.

‖**Putto** (pu·tto). Usu. in pl. **putti** (pu·tti). 1644. [It. pl. *putti* – L. *putus* boy, child.] In *pl.*, Representations of children, nude or in swaddling bands, used in art, esp. in Italy in the 15th–17th c.

Puttock[1] (pɒ·tək). *Obs.* exc. *dial.* late ME. [Of unkn. origin.] A bird of prey; usu. applied to the Kite or Glede (*Milvus ictinus* or *regalis*); sometimes to the Common Buzzard (*Buteo vulgaris*).

†**Puttock**[2]. ME. [Of unkn. origin.] *Naut.* Original name of the small or short shrouds connecting the lower shrouds with the top; also, where there is a top-gallant mast, the similar set connecting the topmast shrouds with the top-gallant top. After 1700 usu. called **p. shrouds,** and now *futtock-shrouds*, from confusion with FUTTOCK.

Putty (pɒ·ti), *sb.* 1633. [– (O)Fr. *potée* jeweller's putty, potter's glaze, loam for moulds, orig. potful (XII), f. *pot* POT *sb.*[1]; see -Y[5].] **1.** A powder of calcined tin (amorphous stannic oxide), or of calcined tin and lead, used for polishing glass or metals; dist. as *jewller's p.*; also *p. powder* 1663. **2.** A fine mortar or cement made of lime and water without sand; dist. as *plasterers' p.* 1633. **3.** A stiff paste composed of powdered whiting, raw linseed oil, used in fixing panes of glass, and for making up inequalities in woodwork, etc. before painting; dist. as *glaziers' p.* 1706. **b.** In full *p. colour*, a light shade of yellowish-grey 1886.

Comb.: **p.-knife,** a knife with a blunt flexible spatulate blade for spreading p. (sense 3); **p. medal,** a fit reward for a small achievement or service; **-root,** a N. American orchid (*Aplectrum hyemale*), the corm of which contains a glutinous matter sometimes used as a cement.

Putty (pɒ·ti), *v.* 1734. [f. prec.] *trans.* To cover, smear, fix, mend, or join with putty; to fill up with putty. Hence **Pu·ttier.**

Put-up, *ppl. a.* 1810. [pa. pple. of *to put up.*] **1.** (Orig. *Thieves' slang.*) Arranged or concocted beforehand, as a burglary, by conspiracy with other persons, as servants in the house; planned in an underhand manner. Often in phr. *a put-up job.* **2.** *transf. Put-up price*, the up-set price at or above which something will be sold at an auction 1895.

‖**Puy** (pwi). 1839. [Fr., hill, mount, hillock :– L. *podium* elevation, height.] A small volcanic cone; *spec.* one of those in Auvergne, France; also, in *Geol.*, generalized.

‖**Puya** (pū·yă). 1866. [mod.L., from the Chilean native name.] (A plant of) a genus of tropical and subtropical plants of Chili and Peru bearing spiny leaves and showy flowers.

Puzzle (pʊ·z'l), *sb.* 1599. [f. next.] **1.** The state of being puzzled; bewilderment, confusion. **2.** A puzzling question; a poser, 'problem', 'enigma' 1655. **3.** A toy or problem contrived for the purpose of exercising one's ingenuity and patience 1814. **b.** = *p.-peg*, a piece of wood, about a foot long, pointed at one end and fastened to the lower jaw of a dog or horse so that the pointed end projects in front, and prevents him from putting his nose close to the ground 1791.

3. *Chinese p.*, one of the ingenious puzzles made by the Chinese, in which the problem is to fit together the dissected pieces of a geometrical or other figure, to disentangle interlocked rings, etc. Hence *fig.* Any specially intricate p. or problem. Hence **Pu·zzledom,** the realm of p.; the state of being puzzled.

Puzzle (pʊ̆·z'l), *v.* 1595. [Of late XVI emergence (*pusle, puzzell*), unless preceded by late ME. pa. pple. *poselet* (rhyming w. *hoselet* houselled), which, except for chronological difficulties, might be f. POSE *v.*² (XVI) + -LE; the origin remains unknown.] **1.** *trans.* †**a.** *orig.* To cause (any one) to be at a loss what to do or where to turn; to perplex, bewilder, confound; said of circumstances, material obstacles, etc. –1735. **b.** To perplex, bewilder (the brain, mind, understanding, will, wit) 1602. **c.** To perplex or embarrass mentally, as or by a difficult problem or question; to pose 1634. **2.** *intr.* To be at a loss how to act or decide; to ponder perplexedly; to exercise oneself with the solution of a puzzle. Const. *over*, formerly *about, upon.* 1605. **b.** To search in a bewildered way; to grope *for* something; to get *through* by perplexed searching 1817. Now *rare.* **3.** *trans.* To make puzzling; to confuse. Now *rare.* 1647. **4.** *To p. out*: to make out by the exercise of ingenuity and patience 1781.

1. The panting Throng In their own Footsteps puzzled, foil'd, and lost 1735. **b.** The dread of something after death..Puzels the will SHAKS. **c.** Men are annoyed at what puzzles them JOWETT. **2.** I my selfe..have pored and pusled vpon many an old Record CAMDEN. **3.** The ways of Heaven are dark and intricate, Puzzled in mazes ADDISON.

Comb.: **p.-mo:nkey,** the Chilian tree *Araucaria imbricata*, from the difficulty which a monkey would have in climbing it. Hence **Pu·zzlingly** *adv.* **Pu·zzle-pate** = PUZZLE-HEAD; so **Pu·zzle-pated** *a.*, **-ness.**

Pu·zzle-hea:ded, *a.* 1784. [f. PUZZLE *sb.*, or put for *puzzled* + HEAD *sb.* + -ED².] Having a puzzled head; having confused ideas. Hence **Puzzlehea·dedness;** so also **Pu·zzlehead,** a p. person.

Puzzlement (pʊ·z'lmĕnt). 1822. [f. PUZZLE *v.* + -MENT.] The fact or condition of being puzzled; perplexity, bewilderment. **b.** A puzzle 1842.

Puzzler (pʊ·zləɹ). 1652. [f. PUZZLE *v.* + -ER¹.] One who or that which puzzles; also, one who occupies himself with puzzles.

‖**Pyæmia** (pəi,ī·miă). Also **pyemia.** 1857. [mod.L., f. Gr. πύον pus + αἷμα blood; see -IA¹.] *Path.* A condition of blood-poisoning accompanied by fever, caused by the presence in the blood of pathogenic bacteria and their toxic products, and characterized by the formation of pus-foci; septicæmia. Hence **Pyæ·mic** *a.* of, pertaining to, or of the nature of p.; affected with p.

‖**Pycnidium** (pikni·diŏm). *Pl.* **-ia.** 1857. [mod.L., f. Gr. πυκνός thick, dense + dim. suff. -ίδιον.] *Bot.* The special receptacle in certain ascomycetous fungi in which the stylospores are produced.

Pycnite (pi·knəit). 1802. [– Fr. *pycnite* (Haüy, 1801), f. Gr. πυκνός thick, dense + -ITE¹ 2b.] *Min.* A variety of topaz occurring in columnar aggregations.

Pycno- (pikno), bef. a vowel **pycn-,** comb. form of Gr. πυκνός thick, dense.

‖**Pycnaspi·deæ** [Gr. ἀσπίς, ἀσπιδ-shield] *Ornith.*, a cohort of scutelliplantar passerine birds, having the planta or back of the tarsus studded with small irregular scales or plates; hence **Pycnaspi·dean** *a.* **Py·cnodont** [Gr. ὀδούς, ὀδοντ- tooth] *a. Ichthyol.*, pertaining to or having the characteristics of the *Pycnodontidæ*, an extinct family of ganoid fishes; *sb.* a pycnodont fish. **Pycno·gonid** [Gr. γόνυ knee] *Zool.*, a marine arthropod of the group *Pycnogonida*, typified by the parasitic genus *Pycnogonum*; a seaspider. **Pycno·meter,** an instrument for determining the specific gravity of a liquid; a specific gravity flask.

Pycnostyle (pi·knostəil), *a.* and *sb.* 1697. [– L. *pycnostylos* – Gr., f. πυκνός dense + στῦλος column.] *Arch.* **A.** *adj.* Having close intercolumniation; having the space between the columns equal to one diameter and a half of a column. **B.** *sb.* A building having such intercolumniation.

Pycnotic (piknǫ·tik), *a.* 1900. [– Gr. πυκνωτικός, f. πυκνοῦν condense; see -IC.] Pertaining or relating to condensation; applied to a theory of the formation of matter.

‖**Pyelitis** (pəi,ėləi·tis). 1842. [mod.L., f. Gr. πύελος trough + -ITIS.] *Path.* Inflammation of the mucous membrane of the pelvis of the kidney. Hence **Pyeli·tic** *a.*

Pygal (pəi·găl), *a.* (*sb.*) 1838. [f. Gr. πυγή rump + -AL¹.] *Zool.* Of or pertaining to the rump or hinder quarters of an animal. **B.** *sb.* (Short for *p. plate* or *shield.*) The posterior median plate of the carapace of a turtle 1889.

Pygarg (pəi·gaɹg). late ME. [– L. *pygargus* – Gr. πύγαργος 'white-rump'; f. πυγή rump + ἀργός white.] **1.** A kind of antelope mentioned by Herodotus and Pliny; by some supposed to be the addax. (In the LXX, etc., used to render Heb. *dīšōn.*) **2.** (In L. form *pygargus.*) The osprey or sea-eagle. late ME.

‖**Pygidium** (pəidʒi·diŏm, pəigi·diŏm). 1849. [mod.L., f. Gr. πυγή rump + dim. suff. -ίδιον.] *Zool.* The posterior part of the body in certain invertebrates, when forming a distinct segment or division; the caudal or pygal segment. Hence **Pygi·dial** *a.*

Pygmæan, -mean (pigmī·ăn), *sb.* and *a.* 1555. [f. L. *pygmæus* (see next) + -AN.] †**A.** *sb.* = PYGMY *sb.* 1. **B.** *adj.* Of or pertaining to the pygmies; of the nature or size of a pygmy; diminutive, dwarfish 1667.

Pygmy, pigmy (pi·gmi), *sb.* and *a.* late ME. [In earliest use pl. *pygmeis* – L. *pygmæi*, pl. of *pygmæus* – Gr. πυγμαῖος dwarf(ish), f. πυγμή measure of length from elbow to knuckles, fist.] **A.** *sb.* **1.** One of a race (or several races) of men of very small size, mentioned in ancient history and tradition as inhabiting parts of Ethiopia or India. *The Pygmies*, the dwarf races existing in equatorial Africa. †**b.** Formerly applied to the chimpanzee and other anthropoid apes –1863. **2.** *gen.* A dwarf 1520. **b.** *fig.* A person of very small importance, or having some specified quality in a very small degree 1592. **c.** *transf.* A thing that is very small of its kind 1838. **3.** An elf, puck, pixy 1611.

2. As very a manne is..a Pigmay as a Geaunt 1532. **b.** These are heathen arts, and we are but pigmies at them 1860.

B. *adj.* **1.** Of or pertaining to the race of pygmies 1661. **2. a.** Of persons and animals: Of very small size or stature, dwarf 1591. **b.** *gen.* Very small, diminutive. In *Nat. Hist.* often used in the names of species of animals that are very small of their kind. 1595.

2. b. A six years' Darling of a pigmy size WORDSW.

Pygo- (pəigo), repr. Gr. πυγο-, comb. form of πυγή rump.

Pygobra·nchiate [Gr. βράγχια gills] *a.*, belonging to the *Pygobranchia*, a group of gastropods having the gills arranged round the anus. **Py·gopod** [Gr. πούς, ποδ- foot], **a.** *adj.* of or pertaining to the *Pygopodes*, an order of aquatic birds, including the auks, grebes, and loons, having the legs set very far back; **b.** *adj.* of or belonging to the genus *Pygopus* of Australian lizards having rudimentary hind legs; *sb.* a lizard of this family, hence **Pygo·podous** *a.*

Pyin (pəi·in). 1845. [f. Gr. πύον pus + -IN¹.] An albuminoid substance found in pus.

Pyjamas, *U.S.* **pajamas** (pidʒā·măs, pă-, pəi-), *sb. pl.* 1800. [– Urdu *pāyejāma* and *pājāma*, f. Pers. *pay(e* leg + Hindi *jāma* clothing, garment.] Loose drawers or trousers, usu. of silk or cotton, tied round the waist, worn by both sexes among the Moslems, and adopted for night wear by Europeans; in England applied to a sleeping suit of loose trousers and jacket. Also *attrib.* (in sing. form) **Pyja·ma.**

Pylagore (pi·lăgoᵊɹ). Also **pylagoras.** 1753. [– Gr. πυλαγόρας, f. Πύλαι Thermopylæ + ἀγορα.] *Gr. Antiq.* The title of one of the two deputies sent by each constituent tribe to the Amphictyonic Council.

Pylangium (pəilændʒəi·ŏm). 1875. [mod. L., f. Gr. πύλη gate + ἀγγεῖον vessel.] *Anat.* The undivided portion of the arterial trunk next the ventricle in the lower vertebrates. Hence **Pyla·ngial** *a.*

‖**Pylon** (pəi·lǫn). 1823. [– Gr. πυλών a gateway, f. πύλη gate.] **1.** *Arch.* A gateway, a gate-tower; *spec.* in recent use, the monumental gateway to an Egyptian temple, usu. formed by two truncated pyramidal towers connected by a lower architectural member containing the gate. **2.** A tower, mast, or post such as is used to mark the course in an aerodrome, to support a long span of telegraph wire, or the like 1909.

Pyloric (pəilǫ·rik), *a.* 1807. [f. PYLORUS + -IC.] *Anat.* Of or pertaining to the pylorus.

Pyloro- (pəilōᵊ·ro), comb. f. next, as in **Pylo·ropla:sty,** plastic surgery of the pylorus 1895.

‖**Pylorus** (pəilōᵊ·rŏs). 1615. [Late L. – Gr. πυλωρός, πυλουρός gatekeeper, f. πύλη gate + οὖρος warder.] *Anat.* The opening from the stomach into the duodenum, which is guarded by a strong sphincter muscle; also, that part of the stomach where it is situated. **b.** An analogous part in invertebrates, as the posterior opening of the stomach in insects 1828.

Pyo- (pəi,o), bef. a vowel **py-,** repr. Gr. πυο-, comb. form of πύον pus.

Pyoco·ccal [Gr. κόκκος grain] *a.*, pertaining to the ‖**Pyoco·ccus,** a microbe or coccus causing suppuration. **Pyocy·anin,** a blue colouring matter, $C_{14}H_{14}NO_2$, obtained from blue or lead-coloured pus; so **Pyocya·nic** *a.* **Pyoge·nesis,** the formation of pus; suppuration; so **Pyogene·tic, Pyoge·nic** *adjs.*, of or pertaining to pyogenesis; producing pus. ‖**Pyopneumotho·rax,** the presence of pus and air in the pleural cavities. **Pyoxa·nthin, Pyoxa·nthose** [Gr. ξανθός yellow], a yellow colouring matter found with pyocyanin in blue suppuration.

Pyoid (pəi·oid), *a.* 1853. [– Gr. πυοειδής like pus, f. πύον; see -OID.] Of the nature of or resembling pus; purulent.

Pyorrhœa (pəi,ŏrī·ă). 1800. [f. PYO- + Gr. ῥοία flux.] Discharge of pus; *spec.* from the gums.

Pyracanth (pəiᵊ·răkænþ), **pyracantha** (pəiᵊrăkæ·nþă). 1664. [– L. *pyracantha* – Gr. πυράκανθα, an unidentified shrub or plant.] An evergreen thorny shrub, *Cratægus pyracantha*, a native of southern Europe, bearing clusters of white flowers and scarlet berries; also called Christ's, Egyptian, or Evergreen Thorn. Hence **Pyraca·nthine** *a.*

Pyral (pəiᵊ·răl), *a. rare.* 1658. [f. L. *pyra* PYRE + -AL¹.] Of or pertaining to a pyre.

‖**Pyralis** (pi·rălis). *Pl.* **pyralides** (piræ·lidīz). 1588. [– Gr. πυραλίς, -ιδ-, f. πῦρ fire.] †**1.** A fabulous fly supposed to live in or be generated by fire –1684. **2.** *Entom.* [mod.L.] A genus of moths typical of the family *Pyralidæ*. So **Py·ralid** *a.* resembling or belonging to the *Pyralidæ*; *sb.* a moth of this family.

Pyramid (pi·rămid), *sb.* late ME. [orig. used in L. form *pyramis*, pl. *pyra·mides*; – L. *pyramis, -id-* – Gr. πυραμίς, pl. πυραμίδες (Herodotus), of alien origin.] **1.** A monumental structure built of stone or the like, with a polygonal (usu. square) base, and sloping sides meeting at an apex; *orig.* and *esp.* one of the ancient structures of this kind in Eygpt 1555. **2.** The form of a pyramid; in *Geom.* a solid figure bounded by plane surfaces, of which one (the base) is a polygon of any number of sides, and the other surfaces triangles having as bases the sides of the polygon, and meeting at a point (the vertex) outside the plane of the polygon. late ME. †**3.** *Arch.* Any structure of pyramidal form, as a spire, pinnacle, obelisk, etc. Also applied to a gable. –1716. **4.** Any material thing, or pile of things, of pyramidal form 1570. **b.** *Gardening.* Applied (orig. *attrib.*, hence also *simply*) to a fruit-tree, etc., trained in a pyramidal form 1712. **5.** *fig.* (from prec. senses) 1593. **6.** *Cryst.* A set of faces belonging to a single crystallographic form, and, if symmetrically developed, meeting in a point 1748. **7.** *loosely.* A plane figure or formation suggesting the profile of a p. 1589. **b.** *Billiards. pl.* A game played (usu.) with fifteen coloured balls arranged in a triangle, and one cue-ball 1850.

3. What needs my Shakespear..that his hallow'd reliques should be hid Under a Star-ypointing P.? MILT. **4.** Smithfield blazing with pyramids of law-books SWIFT. **5.** An unsteddy and sharp-pointed Pyramis of power 1628.

Comb.: **p.-rest** (*Billiards*), a cue-rest the head of which is arched so as to allow it to be placed over a ball which would otherwise be in the way; **-spot,** the spot on a billiard-table where the apex of the p. is placed, between the centre and the top spot. Hence **Py·ramidist,** one who investigates or is specially versed in the structure and history of the Egyptian pyramids.

Pyramidal (piræ·midăl), *a.* (*sb.*) 1571. [– med.L. *pyramidalis*; see prec., -AL[1].] **1.** Of or pertaining to a pyramid; sloping, as an edge or face of a pyramid (*rare*). **2.** Of the nature or shape of a pyramid; resembling a pyramid 1599. **3.** *Cryst.* Used in senses 1 and 2; also applied to the TETRAGONAL system, of which the square pyramid is a characteristic form 1789. **4.** *Arith.* Applied to the several series of numbers, each beginning with unity, obtained by continued summation of the several series of POLYGONAL numbers; so called because each of these numbers, represented (e.g.) by balls, can be arranged according to a certain rule in the form of the corresponding pyramid (on a triangular, square, or polygonal base) 1674. **B.** (as *sb.*) A p. number 1706. Hence **Pyra·midally** *adv.* in a p. manner or form; †*fig.* in allusion to the embalmed bodies of the dead preserved in the pyramids; after the manner of a mummy.

Pyramidic (pirămi·dik), *a. rare.* 1743. [f. PYRAMID + -IC.] Of, like, or proper to a pyramid; heaped up, or lofty and massive, like a pyramid. So **Pyrami·dical** *a.* (now *rare*). = prec. **Pyrami·dically** *adv.*

‖**Pyramidion** (pirămi·diǫn). *Pl.* **-ia, -ions.** 1840. [– Gr. πυραμίς, -ιδ- PYRAMID + dim. suffix -ιον.] A small pyramid; *spec.* in *Arch.*, the pointed pyramidal portion forming the apex of an obelisk.

Pyramidoid (piræ·midoid). *rare.* 1704. [– mod.L. *pyramidoides* (sc. *schema*): see PYRAMID and -OID.] *Geom.* A solid figure in form approaching a pyramid, but of which the edges that meet at the vertex are curves.

Pyramoid (pi·rămoid). *rare.* [– Gr. πυραμοειδής, f. πυραμίς; see -OID.] = prec.

Pyrargyrite: see PYRO- 2.

Pyre (pəiᵊɹ). 1658. [– L. *pyra* – Gr. πυρά, f. πῦρ, πυρ- FIRE.] A pile of combustible material, esp. wood; usu., a funeral pile for burning the dead.

When the Funeral P. was out, and the last Valediction over SIR T. BROWNE.

Pyrene[1] (pəiᵊ·rīn). 1837. [– mod.L. *pyrena*, f. Gr. πυρήν fruit-stone.] *Bot.* The stone of a fruit; *esp.* one of those in a drupaceous pome.

Pyrene[2] (pəiᵊ·rīn). 1839. [f. Gr. πῦρ fire + -ENE.] *Chem.* A solid hydrocarbon ($C_{16}H_{10}$) obtained from the dry distillation of coal, crystallizing in microscopic laminæ. Hence **Pyrenic** (pəire·nik) *a.* designating a yellow crystalline dibasic acid formed by the oxidation of p.

Pyrenean, -æan (pirĕnī·ăn), *a.* and *sb.* 1592. [f. L. *Pyrenæus* (f. *Pyrene* – Gr. Πυρήνη, daughter of Bebryx, beloved of Hercules, said to be buried on these mountains) + -AN. Cf. Fr. *pyrénéen.*] **A.** *adj.* Of or belonging to the Pyrenees. **B.** *sb.* A native of the Pyrenees.

Pyrenoid (pəirī·noid). 1883. [f. PYRENE[1] + -OID.] A small colourless proteid body, resembling a nucleus, found in certain algæ and protozoa.

Pyrethrine (pəire·þrəin). 1838. [– Fr. *pyréthrine* (Parisel, 1833); see next, -INE[5].] *Chem.* The substance to which the sialagogic action of pyrethrum root is due. Hence **Pyre·thric** *a.* as in *p. acid.*

‖**Pyrethrum** (pəirī·þrǒm). 1562. [L. *pyrethrum, -on* (Pliny) – Gr. πύρεθρον feverfew, perh. f. πυρετός fever.] **1.** orig., The plant *Anacyclus pyrethrum*, N.O. *Compositæ*, also called Pellitory of Spain, having a pungent root (*radix pyrethri*) used in medicine. Now so called only in pharmacy. **2.** *Bot.* A genus of composite plants; a plant of this genus, a feverfew 1882. **b.** In full *P. powder*: an insecticide made of the powdered flower-heads of some species of P. 1876.

Pyretic (pəir-, pire·tik), *a.* and *sb.* 1728. [– mod.L. *pyreticus*, f. Gr. πυρετός fever; see -IC.] **A.** *adj.* **1.** Of or pertaining to fever; producing feverish symptoms 1858. **2.** Used for the cure of fever, antipyretic 1868. **B.** *sb.* A febrifuge, an antipyretic 1728.

Pyreto- (pəiᵊ·r-, pi·rěto), bef. a vowel **pyret-**, comb. form of Gr. πυρετός fever; as in **Pyreto·logy** [-LOGY], the branch of medical science which treats of fevers; etc.

‖**Pyrexia** (pəir-, pire·ksiă). *Pl.* **-iæ.** 1769. [mod.L., f. Gr. πύρεξις, f. πυρέσσειν be feverish, f. πῦρ fire; see -IA[1].] *Path.* Febrile disease; fever. Hence **Pyre·xial, Pyre·xic, -al** *adjs.* febrile.

Pyrheliometer (pəɹhīliǫ·mĭtəɹ). 1855. [f. Gr. πῦρ fire + ἥλιος sun + -METER.] An instrument for measuring the amount of heat given off by the sun.

Pyridine (pəiᵊ·ridəin, piᵊ·r-). 1851. [f. Gr. πῦρ, πυρ- fire + -ID[4] + -INE[5].] *Chem.* A colourless volatile liquid alkaloid of offensive odour and poisonous quality, produced in the dry distillation of bone-oil or coal-tar. Hence **Pyri·dic** *a.* of or related to p. **Py·ridyl,** the radical C_5H_4N of p.

Pyriform (pəiᵊ·ri-, pi·rifǭɹm), *a.* 1704. [– mod.L. *pyriformis*, f. *pyrum*, misspelling of *pirum* pear + -FORM.] Pear-shaped; obconic. (Chiefly in scientific and techn. use.)

Pyritaceous (pəiᵊr-, piritēⁱ·ʃəs), *a. rare.* 1794. [f. PYRITES + -ACEOUS.] Of the nature of or containing pyrites.

Pyrite (pəiᵊ·rəit). 1567. [– (O)Fr. *pyrite* or L. *pyrites*; see next.] †**1.** = PYRITES 1. –1791. **2.** *Min.* Native disulphide of iron (FeS_2), crystallizing in isometric forms, esp. in cubes and pyritohedra: one of the forms of *iron pyrites* 1868.

‖**Pyrites** (pirəi·tīz). 1567. [L. (Pliny) – Gr. πυρίτης, subst. use (sc. λίθος stone) of adj., pertaining to fire, f. πῦρ fire; see -ITE[1] 2 b.] †**1.** Vaguely, a 'fire-stone' or mineral which strikes fire –1796. **2.** Either of the two sulphides of iron (FeS_2), pyrite and marcasite, also dist. as *iron p.*; also, the double sulphide of copper and iron ($Cu_2S.Fe_2S_3$), chalcopyrite or *copper p.*

Used also generically to include many related sulphides and arsenides of iron, cobalt, nickel, etc., or of iron with another metal; e.g. **capillary p.,** native sulphide of nickel; **spear p., white iron p.,** varieties of MARCASITE; also HEPATIC *P.* Hence **Pyri·tic, -al** *a.* of or pertaining to p., containing or resembling p. **Pyriti·ferous** *a.* yielding p. **Py·ritous** *a.* of, of the nature of, or containing p.; characterizing, or characterized by the presence of, p.

Pyritize (pəiᵊ·r-, pi·ritəiz), *v.* 1804. [f. prec. + -IZE.] *trans.* To convert into pyrites; to impregnate with pyrites.

Pyrito- (pirəi·to, pəiᵊ·rito), comb. form of PYRITES; as in **Pyritohedron** (-hī·drǫn, -he·drǫn), pl. **-he·dra** [Gr. ἕδρα side], *Cryst.* a form of pentagonal dodecahedron common in crystals of pyrite; hence **Pyritohe·dral** *a.*, pertaining to or the form of a pyritohedron. **Pyrito·logy** [-LOGY], a treatise on, or the study of, pyrites.

Pyritoid (pirəi·toid), *a.* 1895. [f. PYRITES + -OID.] Resembling or allied to pyrites.

Pyro (pəiᵊ·ro). 1879. *Photogr.* Abbrev. of *pyrogallic acid* (see PYRO- 3), used as a developing agent. Often *attrib.*

Pyro- (pəiᵊro, piro), bef. a vowel or *h* sometimes **pyr-**, repr. Gr. πυρο-, πυρ- comb. form of πῦρ fire.

1. In various terms, chiefly scientific or techn., in the sense: Of, relating to, done with, caused or produced by fire. **Pyro-ele·ctric** *a. Min.*, applied to certain crystals which on being heated become electrically polar. **Pyrognostic** (-gnǫ·stik) [Gr. γνωστικός] *a. Min.*, applied to or relating to those characters of a mineral that are ascertained by means of the flame of a blow-pipe or of a Bunsen burner; so **Pyrogno·stics** *sb. pl.*, pyrognostic characters, or the branch of mineralogy that deals with them. **Pyro·graphy** = POKER-WORK. **Pyrolu·site** [Gr. λοῦσις washing, from its use, when heated, for discharging colour from glass], *Min.* native dioxide of manganese, MnO_2. **Pyromagne·tic** *a.*, applied to a dynamo invented by Edison, the working of which depends on the magnetization of iron with increase of temperature. **Pyroma·nia,** insanity characterized by an impulse to set things on fire. **Pyromo·rphous** [Gr. μορφή] *a. Min.*, having the property of crystallizing after fusion by heat. **Pyrophanous** (pəirǫ·fănəs) [Gr. -φανης appearing] *a. Min.*, having the property of becoming transparent or translucent when heated. **Pyro-pho·tograph,** a photographic picture burnt in on glass or porcelain; hence **Pyro-photogra·phic** *a.*; **Pyro-photo·graphy. Py·roscope** [-SCOPE], an instrument for measuring the intensity of radiant heat, consisting of a differential thermometer having one bulb covered with silver.

2. In names of minerals and rocks, usu. indicating some property exhibited or alteration produced by the action of fire or heat; sometimes denoting a fiery red or yellow colour. **Pyrargyrite** (-ā·ɹdʒirəit) [Gr. ἄργυρον], a dark-red silver ore, a native sulphide of silver and antimony. **Py·rochlore** [Gr. χλωρός greenish-yellow], a niobotitanate of calcium, cerium, and other bases, occurring in octahedral crystals of a brown colour, becoming greenish-yellow when strongly heated. **Pyromo·rphite** [Gr. μορφή], chlorophosphate of lead, occurring in green, yellow, or brown crystals; so called because the globule produced by melting assumes a crystalline form on cooling. †**Py·rophane** (-fēⁱn) [Gr. -φανης appearing], a variety of opal which absorbs melted wax, and becomes translucent when heated; also sometimes = FIRE-*opal.*

3. In Chemistry, *pyro-* is prefixed to the name of a substance or to an adj. forming part thereof, in order to name a new substance formed by a destructive distillation or other application of heat.

a. Prefixed to the adj. denominating an acid, to form the name of a new acid, etc. **Pyroga·llic** *acid*, a substance, $C_6H_6O_3$, much used as a reducing agent in photography, etc. **Pyromeco·nic** *acid*, a crystalline bitter acid, $C_5H_4O_3$, obtained by the dry distillation of meconic acid. **Pyromu·cic** *acid*, an acid, $C_5H_4O_3$, metameric with pyromeconic acid, produced by the dry distillation of mucic acid. **Pyrophospho·ric** *acid*, $H_4P_2O_7$, a tetrabasic acid, produced as a glass-like solid, by the action of heat on phosphoric acid. **Pyrotarta·ric** *acid* $C_5H_8O_4$, obtained by the dry distillation of tartaric acid. **Pyru·vic** *acid* [L. *uva* grape), $C_3H_4O_3$, produced by dry distillation of racemic or tartaric acid. Also in the names of salts of these acids, as **Pyrota·rtrate,** etc.

b. Prefixed to a sb. (Now often superseded by other names.) **Pyrocatechin** (pəi:roˌkæ·tĭtʃin), also called *catechol*, *pyro-catechuic acid*, and *oxyphenic acid*, $C_6H_6O_2$, produced by the dry distillation of catechu, kino, etc., forming broad white strongly shining laminæ, and rhombic or small rectangular prisms. **Py·rocoll** [Gr. κόλλα glue], $C_{10}H_6N_2O_2$, a product of the distillation of gelatin when free from fat but containing albumen, casein or gluten. **Pyroxa·nthin** [Gr. ξανθός yellow], a yellow crystalline substance, produced by the action of potash on one of the constituents of the heavy oil of wood-tar.

c. Also in the derivative names of certain hydrocarbon compounds and groups, as **Py·razine, Py·rone.**

Pyro-acid (pəi·roˌæ·sid). 1835. *Chem.* An acid formed from another acid by dry or destructive distillation; see PYRO- 3.

Pyrogen (pəiᵊ·rǒdʒen). *rare.* 1858. [f. PYRO- + -GEN; lit. 'fire-producer', or 'fire-produced'.] †**a.** The 'electric fluid' –1864. **b.** A substance which, when introduced into the blood, produces fever; a pyrogenetic agent 1896.

Pyrogenetic (pəiᵊ:roˌdʒĭne·tik), *a.* 1858. [f. PYRO- 1 + -GENETIC.] **a.** Having the property of producing heat, esp. in the body; thermogenetic. **b.** Having the property of producing fever. So **Pyroge·nic,** *a.* = b.

Pyrogenous (-ǫ·dʒĭnəs), *a.* 1839. [f. as PYROGEN + -OUS.] **1.** Produced by fire or heat. **a.** *Geol.* Of rocks: = IGNEOUS *a.* 2. **b.** *Chem.* Applied to a substance produced by the combustion of another substance. **2.** = prec. 1890.

Pyrolatry (pəirǫ·lătri). 1669. [f. PYRO- + -LATRY.] Fire-worship. Hence **Pyro·later** (**-or**), a fire-worshipper.

Pyroligneous (pəiᵊroˌli·gnĭəs), *a.* 1790. [– Fr. *pyro-ligneux* (De Morveau and Lavoisier, 1787), f. PYRO- + L. *lignum* wood.] Produced by the action of fire or heat upon wood.

P. acid, a crude acetic acid (wood vinegar) obtained by the destructive distillation of wood; so *p. alcohol, ether, spirit,* methyl alcohol. So †**Pyroli·gnic,** †**Pyroli·gnous** *adjs.* **Pyroli·gnate,** a salt of p. acid.

Pyrology (pəirǫ·lŏdʒi). *rare.* 1731. [– mod.L. *pyrologia*; see PYRO- 1, -LOGY.] The science of fire or heat; *spec.* that branch of chemistry which deals with the application of fire to chemical analysis, etc. Hence **Pyro·logist**, one versed in p.

Pyromancy (pəiᵊ·romænsi, pi·ro-). Now *rare.* late ME. [– OFr. *piromance, pyromancie* – late L. *pyromantia* – Gr. πυρομαντεία; see PYRO-, -MANCY.] Divination by fire or signs derived from fire. So **Pyroma·ntic** *a.* pertaining to or practising p.; *sb.* one who divines by fire.

Pyrometer (pəirǫ·mĭtəɹ). 1749. [f. PYRO- + -METER.] †**a.** *orig.* An intrument for measuring the expansion of solid bodies under the influence of heat. **b.** Any instrument for measuring high temperatures, usu. those higher than can be measured by the mercurial thermometer. Hence **Pyrome·tric, -al** *adjs.* pertaining to a p. or to pyrometry; of the nature of, or measurable by, a p. **Pyrome·trically** *adv.* **Pyro·metry,** the measurement of very high temperatures.

Pyrope (pəiᵊ·rōᵘp). ME. [– OFr. *pirope* – L. *pyropus* – Gr. πυρωπός gold-bronze, lit. fiery-eyed, f. πῦρ, πυρ- fire + ὤψ eye, face.] †**1.** Applied vaguely to a red or fiery gem, as ruby or carbuncle –1795. **2.** *Min.* The Bohemian garnet or fire-garnet, a deep-red gem 1804.

Pyrophoric (-fǫ·rik), *a.* 1828. [f. next + -IC.] Of, pertaining to, or of the nature of a pyrophorus; having the property of taking fire on exposure to air. Also **Pyro·phorous** *a.*

‖**Pyrophorus** (pəirǫ·fŏrŏs). *Pl.* **-i** (-əi). 1778. [mod.L. – Gr. πυροφόρος fire-bearing.] **1.** *Chem.* Any substance capable (esp. in a finely divided state) of taking fire spontaneously on exposure to air. **2.** *Entom.* A genus of beetles of the family *Elateridæ*, found in tropical America, containing the most brilliantly luminous 'fire-flies' 1809.

‖**Pyrosis** (pəirōᵘ·sis). 1789. [mod.L. – Gr. πύρωσις, f. πυροῦν set on fire; see -OSIS.] *Path.* An affection characterized by a burning sensation in the stomach and œsophagus, with eructation of watery fluid; water-brash.

Pyrosome (pəiᵊ·rosōᵘm). 1812. [– mod. L. *Pyrosoma*, f. Gr. πῦρ fire (PYRO-) + σῶμα body.] *Zool.* An animal of the genus *Pyrosoma*, consisting of highly phosphorescent compound ascidians, the individuals being united into a free-swimming colony in the form of a hollow cylinder closed at one end.

Pyrotechnic (pəiᵊro,te·knik), *a.* and *sb.* 1704. [f. PYROTECHNY + -IC.] **A.** *adj.* †**1.** Of or pertaining to the use of fire in chemistry, metallurgy, or gunnery –1731. **2.** Of or pertaining to fireworks, or the art of making them; of the nature of a firework 1825. **b.** *fig.*, esp. said of a brilliant display of wit, rhetoric, etc. 1849. **B.** *sb. pl.* **a.** = PYROTECHNY 1, 3. 1729. **b.** A display of fireworks; also *transf.* of lightning 1840. **c.** *fig.* Brilliant displays 1901. So **Pyrote·chnical** *a.*; **-ly** *adv.*

Pyrotechnist (pəiᵊrote·knist). 1791. [f. next + -IST.] One employed or skilled in pyrotechny; a maker or displayer of fireworks.

Pyrotechny (pəiᵊ·rŏtekni). 1579. [– Fr. *pyrotechnie* – mod.L. *pyrotechnia*, f. PYRO- + Gr. τέχνη art.] The art of employing fire. †**1.** (*Military p.*) The manufacture and use of gunpowder, bombs, fire-arms, etc. –1728. †**2.** The use of fire in chemical operations or in metallurgy –1728. **3.** The making and managing of fireworks for scenic display, for military use, or as signals, etc. 1635.

Pyroxene (pəiᵊ·rǫksīn). 1800. [f. Gr. πῦρ, πυρο- fire + ξένος stranger; so named by Haüy, 1796, because it was thought alien to igneous rocks.] *Min.* A species including a large variety of minerals, all bisilicates of lime with one or more of various other bases, most usu. magnesia and iron oxide, but also manganese, potash, soda, and zinc. Hence **Pyroxenic** (-e·nik) *a.* pertaining to, having the character of, consisting of, or containing p. **Pyroxenite** (-ǫ·ksenəit), also **-yte,** a metamorphic rock consisting chiefly of p.

Pyroxyle (pəirǫ·ksil). 1847. [– Fr. *pyroxyle* (Pelouze, 1846), f. PYRO- + Gr. ξύλον wood.] *Chem.* = PYROXYLIN. So **Pyroxy·lic** *a.*, *Chem.* obtained from wood by means of fire, i.e. by dry distillation; chiefly in *p.-spirit*, wood-spirit.

Pyroxylin (pəirǫ·ksilin). 1839. [– Fr. *pyroxyline*, f. as prec. + *-ine* -IN[1].] *Chem.* Any one of the class of explosive compounds, including gun-cotton, produced by treating vegetable fibre with nitric acid, or with a mixture of nitric and sulphuric acids; and used in solution for making lacquers, etc.

Pyrrhic (pi·rik), *sb.*[1] and *a.*[1] 1597. [– L. *pyrrhicha* or Gr. πυρρίχη a dance in armour, said to have been so named from one Πύρριχος the inventor; prop. an adj. (sc. ὄρχησις).] **A.** *sb.* The war-dance of the ancient Greeks, in which the motions of actual warfare were gone through, in armour, to a musical accompaniment. **B.** *adj.* Epithet of this dance; of or pertaining to this dance 1630.

Pyrrhic (pi·rik), *sb.*[2] and *a.*[2] 1626. [– L. *pyrrhichius* – Gr. πυρρίχιος of or pertaining to the Pyrrhic (dance); as sb., short for *pes pyrrhichius*, ποὺς πυρρίχιος pyrrhic foot, a metrical foot used in the war-song.] *Prosody.* **A.** *sb.* A metrical foot, consisting of two short syllables. **B.** *adj.* Consisting of two short syllables; composed of or pertaining to pyrrhics 1749.

Pyrrhic (pi·rik), *a.*[3] 1885. [– Gr. πυρρικός, f. Πυρρός, L. *Pyrrhus*, king of Epirus.] Of, pertaining to, or like that of Pyrrhus.

P. victory, a victory gained at too great a cost; in allusion to the exclamation of Pyrrhus after the battle of Asculum in Apulia, 'One more such victory and we are lost'.

Pyrrhonian (pirōᵘ·niăn), *a.* and *sb.* 1638. [– Fr. *pyrrhonien*, f. L. *pyrrhonius, -eus* (f. *Pyrrho*, Gr. Πύρρων, sceptic philosopher of Elis); see -AN.] **A.** *adj.* = PYRRHONIC *a.* 1651. **B.** *sb.* = PYRRHONIST 1638.

Pyrrhonic (pirǫ·nik), *sb.* and *a.* 1593. [f. Gr. Πύρρων (see prec.) + -IC.] **A.** *sb.* = PYRRHONIST. **B.** *adj.* Of or pertaining to Pyrrho, or to his doctrines; purely sceptical.

Pyrrhonism (pi·rŏniz'm). 1670. [f. as prec. + -ISM. Cf. Fr. *pyrrhonisme* (Pascal).] A system of sceptic philosophy taught by Pyrrho of Elis (*c*300 B.C.); the doctrine of the impossibility of attaining certainty of knowledge; absolute or universal scepticism; hence *gen.*, scepticism, incredulity, philosophic doubt. So **Py·rrhonist,** a follower or disciple of Pyrrho; a professor of P.; a sceptic. **Py·rrhonize** *v. intr.* to practise P.; *trans.* to treat or transform sceptically (*rare*).

Pyrrhotine (pi·rŏtəin). 1849. [– G. *pyrrhotin* (Breithaupt, 1835), f. Gr. πυρρότης redness + *-in* -INE[5].] *Min.* = next.

Pyrrhotite (pi·rŏtəit). 1868. [Altered by Dana from prec.; see -ITE[1] 2 b.] *Min.* A magnetic sulphide of iron, occurring massive and amorphous, having a granular structure, and a colour between bronze and copper-red.

Pyrrol (pi·rǫl). 1835. [f. Gr. πυρρός reddish + L. *oleum* oil (see -OL 3).] *Chem.* A feebly basic, colourless transparent liquid, C_4H_5N, contained in bone-oil and coal-tar, having an odour like chloroform. Hence **Py·rroline** = PYRROL.

Pyruline (pi·riŭləin), *a.* [f. mod.L. *Pyrula*, generic name (f. L. *pirum, pyrum* pear; see next) + -INE[1].] *Zool.* Related to the gastropod genus *Pyrula* or sub-family *Pyrulinæ*, having a pear-shaped shell, the pear-shells or fig-shells.

‖**Pyrus** (pəiᵊ·rŏs). 1894. [med. and mod.L. var. of L. *pirus.*] *Bot.* The genus of rosaceous trees and shrubs which includes the pear, apple, and their congeners; occas. used as the English name of foreign species, esp. the scarlet pyrus, *Pyrus japonica.*

Pythagorean (pəiþægŏrī·ăn), *a.* and *sb.* 1550. [f. L. *Pythagoreus, -ius* – Gr. Πυθαγόρειος, f. proper name Πυθαγόρας Pythagoras + -AN.] **A.** *adj.* Of or pertaining to Pythagoras, an ancient Greek philosopher and mathematician of Samos (6th c. B.C.), or to his system or school. Often with allusion to his belief in the transmigration of souls, or to his abstinence from flesh as food. 1579.

There, love the Fork, thy Garden cultivate, And give thy frugal Frinds a P. Treat DRYDEN. *P. letter*, the Greek Y, used by Pythagoras as a symbol of the two divergent paths of virtue and of vice. *P. proposition* or *theorem*, the 47th of the first book of Euclid, namely, that the square on the hypotenuse of a right-angled triangle is equal to the sum of the squares on the other two sides.

B. *sb.* A disciple or follower of Pythagoras 1550. **b.** *transf.* or *allus.* A person whose doctrine or practice agrees with that of Pythagoras 1599. Hence **Pythagore·anism,** the P. philosophy.

Pythagoric (pəiþăgǫ·rik), *a.* Now *rare.* 1653. [– L. *Pythagoricus* – Gr. Πυθαγορικός.] = PYTHAGOREAN *a.* 1653. So †**Pythago·rical** *a.*

Pythagorize (pəiþæ·gŏrəiz), *v.* 1610. [– Gr. πυθαγορίζειν be a disciple of Pythagoras.] **1.** *intr.* To speculate after the manner of Pythagoras. †**2.** *trans.* To change (one person or thing) into another as by transmigration of souls –1721.

‖**Pythia** (pi·þiă). 1842. [– Gr. Πυθία (sc. ἱέρεια) the priestess of Pythian Apollo at Delphi, fem. of Πύθιος adj. Delphic, f. Πυθώ, place-name.] **1.** *Gr. Antiq.* The priestess of Apollo at Delphi, who delivered the oracles. **2.** *Zool.* A genus of gastropod molluscs.

Pythiad (pi·þiæd). 1842. [– Gr. Πυθιάς, Πυθιαδ-, f. Πύθια pl. (sc. ἱερά) the Pythian games; see -AD 1 b.] The period between two celebrations of the Pythian games.

Pythian (pi·þiăn), *a.* (*sb.*) 1598. [f. L. *Pythius* (– Gr. Πύθιος of Delphi or the Delphic Apollo) + -AN.] **A.** *adj.* Of or pertaining to Delphi, or to the oracle and priestess of Apollo there; also, of or pertaining to the games held near Delphi.

P. games, one of the four national festivals of the Greeks, held near Delphi. *P. meter* or *verse* (L. *versus Pithius*), the dactylic hexameter, perh. so called from its use in the Pythian oracles.

B. *sb.* A native or inhabitant of Delphi; *spec.* the Delphic priestess; hence, one who is ecstatic or frenzied like the priestess; also, an appellation of the Delphic Apollo; hence *transf.* Hence **Py·thic** *a.* = A.

Pythogenic (pəiþo,dʒe·nik), *a.* 1862. [f. Gr. πύθειν to rot + -γεν- producing + -IC.] Generated by or from corruption or filth; esp. in *p. fever*, a name for typhoid or enteric fever.

Python[1] (pəi·þǫn). 1590. [– L. *Python* – Gr. Πύθων.] **1.** *Gr. Myth.* The huge serpent or monster slain near Delphi by Apollo; hence *poet.* any monster or pestilential scourge. **2.** *Zool.* A genus of large non-venomous snakes inhabiting the tropical regions of the Old World, which kill their prey by constriction; the rock-snakes; pop., any large snake which crushes its prey 1836. Hence **Pytho·nic** *a.*[1] of, pertaining to, or resembling the p.; monstrous, huge.

Python[2] (pəi·þǫn). 1603. [– late L. (Vulg.) *pytho, -on-* or late Gr. (N.T.) πύθων familiar spirit.] A familiar or possessing spirit; also, one possessed by such a spirit and acting as its mouthpiece. Hence **Pytho·nic** *a.*[2] prophetic, oracular; **-al** *a.* (now *rare*).

Pythoness (pəi·þŏnės). [In XIV *phitones(se* – OFr. *phitonise* (mod. *pythonisse*) – med.L. *phitonissa*, for late L. *pythonissa* (Vulg., 1 Chron. 10:13), fem. of *pytho* (Deut. 18:11, etc.) – late Gr. πύθων (Acts 16:16), identical with πύθων PYTHON[1]; like the Fr. word finally assim. to the L. form; see -ESS[1].] A woman supposed to have a familiar spirit, and to utter his words; a woman having the power of soothsaying; a witch.

Pythonism (pəi·þŏniz'm). *rare.* 1662. [f. PYTHON[2] + -ISM.] Possession by a pythonic spirit; occult power thence derived; divination.

‖**Pythonissa** (pəiþŏni·să). Now *rare.* late ME. [Late L.; see PYTHONESS.] = PYTHONESS. (Often treated as the proper name of the witch of Endor.)

Pythonomorph (pəiþōᵘ·nomǫɹf). 1880. [– mod.L. *Pythonomorpha* pl., f. PYTHON[1] 2 + Gr. μορφή form.] *Palæont.* One of the *Pythonomorpha*, a division of extinct reptiles allied to the existing *Pythonoidea* (the peropodous snakes); a MOSASAURIAN.

Pyuria (pəiyūᵊ·riă). 1811. [f. PYO- + -URIA.] *Path.* Discharge of pus with urine.

Pyx (piks), *sb.* late ME. [– L. *pyxis* – late Gr. πυξίς Box *sb.*²] **1.** A box; a coffer; a vase (*rare*) 1604. **2.** *Eccl.* The vessel in which the host or consecrated bread of the Sacrament is reserved. late ME. **3.** At the Royal Mint, London, the box or chest in which specimen gold and silver coins are deposited to be tested at the *trial of the p.*, i.e. the final official trial of the purity and weight of the coins, now conducted annually by a jury of the Goldsmiths' Company 1598. **4.** *Anat.* = Pyxis 2. 1894.

Comb. **p.-cloth,** a cloth used to veil the p.

Pyx (piks), *v.* 1546. [f. prec.] *trans.* To place in a pyx. **a.** To reserve (the host) in a pyx. **b.** To deposit (specimen coins) in the pyx (Pyx *sb.* 3); hence, To test (coin) by weight and assay 1561.

Pyxidate (pi·ksideᶦt), *a.* 1753. [– mod. L. *pyxidatus*, f. *pyxis, pyxid-*; see Pyx *sb.*, -ate².] *Bot.* Having the form of a pyxis or pyxidium; opening, as a capsule, with a transverse slit; also, bearing pyxidia.

‖**Pyxidium** (piksi·diŏm). *Pl.* **-ia.** 1832. [mod.L. – Gr. πυξίδιον, dim. of πυξίς a box; see Pyx.] *Bot.* A capsule opening by transverse dehiscence, so that the top comes off like the lid of a box.

‖**Pyxis** (pi·ksis). *Pl.* **pyxides** (pi·ksidīz). late ME. [L.; see Pyx *sb.*] **1.** = Pyx 1, 2. 1536. **2.** *Anat.* The acetabulum or socket of the hip-bone, into which the head of the thigh-bone is inserted. late ME. **3.** (In full *p. nautica.*) The mariners' compass 1686. **4.** *Bot.* **a.** = prec. **b.** A cup-like dilation of the podetium in lichens, having shields on its edge. 1845.

Q

Q (kiū), the seventeenth letter of the English and the sixteenth of the Roman alphabet, was in the latter an adoption of the ϙ (κόππα, *koppa*) of some of the early Greek alphabets. The Phœnician letter from which this was derived had the forms ϙ, φ, Ϙ, and was used as the sign for the more guttural of the two *k*-sounds which exist in the Semitic tongues. In OE. orthography the ordinary symbol for the Com.Teut. initial combination *kw-* was *cw-* (in early use also *cu-*). By the end of the 13th c. *cw-* was entirely discontinued, and *qu-* (or its variants *qv-, qw-*) was the established spelling for all cases of the sound (kw), whether of English, French, or Latin origin. In ordinary mod. English words *q* is employed only in the combination *qu*, whether this is initial as in *quality*, etc., medial as in *equal*, etc., or representing a final (k), as in *cheque, grotesque*, etc.

I. Used to denote serial order, as 'Q Battery', 'Section Q', etc., or as a symbol of some thing or person, a point in a diagram, etc.

II. Abbreviations. **1.** Of Latin words or phrases. **a.** q.v. = *quod vide* 'which see'. †**b.** From the language of medical prescriptions: q.l. = *quantum libet*, q.pl. = *quantum placet* 'as much as one pleases'; q.s. = Quantum sufficit; q.v. = *quantum vis* 'as much as you wish'. **c.** Formulæ placed at the end of mathematical problems or theorems: Q.E.D., Q.E.F., Q.E.I., = *quod erat demonstrandum, faciendum, inveniendum*, 'which was to be demonstrated, done, found'.

2. Of English words or phrases. **a.** Q. = Queen; Q., q. = query, question; q. (in a ship's log) = squalls. **b.** Q.B. = Queen's Bench; Q.C. = Queen's Counsel; Q.M. = Quartermaster; Q.M.G. = Quartermaster-General; Q.T., q.t. = quiet (*slang*); phr. *on the q. t.* **c.** qr. = quarter, quire; qt. = quart, quantity; qu. = query.

Q-boat, Q-ship. 1919. = Mystery-*ship.*

‖**Qua** (kwēᶦ), *adv.* Also **quà, quâ.** 1647. [L., abl. sing. fem. of *qui* who.] In so far as; in the capacity of.

The Apostle commands Wives to submit to their Husbands, surely *quà* Husbands, not *quà* men 1649.

Qua-bird (kwā·bəɹd). *U.S.* 1789. [f. *qua*, imitative of its note + Bird *sb.*] The Night Heron of N. America, *Nycticorax gardeni.*

Quack (kwæk), *sb.*¹ 1638. [abbrev. of Quacksalver. For the shortening cf. Rake *sb.*⁴, Sap *sb.*⁴] **1.** An ignorant pretender to medical skill; one who boasts to have a knowledge of wonderful remedie ; an empiric or imposter in medicine 1659. **2.** *transf.* One who professes a knowledge or skill concerning subjects of which he is ignorant 1638. **3.** *attrib.*, as *quack-doctor*, etc. 1653.

1. Running after Quacks and Mountebanks. . for Medicines and Remedies De Foe. Hence **Qua·ckish** *a.* of the nature of a q. or quackery. **Qua·ckism,** quackery.

Quack (kwæk), *sb.*² 1839. [imit.; cf. Du. *kwak*, G. *quack*, Sw. *qvack* (of ducks or frogs), Icel. *kvak* twittering of birds.] The harsh cry characteristic of a duck; a sound resembling this.

Quack (kwæk), *v.*¹ 1628. [f. Quack *sb.*¹] **1.** *intr.* To play the quack; to talk pretentiously and ignorantly, like a quack. **2.** *trans.* To puff or palm off with fraudulent and boastful pretensions, as a quack-medicine 1651. **3.** To treat after the fashion of a quack; to administer quack medicines to; to seek to remedy by empirical or ignorant treatment 1746.

2. The Politician must be quacked, paragraphed, . . and coteried into notoriety 1830. **3.** A Valetudinarian, who quacked himself to death Bentham.

Quack (kwæk), *v.*² 1617. [Imitative; cf. Du. *kwakken*, G. *quacken* croak, quack. Cf. Quackle.] **1.** *intr.* Of a duck: To utter its characteristic note. **b.** Of a raven or frog: To croak (*rare*) 1727. **2.** *transf.* To make a harsh sound like the note of a duck, make a noisy outcry 1624.

Quackery (kwæ·kəri). 1709. [f. Quack *sb.*¹ + -ery.] The characteristic practices or methods of a quack: charlatanry.

Quackle (kwæ·k'l), *v.* 1564. [In form a deriv. of Quack *v.*², but earlier. Cf. MLG. *quackelen*, G. *quakeln* prattle.] *intr.* To quack, as a duck.

Quack-quack (kwæk,kwæk). 1865. [Imitative; see Quack *sb.*²] An imitation of the note of a duck; a nursery name for a duck.

Quacksalver (kwæ·ksælvəɹ). 1579. [– early mod. Du. *quacksalver* (now *kwakzalver*, whence G. *quacksalber*), of which the second element is f. *salf, zalf* Salve, and the first is prob. the stem of †*quacken, kwakken* prattle.] **1.** = Quack *sb.*¹ 1. **2.** *transf.* = Quack *sb.*¹ 2. 1611. So †**Qua·cksalving** *ppl. a.* belonging to or characteristic of a q.; resembling, acting like, a q.

Quad (kwǫd), *sb.*¹ 1820. Abbrev. (orig. in Oxford slang) of Quadrangle 2.

Quad (kwǫd), *sb.*² 1880. Abbrev. of Quadrat 2.

Quad (kwǫd), *a.* 1888. Abbrev. of Quadruple *a.* c.

Quad (kwǫd), *v.* 1888. [f. Quad *sb.*²] *Printing.* To insert quadrats in (a line of type); to fill with quadrats.

Quadrable (kwǫ·drăb'l), *a.* 1695. [– med.L. *quadrabilis*, f. L. *quadrare*; see Quadrate *v.*, -able.] *Math.* Capable of being represented by an equivalent square, or of being expressed in a finite number of algebraic terms.

Quadragenarian (kwǫ:drădʒĭnēᵊ·riăn), *a.* and *sb.* 1839. [f. late L. *quadragenarius*, f. L. *quadrageni*, distrib. of *quadraginta* forty; see -an.] **A.** *adj.* Forty years old. **B.** *sb.* A person forty years of age. So **Qua:dragena·rious** *a.* 1656.

‖**Quadragesima** (kwǫdrădʒe·simă). 1581. [Late (eccl.) L., subst. use (sc. *dies* day) of fem. of L. *quadragesimus* fortieth, ordinal of *quadraginta* forty.] *Eccl.* †**a.** The forty days of Lent. **b.** (Also *Q. Sunday.*) The first Sunday in Lent. Hence **Quadrage·simal** *a.* of a fast (*esp.* that of Lent), lasting for forty days; belonging or appropriate to the period of Lent.

Quadrangle (kwǫ·dræŋg'l). late ME. [– (O)Fr. *quadrangle* or late L. *quadrangulum*, subst. use of n. of *quadrangulus*; see Quadri-, Angle *sb.*²] **1.** *Geom.* A figure having four angles, and therefore four sides. **2.** A square or rectangular space or court, the sides of which are occupied by parts of a large building, as a palace, college, etc. 1593. **3.** A building containing a quadrangle 1620. Hence **Quadra·ngular** *a.* shaped like a q.; having four angles; **-ly** *adv.*

Quadrant (kwǫ·drănt), *sb.*¹ late ME. [– L. *quadrans, -ant-* quarter, orig. of the as, f. *quadr-*, for **quatr-*, comb. form of *quattuor* four.] †**1.** A quarter of a day; six hours –1646. **2.** A quarter of a circle or circular body, viz. (*a*) an arc of a circle, forming one fourth of the circumference; (*b*) one fourth of the area of a circle, contained within two radii at right angles 1571. **b.** A thing having the form of a quarter-circle 1638. **3.** An instrument, properly having the form of a graduated quarter-circle, used for making angular measurements, *esp.* for taking altitudes in astronomy and navigation. late ME.

2. b. *Q. of altitude*, a graduated strip of brass on an artificial globe, fixed at one end to some point of the meridian, round which it revolves, and extending round one fourth of the circumference.

†**Quadrant,** *sb.*² 1443. [app. alteration of Quadrat or Quadrate *sb.*¹, through assoc. with prec.] **1.** = Quadrangle 2, 3. –1655. **2.** A square; a square thing or piece (also *fig.*); a square picture –1670.

†**Qua·drant,** *a.* 1509. [– L. *quadrans, -ant-*, pr. pple. of *quadrare* square; see Quadrate *sb.*] Square –1618.

Quadrantal (kwǫdræ·ntăl), *a.* 1678. [– L. *quadrantalis*; see Quadrant *sb.*¹, -al¹.] Having the shape of, consisting of, connected with a quadrant or quarter-circle; esp. *q. arc.*

Quadrat (kwǫ·drăt). late ME. [var. of Quadrate *sb.*, in special senses.] †**1.** An instrument formerly used for measuring altitudes or distances, consisting of a square plate with two graduated sides, sights, etc. –1617. **2.** *Printing.* A small block of metal, lower than the face of the type, used by printers for spacing; abbrev. Quad *sb.*² 1683.

Quadrate (kwǫ·dreᶦt), *sb.* 1471. [– L. *quadratum*, subst. use of n. of *quadratus*, pa. pple. of *quadrare* square, f. *quadr-*, Quadri-; see -ate¹.] †**1.** A square; a square area or space; also, a rectangle or rectangular space –1680. †**b.** A square number; the square *of* a number –1646. **2.** A square or rectangular plate or block (*rare*) 1647. †**3.** *Astron.* Quadrate aspect; quadrature –1695. **4.** *Anat.* **a.** The quadrate bone. **b.** A quadrate muscle. 1872.

1. The Powers Militant, That stood for Heav'n, in mighty Q. joyn'd Milt. **2.** His person was a q., his step massy and elephantine Lamb.

Quadrate (kwǫ·drĕt), *a.* late ME. [– L. *quadratus*, pa. pple. of *quadrare*; see prec., -ate².] **1.** Square, rectangular. Now *rare.* †**b.** *Math.* Of numbers or roots: Square –1660. **c.** *Anat.* In the names of parts of the body having an approximately square shape 1856. †**2.** *Astron.* = Quartile *a.* –1685.

1. A strong Castel q. having at eche corner a great Round Tower Leland. **c.** *Q. bone*, a special bone in the head of birds and reptiles, by which the lower jaw is articulated to the skull.

Quadrate (kwǫ·dreᶦt), *v.* 1560. [– *quadrat-*, pa. ppl. stem of L. *quadrare*; see prec., -ate³.] **1.** *trans.* To make (a thing) square (*rare*). **b.** *Math.* To square (a circle, etc.) (*rare*) 1645. **2.** *intr.* To square, agree, correspond, conform *with* (rarely *to*) 1610. **b.** Without const.: To be fitting, suitable, or consistent. Also of two things: To harmonize with each other. Now *rare.* 1664. **c.** *trans.* To make conformable (*to*). *rare.* 1669. **3.** *Artillery.* **a.** *trans.* To adjust (a gun) on its carriage. **b.** *intr.* Of a gun: To lie properly on the carriage. 1706.

2. He had to make a creed which would q. with his immorality 1876.

Quadratic (kwŏdræ·tik), *a.* and *sb.* 1656. [– Fr. *quadratique* or mod.L. *quadraticus*, f. *quadratus*; see Quadrate *a.*, -ic.] **A.** *adj.* **1.** Square (*rare*). **b.** *Cryst.* Of square section through the lateral or secondary axes; characterized by this form 1871. **2.** *Math.* Involving the second and no higher power of an unknown quantity or of a variable; esp. in *q. equation* 1668. **B.** *sb.* **a.** A quadratic equation. **b.** *pl.* The branch of algebra dealing with quadratic equations. 1684. So **Quadra·tical** *a.*

Quadrato- (kwŏdrēᶦ·to), comb. form of L. *quadratus* or *quadratum*; *spec.* in *Zool.*, connected with or pertaining to the quadrate together with some other bone, as **Quadra:to-ju·gal** *a.*

Quadratrix (kwǫdrēⁱ·triks). *Pl.* **-trices.** 1656. [mod.L., fem. agent-n. f. L. *quadrare*; see QUADRATE *v.*, -TRIX. Cf. Fr. *quadratrice* XVII.] A curve used in the process of squaring other curves.

Quadrature (kwǫ·drătiŭɹ). 1563. [– Fr. *quadrature* or L. *quadratura* a square, act of squaring; see QUADRATE *v.*, -URE.] †**1.** Square shape, squareness –1667. **2.** *Math.* The action or process of squaring; *spec.* the expression of an area bounded by a curve, esp. of a circle, by means of an equivalent square 1596. **3.** *Astron.* **a.** One of the two points (in space or time) at which the moon is 90° distant from the sun, or midway between the points of conjunction and opposition 1685. **b.** The position of one heavenly body relative to another when they are 90° apart, *esp.* of the moon to the sun when they are at the quadratures 1591.

Quadrennial (kwǫdre·niăl), *a.* and *sb.* Also **quadriennial.** 1646. [f. next + -AL¹.] **A.** *adj.* **1.** Occurring every fourth year 1700. **2.** Lasting for four years 1656. **B.** *sb.* †**a.** A period of four years (*rare*). **b.** An event happening every four years. 1646. Hence **Quadre·nnially** *adv.*

‖**Quadrennium** (kwǫdre·niŏm). Also **quadriennium.** 1797. [L. *quadriennium*, f. *quadri-* QUADRI- + *annus* year.] A period of four years.

Quadri- (kwǫ·dri), also, before a vowel, **quadr-,** a comb. element (= L. *quattuor* four) with the sense 'having, consisting of, connected with, etc. four (things specified)'.

I. Adjs. with the sense 'having or consisting of four—', 'characterized by the number four', as **qua·driform,** having four forms or aspects; **quadrili·ngual** [late L. *-linguis*], using, written in, etc., four languages; **quadrino·mial, -no·mical, -no·minal,** consisting of four (algebraic) terms.

b. *Bot.* and *Zool.*, as **quadrica·psular, ca·psulate; quadrici·pital,** having four heads or points of origin, as the quadriceps muscle; **quadride·ntate(d),** having four serrations or indentations; **qua·drifid,** cleft into four divisions or lobes; **quadrifo·liate,** consisting of four leaves; **quadrige·minal, -ous,** belonging to the *corpora quadrigemina* at the base of the brain; **quadrilo·bate, -lobed; quadriva·lve, -va·lvular.**

II. Sbs., vbs., and advs., chiefly from adjs. in I: **quadriceps** (extensor) [cf. BICEPS], a large muscle of the leg, having four heads; **qua·dricy:cle,** a four-wheeled cycle; **qua·drifoil** = QUATREFOIL; **quadrise·ction,** a division into four equal parts; **quadrisy·llable,** a word of four syllables; **qua·drivalve,** a plant with a quadrivalvular seed-pod; an instrument, *esp.* a speculum, with four valves.

b. *Math.* Chiefly in sense 'quadric', 'of the second degree or order', as **qua·dricone,** etc.; also **quadrino·mial,** an expression consisting of four terms.

c. *Chem.* In the names of chemical compounds (now superseded by) TETRA-.

Quadric (kwǫ·drik), *a.* and *sb.* 1856. [f. L. *quadra* square; see -IC.] *Math.* **A.** *adj.* Of the second degree. (Used in solid geometry where the variables are more than two.) 1858. **B.** *sb.* A quantic of the second degree; a surface or curve whose equation in three variables is of the second degree 1856.

‖**Quadriga** (kwǫdrəi·gă). 1727. [L.; sing. form for pl. *quadrigæ* contr. of *quadrijugæ*, f. QUADRI- + *jugum* yoke.] A chariot drawn by four horses harnessed abreast; esp. as represented in sculpture or on coins.

Quadrilateral (kwǫdrilæ·tĕrăl), *a.* and *sb.* 1650. [f. late L. *quadrilaterus* + -AL¹; with the sb. cf. med.L. *quadrilaterum* (XIV).] **A.** *adj.* Four-sided; having a four-sided base or section 1656. **B.** *sb.* A figure bounded by four straight lines; a space or area having four sides 1650. **b.** The space lying between, and defended by, four fortresses; *spec.* that in North Italy formed by the fortresses of Mantua, Verona, Peschiera, and Legnano 1859.

Quadriliteral (kwǫdrili·tĕrăl), *a.* and *sb.* 1771. [f. QUADRI- + LITERAL.] **A.** *adj.* Consisting of four letters; *spec.* of Semitic roots which have four consonants instead of the usual three. **B.** *sb.* A word of four letters; a root containing four consonants 1787.

Quadrille (kwǫdri·l, kă-), *sb.*¹ 1726. [– Fr. *quadrille* (1725), perh. – Sp. *cuartillo* (f. *cuarto* fourth), with assim. to next.] A card game played by four persons with forty cards, the eights, nines, and tens of the ordinary pack being discarded.

Quadrille (kwǫdri·l, k(w)ă-), *sb.*² 1738. [– Fr. *quadrille* (1611) – Sp. *cuadrilla*, It. *quadriglia* troop, company, f. *cuadra*, *quadra* square.] **1.** One of four groups of horsemen taking part in a tournament or carousel, each being distinguished by special costume or colours. **2.** A square dance, of French origin, usu. performed by four couples, and containing five sections or figures, each of which is a complete dance in itself. Also called 'a set of quadrilles'. **b.** A piece of music for such a dance. 1773.

Quadrillion (kwǫdri·lyən). 1674. [– Fr. *quadrillion*, f. *quadri-* QUADRI- + (*m*)*illion*; cf. *billion*, *trillion*.] **a.** In Great Britain: The fourth power of a million (1 followed by 24 ciphers). **b.** In U.S. (as in France): The fifth power of a thousand (1 followed by 15 ciphers).

Quadripartite (kwǫdripā·ɹtəit), *a.* and *sb.* late ME. [– L. *quadripartitus*; see QUADRI-, PARTITE.] **A.** *adj.* **1.** Divided into, or consisting of, four parts. Now chiefly in *Bot.*, *Zool.*, and *Arch.* **b.** *spec.* Of a contract, indenture, etc.: Drawn up in four corresponding parts, one for each party 1527. **2.** Divided among or shared by four persons or parties 1594. **B.** *sb.* The Tetrabiblos of Ptolemy 1477. Hence **Quadripa·rtitely** *adv.* So **Qua:dripartiti·tion,** division into or by four.

Quadrireme (kwǫ·drirīm), *a.* and *sb.* 1600. [– L. *quadriremis*, f. *quadri-* QUADRI- + *remus* oar.] **A.** *adj.* Of ancient ships: Having four banks of oars. **B.** *sb.* A vesssel having four banks of oars 1656.

Quadrivial (kwǫdri·viăl), *a.* and *sb.* late ME. [– med.L. *quadrivialis*; see next, -AL¹.] **A.** *adj.* **1.** Having four ways meeting in a point. Of roads: Leading in four directions. 1490. **2.** Belonging to the QUADRIVIUM. **B.** *sb. pl.* The four sciences constituting the QUADRIVIUM. Now *Hist.* 1522.

‖**Quadrivium** (kwǫdri·viŏm). 1804. [L., place where four ways meet; in late L. the four branches of mathematics (Boethius); f. *quadri-* QUADRI- + *via* way.] In the Middle Ages, the higher division of the seven liberal arts, comprising the mathematical sciences (arithmetic, geometry, astronomy, and music).

Quadroon (kwǫdrū·n). 1707. [Earliest forms *quartero(o)n* – (through Fr. *quarteron*) Sp. *cuarterón*, f. *cuarto* fourth, quarter; later assim. to words in *quadr-*.] **1. a.** The offspring of a white person and a mulatto; one who has a quarter of Negro blood. **b.** *rarely.* One who is fourth in descent from a Negro, one of the parents in each generation being white. Also *transf.* 1796. **2.** *attrib.* or as *adj.* 1748.

1. b. *transf.* Koelreuter artificially fertilized hybrid flowers. .and thus obtained a vegetable q. 1879.

Quadru- (kwǫ·dru), var. of QUADRI-; in L. used only in formations where the second element begins with *p*, as *quadrupes*, *quadruplex*, etc. Apart from words based on these L. forms, Eng. has *quadru-* only in *quadrumanous*, etc., and a few 16–17th c. examples.

‖**Quadrumana** (kwǫdrū·mănă), *sb. pl.* 1819. [n. pl. (sc. *animalia*) of mod.L. *quadrumanus* four-handed, f. *quadru-* QUADRU- + *manus* hand.] *Zool.* An order of mammals, including monkeys, apes, baboons, and lemurs, of which the hind as well as the fore feet have an opposable digit, so that they can be used as hands. Hence **Quadru·manal, Quadru·manous** *adjs.* belonging to the Q.; four-handed.

Quadrumane (kwǫ·drumeⁱn), *a.* and *sb.* Also **quadruman** (-mæn). 1828. [– Fr. *quadrumane* (Buffon); see prec.] **A.** *adj.* = QUADRUMANOUS 1835. **B.** *sb.* One of the QUADRUMANA 1828.

Quadruped (kwǫ·drŭped), *sb.* (*a.*) 1646. [– Fr. *quadrupède* or L. *quadrupes, -ped-*, f. *quadru-* QUADRU- + *pes* foot.] **1.** An animal which has four feet. (Usu. confined to mammals, and excluding four-footed reptiles.) **b.** Applied *spec.* to the horse 1660. **2.** *attrib.* or *adj.* Four-footed 1741. **B.** Belonging to, or connected with, four-footed animals 1835. Hence **Quadru·pedal** *a.* four-footed; of, belonging or appropriate to a q.

Quadruple (kwǫ·drup'l), *a.*, *sb.*, and *adv.* late ME. [– (O)Fr. *quadruple* – L. *quadruplus*, f. *quadru-* QUADRU- + *-plus* as in *duplus* DUPLE.] **A.** *adj.* Fourfold; consisting of four parts; four times as great or as many as. Const. *of*, *to*, or without prep. 1557. **b.** *Q. alliance*, an alliance of four powers, *esp.* that of Britain, France, Germany, and Holland in 1718, and of Britain, France, Spain, and Portugal in 1834. 1735. **c.** Applied to printing-papers which are four times the usual size, as *q. crown*, etc. 1889.

Q. rhythm, time, in *Mus.*, rhythm or time having four beats in a measure.

B. *sb.* **1.** Anything fourfold; a sum or quantity four times as great as another. late ME. **2.** *spec.* †**a.** A coin of the value of four pistoles –1695. **b.** A printing machine which prints four copies at once 1890. **C.** *adv.* In a fourfold manner 1840. Hence **Qua·druply** *adv.*

Quadruple (kwǫ·drup'l), *v.* late ME. [– Fr. *quadrupler* or late L. *quadruplare*, f. L. *quadruplus*; see prec.] **1.** *trans.* To make four times as great or as many; to multiply by four. **2.** To amount to four times as many as 1832. **3.** *intr.* (for *refl.*) To grow to four times as many or as much 1776.

3. The exports. .have quadrupled since the relaxation of the monopoly 1833.

Quadruplet (kwǫ·druplet). 1787. [f. QUADRUPLE + -ET, after *triplet*.] **1.** *pl.* Four children born at a birth. Abbrev. *quads.* **2.** Any combination of four things or parts united or working together 1852.

Quadruplex (kwǫ·drupleks), *a.* and *sb.* 1875. [– L. *quadruplex, -plic-* fourfold, f. *quadru-* QUADRU- + *plic-* to fold.] **A.** *adj.* **1.** *Electric Telegr.* Applied to a system by which four messages can be sent over one wire at one time. **2.** *Engineering.* Applied to an engine in which the expansion of the steam is used four times in cylinders of increasing diameter 1896. **B.** *sb.* A telegraphic instrument by means of which four simultaneous messages can be sent over the same wire 1889. Hence **Qua·druplex** *v. trans.* to make (a telegraph circuit, etc.) q.

Quadruplicate (kwǫdrū·plikĕt), *a.* and *sb.* 1657. [– L. *quadruplicatus*, pa. pple. of *quadruplicare*, f. *quadruplex*; see prec. and -ATE²,¹.] **A.** *adj.* **1.** Fourfold; four times repeated. **2.** Forming four exactly similar copies 1807.

1. *Q. proportion, ratio*, the proportion or ratio of fourth powers in relation to that of the radical quantities.

B. *sb.* **1.** *In q.*: in four exactly corresponding copies or transcripts 1790. **2.** *pl.* Four things, *esp.* copies of a document, exactly alike 1883.

Quadruplicate (kwǫdrū·plikeⁱt), *v.* 1661. [– *quadruplicat-*, pa. ppl. stem of L. *quadruplicare*; see prec., -ATE³.] **1.** *trans.* To multiply by four; to quadruple. **2.** To make or provide in quadruplicate 1879. Hence **Quadruplica·tion,** the action of making fourfold, of multiplying by four; also, the result of this.

Quadruplicity (kwǫdrupli·sĭti). 1590. [f. L. *quadruplex* QUADRUPLEX, after *duplicity*, *triplicity*.] Fourfold nature; the condition of being fourfold, or of forming a set of four.

‖**Quære** (kwī^ə·ri), *v. imper.* and *sb.* 1535. [L., imper. of *quærere* to ask, inquire. Now usu. QUERY.] **A.** *v. imper.* Ask, inquire; hence 'one may ask', 'it is a question' (*whether*, etc.). **B.** *sb.* A question, QUERY 1589.

A. Q. more about this HEARNE. Hence †**Quære** *v. trans.* to query –1756.

Quæstor (kwī·stǫɹ). late ME. [– L. *quæstor*, f. **quæs-*, old form of stem of *quærere* (see prec.).] *Rom. Antiq.* **a.** One of a number of Roman officials who had charge of the public revenue and expenditure. **b.** In early times: A public prosecutor in certain criminal cases. Hence **Quæsto·rial** *a.* **Quæ·storship.**

Quaff (kwɑf), *sb.* 1579. [f. next.] An act of quaffing, or the liquor quaffed; a deep draught.

Quaff (kwɑf), *v.* Also †**quaft.** 1523. [In earliest use †*quaft* (More, Coverdale), †*quaght* (Palsgrave); cf. synon. †*quass* (XVI–XVII) – MLG. *quassen* eat or drink immoderately.] **1.** *intr.* To drink deeply; to take a long draught; also, to drink repeatedly in this manner. Const. *of* (†*in*). 1529. **2.** *trans.* To drink (liquor) copiously or in a large draught 1555. **3.** To drain (a cup, etc.) in a copious draught or draughts. Also with *off, out, up.* 1523. **4.** To drive *away*, to bring *down to* or *into* (a certain state) by copious drinking (*rare*) 1714.

1. To day we feast and quaffe in frolique Bowles; To morrow fast QUARLES. **2.** *fig.* They drink, and in communion sweet Q. immortalitie and joy MILT. **3.** I quaffe full bowles of strong enchanting wines DEKKER. Hence **Qua·ffer.**

Quag (kwæg, kwǫg), *sb.* 1589. [Related to next.] A marshy or boggy spot, *esp.* one covered with a layer of turf which shakes or yields when walked on.

Quag (kwæg, kwǫg), *v. Obs.* exc. *dial.* 1611. [Of symbolic origin; cf. WAG *v.*, SWAG *v.* Some dialects have also *quaggle*, corresp. to *waggle*.] *intr.* To shake; said of something soft or flabby.

Quagga (kwæ·gă). 1785. [Said to be orig. Hottentot, but now in Xhosa-Kaffir in the form *iqwara* (with guttural *r*).] **a.** A S. African equine quadruped (*Equus* or *Hippotigris quagga*), related to the ass and the zebra, but less fully striped than the latter. **b.** Burchell's zebra.

Quaggy (kwæ·gi, kwǫ·gi), *a.* 1610. [f. QUAG *sb.* or *v.* + -Y^{1}.] **1.** Of ground: That shakes under the foot; full of quags; boggy, soft. Also of streams: Flowing through boggy soil. **2.** Of things, esp. of the body: Soft, yielding, flabby. Also of persons in respect of their flesh, and *fig.* 1611.

1. O'er the watery strath or q. moss COLLINS.

Quagmire (kwæ·gməiᵊɹ, kwǫ·g-). 1579. [f. QUAG *sb.* or *v.* + MIRE.] **1.** A piece of wet and boggy ground, which quakes or yields under the feet; a quaking bog; a fen, marsh. **2.** *transf.* and *fig.*; *esp.* a position or situation from which extrication is difficult 1635.

2. I have followed Cupid's Jack-a-lantern, and find my self in a q. at last SHERIDAN.

Quahaug, quahog (kwăhǭ·g, kwǭ·hǫg). *U.S.* 1794. [Narraganset Indian.] The common round clam (*Venus mercenaria*) of the Atlantic coast of N. America.

Quaich, quaigh (kwēχ). *Sc.* 1673. [– Gael. *cuach* cup, OIr. *cúach*, prob. – L. *caucus* (Gr. καῦκα).] A kind of shallow drinking-cup formerly common in Scotland, usu. made of small wooden staves hooped together and having two ears or handles.

Quail (kwē^{i}l), *sb.* ME. [– OFr. *quaille* (mod. *caille*) :– med.L. *coacula*, prob. of imit. origin like, if not derived from, synon. MLG., MDu. *quackele* (Du. *kwakkel*), OHG. *wahtala, qua(h)tala* (G. *wachtel*). Cf. AL. *quaila* (XIV).] **1.** A migratory bird allied to the partridge (family *Perdicidæ*), found in the Old World and Australia; *esp.* the European species, *Coturnix communis* or *dactylisonans*, much esteemed for the table. **2.** One of several American gallinaceous birds resembling the European quail, *esp.* the Virginian Quail or colin (*Ortyx virginianus*), and the Californian or Crested Quail (*Lophortyx californicus*) 1817. †**3.** *fig.* A courtesan. (In allusion to the supposed amorous disposition of the bird.) –1694.

attrib. and *Comb.*, as **q.-call** = *q.-pipe*; **-dove,** a dove of the West Indies and Florida (*Starnœnas cyanocephalus*); **-hawk,** a New Zealand species of falcon; **-pigeon,** a pigeon of the genus *Geophaps*; **-pipe,** a pipe on which the note of the q. (usu. the female) can be imitated, in order to lure the birds into a net; †*transf.* the throat; **-snipe,** a S. American plover of the genus *Thinocorys*.

Quail (kwē^{i}l), *v.* ME. [Of unkn. origin. Common in literary use 1520–1650, after which it becomes rare until revived, app. by Scott.] **I.** *intr.* **1.** Of material things: To decline; to fail or give way; to fade, wither, etc. *Obs.* exc. *dial.* 1440. **2.** Of immaterial things. **a.** Of an action, undertaking, etc.: †To fail, break down. In mod. use (transf. from 3): To give way, yield *to* or *before*. ME. **b.** Of courage, etc.: To fail, give way, become faint 1557. **3.** Of persons: To lose heart, be cowed; to give way through fear (*to* or *before*) 1555. **b.** Of the heart or spirit; also of the eyes 1563.

1. Length of time, causeth man and beast to quaile 1568. **2. b.** Perils, which make the courage of the hardiest q. THIRLWALL. **3. b.** Their sharp eyes quailed..before his savage glances BORROW.

II. *trans.* †**1.** To spoil, impair; to overpower, destroy –1669. **2.** To daunt or cow (a person), to bring into subjection by fear; to cause to quail 1526. **b.** To daunt (the heart, courage) with fear or dejection 1567.

1. *Mids. N.* V. i. 292. **2.** He is a stout man whom adversity doth not quaile 1642. Hence **Quai·ler.**

Quaint (kwē^{i}nt), *a.* [ME. *cointe, queinte* – OFr. *cointe, queinte* :– L. *cognitus* known, pa. pple. of *cognoscere* ascertain, f. *co-* COM- + *gnoscere* know.] **I.** †**1.** Of persons: Wise, knowing; skilled, clever, ingenious –1728. †**b.** In bad sense: Cunning, crafty, scheming –1680. †**2.** Of actions, schemes, etc.: Ingenious, clever, cunning –1641. †**3.** Of things: Ingeniously or cunningly designed or contrived; elaborate –1631. †**4.** Of things: Skilfully made, so as to have a good appearance; hence, beautiful, pretty, fine, dainty –1671. †**b.** Of dress: Fine, fashionable, elegant –1627. †**5.** Of persons: Beautiful or handsome in appearance; finely dressed; elegant, foppish –1784. †**6.** Of speech, modes of expression, etc.: Carefully or ingeniously elaborated; highly elegant or refined; clever, smart; affected –1783. †**7.** Strange, odd, curious (in character or appearance) –1808. **8.** Unusual or uncommon in character or appearance, but agreeable or attractive, esp. having an old-fashioned prettiness or daintiness 1795.

1. *Tam. Shr.* III. ii. 149. **b.** Sly, queynt, and fals HOCCLEVE. **4.** In his hand A Scepter or q. staff he bears MILT. **5.** He made himselfe as neate and q. as might be GREENE. **7.** The Flamins at their service q. MILT. **8.** He..knew many a merry ballad and q. tale SOUTHEY.

†**II.** Dainty, fastidious, prim –1678.

Too Queint and Finical in his Expressions 1678. Hence **Quai·nt-ly** *adv.*, **-ness.**

Quake (kwē^{i}k), *sb.* ME. [f. the vb.] The act of quaking or trembling; *spec.* in mod. use, an earthquake.

Quake (kwē^{i}k), *v.* [OE. *cwacian*, rel. to *cweċċan* (:– **kwakjan*), in mod. dial. QUETCH; cf. OS. *quekilīk* waving to and fro.] **1.** *intr.* Of things: To shake, tremble, be agitated, as the result of external shock, internal convulsion, or natural instability. **2.** Of persons, etc., or parts of the body: To shake, tremble, through cold, fear, etc. OE. †**3.** *trans.* To cause to quake –1639.

1. With boughs that quaked at every breath, Grey birch and aspen wept beneath SCOTT. **2.** They reuerence them, and qwake at their presence KNOX. *Cymb.* II. iv. 5. Hence **Qua·kingly** *adv.* with quaking or fear.

Quaker (kwē^{i}·kəɹ). 1653. [f. QUAKE *v.* + -ER^{1}.] A member of the religious society (the Society of Friends) founded by George Fox in 1648–50, distinguished by peaceful principles and plainness of dress and manners. **b.** *transf.* Applied to various plain-coloured birds and moths, with allusion to the colour of the dress usu. worn by Quakers 1775.

attrib. and *Comb.*: **q.-bird,** the sooty albatross; **-buttons** *U.S.*, the seeds of nux vomica; **q. gun** *U.S.*, a dummy gun in a ship or fort; **-ladies** *U.S.*, the small pale-blue flowers of the American plant *Houstonia cærulea*. Hence **Qua·keress,** a female Q. **Qua·kerish** *a.* resembling, characteristic of, or appropriate to, Quakers; **-ly** *adv.* **Qua·kerism,** the principles or practice of the Quakers. **Qua·kerly** *a.* and *adv.* †**Qua·kery,** Quakerism.

Qua·king-gra·ss. 1597. [f. *quaking* ppl. a. of QUAKE *v.*] A pop. name for grasses of the genus *Briza*, esp. *B. media*.

Quaky (kwē^{i}·ki), *a.* 1864. [f. QUAKE *v.* + -Y^{1}.] Inclined to quake; of the nature of quaking.

‖**Quale** (kwē^{i}·li). 1675. [L., n. sing. of *qualis* of what kind.] The quality of a thing; a thing having certain qualities.

Qua·lifiable, *a. rare.* 1611. [f. QUALIFY *v.* + -ABLE.] That may be qualified or modified.

Qualification (kwǫ·lifikē^{i}·ʃən). 1543. [– Fr. *qualification* or med.L. *qualificatio*, f. *qualificat-*, pa. ppl. stem of *qualificare*; see QUALIFY, -FICATION.] The action of qualifying; the condition or fact of being qualified; that which qualifies. **1.** Modification, limitation, restriction; a modifying or limiting element or circumstance. †**2.** The distinctive quality *of* a person or thing; condition, character, nature –1745. †**3.** A quality, attribute, or property (*of*) –1799. †**b.** An accomplishment –1796. **4.** A quality, accomplishment, etc., which qualifies or fits a person *for* some office or function. Also *absol.* 1669. **5.** A necessary condition, which must be fulfilled before a certain right can be acquired, an office held, or the like 1723. **6.** The act of determining the quality or nature of a thing; *spec.* in *Logic*, the expression of quality, or the distinction of affirmative and negative, in a proposition 1891.

1. A promise that hath a q. or condition expressed 1651. **2.** *Oth.* II. i. 282. **4.** Besides his general qualifications for that trust 1669. **5.** A law which fixes a sum of money as the q. of citizenship JOWETT.

Comb. **q. shares,** shares which one must hold in order to be qualified for a directorship in a company.

Qualificative (kwǫ·lifikē^{i}tiv), *a.* and *sb. rare.* 1661. [f. prec., after *predication/predicative*, etc.] **A.** *adj.* Qualifying; denoting some quality. **B.** *sb.* A qualifying word or phrase.

Qualificator (kwǫ·lifikē^{i}təɹ). 1688. [– med.L. *qualificator*, f. *qualificat-*; see QUALIFICATION, -OR 2 b.] One of a board of theologians attached to the Holy Office, who report on the character (heretical or otherwise) of propositions submitted to them.

Qualificatory (kwǫ·lifikē^{i}·təri), *a.* 1805. [f. QUALIFICATION, after *modification/modificatory*.] Having the character of qualifying or modifying; tending to qualify.

Qualified (kwǫ·lifəid), *ppl. a.* 1558. [f. QUALIFY *v.* + -ED^{1}.] †**1.** Furnished with, possessed of (certain) qualities –1681. **2.** Endowed with qualities, or possessed of accomplishments, which fit one for a certain end, office, or function; fit, competent 1558. **3.** Legally, properly, or by custom, capable of doing or being something specified or implied 1559. **4.** Limited, modified, or restricted in some respect; *spec.* in *q. acceptance, fee* (= *base fee*), *negative, oath, property*, etc. 1599. Hence **Qua·lified-ly** *adv.*, **-ness.**

Qualify (kwǫ·lifəi), *v.* 1540. [– Fr. *qualifier* – med.L. *qualificare*, f. *qualis* of what kind, f. base of *qui, quis* WHO + *-alis* -AL^{1}; see -FY.] **I.** To invest with a quality or qualities. **1.** *trans.* To attribute a certain quality or qualities to; to designate in a particular way. (Now current as a gallicism.) 1549. **b.** *Gram.* Of an adj.: To express some quality belonging to (a noun). Of an adv.: To modify. 1837. **2.** To invest (a person) with proper qualities (*for* being something) 1581. **b.** To make fit or competent *for* doing (or *to do*) something, or *for* something. Chiefly *refl.* 1665. **3.** To make legally capable; to give a recognized status to (a person) 1583. **4.** *intr.* (for *refl.*) To make oneself competent *for* something *by* fulfilling some necessary condition 1588.

1. The propositions..have been qualified as heretical 1826. **2. b.** I am qualifying myself to give lessons DICKENS. **4.** All the ministers of state must q., and take this test BURKE.

II. To modify in some respect. **1.** To modify (a statement, opinion, etc.) by any limitation or reservation; to make less strong or positive 1553. **2.** To moderate or mitigate; *esp.* to render less violent, severe, or unpleasant; to lessen the effect of (something disagreeable) 1543. †**b.** To make less wrong –1776. †**3.** To appease, calm, pacify (a person) –1679. †**4.** To bring into, or keep in, a proper condition –1688. **5.** To modify the strength or flavour of (a liquid) 1591. **6.** †**a.** To affect (a person or thing) injuriously. **b.** To abate or diminish (something good); to make less perfect or complete. 1584.

1. Reasons to change or to q. some of my first sentiments BURKE. **2. b.** A falsehood, however qualified by circumstances FIELDING. **5.** Tea, which he drank..qualified with brandy SMOLLETT. **6. b.** *Haml.* IV. vii. 114. Hence **Qua·lifier,** one who, or that which, qualifies; *R. C. Ch.* = QUALIFICATOR.

Qualitative (kwǫ·litĕtiv), *a.* 1607. [– late L. *qualitativus*, f. L. *qualitas*; see QUALITY,

-IVE. Cf. Fr. *qualitatif, -ive.*] Relating to, connected or concerned with, quality or qualities. Now usu. opp. to QUANTITATIVE. Hence **Qua·litatively** *adv.*

Qualitied (kwǫ·litid), *a.* 1600. [f. next + -ED².] Furnished with a quality or qualities.

Quality (kwǫ·lĭti). ME. [– (O)Fr. *qualité* – L. *qualitas* (Cicero, rendering Gr. ποιότης), f. *qualis*; see QUALIFY, -ITY.] **I.** Of persons (in 1 and 2 occas. of animals). **1.** Character, disposition, nature. Now *rare.* **b.** Capacity, ability, or skill, in some respect. (An echo of Shaks. (*Ham.* II. ii. 452), who prob. intended the word in sense 5.) 1856. **c.** Without article or poss. pron.: Excellence of disposition; good natural gifts 1606. **2.** A mental or moral attribute, trait, or characteristic 1533. **b.** An accomplishment or attainment 1584. **3.** Rank or position in (a) society. Now *rare.* late ME. **4.** Nobility, high birth or rank, good social position. Now *arch.* 1579. **b.** *concr.* People of good social position. Now *arch.* or *vulgar* and *dial.* 1693. †**5.** Profession, occupation, business, *esp.* that of an actor. **b.** Fraternity; those of the same profession, *esp.* actors as a body. –1633. **c.** Party, side. SHAKS. **6.** Title, description, character, capacity. Freq. in phr. *in (the) q. of*: in the character of, as. Now chiefly as a gallicism. ME.

1. b. Hal... had given a... touch of his q. by spearing a bird on the wing 1860. **c.** O, sir,.. You are full of q. and faire desert HEYWOOD. **2.** Youre godlye dysposytyon, and vertuous qualityes [illegible] **b.** [illegible] i. 125. **4.** He had all the men of quality his sworn enemies NORTH. **b.** I have looked out among the q. for a future husband for her RICHARDSON. **5.** *Two Gent.* IV. i. 58. **6.** He serv'd his Master in q. of Lutester 1661

II. Of things. **1.** An attribute, property, special feature ME. †**b.** A manner, style [illegible] †**c.** *concretely.* A substance of a certain nature; an essence (*rare*) 1823. **2.** The nature, kind, or character (of something); hence, the degree or grade of excellence, etc. possessed by a thing. late ME. [illegible] Nature, with ref. to origin, hence, cause, occasion SHAKS. **3.** [illegible] That aspect of things under which they are considered in thinking or speaking of their nature, condition, or properties [illegible] [illegible] negative. Of [illegible] distinctness 1594. [illegible] particular [illegible] anything as determined by its qualities [illegible] adjs. [illegible] in the q. of [illegible] measures than in the amount EMERSON. **b.** [illegible] vi. 117.

Qualm ([illegible] kwǭm). 1530. [Of obscure origin; [illegible] corresp. [illegible] either [illegible] pestilence [illegible] (Du. [illegible]) [illegible] sudden feeling [illegible] ness, illness, or sickness. (Now [illegible] cases in which the seat of disorder is in the stomach.) **2.** *transf.* **a.** A fit of sickening fear, misgiving, or depression; a sudden sinking of heart. [illegible] **b.** A painful doubt or consciousness of acting wrongly 1649. **c.** A fit or sudden access of some quality, etc. (Now only with suggestion of [illegible]) [illegible]

1. It makes the stomach sick...and [illegible] It was absurd...to [illegible] this [illegible] FIELDING. **c.** [illegible] W. IRVING.

Qualmish ([illegible]), *a.* [illegible] [f. QUALM + -ISH¹.] [illegible] persons: Affected with a qualm or qualms; tending or liable to be so affected. **2.** Of feelings, etc.: Of the nature of a qualm 1798. Hence **Qua·lmishly** *adv.*, **-ness**. So **Qua·lmy** *a.*

Quamash (kwǫ·mæʃ, kwǫ·mæʃ). See also CAMAS. 1814. [N. Amer. Indian.] A N. Amer. liliaceous plant (*Camassia esculenta*), the bulbs of which are used for food by the American Indians.

Quamoclit (kwæ·moklit) 1731. [Corruption of Mexican *quamo-chitl* [illegible] comb. form of *quauitl* tree.] A subgenus of climbing plants with brilliant flowers found in the tropical parts of America and Asia, belonging to the genus *Ipomœa.*

Quandary (kwǫ·ndări, kwǫndē°·ri), *sb.* 1579. [Also †*quandare*, as if f. L. *quando* when treated as a verbal form with corresp. infin. *quandare*. Cf. †*backare* back!, †*jocundare* merry mood, †*vagare* VAGARY, all XVI.] A state of extreme perplexity or uncertainty; a dilemma causing (great) mental agitation or distress; †a ticklish plight.

Quannet (kwǫ·nĕt). 1842. [Of unkn. origin.] A flat file set in a frame, and used as a plane in filing flat surfaces, as in comb-making.

Quant (kwænt, kwǫnt), *sb.* 1440. [perh. – L. *contus* (Gr. κοντός) boat-pole.] A pole for propelling a boat, esp. one with a prong to prevent it sinking in the mud, used by bargemen on the east coast. Hence **Quant** *v. trans.* to propel a boat with a q.; also *absol.*

Quantic (kwǫ·ntik). 1854. [f. L. *quantus* how great + -IC.] *Math.* A rational, integral, homogeneous function of two or more variables.

Quantification (kwǫ:ntifikē¹·ʃən). 1840. [f. next; see -FICATION.] The action of quantifying.

Q. of the predicate, the expression of the logical quantity of the predicate of a proposition, by applying to the predicate the sign *all* or *some*, or an equivalent.

Quantify (kwǫ·ntifəi), *v.* 1840. [– med.L. *quantificare*, f. *quantus* how great; see QUANTITY, -FY.] **1.** *Logic. trans.* To express the quantity of a term in a proposition, by prefixing *all* or *some* or the like to the term. **2.** To determine the quantity of, to measure 1878. Hence **Quantifier**.

Quantitative (kwǫ·ntitētiv), *a.* 1581. [– med.L. *quantitativus*, f. L. *quantitas*, -*tat*-; see -IVE.] **1.** Possessing quantity or magnitude, or spacial extent. Now *rare.* **2.** Estimated or estimable by quantity 1656. **3.** Relating to or concerned with quantity or its measurement; ascertaining or expressing quantity 1668. **4.** Pertaining to or based on vowel-quantity, as *q. verse* 1790. Hence **Qua·ntitative-ly** *adv.*, **-ness**. So **Qua·ntitive** *a.*, **-ly** *adv.*

Quantity (kwǫ·ntĭti). late ME. [– (O)Fr. *quantité* – L. *quantitas* (tr. Gr. ποσότης), f. *quantus* how great, how much, f. base of *qui*, *quis* who; see -ITY.] **I. 1.** Size, magnitude, dimensions. *Obs.* in gen. sense. **2.** Amount, sum. **a.** Of material things not usu. estimated by spatial measurement. late ME. **b.** Of immaterial things late ME. [illegible] **3.** Length or duration in time. Now only in the phr. [illegible] the right of [illegible] continue. late ME. [illegible] shortness of sounds or syllables [illegible] by the time required to pronounce them [illegible] *Mus.* Length or duration of notes 1591. [illegible] esp. as the subject of mathematics. That property of things which is involved in the question 'how great?' or 'how much?' and is determinable, or regarded as being so, by measurement of some kind; a system of relationships by virtue of which one thing is said to be greater or less than another 1530. **5.** *Logic.* **a.** The extension of a term, dist. as extensive and intensive [illegible] **b.** The degree of extension which a proposition gives to the term forming its subject 1628. **6.** Relative size or amount, proportion [illegible] **7.** Great or considerable amount [illegible] **8.** *Electr.* The strength of a current as dist. from intensity or potential 1837.

1. [illegible] of a surface is called its area, and the q. of a line, its length 1830. **2. a.** [illegible] **3. b.** *False q.*, an incorrect use of a long for a short vowel or syllable, or vice versa. [illegible] see DISCRETE [illegible] **7.** Windsor Castle is a noble instance of the effect of q. HOGARTH.

II. 1. A (specified) portion or amount of an article or commodity. Also *transf.* of immaterial things. ME. **b.** An indefinite (esp. a large or considerable) portion or amount, [illegible] small piece, a fragment ME. [illegible] With *of*, article: The portion or amount (*of* something) present in a particular case or instance 1611.

2. A specified, or indefinite, number of persons or things. late ME. **b.** *pregnantly.* A great number or amount; also *pl.* **3.** A certain space or surface. Const. *of.* Now *rare.* late ME. **4.** *Math.* A thing having q. (I. 4), the number or extension of which is expressible by means of symbols; the symbol itself 1570.

1. A sufficient q. of illusion for the purposes of dramatic interest LAMB. **b.** Away thou Ragge, thou quantitie, thou remnant SHAKS. A q. of wreckage was cast up at Southport 1883. **c.** The q. of sensible heat in a human body BENTHAM. **3.** You would make them a grant of a sufficient q. of your land BURKE. **4.** *transf.* Her husband was an unknown quantity STEVENSON. *Imaginary q.*: see IMAGINARY *a.* 1 c. *Negligible q.* (after Fr. *quantité négligeable*), often *fig.* a person or thing of next to no account, a nonentity.

Comb.: **q.-mark**, a mark indicating the q. of a vowel or syllable; **-surveyor**, a surveyor who estimates the quantities of the materials and labour required for any work.

Quantivalence (kwǫnti·vălĕns). 1871. [f. L. *quanti-*, comb. form of *quantum* how much + *-valence*, after *equivalence*.] = VALENCY 2. **Quanti·valency. Quanti·valent** *a.*

Qua·ntize, *v.* 1921. [f. next + -IZE.] *trans.* To apply quantum mechanics or the quantum theory to; to measure (energy) in quanta. Hence **Quantiza·tion.**

‖**Quantum** (kwǫ·ntŏm). Pl. **quanta.** 1619. [L. n. of *quantus* how much.] **1.** = QUANTITY, in various senses, e.g. I. 2, II. 1, 1c, 4. **2.** *Physics.* A discrete unit quantity of energy, proportional to the frequency of radiation, emitted from or absorbed by an atom 1910.

1. Is there not a sufficient q. of distress and misfortune? 1789. **2.** *Q. theory*, the hypothesis that in radiation the energy of the electrons is discharged in discrete amounts or quanta.

Quantum sufficit (kwǫ·ntŏm sv·fisit). Also abbrev. **quantum suff., quant. suff. (suf.).** 1699. [L., a formula used in medical prescriptions.] 'As much as suffices'; hence, a sufficient quantity, to a sufficient extent, etc.

Quaquaversal (kwē¹kwăvə̄·ısăl), *a.* 1728. [f. late L. *quaqua versus*, -*versum*, f. *quaqua* wherever, whithersoever + *versus* towards; see -AL¹.] Turned or pointing in every direction; chiefly *Geol.* in *q. dip.* Hence **Quaqua·ve·rsally** *adv.*

Quarantine (kwǫ·răntīn), *sb.* 1609. [In sense 1 – med.L. *quarantena*, *quadragena*, f. *quadraginta* [illegible], for L. *quadraginta* forty; [illegible] sense 2 – It. *quarantina*, f. *quaranta* forty; [illegible] -INE¹.] **1.** *Law.* A period of forty days during which a widow, entitled to dower, had right to remain in the chief mansion house of her deceased husband; hence, the right of a widow to remain in the house during this period. **2.** A period (orig. of forty days) during which persons who might spread contagious disease (esp. travellers) are isolated; commonly, the period during which a ship, suspected of carrying contagion, is isolated on arrival at a port. [illegible] the fact or practice of isolating [illegible] isolated [illegible] or isolated [illegible] **3.** Any period, lasting [illegible] seclusion compared to the [illegible] period of forty days; a set of forty [illegible] If she [illegible] within the forty [illegible] her quarantine [illegible] **2.** Anchored [illegible]

Quarantine [illegible], *v.* [illegible] *trans.* To put in quarantine [illegible]

Quare impedit (kwē°·ri [illegible]). [L., 'Why he impedes' [illegible] ME [illegible] A form of writ issued [illegible] disputed presentation to a benefice [illegible] the defendant to state why [illegible] plaintiff from making the [illegible]

Quarenden, quarender [illegible] late ME. [illegible] of the place-name Quarendon [illegible] variety of apple common [illegible] Devon. Also [illegible]

Quarrel (kwǫ·rĕl) [illegible] *quar(r)el* (mod. *carreau*) [illegible] dim. of late L. *quadrus* [illegible] used with the cross [illegible] quarry of [illegible] of glass, [illegible] window. Now [illegible]

Quaff (kwɑf), *v.* Also †**quaft.** 1523. [In earliest use †*quaft* (More, Coverdale), †*quaght* (Palsgrave); cf. synon. †*quass* (XVI–XVII) – MLG. *quassen* eat or drink immoderately.] **1.** *intr.* To drink deeply; to take a long draught; also, to drink repeatedly in this manner. Const. *of* (†*in*). 1529. **2.** *trans.* To drink (liquor) copiously or in a large draught 1555. **3.** To drain (a cup, etc.) in a copious draught or draughts. Also with *off, out, up.* 1523. **4.** To drive *away*, to bring *down to* or *into* (a certain state) by copious drinking (*rare*) 1714.

1. To day we feast, and quaffe in frolique Bowles; To morrow fast QUARLES. **2.** *fig.* They drink, and in communion sweet Q. immortalitie and joy MILT. **3.** I quaffe full bowles of strong enchanting wines DEKKER. Hence **Qua·ffer.**

Quag (kwæg, kwǫg), *sb.* 1589. [Related to next.] A marshy or boggy spot, *esp.* one covered with a layer of turf which shakes or yields when walked on.

Quag (kwæg, kwǫg), *v. Obs.* exc. *dial.* 1611. [Of symbolic origin; cf. WAG *v.*, SWAG *v.* Some dialects have also *quaggle*, corresp. to *waggle*.] *intr.* To shake; said of something soft or flabby.

Quagga (kwæ·gă). 1785. [Said to be orig. Hottentot, but now in Xhosa-Kaffir in the form *iqwara* (with guttural *r*).] **a.** A S. African equine quadruped (*Equus* or *Hippotigris quagga*), related to the ass and the zebra, but less fully striped than the latter. **b.** Burchell's zebra.

Quaggy (kwæ·gi, kwǫ·gi), *a.* 1610. [f. QUAG *sb.* or *v.* + -Y[1].] **1.** Of ground: That shakes under the foot; full of quags; boggy, soft. Also of streams: Flowing through boggy soil. **2.** Of things, esp. of the body: Soft, yielding, flabby. Also of persons in respect of their flesh, and *fig.* 1611.

1. O'er the watery strath or q. moss COLLINS.

Quagmire (kwæ·gməiəɹ, kwǫg-). 1579. [f. QUAG *sb.* or *v.* + MIRE.] **1.** A piece of wet and boggy ground, which quakes or yields under the feet; a quaking bog; a fen, marsh. **2.** *transf.* and *fig.*; *esp.* a position or situation from which extrication is difficult 1635.

2. I have followed Cupid's Jack-a-lantern, and find my self in a q. at last SHERIDAN.

Quahaug, quahog (kwăhǭ·g, kwǭ·hǫg). *U.S.* 1794. [Narraganset Indian.] The common round clam (*Venus mercenaria*) of the Atlantic coast of N. America.

Quaich, quaigh (kwēχ). *Sc.* 1673. [– Gael. *cuach* cup, OIr. *cúach*, prob. – L. *caucus* (Gr. καῦκα).] A kind of shallow drinking-cup formerly common in Scotland, usu. made of small wooden staves hooped together and having two ears or handles.

Quail (kwēⁱl), *sb.* ME. [– OFr. *quaille* (mod. *caille*) :– med.L. *coacula*, prob. of imit. origin like, if not derived from, synon. MLG., MDu. *quackele* (Du. *kwakkel*), OHG. *wahtala, qua(h)tala* (G. *wachtel*). Cf. AL. *quaila* (XIV).] **1.** A migratory bird allied to the partridge (family *Perdicidæ*), found in the Old World and Australia; *esp.* the European species, *Coturnix communis* or *dactylisonans*, much esteemed for the table. **2.** One of several American gallinaceous birds resembling the European quail, *esp.* the Virginian Quail or colin (*Ortyx virginianus*), and the Californian or Crested Quail (*Lophortyx californicus*) 1817. †**3.** *fig.* A courtesan. (In allusion to the supposed amorous disposition of the bird.) –1694.

attrib. and *Comb.*, as **q.-call** = *q.-pipe*; **-dove,** a dove of the West Indies and Florida (*Starnœnas cyanocephalus*); **-hawk,** a New Zealand species of falcon; **-pigeon,** a pigeon of the genus *Geophaps*; **-pipe,** a pipe on which the note of the q. (usu. the female) can be imitated, in order to lure the birds into a net; †*transf.* the throat; **-snipe,** a S. American plover of the genus *Thinocorys*.

Quail (kwēⁱl), *v.* ME. [Of unkn. origin. Common in literary use 1520–1650, after which it becomes rare until revived, app. by Scott.] **I.** *intr.* **1.** Of material things: To decline; to fail or give way; to fade, wither, etc. *Obs.* exc. *dial.* 1440. **2.** Of immaterial things. **a.** Of an action, undertaking, etc.: †To fail, break down. In mod. use (transf. from 3): To give way, yield *to* or *before*. ME. **b.** Of courage, etc.: To fail, give way, become faint 1557. **3.** Of persons: To lose heart, be cowed; to give way through fear (*to* or *before*) 1555. **b.** Of the heart or spirit; also of the eyes 1563.

1. Length of time, causeth man and beast to quaile 1568. **2. b.** Perils, which make the courage of the hardiest q. THIRLWALL. **3. b.** Their sharp eyes quailed..before his savage glances BORROW.

II. *trans.* †**1.** To spoil, impair; to overpower, destroy –1669. **2.** To daunt or cow (a person), to bring into subjection by fear; to cause to quail 1526. **b.** To daunt (the heart, courage) with fear or dejection 1567.

1. *Mids. N.* v. i. 292. **2.** He is a stout man whom adversity doth not quaile 1642. Hence **Quai·ler.**

Quaint (kwēⁱnt), *a.* [ME. *cointe, queinte* – OFr. *cointe, queinte* :– L. *cognitus* known, pa. pple. of *cognoscere* ascertain, f. *co-* COM- + *gnoscere* know.] **I.** †**1.** Of persons: Wise, knowing; skilled, clever, ingenious –1728. †**b.** In bad sense: Cunning, crafty, scheming –1680. †**2.** Of actions, schemes, etc.: Ingenious, clever, cunning –1641. †**3.** Of things: Ingeniously or cunningly designed or contrived; elaborate –1631. †**4.** Of things: Skilfully made, so as to have a good appearance; hence, beautiful, pretty, fine, dainty –1671. †**b.** Of dress: Fine, fashionable, elegant –1627. †**5.** Of persons: Beautiful or handsome in appearance; finely dressed; elegant, foppish –1784. †**6.** Of speech, modes of expression, etc.: Carefully or ingeniously elaborated; highly elegant or refined; clever, smart; affected –1783. †**7.** Strange, odd, curious (in character or appearance) –1808. **8.** Unusual or uncommon in character or appearance, but agreeable or attractive, esp. having an old-fashioned prettiness or daintiness 1795.

1. *Tam. Shr.* III. ii. 149. **b.** Sly, queynt, and fals HOCCLEVE. **4.** In his hand A Scepter or q. staff he bears MILT. **5.** He made himselfe as neate and q. as might be GREENE. **7.** The Flamins at their service q. MILT. **8.** He..knew many a merry ballad and q. tale SOUTHEY.

†**II.** Dainty, fastidious, prim –1678.

Too Queint and Finical in his Expressions 1678. Hence **Quai·nt-ly** *adv.*, **-ness.**

Quake (kwēⁱk), *sb.* ME. [f. the vb.] The act of quaking or trembling; *spec.* in mod. use, an earthquake.

Quake (kwēⁱk), *v.* [OE. *cwacian*, rel. to *cweććan* (:– **kwakjan*), in mod. dial. QUETCH; cf. OS. *quekilīk* waving to and fro.] **1.** *intr.* Of things: To shake, tremble, be agitated, as the result of external shock, internal convulsion, or natural instability. **2.** Of persons, etc., or parts of the body: To shake, tremble, through cold, fear, etc. OE. †**3.** *trans.* To cause to quake –1639.

1. With boughs that quaked at every breath, Grey birch and aspen wept beneath SCOTT. **2.** They reuerence them, and qwake at their presence KNOX. *Cymb.* II. iv. 5. Hence **Qua·kingly** *adv.* with quaking or fear.

Quaker (kwēⁱ·kəɹ). 1653. [f. QUAKE *v.* + -ER[1].] A member of the religious society (the Society of Friends) founded by George Fox in 1648–50, distinguished by peaceful principles and plainness of dress and manners. **b.** *transf.* Applied to various plain-coloured birds and moths, with allusion to the colour of the dress usu. worn by Quakers 1775.

attrib. and *Comb.*: **q.-bird,** the sooty albatross; **-buttons** *U.S.*, the seeds of nux vomica; **q. gun** *U.S.*, a dummy gun in a ship or fort; **-ladies** *U.S.*, the small pale-blue flowers of the American plant *Houstonia cærulea*. Hence **Qua·keress,** a female Q. **Qua·kerish** *a.* resembling, characteristic of, or appropriate to, Quakers; **-ly** *adv.* **Qua·kerism,** the principles or practice of the Quakers. **Qua·kerly** *a.* and *adv.* †**Qua·kery,** Quakerism.

Qua·king-gra:ss. 1597. [f. *quaking* ppl. a. of QUAKE *v.*] A pop. name for grasses of the genus *Briza*, esp. *B. media*.

Quaky (kwēⁱ·ki), *a.* 1864. [f. QUAKE *v.* + -Y[1].] Inclined to quake; of the nature of quaking.

‖**Quale** (kwēⁱ·li). 1675. [L., n. sing. of *qualis* of what kind.] The quality of a thing; a thing having certain qualities.

Qua·lifiable, *a. rare.* 1611. [f. QUALIFY *v.* + -ABLE.] That may be qualified or modified.

Qualification (kwǫ:lifikēⁱ·ʃən). 1543. [– Fr. *qualification* or med.L. *qualificatio*, f. *qual'ficat-*, pa. ppl. stem of *qualificare*; see QUALIFY, -FICATION.] The action of qualifying; the condition or fact of being qualified; that which qualifies. **1.** Modification, limitation, restriction; a modifying or limiting element or circumstance. †**2.** The distinctive quality *of* a person or thing; condition, character, nature –1745. †**3.** A quality, attribute, or property (*of*) –1799. †**b.** An accomplishment –1706. **4.** A quality, accomplishment, etc., which qualifies or fits a person *for* some office or function. Also *absol.* 1669. **5.** A necessary condition, which must be fulfilled before a certain right can be acquired, an office held, or the like 1723. **6.** The act of determining the quality or nature of a thing; *spec.* in *Logic*, the expression of quality, or the distinction of affirmative and negative, in a proposition 1891.

1. A promise that hath a q. or condition expressed 1651. **2.** *Oth.* II. i. 282. **4.** Besides his general qualifications for that trust 1669. **5.** A law which fixes a sum of money as the q. of citizenship JOWETT.

Comb. **q. shares,** shares which one must hold in order to be qualified for a directorship in a company.

Qualificative (kwǫ·lifikēⁱtiv), *a.* and *sb. rare.* 1661. [f. prec., after *predication/predicative*, etc.] **A.** *adj.* Qualifying; denoting some quality. **B.** *sb.* A qualifying word or phrase.

Qualificator (kwǫ·lifikēⁱtəɹ). 1688. [– med.L. *qualificator*, f. *qualificat-*; see QUALIFICATION, -OR 2 b.] One of a board of theologians attached to the Holy Office, who report on the character (heretical or otherwise) of propositions submitted to them.

Qualificatory (kwǫ·lifikēⁱ:təri), *a.* 1805. [f. QUALIFICATION, after *modification/modificatory*.] Having the character of qualifying or modifying; tending to qualify.

Qualified (kwǫ·lifəid), *ppl. a.* 1558. [f. QUALIFY *v.* + -ED[1].] †**1.** Furnished with, possessed of (certain) qualities –1681. **2.** Endowed with qualities, or possessed of accomplishments, which fit one for a certain end, office, or function; fit, competent 1558. **3.** Legally, properly, or by custom, capable of doing or being something specified or implied 1559. **4.** Limited, modified, or restricted in some respect; *spec.* in *q. acceptance, fee* (= *base fee*), *negative, oath, property*, etc. 1599. Hence **Qua·lified-ly** *adv.*, **-ness.**

Qualify (kwǫ·lifəi), *v.* 1540. [– Fr. *qualifier* – med.L. *qualificare*, f. *qualis* of what kind, f. base of *qui, quis* WHO + *-alis* -AL[1]; see -FY.] **I.** To invest with a quality or qualities. **1.** *trans.* To attribute a certain quality or qualities to; to designate in a particular way. (Now current as a gallicism.) 1549. **b.** *Gram.* Of an adj.: To express some quality belonging to (a noun). Of an adv.: To modify. 1837. **2.** To invest (a person) with proper qualities (*for* being something) 1581. **b.** To make fit or competent *for* doing (or *to do*) something, or *for* something. Chiefly *refl.* 1665. **3.** To make legally capable; to give a recognized status to (a person) 1583. **4.** *intr.* (for *refl.*) To make oneself competent *for* something *by* fulfilling some necessary condition 1588.

1. The propositions..have been qualified as heretical 1826. **2. b.** I am qualifying myself to give lessons DICKENS. **4.** All the ministers of state must q., and take this test BURKE.

II. To modify in some respect. **1.** To modify (a statement, opinion, etc.) by any limitation or reservation; to make less strong or positive 1553. **2.** To moderate or mitigate; *esp.* to render less violent, severe, or unpleasant; to lessen the effect of (something disagreeable) 1543. †**b.** To make less wrong –1776. †**3.** To appease, calm, pacify (a person) –1679. †**4.** To bring into, or keep in, a proper condition –1688. **5.** To modify the strength or flavour of (a liquid) 1591. **6.** †**a.** To affect (a person or thing) injuriously. **b.** To abate or diminish (something good); to make less perfect or complete. 1584.

1. Reasons to change or to q. some of my first sentiments BURKE. **2. b.** A falsehood, however qualified by circumstances FIELDING. **5.** Tea, which he drank..qualified with brandy SMOLLETT. **6. b.** *Haml.* IV. vii. 114. Hence **Qua·lifier,** one who, or that which, qualifies; *R. C. Ch.* = QUALIFICATOR.

Qualitative (kwǫ·litĕtiv), *a.* 1607. [– late L. *qualitativus*, f. L. *qualitas*; see QUALITY,

-IVE. Cf. Fr. *qualitatif, -ive.*] Relating to, connected or concerned with, quality or qualities. Now usu. opp. to QUANTITATIVE. Hence **Qua·litatively** *adv.*

Qualitied (kwǫ·litid), *a.* 1600. [f. next + -ED².] Furnished with a quality or qualities.

Quality (kwǫ·lĭti). ME. [– (O)Fr. *qualité* – L. *qualitas* (Cicero, rendering Gr. ποιότης), f. *qualis*; see QUALIFY, -ITY.] **I.** Of persons (in 1 and 2 occas. of animals). **1.** Character, disposition, nature. Now *rare.* **b.** Capacity, ability, or skill, in some respect. (An echo of Shaks. (*Ham.* II. ii. 452), who prob. intended the word in sense 5.) 1856. **c.** Without article or poss. pron.: Excellence of disposition; good natural gifts 1606. **2.** A mental or moral attribute, trait, or characteristic 1533. **b.** An accomplishment or attainment 1584. **3.** Rank or position in (a) society. Now *rare.* late ME. **4.** Nobility, high birth or rank, good social position. Now *arch.* 1579. **b.** *concr.* People of good social position. Now *arch.* or *vulgar* and *dial.* 1693. †**5.** Profession, occupation, business, *esp.* that of an actor. **b.** Fraternity; those of the same profession; *esp.* actors as a body. –1633. **c.** Party, side. SHAKS. **6.** Title, description, character, capacity. Freq. in phr. *in (the) q. of*: in the character of, as. Now chiefly as a gallicism. ME.

1. b. Hans had given me a touch of his q. by spearing a bird on the wing 1856. **c.** O, sir,.. You are full of q. and faire desert HEYWOOD. **2.** Youre godlye dysposytyon, and vertuous qualytyes 1551. **b.** *Timon* I. i. 125. **4.** He had all the men of qualitie his sworne enemies NORTH. **b.** I have looked out among the q. for a future husband for her RICHARDSON. **5.** *Two Gent.* IV. i. 58. **6.** He serv'd his Master In q. of Poetaster 1664.

II. Of things. **1.** An attribute, property, special feature ME. †**b.** A manner, style –1651. †**c.** *concretely.* A substance of a certain nature; an essence (*rare*) –1823. **2.** The nature, kind, or character (*of* something); hence, the degree or grade of excellence, etc. possessed by a thing. late ME. †**b.** Nature, with ref. to origin; hence, cause, occasion SHAKS. **3.** Without article: **a.** That aspect of things under which they are considered in thinking or speaking of their nature, condition, or properties 1533. **b.** *Gram.* Manner of action, as denoted by an adverb; chiefly in phr. *adverb of q.* 1530. **c.** Peculiar excellence or superiority 1874. **4. a.** *Logic.* Of propositions: The condition of being affirmative or negative. Of concepts: Comparative clearness or distinctness. 1594. **b.** *Acoustics* = TIMBRE 1865. **5.** A particular class, kind, or grade of anything, as determined by its quality 1656.

1. *Primary, secondary,* etc. *qualities*: see the adjs. **2.** There is more difference in the q. of our pleasures than in the amount EMERSON. **b.** *Timon* III. vi. 117.

Qualm (kwăm, kwǭm). 1530. [Of obscure origin; phonetically corresp. forms either have inappropriate meanings or cannot be historically connected: OE. *cw(e)alm* pestilence, pain (rel. to QUELL *v.*), MLG. *quallem*, G. *qualm* (Du. *kwalm*) thick vapour or smoke.] **1.** A (sudden) feeling or fit of faintness, illness, or sickness. (Now restricted to cases in which the seat of disorder is in the stomach.) **2.** *transf.* **a.** A fit of sickening fear, misgiving, or depression; a sudden sinking of heart. Now *rare.* 1555. **b.** A painful doubt or consciousness of acting wrongly 1649. **c.** A fit or sudden access *of* some quality, etc. (Now only with suggestion of prec.) 1626.

1. It makes the Stomach sick..and sickish Qualms to arise 1683. **2. b.** It was absurd..to affect any qualms about this trifle FIELDING. **c.** Violent qualms of economy W. IRVING.

Qualmish (kwā·miʃ, kwǭ·miʃ), *a.* 1548. [f. QUALM + -ISH¹.] **1.** Of persons: Affected with a qualm or qualms; tending or liable to be so affected. **2.** Of feelings, etc.: Of the nature of a qualm 1798. Hence **Qua·lmishly** *adv.*, **-ness.** So **Qua·lmy** *a.*

Quamash (kwămæ·ʃ, kwǫ·mæʃ). See also CAMAS. 1814. [N. Amer. Indian.] A N. Amer. liliaceous plant (*Camassia esculenta*), the bulbs of which are used for food by the American Indians.

Quamoclit (kwæ·mǒklit). 1731. [Corruption of Mexican *quamo-chitl* f. *qua-*, comb. form of *quaiutl* tree.] A subgenus of climbing plants with brilliant flowers found in the tropical parts of America and Asia, belonging to the genus *Ipomœa.*

Quandary (kwǫ·ndări, kwǫ̆ndēᵊ·ri), *sb.* 1579. [Also †*quandare*, as if f. L. *quando* when treated as a verbal form with corresp. infin. *quandare.* Cf. †*backare* back!, †*jocundare* merry mood, †*vagare* VAGARY, all XVI.] A state of extreme perplexity or uncertainty; a dilemma causing (great) mental agitation or distress; †a ticklish plight.

Quannet (kwǫ·nět). 1842. [Of unkn. origin.] A flat file set in a frame, and used as a plane in filing flat surfaces, as in comb-making.

Quant (kwænt, kwǫnt), *sb.* 1440. [perh. – L. *contus* (Gr. κοντός) boat-pole.] A pole for propelling a boat, esp. one with a prong to prevent it sinking in the mud, used by bargemen on the east coast. Hence **Quant** *v. trans.* to propel a boat with a q.; also *absol.*

Quantic (kwǫ·ntik). 1854. [f. L. *quantus* how great + -IC.] *Math.* A rational, integral, homogeneous function of two or more variables.

Quantification (kwǫ:ntifikēⁱ·ʃən). 1840. [f. next; see -FICATION.] The action of quantifying.

Q. of the predicate, the expression of the logical quantity of the predicate of a proposition, by applying to the predicate the sign *all*, or *some*, or an equivalent.

Quantify (kwǫ·ntifəi), *v.* 1840. [– med.L. *quantificare*, f. *quantus* how great; see QUANTITY, -FY.] **1.** *Logic. trans.* To express the quantity of a term in a proposition, by prefixing *all* or *some* or the like to the term. **2.** To determine the quantity of, to measure 1878. Hence **Quantifier.**

Quantitative (kwǫ·ntitĕtiv), *a.* 1581. [– med.L. *quantitativus*, f. L. *quantitas, -at-*; see next, -IVE.] **1.** Possessing quantity, magnitude, or spacial extent. Now *rare.* **2.** Estimated or estimable by quantity 1656. **3.** Relating to or concerned with quantity or its measurement; ascertaining or expressing quantity 1668. **4.** Pertaining to or based on vowel-quantity, as *q. verse* 1799. Hence **Qua·ntitative-ly** *adv.*, **-ness.** So **Qua·ntitive** *a.*, **-ly** *adv.*

Quantity (kwǫ·ntĭti). late ME. [– (O)Fr. *quantité* – L. *quantitas* (tr. Gr. ποσότης), f. *quantus* how great, how much, f. base of *qui, quis* who; see -ITY.] **I. 1.** Size, magnitude, dimensions. *Obs.* in gen. sense. **2.** Amount, sum. **a.** Of material things not usu. estimated by spatial measurement. late ME. **b.** Of immaterial things. late ME. †**c.** Of money, payment, etc. –1775. **3.** Length or duration in time. Now only in the legal phr. *q. of estate*, the length of time during which the right of enjoyment of an estate is to continue. late ME. **b.** *Pros.* Length or shortness of sounds or syllables, determined by the time required to pronounce them 1563. **c.** *Mus.* Length or duration of notes 1597. **4.** *esp.* as the subject of mathematics: That property of things which is involved in the questions 'how great?' or 'how much?' and is determinable, or regarded as being so, by measurement of some kind; a system of relationships by virtue of which one thing is said to be greater or less than another 1530. **5.** *Logic.* **a.** The extension or intension of a term, dist. as *extensive* and *intensive q.* **b.** The degree of extension which a proposition gives to the term forming its subject. 1668. †**6.** Relative size or amount, proportion (*rare*) –1602. **7.** Great or considerable amount or bulk 1753. **8.** *Electr.* The strength of a current as dist. from intensity or potential 1837.

1. The q. of a surface is called its area; and the q. of a line..its length 1830. **2. a.** Fern..grew in great Q. there DE FOE. **3. b.** *False q.*, an incorrect use of a long for a short vowel or syllable, or *vice versa.* **4.** *Continuous* and *discrete q.*: see DISCRETE *a.* 2. **6.** *Haml.* III. ii. 177. **7.** Windsor Castle is a noble instance of the effect of q. HOGARTH.

II. 1. A (specified) portion or amount *of* an article or commodity. Also *transf.* of immaterial things. ME. **b.** An indefinite (usu. a fair or considerable) portion or amount; †a small piece, a fragment ME. **c.** With def. article: The portion or amount (*of* something) present in a particular thing or instance 1611. **2.** A specified, or indefinite, number of persons or things. late ME. **b.** *pregnantly.* A great number or amount; also *pl.* **3.** A certain space or surface. Const. *of.* Now *rare.* late ME. **4.** *Math.* A thing having q. (I. 4), the number or extension of which is expressible by means of symbols; the symbol itself 1570.

1. A sufficient q. of illusion for the purposes of dramatic interest LAMB. **b.** Away thou Ragge, thou quantitie, thou remnant SHAKS. A q. of wreckage was cast up at Southport 1883. **c.** The q. of sensible heat in a human body BENTHAM. **3.** You would make them a grant of a sufficient q. of your land BURKE. **4.** *transf.* Her husband was an unknown quantity STEVENSON. *Imaginary q.*: see IMAGINARY *a.* 1 c. *Negligible q.* (after Fr. *quantité négligeable*), often *fig.* a person or thing of next to no account, a nonentity.

Comb.: **q.-mark.** a mark indicating the q. of a vowel or syllable; **-surveyor,** a surveyor who estimates the quantities of the materials and labour required for any work.

Quantivalence (kwǫnti·vălĕns). 1871. [f. L. *quanti-*, comb. form of *quantum* how much + *-valence*, after *equivalence.*] = VALENCY 2. **Quanti·valency. Quanti·valent** *a.*

Qua·ntize, *v.* 1921. [f. next + -IZE.] *trans.* To apply quantum mechanics or the quantum theory to; to measure (energy) in quanta. Hence **Quantiza·tion.**

‖**Quantum** (kwǫ·ntǒm). Pl. **quanta.** 1619. [L. n. of *quantus* how much.] **1.** = QUANTITY, in various senses, e.g. I. 2, II. 1, 1c, 4. **2.** *Physics.* A discrete unit quantity of energy, proportional to the frequency of radiation, emitted from or absorbed by an atom 1910.

1. Is there not a sufficient q. of distress and misfortune? 1789. **2.** *Q. theory*, the hypothesis that in radiation the energy of the electrons is discharged in discrete amounts or quanta.

Quantum sufficit (kwǫ·ntǒm sʊ·fisit). Also abbrev. **quantum suff., quant. suff. (suf.).** 1699. [L., a formula used in medical prescriptions.] 'As much as suffices'; hence, a sufficient quantity, to a sufficient extent, etc.

Quaquaversal (kwēⁱkwăvə̄·ɹsăl), *a.* 1728. [f. late L. *quaqua versus, -versum*, f. *quaqua* where-, whithersoever + *versus* towards; see -AL¹.] Turned or pointing in every direction; chiefly *Geol.* in *q. dip.* Hence **Quaquave·rsally** *adv.*

Quarantine (kwǫ·răntīn), *sb.* 1609. [In sense 1 – med.L. *quarantena, quadrantena*, f. **quadranta*, for L. *quadraginta* forty; in sense 2 – It. *quarantina*, f. *quaranta* forty; see -INE¹.] **1.** *Law.* A period of forty days during which a widow, entitled to dower, had the right to remain in the chief mansion-house of her deceased husband; hence, the right of a widow to remain in the house during this period. **2.** A period (orig. of forty days) during which persons who might spread a contagious disease (esp. travellers) are kept isolated; commonly, the period during which a ship, suspected of carrying contagion, is kept isolated on its arrival at a port. Hence, the fact or practice of isolating or of being isolated in this way; the place where infected or isolated ships are stationed. 1663. **b.** *fig.* Any period, instance, etc., of detention or seclusion compared to the above 1680. **3.** A period of forty days; a set of forty (days) 1639.

1. If she marry within the forty days she loseth her quarentine COKE. **2.** Anchored off q. (*mod.*).

Quarantine (kwǫ·răntīn), *v.* 1804. [f. prec.] *trans.* To put in quarantine.

‖**Quare impedit** (kwēᵊ·ri i·mpĭdit). late ME. [L., 'Why he impedes or hinders'.] *Law.* A form of writ issued in cases of disputed presentation to a benefice, requiring the defendant to state why he hinders the plaintiff from making the presentation.

Quarenden, quarender (kwǫ·rĕnd'n, -dəɹ). late ME. [In XV *quaryndo(u)n*; perh. a use of the place-name *Querendon*, Bucks.] A variety of apple common in Somerset and Devon. Also *attrib.*

Quarrel (kwǫ·rĕl), *sb.*¹ ME. [– OFr. *quar(r)el* (mod. *carreau*) :– Rom. **quadrellus*, dim. of late L. *quadrus* a square.] **1.** A short, heavy, square-headed arrow or bolt formerly used with the cross-bow or arbalest. **2.** A square or (more usu.) diamond-shaped pane of glass, of the kind used in making lattice-windows. Now *rare* exc. *dial.* 1447. **3.** *techn.*

a. A glazier's diamond 1807. **b.** A four-sided graver 1882. **c.** A stonemason's chisel 1882.

Quarrel (kwǫ·rĕl), *sb.*[2] [ME. *querele* – OFr. *querele* (mod. *querelle*) :– L. *querella*, var. of *querela* complaint, f. *queri* complain.] †**1.** A complaint; esp. a complaint against a person; esp. in legal use, an accusation or charge; an action or suit –1641. **2.** A ground or occasion of complaint against a person, leading to hostile feeling or action; also, the state or course of hostility resulting from this. Const. *against*, †*to*, later *with*. Now *rare*. ME. **b.** With poss. pron. or genitive: One's cause, side, or party in a complaint or contest. late ME. †**c.** *transf.* Cause, reason, ground, plea –1633. **3.** A violent contention or altercation *between* persons, or of one *with* another; a rupture of friendly relations 1572. †**b.** Quarrelling; quarrelsomeness (*rare*) –1605.

2. Phr. *To pick a q.*: see PICK *v.*[1] IV. 2. All the q. the squire hath to me is for taking your part FIELDING. **b.** 2 *Hen. VI*, III. ii. 233. In our own q. we can see nothing truly STEVENSON. **c.** So as a Man may have a quarrell to marrye when he will BACON. **3.** A man very valiant of his hands, but hot brained, he had had many quarrels 1639. **b.** *Oth.* II. iii. 52.

Quarrel (kwǫ·rĕl), *v.* late ME. [orig. – OFr. *quereler*, f. *querele* (see prec.); in later use f. the sb.] **1.** *intr.* To raise a complaint, protest, or objection; to find fault; to take exception. **2.** To contend violently, fall out, break off friendly relations, become inimical or hostile. Const. *with* (a person) *for* or *about* (a thing). 1530. †**3.** To dispute, call in question, object to (an act, word, etc.) –1786. **4.** To find fault with (a person); to reprove angrily. *Obs.* exc. *Sc.* 1598. †**5.** With complement: To force or bring by quarrelling –1678.

1. I must not q. with the will Of highest dispensation MILT. Phr. *To q. with one's bread and butter*, to find fault with or give up a means of livelihood for insufficient reasons. **2.** She quarrelled with me for supping with St. John 1829. **3.** I hope you will not q. the words 1745. **4.** I had quarrell'd My brother purposely B. JONS. **5.** You must q. him out o' the house B. JONS. Hence **Qua·rreller,** one who quarrels.

†**Qua·rrelet.** [f. QUARREL *sb.*[1] 2 + -ET.] A small square HERRICK.

Quarrelsome (kwǫ·rĕlsə̆m), *a.* 1596. [f. QUARREL *sb.*[2] + -SOME[1].] Inclined to quarrel; given to, or characterized by, quarrelling.

Men who are . . q. when they are drunk FIELDING. Hence **Qua·rrelsome-ly** *adv.*, **-ness.**

Quarrier (kwǫ·riəɹ). late ME. [– OFr. *quarreour*, *-ieur* (mod. *carrier*), f. *quarrer* (mod. *carrer*) :– L. *quadrare* to square (stones).] One who quarries stone; a quarryman.

Quarry (kwǫ·ri), *sb.*[1] [ME. *quirre*, *querre* – AFr. **quire*, **quere*, OFr. *cuirée* (mod. *curée*), alt., by crossing with *cuir* leather and *curer* cleanse, spec. disembowel (:– L. *curare* CURE *v.*), of *couree* :– Rom. **corata* entrails, f. L. *cor* heart + *-ata* -EE[1], -Y[5].] †**1.** Certain parts of a deer placed on the hide and given to the hounds as a reward –1576. †**2.** A heap made of the deer killed at a hunting –1605. †**b.** *transf.* A heap of dead men –1633. **3. a.** The bird flown at by a hawk, etc. 1486. **b.** The animal pursued by hounds or hunters 1612. **c.** *fig.* An intended prey or victim 1615.

2. *Macb.* IV. iii. 206. **3. a.** As when Joue's . . bird from hye Stoupes at a flying heron . . The stone dead quarrey falls SPENSER. **c.** Folly was the proper Q. of Horace DRYDEN.

Quarry (kwǫ·ri), *sb.*[2] late ME. [– med.L. *quarreia*, shortened var. of *quareria* – OFr. *quarriere* (mod. *carrière*), f. **carre* :– L. *quadrum* a square.] **1.** An excavation from which stone for building, etc. is obtained by cutting, blasting, or the like. **b.** *transf.* Any place from which stones may be obtained as from a quarry 1838. †**2.** A large mass of stone or rock in its natural state, capable of being quarried –1764.

1. b. Houses, temples, the monuments of the dead, were the quarries from which they drew THIRLWALL. Hence **Qua·rryman,** one employed in quarrying; one who works in a q.

Quarry (kwǫ·ri), *sb.*[3] 1555. [alt. of QUARREL *sb.*[1], prob. after †*quarry* adj. square (XIII–XVII) – OFr. *quarré* (mod. *carré*) :– L. *quadratus* QUADRATE.] †**1.** = QUARREL *sb.*[1] 1. –1627. **2.** = QUARREL *sb.*[1] 2. 1611. **3.** A square stone, tile, or brick 1555.

Quarry (kwǫ·ri), *v.*[1] 1575. [f. QUARRY *sb.*[1]] †**1.** *trans.* To teach (a hawk) to seize its quarry –1618. †**2.** *intr.* To pounce *on*, as a hawk on its quarry; to prey or feed *on* –1709. **3.** *trans.* To hunt down or kill (a beast of chase) 1820.

Quarry (kwǫ·ri), *v.*[2] 1774. [f. QUARRY *sb.*[2]] **1.** *trans.* To obtain (stone, etc.) by the processes employed in a quarry. Also with *out*. **b.** *fig.* To extract by laborious methods 1860. **2.** To form a quarry in; to cut into (rock, etc.) 1847. **3.** *intr.* To cut or dig in, or as in, a quarry 1848.

1. b. To q. gold and silver out of the monastic treasuries 1868.

Quart (kwǭɹt), *sb.*[1] ME. [– (O)Fr. *quarte* :– L. *quarta*, subst. use of fem. (sc. *pars* part) of *quartus* fourth, ordinal of *quattuor* four.] **1.** An English measure of capacity, one-fourth of a gallon, or two pints. **b.** A vessel holding a quart; a quart-pot or quart-bottle 1450. †**2.** A quarter, region SPENSER.

1. *attrib.* To sende hom wyn and ij. q. botelys 1454.

Quart (kāɹt), *sb.*[2] 1674. [– Fr. *quarte*; see prec.] **1.** A position in fencing: = QUARTE, CARTE[2] 1692. **2.** A sequence of four cards, in piquet and other card-games 1674.

2. *Q. major*, the ace, king, queen, and knave of a suit.

Quart (kāɹt), *v.* 1692. [– Fr. *quarter*, f. *quarte* QUART *sb.*[2]] **a.** *intr.* To use the position 'quart' in fencing. **b.** *trans.* To draw back (the head and shoulders) in doing so.

Quartan (kwǭ·ɹtăn), *a.* and *sb.* [ME. *quartain* – (O)Fr. *quartaine* (sc. *fièvre* fever) :– L. *quartana* (sc. *febris*), fem. of *quartanus*, f. *quartus*; see QUART *sb.*[1], -AN.] **A.** *adj. Path.* Of a fever or ague: Characterized by the occurrence of a paroxysm every fourth (in mod. reckoning, every third) day.

Ageyn feuerys quarteyn It is medicyn souereyn 1400.

B. *sb.* A (*or* the) quartan ague or fever. late ME.

Quartation (kwǫɹtē[i]·ʃən). 1612. [f. L. *quartus* fourth + -ATION.] The operation of combining three parts of silver with one of gold, as a preliminary to separating and purifying the gold by means of nitric acid.

‖**Quarte** (kāɹt, ‖kart). 1700. [– Fr. *quarte*; see QUART *sb.*[2]] = CARTE[2].

Quarter (kwǭ·ɹtəɹ), *sb.* ME. [– AFr. *quarter*, (O)Fr. *quartier* :– L. *quartarius* fourth part of a measure, gill, f. *quartus* fourth.] **I.** One of four equal or corresponding parts into which anything is or may be divided. **1.** Of things generally. **b.** Const. with sbs. without *of* 1866. **c.** *ellipt.* in contextual uses, as, a *quarter-mile race* 1508. **2.** One of the four parts, each including a leg, into which the carcases of quadrupeds are commonly divided; also of fowls, a part containing a leg or wing ME. **b.** *pl.* The four parts of a human body similarly divided, as in the case of those executed for treason ME. **c.** Of a live person or animal; also freq. = hind-quarter, haunch. late ME. **3.** *Her.* One of the four parts into which a shield is divided by quartering (see QUARTER *v.* 3 b) 1486. **b.** A charge occupying one fourth of the shield, placed in chief 1592. **c.** = QUARTERING *vbl. sb.* 2 b. 1727.

1. The four quarters of the rolling year DRYDEN. Garnish with a Seville orange cut in quarters MRS. GLASSE. Phr. *A bad q. of an hour* [tr. Fr. *un mauvais quart d'heure*], a short but very unpleasant experience. **b.** There is not one-quarter the amount of drunkenness 1897. **2.** They bought a Q. of Lamb PEPYS. *Fifth q.*, the hide and fat of a slaughtered animal. **b.** This morning Mr. Carew was hanged and quartered . . but his quarters . . are not to be hanged up PEPYS. **c.** Two . . walked at each side of the horse's quarter 1806. **3. c.** A baron of sixteen quarters SCOTT.

II. The fourth part of some usual measure or standard. **1.** As a measure of capacity for grain, etc. **a.** The British imperial quarter = 8 bushels; the fifth part of a wey or load; also, local varieties of this ME. **b.** The fourth part of a chaldron. late ME. **2.** As a weight. The fourth part of a hundredweight = 28 lbs. (*U.S.* commonly 25 lbs.). Abbrev. qr. 1481. **3.** As a measure of length or area. **a.** The fourth part of a yard; nine inches. late ME. **b.** *Naut.* The fourth part of a fathom 1769. **4.** As a measure of time. **a.** The fourth part of a year, esp. as divided by the QUARTER-DAYS. Also (esp. in Scotland), the fourth part of the school-year, or of the period during which instruction is usually given, containing about eleven weeks. late ME. **b.** A fourth part of the lunar period. Also, the moon's position when between the first and second or third and fourth quarters; quadrature. late ME. **c.** The fourth part of an hour; the space of fifteen minutes. Also, the moment, as denoted by a mark on the dial, the sound of a bell, etc., at which one quarter of an hour ends and the next begins. late ME. **5.** *U.S.* A silver coin = one fourth of a dollar 1856. **6.** *Naut.* The fourth part of a point on the compass; 2° 48′ 45″. Also *q. point*. 1795. **7.** A quarterly instalment of an allowance or payment 1679.

3. a. *Tam. Shr.* IV. iii. 109. **4. c.** I shall die to-night, A quarter before twelve TENNYSON. 'The quarter's gone!' cried Mr. Tapley DICKENS. **7.** Pay me down the first q. now THACKERAY.

III. Senses denoting locality, and transf. uses of these. **1.** The region lying about or under one of the four principal points of the compass or divisions of the horizon; the point or division itself. late ME. †**b.** Boundary or limit towards one of the cardinal points; side –1611. **c.** A direction or point of the compass when more than four are mentioned or may be implied 1604. **2.** Region, district, place, locality ME. **b.** Indicating a certain portion or member of a community, or some thing or things, without ref. to actual locality 1777. **3.** A particular division or district of a town or city, *esp.* that appropriated to a particular class or race of people 1526. †**b.** A part of a gathering or assembly, army, camp, etc. –1599. **4.** Place of stay or residence; dwelling-place, lodgings, *esp.* of soldiers. Now usu. in *pl.* 1591. **5.** Assigned or appropriate position 1549. †**6.** Relations with, or conduct towards, another; *esp.* in phr. *to keep good* (or *fair*) *quarter(s) with* –1674. **b.** (Good or fair) treatment or terms. *Obs.* exc. *arch.* 1648. **7.** Exemption from being immediately put to death, granted to a vanquished opponent in a battle or fight; clemency shown in sparing the life of one who surrenders 1611. **b.** *transf.* and *fig.* 1647.

1. Vpon Elam I wil bringe the foure wyndes from y[e] foure quarters of heauen COVERDALE *Jer.* 49 : 34. **c.** Winds from all quarters agitate the air COWPER. **2.** A visit to a distant q. 1855. **b.** Even in the highest quarters justice had ceased to be much considered 1856. **3. b.** 1 *Hen. VI*, II. i. 63. Phr. †*To keep good q.*, to keep good watch; to preserve good order. **4.** *Free quarter(s)*: see FREE-QUARTER. *Head-*, *summer-*, *winter-quarters*: see the first element. *To beat up the quarters of*, see BEAT *v.*[1] II. 8. *To take up one's quarters*, to establish oneself (in a place). **5.** Swift to thir several Quarters hasted then The cumbrous Elements MILT. *Quarters*, a name given, at sea, to the several stations where the officers and crew of the ship of war are posted in action FALCONER. **6.** *Com. Err.* II. i. 108. **7.** Many were cut down, the Swedes giving no q. 1659. Phr. †*To cry q.*, to call for q.

IV. Techn. uses, in many of which the original sense is much obscured. **1.** *Carpentry.* A piece of wood, four inches wide by two or four inches thick, used as an upright stud or scantling in partitions and other framing. Chiefly in *pl.* 1497. **2.** *Farriery.* One side of a horse's hoof; one half of the coffin, extending between heel and toe. **b.** The corresponding part of a horse-shoe. 1523. **c.** That part of a shoe or boot lying immediately in front of the back-line, on either side of the foot; the piece of leather, or other stuff, forming this part of the shoe from the heel to the vamp 1753. **3.** *Naut.* **a.** The upper part of a ship's side between the after part of the main chains and the stern 1599. **b.** Of a yard: The part between the slings and the yard-arm 1769. **4.** One of the four parts into which a road is divided by the horse-track and the wheel-ruts 1767.

3. a. The French Admiral's Ship under our q. had lost her foremast 1805. *On the q.*, in a direction midway between astern and on the beam.

Comb.: **q.-aspect,** quartile aspect; **-back,** in American football, a player stationed between the forwards and half-backs; **-bell,** a bell in a clock which sounds the quarters; **-bend,** a section of pipe bent into a quarter-circle; **-binding,** a style of book-binding with narrow leather back and no leather corners; **-block** *Naut.*, a block fitted under the q. of a yard; **-cask,** (*a*) a quarter-hogshead; (*b*) a quarter-butt; **-gallery,** a kind of balcony with windows projecting from the q. of a large vessel; **-guard** *Mil.*, a small guard mounted in front of each battalion in a camp; **-gunner** *Naut.*, an officer subordinate to the gunner; **-ill,** an inflammatory disease of cattle and sheep (*symptomatic anthrax*), causing putrefaction in one or more of the quarters; **-miler,** one who is good at running a quarter-mile race; **-note** *Mus.*, (*a*) = q.-tone; (*b*) *U.S.* a crotchet; **-plate,** a photographic plate measuring $3\frac{1}{4} \times 4\frac{1}{4}$ inches; also, a photograph taken on a plate of this size; **-section** (U.S. and Canada), a quarter of a square mile of land, 160 acres; **-tone** *Mus.*, (the interval of) one half of a semitone; **-track,** a quarter-mile racing course; **-turn,** (*a*) a rifle in which the shot makes a quarter of a revolution in the length of the barrel; (*b*) a bend of a quarter of a circle; **-watch** *Naut.*, a ship's watch composed of one quarter of the crew; **-wheeling,** turning through a quarter of a circle; **-wind,** a wind blowing on a vessel's quarter.

Quarter (kwǭ·ɹtəɹ), *v.* late ME. [f. prec.] **1.** *trans.* To cut into quarters; to divide into four equal or equivalent parts. Also with *out.* **2.** To divide into parts fewer or more than four. Also with *out.* late ME. **3.** *Her.* **a.** To place or bear (charges or coats of arms) quarterly upon a shield; to add (another's coat) to one's hereditary arms; to place in alternate quarters *with.* late ME. **b.** To divide (a shield) into quarters, or into any number of divisions formed by vertical and horizontal lines 1590. **4.** To put (soldiers or others) into quarters; to station, place, or lodge in a particular place. Also *pass.* = to have one's abode, lodging, etc. 1594. **b.** With *on, upon*: To impose (soldiers) upon (a householder, town, etc.) to be lodged and fed. Also *transf.* and *fig.* 1683. **5.** *intr.* To take up (one's) quarters; to stay, reside, lodge 1581. †**6.** *trans.* To give quarters to; to furnish with quarters or lodgings –1682. **7.** *Naut.* To assign (men) to a particular quarter on board ship; to place or station for action 1695. **8.** *Naut. intr.* To sail with the wind on the quarter, *i.e.* between beam and stern 1627. **9.** *trans.* To range or traverse (ground, etc.) in every direction. Said esp. of dogs in search of game. 1698. **b.** *intr.* To range to and fro 1857. **10.** To drive a cart or carriage so that the right and left wheels are on (two of) the quarters of a road, with a rut between. Also, of a horse: To walk with the feet thus placed; hence, to walk in front of the wheel. 1800. **b.** To drive to the side in order to allow another vehicle to pass 1849. **11.** Of the moon: To begin a fresh quarter 1789.

1. Being discovered, betrayed, . . hanged, quartered, etc. DE FOE. Pare and q. your apples and take out the cores MRS. GLASSE. *fig. John* II. i. 506. **2.** Here is a sword. . Will q. you in three 1800. **3. a.** The royal banner of England, quartering the lion, the leopard, and the harp HAWTHORNE. **4.** He was then quartered in Edinburgh as a lieutenant 1882. Soldiers were quartered on recalcitrant boroughs GREEN. **7.** The Captain quartered his Men, and the Decks were cleared 1695. **9.** Just like a Pointer quartering well his ground 1788. **10. b.** Every creature that met us would rely on us for quartering DE QUINCEY. **11.** They would have bad weather until the moon quartered 1789.

Quarterage (kwǭ·ɹtərėdʒ). late ME. [f. QUARTER *sb.* + -AGE, after OFr. *quarterage*; cf. AL. *quarteragium.*] **1.** A quarterly contribution, allowance, pension, or other payment. **2.** Quarters, place of abode; quartering of troops, or the expense of this (*rare*) 1577.

Qua·rter-day·. 1480. One of the four days fixed by custom as marking off the quarters of the year, on which the tenancy of houses usu. begins and ends, and the payment of rent and other quarterly charges falls due.

In England and Ireland the quarter-days are Lady Day (March 25), Midsummer Day (June 24), Michaelmas (Sept. 29), and Christmas (Dec. 25).

Qua·rter-deck. 1627. *Naut.* †**a.** Orig., a smaller deck situated above the HALF-DECK, covering about a quarter of the vessel. **b.** In later use: That part of the upper or spar-deck which extends between the stern and after-mast, and is used as a promenade by the superior officers or cabin-passengers.

Quartering (kwǭ·ɹtəriŋ), *vbl. sb.* 1592. [f. QUARTER *v.* + -ING¹.] **1.** Division into four equal parts; also, division in general 1610. **2.** *Her.* **a.** The dividing of a shield into quarters; the marshalling or bringing in of various coats upon one shield, to denote the alliances of one family with the heiresses of others 1592. **b.** *pl.* The various coats marshalled upon a shield; rarely *sing.*, one of these coats 1719. **3.** The assigning of quarters to a person; the action of taking up quarters; †a place in which one is or may be quartered 1625. **b.** *spec.* The billeting of soldiers; the fact of having soldiers quartered upon one 1646. **4.** *Build.* **a.** The placing or using of quarters in construction. **b.** Work formed of quarters. **c.** Wood in the form, or of the size, of quarters. 1703. **5.** Driving on the quarters of a road 1815. **6.** The moon's passage from one quarter to another 1854.

attrib. and *Comb.*, as *q.-block, -knife.* etc.

Quarterly (kwǭ·ɹtəɹli), *a.* and *sb.* 1563. [f. QUARTER *sb.* + -LY¹.] **A.** *adj.* **1.** That takes place, is done, etc., every quarter of a year; relating to, or covering, a quarter of a year. **2.** Pertaining or relating to a quarter (in other senses) 1769. **B.** *sb.* A quarterly review, magazine, etc. 1818.

A. 1. Q. . . payments 1802. The q. Seasons of Devotion, called the Ember-weeks 1688. **2.** *Q. wind*, a wind on the quarter.

Quarterly (kwǭ·ɹtəɹli), *adv.* (*a., sb.*) 1450. [f. QUARTER *sb.* + -LY²; in 2, after AFr. *esquartelé* (OFr. *quartilé* quarterly), in AL. (app. f. Eng.) *quarteriatim* (XIV).] **1.** Every quarter of a year; once in a quarter 1458. **2.** *Her.* **a.** In the four divisions of a shield formed by a vertical and a horizontal line drawn through the fess point; usu. with ref. to two tinctures, charges, or coats of arms, placed in the diagonally opposite quarters 1450. **b.** With ref. to the division of the shield into quarters, or to blazoning it by quarters 1610. **c.** *ellipt.* as *adj.* = divided quarterly, or (by extension) into any number of parts at right angles to each other, as *q. of eight*; also as *sb.* = a shield divided or charged quarterly 1869.

2. b. *Q.-quartered*, having one or more quarters divided in four; so *q.-quartering.*

Quartermaster (kwǭ·ɹtəɹmɑːstəɹ). late ME. [In sense 1, app. f. QUARTER *sb.* III. 5; in sense 2, f. QUARTER *sb.* III. 4; cf. Du. *kwartiermeester.*] **1.** *Naut.* **a.** A petty officer who attends to the steering of the ship, the binnacle, signals, stowing of the hold, etc. **b.** *transf.* Steering-gear 1882. **2.** *Mil.* An officer attached to each regiment, with the duties of providing quarters for the soldiers, laying out the camp, and looking after the rations, ammunition, and other supplies of the regiment 1600. †**3.** One who shares authority with another to the extent of a fourth –1685.

2. Q.-general, a staff-officer who is chief of the department exercising control over all matters relating to the quartering, encamping, marching, and equipment of troops. **Q.-sergeant,** a non-commissioned officer, ranking as a staff-sergeant, who assists the q. in his duties. Hence **Qua·rtermaːster** *v. intr.* to perform the duties of a q. **Qua·rtermastership.**

Quartern (kwǭ·ɹtəɹn), *sb.* ME. [– AFr, *quartrun*, OFr. *quart(e)ron*, f. *quart(e* fourth. (see QUART *sb.*¹), or *quartier* QUARTER *sb.*] **1.** A quarter *of* anything. *Obs.* exc. *dial.* **2.** A quarter of various weights and measures. late ME. **3.** A quartern-loaf 1844.

Comb. **q.-loaf,** a loaf made of a q. of flour; a four-pound loaf.

Quarter-sessions. 1577. [QUARTER *sb.* II. 4. a.] **1.** In England and Ireland: A court of limited criminal and civil jurisdiction, and of appeal, held quarterly by the justices of peace in the counties (in Ireland by county-court judges), and by the recorder in boroughs. **2.** In Scotland: A court of review and appeal held quarterly by the justices of the peace on days appointed by statute 1661.

Qua·rterstaff. 1550. **1.** A stout pole, from 6 to 8 feet long and tipped with iron, formerly used as a weapon by the English peasantry. **2.** Fighting or exercise with the quarterstaff 1712.

1. My owne Country weapon. What? A Quarter staffe 1626.

Quartet(te (kwǫɹte·t). 1790. [– Fr. *quartette* – It. *quartetto*; see next, -ET, -ETTE.] **1.** *Mus.* A composition for four voices or instruments, *esp.* for four stringed instruments. **2. a.** *Mus.* A set of four singers or players who render a quartette. **b.** *transf.* A set of four persons. 1814. **3.** A set of four things; e.g. of lines in a sonnet, of runs at cricket, etc. 1837.

†‖**Quartetto** (kwǫɹte·to). 1775. [It., f. *quarto* fourth.] = prec. –1842.

Quartic (kwǭ·ɹtik), *a.* and *sb.* 1856. [f. L. *quartus* fourth + -IC.] *Math.* **A.** *adj.* Of the fourth degree. **B.** *sb.* A quantic, curve, or surface of the fourth degree.

Quartile (kwǭ·ɹtil), *a.* and *sb.* 1509. [– med.L. **quartilis*, f. L. *quartus* fourth; see -ILE. Cf. SEXTILE, etc.] *Astr.* and *Astrol.* **A.** *adj. Q. aspect*, the aspect of two heavenly bodies which are 90° distant from each other. **b.** Connected with, relating to, a quartile aspect. 1585. **B.** *sb.* A quartile aspect; a quadrature 1509.

Quarto (kwǭ·ɹto). Also written 4to, 4°. 1589. [L. (*in*) *quarto*, (in) the fourth (of a sheet), abl. sing. of *quartus* fourth.] **1.** The size of paper obtained by folding a whole sheet twice, so as to form four leaves, which, as a rule, are nearly square. Orig. and chiefly in phr. *in q.* **2.** A book composed of paper in this form; a quarto-volume 1642. **3.** *attrib.* or as *adj.* Of paper: Folded so as to form four leaves out of the original sheet; having the size or shape of a quarter-sheet. Of books: Printed on paper thus folded. Of works: Published in q. 1633.

2. The form and magnitude of a q. imposes upon the mind 1769.

Quart-pot. late ME. A pot capable of containing the measure of a quart.

Quartz (kwǭɹts). 1756. [– (M)HG. *quarz* – Westslavic *kwardy* = Czech. *tvrdý*, Pol. *twardy.*] *Min.* A widely diffused mineral, massive or crystallizing in hexagonal prisms; in a pure form consisting of silica or silicon dioxide (SiO_2), but varying greatly in colour, lustre,e tc. Also *attrib.* Hence **Quartzi·ferous.** *a* bearing or containing q. **Qua·rtzoid,** a crystal having the form of a double six-sided pyramid. **Qua·rtzose** *a.* mainly or entirely composed of q.; of the nature of q. **Qua·rtzy** *a.* of the nature of q.; resembling q.

Quartzite (kwǭ·ɹtsəit). 1849. [f. prec. + -ITE¹ 2 b.] *Min.* An extremely compact, granular rock, consisting essentially of quartz.

Quash (kwǫʃ), *v.* [ME. *quasse, quasche* – OFr. *quasser*, (also mod.) *casser* annul – late L. *cassare* (med. L. also *quassare*), f. *cassus* null, void, f. L. *cassare*, frequent. of *quatere* shake. Fr. *-ss-* is repr. by *-sh-* as in *brush, push.*] **1.** *trans.* To annul, to make null or void (a law, decision, election,, etc.); to throw out (a writ, etc.) as invalid; to put an end to (legal proceedings). **2.** To bring to nothing; to crush or destroy; to put down completely; to stifle (a feeling, idea, scheme, etc.) 1609. **3.** To crush, quell, or utterly subdue (a person); to squash. Now *rare.* 1639.

3. This. . resolution. . would in all probability have quashed their enemies HANWAY.

Quashee (kwǫ·ʃi), **quashie** (kwǫ·ʃi). 1833. [Ashantee or Fantee *Kwasi*, a name given to a child born on Sunday.] A Negro personal name, used as a general name for any Negro.

‖**Quasi** (kwēⁱ·səi), *adv.* and *pref.* late ME. [L. = as if, almost.] **1.** Used parenthetically = 'as it were', 'almost', 'virtually' (*rare*) 1485. **2.** Treated (usu.) as a prefix and hyphened: **a.** With sbs.: (A) kind of; resembling or simulating, but not really the same as, that properly so termed 1643. **b.** With adjs., more rarely with advbs. or vbs.: Seemingly, but not really; almost, virtually 1802. **3.** Introducing an etymological explanation of a word: 'As if it were'. Abbrev. *q., qu.* late ME.

2. a. An Empyriall Heaven, a *q. vacuitie* SIR T. BROWNE. **b.** Public or q.-public organisms BRYCE **3.** *L. L. L.* IV. ii. 85.

‖**Quasimodo** (kwēⁱsəiˌmōᵘ·doᵘ). 1706. [f. L. *quasi modo*, the first words of the introit for the first Sunday after Easter.] In *Q. Sunday* = LOW SUNDAY.

Quassia (kwæ·siă, kwæ·ʃ-, kwǫ·ʃiă). 1765. [f. name of a Surinam Negro, Graman (= grand man) *Quassi* or *Quacy* (= QUASHEE), who discovered the virtues of the root.] **1.**

The wood, bark, or root of a S. Amer. tree (*Quassia amara*), found esp. in Surinam, also of the bitter ash (*Picræna excelsa*) of Jamaica, and the bitter damson (*Simaruba amara*) of the W. Indies and S. America. **b.** The bitter decoction prepared from this, used for medicinal and other purposes. **2.** Any of the trees yielding quassia, esp. the *Q. amara* of Surinam 1766.

Quassin (kwæ·sin). 1819. [f. prec. + -IN[1].] The bitter principle of quassia. Also **Qua·ssite.**

Quat (kwǫt). *Obs.* exc. *dial.* 1579. [Of unkn. origin.] **1.** A pustule; a small boil; a stye. †**2.** *transf.* Applied contemptuously to a (young) person –1623.

‖**Quatenus** (kwēⁱ·tĭnŏs), *adv.* 1652. [L., = how far, f. *qua* where + *tenus* up to.] In so far as; in the quality or capacity of; QUA.

Qua:ter-cente·nary (kwætəɹ). 1883. [f. L. *quater* four times.] A 400th anniversary.

Quaternary (kwǫtɔ̈·ɹnări), *a.* and *sb.* late ME. [– L. *quaternarius*, f. *quaterni* four together, by fours.] **A.** *adj.* **1.** Consisting of four things or parts; characterized by the number four. Now chiefly *Chem.* in *q. compound*, a combination of four elements or radicals. 1605. **2.** *Geol.* Used, with the sense of 'fourth in order', as an epithet of the period following on the Tertiary, and of the deposits, animals, etc., belonging to it 1843. **B.** *sb.* A set of four (things); the number four. late ME.

1. *Q. number*, usually = 4, but sometimes taken as = 10 (see B). **B.** *Q. of numbers*, the Pythagorean τετρακτύς, or 1+2+3+4=10.

Quaternate (kwǫtɔ̈·ɹnĕt), *a.* 1753. [f. as prec. + -ATE[2].] Arranged in or forming a set or sets of four; composed of four parts.

Quaternion (kwǫtɔ̈·ɹniən). late ME. [– late L. *quaternio, -on-*, f. *quaterni* four together.] **1.** A group or set of four persons or things. **2.** Of paper or parchment: **a.** A quire of four sheets folded in two. †**b.** A sheet folded twice. 1625. **3.** The number 4 or 10 (cf. QUATERNARY) 1637. **4.** *Math.* **a.** The quotient of two vectors, or the operator which changes one vector into another, so called as depending on four geometrical elements, and capable of being expressed by the quadrinomial formula $w + xi + yj + zk$, in which w, x, y, z are scalars, and i, j, k are mutually perpendicular vectors whose squares are –1. **b.** *pl.* That form of the calculus of vectors in which this operator is employed. 1843. **5.** *attrib.* or as *adj.* Consisting of four persons, things, or parts 1814.

1. This..Elementary Q. of Earth, Air, Water, and Fire 1695. Hence †**Quate·rnioned** *a.* arranged in quaternions.

Quaternity (kwǫtɔ̈·ɹnĭti). 1529. [– late L. *quaternitas*, f. as prec.; see -ITY.] A set of four persons (*esp.* in the Godhead, in contrast to the Trinity) or of four things. Hence **Quaternita·rian** (*rare*), one who believes that there are four persons in the Godhead.

Quatorzain (kæ·tǫɹzēⁱn). 1583. [– Fr. *quatorzaine* a set of fourteen, f. *quatorze*; see next.] A piece of verse consisting of fourteen lines; a sonnet. Now *spec.* a poem of fourteen lines resembling a sonnet, but without strict adherence to sonnet-rules.

‖**Quatorze** (kătǭ·ɹz). 1701. [Fr., :– L. *quatuordecim* fourteen.] In piquet, a set of four similar cards (either aces, kings, queens, knaves, or tens) held by one player, which count as 14.

Quatrain (kwǫ·trēⁱn). 1585. [– Fr. *quatrain*, †*quadrain*, f. *quatre* four + *-ain* -AN.] A stanza of four lines, usu. with alternate rhymes; four lines of verse.

‖**Quatre** (kā·təɹ, Fr. katr). 1550. [Fr., = four.] The number four; the four in dice.

Quatrefoil (kæ·təɹfoil). 1494. [– AFr. **quatrefoil*, f. AFr. *quatre* four + *foil* leaf, FOIL *sb.*[1] Cf. CINQUE-FOIL.] A compound leaf or flower consisting of four leaflets or petals radiating from a common centre; also, a representation or conventional imitation of this, *esp.* as a charge in Heraldry. **b.** *Arch.* An opening or ornament, having its outline so divided by cusps as to give it the appearance of four radiating leaflets or petals.

‖**Quattrocento** (kwattrotʃe·nto). 1875. [It., prop. 'four hundred', but used for 'fourteen hundred'; cf. CINQUECENTO.] The fifteenth century as a period of Italian art, architecture, etc. Hence **Quattroce·ntist,** an Italian artist, author, etc. of the 15th c.; also *attrib.* or as *adj.*

Quaver (kwēⁱ·vəɹ), *sb.* 1570. [f. next.] **1.** *Mus.* A note, equal in length to half a crotchet or one-eighth of a semibreve. **2.** *Mus.* A shake or trill in singing, or (*rarely*) in instrumental music 1611. **3.** A shake or tremble in the voice; a tremulous voice or cry 1748. **4.** A quivering or tremulous movement 1736.

Quaver (kwēⁱ·vəɹ), *v.* late ME. [frequent. (see -ER[5]) of *quave* XIV (in XIII *cwavien*), perh. repr. unrecorded OE. **cwafian*, parallel symbolic formation to *cwacian* QUAKE.] **1.** *intr.* To vibrate, tremble, quiver. Now *rare.* **b.** Of the voice: To shake, tremble 1741. **2.** To use trills or shakes in singing 1538. **3.** *trans.* To sing (a note, song, etc.) with trills or quavers. Also with *forth, out.* 1570.

2. In Singing also the Italians Bleat, the Spaniards Whine, the Germans Howl, and the French Q. 1684. **3.** The Larke..Quaver'd her cleare Notes in the quiet Ayre DRAYTON. Hence **Qua·verer. Qua·very** *a.* apt to q.; somewhat quavering.

Quay (kī), *sb.* 1696. [Later sp. of *kay* KEY *sb.*[2], after Fr. *quai*. Cf. CAY.] An artificial bank or landing-place, built of stone or other solid material, lying along or projecting into a navigable water for convenience of loading and unloading vessels.

But now arrives the dismal day, She must return to Ormond-q. SWIFT. Hence **Quay** *v.*[1] *trans.* to provide with a q. **Quayage** (kī·ĕdʒ), dues levied on goods landed or shipped at a q., or on vessels using the q.; q.-room.

†**Quay,** *v.*[2] [perh. alteration of QUAIL *v.*] *trans.* To depress, subdue, daunt SPENSER.

Queach (kwītʃ). *Obs.* exc. *dial.* 1450. [Of unkn. origin.] A dense growth of bushes; a thicket.

Queachy (kwī·tʃi), *a.* *Obs.* exc. *dial.* 1565. [f. prec. + -Y[1]. For the connection between senses 1 and 2 cf. CARR[2].] †**1.** Forming a dense growth or thicket –1586. **2.** Of ground: Swampy, boggy 1593. **3.** *dial.* Feeble, weak, small 1859.

2. The dampes that rise from out the quechy plots PEELE. **3.** They're poor queechy things, gells is G. ELIOT.

Quean (kwīn). [OE. *cwene* = OS. *cwena* (Du. *kween* barren cow), OHG. *quena, quina*, ON. *kvenna, kvinna* (gen. pl., nom. sing. *kona*), Goth. *qino* woman :– Gmc. **kwenōn*, f. IE. base **gwen-* **gwn-*, repr. by Gr. γυνή. Cf. QUEEN.] **1.** A woman, a female; hence, in disparagement: A bold or ill-behaved woman; a jade; and *spec.* a harlot, strumpet (esp. in 16–17th c.). **2.** *Sc.* A young woman, or girl; a (healthy and robust) lass 1470.

2. I see her yet, the sonsie q. BURNS.

Queasy (kwī·zi), *a.* 1459. [Early forms *coisy, queysy* suggest AFr., OFr. **coisi*, **queisi* or *-ié*, rel. to *coisier* hurt, wound, but there is no evidence.] †**1.** Of the times, etc.: Unsettled, troublous, ticklish –1611. †**b.** Of a matter: Uncertain, hazardous –1605. **2.** Of food: Causing sickness or nausea. Now *rare.* 1496. **3.** Of the stomach: Easily upset; unable to digest strong food. Hence of the body, heart, health, etc. 1545. †**b.** Of the mind, feelings, etc.: Fastidious, nice –1659. **c.** Of conscience, etc.: Tender, scrupulous 1579. **4.** Of pains, etc.: Of the nature of sickness; uneasy, uncomfortable 1589. **5.** Of persons: Having a queasy stomach; liable to turn sick; subject to, or affected with, nausea 1606.

1. The times being queasie, the King wisely forbare to take any seuere reuenge 1611. **b.** A queazie question SHAKS. **5.** *Ant. & Cl.* III. vi. 20. Hence **Quea·si-ly** *adv.*, **-ness.**

‖**Quebracho** (kebrā·tʃo). 1881. [Sp., f. *quebrar* break + *hacha* axe.] Any of several Amer. trees, having extremely hard timber and medicinal bark; esp. the white q. of S. America (*Aspidosperma q.*) and the red q. of Mexico (*Schinopsis lorentzii*). Also *attrib.* as *q. bark, gum.* **b.** = The bark itself.

Queen (kwīn), *sb.* [OE. *cwēn* = OS. *quān*, ON. *kvæn* (also *kván*), Goth. *qēns* (wife) :– Gmc. **kwǣniz*, f. IE. **gwēn-* **gwen-*; see QUEAN.] **1.** A (king's) wife or consort; a lady who is wife *to* a king. **2. a.** The wife or consort of a king. **b.** A woman who is the chief ruler of a state, having the same rank and position as a king. OE. **3.** As a title, placed immed. before or †after a personal name; also *the q.*, before or after the name (now *arch.*) OE. **4.** With specification of the people, country, etc. ruled over by a queen or by the king her consort, as *Q. of Scots*, etc. OE. **5.** *transf.* A female whose rank or pre-eminence is comparable to that of a queen; applied e.g. to the Virgin Mary, to the goddesses of ancient religions or mythologies, or to a woman as a term of endearment and honour OE. **6.** Applied to things personified OE. **7.** The perfect female of bees, wasps, or ants 1609. **8.** In games. **a.** *Chess.* The piece which has greatest freedom of movement, and hence is most effective for defending the king. Also, the position on the board attained by a pawn when it is queened. 1440. **b.** *Cards.* A playing-card bearing the figure of a queen, of which there are four in each pack 1575.

1. Hermione, Queene to the worthy Leontes, King of Sicilia SHAKS. **2. b.** My memorial which was given to the q. SWIFT. The q. of England is either q. regent, q. consort, or q. dowager BLACKSTONE. **5.** Poor q. of love, in thine own law forlorn SHAKS. Mooned Ashtaroth, Heavn's Q. and Mother both MILT. *Q. of hearts* (cf. 8 b). *Q. of the May*: see MAY *sb.*[2] 2. *Q. of glory, grace, heaven, paradise, women*, etc., the Virgin Mary. **6.** May, of myrthfull monethis quene DUNBAR. Venice..the Q. of the Adriatic 1840. *Q. of heaven, the night, the tides*, the moon. *Q. of the meadow(s*, MEADOWSWEET.

Comb.: †**q.-apple**, an early variety of apple; **-bee** (see 7); **-cake**, a small currant-cake; **-conch**, a large marine shell, *Strombus gigas*; †**-gold**, a former revenue of the king's consort, consisting of one-tenth on certain fines paid to the king; **-wasp** (see 7).

b. *Comb.* with **queen's. 1.** In titles or appellations, with the sense of 'belonging to, in the service of, the queen', 'royal', as *Queen's bench, counsel, English, evidence, messenger*, etc.: see these words.

2. queen's colours, one of the pair of colours carried by a regiment, the royal colours; **queen's metal,** an alloy of tin, antimony, bismuth, and lead; **queen's pigeon,** a large and beautiful crested pigeon of the Papuan region, *Gaura victoriæ*; **queen's pipe,** a furnace formerly used for destroying smuggled or damaged tobacco; **queen's shilling,** a shilling formerly given to a recruit on enlisting; **queen's ware,** (*a*) a cream-coloured kind of Wedgwood ware; (*b*) a kind of stone-ware; **queen's yellow,** turpeth mineral, used as a yellow pigment.

3. In names of plants, as †**queen's balm,** alyssum; **queen's cushion,** cut-leaved saxifrage; **queen's delight,** an American euphorbiaceous plant, *Stillingia sylvatica*; **queen's pincushion,** the flowers of the guelder rose; etc. Hence **Quee·ndom. Quee·nhood. Quee·nless** *a.* **Quee·nlike** *a.*

Queen (kwīn), *v.* 1611. [f. prec.] **1.** *To q. it*: to be a queen; to act or rule as a queen; to have pre-eminence like a queen. **2.** *trans.* To make (a woman) a queen. Also *fig.* 1843. **3.** *Chess.* To advance (a pawn) to the opponent's end of the board, where it acquires the power of, and is replaced by, a queen or such other piece as the player may choose. Also *absol.* 1789.

Queen Anne. The Queen of Great Britain and Ireland who reigned from 1702 to 1714. **b.** *attrib.* as an epithet of the style of furniture, buildings, etc., characteristic of Queen Anne's reign, or of things made in this style. Also *absol.* 1881.

Queen Anne is dead, a phr. implying stale news. *Queen Anne's bounty*; see BOUNTY 5.

Queening (kwī·niŋ). late ME. [perh. f. QUEEN *sb.* + -ING[3].] A variety of apple.

Queenly (kwī·nli), *a.* 1540. [f. QUEEN *sb.* + -LY[1].] **1.** Belonging or appropriate to a queen. **2.** Resembling a queen; queenlike 1824.

1. A Q. manner CROMWELL. Hence **Quee·nliness.** So **Quee·nly** *adv.* in the manner of a queen.

Queen-mo·ther. 1577. **1.** A queen dowager who is the mother of the reigning sovereign. **2.** A queen who is a mother. Also applied to a queen-bee, and *fig.* 1602.

Quee·n-post. 1823. [Cf. KING-POST.] One of two upright timbers in a roof-truss, which are framed above into the rafters and below into the tie-beam, at points equidistant from its middle or ends.

Queenship (kwī·nʃip). 1536. [-SHIP.] **1.** The dignity or office of a queen. **2.** The personality of a queen; (her) majesty 1603.

Queer (kwīᵊɹ), *a.*[1] 1508. [poss. – G. *quer* cross, oblique, squint, perverse (MHG. *twer*; see THWART). See next.] **1.** Strange, odd, peculiar, eccentric, in appearance or character. **2.** Not in a normal condition; out of sorts; giddy, faint, or ill; *esp.* in phr. *to feel* (or *look*) *q.* Also *slang*: Drunk. 1800. **3.** *Q. Street*: an imaginary street where people in difficulties reside; hence, any difficulty, fix, or trouble, bad circumstances, debt, illness, etc. 1837.

1. Let me be known all at once for a q. Fellow and avoided STEELE. **3.** Q. Street is full of lodgers just at present DICKENS. Hence **Quee·rish** *a.* **Quee·r-ly** *adv.*, **-ness.**

Queer (kwīᵊɹ), *a.*[2] 1561. [Identical in form with and perh. of the same origin as prec.] *Thieves' cant.* Bad; worthless.

Queer (kwīᵊɹ), *v. slang.* 1790. [f. QUEER *a.*[1] or [2].] **1.** *trans.* **a.** To quiz or ridicule; to puzzle. **b.** To impose upon; to cheat. **2.** To spoil, put out of order 1812. **3.** To put (one) out; to make (one) feel queer 1845.

2. All they dared do they did to 'q.' her Scene 1884. Phr. *To q. the pitch*: to upset the 'game', put obstacles in the way.

Queerity (kwīᵊ·rĭti). 1711. [f. QUEER *a.*[1] + -ITY.] Queerness, oddity.

Queest (kwīst). *Obs.* exc. *dial.* [In XV *quyshte, quyste*, perh. syncopated form of CUSHAT.] The ring-dove, wood-pigeon.

Quelch (kwelʹʃ), *v. rare.* 1659. [Related to SQUELCH as *quash* to *squash*, etc.] *trans.* and *intr.* To squelch.

Quell (kwel), *sb. rare.* late ME. [f. next.] Slaying, slaughter; power or means to quell.

Quell (kwel), *v.* [OE. *cwellan* = OS. *quellian* (Du. *kwellen*), OHG. *quellen* (G. *quälen*), ON. *kvelja* :- Gmc. **kwaljan*, f. **kwal*- **kwel*-, repr. also by OE. *cwalu* death.] **1.** *trans.* To kill, slay, destroy (a person or animal). Now *rare* or *Obs.* **2.** To destroy, put an end to, suppress, extinguish, etc. (a thing or state of things, a feeling, disposition, etc.) late ME. **3.** To crush or overcome (a person or thing); to subdue, vanquish, reduce to subjection or submission 1570. †**4.** *intr.* = QUAIL *v.* I. 2. –1616.

1. Yet him the dart Quell'd not COWPER. **2.** The captain quelled this mutiny DE FOE. We soon succeeded in quelling their fears 1832. **3.** The energy of William has thus thoroughly quelled all his foes FREEMAN. **4.** Winters wrath beginnes to q. SPENSER. Hence **Que·ller**, one that quells.

Quench, *sb. rare.* 1529. [f. the vb.] The act of quenching; the state or fact of being quenched.

Quench (kwenʃ), *v.* [ME. *quenchen* :- OE. **cwenćan* (in *ācwenćan*) :- **kwaŋkjan*, causative of OE. **cwincan* (in *ācwincan*) be extinguished = OFris. *quinka* :- **kweŋkan*.] **I.** *trans.* **1.** To put out, extinguish (fire, flame, or light, *lit.* or *fig.*). Now *rhet.* **b.** To put out the fire or flame of (something that burns or gives light, *lit.* or *fig.*). Now *rhet.* late ME. **c.** To destroy the sight or light of (the eye) 1667. **2.** To extinguish (heat or warmth, *lit.* or *fig.*) by cooling. late ME. **b.** To cool (a heated object) by means of cold water or other liquid. late ME. **3.** *transf.* To put an end to, stifle, suppress (a feeling, act, condition, quality, etc.) ME. **b.** To slake (thirst) completely; †rarely, to satisfy (hunger). late ME. **4.** To destroy, kill (a person); to oppress or crush. Now *rare.* ME. **b.** To put down (in a dispute); to squash 1840.

1. Q. thou his light, Destruction dark SCOTT. **b.** As she turned..To q. the lamp MORRIS. **c.** These eyes..So thick a drop serene hath quencht thir Orbs MILT. **2. b.** Hot bricks, somewhat quenched with water 1612. **3.** How mercifully dyd God q. the fury of the peple 1545. **4.** I, Tyme,..quenche out the ungodly, their memory and fame 1567.

†**II.** *intr.* **a.** Of fire, a burning thing, etc.: To be extinguished, to go out, to cease to burn or shine –1623. Also *transf.* **b.** Of a person: To cool down SHAKS.

b. *Cymb.* I. v. 47. Hence **Que·nchable** *a.* **Que·ncher**, one who, or that which, quenches; *colloq.* a drink. **Que·nchless** *a.* unquenchable, inextinguishable; **-ly** *adv.*, **-ness.**

‖**Quenelle** (kəne·l). 1846. [Fr., of unkn. origin.] A seasoned ball, of which the chief ingredient, usu. meat or fish, has been reduced to a paste.

Quercetin (kwə̄·ɹsĭtin). 1857. [Arbitrarily f. L. *quercus* oak + -IN[1].] *Chem.* A yellow crystalline substance widely distributed in the vegetable kingdom, but now obtained by decomposition of quercitrin.

Quercitannin (kwə̄ɹsitæ·nin). 1845. [f. *querci*-, comb. form of L. *quercus* oak + TANNIN.] *Chem.* A form of tannin obtained from oak-bark. So **Quercita·nnic** *a.* in *quercitannic acid.*

Quercite (kwə̄·ɹsəit). 1857. [f. L. *quercus* oak + -ITE[1] 4 a.] *Chem.* A sweet crystalline alcohol obtained from acorns.

Quercitron (kwə̄·ɹsitrən). 1794. [abbrev. f. *querci-citron*, f. L. *quercus* oak + CITRON.] The black or dyer's oak of N. America (*Quercus tinctoria*); also called *q. oak.* **b.** The inner bark of this, used as a yellow dye and in tanning; also *q. bark.* Hence **Que·rcitrin**, the yellow crystalline colouring matter of q. bark.

Querent (kwīᵊ·rĕnt). 1598. [– *quærent*-, pr. ppl. stem of L. *quærere* inquire; see -ENT.] One who asks or inquires; *spec.* one who consults an astrologer.

Querimonious (kwerimōᵘ·niəs), *a.* 1604. [– med.L. *querimoniosus*, f. L. *quærimonia*; see next, -OUS.] Full of, addicted to, complaining. Hence **Querimo·nious-ly** *adv.*, **-ness.**

Querimony (kwe·riməni). 1529. [– L. *quærimonia*, f. *queri* complain; see -Y[3]. Cf. Fr. †*querimonie* (XVI).] Complaint, complaining.

Querist (kwīᵊ·rist). 1633. [f. L. *quærere* + -IST.] One who inquires; a questioner.

Querl (kwə̄ɹl). *U.S.* 1880. [perh. a blending of *curl* and *twirl.*] A curl, twist, twirl. So **Querl** *v.* to twirl, coil, etc.

Quern (kwə̄ɹn). [OE. *cweorn(e* = OFris., OS. *quern* (Du. *kweern*), OHG. *quirn(a*, ON. *kuern*, Goth. *-qairnus*, f. Gmc. **kvern*-.] An apparatus for grinding corn, usu. consisting of two circular stones, the upper of which is turned by hand; also, a small hand-mill for grinding pepper, mustard, etc.

Comb. **q.-stone**, one of the two stones forming a q.; a millstone.

†**Querula·tion.** 1614. [– med.L. *querulatio* (XV), f. *querulari* complain, f. L. *querulus*; see next, -ATION.] Complaint, complaining. So **Querule·ntal, -le·ntial** *a.* querulous. **Queru·lity, Querulo·sity**, habit or spirit of complaining.

Querulous (kwe·rᶦŭləs), *a.* 1450. [f. L. *querulus* or – late L. *querulosus*, f. *queri* complain; see -OUS.] **1.** Of persons: Complaining, given to complaining, peevish. **b.** Of animals or things: Uttering or producing sounds expressive or suggestive of complaint 1635. **2.** Of the nature of, characterized by, complaining 1540.

1. The q. are seldom received with great ardour of kindness JOHNSON. **b.** One q. rook, unable to sleep, protested now and then DICKENS. **2.** The q. comments of old ladies 1874. Hence **Que·rulous-ly** *adv.*, **-ness.**

Query (kwīᵊ·ri), *sb.* 1635. [Anglicizing of *quere* QUÆRE, with ending assim. to *inquiry*.] **1.** Introducing a question: = QUÆRE A. (Now usu. expressed by the abbreviations *qy., qr., qu.* or the sign ?) 1667. **2.** A question: = QUÆRE B. 1635. **3.** A mark of interrogation (?), or the abbrev. *qy.*, etc., used to indicate a doubt as to the correctness of a statement, phrase, letter, etc. 1836.

1. Q. if purchase money was ever paid 1888. **2.** What News, is the Quæry 1719.

Query (kwīᵊ·ri), *v.* 1639. [f. prec. Cf. QUÆRE *v.*] †**1.** *trans.* To put as a question –1755. **b.** To ask (*whether, if, what*, etc.) 1639. **c.** *absol.* To ask a question or questions 1681. **2.** To question, interrogate (a person). *rare.* 1654. **3.** To call (a thing) in question; to mark as doubtful. Also with *if*, etc. 1772.

1. I do..entreat you to answer all that I have queried on that head BERKELEY. **3.** The returning officer..had queried 76 [votes] 1772.

Quesited (kwĭsəi·tĕd), *a.* and *sb.* 1647. [f. med.L. *quesitum* (L. *quæsitum*, pa. pple. n. of *quærere* seek, inquire) + -ED[1].] †**A.** *adj.* Sought for, asked about, etc. –1674. **B.** *sb. Astrol.* The thing or person inquired about 1647. So **Que·sitive** *a.* interrogative.

Quest (kwest), *sb.* ME. [– OFr. *queste* (mod. *quête*) :- Rom. **quæsita* for L. *quæsita*, subst. use of fem. pa. pple. of *quærere* seek, inquire.] **I. 1.** = INQUEST *sb.* 1. *Obs.* exc. *dial.* **2.** = INQUEST *sb.* 2. Now *rare.* ME. **3.** Any inquiry or investigation made in order to discover some fact; also, the object of such inquiry 1598.

2. One q. of gentlemen, another of yeomen passed upon him FULLER.

II. 1. Search or pursuit, made in order to find or obtain something. Const. *of, for.* ME. †**b.** A person (or set of persons) employed in searching SHAKS. **2.** In mediæval romance: An expedition or adventure undertaken by a knight to procure some thing or achieve some exploit; the knights engaged in such an enterprise. Also *transf.* late ME. **3. a.** The search for game made by hounds. **b.** The baying of hounds in pursuit of game; a peculiar barking uttered by dogs when in sight of game. *Obs.* exc. *dial.* late ME. **4.** *R. C. Ch.* The collection of alms or donations for religious purposes 1528.

1. Whose desire Was to be glorious; 'twas a foolish q. BYRON. Phr. *In q. of* (†*after*, or inf.); The ghost rides forth..in nightly q. of his head W. IRVING. **b.** *Oth.* I. ii. 46. **2.** The q. of the Sancgreal MALORY. **3.** *transf.* Gad not abroad at ev'ry q. and call Of an untrained hope or passion G. HERBERT.

Quest (kwest), *v.* ME. [– OFr. *quester* (mod. *quêter*), f. *queste* (see prec.).] **1.** *intr.* Of hunting dogs, etc.: To search for game. Also with *about.* **b.** Of animals: To search *about* for food 1796. **2.** Of hunting dogs: To break out into a peculiar bark at the sight of game; to give tongue; to bark or yelp. *Obs.* exc. *dial.* late ME. **3.** Of persons: To go about in search of something. Also with *about*, and const. *after, for.* (Chiefly *transf.* from sense 1.) 1624. **b.** *R. C. Ch.* To ask for alms or donations 1748. **4.** *trans.* To search for, pursue, seek *out* 1751.

1. Bevis, questing about, found the body SCOTT. **4.** Flush found a hare, and quested it for two miles MISS MITFORD. Hence **Que·ster**, one who quests. So †**Que·stant**, quester SHAKS.

Question (kwe·styən, kwe·stʃən), *sb.* ME. [– AFr. *questiun*, (O)Fr. *question* – L. *quæstio*, *-on-*, f. *quæst-*, pa. ppl. stem of *quærere* seek, inquire; see -ION.] **I.** The action of inquiring or asking. **1.** The stating or investigation of a problem; inquiry into a matter; discussion of some doubtful point. **2.** The action of questioning, interrogating, or examining a person, or the fact of being questioned, etc.; hence †talk, discourse. late ME. **b.** *spec.* The application of torture as part of a judicial examination 1583.

1. The..vnquiet time Did push it out of farther q. SHAKS. Phr. *Beyond* (*all*) *q., out of, past, without q.*, unquestionably. *In q.*, under consideration, forming the subject of discourse. *To come into q.*, to be thought of as possible. Phr. *To call in* (†or *into*) *q.*, (*a*) to examine judicially, bring to trial; to take to task; (*b*) to question the validity or status of; to raise objections to. †*In q.*, on trial; He that was in q. for the robbery SHAKS. **2.** Others abide our q. Thou art free. M. ARNOLD.

II. What is asked or inquired (about). **1.** The interrogative statement of some point to be investigated or discussed; a problem; hence, a matter forming, or capable of forming, the basis of a problem; a subject involving more or less difficulty or uncertainty ME. **b.** *spec.* A subject or proposal for discussion in a meeting or deliberative assembly, esp. in Parliament; †the putting of this proposal to the vote 1658. **2.** A subject of discussion, debate, or strife *between* parties, or of one party *with* another. late ME. **3.** An interrogation, query, inquiry ME.

1. Phr. *The q.*, the precise matter receiving or requiring deliberation or discussion; But that is not the q.: the q. is concerning your marriage SHAKS. *To beg the q.*: see BEG *v.* 4. **b.** *Question!*, used (*a*) to recall a speaker to the subject under discussion, †(*b*) to demand that the vote be taken. *Previous q.*, see PREVIOUS *a.* *It is a q. of*, what is required or involved is, etc.; It was a q. of time FREEMAN. *Out of the q.*, foreign to the subject; hence, not to be considered or thought of; Retreat was out of the q. 1878. **2.** A q. arose between the heir at law and the younger children, whether it passed by the will CRUISE. Phr. *It is no* (or *not a*) *q.*, *there is no q.*, or simply †*no q.*: There is no room for dis-

pute or doubt (*but, that*). *To make no q.*, to raise or entertain no doubt (*of* or *about* a thing, *but* or inf.). †*No q.* (used parenthetically), no doubt, without q.; This no q. is his meaning CLARENDON. **3.** Ask me no questions and I'll tell you no fibs GOLDSM. If you do not give a plain answer to a plain q., you will be committed 1776.
Comb.: **q.-mark, -stop,** a mark of interrogation.

Question (kwe·styən, -tʃən), *v.* 1470. [– (O)Fr. *questionner*, f. *question* (see prec.).] **1.** *trans.* To ask a question or questions of (a person or *fig.* a thing); to interrogate 1490. **b.** To examine judicially; hence, to call to account, challenge, accuse (*of*). Now *rare.* 1637. †**2.** *intr. To q. with*: To ask questions of; to dispute with –1772. **3.** To ask or put questions 1584. **b.** *trans.* With clause stating the question 1592. **4.** To raise the question (*whether, if*, etc.); hence, to doubt, hold as uncertain 1533. **5. a.** To call in question, dispute, oppose 1632. †**b.** To state as a question SIR T. BROWNE. †**6.** To investigate (a thing) –1655.
1. Her Father..Still question'd me the Storie of my life SHAKS. **3.** Goe wee..to the man that tooke him To q. of his apprehension SHAKS. **b.** They never questioned what crime he had done HOBBES. **4.** Whether the request..can be complied with..may be questioned 1883. Phr. *I do not q.* (*but*, etc.), I have no doubt, I am sure (that); also pass. *it cannot be questioned*, it is certain. **5. a.** Wee q. the truth of your informacion 1632. **6.** *Hen. V*, II. iv. 142.

Questionable (kwe·styənăb'l, -tʃən-), *a.* 1590. [f. prec. + -ABLE.] †**1. a.** Of a person: That may be interrogated. **b.** Of a question: That may be asked or put. **c.** Of a place: Where questions may easily be asked (*rare*) –1607. †**2.** Of persons or acts: Liable to be called to account or dealt with judicially –1685. **3.** Of things, facts, etc.: That may be questioned or called in question (rarely const. *by*); doubtful, uncertain. Freq. in phr. *it is q.* (*whether, if*, etc.). 1607. **b.** Of qualities, properties, etc.: About the existence or presence of which there may be question 1796. **c.** In depreciatory sense: Of doubtful or dubious character or quality 1806.
1. a. Thou com'st in such a q. shape, That I will speake to thee SHAKS. **3.** Whatever rendered property q., ambiguous, and insecure BURKE. **b.** The q. privilege of having as many wives as he could support 1856. **c.** Stick not even at q. means SHELLEY. Hence **Questionabi·lity, Que·stionableness,** the state of being q. **Que·stionably** *adv.*

†**Que·stionary,** *sb. rare.* late ME. [– med.L. **questionarius* = *questionista* QUESTIONIST; see -ARY[1].] **1.** = QUESTIONIST –1787. **2.** = QUESTOR 1. SCOTT.

Questionary (kwe·styənări), *a.* 1653. [app. f. QUESTION *sb.* + -ARY[1].] **1.** Having the form of a question; consisting of questions; conducted by means of questioning. **2.** That asks questions STEELE.

Questioner (kwe·styənəɹ, -tʃən-). 1551. [f. QUESTION *v.* + -ER[1].] One who questions; an interrogator, inquirer.
The curious q., the foolishe answerer CRANMER.

Questionist (kwe·styənist, -tʃən-). 1523. [– med.L. *questionista*; see QUESTION *sb.*, -IST.] **1.** A habitual or professed questioner, *spec.* in theological matters. **2.** Formerly, at Cambridge and Harvard: An undergraduate in his last term before proceeding to the degree of B.A. 1549.

Questionless (kwe·styənlės, -tʃən-), *a.* and *adv.* late ME. [f. QUESTION *sb.* + -LESS.] **A.** *adj.* Not admitting of question; unquestionable, indubitable 1532. **B.** *adv.* Without question; unquestionably; undoubtedly.
B. The first man who came into the world was, q., the most perfect 1760. Hence **Que·stionlessly** *adv.* = B; also, without asking questions.

‖**Questionnaire** (kestyŏnēᵊ·ɹ). 1908. [Fr., f. *questionner* QUESTION *v.* + *-aire* -ARY[1].] A formal list of questions, esp. as used in an official inquiry.

Que·stman. 1854. [f. QUEST *sb.* + MAN *sb.*] A member of a 'quest'; one appointed to make official inquiry into any matter; *spec.* †**a.** a parish or ward official elected annually –1761. **b.** *Eccl.* A churchwarden's assistant; a sidesman. Now *Hist.* 1454.

†**Que·stmonger.** late ME. [f. QUEST *sb.* + MONGER.] One who made a business of conducting inquests –1776.

Questor (kwe·stǫɹ, -əɹ). late ME. [– med.L. *questor*, L. *quæstor* QUÆSTOR.] **1.** *R. C. Ch.* An official appointed by the Pope or by a bishop to grant indulgences on the gift of alms to the Church; a pardoner. **2. a.** In France, one of the treasurers of the National Assembly 1848. **b.** In Italy, a commissary of police 1865.

†**Que·strist.** [f. QUESTER + -IST.] One who goes in quest of another SHAKS.

Quetch, quitch, *v. Obs.* exc. *dial.* [OE. *cweććan*, causative f. **kwak-*; see QUAKE *v.*] †**1.** *trans.* and *intr.* To shake. (OE. and early ME.) **2.** *intr.* To stir; in later use *esp.* to shrink, wince, twitch, as with pain ME. **b.** To utter a sound 1530.

Queue (kiū), *sb.* 1592. [– Fr. *queue* :– L. *cauda* tail.] **1.** *Her.* The tail of a beast. **2.** A long plait of hair worn hanging down behind; a pig-tail 1724. **3.** A number of persons ranged in a line, awaiting their turn to proceed, as at a ticket-office; also, a line of carriages, etc. 1837. **4.** A support for the butt of a lance 1855.

Queue (kiū), *v.* 1777. [f. prec.] **1.** *trans.* To put up (the hair) in a queue. **2.** *intr.* To take one's place in a queue; to form a queue; to form *up* in a queue 1893.

Quibble (kwi·b'l), *sb.* 1611. [f. synon. †*quib* (XVI), prob. f. L. *quibus* (dat. and abl. of *quī, quæ, quod* who, what, which) as a word of frequent occurrence in legal documents and so assoc. with verbal niceties or subtle distinctions; see -LE.] **1.** A play upon words, a pun. **2.** An equivocation, evasion of the point at issue; an argument depending on some likeness or difference between words or their meanings, or on some purely trivial circumstance 1670. **b.** The use of quibbles, quibbling 1710.
2. To a plain understanding his objections seem to be mere quibbles MACAULAY.

Quibble (kwi·b'l), *v.* 1629. [f. prec.] †**1.** *intr.* To pun, to play on words –1751. **2.** To argue in a purely verbal way; to evade the real point by a quibble 1656. **3.** *trans.* With advs.: To cheat or bring *out of*, waste or explain *away*, by quibbling 1713.
1. Nothing is more usual than to see a Hero weeping and quibbling for a dozen Lines together ADDISON. **2.** Quibbling about the meaning of words 1864. Hence **Qui·bbler. Qui·bblingly** *adv.*

Quick (kwik), *a.*, *sb.*, and *adv.* [OE. *cwic(u* = OFris., OS. *quik* (Du. *kwik*), OHG. *quek* (G. *keck*, dial. *kweck* lively, sprightly), ON. *kvikr* :– Gmc. **kwikwaz*; cf. Goth. *qius* (:– **kwiwaz*), f. IE. *base* **qwej-* repr. also in L. *vivus*.] **A.** *adj.* **I.** Characterized by the presence of life. **1.** Living; endowed with life; animate. Now *dial.* or *arch.* †**b.** Of possessions or property: Consisting of animals; (live) stock –1745. **c.** *transf.* or *fig.* OE. **2.** Of persons and animals: In a live state, living, alive. Now *dial.* or *arch.* OE. †**b.** Of the flesh or parts of the body –1649. **c.** *transf.* and *fig.* of qualities, feelings, etc. ME. **3.** Of plants or their parts: Alive, growing OE. **b.** Composed of living plants, esp. hawthorn, as *q. fence, hedge*, etc. 1467. **4.** Const. *with*. **a.** *Q. with child*, said of a female in the stage of pregnancy at which the motion of the fœtus is felt. Now *rare* or *Obs.* †Also *absol.* 1450. **b.** Alive, instinct *with* (life, soul, feeling, etc.) 1837.
1. They could see no quicke things left but onely Owles 1611. **2.** There was a gray Frier burning quicke at S. Markes pillar 1632. Not the q. but dead worthies properly pertain to my pen FULLER. **c.** Strike dead our feare..Rather then keepe it q. CHAPMAN. **3. b.** On the top a palisade and q. hedge 1894. **4.** *L. L. L.* v. ii. 687. **b.** That languid form q. with excitement DISRAELI.

II. Of things: Having some specific quality characteristic or suggestive of a living thing. †**1.** Of the complexion: Having the freshness of life (*rare*) –1693. **2. a.** *Mining.* Of veins, etc.: Containing ore, productive 1676. **b.** Of stock, capital, etc.: Productive of interest or profit 1701. **3.** Of wells, streams, etc.: Running, flowing. Now *rare.* OE. **4.** Of soil, etc.: Mobile, shifting, readily yielding to pressure. Now *rare.* ME. **5.** †**a.** Of coals: Live, burning –1764. **b.** Of fire or flames: Burning strongly. Also of an oven: Exposed to a brisk fire. late ME. †**6.** Of speech, writings, etc.: Lively, full of vigour or acute reasoning –1625. †**7.** Of places or times: Full of activity; busy. Of trade: Brisk. –1746. †**8.** Of sulphur: Readily inflammable, fiery –1661. †**9.** Of wine and other liquors: Brisk, effervescent –1746. **10.** Of colour: Vivid, bright, dazzling (*rare*) 1664. **11.** Of feelings: Lively, vivid, keen, strongly felt 1449. **12.** †**a.** Of a taste or smell: Sharp, pungent; brisk –1797. †**b.** Of speech or writing: Sharp, caustic –1748. **c.** Of air or light: Sharp, piercing (*rare*) 1608.
2. b. The q. assets..amounted on August 31 last to 5,928,338 dols. 1891. **3.** Many quicke and running springs HOLLAND. **4.** The Solway sands, ..as the tide makes,..become q. in different places SMOLLETT. **5. b.** Bake it in a q. oven three hours 1769. **10.** Slain are the poppies that shot their random scarlet Q. amid the wheatears G. MEREDITH. **12. c.** The air is q. there, And it pierces and sharpens the stomach SHAKS.

III. 1. Of persons (or animals): Full of vigour, energy, or activity (now *rare*); prompt or ready to act; acting with speed or rapidity. late ME. **b.** Of qualities, things, etc. late ME. **2.** Of the eye, ear, etc.: Keen or rapid in its function; capable of ready or swift perception. late ME. **b.** So of the senses, perception, feeling, etc. 1548. **3.** Mentally active or vigorous; of ready apprehension, wit, or invention; so of the mind, operations of the mind, etc. OE. **4.** Hasty, impatient, hot-tempered. Now chiefly in comb. *q.-tempered*; so of temper, disposition, etc. 1549. **5.** Moving, or able to move, with speed 1450. **6.** Of movement or succession: Rapid, swift ME. **7.** Of an action, occurrence, process, etc.: That is done, happens, or takes place, rapidly or with speed; *esp.* that is over within a short space of time; that is soon finished or completed 1548. **8.** Of a curve, turn, etc.: Sharp 1725. **9.** With various constructions, viz. *to* and inf., *in, of, at, for, unto* ME.
1. In all thy workes bee quicke *Ecclus.* 31:22. **b.** O true Apothecary: Thy drugs are quicke SHAKS. He was a good patriot, of a q. and clear spirit FULLER. **3.** The quicke Comedians Extemporally will stage vs SHAKS. A man of q. observation and lively fancy 1804. **4.** The Byshop was some what quicke wyth theym, and signified that he was muche offended LATIMER. **5.** Q., cross lightning SHAKS. **6.** Incite them to quicke motion SHAKS. **7.** Give me a q. dispatch one way or other MARVELL. **9.** Quicke is mine eare to heare of good towards him SHAKS. Q. in temper 1837. Q. of foot DICKENS. Your hands then mine, are quicker for a fray SHAKS.

B. Ellipt. or absol. uses passing into sb. **1. a.** *pl.* (Without article or *-s*.) Living persons OE. **b.** *The q.*, the living. Usu. *pl.* and in conjunction with *the dead*. OE. **2.** With *a* and *pl.* A living thing. *rare* (now *dial.*). OE. **3.** *collect.* Living plants, *spec.* of white hawthorn, set to form a hedge 1456. **b.** with *a* and *pl.* = QUICKSET 1 b. 1507. **4.** *The q.*: the tender or sensitive flesh in any part of the body, as that under the nails; also, the tender part of a sore or wound. Usu. in phr. *to the q.* 1523. **b.** *fig.* with ref. to persons, as *touched, galled, stung*, etc. *to the q.* 1526. **c.** *transf.* of things (esp. immaterial things): The central, vital, or most important part 1567. **d.** With *a* and *pl.*: A tender, sensitive, or vital part (*rare*) 1550. **5.** *The q.*: the life (see LIFE *sb.* I. 7.). Chiefly in phr. *to the q.* 1563. *Obs.* or *arch.*
1. a. The Iudge of quicke and dead *Acts* 10:42. **b.** He ascended into Heaven..From thence he shall come to judge the q. and the dead *Bk. Com. Prayer*. **3.** The workes..are curiously hedg'd with q. EVELYN. **4.** He was in the habit of biting his nails to the q. 1862. **b.** Tigranes..was galled to the q., and hit at the heart NORTH. A Tory to the q. TENNYSON. **c.** The point touched the q. of his experience GEO. ELIOT. **5.** To draw to the q. (or to the life) 1727.

C. *adv.* **1.** = QUICKLY ME. **2.** Used imperatively (partly ellipt. for *be quick*) 1596.
1. I am told that you speak very q. CHESTERF. Phr. *As q. as lightning, thought, wink*, etc. **2.** Quicke, quicke, feare nothing; Ile be at thy Elbow SHAKS.
Combs.: **q.-beam** = QUICKEN *sb.*[1]; **-change,** *attrib.* as epithet of an actor, etc. who quickly changes costume or appearance in order to play a different part; also *transf.* and as vb.; **-fire,** *attrib.* of a type of gun which can fire shots in rapid succession; **-firer,** a quick-firing gun; †**-thorn,** thorn used for hedging.

Quick (kwik), *v. arch.* [OE. *cwician*, f.

cwic QUICK *a.*] *intr.* = QUICKEN *v.* 1, 2, 3, 6.

Quicken (kwi·k'n), *sb.*[1] late ME. [app. f. QUICK *a.*] **a.** The mountain-ash or rowan-tree (*Pyrus aucuparia*). **b.** The service-tree (*Pyrus domestica*). †**c.** The juniper.

Quicken (kwi·k'n), *sb.*[2] *Sc.* and *n. dial.* 1684. [f. *quick*, northern f. QUITCH.] Couch-grass: also *pl.* the underground stems of this and other grasses.

Quicken (kwi·k'n), *v.* ME. [f. QUICK *a.* + -EN[5].] **1.** *trans.* To give or restore life to; to animate (as the soul the body). **2.** To give, add, or restore vigour to (a person or thing); to stimulate, excite, inspire. late ME. **3.** To kindle (a fire); to cause or help to burn up ME. †**4.** To make (liquor or medicine) more sharp or stimulant –1799. **5.** To hasten, accelerate, give speed to 1626. **b.** To make (a curve) sharper (*rare*) 1711. **6.** *intr.* To receive life, become living; †also, to revive. late ME. **b.** Of a female: To reach the state of pregnancy at which the child shows signs of life 1530. **7.** *fig.* To come into a state comparable to life. Const. *to*, *into*. ME. **b.** To grow bright 1712. **8.** To become faster 1805.

1. A medicine..able to..Q. a rocke SHAKS. *fig.* It is the spirit that quykeneth, the fleysch profiteth nothing WYCLIF *John* 6:64. **2.** Loue quickened hym day and night LD. BERNERS. This quickened my resolution DE FOE. *absol.* To consider of education and learning, what is good and quickneth 1581. **5.** It had induced him to q. his departure 1838. **6.** As Sommer Flyes..That q. euen with blowing SHAKS. **7.** The hopes that q... Are flowers that wither SHELLEY. **b.** Sees.. keener lightnings q. in her eyes POPE. **8.** Tess's breath quickened T. HARDY. Hence **Qui·ckener**, one who or that which quickens.

Quickhatch (kwi·khætʃ). 1743. [Adaptation of the Cree (Indian) name.] The wolverene.

Qui·cklime. late ME. [f. QUICK *a.* + LIME, after L. *calx viva*, Fr. *chaux vive*.] Lime which has been burned and not yet slaked with water; calcium oxide, CaO.

Quickly (kwi·kli), *adv.* OE. [f. QUICK *a.* + -LY[2].] †**1.** In a living or lively manner; with animation or vigour; also, sensitively –1800. **2.** Rapidly, with haste or speed ME.

2. We may fele our pulses bete quickly and continually 1526. This q. heals even cut Veins and Sinews WESLEY. Retaliation..q. followed 1847.

Quick march. 1752. [In 1 f. QUICK *a.* and MARCH *sb.* In 2 f. QUICK *adv.* and MARCH *v.*] *Mil.* **1.** A march in QUICK TIME. **2.** Used as a command to soldiers to march in quick time 1802.

Quickness (kwi·knės). ME. [f. QUICK *a.* + -NESS.] **1.** Life, vitality, vital principle. Now *rare.* †**2.** Animation, briskness, vigour, freshness, etc. –1656. **3.** Liveliness, readiness, or acuteness of feeling, perception, or apprehension. late ME. **4.** Speed, rapidity (of action, motion, etc.); hastiness (of temper) 1548. †**5.** Sharpness; pungency or acidity of taste; sharpness of speech –1748.

1. The lyfe and quycknesse of the grayne 1545. **3.** Q. of parts FULLER. Q. of sight 1841. **4.** A q. of temper..marred the perfection of his character 1863.

Quicksand (kwi·ksænd). late ME. [f. QUICK *a.* II. 4.] **1.** A bed of extremely loose wet sand, easily yielding to pressure and thus readily swallowing up any heavy object, as a man, a ship, etc. resting upon it. **b.** *fig.* Applied to things (more rarely to persons) of an absorbent, yielding, or treacherous character 1593. **2.** Without article: Loose yielding sand 1838.

1. Conscious that there lay..quicksands in his way COWPER. **b.** He once more tried the quicksands of the Court 1879.

Quickset (kwi·kset), *sb.* and *a.* 1484. [f. QUICK *a.* I. 3 + SET *ppl. a.* and *sb.*] **1. a.** *collect.* Live slips or cuttings of plants, set in the ground to grow, *esp.* those of whitethorn or other shrub of which hedges are made. **b.** With *a* and *pl.* One such slip or cutting 1519. **2.** A quickset hedge or thicket 1573. **B.** *adj.* (or *attrib.*) Of a hedge: Formed of living plants. So also with *fence*, *row*, etc. Also *transf.* and *fig.* 1535. Hence †**Quickset** *v. trans.* to furnish (plant, enclose, etc.) with a q. hedge.

Quick-sighted, *a.* 1552. [f. *quick sight* + -ED[2].] Having quick sight. **Quicksi·ghtedness.**

Quicksilver (kwi·ksi:lvəɹ), *sb.* [OE. *cwicseolfor* = Du. *kwiksilver*, OHG. *quecsilbar* (G. *quecksilber*), ON. *kviksilfr*; tr. L. *argentum vivum* 'living silver' (Pliny), whence also Fr. *vif argent*, It. *argento vivo.*] **1.** The metal mercury, so called from its liquid mobile form at ordinary temperatures. **2.** Used allus. with ref. to the quick motion of which the metal is capable 1562.

2. Thou hast q. in the veins of thee to a certainty SCOTT. Hence **Qui·cksi:lver** *v. trans.* to treat, imbue, or mix with q.; *esp.* to coat (the back of glass) with an amalgam of tin in order to give a reflecting power.

Quick step, qui·ckstep. 1802. **1.** *Mil.* The step used in marching in quick time. Also quasi-*adv.*, at a quick step. **2.** *Mus.* A march in military quick time 1811. **3.** A ballroom dance with short rapid steps 1900.

Quick time. 1802. *Mil.* A rate of marching which in the British army now consists of 128 paces of 33 inches each (= 118 yards) in a minute, or four miles an hour.

Quick-witted, *a.* (Stress variable.) 1530. [f. *quick wit* + -ED[2].] Having a quick or ready wit; mentally acute, sharp, clever.

How likes Gremio these quicke-witted folkes? SHAKS. Hence **Quickwi·ttedness.**

‖**Quicumque vult** (kwəikʊ·mkwĭ vʊlt). 1450. [L. = whosoever will (be saved, *salvus esse*).] The Athanasian Creed, of which these are the opening words.

‖**Quid** (kwid), *sb.*[1] 1606. [L., what, anything, something, n. sing. of *quis* who, anyone, etc.] **1.** That which a thing is. **2.** *U.S.* (abbrev. of *tertium quid.*) A name given to a section of the Republican party in 1805–11.

Quid (kwid), *sb.*[2] *slang.* 1688. [prob. slang use of prec., perh. with allusion to QUID PRO QUO. Cf. Fr. *quibus* 'the wherewithal'.] A sovereign; †a guinea. (*Pl.* usu. without *-s*, as *two q. a week.*)

Quid (kwid), *sb.*[3] 1727. [dial. var. of CUD *sb.*] A piece of something (usu. of tobacco), suitable to be held in the mouth and chewed.

Quid (kwid), *v.* 1775. [f. prec.] **1.** *intr.* To chew tobacco; to chew the cud. **2.** *trans.* Of horses: To let (food) drop from the mouth when half chewed 1831.

‖**Quidam** (kwəi·dæm). *rare.* 1579. [L., f. *qui* who.] Somebody; a certain person.

Qui·ddative, *a. rare.* 1642. Shortened from QUIDDITATIVE.

Quiddit (kwi·dit). Now *arch.* 1592. = QUIDDITY 2.

†**Qui·dditative,** *a.* 1600. [f. med.L. *quidditas*, *quidditat-* (see next) + -IVE; see -ATIVE.] **1.** Pertaining to the quiddity or essence of a thing –1656. **2.** Full of equivocations –1637.

Quiddity (kwi·dĭti). 1539. [– med.L. *quidditas*, f. *quid* what; see -ITY. Cf. *seitas* SEITY, (O)Fr. *quiddité.*] **1.** The real nature or essence of a thing; that which makes a thing what it is 1569. **2.** A captious nicety in argument; a quirk, quibble. (Alluding to scholastic arguments on the 'quiddity' of things.) 1539. **b.** Subtlety (of wit) 1600.

1. The q...of poetry as distinguished from prose DE QUINCEY.

Quiddle (kwi·d'l), *v.* Now chiefly *dial.* and *U.S.* 1567. [prob. f. prec. (sense 2), after *fiddle*, *piddle*, or *twiddle.*] *intr.* **a.** To discourse in a trifling way. **b.** To trifle, waste time (*with*) 1832. Hence **Qui·ddle** *sb.* a fastidious person. **Qui·ddler.**

Quidnunc (kwi·dnʊŋk). 1709. [f. L. *quid* what + *nunc* now.] One who is constantly asking: 'What now?' 'What's the news?'; hence an inquisitive person; a gossip.

Some wretched intrigue which had puzzled two generations of quidnuncs 1874.

‖**Quid pro quo** (kwid prōᵘ kwōᵘ), *sb.* 1565. [L., 'something for something'.] **1.** One thing in place of another; *orig.* and *esp.* one medicinal substance used for another, either intentionally, fraudulently, or by mistake. **b.** The action or fact of using one thing for another; the result of this; a mistake or blunder consisting in such a substitution 1679. **2.** One thing (or action) in return for another; tit for tat 1591.

1. b. A laughable *quid pro quo*..occurred to him in a conversation THACKERAY. **2.** I shall be able..to bestow What you will find a *quid pro quo* 1820.

Quiesce (kwəi,e·s), *v.* 1828. [– L. *quiescere* be still, f. *quies* QUIET.] **1.** *intr.* To become quiescent; to subside *into* 1833. **2.** Of a letter: To become silent: said of the feeble consonants in Hebrew when their sound is absorbed in that of a preceding vowel 1828.

Quiescence (kwəi,e·sĕns). 1631. [– late L. *quiescentia*; see next, -ENCE.] The state of being quiescent; quietness; an instance of this. **b.** *spec.* in Heb. grammar; see prec. 2. 1828.

That there is no such thing in the World as an absolute q. 1664. So **Quie·scency.**

Quiescent (kwəi,e·sĕnt), *a.* and *sb.* 1609. [– L. *quiescens*, *-ent-*, pr. pple of *quiescere* QUIESCE; see -ENT.] **A.** *adj.* **1.** Motionless, inactive, at rest 1646. **2.** Of a letter: Not sounded; silent; *spec.* in Heb. grammar (see QUIESCE *v.* 2) 1609. **b.** Of a person: Silent BOSWELL.

1. The q. and death-like condition of the pupa 1874. **2.** The E silent or q., which yieldeth no sound 1609.

B. *sb.* **1.** A quiescent letter 1727. **2.** A quiescent verb in Heb. grammar 1831. Hence **Quie·scently** *adv.*

Quiet (kwəi·ət), *sb.* ME. [– AFr. *quiete*, which was orig. OFr. *quieté*, whence Sc. †*quiety* XV–XVI, f. *quiet* – L. *quietus*; see next.] **1.** Absence of disturbance or tumult; social or political tranquillity. **b.** Absence of noise or (rapid) motion; calmness, stillness. late ME. **2.** Freedom from external disturbance, molestation, or noise; †freedom from occupation; rest, repose ME. **b.** Freedom from mental agitation; calm or peace of mind 1628. **3.** The condition of remaining quiet 1559.

1. Join with thee calm Peace, and Q. MILT. To whom the care of the Publique q. is committed HOBBES. **2.** An arrant vixen of a wife soured his domestic q. FIELDING.

Quiet (kwəi·ət), *a.* late ME. [– OFr. *quiet(e* – L. *quietus*, pa. pple. of *quiescere* QUIESCE.] **I. 1.** Of persons (or animals): Making no stir, or noise; causing no disturbance; remaining at rest. **b.** (Also of nature or disposition.) Habitually or naturally peaceful or averse to making stir, noise, etc. Of an animal: Gentle. late ME. **2.** Of things: Not active; not moving or stirring; also, making no noise; still 1599. **b.** Free from excess; moderate, gentle; *esp.* of colour, dress, style, etc.: Not obtrusive, glaring or showy 1560.

1. I wish you would be q., you have more tricks than a dancing bear SWIFT. As q. as mice 1843. *Q.!* an injunction to be silent. **b.** A q. horse 1811. **2.** An eye made q. by the power Of harmony WORDSW. **b.** A q. ebb, or a tempestuous flow DRYDEN.

II. 1. Free from disturbance; not interfered or meddled with; left in peace. late ME. **2.** Characterized by the absence of all strife, bustle, stir, or commotion; also, free from noise or uproar, silent, still 1514. **b.** Partaken of, or enjoyed, in q. 1837. **3.** Of the mind, conscience, etc.: Not troubled; free from agitation or excitement. So also of persons in respect of the mind, etc. 1535.

1. A quyete slepe is right necessary and delycious 1532. Anything for a q. life 1626. The grantor may covenant..for the grantee's q. enjoyment BLACKSTONE. **2.** I could be well content To entertaine the Lagge-end of my life With q. houres SHAKS. **b.** A q. cup of tea DICKENS. **3.** Truth hath a q. breast SHAKS.

III. Quasi-*sb.*, in phr. *On the q.*, privately, in secret. (For the abbrev. *q. t.* see Q.) *slang* or *colloq.* 1873. Hence **Qui·et-ly** *adv.*, **-ness.**

Quiet (kwəi·ət), *v.* 1440. [f. prec., partly after late and med.L. *quietare*, f. L. *quietus* QUIET *a.*] †**1.** *trans.* To quit, acquit (oneself or another) –1473. **2.** To make quiet (in various senses); to reduce to quietness 1526. **3.** To settle or establish in quiet. Chiefly *Law.* 1586. **4.** *intr.* To become quiet. Also *to q. down.* 1791.

2. Q. thy Cudgell, thou dost see I eate SHAKS. Those savage nations whom he had quieted HOLLAND. This quieted our apprehensions 1748. Measures which may q. the unhappy divisions of the country BURKE. **3.** The Plaintiffs are entitled..to be quieted in the possession they have had for so many years 1884. **4.** By and by she quieted, and..fell asleep 1865. Hence **Qui·eter,** one who or that which makes quiet.

Quieten (kwəi·ət'n), *v.* 1828. [f. QUIET *a.* + -EN[5].] *trans.* and *intr.* To make or become quiet.

Quietism (kwəi·ətiz'm). 1687. [– It. *quietismo*; see QUIET *a.*, -ISM.] **1.** A form of religious mysticism (originated by Molinos, a Spanish priest), consisting in passive devotional contemplation, with extinction of the will and withdrawal from all things of the senses; also, any similar form of mysticism. **2.** A state of calmness and passivity of mind or body; repose, quietness, tranquillity 1772.

Quietist (kwəi·ətist). 1685. [– It. *quietista*; cf. prec., -IST.] **1.** One who believes in or practises Quietism, or any similar form of mysticism. **2.** One whose attitude towards political or social movements is analogous to Quietism in religion 1798.

2. He was not..a political q. from indifference SOUTHEY. Hence **Quieti·stic** *a.* belonging to, or charasteristic of quietists.

Quietude (kwəi·ətiūd, -ētiūd). 1597. [– Fr. *quiétude* or med.L. *quietudo*, f. *quietus* QUIET *a.*; see -TUDE.] Quietness; rest, calm, tranquillity.

‖**Quietus** (kwəi,ī·tǒs). 1540. [Short for med.L. *quietus est* he is quit.] **1.** An acquittance given on payment of sums due, or clearing of accounts; a receipt. †**2.** A discharge from office or duty –1788. **3.** Discharge or release from life; death, or that which brings death 1602. **b.** Final extinction 1806. **4.** (By assoc. with *quiet.*) Something which quiets or represses 1824.

3. When he himselfe might his q. make With a bare bodkin SHAKS. **4.** The nurse ran to give its accustomed q. to the little screaming infant THACKERAY.

Quiff (kwif). 1902. [Of unkn. origin.] A lock or flat curl of hair coming low on the forehead and sometimes oiled.

‖**Qui-hy** (kwəi,həi). Also **-hi.** 1816. [Urdu (Hindi) *koī hai* 'is any one there?' a call used in India to summon a servant.] An Anglo-Indian, *esp.* one belonging to the Bengal Presidency.

Quill (kwil), *sb.*[1] late ME. [prob. – (M)LG. *quiele*, of unkn. origin, obscurely rel. to synon. MHG. *kil* (G. *kiel*).] †**1.** A hollow stem or stalk, as that of a reed –1688. **b.** A piece of reed or other hollow stem on which yarn is wound; hence, a bobbin, spool, or pirn of any material. late ME. **c.** A musical pipe, made of a hollow stem 1567. **d.** A piece of cinnamon or cinchona bark curled up in the form of a tube 1797. †**2.** A small pipe or tube; *esp.* a small water-pipe –1712. **3.** The tube or barrel of a feather, the part by which it is attached to the skin. Sometimes used loosely in the sense of 'feather' (*esp.* one of the strong wing- or tail-feathers) and *poet.* for 'wing'. 1555. **b.** The feather of a goose, etc., formed into a pen by pointing and slitting the lower end of the barrel 1552. **c.** A plectrum formed of the quill of a feather, used for plucking the strings of a musical instrument 1552. **d.** The float of a fishing line, made of a quill 1606. **e.** A toothpick made of a quill 1784. **4.** One of the hollow sharp spines of a porcupine 1602.

1. c. Who now shall teach to change my oaten q. For trumpet 'larms P. FLETCHER. **3. b.** A q. worn to the pith in the service of the State SWIFT. **e.** He picks clean teeth, and, busy as he seems With an old tavern q., is hungry yet COWPER. **4.** Make..each particular haire to stand an end, Like Quilles upon the fretfull Porpentine SHAKS. *attrib.* and *Comb.*, as **q.-bark,** cinchona bark in the form of quills; **-bit,** a boring-tool for a brace, having a hollow barrel; **-coverts,** the feathers which cover the base of the quill-feathers; **-driver,** one who works with a q. or pen; a clerk or author; **-feather,** one of the stiff, comparatively large, feathers arranged in two rows along the edge of a bird's wing; also, one of the similar feathers of the tail.

†**Quill,** *sb.*[2] *rare.* 1593. [perh. – OFr. **quille* = Fr. *cueille* gathering, harvest, f. *cueillir* (OFr. *quillir*, etc.) gather; cf. CULL *v.*[1], COIL *v.*[1]] *In the* (or *a*) *q.*: in a body; in concert. *To jump in q.*, to act simultaneously or in harmony. –1690.

2 *Hen. VI*, I. iii. 4.

Quill (kwil), *v.* 1710. [f. QUILL *sb.*[1]] **1.** *trans.* To form into cylindrical pleats or folds resembling a quill; to goffer 1712. **2.** To cut the quills off (a wing) SWIFT. **3.** To cover with, or as with, quills 1783. **4.** *intr.* To wind thread or yarn on a quill; to fill spools 1640.

1. His cravat seemed quilled into a ruff GOLDSM. Hence **Qui·lling** *vbl. sb.* the action of the vb.; a ribbon, strip of lace, etc. pleated into small cylindrical folds resembling a row of quills.

‖**Quillaia** (kwilē¹·yă). 1848. [mod.L., f. Chilean *quillai*, f. *quillcan* wash.] **a.** A genus of S. Amer. rosaceous trees, the bark of which possesses soap-like properties. **b.** The soap-bark tree of Chile (*Quillaia saponaria*) or its bark (also *q.-bark*).

Quilled (kwild), *a.* and *ppl. a.* 1727. [f. QUILL *sb.*[1] and *v.* + -ED.] **1.** Having the form of a quill or quills. **2.** Having, or fitted with, a quill or quills, *spec.* of a suture: Having the thread secured to pieces of quill on each side of the wound 1767.

Quillet (kwi·lėt). 1588. [perh. abbrev. of obs. *quillity*, app. an alteration of QUIDDITY.] A verbal nicety or subtle distinction; a quirk.

Some tricks, some quillets, how to cheat the diuell SHAKS.

Quilt (kwilt), *sb.* ME. [– OFr. *coilte*, *cuilte* (mod. *couette*), with var. *coute* :– L. *culcita* mattress, cushion. Cf. COUNTERPOINT *sb.*[2]] **1.** An article of bed-furniture, consisting essentially of two large pieces of woven material having a layer of wool, flock, down, or the like, placed between them; orig. used for lying on; now, a coverlet of similar make, *esp.* one in which the lining is kept in place by lines of stitching passing through the whole; hence, any thick outer bed-covering, a counterpane. **b.** *transf.* A thick covering. †Also applied joc. to a fat person. 1596. **2.** A piece of padded material used to defend the body, as a substitute or lining for armour 1592. †**3.** A pad smeared or stuffed with a medicinal substance, and applied to some part of the body –1684.

1. Let his Bed be hard, and rather Quilts than Feathers LOCKE. **b.** How now blowne Jack? how now Q.? SHAKS.

Quilt (kwilt), *v.*[1] 1555. [f. prec.] **1.** *trans.* To pad, line, or cover (a thing) with some material, after the method employed in making a quilt. **b.** To cover with interlaced cord 1611. **2.** To fasten together (two pieces or thicknesses of woven material) by stitches or lines of stitching so as to hold in position a layer of some soft substance placed between them. Also, to sew (several thicknesses) together. 1555. **b.** *fig.* To compile (a literary work) by putting together scraps from various sources 1605. **3.** To sew up (some object or material) between two pieces of stuff, as in making a quilt 1562. **4.** *intr.* To make a quilt or quilts. *U.S.* 1861.

1. His black velvet bonnet was lined with steel, quilted between the metal and his head SCOTT. **2. b.** Manuals, and Handmaids of Devotion,.. clapt together and quilted out of Scripture phrases MILT. Hence **Qui·lter.**

Quilt (kwilt), *v.*[2] *dial.* and *U.S.* [perh. transf. use of prec.] *trans.* To beat, thrash, flog. Hence **Qui·lting** *vbl. sb.*[2] a flogging.

Quilting (kwi·ltiŋ), *vbl. sb.*[1] 1611. [f. QUILT *v.*[1] + -ING[1].] **1.** The action of QUILT *v.*[1] **2. a.** Quilted material; quilted work. **b.** Material for making a quilt. **c.** A kind of cloth with a diagonal pattern like that of a quilt. 1710. **3.** *dial.* and *U.S.* A quilting-party 1819.

Comb.: **q.-bee, -feast, -frolic, -party** (*U.S.*), a gathering of women held for the purpose of making a quilt, and serving as an occasion for enjoyment.

Quin (kwin). 1840. [Of unkn. origin.] A variety of pecten (*Pecten opercularis*).

Quina (kī·nă, kwəi·nă). 1830. [Sp. spelling of Quichua *kina* bark.] **a.** The bark of several species of *Cinchona* that yield quinine. **b.** *Chem.* = QUININE.

Quinary (kwəi·nări), *a.* and *sb.* 1603. [– L. *quinarius*, f. *quini*, distrib. of *quinque* five; see -ARY[1].] **A.** *adj.* Pertaining to, characterized by, the number five; consisting of five (things or parts).

Q. system, a principle of division in zoology, now discarded.

B. *sb.* A set of five; a compound consisting of five things. Now *rare.* 1651.

Quinate (kwi·n-, kwəi·nět), *sb.* 1836. [f. QUINA + -ATE 1 c.] *Chem.* A salt of quinic acid.

Quinate (kwəi·nět), *a.* 1806. [f. L. *quini* five each, after *binate.*] *Bot.* Of a leaf: Composed of five leaflets; quinquefoliolate.

Quince (kwins). ME. [orig. pl. used collect. of *quoyn* COYN (COYN(E) – Central Fr. *cooin* (mod. *coing*) :– L. *cotoneum* (Pliny), varying with *cydoneum* (apple) of Cydonia (now Canea) in Crete – Gr. μῆλον κυδώνιον.] **1.** The hard, acid, yellowish, pear-shaped fruit of *Pyrus cydonia*, used as a preserve or to flavour other fruits; the seeds are also employed in medicine and the arts. Also, the tree. **2.** Applied to other fruits or trees resembling the quince 1876.

2. *Native Q.*, the Australian bitter-bark, emu-apple, or quinine-tree. *Wild Q.*, the Australian black ash.

Quincentenary (kwinsentī·nări), *a.* and *sb.* 1879. [irreg. f. L. *quin(que* five + CENTENARY. Cf. QUINGENTENARY.] **A.** *adj.* Pertaining to or connected with a five-hundredth year. **B.** *sb.* A five-hundredth anniversary, or the celebration of this. So **Quincente·nnial.**

Quincuncial (kwinkɒ·nʃăl), *a.* 1601. [– L. *quincuncialis*; see next, -AL[1].] Arranged in the form of a quincunx or quincunxes; involving or characterized by this arrangement. **b.** *Bot.* Of æstivation: Having five leaves so disposed that two are exterior and two interior, while the fifth is partly exterior and partly interior. Hence **Quincu·ncially** *adv.* in a q. manner; in the form of a quincunx.

Quincunx (kwi·nkɒŋks). 1647. [– L. *quincunx* five-twelfths, f. *quinque* five + *uncia* twelfth, OUNCE *sb.*[1]] **1.** *Astrol.* An aspect of planets in which these are at a distance of 5 signs or 150 degrees from each other (*rare*). **2.** A disposition of five objects so placed that four occupy the corners, and the fifth the centre of a square or rectangle; a set of five things arranged in this manner 1658. **b.** *spec.* as a basis of arrangement in planting trees; a group of five trees so planted 1664. **c.** *Bot.* Quincuncial æstivation 1832. Hence **Quincu·nxial** *a.* (*rare*).

Quindecagon (kwinde·kăgǫn). 1570. [irreg. f.L. *quindecim*, after *decagon*, etc.; see -GON.] *Geom.* A plane figure having fifteen angles.

Quindecemvir (kwindĭse·mvəɪ). 1601. [L., f. *quindecim* fifteen + *vir* man.] *Rom. Antiq.* A member of a body, commission, etc., of fifteen men; *esp.* one of the priests who had charge of the Sibylline books.

Quindecim (kwi·ndĭsim). 1445. [Alteration of AFr. *quinzisme* QUINZIÈME after L. *quindecim.*] †**1.** A tax or duty of a fifteenth part –1647. **2.** *Eccl. Antiq.* = next 1445.

Quindene (kwi·ndīn). 1494. [– med.L. *quindena*, f. L. *quindeni*, distrib. of *quindecim* fifteen.] *Eccl. Antiq.* The fifteenth (in mod. reckoning, fourteenth) day after a church-festival.

Quingentenary (kwindʒentī·nări), *a.* and *sb.* 1884. [f. L. *quingenti* five hundred, after *centenary*, etc.] = QUINCENTENARY.

Quinhydrone (kwinhəi·drōᵘn). 1865. [f. QUINA + HYDRONE.] *Chem.* A green crystalline substance formed by direct union of quinol and quinone.

Quinia (kwi·niă). 1826. [mod.L., f. QUINA; see -IA[1].] *Chem.* (*Med.*) = QUININE.

Quinic (kwi·nik), **kinic** (ki·nik), *a.* 1814. [f. QUINA + -IC.] *Chem.* Derived from quina. *Q. acid*: a vegetable acid found chiefly in cinchona barks. Hence **Qui·nicine,** an alkaloid, isomeric with quinine and quinidine, from which it is obtained by heating with glycerol.

Quinidine (kwi·nidəin). 1836. [f. QUINA + *-id-* + -INE[5].] *Chem.* An alkaloid found in some cinchona barks along with quinine, with which it is isomeric.

Quinine (kwinī·n, -əi·n, *U.S.* kwəi·nəin). 1826. [f. QUINA + -INE[5].] An alkaloid ($C_{20}H_{24}N_2O_2$) found in the bark of species of cinchona and remigia, and used as a febrifuge, tonic, and antiperiodic, chiefly in the form of the salt, sulphate of quinine, which is popularly termed quinine. Hence **Quini·nic** *a.* pertaining to, derived from, q. **Quini·nism** = next.

Quinism (kwəi·nizm). 1880. [f. QUINA + -ISM.] *Path.* The physical state (giddiness, deafness, loss of sight, etc.) produced by the excessive use of quinine; cinchonism.

Quinnat (kwi·năt). 1829. [N. Amer. Indian.] The king-salmon; the Californian, Columbian, or Chinook salmon (*Oncorhyncus chouicha* or *quinnat*) of the N. Pacific coast.

Quinoa (kī·noˌă, kwinōᵘ·ă). Also **quinua.** 1625. [Sp. spelling of Quichuan *kinua, kinoa.*] An annual plant (*Chenopodium quinoa*) found on the Pacific slopes of the Andes, cultivated in Chile and Peru for its edible farinaceous seeds. Also *attrib.*

Quinoidine (kwinoi·dəin). Also **-ina.** 1836. [f. QUINA + -OID + -INE⁵.] *Chem.* A brownish-black resinous substance, consisting of amorphous alkaloids, obtained as a by-product in preparing salts of quinia.

Quinol (kwi·nǫl). 1881. [f. QUINA + -OL.] *Chem.* = HYDROQUINONE.

Quinoline (kwi·nŏləin). 1845. [f. as prec. + -INE⁵.] *Chem.* = CHINOLINE.

Quinologist (kwinǫ·lŏdʒist). 1869. [f. QUINA + -LOGIST.] One who is versed in the scientific study of quinine. So **Quino·logy,** the scientific study of quinine.

Quinone (kwi·noᵘn, kwinōᵘ·n). 1853. [f. QUINA + -ONE.] *Chem.* **a.** *spec.* A crystalline compound (benzoquinone, $C_6H_4O_2$), the simplest type of the class of quinones. **b.** Any one of a series of aromatic compounds derived from the benzene series of hydrocarbons when two hydrogen atoms are replaced by two of oxygen.

Quinovic (kwinōᵘ·vik), **kino·vic,** *a.* 1838. [f. *quinova-*, shortened form of L. *quina nova* false cinchona bark + -IC.] *Chem. Q. acid,* an acid found in false cinchona bark. So **Quino·vin, kino·vin,** an amorphous bitter compound found in (false and other) cinchona-barks.

Quinquagenarian (kwi:nkwădʒĭnēᵊ·riăn), *sb.* and *a.* 1569. [– L. *quinquagenarius*, f. *quinquageni* distrib. of *quinquaginta* fifty + -AN.] **A.** *sb.* †**1.** A captain of fifty men (*rare*) –1609. **2.** A person aged fifty; or between fifty and sixty 1843. **B.** *adj.* †**1.** Commanding fifty men (*rare*) –1629. **2.** Of fifty years of age; characteristic of one of that age 1822. So **Quinqua·genary** (*rare*). late ME.

‖**Quinquagesima** (kwinkwădʒe·simă). late ME. [med.L., subst. use (sc. *dies* day) of fem. of L. *quinquagesimus* fiftieth, f. *quinquaginta* fifty. So called after QUADRAGESIMA.] †**a.** The period beginning with the Sunday immediately preceding Lent and ending on Easter Sunday. †**b.** The first week of this period. **c.** (Also *Q. Sunday.*) The Sunday before Lent; Shrove Sunday. So **Quinquage·simal** *a.* belonging to a set of fifty; containing fifty days.

†**Qui·nquangle.** 1668. [– late L. *quinquangulum*, subst. use of the n. adj., f. L. *quinque* five + *angulus* angle.] A pentagon –1788. Hence **Quinqua·ngular** *a.* having five angles or corners; pentagonal.

Quinquarticular (kwinkwaɹti·kiŭlăɹ), *a.* 1659. [– mod.L. *quinquarticularis*, f. *quinque* five + *articulus* ARTICLE; see -AR¹.] Relating to the five articles or points of Arminian doctrine condemned by the Calvinists at the Synod of Dort in 1618.

Quinque- (kwi·nkwĭ), comb. form of L. *quinque* five, with the sense 'having, consisting of, etc. five (things specified)', in some words adopted from classical and later L., and in others, chiefly terms of *Bot.* and *Zool.*, of English formation.

Quinquepa·rtite [L. *partitus* divided], *a.* divided into, consisting of, five parts. **Qui·nquesect,** *v. trans.* to cut into five (equal) parts. **Quinque·virate,** an association, board, etc. consisting of five men. **Qui·nquifid,** *a. Bot.* cleft in five.

Quinquenniad (kwinkwe·niăd). 1842. [f. as next + -AD, after *decad.*] = QUINQUENNIUM.

Quinquennial (kwinkwe·niăl), *a.* and *sb.* 1460. [f. L. *quinquennis*, f. *quinque* five + *annus* year; cf. *biennial*, etc.] **A.** *adj.* **1.** Lasting, continuing, holding office, etc. for five years. **2.** Occurring every fifth year 1610. **B.** *sb.* **1.** A period of five years 1890. **2.** A magistrate holding office for five years 1895. Hence **Quinque·nnially** *adv.*

‖**Quinquennium** (kwinkwe·niŏm). *Pl.* **-ia.** 1621. [L., f. *quinque* five + *annus* year.] A period of five years.

Quinquereme (kwi·nkwĭrīm), *a.* and *sb.* 1553. [– L. *quinqueremis*, f. *quinque* five + *remus* oar.] **A.** *adj.* Of ancient ships: Having five banks of oars 1654. **B.** *sb.* A ship having five banks of oars 1553.

Quinquina (kinkī·nă, kwinkwəi·nă). 1656. [Sp. spelling of Quichuan *kinkina* or *kina-kina*, redupl. of *kina* bark, QUINA.] **a.** Peruvian or Jesuits' bark; the bark of several species of cinchona, yielding quinine and other alkaloids. **b.** One or other of the trees producing cinchona-bark.

Quinquivalent (kwinkwi·vălent), *a.* 1877. [f. L. *quinqui-* five + *valent*, as in *bivalent*, etc.] *Chem.* = PENTAVALENT.

Quinsy (kwi·nzi). [In XIV *quinesye* – OFr. *quinencie* – med.L. *quinancia*, f. Gr. κυναγχή CYNANCHE.] Inflammation of the throat or parts of the throat; suppuration of the tonsils; tonsillitis.

Quint (kwint), *sb.*¹ 1526. [– Fr. *quint* or *quinte* :– L. *quintus, -a, -um*, ordinal to *quinque* five.] **1.** A tax of one-fifth. **2.** *Mus.* An interval of a fifth 1806. **b.** (In full *quint-stop.*) An organ-stop giving tones a fifth higher than the normal 1855.

Quint (kint, kwint), *sb.*² 1659. [– Fr. *quinte* fem.; see prec.] **1.** In piquet: A sequence of five cards of the same suit, counting as fifteen. †**2.** *transf.* A set of five persons BUTLER.

1. *Q. major*, the ace, king, queen, knave, and ten of a suit. *Q. minor*, the five cards from the knave to the seven.

Quint-, erron. used in combs. in place of QUINQU(E, as *quintangular*, etc.

Quintain (kwi·ntėn). *Obs.* exc. *Hist.* late ME. [– OFr. *quintaine, -eine*, med.L. *quintana, -ena*, usu. taken to be identical with L. *quintana* market of a camp, f. *quintus* fifth (sc. *manipulus* maniple). See QUINTAN.] A stout post or plank, or some object mounted on such a support, set up as a mark to be tilted at with lances or poles, or thrown at with darts, as an exercise of skill for horsemen or footmen; also, the exercise or sport of tilting, etc. at such a mark.

fig. That which here stands vp Is but a quintine, a meere liuelesse blocke SHAKS.

Quintal (kwi·ntăl), **ki·ntal, ke·ntle.** 1470. [– OFr. *quintal*, med.L. *quintale* – Arab. *ḳinṭār*. Cf. KENTLEDGE.] **a.** A weight of one hundred pounds; a hundredweight (112 pounds). **b.** In the metric system: A weight of 100 kilograms.

Quintan (kwi·ntăn), *a.* and *sb.* 1657. [– med.L. subst. use (sc. *febris* fever) of fem. of L. *quintanus*, f. *quintus* fifth; see -AN, and cf. QUINTAIN.] **A.** *adj.* Of a fever or ague: Having a paroxysm every fifth (= fourth) day. **B.** *sb.* A fever or ague of this kind.

‖**Quinte** (kǣṅt). 1707. [Fr.; see QUINT *sb.*¹] The fifth thrust or parry of the eight taught in fencing-schools.

Quintessence (kwinte·sĕns), *sb.* late ME. [– Fr. *quintessence*, †*quinte essence* – med.L. *quinta essentia* fifth essence.] **1.** The 'fifth essence' of ancient and mediæval philosophy, supposed to be the substance of which the heavenly bodies were composed, and to be actually latent in all things. **2.** The most essential part of any substance; a highly refined essence or extract; *spec.* in older chemistry, an alcoholic tincture obtained by digestion at a gentle heat 1576. **b.** The purest or most perfect form or manifestation of some quality 1570. **c.** The most perfect embodiment of the typical qualities of a certain class of persons, etc. 1590.

2. b. The Law of England, which Lawyers say is the q. of reason MILT. **c.** The q. of bores SCOTT. Hence **Quinte·ssence** *v. trans.* (now *rare*), to extract the q. of; to take *out of* (something) as a q. **Quintesse·ntial** *a.* of the nature of a q.; the purest or most refined of its kind. **Quintessentia·lity. Quintesse·ntially** *adv.*

Quintet(te (kwinte·t). 1811. [– Fr. *quintette* – It. *quintetto*, f. *quinto* fifth.] **1.** *Mus.* A composition for five voices or instruments. **2. a.** *Mus.* A set of five singers or players. **b.** A set of five persons or things. 1882.

Quinti-, prop. a comb. form of L. *quintus* fifth, but sometimes incorrectly used in place of QUINQUE-.

Quintic (kwi·ntik), *a.* and *sb.* 1853. [f. L. *quintus* + -IC.] **A.** *adj.* Of the fifth order or degree. **B.** *sb.* A quantic or surface of the fifth degree 1856.

Quintile (kwi·ntil), *a.* and *sb.* 1610. [– med.L. **quintilis* (in cl. L. *quintilis* (sc. *mensis*) fifth month, July), f. L. *quintus*; see -ILE. Cf. QUARTILE, SEXTILE.] *Q.* (*aspect*): a planetary aspect in which the planets are one-fifth of a circle, or 72 degrees, distant from each other.

Quintillion (kwinti·lyən). 1674. [f. L. *quintus* fifth + (*m*)*illion*; cf. BILLION.] **a.** In Great Britain: The fifth power of a million (1 followed by thirty ciphers). **b.** In U.S. (as in France): The cube of a million (1 followed by 18 ciphers).

Quintole (kwi·ntoᵘl). 1876. [– G. *quintole*, arbitrarily f. L. *quintus* fifth. Cf. SEXTOLE.] *Mus.* A group of five notes to be played in the time of four.

Quintuple (kwi·ntiup'l), *a.* and *sb.* 1570. [– Fr. *quintuple*, f. L. *quintus* fifth, after *quadruple.*] **A.** *adj.* Fivefold; multiplied by five; consisting of five things or parts. **B.** *sb.* A fivefold amount; a group of five (*rare*) 1684.

A. *Q. time, Mus.* having five crotchets in a bar.

Quintuple (kwi·ntiup'l), *v.* 1639. [f. prec.] **1.** *trans.* To multiply by five; to make five times as much or as great. **b.** To produce five times as much as 1824. **2.** *intr.* To become five times as many or as great 1816.

Quintuplet (kwi·ntiuplet). 1873. [f. QUINTUPLE *a.* + -ET, after TRIPLET.] **1.** A set of five things; *Mus.* = QUINTOLE. **2.** *pl.* Five children born at a birth 1889. Abbrev. *quins.*

Quinzaine (kwi·nzeⁱn, Fr. kæṅzẹn). *rare.* 1863. [– Fr. *quinzaine*, f. *quinze*; see next.] *Hist.* = QUINDENE.

Quinze (kwinz, Fr. kǣṅz). 1716. [– Fr. *quinze* :– L. *quindecim.*] A card-game depending on chance, in which the winner is that player who obtains fifteen points, or comes nearest to that number without exceeding it.

Quinzième (Fr. kæṅzyẹm). *Obs.* exc. *Hist.* late ME. [– AFr. *quinzisme, quinzième*, ordinal f. *quinze* (see prec.). Cf. QUINDECIM.] A tax or duty of a fifteenth.

Quip (kwip), *sb.* 1532. [Short f. *quippy* (XVI), perh. – L. *quippe* indeed, forsooth.] **1.** A sharp or sarcastic remark directed against a person; a clever gird or hit. Later, A clever, smart, or witty saying; a verbal conceit. **b.** A verbal equivocation; a quibble 1590. **2. a.** A curious, odd, or fantastic action or feature 1820. **b.** A knick-knack 1820.

1. Quips and Cranks, and wanton Wiles MILT. **b.** Tricks of controversy and quips of law JOWETT.

Quip (kwip), *v.* Now *rare.* 1579. [f. prec.] **1.** *trans.* To assail with a quip or quips 1584. **2.** *intr.* To use a quip or quips; to be wittily sarcastic. Const. *at.*

‖**Quipu** (kī·pu, kwi·pu). 1604. [Quichuan, knot.] A device of the ancient Peruvians for recording events, keeping accounts, sending messages, etc., consisting of cords or threads of various colours, knotted in various ways.

When they go to confession these quipoes serve them to remember their sins 1704.

Quire (kwəiᵊɹ), *sb.*¹ [ME. *quaer*, later *quayer*, etc. – OFr. *qua(i)er* (mod. *cahier* quire, copy-book) :– Rom. **quaternum*, f. L. *quaterni* set of four, f. *quater* four times, f. *quattuor* four.] **1.** A set of four sheets of paper or parchment doubled so as to form eight leaves; hence, any collection or gathering of leaves, one within the other, in a manuscript or printed book. Also twenty-four (sometimes twenty-five) sheets of writing-paper. 1450. **b.** *In quires*: unbound, in sheets 1480. †**2.** A small pamphlet or book, consisting of a single quire; a short poem, treatise, etc., which is or might be contained in a quire –1570.

Quire, *sb.*², *v.*²: see CHOIR *sb.* and *v.*

Quire (kwəiᵊɹ), *v.*¹ 1683. [f. QUIRE *sb.*¹] *trans.* To arrange in quires.

Quirinal (kwi·rinăl). 1838. [– L. *Quirinalis* (sc. *collis* hill), one of the seven hills of Rome, f. *Quirinus* a name of Romulus.] The name of the palace in Rome occupied by the king of Italy; hence, the Italian court or government, or its policy (esp. as contrasted with *Vatican*).

Quiritary (kwi·ritări), *a.* 1865. [– late L. *quiritarius*, f. L. *Quirites* Roman citizens; see -ARY¹.] That is in accordance with Roman civil law; legal, as opp. to equitable (see BONITARIAN). Also of property: Held by legal right or under Roman law. So **Quiri·ta·rian** *a.*

Quirk (kwɔ̄ɹk). 1547. [Of unkn. origin.] **1.** A verbal trick, subtlety, shift, or evasion; a quibble 1565. **b.** Quibbling 1674. **2.** A clever turn or conceit; a quip 1579. **3.** *Mus.* A sudden turn; a fantastic phrase (*rare*) 1579. **4.** A trick in action or behaviour; †a knack, a fad 1601. **5.** A start, sudden stroke SHAKS. **6.** A sudden twist, turn, or curve; *esp.* in drawing or writing: A flourish 1605. **7.** *techn.* or *dial.* **a.** In a stocking = CLOCK *sb.*² 1547. **b.** A piece added to, or taken from, a regular figure, or cut out of a certain surface 1679. **c.** *Arch.* An acute hollow between the convex part of certain mouldings and the soffit or fillet 1816.

1. Not with Syllogisms or Quirks of Wit; but with plain and weighty Reason 1678. **b.** Shiftiness, q., attorney-cunning..fancies itself..to be talent CARLYLE. **2.** I may chance haue some odde quirkes and remnants of witte broken on mee SHAKS. **4.** His manner was full of quirks HAWTHORNE. **5.** I haue felt so many quirkes of ioy and greefe SHAKS. Hence **Quirk** *v. trans.* to assail with quirks; *intr.* to use quirks. **Quirked** (kwɔ̄ɹkt) *ppl. a.* (*Arch.*) furnished with a q. **Qui·rkish** *a.* of the nature of a q.

Quirky (kwɔ̄·ɹki), *a. Sc.* 1806. [f. prec. + -Y¹.] **1.** Full of quirks; tricky. **2.** Full of twists, turns, or flourishes 1885.

1. A quirkie bodie, capable o' making law no law at a' GALT. Hence **Qui·rkiness.**

Quirt (kwɔ̄ɹt), *sb. U.S.* 1851. [– Sp. *cuerda* CORD.] A riding-whip, having a short handle and a braided leather lash about two feet long. Hence **Quirt** *v. trans.*, to strike with a q.

Quit (kwit), *sb.* 1847. [Of unkn. origin.] Pop. name of many small Jamaican birds.

Quit (kwit). *predic. a.* [(i) ME. *quīt, quite* (surviving in QUITE) – L. *quietus* QUIET; superseded by (ii) later ME. or early mod. *quit(te* – (O)Fr. *quitte* – med.L. *quittus*, special development of L. *quietus*.] **1.** Free, clear. **b.** Free, clear, rid *of* (a thing or person) ME. **c.** Const. *from.* Now *rare.* 1471. †**2.** Destitute, deprived *of* (*from*) –1596. †**3.** = QUITS 2. –1757.

1. The judgment shall be against him only..and the other shall go q. 1817. *To be q. for*, to get off with, suffer nothing more than. **b.** To be q. of the trouble and expense 1840. **3.** To be full q. of those my Banishers Stand I before thee heere SHAKS. *Double or q.*: see DOUBLE *adv.*

Quit (kwit), *v.* Pa. t. and pple. **quitted; quit** (now *dial.* and *U.S. colloq.*) [Late ME. *quitte*, repl. earlier *quite* (XIII), pa. t. *quitte* pa. pple. *quit(t*; – (O)Fr. *quitter*, earlier *quiter* (cf. med.L. *quittare, quietare*), f. L. *quietus* QUIET *a.*, QUIT *a.*] **I.** †**1.** *trans.* To set free, release, redeem (usu. a person; also *absol.*). Const. *from, out of*, and occas. with *out* adv. –1652. †**b.** To free, clear, rid of –1798. †**2.** To clear (a suspected or accused person) *from* a charge; to prove (one) innocent *of*. Chiefly *refl.* –1715. †**b.** To absolve, acquit (*of, from*) –1755. **3.** *refl.* To do one's part, behave, bear oneself (usu. in a specified way). Now *arch.* late ME. †**b.** To play (one's part) –1603. †**4.** To remit (a debt, etc.). *rare.* –1693. **5.** To give up, let go, renounce, etc.; to cease to have, use, enjoy, be engaged in or occupied with 1440. **b.** To give up, yield, hand over *to* another. Now *rare* or *Obs.* 1450. **c.** To let go (something held or grasped) 1633. **6.** To cease, stop (doing something). Now *U.S.* 1754. **b.** *absol.* 1641. **7.** To leave, go away or depart from (a place or person); to part or separate from (a thing) 1603. **b.** *absol.* To leave the premises which one occupies as a tenant 1768. **c.** *absol.* To go away. *dial.* and *U.S.* 1839. **8.** *trans.* To remove; to put, take, or send away (also with dat. of person); to dismiss. Now *rare.* 1575.

1. b. She..made me resolve to q. my hands of this office PEPYS. **3.** Q. your selues like men, and fight 1 *Sam.* 4:9. **b.** *Meas. for M.* II. iv. 28. **4.** To q. the fine for one halfe of his goods, I am content SHAKS. **5.** There are very few men who know how to q. any great office 1851. **6. b.** The good old maxim for speech-makers, 'Q. when you've done' 1868. **7.** It is a serious matter to q. country and family and friends 1833. **b.** Giving reasonable notice to q. CRUISE. **c.** He rose at once, and said.. he reckoned he would q. STEVENSON.

II. 1. To repay, reward, requite (a person *with* some return *for* something done). *Obs.* exc. *n. dial.* ME. †**2.** To make a return to (a person) for (something done, a benefit or injury received, etc.) –1548. **b.** To repay (something done to or for one) ME. †**c.** To be a return for, to balance; esp. in phr. *to q. the cost* –1787.

1. We han well deserued hyt, Therfore is ryght that we ben quyt CHAUCER. **b.** On this manner was the Duke of Orleance death quitted 1632.

III. To pay, clear off (a debt, etc.) ME.

A thousand markes..To q. the penalty, and to ransome him SHAKS.

‖**Qui tam** (kwəi· tæm). 1755. [L.; *qui tam* (*pro domino rege quam pro se ipso sequitur*) who as well (for the lord the king as for himself sues).] *Law.* An action brought on a penal statute by an informer, who sues for the penalty both on his own behalf and on that of the crown.

Quitch (kwitʃ). [OE. *cwiće* = MLG. *kweke*; supposed to be rel. to *cwic* QUICK with ref. to the vitality of the grass.] A species of grass = COUCH *sb.*² Also **q.-grass.**

Quitclaim (kwi·tklēⁱm), *sb.* 1450. [– AFr. *quiteclame*, f. *quiteclamer*; see next.] †**a.** A formal discharge or release. **b.** A formal renunciation of a claim.

Quitclaim (kwi·tklēⁱm), *v.* ME. [– AFr. *quiteclamer* declare free, f. *quite* QUIT *a.* + *clamer* proclaim; assoc. later with QUIT *v.* and CLAIM *sb.*] †**1.** *trans.* To declare (a person) free; to release, acquit, discharge, etc. –1609. **2.** To renounce, resign, give up (a possession, right, claim, etc.). late ME. **b.** With *quit* taken as vb. Const. *to.* 1706.

2. b. Having..remitted and quitted claim to the king for all..debts 1886.

Quite (kwəit), *adv.* ME. [adv. use of *quite*, earlier form of QUIT *a.*] **1.** Completely, wholly, altogether, entirely; to the fullest extent or degree. **2.** Actually, really, truly, positively (implying that the case or circumstances are such as to justify the use of the word or phrase thus qualified) 1586. **b.** colloq. *Quite so* (or simply *quite*), used like Fr. *parfaitement*, to express assent. (Cf. *exactly.*) 1896.

1. It speaks a q. other language 1661. My distemper is almost q. gone 1785. Q. by myself 1816. For q. another reason 1845. I spent that day q. alone upon the Mer de Glace TYNDALL. **2.** She was q. ill and restless 1805. That must have been q. a scene 1806. Up to q. a recent period MILL. I q. too awfully near put my foot in it! 1882. It was q. the thing to be in love 1888. You can't q. believe there is a God at all G. MACDONALD. Q. at hand LANDOR. **b.** 'Of course, he's an absolute scoundrel'. 'Oh, quite.' (*mod.*)

Quit-rent (kwi·trent). 1454. [f. QUIT *a.* + RENT *sb.*¹] **1.** A rent, usu. of small amount, paid by a freeholder or copyholder in lieu of services which might be required of him 1460. †**2.** A charge upon an estate for some special purpose –1712.

1. *attrib.* The courtly laureate pays His quitrent ode, his peppercorn of praise COWPER.

Quits (kwits), *a.* and *sb.* 1478. [prob. colloq. use of med.L. *quittus* QUIT *a.*] **A.** *adj.* †**1.** Clear, discharged (of a liability) –1590. **2.** Even or equal (*with* another) by means of repayment or retaliation 1663. **B.** *sb.* **a.** An equivalent, a recompense. **b.** Reprisal, retaliation. *rare.* 1806.

A. 2. I will be quits with him 1675. I shall be content to be q. with fortune for a very moderate portion W. IRVING. Phr. *To cry q.* (cf. QUITTANCE 4). *Double or q.*: see DOUBLE *adv.*

†**Qui·ttal, qui·tal.** 1530. [f. QUIT *v.* + -AL¹.] **a.** Requital. **b.** Acquittal. –1633.

Quittance (kwi·tăns), *sb.* ME. [– OFr. *quitance* (later *quittance*), f. *quiter* QUIT *v.*; see -ANCE.] **1.** The act of freeing or clearing; release; †acquittal. **2.** A release or discharge from a debt or obligation; a document certifying such discharge; a receipt ME. **3.** Recompense or requital; repayment; reprisal 1590. †**4.** *To cry q.*, to declare oneself clear or even *with* another; hence, to make full repayment or retaliation –1679.

2. Hauing paid the custome, it behoueth to haue a q. HAKLUYT. *Prov.* That's all one: omittance is no q. SHAKS. Hence †**Qui·ttance** *v. trans.* to repay, requite (a person, service, injury, etc.) –1624.

Quitter, quittor (kwi·təɹ), *sb.*¹ ME. [perh. – OFr. *quiture, cuiture* cooking, etc.] †**1.** Pus; a purulent discharge from a wound or sore –1689. **2.** *Farriery.* (Also †*q.-bone.*) An ulcer on the coronet of a horse's hoof 1703.

Quitter (kwi·təɹ), *sb.*² *U.S.* 1881. [f. QUIT *v.* + -ER¹.] One who, or that which, 'quits', goes away, shirks, etc.

Quiver (kwi·vəɹ), *sb.*¹ ME. [– AFr. **quiver*, *quiveir*, OFr. *quivre, coivre* – a WGmc. word repr. by OE. *cocor*, OFris. *koker*, OS. *kokar(i* (Du. *koker*), OHG. *kohhar(i* (G. *köcher*); see COCKER *sb.*¹] **1.** A case for holding arrows (sometimes also the bow). **b.** *transf.* and *fig.* late ME. †**c.** A quiverful –1623.

1. His arrowes..he wore in a Woolues skinne at his backe for his Q. 1624. **b.** Like as the arowes in the honde of the giaunte, euen so are the yonge children. Happie is the man, yᵗ hath his quyuer full of them. COVERDALE *Ps.* 126[7]:5.

Quiver (kwi·vəɹ), *a. Obs.* exc. *dial.* [OE. **cwifer* (in *cwiferliće*). Cf. next.] Active, nimble; quick, rapid.

A little quiuer fellow SHAKS.

Quiver (kwi·vəɹ), *v.* 1490. [f. prec. Cf. QUAVER.] **1.** *intr.* To shake, tremble, or vibrate, with a slight but rapid agitation. **2.** *trans.* To cause to vibrate or tremble 1599.

1. Upon the stream the moonbeams q. WORDSW. His hand trembled and his flesh quivered 1869. Hence **Qui·ver** *sb.*² an act of quivering, a tremble; *ellipt.* a trembling of the voice. **Qui·veringly** *adv.*

Quivered (kwi·vəɹd), *a.* and *ppl. a.* 1634. [f. QUIVER *sb.*¹ + -ED².] **1.** Provided with a quiver. **2.** Placed or kept in, or as in, a quiver 1651.

1. Like a quiver'd Nymph with Arrows keen MILT. **2.** The lifted bow he bore, And quiver'd deaths POPE.

Quiverful (kwi·vəɹful). 1861. [f. QUIVER *sb.*¹ + -FUL.] As much as a quiver can hold. Usu. *fig.* with ref. to Ps. 127:5 (see QUIVER *sb.*¹ 1 b).

‖**Qui vive** (ki vīv). 1726. [Fr., lit. '(long) live who?', a sentinel's challenge, intended to discover to which side the party challenged belongs.] *On the q.*, on the alert or look-out.

Quixote (kwi·ksǫ̆t). 1648. [Name of the hero of Cervantes' romance = Sp. *quixote*, now *quijote* a cuisse.] An enthusiastic visionary like Don Quixote, inspired by lofty and chivalrous but unrealizable ideals. **b.** *attrib.* = next 1708.

Quixotic (kwiksǫ·tik), *a.* 1791. [f. prec. + -IC.] **1.** Of persons: Resembling Don Quixote; hence, striving with lofty enthusiasm for visionary ideals. **2.** Of actions, etc.: Characteristic of, appropriate to, Don Quixote 1851.

2. A q. mission to the Indians of Georgia 1874. Hence **Quixo·tical** *a.*, **-ly** *adv.*

Quixotism (kwi·ksǫ̆tiz'm). 1688. [f. as prec. + -ISM.] Quixotic principles, character, or practice; a quixotic action or idea. So **Qui·xotry.**

Quiz (kwiz), *sb.*¹ 1782. [Of unkn. origin. Cf. QUIZ *v.*¹] **1.** An odd or eccentric person, in character or appearance. Now *rare.* **b.** An odd-looking thing JANE AUSTEN. **2.** One who quizzes 1797. **3.** A practical joke; a hoax, a piece of banter or ridicule; a jest or witticism 1807. **b.** The act or practice of quizzing 1819.

1. He's a droll q., and I rather like him MME. D'ARBLAY. **2.** A true Q. is imperturbable 1836.

Quiz (kwiz), *sb.*² *U.S.* 1891. [f. QUIZ *v.*²] An act of quizzing or questioning; *spec.* an oral examination of a student or class by a teacher.

Quiz (kwiz), *v.*¹ 1796. [Of unkn. origin. Cf. QUIZ *sb.*¹] *trans.* To make fun of (a person or thing); *occas.*, to regard with an air of mockery. Hence **Qui·zzer,** one who or that which quizzes. **Qui·zzery,** the practice of quizzing; an instance of this.

Quiz (kwiz), *v.*² *dial.* and *U.S.* 1886. [Of unkn. origin.] *trans.* **a.** To question, interrogate (a person); *U.S.* to examine (a student or class) orally. Also *absol.* **b.** To find *out* (a thing) by questioning.

Quizzical (kwi·zikăl), *a.* 1789. [f. QUIZ *sb.*¹ and *v.*¹ + -ICAL.] **1.** Of the nature of a quiz or oddity; comical. **2.** Given to quizzing;

pertaining to, or characterized by, quizzing 1801. Hence **Qui·zzically** *adv.*

Qui·zzing-glass. *Hist.* 1802. A monocle.

Quo', abbrev. of QUOTH.

‖**Quoad** (kwōᵘ·æd). 1601. [L., 'so far as', 'as much as', 'as to', f. *quo* where, whither + *ad* to.] To the extent of, as regards, with respect to 1742. **b. Quoad hoc,** to this extent, as far as this, with respect to this 1601.

Quod (kwǫd), *sb. slang.* Also **quad.** 1700. [perh. first syll. of QUADRANGLE, but there is no evidence.] Prison. Hence **Quod** *v. trans.* to put in prison.

‖**Quodlibet** (kwǫ·dlibet). late ME. [– med.L. *quodlibet, quodlibetum* (XIV), f. L. *quodlibet*, f. *quod.* what, *libet* it pleases. Cf. (O)Fr. *quolibet.*] **1.** Any question in philosophy or theology proposed as an exercise in disputation; hence, a scholastic debate, thesis, or exercise on a question of this kind (chiefly *pl.* in Univ. use). Now *Hist.* **2.** *Mus.* A fantasia, medley 1845. Hence **Quodlibeta·rian,** †one who does as he pleases; one who discusses quodlibets. **Quodlibe·tic, -al** *a.* of the nature of, connected or concerned with, a q. or quodlibets; **-ly** *adv.*

Quoin (koin), *sb.* 1532. [var. of COIN.] **1.** *Building.* **a.** An external angle of a wall or building; also, one of the stones or bricks serving to form the angle; a corner-stone. **b.** An internal angle or corner, as of a room 1825. **2.** A wedge, or wedge-shaped block, used variously, as: **a.** *Printing.* to lock up a forme 1570; **b.** *Gunnery.* to raise or lower, or fix the breech of, a gun 1627; **c.** *Naut.* to prevent casks from rolling 1711; **d.** *Building.* The key-stone, or any one of the voussoirs of an arch (*rare*). 1730. **3.** An angle, or angular object (*rare*). 1838.

1. b. *Hollow q.*, a recess in the walls at each end of a canal lock, to receive the heel-post of the gate. *Comb.* **q.-post,** the heel-post of a lock-gate. Hence **Quoi·ning,** the stone or brick-work forming the q. of a wall, or the manner in which this is placed.

Quoin (koin), *v.* 1683. [See prec. and COIN *v.*²] **1.** *trans.* To secure or raise with a quoin or wedge. Also with *up.* **2.** To provide with quoins or corners 1834.

Quoit (koit, kwoit), *sb.* late ME. [Of unkn. origin.] **1.** Orig. (now only with ref. to the Greek and Roman discus), a flat disc of stone or metal, thrown as an exercise of strength or skill; *spec.* in mod. use, a heavy flattish ring of iron, with an edge capable of cutting into the ground when it falls. Also, the ring of rope used in *deck-quoits* (see 2). 1440. **2.** *pl.* (rarely *sing.*) The sport of throwing the quoit or of playing with quoits; in the mod. form of this the quoit is aimed at a pin stuck in the ground, and is intended to encircle the pin, or to cut into the ground as near to it as possible. *Deck-quoits*, an imitation of this game, played on shipboard with rings of rope. late ME. **3.** *transf.* The flat covering stone of a cromlech or cist; also, by extension, a cromlech or cist as a whole 1753.

Quoit (koit, kwoit), *v.* 1440. [f. prec.] **1.** *intr.* To play at quoits (rare). **2.** *trans.* To throw like a quoit 1597.

1. To Q., to Run, and Steeds and Chariots drive DRYDEN.

‖**Quomodo** (kwōᵘ·mǒdo), **quo modo** (kwōᵘ mōᵘ·do). 1671. [L., 'in what way?'] *The q.*, the manner, way, means.

Quondam (kwǫ·ndæm), *adv.*, *sb.*, and *a.* 1535. [L., 'formerly'.] **A.** *adv.* At one time, formerly, heretofore (*rare*). 1537. †**B.** *sb.* The former holder of some office or position –1583. **C.** *adj.* That formerly was or existed 1586.

B. Let him be..Jacke out of office, make him a Q. 1583. **C.** My q. friends RUSKIN.

Quop (kwǫp), *v. Obs.* exc. *dial.* 1658. [Later form of †*quap* (XIV–XVI), of imit. origin; cf. G. *quappen* flop, *quappeln* quiver.] To beat, throb, palpitate.

Quorum (kwōᵊ·rǒm). 1455. [L., lit. 'of whom', from the wording of commissions in which persons were designated as members of a body by the words *quorum vos..unum* (*duos*, etc.) *esse volumus* of whom we will that you..be one (two, etc.).] **1.** Orig., certain justices of the peace, usu. of special qualifications, whose presence was necessary to constitute a bench; later applied loosely to all justices. **b.** *transf.* Applied to similarly distinguished members of other bodies; hence, a select company 1602. **2.** A fixed number of members of any body, society, etc., whose presence is necessary for the valid transaction of business 1616.

1. Old Sir John Wellborn, Justice of Peace and Q. MASSINGER. **b.** A Q. of Surgeons..should be ordered to..examine them 1747. **2.** It was order'd that 5 should be a q. for a Council EVELYN.

Quota (kwōᵘ·tă), *sb.* 1668. [med.L. *quota* (sc. *pars* 'how great a part'), fem. of *quotus*, f. *quot* how many.] **1.** The part or share which is, or ought to be, contributed by one to a total sum or amount. **2.** The part or share of a total which belongs, is given, or is due, to one 1700.

Comb. **q.-bill,** a Parliamentary bill passed in March 1795, under which each county and (by a supplementary bill passed in April) each port had to supply its q. of men to the navy. Hence **Quo·ta** *v.* to impose in quotas.

Quotable (kwōᵘ·tăb'l), *a.* 1821. [f. QUOTE *v.* + -ABLE.] Capable of being quoted; suitable for quoting.

Passages of a..q. nature 1821. Hence **Quotabi·lity. Quo·tably** *adv.*

Quotation (kwǒtēⁱ·ʃən). 1532. [– med.L. *quotatio, -on-*, f. *quotat-*, pa. ppl. stem of *quotare*; see QUOTE *v.*, -ION. Cf. Fr. *quotation.*] †**1.** A (marginal) reference to a passage in a book; see QUOTE *v.* 2. –1683. **b.** *Typog.* (ellipt. for *q.-quadrat.*) A large (usu. hollow) quadrat used for filling up blanks (orig. the blanks between marginal references) 1683. **2.** The action or practice of quoting 1646. **b.** A passage quoted 1690. **3.** The amount stated as the price of stocks or any commodity for sale 1812.

2. Classical q. is the *parole* of literary men all over the world JOHNSON.

Comb. **q.-marks,** signs used in writing or printing to mark the beginning and end of a q.; in Eng. the inverted comma and apostrophe are employed. Hence **Quota·tionist,** one who (habitually) quotes.

Quote (kwōᵘt), *sb.* 1600. [f. next.] †**1.** A (marginal) reference; a note –1611. **2.** A quotation 1885. **b.** A quotation mark 1888.

Quote (kwōᵘt), *v.* late ME. [– med.L. *quotare* number, f. *quot* how many, or *quota* QUOTA. Formerly often *cote*, after Fr. *coter.*] **I.** †**1.** *trans.* To mark (a book) with numbers (as of chapters, etc.), or with (marginal) references (*rare*) –1596. †**2.** To give the reference to (a passage in a book) –1651. **3.** †**a.** To cite (a book, author, etc.) for a particular statement or passage. **b.** To copy out or repeat a passage or passages from. 1589. **4.** To copy out or repeat (a passage, statement, etc.) from a book, document, speech, etc., with some indication that one is giving the words of another 1680. **b.** *absol.* To make quotations 1663.

3. He shall q. and recite one Author against another STEELE. **4.** He quotes verses without mercy 1771. **b.** He..quotes largely from state documents J. R. GREEN.

II. †**1.** To write down; to make a note of in writing –1635. †**b.** To take mental note of; to notice –1640. **2.** †**a.** To take, note, *as* or *for* something; to mention *for* having done something –1722. **b.** To cite *as* an instance of or *as* being something 1806. **3.** To state the price of (a commodity) 1866.

1. *fig.* A fellow by the hand of Nature mark'd, Quoted, and sign'd to do a deede of shame SHAKS. **b.** *Rom. & Jul.* I. iv. 31. **2. a.** He's quoted for a most perfidious slaue SHAKS. **b.** This has..been quoted as an excuse 1858. **3.** No shingles are quoted 1866. Hence **Quo·ter.**

Quoth (kwōᵘþ), *v.* (*pa. t.*) Now *arch.* or *dial.* ME. [OE. *cwæþ*, pa. t. of *cweþan* say, = OFris. *qwetha*, OS. *queðan*, OHG. *quedan*, ON. *kveða*, Goth. *qiþan* :– Gmc. **kweþan*; early ME. *cwað, quaþ* became *quoþ* by rounding of *a* in contiguity with w in unstressed positions; a common var. (XIV–XVI) was *quod.*] Said. **1.** Used with sbs., or pronouns of the first and third persons, to indicate that the words of a speaker are being repeated. †**2.** Used interrog. with a pronoun of the second person, with the same force as QUOTHA –1681.

1. Q. Mrs. Gilpin, 'That's well said' COWPER.

Quotha (kwōᵘ·þă), *interj.* Now *arch.* 1519. [For *quoth he* (see A *pron.*).] The phr. 'said he', used with contemptuous or sarcastic force in repeating a word or phrase used by another; hence = indeed! forsooth!

Learning, q.! a mere composition of tricks and mischief GOLDSM. The 'fickle moon', q.! I wish my friends were half as constant 1835.

Quotidian (kwǒti·diăn), *a.* and *sb.* [ME. *cotidien* – OFr. *cotidien* (mod. *quotidien*), early assim. to L. *quotidianus*, earlier *cott-*, *cotidianus*, f. *cotidie* every day; see -IAN.] **A.** *adj.* **1.** Of things, acts, etc.: Of or pertaining to every day; daily. late ME. **b.** *spec.* of an intermittent fever or ague, recurring every day ME. **2.** Of persons: Performing some act, or sustaining some character, daily (*rare*) 1456. **3.** Of an everyday character; ordinary, trivial 1461.

3. Common and q. thoughts are beneath the grace of a Verse 1665.

B. *sb.* **1.** A quotidian fever or ague. late ME. **2.** A daily allowance or portion (*rare*) 1828. Hence **Quoti·dianly** *adv.* daily.

Quotient (kwōᵘ·ʃĕnt). late ME. [f. L. *quotiens* how many times (f. *quot* how many), erron. taken as a ppl. form in *-ens, -ent-*. Cf. Fr. *quotient.*] *Math.* The result obtained by dividing one quantity by another; the number of times one quantity is contained by another as ascertained by division.

Quotiety (kwotəi·ĕti). 1862. [f. L. *quot*, after words in *-iety.*] Condition in respect of number; relative frequency.

‖**Quotum** (kwōᵘ·tǒm). 1660. [L., n. sing. of *quotus*; see QUOTA.] A number or quantity considered in its proportional relationship to a larger number or quantity; a quota.

‖**Quo warranto** (kwōᵘ wǫræ·nto). 1535. [Law Latin 'by what warrant', abl. sing. of *quod* what and *warrantum* WARRANT *sb.*] A King's Bench writ formerly in use, by which a person or persons were called upon to show by what warrant he or they held, claimed, or exercised an office or franchise.

Qy., abbrev. of QUERY.

R

R (ɑ̄ɹ), the eighteenth letter of the modern and seventeenth of the ancient Roman alphabet, is derived through early Greek ᚱ, ᚹ from the Phoenician 𐤓. In general the character denotes an open voiced consonant, in the formation of which the point of the tongue approaches the palate a little way behind the teeth; in many languages this is accompanied by a 'trill' or vibration of the tongue. This trill is almost absent in the *r* of modern standard English, which moreover retains its consonantal value only when it precedes a vowel; in other positions it has been vocalized to an ə-sound, here denoted by (ɹ), and even this is entirely lost after certain vowels. By southern speakers *r* is frequently introduced in hiatus, as in *the idea(r) of, Asia(r) and Africa.*

I. 1. *The 'r' months*: those months with an *r* in their name (Sept. to April), during which oysters are in season. **2.** Used to denote serial order, as 'R Battery', 'MS. R', etc., or as a symbol of some thing or person, a point in a diagram, etc.

II. *Abbreviations.* **1.** Of Latin words and phrases. **a.** R. = *rex* king, *regina* queen. In medical prescriptions: R, ℞, = *recipe* take. **b.** R.I.P. = *requiescat* (*-ant*) *in pace* may he or she (they) rest in peace. **2.** Of English words and phrases: **a.** R. = Rabbi, radius, Railway, Reaumur, right, River, Royal, rupee; also various proper names, as Richard, Robert, etc.; r (*Naut.* in log-book) = rain; *r* = radius vector. R.A. = Rear-Admiral, Royal Academy or Academician, (*Astron.*) right ascension; R.A.M.C. = Royal Army Medical Corps; R.A.S.C. = Royal Army Service Corps; R.C. = Roman Catholic; R.E. = Royal Engineers; R.H. = Royal Highness; R.M. = Resident Magistrate; R.M.A. = Royal Marine Artillery; R.N. = Royal Navy; R.N.A.S. = Royal Naval Air Service; R.N.R. = Royal Naval Reserve; R.S. = Royal Society; R.T.O. = Railway Transport Officer; R.V. = Revised Version (of the Bible); R.W. = Right Worthy or Worshipful. **b.** *The three R's*: Reading, (W)riting, (A)rithmetic. **3.** R.S.V.P., abbrev. of the French phrase *répondez, s'il vous plaît*, 'reply, if you please': commonly placed in one of the corners of invitation-cards. R.D. = Refer to drawer.

Rab (ræb). 1825. [– Fr. *rabot* in same sense.] A wooden beater, formed like a crutch, used for mixing the ingredients of mortar.

Rabatine. [app. f. Fr. *rabat* REBATO + -INE[1].] A low collar SCOTT.

Rabbet (ræ·bĕt), *sb.* late ME. [– OFr. *rab(b)at*, f. *rabattre* beat back or down; see REBATE *v.*[1] The ending has been assim. to -ET.] **I. 1. a.** A channel, groove, or slot cut along the edge or face of a piece (or surface) of wood, stone, etc., and intended to receive the edge or end of another piece or pieces, or a tongue to fit the groove. **b.** A rectangular recess made along a projecting angle or arris. **2.** †**a.** A tongue to fit into a groove. **b.** One of the sides of a rabbet made in an arris; a shoulder, a ledge. 1678. **II.** An elastic beam fixed so as to give a rebound to a large fixed hammer; a spring-pole 1825.

Rabbet (ræ·bĕt), *v.* 1565. [app. f. prec., but found earlier in vbl. sb. *rabityng* (Wyclif).] **1.** *trans.* To join or fix by means of a rabbet or rabbets. Also with *in*.. **2.** To form a rabbet in; to cut *away* or *down* as in making a rabbet 1572. **3.** *intr.* To join *on* or lap *over* by means of a rabbet 1850. Hence **Ra·bbeting** *vbl. sb.* the process of cutting rabbets, or of fitting rabbeted boards together; the groove or rabbeted portion of such boards. late ME.

Rabbi (ræ·bəi, ræ·bi). [Late OE. *rabbi*, ME. *rabi* XIV – eccl.L. *rabbi* (Gr. ῥαββί) – Heb. *rabbî* my master, f. *rab* master, with pronominal suffix.] **1.** A title of respect (in use since the first century B.C.) given by the Jews to doctors of the law. **2.** A Jewish doctor of the law. In mod. Jewish use applied only to one who is authorized by ordination to deal with questions of law and ritual, and to perform certain functions. 1484. †**b.** *transf.* One whose learning, authority, or office is comparable to that of a Jewish rabbi. (Freq. contempt.) –1855.

1. Raby Moyses says alle þis HAMPOLE. Ye shall not suffre youre selves to be called Rabi TINDALE *Matt.* 23:8. **2.** The gowned Rabbies.. were of opinion that hee was a friend of Beelzebub MILT. *The rabbis = the rabbins* (see next).

Rabbin (ræ·bin). 1531. [– Fr. *rabbin* (XVI) or mod.L. *rabbinus* (XVI), vars. of *rabbi*; the *n* may be due to a Semitic pl. form.] = RABBI 2 (but mainly used in *pl.* to designate the chief Jewish authorities on matters of law and doctrine, most of whom flourished between the 2nd and the 13th centuries of the Christian era) 1579. †**b.** = RABBI 2 b –1632. **c.** Used as *pl.* 1826. Hence **Ra·bbinate,** the office or dignity of a rabbi; the period during which some one is a rabbi; *collect.* rabbis as a class. Hence **Ra·bbinite** = RABBINIST.

Rabbinic (răbi·nik), *a.* and *sb.* 1612. [f. prec. + -IC. Cf. Fr. *rabbinique*.] **A.** *adj.* = next. **B.** *sb.* Rabbinical Hebrew 1832.

Rabbinical (răbi·nikăl), *a.* 1622. [f. as prec.; see -ICAL.] **1.** Of things: Pertaining to, or characteristic of, the rabbins, their learning, writings, etc. **b.** *spec.* of the later form of the Hebrew language or character used by the rabbins 1727. **2.** Of persons: Belonging to the class of rabbis or rabbins; resembling a rabbi; occupied with or skilled in r. literature 1642.

1. A R. opinion concerning Manna 1779. **2.** The Masoreths and Rabbinicall Scholiasts MILT. Hence **Rabbi·nically** *adv.*

Rabbinism (ræ·biniz'm). 1652. [f. RABBIN + -ISM. Cf. Fr. *rabbinisme*.] **1.** The teaching or doctrine of the rabbins. **2.** A rabbinical expression; a peculiarity of the language of the rabbins 1832.

Rabbinist (ræ·binist). 1599. [f. as prec. + -IST. Cf. Fr. *rabbiniste*.] An adherent or follower of the rabbins; *esp.* among the Jews, one who accepts the teaching of the Talmud and the rabbins, in contrast to the Karaites, who reject tradition. Hence **Rabbini·stic, -al** *a.*

Rabbit (ræ·bit), *sb.* [In XIV *rabet(te*, perh. – an OFr. form repr. by Fr. dial. *rabotte*, *rabouillet* young rabbit, *rabouillère* rabbit burrow, possibly of LDu. origin (cf. Flem. *robbe*, dim. *robbeke*, Du. †*robett*, Walloon *robète*).] **1.** A common burrowing rodent of the hare family (*Leporidæ*), esp. the common European species, *Lepus cuniculus*, which is naturally brownish-grey, but in domestication also white, black, or pied. †Orig. applied only to the young animal, the full-grown one being called a CONY. **2.** *transf.* Applied contempt. to a person, *spec.* to one who plays games (esp. cricket or tennis) badly 1597.

1. Rabbets will breed seven times a year PENNANT. **2.** Away, you horson, upright Rabbet, away SHAKS.

attrib. and *Comb.* as *r.-burrow*, *-hole*, *-hutch*, *-warren*, etc.; *r.-breeder*, *-fancier*, *-trapper*, etc.; **r.-fish,** a name for fishes having points of resemblance to a rabbit, as (*a*) the British fishes *Chimæra monstrosa* and the striped rock-gurnard, (*b*) an American fish of the genus *Lagocephalus* with teeth resembling a rabbit's incisors; **-foot** (clover) = HARE'S-FOOT 1. Hence **Ra·bbitry,** a place in which rabbits are kept; a collection of rabbits. **Ra·bbity** *a.* abounding in rabbits; resembling a r.

Rabbit (ræ·bit), *v.*[1] 1852. [f. prec.] **1.** *intr.* To hunt for or catch rabbits. Chiefly in *pres. pple.* **2.** To crowd *together* like rabbits 1892. Hence **Ra·bbitter,** a man or a dog that hunts rabbits.

Rabbit (ræ·bit), *v.*[2] *vulgar.* 1742. [prob. an alteration of *rat*, in *od rat*, *drat*.] A meaningless word used as an imprecation. Also *drabbit*, *od(d) rabbit*.

Rabble (ræ·b'l), *sb.*[1] (and *a.*) late ME. [perh. conn. w. RABBLE *v.*[1]] **A.** †**1.** A pack, string, swarm (of animals) –1634. **2.** A disorderly crowd of people, a mob. late ME. **b.** Applied contempt. to a class or body of persons imagined as a mob 1529. **c.** Without article: Persons of the lowest class 1687. **3.** A disorderly collection, a confused medley (of things) 1514. †**4.** A long string *of* words, etc., having little meaning or value –1656. **b.** A rigmarole. Now *dial.* 1592.

2. At last the r. broke up and so I away PEPYS. Rather a confused r. than a regular army BERKELEY. Phr. *The r.*, the common, low, or disorderly part of the populace; the mob. **c.** You live in Dublin among a parcel of r. 1734. **3.** A r. of books of all ages, sizes [etc.] 1803. A seditious r. of doubts 1847.

B. *attrib.* or *adj.* **1.** Of persons: Forming a rabble; of or belonging to the rabble 1549. **2.** Of things, actions, etc.: Characteristic of, appropriate to, the rabble 1603.

2. To burn the jails..was a good r. trick JOHNSON.

Rabble (ræ·b'l), *sb.*[2] 1664. [– Fr. *râble*, earlier *roable* :– med.L. *rotabulum* = L. *rutabulum* fire-shovel, oven rake, f. *ruere* rake up.] †**1.** A kind of shovel used by charcoal-burners for taking off the covering from the burned pile EVELYN. **2.** An iron bar sharply bent at the end, used for stirring and skimming molten metal in puddling; also, a steam-pipe used for the same purpose 1861.

Rabble (ræ·b'l), *v.*[1] *Obs.* exc. *dial.* late ME. [prob. – MDu. *rabbelen*, LG. *rabbeln*, of imit. origin.] **1. a.** *trans.* To utter (words or speech) in a rapid confused manner. Also with *forth*, *off*, *out*, *over*. **b.** *intr.* To speak or read in this fashion; to gabble. **2.** To work in a hurried slovenly manner (*dial.*). **b.** *trans.* To rattle *up*. 1862.

Rabble (ræ·b'l), *v.*[2] 1644. [f. RABBLE *sb.*[1] 2.] **1.** *trans.* To attack or assail (a person or his property) as, along with, or by means of, a rabble; to mob. **2.** *intr.* To become a rabble 1813.

1. Some..were..active in rabbling the Clergy 1690.

Rabble (ræ·b'l), *v.*[3] 1860. [f. RABBLE *sb.*[2]] To stir, skim, or rake with a rabble. Hence **Ra·bbler,** one who uses a rabble; an instrument for rabbling.

Rabblement (ræ·b'lmĕnt). 1545. [f. RABBLE *sb.*[1] + -MENT.] **a.** = RABBLE *sb.*[1] in various senses. **b.** Tumult or disturbance like that of a rabble; riotous conduct (*rare*) 1590.

a. As hee refus'd it, the r. howted SHAKS. A r. at the heels of Rosinante LAMB. **b.** The raskall many..Heaped together in rude rablement SPENSER.

Rabble rout (ræ·b'lraut). 1599. [f. RABBLE *sb.*[1] + ROUT *sb.*] = RABBLE 2, 2 b.

Rabelaisian (ræbĕlē[i]·ziăn), *a.* (and *sb.*). 1817. [f. name of François *Rabelais* (c1490–1553) + -IAN.] **A.** *adj.* Pertaining to, characteristic of, or resembling Rabelais or his writings, which are distinguished by exuberance of imagination and language, combined with extravagance and coarseness of humour and satire. **B.** *sb.* A student or admirer of Rabelais 1893. Hence **Rabelai·sianism,** the characteristic style or attitude of Rabelais.

Rabid (ræ·bid), *a.* 1611. [– L. *rabidus*, f. *rabere* be mad; see -ID[1].] **1.** Furious, raging; madly violent in nature or behaviour. Also *transf.* of things or parts of the body. **2.** *spec.* Of beasts (rarely of human beings): Affected with rabies; mad 1804. **b.** Pertaining to, of the nature of, rabies 1806.

1. All the rabide flight Of winds that ruine ships CHAPMAN. R. Hunger DRYDEN. A r. pedant LAMB. **2.** Bites of r. animals 1880. **b.** An accompaniment of the r. virus 1887. Hence **Rabi·dity. Ra·bid-ly** *adv.*, **-ness.**

Rabies (rē[i]·bi,īz, -bīz). 1661. [– L. *rabies*, f. *rabere* (see prec.).] Canine madness; hydrophobia.

Ra·binet. *Obs.* exc. *Hist.* 1587. [app. later f. ROBINET.] A small variety of cannon.

†**Raccommo·de,** *v.* 1673. [– Fr. *raccommoder*, f. *re-* + *accommoder* ACCOMMODATE.] *trans.* To restore to good relations (*with* a person); to set right –1756.

Raccoon, var. of **Racoon.**

Race (rē[i]s), *sb.*[1] ME. [– ON. *rás* = OE. *rǣs*, MLG. *rās* current.] **I. 1.** The act of running; a run. Now *Sc.* **b.** *fig.* The course of life or some portion of it 1513. †**2.** The act of riding rapidly on horseback; a course in a tournament –1600. †**b.** A journey or voyage –1557.

1. b. My r. of glory run, and r. of shame MILT.

II. †**1.** Onward movement, e.g. of the heavenly bodies, a vehicle, etc.; running or rush of water –1670. **b.** *esp.* The daily (or annual) course of the sun through the heavens. Similarly of the moon. 1590. **c.** The course of time 1595. †**d.** The course of events, or of a narrative –1626. **2.** A strong current in the sea or in a river. late ME.

1. b. The Sun..ere half his r. be run 1662. **c.** Fly envious Time, till thou run out thy r. MILT. **2.** A short cockling Sea, as if it had been a R. or place where two Tides meet DAMPIER. The R. (or Ras) of Alderney 1862.

III. As a portion of time or space. **1.** A piece of ground suitable for running or racing (*rare*) 1612. †**2.** The course, line, or path taken by a person or a moving body –1585. **b.** The channel or bed (of a stream); *esp.* an artificial channel, as in a mill or mining claim. Now chiefly *U.S.* See also HEAD-, MILL-, TAIL-RACE. 1565. **c.** *Weaving.* The channel along which the shuttle moves in crossing the web 1855. **d.** *Mech.* The space in which a drum or wheel revolves 1883. **3. a.** *Mining.* 'A small thread of spar or ore' (Raymond) 1580. **b.** A row or series. *dial.* and *techn.* 1877.

1. Nor yet the level South can shew a smoother r. DRAYTON.

IV. The act of running, riding, sailing, etc. in competition with one or more rivals; a contest of speed; in *pl.* usu. denoting a series of horse-races held at a fixed time on a regular course 1513.

To indite Warrs..or to describe Races and Games MILT. We're going on to the races DICKENS.

attrib. and *Comb.* as *r.-meeting*, *-week*, etc.: **r.-ball,** a ball held in connection with a race-meeting; **-card,** a printed card giving information about races; **-day,** the day on which a race or set of races is held; **-glass,** a field-glass for use at races; **-way,** *U.S.* a passage or channel for water; the bed of a canal, etc.

Race (rē[i]s), *sb.*[2] 1500. [– Fr. *race* – It. *razza*; of unkn. origin.] **I.** A group of persons, animals, or plants, connected by common descent or origin. **1.** The offspring or posterity *of* a person; a set of children or descendants. Chiefly *poet.* Also *transf.* and *fig.* 1570. †**b.** Breeding, the production of offspring –1667. †**c.** A generation (*rare*) –1741. **2.** A limited group of persons descended from a common ancestor; a house, family, kindred 1581. **b.** A tribe, nation, or people, regarded as of common stock 1600. **c.** A group of several tribes or peoples, forming a distinct ethnical stock 1842. **d.** One of the great divisions of mankind, having certain physical peculiarities in common 1774. **3.** A breed or stock of animals; a particular variety of a species 1580. †**b.** A stud or herd (of horses) –1667. **c.** A genus, species, kind of animals 1605. **4.** A genus, species, or variety of plants 1596. **5.** One of the great divisions of living creatures: **a.** Mankind. In early use always *the human race, the race of men* or *mankind*, etc. 1580. **b.** A class or kind of beings other than men or animals 1667. **c.** One of the chief classes of animals (as beasts, birds, fishes, etc.) 1726. **6.** Without article: **a.** Denoting the stock, family, class, etc. to which a person, animal, or plant belongs, chiefly in phr. *of* (*noble*, etc.) *r.* 1559 **b.** The fact or condition of belonging to a particular people or ethnical stock; the qualities, etc. resulting from this 1849. †**7.** Natural or inherited disposition SHAKS.

1. I will take some savage woman, she shall rear my dusky r. TENNYSON. **b.** Male he created thee, but thy consort Femal for R. MILT. **2.** The Bourbon is by no means a cruel r. STERNE. **b.** That Pigmean Race Beyond the Indian Mount MILT. **d.** The second great variety in the human species seems to be that of the Tartar r. GOLDSM. **3.** The plains..bred a generous r. of horses GIBBON. **b.** *Merch. V.* v. i. 72. **c.** I wish the r. of cows were perished SHELLEY. **5.** That every tribe..Might feel themselves allied to all the r. COWPER. **b.** A R. of Demi-Gods DRYDEN. **6.** Two Coursers of ethereal r. GRAY. **b.** R. in the negro is of appalling importance EMERSON. **7.** I giue my sensuall r., the reine SHAKS.

II. A group or class of persons, animals, or things, having some common feature or features. **1.** A set or class of persons 1500. **b.** One of the sexes (*poet.*) 1590. **2.** A set, class, or kind of animals, plants, or things. Chiefly *poet.* 1590. †**b.** One of the three 'kingdoms' of nature (*rare*) –1707. **3.** A particular class of wine, or the characteristic flavour of this, due to the soil 1520. **b.** *fig.* Of speech, writing, etc. A peculiar and characteristic style or manner, *esp.* liveliness, piquancy 1680.

1. The r. of learned men, Still at their books THOMSON. **2.** I hope [her disease] is not of the cephalick r. JOHNSON. **3.** A pipe Of rich Canary.. Is it of the right r.? MASSINGER. **b.** His conversation had a r. and flavour peculiarly its own 1875.

Comb.: **r. suicide,** term for voluntary restriction of child-birth 1901.

Race (rēⁱs), *sb.*³ 1450. [– OFr. *rais, raiz* :– L. *radix, radic-* root; see RADISH, RADIX.] A root (of ginger).

Race (rēⁱs), *v.*¹ 1672. [f. RACE *sb.*¹] **1.** *intr.* To run a race (*with*), to compete (*with*) in speed. **b.** To practice or engage in horse-racing 1827. **2.** To run, ride, sail, etc. swiftly 1757. **b.** Of inanimate things 1808. **c.** Of a steam engine, screw propeller, wheel, etc.: To run or revolve with uncontrolled speed, when resistance is diminished while the driving power continues the same 1862. **3.** *trans.* To race with 1809. **4.** To cause to move swiftly; to cause to run a race or races 1860. **5.** To suspend (a wheel, grindstone, etc.) in the proper position for running 1870.

1. I who..would r. With my own steed from Araby KEATS. **b.** I have been racing now getting on fifty years 1881. **2.** Run, Pheidippides, run and r., reach Sparta for aid! BROWNING. **b.** Like streamlet..racing forth SCOTT. **3.** Fought cocks, and raced their neighbours' horses W. IRVING.

Race (rēⁱs), *v.*² 1440. [var. of RASE *v.*¹, now only techn. in sense 1.] **1.** *trans.* To scratch or tear with something sharp; to cut or slash. †**2.** To scrape *out*, erase. (Now written RASE or RAZE.) –1705. †**3.** To level with the ground; to RAZE –1679.

2. *fig.* To massacre them all, And r. their faction, and their familie SHAKS.

Ra·ce-course. 1764. [f. RACE *sb.*¹ + COURSE.] **1.** A piece of ground laid out with a track for racing. **2.** A water-way, mill-race 1841.

Ra·ce-horse. 1626. [f. RACE *sb.*¹ + HORSE.] **1.** A horse bred or kept for racing. **2.** A logger-head or steamer duck 1773.

Racemate (ræ·sĭmět). 1838. [f. RACEMIC + -ATE⁴.] *Chem.* A salt of racemic acid.

Raceme (răsī·m). 1785. [– L. *racemus* cluster of grapes.] *Bot.* A simple inflorescence in which the flowers are arranged on short, nearly equal, pedicels, at equal distances on an elongated axis.

Compound r., one having the lower pedicels developed into secondary racemes. Hence **Race·med** *a.* disposed in racemes. So **Racemi·ferous** *a.* bearing racemes or clusters. **Race·miform** *a.* having the form of a r.

Racemic (răse·mik, răsī·mik), *a.* 1835. [f. prec. + -IC.] *Chem.* Derived from grapes or grape-juice.

Racemo- (răsī·mo), comb. form of L. *racemus* RACEME, with sense 'containing a proportion of racemic acid', as *r.-carbonate*; *r.-carbonic* adj., etc.

Racemose (ræ·sĭmōᵘs), *a.* 1698. [– L. *racemosus*, f. *racemus*; see -OSE¹.] **1.** *Bot.* **a.** Of flowers: Arranged in racemes. **b.** Of an inflorescence or vegetable growth: Having the form of a raceme. **2.** *Anat.* Having the form of, arranged as, a cluster (esp. as an epithet of compound glands) 1835. So **Ra·cemous** *a.* (*rare*) = 1.

Racemule (ræ·sĭmiul). 1882. [dim. of L. *racemus*; see -ULE.] *Bot.* A small raceme. So **Race·mulose** *a.* resembling a r.; somewhat racemose 1864.

Racer (rēⁱsəɹ). 1649. [f. RACE *v.*¹ + -ER¹.] **1.** One who races or takes part in a race. **2.** A race-horse 1670. **b.** Any animal having great speed; *spec.* as the name of species of American snakes, of a sand-crab, etc. 1699. **3.** Anything used for racing, as a bicycle, yacht, etc.; anything capable of great speed 1793. **4.** *Gunnery.* A rail, forming a horizontal arc, on which the carriage or traversing-platform of a gun is moved 1861.

2. As much difference..as..between a r. and a cart-horse 1833.

Rache, ratch (rætʃ). *Obs.* exc. *arch.* [OE. *ræćć*, related to ON. *rakki* dog.] A hunting-dog which pursues its prey by scent.

Rachi- (rēⁱ·ki), **rachio-** (rēⁱ·kio), comb. forms of RACHIS, used in some terms of *Anat.* and *Path.* relating to the spine or vertebral column. (Also occas. written with *rh-*.) **Rachia·lgia** [Gr. -αλγία pain], pain in or due to the spine; painter's colic; hence **Rachia·lgic** *a.* **Ra·chiodont** [Gr. ὀδοντ- tooth] *a.*, of a genus of serpents (*Rachiodon*): having vertebral processes which penetrate the gullet and serve as teeth. **Ra·chiotome** [Gr. -τόμος cutting], a dissecting instrument for cutting open the spinal canal. **Rachio·tomy** [Gr. -τομία], the operation of cutting into the spinal canal.

Rachidian (răki·diăn), *a.* Also **rha-**. 1848. [f. *r(h)achid-*, assumed stem of Gr. ῥάχις RACHIS + -IAN.] Of or pertaining to a rachis.

‖**Rachis** (rēⁱ·kis). Also **rha-**. *Pl.* **rachides** (rēⁱ·kidīz). 1693. [mod.L. – Gr. ῥάχις spine, ridge, rib (of a leaf), etc. The pl. *rachides* is erroneous, as the stem is ῥαχι-.] **1.** *Anat.* The vertebral column, or the cord from which it develops. **b.** The median part of the odontophore of a mollusc, resembling a series of vertebrae 1851. **c.** A cord of protoplasmic matter in the ovary of nematoid worms, round which ova are developed 1877. **2.** *Bot.* **a.** The axis of an inflorescence in which flower-stalks occur at short intervals from each other, as in grasses 1785. **b.** The axis of a pinnately compound leaf or frond, corresponding to the midrib of a simple leaf 1832. **3.** *Ornith.* The stem or shaft of a feather, esp. the part bearing the vexillum 1874.

‖**Rachitis** (rækəi·tis). 1655. [mod.L. – Gr. ῥαχῖτις (f. ῥάχις + -ιτις -ITIS), prop. meaning 'inflammation of the spine'.] = RICKETS. Hence **Rachitic** (ræki·tik) *a.* affected with rickets; connected with, or pertaining to, rickets.

Racial (rēⁱ·ʃăl), *a.* 1862. [f. RACE *sb.*² + -IAL.] Belonging to, or characteristic of, race. Hence **Ra·cially** *adv.*

Racing (rēⁱ·siŋ), *vbl. sb.* 1680. [f. RACE *sb.*¹ or *v.*¹ + -ING¹.] The action of RACE *v.*¹

attrib. and *Comb.* as *r.-boat*, etc.; **R. Calendar,** a yearly publication giving particulars of races run or to be run; **r.-tail,** the tail of natural length worn by race-horses.

Rack (ræk), *sb.*¹ ME. [prob. of Scand. origin; cf. Norw. and Sw. dial. *rak* (Sw. *vrak*, Da. *vrag*) wreck, wreckage, refuse, f. *reka* drive (cf. ON. *reki* flotsam).] †**1.** A rush, shock, collision. Also, a noise as of a shock; a crash. –1513. **2.** Clouds, or a mass of cloud, driven before the wind in the upper air ME. †**b.** Driving mist or fog –1610.

2. The Windes in the Vpper Region (which moue the Clouds aboue which we call the Racke) BACON. **b.** *Ant. & Cl.* IV. xiv. 10. *fig.* The great Globe it selfe..shall dissolue, And..Leaue not a racke behinde SHAKS.

Rack (ræk), *sb.*² [ME. *rakke*, occas. *rekke*, – Du. *rak*, LG. *rack*, also MDu. *rek* (Du. *rek, rekke*), MLG. *rek(ke* horizontal bar, shelf, prob. f. *recken* stretch (see RACK *v.*³).] **1.** app. An iron bar to which prisoners were secured –1590. **2.** A bar (usu. in *pl.*) or set of bars used to support a spit or other cooking utensil. *Obs.* exc. *dial.* late ME. **3.** A frame made with upright bars of wood or metal to hold fodder for horses or cattle, either fixed in a stable or movable ME. **4.** A framework in or on which articles are placed or suspended. Freq. differentiated, as *bottle-, case-, hat-, plate-r.*, etc. 1537. **5.** *spec.* or *techn.*: **a.** *Naut.* = FIDDLE 3 a. 1769. **b.** An inclined frame or table on which tin-ore is washed 1839. †**c.** An open-work side for a cart or wagon –1687. **d.** In organ-building = PIPE-*rack*. **6.** *Mech.* A bar having teeth or indentations on the side or edge, which gear into those of a wheel, pinion, or worm, or serve to hold something in a desired (and easily alterable) position. Often coupled with *pinion.* 1797.

3. Phr. *At r. and manger*, in the midst of abundance or plenty, wanting for nothing. Hence *R. and manger*, want of proper management, waste and destruction (now *dial.*).

Comb.: **r.-calipers,** calipers fitted with a r. and pinion; so **-compass, -easel; -rail,** a cogged rail, into which a cogged wheel on a locomotive works; **r. railway,** a railway having a r.-rail laid between or beside the bearing-rails; **r. saw,** a saw with wide-set teeth; **-wheel,** a cog-wheel; **-work,** mechanism of the nature of, or containing, a r.

Rack (ræk), *sb.*³ 1460. [prob. spec. use of prec.] **1.** An instrument of torture formerly in use, consisting (usu.) of a frame having a roller at each end; the victim was fastened to these by the wrists and ankles, and had the joints of his limbs stretched by their rotation. **b.** *transf.* and *fig.* That which (*rarely* one who) causes acute suffering, physical or mental; also, the result of this; intense pain or suffering 1591. **2.** A frame on which cloth is stretched. *Obs.* exc. *dial.* 1519. †**3.** A windlass or winch for bending a cross-bow –1687. **4.** = RACK-RENT. Now *rare* or *Obs.* 1605. **5.** That which racks or strains; stress of weather; a storm 1806.

1. The r. seldom stood idle in the Tower for all the latter part of Elizabeth's reign HALLAM. **b.** The r. of publicke censure DEKKER. Phr. *On the r.*, in a state of acute physical or mental suffering; in keen suspense. *To put* or *set* (faculties, †words, etc.) *on the r.*, to strain to the utmost. So *to be on the r.*, to be at full stretch or strain. **5.** A strong voice, unworn by age and the r. of various seas 1891.

Rack (ræk), *sb.*⁴ 1599. [var. of WRACK, WRECK.] Destruction; chiefly in phr. *to go to r. and ruin.* †**b.** A crash as of something breaking MILT.

Rack (ræk), *sb.*⁵ 1580. [perh. ult. of Arab. origin (cf. Arab. *faras rikwa* an easy paced mare, and mod. Gr. (Chios) ῥαχβάν amble).] A horse's gait in which the two feet on each side are lifted simultaneously, and all four feet are off the ground together at certain moments.

Rack (ræk), *sb.*⁶ 1602. Aphetic f. ARRACK. Also *attrib.*, as *r.-punch*, etc.

Rack (ræk), *v.*¹ 1590. [f. RACK *sb.*¹ 2.] *intr.* Of clouds: To drive before the wind.

Rack (ræk), *v.*² 1577. [f. RACK *sb.*²] †**1.** *trans.* To fit up (a stable) with racks (*rare*) –1583. **2.** *To r. up.* **a.** *intr.* To fill a stable-rack with hay or straw before leaving the horse or horses for the night 1778. **b.** *trans.* To fill the rack for (a horse) 1798. **c.** To fasten (a horse) to the rack 1856. **3.** To place (a thing) in or on a rack 1855. **b.** *Mining.* To wash on the rack (RACK *sb.*¹ 5 b) 1891. **4.** *trans.* and *intr.* To move, or be moved, by means of a rack and pinion 1867.

Rack (ræk), *v.*³ late ME. [– MLG., MDu. *racken*, also *recken* = OE. *reććan*, OS. *rekkian*, OHG. *recchan* (G. *recken*), ON. *rekja*, Goth. *ufrakjan* stretch, Gmc. **rakjan*.] **1.** *trans.* To stretch the joints of (a person) by tugging or pulling, *esp.* by means of a rack (see RACK *sb.*³). **b.** To affect with pain similar to that caused by the use of the rack. (Said esp. of diseases.) 1588. **c.** To torture, distract, lacerate (the mind, soul, etc.) 1576. †2. To stretch, pull out, increase the length of (a thing, period of time, etc.) –1642. **b.** To pull apart, to separate by force, to break up. *Obs.* exc. *dial.* 1549. **c.** To shake (a thing) violently; to strain 1840. **d.** *intr.* To undergo stretching, strain, or dislocation. Chiefly *Sc.* 1508. †**3.** To strain the meaning of (words, etc.); to give a forced interpretation to –1711. **b.** To strain, task severely (the mind, brain, etc.) 1583. †**c.** To stretch or raise beyond the normal –1618. **4.** To raise (rent) above a fair or normal amount. Cf. RACK-RENT. 1553. †**b.** To charge an excessive rent for (land) –1766. **c.** To oppress (a person) by extortions or exactions, *esp.* of excessive rent; to bear hard upon (one's purse, etc.) 1584. †**d.** To extort (money, etc.). Also *absol.* –1680. **e.** To exhaust (tenants, land, etc.) by exactions or excessive use. Also with *out.* 1778.

1. Some drowned,..some racked, some hanged on a gybet 1526. **b.** Ile racke thee with old Crampes, Fill all thy bones with Aches SHAKS. **c.** How must she be racked with Jealousy STEELE. **2. c.** A dreadful cough, which seemed to r. his whole shattered system 1840. **3.** Grant that I may never r. a Scripture simile beyond the true intent thereof FULLER. **b.** Racking his wits to contrive exquisite compliments 1880. **4.** They racke their rents vnto a treble rate 1598. **c.** Here are no hard Landlords to racke vs with high rents 1624.

Rack (ræk), *v.*[4] 1530. [Goes with RACK *sb.*[6]] *intr.* Of animals, *esp.* horses: To move with the gait called a rack. Hence **Ra·cker,** a racking horse.

Rack (ræk), *v.*[5] 1460. [– Prov. (Gascon) *arracar*, f. *raca* the stem and husks of grapes, thick dregs.] **1.** *trans.* To draw off (wine, cider, etc.) from the lees. Also with *off.* †**2.** To empty (a cask) by racking. *rare.* –1703.

Rack, *v.*[6] 1769. [Of unkn. origin.] *Naut.* To bind two ropes together with cross-turns. Hence **Ra·cking** *vbl. sb.*, spun yarn, etc. used for this 1711.

Racket (ræ·kėt), *sb.*[1] 1500. [– Fr. *raquette* – It. *racchetta*, f. Arab. *rāḥat*, construct form of *rāḥa* palm of the hand.] **1.** A bat used in rackets, tennis, etc., consisting of a network of cord, catgut, or steel wire stretched across a somewhat elliptical frame formed of a bent strip of wood or steel, to the base of which a handle is attached. **b.** A game of ball for two or four persons, played with rackets in a plain four-walled court. Now always *pl.* 1529. **2.** A snow-shoe made after the fashion of a racket, as used in Northern America 1613. **b.** A broad wooden shoe for man or horse to enable them to walk over marshy ground 1864.

1. The main object of modern lawn tennis is to meet the ball with a full r. 1890.
attrib. and *Comb.*, as *r.-court*, etc.; **r.-press,** a contrivance to keep a r. from warping.

Racket (ræ·kėt), *sb.*[2] 1565. [perh. imit. of a clattering noise.] **1.** Disturbance, loud noise, uproar, din. **b.** With *a* and *pl.* An instance of this 1622. **c.** Clamour, outcry; excitement or fuss (*about* something, or *with* a person) 1652. **2.** The whirl of society; excessive social excitement or dissipation 1784. **b.** A large or noisy social gathering 1745. **3.** *slang.* A trick, dodge, scheme, game, line of business or action 1812. Now usually, any scheme for obtaining money, or effecting some other object, by illegal, and often violent, means (*U.S. colloq.*) 1928. **4.** A trying experience; an ordeal 1823.

1. A quiet country life—no r. except the roosters in the morning 1877. **4.** Phr. *To stand the r.*, (*a*) to hold out against strain or wear and tear; (*b*) to face the consequences of an action.

†**Ra·cket,** *v.*[1] 1603. [f. RACKET *sb.*[1]] *trans.* To strike with, or as with, a racket; to toss or bandy about. Chiefly *fig.* –1705.

Racket (ræ·kėt), *v.*[2] 1753. [f. RACKET *sb.*[2]] **1.** *intr.* To live a gay life, to take part in social excitement. Also with *about.* 1760. **2.** To make a noise or racket; to move about in a noisy way 1827. **3.** *trans.* To keep lively, to disturb, destroy by racketing 1753.

Racketeer (rækėtīᵊ·ɹ), *sb. U.S.* 1927. [f. RACKET *sb.*[2] 3 + -EER.] One of an organized gang who blackmail traders by intimidation and violence. Hence **Racketee·r** *v.*, **-ee·ring** *vbl. sb.*

Ra·cket-tail. 1851. [f. RACKET *sb.*[1]] A (bird's) tail shaped like a tennis-racket; hence, a name for various humming birds and motmots having such tails So **Ra·cket-tailed** *a.* having a r.

Ra·ckety, *a.* 1773. [f. RACKET *sb.*[2] + -Y[1].] **1.** Addicted to making a racket. **2.** Characterized by noise, excitement, etc. 1827.

Ra·ck-rent, *sb.* 1591. [f. RACK *v.*[3] + RENT.] A very high, excessive, or extortionate rent; a rent equal (or nearly equal) to the full annual value of the land. Also *transf.* and *fig.* Hence **Ra·ck-rent** *v. trans.* to subject (a person) to the payment of r. **Ra·ck-re:nter,** one who pays, or one who exacts, r.

Ra·ck-stick. 1859. [f. RACK *v.*[3]] A stick used for tightening a rope placed round anything. So **Ra·ck-pin.**

‖**Raconteur** (rakoṅtör). 1829. [Fr., f. *raconter* relate; see RECOUNT *v.*[1]] One skilled in relating anecdotes or stories. So **Raconteuse** (-tǫ̈z), a female r.

Racoon, raccoon (răkū·n, rækū·n). 1608. [Powhatan (Virginia) dialect of Algonquian.] An American nocturnal carnivore of the genus *Procyon.* The common N. Amer. species is *P. lotor*, a greyish-brown furry animal with bushy tail and sharp snout.

Racovian (răkōᵘ·viăn), *a.* and *sb.* 1652. [f. mod.L. *Racovia*, f. *Rakow*, a town in Poland + -IAN.] **A.** *adj.* Of or pertaining to Rakow, or to the Unitarians (Socinians) who made it their chief centre in the 17th c. **B.** *sb.* An adherent of the doctrines taught at Rakow.

Racquet, -ette, var. ff. RACKET *sb.*, RAQUETTE.

Racy (rēⁱ·si), *a.* 1650. [f. RACE *sb.*[2] II. 3 + -Y[1].] **1.** Of wine, fruits, etc.: Having a characteristically excellent taste, flavour, or quality. So of taste, flavour, etc. Also *fig.* **2. a.** Of persons: Having a distinctive quality or vigour of character or intellect; lively, full of 'go'. So of actions, qualities, etc. 1668. **b.** Of animals or their parts: Showing high breeding or good blood 1841. **3.** Of speech, writing, etc.: Having a characteristic sprightliness, liveliness, or piquancy 1667. **b.** *U.S.* Salacious. **4.** Of pleasure, etc.: Peculiarly agreeable 1690.

1. The r. flavour and strong body of this wine 1756. **2. a.** Yorkshire has such families here and there..peculiar, r., vigorous C. BRONTË. **3.** Brisk r. Verses, in which we The Soil from whence they came, tast, smell, and see COWLEY. Phr. *R. of the soil*, characteristic of a certain country or people (usu. with ref. to Ireland). Hence **Ra·cily** *adv.* **Ra·ciness.**

Rad (ræd). 1831. Abbrev. of RADICAL.

Raddle (ræ·d'l), *sb.*[1] *Obs.* exc. *dial.* 1577. [– AFr. *reidele*, OFr. *reddalle*, (also mod.) *ridelle* rail of a cart.] **1.** *n. dial.* and *U.S.* A wooden bar with upright pegs, used to keep the threads of the warp in place while it is being wound upon the beam 1848. **2.** A slender rod, wattle, or lath, fastened to or twisted between upright stakes or posts to form a fence, partition, or wall 1577. **3.** A piece of wattled work; a hurdle, door, etc. made with intertwined raddles 1886.

Raddle (ræ·d'l), *sb.*[2] 1523. [var. of RUDDLE.] Red ochre, RUDDLE.

Raddle (ræ·d'l), *v.*[1] 1671. [f. RADDLE *sb.*[1]] *trans.* To weave or twist together (like raddles), to intertwine, interlace.

Raddle (ræ·d'l), *v.*[2] 1631. [f. RADDLE *sb.*[2]] *trans.* To paint or mark with raddle; to colour coarsely with red or rouge.

‖**Radeau** (rado). 1759. [Fr. – Prov. *radel* :– L. **ratellus*, dim. of *ratis* raft.] A raft; *spec.* a floating battery.

Radial (rēⁱ·diăl), *a.* and *sb.* 1570. [– med.L. *radialis*, f. *radius*; see RADIUS, -AL[1].] **A.** *adj.* **1.** Of light, beams, etc.: Proceeding or issuing as rays from a common centre; also, of or pertaining to light in the form of rays. Now *rare.* **2.** Arranged like rays or the radii of a circle; having the position or direction of a radius 1750. **3.** Having spokes, bars, lines, etc., extending from a centre; *spec.* applied to apparatus or machines having a part or parts thus arranged, as *r. drill, plane*, etc. 1762. **4.** Of immaterial things: Characterized by the divergence of lines or parts from a centre; taking the direction of such lines 1833. **5.** *Anat.* Pertaining to the radius or chief bone of the forearm, esp. in *r. artery, nerve, vein* 1741.

2. *R. axle*, an axle (of a railway carriage, tramway car, etc.) which on a curve of the track assumes the position of a radius to that curve; so *r. axle box.* **4.** Another form of symmetry which is entirely absent in Man is r. symmetry MIVART. Hence **Ra·dially** *adv.*

B. *sb. Anat.* **1.** A radiating segment of a crinoid, between the stem and the brachials 1872. **2.** A radial nerve or artery 1871.

‖**Radiale** (rēⁱdiˌēⁱ·li). *Pl.* **-alia.** 1877. [mod.L., subst. use (sc. *os* bone) of n. of med.L. *radialis*; see prec.] **1.** = prec. B 1. **2.** The carpal bone or element which lies on the radial side of the carpus 1888.

Radian (rēⁱ·diăn). 1879. [f. RADIUS + -AN.] *Trig.* An angle which subtends, at the centre of a circle, an arc whose length is equal to the radius.

Radiance (rēⁱ·diăns). 1601. [f. next; see -ANCE.] **1.** Light shining with diverging rays; hence, brilliant light, vivid brightness, splendour. **b.** Brightness of the eye or look 1748. **2.** = RADIATION 1800.

1. The Son..with r. crown'd Of majesty divine MILT. **b.** Sweet love their looks a gentle r. lends THOMSON. So **Ra·diancy.**

Radiant (rēⁱ·diănt), *a.* and *sb.* 1450. [– L. *radians, -ant-*, pr. pple. of *radiare* emit rays; see -ANT.] **A.** *adj.* **1.** Sending out rays of light; shining brightly. **b.** Represented as sending out rays of light, or having radial projections resembling this. In *Her.* = RAYONNÉ. 1610. **c.** Of the eyes or looks: Bright, beaming with joy or hope 1794. **2.** Issuing or appearing in the form of rays (of light); hence, bright, shining, splendid. Also *transf.* of beauty, etc. 1509. **3.** Moving or operating in a radial manner 1800. **4.** (Chiefly *Bot.*) Extending in a radial manner; having parts so extending 1828. **5.** Characterized by radiation 1825. **6.** *R. point*: **a.** Any point forming a centre from which rays or radii proceed 1726. **b.** *Astron.* The apparent focal point of a meteoric shower. So *r. region.* 1864.

1. On his right The r. image of his Glory sat. His onely Son MILT. **2.** With scintillations, or r. Halo's about their heads SIR T. BROWNE. **3.** *R. heat*: see HEAT *sb.* 2.

B. *sb.* **1.** *Physics.* A point or object from which light or heat radiates 1727. **2.** *Geom.* 'A straight line proceeding from a given point or fixed pole about which it is conceived to revolve' (Brande) 1842. **3.** *Astron.* A radiant point 1864. Hence **Ra·diantly** *adv.*

Radiary (rēⁱ·diări). 1835. [– Fr. *radiaire* or mod.L. *Radiaria* (pl.), f. L. *radius* ray; see -ARY[1].] *Zool.* An animal of the class *Radiaria* (comprising certain Invertebrates).

‖**Radiata** (rēⁱdiˌēⁱ·tă), *sb. pl.* 1828. [mod.L., n. pl. of L. *radiatus*; see next, -ATE[1].] *Zool.* One of the great divisions of the animal kingdom according to Cuvier (now discarded), consisting of animals with radial structure, as sea urchins, sea anemones and polyps.

Radiate (rēⁱ·diět), *a.* (*sb.*) 1668. [– L. *radiatus*, pr. pple. of *radiare*; see next, -ATE[2].] **1.** Having rays proceeding from a centre, or having parts arranged in this manner. **2.** Arranged like rays, diverging from a centre 1822. **3.** = RADIAL *a.* 4. 1859. †**B.** *sb.* A radiate animal; one of the Radiata –1863.

1. *R. crown*; see RADIATED *ppl. a.* 1. *R. flower*, a composite flower-head having radial (usu. ligulate) florets.

Radiate (rēⁱ·diˌeⁱt), *v.* 1619. [– *radiat-*, pa. ppl. stem of L. *radiare* furnish with rays, emit rays, f. *radius* ray; see -ATE[3].] **1.** *intr.* To emit rays (of light or heat); to shine brightly 1649. **b.** *spec.* To transmit electromagnetic waves 1927. **2.** Of light or heat: To issue in rays 1704. **3.** To spread or move in all directions from a centre; to diverge from a central point 1619. **b.** To converge to or towards a centre (*rare*) 1835. **4.** *trans.* To emit (light or heat) in rays 1794. **b.** To spread as from a centre 1821. **c.** To transmit by wireless. **5.** To irradiate (*rare*) 1658.

3. The..valleys that r. from the uplands 1856.

Radiated (rēⁱ·diˌeⁱtėd), *ppl. a.* 1658. [f. prec. + -ED[1].] **1.** Furnished with rays; made or depicted with rays issuing from it, esp. *r. crown.* **2.** Having or consisting of parts arranged like rays or radii 1731. **b.** *spec.* in

Ornith. of the plumage or markings of birds 1781. **3.** = RADIATE *a.* 2. 1748. **4.** = RADIAL *a.* 4. 1798.

Radiation (rēⁱdiˌēⁱ·ʃən). 1570. [– L. *radiatio*; see RADIATE *v.*, -ION. Cf. Fr. *radiation*.] **1.** The action or condition of sending out rays of light. Now *rare*. 1626. **b.** A ray or quantity of light emitted by a radiant body. Usu. *pl.* 1570. **2.** The manner in which the energy of a vibrating body is transmitted in all directions by a surrounding medium; the emission and diffusion of heat-rays; the process by which heat passes from a heated body 1812. **b.** The emission of Röntgen or X rays, or the rays characteristic of radio-active substances 1896. **3.** Divergence from a central point; radial arrangement or structure 1658. **b.** One of a set of radiating things or parts 1843.

Comb.: **r.-fog,** a fog caused by r. of heat on low grounds; **-thermometer,** a thermometer specially adapted for measuring the effects of r.

Radiative (rēⁱ·diětiv), *a.* 1837. [f. RADIATE *v.* + -IVE.] Pertaining to, or connected with, radiation; having the quality of radiating.

Radiato- (rēⁱ·diˌēⁱto), comb. form of RADIATE *a.*, with the meaning 'in a radial direction, in the manner of rays', as *r.-striate*, etc.

Radiator (rēⁱ·diˌeⁱtəɹ). 1836. [f. RADIATE *v.* + -OR 2.] One who or that which radiates; *esp.* anything which radiates light or heat. **b.** A small chamber or compartment heated by means of steam or hot air, and radiating warmth into a room, etc. 1875. **c.** In a motor-car: A device for keeping the engine cool, consisting of tubes having a large radiating surface, through which water circulates 1902.

Radical (ræ·dikăl), *a.* and *sb.* late ME. [– late L. *radicalis* (Augustine), f. L. *radix* root; see -AL¹.] **A.** *adj.* Of or pertaining to a root or to roots. **1.** *R. humour, moisture*: In mediæval philosophy, the moisture naturally inherent in all plants and animals, its presence being a necessary condition of their vitality. **b.** Of qualities: Inherent in the nature or essence of a thing or person; fundamental 1562. **2.** Forming the root, basis, or foundation; original, primary 1560. **3.** Going to the root or origin; thorough; esp. *r. change, cure* 1651. **4.** *Math.* **a.** Pertaining to or forming the root of a number or quantity 1557. **b.** *Geom.* Used in several terms relating to the intersection of circles and planes, esp. *r. axis, centre*, etc. 1848. **5.** *Philol.* Of or belonging to the roots of words; connected with, based on, roots 1577. **b.** *R. letter*: (*a*) an original unchanged letter (so also *r. sound*) 1645; (*b*) a letter belonging to the root of a word 1653. **6.** *Mus.* Belonging to the root of a chord 1753. **7.** *Bot.* Of or belonging to the root of a plant; *esp.* of leaves or stalks: Springing directly from the root-stock or the stem close to the root 1753.

1. b. The r. diversity of these rival maladies 1806. The r. rottenness of human nature 1871. **2.** The r. articles of the French creed of the eighteenth century MORLEY. **3.** *R. reform*, a thorough reform; *esp.* as a phr. of English politics. So *R. reformer* = sense B. 5. **4. a.** *R. sign*, the sign $\surd$ used to indicate a root of the number to which it is prefixed. **5.** *R. word*, a simple uncompounded word having the form of, or directly based on, a root. **6.** By the root of a chord, or its R. Bass, is meant its Bass-note in its original, uninverted form 1873.

B. *sb.* **1.** *Philol.* A root; a word or part of a word which cannot be further analysed 1641. **b.** A radical letter 1652. **2.** A basis, a fundamental thing or principle 1657. **b.** A root or radicle 1850. **3.** *Math.* **a.** A quantity forming or expressed as a root of another quantity 1738. **b.** The radical sign 1780. **4.** *Chem.* An element or atom (*simple r.*), or a group of these (*compound r.*), forming the base of a compound and remaining unaltered during the ordinary chemical reactions to which this is liable 1816. **5.** *Politics.* An advocate of 'radical reform'; one who holds the most advanced views of political reform on democratic lines, and thus belongs to the extreme section of the Liberal party 1802.

1. The Welsh, the Cornish and the Armoric dialects, whose radicals are so much alike 1797. **5.** It is manifest to the Tory that the R. does not see the benefit there is in that which he wishes to destroy H. SPENCER. Hence **Ra·dicalism,** the political views characteristic of Radicals; *transf.* thoroughness of method. **Radica·lity,** r. state or condition; the fact of being r. **Ra·dicalize** *v. trans.* and *intr.* to make or become R. in politics. **Ra·dical-ly** *adv.*, **-ness.**

Radicant (ræ·dikănt), *a. rare.* 1753. [L. *radicans, -ant-*, pr. pple. of *radicare*; see next, -ANT.] *Bot.* Producing roots; usu. said of parts of a plant which produce adventitious roots.

Radicate (ræ·dikeⁱt), *v.* Now *rare.* 1448. [– *radicat-*, pa. ppl. stem of L. *radicare, -ari* strike root, f. *radix, -ic-* root; see -ATE³.] **1.** *trans.* To cause to take root; to plant or establish firmly. Usu. *fig.* with ref. to qualities. †**2.** *intr.* To take root, become established –1681.

1. My regard for you is so radicated and fixed, that it is become part of my mind JOHNSON. Hence **Ra·dicated** *ppl. a.* rooted, established; *esp.* of qualities. **Radica·tion,** the process of taking root; the fact of being rooted, established, etc.; an arrangement or system of roots.

Radicel (ræ·disel). 1819. [– mod.L. *radicella*, dim. of RADIX; see -EL. Cf. Fr. *radicelle*.] *Bot.* A rootlet.

Radici-, comb. f. L. *radix, radic-* RADIX, as in **Ra:diciflo·rous** *a.*, flowering from the root. **Radi·ciform** *a.*, having the form of a root.

Radicle (ræ·dik'l). 1671. [– L. *radicula* RADICULE.] **1.** *Bot.* **a.** That part of the embryo of a plant which develops into the primary root. **b.** A rootlet 1829. **2.** *Anat.* One of the branching subdivisions of veins, nerves, etc. resembling a part of a root 1830. **3.** *Chem.* = RADICAL *sb.* 4. 1857.

Radicular (rădi·kiŭlăɹ), *a.* 1819. [f. next + -AR¹.] **1.** *Bot.* Belonging to the radicle. **2. a.** *Path.* Affecting the roots (of a tooth, nerve, etc.) 1878. **b.** *Anat.* Belonging to the roots of an artery, nerve, etc. 1897.

Radicule (ræ·dikiul). 1814. [– L. *radicula*, dim. of RADIX; see -CULE.] *Bot.* = RADICLE. Hence **Radi·culose** *a.* having radicles.

Radio (rēⁱ·dioᵘ). orig. *U.S.* 1910. [Short for *radio-telegraphy, -telephony*; see next.] Wireless telegraphy or telephony; a message transmitted by these; wireless broadcasting; a wireless receiving-set. Also *attrib.* and *Comb.*, as *r. announcer, r.-communication*, etc. Hence **Ra·dio** *v. trans.* and *intr.* to broadcast by wireless telephony; to send (a message etc.) by wireless telegraphy.

Radio- (rēⁱ·dio), comb. form of RADIUS. **1.** *Anat.* Belonging to the radius in conjunction with some other part, as **Ra:dio-ca·rpal, -mu·scular, -u·lnar** *adjs.* **2.** *Physics.* Connected with rays or radiation, as **Ra:dio-condu·ctor,** part of the receiver of a wireless telegraphy apparatus (usu. a tube containing iron filings), which is converted into a conductor by the impact of the electric waves on the collecting wire; a 'coherer'. **Ra:dio-tele·graphy, -tele·phony,** wireless telegraphy or telephony; so **Ra:dio-te·le·gram,** etc.

Ra:dioa·ctive, *a.* 1900. [f. prec. + ACTIVE.] Capable (as radium) of emitting spontaneously rays consisting of material particles travelling at high velocities; so **Ra:dioacti·vity.**

Radiogram (rēⁱ·diogræm). 1896. [f. as prec. + -GRAM.] **1.** = next 2. **2.** A message transmitted by wireless telegraphy 1907.

Radiograph (rēⁱ·diograf), *sb.* 1881. [f. as prec. + -GRAPH.] **1.** An instrument for measuring and recording the duration and intensity of sunshine. **2.** An impression or image of an object produced on a sensitive plate by means of the Röntgen rays 1896. So **Ra·diograph** *v. trans.* to make a r. of (a thing). **Ra:diogra·phic, -al** *adjs.* relating to radiography; of or connected with wireless telegraphy; **-ly** *adv.* **Radio·graphy,** the production of images on sensitized plates by means of the Röntgen rays.

‖**Radiolaria** (rēⁱ:diŏlēᵊ·riă), *sb. pl.* 1872. [mod.L., f. L. *radiolus*, dim. of RADIUS; see -ARY¹.] *Zool.* A class of rhizopods. Hence **Ra:diola·rian** *a.* of or pertaining to the R.; *sb.* one of the R.

Radiolite (rēⁱ·diolait). 1842. [f. RADIO- + -LITE.] *Palæont.* A cretaceous fossil bivalve of the family *Rudista*.

Radiology (rēⁱdiǫ·lŏdʒi). 1905. [f. RADIO- + -LOGY.] The theory of radioactivity; the method of curing disease, etc. by means of Röntgen rays. So **Radiolo·gical** *a.* **Radio·-logist,** one who operates a Röntgen-ray apparatus.

Radiometer (rēⁱdiˌǫ·mĭtəɹ). 1727. [f. RADIO- + -METER.] †**1.** An instrument formerly used for measuring angles; a cross-staff, fore-staff –1802. **2.** An instrument designed to illustrate the transformation of radiant energy into mechanical force 1875. So **Ra:diomicro·meter,** an instrument for measuring minute degrees of radiation.

Radiophone (rēⁱ·diofōᵘn). 1881. [f. RADIO- + -PHONE.] An instrument for the production of sound by intermittent radiant energy, such as light or heat; the photophone is a special form. So **Radio·phony,** the theory or method of producing sound by radiant light or heat.

Radioscopy (rēⁱdiˌǫ·skŏpi). 1898. [f. as prec. + -SCOPY.] The examination of objects by means of the Röntgen rays.

†**Ra·dious,** *a.* 1500. [– med.L. (also L.) *radiosus*, f. RADIUS; see -OUS. Cf. Fr. *radieux*.] Radiant, bright –1692. **b.** Forming rays of light. BERKELEY.

Radish (ræ·diʃ). [OE. *rædić* (ME. *redich, radich*) – L. *radix, radic-* root; in late ME., *radish* (XV), alt. of this, perh. by blending with Fr. *radis*.] **a.** The fleshy, slightly pungent, root of a cruciferous plant (*Raphanus sativus*), commonly eaten raw as a relish or in salads. **b.** The plant of which this is the root.

Wild r., a field-weed (*R. raphanistrum*), also called *jointed charlock*.

Comb. **r.-fly** (U.S.), a small dipterous insect, *Anthomyia raphani*, whose larvæ burrow in radishes.

Radium (rēⁱ·diŏm). 1900. [f. L. *radius* ray, RADIUS + -IUM.] A highly radioactive metallic element found in minute quantities in combination in pitchblende; its chemical symbol is Ra and atomic weight 226·4.

Radius (rēⁱ·diŏs). *Pl.* **radii** (rēⁱ·diˌəi). 1597. [– L. *radius*.] **1.** A staff, rod, bar, or other straight object. †**a.** The staff of a cross –1742. **b.** *Anat.* The thicker and shorter of the two bones of the forearm in man; also, the corresponding bone of the foreleg in quadrupeds, and of the wing in birds 1615. **2.** A rod, bar, etc., forming one of a set extending in several directions from one point; a wheel-spoke, a radiating part or filament, etc. 1726. **b.** *Bot.* (*a*) The ray or outer whorl of ligulate florets surrounding the disc in a composite flower-head; the border of enlarged petals on a partial umbel; (*b*) a peduncle supporting a partial umbel; (*c*) a medullary ray 1775. **c.** *Ornith.* One of the processes on the barb of a feather, a barbule 1893. **3.** *Math.* A straight line drawn to the circumference of a circle or the surface of a sphere from the centre, all lines so drawn being equal in length 1656. **b.** A radial line of a curve, drawn from a certain point such as the focus to any point on the curve 1836. **c.** Any line in an arrangement of straight lines diverging from a point, and resembling the radii of a circle 1774. **d.** *R. vector*, a variable line drawn to a curve from a fixed point as origin; in astronomy usu. from the sun or a planet round which a satellite revolves 1753. **4.** A circular area of which the extent is measured by the length of the radius of the circle which bounds it 1853. **b.** *spec.* in London, a circle of four miles in all directions from Charing Cross 1889.

Comb.: **r.-bar,** a bar pivoted at one end so that it can move in a circle or arc of a circle, used esp. in the parallel motion of a steam engine.

Radix (rēⁱ·diks). Pl. **radices** (rēⁱ·disīz), **radixes.** 1571. [– L. *radix, radic-* root of a plant.] = ROOT. **1.** *Math.* †**a.** A root of a number –1719. **b.** A number or quantity, etc. which is made the basis of a scale of numeration 1798. **2.** The source or origin; that in which anything originates 1607. †**3.** *Philol.* = ROOT *sb.* III. 2 b. –1771. **4.** *Bot.* The root of a plant 1727.

Radon (rēⁱ·dǫn). 1925. [f. RADIUM, and the termination of ARGON, NEON, XENON.]

Chem. A gaseous radioactive element arising from the disintegration of radium, discovered in 1900. Symbol Rn.

‖**Radula** (ræ·diŭlă). 1877. [L., scraper, f. *radere* scrape; see -ULE.] *Zool.* = ODONTOPHORE. **Ra·dular** *a.* **Ra·duliform** *a.* rasp-like.

Raff[1] (ræf). ME. [perh. of Scand. origin (cf. Sw. *rafs* rubbish, tag-rag). See RIFF-RAFF.] **1.** *Sc.* and *north.* Abundance, plenty; a large number or collection. **2.** Worthless material, trash, rubbish, refuse. Now only *dial.* late ME. **3.** *collect.* The common run (of people); the lowest class 1673. **4.** A low worthless fellow 1785.

Raff[2] (ræf). 1440. [perh. – G. *raf, raff(e,* obs. or dial. ff. *rafe* rafter, beam.] Foreign timber, usu. in the form of deals.

Raffaelesque, var. of **Raphaelesque.**

Raffia (ræ·fiă). Also **rafia.** 1882. [Also RAPHIA; a Malagasy word.] **1.** A palm of the genus *Raphia* 1897. **2.** The soft fibre from the leaves of *Raphia ruffia* and *R. tædigera,* used for tying up plants, cut flowers, etc., embroidering, and plaiting or weaving into baskets, etc. 1882. Also *attrib.*

Raffinose (ræ·finōᵘs). 1881. [f. Fr. *raffiner* refine + -OSE².] *Chem.* A colourless crystalline compound with a sweetish taste found in various substances, as the sugar-beet, etc.

Raffish (ræ·fiʃ), *a.* 1801. [f. RAFF¹ + -ISH¹.] Disreputable, low. **Ra·ffish-ly** *adv.*, **-ness.**

Raffle (ræ·f'l), *sb.*[1] late ME. [– OFr. *raffle,* (also mod) *rafle* (in med.L. *raffla*), of which †*raffe,* †*raphe* were synonyms in the senses 'throw at dice of all three alike', 'clean sweep'; of unkn. origin.] **1.** A game of chance played with three dice, in which the winner was the one who threw the three all alike, or, if none did so, the one who threw the highest pair; also, the throwing of a doublet or triplet in this game. *Obs.* exc. *dial.* **2.** A form of lottery in which an article is assigned by drawing of lots (prop. by casting of dice) to one person of a number who have each paid a certain part of its value 1766.

Raffle (ræ·f'l), *sb.*[2] 1470. [perh. – OFr. *raf(f)le* in phr. *rifle ou rafle* anything whatsoever, *ne rifle ne rafle* nothing at all. See RAFF¹, RIFF-RAFF.] †**1.** A rabble; riff-raff –1670. **2.** Rubbish, refuse 1848. **b.** *Naut.* Lumber, débris, a confused tangle of ropes, canvas, broken spars, etc. 1881.

2. *transf.* The r. of conversation that a man picks up as he passes KIPLING.

Raffle (ræ·f'l), *v.*[1] 1680. [f. RAFFLE *sb.*¹ or – Fr. *rafler* in same sense.] **1.** *intr.* To cast dice, draw lots, etc. *for* something; to take part in a raffle. **2.** *trans.* To dispose of by means of a raffle 1851.

1. Will you please to r. for a tea pot 1389.

Ra·ffle, *v.*[2] *rare.* 1712. [perh. var. of RUFFLE *v.*] *trans.* **a.** To indent, serrate (a leaf). **b.** To crumple 1728. **c.** *dial.* To ruffle 1868.

a. The best examples have all some trifling difference, principally in the raffling of the leaves 1817.

Rafflesia (ræflī·ʒiă, -ī·ziă). 1820. [mod.L., f. name of Sir T. Stamford *Raffles* (1781–1826), British governor in Sumatra; see -IA¹.] *Bot.* A stemless, leafless plant of the order *Cytinaceæ,* found in Java and Sumatra growing as a parasite on the stems of various species of grape-vine, and remarkable for the size of its flowers.

Raft (raft), *sb.*[1] late ME. [– ON. *raptr* rafter, rel. to OHG. *ravo,* ON. *ráfr, ræfr*; cf. RAFTER *sb.*¹] **1.** A beam, spar, rafter. Now only *arch.* **2.** A collection of logs, planks, casks, etc., fastened together in the water for transportation by floating 1497. **3.** A flat structure of logs, inflated skins, etc., for the conveyance or support of persons or things on water 1590. **b.** *Mil.* A floating bridge 1802. **4.** (Chiefly *U.S.*) A large floating mass or accumulation of fallen trees, logs, vegetation, ice, etc. Also, a dense flock of swimming birds. 1718.

attrib. and *Comb.*: **r.-bridge,** a bridge made of a r., or supported by rafts; **-duck,** *U.S.* the scaup or blackhead duck, so called from its flocking closely on the water; **-port,** a square hole cut in the sides of some ships for loading or unloading planks or pieces of timber.

Raft, *sb.*[2], var. of **Raff**².

Raft (raft), *v.* 1706. [f. RAFT *sb.*¹] **1.** *trans.* To transport by water: **a.** in the form of a raft; **b.** on, or by means of, a raft 1766. **2.** To form into a raft or rafts 1745. **3.** To go upon or cross (a river) by means of a raft 1765. **4.** *intr.* To work on or direct a raft 1741.

1. Phr. *To r. off,* to float off (water-casks, or the water in them) from the shore to a ship.

Rafter (ra·ftəɹ), *sb.*[1] [OE. *ræfter* = OS. *rehter,* MLG. *rafter, rachter,* rel. to RAFT *sb.*¹] One of the beams which give slope and form to a roof, and bear the outer covering of slates, tiles, thatch, etc. †**b.** A large beam such as is used for a rafter –1697.

Principal r., a strong beam in a truss, lying under the *common* or *ordinary rafters.*

Rafter (ra·ftəɹ), *sb.*[2] 1809. [f. RAFT *sb.*¹ or *v.* + -ER¹.] One who is employed in rafting timber.

Rafter (ra·ftəɹ), *v.* 1538. [f. RAFTER *sb.*¹] **1.** *trans.* To build or furnish with rafters. **2.** *Agric.* To plough (land), leaving a space between the furrows 1733. **3.** To form into rafters 1846.

Raftsman (ra·ftsmæ̆n). 1776. [f. gen. sing. of RAFT *sb.*¹ + MAN.] One who works on a raft.

Rag (ræg), *sb.*[1] [ME. *ragge,* prob. back-formation from RAGGED *a.* or RAGGY *a.*] **1.** A small worthless fragment or shred of some woven material; *esp.* one of the irregular scraps into which a piece of such material is reduced by wear and tear. **b.** *pl.* Ragged or tattered garments or clothes; freq. in phr. *in rags* ME. **c.** In neg. phrases, etc., the smallest scrap of cloth or clothing 1590. **d.** Similarly, the smallest scrap *of* sail 1653. **e.** In *sing.* without article, as a material 1808. **2.** *transf.* A fragment, scrap, bit, remnant; a torn or irregularly shaped piece 1440. †**b.** Of money. Hence in *Cant,* a farthing. –1700. **3.** Applied contempt. to things, e.g. a torn or scanty garment, a flag, handkerchief, newspaper, etc. 1549. **b.** Similarly applied to persons 1566. **4.** A sharp or ragged projection (*rare*) 1664.

1. Cowles, Hoods and Habits..tost And flutterd into Raggs MILT. **b.** Going in rags through the winter RUSKIN. *fig.* I begin, In virtue cloathed, to cast the rags of sin DRYDEN. **c.** Won't leave him a r. to his back, nor a penny in his pocket 1782. **d.** With every r. of sail set 1804. **2.** Volumes and flying rags of cloud 1873. They have no r. of evidence to uphold them 1893. **b.** *Com. Err.* IV. iv. 89. **3.** Every rubbishy r. now contains the 'news' 1889. **b.** You Witch, you Ragge, you Baggage SHAKS. **4.** File off the rags left by the saw 1872.

attrib. and *Comb.*, as *r.-basket*; *r.-carpet, -doll, -paper,* etc.; *r.-made* adj.; *r.-picker, -seller,* etc.; also, **r.-engine,** a machine for reducing rags to pulp, used in paper-making; **-merchant,** a dealer in rags; **-money** (contempt.), paper-money; **-shop,** a shop for rags and old clothes; **-wool,** wool obtained by tearing rags to pieces.

Rag (ræg), *sb.*[2] ME. [Of unkn. origin, but later assoc. with prec.] **1.** A piece (mass or bed) of hard, coarse or rough stone. *Obs.* exc. *dial.* **b.** A large coarse roofing-slate 1825. **2.** A name for certain kinds of stone, chiefly of a hard coarse texture, and breaking up in flat pieces several inches thick ME.

Rag (ræg), *sb.*[3] *Univ. slang.* 1892. [f. RAG *v.*²] An act of ragging; *esp.* an extensive display of noisy disorderly conduct, carried on in defiance of authority or discipline.

Rag (ræg), *v.*[1] 1440. [f. RAG *sb.*¹] **1.** *trans.* †**a.** To tear in pieces. **b.** To make ragged. †**2.** *intr.* To become ragged (*rare*) –1683.

Rag (ræg), *v.*[2] *dial.* and *slang.* 1796. [Of unkn. origin; cf. BULLYRAG.] **1.** *trans.* **a.** To scold, rate, talk severely to. **b.** To annoy, tease, torment; *spec.* in *Univ. slang,* to assail in a rough or noisy fashion; to create wild disorder in (a room). Also *absol.* 1808. **2.** *intr.* To wrangle *over* a subject 1889.

Rag (ræg), *v.*[3] 1875. [Of unkn. origin.] *trans.* To break up (ore) with a hammer, preparatory to sorting.

Ragabash (ræ·găbæʃ), *sb.* and *a.* *Sc.* and *n. dial.* 1609. [app. f. RAG *sb.*¹, with fanciful ending.] **1.** An idle worthless fellow; a ragamuffin. **2.** *collect.* Rabble, riff-raff 1824. **B.** *adj.* Beggarly 1818.

Ragamuffin (ræ·gămɒfin), *sb.* and *a.* late ME. [prob. f. RAG *sb.*¹, with fanciful ending.] †**1.** The name of a demon. LANGLAND. **2.** A ragged, dirty, disreputable man or boy 1581. **b.** *attrib.* or as *adj.* Rough, beggarly, good-for-nothing, disorderly 1602.

Ra·g-bag. 1861. A bag in which rags or scraps of cloth are collected or stored. **b.** *transf.* and *fig.* A motley collection 1864.

b. The Convention was a r. of dissent LOWELL.

Ra·g-bolt. 1627. [perh. f. RAG *sb.*¹ 4.] A bolt having barbs directed towards the head, so that it cannot be easily withdrawn after it is driven in; a jag-bolt or barb-bolt.

Rage (rēⁱdʒ), *sb.* ME. [–(O)Fr. *rage* :– Rom. **rabia,* for L. *rabies*; see RABIES.] **1.** Madness; insanity; a fit or access of mania. *Obs.* exc. *poet.* **2.** Violent anger, furious passion; a fit or access of such anger; †angry disposition ME. **3.** *transf.* Violent operation or action, 'fury' (of wind, the sea, fire, etc.) ME. **b.** A flood, high tide, sudden rising of the sea. late ME. **4.** A violent feeling, passion, or appetite. Also, violence (*of* a feeling, etc.). late ME. †**b.** Violent desire; sexual passion; heat –1697. **5.** A vehement passion *for,* desire *of,* a thing. Also const. *infin.* and *absol.* 1593. **6.** Poetic or prophetic inspiration; musical excitement 1600. **7.** Martial or high spirit, ardour, fervour, manly enthusiasm or indignation 1591. **8.** Excitement or violence *of* an action, operation, etc.; also, the acutest point or heat of this 1593.

1. *Com. Err.* IV. iii. 88. **2.** [The horse] swalloweth the ground with fiercenesse and r. *Job* 39:24. His green Eyes, that sparkled with his R. DRYDEN. **3.** Bodies..exposed to the Sunnes fiery r. 1634. **4.** The present r. of your sorrow 1691. In the R. of the Distemper STEELE. **b.** *Haml.* III. iii. 89. **5.** The earth-consuming r. Of gold and blood SHELLEY. Phr. (*All*) *the r.,* said of the object of a widespread and usu. temporary enthusiasm. **7.** The soldiers shout around with generous r. DRYDEN. **8.** Great carnage did..ever attend the first r. of conquest BURKE.

Rage (rēⁱdʒ), *v.* ME. [– (O)Fr. *rager,* f. *rage* (see prec.).] †**1.** *intr.* To go mad; to be mad; to act madly or foolishly –1567. **2.** To show signs of madness or frenzy; to rave; to act or speak wildly or furiously; to storm; *Sc.* to scold. Also, to be full of anger ME. †**3.** To behave wantonly or riotously; to take one's pleasure. Const. *with* (a person), *in* (an action, practice, etc.). –1645. **4.** *transf.* of things (e.g. wind, the sea, etc.): To be violent and boisterous; to move or rush furiously 1535. **b.** Of passions, feelings, etc.: To have or reach a high degree of intensity 1583. **c.** Of a storm, battle, etc.: To have course without check or with fatal effect; to be at the height 1667. **d.** Of a disease or pain: To be violent. Also *transf.* 1602. **5.** To be widely prevalent, or to spread widely, in a violent or virulent form 1563. **6.** To act with fury, ardour, or vehemence; to move furiously *over* (a place), or *about* 1593. †**7.** To be violently bent *upon,* to be furiously eager *to* (with inf.), to be impatient *for. rare.* –1671. **8.** *trans.* (in *pa. pple.*) To enrage. SHAKS.

2. Whereat hee inlie rag'd MILT. I raged against the public liar TENNYSON. **4.** Come vp ye horses, and r. yee charets *Jer.* 46:9. R. on, ye elements! WORDSW. **b.** The passion for play raged in him without measure MACAULAY. **c.** The gale..raged above our heads 1871. **d.** Some fever rages in thy blood 1611. **5.** Sickness..raged throughout the camp 1893. **6.** Why stand we..heere, Wayling our losses, while the Foe doth R. SHAKS.

Rageful (rēⁱ·dʒfŭl), *a.* 1580. [f. RAGE *sb.* + -FUL.] †**1.** Mad, frantic, frenzied –1635. **2.** Full of furious anger 1580. **3.** *transf.* of things: Full of furious activity 1597.

2. With ragefull eyes shee bad him defend himselfe SIDNEY. **3.** Ragefull windes 1619. Hence **Ra·gefully** *adv.*

Rag-fair. 1722. [f. RAG *sb.*¹ + FAIR *sb.*¹] A market for the sale of old clothes, held at Houndsditch in London. Also *attrib.*

Ragged (ræ·gĕd), *a.* ME. [– ON. *rǫggvaðr* tufted (cf. Norw. *raggct* shaggy); see RAG *sb.*¹] **I. 1.** Of animals, their fur, etc.: Rough, shaggy, hanging in tufts. **2.** Of a rough, irregular, or straggling form; having a broken jagged outline or surface; full of rough or sharp projections. late ME. **3.** *transf.* of immaterial things: **a.** Faulty, imperfect, irregular 1500. **b.** Of sounds; Harsh, discordant, rough 1600.

1. What Shepherd owns those r. Sheep? DRY-

DEN. **2.** Herne the Hunter..with great rag'd-hornes SHAKS. Yon r. cliff COLLINS. A r. thorn COWPER. The thick r. skirts Of the victorious darkness SHELLEY. **3. a.** My r. rhimes QUARLES. **b.** My voice is r.; I know I cannot please you SHAKS.

II. 1. Of cloth, garments, etc.: Rent, torn, frayed, in rags ME. **2.** Of persons: Wearing ragged clothes; dressed in rags. Hence of appearance, etc. late ME.

1. He draws back the r. curtain DICKENS. **2.** A swarm of dirty and r. plebeians GIBBON.

Comb.: **r. hip,** in a horse: a hip standing away from the backbone; **R. Robert,** *Geranium robertianum*; **r. school,** a free school for children of the poorest class. Hence **Ra·gged-ly** *adv.*, **-ness.**

Ragged Robin. 1741. [See ROBIN.] A pop. name of a well-known English flower, *Lychnis floscuculi*. Also *attrib.*

Ragged staff. 1449. [RAGGED *a.* I. 2.] A staff with projecting stumps or knobs; chiefly in ref. to the badge or crest of the Earls of Warwick.

Old Neuils Crest, The rampant Beare chain'd to the ragged staffe SHAKS.

Raggle-taggle, *a.* Extended form of RAG-TAG, used *attrib.*

Raggy (ræ·gi), *a.* [OE. *racgiġ* 'setosus' (cf. Sw. *raggig* shaggy), f. **racg-* – ON. *rǫgg* (**raggw-*) tuft or strip of fur (cf. Norw., Sw. *ragg* rough hair); of unkn. origin. Cf. RAGGED *a.*] = RAGGED *a.*

Raglan (ræ·glăn). 1864. [f. name of Lord *Raglan*, the British commander in the Crimean war.] An overcoat without shoulder seams, the sleeve going right up to the neck. Also *attrib.*

Ragman[1] (ræ·gmæ̆n). late ME. [f. RAG *sb.*[1] + MAN.] †**1.** A name given to the Devil, or one of the devils –1600. **2.** A rag-gatherer, rag-dealer 1586.

†**Ra·gman**[2]. ME. [Earliest form *rageman* (three syll., as in AL. *ragemannus* XIV) later *ragman* (two syll.) XIV; of unkn. origin.] **1.** The name given to a statute of 4 Edw. 1, and to certain articles of inquisition associated with proceedings of *Quo warranto* under this statute. **2.** A roll, list, catalogue –1460. **3.** A document (contract, agreement, indenture, etc.) with seals attached –1470.

Ragman('s) roll. *Obs.* exc. *Hist.* 1523. [f. prec. + ROLL.] †**1.** RAGMAN 2. –1610. **2.** A set of rolls, now in the Public Record Office in which are recorded the instruments of homage made to Edw. I by the Scottish King (Balliol), nobles, etc., in 1296. 1710.

Ragout (rĕgū·), *sb.* 1664. [– Fr. *ragoût*, f. *ragoûter* revive the taste of, f. GOÛT.] **1.** A dish of meat cut in small pieces, stewed with vegetables and highly seasoned. **b.** *transf.* or *fig.* 1672. †**2.** A sauce or relish –1750.

Ragout (rægū·), *v.* 1710. [f. prec.] **1.** *trans.* To make a ragout of, to stew with highly flavoured seasoning. †**2.** *transf.* To give piquancy or variety to –1753.

1. To r. a Leg of Mutton 1756.

Ra·gstone. ME. [f. RAG *sb.*[2]] = RAG *sb.*[2] 1, 2.

Rag-tag (ræ·g,tæg). 1820. [f. RAG *sb.*[1] + TAG *sb.*[1]; for older TAG-RAG.] **1. a.** *collect.* The raff or rabble of the community. **b.** One of the individuals forming this class. 1879. **2.** *Rag-tag* (or *rag, tag*) *and bob-tail* = 1 a. Also *transf.*; sometimes = 'the whole lot'. 1820.

Ra·g-time. Orig. *U.S.* 1901. Music in which there is frequent syncopation, as in many Negro melodies. Also *attrib.*

Raguly (ræ·giŭli), *a.* 1658. [perh. based on RAGGED *a.* I. 2 (see also RAGGED STAFF), after *nebuly* (see NEBULÉ); see -Y[5].] *Her.* Of a cross or other bearing. Having short oblique projections resembling the stumps of branches cut off close to the stem. Hence of a division between parts of the field: Having alternate projections and depressions like a battlement, but set obliquely.

Ra·gweed. 1658. [f. RAG *sb.*[1] + WEED *sb.*[1]; see RAGWORT.] **1.** = RAGWORT. **2.** *U.S.* A plant belonging to the genus *Ambrosia*, esp. *A. trifida* and *A. artemisiæfolia* 1866.

Ra·g-wheel. 1829. [f. RAG *sb.*[1]] **1.** A wheel having projections which catch into the links of a chain passing over it, as in a chain-pump; a sprocket-wheel. **2.** A polishing wheel composed of rags 1884.

Ra·gwork. 1840. [f. RAG *sb.*[2]] Masonry composed of flattish pieces of ragstone, having an undressed surface.

Ra·gworm. 1865. [f. RAG *sb.*[1]] A sand-worm (*Nephthys cæca*) of the British coasts, also called *white-rag worm* and *lurg.*

Ra·gwort. 1450. [f. RAG *sb.*[1] + WORT[1], in ref. to the ragged form of the leaves.] The pop. name of several species of the genus *Senecio*, esp. the Common Ragwort, *S. jacobæa.*

‖**Raia** (rēi·ă). Also **raja.** 1633. [L. *raia* (pl. *raiæ*).] *Zool.* = RAY *sb.*[2]

Raid (rēid), *sb.* late ME. [Sc. f. OE. *rād* ROAD, revived by Scott, and subseq. extended in meaning.] **1.** A military expedition on horseback; a predatory excursion, prop. of mounted men; a foray, INROAD. **2.** *transf.* and *fig.* **a.** An invading troop, as of raiders 1826. **b.** A rush 1861. **c.** A sudden or vigorous descent, onset, or attack *upon* something to be seized, suppressed, or destroyed 1873. †**3.** A roadstead for ships –1636.

1. The Scottis maid dywerse incurtiouns and raidis in Ingland 1578. **2. b.** A rapid r. into some of the nearest shops, for things remembered at the last moment 1877. **c.** A general r. upon Protestant literature all over France 1873.

Raid (rēid), *v.* 1824. [f. prec.] **1.** *intr.* To go upon, or take part in a raid. **b.** *Stock Exchange*, etc. To act so as to depress prices or create uncertainty as to values 1889. **2.** *trans.* To make a raid on (a place, person, cattle, etc.) 1880.

2. Phr. *To r. the market*: see 1 b. Hence **Rai·der,** one who raids.

†**Rail,** *sb.*[1] [OE. *hræġ(e)l* = OFris. *(h)reil*, OHG. *(h)regil*, of unkn. origin.] **1.** A garment, dress –1552. **2.** A neckerchief formerly worn by women. See also NIGHT-RAIL. –1710.

Rail (rēil), *sb.*[2] [ME. *reyle, raile* – OFr. *reille* iron rod :– L. *regula* staff, rod, RULE.] **1.** A bar of wood, fixed in a horizontal position for hanging things on, etc., as *hat-, towel-r.* **b.** Used to support vines or other plants. late ME. **c.** Forming part of the sides of a cart 1530. **2.** A horizontal bar of wood or metal, fixed upon upright supports (posts) as part of a fence. (In *pl.* freq. = b.) 1464. **b.** A continuous series of bars forming the horizontal part of a fence; hence, a fence or railing, whether constructed of posts and rails, or of some other form 1541. **c.** The HAND-RAIL of a stair 1453. **d.** An altar-rail 1641. **e.** *Naut.* (*pl.*) Narrow pieces of wood nailed for ornament on parts of a ship's upper works 1750. **3.** *Carpentry.* One of the horizontal pieces in a door or other frame-work 1678. **4.** A bar or continuous line of bars (now usu. of iron or steel) laid on or near the ground (commonly in pairs) to bear and guide the wheels of a vehicle, and enable them to run more easily 1598. **5.** = RAILWAY, now chiefly in phr. *by r.* 1843. **b.** On the Stock Exchange in *pl.* = railway shares 1893.

4. Phr. *Off the rails* (freq. *fig.* = out of the proper or normal condition; morally or mentally astray).

attrib. and *Comb.* **a.** In senses 1 and 2, as *r.-fence* (U.S.), *-post, -splitter* (U.S.), etc.; **r.-bird,** the American spotted cuckoo. **b.** In sense 4, in many recent compounds, as *r.-chair, -joint, -layer, -mill,* etc. **c.** In sense 5, as *r.-head, track,* etc. **r.-motor** *a.* pertaining to motor vehicles running on a rail-way.

Rail (rēil), *sb.*[3] 1450. [– Norman-Picard *raille* :– Rom. **rasc(u)la*, perh. of imit. origin.] A bird of the family *Rallidæ* and esp. of the genus *Rallus*: see LANDRAIL, WATER-RAIL.

Rail (rēil), *sb.*[4] *rare.* 1529. [f. RAIL *v.*[4]] An act of railing or reviling.

Rail (rēil), *v.*[1] *Obs.* exc. *Sc.* ME. [– OFr. *reiller* :– L. *regulare*, f. *regula* RAIL *sb.*[2]] †**1.** *trans.* To set in order or array; to arrange; to regulate –1530. †**b.** To tie or fasten in a string or row (*rare*) –1634. **2.** To array, adorn, set (*with* something) ME.

1. b. Whiche rebelles were brought..to London railed in ropes like horses drawyng in a carte 1548.

Rail (rēil), *v.*[2] late ME. [f. RAIL *sb.*[2]] **1.** *trans.* To furnish or enclose (a place) with rails. **2.** To provide (a hedge, bench, etc.) with a rail or rails. Also with *about, in. rare.* 1577. **3.** To lay with rails 1888. **4.** To convey by rail 1865. **5.** *intr.* To travel by rail 1842.

1. *To r. in*, to enclose (a space or thing) with rails; A space was railed in for the reception of the..jurors 1802. *To r. off*, to separate by a railing.

†**Rail,** *v.*[3] ME. [Of unkn. origin.] *intr.* To flow, gush (*down*) –1600.

A tempest railed downe her cheecks amaine 1600.

Rail (rēil), *v.*[4] 1460. [– Fr. *railler*, †*ragler* – Pr. *ralhar* jest :– Rom. **ragulare*, f. **ragere* roar, bray, neigh, crossing of L. *rugire* bellow with Rom. **bragere* BRAY. Cf. RALLY *v.*[2]] **1.** *intr.* To utter abusive language. †**2.** To jest, to rally. Also const. *with.* –1685. **3.** *trans.* To bring (a person) *into* a certain condition by railing. Also rarely with a thing as obj. in other constructions. 1596.

1. To see you r. and rage at the rate you do BERKELEY. Don't r. against the women MISS BRADDON. **3.** I shal sooner rayle thee into wit and holiness SHAKS.

Railing (rēi·liŋ), *vbl. sb.* 1471. [f. RAIL *v.*[2]] **1.** The action of making fences or enclosing ground with rails. Also *railing-in.* 1543. **b.** *concr.* (also in *pl.*) A fence or barrier made of rails or in some other fashion 1471. **c.** Material for railings 1812. **2.** The laying of rails; a set or line of rails 1624.

Railing (rēi·liŋ), *ppl. a.* 1526. [f. RAIL *v.*[4] + -ING[2].] That rails; characterized by railing.

The r. Eloquence of Cicero in his Philipics DRYDEN. Hence **Rai·lingly** *adv.* in a r. manner.

Raillery (rēi·ləri). 1653. [– Fr. *raillerie*, f. *railler*; see RAIL, *v.*[4], RALLY *v.*[2], -ERY. A var. †*rallery* (XVII–XVIII) is repr. by the pronunc. (ræ·leri) still used by some (esp. U.S.) speakers.] Good-humoured ridicule, banter. **b.** With *a* and *pl.* An instance of this 1654.

By saying this of others, I expose my self to some R. COWLEY. **b.** There is a shocking familiarity both in his railleries and civilities ADDISON.

†‖**Railleur** (rayŏr). 1667. [Fr., f. *railler*; see prec.] One who practises raillery –1751.

Railroad (rēi·lroud). (Now chiefly *U.S.*) 1775. [f. RAIL *sb.*[2] 4.] = next. Hence **Rai·l-road** *v. trans.* (*U.S.*) to rush (a person or thing) *to* or *into* a place, *through* a process 1884. **Rai·lroading** *vbl. sb.* travelling by rail; the business of making or working rail-roads.

Railway (rēi·lwei), *sb.* 1756. [f. RAIL *sb.*[2] 4 + WAY.] **1.** A way or road laid with rails (orig. of wood, subseq. of iron or steel), on which the wheels of wagons containing heavy goods are made to run for ease of transport; also the way composed of rails thus laid. **2.** *spec.* A line or track consisting of iron or steel rails, on which carriages or wagons conveying passengers or goods are moved by a loco-motive engine. Hence also, the whole organization necessary for the working of this, and the company of persons owning or managing it. 1832.

attrib. and *Comb.*, as *r. accident, engine, man, station, train,* etc.; **r. novel,** a light novel, suitable for reading on a r. journey; **r. rug,** a rug used for warmth on a r. journey; **-spine,** an affection of the spine produced by concussion in a r. accident. Hence **Rai·lway** *v. intr.* to make railways; to travel by rail; *trans.* to supply with railways.

Raiment (rēi·mĕnt). 1440. [aphet. f. ARRAY-MENT; cf. RAY *v.*[2]] Clothing, clothes, dress, apparel. Now *rhet.* †**b.** With *a* and *pl.* A garment, a dress –1665.

The white r. destined to the saints CARY.

Rain (rēin), *sb.* [OE. *reġn, rēn* = OFris. *rein*, OS., OHG. *regan* (Du., G. *regen*), ON. *regn*, Goth. *rign.*] **1.** The condensed vapour of the atmosphere, falling in drops large enough to attain a sensible velocity; the fall of such drops. **2.** *pl.* Showers of rain; rainfalls OE. **b.** In India, the rainy season 1616. **c.** *Naut.* A part of the Atlantic ocean, in which rain is frequent 1727. **3.** With indef. article: †**a.** A shower of rain –1597. **b.** A (specified) kind of rain (or shower) 1699. **4.** *transf.* The descent of liquid or solid particles or bodies falling in the manner of rain; the collective particles or bodies thus falling. Also *fig.* late ME. **b.** *spec.* A composition used in rockets, producing a shower of bright-coloured sparks 1749.

1. We may fairly expect the formation of rain to be preceded by that of cloud HUXLEY. **2. b.** One rains he died 1895. **3. b.** Set off in a mizzling r. 1853.

Comb.: **r.-band,** a dark band in the solar spectrum, caused by the presence of water-vapour in the atmosphere; **-cap, -coat,** etc. worn as a protection against rain; **-gauge,** an instrument measuring the amount of the rainfall; **-glass,** a barometer; **-goose,** the red-throated diver (*Colymbus septentrionalis*); **-map,** a map showing the distribution of the rainfall over a certain area; **-mark, -pit,** an indentation made in the ground by a raindrop; **-quail,** the Indian and African quail (*Coturnix coromandelicus*), abundant in some parts of India during the rainy season; **-wash,** the effect of rain in washing away earth, etc.; also, the matter thus washed away; **-worm,** the common earthworm. Hence **Rai·nless** *a.* destitute of rain.

Rain (rēin), *v.* [OE. *reġnian* (rare), f. *reġn*; see prec.] **I.** *intr.* **1.** *It rains*: Rain falls ME. **2.** Of the Deity, the sky, clouds, etc.: To send or pour down rain OE. **3.** Of rain: To fall ME. **b.** Of tears, immaterial things, etc.: To descend, fall, come, etc. like rain. late ME. **4.** *It rains in*: Rain enters or penetrates. Also *transf.* with other subjects. 1596.

1. It rained very hard DAMPIER. *Prov.* It never rains but it pours. **2.** Heavily the low sky raining Over tower'd Camelot TENNYSON. *fig.* To raine vpon Remembrance with mine Eyes, That it may grow SHAKS. **3.** The raine it raineth every day SHAKS. **b.** Manna also y[t] in desert reynyde 1450. As from a giant's flail, The large blows rain'd TENNYSON.

II. *trans.* **1.** *It rains*: There is a shower of (something falling from above) ME. **2.** To pour down (something falling through the air like rain) ME. **b.** To shed (tears) copiously 1588. **c.** *fig.* To pour down ME. **3.** To bring into a specified condition by raining ME.

1. It rayned fyre and brymstone from heauen COVERDALE *Luke* 17:29. *fig. Ant. & Cl.* III. xiii. 85. *To r. cats and dogs* (colloq.): to r. very heavily. **2.** He rained shells and redhot bullets on the city MACAULAY. **b.** His eyes r. tears JOWETT. **c.** Ladies, whose bright eies R. influence MILT.

Ra·in-bird. 1555. [f. RAIN *sb.* + BIRD.] **1.** The green woodpecker, *Gecinus viridis*. **2.** A Jamaican cuckoo 1725.

Rainbow (rēi·nbou), *sb.* [OE. *reġnboga* = OHG. *reginbogo*, ON. *regnbogi*; see BOW *sb.*[1]] **1.** A bow or arch exhibiting the prismatic colours in their order, formed in the sky opposite the sun by the reflection, double refraction, and dispersion of the sun's rays in falling drops of rain. Also, a similar arch formed in the spray of cataracts, etc. **2.** *transf.* A brightly coloured arch, ring, etc. resembling a rainbow 1715. **3.** Short for *r.-trout* 1897.

1. I was beaten..into all the colours of the Rainebow SHAKS. *fig.* (cf. *Gen.* 9:13–16) A new r. of hope 1876. *Lunar r.*, one formed by the moon's rays, rarely seen. *Marine* or *sea r.*, one formed on sea spray. *Secondary* or *supernumerary r.*, a fainter one formed inside or outside the primary by double reflection and double refraction, and exhibiting the spectrum colours in the opposite order to that of the primary. **2.** The peacock sends his heavenly dyes, His rainbows and his starry eyes COWPER.

Comb.: **r. trout,** a Californian species of trout, *Salmo irideus*; **r. wrasse,** a brilliantly coloured labroid fish (*Julis vulgaris* or *Coris julis*). Hence **Rai·nbow** *v. trans.* to brighten or span with, or as with, a rainbow; to produce like a rainbow.

Rai·ndrop, ra·in-drop. [OE. *reġndropa*; see DROP *sb.*] **1.** A single drop of rain. **2.** The dropping of rain or rain-water. *rare.* late ME.

Rai·nfall. 1848. [f. RAIN *sb.* + FALL *sb.*] **1.** A fall or shower of rain. **2.** The quantity of rain falling in a certain time within a given area, usu. estimated by inches (in depth) per annum 1854.

2. There is one arid region, with a normal r. of less than fifteen inches 1880.

†**Rai·n-fowl.** 1440. **1. a.** = RAIN-BIRD 1. –1769. **b.** The Mistletoe Thrush –1817. **2.** = RAIN-BIRD 2. –1694.

Rai·n-wa:ter. [OE. *reġnwæter* = MHG. *regenwazzer*, ON. *regnvatn*.] Water that falls from the clouds as rain. Also *attrib.*

Rainy (rēi·ni), *a.* OE. [f. RAIN *sb.* + -Y[1].] **1.** Of weather or climate: Characterized by rain. **2.** Of periods of time: During or within which rain is falling, or usually falls OE. **b.** fig. *A r. day*: a time of need 1580. **3.** Of places: In which it rains or is raining; subject to rain. late ME. **b.** Of an action: Done in the rain. SHAKS. **4.** Of clouds, mist, etc.: Bringing rain; laden with rain; of the nature of or connected with rain. late ME. **b.** *fig.* Of the eyes: Tearful 1563.

2. The r. season came on DE FOE. **b.** In the Time of Plenty, they lay up for a Rainy-day 1677. Hence **Rai·nily** *adv.* **Rai·niness.**

Raisable (rēi·zăb'l), *a.* Also **-eable.** 1644. [f. RAISE *v.* + -ABLE.] Capable of being raised.

Raise (rēiz), *sb.*[1] 1538. [f. RAISE *v.*] †**1.** The act of raising; elevation –1626. **2.** A rising passage or road 1877. **3.** An increase in amount 1891.

Raise (rēiz), *sb.*[2] *n. dial.* 1695. [– ON. *hreysi* cairn.] A pile of stones, a cairn. (Freq. in place-names.)

Raise (rēiz), *v.* ME. [– ON. *reisa* = OE. *rǣran* REAR *v.*] **I.** To set upright; to make to stand up. **1.** *trans.* To set (a thing) on end; to restore (a fallen thing) to its usual position. Also *fig.* **b.** *spec.* To set up (paste, crust) without the support of a dish 1594. **2.** To lift (a person or animal) and place in a standing posture; to assist (one) to rise from the ground, etc. ME. **b.** *refl.* To rise, get up ME. **3.** *trans.* To restore (a dead person or animal) to life ME. **4.** To cause (a person or animal) to rise or stand up: †**a.** To make (one) waken or get out of bed ME. **b.** To rouse (a beast or bird) from a lair, retreat, or covert. late ME. **c.** To cause or compel (a person) to rise from a seat 1460. **5.** To rouse (a number of persons, a district, etc.) for the purpose of common action, esp. for attack or defence. late ME. **b.** To stir up, incite, instigate (one or more persons) *to* do something or *to* some feeling 1581. **6.** To rouse up, to give vigour to (the mind, spirit, etc.); to animate, stimulate. late ME. †**b.** To inspire (a person) *with* courage, hope, etc. –1697. **7.** *To r. the wind*: To cause the wind to blow ME.; hence *fig.* (with ref. to wind as a motive power), to procure money or necessary means 1789.

1. Stones of power By Druids raised in magic hour SCOTT. **b.** Miss Liddy can dance a Jig, r. Paste STEELE. **2.** If you fall you shall nat be reysed for me 1530. **3.** God was able to r. him from the dead 1770. **4. a.** Raising the people at midnight 1781. **b.** This being effected, they r. the Bear 1607. **5.** Danvers undertook to r. the City MACAULAY. **b.** That fixt mind And high disdain.. That with the mightiest rais'd me to contend MILT. **6.** His spirits being a little raised with the dram I had given him, he was very cheerful DE FOE.

II. To build up, construct, create, produce, etc. **1.** To lift up and put in position the parts of (a structure); to construct by piling up, building, or fitting together; *spec.* in *U.S.*, to set up the wooden framework of (a house or other building) ME. †**b.** To found, build up (a scheme, plan, description, etc.) –1802. **c.** To form (a small projection or elevation), to cause (a blister, etc.) to rise or form 1551. **2.** To bring into existence, to produce, beget (offspring). Now *rare.* ME. **b.** To produce a supply of (persons of a certain class); to breed (animals) 1601. **3.** To foster, rear, bring up (a person). Now chiefly *U.S.* 1744. **b.** To rear or bring up (animals) 1767. **c.** To promote the growth of (plants), to grow (fruit, vegetables, flowers, etc.) 1669. **4.** To cause (a person of specified character) to come into existence or appear. late ME. **5.** To produce, bring into existence or action (various natural phenomena or forces; also *fig.*) late ME. **6.** To utter (a cry, etc.) with loud voice; to produce (a loud noise) by shouting or otherwise ME. **b.** Hence simply, to utter or produce (a sound) 1590. **c.** To sing; also, to strike up 1653. **7.** To cause, originate, give rise to, bring about, set going ME. **8. a.** *Law.* To draw up (a letter, summons, etc.), institute (an action or suit), establish (a use) 1632. **b.** To bring up (a question, point, etc.); to bring forward (a difficulty, objection, etc.); to advance (a claim) 1647.

1. Of Parian Stone a Temple will I r. DRYDEN. **2.** God..from him will r. A mightie Nation MILT. **b.** From this one, this single ewe, Full fifty comely sheep I raised WORDSW. **3.** I was raised.. among the mountains of the north 1817. **4.** Thi Lord God schal reise a prophete of thi folk WYCLIF *Deut.* 18:15. Her gentleness had never raised her an enemy H. WALPOLE. **5.** To r. a storm in a tea-cup 1884. **6. b.** He rais'd a sigh SHAKS. **c.** An old negro..who raised a hymn 1856. **7.** A groundless Report that has been raised, to a Gentleman's Disadvantage ADDISON. Liberty.. Shall r. no feuds for armies to suppress COWPER. Such manures as r. a fermentation 1765. **8.** A use could not be raised without a sufficient consideration BLACKSTONE.

III. To remove to a higher position. **1.** To lift as a whole, to put or take higher, to elevate. Also, to hoist (sail, etc.) ME. **b.** *spec.* To draw or bring up (water, minerals, etc.) to the surface of the ground 1745. **c.** To turn (the eyes or look) upwards. late ME. **2.** *fig.* To promote or advance (a person, people, etc.) to a higher rank, office, or position; to exalt in dignity or power ME. **b.** To exalt (one's name, state, etc.). *rare.* late ME. **c.** To extol, laud (*rare*) 1631. **3.** *fig.* To elevate (persons) to a higher moral or mental condition ME. **b.** To elevate (the thoughts, mind, etc.) ME. **c.** To elevate (a subject, style, diction) 1668. **4.** To cause (a spirit) to appear, esp. by means of incantations ME. **5.** To make (the voice) heard. late ME. **6.** To cause (dust, vapour, smoke, water, etc.) to ascend or rise; to send or force up, to stir up. late ME. **7.** *Naut.* **a.** To come in sight of (another ship, land, a whale, etc.) 1556. **b.** To give a higher appearance to (a ship, etc.) by coming nearer 1574. **8.** To levy (a tax, etc.); to collect (rents or other charges); hence, to bring together, obtain, procure by means of collecting or in any other way ME. **b.** *transf.* To obtain, procure (advantage, pleasure, praise, etc.) 1633. **c.** To succeed in producing 1841. **9.** To levy, collect, gather, bring together (an army, troops, etc.). late ME. **10.** To put an end to (a siege or blockade) by withdrawing the investing forces. late ME. **b.** To remove, rescind (a prohibition, etc.) 1887. **11.** To end (a siege, etc.) by compelling the investing forces to desist or remove 1489. **12.** To set in motion (an army or camp) 1470.

1. Then will I r. aloft the Milke-white-Rose SHAKS. **c.** I reiside myn iȝen to the hillis WYCLIF *Ps.* 120:1. **2. c.** Fame that her high worth to r. Seem'd erst so lavish MILT. **3. b.** What in me is dark Illumine, what is low r. and support MILT. **4.** Phr. *To r. the Devil, Cain, the mischief*, to create trouble, uproar, or confusion. **5.** Not a voice was raised in opposition 1868. **6.** They doe nothing else but r. a dust 1581. **7. a.** The last of June we raised the Antarticke Pole SIR T. HERBERT. **b.** In going to the North, you doe rayse the Pole, and lay the Equinoctiall 1574. **8.** The difficulty of raising Mony, for the necessary uses of the Common-wealth HOBBES. **11.** He is besieg'd, the Siege that came to r. DRAYTON.

IV. 1. To increase in height or bulk; to cause to rise up or swell; to give a higher level to 1450. **2.** *techn.* **a.** To bring up (the nap of cloth) by carding with teazles, etc.; to make a nap on (cloth) 1481. **b.** To cause (dough, bread) to expand and become light, as by the use of yeast. Also *absol.* late ME. **c.** To give (metal), a rounded form 1846. **3.** To increase the amount of, to heighten (rent, taxes, prices, etc.) 1500. **b.** To increase, add to (one's reputation, interest, credit, etc.) 1654. **c.** *Math.* To increase (a number or quantity) by multiplication into itself 1706. **4.** To increase the value, price, or rate of 1535. **5.** To increase the degree, intensity, or force of (the voice, sensations, colours, the pulse, etc.) 1638.

3. This making of Christians will r. the price of Hogs SHAKS. **4.** *To raise the market*, to charge a higher price.

†**V.** *intr.* To rise, in various senses –1761.

Raised (rēizd), *ppl. a.* 1582. [f. RAISE *v.* + -ED[1].] In various senses of RAISE *v.*

R. pie, a pie having a 'raised' crust (see prec. I. 1 b). *R. beach*, a former beach, now situated above sea-level. *R. upon* (*Naut.*), having a framework added to increase the height of the sides.

Raisin (rēi·z'n). ME. [– (O)Fr. *raisin* grape :– Rom. **racimus* for L. *racēmus* cluster of grapes (see RACEME).] †**1.** A cluster of grapes; a grape –1669. **2.** A grape partially dried, either in the sun or artificially. (Chiefly *pl.*) ME. **b.** *Raisins of the sun*, sun-dried grapes 1544.

Raising (rēi·ziŋ), *vbl. sb.* ME. [f. RAISE *v.* + -ING[1].] **1.** The action of RAISE *v.*; *spec.* in *Curling*, driving a partner's stone into one of the circles round the tee. **b.** With *a* and *pl.* An instance of this; *spec.* in *U.S.*, a house-raising. late ME. **2.** Anything that is raised; a raised place 1572. **3.** A crop raised 1869.

Comb.: **r.-bee** (*U.S.*), a gathering of neighbours to give assistance in raising the framework of a house, etc.; **-hammer,** a hammer used in giving metal a rounded form; **-room,** a room where cloth is raised.

Rai·sing-piece. 1548. [f. RASEN, assoc. with prec.] A wall-plate. So **Rai·sing-plate.**

‖**Raison d'être** (rę̄zoṅ dę̄tr). 1867. [Fr.] Rational ground for existence.

‖**Raisonné** (rę̄zone), *a.* 1777. [Fr., pa. pple. of *raisonner* to reason, f. *raison* REASON.] Reasoned out, logical or systematical.
Catalogue r., a catalogue (of books, pictures, etc.) arranged according to subjects, and giving information beyond mere names or titles.

‖**Raj** (rādʒ). 1800. [Hindi *rāj* reign; cf. next.] Sovereignty, rule; kingdom.

Raja, rajah (rā·dʒă). 1555. [– (prob. through Pg. *raja*) Hindi *rājā* :– Skr. *rājan* king, etc., cogn. with L. *rex, reg-*, OIr. *rī, rīg* king. See RICH.] Orig. the title given in India to a king or prince; later extended to petty chiefs or dignitaries (as Zemindars) or conferred as a title of nobility on Hindus, and adopted as the usual designation of Malay and Javanese rulers or chiefs. Hence **Ra·jahship,** the territory, rank, or power of a r.; also as a title.

‖**Rajpoot, rajput** (rā·dʒpūt). 1598. [Hindi *rājpūt*, f. Skr. *rājan* king (see prec.) + *putrá* son.] A member of a Hindu tribe or class, claiming descent from the original Kshatriyas and distinguished by its military spirit.

Rake (rēɪk), *sb.*[1] [OE. *raca, racu* = MLG., MDu. *rāke* (Du. *raak*), rel. to Goth. *uf/rakjan* stretch out, and by gradation to MLG., MDu. *rēke* (Du. *reek*), OHG. *rehho* (G. *rechen*), ON. *reka*, and OHG. *rehhan*, Goth. *rikan* heap up; Gmc. **rak-* **rek-*.] **1.** An implement, consisting of a bar fixed across a long handle and fitted with teeth pointing downwards, used for drawing together hay, grass, or the like, or for breaking up, levelling, or smoothing the surface of the ground (a *hand-rake*). Also, a large implement of the same character, mounted on wheels and drawn by a horse (a *horse-rake*) or tractor, or one of the bars with teeth in a tedding-machine. **b.** *transf.* A very lean person 1582. **2.** A similar implement, used for various purposes, sometimes having a flat blade in place of the bar with teeth 1530. **b.** A kind of rasp or scraper 1727.
1. Phr. *As lean* (also *thin*, †*rank*) *as a r.* **b.** Let vs reuenge this with our Pikes, ere we become Rakes SHAKS.

Rake (rēɪk), *sb.*[2] *Sc.* and *n. dial.* late ME. [– ON. *rāk* stripe, streak (Norw dial. *raak* foot-path, channel, etc.), f. **rak-*, ablaut-var. of *rek* -drive; cf. RACK *sb.*[1]] **1.** A way, path. **2.** Course or path, *esp.* of cattle in pasturing; hence, pasture-ground, right of pasture 1640. **3.** A leading vein of ore, having a more or less perpendicular lie. Also *r.-vein.* 1556. **4.** A rut, groove 1691.

Rake (rēɪk), *sb.*[3] 1626. [f. RAKE *v.*[3]] **1.** *Naut.* **a.** The projection of the upper part of a ship's hull at stem and stern beyond the corresponding extremities of the keel (dist. as *forerake* and *sternrake*). **b.** The deviation (usu. towards the stern) of a ship's masts from a perpendicular to the keel 1815. **2.** *transf.* The inclination of any object from the perpendicular or to the horizontal; slope 1802.
2. The arrangement of the plants follows the r. of the roof 1881.

Rake (rēɪk), *sb.*[4] 1653. [Clipped form of *rakel* (XVII), dial. var. of RAKE-HELL.] A man of loose habits and immoral character; an idle dissipated man of fashion. **b.** A woman of like character 1712.
An old r. who has survived himself is the most pitiable object in creation 1836.

Rake (rēɪk), *v.*[1] ME. [– ON. *raka* scrape, shave, rake; also f. RAKE *sb.*[1]] **I. 1.** To draw together, collect, gather (scattered objects) with, or as with, a rake. **b.** So with *together* 1550. **2.** To draw or drag in a specified direction with, or as with, a rake. late ME. **b.** With *up*. Used *esp.* of searching for and bringing forward all that can be said against a person 1581.
1. Her exceeding greedines in raking mony 1598. **2.** All the bad things..which Prynne could pick and r. out of Histories 1691. To see that your fire was safely raked out at night 1853. **b.** The old charges..were again raked up against him FREEMAN.

II. †**1.** To cover with, or bury under, something brought together with, or as with, a rake –1786. **2.** *spec.* To cover (a fire) with ashes or small coal in order to keep it in without active burning. Also with *up*. Now *dial.* late ME.
2. To work by Night, and r. the Winter Fire DRYDEN.

III. 1. To go over with a rake, so as to make clean, smooth, etc., or to find something. Also with *up, over*. 1523. **b.** *transf.* To search, etc., as with a rake 1618. **2.** To scratch or scrape. Also *intr.* or *absol.* 1609. **3.** *Farriery.* To clean (a costive horse or its fundament) from ordure by scraping with the hand 1575. **4.** *Mil.* and *Naut.* To sweep or traverse with shot; to enfilade; *spec.* to send shot along (a ship) from stem to stern (in full *to r. fore and aft*) 1630. **b.** To command, overlook 1842. **c.** To sweep with the eyes; to look all over 1848. **d.** *Hawking.* Of a hawk: To strike (the game) in the air. Also *to r. off.* 1773. **5.** *Dyeing.* To stir or mix (liquor) with a rake 1816.
1. R. the surface perfectly level 1856. **b.** The statesman rakes the town to find a plot SWIFT. Phr. †*To r. hell*; Suche a feloe as a manne should r. helle for UDALL. **2.** Sand raked his sores from heel to pate M. ARNOLD. *absol.* Thou..rakest like a Wolfe BURTON. **4.** Captain Peard..lay across his hawse, and raked him with several broadsides NELSON. *transf.* [Pictures hung] with their sides to the light, so that it 'rakes' them RUSKIN. **c.** George took the glass again and raked the vessel THACKERAY.

IV. *intr.* or *absol.* **1.** To use a rake; to scrape with the fingers or similar means; to make search with, or as with, a rake 1440. **b.** *fig.* To make search; to poke *into* 1637. **2.** To move *on* or *over* like, or with the effect of, a rake; to scrape *against* 1598. **3.** To come *up* when raked (*rare*) 1778.
1. The Cock..raked in golden barley TENNYSON. **b.** To r. into the histories of former ages BURKE.

Rake (rēɪk), *v.*[2] [OE. *racian*, perh. = Sw. *raka* run, rush, slip, etc.] **1.** *intr.* To proceed, make one's way; to walk, stroll, wander. Now *dial.* **2.** *spec.* **a.** Of hawks; To fly along after the game; also = *to r. out* (*off, away*), to fly wide of (or away from) the game; sometimes said of the game itself 1575. **b.** Of hunting dogs: To run with their noses close to the ground

Rake (rēɪk), *v.*[3] 1627. [prob. rel. to G. *ragen* project (whence Sw. *raka*, Da. *rage*), of unkn. origin.] **1.** *intr.* **a.** Of a ship, its hull, timbers, etc.: To have a rake at stem or stern. **b.** Of masts or funnels: To incline from the perpendicular 1691. **2.** *trans.* To cause to incline. In *pa. pple.* 1842.
1. Two lines of masts, one raking one way, the other the other 1883.

Rake (rēɪk), *v.*[5] 1700. [f. RAKE *sb.*[4]] *intr.* To be a rake; to live a dissipated life.

Rake-hell (rēɪ·khel). Now *arch.* 1547. [See RAKE *v.*[1] III. 1. b, HELL *sb.*] **1.** A thorough scoundrel or rascal; an utterly immoral or dissolute person; a vile debauchee or rake 1554. **2.** *attrib.* or as *adj.* = RAKE-HELLY *a.*
1. Al the rake-hels and loose vagabonds in a countrey 1603.

Rakehelly (rēɪ·khe:li), *a.* and *sb.* 1579. [f. prec. + -Y[1].] **1.** Of persons. Of the nature of, or resembling, a rakehell or rakehells. **2.** Characteristic of rakehells 1594. **B.** *sb.* = prec. 1. 1762.

Raker[1] (rēɪ·kəɹ). late ME. [f. RAKE *v.*[1] + -ER[1].] **1.** One who rakes. Also with *after, up.* 1563. **2.** *spec.* A scavenger, street-cleaner. Now *arch.* late ME. **3.** An implement for raking. **b.** *spec.* A gill-raker (see GILL *sb.*[1]). 1727.

Raker[2] (rēɪ·kəɹ). *colloq.* 1876. [f. RAKE *v.*[2] + -ER[1] 1.] An extremely fast pace.

Rakery (rēɪ·kəri). Now *rare.* 1728. [f. RAKE *sb.*[4] + -ERY.] Rakish conduct; debauchery, dissoluteness; social excitement.
He..instructed his Lordship in all the r. and intrigues of the lewd town NORTH.

Rakeshame (rēɪ·kˌʃēɪm). Now *rare.* 1599. [f. RAKE *v.*[1] + SHAME *sb.* Cf. RAKEHELL.] One who covers himself with shame; an ill-behaved, disorderly, or dissolute fellow.

Rakish (rēɪ·kiʃ), *a.*[1] 1706. [f. RAKE *sb.*[4] + -ISH[1].] **1.** Having the character, appearance, or manners, of a rake. **2.** Characteristic of, appropriate to, a rake 1706.
1. A..r. youngster wild from school BYRON. **2.** R. talk 1722. The r. swagger..of the coxcombs KINGSLEY. Hence **Ra·kish-ly** *adv.*, **-ness.**

Rakish (rēɪ·kiʃ), *a.*[2] 1824. [f. RAKE *sb.*[3] + -ISH[1]; partly assoc. with RAKE *sb.*[4]] **1.** *Naut.* Of a ship: Having an appearance indicative of smartness and fast sailing, freq. with suggestion of piratical character. **2.** Of a hawk's wings: Smart-looking 1855.

‖**Râle** (rāl). 1829. [Fr., vbl. sb. f. *râler*; etym. unkn.] *Path.* An abnormal sound additional to that of respiration, heard on auscultation of the lungs when these are not perfectly healthy.

‖**Rallentando** (rælĕntæ·ndoᵘ). 1800. [It., pres. pple. of *rallentare* slow down.] *Mus.* A direction indicating that a passage is to be played or sung in a time growing gradually slower.

Ralli-car, -cart. 1890. A form of light two-wheeled driving-trap for four persons, named after the first purchaser.

Ralline (ræ·ləin), *a.* 1885. [f. mod.L. *rallus* RAIL *sb.*[3] + -INE[1].] *Ornith.* Pertaining to, related to, or resembling the rail, or the family *Rallidæ*.

Rally (ræ·li), *sb.*[1] 1651. [f. RALLY *v.*[1]] **1.** A rapid reunion for concentrated effort, *esp.* of an army after repulse or disorganization. **b.** *Mil.* The signal for rallying 1897. **2.** A quick recovery from a state of exhaustion, a renewal of energy, *esp.* a (temporary) recovery of strength during illness 1826. **3. a.** *Theatr.* A general mêlée, scramble, or chase, of the characters in a pantomime 1870. **b.** *U.S. colloq.* A political mass-meeting 1878. **4. a.** *Boxing.* A separate bout 1825. **b.** *Lawn Tennis.* The series of strokes made by both players between the service and failure to return the ball 1887.
1. They yielded at last..with frequent rallies, and sullen submission JOHNSON. **2.** I made a r. to-day and wrote four pages SCOTT.

Rally (ræ·li), *sb.*[2] 1832. [f. RALLY *v.*[2]] A piece of rallying or banter.

Rally (ræ·li), *v.*[1] 1603. [– Fr. *rallier*, f. *re-* RE- + *allier* ALLY *v.* Cf. RELY *v.* 1.] **I.** *trans.* **1.** To reassemble, bring together again (an army or company which has been, or is, scattered) 1604. **2.** To collect (persons) to one's assistance, or for concentrated action 1603. **3.** To concentrate or revive (a faculty, etc.) by a strong effort of the will 1667. **b.** To pull together, revive, rouse, stimulate (a person or animal) 1624.
1. Their troops, being rallied by the dexterity of their generals, came on again to the charge DE FOE. **2.** Even this blow failed to r. the Country round the Queen 1874. **3.** She rallied her drooping spirits 1791.

II. *intr.* **1.** To come together again, to reassemble, *esp.* in order to renew the conflict; to return in a body to the fray or contest 1655. **b.** Of a single person: To return and renew the attack; *spec.* in *Boxing* 1813. **2.** Of persons: To come together in a body; to unite for a common purpose, *esp.* to assist or support some one. Usu. const. *round*. 1818. **b.** Const. *to*. (Also said of a single person). 1879. **3.** To revive, recover, acquire or assume fresh vigour or energy 1840. **b.** To recover in part from an illness 1853.
1. The battalions rallied and came boldly on to charge a second time DE FOE. **2. b.** Mr. Gladstone..rallied to the support of the Government 1879. **3.** At last his flagging powers rallied 1871. Hence **Ra·llying** *vbl. sb.*, often *attrib.*, as *rallying cry, point*, etc.

Rally (ræ·li), *v.*[2] 1665. [– Fr. *railler*; see RAIL *v.*[4]] **1.** *trans.* To treat or assail with banter, pleasantry, or good-humoured ridicule; to make fun or game of. †**2.** *absol.* or *intr.* To employ banter or pleasantry against one. Also const. *at, with* (a person), *upon* (a thing). –1792.
1. They rally'd next Vanessa's dress SWIFT. He rallied Simonides for his absurdity 1770. **2.** I see Madam you are disposed to r. 1676.

Ralstonite (rǭ·lstənəit). 1875. [f. name of J. G. *Ralston* its discoverer; see -ITE[1] 2 b.] *Min.* A hydrated aluminium fluoride containing traces of sodium and calcium.

Ram (ræm), *sb.*[1] [OE. *ram(m*, corresp. to Fris. *ram, room*, (M)LG., (M)Du. *ram*, OHG., MHG. *ram* ram (G. *ramme* rammer), perh. rel. to ON. *ram(m)r* strong.] **1.** A male sheep; in domestication, one kept for breeding purposes, a tup. **2.** *Astron.* (with cap.) The zodiacal sign ARIES OE. **3.** = BATTERING-RAM OE. **b.** *Naut.* A solid point or beak projecting from the bows of a war-vessel, and enabling it to ram and batter in the sides of an opponent 1865. **c.** *Naut.* A battleship fitted with a ram 1862. **4.** The weight of a pile-driving machine; a monkey 1440. **b.** A steam-hammer used in setting-up a bloom of metal 1875. **c.** A paviour's RAMMER 1885. **5. a.** An automatic water-raising machine, in which the raising power is supplied by the concussion of a descending body of water in a pipe 1808. **b.** The piston of the large cylinder of a hydrostatic press 1816. **c.** A hydraulic lifting-machine 1861. **d.** The plunger of a force-pump 1883.

3. *fig.* The iron and rock, Which tryes, and counterstands the shock, And ramme of time HERRICK.

Ram, *sb.*[2] 1723. [Cf. RAM-LINE.] *Naut.* Length 'over all' of a boat.

Ram (ræm), *v.* ME. [f. RAM *sb.*[1]] **1.** *absol.* To beat down earth with a heavy implement, so as to make it hard and firm. **b.** *trans.* To beat down (earth) thus 1596. **c.** To fix or make (a thing) firm by ramming the surrounding soil 1565. **2.** To force or drive *down* or *in* by heavy blows; to drive (piles, etc.) *into* the soil in this way 1519. **b.** To force (a charge) into a fire-arm by means of a ram-rod 1598. **c.** To cram, stuff, thrust (a person or thing) *into* something 1582. **d.** To push firmly *down*; to pen *up* closely 1602. **3.** To force in or compress the charge or contents of (a gun, etc.) by ramming 1581. **b.** To cram or stuff hard *with* something 1590. **4.** To stop, stuff, or block *up* 1548. **5.** To dash violently against, to strike with great force; esp. *Naut.* to strike (a ship) with the ram 1864. **6.** To dash, force, or drive (one thing *on, at,* or *into* another) 1715.

2. We r. some concrete between the piles 1840. **d.** He rams his old hat down on his head 1887. **5.** The Tennessee was rammed by the Hartford 1864. **6.** Ramming his horse well at it, he gets through 1858.

‖**Ramadan** (ræmădā·n), **ramazan** (-zā·n). 1599. [– Arab. *ramaḍān* (hence Turk. and Pers. *ramazān*), f. *ramaḍa* be parched or hot.] The ninth month of the Moslem year, rigidly observed as a thirty days' fast, during the hours of daylight, by all Moslems.

Ramage (ræ·mĕdʒ), *sb. arch.* 1616. [– Fr. *ramage* :– Gallo-Rom. **ramaticum*, f. L. *ramus* branch; see -AGE.] **1.** The collective branches of trees 1656. †**2.** The song or cry of birds –1693.

†**Ra·mage,** *a.* ME. [– OFr. *ramage* (whence also AL. *ramagius*, in sense 1) :– Gallo-Rom. **ramaticus*; see prec.] **1.** Of hawks: Having left the nest, and begun to fly from branch to branch; hence, wild, untamed, shy. Also *transf.* of persons. –1773. **2.** Of animals: Wild, untamed, unruly, violent –1639.

Ramal (rēⁱ·măl), *a.* 1856. [f. L. *ramus* branch + -AL[1].] **1.** *Bot.* Of or belonging to a branch; growing on or out of a branch. **2.** *Anat.* and *Zool.* Pertaining to, or of the character of, a ramus 1891.

Ramble (ræ·mb'l), *sb.*[1] 1654. [f. the vb.] **1.** An act of rambling; a walk (†excursion or journey) without definite route, for pleasure or recreation. **2.** Rambling, incoherence 1716.

Ra·mble, *sb.*[2] 1851. [Cf. Sw. *ramla* fall down.] *Coal-mining.* A thin bed of shale lying above a coal-seam, which falls down as the coal is taken out, and requires to be separated from it.

Ramble (ræ·mb'l), *v.* 1620. [prob. – MDu. *rammelen* (of cats, rabbits, etc.) be excited by sexual desire and wander about, frequent. f. *rammen* copulate with, cover, corresp. to OHG. *rammalōn* (G. *rammeln*); ult. f. *ram* RAM *sb.*[1]; see -LE.] **1.** *intr.* To wander, travel (now usu. to walk) about from place to place without definite aim or direction. **b.** *fig.* with ref. to mental pursuits or studies 1650. **2.** To wander in discourse; to write or talk incoherently or without natural sequence of ideas 1640.

1. I go tomorrow towards Italy, where I will r. for two or three months 1672. The stream..As through the glen it rambles WORDSW. **2.** He rambled on in a childish sort of way COBBETT. Hence **Ra·mbler,** one who rambles; *spec.* a rose which straggles or climbs freely, esp. the *Crimson R.*

Rambling (ræ·mbliŋ), *ppl. a.* 1623. [f. prec. + -ING[2].] That rambles, in various senses. **1.** Wandering, moving about, straying from place to place. **b.** Of life, etc.: Characterized by wandering 1699. **2.** Of the thoughts, mind, speech, etc.: Straying from one subject to another, unsettled 1635. **b.** Of persons: Given to wandering in thought or discourse 1693. **3.** Of plants: Straggling, spreading or climbing freely and irregularly 1728. **4.** Having a straggling irregular form or plan 1849.

1. A kind of r. rheumatism 1741. **b.** Life's r. journey COWPER. **2.** A long r. ghost story 1837. **3.** The r. briar CRABBE. **4.** [The house] was antique, r., and incommodious C. BRONTË. Hence **Ra·mbling-ly** *adv.*, **-ness.**

Rambunctious (ræmbɒ·ŋkʃəs), *a. U.S. slang.* 1854. [Of unkn. origin.] Wild or unruly of behaviour.

Rambutan, -bootan (ræmbū·tăn). 1707. [– Malay *rambūtan*, f. *rambut* hair, in allusion to its villose covering.] The fruit of *Nephelium lappaceum*, a tree of the Malay archipelago, having a reddish coat, covered with soft spines or hairs, and pulp of a subacid flavour.

Ra·m-cat. Now *dial.* 1672. [f. RAM *sb.*[1]] A male cat.

Rame (rēⁱm). *rare.* 1578. [– Fr. *rame* :– L. *ramus* branch.] A branch of a tree or shrub; also *transf.* of a nerve, etc.

Rameal (rēⁱ·miˌăl), *a. rare.* 1852. [var. (by suffix-substitution) of earlier RAMEOUS, or var. of contemp. RAMAL.] *Bot.* = RAMAL.

Ramean (rēⁱ·miˌăn), *a.* and *sb.* 1710. [f. *Ramus* (see RAMIST) + -(E)AN.] **A.** *adj.* Belonging to, connected with, Ramus. **B.** *sb.* A Ramist.

Ramekin, ramequin (ræ·mĕkin). 1706. [– Fr. *ramequin* (XVII), of LDu. origin (cf. Flem. †*rameken* toasted bread); perh. – MDu. **ramkin* (cf. G. *rahm* cream, -KIN).] A small quantity of cheese, with bread-crumbs, eggs, etc., usu. baked and served in a special mould. Chiefly *pl.*

Ramentaceous (ræmĕntēⁱ·ʃəs), *a.* 1816. [f. RAMENTUM + -ACEOUS.] *Bot.* **1.** Covered with ramenta. **2.** Resembling ramenta 1861.

‖**Ramentum** (răme·ntɒ̆m). Chiefly in pl. **ramenta.** 1662. [L., f. *radere* scrape; see -MENT.] **1.** A fragment scraped off; †an atom, mote. **2.** *Bot.* A thin membraneous scale formed on the surface of leaves and stalks 1819.

Rameous (rēⁱ·miˌəs), *a.* 1760. [f. L. *ramus* branch + -EOUS.] *Bot.* Of or belonging to branches.

Ramessid (ræ·mĕsid), **-ide** (-əid). 1854. [– G. *Ramesside*, f. Gr. Ῥαμέσσης Rameses + -*ide*, patronymic suffix = -ID[3].] A member of the Egyptian royal family during the 19th and 20th dynasties. Also *attrib.* or as *adj.*

Ramie (ræ·mi). Also **ramee.** 1888. [Malay *rāmī*.] **a.** A Chinese and East Indian plant of the nettle family, *Bœhmeria nivea*, called also *Rhea* and *grass-cloth plant.* **b.** The fine fibre of this plant, extensively employed in weaving.

Ramiferous (rămi·ferəs), *a. rare.* 1819. [f. L. *ramus* branch + -FEROUS.] Bearing branches.

Ramification (ræ:mifikēⁱ·ʃən). 1677. [– Fr. *ramification*, f. *ramifier*; see RAMIFY, -FICATION.] **1.** The action or process of ramifying 1760. **b.** The branches of a tree collectively 1821. **2.** A subdivision or single part of a complex structure analogous to the branches of a tree, *esp.* of veins, arteries, and other parts in animals and plants, and of rivers 1677. **b.** *transf.* Of immaterial things 1755.

2. b. One of the ramifications of the Whig plot MACAULAY.

Ramiform (ræ·mifǭɹm), *a.* 1822. [f. L. *ramus* branch + -FORM.] Branch-like; ramified.

Ramify (ræ·mifəi), *v.* 1541. [– (O)Fr. *ramifier* – med.L. *ramificare* branch out, f. L. *ramus* branch; see -FY.] **1** *intr.* Of trees and plants or their parts: To form branches, to branch out, extend in the form of branches 1576. **2.** To extend or spread in a number of subdivisions or offshoots analogous to branches; esp. *Anat.* of veins, nerves, etc. 1578. **3.** To break up, divide, into branches or analogous parts 1541. **4.** *trans.* To cause to shoot out, spread, or extend after the manner of branches 1565. **5.** To separate into branches or analogous divisions. Also *absol.* 1800.

1. When they [asparagus plants] are older, and begin to r., they lose this Quality 1735. **2.** Dissent had grown and spread and ramified throughout the land 1861. **3.** The road..soon began to r. 1856. **4.** Railways..may be ramified over a whole country 1825.

Ramillie (ræ·mili). *Obs.* exc. *Hist.* 1740. [From *Ramillies* in Belgium, the scene of Marlborough's victory in 1706.] **1.** *attrib.* Applied **a.** to a wig having a long plait behind tied with a bow at top and bottom (so also with *tail*); **b.** to a method of cocking the hat. **2.** *absol.* A Ramillie wig or tail 1752.

2. A head of fine flaxen hair..braided into a r. 1752.

Ramism (rēⁱ·miz'm). 1710. [f. *Ramus* (see next) + -ISM.] The logical system of Ramus.

Ramist (rēⁱ·mist), *sb.* (and *a.*) 1605. [f. the name of *Ramus* (Pierre de la Ramée, 1515–1572) + -IST.] **A.** *sb.* A follower of Ramus, as the author of a system of logic opposed in various respects to the Aristotelian. **B.** *attrib.* or as *adj.* Of, pertaining to, characteristic of, Ramists or Ramism 1863.

Ra·m-ja·m, *adv. dial.* and *slang.* 1879. [f. RAM *v.* + JAM *v.*] *R. full*, crammed full.

Ram-line. 1664. [Cf. RAM *sb.*[2]] *Naut.* A line used to gain a straight middle-line upon a tree or mast.

Rammer (ræ·məɹ). 1497. [f. RAM *v.* + -ER[1].] **1.** An instrument consisting of a heavy piece of wood held upright, for ramming or beating down earth, or forcing stones into the ground. **b.** A similar implement used for other purposes; a pestle or stamp 1643. **2.** A cylindrical block of wood fixed at the end of a staff, used to drive home the charge of a cannon; †the ramrod of a fire-arm 1497. **b.** A ramming instrument used in chemical experiments, or in blasting operations 1660. **3.** A pile-driver, or similar device 1688. **4.** One engaged in ramming earth 1876.

Rammish (ræ·miʃ), *a.* Now *dial.* late ME. [f. RAM *sb.*[1] + -ISH[1].] Rank, strong; having a rank smell or taste.

Hir sauour is so rammyssh and so hoot CHAUCER. Hence **Ra·mmish-ly** *adv.*, **-ness.**

Rammy (ræ·mi), *a.* Now chiefly *n. dial.* 1607. [f. RAM *sb.*[1] + -Y[1].] Characteristic of, resembling (that of) a ram; *esp.* = prec.

Ramoon (rămū·n). Also **ramon.** 1756. [– Sp. *ramon*, f. *ramo* branch :– L. *ramus*; see -OON.] The tops and leaves of a W. Indian and Central Amer. tree (*Trophis americana*), used as fodder for cattle. Chiefly in comb. *r.-tree.*

Ramose (rămōᵘ·s), *a.* 1689. [– L. *ramosus*, f. *ramus* branch; see -OSE[1].] = next 1. Hence **Ramo·sely** *adv.*

Ramous (rēⁱ·məs), *a.* Now *rare.* 1562. [– L. *ramosus*; see prec., -OUS.] **1.** Branching, as plants or plant-like forms. **b.** Applied (after ancient physics) to the particles of viscous or rigid bodies 1674. **2.** Belonging to, characteristic of, branches 1813.

†**Ramp,** *sb.*[1] 1440. [perh. f. RAMP *v.*[1] 5.] A bold, vulgar, ill-behaved woman or girl –1728.

Ramp (ræmp), *sb.*[2] 1671. [f. RAMP *v.*[1]] The act of ramping.

The bold Ascalonite Fled from his Lion r. MILT.

Ramp, *sb.*[3] *slang.* 1888. [f. RAMP *v.*[2] 2.] A swindle, esp. one depending upon an artificial boom in prices.

A Christmas ramp in food prices 1922.

Ramp (ræmp), *sb.*[4] 1725. [– Fr. *rampe*, f. *ramper* RAMP *v.*[1]] **1.** A slope; an inclined plane connecting two different levels, *esp.* in fortifications, or at the end of a railway station platform 1779. **2.** The difference in level between the abutments of a rampant arch 1725. **3. a.** Part of the handrail of a stair, having a concave or upward bend (freq. continued in a knee or convex bend), as at a landing 1778. **b.** A slanting (straight or curved) shoulder connecting two levels of the coping of a wall. Also, the sloping part of a stair parapet. 1842.

Ramp (ræmp), *v.*[1] ME. [– (O)Fr. *ramper* creep, crawl, climb = It. *rampare*; ult. origin unc.] †**1.** *intr.* To creep or crawl on the ground (*rare*) –1594. **2.** To climb, scramble. Now *dial.* 1523. **b.** Of plants: To climb (*up* or *upon* some support). Now chiefly *dial.* 1597. **c.** Of non-climbing plants: To grow rankly, to shoot up rapidly. Now *dial.* 1607. **3.** Of beasts (esp. in *Her.*): To rear or stand on the hind legs, as if in the act of climbing; to raise the fore-paws in the air; hence, to assume, or to be in, a threatening posture. (Chiefly said of lions.) Also of persons: To raise, or gesticulate with, the arms; †to clutch wildly *at*. ME. **4.** Of persons: To storm or rage with violent gestures; to act in a furious or threatening manner. Also *transf.* late ME. †**5.** To go about in a loose, immodest way –1611. **b.** = ROMP *v.* Now *dial.* 1657. **6.** To bound, rush, or range about in a wild or excited manner 1627. **b.** To sail swiftly, to scud 1872. **7.** *Arch.* Of a wall: To ascend or descend from one level to another 1855. **8.** *trans. Mil.* and *Arch.* To furnish with a ramp, to build with ramps 1848.

2. b. Ramping upon Trees, Shrubs, Hedges or Poles, they mount up to a great height RAY. **3.** Their bridles they would champ, And trampling the fine element would fiercely r. SPENSER. **4.** By this time the long dormant Usurer ramps for the payment of his money FULLER.

Ramp (ræmp), *v.*² 1567. [Of unkn. origin.] †**1.** *trans.* To snatch, tear, pluck –1633. **2.** *slang.* To rob or swindle; *spec.* to force (one) to pay a pretended bet 1812.

Rampage (ræmpēⁱ·dʒ), *sb.* 1861. [f. next.] A state of excitement or violent passion; the act of behaving or rushing about in a reckless or riotous fashion; esp. in phr. *on the r.*

Rampage (ræmpēⁱ·dʒ), *v.* 1715. [Of unkn. origin; poss. based on RAMP *v.*¹] **1.** *intr.* To behave violently or furiously; to storm, rage wildly. **2.** To go about in an excited, furious, or violent manner; to rush wildly hither and thither 1808.

Rampageous (ræmpēⁱ·dʒəs), *a.* 1822. Also occas. **-acious.** [f. RAMPAGE *sb.* + -OUS.] **1.** Violent; unruly; boisterous. **2.** *transf.* Glaring, outrageous 1889.

1. The primitive ages of a r. antiquity GALT. Hence **Rampa·geous-ly** *adv.*, **-ness.**

†**Rampa·llion.** 1593. [perh. based on RAMP *v.*¹ Cf. the later RASCALLION.] A ruffian, villain, scoundrel; occas. of a woman –1822.

Rampancy (ræ·mpănsi). 1664. [f. next; see -ANCY.] The fact or condition of being rampant.

Rampant (ræ·mpănt), *a.* late ME. [– (O)Fr. *rampant*, pr. pple. of *ramper*; see RAMP *v.*¹, -ANT.] **1.** Of beasts, esp. lions: Rearing or standing with the fore-paws in the air. **b.** *spec.* in *Her.* 'Standing on the Sinister hind-leg, with both forelegs elevated, the Dexter above the Sinister, and the head in profile' (Cussans). late ME. **c.** Given to ramping; of a fierce disposition. late ME. **d.** Exhibiting fierceness or high spirits by ramping or similar movements. Also const. *with.* 1529. **2.** *transf.* **a.** Of persons: Violent and extravagant in action, opinion, etc. 1628. **b.** Of things: Unchecked, unrestrained, aggressive, etc. 1619. †**3.** Lustful; vicious –1812. **4.** Of plants or their growth: Rank, luxurious 1733. **5.** *Arch.* Of an arch or vault: Having the abutments or springing lines on different levels 1725.

1. The Tawnie Lion..R. shakes his Brinded main MILT. **b.** Lillies, and Lions R., and Spread Eagles in Fields d'Or COWLEY. **2. a.** The Whiggs are r., and thinke to carry all before them 1709. **b.** It grieved him to see ignorance and impiety so r. FULLER. Hence **Ra·mpantly** *adv.*

Rampart (ræ·mpaɹt), *sb.* 1583. [– Fr. *rempart*, †*rampart*, alt. (after *boulevart* BOULEVARD) of †*rempar*, f. *remparer* fortify; see RAMPIRE *v.*] *Fortif.* A mound of earth raised for the defence of a place, capable of resisting cannon-shot, wide enough on the top for the passage of troops, guns, etc., and usu. surmounted by a stone parapet.

This daie was begunne a R., at Northe newe Gate 1583. *transf.* That had the waters round about it, whose r. was the sea *Nahum* 3:8. So **Ra·mpart** *v. trans.* to fortify or surround (as) with a r. 1557.

Rampion (ræ·mpiən). 1573. [f. some var. of the Rom. forms derived from med.L. *rapuncium, rapontium* (It. *raperonzo*, Fr. *raiponce*, Sp. *reponcha*; cf. G. *rapunzel*), presumably f. L. *rapum* RAPE *sb.*³] **1.** A species of bellflower, *Campanula rapunculus*, of which the white tuberous roots are sometimes used as a salad. **2.** A plant of the genus *Phyteuma* 1760. †**3.** The Lobelia –1760.

Rampire, -pier (ræ·mpəiᵊɹ), *sb.* Now *arch.* 1548. [In forms †*rampar*, †*rampere* – Fr. †*rempar*, †*ramper*, f. *remparer* (XV); see next.] **1.** = RAMPART. †**b.** A dam, barrier –1764. **2.** *transf.* and *fig.* A thing or person resembling or comparable to a rampart 1567.

1. Buttress, and rampire's circling bound SCOTT. **2.** The son of Thetis, r. of our hosts DRYDEN.

Rampire, -pier (ræ·mpəiᵊɹ), *v.* Now *arch.* 1550. [In forms †*rampar*, †*rampere* – Fr. *remparer* fortify, f. *re-* RE- + *emparer* take possession of – Pr. *amparer* :– Rom. **anteparare* put in position before another, f. L. *ante* ANTE- + *parare* PREPARE. The origin of the forms in *-ire, -ier* of the vb. and sb. is not clear.] †**1.** *trans.* To strengthen (a bulwark, gate, etc.) against attack; to block *up* (a gate) for this purpose, *esp.* by piling earth behind it; to close *up* (an opening) –1709. **2.** To fortify, strengthen, or protect (a place), *esp.* by a rampart 1550.

2. R. with abundant power Long Alba 1855.

Ram-rod (ræ·mrǫd). 1797. [f. RAM *v.* + ROD.] A rod used for ramming down the charge of a muzzle-loading fire-arm.

Ramshackle (ræ·mʃæk'l), *a.* 1830. [Later form of next.] **1.** Loose and shaky; rickety, crazy, tumble-down. **2.** Of persons, actions, etc.: Unsteady, irregular, disorderly, rude. (Chiefly *dial.*) 1855.

1. A huddle of r. lath-and-plaster houses 1865. Hence **Ra·mshackle** *v. trans.* to 'rattle up'.

Ramshackled (ræ·mʃæk'ld), *ppl. a.* 1675. [orig. pa. pple. of †*rans(h)ackle* ransack, f. RANSACK *v.* + -LE.] = prec. 1.

Ram's-horn. ME. [f. RAM *sb.*¹] **1.** The horn of a ram; the material of this. †**2.** An ammonite or nautilus (*Nautilus spirula*) –1798. **3.** A vessel in which fish are washed 1809.

Ramson (ræ·msən). [OE. *hramsan*, pl. of *hramsa, -se* wild garlic, but in later use a sing., with pl. *ramsons.*] The broad-leaved garlic, *Allium ursinum*; the bulbous root of this plant, used as a relish. Chiefly in *pl.*

Ramulose (ræ·miŭlōᵘs), *a.* 1753. [– L. *ramulosus*, f. *ramulus*; see next, -OSE¹.] *Bot.* and *Zool.* Characterized by ramuli. So **Ra·mulous** *a.*

‖**Ramulus** (ræ·miŭlŏs). Pl. **-li** (-ləi). 1783. [L., dim. of *ramus.*] *Bot.* and *Anat.* A small branch or ramus.

‖**Ramus** (rēⁱ·mŏs). Pl. **-mi** (-məi). 1803. [L., = branch.] **1.** *Anat.* A process of a bone, *esp.* of the ischium and pubes, and of the jaw-bone. **2.** *Ornith.* = BARB *sb.*¹ 6. 1882.

Ramuscule (rămʊ·skiul). 1831. [– late L. *ramusculus*, dim. of *ramus* RAMUS; see -CULE.] *Biol.* A small branch.

Ran (ræn). 1794. [Of unkn. origin.] A certain length of twine.

Ran, pa. t. and obs. pa. pple. of RUN *v.*

Rance (rɑns), *sb.*¹ 1598. [prob. of Fr. origin.] A kind of marble, of a red colour varied with veins and spots of blue and white.

Rance, ranse (ræns), *sb.*² Chiefly *Sc.* 1808. [perh. – (O)Fr. *ranche* pole, bar, etc., of unkn. origin.] A bar or baton; a prop or support.

Ranch (rɑntʃ, rɑnʃ), *sb. U.S.* 1808. [Anglicized f. RANCHO.] **1.** A hut or house in the country. **2.** A cattle-breeding establishment, farm, or estate. Also, the people employed or living on this. 1872. Hence **Ranch** *v.*¹ *intr.* to conduct a r. (whence **Ra·ncher,** a ranchman; **Ra·nching,** stock-raising or cattle-breeding on a r.). **Ra·nchman,** the owner of a r.; a man employed on a r.

Ranch (rɑnʃ), *v.*² *Obs.* exc. *dial.* late ME. [Nasalized f. RACE *v.*²] *trans.* To tear, cut, scratch, etc.

‖**Ranchero** (rɑntʃē·ro). 1840. [Sp., f. *rancho* RANCHO.] One employed on a ranch as herdsman or overseer; the owner of a ranch; a ranchman.

Rancho (rɑ·ntʃo). 1648. [Sp., = a mess, a company of persons who eat together.] **1.** In Spanish America: A rudely-built house, a hut or hovel; also, a collection of huts, a hamlet or village 1845. **b.** *spec.* A hut or shed, or a collection of these, put up for the accommodation of travellers 1648. **2.** In Western U.S., a cattle-farm, a ranch 1840.

Rancid (ræ·nsid), *a.* 1646. [– L. *rancidus*, f. **rancēre* (in pr. pple. *rancens*) be putrid; see -ID¹.] Having the rank unpleasant taste or smell of oils and fats when no longer fresh. Hence of tastes or smells.

The black wet bread, with r. butter spread 1813. Hence **Ra·ncid-ly** *adv.*, **-ness.** **Ranci·dity,** r. state or quality.

Rancorous (ræ·ŋkŏrəs), *a.* 1590. [f. next + -OUS.] **1.** Of feelings: Having, or partaking of, the nature of rancour. Also *transf.* **2.** Of actions, etc.: Proceeding from, or characterized by, rancour 1590. **3.** Of persons, the mind, heart, etc.: Feeling or displaying rancour 1592.

1. So flam'd his eyne with rage and r. yre SPENSER. **3.** In that age of harsh and r. tempers M. ARNOLD. Hence **Ra·ncorous-ly** *adv.*, **-ness.**

Rancour (ræ·ŋkəɹ). ME. [– OFr. *rancour* (mod. *rancœur*) :– late L. *rancor* rankness, (in Vulg.) bitter grudge, f. **rancēre*; see RANCID, -OUR, -OR 1.] **1.** Inveterate and bitter ill-feeling, grudge, or animosity; malignant hatred or spitefulness. **b.** *transf.* and *fig.* of things 1582. †**2.** Rancid smell; rancidity; rankness (*rare*) –1567.

1. Peace in their mouthes, and all rancor and vengeaunce in their hartes 1547. **b.** Through the rancor of the poyson, the wound was iudged incurable CAMDEN.

Rand (rænd), *sb.* [OE. *rand*, corresp. to OFris. *rond*, OS. *rand* 'umbo', OHG. *rant* (G. *rand*), ON. *rǫnd* edge, rim of a shield :– Gmc. **rand-*.] **1.** A border, margin, or brink (*esp.* of land). *Obs.* exc. *dial.* **2.** A strip or long slice: **a.** of meat. Now *dial.* late ME. **b.** of fish (esp. sturgeon). Now *rare.* 1572. **3. a.** A strip of leather placed under the quarters of a boot or shoe, to make this level before the lifts of the heel are attached 1598. **b.** A strip of iron 1831.

†**Rand,** *v. rare.* 1601. [– Du. †*randen*, var. of †*tranten* RANT *v.*] **1.** *intr.* To rave, to rant –1607. **2.** *trans.* (with *out*). To utter in a furious manner –1609.

Randan (ræ·nˌdæn), *sb.*¹ 1662. [perh. var. of *randon* RANDOM, with assim. of the vowels.] **1.** Riotous or disorderly behaviour; a spree. **2.** A riotous person (*rare*) 1809.

1. Phr. *On the r.*; They were a' on the ran-dan last nicht! STEVENSON.

Randan (rænˌdæ·n), *adv., sb.*² (and *a.*). 1828. [prob. transf. use of *randem* style of driving in which three horses are harnessed tandem (*randem-tandem* c1805, jingling formation on TANDEM); but the stress is then difficult to account for.] **A.** *adv.* Applied to a style of rowing in which the middle one of three rowers pulls a pair of sculls, stroke and bow an oar each. **B.** *sb.* A boat for rowing in this fashion 1885. **C.** *attrib.* or *adj.* 1884.

Randing (ræ·ndiŋ). 1834. [perh. f. RAND *sb.*] *Mil.* A kind of basket-work used in fortifications in making gabions.

Random (ræ·ndəm), *sb., a.,* and *adv.* [ME. *rand(o)un* – OFr. *randon*, rel. to *randir* run impetuously, gallop, f. Gmc. **rand-* RAND *sb.* For the dissimilation of *n..n* to *n..m* cf. RANSOM.] **A.** *sb.* **I.** †**1.** Impetuosity, great speed, force, or violence (in riding, running, striking, etc.). Also with *a*, an impetuous rush, a rapid head-long course. –1611. **2.** Phr. *At r.*, orig. at great speed, without consideration, care, or control; hence a. At haphazard; without aim, purpose, or fixed principle; heedlessly, carelessly 1565. **b.** So with sbs. (*rare.*) 1653. **c.** (*To leave*) in a neglected or untended condition. Now *rare.* 1582. **c.** A random course. Now *rare.* 1561.

1. The frenchmen..came on them with great randon, their speares in their restes 1523. **2. a.** He talkes at randon: sure the man is mad SHAKS. **b.** Thy words at r., as before, Argue thy inexperience MILT.

II. *techn.* †**1.** *Gunnery.* The range of a piece of ordnance; properly, long or full range obtained by elevating the muzzle of the piece; hence, the degree of elevation given to a gun, and *spec.* that which gives the utmost range

–1803. **2.** *Mining.* The direction (*of* a rake vein, etc.) 1653.

1. Phr. †*At r.*, at any range other than point-blank.

B. *adj.* (from phr. *at r.*). **1.** Not sent or guided in a special direction; having no definite aim or purpose; made, done, occurring, etc. at haphazard 1655. **2.** Of persons: Living irregularly (*rare*) 1825. **3.** *techn.* Said of masonry, in which the stones are of irregular sizes and shapes 1823. **4.** *R. shot*, a shot fired at random (orig. in sense A II. 1, but now taken as sense B. 1) 1693.

1. Leaving the poor to be supported by r. charity 1764. **2.** Men who were r. grow steady when they have children to provide for H. SPENCER. **4.** *fig.* The r. shot of..self-created guides in matters of taste 1809.

C. *adv.* †**1.** = At random (*rare*) –1619. **2.** *Comb.*, as *r.-cast*, *-wise*, *-jointed*. Hence **Ra·ndom-ly** *adv.*, **-ness.**

‖**Ranee** (rā·nī). 1698. [Hindi *rānī* = Skr. *rājnī*, fem. of *rājan* RAJAH.] A Hindu queen; a rajah's wife.

Rang, see RING *v.*[1] and [2].

Range (rēⁱndʒ), *sb.*[1] ME. [– OFr. *range* row, rank, file, f. *ranger* RANGE *v.*[1]] **I. 1.** A row, line, file or rank of persons or animals. Now *rare.* **2.** A row, line, or series of things; *esp.* of mountains 1511. **b.** *spec. U.S.* A series of townships six miles in width 1843. **c.** *Math.* A set of points on a straight line 1858. **3.** Rank, class, order (*rare*) 1625. **4.** Line, direction, lie 1677.

2. The New-Street is a double R. of Palaces from one end to the other ADDISON. A magnificent r. of cliffs 1859. **3.** The cohesion of the nation was greatest in the lowest ranges 1874. **4.** Keeping the two Buoys in r. with the Lighthouse 1858.

II. 1. The act of ranging or moving about. Now *rare* in literal sense. 1470. **b.** Opportunity or scope for ranging; liberty to range 1793. **2.** An area, space, or stretch of ground, over which ranging takes place or is possible; *spec.* in *U.S.*, an extensive stretch of grazing or hunting ground 1470. **b.** *U.S.* Without article: Grazing ground 1766. **3.** *Bot.* and *Zool.* The geographical area over which a plant or animal is distributed. Also, the period of time during which it has existed on the earth; the limits of depth between which a marine animal is found. 1856. **b.** The area or period over or during which the occurrence of something is possible 1830. **4.** The area or extent covered by, or included in, some thing or concept 1661. **b.** A series, number, or aggregate 1847. **5.** Sphere or scope of operation or action; the extent to which energy may be exerted, a function discharged, etc. **a.** of immaterial things 1666. **b.** of instruments; *esp.* of musical instruments (and so of the voice); compass, register 1825. **c.** of persons, in respect of knowledge, ability, etc. 1847. **6.** The limits between which a thing may vary in amount or degree 1818. **b.** A series or scale (of sounds, temperatures, prices, etc.) extending between certain limits 1812. **7.** The distance to which a gun, rifle, etc. is capable of sending a ball or bullet. Also, the distance of the object aimed at. 1591. **b.** The position of a gun in firing 1669. **c.** A place fitted with targets, etc., used for practice in shooting 1873.

1. *fig.* This blest exchange Of modest truth for wit's eccentric r. COWPER. **4.** Far as Creation's ample r. extends, The scale of sensual, mental pow'rs ascends POPE. **b.** The English derive their pedigree from such a r. of nationalities EMERSON. **5. a.** He would not suffer them to fall without the r. of Mercy BUNYAN. **b.** Her..voice, a lyre of widest r. TENNYSON. **7.** The enemy have got the r. of our camp 1860.

III. 1. A form of fire-grate, fire-place, or cooking apparatus. Now *spec.* a fire-place having one or more ovens at the sides, and closed on the top with iron plates having openings for carrying on several cooking operations at once. 1446. **2.** *Naut.* (*pl.*) Pieces of timber for fastening ropes to 1644. **3.** A length or stretch of something, e.g. of glass, of leather, cable, etc. 1537. **4.** *Shoe-making.* The lie or line of the upper edge of the counter in a top-boot, corresponding to (and continued in) that of the vamp 1840.

attrib. and *Comb.*, as *r.-finder*, etc.; **r.-heads** *Naut.*, the windlass bitts; **r. work,** (*a*) work having a straight face; (*b*) masonry laid in level courses.

Range (rēⁱndʒ), *sb.*[2] *Obs.* exc. *dial.* 1615. [Of unkn. origin. Cf. RANGE *v.*[2]] A kind of sieve or strainer.

Range (rēⁱndʒ), *v.*[1] late ME. [– Fr. *ranger*, f. *rang* RANK *sb.*] **I.** *trans.* **1.** To place, set, or station (persons, rarely animals) in a row, line, or rank; to draw up, arrange (an army, etc.) in ranks. Chiefly *pass.* and *refl.* **b.** To place (a person or persons) in a specified position, situation, or company. Chiefly in *pass.* and *refl.*, and commonly *fig.* 1598. †**c.** To bring *under* obedience, or *to* something –1659. **2.** To set or dispose (things) in a line or lines; hence, to arrange, put in order. late ME. **b.** *Naut.* To lay out (a cable) so that the anchor may descend without check 1833. **3.** To place (persons or things) *in* a certain class or category; to divide *into* classes; to classify, arrange, etc. 1601. **4.** *refl.* (– Fr. *se ranger.*) To adopt a more regular mode of life 1855.

1. A double file of men..ranged themselves along the ropes 1877. **b.** To r. myself on the side of the Duke of Bedford BURKE. **2.** Her Books..were ranged together in a very beautiful Order ADDISON. **3.** To r. the faculties In scale and order WORDSW.

II. *intr.* **1.** Of buildings, large natural objects, etc.: To stretch out or run in a line, to extend 1607. **b.** To extend or lie in the same line or plane (*with*); esp. in *Printing*, of type, lines, or pages 1599. **2.** To take up or occupy a place or position. Also, of a number of persons: To draw up in rank or order (*rare*) 1596. **b.** *Naut.* of ships 1709.

1. b. Whatsoeuer comes athwart his affection, ranges euenly with mine SHAKS. **2.** When all the full-faced presence of the Gods Ranged in the halls of Peleus TENNYSON. **b.** The Excellent ranged up within two feet of the San Nicholas NELSON.

III. 1. To move hither and thither over a comparatively large area; to rove, roam, wander, stray 1547. **b.** *Gunnery.* Of projectiles: To traverse, go (a specified distance) 1644. **2.** To change from one attachment to another; to be inconstant 1596. **3.** *Bot.* and *Zool.* Of plants and animals: To extend (i.e. to occur, be found) over a certain area or throughout a certain period of time 1859. **4.** To vary within certain limits 1835.

1. Brave beasts..In the wilde forrest raunging fresh and free SPENSER. As far as the eye can r. 1872. **2.** My Mind is fixt, I will not r., I like my Choice too well to change 1706. **4.** The thermometer..ranged from 42° to 52°. 1857.

IV. *trans.* **1.** To traverse, to go over or through (a place or area) in all directions 1533. **b.** *Naut.* To sail along or about (a country, the coast, etc.) 1603. **2. a.** To pasture (cattle) on a range 1857. **b.** To place (a telescope) in position 1860. **c.** To throw (a projectile) a specified distance 1858. **d.** *absol.* To give a gun a certain range 1892.

1. To traverse seas, r. kingdoms COWPER.

Range (rēⁱndʒ), *v.*[2] *Obs.* exc. *dial.* 1538. [Of unkn. origin. Cf. RANGE *sb.*[2]] *trans.* To sift (meal).

Ranger (rēⁱ·ndʒəɹ). late ME. [f. RANGE *v.*[1] + -ER[1].] One who or that which ranges. **1.** A rover, wanderer; †a rake 1593. **b.** Applied *spec.* to certain animals 1686. **2.** A forest officer, a gamekeeper. Now only *arch.*, and as the official title of the keepers of the royal parks. late ME. **3.** *pl.* A body of mounted troops, or other armed men, employed in ranging over a tract of country. Chiefly *U.S.* 1742. **4.** One who sets in order (*rare*) 1611.

1. b. I had two horses; one was an old..'Texian R.' 1855. **3.** The 'Sarawak Rangers'..are recruited from Malays and Dyaks 1882. Hence **Ra·ngership,** the office of r. of a forest or park.

Rangy (rēⁱ·ndʒi), *a.* Chiefly *U.S.* 1880. [f. RANGE *sb.*[1] or *v.*[1] + -Y[1].] **1.** Of animals: **a.** Adapted for or capable of ranging 1891. **b.** Of a long slender form 1886. **2.** Of places: Giving scope for ranging; spacious 1880. **3.** *Austral.* Mountainous 1880.

Rani, var. of RANEE.

Raniform (rēⁱ·nifǭɹm), *a.* 1852. [f. L. *rana* frog + -FORM.] Frog-shaped.

Ranine (rēⁱ·nəin), *a.* 1819. [f. L. *rana* frog + -INE[1].] **1.** *Anat.* Belonging to the under side of the tip of the tongue (the part liable to be affected by RANULA); in *r. artery* (the terminal branch of the lingual artery), *r. vein.* **2.** Pertaining to a frog; frog-like (*rare*) 1840.

Rank (ræŋk), *sb.* 1547. [– OFr. *ranc*, var. of *renc* (now *rang*) – Gmc. **xrengaz* RING *sb.*[1]] **1.** A row, line, or series of things. **2.** A row or line of persons. Now *rare.* 1571. †**b.** Movement in line or file SHAKS. **3.** *Mil.* A number of soldiers drawn up in line abreast; *pl.* (with *the*) = forces, battalion, army. 1574. **b.** *pl.* (with *the*) The body of private soldiers; the rank and file 1809. **c.** *Chess.* One of the lines of squares stretching across the board from side to side 1597. **d.** *fig.* of things 1593. **4.** Without article: Line, order, array 1572. **5.** *R. and file*: see quot. and FILE *sb.*[2] II. 1. Chiefly *pl.* or without article in phr. *in r. and file.* 1598. **b.** *collect.* (The) common soldiers; (the) privates and non-commissioned officers 1796. †**6.** One of several rows of things placed at different levels –1734. **7.** A number of persons forming a distinct class in the social scale, or in any organized body; a grade of station or dignity, an order; hence, (a person's) social position or standing 1596. **b.** High station in society, etc.; social distinction. Also *concr.* persons of high position. 1742. **8.** A class (of persons, animals, or things) in a scale of comparison; hence, relative position or status, place 1605.

1. A r. of cabs 1903. Also, the place where these stand; a cab-rank, or -stand. **2. b.** *A. Y. L.* III. ii. 103. **3. b.** Phr. *To rise from the ranks.* **d.** Simois..Whose waves to imitate the battle sought..and their ranks began To break upon the galled shore SHAKS. **4.** Phr. *In* (*into*) *r.*, *out of r.*, *to keep* or *break r.* **5.** *Ranks and files*, are the horizontal and vertical lines of soldiers when drawn up for service 1802. **b.** Unless the R. and File are interested in their work, there will be no enthusiasm 1894. **6.** Ranks of oars in the modern galleys 1734. **7.** Reasonable and well-educated men of all ranks BERKELEY. **b.** The r. and fashion of the..country 1883. **8.** The Convertine, a Ship of the second R., that carried seventy Guns CLARENDON.

Rank (ræŋk), *a.* and *adv.* [OE. *ranc* = (M)LG. *rank* long and thin, ON. *rakkr* erect, f. Gmc. **raŋkaz.*] **A.** *adj.* **I.** †**1.** Proud, high-minded, haughty; froward, rebellious –1560. **2.** Stout and strong. *Obs.* exc. *dial.* OE. **3.** Having great speed or force; swift; impetuous; violent. Also const. *of.* ME.

3. †*R. rider*, a rapid, headlong, or reckless rider; a moss-trooper, highwayman.

II. Full, large or gross in size, quantity, etc. †**1.** Full-grown; mature (*rare*) –1536. **2.** Vigorous or luxuriant in growth. In later use: Growing too luxuriantly; large and coarse. Hence of growth, etc. ME. †**3.** Excessively great or large; *esp.* swollen, puffed up, grossly fat, too highly fed –1631. **b.** High or excessive in amount. *Obs.* exc. *Law.* 1602. †**4.** Abundant, copious –1632. **5. a.** In close array, crowded together; thick, dense. *Obs.* exc. *n. dial.* late ME. **b.** Numerous, frequent. *Obs.* exc. *n. dial.* 1545. **6.** *techn.* Projecting, standing out 1678.

2. The woods are choked with its r. luxuriance 1777. The male lion is adorned with a long r., shaggy mane 1850. **3. b.** The *modus* must not be too large, which in law is called a *r. modus* BLACKSTONE. **5. a.** Where the sheep are 'r.' on the fell sides 1864. **6.** When a ship has a deep keel, she is said to have a r. keel 1727.

III. Of a luxuriant, gross, or coarse quality. **1.** Covered or filled with a luxuriant (and coarse) growth of grass or plants. late ME. **2.** Grossly rich, heavy, or fertile; liable to produce rank vegetation. late ME. **3.** Having an offensively strong smell; rancid 1529. **b.** Of smell: Offensively strong 1570. †**4.** Lustful, licentious; in heat –1765. **5.** Gross, highly offensive or loathsome; in later use *esp.* coarse or indecent ME. **b.** Corrupt, foul; festering 1579. **6.** Of a strongly marked, violent, or virulent type; absolute, downright, gross. (Used as an intensive of the bad qualities implied by the qualified sb.) 1513. **b.** Grossly apparent (*rare*) 1624.

1. The patch..now r. with weeds 1890. **2.** A r. clay that requires the labour of years to make it mellow G. WHITE. **3.** Our men made some butter ..but it grew r. DE FOE. *fig.* Oh my offence is ranke, it smels to heauen SHAKS. **4.** *Cymb.* II. v. 24. **5.** The r. vocabulary of malice and hate MORLEY. **6.** 'Tis a most r. untruth MIDDLETON. The rankest Idiot MARVELL. R. treason against the royalty of Virtue 1766.

B. *adv.* †1. In a rank manner SPENSER. 2. With adjs.: Completely, extremely 1607.

2. He's irrecoverable; mad, ranke madde MARSTON. Hence **Ra·nk-ly** *adv.*, **-ness.**

Rank (ræŋk), *v.* 1573. [f. RANK *sb.*] 1. *trans.* To arrange or draw up (persons, *esp.* soldiers) in a rank or in ranks. 2. To arrange (things) in a row or rows; to set in line; to put in order 1590. †b. To divide or form *into* ranks or classes –1690. †c. In *pa. pple.*, of a place: Surrounded or bounded with rows or ranks –1698. 3. To place, locate; to give a certain position or station to; to class or classify. Also *refl.* 1592. 4. *U.S.* To take precedence of 1865. 5. *intr.* To form a rank or ranks; to stand in rank; to take up a position in a rank 1582. b. To take or have a place in a certain rank or class; to have rank or place 1599. c. *Law.* Of creditors or claims: To have a place on the list of claims, or of those having claims, on a bankrupt estate 1883. 6. To move or march in rank; chiefly *Mil.* 1832.

1. In view Stood rankt of Seraphim another row MILT. 2. He knew to r. his Elms in even Rows DRYDEN. c. *Timon* I. i. 65. 3. Those who r. Lucan rather among historians in verse than epic poets DRYDEN. 5. b. Also (*U.S.*), to have the highest rank; to be supremely eminent.

Ranker (ræ·ŋkəɹ). 1832. [f. RANK *sb.* and *v.* + -ER[1].] 1. One who arranges in ranks. 2. One (esp. a soldier) in the ranks 1890. 3. An officer who has risen from the ranks 1878.

Rankle (ræ·ŋk'l), *v.* ME. [– OFr. *rancler*, *raoncler* (cf. med.L. *ranclare*, *ranquillare*), var. of *draoncler* (mod. dial. *drancler*), f. *rancle*, *raoncle*, var. of *draoncle* ulcer, festering sore – med.L. *dranculus*, for L. *dracunculus*, dim. of *draco* serpent, DRAGON.] I. *intr.* 1. To fester, esp. to a degree that causes pain. †2. To inflict a festering wound; to cause a painful festering –1698. 3. a. Of persons: To fret or chafe angrily (*rare*) 1582. b. Of a bitter or malignant feeling: To have course, or continue in operation, like a festering sore 1508. c. Of experiences, events, etc.: To continue to cause painful, bitter, or venomous feelings 1735. 4. To change *to* or *into*, by or as by festering 1741.

1. Therewithal their knees would r. MARLOWE. The wound..is but skinned over, and rankles still at the bottom 1741. 3. b. A bitter feeling rankled in his heart 1874. c. The sight of the palace of the English King..rankled in his soul FREEMAN. 4. Discontent will r. into disaffection 1831.

II. *trans.* To cause (flesh, wounds, etc.) to fester; to make painful 1530. b. To embitter, envenom (feelings); to cause painful irritation in (a person) 1606.

b. A fierce reformer once, now ranckl'd with a contrary heat MILT. Hence **Ra·nkle** *sb.* (*rare*).

Ranny (ræ·ni). *Obs.* exc. *dial.* 1559. [app. – L. *araneus mus.*] The shrew mouse or field mouse.

Ransack (ræ·nsæk), *v.* ME. [– ON. *rannsaka* search for stolen goods, f. *rann* house (= OE. *ærn*; see BARN) + *-saka*, rel. by gradation to *sækja* SEEK.] †1. *trans.* To search (a person) for something stolen or missing –1493. 2. To make thorough search in or throughout (a place, receptacle, collection of things, etc.) *for* something (in early use, something stolen) ME. b. *absol.* To make thorough search. Now *rare.* late ME. 3. To examine thoroughly; to overhaul and investigate in detail ME. 4. To search (a place, person, etc.) with intent to rob; hence, to rob, plunder, pillage (*of*). late ME. b. To search for and take (*away*) or carry off as plunder. Now *rare.* late ME.

2. I am ransacking my memory for..scraps of theatrical history CIBBER. 3. She ransacked her conscience..and took herself to task..for a thousand imaginary faults HAWTHORNE. 4. The palaces were ransacked of their valuables and then ruthlessly set on fire 1878. Hence **Ra·nsack** *sb.* 1589, **Ra·nsacker**, a pillager.

Ransom (ræ·nsəm), *sb.* [ME. *rans(o)un* – OFr. *ransoun*, *raençon* (mod. *rançon*) :– L. *redemptio*, *-on-* REDEMPTION.] 1. The action of procuring the release of a prisoner or captive by paying a price, or of obtaining one's own freedom in this way; the fact or possibility of being set free on this condition; the paying of money to this end. 2. The sum or price paid or demanded for the release of a prisoner or the restoration of captured property ME. b. *fig.* in religious use, of Christ or His blood ME. †3. The action or means of freeing oneself from a penalty; a sum of money paid to obtain pardon for an offence; a fine, mulct –1769.

1. Phr. *To hold to r.*; Gweskien, taken prisoner by Chandos, was held by him to r. 1859. 2. *A king's r.*, a large sum; I'll not speak another word for a King's r. MARLOWE. b. Sending thee..his Mediator..Both R. and Redeemer voluntarie MILT. 3. This is the reason why fines in the king's court are frequently denominated ransoms BLACKSTONE.

Comb. **r.-bill, -bond,** an engagement to redeem or pay r., in later use esp. for a vessel captured by the enemy. Hence **Ra·nsomless** *a.* without r.

Ransom (ræ·nsəm), *v.* ME. [– OFr. *ransouner* (mod. *rançonner*), f. *ransoun*; see prec. For the dissimilation of *n..n* to *n..m* cf. RANDOM.] 1. *trans.* To redeem (from captivity or punishment); to procure the release of (a person) or restoration of (a thing) by payment of the sum or price demanded. late ME. b. To redeem, deliver, in religious sense ME. c. To purchase (life or liberty) by a ransom 1630. d. To atone or pay for, to expiate; †to procure respite of (time); to bring *into* by ransoming ME. 2. a. To permit to be ransomed; to admit to ransom; to set free on payment of a sum of money. late ME. b. To demand ransom from or for; to exact payment from; †hence, to oppress with exactions. Also *absol.* late ME. 3. To pay ransom to (a person). *rare.* 1722.

1. They were obliged to r. not only their prisoners but their dead THIRLWALL. b. His Brethren, ransomd with his own dear life MILT. d. Those tears are..rich and r. all ill deeds SHAKS. 2. b. These gentlemen contend that unfortified towns will never be bombarded or ransomed 1888. Hence **Ra·nsomable** *a.* **Ra·nsomer,** one who ransoms; a redeemer; (with cap.) a member of the R. C. Guild of Our Lady of Ransom which works for the conversion of England.

Rant (rænt), *sb.* 1649. [f. the vb.] 1. A high-flown, extravagant, or bombastic speech or utterance; a piece of turgid declamation; a tirade. †b. A violent scolding (*rare*) –1725. c. A ranting state or condition 1722. 2. Extravagant or bombastic language or sentiments; empty declamation 1708. b. A declamatory way of speaking. JOHNSON. 3. *n. dial.* and *Sc.* A noisy merrymaking; a spree 1675.

1. A R. Against the Envious, and the Ignorant DRYDEN. 2. The following passages are pure r. 1762. b. The players, Sir, have got a kind of r., with which they run on, without any regard either to accent or emphasis 1742.

Rant (rænt), *v.* 1598. [– Du. *ranten* talk foolishly, rave. See RAND *v.*] 1. *intr.* (†or with *it*). To talk or declaim in an extravagant high-flown manner; to use bombastic language 1602. †b. To storm or scold violently. Const. *at*, *against*. –1710. 2. To be jovial, boisterous, uproariously gay or merry; also, to sing loudly 1598. 3. *trans.* To utter in a declamatory and bombastic manner; to mouth. Also with *out.* 1650.

1. Nay, and thou'lt mouth, Ile r. as well as thou SHAKS. b. They say you're angry, and r. mightily COWLEY. 3. Ranting Carlyle and Emerson by the volume MORLEY. Hence **Ra·ntingly** *adv.* †**Ra·ntism** (*rare*), the practice of ranting; *spec.* = RANTERISM.

Ranter (ræ·ntəɹ), *sb.* 1649. [f. RANT *v.* + -ER[1].] 1. One who rants, esp. in preaching. †2. A noisy, riotous, dissipated fellow; a rake –1828. 3. *spec.* (chiefly *pl.*) a. A member of a sect of Antinomians which arose *c*1645. Now only *Hist.* 1651. b. A member of the Primitive Methodist body, which originated in 1807–1810. 1823.

1. There went also, with this party, Sir Thomas Armstrong, Colonel Trevor, and most of their great ranters CROMWELL. Hence **Ra·nterism,** the practices or doctrines of Ranters.

Rantipole (ræ·ntipōᵘl), *sb.* (and *a.*) Now *rare.* 1700. [Of unkn. origin. Cf. RAMP *sb.*[1]] 1. A romp; a wild, ill-behaved or reckless person; a scold, termagant. 2. *attrib.* or as *adj.* Wild, disorderly, rakish 1700.

Rantipole (ræ·ntipōᵘl), *v.* 1712. [f. prec.] *intr.* To go *about*, or behave, in a romping, rude or noisy fashion.

She used to R. about the House, pinch the Children, kick the Servants 1712.

‖**Ranula** (ræ·niŭlă). 1657. [L. *ranula* little frog, little swelling on the tongue of cattle (Vegetius), dim. of *rana* frog; see -ULE.] *Path.* A cystic tumour under the tongue, caused by the obstruction of the salivary ducts or glands. Hence **Ra·nular** *a.*

Ranunculaceous (rănɒŋkiŭlēⁱ·ʃəs), *a.* 1833. [f. next + -ACEOUS.] *Bot.* Belonging to the *Ranunculaceæ*, of which Ranunculus is the typical genus.

‖**Ranunculus** (rănɒ·ŋkiŭləs). *Pl.* **-culuses, -culi.** 1578. [L., a little frog, tadpole; also a medicinal plant; dim of *rana* frog.] *Bot.* A genus of plants (also called CROWFOOT); the common species with yellow flowers are popularly called BUTTERCUPS; the usual cultivated species is *R. asiaticus.* b. A plant belonging to this genus.

‖**Ranz-des-vaches** (rań(s) de vaʃ). 1801. [Swiss dial. of Fribourg.] One of the melodies peculiar to Swiss herdsmen, usu. played on an Alpine horn, and consisting of irregular phrases made up of the harmonic notes of the horn.

Rap (ræp), *sb.*[1] ME. [Goes with RAP *v.*[1] Cf. Sw. *rapp*, Da. *rap.*] A blow or stroke, esp. one inflicted on a person. Now restricted to a sharp or smart stroke with a stick or the like, not causing serious hurt. b. A sharp knock such as is produced by striking on a wooden surface with something hard; esp. a knock at a door, or (in recent use) one supposed to be made by a spirit 1637.

Rap (ræp), *sb.*[2] 1724. [Shortening of Ir. *ropaire.*] A counterfeit coin, worth about half a farthing, which passed current for a halfpenny in Ireland in the 18th c., owing to the scarcity of genuine money. Now *Hist.* b. Taken as a type of the smallest coin 1823. c. *fig.* An atom, the least bit. Chiefly in neg. phrases, and esp. *not to care a r.* 1834.

Rap (ræp), *v.*[1] late ME. [prob. imit.; perh. of Scand. origin; cf. Sw. *rappa* beat, drub, and *clap*, *flap*, *slap*, *tap.*] 1. *trans.* To strike, smite (*esp.* a person); now, to strike smartly without causing serious hurt. 2. To drive, dash, knock, etc. with a rap. Chiefly *Sc.* late ME. 3. Usu. with *out.* To utter (*esp.* an oath) sharply, vigorously, or suddenly 1541. †b. *slang.* To swear (a thing) *against* a person. Also *intr.* To swear; to perjure oneself. –1818. 4. *intr.* To knock sharply (*esp.* at a door) 1440. b. *trans.* To strike with a rap; to rap at or on 1712. c. *To r. out*, to knock out; also (*esp.* of spirits) to declare by means of raps 1841.

1. Phr. *To r.* (a person's) *fingers* or *knuckles*, to check or punish him smartly. b. *U.S.* To criticize adversely; to reprove 1906. 3. Out he rapped Such a round of oaths BROWNING.

Rap (ræp), *v.*[2] Now *rare.* 1528. [In sense 1 perh. related to MLG. *rappen* seize, snatch; in 2 app. a back-formation from RAPT *pa. pple.*] †1. *trans.* To seize or snatch for oneself; to take or get by snatching or stealing –1754. 2. To take up and carry off, to transport, remove 1599. b. To affect with rapture; to transport, ravish (with joy, etc.) 1599.

1. Phr. *To r. and rend* (common in 16–17th c.; now *arch.* or *dial.*); From foe and from friend He'd 'r. and he'd rend' BARHAM. 2. b. Is't a prognostication raps him so? B. JONS.

Rapacious (răpēⁱ·ʃəs), *a.* 1651. [f. L. *rapax*, *rapac-* grasping, f. *rapere* snatch; see -OUS, -IOUS.] 1. Given to grasping or taking for oneself; inordinately greedy. Also const. *of* and *inf.* 2. Of animals: Subsisting by the capture of living prey; raptorial 1661.

1. Who more r. in robbing, who more profuse in giving? COWLEY. Deliver me from this r. deep KEATS. The r. domination of the Fanariotes 1847. 2. Of R. Birds in General GOLDSM. Hence **Rapa·cious-ly** *adv.*, **-ness.**

Rapacity (răpæ·sĭti). 1543. [– Fr. *rapacité* or L. *rapacitas*, f. as prec.; see -ITY.] The quality or fact of being rapacious; the exercise of rapacious tendencies.

The rapacite of wolues 1543. An act of wanton r. FREEMAN.

Rape (rēⁱp), *sb.*[1] late ME. [– AFr. *ra(a)p*, *rape* (Britton), f. *raper*; see RAPE *v.*] †1. The act of taking anything by force; violent seizure (of goods), robbery. Also with *a*: A case or instance of this. –1712. 2. The act of carrying away a person (*esp.* a woman) by force. late ME. 3. Violation or ravishing of a woman 1481. b. With *a* and *pl.* An instance of this 1577. †4. *concr.* One who is raped –1683.

1. The R. of the Lock (*title*) POPE. **2.** The r. of the Sabines SCOTT. **3.** Marrying or prostituting, as befell, R. or Adulterie MILT. **b.** An assault, with intent to commit a r. 1834. *fig.* A r. Vpon the maiden vertue of the Crowne SHAKS.

Rape (rēⁱp), *sb.*² OE. [Identical with OE. *rāp* ROPE (the var. *rope* is found occas. in XIV), the reference being to the fencing-off of land with a rope. In AL. *rapum, rapa.* Cf. the similarly used cogn. OHG., MHG. *reif.*] One of the six administrative districts into which Sussex is divided, each comprising several hundreds.

Rape (rēⁱp), *sb.*³ late ME. [– L. *rapum, rapa* turnip.] †**1.** (With *a* or in *pl.*) **a.** A turnip (? or radish). **b.** A plant of rape –1714. **2.** As a plant-name. †**a.** The common turnip. **b.** The plant *Brassica napus*, usu. grown as food for sheep. **c.** The plant *Brassica campestris oleifera*, from the seed of which oil is made; coleseed. late ME. **3.** *Wild r.*, Charlock or Field-Mustard 1551.

Comb.: **r.-cake,** a flat cake made of rapeseed after the oil has been extracted from it; **-oil,** a thick brownish-yellow oil expressed from rapeseed, used for lubricating, etc.; **-seed,** (*a*) the seed of the r. (esp. *Brassica campestris oleifera*); (*b*) as a name for the plant (now *rare*).

Rape (rēⁱp), *sb.*⁴ 1600. [In branch I – (O)Fr. *râpe*, med.L. *raspa*. In II prop. *rapé* – (O)Fr. *râpé*, f. *râpe*. Cf. AL. *raspatum* (XII), *vinum raspatum* (XIII).] **I. 1.** The stalks of grape-clusters, or refuse of grapes from which wine has been expressed, used in making vinegar. Also *pl.* in same sense. 1657. **2.** A vessel used in the manufacture of vinegar 1805. †**II.** (In full *R. wine* = Fr. *vin râpé.*) Wine made either from the rape (sense 1 above) by addition of water, or from fresh grapes and light wine placed together in a cask –1733.

Rape (rēⁱp), *v.* late ME. [– AFr. *raper* – L. *rapere* seize, snatch, take by force.] **1.** *trans.* To take (a thing) by force. Also *absol.* **b.** To rob, strip, plunder (a place). *rare.* 1721. †**2.** To carry off (a person, *esp.* a woman) by force –1720. **3.** To ravish, commit rape on 1577. **4.** To transport, ravish, delight. Now *rare.* 1613.

Raphaelesque (ræ:fĕĭĕle·sk), *a.* Also **raffaell-.** 1830. [f. name of *Raphael* (It. *Raffaello*) the painter (1483–1520) + -ESQUE.] After the style of Raphael. Hence **Ra·phaelism,** the principles of art introduced by Raphael; his style or method. **Ra·phaelite,** one who adopts the principles or follows the style of Raphael.

‖**Raphanus** (ræ·fănŏs). 1730. [L. – Gr. ῥάφανος – ῥαφανίς radish.] *Bot.* A genus of cruciferous plants, of which the common radish (*R. sativus*) is the most important species.

‖**Raphe** (rī·fi). 1706. [mod.L. – Gr. ῥαφή seam, suture (of the skull, a wound, etc.).] **1.** *Anat.* A line of union between the two halves of an organ or part of the body, having the appearance of a seam. **2.** *Bot.* **a.** In certain ovules, a cord connecting the hilum with the chalaza, and usu. appearing as a ridge. **b.** In the Umbelliferæ, the line of junction or suture between the carpels. **c.** A median line or rib on the valves of diatoms. 1830. **3.** *Ornith.* The groove along the under-side of the rachis of a feather 1859.

Raphia (rēⁱ·fiă). 1866. [Malagasy, var. of RAFFIA.] *Bot.* A palm of the genus so named, having short stems and long pinnate leaves. *attrib.*: *R. grass* = RAFFIA.

Raphide (rēⁱ·fəid). 1884. [– Fr. *raphide*, f. stem of Gr. ῥαφίς; see next.] *Bot.* = next.

‖**Raphis** (rēⁱ·fis). Also **rha-.** *Pl.* **raphides** (ræ·fidīz). 1842. [Gr. ῥαφίς, ῥαφιδ- needle.] *Bot.* One of the minute crystals, usu. of acicular form, found in the cells of many plants.

Rapid (ræ·pid), *a.* (*adv.*), and *sb.* 1634. [– L. *rapidus*, f. *rapere*; see RAPE *v.*, -ID¹.] **A.** *adj.* **1.** Moving, or capable of moving, with great speed; swift, very quick. **2.** Of movement: Characterized by speed 1697. **3.** Quick in action, discourse, etc. 1791. **b.** *techn.* Said of photographic lenses, plates, or subjects, requiring only a short exposure 1878. **4.** Taking place with speed; coming quickly into existence or to completion 1780. **b.** Of a slope: Descending quickly 1890. **5.** quasi-*adv.* Rapidly 1791.

1. Part..shun the Goal With r. wheels MILT. On r. feet COWPER. **2.** Fancy's r. flight 1730. I heard my name among those r. words BROWNING. **3.** Homer is eminently r. M. ARNOLD. **4.** The r. victories of these Eastern conquerors 1780.

B. *sb.* A part of a river where the bed forms a steep descent, causing a swift current. (Orig. *U.S.*, and usu. in *pl.*). 1776.

Mortal boat In such a shallow r. could not float SHELLEY. Hence **Rapi·dity,** the quality of being r. **Ra·pid-ly** *adv.*, **-ness** (now *rare*).

Rapier (rēⁱ·piəɹ). 1547. [prob. – Du. *rapier* or LG. *rappir* – Fr. *rapière*, orig. *espee rapiere* (XV) 'rapier sword', of unkn. origin.] Orig., a long, pointed, two-edged sword adapted either for cutting or thrusting, but chiefly used for the latter. Later, a light, sharp-pointed sword designed only for thrusting; a small sword. Hence **Ra·piered** *a.* wearing or furnished with a r.; sharp-pointed.

‖**Rapilli** (rapi·lli). 1809. [It., pl. of *rapillo.*] Small fragments of pumice-stone.

Rapine (ræ·pəin), *sb.* late ME. [– (O)Fr. *rapine* or L. *rapina*, f. *rapere* seize; see RAPE *v.*, -INE⁴.] The act or practice of seizing and taking away by force the property of others; plunder, pillage, robbery. **b.** *pl.* Acts of violent robbery or pillage (now *rare*) 1494. **c.** *Beast* (etc.) *of r.*: Beast of prey 1612.

The lawless r. of banditti 1769. Hence †**Ra·pine** *v. intr.* to commit r.; *trans.* to plunder, or carry away, by r. †**Ra·pinous** *a.* given to r.; rapacious.

Rapparee (ræpărī·). 1690. [– Ir. *rapaire*, pl. *rapairidhe* (-i·yə) short pike.] †**1.** A half-pike (*rare*). **2.** *Hist.* An Irish pikeman or irregular soldier, of the kind prominent during the war of 1688–92; hence, an Irish bandit, robber, or freebooter 1690.

Rappee (ræpī·). 1740. [– Fr. (*tabac*) *râpé*, pa. pple. of *râper* RASP *v.*¹] A coarse kind of snuff made from the darker and ranker tobacco leaves, and orig. obtained by rasping a piece of tobacco.

‖**Rappel** (rapę̄l). 1848. [Fr., f. *rappeler* to recall.] The roll or beat of a drum to summon soldiers to arms.

Rapper (ræ·pəɹ). 1611. [f. RAP *v.*¹ + -ER¹.] **1.** One who raps or knocks; a spirit-rapper 1755. **2.** Anything used for rapping; *spec.* †a door-knocker 1640. **3. a.** An arrant lie. Now *dial.* 1611. **b.** A great oath. Now *dial.* 1678. †**4.** Something remarkably good or large –1672.

Rapport (ræpōᵊ·ɹt, Fr. rapōr). 1455. [Fr., f. *rapporter*; see RE- and APPORT *v.*] †**1.** Report, talk –1539. **2.** Reference, relationship; connection, correspondence 1661. **b.** *spec.* A state in which mesmeric action can be exercised by one person on another 1848. **3.** In Fr. phr. *en rapport*, in connection, etc. 1818.

2. Between whose Languages there is no more r., then the English hath to the Greek and Arabian 1662.

‖**Rapprochement** (raproʃmaṅ). 1809. [Fr., f. *rapprocher* (f. *re-* + *approcher* APPROACH) + -MENT.] A coming or bringing together, an establishment of harmonious relations.

Rapscallion (ræpskæ·liən). 1699. [Later f. RASCALLION.] A rascal, rogue, vagabond, scamp. Also *attrib.* or as *adj.*

†**Rapt** (ræpt), *sb.* 1440. [– (O)Fr. *rapt* or L. *raptus*, f. *rapere* RAPE *v.*] **1.** *Sc.* = RAPE *sb.*¹ 3. –1693. **2.** A trance, ecstasy, rapture –1826. **3.** The act or power of carrying forcibly away; sweep; force, current –1682.

Rapt (ræpt), *pa. pple.* (and *pa. t.*). late ME. [– L. *raptus*, pa. pple. of *rapere* seize, RAPE.] **I.** As *pa. pple.* passive. **1.** (Also with *up.*) Taken and carried up *to* or *into* heaven (either in literal or mystical sense). **2.** Carried away *in spirit*, without bodily removal 1470. **3.** Transported with some emotion, ravished, enraptured. Also const. *with* or *by*. 1539. **4.** Deeply engaged or buried *in* (a feeling, subject of thought, etc.): intent *upon* 1509. **5.** Of a woman: Carried away by force; raped. late ME. **6.** Carried away from one place, position, or situation to another. (Chiefly said of persons). 1552. **b.** Taken *away* by death 1820.

1. They are..r., perhaps, like Elijah, alive into Heaven 1760. **2.** St. Paul when he was r. in the spirit into Paradise 1878. **3.** Nor r., nor craving, but in settled peace WORDSW. **4.** For a woman r. in love so marveylously 1509.

II. As *pa. pple.* active (*rare*) 1509.

What accident Hath r. him from us? MILT.

III. As *pa. t.* Chiefly *poet.*; now *rare.* 1594.

Sorrow and fear So struck, so roused, so r. Urania SHELLEY.

Rapt (ræpt), *ppl. a.* 1555. [See prec.] **1.** Entranced, ravished, enraptured. **2.** Indicating, proceeding from, characterized by, a state of rapture 1797.

1. Thy r. soul sitting in thine eyes MILT. **2.** He listened..with a r. attention 1797.

†**Rapt,** *v.* 1577. [f. RAPT *pa. pple.*] **1.** *trans.* To carry away by force –1619. **2.** To transport, enrapture –1619. Hence †**Ra·pter,** a ravisher DRAYTON.

Raptor (ræ·ptǫ̆ɹ). 1609. [– L. *raptor*, f. *rapt-*, pa. ppl. stem of *rapere* RAPE *v.*; see -OR 2.] **1.** A ravisher. †**2.** A plunderer, robber –1720. **3.** *Ornith.* One of the *Raptores* (see 4) 1873. **4.** In L. pl. **raptores** (ræptōᵊ·rīz), as the name of an order of birds of prey, including the eagle, hawk, buzzard, owl, etc. 1823.

Raptorial (ræptōᵊ·riăl), *a.* 1825. [f. prec. + -IAL.] **1.** Given to seizing prey, predatory; esp. *r. birds* = prec. 4. **2.** Pertaining to, or characteristic of, predatory birds or animals; adapted for seizing prey 1839. So **Rapto·rious** *a.*

Rapture (ræ·ptiŭr, -tʃəɹ), *sb.* 1600. [– Fr. †*rapture* or med.L. *raptura*; partly infl. by RAPT *pa. pple.*; see -URE.] †**1.** The act of seizing and carrying off as prey or plunder –1639. **2.** The act of carrying, or state of being carried, onwards; force of movement. Now *rare.* 1615. †**3.** The act of carrying off a woman –1728. †**b.** = RAPE *sb.*¹ 3. –1649. **4.** The act of conveying a person from one place to another, *esp.* to heaven; the fact of being so conveyed 1647. **5.** Transport of mind, ecstasy; now *esp.* ecstatic delight or joy 1629. **b.** With *a* and *pl.* An instance of this 1605. **c.** A state of passionate excitement; a paroxysm, fit. *rare.* (now *dial.*). 1607. **d.** A strong fit *of* (some emotion or mental state) 1795. **6.** The expression of ecstatic feeling in words or music; a rhapsody 1620.

1. *Per.* II. i. 161. **2.** Our Ship..'gainst a Rocke, or Flat, her Keele did dash, With headlong r. CHAPMAN. **3.** The r. of Proserpine by a Centaure 1662. **5.** Such musick sweet..As all their souls in blisfull r. took MILT. **b.** Phr. *To be in*, or *to go into raptures*; A place that strangers fell into raptures with 1862. **c.** *Cor.* II. i. 223. **d.** A r. of forgetfulness WORDSW. Hence **Ra·pture** *v. trans.* to enrapture (now *rare*). **Ra·ptured** *ppl. a.* ecstatic, enraptured.

†**Ra·pturist.** *rare.* 1663. [f. prec. + IST.] An enthusiast –1783.

Rapturize (ræ·ptiŭrəiz), *v.* 1882. [f. RAPTURE *sb.* + -IZE.] *intr.* To fall into ecstasies.

Rapturous (ræ·ptiŭrəs, -tʃərəs), *a.* 1678. [f. as prec. + -OUS.] **1.** Characterized by, expressive or partaking of, rapture. **2.** Feeling or exhibiting rapture 1754.

1. A shout of r. applause 1853. **2.** A r. imaginative girl 1851. Hence **Ra·pturous-ly** *adv.*, **-ness.**

‖**Raquette.** 1861. = RACKET *sb.*¹

‖**Rara avis** (rēᵊ·ră ēⁱ·vis). 1654. [L., = 'rare bird'.] A remarkable person; a paragon.

Rare (rēᵊɹ), *a.*¹ late ME. [– L. *rarus.* Cf. Fr. *rare.*] **1.** Having the constituent particles not closely packed together. (Opp. to *dense.*) In later use chiefly of the air or gases. †**2. a.** Having the component parts widely set; of open construction; in open order (*rare*) –1647. **b.** Thinly attended or populated (*rare*) –1789. †**3.** Placed or stationed at wide intervals; standing or keeping far apart –1667. **4.** (With pl. sbs.) Few in number and widely separated from each other (in space or time); forming a small and scattered class 1555. **5.** Of a kind, class, or description seldom found, met with, occurring; unusual, uncommon, exceptional 1542. **6.** Unusual in respect of some good quality; remarkably good or fine 1483. **b.** *colloq.* Splendid, excellent, fine 1596. †**c.** Interjectionally in *O rare!* –1786. **d.** *colloq.* as an intensive, with sbs. and adjs. (also *r. and* with adjs.) 1833.

1. All pure and r. bodies ascend, as the Fire more than the Air 1669. **3.** Among the trees in pairs they rose, they walk'd; Those r. and solitarie, these in flocks MILT. **4.** I never saw but one Grey-ey'd, and therefore I suppose them r. 1698. **5.** Gathering r. shells, delighted children stray 1812. Phr. *It is r. that*..(cf. Fr. *il est rare que*..).

6. A boat of r. device, which had no sail SHELLEY. **b.** He's a r. Fellow for giving a bad Captain a good Word 1706. **c.** 1 *Hen. IV*, I. ii. 72. Hence **Ra·re-ly** *adv.*, **-ness.**

Rare (rēᵊɹ), *a.*[2] 1655. [Later f. REAR *a.*[2]] †**a.** Of eggs: Left soft in cooking. **b.** Of meat: Underdone 1784.

b. The same flesh, rotten-roasted or r., on the Tuesdays LAMB.

Rare (rēᵊɹ), *a.*[3] and *adv. Obs.* exc. *dial.* 1574. [var. of RATHE *a.*] Early.

Rude mechanicals, that r. and late Work in the market-place CHAPMAN.

Rarebit: see WELSH RAREBIT.

Raree-show (rēᵊ·rī,ʃōᵘ). 1681. [app. the Savoyard showmen's pronunciation of *rare show.*] A show contained or carried about in a box; a peep-show; *transf.* a show or spectacle of any kind.

Rarefaction (rēᵊrǐfæ·kʃən). 1603. [– med.L. *rarefactio, -ion-*, f. *rarefact-*, pa. ppl. stem of *rarefacere*; see RAREFY, -FACTION.] The action of rarefying or process of being rarefied; diminution of density. (Now chiefly of the air or gases, or *Path.* of bones.)

There is..thickening or r. of skull bones 1898.

Rarefa·ctive, *a.* 1656. [– med.L. *rarefactivus*, f. as prec.; see -IVE.] Having the quality of rarefying; characterized by rarefaction. (In recent use only *Path.* of diseases of bones.)

Rarefy (rēᵊ·rǐfəi), *v.* late ME. [– (O)Fr. *raréfier* or med.L. *rarificare*, extension of L. *rarefacere*, f. *rarus* RARE *a.*[1]; see -FY.] **1.** *trans.* To make rare or thin, esp. by expansion; to lessen the density or solidity of (a substance, now usu. air, or, in *Path.*, bone). **2.** *fig.* To make less gross or material, to refine, to purify 1599. **b.** To make (an idea) subtle 1699. †**3.** To thin (a wood). FULLER. **4.** *intr.* To become less dense; to be thinned (*rare*) 1658.

1. Water rarified becomes Ayre againe 1477. The hot wire rarefied the air in contact with it TYNDALL. **4.** Like the mist sometimes rarefying into sunny gauze 1847. Hence †**Rarefiable** *a.* (*rare*). **Rarefica·tion** (*rare*) = RAREFACTION.

Ra·re-ripe, *a.* and *sb. dial.* and *U.S.* 1799. [f. RARE *a.*[3] + RIPE.] **A.** *adj.* Rathe-ripe. **B.** *sb.* An early fruit or vegetable. **b.** *attrib.* Of the colour of a peach called the *rare-ripe*.

Rarity (rēᵊ·rīti). 1560. [– Fr. *rareté*, †*rarité* or L. *raritas*, f. *rarus* RARE *a.*[1]; see -ITY.] **1.** Of substances (now chiefly of air): Thinness of composition or texture. (Opp. to *density.*) 1644. **2.** Relative fewness in number; the fact of occurring seldom or in few instances 1560. **3.** Unusual or exceptional character, esp. in respect of excellence 1601. **4.** A rare or uncommon thing or occurrence 1592.

4. It was a fine day, which is a r. with us SWIFT.

Rasant (rēⁱ·zănt), *a.* Now *rare* or *Obs.* 1696. [– (O)Fr. *rasant*, pr. pple. of *raser* shave close; see RASE *v.*[1], -ANT.] *Mil.* In fortification: Sweeping, grazing.

Rascal (ra·skăl), *sb.* and *a.* ME. [– OFr. *rascaille* (mod. *racaille*), prob. f. ONFr. **rasque* = OFr. *rasche*, Pr. *rasca* scab, scurf :– Rom. **rasica*, f. **rasicare*, f. *ras-*, pa. ppl. stem of L. *radere* scrape, scratch, shave.] **A.** *sb.* †**1.** *collect.* The rabble of an army or of the populace; persons of the lowest class. *Obs.* exc. *arch.* †**b.** A rabble or mob (*rare*) –1532. †**2.** One belonging to the rabble; a man of low birth or station –1674. **3.** A rogue, knave, scamp 1586. **b.** Used playfully, or as a mild term of reproof 1610. †**4.** *collect.* The young, lean, or inferior deer of a herd, dist. from the full-grown antlered bucks or stags –1607. **b.** Similarly applied to other animals 1530.

3. The Whip..is a Punishment inflicted upon all Vagabonds, Wandering Beggars and Idle Rascals 1688. **b.** You are a lucky r., and I wish..I were in your shoes 1899.

B. *adj.* **1.** Belonging to, or forming, the rabble. Also *rarely*, rascally, knavish. late ME. †**b.** Common, private (soldiers) –1581. **c.** Pertaining or appropriate to (†the rabble, or) rascals 1566. †**2.** Wretched, miserable, mean –1748. †**3.** Of deer, etc.: see A. 4. –1664.

1. The R. Rabble DRYDEN. **c.** The Rascall humours of the vaine And giddy multitude 1618. **2.** On what r. foundations were built up all the pretences to virtue which were set up in opposition to him H. WALPOLE. Hence **Ra·scaldom,** the world or body of rascals; rascally conduct, a rascally act. †**Ra·scaless** (*nonce-wd.*), a female r.

Rascality (raskæ·lĭti). 1577. [f. RASCAL *sb.* + -ITY.] **1.** = prec. A. 1. **2.** Rascally character or conduct; a rascally act or practice 1592.

1. The Chief Heads of their Clans, with all the several Rascalities depending on them 1652.

Rascallion (raskæ·liən). 1649. [perh. f. RASCAL with fanciful ending, after RAMPALLION.] A low mean wretch or rascal.

Rascally (ra·skăli), *a.* 1596. [f. RASCAL *sb.* + -LY[1].] †**1.** = RASCAL *a.* 1. –1687. **2.** Low, mean, or unprincipled in character or conduct; knavish 1598. **3.** = RASCAL *a.* 1 c. 1596. **4.** = RASCAL *a.* 2. 1606.

1. There was none of any quality, but poor and r. people PEPYS. **2.** Our common soldiers are such a low r. set of people HUME. **3.** Vile..r. verses B. JONS. **4.** A whorson r. tisicke SHAKS. So **Ra·scally** *adv.*

†**Rase,** *sb.* 1530. [f. next.] **1.** The act of scraping or scratching; the fact of being scratched or cut –1628. **2.** A scratch, cut, slit –1677.

Rase (rēⁱz), *v.*[1] late ME. [– (O)Fr. *raser* shave close :– Rom. **rasare*, (AL. XIII) f. *ras-*, pa. ppl. stem of L. *radere.*] †**1.** *trans.* To scratch or tear with something sharp; to cut, slit, or slash (esp. the skin or clothing) –1714. †**b.** *intr.* To slash; to make way or penetrate; to make an incised mark –1677. **c.** *trans.* To incise (a mark or line) 1815. **2.** To remove by scraping or rasping. Somewhat *rare* in literal sense. late ME. **b.** *esp.* To erase (something written). late ME. **3.** (Without const.) To erase, obliterate (writing), orig. by scraping with a knife. Now *rare* or *Obs.* late ME. †**4.** To scrape (a thing) so as to remove something from its surface; also, to scrape down into small particles –1743. †**b.** To alter (a writing) by erasure –1703. **5.** To level with the ground; to RAZE. Now *rare.* 1537. †**6.** To graze –1786.

2. b. Unlesse you can r. these words..out of the Statute 1658. **3.** To r. all records in their journals of that matter MARVELL. **4. b.** Counterfeiting Rasing or Falsifying any Cocquet Certificate 1697. **5.** They..rased the noblest Structures in the Land, to sell the Materials 1680. **6.** Sometimes his feet rased the surface of the water 1786.

†**Rase,** *v.*[2] late ME. [var. f. *race*, aphet. f. ARACE.] *trans.* To pull or pluck –1594.

He dreamt, the Bore had rased off his Helme SHAKS.

†**Ra·sen.** [OE. *ræsn*, of unkn. origin.] = RAISING-PIECE –1703.

Rash (ræʃ), *sb.*[1] Now *Hist.* 1578. [– Fr. *ras* (XVI), subst. use of adj. corresp. to L. *rasus* scraped, shaven, smooth, f. *radere*; see RASE *v.*[1]] A smooth textile fabric made of silk (*silk r.*), or worsted (*cloth r.*).

Rash (ræʃ), *sb.*[2] 1709. [corresp. in form to OFr. *ra(s)che* skin eruption = It. *raschia* itch, but the late emergence of the word is against direct connection.] A superficial eruption or efflorescence of the skin in red spots or patches, as in measles, scarlet fever, etc.

Rash (ræʃ), *sb.*[3] 1668. [imit.] A rustling noise. DRYDEN.

Rash (ræʃ), *a.* and *adv.* ME. [:– OE. **ræsc* = (M)Du. *rasch*, OHG. *rasc* (G. *rasch*), ON. *rǫskr* doughty, brave :– Gmc. **raskuz*, perh. for **raþskuz*, f. **raþ-* RATHE.] **A.** *adj.* **1.** *Sc.* and *n. dial.* Active, fresh, vigorous; brisk, nimble, quick; eager. **2.** Hasty, impetuous, reckless, acting without due consideration or regard for consequences 1509. †**b.** Of things: Operating quickly and strongly. SHAKS. **3.** Of speech, actions, qualities, etc.: Characterized by, or proceeding from, undue haste and want of consideration 1558. †**b.** Urgent. SHAKS.

2. I was a fool, too r., and quite mistaken MILT. **b.** Though it doe worke as strong As Aconitum, or r. Gun-powder SHAKS. **3.** R. adventures speed not always best HOLLAND. **b.** I scarce haue leisure to salute you, My matter is so r. SHAKS. Hence **Ra·sh-ly** *adv.*, **-ness.**

†**B.** *adv.* = RASHLY –1777.

Why do you speake so startingly and r.? SHAKS.

Rash (ræʃ), *v.*[1] Chiefly *Sc.* Now *rare* or *Obs.* late ME. [prob. imit; cf. *clash, crash, dash*, etc.] **1.** *intr.* To dash or rush hastily or violently. †**2.** *trans.* To dash (things *together*, or one thing *against, in*, or *through* another) –1666. †**3.** *To r. up*: To put together hurriedly; to rush or run up –1650.

Rash, *v.*[2] 1500. [Alteration of RASE *v.*[1], perh. after prec. or next.] **1.** *trans.* To cut, slash –1599. **2.** To scrape out, erase –1650.

1. They..shields did share, and mailes did r., and helmes did hew SPENSER.

†**Rash,** *v.*[3] 1523. [Aphetic f. *arrache* = RASE *v.*[2]] *trans.* To pull, drag (*down, off, out,* etc.), to tear *away* –1697.

Rasher (ræ·ʃəɹ). 1592. [Of unkn. origin.] A thin slice of bacon or ham, cooked (or intended to be cooked) by broiling or frying.

‖**Raskolnik** (ræskǫ·lnik). 1799. [– Russ. *raskól'nik*, f. *raskól* split, schism.] A dissenter from the Orthodox Church of Russia.

Rasp (rasp), *sb.*[1] 1541. [– OFr. *raspe* (mod. *râpe*), f. *rasper*; see RASP *v.*[1]] **1.** A coarse kind of file, having separate teeth raised on its surface by means of a pointed punch; also, any similar tool or implement used for scraping or rubbing down. **2.** *transf.* **a.** A rough surface like that of a rasp 1869. **b.** *Zool.* The radula of a mollusc, or one of the teeth on this 1826. **3.** A rough sound as of a rasp 1851.

Comb.: **r.-palm,** a Brazilian palm (*Iriartea exorhiza*), having exposed roots which are used by the natives as rasps; **-punch,** a punch for raising the teeth of rasps.

Rasp (rasp), *sb.*[2] 1555. [Shortened form of RASPIS.] = RASPBERRY 1, 2.

Rasp (rasp), *v.*[1] ME. [– OFr. *rasper* (mod. *râper*) :– Rom. **raspare* (cf. med.L. *raspare* scratch, XIII) – WGmc. (= OHG.) *raspōn* scrape together. In later use from RASP *sb.*[1]] **1.** *trans.* To scrape or abrade with a rasp or the like. **b.** To scrape or rub in a rough manner 1715. **c.** *fig.* To grate upon, to irritate 1810. **2.** To scrape *off* or *away* 1789. **3.** *intr.* or *absol.* **a.** To scrape or grate, *esp.* on a stringed instrument 1842. **b.** To make a grating sound 1868.

1. The fuze must be rasped if necessary 1859. **c.** Her hard, metallic voice had rasped the invalid's nerves 1887. **2.** I began to r. off the bark 1789. **3. a.** Sorrily rasping on an execrable fiddle 1870. **b.** A loud, harsh, sharp tone, that rasps like a file 1868.

Rasp (rasp), *v.*[2] Now *dial.* 1626. [imit.] *intr.* and *trans.* To belch.

Raspatory (ra·spătəri). 1562. [– Fr. †*raspatoire*, or its possible source, med. (mod.)L. **raspatorium* form of rasp used in surgery, f. *raspat-*, pa. ppl. stem of med.L. *raspare* RASP *v.*[1]; see -ORY[1].] A form of rasp used in surgery.

Raspberry (ra·zběri). 1623. [f. RASP *sb.*[2] + BERRY.] **1.** The fruit of several plants of the genus *Rubus*, esp. *R. idæus*, consisting of many small juicy grains or drupes of a subacid flavour arranged on a conical receptacle, from which the ripe fruit, usu. of a red colour, but also white or yellow, is easily detached. **2.** The plant which produces the raspberry, or other similar plants of the genus *Rubus*. Also **r. cane.** 1733. **3.** Raspberry wine 1768. **4.** *slang.* A sound or manifestation of dislike or contempt; disapproval; dismissal 1915.

Rasper (ra·spəɹ). 1725. [f. RASP *v.*[1] + -ER[1].] **1.** One who or that which rasps; a rasping-machine for beetroot, etc. **2.** *Hunting.* A high difficult fence 1812. **3.** *slang.* A person or thing that rasps or irritates; also, anything extraordinary in its own way 1839.

3. He's what you may a-call a r. DICKENS.

†**Ra·spis.** 1532. [Also †*raspes*, †*respis*, used as collect. pl. or as sing.; it is of unkn. origin, but is identical in form with †*raspis* (XV–XVI) kind of wine. See RASP *sb.*[2]] **1. a.** *collect.* Raspberries –1688. **b.** (With pl. in *-es.*) A raspberry –1678. **2.** The raspberry plant –1682.

Raspy (ra·spi), *a.* 1838. [f. RASP *v.*[1] + -Y[1].] **1.** Of a rasping nature; harsh, grating. **2.** Irritable 1877.

Rasse (ræ·se, ræs). 1817. [Javanese *rase.*] A kind of civet-cat (*Vivernicula malaccensis*) found in India, the Malay Peninsula, Java, China, etc., and frequently kept in captivity for the sake of the perfume obtained from it.

Rasure (rēⁱ·ziŭɹ, -ʒəɹ). Now *rare.* late ME. [–(O)Fr. *rasure* or L. *rasura*, f. *ras-*; see RASE *v.*[1], -URE.] †**1.** The act of scraping or shaving; a scratch, mark, cut, slit –1721. †**b.** A particle, or the particles, scraped off –1669. †**2.** The act of shaving (the head, hair, etc.); tonsure –1737. **3.** The act of scraping out something written; an erasure 1508. **b.** *transf.* Obliteration, effacement; cancelling 1603.

3. A specimen of his continual corrections and critical rasures D'ISRAELI. **b.** A forted residence 'gainst the tooth of time And razure of obliuion SHAKS.

Rat (ræt), *sb.* [OE. *ræt* – Rom. **rattus*, whence other Gmc. forms; ult. origin unkn. and historical details unc. In late ME. reinforced from (O)Fr. *rat*. Cf. RATTON.] **1.** Any rodent of certain of the larger species of the genus *Mus*, esp. *M. rattus*, the black rat (now almost extinct), and *M. decumanus*, the common grey, brown, or Norway rat. (See also LAND-, MUSK-, WATER-RAT.) **b.** *transf.* Applied to animals of other species resembling the rat 1598. **2.** With ref. to the alleged killing or expulsion of Irish rats by riming 1600. **b.** *slang.* Used ironically in *pl.* to express incredulity: 'humbug', 'nonsense' 1816. **3.** As an opprobrious or familiar epithet 1594. **4.** *spec.* †**a.** A pirate –1673. **b.** In politics, one who deserts his party 1788. **c.** A workman who refuses to strike along with others, or takes a striker's place; also, one who works for lower wages than the ordinary (or trade-union) rate 1881. **5.** [f. RAT *v.*^{1}] The act of ratting or changing one's side 1838.

1. It is the Wisedome of Rats, that will be sure to leaue a House, somewhat before it fall BACON. Phr. *To smell a r.*, to suspect something. *Like* (or *as wet as*) *a drowned r.* **b.** *Marsupial r.*, the opossum. *Pharaoh's r.*, the ichneumon. **2.** I was neuer so berim'd since..I was an Irish R. SHAKS. **3.** *Rich. III*, v. iii. 331.

Comb.: **r.-firm,** a firm which employs 'rats' or non-union workmen; **-fish,** a chimæra of the Pacific coast of America; **-kangaroo** = KANGAROO-RAT; **-mole** = MOLE-*rat*; **-pit,** a pit in which rats are confined to be worried by dogs; **-poison,** poison for destroying rats; **-snake,** a snake which kills rats, *esp.* a species found in Ceylon, frequently kept in domestication for this purpose.

Rat (ræt), *v.*^{1} 1815. [f. prec.] **1.** *intr.* (chiefly *pres. pple.*) To catch or hunt rats 1864. **2. a.** To desert one's party, side, or cause, *esp.* in politics; to go *over* as a deserter 1815. **b.** To act as a 'rat' (sense 4 c) 1847.

2. a. If you have a mind to r., r. *sans phrase* 1817.

Rat (ræt), *v.*^{2} *vulgar.* 1696. [Minced pronunciation of ROT *v.*; cf. DRAT.] A form of imprecation, = DRAT.

Rata (rā·tă). 1835. [Maori.] A large and handsome forest-tree of New Zealand, bearing crimson flowers and yielding a hard red wood.

Ratable, etc.: see RATEABLE, etc.

Ratafia (rætăfī·ă). 1699. [– Fr. *ratafia* (Boileau), prob. of Creole origin and rel. to TAFIA.] **1.** A cordial or liqueur flavoured with almonds or peach-, apricot-, or cherry-kernels. **2.** A kind of cake or biscuit having the flavour of ratafia, or made to be eaten along with it 1845. **3.** A variety of cherry 1835.

Ratal (rē^i·tăl). 1859. [f. RATE *sb.*^{1} + -AL^1, prob. after *rental*.] The amount on which rates are assessed. Also *attrib.* or as *adj.*

Rataplan (rætăplæ·n). 1847. [– Fr. *rataplan*, of imit. origin.] A drumming or beating noise; a tattoo, rub-a-dub.

Ra:t-a-ta·t. 1681. [Echoic.] = RAT-TAT.

Ra·t-ca:tcher. 1592. [f. RAT *sb.*] One whose business it is to catch rats. **b.** Unconventional hunting dress 1930.

Ratch (rætʃ), *sb.* 1620. [May depend on G. *ratsche*, *rätsche* ratchet-wheel. Cf. RATCHET.] †**1.** *Sc.* = FIRELOCK 1 (*rare*) –1657. **2.** A ratchet 1721. **3.** A ratchet-wheel 1696.

Ratch (rætʃ), *v.* 1777. [f. prec.] *Mech. trans.* To cut into teeth like those of a ratch; to turn *round* in the process of doing this.

Ratchel (ræ·tʃĕl). *techn.* or *dial.* 1747. [Of unkn. origin.] Fragments of loose shivery stone lying above the firm rock.

Ratchet (ræ·tʃĕt), *sb.* 1659. [Earliest *rochet* – Fr. *rochet* (in OFr.) blunt lance-head, (later) bobbin, spool, ratchet (wheel), corresp. to or partly – It. *rocchetto* spool, ratchet, dim. f. Rom. **rokk-*; see ROCK *sb.*^{2} Later assim. to synon. RATCH.] **1.** A set of angular or saw-like teeth on the edge of a bar or rim of a wheel, into which a cog, tooth, click, or the like may catch, usu. for the purpose of preventing reversed motion; also, a bar or wheel (*r.-wheel*) provided with such teeth. **b.** *pl.* in same sense (*rare*) 1721. **2.** A click or detent, catching into the teeth of a ratchet-wheel 1846. Hence **Ra·tchet** *v. intr.* to move by means of a r.

Rate (rē^{i}t), *sb.*^{1} late ME. [– OFr. *rate* – med.L. *rata* (evolved from phr. *pro rata*, short for *pro rata parte* or *portione* according to an estimated or fixed part, proportionally), fem. of *ratus* (see RATIFY).] **I.** †**1.** The (total) estimated quantity, amount, or sum *of* anything, usu. as forming a basis for calculating other quantities or sums –1597. †**b.** A fixed portion or quantity (*rare*)–1611. **2.** Estimated value or worth (of individual things or persons). late ME. †**b.** Estimation, consideration –1727. **3.** Price, the sum paid or asked for a single thing 1590.

2. The low r. at which you seem to value my understanding '*Junius' Lett.* **b.** *Temp.* II. i. 109. **3.** To purchase heaven for repenting, Is no hard r. G. HERBERT. Phr. †*At the r. of*, at the cost of. *At an easy r.*, without great expense; also *transf.* without great loss or suffering.

II. 1. The amount or number of one thing which corresponds or has relation to a certain amount or number of some other thing. Chiefly in phr. *at the r. of*. 1497. **2.** Value (of money, goods, etc.) as applicable to each individual piece or equal quantity 1488. **b.** The basis of equivalence on which one form of currency is exchanged for another 1727. **3.** The amount *of* a charge or payment (such as interest, discount, wages, etc.) having relation to some other amount or basis of calculation 1540. **b.** A fixed charge applicable to each individual instance; *esp.* the (*or* an) amount paid or demanded for a certain quantity of a commodity, material, work, etc. 1526. †**c.** Relative cost or expense, (of living) –1646. **d.** (Usu. *pl.*) Amount of assessment on property for local purposes. (Cf. POOR-RATE, etc.) 1712. **4.** Degree of speed in moving from one place to another; the ratio between the distance covered and the time taken to traverse it. Chiefly in phr. (*to go*, etc.) *at a..rate*. Also const. *of* (travelling, etc.). 1652. **b.** Relative speed of working, acting, etc. 1751. **c.** Of time-pieces: Amount of gain or loss on the correct time during twenty-four hours 1833. **5.** Relative amount of variation, increase, decrease, etc. 1816.

1. [Interest] after the r. of six pounds per cent 1660. Although we were going at the r. of nine knots, the ship made no noise 1860. **2.** The legal r. of an ounce of either of these metals in coin is called the mint price 1758. **3.** It is not on this that the r. of wages depends 1833. **b.** The high rates of the railway companies prevented the cheaper kinds of fish from being sent to the markets 1883. **d.** Rates have increased in towns with great rapidity GLADSTONE. **4.** The motion.. swiftly augmented to the r. of an avalanche TYNDALL. **5.** Three millions of paupers..increasing at a frightful r. per day CARLYLE.

III. †**1.** Standard or measure in respect of quality or condition; hence, class, kind, sort –1815. **b.** *Naut.* Class of vessels, *esp.* war-vessels, according to their size or strength 1649. **c.** Class or sub-class of buildings, in respect of purpose or size 1774. †**2.** Standard of conduct or action; hence, manner, style. Chiefly with *after*. –1792. **3.** Degree or extent of action, feeling, etc. Chiefly in phr. *at a..rate*. 1523.

1. He was very learned, according to the r. of that age FULLER. **2.** They behaved themselves after another r. in private 1702. **3.** I swore and curst at that most fearful R., that she was made to tremble to hear me BUNYAN.

Phrases. **At any r.** †**a.** On any terms. †**b.** (With negatives.) On any account. **c.** Under any circumstances; in any or either case. **d.** At all events; at least. †**e.** By any means. **At all rates.** †**a.** At any cost or by any means. **b.** At all events. **At that** (or **this**) **r.**, in that case, things being so, under these circumstances.

Rate (rē^{i}t), *sb.*^{2} 1575. [f. RATE *v.*^{2}] *Hunting.* A reproof to a dog.

Rate (rē^{i}t), *v.*^{1} 1477. [f. RATE *sb.*^{1}] †**1.** *trans.* To fix, assign, settle the amount of (a payment, fine, etc.) –1623. †**b.** To divide proportionally; to allot or apportion (*between* or *to* persons) as an amount or sum to be received or paid; also, to give or assign (one) his share –1661. **2.** To reckon, estimate the amount or sum of. Now *rare*. 1597. **3.** To estimate the (†nature) worth or value of; to appraise, value, †price 1599. **b.** To value *at* a certain sum 1570. **c.** To assign a certain value to (coin or metals) as, or in relation to, monetary standards. (Chiefly in *pass.*; also const. to.) 1758. **4.** To reckon, esteem, consider, count 1565. **5.** In *pass.* To be subjected or liable to payment of a certain rate; to be valued for purposes of assessment, taxation, etc. 1498. **b.** Const. *to* (the payment required) 1642. **6.** Chiefly *Naut.* To place in a certain class or rank; to give rating to 1706. **b.** *intr.* To be rated *as* 1809. **7.** *trans.* **a.** To calculate or fix at a certain rate 1845. **b.** To ascertain the variation of (a chronometer) from true time 1853.

1. b. *Ant. & Cl.* III. vi. 25. **2.** To r. What millions died—that Cæsar might be great! CAMPBELL. **3.** Instead of rating the man by his performance, we r. too frequently the performance by the man JOHNSON. **b.** You r. yourself too humbly 1884. **c.** Copper is rated very much above its real value ADAM SMITH. **4.** Surely I may r. myself among their benefactors JOHNSON. **6.** On board that ship I was rated as surgeon 1887. **b.** To r. as a full journeyman 1854. **7. b.** The watch used in rating chronometers, should..be carried in a box 1875.

Rate (rē^{i}t), *v.*^{2} late ME. [Of unkn. origin.] **1.** *trans.* To chide, scold, reprove vehemently or angrily. Const. *for*, †*of*. †**2.** To drive *away*, *back*, *from*, or *off*, by rating –1702. **3.** *intr.* To utter strong or angry reproofs. Chiefly const. *at*. 1593.

1. The Bishop being angrie, rated the fellow roughly CAMDEN. When hounds are rated and do not answer the rate, they should be coupled up immediately 1781. **2.** He..Rated my Vnckle from the Councell-Boord SHAKS. **3.** Such a one As all day long hath rated at her child TENNYSON. Hence **Ra·ter**^{2}, one who rates or scolds. **Ra·ting** *vbl. sb.*^{2} the action of reproving; an instance of this.

Rateable (rē^i·tăb'l), *a.* Also **ratable.** 1503. [f. RATE *v.*^{1} + -ABLE.] **1.** Capable of being rated, estimated, or calculated, esp. in accordance with some scale; proportional. **2.** Liable to payment of rates 1760.

1. A r. distribution being made of their estates to the Kings well-deseruing friends 1611. **2.** The r. property of the citizen 1846. Hence **Rateabi·lity,** the quality of being r. **Ra·teably** *adv.* proportionately 1490.

Ratel (rē^i·tĕl). 1777. [– S. Afr. Du. *ratel*, of unkn. origin.] A carnivorous quadruped of S. Africa, *Mellivora capensis*, of the family *Mustelidæ*; the honey-badger or honey-ratel. Also, the Indian species, *M. indica*.

Rater^1 (rē^i·tɘɹ). 1611. [f. RATE *v.*^{1} + -ER^1.] **1.** One who (or a thing which) rates, estimates, measures, etc. Now *rare*. **2.** A vessel, etc. of a specified rate. (In recent use with ref. to the tonnage of racing vessels.) 1806.

Rath (rɑþ). 1596. [– Ir. *rath* (now pronounced rā) = Gael. †*ráth*, Gaul. (acc.) *rātin*, *-rātum* in place-names (e.g. *Argentoratum*, Strasburg).] *Irish Antiq.* An enclosure (usu. circular) made by a strong earthen wall, and serving as a fort and place of residence for the chief of a tribe; a hill-fort. (Often erron. ascribed to the Danes.)

Rathe (rē^{i}ð), **rath** (rɑþ), *a. poet.* and *dial.* [OE. *hræþ*, var. of *hræd* (ME. and dial. *rad*) = OHG. (*h*)*rad*, ON. *hraðr*, Goth. **raþs* :– Gmc. **χraþaz*; cf. RASH *a.* The form *rathe* is from OE. obl. cases.] **1.** Quick in action, speedy, prompt; eager, earnest, vehement. **2.** Done, occurring, etc. before the natural time. (Orig. with *too*.) late ME. **b.** esp. of fruits, flowers, etc., which bloom or ripen early in the year 1572. **3.** Early in the day; belonging to the morning 1596. **4.** Belonging to the first part of some period of time 1850.

2. A r. December blights my lagging May 1833. **b.** The r. Primrose that forsaken dies MILT. **3.** The r. Morning newly but awake DRAYTON. Hence †**Ra·thely** *adv.* = next 1.

Rathe (rē^{i}ð), *adv. poet.* and *dial.* [OE. *hraþe*, *hræþe* = MLG. *rade*, OHG. (*h*)*rado*. See prec.] †**1.** Quickly, rapidly, swiftly; *esp.* without delay, promptly, soon –1649. †**b.** With *too*: Too quickly, too soon; hence, too early; before the fitting or natural time –1541. **2.** Early (in the morning or day). late ME.

2. I am the hunte, which r. and earely ryse 1575.

†**Ra·ther,** *a.* ME. [Comparative of RATHE *a.*; see -ER^3.] **1.** Earlier –1620. **b.** Antecedent, prior; of greater importance (*rare*) –1668. **2.** The earlier (of two persons or things); the former –1484.

1. The r. Lambes bene starved with cold SPENSER.

Rather (rā·ðəɹ), *adv.* OE. [OE. *hraþor* (= Goth. *raþizo*), compar. of *hræþe* RATHE *adv.*; see -ER³. The pronunc. rē̆ⁱ·ðəɹ, which shows normal development of ME. *ă* in an open syll., is now only dial., as are also pronuncs. with æ, a; cf. *father, gather, lather.*] **I.** Denoting precedence in time. †**1.** (*The*) *r.*, (all) the more quickly, (all) the sooner –1605. **2.** Earlier, sooner; at an earlier time, season, day, hour, etc. Now *dial.* OE. **3.** Previously, formerly. Now *dial.* ME.

1. When Duncan is asleepe (Whereto the r. shall his dayes hard Iourney Soundly inuite him) SHAKS.

II. Denoting priority in nature or reason. **1.** *The r.*, the more readily; (all) the more OE. **2.** More truly or correctly; more properly speaking. late ME. **3.** More (so) than not; more than anything else; hence, in a certain degree or measure; somewhat, slightly 1597. **4.** *colloq.* Used as a strong affirmative in answer to a question: = 'I should rather think so'; very much so; very decidedly 1836.

1. A Case..which I the r. mention, because both Sexes are concerned in it 1710. **2.** The Inhabitants..build their dwellings, rather like stoves then houses 1657. Say r., that he loves all the world GOLDSM. Last night, or r. very early this morning 1875. **3.** His Appearance at the Baronet's must have been r. a silly one 1778. I r. think that you know him JOWETT. **4.** 'Do you know the young lady?' 'Rather!' 1856.

III. Denoting prior eligibility or choice. **1.** Sooner (as a matter of fitness, expediency, etc.); with better reason or ground; more properly or justly. With *than.* ME. **2.** Sooner (as a matter of individual choice); more readily or willingly; with or in preference ME. **b.** Without *than,* in contrast to a preceding statement. Also rarely *the r.* ME. **c.** (One) *had r.* = (one) would rather. (See HAVE *v.* A. III.) 1450. †**d.** (One) *would r.* = (one) would rather have or choose –1675.

1. Therefore I r. deserve death than he 1573. **2.** They would r. have died than refused MME. D'ARBLAY. Painting cheeks with health r. than rouge RUSKIN. **b.** Ye..wol not applie you..unto the said marriage..but r. induce yoʳ said doghter to the contrarye 1480.

Ra·therest, *adv.* (and *a.*) late ME. [f. prec. + -EST.] **1.** Most of all, most particularly. Now *dial.* **2.** *Rather of the r.*, just a little too much or too little 1787.

1. His..vntrained, or rather vnlettered, or r. vnconfirmed fashion SHAKS.

Rathe-ripe, rath-ripe (rē̆ⁱ·ð-, rɑ·þ-), *a.* and *sb.* Now *poet.* and *dial.* 1578. [f. RATHE *a.* + RIPE *a.* With ref. to grain usu. spelt *rath-*. Cf. RARE-RIPE.] **A.** *adj.* **1.** Of fruits, grain, etc.: Coming early to maturity; ripening early in the year. **2.** *fig.* Precocious. Now *dial.* 1617. **B.** *sb.* Applied to early peas, apples, etc. 1677.

A. 1. Fruits like the fig-tree's, r., rotten-rich BROWNING.

‖**Rathskeller** (rā·tskeləɹ). *U.S.* 1900. [G., town-hall cellar.] A beer-saloon or restaurant, usu. in a basement.

Ratification (rætifikē̆ⁱ·ʃən). 1450. [– (O)Fr. *ratification* or med.L. *ratificatio, -on-*, f. *ratificat-*, pa. ppl. stem of *ratificare*; see next, -ION.] The action of ratifying or confirming; sanction, confirmation.

Ratify (ræ·tifəi), *v.* ME. [– (O)Fr. *ratifier* – med.L. *ratificare*, f. L. *ratus* fixed, established, pa. pple. of *reri* reckon, think; see RATE *sb.*¹] **1.** *trans.* To confirm or make valid (an act, compact, promise, etc.) by giving consent, approval, or formal sanction (esp. to what has been done or arranged for by another). †**b.** To confirm, to guarantee the fulfilment of (a purpose, hope, etc.) –1649. †**c.** To confirm the possession of –1611. **2.** To declare or confirm the truth or correctness of (a statement, etc.). Now *rare* or *Obs.* late ME. †**3.** To bring to fulfilment or completion (*rare*) –1720.

1. To ratifie..the auncient friendship with a new peace 1579. **b.** God..onely can ratifie all our pious resolutions 1649. **2.** The prophesie..thus ratified by the euent 1631. Hence **Ra·tifier,** one who or that which ratifies.

Ratihabition (rætihăbi·ʃən). 1561. [– late L. *ratihabitio, -on-*, f. *ratum* confirmed (see prec.) + *habēre* have, hold; see -ION.] *Law.* Approval, sanction.

Rating (rē̆ⁱ·tiŋ), *vbl. sb.*¹ 1534. [f. RATE *v.*¹ + -ING¹.] **1.** The action of RATE *v.*¹ **b.** The (*or* an) amount fixed as a rate 1887. **2.** *Naut.* 'The station a person holds on the ship's books' (Smyth); also *transf.*, position, class, etc., in general 1702. **b.** *Naut.* in *pl.* Men of a certain rating 1893.

Ratio (rē̆ⁱ·ʃio). 1636. [– L. *ratio*, f. *rat-*, pa. ppl. stem of *reri*; see RATIFY.] †**1.** Reason, rationale (*rare*) –1752. **2.** *Math.* The relation between two similar magnitudes in respect of quantity, determined by the number of times one contains the other (integrally or fractionally) 1660. **b.** The corresponding relationship between things not precisely measurable 1808. **3.** *spec.* In monetary science, the quantitative relation in which one metal stands to another in respect of their value as money or legal tender 1879. †**4.** = RATION *sb.* 3. –1824.

2. The r...is exactly one to a hundred '*Junius' Lett.* **b.** Executorships..which excited his spleen or soothed his vanity in equal ratios LAMB. **4.** A cow..eat up two ratios and half of dried grass STERNE.

Ratiocinate (rætiọ·sineⁱt), *v.* 1643. [– *ratiocinat-*, pa. ppl. stem of L. *ratiocinari* calculate, deliberate, f. *ratio* REASON *sb.*; see prec., -ATE³. Cf. Fr. *ratiociner.*] *intr.* To reason, to carry on a process of reasoning. (Now *rare* in serious use.)

Ratiocination (ræ:tiọsinē̆ⁱ·ʃən). 1530. [– L. *ratiocinatio*, f. *ratiocinari*; see prec., -ION.] **1.** The process of reasoning. **2.** With *a* and *pl.* An instance of this; also, a conclusion arrived at by reasoning 1620. **3.** Power or habit of reasoning (*rare*) 1647.

Ratiocinative (rætiọ·sinĕtiv), *a.* 1620. [– L. *ratiocinativus*, f. as prec.; see -IVE. Cf. (O)Fr. *ratiocinatif.*] Characterized by, given to, or expressive of, ratiocination. So **Ratio·cinatory** *a.*

Ration (ræ·ʃən, *U.S.* rē̆ⁱ·ʃən), *sb.* 1550. [– Fr. *ration* – It. *razione* or Sp. *ración* (cf. med.L. *ratio* soldier's ration, in ref. to Spain) – L. *ratio, ration-* reckoning, computation, sum or number. Senses 1 and 2 were immed. from L. See RATIO, REASON.] †**1.** Reasoning 1550. †**2.** = RATIO 2, 3, –1815. **3.** A fixed allowance or share of provisions; *spec.* in the army and navy, the daily amount of certain articles of food allotted to each officer and man. (Sometimes, esp. *pl.*, simply = provisions, food.) 1702. **b.** *Mil.* The daily allowance of forage or provender assigned to each horse or other animal 1727. **c.** An allowance, share, portion *of* provisions or other supplies 1727.

3. A 'ration' in the literal military sense of the word means 1 lb. of bread and ¾ lb. of meat 1885.

Ration (ræ·ʃən, *U.S.* rē̆ⁱ·ʃən), *v.* 1859. [f. prec.] **1.** *trans.* To supply (persons) with rations; to provision; to put on a fixed allowance. **2.** To divide (food, etc.) into rations; to serve *out* in fixed quantities 1870. **3.** *intr.* (for *refl.*) To obtain a supply of food 1859.

Rational (ræ·ʃənăl), *a.* and *sb.*¹ late ME. [– L. *rationalis*, f. *ratio* REASON *sb.*; see RATIO, -AL¹. Cf. Fr. †*rational*, mod. *-el.*] **A.** *adj.* **1.** Having the faculty of reasoning; endowed with reason. **b.** Exercising one's reason in a proper manner; having sound judgement; sensible, sane 1632. **2.** Of, pertaining or relating to, reason 1601. **3.** Based on, derived from, reason or reasoning 1531. **4.** Agreeable to reason; reasonable, sensible; not foolish, absurd, or extravagant 1601. **5.** *Math.* Applied to quantities or ratios which can be expressed without the use of radical signs 1570.

1. We are r.: but we are animal too COWPER. **b.** R. and experienced men tolerably well know,..how to distinguish between true and false liberty BURKE. **2.** *R. faculty, nature, power*, etc.: Our r. faculty is the gift of God 1788. **4.** *R. dress*, a form of dress for women, proposed as more sensible than that in general use; usu. the use of knickerbockers in place of a skirt, esp. for cycling. **5.** *R. horizon*: see HORIZON 3.

B. *sb.*¹ The adj. used absol. **1. a.** A rational being. Chiefly in *pl.* = human beings, men. Now *Obs.* or *rare.* 1606. **b.** An advocate of something 'rational' 1756. †**2.** *Math.* A rational quantity (*rare*) –1797. **3.** *pl.* 'Rational' dress; knickerbockers for women 1889. Hence **Ra·tional-ly** *adv.*, **-ness** (now *rare*).

Rational (ræ·ʃənăl), *sb.*² late ME. [– L. *rationale*, n. of *rationalis* adj.; used in the Vulg. to translate Hebrew *ḥōšen*, after the LXX. λογεῖον oracle, oracular instrument.] †**1.** The breastplate worn by the Jewish high-priest –1674. **b.** An ornament formerly worn on the breast by bishops during the celebration of mass 1849. †**2.** = next 2. –1676.

1. The twelve stones in the Rationall or breast-plate of Aaron SIR T. BROWNE.

‖**Rationale** (ræʃⁱŏnē̆ⁱ·li). 1657. [mod.L., subst. use of n. of L. *rationalis*; see prec.] **1.** A reasoned exposition of principles; a statement of reasons. **2.** The fundamental reason, the logical or rational basis (*of* anything) 1688.

Rationalism (ræ·ʃənăliz'm). 1827. [f. RATIONAL *a.* + -ISM, after Fr. *rationalisme*, G. *rationalismus.*] **1.** *Theol.* **a.** The practice of explaining in a manner agreeable to reason whatever is apparently supernatural in the records of sacred history. **b.** The principle of regarding reason as the chief or only guide in matters of religion. **2.** *Metaph.* A theory (opp. to *empiricism* or *sensationalism*) which regards reason, rather than sense, as the foundation of certainty in knowledge 1857.

Rationalist (ræ·ʃənălist), *sb.* and *a.* 1626. [f. as prec. + -IST, after Fr. *rationaliste* (XVI).] **1.** One who forms his opinions by pure or *a priori* reasoning. **2.** *Theol.* One who rationalizes in matters of religion or sacred history; an adherent of rationalism 1640. **b.** *attrib.* or as *adj.* = next 1828.

Rationalistic (ræ:ʃənăli·stik), *a.* 1830. [f. prec. + -IC.] Characterized by rationalism, given or inclined to rationalism. Hence **Rationali·stical,** *a.*, **-ly** *adv.*

Rationality (ræʃənæ·lĭti). 1570. [– late L. *rationalitas*; see RATIONAL, -ITY.] **1.** The quality of possessing reason; the power of being able to exercise one's reason 1628. **2.** The fact of being based on, or agreeable to, reason 1651. **b.** A rational or reasonable view, practice, etc. 1660. **3.** The tendency to regard everything from a purely rational point of view 1791. †**4.** *Math.* The quality of being rational 1570. †**5.** = RATIONALE 2. 1646.

1. Some kind of brute Force within, prevails over the Principle of R. 1726. **5.** Many well directed intentions, whose rationalities will never beare a rigid examination SIR T. BROWNE.

Rationalization (ræ:ʃənăləizē̆ⁱ·ʃən). 1846. [f. next + -ATION.] **1.** The act of making rational or intelligible, or the result of this. **2.** *Math.* The process of clearing from irrational quantities 1853. **3.** *Econ.* The scientific organization of industry to ensure the minimum waste of labour, the standardization of production, and the consequent maintenance of prices at a constant level 1928.

Rationalize (ræ·ʃənăliz), *v.* 1816. [f. RATIONAL *a.* + -IZE.] **1.** *trans.* To render conformable to reason; to explain on a rational basis 1817. **2.** *Math.* To clear from irrational quantities 1816. **3.** *intr.* To employ reason or rationalism; to think rationally or in a rationalistic manner 1835. **4.** *trans.* To organize (industry) in the manner defined in prec. 3. 1928.

3. When we ask for reasons when we should not, we rationalise J. H. NEWMAN.

Ratite (ræ·təit), *a.* 1877. [f. L. *ratis* raft + -ITE².] *Ornith.* Of or belonging to the *Ratitæ*, a class of birds having a keelless sternum, as the ostrich, emu, cassowary, etc. (opp. to *carinate.*)

Ratlin(e, ratling (ræ·tlin, -liŋ). 1481. [Of unkn. origin.] **1.** Thin line or rope such as is used for the ratlines (see 2). **2.** (Chiefly *pl.*) One of the small lines fastened horizontally on the shrouds of a vessel, and serving as steps to go up and down the rigging 1611.

Ratoon (rătū·n), *sb.* Also **ratt-**. 1777. [– Sp. *retoño* a fresh shoot or sprout.] A new shoot or sprout springing up from the root of the sugar-cane after it has been cropped. Hence **Ratoo·n** *v. intr.* (of the sugar-cane, etc.) to send up new shoots after being cut down or cropped.

Ratsbane (ræ·tsbē̆ⁱn). 1523. [f. RAT *sb.* + BANE.] **1.** Rat-poison; †*spec.* arsenic. (Now only *literary.*) **2.** Applied to certain plants

1846. Hence **Ra·tsbaned** *ppl. a.* poisoned with r.

Ra·t's-tail. 1580. [f. RAT *sb.*] **1.** *pl.* in *Farriery*: †**a.** Chaps or cracks on the back of a horse's hind legs. **b.** Warty or suppurating excrescences on the same part. **2.** Applied to various things resembling a rat's tail in shape; e.g. the tapering end of a rope; a lank lock of hair, etc. 1869. **3.** A rat-tail file 1827.

Ra·t-tail. 1705. [f. as prec.] **1.** *pl.* = RAT'S-TAIL 1. 1753. **2.** A tail resembling that of a rat; *esp.* a horse's tail with little or no hair; also, a horse having a hairless tail, or the diseased condition which causes the hair of the tail to fall off 1705. **3.** A fish of the genus *Macrurus*, esp. *M. fabricii* 1882.

attrib.: *r. file*, a fine round file used for enlarging holes in metal, etc.

Ra·t-tailed, *a.* 1684. [f. RAT *sb.* + -ED².] **1.** Having the tail like that of a rat; *esp.* of horses, having a rat-tail. **b.** Of the larva of a drone-fly (*Eristalis*) having a long slender tail 1753. **c.** *spec.* in the names of certain animals 1846. **2.** Of a spoon: Having a tail-like prolongation of the handle along the back of the bowl 1881.

1. c. *R. serpent*, an American viper. *R. shrew*, the Musk-rat. *R. snake*, the fer-de-lance.

Rattan, ratan (rătæ·n). 1660. [var. of earlier *rot(t)ang* – Malay *rōtan*, prob. f. *raut* pare, trim, strip.] **1.** One of several species of the genus *Calamus*, climbing palms growing chiefly in the East Indies, and to a small extent in Africa and Australia, and notable for their long thin jointed and pliable stems; also, a plant belonging to one of these species 1681. **2.** A portion of the stem of a rattan, used as a switch or stick, or for other purposes 1660. **3.** Without article, as a material 1748.

Rat-tat (ræ·t,tæ·t). 1774. [imit.] A sharp rapping sound, *esp.* of a knock at a door. So **Rat-tat-tat,** etc. (cf. RAT-A-TAT).

Ratteen (rătī·n). 1685. [– Fr. *ratine*, of unkn. origin.] A thick twilled woollen cloth, usu. friezed or with a curled nap, but sometimes dressed; a frieze or drugget. Now *Hist.* **b.** A piece of ratteen 1706.

Ratten (ræ·t'n), *v.* 1867. [Back-formation from next.] **a.** *trans.* To molest (a workman or employer) by rattening. **b.** *intr.* To practise rattening. Hence **Ra·ttener.**

Ra·ttening, *vbl. sb.* 1843. [Of unkn. origin.] The act or practice of abstracting tools, destroying machinery, etc., as a means of enforcing compliance with the rules of a trade union, or of venting spite. Also *transf.*

Ratter (ræ·təɹ). 1834. [f. RAT *sb.* and *v.*¹ + -ER¹.] **1.** A ratcatcher; a dog or other animal which hunts rats 1858. **2.** One who 'rats': **a.** One who deserts his party. **b.** A workman who refuses to join a strike, etc. 1834.

Ratting (ræ·tiŋ), *vbl. sb.* 1816. [f. RAT *v.*¹ + -ING¹.] **1.** Desertion of one's party or principles. Also with *over*. **2.** The catching or killing of rats 1828.

Rattle (ræ·t'l), *sb.* 1500. [f. next; cf. LG., Du. *rattel*.] **I. 1.** An instrument used to make a rattling noise; *esp.* a child's toy; also, one formerly used by watchmen to give an alarm 1519. **2.** A set of horny, loosely-connected rings forming the termination of the tail in the rattlesnake, by shaking which it produces a rattling noise. Also *pl.* 1624. **3.** Applied to certain plants having seeds which rattle in their cases when ripe: **a.** Yellow rattle, *Rhinanthus Crista-galli* = COCK'S-COMB 5; **b.** Red rattle, *Pedicularis sylvatica* 1578.

1. I wyll bye a rattell to styll my baby for cryenge 1519. *transf.* Such rattles as drums and trumpets H. WALPOLE.

II. 1. A rapid succession of short sharp sounds, caused by the concussion of hard bodies 1500. **b.** *transf.* Racket, uproar, noisy gaiety, stir 1691. **c.** A rattling sound in the throat, caused by partial obstruction; see RÂLE, and DEATH-*rattle*. Also in *pl.* (spec. as a pop. name for croup). 1752. †**2.** A sharp reproof –1711. **3. a.** A noisy flow of words 1627. **b.** Without article: Lively talk or chatter of a trivial kind 1780. **4.** A constant chatterer; one who talks incessantly in a lively or thoughtless fashion 1742.

1. Sent bounding down the slope with peal and r. TYNDALL. **b.** She cannot bear a place without some cheerfulness and r. JOHNSON. **4.** My companion turned out to be a lively amusing r. 1859.

attrib. and *Comb.*: **r.-bag,** a r. in the form of a bag; also as *adj.*, rattling, reckless; **-box,** (*a*) a r. in the form of a box or case; (*b*) = RATTLE I. 3; (*c*) a species of rattlewort (*Crotalaria sagittalis*); **-brain,** an empty-headed noisy fellow; so **-brained** *a.*; **-weed,** (*a*) *U.S.* loco-weed; (*b*) *dial.* Bladder Campion; **-wort,** the genus *Crotalaria*.

Rattle (ræ·t'l), *v.*¹ ME. [prob. –(M)LG., MDu. *ratelen*, of imit. origin.] **I.** *intr.* **1.** Of things: To give out a rapid succession of short sharp sounds, usu. in consequence of rapid agitation and of striking against each other or against some hard dry body. **b.** Of sounds having this character 1587. **c.** Of places: To resound, be filled, with a noise of this kind 1622. **d.** Of an agent: To produce a succession of sharp sounds by striking or knocking on something, or by causing hard bodies to strike against each other 1676. **2.** To produce an involuntary sound of this kind, *esp.* in the throat. late ME. **3.** To talk rapidly in a thoughtless, noisy, or lively manner (esp. with *on, along*, etc.); to chatter 1594. **4.** To move, fall, etc. rapidly and with a rattling noise. Usu. with advs., as *along, by, in, out*, or advb. phr. 1555. **b.** To drive in a rapid rattling fashion 1838.

1. The stones did r. underneath COWPER. **b.** Rowling Thunder rattl'd o'er his Head DRYDEN. **d.** The storm that blows Without, and rattles on his humble roof THOMSON. **3. b.** A resolution to break the ice, and r. away at any rate GOLDSM. **4.** The car rattling o'er the stony street BYRON. **b.** All..entered the coach, and rattled off THACKERAY.

II. *trans.* **1.** To make (a thing or things) rattle 1560. †**b.** To assail with a rattling noise SHAKS. **2.** To say or utter in a rapid or lively manner. late ME. **b.** To play (music) in a rattling fashion on a piano 1848. †**3.** To scold, rate, or rail at, volubly –1736. †**b.** So with *up* or *off*, or complement –1722. **4.** *Sporting.* To beat up or chase vigorously 1829. **5.** To impel, drive, drag, bring, etc., in a rapid rattling manner 1825. **6.** orig. *U.S.* To shake or agitate (a person) by fear or consternation 1887.

1. To r. his chains by way of lullaby CARLYLE. **2. b.** She rattled away a triumphant voluntary on the keys THACKERAY. **4.** A fox well rattled, up to the first check,..is as good as half killed 1860. **5.** The anchor was rattled up in a minute 1867.

Rattle (ræ·t'l), *v.*² 1729. [Back-formation from *rattling* RATLIN(E, taken as a vbl. sb.] *trans.* To furnish with ratlines. Usu. with *down*.

†**Ra·ttle-head.** 1641. **1.** An empty-headed noisy fellow –1788. **2.** *spec.* A Cavalier (in contrast to a ROUNDHEAD) –1649. So **Ra·ttle-headed** *a.*

Ra·ttle-pate. 1643. = RATTLE-HEAD 1. So **Ra·ttle-pated** *a.* 1633.

Rattler (ræ·tləɹ). 1449. [f. RATTLE *v.*¹ + -ER¹.] **1.** = RATTLE *sb.* II. 4. **2.** A thing which rattles 1594. **b.** *U.S.* A rattlesnake 1827. **3.** A sharp or severe blow, fall, storm, etc. 1812.

Rattlesnake (ræ·t'l,snēⁱk). 1630. [f. RATTLE *sb.* or *v.*¹ + SNAKE.] A venomous American snake, having a series of horny rings at the end of the tail which make a rattling noise when the tail is vibrated. Also *attrib.*

Comb., in names of American plants, as **r.-fern,** a species of moonwort or grape-fern, *Botrychium virginianum*; **-grass,** a kind of quaking-grass, *Glyceria canadensis*; **-herb,** the Bane-berry, *Actæa rubra* or *alba*, and some other plants; **rattlesnake('s) master,** the Button-snakeroot, *Liatris scariosa* or *squarrosa*, and other plants; **r. plantain,** one of three species of *Goodyera*, esp. *G. pubescens*; **-root,** (*a*) the root of a species of milkwort, *Polygala senega* (see SENEGA); (*b*) one of several species of *Prenanthes*, esp. *P. serpentaria*; **r. weed,** (*a*) a species of *Eryngium*; (*b*) a species of hawk-weed, *Hieracium venosum*; **-wort** = *r.-root* (a).

Ra·ttletrap, *sb.* and *a.* 1766. [f. RATTLE *sb.* or *v.*¹ + TRAP *sb.*¹] **A.** *sb.* **1.** *pl.* Knick-knacks, trifles, odds and ends, curiosities, or the like. Also *sing.*, one such article. **2.** A rattling rickety coach or other vehicle 1822. **3.** Any rickety or shaky thing 1833. **4.** *slang.* The mouth 1824. **B.** *adj.* Rickety, shaky 1834.

Rattling (ræ·tliŋ), *ppl. a.* late ME. [f. RATTLE *v.*¹ + -ING².] **1.** That rattles or makes a rattle. **2.** Of persons: Extremely lively 1727. **3.** Remarkably good, fine, fast, etc. 1690. **b.** advb. with adjs.: Remarkably, extremely 1829.

Rattling, var. of RATLIN(E.

Ratton (ræ·t'n). Now *Sc.* and *n. dial.* ME. [– OFr. *raton*, f. *rat* RAT (with augm. suffix -OON). In ME. more frequent than *rat*.] A rat.

†**Rattoon.** 1656. [Cf. Fr. *raton* in same sense.] var. of RACOON –1755.

Ra·t-trap. 1469. [f. RAT *sb.* + TRAP *sb.*¹] **1.** A trap for catching rats. **2.** Applied to a cycle pedal consisting of two parallel iron plates with teeth cut in them 1885.

Ratty (ræ·ti), *a.* 1865. [f. RAT *sb.* + -Y¹.] **1. a.** Characteristic of a rat or rats 1888. **b.** Infested with rats 1865. **2.** *slang.* Wretched, mean, miserable. **b.** Angry, irritated. 1885.

Rau·cid, *a.* [f. L. *raucus* hoarse + -ID¹.] Raucous. LAMB.

Raucity (rǭ·sĭti). *rare.* 1607. [– Fr. *raucité* or L. *raucitas*, f. *raucus*; see next, -ITY.] Harshness, roughness, hoarseness.

Raucous (rǭ·kəs), *a.* 1769. [f. L. *raucus* hoarse + -OUS.] Hoarse, rough, harsh-sounding. Hence **Rau·cous-ly** *adv.*, **-ness.**

Raughty, variant of RORTY.

Ravage (ræ·vėdʒ), *sb.* 1611. [– (O)Fr. *ravage*, alt., by substitution of -AGE, of *ravine* RAVINE, both being used in the sense 'rush of water'.] The act or practice of ravaging, or the result of this; destruction, devastation, extensive damage, done by men or beasts. **b.** *pl.* Extensive depredations 1697. **c.** *transf.* 1704.

Noise of r. wrought by beast and man TENNYSON. **c.** If Mrs. Evergreen does take some pains to repair the ravages of time SHERIDAN. The ravages of the pestilence 1838. The r. of four years J. H. NEWMAN.

Ravage (ræ·vėdʒ), *v.* 1611. [– Fr. *ravager*, f. *ravage*; see prec.] **1.** *trans.* To devastate, lay waste, despoil, plunder (a country). Also *transf.* and *fig.* **2.** *intr.* To commit ravages; to make havoc or destruction 1627.

1. The barbarians who ravag'd Greece and Italy 1704. That sweet face so sadly ravaged by grief and despair THACKERAY. Hence **Ra·vager,** one who or that which ravages.

Rave (rēⁱv), *sb.*¹ 1530. [var. of *rathe* (XV, now dial.) in same sense.] A rail of a cart; esp. *pl.* a framework of rails or boards (permanent or removable) added to the sides of a cart to enable a greater load to be carried. **b.** *U.S.* One of the vertical side-pieces in the body of a wagon or sleigh.

Rave (rēⁱv), *sb.*² 1598. [f. next.] The (*or* an) act of raving; frenzy, great excitement.

Rave (rēⁱv), *v.* late ME. [prob. – ONFr. *raver*, rel. obscurely to (M)LG. *reven* be senseless, rave, Du. †*ravelen, ravotten*.] **1.** *intr.* †To be mad, to show signs of madness or delirium; hence, to talk or declaim wildly or furiously in consequence of madness or some violent passion. Occas. (now *dial.*) to shout or brawl. **2.** *transf.* Of the sea, storms, etc.: To rage; to dash, rush, roar, etc., in a furious manner 1559. **3.** To talk or declaim with enthusiasm or poetic rapture 1704. **4.** *trans.* To utter in a frenzied or enthusiastic manner 1602. **5.** quasi-*trans.* with complement: To bring (into a specified state) by raving 1812.

1. She talks like one who raves in fever 1871. The *Times* is already raving about our having reached 'a crisis' 1884. **2.** The milde Ocean, Who now hath quite forgot to r. MILT. When the pibroch bids the battle r. SCOTT. **3.** Solitude, however some may r., Seeming a sanctuary, proves a grave COWPER. How people can r. about Italy, I can't think 1838. **4.** For he now raved enormous folly SHELLEY. Hence **Ra·ver,** one who raves, a madman; an extravagant speaker. **Ra·ving** *vbl. sb.* the action of the verb; wild or delirious talk or declamation; an utterance of this kind.

Ravel (ræ·v'l), *sb.* 1634. [f. next.] **1.** A tangle, complication, entanglement. **2.** A broken thread, a loose end. Also *fig.* 1832.

Ravel (ræ·v'l), *v.* 1582. [poss. – Du. *ravelen* tangle, fray out, unweave, obscurely corresp. to LG. *reffeln, rebbeln*.] **I.** *intr.* **1.** To become entangled or confused. *rare* exc. *dial.* 1585. **2.** Of a fabric: To fray *out*, to suffer disintegration 1611. **3.** Of a clue or thread: To unwind; to come off the clue, reel, etc. *rare.* (now *dial.*) 1649. †**4.** To examine or inquire *into* a thing –1710.

1. By thir own perplexities involv'd They r. more

MILT. **2.** The hem of a garment is that which binds it round, and prevents it from ravelling out 1860. **4.** The malicious. .r. into the conduct of a man of honour in the dark 1710.

II. *trans.* **1.** To entangle, confuse, perplex 1598. **2.** To unwind or unweave; to unravel 1607. **b.** *fig.* To take to pieces; to disentangle 1582. **3.** *To r. out*: To draw or pull out by unwinding or unweaving 1623. †**b.** To destroy, spoil, or waste, as by pulling a fabric into threads –1708. **c.** To disentangle, make plain or clear 1593.

1. It ravels and complicates the meaning of the prophecies 1845. **2.** The night still ravell'd, what the day renew'd POPE. **3.** A stitch in a man's stocking not taken up in time, ravels out all the rest 1623. **c.** Must I rauell out My weau'd-vp follyes? SHAKS. Hence **Ra·veller,** one who ravels.

Ravelin (ræ·vlin). 1589. [– Fr. *ravelin* – It. †*ravellino*, now *rivellino*, of unkn. origin.] *Fortif.* An outwork consisting of two faces which form a salient angle, constructed beyond the main ditch and in front of the curtain.

Ravelling (ræ·v'liŋ), *vbl. sb.* 1658. [f. RAVEL *v.* + -ING[1].] **1.** The action of RAVEL *v.* 1673. **2.** *concr.* A thread from a woven fabric which is frayed or unravelled 1658.

Raven (rēi·v'n), *sb.*[1] (*a.*) [OE. *hræfn* = OS. *naht|hraban* 'nocticorax', MLG., MDu. *rāven* (Du. *raaf*), OHG. (*h*)*raban*, ON. *hrafn*, beside MDu. *rave*, OHG. *rabo* (G. *rabe*) :– Gmc. **χrabnaz*, **χraban.*] **1.** A widely distributed corvine bird (*Corvus corax*) of Europe and Asia, of large size, with black lustrous plumage and raucous voice, which feeds chiefly on carrion or other flesh. Applied also to birds belonging to other species of *Corvus*, esp. the American raven (*Corvus carnivorus*). **b.** *fig.* A croaker 1814. **2.** The figure of a raven on the flag of the Danish vikings; also, the flag itself or the warlike power typified by this OE. †**3.** *Astron.* The southern constellation Corvus (*rare*) –1551. **4.** *attrib.* or *adj.* Of the colour of a raven; glossy black; intensely dark or gloomy 1601.

1. The sad-presaging r., that tolls The sick man's passport in her hollow beak MARLOWE. **4.** Smoothing the R. doune Of darknes MILT.

Comb.: **r.-duck** [– G. *rabentuch*], a kind of canvas (also **raven's duck**); **r. standard:** cf. sense 2; **-stone** [– G. *rabenstein*], the place of execution, the gallows or gibbet.

Raven *sb.*[2]: see RAVIN.

Raven (ræ·v'n), *v.* 1494. [– (O)Fr. *raviner* rush, ravage, (now) hollow out, furrow :– Rom. **rapinare*, f. L. *rapina* RAPINE.] †**1.** *trans.* To take (goods) away by force; to seize or divide as spoil –1593. **b.** *absol.* or *intr.* To plunder; to seek *after*, to go *about*, with intent to plunder 1603. **2.** To devour voraciously 1560. **b.** So with *up, down, in.* Now *rare.* 1598. **3.** *intr.* or *absol.* To eat voraciously; to prey *on* or *upon* 1530. **b.** To have a ravenous appetite or desire *for* 1667. **c.** To have an intense longing for food 1858. **4.** *intr.* To prowl ravenously; to go about in search of food 1560.

1. b. His Croats and loose hordes went openly ravening about CARLYLE. **2.** Like a roaring lion rauening the pray BIBLE (Geneva) *Ezek.* 22:25. **3.** For Greedy Cormorants to r. upon 1575. **b.** The more they fed, they ravened still for more DRYDEN. **c.** You must have been ravening hours ago 1881. **4.** Beniamin shall rauine (as) a wolfe BIBLE (Geneva) *Gen.* 49:27. *fig.* The unclean pestilence ravins in your streets RUSKIN. Hence **Ra·vener.**

Ravening (ræ·v'niŋ), *ppl. a.* 1526. [f. prec. + -ING[2].] That ravens, in the senses of the vb. (In early use esp. of wolves.) †**2.** Rabid, mad –1696. Hence **Ra·veningly** *adv.*

Ravenous (ræ·v'nəs), *a.* late ME. [– OFr. *ravinos, -eus*, f. *raviner*; see RAVEN *v.*, -OUS. Cf. AL. *rapinosus* thievish.] **1.** Addicted to plundering or taking by force; extremely rapacious. **2.** Of animals: Given to seizing in order to devour; voracious, gluttonous. Hence of appetite, hunger, etc. late ME. **3.** Excessively hungry 1719.

1. Nations who were r. . .treacherous and fierce DE FOE. **2.** *transf.* Thy desires Are Woluish, bloody, steru'd, and rauenous SHAKS. **3.** I got up r. DE FOE. Hence **Ra·venous-ly** *adv.*, **-ness.**

Ravin (ræ·vin), **raven**[2] (ræ·v'n). ME. [– (O)Fr. *ravine* :– L. *rapina* RAPINE.] **1.** Robbery, rapine. †**b.** With *a* and *pl.*: An act of rapine –1593. **2.** The act or practice of seizing and devouring prey or food; hence, voracity, gluttony. late ME. **3.** *concr.* That which is taken or seized; plunder; prey (of men or beasts) ME. **4.** *attrib.* as *adj.* = prec. late ME.

1. Blood, and ravin, and robbery are their characteristics RAWLINSON. **2.** *Beast* (etc.) *of r.*: Beast of prey. **4.** I met the rauine Lyon SHAKS.

Ravine (răvī·n), *sb.* 1450. [– (O)Fr. *ravine* violent rush (now only of water), ravine; identical with prec.] †**1.** Impetus, violence, force –1450. **2.** A deep narrow hollow or gorge, a mountain cleft, prop. one worn by a torrent 1802. Hence **Ravi·ne** *v. trans.* to score with ravines; to hollow *out.*

Raving (rēi·viŋ), *ppl. a.* 1475. [f. RAVE *v.* + -ING[2].] Delirious, frenzied; raging. **b.** quasi-*adv.* with adjs., esp. *mad* 1786. Hence **Ra·vingly** *adv.*

Ravish (ræ·viʃ), *v.* ME. [– *raviss-*, lengthened stem of (O)Fr. *ravir* :– Rom. **rapire*, for L. *rapere* seize; see RAPE *v.*, -ISH[2].] **1.** *trans.* To seize and carry off (a person); to take by violence; to tear or drag away *from* (a place or person). Now *rare.* †**2.** To carry away (a woman) by force. (Sometimes implying subsequent violation). –1665. **b.** To commit rape upon (a woman), to violate. late ME. †**c.** To spoil, corrupt SHAKS. **3.** To carry away or remove from earth (esp. to heaven) or from sight. Now *rare.* ME. **b.** To transport *in spirit* without bodily removal ME. **c.** To transport with the strength of some feeling; to carry away with rapture; to entrance ME. **4.** To seize and take away as plunder or spoil; to seize upon (a thing) by force or violence; to make a prey of. late ME. †**b.** To remove by force –1698. †**5.** To ravage, despoil, plunder –1619. †**b.** To despoil (a person) *of* something –1803.

2. c. O hateful, vaporous, and foggy Night. . With rotten damps r. the morning air SHAKS. **3. c.** She had suche ioye that of a great spase she coude speke no word, she was so rauysshyd LD. BERNERS. **4.** I. .am not. .obliged to r. my bread out of the mouths of others DE FOE. The Freebooters had used to r. away their lives and their cattle 1731. **b.** These are the ways of all soch as be covetous, that one wolde rauysh anothers life COVERDALE *Prov.* 1:12. Hence **Ra·visher. Ra·vishingly** *adv.*

Ravishment (ræ·viʃmĕnt). 1477. [– (O)Fr. *ravissement*; see prec., -MENT.] †**1.** The act of carrying off a person; in *r. of ward* or *de gard*, the taking away of a ward; also, the writ issued in consequence of this –1700. **2.** Forcible abduction or violation of a woman 1529. **b.** With *a* and *pl.* An instance of this 1576. **3.** Transport, rapture, ecstasy. Also with *a* and *pl.* 1477.

3. A melody That, indistinctly heard, with r. Possess'd me CARY.

Ra·vissant, *a.* ME. [– Fr., pr. pple. of *ravir*; see RAVISH.] †**1.** Of beasts: Ravening (*rare*) –1549. **2.** Ravishing, delightful 1653.

Raw (rǭ), *a.* (*sb.*). [OE. *hrēaw* = OS. *hrāo* (Du. *rauw*), OHG. (*h*)*rāo* (G. *roh*), ON. *hrár* :– Gmc. **χrawaz* :– IE. **krowos*, repr. by Gr. κρέας raw flesh.] **A.** *adj.* **1.** Uncooked, not prepared for use as food by the action of fire or heat. **b.** Unburnt, unbaked; not hardened or fused by fire 1634. **2.** In a natural or unwrought state; not yet subjected to any process of dressing or manufacture: **a.** of the materials of textile fabrics; esp. *r. silk*, silk simply drawn from the cocoons by reeling ME. **b.** of cloth: Unfulled. late ME. **c.** of leather or hides: Untanned, undressed. Also *rawhide*, a rope or whip of undressed hide. 1489. **d.** of other substances (or their qualities), e.g. undiluted (spirits), unrefined (oil), unmalted (grain); etc. 1567. **e.** with general terms, as *r. material, produce*, etc. 1738. **3.** Crude, not brought to perfect composition, form or finish. (In mod. use chiefly of colouring). late ME. **b.** Uncultivated, uncivilized, brutal (*rare*) 1577. †**4.** Unripe, immature –1652. **5.** Of persons: Inexperienced, unskilled, untrained; quite new or fresh to anything 1561. **b.** *esp.* of soldiers without training or experience in fighting 1577. **c.** of things, qualities, actions, etc. (*rare*) 1602. **6.** Having the skin removed, so that the flesh is exposed; excoriated. late ME. **b.** Painful, as when the raw flesh is exposed 1590. **c.** †Showing through the skin; raw-boned 1596. †**d.** Affected with indigestion –1621. **7.** Of the weather, etc.: Damp and chilly 1546.

1. b. R. glazes are employed for the common pottery 1825. **2. c.** The r. materials, or necessary instruments of all manufactures 1796. **3. b.** The man. .R. from the prime, and crushing down his mate TENNYSON. **5.** A r., innocent, young Creature, who thinks all the World as sincere as herself STEELE. **b.** With a r. and inexperienced army he engaged legions in perfect discipline FROUDE. **6.** They were both flogged till their backs were r. 1788. **7.** You shan't venture out this r. evening GOLDSM.

B. ellipt. or absol. uses passing into sb. **1. a.** *The r.*, the exposed flesh. Chiefly in phr. *to touch* (a person) *on the r.* (usu. *fig.*) 1823. **b.** A raw place in the skin, a sore or sensitive spot 1825. **2.** *The r.*, applied to any raw article (esp. raw spirits), or quality 1844. **3.** A raw person, article, product, etc.; *spec.* in *pl.* raw sugars, or raw oysters 1868. Hence **Raw** *v. trans.* to make r. **Raw-ly** *adv.*, **-ness.**

†**Raw·-bone,** *a.* and *sb.* 1593. [f. RAW *a.* 6 c.] **A.** *adj.* = next –1772. **B.** *sb.* A very lean or gaunt person, a mere skeleton; *pl.* Death –1784.

Raw·-boned, *a.* 1591. [f. as prec. + -ED[2].] Having projecting bones, barely covered with flesh; excessively lean or gaunt.

Raw·-head. 1550. [f. RAW *a.* 6 + HEAD *sb.*] The name of a nursery bug-bear, usu. coupled with BLOODY-BONES.

Rawhide: see RAW *a.* 2 c.

Rawish (rǭ·iʃ), *a.* 1602. [-ISH[1].] Somewhat raw.

Ray (rēi), *sb.*[1] ME. [– (O)Fr. *rai* :– L. *radius* RADIUS.] **I. 1.** A single line or narrow beam of light; in mod. scientific use, the straight line in which the radiant energy capable of producing the sensation of light is propagated to any given point. **b.** A representation of a ray (esp. *Her.*); a brilliant stretch (of something) 1729. **c.** *fig.* of mental and moral influences, etc., comparable to light 1634. **d.** A trace of anything. (Chiefly with negs.) 1773. **2.** (Chiefly *poet.*) Light, radiance; (freq. also implying heat) 1592. **3. a.** (Chiefly *poet.*) A beam or glance of the eye; †also, sight 1531. **b.** A line of sight 1700. **4.** Used in ref. to the emission or transmission of non-luminous physical energies propagated in radiating straight lines after the manner of light 1664.

1. 'Tis as conceivable as how the Rays of Light should come in a direct line to the eye GLANVILL. The rays of the moon stole through the leafless branches 1849. *Röntgen* (rö·ntyəĕn) *rays*, a form of radiation discovered by Prof. Röntgen, having the power of penetrating many substances impervious to the rays of ordinary light. Also called *X-rays*. **c.** Only one r. of hope broke the gloom of her prospects 1838. **d.** Isn't it enough that you were seven boys before, without a r. of gal DICKENS. **2.** Lamps, that shed at Ev'n a cheerful r. GRAY. **3. a.** The Aire, No where so cleer, sharp'nd his visual r. To objects distant farr MILT. All eyes direct their rays On him POPE. **4.** There are rays transmitted from the sun which do not illuminate SIR H. DAVY.

II. 1. *Math.* **a.** = RADIUS 3. Now *rare.* 1690. **b.** Any one of the lines forming a pencil or set of straight lines passing through a point 1879. **2.** One of any system of lines, parts, or things radially disposed 1668. **3.** *Bot.* **a.** The marginal portion of a composite flower, consisting of ligulate florets arranged radially 1766. **b.** A pedicel or branch of an umbel 1785. **4.** *Zool.* **a.** = *fin-ray*, FIN *sb.* 1668. **b.** One of the radial divisions of a star-fish 1753.

Comb.: **r.-filter,** a means of separating the obscure from the luminous rays of electric light; **-fungus,** a fungus (*Actinomyces*) which enters the body and produces the disease *actinomycosis.*

Ray (rēi), *sb.*[2] ME. [– (O)Fr. *raie* :– L. RAIA.] A selachian fish of the family *Raiidæ*, having a broad flat body and inferior gill-openings; *esp.* a skate. **b.** Dist. as *eagle-, rock-, shark-, sting-, whip-r.*; see these words.

†**Ray,** *sb.*[3] ME. [Aphetic form of ARRAY *sb.*] **1.** Order, array, *esp.* of soldiers –1632. **2.** A line or rank –1587. **3.** Dress –1760.

3. *transf.* As a ship, whom cruell tempest drives Upon a rocke. ., spoyling all her. .goodly r. SPENSER.

Ray (rēi), *sb.*[4] (and *a.*). *Obs.* exc. *Hist.* ME. [– OFr. **raié*, f. *raie* stripe, streak.] **1.** A kind of striped cloth. So *cloth of r.* (cf. Fr. *étoffe de* raies). **2.** *attrib.* or as *adj.* Striped; made of striped cloth. late ME.

Ray (rēⁱ), *v.*¹ 1598. [f. RAY *sb.*¹, or – Fr. *rayer*, OFr. *raier* :– L. *radiare*, f. RADIUS.] **1.** *intr.* Of light: To issue from some point in the form of rays. **2.** Of luminous bodies or points: To emit light in rays 1647. **3.** To radiate, extend in the form of radii 1659. **4.** *trans.* To send *out* or *forth*, to emit (light) in rays 1789. **5. a.** To furnish *with* rays or radiating lines. **b.** To irradiate. 1750.

Ray (rēⁱ), *v.*² *Obs.* exc. *dial.* late ME. [aphet. f. ARRAY *v.*] †**1.** *trans.* To put (men) in order or array –1600. †**2.** To arrange, dispose, or deal with, in any fashion –1509. **3.** To dress (oneself or another). Also *absol.* late ME. †**4.** To BERAY –1663.

‖**Rayah** (rai·ă). 1813. [– Turk. *râya*, pl. of *raiyye* – Arab. *ra'īya* flock or herd, peasants, subjects, f. *ra'ā* to pasture.] A non-Moslem subject of the Sultan of Turkey, subject to payment of the poll-tax.

Ray·-grass. 1677. = RYE-GRASS (now the usual form).

Rayless (rēⁱ·lės), *a.* 1742. [f. RAY *sb.*¹ + -LESS.] **1.** Devoid of, not illumined by, any ray of light; dark, gloomy. **2.** That sends out no rays; dull 1832. **3.** Excluding, dispensing with, rays of light 1896. **4.** Having no rays or ray-like parts 1769.

Rayon¹ (rēⁱ·ǫn, Fr. rẹyoṅ). 1591. [– Fr. *rayon*, dim. of *rai*; see RAY *sb.*¹] **1.** A ray of light (*rare*). ‖**2.** = RADIUS 4. 1878.

Rayon² (rēⁱ·ǫn). 1924. [Arbitrary; with suggestion of *ray* beam of light.] Trade name for artificial silk.

‖**Rayonné** (rẹyone), *a.* 1780. [Fr., pa. pple. of *rayonner*, f. *rayon* RAYON¹.] *Her.* Of a division between parts of the field: Having alternate pointed projections and depressions, whose sides are formed by wavy lines.

Raze (rēⁱz), *v.* 1547. [var. RASE *v.*¹] **1.** = RASE *v.*¹, in various senses. **b.** *esp.* To cut or wound slightly, to graze 1586. †**2.** *spec.* To erase or obliterate (writing, etc.) by scraping or otherwise –1709. †**3.** To alter by erasure –1724. **4. a.** To sweep away, efface, or destroy (a building, town, etc.) completely. In later use esp. to *r. to the ground.* 1547. **b.** To take away, remove (*from* a place), in a thorough manner 1580.

2. The clause formerly razed..is agreed to be kept in the bill 1709. **4.** The fortifications were razed to the ground GIBBON. Hence †**Raze** *sb.* a slash, scratch, slit –1766.

Razee (răzī·), *sb.* 1803. [– Fr. *rasé(e*, pa. pple. of *raser* RASE *v.*¹; see -EE¹.] *Naut.* A warship or other vessel reduced in height by the removal of her upper deck or decks.

Razee (răzī·), *v.* 1837. [f. prec.] **1.** *trans.* To cut down (a ship) to a lower size by reducing the number of decks 1842. **2.** *fig.* To abridge, prune, dock 1837.

1. The Merrimac..has been razed and iron-plated 1862.

Razor (rēⁱ·zəɹ), *sb.* [ME. *raso(u)r* – OFr. *rasor, -ur* (superseded by *rasoir*), f. *raser* RASE *v.*¹; see -OR 2.] **I. 1.** A sharp-edged instrument, specially used for shaving the beard or hair. **2.** = RAZOR-FISH, RAZOR-SHELL 1610.

1. His little weezen face as sharp as a r. 1765. *fig.* Phr. *On the razor's edge* (after Gr. ἐπὶ ξυροῦ ἀκμῆς), in a precarious position; Now on the eager razors edge, for life or death we stand CHAPMAN. *Occam's razor*, the leading principle of the nominalism of William of Occam, that for the purposes of explanation things not known to exist should not, unless it is absolutely necessary, be postulated as existing.

Comb.: **r.-bridge**, the bridge believed by Moslems to lead over hell; **-edge,** a keen edge, *fig.* a narrow foothold, a critical situation; **-grass,** a W. Indian sedge (*Scleria scindens*) with sharp-edged leaves and stems; **-paper,** paper specially made for sharpening razors on; **-paste,** a paste of emery- or crocus-powder for improving razor-strops. Hence **Ra·zor** *v. trans.* to shave as with a r.; to cut *down.* †**Ra·zorable** *a.* capable of, or fit for, being shaved SHAKS.

Ra·zor-back, *sb.* (and *a.*). 1823. [f. prec.] **A.** *sb.* **1.** A sharply-ridged back, like a razor 1844. **2.** The Razor-back whale or Rorqual 1823. **3.** A pig having a sharp ridge-like back 1849. **B.** *adj.* Having a very sharp back or ridge 1836. So **Ra·zor-backed** *a.*

Ra·zor-bill. 1674. [f. RAZOR *sb.* + BILL *sb.*²] **a.** A species of Auk (*Alca torda*). **b.** *U.S.* The Cut-water or Skimmer 1794. **c.** The red-breasted Merganser, *Mergus serrator* 1883. So **Ra·zor-billed** *a.* having a bill resembling a razor.

Ra·zor-fish. 1602. [f. RAZOR *sb.*] Any bivalve mollusc of the genus *Solen* or family *Solenidæ*, having a long narrow shell like the handle of a razor; esp. the European species *Solen ensis* or *siliqua*, common on sandy shores.

Ra·zor-gri:nder. 1825. [f. RAZOR *sb.*] **1.** One who grinds or sharpens razors 1833. **2.** A name of various birds: **a.** The Australian Dishwasher or Restless Fly-catcher (*Seisura inquieta*) 1825. **b.** *dial.* The Night-jar 1895. **c.** *dial.* The Grasshopper Warbler 1895.

Ra·zor-shell. 1752. [f. RAZOR *sb.*] The shell of a Razor-fish, or the mollusc together with its shell.

‖**Razzia** (ræ·ziă). 1845. [Fr. – Algerian Arab. *ġazīa*, var. Arab. *ġazwa*, f. *ġazw* make raids.] A hostile incursion, foray or raid, for purposes of conquest, plunder, capture of slaves, etc., as practised by the Moslem peoples in Africa; also *transf.* of similar raids by other nations.

Ra·zzle-da·zzle. *slang*, orig. *U.S.* 1890. A rhyming formation on DAZZLE denoting bewilderment or confusion, rapid stir and bustle, riotous jollity or intoxication, etc. Also abbrev. *razzle*, esp. in phr. *on the razzle.*

Re (rēⁱ), *sb.* ME. [See UT.] **a.** The second note of Guido's hexachords, and of the octave in modern solmization. **b.** (As in Fr. and It.) The note D, the second of the natural scale of C major (*rare*). Hence †**Re** *v.* (nonce-use) SHAKS.

‖**Re** (rē), *prep.* 1707. [abl. of L. *res* thing, affair.] In the matter of, with references to. The L. phr. *in re* is similarly used.

Re-, *prefix*, of L. origin, with the general sense of 'back, or 'again', occurring in a large number of words adopted from L., or of later Rom. origin, and on the model of these freely employed in English.

In earlier L. *re-* was used bef. consonants, and *red-* bef. vowels or *h-*, as in *redire, redhibere* (rarely in other cases, as in *reddere*). In later L. *re-* was employed bef. vowels as well as consonants, as in *reagere*, etc. **2.** The original sense of *re-* in Latin is that of 'back' or 'backwards', but in use the prefix acquires various shades of meaning. **a.** 'Back from a point reached', 'back to or towards the starting-point', as in *recedere, revocare*, etc. **b.** 'Back to the original place or position', as in *reponere, restituere*, etc.; freq. implying 'back to one's hands or possession', as in *recipere, resumere*, etc. **c.** 'Again', 'anew', as in *recreare, regenerare*, etc. **d.** In some cases *re-* has the same force as Eng. *un-*, as in *recingere* to ungird, *recludere* to unclose, *revelare* to unveil. In *reprobare* to disapprove of, it expresses direct negation. **e.** 'Back in a place', i.e. 'from going forward', with verbs of keeping or holding, as *retinere*, etc.; or 'without going on or forward', with verbs of rest, as *remanere; residere*, etc. **3.** Words formed with the prefix *re-* first make their appearance in English about the year 1200. Towards the end of the 16th c. *re-* begins to rank as an ordinary English prefix, chiefly employed with words of Latin origin, but also freely prefixed to native verbs. Since 1600 the use of the prefix has been very extensive. **4.** In English formations, whether on native or Latin bases, *re-* is almost exclusively employed in the sense of 'again'. In all words of this type the prefix is pronounced with a clear *e* (rī), and frequently with a certain degree of stress, whereas in words of L. or Rom. origin the vowel is usu. obscured or shortened, as in *repair* (rĭpēᵊ·ɹ), *reparation* (repărēⁱ·ʃən). In this way double forms arise, with difference of meaning, which in writing are usually distinguished by hyphening the prefix, as *recoil* and *re-coil, recover* and *re-cover*, etc. The hyphen is also freq. employed, when stress is laid on the idea of repetition, esp. when the simple word precedes the compound, as in *make and re-make, state and re-state*; also, when the main element begins with a vowel; before *e* it is usual to insert the hyphen, as *re-enter*, etc. **b.** *Re-* is occas. doubled or even trebled (usu. with hyphens inserted) to express further repetition, but not in serious writing. **5.** The number of forms resulting from the use of this prefix in English during the 19th c. is infinite, but they nearly all belong to one or other of three classes. **a.** Prefixed to ordinary verbs of action (chiefly trans.) and to derivatives from these, sometimes denoting that the action itself is performed a second time, and sometimes that its result is to reverse a previous action or process, or to restore a previous state of things; as *reaccept, reaccuse, reacknowledge, reacquire, readapt, readjourn, readminister, readopt, readorn, readvance, readvise, reaffim, reafforest, re-allot, re-apply, re-appoint, re-approach, re-arrange, rebind, re-celebrate, re-clasp, recoin, recombine, recommission, reconduct, reconfirm, reconquer, reconsecrate, reconstitute, recross, recrystallize, redeliver, redemand, re-descend, redirect, rediscover, redispose, redistil, re-edit, re-elect, re-embark, re-embody, re-emerge, re-enact, re-endow, re-engage, re-engrave, re-enjoy, re-enlist, re-erect, reface, refashion, refasten, refind, refix, refloat, reflower, refold, reforge, refortify, reframe, refurbish, refurnish, regild, regrow, reheat, reillume, reillumine, reimpose, reimpress, reimprison, reincur, reinduce, reinfect, reinhabit, reinspire, reinstruct, reinterpret, reinterrogate, re-introduce, reinvigorate, reissue, rejudge, re-lay, re-let, relocate* (U.S.), *remake, re-mark, remelt, remix, remodel, remould, rename, renumber,* †*renumerate, reoccupy, reopen, reordain, reorder, reorganize, repack, repaint, reperuse, replate, repleat, repolish, repopulate, re-present, repurchase, re-rate, re-resolve, reseat, resell, reshape, reship, re-sign, re-sound, re-sow, respell, restock, re-strengthen, resubject, resummon, resupply, resurvey, retell, re-trace, retransform, retranslate, retransmit, retype, revaccinate, revalue, revictual, revisit, rewake, rewaken, rewire, reword, rewrite*, etc. vbs.; *reaccess, readvancement, re-application, reconquest, redelivery, re-election, re-enactment, refoundation, regenesis, re-hire, reissue, replantation, representation, re-presentment, repurchase, resale, resolution, resurvey, retransmission, retrial, revaluation*, etc. sbs.; *re-eligible, reincarnate, remade, re-orient, re-soluble*, etc. adjs. **b.** Prefixed to vbs. and sbs. which denote 'making (of a certain kind or quality)', 'turning or converting into—', esp. those formed on adjs. by means of the suffix *-ize*, as *rebarbarize* vb., etc. **c.** Prefixed to vbs. and sbs. which denote fitting, furnishing, supplying, or treating with something, as *re-type*, etc. (Freq. in recent technical use.)

Reabso·rb, *v.* 1768. [RE- 5 a.] *trans.* To absorb anew or again; to take in again by absorption. So **Reabso·rption,** *spec.* in *Path.* = RESORPTION.

Reach (rītʃ), *sb.* 1526. [f. next.] **I.** An act of reaching. **1.** An (*or* the) act of reaching out with the arm, or with something held in the hand 1570. **b.** With indication of, or ref. to the space or distance covered in the act of reaching 1607. †**2.** *fig.* An attempt to attain or achieve something; a device, scheme, plan, contrivance –1785. **3.** A single stretch or spell of movement, travel, flight, etc. 1652. **b.** *Naut.* A run on one tack; a board 1830.

1. b. You needn't take quite such long reaches with your rake T. HARDY. **2.** In India this is a r. of deep policy BURKE.

II. Power of, or capacity for, reaching. **1.** The extent to which a person can stretch out the arm or hand, *esp.* so as to touch or grasp something; the distance to which an animal can extend a limb or other part, or to which any limb can be extended 1579. **b.** In prep. phrases, esp. *within, above*, or *out of* (one's) *r.* 1548. **c.** *transf.* of things 1586. **2.** Capacity or power to achieve some action, attain to some state or condition, etc. 1576. †**b.** Of the voice: Range, compass –1680. **3.** Capacity or power of comprehension; extent of knowledge or of the ability to acquire it; range of mind or thought 1542. **4.** Of the mind or mental powers: Range of efficiency in speculation, acquisition of knowledge, penetration, etc. 1580. **5.** Range, scope; extent of application, effect, influence, etc. 1546. **6.** Range (of carrying or traversing): **a.** of a gun, or shot 1591; **b.** of the eye or sight 1623; **c.** of the voice 1797. **7.** Power or possibility of getting to (or as far as) some place, person, or object; distance or limit from which some point may be reached 1784.

1. High from ground the branches would require Thy utmost r. MILT. **b.** The Tigre seeing them out of his r...falls a Roaring 1698. **c.** No lawful meanes can carrie me Out of his enuies r. SHAKS. **2.** His Learning was above yᵉ common R. 1711. The highest r. of science is, one may say, an inventive power M. ARNOLD. **3.** Nothing beyond the r. of any man of good parts MACAULAY. **4.** The 'Utopia' of Sir Thomas More..shows a r. of thought far beyond his contemporaries JOWETT. **5.** My simple wit Can never found a judgment of such r. HEYWOOD. **6. b.** Above the r. of mortall ey MILT. **7.** Within r. of markets 1833. All the people within r. had suspended their business DICKENS.

III. That which reaches or stretches. **1.** A continuous stretch, course, or extent 1609. **2.** *spec.* **a.** That portion of a river, channel, or lake which lies between two bends; as much as can be seen in one view. Also, the portion of a canal between two locks. 1536. †**b.** A bay –1736. **c.** A headland or promontory. *Obs.* exc. *U.S.* (local). 1562.

1. Darksome night..dimming the spacious r. of heaven 1638. **2. a.** The king..examined every r. and turning of the river DE FOE.

Reach (rītʃ), *v.*¹ Pa. t. **reached, †raught.** [OE. *rǣćan* = OFris. *rēka*, *rēts(i)a*, MLG., (M)Du. *reiken*, OHG. (G.) *reichen* :– WGmc. **raikjan*.] **I.** *trans.* **1.** To stretch out, extend, hold *out* or *forth* (one's hand, arm, etc.). **b.** Of a tree: To extend (its branches) 1613. **2.** To hold out (a thing) and give (it) *to*, to hand *to* a person OE. **3.** To deal or strike (a blow). *rare* or *Obs.* late ME. **4.** To succeed in touching or grasping with the outstretched hand (or with something held in it) or by any similar exertion OE. †**b.** To obtain by seizure or otherwise –1612. †**c.** To take or lay hold of; to carry off –1667. **5. a.** To take or snatch *from* a person or thing; to take *away*, *hence*, *out*, *up*. Now *arch.* late ME. **b.** To draw or bring towards oneself (esp. to take down) *from* a certain place or position; to lift *up*, take *down*, etc. 1450. **6.** To succeed in touching with a weapon or with the hand in delivering a blow OE. **b.** To succeed in affecting or influencing by some means; to impress, convince, win over, etc. 1667. **7. a.** Of things (or of persons in respect of some part of the body): To come into contact with, to touch; to extend so far as to touch ME. **b.** Of immaterial things, *esp.* to succeed in affecting or influencing. late ME. **8.** To come to (a person, place, object, or point in space), to get up to or as far as ME. **b.** Of sounds: To come to (the ear, a person or place) 1649. **c.** Of the eye, a gun, etc.: To carry to (a point) 1667. **9.** To arrive at, to attain or come to (a point in time, a condition, quality, etc.) 1590. **10. a.** To succeed in understanding or comprehending. *Obs.* or *poet.* 1605. **b.** To succeed in acquiring or obtaining 1638. **11.** To stretch; to draw or pull *out* †or *in*. *Obs.* exc. *dial.* OE.

1. He raught out his right foot and dubbed me in the necke CAXTON. **b.** Where any row Of fruit-trees..reached too far Thir pamperd boughes MILT. **2.** I..bade one reche me a booke CHAUCER. **4.** Wilt thou r. stars, because they shine on thee? SHAKS. **c.** The hand of death hath raught him SHAKS. **6. b.** Men's opinions must be reached by reason, not by force 1851. **7. a.** His stature reacht the Skie MILT. **b.** Liberty should r. every Individual of a People ADDISON. **8.** You may easily r. Harwich in a Day STEELE. **b.** My name, perhaps, hath reach'd your ear GAY. **9.** Till ryper yeares he raught SPENSER. This little work reached a second edition 1888. **10. a.** The words are twisted in some double sense That I r. not SHELLEY.

II. *intr.* **1.** To make a stretch *with* the arm or hand; to extend the arm, hold out the hand. Also of the arm or hand: To stretch out. OE. **b.** To grasp or clutch *at* 1562. **c.** *fig.* of mental striving 1646. **2.** To succeed in stretching one's arm, etc., so far ME. **3.** To stretch out (continuously), to extend; to project a certain distance (*above*, *beyond*, etc.) OE. **b.** Of a period of time, or with ref. to duration of time ME. †**c.** To suffice, be adequate or sufficient *to* (also with *infin.*). Chiefly of money. –1733. **d.** To amount *to* 1596. **4.** *Naut.* To sail on a reach 1832. **5.** To attain or succeed in coming *to* a place, point, person, etc. 1632. **b.** Of the eye, a gun, etc.: To carry 1632. **6.** To attain *to* an achievement, condition, etc. Now *rare* or *Obs.* ME. †**b.** To attain *to* (knowledge of) –1653.

1. What hinders then To r., and feed at once both Bodie and Mind? MILT. **b.** Put forth thy hand, r. at the glorious Gold SHAKS. **2.** By reaching beyond his reach, he reacheth nothing at all 1581. This woman hath herein reached beyond your conceit 1633. **3.** These vast domains, reaching from the Ebro to the Carpathian mountains BRYCE. **b.** The wyne haruest shal reache vnto the sowynge tyme COVERDALE *Lev.* 26:5. **d.** 1 *Hen. IV*, IV. i. 129. **5. b.** As far as the eye could r. in either direction 1885. Hence **Rea·chable** *a.* that may be reached. **Rea·cher,** one who or that which reaches; †an exaggerated statement.

Reach (rītʃ), *v.*² Now *dial.* [OE. *hrǣćan* = ON. *hrækja* spit, f. Gmc. **χraik-*, repr. also by OE. *hrāca*, ON. *hráki* spittle; of imit. origin.] †**1. a.** *intr.* To spit; also, to hawk –1565. †**b.** *trans.* To spit or bring *up* (blood or phlegm) –1606. **2.** *intr.* To make efforts to vomit; to RETCH 1575.

Reachless (rī·tʃlės), *a.* 1599. [f. REACH *v.*¹ + -LESS.] That cannot be reached.

Rea·ch-me-dow:n, *a.* and *sb.* 1862. [f. REACH *v.*¹ I. 5 b.] **A.** *adj.* Of clothes: Ready-made; also, second-hand. **B.** *sb.* Chiefly *pl.* **1.** A ready-made or second-hand garment. 1862. **2.** orig. *U.S.* Trousers 1905.

React (ri,æ·kt), *v.*¹ 1644. [f. RE- 2 a + ACT *v.*, in XVII after med.L. *reagere*, f. L. *re-* RE- + *agere* do, act.] **1.** *intr.* To act in return, or in turn, *upon* some agent or influence. **b.** *spec.* in *Chem.* of the action of reagents 1797. **2.** To act, or display some form of energy, in response to a stimulus; to undergo a change under some influence. Const. *to* (in recent use). 1656. **3.** To act in opposition to some force 1861. **4.** To move or tend in a reverse direction; to return towards a previous condition 1875.

Re-act (rī,æ·kt), *v.*² 1648. [f. RE- 5 a + ACT *v.*] *trans.* To act, do, or perform again.

Reactance (ri,æ·ktăns). 1896. [f. REACT *v.*¹ + -ANCE.] *Electr.* That part of the impedance of an alternating-current circuit which is due to capacitance or inductance or both.

Reaction (ri,æ·kʃən). 1643. [f. REACT *v.*¹ + -ION; in XVII after med.L. *reactio*. Cf. Fr. *réaction*.] **1.** Repulsion or resistance exerted by a body in opposition to the impact or pressure of another body. **2.** The influence which a thing, acted upon or affected by another, exercises in return upon the agent, or in turn upon something else 1771. **b.** *Chem.* The action of one chemical agent upon another, or the result of such action 1836. **3.** *Phys.* and *Path.* **a.** The supervention of an opposite physical condition, as the return of heat after cold, or of vitality after shock 1805. **b.** The response made by the system or an organ to an external stimulus 1896. **c.** *Wireless.* Method by which weak signals are strengthened 1923. **4.** A movement towards the reversal of an existing tendency or state of things, esp. in politics, a return, or desire to return, to a previous condition of affairs; a revulsion of feeling 1801.

1. The r. of the sides of the vessel against the fluid 1800. *fig.* It is the method of Charity to suffer without r. SIR T. BROWNE. **2.** Action and r. have thus gone on from prehistoric ages to the present time TYNDALL. **3. a.** The cold bath, when not followed by a healthy r., is anything but a tonic 1875. **b.** The r. to light was lost in both eyes 1899. **4.** In the ancient as well as the modern world there were reactions from theory to experience JOWETT.

attrib. and *Comb.*, as (sense 3) *r. period*, *stage*, *time*; **r. engine** or **machine,** a small apparatus in which the motive power is derived from the r. exerted by escaping steam; **r. wheel,** a water-wheel impelled by the r. of escaping water.

Reactionary (ri,æ·kʃənări), *a.* and *sb.* 1847. [f. prec. + -ARY¹, partly after Fr. *réactionnaire* (XVIII in political sense).] **A.** *adj.* **1.** Of, pertaining to, or characterized by, reaction. **2.** Inclined or favourable to reaction 1858. **B.** *sb.* One who favours or is inclined to reaction 1858.

Rea·ctionist, *sb.* and *a.* 1858. [f. as prec. + -IST.] **A.** *sb.* A professed reactionary 1862. **B.** as *adj.*

So **Rea·ctionism.**

Reactive (ri,æ·ktiv), *a.* and *sb.* 1790. [f. REACT *v.*¹ + -IVE. Cf. Fr. *réactif*.] **A.** *adj.* **1.** Active or operative in return 1794. **2.** *Path.* **a.** Supervening on a previous opposite state; due to reaction 1822. **b.** Recuperative; responsive (*to* a stimulus) 1822. **3.** Characterized by reaction (sense 4) 1868. **4.** Possessing electrical reactance 1902. **B.** *sb.* *Chem.* [– Fr. *réactif*.] A reagent (*rare*) 1790. Hence **Rea·ctive-ly** *adv.*, **-ness.**

Reactor (ri,æ·ktəɹ). 1926. [f. as prec. + -OR 2.] **1.** *Electr.* An apparatus possessing electrical reactance. **2.** *Med.* An animal or patient reacting positively to a foreign substance 1928.

Read (rīd), *sb.* 1838. [f. next.] An act of perusal; a spell of reading.

Read (rīd), *v.* Pa. t. and pple. **read** (red). [OE. *rǣdan* = OFris. *rēda*, OS. *rādan* (Du. *raden*), OHG. *rātan* (G. *raten*), ON. *ráða* advise, plan, contrive, explain, read, Goth. *-rēdan* :– Gmc. **rǣðan*.] **I.** *trans.* **To consider, interpret, discern*, etc. †**1. a.** To have an idea; to think or suppose *that*, etc. (*rare*) –1768. †**b.** To guess *what*, *who*, *why*, etc. –1590. **2.** To make out the meaning of (a dream, riddle, etc.); to declare or expound this to another OE. **b.** To foresee, foretell, predict. Chiefly in *to r. one's fortune*. 1591. †**3.** To see, discern. SPENSER.

***To peruse, without uttering in speech.* **4.** To inspect and interpret in thought (any signs which represent words or discourse); to look over or scan (something written, printed, etc.) with understanding of what is meant by the letters or signs; to peruse (a document, book, author, etc.). Also with advs., as *through*, *over* OE. **b.** To peruse books, etc. written in (a certain language); *esp.* to have such knowledge of (a language) as to be able to understand works written in it 1530. **c.** *transf.* and *fig.*; *gen.* of interpretation of signs or marks; *esp.* to make out the character or nature of (a person, the heart, etc.) by scrutiny or interpretation of outward signs 1611. **d.** To peruse (printer's proofs), comparing them with the copy; to examine as a proof-reader 1808. **e.** *To r. off*: to note in definite form (the result of inspection, esp. of a graduated instrument) 1812. **5.** To take in a particular way (what is read) 1624. **b.** *transf.* To regard (a person, thing, event, etc.) in a certain light 1847. **6.** Const. with preps. **a.** *refl.* To bring oneself *into* or *to* (a certain state) by reading 1676. **b.** To introduce (an additional idea or element) *into* what is being read or considered. (Freq. implying that the insertion is unwarranted or erroneous.) 1879. **7.** To adopt, give, or exhibit as a reading in a particular passage 1538.

4. Auld storys that men redys, Representis to thaim the dedys of stalwart folk BARBOUR. **b.** He read all the languages which are considered either as learned or polite JOHNSON. **c.** He reads the skies COWPER. One of the greatest of all difficulties in reading the hand 1867. This they call..reading men and manners SWIFT. You read us like books 1902. **e.** Before the height of the mercury is read off 1816. **5.** R. it how you will, it is not to purpose 1624. **6. b.** Men r. back developed ideas into undeveloped minds H. SPENCER. **7.** For *Lovaine* some copies of Wace r. *Alemaigne* 1847.

****To learn by perusal.* **8.** To see or find (a statement) in a written or otherwise recorded form; to learn by perusal of a book or other document OE. **b.** To discern or discover (something) *in* (or *on*) the face, look, etc. of a person 1590.

8. I haue read the cause of his effects in Galen SHAKS. *transf.* Her quick eye seemed to r. my thoughts DICKENS. **b.** Muffle your false loue.. Let not my sister r. it in your eye SHAKS.

*****To peruse and utter in speech.* **9.** To utter aloud; to render in speech (the words of written or printed matter). Often, *to r. aloud.* Also *reading* = being read. **b.** Used of submitting a proposed measure to a legislative assembly by reading the whole or some part of it 1459. †**10.** To teach or impart (some art or branch of knowledge) *to* another by (or as by) reading aloud –1662. **11. a.** *To r. oneself in*: to enter upon office as incumbent of a benefice in the Church of England, by reading publicly the Thirty-nine Articles and making the Declaration of Assent 1857. **b.** *To r. out of*: to expel from (a body, party, etc.), properly by reading out the sentence of expulsion. Chiefly in *pass.* 1865. †**12.** To declare, as by reading aloud; to relate, tell, say –1591. †**b.** To speak of or mention; to describe; to name or call –1617.

9. R. the Will; wee'l heare it Antony SHAKS. The clerk and sexton read out the askings for the marriage 1890. Phr. *To r. a lesson* or *lecture*, freq. *fig.* to teach (a person) something, to administer a reprimand or check (to a person).

II. *intr.* or *absol.* **1.** To apprehend mentally the meaning of written or other characters; to be engaged in doing this; to be occupied in perusing a book, etc. OE. **b.** Coupled with *write*, usu. with ref. to rudimentary education 1490. **c.** To study, esp. with a view to examination. Also *to r. up*, to collect information by reading. 1826. **2.** To find mention or record *of* something by, or in the course of, reading ME. **3. a.** To bear reading;

to be readable 1668. **b.** To turn out (well or ill), or have a specified character, when read; to produce a certain impression on the reader 1731. **c.** To admit of interpretation 1866. **4.** To render in speech the words one is reading (in sense I. 4) OE. **b.** *To r. in* = I. 11 a. 1828. †**5.** To give instruction by means of reading aloud; to lecture or discourse *upon* a subject –1700.

1. Who reads Incessantly..Uncertain and unsettl'd still remains MILT. *fig.* Phr. *To r. between the lines*: see LINE *sb.*[2] III. 5 a. **c.** [He] was reading for honours 1859. **2.** I have read of Caligula's Horse, that was made Consul 1645. **3. b.** Whose productions..r. better than they act 1789. **4.** Then he went up to his study to be read to till six 1879. **b.** I read in—i.e. read the Thirty-nine Articles J. H. NEWMAN.

Read (red), *ppl. a.* 1586. [f. prec.] **1.** That is read, *esp.* that is read out 1590. **2.** In pred. use: Experienced, versed, or informed *in* a subject by reading 1586. **3.** (Chiefly pred.) Informed by reading, acquainted with books or literature, learned. (Now only with advs., esp. WELL-READ.) 1588.

1. The trouble of attending the meeting to hear a r. speech 1901. **2.** An Oxford Man, extreamly r. in Greek PRIOR.

Readable (rī·dăb'l), *a.* 1570. [f. READ *v.* + -ABLE.] **1.** Capable of being read, legible. **2.** Capable of being read with pleasure or interest. Usu. of literary work: Agreeable or attractive in style. 1826. Hence **Readabi·lity, Rea·dableness.**

Readdre·ss, *v.* 1611. [RE- 5 a.] **1.** *refl.* To address (oneself) anew. **2.** *trans.* To put a new address on (a letter, etc.) 1884.

1. Didymus..readdressed himself to her BOYLE.

Reader (rī·dəɹ). OE. [f. READ *v.* + -ER[1].] †**1.** An interpreter (of dreams) –1440. **2.** One who reads or peruses OE. **b.** A proof-reader employed by a printer 1808. **c.** One employed by a publisher to read works offered for publication and to report on their merits 1871. **3.** One who reads aloud; *spec.* one who reads parts of the service in a place of worship OE. **4.** One who reads (and expounds) to pupils or students; a teacher, instructor; *spec.* in some Universities, as the title of certain instructors 1519. **b.** In the Inns of Court, a lecturer on law 1517. **5.** A title for books containing passages for instruction or exercise in reading 1799. Hence **Rea·dership,** the office of a r.

3. *Lay reader*: see LAY *a.*

Readily (re·dili), *adv.* ME. [f. READY *a.* + -LY[2].] In a ready manner. **1.** Promptly, in respect of the voluntariness of the action; hence, willingly, cheerfully. **2.** Quickly, without delay; also, without difficulty, with ease or facility. late ME.

2. Her gratitude may be more r. imagined than described GOLDSM.

Readiness (re·dinės). late ME. [f. as prec. + -NESS.] **1.** Promptness in voluntary action; prompt compliance, willingness, etc. **2.** The quality of being prompt or quick in action, performance, expression, etc. late ME. **b.** The quickness or facility with which something is done 1585. **3.** A state of preparation, in phr. *in r.* 1541. **4.** The condition or fact of being ready or fully prepared (*rare*) 1548.

1. The r. of all the country to take arms was very singular SCOTT. **2.** His r. in the French tongue GEO. ELIOT.

Reading (rī·diŋ), *vbl. sb.* OE. [f. READ *v.* + -ING[1].] **1.** The action of perusing written or printed matter; the practice of occupying oneself in this way. Also with *up, off.* **b.** The extent to which one reads or has read; literary knowledge, scholarship 1593. **c.** Ability to read; the art of reading 1599. **d.** A single or separate act or course of perusal 1757. **2.** The action of uttering aloud the words of written or printed matter OE. **b.** The delivery in this manner of a specified portion of matter; a single act or spell of this; also, the portion so read at one time OE. **c.** The formal recital of a bill before a legislative assembly 1647. **d.** A social or public entertainment at which the audience listens to a reader 1858. †**3.** The act of lecturing or commenting upon some subject, *esp.* a law text; also, the matter of such lecture or comment, a commentary or gloss –1741. **4.** The form in which a given passage appears in any copy or edition of a text; the actual word or words used in a particular passage 1557. **5.** Matter for reading, esp. with ref. to its quality or kind 1706. **6.** That which presents itself to be read; *spec.* the indication of a graduated instrument. So *r. off.* 1808. **7.** The interpretation or meaning one attaches to anything, or the view one takes of it; in recent use *esp.* the rendering given to a play or a character, a piece of music, etc. 1792.

1. R. is to the Mind, what Exercise is to the Body STEELE. **b.** A man of some r. 1797. **2.** It was genuine r., not dramatic recitation 1878. **b.** They had their weekly Readings of the Law of Moses 1673. **4.** *Various readings*: see VARIOUS. **7.** She gave him her r. of the matter 1860.

attrib. and *Comb.*, as **r.-book,** a book containing passages for instruction in reading; **-desk,** a desk for supporting a book while it is being read, *spec.* a lectern; **-glass,** a large magnifying glass for use in reading; **r. room,** a room devoted to reading, *esp.* one in the premises of a club or library, or intended for public use; also, the proof-readers' room in a printing-office.

Reading (rī·diŋ), *ppl. a.* 1673. [f. READ *v.* + -ING[2].] **1. a.** *R. clerk*, the designation of one of the clerks to the House of Lords 1788. **b.** *R. boy*, a boy who reads copy aloud to the corrector of the press 1808. **2.** Given to reading; studious 1673.

2. *R. man*, applied *spec.* to a university student who makes reading his chief occupation.

Readju·st, *v.* 1611. [RE- 5 a.] *trans.* To adjust again or afresh; to put in order again. Hence **Readju·stment.**

Readju·ster. 1862. [f. prec. + -ER[1].] One who readjusts. **b.** *U.S.* A member of a political party (formed in 1877–1878) in Virginia, which advocated a legislative readjustment of the State debt 1879.

Readmission (rī,ædmi·ʃən). 1655. [RE- 5 a.] The action of admitting again.

Readmit (rī,ædmi·t), *v.* 1611. [RE- 5 a.] *trans.* To admit again. So **Readmi·ttance.**

Ready (re·di), *a., adv.,* and *sb.* [Early ME. *rædi(ȝ, readi, redi,* extended forms (with -Y[1]) of OE. *rǣde* (usu. *ġerǣde*) = OFris. *rēde*, MLG. *rēde* (Du. *gereed*), OHG. *reiti*, ON. *reiðr* ready, Goth. *garaiþs* arranged, f. Gmc. **raið-* prepare, arrange.] **A.** *adj.* **I. 1.** In a state of preparation for performing (or becoming the object of) such action as is implied or expressed in the context. **b.** *spec.* Properly dressed or attired; having finished one's toilet. late ME. †**c.** Used in replying to a call or summons SHAKS. **d.** *Mil.* and *Naut.* As a word of command 1802. **2.** Prepared, or having all preparations made, *to* do something ME. **b.** Willing; feeling or exhibiting no reluctance ME. **c.** Easily inclined or disposed 1596. **d.** Sufficiently angry to be on the point of (doing something violent) 1535. **3. a.** That has passed, or has been brought, into such a condition as to be immediately likely or liable (*to* do something). late ME. **b.** Likely, liable, 'fit' 1596. **4.** Const. with preps.: †**a.** With *to* or *unto* (rarely *into*): Prepared, inclined, or willing to do, give, suffer, etc. (what is indicated by the sb.) –1591. **b.** Prepared *for* (an event, action, state, etc.) 1591. **5.** Prompt, quick, expert, dexterous ME. **6. a.** Of the mind or mental powers: Quick to devise, plan, comprehend, observe, etc. ME. **b.** Of persons, etc.: Prompt or quick in speech, discourse, or writing ME. **c.** Proceeding from, delivered with, promptness of thought or expression 1583. **7.** Of action, etc.: Characterized by promptness or quickness. late ME. **b.** Characterized by alacrity or willingness in some respect 1548. **c.** Taking place easily or quickly 1596.

1. Some one be readie with a costly suite SHAKS. **b.** Whan thou arte vp and redy, than first swepe thy house 1523. **c.** *Mids. N.* III. i. 165. **2.** My nephew was r. to sail DE FOE. **b.** Thou Lord art the God most mild Readiest thy grace to shew MILT. **c.** You are too r. to speak evil of men JOWETT. **d.** They are almost r. to stone me COVERDALE *Exod.* 17:4. **3.** Cordials to take when r. to faint 1748. **b.** Winds..r. to cut you through 1698. **4. b.** *Meas. for M.* III. i. 107. **5.** My tonge is yᵉ penne of a r. writer COVERDALE *Ps.* 44:1. R. in gybes, quicke-answered, sawcie SHAKS. How r. he is at all these sort of things SHERIDAN. **6. b.** Reading maketh a full man, conference a readye man BACON. **7.** A r., tho' unwilling Obedience 1754. **b.** Open speech, and r. hand BYRON. **c.** That when at Market they may find a readier sale 1730.

II. 1. In the condition of having been prepared or put in order for some purpose ME. **2.** Close at hand; handy, convenient for use ME. **3.** Immediately available as currency; having the form of coin or money ME. **4.** Of a way, path, etc.: Lying directly before one; straight, direct, near. *Obs.* exc. *dial.* ME. **b.** Hence with *way* in the sense of 'method', 'means', etc.; and so *r. means* 1542. †**5.** Of payment or pay: Made or given promptly; not delayed or deferred. –1697.

1. A servant came to tell us the tea was r. BERKELEY. **2.** The slightest, easiest, readiest recompence MILT. Phr. *R. to* (one's) *hand(s), r. to* hand. **3.** What advantage might be made of the r. Cash I had STEELE. **4. b.** Teaching covetousness ..a r. way to assault them FULLER.

Phr. **To make ready. a.** *refl.* To prepare (oneself); †*spec.* to array, attire or dress (oneself). **b.** *trans.* To prepare or put in order (a thing or things); †to dress (a person). (Cf. MAKE-READY.) **c.** *absol.* To make preparations.

Comb. Prefixed to pa. pples. to emphasize the completion of the process expressed by these, as *r.-cooked, -dressed, -prepared,* etc. **b.** *r.-for-service, -to-eat.*

B. *adv.* = READILY. (Now only in compar. and superl.) ME.

There was not..A child who..answered readier through his Catechism SOUTHEY.

C. *sb.* **1.** (usu. with *the.*) Ready money, cash. (*slang* or *colloq.*) 1688. **2.** (Usu. with *the.*) The position of a fire-arm when the person holding or carrying it is ready to raise it to the shoulder and aim or fire 1837.

1. He was not flush in r., either to go to law, or clear old debts ARBUTHNOT. **2.** I..found the guard with his musket at the 'r.' 1837.

Ready (re·di), *v.* ME. [f. READY *a.*] **1.** *refl.* To make (oneself) ready in any way. **2.** *trans.* To make (a thing) ready; to prepare; put in order. Now *dial.* ME. **3.** *slang. Racing.* To prevent (one's horse) from winning, in order to secure a handicap in another race 1887.

Ready-made (stress var.), *ppl. phr., a.,* and *sb.* late ME. [f. READY *a.* + MADE.] †**1.** Made ready, prepared –1588. **2.** Of made and manufactured articles: In a finished state, immediately ready for use; now *spec.* of articles which are offered for sale in this state 1535. **3.** Hence applied to any thing or person which exists in a finished or complete form; freq. used with depreciatory force, in allusion to the inferiority of 'ready-made' goods 1738. **b.** In *attrib.* use 1797. **4.** Pertaining to, dealing in, ready-made articles 1809. **B.** *sb.* A ready-made article; *esp.* a ready-made garment, etc. 1882.

3. A good Wife must be bespoke, for there is none ready made SWIFT. **b.** Some ready-made face Of hypocritical assent SHELLEY.

Rea·dy mo·ney. late ME. [READY *a.* II. 3.] **1.** Coined money, cash, as being immediately available for use; also, immediate payment in coin for anything bought. Hence **2.** *attrib. phr.* Characterized by immediate payment in money for articles bought 1712. **3.** Paying ready money 1796.

2. The landlord carried on a ready-money business 1898.

Rea·dy re·ckoner. 1757. [READY *a.*] A table, or tables, showing at a glance the results of such arithmetical calculations as are most frequently required in business, etc.

Ready-to-wear. Also **-for-.** 1905. = READY-MADE *a.* 2, *sb.*

Ready-witted, *a.* 1581. [READY *a.* I. 6 a.] Of a ready wit or intelligence; quick of apprehension.

Reagency (ri,ē̆i·dʒĕnsi). 1842. [RE- 2 a.] Reactive power or operation.

Reagent (ri,ē̆i·dʒĕnt). 1797. [RE- 2 a; cf. REACT *v.*[1]] **1.** *Chem.* A substance employed as a test to determine the presence of some other substance by means of the *reaction* which is produced. **2.** A reactive substance, force, etc. 1856.

2. Mind is a r. against society 1865.

Re:aggrava·tion. 1611. [– med.L. *reaggravatio*; see AGGRAVATION 3. Cf. Fr. †*réaggravation* (XV).] *Eccl.* The second warning given to a person before final excommunication.

†**Reaks,** *sb. pl.* 1575. [Of unkn. origin; cf. FREAK *sb.*[1], REX[1].] Pranks –1818.

Real (rī·ăl, rē·ăl), *sb.*[1] 1588. [– Sp. *real*,

subst. use of *real* ROYAL; in full *real de plata* 'royal coin of silver'.] **1.** A small silver coin and money of account in use in Spain and Spanish-speaking countries. †**2.** *R. of eight* = *piece of eight* (EIGHT A.) –1818.

†**Real,** *a.*^{1} ME. [– OFr. *real* (mod. *royal*); see ROYAL, and cf. LEAL.] Royal, regal, kingly –1602. Hence †**Re·ally** *adv.*^{1} royally –1578.

Real (rī·al), *a.*^{2}, *adv.*, and *sb.*^{2} 1448. [orig. – AFr. *real* = (O)Fr. *réel*; later – its source, late L. *realis*, f. L. *res* thing, acc. *rem*; see -AL^{1}.] **A.** *adj.* **I. 1.** Having an objective existence; actually existing as a thing 1601. **b.** In *Philosophy* applied to whatever is regarded as having an existence in fact and not merely in appearance, thought, or language, or as having an absolute and necessary, in contrast to a merely contingent, existence 1701. **c.** *Math.* Of quantities. (Opp. to IMAGINARY, or IMPOSSIBLE.) 1727. **d.** *Optics* (see quot.) 1859. **2.** Actually existing or present as a state or quality of things; having a foundation in fact; actually occurring or happening 1597. **3.** That is actually and truly such as its name implies; possessing the essential qualities denoted by its name; hence, genuine, undoubted 1559. **b.** Natural, as opp. to artificial or depicted 1718. **4. a.** That is actually present or involved, as opp. to *apparent, ostensible*, etc. 1716. **b.** The actual (thing or person); that properly bears the name 1631. **5.** †**a.** Sincere, straightforward, honest –1709. **b.** Free from nonsense or affectation; 'genuine' 1847.

1. Whereat I wak'd, and found Before mine Eyes all r., as the dream Had lively shadowd MILT. **d.** If an image consist of points through which the light actually passes it is called r.; —in other cases virtual 1859. **2.** He can imagin'd pleasures find, To combat against r. cares PRIOR. *R. presence*, the actual presence of Christ's body and blood in the sacrament of the Eucharist. **3.** It was evidently r. and not affected doubt 1866. **4. a.** There lurks the r. reason at the bottom of the ostensible one BENTHAM. Phr. *The r. thing*, the thing itself, as contrasted with imitations or counterfeits; hence *slang*, the 'genuine article'. **5. b.** She had been so near r. people 1880.

II. 1. *Law.* (Opp. to PERSONAL.) **a.** Of actions, causes, etc.: Relating to things, or *spec.* to real property 1448. **b.** Connected in some way with things or real property 1467. **c.** Consisting of immovable property, as lands and houses; esp. *r. estate* 1641. **d.** *Chattels r.*: see CHATTEL 2. **2. a.** Relating to, concerned with, things 1593. †**b.** Of written characters: Representing things instead of sounds –1741. **c.** Corresponding to actuality; true 1657. **3.** Attached or pertaining to scholastic Realism 1528.

B. *adv.* (usu. with adjs.) Really, genuinely. Also (chiefly *Sc.* and *U.S.*): Very, extremely. 1658.

C. *absol.* or as *sb.* †**1.** = REALIST 1. –1684. **2.** A real thing; a thing having a real existence, either in the ordinary or in a metaphysical sense 1626. **3.** *The r.*: that which actually exists, contrasted (*a*) with a copy, counterfeit, etc., (*b*) with what is abstract or notional 1818. Hence **Re·alness,** the fact or quality of being r.; reality, truth.

Realgar (ri,æ·lgār). late ME. [– med.L. *realgar* – Arab. *rahj al-ġār* 'powder of the cave or cavern' (*rahj* powder, *al* AL-^{2}, *ġār* cave). Cf. Fr. *réalgar*.] The native or factitious disulphide of arsenic, also called *red* (*sulphide* or *sulphuret of*) *arsenic* and *red orpiment*, used as a pigment and in pyrotechnics.

Realism (rī·ăliz'm). 1817. [f. REAL *a.*^{2} + -ISM 2 b, orig. after G. *realismus* or Fr. *réalisme*.] **1.** *Philos.* **a.** The scholastic doctrine of the objective or absolute existence of universals, of which Thomas Aquinas was the chief exponent. (Opp. to NOMINALISM and CONCEPTUALISM.) Also in later use: The attribution of objective existence to a subjective conception 1838. **b.** Belief in the real existence of matter as the object of perception (*natural r.*); also, the view that the physical world has independent reality, and is not ultimately reducible to universal mind or spirit. (Opp. to IDEALISM 1.) 1836. **2.** Inclination or attachment to what is real; tendency to regard things as they really are; any view or system contrasted with IDEALISM 2. 1817. **3.** Close resemblance to what is real; fidelity of representation, rendering the precise details of the real thing or scene: in ref. to art and literature, often with implication that the details are of an unpleasant or sordid character 1856.

Realist (rī·ălist), *sb.* (and *a.*) 1605. [f. REAL *a.*^{2} + -IST, after Fr. *réaliste*.] †**1.** One who occupies himself with things rather than words (*rare*) –1623. **2.** *Philos.* An adherent or advocate of Realism (as opp. either to NOMINALIST or to IDEALIST) 1695. **3. a.** One devoted to what is real, as opp. to what is fictitious or imaginary 1847. **b.** An artist or writer addicted to realism 1870. **4.** *attrib.* or as *adj.* Pertaining to, characteristic of, realists 1845.

3. b. [Fielding] is..as hearty a r. as Hogarth 1874.

Realistic (ri,ăli·stik), *a.* 1856. [f. prec. + -IC.] **1.** Characterized by artistic or literary realism; representing things as they really are. **2.** Concerned with, or characterized by, a practical view of life 1862. **3.** Of or pertaining to realists in philosophy; of the nature of philosophical realism 1874.

3. The r. tendency—the disposition to mistake words for things—is a vice inherent in all ordinary thinking 1874. Hence **Reali·stically** *adv.*

Reality (ri,æ·lĭti). 1550. [– (O)Fr. *réalité* or med.L. *realitas*; see REAL *a.*^{2}, -ITY.] **1.** The quality of being real or having an actual existence. †**b.** Correspondence to fact; truth –1793. **c.** Suggestion of, resemblance to, what is real 1856. †**2.** Sincere devotion or loyalty *to* a person; sincerity or honesty of character or purpose –1761. **3.** Real existence; what is real; the aggregate of real things or existences; that which underlies and is the truth of appearances or phenomena 1647. **4.** A real thing, fact, or state of things 1646. **5.** The real nature or constitution *of* something; also without const., the real thing or state of things 1690. **b.** That which constitutes the actual thing, as dist. from what is merely apparent or external 1840. †**6.** *Law.* = REALTY^{2} 3. –1706.

1. Lucretius..makes no doubt of the R. of Apparitions ADDISON. **2.** We..wait a time, to expresse our reallity to the Emperour FULLER. **3.** To carry it on from Discourse and Design to R. and Effect COWLEY. Phr. *In r.*, really, actually, in fact. **5. b.** A formal grant of the powers of which he already possessed the r. MACAULAY.

Realization (rī:ăləizēⁱ·ʃən). 1611. [f. next + -ATION, after Fr. *réalisation*.] The action or result of realizing. **1.** The action of making real; the process of becoming real; conversion into real fact. **b.** A case or instance of this 1837. **2.** The action of forming a clear and distinct concept, or the concept thus formed 1828. **3. a.** The action of converting (paper money, property, etc.) into a more available form; in later use chiefly applied to the sale of stock, or of a bankrupt's estate, in order to obtain the money value. **b.** The action of obtaining or acquiring (a sum of money, a fortune, etc.). 1796.

Realize (rī·ălәiz), *v.* 1611. [f. REAL *a.*^{2} + -IZE, after Fr. *réaliser*.] **1.** *trans.* To make real, give reality to (something merely imagined, planned, etc.); to convert into reality. **b.** To make realistic or apparently real 1779. **2.** To make real as an object of thought; to present as real; to bring vividly or clearly before the mind 1646. **3.** To conceive, or think of, as real; to understand or grasp clearly 1775. **b.** *U.S.* To have actual experience of 1776. **4.** To convert (securities, paper money, etc.) into cash, or (property of any kind) into money 1727. **b.** *absol.* To realize one's property; to sell out 1781. **5.** To obtain or amass (a sum of money, a fortune, etc.) by sale, trade, or similar means; to acquire for oneself or by one's own exertions; to make (so much) out of something 1753. **b.** Of property or capital: To bring (a specified amount of money or interest) when sold or invested; to fetch (so much) as a price or return 1836.

1. Ideals are none the worse because they cannot be realized in fact JOWETT. **2.** An Act of the Imagination, that realises the Event however fictitious, or approximates it however remote JOHNSON. **3.** She cannot r. the change we must undergo W. IRVING. **4.** Substantial securities..to be realised and converted into cash 1768. **b.** He realised with great prudence while this mine was still at its full vogue THACKERAY. **5.** You, sir, who have realized a fortune 1775. **b.** His duty was to see that the property realised its full value 1885. Hence **Re·alizable** *a.* that may be realized. **Re:alizabi·lity. Re·alizer,** one who or that which realizes. **Re·alizingly** *adv.*

†**Re-ally·**, *v.* 1456. [– Fr. †*real(l)ier*, var. *ral(l)ier* RALLY *v.*^{1}; see RE- 2 and ALLY *v.*] **1.** *trans.* and *refl.* **a.** = RALLY *v.*^{1} 1. Also with *up*. –1645. **b.** To connect, unite (again) *to* or *with* –1653. **2.** *intr.* (for *refl.*) = RALLY *v.*^{1} II. 1. –1647. **3.** *trans.* To form (plans) again SPENSER.

Really (rī·ăli), *adv.*^{2} late ME. [f. REAL *a.*^{2} + -LY^{2}.] **1.** In a real manner; in reality; in point of fact; actually. **b.** Used to emphasize the truth or correctness of an epithet or statement; hence, positively, indeed 1610. **2.** In isolated position: **a.** As a term of asseveration or protest 1602. **b.** Interrogatively 1815.

1. The Account of such things as have r. happened ADDISON. **b.** This last Bill was r. frightful DE FOE. The king is r. and truly a Catholic MACAULAY. **2.** Why r., I said, the truth is that I do not know JOWETT. **b.** She exclaimed, 'R.? It is r. true?' 1893.

Realm (relm). [ME. *reaume*, later *realme* (XIV) – OFr. *reaume*, *realme* (mod. *royaume*) – L. *regimin-* REGIMEN; the forms with *-l-* are due to blending with OFr. *reiel* ROYAL.] **1.** A kingdom. Now chiefly *rhet.*, and in such phrases as 'Statutes of the R.'. **2.** *transf.* and *fig.* **a.** The kingdom of heaven, or of God ME. **b.** Any sphere or region. (Occas. with suggestion of a ruling power.) late ME. **c.** The sphere, domain, or province *of* some quality, state, or other abstract conception 1667. **d.** A primary zoogeographical division of the earth's surface 1876.

1. The Duke of Argyle is to be created a Peer of this Realme 1705. **2. a.** The avenging God! Who..sits High in heaven's r. SHELLEY. **b.** The realms of Hell are gleaming fiery bright 1816. **c.** Thir legions..Scout farr and wide into the R. of night MILT. Hence **Rea·lmless** *a.* destitute of a r.

Realtor (rī·ăltọɹ). *U.S.* 1922. [f. REALTY^{2} + -OR 2.] A dealer in real estate; prop., a member of the National Association of Real Estate Boards.

†**Re·alty**^{1}. ME. [– (O)Fr. *realté*, *reauté* :– med.L. *regalitas, -tat-*, f. L. *regalis* REGAL; see -TY^{1}. Superseded by ROYALTY.] Royalty; royal state, dignity, or power –late ME.

Realty^{2} (rī·ălti). 1440. [f. REAL *a.*^{2} + -TY^{1}.] †**1.** Reality –1644. †**2.** Sincerity, honesty –1667. **3.** *Law.* Real property or estate 1544.

Ream (rīm), *sb.*^{1} *Obs.* exc. *dial.* [OE. *rēam* = MLG. *rōm(e*, (M)Du. *room*, MHG. *milch|roum* (G. *rahm*, dial. *raum*, *rohm*) :– WGmc. **rauma*.] **1.** = CREAM *sb.*^{2} 1. **2.** *transf.* A scum or froth upon any liquid 1460.

Ream (rīm), *sb.*^{2} [In XIV *rēm* and *rīm* – OFr. *raime*, etc. (mod. *rame*), ult. – Arab. *rizma* bale or bundle (of clothes, paper, etc.).] A quantity of paper, properly 20 quires or 480 sheets, but frequently 500 or more, to allow for waste; of paper for printing, $21\frac{1}{2}$ quires or 516 sheets (a *printer's r.*). **b.** A large quantity of paper, without ref. to the precise number of sheets 1597.

b. More fire than warms whole reams of modern plays SCOTT.

Ream, *v.*^{1} *Obs.* exc. *dial.* [ME. *ræmien*; origin obsc.] **1.** *intr.* To stretch oneself after sleep or on rising. **b.** To reach after ME. **2.** *trans.* To draw out, stretch. late ME.

Ream (rīm), *v.*^{2} Chiefly *Sc.* 1440. [f. REAM *sb.*^{1}] **1.** *intr.* To froth or foam. Also const. *over*. **2.** *trans.* To take the cream off; to skim. Also *intr.*, to be skimmed. 1768.

Ream (rīm), *v.*^{3} *techn.* Also **reem.** 1815. [Origin obsc.] **1.** *trans.* To enlarge or widen (a hole) with an instrument. **2.** To enlarge the bore of (a gun) by the use of a special tool. Chiefly with *out*. 1867. **3.** With *out*: To remove (a defect) by reaming 1861. Hence **Rea·mer** an instrument used to enlarge a hole or boring.

Reanimate (ri,æ·nimeⁱt), *v.* 1611. [RE- 5 a.] **1.** *trans.* To animate with new life, to make alive again, to restore to life or consciousness. **2. a.** To give fresh heart or courage to (a person); to stimulate anew

1706. **b.** To impart fresh vigour, energy, or activity to (a thing) 1762. **3.** *intr.* To recover life or spirit 1645.

1. Fame that will scarce re-animate their clay BYRON. **2. a.** His late Majesty could not re-animate the Dutch with the love of liberty 1792. **b.** He reanimated the textile manufactures 1872. Hence **Re·anima·tion,** the action of restoring to life (also *fig.*); the fact or process of returning to life; renewal of vigour or liveliness.

†**Rea·nswer,** *v.* 1523. [f. RE- + ANSWER *v.*, prob. after *reply*, etc.] *trans.* **a.** To answer –1599. **b.** To meet, be sufficient for, or equivalent to –1630.

b. *Hen. V*, III. vi. 136.

Reap (rīp), *sb.* [OE. *reopa, rypa*, related to *ripan* REAP *v.*] A bundle or handful of grain or any similar crop; a sheaf, or the quantity sufficient to make a sheaf.

Reap (rīp), *v.* [ME. *repen, reopen*, repr. OE. (i) *reopan*, **riopan*, var. of *ripan*, and (ii) **repan* (pa. t. pl. *ræpon*); no certain cognates are known.] **1.** *intr.* and *trans.* To perform the action of cutting grain (or any similar crop) with the hook or sickle, esp. in harvest; hence, to gather or obtain as a crop (usu. of grain) by this or some other process. **b.** *transf.* To cut (plants, flowers, etc.) after the fashion of reaping 1721. **2.** *fig.* To get in return; to obtain (esp. some profit or advantage) for oneself; to gain, acquire ME. **3.** *trans.* To cut down or harvest the crop or produce of (a field, etc.). late ME.

1. They dyd sowe, & we do repe 1526. Labouring the soile, and reaping plenteous crop MILT. *fig.* To r. the fullest fruits of a victory 1853. See also *Matt.* 25:24, *Luke* 19:21, *Hosea* 8:7. **b.** Compared with which The laurels that a Cæsar reaps are weeds COWPER. **2.** Why do I..suing For peace, r. nothing but repulse and hate? MILT. **3.** *transf.* His Chin new reapt, Shew'd like a stubble Land at Haruest home SHAKS. Hence **Reaped** *ppl. a.* **Rea·ping** *vbl. sb.*, often *attrib.*, as *reaping-hook, -machine*, etc.

Reaper (rī·pəɹ). OE. [f. prec. + -ER¹.] **1.** One who reaps. **2.** A mechanical device for cutting grain without manual labour 1862.

1. A Reper and Carter..iij d. by the day 1495.

Reappear (rīˌăpīᵊ·ɹ), *v.* 1611. [RE- 5 a.] *intr.* To appear again. So **Reappea·rance,** the act of appearing again; a second or fresh appearance.

Rear (rīᵊɹ), *sb.* (and *a.*¹) 1600. [prob. extracted from phr. *in the rearward* (XV) or simply a shortening of *rearward* or *rear-guard*, as the somewhat later VAN *sb.*² is of VANGUARD.] **1.** *Mil.* (and *Naval*). The hindmost portion of an army (or fleet); that division of a force which is placed, or moves, last in order 1606. **2.** The back (as opp. to the front); of an army, camp, or person; also the space behind or at the back; the position at or towards the back 1600. **3.** *gen.* The back, back part 1641. **4.** *slang.* A latrine, W.C. 1900.

1. When the fierce Foe hung on our brok'n R. Insulting MILT. *fig.* While the Cock..Scatters the r. of darkness MILT.

Phrases. *In the r.* (less freq. *in r.*), in the hindmost part (of an army, etc.); hence, at or from the back, behind. *In* (or *on*) *one's r.*, behind one. *In the r. of*, at the back of, behind. *To bring up* (or *close*) *the r.*, to come last in order. *To hang on one's r.*, to follow closely, in order to attack or harass. *Front and r.*, used advb. = in front and behind.

B. *attrib.* passing into adj. **1.** Placed or situated at the back; hindmost, last 1600. **2.** With adverbial force: **a.** Towards the rear. **b.** From the rear. 1855.

Comb.: **r.-driver,** a cycle driven by means of the r. wheel; **-steerer,** a tricycle steered from the back.

Rear (rīᵊɹ), *a.*² [OE. *hrēr*, of unkn. origin. Cf. RARE *a.*²] Slightly or imperfectly cooked, underdone. In early use only of eggs.

Rear (rīᵊɹ), *v.* [OE. *rǣran* = ON. *reisa*, Goth. *ur/raisjan* awaken :– Gmc. **raizjan*, causative of **reisan* RAISE *v.*] **I.** To set up on end; to make to stand up. **1.** *trans.* = RAISE *v.* I. 1. **b.** *spec.* of setting up the crust of a pie. Now *dial.* late ME. **2.** To lift (a person or animal) to or towards an erect or standing posture; usu., to set (one) on one's feet, assist to rise. Now chiefly *dial.* 1590. **b.** *refl.* To get up on one's feet, to rise up (*rare*); also of animals, to rise on the hind feet 1580. **c.** So with body, etc. as obj. 1588. **3.** To cause to rise: **a.** = To rouse from bed or sleep. *Obs.* exc. *dial.* OE. †**b.** = RAISE I. 4 b. –1846. **4.** = RAISE I. 5. *Obs.* exc. *dial.* late ME. †**5.** = RAISE I. 6. –1647.

1. The May-pole was reared on the green W. IRVING. **2.** Till gently reard By th' Angel, on thy feet thou stood'st at last MILT. **c.** Upright he rears from off the Pool His mighty Stature MILT.

II. To build up, create, bring into existence. **1.** To construct by building up OE. †**b.** To bring into existence –1591. †**2.** = RAISE II. 5, 7. –1590. **b.** To make (a noise) by shouting; to utter (a cry). *rare.* ME. **3.** To bring (animals) to maturity or to a certain stage of growth by giving proper nourishment and attention; *esp.* to raise (cattle, etc.) as an occupation. late ME. **b.** To bring up (a person), to foster, nourish, educate 1590. **c.** To attend to, promote, or cause the growth of (plants); to grow (grain, etc.) 1581.

1. A tower..rered by great crafte HALL. **b.** From their ashes shall be reard A Phœnix SHAKS. **3.** It is a common saying, the worst housewife will r. the best pigs 1759. **b.** The gentle hand That reared us COWPER. **c.** *transf.* Delightful task! to r. the tender thought, To teach the young idea how to shoot THOMSON.

III. 1. To lift up or upwards as a whole OE. **b.** To have, hold, or sustain (some part) in an elevated or lofty position. Also quasi-*refl.* 1667. **c.** *refl.* To raise up to a height, to tower 1774. **2.** To lift up, raise, elevate, exalt, in various fig. applications. Now *rare* or *Obs.* late ME. **3.** To turn or direct (*esp.* the eyes) upwards 1596. **4.** To cause to rise: **a.** *Naut.* = RAISE *v.* III. 7 a. late ME. †**b.** To make (the voice) heard –1818. †**5.** To levy, raise, gather, collect (fines, rents, etc.) –1599.

1. High in his hands he rear'd the golden bowl POPE. **b.** Sublime their starry fronts they r. GRAY. **3.** Up to a hill anon his steps he rear'd MILT. **4. b.** His voice then did the stranger r. SHELLEY.

IV. *intr.* To rise up; to rise high, to tower ME. **b.** Of a quadruped, *esp.* a horse: To rise on the hind feet. late ME.

b. Sometimes he trots,..Anon he reres vpright, curuets, and leaps SHAKS.

†**Rear,** *adv.* = RARE *adv.* GAY.

Rear-, comb. form, partly of OFr. or AFr. origin, as in *rearward*, etc. (and hence by analogy in *rear-admiral*, etc.), partly – Fr. *arrière-*, as in *rear-vassal*, etc., and partly attrib. use of REAR *sb.* In recent use occas. spelt RERE-, esp. in archaic or architectural terms (see REAR-ARCH, etc.).

Rea·r-a:dmiral. 1587. [REAR-.] **1.** A flag-officer in the navy, the next in rank below a vice-admiral 1589. †**2.** A ship carrying a rear-admiral's flag –1690.

Rear-arch. Also **rere-.** 1849. [f. REAR- + ARCH *sb.*] *Arch.* The inner arch of a window- or door-opening, when differing in size or form from the external arch.

Rearer (rīᵊ·rəɹ). late ME. [f. REAR *v.* + -ER¹.] One who rears; *spec.* a horse that rears, or has a habit of rearing.

Rear-guard (rīᵊ·ɹgāɹd). 1481. [– OFr. *rereguarde* (cf. Fr. *arrière-garde*), f. *rer, riere* :– L. *retro* back (see RETRO-) + *guarde* GUARD *sb.* Cf. ARREAR-GUARD, REARWARD *sb.*] *Mil.* †**1.** = REAR *sb.* 1. –1636. **2.** A body of troops detached from the main force to bring up and protect the rear 1659.

2. *attrib.* The worst of all battles to fight—a rear-guard action 1898.

Reargue (rīˌā·ɹgiu), *v.* 1776. [RE- 5 a.] *trans.* To argue (*spec.* a case in law) a second time; to debate over again. So **Rea·rgument.**

Rea·r-horse. 1884. [f. REAR *v.* IV. b.] *Entom.* A mantis.

†**Rea·rly,** *adv. rare.* 1612. [For *rarely*, f. RARE *a.*³ + -LY².] Early –1714.

Rearm (rīˌā·ɹm), *v.* 1871. [RE- 5 a.] *Mil. trans.* To arm again; *esp.* to arm afresh with more modern weapons. So **Rea·rmament.**

Rearmost (rīᵊ·ɹmoᵘst), *a.* 1718. [f. REAR *a.*¹ + -MOST.] Farthest in the rear, coming last.

Rearmouse, reremouse (rīᵊ·ɹmaus). Now *arch.* or *dial.* [OE. *hrēremūs*, the first element of which is of unkn. origin, the second MOUSE; poss. alt. of synon. *hrēademūs.*] = BAT *sb.*¹

Rear-vassal. Also **rere-.** 1728. [f. REAR- + VASSAL, after Fr. *arrière-vassal.*] *Hist.* A sub-vassal; one who does not hold directly of the sovereign.

Rear-vault. Also **rere-.** 1844. [f. REAR-, after Fr. *arrière voussure.*] *Arch.* The vaulted space connecting an arched window- or door-head with the arch in the inner face of the wall.

Rearward (rīᵊ·ɹwǭɹd), *sb.* ME. [– AFr. *rerewarde*, var. of *reregarde* REARGUARD.] **1.** *Mil.* (and *Naval*). That part of an army (or fleet) which is stationed behind the main body; the third division in a force drawn up for battle. *Obs.* exc. *arch.* **2.** *transf.* The hinder parts, posteriors. late ME.

1. *In* (or *at*) *the r.*, in the rear. *In the r. of*, in the rear of; Hee was the very Genius of Famine: he came euer in the rere-ward of the Fashion SHAKS.

Rearward (rīᵊ·ɹwǭɹd), *a.* 1598. [f. REAR- + -WARD.] **1.** Situated in the rear. **2.** Directed towards the rear; backward 1861.

Rearward (rīᵊ·ɹwǭɹd), *adv.* 1625. [f. as prec.] Towards the rear; backward. **b.** At the back *of* 1880. So **Rea·rwards** *adv.*

Reascend (rīˌăse·nd), *v.* 1450. [RE- 5 a.] *trans.* and *intr.* To ascend again.

To re-ascend that glorious height we fell from MASSINGER. So **Reasce·nsion. Reasce·nt,** the act of reascending; the way by which one reascends; the distance to which one reascends.

Reason (rī·z'n), *sb.* [ME. *res(o)un, reson, reisun* – OFr. *reisun, res(o)un* (mod. *raison*) :– Rom. **ratione*, L. *ratio, ration-* reckoning, account, etc., f. *rat-*, pa. ppl. stem of *reri* think, reckon; see -TION.] **I. 1.** A statement of some fact (real or alleged) employed as an argument to justify or condemn some act, prove or disprove some assertion, idea, or belief. (Since 1600 somewhat *rare.*) **b.** *Logic.* One of the premises in an argument; *esp.* the minor premise when placed after the conclusion 1826. †**2.** A statement, narrative, or speech; a saying, observation, or remark; an account or explanation *of*, or answer *to*, something. Also, without article, talk or discourse. –1635. †**3.** A sentence –1530. †**b.** A motto, posy –1548.

1. Strengthning their reasons with many examples 1600. Phr. *A woman's r.*; I haue no other but a woman's r.: I thinke him so, because I thinke him so SHAKS. *To give, yield,* or *render* (*a*) *r.*, to give an account (of one's acts or conduct). **2.** *L. L. L.* v. i. 2.

II. 1. A fact or circumstance forming, or alleged as forming, a ground or motive leading, or sufficient to lead, a person to adopt or reject some course of action or procedure, belief, etc. Const. *why, wherefore, that*; *of, for*; *to* with inf. ME. **2.** A ground or cause of, or for, something: **a.** of a fact, procedure, or state of things in some way dependent upon human action or feeling ME. **b.** Of a fact, event, or thing not dependent on human agency. late ME. †**3.** Rationale, fundamental principle, basis –1678.

1. He made a Voyage to Grand Cairo for no other R., but to take the Measure of a Pyramid ADDISON. Phr. *R. of state*, a purely political ground of action on the part of a ruler or government, esp. as involving some departure from strict justice, honesty, or open dealing 1600. **2. a.** Custom it self, without a r. for it, is an argument only to fools 1698. **b.** There is not a hair or a line, not a spot or a color, for which there is not a r. 1879.

Phrases. *By r. of*, on account of. *By r.* (*that*), for the reason that, because (now *rare*). *There is* (*good*, etc.) *r.*; also with omission of vb. *To have r. for*, or *to* do, something; also *ellipt.*, without construction. *To see r.* (*to* do something). *With* or *without r.*

III. 1. That intellectual power or faculty (usu. regarded as characteristic of mankind, but sometimes also attributed in a certain degree to the lower animals) which is ordinarily employed in adapting thought or action to some end; the guiding principle of the human mind in the process of thinking ME. **b.** So (†*good* or) *right r.* Now *rare.* ME. **c.** In the Kantian philosophy: The power (*Vernunft*) by which first principles are grasped *a priori*, as dist. from UNDERSTANDING (*Verstand*) 1809. **2.** The ordinary thinking faculty of the human mind in a sound condition; sanity. late ME. **b.** A reasonable or sensible view of a matter; chiefly in phr. *to bring to r.* ME. **3.** In verbal phrases denoting the conformity of something to the dictates of reason: †**a.** *R. will* or *would* –1597. **b.** *It stands to r.* 1632. **4.** In prep. phrases, denoting agreement with, or opposition to, what reason directs or indicates (see quots.) ME. **5.** A matter, act, proceeding, etc., agreeable to reason. Now *rare*. ME. †**6.** That treatment which may with reason be expected by, or required from, a person; justice; satisfaction; chiefly in phr. *to do* (one) *r.* (tr. Fr. *faire raison*) –1662. **b.** With ref. to drinking. Now only *arch.* 1594. †**7.** A reasonable quantity, amount, or degree –1675. †**8.** *To have r.* (tr. Fr. *avoir raison*): to be right (esp. in making a statement) –1771. **9.** The fact or quality of being agreeable to the reason; such a (†procedure or) view of things as the reason can approve of 1470.

1. Of all the faculties of the human mind, it will, I presume, be admitted that R. stands at the summit DARWIN. **2.** So now my r. was restored to me SHELLEY. **4.** †*By r.* (= OFr. *par raison*). *In r.*; If you want a cheque for yourself..you can name any figure you like—in r. G. B. SHAW. Also *in all r.*; in the opposite sense, *out of all r.* **5.** Phr. *It is r.* or *r. is* (also with *good, great*), *it is no* (or *not*) *r.*; It is, however, but r. that I should rejoice 1864. †*And r.*, placed after a statement. So †*and good r.* **6.** *Tit. A.* I. i. 278. **b.** I pray you..to do me r. in a cup of wine SCOTT. **7.** *Much Ado* V. iv. 74. **8.** The Objectors have R., and their Assertions may be allowed SWIFT. **9.** There is r. in what you say BERKELEY. Phr. *To hear, listen to, speak r.*; Your wife will listen to r. T. HARDY.

†**IV. 1.** The act of reasoning or argumentation –1647. **2.** Consideration, regard, respect –1533. **3.** Way, manner, method; *spec.* the method of science –1643. **b.** Possibility of action or occurrence. Const. *but. rare.* –1596. **4.** *Math.* = RATIO 2. –1713.

3. b. When I looke on her perfections, There is no r., but I shall be blinde SHAKS.

Reason (rī·z'n), *v.* ME. [– OFr. *raisoner* (mod. *-onner*), f. *raison*, after med.L. *rationare*; see prec.] †**1.** *trans.* To question (a person); to call (one) to account (*rare*) –1578. †**2.** *intr.* To hold argument, discussion, discourse, or talk *with* another –1671. †**b.** To argue, discourse, converse, talk –1667. **c.** To employ reasoning or argument *with* a person in order to influence his conduct or opinions 1847. **3.** To think in a connected, sensible, or logical manner; to employ the faculty of reason in forming conclusions 1593. **4.** With object-clause: **a.** To question, discuss *what, why*, etc. 1529. **b.** To argue, conclude, infer *that*, etc. 1527. **5.** *trans.* **a.** To discuss or argue (a matter). Now *rare.* 1526. **b.** To explain, support, infer, deal with, by (or as by) reasoning 1605. **6. a.** To bring (a person) *into, out of* (a state of mind, etc.) by reasoning 1599. **b.** To put *down* by reasoning 1686. **7.** To think *out*, to arrange the thought of in a logical manner 1736.

2. Now therefore stand still, that I may r. with you before the Lord 1 *Sam.* 12:7. **b.** And they reasoned among themselves, saying, It is because we haue taken no bread *Matt.* 16:7. Others.. reason'd high Of Providence, Foreknowledge, Will, and Fate MILT. **c.** All he could do was..to r. with him 1847. **3.** Reasoning at every step he treads, Man yet mistakes his way COWPER. Whilst we enjoy, he reasons of enjoyment SHELLEY. Reasoning from experience of the past abuses..they anticipated a like result from the present 1844. **5. b.** *Lear* I. ii. 114. **6. a.** David tried to r. him out of his fears 1893. **b.** Love is not to be reason'd down ADDISON. Hence **Rea·soner,** one who reasons.

Reasonable (rī·z'năb'l), *a.*, *adv.*, and *sb.* ME. [– OFr. *raisonable* (mod. *-nn-*), f. *raison*, after L. *rationabilis*; see REASON *sb.*, -ABLE.] **A.** *adj.* **1.** Endowed with reason. Now *rare.* **2.** Having sound judgement; sensible, sane. Also, not asking for too much ME. **b.** Requiring the use of reason (*nonce-use*). SHAKS. **3.** Agreeable to reason; not irrational, absurd or ridiculous ME. **4.** Not going beyond the limit assigned by reason; not extravagant or excessive; moderate ME. **b.** Moderate in price; inexpensive 1667. **5.** Of such an amount, size, number, etc., as is judged to be appropriate or suitable to the circumstances or purpose. late ME. †**b.** Of a fair, average, or considerable amount, size, etc. –1726.

1. For man is by nature r. BURKE. **2.** If mankind were r. they would want no government 1802. **3.** The conviction would be r., for it would be based upon universal experience 1877. **4.** The r. wishes of the whole people 1832. Doing a great service on r. terms to the Church of which he was a member MACAULAY. **5.** All..forage..is to be taken for the use of the army and a r. price paid for the same 1755.

B. *adv.* Reasonably 1470.

The minister..made a r. long exhortation 1583.

†**C.** *absol.* as *sb.* A reasonable being –1633. Hence **Rea·sonableness,** the fact or quality of being r. **Rea·sonably** *adv.* in a r. manner; sufficiently, fairly.

Reasoning (rī·z'niŋ), *vbl. sb.* late ME. [f. REASON *v.* + -ING[1].] The action of REASON *v.*, *esp.* the process by which one judgement is deduced from another or others which are given. **b.** With *a* and *pl.* An instance of this 1552. **c.** *attrib.*, as *r. power*, etc. 1728.

There is no reazoning against those which denie the Principles 1587. **b.** Socrates is a man, and therefore a living creature, is a right r., and that most evident HOBBES.

Reasonless (rī·z'nlės), *a.* late ME. [f. REASON *sb.* + -LESS.] **1.** Not endowed with, acting without the aid of, reason; irrational. **2.** Devoid of ordinary reason; senseless. late ME. **3.** Not grounded upon reason or reasons; not supported by any reason 1553.

1. Reasonlesse creatures 1581. A purely r. concourse of atoms 1895. **3.** This proffer is absurd, and reasonlesse SHAKS. Hence **Rea·sonless-ly** *adv.*, **-ness.**

Reasse·mblage. 1744. [RE- 5 a.] A collecting, meeting, or gathering together again. So **Reasse·mbly.**

Reassemble (rīˌăse·mb'l), *v.* 1494. [RE- 5 a.] *trans.* and *intr.* To bring, or come, together again.

Reassert (rīˌăsǝ̄·ɹt), *v.* 1665. [RE- 5 a.] **1.** *trans.* To assert (a statement, claim, etc.) again. **2.** To claim (a thing) again (*rare*) 1725.

1. You replied with abuse, and reasserted your charge '*Junius*' *Lett.* So **Reasse·rtion,** a repeated assertion, a reaffirmation.

Reassume (rīˌăsiū·m), *v.* 1494. [f. RE-5 a + ASSUME *v.*] **1.** *trans.* To take, or take up, again (a material laid down or handed to another). **b.** To revoke, take back (a grant, gift, etc.) 1609. **2.** †**a.** To take back (a person) into close relationship with oneself –1667. **b.** To take back (a thing) as a constituent part 1692. **3.** To take again upon oneself 1624. **4.** To take, resume (one's place) again 1640. **5.** To recommence, take up again, resume 1608. †**b.** *intr.* To resume, continue speaking, after a pause –1796.

2. a. Into his blissful bosom reassum'd In glory as of old MILT. **3.** At last, reason reassumed her empire 1774. He had re-assumed his hereditary name LYTTON. **5. b.** I own it is necessary, reassumed the master of the hotel, that [etc.] STERNE. So **Reassu·mption.**

Reassurance (rīˌăʃūᵊ·răns). 1611. [RE-5 a.] **1.** Renewed or repeated assurance. **2.** Renewed or restored confidence 1875. **3.** Reinsurance 1745.

Reassure (rīˌăʃūᵊ·ɹ), *v.* 1598. [RE- 5 a.] †**1.** *trans.* To re-establish, confirm (a thing). Also const. *to* (a person). **b.** To confirm (one) again in (an honour). –1764. **2.** To restore (a person, the mind, etc.) to confidence 1598. **b.** To confirm again in an opinion or impression. Const. *of.* 1811. **3.** To reinsure 1826.

2. This was a sort of explanation more likely to alarm than to r. the public 1879. **b.** And long he paused to r. his eyes BYRON. Hence **Reassu·rer. Reassu·ring** *ppl. a.*, **-ly** *adv.*

Reasty (rī·sti), *a.* Now *techn.* 1573. [Later form of RESTY *a.*[2]] Rancid.

Reata: see RIATA.

Reattach (rīˌătæ·tʃ), *v.* 1607. [RE- 5 a.] †**1.** *trans. Law.* To seize (a person) by authority of a writ of reattachment. **2.** To attach again. Const. *to.* Also *refl.* 1813. So **Reatta·chment,** a fresh attachment, esp. in *Law.* 1574.

‖**Réaumur** (rēⁱ·omür). 1782. The name of a French physicist (1683–1757), used *ellipt.* to denote the thermometer or thermometric scale introduced by him, in which the freezing point of water is 0° and the boiling point 80°.

Reave (rīv), *v.*[1] Pa. t. and pa. pple. **reft.** Now only *arch.* or *poet.* [OE. *rēafian* = OFris. *rāvia, rāva*, OS. *rōbon* (Du. *rooven*), OHG. *roubōn* (G. *rauben*), Goth. *bi/raubōn* :– Gmc. **raubōjan*, f. **raub-*; see ROB *v.*] **1.** *intr.* To commit spoliation or robbery; to plunder, pillage. Const. *from.* (In later use chiefly *Sc.*, often written *reive, rieve.*) †**2.** *trans.* To spoil, rob, or plunder –1567. **3.** To despoil, rob, or forcibly deprive (usu. a person) *of* something. (In mod. use chiefly in pa. pple. *reft*) ME. †**4.** To take (a thing or person) from (one) by, or as by, robbery or violence; to deprive (one) of (a possession, quality etc.) –1594. **5.** To take forcible possession of (something belonging to another); to take away from another for oneself OE. **b.** To take away (life, rest, sight, etc.) ME. **6.** To take or carry away (a person) *from* another, *from* earth, *to* heaven, etc.; also *ellipt.* to carry off to heaven; to take *away* from earth or this life ME.

1. Thor the strong could r. and steal LOWELL. **3.** Reft of a crown, he yet may share the feast GRAY. **5.** Lands reft from Canterbury 1884. **b.** Sith that false traytour did my honour r. SPENSER. **6.** Who hath reft (quoth he) my dearest pledge? MILT. Hence **Rea·ver, rei·ver,** a robber, plunderer; †a pirate, sea-robber.

Reave, *v.*[2] Pa. t. and pa. pple. **reft.** Now *dial.* or *arch.* ME. [app. a confusion of prec. with RIVE *v.*] *trans.* To tear; to split, cleave.

The patriot's burning thought..Of England's roses reft and torn SCOTT.

Rebaptism (rībæ·ptiz'm). 1795. [RE- 5 a.] A second baptism; rebaptizing. So †**Reba·ptist,** *spec.* = ANABAPTIST.

Rebaptize (rībæptəi·z), *v.* 1460. [– late L. *rebaptizare*; see RE- 5 a, BAPTIZE. Cf. (O)Fr. *rebaptiser*.] **1.** *trans.* To baptize again or anew. **2.** To give a new name to 1596. So †**Rebaptiza·tion,** the act or practice of baptizing again. **Rebapti·zer,** one who rebaptizes.

Rebarbative (rībā·ɹbătiv), *a. rare.* 1892. [– Fr. *rébarbatif, -ive*, f. *barbe* beard.] Crabbed, unattractive, repellent.

Rebate (rī·bēⁱt, rībeⁱ·t), *sb.*[1] 1656. [f. REBATE *v.*[1]; cf. Fr. *rabat.*] A reduction from a sum of money to be paid, a discount; also, a repayment.

Rebate (rībēⁱ·t), *sb.*[2] 1674. [Respelling of RABBET *sb.*, after prec. In techn. use pronounced as if written *rabbet.*] A rabbet. Also *attrib.*, as *r.-plane.*

Rebate (rībēⁱ·t), *v.*[1] [Late ME. *rabat* – (O)Fr. *rabattre*, f. *re-* RE- + *abattre* ABATE; later alt. by substitution of *re-* for the first syll.] †**1.** *trans.* **a.** To deduct (a certain amount from a sum); to subtract (one quantity or number from another) –1675. †**b.** To reduce or diminish (a sum or amount) –1677. †**c.** To give or allow a reduction to (a person) –1670. **2.** To reduce, lessen, diminish (a condition, quality, feeling, activity, etc.). Now *rare.* 1450. **b.** To reduce the effect or force of (a blow, stroke, etc.). Now *rare.* 1579. †**c.** To lessen the vigour or activity of (the mind, etc.); to repress, stop (a person or action) –1788. **3.** To make dull, to blunt 1467. **4.** *Her.* To diminish (a charge) by removal of a portion, esp. a point or projection. **b.** To remove (a point, etc.) from a charge. 1562.

2. To pacify her, or, at least, to r. her first violence RICHARDSON. **3.** Takes he his weapon? thou the edge rebatest C'TESS PEMBROKE. This shirt of mail worn near my skin Rebated their sharp steel 1625. *fig.* Compassion so rebated the edge of Choler SIDNEY. Hence **Reba·ter.**

Rebate, *v.*[2] 1475. [Later spelling of RABBET *v.*, after prec. For pronunc. see REBATE *sb.*[2]] **1.** *trans.* To make a rebate or rabbet in. **2.** To join *together* with a rebate 1838.

†**Reba·tement.** 1542. [– OFr. *rebatement*; see REBATE *v.*[1] and -MENT.] **1.** A sum to be deducted from another; a discount –1727. **2.** Diminution in amount, force, etc. –1701. **3.** *Her.* = ABATEMENT 3. –1727.

†**Reba·to.** 1591. [f. Fr. *rabat* collar, etc., after It. words in *-ato.*] A kind of stiff collar worn by both sexes –1630. **b.** A collar of this kind used to support a ruff, or a frame of wire serving the same purpose –1634.

Rebeck (rī·bek). Now only *Hist.* or *poet.* 1509. [– Fr. *rebec*, †*rabec*, unexpl. alt. of OFr. *rebebe, rubebe* RIBIBE.] A mediæval musical instrument, having three strings and played with a bow; an early form of the fiddle.

When..the jocond rebecks sound MILT.

Rebel (re·bĕl), *a.* and *sb.*[1] ME. [– (O)Fr. *rebelle* adj. and sb. – L. *rebellis* adj. and sb. (said orig. of the conquered making war afresh), f. *re-* RE- + *bellum* war.] **A.** *adj.* (Now only attrib.) **1.** Refusing obedience or allegiance, or offering armed opposition, to the rightful or actual ruler or ruling power of the country. **b.** Consisting of, belonging or falling to, in command of, rebels 1682. **2.** Disobedient to a superior or to some higher power; contumacious, refractory ME. **3.** Characterized by rebelliousness; characteristic of a rebel or rebels. late ME.

1. Amaze..and terrour seis'd the r. Host MILT. The R. States LOWELL. **b.** The r. ranks were broken GIBBON. **2.** To speak in thunder to the r. world SHELLEY. *transf.* From a pure heart command thy rebell will SHAKS.

B. *sb.*[1] **1.** One who resists, or rises in arms against, the established governing power; one who refuses or renounces allegiance or obedience to his sovereign or the government of his country. late ME. **b.** *Law* (now only *Sc. Law*). One who resists or disobeys a legal command or summons 1592. **2.** One who, or that which, resists authority or control of any kind ME.

1. For such sentiments I am called a r. 1778. **2.** Our Wills controul; Subdue the R. in our Soul WESLEY.

†Rebel, *sb.*[2] late ME. [f. next.] Rebellion –1618.

Rebel (rĭbe·l), *v.* ME. [– (O)Fr. *rebeller* – L. *rebellare*, f. *re-* RE- 2 c + *bellare* make war, f. *bellum* war.] *intr.* To rise in opposition or armed resistance against the rightful or established ruler or government of one's country. Const. *against*, †*from*, †*to*. late ME. **b.** To resist, oppose, or be disobedient to, some one having authority or rule ME. **c.** *transf.* or *fig.* To offer resistance, exhibit opposition, to feel or manifest repugnance, etc. late ME.

It is astonishing..the People should ever rebell for Slavery 1718. **b.** Rebellyng agaynst theyr prelates & curates 1526. **c.** Thus Conscience pleads her cause..Though long rebelled against, not yet suppressed COWPER. Hence **†Rebe·lled** *ppl. a.* in active sense. MILT.

Rebeldom (re·bĕldəm). 1859. [f. REBEL *sb.*[1] + -DOM.] **1.** The domain of rebels. (Chiefly applied by their opponents to the Confederate States during the American Civil War.) 1862. **2.** Rebellious behaviour 1859.

Rebe·ller. Now *rare.* late ME. [f. REBEL *v.* + -ER[1].] A rebel, one who rebels.

Rebellion (rĭbe·lyən). ME. [– (O)Fr. *rébellion* – L. *rebellio, -on-*, f. *rebellis*; see REBEL *a.*, -ION.] **1.** Organized armed resistance to the ruler or government of one's country; insurrection, revolt 1440. **b.** With *a* and *pl.* An instance of this. late ME. **c.** *Law* (now only *Sc. Law*). Disobedience to a legal summons or command; also *ellipt.*, the fact of being regarded as a rebel on account of such disobedience 1550. **2.** Open or determined defiance of, or resistance to, any authority or controlling power ME.

1. There can be no doubt that r. is the last remedy against tyranny BUCKLE. **b.** *The Great R.*, the civil war of 1642–9 and the Commonwealth Government of 1649–60. **2.** Contempt of God, and r. against your parents DE FOE.

Rebellious (rĭbe·lyəs), *a.* late ME. [f. prec. + -OUS, or f. earlier †*rebellous*, by substitution of suffix.] **1.** Insubordinate, defying lawful authority; belonging to a party of rebels. **2.** Of actions, etc.: Characteristic of a rebel or of rebels; marked by rebellion 1492. **3.** Of things: Offering resistance to treatment; refractory 1578.

1. My weak heart..Will beat, r. to its own resolves SOUTHEY. *absol.* Let not the r. exalt themselues *Ps.* 66:7. *transf.* Hot and r. liquors SHAKS. A r. spear SCOTT. **3.** Very good against..r. old sores 1578. Hence **Rebe·llious-ly** *adv.*, **-ness.**

Rebellow (rĭbe·lo[u]), *v.* 1590. [f. RE- 2 a + BELLOW *v.*, after L. *reboare.*] **1.** *intr.* Of cattle: To bellow in reply or in turn 1596. **b.** Of places or material objects, sounds, etc.: To re-echo loudly 1590. **2.** *trans.* To return or repeat (a sound) in a bellowing tone 1765.

1. b. The earth Rebellow'd to the feet of steeds and men COWPER.

Rebirth (rībə̄·ɹþ). 1837. [RE- 5 a.] A second birth (physical or spiritual); also *fig.* of things.

Rebite (rībəi·t), *v.* 1816. [RE- 5 a.] *trans.* To bite again (in sense 9 of the vb.).

Reboant (re·bo[u]ănt), *a.* Chiefly *poet.* 1830. [– L. *reboans, -ant-*, pr. pple. of *reboare*, f. *re-* RE- 2 a + *boare* roar, resound; see -ANT.] Rebellowing, re-echoing loudly. So **Reboa·ntic** *a.*

†Reboi·l, *v.*[1] 1444. [– OFr. *rebouillir* :– L. *rebullire* bubble up; see BOIL *v.*] **1.** *intr.* Of wine: To ferment a second time –1601. **2.** To boil up or over –1601.

2. Some of his compnanyons therat reboyleth. ELYOT.

Reboil (rīboi·l), *v.*[2] 1615. [RE- 5 a.] *trans.* To boil again.

Reboisement (rĭboi·zmĕnt). 1882. [– Fr. *reboisement*, f. *reboiser*, f. *re-* RE- + *bois* wood; see -MENT.] Reafforestation.

Re-book, *v.* 1864. [RE- 5 a.] *trans.* and *intr.* To book again (BOOK *v.* 4 b).

Reborn (rībǭ·ɹn), *pa. pple.* and *ppl. a.* 1598. [RE- 5 a.] Born again (physically or spiritually). Also *transf.* of things.

Rebound (rĭbau·nd, rī·baund), *sb.* 1530. [f. next, or – Fr. *rebond* (XVI).] The act of bounding back after striking; resilience, return, recoil. Also *transf.* and *fig.*

His head..made three rebounds upon the scaffold 1732. Phr. *To take, catch*, etc. *on the r.*

Rebound (rĭbau·nd), *v.* late ME. [– OFr. *rebonder*, (also mod.) *rebondir*, f. *re-* RE- 2 a + *bondir* BOUND *v.*[2]] **1.** *intr.* To spring back from force of impact, to bound back. Also *transf.* or *fig.* of immaterial things. **2.** To re-echo, reverberate, resound. Now *rare* or *Obs.* 1440. **3. a.** To bound or leap, esp. in return or response to some force or stimulus. Now *rare* or *Obs.* late ME. **b.** To bound back (without impact) 1513. **4.** *trans.* To cause to bound back; to cast or throw back, to return. Now *rare.* 1560. **5.** To re-echo, return (a sound). Now *rare.* 1555.

1. An evil example, that would r. back on themselves BURKE. When shell and ball Rebounding idly on her strength did light BYRON. **2.** With hoarse allarms the hollow Camp rebounds DRYDEN. **3.** At once with joy and fear his heart rebounds MILT. **5.** The hollow hills..Were wont redoubled Echoes to r. SPENSER.

Reboundant (rĭbau·ndănt), *a.* 1688. [f. prec. + -ANT.] *Her.* = REVERBERANT *a.* 1.

Rebuff (rĭbʋ·f), *sb.* 1611. [– Fr. †*rebuffe* – It. *ribuffo*; see next.] **1.** A peremptory check given to one who makes an advance of any kind; a blunt refusal of a request or offer; a snub. **b.** A check to further action or progress, due to circumstances 1672. **2.** A repelling puff or blast (*rare*) 1667.

1. The..insolent rebuffs Of knaves in office COWPER. **2.** The strong r. of som tumultuous cloud Instinct with Fire and Nitre MILT.

Rebuff (rĭbʋ·f), *v.* 1586. [– Fr. †*rebuffer* – It. *ribuffare, rabbuffare*, f. *ribuffo, rabbuffo*, f. *ri-* RE- + *buffo* gust, puff, of imit. origin.] **1.** *trans.* To repel bluntly or ungraciously; to give a rude check or repulse to. **2.** To blow or drive back (*rare*) 1747.

Rebuild (rībi·ld), *v.* 1490. [RE- 5 a.] *trans.* To build again; to reconstruct. Also *absol.* **b.** *Rebuilding* = being rebuilt 1668.

b. That most stately and magnificent structure now re-building 1668. Hence **Rebui·lder.**

Rebuke (rĭbiū·k), *sb.* late ME. [f. next.] **†1.** A shameful or disgraceful check; a shame or disgrace –1485. **†b.** Without *a* or *pl.*: Shame, disgrace, reproach –1590. **2.** Reproof, reprimand. late ME. **b.** With *a* and *pl.* A reproof, a reprimand 1514.

1. b. For great r. it is love to despise SPENSER. **2.** A wise sonne heareth his fathers instruction: but a scorner heareth not r. *Prov.* 13:1. **b.** Shee's a Lady So tender of rebukes, that words are stroke[s] SHAKS.

Rebuke (rĭbiū·k), *v.* ME. [– AFr., ONFr. *rebuker* = OFr. *rebuchier*, f. *re-* RE- + *buschier, buchier, bukier* beat, strike, prop. cut down wood, f. *busche* (mod. *bûche*) log.] **†1.** *trans.* To beat down or force back; to repress or check; to repulse –1605. **2.** To reprove, reprimand, chide severely ME. **b.** To express blame or reprehension of (a quality, action, etc.) by reproof or reprimand addressed to persons. Also *transf.* and *fig.* 1529.

1. Wee could haue rebuk'd him at Harflewe SHAKS. **2.** He rebuked them for their cowardice and want of faith 1883. **b.** The Palmer..much rebukt those wandring eyes of his SPENSER. Hence **Rebu·keable** *a.* (now *rare*) that may be rebuked; deserving of rebuke. **Rebu·ker. Rebu·kingly** *adv.*

Rebukeful (rĭbiū·kfŭl), *a.* 1523. [f. REBUKE *sb.* + -FUL.] **1.** Of words: Of a rebuking character. **b.** Of persons: Full of, given to, rebuke 1868. **†2.** Deserving of rebuke; disgraceful, shameful –1570. Hence **Rebu·keful-ly** *adv.*, **-ness.**

Rebus (rī·bŏs), *sb.* 1605. [– Fr. *rébus* – L. *rebus*, abl. pl. of *res* thing, in the phr. *de rebus quæ geruntur* 'concerning things that are taking place', title given by the guild of lawyers' clerks of Picardy to satirical pieces containing riddles in picture form.] An enigmatical representation of a name, word, or phrase by figures, pictures, arrangement of letters, etc., which suggest the syllables of which it is made up. **b.** In later use, a puzzle in which a punning application of each syllable of a word is given, without pictorial representation. Hence **Re·bus** *v. trans.* to mark or inscribe with a r. or rebuses.

Rebut (rĭbʋ·t), *v.* ME. [– AFr. *rebuter*, OFr. *reboter, -bouter*, f. *re-* RE- + *boter* BUTT *v.*[1]] **†1.** *trans.* To assail (a person) with violent language; to revile, rebuke, reproach –1470. **†2.** To repel, repulse, drive back (a person, or an attack) –1590. **b.** *transf.* 1536. **3.** To force or turn back (a thing, now usu. something abstract); to give a check to 1490. **4.** *Law.* To repel by counter-proof, refute (evidence, a charge, etc.). Hence *gen.* To refute, disprove (any statement, theory, etc.). 1817. **†5.** *intr.* or *absol.* **a.** To draw back, retire, retreat, recoil –1624. **b.** *Law.* To bring forward a rebutter –1768.

2. But he..Their sharp assault right boldly did r. SPENSER. **3.** Their points rebutted backe againe Are duld SPENSER. **5. b.** The plaintiff may answer the rejoinder by a sur-rejoinder; upon which the defendant may r. BLACKSTONE. So **Rebu·tment** = REBUTTAL. **Rebu·ttable** *a.* that may be rebutted.

Rebuttal (rĭbʋ·tăl). 1830. [f. prec. + -AL[1].] Refutation, contradiction; *spec.* in *Law* (cf. prec. 4).

Rebutter (rĭbʋ·təɹ). 1540. [In sense 1 – AFr. *rebuter* (see REBUT *v.*, -ER[4]); in sense 2 partly f. REBUT *v.* + -ER[1].] **1.** *Law.* An answer made by a defendant to a plaintiff's surrejoinder. **2.** That which rebuts, repels, refutes, etc.; a refutation 1794.

‖Recado (rekā·do). 1615. [– Sp. or Pg. *recado* message, gift, etc.; origin unkn.] **†1.** A present; a message of compliment –1698. **2.** A S. Amer. saddle 1826.

Recalcitrance (rĭkæ·lsitrăns). 1856. [See next and -ANCE.] Recalcitrant temper or conduct.

Recalcitrant (rĭkæ·lsitrănt), *a.* and *sb.* 1843. [– Fr. *récalcitrant* – L. *recalcitrans, -ant-*, pr. pple. of *recalcitrare*; see next, -ANT.] **A.** *adj.* **1.** 'Kicking' against constraint or restriction; obstinately disobedient or refractory. Also const. *to*. **2.** Characterized by refractoriness 1865. **B.** *sb.* A recalcitrant person 1865.

Recalcitrate (rĭkæ·lsitre[i]t), *v.* 1623. [– *recalcitrat-*, pa. ppl. stem of L. *recalcitrare* kick out, (later) be refractory; see RE-, CALCITRATE *v.*] **1.** *intr.* To kick out, kick backwards (*rare*). **b.** To 'kick out' *against* or *at* a thing; to show strong objection or repugnance; to be obstinately disobedient or refractory 1767. **2.** *trans.* To kick back (*rare*) 1832.

1. b. Those who..r. at their caresses, they threaten with Tartarus LANDOR. **2.** The more heartily did one disdain his disdain, and r. his tricks DE QUINCEY. Hence **Recalcitra·tion.**

Recalesce (rīkăle·s), *v.* 1887. [– L. *recalescere*, f. *re-* RE- 2 c + *calescere* grow hot. See CALESCENT.] *intr.* To grow hot again. So **Recale·scence.**

Recall (rĭkǭ·l), *sb.* 1611. [f. RE- + CALL *sb.*, after the vb.] **1.** The act of calling back; *spec.* the calling back of an actor, etc. to the stage or platform; an encore. **b.** *Naut.* A signal flag used to call back a boat to a ship, or a vessel to a squadron 1832. **c.** Any sound made as a signal to return; esp. *Mil.* a signal sounded on a musical instrument to call soldiers back to rank or camp 1855. **2.** The act or possibility of recalling, revoking, or annulling something done or past 1667.

1. The admiral..gave the signal of recal 1806. **2.** Phr. *Beyond, past r.*; 'Tis done, and since 'tis done, 'tis past r. DRDYEN.

Recall (rĭkǭ·l), *v.* 1575. [f. RE- + CALL *v.*, after L. *revocare* or Fr. *rappeler.*] **1.** *trans.* To call back, to summon (a person, or *fig.* a thing) to return to or from a place 1591. **b.** To bring back by (or as by) calling upon 1582. **c.** To bring back (the attention, mind, etc.) *to* a subject. Also without const. 1667. **2.** To call or bring back *to* (or *from*) a certain state, occupation, etc. 1575. **3.** To call or bring back (a circumstance, person, etc.) *to* the mind, memory, thoughts, etc. 1611. **b.** To bring back to the mind; to cause one to remember 1651. **c.** To recollect, remember 1690. **4.** To bring back, restore, revive, resuscitate (a feeling, quality, or state) 1593. **5.** To revoke, undo, annul (a deed, sentence, decree, etc.) 1588. **b.** To revoke, take back (a gift) 1608.

1. Let them be recall'd from their Exile SHAKS. **b.** But past who can r., or don undoe? MILT. **2.** If Henry were recall'd to life againe SHAKS. **3.** The name does not r. any one to me 1875. **4.** Once gone, You cannot now r. your sister's peace SHELLEY. **5. b.** The Gods themselves cannot r. their gifts TENNYSON. Hence **Reca·llable** *a.* that can be recalled. **Reca·llment** = RECALL *sb.*

Recant (rĭkæ·nt), *v.* 1535. [– L. *recantare* recall, revoke, f. *re-* RE- 2 d + *cantare* sing, CHANT, after Gr. παλινῳδεῖν (see PALINODE).] **1.** *trans.* To withdraw, retract, or renounce (a statement, opinion, belief, etc.) as erroneous, and *esp.* with formal or public confession of error in matters of religion. †**b.** To renounce (a course of life or conduct) as wrong or mistaken –1701. **2. a.** To withdraw, retract (a promise, vow, etc.). Now *rare.* 1596. **b.** To renounce, give up (a design or purpose) 1652. **3.** *intr.* To retract, renounce, or disavow a former opinion or belief; *esp.* to make a formal or public confession of error 1553.

1. He was content to r. his opinions at Paules crosse 1601. **2. a.** He shall doe this, or else I doe r. The pardon that I late pronounced heere SHAKS. **3.** Here I r., and of those words repent me 1633. Hence **Recanta·tion,** the action of recanting; an instance of this. **Reca·nter.**

Recapa·citate, *v. rare.* 1702. [RE- 5 a.] *trans.* and *refl.* To make (legally) capable again.

Recapitulate (rĭkăpi·tiŭleᶦt), *v.* 1570. [– *recapitulat-*, pa. ppl. stem of L. *recapitulare*, f. *re-* + *capitulum* CHAPTER; see RE-, CAPITULATE *v.*] **1.** *trans.* To go over or repeat again, properly in a more concise manner; to summarize, restate briefly. Also *absol.* **b.** *transf.* in *Biol.* of young animals: see next b. Also *absol.* 1879. **2.** To bring together again; to sum up or unite in one (*rare*) 1607. Hence **Recapi·tulator. Recapi·tulatory** *a.* of the nature of, characterized by, recapitulation.

Recapitulation (rĭkăpitiŭlēᶦ·ʃən). late ME. [–(O)Fr. *récapitulation* or late L. *recapitulatio, -on-*, f. as prec.; see -ION.] The action of recapitulating; a summing up or brief repetition. **b.** *Biol.* The repetition of evolutionary stages in the growth of a young animal. Also *attrib.* 1875. Hence **Recapitula·tionist,** an adherent of the doctrine of r. in Biology.

Recaption (rĭ-, rīkæ·pʃən). 1607. [f. RE- + CAPTION.] **1.** *Law.* **a.** A second distraint. **b.** (Also *writ of r.*) A writ issued in favour of one who has been distrained twice 1607. **2.** *Law.* The peaceful seizure without legal process of one's own property wrongfully taken or withheld 1768.

Recaptor (rīkæ·ptǫɹ). 1752. [f. RE- + CAPTOR.] **1.** One who retakes by capture; *esp.* one who makes a recapture at sea. **2.** *Law.* One who takes goods by a recaption or second distraint 1841.

Recapture (rīkæ·ptiŭɹ, -tʃəɹ), *sb.* 1752. [f. RE- + CAPTURE.] **1.** The fact of taking, or being taken, a second time; recovery or retaking by capture. **2.** That which is captured again 1861.

Recapture (rīkæ·ptiŭɹ), *v.* 1799. [RE- 5 a.] *trans.* To capture again; to recover by capture.

Recarriage (rīkæ·ridʒ). 1541. [f. RE- + CARRIAGE.] The act of carrying or conveying back again, *esp.* conveyance back of merchandise; also, the fact of being carried back.

Recast (rīkɑ·st), *sb.* 1840. [RE- 5 a.] An act or instance of recasting; the new thing or form produced by recasting.

Recast (rīkɑ·st), *v.* 1603. [RE- 5 a + CAST *v.*; sense 2 after (O)Fr. *refondre.*] **1.** *trans.* To cast or throw again. *rare.* **2.** To cast or found (metal) again. Also *fig.* 1768. **b.** To refashion, remodel, reconstruct (a thing, *esp.* a literary work, a sentence, etc.); to invest with new form or character 1790. **3.** To supply new actors for (a play) 1911.

2. b. I have recast and rewritten the chapters MALTHUS. Buonaparte recast the art of war 1840.

Recaulescence (rīkǫle·sĕns). 1880. [RE- 5 a; see CAULESCENT *a.*] *Bot.* The adhesion throughout its whole length of a bract or leaf to its stem.

Recede (rĭsī·d), *v.*[1] late ME. [– L. *recedere*, f. *re-* RE- 2 a + *cedere* go, CEDE.] **1.** *intr.* To go back or further off; to retreat; retire. late ME. **b.** To become more distant; to lie further back or away; to slope backwards 1777. †**2.** To depart *from* some usual or natural state, an authority, standard, principle, etc. –1796. **b.** Of things: To depart, differ, or vary *from* something else. Now *rare* or *Obs.* 1576. **3.** To draw back, withdraw *from* a bargain, promise, position, opinion, etc. 1648. **4.** To go away, depart, retire (*from* or *to* a place or scene). *rare.* 1440. **5. a.** To go back or away in time 1831. **b.** To decline in character or value 1828.

1. As the sun recedes, the moon and stars discouer themselues GLANVILL. **2.** Receding from custome when their interest requires it HOBBES. **3.** How could I r. from such an engagement? 1792. **5. b.** Foreign Government stocks receded fractionally 1883.

Recede (rīsī·d), *v.*[2] 1771. [f. RE- 5 a + CEDE *v.*] *trans.* To cede again, give up to a former owner.

Receipt (rĭsī·t), *sb.* [In XIV *receit(e* – AFr. (ONFr.) *receite* = OFr. *reçoite*, var. of *recete* (mod. *recette*) – med.L. *recepta*, subst. use of fem. pa. pple. of L. *recipere* RECEIVE. The sp. with *p* appears in OFr. *recepte* (XIV), a latinized form of *recete.*] **I. 1.** A formula or prescription, a statement of the ingredients (and mode of procedure) necessary for the making of some preparation, esp. in *Med.* (now *rare*) and *Cookery*; a RECIPE. **b.** The formula or description of a remedy *for* a disease; also *absol.* a remedy, means of cure 1586. **c.** The means to be adopted *for* attaining some end 1621. †**2.** A drug or other mixture compounded in accordance with a receipt –1773.

1. *fig.* Some.. Write dull receipts how poems may be made POPE. **b.** Euery defect of the mind may haue a speciall receit BACON. **c.** From the knowledge of simples shee had a r. to make white haire black SIR T. BROWNE.

II. That which is received; the amount, sum, or quantity received. late ME.

An excess of actual revenue over estimated receipts 1863.

III. 1. The act of receiving something given or handed to one; the fact of being received. late ME. **b.** A written acknowledgement of money or goods received into possession or custody 1602. **2.** The act of receiving or taking in; admittance (of things) to a place or receptacle. *Obs.* or *arch.* late ME. †**3.** The act of receiving or admitting (a person) to a place, shelter, accommodation, assistance, etc.; the fact of being so received; reception –1676. †**b.** The ordinary or habitual reception of strangers or travellers; esp. in *place of r.* –1650. †**4.** Acceptance of a person or thing (*rare*) –1621. **5.** The fact of receiving (a blow, wound). *Obs.* or *arch.* 1533.

1. The r. and expenditure of large sums of money 1848. **b.** Make a receit for the same on the backside of the said Bill 1651. **2.** Ample cisternes for the receit of raine 1615. **3. b.** The greatest place of r. in Samaria FULLER.

IV. 1. The chief place or office at which moneys are received on behalf of the Crown or government; the public revenue-office. Also, *R. of the (King's) Exchequer.* Now only *Hist.* 1442. **b.** The receiving-place *of* custom. Hence *fig.* 1539. †**2.** A place for the reception of things; a receptacle –1605. †**b.** *esp.* A basin or other part of a fountain; a reservoir –1646. †**3.** A place of refuge –1625. †**b.** A chamber, apartment (*rare*) –1615. †**4.** *Hunting.* A position taken up to await driven game with fresh hounds; a relay of men or dogs placed for this purpose –1688.

1. b. He sawe a man (named Mathew) syttyng at the receate of custome BIBLE (Great) *Matt.* 9:9. **3. b.** Atrides, and his..spouse,..In a retired receit, together lay CHAPMAN.

V. †**1.** Capability of receiving, accommodating, or containing; capacity, size –1703. †**b.** Mental capacity –1628. †**2.** Accommodation or space provided –1627.

1. *fig.* His popular manner was of such r. that he had room to lodge all comers FULLER.

Comb.: **r.-book,** (*a*) a book of medical or cooking receipts; (*b*) a book containing printed forms for receipts for payments made.

†**Recei·pt,** *v.*[1] ME. [–(O)Fr. *receiter*, var. of *receter* RESET *v.*[1]] *trans.* To receive, harbour (a person, esp. a criminal) –1733. So †**Recei·pter,** one who receives or harbours criminals or stolen goods.

Receipt (rĭsī·t), *v.*[2] 1787. [f. RECEIPT *sb.*] **1.** *trans. U.S.* To acknowledge in writing the receipt of (a sum of money, etc.). **2.** To mark (an account) as paid 1844. **3.** *intr. U.S.* To give a receipt *for* (a sum of money, etc.) 1880. Hence **Recei·ptor** *U.S.* a person who receipts property attached by a sheriff; a bailee.

Receivable (rĭsī·văb'l), *a.* late ME. [orig. – AFr. *receivable*, var. of OFr. *recevable*; in later use f. RECEIVE *v.* + -ABLE.] **1.** Capable of being received. **b.** Of certificates, paper money, etc.: That is to be received as legal tender 1790. **2.** Capable of receiving (*rare*) 1530.

1. The general rule of English law is, that hearsay evidence is not r. 1880. Hence **Receivabi·lity. Recei·vableness.**

Receival (rĭsī·văl). Now *rare.* 1637. [f. RECEIVE *v.* + -AL[1].] Receipt, reception.

Receive (rĭsī·v), *v.* [ME. *receive, receve* – OFr. *receivre*, var. of *reçoivre* or later (refash.) *recevoir*, ult. :– L. *recipere*, f. *re-* RE- + *capere* take.] **I. 1.** *trans.* To take in one's hand, or into one's possession (something held out or offered by another); to take delivery of (a thing) from another, either for oneself or for a third party. **b.** Of God: To take (a soul) to himself ME. **c.** To take (stolen goods) into one's keeping 1583. **d.** To take from another by hearing; to attend or give heed to. late ME. **2.** To accept (something offered or presented) ME. **3.** To become the support of (something superimposed). late ME. **b.** To catch (a person or thing descending) in the arms or otherwise 1470. **c.** To catch or intercept (a missile, blow, etc.); to encounter the force or effect of 1560. **d.** To catch (a sound) by hearing. late ME. **4.** To permit oneself to be the object of (some action, etc.); to allow (something) to be done to, or (some quality, etc.) to be conferred on, oneself; to submit to ME. **b.** To admit (an impression, etc.) by yielding or by adaptation of surface. late ME. **c.** To allow (something) to be applied to, or placed on, oneself 1549. **d.** Of recording instruments: To be affected, or operated on, by (the thing transmitted) 1862. **5.** To take in; to admit as to a receptacle or containing space; to allow to enter or penetrate ME. **b.** Of a place or building: To admit (a person); to give accommodation or shelter to ME. **c.** To afford proper room or space to; to hold or contain conveniently 1440. **5.** To take in by the mouth; to swallow. *Obs.* or *arch.* late ME. **b.** To participate in, take (the sacrament or holy communion) ME. **6.** To take into the mind; to understand; to learn 1603.

1. He..Received it, and at one draught drank it off SHELLEY. **b.** Jesu, do Thou my soul r. KEBLE. **d.** A wyse man wil receaue warnynge COVERDALE *Prov.* 10:8. **2.** We cannot r. parole evidence of their contents 1776. **3.** Make broad thy shoulders to r. my weight TENNYSON. **c.** The son..received the first discharge of her fury SMOLLETT. **4. b.** His tendrer cheeke receiues her soft hands print SHAKS. **c.** Egypt has since Received his yoke, and the whole Nile is Cæsar's ADDISON. **d.** Also, of wireless receiving-sets or the operators of these. **5. b.** Innes ordeyned..to resceyve bothe Man and Hors MAUNDEVILLE.

II. 1. To admit (a person) into some relation with oneself, esp. to familiar or social intercourse; to treat in a friendly manner ME. **b.** In religious use ME. **2.** To meet (a person) with signs of welcome or salutation; to pay attention or respect to (one who comes to a place); to greet upon arrival or entrance ME. **3.** To meet, welcome, or greet (a person) in a specified manner ME. **b.** *Mil.* To meet with resistance (an enemy, his attack, etc.). late

ME. **4.** To admit (a person) to a place; *esp.* to give accommodation or shelter to; to harbour. late ME. **5.** To admit (a person or thing) *to, into* a state, condition, privilege, occupation, etc. late ME. **b.** To admit to membership of a society or class or to partnership in work; to take in *among* other persons or things. late ME. **6.** To take or accept (a person) in some capacity. late ME. **b.** To admit (a person) to plead or give evidence 1607. **7.** To take, accept, regard, hear, etc. (anything offered or presented, or to which attention is given) in a specified manner or with a specified expression of feeling. late ME. **8.** To accept as an authority, rule, or practice; to admit the truth or validity of; to make use of. late ME. **b.** To give credit to; to believe. Also *absol.* late ME.

1. He is a Gentleman so Receiv'd, so Courted, and so Trusted STEELE. **b.** God accept him, Christ r. him TENNYSON. **2.** Preparations to r. the King CLARENDON. **4.** Take heede what Guests You receiue SHAKS. **4.** R. me, at my death, to everlasting happiness JOHNSON. **b.** Forty-five persons have been received by immersion into the church 1843. **7.** But how hath she receiu'd his Loue? SHAKS. **8.** An axiom universally received BERKELEY. **b.** They..speak in ears That hear not or r. not their report COWPER.

III. 1. To have (a thing) given or handed to oneself; to get from another, or others ME. **b.** To get (a letter, etc.) brought to oneself. late ME. **c.** To get by communication from another; to learn, ascertain, etc., in this way 1526. **2. a.** To get (a person) into one's custody, control, vicinity, society, etc. Now *rare* or *Obs.* ME. **b.** To get, or come into possession of (a town, country, etc.) *rare.* 1568. **c.** To get or acquire (some feature) 1789. **3.** To have (some quality, attribute, or property) given, bestowed, conferred, or impressed ME. **4.** To be the object of (some action); to experience or meet with (some treatment, etc.) ME. **5.** To have (a blow, wound, mark, etc.) inflicted or made upon one or *in* some part; to get (a specified injury). late ME. **b.** To come in the way of and suffer from (a missile, gun, etc.) 1715. **6.** To have (a law, etc.) imposed or laid on one; to get as a charge. late ME.

1. His mother..residing in one of them..and receiving rent for the others 1818. **b.** I receyved but one letter from my father 1530. **c.** On Mr. Anson's receiving any other intelligence 1748. **3.** Such collections of stony fragments..r. the name of Moraines 1813. **4.** The affronts she had received DICKENS. The proposal..deserves more attention than it is likely..to r. 1891. **5.** I stood like one that had received a blow TENNYSON. **b.** His bended arm received the falling stone POPE.

IV. Absol. uses. **1.** To take, accept, or get, in various senses; to be or become a recipient. late ME. **2.** To take the sacrament or holy communion; to communicate 1560. **3.** To hold receptions 1854.

Hence **Recei·ving** *vbl. sb.* (also *attrib.* as *r.-office, -room,* etc.; *r.-set* in Wireless) and *ppl. a.*

Receiver (rǐsī·vəɹ). ME. [– AFr. **receivere, -our* = OFr. *recevere, -our*. In later use also f. the verb + -ER¹.] **1.** One who receives (see the vb.). **2.** One who receives on behalf of others: **a.** An official, officer, or servant appointed to receive money due; a treasurer, collector. Also †*general r.*: see RECEIVER-GENERAL. Now chiefly *Hist.* ME. **b.** A person appointed by a court to administer the property of a bankrupt, or property which is the subject of litigation, pending the suit. In recent use also *official r.* 1793. **3.** One who knowingly receives stolen goods or harbours offenders; a resetter ME. **4.** That which receives; a receptacle. late ME. **b.** A tank or reservoir; a vessel to hold anything 1538. **c.** A mould to receive molten metal 1846. **4.** As the name of certain parts of apparatus or machinery intended to receive and contain something; e.g. *Chem.* a vessel for receiving and condensing the product of distillation; the receptacle for mercury in a barometer 1576. **6. a.** A device or instrument which receives an electric current or a telegraphic message 1873. **b.** An apparatus which receives and reproduces sounds from another part of an electric circuit; that part of a telephone which is applied to the ear 1877. **c.** An apparatus for transforming broadcast waves into sound or light; a wireless receiving-set 1890. **Recei·vership** (sense 2).

Recei·ver-gen·eral. 1439. [– AFr. *receivour* (see prec.) *general*, in AL. *receptor generalis.*] A chief receiver, esp. of public revenues. (See RECEIVER 2 a).

In Great Britain now only as the title of an official of the Duchy of Lancaster.

Recency (rī·sěnsi). 1612. [f. RECENT; see -ENCY.] The state or quality of being recent.

Recense (rǐse·ns), *v.* 1597. [– (O)Fr. *recenser* or L. *recensēre*, f. *re-* RE- + *censēre* CENSE *v.*²] *trans.* To survey, review, revise (now *spec.* a text).

Recension (rǐse·nʃən). 1638. [– L. *recensio, -on-*, f. *recensēre* reckon, survey, revise; see prec., -ION.] **1.** An enumeration, survey, review. Now *rare.* **b.** A review (of a book). GEO. ELIOT. **2.** The revision of a text, esp. in a careful or critical manner; a particular version of a text resulting from such revision 1818. **b.** *transf.* A revised or distinct form of anything 1835. Hence **Rece·nsionist,** one who makes a r.

Recent (rī·sěnt), *a.* 1533. [– Fr. *récent* or L. *recens, recent-*.] **1.** Lately done or made; that has lately happened or taken place, etc. **2.** Lately formed, created, originated, or begun; †new-born 1676. **b.** Fresh; not yet affected by decay, decomposition, or loss of moisture 1558. **c.** *poet.* Lately or freshly come or arrived *from* a place 1715. **3.** Belonging to a (past) period of time comparatively near to the present. (Opp. to *ancient* †or *antique.*) 1622. **b.** *Geol.* Of or pertaining to the present geological epoch 1830. **4.** Of a point or period of time: Not long past 1823. **b.** *Geol.* Applied to the later portion of the Quaternary or Post-Pliocene period 1833.

1. R. translations I have seen of it in French 1661. The bright drops of a r. shower 1837. **2.** Lorraine and Arles, two r. and transitory kingdoms GIBBON. **c.** R. from the roar of foreign foam SWINBURNE. **3.** Though it be an action of so r. memorie BACON. **b.** An intermixture of extinct and r. species of quadrupeds 1833. **4.** Up to a very r. period 1823. Hence **Re·cently** *adv.* at a r. date; lately, newly 1533. **Re·centness.**

Receptacle (rǐse·ptăk'l). late ME. [– (O)Fr. *réceptacle* or L. *receptaculum*, f. *receptare*, f. *recept-*, pa. ppl. stem of *recipere* RECEIVE.] **1.** That which receives and holds a thing; a containing vessel, place, or space; a repository. **2.** Any place into which persons (ships, animals, etc.) are received or retire, esp. for shelter or security. late ME. **3.** *spec.* in scientific use. **a.** *Anat.* and *Bot.* An organ or space which receives a secretion, esp. *r. of chyle* (the dilated lower portion of the thoracic duct), *of secretion* (in plants) 1543. **b.** *Bot.* The common base which supports the floral organs, the torus or thalamus (*floral r.*). Also, the axis or rachis of a head, spike, or other cluster (*r. of inflorescence*). 1753. **c.** *Bot.* In Ferns, Mosses, Algæ, and Fungi, the support of the fructification or reproductive organs; an apothecium, pycnidium, sporophore, etc. 1842.

1. *fig.* The soule of man is the r. of Christ's presence HOOKER. **2.** Holy-wells, rocks and caves, which have been the reputed cells and receptacles of men reputed saints 1672. So **Recepta·cular** *a. Bot.* pertaining to the r. of a flower; also, of the nature of, or serving as, a r.

†**Rece·ptary,** *sb.* and *a. rare.* 1611. [In sense 1 – Fr. †*réceptaire* – med.L. **receptarium* (f. *recepta*; see RECEIPT *sb.*, -ARY¹); in other senses a different application of the med.L.] **A.** *sb.* **1.** A book or collection of receipts –1656. **2.** An accepted notion or belief. **B.** *adj.* Merely accepted as true, without proof. –1646.

Receptible (rǐse·ptib'l), *a.* Now *rare.* 1574. [– Fr. †*réceptible*, or its source med.L. *receptibilis*, f. *recept-* (see RECEPTACLE); see -IBLE.] **1.** That may be received, receivable. **2.** Capable of receiving. Const. *of.* 1656. So **Rece:ptibi·lity,** the quality or state of being r.

Reception (rǐse·pʃən). late ME. [– (O)Fr. *réception* or L. *receptio, -on-*, f. as prec.; see -ION.] **1.** The action or fact of receiving or getting 1489. **2. a.** *Astrol.* The fact of each of two planets being received into the other's house, exaltation, or other dignity. late ME. **b.** The action of receiving (esp. persons), or fact of being received, into a place, company, state, etc. 1650. **c.** The action of receiving, or fact of being received, in a formal or ceremonious manner 1662. **d.** An occasion of ceremonious receiving; an assemblage of persons for this purpose 1882. **3.** The action of receiving, or taking in, physically or spatially. late ME. **4.** The action of accepting or admitting; acceptance, admittance, approbation 1660. †**b.** An idea accepted without evidence of its truth –1691. **5.** The action of receiving, or fact of being received, in a certain manner; kind or manner of reception 1647. **6.** The action of receiving or taking 1863. †**7.** Capacity for receiving –1698. †**8.** A receptacle –1696. †**9.** Recovery, recapture. BACON.

1. The prospect of the wealth which awaits man's r. 1834. **2. b.** All hope is lost of my r. into grace MILT. **c.** The r. of a deputation 1886. **3.** Towers for the r. of the bells 1868. **4.** To persuade us into a R. of Divine Truth ATTERBURY. **5.** *spec.* The receiving of wireless signals, or the efficiency with which they are received 1907.

Comb.: **r.-order,** an order authorizing the r. and detention of a person in a lunatic asylum. Hence **Rece·ptionist,** *(a) Theol.* applied attrib. to a view of the Eucharist which makes the presence of Christ depend on the disposition of the communicant. *(b)* a person employed by a photographer, dentist, etc. to receive clients.

Receptive (rǐse·ptiv), *a.* 1547. [– Fr. *réceptif* or med.L. *receptivus*, f. as prec.; see -IVE.] **1.** Having the quality of, or capacity for, receiving; able to receive; pertaining to, of the nature of, reception. **2.** *spec. R. spot*, the spot in an oosphere at which the male gamete is admitted 1875.

1. The passive r. work of the mind 1875. I should wish the citizens to be as r. of virtue as possible 1875. Hence **Rece·ptive-ly** *adv.*, **-ness. Receptivity** (rǐsepti·vĭti), ability or readiness to receive or take in.

‖**Recercelé** (rǐsō·ɹsěli). 1766. [OFr. *recercelé, -lée* circular, curled, f. *re-* RE- + *cercel* circle.] *Her.* Of a cross: Having the ends of the arms curling into divergent spirals.

Recess (rǐse·s), *sb.* 1531. [– L. *recessus*, f. *recess-*, pa. ppl. stem of *recedere* RECEDE.] †**1.** The act of retiring, withdrawing, or departing; withdrawal, departure. (Freq. in phr. *access and r.*) –1692. †**2.** The (or an) act of retirement from public life or into privacy; the fact of living retired; a period of retirement –1762. **3.** The act of retiring for a time from some occupation; a period of cessation from usual work or employment 1642. †**b.** Cessation from work; relaxation –1781. †**4.** Delay, respite (*rare*) –1706. **5.** A place of retirement, a remote, secret, or private place 1636. **6.** The act of receding, of going back or away, from a certain point. (Used chiefly of the motion of things, and *esp.* of water, the sea, or the heavenly bodies.) 1607. **7.** A retired or inner place or part; one of the remotest or innermost parts or corners of anything 1616. **8.** A receding part or indentation in the line of some natural feature or object, as a coast, range of hills, etc. 1697. **b.** *spec.* A niche or alcove 1774. **c.** Any small depression or indentation; also *Anat.* a sinus or fold in an organ or part 1839. **8.** *Hist.* A resolution, decree, or act of the Imperial Diet of Germany or of the Diet of the Hanseatic League. [After med.L. *recessus.*] 1706.

3. In this r. of action, we had several treaties about prisoners 1671. In the r.,..or interval of suspended studies in the middle of the forenoon 1860. We are in a Parliamentary r. 1881. *The r.*: spec. the interval between two sessions of parliament. **5.** The last retreat, and r., of his every-day waning grandeur LAMB. **6.** An alternate r. and advance of the apsides 1834. *transf.* Painting the access and r. of his thought 1843. **7.** The gloomy recesses of the cloister 1801. *fig.* Deep in the close recesses of my soul POPE. **8.** His dwelling a r. in some rude rock COWPER.

Recess (rǐse·s), *v.* 1809. [f. prec.] **1.** *trans.* To place in a recess or in retirement; to set back or away. **b.** *spec.* To set (part of a wall or other structure) in a recess 1845. **2.** To make a recess or recesses in; to cut away, so as to form a recess 1876. **3.** *intr. U.S.* To take a recess or interval 1893.

1. b. The arches,..one recessed within the other 1845. Hence **Rece·ssed** *ppl. a.* set in a recess; as *recessed arch*, an arch set within another arch.

Recession (rǐse·ʃən). 1652. [– L. *recessio,*

f. *recess-*; see RECESS *sb.*, -ION.] **1.** The action of receding; withdrawal, retirement. **b.** A setting or going back in time (*rare*) 1646. **2.** The action of receding, retiring or departing, in various *transf.* or *fig.* senses. Const. *from*. 1647.

Recessional (rĭse·ʃənăl), *a.* and *sb.* 1867. [f. prec. + -AL[1].] **A.** *adj.* **1.** Of or belonging to the recession or retirement of the clergy and choir from the chancel to the vestry at the close of a service; esp. *r. hymn*, a hymn sung while this retirement is taking place. **2.** Belonging to a recess (of Parliament) 1895. **B.** *sb.* A recessional hymn 1867.

Recessive (rĭse·siv), *a.* (and *sb.*) 1672. [f. RECESS *sb.*, after *exceed*/*excess*/*excessive*.] Tending to recede; *spec.*, in the Mendelian theory of heredity, opp. to *dominant*. As *sb.* = a recessive character.

Rechabite (re·kăbəit). late ME. [– eccl.L. (Vulg.) *Rechabita*, used in pl. to render Heb. *rēkābîm*, f. *rēkāb*; (*Jer.* 35); see -ITE[1].] One of a Jewish family descended from Jonadab, son of Rechab, which refused to drink wine or live in houses. Hence (*a*) one who abstains from intoxicating liquors; now *spec.* a member of the Independent Order of Rechabites, a benefit society founded in 1835; (*b*) a dweller in tents. Hence **Re·chabitism.**

Rechange (rītʃē[i]·ndʒ). 1487. [f. RE- 5 a + CHANGE *sb.*] †**1.** The RE-EXCHANGE on a bill –1682. †**2.** The act of re-exchanging (money or goods) –1625. **3.** The act of changing or altering again 1550.

Recharge (rītʃā·ɹdʒ). *sb.* 1603. [f. RE- + CHARGE *sb.*, partly after Fr. *recharge*.] **1.** A fresh charge or load 1611. **2.** A renewed or return charge in battle 1603.

Recharge (rītʃā·ɹdʒ), *v.* late ME. [f. RE- + CHARGE *v.*, partly after (O)Fr. *recharger*.] **1.** *trans.* †**a.** To reload (a vessel). Also *absol.* –1615. **b.** To put a fresh charge in; to refill, reload 1839. **2.** †**a.** To charge or accuse in return –1697. **b.** To make a new charge against 1895. **3.** To lay or impose again as a charge (*rare*) 1611. **4.** *intr.* To charge (in battle) again or in return 1598.

2. b. The magistrate..then directed that she should be re-charged for the assault on the.. gaoler 1895.

Recha·se, *v.* *Obs.* exc. *dial.* late ME. [– (O)Fr. *rechasser*; see RE-, CHASE *v.*[1]] †**1.** *trans.* To chase or drive back; to chase in turn –1614. **2.** †**a.** *Hunting.* To chase (a deer) back into the forest –1741. **b.** To drive back (cattle or sheep) from one pasture to another 1618.

‖**Réchauffé** (reʃofe). 1805. [Fr., pa. pple. of *réchauffer* warm up again, f. *re-* RE- + *échauffer*; see CHAFE *v.*] A warmed-up dish; hence *fig.* something old served up again, esp. a rehash of literary matter.

It is really wasting time to confute this *r.* of a theory 1805.

Recheat (rĭtʃī·t), *sb.* *Obs.* exc. *arch.* 1470. [f. *recheat* v. (see below) – OFr. *racheter*, *rachater* reassemble, rally.] †**a.** The act of calling together the hounds to begin or continue the chase of a stag, or at the close of the hunt (*rare*). **b.** The series of notes sounded on a horn for one or other of these purposes. †**Recheat** *v.* (XIV) *intr.* to blow a r. –1612.

‖**Recherché** (rəʃɛrʃe), *a.* 1722. [Fr., pa. pple. of *rechercher*, f. *re-* RE- + *chercher* seek.] Carefully sought out; hence, extremely choice or rare.

†**Recidivate,** *pa. pple.* and *v.* *rare.* 1528. [– med.L. *recidivatus*, pa. pple. of *recidivare*, f. L. *recidivus*, f. *recidere* fall back, f. *re-* RE- + *cadere* fall; see -ATE[2,3].] **A.** *pa. pple.* Fallen back. **B.** *v.* *intr.* To fall back, relapse. –1677.

†**Recidivation.** late ME. [– Fr. *récidivation* or med.L. *recidivatio*, *-on-*, f. *recidivare*; see prec., -ION.] **1.** Relapse into sin, error, crime, etc.; backsliding, apostasy –1693. **2.** A relapse in a sickness or disease –1706.

Recidive (re·sidiv), *a.* and *sb.* *rare.* 1537. [– L. *recidivus* (see RECIDIVATE); in sense B. a = Fr. *récidive*, med.L. *recidiva*.] †**A.** *adj.* Falling back, relapsing –1659. **B.** *sb.* †**a.** = RECIDIVATION 2. –1600. **b.** = next 1854.

Recidivist (rĭsi·divist). 1880. [– Fr. *récidiviste*, f. *récidiver* – med.L. *recidivare*; see RECIDIVATE, -IST.] One who relapses; *esp.* one who habitually relapses into crime. So **Reci·divism,** the habit of relapsing into crime.

Recidivous (rĭsi·divəs), *a.* 1658. [f. L. *recidivus* RECIDIVE + -OUS.] Liable to fall back or relapse.

Recipe (re·sipi), *v.* *imper.* and *sb.* late ME. [– L. *recipe*, imper. sing. of *recipere* take, RECEIVE, used by physicians (abbrev. R., ℞) at the head of prescriptions, and hence applied to these and similar formulæ.] †**A.** *v. imper.* = Take –1652. **B.** *sb.* **1.** *Med.* A formula for a medical prescription; a prescription, or the remedy prepared in accordance with this 1584. **2.** A statement of the ingredients and procedure necessary for the making or compounding of some preparation, esp. of a dish in cookery; a receipt 1743. **3.** *transf.* A means (actual or suggested) for attaining or effecting some end 1643.

Recipience (rĭsi·piĕns). *rare.* 1882. [f. as next; see -ENCE.] The act or process of receiving.

Recipiency (rĭsi·piĕnsi). 1822. [f. next; see -ENCY.] Receptivity; reception.

Recipient (rĭsi·piĕnt), *a.* and *sb.* 1558. [– Fr. *récipient* – It. *recipiente* or L. *recipiens*, *-ent-*, pr. pple. of *recipere* RECEIVE; see -ENT.] **A.** *adj.* That receives or is capable of receiving; receptive 1610. **B.** *sb.* **1.** One who or that which receives 1615. †**2. a.** *Chem.* A receiver; a (glass) vessel for receiving or holding a liquid –1794. **b.** The receiver of an air-pump –1815. **3.** A re-entrant angle 1811.

Reciprocal (rĭsi·prŏkăl), *a.* and *sb.* 1570. [f. L. *reciprocus* (see RECIPROQUE) + -AL[1].] **A.** *adj.* †**1.** Having, or of the nature of, an alternate backward and forward motion. (Said *esp.* of tides.) –1726. †**b.** Of actions: Alternating –1758. **2.** Of the nature of or pertaining to a return made for something; given, felt, shown, etc., in return 1596. **b.** Existing on both sides; felt or shared by both parties; mutual 1579. **3.** Inversely correspondent or related; correlative, complementary; †opposed. Now chiefly *Math.* 1570. **b.** *Math.* Based upon an inverse relationship 1823. **4.** Corresponding or answering to each other, as being either similar or complementary 1570. †**5.** Convertible, synonymous –1733. **6.** *Gram.* Of pronouns and verbs, or their signification: Reflexive; now, more usu. expressing mutual action or relationship 1611.

2. He had a right to expect from them a r. demonstration of firmness '*Junius' Lett.* **b.** Kindness is generally r. JOHNSON. Phr. *R. defence*, in *Fortif.*, a form of flanking defence. **3. b.** *R. equation*, one of those which contain several pairs of roots, which are the r. of each other..*R. proportion* is when the reciprocals of the two last terms have the same ratio as the quantities of the first terms..*R. ratio* is the ratio of the reciprocals of two quantities. 1823. **4.** Reciprocall figures are those, when the termes of proportion are both antecedentes and consequentes in either figure 1570. Let our reciprocall vowes be remembred SHAKS. Allegiance and Protection are r. in all Countries 1718. R., in mathematics, is applied to quantities which multiplied together produce unity 1797. **6.** A Pronoun or a Verb r. 1727. *One another, each other*, are sometimes called r. pronouns 1872.

B. *sb.* †**1.** One who is sent back. CHAPMAN. **2.** A thing corresponding in some way or other; a return, equivalent, counterpart, etc. 1570. †**3.** *Gram.* A reflexive verb –1766. **4.** *Math.* A function or expression so related to another that their product is unity; the inverse 1685.

2. Corruption is a Reciprocall to Generation BACON. Hence **Reciproca·lity,** †**Reci·procalness,** reciprocity.

Reciprocally (rĭsi·prŏkăli), *adv.* 1570. [f. prec. + -LY[2].] In a reciprocal manner; with reciprocity.

As the mind affects the body, the body r. affects the mind 1756. The existence of our kind is continuous, and its ages are r. dependent 1876. You must vnderstand it r., the battel is not alwayes to the strong, therefore it is sometimes to the weake 1628.

Reciprocate (rĭsi·prŏke[i]t), *v.* 1611. [– *reciprocat-*, pa. ppl. stem of L. *reciprocare*, f. *reciprocus*; see RECIPROQUE, -ATE[3].] **1.** *intr.* †**a.** To go back, return; to have a backward direction –1661. **b.** To move backwards and forwards (now *Mech.*); †to go up and down, to vary 1678. **c.** *trans.* To alternate the direction of; to cause to move backwards and forwards 1653. **2. a.** To give and receive in return or mutually; to interchange 1611. **b.** To return, requite; to do, feel, etc., in or by way of return 1820. **3.** *intr.* To make a return or interchange *with* (another or others). Now *rare* or *Obs.* 1626. **b.** *spec.* To make a return or exchange of good wishes 1779. †**4. a.** *trans.* To make correspondent or convertible *with*; to convert –1788. **b.** *intr.* To be correspondent or in agreement (*with* something); to be equivalent or convertible 1683. **5.** *Math.* **a.** *trans.* To find the reciprocal to (a curve) 1861. **b.** *intr.* To pass *into* by reciprocation 1861.

1. c. Vainly reciprocating the saw of endless contention 1677. **2. a.** The waters reciprocating their tides with the neighbouring sea EVELYN. **3. b.** Then when the two glassés of water were brought ..he said, 'Madam, let us r.' JOHNSON. Hence **Reci·procating** *ppl. a.* that reciprocates; *spec.* in *Mech.* (of machines, etc.) having a reciprocating part or parts. **Reci·procator,** one who, or that which, reciprocates.

Reciprocation (rĭsiprŏkē[i]·ʃən). 1530. [– Fr. *réciprocation* or L. *reciprocatio*, *-on-*, f. as prec., see -ION.] †**1.** Reflexive action; a reflexive mode of expression –1631. **2.** Motion backwards and forwards. Now *Mech.* 1646. **b.** Alternate action or operation (*rare*) 1656. †**c.** Alternation; vicissitude –1794. **3.** The action of making a return, or doing something in return; *esp.* a mutual return or exchange of acts, feelings, etc. 1561. **4.** The state of being in a reciprocal or harmonious relation; correspondence 1605. †**b.** *Logic.* The conversion of terms or propositions, or the relation involved by this –1677.

3. With a sincere r. of all your kindly feeling DICKENS.

Reciprocity (resiprǫ·sĭti). 1766. [– Fr. *réciprocité*, f. *réciproque*; see next, -ITY. Cf. late L. *reciprocitas*.] **1.** The state or condition of being reciprocal; a state or relationship in which there is mutual action, influence, giving and taking correspondence, etc., between two parties or things. **2.** *spec.* **a.** Mutual or correspondent concession of advantages or privileges, as forming a basis for the commercial relations between two countries 1782. **b.** In the Kantian philosophy: Mutual action and reaction 1883.

2. a. New arrangements of trade, on the footing of r. and mutual convenience 1783.

†**Reciproque,** *a.* and *sb.* 1532. [– (O)Fr. *réciproque* – L. *reciprocus* moving backwards and forwards, f. (ult.) *re-* back, *pro* forward.] **A.** *adj.* = RECIPROCAL *a.* –1619. **B.** *sb.* A return or equivalent. Also with *the*: The natural return, the like. –1648.

B. It is a true rule that loue is euer rewarded either with the r. or with an inward..contempt BACON.

Recision (rĭsi·ʒən). Now *rare.* 1611. [– L. *recisio*, *-on-*, f. *recis-*, pa. ppl. stem of *recidere* cut back; see -ION.] **a.** The action of cutting back or pruning. †**b.** The action of rescinding –1706.

Recital (rĭsəi·tăl). 1512. [f. RECITE *v.* + -AL[1].] **1.** A rehearsal, account, or description *of* some thing, fact, or incident; also (esp. in early use), a relation of the particulars or details *of* something 1550. **b.** A discourse, account, relation, narrative 1565. **2.** *spec.* The rehearsal or statement in a formal or legal document of some fact or facts closely connected with the matter or purpose of the document itself; the part containing this statement 1512. **3.** An (*or* the) act of (†reading or) reciting 1612. **b.** *Mus.* A musical performance given by one person; a concert consisting of selections from one composer 1811.

2. The particular r. prefixed, by way of preamble, to this very clause BENTHAM. **3. b.** M. Liszt will also give a r. of one of his great fantasias 1840. *Opera r.*, a performance of the music and words of an opera without appropriate costume or acting. Hence **Reci·talist,** one who gives musical recitals.

Recitation (resitē[i]·ʃən). 1484. [– (O)Fr. *récitation* or L. *recitatio*, *-on-*, f. *recitat-*, pa. ppl. stem of *recitare*; see RECITE *v.*, -ION.] **1.** The action of rehearsing, detailing, †or enumerating; recital. **b.** An instance of this; an account, narrative 1641. **2.** The action of reciting (†or reading aloud); the repetition of something got by heart 1623. **b.** An instance of this; an act of reciting; also, a piece to be recited 1841. **3.** *U.S.* The repetition of a prepared lesson or exercise; an examination on something previously learned or explained 1824.

Recitative (re:sitătī·v), *a.*[1] and *sb.* 1645. [– It. *recitativo* RECITATIVO.] *Mus.* **A.** *adj.* **1.** Of the nature of, in the style of, recitative. **†2.** Employing a recitative style –1660. **B.** *sb.* **1.** A style of musical declamation, intermediate between singing and ordinary speech, commonly employed in the dialogue and narrative parts of operas and oratorios 1656. **†b.** The tone or rhythm peculiar to any language –1791. **2.** Words or passages intended to be delivered in recitative 1716. **3. a.** A part rendered in recitative, or a piece of music intended for such a part 1754. **b.** A performance in r. 1873.

1. b. Some gentlemen of Ireland, to whom a slight proportion of the accent and r. of that country is an advantage BOSWELL. Hence **†Recitatively** *adv.*

Recitative (re·siteitiv, rĭsi·tătiv), *a.*[2] *rare.* 1860. [f. RECITE *v.* + -ATIVE.] Of the nature of a recital or repetition.

Recitativo (re:sitătī·vo). 1645. [– It. *recitativo* (orig. in *stile recitativo*), pa. ppl. stem of *recitare* RECITE *v.* + *-ivo* -IVE.] = RECITATIVE *sb.* 1.

†Recite (rĭsəi·t), *sb. rare.* 1685. [f. next.] A recital.

Recite (rĭsəi·t), *v.* late ME. [–(O)Fr. *réciter*, or L. *recitare* read out, f. *re-* RE- + *citare* CITE.] **1.** *trans.* To repeat or utter aloud (something previously composed, heard, or learned by heart); now *spec.* to repeat to an audience (a piece of verse, etc.) from memory and in an appropriate manner. Also, to read out or aloud (now *rare*). 1481. **2.** To relate, rehearse, narrate, tell, declare; to give an account of; to describe in detail. *Obs.* or *arch.* 1483. **b.** *Law.* To rehearse or state in a deed or other document (some fact bearing closely upon the matter in hand). late ME. **†3.** To compose; to write *down* (*rare*) –1654. **4.** To go through or over in detail; to enumerate, give a list of. Now *rare.* 1533. **†5.** To cite, quote –1793. **†b.** To cite or mention, to quote from (a book) –1807. **6.** *intr.* To repeat something from memory; *U.S.* to repeat a lesson, or be examined on one 1735.

1. I recited some Heroick Lines of my own STEELE. **2. b.** John Ivy, reciting that he had made a former will in the life of his wife 1818. **3.** Such as found out musical tunes, and recited verses in writing *Ecclus.* 44:5. **4.** By reciting the sins of their neighbours, men indulge their own foolish.. desires WESLEY. Hence **Reci·ter,** one who recites; also used as the title of books containing passages for recitation.

Reck (rek), *sb. Obs.* exc. *poet.* 1568. [f. next.] Care, heed, consideration, regard.

Reck (rek), *v.* Now chiefly *rhet.* or *poet.* [OE. (i) **rēcan*, pa. t. *rōhte* = OS. *rōkjan*, OHG. *ruohhen*, ON. *rœkja* :– Gmc. **rōkjan*; (ii) *reċċan*, of obscure origin (see next). The present form is due partly to the generalization of the *k* of ME. 3rd. sing. pres. ind. *rekþ*, partly to the infl. of ON. *rœkja.*] **1.** *intr.* **a.** To take care, heed, or thought *of* some thing (or person) with desire or favour towards it, interest in it, or the like; to set store or account *by*; to care *for*. Also with *inf.* **b.** To take head or have a care *of* some thing (or person), so as to be alarmed or troubled thereby, or to modify one's conduct or purpose on that account. Also with *inf.* or dependent clause. OE. **c.** To know, be aware, or think *of* 1813. **2.** Without const. (usu. *ellipt.*): To care, heed, mind, etc. OE. **3.** *trans.* To heed, regard, care for, etc. ME. **4.** In impers. use: To concern or trouble (a person); to interest ME. **b.** *absol.* To matter; to be of importance or interest ME.

1. My master..little wreakes, to finde the way to heauen By doing deeds of hospitalitie SHAKS. Little recked he of flowers—save cauliflowers BARHAM. **b.** Then it was, old Father Care, Little reck'd I of thy frown SHERIDAN. **c.** Little recked Mr. Podsnap of the traps and toils besetting his Young Person DICKENS. **2.** I wreake not, though thou end my life to day SHAKS. Revenge..back on itself recoiles; Let it; I r. not MILT. **3.** Himself.. reaks not his owne reade SHAKS. **4.** Of night, or loneliness it recks me not MILT.

Reckless (re·klės), *a.* [OE. *reċċelēas*, *reċe-*, earlier *reċċilēas*, whence ME. *rech-*, *retch(e)-less* (to XVII), corresp. to MLG. *rōkelōs*, (M)Du. *roekeloos*, OHG. *ruahhalōs* (G. *ruchlos*); f. base of RECK *v.* + -LESS; the forms with -*(c)k-* are by assoc. with the verb (*rekken*).] **1.** Of persons: Careless of the consequences of one's actions; heedless (*of* something); lacking in prudence or caution. **2.** Of actions, conduct, things, etc. Characterized or distinguished by (†carelessness or) heedless rashness ME. **3.** Quasi-*adv.* Recklessly. late ME.

1. R. of life GROTE. A rough and r. soldier, caring for nothing but a fight 1879. **2.** A r. increase of population 1863. Hence **Re·ckless-ly** *adv.*, **-ness.**

Reckling (re·kliŋ). Also **wreck-.** 1611. [Of unkn. origin.] The smallest and weakest animal of a litter; the youngest or smallest child in a family.

Reckon (re·k'n), *v.* [OE. *ġerecenian* = OFris. *rek(e)nia*, (M)LG., (M)Du. *rekenen*, OHG. *rehhanōn* (G. *rechnen*) :– WGmc. **(ʒa)rekenōjan.*] **I.** *trans.* **†1.** To enumerate serially or separately; to go over or through (a series) in this manner ME. **b.** So with *up*, rarely *over* ME. **†c.** To recount, relate, narrate, tell –1586. **†d.** To mention –1596. **2.** To count, so as to ascertain the number or amount of; to ascertain (a number, quantity, etc.) by counting or calculating; to compute. Also with *out.* ME. **b.** To calculate or keep count of, in relation to some starting-point 1540. **†c.** To count out, to pay –1713. **d.** To count *up*; also, to sum *up*, to estimate the character of (a person) 1836. **3.** To include in a (*or* the) reckoning; hence, to place or class. late ME. **b.** To accept or state as a total 1563. **†4. a.** To estimate, value –1667. **b.** To take into consideration (*rare*) –1686. **5.** To consider, judge, or estimate by, or as the result of, calculation 1555. **b.** To set down or consider as being of a specified character, importance or value, or (rarely) as being in a certain condition ME. **c.** With *inf.* To regard as doing something 1513. **6.** To consider, think, suppose, be of opinion *that* 1513. **b.** *I reckon*, used parenthetically or finally. (Now *dial.* and Southern *U.S.*) 1603. **†7.** To account, assign, or attribute *to* (a person or thing) –1719.

1. b. I shall r. up only such authors whose records ..are lost and gone 1638. **2.** I am ill at these Numbers; I haue not Art to r. my grones SHAKS. **3.** In this class we may r. the Georgians, Circassians, and Mingrelians GOLDSM. **5.** They r. that this..Work will be finish'd in about fifty Years 1745. **6.** I r., said Socrates, that no one..could accuse me of idle talking JOWETT.

II. *intr.* **†1.** *To r. right*: to judge correctly –1667. **2.** To count, to make a calculation; to cast up an account or sum ME. **3.** To go over or settle accounts *with* one, or *together* ME. **b.** *To r. with*: to take into consideration; to be prepared for 1885. **4.** To calculate, design, or expect *to* do something. Now *dial.* 1550. **b.** To look *for* something 1848. **5.** To account or think (much, etc.) *of*; to take account *of*, think highly or approve *of*. Now *rare* exc. *dial.* 1594. **6.** To count, depend, or rely *on* or *upon* 1632. **7.** To count, have a place or value 1879.

1. This to attain, whether Heav'n move or Earth, Imports not, if thou reck'n right MILT. **2.** Phr. *To r. without one's host*: see HOST *sb.*[2] 2. **3.** God..Will r. with us roundly for the abuse COWPER. **b.** A contingency to be reckoned with 1885. **4.** You may have more to bear than you r. for J. H. NEWMAN. **6.** He could r. on no support within England itself J. R. GREEN. Hence **Re·ckoner,** one who reckons; an aid to reckoning (see READY RECKONER).

Reckoning (re·k'niŋ), *vbl. sb.* ME. [f. prec. + -ING[1].] **1.** The action of RECKON *v.*; enumeration, calculation, computation. **b.** Manner of computing or numbering. late ME. **2.** An enumeration, calculation, or account. Also with *up.* ME. **b.** The process or result of (one's) counting. Freq. in phrases, as *to be out, in or of, to leave out of, to lose one's r.* 1585. **c.** *spec.* The calculated period of pregnancy 1638. **d.** *Naut.* The estimate made of a ship's position by calculation from the log, the course steered, observation of the sun, etc. See also DEAD RECKONING. 1577. **3.** A computation or account of the sum owing by, or due to, a person; a bill, *esp.* at an inn or tavern. late ME. **b.** *Dutch r.*: see quot. **4.** The action of rendering an account of property entrusted to one's charge, etc.; an account so rendered ME. **b.** *spec.* With ref. to rendering an account of one's life or conduct to God at death or judgment ME. **5.** The settlement of accounts or differences between parties 1470. **6.** The action of calculating chances or contingencies; (an) anticipation or expectation 1568. **†7. a.** Mode of regarding a matter –1649. **b.** *To be*, or *come to*, *one r.*: to be equivalent –1674. **†8.** Estimation, consideration, distinction –1653.

1. b. The r. by Olympiads was not yet in use NEWTON. **2. b.** I should lose my r. of time DE FOE. **3.** They liked the wine, but not the r. which was to be paid for it FULLER. **b.** A Dutch r., wherein if you dispute the..exorbitance of the bill, the land lord shall bring it up every time with new additions SWIFT. **4.** Howbeit, there was no r. made with them, of the money that was deliuered into their hand 2 *Kings* 22:7. There will be a day of r. sooner or later DICKENS. **5.** A firm bargain and a right r. make long friends 1776.

Reclaim (rĭklēi·m), *sb.* Now *rare.* ME. [– OFr. *reclaim*, f. *reclamer*; see next.] **†1.** The act of recalling a hawk –1486. **†b.** The recall or bringing back of a person –1590. **2.** The act of recalling, or state of being recalled, to right conduct ME. **b.** The reclamation of land 1799. Hence **Reclai·mless** *a.* (*rare*) that cannot be reclaimed.

Reclaim (rĭklēi·m), *v.* ME. [– OFr. *reclaim-*, tonic stem of (O)Fr. *réclamer* – L. *reclamare* cry out, exclaim; see RE-, CLAIM *v.*] **I.** *trans.* **†1. a.** *Falconry.* To call back (a hawk which has been let fly) –1741. Also *transf.* **b.** To call back; to recall –1741. **c.** To restrain, check, hold back –1700. **d.** To withdraw (a statement); to revoke (*rare*) –1741. **2.** To recall, bring back (a person or animal) *from* a wrong course of action, etc., *to* a proper state. late ME. **b.** To call back from wrong-doing or error; to reform 1577. **c.** To win back, win over (again). Also with *inf.* (*rare*) 1587. **d.** To put right, to remedy, correct, amend (an error, fault, etc.). *rare.* 1596. **3.** To reduce to obedience, tame, subdue (*esp.* a hawk, also rarely a person). late ME. **†b.** To keep the growth of (wood or trees) within bounds –1697. **c.** To remove (rude qualities) by means of instruction or culture; to bring (savage people) to a state of civilization 1760. **d.** To bring (waste land, etc.) under, or into a fit state for, cultivation 1764. **4.** To claim the restoration of, to demand or take back (a person or thing) 1450. **†5.** To cry out against (a thing or person); to gainsay –1650.

2. Henrietta had reclaimed him from a life of vice MACAULAY. **c.** Once alienated, [I doubt] whether he were ever to be reclaimed C. BRONTË. **d.** In reclaiming vulgar errors BACON. **3. c.** A fair field, ..with no aborigines to be protected or reclaimed 1865. **5.** Herod..in stead of reclaiming what they exclaimed,..hug'd their praises as proper to himself FULLER.

II. *intr.* **1.** To exclaim, protest. Now *rare.* 1440. **b.** With obj. clause. To declare or say in protest. 1449. **c.** *Sc. Law.* To appeal 1578. **†2.** To call out, cry loudly (*rare*) –1700. **†3. a.** To draw back; to recant (*rare*) –1604. **b.** To reform –1757.

1. The whole Context in Dionysius reclaims against this Emendation BENTLEY. **2.** One whisper'd soft, and one aloud reclaim'd DRYDEN. Hence **Reclai·mable** *a.* **Reclai·mant, Reclai·mer,** one who reclaims.

Reclamation (reklămēi·ʃən). 1533. [– Fr. *réclamation* or L. *reclamatio*, *-on-*, f. *reclamat-*, pa. ppl. stem of *reclamare*; see prec., -ION.] **1.** The action of protesting; a protest. **2.** The action of calling or bringing back from wrong-doing, reformation 1633. **b.** The action of reclaiming *from* barbarism 1868. **c.** The making (of land) fit for cultivation 1861. **3.** The action of claiming the return of something taken away; a claim *for* something 1787.

1. An act..done against the r. of the Law of Nature 1650.

‖**Réclame** (reklam). 1883. [Fr., f. *réclamer.*] The attainment of notoriety by 'puff' or advertisement.

Reclinant (rĭklai·nănt), *a.* 1850. [f. RECLINE + -ANT.] *Her.* Bending or bowed.

Reclinate (re·klineⁱt), *a.* 1753. [– L. *reclinatus*, pa. pple. of *reclinare* RECLINE; see -ATE².] Bending downward; esp. *Bot.* of stems, branches, leaves, etc.

Reclination (reklinēⁱ·ʃən). 1578. [– OFr. *reclination* or late L. *reclinatio*, f. *reclinat-*, pa. ppl. stem of L. *reclinare*; see prec., -ION.] **1.** The action, posture, or practice of reclining. Now *rare*. **†2.** *Dialling.* The angle made by the plane of the dial with a vertical point intersecting it –1797. **3.** *Surg.* An operation formerly used for cataract 1820.

3. 'R.' disposes of the cataract by tilting it backwards 1875.

Recline (rĭklai·n), *sb. rare.* 1753. [f. the vb.] A recumbent or reclining posture.

†Recli·ne, *a.* 1667. [– L. *reclinis*, f. *reclinare*; see next.] Recumbent, reclining. MILT.

Recline (rĭklai·n), *v.* late ME. [– OFr. *recliner* (in sense 2), reinforced from its source L. *reclinare* bend back, lay aside, recline, f. *re-* RE- + *-clinare* (cf. DECLINE, INCLINE).] **1.** *trans.* To lay down, or make to lie down (properly on the back); to cause to incline (backwards); to rest (the head, etc.) in this way. **†2.** *intr.* Of a dial: To have a backward inclination, to lie away back from the vertical –1797. **3.** To rest in a recumbent or inclined position, lean or repose *on* or *upon* something 1697. **b.** *Mil.* Of one extremity of an army: To rest *upon* a place (*rare*) 1850. **†4.** To fall backwards or down. GOLDSM.

1. The sonne of man haþe not wer he may reclyne ..his hede 1440. Thus oft, reclined at ease, I lose an hour At evening COWPER. **3.** The wood-crowned cliffs that o'er the lake r. WORDSW. Hence **Recli·ned** *ppl. a.* placed in a reclining position; characterized by recumbency. **Recli·ner**, one who or that which reclines; *spec.* a reclining dial or plane.

Reclining (rĭklai·niŋ), *ppl. a.* 1668. [f. prec. + -ING².] That reclines.

Dials..are called inclining or r. dials, according as their planes make acute or obtuse angles with the horizon 1797.

†Reclu·de, *v.* late ME. [– L. *recludere*; see next.] **1.** *trans.* To open (a gate, etc.) –1665. **2.** To shut up (a thing or person); to close –1843. **b.** To shut (a person) off *from* a thing –1657.

Recluse (rĭklū·s), *a.* and *sb.* ME. [– (O)Fr. *reclus*, fem. *recluse*, pa. pple. of *reclure* :– L. *recludere* (pa. pple. *reclusus*) shut up, (earlier) open, f. *re-* RE- + *claudere* CLOSE.] **A.** *adj.* **1.** Of persons: Shut up, secluded from society, esp. as a religious discipline. **2.** Of life, condition, etc.: Characterized by seclusion or close retirement 1645. **3.** Of places: Secluded, solitary. Now *rare*. 1652. **†b.** Of things, actions, etc.: Hidden, private –1783.

1. I have lived r. in rural shades COWPER. The example of r. philosophers 1865. **2.** His private habits were sober and r. GROTE. **3.** The most r. retreats 1782.

B. *sb.* **1. a.** A person shut up from the world for the purpose of religious meditation; a monk, anchorite or anchoress, *spec.* one who remains perpetually shut up in a cell under a vow of strict seclusion. **b.** One who mixes little with society. ME. **†2.** A place of seclusion –1772.

†Reclu·se, *v.* late ME. [– *reclus-*, pa. ppl. stem of L. *recludere*; see prec.] *trans.* To shut up, seclude –1713.

Reclusion (rĭklū·ʒən). late ME. [– med.L. *reclusio* shutting up, (monastic) seclusion, state of recluse, f. as prec.; see -ION.] **1.** The action of shutting up, or fact of being shut up, in seclusion; a state of retirement. **b.** The fact of being shut up as a prisoner, esp. in solitary confinement 1872. **2.** A place of religious retreat 1797.

Reclusive (rĭklū·siv), *a.* 1599. [f. RECLUSE *v.* + -IVE.] Marked by reclusion or retirement.

In some reclusiue and religious life, Out of all eyes SHAKS.

Reclusory (rĭklū·səri). 1821. [– med.L. *reclusorium*, f. *reclus-* (see RECLUSE *a.*) + *-orium* -ORY¹.] The cell of a recluse.

Recoct (rĭkǫ·kt), *v.* 1562. [– *recoct-*, pa. ppl. stem of L. *recoquere*, f. *re-* RE- + *coquere* cook.] *trans.* To boil or cook a second time; also *fig.* to vamp or furbish up anew. So **Reco·ction.**

Recognition (rekǫgni·ʃən). 1450. [– L. *recognitio*, *-on-*, f. *recognit-*, pa. ppl. stem of *recognoscere*; see RECOGNOSCE, -ION.] The act of recognizing. **†1.** Payment on the conclusion of a bargain. **†2.** *Sc. Law.* The resumption of lands by a feudal superior –1765. **†3.** Revision, recension –1862. **b.** *Hist.* The form of inquest by jury in use in England under the early Norman kings 1609. **4.** The action of acknowledging as true, valid, or entitled to consideration; formal acknowledgement as conveying approval or sanction of something; hence, notice or attention accorded to a thing or person 1597. **b.** The formal acknowledgement by subjects of (the title of) a sovereign or other ruler; *spec.* as the name of a part of the Coronation ceremony 1558. **5.** The acknowledgement or admission of a kindness, service, obligation, or merit, or the expression of this in some way. Now chiefly in phr. *in r. of.* 1570. **6.** The action or fact of perceiving that some thing, person, etc., is the same as one previously known; the mental process of identifying what has been known before; the fact of being thus known or identified 1798. **b.** The action or fact of apprehending a thing as having a certain character or belonging to a certain class 1881.

4. A fourth kind of publick reading, whereby the lives of such saints had..solemn r. in the church of God HOOKER. **6.** I could not escape r. 1866. **b.** The r. that certain things were not true 1881.

Recognitor (rĭkǫ·gnitǫɹ). Now *Hist.* 1574. [– AL. *recognitor*, f. as prec.; see -OR 2.] A member of a jury impanelled on an assize or inquest.

Recognitory (rĭkǫ·gnitəri), *a.* 1822. [app. f. RECOGNITION + -ORY².] Of or pertaining to recognition or acknowledgement.

Recognizable, -isable (re·kǫgnaizăb'l), *a.* 1799. [f. RECOGNIZE + -ABLE.] Capable of being recognized; that admits of recognition. Hence **Recognizabi·lity**, r. quality. **Re·cognizably** *adv.*

Recognizance, -isance (rĭkǫ·nizăns, rĭkǫ·gn-). late ME. [– OFr. *recon(n)issance* (mod. *reconnaissance*); see RE-, COGNIZANCE.] **1.** *Law.* A bond or obligation, entered into and recorded before a court or magistrate, by which a person engages himself to perform some act or observe some condition (as to appear when called on, to pay a debt, or to keep the peace); also, a sum of money pledged as a surety for such performance, and rendered forfeit by neglect of it. Usually *pl.* **2.** Recognition or acknowledgement (of a person as holding a certain position, of a fact, duty, right, service, etc.). Now *rare.* late ME. **b.** Recognition (of a person) as the same, or as having a known character. Now *rare.* 1489. **3.** A token, badge, emblem; a cognizance. Now *arch.* 1477.

3. That R. and pledge of Loue Which I first gaue her SHAKS.

Recognize, -ise (re·kǫgnaiz), *v.* 1531. [– OFr. *recon(n)iss-*, pr. stem of *reconnaistre* (mod. *reconnaître*) :– L. *recognoscere*; see RECOGNOSCE. Early forms *-nis*, *-nish* soon assim. to verbs in -IZE.] **†1.** *trans.* To look over again; to revise, correct, amend –1715. **†b.** To reconnoitre. Also *absol.* (*rare*) –1814. **†2.** To acknowledge by admission, confession, etc.; to admit (to oneself or another) –1641. **3.** To acknowledge by special notice, approval or sanction; to treat as valid, as having existence or as entitled to consideration; to take notice of (a thing or person) in some way 1548. **4.** To know again; to perceive to be identical with something previously known 1533. **b.** To know by means of some distinctive feature; to identify from knowledge of appearance or character 1725. **c.** To perceive clearly, realize 1865. **5.** *Law.* (rĭkǫ·gnaiz) **a.** *U.S. refl.* and *intr.* To enter into a recognizance 1699. **†b.** *trans.* To bind over by a recognizance –1809.

3. The only army which the law recognized was the militia MACAULAY. **4. b.** Without being able to express accurately all we mean by love, we r. it when we meet it 1876. **c.** Linnell has made us r. a new beauty in the heather 1865. Hence **Re·cognizer.**

Recognizee (rĭkǫg-, rĭkǫnizī·). 1544. [f. RECOGNIZE *v.* + -EE¹.] *Law.* The person to whom one is bound in a recognizance.

Recognizor (rĭkǫg-, rĭkǫnizǫ·ɹ). 1531. [f. as prec. + -OR 2 a.] *Law.* One who enters into a recognizance.

†Recognosce, *v.* 1533. [– L. *recognoscere*; see RE-, COGNOSCE.] *trans.* To recognize or acknowledge –1671.

Recoil (rĭkoi·l), *sb.* ME. [f. next.] **1.** The act of retreating, retiring, or going back. Now *rare.* **2.** The act of bounding or springing back, esp. through impact or elasticity; resilience 1613. **b.** *fig.* of feelings; *esp.* with ref. to shrinking *from* something 1643. **3.** *spec.* The rebound or 'kick' of a gun or firearm when discharged 1575.

2. We strain a bow and let its r. propel the arrow H. SPENCER. **b.** Indignant r. from ugliness RUSKIN.

Comb.: **r. escapement**, an escapement in clocks and watches, in which the teeth of the crown- or balance-wheel act on the pallets by r.; **r. pallet** a pallet in a r. escapement; **r. wave**, a dicrotic wave.

Recoil (rĭkoi·l), *v.* [ME. *recule*, etc. – (O)Fr. *reculer* – Rom. **reculare*, f. *re-* RE- + L. *culus* posteriors.] **†1.** *trans.* To beat, drive, or force back; to cause to retreat or retire –1713. **†b.** To return or retort (a thing) *upon* a person –1662. **2.** *intr.* To retreat, retire, go or draw *back* (or *aback*) before an enemy or opposite force. late ME. **b.** To stagger back (from a blow) 1533. **†3.** To go back (or backwards); to recede, retire, retreat, return –1651. **†b.** To fall back or away (from some state or condition), to degenerate (*rare*) –1611. **†c.** To go back in memory or in a narrative (*rare*) –1655. **†4.** To retire, withdraw oneself *to* a place –1627. **†b.** *fig.* To draw back *from* an act or course of action, a promise, etc. –1761. **5.** To start or spring back in fear, horror, disgust, or the like 1513. **6. a.** To rebound, to spring or fly back through force of impact 1581. **b.** Of firearms or artillery: To spring back by the force of the discharge 1530. **7.** To rebound, spring *back*, or return, to the starting-point or source. Chiefly *fig.* (now with *on*). 1599.

2. Skilfull darters who by recoyling are wont to gaine the day 1637. **b.** Ten paces huge He back recoild MILT. **3. c.** *Wint. T.* I. ii. 154. **4.** A whyle I read you rest, and to your bowres recoyle SPENSER. **5.** Back they recoild affraid At first, and call'd me Sin MILT. *fig.* The age..recoiled from the cool cynicism of his crimes 1874. **7.** The good or evil we confer on others, very often..recoils on ourselves FIELDING. Hence **Recoi·ler. Recoi·lingly** *adv.* **†Recoi·lment**, dismissal; the act of recoiling or springing back.

Recollect (re·kǫlekt), *sb.* 1626. [– med.L. *recollectus*, pa. pple. of L. *recolligere*; see next. Cf. Fr. *récollet* RECOLLET.] A member of an Observantine branch of the Franciscan order, which originated in Spain in the end of the 15th c., and was so named 'from the detachment from creatures and recollection in God which the founders aimed at' (*Catholic Dict.*).

Recollect (rĭkǫle·kt), *v.*¹ 1513. [– *recollect-*, pa. ppl. stem of L. *recolligere*, f. *re-* RE- + *colligere* COLLECT *v.* Later occas. written *re-collect*, as if f. RE- 5 a + COLLECT *v.*; see next.] **†1.** *trans.* To collect, gather –1670. **†b.** To collect *again* –1693. **2.** To collect, gather, or bring together (things or persons) again 1615. **b.** *intr.* To come together again (*rare*) 1631. **3.** *trans.* To collect (one's spirits, thoughts, mind, etc.) 1614. **4.** To gather or summon up (strength, courage, etc.); to rally; to recover by an effort 1655. **†5.** To bring back again *to* or *from* some position or state; to withdraw (oneself) *from* –1655.

2. How dust scattered and blown up and down should be recollected 1655. **3.** He was timorous and bashful; but, when the talk became regular, he recollected his powers JOHNSON. **4.** Then soon Fierce hate he recollects, and all his thoughts Of mischief..thus excites MILT.

Recollect (rekǫle·kt), *v.*² 1559. [f. as prec., but now differentiated by the pronunciation.] **1.** *trans.* To call or bring back (something) to one's mind; to recall the knowledge of (a thing, person, etc.). **†2.** To reflect *with* (oneself) –1719. **3.** To concentrate or absorb (the mind, oneself, etc.) in contemplation; *spec.* in mystical religious use 1671. **4.** *refl.* To bring (oneself) back to a state of composure; to recover (oneself). Also const. *from*. Now *rare*. 1639.

1. Recollecting still that he is man, We trust him not too far COWPER. *absol*. To remember and to r. are different things JOHNSON. 'I can't remember.' 'But try and recollect' (*mod*.). 4. His heart beat violently, and he..stopped, to r. himself MAR. EDGEWORTH. Hence **Recolle·ctable** *a*.

Recollection[1] (rīkǫle·kʃən). 1598. [– Fr. *récollection* or med.L. *recollectio, -on-*, f. *recollect-*; see RECOLLECT *v.*[1], -ION.] **1.** A gathering together again. **2.** A recapitulation –1659.

Recollection[2] (rekǫle·kʃən). 1642. [Same wd. as prec. in special senses]. **1.** Religious or serious concentration of thought; †conduct regulated by this. **2.** Composure, calmness of mind, self-possession 1757. **3.** The act of recalling to the memory; the mental operation by which objects or ideas are revived in the mind; also, an instance of this 1683. **b.** The power of recalling to the mind; the sphere or period over which such power extends; the memory 1732. **4.** A thing or fact recalled to the mind; the memory *of* something 1781. **5.** *pl.* A message expressing recollection of, or a desire to be recollected by, another 1816.

3. The power of r. seems to depend on the intensity or largeness of the perception JOWETT. **b.** The scene of the preceding night ran in his r. SCOTT. 4. A r. or a fresh tradition 1883.

Recollective (rekǫle·ktiv), *a*. 1789. [f. RECOLLECT *v.*[2] + -IVE.] **1.** Relating to, characterized by, concerned with, recollection. **2.** Given to, distinguished by (the power of), occupied with, recollection 1813.

‖**Recollet** (rekole). 1695. [Fr. *récollet*; see RECOLLECT *sb.*] = RECOLLECT *sb.*

†**Reco·mfort**, *sb.* late ME. [– (O)Fr. *reconfort*; see RE-, COMFORT *sb.*] Comfort, support, consolation –1605. Hence †**Reco·mfortless** *a.* without comfort.

Recomfort (rīkɒ·mfəɹt), *v. Obs.* exc. *arch.* late ME. [– (O)Fr. *reconforter*; see RE-, COMFORT *v.*] **1.** *trans.* †**a.** To strengthen or inspire with fresh courage –1667. **b.** To soothe, console, or relieve in distress or trouble. Now *rare*. late ME. †**c.** *refl.* and *absol.* To take courage or heart again –1654. **2.** *trans.* (Usu. of things): To strengthen or invigorate physically; to refresh. Also *absol.* Now *rare*. late ME.

1. **a.** As one from sad dismay Recomforted MILT. 2. My weary frame After short pause recomforted, again I journey'd CARY. Hence †**Reco·mforture**, consolation, comfort SHAKS.

Recommence (rīkǫme·ns), *v.* 1481. [– (O)Fr. *recommencer*; see RE-, COMMENCE *v.*] **1.** *intr.* To begin again. **b.** With complement 1778. **2.** *trans.* To cause to begin again; to renew 1494.

2. The two brothers r. their exhortation to virtue JOWETT. So **Recomme·ncement**, a second commencement.

Recommend (rekǫme·nd), *v.* late ME. [– med.L. *recommendare*, f. *re-* RE- + L. *commendare* COMMEND.] **1.** To commend or commit (oneself or another, one's soul or spirit) *to* God, his keeping, etc. Also (rarely) without const. **b.** (Chiefly *refl.*) To commit (oneself or another) *to* a person (or thing), or *to* some one's care, prayers, etc. late ME. †**c.** To give in charge, consign, commit, submit (a thing) *to* a person or thing –1601. †**d.** To communicate (a thing) *to* a person. Also without const., to mention. –1641. †**c.** To inform (a person). SHAKS. †**2.** *refl.* and *absol.* To commend (oneself) to the kindly remembrance of another –1572. †**b.** To speak of (a person) to another, with a view to exciting kindly remembrance –1773. †**3.** To praise, commend –1738. **4. a.** To name or speak of (a person) as fit or worthy to hold some position or employment 1641. **b.** To present or bring forward (a person) as worthy of notice, favour, care, etc. Const. *to* (a person, etc.) *for* (the thing desired). 1647. **5.** To mention or introduce (a thing) with approbation or commendation (*to* a person), in order to induce acceptance or trial 1581. **6.** To make (a person or thing) acceptable. (Chiefly of qualities, circumstances, or things). Also *refl.* 1605. **7.** To counsel, advise 1733.

1. When I lay me down to Sleep, I r. myself to his Care ADDISON. **c.** *Twel. N.* V. i. 94. 2. **b.** R. me to the poor dear lady JOHNSON. 4. **b.** The trouble I gave in recommending a gentleman to your protection SWIFT. 5. Allow me..to r. this dish SHELLEY. We will conclude by recommending his work to our readers 1863. 6. That man has little enough to r. him whom women dislike 1863. 7. He recommended, that the whole disposition of the camp should be changed 1829. Hence **Recomme·ndable** *a.* that may be recommended. **Recomme·ndableness. Recomme·ndably** *adv.* **Recomme·nder.**

Recommendation (re:kǫmendēⁱ·ʃən). 1450. [– OFr. *recommendation* (mod. *-and-*) or med.L. *recommendatio, -on-*, f. *recommendat-*, pa. ppl. stem of *recommendare*; see prec., -ION.] †**1.** The action of recommending oneself to another's remembrance; a message of this nature –1634. †**2.** Commendation, favour, repute, esteem –1585. **3.** The action of recommending a person or thing as worthy or desirable 1578. **b.** A letter or certificate of recommendation 1645. **4.** That which procures a favourable reception or acceptance 1647. **5.** Exhortation, advice 1585.

3. Buying at his Shop upon my R. STEELE. *Letter of r.*, a letter recommending a person; in later use, a letter of introduction. 4. Upon no other..r., than of the Beauty..of his Person CLARENDON.

†**Recomme·ndative**, *a.* and *sb. rare*. 1611. [f. RECOMMEND *v.* + -ATIVE.] **A.** *adj.* That recommends. **B.** *sb.* That which recommends. –1727.

Recommendatory (rekǫme·ndătəri), *a.* 1611. [f. RECOMMEND *v.*, after COMMENDATORY *a.*] **1.** Having the attribute of recommending; expressing or conveying a recommendation. **2.** Of a quality, feature, etc.: That recommends its possessor 1709. **3.** Of a resolution, appointment, etc.: In the form of a recommendation, without binding force 1690.

1. *R. letter*, a letter of recommendation.

Recommit (rīkǫmi·t), *v.* 1621. [RE- 5 a.] **1.** *trans.* To send or refer (a bill, etc.) back to a committee. **b.** To entrust (a person or thing) again *to* a person 1783. **2.** To commit (a person) again (*to* a court, prison, etc.) 1647. **3.** To commit or do (an action) again 1647.

1. Ordered, That the said Act be re-committed for several Amendments 1729. So **Recommi·tment, Recommi·ttal**, a renewed commitment or committal.

Recompensation (rī:kǫmpĕnsēⁱ·ʃən). late ME. [– OFr. *recompensacion* – late L. *recompensatio, -on-*, f. *recompensat-*, pa. ppl. stem of *recompensare*; see RECOMPENSE *v.*, -ION.] †**1.** = next 1715. **2.** *Sc. Law.* In actions for debt, a counter-plea of compensation raised by a pursuer to meet the defendant's plea of compensation 1681.

Recompense (re·kǫmpens), *sb.* Also **-pence.** late ME. [– (O)Fr. *récompense*, f. *récompenser*; see next. Cf. med.L. *recompensa* (XIII).] **1.** Reparation or restitution made to another for some wrong done to him; atonement or satisfaction for some misdeed or offence. **2.** Compensation (received or desired) for some loss or injury sustained 1508. **3.** Return or repayment for something given or received 1473. **4.** Compensation or return for trouble, exertion, services or merit 1500. **5.** Retribution for some injury or offence 1538.

1. Sin cannot be taken away by recompence HOBBES. 2. Have you secured no r. for such a waste of honour? '*Junius' Lett.* 4. His lovely words her seem'd due r. Of all her passed paines SPENSER. 5. Such is the tyrant's r.: 'tis just: He who is evil can receive no good SHELLEY.

Recompense (re·kǫmpens), *v.* Also **-pence.** late ME. [– (O)Fr. *récompenser* – late L. *recompensare*, f. *re-* RE- + L. *compensare* COMPENSATE.] **1.** *trans.* To reward, requite, repay (a person) for something done or given. **b.** To compensate (a person) *for* some loss or injury sustained 1477. **2. a.** To make up for (some loss, injury, defect, etc.); †to take the place of. late ME. **b.** To make compensation or atonement for (a misdeed, wrong, etc.) 1450. **c.** To make a return or requital for (something done or given) 1530. †**3.** To mete out in requital –1535. **4.** *intr.* To make repayment, return, or amends. late ME.

1. *absol.* Be his To r., who sees and can reward thee CARY. 2. **a.** The length of the journey will be recompensed by the goodness of the way FULLER. **b.** In some part to r. My rash but more unfortunate misdeed MILT. 3. Recompence to no man evyll for evyll TINDALE *Rom.* 12:17. Hence **Re·compenser** (*rare*), one who or that which recompenses. **Re·compensive** *a.* (*rare*) that recompenses.

Recompose (rīkǫmpōᵘ·z), *v.* 1611. [RE- 5 a. Cf. Fr. *récomposer*.] **1.** *trans.* To put together again; to form again by composition. Chiefly in antithesis to *decompose*. **2.** To put together in a new form or manner; to rearrange 1816. **3.** To restore to composure. Also *refl.* 1649. **4.** To restore to harmony 1856.

1. Whatever is decomposed may be recomposed by the being who first composed it PRIESTLEY. 3. I shall never r. my features to receive Sir Rowland CONGREVE. Our spirits, when disordered, are not to be recomposed in a moment FIELDING. 4. To r. the quarrels in the church 1856. Hence **Recompo·ser** (*rare*). **Recomposition** (rī:kǫmpǒzi·ʃən), the action or process of recomposing.

Reconcilable (re·kǫnsəilăb'l), *a.* Also **-cileable.** 1612. [f. next + -ABLE.] **1.** Of statements, opinions, facts, etc.: Capable of being mutually reconciled. **2.** Capable of being reconciled *with* something 1640. Also const. *to* (now *rare*), and †*ellipt.* without const. **3.** Of persons, their natures, etc.: Easily conciliated or reconciled. Now *rare*. 1621. **4.** Admitting of reconciliation MILT.

1. The opposite yet reconcileable vices of rapaciousness and prodigality GIBBON. 3. A peaceable and r. inclination 1621. Hence **Re·concilableness. Re·concilably** *adv.*

Reconcile (re·kǫnsəil), *v.* ME. [– (O)Fr. *réconcilier* or L. *reconciliare*, f. *re-* RE- + *conciliare* CONCILIATE.] **I. 1.** *trans.* To bring (a person) again into friendly relations *to* or *with* (oneself or another) after an estrangement. †**b.** To recommend, make agreeable CLARENDON. **2.** To win over (a person) again to friendship with oneself or another. late ME. **3.** To set (estranged persons or parties) at one again; to bring back into concord, to reunite (persons or things) in harmony. late ME. †**4.** To bring (a person) back *to*, *into* peace, favour, etc. Also *refl.* –1594. †**5.** To bring back, restore, or readmit to the Church, *spec.* the Church of Rome –1715. **b.** *pass.* and *refl.* To become united *to* a church 1639. **6.** *Eccl.* To purify (a church, etc.) by a special service after profanation. late ME. †**7.** To conciliate, recover (a person's favour, etc.); to gain (credit) –1665. **8.** To bring into a state of acquiescence (†*with*) or submission *to* a thing. Also *refl.* and with *inf.* 1606.

1. *refl.* Thou mightst..r. thyself with thine own heart And with thy God SHELLEY. **b.** His courtesy and affability..marvellously reconciled [him] to all men 1647. 2. The Gods are hard to r. TENNYSON. 3. Let it be mine honour..That I haue reconcil'd your friends and you SHAKS. 8. Trials often r. us to that, which..we looked on with aversion LOCKE.

II. 1. To adjust, settle, bring to agreement (a controversy, quarrel, etc.). late ME. **2.** To make (discordant facts, statements, etc.) consistent, accordant, or compatible with each other 1560. **3.** To make (an action, condition, quality, etc.) compatible or consistent in fact or in one's mind *with* another; to regard as consistent *with*. Also const. *to*. 1624. **b.** To make (a theory, statement, author, etc.) agree *with* another or with a fact; to show to be in agreement *with*. Const. *to*. 1613. **4.** To make even or smooth, or fit together so as to present a uniform surface 1687.

1. The quarrel was..reconciled FIELDING. 2. Such welcome, and vnwelcom things at once, 'Tis hard to r. SHAKS. 3. A soul..That reconciled the sword unto the pen, Using both well 1624. **b.** A plain matter of fact, which men cannot r. with the general account they think fit to give of things BUTLER. Hence **Re·concilement**, reconciliation. **Re·conciler**, one who or that which reconciles; *spec.* applied to Christ.

Reconciliation (re:kǫnsili,ēⁱ·ʃən). ME. [– Fr. *réconciliation* or L. *reconciliatio, -on-*, f. *reconciliat-*, pa. ppl. stem of *reconciliare*; see prec., -ION.] **1.** The action of reconciling persons or the result of this; the fact of being reconciled. late ME. **b.** *spec.* in religious use, of God and man ME. **2.** Reunion of a person to a church 1625. **3.** The purification, or restoration to sacred uses, of a church, etc., after desecration or pollution 1533. **4.** The action of bringing to agreement, concord, or harmony 1560.

1. And so kissed me as a mark of r. RICHARDSON. 4. The absence of any appearance of r. between the theory and practice of life EMERSON.

Reconciliatory (rekǫnsi·liătəri), *a.* 1586.

[– Fr. †*réconciliatoire* (XVI), or f. †*reconciliate* vb. (XVIII); see -ORY². Cf. eccl.L. *reconciliatorius*.] Of words, actions, etc.: Tending to reconciliation.

Recondite (re·kǫ̆ndəit, rĭkǫ·ndəit), *a.* 1649. [– L. *reconditus*, pa. pple. of *recondere* put away, hide, f. *re-* RE- + *condere* put together, compose, hide.] **1.** Of things: Removed or hidden from view; kept out of sight. Now *rare*. **2.** Removed from ordinary apprehension, understanding, or knowledge; deep, profound, abstruse 1652. **b.** Of learning, investigation, discussion, etc.: Consisting in, relating to, uncommon or profound knowledge 1654. **c.** Of writers, sources, etc.: Obscure, little known 1817. **3.** Of persons: Writing in an obscure fashion 1788.

2. The r. principles of philosophy 1772. **c.** The traditional edition of a r. classical author 1865. Hence **Re·condite-ly** *adv.*, **-ness.**

†**Reco·nditory.** 1633. [– med.L. *reconditorium* repository for documents, relics, etc., storehouse, f. as prec.; see -ORIUM, -ORY¹.] A store-house, repository –1685.

Reconnaissance (rĭkǫ·nĕsăns). 1810. [– Fr. *reconnaissance*, †*-oissance*, f. stem of *reconnaître*, later form of †*reconnoître*; see RECONNOITRE *v.*, -ANCE]. **1.** *Mil.* An examination or survey of a tract of country, made with a view to ascertain the position or strength of an enemy, or to discover the nature of the ground or resources of a district before making an advance. Also *Naval*, a survey of a coast, etc. made for similar purposes. **b.** A body of troops sent to reconnoitre 1811. **2.** *transf.* A survey of a district made for practical or scientific purposes 1838. **3.** Without article: Reconnoitring, surveying 1887.

1. *R. in force*, an advance made with a considerable body of troops to discover the position of the enemy.

Reconnoissance (rĭkǫ·nisăns). 1672. Older spelling (now disused) of prec., used in senses of RECOGNIZANCE and RECONNAISSANCE.

Reconnoi·tre, *sb.* 1799. [f. next.] An act of reconnoitring; a reconnaissance.

Reconnoitre (rekǫ̆noi·təɹ), *v.* 1707. [– Fr. *reconnoître* (now *reconnaître*) :– L. *recognoscere* look over, inspect; see RECOGNIZE.] **1.** *trans. Mil.* (and *Naval*). To make an inspection or take observations of (an enemy, his strength, position, etc.). Also *transf.* **2.** *Mil.* To inspect, examine, or survey (a district or tract of ground) in order to discover the presence or position of an enemy, or to find out the resources or military features of the country. Also *transf.* 1726. **3.** *absol.* or *intr.* To make a reconnaissance 1712. †**4.** *trans.* To recollect, remember, recognize –1787.

4. Whether, if the dead of past ages could revive, they would be able to r. the events of their own times, as transmitted to us H. WALPOLE.

Reconsider (rīkǫ̆nsi·dəɹ), *v.* 1571. [f. RE- 5 a + CONSIDER. Cf. Fr. *reconsidérer* (XVI).] **1.** *trans.* To consider (a matter or thing) again. **b.** To consider (a decision, etc.) a second time with a view to changing or amending it; to rescind, alter 1849. **2.** *refl.* To reflect on one's conduct, with a view to repentance or amendment (*rare*) 1855. **Re-considera·tion.**

Reconstitution (rī:kǫnstitiū·ʃən). 1853. [RE- 5 a. Cf. Fr. *reconstitution.*] A fresh constitution. **b.** In French criminal procedure, the action of going over the supposed details of a crime at the place where it was committed 1897.

Reconstruct (rĭkǫ̆nstrɒ·kt), *v.* 1768. [RE- 5 a.] **1.** *trans.* To construct anew. **2.** To construct anew in the mind; to restore (something past) mentally 1862. **3.** *U.S.* To win over or reconcile to the Federal system of government 1904.

Reconstruction (rĭkǫ̆nstrɒ·kʃən). 1791. [RE- 5 a.] **1.** The action or process of reconstructing. **b.** *U.S. Hist.* The process by which after the Civil War the States which had seceded were restored to the rights and privileges of the Union 1865. **2.** An instance or example of reconstructing; a thing reconstructed 1795.

Reconstructive (rī:kǫnstrɒ·ktiv), *a.* and *sb.* 1862. [f. RECONSTRUCT + -IVE.] **A.** *adj.* Related to, concerned with, reconstruction. **B.** *sb.* That which reconstructs, a reconstituent 1890.

†**Reconti·nuance.** 1540. [f. RECONTINUE *v.* + -ANCE.] The act of recontinuing; resumption –1631.

Reconti·nue, *v. rare.* late ME. [– OFr. *recontinuer*; see RE- 5 a, CONTINUE.] *trans.* To go on again with (an action, occupation, state, etc., which has been discontinued).

Reconvention (rīkǫ̆nve·nʃən). 1449. [– (O)Fr. *reconvention* or med.L. *reconventio, -on-*; see RE-, CONVENTION.] †**1.** An agreement made in return PECOCK. **2.** *Law.* A counter-charge; a counter-action brought against the plaintiff by the defendant in a suit 1538. †**3.** The reassembling (of Parliament, etc.) –1664.

Reconvert (rīkǫ̆nvɔ̄·ɹt), *v.* 1611. [RE- 5 a. Cf. Fr. *reconvertir* (XVI), med.L. *reconvertere.*] **1.** *trans.* To convert back to a previous state. **2.** *Logic.* To transpose again the subject and predicate of (a proposition) 1864. **3.** *Law.* To change back again into something of equivalent value 1884.

1. I myself having known many Papists..reconverted WESLEY. The air was re-converted into water 1783. So **Reconve·rsion. Reconve·rtible** *a.* capable of being reconverted.

Reconvey (rīkǫ̆nvē¹·), *v.* 1506. [RE- 5 a.] **1.** *trans.* To convey (†or escort) back to a previous place or position; to convey in a reverse direction. Now *rare*. **2.** *Law.* To make over again or restore to a former owner 1665.

1. The water..would be reconveyed to the sea at ebb tide 1846. So **Reconvey·ance,** the act of reconveying; *spec.* in *Law*, restoration to a former owner.

Record (re·kǫɹd), *sb.* ME. [– (O)Fr. *record* remembrance, f. *recorder*; see next.] **I. 1.** *Law.* The fact or attribute of being, or of having been, committed to writing as authentic evidence of a matter having legal importance, *spec.* as evidence of the proceedings or verdict of a court of justice; evidence which is thus preserved, and may be appealed to in case of dispute. **2.** The fact or condition of being preserved as knowledge, *esp.* by being put into writing; knowledge or information preserved or handed down in this way. Freq. in phrases (†*of*,) *on* or *upon r.* late ME. †**3.** Attestation or testimony of a fact; witness, evidence, proof –1646. †**b.** A witness –1768.

1. These Estates are created by word, by writing, or by r. BACON. Phr. *Matter* (*thing, debt*, etc.) *of r. Court of r.*, a court whose proceedings are formally enrolled and valid as evidence of fact, being also a court of the sovereign, and having the authority to fine or imprison. So †*Judge of r.* **2.** Having beaten the highest break on r. 1884. **3.** *To bear r.*, to bear witness; Iohn bare r., saying [etc.] *John* 1:32. *To take* or *call to r.*, to call to witness. **b.** God is my r.,..that I do not speak it vauntingly STERNE.

II. 1. *Law.* An authentic or official report of the proceedings in any cause coming before a court of record, together with the judgement given thereon, entered upon the rolls of court and affording indisputable evidence of the matter in question 1455. **b.** A copy of the material points, pleadings, and issue between defendant and plaintiff on a matter of law, constituting the case to be decided by the court; hence, a case so constituted or presented 1627. **2.** An account of some fact or event preserved in writing or other permanent form; a document, monument, etc., on which such an account is inscribed; also *transf.* any thing or person serving to indicate or give evidence of, or preserve the memory of, a fact, or event; a memorial. Freq. in *pl.* a collection of such accounts, etc. Also, in recent use, a tracing or series of marks, made by a recording instrument. 1611. **b.** In full *gramophone r.*, the disc of wax, etc., bearing the record of the sounds to be reproduced by the gramophone 1896. **c.** The leading facts in the life or career of a person, *esp.* of a public man; the sum of what one has done or achieved (orig. *U.S.*) 1856. **d.** A performance or occurrence going beyond others of the same kind; *spec.* the best recorded achievement in any competitive sport. Freq. in phr. *to beat* or *break the r.*: to surpass all previous performances. 1883.

1. Phr. *To travel out of the r.*, to take notice of any thing that does not appear in it. Also *transf.*, to go off the subject. So *to keep to the r.* **2.** *Ezra* 6:2. **e.** Phr. (Chiefly *U.S.*) *To put* (oneself) *on r.*, to give (oneself) a place among recorded things; to express one's opinion; also *to go on r.*

†**III. 1.** Reputation, repute, account –1470. **2.** Memory, remembrance, recollection –1601.

2. O that r. is liuely in my soule SHAKS.

IV. *Comb.* as *r.-breaker, -breaking, -maker, -making.* **b.** passing into *adj.* = largest, best, etc. recorded or on record 1893.

Record (rĭkǭ·ɹd), *v.* ME. [– (O)Fr. *recorder* bring to remembrance :– L. *recordare*, usu. *-ari* think over, be mindful of, f. *re-* RE- + *cor, cord-* heart.] **I.** †**1.** *trans.* **a.** To get by heart, to go over in one's mind. **b.** To say over as a lesson, to recite. –1656. **2.** To practise (a song, tune, etc.). In later use only of birds. late ME. †**b.** To sing of or about (something); to render in song –1597. **3.** *intr.* Of birds (rarely of persons): To practise or sing a tune in an undertone; to go over it quietly or silently. Now *techn.* 1510. †**b.** To sing or warble –1616.

2. **b.** Here can I..to the Nightingales complaining Notes Tune my distresses, and r. my woes SHAKS. **3.** The young males continue practising, or, as the bird-catchers say, recording, for ten or eleven months DARWIN.

†**II. 1.** *trans.* To call to mind, to recall, remember –1460. **2.** To meditate, ponder (something) *with* oneself –1586. **3.** To think or meditate *on* a thing or person –1604.

3. Recorde on..Parys the fayre citee LYDG.

III. †**1.** *trans.* To relate in words; to tell or narrate orally –1738. **2.** To relate in writing; to put or set down in writing; to put on record. Also, in recent use, of telegraphic and other instruments: To set down (a message, etc.) in some permanent form; also *absol.*, of an instrument, etc., to be recorded thus for reproduction by a gramophone. ME. **b.** To have properly recorded; to give (a verdict or vote) 1596. †**3.** To bear witness to (a fact, etc.); to attest, confirm. Also *absol.*, To testify. –1607. †**b.** To call to witness. MARLOWE.

2. The last words of his that are recorded, are worthy the greatness of his soul W. IRVING. **b.** There is only one verdict which those who disapprove of it can r. 1884. **3.** *Timon* IV. ii. 4. Hence **Reco·rdable** *a.* capable of being recorded.

†**Reco·rdance.** *rare.* 1450. [– OFr. *recordance*, or f. RECORD *v.* + -ANCE.] Recording, setting on record; remembrance –1630.

Recordation (rekǫɹdē¹·ʃən). late ME. [– OFr. *recordation* or L. *recordatio, -on-*, f. *recordat-*, pa. ppl. stem of *recordari*; see RECORD *v.*, -ION.] †**1.** The faculty of remembering or recollecting –1666. †**2.** Remembrance or recollection *of* something –1748. †**3.** An act of commemorating or making mention; a commemorative account –1670. **4.** The action or process of recording or committing to writing 1802.

Recordative (rĭkǭ·ɹdătiv), *a.* 1551. [– Fr. †*recordatif* (XVI) or late and med.L. *recordativus*, f. as prec.; see -IVE.] Commemorative.

Recorder¹ (rĭkǭ·ɹdəɹ). late ME. [– AFr. *recordour*, OFr. *-eur, f. recorder*; see RECORD *v.*, -ER² 3; later, partly f. RECORD *v.* + -ER¹.] **1.** A certain magistrate or judge having criminal and civil jurisdiction in a city or borough.

The Recorder was orig. a person with legal knowledge appointed by the mayor and aldermen to 'record' or keep in mind the proceedings of their courts and the customs of the city, his oral statement of these being taken as the highest evidence of fact. The Recorder of London is still appointed by the court of aldermen; in other cities and boroughs the appointment is made by the crown.

†**b.** The chief justice of an East Indian settlement –1800. **2.** One who records or sets down in writing 1537. **3.** A recording apparatus; *esp.* a device in a telegraphic instrument for recording the signals received 1873. Hence **Reco·rdership,** the office, or term of office, of a r. 1484.

Reco·rder². late ME. [f. RECORD *v.* (I. 2, 3) + -ER¹.] A wind instrument of the flute or flageolet kind. †**b.** One of the pipes of an organ –1650.

One of them plaied on a Lute;..another made a maruellous sweet countertenour vpon a R. 1598.

Recording (rĭkǭ·ɹdiŋ), *ppl. a.* 1761. [f.

RECORD *v.* + -ING².] That records, now *esp.* in phr. *r. angel.*

Recount (rī·kau·nt, rī·kaunt), *sb.* 1884. [RE- 5 a.] A new count; a second or subsequent enumeration (*esp.* of votes in an election). So **Re:cou·nt** *v.*² *trans.* to count or reckon over again 1764.

Recount (rĭkau·nt), *v.*¹ 1456. [– AFr., ONFr. *reconter*, f. *re-* RE- + *conter* COUNT *v.*] **1.** *trans.* To relate or narrate; to give a full or detailed account of (some fact, event, etc.). **b.** (With pl. obj.) To relate in order; to enumerate by particulars 1483. †**2.** To regard, consider, or account (a person or thing) as possessing a certain character or quality –1661. †**3.** *intr.* and *trans.* To reckon, count *up* –1647.

1. b. To r. Almightie works What words or tongue of Seraph can suffice? MILT. Hence †**Recou·ntment**, relation, recital SHAKS.

Recoup (rĭkū·p), *v.* late ME. [– OFr. *recouper* retrench, cut back, f. *re-* RE- + *couper* cut.] †**1.** *trans.* To cut short, interrupt –late ME. **2.** *Law.* To deduct; to take off or keep back. Also *absol.* to make a deduction. 1628. **3.** (With double obj.) To recompense (a person) for (some loss or outlay); to make up or make good (loss, etc.) to (a person) 1664. **b.** To recompense, repay (a person). Freq. *refl.* to recover what one has expended or lost. 1862. **4.** To make up for, make good 1860. **b.** To yield in return 1868.

2. The defendant might r. damages for a breach of warranty for the thing sold 1869. **4.** How to r. the loss occasioned to the State revenue by the abolition of the salt tax 1880. Hence **Recou·pment**, the act of recouping or recompensing; the fact of being recouped for loss or expense.

Recourse (rĭkō³·ɹs), *sb.* late ME. [– (O)Fr. *recours* :– L. *recursus*; see RE-, COURSE *sb.*] †**1.** A running, coming, or flowing back, a return, refluence; also, opportunity or passage to return –1694. †**b.** A periodical recurrence –1677. †**2.** Course, movement, or flow in some direction; a course, passage, or path *to* or *into* something –1653. †**b.** The ebb and flow of the tide –1622. **3.** Resort *to* some person or thing for assistance, help, or safety. late ME. **4.** The thing, means, or person applied or resorted to for help, etc. 1440. **b.** *Law* (chiefly *Sc.*). The right to demand pecuniary compensation from some one; *esp.* the right when the holder of a bill of exchange has to come back upon the drawer and endorsers if the acceptor fails to meet it 1747. †**5.** Usual or habitual going or resorting to a particular place –1705. †**b.** Gathering or concourse (of people) at a particular time –1656. †**6.** Opportunity of resorting *to* a person; access, admission –1594.

1. The r. of the Blood into the Heart is hindred 1668. **3.** *To have* (*a*) *r. to*, to apply to (a person, etc.) for help, advice, or information; If threats.. proved ineffectual, he had often r. to violence GIBBON. **4.** This is their usual r., when they are hard pressed by inconsistencies 1774. **5.** They had their place of r. or rendevouz 1658. **6.** I, but the doores be lockt,..That no man hath r. to her by night SHAKS. Hence †**Recou·rseful** *a.* flowing back; ebbing and flowing.

Recourse (rĭkō³·ɹs), *v.* 1500. [f. prec.] †**1.** *intr.* To run back, return (*to* a place) –1632. **2.** Const. *to.* To have recourse to, to fall back on. Now *rare* or *Obs.* 1586.

1. The flame departyng and recoursing thrise ere the woode tooke strength..to consume him FOXE.

Recover (rĭkʊ·vəɹ), *sb.* ME. [orig. – OFr. *recovre*, f. *recovrer* RECOVER *v.*¹; later, f. the vb.] †**1.** Recovery, or means of recovery –1631. **2.** The act of bringing or coming back to a former position 1819. †**b.** *Mil.* (chiefly in phr. *at, on,* or *to the r.*). A position of the firearm forming part of the manual exercise –1847.

Recover (rĭkʊ·vəɹ), *v.*¹ ME. [– AFr. *recoverer*, OFr. *recovrer* (mod. *recouvrer*) – L. *recuperare* RECUPERATE.] **I.** *trans.* **1.** To get (†occas., to take) back again into one's hands or possession; to regain possession of (something lost or taken away). late ME. **b.** To regain (country, territory, etc.) by conquest or main force; to win back (ground lost in fighting). late ME. **c.** To find again, come upon a second time 1611. **d.** To reclaim (land) *from* the sea 1793. **2.** To regain, acquire again, resume, return to (health, strength, one's feet, etc.) ME. **3.** To bring, draw, or win back (a person) to friendship or willing obedience; to reconcile 1576. †**4.** To get in place of, or in return for, something else –1525. **5.** *Law.* To get back or gain by judgement in a court of law; to obtain possession of, or a right to, by legal process. late ME. **b.** To have (a judgement or verdict) given in one's favour 1768. †**6.** To get or obtain; to get hold of –1661. **b.** To get (the wind of one). *Obs.* exc. *arch.* 1602. **7.** To get to, reach, arrive at, gain (some place or point). Now *rare.* ME. **8.** To get back for another; to bring back, restore. Const. *to* or *unto* a person, country, etc. 1484. **9.** To restore or bring back (usu. a person) to life or consciousness, late ME. **b.** To restore (a person or animal) to health or strength; to cure, heal 1579. **c.** In passive, *To be recovered*, to be well again ME. †**10.** To restore (a person or thing) to a good or proper estate or condition; to set or make right again –1731. **11.** To rescue or reclaim (a person) *from* or *out of* a state, etc. 1614. **12. a.** To bring back (a weapon) to a certain position 1594. **b.** To pull back (a horse) on to its feet again 1646. **13.** To get over, get better from (a sickness, misfortune, or affliction) ME. **b.** To annul the effect of (a slip, stumble, etc.) 1748. **14.** To retrieve, make good, make up for (loss, damage, etc. to oneself). late ME. **15.** To put right, remedy (something wrong, a fault, etc.). Now *rare.* late ME.

1. For tyme y-lost..Be no way may recoverd be CHAUCER. Humanity had lost its title-deeds, and he had recovered them MORLEY. **2.** The Lead.. will not of it self r. its Sphæricity BOYLE. They stopped to r. their wind MARRYAT. I had by this time recovered my usual health 1849. **3.** Harold's way of recovering rebels differed widely from William's FREEMAN. **4.** For every wo ye shall r. a blisse CHAUCER. **5.** This Law..enabled the Clergy to..r. Tithes 1710. An action to r. damages for false imprisonment 1891. **b.** A defendant, against whom judgment is recovered BLACKSTONE. **7.** Without a pocket-compass..I should never have recovered the Fair Isle, for which we run SCOTT. **8.** So had the glory of Prowess been recover'd To Palestine MILT. **9.** From Death to Life, thou mights't him yet r. DRAYTON. The squire suddenly recovered her by calling for..a bucket of water 1841. **11.** So men will be well guarded, or recovered from false Religions LOCKE. **12.** *To r. arms*, a position of the firelock when the piece is held with the lock equal to the left shoulder, and the sling to the front 1802. **13. b.** To r. so terrible a stumble 1768. **14.** Many..losses..which he was not able to r. 1682. **14.** To r. the mischief he had done..was difficult 1869.

II. *refl.* **1. a.** To regain one's natural position or balance. late ME. **b.** To return to life or consciousness 1597. **c.** To get over a loss or misfortune; to recoup oneself (*rare*) 1645. **d.** To get over fatigue or illness. †Also const. *of.* 1745. **2.** †**a.** To retreat, retire *into* a place; to fall back *on* one as an authority –1655. **b.** To withdraw or escape *from* or *out of*, to return *to*, a position, state, or condition. Now *rare.* 1611.

1. a. We daily see..rope-dauncers..handsomly r. themselves after a perillous staggering and reeling 1638. **2. b.** That they may recouer themselues out of the snare of the deuill 2 *Tim.* 2:26.

III. *intr.* or *absol.* **1.** To regain health after a wound or sickness; to get well again ME. **2.** To regain life, consciousness, or composure. Also const. *of, from, out of.* ME. †**3.** To rally, to return; to make one's way; to succeed in coming or passing (again) –1680. **4.** To regain one's footing, position, or balance; also, to make a return *from*, †to get the better *of*, a slip, etc. 1494. **b.** *Fencing.* To return to a position of guard after a thrust 1705. **c.** To rise again after bowing or curtseying 1711. **5.** *Law.* To obtain, by legal process, possession or restoration of the thing claimed; to succeed in a claim or suit of recovery. late ME.

1. If hee be sicke with Ioy, Hee'le recouer without Physicke SHAKS. The man recovered of the bite, The dog it was that died GOLDSM. **2.** I soon r. from these needless frights COWPER. **5.** The plaintiff shall r. according to the verdict 1817.

Recover (rī:kʊ·vəɹ), *v.*² Also **re-cover.** late ME. [RE- 5a.] *trans.* To cover again.

Recoverable (rĭkʊ·vĕrăb'l), *a.* 1470. [f. RECOVER *v.*¹ + -ABLE.] **1.** Capable of being recovered or regained. **b.** Capable of being legally recovered or obtained 1590. **2.** Capable of being restored to a sound, healthy, or normal condition 1596. **b.** That may be amended; curable 1616. **c.** Capable of being retrieved or made good 1797. †**3.** Capable of being retraced. SHAKS.

1. b. That mere debts should not be r. by law JOWETT. **2.** Having nowe both sowle and bodye greatly diseased, yet both r. SPENSER. **3.** A Prodigall course Is like the Sunnes, but not like his recouerable SHAKS. Hence **Reco·verableness.**

Recoverance (rĭkʊ·vĕrăns). Now *arch.* late ME. [– OFr. *recoverance*; see RECOVER *v.*¹, -ANCE.] Recovery.

Recoveree (rĭkʊvəri·). Now *rare* or *Obs.* 1531. [f. RECOVER *v.*¹ + -EE¹.] *Law.* The person from whom some property is recovered; *spec.* the defendant in an action of common recovery.

Recoverer (rĭkʊ·vərəɹ). late ME. [f. as prec. + -ER¹.] One who recovers, regains, restores, etc.

Recoveror (rĭkʊ·vərəɹ). Also **-er** (-ER⁴). 1628. [f. as prec. + -OR 2.] *Law.* The demandant who recovers a judgement, esp. in an action of common recovery.

Recovery (rĭkʊ·vəri). late ME. [– AFr. *recoverie*, OFr. *reco(u)vree*, f. the verb; see RECOVER *v.*¹, -ERY.] **I.** †**1.** Possibility or means of recovering, or of being restored to, a normal state; remedy –1686. **2.** The act of recovering oneself from a mishap, mistake, fall, etc. 1525. **b.** The act of regaining the natural position after curtseying 1712. **c.** *Rowing.* The act of returning to the proper position for making a fresh stroke 1856. **3.** Restoration or return to health from sickness 1599.

1. On purpose to ruine past r. a country that.. subsists by making of silk 1686. **3.** Phr. †*On the r.*, recovering.

II. 1. *Law.* The fact or procedure of gaining possession of some property or right by a verdict or judgement of court; *spec.* the process, based on a legal fiction, by which entailed estate was commonly transferred from one party to another (also called *common r.*) 1472. **2.** The recovering *of* something lost or taken away; the possibility of recovering such a thing 1538. **3.** The restoration or bringing back *of* a person (or thing) to a healthy or normal condition or to consciousness 1590. **4.** Restoration to a higher or better state: **a.** of persons 1593; **b.** of land (*rare*) 1853. **5.** The action of bringing back (an oar) to the original position 1856.

1. *Single r.*, a suit of r. in which a single vouchee was called (so *double, treble r.*). **3.** What? doth shee swowne? vse meanes for her recouerie SHAKS.

Recreance¹ (re·krĭ,ăns). 1475. [f. RECREATION¹, by substitution of suffix -ANCE.] Recreation, refreshment.

Re·creance². 1879. [f. RECREANT *a.*; see -ANCE.] = next.

Recreancy (re·krĭ,ănsi). 1602. [f. as prec.; see -ANCY. Cf. med.L. *recredentia* (XII).] The quality of being recreant; mean-spiritedness, apostasy.

Recreant (re·krĭ,ănt), *a.* and *sb.* Now *poet.* and *rhet.* ME. [– OFr. *recreant* adj. and sb., uses of pr. pple. of *recroire* yield, surrender :– med.L. (*se*) *recredere* surrender (oneself), f. *re-* RE- + *credere* entrust, believe; see -ANT, and cf. MISCREANT.] **A.** *adj.* **1.** Confessing oneself to be overcome or vanquished; surrendering, or giving way, to an opponent; hence, cowardly, faint-hearted, craven, afraid. **2.** Unfaithful to duty; false, apostate 1643.

1. The loud r. wretch who boasts and flies BYRON. **2.** Who..Turn'd r. to God, ingrate and false MILT. To rebuke the r. American 1863.

B. *sb.* **1.** One who yields in combat; a cowardly or faint-hearted person. late ME. **2.** One who breaks allegiance or faith; an apostate, deserter, villain 1570.

1. Hold! recreants! cowards! What, fear ye death, and fear not shame? SHERIDAN. Hence **Re·creant-ly** *adv.*, **-ness.**

Recreate (re·krĭ,eⁱt), *v.*¹ 1470. [– *recreat-*, pa. ppl. stem of L. *recreare*, f. *re-* RE- + *creare* CREATE; see -ATE³.] **1.** To invest with fresh vigour or strength; to refresh, reinvigorate (nature, strength, a person or thing) 1535. †**2.** To refresh (a sense or its organ) by means of some agreeable object or impression –1710. †**b.** To refresh or enliven (the spirits, mind, a person) by some sensuous or purely physical influence; to affect agreeably in this way –1778. **3.** To refresh or cheer (a person) by giving comfort, consolation or encouragement. Now *rare*. 1470. **4.** To refresh or enliven (the mind, the spirits, a person) by some pastime, amusement, occupation, agreeable news, etc. Also *refl.* 1530. †**b.** To enliven or gratify (a feeling) –1686. **5.** *intr.* To take recreation 1587. †**6.** *trans.* To relieve (an occupation, state, etc.) by means of something of a contrary nature –1653.

1. Each living being requires a certain portion of air to r. itself with 1862. **2.** Speckled with little red spots that r. the Sight EVELYN. **4.** No busy faces to r. the idle man who contemplates them ever passing by LAMB. **b.** The other Attribute wherewith I r. my devotion, is His Wisdom SIR T. BROWNE.

Recreate (rīkri,ēⁱ·t), *v.*² Also **re-create.** 1587. [f. RE- 5 a + CREATE *v.*] *trans.* To create anew. Hence **Recrea·tion**² (rīkri,ēⁱ·ʃən), the action of creating anew; a new creation.

Recreation¹ (rekri,ēⁱ·ʃən). late ME. [– O)Fr. *récréation* – L. *recreatio, -on-*; see RE-, CREATION.] †**1.** Refreshment by partaking of food; a refection; nourishment –1600. **2.** The action of recreating (oneself or another), or fact of being recreated, by some pleasant occupation, pastime or amusement. late ME. **b.** An instance of this; a pleasurable exercise or employment. late ME. **c.** One who or that which supplies recreation 1601.

2. c. If I do not gull him into an ayword, and make him a common r. [etc.] SHAKS.

attrib.: **r. ground,** a public ground with facilities for games, etc.

Recreative (re·kri,eⁱtiv), *a.*¹ and *sb.* 1549. [f. RECREATE *v.*¹ + -IVE, after Fr. *récréatif.*] **A.** *adj.* Tending to recreate or refresh in a pleasurable manner; amusing, diverting. †**B.** *absol.* as *sb.* A recreative thing or pursuit –1620.

A. The r. literature of the day 1887. Hence **Re·creative-ly** *adv.*, **-ness**¹.

Recreative (rīkri,ēⁱ·tiv), *a.*² 1861. [RE- 5 a.] That creates anew. Hence **Recrea·tiveness**².

Recrement (re·krĭmĕnt). 1599. Now *rare*. [– Fr. *récrément* or L. *recrementum*, f. *re-* RE- + *cre-*, pa. ppl. stem of *cernere* separate; see -MENT. Cf. EXCREMENT¹.] **1.** The superfluous or useless portion of any substance; refuse, dross, scum, off-scouring. **2.** *spec.* **a.** A waste product or excretion of an animal or vegetable body; also *Phys.*, a fluid which is separated from the blood and again absorbed into it, as the saliva or bile (opp. to *excrement*) 1615. **b.** The dross or scoria of metallic substances 1611.

1. *fig.* A r. of ancient tradition 1882. **2. b.** Slag.. is the R. of Iron 1678. Hence †**Recreme·ntal** *a.* **Recrementi·tious** *a.* of the nature of r.

Recriminate (rīkri·mineⁱt). 1603. [– *recriminat-*, pa. ppl. stem of med.L. *recriminare*, f. *re-* RE- 2 + L. *criminari* accuse, f. *crimen, crimin-*; see CRIME, -ATE³.] **1.** *intr.* To retort an accusation; to bring a charge or charges in turn against one's accuser 1611. **2.** *trans.* **a.** To accuse (a person) in return; to make a counter-charge against (the accuser). Now *rare.* 1621. †**b.** To return or retort (a charge or accusation) *against, upon* a person –1653.

1. To criminate and r. never yet was the road to reconciliation, in any difference amongst men BURKE. To re-criminate on my base accuser 1786. Hence **Recri·minative, Recri·minatory** *adjs.* involving, of the nature of, recrimination. **Recri·minator.**

Recrimination (rīkriminēⁱ·ʃən). 1611. [– Fr. *récrimination* or med.L. *recriminatio, -on-*, f. as prec.; see -ION.] **1.** The action of bringing a counter-accusation against a person. **2.** A counter-accusation; an accusation brought in turn by the accused against the accuser 1621.

Recru·dency. 1603. [perh. a syncopation of contemp. RECRUDESCENCY.] = RECRUDESCENCE (*rare*).

Recrudesce (rī-, rekrude·s), *v.* 1884. [Back-formation from *recrudescence, recrudescent.*] To break out again (*lit.* and *fig.*).

Recrudescence (rī-, rekrude·sens). 1721. [f. L. *recrudescere*, f. *re-* RE- + *crudescere* become raw, f. *crudus*; see CRUDE, -ESCENCE.] The state or fact of breaking out afresh. **a.** *fig.* Of a quality or state of things (usu. one regarded as bad), a disease, epidemic, etc. **b.** Of a wound or sore 1865.

a. The fears of a r. of the epidemic 1884. So **Recrude·scency.**

Recrudescent (rī-, rekrude·sĕnt), *a.* 1727. [f. as prec.; see -ESCENT.] Breaking out again.

Recruit (rĭkrū·t), *sb.* 1643. [– Fr. dial. (Hainault) †*recrute* = Fr. *recrue*, subst. use of fem. pa. pple. of *recroître* :– L. *recrescere*, f. *re-* RE- + *crescere* grow. Cf. CREW.] **I.** †**1.** *Mil.* A fresh or auxiliary body of troops, added as a reinforcement to an army, regiment, garrison, etc., either to increase or to maintain its strength –1728. **b.** *pl.* †Fresh or auxiliary troops, reinforcements; the men composing such forces. Hence (in later use) also in *sing.*: One of a newly-raised body of troops; one newly or recently enlisted for service in the army. 1645. †**2.** A fresh supply or number of persons (or animals), either as additional to the previous number, or to make up for a decrease –1769. **3.** A fresh or additional supply of something. Now *rare.* 1650.

1. b. A r. remains a r. from the date of his enlistment until he has passed his drill 1876. *transf.* Recruits from our schools of art 1885. **3.** This r. to my finances was not a matter of indifference to me SCOTT.

II. †**1.** *Mil.* Increase or reinforcement (of an army) by the addition or accession of fresh men –1724. **2.** Renewal or repair of something worn out 1691. **3.** Renewal of strength or vigour; restoration to a normal state or condition; recovery 1643. **4.** A means of recruital. Now *rare.* 1655.

4. Little quarrels often prove To be but new recruits of love BUTLER.

Recruit (rĭkrū·t), *v.* 1635. [– Fr. *recruter*, f. †*recrute*; see prec.] **I.** *trans.* **1.** *Mil.* To strengthen or reinforce (an army, etc.) with fresh men or troops 1643. **b.** To add to or keep up the number of (a class or body of persons or things) 1770. **2.** To furnish *with* a fresh supply of something; to replenish. Now *rare.* 1661. **3.** To replenish the substance of (a thing) by addition of fresh material 1661. **b.** To increase or maintain (a quality) by fresh influence or operation 1678. **4.** To increase or restore the vigour or health of (a person or animal); to refresh, re-invigorate (one's spirits, etc.). Also occas. with inanimate object. 1676. **5.** To renew, or add to, one's supply of (a thing) 1748. **6.** *Mil.* (and *Naval*). To raise (men) as recruits; to enlist as soldiers (or sailors); to raise (a regiment, etc.) in this way 1814.

1. Public and private distress recruited the armies of the state GIBBON. **2.** The contributions offered by the English Catholics did little to r. the Exchequer GREEN. **3. b.** Since the Crimean War.. Russia has been carefully engaged in recruiting her strength 1870. **4.** Thy Rains from Heav'n parch'd Hills r. WESLEY. Our guide recruited himself with a large dish of thick sour milk 1856.

II. *intr.* **1. a.** *Mil.* To enlist new soldiers; to get or seek for fresh supplies of men for the army 1655. †**b.** To take fresh stores on board ship. DE FOE. **2.** To recovery vigour or health; to employ means for recovering from exhaustion, etc. 1635. †**3.** To recover what one has expended in trade –1727.

2. Leaving four of my party to r. at this station KANE. Hence **Recrui·tal,** †a new or fresh supply; restoration to health. **Recrui·ter,** one who or that which recruits; *esp.* one who seeks to enlist recruits. **Recrui·tment,** a reinforcement; also, the act or process of recruiting.

Rectal (re·ktăl), *a.* 1872. [f. RECTUM + -AL¹.] *Anat.* and *Med.* Of or belonging to the rectum.

Rectangle (re·ktæŋg'l). 1571. [– Fr. *rectangle* or med.L. *rectangulum*, for earlier *rectiangulum* (Isidore), subst. use of n. sing. of *rect(i)angulus* (after Gr. ὀρθογώνιος), f. L. *rectus* straight + *angulus* ANGLE *sb.*²] **1.** *Geom.* A plane rectilineal four-sided figure having all its angles right angles, and therefore its opposite sides equal and parallel. †**b.** The product of two quantities –1763. †**2.** A right angle –1795. Hence **Re·ctangled** *a.* (now *rare*) right-angled.

Rectangular (rektæ·ŋgiŭlăɹ), *a.* 1624. [f. ANGULAR, after Fr. *rectangulaire*; see -AR¹.] **1.** Shaped like a rectangle; having four sides and four right angles. **b.** Of a solid body: Having the sides, base, or section in the form of a rectangle, or with right-angled corners 1624. †**2.** Of a triangle: Right-angled –1678. **3.** Placed or lying at right angles. (Said also of the relative position of two things). 1646. **4.** Having parts, lines, etc. at right angles to each other; characterized or distinguished by some arrangement of this kind 1727. **Rectangula·rity,** the quality or state of being r. **Recta·ngularly** *adv.*

Rectifiable (re·ktifəiăb'l), *a.* 1646. [f. RECTIFY *v.* + -ABLE.] Capable of being rectified; *spec.* in *Math.* (see RECTIFY *v.* 7 b).

Rectification (rektifikēⁱ·ʃən). 1460. [– (O)Fr. *rectification* or late L. *rectificatio, -on-*, f. *rectificat-*, pa. ppl. stem of med.L. *rectificare*; see RECTIFY, -ION.] The action of rectifying. **1.** The correction of error; a setting straight or right; amendment, improvement, correction. **2.** *Chem.* The purification or refinement of any substance by renewed distillation or other means 1605. **3.** *Geom.* The finding of a straight line equal in length to a given curve 1685. **4.** *Electr.* (cf. RECTIFY *v.* 7 c) 1903.

1. They haue done more cures in this kind by r. of Diet, then all other Physick BURTON. **2.** The Oil of Sugar that remains after R. 1712.

Rectifier (re·ktifəiəɹ). 1611. [f. RECTIFY *v.* + -ER¹.] **1.** One who, or that which, rectifies. **2.** †**a.** An instrument for ascertaining the variation of the compass –1704. **b.** A device for converting an alternating electric current into a direct or continuous one 1898. **3.** One who, or an apparatus which, rectifies spirit 1727.

Rectify (re·ktifəi), *v.* late ME. [– (O)Fr. *rectifier* – med.L. *rectificare*, f. *rectus* right; see -FY.] **1.** *trans.* To put or set right, to remedy (a bad or faulty condition or state of things); to correct, amend, make good (an error, omission, etc.) 1659. **2.** †**a.** To restore (an organ) to a sound or healthy condition –1694. **b.** To put or set (a person or thing) right 1529. **3.** *Chem.* To purify or refine (any substance) by a renewed or repeated distillation, or by some chemical process; to raise *to* a required strength in this way; also, to flavour (a liquor) with some substance during rectification 1450. **4.** To correct or reform (a person, one's nature, mind, etc.) from vice or moral defect 1450. †**b.** To correct (one who is mistaken or in error); to set right –1711. **5.** To correct by removal of errors or mistakes; to amend or improve in this way 1494. **b.** To correct or emend (a text). *rare.* 1730. **6.** To put right by calculation or adjustment 1559. **b.** To set right, adjust (an instrument or apparatus) 1669. **c.** *spec.* To adjust (a globe) for the solution of a problem. Also *absol.* 1646. †**7.** To make straight, straighten out (anything crooked, etc.); to bring into line –1793. **b.** *Geom.* To equate (a curve) with a straight line 1673. **c.** To transform (an electric current) from an alternating to a continuous 1893. †**8.** To guide or direct aright (*rare*) –1618.

1. Payne is good, for by it god rectifyeth synne 1526. The slight omission was rectified DICKENS. **2. b.** Rectifying his position 1882. **3.** *transf.* The Sunne, which rectifieth the aire 1620. **4.** Rectifie a noþer if that ye may,..And rectifie youre selfe first euery day 1460. **5.** Some Oracle Must rectifie our knowledge SHAKS. **7.** O Conscience,..Check me, and r. my devious Lines KEN. Hence **Re·ctified** *ppl. a.* esp. of spirit: purified or refined by renewed distillation; redistilled.

Rectilineal (rektili·nĭ,ăl), *a.* 1646. [f. late L. *rectilineus*, f. L. *rectus* straight + *linea* LINE *sb.*²; see -AL¹. Cf. CURVILINEAL.] = next *a.*

Rectilinear (rektili·nĭ,ăɹ), *a.* and *sb.* 1659. [f. as prec. + -AR¹. Cf. CURVILINEAR.] **A.** *adj.* **1.** Of motion, course or direction: Taking or having the course of a straight line; tending always to the same point. **2.** Lying in, or forming, a straight line 1704. **3.** Of a figure or angle: Bounded or formed by straight lines 1728. **4.** Characterized by straight lines 1727. **b.** Of a lens: see quot. 1874.

4. b. *Rectilinear*, a term applied to lenses which have been corrected for aberration as much as possible, so that in photographing architectural subjects the lines appear perfectly straight in the image 1890.

B. *sb. Photogr.* A rectilinear lens 1890.

Hence **Rectilinea·rity,** the quality of being r.

Rection (re·kʃən). *rare.* 1637. [– L. *rectio, -on-* government, f. *regere, rect-* rule; see -ION.] *Gram.* Syntactical government; regimen.

Rectiserial (rektisīə·riăl), *a.* 1861. [f. *recti-*, comb. form of L. *rectus* straight + SERIAL.] *Bot.* (See quot.)

The leaves..in strict vertical ranks, or..r. 1880.

Rectitude (re·ktitiūd). late ME. [– (O)Fr. *rectitude* or late L. *rectitudo*, f. L. *rectus* right; see -TUDE.] **1.** The quality or fact of being straight; straightness. Now *rare* or *Obs.* **b.** Straight line; direction in a straight line 1578. **2.** Moral straightness or uprightness; goodness, integrity; virtue, righteousness 1533. **3.** Correctness of the judgement, or of its conclusions 1651. **4.** Correctness of nature, procedure, or application. Also with *pl.*, an instance of this. 1656.

2. A man of singular piety, r., and virtue BURKE.

Recto (re·kto), *sb.* and *adv.* (Abbrev. r°.) 1824. [– L. *recto* (sc. *folio*), abl. of *rectus* right.] **A.** *sb.* In *Printing*, the right-hand page of the open book; hence, the front of a leaf as opp. to the back or VERSO. **B.** *adv.* On or to the right-hand side 1888.

Recto-, used as comb. form of RECTUM in terms of *Anat.* and *Path.*, with the sense 'relating to the rectum in conjunction with some other part of the body', as **r.-ure·thral, -vagi·nal, -ve·sical,** etc.

Rector (re·ktəɹ). late ME. [– OFr. *rectour* (mod. *recteur*) or L. *rector, -ōr-*, f. *rect-*, pa. ppl. stem of *regere* rule; see -OR 2.] †**1.** The ruler or governor of a country, city, state, or people –1685. †**b.** Applied to God as the ruler of the world, of mankind, etc. –1741. **2.** One who, or that which, has or exercises supreme or directive control in any sphere. Now *rare*. 1482. **3.** A parson or incumbent of a parish whose tithes are not impropriate. (Cf. VICAR.) In Roman Catholic use, the head priest of a parish. late ME. **4.** In scholastic use: **a.** The permanent head or master of a university, college, school, or religious institution (esp. a Jesuit college or seminary). In Eng. use now applied only to the heads of Exeter and Lincoln Colleges, Oxford. 1464. **b.** In Scottish universities: The holder of one of the higher offices 1522. **c.** The acting head, and president of the administrative body, in continental universities 1548.

3. *Lay r.*, a layman receiving the rectorial tithes, or in whom the rectory is vested. **b.** *U.S.* A Protestant Episcopal clergyman in charge of a parish. **Re·ctoral** *a.* of or pertaining to a r. or ruler (Said only of God). **Re·ctorate,** the office or position of a r.; the period during which the office is held. **Re·ctoress,** †a female ruler; *colloq.* the wife of the r. of a parish. **Re·ctorship,** the office of ruler or governor; government, rule (now *rare*); the office of r.

Rectorial (rektōə·riăl), *a.* (*sb.*) 1611. [f. RECTOR + -IAL.] **1.** Of or pertaining to a university rector. **2.** Of or belonging to the rector of a parish (esp. *r. tithes*); held by a rector 1769. **3.** Of or pertaining to a ruler or governor 1679. **B.** as *sb.* In Scottish and other universities: A rectorial election 1920.

Rectory (re·ktŏri). 1594. [– AFr., OFr. *rectorie* or med.L. *rectoria*; see RECTOR, -Y³.] **1.** A benefice held by a rector. **b.** The residence appertaining to a rector 1849. †**2.** Rectorship; administration –1675.

Rectress (re·ktrės). 1603. [f. RECTOR + -ESS¹.] †**1.** A female ruler or governor –1656. **2.** The female head of a school or institution 1843. **3.** The wife of a rector 1906.

Rectrix (re·ktriks). 1611. [– L. *rectrix*, fem. of RECTOR; see -TRIX.] **1.** = RECTRESS 1 (*rare*). **2.** *Ornith.* in *pl.* **rectrices** (rektrəi·sīz). The strong feathers of the tail in birds, by which their flight is directed 1768.

‖**Rectum** (re·ktŏm). 1541. [L., n. of *rectus* straight, short for *intestinum rectum* the straight gut (Celsus).] *Anat.* and *Med.* The final section of the large intestine (so called from its form in some animals), extending in man from the sigmoid flexure of the colon to the anus.

‖**Rectus** (re·ktŏs). *Pl.* **recti** (re·ktəi). 1704. [L. (sc. *musculus* muscle); see prec.] *Anat.* The name of various muscles, esp. of the abdomen, thigh, neck, and eye, so called from the straightness of their fibres. So *r. muscle.*

†**Recuba·tion.** [f. L. *recubare* recline, f. *re-* RE- + *cubare* recline, sleep; see -ATION.] The action of reclining, recumbency SIR T. BROWNE.

Recueil (rəköy), *sb.* 1474. [– (O)Fr. *recueil*, f. *recueillir*; see next.] **1.** A literary compilation or collection. (Now only as Fr.) †**2.** Reception, welcome; reset –1588.

†**Recueil,** *v.* 1474. [– (O)Fr. *recueillir* :– L. *recolligere* collect, gather up, f. *re-* RE- + *colligere* CULL *v.*¹] **1.** *trans.* To gather together –1566. **2.** To receive hospitably, entertain. CAXTON. **3.** To receive, catch. CAXTON.

†**Recu·mb,** *v.* 1677. [– L. *recumbere*; see RECUMBENT *a.*] *intr.* To lean, recline.

Recumbence (rĭkɒ·mbĕns). Now *rare.* 1676. [f. as next + -ENCE.] = RECUMBENCY.

Recumbency (rĭkɒ·mbĕnsi). 1642. [f. next; see -ENCY.] **1.** The state of lying or reclining; a recumbent posture 1646. **b.** *fig.* Repose 1653. **2.** *fig.* Reliance *on* or *upon* a person or thing. Chiefly in religious use. Now *rare.* 1646. **b.** Without const. Also *pl.* 1642.

1. The Tricliniums, or places of festivall R. SIR T. BROWNE.

Recumbent (rĭkɒ·mbĕnt), *a.* 1705. [– L. *recumbens, -ent-*; pr. pple. of *recumbere* recline, f. *re-* RE- + *-cumbere* (cf. INCUMBENT).] **1.** Of persons or animals: Lying down, reclining, reposing 1774. **2.** Of posture: Reclining, leaning or lying 1705. Hence **Recu·mbently** *adv.*

Recuperate (rĭkiū·pĕreᵗt), *v.* 1542. [– *recuperat-*, pa. ppl. stem of L. *recuperare*, f. *re-* RE- + **cup-* (see OCCUPY), var. of **cap-* (see CAPTURE); see -ATE³. Cf. RECOVER.] †**1.** *trans.* To recover (a thing) –1661. **2.** To restore (a person) to health or vigour 1864. **3.** *intr.* To recover from exhaustion, ill-health, pecuniary loss, etc. 1864. So †**Recu·perable** *a.* recoverable.

Recuperation (rĭkiūpĕrēᵗ·ʃən). 1481. [– L. *recuperatio, -on-*, f. as prec.; see -ION.] †**1.** The recovery or regaining *of* a thing –1685. **2.** Restoration to health, vigour, etc. 1865.

Recuperative (rĭkiū·pĕrătiv), *a.* (and *sb.*) 1623. [– late L. *recuperativus*, f. as prec.; see -IVE.] †**1.** Recoverable. †**2.** Belonging to, concerned with, the recovery of something lost –1858. **3.** Having the power of restoring (a person or thing) to a proper state 1861. **b.** Of or belonging to recovery of health, vigour, etc. 1860. **B.** *sb.* A substance which restores land to fertility 1883.

Recuperator (rĭkiū·pĕreᵗtəɹ). 1706. [– L. *recuperator*, f. as prec.; see -OR 2.] **1.** *Rom. Law.* A member of a commission for trying certain cases. **2.** *Mech.* The regenerator of a hot-air engine, gas-burning furnace, etc. 1884.

Recu·peratory, *a.* *rare.* 1656. [– L. *recuperatorius*, f. *recuperator*; see prec., -ORY².] Of or belonging to recovery or recuperators.

Recur (rĭkō·ɹ), *v.* 1468. [– L. *recurrere*, f. *re-* RE- + *currere* run.] **1.** †*intr.* To move or run back, recede (*rare*) –1788. **b.** To return *into* or *to* a place (*rare*) 1468. **2.** To return, go back, in thought, memory, or discourse. Usu. const. *to*. 1620. **3.** To go back, resort *to* a thing (rarely a person), for assistance or argument 1529. **4.** Of something known, an idea, thought, etc.: To come back or return (†*into*, *in* or) *to* one's thoughts, mind or memory 1704. **b.** Without const.: To return to the mind 1711. **c.** Of questions, difficulties, etc.: To come up again for consideration; to present themselves, or confront one, again 1651. **5.** To occur, happen, take place, appear, again 1673. **b.** *Math.* Of a figure or figures in a decimal fraction: To return or come again (in the same order), to repeat 1801.

2. I know it is painful to her to r. to that terrible time 1833. **3.** If to avoid Succession in eternal Existence, they r. to the *Punctum Stans* of the Schools LOCKE. **4. b.** Wherever I have heard A kindred melody, the scene recurs COWPER. **c.** But still, the question recurs, whether man be free? BERKELEY. **5.** In some..the disease has appeared to r. 1851.

†**Recu·re,** *sb.* late ME. [f. next.] Recovery; remedy, succour; cure –1626.

Phr. *But, past*, or *without r.*, past or without hope or possibility of recovery.

†**Recu·re,** *v.* late ME. [– L. *recurare*, f. *re-* RE- + *curare* CURE *v.*¹, but also in part repr. RECOVER *v.*¹] **1.** *trans.* To cure (a person) *of* or *from* a disease, wound, trouble, etc.; to restore to health. Also *absol.* –1647. **b.** To restore after loss, damage, exhaustion, etc. Also const. *to* (a better state). –1667. **2.** To cure (a disease, sickness, etc.); to heal, make whole (a wound or sore) –1667. **b.** To remedy (a wrong, defect, etc.) –1631. **3.** *intr.* Of persons: To become whole; to regain health or a former state –1547. **4.** *trans.* To recover (something lost); to get, obtain, win –1746.

1. b. No Physick can r. my weaken'd State COWLEY. **4.** So hard was this lost Isle, so hard to be recur'd P. FLETCHER. Hence †**Recu·reless** *a.* incurable.

Recurrence (rĭkɒ·rĕns). 1646. [f. next; see -ENCE.] **1.** Return (of a thing, state, event, etc.); renewed, frequent, or periodical occurrence. Also, with *a* and *pl.*, an instance of this. **2.** Resort, recourse, reference *to* something. Also without const. 1667. **3.** The action of going back mentally or in discourse *to* something. Also with *a* and *pl.*, an instance of this. 1751. **4.** Return or reversion *to* a state, occupation, etc. 1812.

1. The r. of the same follies 1877. Atavism,..the name given to the r. of ancestral traits H. SPENCER. **2.** Such an alliance will occasion frequent r. to arms 1804. **3.** The announcement..effectually put a stop to any r. to the subject 1862. So †**Recu·rrency** (in sense 1).

Recurrent (rĭkɒ·rĕnt), *a.* and *sb.* 1597. [– L. *recurrens, -ent-*, pr. pple. of *recurrere* RECUR; see -ENT.] **A.** *adj.* **1.** *Anat.* and *Bot.* Of a nerve, vein, artery, branch, etc.: Turned back so as to run or lie in a direction opposite to the former one 1611. **b.** *Path. R. sensibility*, the sensibility manifested by the anterior roots of the spinal cord owing to the recurrent course of the sensory fibres from the corresponding posterior roots 1873. **2.** Occurring or coming again (esp. frequently or periodically); reappearing 1666.

1. *R. nerves*, the laryngeal and meningeal branches of the pneumogastric nerve.

B. *sb.* A recurrent artery or nerve; *esp.* the right or left recurrent laryngeal nerve 1597. Hence **Recu·rrently** *adv.*

Recursant (rĭkō·ɹsănt), *a.* 1828. [– L. *recursans, -ant*, pr. pple. of *recursare* hasten back, return, f. *recurs-*, pa. ppl. stem of *recurrere* RECUR; see -ANT.] *Her.* Of an eagle: Having the back towards the spectator.

Recursion (rĭkō·ɹʃən). Now *rare* or *Obs.* 1616. [– late L. *recursio, -on-*, f. as prec.; see -ION.] A backward movement, return.

Recurvate (rĭkō·ɹvĕt), *a.* 1776. [– L. *recurvatus*, pa. pple. of *recurvare* RECURVE; see -ATE².] Recurved.

Recurvate (rĭkō·ɹveᵗt), *v.* Now *rare.* 1597. [– *recurvat-*, pa. ppl. stem of L. *recurvare* RECURVE; see -ATE³.] **1.** *trans.* To bend (a thing) back (*rare*). **b.** In pa. pple. Bent backwards 1597. **2.** *intr.* Of a thing: To bend back; to recurve 1822.

Recurvation (rīkɒɹveᵗ·ʃən). Now *rare.* 1597. [f. next + -ATION.] The fact of being bent or curved back; a backward bend or curve. So **Recu·rvature.**

Recurve (rĭkō·ɹv), *v.* 1597. [– L. *recurvare* bend (a thing) backwards, f. *re-* RE- + *curvare* CURVE *v.*] **1.** *trans.* To bend (a thing) back or backwards. **2.** *intr.* (Chiefly of a wind or current): To turn back in a curve upon its previous direction 1850. Hence **Recu·rved** *ppl. a.* bent back; having a backward curve.

†**Recu·rvity.** 1668. [– med.L. *recurvitas*, f. L. *recurvus* curved back; see -ITY.] The fact of being recurved. SIR T. BROWNE.

Recurvo-, used in *Bot.* as comb. form of L. *recurvus*, as **recu:rvo-pa·tent,** bent back and spreading, etc.

Recurvous (rĭkō·ɹvəs), *a.* *rare.* 1713. [f. L. *recurvus* curved back + -OUS.] Recurved, bent back.

Recusance (re·kiuzăns, rĭkiū·zăns). 1597. [f. as next; see -ANCE.] = next.

Recusancy (re·kiuzănsi, rĭkiū·zănsi). 1563. [– AL. *recusantia* (XVI), f. as next; see -Y³,

-ANCY.] **1.** *Hist.* Refusal, esp. on the part of Roman Catholics, to attend the services of the Church of England 1600. **2.** Refusal to obey some authority or command 1563.

Recusant (re·kiuzănt, rĭkiū·zănt), *sb.* and *a.* 1552. [– L. *recusans, -ant-*, pr. pple. of *recusare* refuse, f. *re-* RE- + *causa* CAUSE *sb.* (cf. *accuse, excuse*); see -ANT.] **A.** *sb.* **1.** *Hist.* One, esp. a Roman Catholic (*Popish r.*), who refused to attend the services of the Church of England. **b.** Applied to other religious dissentients 1777. **2.** One who refuses to submit to some authority, comply with some regulation or request, etc. 1584.

1. It appears that this remote county was full of Popish recusants SCOTT. 2. Dealing with the dominions of the r. as being a forfeited fief FREEMAN.

B. *adj.* **1.** Refusing to attend the parish church; dissenting 1611. **2.** Refusing to acknowledge authority or to do something commanded or desired 1659.

1. The R. Lords 1647. 2. Those R. Jews MILT.

Recusation (rekiuzēⁱ·ʃən). Now *rare.* 1529. [– (O)Fr. *récusation* or L. *recusatio, -on-*, f. *recusat-*, pa. ppl. stem of *recusare* (see prec.); see -ION.] *Civil* and *Canon Law.* The interposition of an objection or appeal; *esp.* an appeal grounded on the judge's relationship or personal enmity to one of the parties.

†**Recu·sative,** *a. rare.* [– late L. *recusativus,* f. as prec.; see -IVE.] That tends to refuse or prohibit. JER. TAYLOR.

Recuse (rĭkiū·z), *v.* Now *rare.* late ME. [– L. *recusare*; see RECUSANT. Cf. (O)Fr. *récuser.*] **1.** To reject, renounce (a person, his authority, etc.); to object to (a judge) as prejudiced. †**2.** To refuse *to* do something –1542.

Red (red), *a.* and *sb.* [OE. *rēad* = OFris. *rād,* OS. *rōd* (Du. *rood*), OHG. *rōt* (G. *rot*), ON. *rauðr,* Goth. *rauþs* :- Gmc. **rauðaz* :- IE. **roudhos.* Cf. L. *rufus, ruber,* Gr. ἐρυθρός, Skr. *rudhirás* red.] **A.** *adj.* **I. 1.** Having, or characterized by, the colour which appears at the lower or least refracted end of the visible spectrum, and is familiar as that of blood, fire, the poppy, the rose, and ripe fruits. (The shades of colour to which the name is applied vary from bright scarlet or crimson to reddish yellow or brown.) **2.** As an epithet (chiefly *poet.*) of blood ME. **b.** In pregnant uses, implying superior quality or value 1596. **3.** As a conventional (chiefly *poet.*) epithet of gold. Now only *arch.* OE. **b.** Golden, made of gold. Now only *thieves' slang.* late ME. **c.** *U.S.* As an epithet of the cent (formerly made of copper), usu. in negative expressions 1852. **4.** Of cloth, clothing, etc.: Dyed with red OE. **b.** *R. flag,* as a sign of battle, etc. 1602. **5.** Of persons: Having red hair; †of a red or ruddy complexion OE. **b.** Of animals: Having red or reddish hair; tawny, chestnut, or bay. late ME. **c.** Of certain peoples, esp. the N. American Indians: Having (or regarded as having) a reddish skin. See also RED MAN, RED SKIN. 1587. **6.** Wearing red clothing (uniform, livery) or armour. Now *rare.* late ME. **7.** Of the face, or of persons in respect of it: Temporarily suffused with blood, esp. as the result of some sudden feeling or emotion; flushed or blushing *with* (anger, shame, etc.) ME. **b.** Exceptionally high in colour. late ME. **8.** Stained or covered with blood ME. **b.** Of meat: Full of, coloured with, blood 1837. **c.** Consisting of blood 1816. **9.** Marked or characterized by blood or fire, or by violence suggestive of these ME. **b.** Extremely radical or revolutionary, *esp.* communistic 1854. **10.** Red-hot, glowing ME. **11.** Of eyes: (*a*) Naturally of a red colour. (*b*) Bloodshot. (*c*) Inflamed as with weeping. late ME.

1. Like a r. morne that euer yet betokend Wracke to the sea man SHAKS. The Thunder, Wing'd with r. Lightning MILT. Women with big black Eyes, and r. Cheeks 1687. One with a r. beard KINGSLEY. Phr. *R. as blood, fire, a rose, cherry, fiery r.,* etc. *To paint the town r.,* to behave riotously or uproariously; to go 'on the spree'. 2. I have . . Seen through r. blood the war-horse dashing SCOTT. b. *Merch. V.* II. i. 7. 3. c. I don't care a r. cent what you say 1889. 4. The r. shirt of Garibaldi's troops 1868. *R. hat* (of cardinals): see HAT *sb.* 2. 5. The R. O'Donnell and others 1849. b. Master had the r. setter with him this morning 1882. 7. Mine enemies shall . . then grow r. with shame MILT. b. As R. in the Gills as a Turkey-cock 1689. 8. Sad Philippi, r. with Roman Gore GRAY. b. Avoid altogether r. meat 1898. 9. Ye shal be deed by myghty Mars the rede CHAUCER. b. *Red flag,* a symbol of revolution, communism, etc. (see also sense 4 b above); the title of a revolutionary song. 10. A waking dream of houses, towers . . expressed In the r. cinders COWPER.

II. In special applications. **a.** As a distinctive epithet of things in which the colour forms a natural or obvious mark of kind or class OE. **b.** Applied to various diseases marked by evacuation of blood or cutaneous eruptions. late ME. **c.** *R. squadron,* one of the three squadrons into which the Royal Navy was formerly divided 1702.

Comb. and collocations. **a.** used with the names of beasts, birds, fishes, plants and minerals, as **r. ant,** any ant of this colour, esp. (*a*) a common small British ant *Formica* (*Myrmica*) *rubra*; (*b*) the hill- or horse-ant, *F. rufa*; (*c*) the American house-ant, *Monomorium pharaonis*; **r. antimony (ore)** = KERMESITE; **r. ash,** (*a*) a N. Amer. ash, *Fraxinus pubescens*; (*b*) an Australian tree, *Alphitonia excelsa*; (*c*) the silky oak of Australia, *Orites excelsa*; **r. bass,** *U.S.* the red-drum or red-fish, *Sciæna ocellata*; **r. bay,** *U.S.* a lauraceous tree, *Persea carolinensis*; **r. birch,** an American birch, *Betula nigra*; **r. bird,** any of various small American birds with red plumage, esp. the scarlet tanager (*Piranga rubra*), Baltimore oriole, and cardinal grosbeak; **r. bug,** *U.S.* (*a*) the cotton-stainer, *Dysdercus suturellus*; (*b*) one of several red harvest-ticks; **r. chalk,** (*a*) ruddle; (*b*) *Geol.* a bed of chalk of a red colour, occurring in Norfolk and elsewhere; **r. cock,** the grouse; **r. copper ore,** CUPRITE; **r. coral** (see CORAL 1 a); **r. fir,** (*a*) *Picea morinda*; (*b*) a N. Amer. fir, *Abies nobilis*; (*c*) the Oregon Pine, *Pseudotsuga douglasii*; **r. fox,** (*a*) the common European fox, *Vulpes vulgaris*; (*b*) the common N. Amer. fox, *V. fulvus*; (*c*) the kit-fox of N. America; **r. grouse** (see GROUSE 1 b); **r. kite,** the common kite; **r. lead ore,** CROCOITE; **r. maggot** (see MAGGOT 1); **r. manganese (ore),** DIALOGITE; **r. maple,** a species of maple, *Acer rubrum,* with crimson flowers; **r. pepper,** capsicum; **r. perch,** the rose-fish, *Sebastes marinus*; **r. ptarmigan,** the grouse; **r. robin,** (*a*) the redbreast; (*b*) the scarlet tanager; **r. spider,** a small red spider-like mite (*Tetranychus* or *Acarus telarius*) infesting plants, esp. in hothouses; **r. squirrel,** the chickaree; **r. viper,** (*a*) a species of British viper; (*b*) *U.S.* the copperhead; **r. weed,** (*a*) an Amer. plant or plants; now applied to a species of *Phytolacca*; (*b*) the corn-poppy; **r. wheat,** a varity of the common wheat, of a reddish colour; **r. worm,** (*a*) a variety of earthworm much used as bait in angling; (*b*) a worm or grub attacking grain; **r. zinc (ore),** zincite.

b. prefixed to the name of a part (or some distinctive feature) used to denote the whole; (*a*) of persons, as **r.-hat,** a cardinal; **-shirt,** a revolutionary, an anarchist; (*b*) *spec.* forming the names of certain birds, fishes, plants, etc., as **r.-back,** *U.S.* the American dunlin or red-backed sandpiper, *Tringa americana*; **-belly,** (*a*) a species of lake-trout; (*b*) the Welsh char; (*c*) *U.S.* the red-bellied perch or sunfish; **-bud,** a tree belonging to any Amer. species of *Cercis,* esp. *C. canadensis*; the Judas-tree; **-eye,** (*a*) the rudd, *Leuciscus erythrophthalmus*; (*b*) one of several American fishes, as the rock-bass, the red-fish; **-fin,** *U.S.* the shiner and various other American fishes; **-root,** *U.S.* (*a*) New Jersey tea, *Ceanothus americanus*; (*b*) the blood-root, *Sanguinaria canadensis*; (*c*) the stone-weed, *Lithospermum arvense*; (*d*) a plant of the blood-wort family, *Lacnanthes tinctoria*; **-tail,** (*a*) = REDSTART 1; (*b*) *U.S.* the red-tailed buzzard, *Buteo borealis*; **r. throat,** an Australian singing bird, *Pyrrholæmus brunneus*; **-underwing,** a species of moth, *Catocala nupta.*

c. with miscellaneous sbs., as **r. admiral,** a butterfly, *Vanessa atalanta*; see also ADMIRAL 6; **r. ash,** *U.S.* a coal producing a red ash (also *attrib.*); **r. bark,** a variety of cinchona-bark; **r. body,** in fishes, an aggregation of capillaries on the inside of the swimming-bladder; **r. box,** a box (covered with red leather) used by ministers of state for holding official documents; **R. Crescent,** the Turkish ambulance society answering to the RED CROSS; **r. fire,** a pyrotechnic effect, or the mixture ignited to produce it; **r. fog,** a sea-haze due to the presence of sand or dust in the air; **r. game,** the red grouse *Lagopus scoticus*; **r. lac,** a species of sumach (*Rhus succedanea,* also called *red lac sumach*), from the fruit of which Japan wax is obtained; **r. lamp,** a lamp having red glass, used as a doctor's sign; in the war of 1914–18, the sign of a licensed brothel; **r. lane,** *colloq.* the throat; **r. lattice** (now *arch.*), a lattice painted red as the sign of an alehouse; hence *transf.* an alehouse, inn; **r. light (district),** *U.S.* quarters of licensed prostitutes; phr. *to see the r. light,* to suspect danger; **r. liquor,** a mordant used in calico-printing; **r. mass** [after Fr. *messe rouge*], a mass (usu. one of the Holy Ghost) at which red vestments are worn by the priest; **r. metal,** a name given to various alloys of copper having a reddish colour; **r. precipitate,** red oxide of mercury, prepared by solution (and repeated distillation) with nitric acid; **r. ribbon,** †(*a*) the crimson ribbon worn by Knights of the Order of the Bath, hence, membership of this Order, or the Order itself; (*b*) the band-fish; **r. sanders,** red sandal-wood; the wood of an E. Indian tree *Pterocarpus santalinus,* used in dyeing, and formerly as an astringent and tonic; **r. scale,** a scale-insect, *Aonidia aurantii,* infesting orange trees; **r. softening,** a variety of acute softening of the brain, marked by extravasation of blood in the tissue; **r. stuff,** an iron oxide, as crocus or rouge, used in grinding or polishing; **r. triangle,** a form of danger sign; **r. twig,** red root (*Ceanothus*); **r. water,** (*a*) a disease in cattle and sheep characterized by the presence of free hæmoglobin in the urine; (*b*) the poisonous red juice of the sassy-tree of W. Africa.

d. with adjs., as **r.-blind,** colour-blind in respect of red; **-ripe,** fully ripe, as indicated by the red colour.

e. parasynthetic (chiefly in the names of animals, birds, fishes, etc.), as *r.-blooded* (also *fig.* = strong, vigorous, virile), *-eyed, -legged, -necked, -nosed, -tailed, -throated,* etc.

B. *sb.* **1.** Red colour (dye, stain, etc.); redness. Often with defining terms prefixed, as *alizarin, cherry,* etc. ME. **b.** The red colour in roulette or rouge-et-noir 1849. **c.** The red ball in billiards 1866. **2. a.** Stuff, cloth, or the like, of a red colour (usu. as the material of a dress). late ME. **b.** Ruddle (now *dial.*); †rouge, late ME. **3.** Red wine. late ME. **4.** = *Red Squadron* (cf. A. II. c.) 1690. **5.** *pl.* (rarely *sing.* with *a*). **a.** Shades or tints of red 1633. **b.** Red kinds or varieties of cloth, wine, wheat, etc.; red cattle, ants, herrings, etc. 1566. **6. a.** *pl.* Red men; North American Indians 1804. **b.** An extreme radical or revolutionary; latterly *esp.* a communist 1864.

1. MILT. *Nativity* 230. *Red, white, and blue,* (the three colours of) the Union Jack. *To see red* (colloq.), to be overcome with rage, to lose control of one's temper or actions. *To come* (or *be*) *out of the r.* (U.S.), to (begin to) show a profit; to be on the credit side; so *to be in the r.,* to show a loss. (From the practice of recording debit balances in red ink.) Hence **Re·d-ly** *adv.,* **-ness.**

†**Red,** *v.* [OE. *rēadian,* f. *rēad* RED *a.*] **1.** *intr.* **a.** To be red. **b.** To become or grow red; to blush. late ME. **2.** *trans.* To make red –1736.

-red, *suffix,* repr. OE. *rǣden* condition. In ME. the full form *-ræden, -reden, -raden,* was by the general dropping of final *-n* reduced to *-rede,* and this was subseq. shortened to *-red.* See GOSSIPRED, HATRED, KINDRED.

Redact (rĭdæ·kt), *v.* late ME. [– *redact-*, pa. ppl. stem of L. *redigere* bring back, collect etc., f. *re*(*d*)- RE + *agere* drive, etc.] †**1.** *trans.* To bring (matter of reasoning or discourse) *into* or *to* a certain form; to put *together* in writing –1639. †**2.** To bring together *into* one body –1550. †**3.** To reduce (a person or thing) *to, into* a certain state, condition, or action –1731. **4. a.** To draw up, frame (a statement, decree, etc.) 1837. **b.** To put (matter) into proper literary form; to work up, arrange, or edit 1851.

4. a. The House of Commons . . was busy redacting a 'Protestation' CARLYLE. So **Reda·ctor,** one who redacts; an editor 1816.

‖**Rédacteur** (redaktör). 1804. [Fr.] = REDACTOR (see above).

Redaction (rĭdæ·kʃən). 1621. [In sense 1 – late L. *redactio, -on-*, f. *redact-*; see REDACT, -ION. In sense 2 – Fr. *rédaction.*] †**1.** The action of driving back, resistance, reaction –1659. **2.** The action or process of preparing for publication; reduction to literary form; revision, rearrangement 1803. **b.** The result of such a process; a new edition 1810.

Redan (rĭdæ·n). 1684. [– Fr. *redan,* for *redent,* notching as of a saw, f. *re-* RE- + *dent* tooth.] *Fortif.* A simple form of field-work, having two faces which form a salient angle. Also *attrib.*

Redargue (redā·ɹgiu), *v.* Now *Sc.* late ME. [– L. *redarguere* disprove, etc., f. *re*(*d*)- RE- + *arguere* ARGUE. Cf. (O)Fr. *rédarguer.*] †**1.** *trans.* To blame, reprove (a person or persons, an action, etc.). Also const. *of, for.* –1677. **2.** To confute (a person) by argument. late ME. **3.** To refute or disprove (an argument, statement, etc. Since *c* 1700 only *Sc.*, chiefly *Law.*) 1627. **4.** *absol.* or *intr.* To reprove or refute; to employ argument for the purpose of refuting 1641.

1. Basil..severely redargues Origen's allegoric mode of Theologising 1677. **3.** I may..r. your claim and statements, as the result of a mistake HAMILTON. Hence †**Reda·rgutory** *a.* (*rare*) pertaining to refutation or reproof.

Redargution (redaɹgiū·ʃən). 1483. [– eccl.L. *redargutio* reproof, f. L. *redarguere*; see prec. Cf. OFr. *redargucion.*] †**1.** Reproof, reprehension (of a person, an action, etc.) –1690. **2.** Confutation (of a person); refutation, disproof (of a statement, etc.). Now *rare.* 1529.

Red-backed, *a.* 1768. Having a red back; chiefly of birds, *esp.* the red-backed butcher-bird or shrike (*Lanius collurio*), and the red-backed sandpiper (*Tringa americana*).

Re·d book, re·d-book. 1479. A book bound in red. **1.** As the name of individual books of an official character, or otherwise important. †**b.** A book containing the names of all persons holding office under the State or receiving pensions from it –1820. **2.** A popular name for the 'Royal Kalendar, or Complete..Annual Register' (published from 1767 to 1893); also, the title of a similar work of later date 1788.

1. *Red Book of the Exchequer*, a miscellaneous volume, containing copies of charters, statutes, surveys, etc.; orig. compiled in the 13th c. *Red book of Hergest*, a Welsh MS. of the 14–15th c., containing the tales known as the Mabinogion and other pieces.

Re·dbreast. late ME. The robin. **b.** Applied to other red-breasted birds, esp. *U.S.* to the migratory thrush (also called *robin*) 1775.

Re·dcap, red-cap, red cap. 1539. **1.** Applied to one who wears a red cap 1550. **b.** *spec.* as the name of a sprite or goblin 1802. **c.** *slang.* A military policeman. †**2.** A red-hat, a cardinal –1609. **3.** The goldfinch 1785.

Red cedar. 1717. **a.** An American evergreen tree, *Juniperus virginianus*, the wood of which is widely used for pencils. **b.** The toon-tree or Moulmein cedar, *Cedrela toona*. **c.** An Australian timber-tree, *Flindersia australis*.

Re·dcoat, red-coat, red coat. 1520. One who wears a red coat; *spec.* a soldier in the British army.

Red cross, red-cross. late ME. **1.** A cross of a red colour; *esp.* **a.** as the national emblem of England; St. George's Cross. **b.** as the mark made on the doors of infected houses during the London plagues of the 17th c. 1603. **c.** as the badge of an ambulance service; the Geneva cross 1863. **2.** *transf.* **a.** The Christian side in the Crusades 1801. **b.** An ambulance or hospital service organized in accordance with the Geneva convention of 1864, and distinguished by a cross (see 1 c); a person attached to an ambulance or hospital of this kind 1877. **3.** *attrib.*, as (sense 1) *red cross knight*, etc., (sense 1 c or 2 b) *Red Cross hospital, Society*, etc. 1590.

Red currant. 1629. The fruit of the *Ribes rubrum* (see CURRANT 2) or the shrub itself. Also *attrib.*, as *red currant jelly, wine*.

Redd (red), *v. Sc.* and *n. dial.* late ME. [= MLG., Du. *redden* in the same senses, but the origin and relationship of the forms is not clear. Most of the senses of the word are also repr. under RID *v.*] *trans.* To clear, put in order; to clean *up* (also *U.S.*).

Red deer. 1470. **a.** A species of deer, *Cervus elaphus*, so named from its reddish-brown colour, still existing in a wild state in the Highlands of Scotland and some other parts of Great Britain. **b.** The Virginia deer, *Cariacus virginianus*, the common deer of N. America. **c.** The Caspian or Persian deer, *Cervus maral*.

Redden (re·d'n), *v.* 1611. [f. RED *a.* + -EN[5] 1.] *trans.* and *intr.* To make or become red. **b.** *intr.* To become red (in the face) *with* shame, rage, etc.; to flush, blush 1648.

Bright leaves, reddening ere they fall KEBLE. **b.** He would r. with Rage 1701.

‖**Reddendum** (rĕde·ndŏm). 1607. [L., neut. sing. of *reddendus*, gerundive of *reddere* give in return, RENDER.] *Law.* A reserving clause in a deed.

Reddish (re·diʃ), *a.* late ME. [f. RED *a.* -ISH[1].] Somewhat red, red-tinted. Hence **Re·ddishness.**

†**Reddi·tion.** 1449. [– L. *redditio, -on-*, f. *reddit-*, pa. ppl. stem of *reddere* give back, RENDER. Cf. (O)Fr. *reddition.*] **1.** Restoration of something taken or received; also, surrender of a thing, a town, army, etc. –1794. **2.** The application of a comparison, or the clause containing the application –1786. **3.** Rendering, translation –1685.

2. We know that al Parables consiste of two parts, the proposition and R. or moral 1678.

†**Re·dditive,** *a.* and *sb.* 1590. [– late L. *redditivus*, f. as prec.; see -IVE.] **A.** *adj.* That answers to something already said; corresponding, correlative –1659. **B.** *sb. Gram.* A correlative word –1668.

Reddle (re·d'l), *sb.* 1668. [var. of RUDDLE; cf. RADDLE *sb.*[2]] Red ochre, ruddle. Hence **Re·ddle** *v. trans.* to paint or wash over with r. **Re·ddleman,** a dealer in r.

Rede (rīd), *sb.* Now *arch.* or *poet.* and *dial.* [OE. *rǣd*, corresp. to OFris. *rēd*, OS. *rād* (Du. *raad*), OHG. *rāt* (G. *rat*), ON. *ráð* :– Gmc. **rǣðaz, -am*, f. base of **rǣðan* READ *v.*] **1.** Counsel or advice given by one person to another. **2.** Counsel, decision, or resolve taken by one or more persons; a plan, design, or scheme devised or adopted OE. **3.** Tale, narrative, story; †a saying, proverb. late ME. †**b.** Speech. SPENSER. **c.** Interpretation. BROWNING.

2. Therefore swift r. I take with all things here MORRIS. **3.** A final note..to bid the gentles speed Who long have listened to my r. SCOTT.

Rede (rīd), *v.* Now *arch.* or *poet.* and *dial.* OE. [Same word as READ *v.*, the common ME. spelling being retained for the archaic senses of the word.] **I.** †**1.** *intr.* To take counsel together or *with* another, to deliberate. Also of one person: To take counsel *for* others. –1494. †**2.** *trans.* To agree upon, resolve, decide, after consultation or deliberation –1559. **II. 1.** To advise or counsel (a person) OE. †**2.** To advise (a thing); to give as advice or counsel –1650. †**3.** *intr.* To give advice –1591. **4.** *Sc.* To think, imagine, guess 1768. **5.** To interpret, explain 1725. **6.** To relate, tell 1840.

1. I can mine selue In this case nat r. CHAUCER. **2.** Now read..What course ye weene is best for us to take SPENSER. **5.** The secret of Man's being is still..a riddle that he cannot r. CARLYLE. **6.** I'll r. ye a lay of Grammerye BARHAM.

Redeem (rĭdī·m), *v.* late ME. [– Fr. *rédimer* or L. *redimere*, f. *re(d)-* RE- + *emere* buy.] **1.** *trans.* To buy back (a thing formerly possessed); to make payment for (a thing held or claimed by another). Also *absol.* **b.** To regain, recover (an immaterial thing) 1526. **c.** To regain or recover by force 1666. **2. a.** To free (mortgaged property), to recover (a person or thing put in pledge), by payment of the amount due, or by fulfilling some obligation 1470. **b.** To buy off, compound for (a charge or obligation) by payment or some other way 1494. **c.** To fulfil, perform (a pledge, promise, etc.) 1840. **3.** To ransom, liberate, free (a person) from bondage, captivity, or punishment; to save (a person's life) by paying a random. late ME. **4.** To rescue, save, deliver 1470. **b.** To reclaim (land) 1721. **5.** To free from a charge or claim 1494. **6.** Of God or Christ: To deliver from sin and its consequences 1500. †**7.** To obtain by purchase, to buy –1645. **8.** To save (time) from being lost 1526. **9.** Of persons: To make amends or atonement for, to compensate (an error, fault, etc.) 1526. †**b.** To repay (some wrong sustained). SHAKS. **c.** To make good (a loss). *rare.* 1629. **10.** Of qualities, actions, etc.: To make up for, compensate for, counterbalance (some defect or fault) 1586. **b.** To save (a person or thing) *from* some defect or blot 1601. **11.** To restore, set right again (*rare*) 1575. †**12.** To gain, reach (a place). HERRICK.

1. That precious Time, which no sum..can either purchase or r. BOYLE. **b.** To r. his Honour DRYDEN. **c.** The Gael..Shall with strong hand r. his share SCOTT. **2. a.** *fig.* My Honor is at pawne, And but my going, nothing can redeeme it SHAKS. **b.** To r. incumbrances 1818. **3.** Wanting gilders to redeeme their liues SHAKS. **4.** Redeeme Israel, O God, out of all his Troubles *Ps.* 25:22. *absol.* Is my hande shortened at all, that it cannot redeeme? *Isa.* 50:2. **6.** Subiecte your selues whollye to God: for he hath redemed you 1558. **7.** 1 *Hen. VI*, II. v. 108. **8.** Walke wysely to them that are with out, and redeme the tyme TINDALE *Col.* 4:5. **9.** Which of ye will be mortal to r. Man's mortal crime? MILT. **c.** The Babe..That on the bitter cross Must r. our loss MILT. **10.** His bravery had redeemed much of his earlier ill-fame GREEN. **11.** With his barb'd horse..Stout Cromwell has redeem'd the day SCOTT. Hence **Redee·mless** *a.* irrecoverable; admitting of no redemption.

Redeemable (rĭdī·măb'l), *a.* and *sb.* 1611. [f. prec. + -ABLE.] **A.** *adj.* Capable of being redeemed. **b.** *spec.* Of property sold or mortgaged, bonds, stock, annuities, etc.: Capable or admitting of being repurchased or bought in again 1646.

b. The same is hereby created to the amount of £600,000 as a r. stock 1882.

B. *sb. pl.* Redeemable property, stocks, annuities, etc. Now *rare.* 1720. Hence **Redeemabi·lity** (*rare*). **Redee·mableness,** capability of being redeemed. **Redee·mably** *adv.*

Redeemer (rĭdī·məɹ). ME. [f. REDEEM *v.* + -ER[1].] **1.** One who redeems, in religious sense; God or Christ regarded as saving man from sin or its effects. **2.** One who redeems, in other senses of the vb. 1552.

1. Mans Friend, his Mediator, his design'd Both Ransom and R. voluntarie MILT.

Redeless (rī·dlės), *a. Obs.* exc. *arch.* [OE. *rǣdlēas*; see REDE *sb.*, -LESS.] Devoid or destitute of counsel; *esp.* of persons, having no resource in a difficulty or emergency, not knowing what to do.

Redemise (rīdĭməi·z), *sb.* 1797. [RE-.] *Law.* The retransfer of land to one who has demised it. So **Redemi·se** *v. trans.* to demise (land) back again.

Redemption (rĭde·mpʃən). ME. [– (O)Fr. *rédemption* – L. *redemptio, -on-*, f. *redempt-*, pa. ppl. stem of *redimere*; see REDEEM, -ION. Cf. RANSOM.] **1.** Deliverance from sin and its consequences by the atonement of Jesus Christ. **2.** The action of freeing a prisoner, captive, or slave by payment; ransom. late ME. **b.** *Jewish Law.* The ceremony of redeeming the eldest son by an offering (Num. 18:15). late ME. **3.** The action of freeing, delivering, or restoring in some way 1470. **b.** That which redeems; a redeeming feature 1860. **4.** The action of redeeming oneself from punishment; way or means of doing this; atonement 1468. †**b.** A recompense. BACON. **5.** The fact of obtaining a privileged status, or admission to a society, by means of purchase 1500. **6.** The action of clearing off a recurring liability or charge by payment of a single sum 1494. **7.** The action of redeeming or buying back from another, in various applications 1548.

1. Proclaiming Life to all who shall believe In his r. MILT. *Year of Redemption* = ANNO DOMINI. **2.** The r. of captives..is esteemed an act of piety MILMAN. **3.** Phr. *Without* or *past r.*, without or beyond the possibility of deliverance, recovery, or restoration. **6.** R. of the tolls 1867. **7.** An Act for the more easy R. and Foreclosure of Mortgages 1734. *Equity of r.*: see EQUITY 5. Hence **Rede·mptional** *a.* of or belonging to r. †**Rede·mptionary,** one who enters a society by purchase. **Rede·mptionist,** †(*a*) a redeemer; (*b*) = RANSOMER 2 a. **Rede·mptionless** *a.* incapable of r.

Redemptioner (rĭde·mpʃənəɹ). 1617. [f. prec. + -ER[1].] †**1.** = REDEMPTIONARY. **2.** *U.S.* An emigrant who received his passage to America on the condition that his services there should be disposed of by the master or owners of the vessel, until the passage-money and other expenses were repaid out of his earnings 1775. **3.** One who clears off a charge by redemption 1897.

Redemptive (rĭde·mptiv), *a.* 1647. [In XVII – Fr. †*redemptif, -ive*; later f. REDEMPTION + -IVE. Cf. med.L. *redemptivus* subject to ransom.] Tending to redeem, redeeming.

Redemptor (rĭde·mptǒɹ). Now *r*... ME. [– OFr. *redemptor* (mod. *rédem*... its source, L. *redemptor*, f. *re*... REDEMPTION) + *-or* -OR 2.] †**1.** ... 1 –1634. **2.** A redeemer, in oth... word (*rare*) 1880.

1. I wote ryght well tha... Lyueth yet 1400.

Redemptorist (rĭde·mᵖtŏrist). 1835. [– Fr. *rédemptoriste*; see prec., -IST.] **1.** A member of the Roman Catholic Congregation of the Most Holy Redeemer, founded at Naples in 1732 by St. Alphonsus Liguori, and devoted chiefly to work among the poor. **2.** *attrib.* or *adj.* Belonging to this Order 1863.

Redemptory (rĭde·mᵖtŏri), *a.* Now *rare.* 1598. [app. f. REDEMPTION + -ORY².] Of or pertaining to redemption; redemptive.

Redevable, *a.* (and *sb.*). 1502. [– Fr. *redevable*, f. *redevoir* (see RE-, DEVOIR) + -ABLE.] Beholden, indebted. Also as *sb.*, a debtor. –1711.

Red fish, re·d-fish. late ME. **1.** A male salmon in the spawning season, when it assumes a red colour. **b.** The salmon, in contrast to 'white' fish 1851. **2. a.** The red gurnard, *Trigla cuculus* 1611. **b.** Any of various American fishes, *esp.* the blue-backed salmon (*Oncorhyncus nerka*) and the red perch or rose-fish 1876.

Re·d gum, re·d-gum¹. 1597. [Alteration of earlier *radegounde*, *red-gown(d*, *-gown*, the second element of which is OE. *gund* pus.] **1.** A papular eruption or rash (*Strophulus intertinctus*) incident to young children, esp. during dentition, consisting of red pimples and patches irregularly disposed on the skin. *Rank red gum*, a virulent form of this (*Strophulus confertus*). **2.** A form of rust in grain 1807.

Re·d gum, re·d-gum². 1738. **1.** A reddish resinous substance exuded from the bark of various tropical or semi-tropical trees and shrubs, esp. that obtained from various Australian species of Eucalyptus. **2.** A tree of one or other of the Australian species yielding a red gum; also, the wood of these trees 1802.

Red hand, red-hand, *a.* and *sb.* late ME. **A.** *adj.* **1.** *Sc.* (orig. *Law*). = next 1. **2.** = next 1 c. 1894. **B.** *sb.* **1.** In phr. *with (the) red hand* = A. 1. Now *rare.* 1577. **2.** *Her.* (See quot.) 1856.

2. The open red hand..the noted *Lamh derg Eirin*, or red hand of Ulster 1863.

Red-handed, *a.* 1805. **1.** In the very act of crime, having the evidences of guilt still upon the person, esp. in phr. *to take*, or *be taken, red-handed* 1819. **b.** Having the hands red with blood 1861. **c.** That sheds or has shed blood; bloody, sanguinary, violent 1879. **2.** Having red hands 1805.

Re·d-head, re·dhead. ME. **1.** *attrib.* Having a red head or hair 1664. **2.** One who has a red head or hair ME. **3.** Applied to various birds, *esp.* the American pochard and red-headed woodpecker 1814. So **Red·-headed** (stress var.) *a.* having red hair; having a red head, esp. in names of birds, as **red-headed woodpecker,** *Melanerpes erythrocephalus.*

Red heat, red-heat. 1686. The state or condition of being red-hot; the degree of heat present when a substance is red-hot.

Red herring. late ME. *collect.* Herring to which a red colour is imparted in the process of curing them by smoke. **b.** A single herring cured in this way 1460.

Phr. *Neither fish, (nor) flesh, nor good red herring*, etc.: see FISH *sb.*¹ 3. *To draw a red h. across the track*, to attempt to divert attention from the real question; hence *red-herring*, a subject intended to have this effect.

Red-hot (stress var.), *a.* (and *sb.*). late ME. **1.** Heated to redness. **b.** *absol.* as *sb.* Red-hot metal 1832. **2.** *fig.* **a.** Of persons: Highly inflamed or excited; fiery; violently enthusiastic, extreme (in some view or principle). Also as *sb.* 1608. **b.** Of things, actions, etc.: Burning, scorching, urgent, violent, furious, etc. 1647. **c.** Very warm (as the favourite for a race) 1882. **3.** *Red-hot poker*, the flame-flower (*Tritoma*) 1897.

1. Showers of r. ashes 1878. **2.** A r. Predestinarian WESLEY. **b.** A r. flirtation 1879.

‖**Redia** (rī·diă). *Pl.* **rediæ** (rī·diī). 1877. [mod.L., f. *Redi*, name of an Italian naturalist.] *Zool.* An asexual stage in some trematodes, as the liver-fluke (*Distomum hepaticum*), hatched from eggs formed within the sporocyst, and in turn developing into a cercaria.

Redingote (re·dingoᵘt). 1835. [– Fr. *redingote*, repr. Eng. *riding-coat.*] **a.** In France: A double-breasted outer coat for men, with long plain skirts not cut away in the front. **b.** A similar garment worn by women, sometimes cut away in front.

†**Redintegrate,** *pa. pple.* 1501. [– L. *redintegratus*, pa. pple. of *redintegrare*; see next, -ATE².] Restored to a perfect state, renewed –1819.

Redintegrate (redi·ntĭgreᵗt), *v.* late ME. [– *redintegrat-*, pa. ppl. stem of L. *redintegrare*, f. *re(d)-* RE- + *integrare* INTEGRATE; see -ATE³.] **1.** *trans.* To restore to a state of wholeness, completeness or unity; to renew, re-establish, in a united or perfect state. †**2.** To re-establish (a person) *in* a place (*rare*) –1649. **b.** To re-establish (a person) *in* (†*into*) a position, condition, etc. Chiefly *pass.* Now *rare.* 1622.

1. To r. the Honour and Credit of that exploded Faction 1734. **2. b.** I..had to pay the..taxes..before I could be redintegrated in my own property THACKERAY.

Redintegration (redintĭgrēⁱ·ʃən). 1471. [– AFr. *redintegracioun* or L. *redintegratio*, *-on-*, f. as prec.; see -ION.] **1.** The action of redintegrating; restoration, re-establishment, reconstruction, renewal 1501. **2.** *spec.* †**a.** *Chem.* The restoration of any body or matter to its former state –1802. **b.** *Psychol.* (See quot.) 1836. †**3.** The restoration of a person to a previous condition –1741. †**4.** Reconciliation –1667.

1. A r. of love THACKERAY. **2. b.** The law of R. or Totality..Those thoughts suggest each other which had previously constituted parts of the same entire or total act of cognition SIR W. HAMILTON.

Redire·ct, *a.* 1891. [RE- 5 a.] *U.S. Law.* The term applied to the further examination of a witness by the party calling him, after cross-examination by the opposing party.

Redisseisin (rīdisī·zin). 1535. [– AFr. *redisseisine*; see RE-, DISSEISIN.] *Law.* Repeated disseisin.

Redistri·bute, *v.* 1611. [RE- 5 a.] *trans.* To distribute anew. So **Redistribu·tion,** a fresh distribution, esp. of Parliamentary seats.

Redi·strict, *v. U.S.* 1850. [RE- 5 a.] *trans.* To divide or apportion anew into districts.

†**Redi·tion.** *rare.* 1595. [– L. *reditio*, *-on-*, f. *redit-*, pa. ppl. stem of *redire* go or come back, f. *re(d)-* RE + *ire* go; see -ION.] The action of going or coming back; return –1656.

Red lead, red-lead (-led). 1450. A red oxide of lead, largely used as a pigment.

Re·d-legs, re·d-leg. 1802. **1.** *Ornith.* Any of various birds with red legs; *esp.* the redshank (*Totanus calidris*), the red-legged partridge (*Caccabis rufa*), and (*U.S.*) the turnstone (*Strepsilas interpres*). **2.** The plant bistort (*Polygonum bistorta*) 1820.

Red letter. late ME. **1.** (Chiefly *pl.*) A letter made with red ink, or with some red pigment, esp. as used in eccl. calendars to indicate saints' days and church festivals. **2.** *attrib.* as *red-letter almanac*, etc.; †**red-letter man,** a Roman Catholic 1677. **b. Red-letter day,** a saint's day or church festival indicated in the calendar by red letters; hence, any memorable, fortunate, or specially happy day 1776.

Re·d man, red-màn, 1610. †**1.** *Alchemy.* Red sulphide of mercury. B. JONS. **2.** A. N. American Indian; a redskin 1744.

Re-do·, redo, *v.* 1597. [RE- 5 a.] **1.** *trans.* To do over again or afresh. **b.** To redecorate (a room) 1864. †**2.** To do back or in return –1650.

Red ochre. 1572. A variety of ochre commonly used for colouring with; reddle or ruddle. Also *attrib.* Hence **Red-ochre** *v. trans.*

Redolence (re·dŏlĕns). late ME. [– OFr. *redolence*, f. *redolent*; see next, -ENCE.] Sweet smell, fragrance, perfume. Also *fig.* So †**Re·dolency.**

Redolent (re·dŏlent), *a.* late ME. [– OFr. *redolent* or L. *redolens*, *-ent-*, pr. pple. of *redolēre*, f. *re(d)-* RE- + *olēre* emit a smell; see -ENT.] **1.** Having or diffusing a pleasant odour; sweet-smelling, fragrant, odorous. Now *rare.* **2.** Of smell, odour, etc.: Pleasant, sweet, fragrant 1450. **3.** Odorous or smelling *of* or *with* something; full of the scent or smell *of* 1700.

1. The r. breath Of the warm seawind TENNYSON. **2.** All manner of r. Odors 1629. **3.** The gales..seem.., r. of joy and youth, To breathe a second spring GRAY. *fig.* On every side Oxford is r. of age and authority EMERSON.

Redouble (rĭdʊ·b'l), *v.*¹ 1477. [– Fr. *redoubler*, f. *re-* RE- + *doubler* DOUBLE.] **1.** *trans.* To double (a thing); to make twice as great or as much. **b.** *intr.* To be doubled. Also, to become doubly strong *in* some respect. 1490. **2.** *trans.* To repeat; to do, say, etc., a second time 1581. **b.** *esp.* To repeat (a blow, etc.) 1593. †**3.** To repeat (a sound); to return, reproduce, re-echo –1679. **b.** *intr.* To re-echo, resound 1725. **4.** *trans.* To duplicate by reflection 1827.

1. This made our people r. their efforts 1748. **2. b** Let thy blowes doubly redoubled, Fall like amazing thunder SHAKS. **3.** Their moans The Vales redoubl'd to the Hills, and they To Heav'n MILT.

Redouble (rĭdʊ·b'l), *v.*² 1530. [RE- 5 a.] To double again (esp. in *Bridge*).

Redoubt (rĭdau·t), *sb.* †Also **redout(e.** 1608. [– Fr. *redoute*, †*ridotte* – It. †*ridotta*, now *ridotto* – med. L. *reductus* refuge, retreat, f. pa. ppl. stem of L. *reducere* draw-off, withdraw. The intrusive *b* is due to assoc. with next.] **1.** *Fortif.* †**a.** A small work made in a bastion or ravelin of a permanent fortification, or (*detached r.*) at some distance beyond the glacis, but within musket-shot from the covert-way. **b.** A species of out-work or field-work, usu. of a square or polygonal shape, and with little or no means of flanking defence. **2.** *Fortif.* = REDUIT 1802.

1. b. *fig.* Conservatism, entrenched in its immense redoubts EMERSON.

Redoubt (rĭdau·t), *v.* Now *rhet.* late ME. [– (O)Fr. *redouter*, †*redoubter* fear, dread, f. *re-* RE- + *douter* DOUBT.] *trans.* To dread, fear, stand in awe or apprehension of. Hence **Redou·bted** *ppl. a.* feared or dreaded; reverenced; noted, distinguished.

Redoubtable (rĭdau·tăb'l), *a.* (and *sb.*) late ME. [– (O)Fr. *redoutable*, f. *redouter*; see prec., -ABLE.] To be feared or dreaded; formidable. †Also, of persons: Commanding respect.

That you marry this r. couple together—Righteousness and Peace CROMWELL. That spear, r. in war BURNS.

Redound (rĭdau·nd), *v.* late ME. [– (O)Fr. *redonder*:–L. *redundare*, f. *re(d)-* RE- + *undare* surge, f. *unda* wave. See REDUNDANT.] **I.** *intr.* †**1.** Of water, waves, etc.: To swell or surge up, to overflow –1725. †**b.** *transf.* To be in excess or superfluous –1667. †**2.** To be plentiful, abound –1581. †**3.** To flow, come, or go back; to return (*to* a place or person); to come again –1596. †**4.** To resound, reverberate, re-echo –1632. **5.** To result in contributing or turning *to* some advantage or disadvantage for a person or thing. late ME. **b.** To turn *to* one's honour, disgrace, etc. 1474. **6.** Of advantage, damage, praise, etc.: To result, attach, accrue *to*, *unto* (a person) 1500. **7.** Of honour or disgrace, advantage, etc.: To recoil or come back, to fall, *upon* a person 1589. †**8.** To proceed, issue, arise *from* or *out of* something –1796.

1. Round the descending nymph the waves redounding roar POPE. **5.** Which could not but mightily r. to the good of the Nation MILT. **b.** Affyrming that it would redounde to the perpetuall shame of Germany 1560. **6.** The clear gain redounding to the Commonwealth SWIFT. **8.** The anxietie of spirit which redoundeth from knowledge BACON.

†**II.** *trans.* **1.** To reflect (honour, blame, etc.) *in, to, upon* a person –1712. **2.** To add, yield, cause to accrue –1690.

1. For fear they should r. Dishonour upon the Innocent STEELE. Hence **Redou·nd** *sb.* (*rare*) reverberation, echo; a resounding cry; also, the fact of redounding.

‖**Redowa** (re·dŏvă). Also **redowak.** 1860. [– Fr. or G. *redowa* – Czech *rejdovák*, f. *rejdovati* turn or whirl round.] A slow waltz, of Bohemian origin, resembling the mazurka; also, the music for such a dance.

Re·dpoll[1], **-pole.** 1738. [f. RED *a.* + *pole* POLL *sb.*[1]] **1.** Any of several species of the family *Fringillidæ* characterized by bright red feathers on the crest. **a.** The greater r., the male of the common linnet in summer plumage. **b.** The lesser or common r., a common British cagebird, *Linota rufescens* or *Ægiothus linaria*. **c.** The mealy or stone r., *Ægiothus canescens*. Also the allied American species (*Æ. exilipes*). **2.** *Yellow r.*, an American warbler, *Dendræca palmarum*; the palm-warbler 1758. So **Re·d-polled** *a.* red-headed.

Re·dpoll[2], **-polled.** 1895. *pl.* Red-haired polled cattle.

Redraft (rīdra·ft), *sb.* 1682. [RE- 5 a.] **1.** A bill of re-exchange. **2.** A second or new draft 1847.

Redraft (rīdra·ft), *v.* 1798. [RE- 5 a.] *trans.* To draft again (a writing or ducument).

Red rag, red-rag. 1700. **1.** *slang.* The tongue. **2.** A variety of rust in grain 1851. **3.** (From the phr. *like a red rag to a bull.*) A source of extreme provocation or annoyance 1885.

Redraw (rīdrǭ·), *v.* 1692. [RE- 5 a.] **1.** *intr.* To draw a fresh bill of exchange to cover a former one. **2.** *trans.* To draw or take out again 1805. **3.** To draw (a picture, etc.) again 1830. Hence **Redraw·er.**

Redress (rīdre·s), *sb.* late ME. [– AFr. *redresse, -esce*, f. *redresser*; see next.] **1.** Reparation of, satisfaction or compensation for, a wrong sustained or the loss resulting from this. †**2.** Remedy for, or relief from, some trouble; assistance, aid, help –1759. †**b.** Correction, amendment, or reformation of something wrong –1764. †**3.** With *a* and *pl.* A means or way of redress; an act or arrangement whereby a person or thing is redressed; an amendment, improvement –1728. †**b.** One who, or that which, affords redress –1697. **4.** The act of redressing; correction or amendment *of* a thing, state, etc. 1538.

1. He who gives credit, and is cheated, will have no r. 1875. **2.** My griefs..finding no r., ferment and rage MILT. Phr. †*Beyond, past, without r.*, beyond the possibility of remedy, aid, or amendment. **3. b.** Fair majesty, the refuge and r. Of those whom fate pursues and wants oppress DRYDEN. **4.** The great principle that r. of wrongs precedes a grant to the Crown GREEN.

Redress (rīdre·s), *v.*[1] late ME. [– (O)Fr. *redresser*, †*-drecier* (cf. med.L. *redirectiare, redreçare*, etc.); see RE-, DRESS *v.*] †**1.** *trans.* To set (a person or thing) upright again; to raise again to an erect position –1711. †**2.** *fig.* To bring back to the right course; to correct or direct aright –1689. †**b.** To direct or amend (one's acts or ways) –1635. †**3.** To put (things) in order; to arrange –1585. †**4.** To put right, or in good order, again; to mend, repair; to reform, amend –1764. **b.** To correct, emend (*rare*) 1710. **c.** To adjust again. (Chiefly with *balance.*) 1847. †**5.** To restore (a person) to happiness or prosperity; to save, deliver *from* misery, death, etc. –1583. **6.** To set (a person) right, by obtaining, or (occas.) giving, satisfaction or compensation for the wrong or loss sustained. late ME. **7.** To remedy or remove (trouble or distress of any kind). late ME. **8.** To set right, repair, rectify (a wrong, injury, grievance, etc.). late ME. **9.** To correct, amend, reform or do away with (a bad or faulty state of things, now *esp.* an abuse). late ME. †**10.** To repair (an action); to atone for (a misdeed or offence) –1597.

1. To..r. a leaning Wall SHAFTESB. **2. b.** Wherewith shal a yong man redresse his waie? BIBLE (Genev.) *Ps.* 119:9. **4.** Rise God, judge thou the earth in might, This wicked earth r. MILT. **b.** The material estimate of worth should be redressed by a moral standard 1868. **6.** 'Tis thine, O King, the afflicted to r. DRYDEN. **7.** Such carbuncles..As no Hungarian water can r. 1687. You will..r. a Misfortune 1714. **8.** To r. grievances HUME. To prevent or r. the threatened outrage 1863. **9.** In a vigorous campaign he pacified Ireland while redressing the abuses of its government GREEN. Hence **Redre·ssable** *a.* **Redre·ssal,** redress. **Redre·sser,** one who redresses (*esp.* a wrong). **Redre·ssive** *a.* (*rare*) seeking to redress; bringing redress. **Redre·ssment,** the act of redressing; redress.

Redress (rīdre·s), *v.*[2] 1739. [RE- 5 a.] *trans.* and *intr.* To dress again.

Redre·ssor. 1884. [f. REDRESS *v.*[1] + -OR 2.] One who, or that which, redresses; *spec.* in *Surg.* (see quot.).

Redressor, a replacing instrument, e.g. the uterine r. 1884.

Red-sha·nk(s, re·dshank. 1500. **1.** One who has red legs; *spec.* (chiefly in *pl.*) one of the Celtic inhabitants of the Scottish Highlands and of Ireland. Now *Hist.* 1542. **2.** *Ornith.* A wading bird (*Totanus calidris*) of the snipe family (*Scolopacidæ*), so called from the colour of its legs 1500. **b.** Applied also, with defining word, to *Tetanus fuscus*, the Black, Dusky, or Spotted R. 1776.

attrib.: **red-shank gull,** the black-headed gull, *Larus ridibundus.*

†**Re·dshire, -share,** *a.* 1665. [– Sw. *rödskör*; see next.] *Metall.* = next –1794.

Re·d-short, *a.* 1730. [– Sw. *rödskört* (sc. *jern* iron), n. of *rödskör*, f. *röd* red + *skör* brittle; cf. COLD-SHORT.] *Metall.* Of iron: Brittle while in a red-hot condition, owing to excess of sulphur in the metal. Hence **Re·d-shortness,** the quality or state of being r.

Re·dskin. 1699. [See RED A. 5 c.] A North American Indian.

Red snow. 1678. **1.** Snow reddened by a kind of alga (*Protococcus nivalis*), common in Arctic and Alpine regions. **2.** *transf.* The alga which gives a red colouring to snow 1825.

Redstart (re·dstāɹt). 1570. [f. RED *a.* + START *sb.*[1]] *Ornith.* **1.** A common European singing-bird (*Ruticilla phœnicurus*), so named from its red tail, which it has a habit of moving quickly from side to side. **b.** *Black r.*, a related species, *Ruticilla titys*, occurring in southern England and common on the European continent 1836. **2.** An American fly-catching warbler, *Setophaga ruticilla*, outwardly resembling the common European redstart but generically distinct from it 1796.

Re·d-streak. Also †**-strake.** 1664. **1.** A red-streaked apple formerly highly esteemed for making cider. **b.** The cider made from this 1671. **2.** *transf.* A girl with red cheeks 1771.

Red-tape, red tape. 1696. **a.** Tape of a pinkish-red colour such as is commonly used in securing legal and other documents. Hence **b.** Excessive formality or attention to routine; rigid or mechanical adherence to rules and regulations. Also *attrib.*

His brain was little better than red tape and parchment W. IRVING. Hence **Red-ta·pism, -ta·peism,** the system or spirit of red-tape. **Red-ta·pist, -ta·peist,** one who adheres strictly or mechanically to official routine.

Re·d-top. 1800. **1.** *attrib.* Having a red top; red-topped. **2.** *U.S.* A kind of bent-grass, *Agrostis vulgaris*, highly valued for pasture. *Tall red-top*, a tall reddish grass, *Triodea cuprea.* 1819. **3.** A variety of turnip 1830.

†**Redu·b,** *v.* 1522. [– AFr. *redubber*, f. *re-* RE- + *dubber* DUB *v.*[1]. Cf. AL. *redubbare* (XIII).] *trans.* To repair or restore; to put right, remedy, improve, amend, redress –1568.

Reduce (rĭdiū·s), *v.* late ME. [– L. *reducere* bring back, restore, f. *re-* RE- + *ducere* lead, bring.] **I.** *trans.* †**1.** To bring back, recall (a thing or person) *to* the memory, mind, etc. –1624. †**b.** To bring back, recall (the mind, thoughts, etc.) *from* or *to* a subject –1706. †**2.** To lead or bring back *to, into, from*, etc. a place or way, or *to* a person –1731. †**3.** To take back, refer (a thing) *to* its origin or author –1660. **4.** To bring back, restore (a condition, state of things, time, etc.). Now *rare.* 1477. **5.** *Surg.* To restore (a dislocated, fractured, or ruptured part) to the proper position 1541. **b.** To adjust, set (a dislocation or fracture) 1836.

4. Abate the edge of Traitors..That would r. these bloudy dayes againe SHAKS.

II. †**1.** To lead or bring back from error in action, conduct, or belief; to restore to the truth or the right faith –1788. †**2.** To bring back or restore (a person, etc.) *from* or *to* a state or condition –1741. †**b.** To bring back (a thing, institution, etc.) *to* a former state. Also without const. –1765. †**3.** To bring (a person or thing) *to* or *into* a certain state or condition or *to* do something –1719. **b.** To bring (a theory, etc.) *to* (or *into*) practice or action 1625. †**4.** To adapt (a thing) *to* a purpose. *rare.* –1609. **b.** *Astron.* To adapt (an observation) *to* a particular place or point 1633. †**5. a.** To bring *into* another language; to render, translate –1581. **b.** To set down or record in writing; to put down or draw in a map –1603. **6.** To bring (†*into* or) *to* a certain order or arrangement 1570. **b.** To bring *to* (†*into* or *under*) a specified number of classes or heads; also, to assign or refer *to* a certain class 1526. **7.** To bring (†*into* or) *to* a certain form or character 1592. **b.** To put *into*, commit *to*, writing 1659. **8. a.** *Arith.* To change (a number or quantity) from one denomination *into* or *to* another 1579. **b.** To change (a quantity, figure, etc.) *into* or *to* a different form. Also *absol.* 1579. **c.** To resolve by analysis. Const. *to.* 1860. **9.** To turn *to*, convert *into*, a different physical state or form; esp. to break down, grind, or crush *to* powder, etc. 1605. **b.** *Metall.* To convert (ore) into metal; to smelt 1758. **c.** *Chem.* To remove oxygen from (a compound); also to diminish the valency of (an atom, an element) towards electro-negative radicals 1741. **d.** To break up (soil) into fine particles 1763. **10.** *Logic.* To bring a syllogism (†or proposition) into a different but equivalent form, *spec.* to one of the moods of the first figure 1727.

6. The infinite would be no longer infinite, if limited or reduced to measure JOWETT. **b.** Those who set up for Criticks in Poetry..may be reduced to two Classes STEELE. **7.** A second Word,..reducing it to the English Orthography may be spelt thus, Houyhnhnm SWIFT. **8. b.** To R. an Integer to the Form of a Fraction 1797. **9. b.** Several attempts had been made to r. iron ore with coaked coal 1839.

III. 1. To bring *to* (or *into*) order, obedience, reason, etc., by constraint or compulsion 1490. †**b.** To make subject *to* a person; to cause to give obedience or adherence *to*; to bring *into* or *under* a person's power, *within* bounds, etc. –1833. **c.** *Law.* To bring (a thing or right) *into* (†*to*) possession 1766. **2.** To bring (a place) into subjection, to subdue, conquer; *spec.* to capture (a town, fortress, etc.); to compel to submit or surrender 1612. **b.** To subdue, conquer (a person) 1598. **c.** To constrain, compel, force (a person) *to* do something 1622. †**d.** To subdue, repress, moderate (a desire, temper, etc.) –1725. **3.** To bring down *to* a bad or disagreeable condition 1572. **b.** In *pass.*, with *inf.* To be compelled by want *to* do something; also, to be hard put to it 1693. **c.** To weaken physically 1734. **d.** To diminish the strength of (spirit) 1880. **4.** To bring down *to* a lower rank or position, dignity, etc. 1641. †**5.** *Mil.* To break up, disband (an army or regiment) –1802. **b.** To break up (a square, etc.) and restore the component parts to line or column 1672.

1. The clergy could not be allowed to r. Crown and barons into entire submission to their own pleasure FROUDE. **2.** Chester was reduced by famine DE FOE. **c.** A blow..reduced him to measure his length on the ground FIELDING. **3.** Reduced almost to penury 1820. **b.** Poor creature! he was reduced..to borrow five guineas of Sir Francis Dashwood H. WALPOLE. **4.** Phr. *To r. to the ranks* (*Mil.*), to degrade (a non-commissioned officer) to the rank of private.

IV. 1. To bring or draw together. (In later use only as implying diminution of bulk.) late ME. **2.** To bring down, diminish *to* a smaller number, amount, extent, etc., or *to* a single thing 1560. **b.** To lower, diminish, lessen 1787. **c.** *intr.* To become lessened or limited 1811.

1. Tom reduced himself into the least possible space DICKENS. **2.** Thus incorporeal Spirits to smallest forms Reduc'd thir shapes immense MILT. Reduced to half-price 1762. Hence †**Redu·ceable** *a.* = REDUCIBLE. †**Redu·cement,** reduction. **Redu·cer,** one who, or that which, reduces.

Reducent (rĭdiū·sěnt), *a.* (and *sb.*). 1805. [f. prec. + -ENT, after *abducent, adducent.*] **A.** *adj.* **1.** *Bot.* and *Zool.* Of a vein, channel, etc.: That carries something back from a certain part. (Opp. to *adducent.*) **2.** *Med.* Lowering 1822. **B.** *sb.* That which reduces 1847.

Reducible (rĭdiū·sĭb'l), *a.* 1450. [In early use – med.L. *reducibilis*; later, f. REDUCE *v.* + -IBLE.] That may be reduced. Hence

Reducibi·lity. Redu·cibleness. Redu·cibly *adv.*

Reducing (rĭdiū·siŋ), *vbl. sb.* 1488. [f. REDUCE *v.* + -ING¹.] The action of REDUCE *v.*; reduction.

Comb.: **r. compasses,** compasses adapted for copying figures on a smaller scale; **r. coupling** or **piece,** a pipe-coupling with ends of different diameters, used in joining pipes of different sizes; **r. valve,** a valve serving to reduce the pressure in a steam-engine; **r. works,** a place at which metallic ore is reduced.

†**Redu·ct,** *v.* 1558. [– *reduct-*, pa. ppl. stem of L. *reducere* REDUCE.] **1.** *trans.* To bring, lead, lead back –1816. **2.** To deduct (a sum) –1738.

‖**Reductio ad absurdum** (rĭdɒ·kʃio æd æbsɒ̄·ɹdɒ̆m): see REDUCTION II. 4.

Reduction (rĭdɒ·kʃən). 1474. [– (O)Fr. *réduction* or L. *reductio*, f. *reduct-*; see REDUCT, -ION.] **I.** †**1.** The action of bringing (back) *to* or *from* a state, condition, belief, etc. –1677. †**2.** The action of bringing back (a person, thing, institution, etc.) to a place previously occupied; restoration –1741. **3.** *Surg.* The restoration of a dislocated part to its normal position; the action of reducing a displacement, etc. 1656.

2. The whole History of their R. out of Egypt WARBURTON.

II. 1. Conquest or subjugation *of* a place, esp. a town or fortress 1474. **b.** The action of reducing *into* possession. Also without const. 1647. **c.** [– Sp. *reduccion*.] A settlement or colony of S. Amer. Indians converted and governed by the Jesuits 1712. **2. a.** *Arith.* (*a*) The process of changing an amount from one denomination to another. (*b*) The process of bringing down a fraction to its lowest terms. 1542. **b.** *Alg.* (See quot.) 1702. **c.** *Astron.* The correction of observations by allowance for modifying circumstances, as parallax, refraction, etc. 1812. **3.** *Logic.* The process of reducing a syllogism (†or proposition) to another, esp. to a simpler or clearer, form; *spec.* by expressing it in one of the moods of the first figure (*direct* or *ostensive r.*). Also, the process of establishing the validity of a syllogism by showing that the contradictory of its conclusion is inconsistent with its premisses (*indirect* or *apagogical r.*). 1551. **4.** Conversion *into* or *to* a certain state, form, etc. 1605. **5.** The action or process of reducing (a substance) to another (usu. a simpler) form, *esp.* by some chemical process 1650. **b.** The conversion of ore into metal; smelting 1797. **6.** Diminution, lessening, cutting down 1676. **b.** The action or process of making a copy on a smaller scale; also, a copy of this kind 1727.

1. The r. of Syracuse THIRLWALL. **2. b.** *R. of equations*..is the reducing them into a fit and proper Order or Disposition for a Solution 1702. **4.** Phr. *R. to the absurd* or *to absurdity* (= L. *reductio ad absurdum*), a method of proving the falsity of a premiss, principle, etc., by showing that the conclusion or consequence is absurd; also, loosely, the pushing of anything to an absurd extreme. **6.** Not one shilling towards the r. of our debt BURKE.

Comb.: **r. compasses,** reducing compasses; **-works,** works for the reduction of metallic ore.

Reductive (rĭdɒ·ktiv), *a.* and *sb.* Now *rare.* 1633. [– med.L. *reductivus*, f. as prec.; see -IVE. Cf. (O)Fr. *réductif*.] **1.** That leads or brings back. Also with *of.* 1655. **2.** That reduces, or serves to reduce; connected with, of the nature of, reduction. Also with *of.* 1633. †**3.** That may be referred to or derived from something else; reducible –1691. **4.** *absol.* as *sb.* That which tends to reduce 1676. Hence **Redu·ctively** *adv.* (now *rare*), by reduction; by consequence or interference 1624.

‖**Reduit** (redwi). 1604. [Fr., ult. – med.L. *reductus*; see REDOUBT *sb.*] *Fortif.* A keep or stronghold into which a garrison may retire when the outworks are taken.

Redundance (rĭdɒ·ndăns). 1596. [f. as next; see -ANCE.] = next.

Redundancy (rĭdɒ·ndănsi). 1601. [– L. *redundantia*, f. as next; see -ANCY.] The state or quality of being redundant; superabundance, superfluity. Also with *a* and *pl.*, an instance of this. **b.** A redundant thing or part 1631. **c.** That which is redundant; the surplus 1733.

c. It is not the whole of the people..It is only the r. that we have to take care of. 1832.

Redundant (rĭdɒ·ndănt), *a.* and *sb.* 1596. [– L. *redundans*, *-ant-*, pr. pple. of *redundare*; see REDOUND, -ANT.] **1.** Superabundant, superfluous, excessive. **b.** Characterized by superfluity or excess in some respect. Also const. *in.* 1638. **2.** Abounding to excess or fullness; plentiful, copious, exuberant 1671. **b.** Characterized by copiousness, fullness, or abundance. Also const. *of*, *with.* 1653. †**3. a.** Flowing or swelling, wave-like –1726. †**b.** Swelling up, overflowing –1774. †**B.** *sb.* Something redundant –1797.

1. The employment of r. capital MACAULAY. **b.** Milton frequently uses..the hypermetrical or r. line of eleven syllables JOHNSON. **2.** These r. locks Robustious to no purpose clustring down MILT. **3. a.** The vest unbound Floats in bright waves r. o'er the ground POPE. **b.** R. Nile, Broke from its channel, overswells the pass 1719. Hence **Redu·ndantly** *adv.*

Reduplicate (rĭdiū·plikĕt), *a.* and *sb.* 1647. [– late L. *reduplicatus*, pa. pple. of *reduplicare*; see next, -ATE¹,².] **A.** *adj.* **1.** Doubled, repeated. **b.** *Gram.* Reduplicated; connected with or involving reduplication 1841. **2.** *Bot.* Valvate, with the edges reflexed 1856. **B.** *sb.* A double (one), a duplicate 1657.

Reduplicate (rĭdiū·plikeˈt), *v.* 1570. [– *reduplicat-*, pa. ppl. stem of late L. *reduplicare*, f. *re-* RE- + L. *duplicare* DUPLICATE *v.*] **1.** *trans.* To make double; to repeat, redouble. **b.** *Gram.* To repeat (a letter or syllable); to form (a tense) by reduplication 1832. **2.** *intr.* To become double or doubled (*rare*) 1709.

Reduplication (rĭdiūplikēˈ·ʃən). 1589. [– late L. *reduplicatio*, *-on-*, f. as prec.; see -ION. Cf. Fr. *réduplication*.] †**1.** The action of doubling or folding. PUTTENHAM. **b.** A double or fold (*rare*) 1698. **2.** The action of making or becoming double or two-fold; repetition; also, a double or counterpart 1649. **b.** Repetition of a word (or phrase) 1619. †**3.** *Logic.* The repetition of a term with a limiting or defining force; the addition of some limiting term to one already used, or the sense of a term as thus limited –1741. **4.** *Gram.* Repetition of a syllable or letter, *esp.* in the perfect tense of verbs in Greek and other Indo-European languages 1650. **b.** A word-form produced by repetition of a syllable 1862.

4. *Attic r.*, the form exemplified in Gr. ἀκήκοα from ἀκούω, ἤγαγον from ἄγω.

Reduplicative (rĭdiū·plikĕtiv), *a.* 1605. [– med.L. *reduplicativus*, f. as prec.; see -IVE.] **1.** Of the nature of, pertaining or relating to, expressing or implying, reduplication of terms. (See prec. 3.) Now *rare.* **b.** Of propositions: Having a limiting repetition of the subject expressed 1704. **2.** Formed by reduplication 1833. **3.** *Bot.* = REDUPLICATE *a.* 2. 1866.

1. b. *R. Propositions*, are such wherein the Subject is repeated: Thus, Men, as Men, are Rational 1704. Hence **Redu·plicatively** *adv.*

Re·dwing, re·d-wing. 1645. *Ornith.* **a.** A common variety of thrush (*Turdus iliacus*), characterized by its red wings. **b.** The red-winged blackbird (*Agelæus phœniceus*) of N. America 1831. So **Red-winged** *a.* having red wings, as *red-winged blackbird* = b.

Re·dwood, *sb.* Also **red wood, red-wood.** 1633. **1.** Wood of a red colour, obtained from many tropical trees; formerly applied esp. to such as were used for dyeing. **2.** Any of various trees having a red wood, *esp.* a tall Californian timber-tree, *Sequoia sempervirens* 1716.

Ree (rī), *sb.* 1550. [var. of REEVE *sb.*²] The female of the ruff.

Ree (rī), **rye** (rəi), *v. dial.* late ME. [Of unkn. origin.] *trans.* To clean or sift (winnowed grain, peas, etc.), *spec.* by giving a circular motion to the contents of the sieve, so that the chaff, etc. collects in the centre.

‖**Reebok** (rē·bǫk). 1775. [Du., = ROE-BUCK.] A small S. African antelope, *Pelea capreola*, with sharp horns.

Re-e·cho, *v.* 1590. [f. RE- + ECHO *v.*] **1.** *intr.* To echo (again), resound. **2.** *trans.* **a.** To echo back; to return (a sound), reverberate, multiply by repetition 1595. **b.** To repeat like an echo 1636.

1. The thunder of the avalanche Re-echoes far behind SOUTHEY. **2. a.** Severn shall reecho with affright The shrieks of death GRAY. **b.** Those who still r. Ricardo and Malthus 1875. So **Re-e·cho** *sb.* an echo; also a second or repeated echo.

Reechy (rī·tʃi), *a. Obs.* exc. *dial.* 1460. [f. *reech* REEK *sb.* + -Y¹.] Smoky; squalid, dirty; rancid.

Reed (rīd), *sb.* [OE. *hrēod* = OFris. *hriad*, OS. *hriod*, MDu. *ried*, *riet* (Du. *riet*), OHG. (*h*)*riot* (G. *ried*) :– WGmc. **χreuđa*.] **I. 1.** One of the tall straight stalks or stems formed by plants of the genera *Phragmites* and *Arundo*; †also, a cane. **2.** *collect.* Reeds (as plants); a growth or bed of reeds OE. **b.** Reeds employed for firing or thatching, or for plastering upon 1494. **c.** *transf.* Wheat-straw prepared for thatching. late ME. **3.** Without article, as a material ME. **4.** With *the*, as the distinctive name of the class of plants forming the genera *Phragmites* and *Arundo*, having a firm stem and growing in water or marshy ground; *esp.* the common species *Phragmites communis*, abundant in Britain and on the Continent; †also, the sugar-cane. late ME.

4. Up stood the cornie Reed Embattel'd in her field MILT.

II. 1. a. A reed used as a dart or arrow; hence *poet.* an arrow. late ME. **b.** in biblical use: A reed employed as a measuring-rod; hence, a Jewish measure of length (also called *Ezekiel's r.*), equal to six cubits. late ME. **2.** A reed made into a rustic musical pipe. Also *transf.*, esp. in *oaten r.* late ME. **b.** *fig.* as the symbol of rustic or pastoral poetry 1582. **3.** A part of various musical instruments. **a.** In the oboe and bassoon: A part of the mouthpiece, consisting of two slightly concave wedge-shaped pieces of reed or cane fixed face to face on the end of a metal tube. Also, a similar device fixed in the chanter of a bagpipe. (Now freq. called a *double r.*) 1530. **b.** In the organ: A small metal tube fixed at the lower end of a pipe, having a longitudinal opening covered or closed by a metal tongue, which is made to vibrate by the air entering the tube 1727. **c.** (*a*) A metal tongue used to produce sound by vibration, *esp.* that used in an organ-pipe; (*b*) a slip of cane used for the same purpose, as in the clarinet. (Sometimes called *single r.*; cf. a.) 1811. **4.** *Mining.* A tube containing the powder-train for igniting the charge in blasting 1875. **5.** A weaver's instrument for separating the threads of the warp and beating up the weft, formerly made of thin strips of reed or cane, but now of metal wires, fastened by the ends into two parallel bars of wood 1611. **6.** *Arch.* One of a set of small semicylindrical mouldings 1745.

1. b. He measured the East side with the measuring reede, fiue hundreth reedes *Ezek.* 42:16. **2.** The..sound of pastoral r. with oaten stops MILT. **3. c.** *Beating* or *striking r.*, one which strikes against its seat; in the organ, against the edges of the opening in the tube. *Free r.*, one which produces sound by vibration only, esp. one which vibrates in the opening of a tube without touching the edges, as in instruments of the reed-organ type.

Comb.: **r.-babbler** = REED-WARBLER; **-bird,** a bird which frequents reeds; *spec.* a N. Amer. bobolink, *Dolichonyx oryzivorus*; **-buck,** the rietbok, or other antelope frequenting reeds; **-bunting,** the r.-sparrow, *Emberiza schœniclus*; **-grass,** any of various reed-like grasses, as the bur-r., bent, etc.; **-organ,** a musical instrument of the organ type in which the sounds are produced by means of reeds; **-pipe,** (*a*) a musical pipe made of r.; (*b*) an organ-pipe fitted with a r.; **-sparrow,** (*a*) a common British bird, *Emberiza schœniclus*, frequenting reedy places; (*b*) the sedge-warbler; **-stop,** an organ-stop composed of r.-pipes; **-wren,** the r.-warbler; also, any of various allied American birds.

Reed (rīd), *v.* 1440. [f. prec.] **1.** *trans.* To thatch with reed. Chiefly *pass.* **2.** To make (straw) into reed 1817. **3.** To fashion into, or decorate with, reeds; to furnish with a reed-moulding 1823.

Reeded (rī·dėd), *ppl. a.* 1819. [f. REED *v.* and *sb.* + -ED.] **1.** Overgrown with reeds 1876. **2.** Thatched with reed 1819. **3.** Ornamented with reed-moulding 1833.

Reeden (rī·d'n), *a.* Now *rare.* late ME. [f. REED *sb.* + -EN⁴.] Made or consisting of reed; reed-like.

Re:-edifica·tion. 1473. [– (O)Fr. *réédification* or late L. *reædificatio, -on-*, f. pa. ppl. stem of *reædificare*; see RE-, EDIFICATION.] The action of rebuilding or state of being rebuilt. Now *rare* or *Obs.*

Re-edify (rī,e·difəi), *v.* late ME. [– (O)Fr. *réédifier* – late L. *reædificare*; see RE-, EDIFY.] **1.** *trans.* To rebuild (a house or other building, a wall, city, etc.). **2.** *fig.* To rebuild, restore, re-establish 1540. **3.** *transf.* To build up again physically 1897.

Reeding (rī·diŋ), *vbl. sb.* 1440. [f. REED *v.* + -ING¹.] **1.** The action of REED *v.* **2. a.** A small semicylindrical moulding; ornamentation of this form 1815. **b.** The milling on the edge of coins 1875.

Comb.: **r.-plane,** a plane used for making reeds in wood.

Reedling (rī·dliŋ). 1840. [f. REED *sb.* + -LING.¹] The bearded titmouse, *Panurus biarmicus*. Also called *bearded r.*

Reed-mace. 1548. [REED *sb.*] **a.** An aquatic plant, *Typha latifolia*, common on the margins of ponds and lakes, having long ensiform leaves and tall stems, the latter terminated by dense cylindrical spikes of small brownish flowers. (Also called *cat's-tail, cat-tail*, and *bulrush*.) **b.** The smaller species, *T. augustifolia*.

Reed-warbler. 1802. [REED *sb.*] **a.** A common British sylvioid bird, *Acrocephalus streperus*, frequenting reed-beds. **b.** A related species, *A. arundinaceus* (also called *reed-thrush* and *great reed-warbler*), occas. seen in Britain.

Reedy (rī·di), *a.* late ME. [f. REED *sb.* + -Y¹.] **1.** Abounding with, full of, or characterized by the presence of reeds. **2.** Made or consisting of reed or reeds; reeden 1763. **3.** Resembling a reed or reeds 1628. **4.** Having a tone resembling that produced by a musical reed 1811. **b.** Having a reedy voice 1855.

1. To Simois reedie bankes the red bloud ran SHAKS. **3.** The leek with crown globose and r. stem CRABBE. R. coarse grass 1863. Hence **Ree·diness.**

Reef (rīf), *sb.*¹ *Pl.* **reefs, †reeves.** [In XV *riff, refe* – (M)Du. *reef, rif* – ON. *rif* (RIB) in same sense; cf. next.] **1.** *Naut.* One of the horizontal portions of a sail which may be successively rolled or folded up in order to reduce the extent of canvas exposed to the wind. Freq. in phr. *to take in a r.* (also in fig. context). **2.** A mode of reefing 1829.

1. He is wasting away, and is obliged to take in reefs in his waistcoat 1885. **2.** We tried a Spanish r., that is, let the yards come down on the cap MARRYAT.

Comb.: **r.-band,** a long piece of canvas sewn across the sail, for strengthening it in the place where the reef-holes are made; **-knot,** *(a)* a knot made in tying the reef-points; *(b)* a certain form of knot used for this and other purposes; hence **r. knot** *v. trans.*, to tie with a reef-knot; **-point,** one of a set of short ropes fixed in a line along a reef-band to secure the sail when reefed.

Reef (rīf), *sb.*² 1584. [In XVI–XVIII *riff(e*, in nautical use – MLG. *ref, rif*, pl. *reves*, MDu. *rif, ref* – ON. *rif* (RIB) in same sense; cf. prec.] **1.** A narrow ridge or chain of rocks, shingle, or sand, lying at or near the surface of the water. **2.** *Gold-mining* (orig. *Austral.*). **a.** A lode or vein of auriferous quartz 1858. **b.** The bed-rock 1869. Short for *r.-sponge* 1883.

1. CORAL R., BARRIER-*r.*, etc.: see these words.

Comb.: **r.-builder,** a coral insect which builds reefs; **-heron,** an Australian heron of the genus *Demi-egretta*, as *D. jugularis* or *D. sacra*; **-sponge,** a kind of sponge obtained in the W. Indies. Hence **Reef** *v.*² *intr.* to work at a (mining) reef. **Ree·fy** *a.* full of reefs.

Reef (rīf), *v.*¹ 1667. [f. REEF *sb.*¹] **1.** *trans.* To reduce the extent of (a sail) by taking in or rolling up a part and securing it. Also *absol.* **2. a.** To shorten (a topmast) by lowering, or (a bowsprit) by sliding inboard 1704. **b.** To alter (a paddle) by moving the float-boards nearer to the centre of the wheel, in order to diminish the dip when the vessel is deep 1838. Hence **Reefed** (rīft) *ppl. a.*

Reefer (rī·fəɪ). 1829. [f. REEF *v.*¹ + -ER¹.] **1.** One who reefs; *spec.* a slang name given to midshipmen 'because they have to attend in the tops during the operation of taking in reefs' (Smyth). **2.** A reefing jacket 1883.

Reefing (rī·fiŋ), *vbl. sb.* 1750. [f. REEF *v.*¹ + -ING¹.] *Naut.* The action of REEF *v.*¹ **b.** *attrib.*, as *r. breeze, point*, etc.; **r.-jacket,** a particular form of close-fitting jacket made of stout heavy cloth 1856.

Reek (rīk), *sb.* [OE. *rēc*, **rieć* = OFris. *reek*, OS. *rōk* (Du. *rook*), OHG. *rouh* (G. *rauch*), ON. *reykr* :– Gmc. **raukiz*, f. **rauk-* **reuk-* (see next). The normal repr. of the OE. sb. is ME. and dial. *reech* (cf. dial. *smeech, smeek*); the *k*-form is due partly to Scand. infl., partly to assoc. with the native verb.] **1.** Smoke from burning matter. (Now *Sc.* and *n. dial.* In standard Eng. only in literary use, and chiefly applied to dense or unctuous smoke.) **2.** Vapour or steam arising from, or given off by, something in a moist or heated state, as wet or marshy ground, wet clothes, boiling water, etc. late ME. **b.** *spec.* The vapour given off by hops in drying 1846. **3.** An exhalation; a fume emanating from some body or substance; in mod. use a strong and disagreeable fume or smell 1659. **b.** Impure, fetid atmosphere 1873.

3. A r. of gin and powder filled the chamber 1871.

Reek (rīk), *v.* [OE. *rēocan* = OFris. *riāka*, (M)Du. *rieken*, OHG. *riohhan* (G. *riechen*), ON. *rjúka*, f. Gmc. **reuk-*; see prec.] **1.** *intr.* To emit smoke. **2.** To emit hot vapour or steam; to smoke with heat; to exhale vapour (or fog). *dial.* OE. **3.** To emit an unwholesome or disagreeable vapour or fume; hence, to smell strongly or unpleasantly; to stink 1679. **†4.** Of smoke, vapour, perfume, etc.: To be emitted or exhaled; to rise, emanate, etc. –1599. **5.** *trans.* To expose to smoke; to dry or taint with smoke; to fumigate. Also *techn.*, to coat (moulds for steel) with soot. OE. **6.** To emit (smoke, steam, etc.) 1598.

1. The kilne began to reeke 1500. While temples crash, and towers in ashes r. KEBLE. **2.** The Violence of Action hath made you r. as a Sacrifice SHAKS. **3.** She literally reeked of garlic 1881. **4.** *fig.* I heard your guilty Rimes..Saw sighes reeke from you SHAKS.

Reeky (rī·ki), *a.* late ME. [f. REEK *sb.* + -Y¹.] **1. a.** That emits vapour; steamy; full of rank moisture. **b.** Emitting smoke, smoky 1604. **2.** Consisting of or resembling smoke 1513. **3.** Full of smoke 1576. **b.** Blackened with smoke 1859.

1. b. A reekie cole JAS. I.

Reel (rīl), *sb.*¹ [OE. *hrēol*; not repr. in cogn. langs.] **1.** A rotatory instrument on which thread is wound after it is spun, or silk as it is drawn from the cocoons. **b.** A similar framework on which other materials are wound at some stage in the process of manufacture, as the separate spun-yarns in rope-making, paper as it comes from the machine, etc. 1797. **2.** An apparatus by which a cord, line, etc., may be wound up and unwound as required 1727. **b.** A device of this kind attached to a fishing-rod, on which the line is wound up 1726. **c.** *Off the r.*, in an uninterrupted course or succession 1837. **3.** A small cylinder usu. of wood, with a rim or wider part at each end, on which thread is commonly wound for ordinary use; a quantity of thread made up in this way 1784. **b.** A small cylinder on which any flexible substance is wound 1839. *spec.* A quantity of positive cinematographic film rolled on one reel 1926. **4.** A rotatory apparatus in various machines; *esp.* in a reaping-machine, an arrangement of radial arms with horizontal bars at their extremities, which by its rotation presses the grain against the knives 1839.

Reel (rīl), *sb.*² 1572. [f. REEL *v.*¹] A whirl or whirling movement; an act of reeling; a roll or stagger. **†b.** *pl.* Revels, revelry (*rare*).

The drunken r. Of vice and folly round him BROWNING. **b.** Drinke thou: encrease the Reeles SHAKS.

Reel (rīl), *sb.*³ 1585. [perh. same word as prec.] **1.** A lively dance, chiefly associated with Scotland, usu. danced by two couples facing each other, and describing a series of figures of eight. **b.** *trans.* (perh. sometimes assoc. w. prec. sb.) 1768. **2.** The music for such a dance 1591.

1. *Virginia r.*, an American country-dance supposed to be derived from the English *Sir Roger de Coverley*. **b.** About, about, in r. and rout The death-fires danced at night COLERIDGE.

Reel (rīl), *v.*¹ late ME. [f. REEL *sb.*¹] **1.** *intr.* To whirl round or about; to go with a whirling motion. **2.** Of the eyes; To whirl, with dizziness or excitement 1513. **b.** Of the mind, head, etc.: To be in a whirl, to be or become giddy or confused 1796. **c.** To have, or seem to have, a rapid quivering motion 1847. **3.** Of an army, rank, line of battle, etc.: To waver, become unsteady, give way, late ME. **b.** Of persons (or animals): To sway or stagger as the result of a blow or encounter. Often with *back, backward*. late ME. **4.** Of persons (or animals): To sway unsteadily from side to side, as if about to fall; to swing about with the whole body in trying to walk or stand, as the result of intoxication, faintness, etc. 1477. **b.** *transf.* of parts of the body, etc. 1590. **5.** Of things: To shake, rock, or swing violently; to totter, tremble 1495. **b.** *fig.* Of kingdoms or institutions 1577. **c.** To fall or roll hurriedly (*rare*) 1593. **6.** To walk with the body swinging violently from side to side; to make one's way in a swaying or staggering manner, esp. under the effects of intoxication 1607. **b.** To move, fly, or dash, rapidly and unsteadily 1727. **7.** *trans.* To cause to roll, whirl, or stagger; to impel violently. Now *rare*. late ME. **8.** To reel through or along (a street) SHAKS.

1. Thus the World doth, and evermore shall Reele DRAYTON. **2. b.** My head reels, doctor 1881. **3. b.** Cossack and Russian Reel'd from the sabre-stroke Shatter'd and sunder'd TENNYSON. **4. b.** Knees which r. as marches quicken KINGSLEY. **5.** So quick the run, We felt the good ship shake and r. TENNYSON. **6.** To r. drunk about the streets 1849.

Reel (rīl), *v.*² late ME. [f. REEL *sb.*¹] **1.** *trans.* To wind (thread, silk, etc.) on a reel. Also *absol.* **b.** *Angling.* To wind (the line) on the reel. Also with *up*, and *absol.* 1854. **2.** To take *off* by reeling 1530. **b.** *transf.* To rattle *off* (a story, song, etc.) without pause or effort 1837. **3.** To draw *out*, as with a reel; to draw *through* (something), or cause to move, by means of a reel 1855. **b.** *Angling.* To draw in (a fish, etc.) by reeling up the line 1881.

2. b. General Butler..can r. off nautical stories by the yard 1885.

Reel (rīl), *v.*³ 1768. [f. REEL *sb.*³] *intr.* and *trans.* To dance a reel.

Reeler (rī·lər). 1598. [f. REEL *v.*² + -ER¹.] **1.** One who reels or winds yarn, cord, etc., upon a reel; also, one who employs such workers. **b.** The grasshopper-warbler, *Locustella nævia* 1871. **†2.** An instrument for reeling (*rare*) –1629.

‖**Reem** (rīm). 1719. [– Heb. *rᵉēm*, rendered in the Vulgate by *rhinoceros* and *unicornis*.] An animal mentioned in the O.T., now identified with the wild ox.

Re-enfo·rce, *v.* 1586. [f. RE- + ENFORCE *v.* Now rare in English, but common in American use.] **1.** *trans.* To strengthen, give fresh or additional strength to. **2.** = REINFORCE 1. 1596. **†b.** To reassemble –1599. **†3.** *intr.* To renew one's efforts; to insist –1642.

1. Thou, Jehova,..With strength my weakness r. 1586. **2. b.** The French haue re-enforc'd their scatter'd men SHAKS. So **Re-enfo·rcement,** the act of re-enforcing, or the state of being re-enforced; that which re-enforces; a fresh supply.

Re-enter (rī,e·ntəɪ), *v.* 1442. [RE- 5 a + ENTER *v.*] **1.** *intr.* To enter again. Const. *†in, into, upon.* 1483. **b.** *Law.* To enter again upon possession of lands or tenements 1461. **2.** *trans.* To enter (a place, etc.) again 1442. **3.** To enter again in a book or register 1839. **4.** *techn.* **a.** In hand calico-printing: To apply (the secondary colours), to ground in 1839. **b.** In engraving: To cut (imperfect or worn lines) deeper in the plate 1854.

Re-e·ntering, *ppl. a.* 1696. [f. prec. + -ING².] **1.** = next adj. **2.** Returning into a place 1850.

Re-e·ntrant, *a.* (and *sb.*) 1781. [f. RE- + ENTRANT, after Fr. *rentrant*.] **A.** *adj. R. angle*, an angle pointing inward. **B.** *sb.* A re-entrant angle in a fortification 1900.

Re-entry (rī,e·ntri). 1450. [RE- 5 a.] **1.** *Law.* The act of re-entering upon possession of lands, tenements, etc., previously granted or let to another 1461. **2.** The act of re-entering or coming back into a place, etc.; a second or new entry 1450. **3.** The act of setting down or recording again; the fact of being so set down; the entry thus made 1839.

2. *Card of re-entry*, in whist and bridge, a card which by winning a trick gives the lead to a player at an advanced stage of the hand.

Re-establish (rīˌestæ·bliʃ), *v.* 1483. [RE- 5 a.] *trans.* To establish again. **1.** To establish (a person or thing) again *in* a former place, position, or state; to restore to a previous place or position. **b.** To fix or set up again (*rare*) 1669. **2.** To set up again in a status or condition similar to the former one; to restore 1559. **3.** To restore (one's health or strength) to the usual state. Usu. in *pass.* 1697. **b.** To restore to a proper condition 1812. **4.** To reassure. DE FOE.

1. He could now deliuer them..and r. them in their former peace 1606. **2.** America was..re-establishing a metallic currency 1866. **3.** The jeweller..felt his strength re-established 1850. Hence **Re-esta·blisher. Re-esta·blishment,** the act of re-establishing; the fact or condition of being re-established.

Reeve (rīv), *sb.*[1] Now chiefly *Hist.* [OE. *rēfa*, aphetic var. of *ġerēfa*, earlier *ġirǣfa* (see GRIEVE *sb.*), f. *ġe-* Y- + **rōf* in *seċġrōf* host of men, *stæfrōf* alphabet = OHG. *ruova, ruoba*, ON. *stafróf*. See PORTREEVE, SHERIFF.] **1.** *Hist.* An Old English official of high rank having a local jurisdiction under the king; the chief magistrate of a town or district. **2.** †**a.** A bailiff, steward, or overseer; a minor officer appointed by a landowner to superintend his estates, tenants, or workmen. **b.** A local official of minor rank; an overseer of a parish, a churchwarden, or the like. ME. **c.** In Canada, the president of a village- or town-council 1890.

Reeve (rīv), *sb.*[2] 1634. [Of unkn. origin. Cf. REE *sb.*] The female of the ruff, *Tringa pugnax.*

Reeve (rīv), *v.* Chiefly *Naut.* 1627. [prob. – Du. *rēven* reef, with shift of meaning.] **1.** *trans.* To pass (a rope) through a hole, ring, or block. Also const. *through.* **b.** *transf.* To thrust or pass (a rod, etc.) *through* any aperture or opening 1681. **c.** *intr.* Of a rope: To pass *through* a block, etc. 1860. **2.** *trans.* To place *in, on,* or *round,* to fix *to* something by reeving 1667. **3.** To fit (a block) with a rope by reeving; to attach in this way; to tie 1639. **b.** Of a rope: To pass through (a block) 1775. **c.** *transf.* Of a ship: To thread (shoals or ice-pack) 1860.

Re-exa·mine, *v.* 1594. [RE- 5 a.] *trans.* To examine again; *spec.* in legal use, of a counsel, to examine (a witness) again, after cross-examination by the opposing counsel. So **Re-exa·minable** *a.* **Re:-examina·tion.**

Re-excha·nge. 1480. [RE- 5 a.] **1.** *Comm.* (See quot.) **2.** A second or fresh exchange 1856.

1. R. means the damages incurred by non-acceptance and non-payment, and they consist of protest charges on the amount of the bill, commission, bill brokerage, interest, stamps, and postages 1809.

Re-e·xport, *sb.* 1761. [RE- 5 a.] *Comm.* **1.** A commodity re-exported. Also (chiefly in *pl.*), the amount (*of* something) re-exported. **2.** = RE-EXPORTATION 1792.

Re-expo·rt, *v.* 1690. [RE- 5 a.] *Comm. trans.* To export (imported goods) again. So **Re-exporta·tion,** the exportation of imported goods.

†**Refa·ction.** 1640 [– Fr. *réfaction*; see RE-, FACTION.] Recompense, satisfaction –1755.

†**Refe·ct,** *pa. pple.* late ME. [– L. *refectus*, pa. pple of *reficere*; see next.] Refreshed, restored –1456.

Refect (rīfe·kt), *v.* Now *rare* or *Obs.* 1470. [– *refect-*, pa. ppl. stem of L. *reficere* remake, renew, f. *re-* RE- + *facere* make; in later use a back-formation from next.] *trans.* To refresh, esp. with food or drink; to restore after fatigue. Often *refl.*

Refection (rīfe·kʃən). ME. [– (O)Fr. *réfection* – L. *refectio, -on-*, f. as prec.; see -ION.] **1.** Recreation or refreshment received through some spiritual or intellectual influence. **2.** The action of refreshing or partaking of refreshment; the fact of being refreshed, or of refreshing oneself, with food or drink after hunger or fatigue. Also, an instance or case of this. late ME. **b.** Entertainment with food and drink; the right of demanding, or duty of supplying, such entertainment. Now *Hist.* 1601. **3.** An occasion of partaking of food; a meal. late ME. **b.** A portion of food or drink; a slight repast 1482.

1. The only sight of God is the true food and r. of our minds 1630. **2.** She..toke only for her r. brede and water CAXTON. **3. b.** A miserable r. of weak tea and tough toast MRS. CARLYLE. Hence **Refe·ctioner,** in a monastery or convent, the person having charge of the refectory and supplies of food.

†**Refective** (rīfe·ktiv), *a.* and *sb.* 1611. [– Fr. †*réfectif, -ive* refreshing, etc.; see REFECT *v.*, -IVE. Cf. AL. *refectivus.*] **A.** *adj.* Refreshing, restoring, nourishing –1665. **B.** *sb.* A medicine that restores the strength –1706.

Refectory (rīfe·ktəri), *sb.* 1483. [– late L. *refectorium* (Gregory), f. L. *reficere*; see REFECT *v.*, -ORY[1].] A room for refreshment; *esp.* in religious houses and colleges, the hall or chamber in which the meals take place.

†**Refe·l,** *v.* 1451. [– L. *refellere* disprove, refute, f. *re-* RE- + *fallere* deceive, etc.] **1.** *trans.* To refute, confute, disprove. Also *absol.* –1734. **2.** To reject (a request, a thing offered, etc.) –1603. **3.** To repel, force or drive back, repress –1652.

Refer (rĭfə̄·ɹ), *v.* late ME. [–(O)Fr. *référer* – L. *referre* carry back, f. *re-* RE- + *ferre* bear, carry.] **I.** *trans.* **1.** To trace (back), assign, attribute, impute (something) *to* a person or thing as the ultimate cause, origin, author, or source. **2.** To assign *to* a thing, or class of things, as being properly included or comprehended in this; to regard as naturally belonging, pertaining, or having relation *to*; to attach or attribute *to.* late ME. **b.** To assign *to* a particular place or date 1604. **3.** *refl.* To betake, commit, commend, entrust (oneself) *to* some person or thing for assistance, advice, etc., or in a spirit of submission, acquiescence, or confidence. Now *rare* or *Obs.* 1450. **4.** To commit, submit, hand over (a question, cause, or matter) *to* some special or ultimate authority for consideration, decision, execution, etc. Also rarely without const. 1456. †**5.** To defer, postpone, put off (something) –1751. **b.** To reserve (a subject, etc.) for later treatment. Also const. *to* and with *inf.* Now *rare.* 1559. **6.** To send or direct (a person) *to* a person, a book or its author for information 1601. **b.** To direct (a person) *to* a fact, event, or thing, by drawing attention to it or pointing it out 1605. **7.** To relate, recount, report, record. Now *rare.* 1568. †**8.** To hand over, give, transfer –1705.

1. Thanne folweth it that owre vices ben referred to the makere of alle good CHAUCER. **2.** Thys law ys the ground and end of the other, to the wych hyt must euer be referryd 1538. **3.** I doe referre me to the Oracle: Apollo be my Iudge SHAKS. **4.** The King referred the matter to the council 1769. Bankers' phr. *Refer to drawer.* **5. b.** My Account of this Voyage must be referred to the Second Part of my Travels SWIFT. **6.** My wife..referred her to all the neighbours for a character GOLDSM. **8.** *Cymb.* I. i. 6.

II. *intr.* **1.** To have reference or relation *to* a thing; *esp.* to have allusion, to apply, *to.* late ME. **b.** To make reference or allusion, to give a reference, direct the attention, *to* something 1691. †**2.** To suggest, or leave, *to* a person to do something (*rare*) –1645. **3.** To have recourse, make application, *to* a thing; to turn or appeal *to* for some purpose 1595.

1. My measurements r. to the ice at and near the surface TYNDALL. **b.** He refers to passages of his personal history JOWETT. **3.** He is to r. to and obey all orders of the army referrible to the mode of treating the Spanish Colonel WELLINGTON. Hence **Referable** (re·fĕrăb'l) *a.* capable of being referred or assigned *to* (some person or thing); assignable, ascribable.

Referee (refĕrī·), *sb.* 1621. [f. REFER *v.* + -EE[1].] †**1.** One appointed by Parliament to examine and report on applications for monopolies or letters patent –1663. **b.** One to whom the management or superintendence of something is entrusted 1705. **c.** A member of certain committees and courts appointed by the House of Commons to deal with private bills 1865. **2.** *Law.* A person to whom (either alone or with others) a dispute between parties is referred by mutual consent; an arbitrator 1565. **3.** One to whom any matter or question in dispute is referred for decision; an umpire 1670. **b.** In games or sports 1860.

3. Clear-sighted, unprejudiced, sagacious;..he was the universal r. DISRAELI. Hence **Referee·** *v. trans.* to preside over (a match) as r.

Reference (re·fĕrĕns), *sb.* 1589. [f. REFER *v.* + -ENCE.] **1.** The act or expedient of referring or submitting a matter, esp. a dispute or controversy, to some person or authority for consideration, decision, or settlement (in legal use *spec.* to the Masters in Ordinary of the Court of Chancery). Also, the scope allowed to persons conducting an inquiry, of any kind. †**2.** Assignment. SHAKS. **3.** Relation, relationship, respect, regard *to* some thing or person 1593. **4.** An illusion or directing of attention *to* some thing or person 1613. **5.** A direction to a book, passage, etc. where certain information may be found. Also without article. 1612. **b.** A mark or sign referring the reader to another part of a page or book (*esp.* from the text to a note), or serving to indicate the part of a figure or diagram referred to 1678. **6.** The act of referring one person to another for information or an explanation 1815. **b.** The name of a person given as one prepared to vouch for the character of a person seeking employment or of goods offered for sale, etc.; the person himself, or (loosely) the testimonial given 1865. **7.** *Book,* etc. *of r.*, one intended to be, or suitable for being, referred to or consulted 1836.

1. If the arbitrator refuses or ceases to act, the r. is at an end 1834. **2.** *Oth.* I. iii. 238. **3.** The world is a..system, whose parts have a mutual r. to each other 1736. *In* or *with r. to*, with respect or regard to; †with a view to, according to. *Without r. to*, without regard to, without consideration of or for. **4.** No r. had been made to the former conversation 1865. **5.** See also CROSS-REFERENCE. *Legislation by r.* (= by reference to previous statutes instead of by restatement). **6.** I don't ask you to trust me, without offering a respectable r. DICKENS. **7.** Books of r. such as..Encyclopædias, Lexicons, Dictionaries, etc. 1859. *For r.*, for the purpose of consulting or being consulted.

attrib.: **r. bible,** a bible furnished with marginal cross-references to parallel passages; **r. library,** a library where books may be consulted without being removed from it; **r. mark,** a mark or sign (as *†¶ or superior numbers) used to refer the reader to notes.

Reference (re·fĕrĕns), *v.* 1621. [f. prec.] †**1.** *trans.* To refer, assign *to* a thing (*rare*) –1627. **2.** To provide with references; to give a reference to (a passage); to find by reference 1891. **3.** *intr.* To make out a return of the number of people to be displaced by proposed railway extension. Also *trans.* to schedule (property) for this purpose. 1884. Hence **Re·ferencer.**

Referendary (refĕre·ndări). 1528. [– late L. *referendarius*; see next, -ARY[1]. Cf. (O)Fr. *référendaire.*] **1.** One to whom a matter in dispute is referred for decision; a referee. Now *rare.* 1546. **2.** *spec.* A title given at various times to certain officials in the papal, imperial, and some royal courts, charged with the duty of examining and reporting on petitions, requests, use of the seal, and similar matters 1528. †**3.** One who, or that which, furnishes news or information; a reporter –1636.

3. Sir, when these places afford anything worth your knowledge, I shall be your r. DONNE.

‖**Referendum** (refĕre·ndŏm). 1882. [Gerund or n. gerundive of L. *referre* REFER.] **1.** The act, practice, or principle (chiefly associated with the Swiss constitution) of submitting the direct decision of a question at issue to the whole body of voters. **2.** A note from a diplomatic agent to his government, requesting instructions on a particular matter 1891.

Referent (re·fĕrĕnt), *sb.* and *a. rare.* 1844. [– L. *referens, -ent-*, pr. pple. of *referre* REFER;

see -ENT.] A. *sb.* 1. One who is referred to or consulted. 2. A word referring to another 1899. B. *adj.* Referring, containing a reference 1899.

Referential (refĕre·nʃăl), *a.* 1660. [f. REFERENCE, after *inferential*, etc.] Having reference (*to* something); belonging to, or of the nature of, (a) reference; containing a reference or references.

The r. mark..referring to the note annexed 1806. Hence **Refere·ntially** *adv.*

†**Refe·rment.** 1558. [f. REFER *v.* + -MENT.] Reference –1655.

Referrer (rĭfə̄·rəɹ). 1683. [f. REFER *v.* + -ER[1].] One who refers.

Referrible (rĭfə̄·rĭb'l), *a.* 1596. [– med.L. *referibilis* in same sense; see REFER, -IBLE. *Referable* (see REFER), *referrable*, are somewhat later.] = REFERABLE.

Refigure (rīfi·gər, -iŭɹ), *v.* late ME. [– med.L. *refigurare* recall in imagination, refashion; see RE-, FIGURE *v.* Cf. Fr. †*réfigurer*.] 1. *trans.* To figure again; to represent anew. 2. *spec.* To restore (a metallic speculum) to the original parabolic figure 1888.

Refill (rī:fi·l, rī·fil), *sb.* 1886. [RE- 5 a.] That which serves to refill anything; a fresh fill for a memorandum or pencil case, etc.

Refi·ll, *v.* 1687. [RE- 5 a.] *trans.* and *intr.* To fill again.

Refine (rĭfəi·n), *v.* 1582. [f. RE- + FINE *v.*[3], partly after Fr. *raffiner*.] 1. *trans.* To purify or separate (metals) from dross, alloy, or other extraneous matter; in iron-working, to convert grey pig-iron into white or plate metal by partial decarburization. 2. To free from impurities; to purify or cleanse 1601. b. *spec.* To purify or clarify (a substance or product) by means of some special process; to make purer or of a finer quality; *esp.* to subject (raw sugar) to the processes of clarifying, condensing, and crystallizing 1613. †3. a. To clear (the spirits, mind, etc.) from dullness; to make clearer or more subtle –1728. b. To free or cleanse from moral imperfection; to raise to a higher spiritual state –1711. 4. To free from imperfections or defects; to bring to a more perfect or purer state 1670. b. To polish or improve (a language, composition, etc.); to make more elegant or cultured 1617. 5. To free from rudeness, coarseness, or vulgarity; to imbue with culture or polish, delicate feelings or instincts, etc. 1667. 6. *intr.* To become pure; to grow clear or free from impurities 1604. 7. To improve in polish, elegance, or delicacy 1620. 8. To employ or affect a subtlety of thought or language 1713. 9. To improve *on* or *upon* something, by introducing refinements 1662.

1. So doth the Fire the drossy Gold r. 1592. 2. To ..raise From the conflagrant mass, purg'd and refin'd, New Heav'ns, new Earth MILT. b. The Table was furnished with fat things, and with Wine that was well refined BUNYAN. 3. b. Tri'd in sharp tribulation, and refin'd By Faith and faithful works MILT. 4. They may as well r. the speech as the sentiments of their personages JOHNSON. 5. Love refines The thoughts, and heart enlarges MILT. 6. The pure stream..Works it self clear, and, as it runs, refines ADDISON. 7. Let a Lord once own the happy lines, How the wit brightens! how the style refines! POPE. 8. Who, too deep for his hearers, still went on refining, And thought of convincing, while they thought of dining GOLDSM. Hence **Refi·nable** *a.*

Refined (rĭfəi·nd), *ppl. a.* 1574. [f. prec. + -ED[1].] 1. Purified; freed from impurities or extraneous matter 1595. 2. Characterized or distinguished by the possession of refinement in manners, action, or feeling 1588. b. Free from rude, gross, or vulgar elements 1650. c. Of language, speech, etc.: Cultivated, polished, elegant 1611. 3. †a. Having or affecting a subtlety of mind or judgement –1714. b. Raised to a high degree of subtlety, nicety, precision, etc. 1668.

1. To gilde r. Gold, to paint the Lilly..Is wastefull, and ridiculous excesse SHAKS. 2. Modern taste Is so r. and delicate and chaste COWPER. c. She spoke with a r. accent GEO. ELIOT. 3. Nothing subtle or r. should enter into the views of a Christian missionary 1812. Hence **Refi·nedly** (-ĕdli) *adv.*

Refinement (rĭfəi·nmĕnt). 1611. [f. REFINE *v.* + *-ment*, after Fr. *raffinement*.] 1. The act or process of refining; the result of refining, or the state of being refined. 2. Fineness of feeling, taste, or thought; elegance of manners; culture, polish 1710. b. An instance of this 1708. 3. The act or practice of refining in thought, reasoning, or discourse; an instance of this 1712. b. A piece of subtle reasoning; a subtlety 1694. 4. An instance of improvement or advance towards something more refined or perfect; the state or thing thus arrived at or obtained 1710.

1. The renovation and r. of the present world by the last fire BOYLE. 2. That sensibility of pain with which R. is endued COWPER. b. The refinements of highly cultivated society W. IRVING. 4. For Emulation..is..but a r. upon envy LAW.

Refiner (rĭfəi·nəɹ). 1586. [f. REFINE *v.* + -ER[1].] One who or that which refines; *spec.* one who makes a business or refining (metal, sugar, etc.).

Refinery (rĭfəi·nəri). 1727. [f. as prec. + -ERY, after Fr. *raffinerie*.] A place, building, or establishment, where refining (of sugar, oil, metal, etc.) is carried on. b. A furnace for the conversion of cast into malleable iron 1825.

Refit (rīfi·t), *v.* 1666. [RE- 5 a.] 1. *Naut.* a. *trans.* To fit out (a ship, fleet, etc.) again; to restore to a serviceable condition by renewals and repairs. b. *intr.* To get refitted 1669. 2. a. *trans.* To fit up or fit out afresh 1676. b. *intr.* To renew supplies or equipment 1802.

1. b. The Portland has come in to r., having lost her masts 1669. So **Refit** (stress var.) *sb.* an act or instance of refitting (*esp.* of a ship). **Refi·tment**, the act of refitting; a refit.

Reflation (riflē·ʃən). 1932. [f. RE- 2 a, after *inflation*, *deflation*.] Inflation undertaken after deflation to restore the previous position.

Refle·ct, *sb.* 1596. [f. next.] Reflection –1829.

Reflect (rĭfle·kt), *v.* late ME. [– OFr. *reflecter* or L. *reflectere*, f. *re-* RE- + *flectere* bend.] I. *trans.* 1. To turn or direct in a certain course, to divert; to turn away or aside, to deflect. 2. To bend, turn, or fold back; to give a backward bend or curve to (a thing); to recurve. (Chiefly in *pa. pple.*, denoting the position of parts.) 1578. †3. To turn (back), cast (the eye or thought) *on* or *upon* something –1677. 4. To throw or cast back again; to cause to return or rebound 1611. b. *spec.* Of bodies or surfaces: To cast or send back (heat, cold, or sound) after impact 1718. 5. Of (smooth or polished) bodies or surfaces: To turn, throw, or cast back (beams, rays, or light) 1573. 6. Of mirrors or other polished surfaces: To give back or exhibit an image of (a person or thing); to mirror. Also *absol.* 1592. 7. To throw or cast (blame, dishonour, etc.) *on* or *upon* a person or thing 1670.

2. The bill is..not quite strait, but a little reflected upwards PENNANT. 3. Let me minde the Reader to r. his eye on our Quotations FULLER. 4. b. A cloud..reflects or throws back upon the earth the heat HUXLEY. 5. The Light of the Moon reflected from frozen Snow BENTLEY. 6. The glass..Reflected now a perfect fright GOLDSM. *fig.* The law..reflects the plain sentiments of the better order of average men FROUDE. 7. This..reflects the greatest dishonour on his reputation ROBERTSON.

II. *intr.* †1. Of beams or rays of light: To return, turn back, after striking or falling upon a surface –1703. †b. To shine, cast a light –1653. †2. To return; to turn, come, or go back –1717. †3. To cast a look or glance *upon* a thing; to have a bearing *upon*, etc. –1662. †b. To bestow attention or regard *upon* a person or thing; to set a value *on* (*rare*) –1661. 4. To turn one's thoughts (back) *on*, to fix the mind or attention *on* or *upon* a subject; to ponder, meditate *on* 1605. b. Without const.: To employ reflection 1704. 5. To cast a slight or imputation, reproach or blame, *on* or *upon* a person or thing; to pass a censure *on* 1631. 6. Of actions, circumstances, etc.: To cast or bring reproach or discredit *on* a person or thing 1647. b. To cast a certain light or character *on* 1856.

1. b. *Tit. A.* I. ii. 226. 3. b. *Cymb.* I. vi. 24. 4. We are..constituted such sort of creatures as to r. upon our own nature 1726. b. It is necessary.. that we think and r. before we act PRIESTLEY. 5. I would not be thought to r. upon this very eminent physician's practice 1756. 6. Ill Language, and brutal Manners, reflected only on those who were guilty of 'em STEELE. Hence **Refle·cted** *ppl. a.*, **-ly** *adv.* **Refle·ctible** *a.* that may be reflected.

Reflecting (rĭfle·ktiŋ), *ppl. a.* 1590. [f. prec. + -ING[2].] 1. That reflects, or casts back, light or images of things. b. Provided or fitted with some arrangement or apparatus serving to reflect light or images; esp. *r. telescope* 1704. 2. Casting reflections on a person or thing 1687. 3. Having or exercising reflection or thought; characterized by reflection 1711.

1. †*R. glass*, a mirror. 3. Grave and r. men MACAULAY. Hence **Refle·ctingly** *adv.*

Reflection, reflexion (rĭfle·kʃən). late ME. [– (O)Fr. *réflexion* or late L. *reflexio*, *-on-* (med.L. also *-flect-*); see REFLECT *v.*, FLEXION. Except in scientific use, the form with *ct* is the prevailing one.] 1. The action, on the part of surfaces, of throwing back light or heat (rays, beams, etc.) falling upon them; the fact or phenomenon of light and heat being thrown back in this way. b. Reflected light or heat 1555. 2. The action of a mirror or other polished surface in exhibiting or reproducing the image of an object; the fact or phenomenon of an image being produced in this way. late ME. b. An image or counterpart thus produced 1587. c. The fact of colour being thrown by one thing upon another; a colour, hue, or tint received in this way; also *Zool.* an iridescence 1614. 3. The action of bending, turning, or folding back; recurvation 1553. †b. The action of turning back from some point –1662. 4. The action of throwing back, or fact of being thrown or driven back, after impact. late ME. b. *Phys.* Reflex action 1836. 5. Animadversion, blame, censure, reproof 1651. b. A remark or statement reflecting on a person 1647. c. An imputation; a fact or procedure casting an imputation or discredit *on* one 1663. 6. The action of turning (back) or fixing the thoughts on some subject; meditation, deep or serious consideration 1674. †b. Recollection or remembrance *of* a thing. Also without const. –1704. c. *Philos.* The mode, operation, or faculty by which the mind has knowledge of itself and its operations, or by which it deals with the ideas received from sensation and perception 1690. 7. A thought or idea occurring to, or occupying, the mind 1647. b. A thought expressed in words; a remark made after reflection on a subject 1659.

1. Phr. *Angle of r.*, the angle which the reflected ray makes with a perpendicular to the surface (†or with the surface itself). b. *fig.* Shee's a good signe, but I haue seene small r. of her wit SHAKS. 2. The eye sees not it selfe but by r., By some other things SHAKS. c. Feathers..golden-green, with grey edges, and all are glossed with brilliant metallic reflections 1840. 3. b. *Macb.* I. ii. 25. 5. For in English, to say Satire, is to mean R., as we use that Word in the worst sence DRYDEN. b. May no r. shed Its poisonous venom on the royal dead PRIOR. 6. Mankind act more from habit than r. PALEY. b. Though it made you a little uneasy for the present, yet the r. of it must needs be entertaining CONGREVE. c. R..., that notice which the Mind takes of its own Operations, and the manner of them LOCKE. 7. These reflections draw after them others that are too melancholy 1716.

Reflective (rĭfle·ktiv), *a.* 1627. [f. REFLECT *v.* + -IVE.] 1. a. That gives back an image or reflection of an object; that mirrors or reproduces. b. That throws back something striking or falling on the surface; *esp.* that reflects light 1742. c. *Gram.* = REFLEXIVE 5. 1843. 2. Of light: Produced by reflection, reflected, borrowed 1666. †3. That makes or contains reflections or censures *on* or *upon* a person –1677. 4. Of mental faculties: Of or pertaining to reflection (on what is presented to the mind) 1678. b. Meditative, thoughtful 1820.

1. The polished floor..as r. as a mahogany table RUSKIN. 3. Little said r. on me, though W. Pen and J. Minnes do mean me in one or two places PEPYS. 4. b. Elegy is the form of poetry natural to the r. mind COLERIDGE. Hence **Refle·ctive-ly** *adv.*, **-ness.**

Reflector (rĭfle·ktə̆ɹ). 1665. [f. REFLECT *v.* + -OR 2.] †1. One who reflects or meditates BOYLE. †2. One who casts reflections; a censor, critic –1748. 3. A reflecting telescope, microscope, etc. 1767. 4. A body or surface which reflects (rays of) light, heat, sound, etc. 1800. **b.** *spec.* A specially prepared surface of metal or glass (usu. of a curved or concave form), for the purpose of reflecting rays of light, heat or sound in a required direction 1797. **5.** A polished surface exhibiting images of objects 1831. **b.** *spec.* The speculum of a reflecting telescope 1815. **6.** That which reflects, in other senses 1840.

Reflex (rī·fleks), *sb.* 1508. [– L. *reflexus* a bending back, f. as next.] **1.** Reflection of light (or heat); reflected light; light or colour resulting from reflection. Now *rare.* **b.** *spec.* in *Art* and *Arch.* The light reflected, or supposed to be reflected, from a surface in light to one in shade 1695. **2.** The reflection or image of an object, as seen in a mirror or surface acting as such 1638. **b.** *fig.* An image, reproduction; something which reproduces certain essential features or qualities of another thing 1683. †**3.** The act of bending or turning the mind (back) *upon* a subject; reflection –1658. †**4.** A glance or side look (*lit.* and *fig.*); indirect reference or allusion –1650. †**5.** Return, rebound; indirect action or operation –1683. **6.** *Phys.* A reflex action 1877. **7.** *Wireless.* Ellipt. for *reflex set* (see next 7).

1. The r. from the window..lit his face C. BRONTË. **b.** Gradations of middle tint, local colour, and reflexes 1807. **2.** To cut across the r. of a star That..gleamed Upon the glassy plain WORDSW. **5.** Let us abstain from railery least it return by r. upon our selves 1683.

Reflex (rī·fleks), *a.* 1649. [– L. *reflexus*, pa. pple. of *reflectere* REFLECT.] **1.** Bent or turned back; recurved 1658. **2.** Of light, rays, etc.: Reflected 1681. **3.** Of acts of thought: Directed or turned back upon the mind itself or its operations. Chiefly in *r. act.* 1649. **b.** Derived from, consisting in, the conversion of the mind or thought upon itself 1652. **4.** Coming by way of return or reflection 1822. **5.** *Phys.* **a.** *R. action*, involuntary action of a muscle, gland, or other organ, caused by the excitation of a sensory nerve being transmitted to a nerve-centre, and thence 'reflected' along an efferent nerve to the organ in question 1833. **b.** Of the nature of, characterized by, or connected with, such action 1833. **6.** *Gram.* Reflexive 1873. **7.** *Wireless. R. circuit*: a circuit in which the same valve gives high-frequency and low-frequency amplification; *r. receiver, set*, one acting by means of a r. circuit 1924.

3. Which I call the r. act of the Soul, or the turning of the intellectual eye inward upon its own actions HALE. **b.** This r. knowledge whereby we know what it is to know 1652. **5. a.** Coughing and sneezing are familiar instances of r. actions DARWIN. Hence **Refle·xly** *adv.*

Reflex (rĭfle·ks), *v.* late ME. [– *reflex-*, pa. ppl. stem of L. *reflectere* REFLECT.] **1.** *trans.* = REFLECT *v.* I. 2. Chiefly *Her.* and *Bot.*, and only in pa. pple. 1572. †**2.** To reflect (light, an object, etc.) –1658.

1. The petals are reflexed, and turn over 1861. **2.** For neither rain can fall upon the earth, Nor sun r. his virtuous beams thereon MARLOWE. Hence **Reflexed** (rĭfle·kst) *ppl. a.* in the senses of the vb.; also, †directed backwards.

Reflexible (rĭfle·ksĭb'l), *a.* 1706. [f. prec. + -IBLE.] Capable of being reflected.

The Light of the Sun consists of Rays that are differently R. and Refrangible 1706. Hence **Reflexibi·lity.**

Reflexion: see REFLECTION.

Reflexive (rĭfle·ksiv), *a.* and *sb.* 1588. [f. REFLEX *v.* + -IVE; cf. med.L. *reflexivus* (XIII) caused by reflexion (of light).] **A.** *adj.* **1.** Capable of bending or turning back (*rare*). †**2.** Of mental operations: Turned or directed back upon the mind itself –1708. †**b.** Reflective –1752. †**3.** Reciprocal, correspondent –1681. †**4.** Reflecting on a person –1716. **5.** *Gram.* Of pronouns, verbs, and their signification: Characterized by, or denoting, a reflex action on the subject of the clause or sentence 1837. **6.** Of a reflex character 1871.

2. Being not capable of a r. act, they know it not BEVERIDGE. **4.** I would fain know what man.. there is that does not resent an ugly r. word 1716.

B. *sb.* A reflexive verb or pronoun 1866. Hence **Refle·xive-ly** *adv.*, **-ness.**

†**Refloa·t.** *rare.* 1594. [– Fr. †*reflot*; see RE- 2 a, FLOAT *sb.* I. 2.] A flowing back; reflux, ebb (of the tide) –1626.

Reflow·, *sb.* 1610. [RE- 2 a.] A reflux, refluence, ebb of the tide.

Reflow·, *v.* Now *rare.* late ME. [RE- 2 a.; orig. after L. *refluere.*] *intr.* To flow back; *esp.* of the tide, to ebb. Freq. in phr. *flow and r.*

Refluence (re·fluĕns). 1592. [See next and -ENCE.] A flowing back; a reflux. So †**Re·fluency** (*rare*).

Refluent (re·fluĕnt), *a.* late ME. [– L. *refluens, -ent-*, pr. pple. of *refluere* flow back, f. *re-* RE- 2 a + *fluere* flow; see -ENT.] **1.** Flowing back, reflowing. **2.** Characterized by refluence, *esp.* tidal 1741. †**3.** Directed backwards. SHENSTONE.

1. *transf.* The once triumphant Peninsular hosts, r. through the passes of the Pyrenees 1842. **2.** A phantom colony smoulder'd on the r. estuary TENNYSON.

Reflux (rī·flɒks). late ME. [f. RE- 2 a + FLUX. Cf. Fr. *reflux* (XVI).] A flowing back, return, refluence.

Ill-contrived sewers permitting a large r. of air into the houses 1869. Phr. *Flux and r.*

Refo·cillate, *v.* Now *rare.* 1611. [– late L. *refocillare* warm with life again, revive. Cf. Fr. †*refociller.*] *trans.* To revive, refresh, reanimate. So **Refocilla·tion,** refreshment, reanimation, reinvigoration 1576.

Reform (rĭfǭ·ɹm), *sb.* 1663. [f. next, or – Fr. *réforme.*] **1.** The amendment of some faulty state of things, *esp.* of a corrupt or oppressive political institution or practice; the removal of some abuse or wrong. **b.** An instance of this; a change for the better 1781. **2.** Amendment of conduct; reformation of persons or character 1784. **3.** Improvement or rectifying of something faulty or inexact 1856. **4.** A religious order created by the reduction of another to stricter observances 1727.

1. He said when any change was brewing, R. was a fine name for ruin 1786. **b.** The public..calling for sweeping reforms 1883. **2.** Remorse begets r. COWPER. **3.** The r. of the calendar EMERSON. *attrib.*: **R. Act** or **Bill**, an act or bill to amend the system of parliamentary representation, esp. those brought in and passed in 1831–2.

Reform (rĭfǭ·ɹm), *v.*[1] ME. [–(O)Fr. *réformer* or L. *reformare*, f. *re-* RE- + *formare* FORM *v.*] †**1.** *trans.* To renew, restore, re-establish (peace) –1556. †**2.** To convert, bring back, or restore (a thing or person) to the original form or state, or to a previous condition –1579. †**3.** To rebuild, repair (a building) –1667. **4.** To convert into another and better form; to free from previous faults or imperfections. Now *rare.* late ME. †**b.** To correct, emend (a book, writing, chart, etc.); to recast –1779. **c.** *Law.* To allow an instrument to be corrected or construed according to the original intention, when an error has been committed in it 1586. **5.** To amend or improve (an arrangement, state of things, institution, etc.) by removal of faults or abuses. late ME. **6.** To put a stop or end to (an abuse, disorder, malpractice, etc.) by enforcing or introducing a better procedure or conduct. late ME. †**b.** To correct, put right (an error or mistake) –1784. **7.** To bring, lead, or force (a person) to abandon a wrong or evil course of life, conduct, etc., and adopt a right one; to bring about a thorough amendment in (a person, his conduct, oneself, etc.) late ME. †**8.** To cut down or back to a desired length; to trim, prune –1697. †**9.** *Mil.* [After Fr. *réformer.*] To form into a new regiment or company; to break up, partially or completely, for this purpose; hence also, to disband, dismiss from the service –1768. **10.** *intr.* (for *refl.*) To abandon wrongdoing or error; to free oneself from misconduct or fault 1582.

4. Romulus's calendar was reformed by Numa, who added two more months 1727. **5.** To r. the administration of justice 1845. **7.** A man is never thoroughly reformed till a new principle governs his thoughts BURNET. **8.** Shall we doubt..To sow, to set, and to r. their growth? DRYDEN. **9.** If you must r. two of them, be sure let him command the troop that is left PEPYS. **10.** It is possible the young man may, in time, grow wiser and r. *'Junius' Lett.* Hence **Refo·rmable** *a.* capable of being reformed; admitting or susceptible of reformation.

Re-form, reform (rĭfǭ·ɹm), *v.*[2] ME. [orig. same as prec. but in later use f. RE- 5 a + FORM *v.* In Fr., *reformer.*] *trans* and *intr.* To form a second time, form over again.

Reformado (refǭɹmē¹·do). Also †**-ade.** 1616. [– Sp. *reformado*, subst. use of pa. pple. of *reformar* REFORM *v.*[1]] **1.** *Mil.* Now *Hist.* **a.** An officer left without a command (owing to the 'reforming' or disbanding of his company) but retaining his rank and seniority, and receiving full or half pay. **b.** A volunteer serving in the army (or navy) without a commission, but with the rank of an officer. **2.** One who is (or has) reformed in some respect; also, one who favours reform; a reformer 1632.

Reformation (refǫɹmē¹·ʃən). late ME. [– (O)Fr. *réformation* or L. *reformatio*; see RE-, FORMATION.] **1.** Improvement in form or quality; alteration to a better form; correction or removal of faults or errors; †rebuilding. **b.** Improvement in health. JOHNSON. **2.** Improvement of (or in) an existing state of things, institution, practice, etc.; a radical change for the better effected in political, religious, or social affairs 1460. **b.** *spec.* (with capital). The great religious movement of the 16th century, having for its object the reform of the doctrines and practices of the Church of Rome, and ending in the establishment of the various Reformed or Protestant Churches of central and north-western Europe 1563. **3.** The action of reforming (one's own or another's) conduct or morals; improvement or amendment in this respect; correction 1509. †**4.** Phr. *Under* (or *saving*) *your r.*: subject to your amendment or correction –1617. †**5.** A disbanding, dismissal (of troops); the removal of an officer from the active list –1670.

1. The late r. of the gold coin of Great Britain ADAM SMITH. **2.** The r. of the church and that of learning began together BERKELEY. **3.** My trouble came tumbling upon me again, and that over the neck of all my Reformations BUNYAN. *House of r.*, a reformatory.

Re-formation (rīfǫɹmē¹·ʃən). late ME. [orig. same word as prec.; in later use f. RE- 5 a + FORMATION.] The action of forming again; a second or new formation.

Reformative (rĭfǭ·ɹmătiv), *a.* 1593. [– OFr. *reformatif* or med.L. *reformativus*, f. pa. ppl. stem of L. *reformare* REFORM *v.*[1]; see -IVE.] Inclined to reform; that tends to, or makes for, reform.

Reformatory (rĭfǭ·ɹmătəri), *a.* and *sb.* 1589. [f. REFORMATION + -ORY.] **A.** *adj.* Having a desire or tendency to reform (a person or thing); designed for reforming. **B.** *sb.* An institution to which juvenile incorrigibles or offenders against the law are sent with a view to their reformation 1837.

attrib. The average r. population [in the United States] is about 15,000. 1885.

Reformed (rĭfǭ·ɹmd), *ppl. a.* and *sb.* 1563. [f. REFORM *v.*[1] + -ED[1].] **A.** *ppl. a.* **1. a.** Of religion, churches, etc.: Brought to a better or purer state by the removal of errors or abuses, esp. those imputed to the Church of Rome. Also *transf.* of persons, times, etc. **b.** Of parliament, *spec.* of that which met after the Reform Act of 1832. 1822. **2.** Improved in character, conduct or morals 1579. **3.** Altered in form or content; *esp.* put into a better form, corrected, amended 1584. †**4.** *Mil.* Of officers: Left without a command (see REFORMADO 1) 1629. †**B.** *sb.* **a.** as *pl.* Adherents of the Reformed religion; Protestants. **b.** *sing.* A Protestant (*rare*). –1772.

A. 1. The name of *R. Church(es)* sometimes includes all the Protestant churches, and sometimes is specifically restricted to the Calvinistic bodies as contrasted with the Lutheran. O.E.D.

Reformer (rĭfǭ·ɹməɹ). 1526. [f. as prec. + -ER[1].] **1.** One who reforms another (*rare*). **2.** One who reforms, or effects a reform in, a state of things, practice, etc. 1548. **3.** *spec.* **a.** One of the leaders in the reformation of religion in the 16th c. 1561. **b.** An advocate or supporter of political or parliamentary reform; *esp.* one who took part in the reform movement of 1831–2. 1785. **4.** A reviser, corrector, improver (*rare*) 1656.

2. Ambroise Paré was a great R. of Surgery 1767.

Reformist (rĭfǭ·ɹmist). 1589. [f. REFORM *v.*[1] + -IST.] **1.** One who advocates reform.

†2. A member of a reformed religious order –1706. So **Refo·rmism.**

Refound (rĭfau·nd), *v.*¹ 1500. [f. RE- 5 a + FOUND *v.*¹ Cf. OFr. *refonder.*] *trans.* To found (a town, etc.) again; to re-establish. Hence **Refou·nder**, one who refounds.

Refound (rĭfau·nd), *v.*² 1649. [f. RE- 5 a + FOUND *v.*² Cf. OFr. *refondre.*] *trans.* To cast (objects of metal) again; to recast.

Refract (rĭfræ·kt), *v.* 1612. [– *refract-*, pa. ppl. stem of L. *refringere*, f. *re-* RE- + *frangere* break.] **1.** *trans. Physics.* Of substances: To break the course of (light, etc.) and turn (it) out of the direct line; *esp.* to deflect at a certain angle at the point of passage from one medium into another of different density. **b.** To produce by refraction (*rare*) 1728. †**2.** To throw back; to reflect –1694. †**3.** To break up; to impair (*rare*) –1676. **b.** *Chem.* To analyse (nitre) in order to discover the percentage of impurities 1842.

1. Glass refracts light more strongly than water does HUXLEY. Hence **Refra·ctable** *a.* refrangible. **Refra·cted** *ppl. a.* bent aside, deflected; connected with or produced by refraction.

†**Refra·ctary**, *a.* and *sb.* 1599. [– L. *refractarius*, f. as prec.; see -ARY¹. Cf. Fr. *réfractaire.*] **A.** *adj.* = REFRACTORY –1694. **B.** *sb.* A refractory person –1657. Hence †**Refra·ctariness.**

Refractile (rĭfræ·ktil, -təil), *a.* 1847. [f. REFRACT *v.* + -ILE.] Capable of producing refraction.

Refracting (rĭfræ·ktiŋ), *ppl. a.* 1704. [f. as prec. + -ING².] Causing refraction; refractive. **b.** Provided with some apparatus or arrangement for refracting light; esp. *r. telescope*, a telescope in which the rays of light are converged to a focus by an object glass 1764. **c.** *R. angle*, the angle between two faces of a prism or lens 1796.

Refraction (rĭfræ·kʃən). 1578. [– Fr. *réfraction* or late L. *refractio, -on-*, f. *refract-*; see REFRACT, -ION.] †**1. a.** The action of breaking open or breaking up (*rare*) –1661. †**b.** Rebound, recoil (*rare*) –1661. **2.** The fact or phenomenon of a ray of light, heat, (†the sight,) etc., being diverted or deflected from its previous course in passing obliquely out of one medium into another of different density, or in traversing a medium not of uniform density 1603. Also with *a* and *pl.*, an instance of this. †**b.** Refracted beams –1649. **3. a.** *Astron.* The deflection of the beams or light from heavenly bodies when not in the zenith, due to the refracting power of the atmosphere, which increases their apparent elevation. (Spec. called *atmospheric* and *astronomical r.*) 1603. **b.** The effect of the atmosphere in making terrestrial objects appear higher than they are. (Spec. called *terrestrial r.*) 1698. **4.** The action *of* a medium in refracting light; refractive power or effect 1664. **5.** The ascertainment of the percentage of impurities contained in a sample of nitre; the sum of the impurities as thus ascertained 1842.

2. Phr. *Angle of r.*, the angle between the refracted ray and the perpendicular to the surface of the refracting medium at the point of incidence (†or that between the refracted ray and a continuation of the incident ray). *Double r.*, the fact of a ray of light being split up by certain minerals into two divergent, unequally refracted rays. *Index of r.*: see INDEX *sb.* 9.

Comb.: **r.-circle**, one of two or more graduated circles attached to a refracting telescope in order to adjust its direction.

Refractive (rĭfræ·ktiv), *a.* 1673. [f. REFRACT *v.* + -IVE.] **1.** That refracts light, etc.; possessed of, characterized by, the power of refracting. **2. a.** Due to, caused by, refraction 1717. **b.** Refrangible 1890. **3.** Relating to refraction 1727.

1. Tourmaline is a doubly r. substance 1854. Phr. *R. power*, the power which a transparent body has of refracting the light passing through it. *R. index* (see INDEX *sb.* 9). **2. a.** R. aberration 1879. Hence **Refra·ctiveness, Refracti·vity.**

Refractometer (rĭfræktǫ·mĭtəɹ). 1876. [f. REFRACT *v.* + -METER.] An instrument for measuring the indices of refraction of various substances.

Refractor (rĭfræ·ktǫɹ). 1769. [f. REFRACT *v.* + -OR 2.] A medium which refracts light; a refracting lens 1836. **b.** A refracting telescope 1769.

Refractory (rĭfræ·ktəri), *a.* and *sb.* 1599. [alt. of REFRACTARY by substitution of -ORY.] **A.** *adj.* **1.** Stubborn, obstinate, perverse; unmanageable, rebellious 1606. †**2.** Strongly opposed, refusing compliance, *to* something –1723. **3.** *Med.* Of wounds, diseases, and the like: Obstinate, not yielding *to* treatment 1663. **b.** Able to offer resistance *to* a disease; not susceptible to morbid agencies 1884. **4.** Resisting the action of heat; difficult to fuse (or to work in any way) 1758.

A. 1. They were a parcel of r., ungovernable villains DE FOE. The r. proceedings of the crew 1748. **2.** A People..so r. to all Culture 1723. **3.** The wound was at first r. 1836. Hence **Refra·ctori-ly** *adv.*, **-ness.**

†**B.** *sb.* **1.** A refractory person –1633. **2.** A piece of refractory ware employed in the process of glazing pottery 1839.

†**Refragate**, *v.* 1593. [– *refragat-*, pa. ppl. stem of L. *refragari* resist; see -ATE³.] *intr.* To oppose, controvert –1661.

Refrain (rĭfrēⁱ·n), *sb.* late ME. [– (O)Fr. *refrain*, †*refrein*, succeeding to earlier *refrait, -eit*, prob. – Pr. *refranh* bird's song, f. *refranhar* – Rom. **refrangere*, for L. *refringere*, f. *re-* RE- + *frangere* break.] A phrase or verse recurring at intervals, esp. at the end of each stanza of a poem or song; a burden, chorus.

Refrain (rĭfrēⁱ·n), *v.* late ME. [– (O)Fr. *refréner* – L. *refrenare* to bridle, f. *re-* RE- + *frenum, frænum* bridle.] **I.** *trans.* †**1.** To restrain, hold back, check (a person or thing) –1645. **b.** *refl.* To restrain, put restraint upon (oneself); to repress any manifestation of emotion, impatience, etc. Now *arch.* late ME. **2.** To hold back, restrain (a person or thing) *from* something, esp. some act or course of action. Now *rare.* late ME. †**3.** To restrain, curb, check, stay (an action, proceeding, feeling, quality, etc.) –1683. **4.** To put a restraint or check upon (one's own desires, feelings, actions, etc.). late ME. †**5.** To keep from (an action), desist from, give up –1725. †**6.** To abstain from (a habit or practice); to give up, avoid, eschew –1751. †**7.** To avoid, shun, eschew (a person's company) –1716. †**b.** To avoid, keep away from (a place); also, to go away from, to leave –1748.

1. b. And thou, O human heart of mine, Be still, r. thyself, and wait CLOUGH. **2.** Nor from the Holie One of Heav'n Refrein'd his tongue blasphemous MILT. **4.** When we heard that, we were ashamed, and refrained our tears JOWETT.

II. *intr.* **1.** To abstain, forbear. late ME. **2.** To abstain, keep oneself, *from* some act or feeling, †using or partaking of something, interference with a person, etc. 1538.

1. Who could refraine, That had a heart to loue? SHAKS. **2.** And now I say vnto you, refraine from these men, and let them alone *Acts* 5 : 38. Hence †**Refrai·ner** (*rare*), one who restrains. **Refrai·nment** (*rare*), refraining, abstinence.

Refrangent (rĭfræ·ndʒĕnt), *a. rare.* 1880. [irreg. var. of REFRINGENT, after L. *frangere.*] Refracting; breaking up again.

Refrangible (rĭfræ·ndʒib'l), *a.* 1673. [– mod.L. *refrangibilis* (Newton), f. *refrangere*, for cl.L. *refringere*; see REFRACT *v.*, -IBLE.] Capable of being refracted; admitting of, susceptible to, refraction. Hence **Refrangibi·lity, Refra·ngibleness.**

†**Refrenation.** 1450. [– L. *refrenatio, -on-*, f. *refrenat-*, pa. ppl. stem of *refrenare*; see REFRAIN *v.*, -ION.] **1.** The action of refraining or restraining –1652. **2.** *Astrol.* The prevention of a conjunction by the retrogression of one of the planets –1706.

Refresh (rĭfre·ʃ), *sb.* Now *colloq.* 1592. [f. next.] †**1.** The act of refreshing; refreshment; renewal of supplies –1648. **2.** A refreshment (esp. of liquor) taken by a person; a refresher 1884.

Refresh (rĭfre·ʃ), *v.* late ME. [– OFr. *refreschier, refreschir* (mod. *rafraîchir*), f. *re-* RE- + *fres*, fem. *fresche* fresh.] **1.** *trans.* Of physical agents (esp. water): To impart freshness to (a place or thing, the air, etc.) by means of cooling or wetting. **2.** To make (a person) feel fresher than before; to reanimate, reinvigorate physically, mentally, or spiritually; to provide with refreshment. late ME. **b.** *refl.* (of persons): To make (oneself) fresher, by partaking of food or drink, by resting, etc. late ME. †**c.** To relieve *of* –1760. **3.** To freshen up (the memory), to make clear or distinct again 1542. †**4.** To restore, renovate (a building). *rare.* –1548. **5.** To restore to, or keep at, a certain level or condition by furnishing a fresh supply of something 1450. **6.** †**a.** To restore (a thing) to a fresh or bright condition; to brighten or freshen up –1818. **b.** To make (a surface) fresh, esp. by cutting 1658. **7.** *intr.* (for *refl.*) To refresh oneself; to take refreshment in some way; now *spec.* to partake of some refreshing liquor 1650. **b.** To lay in fresh supplies 1685.

1. Pearly Rains Descend in silence to r. the Plains DRYDEN. **2.** We rose with the sun, refreshed and strong TYNDALL. **5.** They went into the hut, and they refreshed the fire 1895. **6. a.** The rest r. the scaly Snakes, that fold The Shield of Pallas, and renew their Gold DRYDEN. **7. b.** It was not the most eligible place for a ship to r. at 1748.

Refresher (rĭfre·ʃəɹ). late ME. [f. REFRESH *v.* + -ER¹.] **1.** One who or that which refreshes. **b.** A refreshment; *colloq.* a drink 1822. **2.** A reminder 1837. **3.** In legal use: An extra fee paid to counsel in prolonged or frequently adjourned cases. Also *attrib.* 1850.

3. Daily refreshers should be abolished, as being one of the principal causes of the undue lengthening of trials 1881.

attrib.: **r. course**, a course of instruction for officers or men during intervals between fighting.

Refreshful (rĭfre·ʃfŭl), *a.* 1637. [f. REFRESH *v.* + -FUL.] Full of refreshment, refreshing. Hence **Refre·shfully** *adv.*

Refreshment (rĭfre·ʃmĕnt). late ME. [– OFr. *refreschement*, f. *refrescher*; see REFRESH *v.*, -MENT, or f. REFRESH *v.*] **1.** The act of refreshing, or fact of being refreshed. Also, that which refreshes; the means of restoring strength or vigour, mental or physical. Freq. in phr. *to take r.* **2.** With *a* and *pl.* late ME. **b.** Applied to food and drink; now, of a light repast, and often *spec.* of drink. 1665. †**3.** *pl.* Fresh supplies of men or provisions –1803.

1. With singleness of heart to His glory, and the r. of His people CROMWELL. **2. b.** To ..allow of no refreshments but such as are consistent with the strictest rules of Christian Sobriety LAW. **4.** *attrib.*, as *r. car, house, stall*, etc.; **R. Sunday,** mid-Lent Sunday.

†**Re·fricate**, *v. rare.* 1570. [– *refricat-*, pa. ppl. stem of L. *refricare*, f. *re-* RE- + *fricare* rub; see -ATE³.] *trans.* To open up again, renew (a wound or grief); to stimulate (the memory) afresh –1657. Hence †**Refrica·tion.**

Refrigerant (rĭfri·dʒĕrănt), *a.* and *sb.* 1599. [– Fr. *réfrigérant* or L. *refrigerans, -ant-*, pr. pple. of *refrigerare*; see next, -ANT.] **A.** *adj.* **1.** Of medicinal agents or appliances: Cooling the body or part; allaying heat or fever. Also with *property*, etc. †**b.** Refreshing, otherwise than by cooling. BACON. **2.** *gen.* Cooling, producing coolness 1766. **B.** *sb.* **1. a.** A medicinal agent or appliance employed to reduce abnormal heat, as in inflammation or fever; a cooling medicine 1676. **b.** *transf.* or *gen.* A means of cooling, *esp.* a cooling or refreshing drink 1826. †**2.** In distillation, a cooling vessel or apparatus at the head of a still –1727. **3.** A freezing agent 1885.

1. *fig.* This..never fails to prove a r. to passion 1783.

Refrigerate (rĭfri·dʒĕrēⁱt), *v.* 1534. [– *refrigerat-*, pa. ppl. stem of L. *refrigerare*, f. *re-* RE- + *frigus, frigor-* cold; see -ATE³.] **1.** *trans.* To cause to become cold, to make or keep cool. Also *absol.* **b.** To expose to extreme cold for the purpose of freezing or preserving 1875. **2.** *intr.* To grow cold 1563.

2. I will make a fire, and leave them to r. as much longer as they please LOWELL.

Refrigeration (rĭfridʒĕrēⁱ·ʃən). 1471. [– L. *refrigeratio, -on-*, f. as prec.; see -ION.] **1.** The action of refrigerating, cooling, or freezing; the process of becoming cold. **b.** *Geol.* The gradual cooling of the earth from natural causes 1794. **c.** The freezing of provisions for the purpose of preserving them 1881. **2.** Reduction of heat in the body (now only *Med.*); †cooling and refreshing of the blood or spirits 1502.

Refrigerative (rĭfri·dʒĕrătiv), *a.* and *sb.* 1558. [– late and med.L. *refrigerativus* cooling, f. as prec.; see -IVE. Cf. (O)Fr *réfrigératif.*] **A.** *adj.* Tending to cool, refrigerant. **B.** *sb.* A cooling medicine (*rare*) 1706.

Refrigerator (rĭfri·dʒĕreⁱtəɹ). 1611. [f. REFRIGERATE *v.* + -OR 2.] **1.** That which refrigerates or cools. **2.** An apparatus, vessel, or chamber for producing or maintaining a low degree of temperature; *esp.* **a.** any vessel, chamber, or apparatus in which the contents are preserved by maintaining a temperature, near, at, or below freezing-point, esp. in the cold storage of food; **b.** = next 1. 1824.

Refrigeratory (rĭfri·dʒĕrătəri), *sb.* 1605. [– mod.L. *refrigeratorium*, subst. use of n. of L. adj. *refrigoratorius*; see next, -ORY[1].] **1.** A vessel at the head of a still filled with cold water through which the worm passes, for condensing alcoholic and other vapours; any vessel or apparatus employed for a similar purpose. **2.** Any appliance, vessel or chamber by or in which the process of cooling or freezing is effected 1653.

Refrigeratory (rĭfri·dʒĕrătəri), *a.* 1721. [– L. *refrigeratorius*; see REFRIGERATE *v.*, -ORY[2].] Tending to cool or make cold; cooling.

†**Refrige·rium.** 1645. [L., lit. 'cooling', in eccl.L. mitigation, consolation, f. *refrigerare* REFRIGERATE.] A respite granted to the souls of the damned; also *transf.* hymns or prayers for such a respite –1667.

Refringency (rĭfri·ndʒĕnsi). 1882. [f. next; see -ENCY.] = REFRACTIVITY.

Refringent (rĭfri·ndʒĕnt), *a.* 1778. [– L. *refringens, -ent-*, pr. pple. of *refringere*; see REFRACT *v.*, -ENT. Cf. Fr. *refringent* (XVIII).] = REFRACTIVE.

Reft (reft), *ppl. a.* 1847. [See REAVE *v.*[1]] Robbed, bereft of something.

Refuge (re·fiūdʒ), *sb.* late ME. [– (O)Fr. *refuge* – L. *refugium*, f. *re-* RE- + *fugere* flee.] **1.** Shelter or protection from danger or trouble; succour sought by, or rendered to, a person. **2.** One who, or that which, serves to give shelter, protection, aid, comfort, etc. late ME. **3.** A place of safety or security; a shelter, asylum, stronghold. late ME. **b.** A portion of the roadway marked off at busy crossings, for securing the safety of foot passengers 1881. **4.** †**a.** A resource; recourse *to* a practice –1734. **b.** A plea, pretext, excuse, or answer, in which one takes refuge 1549.

1. So violence Proceeded..Through all the Plain, and r. none was found MILT. Phr. *Of r.*, adapted or intended for shelter or protection, as in *city, country, harbour, place, port of r.*; also *house of r.*, an institution for sheltering the homeless or destitute. *To take r.*, to seek safety or shelter *in* (or *at*) a place; also *transf.* (const. *in*), to have recourse to (something) as a means of escape, consolation, etc. **2.** Books—the r. of the destitute KIPLING. **3.** And like a dowve fle to his r. 1450. **4. b.** 1 *Hen. VI*, v. iv. 69.

Refuge (re·fiūdʒ), *v.* Now *rare.* 1594. [f. prec., or – Fr. *réfugier*, †*refuger* (XV), usu. *se réfugier* take refuge.] **1.** *trans.* To afford a refuge, asylum, or retreat to (a person); to shelter, protect. †**b.** *refl.* To take refuge; to flee for refuge *to* a place –1748. **2.** *intr.* To take refuge; to seek shelter or protection 1638.

Refugee (refiudʒī·), *sb.* 1685. [– Fr. *réfugié*, pa. pple. of (*se*) *réfugier*, f. *refuge* (see prec.); the ending was early assim. to -EE[1].] **1. a.** One who, owing to religious persecution or political troubles, seeks refuge in a foreign country; orig. applied to the French Huguenots who came to England after the revocation of the Edict of Nantes in 1685. **b.** A runaway; a fugitive from justice, etc. (*rare*) 1760. **2.** *U.S.* A name given, esp. in New York State, to parties of marauders in the American revolutionary war who claimed British protection. *Obs.* exc. *Hist.* 1780.

Refulgence (rĭfɒ·ldʒĕns). 1634. [– L. *refulgentia*, f. *refulgens*; see next, -ENCE.] The quality of being refulgent, splendour, brightness, radiance. So †**Refu·lgency** –1796.

Refulgent (rĭfɒ·ldʒĕnt), *a.* 1509. [– L. *refulgens, -ent-*, pr. pple. of *refulgēre*, f. *re-* RE- + *fulgēre* shine; see -ENT.] Shining with, or reflecting, a brilliant light; radiant, resplendent, gleaming.

There will be no clouds or fogs; but one bright r. day WESLEY. A most r. smile DICKENS. Hence **Refu·lgent-ly** *adv.*, **-ness.**

Refund (rĭfɒ·nd), *v.*[1] late ME. [– OFr. *refonder* or L. *refundere*, f. *re-* RE- + *fundere* pour; in later use based on FUND *v.*] **1.** *trans.* To pour back, pour in or out again. Now *rare* or *Obs.* **b.** To give back, restore. Also *absol.* late ME. **2.** To make return or restitution of (a sum received or taken); to hand back, repay, restore 1553. **3.** To reimburse, repay (a person) 1736. **4.** *absol.* To make repayment 1655.

1. One may as easily perswade the thirsty earth to r. the water she has suckt into her veins 1674. **2.** Whatever charges you are at in copying I shall willingly r. 1723. Hence **Refu·nd** *sb.* repayment. **Refu·nder**, one who refunds. **Refu·ndment**, the act of refunding.

Refu·nd (rī-), *v.*[2] 1860. [RE- 5a.] *trans.* To fund again or anew.

Refusable (rĭfiū·zăb'l), *a.* Now *rare.* 1570. [f. REFUSE *v.* + -ABLE.] That may be refused.

Refusal (rĭfiū·zăl). 1474. [f. REFUSE *v.* + -AL[1] 2.] **1.** The act of refusing; a denial or rejection of something demanded or offered. **b.** *spec.* in the game of écarté, the action of the dealer in refusing to allow a discard. Hence *r. hand*, a hand on which the dealer should so refuse. 1877. **c.** Of a horse: The action of stopping short (at a hedge, water, etc.) instead of leaping 1856. **2.** The chance of refusing some thing, office, or the like before it is offered to others; the privilege or right of having it placed at one's disposal for acceptance; *esp.* in phr. *to have the r. of* 1563. **3.** That which has been refused or rejected 1618.

1. Do they not seek occasion of new quarrels, On my r., to distress me more? MILT. **2.** They had the first r. of any concessions he might obtain 1887.

†**Refu·se,** *sb.*[1] late ME. [– (O)Fr. *refus*, f. *refuser*; see next.] = prec. 1 and 2. –1753.

Refuse (re·fiūs), *a.* and *sb.*[2] ME. [perh. – OFr. *refusé*, pa. pple. of *refuser* REFUSE *v.* For the loss of *é* cf. COSTIVE, SIGNAL *a.*, TROVE.] **A.** *adj.* †**1.** Refused or rejected (*rare*) –1508. **2.** Rejected or thrown aside as worthless or of little value 1464. **B.** *sb.* That which is cast aside as worthless; rubbish or worthless matter of any kind; the rejected or rubbishy part of anything 1440. **b.** The scum, off-scourings, dregs, etc. *of* some class of persons 1603. **c.** The leavings *of* something 1665.

A. 2. Certain trades pour their r. water into rivers 1869. **B.** The stones and r. on the shore DICKENS. **c.** Some Carcass half devour'd, the R. of gorg'd Wolves SWIFT.

Comb.: **r. consumer, destructor,** a furnace in which r. of various kinds is burned.

Refuse (rĭfiū·z), *v.* ME. [– (O)Fr. *refuser* – Rom. **refusare*, prob. alt. of L. *recusare* refuse (see RECUSANT), after *refutare* REFUTE.]

I. †**1.** To avoid, keep clear of or free from (sin, vice, etc.) –1691. **2.** To decline to take or accept (something offered or presented); to reject the offer of (a thing) ME. **b.** To reject (a thing or person) in making a choice or selection. Now *rare.* 1526. **3.** To decline to accept or submit to (a command, rule, instruction, etc.) or to undergo (pain or penalty). late ME. **b.** Of a horse: To stop short at (a hedge, water, etc.) instead of leaping 1840. **4.** †**a.** To reject (a person); to decline to admit to a certain position, or to some relationship with oneself –1683. **b.** To reject, decline to have, as a wife or (now usu.) a husband. late ME. †**c.** To decline to meet (an opponent) –1606.

2. Lord Halifax began a health to me to-day;.. which I refused SWIFT. **b.** That hee may know to r. the euill, and choose the good *Isa.* 7:15. **4. a.** This Moses whom they refused, saying, Who made thee a ruler and a Iudge? *Acts* 7:35.

†**II. 1.** To renounce –1684. **2.** To renounce (God or Christ); to cast off (a person); to divorce (a wife) –1599. **3.** To put or drive away, get rid of (*rare*) –1483. **4.** To deny (a charge or allegation). *rare.* –1753.

1. Denie thy Father and r. thy name SHAKS. They still R. this World, to do their Father's will BUNYAN.

III. 1. With *inf.* To decline positively, to express or show a determination not *to* do something. Also *transf.* of things. late ME. **2.** To decline to give or grant; to deny (something asked) *to* a person (or thing) 1585. **b.** *Mil.* To decline to oppose (troops) to the enemy; to withdraw or move back from the regular alignment 1796. **3.** With double acc.: To decline to give, deny (something) to (a person or thing) 1621. **b.** With personal object only 1784. †**4.** To refuse (one) leave *to* do something; to prohibit or keep back *from* something –1688.

1. Seeing kindly sleep r. to doe His office SPENSER. Eliot refused to move from his constitutional ground GREEN. **2.** He could not r. his tears to the unhappy fate of Carthage 1734. **b.** The French during the whole of the action..refused their right wing 1802. **3.** I feel already that I can r. you nothing MISS BURNEY. **b.** Soon I could not have refused her SHELLEY.

IV. *intr.* To make refusal; to decline acceptance or compliance; to withhold permission; *spec.* in écarté (see REFUSAL 1 b). late ME. **b.** Of a horse: (see I. 3 b above) 1525.

But he refused, and sayde, I wil not eate COVERDALE 1 *Sam.* 28:23. Hence **Refu·ser,** one who refuses; *esp.* a recusant.

†**Refu·sion.** *rare.* 1656. [– Fr. †*réfusion* – late L. *refusio*; see RE-, FUSION.] The action of pouring back; re-infusion (of the soul) –1741.

Refutable (re·fiŭtăb'l, rĭfiū·tăb'l), *a.* 1560. [– late L. *refutabilis*, f. L. *refutare*; see REFUTE *v.*, -ABLE.] That may be (†rejected,) refuted, or disproved. Hence **Refutabi·lity** (*rare*), capability of being refuted. **Refu·tably** *adv.*

Refutal (rĭfiū·tăl). 1605. [f. REFUTE *v.* + -AL[1] 2.] = next.

Refutation (refiuteⁱ·ʃən). 1548. [– L. *refutatio, -on-*, f. *refutat-*, pa. ppl. stem of L. *refutare*; see REFUTE *v.*, -ION.] The action of refuting or disproving a statement, charge, etc.; confutation.

An effectual r. of his own Principles BENTLEY.

Refutative (re·fiŭteⁱtiv, rĭfiū·tătiv), *a. rare.* 1652. [f. as prec. + -IVE.] That tends to refute; belonging to refutation. So **Refu·tatory** *a.*

Refute (rĭfiū·t), *v.* 1545. [– L. *refutare* repel, rebut.] **1.** *trans.* To prove (a person) to be in error, to confute. **2.** To disprove, overthrow by argument, prove to be false 1597. **3.** *absol.* To demonstrate error 1742.

2. An errour so gross..that it needs not the Microscope to r. it 1664. The surest way to r. such calumnies THIRLWALL. Would you not seek everywhere for proofs to r. the accusation? MANNING. Hence †**Refute** *sb.* refutation. **Refu·ter,** one who refutes.

Regain (rĭgēⁱ·n, rī-), *v.* 1548. [– (O)Fr. *regagner*; see RE-, GAIN *v.*] **1.** *trans.* To gain or get anew; to recover possession of (something). Also *absol.* †**2.** To win or bring back *to* a state or condition –1679. **3.** To get back to, succeed in reaching (a place) again; to rejoin (a person) 1634. **b.** To recover (one's feet) 1814.

1. I began by degrees to r. confidence JOWETT. Hence **Regai·nment.**

Regal (rī·găl), *a.* and *sb.*[1] ME. [– OFr. *regal* or L. *regalis*, f. *rex, reg-* king; see -AL[1].] **A.** *adj.* **1.** Of or belonging to a king; royal. †**2.** Ruling, governing (*rare*) –1656. **3.** Befitting, or resembling, a king; kingly; hence, splendid, magnificent, stately, etc. 1799.

1. When they see all R. Power Giv'n me to quell thir pride MILT. The r. title GIBBON.

†**B.** *sb.* **1.** Royalty, sovereignty, royal authority –1460. **2.** A prince, ruler (*rare*) –1821. **3.** The chalice used for the communion at the coronation of British sovereigns –1662. †**4.** *pl.* = REGALIA[1] 2. –1604. Hence **Re·gally** *adv.*

Regal (rī·găl), *sb.*[2] 1541. [– Fr. *régale* (XVI), of obsc. origin.] **1.** Chiefly *pl.* A small portable organ, having one, or sometimes two, sets of reed-pipes played with keys by the right hand, while a small bellows was worked by the left hand. Now chiefly *Hist.* **2.** One of certain reed-stops (*esp.* the *vox humana*) in organs 1799.

‖**Regale** (rĭgēⁱ·li, Fr. regal), *sb.*[1] 1611. [– Fr. *régale* (OFr. *regales*), f. med.L. *regalia* (sc. *jura* prerogatives), subst. use of n. pl. of L. *regalis* REGAL *a.*] **1.** *Eccl. Hist.* The right, on the part of the kings of France, of enjoying the revenues of vacant bishoprics or abbacies, and of presenting to benefices dependent on these. †**2.** A privilege or prerogative of royalty –1797.

Regale (rĭgēⁱ·l), *sb.*[2] 1670. [– Fr. †*regale* XV (mod. *régal*), f. OFr. *gale*; cf. next.] **1.** A choice repast, feast, or banquet; †an entertainment or fête. Also *transf.* or *fig.* **2.** A choice article of food or form of refreshment; a dainty 1673. **3.** Refreshment 1753. †**4.** A complimentary present (*rare*) –1744.

2. I may therefore hope..to see the tables adorned with the r. of Devonshire cream 1791. **4.** I had been threatened with a r. of hams and Florence wine H. WALPOLE.

Regale (rĭgēⁱ·l), *v.* 1656. [– Fr. *régaler*, f. *re-* RE- + OFr. *gale* pleasure, joy; see GALE *sb.*[2], GALLANT.] **1.** *trans.* To entertain or feast (a person, etc.) in a choice manner. **b.** Of things: To furnish (one) with a choice feast or refreshment 1721. **2.** To gratify or delight (the mind) by some pleasing influence or occupation; to entertain (a person) in a highly agreeable manner 1671. **b.** To affect with a pleasurable sensation 1703. **3.** To gratify, please, delight, by a gift, deference, etc. (*rare*) 1671. **4.** *refl.* To entertain or recreate (oneself) with food, drink, or amusement 1719. **5.** *intr.* To feast; const. *on, upon, with* 1678.

1. Regaling each other in the best style their respective camps afforded W. IRVING. **2. b.** The peach's vernal bud regal'd his eye SHENSTONE. Hence **Rega·lement,** the act of regaling; a dainty.

‖**Regalia**[1] (rĭgēⁱ·liă). 1540. [med.L., royal residence, royal rights, n. pl. of L. *regalis* REGAL *a.*; see -IA[2].] **1.** Rights appertaining to a king; royal powers or privileges. **2.** The emblems or insignia of royalty; the crown, sceptre, and other distinctive ornaments of a king or queen which are used at coronations 1626. **3.** The decorations or insignia of an order 1676.

Regalia[2] (rĭgēⁱ·liă). 1819. [– Sp. *regalia* royal privilege.] A Cuban or other large cigar of superior quality.

Regalian (rĭgēⁱ·liăn), *a.* 1818. [– Fr. *régalien*; see REGAL *a.*, -IAN.] Pertaining to a sovereign; regal.

Regalism (rī·găliz'm). 1869. [f. REGAL *a.* + -ISM.] The doctrine or practice of the supremacy of the sovereign in ecclesiastical matters. So **Re·galist,** a supporter of r.

Regality (rĭgæ·lĭti). late ME. [– OFr. *regalité* or med.L. *regalitas, -tat-*, f. L. *regalis* REGAL *a.*; see -ITY.] **1.** Royalty, kingship, sovereign rule or jurisdiction. **2.** *Sc.* Territorial jurisdiction of a royal nature granted by the king. Now *Hist.* late ME. **3.** *Sc.* A particular territory or area subject to a lord of regality. late ME. **4.** A country or district subject to royal authority, a kingdom; a monarchical state 1486. **5.** A right or privilege pertaining or appropriate to a king. Chiefly *pl.* 1523.

1. When raging Passion with fierce tyranny Robs Reason of her dew regalitie SPENSER. **2.** *Lord of r.*, the person to whom r. was granted. **5.** Before Ile be halfe a king, and contrould In any r., ile hazard all 1592.

‖**Regalo** (rega·lo). Now *rare.* 1622. [– It. (also Sp. and Pg.) *regalo* a gift, related to *regalare* to REGALE.] A present, esp. of choice food or drink; a choice or elegant repast or entertainment, etc. (see REGALE *sb.*[2]).

Re·galty. ME. [prob. – AFr. **regalté*, *regauté*; see REGAL and cf. ROYALTY.] = REGALITY –1703.

Regard (rĭgā·ɹd), *sb.* late ME. [– (O)Fr. *regard*, f. *regarder*; see next.] **I. 1.** †Aspect, appearance; look (of persons); habit or manner of looking; air. **2.** A look, glance, or gaze 1477. †**b.** An object of sight (*rare*) –1604. **3.** The official inspection of a forest in order to discover whether any trespasses have been committed in it; the right of such inspection, or the office of one appointed to make it. *Obs.* exc. *Hist.* 1502. **b.** The district within the jurisdiction of the official regarders 1594. **4.** †**a.** Reference *to* a person or thing. Chiefly in phr. *to have* (*a*) *r. to*. –1677. **b.** Respect, point, particular 1602. †**c.** ? Intention, purpose, design. SHAKS.

1. To whom with stern r. thus Gabriel spake MILT. **2.** He..bites his lip with a politique r. SHAKS. **b.** To throw-out our eyes for braue Othello, Euen till we make the Maine,..An indistinct r. SHAKS. **4. b.** I will pay every possible attention to your instructions in this r. SHELLEY. **c.** *Jul. C.* III. i. 224.

II. †**1.** Repute, account, or estimation, in which anything is held –1785. **2.** Observant attention or heed bestowed upon or given *to* a matter. †Also *pl.* 1456. **b.** Care in doing something; close attention *to* some principle or method 1575. **3.** Care or concern *for* something 1836. **4.** Attention, heed, or consideration, given to a thing or person, as having an effect or influence on one's actions or conduct; respect or deference paid *to*, or entertained *for*, some authority, principle, etc. Orig. in phr. *to have* (†*make* or *take*) *r. to*; in later use also const. *of, for.* 1477. **5.** A thing or circumstance looked to, or taken into account, in determining action; a consideration, a motive 1579. †**b.** A looking *to* another in order to direct one's actions or conduct (*rare*) –1732. **6.** Esteem, affection, kindly feeling 1591. **b.** *pl.* in epistolary expressions of good-will 1775.

1. What things there are Most abiect in r., and deare in vse SHAKS. †*Of..r.*, of (small, great, etc.) account, estimation, or value. †*In* (one's) *r.*, in one's opinion, estimation, or judgement (*rare*). **2.** The conduct pursued by the Governor-General is the next object of r. 1818. **3.** R. for the safety of the hostages FREEMAN. **4.** A religious r. was paid to fire BERKELEY. *Without r.* (†*of* or) *to*, without giving consideration or weight *to* a thing; without reference *to*. **5.** A benevolence which shall lose all particular regards in its general light EMERSON. **6.** There is no guide..for whom I have a stronger r. TYNDALL.

Phrases. *In r. of*, in comparison with (now *arch.*) *In r. of* or *to, with r. to*, in respect of, with respect or reference to. *In one's r.*, with regard, respect, or reference to one. †*In r. of* or *to*, out of consideration for. †*In r.* (*that*), since, because, inasmuch as, considering that.

Regard (rĭgā·ɹd), *v.* late ME. [– (O)Fr. *regarder*, f. *re-* RE- + *garder* GUARD *v.*] **I.** *trans.* **1.** To look at, gaze upon, observe 1523. †**b.** Of places, etc.: To look or face toward –1750. **2.** To take notice of, bestow attention or notice upon; to take or show an interest in; to give heed to; †to take care of. late ME. †**3.** To look to, have a care of or for (oneself, one's own interest, health, etc.) –1671. **b.** To look to, consider, take into account 1591. †**4.** To take notice of (a thing) as being of special value, excellence, or merit; to value or set store by –1656. **b.** To hold (a person) in great esteem; to have a regard for (a person) 1513. **5.** To heed, or take into account, in regulating one's actions or conduct 1512. **b.** To have respect for or dread of (a person) 1526. **c.** To pay heed or attention to (one speaking or something said) 1535. **d.** To show consideration for (a thing or person) 1513. **6.** To consider, look on, *as* being something 1607. **b.** To look upon *with* some feeling 1615. **7.** To concern, have relation or respect to 1603. **b.** In *pres. pple.* Concerning, relating to 1793. **c.** *As regards*, so far as relates to 1819.

1. Your neece regards me with an eye of fauour SHAKS. **2.** R. the weak and fatherless MILT. **3. b.** *Two Gent.* III. i. 256. **4. b.** I have in vain done all I can to make her r. me STEELE. **5.** They that r. not the Law are a dishonourable seed *Ecclus.* 10:19. **b.** Here's Beauford, that regards not God nor King SHAKS. **c.** Hee talk'd very wisely, but I regarded him not SHAKS. **d.** We may be led to think that the rights of England were..strictly regarded FREEMAN. **6.** He regarded his submission as the end of the dispute FROUDE. **b.** The stamp of artless piety..The youth..Regards with scorn COWPER. **7.** Morals and criticism r. our tastes and sentiments HUME.

II. 1. *absol.* or *intr.* **a.** To look, gaze (*rare*) 1523. **b.** To pay attention, give heed; to bestow attention *on* a thing 1611. †**2.** To look *to*; to refer *to* –1659. **3.** To look, appear. SHELLEY.

1. a. We with blind surmise Regarding, while she read TENNYSON. **b.** I haue stretched out my hand, and no man regarded *Prov.* 1:24. **3.** The hills and woods..R. like shapes in an enchanter's glass 1819.

Rega·rdable, *a.* Now *rare.* 1591. [f. prec. + -ABLE.] Worthy of being regarded, noticeable.

Regardant (rĭgā·ɹdănt), *a.* and *sb.* 1443. [– AFr., (O)Fr. *regardant*, pr. pple. of *regarder*; see REGARD *v.*, -ANT.] **A.** *adj.* **1.** *Law.* (now *Hist.*) Attached to a manor. **2.** *Her.* Looking backward 1500. **3.** Observant, watchful, contemplative 1588. †**B.** *sb.* A villein regardant, a serf –1795.

A. 3. The look..was rather cogitative than r. SOUTHEY.

Regarder (rĭgā·ɹdəɹ). 1502. [f. REGARD *v.* + -ER[1], in early use after AFr. *regardour*, AL. *regardor, -ator* (XII).] **1.** An officer charged with the supervision of a forest. Now *local* and *Hist.* **2.** One who or that which regards 1525.

Regardful (rĭgā·ɹdfŭl), *a.* 1586. [f. REGARD *sb.* + -FUL.] **1.** Heedful, attentive, observant. **2.** Respectful; indicative of regard or esteem 1607. †**3.** Worthy of regard or attention –1650.

1. They ar more r. of their worldly gain..then they ar of a good conscience 1653. Hence **Rega·rdful-ly** *adv.*, **-ness.**

Regardless (rĭgā·ɹdlės), *a.* 1591. [f. as prec. + -LESS.] **1.** Heedless, indifferent, careless; without regard *of*. **2.** Unregarded, slighted; unworthy of regard 1591. **3.** advb. in *r. of*, without regard to; also *ellipt.* (orig. *U.S.*) 1872.

1. R. of the Bliss wherein hee sat MILT. Treading the May-flowers with r. feet WHITTIER. Hence **Rega·rdless-ly** *adv.*, **-ness.**

Regatta (rĭgæ·tă). 1652. [– It. (orig. Venetian) †*regatta*, †*rigatta*, *regata* 'a strife or contention or struggling for the maistrie' (Florio).] **1.** The name given at Venice to certain boat-races held on the Grand Canal. **2.** A boat- or yacht-race, or (usu.) an organized series of such races, forming a more or less sporting and social event 1775.

Regelate (rī·dʒėlēⁱt), *v.* 1860. [f. RE- 5 a + pa. ppl. stem of L. *gelare* freeze.] *intr.* (and *refl.*) To freeze together again.

Regelation (rīdʒėlēⁱ·ʃən). 1857. [See prec. and GELATION.] The action of freezing together again; *spec.* the fusion of two pieces of ice, having moist surfaces, at a temperature above freezing-point.

†**Re·gence.** *rare.* 1457. [– Fr. *régence* (XVI), f. *régent* REGENT *sb.*; see -ENCE.] = next –1678.

Regency (rī·dʒĕnsi). late ME. [– med.L. *regentia*, f. L. *regens, regent-*; see REGENT *sb.*, -ENCY.] **1.** The position or office of ruler; exercise of rule or authority; government, dominion, control. Now *rare* or *Obs.* 1485. **2.** The office and jurisdiction of a regent or vice-regent; government by a regent or by a body exercising similar authority. late ME. **3.** †**a.** The governing body of certain (chiefly European) towns and Moslem states –1796. **b.** A body of men appointed to carry on the government during the absence, minority, or incapacity of the sovereign or hereditary ruler; a Government so constituted 1721. **4.** A district under the control of a regent or regency 1667. **5.** The period during which a regent governs; *spec.* the period during which George, Prince of Wales (the Prince Regent, 1810–20) acted as regent 1727. **6.** The office or function of a university regent 1639.

3. b. We expect some chagrin on the new R. at the head of which is to be the Duke H. WALPOLE.

Regeneracy (rĭdʒe·nĕrăsi). 1626. [f. next + -ACY.] The state of being regenerate.

Regenerate (rĭdʒe·nĕrĕt), *ppl. a.* and *sb.* 1471. [– L. *regeneratus*, pa. pple. of *regenerare*; see next, -ATE[2].] **A.** *ppl. a.* †**1.** Re-born; brought again into existence; formed anew –1610. **2.** In religious use: Spiritually re-born 1526. **b.** Restored to a better state, reformed 1647. **c.** Of nations: Restored or raised again from a sunk or base condition 1811. †**3.** Degenerate, renegade (*rare*) –1607. †**B.** *sb.* A regenerate person –1652.

A. 1. The earthy author of my blood, Whose youthfull spirit in me r., Doth with a two-fold rigor lift mee vp SHAKS.

Regenerate (rĭdʒe·nĕreⁱt), *v.* 1541. [– *regenerat-*, pa. ppl. stem of L. *regenerare*; see RE-, GENERATE *v.*] **1.** *trans.* In religious use: To cause to be born again in a spiritual sense; to invest with a new and higher spiritual nature 1557. **b.** To reform completely (a person or state of things, etc.) 1849. **2.** *Path.* To reproduce, form afresh (some part of the body). Chiefly in *pass.* 1597. **3.** To reproduce, re-create; to form or bring into existence again 1608. **4.** To reconstitute on a higher plane; to place on a new basis 1789. **5.** *intr.* **a.** To form again. Chiefly *Path.* 1541. **b.** To reform, become regenerate 1786. **6.** *Electr.* To increase the amplification of (an electron current) by causing a part of the power in the output circuit to act upon the input circuit.

Regeneration (rīdʒenĕrē[1]·ʃən). ME. [– (O)Fr. *régénération* or L. *regeneratio, -on-*, f. as prec.; see -ION.] **1.** The action of regenerating; the process or fact of being regenerated; re-creation, re-formation, etc. **b.** *fig.* Revival; renascence, re-constitution on a higher level 1627. **2.** In religious use: The process or fact of being born again spiritually; the state resulting from this. late ME. **3.** *Path.* The formation of new animal tissue; the reproduction of lost parts or organs. late ME. **4.** *Electr.* (cf. prec. 6).

1. b. All great regenerations are the universal movement of the mass LYTTON. **2.** Spiritual r. begins naturally among the poor and the humble FROUDE. **3.** The local death of some tissues is followed by their r. HUXLEY.

Regenerative (rĭdʒe·nĕrĕtiv), *a.* late ME. [– (O)Fr. *régénératif* or med.L. *regenerativus*, f. as prec.; see -IVE.] **1.** Tending to or characterized by regeneration. **2.** *Mech.* Constructed on, or employing the principle of the REGENERATOR 1861.

1. The great r. work which he undertook 1871. *spec.* (*Electr.*) cf. REGENERATE *v.* 6, REGENERATION 4. **2.** Mr. Siemens, the inventor of the so-called r. furnaces 1864. Hence **Rege·neratively** *adv.*

Regenerator (rĭdʒe·nĕrē[1]təɹ). 1740. [f. REGENERATE *v.* + -OR 2. Cf. (O)Fr. *régénérateur.*] **1.** One who or that which regenerates. **2.** *Mech.* A fuel-saving device attached to a furnace, consisting of layers of fire-brick which, becoming heated by the hot air and gases from the furnace, impart the heat to an incoming current of cold air or combustible gas acting alternately with the outgoing current 1835.

Regeneratory (rĭdʒe·nĕrătəri), *a.* 1803. [f. as REGENERATE *v.* + -ORY[2].] Of the nature of regeneration; regenerative.

Regent (rī·dʒĕnt), *sb.* late ME. [– (O)Fr. *régent* or L. *regens, regent-*, subst. use of the pr. pple; see next.] **1. a.** That which rules, governs, or has supremacy; a ruling power or principle. Now *rare.* **b.** One who rules or governs; a ruler, governor, director. Now *rare* or *Obs.* 1480. **2. a.** One who is invested with royal authority by, or on behalf of, another; *esp.* one appointed to administer a kingdom during the minority, absence, or incapacity of the sovereign. late ME. **b.** The name given to the municipal authorities of some continental cities (*obs.*), and to the native chiefs in Java 1724. **3.** In the Universities: **a.** At Oxford and Cambridge, a Master of Arts ruling or presiding over disputations in the Schools, a duty orig. discharged for one, and afterwards for five, years after graduation; hence, in later use, a Master of not more than five years standing. Now *Hist.* late ME. **b.** In France, the title usu. given to those who taught the more elementary classes; an instructor in arts or science 1611. **c.** *U.S.* A member of the governing board of a State University (and of the Smithsonian Institute, Washington) 1817. †**4.** The head master of a school –1796.

attrib.: **R. bird** or **oriole,** an Australian bird, *Sericulus melinus*, named in compliment to the Prince Regent, afterwards George IV. **R.** (**congregation** or) **house,** the upper of the two houses into which the Senate of Cambridge University was formerly divided. Hence **Re·gentess,** a female regent. **Re·gentship,** the office or position of a regent.

Regent (rī·dʒĕnt), *a.* ME. [– (O)Fr. *régent* or L. *regens, regent-*, pr. pple. of *regere* rule; see -ENT.] **1.** In spec. senses (usu. placed after the sb.). **a.** Holding the position of a University regent. Now *Hist.* **b.** Acting as, having the position of, regent of a country, esp. *Queen r.* 1555. **2.** Ruling, governing, controlling. Now *rare.* 1613.

2. The r. helm her motion still commands 1762.

Regent (rī·dʒĕnt), *v.* Now *rare.* 1623. [f. REGENT *sb.*] **1. a.** *trans.* To superintend or teach (a college, class, etc.), as a regent. **b.** *intr.* To act as a University regent 1631. **2.** *trans.* To control (a person) as a regent 1797.

†**Rege·st,** *sb. rare.* 1670. [– late L. *regesta* list, n. pl. of pa. pple. of L. *regerere* enter, transcribe, record, register (Quintilian); cf. DIGEST *sb.* and REGISTER *sb.*[1]] A register. MILT.

†**Re·gian.** 1653. [f. L. *regius* royal + -AN.] An upholder of regal authority; a royalist –1670.

Regicidal (re·dʒisəidăl), *a.* 1779. [f. REGICIDE[2] + -AL[1].] Pertaining to, characterized by, inclined to, regicide.

Regicide[1] (re·dʒisəid). 1548. [f. *rex, reg-* king + -CIDE 1, prob. after Fr. *régicide.*] **1.** One who kills a king, esp. his own king; one who commits the crime of regicide. **2.** *spec.* **a.** *Eng. Hist.* One of those who took part in the trial and execution of Charles I. 1654. **b.** *Fr. Hist.* One of those Revolutionists concerned in the execution of Louis XVI. 1796. **3.** *attrib.* or *adj.* 1645.

Regicide[2] (re·dʒisəid). 1602. [f. as prec. + -CIDE 2.] The killing or murder of a king. Hence **Re·gicidism,** the practice or principle of r.

‖**Régie** (reʒi). 1883. [Fr., fem. pa. pple. of *régir* to rule.] The revenue department established in some European countries for the entire control of the importation and manufacture of tobacco, salt, etc.

Regifuge (re·dʒifiūdʒ). 1654. [– L. *regifugium*, f. *rex, reg-* king; see -FUGE.] *Rom. Hist.* The flight or expulsion of the kings from Rome.

‖**Régime, regime** (reʒī·m). 1776. [Fr. – L. *regimen*; see next.] **1.** = next 2. **2.** A manner, method, or system of rule or government; a system or institution having widespread influence or prevalence 1792.

1. Regime is better than physic 1776. **2.** Phr. *The ancient*, or *old, r.* (tr. Fr. *l'ancien régime*), the system of government in France before the Revolution of 1789. Also *transf.*, the old system or style of things.

Regimen (re·dʒimen). late ME. [– L. *regimen*, f. *regere* rule, direct.] **1.** The act of governing; government, rule 1456. **b.** A particular form or kind of government; a regime; a prevailing system 1734. **2.** *Med.* The regulation of such matters as have an influence on the preservation or restoration of health; a particular course of diet, exercise, or mode of living, prescribed or adopted for this end. late ME. **3.** *Gram.* The government of one word by another; the relation which one word in a sentence has to another depending on it 1600.

1. b. Nothing is so apt to follow as sedition from a popular r. HALLAM. **2.** Things.. Very behoofull to the R. Of health 1646. Hence **Regi·menal** *a.* = REGIMINAL.

Regiment (re·dʒmĕnt, re·dʒimĕnt), *sb.* late ME. [– (O)Fr. *régiment* – late L. *regimentum* rule, f. *regere* rule, direct; see -MENT.] **1.** Rule or government over a person, people, or country; *esp.* royal or magisterial authority. Now *rare.* †**b.** Manner, method, or system of ruling or governing; a form of polity, a regime –1676. †**2. a.** The office or function of a ruler –1630. **b.** The time or period during which one rules; a reign –1630. †**3.** Government or control over oneself, one's feelings or actions –1679. †**b.** Control or influence exercised by one thing over another, or over a person –1674. †**4.** The ruling or governing *of* a person, people or place –1702. †**b.** The management, guidance, or control *of* a thing or affair (*rare*) –1741. †**5.** = REGIMEN 2. –1768. †**6.** A place or country under a particular rule; a kingdom, province, domain, district –1662. **7.** *Mil.* A considerable body of troops, more or less permanently organized under the command of a superior officer, and forming a definite unit of an army or military force; since the 17th c. the specific name of the largest permanent unit of the cavalry, infantry, and foot-guards of the British Army 1579. **b.** *transf.* and *fig.*: *esp.* a large array or number (of anything) 1605. †**c.** A class or kind –1656. †**8.** *pl.* Regimentals. H. WALPOLE.

3. The R. & gouernment of euery man, over himself BACON. **4. b.** The greatest Lords thought the R. of Sea-affairs worthy of the best of their Rank 1651. **6.** *transf.* Men who never saw the sea, yet desire to behold that r. of waters 1623. **7.** The.. strength of a r. of infantry of a single battalion is 750. 1853.

Regiment (re·dʒmĕnt, re·dʒimĕnt), *v.* 1617. [f. prec.] **1.** *trans. Mil.* To form into a regiment or regiments. (Chiefly in *pass.*) **b.** To form (persons, now esp. workers) into a definitely organized body or group 1718. **c.** To bring or put (things) *into* some definite order or system; to organize, systematize 1698. **2.** To assign to a regiment or group 1774. Hence **Re:gimenta·tion,** the action or process of regimenting or organizing.

Regimental (redʒme·ntăl, redʒime·ntăl), *a.* and *sb.* 1702. [f. REGIMENT *sb.* + -AL[1].] **A.** *adj.* Of or belonging to, associated with, a regiment, or with some particular regiment. **B.** *sb. pl.* The dress proper to or characteristic of any particular regiment; military uniform 1708.

A. R. hospitals are of the greatest importance 1753. Hence **Regime·ntally** *adv.*

Regiminal (rĭdʒi·minăl), *a.* 1832. [f. REGIMEN, after L. types, as *criminal.*] *Med.* Of or pertaining to, of the nature of, regimen.

Reginal (rĭdʒəi·năl), *a.* 1568. [– med.L. *reginalis*, f. L. *regina* queen + -AL[1]. Cf. Fr. †*réginal.*] **a.** Queenly, queenlike. **b.** Taking the side of the queen.

Region (rī·dʒən). ME. [– (O)Fr. *région* – L. *regio, -on-* direction, line, boundary, district, province, f. *regere* direct, guide, rule; see -ION.] **1.** †**a.** A realm or kingdom. **b.** A large tract of land; a country; a more or less defined portion of the earth's surface, now esp. as distinguished by certain natural features, climatic conditions, a special fauna or flora, or the like. **c.** An area, space, or place, of more or less definite extent or character 1726. **2.** A separate part or division of the world or universe, as the air, heaven, etc. ME. **b.** *fig.* A place, state or condition, having a certain character or subject to certain influences; the sphere or realm *of* something 1526. **3.** One of the successive portions into which the air or atmosphere is theoretically divided according to height. Also similarly of the sea according to depth. 1563. **4.** An administrative division of a city or district 1593. **5.** A part or division of the body or its parts. late ME. **6.** A space occupied by a thing 1664. **7.** *attrib.* 1600.

1. b. Nauigatours haue discouered few or no Regions wanting inhabitants 1625. **2.** Anon the dreadfull Thunder Doth rend the R. SHAKS. **b.** That he escaping the.. paynes of eternall derkenes May euer dwel in the r. of lighte *Bk. Com. Prayer.* **3.** Regions of the Air, are distinguished into Upper, Middle, and Lower 1704. *fig.* He is of too high a R., he knows too much SHAKS. **5.** Let it fall rather, though the fork invade The r. of my heart SHAKS. **7.** The r. cloude hath mask'd him from me now SHAKS. Hence **Re·gional** *a.* of or pertaining to a particular r. or district; pertaining to a special part of the body.

Regionalism (rī·dʒənăliz'm). 1881. [f. REGIONAL + -ISM.] Tendency to, or practice of, regional systems or methods; localism on a regional basis. So **Re·gionalist. Regionali·stic** *a.* **Re·gionalize** *v.* to organize on a regional basis; **Re:gionaliza·tion.**

Regionary (rī·dʒənări), *a.* and *sb.* 1657. [– late and med.L. *regionarius*; see REGION, -ARY.] **A.** *adj.* Of or pertaining to a region. **B.** *sb.* An account or description of the regions of Rome 1818.

A. *R. bishop*, a bishop without any particular diocese.

Register (re·dʒistəɹ), *sb.*[1] [Late XIV *registre, -estre* – (O)Fr. *registre*, †*regestre* or med.L. *registrum, -estrum*, alt. of *regestum*, sing. of late L. *regesta*; see REGEST.] **I. 1.** A book in which regular entry is made of details of any kind sufficiently important to be exactly recorded; a written record thus formed; †a list, catalogue. †**2.** As the title of a compilation containing the forms of writs of the Common Law, cited by English lawyers of the 16–17th c. –1628. **3.** As the name of certain official or authoritative records or books of record: e.g. **a.** of the baptisms, marriages, and burials in a parish, kept by the clergyman; or (in later use) of births, marriages, and deaths, kept by an official (a REGISTRAR) appointed for the purpose 1538. **b.** of seamen in the British mercantile marine 1695. **c.** of shipping, containing particulars of construction, materials, size, ownership, etc.; also, a certificate issued by the registering official, esp. as evidence of the nationality of the vessel 1825. **d.** of those entitled to vote in Parliamentary or municipal elections 1832. **4.** An entry in a register (esp. in sense 3 a) 1535. **5.** Registration, registry 1653.

1. He kept a r. of all the King's promises BURNET. *fig.* As you haue one eye vpon my follies,..turne another into the R. of your owne SHAKS. **4.** There being no R. of his Christening ARBUTHNOT.

II. 1. a. An index; a table of contents (*rare*) 1585. **b.** The series of signatures in a printed book; the list of these at the end of early printed books 1885. **2.** *Mus.* A slider in an organ; a set of pipes controlled by a slider, a stop; also, a stop-knob 1585. **b.** The compass of a voice or instrument; now *spec.* the particular range of tones which can be produced in the same way and with the same quality 1811. **3.** A contrivance, usu. consisting of a metal plate or plates by which an opening may be wholly or partially closed, used for regulating the passage of air, heat, or smoke 1610. **4.** A registering device; a mechanical contrivance or apparatus by which data of some kind are automatically recorded; an indicator 1830. **5.** *Printing.* †**a.** An inner part of a type-mould –1738. **b.** Precise adjustment of the type or printing; *esp.* exact correspondence of the printed matter on the two sides of a leaf 1683. **c.** *Photogr.* In a camera, proper correspondence between the focussing screen and the sensitive plate or film 1890.

2. b. The 'soprano register', the 'tenor register', denote that part of the scale which forms the usual compass of those voices; the 'head register' means the notes which are sung with the head voice; the 'chest register' those which are sung from the chest GROVE. **3.** Looke well to the r., And let your heat, still, lessen by degrees B. JONS. *Comb.*: **r. book** = sense I. 1; **r.-ship,** a Spanish ship having a registered licence to trade with the Spanish possessions in America (now *Hist.*).

Register (re·dʒistəɹ), *sb.*[2] Now *rare* exc. in U.S. 1531. [Ostensibly alt. of REGISTRER.] The keeper of a register; a REGISTRAR. Hence †**Re·gistership,** the office of registrar.

Register (re·dʒistəɹ), *v.* late ME. [– (O)Fr. *registrer* or med.L. *registrare*, f. *registrum* REGISTER *sb.*[1]] **1.** *trans.* To set down (facts, names, etc.) formally in writing; to enter or record in a precise manner. †**b.** To set (a person) down *for*, or as, something –1611. **2.** *spec.* To make formal entry of (a document, fact, name, etc.) in a particular register; also, to get (a document, etc.) entered in the register by the person entitled to do so 1463. **3.** Of instruments: To record by some automatic device; to indicate 1797. **b.** Of a cinema actor or actress: To express (an emotion) by facial expression, etc. Also *transf.* 1901. **4.** *intr.* To coincide or correspond exactly 1839. **b.** *trans.* To adjust with precision, so as to secure the exact correspondence of parts 1839. **5.** *intr.* To manipulate the registers of an organ 1891.

1. Such follow him, as shall be registerd Part good part bad, of bad the longer scrowle MILT. **2. b.** *intr.* (U.S.) To have one's name entered on the list of qualified voters; also, to enter one's name in the register of an hotel or lodging-house 1850.

Re·gister o·ffice. 1760. An office at which a register of any kind is kept, or where registration is made; a registry.

Registrar (redʒistrā·ɹ, re·dʒistrāɹ). 1675. [– med.L. *registrarius*, f. *registrum* REGISTER *sb.*[1]; see -AR[2]. Superseding next in gen. Eng. use.] One whose business it is to keep an official register.

R.-General, the chief officer of the General Register Office, Somerset House.

Registrary (re·dʒistrări). 1541. Retained only at Cambridge. [– med.L. *registrarius*; see prec., -ARY[1].] A registrar.

†**Re·gistrate,** *v.* Chiefly *Sc.* 1570. [– *registrat-*, pa. ppl. stem of med.L. *registrare*; see REGISTER *v.*, -ATE[3].] *trans.* To register –1776.

Registration (redʒistrēi·ʃən). 1566. [– Fr. †*régistration* (XVI) or med.L. *registratio*, f. as prec.; see -ION.] **1.** The act of registering or recording. **b.** With *a* and *pl.* An instance of this; an entry made in a register 1611. **c.** *attrib.*, as *r. act, fee*, etc. 1843. **2.** *Printing.* Adjustment 1890.

Re·gistrer. Now *rare.* late ME. [– AFr. *registrere = OFr. *registreur*, med.L. *registrator*, f. as prec.; see -ER[2] 3. See REGISTER *sb.*[2]] †**a.** A registrar. **b.** = REGISTER *sb.*[1] II. 4.

Registry (re·dʒistri). 1589. [Reduced form of †*registery* (XV–XVI) – med.L. *registerium*.] **1.** The act of registering, registration. **2.** A place where registers are kept; now often used (*a*) colloq. = district register office, where marriages take place, (*b*) short for *servants registry*, an office where the names of domestic servants seeking employment are registered 1603. **3.** A register, a book of record; also, an entry in a register 1622. **4.** *attrib.*, as *r. fee* (U.S.), *office*, etc. 1721.

Regius (rī·dʒiŏs). 1621. [L. = royal, f. *rex, reg-* king.] The designation of certain university professors of royal foundation and (for the most part) appointed by royal mandate.

†**Regle, reigle,** *v.* 1591. [– (O)Fr. *régler*, †*reigler* – late L. *regulare* REGULATE *v.*] *trans.* To rule, regulate –1670.

‖**Re·glement** (rẹgləmaṅ), †**reiglement.** 1598. [– Fr. *règlement*, †*reigle-*, f. *régler*; see prec., -MENT.] †**1.** The act of regulating or controlling –1734. **2.** A regulation. (Now only as Fr.) 1625.

1. The Reformation and Reiglement of Vsury BACON.

Regleme·ntary, *a. rare.* 1870. [– Fr. *réglementaire*; see prec., -ARY[1].] Regular, according to regulations.

Reglet (re·glėt), †**triglet.** 1576. [– (O)Fr. *réglet*, also *-ette*, dim. of *règle* RULE *sb.*; see -ET; in sense 2 – It. *regoletto*, f. *regola* rule.] †**1.** A narrow division of a page of a book; a column –1576. **2.** *Arch.* A narrow flat band used to separate mouldings or other parts from each other 1664. †**3.** A thin, flat piece or strip of wood used in carpentry or frame-making (*rare*) –1683. **b.** *Printing.* A thin, narrow strip of wood or metal, used to make wide blanks between lines of types 1683. **c.** Collectively, or as a material. Also *attrib.*, as *r. plane*. 1846.

‖**Regma** (re·gmă). *Pl.* **re·gmata.** 1839. [– Gr. ῥῆγμα fracture.] *Bot.* In Mirbel's classification, a dry fruit formed of three or more cells which break open when ripe.

Regnal (re·gnăl), *a.* 1612. [– AL. *regnalis*, f. L. *regnum* kingdom; see -AL[1].] **1. a.** *R. year*, any year of a sovereign's reign, reckoned from the date of his accession. **b.** *R. day*, the anniversary of a sovereign's accession 1877. **2.** Of or pertaining to a reign, kingdom, or king 1643.

Regnant (re·gnănt), *ppl. a.* 1600. [– L. *regnans, -ant-*, pr. pple. of *regnare* reign; in sense 2 after Fr. *régnant*.] **1.** Reigning, ruling. **2.** Of things, qualities, etc.: Ruling, exercising sway or influence, predominant, dominating 1621. **b.** Prevalent, wide-spread 1625.

1. Queens r. WOTTON. The r. house 1856. **2. b.** The belief in witchcraft and diabolical contracts which was r. in his day M. ARNOLD.

Regorge (rīgǭ·ɹdʒ), *v.* 1605. [– (O)Fr. *regorger*, or f. RE- + GORGE *v.*] **1.** *trans.* To disgorge or cast up again; to throw or cast back (*lit.* and *fig.*). **b.** *intr.* To gush or flow back again 1654. **2.** *trans.* To engorge or swallow again (*rare*) 1700.

2. And tides at highest mark r. the flood DRYDEN.

Regrate (rĭgrēi·t), *v. Obs.* exc. *Hist.* 1467. [– OFr. *regrater*, supposed to be f. *re-* RE- + *grater* (mod. *gratter*) scratch, of Gmc. origin.] **1.** *trans.* To buy up (market commodities, esp. victuals) in order to sell again at a profit in the same or a neighbouring market. **2.** To sell again (articles so bought), to retail 1582. Hence **Regra·ter, Regra·tor,** one who regrates victuals, etc.; a retailer; a middleman. †**Regra·tery,** the practice of regrating.

Regrede (rĭgrī·d), *v.* 1865. [– L. *regredi*, f. *re-* RE- + *gradi* go.] *intr.* To retrograde, go back. So †**Regre·dience,** return.

†**Regree·t,** *sb.* 1595. [f. next.] A (return of a) greeting –1665. **b.** *pl.* Greetings –1639.

Regree·t, *v.* Now *rare.* 1586. [f. RE- + GREET *v.*[1]] **1.** *trans.* To greet again or anew. **2.** To greet (a person) in return; also simply, to greet, give salutation to 1593.

Regress (rī·gres), *sb.* late ME. [– L. *regressus*, noun of action f. *regredi*; see next.] **1.** The act of going or coming back; a return or withdrawal; re-entry *to* or *into* the place of issue or origin. Freq. in the phrases (orig. legal) *egress*, or *ingress, and r.* **2.** *Law.* †**a.** Return to possession; re-entry (*rare*) –1628. **b.** *Canon Law.* 'Right of returning to a benefice vacated in case of death, &c., of the actual incumbent' 1710. **3.** The fact of going back from, or in respect of, a state or condition 1590. **4.** The act of working back in thought from one thing to another, *spec.* from an effect to a cause 1620. **5.** *Astr.* = RETROGRADATION 1. 1642.

1. *fig.* The standing is slipery, and the regresse is either a downefall, or..an Eclipse BACON.

Regress (rĭgre·s), *v.* 1552. [– *regress-*, pa. ppl. stem of L. *regredi*; see REGREDE.] **1.** *intr.* To recede *from*; to return *to* a subject or place, or *into* a former state. **2.** To move in a backward direction. Chiefly *Astron.* 1823.

Regression (rĭgre·ʃən). 1520. [– L. *regressio, -on-*, f. as prec.; see -ION.] †**1.** Return to a subject –1620. **2.** The action of returning to or towards a place or point of departure 1597. **b.** *Geom.* Return of a curve 1727. **3.** Return *to* or *into* a state or condition; relapse; reversion to a less developed form 1646. **4.** = REGRESS *sb.* 4. 1637. **5.** *Astr.* = RETROGRADATION 1. 1823.

Regressive (rĭgre·siv), *a.* 1634. [f. REGRESS *v.* + -IVE.] **1.** Retrogressive; returning, passing back. **b.** Acting in a backward direction; retroactive 1888. **2.** *Philos.* Proceeding from effect to cause, or from particular to universal 1836. **3.** *Med.* Tending towards, of the nature of, degeneration or decomposition 1865.

1. b. *R. assimilation*, assimilation of a sound to one following it, as in *comp-* from *conp-*. Hence **Regre·ssive-ly** *adv.*, **-ness.**

Regret (rĭgre·t), *sb.* 1533. [– (O)Fr. *regret*, f. the verb; see next.] †**1.** Complaint, lament –1547. **2.** Sorrow or disappointment due to some external circumstance or event 1590. **b.** (*pl.*) An intimation of regret for inability to do something, *esp.* to accept an invitation 1859. **3.** Sorrow or pain due to reflection on something one has done or left undone 1641. **4.** Sorrow at, or *for*, some loss or deprivation or a lost thing or person. Also const. *of*. 1647.

2. The protestants beheld with r. the Earl of Argyll..still adhering to the queen 1759. **3.** Pining regrets, and vain repentances SHELLEY. **4.** When for a friend long lost wakes some unhappy r. 1871.

Regret (rĭgre·t), *v.* late ME. [– OFr. *regreter* bewail (the dead), mod. *regretter*, perh. f. *re-* RE- + Gmc. *ʒrētan weep, GREET *v.*[2]] **1.** *trans.* To remember, think of (something lost), with distress or longing; to feel (†or express) sorrow for the loss of (a person or thing). **2.** To grieve at, feel distress on account of (some event, fact, action, etc.) 1553.

1. He died at length regretted of all men DRYDEN. **2.** Poets, of all men, ever least r. Increasing taxes and the nation's debt COWPER. So **Regre·ttable** *a.* deserving of, calling for, regret. **Regre·ttably** *adv.*

Regretful (rĭgre·tfŭl), *a.* 1647. [f. REGRET *sb.* + -FUL.] Full of sorrow or regret. Hence **Regre·tfully** *adv.*

Regue·rdon, *v. rare.* late ME. [– OFr. *reguerdoner*; see RE-, GUERDON *v.*] *trans.* To reward. So †**Regue·rdon** *sb.* (*rare*) recompense, reward –1591.

‖**Regula** (re·giŭlă). 1563. [L., = ruler, rule, f. *regere* make or lead straight.] *Arch.* A fillet or reglet; *spec.* a short band, with guttæ on the lower side, placed below the tænia in Doric Architecture.

Regulable (re·giŭlăb'l), *a.* 1660. [f. REGULATE *v.* + -ABLE.] Capable of being regulated.

Regular (re·giŭlăɹ), *a.*, *adv.*, and *sb.* [Late XIV *reguler* (later with ending assim. to Latin: see -AR[1], -ER[2] 1) – OFr. *reguler* (mod. *régulier*, with change of suffix) – L. *regularis*, f. *regula* RULE *sb.*] **A.** *adj.* **1.** *Eccl.* Subject to, or bound by, a religious rule; belonging to a religious or monastic order. (Opp. to *secular*.) **2.** Having a form, structure, or arrangement which follows, or is reducible to, some rule or principle; characterized by harmony or proper correspondence between the various parts or elements; symmetrical 1584. **b.** *Geom.* Of plane figures: Equilateral and equiangular; of solids; of which all the faces are equal in size and shape 1665. **c.** *Bot.* Having all the parts or organs of the same kind normally alike in form and size 1785. **3.** Characterized by the presence or operation of a definite principle; marked by steadiness or uniformity of action, procedure, or occurrence 1594. **b.** Recurring or repeated at fixed times or uniform intervals 1756. **c.** Habitually or customarily used, received, observed, etc.; habitual, constant 1797. **4.** Pursuing a definite course, or observing some uniform principle, of action or conduct; adhering to rule; now *esp.* observing fixed times for, or never failing in, the performance of certain actions or duties 1602. **b.** Orderly, well-ordered, well-behaved, steady 1705. **c.** Acting at the proper intervals 1783. **5.** Conformable to some accepted or adopted rule or standard; recognized as formally correct 1647. **b.** *Gram.* Of parts of speech, esp. verbs: Following some usual and uniform mode of inflection or conjugation 1611. **6.** Properly constituted; normal 1638. **b.** Of persons: Properly qualified or trained 1712. **c.** *colloq.* Thorough, complete, absolute, perfect 1821. **7.** *Mil.* Of forces or troops: Properly and permanently organized; constituting the standing army 1706.

2. I cannot, however, tell you that her features are r. 1716. A r. and appropriate nomenclature 1815. Small r. teeth 1863. **b.** R. Figures are those where the Angles and Lines or Superficies are equal 1679. *R. Curves*, are such Curves as the Perimeters of the Conick Sections, which are always curved after the same R. Geometrical Manner 1704. **3.** He supposes the philosopher to proceed by r. steps, until he arrives at the idea of good JOWETT. **b.** How r. his meals, how sound he sleeps! COWPER. Her r. pulses SHELLEY. **c.** It's past my r. time for going to bed DICKENS. **4.** The Herr Doctor was a r. man, and always appeared at his window at the same hour 1883. **b.** He grew first r., and then pious JOHNSON. **5.** Making acquaintances..without r. introductions 1831. **6. b.** A r. doctor JOHNSON. **c.** On Wednesday we had a r. flood, and it has been raining..ever since 1846. **7.** His Majesty's r. forces 1756.

B. *adv.* Regularly, steadily; thoroughly 1710.

C. *sb.* **1.** *Eccl.* A member of a religious order observing a RULE; one of the regular clergy 1563. **2.** A soldier belonging to the standing army; a member of the regular forces. Usu. *pl.* 1756. Hence **Re·gular-ly** *adv.*, **-ness.**

Regularity (regiŭlæ·rĭti). 1603. [f. prec. + -ITY. Cf. (O)Fr. *régularité*.] The state or character of being regular.

Regularize (re·giŭlăraiz), *v.* 1780. [f. REGULAR + -IZE, after Fr. *régulariser* (XVIII); see -IZE.] *trans.* To make regular. Hence **Re:gulariza·tion.**

†**Re·gulate,** *ppl. a.* 1577. [– late L. *regulatus*, pa. pple. of *regulare*; see next, -ATE².] Regulated; regular –1644.

Regulate (re·giŭleⁱt), *v.* 1630. [– *regulat-*, pa. ppl. stem of late L. *regulare*, f. L. *regula* RULE *sb.*; see -ATE³.] **1.** *trans.* To control, govern, or direct by rule or regulations; to subject to guidance or restrictions; to adapt to circumstances or surroundings. †**b.** To bring or reduce (a person or body of persons) to order –1839. †**c.** To correct by control –1682. **2.** To adjust, in respect of time, quantity, etc., with reference to some standard or purpose; *esp.* to adjust (a clock, etc.) so that the working may be accurate 1662.

1. Can freedom be regulated without being..in some part destroyed? 1792. **c.** To r. the Errors of the Mind 1680. **2.** Clocks ought to be regulated by the mean solar time 1812.

Regulation (regiŭlēⁱ·ʃən). 1672. [f. prec.; see -ATION.] **1.** The act of regulating, or the state of being regulated. Also, an instance of this. **2.** A rule prescribed for the management of some matter, or the regulating of conduct; a governing precept or direction; a standing rule 1715. **3.** *attrib.* That is prescribed by, or in accordance with, a regulation or regulations; hence, regular, ordinary 1836.

1. The advancement and r. of manufactures and commerce BLACKSTONE. **2.** It's against regulations for me to call at night DICKENS. **3.** He can't afford more than his r. chargers THACKERAY.

Regulative (re·giŭleⁱtiv), *a.* 1599. [f. REGULATE *v.* + -IVE.] Tending to regulate. Chiefly *Philos.*

Logic is not useless; it has a r., not a creative virtue 1874. Hence **Re·gulatively** *adv.*

Regulator (re·giŭleⁱtəɹ). 1655. [f. REGULATE *v.* + -OR 2.] **1.** One who regulates. **b.** *Eng. Hist.* A member of a commission appointed in 1687 to investigate and revise the constitution of various boroughs, for the purpose of influencing the election of members of parliament 1688. **c.** *U.S.* A member of one of the bands formed at various times in wild parts of the country, with the professed object of supplying the want of the regular administration of justice 1767. **2.** *techn.* A device for controlling machinery in motion, or for regulating the passage of air, electricity, gas, steam, water, etc. 1702. **b.** A device for adjusting the balance of a clock or watch, in order to regulate its speed 1696. **3.** A clock or watch keeping accurate time, by which other timepieces may be regulated 1758. **4.** Something which regulates; a regulating principle or power 1766.

1. c. The lynchers, or 'regulators' as they are often called, soon find that their foes organize also 1847.

Reguline (re·giŭləin), *a.* 1669. [f. REGULUS + -INE¹.] *Chem.* Of, or pertaining to, of the nature of, regulus.

Re·gulize, *v. rare.* 1778. [f. as prec. + -IZE.] *trans.* To reduce to regulus.

‖**Regulus** (re·giŭlŏs). *Pl.* **-li** (-ləi). 1559. [L., dim. of *rex, reg-* king; see -ULE.] **1.** *Astron.* A bright star (α Leonis) in the constellation Leo, called also *Cor Leonis*. **2.** *Chem.* †**a.** The metallic form of antimony, so called by early chemists, app. on account of its ready combination with gold. **b.** The purer or metallic part of a mineral, which sinks to the bottom of a crucible or furnace and is thus separated from the remaining matter. **c.** A product of the smelting of various ores, as copper, lead, and silver, consisting of metal in a still impure state. 1594. **3.** A petty king or ruler 1682. **4.** The golden-crested (and fire-crested) wren 1824.

Regurgitant (rĭgɔ̄·ɹdʒităn̆t), *ppl. a.* 1866. [See next and -ANT.] *Path.* Regurgitating; characterized by regurgitation.

Regurgitate (rĭgɔ̄·ɹdʒiteⁱt), *v.* 1653. [– *regurgitat-*, pa. ppl. stem of med.L. *regurgitare*, f. *re-* RE- + late L. *gurgitare*.] **1.** *intr.* Of fluids, air, or gases: To gush, rush, or pour back (again). **b.** *transf.* of the containing vessel. BOYLE. **2.** *trans.* To pour or cast out again from a receptacle, *esp.* from the stomach 1753.

2. *absol.* The Whale that swallowed Jonah found him hard meat, and..was forced to r. 1657.

Regurgitation (rĭgɔ̄ɹdʒitēⁱ·ʃən). 1601. [– med.L. *regurgitatio, -on-*, f. as prec.; see -ION.] The act of pouring or gushing back; the fact of reissuing or being ejected again from a receptacle. Chiefly *Med.* with ref. either to the blood or to food.

Rehabilitate (rĭhăbi·liteⁱt), *v.* 1580. [– *rehabilitat-*, pa. ppl. stem of med.L. *rehabilitare*; see RE-, HABILITATE *v.*] **1.** *trans.* To restore by formal act or declaration (a person degraded or attainted) to former privileges, rank, and possessions; to re-establish (a person's good name or memory) by authoritative pronouncement. **b.** To re-establish the character or reputation of (a person or thing) 1847. **2.** To restore to a previous condition; to set up again in proper condition 1845.

1. The king alone can r. an officer noted, condemned, and degraded; or a gentleman who has derogated from his rank 1727. **2.** The unwearied Lord Lieutenant..has been rehabilitating Courts of Justice in Dublin CARLYLE. Hence **Re:habilita·tion,** the action of rehabilitating, or state of being rehabilitated.

Rehash (rĭhæ·ʃ), *sb.* 1849. [f. RE- 5 a + HASH *sb.* 2.] A mere restatement in different words of opinions previously expressed; something served up afresh under a different form or name.

Reha·sh, *v.* 1822. [RE- 5 a.] *trans.* To restate (old ideas or opinions) in new language. All they did was to r. the old..arguments 1884.

Rehearsal (rĭhɔ̄·ɹsăl). late ME. [f. next + -AL¹.] **1.** The act of rehearsing; a recounting or recital; a repetition of words or statements; recitation. **2.** The practising of a play or musical composition preparatory to performing it in public; a private meeting of actors or performers held for this purpose 1579.

1. Many..made it a pretext for r. of old grievances 1842. **2.** The second part of the *Beggar's Opera*..was almost ready for r. GAY. *Dress r.*, a final r. in full costume. *In r.*, in process of being rehearsed.

Rehearse (rĭhɔ̄·ɹs), *v.* [ME. *reherce, -erse* – AFr. *rehearser*, OFr. *reherc(i)er*, perh. f. *re-* RE- + *hercer* harrow (see HEARSE, HERSE).] **1.** *trans.* To recite or repeat aloud in a formal manner; to say over, or read aloud, from beginning to end. **b.** To repeat, say over again (something previously said or heard) ME. †**c.** To say, utter, speak –1567. **2.** To give an account of; to relate, narrate, recount, describe at length. Now *rare*. ME. **3.** To recount in order; to name or mention one after another; to enumerate, reckon up, †number. late ME. †**b.** To mention, make mention of; to cite, quote –1562. **4.** To go through or practise (a play, scene, part, etc.) in private, in preparation for a more formal or public performance 1579. **b.** To exercise, train, or make proficient by rehearsal 1768. **5.** To perform, practise, as in rehearsing (*rare*) 1700. **6.** *intr.* To recite; to engage in rehearsal 1693.

1. Words learned by rote a parrot may r. COWPER. **b.** The critic brings thee praise, which all r. 1822. **2.** First of all we shall r...The Nativity of our Lord LONGF. **3.** I will r. the captains and their fleets COWPER. **4.** Sit downe..and r. your parts SHAKS. **6.** We got together, in order to r. GOLDSM. Hence **Rehea·rser.**

Rei, assumed sing. of REIS¹.

‖**Reich** (raiχ). 1924. [G., kingdom, empire, state.] The German state or commonwealth.

Reif (rīf). Chiefly *Sc.* [OE. *rēaf* = OFris. *rāf*, OS. *rōf*, OHG. *roub* :- Gmc. **raub-*; see REAVE *v.*¹] †**1.** Spoil, plunder –1557. **2.** The act or practice of robbery; spoliation. *Obs.* exc. *arch.* ME.

Reify (rī·ifəi), *v.* 1854. [f. L. *res, re-* thing + -FY.] *trans.* To convert mentally into a thing; to materialize. Hence **Reifica·tion.**

Reign (rēⁱn), *sb.* ME. [– OFr. *reigne* (also mod.) *règne*, in OFr. always 'kingdom' – L. *regnum*, rel. to *rex, reg-* king.] **1.** Royal power or rule; kingdom, sovereignty; also *transf.* power or rule comparable to that of a king. Now *rare*. **b.** *transf.* Influence, dominion, sway (of something immaterial). late ME. †**2.** A kingdom or realm; a territory ruled over by a king –1725. †**b.** The kingdom of heaven or of God –1594. **c.** *poet.* A place or sphere under the rule of some specified person or thing, or having a specified character. Now *rare*. late ME. †**d.** = KINGDOM 5. (*rare*) –1781. **3.** The period of a sovereign's rule ME.

1. Under the r. of Queen Victoria THACKERAY. **b.** The owlet Night resumes her r. SHELLEY. **2. c.** A shout that..Frighted the R. of Chaos and old Night MILT. **d.** The vegetable and the mineral reigns THOMSON. **3.** After a r. of seventy years, he died 1841. Phr. *R. of Terror*: see TERROR.

Reign (rēⁱn), *v.* ME. [– OFr. *reignier* (mod. *régner*) – L. *regnare*, f. *regnum* (see prec.).] **1.** *intr.* To hold or exercise the sovereign power or authority in a state; to rule or govern as king or queen. Also *transf.* or *fig.* **2.** Of persons: To exercise authority of any kind; to hold sway; to rule ME. **3.** Of things: To have power, sway, or predominance; to prevail or be prevalent ME.

1. During the time Edward the third did raigne SHAKS. Who reigned'st in thy heaven, yet felt'st our hell 1633. While..Reigns in pomp the perfect moon 1871. **2.** Yet he who reigns within himself, and rules Passions, Desires, and Fears, is more a King MILT. **3.** Lord, Lord: to see what folly raignes in vs SHAKS. In thy heart eternal winter reigns POPE. Famine has long reigned CARLYLE. Hence †**Rei·gner,** a ruler.

‖**Reim** (rīm). *S. Afr.* 1865. [– Du. *riem*.] A strip of ox-hide, a thong, strap.

Reimburse (rīˌimbɔ̄·ɹs), *v.* 1611. [f. RE- 5 a + IMBURSE, after Fr. *rembourser*.] **1.** *trans.* To repay or make up to a person (a sum expended). **2.** To repay, recompense (a person) 1637. **3.** With double object 1624.

1. The tardy sale of so voluminous a work could not have reimbursed the cost HALLAM. **2.** I will see you fully and thankfully reimbursed for what charges shall attend the same PEPYS. **3.** To r. him the costs of his trial 1841. Hence **Reimbu·rsable** *a.* that is to be reimbursed, repayable. **Reimbu·rsement,** the act of reimbursing, repayment. **Reimbu·rser.**

Reim-kennar (rəi·mˌke:naɹ), *pseudo-arch.* 1821. [app. formed by Scott on G. *reim* rhyme

+ *kenner* knower.] One skilled in magic rhymes.

Rein (rēⁱn), *sb.*¹ [ME. *rene* – OFr. *rene*, *reigne*, earlier *resne*, (AFr.) *redne* (mod. *rêne*) :– Rom. **retina*, f. L. *retinēre* RETAIN, repl. L. *retinaculum* halter, tether.] **1.** A long narrow strap or thong of leather, attached to the bridle or bit on each side of the head, by which a horse, etc., is controlled and guided by the rider or driver; any similar device used for the same purpose. (The *pl.* has freq. the same sense as the *sing.*) **2.** *fig.* Any means of guiding, controlling, or governing; a curb, check, or restraint of any kind. late ME.

1. His horse in his hond held by the reyne 1400. In this Country they never use reins to their Oxen 1785. *Bearing-*, *bridle-*, *coupling-*, *gag-r.*, etc.: see the first element. Phr. *To give* (a horse) *the rein(s)*, to allow (it) free motion. *To draw r.*, to bring one's horse to a stand. **2.** The council of state assumed the reins of government 1777. Phr. *To give the rein(s) to*, to allow full course or scope to.

Comb.: **r.-orchis**, an orchis of the genus *Habenaria*, the Fringed Orchis.

Rein (rēⁱn), *sb.*² 1555. [– Sw., Da. *ren*, †*reen* :– ON. *hreinn* = OE. *hrān*, according to some of Finnish-Lappish origin.] The reindeer.

Rein (rēⁱn), *v.* ME. [f. REIN *sb.*¹] †**1.** *trans.* To tie (a horse or its head) *to* something by the rein; to tie up in this way –1592. **2.** To fit or furnish with a rein or reins 1483. **3.** To check or stop, by pulling at the rein 1530. **b.** *fig.* To put a check or restraint upon (something); to restrain *from* something 1588. **4.** To govern, control, manage, or direct, by means of reins. Now *rare*. 1590. **b.** *fig.* To rule, guide, or govern 1581. **5.** To pull *up* or *back*, to check and hold *in*, by means of the reins 1552. **6.** *U.S.* To preserve or keep enclosed *from* stock. Also with *up*. 1799. **7.** *intr.* Of a horse: **a.** To bear, or submit to (the rein) in a specified manner 1565. **b.** To move *back*, etc. under the rein 1627. Also *fig.*

3. Sudden his steed the leader rein'd SCOTT. **b.** My tongue within my lips I r. GAY. **4. b.** Lawes and statutes..Wherby good subjects easily are rain'd 1614. **5.** *absol.* We reined in at last to a walk 1888. **7. a.** Hee will beare you easily, and raines well SHAKS.

Reinca·rnate, *v.* 1858. [RE- 5 a.] *trans.* To incarnate anew. So **Re:incarna·tion** 1858.

Reindeer (rēⁱ·ndīᵊɹ). late ME. [– ON. *hreindýri*, f. *hreinn* (see REIN *sb.*²) + *dýr* DEER.] An animal of the deer kind, *Rangifer tarandus*, having large branching or palmated antlers, now confined to sub-arctic regions, where it is used for drawing sledges, and is kept in large herds for the sake of the milk, flesh, and hides.

Comb.: **r. lichen, moss**, a species of lichen, *Cladonia rangiferina*, which constitutes the winter food of the r.; **r. period, epoch**, a name sometimes given to the more recent stage of the Palæolithic period.

‖**Reinette** (rēⁱne·t). 1583. [Fr.; see RENNET *sb.*²] A variety of apple, the rennet.

Reinforce (rī,infōᵊ·ɹs), *sb.* 1648. [f. next.] †**1.** *Mil.* A reinforcement of troops. EVELYN. **2.** A part (or one of two parts) of a gun next the breech, made stronger than the rest in order to resist the explosive force of the powder 1769. **3.** Any thing or part added to an object to strengthen it 1869.

attrib. (sense 2): **r. band, ring**, a flat ring or moulding round a gun at the points where the reinforces meet or terminate.

Reinforce (rī,infōᵊ·ɹs), *v.* 1600. [alt., by analysis into RE- and *inforce* ENFORCE, of †*renforce* (XVI), often (XVI–XVII) sp. *re'n-*, *r'en-*, *r'in-*, – (O)Fr. *renforcer*, in mil. use prob. – It. *rinforzare*.] **I. 1.** *trans.* To strengthen (a military or naval force) by means of additional men. **b.** To increase the number or amount of 1839. **2.** To strengthen, make stronger; to furnish with additional support 1635. **b.** To strengthen (some material thing) by additional support, added thickness, etc. 1692. **3.** To make more forcible or cogent 1629. **b.** To increase by giving fresh force to; also simply, to increase 1659. **4.** *intr.* To obtain reinforcements (*rare*) 1611.

1. Fresh troops continually came up to r. those who were exhausted with fatigue 1849. **3.** It is said, he reinforced the proposal by promising a liberal share of the proceeds of it 1843. **4.** *Cymb.* v. ii. 18.

†**II. 1.** To renew or repeat with fresh force –1662. **2.** To enforce, or put in force, again –1720.

2. [To] attend his Majesty, desiring him to r... the laws against Conventicles MARVELL. Hence **Re·inforced** *ppl. a.*, *spec.* in **reinforced cement, concrete**, cement or concrete with metal bars, gratings, or wire embedded in it.

Reinforcement (rī,infōᵊ·ɹsmĕnt). 1607. [f. prec. + -MENT.] †**1.** A renewal of force; a fresh assault. SHAKS. **2.** The act of reinforcing with fresh troops 1617. **b.** A fresh supply of men to assist or strengthen a military or naval force 1646. **3.** Augmentation of strength or force; the act of strengthening or increasing in any way 1651. **4.** The act of enforcing anew. Now *rare*. 1641.

1. *Cor.* II. ii. 117. **3.** What r. we may gain from Hope MILT.

†**Reinfu·nd**, *v.* [f. RE- 5 a + †*infund* (XVI–XVII) – L. *infundere* pour in.] *intr.* To pour in again. SWIFT.

Reinless (rēⁱ·nlės), *a.* 1559. [f. REIN *sb.*¹ + -LESS.] **1.** Without a rein or reins. **2.** *transf.* and *fig.* Unchecked, unrestrained 1566.

1. The r. steed SOUTHEY. The r. rider 1892. **2.** R. speed SHELLEY.

Reins (rēⁱnz), *sb. pl.* Now *arch.* late ME. [– (O)Fr. *reins* :– L. *renes* pl.] **1.** The kidneys. **2.** The region of the kidneys; the loins. late ME. **b.** *Arch.* (See quot.) 1727. **3.** In or after Biblical use: The seat of the feelings or affections. late ME.

2. b. R., or fillings up of a Vault, are the sides which sustain it 1727. **3.** I am nere to theyr mouthes, but I am ferre from theyr raynes 1526. Yea my reines shall reioyce, when thy lippes speake right things *Prov.* 23:16.

Reinstate (rī,instēⁱ·t), *v.* 1599. [RE- 5 a.] **1.** *trans.* To reinstall or re-establish (a person or thing *in* a place, station, condition, etc.). **2.** To restore to its proper or original state; to instate afresh 1793.

1. The said archbishop is now reinstated in his majesty's favour 1628. The senators could not r. him by force 1878. **2.** To r. the streets..so opened by them 1833. So **Reinsta·tement, Reinsta·tion**, the action of reinstating; re-establishment.

Reinsu·rance. 1755. [RE- 5 a.] A renewed or second insurance; *spec.* one in which an insurer or underwriter secures himself (wholly or in part) against the risk he has undertaken.

Reinsu·re, *v.* 1828. [RE- 5 a.] *trans.* To insure again; *spec.* to devolve the risk of an insurance on another insurer. So **Reinsu·rer.**

Reintegrate (rī,i·ntigrēⁱt), *v.* 1581. [var. of REDINTEGRATE, after (O)Fr. *réintégrer* or med.L. *reintegrare* (IX).] †**1.** *refl.* To reinstate (oneself) –1648. **2.** *transf.* = REDINTEGRATE *v.* 2 b. Now *rare*. 1605. **3.** = REDINTEGRATE *v.* 1. 1626.

3. The atmosphere alone will r. a soil rested in due season 1798. So **Reintegra·tion.**

Reinvest (rī,inve·st), *v.* 1611. [RE- 5 a.] **1.** *trans.* To invest again with or as with a garment. **b.** To re-endow *with* a possession, power, etc. 1648. **2.** To replace, re-establish. Const. *in.* 1617. **3.** To invest (money) again 1848.

3. The proceeds of sale have been..reinvested in land 1885. So **Reinve·stment**, a fresh investment.

‖**Reis**¹ (rēⁱs), *sb. pl.* 1555. [Pg. *reis* for **reaes*, pl. of *real* = Sp. *real* REAL *sb.*¹] A Pg. money of account equal to about one-twentieth of a penny in Portugal and one-fortieth in Brazil.

‖**Reis**², **rais** (rəis, rais). 1585. [– Fr. *réis*, *rais* – Arab. *rā'is* chief, f. *rā's* head.] **1.** The captain of a boat or vessel. **2.** A chief or governor 1678.

2. *R. Effendi*, the title of a former officer of state in the Turkish empire, who acted as chancellor and minister of foreign affairs.

Reisner (rəi·snəɹ). 1833. [f. name of a German artist in wood, of the time of Louis XIV.] *R.-work* (also simply *R.*), a method of inlaying in wood of different colours.

†**Reit.** 1538. [Of unkn. origin.] Chiefly *pl.* Sea-weed –1661.

Reiter (rəi·təɹ). Now *Hist.* 1584. [– G. *reiter* rider, trooper, f. *reiten* RIDE *v.*] A German cavalry soldier, *esp.* one of those employed in the wars of the 16th and 17th c.

Reiterant (ri,i·tĕrănt), *a.* 1610. [f. REITERATE *v.* + -ANT.] Reiterating, repeating. So **Rei·terance**, repetition.

Reiterate (ri,i·tĕrĕt), *pa. pple.* and *ppl. a.* 1471. [– L. *reiteratus*, pa. pple. of *reiterare*; see next, -ATE².] Reiterated.

Reiterate (ri,i·tĕrēⁱt), *v.* 1526. [– *reiterat-*, pa. ppl. stem of L. *reiterare*; see RE-, ITERATE.] **1.** *trans.* To repeat (an action); to do over again. **2.** To repeat (a request, statement, word, etc.); to give renewed expression to (a feeling) 1560. †**3.** To walk over (a place) again. HERRICK.

1. Which Sentence was barbarously executed, and afterwards reiterated upon others CLARENDON. **2.** My father..reiterated his orders, that no one should presume to fire until he gave the word SCOTT. Hence **Rei·teratedly** *adv.*

Reiteration (ri,itĕrēⁱ·ʃən). 1560. [– Fr. *réitération* (XVI) or med.L. *reiteratio*; see RE-, ITERATION.] The (*or* an) act of reiterating.

Reiterative (ri,i·tĕrĕtiv), *a.* and *sb.* 1813. [f. REITERATE *v.* + -IVE.] **A.** *adj.* Characterized by reiteration. **B.** *sb.* A word expressing reiteration. So **Rei·teratively** *adv.* 1619.

Reive(r, var. of REAVE(R.

Reject (rī·dʒekt, rĭdʒe·kt), *sb.* 1555. [f. next.] One who, a thing which, is rejected.

Reject (rĭdʒe·kt), *v.* 1494. [– *reject-*, pa. ppl. stem of L. *reicere* throw back, f. *re-* RE- + *jacere* throw. Cf. Fr. †*rejecter*, var. of †*rejetter*, mod. *rejeter*; see JET *v.*²] **1.** *trans.* To refuse to recognize, acquiesce in, submit to, or adopt (a rule, command, practice, etc.); to refuse credit to (a statement). **2.** To refuse to have or take for some purpose; to set aside or throw away as useless or worthless 1531. **3.** To refuse (something offered); to decline to receive or accept 1671. **4.** To expel from the mouth or stomach 1667. **5.** To repel or rebuff (one who makes advances); to refuse to accept, listen to, admit, etc. 1561. **b.** Of a woman: To refuse (a man) as lover or husband 1581. **6.** To refuse to grant, entertain, or agree to (a request, proposal, etc.) 1602. †**7.** To cast (a fault, etc.) back *upon* a person –1678. **8.** To throw or cast back 1603.

1. Nor perhaps ought we to r. the farther account ..as a groundless fiction THIRLWALL. **2.** The stone which the builders reiected, the same is become the head of the corner *Matt.* 21:42. **3.** Good counsel rejected, returns to enrich the giver's bosom GOLDSM. **5.** Not to r. The penitent, but.. to forgive MILT. **6.** I could not r. his proposal SWIFT. Hence **Reje·ctable** *a.* that may, or ought to be rejected. **Reje·cter.**

‖**Rejectamenta** (rĭdʒektăme·ntă). 1816. [mod.L., pl. of *rejectamentum*; see REJECT *v.* and -MENT.] **1.** Things rejected as useless or worthless; refuse. **2.** Wrack or rubbish cast up by the sea 1819. **3.** *Phys.* Excremental matter 1879.

†**Rejecta·neous**, *a.* 1657. [– L. *rejectaneus*, f. *rejicere* to REJECT.] Deserving rejection, rejectable –1734.

Rejection (rĭdʒe·kʃən). 1552. [– Fr. *réjection* or L. *rejectio*, *-on-*, f. *reject-*; see REJECT *v.*, -ION.] The action of rejecting or the state of being rejected. **b.** *concr.* That which is rejected; excrement 1605.

Rejectment (rĭdʒe·ktmĕnt). 1677. [f. REJECT *v.* + -MENT.] †**1.** Rejection (*rare*) –1690. **2.** *concr.* Rejected matter, excrement. Also *pl.* 1828.

†**Rejoi·ce**, *sb.* 1445. [f. next.] Joy, rejoicing; a cause of joy –1682.

Rejoice (rĭdʒoi·s), *v.* [ME. *reioshe*, *reioische*, *reioyse*, f. *rejoiss-*, lengthened stem of OFr. *re(s)joir*, later *réjouir*, f. *re-* RE- + *esjoir* (*éjouir*), f. *es-* EX-¹ + *joir* JOY *v.*] †**1.** *trans.* To enjoy by possessing; to have full possession and use of (a thing) –1577. **2.** To gladden, make joyful, exhilarate (a person, his spirits, etc.). late ME. **3.** *refl.* To make (oneself) glad or joyful; hence = sense 5. Now *rare*. late ME. †**4.** To feel joy on account of (an event) –1611. **5.** *intr.* To be full of joy; to be glad or greatly delighted; to exult. late ME.

2. I love to r. their poor Hearts at this season ADDISON. The King was rejoiced at seeing him 1841. **3.** R. myself with a glance at the volutes of the Erectheium RUSKIN. **4.** Nere Mother Reioyc'd deliuerance more SHAKS. **5.** O reioyce Beyond a common ioy SHAKS. Rejoicing at that answer to his prayer TENNYSON. Hence **Rejoi·cement**, joy, exultation, rejoicing. **Rejoi·cer**, one who rejoices; one who or that which causes rejoicing. **Rejoi·cingly** *adv.*

Rejoicing (rĭdʒoi·siŋ), *vbl. sb.* late ME. [f. prec. + -ING¹.] **1.** The action of REJOICE *v.*; the feeling and expression of joy. **b.** With *a* and *pl.*: An instance, occasion, or expression of rejoicing; a festival 1540. †**2.** A cause or source of rejoicing or gladness –1611. **3.** *attrib.*, as *r.-fire*, etc. 1611.

1. My reioycing At nothing can be more SHAKS. **b.** The rejoycings upon this occasion were of short continuance 1707. **2.** Thy word was unto me, the ioy and reioycing of my heart *Jer.* 15:16.

Rejoin (rĭdʒoi·n), *v.*[1] 1456. [f. *rejoign-*, stem of (O)Fr. *rejoindre*; see RE-, JOIN *v.*] **1.** *intr. Law.* To reply to a charge or pleading; *spec.* to answer the plaintiff's replication. †**2.** To answer a reply; also more loosely, to reply. Const. *to, with.* –1665. **3.** *trans.* To say in answer 1637.

2. Vnto whom..wee shall not contentiously rejoyne 1646.

Rejoin (rī-, rĭdʒoi·n), *v.*[2] 1541. [– (O)Fr. *rejoign-* (see prec.), or f. RE- 5 a + JOIN *v.*] **1.** *intr.* Of things: To come together, or unite again. **2.** *trans.* To join again, reunite (persons or things, *to* or *with* another) 1570. **3.** To join (a person, company, etc.) again 1611.

2. As tin-soder doth knit and rejoyne a crackt peece of brasse 1603.

Rejoinder (rĭdʒoi·ndəɹ). 1450. [– AFr. **rejoinder*, infin. used as sb.; see REJOIN *v.*[1], -ER[4].] **1.** *Law.* The defendant's answer to the plaintiff's replication. **2.** An answer to a reply; also simply, a reply 1566. **b.** Without article, in phr. *in r.* 1556.

†**Rejoi·ndure.** [app. f. REJOIN *v.*[2] (infl. by prec.), or f. RE- + JOINDER with substitution of suffix -URE (cf. contextual EMBRASURE *sb.*[1]).] Reunion. SHAKS.

†**Rejou·rn,** *v.* 1513. [f. RE- + AD)JOURN.] **1.** *trans.* To adjourn, postpone, put off –1647. **2.** To refer (a person) *to* something. BURTON. So †**Rejou·rnment,** adjournment.

Rejuvenate (rĭdʒū·vĭneⁱt), *v.* 1807. [irreg. f. RE- + L. *juvenis* young + -ATE[3], after Fr. *rajeunir.*] *trans.* To restore to youth; to make young or fresh again. Also *absol.* Hence **Rejuvena·tion.**

Rejuvenesce (rĭdʒūvĭne·s), *v.* 1879. [– late L. *rejuvenescere*, f. *re-* RE- + *juvenis* young; see -ESCENT.] **a.** *intr.* To become young again; *spec.* in *Biol.* of cells: To acquire renewed vitality. **b.** *trans.* To impart fresh vitality to (a cell).

Rejuvenescence (rĭdʒūvĭne·sĕns). 1631. [f. as prec. + -ENCE.] A renewal of youth, physical, mental, or spiritual. **b.** *spec.* in *Biol.* and *Bot.* The process by which a vegetative cell transforms itself into a new one 1855. So †**Rejuvene·scency.**

Rejuvenescent (rĭdʒūvĭne·sĕnt), *a.* 1763. [f. as prec. + -ENT.] **1.** Becoming young again 1807. **b.** *spec.* in scientific use 1859. **2.** Rejuvenating 1763.

1. The Crawley House in Great Gaunt Street was quite r. THACKERAY.

Rejuvenize (rĭdʒū·vĭnəiz), *v.* 1816. [app. f. REJUVENATE *v.* with substitution of suffix -IZE.] *trans.* To rejuvenate, make young again.

Rekindle (rīki·nd'l), *v.* 1593. [RE- 5 a.] **1.** *trans.* To kindle again, set fire to afresh. **b.** *fig.* To inflame afresh, rouse anew 1652. **2.** *intr.* To take fire again 1597.

-rel, -erel (also formerly *-ral, -ril*), a diminutive and depreciatory suffix, repr. OFr. *-erel* (mod. Fr. *-ereau*) or *-erelle*, in derivation from Fr.; hence suffixed to various native stems, and in other formations of uncertain origin, as *cockerel, mackerel, doggerel, mongrel, scoundrel.*

Relapse (rĭlæ·ps), *sb.*[1] 1533. [f. RELAPSE *v.*, after LAPSE *sb.*, or – Fr. *relaps* sb. and adj. – med.L. *relapsus*, pa. pple. of L. *relabi* RELAPSE *v.*] **1.** A falling back into error, heresy, or wrong-doing; back-sliding. **2.** The fact of falling back again into an illness after a partial recovery; return of a disease or illness during the period of convalescence 1584. **3.** The act of falling or sinking back again 1876.

1. Which would but lead me to a worse r., And heavier fall MILT.

Relapse (rĭlæ·ps), *sb.*[2] Now *rare.* 1546. [– med.L. *relapsus, -a* relapsed heretic, L. *relapsus*, pa. pple. of *relabi*; see prec. So Fr. *relaps.*] A relapsed person; one who has fallen again into error or heresy.

Relapse (rĭlæ·ps), *v.* 1548. [– *relaps-*, pa. ppl. stem of L. *relabi*, f. *re-* RE- + *labi* slip.] **1.** *intr.* To fall back into wrong-doing or error; to backslide; *spec.* to fall again into heresy after recantation 1570. **2.** To fall back into an illness after partial recovery or from a convalescent state 1548. **b.** Of stock: To fall again in value 1896. **3.** To fall back or sink again *into* any state, practice, etc. 1593. †**b.** To fall away *from* a person –1687. †**4.** *trans.* To cause to fall back –1773.

1. The Children of Israel..relapsed into the Idolatry of the Egyptians HOBBES. **2.** *transf.* The red fire..Rallies, relapses, dwindles, deathward sinks! BROWNING. **3.** He relapsed into a musing mood 1864. Hence **Rela·pser,** one who relapses, esp. into error or sin. **Rela·psing** *ppl. a.* that relapses; *r. fever*, a fever characterized by relapses.

Relate (rĭlēⁱ·t), *sb.* 1633. [– L. *relatus, -a, -um*, pa. pple. of *referre* REFER, taken substantivally; cf. med.L. *relata* (n. pl.) relative terms. See CORRELATE *sb.*] †**1.** A relation, relative –1656. **2.** *Logic.* One of two objects of thought between which a relation subsists 1633.

Relate (rĭlēⁱ·t), *v.* 1530. [– stem of L. *relatus*, functioning as pa. pple. of *referre* REFER; see -ATE[3]. Cf. (O)Fr. *relater*, whence sense 1.] **I.** *trans.* **1.** To recount, narrate, tell, give an account of. †**2.** To bring back, restore. SPENSER. †**3.** To refer (a person) *to* a book, etc. –1657. **4.** To bring (a thing or person) into relation *to* another 1697. **b.** To connect, establish a relation between 1771.

1. Letters..wherein hee related..what hee had seene in the Indias 1582. What thought can measure thee or tongue R. thee? MILT. **4. b.** Volta..first enabled us definitely to r. the forces of chemistry and electricity 1846.

II. *intr.* **1.** *Law.* To refer *back*, to have application *to* an earlier date 1596. **2.** To have reference *to* 1606. †**3.** Of persons: To make reference *to* –1655. **4.** To be related, have relation, stand in some relation, *to* another thing (†person or place) 1646. †**5.** To discourse; to give an account –1747.

2. Old persons are quick to see and hear all that relates to them JOWETT. **4.** The critic Eye.. examines bit by bit: How parts r. to parts, or they to whole POPE. **5.** Adam relating, she sole Auditress MILT. Hence **Rela·ter,** one who relates; a narrator, historian.

Related (rĭlēⁱ·tĕd), *ppl. a.* 1604. [f. prec. + -ED[1].] **1.** Narrated, recited; †referred to (*rare*). **2. a.** Having relation *to*, or relationship *with*, something else, Also *attrib.* without const. 1662. **b.** Having mutual relation or connection 1671. **3.** Of persons: Connected by blood or marriage (*to* another, or with each other) 1702.

2. a. Saw Twelfth-Night acted well, though it be but a silly play, and not related at all to the name. or day PEPYS. **b.** Whenever two things are said to be r. there is some fact or series of facts into which they both enter 1843. **3.** A Persian of the highest rank, related to the royal family 1837. Hence **Rela·tedness,** the state or condition of being r.

Relation (rĭlēⁱ·ʃən). late ME. [– (O)Fr. *relation* or L. *relatio, -on-*, f. *relat-*; see RELATE *v.*, -ION.] **1.** The action of relating in words; narration, recital, account; report. **b.** *Law.* The action of a relator. (Cf. INFORMATION 5 b.) 1632. **2.** A particular instance of relating or narrating; a (or one's) narrative, account, statement 1500. **3.** That feature or attribute of things which is involved in considering them in comparison or contrast with each other; the particular way in which one thing is thought of in connection with another; any connection, correspondence, or association, which can be conceived as naturally existing between things. late ME. **4. a.** *To have* or *make r.*: to have or make reference or allusion *to* something. late ME. **b.** *Law* (in phr. *to have r.*). Reference or application *to* an earlier date 1491. †**c.** A fiction of law by which two times or other things are identified, and, for legal purposes, regarded as one and the same –1749. **5.** Connection between persons arising out of the natural ties of blood or marriage; kinship 1660. **b.** A person related to one by blood or marriage; a kinsman or kinswoman; a relative. Also freq. in *pl.*, kinsfolk, relatives. 1502. **6.** The position which one person holds with respect to another on account of some social or other connection between them; the particular mode in which persons are mutually connected by circumstances 1650. **b.** *pl.* The aggregate of the connections, or modes of connection, by which one person is brought into touch with another or with society in general 1687. **c.** *pl.* The various modes in which one country, state, etc., is brought into contact with another by political or commercial interests 1797.

1. I like no R. so well, as what mine eye telleth me 1601. **2.** A r. of the great and Golden Citie of Manoa RALEGH. **3.** The Nature of R. consists in the referring or comparing two things one to another LOCKE. Phr. *In* or *with r. to.* **5.** The r. is as real as that of husband and wife 1758. **b.** Their Friends attend the Herse, the next Relations mourn DRYDEN. **6.** The r. of ruler and subject MACAULAY. The r. of every man to his lord FREEMAN. **b.** Our relations to each other are various and infinite GIBBON. **c.** Our commercial relations with the Baltic cities 1861.

Relational (rĭlēⁱ·ʃənăl), *a.* 1662. [f. prec. + -AL[1].] **1.** Of or belonging to human relationship. **2.** Of, belonging to, or characterized by relation in general 1840.

Rela·tionism. 1858. [f. RELATION *sb.* + -ISM.] *Philos.* **a.** The doctrine of the relativity of knowledge; relativism. **b.** The doctrine that relations have a real existence. So **Rela·tionist,** one who maintains a theory based on a relation between ideas.

Relationship (rĭlēⁱ·ʃənʃip). 1744. [f. as prec. + -SHIP.] The state of being related; a condition or character based upon this; kinship.

Relatival (relătəi·văl), *a.* 1869. [f. next + -AL[1].] Of or pertaining to a relative or relation. Chiefly *Gram.*

Relative (re·lătiv), *a.* and *sb.* late ME. [– (O)Fr. *relatif, -ive* or late L. *relativus* having reference or relation; see RELATE *v.*, -IVE.] **A.** *adj.* **1.** *Gram.* Relating or referring to an antecedent term; applied to a class of words (pronouns, adjectives, adverbs) having the function of introducing adjectival clauses 1530. **2.** Having mutual relationship; related to, or connected with, each other 1594. **b.** Corresponding 1849. **c.** *Mus.* Of a minor key in relation to a major key: Having the same key-signature 1818. **3.** Having relation to the question or matter in hand; pertinent, relevant 1602. **4.** Arising from, depending on, or determined by, relation to something else or to each other; comparative 1611. **b.** Constituted, or existing, only by relation to something else; not absolute or independent 1704. **5.** Of worship: Offered indirectly by means of or through an image 1624. **6.** Of terms, etc.: Involving or implying relation; depending for meaning or significance upon some relationship of things or persons 1678. **7.** Having, or standing in, a relation *to* something else; correspondent or proportionate *to* 1660. **b.** In proportion *to* something 1789. **8.** Having application or reference *to* a thing 1765. **b.** Relating *to* a matter of fact, event, person, etc.; with reference *to* 1763.

1. The r. pronouns are *who, which, that, as* 1872. **3.** Ile haue grounds More Relatiue then this SHAKS. **4.** They were..so marked, that..they could..be restored to the same r. position SMEATON. **b.** Certainty is positive, evidence r. COLERIDGE. **6.** A name is r. when, being the name of one thing, its signification cannot be explained but by mentioning another MILL. **7. b.** Naples, the most populous of cities, r. to its size GIBBON. **8.** Things r. to immediate Want 1765. **b.** I write to the Admiralty r. to my health NELSON.

B. *sb.* **1.** *Gram.* A relative word; *esp.* a relative pronoun. late ME. **2.** A thing (†or person) standing in some relation to another. late ME. **b.** A relative term. (See A. 6.) 1551. **c.** *Mus.* A relative major or minor key (see A 2 c) 1811. **3.** One who is connected with another or others by blood or affinity; a kinsman 1657. †**4.** A relationship –1675. **5.** *The r.*, that which is relative (in sense A. 4 b) 1856.

2. b. Some Terms which seem Absolute are Relatives 1697. **3.** He had received intelligence of the death of a near r. TYNDALL. Hence **Re·latively** *adv.*, **-ness.**

Relativism (re·lătiviz'm). 1885. [f. prec. + -ISM.] *Philos.* The doctrine that knowledge is only of relations. So **Re·lativist,** one who holds this doctrine.

Relativity (relăti·vĭti). 1834. [f. as prec. + -ITY.] The fact or condition of being relative, relativeness. **b.** Applied to various theories which assert the dependence of individuals or the reciprocal dependence of the individual and society 1890. **c.** The theory of the universe propounded by Albert Einstein, that all motion is relative 1905.

R. of knowledge: (*a*) *Philos.* the doctrine that human knowledge is only relatively true or certain; (*b*) *Psychol.* the doctrine that sensations are significant only in relation to other sensations.

Relator (rĭlēⁱ·tǫɹ). 1591. [– L. *relator*, f. *relat-*; see RELATE *v.*, -OR 2.] **1.** A relater, narrator. †**b.** (One's) informant –1610. **2.** *Law.* An informer; *spec.* one who supplies the materials for an information by the Attorney General 1603.

†**Rela·x**, *sb.* 1627. [f. the vb.] Relaxation; an instance of this –1773.

Rela·x, *a. rare.* 1609. [f. next, after LAX *a.*] **1.** Lax, wanting in strictness. †**2.** Relaxed, slack. BACON.

Relax (rĭlæ·ks), *v.* late ME. [– L. *relaxare*, f. *re-* RE- + *laxus* LAX *a.* Cf. (O)Fr. *relaxer.*] **I.** *trans.* †**1.** To make (a thing) less compact or dense; to loosen or open up by separation of parts –1676. **b.** *spec.* To render (a part of the body) less firm or rigid; to make loose or slack; to enfeeble or enervate. Also *absol.* 1620. **c.** To diminish the force or tension of; *esp.* to loosen (one's hold or grasp) 1781. **2.** To make less strict, severe, or rigid; to mitigate, tone down, modify 1662. **b.** To slacken, abate, diminish (an effort, etc.) 1774. **c.** To cause to abate in zeal or force (*rare*) 1660. **3.** Of the Inquisition: To hand over (heretics) to the secular power for execution 1838.

1. To r. thir serried files MILT. **b.** The heat relaxed my muscles TYNDALL. **c.** Charity may r. the miser's fist COWPER. **2.** The old woman seemed somewhat to r. her tone of severity SCOTT.

II. *intr.* **1.** To become loose or slack; to grow less tense or firm 1720. **b.** Of the features: To become less rigid or stern 1797. **2.** To abate in degree or force 1701. **3.** To become less severe, strict, or exacting; to grow milder 1749. **b.** Of persons: To become less stiff or distant; to assume a friendlier manner 1837. **4.** To slacken in zeal or application; to seek or take relaxation *from* work or occupation 1760.

1. Tired by the tides, his knees r. with toil POPE. **b.** His features would r. into a look of fondness DICKENS. **3.** It was hoped..the Court would r. in its opposition 1789. **4.** He did not however r. in his perseverance 1833. Hence †**Rela·xable** *a.* admitting of remission.

Relaxant (rĭlæ·ksănt), *a.* and *sb.* 1771. [– L. *relaxans, -ant-*, pr. pple. of *relaxare*; see prec., -ANT.] *Med.* **A.** *adj.* Causing, or distinguished by, relaxation. **B.** *sb.* A practice or drug serving to produce relaxation 1832.

Relaxation (rĭlæksēⁱ·ʃən). 1526. [– L. *relaxatio, -on-*, f. *relaxat-*, pa. ppl. stem of *relaxare*; see RELAX *v.*, -ION. Cf. (O)Fr. *relaxation.*] **1.** Partial (†or complete) remission *of* some penalty, burden, duty, etc.; †also, the document granting such remission. **b.** The action of RELAX *v.* I. 3. 1826. **2.** The action of unbending the mind from severe application; release from ordinary occupations or cares; recreation 1548. **3.** *Path.* A loosening or slackening of the fibres, nerves, joints, etc., of the body 1626. **4.** Diminution of, release or freedom from, strictness or severity 1626. **5.** Abatement of intensity, vigour, or energy 1695.

2. To thy bent mind some r. give, And steal one day out of thy life to live COWLEY. **3.** Bathing or Anointing gives a R. or Emollition BACON. **4.** These are not times to admit of any r. in the little discipline we have left '*Junius' Lett.*

Relaxative (rĭlæ·ksătiv), *a.* and *sb.* 1611. [f. RELAX *v.*, after LAXATIVE. As sb., – med.L. *relaxativa* n. pl.] **A.** *adj.* Tending to relax; of the nature of relaxation (*rare*). †**B.** *sb.* A means of relaxing; *esp.* a relaxing medicine –1671.

Relay (rĭlēⁱ·), *sb.* late ME. [– OFr. *relai* (mod. *relais*), f. *relayer*; see next.] **1.** A set of fresh hounds (and horses) posted to take up the chase of a deer in place of those already tired out; †also, the place where these are posted. *Obs.* exc. *arch.* **2.** A set of fresh horses obtained, or kept ready, at various stages along a route to expedite travel 1659. **b.** The place where a fresh relay is obtained 1706. **3.** A set of persons appointed to relieve others in the performance of certain duties; a relief-gang 1808. **4.** An apparatus used in long-distance telegraphy, wireless telephony, etc. to enable an electric current which is too weak to influence recording instruments, or to transmit a message, etc., to the required distance, to do so indirectly by means of a local battery brought into connection with it 1860.

2. A traveller may have relays of horses to carry him day and night at the rate of ten miles an hour 1879.

Comb.: **r.-race**, a team-race, in which the second and succeeding members of every team take up the race as the preceding members finish, each member at the end of his lap handing on to the next an object which has to be carried throughout the race.

Relay (rĭlēⁱ·), *v.* late ME. [f. prec. or – (O)Fr. *relayer*, f. *re-* RE- + *laier*, ult. repr. L. *laxare*; see LEASE *sb.*³ and cf. DELAY *v.*¹] †**1.** *trans.* Of a hunter: To let go (the fresh hounds) upon the track of the deer. late ME. only. **2.** To place in relays; to provide with, or replace by, fresh relays 1788. **3.** In wireless broadcasting, etc.: To retransmit (a programme, message, etc.) by means of a relay (sense 4) 1923. **4.** *intr.* To get a fresh relay 1829.

Release (rĭlī·s), *sb.* ME. [– OFr. *reles*, f. *relesser*; see next.] **1.** Deliverance or liberation from trouble, pain, sorrow or the like. **2.** The act of freeing, or fact of being freed, from some obligation, duty, or demand; remission; discharge ME. **b.** A written discharge, acquittance, or receipt 1440. **3.** *Law.* The act of conveying or making over an estate or right to another, or disposing of it in some legal fashion; a deed or document made for this purpose. late ME. **4.** The action of setting free, or the fact of being set free, from restraint or confinement; permission to go free; also, a document giving formal discharge from custody 1586. **b.** The act of letting go something fixed or held in a certain position, or confined in some way; also, any device by which this is effected 1871. **5.** The action of 'releasing' a cinema film, etc.; the fact of being so released; an article so released 1907.

1. Nowthir frende nor foo Shulde fynde reles in helle 1440. **3.** *Lease and r.*, 'a conveyance of the fee-simple, right, or interest in lands or tenements..giving first the possession, and afterwards the interest in the estate conveyed'. **4.** All prisoners..They cannot boudge, till your r. SHAKS.

Release (rĭlī·s), *v.* [ME. *relese, -esse* – OFr. *relesser, relaiss(i)er* :– L. *relaxare* RELAX *v.*] **I.** †**1.** *trans.* To withdraw, recall, revoke, cancel (a sentence, punishment, condition, etc.) –1671. †**2.** To relieve, alleviate, or remove (labour, pain, etc.) –1597. **3.** To remit; to grant remission or discharge of or for (something); *esp.* a debt, tax, tribute, etc. Now *Law.* late ME. **4.** To give up, resign, relinquish, surrender (*esp.* a right or claim in favour of another person). late ME. **b.** *spec.* To surrender, make over, transfer (land, etc.) to another. Chiefly *Law.* late ME. †**5.** To relax, mitigate –1677.

3. Sire, I releesse thee thy thousand pound...I wol nat take a peny of thee CHAUCER. **4.** That we should at once r. our claims JOHNSON. **b.** 2 *Hen. VI*, I. i. 51.

II. To set or make free; to liberate, deliver, *of* (now *rare*) or *from* pain, bondage, obligation, etc. Also without const. ME. **b.** To unfix, free (a thing) from some fastening 1833. **c.** To permit the public performance, exhibition, publication, or sale of (a play, cinema film, book, or the like) for the first time 1904.

The Duke of Buckingham and Marquesse of Dorchester are again releast from the Tow'r MARVELL. A mind released From anxious thoughts COWPER. *absol.* He that can bind, can r. HOBBES. Hence **Relea:see·** (*Law*), one to whom an estate is released. **Relea·ser**, one who or that which, releases or sets free. **Relea·sor** (*Law*), one who releases a claim or estate in favour of another.

Releasement (rĭlī·smĕnt). 1548. [f. prec. + -MENT.] **1.** The act of releasing, or the fact of being released, from prison, obligation, debt, trouble, etc. †**2.** Relaxation, remission, or removal *of* a thing –1647.

Relegate (re·lĭgeⁱt), *v.* 1599. [– *relegat-*, pa. ppl. stem of L. *relegare* send away, refer, f. *re-* RE- + *legare* send; see LEGATE *sb.*, -ATE³.] **1.** *trans.* To send (a person) into exile; to banish *to* a particular place. **2.** To consign *to* a place or position, esp. one of inferiority 1790. **b.** To consign (a subject) *to* some province, sphere, domain, etc. 1866. **c.** To assign or refer (a thing) *to* a class or kind 1870. **3.** To refer (a matter) *to* some authority for decision 1846. **b.** To commit, hand over (a thing), *to* another to carry out or deal with 1864.

2. b. If occasionally we come across difficulties.. we r. some of them to the sphere of mystery JOWETT.

Relegation (relĭgēⁱ·ʃən). 1586. [– L. *relegatio, -on-*, f. as prec.; see -ION.] **1.** The action of banishing; the state of temporary exile or banishment. In *Rom. Antiq.* banishment to a certain place, or to a specified distance from Rome, for a limited time and without loss of civil rights. **b.** Banishment or consignment *to* a place or position 1829. **2.** The action of referring, consigning, etc., a thing *to* others for some purpose 1844.

†**Rele·nt**, *sb. rare.* 1590. [f. the vb.] **I.** Slackening of speed. SPENSER. **2.** Relenting, giving way –1686.

Relent (rĭle·nt), *v.* late ME. [– med.L. **relentare* (cf. L. *relentescere* slacken), f. *re-* RE- + L. *lentare* bend, med.L. soften, f. *lentus* flexible.] †**1.** *intr.* To melt under the influence of heat; to assume a liquid form; to dissolve into water. Also *fig.* –1784. †**b.** To become soft or moist –1620. **2.** To soften in temper; to grow more gentle or forgiving 1526. †**b.** To yield, give way; to give up a previous determination or obstinacy –1667. †**3.** *trans.* To dissolve, melt, soften –1661. †**b.** To soften (one's heart, mind, etc.); to cause (a person) to relent –1787. †**4.** To lessen, abate; to slacken –1667. †**b.** To relinquish, abandon, give over –1684. †**5.** To repent (an action, etc.). SPENSER.

1. All nature mourns, the Skies r. in show'rs POPE. **2.** Perhaps God will r., and quit thee all his debt MILT. **3. b.** Yet pitty often did the gods r. SPENSER. **4.** Nothing might r. her hasty flight SPENSER. Hence **Rele·ntment** (now *rare*), the act of relenting; softening of rigour.

Relentless (rĭle·ntlĕs), *a.* 1592. [f. prec. + -LESS.] Incapable of relenting; pitiless.

Onely in destroying I finde ease To my r. thoughts MILT. Hence **Rele·ntless-ly** *adv.*, **-ness.**

Rele:ssee·. *rare.* 1766. [f. RE- 5 a + LESSEE after *release.*] *Law.* One to whom a release is executed. So **Rele:sso·r**, one who executes a release.

Re·levance. 1733. [f. RELEVANT; see -ANCE.] Relevancy.

Relevancy (re·lĭvănsi). 1561. [f. next; see -ANCY.] The quality or fact of being relevant.

His answer..would thus come with more r. and effect 1826.

Relevant (re·lĭvănt), *a.* 1560. [– med.L. *relevans, -ant*, pr. pple. of L. *relevare* raise up, RELIEVE, in med.L. take up, take possession of (a fief), pay a relief for, hold of a landlord; see -ANT.] **1.** Bearing upon, connected with, pertinent *to*, the matter in hand. **2.** *Sc. Law.* Legally pertinent or sufficient 1561. †**3.** Relieving, remedial (*rare*) –1762.

1. Many things in a controversy might seem r., if we knew to what they were intended to refer JOWETT. Hence **Re·levantly** *adv.*

†**Releva·tion.** late ME. [– OFr. *relevacion* or L. *relevatio, -on-*, f. *relevat-*, pa. ppl. stem of *relevare* RELIEVE; see -ION.] The action of raising, lifting up, supporting, relieving, etc. –1658.

Reliability (rĭlaiăbi·lĭti). 1816. [f. next + -ITY.] The quality of being reliable, reliableness.

Comb., as *r. test, trial*, etc.

Reliable (rĭlai·ăb'l), *a.* 1569. [f. RELY *v.* + -ABLE.] That may be relied upon; in which reliance or confidence may be put; trustworthy, safe, sure.

A very r. medicine 1792. Macaulay may not have been a r. guide in the regions of high art 1876. Hence **Reli·ableness. Reli·ably** *adv.*

Reliance (rĭlai·ăns). 1607. [f. RELY *v.* + -ANCE.] **1.** The (†or an) act of relying; the condition or character of being reliant; dependence, confidence. **2.** That on which one relies or depends 1798.

1. Little r. can be placed on statements unconfirmed by writing 1877. **2.** The dogs, the indispensable r. of the party, were in bad working trim KANE.

Reliant (rĭlɔi·ănt), *a.* 1856. [f. as prec. + -ANT.] Having reliance or confidence; confident, trustful.

Relic (re·lik). [ME. *relike* – (O)Fr. *relique*, orig. pl. – L. RELIQUIÆ.] **1.** In Christian use: An object (as a part of the body or clothing, an article of personal use, or the like) which remains as a memorial of a departed saint, martyr, or other holy person, and as such is carefully preserved and venerated. †**b.** Applied to the sacred objects of the ancient Jewish and pagan religions –1606. †**c.** A precious or valuable thing (*rare*) –1470. **d.** Something kept as a remembrance or souvenir; a memento 1601. **2.** *pl.* The remains of a person; the body, or part of the body, of one deceased. (Sometimes implying sense 1.) ME. **b.** *sing.* in the same sense (*rare*) 1635. **3.** *pl.* That which remains or is left behind, in later use esp. after destruction or wasting away; the remains or remaining fragments (of a thing); the remnant, residue (of a nation or people). Also occas. in *sing.* of a single thing or person. ME. **4.** A surviving trace *of* some practice, fact, idea, quality, etc. In early use chiefly *pl.* 1586. **b.** A surviving memorial *of* some occurrence, people, period, etc. 1695. **5.** An object invested with interest by reason of its antiquity or associations with the past 1596.

1. The Friars keepe for a holy relike the Thorne wherewith Christ was crowned 1617. **d.** Luther's ..apartment..contains his portrait, bible, and other relics 1838. **2.** Men took a lasting adieu of their interred Friends,..having no old experience of the duration of their Reliques SIR T. BROWNE. **3.** The relikes of a Church 1615. Treat the poor, as our Saviour did the Multitude, to the reliques of some baskets SIR T. BROWNE. After a bloody conflict of eight years.., the relics of the nation submitted GIBBON. **4.** A Relique of a certain Pagan Worship 1712. **b.** Curious relics of ancient times 1832.

Relict (re·likt), *sb.* 1450. [– L. *relictus*, pa. pple. of *relinquere* leave behind, RELINQUISH; in sense 2 – OFr. *relicte*, late L. *relicta*.] **1.** = RELIC 1, 1 d, and 5. Now *rare* or *Obs.* 1535. **2.** The widow *of* a man 1450. **3.** *pl.* Remains, remnants, residue. Also *sing.* a surviving part; †a survivor. 1598. **b.** A surviving trace, survival 1646. **c.** *pl.* The remains of one deceased (*rare*) 1649. †**4.** Leavings; refuse (*rare*) –1748.

2. He married the Earl of March's R. 1610. To the great prejudice of a poor r. and her helpless child 1776.

†**Reli·ct,** *a.* 1649. [f. as prec.; cf. DERELICT.] **1.** Left by death, surviving –1661. **2.** Of lands: **a.** Left by the recess of the sea. **b.** Abandoned, deserted. –1687.

1. His R. Lady..lived long in Westminster FULLER.

Relief¹ (rĭlī·f). ME. [– AFr. *relef*, (O)Fr. *relief*, f. *relever* (tonic stem *reliev-*) RELIEVE.] **1.** A payment, varying in value and kind according to rank and tenure, made to the overlord by the heir of a feudal tenant on taking up possession of the vacant estate. Now *Hist.* exc. in *Sc. Law.* **b.** *Hist.* Formal acknowledgement of feudal tenure made by a vassal to his lord (*rare*) ME. **2.** Ease or alleviation given to or received by a person through the removal or lessening of some cause of distress or anxiety; deliverance from what is burdensome or exhausting to the mind; mental relaxation. late ME. **b.** Ease from, or lessening of, physical pain or discomfort 1691. **c.** An agreeable change of object, esp. to the sense of sight 1712. **d.** A gradual widening in the bore of a gun-barrel towards the muzzle 1824. **3.** Aid, help, or assistance given to a person or persons in a state of poverty or want; now *spec.* assistance in money or necessary articles given to the indigent from funds administered under the Poor Law or from parish doles. late ME. †**b.** Sustenance –1613. †**c.** A fresh supply or supplies of some article of food or drink –1725. **4.** Assistance in time of danger, need, or difficulty; aid, help, or succour 1500. **b.** Aid or succour rendered to persons or places endangered by war; in later use *esp.* deliverance *of* a besieged town, etc. from the attacking force 1548. †**c.** A body of men coming to the relief of a person or place (*rare*) –1670. **5.** Release from some occupation or post of duty; in later use *spec.* of the replacing of a sentinel or watch by a fresh man or body of men 1513. **b.** One who relieves another on duty 1822. **6.** Deliverance (esp. in *Law*) from some hardship, burden, or grievance; remedy, redress 1616. **7.** Alleviation *of* some pain, burden, etc.; remission *of* a tax (*rare*) 1526. †**8.** *Hunting.* Of the hare or hart: The act of seeking food; feeding or pasturing –1668. **9.** *R. Church,* A Scottish sect founded in 1761 in assertion of the right of congregations to elect their ministers; in 1847 amalgamated with the United Secession to form the United Presbyterian Church.

2. It is a r. to turn from so painful a subject BUCKLE. **c.** A clump of beeches..was a r. to the eye 1833. **3.** In their idea of r., there is always included something of punishment BURKE. **4.** At night Boats and Pilots went off to her R. 1698. *R. works,* public works undertaken for the r. of unemployment. **b.** Stilicho..advanced..to the r. of the faithful city GIBBON. **5.** For this releefe much thankes SHAKS. Hence **Relie·f-ful** *a.*, **-less** *a.*

Relief² (rĭlī·f). 1606. [– Fr. *relief* – It. *rilievo*, †*rilevo*, f. *rilevare* raise; see RELIEVE *v.*] **1.** In the plastic arts, the elevation or projection of a design, or parts of a design, from a plane surface in order to give a natural and solid appearance; also, the degree of such projection; the part which so projects. **b.** A composition or design executed in relief 1682. **2.** The appearance of solidity or detachment given to a design or composition on a plane surface by the arrangement and disposition of the lines, colours or gradations of colour of which it is composed; hence, distinctness of outline due to contrast of colour 1789. **b.** *fig.* Vividness, distinctness, or prominence due to contrast or artistic presentation 1781. **3. a.** *Fortif.* The height to which works are raised above the bottom of the ditch 1834. **b.** *Phys. Geog.* The contour of some part of the surface of the earth considered with ref. to variations in its elevation 1865.

1. *High* (†or *great*), *low,* and *middle r.*: see ALTO-, BASSO-, MEZZO-RELIEVO, and BAS-RELIEF. **2.** A church with its dark spire in strong r. against the clear cold sky W. IRVING.

attrib.: **r. map,** a map in which the conformation of an area of the earth's surface is shown by elevations and depressions or by suitable colouring.

Relier (rĭlɔi·əɹ). *rare.* 1593. [f. RELY *v.* + -ER¹.] One who relies (*on* a person or thing).

Relievable (rĭlī·văb'l), *a.* 1670. [f. RELIEVE *v.* + -ABLE.] **a.** Capable of receiving, admitting of, legal relief; also const. *against.* **b.** That may be relieved or assisted 1707.

Relieve (rĭlī·v), *v.* [Late ME. *releve* – (O)Fr. *relever* :– L. *relevare* raise again, succour, alleviate, f. *re-* RE- + *levare* raise, f. *levis* light.] **I.** *trans.* **1.** To raise (a person) out of some trouble, difficulty, or danger; to rescue, succour, aid or assist in straits; to deliver *from* something troublesome or oppressive. Now somewhat *rare.* **b.** To bring assistance to (a besieged town); to free from siege 1586. **c.** *Law.* To free or clear (a person) from an obligation; to give (a person) legal relief. Also *absol.* 1562. **2.** To assist (the needy) by gifts of money or necessary articles; to help in poverty or necessity. late ME. **3.** To ease or free (a person, the mind, etc.) from sorrow, fear, doubt, or the like. late ME. **b.** To give (a person, part of the body, etc.) ease or relief from physical pain or discomfort. late ME. **c.** To widen or open up; to ease (some mechanical device) by making slacker or wider 1824. **4.** To ease or mitigate (what is painful or oppressive); to render less grievous or burdensome. late ME. **b.** To make less tedious, monotonous, or disagreeable by the introduction of variety or of something striking or pleasing 1771. **5.** *spec.* To release (a person) from guard, watch, or other duty by becoming or providing a substitute 1601. **b.** To set (a person) free *from,* to ease (a person) *of,* any task or burden 1671; *joc.* to rob *of* a thing (e.g. *He was relieved of his watch*).

1. b. Soon after Prince Rupert came to r. the Town We raised the siege LD. FAIRFAX. **2.** To r. the Confederate prisoners in the Northern prisons 1864. **3.** Proofs which should r. my mind of all doubt upon the subject TYNDALL. **b.** *To r. nature*: to evacuate urine or fæces. **4.** The final cause of compassion is much more to r. misery 1729. **b.** No great work relieved the barrenness of the time 1869.

†**II. 1.** To lift or raise up again –1533. **2.** *intr.* **a.** To rise again –1533. **b.** To return or rally in battle –1513. **3.** *trans.* To take up or hold (a feudal estate) from the superior –1525. **III.** †**1.** To bring (a matter) into prominence; to make clear or evident (*rare*) –176.. **2.** To make (a thing) stand out; to render prominent or distinct; to bring into relief 1778. **b.** *intr.* To stand out in relief 1812.

2. To Ariadne is given (say the critics) a red scarf, to r. the figure from the sea which is behind her SIR J. REYNOLDS. Hence **Relie·ver,** one who or that which relieves.

†**Relie·vement.** 1443. [– OFr. *releve-*, *relievement*, f. *relever* RELIEVE; see -MENT.] The act of relieving; relief –1631.

Relieving (rĭlī·viŋ), *ppl. a.* 1681. [f. RELIEVE *v.* + -ING².] That relieves or gives relief.

R. officer, an officer appointed by a parish or union to administer relief to the poor. *R. tackle,* one of two strong tackles used to prevent a ship from overturning on the careen; also, one of those which are occasionally hooked to the tiller in bad weather, or in action, when the wheel or tiller-rope is broken or shot away. *R. arch* (Arch.), an arch formed in the substance of a wall to relieve the pressure or weight upon the wall. Hence **Relie·vingly** *adv.*

Relievo (rĭlī·vo). 1625. [– It. *rilievo*; see RELIEF².] = RELIEF² 1, 1 b, 2. *In r.*, in relief.

Religate (re·ligeⁱt), *v. rare.* 1651. [– *religat-*, pa. ppl. stem of L. *religare* bind up or back; see RE-, LIGATE *v.*] *trans.* To bind together or unite. So **Religa·tion,** the action of tying or binding up.

‖**Religieuse** (rəliʒyǒz). 1796. [Fr., fem. of next.] A woman bound by religious vows, or devoted to a religious life; a nun.

‖**Religieux** (rəliʒyö). Now *rare* or *Obs.* 1654. [Fr. – L. *religiosus* RELIGIOUS.] A man vowed to a religious life; a monk.

Religio-, mod. comb. form of RELIGION or RELIGIOUS, as in *r.-educational, -magical,* etc.

Religion (rĭli·dʒən). ME. [– AFr. *religiun*, (O)Fr. *religion* – L. *religio, -on-*, obligation (as of an oath), bond between man and the gods, scrupulousness, scruple(s), reverence for the gods; in late L. (from V) religious (monastic) life; of disputed origin.] **1.** A state of life bound by monastic vows; the condition of one who is a member of a religious order; the religious life. **2.** A particular monastic or religious order or rule; †a religious house. Now *rare.* ME. **3.** Action or conduct indicating a belief in, reverence for, and desire to please, a divine ruling power; the exercise or practice of rites or observances implying this. Also *pl.*, religious rites. Now *rare,* exc. as implied in 5. ME. **4.** A particular system of faith and worship ME. †**b.** *The R.* [after Fr.]: the Reformed Religion, Protestantism –1674. **5.** Recognition on the part of man of some higher unseen power as having control of his destiny, and as being entitled to obedience, reverence, and worship; the general mental and moral attitude resulting from this belief, with ref. to its effect upon the individual or the community; personal or general acceptance of this feeling as a standard of spiritual and practical life 1535. †**6.** *transf.* Devotion to some principle; strict fidelity or faithfulness; conscientiousness; pious affection or attachment –1691. †**7.** The religious sanction or obligation *of* an oath, etc. –1704.

1. My father..was retired into r. in the Kingdom of Naples H. WALPOLE. †*Man of r.*, one bound by monastic vows or in holy orders. †*House,* etc. *of r.*, a religious house, a monastery or nunnery. **2.** Some ships of the r. of Malta 1769. **3.** The public r. of the Catholics was uniformly simple and spiritual GIBBON. **4.** I wonder what r. he is of B. JONS. All important religions have sprung up in the East 1862. *transf.* We hear men speak of a r. of art, of a r. of work, of a r. of civilization 1872. **5.** There are no signes..of R., but in Man onely HOBBES. Therfore on thy firme hand r. leanes In peace, & reck'ns thee her eldest son MILT. Phr.

To get r.: see GET *v.* I. 10. **6.** *Rom. & Jul.* I. ii. 93. Phr. *To make (a) r. of* or *to make (it) r. to*, to make a point of, to be scrupulously careful (†not) to do something. Hence **Reli·gionless** *a.* destitute of r.

Religionary (rĭli·dʒənări), *a.* and *sb.* 1663. [f. prec. + -ARY[1], or – Fr. *religionnaire* Protestant, Calvinist.] **A.** *adj.* Relating to religion; religious. Now *rare.* 1691. †**B.** *sb.* **a.** A person 'in religion'. **b.** A Protestant. –1760.

Religioner (rĭli·dʒənəɹ). 1812. [f. as prec. + -ER[1].] **a.** A person 'in religion'. **b.** = RELIGIONIST.

Religionism (rĭli·dʒeniz'm). 1791. [f. RELIGION + -ISM.] Marked or excessive inclination to religion; exaggerated or affected religious zeal.

Religionist (rĭli·dʒənist). 1653. [f. as prec. + -IST.] One addicted or attached to religion; one imbued with, or zealous for, religion. Occas., a religious zealot or pretender.

These pretended religionists are really a kind of superstitious atheists HUME. A dispassionate, placid, and mild r. 1812.

Religionize (rĭli·dʒənəiz), *v.* 1716. [f. as prec. + -IZE.] **a.** *trans.* To imbue with religion, to render religious. **b.** *intr.* To be addicted to, to affect, religion.

Religiose (rĭlidʒiō^u·s), *a.* 1853. [– L. *religiosus* RELIGIOUS; see -OSE[1].] Religious to excess; unduly occupied with religion; morbidly or sentimentally religious.

Religiosity (rĭlidʒiǫ·sĭti). late ME. [– L. *religiositas*, f. *religiosus*, see next, -ITY; in more recent use perh. after Fr. *religiosité*.] Religiousness, religious feeling or sentiment. **b.** Affected or excessive religiousness 1799.

Religious (rĭli·dʒəs), *a.* and *sb.* ME. [– AFr. *religius*, OFr. *religious* (mod. *-eux*) – L. *religiosus*; see RELIGION, -OUS.] **A.** *adj.* **1.** Imbued with religion; exhibiting the spiritual or practical effects of religion; pious, godly. **2.** Of persons: Bound by monastic vows; belonging to a religious order ME. **b.** Of things, places, etc.: Of, belonging to, or connected with, a monastic order ME. **3.** Of the nature of, pertaining or appropriate to, concerned or connected with, religion 1538. **b.** (Chiefly *poet.*) Regarded as sacred 1618. **4.** *transf.* Scrupulous, exact, strict, conscientious 1599.

1. That sober Race of Men, whose lives R. titl'd them the Sons of God MILT. Phr. *Most r.*, used as an epithet of royalty. **2.** Houses of r. women 1745. **b.** Those r. places that are neare Oxford WOOD. **3.** Storied Windows richly dight, Casting a dimm r. light MILT. Prayer is the most directly r. of all our duties J. H. NEWMAN. **b.** Thy Shrine in some r. wood COLLINS. **4.** A Coward, a most deuout Coward, r. in it SHAKS. His library is preserved with the most r. neatness GOLDSM.

B. *sb.* **1.** As *pl.* Persons bound by monastic vows or devoted to the religious life according to the rules of an order or congregation in a Christian church ME. **b.** With ref. to non-Christian religions 1585. **2.** *sing.* A person devoted to the religious life, as a monk or nun ME. Hence **Reli·gious-ly** *adv.*, **-ness**.

Reli·ne (rī-), *v.*[1] 1851. [f. RE- 4 + LINE *v.*[1]] *trans.* To provide with a new lining.

Reli·ne (rī-), *v.*[2] 1875. [f. RE- 4 + LINE *v.*[2]] *trans.* To renew the lines of.

Relinquent (rĭli·ŋkwĕnt), *a.* and *sb.* *rare.* 1847. [– L. *relinquens, -ent-*, pr. pple. of *relinquere*; see next, -ENT. Cf. DELINQUENT.] **A.** *adj.* Relinquishing; vanquishing. **B.** *sb.* One who relinquishes.

Relinquish (rĭli·ŋkwiʃ), *v.* 1472. [f. *relinquiss-*, lengthened stem of OFr. *relinquir* – L. *relinquere*, f. *re-* RE- + *linquere* leave; see -ISH[2].] †**1.** *trans.* To withdraw from, desert, abandon (a person). *rare.* –1552. †**b.** To give up as incurable. SHAKS. **2.** To give up or give over, to abandon, desist from (an idea, action, practice, etc.); to cease to hold, adhere to, or prosecute 1497. †**b.** To desist from putting forward for office. H. WALPOLE. **3.** To give up, resign, surrender (a possession, right, etc.). Also const. *to.* 1560. **b.** To let go (something held) 1850. †**4.** To leave behind (*rare*) –1679. †**5.** *intr.* To disappear, pass away. B. JONS.

1. I..shall vtterlye renounce, refuse, r., & forsake the bishop of Rome *Bk. Com. Prayer.* **2.** Alarmed by this intelligence, he hastily relinquished the siege GIBBON. **3.** They know my disinclination to r. the command WELLINGTON. Hence **Reli·nquishment**, the act of relinquishing; abandonment, giving up, surrender.

‖**Reliquaire** (re·likwē^əɹ). 1769. [Fr.; see next.] = next.

Reliquary (re·likwări), *sb.* 1656. [– (O)Fr. *reliquaire*, f. *relique* RELIC; see -ARY[1]. Cf. med.L. *reliquiarium*.] A small box, casket, shrine, etc., in which a relic or relics are kept.

Re·liquary, *a.* *rare.* 1826. [attrib. use of prec.] Belonging to a relic or relics.

‖**Reliquiæ** (rĭli·kwi,ī), *pl.* 1835. [L. fem. sb. pl., f. *reliquus* remaining, f. *re-* RE- + *liq-* stem of *linquere* leave.] **1.** Remains of any kind; *spec.* in *Geol.* remains of early animals or plants 1840. **2.** *Bot.* 'The withered remains of leaves, which, not being articulated with the stem, cannot fall off, but decay upon it' 1835.

Relish (re·liʃ), *sb.*[1] 1530. [alt., with assim. to -ISH[2], of ME. *reles*, corresp. formally to OFr. *reles*, var. of *relais* remainder, f. *relaisser* leave behind (cf. RELEASE *v.*), but the senses of the Eng. word are not recorded in OFr.] **1.** A taste or flavour; the distinctive taste *of* anything. **b.** *transf.* A trace or tinge *of* some quality; a suggestion; a sample or specimen; a small quantity 1597. †**2.** An individual taste or liking –1758. **3.** An appetizing or pleasing flavour; a savoury or piquant taste 1665. **b.** A savoury addition to a meal; an appetiser 1798. **4.** Enjoyment of the taste or flavour of something; liking, zest 1649. †**5.** Sense of taste; power of relishing. GOLDSM.

1. A Laplander or Negro has no notion of the r. of wine HUME. **b.** Your Lordship..hath yet some smack of age in you; some rellish of the saltnesse of Time SHAKS. **3.** The tired glutton..finds no r. in the sweetest meat POPE. **b.** A r. they shall have—salt and olives and cheese JOWETT. **4.** Cranmer.. seems to have done this with great r. 1882. A moral r. for veritable proofs of honesty MORLEY.

†**Re·lish**, *sb.*[2] 1561. [perh. ult. the same as prec.] *Mus.* A grace, ornament, or embellishment –1668.

Relish (re·liʃ), *sb.*[3] *rare.* 1611. [– OFr. *relais.*] A projection; now *spec.* in *Joinery*, the projection of the shoulder of a tenon.

Relish (re·liʃ), *v.*[1] 1586. [f. RELISH *sb.*[1]] **1.** *trans.* **a.** To give or impart a relish to (a thing); to make pleasant to the taste. †**b.** To have a taste, tinge, or trace of (some quality or thing), to partake of –1702. †**c.** To provide with something relishing; to please, gratify, delight –1794. †**2.** To taste, take a taste of; to distinguish by tasting (*rare*) –1633. †**b.** To feel. SHAKS. **3.** To enjoy, take pleasure or delight in 1599. **b.** To like, have a liking for; to care for, be pleased or satisfied with; to approve of 1594. **c.** To take or receive in a particular manner. Now *rare.* 1600. †**d.** To appreciate, understand (*rare*) –1611. **4.** *intr.* To have a (or the) taste *of* something; to savour or smack *of*, have a touch or trace *of* 1602. **5.** To taste in a particular way; to have a specified taste or relish. Now *dial.* and *U.S.* 1600. †**6.** *fig.* To be agreeable or pleasant; to find acceptance or favour (*with* a person) –1740.

1. I have also a novel..,to r. my wine MACAULAY. **c.** They send her many dainty dishes..to rellish her palate 1626. **3.** I once more smell the dew and rain, And r. versing G. HERBERT. **b.** They do not r. the prospect before them 1885. **5.** To be thus affected, would r. too much of a Cynical Humour 1703. **5.** Afflictions r. sour and bitter even to the palates of the best saints FULLER. **6.** Indeed, if a Man sets up for a Sceptick, I don't expect the Argument should R. 1697. Hence **Re·lishable** *a.* **Re·lisher.**

†**Re·lish**, *v.*[2] 1591. [app. f. RELISH *sb.*[2]] *trans.* To sing, warble –1608.

Relish (re·liʃ), *v.*[3] *rare.* 1611. [Cf. RELISH *sb.*[3]] †**1.** *intr.* To project, jut out. COTGR. **2.** *trans.* To make shoulders on (wood) in shaping tenons 1884.

Relive (rĭli·v), *v.* 1548. [f. RE- 5 a + LIVE *v.*, in early use after *revive.*] †**1.** *trans.* To raise or restore again to life; to resuscitate –1592. **2.** *intr.* To come to life again; to live anew 1548. **3.** *trans.* To live (a period of time) over again 1711.

2. Will you deliuer how this dead Queene relives? SHAKS.

†**Reli·ver**, *v.* *rare.* 1456. [– OFr. *relivrer*, f. *re-* RE- + *livrer* deliver.] *trans.* To give up again, restore –1603.

Reloa·d (rī-), *v.* 1778. [RE- 5 a.] **1.** *trans.* To make up again as a load; to furnish with a fresh load. **2. a.** *absol.* To put in a fresh gun-charge 1784. **b.** To load (a fire-arm or cartridge) again 1853.

Relocation (relokē^i·ʃən, rī-). 1575. [In sense 1 f. late L. *relocare* to relet (cf. Fr. *relocation*); in sense 2 f. RE- 5 a + LOCATION.] **1.** *Sc. Law.* *Tacit r.*, the implied renewal of a lease when the landlord allows a tenant to continue without a fresh agreement, after the original lease has expired. **2.** The action of locating afresh; a new allocation 1877.

Relucent (rĭl^iū·sĕnt), *a.* Now *rare.* 1507. [– L. *relucens, -ent-*, pr. pple. of *relucēre* shine back, or f. contemp. LUCENT; see -ENT.] Casting back light; shining, gleaming, bright, refulgent.

In brighter mazes the r. stream Plays o'er the mead THOMSON. So **Relu·cence, -ency.**

Reluct (rĭlɒ·kt), *v.* 1526. [– L. *reluctari* struggle against, f. *re-* RE- + *luctari* struggle.] †**1.** *intr.* To strive or struggle *to* do something –1633. **2.** To struggle, strive, or rebel *against*, to show dislike, to revolt *at*, to offer opposition *to*, a thing 1547. **b.** Without prep.: To offer opposition; to manifest or express reluctance; to object 1648.

2. I..r. at the inevitable course of destiny LAMB.

Reluctance (rĭlɒ·ktăns). 1641. [f. RELUCTANT; see -ANCE.] **1.** The act of struggling *against* something; resistance, opposition. Now *rare.* **b.** *Electr.* The property, in a magnetic circuit, of opposing to a certain extent the passage of the magnetic lines of force 1888. **2.** Unwillingness, disinclination. Freq. in phr. *with* (or *without*) *r.* 1667. †**3.** A struggle or qualm of conscience. PEPYS.

1. Untam'd r., and revenge MILT. **2.** There is nothing which we receive with so much R. as Advice ADDISON. Your r. to put the vanity of an author out of countenance CIBBER.

Reluctancy (rĭlɒ·ktănsi). Now *rare.* 1621. [See next and -ANCY, and cf. prec.] †**1.** An internal or mutual struggle or contest –1662. †**2.** Resistance or opposition of one thing *to* another –1665. †**b.** Resistance or opposition on the part of persons *against* or *to* something. Also *pl.* –1679. **3.** = RELUCTANCE 2. 1634.

3. The slowness and r. with which errors yield to conviction 1826.

Reluctant (rĭlɒ·ktănt), *a.* 1667. [– L. *reluctans, -ant-*, pr. pple. of *reluctari*; see RELUCT, -ANT.] **1.** Struggling; writhing (*rare*). **b.** Offering resistance or opposition *to* something (*rare*) 1726. **2.** Unwilling, averse, disinclined 1706. **b.** *transf.* of things 1667. **3.** Characterized by unwillingness, disinclination, or distaste 1725.

1. Down he fell A monstrous Serpent on his Belly prone, R., but in vaine MILT. **2.** Edward was still r. to begin the war GREEN. **b.** R. on its rusty hinge Revolved an iron door SCOTT. **3.** R. consent BURKE. Hence **Relu·ctantly** *adv.*

Reluctate (rĭlɒ·ktē^it), *v.* 1643. [– *reluctat-*, pa. ppl. stem of L. *reluctari*; see RELUCT, -ATE[3].] **1.** *intr.* To offer resistance; to strive or struggle *against* something; to show reluctance. **2.** *trans.* To strive against, refuse, reject (*rare*) 1681.

1. Having..something within him, which reluctated against those superstitions FULLER. So **Relucta·tion**, struggle, resistance, opposition; †reluctance, unwillingness.

Reluctivity (relɒkti·vĭti). 1888. [f. RELUCTANCE 1 b, after *conductance/conductivity*; cf. *resistance, resistivity*.] *Electr.* Degree of magnetic reluctance.

Relume (rĭl^iū·m), *v.* 1604. [f. RE- 4 + *-lume* of ILLUME, partly after Fr. *rallumer* or late L. *reluminare.*] **1.** *trans.* To relight, rekindle; to cause to burn afresh. **2.** To make clear or bright again 1746. **3.** To light up again; to re-illuminate; to shine upon anew 1786.

1. I know not where is that Promethean heate That can thy Light re-Lume SHAKS. **3.** And Shakspeare's sun relumes the clouded stage 1786.

Relu·mine, *v.* *rare.* 16.. [– late L. *reluminare*; see RE- and ILLUMINE.] *trans.* = prec.

Rely (rĭləi·), *v.* ME. [– OFr. *relier* bind together :– L. *religare* bind closely, f. *re-* RE- + *ligare* bind.] †**1.** *trans.* To gather (soldiers, followers, etc.) together; to assemble, to rally –1608. **2.** *intr.* To depend *on* a person or thing with full trust or confidence; to rest *upon* with assurance 1574. **b.** With ref. to facts or statements 1809. †**c.** To rest *upon* a support –1683. **3.** To put trust or confidence *in* a person or thing. Somewhat *rare.* 1606. †**4.** *refl* and *trans.* To repose (oneself, one's soul, faith, etc.) *on, upon,* or *in* some person or thing –1641.

2. Go in thy native innocence, relie On what thou hast of vertue MILT. Can I r. upon your secrecy? DICKENS. **3.** Asdrubal placed his Gauls (in whom he least rely'd) in the Left Wing 1654.

Remain (rĭmēⁱ·n), *sb.*[1] 1456. [Partly – OFr. *remain,* f. *remaindre* (see REMAIN *v.*); partly immed. f. the vb.] **I.** †**1.** Those left, surviving, or remaining out of a number of persons; the remainder or rest –1671. **2.** That which remains or is left (unused, undestroyed, etc.) of some thing or quantity of things; also, that which remains to be done. Now *rare.* 1529. †**b.** (Also *pl.*) The balance or unpaid remainder of a sum of money –1669. **3.** A remaining or surviving part or fragment of something. Now *rare.* 1570. **4.** (With *pl.*) **a.** A survival; a relic *of* some obsolete custom or practice; a surviving trait or characteristic. Now *rare.* 1641. **b.** A material relic (*of* antiquity, etc.); an ancient monument, building, or other structure; an object which has come down from past times 1687. †**c.** A literary relic –1738.

1. I believe the number of these sent will be about a hundred; the r. also being forty or fifty CROMWELL. **2.** *Cymb.* III. i. 87. **3.** When this r. of horror has entirely subsided BURKE. Every yet inedited r. of Anglosaxon 1843. **4. b.** The supposition..that Low Hill is a Druidical r. 1864.

II. *pl.* **1.** Surviving members of a company, family, or other body of persons. Also rarely of a single person. 1456. **2.** The remaining parts *of* some thing or things; all that is left of something; articles remaining from a store or stock 1500. **b.** Const. *of* the destroying force (*rare*) 1715. **c.** Const. as *sing.* 1801. **3. a.** The literary works (*esp.* the unpublished ones) left by an author; also, the fragments of an ancient writer 1652. **b.** That which is left of a person when life is extinct; the (dead) body, corpse 1700. **c.** Substances of organic origin preserved in the earth in a fossilized condition 1799.

2. The wretched remains of a ruined reputation '*Junius' Lett.* **c.** This short remains of happiness 1801. **3. a.** The remains of Clement and Polycarp 1873. **b.** I saw..her poor remains laid at rest in the convent garden 1797.

†**Remai·n,** *sb.*[2] *rare.* 1470. [f. the vb.] Stay –1605.

A..worke..Which often since my heere remaine in England, I haue seene him do SHAKS.

Remain (rĭmēⁱ·n), *v.* late ME. [f. *remain-, remein-,* tonic stem of OFr. *remanoir* :– L. *remanēre,* f. *re-* RE- + *manēre* remain; or – OFr. *remaindre* :– Rom. **remanere,* for L. *remanēre.*] **1.** *intr.* To be left after the removal or appropriation of some part, number, or quantity. **2.** To be left over and above what has already been done or dealt with in some way. late ME. †**3.** To continue to belong *to* one –1605. **4.** To continue in the same place (or with the same person); to abide, stay 1439. †**b.** To dwell –1611. **5.** With complement: To continue to be 1509. **b.** To continue in the same state; to lie untouched or undisturbed 1839. **6.** To continue to exist; to have permanence; to be still existing or extant. late ME. †**b.** To stick in the mind. Const. *with.* SHAKS. **c.** To continue with (a person). MILT. **7.** To await, be left for (a person). *rare.* 1579.

1. There is not Sap enough remaining to nourish the Leaves 1707. **2.** Nothing remaines, but that I kindle the boy thither SHAKS. What remains to tell TENNYSON. **3.** *Lear* I. i. 82. **4.** Charles remained six days in Paris ROBERTSON. **b.** But for my Mistris, I nothing know where she remaines SHAKS. **5.** I formed them free, and free they must r. MILT. *I r.,* as the concluding formula of a letter; I r., my dear friend, Affectionately yours, W.C. 1793. **6.** A little Verse my All that shall r. GRAY. **7.** If thence he scape.., what remains him less Then unknown dangers and as hard escape MILT.

Remainder (rĭmēⁱ·ndəɹ), *sb.*[1] late ME. [– AFr. *remainder* = OFr. *remaindre* (see prec.) subst. use of infin.; see -ER[4].] **1.** *Law.* The residual or further interest remaining over from an estate, coming into effect when this has determined, and created by the same conveyance by which the estate was granted. **b.** So *r. over.* Sometimes = a further remainder. 1544. **c.** *transf.* The right to succeed to a title or position on the death of the holder; *esp.* the right of succession to a peerage expressly assigned to a certain person or line of descent in default of male issue in the direct line 1809. **2. a.** Those still left out of a number of persons; the rest 1547. **b.** That which is left when part has been taken away, used, dealt with, etc.; the residue 1560. **3.** †**a.** A single person, or a few persons, remaining out of a number –1697. **b.** A remaining (†or still existing) part or fragment; chiefly *pl.* = remains, *esp.* of ancient buildings 1604. **c.** A remaining trace *of* some practice, quality, feeling, etc. Now *rare.* 1641. **4. a.** *Arith.* The number which remains after subtraction of a lesser from a greater; the excess after a process of division 1571. **b.** = REMAIN *sb.*[1] I. 2 b. SHAKS. **5.** In the book-trade: A number of copies remaining unsold out of an edition (esp. after the demand for it has fallen off or ceased), and frequently disposed of at a reduced price 1791. **6.** *attrib.* or *adj.* Remaining, left over; reserve 1567.

1. *Cross remainders,* estates in r. arising where lands are devised to two or more persons in tail, with r. to either upon failure of the other's issue. *R. man.* the person to whom a r. is devised. **2. a.** We drove the R. headlong off the Deck 1737. **b.** He should be permitted to pass the r. of his life in..exile GIBBON. **3. c.** If you have any remainders of modesty or truth cry God mercy MILT. **6.** His braine..is as drie as the r. bisket After a voyage SHAKS. Hence **Remai·nder** *v. trans.* to sell (a number of books, etc.) as remainders. **Remai·ndership** (*Law*) the possession of a r.; the fact of there being a r.

†**Remai·nder,** *sb.*[2] *rare.* 1594. [f. as prec.] Stay; time of staying or remaining –1646.

†**Remai·ndment.** 1596. [irreg. f. REMAINDER *sb.*[1]] *Law.* A remainder. BACON.

Remand (rĭma·nd), *sb.* 1771. [f. the vb.] **1.** The act of remanding, or the fact of being remanded; now *spec.* recommittal of an accused person to custody. **2.** A remanded prisoner 1888.

Remand (rĭma·nd), *v.* late ME. [– late and med.L. *remandare,* f. *re-* RE- + L. *mandare* command, send word.] **1.** *trans.* To send (a thing) back again *to* a place; to reconsign; also, to remit, consign. **2.** To send back (a person); to command or order to go back *to* a place 1588. **b.** Of a court or magistrate: To send back (a prisoner) into custody, now *spec.* in order that further evidence on the charge may be obtained 1643. **3.** To call or summon back, to recall. Now *rare* or *Obs.* 1525. †**4.** To demand back from another –1677.

1. Both dissuaded me from suffering it to be represented on the stage; and accordingly it was remanded back to my shelf FIELDING. **2. b.** The said A. is remanded into custody 1794. **3.** He remanded his own [men] from the pursuit 1656.

Remanence (re·mănĕns). 1666. [– med.L. *remanentia* (XII) remnant, remainder; see REMAIN *v.,* -ENCE.] **1.** That which remains; residuum (*rare*). **2.** The fact of remaining; permanence. COLERIDGE. So †**Re·manency.**

†**Re·manent,** *sb.* late ME. [subst. use of next; but cf. med.L. *remanens* (XI) remnant.] The remainder, the remaining part, the rest –1651. **2.** A remaining part or amount; a remnant; *pl.* remains –1632. **3.** *Arith.* A remainder –1559.

Remanent (re·mănĕnt), *a.* Now *rare.* late ME. [– L. *remanens, -ent-,* pr. pple. of *remanēre*; see REMAIN, -ENT.] †**1.** In predicative use: Remaining, staying, abiding; continuing to exist –1649. **2.** Left behind, remaining, when the rest is removed, used, done, etc. Now *rare.* late ME. **3.** *Law.* = next 2 a. 1808.

1. There is no effect r. upon the body JER. TAYLOR.

Remanet (re·mănet). 1511. [app. a med.L. subst. use of L. *remanet* 'there, or it, remains', 3rd sing. pr. ind. of *remanēre* REMAIN *v.*] **1.** A remainder. **2. a.** *Law.* A cause or suit of which the hearing is postponed to another day or term 1734. **b.** A parliamentary bill left over till another session 1870.

Remark (rĭmā·ɹk), *sb.*[1] 1654. [– Fr. *remarque,* f. *remarquer* REMARK *v.*] †**1.** The fact or quality of being worthy of notice or comment –1702. **2.** Observation, notice; comment 1680. **b.** Air of observation; look. THOMSON. **3. a.** An act of observing or noticing; an observation. Now *rare.* 1660. **b.** A verbal or written observation; a comment; a brief expression of opinion or criticism 1673. †**4.** A sign, mark, indication –1709.

1. In which there were three Women, but of no great r. 1702. **2.** Lord R. Churchill's latest escapade..is the theme of general r. 1885. **3. b.** He could not bear to hear Mr. Barker's chaffing remarks 1883.

Remark (rĭmā·ɹk), *sb.*[2] Also **re-mark.** 1880. Anglicized f. REMARQUE.

Remark (rĭmā·ɹk), *v.* 1633. [– Fr. *remarquer*; see RE-, MARK *v.*] †**1.** *trans.* To mark out, distinguish –1671. †**b.** To point out, indicate –1742. **2.** To observe, take notice of, perceive 1675. **3.** To say, utter, or set down, as an observation or comment 1704. **b.** *intr.* To make a remark *on* a thing 1859.

1. His manacles r. him, there he sits MILT. **2.** Has not your highness remarked it? H. WALPOLE. **b.** The singular fact remarked on by several observers DARWIN.

Remarkable (rĭmā·ɹkăb'l), *a.* and *sb.* 1604. [– Fr. *remarquable*; see prec., -ABLE.] **A.** *adj.* **1.** Worthy of remark, notice, or observation; hence, extraordinary, unusual, singular. †**2.** Perceptible; admitting of being observed or noted –1766. †**b.** Conspicuous, noticeable –1801.

1. The oddes is gone, And there is nothing left remarkeable Beneath the visiting Moone SHAKS. **2.** A demure look, and some other r. signs of grace 1704.

B. *sb.* A noteworthy thing or circumstance; something extraordinary or exceptional. Chiefly in *pl.* Now *arch.* 1639.

After lunch to-day we..set forth to see the remarkables of Oxford HAWTHORNE. Hence **Remarkabi·lity, Rema·rkableness,** the fact or character of being r. **Rema·rkably** *adv.* in a r. manner.

Remarker (rĭmā·ɹkəɹ). Now *rare.* 1684. [f. REMARK *v.* + -ER[1].] †**1.** One who makes or publishes remarks on a literary work; a reviewer or critic; also, an author of 'Remarks' on some subject –1795. **2.** One who makes observations; an observer, commenter 1684.

‖**Remarque** (rəmark). 1882. [Fr.] *Engraving.* A distinguishing feature indicating a certain state of the plate, usu. consisting in the insertion of a slight sketch in the margin. Also *attrib.* in *r.-proof.*

‖**Remblai** (raṅblę). Also in pl. form **remblais.** 1794. [Fr., f. *remblayer* embank, f. *re-* RE- + *emblayer* heap up. Cf. DÉBLAI.] **1.** *Fortif.* The earth used to form a rampart, or embankment. **2.** *Mining.* Material used to fill up the excavations made in a thick seam of coal 1867.

Rembrandtesque (rembrante·sk), *a.* 1879. [f. name of *Rembrandt,* the Du. painter and etcher (1608–1669), + -ESQUE.] Resembling the manner or style of Rembrandt. So **Re·mbrandtish** *a.* 1860.

Remeant (rĭ·miănt), *a. rare.* 1848. [– L. *remeans, remeant-,* pr. pple. of *remeare* return, f. *re-* RE- + *meare* pass; see -ANT.] Returning.

Remede, remeid (rĭmī·d). Now *arch.* late ME. [– (O)Fr. *remède* – L. *remedium* REMEDY *sb.*] Remedy, redress.

Remediable (rĭmī·diăb'l), *a.* 1491. [– (O)Fr. *remédiable* or L. *remediabilis* curable, (later) curative; see REMEDY *v.,* -ABLE.] †**1.** Capable of remedying; remedial –1596. **2.** Capable of being remedied or redressed 1570. Hence **Reme·diableness. Reme·diably** *adv.*

Remedial (rĭmī·diăl), *a.* 1651. [– late L. *remedialis,* f. L. *remedium* REMEDY *sb.*; see -AL[1].] Affording a remedy, tending to relieve or redress.

Every good political institution must have a preventive operation as well as a r. BURKE. Suffering is a medicine, r. though bitter 1862. Hence **Reme·dially** *adv.*

Remediless (re·mĭdilės), *a.* late ME. [f. next + -LESS; orig. stressed *remē·diless.*] **1.** Of persons, etc.: Destitute of remedy; having no prospect of aid or rescue. Now *rare* or *Obs.* **2.** Of trouble, disease, etc.: Not admitting of remedy; incapable of being remedied, cured, or redressed 1513.

1. I'll rear up Malta, now r. MARLOWE. **2.** Grief—deep r. grief SHELLEY. Hence **Re·mediless-ly** *adv.,* **-ness.**

Remedy (re·mĭdi), *sb.* ME. [– AFr. *remedie* = (O)Fr. *remède* – L. *remedium* medicine, means of relief, in med.L. concession, f. *re-* RE- + *med-*, stem of *mederi* heal.] **1.** A cure for a disease or other disorder of body or mind; any medicine or treatment which alleviates pain and promotes restoration to health. **2.** A means of counteracting or removing an outward evil of any kind; reparation, redress, relief ME. **3.** Legal redress 1450. **4.** *Coining.* The small margin within which coins as minted are allowed to vary from the standard fineness and weight. Also called *tolerance*. late ME. **5.** At various schools (as still at St. Paul's and Winchester): A time specially granted for recreation; a half-holiday 1518.

1. The only R. is to lay the Bone open 1702. *fig.* Withdraw thy Action, and depart in Peace; The R. is worse than the Disease DRYDEN. The only r. for superstition is knowledge 1862. **2.** A r. against those optical deceptions 1837. Phr. *There is no r.* (= way out of it, help for it, alternative) *but*, etc. †*No r.*, unavoidably. **3.** Left to the remedie, which the Law of the place alloweth them HOBBES.

Remedy (re·mĭdi), *v.* late ME. [– (O)Fr. *remédier* or L. *remediare*, f. *remedium* REMEDY *sb.*] **1.** *trans.* †**a.** To grant (a person) legal remedy; to right (a person) in respect of a wrong suffered –1662. **b.** To bring remedy to (a person, diseased part, etc.); to heal, cure, make whole again. Now *rare*. 1470. **2.** To cure (a disease, etc.); to put right, reform (a state of things); to rectify, make good. late ME.

1. b. Into the woods..shee went, To seeke for hearbes that mote him r. SPENSER. **2.** They tooke up Armes to remedie their wrong DRAYTON. A great deal has been done to r. the deficiency 1853.

Remember (rĭme·mbəɹ), *v.* ME. [– OFr. *remembrer* :– late L. *rememorari* call to mind, f. *re-* RE- + *memor* mindful.] **I. 1.** *trans.* To retain in, or recall to, the memory; to bear in mind. **b.** With *inf.* To bear in mind, not to forget, *to* do something. late ME. **2.** To think of, recall the memory of (a person) with some kind of feeling or intention. late ME. **b.** To bear (a person) in mind as entitled to a gift, recompense, or fee, or in making one's will; hence, to fee, reward, 'tip' 1470. †**3.** To record, mention, make mention of (a thing, person, etc.) –1749. †**b.** To commemorate –1658. **c.** To have mind *of* and mention (a person, his condition, etc.) in prayer 1602. **4.** *absol.* or *intr.* To have or bear in mind; to recall to the mind; also, to exercise or possess the faculty of memory. late ME. **5.** *refl.* To bethink or recollect, †to think or reflect upon (oneself). Now *rare*. late ME. **6. a.** *impers.* (*It*) *remembers me* [after OFr. (*il*) *me remembre*], I remember. Now *arch.* late ME. **b.** *To be remembered*, to remember; also const. *of*. *Obs.* exc. *dial.* 1440.

1. I was..left by my father, whom I cannot r., to the care of an uncle JOHNSON. Phr. †*R. your courtesy*, be covered. **b.** You will also r. to take bonds for the money BERKELEY. **2.** Remembre thy maker in thy youth, or euer the dayes of aduersite come COVERDALE *Eccl.* 12:1. **b.** Anon, anon, I pray you r. the Porter SHAKS. **3. b.** *Temp.* I. ii. 405. **c.** Nimph, in thy Orisons Be all my sins rememberd SHAKS. **4.** That shallow vassall.. which as I r., hight Costard SHAKS. **b.** To have mind, memory, or recollection *of* something (now *rare* exc. in U.S.) CHAUCER. **5.** *Lear* IV. vi. 233. **6. a.** Whan that it remembreth me Up-on my yowthe CHAUCER.

II. 1. To remind (a person); esp. to put (one) in mind *of* a thing or person. Now *arch.* or *dial.* late ME. †**2.** To recall (a thing or person) *to* a person. Also with double obj., obj. clause, and without const. –1672. **b.** To mention (a person) *to* another as sending a friendly greeting. Also without const. 1560.

1. Emanuel..remember'd Azem of his Promises 1745. **2.** By onely remembring them the truth of what they themselves know to be heer missaffirmed MILT. **b.** R. me In all humilitie vnto his Highnesse SHAKS. Katty Tatham desires to be remembered to you all 1872. Hence **Reme·mberable** *a.* capable or worthy of being remembered. **Reme·mberably** *adv.* **Reme·mberer,** one who, or that which, remembers (†or reminds).

Remembrance (rĭme·mbrăns). ME. [– OFr. *remembrance* (AFr. *-aunce*), f. *remembrer*; see prec., -ANCE.] **1.** Memory or recollection in relation to a particular thing. **2.** That operation of the mind which is involved in recalling a thing or fact; recollection. Freq. personified, or in fig. context. late ME. †**b.** Faculty or power of remembering or calling to mind –1631. **3.** With possess. pron. (A person's) memory or recollection; also, in later use, (a person's) power of remembering (cf. prec.). late ME. **b.** The point at which one's memory of events begins, or the period over which it extends 1565. **4.** The memory (†or thought) which one has *of* a thing or person. late ME. **b.** With *a* and *pl.* A recollection, reminiscence 1601. **c.** The surviving memory of a person 1579. **d.** *pl.* Greetings expressive of remembrance 1789. †**5.** Mention, notice –1631. †**b.** A memorial inscription –1599. †**6.** The act of reminding or putting in mind –1659. †**7.** A memorandum –1676. †**b.** A reminder; a remark intended to remind –1638. **8.** A keepsake, souvenir; a token. late ME. **b.** A memorial or record of some fact, person, etc. Now *rare*. 1470.

1. This ever grateful in r. bear POPE. R. rises faint and dim Of sorrows suffer'd long ago 1816. Phr. *To have in r., to call to r.* **2.** Not for thy life, lest fierce r. wake My sudden rage MILT. **b.** This Lord of weake r. SHAKS. **3.** But now is my r. weak with eld 1864. **b.** Thee I have heard relating what was don Ere my r. MILT. **4.** The dear r. of his native coast POPE. **b.** How sharpe the point of this r. is SHAKS. **5. b.** *Hen. V.* I. ii. 229. **7. b.** 2 *Hen. IV*, V. ii. 115. **8. b.** On his brest a bloodie Crosse he bore, The deare r. of his dying Lord SPENSER.

Remembrancer (rĭme·mbrănsəɹ). 1455. [– AFr. *remembrauncer*, f. *remembraunce*; see prec., -ER[2] 2.] **1.** The name of certain officials of the Court of Exchequer. **b.** An official of the Corporation of the City of London, whose chief duty now is to represent that body before parliamentary committees and at Council and Treasury Boards 1710. **2.** One who reminds another; in former use, *esp.* one engaged or appointed for that purpose 1523. **3.** *fig.* of things; also, a thing serving to remind one; a reminder; a memento, souvenir 1589. **b.** A memorandum-book. THACKERAY. †**4.** One who sends remembrances to another. PEPYS.

1. The *King's* (or *Queen's*) *R.*, an officer responsible for the collection of debts due to the Sovereign; now an officer of the Supreme Court. **3.** Premature consolation is but the r. of sorrow GOLDSM.

†**Reme·morate,** *v.* 1460. [– *rememorat-*, pa. ppl. stem of late L. *rememorari*; see RE-, MEMORATE *v.*] **a.** *trans.* To remind, put in mind (of). Also *absol.* **b.** *intr.* To remember. –1685. So **Rememora·tion** (now *rare*), the action of remembering (†or reminding); an instance of this.

†**Reme·morative,** *a.* and *sb.* 1449. [– Fr. *remémoratif* or med.L. *rememorativus*, f. as prec.; see -IVE.] **A.** *adj.* Serving to remind –1641. **B.** *sb.* A reminder –1676.

†**Re·menant.** ME. [– OFr. *remenant*, subst. use of pr. pple. of *remenoir* REMAIN; see -ANT, REMNANT.] **1.** The rest or remainder. Also *pl.* –1573. **2.** A remaining thing or part; a remnant –1433.

†**Reme·rcy,** *v.* 1477. [– Fr. *remercier*, f. *re-* RE- + *merci* thanks; see MERCY.] To thank –1592.

She him remercied as the Patrone of her life SPENSER. So †**Reme·rcy** *sb.* thanks –1606.

‖**Remex** (rī·meks). *Pl.* **remiges** (re·midʒīz). 1767. [L., f. *remus* oar.] *Ornith.* One of the principal feathers of a bird's wing, by which it is sustained and carried forward in flight; a wing-quill. Chiefly *pl.* Hence **Remi·gial** *a.* (*rare*) serving to propel; of or pertaining to the remiges.

Remiform (re·mifǭɹm), *a.* *rare.* 1860. [f. L. *remus* oar + -FORM] Shaped like an oar.

Remigrate (re·migreit, rĭməi·greit), *v.* 1601. [orig. – *remigrat-*, pa. ppl. stem of L. *remigrare* journey back; later, f. RE- 5 a + MIGRATE *v.*] †**1.** *intr.* To change back again –1680. **2.** To migrate again or back 1623. So **Remigra·tion,** the action of remigrating; return.

Remind (rĭməi·nd), *v.* 1645. [f. RE- 5 a + MIND *v.*, prob. after REMEMORATE, still current in XVII.] **1.** *trans.* To recall (a thing) to one's own mind; to remember, recollect. Now *rare* or *Obs.* †**b.** To recall to another's mind (*rare*) –1669. **2.** To put (a person) in mind *of* something, *to do* something, etc. 1660.

2. The time of year reminds me how the months have gone DICKENS.

Reminder (rĭməi·ndəɹ). 1653. [f. prec. + -ER[1].] Something which reminds one; mention made for the purpose of reminding. **b.** *Path.* in *pl.* Secondary syphilitic symptoms 1897.

Remi·ndful, *a.* 1810. [f. as prec. + -FUL.] **1.** Mindful, retaining the memory, *of*. **2.** Reminiscent, reviving the memory, *of* 1864.

Reminisce (remini·s), *v.* *colloq.* or *joc.* 1829. [Back-formation from next.] **1.** *trans.* and *intr.* To recollect, remember. **2.** *intr.* To indulge in reminiscences 1882.

Reminiscence (remini·sĕns). 1589. [– late L. *reminiscentia* (Tertullian), f. L. *reminisci* remember, f. *re-* RE- + **men-* (see MIND *sb.*). Cf. (O)Fr. *réminiscence*.] **1.** The act, process, or fact of remembering or recollecting; sometimes *spec.* the act of recovering knowledge by mental effort. **2.** (Chiefly *pl.*) **a.** A recollection or remembrance, as a mental fact 1813. **b.** A recollection or remembrance of some past fact or experience related to others; freq. (in *pl.*), the collective memories or experiences of a person put into literary form 1811. **3.** A feature, fact, etc., which recalls something else 1860.

1. The other part of memory, called R.: which is the Retreiving of a thing, at present forgot, or but confusely remembred 1692. **2. b.** As he listened to these reminiscences of the sailors PRESCOTT.

†**Remini·scency.** 1655. [f. as prec.; see -ENCY.] The faculty of reminiscence –1732.

Reminiscent (remini·sĕnt), *sb.* 1822. [subst. use of next.] A relater or writer of reminiscences.

Reminiscent (remini·sĕnt), *a.* 1765. [– L. *reminiscens, -ent-*, pr. pple. of *remininisci*; see REMINISCENCE, -ENT.] **1.** Pertaining to, characterized by, reminiscence. **b.** Having reminiscence *of* something 1830. **2.** Of the nature of reminiscence or reminiscences 1863. **3.** Evoking a reminiscence *of* a person or thing 1880.

1. b. Some other state of existence, of which we have been previously conscious and are now r. 1836. Hence **Remini·scently** *adv.*

Reminiscential (re:minise·nʃăl), *a.* 1646. [f. REMINISCENCE; cf. *essential*.] Of the nature of, pertaining to, reminiscence; of a reminiscent character.

Remiped (re·miped), *sb.* and *a.* 1826. [– Fr. *rémipède*, f. L. *remus* oar + *pes, ped-* foot.] *Zool.* **A.** *sb.* One of an order of coleopterous insects having tarsi adapted for swimming; also, a crustacean of the genus *Remipes*. **B.** *adj.* Having feet that are oar-shaped, or used as oars 1864.

†**Remi·se,** *sb.*[1] 1473. [– Fr. *remise*, identical w. next.] **1.** *Law.* A transfer of property –1766. **2.** A remission or cessation of sickness. FLORIO. **3.** The act of remitting money; a remittance –1689.

‖**Remise** (rəmī·z), *sb.*[2] 1698. [Fr., f. *remis, -e* pa. pple. of *remettre* put back or up. Cf. REMIT.] **1.** A coach-house. **b.** (Ellipt. for *voiture de remise*.) A carriage hired from a livery stable, of a better class than the ordinary hackney-carriage 1698. **2.** *Fencing.* A second thrust made after the first has missed and while still upon the lunge; the act of making a thrust of this kind 1823. **3.** A wired-in space planted to attract game-birds 1905.

Remise (rĭməi·z), *v.*[1] 1481. [f. Fr. *remis(e*; see prec.] †**1.** *trans.* To put back again *in* or *into* a place or state; to replace; to convert again *into*; to send back *to* a place –1623. **2.** *Law.* To give up, surrender, make over to another, release (any right, property, etc.) 1487.

Remi·se, *v.*[2] 1889. [f. REMISE *sb.*[2] 2.] *Fencing. intr.* To make a remise.

Remiss (rĭmi·s), *a.* late ME. [– L. *remissus*, adj. use of pa. pple. of *remittere* slacken, relax; see REMIT.] †**1.** *Med.* Weakened; dilute –1625. **2.** Of persons: Slack in the discharge of a task or duty; careless, negligent 1450. **b.** Of conduct, actions, etc.: Characterized by carelessness, negligence, or inattention 1502. †**3.** Characterized by a lack of strictness or proper restraint; lax, loose –1751.

†**b.** Lenient –1651. **4.** Free from vehemence or violence; also, lacking in force or energy 1550. †**b.** Not intense or strong; moderate, mild (esp. of heat and cold) –1686. †**5.** Diminished in tension; loose, relaxed –1667.

2. R. in the duties..of Religion BENTLEY. A very r. correspondent 1893. **b.** What had been r. in the conduct of his predecessor 1817. **3.** A r. discipline JER. TAYLOR. **4.** The passion must neither be too violent nor too r. HUME. **5.** Pain Which..makes r. the hands of Mightiest MILT. Hence **Remi·ss-ly** *adv.*, **-ness.**

Remiss (rĭmi·s), *v. rare.* 1500. [– *remiss-*, pa. ppl. stem of L. *remittere* REMIT. Cf. REMISE *v.*[1]] †**1.** *trans.* To remit; to resolve or dissolve; to mitigate; to let go, pass over –1656. **2.** *Law.* = REMISE *v.*[1] 2. 1809.

Remi·ssful, *a. rare.* 1603. [f. REMISS *v.* or *a.* + -FUL.] †**1.** Full of remission; merciful. DRAYTON. **2.** Full of remissness; negligent 1836.

Remissible (rĭmi·sĭb'l), *a.* 1577. [– Fr. *rémissible* or late L. *remissibilis* (Tertullian); see REMISS *v.*, -IBLE.] Capable or admitting of remission; that may be remitted. Hence **Remissibi·lity, Remi·ssibleness,** r. state or condition.

Remission (rĭmi·ʃən). ME. [– (O)Fr. *rémission* or L. *remissio, -on-*, f. *remiss-*; see REMISS *v.*, -ION.] **1.** Forgiveness or pardon *of* sins or other offences. **2.** Forgiveness or pardon granted for sins or offences against divine law; the cancelling of, or deliverance from, the guilt and penalties of sin ME. **b.** Pardon for a political, legal, or other offence. Now *Hist.* late ME. †**3. a.** Release from a debt or payment –1608. **b.** Liberation from captivity, etc.; respite –1761. **4.** The action of remitting or giving up partially or wholly (a debt, tax, penalty, etc.). late ME. †**5.** Relaxation; lessening of tension; slackening of energy or application –1741. **6.** Diminution of force or effect; lowering or decrease of a condition or quality, esp. of heat or cold 1603. **b.** *Path.* A decrease or subsidence (esp. a temporary one) in the violence of a disease or pain; also *transf.* of violent emotions 1685. **7.** The action of remitting or sending (back); a remittal (*rare*) 1724.

1. In..Scripture, R. of Sinne, and Salvation from Death and Misery, is the same thing HOBBES. **2.** He gives repentance and r. DE FOE. **b.** *Two Gent.* I. ii. 65. **6.** The r. of the cold did not continue long enough to afford me much relief JOHNSON. **7.** The r. of a million every year to England SWIFT.

Remissive (rĭmi·siv), *a.* 1514. [– med.L. *remissivus*; see REMISS *v.*, -IVE.] †**1.** Careless, remiss (*rare*) –1640. **2.** Inclined to, of the nature of, productive of, remission or pardon. Now *rare.* 1611. †**3.** Producing or allowing decrease *of* something –1718. **4.** Characterized by remission or abatement 1686.

2. No contrition alone is r. of sins JER. TAYLOR.

Remissory (rĭmi·sŏri), *a. rare.* 1548. [– med.L. *remissorius*; see REMISS *v.*, -ORY[2].] Tending to, of the nature of, remission.

Remit (rĭmi·t), *v.* late ME. [– L. *remittere* send back, slacken, relax, postpone, f. *re-* RE- + *mittere* send.] **I.** *trans.* **1.** To forgive or pardon (a sin, offence, †a person, etc.). †**2.** To give up, resign, surrender (a right or possession) –1670. **3.** To abstain from exacting (a payment or service of any kind); to allow to remain unpaid (or unperformed) 1463. **b.** To refrain from inflicting (a punishment) or carrying out (a sentence); to withdraw, cancel; to grant remission of (suffering) 1483. †**4.** To discharge, set free, release, liberate (a person) –1647.

1. Whose synnes soeuer ye remytte they are remytted vnto them COVERDALE *John* 20:23. **2.** Th' Ægyptian Crown I to your hands r. DRYDEN. **3.** She remitted the Arrears that were owing 1701. **b.** The queen remitted the quartering of his body 1693.

II. 1. To give up, lay aside (anger, etc.) entirely or in part. late ME. **b.** To give up or over, abandon, desist from (a pursuit, occupation, etc.) 1587. **2.** To allow (one's diligence, attention, etc.) to slacken or abate 1510. †**b.** To mitigate, diminish, or abate. –1750. †**3.** To relax, relieve from tension –1711.

1. Our Supream Foe in time may much r. His anger MILT. **b.** Engaged..in a siege which they could not r. KINGLAKE. **2.** Do not r. your care JOHNSON.

III. 1. To refer (a matter) for consideration, decision, performance, etc., *to* a person or body of persons, now usu. to one specially empowered or appointed to deal with it; also *spec.* in *Law*, to send back (a case) to an inferior court. late ME. **b.** To send (a person) from one tribunal *to* another for trial or hearing (*rare*) 1538. †**c.** To commit (a person) *to* the charge or control of another. Also *refl.* –1741. **2.** To refer (a person) *to* a book, another person, etc., for information. late ME. **3. a.** To send (a person) back to prison, or to other custody; to recommit. Now *rare.* late ME. †**b.** To emit or send out again. DRYDEN. **4.** †**a.** *Law.* To restore to a former and more valid title; see REMITTER[2] 1. –1768. **b.** To put back *into*, to admit or consign again *to* a previous position, state, or condition 1591. **5.** To postpone, put off or defer 1635. **6.** To refer, assign, or make over *to* a thing or person 1641. †**b.** To enter or insert *in* (or *into*) a book –1716. **7.** To send or transmit (money or articles of value) *to* a person or place. Also *absol.* 1640.

1. Wheche mater I remytte..to youre ryght wyse discrecion 1455. **2.** Let us hear Du Cange, to whom Robertson remits us 1835. **4. b.** You propose to r. to slavery three millions of negroes BRIGHT. **7.** We parted; and he remitted me a small annuity JOHNSON.

IV. *intr.* **1.** To abate, diminish, slacken 1629. **2.** To relax *from* labour; to give over 1760.

1. How often have I blest the coming day, When toil remitting lent its turn to play GOLDSM. **2.** Their enemies will not r.; rust, mould, vermin.. all seize their own EMERSON. Hence **Remi·tment** †remission, pardon; remitting of money. **Remi·ttal,** remission *for* sin, or *of* a debt, penalty, etc.; *Law*, the act of referring a case from one court to another. **Remi:ttee·**, one to whom a remittance is made or sent. **Remi·tter**[1], one who forgives or pardons (*rare*); one who sends a remittance.

Remittance (rĭmi·tăns). 1705. [f. REMIT *v.* + -ANCE.] A sum of money sent from one place or person to another; a quantity of some article sent in this way; also, the act of sending money, etc., to another place.

R.-man, an emigrant who is supported or assisted by remittances from home.

Remittent (rĭmi·tĕnt), *a.* and *sb.* 1693. [– L. *remittens, -ent-*, pr. pple. of *remittere*; see REMIT, -ENT.] **A.** *adj.* That remits or abates for a time; *spec.* in *Path.* of a type of fever, the symptoms of which abate at intervals (without disappearing entirely as in the *intermittent* type). **B.** *sb.* **1.** *Path.* A remittent fever 1693. **2.** One who remits money 1855.

Remitter[2] (rĭmi·təɹ). 1445. [See REMIT *v.* and -ER[4].] **1.** *Law.* **a.** A principle or operation by which one having two titles to an estate, and entering on it by the later or more defective of these, is adjudged to hold it by the earlier or more valid one. **b.** The act of remitting a case to another court for decision 1726. **2.** Restoration to rights or privileges, or to a previous state (*rare*) 1623.

Remnant (re·mnănt), *sb.* and *a.* ME. [contr. f. REMENANT.] **A.** *sb.* **1.** With *the.* That which remains after the removal of a portion; the remainder, rest, residue. Now applied only to a small remaining number or part. **2.** With *a* and *pl.* A (small) remaining number, part, or quantity 1611. **b.** Of a single person: A survivor (*rare*) 1594. **3.** A remaining trace or survival *of* some quality, belief, condition, or state of things 1560. **4.** A fragment, a small portion, a scrap. late ME. **b.** *spec.* among drapers and clothiers: An end of a piece of goods, left over after the main portion has been used or sold. late ME. †**c.** A scrap or tag of quotation. B. JONS.

1. The remnaunt of the captiuyte COVERDALE *Neh.* 1: 3. The r. of my tale is of a length To tire your patience DRYDEN. **2.** The remnants of their provisions on the voyage 1888. **b.** *Rich. III*, I. ii. 7.

B. *adj.* Remaining 1550.

Act through thy r. life the decent part PRIOR.

‖**Remolade** (remolad). 1702. [– Fr. †*rémolade, rémoulade* – It. *remolata.*] **1.** An unguent used in farriery. **2.** A piquant salad-dressing resembling mayonnaise 18..

Remonetize (rīmǫ·nĭtəiz), *v.* 1878. [f. RE- 5 a + MONETIZE.] *trans.* To restore (a metal or other substance) to its former use as full legal tender. So **Remonetiza·tion.**

Remonstrance (rĭmǫ·nstrăns). 1477. [– Fr. †*remonstrance* (mod. *remontrance*) or med.L. *remonstrantia*, f. *remonstrare*; see REMONSTRATE, -ANCE.] †**1.** An appeal, request –1490. †**2.** Demonstration, proof, evidence, manifestation of some fact, quality, etc.; also, a ground *of* some belief –1774. **3.** †**a.** A (written or spoken) demonstration, statement, account, or representation. Usu. const. *of* (the matter declared or brought forward). –1772. **b.** A formal statement of grievances or similar matters of public importance, *esp.* the *Grand R.* presented by the House of Commons to the Crown in 1641. Now *Hist.* 1626. **c.** *Eccl. Hist.* A document presented in 1610 to the States of Holland by the Dutch Arminians, relative to the points of difference between themselves and the strict Calvinists 1662. **4.** The action of remonstrating; expostulation 1603. **b.** With *a* and *pl.* An instance of this 1729. **5.** A monstrance 1656. *Obs.* or *rare.*

2. The externall and visible remonstrances of religion JER. TAYLOR. **4. b.** The remonstrances of the people were disregarded 1774.

Remonstrant (rĭmǫ·nstrănt), *a.* and *sb.* 1618. [– med.L. *remonstrans, -ant-*, pr. pple. of *remonstrare*; see next, -ANT.] **A.** *adj.* **1.** *Eccl. Hist.* Of or belonging to the Arminian party in the Dutch Reformed Church. **2.** That remonstrates or expostulates 1641. **B.** *sb.* **1.** *Eccl. Hist.* A member of the Arminian party in the Dutch Reformed Church (see REMONSTRANCE 3 c.) 1618. **2.** One who remonstrates; †the author, or a supporter, of a remonstrance (in senses 3 a, b) 1641. Hence **Remo·nstrantly** *adv.* in a r. manner.

Remonstrate (rĭmǫ·nstreit, re·mǫnstreit), *v.* 1599. [– *remonstrat-*, pa. ppl. stem of med.L. *remonstrare* demonstrate, f. *re-* RE- + L. *monstrare* show; see -ATE[3].] †**1.** *trans.* To make plain or manifest, demonstrate, exhibit, show –1742. †**2.** To point out (a fault, etc.) to another by way of reproof, disapprobation, or complaint; to protest against (a wrong) –1751. †**b.** To point out, state, or represent (a grievance, etc.) to some authority. Also const. *to.* –1741. †**3.** *intr.* To raise an objection *to* a thing; to address a remonstrance *to* a person –1792. **4.** To urge strong reasons *against* a course of action, to protest *against*; to expostulate *with* a person, *on* or *upon* an action. Also *absol.* 1695. **5.** *trans.* To say, assert, or plead in remonstrance 1758.

1. Mr. Edw. Wood was the spokes-man: remonstrated that they were Oxon. scholars 1680. **2. b.** The Parliament sent but six or seven, to r. their complaints 1647. **4.** Corporal Trim, by being in the service, had learned to obey,—and not to r. STERNE. **5.** 'I am a mortal', Scrooge remonstrated, 'and liable to fall' DICKENS. Hence **Remonstra·tion,** the action of remonstrating, expostulation; an instance of this. **Remo·nstrative** *a.* of or characterized by remonstrance. **Remo·nstrator,** one who remonstrates, a remonstrant. **Remo·nstratory** *a.* expostulatory.

Remontant (rĭmǫ·ntănt), *a.* and *sb.* 1883. [– Fr. *remontant*, pr. pple. of *remonter* REMOUNT *v.*] **A.** *adj.* Of roses: Blooming a second time or oftener in a season. **B.** *sb.* A hybrid perpetual rose blooming more than once in a season 1883.

‖**Remontoir** (rəmoṅtwār). 1801. [Fr., f. *remonter* REMOUNT *v.*] *Clock-making.* A device by which an exactly uniform impulse is given to the pendulum or balance. Also *attrib.*

Remora (re·mŏră). 1567. [– L. *remora* delay, hindrance, f. *re-* RE- + *mora* delay.] **1.** The sucking-fish (*Echeneis remora*), believed by the ancients to have the power of staying the course of any ship to which it attached itself. **2.** An obstacle, hindrance, impediment, obstruction 1604. **3.** *Surg.* An instrument used to retain bones or other parts in place (*rare*) 1688.

1. Like the r., of which mariners tell marvels, it counteracts, as it were, both oar and sail LANDOR. **2.** These numerous demands are likely to operate as a *r.*, and to keep us fixed at home COWPER.

†**Re·morate,** *v. rare.* 1638. [– *remorat-*, pa. ppl. stem of L. *remorari*, f. *re-* RE- + *morari* delay.] *trans.* To detain, delay, obstruct –1657.

Remo·rd, *v. Obs.* (exc. as *nonce-wd.*). late ME. [- (O)Fr. *remordre* :- Rom. **remordere*, for L. *remordēre*, f. *re-* RE- + *mordēre* bite, sting, etc.] **1.** *trans.* To visit with affliction. CHAUCER. **2.** To afflict (a person, the mind, etc.) with remorse or painful feelings. late ME. **b.** To afflict (oneself) with remorseful thoughts; also, to unburden with contrition; to examine in a penitent spirit 1450. **3.** To recall to mind with remorse or regret. late ME. **4.** *intr.* To feel remorse 1440. **5.** *trans.* To blame, rebuke 1523.

2. b. Others thought he must. .have pillaged a church;. .and now was committing the mistake of remording himself about it READE.

Remorse (rĭmǭ·ɹs), *sb.* late ME. [- OFr. *remors* (mod. *remords*) - med.L. *remorsus*, f. *remors-*, pa. ppl. stem of L. *remordēre* vex, torment; see prec.] **1.** *R. of conscience* (or *mind*) = 2. Now somewhat *rare* and *arch.* **2.** A feeling of compunction, or of deep regret and repentance, for a sin or wrong committed. late ME. **b.** With *a* and *pl.* A fit of remorse –1761. †**3.** Sorrow, pity, compassion; also *pl.* signs of tender feeling –1700. †**4.** Regretful or remorseful remembrance or recollection *of* a thing –1695. †**b.** A solemn obligation. SHAKS. **5.** Biting or cutting force. SPENSER.

1. One of these Lieutenants, having a R. of Conscience, discovered the. .Mater 1704. **2.** The fruit of our own ill-doing is r. HOOKER. **3.** Curse on th' unpard'ning Prince, whom Tears can draw To no R. DRYDEN.

†**Remo·rse**, *v.* 1483. [f. L. *remors-*; see prec.] *trans.* and *intr.* To affect with, or feel, remorse –1690.

Remorseful (rĭmǭ·ɹsfŭl), *a.* 1591. [f. REMORSE *sb.* + -FUL.] **1.** Affected with or characterized by remorse; impressed with a sense of, and penitent for, guilt 1592. †**2.** Compassionate, full of pity –1611. †**3.** Pitiable. CHAPMAN.

1. Many a bitter hour and year of r. sorrow CARLYLE. **2.** *Two Gent.* IV. iii. 13. Hence **Remo·rseful-ly** *adv.*, **-ness.**

Remorseless (rĭmǭ·ɹslės), *a.* 1593. [f. as prec. + -LESS.] Devoid of remorse; pitiless, cruel. **b.** quasi- *adv.* Without remorse 1593.

Remorsles cruelty MILT. A r. foe 1853. Hence **Remo·rseless-ly** *adv.*, **-ness.**

Remote (rĭmōᵘ·t), *a.* late ME. [- L. *remotus*, pa. pple. of *removēre* REMOVE.] **1.** Placed or situated at a distance or interval from each other; far apart. **2.** Far away, far off, distant *from* some place, thing, or person; removed, set apart 1586. **3.** Far-off, far-distant 1533. **b.** Out-of-the-way, retired, secluded 1611. **c.** In quasi-*adv.* use: At a distance, far off 1667. **d.** Distant in (past or future) time 1712. **4.** Far off, or distant, in various *transf.* uses: *esp.* not immediately or closely related to, connected with, bearing upon, or affecting something else 1599. †**b.** Far-fetched; unusual (*rare*) –1781. **c.** Not closely related by blood or kinship 1760. †**5.** Antecedent; ultimate (*rare*) –1697. **6.** Slight, faint. In later use, esp. *not the remotest*, not the slightest, not the least (idea, etc.) 1711.

1. Hearts r., yet not asunder SHAKS. **2.** Some. . Hermitage, R. from all the pleasures of the world SHAKS. **3.** To grace the Gentry of a Land r. SHAKS. **b.** Places r. enough are in Bohemia, There. .leaue it crying SHAKS. **c.** The sound Of Thunder heard r. MILT. **4.** Their nimble nonsense . .gains r. conclusions at a jump COWPER. They had not foreseen how the remoter consequences would affect their own safety THIRLWALL. **b.** Words too familiar or too r., defeat the purpose of a poet JOHNSON. **6.** It had a bearing—r. indeed, but real—on what is being done now 1861. Hence **Remo·te-ly** *adv.*, **-ness.**

†**Remoted**, *a.* 1580. [f. as prec. + -ED¹ 2.] Remote, distant; removed –1683.

Remotion (rĭmōᵘ·ʃən). Now *rare.* late ME. [- Fr. †*remotion* or L. *remotio, -on-*; see RE-, MOTION *sb.*] **1.** Remoteness. Now *rare.* **2.** The action of removing; removal; putting or taking away 1449. †**b.** The process of arriving at some conception (*spec.* that of God) by removal of everything which is known not to be included in it –1677. †**3.** The action of removing or departing –1692.

1. Its utter solitude and r. from men or cities DE QUINCEY. **3.** *Lear* II. iv. 115.

Remo·tive, *a. rare.* 1819. [f. L. *remot-* (see REMOTE) + -IVE.] †**1.** *Bot.* Characterized by removal of the episperm from the sheath of the cotyledon. LINDLEY. **2.** That may be removed 1834.

Remount (rī-, rĭmau·nt), *sb.* 1802. [f. the vb.] *Mil.* **1. a.** A supply of fresh horses for a cavalry regiment. **b.** A horse used to replace another which is worn out or killed 1829. **2.** *attrib.*, as *r. depot*, etc. 1812.

Remount (rī-, rĭmau·nt), *v.* late ME. [In early use - (O)Fr. *remonter*, f. *re-* RE- + *monter* MOUNT *v.*; in later use in part a new formation on MOUNT *v.*] **I.** *trans.* †**1.** To raise or lift up again –1577. **b.** To set up in place again; *esp.* to mount (a gun) again 1627. **c.** To mount, put together, again 1888. **2. a.** To replace, to assist or enable (a person) to mount again, on horseback. late ME. **b.** To provide (cavalry) with fresh horses 1688. **3. a.** To ascend or go up (a place or thing) again 1621. **b.** To mount (a horse, etc.) again 1788.

3. a. To r. the stream to its ancient source 1884.

II. *intr.* **1.** To mount, rise, or move upwards again 1490. **2.** To get on horseback again 1500. **3.** To go back, in the course of an investigation or study, *to* a certain point, period, etc. 1738. **b.** To go back in time *to* a certain date 1831. **c.** To go back *to* a source 1839.

3. We soon r. to facts which lie beyond our powers of analysis and observation 1837. **b.** A practice which remounts to the first ages of Christianity 1844.

Removable (rĭmū·văb'l), *a.* and *sb.* 1534. [f. REMOVE *v.* + -ABLE.] **1.** Subject to removal. **2.** Capable of being removed (from one place to another, or entirely) 1564. **B.** *sb.* A removable resident magistrate in Ireland 1888. Hence **Remo:vabi·lity. Remo·vableness.**

Removal (rĭmū·văl). 1597. [f. REMOVE *v.* + -AL¹ 2.] **1.** The act of taking away entirely. **2.** Dismissal from an office or post; also, transference to another office, etc. 1647. **3.** The act of conveying or shifting to another place; the fact of being so transferred 1639. **4.** The act of changing one's ground, place, or position; *esp.* change of habitation 1642.

2. The appointment and r. of magistrates 1863.

Remove (rĭmū·v), *sb.* 1553. [f. the vb.] †**1.** Removal of a person from a position or office; dismissal –1799. †**b.** The act of removing a person by death; murder –1653. **2.** †**a.** The act of taking away, or doing away with, a thing –1676. **b.** *Farriery.* The act of taking off a horse's shoe in order to dress the hoof and replace the shoe on the same or another foot; hence, an old shoe used over again. Now *dial.* 1549. **c.** The act of taking away a dish or dishes at a meal in order to put others in their place; hence, a dish thus removed, or brought on 1773. **3.** The act of removing a thing from one place to another 1582. †**4.** The act of transferring a person from one office or post to another; the fact of being so transferred –1751. **b.** Promotion, at school, to a higher class or division 1662. **c.** At some schools: An intermediate form or class 1718. **5.** The (*or* an) act of changing one's place, *esp.* one's place of residence; departure to another place. Now *rare.* 1586. †**b.** A period of absence from a place. SHAKS. **6.** Distance, in time, place, condition, etc. 1628. **b.** A step or stage in gradation of any kind; esp. in phr. *but one* (or *a*) *r. from* 1633. **c.** A degree in descent or consanguinity 1766.

1. b. He most violent Author Of his owne iust remoue SHAKS. **3.** An Elephant for the r. of our baggage and commodities 1660. **4. b.** Surprising I didn't get my r. this term 1894. **c.** Some unhappy wight in the r. DISRAELI. **5.** Three removes are as bad as a fire FRANKLIN. **6. b.** Yet nascent feudality was but one r. from anarchy BRYCE.

Remove (rĭmū·v), *v.* [ME. *remeve, remove* - OFr. *remeuv-, remov-*, stressed and unstressed stems respectively of *removeir* (mod. *remouvoir*) :- L. *removēre*; see RE-, MOVE *v.* For the vocalism, cf. PROVE.] **I.** *trans.* **1.** To move from or out of the place occupied; to lift or push aside, lift up and take away, take off, withdraw. **b.** To put (a person) out of the way; to assassinate, murder 1653. **c.** *pass.* Of dishes: To be replaced or followed *by*, after removal 1840. **2.** To move, shift, or convey from one place to another; to change the place or situation of ME. †**b.** *Law.* To transfer (a cause or person) for trial from one court of law to another –1744. **3.** To send or put (a person) away; to compel (a person) to go from, or quit, a place. late ME. **b.** To depose, dismiss from a position or office. late ME. **4.** To take away (*from* a person), to relieve or free one from, some feeling, quality, condition, etc., esp. one of a bad or detrimental kind; †to do away with (a practice). late ME. †**b.** To put away (a feeling, etc.) *from* oneself –1703. †**5.** To move or persuade (a person) *out of* or *from* a purpose or resolve –1654.

1. God to r. his wayes from human sense, Plac'd Heav'n from Earth so farr MILT. *To r. mountains*: to perform miracles: after Matt. 17:20, etc. **c.** Boiled haddock, removed by hashed mutton THACKERAY. **2.** Elizabeth was now removed to Canterbury 1839. **3.** To r. him I decree, And send him from the Garden MILT. **b.** None of the sheriffs now removed were employed again STUBBS. **4.** The death of Norfolk. .removed the dread of. .war 1874.

II. *intr.* **1.** To go away or depart from a place; to move off to somewhere else ME. **b.** *spec.* To change one's place of residence; also of a tenant, to quit a house or holding. late ME. †**c.** To shift one's place or position –1656. **2.** Of things: To change place; to move off or away; to disappear, etc. late ME. †**3.** To move, stir; to be in motion –1601.

1. He said, he'd r. into another room GLANVILL. **b.** One who, having liv'd in Long-Acre. .had removed for fear of the Distemper DE FOE. **2.** The mountaynes shall remoue, & the hilles shal fall downe COVERDALE *Isa* 54:10.

Removed (rĭmū·vd), *ppl. a.* 1548. [f. prec. + -ED¹.] **1.** Distant in relationship by a certain degree in descent or consanguinity. **2.** †**a.** Remote; retired, secluded –1632. †**b.** Separated by time or space (*rare*) –1628. **c.** Lifted or taken away 1625. **3.** *predic.* Remote, separated, or distant *from* something 1617.

1. He is a cousin, several time r. DICKENS. **2. a.** Som still r. place MILT. **b.** *Twel. N.* V. i. 92. Hence **Remo·vedness.**

Remover (rĭmū·vəɹ). 1594. [f. REMOVE *v.* + -ER¹.] **1.** One who or that which removes or takes away; *spec.* a furniture-remover. **2.** One who changes his place (*rare*) 1690.

2. Loue is not loue Which. .bends with the remouer to remoue SHAKS.

†**Remuable**, *a. rare.* late ME. [- (O)Fr. *remuable*, f. *remuer*; see next, -ABLE.] Changeable, unstable; mobile. late ME. only.

†**Remue·**, *v.* ME. [- (O)Fr. *remuer*, f. *re-* RE- + *muer* :- L. *mutare* change.] **1.** *trans.* To remove or transfer to another place –1600. **2.** *intr.* To move off or away, depart –1482.

Remu·nerable, *a. rare.* 1593. [f. next + -ABLE.] That may be rewarded; deserving of reward. Hence **Remunerabi·lity** (*rare*).

Remunerate (rĭmiū·nĕreⁱt), *v.* 1523. [- *remunerat-*, pa. ppl. stem of L. *remunerari* (later *-are*), f. *re-* RE- + *munerari, -are*, f. *munus, muner-* gift; see -ATE³.] **1.** *trans.* To repay, requite, make some return for (services, etc.). **2.** To reward (a person); to pay (a person) for services rendered or work done 1588. **b.** Of things: To recompense or repay (a person) 1849.

2. b. The principle that our exclusive trade with the colonies remunerates us for the expense of colonial establishments COBDEN. Hence **Remunera·tion,** reward, recompense, repayment; payment, pay. **Remu·nerator** (*rare*), one who remunerates. **Remu·neratory** *a.* serving to r.; affording remuneration.

Remunerative (rĭmiū·nĕrĕtiv), *a.* 1626. [In XVII - med.L. *remunerativus*; in later use a new formation on the verb.] †**1.** Inclined to remunerate (*rare*) –1626. **2.** That remunerates or rewards 1677. **3.** That brings remuneration; profitable 1853.

2. R. justice 1677. **3.** The scheme did not prove r. 1865. Hence **Remu·nerative-ly** *adv.*, **-ness.**

Remurmur (rĭmɔ̄·ɹmŏɹ), *v.* Chiefly *poet.* 1697. [- L. *remurmurare*; see RE-, MURMUR *v.*] **1.** *intr.* **a.** To give back or give forth a murmuring sound; to resound with murmurs. **b.** To answer with murmurs *to* a sound 1697. **c.** Of sounds: To echo in murmurs 1717. **2.** *trans.* To repeat in murmurs 1704.

1. b. Eurota's banks remurmur'd to the noise POPE. **2.** The trembling trees. .Her fate r. to the . .flood POPE.

Ren, obs. f. RUN *v.*

Renable (re·năb'l), *a. Obs.* exc. *dial.* ME. [- OFr. *re(s)nable* :- L. *rationabilis*; see

REASONABLE.] **a.** Of persons: Ready of speech, eloquent; †esp. in phr. *r. of tongue.* **b.** Of speech: Ready, fluent, plain. late ME.

Renaissance (rĭnē·sāns, Fr. rənɛsaṅs). 1840. [– Fr. *renaissance* (in spec. use, short for *r. des arts, r. des lettres*), f. *re-* RE- + *naissance* birth :– L. *nascentia*, f. *nasci* be born, or f. *naiss-*, pres. stem of *naître* :– Rom. **nascere*; see -ANCE. Cf. RENASCENCE.] **1.** The revival of art and letters, under the influence of classical models, which began in Italy in the 14th c.; the period during which this movement was in progress 1845. **b.** *ellipt.* The style of art or architecture developed in, and characteristic of, this period 1840. **2.** Any revival in art, literature, etc. 1872.

2. Voltairism may stand for the name of the R. of the eighteenth century 1872.

Renaissant (rĭnē·sănt), *a. rare.* 1864. [– Fr. *renaissant*, pr. pple. of *renaître*; see prec., -ANT.] Of or belonging to, characteristic of, the Renaissance.

Renal (rī·năl), *a.* 1656. [– Fr. *rénal* – late L. *renalis*, f. L. *renes* REINS; see -AL¹.] Of or pertaining to the reins or kidneys.

Re·nardine, *a. rare.* 1866. [f. *Renard*, var. of REYNARD; see -INE¹.] Pertaining to Reynard the Fox.

Renascence (rĭnæ·sĕns). 1727. [f. next + -ENCE. In sense 2 substituted by Matthew Arnold for RENAISSANCE.] **1.** The process or fact of being born anew; re-birth, renewal, revival. **2.** = RENAISSANCE 1. 1869. So **Rena·scency** = sense 1. 1664.

Renascent (rĭnæ·sĕnt), *a.* 1727. [– L. *renascens, -ent-*, pr. pple. of *renasci*, f. *re-* RE- + *nasci* be born; see -ENT.] That is being born again, reviving, springing up afresh.

†**Rena·te,** *ppl. a. rare.* 1570. [– L. *renatus*, pa. pple. of *renasci*; see prec., -ATE².] Reborn, reincarnate –1660.

†**Renay·, reny·,** *v.* ME. [– OFr. *reneier* (mod. *renier*) :– med.L. *renegare* RENEGUE.] **1.** *trans.* To renounce, abjure (one's faith, God, lord, etc.). **2.** To deny, disown –1512. **3.** To refuse *to* do something. SKELTON.

Rencontre (renkǫ·ntəɹ, Fr. raṅkoṅtr'). 1619. [– Fr. *rencontre*; see next.] = next 1, 1 b, 1 c, 3.

Rencounter (renkau·ntəɹ), *sb.* 1523. [– (O)Fr. *rencontre*, f. *rencontrer*; see next.] **1.** An encounter or engagement between two opposing forces; a battle, skirmish, conflict. **b.** A hostile meeting between two adversaries; a duel 1590. **c.** An encounter or contest of any kind; in early use, esp. a contest in wit or argument 1632. †**2.** An unpleasant experience –1682. **3.** A chance meeting of two persons, or of a person with a thing 1632. **b.** A meeting of two things or bodies; an impact, collision. Now *rare* or *Obs.* 1662.

1. Three little rencounters have happened with the enemy 1781. **3. b.** My nose and this very Post should have a R. SWIFT.

Rencounter (renkau·ntəɹ). *v.* Now *rare.* 1463. [– (O)Fr. *rencontrer*, f. *re-* RE- + OFr. *encontrer*; see ENCOUNTER *v.*] **1.** *trans.* To meet or encounter (an army, person, etc.) in hostile fashion; to engage (a person) in fight. **2.** To meet or fall in with (a person) 1549. †**b.** *intr.* Const. *with.* –1676. †**3.** *trans.* To come into contact or collision with –1695. **b.** *intr.* To come together, collide 1712.

Rend (rend), *v. Pa. t.* and *pple.* **rent.** [OE. *rendan* = OFris. *renda*, rel. to MLG. *rende.*] **1.** *trans.* To tear, to pull violently or by main force, *off, out of,* or *from* a thing or place; to tear *off* or *away.* **2.** To tear, wrench, drag *up* or *down* ME. **3.** To tear apart (*asunder*) or in pieces OE. **b.** To wear *out* (clothes) by tearing. SHAKS. **c.** *techn.* To make (laths) by cleaving wood along the grain into thin strips; also, to strip (trees) of bark 1688. **4.** To tear apart or in pieces, in later use, esp. to split into parties or factions. late ME. **5.** *absol.* To tear; to act by tearing ME. **6.** *intr.* To burst, break, or tear ME.

1. The Rocks are from their old Foundations rent DRYDEN. Phr. *To rap* (or *rive*) *and r.*: see RAP *v.*² 1 and RIVE *v.* **2.** God rent them up by the roots in the days of Pekah FULLER. **3.** A banner that was many a time rent but was never out of the field MORLEY. Lo, they will weep, and r. their hair 1839. **4.** Anon the dreadfull Thunder Doth r. the region SHAKS. The Commons live, by no Divisions rent DRYDEN. Her heart was rent by contending emotions 1891. **5.** Whose Rage doth r. Like interrupted Waters SHAKS. **6.** He laid hold vpon the skirt of his mantle, and it rent 1 *Sam.* 15:27. Hence †**Rend** *sb.* a rent, split, division –1674. **Re·nder** *sb.*¹ one who rends.

Render (re·ndəɹ), *sb.*² ME. [f. next.] †**1.** A lesson, repetition. ME. only. †**2.** The act of rendering up, or making over to another; surrender (of a person or place) –1670. **3.** *Law.* **a.** (Usu. *grant and r.*) A return made by the cognizee to the cognizor in a fine; a conveyance of this nature 1594. **b.** A return in money or kind, or in some service, made by a tenant to the superior 1647. †**4.** The act of rendering an account, statement, etc.; an account of expenses –1768. **5.** The first coat of plaster or the like applied to a brick or stone surface 1833.

3. b. Payments in money and renders in kind 1897. **4.** *Cymb.* IV. iv. 11.

Render (re·ndəɹ), *v.* ME. [– AFr. *render*, (O)Fr. *rendre* :– Rom. **rendere*, alt., after **prendere* (L. *præhendere*), of L. *reddere* give back, etc., f. *red-* RE- + *dare* give. For the unusual retention in Eng. of the Fr. inf. ending cf. TENDER *v.*¹] **I.** †**1.** *trans.* To repeat (something learned); to say over, recite –1565. **2.** To give in return, to make return of. Now somewhat *rare.* 1477. **b.** To return (thanks) 1484. †**3.** To give (†or hand) back, to restore. Also with *again* or *back.* 1513. **b.** *Law.* (usu. *grant and r.*) Of a cognizee: To make over as a return to the cognizor in a fine 1594. **c.** To give back, return (a sound, image, etc.) by reflection or repercussion. Also with *back.* 1600. **4.** To reproduce or represent, esp. by artistic means; to depict 1599. **b.** To play or perform (music) 1676. †**5.** To give or make (a person) out to be of a certain character or in a certain state –1726. **6.** To reproduce or express in another language, to translate 1610.

2. Receiving benefits and rendering none COWPER. **b.** To rendre thankes for the greate benefytes that we haue receyued at his handes *Bk. Com. Prayer.* **3.** I r. agayne to you all your londes LD. BERNERS. **c.** Who. . like a gate of steele, Fronting the sunne, receiues and renders backe His figure, and his heate SHAKS. **4.** A fearefull Battaile rendred you in Musique SHAKS. **5.** *A. Y. L.* IV. iii. 123. **6.** The word has been rendered in different places either Temperance or Wisdom JOWETT.

II. 1. To hand over, deliver, commend, or commit, to another; to give, in various senses. late ME. **2.** To give *up*, surrender, resign, relinquish. late ME. †**3.** To give out, emit, discharge –1730. **4.** To give (an account, reason, answer, etc.); to submit to, or lay before, another for consideration or approval; also, in mod. use, to send in (an account) to a customer or purchaser 1481. †**b.** To declare, state. SHAKS. **5.** To pay as a rent, tax, tribute, or other acknowledgement of dependence 1526. **6.** To give, pay, exhibit, or show (obedience, honour, attention, etc.); to do (a service) 1588. **7.** *refl.* To present (oneself), take steps to be *at* (†or *in*) a certain place 1619.

1. Of all the treasure in this field atcheiued. . We r. you the Tenth SHAKS. **2.** I r. my cause, as the sword-men would have it 1673. In the city rendered by compact, and not taken by storm 1865. **4.** By this hand, Claudio shall r. me a deere account SHAKS. *Account rendered*: entry describing the sum of an account that has been previously sent in. **b.** *Cymb.* V. v. 135. **5.** R. to Cesar the things that are Cesars *Mark* 12:17. **6.** There were personal attentions to be rendered C. BRONTË.

III. 1. †To bring (a person) *into* a state or condition; to cause to be *in* a certain state (*rare*) 1490. †**b.** To present or expose *to*, to bring *under*, something –1661. **2.** To make, cause to be or become, of a certain nature, quality, etc. †Const. with *as* or *to be* 1560.

2. O ye Gods! R. me worthy of this Noble Wife SHAKS.

IV. *techn.* **a.** To melt (fat, etc.); to obtain or extract by melting; to clarify. late ME. **b.** *Plastering.* To cover (stone or brickwork) with a first coating of plaster 1750. **c.** *Naut.* (See next 3 b.) 1841. Hence **Re·nderable** *a.* (*rare*) capable of being rendered. **Re·nderer.**

Rendering (re·ndəriŋ), *vbl. sb.* 1440. [f. prec. + -ING¹.] **1.** The action of restoring, surrendering, yielding, etc.; also, that which is yielded or given. **2. a.** Translation, interpretation 1641. **b.** Reproduction, representation, performance 1862. **3.** *techn.* **a.** *Plastering.* The action of plastering with a first coat; the work so done; the plaster thus applied 1659. **b.** Yielding, slipping, or running out of tackle or lines 1769. **c.** Extracting or melting of fat, etc. 1865.

2. b. The painter has shown himself extremely skilful in his r. of curious effects of light 1893.

Rendezvous (re·ndĕvū, Fr. raṅdevu), *sb. Pl.* **rendezvous.** 1591. [Fr., subst. use of *rendez vous* 'present or betake yourselves'.] **1.** *Mil.* A place appointed for the assembling of troops or armed forces. **b.** A place or port fixed upon, or suitable, for the assembling of a fleet or number of ships; also, instructions concerning a rendezvous 1600. **2.** *gen.* An appointed place of meeting or gathering; a place of common resort 1594. †**3.** A retreat, refuge –1645. †**b.** A last resort. SHAKS. **4.** A meeting or assembly held by appointment or arrangement 1600. †**b.** The assembling, or an assemblage, of things –1680. **5.** Without article, in *place* (*point, port,* etc.) *of r.* 1600.

1. He proclaimed the Rendez-vous at Sora, for his Soldiers there to meete HOLLAND. **2.** A tauerne is the Randeuous, the Exchange, the staple for good fellowes LYLY. Phr. †*To make* or *keep* (one's) *r.*, to meet, or be in the habit of meeting, in or at a place.

Rendezvous (re·ndĕvū, -vūz, Fr. raṅdevu), *v.* 1645. [f. prec.] **1.** *intr.* To assemble at a place previously appointed; also, gen., to assemble, come together, meet. †**2.** Of a commander: To assemble his troops or fleet –1745. **3.** *trans.* To bring together (troops or ships) at a fixed place. Now *U.S.* 1654. †**b.** To bring together, collect, assemble (persons or things) –1719.

Rendition (rendi·ʃən). 1601. [– Fr. †*rendition*, f. *rendre* RENDER *v.*; see -ITION.] **1.** The surrender of a place, garrison, possession, etc. **b.** The surrender of a person 1649. **2.** Translation, rendering. Now *U.S.* 1659. **3.** orig. *U.S.* The action of rendering, giving out or forth, acting, performing, etc. 1858. **4.** *U.S.* The amount produced or rendered 1889.

1. The r. of Oxford to the Parliament forces 1691. **b.** His r. afterward to the Scotch Army MILT. **2.** Calverley's complete r. of Theocritus 1875.

Rendrock (re·ndrǫk). 1880. [f. REND *v.* + ROCK *sb.*] A kind of explosive.

Renegade (re·nĭgeⁱd), *sb.* (and *a.*) 1583. [Anglicized f. RENEGADO; see -ADE 3.] **1.** An apostate from any form of religious faith, *esp.* a Christian who becomes a Moslem. **2.** One who deserts a party, person, or principle, in favour of another; a turn-coat 1665. **3.** *attrib.*, passing into adj. 1705.

1. Like all renegades, he was a bitter and furious persecutor 1873. Hence **Re·negade** *v. intr.* to turn r.; to go over *from* a religion, party, etc.

Renegado (renĭgē·do), *sb.* (and *a.*) 1599. [– Sp. *renegado* – med.L. *renegatus*, subst. use of pa. pple. of *renegare*; see RENEGUE, -ADO.] = prec. Hence **Renega·do** *v. intr.* to turn r.

Renegate (re·nĭgĕⁱt), *sb.* (and *a.*) *Obs.* exc. *dial.* late ME. [– med.L. *renegatus*; see prec.] **1.** A renegade, deserter. **2.** *attrib.* or as adj. 1485.

Renegation (renĭgēⁱ·ʃən). 1615. [f. next + -ATION.] The action of renouncing or renegading.

Renegue (rĭnī·g), *v.* 1548. Also *U.S.* **renig.** [– med.L. *renegare*, f. *re-* RE- + *negare* deny, NEGATE.] **1.** *trans.* To deny, renounce, abandon, desert (a person, faith, etc.). Now *arch.* †**2.** *intr.* or *absol.* To make denial –1689. **3.** To refuse, decline (*rare*) 1582. **4.** *Card-playing.* To refuse or fail to follow suit; to revoke. Now *local* and *U.S.* 1680.

1. Those of this reformed Religion, who will not reneague it 1857. **2.** *Lear* II. ii. 84.

Renew (rĭniū·), *v.* late ME. [f. RE- + NEW *a.*, after earlier RENOVEL, L. *renovare* RENOVATE.] **1.** To make new, or as new, again; to restore to the same condition as when new, young, or fresh. **b.** To make spiritually new; to regenerate. late ME. **c.** To assume anew, to recover (one's original strength, youth, etc.) 1481. **2.** To restore, re-establish, set up again, bring back into use or existence. late ME. **3.** To take up again or afresh; to resume; to begin again, recommence. late ME. **b.** To say in resumption 1687. **4.** To go, or do, over again, repeat. late ME. **5.** To replace by some new or fresh thing of the same kind; to restore by means of substitution or a fresh supply; to fill (a vessel) again 1439. **6.** To revive, reawaken, resuscitate 1484. **7.** To grant anew, *esp.* to grant or give (a lease, bill, etc.) for a fresh period; also, to take afresh, to obtain an extension of 1617. **8.** *intr.* To grow afresh, become new again. late ME. †**9.** To begin a fresh attack, to return or come back, *upon* one; to renew the fight –1656. **10.** To begin again, recommence 1523.

1. In such a night Medea gathered the inchanted hearbs That did r. old Eson SHAKS. **b.** Graunt that we..maye dallye be renued by thy holy spirite *Bk. Com. Prayer.* **c.** Heav'n his wonted face renewed MILT. **2.** We..In pleasing dreams the blissful age r. JOHNSON. **3.** Socrates renews the attack from another side JOWETT. **4.** The Lady renewed her Excuses STEELE. **5.** The earth doth like a snake r. Her Winter weeds outworn SHELLEY. **6.** My fayre Frend, renewe not my sorowe CAXTON. **7.** The lease expired..and she did not care to r. it RUSKIN. *absol.* 'Won't the party r.?' THACKERAY. **8.** R. I could not like the Moone SHAKS. **9.** *Tr. & Cr.* v. v. 6. **10.** Whereupon the combat renewed with more cruelty than before 1640. Hence **Renewabi·lity. Renew·able** *a.* **Renew·al,** the act of renewing, or the state of being renewed; an instance of this. **Renew·ed-ly** *adv.*, **-ness. Renew·er. Renew·ment** (now *rare* or *Obs.*) renewal.

†**Renfo·rce,** *v.* 1525. [– (O)Fr. *renforcer*, f. *re-* RE- + OFr. *enforcier* ENFORCE *v.*] **1.** *trans.* To reinforce, strengthen –1652. **2.** To compel (a person) *to* do a thing again. SPENSER.

Reni-, comb. form of L. *ren* kidney (see REINS), used in some scientific terms, as *renicapsular.*

Reniform (rī·nifǭɹm), *a.* 1753. [f. RENI- + -FORM.] Having the form of a kidney; kidney-shaped.

†**Renitence.** 1652. [– Fr. *rénitence* (Paré); see RENITENT, -ENCE.] = next –1743.

Renitency (rĭnəi·tĕnsi, re·nitĕnsi). Now *rare.* 1613. [f. as prec.; see -ENCY. Cf. med.L. *renitentia.*] †**1.** Physical resistance, *esp.* the resistance of a body to pressure –1704. **2.** Resistance to constraint; opposition, reluctance 1626.

2. Nature has form'd the mind of man with the same..backwardness and r. against conviction STERNE.

Renitent (rĭnəi·tĕnt, re·nitĕnt), *a.* Now *rare.* 1701. [– Fr. *rénitent* (Paré), later – L. *renitens, -ent-*, pr. pple. of *reniti* struggle against, resist; see -ENT.] **1.** That offers physical resistance; hard. **2.** Recalcitrant 1847.

Rennet (re·nėt), *sb.*[1] late ME. [prob. south-eastern repr. of an OE. **rynet* (f. **run-* RUN), corresp. to dial. *runnet* (XV).] **1.** A mass of curdled milk found in the stomach of an unweaned calf or other animal, used for curdling milk in making cheese, etc.; also, a preparation of the inner membrane of the stomach, used for this or other purposes. **2.** Anything used to curdle milk, *esp.* the plant *Galium verum*, Lady's Bedstraw 1577.

attrib.: **r.-bag,** the stomach of a calf used as r.; **r. stomach,** the fourth stomach of a ruminant; **r. wort,** the plant *Galium aparine.*

Rennet (re·nėt), *sb.*[2] 1568. [– Fr. *reinette*, also *rainette*, prob. f. *raine* tree-frog (:– L. *rana* frog), the fruit being so named from the spotted markings of some varieties. See REINETTE.] One of a large class of dessert apples of French origin; †formerly applied to a pippin grafted on a pippin-stock.

†**Re·nnet,** *v. rare.* 1624. [f. RENNET *sb.*[1]] *trans.* To curdle (milk) with rennet; to supply with rennet –1648.

Men,..like Cheese o're-rennetted HERRICK.

Renounce (rĭnau·ns), *sb.* 1747. [– Fr. *renonce*, f. *renoncer*; see next.] *Card-playing.* An act or instance of renouncing (cf. next 5). **b.** A chance of renouncing, by having no cards of a particular suit 1830.

Renounce (rĭnau·ns), *v.* late ME. [–(O)Fr. *renoncer* :– L. *renuntiare* announce, proclaim, protest against, f. *re-* RE- + *nuntiare* bring news.] **1.** *trans.* To give up, resign, or surrender (†*to* another); *esp.* to give up in a complete and formal manner. **b.** To abandon, cast off, repudiate; to decline to recognize, hold, observe, etc. 1533. **2.** To abandon, give up (a practice, habit, intention, etc.) 1484. **b.** To abandon or give up (a belief or opinion) by open profession or recantation 1535. **3.** To cast off, disclaim or disown obedience, allegiance, or relationship to (a person) 1502. **4.** *intr.* or *absol.* †**a.** To make renunciation. Const. *to* (the thing renounced). –1728. **b.** *Law.* To make formal resignation of some right or trust, esp. of one's position as heir or executor 1604. **5.** *Card-playing.* To fail to follow suit; orig. implying the possession of, but now usu. the want of, a proper card. In the former case REVOKE is the current term. 1579.

1. I should require them..to r. in writing all claims upon myself 1856. Phr. *To r. the world*, to withdraw from worldly interests in order to lead a spiritual life. **b.** Napoleon renounced, once for all, sentiments and affections EMERSON. **2.** He was compelled to r. the attempt GROTE. **b.** All others must..submit and r. their errors BLACKSTONE. **3.** Your kindred r. you DICKENS. **4. a.** He of my sons who fails to make it good, By one rebellious act renounces to my blood DRYDEN. **b.** Where there is a Will and the Executor renounces 1695. Hence **Renou·nceable** *a.* that may be renounced. **Renou·ncement,** the act of renouncing; a renunciation. **Renou·ncer.**

Renovate (re·nŏvᵉⁱt), *v.* 1535. [– *renovat-*, pa. ppl. stem of L. *renovare*, f. *re-* RE- + *novare* make new, f. *novus* new.] †**1.** *trans.* To renew, resume (an action or purpose) –1796. **2.** To renew materially; to repair; to restore by replacing lost or damaged parts; to create anew 1552. **b.** To restore to vigour; to refresh 1671. **c.** To regenerate 1800.

2. Ethelwolde..did clerely r. and augmentid this Abbay LELAND. So **Re·novate** *pa. pple.* and *ppl. a.* renewed 1520. **Re·novator.**

Renovation (renŏvēⁱ·ʃən). late ME. [– Fr. *rénovation* or L. *renovatio, -on-*, f. as prec.; see -ION.] **1.** The action of renovating, or the condition of having been renovated; renewal; restoration; an instance of this, a change effected by renewal. †**b.** Renewal of the body at the resurrection –1667. **2.** *Theol.* Renewal wrought by the Holy Ghost; the creation of a new spirit within one 1543. †**3.** The renewal or resumption of an action, agreement, condition, etc. –1798.

1. The regular return of genial months, And r. of a faded world COWPER.

†**Reno·vel,** *v.* ME. [– OFr. *renoveler* (mod. *renouveler*), f. *re-* RE- + L. *novellus* young, new, f. *novus* new. See NOVEL *a.*] To renew –1537.

Renown (rĭnau·n), *sb.* ME. [– AFr. *renoun, renun*, OFr. *renon, renom*, f. *renomer* make famous, f. *re-* RE- + *nomer* name (:– L. *nominare* NOMINATE).] **1.** *Of r.*, of fame or distinction; widely known or celebrated; esp. *of great* (*high*, etc.) *r.* **2.** The fact or condition of being widely celebrated or held in high repute; celebrity, fame, honourable distinction ME. **b.** The fame or reputation attaching to a particular person, place, etc. late ME. †**3.** Report, rumour (sometimes implying sense 2.) –1610. †**b.** Reputation of a specified kind (*rare*) –1608. †**c.** Good name, reputation. SHAKS.

1. Mightie men, which in olde time were men of renoume BIBLE (Genev.) *Gen.* 6:4. **2.** The inheritors of unfulfilled r. Rose from their thrones SHELLEY. **b.** The r. of the Spanish infantry had been growing GREEN. **3. b.** A young Gentlewoman..of a most chaste r. SHAKS. **c.** *Cymb.* v. v. 202. Hence **Renow·nful, Renow·nless** *adjs.* (*rare*).

Renown (rĭnau·n), *v.* Now *rare.* 1530. [In XVI also *renoume* – OFr. *renoumer*, var. of *renomer*; see prec. The form *renown* has been assim. to the sb.] *trans.* To make famous, spread the fame of; to celebrate.

The Bard whom pilfer'd Pastorals r. POPE. Hence **Renow·ner,** one who celebrates or makes famous.

Renowned (rĭnau·nd), *ppl. a.* late ME. [f. as prec. + -ED[1], after earlier †*renomed* – OFr. *renomé* (mod. *renommé*).] Full of or covered with renown.

Peace hath her victories No less renownd then warr MILT. Hence **Renow·ned-ly** *adv.*, **-ness.**

Rensselaerite (rensĕlēᵊ·rəit, re·nsĕlĕrəit). 1846. [f. name of Gov. Stephen van *Rensselaer*; see -ITE[1] 2 b.] *Min.* A variety of talc found in parts of New York State and Canada, capable of being worked on a lathe and manufactured into various articles.

Rent (rent), *sb.*[1] ME. [– (O)Fr. *rente* :– Rom. **rendita*, f. **rendere* RENDER *v.*] †**1.** (In *pl.*) A source or item of revenue or income (e.g. a piece of property) –1611. †**b.** Revenue, income –1783. †**2.** A tribute, tax, or similar charge, levied by or paid to a person –1703. **3.** The return or payment made (in money or in kind) by a tenant to the owner or landlord, at certain specified or customary times, for the use of lands or houses ME. Called spec. *commercial r.* See also GROUND-RENT. **b.** The sum paid for the use of machinery, etc., for a certain time. **4.** A piece of property for which an annual rent is received or charged; esp. *pl.* a number of tenements or houses let out to others. Now *U.S. colloq.* (except in surviving proper names of such properties). 1466.

1. What are thy Rents? what are thy Commings in? SHAKS. **b.** To allow each of them such a r., as.. would make them easy SWIFT. **3.** Some of them pay more r. yerely than theyr Fermes be worth 1560. *Economic* (*Ricardian, true*) *r.*: the annual value of the powers of production which are inherent in the soil; the difference between the return from a given piece of land and from land of equal area which is on the margin of cultivation; also, more widely, the differential advantage for production due to the pre-eminent qualities of a person, factory, etc.

Rent (rent), *sb.*[2] 1535. [f. RENT *v.*[2]] **1.** The result of rending; a separation of parts produced by tearing or the like; *esp.* a large tear in a garment or piece of woven stuff. **2.** A breach, split, schism, or dissension in a society or party or between persons (*rare*) 1608. **3.** A cleft, fissure, breach 1705. **b.** *Coal-mining.* A plane of cleavage running across a seam 1883. **4.** The act of rending or fact of being rent 1836.

1. See what a r. the enuious Casca made SHAKS. **2.** It occasions..Rents, Confusions and Divisions in Families 1679.

Rent (rent), *v.*[1] late ME. [– (O)Fr. *renter*, f. *rente*; see RENT *sb.*[1]] †**1.** *trans.* To provide with revenues; to endow –1485. **2.** To pay rent for (land, houses, etc.); to take, hold, occupy or use, by payment of rent 1530. **3.** To let (*out*) for rent or payment; to hire out 1546. **4.** *intr.* To let *at* a certain rent 1538. **5.** *trans.* To charge (a person) with rent; to impose a certain rent on 1881.

2. If I can r. rooms in town to lodge in 1763. **b.** *intr.* (U.S.) To secure the use of a house in return for rent 1911. **4.** Arable land rents at £3 and £4, or even £6 an acre 1815. **5.** The power..to r. a man upon his own improvements 1894. Hence **Re·ntable** *a.* liable to pay rent; that may be rented, or let out for hire.

Rent (rent), *v.*[2] *Obs.* exc. *dial.* late ME. [var. of REND *v.* based on pa. t. and pa. pple. *rent.*] **1.** *trans.* To rend, tear, pull asunder or in pieces. **2.** *intr.* To tear; to give way or separate by tearing or splitting 1526.

1. Rente youre clothes, and gyrd sack cloth aboute you COVERDALE 2 *Sam.* 3:31. Rente your hertes, & not youre clothes COVERDALE *Joel* 2:12.

Rent (rent), *ppl. a.* late ME. [pa. pple. of REND *v.*] Torn, in various senses.

Rentage (re·ntėdʒ). 1633. [f. RENT *sb.*[1] + -AGE.] Rent, rental, or renting; also, that which is held for rent.

Rental (re·ntăl). late ME. [– AFr. *rental* or AL. *rentale* (XIII); see RENT *sb.*[1], -AL[1].] **1.** A rent-roll. Now *rare.* **b.** An income arising from rents received. late ME. **2.** The amount paid or received as rent 1637. **b.** *U.S.* Returns from the lending of books; *Comb.* **r. library** 1928.

1. b. Emily's..r. offered a mark to his ambition 1801.

Re·nt-charge. Also **rent charge.** 1443. [f. RENT *sb.*[1] + CHARGE *sb.*] *Law.* A rent forming a charge upon lands, etc., granted or reserved by deed to one who is not the owner, with a clause of distress in case of arrears. Hence **Re·nt-cha:rger,** one in receipt of, or who benefits by, a rent-charge.

Renter (re·ntəɹ), *sb.* late ME. [f. RENT *v.*[1] + -ER[1].] **1.** One who owns or lets lands, tenements, etc. (now *U.S.*). †**2.** A collector of rents, taxes, or tribute –1762. **3.** A farmer of tolls or taxes (*rare*) 1598. **4.** A holder of lands, houses, or other property, by payment of rent 1655. †**b.** *spec.* A tenant-farmer –1792.

Rent-free, *a.* 1631. [RENT *sb.*[1]] Exempt from payment of rent.

‖**Rentier** (rañtye). 1881. [Fr., f. *rente* RENT *sb.*[1] + *-ier* -IER 2.] One whose income is derived from investments.

Re·nt-roll. 1534. [RENT *sb.*[1]] A roll or register of rents; a list of lands and tenements belonging to a person, together with the rents paid on them; hence, the sum of a person's income as shown by such a list.

Rent-seck. 1472. [– AFr. *rente secque* lit. dry rent.] *Law.* A rent reserved by deed in favour of some person, without a clause of distress in case of arrears (abolished in 1731).

Re·nt-se:rvice. 1477. [RENT *sb.*[1]] Personal service by which lands or tenements are held in addition to, or in lieu of, money payment; tenure of this kind.

Renule (re·niul), *sb.* 1847. [f. L. *ren* kidney + -ULE.] *Anat.* One of the separate lobules of which the kidneys in some animals are composed.

Renunciate (rǐnɒ·nʃieᶦt), *v.* 1656. [Back-formation from next.] †**1.** *trans.* To proclaim or declare openly. BLOUNT. **2.** To renounce, give up (*rare*) 1814.

Renunciation (rǐnɒnsi,ēᶦ·ʃən). late ME. [– (O)Fr. *renonciation* or late and med.L. *renuntiatio, -on-,* (cl.L. = announcement, etc.), f. *renuntiat-* pa. ppl. stem of L. *renuntiare* RENOUNCE; see -ION.] **1.** The action of renouncing, giving up, or surrendering (a possession, right, title, etc.); an instance of this; a document expressing this. **b.** The action of giving up something naturally attractive 1526. **2.** The action of rejecting, disowning, or disclaiming; repudiation, formal rejection. late ME.

1. The queen's r. of her right of succession HALLAM. b. A r. of my old and more favourite pursuits TYNDALL.

Renunciative (rǐnɒ·nʃiětiv), *a.* late ME. [In sense 1 perh. f. *renunciat-*, pa. ppl. stem of L. *renuntiare* announce (see RENOUNCE); in sense 2 f. RENUNCIATION + -IVE.] †**1.** Serving to announce or enunciate –1622. **2.** Characterized by renunciation 1850. So **Renu·nciatory** *a.*

†**Renve·rse,** *v.* 1590. [– (O)Fr. *renverser*, f. *re-* RE- + *enverser* overturn.] **1.** *trans.* To reverse; to turn upside down, turn the wrong way, turn back –1681. **2.** To overturn or overthrow; to bring to confusion –1728.

1. Whose shield he beares renverst, the more to heap disdayn SPENSER. Hence †**Renve·rsement,** the act of reversing; the result of this.

Renversé (raṅverse), *a.* 1725. [– Fr., pa. pple. of *renverser*; see prec.] *Her.* Inverted; reversed.

†**Renvoy,** *sb.* 1600. [– Fr. *renvoi*, f. *renvoyer*; see next.] The act of sending back; discharge, dismissal –1654.

†**Renvoy,** *v. rare.* 1477. [– (O)Fr. *renvoyer*, f. *re-* RE- + *envoyer*; see ENVOY *sb.*[1]] *trans.* To send back –1622.

I doo Renvoye the..palmer thither agayn CROMWELL.

Reo·pen (rī-), *v.* 1733. [RE- 5 a.] **1.** *trans.* To open again. **b.** To open up again, to renew 1848. **2.** *intr.* To open again 1830.

Reordai·n (rī-), *v.* 1611. [RE- 5 a. Cf. Fr. *réordonner* (XVI).] *trans.* To ordain again. So **Reordina·tion** 1597.

Reorganiza·tion (rī-). 1813. [RE- 5 a.] The action or process of reorganizing; a fresh organization.

A re-organization of the cavalry WELLINGTON.

Reo·rganize (rī-), *v.* 1681. [RE- 5 a.] *trans.* To organize anew.

Rep[1]. 1705. Now *U.S.* Abbrev. of REPUTATION.

Rep[2] (rep). Now *rare.* 1747. [perh. abbrev. of REPROBATE *sb.* The relation to DEMI-REP is not clear. Cf. RIP *sb.*[4]] **1.** A man (†or woman) of loose character. **2.** An inferior article 1786.

Rep[3] (rep). Also **repp.** 1860. [– Fr. *reps*, of unkn. origin.] A textile fabric (of wool, silk, or cotton) having a corded surface.

Repair (rǐpēᵊ·ɹ), *sb.*[1] ME. [– OFr. *repaire, repeire* (mod. *repaire, repère*), f. *repairer*; see REPAIR *v.*[1]] **1.** (Chiefly in phr. *to make* or *have r.*) Resort, frequent or habitual going, *to* a place. Now *arch.* or *Obs.* **2.** The place to which one repairs; *esp.* a haunt, usual abode or dwelling-place. late ME. †**b.** So *place, house,* etc. *of r.* –1611. **3.** Concourse or confluence of people in or at a place; common or extensive resort of persons *to* a place. Now *rare* or *Obs.* ME. †**b.** Following, retinue, company (*rare*) –1548. †**4.** The act of (†returning) going or making one's way *to* a place –1698.

1. Peter Heylin..was furnished with Books..by his r. to Bodlies Library WOOD. 2. b. Jehova is my fort, My place of safe repaire 1586. 4. At my..repayre thither it pleased his highnes to call for me 1531. Phr. *To make* (one's) *r. to* (a place or person). Now *arch.*

Repair (rǐpēᵊ·ɹ), *sb.*[2] 1595. [f. REPAIR *v.*[2]] **1.** The act of restoring to a sound or unimpaired condition; the process by which this is accomplished; the result attained. **b.** *spec.* Restoration of some material thing or structure by the renewal of decayed or worn out parts, by refixing what has become loose or detached; the result of this. Also *pl.* 1661. **2.** Relative state or condition of something admitting or susceptible of restoration in the event of damage or decay; chiefly in phr. *in good* (or *bad*) *r.* 1600.

1. I,..Dazl'd and spent, sunk down, and sought r. Of sleep MILT. 2. A Country-House in no very good R. SWIFT. Phr. *In r.*, in good or proper condition. *Out of r.*, in bad condition, requiring repairs.

Repair (rǐpēᵊ·ɹ), *v.*[1] ME. [– OFr. *repair(i)er* (mod. *repairer, repérer*) :– late L. *repatriare* return to one's country; see REPATRIATE.] **1.** *intr.* To go, betake oneself, make one's way. **b.** To resort *to* a place or person; to go commonly, frequently, or in numbers. late ME. †**2.** To return (*again*), to come or go back (*to* or *from* a place, person) etc. Also without const. –1633. †**3.** To be present, temporarily or habitually; to have one's resort; to dwell, reside –1560. †**4.** *trans.* To draw *back*, to recover. SPENSER.

1. To those Places straight r. Where your respective Dwellings are 1663. b. The people of Calais r. hither for their evening dance 1809. 2. *Mids. N.* IV. i. 72. If I might beseech you Gentlemen, to repayre some other houre SHAKS.

Repair (rǐpēᵊ·ɹ), *v.*[2] late ME. [– (O)Fr. *réparer* – L. *reparare*, f. *re-* RE- + *parare* make ready, put in order.] **1.** *trans.* To restore (a composite thing, structure, etc.) to good condition by renewal or replacement of decayed or damaged parts, or by refixing what has given way; to mend. **b.** To heal or cure (a wound). Also *intr.* of a wound: To mend, heal up. 1590. **2.** *trans.* To renew, renovate (some thing or part); to restore to a fresh or sound condition by making up in some way for previous loss, waste, decay, or exhaustion. late ME. †**b.** To revive, recreate (a person). SHAKS. **3.** To restore (a person) to a previous state; to reinstate, re-establish, rehabilitate –1738. **4.** To remedy, make up (loss, damage, etc.); to set right again 1533. **b.** To make good, make amends for (harm done, etc.) 1562.

1. He repaired his navie and returned to Constantinople 1560. b. The wound was not repairing 1881. 2. So sinks the day-star in the Ocean bed, And yet anon repairs his drooping head MILT. The fair..Repairs her smiles, awakens ev'ry grace POPE. b. *Two Gent.* V. iv. 11. 4. Unskilful either in improving their victories, or repairing their defeats BURKE. The loss of such a man could not be easily repaired MACAULAY. b. The emperor seemed impatient to r. his injustice GIBBON. Hence **Repai·rable** *a.* capable of being repaired; that is to be repaired. **Repai·rer,** one who or that which restores or mends.

Repand (rǐpæ·nd), *a.* 1760. [– L. *repandus* bent backwards, f. *re-* RE- + *pandus* bent.] *Bot.* and *Zool.* Having an undulating margin, wavy.

Reparable (re·părăb'l), *a.* 1570. [– (O)Fr. *réparable* – L. *reparabilis*; see REPAIR *v.*[2], -ABLE.] **1.** Capable of being repaired, mended or set right again. **2.** Liable to be repaired *by* some one 1864.

1. Twenty r...spare wheels 1809. Only slight and r. injuries 1884. 2. New streets..r. by the local authorities 1864. Hence **Re:parabi·lity. Re·parably** *adv.*

Reparation (repărēᶦ·ʃən). late ME. [– (O)Fr. *réparation* – late L. *reparatio, -on-,* – *reparat-*, pa. ppl. stem of L. *reparare*; see REPAIR *v.*[2], -ION.] **1.** The action of restoring to a proper state; restoration or renewal (*of* a thing or part). †**b.** Spiritual restoration, salvation; an instance of this –1725. **2.** The action of repairing or mending, or the fact of being repaired. (Now more usu. expressed by REPAIR *sb.*[2] 1 b.) ME. **3.** *pl.* Repairs. Now *rare.* 1439. **4.** The action of making amends for a wrong done; amends; compensation. Now usu. *pl.* late ME.

2. The original charter records the r. of the Church FREEMAN. 4. Willing to make reasonable r. 1877.

Reparative (rǐpæ·rătiv), *a.* 1656. [f. prec. + -IVE; see -ATIVE.] **1.** Capable of effecting, or tending to effect, repair; relating to repair. **2.** Pertaining to the making of amends, or the remedying of some wrong 1695.

†**Repa·rel,** *v.* ME. [– OFr. *repareill(i)er, -aill(i)er*, f. *re-* RE- + *apareill(i)er* (mod. *appareiller*); see APPAREL *v.*] **1.** *trans.* To repair (a thing or structure) –1560. **2.** To restore *to* some state or condition, set right again; to recover (*rare*) –late ME. **3.** To fit up, array, apparel (*rare*) –1579. So †**Repa·rel** *sb.* furniture, apparel.

†**Repa·rt,** *v.* 1574. [– (O)Fr. *répartir*, f. *re-* RE- + *partir* PART *v.*] *trans.* To divide or distribute, esp. *among* a number of persons –1755.

Repartee (repaɹtī·), *sb.* 1645. [– (O)Fr. *repartie*, subst. use of fem. pa. pple. of *repartir* set out again, reply readily, f. *re-* RE- + *partir* PART *v.*] **1.** A ready, witty, or smart reply; a quick and clever retort. **2.** Sharpness or wit in sudden reply; such replies collectively; the practice or faculty of uttering them 1668.

1. The Grave abound in Pleasantries, the Dull in Repartees and Points of Wit ADDISON. 2. Skill'd in no other arts..But dressing, patching and r. GOLDSM.

Repartee (repaɹtī·), *v.* 1668. [f. prec.; cf. Fr. *repartir.*] **1.** *intr.* To make witty or smart replies. Now *rare.* †**2.** *trans.* To say by way of repartee or retort –1686. †**3.** To answer (a person or something said) with a repartee or retort (*rare*) –1743.

Repartition (repaɹti·ʃən, rī-). 1555. [f. RE- + PARTITION *sb.*] **1.** Partition, distribution, allotment (in former use *esp.* of troops or military quarters). With *a* and *pl.* An instance of this. **2.** A fresh distribution or allotment 1835.

1. No fair r. of burthens upon all the orders could possibly restore them BURKE.

Repass (rǐpɑ·s), *v.* 1456. [– (O)Fr. *repasser*; see RE-, PASS *v.*] **1.** *intr.* To pass again in the contrary direction; to return. Chiefly in *pass and r.* **2.** *trans.* To cross (the sea, a river, etc.) again in the contrary direction 1500. **b.** To pass again over, through, or by (a way, gate, place, etc.); to go past again 1618. **3.** To cause to pass again; to put *through* again 1565. **b.** To pass (a bill, resolution) again 1796.

1. A lawn terminated by water, with objects passing and repassing upon it 1785. *Hey pass, r.*, a conjurer's formula. 2. In repassing the mountains, great numbers of soldiers perished GIBBON. b. I..passed and repassed the spot many times 1898. So **Repassage** (ripæ·sédʒ), [– Fr. *repassage*] the act of repassing; passage back; liberty or right to repass. late ME.

Repassant (rǐpæ·sănt), *a.* 1828. [See RE-, PASSANT.] *Her.* Passant in opposite directions; counterpassant.

Repast (rǐpɑ·st), *sb.* ME. [– OFr. *repast* (mod. *repas*), f. *repaistre*, mod. *repaître* (:– late L. *repascere*), after OFr. *past* (:– L. *pastus* fodder, food); see RE-, PASTURE *sb.*] **1.** A quantity of food and drink forming, or intended for, a meal or feast. †**2.** Food, supply of food or victuals –1732. **3.** The action or fact of taking food; the refreshment of food. Now *arch.* 1588. **b.** An occasion of taking or partaking of food; a meal or feast in this sense 1639. †**4.** Refreshment; repose –1615.

1. What neat r. shall feast us, light and choice,..with Wine? MILT. 2. A Buck was then a week's r. POPE. 3. If (before r.) it shall please you to gratifie the table with a Grace SHAKS.

Repast (rǐpɑ·st), *v.* Now *rare.* 1470. [f. prec.] †**1.** *refl.* To refresh (oneself) with food –1617. †**2.** *trans.* To feed, supply with food –1669. **3.** *intr.* To feed, feast 1520.

2. *Haml.* IV. v. 147. Hence †**Repa·ster,** one who takes a repast.

†**Repa·sture.** *rare.* 1588. [f. prec. + -URE. Cf. OFr. *repaisture* food.] Food; a repast –1614.

Foode for his rage, r. for his den SHAKS.

Repatriate (rǐpæ·trieᶦt, -pēᶦ·t-), *v.* 1611. [– *repatriat-*, pa. ppl. stem of late L. *repatriare* go back home, in med.L. causative, f. *re-* RE- + L. *patria* native land; see -ATE³.] **1.** *trans.* To restore (a person) to his own country. **2.** *intr.* To return to one's own country (*rare*) 1656. Hence **Repatria·tion,** return or restoration to one's own country.

Repay (rĭpē¹·), *v.* 1530. [– OFr. *repaier*; see RE-, PAY *v.*¹] **1.** *trans.* To refund, pay back (a sum of money, etc.). Also with double obj. **b.** To return (a blow, visit, salutation, etc.) 1593. **c.** To give (a thing) in return or recompense (*for* something) 1560. **2.** To make repayment or return to (a person); to pay (a person) back in some way 1542. **3.** To requite (an action, etc.) 1596. **4.** *intr.* To make repayment or return 1557.

1. What so ever you lay out it shalbe repayed you 1530. **b.** 3 *Hen. VI*, II. iii. 3. **c.** Euill pursueth sinners: but to the righteous, good shall be repayd *Prov.* 13:21. **2.** Let me now you pray,..Ye will me now with like good turne r. SPENSER. **4.** Vengeance is mine: I will repaye, saith the Lord N.T. (Genev.) *Rom.* 12:19. Hence **Repay·able** *a.* that may be, or is to be, repaid.

Repayment (rĭpē¹·mĕnt, rĭ-). 1435. [f. prec. + -MENT.] **1.** The (*or* an) act of repaying; payment back (of money lent, etc.). **2.** Requital, return (of services, etc.) 1574.

Repeal (rĭpī·l), *sb.* 1483. [– AFr. *repel* = OFr. *rapel* (mod. *rappel*), f. *rapeler*; see next.] †**1.** Recall, as from banishment –1658. **2.** The (*or* an) act of repealing (a law, resolution, sentence, etc.); abrogation 1503. **b.** *spec.* The cancelling of the Union between Great Britain and Ireland as an Irish political demand. Now *Hist.* 1831. **3.** Means or possibility of release (*from* punishment). *rare.* 1594.

1. The decree of repeale was authorized by the people, and the banished men returned to Syracvsa 1612. **3.** That deep gulf without r. BYRON.

Repeal (rĭpī·l), *v.* ME. [– AFr. *repeler*, for OFr. *rapeler* (mod. *rappeler*), f. *re-* RE- + *ap(p)eler* APPEAL *v.*] **1.** *trans.* To revoke, rescind, annul (a resolution, law, sentence, etc.). †**b.** To recall, withdraw (a privilege, grant, etc.) –1598. †**2.** To withdraw or retract (a statement); to give up, abandon (a thought, feeling, etc.) –1667. †**3. a.** To recall (a person) from exile –1662. **b.** To call or summon back –1727.

1. The Soveraign..having power to make, and repeale Lawes HOBBES. **2.** Adam soon repeal'd The doubts that in his heart arose MILT. **3. a.** The banish'd Bullingbrooke repeales himselfe, And.. is..arriu'd At Rauenspurg SHAKS. **b.** His scar'd Senses returning to their proper Seat, and his stray'd Reason repeal'd 1727. Hence **Repea·lable** *a.* that may be repealed or revoked. **Repealabi·lity. Repea·lableness.** †**Repea·lment,** recall from banishment.

Repealer (rĭpī·ləɹ). 1765. [f. prec. + -ER¹.] One who repeals or advocates repeal. **b.** *spec.* An advocate of the repeal of the Union between Great Britain and Ireland. Now *Hist.* 1831.

Repeat (rĭpī·t), *sb.* 1450. [f. the vb.] **1.** The (*or* an) act of repeating, repetition 1556. **b.** A repetition of a musical piece or performance, or of some part of these 1853. **2.** *Mus.* **a.** A passage repeated or performed twice; the repetition of a passage 1450. **b.** A sign directing that a passage is to be performed twice 1667. **3.** A duplicate of something 1842. **b.** A device or pattern on cloth, paper, etc., which is repeated uniformly over the surface 1845. **c.** *Comm.* A second or fresh supply of goods similar to one already received; also, an order for such a supply 1885.

3. c. We can tell how trade is going by the 'repeats' we get 1895. *attrib.* R. orders are coming in 1891.

Repeat (rĭpī·t), *v.* [Late XIV *repete* – (O)Fr. *répéter* – L. *repetere*, f. *re-* RE- + *petere* attack, make for, demand, seek, etc.] **I. 1.** *trans.* To say or utter over again, to reiterate. **2.** To say over, recite; also, to say or enunciate in a formal manner or in due order; to relate, recount. Also *absol.* 1559. †**b.** To celebrate, speak of (as). *rare.* –1671. **3.** To say or utter again after another or others 1595.

1. His still refuted quirks he still repeats COWPER. **2.** R. me these verses again, slowly and deliberately SCOTT. **b.** Reserv'd alive to be repeated The subject of thir cruelty, or scorn MILT. **3.** I do but r. what has been said a thousand times STEELE.

II. †**1.** To seek again, return to, encounter, or undergo again –1697. **2.** To do, make, perform, or execute over again 1560. **b.** To cause to appear, to bring up or present again. Also freq. in *pass.*, denoting recurrence. 1714. **c.** *intr.* To recur 1714. **3.** *spec.* **a.** Of clocks and watches: To strike (the last hour or quarter) again. Also *absol.* 1727. **b.** *Naut.* To reproduce (signals made by the admiral). Also *absol.* 1769. **c.** *absol.* Of food: To rise in the gullet, so as to be tasted again 1879. **4.** *refl.* **a.** To reproduce or present (oneself) again; to reappear in the same form 1850. **b.** To say again what one has already said 1864.

2. There is scarce a painter but has repeated some one of his works 1706. **4. b.** He spoke more than an hour without a note—never repeating himself FROUDE.

†**III.** Chiefly *Sc. Law.* To ask back, to demand the restitution of (money or goods); to claim, require –1649. Hence **Repea·tedly** *adv.* more than once, frequently.

Repeater (rĭpī·təɹ). 1577. [f. prec. + -ER¹.] †**1.** A rehearser, trainer. HOLINSHED. **2.** One who repeats something heard or learned; a relater, reciter 1598. **3. a.** A repeating watch or clock 1760. **b.** *Naut.* A repeating ship 1829. **c.** A repeating fire-arm 1868. **d.** *Telegraphy.* A device for automatically retransmitting signals from one circuit to another 1860. **4.** *Arith.* A recurring decimal 1773. **5.** *U.S.* **a.** One who votes, or attempts to vote, more than once at an election 1884. **b.** One who is frequently committed to prison 1884.

Repea·ting, *ppl. a.* 1688. [f. as prec. + -ING².] That repeats. **1. a.** Of watches and clocks, or parts of these. **b.** Of ships (see REPEAT *v.* II. 3 b) 1802. **c.** *R. circle*, an instrument for measuring angles, in which accuracy is obtained by repeated measurements on a graduated circle. So *r. instrument*, etc. 1815. **d.** Of fire-arms: Capable of firing a number of shots in succession without reloading 1824. **2.** *Arith.* Of decimals: Recurring 1773. **3.** That repeats a sound 1709.

Repel (rĭpe·l), *v.* late ME. [– L. *repellere*, f. *re-* RE- + *pellere* drive.] †**1.** *trans.* To drive or put away; to remove, extinguish, quench –1586. **2.** To drive or force back (an assailant or invader, an attack, etc.); to repulse 1450. **b.** To resist, repress (a feeling, incentive, etc.) 1586. **c.** *Med.* To force back into the blood or system; to repress (a morbid humour, swelling, eruption, etc.). Now *rare* or *Obs.* 1719. †**3.** To reject or debar (a person *from* an office, right, etc.) –1766. †**b.** To stop, hinder, or restrain (a person) *from* an action or manner of acting –1617. **4.** To turn back, ward off (a weapon, blow, or wound) 1526. **b.** To ward off, resist (some outward evil) 1600. **5.** To drive or force back, esp. by physical resistance 1605. **b.** To force away by the operation of natural laws of matter 1710. **c.** To refuse to mix with (one another), or to admit (moisture) 1744. **6.** To refuse to accept or receive; *esp.* to reject (a statement, plea, etc.) as unfounded or invalid 1561. **7.** To drive away or repulse with harsh words or treatment, or by denial; to reject (a suit) 1571. **b.** To affect (a person) with distaste or aversion. Also *absol.* 1817.

2. So turn'd stern Ajax, by whole hosts repell'd POPE. **5.** As the Rocks r. the greatest waves 1657. **c.** Why oil and water, mercury and iron, r...each other BERKELEY. **7.** Like suitors that will not be repelled TYNDALL. **b.** A study which repels you is invaluable 1878.

Repellant (rĭpe·lănt), *a.* and *sb.* 1689. [f. REPEL + -ANT.] **A.** *adj.* = next A. 2, 3. 1768. **B.** *sb.* = next B. So **Repe·llance, -ancy,** the act of repelling; a repellent feature or trait.

Repellent (rĭpe·lĕnt), *a.* and *sb.* 1643. [– L. *repellens, -ent-*, pr. pple. of *repellere*; see REPEL, -ENT.] **A.** *adj.* **1.** Of medicines: Having the effect of repelling morbid humours, etc. Now *rare.* **2.** Having the power of repelling other bodies; characterized by repulsion 1744. **3.** Repelling by coldness of demeanour, or by some disagreeable feature; affecting one with distaste or aversion 1797.

1. All those means are said to be r., which check the Growth of the Tumour 1719.

B. *sb.* **1.** *Med.* An application serving to repel humours, etc. Now *rare.* 1661. **2.** A repelling power or influence 1802. Hence **Repe·llence, -ency,** the quality of being r.; repelling power. **Repe·llently** *adv.*

Repe·ller. 1611. [f. REPEL *v.* + -ER¹.] **1.** One who repels. †**2.** = prec. B. 1. –1753.

†**Repe·nt,** *sb.* 1590. [f. the vb.] Repentance; an act of repentance –1611.

Repent (rī·pĕnt), *a.* 1669. [– L. *repens, repent-*, pr. pple. of *repere* creep; see -ENT.] **1. a.** *Bot.* Creeping; *esp.* growing along the ground, or just under the surface, and sending out roots at intervals. **b.** *Zool.* Creeping, crawling, reptant 1836. †**2.** *fig.* Unable to rise to high ideas. EVELYN.

Repent (rĭpe·nt), *v.* ME. [– (O)Fr. *repentir*, f. *re-* RE- + *pentir* :– Rom. **pœnitire*, for L. *pœnitēre*; see PENITENT.] **1.** *refl.* To be affected with contrition or regret for something done. Now *arch.* **2.** *impers.* To cause (a person) to feel regret, etc. ME. **3.** *intr.* To feel contrition, compunction, sorrow, or regret for something one has done or left undone; to change one's mind with regard to past action or conduct through dissatisfaction with it or its results ME. †**b.** To be sad, to mourn (for an event). SPENSER. **4.** *trans.* To view or think of (any action, etc.) with dissatisfaction and regret; to be sorry for ME. **b.** *esp.* To feel regret, sorrow, or contrition for (some fault, misconduct, sin, or other offence). late ME. †**5.** To live *out* in repentance. SHAKS.

1. I r. me that the Duke is slaine SHAKS. **2.** It salle r. vs..sore and we ryde forthire! late ME. **3.** If your purpose is evil, pause a moment, and r. MRS. RADCLIFFE. Nor do I now r. of the manner of my defence JOWETT. **4.** I do r. The tedious minutes I with her haue spent SHAKS. **b.** For a few minutes I repented my temerity SOUTHEY. Hence **Repe·nter,** one who repents. **Repe·ntingly** *adv.*

Repentance (rĭpe·ntăns). ME. [– (O)Fr. *repentance*; see next, -ANCE.] The act of repenting or the state of being penitent; sorrow, regret, or contrition for past action or conduct; an instance of this.

R. is never too late, but it is a true saying, r. is never too soon 1591. Phr. *Stool of r., r.-stool*, a stool formerly placed in a conspicuous position in Scottish churches for the use of offenders (esp. against chastity) making public repentance; also called CUTTY-STOOL.

Repentant (rĭpe·ntănt), *a.* and *sb.* ME. [– (O)Fr. *repentant*, pr. pple. of *repentir*; see REPENT *v.*, -ANT.] **A.** *adj.* **1.** Experiencing repentance; sorrowful for past sins, penitent. **2.** Expressing or indicating repentance 1594. †**B.** *sb.* One who repents, a penitent –1814.

A. 1. Thus they in lowliest plight r. stood MILT. **2.** R. sighs POPE. Hence **Repe·ntantly** *adv.*

Repercuss (rĭpəɹkʊ·s), *v. Obs.* or *rare.* 1501. [f. *repercuss-*, pa. ppl. stem of L. *repercutere*, f. *re-* RE- + *percutere* PERCUSS.] *trans.* †**a.** To beat or drive back (air, fluids, etc.) –1773. †**b.** To reflect (beams or rays of light) –1686. **c.** To return, reverberate (a sound). *rare.* 1585.

c. Whether a Man shall heare better, if he stand aside the Body Repercussing BACON.

Repercussion (rĭpəɹkʊ·ʃən). late ME. [– (O)Fr. *répercussion* or L. *repercussio, -on-*, f. as prec.; see -ION.] **1.** The action of a thing in forcing or driving back an impinging or advancing body; also, the power of doing this. Now *rare.* 1536. †**2.** *Med.* The action of forcing back or driving away by the application of remedies; the operation of repelling (humours, swellings, etc.) from a particular part of the body; also, a medicine or application used for this purpose –1727. **3.** Repulse or recoil of a thing after impact; the fact of being forced or driven back by a resisting body 1553. **b.** *Med.* A method of diagnosing pregnancy in which, upon a sudden push with the finger upon the uterine wall, the fœtus is felt to move away and return again 1860. **4.** The return or reverberation of a sound; echo, echoing noise 1595. **b.** *Mus.* (*a*) Repetition of a chord or note; (*b*) the reappearance of the subject of a fugue after the exposition 1872. **5.** The action of a substance in reflecting light; †colour resulting from such reflection 1601. **b.** Reflection *of* beams, rays, etc. 1601. **6.** A blow or stroke given in return; also *fig.* a return of any kind of action, a responsive act 1603. †7. A repeated attack *of* pain. BURNS.

3. The waters are violently carried against the rocks: and in their r., form dangerous whirlpools 1760. 4. Like the echo which is a r. of the original voice J. H. NEWMAN.

Repercussive (rīpəɹkɒ·siv), *a.* and *sb.* late ME. [– (O)Fr. *répercussif, -ive* or med.L. *repercussivus*, f. as prec.; see -IVE.] **A.** *adj.* †**1.** Of medicines or medical applications: Serving to repel humours or reduce swellings –1694. **2. a.** Of sounds: Reverberating or reverberated; echoing, resounding; repeated 1598. **b.** Of things or places: Returning a sound 1695. †**3.** Of light: Reflected –1639.

1. Besides this, it is very drying, r., and anodyn 1694. 2. a. Amid Carnarvon's mountains rages loud The r. roar THOMSON. b. Ye noisie Waves Strike with Applause the r. Caves 1712.

†**B.** *sb. Med.* A repellent –1725.

Hence **Repercu·ssive-ly** *adv.*, **-ness.**

‖**Repertoire** (re·pəɹtwāɹ, Fr. repertwar). Also **ré-**. 1847. [Fr. – late L. REPERTOR-IUM.] A stock of dramatic or musical pieces which a company or player is accustomed or prepared to perform; one's stock of parts, tunes, songs, etc. *R. theatre* = REPERTORY *t.*

‖**Repertorium** (repəɹtō°·riŏm). 1667. [Late L.; see next.] †**a.** A catalogue. **b.** A storehouse, repository.

Repertory (re·pəɹtəri). 1552. [– late and med.L. *repertorium* inventory, catalogue, summary, f. *repert-*, pa. ppl. stem of L. *reperire* find; see -ORY¹.] †**1.** An index, list, catalogue or calendar –1761. **2.** A storehouse, magazine, or repository, where something may be found 1593. **3.** = REPERTOIRE 1845.

attrib. (sense 3) as *r. company, players*, etc.; **r. theatre,** a theatre to which is attached a permanent company of actors who perform plays belonging to a certain repertory or of the same class as these.

Repetend (re·pĭtend, repĭte·nd). 1714. [– L. *repetendum*, n. gerundive of *repetere* REPEAT *v.*] **1.** *Arith.* The recurring figure or figures in an interminate decimal fraction. **2.** A recurring note, word, or phrase; a refrain 1874.

Repetition (repĭti·ʃən). 1526. [– (O)Fr. *répétition* or L. *repetitio, -on-*, f. *repetit-*, pa. ppl. stem of *repetere*; see REPEAT *v.*, -ION.] **1.** The action of repeating or saying over again; reiteration; an instance of this. **b.** *Rhet.* The use of repeated words or phrases 1553. **2.** The action of saying over something in order to retain it in the memory; †the rehearsal of a play 1581. **b.** The action of reciting in a formal manner, *esp.* recitation of something learned by heart; a piece set to be learned and recited 1597. **3.** Recital, narration, mention 1594. **4.** The action or fact of doing something again; renewal or recurrence of an action or event; repeated use, application, or appearance 1597. **b.** *Mus.* The action or fact of repeating; the rapid reiteration of a note 1597. **c.** The comparative ability of a musical instrument to repeat the same note in quick succession 1881. **5.** A copy or replica of a thing 1853.

1. When ye pray, vse no vaine repetitions as the heathen BIBLE (Genev.) *Matt.* 6:7. 2. It is now in r. at the French comedy FOOTE. 3. A name Whose r. will be dogg'd with Curses SHAKS. Hence **Repeti·tional, Repeti·tionary** *adjs.* characterized by, of the nature of r.

Repetitious (repĭti·ʃəs), *a.* 1675. [f. as prec. + -IOUS.] Abounding in, or characterized by, repetition, esp. of a tedious kind; tiresomely iterative. Hence **Repeti·tious-ly** *adv.*, **-ness.**

Repetitive (rĭpe·titiv), *a.* 1839. [f. as prec. + -IVE.] Characterized by, of the nature of, repetition; repetitious.

†**Repi·ne,** *sb.* 1592. [f. the vb.] The (*or* an) act of repining; discontent, grudge –1615.

Repine (rĭpəi·n), *v.* 1530. [f. RE- + PINE *v.*, after *repent.*] **1.** *intr.* To feel or manifest discontent or dissatisfaction; to fret, murmur, or complain. **b.** To long discontentedly *for* something (*rare*) 1742. †**2.** *trans.* To regard with discontent or dissatisfaction; to fret or murmur at –1793.

1. Through the long and weary day he repines at his unhappy lot W. IRVING. b. These Ears, alas, for other Notes r. GRAY. 2. In signe Of servile yoke That nobler harts r. SPENSER. Hence **Repi·ner,** one who repines; a grumbler. **Repi·ningly** *adv.*

Repique (rĭpī·k), *sb.* 1668. [– Fr. *repic* = It. *ripicco*; see RE-, PIQUE *sb.*²] In *Piquet*, the winning of thirty points on cards alone before beginning to play (and before the adversary begins to count), entitling the player to begin his score at ninety.

Repique (rĭpī·k), *v.* 1659. [f. prec.] **1.** *trans.* In *Piquet*, to score a repique against (the opposing player). **2.** *intr.* To score a repique 1719.

Replace (rĭplē^i·s), *v.* 1595. [f. RE- 5 a + PLACE *v.*, prob. after Fr. *remplacer* (XVI).] **1.** *trans.* To restore to a previous place or position; to put back again *in* a place. **2.** To take the place of, become a substitute for (a person or thing) 1753. **3.** To fill the place of (a person or thing) *with* or *by* a substitute 1765. **b.** To provide or procure a substitute or equivalent in place of (a person or thing) 1796.

1. To chaste th' vsurper and r. their king 1595. 2. Sir Edward Hawke, and Captain Saunders..went to r. Admirals Byng and West 1756. The paper [money] would be seasonably replaced by a metallic currency 1823. 3. b. The loss of such a treasure as he will not easily r. 1802. Hence **Repla·ceable** *a.* **Repla·ced** *ppl. a.* spec. applied to a crystal that has each of its edges or angles replaced by one or more planes. **Repla·cement,** the act or process of replacing; the fact of being replaced.

Replant (rĭplɑ·nt), *v.* 1575. [RE- 5 a.] **1.** *trans.* To plant (a tree, plant, etc.) again. **2.** To plant (ground, etc.) again; to furnish with new plants (or inhabitants) 1652. **3.** *intr.* To provide and set fresh plants 1712.

1. *transf.* I will..r. Henry in his former state SHAKS. Hence **Repla·ntable** *a.*

Replay· (rĭ-), *v.* 1884. [RE- 5 a.] *trans.* To play (a match, etc.) again. Hence **Re·play** *sb.* a replayed match.

Replea·der. 1607. [RE- 5 a; see -ER⁴.] *Law.* The action of, right to, a second pleading.

Replenish (rĭple·niʃ), *v.* ME. [f. *repleniss-*, lengthened stem of OFr. *replenir*, f. *re-* RE- + *plenir* PLENISH.] **I.** *pass.* (*Obs.* exc. as direct pass. of II.) **1.** To be fully or abundantly stocked *with.* **b.** To be provided or furnished *with.* 1533. †**2.** To be filled, or fully imbued *with* some quality or condition –1702. **3.** To be physically or materially filled *with* 1490.

1. b. His intellect is not replenished, hee is onely an animall SHAKS. 3. Generally all the earth is replenished with Brimstone 1612.

II. †**1.** *trans.* To make full *of*, to fill, stock or store abundantly *with*, persons or animals –1596. †**2.** To occupy (a place) as inhabitants or settlers, to inhabit, people –1788. **b.** To occupy the whole of (a space or thing). Now *rare.* 1563. †**3.** To fill with food; to satiate –1665. †**4.** To fill (a place or space) *with* something –1615. **5.** To fill up again; to restore to the former amount or condition 1612. **6.** *intr.* To become filled; to attain to fullness; to increase (*rare*) 1579.

2. The vacant habitations were replenished by a new colony GIBBON. 5. Full of wants of money and much stores to buy, for to r. the stores, and no money to do it with PEPYS. 6. Her Coffers began to r., Her Subjects were rich 1673. Hence **Reple·nisher,** one who or that which replenishes; *spec.* in *Elect.* a device for increasing or maintaining a charge in certain apparatus. **Reple·nishment,** the act of replenishing; that which replenishes; a fresh supply.

Replete (rĭplī·t), *a.* late ME. [– (O)Fr. *replet*, fem. *-ète*, or L. *repletus*, pa. pple. of *replēre* fill.] **1.** Filled *with* (†or full *of*) some thing or substance. **b.** Filled to satisfaction *with*, full *of*, food or drink; sated, gorged. late ME. †**c.** Plethoric, fat –1758. **2.** Filled *with* (†full *of*), abundantly supplied or provided *with*, in various uses. late ME. **3.** Full, entire, perfect, complete 1601.

1. Sweet Gardens, repleat with fragrant flowres 1634. b. Herodes,..Whan he of wyn was repleet at his feeste CHAUCER. c. Of a strong and r. Habit of Body 1758. 2. Proceedings..r. with irregularity and injustice 1817. Hence **Reple·teness.**

Repletion (rĭplī·ʃən). late ME. [– (O)Fr. *réplétion* or late L. *repletio, -on-*, f. *replet-*, pa. ppl. stem of *replēre*; see prec., -ION.] **1.** The action of eating or drinking to excess; the condition of body arising from this. **2.** The fact or condition of being filled up, stuffed full, or crowded. late ME. **3.** The action of filling up; the filling *of* a cavity or receptacle 1646. **4.** The satisfaction of a desire or want 1654.

1. Repleccion ne made hire neuere sik, Attempree diete was al hir phisik CHAUCER. *fig.* Your malady, in this respect, is a disorder of r. BURKE. 2. The body of the house was filled to r. by adults 1870.

†**Reple·tive,** *a.* 1611. [– (O)Fr. *réplétif*, f. as prec.; see -IVE. Cf. med.L. *repletivus* capable of filling.] Causing repletion, replenishing –1733. So †**Reple·tively** *adv.* 1601.

†**Reple·ve,** *v.* 1592. [– OFr. *replevir* REPLEVY *v.*] *Law. trans.* To replevy; to bail out –1644.

Repleviable (rĭple·viăb'l), *a.* 1755. [f. REPLEVY *v.* + -ABLE.] *Law.* Replevisable.

Replevin (rĭple·vin), *sb.* 1461. [– AFr. *replevin*, f. OFr. *replevir* recover; see REPLEVY *v.*] *Law.* **1.** The restoration to, or recovery by, a person of goods or chattels distrained or taken from him, upon his giving security to have the matter tried in a court of justice and to return the goods if the case is decided against him. †**b.** The bailing of, or bail for, a person –1651. **2.** A writ empowering a person to recover his goods by replevin 1465. **3.** An action arising out of a case in which goods have been distrained or taken and replevied 1515.

Replevin (rĭple·vin), *v.* 1659. [f. prec.] *Law.* †**1.** *trans.* = REPLEVY *v.* 1, 2 b –1720. 2. = REPLEVY *v.* 2. Now *U.S.* 1678.

Replevisable (rĭple·visăb'l), *a.* 1532. [– AFr. *replevis(s)able*, f. *repleviss-*, lengthened stem of *replevir* REPLEVY *v.*; see -ABLE.] *Law.* That may be replevied.

Replevy (rĭple·vi), *sb.* Now *rare.* 1451. [f. next.] = REPLEVIN *sb.* 1, 1 b, 2.

Replevy (rĭple·vi), *v.* 1554. [– OFr. *replevir* recover, f. *re-* RE- + *plevir* – Gmc. **plezjan*; see PLEDGE sb.] *Law.* **1.** *trans.* To bail (a person), or admit to bail. **2.** To recover (cattle or goods) by replevin 1596. †**b.** Of the sheriff or bailiff: To recover for, or restore to, the owner by replevin –1683. **3.** *intr.* or *absol.* To carry out the act of replevin 1607.

Replica (re·plikă). 1824. [– It. *replica*, f. *replicare*; see REPLY *v.*] A copy, duplicate, or reproduction of a work of art; *prop.*, one made by the original artist. **b.** *transf.* A copy, reproduction, facsimile 1865.

†**Re·plicant.** 1631. [– L. *replicans, -ant-*, pr. pple. of *replicare*; see REPLICATE *v.*, -ANT.] One who replies –1755.

Replicate (re·plikĕt), *sb.* 1730. [f. as next.] *Mus.* A tone one or more octaves above or below a given tone.

Replicate (re·pliket), *a.* 1832. [– L. *replicatus*, pa. pple. of *replicare*; see next, -ATE².] **1.** *Bot.* Of a leaf, etc.: Folded back upon itself; also, folded so as to form a groove or channel. **2.** *Entom.* Of the wings of certain insects: Provided with a joint by means of which the outer part folds back on the base 1891.

Replicate (re·plikeᶦt), *v.* 1535. [– *replicat-* pa. ppl. stem of L. *replicare* unfold, reflect on, (later) reply, f. *re-* RE- + *plicare* fold; see -ATE³. Cf. PLY *v.*¹, REPLY *v.*] **1.** To answer, say in reply (*rare*). **2. a.** To repeat, reproduce (an action) *rare.* 1607. **b.** To make a replica of (a picture) 1882. **3.** To fold or bend back 1777.

Replication (replikē^i·ʃən). late ME. [– OFr. *replicacion* – L. *replicatio, -on-*, f. as prec.; see -ION.] **1.** The action of folding up or back; a fold (*rare*). **2.** Reply, answer, rejoinder. Also with *a* and *pl.* late ME. **3.** *spec.* A reply to an answer 1440. **b.** *Law.* The reply of the plaintiff to the plea or answer of the defendant, being the third step in common pleadings. (Superseded since the Judicature Act of 1875 by *reply.*) 1453. †**4.** Repetition –1683. **5.** Return of a sound; reverberation, echo 1601. **6.** A copy, reproduction. Also, the action of reproducing. 1692.

2. Your Discrete answers and replicacions made in that behalf 1535. Phr. †*Without* (*any*) *r.*, without reply being allowed; without protest or

opposition. **5.** Tyber trembled vnderneath her bankes To heare the r. of your sounds SHAKS.

Replier (rĭpləi·əɹ). 1549. [f. REPLY *v.* + -ER¹.] One who replies or answers.

‖**Replum** (re·plŏm, rĭ·plŏm). *Pl.* **repla.** 1830. [L. *replum* 'a bolt for covering the commissure of the folding-door'.] *Bot.* The central frame or placenta left in certain fruits when the valves fall away by dehiscence.

Reply (rĭpləi·), *sb.* 1560. [f. the vb.] **1.** An answer or response made in words or writing; *transf.*, a response made by an act, gesture, etc. **b.** *Law.* (*a*) The final speech of counsel in a trial; (*b*) a pleading delivered by the plaintiff after the delivery of the defence 1875. **c.** *Mus.* The answer or response in a fugue 1597. **d.** *attrib.*, as *r.-paid* adj., etc. 1884. **2.** A counter-answer, a replication 1702.

1. How pregnant..his Replies are! SHAKS.

Reply (rĭpləi·), *v.* late ME. [– OFr. *replier* turn back, reply :– L. *replicare*; see REPLICATE *v.*] **1.** *intr.* To answer or respond in words or writing. **b.** To respond by some gesture, act, or performance; *esp.* to return gun-fire 1818. **2.** To return a sound; to echo. late ME. **3.** To make counter-answer; *spec.* in *Law*, to answer a defendant's plea; to make a replication; also, to make the final speech in a trial 1453. **4.** *trans.* To return as an answer; to say in reply. late ME. **b.** To return, re-echo (a cry) 1650.

1. R. not to me, with a Foole-borne Iest SHAKS. **b.** The besieged replied..sharply 1829. **2.** Blow, let us hear the purple glens replying TENNYSON. **4.** Lords, vouchsafe To giue me hearing what I shall r. SHAKS. **b.** With his last Voice, Eurydice, he cry'd. Eurydice, the Rocks and River-banks reply'd DRYDEN.

Repone (rĭpōᵘ·n), *v. Sc.* 1525. [– L. *reponere*; see REPOSE *v.*¹]. **1.** *trans. Law.* To restore a person to a position or office previously held; in later use *spec.* to restore to the ministry or a ministerial charge. **b.** To restore to a certain legal status, to rehabilitate (a person), esp. *against* a decree or sentence, so that the case may be tried afresh 1574. †**2.** To put (a person or thing) back *in* a place (*rare*) –1640.

Report (rĭpōᵊ·ɹt), *sb.* late ME. [– OFr. *report*, f. *reporter*; see next.] **1.** Rumour, common talk. Now *rare.* **b.** With *a* and *pl.* A rumour; a statement generally made or believed. late ME. **c.** Repute, fame, reputation. (Now only with *good*, etc., as an echo of Biblical passages.) 1514. **2.** An account brought by one person to another, esp. of some matter specially investigated. late ME. **b.** Without article, in phr. *to make r.* 1534. **c.** A formal statement of the results of an investigation, or of any matter on which definite information is required, made by some person or body instructed or required to do so 1661. **d.** In Parliamentary practice, the account of a bill, etc., given to the House by the Committee appointed to consider it 1628. **3.** A statement made by a person; an account, more or less formal, *of* some person or thing. late ME. †**b.** Testimony *to*, or commendation of, a person or quality. SHAKS. **c.** *Law.* A formal account of a case argued and determined in any court, giving the important points in the pleadings, evidence, etc. Freq. in *pl.* 1617. **d.** An account, more or less complete, of the statements made by a speaker or speakers (as in a debate, lecture, etc.), of the proceedings at a meeting, or of any occurrence or event, *esp.* with a view to publication in a special form, or in the newspaper press 1812. †**4.** Relation, reference, bearing, connection (*rare*) –1738. †**5.** *Mus.* A response; a note or part answering to or repeating another; loosely, a note, a musical sound –1662. **6.** A resounding noise, esp. that caused by the discharge of fire-arms or explosives 1590.

1. As that dishonest victory..Kil'd with r. that Old man eloquent MILT. **b.** He will..perhaps Ruine himself..by spreading Reports BOYLE. **2. c.** The rest of the Committee did not think fit to sign the r.. BURNET. **d.** Report—that is, the intermediate stage between the second and third reading 1886. **3. b.** *L. L. L.* II. i. 64. **c.** The reports are extant in a regular series from the reign of king Edward the second inclusive BLACKSTONE. **4.** The kitchen and stables are ill-placed..having no r. to the wings they joyne to EVELYN. **6.** They..exploded with a very loud r. in the air TYNDALL.

Report (rĭpōᵊ·ɹt), *v.* late ME. [– OFr. *reporter* :– L. *reportare* carry back, bear away (spec. an account), f. *re-* RE- + *portare* carry.] **I.** *trans.* **1.** To relate, narrate (a fact, event, etc.). Now *rare.* **2.** To carry, convey, or repeat (something said, a message, etc.) *to* another. late ME. **b.** To repeat (something heard); to relate as having been spoken by another. late ME. **c.** *spec.* To take down (a law-case, speech, discussion, etc.) in writing, now esp. for publication in a newspaper; to prepare a written account of (any meeting, event, etc.) 1600. **3.** To make a formal report on (some matter or thing); to state (something) in such a report 1580. **b.** To relate, state, or notify (something) as the result of special observation or investigation; to bring in a report of (something observed) 1631. **c.** To name (a person) to a superior authority as having offended in some way 1885. **d.** *refl.* To make known to some authority that one has arrived or is present at a certain place 1802.

1. He..found Already known what he for news had thought To have reported MILT. Phr. *It is reported*, it is commonly said or stated; On the Alpes, It is reported thou did'st eate strange flesh SHAKS. **2.** I wyll reporte this tale unto Duke Maurice 1560. You would aske mee newes, in a time, when reporting it is dangerous 1638. **3.** All goods not duly reported..shall be forfeited 1833. **b.** If the Herald r. him a Gentleman 1631. **d.** Every officer on his arrival..must r. himself to the governor 1802.

II. *intr.* or *absol.* **1. a.** To make a report *of*, to speak or talk in a certain way *of*, a person or thing 1432. **b.** To act as a (newspaper) reporter 1850. **2.** To make report (*on* a person or thing) 1450. **b.** To make or draw up, to give in or submit, a formal report 1628. **c.** To report oneself (see I. 3 d.) 1864.

1. *All's Well* III. v. 60. **2.** This Pitch (as ancient Writers doe r.) doth defile SHAKS. **b.** The committee will r. at twelve o'clock 1828. **c.** I reported for duty at Jefferson Barracks 1885.

†**III.** *trans.* **1. a.** *refl.* To betake (oneself) for support, to appeal *to* a person or thing –1639. **b.** To refer *to*, esp. for information –1639. **2.** To bring or convey; to carry (news) –1590. **3.** To cause to re-echo or resound –1673. **b.** To send back, re-echo (a sound). *rare* –1626. Hence **Repo·rtable** *a.* capable or worthy of being reported. **Repo·rtage**, †report, gossip. †**Repo·rtingly** *adv.* by hearsay.

Reporter (rĭpōᵊ·ɹtəɹ). late ME. [orig. – AFr. *reportour = OFr. *reporteur* (mod. *rapporteur*); see REPORT *v.*, -ER² 3. In later use from the vb. + -ER¹.] **1.** One who reports or relates; a narrator. Now *rare.* **b.** One specially appointed to make or draw up a report, or to give information of something 1625. **2. a.** One who takes down reports of law-cases 1617. **b.** One who reports debates, meetings, speeches, etc., esp. for a newspaper; a person specially employed for this purpose 1813. †**3.** A pistol –1865.

1. Ther-of was I noon Auctour; I was..but a reportour Of folkes tales HOCCLEVE. **2. b.** His father ..was..seeking employment as a r. 1882.

Reportorial (repoɹtōᵊ·riăl), *a.* Chiefly *U.S.* 1860. [irreg. f. REPORTER; see -ORIAL.] Consisting of, pertaining to, or characteristic of, reporters.

Reposal (rĭpōᵘ·zăl). 1605. [f. REPOSE *v.*¹ and *v.*² + -AL¹.] **1.** The act of reposing (trust, confidence, etc.); †trust or reliance *in* something (*rare*). †**2.** The fact or state of reposing or resting –1642. †**b.** That on which one reposes. BURTON.

Repose (rĭpōᵘ·z), *sb.* 1509. [f. REPOSE *v.*² or – (O)Fr. *repos*, f. *reposer.*] **1.** Temporary rest or cessation from activity; *esp.* the rest given by sleep. **b.** *Eccl.* Death, decease (of a saint) 1869. **2.** Relief or respite from exertion, toil, trouble, or excitement 1529. †**3. a.** A place of rest –1671. **b.** *Painting.* A large mass of shadow –1738. **4.** A state of quiet or peaceful inaction or of freedom from disturbing influences 1651. †**b.** Peace of mind (*rare*) –1718. **5.** Quiet, calm or calmness, tranquillity 1717. **b.** *Painting.* Harmonious arrangement of figures or colours, having a restful effect on the eye 1695. **c.** Composure, quiet, ease of manner 1833. **6.** Absence of activity (in things); cessation of natural forces; quiescence 1757. **b.** Undisturbed or unagitated condition 1855. **c.** The fact of being left undisturbed 1844. **7.** Trust, confidence 1629.

1. So forth she rode, without r. or rest, Searching all lands SPENSER. Phr. *Altar of R.*, the altar on which the reserved sacrament rests after the mass of Maundy Thursday. *To take, seek, r.* **2.** The state had need of some r. BYRON. **4.** The Felicity of this life, consisteth not in the r. of a mind satisfied HOBBES. **5. b.** The piece wants r. SIR J. REYNOLDS. **c.** That r. Which stamps the caste of Vere de Vere TENNYSON. **6.** Vesuvius was virtually in r. RUSKIN. In Engineering, *angle of r.*, the greatest angle between two planes which is consistent with stability.

Repose (rĭpōᵘ·z), *v.*¹ late ME. [f. RE- + POSE *v.*¹, after L. *reponere* replace, restore, store up, lay aside or to rest, f. *re-* RE- + *ponere* place.] †**1.** *trans.* To replace, put back into the same place –1660. **2.** To place or put; *esp.* to deposit or lay up *in* a place. Now *rare.* 1548. **3.** To set or place (confidence, trust, etc.) *in* a thing or person 1560. **b.** To place or leave (something) *in* the control or management of another 1589. †**c.** To regard as existing *in* something –1614.

2. The brass cannon and mortars..were reposed for some days in Hyde Park H. WALPOLE. **3.** Herein mainly should we r. our hopes DISRAELI.

Repose (rĭpōᵘ·z), *v.*² 1470. [–(O)Fr. *reposer*, earlier *repauser* :– late L. *repausare*, f. *re-* RE- + *pausare* PAUSE *v.*] **1.** *refl.* To rest oneself; to lay oneself to rest. †**b.** *fig.* To settle oneself with confidence *on* something –1770. **2.** *trans.* To lay to rest or repose *on* or *in* something. In later use only *fig.* 1535. **b.** In pa. pple.: Rested, reclining, lying 1674. **3.** To give or afford rest to (a person), to refresh by rest 1549. **4.** *intr.* To take rest; to cease from exertion or travel; to enjoy freedom from disturbance 1548. **b.** To take rest by sitting or lying down; to lie down to rest; *transf.* to rest in death 1535. **c.** To remain still; to lie in quiet 1817. †**5.** To confide or place one's trust *in*, to rely *on*, a thing or person –1781. **6.** To rest *on* or *upon*, in various senses 1611.

1. Now may I r. me: Custance is mine owne UDALL. **b.** I can r. myself very confidently upon your prudence JOHNSON. **3.** Have ye chos'n this place After the toyl of Battel to r. Your wearied vertue..? MILT. **4. c.** When the centuries behind me like a fruitful land reposed TENNYSON. **6.** Almost every glacier reposes upon an inclined bed TYNDALL.

Reposed (rĭpōᵘ·zd), *ppl. a.* 1533. [f. prec. + -ED¹.] Settled, free from agitation or movement. Hence **Repo·sed-ly** *adv.* (*rare*), **-ness.**

Reposeful (rĭpōᵘ·zfŭl), *a.* 1852. [f. REPOSE *sb.* + -FUL.] Full of repose; having an air of repose; quiet. Hence **Repo·seful-ly** *adv.* **-ness.**

Reposit (rĭpǫ·zit), *v.* 1641. [– *reposit-*, pa. ppl. stem of L. *reponere* REPONE.] **1.** *trans.* To put or deposit (a thing) *in* a place; to lay up, store. **2.** To replace (*rare*) 1884.

Some reposite their Eggs or Young in the Earth 1713.

Reposition (rĭpŏzi·ʃən). 1588. [In sense 1 prob. f. POSITION *sb.* (but cf. med.L. *repositio* placing, arranging); in sense 2 = late L. sense 'storage, etc.', perh. through REPOSIT *v.* and REPOSITORY.] **1.** *Surg.* The operation of restoring to the normal position; replacement. **b.** Replacement (of a thing), in other senses 1874. **2.** The action of repositing, laying up or aside 1617.

Repositor (rĭpǫ·zitǫɹ). 1875. [f. REPOSIT *v.* + -OR 2.] A replacing instrument.

Repository (rĭpǫ·zitəri), *sb.* 1485. [– Fr. †*repositoire* or L. *repositorium*, f. *reposit-*; see REPOSIT *v.*, -ORY¹.] **1.** A vessel, receptacle, chamber, etc., in which things are, or may be placed, deposited, or stored. **b.** A place, room, or building, in which specimens, curiosities, or works of art are collected; a museum. Now *rare.* 1658. **c.** A place where things are kept or offered for sale; a warehouse, store, shop, mart 1785. **2.** A vault or sepulchre 1663. **3.** A place or thing within which something immaterial is thought of as deposited or contained 1645. **4.** A part or place in which something is accumulated or exists in quantities 1672. **5.** A person to whom some matter is entrusted or confided 1697.

1. c. The Fine Art R. THACKERAY. 4. Cornwall is..an immense subterranean r. of copper and tin 1855. 5. Make me the r. of your sorrows SHELLEY.

Reposse·ss (rī-), *v.* 1494. [RE- 5 a.] **1.** *trans.* To recover possession of (a place, etc.); to reoccupy. **2.** To put (a person) in possession *of* something again 1591. **b.** *refl.* To regain possession *of* something 1670.

1. Earth repossesses Part of what she gave YOUNG. 2. b. When..the Hamburg banker wishes to r. himself of his money 1861. So **Reposse·ssion,** recovery; renewed possession.

‖**Repoussé** (rəpuse), *a.* (and *sb.*) 1851. [Fr., pa. pple. of *repousser*, f. *re-* RE- + *pousser* PUSH *v.*] **A.** *adj.* Of metal work: Raised or beaten into relief, ornamented in relief, by means of hammering from the reverse side. **B.** *ellipt.* as *sb.* Metal-work of this kind; the process of hammering into relief 1875.

Reprehend (reprĭhe·nd), *v.* ME. [– L. *reprehendere*, f. *re-* RE- + *prehendere* seize.] **1.** *trans.* To reprove, reprimand, rebuke, censure, find fault with. Also *absol.* †**2.** To refute. BACON. ¶**3.** Misused by ignorant speakers for 'represent' and 'apprehend' 1588.

1. He reprehended me afore al the companye 1530. I nor advise, nor r. the Choice 1708. 3. *L. L. L.* I. i. 184. Hence **Reprehe·nder.**

Reprehensible (reprĭhe·nsĭb'l), *a.* late ME. [– late L. *reprehensibilis*, f. *reprehens-*, pa. ppl. stem of L. *reprehendere*; see prec., -IBLE. Cf. (O)Fr. *répréhensible.*] Deserving of reprehension, censure, or rebuke; reprovable; blameworthy.

In a meane man prodigalitie and pride are faultes more r. then in Princes PUTTENHAM. Hence **Reprehe·nsibleness. Reprehe·nsibly** *adv.*

Reprehension (reprĭhe·nʃən). late ME. [– L. *reprehensio, -on-*, f. as prec.; see -ION. Cf. (O)Fr. *répréhension.*] **1.** The action of reprehending; censure, reproof, rebuke, reprimand. **b.** With *a* and *pl.* An instance of this 1574. †**2.** Refutation; proof of fallacy –1620.

1. If they are corrupt, they merit. .blame and r. BURKE.

Reprehensive (reprĭhe·nsiv), *a.* 1589. [– Fr. *répréhensif* or med.L. *reprehensivus*, f. as prec.; see -IVE.] Of the nature of reprehension; containing reproof. Now *rare.* Hence **Reprehe·nsively** *adv.* So **Reprehe·nsory** *a.* (now *rare*).

Represent (reprĭze·nt), *v.* late ME. [– (O)Fr. *représenter* or L. *repræsentare*, f. *re-* RE- + *præsentare* PRESENT *v.*] †**1.** *trans.* To bring into presence; *esp.* to present (oneself or another) *to* or *before* a person –1649. **2.** To bring clearly and distinctly before the mind, esp. by description or by an act of imagination. late ME. **b.** To place (a fact) clearly before another; to state or point out explicitly or seriously *to* one, with a view to influencing action or conduct, freq. by way of expostulation or remonstrance 1582. **c.** *absol.* To protest *against* something. Now *rare.* 1717. **3.** To describe as having a specified character or quality; to give out, assert, or declare to be of a certain kind 1513. **4.** To show, exhibit, or display to the eye; to make visible or manifest. Now *rare.* late ME. **b.** *spec.* to exhibit by means of painting, sculpture, etc.; to portray, depict, delineate. late ME. **c.** Of pictures, etc.: To exhibit by artificial resemblance or delineation. late ME. **5.** To exhibit or reproduce in action or show; to perform or produce (a play, etc.) upon the stage 1460. **b.** To exhibit or personate (a character) on the stage; to act the part of (some one) 1662. **6.** To symbolize, serve as an embodiment of (some quality, fact, or other abstract concept). late ME. **b.** Of quantities: To indicate or imply (another quantity) 1860. **7.** Of things: To stand for or in place of (a person or thing); to be the figure or image of (something). late ME. **b.** To be the equivalent of, to correspond to, to replace (*esp.* another animal or plant in a given region) 1855. **8.** To take or fill the place of (another) in some respect or for some purpose; to be a substitute in some capacity for (a person or body); to act for (another) by a deputed right 1509. **b.** *spec.* To be accredited deputy or substitute for (a number of persons) in a legislative or deliberative assembly; to be member of Parliament for (a certain constituency); hence in *pass.*, to be acted for in this respect *by* some one; to have a representative or representatives 1655. **9.** To serve as a specimen or example of (a class or kind of things); hence, in *pass.*, to be exemplified (*by* something) 1858.

2. Of all external things, Which the five watchful Senses r., She forms Imaginations MILT. b. It would have been useless to r. these things to James MACAULAY. 3. Sunderland they represented as the chief conspirator MACAULAY. 4. b. My wife desired to be represented as Venus GOLDSM. c. Two allegorical pieces by..Holbein, representing the Triumph of Riches and the Triumph of Poverty respectively 1861. 5. b. Persons who r. Heroes in a Tragedy STEELE. 6. No sovereign has ever represented the majesty of a great state with more dignity and grace MACAULAY. b. I knew the immense amount of mechanical force represented by four ounces of bread and ham TYNDALL. 8. Men who are in absolute liberty may..give Authority to One man to r. them every one HOBBES. b. I do not wish to r. Bristol, or to r. any place, but upon terms that shall be honourable BURKE. 9. A soup in which twenty kinds of vegetables were represented HAWTHORNE. Hence **Represe·ntable** *a.* capable of being represented.

Representant (reprĭze·ntănt). 1651. [– Fr. *représentant*, pr. pple. of *représenter*; see prec., -ANT.] **1.** A person representing another or others; a representative (*rare*). **2.** An equivalent 1863.

Representation (reprĭzentē¹·ʃən). late ME. [– (O)Fr. *représentation* or L. *repræsentatio, -on-*, f. *repræsentat-* pa. ppl. stem of *repræsentare*; see REPRESENT, -ION.] †**1. a.** Presence, bearing, air –1640. **b.** Appearance –1664. **2.** An image, likeness, or reproduction in some manner *of* a thing. late ME. **b.** A material image or figure; in later use *esp.* a drawing or painting (*of* a person or thing) 1477. **c.** The action or fact of exhibiting in some visible image or form 1483. **3.** The exhibition of character and action upon the stage; the (*or* a) performance of a play 1589. **4.** The action of placing a fact, etc., before another or others by means of discourse; a statement or account, *esp.* one intended to influence opinion or action 1553. **b.** *Insurance.* A special statement of facts relating to the risk involved, made by the insuring party to the insurer or underwriter before the subscription of the policy 1838. **5.** A formal and serious statement of facts, reasons or arguments, made with a view to effecting some change, preventing some action, etc.; hence, a remonstrance, protest, expostulation 1679. **6.** The action of presenting to the mind or imagination; an image thus presented; a clearly-conceived idea or concept 1647. **b.** The act or process by which the mind forms an image or concept; the faculty of doing this; the product of such an act 1836. **7.** The fact of standing for, or in place of, some other thing or person, esp. with a right or authority to act on their account; substitution of one thing or person for another 1624. **b.** *Law.* The assumption by an heir of the position, rights, and obligations of his predecessor 1693. **8.** The fact of representing or being represented in a legislative or deliberative assembly, *spec.* in Parliament; the position, principle, or system implied by this 1769. **b.** The aggregate of those who thus represent the elective body 1789.

1. a. This yoong man of a noble birth, of a manly r. 1598. 2. The Play-House is a R. of the World in nothing so much as in this Particular STEELE. c. Fidelity of r. being..adhered to 1830. 3. Never having been before at a theatrical r. THACKERAY. 4. Drawing up a r. of the state of my victualling-business PEPYS. 5. Ferdinand.. instructed his ambassador to make the strongest representations to the Pope 1841. 6. The word r...I have restricted to denote..the immediate object or product of Imagination 1838. 7. So cannot these Members be formed into a body by the King, either by his Royal presence or r. 1660. b. *Right of r.*, the right whereby the son of an elder son deceased succeeds to his grandfather in preference to the latter's immediate issue. 8. We ought not to be quite so ready with our taxes, until we can secure the desired r. in parliament BURKE. Hence **Representa·tional** *a.* pertaining to, or of the nature of, r.; also, holding the doctrine of representationism. **Representa·tionary** *a.* (*rare*) representative.

Representationism (re:prĭzentē¹·ʃəniz'm). 1842. [f. prec. + -ISM.] The doctrine that the immediate object of the mind in perception is only a representation of the real object in the external world. So **Representa·tionist,** an adherent of this doctrine.

Representative (reprĭze·ntătiv), *a.* and *sb.* late ME. [– (O)Fr. *représentatif, -ive* or med.L. *repræsentativus*, f. as REPRESENTATION; see -IVE.] **A.** *adj.* **1.** Serving to represent, figure, portray, or symbolize. **b.** Presenting, or capable of presenting, ideas of things to the mind 1753. **c.** Relating to mental representation 1847. **2.** Standing for, or in place of, another or others, *esp.* in a prominent or comprehensive manner 1624. **b.** *spec.* Holding the place of, and acting for, a larger body of persons (*esp.* the whole people) in the work of governing or legislating; pertaining to, or based upon, a system by which the people is thus represented 1628. **c.** Connected with, or based upon, the fact of one person representing another 1766. **3.** Typical of a class; conveying an adequate idea of others of the kind 1788. **4.** Taking the place of, replacing, other forms or species 1845.

1. b. The distinction between perception as a presentative, and Memory,..as a r., cognition 1842. 2. A king or queen, as r. persons in a nation 1861. b. The two Houses of Parliament being the R. Body of the Kingdome 1643. 3. This experiment is r., and it illustrates a general principle TYNDALL. 4. Many of these were 'r. forms' (species or races which take the place of other allied species or races) of others found on the opposite banks 1863.

B. *sb.* **1.** A person (or thing) representing a number or class of persons (or things); hence, a sample or specimen 1647. **b.** A typical embodiment *of* some quality or abstract concept 1715. **2.** One who (†that which) represents a number of persons in some special capacity; *spec.* one who represents a section of the community as member of a legislative body; a member of Parliament or (*U.S.*) of the House of Representatives 1658. †**3.** A representative body or assembly –1761. **4.** One who represents another as agent, delegate, substitute, successor, or heir; also *spec.* a person appointed to represent his sovereign or government in a foreign court or country 1691. **b.** One who or that which in some respect represents another person or thing 1691.

1. Noah and his sons..were..the..representatives of all mankind 1676. b. An ideot..who was the r. of Credulity ADDISON. 2. The English nation declare they are grossly injured by their representatives '*Junius*' *Lett. House of Representatives*, the lower or popular house of the United States Congress or of a State legislature. 4. Lord lieutenants began to be introduced, as standing representatives of the crown BLACKSTONE. b. Money is only a commodious r. of the commodities which may be purchased with it 1788. Hence **Represe·ntative-ly** *adv.*, **-ness.**

Representer (reprĭze·ntəɹ). 1570. [f. as prec. + -ER¹.] **1.** One who represents by acting; †an exhibitor; †an actor. **2.** One who makes a representation, or states a matter in a certain light. Now *rare* or *Obs.* 1847. †**3.** A representative of a thing or person –1691. †**b.** *spec.* = REPRESENTATIVE B. 2. –1726.

Representment (reprĭze·ntmĕnt). 1594. [f. as prec. + -MENT. Cf. Fr. †*représentement.*] **1.** The act of representing in some form or figure; the fact of being so represented, or the result of such representation. Now *rare.* †**2.** Representation by discourse or argument –1680.

Repress (rĭpre·s), *v.* late ME. [f. *repress-*, pa. ppl. stem of L. *reprimere*; see RE-, PRESS *v.*] **1.** *trans.* To check, restrain, put down or keep under (something bad or objectionable). **b.** To check by some special treatment; to cure, stanch 1493. **2.** To check or withstand (some passion, feeling, etc.) in another by opposition or control. late ME. **b.** To keep or hold back, to restrain or check (a person) from action or advance 1638. **3.** To keep down, suppress (one's desires, feelings, etc.); to restrain, refrain from (an action); *spec.* in *Psychol.*, to suppress (a painful or otherwise undesirable memory, desire, etc.). late ME. **4.** To reduce (troublesome persons) to subjection or quietness; to put down by force, suppress. late ME. **b.** To put down (a rebellion, riot, etc.) 1475. **5.** To keep under, check, curb 1557. †**6.** To force or drive back –1662.

1. Authorised by law to r. spiritual abuses MACAULAY. **b.** When now the rage of hunger was represt POPE. **2.** To r. the self-seeking tendencies in the mercantile classes FROUDE. **3.** Desire of wine..Thou couldst r. MILT. **4. b.** The duty of repressing riots..in England lay with the nobility in their several districts FROUDE. Hence **Repre·sser.** **Repre·ssive** *a.* having the nature of, or tending to, repression; **-ly** *adv.*, **-ness.**

Repression (rĭpre·ʃən). late ME. [– late L. *repressio, -on-*, f. as prec.; see -ION.] †**1.** Power of repressing. CHAUCER. **2.** The action of repressing; an instance of this 1533.

2. The r. and punishment of Malefactors 1553.

Reprieval (rĭprī·văl). 1586. [f. REPRIEVE *v.* + -AL[1] 2.] = next. Now *rare.*

Reprieve (rĭprī·v), *sb.* 1598. [f. the vb.] **1.** The act of reprieving; the fact of being reprieved 1607. **b.** An instance of this; a formal suspension of the execution of a sentence; a remission or commutation of a capital sentence 1598. †**c.** The time during which one is reprieved. SHAKS. **2.** A warrant granting or authorizing the suspension or remission of a capital sentence 1602. **3.** *transf.* Respite from a natural or violent death 1633. **b.** A respite, or temporary escape, from some trouble, calamity, etc. 1635.

1. Without R. adjudg'd to death MILT. **b.** Like the felon, that feels there is no chance of a r. 1843. **2.** A r. was brought to Newgate for Dr. Hensey, respiting his sentence for a fortnight 1758. **3.** The sense of r. from approaching and apparently inevitable death had its usual effect SCOTT.

Reprieve (rĭprī·v), *v.* 1494. [First in pa. pple. *reprived*, for earlier *repryed* – AFr., OFr. *repris*, pa. pple. of *reprendre*; see REPRISE *v.* The change (XVI) of *repry* to *reprive*, and hence to *repre(e)ve, reprieve*, is unexplained.] †**1.** *trans.* To take or send back *to* prison; to remand; to detain on remand –1588. †**2.** To postpone, delay, put off (*rare*) –1664. **3.** To respite or rescue (a person) from impending punishment; *spec.* to suspend or delay the execution of (a condemned person) 1596.

3. He who escapes from death is not pardoned, he is only reprieved, and reprieved to a short day FIELDING. Hence †**Reprie·vement**, the action of reprieving; a reprieve –1647.

Reprimand (re·primand), *sb.* 1636. [– Fr. *réprimande*, †*-ende* – Sp. *reprimenda* – L. *reprimenda*, n. pl. of gerundive of *reprimere* REPRESS.] A sharp rebuke, reproof, or censure, esp. one given by a person or body having authority, or by a judge or magistrate to an offender.

Reprimand (reprimā·nd), *v.* 1681. [– Fr. *réprimander*, f. *réprimande*; see prec.] *trans.* To rebuke, reprove, or censure (a person) sharply or severely.

The Captain..reprimanded the sentinel for deserting his post W. IRVING. Hence **Reprima·nder.**

Re·print (rī-), *sb.* 1611. [f. the vb.] **1.** A reproduction in print of any matter already printed; a new impression of a work previously printed; without alteration of the matter. **2.** *Typog.* Printed matter used as copy to be set up and printed again; also *r. copy* 1824.

1. An uniform r. of the Novels LOCKHART.

Repri·nt (rī-), *v.* 1551. [RE- 5 a.] **1.** *trans.* To print (a work) again in a new edition; to print (matter) a second time. **b.** To print again in a different form 1693. **2.** To impress or stamp again 1662. Hence **Repri·nter,** one who reprints or who publishes a reprint.

Reprisal (rĭprəi·zăl). 1447. [– AFr. *reprisaille* (XIV) – med.L. *reprisalia, represalia* n. pl., (also *-alie* fem. pl.), contr. of *repræ(h)ensalia, -aliæ*, f. *repræhens-*, pa. ppl. stem of L. *repræhendere*, f. *re-* RE- + *præhendere* take; see -AL[1] 2.] **I. 1.** (Without article or plural.) The act or practice of seizing by force the property (or persons) of subjects of another nation, in retaliation for loss or injury suffered from these or their countrymen. Now *Hist.* **2.** An act or instance of seizing property or persons belonging to another state by way of indemnity or recompense for loss sustained 1611. †**3. a.** The taking *of* a thing as a prize –1596. **b.** A prize (*rare*) –1611. †**c.** Regaining, recapture –1867. **4.** An act of retaliation for some injury or attack; *spec.* in warfare, the infliction of similar or severer injury or punishment on the enemy, e.g. by the execution of prisoners taken from them 1710.

1. *Letters* (or *Commission*) *of r.*, an official warrant authorizing an aggrieved subject to exact forcible reparation from the subjects of another state. **2.** And indeed this custom of reprisals seems dictated by nature herself BLACKSTONE. *transf.* In the winter, when the sea is making reprisals on the delta 1849.

II. 1. (Chiefly *pl.*) A return or compensation; a sum or amount paid or received as compensation. Now *rare.* 1668. †**2.** = REPRISE *sb.* 3. H. WALPOLE.

Reprise (rĭprəi·z), *sb.* late ME. [– (O)Fr. *reprise*, subst. use of pa. pple. fem. of *reprendre*; see next.] **1.** A deduction, charge, or payment falling to be made yearly out of a manor or estate. Chiefly *pl.* †**b.** A charge, duty, or tax. EVELYN. †**2. a.** A return or compensation received or paid –1736. **b.** Reprisal –1700. **3.** A resumption or renewal of an action; a separate occasion of doing something. Chiefly in phr. *at* or *in..reprises.* Somewhat *rare.* 1685. **II. 1.** *Arch.* A return (RETURN *sb.* II. 1) in an internal angle 1501. **2.** *Mus.* †**a.** A refrain –1702. †**b.** A cadence –1811. **c.** The recurrence of the first theme or subject of a movement after the development 1879.

Repri·se, *v. Obs.* exc. *arch.* 1481. [f. (O)Fr. *repris*, pa. pple. of *reprendre*, f. *re-* RE- + *prendre* take.] †**1.** *trans.* To begin again, resume –1603. †**b.** To take anew. SPENSER. **2.** To take back again, esp. by force; to recapture (a thing or person), to recover 1481. **3.** To take or hold back out of a sum 1559. **4.** To compensate (a person) 1662.

Reproach (rĭprōᵘ·tʃ), *sb.* late ME. [– (O)Fr. *reproche*, f. *reprocher*; see next.] **1.** A source or cause of disgrace or shame (*to* a person, etc.). **b.** A thing, animal, or person forming a source of disgrace or discredit 1712. **2.** Shame, disgrace, opprobrium, or blame, incurred by or falling upon a person or thing 1484. **3.** Blame or censure directed against a person (in mod. use, often applied to mild upbraiding or rebuke) 1477. **4.** An expression of disapproval, censure, reproof, or upbraiding; †a verbal insult 1548. **b.** *pl.* [tr. eccl. L. *improperia*, n. pl.] A series of antiphons and responses, in which Christ is represented as reproaching his people, sung in the Western Church on Good Friday 1884.

1. I pray'd for Children, and thought barrenness In wedlock a r. MILT. **2.** Many good knyghtes and squyers..hadde rather a dyed, than to haue had any reproche 1523. And shee..bare a sonne, and said; God hath taken away my reproch *Gen.* 30:23. **3.** I was sorry to see this way of r. taken against us PEPYS. *Term*, etc. *of r.*, one expressing strong censure or condemnation. **4.** Thrice she assay'd with..amorous reproaches to win from me My capital secret MILT. Hence **Reproa·chless** *a.* irreproachable 1826.

Reproach (rĭprōᵘ·tʃ), *v.* 1489. [– OFr. *reprochier* (mod. *reprocher*) :– Rom. **repropiare* 'bring back near', f. *re-* RE- + L. *prope* near.] **1.** *trans.* To object or cast up (a thing) *to*, or bring (up) *against*, a person as a reproach or fault. Now *rare.* **2.** To upbraid, reprove, or rebuke (a person) 1513. **b.** To upbraid (a person) *with* something 1725. **c.** To censure or reprove (a thing, act, etc.) 1660. **3.** To bring (a thing) into reproach or discredit; to be a reproach to (a person) 1593.

1. He failed not to r. unto the Pope his assisting of Francis 1648. **2.** He reproached Fitzurse for ingratitude for past kindness FROUDE. **b.** The Duke..reproached him in plain terms with his duplicity '*Junius' Lett.* **c.** His last sighs r. the faith of Kings JOHNSON. **3.** Imputation, for that he knew you, might r. your life SHAKS. Hence **Reproa·chable** *a.* (now *rare*) deserving of, or liable to, reproach; †reproachful; **-ness.** **Reproa·chably** *adv.* (*rare*). **Reproa·cher.**

Reproachful (rĭprōᵘ·tʃfŭl), *a.* 1548. [f. RRPROACH sb. + -FUL.] †**1.** Full of reproach or shame; shameful, disgraceful. Also, deserving of reproach or censure; blameworthy. –1796. **2.** Full of reproach, reproof, or censure; upbraiding, †abusive 1548. †**3.** Derogatory *to* a person, etc. (*rare*) –1645.

1. To be Ignorant, and to be deceived, we look upon as a wretched, and a r. thing 1681. **2.** Not I, till I haue..Thrust these reprochfull speeches downe his throat SHAKS. Hence **Reproa·chful-ly** *adv.*, **-ness.**

Re·probacy. 1594. [f. REPROBATE *a.*; see -ACY.] The state or condition of being reprobate. So †**Re·probance.** SHAKS.

Reprobate (re·prŏbĕt, -eᶦt), *sb.* 1545. [– late L. *reprobatus*, subst. use of pa. pple. of L. *reprobare* REPROBATE *v.*; see -ATE[1].] **1.** One rejected by God; one lost in sin. **2.** An abandoned or unprincipled person; a scamp 1592.

2. Come from him, hee's a r. HEYWOOD.

Reprobate (re·prŏbĕt), *a.* 1545. [– late L. *reprobatus*, pa. pple. of L. *reprobare*; see next, -ATE[2].] **1.** Rejected or condemned as worthless, inferior or impure. Now *rare.* †**2.** Depraved, morally corrupt –1671. **3.** Rejected by God; lost or hardened in sin 1561. **b.** Of abandoned character; lost to all sense of religious or moral obligation; unprincipled 1660. **4.** *absol.* Those who are rejected by God, and thus excluded from participation in eternal life with Him. (Opp. to *the elect.*) 1563. †**5.** Deserving or worthy of condemnation or reproof; appropriate to reprobates –1771.

1. Thei shal call them r. siluer, because the Lord hathe reiected them BIBLE (Genev.) *Jer.* 6:30. **2.** *L. L. L.* I. ii. 64. **3.** Thir..Strength and Art are easily outdone By spirits r. MILT. **4.** Can the predestinate be lost, or the r. saved? 1833. Hence **Re·probateness.**

Reprobate (re·prŏbeᶦt), *v.* late ME. [– *reprobat-*, pa. ppl. stem of L. *reprobare* disapprove, f. *re-* RE- + *probare* approve; see PROVE, -ATE[3].] **1.** *trans.* To disapprove of, censure, condemn. **2.** Of God: To reject or cast off from Himself; to exclude from participation in future bliss 1451. **3.** To reject, refuse, put away, set aside 1609. **b.** *Law.* To reject (an instrument or deed) as not binding on one. (Chiefly in *Sc. Law.*) Also *absol.* 1726. **c.** To repudiate, cast off. *Obs.* or *arch.* 1748.

1. His neighbours reprobated his method of proceeding 1787. **2.** For theyr synne they be reprobate & forsaken of god 1526. **3.** Reprobated and rejected Was this Stone 1850. **b.** You cannot approbate and r. the same instrument 1836. Hence **Re·probater** (*rare*), one who reprobates.

Reprobation (reprŏbēᶦ·ʃən). late ME. [– (O)Fr. *reprobation* or late L. *reprobatio, -on-*, f. as prec.; see -ION.] †**1.** Reproof, shame. late ME. only. **2.** The action of raising objections or exceptions (*against* a thing or person); a legal objection or exception (*rare*) 1485. **3.** *Theol.* Rejection by God; the state of being so rejected or cast off, and thus ordained to eternal misery. (Opp. to *election.*) 1532. **4.** Rejection of a person or thing; condemnation as worthless or spurious 1582. **b.** Disapproval, censure, reproof 1727.

3. Austine doth call r. predestination to destruction 1651. **4.** You are empowered to..set a brand of r. on clipt poetry, and false coin DRYDEN. **b.** The fear of public r. 1883. Hence †**Reproba·tioner,** a believer in the doctrine of r.

Reprobative (re·prŏbeᶦtiv), *a.* 1835. [f. REPROBATE *v.* + -IVE.] Conveying or expressing disapproval or reprobation.

Reprobator (re·prŏbeᶦtǫɹ). 1666. [In 'action of reprobator' repr. med.L. *actio* **reprobatoria*, f. *reprobat-* (see REPROBATE *v.*) + *-oria* -ORY[2]. Cf. DECLARATOR, INTERLOCUTOR[2].] *Sc. Law.* An action for the purpose of proving a witness to be liable to valid objections or to a charge of perjury.

Re·proba:tory, *a.* 1823. [f. REPROBATE *v.* + -ORY[2].] Reprobative, condemnatory.

Reproduce (rĭprŏdiū·s), *v.* 1611. [f. RE- 5 a + PRODUCE *v.*, after Fr. *reproduire.*] **1.** *trans.* To bring again into existence; to create or form anew; *spec.* in *Biol.* to form (a lost limb or organ) afresh; to generate (new individuals). **b.** *absol.* To multiply by generation 1894. **2.** To produce again by means of combination or change 1666. **3.** To bring about again; to effect, exhibit, or present anew; to repeat in some fashion 1688. **b.** To repeat in a more or less exact copy; to produce a copy of (a work of art, etc.), now *esp.* by means of engraving, photography, or similar processes 1850. **c.** *intr.* To turn out (well, etc.) in a copy 1891. **4.** To present again in writing or print 1860. **5.** To create again by a mental effort; to represent clearly to the mind 1869.

1. Man..reproduces his kind; and he vanishes into darkness 1800. **b.** It reproduces at the rate of hundreds per day 1894. **2.** When the vapour of water is condensed it reproduces pure water HUXLEY. **3. b.** The rude art of English masons strove to r. the campaniles of Northern Italy FREEMAN. **5.** The novels of the eighteenth century enable us to r. the parson of the time with ease 1870. Hence **Reprodu·ceable** *a.* reproducible. **Reprodu·cer. Reprodu·cible** *a.* that may be reproduced.

Reproduction (rīprǒdɒ·kʃən). 1659. [f. prec., after *production.*] **1.** The action or process of forming, creating or bringing into existence again. **b.** The process, on the part of certain animals, of reproducing parts of the organism which have been destroyed or removed. (Now freq. called *regeneration.*) 1727. **c.** The process of producing new individuals of the same species by some form of generation; the generative production of new animal or vegetable organisms by or from existing ones; also, power of reproducing in this way 1785. **d.** The action or process of bringing again before the mind in the same form 1800. **e.** The action or process of repeating in a copy 1883. **2.** A copy or counterpart; in recent use *esp.* a copy of a picture or other work of art by means of engraving or some other process 1807. **b.** A representation in some form or by some means of the essential features of a thing 1844.

Reproductive (rīprǒdɒ·ktiv), *a.* 1753. [f. as prec., after *productive.*] **1.** Of the nature of, pertaining to, or effecting, reproduction. **2.** *spec.* in *Biol.* Connected with or effecting generative reproduction in animals or plants 1836. Hence **Reprodu·ctive-ly** *adv.*, **-ness. Reproducti·vity.**

Reproof (rīprū·f). Also †**repref(e, -preve.** [ME. *reprove, reprof(e* – OFr. *reprove*, f. *reprover* REPROVE.] †**1.** Shame, disgrace, ignominy, or reproach, adhering or resulting to a person in consequence or by reason of some fact, event, conduct, etc. (Occas. with *a* and *pl.*) –1631. †**2.** Insulting or opprobrious language or action used against a person; insult, contumely, scorn –1596. †**b.** With *a* and *pl.* An instance of this –1597. †**c.** An object of scorn or contempt –1535. **3.** Censure, rebuke, reprimand, reprehension ME. **b.** With *a* and *pl.* An instance of this 1513. **4.** Disproof, refutation. Now *rare* or *Obs.* 1529.

3. A foole despiseth his fathers instruction: but hee that regardeth reproofe, is prudent *Prov.* 15:5. Those best can bear r., who merit praise POPE. **b.** How have I deserved these reproofs? 1794.

Reprovable (rīprū·văb'l), *a.* ME. [f. REPROVE *v.* + -ABLE, after late L. *reprobabilis* and (O)Fr. *réprouvable* (XIV).] Deserving of reproof or censure; blameworthy, reprehensible.

Reproval (rīprū·văl). 1846. [f. next. + -AL[1] 2.] The act of reproving; reproof.

Reprove (rīprū·v), *v.* Also †**repreve, reprieve.** ME. [– OFr. *reprover* (mod. *réprouver*) :– late L. *reprobare*; see REPROBATE *v.*] †**1.** *trans.* To reject –1604. **2.** To express disapproval of (conduct, actions, beliefs, etc.); to censure, condemn. Now *rare.* ME. **3.** To reprehend, rebuke, blame, chide, or find fault with (a person) ME. **4.** *absol.* To employ reprehension or rebuke ME. †**5.** To disprove; to prove (an idea, statement, etc.) to be false or erroneous –1691. †**b.** To refute or confute (a person) –1601.

2. Envy loves That humor best, which bitterly reproves All states 1615. **3.** What if thy Son Prove disobedient, and reprov'd, retort, Wherefore didst thou beget me? MILT. **5.** 2 *Hen. VI*, III. i. 40. **b.** Deceived they are,and may be reproved by the instance of fig-trees HOLLAND. Hence **Repro·ver. Repro·vingly** *adv.*

Reps (reps), var. of REP[3]. 1867.

Reptant (re·ptănt), *a.* 1657. [– L. *reptans, -ant-*, pr. pple. of *reptare* creep; see -ANT.] Creeping, crawling.

Reptation (reptēi·ʃən). 1842. [– L. *reptatio, -on-*, f. *rept-*; see REPTILE *a.*, -ION.] The action of creeping or crawling.

Reptile (re·ptəil), *sb.* late ME. [– (O)Fr. *reptile* or late L. (Vulg.), *reptile* n. of *reptilis*; see next.] **1.** A creeping or crawling animal; *spec.* an animal belonging to the class REPTILIA. **2.** *transf.* A person of a low, mean, grovelling, or repulsive character 1749.

1. *collect.* God said, let the Waters generate Reptil with Spawn abundant MILT. **2.** These reptiles publish. .a newspaper COBBETT. Hence **Reptili·ferous** *a.* containing fossil reptiles.

Reptile (re·ptəil), *a.* 1607. [– late L. *reptilis*, f. *rept-*, pa. ppl. stem of L. *repere* creep, crawl; see -ILE.] **1. a.** Of animals: Creeping, crawling; reptant. †**b.** Of plants: Repent (*rare*) –1738. **2.** Of the nature of, characterized by, pertaining to, the action of creeping or crawling 1727. **3.** *transf.* Grovelling, mean, low, malignant 1654.

‖**Reptilia** (repti·liă), *sb. pl.* 1627. [L., pl. of *reptile* REPTILE *sb.*; see -IA[2].] *Zool.* Those animals which creep or crawl; *spec.* in mod. use, that class of vertebrate animals which includes the snakes, lizards, crocodiles, turtles and tortoises.

Reptilian (repti·liăn), *a.* and *sb.* 1846. [f. prec. + -AN I. 1.] **A.** *adj.* **1.** Resembling a reptile; having the characteristics of the Reptilia. **b.** Consisting or composed of reptiles 1851. **2.** Of or pertaining to, characteristic of, a reptile or the Reptilia 1849. **3.** *transf.* Mean, malignant, underhand 1859. **B.** *sb.* A member of the class Reptilia 1847.

Republic (rīpɒ·blik), *sb.* (and *a.*) 1603. [– Fr. *république* – L. *respublica*, f. *res* affair, thing + fem. of *publicus* PUBLIC *a.*] †**1.** The state, the common weal –1684. **2.** A state in which the supreme power rests in the people and their elected representatives or officers, as opp. to one governed by a king or the like; a commonwealth 1604. **b.** Applied to particular states having this form of constitution 1631. **3.** *transf.* and *fig.* Any community of persons, animals, etc., in which there is a certain equality among the members 1651. **4.** *attrib.* or as *adj.* Of the nature of, characteristic of or pertaining to, a republic or republics; republican. Now *rare* or *Obs.* 1638.

2. The Army..would depose the King, change the Government, and settle a Republick by their own Rules 1674. **3.** *The r. of letters*, the collective body of those engaged in literary pursuits; the field of literature itself.

Republican (rīpɒ·blikăn), *a.* and *sb.* 1659. [f. prec. + -AN I. 1, partly after Fr. *républicain.*] **A.** *adj.* **1.** Of or belonging to a republic; having the form or constitution of a republic; characteristic of a republic or republics. **b.** Of persons or parties: Favouring, supporting, or advocating the form of state or government called a republic 1683. **2.** *U.S. politics* (with capital): **a.** Orig. applied to the *Anti-Federal* party, later to the *Democratic-R.* (see DEMOCRATIC 2). **b.** The name of a party opposed to the *Democratic*, formed in 1854 to resist the extension of slave territory, and favouring a liberal interpretation of the constitution, extension of the central power, and a protective tariff. 1806. **3.** *Ornith.* Living, nesting, or breeding, in large flocks or communities, applied esp. to the N. Amer. *r. swallow*, and the S. African *r. grosbeak* or *weaver-bird* 1829.

1. I would have the manners of the people purely and strictly r. '*Junius' Lett. R. calendar*, the calendar adopted for a short time by the French Republic; so *r. era*, dating from 22 Sept. 1792.

B. *sb.* **1.** One who believes in, supports, or prefers a republican form of government 1659. **2.** *U.S. politics.* A member of the Republican party 1782. **3.** *Ornith.* A republican weaver-bird or swallow 1801.

1. *Red. r.*, one bent on maintaining extreme r. doctrines, even at the expense of blood 1864.

Republicanism (rīpɒ·blikăniz'm). 1689. [f. prec. + -ISM.] Republican spirit; attachment to republican principles; republican government or institutions, etc.

Republicanize (rīpɒ·blikănəiz), *v.* 1797. [– Fr. *républicaniser*; see REPUBLICAN, -IZE.] **1.** *trans.* To render republican in principles or character, convert into republican form. **2.** *intr.* To show republican tendencies 1834.

1. Agents commissioned..to republicanise the country 1871. *trans.* To r. our orthography and our syntax 1858. Hence **Repu·blicaniza·tion.**

Republication (rīpɒblikēi·ʃən). 1730. [RE- 5 a.] **1.** A fresh promulgation *of* a religion or law. **2.** A fresh publication *of* a will 1743. **3.** The action of republishing (a work), or the fact of being republished 1783. **b.** A work published again 1796.

2. The r. of a former will revokes one of a later date BLACKSTONE. **b.** Much of the correspondence would bear r. in a permanent form 1868.

Republish (rīpɒ·bliʃ), *v.* 1625. [RE- 5 a.] *trans.* To publish again.

No after-purchased lands will pass under such devise, unless..the devisor republishes his will BLACKSTONE. Hence **Repu·blisher,** one who republishes.

Repu·diable, *a. rare.* 1611. [See REPUDIATE *v.*, -ABLE.] That may be repudiated.

Repudiate (rīpiū·dieit), *v.* 1545. [– *repudiat-*, pa. ppl. stem of L. *repudiare*, f. *repudium* divorce; see -ATE[3].] **1.** *trans.* **a.** Of a husband: To put away or cast off (his wife); to divorce, dismiss. **b.** To cast off, disown (a person or thing) 1699. **2.** To reject; to refuse to accept or entertain (a thing), or to have dealings with (a person) 1548. **b.** To reject (opinions, conduct, etc.) with condemnation or abhorrence 1824. **c.** To reject (a charge, etc.) with denial, as being quite unfounded or inapplicable 1865. **3.** To reject as unauthorized or as having no binding force on one 1646. **b.** To refuse to discharge or acknowledge (a debt or other obligation). Chiefly of states disowning a public debt, and freq. *absol.* 1837.

1. a. His separation from Terentia, when he repudiated not long afterward 1716. **b.** To r. and denounce his father DICKENS. **2.** If they repudiated the empire placed within their reach, some other power would certainly seize it 1862. **b.** I r. the dreams of Pantheism 1865. **3.** He hath obtained with some to r. the books of Moses SIR T. BROWNE. Hence **Repu·diator,** one who repudiates.

Repudiation (rīpiūdiēi·ʃən). 1545. [– L. *repudiatio, -on-*, f. as prec.; see -ION.] The action of repudiating or fact of being repudiated. **1.** Divorce (of a wife). **2.** The action of rejecting, disowning, disavowing, etc. 1848. **b.** *spec.* of a debt 1843. Hence **Repudia·tionist** *U.S.*, one who advocates the r. of a public debt.

Repugn (rīpiū·n), *v.* late ME. [– L. *repugnare*, f. *re-* RE- + *pugnare* fight.] †**1.** *intr.* To be contradictory or inconsistent; to be contrary *to*, to stand *against* something –1673. **2.** To offer opposition or resistance; to resist; to be recalcitrant; to object. Now *rare.* late ME. **3.** *trans.* To oppose, resist, or contend against (a thing or †person). Now *rare.* late ME. †**4.** To be contrary or opposed to (a thing) –1681. **5.** To affect (a person) with repugnance or aversion. Also *absol.* 1868.

2. To r...against a domineering Ritterdom CARLYLE. **3.** The very nature of his Subject..repugns any such Suspicion 1731. Hence †**Repu·gnable** *a.* capable of being repugned; contrary, opposed. **Repu·gner.**

Repugnance (rīpɒ·gnăns). late ME. [– (O)Fr. *répugnance* or L. *repugnantia*, f. *repugnant-*; see next, -ANCE.] **1.** Contradiction, inconsistency; contradictory opposition or disagreement of ideas or statements. Also with *a* and *pl.* †**2.** Resistance –1547. †**b.** Opposition or contrariety between or of things –1654. **3.** Strong dislike, distaste, antipathy, or aversion (*to* or *against* a thing). Also *pl.* 1592.

1. In it there is more than the usual r. between the title and the purport 1824. **3.** Those national repugnances do not touch me SIR T. BROWNE. A deep r. against ecclesiastical tyranny 1854. So **Repu·gnancy,** in senses 1, 3.

Repugnant (rīpɒ·gnănt), *a.* late ME. [– Fr. *répugnant* or L. *repugnans, -ant-*, pr. pple. of *repugnare*; see REPUGN, -ANT.] **1.** Contrary or contradictory (*to*), inconsistent or incompatible (*with*). **2.** Making or offering resistance (*to* a person or thing); opposing, resisting, hostile, antagonistic, refractory 1460. **3.** Distasteful or objectionable *to* one 1777.

1. A condition either impossible, illegal, or r. 1766. The clause was void, because it was r. to the body of the act 1818. **3.** Characters in comedy ..which involve some notion r. to the moral sense LAMB. Hence **Repu·gnant-ly** *adv.*, **-ness.**

Repullulate (rīpɒ·liŭleit), *v.* 1623. [– *repullulat-*, pa. ppl. stem of L. *repullulare* sprout again; see RE-, PULLULATE *v.*] **1.** *intr.* To bud or sprout again. **2.** *Path.* Of a disease: To start afresh; to recur 1762.

1. Whose branches I fear are withered, never to r. again 1822. Hence **Repullula·tion.**

Repulse (rĭpʊ·ls), *sb.* 1533. [– L. *repulsus, repulsa*, f. *repuls-*; see next.] **1.** The act of repelling an assailant or hostile force; the fact of being driven back in an engagement or assault 1540. **2.** Refusal (of a request, suit, etc.); denial, rejection, rebuff 1533. **3.** The act of forcing or driving back; the fact of being forced back. Now *rare* or *Obs.* 1578.

1. The r. of the Turks before the City of Zenta 1879. 2. Applications for Places, with their respective Successes or Repulses ADDISON.

Repulse (rĭpʊ·ls), *v.* 1533. [– *repuls-*, pa. ppl. stem of L. *repellere* REPEL.] **1.** *trans.* To drive or beat back (an assailant); to repel by force of arms. †**b.** To repel or ward off (an injury) –1606. †**c.** To force back (a thing) –1664. **2.** To repel with denial; to reject, refuse, rebuff 1533. †**3.** To shut out, exclude *from* something –1602. **4.** To affect with repulsion (*rare*) 1845.

1. His valour withstood and repulsed the superior numbers of the Christians GIBBON. 2. Eve Not so repulst..at his feet Fell humble MILT.

Repulsion (rĭpʊ·lʃən). late ME. [– late L. *repulsio, -on-*, f. as prec.; see -ION. Cf. Fr. *répulsion.*] †**1.** Repudiation, divorce –1450. **2.** The action of forcing or driving back or away 1547. **b.** *Med.* The action of repelling humours, eruptions, etc., from the affected parts; †a means of effecting this 1725. **3.** *Physics.* The action of one body in repelling another; tendency of bodies to increase their mutual distance. (Opp. to ATTRACTION 5.) 1725. **b.** *transf.* Tendency to separate or put further apart, to introduce division or difference, etc. 1843. **4.** Influence tending to repel one from a person or thing; dislike, aversion 1751.

3. The production of motion by the mutual attractions and repulsions of distant or contiguous masses HERSCHEL. *Capillary r.*, the apparent r. of a liquid caused by capillarity. 4. There are many natures which..seem to start back from each other by some invincible r. JOHNSON.

Repulsive (rĭpʊ·lsiv), *a.* 1611. [– (O)Fr. *répulsif, -ive* or f. REPULSE *v.* + -IVE.] **1.** Having the character of repelling; driving or forcing back; returning a sound; resisting moisture, etc. **2.** *Physics.* Of the nature of, characterized by, repulsion. (Opp. to ATTRACTIVE.) 1704. **3.** Intended or tending to repel by denial, coldness of manner, etc.; repellent 1598. **4.** Repellent to the mind; disgusting 1816.

1. R. of his might the weapon stood POPE. The desolation of the spot was r. to his wishes 1791. 3. Mary was not so r. and unsisterly as Elizabeth JANE AUSTEN. 4. There was something so r. about the woman 1866. Hence **Repu·lsive-ly** *adv.*, **-ness.**

†**Repu·re,** *v. rare.* 1606. [f. RE 5 a + PURE *v.*] *trans.* To purify again –1635.

Reputable (re·piŭtăb'l), *a.* 1611. [– Fr. †*reputable* or med.L. *reputabilis* (XIII); see REPUTE *v.*, -ABLE.] †**1.** Capable of being regarded or taken into account. **2.** Having a good reputation; of good repute; estimable, honourable, respectable 1674.

2. His Imployment, as a Bookseller, I think a very r. one BENTLEY. The jury were men of fair and r. characters HUME. So **Re:putabi·lity. Re·putableness. Re·putably** *adv.*

Reputation (repiutēⁱ·ʃən). late ME. [– L. *reputatio, -on-* computation, consideration, f. *reputat-*, pa. ppl. stem of *reputare*; see REPUTE *v.*, -ION.] **1.** The common or general estimate of a person with respect to character or other qualities; the relative estimation or esteem in which a person is held. **2.** The condition, quality, or fact, of being highly regarded or esteemed; also, respectability, good report. late ME. **b.** With *a* and *pl.* Also, †a source of honour and credit; a person of note or distinction. 1653. **3.** The honour or credit *of* a particular person or thing; one's good name, good report, or fame in general 1553. **b.** With *a* and *pl.* Some one's good name, etc. 1712. **4.** The estimation, credit, or ascription *of* being or possessing something 1570.

1. Phrases. †*In* (or *of*) *r.*; in later use applied to titles given by courtesy. *To be, have, hold in no, great*, etc., *r.* (now *rare*). *Of no, great, small*, etc. *r.*; Other men, of slender r. SHAKS. 2. But in the company of women of r. I never saw such an idiot GOLDSM. Thus r. is a spur to wit COWPER. b. A great r. for learning THACKERAY. 3. The r. of the state was the first consideration BUCKLE. b. At ev'ry word a r. dies POPE. 4. The r. of Wisedome HOBBES. This very old Woman had the R. of a Witch all over the Country ADDISON.

Reputative (rĭpiŭ·tătiv), *a.* 1656. [– med.L. *reputativus*, f. as prec.; see -IVE.] Considered or regarded as such; putative. Hence **Repu·tatively** *adv.* by repute.

Repute (rĭpiŭ·t), *sb.* 1551. [f. the vb.] †**1.** Opinion, estimate (*rare*) –1711. **2.** Reputation of a specified kind 1551. †**b.** The reputation *of* (having or being) something –1699. †**3.** Relative estimation; rank or position –1700. **4.** Reputation, distinction, honour, credit 1615. **5.** The reputation of a particular person. Freq. in phr. *by r.* 1662.

2. Let them be men of good r. and carriage SHAKS. 4. Ceremony which giueth r. vnto things in themselues but triuiall 1615. 5. Omitting nothing that rage can invent to black his r. 1683. I know him well, by r. 1838. Hence †**Repu·teless** *a.* devoid of r.; inglorious. SHAKS.

Repute (rĭpiŭ·t), *v.* late ME. [– (O)Fr. *réputer* or L. *reputare*, f. *re-* RE- + *putare* reckon.] **1.** *trans.* To consider, think, esteem, reckon (a person or thing) to be, or as being, something 1460. †**2. a.** To take *for* something; to reckon, account *as* something –1670. **b.** To consider to be *in* a person or thing –1533. †**3.** To assign, attribute, impute, or reckon *to* a person –1659. †**4.** To have or hold (a person) in repute or esteem; to think (well, etc.) of; to value –1665. †**5.** *intr.* To think (highly, etc.) *of* a thing or person –1698.

1. To thende that they may be reputed and holden sage and wyse CAXTON. Ingratitude, which Rome reputes to be a hainous sinne SHAKS. 2. a. He..is content to r. me for Pious 1670. 3. It was reputed to him for righteousness 1659. Hence **Repu·tedly** *adv.* by repute or common estimation.

Request (rĭkwe·st), *sb.* ME. [– OFr. *requeste* (mod. *requête*) :– Rom. **requæsita*, subst. use of fem. of pa. pple. of L. *requærere* REQUIRE.] **1.** The act, on the part of a specified person, of asking for some favour, service, etc.; the expression of one's desire or wish directly addressed to the person or persons able to gratify it. **2.** An act or nstance of asking for something; a petition or expressed desire; a writing or document of this nature; also, that which is asked for. late ME. **3.** Without article. †**a.** *To make r.*, to ask or beg –1700. **b.** The act of asking or fact of being asked (to do something). Now esp. n *by r.*, in response to an expressed wish. 1460. **4.** The state, fact, or condition of being asked for or sought after; demand; †vogue, fashion. Chiefly in phr. *in* or *into r.* 1586.

1. At my r...they let her go a drift 1687. Consider, 'tis my first r. POPE. 2. The r. made in the foregoing letter was conceded 1838. 3. a. Then yᵉ king said.., For what doest thou make r.? *Neh.* 2:4. b. Where one is bound to levy a Fine upon R. 1683. 4. Idiots are still in R. in most of the Courts of Germany ADDISON.

Phr. *Courts of Request(s)*: †**a.** a former court of record, technically forming part of the king's council, held by the Lord Privy Seal and the Masters of Requests for the relief of persons petitioning the king; also, in later use, the hall at Westminister in which the court was held; **b.** a local court for the recovery of small debts. †*Master of (the) Request(s)*, one of the leading officers of the Court of Requests.

Request (rĭkwe·st), *v.* 1533. [f. prec., or – OFr. *requester*, f. *requeste* (prec.).] **1.** With *infin.* To express a wish or desire *to* have, etc.; to beg the favour or permission to be allowed *to do* something 1565. **2.** *trans.* To ask, or ask for (something) 1594. **3.** To ask (a person) *to do* something 1533. †**b.** *ellipt.* To ask (a person) to act *against* another, to come or go *to* a place, etc. (*rare*) –1613.

1. He requested to heare Erasmus judgement concerning Luther 1641. 2. To tell the ladies That I r. their presence SHELLEY. 3. Butler requested them to open the gate SCOTT. b. I was requested to supper last night B. JONS. Hence **Reque·ster.**

Requiem (re·kwiĕm). ME. [L., acc. of *requies* 'rest', from the Introit in the Mass for the Dead, 'Requiem eternam dona eis, Domine'.] **1.** A special mass for the repose of the souls of the dead. Also *Mass of R.* **b.** A musical setting of a mass for the dead 1789. **2.** Any dirge or solemn chant for the repose of the dead. Chiefly *poet.* 1611. †**3.** An invitation to rest or repose –1684. **4.** Rest, repose, peace, quiet 1616.

1. Behind, four priests, in sable stole, Sung r. for the warrior's soul SCOTT. 4. Repose denies her r. to his name BYRON.

‖**Requiescat** (rekwiˌe·skæt). 1824. [L., the first word of *requiescat in pace* 'may he rest in peace'.] A prayer for the repose of the dead.

Requiescence (rekwiˌe·sĕns). 1654. [f. L. *requiescere*, after QUIESCENCE.] A state of quiescence, rest, repose.

†**Requi·rable,** *a.* late ME. [orig. – OFr. *requerable*; later, f. REQUIRE *v.* + -ABLE.] Capable of being required; that may properly be asked for –1676.

Require (rĭkwəiᵊ·ɹ), *v.* late ME. [In XIV *requere, require* – OFr. *requer-, requier-*, stem of *requere* (now refash. as *requérir*) :– Rom. **requærere*, for L. *requirere*, f. *re-* RE- + *quærere* seek, ask.] **I.** †**1.** *trans.* To ask (a person) a question; to inquire of (a person) *why, if*, etc. (*rare*) –1579. †**2.** To ask or request (a person) for something –1583. †**3.** To ask, request, or desire (a person) to do something –1641. **4.** To demand of (any one) *to do* something 1751.

3. Defend vs mighty Lord wee thee r. 1584. 4. The government required each county to find its quota of ships FREEMAN.

II. 1. a. To ask for (some thing or person) authoritatively or imperatively, or as a right; to demand, claim, insist on having. late ME. **b.** To ask for (something) as a favour; to beg, entreat, or request. Now *rare.* late ME. **c.** *intr.* To make request or demand. late ME. **2.** *trans.* To demand as necessary or essential on general principles, or in order to comply with some regulation. late ME. **b.** To call for or demand as appropriate or suitable in the particular case; to need for some end or purpose. late ME. **c.** To demand as a necessary help or aid; hence, to stand in need of; to need, want. late ME. **d.** *It requires*, there is need of 1820. **3.** *intr.* To be requisite or necessary. Now *rare.* 1500. **4.** To feel, or be under, a necessity *to* do something 1805. **b.** To fall necessarily, to need, *to be* done, etc. 1842.

1. Oliver Cromwell..requir'd, both of the Soldiers and others, the Oath of Fidelity 1720. b. They go commission'd to r. a Peace DRYDEN. 2. b. An acre of ground will r. ten pound of seed 1759. c. Light labour..Just gave what life required, but gave no more GOLDSM. 4. b. The wicked are miserable because they r. to be punished JOWETT.

†**III.** *trans.* To seek after, search for; to inquire after; to call upon, summon –1797.

A different Object do these Eyes r. GRAY. Hence **Requi·rer** (now *rare*), one who requires.

Requirement (rĭkwəiᵊ·ɹmĕnt). 1530. [-MENT.] †**1.** The act of requiring; a requisition, request. **2.** That which is required; a want, need 1662. **b.** That which is called for or demanded; a condition which must be complied with 1841.

2. £15,000 would have amply met the requirements of the county 1878. b. The other professors are under more stringent requirements to teach 1868.

Requisite (re·kwizit), *a.* and *sb.* 1470. [– L. *requisitus*, pa. pple. of *requirere* search for, pass., be necessary; see REQUIRE, -ITE².] **A.** *adj.* Required by circumstances or the nature of things. **B.** *sb.* Something that is requisite 1602.

A. There are..two poyntes r. vnto saluacion MORE. B. The two requisites of efficacy and economy 1880. Hence †**Re·quisite-ly** *adv.*, **-ness.**

Requisition (rekwizi·ʃən), *sb.* 1503. [– (O)Fr. *réquisition* or L. *requisitio, -on-*, f. *requisit-*, pa. ppl. stem of *requirere*; see prec., -ION.] **1. a.** The action of requiring; a demand made by a person. **b.** A requirement, necessary condition 1836. **2.** The (*or* an) action of formally requiring one to perform some action, discharge some duty, etc.; †the fact of being so called upon. Also, a written demand of this nature. 1553. **3.** The action of requiring a certain amount or number of anything to be furnished; a demand or order of this nature, *esp.* one made upon a town, district, etc., to furnish or supply anything required for military purposes 1776. **4.** The state or condition of being called or pressed into service or use 1796.

1. a. I obey your r., and inquire the purpose of it 1797. **2.** There can be no ballot except on a r. signed by nine proprietors 1840. **3.** After the battle of Jena..the r. upon humbled Prussia was more than a hundred millions of francs 1860. **4.** Phr. *To put (place, call) in* (or *into*) *r.* (*To be*) *in* (constant, etc.) *r.*; The guillotine was..in constant r. 1817. Hence **Requisi·tionist**, one who makes a r.

Requisition (rekwizi·ʃən), *v.* 1837. [f. prec., after Fr. *réquisitionner*.] **1.** *trans.* **a.** To require (anything) to be furnished for military purposes; to put in requisition. **b.** To make demands upon (a town, etc.) 1870. **2.** To make requisition for; to demand, call for, request to have or get 1874. **b.** To call in for some purpose 1887.

1. a. To r. such horses as might be needed 1870. **b.** When it is intended to r. a village or town, all the outlets should be guarded 1897. **2. b.** The military had to be requisitioned 1887.

Requisitor (rĭkwi·zitǫɹ). *rare.* 1790. [f. L. *requisit-* (REQUISITION *sb.*) + -OR 2.] One who makes a requisition or requisitions.

Requisitory (rĭkwi·zitəri), *sb. rare.* 1824. [– Fr. *réquisitoire*; cf. next and see -ORY[1].] In French legal practice, the demand made by a public prosecutor for the punishment of the accused on the charges stated.

Requisitory (rĭkwi·zitəri), *a. rare.* 1447. [– med.L. *requisitorius* (spec. in *litteræ requisitoriæ*) or Fr. †*réquisitoire*; see REQUISITE, -ORY[2].] **a.** Of the nature of, expressing or conveying, a request or requisition. **b.** Capable of making a requisition 1825.

Requitable (rĭkwəi·tăb'l), *a.* Now *rare* or *Obs.* 1610. [f. REQUITE *v.* + -ABLE.] Capable of being requited.

Requital (rĭkwəi·tăl). 1579. [f. REQUITE *v.* + -AL[1] 2.] **1.** Return for some service, kindness, etc.; recompense or reward for action or exertion. **b.** With *a* and *pl.* A return or repayment (*for* or *of* something) 1591. **2.** Return of an injury, etc.; retaliation, revenge 1582.

1. Whose bold perseverance at length reap'd r. 1815. Phr. *In* (rarely †*for*) *r.* (*of*); In r. whereof, henceforth, carry your letters your selfe SHAKS. **2.** In r. of that shameful act of perfidy 1885.

Requite (rĭkwəi·t), *v.* 1529. [f. RE- + *quite*, var. of QUIT *v.*] **1.** *trans.* To repay, make return for, reward (a kindness, service, etc.). **b.** To make retaliation or return for, to avenge (a wrong, injury, etc.) 1555. **2.** To repay (a person) for some service, etc. 1560. b. To pay back, make retaliation on (a person) for some injury, etc. 1590. †**3.** To repay with the like; to return (a visit) –1648. **4.** To make return of; to give or do in return *for* something 1547. †**5.** To take the place of, make up for, to counterbalance or compensate –1697.

1. Requiting years of care with contumely SHELLEY. **b.** *absol.* The Lord God of recompenses shall surely r. *Jer.* 51:56. **2.** I am so poore to r. you, you must looke for nothing but thankes of me 1611. **b.** Hee payes vs shot for shot; Well, wee shall r. him 1627. **4.** In case of *talio*, or requiting like for like 1631. Hence **Requi·tement**, requital, revenge. **Requi·ter.**

Rere-, comb. form; see REAR-.

Re·re-brace. *Obs.* exc. *Hist.* ME. [– AFr. **rerebras*, f. *rere-* back + *bras* arm.] Armour for the upper arm from the shoulder to the elbow (orig. a plate protecting the back of the arm only).

Re·re-do:rter. *rare.* 1450. [f. RERE- + DORTOUR, DORTER.] A privy situated at the back of the dormitory in a convent or monastery.

Reredos (rīᵊ·ɹdǫs). late ME. [– AFr. **reredos*, aphet. f. OFr. *areredos*, f. *arere* back (see ARREAR, REAR-) + *dos* back.] **1.** *Eccl.* **a.** An ornamental facing or screen of stone or wood covering the wall at the back of an altar. **b.** A choir-screen 1446. †**2.** A hanging of velvet or silk for covering the wall at the back of an altar –1552. **3.** The brick or stone back of a fire-place or open hearth; an iron plate forming a fire-back. *Obs.* exc. *arch.* late ME.

Re·re-su:pper. *Obs.* exc. *arch.* ME. [–AFr. *rere-super*; see RERE-, SUPPER.] A supper (usu. of a sumptuous nature) following upon the usual evening meal, and thus coming very late at night.

Guilty of the enormity of rere-suppers SCOTT.

†**Resa·lgar.** late ME. [– Arab. *rahj al-ḡār* (see REALGAR).] Realgar, disulphide of arsenic –1610.

Resalute (rīsăl[i]ū·t), *v.* Now *rare.* 1493. [– L. *resalutare*, or (in sense 2) f. RE- 5 a + SALUTE *v.*] **1.** *trans.* To salute in return. **2.** To salute again or anew 1586.

Resa·rcelée, Resa·rcelled, *a. Her.* 1586. [– (O)Fr. *recercelé* hooped, curled, etc., f. *re-* + *cercelé* SARCELLY.] Applied to a cross surcharged with another of a different colour.

Rescind (rĭsi·nd), *v.* 1637. [– L. *rescindere*, f. *re-* RE- + *scindere* split, divide.] **1.** *trans.* To cut off, take away, remove. Chiefly *fig.* †**2.** To cut through, sever. JER. TAYLOR. **3.** To abrogate, annul, repeal 1637.

1. His unnecessary expences are rescinded, his superfluous cut off PRYNNE. **3.** It required a particular Act of Parliament to r. this bye-law 1776. The vendor shall have the power of rescinding the contract 1846. Hence **Resci·ndable** *a.* **Resci·ndment.**

Rescission (rĭsi·ʒən). 1611. [– late and eccl. L. *rescissio, -on-*, f. *resciss-*, pa. ppl. stem of *rescindere*; see prec., -ION.] †**1.** The action of cutting off (*rare*) –1626. **2.** The action of annulling or abrogating 1651.

2. A thing's being found damaged, or sold at above double the just value, is a good cause of r. 1727.

Rescissory (rĭsi·səri), *a.* 1605. [– late L. *rescissorius*, f. as prec.; see -ORY[2].] Of the nature of, or having the effect of, rescinding or revoking; connected with, or characterized by, rescission.

Next they fell upon forming an Act R., whereby former Acts..should be nulled 1654.

†**Rescou·nter**, *sb.* 1543. [– It. *riscontro* comparison, balancing, f. *ri-* RE- + *scontro* encounter.] **1.** Encounter, hostile meeting (*rare*). **2.** Balancing of contra-accounts; settlement or payment of differences on accounts, in later use *spec.* on the Stock Exchange –1796. **3.** An engagement to pay the sum due on a balance of accounts –1682. So †**Rescou·nter** *v. intr.* to encounter *with* an enemy; *trans.* to balance or settle in the way of business.

†**Rescous**, *sb.* ME. [– OFr. *rescousse*, f. *rescourre* RESCUE *v.*] **1.** Rescue, assistance, aid –1602. **2.** *Law.* = RESCUE *sb.* 2. –1768. So **Rescous** *v. trans.* to rescue –1625.

Rescribe (rĭskrəi·b), *v.* 1462. [– L. *rescribere*, f. *re-* RE- + *scribere* write.] †**1.** To write back, write in reply –1726. **2.** To write again or anew; to rewrite. Now *rare.* 1565.

Rescript (rī·skript). 1528. [– L. *rescriptum*, subst. use of n. of pa. pple. of *rescribere* reply in writing to a petition, etc.; see prec.] **1. a.** A decretal epistle from the Pope in reply to some question or difficulty referred to him; also, any Papal decision, decree, or edict. **b.** The reply sent by a Roman emperor to a magistrate or other person consulting him on a doubtful point of law or as to the action to be taken in particular circumstances 1589. **2.** Any edict, decree, order, or formal announcement made by a ruler or governing body, or having an official character 1545. **3.** Something written over again; a re-writing 1820. **b.** *U.S. Law.* A duplicate or counterpart 1843. **4.** A palimpsest writing 1817.

1. The summes of money which the Pope receiveth for first fruits,..Indulgences, Bulls,.. Rescrips,..cannot be counted 1635. **3.** I wrote it three times..subduing the phrases at every r. C. BRONTË.

†**Rescri·ption.** 1588. [– (O)Fr. *rescription* or late L. *rescriptio, -on-* (var. of *rescriptum* RESCRIPT), f. *rescript-*; see prec., -ION.] **1.** A rewriting, writing over again –1697. **2.** The action of replying in writing; a written reply –1657. **3.** A promissory note issued by a Government –1798.

Re·scuable, *a. rare.* 1611. [f. RESCUE *v.* + ABLE.] Capable of being rescued.

Rescue (re·skiu), *sb.* late ME. [f. the vb., superseding RESCOUS.] **1.** The (*or* an) act of rescuing (esp. persons) from enemies, saving from danger or destruction, etc.; succour, deliverance. **2.** *Law.* The forcible taking of a person or goods out of legal custody; forcible recovery (by the owner) of goods distrained 1450. **b.** A person rescued from custody 1888.

1. R. would be out of the question, should the climber go over the edge TYNDALL. **2.** Precautions..justifiable..from the apprehensions so generally entertained of an expected r. SCOTT.

attrib. esp. in sense 'directed to, aiming at, the raising of fallen or degraded women', as *r. home, work, worker.* **R.-bid** (Bridge), a bid made to get one's partner out of a difficult situation.

Rescue (re·skiu), *v.* [ME. *rescowe, reskewe, rescou-, reskeu-*, stem of OFr. *rescoure, reskeure* (mod. *recourre*) :– Rom. **reexcutere*, f. *re-* RE- + *excutere* shake out, discard, f. *ex* EX-[1] + *quatere* shake.] **1.** *trans.* To deliver (a person) from the attack of, or out of the hands of, assailants or enemies. **b.** To liberate by unlawful force from legal custody 1600. **2.** To deliver (a castle, town, etc.) from siege ME. **b.** To recover, take back by force 1450. **3.** To deliver or save (a person or thing) *from* some evil or harm ME. **4.** *refl.* To save oneself in some respect ME. **5.** *absol.* To afford deliverance or safety (*rare*). late ME.

1. He took..many horse and arms, and rescued all their prisoners 1643. **2.** Rescu'd is Orleance from the English Wolves SHAKS. **3.** To r. Mankind from Tyranny and Oppression 1718. Hence **Re·scuer.**

Re·scusser. *rare.* 1632. [f. RESCOUS *v.* + -ER[1].] *Law.* One who makes a rescue.

Research (rĭsə̄·ɹtʃ), *sb.* 1577. [– Fr. †*recerche* (now *recherche*); see RE-, SEARCH *sb.*] **1.** The act of searching (closely or carefully) *for* or *after* a specified thing or person. **2.** An investigation directed to the discovery of some fact by careful study of a subject; a course of critical or scientific inquiry. Freq. in *pl.* 1639. **b.** Without article: Investigation, inquiry into things. Also, habitude of carrying out such investigation. 1694.

1. Researches after gold and other precious metals 1889. **2.** Cuvier was usually engaged for seven hours daily in his scientific researches 1850. **b.** A writer of painstaking r. 1861. *attrib.*, as *r. degree, student, work.* Hence **Resea·rchful** *a.* devoted to, characterized by, replete with, r.

Research (rĭsə̄·ɹtʃ), *v.* 1593. [– OFr. *recercher* (mod. *rechercher*); see RE-, SEARCH *v.*] **a.** *trans.* To search into (a matter or subject); to investigate or study closely. Now *rare* or *Obs.* **b.** *intr.* To make researches; to pursue a course of research 1801.

b. On these three subjects he is directed to read and r.—corn-laws, finance, tythes SOUTHEY.

Researcher (rĭsə̄·ɹtʃəɹ). 1615. [f. prec. + -ER[1].] One who researches; an investigator, nquirer. **b.** One who devotes himself to scientific or literary research 1883. **c.** *Psychical R.*, a member of the Society for Psychical Research; one who investigates psychical phenomena.

Resect (rĭse·kt), *v.* 1653. [– *resect-*, pa. ppl. stem of L. *resecare* cut off, f. *re-* RE- + *secare* cut.] †**1.** *trans.* To cut off or away; to remove –1686. **2.** *Surg.* To cut or pare down; to remove a portion of (bone, cartilage, nerve, etc.) in this way; to cut out (in part) 1846.

Resection (rĭse·kʃən). 1611. [– L. *resectio, -on-*, f. as prec.; see -ION.] †**1.** The action of cutting off or away –1662. **2.** *Surg.* The operation of cutting or paring away a portion of bone, etc., esp. the articular ends of bones 1775.

2. Compound fracture about the elbow-joint, which rendered primary r. of the articulation necessary.

‖**Reseda.** 1753. [L., acc. to Pliny f. the imper. of *resedare* assuage, allay (the words *reseda morbis* having been used as a charm when applying the plant to the reduction of tumours).] **1.** (rĭsī·dă) *Bot.* An extensive genus of herbaceous plants (typical of the *Resedaceæ*); including Mignonette (*R. odorata*) and Dyer's Weed (*R. luteola*). **2.** (re·zedă, or as Fr. rezeda) A pale green colour similar to that of mignonette 1883.

Reseize (rīsī·z), *v.* late ME. [– OFr. *resaisir* (mod. *ressaisir*); see RE-, SEIZE *v.*] †**1.** *trans.* To invest or endow (a person) again *with*, put again in possession *of*, something; to replace *in*, or restore to, a former position or dignity –1647. **2.** To seize, take hold or possession of (something or person) again 1567. Hence **Resei·zer.** So †**Resei·zure**, the act of seizing or taking back again –1683.

†**Rese·mblable**, *a.* late ME. [– OFr. *resemblable*; see RESEMBLE *v.*[1], -ABLE.] Capable of being compared or likened; comparable, similar (*to* some person or thing); like –1665.

Resemblance (rĭze·mblăns). late ME. [– AFr. *resemblance* (mod. *ress-*); see RESEMBLE *v.*[1], -ANCE.] **1.** The quality of being like or similar; likeness or similarity in any respect; the fact of some likeness existing or being present. **2.** The external appearance, or characteristic features, peculiar to an individual or a class of persons or things. late ME. †**3.** A symbol or figure *of* something –1669. †**b.** A simile or comparison; a thing compared to another –1694. **4.** A likeness, image, representation or reproduction of some person or thing. late ME. †**b.** An appearance or show *of* some quality; a likelihood or probability –1603.

1. A vague comparison between two things which have little or no r. to each other *'Junius' Lett.* **2.** His r. being not like the Duke SHAKS. A garden.. which..had the r. of a vast mosaic DISRAELI. **4.** Fairest r. of thy Maker faire MILT.

Resemblant (rĭze·mblănt), *a.* Now *rare.* late ME. [OFr. *resemblant* (mod. *ress-*); see next, -ANT.] **1.** Similar, having resemblance or likeness, *to* something. **2.** Characterized by resemblance or similarity; similar, like 1581. **3.** Aiming at the production of resemblances 1870.

3. The object of the great R. Arts is..to resemble as closely as possible RUSKIN.

Resemble (rĭze·mb'l), *v.*[1] ME. [– OFr. *resembler* (mod. *ress-*), f. *re-* RE- + *sembler* seem :– L. *similare*, f. *similis* like.] **1.** *trans.* To be like, to have likeness or similarity to, to have some feature or property in common with (another person or thing). **2.** To compare or liken (a person or thing) *to* another. Now *arch.* late ME. †**b.** To compare together, or *with* another thing –1673. †**3.** To represent, depict, make an image or likeness of (a person or thing); to figure, typify –1705. **4.** To make like *to* some person or thing. Also in *pa. pple.*, made like, similar. Now *rare.* 1460. †**5.** *intr.* To seem, appear –1510. **6.** To be like in some respect *to* another person or thing. Now *rare.* late ME. **b.** To have mutual likeness; to be like or similar to each other 1751.

1. Cunning resembles Prudence, as an Ape resembles a Man 1718. **2.** Thus Solomon resembles the Nose of his Beloved to the Tower of Libanon ADDISON. **4.** I hope we are resembled, Vowing our loves to equal death and life MARLOWE. **6. b.** In one feature or two, nations r., which are placed at stages considerably remote 1817. Hence **Rese·mbler.** †**Rese·mblingly** *adv.*

†**Rese·mble,** *v.*[2] 1450. [f. RE- + *semble*, aphet. var. of ASSEMBLE *v.*] **1.** *intr.* To assemble, collect, come together –1596. **2.** *trans.* To bring together or collect –1494.

Resent (rĭze·nt), *v.* 1605. [– Fr. †*resentir* (now *ressentir*), f. *re-* RE- + *sentir* feel.] †**I. 1.** *refl.* [= Fr. *se ressentir.*] To have a feeling *of* pain; to feel pain or distress; to regret, repent –1654. **2.** *trans.* To feel (something) as a cause of depression or sorrow; to feel deeply or sharply –1728. **b.** To repent, regret (an action) –1676. **3.** To feel or experience (joy, sorrow, pain, etc.) –1734. **4.** *fig.* To smell out, perceive –1665. **II.** †**1.** *refl.* To express one's resentment; to avenge oneself –1656. **2.** *trans.* To feel injured or insulted by (some act or conduct on the part of another); to show displeasure or anger at (some wrong, injury, etc. sustained) 1628. †**3.** To take or receive in a certain way or with certain feelings; to take *well* or *ill* –1734. †**4.** To appreciate, be sensible of, feel grateful for (a kindness, favour, etc.); to remember with gratitude –1765.

2. It is best to be plain at once—r. my refusal as you will SCOTT. **3.** It was mighty well resented and approved of PEPYS. **4.** If she gratefully resented that small thing for the sake of the hand it came from 1702.

†**III. 1.** To give forth, exhale (a perfume), to have an odour or suggestion of, to show traces of (some quality, etc.). *rare.* –1633. **2.** To savour *of*, have a touch or taste *of* (a person or thing) –1826.

2. Some works resent too much of their authour FULLER. Hence **Rese·nter,** †one who has a feeling or appreciation of something; one who feels or shows resentment (*rare*).

Rese·ntful, *a.* 1656. [f. prec. + -FUL.] Full of, inspired by, resentment.

A look of r. mortification 1782. Hence **Rese·ntful-ly** *adv.*, **-ness.**

†**Rese·ntiment.** *rare.* 1595. [– Fr. †*resentiment*; see RESENTMENT.] = RESENTMENT –1661.

†**Rese·ntive,** *a.* 1662. [f. RESENT *v.* + -IVE.] Apt or inclined to resent –1735.

Resentment (rĭze·ntmĕnt). 1619. [– Fr. †*resentiment*, now *ress-*, f. *res(s)entir*; see RESENT, -MENT.] **1.** An indignant sense *of* injury or insult received, or *of* wrong or affront done to some person or thing to which one is attached. Now *rare.* **2.** A strong feeling of ill-will or anger against the author or authors of a wrong or affront; the manifestation of such feeling against the cause of it. Also in *pl.* 1634. †**3.** A feeling or sense *of* some trouble, or loss; *of* something enjoyed, etc. –1698. †**4.** A feeling or emotion of any kind. Also without article. –1748. †**5.** Feeling or sensation; susceptibility to sensuous or mental impressions –1704. †**6.** An appreciation or understanding *of* something –1678. †**b.** Interest in a thing; regard *for*, care *of*, something (*rare*) –1751. †**7.** Grateful appreciation or acknowledgement (*of* a service, kindness, etc.); a feeling or expression of gratitude –1849. †**8.** A particular idea, opinion, or view *of* or *upon* something (*rare*) –1748.

2. The shocked conscience of mankind..was already kindling into r. FROUDE. **3.** Hearts being ever tender in the ressentment of calamities 1632. **4.** Deep impressions, and ravishing refreshing resentments 1658.

†**Reserate,** *v.* 1597. [– *reserat-*, pa. ppl. stem of L. *reserare* unlock, f. *re-* RE- + *sera* bar, bolt; see -ATE[3].] *trans.* To open up –1710. So †**Resera·tion,** the action of opening; that which opens up.

Reservation (rezəɹvēⁱ·ʃən). late ME. [– (O)Fr. *réservation* or late L. *reservatio*, *-on-*, f. *reservat-*, pa. ppl. stem of L. *reservare*; see RESERVE *v.*, -ION.] **I. 1.** *Eccl.* **a.** The action of reserving as a tithe. **b.** The action, on the part of the Pope, of reserving to himself the right of nomination to a vacant benefice, or the fact of this being reserved to him by some rule or constitution of the Church. late ME. **2.** *Law.* The action or fact of reserving or retaining for oneself some right or interest in property which is being conveyed to another; an instance of this; a right or interest so retained; the clause or part of a deed by which something is thus reserved 1487. **3.** The action or fact of reserving (for oneself or another) some right, power, privilege, etc.; a right, etc., thus reserved 1605. **b.** *U.S.* A tract of land set apart by Government for some special purpose, or for the exclusive use of certain persons, esp. of a native tribe 1789. **4.** An expressed or tacit limitation or exception made with regard to something; the action of making an exception of this kind 1614. †**5.** The action of keeping back or concealing from others; something thus kept back or concealed; a secret; a deceptive answer or excuse –1645. †**b.** The fact or habit of being reticent; reservedness (*rare*) –1674.

2. The *reddendum* or r., whereby the grantor doth create or reserve some new thing to himself out of what he had before granted BLACKSTONE. **3.** *Lear* II. iv. 255. **c.** The action or fact of engaging seats, rooms, places, etc. in advance; a seat or room reserved thus (*U.S.*) 1907. **4.** Phr. *Mental r.*, a qualification tacitly introduced in making a statement, taking an oath, etc., when it is thought inexpedient or unnecessary to speak or dissent openly; also, the fact or practice of making such qualifications; This looks very much like lying, but..it is speaking the truth under a..mental r. 1888. **5.** To make some reseruation of your wrongs *All's Well* II. iii. 260.

II. 1. *Eccl.* The action or practice or retaining or preserving for some purpose a portion of the eucharistic elements (esp. the bread) after the celebration of the sacrament; †also, a part of the elements thus reserved 1551. †**2.** The action or fact of keeping back a matter for further action or later decision –1659. †**b.** The action or fact of keeping back something from others or for one's own use –1634.

†**Rese·rvatory.** 1662. [– med.L. *reservatorium*, f. as prec.; see -ORY[1].] **1.** A receptacle for food; a cupboard; a store-room or storehouse –1807. **2.** A vessel for liquids (*rare*) –1720. **3.** A reservoir for water, etc. –1790. **b.** A receptacle for fluids in animals or plants –1731.

Reserve (rĭzə̄·ɹv), *sb.* 1644. [f. next.] **I. 1.** Something stored up, kept back, or relied upon, for future use or advantage; a store or stock; an extra quantity 1658. **b.** The amount of capital kept on hand by a banker, insurance company, etc., in order to meet ordinary or probable demands. Also *pl.* 1866. **2.** *Mil.* **a.** *pl.* Those troops or portions of an army which are withheld from action in order to serve as reinforcement, or, in case of retreat, as cover to the main body. Also *sing.* in same sense. 1648. **b.** That portion of the military or naval forces of a state which is maintained as a further means of defence in addition to the regular army and navy, and is liable to be called out in time of war or emergency; also, in recent use, a member of this force, a reservist 1866. †**3. a.** A certain amount *of* some quality, feeling, etc., still retained or remaining (*rare*) –1714. **b.** A place or thing in which something is preserved or stored –1659. **c.** A thing or means to which one may have recourse; a refuge (*rare*) –1715.

1. There are three reserves of ammunition 1876. **b.** The banker does not lend all he receives. The difference is called his r. 1880. **3. a.** A r. of Puerility we have not shaken off from School SIR T. BROWNE.

Phr. *In r.*, kept or remaining unutilized; still available. *Of r.* (after Fr. *armée* or *corps de réserve*), acting as, or destined for, a support or recourse; chiefly *Mil.* in *army, body*, or *corps of r.*

II. 1. Something reserved or set apart for some reason or purpose 1649. **b.** A district or place set apart for some particular use, or assigned to certain persons 1853. **c.** A distinction given to an exhibit at a show, indicating that it will receive a prize in the event of another being disqualified 1867. **2.** An expressed limitation, exception, or restriction made concerning something. Now *rare.* 1654. **b.** A mental limitation or qualification of the adherence given to some principle, article of belief, etc. 1679. **3.** *techn.* **a.** A preparation used to prevent or modify the action of colouring matter upon textile fabrics; a resist 1836. **b.** A preparation used for similar purposes in electro-plating 1873.

1. A r. of Corn rent paid to Secular Priests, or to the Religious 1695. **c.** The Duke of York had a r. for a red-polled cow 1895. **2.** How many reserves must be made in praising either his poetry, or his criticism! M. ARNOLD. Phr. *Without r.*, without limitation or restriction of any kind (in mod. use chiefly with ref. to sales by auction.)

III. 1. Self-restraint; self-control; imposition of some limit to one's action 1665. **b.** Reticence; also *spec.* in casuistry, an intentional suppression of truth in cases where it might lead to inconvenience 1704. **c.** Avoidance of too great familiarity; want of cordiality or open friendliness 1721. †**2.** An instance of keeping some knowledge from another person; a fact or item of information kept or disguised; a secret –1805.

1. b. A furious critic, whose age, rank, or fortune gives him confidence to speak without r. JOHNSON. **c.** This frigid r. somewhat disgusted me JOHNSON. **2.** Consult Mr. Grattan, with whom I have no reserves, and I wish you to have none BURKE.

IV. *attrib.* or as *adj.* Kept in reserve, constituting a reserve 1719.

The r. ammunition of a regiment 1876. *R. price*, the price set upon an object to be sold, which is the lowest that will be accepted by the seller.

Reserve (rĭzə̄·ɹv), *v.* ME. [– (O)Fr. *réserver* – L. *reservare*, f. *re-* RE- + *servare* keep, save.] **1.** *trans.* To keep for future use or enjoyment; to store up *for* some time or occasion; to refrain from using or enjoying at once. **b.** To keep back or hold over to a later time or place or for further treatment; to postpone the discussion, decision, or declaration of (a matter). late ME. **c.** *refl.* To keep (oneself) in reserve *for* some occasion, etc. 1605. **2.** To retain as one's own; to keep *to* or *for* oneself. late ME. †**b.** To keep (a matter) from the knowledge of others –1738. **3.** To set apart, keep (†*to* or) *for* another. late ME. **4.** *Eccl.* To set apart, keep back (cases for absolution) to be dealt with by a superior authority. late ME. **5. a.** To retain or secure (some right or profit) for oneself or another by formal stipulation; †to provide or stipulate *that.* (Chiefly in legal use.) late ME. **b.** To set apart (a portion of rent) for payment *in* corn, etc. 1575. **6.** To set (a thing) apart for some purpose or with some end in view; to keep *for* some use. late ME. **b.** To set (a person) apart *for* some fate, destiny, end, etc. Now *rare.* late ME. †**c.** To make an exception of (a thing or person); to exempt (a person) *from* something –1806. **7.** To retain or preserve alive; to exempt from slaughter; to save *from* death. Now *rare.* late ME. †**8.** To keep or maintain (a person or thing) in a certain state or condition –1633. †**9.** To keep in store; to lay up as a store or stock; to deposit for preservation –1692. †**b.** To keep, preserve (things liable to decay or destruction) –1750. †**10. a.** To keep in one's possession –1604. **b.** To keep, preserve (antiquities, relics, etc.) –1708. **11.** *Eccl.* To retain or preserve (a portion of the consecrated species) for certain purposes 1548. †**12.** To retain or preserve, to continue to have, possess, or show (a characteristic, quality, mark, etc.) –1726.

1. I shall r. the rest of my threatnings till further provocation SWIFT. **b.** Take each mans censure; but reserue thy iudgement SHAKS. **2.** Man over men He made not Lord; such title to himself Reserving MILT. **3.** The Fader..for the thirde, Cordeilla, reserued no thynge 1494. This discovery was reserved to our times BERKELEY. **6.** Euery Printer shall reserue one Book..and shall..deliuer it to the Officer..to be sent to the Librarie at Oxford 1637. **b.** We are decreed, Reserv'd and destin'd to Eternal woe MILT. **7.** *M. for M.* v. i. 472. **10. a.** SHAKS. *Sonn.* xxxii.

Reserved (rǐzə̄·ɹvd), *ppl. a.* 1474. [f. RESERVE *v.* + -ED[1].] †**1.** Excepted. Chiefly in prep. use: With the exception of, except, save. –1591. **2.** Averse to showing familiarity or to open expression of thought or feeling; cold or distant; reticent, uncommunicative 1601. **3.** Restrained or restricted in some way 1654. **4.** Set or kept apart; specially retained for some person or purpose 1616.

2. All her deseruing Is a reserued honestie SHAKS. As a statesman he was r., seldom showing his own thoughts FROUDE. **4.** *R. sacrament*: see 11 above and RESERVATION II. 1. *R. seats*, those seats at a public entertainment or meeting which may be specially engaged beforehand. *R. list*, a list of naval officers removed from active service but liable to be called out in the event of their being required. So *r. officer, pay*, etc. Hence **Rese·rvedly** *adv.*, **-ness.**

Reservist (rǐzə̄·ɹvist). 1876. [f. RESERVE *sb.* + -IST, after Fr. *réserviste.*] One who belongs to or serves in the reserve forces.

Reservoir (re·zəɹvwāɹ), *sb.* 1690. [– Fr. *réservoir*, f. *réserver* RESERVE *v.* + *-oir*; see -ORY[1].] **1.** A receptacle (of earthwork, masonry, etc.) specially constructed to contain and store a large supply of water for ordinary uses 1705. **b.** A place or area in which water naturally collects in large quantities 1730. **c.** *fig.* A place where something is collected or tends to collect 1690. **2.** A part of an animal or plant in which some fluid or secretion is collected or retained 1727. **b.** A part of some apparatus in which a fluid or liquid is contained 1784. **3.** Any receptacle for fluids (or vapours) 1774. †**b.** A receptacle or repository for things or articles –1836. **c.** A store or collection, a reserve supply, *of* something 1784.

1. c. Rome—the r., as Tacitus says, into which all things infamous and shameful flowed 1882. **3. c.** The labours of others have raised for us an immense r. of important facts DICKENS. Hence **Re·servoir** *v. trans.* to store up, keep in or as in a r.

Reset (rī·se·t), *sb.*[1] ME. [– OFr. *recet* :– L. *receptum*, f. *recipere* RECEIVE.] †**1.** The opportunity, advantage, privilege, etc., of being received or sheltered in a place; refuge, shelter, succour –1685. †**b.** A place of reception, refuge, or accommodation; an abode, haunt, usual retreat –1582. **2.** *Sc. Law.* **a.** Reception or shelter given to another, *spec.* to a thief, criminal, or proscribed person; the act or practice of receiving or harbouring such persons. Now *arch.* 1456. **b.** The act or practice of receiving stolen goods 1768.

Reset (rī·set, rī·se·t), *sb.*[2] 1847. [f. RESET *v.*[2]] The act of resetting; matter set up again in type.

Reset (rī·se·t), *v.*[1] ME. [– OFr. *receter, recetter* :– L. *receptare*, f. *recept-*, pa. ppl. stem of *recipere* RECEIVE.] **1.** *trans.* To harbour (a person, *esp.* an offender against the law). Now *arch.* (in later use *Sc.*). **2.** *Sc. Law.* To receive (stolen goods) from a thief with intent to cover or profit by the theft 1609.

1. You knew, that,..you were prohibited to r., supply, or intercommune with this..traitor SCOTT.

Reset (rī·se·t), *v.*[2] 1655. [RE- 5 a.] *trans.* To set again; esp. *Typog.* to set up, compose (type) again.

Resetter (rī·se·təɹ). late ME. [– OFr. *recetour, -eur*; see RESET *v.*[1], -ER[2].] †**a.** A harbourer of criminals, thieves, etc. –1632. **b.** A receiver of stolen goods. Now *Sc.* 1440.

†**Re·siance.** 1577. [– Fr. †*res(s)eance*; see next, -ANCE.] Abode, residence –1632. So †**Re·siancy** –1673.

Resiant (re·ziănt), *a.* and *sb.* late ME. [– OFr. *reseant*, pr. pple. of *reseoir* :– L. *residēre*; see next, -ANT.] **A.** *adj.* †**1.** *predic.*, or placed after the sb. Resident; abiding –1752. †**2. a.** Of residence or stay. **b.** = RESIDENT *a.* 2. (*rare*) –1600. **B.** *sb.* A resident. Now *rare.* late ME.

A. 1. A King..that hath the Spirit of the liuing God r. in him 1624.

Reside (rǐzəi·d), *v.*[1] 1456. [prob. orig. back-formation from *resident* but later infl. by Fr. *résider* and L. *residēre*; see RESIDENT *a.*] †**1.** *intr.* To settle; to take up one's abode or station (*rare*) –1657. **2.** To dwell permanently or for a considerable time, to have one's settled or usual abode, to live, *in* or *at* a particular place 1578. **b.** To live (at a place) for the discharge of official duties; to be 'in residence' 1456. **3. a.** Of power, rights: To rest or be vested *in* a person 1607. **b.** Of qualities, attributes, etc.: To be present or inherent *in* a person or thing 1611. **c.** To be physically present *in* a thing. Now *rare.* 1620. †**4.** Of things: To lie, be placed, somewhere (*rare*) –1742.

2. There at the moated-Grange recides this deiected Mariana SHAKS. **3. a.** Power—physical power—resides in the people BERKELEY. **b.** Cogitation Resides not in that man, that do's not thinke SHAKS. Hence **Resi·der**, a resident.

†**Resi·de**, *v.*[2] 1586. [– L. *residere* subside, f. *re-* RE- + *sidere* sink.] *intr.* To sink down; to settle down as a deposit –1702.

Residence[1] (re·zidĕns). late ME. [– (O)Fr. *résidence* or med.L. *residentia*; see RESIDENT *a.*, -ENCE.] **1. a.** *To have* (†*hold, keep, make*) *one's r.*, to have one's usual dwelling-place or abode; to reside. *To take up one's r.*, to establish oneself; to settle. **b.** The circumstance or fact of having one's permanent or usual abode in or at a certain place; the fact of residing or being resident 1480. **2.** The fact of living or staying regularly at or in some place for the discharge of special duties, or to comply with some regulation; also, the period during which such stay is required of a person. Now freq. in phr. *in r.* late ME. **3.** The place where a person resides; his dwelling-place; the abode *of* a person (esp. one of some rank or distinction) 1595. **b.** A dwelling, *esp.* one of a superior kind; a mansion 1603. **4.** *fig.* The (*or* a) seat *of* power, liberty, etc. 1642. **5.** The time during which a person resides in or at a place 1683. **b.** A period of residing; a stay 1686.

1. The arts and sciences took up their r...at Rome 1788. **b.** *Haml.* II. ii. 343. **2.** The Canon in R... gave orders that the Rolls..should be thrown into the fire 1892. At Oxford r. will not be resumed until the end of next week 1896. **3.** Not many furlongs thence Is your Fathers r. MILT. **b.** A r. was assigned him at Bithur 1844. **4.** The r. of the supreme authority,..the..Junta SCOTT.

†**Residence**[2]. 1541. [f. RESIDE *v.*[2] + -ENCE.] That which settles as a deposit; the residuum or deposit left after any chemical process –1685.

Residency (re·zidĕnsi). 1579. [f. as RESIDENCE[1]; see -ENCY.] †**1.** = RESIDENCE[1] –1670. **2.** The official residence of a representative of the Governor-general (formerly of the East India Company) at an Indian native court 1800. **3.** An administrative division in the Dutch East Indies 1814.

Resident (re·zidĕnt), *a.* and *sb.*[1] late ME. [– (O)Fr. *résident* or L. *residens, -ent-*, pr. pple. of *residēre* remain behind, rest, f. *re-* RE- + *sedēre* settle, sit; see -ENT.] **A.** *adj.* **1.** Resting, dwelling, or having an abode in a place. **b.** Of animals or birds: Non-migratory 1828. **2.** Staying in or at a place in discharge of some duty or in compliance with some regulation. late ME. **3.** Of qualities, etc.: Abiding, inherent, prevalent, established 1525. †**4.** Of things: Situated, lying –1695. †**b.** Remaining still; firm, abiding –1653.

1. He considered r. county gentlemen the greatest blessing of this country 1817. **2.** Mr. Wachsell, the r. surgeon 1803. **4. b.** The watry pavement is not stable and r. like a rock JER. TAYLOR.

B. *sb.* **1.** One who resides permanently in a place; sometimes *spec.* applied to inhabitants of the better class 1487. **b.** A resident incumbent 1812. **2.** A diplomatic representative, inferior in rank to an ambassador, residing at a foreign court. Now *Hist.* 1650. **b.** A representative of the (†East India Company or) Governor-general of India residing at a (†commercial station or) native court 1786. **c.** The governor of a residency in the Dutch East Indies 1814. Hence **Re·sidentship,** the office or post of a R.

†**Resident,** *sb.*[2] *rare.* 1625. [f. RESIDE *v.*[2]; parallel to RESIDENCE[2]. See -ENT.] Deposit or sediment –1666.

Residenter (re·zidentəɹ, *Sc.* rezide·ntəɹ). 1446. [var. of contemp. †*residencer* – AFr. *residencer*, OFr. *-ier* – med.L. *residentiarius* RESIDENTIARY.] †**1.** *Eccl.* A residentiary –1719. **2.** *Sc.* and *U.S.* A resident, inhabitant 1678.

Residential (rezide·nʃăl), *a.* 1654. [f. RESIDENCE[1] + -IAL, after *presidential.* Cf. AL. *residentialis* (XV).] †**1.** Serving or used as a residence; in which one resides –1740. **b.** Adapted or suitable for the residence of those belonging to the better class; characterized by houses of a superior kind 1878. **2.** Connected with, pertaining or relating to, residence or residences 1856. **3.** Of or belonging to a Resident (*rare*) 1885.

1. b. A considerable r. estate 1878. **2.** The r. qualification of voters 1881.

Residentiary (rezide·nʃări), *sb.* and *a.* 1525. [– med.L. *residentiarius*, f. *residentia* RESIDENCE[1] + *-arius* -ARY[1].] **A.** *sb.* **1.** An ecclesiastic who is bound to official residence, *esp.* a canon of a cathedral or collegiate church. **2.** One who or that which is resident 1615.

2. The r., or the frequent visitor of the favoured spot COLERIDGE.

B. *adj.* **1.** *Canon r.*, a canon of whom residence is required 1632. **b.** Involving, relating or pertaining to, official residence 1662. **2.** Residing or resident in a place 1640. **b.** Connected with residence 1871. Hence **Reside·ntiaryship,** the office of a (canon) r.

Residual (rǐzi·diu,ăl), *sb.* 1557. [subst. use of next.] **1.** *Math.* **a.** A residual quantity. **b.** Either of two systems of points which together make up all the intersections of any given curve with a plane cubic curve 1867. **2.** A remainder; an amount remaining after the main part is subtracted or accounted for 1860. **3.** A substance or product of the nature of a residuum 1885.

Residual (rǐzi·diu,ăl), *a.* 1570. [f. RESIDUE + -AL[1]. Cf. Fr. *résiduel.*] **1.** *Math.* Resulting from, formed by, the subtraction of one quantity from another. **2.** Remaining; still left; left over 1609. **b.** In the physical sciences: Left as a residuum, *esp.* at the end of some process 1757. **c.** Left unexplained or uncorrected 1830.

1. *R. analysis*, a calculus proposed by the inventor, Mr. Landen, as a substitute for the method of fluxions 1801. *R. calculus*, the calculus of residuals or residues 1890. **2. b.** The heat referred to is mainly..the r. heat of a cooling globe 1896. **c.** The r. error in our observations 1871.

Residuary (rǐzi·diu,ări), *a.* and *sb.* 1726. [f. RESIDUUM + -ARY[1].] **A.** *adj.* **1.** *Law.* Of the nature of the residue of an estate. **2.** Of the nature of a residuum or remainder of any kind; *esp.* with ref. to chemical processes, scientific observations, etc. 1793.

1. *R. legatee* or *devisee*, one to whom the residue of an estate is left. *R. clause*, a clause by which a residue is devised. **2.** We celebrated it by an extra dinner..and a couple of our r. bottles of wine 1853.

B. *sb.* A residuary legatee (*rare*) 1817.

Residue (re·zidiu). late ME. [– (O)Fr. *résidu* – L. *residuum* RESIDUUM.] **1.** The remainder, rest; that which is left. **2.** *Law.* That which remains of an estate after all charges, debts, and bequests have been paid. late ME. **3.** *Math.* = REMAINDER *sb.*[1] 4 a. *Obs.*

exc. as in *quadratic r.*, the remainder left on dividing the square of a number by a given number; so *cubic r.*, etc. late ME. **4.** = RESIDUUM 3. 1807. **5.** *Chem.* The atom or group of atoms remaining after part of a molecule has been removed 1873.

1. *Method of Residues*: see Mill *Logic* (1843) III. viii. § 5. The resydew of our lyucs LD. BERNERS. The R. of the conquer'd People fled to their Canoes DE FOE. †*In, for the r.*, as to the remainder.

Residuous (rĭzi·diu,əs), *a.* Now *rare.* 1626. [– L. *residuus*,; see next, -OUS.] Remaining.

Residuum (rĭzi·diu,ŏm). *Pl.* **residua** (rĭzi·diu,ă). 1672. [– L. *residuum*, subst. use of n. of *residuus* remaining, f. *residēre* RESIDE *v.*[1]] **1.** That which remains; a residue. (Chiefly of immaterial things.) **b.** Applied to persons of the lowest class 1867. **2.** *Law.* = RESIDUE 2. 1743. **3.** *spec.* That which remains after a process of combustion, evaporation, etc.; a deposit or sediment; a waste or residual product 1756.

1. b. The r., which there is in every constituency, of almost hopeless poverty and dependence BRIGHT.

Resign (rĭzəi·n), *v.* late ME. [– (O)Fr. *résigner* – L. *resignare* unseal, cancel, give up, f. *re-* RE- + *signare* SIGN *v.*] **I.** *trans.* **1.** To relinquish, surrender, give up, or hand over (something); *esp.* an office, position, right, claim, etc. Also with *up* (now *rare*). **2.** To give up, make over, abandon, consign *to* a person, thing, or condition. late ME. **b.** To yield up (oneself, etc.) with confidence *to* another for care or guidance. late ME. **c.** To make surrender of (one's will, reason, etc.) in reliance upon another 1585. **d.** To give (oneself, one's mind, etc.) up *to* some emotion, condition, or state 1718. †**3.** To give over, desist or refrain from –1590.

1. Upon his resigning the great seal 1818. The commonwealth was required..to r...its foreign possessions 1839. **2. b.** He..vows to r. himself to her direction 1869. **d.** I will r. myself to rest COWPER.

II. *intr.* **1.** To give up an office or position; to retire; †to abdicate 1450. **2.** To submit or yield, *to* a person or thing. Now *rare.* 1450. **3.** To make surrender or relinquishment 1738.

1. If my Lord bishop wants to r. 1860. Hence †**Resignee·**, one to whom anything is resigned. **Resi·gner,** one who resigns. **Resi·gnment,** the act of resigning; resignation (now *rare*).

Resignation (rezignē·ʃən). late ME. [– (O)Fr. *résignation* – med.L. *resignatio*, *-on-*; see RESIGN *v.*, -ATION.] **1.** The (*or* an) action of resigning an office, etc.; also, the document conveying this. **2.** A giving up *of* oneself (to God) 1450. **3.** The fact of resigning oneself or of being resigned; acquiescence, submission, compliance 1647.

1. Archbishopricks and bishopricks may become void..by r. BLACKSTONE. They..gave in their r. 1848. **3.** Proba supported, with Christian r., the loss of immense riches GIBBON.

Resigned (rĭzəi·nd), *ppl. a.* 1654. [f. RESIGN *v.* + -ED[1].] †**1.** Given *up*, abandoned, surrendered –1666. **2.** Full of resignation; submissive, acquiescent; characterized by resignation 1699. **3.** That has retired from a position 1896.

2. Sufficiently philosophical to be r., he was yet too ambitious to be contented 1894. Hence **Resi·gned-ly** *adv.*, **-ness.**

Resile (rĭzəi·l), *v.* 1529. [– Fr. †*resilir* or L. *resilire* leap back, recoil, f. *re-* RE- + *salire* leap. In sense 1 = med.L. *resilire* (*ab*) repudiate.] **1.** *intr.* To draw back *from* an agreement, contract, statement, etc.; to shrink, retreat, *from* something with aversion or non-acceptance. **2.** Of material things: To recoil or rebound after contact. **b.** Of elastic bodies: To return to their original position after being stretched or compressed 1709. **3. a.** To turn back from a point reached 1887. **b.** To return to one's original position 1889. Hence **Resi·lement.**

Resilience (rĭzi·liĕns). 1626. [f. as RESILIENT; see -ENCE.] **1.** The (*or* an) act of rebounding or springing back; rebound, recoil. **2.** Elasticity; the power of resuming the original shape or position after compression, bending, etc. 1824.

1. Whether there be any such R. in Eccho's BACON.

Resiliency (rĭzi·liĕnsi). 1668. [f. as prec.; see -ENCY.] **1.** Tendency to rebound or recoil. **2.** = RESILIENCE 2. 1835. **3.** Buoyancy, power of recovery 1857.

Resilient (rĭzi·liĕnt), *a.* 1644. [– L. *resiliens*, *-ent-*, pr. pple. of *resilire*; see RESILE, -ENT.] **1.** Returning to the original position; springing back, recoiling, etc. **2.** Resuming the original shape or position after being bent, compressed, or stretched 1674. **3.** *fig.* Of persons, etc.: Rising readily again after being depressed; hence, cheerful, buoyant, exuberant 1830.

3. The r. spirit of roving Englishmen 1859.

†**Resili·tion.** 1658. [f. RESILE *v.* + -ITION. Cf. DISSILITION.] The (*or* an) act of springing back; recoil, rebound, resilience –1738.

Resin (re·zin), *sb.* [Late ME. *recyn*, *resyn*, *rosyn*, *rosine* – L. *resina* and med.L. *rosinum* (XIII), *rosina* (XIV), prob. collateral adoption, with Gr. ῥητίνη, from some IE. source. Cf. ROSIN.] **1.** A vegetable product, formed by secretion in special canals in almost all trees and plants, from many of which (as the fir and pine) it exudes naturally, or can be readily obtained by incision; extensively used in making varnishes, etc., and in pharmacy. **b.** With *a* and *pl.* A particular kind of resin 1801. **2.** A resinous precipitate obtained by special treatment of certain vegetable products; a similar substance obtained from bile 1681.

Comb.: **r.-bush,** a South African shrub, *Euryops speciosissimus*, so named because of a gummy exudation often seen on the stem and leaves; **-weed,** = ROSIN-WEED. Hence **Re·sin** *v.* to rub or treat with r. **Resina·ceous** *a.* (*rare*) that yields r. **Resi·nic** *a.* of, belonging to, or derived from r. **Resini·ferous** *a.* yielding or containing r. **Re·siniform** *a.* having the character of r. **Re·siny** *a.* resinous.

Resinate (re·zinĕt). 1838. [f. prec. + -ATE[1] 1 c.] *Chem.* A salt formed by the action of a resinous acid on a base.

Resinify (re·zinifəi), *v.* 1816. [– Fr. *résinifier*; see RESIN *sb.*, -FY.] **1.** *trans.* To change into resin. **2.** *intr.* To become resinous 1856. So **Re:sinifica·tion** [Fr. *résinification*] 1800.

Resino-, comb. form of RESIN *sb.*, as in **r.-electric** *a.*, containing or exhibiting resinous or negative electricity.

Resinoid (re·zinoid), *a.* and *sb.* 1830. [f. RESIN *sb.* + -OID.] **A.** *adj.* Resembling resin. **B.** *sb.* A resinous substance 1880.

Resinol (re·zinǫl). 1893. [f. RESIN *sb.* + -OL 1.] **1.** *Chem.* Any of various alcohols found in resin. **2.** = RETINOL 1893.

Resinous (re·zinəs), *a.* 1646. [– Fr. *résineux* – L. *resinosus*; see RESIN *sb.*, -OUS.] **1.** Of the nature of resin. **2.** Of plants or their parts: Containing resin 1656. **3.** Of properties, etc.: Properly belonging to, or characteristic of, resin 1811. **4.** Made or compounded of resin; affected or produced by the burning of resin 1808. **5.** *Electr.* = NEGATIVE *a.* II. 3. 1797.

4. I can smell the heavy r. incense as I pass the church DICKENS. Hence **Re·sinous-ly** *adv.*, **-ness.**

Resipiscence (resipi·sĕns). 1570. [– Fr. *résipiscence* or late L. *resipiscentia*, f. L. *resipiscere* come to oneself again, f. *re-* RE- + *sapere* know; see -ENCE.] Repentance for misconduct; recognition of errors committed; return to a better mind or opinion. So †**Resipi·scency. Resipi·scent** *a.* returning to a sound state of mind.

Resist (rĭzi·st), *sb.* 1535. [f. the vb.] †**1.** Resistance –1630. **2.** In calico-printing, a preparation applied to those parts of the fabric which are not to be coloured, in order to prevent the dye from affecting them 1836. **3.** Any composition applied to a surface to protect it from the effects of an agent employed on it for some purpose. Also *r.-varnish.* 1839.

Resist (rĭzi·st), *v.* late ME. [– (O)Fr. *résister* or L. *resistere*, f. *re-* RE- + *sistere* stop, redupl. f. *stare* stand.] **1.** *trans.* Of things: To stop or hinder (a moving body); to succeed in standing against; to prevent (a weapon, etc.) from piercing or penetrating. **b.** To withstand the action or effect of, fail to be affected by (a natural force, physical agency, etc.) 1567. **2.** Of persons: To withstand, strive against, oppose. late ME. †**3.** To affect with distaste. SHAKS. **4.** *intr.* †**a.** To stand *against*, make opposition *to*, a person or thing –1651. **b.** To offer resistance 1547.

1. Spiritual Armour, able to r. Satans assaults MILT. **b.** Able to r. fire 1567. *To r. a joke* (with neg.): to help making, or fail to be amused by, it. **2.** Fleshly weaknesse, which no creature may Long time r. SPENSER. That mortal dint, Save he who reigns above, none can r. MILT. O King of Glory! thou alone hast power! Who can r. thy will? SHELLEY. **4. b.** *Oth.* I. ii. 80.

Resistance (rĭzi·stăns). late ME. [– Fr. *résistance*, later form of †*résistence* – late L. *resistentia*; see RESIST *v.*, -ANCE.] **1.** The act, on the part of persons, of resisting, opposing, or withstanding. **2.** Power or capacity of resisting 1590. **3.** Opposition of one material thing to another material thing, force, etc. 1625. **b.** *esp.* in the physical sciences, the opposition offered by one body to the pressure or movement of another 1656. **4.** Non-conductivity in respect of electricity, magnetism, or heat 1860. **b.** A part of an electrical apparatus used to offer a definite resistance to a current 1878. **5.** *Piece of r.*, = Fr. *pièce de résistance*: see PIÈCE b. 1797.

1. There is yet a spirit of r. in this country, which will not submit to be oppressed '*Junius' Lett.* Phr. *Passive r.*, simple refusal to comply with some demand, without active opposition; *spec.* refusal to pay voluntarily the education rate imposed by the Education Act of 1902. **3.** The Heauens in their motion find no r. 1625. **b.** All the Bodies in the World, pressing a drop of Water on all sides, will never be able to overcome the R. it will make LOCKE. Phr. *Line of r.* **5.** The good girl liked a piece of r., a solid tome 1858.

attrib. and *Comb.*, as **r.-box** (*Electr.*) a box containing one or more r. coils, also *transf.*; **r. coil,** a coil introduced into an electric circuit, so as to increase the r.

Resistant (rĭzi·stănt), *a.* and *sb.* 1600. [– Fr. *résistant*, pr. pple. of *résister* RESIST *v.*; see -ANT.] **A.** *adj.* That makes resistance or opposition 1610. **B.** *sb.* One who or that which resists; a resister. Now *rare.* 1600. **b.** In calico-printing, = RESIST *sb.* 2. 1879.

†**Resi·stence.** [Late ME. – OFr. *resistence*; see RESISTANCE, -ENCE.] = RESISTANCE –1738. So †**Resi·stency.**

Resistent (rĭzi·stĕnt), *a.* and *sb.* 1600. [– L. *resistens*, *-ent-*, pr. pple. of *resistere* RESIST *v.*; see -ENT.] **A.** *adj.* = RESISTANT *a.* 1640. †**B.** *sb.* = RESISTANT *sb.* –1644.

Resister (rĭzi·stəɹ). late ME. [f. RESIST *v.* + -ER[1].] One who, or that which, resists. *Passive r.*: see RESISTANCE 1.

Resi·stful, *a.* 1614. [f. RESIST *sb.* and *v.* + -FUL.] Capable of, or inclined to, resistance.

Resistibility (rĭzistĭbi·lĭti). 1617. [f. as next + -ITY.] **1.** The quality of being resistible. **2.** Power of offering resistance 1646.

Resistible (rĭzi·stĭb'l), *a.* 1643. [f. RESIST *v.* + -IBLE.] Capable of being resisted.

Earthquakes themselves, the least r. of natural violence JOHNSON. Hence **Resi·stibleness. Resi·stibly** *adv.*

Resi·sting, *ppl. a.* 1593. [f. as prec. + -ING[2].] That resists or offers resistance. Hence **Resi·stingly** *adv.*

Resistive (rĭzi·stiv). 1603. [In XVII – med.L. *resistivus*; in later use, f. RESIST *v.* + -IVE.] Capable of or inclined to resistance. Hence **Resi·stive-ly** *adv.*, **-ness. Resisti·vity** (*Electr.*) the specific resistance of a substance.

Resistless (rĭzi·stlĕs), *a.* 1586. [f. RESIST *sb.* and *v.* + -LESS.] **1.** That cannot be resisted; irresistible. **2.** Powerless to resist 1591.

1. Try to Imprison the r. Wind 1693. Hence **Resi·stless-ly** *adv.*, **-ness.**

Resoluble (re·zǫliŭb'l), *a.* 1602. [– Fr. *résoluble* (XVI) or late and med.L. *resolubilis*; see RE-, SOLUBLE.] Capable of being resolved; resolvable. Hence **Resolubi·lity, Re·solubleness.**

†**Re·solute,** *sb. rare.* 1534. [subst. use of next.] **1.** A payment –1610. **2.** A resolute or determined person –1800.

2. A List of Landlesse Resolutes SHAKS.

Resolute (re·zŏl[1]ut), *a.* (and *pa. pple.*). late ME. [– L. *resolutus*, pa. pple. of *resolvere* RESOLVE *v.*] †**1.** Dissolved. late ME. only. †**2.** Of rents: Paid, rendered –1670. †**3.** Determinate, decided, positive, absolute, final; esp. *r. answer* –1656. **4.** Of persons, their minds, etc.: Determined, having a fixed resolve, constant, firm 1533. **5.** Of actions:

Characterized by determination or firmness of purpose 1603.

4. I am determined to continue r. in well doing 1634. They were few, but r. SHELLEY. R. for peace GREEN. 5. He..leads Invincibly a life of r. good SHELLEY. Hence **Re·solute-ly** *adv.*, **-ness.**

Resolute (re·zŏl[1]ut), *v.* Now *U.S.* 1548. [– *resolut-*, pa. ppl. stem of L. *resolvere*; in mod. use a back-formation from next.] †1. *refl.* To resolve, decide (oneself) *upon* a person –1548. †2. *trans.* To resolve, dissolve *into* something –1727. 3. *U.S. intr.* To draw up or pass resolutions 1860.

Resolution (rezŏl[1]ū·ʃən). late ME. [– L. *resolutio, -on-*, f. as prec.; see -ION. Cf. (O)Fr. *résolution.*] I. †1. = Dissolution, death –1582. 2. The process by which a material thing is reduced or separated into its component parts or elements; a result of this. late ME. b. Const. *to, into.* Also, conversion *into* something else, or *into* a different form. 1519. c. The effect of an optical instrument in making the separate parts of an object (*esp.* the stars of a nebula) distinguishable by the eye 1860. 3. *Med.* †a. Dissolution or dispersion of humours or of morbid matter in the body –1778. b. Disappearance of inflammation without coming to suppuration 1783. †4. Conversion to a fluid state –1686. 5. Relaxation or weakening of some part of the body. Now *rare.* 1547.

1. The tyme of my resolucioun..is nyȝ WYCLIF 2 *Tim.* 4:6.

II. 1. The process of resolving or reducing a non-material thing into simpler forms, or of converting into some other thing or form. late ME. b. In prosody, the substitution of two short syllables for a long one 1884. †2. *Math.* and *Logic.* = ANALYSIS 7, 8. –1738. 3. *Mus.* The process by which a discord is made to pass into a concord 1727. 4. *Mech.* The substitution for a single force of two or more forces, to which it is mechanically equivalent, or of which it is the resultant 1798. III. 1. The answering *of* a question; the solving *of* a doubt or difficulty. Now *rare.* 1548. b. The solution *of* an arithmetical or mathematical problem. Now *rare* or *Obs.* 1579. 2. A statement upon some matter; a decision or verdict on some point. Now *rare* or *Obs.* 1581. b. A formal decision, determination, or expression of opinion, on the part of a deliberative body or other meeting; a proposal of this nature submitted to an assembly or meeting 1604. †3. An explanatory account *of* something –1658.

1. Of this question..we must be content to live without the r. JOHNSON. b. Of the R. of Equations 1797. 2. b. The passing by the House of Commons of such a r. as this FREEMAN.

IV. †1. a. The removal of a doubt on some point from a person's mind (*rare*) –1644. b. Confidence; conviction, certainty, positive knowledge (*rare*) –1637. 2. The (*or* an) act of resolving or determining; anything resolved upon; a fixed determination 1590. 3. Determination; firmness or steadiness of purpose; unyielding temper 1588.

1. b. *Lear* I. ii. 108. 2. To be praised then every man resolves; but resolutions will not execute themselves JOHNSON. 3. He comes, and settl'd in his face I see Sad r. and secure MILT. Hence **Resolu·tionist,** one who makes, or joins in, a r.

Resolutioner (rezŏl[1]ū·ʃənəɹ). 1693. [f. RESOLUTION + -ER[1].] 1. *Hist.* A member of that party in Scotland which accepted the resolutions passed in 1650 for rehabilitating those persons who had not taken part in the struggle against Cromwell. 2. One who joins in or subscribes to a resolution. Now *Obs.* or *rare.* 1816.

Resolutive (re·zŏl[1]utiv), *a.* and *sb.* late ME. [– med.L. *resolutivus* (XIII), f. L. *resolut-*; see RESOLUTE *v.*, -IVE. Cf. (O)Fr. *résolutif, -ive.*] A. *adj.* 1. a. Having the power to dissolve. b. *Path.* Terminating by resolution 1861. 2. *Law. R. condition,* a condition by the happening of which a contract or obligation is terminated 1623. †3. *Logic.* Analytical –1656. B. *sb.* A medical application or drug which serves to resolve or disperse morbid matter. late ME.

Resolutory (re·zŏl[1]utəri), *a. rare.* 1609. [– late L. *resolutorius*, f. as prec.; see -ORY[2]. In sense 2 var. of prec. by suffix-substitution.] †1. Explanatory, enlightening –1669. 2. *Law.* = RESOLUTIVE *a.* 2. 1818.

Resolvable (rĭzǫ·lvăb'l), *a.* 1646. [f. RESOLVE *v.* + -ABLE.] Capable of being resolved.

R. nebula, a nebula which admits of resolution by a powerful telescope. Hence **Resolvabi·lity. Reso·lvableness,** the capability of being resolved into parts.

Resolve (rĭzǫ·lv), *sb.* 1591. [f. the vb.] 1. A determination or resolution 1592. 2. Firmness or steadfastness of purpose 1591. 3. A determination of a deliberative body; a formal resolution. Now *U.S.* 1656. †4. Answer, solution –1670.

1. She made up her mind never to marry again, and she kept her r. 1889. 2. We must be stiffe and steddie in r. MARSTON. 3. Cæsar's approach has summon'd us together, And Rome attends her fate from our resolves ADDISON.

Resolve (rĭzǫ·lv), *v.* late ME. [– L. *resolvere*, f. *re-* RE- + *solvere* loosen, dissolve.] I. †1. *trans.* To melt, dissolve, reduce to a liquid or fluid state –1732. 2. To disintegrate; to break up or separate into constituent or elementary parts. Now *rare* or *Obs.* late ME. †b. *Math.* To solve (an equation) –1798. c. To analyse (a force or velocity) into its components 1825. d. Of optical instruments (or persons using them): To separate, break up (an object) into distinguishable parts 1785. 3. *Med.* To soften (a hard tumour); to disperse or dissipate (humours, swellings, etc.). Now *rare* or *Obs.* late ME. b. To remove (inflammation) by resolution 1732. †4. To slacken, relax (the limbs, etc.); to weaken –1715. †b. To render lax in feeling or conduct –1611. 5. *Mus.* To cause (a discord) to pass into a concord 1727.

2. A mellow ground that is fat, and will soone be resolved 1577. 2. d. When he resolves one nebula into stars, he discovers ten new ones which he cannot r. HERSCHEL.

II. 1. To separate (a thing) *into* its component parts or elements; to dissolve *into* some other physical form. late ME. b. To convert, transform, alter (a thing) *into* some other thing or form 1570. 2. To reduce by mental analysis *into* more elementary forms, principles, or relations. late ME. 3. *refl.* Of things: To pass, by dissolution, separation, or change, *into* another form or *into* simpler forms 1602. b. Of a deliberative body: To convert (itself) *into* a committee 1710. 4. To reduce, transform, or change (a thing) *to* something else. Also *refl.* Now *rare.* 1538.

1. To r. the German Empire back again into its elements 1891. b. That the House be resolved into a Committee 1641. 2. Why may we not..r. Christianity into a system of practical Morality? 1841. 3. The argument..resolves itself into four parts 1814.

III. †1. To untie, loosen –1609. 2. To answer (a question, argument, etc.); to solve (a problem of any kind) 1577. b. To explain; to make clear 1585. 3. To remove, clear away, dispel (a doubt, difficulty, or obscurity) 1571. 4. To decide, determine, settle (a doubtful point) 1586. †b. To conclude, settle (a thing) in one's mind –1702. 5. To determine or decide upon (a course of action, etc.); often with obj. clause 1523. b. To adopt or pass as a resolution 1590. †6. To free (a person) from doubt or perplexity; to bring to certainty or clear understanding; to convince or assure *of* something –1767. †7. To inform, tell (a person) *of* a thing; to advise as to a decision; also with obj. clause –1697. b. To determine (a person) *on* a course of action 1836. 8. *refl.* †To make up one's mind, †free oneself *of* a doubt; to satisfy or convince oneself (*arch.*) 1528.

2. After a great part of life spent in enquiries which can never be resolved JOHNSON. 3. Myself can shew a catalogue of Doubts which are not resolved at the first hearing SIR T. BROWNE. 4. Happiness, it was resolved by all, must be some one uniform end 1719. 5. Warr Open or understood must be resolv'd MILT. b. Resolved unanimously, that this meeting [etc.] 1806. 6. Yet you are amaz'd, but this shall absolutely resolue you SHAKS. 1 *Hen. VI,* III. iv. 20. 7. My Letter will resolue him of my minde SHAKS. 8. He must r. himself on the question 1869.

IV. *intr.* †1. To melt, dissolve, become fluid –1759. 2. To undergo dissolution or separation into elements; to pass *into,* return or change *to,* some form or state. late ME. b. *Path.* To undergo resolution 1822. c. *Mus.* To change from discord to harmony 1889. 3. To come to a determination; to make up one's mind. Now usu. const. inf. or (*up*)*on.* 1570. †b. To decide to make *for* a place –1760. †4. To be satisfied or convinced –1659. †b. To consult, take counsel –1719.

1. Euen as a forme of waxe Resolueth from his figure 'gainst the fire SHAKS. 2. The phantom.. Resolves to air POPE. It would r. into an equitable claim SCOTT. 3. He had resolved..to give way 1856. b. I will resolue for Scotland SHAKS.

Resolved (rĭzǫ·lvd), *ppl. a.* 1497. [f. prec. + -ED[1].] In the senses of the vb. *esp.* 1. Of persons: Determined, decided, settled in purpose 1520. 2. Of actions, states of mind, etc.: Deliberate 1595. 3. Of persons, the mind, etc.: Characterized by determination or firmness of purpose; resolute 1586.

1. I am resolued what to doe *Luke* 16:4. 2. A resolu'd and honourable warre SHAKS. 3. The hat pulled over his r. brows SCOTT. Hence **Reso·lved-ly** *adv.*, **-ness.**

Resolvend (rĭzǫ·lvĕnd), *sb.* 1673. [– L. *resolvendum*, n. gerundive of *resolvere* RESOLVE *v.*] *Arith.* The number formed by extending the remainder after subtraction in the process of extracting the square or cube root.

Resolvent (rĭzǫ·lvĕnt), *a.* and *sb.* 1676. [– L. *resolvens, -ent-*, pr. pple. of *resolvere* RESOLVE *v.*] A. *adj.* 1. Chiefly *Med.* Having the power to resolve; causing solution. 2. Of a proposition: That merely asserts what is already included in the conception of the subject 1856. B. *sb.* 1. *Med.* A medicine or application to cause the resolution of a swelling; a discutient 1676. 2. Something capable of resolving; a solvent 1706. 3. A means of removing difficulties, settling problems, etc. 1851.

Resolver (rĭzǫ·lvəɹ). late ME. [f. RESOLVE *v.* + -ER[1].] †1. A resolvent substance –1756. 2. One who, or that which, answers a question or solves a doubt or difficulty 1609. 3. One who makes a resolve; one who supports a resolution 1749.

Resonance (re·zŏnăns). 1491. [– Fr. †*reson(n)ance* (mod. *résonnance*) – L. *resonantia* echo (Vitruvius), f. *resonant-*; see next, -ANCE.] 1. The reinforcement or prolongation of sound by reflection, or *spec.* by synchronous vibration. b. *Path.* The sound heard in auscultation of the chest while the person is speaking, or that elicited by percussion of parts of the body 1822. c. *Electr.* The effect produced by an oscillatory current upon one of equal period 1889. 2. The quality of reinforcing or prolonging a sound by vibration 1669.

Resonant (re·zŏnănt), *a.* and *sb.* 1592. [– (O)Fr. *résonnant* or L. *resonans, -ant-*, pr. pple. of *resonare*; see RESOUND *v.*, -ANT.] A. *adj.* 1. Of sounds: Re-echoing, resounding; continuing to sound or ring. 2. Of bodies: Causing reinforcement or prolongation of sound, esp. by vibration 1685. 3. Of places: Echoing or resounding *with* something 1813.

3. Fertile valleys, r. with bliss SHELLEY.

B. *sb.* A nasal consonant 1875. Hence **Re·sonantly** *adv.*

Resonate (re·zŏne[1]t), *v.* 1873. [– *resonat-*, pa. ppl. stem of L. *resonare*; see RESOUND *v.*, -ATE[3].] *intr.* To produce or exhibit resonance.

Resonator (re·zŏnē[1]təɹ). 1869. [f. prec. + -OR 2.] 1. An instrument responding to one single note, and used for its detection when combined with other sounds. 2. An appliance for increasing sound by resonance; a body or object which produces resonance 1871. 3. *Electr.* An apparatus used for the detection of Hertzian waves 1893.

Resorb (rĭsǭ·ɹb), *v.* 1640. [– L. *resorbēre*, f. *re-* RE- + *sorbēre* drink in.] To absorb again.

The extravasated blood was resorbed 1902. So **Reso·rbence,** reabsorption. **Reso·rbent** *a.*

Resorcin (rezǭ·ɹsin). Also **-ine.** 1866. [f. RES(IN + ORCIN.] *Chem.* A colourless crystalline compound, formerly produced by the action of potash upon galbanum or other resins, now usu. prepared synthetically. It is used as a dye-stuff, and in medicine and photography. Hence **Reso·rcinol,** a form of r.; a compound of r. with other substances. **Resorcylic** (rezǫɹsi·lik) *a.* pertaining to, derived from r.

Resorption (rǐsǭ·ɹpʃən). 1818. [f. RESORB *v.*, after *absorb, absorption.*] The fact or process of reabsorption, *spec.* of an organ, tissue, or excretion.

Resort (rǐzǭ·ɹt), *sb.* late ME. [– (O)Fr. *resort*, f. *resortir*; see next.] **I. 1.** That to which one has recourse for aid or assistance, or in order to accomplish some end. **2.** Recourse *to* some person, thing, or expedient, for aid or assistance, for the settlement of some difficulty, or the attainment of some end 1474. **3.** General or habitual repair of persons to some place or person. late ME. †**4.** Concourse or assemblage of people –1700. **b.** An assemblage, gathering, throng, crowd 1550. **5.** A place to which people repair, as for holiday-making, restoration of health, etc. (*health, seaside r.*, etc.) 1754.

1. A fit one [*sc.* sledge] was not to be found, and a carriage was..the only r. TYNDALL. **2.** It will be impossible to close the Committee to-night without r. to a sitting of unusual length 1884. Phr. *In the last r.* [after Fr. *en dernier ressort*], orig. as a judge or court from which there is no appeal; hence, as a last expedient, in the end, ultimately. *Without r.*, without appeal (*rare*). **3.** To build Houses, Temples, and Places of Publick R. 1683. **6.** This intellectual cloud, which hangs, like a fog, over every gay r. of our moral invalids 1754.

†**II.** A mechanical spring –1714.

Resort (rǐzǭ·ɹt), *v.* late ME. [– OFr. *resortir* (mod. *ressortir*), f. *re-* RE- + *sortir* go out.] †**1.** *intr.* To issue, come out, again –1480. †**2. a.** To return *to* oneself; to revert *to* a former condition or custom –1589. **b.** To return *to* a subject or matter; also, to go back in a discourse or in time –1749. **c.** To revert or fall *to* a person's lot or share –1676. †**3.** To turn, direct one's attention, *to* a subject –1581. **4.** To betake oneself, repair or go, *to* a person for aid 1460. **b.** To have recourse *to* something for assistance or furtherance of an object 1647. **5.** To repair, make one's way, come or go, esp. habitually or frequently *to* a person or place; to respond to a summons 1447. **6.** To proceed or go *to* (or *towards*) a place 1450. **7.** To have one's or its abode, stay 1453. †**8.** *trans.* To frequent or haunt (a place) –1756.

4. b. At length we r. to actual experiment TYNDALL. **5.** Crowes will to carrion still, Like euer vnto like r. 1607. The chop-house here, To which I most r. TENNYSON. **6.** The Sons of Light Hasted, resorting to the Summons high, And took thir Seats MILT. **7.** 'Tis pitty that thou liu'st To walke where any honest men r. SHAKS. Hence **Reso·rter**, a frequenter or visitor.

†**Resou·nd**, *sb.* 1586. [f. the vb.] A returned or re-echoed sound; a resonance –1701.

Resound (rǐzau·nd), *v.* [Late XIV *resoune*, f. *re-* RE- + *soune* SOUND *v.*[1], after OFr. *resoner* or L. *resonare.*] **I.** *intr.* **1.** Of places: To ring, re-echo (*with* or †*of* some sound). **2.** Of things: To make or produce an echoing sound 1530. **3.** Of sounds: To echo, ring 1547. **b.** To be mentioned or repeated; to be celebrated or renowned 1578.

1. Together rush'd Both Battels maine..all Heav'n Resounded MILT. The dome resounded with the acclamations of the people GIBBON. **2.** His arms resounded as the boaster fell POPE. **3.** And echoing praises..r. at your return COWPER. **b.** Milton, a name to r. for ages TENNYSON.

II. *trans.* **1.** To proclaim, repeat loudly (a person's praises, etc.); to celebrate (a person or thing) 1561. **2.** To repeat or utter (words, etc.) in a loud or echoing manner. Now *rare*. 1594. **3.** Of places: To re-echo 1579.

1. Let us..in our Mother Tongue r. his Praise DRYDEN. **3.** Hell..sigh'd From all her Caves, and back resounded 'Death!' MILT. Cliffs, woods and caves, her viewless steps r. WORDSW.

Resource (rǐsōə·ɹs). 1611. [– Fr. *ressource*, †*-ourse*, subst. use of fem. pa. pple. of OFr. (dial.) *resourdre* rise again, recover :– L. *resurgere*; see RESURGE.] **1.** A means of supplying some want or deficiency; a stock or reserve upon which one can draw when necessary. Now usu. *pl.* **b.** *pl.* The collective means possessed by any country for its own support or defence 1779. **2.** Possibility of aid or assistance. (Chiefly in phr. *without r.*) 1697. **3.** An action or procedure to which one may have recourse in a difficulty or emergency; an expedient, device, shift 1697. **4.** A means of relaxation or amusement 1776. **5.** Capability in adapting means to ends, or in meeting difficulties 1853.

1. *sing.* The treasure of the Hotel de Ville presented an immediate r. 1849. *pl.* It was limited with respect to pecuniary Resources 1800. **2.** Vanquish'd without r.; Laid flat by fate DRYDEN. **3.** Us'd threatnings, mix'd with pray'rs, his last r. DRYDEN. **4.** Reading had been her chief r. DISRAELI. **5.** R. in difficulties is the distinction of great generals FROUDE. Hence **Resou·rceful** *a.* full of r.; abounding in resources; **Resou·rcefulness. Resou·rceless** *a.* without r.; destitute of resources; **Resou·rcelessness.**

Respect (rǐspe·kt), *sb.* late ME. [– (O)Fr. *respect* or L. *respectus*, f. pa. ppl. stem of *respicere* look (back) at, regard, consider, f. *re-* RE- + *specere* look.] **I. 1.** †**a.** An aspect of a thing; a relative property or quality; a relationship –1753. **b.** A particular, point, detail. Only in phrases with *in*, as *in all, many*, or *some respects*. 1581. **2.** A relationship of one person or thing *to* another; a reference *to* some thing or person 1551. †**3.** Relationship, reference –1662. †**b.** Bearings, results. DRYDEN.

1. a. Doth Relation to us alter the Case, and that R. alone impart Worth? 1748. **b.** I should like to know in what r. the argument is not sufficient 1875. **2.** A worldly morality which has no r. to God 1850.

II. †**1.** A view; a backward survey (*rare*) –1661. **2.** Regard, consideration. Const. *of* or *to*. 1530. **b.** Discrimination, partiality, or favour in regard *of* persons or things 1535. †**c.** Heed, care, attention –1647. †**d.** *pl.* Attention or consideration given to more than one point or matter –1656. **3.** A consideration; a fact or motive which assists in, or leads to, the formation of a decision; an end or aim 1549.

1. Taking a prospect (or r. rather) of the Country they have passed FULLER. **2.** R. and reason, wait on wrinkled age! SHAKS. **b.** Is there no r. of place, persons, nor time in you? SHAKS. **c.** When men shall carry a r. not to descend into any course that is corrupt BACON. **3.** These Respects gave the first Rise to a Treaty of Peace 1673.

III. 1. Deferential regard or esteem felt or shown towards a person or thing 1586. **b.** The condition or state of being esteemed or honoured 1597. †**c.** Rank, standing, station in life –1652. **2.** *pl.* †**a.** Deferential or courteous attentions; actions expressive of respect for a person; politenesses, courtesies –1707. †**b.** Deferential salutations. CLARENDON. **c.** In complimentary formulæ, usu. conveying a message expressive of regard or esteem 1645. **d.** *To pay one's respects*, to show polite attention *to* a person by presenting oneself or by making a call 1668.

1. Zeale to promote the common good..deserueth certainly much r. and esteeme 1611. **b.** Youth without honour, age without r. BYRON. **c.** *Jul. C.* I. ii. 59. **2. c.** Pray give my respects to him MISS BURNEY. **d.** He expressed great eagerness to pay his respects to his master SMOLLETT.

Phrases. *To have r. to*: **a.** To have regard or relation *to*, or connection with, something. **b.** To have reference, to refer, to something. †**c.** To have an eye *to*, to give heed *to*, by looking at. **d.** To give heed, attention, or consideration to something; to have regard *to*; to take into account. Also const. ellipt. with *that*. **e.** To have in view; to allude *to*. †*In r. of*, in comparison with. †*In r.*, in comparison. *In r.* (*of*): **a.** With reference to; as relates to or regards. †**b.** In view of, by reason or because of. **c.** Considering, seeing, since (*that*). *Without r.*: †**a.** Without discrimination or consideration. **b.** Without consideration *of*, or regard *to*, something. *With r.*, with reference or regard *to* something.

Respect (rǐspe·kt), *v.* 1542. [– *respect-*, pa. ppl. stem of L. *respicere*, or its frequent. deriv. *respectare*; see prec.] †**1.** *trans.* To respite; to put off, neglect –1620. †**2.** To regard, consider, take into account –1668. †**b.** To pay attention to; to observe carefully –1662. †**c.** To regard as being of a certain kind, etc. (*rare*) –1602. **3.** To be directed to; to refer or relate to; to deal or be concerned with 1563. **b.** In *pres. pple.* used as *prep.* With reference or regard to 1732. **4.** To treat or regard with deference, esteem, or honour; to feel or show respect for 1560. †**b.** To esteem, prize, or value (a thing) –1638. **c.** To treat with consideration; to refrain from interfering with; to spare 1621. †**5.** To expect, anticipate, look (for). *rare.* –1623. **6. a.** *Her.* Of charges: To look at, face (*esp.* each other) 1562. †**b.** To regard; to look upon –1620. †**c.** To look towards; to face –1734. **d.** *intr.* To face or look *to* or *towards* (*rare*) 1585.

2. c. To whom my father gave this name of Gasper, And as his own respected him B. JONS. **3.** The greatest wits want perspicacity in things that r. their own interest 1663. *As respects*, with reference or regard to, concerning. **b.** He could not agree with him respecting the price 1802. **4.** I always loved and respected him very much SWIFT. **b.** *Two Gent.* I. ii. 134. **c.** Lewis had,..repeatedly promised to r. the privileges of his Protestant subjects MACAULAY. **6. b.** Wise men will not view such persons but with scorn, nor r. them but with disesteem 1620. **c.** The latter stands on a sharp cliff respecting the north 1734.

Respectability (rǐspektăbi·lǐti). 1785. [f. RESPECTABLE *a.* + -ITY.] **1.** The state, quality, or condition of being respectable in point of character or social standing. **b.** *concr.* Those who are respectable 1808. **2. a.** A person of respectable character 1840. **b.** *pl.* Those features of life and conduct which are regarded as respectable 1843. †**3.** Importance (*rare*) 1824.

1. A model of elderly English r. C. BRONTË. **2. b.** Out of a regard to the respectabilities of life JOWETT.

Respectable (rǐspe·ktăb'l), *a.* and *sb.* 1586. [f. RESPECT *sb.* + -ABLE. Cf. Fr. *respectable.*] **A.** *adj.* †**1.** Worthy of notice, observation, or consideration (*rare*) –1605. **2.** Worthy or deserving of respect by reason of some inherent quality or qualities 1599. **b.** Considerable in number, size, quantity, etc. 1755. **c.** Of comparative excellence; tolerable, fair 1775. **d.** Of writers, in respect of authority or literary merit 1781. **3.** Of persons: Worthy of respect by reason of moral excellence 1755. **4.** Of persons: Of good or fair social standing, and having the moral qualities naturally appropriate to this. Hence, in later use, honest and decent in character or conduct, without ref. to social position. Similarly of appearance, character, etc. 1758. **b.** Of decent or presentable appearance 1775. †**c.** Creditable; of a good or superior kind –1800.

2. Your studies, the r. remains of antiquity CHESTERF. **c.** Very r. literary talents 1799. **d.** The more r. English essayists 1866. **4.** The r. middle classes, who had no sympathy with revolutionists FROUDE.

B. *sb.* A respectable person 1814. Hence **Respe·ctableness. Respe·ctably** *adv.*

Respectant (rǐspe·ktănt), *a. rare.* 1688. [f. RESPECT *v.* + -ANT.] **1.** *Her.* Of animals: Facing each other. **2.** Looking backward 1830.

Respe·cter. 1611. [f. RESPECT *v.* + -ER[1].] One who respects.

R. of persons: (after *Acts* 10:34), one who pays undue regard to wealth or exalted position.

Respectful (rǐspe·ktfŭl), *a.* 1598. [f. RESPECT *sb.* + -FUL.] †**1.** Mindful, heedful, careful (*of* something) –1663. †**2.** Worthy of, or commanding, respect –1702. **3.** Full of, exhibiting, or marked by respect 1687.

3. The r. attention shown to him by Socrates JOWETT. A moderate man, r. of tradition 1892. Hence **Respe·ctful-ly** *adv.*, **-ness.**

†**Respe·ction.** late ME. [– late and med.L. *respectio*, f. *respect-*; see RESPECT *v.*, -ION.] Sight; aspect; regard; respect (of persons) –1527.

Respective (rǐspe·ktiv), *a.* 1525. [– Fr. *respectif, -ive* or med.L. *respectivus*, f. as prec.; see -IVE.] †**1.** Of persons: Regardful, attentive, considerate, careful –1643. **b.** Careful or regardful *of* something. Now *rare*. 1599. **2.** Of conduct, etc.: Marked by regardful care or attention; heedful. Now *rare*. 1598. †**b.** Discriminating; partial –1643. †**3.** Respectful, courteous (*to* or *towards* a person) –1785. †**4.** Worthy of respect or deference; respectable –1633. †**5.** Having relationship or reference *to* something; correspondent; also *absol.* relative –1865. **6.** Properly pertaining to, or connected with, each individual, group, etc., of those in question 1646.

1. b. All such as are respectiue of their health 1620. **2. b.** *Rom. & Jul.* III. i. 128. **4.** What should it be that he respects in her, But I can make respectiue in my selfe? SHAKS. **6.** To those places straight repair Where your r. dwellings are 1663. We cannot fix the r. amounts of truth and falsehood FREEMAN. Hence **Respe·ctiveness** (now *rare* or *Obs.*).

Respectively (rǐspe·ktivli), *adv.* 1556. [f.

prec. + -LY².] †1. Carefully, attentively –1620. †2. Respectfully; with becoming respect, deference, or courtesy –1720. †3. Relatively; comparatively –1664. 4. Relatively to each of several persons or things; individually, singly, separately; each to each, severally 1626.

4. Of the three defendants..two were r. president and secretary of the..Society 1891.

Respectless (rĭspe·ktlĕs), *a.* 1542. [f. RESPECT *sb.* + -LESS.] †1. Regardless; heedless, reckless; unheeding, careless –1639. 2. Devoid of respect or deference; discourteous, disrespectful. Now *rare.* 1591. †3. Impartial, unbiassed (*rare*) –1612.

2. This fellow being in drinke, gave us manie insolent r. speeches 1617. Hence †**Respe·ctlessly** *adv.*, †**-ness.**

†**Respe·ctuous,** *a.* 1603. [f. RESPECT *sb.* + -UOUS, after Fr. *respectueux.*] 1. Worthy of respect –1686. 2. Respectful, deferent –1683.

Respirable (re·spirăb'l), *a.* 1779. [– Fr. *respirable* or late L. *respirabilis*, f. *respirare*; see RESPIRE *v.*, -ABLE.] 1. Capable of, or fit for, being respired. 2. Capable of respiring 1822. Hence **Respirabi·lity, Re·spirableness,** the quality of being r.

Respiration (respirēⁱ·ʃən). late ME. [– Fr. *respiration* or L. *respiratio, -on-*, f. *respirat-*, pa. ppl. stem of *respirare*; see RESPIRE *v.*, -ION.] 1. The action of breathing (†out); the inspiration and expiration of air. b. *Bot.* The process by which a plant absorbs oxygen from the air, and gives out carbon dioxide 1831. 2. A single act of breathing 1611. †3. Opportunity for breathing again; a breathing-space; a respite –1752.

1. *transf.* The r. of the sea, The soft caresses of the air LONGF. 2. Measuring the Number of Pulses by the Number of Respirations 1707. 3. A short r. from the fatigues of war JOHNSON. Hence **Respira·tional** *a.* relating to r.

Respirato-, used as comb. form with the sense 'respiratory as well as'.

Respirator (re·spireⁱtəɹ). 1792. [f. RESPIRE *v.* + -ATOR.] †1. *Chem.* An apparatus used for testing the composition of exhaled air –1792. 2. A device of gauze or wire, covering the mouth, or mouth and nose, and serving to warm the inhaled air; in *Mil.* use, a chemical filtering apparatus to prevent the inhalation of dust, poisonous gases, etc. 1836.

Respiratory (rĭspəiᵊ·rătəri, re·spireⁱtəri), *a.* 1790. [– mod.L. *respiratorius* or Fr. *respiratoire*; see RESPIRATION, -ORY².] Of, pertaining to, or serving for respiration.

Respire (rĭspəiᵊ·ɹ), *v.* late ME. [– (O)Fr. *respirer* or L. *respirare*, f. *re-* RE- + *spirare* breathe.] I. *intr.* †1. To come up to the surface to breathe. T. USK. 2. To breathe; to inhale and exhale air 1599. †b. To draw breath, to live. DRAYTON. 3. *fig.* To breathe again, after distress, trouble, etc.; to recover hope, courage, or strength. late ME. 4. To take breath; to rest or enjoy relief from toil or exertion 1590. †5. Of wind: To blow (*rare*) –1762.

2. The ordinary Air in which we live and r. BENTLEY. b. Yet the braue Barons, whilst they do r., With Courage charge 1619. 3. Then shall the Britons..From their long vassalage gin to r. SPENSER. 4. But let our weary Muse a while r. P. FLETCHER.

II. *trans.* 1. To breathe; to inhale and exhale (air, etc.) 1548. 2. To breathe or give out, to exhale (an odour, etc.). Chiefly *fig.* 1577. 3. To breathe (a thing) *into* a person's ear 1846.

1. *fig.* I seemed to r. hope and comfort with the free air W. IRVING. 2. The ayre respires the pure elyzian sweets, In which she breathes B. JONS.

Respite (re·spit, -əit), *sb.* ME. [– OFr. *respit* (mod. *répit*) :– L. *respectus* RESPECT *sb.*] 1. Delay, or extension of time, asked or granted for some reason (orig. for further consideration of a matter). b. Delay specially granted in the carrying out of a capital sentence; a reprieve 1722. 2. Temporary cessation of labour, suffering, war, etc.; (an) interval of rest ME. †3. Delay in action; stay –1591. †4. Leisure; opportunity for doing something –1611. †5. Time granted to one until the coming *of* a certain date. MILT.

1. Give me some Respight, I'll discharge the Debt DRYDEN. Phr. *To put in r.*, to delay, postpone. b. *transf.* The annihilation of those hordes had given Rome a passing r. FROUDE. 2. Frequent respites from toil are the..safety-valves of professional men 1873. Hence **Re·spiteless** *a.* without r. or relief.

Respite (re·spit), *v.* late ME. [– OFr. *respitier* :– L. *respectare* RESPECT *v.*] I. 1. *trans.* To grant a respite to (a person); *esp.* from death or execution. †b. To save or prolong (a person's life) –1603. †2. To relieve by an interval of rest –1670.

1. Forty days longer we do r. you SHAKS. b. *Meas. for M.* II. iii. 41. 2. From the heat of Noon retir'd, To respit his day-labour with repast MILT.

II. 1. To grant delay or postponement of (a sentence, punishment, obligation, etc.). late ME. 2. To delay, postpone, put off. late ME. 3. †To cease from, give up; to suspend. late ME. 4. *Mil.* a. To suspend (a person) from pay 1705. b. To keep back, withhold (pay) 1802. †5. To rest; to recover *from* something –1769.

2. If you please..to respit your other Business,.. I will relate some Passages that will not be unpleasant 1707. 5. For I and mine will r. here a space 1575.

Resplend (rĭsple·nd), *v.* 1492. [– L. *resplendēre*, f. *re-* RE- + *splendēre* shine.] *intr.* To be resplendent or radiant; to shine brightly.

Resplendence (rĭsple·ndĕns). late ME. [– late L. *resplendentia*; see prec., -ENCE.] Brightness, brilliance, lustre, splendour.

The r...of the sonne 1561. The r. of those evident Truths MARVELL. So **Resple·ndency.**

Resplendent (rĭsple·ndĕnt), *a.* 1448. [– L. *resplendens, -ent-*, pr. pple. of *resplendēre*; see RESPLEND, -ENT.] Shining, brilliant, splendid.

A temple..r...in colours and gold 1883. Hence **Resplen·dently** *adv.*

†**Resple·ndish,** *v.* 1475. [– *resplendiss-*, lengthened stem of (O)Fr. *resplendir*; see RESPLEND, -ISH².] *intr.* To be resplendent –1549.

Respond (rĭspǫ·nd), *sb.* late ME. [– OFr. *respond*, f. *respondre* (mod. *répondre* :– Rom. **respondere*, for L. *respondēre*; see next.] 1. *Eccl.* a. = RESPONSORY *sb.* b. A response to a versicle 1555. 2. An answer, a response. Now *rare.* 1600. 3. *Arch.* A half-pillar or half-pier attached to a wall to support an arch 1448.

Respond (rĭspǫ·nd), *v.* 1600. [– L. *respondēre*, f. *re-* RE- + *spondēre* make a solemn engagement.] 1. *trans.* To answer or correspond to (something); to reciprocate. Now *rare* or *Obs.* b. *U.S.* To answer, satisfy 1890. 2. *intr.* a. To correspond *to* something (*rare*) 1591. b. To make answer or give a reply, in words 1719. c. To answer by some responsive act; to act in response *to* some influence 1726. d. *U.S.* To give satisfaction 1890.

2. b. I remember him in the divinity school responding and disputing with a perspicuous energy 1734. c. To every Theme responds thy various Lay 1726. d. The defendant is held to r. in damages 1890.

Respondence (rĭspǫ·ndĕns). 1590. [– Fr. †*respondence*; see RESPOND *v.*, -ENCE.] †1. Answer, response, to a sound –1600. 2. Correspondence, agreement, concord 1598. b. Response *to* some stimulus 1867.

1. Th' Angelicall soft trembling voyces made To th' instruments divine r. meet SPENSER. So **Respo·ndency,** correspondence, congruence.

Respondent (rĭspǫ·ndĕnt), *sb.* 1528. [f. as next.] 1. One who answers; *spec.* one who defends a thesis against one or more opponents. 2. A defendant in a lawsuit; now *spec.* in a divorce case 1562.

Respondent (rĭspǫ·ndĕnt), *a.* 1533. [– L. *respondens, -ent-*, pr. pple. of *respondēre*; see RESPOND *v.*, -ENT. Cf. Fr. †*respondant* (mod. *répondant*); see -ENT.] †1. Correspondent (*to* something else) –1726. 2. Answering; making reply. Also, having the position of defendant in an action. 1726. 3. Responsive *to* some influence 1766.

2. To hear the King's Speech, and the r. Address read H. WALPOLE.

‖**Respondentia** (respǫnde·nʃⁱă). 1727. [mod.L.] A loan upon the cargo of a vessel, to be repaid (with maritime interest) only if the goods arrive safe at their destination. (Cf. BOTTOMRY.)

†**Respo·nsal,** *sb.* late ME. [– late L. *responsalis*, subst. use of the adj.; see next.] 1. A response –1652. b. A liturgical response or respond –1753. 2. The respondent in a disputation –1574. 3. One appointed by a prelate to give or send replies to questions; an apocrisiary –1610.

†**Respo·nsal,** *a.* late ME. [– late L. *responsalis*, f. *respons-*; see next, -AL¹.] 1. Answerable, responsible –1797. 2. Responsive; of the nature of responses –1738.

Response (rĭspǫ·ns). [ME. *respons* (not continuous with OE. *respons*) – OFr. *respons* (mod. *répons*) or *response* (mod. *réponse*) or L. *responsum* (pl. *-a*), f. pa. pple. of *respondēre* RESPOND.] 1. An answer, a reply. b. *transf.* and *fig.* An action or feeling which answers to some stimulus or influence 1815. 2. *Eccl.* a. = RESPONSORY *sb.* 1450. b. A part of the liturgy said or sung by the congregation in reply to the priest. (Correl. to VERSICLE.) 3. An oracular answer 1513. 4. *Mus.* In contrapuntal music, the repetition by one part of a theme given by another part 1797.

3. The ancient oracle..from which..the Greeks of his time used to seek responses 1869. Hence **Respo·nseless** *a.* giving no r. or reply.

Responsibility (rĭspǫnsĭbi·lĭti). 1787. [f. next + -ITY.] 1. The state or fact of being responsible. 2. With *a* and *pl.* A charge, trust, or duty, for which one is responsible 1796. b. A person or thing for which one is responsible 1832.

2. Anxious to be relieved of a r. that was becoming irksome C. BRONTË.

Responsible (rĭspǫ·nsib'l), *a.* 1599. [– Fr. †*responsible*, f. L. *respons-*; see next, -IBLE.] †1. Correspondent or answering *to* something –1698. 2. Answerable, accountable (*to* another *for* something); liable to be called to account 1643. b. Morally accountable for one's actions; capable of rational conduct 1836. 3. *U.S.* Answerable to a charge 1650. 4. Capable of fulfilling an obligation or trust; reliable, trustworthy; of good credit and repute 1691. b. Of respectable appearance 1780. 5. Involving responsibility or obligation 1855.

1. The Mouth large, but not r. to so large a Body 1698. 2. Being r. to the King for what might happen to us 1662. b. The great God has treated us as r. beings 1836. 4. Very r. tenants 1817. b. He is wrapped in a r. dressing-gown DICKENS. 5. High and r. positions 1880. Hence **Respo·nsibleness. Respo·nsibly** *adv.*

Responsion (rĭspǫ·nʃən). 1470. [– Fr. †*responsion* or L. *responsio, -on-*, f. *respons-*, pa. ppl. stem of *respondēre* RESPOND; see -ION. Sense 3 in AL. *responsio* (XIV).] 1. An answer or reply; a response. Now *rare* 1502. †2. A sum due to be paid; *esp.* an annual payment which was required from knights of the military orders –1738. 3. *pl.* The first of the three examinations which candidates for the B.A. degree at Oxford are required to pass 1813. 4. A public university disputation 1841.

Responsive (rĭspǫ·nsiv), *a.* 1529. [– (O)Fr. *responsif, -ive* or late L. *responsivus*, f. as prec.; see -IVE.] 1. Answering, responding; making answer or reply. 2. Correspondent or corresponding (*rare*) 1602. 3. Responding readily to some influence 1762. 4. Characterized by the use of responses 1778. †5. Responsible, answerable. JER. TAYLOR.

1. Celestial voices..Sole, or r. each to others note MILT. 3. Thus, and so quick, the helm r. flew 1762. Hence **Respo·nsive-ly** *adv.*, **-ness.**

Responsorial (respǫ̆nsōᵊ·riăl), *a.* 1820. [See next and -AL¹ 1.] 1. Making answer or reply; responsive. 2. Pertaining to, of the nature of, responses 1832.

Responsory (rĭspǫ·nsəri), *sb.* ME. [– late L. *responsorium*, subst. use of the adj.; see next, -ORY¹.] *Eccl.* An anthem said or sung after a lesson by a soloist and choir alternately.

†**Respo·nsory,** *a.* 1586. [– late L. *responsorius*, f. L. *respons-*; see RESPONSION, -ORY².] Of the nature of an answer or reply; relating or pertaining to answering –1737.

‖**Ressalah** (rĕsā·lă). 1758. [Urdu (Arab.) *risāla*, f. Arab. *arsala* he sent.] In India, a squadron of native cavalry. Also **Ressaldar** (resăldā·ɹ), [Urdu *risāladār*], a native captain in an Indian cavalry regiment.

Rest, *sb.*¹ [OE. *ræst, rest* repose, bed, corresp. to OFris. *rasta*, OS. *rasta* place of rest, OHG. *rasta* rest, league (G. *rast*), ON.

rǫst, Goth. *rasta* mile.] **I. 1.** The natural repose or relief from daily activity which is obtained by sleep. **2.** Intermission of labour or exertion of any kind; repose obtained by ceasing to exert oneself. Also, later, with *a* and *pl.* OE. **3.** Freedom from or absence of labour, exertion, or activity of any kind OE. **b.** The freedom from toil or care associated with the future life OE. **c.** Freedom from distress, molestation, or aggression OE. **d.** Spiritual or mental peace OE. **e.** Quietness, peacefulness, or tranquillity in nature 1820. **4.** Place of resting or abiding; residence, abode. †Also, abiding, stay. OE. **b.** An establishment providing shelter or lodging for certain classes of persons during their spare time, or when unemployed 1892. **5.** The repose of death or of the grave. Chiefly in phrases, as *to go, be laid, to r.* late ME. **6. a.** *Mus.* An interval of silence occurring in one or more parts during a movement, frequently of all the parts together; a pause; also, the character or sign by which this is denoted 1579. **b.** A pause in speaking or reading 1612. **7.** Absence, privation, or cessation of motion; continuance in the same position or place 1475. **8.** *At r.* In a state of (physical or mental) repose, quiescence, or inactivity. Also, dead. late ME. **b.** *To set at r.*, to satisfy, assure; to settle, decide finally. *At r.*, settled 1590.

1. Mans ore-labor'd sense Repaires it selfe by rest SHAKS. Phr. *To go to* (one's) *r.*, to betake oneself to repose for the night; This floure gan close, and goon to r. CHAUCER. *To take* (one's) *r.* **2.** Vnto hys chambre was he led anon, To take hys ease, and for to haue hys r. CHAUCER. After several rests, we got to the top 1687. Phr. *At r.* temporarily withdrawn from active warfare to r. and recuperate. *Day of r.* = SABBATH 1 a, b. **3.** *transf.* The gale had sigh'd itself to r. SCOTT. **b.** There remaineth therefore a r. to the people of God *Heb.* 4:9. **c.** And the land had r. from warre *Josh.* 14:15. **d.** The truth wherein r. is For every mind CARY. **4.** Till we end In dust, our final r. and native home MILT. **7.** The common Centre of Gravity..does not change its state of Motion or Rest 1715.

II. 1. a. A support for a fire-arm, employed in steadying the barrel to ensure accuracy of aim 1590. **b.** A support for a cue in billiards 1868. **2.** A thing upon which something else rests; *esp.* that part of a lathe on which the cutting-tool is supported in the operation of turning 1609. **3.** Something upon which one rests (*rare*) 1641. **b.** A projection for the foot to rest on 1869.

2. Seasoned board of oak layd uppon sufficient rests of oake tymber for the grounde floare 1617.

attrib.: **r. camp,** a camp to which an army retires to recuperate after fighting; **r. cure,** a medical cure of which complete rest from all activity is the chief feature; **r. gown,** a loose-fitting garment worn by women on informal occasions; **r. house,** a dawk bungalow; a boarding-house for persons requiring rest.

Rest, *sb.*[2] late ME. [– (O)Fr. *reste*, f. *rester*; see REST *v.*[2]] †**1.** That which remains over; a remainder or remnant –1693. **b.** *pl.* Remains, remnants, relics. Now *rare.* 1467. **2. a.** The reserve or surplus fund of a bank, esp. of the Bank of England 1844. **b.** *Comm.* The striking of a balance in an account; the amount of a balance 1825. **3.** The remainder or remaining part(s) *of* something 1530. **b.** The remainder *of* a number of persons, animals, or things 1535. **4.** The remainder of something specified or implied in the context 1530. **b.** The remaining persons or things; the others 1535. **5.** In tennis and battledore, a spell of quick and continuous returning of the ball or shuttlecock maintained by the players 1600.

1. Thou hast too, yet, I hope, a R. of Reputation 1693. **3.** When England, in common with the r. of Europe, was Catholic 1861. **b.** The r. of us went to church BERKELEY. **4.** In her tone and look he read the r. KEATS. **b.** The Duchess would drive over..The r. were to ride DISRAELI. Phrases. (*As*) *for the r.*, as regards, with regard to, what remains. *As to the r.*, in other respects, otherwise. †*Above the r.*, especially. †*To set up one's r.* **a.** To venture one's final stake or reserve; from the old game of cards called primero, in which the loss of the 'rest', i.e. the stakes kept in reserve, and agreed upon at the beginning, terminated the game. **b.** *fig.* To stake, hazard, or venture one's all. **c.** To have or take a resolution; to be resolved. **d.** To fix or settle *upon* something. **e.** To take up one's (permanent) abode. †*To set down one's r.*, to stop, make an end; to take up one's residence.

Rest, *sb.*[3] late ME. [Aphetic f. *arest* ARREST *sb.*[1]] †**1.** Arrest of persons or goods –1587. **2.** In mediæval armour, a contrivance fixed to the right side of the cuirass to receive the butt-end of the lance when couched for the charge, and to prevent it from being driven back upon impact. late ME. **b.** *Her.* A charge supposed to represent the above 1661.

2. A knight..who laid his lance In r., and made as if to fall upon him TENNYSON.

Rest, *v.*[1] [OE. *ræstan, restan* = OFris. *resta*, OHG. *restan.*] **I.** *intr.* **1.** To take repose by lying down, and *esp.* by going to sleep; to lie still or in slumber. **b.** To lie in death or in the grave OE. **2.** To take repose by intermission of labour or exertion of any kind; to desist from effort or activity; to become or remain inactive. Also, in recent use, with *up.* OE. **b.** Of things OE. **c.** To cease *from*, to have intermission or cessation †*of*, something. late ME. **3.** To be at ease or in quiet; also (of persons or things), to continue without change or removal; to stay, remain, lie, have place or station OE. **b.** To stop or cease at a certain point and remain otherwise inoperative or inactive 1577. **c.** To be at peace; to have quiet of mind 1782. **4.** To have place or position, to settle, lie, be diffused, etc., *on* or *upon* some person or thing OE. **b.** Of the eyes in relation to the object looked at 1813. **c.** Of a wing or division of an army 1844. **d.** To lie as a charge or stigma *on* a person 1678. **5.** To lie or lean *on, upon,* or *against* a person or thing to obtain repose or support. late ME. **b.** To rely *on* or *upon*, to trust *to*, some thing or person. late ME. **c.** To depend *upon*, to be based or founded *on*, something 1530. **d.** To decide *on* (a person). DRYDEN. **6. a.** To remain confident or hopeful, to put trust, *in* something. late ME. **b.** To lie *in* or remain *with* one, as something to be accomplished or determined 1593.

1. Now good my Lord, lye heere, and r. awhile SHAKS. **b.** Thus rested Salomon with his fathers COVERDALE *Ecclus.* 47:23. **2.** I have often heard of the Pyramids, and shall not r. till I have seen them JOHNSON. Our men..had orders not to let the enemy r. 1896. **b.** The land was allowed 'to r.'—i.e. to remain unploughed for a period of years 1831. **c.** And he rested on the seuenth day from all his worke *Gen.* 2:2. **3.** This way the King will come..Here let vs r. SHAKS. Phr. *R. you merry, happy, fair.* **b.** The matter could not r. here 1782. *To let..rest*, to pursue or prosecute no further. **4.** His indignation resteth vpon sinners *Ecclus.* 5:6. The roof..rested upon four concentric arches SCOTT. **b.** Her eyes resting on a lace cap she had been making 1813. **c.** Their left resting on the hills 1844. **5. c.** Science rests on phenomena observed by the senses 1884. **6. a.** Nor did he doubt her more, But rested in her fealty TENNYSON. **b.** It rested in your Grace To vnloose this tyde-vp Iustice SHAKS.

II. 1. *refl.* To give oneself rest or repose OE. **2.** *trans.* To give (a person) rest; to relieve or refresh by rest; to lay to rest ME. **b.** To allow (a thing) to rest; to permit to remain undisturbed or quiescent 1580. **c.** To hold (a weapon) in an easy position 1682. **d.** *Law.* To cease voluntarily from presenting evidence on (a case). **3.** To lay (the head, etc.) *on* or *upon* something for support ME. **b.** To place (a thing) *upon* something to support it or keep it in position. late ME. **c.** To throw (some weight) *on* a thing 1809. **d.** To make or allow to depend, to base *on* something 1732. **4.** To place or settle *in* something. late ME.

1. I was very glad to stay there a day to r. myself 1716. **2.** He rests me in greene pasture SIDNEY. Phr. (*God* or *heaven*) *r. his soul, him,* etc. Now *arch.* †*God rest you merry.* **3.** I vpon this banke will r. my head SHAKS. **b.** Its ground-sill was rested upon a bed of lead SMEATON. **d.** The plaintiff..rested her case on equitable grounds 1885. **4.** 1 *Hen. VI*, I. i. 44.

Rest, *v.*[2] 1463. [– (O)Fr. *rester* :– L. *restare*, f. *re-* RE- + *stare* stand.] *intr.* **1.** †**a.** Chiefly *Sc.* To remain due or unpaid –1781. †**b.** To remain after subtraction, diminution, etc. –1700. **c.** To be left still undestroyed or unremoved. Now *rare.* 1495. **2.** With complement. To remain or be left in a specified condition 1472. **b.** In valedictory formulæ. Now *arch.* 1580. †**3. a.** To remain to be done –1667. **b.** To remain to be dealt with –1636.

1. c. What rested of a goodly face 1867. **2.** R. equal happy both DRYDEN. Phr. *To r. assured, satisfied,* etc.; That I may r. assur'd Whether yond Troopes, are Friend or Enemy SHAKS. **b.** I r. thy affectionate brother, Walter Shandy STERNE.

Rest, *v.*[3] Now *dial.* late ME. [Aphetic f. *arest* ARREST *v.*] †**1.** *trans.* To stop, check, arrest (*rare*) –1471. **2.** To arrest or apprehend (a person). late ME. **3.** To arrest or seize (goods). Chiefly *Sc.* 1565.

2. *Com. Err.* IV. iv. 3.

†**Resta·gnate,** *v.* 1655. [– *restagnat-*, pa. ppl. stem of L. *restagnare* overflow.] *intr.* To stagnate; to become or remain stagnant –1676. Hence †**Restagna·tion,** an overflow; stagnation –1706.

Restant (re·stănt), *a.* 1828. [– Fr. *restant* or L. *restans, -ant-*; see REST *v.*[2], -ANT.] *Bot.* Persistent.

Restaurant (re·stǫrănt, Fr. rẹstoraṅ). 1827. [– Fr. *restaurant*, subst. use of pr. pple. of *restaurer* RESTORE.] An establishment where refreshments or meals may be obtained.

‖**Restaurateur** (rẹstoratǫ̈r). 1796. [Fr., f. *restaurer*; see prec.] **1.** A keeper of a restaurant. **2.** A restaurant 1804.

Restauration (restǫrēⁱ·ʃən). Now *rare.* late ME. [– (O)Fr. *restauration* or late and med.L. *restauratio, -on-*, f. pa. ppl. stem of L. *restaurare* RESTORE.] †**1.** The restoration of a person to a former status or position, as of man to the divine favour or a state of innocence –1718. **2.** The restoration of a thing, institution, etc. to its proper or pristine condition. late ME. **3.** A restaurant [So G. *restauration.*] 1862.

Rest-balk (re·st,bǫk), *sb.* 1523. [f. REST *sb.*[1] or *v.*[1] + BALK *sb.* 3.] A ridge left unploughed between two furrows, *esp.* in the process of raftering or ribbing. Hence **Re·st-balk** *v. trans.* to plough (land) with rest-balks.

Re·stful, *a.* ME. [f. REST *sb.*[1] + -FUL.] **1.** Characterized by, of the nature of, productive of, rest or repose; free from strife or disturbance. **2.** Quiet; peaceful; taking or enjoying rest. late ME.

1. Tyr'd with all these for restfull death I cry SHAKS. Hence **Re·stful-ly** *adv.*, **-ness.**

Re·st-harrow. 1550. [f. REST *sb.*[3] or *v.*[3] + HARROW.] A field-shrub (*Ononis arvensis*), with tough roots, also called CAMMOCK.

Restiff (re·stif), *a.* late ME. [Earlier f. RESTIVE *a.*] = RESTIVE *a.*

Restiform (re·stifǫ̈m), *a.* 1831. [f. L. *restis* cord + -FORM.] Cord-like; in *r. body*, one or other of two rounded bundles of fibrous matter lying on each side of the medulla oblongata and connecting it with the cerebellum. So *r. column, tract.*

†**Re·stiness.** 1540. [f. RESTY *a.*[1] + -NESS.] The quality of being restive; restiveness –1708.

Re·sting, *ppl. a.* late ME. [f. REST *v.*[1] + -ING[2].] **1.** That rests or is taking a rest. **b.** *Bot.* in *r. spore, cell,* etc. 1857. **2.** Remaining stationary. SHAKS.

1. b. Seeds and resting-spores..are organized in a manner especially adapted to preserve the latent vitality from injury by external influences 1857.

Restitute (re·stitiūt), *v.* 1500. [– *restitut-*, pa. ppl. stem of L. *restituere* restore, f. *re-* RE- + *statuere* set up, establish.] **1.** *trans.* To restore to a position or status; to reinstate, rehabilitate. Now *rare.* **2.** To restore, refund. Also *absol.* To make restitution. 1727. So **Re·stitutor,** a restorer (*rare*). **Resti·tutory** *a.* of or relating to restitution.

Restitution (restitiū·ʃən). ME. [– (O)Fr. *restitution* or L. *restitutio, -on-*, f. as prec.; see -ION.] **1.** The action of restoring or giving back something to its proper owner, or of making reparation to a person for loss or injury inflicted. **2.** With *a* and *pl.* A restoration of something taken from another 1440. **3.** The action of restoring a person or persons to a previous status or position; the fact of being restored or reinstated; a document authorizing such restoration. Now *rare.* late ME. **4.** The action of restoring a thing or institution to its original state or form. (In later use only in echoes of, or with ref. to,

Acts 3:21). late ME. **5.** †**a.** Reposition, replacement (*rare*) –1658. **b.** Tendency to return to a previous position by virtue of elasticity or resilience 1656.

1. Euer the Frenche Ambassadours promised restitucion of euery thyng, but none was restored 1548. Phr. *To make r.*; They had wronged her.., therefore they ought to make her r. 1720. **2.** David passes sentence..that there should be a fourfold r. made 1729. **3.** After the R. of King Charles the Second DE FOE. Phr. *R. in blood*, re-admission to the privileges of birth and rank of one under sentence of corruption of blood (see CORRUPTION 2), or of his heirs. **4.** The R. of all Things to their first State of Perfection 1781.

Restive (re·stiv), *a.* 1599. [Later form (by assim. to -IVE) of RESTIFF – OFr. *restif* (mod. *rétif*) :– Rom. **restivus* 'inclined to remain stationary', f. *restare* REST *v.*² See RESTY *a.*¹] †**1.** Inclined to rest or remain still; inactive, inert –1833. †**2.** Persistent, obstinate, settled or fixed *in* an opinion or course of action –1826. **3.** Of horses: Refusing to go forward; stubbornly standing still; obstinately moving backwards or to the side when being driven or ridden; hence, intractable, refractory 1656. **b.** *transf.* Of persons or things 1687. **4.** Of actions: Characterized by unwillingness or resistance to control 1806.

1. What great imployment with stirring and mettald spirits, what perpetuall quiet with heavie and r. bodies 1599. **2.** Every one being r. in his opinion, there can nothing..be concluded 1660. **3.** The beasts..became r. and went back MACAULAY. **b.** He turned r. at the least attempt at coercion 1863. **4.** The outward man yielded a reluctant and r. compliance SCOTT. Hence **Re·stive-ly** *adv.*, **-ness.**

Restless (re·stlės), *a.* OE. [f. REST *sb.*¹ + -LESS.] **1.** Deprived of rest; finding no rest; *esp.* uneasy in mind or spirit. **b.** Marked by unrest; affording no rest 1605. **2.** Constantly stirring or active, or desirous to be so; averse to being quiet or settled 1475. †**b.** Const. *to* (with inf.) or *of*: Impatient –1725. **c.** *spec.* in names of animals, as *r. cavy, thrush*, etc. 1771. **3.** Of conditions: Unceasing, continuous. late ME. **b.** Of things: Never ceasing or pausing 1596. **4.** quasi-*adv.* Restlessly. late ME.

1. R. he passed the remnants of the night DRYDEN. **b.** R. was the chair; the back erect Distress'd the weary loins COWPER. **2.** Cities, humming with a r. crowd COWPER. All the reason ..For so much rambling, was, a r. mind CRABBE. **3.** A world of restlesse Cares SHAKS. **b.** That Goddesse blind, that stands vpon the rolling restlesse Stone SHAKS. Hence **Re·stless-ly** *adv.*, **-ness.**

Restorable (rĭstōᵊ·răb'l), *a.* 1611. [f. RESTORE *v.* + -ABLE.] That can be restored or brought back to a former condition.

Restoral (rĭstōᵊ·răl). 1611. [f. RESTORE *v.* + -AL¹ 2.] Restoration, restitution.

Restoration (restŏrē¹·ʃən). 1660. [Later f. RESTAURATION, after RESTORE *v.*] **1.** The action of restoring to a former state or position; the fact of being restored or reinstated. **b.** *Theol.* = RESTITUTION 4. 1781. **2.** *Hist.* **a.** The re-establishment of the monarchy in England with the return of Charles II in 1660; also, the period marked by this event 1718. **b.** The reinstatement, in 1814, of the Bourbons in the sovereignty of France 1839. **3.** The action of restoring a person to health or consciousness; recovery of physical strength 1605. **4.** The action or process of restoring something to an unimpaired or perfect condition 1801. **b.** *Arch.* The process of carrying out alterations and repairs with the idea of restoring a building to something like its original form; a general renovation 1824. **c.** A representation of the original form of a ruined building, extinct animal, etc. 1836. **5.** The action of restoring something to one who has been previously deprived of it 1788.

1. The happy R. of his Majesty to his People and Kingdoms 1660. That period which has been distinguished as the r. of letters 1841. **4.** The r. of disfigured and decayed works of art 1835. The passages which defy r. 1874. **b.** Under the name of 'r.' the ruin of the noblest architecture..is constant throughout Europe RUSKIN. **c.** Fig. 81 represents a r. of this extinct elephant 1878. **5.** The r. of estates that his predecessors had alienated 1877. Hence **Restora·tioner,** = RESTORATIONIST.

Restora·tionism. 1834. [f. prec. + -ISM.] The doctrine that all men will ultimately be restored to a state of happiness in the future life. So **Restora·tionist,** a believer in r.

Restorative (rĭstōᵊ·rătiv, -ǫ·rătiv), *a.* and *sb.* late ME. [var. of †*restaurative* (XIV–XVII) – OFr. *restauratif, -ive*; cf. RESTAURATION and see -IVE. Cf. med.L. *restaurativus* (in medical use, XIII).] **A.** *adj.* Pertaining to restoration (of strength or health); capable of restoring or renewing.

To try if there was any r. quality in the more genial air of that climate 1807.

B. *sb.* A food, cordial, or medicine, which has the effect of restoring health or strength. late ME. **b.** A means of restoring one to consciousness 1852. Hence **Resto·ratively** *adv.*

†**Resto·re,** *sb.* 1450. [f. next.] Restoration –1646.

Restore (rĭstōᵊ·ɹ), *v.* ME. [– OFr. *restorer* (mod. *restaurer*) :– L. *restaurare.*] **1.** *trans.* To give back, to make return or restitution of (anything previously taken away or lost). **2.** To make amends for; to compensate, make good (loss or damage). Now *rare* or *Obs.* ME. **b.** To set right, repair (decay, etc.). *rare.* 1567. **3.** To build up again; to re-erect or reconstruct. Now *spec.* to repair and alter (a building) so as to bring it as nearly as possible to its original form ME. **b.** To bring back to the original state; to improve, repair, or retouch (a thing) so as to bring it back to its original condition 1679. **c.** To reproduce or represent (an extinct animal, etc.) in its original form 1771. **4. a.** To replace (mankind) in a state of grace; to free from the effects of sin ME. **b.** To reinstate or replace (a person) in a former office, dignity, or estate 1450. **c.** To bring (a person or part of the body) back to a healthy or vigorous state. late ME. **d.** To bring back to mental calm. Now *rare.* 1582. **5.** To renew; to set up or bring into existence again; to re-establish, bring back into use, etc. ME. **b.** To replace or insert (words or letters which are missing or illegible in a text) 1855. **6.** To bring back (a person or thing) *to* a previous, original, or normal condition ME. **b.** To grant to or obtain for (a person) reinstatement *to* former rank, office, or possessions 1533. **c.** To take or put back *into*, to convey or hand back *to*, a place 1450.

1. Your helthe shall be restored to yow CAXTON. **2.** Time may r. some losses FULLER. **3.** At Winchester, where they are restoring the cathedral 1820. **4. a.** R. thou them that be penitent *Bk. Com. Prayer.* **b.** *To r. in blood*: see BLOOD *sb.* III. 5. **c.** The quiet place, the pure air..will r. you in a few days DICKENS. **5.** It was with great difficulty that the..man in the cocked hat restored order 1820. **6.** The application of faradic electricity quickly restored the patient to consciousness 1882. **b.** The innocent were restored to their rank and fortunes GIBBON. Hence **Resto·rement,** the act of restoring; restoration, restitution. **Resto·rer,** one who restores.

Restrain (rĭstrē¹·n), *v.* [ME. *restreyne, restrayne* – OFr. *restrei(g)n-, -ai(g)ne-*, pr. stem of *restreindre, restraindre* :– L. *restringere* bind fast, confine, f. *re-* RE- + *stringere* draw tight.] **1.** *trans.* To check, hold back, or prevent (a person or thing) *from* some course of action. **b.** Without const. To keep (a person) in check or under control. Freq. *refl.* late ME. **c.** To place under arrest or in confinement; to deprive of personal liberty or freedom of action; also, to shut in by material barriers 1494. **d.** To deprive (a person) *of* liberty by restraint 1530. **2.** To check, to put a check or stop upon, to repress, keep down (a desire, feeling, activity, physical agent, force, etc.) ME. **3.** To restrict, limit, confine ME. †**4.** To withhold, keep back, *from* a person –1594. †**5.** To forbid or prohibit (a person) *to* do something; to keep back *from* something desired –1791. †**6. a.** To draw tightly (*rare*) –1596. **b.** To compel or constrain (*rare*) –1655. **7.** *intr.* To refrain (*from* something; †also with infin.). Now *rare.* 1594.

1. This faculty tends to r. men from doing mischief to each other 1729. **b.** If I want skill or force to r. the Beast that I ride upon COWLEY. **2.** I could hardly r. my feelings 1839. The necessity of restraining population MILL. **6. a.** *Tam. Shr.* III. ii. 59. **b.** By antient custome no Vestal Virgin or Flamen of Jupiter was restrained to swear FULLER. Hence **Restrai·nable** *a.* capable of being restrained. **Restrai·nedly** *adv.* with restraint. **Restrai·ner. Restrai·ningly** *adv.* †**Restrai·nment,** restraint –1688.

Restraint (rĭstrē¹·nt), *sb.* late ME. [– (O)Fr. *restreinte*, fem. pa. pple. of *restreindre*; see prec.] **1.** The action of restraining or checking a thing, operation, etc.; an instance of this, a stoppage. **2.** A means of restraining or checking persons from a course of action, or of keeping them under control; any force or influence which has a restraining effect; an instance of restraining or of being restrained. late ME. **b.** Without article. Restraining action or influence, as applied to persons 1567. **c.** The state or condition of being restrained; *esp.* abridgement of liberty, confinement 1547. **3.** †**a.** A prohibition –1594. **b.** An embargo. Usu. *r. of princes.* 1475. **4.** Constraint; reserve 1601. †**5.** Restriction or limitation –1746.

1. A bill for the r. of the Press 1863. *Without r.*, freely, copiously. **2.** All Government is a R. upon Liberty 1672. **b.** R. she will not brook MILT. **c.** 'Tis not R. or Liberty That makes Men prisoners or free BUTLER. **4.** She..did angle for mee, Madding my eagernesse with her r. SHAKS. **5.** This r. of Easter to a certaine number of dayes HOOKER.

Restrict (rĭstri·kt), *v.* 1535. [– *restrict-*, pa. ppl. stem of L. *restringere* RESTRAIN.] *trans.* To confine (some person or thing) *to* or *within* certain limits; to limit or bound. **b.** To restrain by prohibition 1835.

The power of preaching was restricted by the issue of licences only to the friends of the Primate 1874. **b.** The act..which restricted the Bank from making payments in gold 1835. Hence **Restri·ctedly** *adv.*

Restriction (rĭstri·kʃən). late ME. [– (O)Fr. *restriction* or L. *restrictio, -on-*, f. as prec.; see -ION.] **1.** A limitation imposed upon a person or thing; a condition or regulation of this nature. **b.** The action or fact of limiting or restricting 1629. **2.** *Logic.* Limitation or qualification of a term 1551. **3.** Constriction (*rare*) 1758.

1. The restrictions under which our first parents were laid 1772. **b.** Yet this must be understood with some r. BLACKSTONE. **3.** Severe r. of the waist 1871. Hence **Restri·ctionary** *a.* imposing restrictions.

Restri·ctionist. 1849. [f. prec. + -IST.] One who advocates the restriction of some practice, institution, etc., such as the liquor-trade.

Restrictive (rĭstri·ktiv), *a.* and *sb.* late ME. [– (O)Fr. *restrictif, -ive* or med.L. *restrictivus*, f. as RESTRICT *v.*; see -IVE.] **A.** *adj.* †**1.** = RESTRINGENT *a.* 1. –1727. **2.** Of terms, expressions, etc.: Implying, conveying, or expressing restriction or limitation 1579. **3.** Restricting; limitative *of* the power or scope of some thing or person 1652.

1. This Plaister being r. 1607. **2.** In order to restrain the devise..it was necessary to shew r. words 1827. **3.** The r. negative power of conscience CLARENDON.

B. *sb.* A term or expression having the force of, or implying, a restriction or qualification 1671.

The indeterminate character of the restrictives, *alone* and *only* BENTHAM. Hence **Restri·ctive-ly** *adv.*, **-ness** (*rare*).

Restringe (rĭstri·ndʒ), *v.* 1597. [– L. *restringere* bind fast, confine, f. *re-* RE- + *stringere* draw tight.] †**1.** *trans.* To affect (a person) with costiveness; to have an astringent effect upon (a part of the body) –1758. **2.** To confine, limit, restrict. Now *rare.* 1604.

2. Of Passions..some..dilate, and some compresse and r. the heart 1604.

†**Restri·ngent,** *a.* and *sb.* 1578. [– L. *restringens, -ent-*, pr. pple. of *restringere*; see prec., -ENT.] **A.** *adj.* **1.** Having astringent or binding properties; *esp.* tending to restrain the action of the bowels –1799. **b.** Of outward applications: Styptic –1834. **2.** Constipated, costive (*rare*) –1635. **B.** *sb.* **1.** A word which has a limitative or restricting force –1671. **2.** A medicine or application which possesses astringent or styptic properties –1792. So †**Restri·ngency,** the quality or property of being r.

Resty (re·sti), *a.*¹ *Obs.* exc. *dial.* 1515. [var. of RESTIFF, RESTIVE; cf. *hasty, tardy.*] **1.** = RESTIVE *a.* 3. †**2.** Disinclined for action or exertion; sluggish, indolent, lazy –1711. †3. Of land: Fallow, untilled (*rare*) –1649.

2. Some great household..where the Maister is too restie or too rich to say his own prayers MILT. Hence **Re·stily** *adv.* stubbornly.

†**Re·sty**, *a.*² ME. [– OFr. *resté* left over, pa. pple. of *rester* remain; see REST *v.*², -Y⁵. Later vars. are REASTY, RUSTY *a.*²] Rancid, REASTY –1671.

Result (rĭzɒ·lt), *sb.* 1626. [f. the vb.] †1. The action of springing back again *to* a former position or place. BACON. 2. A decision or resolution; the outcome of the deliberations of a council or assembly. Now *U.S.* 1647. b. The effect, issue, or outcome of some action, process, design, etc. 1651. c. The quantity, formula, etc., obtained by calculation in arithmetic or algebra 1771.

1. The sound being produced betweene the String and the Aire..by the Returne or the R. of the String 1626. 2. If our proposals once again were heard We should compel them to a quick r. MILT. b. The whole proceedings of the said resident were the natural r. of the treaty of Chunar BURKE. c. If you substitute 2 for *x*, the r. will be 24. 1771. Hence **Resu·ltful, Resu·ltless** *adjs.*

Result (rĭzɒ·lt), *v.* late ME. [– med.L. (AL.) *resultare*, fig. use of L. *resultare* spring back, reverberate, f. *re-* RE- + *saltare* leap.] 1. *intr.* To arise as a consequence, effect, or conclusion *from* some action, process, etc.; to end or conclude *in* a specified manner. †2. To recoil; to rebound or spring back –1784. 3. a. *Law.* To revert *to* a person 1768. †b. To appertain or fall *to* a person –1793.

1. Crevasses..r. from the motion of the glacier TYNDALL. 2. The huge round stone resulting with a bound Thunders impetuous down POPE.

Resultance (rĭzɒ·ltăns), Now *rare.* 1440. [prob. – med. L. **resultantia*; f. *resultare*; see prec., -ANCE.] †1. Origin, beginning. CAPGRAVE. †2. The sum or gist *of* something –1640. 3. †a. Something which issues, proceeds, or emanates from another thing –1680. †b. A reflection (of light) –1652. c. A result, effect, or outcome. Now *rare.* 1635. †4. The fact of issuing or resulting (*from* something); esp. *by r.*, derivatively –1680. So †**Resu·ltancy** –1701.

Resultant (rĭzɒ·ltănt), *sb.* late ME. [subst. use of next.] †1. *Arith.* The total or sum. late ME. only. 2. *Mech.* That force which is the equivalent of two or more forces acting from different directions at one point; *gen.* the composite or final effect of any two or more physical forces. Also *transf.* of other than physical forces. 1815. b. The product or outcome *of* something 1847. 3. *Math.* = ELIMINANT B. 1856.

2. b. Collective social action is the mere r. of many individual actions 1871.

Resultant (rĭzɒ·ltănt), *a.* 1615. [– L., (med.L.) *resultans, -ant-*, pr. pple. of *resultare*; see RESULT *v.*, -ANT.] †1. Issuing or shining by reflection –1661. 2. That results, resulting; consequent 1639. Hence **Resu·ltantly** *adv.*

Resumable (rĭzⁱū·măb'l), *a.* 1644. [f. RESUME *v.* + -ABLE.] Capable of being resumed.

Resume (rĭzⁱū·m), *v.* late ME. [– (O)Fr. *résumer* or L. *resumere*, f. *re-* RE- + *sumere* take.] I. *trans.* 1. To assume, put on, or take to oneself anew (something previously lost, given up, or discarded). b. To take again, reoccupy (a place or seat) 1633. 2. To take up or begin again, recommence (some interrupted practice or occupation) 1440. b. *esp.* To go on again with (a discourse, discussion, remark) 1600. 3. To take back to oneself (something previously given or granted) 1450. 4. a. To take back (a person) to, or into some relation with, oneself 1494. b. To take or pick up (a thing) again; to return to the use of 1596. 5. To recapitulate or summarize (facts) 1676.

1. Ile r. the shape which thou dost thinke I haue cast off for euer SHAKS. Thus they out of their plaints new hope r. MILT. Could I see your natural good sense r. its influence over passion 1791. b. Reason resum'd her place, and passion fled DRYDEN. 2. I resumed some work I had dropped C. BRONTË. b. The Senate resumed the consideration of the Treaty 1795. 3. Gods..R. not, what themselves have giv'n SWIFT. 4. a. R. thy spirit from this world of thrall VAUGHAN. b. He was content to r. his pipe and listen 1873. 5. A philosophy which should r. all his views upon nature, man, and society 1878.

II. *absol.* 1. To reassume possession 1565. 2. To give a résumé 1770. 3. a. To begin to speak again 1802. b. To recommence work or business 1817. c. To continue; to begin again 1815.

1. *Cymb.* III. i. 15. 3. a. When he could again be heard.., he resumed, as follows 1802. b. The House then resumed 1817.

‖**Résumé** (rezüme). 1804. [Fr., pa. pple. of *résumer* RESUME.] A summary, epitome.

Resu·mmons (rĭ-). Now *Hist.* 1495. [– AFr. *resomons*; see RE-, SUMMONS.] *Law.* A second or renewed summons.

Resumption (rĭzɒ·mᵖʃən). 1449. [– (O)Fr. *résumption* or late and med.L. *resumptio, -on-*, f. *resumpt-*, pa. ppl. stem of L. *resumere*; see RESUME, -ION.] 1. *Law.* The action, on the part of the Crown or other authority, of reassuming possession of lands, rights, etc., which have been bestowed on others; a case or instance of this. b. *gen.* The action of taking back or recovering something 1702. 2. The action of resuming, taking up, or beginning again 1589. b. *Banking.* A return to specie payments 1866. 3. Recapitulation, résumé (*rare*) 1727.

1. b. Resumptions are as ordinary with this lady [fortune] as with a House of Commons 1702. 2. The hour's past..For the r. of his trial BYRON. 3. A theory, in fact, which is the r. and complement of them all 1836.

Resumptive (rĭzɒ·mᵖtiv), *a.* late ME. [In sense 1 – late and med.L. *resumptivus*, f. as prec.; see -IVE. In sense 2 f. RESUMPTION, after *presumptive, consumptive*, etc.] †1. *Med.* Restorative (*rare*) –1657. 2. That repeats, or summarizes 1854.

2. The statement is r. 1884. Hence **Resu·mptively** *adv.*

Resupinate (rĭsⁱū·pineⁱt), *a.* 1776. [– L. *resupinatus*, pa. pple. of *resupinare* bend back; see RE-, SUPINE *a.*, -ATE².] Chiefly *Bot.* Turned or twisted upwards. So **Resu·pinated** *ppl. a.* 1661.

Resupination (rĭsⁱūpinēⁱ·ʃən). 1624. [See prec., -ATION.] †1. a. The effect of height upon the proportions of a standing figure (*rare*) –1638. b. The fact of lying on, or the action of turning upon, the back –1661. 2. *Bot.* Inversion of parts 1760.

Resupine (rĭsⁱupəi·n), *a.* 1628. [– L. *resupinus*; see RE- and SUPINE *a.*] †1. Listless, apathetic –1643. 2. Lying on the back; inclined backwards 1669.

2. One, r., Upcast it high toward the dusky clouds COWPER.

Resurge (rĭsɒ̄·ɹdʒ), *v.* 1575. [– L. *resurgere*, f. *re-* RE- + *surgere* rise.] *intr.* To rise or come back again.

Resurgence (rĭsɒ̄·ɹdʒĕns). 1834. [f. next; see -ENCE.] The act of rising again.

Resurgent (rĭsɒ̄·ɹdʒĕnt), *sb.* and *a.* 1768. [– L. *resurgens, -ent-*, pr. pple. of *resurgere*; see RESURGE, -ENT.] A. *sb.* One who has risen again. B. *adj.* That rises, or tends to rise, again 1808.

R. Poland, he says, means r. Hungary, and even r. Italy 1854.

Resurrect (rezɒ̆re·kt), *v.* 1772. [Back-formation from RESURRECTION.] 1. *trans.* To raise (a person) from the dead or from the grave; to restore to life or to view again. 2. *intr.* To rise again from the dead 1823.

1. *fig.* Slavery is already dead, and cannot be resurrected 1863.

Resurrection (rezɒ̆re·kʃən). ME. [– (O)Fr. *résurrection* – late L. *resurrectio, -on-*, f. *resurrect-*, pa. ppl. stem of L. *resurgere*; see RESURGE, -ION.] 1. (Now with cap.) The rising again of Christ after his death and burial. 2. The rising again of men at the Last Day ME. 3. The action or fact of rising again from sleep, disuse, etc.; revival; restoration to previous status or vogue. late ME. 4. A resurrected thing (*rare*) 1771.

1. Forty dayes after his resurreccyon that blessed lorde ascended 1526. 2. So shalt thou ioyefully abide the general resurection. late ME. 3. See we not a yearly R. of grasse, herbs, grain,.. every Spring tide? 1657. 4. His horse was..a r. of dry bones SMOLLETT.

attrib. and *Comb.*, as **r. flower** = *r. plant* b; **-man**, one who made a trade of exhuming bodies in order to sell them to anatomists; **r. pie**, a pie made out of remains from previous meals; **r. plant** (*a*) a Californian plant, *Selaginella lepidophylla*, the dried fronds of which unfold again when moistened; (*b*) the Rose of Jericho, an Eastern plant having similar properties. Hence **Resurre·ctional** *a.* relating to, or concerned with, r. **Resurre·ctionary** *a.* restoratory; concerned or connected with the disinterment of bodies for anatomical purposes. **Resurre·ctionize**, *v. trans.* to resurrect.

Resurre·ctionist. 1776. [f. prec. + -IST.] 1. An exhumer and stealer of corpses; a resurrection-man. 2. One who revives or brings to light again. (Chiefly *transf.* from prec.) 1834.

†**Resu·scitate**, *pa. pple.* 1520. [– L. *resuscitatus*, pa. pple. of *resuscitare*; see next, -ATE².] Revived, restored to life –1680.

Resuscitate (rĭsɒ·siteⁱt), *v.* 1532. [– *resuscitat-*, pa. ppl. stem of L. *resuscitare*, f. *re-* RE- + *suscitare* raise, revive; see -ATE³.] 1. *trans.* To restore (a person) to life (physical or spiritual) or to consciousness. 2. To revive, renew, restore (a thing) 1532. 3. *intr.* To revive, come to life again 1652.

1. Her mother..took means to r. her child 1839. 2. No one discovery resuscitates the world 1851. 3. Every plant will earlier or later r. 1787. So **Resu·scitable** *a.* capable of being resuscitated. **Resu·scitative** *a.* revivifying, reviving. **Resu·scitator**, one who resuscitates or revives.

Resuscitation (rĭsɒsitēⁱ·ʃən). 1526. [– late L. *resuscitatio, -on-*, f. as prec.; see -ION.] 1. Restoration to life. b. *spec.* Restoration of life or consciousness in one almost or apparently drowned or dead 1788. 2. Revival, renewal, restoration (of something) 1663.

1. b. Efforts at r. should be kept up for at least two hours 1875. 2. The r. of their national life 1874.

Ret, *v.* 1440. [The E. Anglian forms *reten, retten* correspond to MDu. *reeten*, (also mod.) *reten*; but the north. forms *rayte, rate* point to an ON. **reyta*, corresp. to MLG. *rōten*, MDu. *rooten, roten*; rel. to ROT *v.*] 1. *trans.* To soak (esp. flax or hemp) in water, or expose to moisture, in order to soften or season. 2. Of hay, etc. *pass.*: To be spoiled by exposure to wet 1641. 3. *trans.* and *intr.* To rot 1846.

Retable (rĭ·tēⁱb'l). 1823. [– Fr. *rétable, retable* – Sp. *retablo* – med.L. **retabulum*, for *retrotabulum* (XIII) 'structure at the back of an altar-table', f. L. *retro* RETRO- + *tabula* TABLE.] *Eccl.* A shelf or ledge (on which ornaments may be placed), or a frame enclosing decorated panels, above the back of an altar. So ‖**Reta·blo**, ‖**Reta·bulum.**

Retail (rī·teⁱl), *sb.* late ME. [– AFr. **retaille* (AL. *retallia*, also in phr. *ad retalliam vendere* sell by retail XIV), spec. use of OFr. *retaille* piece cut off, shred, f. *retaillier*, f. *re-* RE- + *taillier* cut (see TAIL *v.*²).] 1. The sale of commodities in small quantities. (Often in adv. phrases, with *by, at*, or used advb. without prep.) †2. Detail (of a matter) –1678. 3. A retailer 1884. 4. *attrib.* or as *adj.* Of or pertaining to, connected with, engaged in, the sale of commodities in small quantities 1601.

1. What barbarous parents,..to oblige a person of my figure to deal out tea and sugar r.! 1784.

Retail (rĭtēⁱ·l), *v.* late ME. [See prec.] 1. *trans.* To sell (goods, etc.) in small quantities. b. *intr.* To be sold by retail 1881. 2. To recount or tell over again; to relate in detail; to repeat to others 1594.

1. He is Wits Pedler and retailes his Wares, At Wakes, and Wassels SHAKS. b. Turbot, brill, and halibut r. at 9*d.* per lb. 1897. 2. The licensed fool retail'd his jest SCOTT. Hence **Retai·ler**, one who retails goods, a small dealer or trader; one who repeats or relates. **Retai·lment**, the act of retailing.

Retain (rĭtēⁱ·n), *v.* late ME. [– AFr. *retei(g)n-*, repr. tonic stem of (O)Fr. *retenir* :– Rom. **retenēre*, for L. *retinēre*, f. *re-* RE- + *tenēre* hold.] I. *trans.* †1. To restrain; to hold back, check, or stop; to prevent or hinder –1737. b. To keep in custody or under control; to prevent from departing, issuing, or separating; to hold fixed in some place or position 1533. 2. †a. To entertain (*rare*) –1585. b. To keep attached to one's person or engaged in one's service 1450. c. To engage (a barrister) by the payment of a preliminary fee, in order to secure his services for one's own cause if necessary 1548. 3. To keep hold or possession of; to continue to have or keep, in various senses 1450. **b.** To continue to use, practise, etc. 1548. **c.** To continue to have or possess (some attribute, quality, etc.) 1582. **d.** To allow to remain, in place of discarding or removing; to preserve 1802. **4.** To keep or bear in mind; to remember 1474.

1. b. Two Mils to retaine the water when the Sea ebs 1617. **2. b.** A great number of knights were retained in his service HUME. **c.** *Cliens*..is also he whiche hath retayned a lawyer to susteyne his matter ELYOT. **3.** His Power..he seem'd Above the rest still to r. MILT. He still aimed at retaining the most lucrative of his benefices FROUDE. **c.** A kind of Stone that long retains its whiteness 1687. **4.** It requires a..good memory to r. these distinctions 1782.

II. *intr.* †**1.** To refrain *from* something –1602. **2.** To adhere, belong, be attached, or be a retainer *to* one –1711. **3.** To continue, remain. DONNE.

2. Most of the Members..thought it an honour to r. to some great Lord, and to wear his blew Coat 1681. Hence **Retai·nable** *a.* capable of being retained; whence **Retainabi·lity, Retai·nableness. Retai·nal,** retention. **Retai·nment,** the (*or* an) act of retaining; retention; †maintenance.

Retainer[1] (rĭtē[i]·nəɹ). 1453. [f. RETAIN *v.* + -ER[4].] **1.** The act or fact of retaining, withholding, or keeping for oneself; an authorization to do this. Now *rare.* **2. a.** The fact of being retained in some capacity 1775. **b.** An authorization given to an attorney to act in a case. Chiefly *U.S.* 1816. **3.** A fee paid to a barrister to secure his services; engagement by a retaining-fee 1818. **b.** A sum paid to secure special services if required 1859.

3. b. Half-pay to the disbanded officers..was meant to be a r. as well as a reward MACAULAY.

Retainer[2] (rĭtē[i]·nəɹ). 1540. [f. RETAIN *v.* + -ER[1].] **1.** One who or that which retains or holds; a maintainer, preserver 1548. **2.** A dependent or follower of some person of rank or position; one attached to a house or owing it service. Now *Hist.* or *arch.* 1540. **b.** *U.S.*: A person irregularly attached to an army; a sutler, camp-follower 1890.

2. A swarm of armed retainers whom the lord could not control, and whom he conceived himself bound to protect STUBBS. *transf. Hen. VIII,* II. iv. 113. Hence **Retai·nership.**

Retaining (rĭtē[i]·niŋ), *ppl. a.* 1611. [f. as prec. + -ING[2].] That retains; serving to retain or hold by physical force or resistance.

R. fee = RETAINER[1] 3. *R. wall,* a wall built to support a mass of earth or water.

Retaliate (rĭtæ·li,ē[i]t), *v.* 1611. [– *retaliat-*, pa. ppl. stem of L. *retaliare,* f. *re-* RE- + *talis* of such a kind; see -ATE[3].] **1.** *trans.* To requite, repay in kind, make return for: **a.** kindness, etc. Now *rare.* **b.** injury, ill-treatment, etc. 1631. **c.** Const. *upon* (a person). Also, to inflict in return, to cast back, *upon* (a person). 1676. **2.** *intr.* To make return or requital (now only of injury, insult, etc.) 1658.

1. a. Our Ambassador sent word..to the Dukes son, his visit should be retaliated 1638. **c.** Thus did the Lord..r. upon him the innocent blood which he had shed 1676. So **Reta·liative** *a.* tending to, or of the nature of, retaliation; revengeful. **Reta·liatory** *a.* pertaining to, of the nature of, retaliation.

Retaliation (rĭtæli,ē[i]·ʃən). 1581. [app. f. prec. + -ION; but cf. contemp. TALIATION.] **1.** The action of retaliating; the return of like for like; repayment in kind; requital, reprisal. **2.** An instance of this; a return or requital, *esp.* of injuries 1645.

1. Contentiousness and Cruelty seldom fail of R. BENTLEY. **2.** This sanguinary r. on the Turks 1847.

‖**Retama** (retā·mă). 1852. [Sp. *retama* – Arab. *ratama,* a plant of the genus *Genista.*] A class of shrubby plants, chiefly found in the Mediterranean region, related to the broom, and usu. referred to the genus *Genista.* Hence **Reta·mine** (*Chem.*), an alkaloid extracted from *Retama sphærocarpa.*

Retard (rĭtā·ɹd), *sb.* 1788. [– Fr. *retard,* f. *retarder*; see next.] **1.** Retardation, delay. **2.** *R. of the tide* or *of high water,* the interval between the moon's transit and the high water following upon this 1833.

1. *In r.,* retarded, delayed; in the rear *of*; I was far in r. of them in real knowledge RUSKIN.

Retard (rĭtā·ɹd), *v.* 1489. [– (O)Fr. *retarder* :– L. *retardare,* f. *re-* RE- + *tardus* slow.] **1.** *trans.* To keep back, delay, hinder, impede (a person or thing in respect of progress, movement, action, or accomplishment). **2.** To delay the progress or accomplishment, to impede the course, of (an action, movement, etc.) 1572. **b.** To defer, put off (*rare*) 1735. **3.** *intr.* To be delayed; to come, appear, or happen later; to undergo retardation 1646.

1. This fleet..was extremely retarded by the winds 1732. **2.** They would r. instead of accelerating the further increase ADAM SMITH. **b.** To advance or r. the hour of refection SCOTT. **3.** Putrefaction..shall r. or accelerate according to the subject and season of the year SIR T. BROWNE. So †**Reta·rdate** *v.* **Reta·rdative** *a.* tending or having power to r. **Reta·rdatory** *a.* having a retarding effect or influence. **Reta·rder,** one who or that which checks or delays. **Reta·rdment,** retardation; delay, check.

Retardation (rĭtaɹdē[i]·ʃən). late ME. [– (O)Fr. *retardation* or L. *retardatio, -on-*, f. pa. ppl. stem of *retardare*; see prec., -ION.] **1.** The action of retarding in respect of action or movement, or making later in happening; an instance of this. **2.** In the physical sciences: **a.** of motion or moving bodies. (Opp. to *acceleration.*) 1642. **b.** of the tides: (*a*) The excess of periods of high water above the solar day. (*b*) = RETARD *sb.* 2. 1797. **c.** of celestial bodies 1812. **d.** of rays or waves of light, heat, etc. 1831. **3.** *Mus.* **a.** Delay in the progression of a part or note 1818. **b.** A slackening of the tempo 1853.

1. Causing a r. of reading, and some sloth or relaxation of memory BACON. This r. or decreased rate of growth 1891. **2. a.** In an elliptical orbit there is now acceleration and now r. 1862. **3. a.** When an interval of a melody (or of an inner part) is kept back in ascending, it is called a r. 1868.

Retch (retʃ, rĭtʃ), *v.* 1548. [var. of REACH *v.*[2]] †**1.** *intr.* To hawk, bring *up* phlegm –1623. **2. a.** To make efforts to vomit 1850. **b.** *trans.* To throw up in vomiting 1888.

†**Retchless,** var. of RECKLESS *a.* q.v.

‖**Rete** (rī·ti). *Pl.* **retia** (rī·tiă, rī·ʃia). late ME. [L., = net.] †**1. a.** An open-work metal plate, affixed to an astrolabe, and serving to indicate the positions of the principal fixed stars –1613. **b.** A graduated scale affixed to an astronomical telescope –1677. **2.** *Anat.* **a.** *R. mirabile,* an elaborate network or plexus of blood-vessels 1541. **b.** The under portion of the epidermis, in which the pigment-cells are situated. Usu. in full, *r. mucosum* or *r. Malpighii.* 1797.

Retene (retī·n). 1867. [f. Gr. ῥητίνη resin; see -ENE.] *Chem.* A hydrocarbon, polymeric with benzene, obtained from resinous (esp. fossil) pine-wood.

Retention (rĭte·nʃən). late ME. [– (O)Fr. *retention* or L. *retentio, -on-*, f. *retent-*, pa. ppl. stem of *retinēre*; see RETAIN, -ION.] **1.** *Med.* The fact of retaining within the body one of the secretions (esp. the urine) which are normally evacuated; a case or instance of this. **2. a.** The fact of retaining things in the mind; the power or ability to do this; memory 1483. **b.** The fact of maintaining, keeping up, or continuing to use something 1625. **3.** The action or fact of keeping to oneself or in one's own hands, under one's power or authority 1540. **4.** †**a.** Detention of persons by forcible or other means –1615. **b.** The action or fact of holding fast or keeping fixed in a place or position; the fact or property of being kept, or remaining, in place 1597. †**c.** Restraint –1633. **5.** Power to retain; capacity for holding or keeping something 1601.

3. *Twel. N.* v. i. 84. **5.** No womans heart So bigge, to hold so much, they lacke r. SHAKS.

†**Rete·ntive,** *sb.* late ME. [– OFr. *retentive,* or f. next.] **1.** Recollection, memory –1454. **2.** A restraining force; a means of restraint –1650. **3.** *pl.* The organs by which the natural excretions of the body are regulated –1717.

Retentive (rĭte·ntiv), *a.*[1] late ME. [– (O)Fr. *retentif, -ive* or med.L. *retentivus,* f. as RETENTION; see -IVE.] **1.** Of the mind or memory: Tenacious; good at remembering. **b.** Of persons: Possessed of a good memory 1758. †**2.** *The r. virtue* or *faculty,* the ability to retain the physical secretions, or to keep food within the stomach –1683. †**3.** Sparing, niggardly –1678. **4.** Having the property of, tending or inclinded to, the retention or keeping *of* something 1582. **5.** Holding or confining; keeping firm hold 1601. **b.** *Surg.* Serving to keep (a dressing, organ, etc.) in the proper place 1597. **c.** Apt to retain or hold moisture 1730. †**6.** Restrained, cautious, reticent –1626.

1. The memory of the peple is not retentyf CAXTON. **3.** Never was King more frugal, never King more r. in his largesses 1654. **5.** *Jul. C.* I. iii. 95. Hence **Rete·ntive-ly** *adv.*, **-ness.**

†**Rete·ntive,** *a.*[2] [f. Fr. *retentir* + -IVE.] That reverberates or resounds. POPE.

Retenti·vity. 1881. [f. RETENTIVE *a.*[1] + -ITY.] *Electr.* The capacity for retaining magnetism after the action of the magnetizing force has ceased; also = coercive force (see COERCIVE *a.*).

‖**Retenue** (rətənü). 1748. [Fr., pa. pple. fem. of *retenir* restrain, used subst.] Reserve, restraint, caution, self-control.

Retepore (re·tĭpō[ə]ɹ). 1878. [– mod.L. *Retepora,* f. L. *rete* net + *porus* PORE *sb.*] An ectoproctous polyzoan of the genus *Retepora.*

‖**Retiarius** (rĭti,ē[ə]·riŏs, rĭʃ-). 1647. [L., f. *rete* a net + *-arius* -ARY[1].] A Roman gladiator who carried a net with which to entangle his adversary.

Retiary (rī·ʃiări), *a.* 1646. [used adjectivally – L. *retiarius*; see prec.] **1.** Pertaining or relating to the making of webs, nets, or the like 1658. **2.** Fighting with a net; using a net like a retiarius 1658. **3.** *R. spider,* a spider which constructs a web; a geometrical spider. Also *ellipt.* as *sb.* 1646.

1. This kinde of Work in Retiarie and hanging tectures SIR T. BROWNE. **2.** His scholastic r. versatility of logic COLERIDGE.

Reticence (re·tisĕns), *sb.* 1603. [– L. *reticentia,* f. *reticēre* keep silence, f. *re-* RE- + *tacēre* be silent; see -ENCE. Cf. Fr. *réticence.*] Maintenance of silence; avoidance of speaking freely; disposition to say little. **b.** *pl.* Instances of silence or reserve 1814.

A man so known for impenetrable r. as Teufelsdröckh CARLYLE. Surprised at her unusual r. of epithets 1856. So **Re·ticency.**

Reticent (re·tisĕnt), *a.* 1834. [– L. *reticens, -ent-*, pr. pple. of *reticēre*; see prec., -ENT.] Reserved; disinclined to speak freely; given to silence or concealment. Hence **Re·ticently** *adv.*

Reticle (re·tik'l). 1656. [– L. RETICULUM.] †**1.** A little net, a structure resembling a net –1790. **2.** A set of parallel wires, threads, etc., with others intersecting them at right angles, or of lines similarly ruled upon a sheet of glass, placed in the object-glass of a telescope, in order to facilitate accurate observations 1731.

Reticular (rĭti·kiŭlăɹ), *a.* 1597. [– mod.L. *reticularis,* f. L. RETICULUM; see -AR[1].] **1.** Resembling a net in appearance or construction; net-like. **2.** *Arch.* Of masonry: Constructed of lozenge-shaped stones, bricks, etc., or of square pieces set diagonally 1797. **3.** Resembling a net in effect or operation; intricate, entangled 1818.

1. The r. covering of a coco-nut 1769. A delicate r. membrane 1805. Hence **Reti·cularly** *adv.*

Reticulate (rĭti·kiŭlĕt), *a.* 1658. [– L. *reticulatus,* f. RETICULUM; see -ATE[2].] Reticulated. Hence **Reti·culately** *adv.*

Reticulate (rĭti·kiŭle[i]t), *v.* 1787. [Back-formation from next.] **1.** *trans.* To divide or mark in such a way as to resemble network. **2.** *intr.* To divide so as to form a network, or something having that appearance 1862.

Reticulated (rĭti·kiŭle[i]tėd), *a.* 1728. [f. RETICULATE *a.* + -ED[1].] **1.** Constructed or arranged like a net; made or marked so as to resemble a net or network. **2.** *Arch.* **a.** = RETICULAR *a.* 2. 1823. **b.** Of tracery: Formed by the repetition of the same foliated opening 1847. **3.** Divided into small squares 1867.

1. *Network,* any thing r. or decussated, at equal distances, with interstices between the intersections JOHNSON. The r. rivers in the central valley LIVINGSTONE. Bodies..with the surface r. 1877.

Reticulation (rĭtikiŭlē[i]·ʃən). 1671. [f. RETICULATE *a.*; see -ATION.] A network; an arrangement of lines, etc., resembling a net; reticulated structure or appearance.

fig. The minute reticulations of tyranny which he had begun..to spin about a whole people 1855.

Reti·culato-, comb. form of RETICULATE *a.*, as in *r.-ramose,* etc.

Reticule (re·tikiŭl). 1727. [– Fr. *réticule* – L. RETICULUM.] **1.** = RETICLE 2. **2.** A small bag, usu. made of some woven material, for carrying on the arm or in the hand, used by ladies as a pocket or workbag 1824. **3.** *Astr.* One of the southern constellations, situated near Hydra 1868.

2. *R.-basket*, a small basket resembling, or serving the purpose of, a r.

Reti·culo-, comb. form of L. *reticulum*, as in *r.-ramose*, etc.

Reticulose (rĭti·kiŭlōᵘs), *a.* 1826. [f. next + -OSE.[1]] Of the nature of, resembling, network.

‖**Reticulum** (rĭti·kiŭlŏm). 1658. [L., dim. of *rete* net; see -CULE.] **1.** *Anat.* **a.** The second stomach of a ruminant. †**b.** The omentum or mesentery –1738. **2. a.** *arch.* Reticulated work (*rare*) 1797. **b.** *Bot.* The fibrous sheath at the base of the leaves in palms 1835. **c.** A net-like structure; a membrane, etc., having a reticulated form or appearance 1858. **3.** *Astr.* = RETICULE 3. 1841.

Retiform (rī·tifǭɹm), *a.* 1636. [f. L. *rete* net + -FORM.] Having the form of a net.

Retina (re·tină). late ME. [– med.L. *retina*, f. L. *rete* net.] The innermost layer or coating at the back of the eyeball (esp. of vertebrates), which is sensitive to light, and in which the optic nerve terminates. Hence **Re·tinal** *a.* pertaining or relating to the r. **Retini·tis** (*Path.*), acute inflammation of the r.

‖**Retinaculum** (retinæ·kiŭlŏm). *Pl.* **-ula.** 1825. [L., f. *retinēre* hold back; see -CULE.] *Ent.* and *Bot.* Anything serving to keep something in position; in various *spec.* uses. Hence **Retina·cular** *a.* relating to, of the nature of, a r.

Retinalite (re·tinălait). 1836. [f. Gr. ῥητίνη resin + -LITE.] *Min.* A variety of serpentine which has a resinous lustre.

Retinasphalt (retinæ·sfælt). Also **-asphaltum.** 1804. [f. as prec. + L. *asphaltum* ASPHALT.] A fossil resin found with lignite.

Retinic (rĕti·nik), *a.* 1844. [f. as prec. + -IC.] *Chem.* In *r. acid*, an acid found in retinasphalt.

Retinite (re·tinait). Also **-it.** 1821. [– Fr. *rétinite* (1795), f. Gr. ῥητίνη resin + -ITE[1] 2 b.] *Min.* **a.** Retinasphalt. **b.** A mineral resin derived from brown coal. **c.** Pitchstone.

Retino-, used as comb. form of RETINA, as in *r.-cerebral*, etc.

Retinol (re·tinǫl). Also **-ole.** 1838. [f. Gr. ῥητίνη resin + -OL.] *Chem.* A hydrocarbon, obtained from resins.

Retinoscopy (retinǫ·skŏpi). 1884. [f. RETINA + -SCOPY.] The method of examining the eye, for refraction, by the observation of the movement of a shadow on the retina, caused by the rotation of the mirror of the ophthalmoscope. Hence **Retinosco·pic** *a.* of or pertaining to, performed by, r. **Retinosco·pically** *adv.*

Retinue (re·tiniŭ), *sb.* late ME. [– OFr. *retenue* RETENUE.] †**1.** The fact of being retained in the service of another; a relationship of service or dependency –1607. **2.** A number or company of persons retained in the service of, or attached to and following some one, esp. a sovereign, noble, or person in authority; a train or suite. late ME. **b.** Collectively, without article or pronoun 1665.

2. So many Nymphs, which she doth hold In her retinew SPENSER. An enormous r. of officers and servants 1878. **b.** Worth is not to be judg'd by Success, and R. GLANVILL. Hence **Re·tinue** *v. trans.* to furnish with a r.; to accompany as a r. 1827.

Retinula (reti·niŭlă). *Pl.* **-ulæ.** 1878. [dim., on L. types, of RETINA; see -ULE.] *Biol.* One of the pigmented cells from which, in certain compound eyes of Arthropods, the rhabdom arises. Hence **Reti·nular, Reti·nulate** *adjs.*

Retiracy (rĭtaiᵊ·răsi). *U.S.* 1842. [f. RETIRE *v.* + -ACY, after *privacy*.] **1.** Retirement, seclusion, privacy. **2.** A sufficient fortune to retire upon 1859.

1. I enjoy a considerable portion of r. 1842.

Retiral (rĭtaiᵊ·răl). 1611. [f. RETIRE *v.* + -AL[1] 2.] **1.** The act of retreating or withdrawing (*rare*). **2.** The act or fact of withdrawing from, or of giving up an office, position, or vocation 1879.

Retire (rĭtaiᵊ·ɹ), *sb.* 1540. [f. the verb.] **1.** Retirement; withdrawal from the world or the society of others. Now *rare.* †**2.** The act of retiring or withdrawing to or from a place or position –1676. †**3.** The act of drawing back or yielding ground in warfare –1606. **4.** A place of retirement; a retreat. Now *rare.* 1595.

1. Eve..with audible lament Discover'd soon the place of her r. MILT. **3.** Phr. *To sound a* (or *the*) *r.* (In mod. use the imper. of the vb. used subst.) **4.** What r. or retreat could he find in any place? 1620.

Retire (rĭtaiᵊ·ɹ), *v.* 1533. [– (O)Fr. *retirer* withdraw, f. *re-* RE- + *tirer* draw.] **I.** *intr.* **1.** To withdraw *to* or *into* a place (or way of life) for seclusion, shelter, or security 1538. **b.** To withdraw *to* one's usual place of abode, or some customary occupation 1584. **c.** To withdraw from company and betake oneself *to* rest or bed. Also *ellipt.* in same sense. 1670. **d.** To withdraw from office or an official position; to give up one's business or occupation in order to enjoy more leisure or freedom (esp. after having made a competence or earned a pension) 1667. **e.** *Cricket.* To go out 1884. **2.** Of an army, commander, etc.: To withdraw, fall back, or retreat, esp. in the face of opposition or superior force 1533. **b.** *Fencing.* To give ground before one's adversary; to take one or more steps backward 1594. **3.** To withdraw, go away, remove oneself (*from* a place, etc.) 1585. **b.** To move back or away; to recede, or have the appearance of doing this 1585. **c.** To disappear *from* sight; to vanish 1697. †**4.** To return; to come back –1613. **5.** In *pa. pple.* having retired 1610.

1. Shakspeare..retired to his native place before he was old L. HUNT. **b.** I'll r. to my own chamber, and think of what you have said CONGREVE. **c.** At their usual time the old couple r. to bed 1775. When most of the..people had 'retired', or, in vulgar language, 'gone to bed' 1860. **d.** He felt as a trader feels when he retires from business 1863. **e.** G. B. Studd retiring for six 1884. **2.** The task of a rear guard retiring before a victorious enemy..is one of the most delicate of operations 1888. **3.** When the ladies retired from the dinner table LOCKHART. **5.** All things now retir'd to rest Mind us of like repose MILT.

II. *refl.* To withdraw or remove (oneself); to betake (oneself) away. Now *rare.* 1539. **III.** *trans.* **1.** To withdraw, lead back (troops, etc.), esp. before a superior force 1550. †**2.** To put away; to withdraw, remove, lead away (a person or thing) –1719. †**b.** To withdraw the mind, thoughts, etc., *from* some object or sphere –1699. **c.** To withdraw (a thing) from notice; to hide away, put into obscurity 1605. **3.** To draw or pull (a thing) back (again) 1593. **4.** To withdraw from operation or currency; to take up or pay (*esp.* a bill) 1681. **5.** To remove (an officer) from active service 1870. **b.** To remove from the usual sphere of activity; to take off 1883.

1. The French were soon seen to r. their heavy guns LEVER. **4.** Two of his notes for £100..which he thinks nae mair of retiring than he does of paying the national debt SCOTT. **4.** Admiral.. Hamilton..was retired from the active list under the age clause 1894. Hence **Reti·rer**, one who retires or retreats. **Reti·ring-ly** *adv.*, **-ness.**

Retired (rĭtaiᵊ·ɹd), *ppl. a.* 1590. [f. prec. + -ED[1].] **1.** Withdrawn into seclusion or away from contact with the world. **2.** Secluded, sequestered; removed from places frequented by people 1593. **3.** Withdrawn into oneself; reserved 1611. **4. a.** That has receded or subsided. SHAKS. **b.** *R. flank*, in fortification, one bent back towards the rear of the work 1696. **5.** Withdrawn from, no longer occupied with, business or official duties 1824.

1. The r. and solitary Student 1691. **2.** An obscure, little, r. street WYCHERLEY. **5.** *R. List*, a list of r. officers. *R. allowance* or *pay*, the pension given to a r. officer or official. Hence **Reti·red-ly** *adv.*, **-ness.**

Retirement (rĭtaiᵊ·ɹmĕnt). 1596. [f. RETIRE *v.* + -MENT. Cf. Fr. *retirement.*] **1.** The act of falling back, retreating, or receding from a place or position. (In mod. use chiefly *Mil.*) **2.** The act of withdrawing into seclusion or privacy; withdrawal *from* something 1599. **b.** Withdrawal from occupation or business activity 1648. **3.** The state or condition of being withdrawn from society or publicity; seclusion, privacy 1603. **b.** A time or occasion of seclusion or privacy 1632. **4.** A place or abode characterized by seclusion or privacy; a retreat 1652. **5.** The act of withdrawing from circulation 1865.

1. On the r. of the Lacedæmonian force, the Samian exiles were left destitute GROTE. **2.** For solitude..is best societie, And short r. urges sweet returne MILT. **b.** R. is as necessary to me as it will be welcome WASHINGTON. **3.** As the Duchess lived in close r. SCOTT. **b.** Dearly did he enjoy these retirements 1852. **4.** Exmouth; where he has, as they say, a sweet country r. WILKES. **5.** The r. of all paper currency of a lower denomination than ten dollars 1897.

Retorsion (rĭtǭ·ɹʃən). Now *rare.* 1657. [– (O)Fr. *rétorsion* – med.L. **retorsio*; see RE-, TORSION.] Retortion (of an argument, etc.).

Retort (rĭtǭ·ɹt), *sb.*[1] 1600. [f. RETORT *v.*[1]] **1.** A sharp or incisive reply, esp. one by which the first speaker's statement or argument is in some way turned against himself, or is met by a counter-charge. **2.** The act or practice of replying in a sharp or incisive manner 1791.

1. *A. Y. L.* v. iv. 76. **2.** Johnson's dexterity in r...was very remarkable BOSWELL. Nothing is so easy..as the r. of abuse and sarcasm W. IRVING.

Retort (rĭtǭ·ɹt), *sb.*[2] 1605. [– Fr. *retorte* – med.L. *retorta*, subst. use of fem. pa. pple. of L. *retorquēre*; see next.] **1.** A vessel usu. made of glass, and provided with a long neck, bent downwards, in which liquids, etc., subjected to distillation are heated. **2.** A vessel in which mercury is separated from amalgam or impurity by volatilization 1683. **3.** A clay or iron receptacle, forming a cylinder or segment of one, in which coal is heated for the production of gas 1808. **4.** A furnace in which iron is heated with carbon, in order to produce steel 1868.

attrib.: **r. carbon,** carbon which remains as a residue in the retort when gas has been extracted from coal.

Retort (rĭtǭ·ɹt), *v.*[1] 1557. [f. *retort-*, pa. ppl. stem of L. *retorquēre*, f. *re-* RE- + *torquēre* twist.] **I. 1.** *trans.* To make return of (something done to one, *esp.* an injury); to repay or pay back; to requite by retaliation. **b.** To cast back, cause to return, *upon* or *against* the offending party 1559. **2.** To cast or hurl back (a charge, epithet, etc.) 1596. **3.** To reply in kind to (a jest, sarcasm, etc.); to answer with the like 1602. **b.** To say or utter by way of (sharp or aggressive) reply 1625. **c.** *intr.* To make a retort or retorts 1838. **4.** To meet or answer (an argument, etc.) by a similar argument to the contrary; to turn or direct (his own statement) *against* an opponent 1610.

1. It was now his time to r. the humiliation 1817. **b.** They..r. upon the Aggressour the Injury, which they parry from themselves 1718. **2.** He asserted that I was heterodox; I retorted the charge GOLDSM. **3.** R. their raillery with raillery, always tempered with good breeding CHATHAM. **c.** He must smile and r., and look perfectly at his ease GEO. ELIOT. **4.** Not a single voice was raised in either House..to r. the argument 1852.

†**II. 1.** To throw or hurl back (a weapon); to turn back (a blow) upon the striker –1771. **2.** To reflect (heat or light); to return or re-echo (a sound); to drive back, etc. –1662. †**3.** To reject or refuse (an appeal). SHAKS. **4.** To turn back or backwards; to bend or twist back –1718. **5.** *intr.* To spring or fly back; to rebound, recoil; to twist –1710.

2. As when his vertues shining vpon others, Heate them, and they r. that heate againe To the first giuer SHAKS. Hence **Reto·rter** (*rare*) one who retorts.

Retort (rĭtǭ·ɹt), *v.*[2] 1879. [f. RETORT *sb.*[2]] *trans.* To purify (an amalgam, mercury, etc.) by subjecting to heat in a retort.

Retorted (rĭtǭ·ɹtėd), *ppl. a.* 1599. [f. RETORT *v.*[1] + -ED[1].] **1.** Recurved; twisted or bent backwards. **2.** Thrown or cast back; returned 1621. **3.** Reverted; turned in a backward direction 1720.

Retortion (rĭtǭ·ɹʃən). 1591. [In sense 1 perh. f. *contortion* with substitution of prefix, after L. *retorquēre, retort-*; in other senses f. RETORT *v.*[1]] **1.** The action or fact of bending or turning backwards; an instance of this. †**2. a.** A reply of the nature of a retort –1682. **b.** An answer made to an argument by converting it against the person using it –1741. **c.** The method or device of meeting an argument, etc., by retorting it –1732. **3.** Return for something done; retaliation. Now *spec.* in international law. 1654.

Retortive (rĭtǭ·ɹtiv), *a. rare.* 1807. [f. L. *retort-* (see RETORT *v.*[1]), or RETORT *v.*[2], + -IVE.] **1.** Turned backwards. **2.** Of the nature of a retort 1826.

Retouch (rītʊ·tʃ), *sb.* 1703. [prob. – Fr. *retouche* (1507), f. *retoucher*; see next.] A second or further touch given to some part of a picture, composition, etc., with a view to improving it.

Retouch (rītʊ·tʃ), *v.* 1650. [prob. – (O)Fr. *retoucher*; see RE-, TOUCH *v.*] **1.** *trans.* To touch again with a view to improving; to amend or improve by fresh touches; to touch up. Also *absol.* **2.** To touch upon, to speak of, to introduce or bring in, again (*rare*) 1701. Hence **Retou·cher,** one who retouches, *esp.* one whose occupation is to retouch photographs.

Retrace (rĭtrē¹·s), *v.* 1697. [– Fr. *retracer*; see RE-, TRACE *v.*] **1.** *trans.* To trace back to an origin or source; to track through preceding stages. **2.** To trace again with the eyes; to look over again with care or close attention 1726. **b.** To trace again in memory; to recall 1748. **3.** To go back upon (one's steps, way, etc.) 1794.

1. Then if the Line of Turnus you r.; He springs from Inachus of Argive Race DRYDEN. **2.** The chief divine Gaz'd o'er his sire, retracing ev'ry line POPE. **3.** With purpose to r. my steps, I turned CARY.

†**Retra·ct,** *sb.* 1553. [f. the vbs.] **1.** Retractation (of errors, statements, etc.) –1656. **2.** Retreat on the part of an army or force –1614.

Retract (rĭtræ·kt), *v.*[1] late ME. [f. *retract-*, pa. ppl. stem of L. *retrahere*, f. *re-* RE- + *trahere* draw.] **I.** *trans.* **1.** To draw or pull (something) back. **b.** To draw back or in (some part of the body) 1664. †**2.** To restrain; to hold back or prevent *from* some course. Also *absol.* –1670. †**3.** To withdraw, remove, or take away (a person or thing) –1728.

1. b. Birds which have sharp claws..r. them when they hope to prevent their being blunted 1835.

II. *intr.* To undergo or exhibit retraction; to admit of being drawn back 1784.

In non-military rifles, the foresight..retracts within a strong sheath 1862.

Retract (rĭtræ·kt), *v.*[2] 1545. [– (O)Fr. *rétracter* or L. *retractare*, f. *re-* RE- + *tractare* draw, pull, frequent. of *trahere*; cf. prec.] **1.** *trans.* **a.** To withdraw, recall, revoke, rescind (a decree, declaration, promise, etc.). **b.** To withdraw (a statement, etc.) as being erroneous or unjustified 1560. **2.** *intr.* **a.** To make withdrawal or disavowal 1645. **b.** To draw back (from a promise, resolve, etc.) 1700. **c.** *Card-playing.* To draw back, change one's mind, after having agreed or declined to play with a certain hand 1830.

1. The permission..has been given, and cannot be retracted JOWETT. **b.** He had nothing, he said, to r. 1879. **2. a.** The affront once given,..they fight first and r. afterwards 1833. **b.** She grants, denies, Consents, retracts, advances, and then flies 1735.

Retractable (rĭtræ·ktăb'l), *a.* 1620. [f. RETRACT *v.*[1] and *v.*[2] + -ABLE.] **1.** That may be retracted or disavowed. **2.** Retractile 1769.

Retractation (rĭtræktē¹·ʃən). 1451. [In sense 1 – late L. *retractationes* pl. (see def.); f. RETRACT *v.*[2] + -ATION. cl.L. *retractatio* is used in other senses.] **1.** *pl.* The title of a book written by St. Augustine containing further treatment and corrections of matters treated in his former writings. **2. a.** Withdrawal or recantation of an opinion, statement, etc., with admission of error 1548. **b.** Withdrawal from an engagement, promise, etc. 1654.

Retra·cted, *ppl. a.* 1643. [f. RETRACT *v.*[1] + -ED[1].] Drawn or pulled back; drawn or turned inwards. **b.** Of accent: Thrown back towards the beginning of a word 1888. **c.** *Phonetics.* Of a vowel sound: Pronounced with the tongue drawn back 1902.

Men not of r. Looks, but who carry their Hearts in their Faces SIR T. BROWNE.

Retractile (rĭtræ·ktəil), *a*, 1777. [f. RETRACT *v.*[1] + -ILE, after *contractile.*] Admitting of retraction; capable of being drawn in or back; exhibiting the function or power of retraction.

The tongue..is attached by a very elastic r. membrane to the base of the right nostril 1808. Hence **Retracti·lity,** the fact of being r.

Retraction (rĭtræ·kʃən). late ME. [– L. *retractio, -on-*, f. *retract-*; see RETRACT *v.*[1], -ION.] **1.** = RETRACTATION 2 a, b. †**2.** *pl.* = RETRACTATION 1. –1734. **3.** Withdrawal, revocation or recall, *of* something decreed, determined, advanced, etc. 1583. **4.** The action of drawing or pulling back or in; the fact or condition of being drawn in or contracted; retractile power 1550. **b.** The placing of the accent as far from the end of a word as possible 1888. **c.** *Phonetics.* The drawing back of the tongue in the utterance of a sound; the modification (of a vowel) by means of this 1890.

3. He thought the r. of an error a deviation from honour 1756. **4.** *fig.* There is a spirit of r. of one to his native country FULLER.

Retractive (rĭtræ·ktiv), *a.* and *sb.* late ME. [In sense 1 – med.L. *retractivus* (XIV); later f. RETRACT *v.*[1] and [2] + -IVE.] **A.** *adj.* **1.** Serving to retract or pull back. **2.** Inclined to draw back; †backsliding (*rare*) 1509. †**B.** *sb.* A dissuasive –1644.

Retractor (rĭtræ·ktəɹ). 1837. [f. RETRACT *v.*[1] + -OR 2.] **1.** *Surg.* A bandage or other appliance, used, in various operations, to hold back parts that would impede the operator 1846. **2.** *Anat.* A muscle that serves to retract a limb or member. So *r. muscle.* 1837.

Retrad (rī·træd). 1891. [f. L. *retro* + -AD II; cf. *dextrad.*] To or towards the rear.

†**Retraict.** 1570. [– Fr. *retraict(e*, obs. vars. of *retrait(e*; see next.] **1.** The act of retreating, in various senses –1640. **b.** Possibility of retreat 1622. **2.** A place of retreat 1596.

†**Retrai·t,** *sb.*[1] 1481. [– (O)Fr. *retrait* masc., or *retraite* fem., pa. pple. of *retraire*; see RETREAT *sb.*] **1.** A place of retreat or refuge –1626. **2.** *Mil.* The signal for retiring –1648. **3.** Retirement, retreat –1658.

†**Retrai·t,** *sb.*[2] *rare.* 1590. [– It. *ritratto*, perh. after *portrait*, or infl. by prec.] Portraiture.

†**Retrai·t,** *v.* 1548. [f. pa. ppl. stem of (O)Fr. *retraire*; see RETRAIT *sb.*[1]] **1.** *trans.* To withdraw, take away, remove –1614. **2.** *intr.* To retreat, retire –1624. **b.** To have recourse *to* something. FULLER.

Retral (rī·trăl), *a.* 1875. [f. RETRO- + -AL[1].] **1.** Posterior; directed backwards. **2.** Taking a backward direction 1885. **Re·trally** *adv.*

†**Retra·xit.** 1579. [L., 3rd pers. sing. perf. ind. of *retrahere* RETRACT *v.*] *Law.* The formal withdrawal of his suit by a plaintiff –1768.

Retrea·d (rī-), *v.*[1] 1598. [RE- 5 a.] To tread again.

Re-trea·d, *v.*[2] 1908. [f. RE- 5 c + TREAD *sb.* II. 5.] To furnish (a tire) with a new tread.

Retreat (rĭtrī·t), *sb.* [In XIV *retret* – OFr. *retret*, etc., vars. of *retraite*, etc., subst. use of masc. and fem. of pa. pple. of (O)Fr. *retraire* :– L. *retrahere* RETRACT *v.*[1]] **1.** *Mil.* **a.** The signal to retire. Chiefly in phr. *to blow* or *sound the* (or *a*) *r.* †**b.** The recall of a pursuing force. SHAKS. **c.** A signal given by sounding a bugle, drum, etc., at sunset 1753. **2.** The act of retiring or withdrawing in the face of opposition, difficulty, or danger. late ME. **b.** *esp.* of an army or armed force after defeat or to avoid an engagement 1579. **c.** Recession, retrogression (*rare*) 1781. **3.** The act of retiring or withdrawing into privacy, or into some place of safety. Also in *place*, etc., *of r.* 1475. **b.** Retirement, seclusion 1646. **c.** *Eccl.* A period of seclusion or retirement from one's ordinary occupations devoted to religious exercises 1756. **4.** A place of seclusion or privacy; a retired place or residence. late ME. **b.** A place of refuge or resort 1662. **c.** A hiding-place; a lair or den 1774. **d.** An establishment to which insane persons or habitual inebriates are admitted in order that they may be under proper supervision or control 1797. **5.** *Arch.* Recessed work; a recess or recessed part in a wall, etc. 1687.

2. b. The famous R. of Xenophon..at the Head of ten thousand Greeks 1690. **3.** I saw the great towns..famous for the r. of the imperial court when Vienna was besieged 1716. **4.** I am promised a retreate three miles from Bloys 1638. **b.** The building..should be a r. for seamen disabled in the service of their country MACAULAY. Hence †**Retrea·tful** *a.* (*rare*) serving as a r. CHAPMAN.

Retreat (rĭtrī·t), *v.* late ME. [In XV f. as prec., or – (O)Fr. *retraiter*, with accommodation to the sb.] **1.** *intr.* To withdraw, retire, draw back. **b.** Of an army or a combatant: To retire before superior force or after a defeat 1596. **c.** In *pa. pple.* with *is, was*, etc. 1648. **d.** To recede 1863. **2.** *trans.* To draw or lead back; to remove, take away. Now chiefly in *Chess*, to move (a piece) back from a forward or threatened position. 1523. †**b.** To diminish, reduce. LOCKE.

1. You have now carried things too far to r. '*Junius' Lett.* **c.** Others..Retreated in a silent valley, sing..Thir own Heroic deeds and hapless Fall MILT. **d.** The forehead..retreats somewhat HAWTHORNE. **2.** He had no choice but to r. the bishop 1886.

Retreatant (rĭtrī·tănt). 1880. [f. prec. + -ANT.] One who takes part in a religious retreat.

Retrench (rĭtre·nʃ). *v.*[1] 1607. [– Fr. †*retrencher*, early form of *retrancher*; see RE-, TRENCH *v.*] †**1.** *trans.* To cut short, check, repress –1688. †**2.** To cut off, bar (a way or passage) –1618. **3.** To cut down, reduce, diminish; *esp.* to curtail (one's expenses) by the exercise of economy 1625. †**4.** To cut short, reduce in size –1784. **5.** To cut off, remove, take away 1650. **b.** To do away with (an item of expense) 1647. **c.** To cut out, omit, delete (some portion of a book or document) 1645. **6.** *intr.* To reduce expenditure 1663. **b.** To make excisions or diminutions (*rare*) 1700.

3. Forced to r. my expensive Way of Living 1709. To r. the Evils of Life by the Reasonings of Philosophy ADDISON. **4.** The very Lowness of your Subject has retrenched your Wings COWLEY. **5.** To r. what is Superfluous 1718. **b.** To r. one Dish at my Table 1714. **6.** If rich, they go to enjoy; if poor, to r. ROGERS. Hence **Retre·ncher.**

Retrench (rĭtre·nʃ), *v.*[2] 1598. [f. as prec.] *trans.* and *refl.* To protect by, to furnish with, a retrenchment. Also *absol.*

They perceived how the Turks were retrenched within 1600.

Retrenchment[1] (rĭtre·nʃmĕnt). 1600. [– Fr. *retrenchement*, obs. var. of *retranchement*; see RETRENCH *v.*[1], -MENT.] **1.** The act of cutting down, off, or out; curtailment, limitation, reduction. **b.** The act of excising, deleting, or omitting; an instance of this 1691. **2.** The act of economizing or cutting down expenditure; an instance of this 1667.

1. It was not a r. of superfluities DRYDEN. **b.** This one r. of the text 1867. **2.** Reform has gone too far in the way of r. 1868.

Retrenchment[2] (rĭtre·nʃmĕnt). 1589. [f. as prec.] *Mil.* A work, usu. consisting of a trench and parapet, constructed for the defence of a position; *esp.* an inner line of defence within a large work.

Retribute (re·trĭbiut), *v.* Now *rare.* 1575. [f. *retribut-*, pa. ppl. stem of L. *retribuere*, f. *re-* RE- + *tribuere* assign; see TRIBUTE.] **1.** *trans.* To give in return; to make return of; to retaliate (something) *on* a person. **2.** To make return for; to repay 1612. **3.** *intr.* To make a return or requital 1612.

1. To whom in particular were retributed no small rewardes 1579. **3.** A just God who will r. to every one according to the deeds done in the body DE FOE. So **Re·tributor,** one who makes retribution; a repayer.

Retribution (retribiū·ʃən). late ME. [– Chr.L. *retributio, -on-*, f. as prec.; see -ION. Cf. (O)Fr. *rétribution.*] **1.** Repayment, recompense, return, for some service, merit, etc. Now *rare.* **2.** *Day of r.*, the day on which divine reward or punishment will be assigned to men (now usu. assoc. w. sense 3); also generally any day of punishment or nemesis 1526. **b.** Recompense, in another life, for one's good or bad deeds in this world 1633. **3.** A recompense for, or requital of, evil done; return *of* evil, etc. 1570.

1. Never did a charitable act go away without the r. of a blessing 1612. **2.** I..am led to believe that even in this world the day of r. rarely fails to come at last 1856. **b.** All who have thir reward on Earth..here find Fit r., emptie as thir deeds MILT. **3.** In Revenges (that is, r. of Evil for Evil) HOBBES.

Retributive (rĭtri·biŭtiv), *a.* 1678. [f. as RETRIBUTE *v.* + -IVE. Cf. Fr. †*rétributif.*]

Characterized by, of the nature of, retribution. Freq. with *justice*. Hence **Retri·butively** *adv.*

Retributory (rĭtri·biŭtəri), *a.* 1612. [f. as RETRIBUTE *v.* + -ORY².] Involving, producing, or characterized by retribution or recompense.

That sect, which in their prosperity shewed no mercy, now met with r. vengeance 1771.

Retrievable (rĭtrī·văb'l), *a.* 1711. [f. RETRIEVE *v.* + -ABLE.] Capable or admitting of being retrieved.

Retrieval (rĭtrī·văl). 1643. [f. RETRIEVE *v.* + -AL¹ 2.] **1.** The act of retrieving or recovering; an instance of this. **2.** = next 2. 1707.

2. Matrimony clenches ruin beyond r. FIELDING.

Retrieve (rĭtrī·v), *sb.* 1575. [f. the vb.] †**1.** The second discovery and flight of a bird (esp. a partridge) which has already been sprung –1673. **2.** Possibility of recovery. With *beyond, past, †without.* 1697. **b.** The act of recovering. Now *rare.* 1701.

2. We're ruin'd and undone, past all r. 1700.

Retrieve (rĭtrī·v), *v.* [In XV *retreve* – OFr. *retroev-, -euv-*, tonic stem of *retrover* (mod. *retrouver*), f. *re-* RE- + *trover* (*trouver*) find. For the vocalism cf. CONTRIVE.] **I.** *trans.* **1.** Of dogs: **a.** To find or discover again (game which has been temporarily lost); *esp.* to flush or set up (partridges) a second time. **b.** To find and bring in (a bird, etc.) that has been wounded or killed 1856. **2.** To recover by study or investigation, esp. of the past; to restore to knowledge. Now *rare.* 1567. **b.** To recover by an effort of memory; to recall to mind 1644. †**c.** To find again –1660. **3.** To recover, get or take possession of (a thing, etc.) again 1589. †**4.** To bring back; to cause to turn back or return –1662. **b.** To rescue or save *from* or *out of* a place or state 1611. **c.** To save (time) from other occupations 1687. **5.** To restore, revive; to bring back to the original state or to a flourishing condition (*esp.* one's fortunes, honour, credit, etc.) 1676. **6.** To make good, repair, set right again (a loss, disaster, error, etc.) 1688.

1. *fig.* Popes vse Potentates but to retriue their Game 1592. **2.** An ancient word..grown so obsolete that the original purport could not be retrieved 1774. **3.** A warrant..to search for and r. the fugitive SMOLLETT. **5.** The spirit of the country was broken, and nothing could r. it 1861. No courage..could now r. the fortunes of the field 1880. **6.** He endeavoured to r. the error he had committed by the most solemn assurances 1844.

II. *intr.* **1.** Of dogs: †**a.** To find and set up game again (*rare*) –1635. **b.** To find and bring in wounded or dead game 1856. **2.** To recuperate; to recover 1675.

1. b. A little rough terrier, expressly broken to r. 1856. Hence **Retrie·vement,** (*rare*) retrieval.

Retriever (rĭtrī·vəɹ). 1486. [f. RETRIEVE *v.* + -ER¹.] **1.** A dog used for the purpose of retrieving; *esp.* one of a breed specially adapted for finding and bringing in dead or wounded game. **2.** One who retrieves or recovers 1658.

‖**Retro-** (rī·tro), *adv. rare.* 1768. [L.; see next.] Backwards; into past time.

It is of the nature of all confirmations to operate *r.* 1768.

Retro- (rī·tro, re·tro), *prefix*, repr. the L. adverb *retro* backwards, back, which in post-cl.Latin appears in comb. with various vbs. and verbal nouns, as *retroagere*, etc. and rarely in adjectival forms, as *retrogradus*. From the 19th c., esp. the latter part of it, *retro-*, has been very freely used as a prefix, chiefly in scientific terms. In most words the pronunciation of the prefix may be either (rĭtro) or (retro); recent dictionaries usu. prefer (rītro), exc. in *retrograde* and *retrospect*.

a. Miscellaneous terms, as **Retrocogni·tion,** knowledge of the past supernaturally acquired; so **Retroco·gnitive** *a.* **Retroco·pulant** *a.* (*rare*) that copulates backwards. **Retrocopula·tion,** the action or fact of copulating backwards. **Re·trofracted** *a.* (*Bot.*), sharply bent back, as if broken. **Retroge·nerative** *a.* retrocopulant. **Retromi·ngent** *a.*, that urinates backwards; also as *sb.*, an animal which does this; so †**Retromi·ngency. Retro-o·perative** *a.*, having a retrospective effect. **Retropu·lsion** (*Path.*), transference of an external disease to some internal part or organ. **Retropu·lsive** *a.* (*rare*) causing backward or reverse movements. **Retrovaccina·tion,** inoculation of cows with vaccine lymph from a human being.

b. Terms of *Anat.* and *Path.*, in which *retro-* is combined with an adj. denoting some part of the body, and has the sense 'situated behind' (the part in question), as *r.-mastoid, -ocular, -uterine,* etc.

Retroa·ct, *v.* 1795. [f. RETRO- + ACT *v.*] *intr.* To react; also, to operate in a backward direction or towards the past.

Retroa·ction. 1727. [f. RETRO- + ACTION. Cf. Fr. *rétroaction* (XVIII).] **1.** A retrospective action. **2.** Return action; reaction 1829.

Retroa·ctive, *a.* 1611. [f. RETRO- + ACTIVE (cf. *retrospective*), prob. after Fr. *rétroactif* (XVI).] **1.** Of enactments, etc.: Extending in scope or effect to matters which have occurred in the past; retrospective. **b.** Directed backwards in time 1822. **2.** Operating in a backward direction (*rare*) 1611. †**3.** Reactive (*rare*) –1802.

1. The r. clause in the..Bill will be either cancelled or amended 1897. Hence **Retroa·ctively** *adv.* So **Retroacti·vity,** the condition or fact of being r.

Re·trocede, *v.*¹ 1654. [– L. *retrocedere*; see RETRO-, CEDE.] **1.** *intr.* To go back, retire, recede. **2.** *Med.* Of gout: To strike inwardly 1866.

Retroce·de, *v.*² 1818. [– Fr. *rétrocéder* (XVI); see RETRO-, CEDE.] *trans.* To cede (territory) back again *to* a country, etc. So **Retroce·ssion**², the action or fact of ceding territory back.

Retrocedent (-sī·dĕnt), *a.* 1583. [– L. *retrocedens, -ent-*, pa. pple. of *retrocedere*; see RECEDE *v.*¹, -ENT.] **1.** *Astr.* = RETROGRADE *a.* 1. (*rare*). **2.** *Med.* **a.** Of gout: Striking inward 1776. **b.** Of tubercle: Retrograding or caseating 1898. So **Retroce·dence,** retrogression; retrocession.

Retrocession (-se·ʃən)¹. 1646. [– late L. *retrocessio*; see RETRO-, CESSION.] **1.** The action or fact of moving backward, retiring, or receding; retrogression. †**2.** *Astr.* = PRECESSION –1738. **3.** *Path.* The action or fact, on the part of a disease, of striking inwards, so as to affect the internal organs; the 'going in' of an eruption 1771.

Retrochoir (rī·troˌkwəiᵊɹ). 1802. [– med.L. *retrochorus*; see RETRO-, CHOIR.] *Eccl.* That part of a cathedral or large church which lies behind the high altar.

Re·troflex, *a.* 1776. [mod. use of L. *retroflexus*, pa. pple. of L. *retroflectere* bend back.] Bent or turned backwards; retorted. Chiefly *techn.* So **Re·troflexed** *a.*

Retrofle·xion. 1845. [f. RETRO- + FLEXION.] The fact or state of being turned back or retorted. Chiefly *Path.*, retroversion.

Retrogradation (rī:tro-, re:trogrădēⁱ·ʃən). 1554. [– late and med.L. *retrogradatio, -on-*; see RETRO-, GRADATION.] **1.** *Astr.* The apparent backward motion of a planet in the zodiac; motion of a heavenly body from east to west; a case or instance of this. **b.** The backward movement of the lunar nodes on the ecliptic 1727. **2.** The action or process of going back towards some point in investigation or reasoning 1577. **3.** The action or fact of moving or drawing back or backwards; retirement, retreat 1644. **4.** The action, fact, or condition of falling back in development; retrogression, decline 1748.

Retrograde (re·trogreⁱd), *a.* and *sb.* late ME. [– L. *retrogradus*, f. *retro-* RETRO- + *grad-* step; see GRADE *sb.*] **A.** *adj.* **1.** *Astr.* Of the planets: Apparently moving in a direction contrary to the order of the signs, or from east to west. **2.** Of movement: **a.** *Astr.* Apparently or actually contrary to the order of the signs; directed from east to west. late ME. **b.** Directed backwards; in a direction contrary to the previous motion; retiring, retreating 1622. **3.** Tending or inclined to go back or to revert; moving or leading backwards, *esp.* towards an inferior or less flourishing condition 1530. **4.** Moving backwards (in literal sense); returning upon the previous course 1564. **b.** Of order in enumeration, etc.: Inverse, reversed 1664. †**5.** Opposed, contrary, or repugnant *to* something –1797. **6.** As quasi-*adv.* In a backward or reverse direction 1619.

1. I would have sworn some r. planet was hanging over this unfortunate house of mine STERNE. **2. b.** A r. movement is always bad in this country WELLINGTON. **3.** The capital of a country may be stationary, progressive, or r. 1868. **5.** For your intent In going backe to Schoole in Wittenberg, It is most r. to our desire SHAKS. **6.** The reformation begun to go r. in Q. Elizabeth's time 1709.

B. *sb.* **1.** One who falls away or degenerates 1593. **2.** A backward movement or tendency (*rare*) 1613.

Retrograde (re·trogrēⁱd), *v.* 1582. [– L. *retrogradi*, later *retrogradare*, f. *retro-* RETRO- + *gradi* walk, etc.] **1.** *trans.* To turn back, reverse, revert; to make, or cause to become, retrograde. Now *rare.* **2.** *intr. Astr.* Of the planets, etc.: To go backward (in apparent motion) in the zodiac; to seem to travel from east to west 1601. **3.** To move backwards, to take a backward course; to retire, recede 1598. **4.** To fall back or revert towards a lower or less flourishing condition 1613.

1. We see, now, events forced on, which seem to retard or r. the civility of ages EMERSON. **4.** All that is human must r. if it do not advance GIBBON.

Re·trogress, *sb. rare.* 1814. [f. after PROGRESS *sb.* by prefix-substitution.] A retrogression.

Retrogre·ss, *v.* 1819. [f. after PROGRESS *v.* by prefix-substitution.] *intr.* To move backwards; to go back.

Retrogression (-gre·ʃən). 1646. [f. RETRO- + PRO)GRESSION, perh. as a var. of RETROGRADATION.] **1.** *Astr.* = RETROGRADATION 1. **2.** Movement in a backward or reverse direction. In early use *Math.* 1704. **3.** The action or fact of going back in respect of development or condition; return to a less advanced state or stage; a case or instance of this 1768. **b.** *Path.* The disappearance of an eruption 1899.

3. We find at best a very slow progress and on the whole a r. MACAULAY.

Retrogre·ssive, *a.* and *sb.* 1802. [f. after PROGRESSIVE by prefix-substitution.] **A.** *adj.* **1.** Working back in investigation or reasoning 1817. **2.** Moving or directed backwards 1830. **3.** Retrograde; tending to return to an inferior state; going back to a worse condition 1802. **b.** *spec.* in *Path.* or *Anat.* of changes in tissues or organs 1871. **B.** *sb.* One who has retrograde tendencies 1892. Hence **Retrogre·ssively** *adv.*

Retrorse (rĭtrǭ·ɹs), *a. rare.* 1825. [– L. *retrorsus*, contr. f. *retroversus*; see RETROVERSE *a.*] Turned backwards; reverted.

Retrospect (re·trospekt, rī·tro-), *sb.* 1602. [f. after PROSPECT *sb.* by prefix-substitution.] **1. a.** A regard or reference *to* some fact, authority, precedent, etc. **b.** Application to past time 1727. **2.** A backward look or view (*rare*) 1675. **b.** A view or survey of past time, *esp.* with ref. to one's own life or experiences 1678. **c.** A survey or review of some past course of events, acts, etc.; *esp.* in a particular sphere or line of things 1663. **3.** *attrib.* or as *adj.* Retrospective 1709.

1. b. The deed given in 1762..becomes good..by r. 1792. **2. b.** The most auspicious moment..for indulging in a r. 1807. **c.** A short r. is now necessary to view what Congress determined upon 1865.

Re·trospect, *v.* 1659. [app. f. prec.; cf. PROSPECT *v.*] **1.** *intr.* To indulge in retrospection. **b.** To look or refer back *to*; to reflect *on* 1689. **2.** *trans.* To consider, regard, or think of (some person or thing) retrospectively 1734.

1. b. To give a correct idea of the circumstances.., it may be useful to r. to an early period 1804.

Retrospection (retrŏspe·kʃən, rītrŏ-). 1633. [prob. f. RETROSPECT *v.*; see -ION. Cf., however, contemp. PROSPECTION.] **1.** The action of looking back (*rare*). **2.** The action of looking back or referring *to* something; reference or allusion to past events 1674. **3.** The action or fact of looking back upon, or surveying, past time 1729. **b.** An instance of this; *esp.* a survey of past life or experiences 1697. **c.** A review of past events or of some matter 1753. **4.** A retrogressive course of thought 1870.

4. The long r. lodges us at length at..first principles J. H. NEWMAN.

Retrospe·ctive, *a.* 1664. [f. RETROSPECT *sb.* + -IVE.] **1.** Directed to, contemplative of, past time. **2.** Of statutes, etc.: Operative with regard to past time; retroactive 1768. **3.** Backward; lying to the rear 1796.

1. The Sage, with r. eye POPE. R. researches 1873. **2.** Sentencing a man to death by r. law MACAULAY. **3.** R. views of Ambleside 1872. Hence **Retrospe·ctively** *adv.*

||**Retroussé** (rətruse), *a.* 1837. [Fr., pa. pple. of *retrousser*, f. *re-* RE- + *trousser* TRUSS *v.*] Turned up. (Chiefly of the nose.)

Re·troverse, *a. rare.* 1849. [– L. *retroversus*, f. *retro-* RETRO- + *versus* turned.] Turned or directed backwards; reversed.

Retroversion (-vɔ̄·ɹʃən). 1776. [In sense 1 f. contemp. *retroverted*, after *inverted*; in sense 2 app. f. RETROVERT *v.* after similar pairs; in sense 3 f. RETRO- + VERSION.] **1.** *Path.* The fact of (the uterus) becoming retroverted. **2.** The action of turning or looking back 1820. **3.** Retranslation into the original language 1888.

Retrove·rt, *v. rare.* 1639. [– late and med.L. *retrovertere*, f. *retro-* RETRO- + *vertere* turn.] *intr.* and *trans.* To turn back; to revert. Hence **Re·troverted** *ppl. a.* turned backwards, reverted; *spec.* in *Path.*, of the uterus.

†**Retru·se,** *a.* 1635. [– L. *retrusus*, pa. pple. of *retrudere* thrust back.] Concealed, recondite –1697.

Retrusion (rĭtrū·ʒən). *rare.* 1657. [orig. – med.L. *retrusio, -on-*, f. *retrus-* (see prec., -ION); in later use app. after *protrusion* or *intrusion* with substitution of prefix.] The action of putting away or back.

Rettery (re·təri). 1853. [f. RET *v.* + -ERY 2.] A place where flax is retted.

Re·tting, *vbl. sb.* 1727. [f. RET *v.* + -ING[1].] The preparation of flax, etc., by steeping or watering. Also *attrib.*

Retund (rĭtʊ·nd), *v.* Now *rare* or *Obs.* 1634. [– L. *retundere*, f. *re-* RE- + *tundere* beat.] **1.** *trans.* To weaken (some physical quality or agent); to diminish the strength or effect of. **2.** To beat back, repress (malice, etc.) 1642. **b.** To put down or refute 1653. **3.** To dull or blunt (the edge of a weapon) 1691. **4.** To drive or force back 1654.

3. *fig.* None of all these things could r. the edge of his expectations to find the wreck 1702.

Return (rĭtɔ̄·ɹn), *sb.* late ME. [– AFr. *retorn, return*, f. *retorner*; see next.] **I. 1.** The act of coming back to or from a place, person, or condition. **b.** *ellipt.* A return-ticket 1868. **c.** *ellipt. Mining.* A passage through which the ventilating air returns to the upcast shaft 1883. **2.** The fact of (a certain time or thing) recurring or coming round again; †a spell of some action 1589. **3.** The recurrence or renewal of some condition; *esp.* of illness or indisposition 1648.

1. Uppon the King's returne from his recreations att Newmarkett 1670. Phr. *By* (*†the*) *r.*, *by r. of post*: see POST *sb.*[2] III. **2.** At the returne of the yeere, the king of Syria will come vp against thee 1 *Kings* 20:22. Phr. *To wish* (one) *many* (*happy*) *returns* (*of the day*). **3.** The King had yesterday some returns of his ague 1694.

II. 1. A side or part which falls away, usu. at right angles, from the front or direct line of any work or structure. **a.** In cornices, pilasters, windows, etc. 1450. **b.** In appendages to, or minor parts of, buildings, walls, or other structures 1463. **c.** A wing or side of a building; †a side-street 1625. **2.** A bend or turn (in a line, etc.); a portion extending between two bends 1655. †**b.** A bend, turn, or winding in a stream, trench, gallery, etc. –1802. **3.** A consignment or cargo, an aggregate or class of commodities, which comes back (to a person) in exchange for merchandise sent out as a trading venture; the value or profits represented by this. (Now merged in b.) 1543. **b.** Pecuniary value resulting to a person from the exercise of some trade or occupation; gain, profit, or income, in relation to the means by which it is produced; also (in *pl.*), proceeds, results 1691. **c.** The fact of bringing value in exchange 1753.

2. We then put up a Line that was 666 Feet in Length, by eight Returns 1731. **3.** He had also six rich Returnes from the East India 1614. **b.** If the Merchant's R. be more than his Vse, (which 'tis certain it is, or else he will not Trade) LOCKE. **c.** What maketh rich, is a small profit and a quick r. 1753.

III. 1. The act, on the part of a sheriff, of sending back a writ to the court from which it issued, together with a statement of how far he has been able to carry out its instructions; hence, the report of a sheriff upon any writ directed to him. late ME. **b.** *ellipt.* for RETURN-DAY 1577. **2.** The official report made by a returning officer (orig. the sheriff) as to the election of a member or members of Parliament; hence, the fact of being elected to sit in Parliament 1459. †**b.** A response to a demand; a reply to a letter or dispatch –1655. **c.** A report of a formal or official character giving information as to the numbers, amounts, etc., of the subjects of inquiry; a set of statistics compiled by order of some authority 1756. **3.** Restoration *of* something to a person; *spec.* in *Law* 1641. **4.** The act of giving, or (more usu.) that which is given or received, by way of recompense, acknowledgement, or reciprocity 1542. **b.** The yield of some productive thing considered in relation to the original amount or expenditure 1626. **5.** A reply, answer, or retort. Now *rare* or *Obs.* 1599. **b.** A thrust, stroke, volley, etc., given in reply to one from an opponent or enemy 1705. **c.** *gen.* The act of sending back 1841. **d.** The act of returning a ball to an opponent or to another player; skill in doing this 1886. **6.** The act of bringing a thing back to a former position 1638. **7.** *pl.* †Refuse-tobacco. Later, a mild light-coloured tobacco for smoking 1789. **8.** A thing or person sent back. Chiefly *pl.* 1875.

2. c. A r. of the stores at this place is enclosed WASHINGTON. **4.** A grateful r. is due to the author of a benefit GIBBON. Phr. *In r.*; As rich men deale Guifts, Expecting in returne twenty for one SHAKS. *In r. for*; A present is usually given in r. for the hospitality 1857. **b.** In the course of a year they give two returns,—the lamb, and the fleece 1886. **5.** *Hen. V*, II. iv. 127. **8.** Any cheques or bill refused payment are called 'returns' 1875.

attrib. and *Comb.*, as *r. angle, cargo, current, journey, match*, etc.; **r. bend,** a U-shaped coupling for uniting the ends of pipes; **r. pipe,** a pipe through which water of condensation from a heater or radiator returns to the boiler; **-ticket,** a railway (or other) ticket available for the journey back from, as well as to, the place specified upon it. Hence **Retu·rnless** *a.* devoid of, not admitting of, a r.; that is without r.

Return (rĭtɔ̄·ɹn), *v.* ME. [– OFr. *retorner, returner* (mod. *retourner*) :– Rom. **retornare*; see RE-, TURN *v.*] **I.** *intr.* **1.** To come or go back to a place or person. **b.** *transf.* Of immaterial things, as time, etc. late ME. **2.** To go back in discourse; to revert *to* or resume a topic or subject. late ME. **3.** To revert, go back again, *to* (or *into*) a previous condition or state; to come back *to* oneself 1484. **b.** To revert *to* some practice, opinion, etc. 1534. **4.** To go back or revert *to* a previous owner 1460.

1. He returned, and I went on alone TYNDALL. Aristotle..returned to Athens after the death of Plato JOWETT. **b.** Till many years over thy head r.; So maist thou live MILT. **2.** I r. to the Story DE FOE. **3.** Dust thou art, and vnto dust shalt thou returne *Gen.* 3:19. **b.** They..retourned..to their errours agayne 1534.

II. 1. *trans.* To take or lead back upon the former direction; to turn at an angle to the previous course 1613. **2.** To turn or direct (one's eyes, sight, mind) back, or towards something 1509. **3.** To bring or convey back to a place or person. late ME. **b.** To bring back or restore (something) *to* or *into* a former position or state; to restore to a normal state 1462. **4.** To bring back in exchange; to yield in return. Now *rare.* 1596. †**b.** To turn over in business (*rare*) –1761. **5.** To put back *in* or *into* something; to restore *to* some receptacle 1611. **b.** *Mil.* To replace (arms, etc.) in the usual receptacle 1696.

1. I propose that the upper row of stalls should be returned at the west end of the chancel 1874. **2.** The King..then returns his thoughts for France 1647. **3.** Thou shalt my people returne from farre exyle 1538. **b.** Of a man turned into an asse, and returned againe into a man by one of Bodins witches 1584. **5.** Arbaces and Salemenes r. their swords to the scabbards BYRON.

III. 1. To send (a person or thing) back again 1459. **b.** To send back or reflect (sound or light) 1693. **2.** To report in answer to a writ or to some official demand for information; to state by way of a report or verdict. late ME. **b.** Of a sheriff: To report (certain persons) as having been appointed to serve on a jury or to sit in Parliament. Hence, in later use, of constituencies: To elect as a member of Parliament or some other administrative body. late ME. **3.** To send or turn back, to visit (something) *upon* a person. Now *rare.* 1547. †**b.** To retort (a charge, argument, etc.) *to* or *upon* a person –1719. **c.** *absol.* To retort or reply (*to* or *upon* a person) 1652.

1. b. And lake and fell Three times return'd the martial yell SCOTT. **2.** To be returned upon the surgeon's list as unfit for duty 1802. **b.** Hyde.. was returned both by Shaftesbury and Wootton Basset 1845. **3.** The Lord shall returne his blood vpon his owne head 1 *Kings* 2:32.

IV. 1. To give or render back (*to* a person) 1607. **b.** To give or send in return; to reply with 1599. **2.** To give or send (an answer) 1591. **b.** To say or state by way of reply or answer 1593. **3.** To give or render (thanks) 1591. **4.** To repay or pay back in some way, esp. with something similar 1599. **b.** To repay, or respond to, by a similar courtesy, compliment, etc. 1674. **c.** In games: To respond to (the play of one's partner or opponent) 1742.

1. Weight is returned for weight, to any person who carries their gold and silver to the Tower 1771. **b.** When Tierce is thrusted, r. Tierce or Sagoone 1705. **2.** Answer was return'd, that he will come SHAKS. **b.** He returned, that learning was beneath the greatness of a prince FULLER. **4.** He returns my Envy with Pity STEELE. Herbert did not r. the blow SCOTT. **b.** To r. a visit GOLDSM. **c.** He returns his Partner's Lead 1742.

Returnable (rĭtɔ̄·ɹnăb'l), *a.* late ME. [– AFr. *retornable*, OFr. *retournable*; see RETURN *v.*, -ABLE.] **1.** Of writs, etc.: Appointed to be returned (to the issuing court). **b.** That is (or are) to be returned 1658. **2.** Capable of being returned 1542. **3.** Able to return (*rare*) 1654. **4.** Admitting of return 1853.

1. b. The said letter..being..indorsed, r. to the pay-office 1758. **4.** Return tickets at one fare.. r. by the 7.30, 8.20 and 8.55 a.m. trains only 1856.

Retu·rn-day. 1651. [See RETURN *sb.* III. 1.] *Law.* The day on which a writ is appointed to be returned.

Retu·rned, *ppl. a.* late ME. [f. RETURN *v.* + -ED[1].] **1.** Bent or turned back in some way; *esp.* made with a return. **2.** That has come back 1600. **3.** Sent or brought back 1722.

3. *R. empty*, an empty cask, case, etc., returned to the sender; *transf.* a colonial clergyman who has come back to England.

Retu·rner. 1611. [f. as prec. + -ER[1].] **1.** One who, or that which comes back or returns. **2.** One who or that which gives or brings back 1691.

Retuse (rĭtiū·s), *a.* 1753. [– L. *retusus*, pa. pple. of *retundere* RETUND.] *Bot.* and *Ent.* Terminating in a broad or rounded end with a depression in the centre.

Reunion (rī,yū·niən). 1610. [– Fr. *réunion*, f. *réunir* or AL. *reunio, -on-*, f. *reunire* unite; see RE- 5 a, UNION.] **1.** The action of reuniting or coming together again; the state of being reunited. **2.** The fact of (persons) meeting again after separation 1703. **3.** A meeting or social gathering of persons acquainted with each other, or having some previous link of connection. Often in Fr. form. 1820.

1. The re-union to the state, of all the Catholicks of that country BURKE. **2.** His r. with his disciples 1843. Hence **Reu·nionist,** one who desires reunion; esp. of the Anglican with the Roman Catholic Church.

Reunite (rī,yunəi·t), *v.* 1591. [– *reunit-*, pa. ppl. stem of AL. *reunire* XIV; in later use, f. RE- + UNITE *v.*] **1.** *trans.* To unite or bring together again; to join together after separation. **2.** *intr.* To come together again and unite 1660. Hence **Reuni·table** *a.* **Reuni·tedly** *adv.*

Rev., abbrev. f. REVEREND.

Rev. (rev), abbrev. f. REVOLUTION 4 c. Hence **Rev** *v. trans.* to work *up* (an engine), to a high number of revolutions per minute; also *intr.* of the engine. 1901.

Revalenta (revăle·ntă). 1850. [Arbitrary alteration of *ervalenta*, f. *ervum lens* LENTIL.] A preparation of lentil and barley flour.

Revalorization (rīvæ:lŏrəizē[1]·ʃən). 1926. [– Fr. *révalorisation*; see RE-, VALORIZATION.] Establishing a fresh price or value of a commodity, etc.; *esp.* restoration of currency to its former or normal value. So **Reva·lorize** *v. trans.*

Reveal (rǐvī·l), *sb.*[1] *rare.* 1629. [f. REVEAL *v.*] A revealing, revelation, disclosure.

Reveal (rǐvī·l), *sb.*[2] 1688. [f. †*revale* (XV) lower, bring down – OFr. *revaler*, f. *re-* RE- + *avaler* lower; see AVALE *v.*] A side of an opening or recess which is at right angles to the face of the work; *esp.* the vertical side of a doorway or window-opening between the door- or window-frame and the arris.

Reveal (rǐvī·l), *v.* late ME. [– (O)Fr. *révéler* or L. *revelare*, f. *re-* RE- + *velum* VEIL.] **1.** *trans.* To disclose, make known (*to* a person) in a supernatural manner. **2.** To disclose, divulge, make known (*to* a person) by discourse or communication. late ME. †**b.** To betray –1657. **3.** To display, show, make clear or visible, exhibit 1494.

1. A matter revealed and prefigured unto Domitian in a dream BACON. **2.** Did not she..r. The secret wrested from me? MILT. **3.** In compleat Glory shee reueal'd her selfe SHAKS. Our inward loue, let outward deedes reueale it 1605. Hence **Revealabi·lity.** **Revea·lable** *a.* capable of being revealed, **-ness.** **Revea·ler,** one who or that which reveals. **Revea·lment,** the act of revealing; revelation.

Revealed (rǐvī·ld), *ppl. a.* 1562. [f. prec. + -ED[1].] Brought to light, disclosed; *esp.* made known by divine or supernatural agency, as *r. religion.*

Reveille (rǐvæ·li, rǐve·li). Also †**reveillez.** 1644. [– Fr. *réveillez*, imper. pl. of *réveiller* awaken, f. *re-* RE- + *veiller* :– L. *vigilare* keep watch.] A morning signal given to soldiers, usu. by beat of drum or by bugle, to waken them and notify that it is time to rise.

Sound a R., Sound, Sound, The Warrior God is come DRYDEN. While our slumbrous spells assail ye, Dream not..Bugles here shall sound reveillé SCOTT. vars. **Reveil, reveil** (*rare*) So **Reveillez.**

Revel (re·věl), *sb.* ME. [– OFr. *revel*, noisy mirth, etc., f. *reveler*; see next.] **1.** Riotous or noisy mirth or merry-making. late ME. **2.** An occasion or course of merry-making or noisy festivity, with dancing, games, masking, acting, or other forms of lively entertainment ME. **b.** *spec.* In the south-western counties, a parish festival or feast; a fair 1478.

1. The brief night goes In babble and r. and wine TENNYSON. **2.** Faerie Elves, Whose midnight Revels..some belated Peasant sees MILT. Phr. *Master of the Revels*, a person (permanently or temporarily) appointed to organize or lead revels, esp. in the Royal Household or the Inns of Court.

Revel (re·věl), *v.*[1] ME. [– OFr. *reveler* (refl.) rebel, rejoice noisily :– L. *rebellare* REBEL *v.*] **1.** *intr.* To make merry; to indulge in pastime or festivities; to take part in a revel. **b.** To enjoy oneself greatly, to take intense pleasure or delight, *in* something 1754. **2.** *trans.* **a.** To spend or waste (time) in revelry 1628. **b.** To squander (money) in revelling 1813.

1. Antony that Reuels long a-nights SHAKS. Thou must..leave duty to r. it gaily with the wild and with the wicked SCOTT. **b.** Maggots r. in putrefaction PALEY. Hence **Re·velment,** the act of revelling; revelry.

†**Reve·l,** *v.*[2] 1597. [– L. *revellere*, f. *re-* RE- + *vellere* pull.] *trans.* To draw back (humours or blood) from some part of the system –1752.

Revelation (revél-, revělē[i]·ʃən). ME. [– (O)Fr. *révélation* or Chr.L. *revelatio, -on-*, f. *revelat-*, pa. ppl. stem of L. *revelare*; see REVEAL *v.*, -ION.] **1.** The disclosure of knowledge to man by a divine or supernatural agency. **2.** Something disclosed or made known by divine or supernatural means. late ME. **b.** A striking disclosure of something previously unknown or not realized 1862. **3.** *The R.* (*of St. John*), the last book of the New Testament; the Apocalypse. So in pl. (*the*) *Revelations.* late ME. **4.** Disclosure of facts made by a person; exposure of something previously disguised or concealed 1475.

1. He sayd, how he had all thinges shewed him by r. 1560. **2. b.** We have a veritable r. in Science H. SPENCER. **4.** This astounding r. excited alarm and anger 1880. Hence **Revela·tionist,** one who makes a r., *esp.* the author of the Apocalypse; one who believes in r. **Revela·tor,** one who or that which makes a r. **Re·velatory** *a.* serving to reveal.

Reve·llent, *a.* (*sb.*) *rare.* 1661. [– L. *revellens, -ent-*, pr. pple. of *revellere*; see REVEL *v.*[2], -ENT.] **A.** *adj.* Revulsive 1822. **B.** as *sb.* A revulsive agent.

Reveller (re·vĕlə). late ME. [f. REVEL *v.*[1] + -ER[1].] One who takes part in a revel; one who is given to revelling, or leads a disorderly life.

The barbarous dissonance Of Bacchus and his Revellers MILT.

Re·velous, *a. rare.* late ME. [– OFr. *revelous*, f. *revel*; see REVEL *sb.*, -OUS.] Given to or marked by revelling.

Re·vel-rout. *arch.* or *Obs.* 1553. [f. REVEL *sb.* + ROUT *sb.*] **1.** Uproarious revelry; boisterous merriment. **b.** An occasion of revelling; a revel 1652. **2.** A crowd or party of revellers (*rare*) 1655.

1. Then made they revell route and goodly glee SPENSER.

Revelry (re·vělri). late ME. [f. REVEL *sb.* + -RY.] The act of revelling, merry-making; boisterous gaiety or mirth.

Mean while welcom Joy, and Feast, Midnight shout, and R. MILT. There was a sound of r. by night BYRON.

‖**Revenant** (rəvnaṅ). 1828. [Fr., pr. pple. of *revenir* return.] **1.** One who returns from the dead; a ghost. **2.** One who returns to a place 1886.

Revendication (rǐvendikē[i]·ʃən). 1760. [– Fr. *revendication*, f. *revendiquer* claim back.] The action of claiming back or recovering by a formal claim.

Revenge (rǐve·ndʒ), *sb.* 1547. [f. next. Cf. Fr. †*revenge*, var. of *revenche* (mod. *revanche*).] **1.** The act of doing hurt or harm to another in return for wrong or injury suffered; satisfaction obtained by repayment of injuries 1566. **b.** A desire to repay injuries by inflicting hurt in return 1586. **2.** With possess. pron. **a.** One's desire to be revenged, or the gratification of this 1547. †**b.** The avenging of a person (*rare*) –1653. **3.** A particular act of repaying injuries or wrongs 1582. **4.** Repayment *of* some wrong, injury, etc., by the infliction of hurt or harm 1615. †**5.** Punishment; chastisement –1697. **6.** An opportunity of retaliation or retrieval; *spec.* in cards, chess, etc., a return game, esp. in phr. *to give one* (*his*) *r.* 1672.

1. Reuenge now goes To lay a complot to betray thy Foes SHAKS. A desire of r. upon the plunderers of his country GOLDSM. **b.** Fury in his eyes and reuenge in his heart SIDNEY. **2.** I..vowed to have my r. 1887. **b.** 1 *Hen. VI*, I. v. 35. **4.** The Reuenge of that wrong, putteth the Law out of Office BACON. **6.** I'll give you R. whenever you please SWIFT. Hence **Reve·ngeful** *a.* vindictive; **-ly** *adv.* **Reve·ngeless** *a.* unrevenging; unavenged.

Revenge (rǐve·ndʒ), *v.* late ME. [– OFr. *revenger*, var. of *revencher* (mod. *revancher*) :– late L. *revindicare*, f. *re-* RE- + *vindicare* VENGE.] **1.** *refl.* To avenge oneself; to take revenge *on* a person *for* a wrong, injury, insult, etc., received or resented. Also in *pass.* **2.** *trans.* To inflict punishment or exact retribution for (an injury, harm, wrong, etc., done to oneself or another) 1456. **b.** To maintain, uphold, or vindicate (one's cause, etc.) by some act of retribution or punishment 1526. **3.** To avenge (a person, etc.) 1470. †**4.** To punish, exact punishment for (a wrong, crime, or sin) –1713. **5.** *absol.* To take vengeance or revenge 1456.

1. Methinks I should r. me of my wrongs MARLOWE. **b.** Now Ile doo't, and so he goes to Heauen, And so am I reueng'd SHAKS. **2.** When my Betters give me a Kick I am apt to r. it with six upon my Footman SWIFT. Her brother..was slain, and she revenged his death 1727. **3.** The brother..immediately took up arms to r. him 1841. **4.** The Lord will surely reuenge thy pride *Ecclus.* 5:3. **5.** The Lord reuengeth, and is furious *Nahum* 1:2. Hence **Reve·ngeable** *a.* †revengeful; worthy or capable of being revenged. †**Reve·ngeance,** revenge, vengeance. **Reve·ngement,** revenge, retribution; †punishment. **Reve·nger.** **Reve·ngingly** *adv.*

Revengeful (rǐve·ndʒful), *a.* 1586. [f. REVENGE *sb.* + -FUL 1.] Full of revenge; vindictive. Hence **Reve·ngeful-ly** *adv.*, **-ness.**

Revenue (re·věniu). late ME. [– (O)Fr. *revenu*, †*revenue*, subst. use of masc. and fem. pa. pple. of *revenir* :– L. *revenire* return, f. *re-* RE- + *venire* come. Cf. AL. *reventus* (pl.) revenues.] †**1.** Return to a place (*rare*) –1532. †**2.** The return, yield, or profit *of* any lands, property, or other important source of income. Also *pl.* in same sense. –1654. **3.** That which comes in to one as a return from property or possessions, esp. of an extensive kind; income from any source (but esp. when large and not directly earned). late ME. **4.** *pl.* The collective items or amounts which constitute an income, *esp.* that of a person having extensive landed possessions, a ruler, city, state, etc. late ME. **5.** An income; an amount of money regularly accruing to a person 1614. **b.** A separate source or item of (private or public) income 1624. **6.** The annual income of a government or state, from all sources, out of which the public expenses are defrayed 1690. **b.** The department of the civil service which deals with the collection of the national funds 1700.

2. *Rich. II*, I. iv. 46. **3.** I haue a Widdow Aunt, a dowager, Of great reuennew SHAKS. **4.** They took Care of the Church's Revenues 1704. **5. b.** This..supplied a r. to the crown 1879. **6.** *Inland r.*: see INLAND *a.* 2. **b.** When I was employ'd in the R. SWIFT.

attrib. and *Comb.*, as *r. act, officer*, etc.; *r.-earning, -producing.* Hence **Re·venued** *a.* having (large or rich) revenues.

Reverb (rǐvɔ̄·ɹb), *v.* 1605. [irreg. – L. *reverberare*; in modern use, after Shakespeare.] *trans.* and *intr.* To reverberate, re-echo.

Reverberant (rǐvɔ̄·ɹbĕrănt), *a.* 1572. [– Fr. *réverbérant*, pr. pple. of *réverbérer*; in sense 2 also f. REVERBERATE *v.* + -ANT.] **1.** *Her.* Of a lion's tail: Turned up like the letter S, with the end outwards. **2.** Reverberating; resonant 1807.

Reve·rberate, *pa. pple.* and *ppl. a.* 1589. [– L. *reverberatus*, pa. pple. of *reverberare*; see next, -ATE[2].] **1.** Reverberated. †**2.** Reverberating –1605.

2. Hallow your name to the reuerberate hilles SHAKS.

Reverberate (rǐvɔ̄·ɹbĕre[i]t), *v.* 1547. [– *reverberat-*, pa. ppl. stem of L. *reverberare*, f. *re-* RE- + *verberare* strike, beat, f. *verbera* rods, scourge; see -ATE[3].] **I.** *trans.* **1.** To beat, drive, or force back; to repel, repulse. Now *rare* or *Obs.* **b.** To send back, return, re-echo (a sound or noise) 1591. **c.** To cast back, reflect (light, heat, etc.) 1638. **d.** *absol.* To cause reverberation 1763. **2.** *trans.* To subject to the heat of a reverberatory furnace. Also *absol.* 1610.

1. b. The hilles, to heav'n, r. their voyce FLORIO. **c.** On which the Sun shining..,its Rays were reverberated as from another Sun 1745. **2.** Steel corroded with Vinegar,..and after reverberated by fire 1646.

II. *intr.* **1.** †**a.** To turn or bend back (*rare*) –1608. **b.** To recoil *upon*, to have a respondent effect *on*, to appeal responsively *to*, something (*rare*) 1713. **c.** Of material objects: To rebound 1837. **2.** To shine or reflect *from* a surface, etc. 1598. †**b.** To shine or glow *on* (something) with reflected beams –1650. **3.** Of sound: To resound, re-echo 1613. **4.** Of flames, etc.: To strike *upon*, to pass *over* or *into*, as the result of being forced back 1704.

1. c. Our rifle-balls reverberated from their hides like cork pellets from a pop-gun target 1856. **3.** The shock, the shout, the groan of war, R. along that vale BYRON.

Reverberation (rǐvɔ̄ɹbĕrē[i]·ʃən). late ME. [– (O)Fr. *réverbération* or med.L. *reverberatio, -on-*, f. as prec.; see -ION.] **1. a.** The fact, on the part *of* a thing, of being driven or forced back, esp. after impact (*rare*). **b.** Reflection *of* light or heat 1460. **c.** Return or re-echoing *of* sounds 1626. †**2. a.** The action *of* something in reflecting light or heat –1686. †**b.** The action *of* a thing in returning a sound, or the result of this –1657. **3.** The action of driving or sending back, reflecting light, returning a sound, etc.; the fact of being reflected, returned, etc.; an instance of this 1597. **b.** The fact or process of subjecting to heat in a reverberatory furnace 1460. **4. a.** A re-echoing sound 1845. **b.** A reflection of light or colour 1860.

1. a. The sound made by r. of the aire, which men call Eccho HOLLAND. **b.** Like the several Reverberations of the same Image from two opposite Looking-Glasses ADDISON.

Reverberative (rǐvɔ̄·ɹbĕre[i]tiv), *a.* 1716.

[f. Reverberate *v.* + -ive.] Inclined to reverberate; having the nature of a reverberation.

Reverberator (rĭvə̄·ɹbĕreˡtəɹ). 1794. [f. as prec. + -or 2. Cf. Fr. *réverbère.*] **1.** A reflector; a reflecting lamp. **2.** One who reverberates 1803.

Reverberatory (rĭvə̄·ɹbĕrătəri), *sb.* 1651. [– mod.L. *reverberatorium*, subst. use of the adj; see next, -ory¹.] A reverberatory furnace or kiln.

Reverberatory (rĭvə̄·ɹbĕrătəri), *a.* 1605. [– mod. L. *reverberatorius*, f. *reverberare;* see Reverberate *v.*, -ory.²] **1.** Of fire: Forced or driven back by some contrivance upon the substance which is subjected to its operation. **b.** Of heat: Produced by reverberation 1799. **2.** Of a furnace, kiln, etc.: So constructed that the flame is forced back upon the substance exposed to it 1672.

†**Reverdure,** *v.* 1525. [– OFr. *reverdurer* (mod. *reverdir*); see Re-, Verdure.] *trans.* To clothe again with verdure.

Revere (rĭvīᵊ·ɹ), *v.* 1611. [– Fr. *révérer* or L. *reverēri*, f. *re-* Re- + *verēri* feel awe of, fear.] *trans.* To hold in, or regard with, deep respect or veneration. Also *absol.*

For all..revered the name of Cæsar Bryce. Hence **Reve·rable** *a.* (*rare*). **Reve·rer,** one who reveres.

Reverence (re·vĕrĕns), *sb.* ME. [– (O)Fr. *révérence* – L. *reverentia*; see Reverent, -ence.] **1.** Deep or due respect felt or shown towards a person on account of his or her position or relationship; deference. Now *rare* or *Obs.* **b.** Deep respect and veneration for some thing, place, or person regarded as having a sacred or exalted character ME. **2.** A gesture indicative of respect; an obeisance; a bow or curtsy. late ME. **3.** The condition or state of being respected or venerated. late ME. **4.** *Your r.*, A respectful form of address, now only used by the lower classes, esp. in Ireland, in speaking to a clergyman ME. **b.** *His r.*, as the designation of a clergyman 1762.

1. In speakynge of my Princes I must use a due r. and regarde 1572. **b.** I hold the church in holy r. Lytton. Women are notably deficient in real r. for authority 1897. Phr. *To do r. to*, to show respect or veneration for (a person or thing) by some action. **2.** [He] had never seen his friend offer so low a r. 1833. **3.** Two reigns..passed in external glory and domestic r. Hallam. Phr. †*Save* (a person's) *r.*, an apologetic phrase introducing a criticism, contradiction, etc., that might offend the hearer; so †*saving* (a person's) *r.*

Reverence (re·vĕrĕns), *v.* ME. [– AFr. *reverencer* (Gower), f. *reverence*; see prec.] †**1.** *trans.* To salute (a person) with deep respect; to show respect for (a person) by bowing, kneeling, etc.; to make obeisance to –1686. †**b.** To treat with respect or deference –1592. **2.** To regard with reverence or veneration as having a divine or sacred character; †to worship in some manner ME. **b.** To hold in high respect; to venerate 1548.

2. Ye shall keepe my Sabbaths, and reuerence my Sanctuary *Lev.* 19:30. **b.** So prone To rev'rence what is ancient Cowper. Hence **Re·verencer,** one who reverences; a respecter *of* some thing or person.

Reverend (re·vĕrĕnd), *a.* (and *sb.*) 1449. [– (O)Fr. *révérend* or L. *reverendus*, gerundive of *reverēri* Revere.] **1.** Of persons: Worthy of deep respect or reverence on account of (†rank), age, or character; †commanding respect by personal ability or great learning. **b.** As a courteous or respectful form of address 1486. **2.** As a respectful epithet applied to members of the clergy. Also *Very R.* (of deans), *Right R.* (of bishops), *Most R.* (of archbishops). 1485. **b.** Prefixed to the name (and designation) of the person, and frequently abbreviated as *Rev.* 1642. **c.** *sb.* A clergyman; a cleric or divine. Also *Right R.*, a bishop. Now *illiterate.* 1608. **3.** Of things, places, etc.: Worthy of, or inspiring, reverence 1586. **4.** Connected with, characteristic of, belonging to, the clergy 1645. **5.** = Reverent *a.* 2. Now somewhat *rare.* 15..

1. Next Camus, r. Sire, went footing slow Milt. **b.** Yet Reuerend Madame, but forget what's past Heywood. **2. c.** We are not so meddlesome as you reverends are 1894. **3.** The big tears..straying down his r. cheeks Richardson. **4.** A r. ignorance in fear to be convicted Milt. Hence **Re·verendly** *adv.* reverently; in a way, to a degree, that inspires reverence.

Reverent (re·vĕrĕnt), *a.* late ME. [In sense 1 – OFr. *reverent* or f. after med.L. *reverentissimus* most reverend (of bishops); in sense 2 – L. *reverens, -ent-*, pr. pple. of *reverēri* Revere.] **1.** = Reverend *a.* Now *illiterate.* **2.** Characterized by, exhibiting or feeling, reverence; deeply respectful 1486.

1. No harm is intended to the r. sage of the mountain 1796. **2.** Lowly r. Towards either Throne they bow Milt. Hence **Re·verent-ly** *adv.*, **-ness** (*rare*).

Reverential (revĕre·nʃăl), *a.* 1555. [– Fr. †*révérencial, révérentiel* or med.L. *reverentialis*, f. as prec.; see -ial.] **1.** Of the nature of, inspired or characterized by, reverence; reverent. **2.** Inspiring reverence; venerable, reverend (*rare*) 1654.

1. He did it for a r. fear he had of his father 1555. **2.** [A] fatherly, prolixe, and reverentiall beard 1656. Hence **Revere·ntial-ly** *adv.*, **-ness.**

Reverie (re·vĕri), *sb.* late ME. [In xiv – OFr. *reverie* rejoicing, revelry, wildness, rage, f. *rever* (mod. *rêver* dream), of unkn. origin. In xvii–xviii (often *resverie*) – later Fr. *resverie*, now *rêverie*; see -ery.] †**1.** A state of delight. Chaucer. †**2.** Violent or rude language. late ME. only. **3.** A fantastic, fanciful, unpractical, or purely theoretical idea or notion 1653. **4.** A fit of abstracted musing; a 'brown study' or day-dream 1657. **b.** *Mus.* An instrumental composition suggestive of a dreamy or musing state 1880. **5.** The fact, state, or condition of being lost in thought or engaged in musing 1690.

3. I indeed desire Men to look upon [this] rather as a Dream or Resvery than a rational Proposition 1687. **4.** Walking about in a sad r.,..unconscious of the world around her W. Irving. **5.** His fits of r. were..frequent 1762.

‖**Revers** (rĭvīᵊ·ɹz, ri·vəɹz, Fr. rəvę̄r). 1838. [Fr., = Reverse *sb.*] A part of a coat, vest, bodice, etc., of which the edge is turned back so as to exhibit the under surface; the material covering this reversed edge. (Freq. used as a *pl.*)

Reversal (rĭvə̄·ɹsăl), *sb.* 1488. [f. Reverse *v.* + -al¹ 2.] **1.** *Law.* The act of reversing or annulling a decree, sentence, punishment, etc.; the fact of being reversed or annulled. **2.** The act or process of reversing; an instance of this 1698. **3.** Reversion *to* some practice, etc. (*rare*) 1862.

1. The effect of the r. of an outlawry in a civil action 1797. **2.** The effects of the r. of the poles of magnets, as caused by lightning 1794.

†**Reve·rsal,** *a. rare.* 1656. [– Fr. *réversal* or med.L. *reversalis*; see next, -al¹.] Revocatory –1715.

Reverse (rĭvə̄·ɹs), *sb.* late ME. [– (O)Fr. *revers* or †*reverse* – subst. uses of L. *reversus*; see next.] **I. 1.** The opposite or contrary of something. **2.** The opposite or contrary *of* or *to* something specified. late ME. **b.** Used with general terms or with adjs. to express more than a mere negation 1783. **3.** That side of a coin, medal, or seal which does not bear the main device or inscription; the back. (Opp. to Obverse B 1.) 1625. **b.** The design, etc., on the reverse side 1623. **c.** The back or verso of a leaf (in a book) 1824. **d.** In general use as the correlative of *obverse* 1831. **4.** The back of a mountain, mound, etc. 1777. **5.** *In r.* **a.** *Mil.* In the rear 1781. **b.** Contrary to the usual manner; of a motor-car, etc.: On the reverse gear 1875.

1. The r. also happens; and very plausible schemes..have often shameful and lamentable conclusions Burke. **2. b.** Remarks which are the r. of complimentary 1860. **5. a.** To take the enemy in r., and intercept their retreat 1781.

II. †**1.** A back-handed stroke or cut –1656. **2.** An adverse change of fortune; a disaster; esp. in mod. use, a defeat in battle 1526. **3.** = Reversal *sb.* Now *rare* or *Obs.* 1589. **4.** The act of reversing in dancing 1888.

2. Some reverses which happened in the beginning of that war Burke. Hence **Reve·rseless** *a.* (*rare*) incapable of being reversed.

Reverse (rĭvə̄·ɹs), *a.* and *adv.* ME. [– OFr. *revers(e* – L. *reversus, -a*, pa. pple. of *revertere* Revert *v.*] **A.** *adj.* **1.** Opposite or contrary (*to* something else, or to each other) in character, order, succession, etc. **b.** Lying behind or to the back 1851. †**2.** Of blows, etc.: Back-handed –1667. **3.** *Mil.* Connected with, commanding, or facing towards the rear 1702. **4.** Acting in a way contrary or opposite to that which is customary 1860.

1. The..story is the contrary to truth, and happened in the very r. manner Burke. **3.** The flank at the other extremity from the pivot of a division is termed the r. flank 1867.

B. *adv.* In a reverse way; reversely. late ME. The edg of their own Proverb falls r. upon themselves Milt. Hence **Reve·rsely** *adv.*

Reverse (rĭvə̄·ɹs), *v.* ME. [– OFr. *reverser* (now *ren-*) – late L. *reversare*, f. L. *reversus*; see prec.] **I.** *trans.* †**1. a.** To bring back *to* or *into* a state or condition, a place, the mind, etc. –1590. **b.** To remove or put away; to divert or turn away (*rare*) –1639. †**2.** To overthrow, overturn, upset, or throw down (a person or thing) –1587. †**b.** To confute –1581. **3.** To turn or place upside down; to invert. late ME. **b.** To hold or carry (a weapon) in the position contrary to that in which it is ready for use 1650. †**4.** To turn back or trim (a garment) *with* some other material –1523. **5.** To revoke, abrogate, annul (a decree, act, measure, etc.) *esp.* in legal use. late ME. **b.** To undo (work) 1725. **6.** To turn the other way, in respect of position or aspect; to transpose, turn inside out. late ME. **7.** To convert into something of an opposite character or tendency; to turn the contrary way; to alter or change completely 1500. **b.** To employ, perform, in a way opposite to the former or usual method 1728. **8.** To turn in the opposite direction; to send on a course contrary to the previous one 1509. **b.** To cause (an engine) to work or revolve in the contrary direction. Also *absol.* 1860.

1. The knight..to his..remembraunce did r. The ugly vew of his deformed crimes Spenser. **b.** That old Dame said many an idle verse, Out of her daughters hart fond fancies to r. Spenser. **3.** Without his rod revers't,..We cannot free the Lady Milt. **5.** It was hoped..to get my Lord Chancellor to r. a decree of his Pepys. As she could not r. the curse..she did what she could to mitigate it 1869. **b.** The work she plied; but, studious of delay, By night reversed the labours of the day Pope. **7.** I like not this charitie reversed, when it begins farre off and neglects those at home Fuller. **8.** The ingenious mode of consuming smoke by reversing the flame 1824. **b.** The engines..were stopped and reversed full speed 1883.

II. *intr.* **1.** To draw back or away; to move backwards (*rare*). late ME. **b.** In dancing, *esp.* waltzing: To move or turn in a contrary direction 1884. †**2.** To fall over, fall down –1530. †**3.** To return *back* or *home* –1647. So **Reve·rsement,** the act of reversing, or fact of being reversed. **Reve·rser** (*spec.* in *Electr.*).

Reversed (rĭvə̄·ɹst), *ppl. a.* late ME. [f. Reverse *v.* + -ed¹.] Turned backwards, or placed the contrary way; inverted. **b.** In various special uses 1682.

b. When the spire of a shell turns in a direction opposite to what is normal, it is said to be 'r.' 1888. Hence **Reve·rsedly** *adv.*

Reversible (rĭvə̄·ɹsĭb'l), *a.* and *sb.* 1648. [f. Reverse *v.* + -ible.] **A.** *adj.* Admitting of being reversed; capable of reversing. **B.** *sb.* A cloth which is faced on both sides to allow of its being turned 1860. Hence **Reversibi·lity.**

Reve·rsing, *ppl. a.* 1864. [f. Reverse *v.* + -ing².] **1.** That reverses or causes reversal. **2.** Of the nature of, characterized by, reversal (of an action, process, etc.) 1878.

1. *R. layer* or *stratum*, a stratum of the solar atmosphere, reversing the dark lines of the ordinary solar spectrum.

Reversion (rĭvə̄·ɹʃən). late ME. [– (O)Fr. *réversion* or L. *reversio, -on-*, f. *revers-*, pa. ppl. stem of *revertere*; see Revert *v.*, -ion.] **I. 1.** *Law.* That part of an estate which remains undisposed of after the determination of the particular estate, and falls into the possession of the original grantor or his representative. late ME. **2.** *Sc. Law.* The power to redeem an estate that is security for a debt or a judgement 1469. **3.** *transf.* The right of succeeding to the possession *of* something after another is done with it, or simply of obtaining it at some future time; a thing or possession which one expects to obtain 1530. **b.** The right of succession to an office or place of emolument, after the death or retirement of the holder 1623. **4.** A deferred or reversionary annuity 1771.

1. A r. of the best lease 1587. 3. Is there no bright r. in the sky, For those who greatly think, or bravely die? POPE.

Phr. **In r.**: (*a*) conditional upon the expiry of a grant or the death of a grantee; (*b*) destined to come into a person's possession or to be realized in the future. Were our England in reuersion his, And he our subjects next degree in hope SHAKS. The prospect of too good a fortune in r. when I married her JOHNSON. An annuity is said to be in r., when the purchaser..does not immediately enter upon possession 1771. The whole capital which Nicholas found himself entitled to either in possession, r., remainder, or expectancy DICKENS.

II. †**1.** The residue or remainder *of* something; also, a remnant, a small number –1824. †**2.** The action or fact of returning to or from a place –1741. **b.** The action or fact of returning to a certain condition, practice, or belief; an instance of this 1582. **c.** *Biol.* The fact or action of reverting to a primitive or ancestral type or condition; an instance of this 1859. **3.** The act of turning something or fact of being turned the reverse way 1677. **b.** *Math.* (See quot.) 1698.

3. b. R. of series is the method of finding the value of the quantity whose several powers are involved in a series, in terms of the quantity which is equal to the given series 1797.

Reve·rsional, *a.* 1675. [f. prec. + -AL¹ 1.] = next 2.

Reversionary (rĭvə̄·ɹʃənări), *a.* and *sb.* 1651. [f. as prec. + -ARY¹.] **1.** Entitled to the reversion of something (*rare*). **2.** Of the nature of, connected with, a reversion 1720. **3.** *Biol.* Relating to reversion to type; tending to revert; atavistic 1873.

2. A r. grant of the Mastership of the Rolls 1845. 3. What may be termed r. degeneration 1896.

B. *sb.* A reversioner (*rare*) 1660.

Reversioner (rĭvə̄·ɹʃənəɹ). 1614. [f. REVERSION + -ER¹.] One who possesses the reversion to an estate, office, etc.; an heir in reversion.

‖**Reversis.** Now *Hist.* 1814. [Fr., var. of *reversi*, earlier *reversin* – It. *rovescina*, f. *rovesciare* reverse.] An obsolete card game in which the object was to avoid winning the tricks.

Revert (rĭvə̄·ɹt, rī·vəɹt), *sb.* 1655. [f. next; in sense 2, after *convert, pervert.*] **1.** A return *to* some means, etc. 1895. **2.** One who returns to his previous faith 1655.

Revert (rĭvə̄·ɹt), *v.* ME. [– OFr. *revertir* or L. *revertere*, f. *re-* RE- + *vertere* turn.] **I.** *intr.* †**1.** To recover consciousness; to come to oneself again –1560. **3.** To return, to come or go back, to or from a place or position. Now *rare.* late ME. **3.** *Law.* To return to the former possessor or his heirs 1447. **4.** To return *to* a custom, practice, idea, etc. 1612. **5.** To go back, recur, *to* a former subject of discourse 1587. **b.** To return *to* a subject of thought 1822. **6.** To return *to* a former condition 1638. **b.** To return *to* an earlier or primitive form; to reproduce the characteristics of an ancestral type 1859. **c.** To fall back into a wild state 1884.

4. The Christians..had reverted to the habit of wearing the white turban 1836. 5. b. His ideas.. naturally reverted to his neighbour SCOTT. 6. b. That our domestic varieties, when run wild, gradually..r. in character to their aboriginal stocks DARWIN.

II. *trans.* †**1.** To cause to return, *esp.* to bring back or restore, to a person, place, etc. –1651. **2.** To turn (one's eyes or steps) back; to direct backwards 1632. **3.** To turn the other way; to reverse, invert, turn up. Now *rare* or *Obs.* late ME. **b.** *Math. To r. a series*, to determine the value of a quantity whose several powers are involved in a series, in terms of the quantity which is the sum of the series 1737. †**4.** To reverse, revoke, recall, annul –1639.

2. But I my steps toward the ancient bard Reverting, ruminated on the words CARY. 3. I apply my Finger..upon the Top of the Tube, and then invert it;..then I r. the Tube, or turn it up again 1755. Hence **Reve·rter²**, one who or that which reverts. **Reve·rtible** *a.* capable of reverting; admitting of reversion.

Reverted (rĭvə̄·ɹtĕd), *ppl. a.* 1590. [f. prec. + -ED¹.] **1.** Turned backwards or the wrong way; bent back; reversed. **2.** Of the eyes, steps, etc.: Directed backwards 1741.

Reverter¹ (rĭvə̄·ɹtəɹ). 1491. [f. REVERT *v.* + -ER⁴.] *Law.* Reversion (of lands, etc.).

†**Reve·st**, *v.¹* ME. [– OFr. *revestir* (mod. *revêtir*) :– late L. *revestire*, f. *re-* RE- + *vestire* clothe.] **1.** *trans.* **a.** In *pa. pple.* Of priests, etc.: Arrayed in ecclesiastical vestments, esp. for the purpose of performing mass or other office –1609. **b.** *gen.* To clothe, apparel, attire –1664. **2.** *refl.* To dress or apparel (oneself), esp. in ecclesiastical vestments –1652. **3.** *trans.* To put on (attire) again –1867.

3. R. (yee States) your Robes of dignitie SYLVESTER. So †**Reve·sture** (*rare*), vesture, vestments –1621.

Revest (rīve·st), *v.²* 1561. [f. RE- 5 a + VEST *v.*] **1.** *trans.* To reinvest (a person) with power, ownership, or office; to reinstate. **2.** To vest (something) again *in* a person, etc. 1697. **3.** *intr.* To become reinvested (*in* a person) 1651.

2. A Bill to r. in the Universities the monopoly in Almanacks 1799. So **Reve·stment.**

Revestry (rĭve·stri). late ME. [– (O)Fr. *revestiaire* or med.L. *revestiarium*, after *vestry*; see REVEST *v.¹*, VESTIARY, VESTRY.] The vestry of a church (†or temple). So **Reve·stiary**, in same sense.

Revet (rĭve·t), *v.* 1812. Also in pseudo-Fr. form **revête.** [– Fr. *revêtir*; see REVEST *v.¹*] *trans.* To face (an embankment or wall) with masonry or other material, *esp.* in fortification.

Revetment (rĭve·tmĕnt). 1779. Also in Fr. or quasi-Fr. form (1771). [– Fr. *revêtement*, f. *revêtir*; see REVEST *v.¹*, -MENT.] **1.** *Fortif.* A retaining-wall (of masonry, etc.) supporting the face of an earthen rampart or the side of a ditch. **2.** *Civil Eng.* A facing of masonry, concrete, sods, etc., supporting or protecting a bank or embankment 1838. **3.** *Arch.* A facing of stone or other hard material over a less durable substance 1891.

†**Revie·**, *sb.* 1588. [– Fr. *renvi*, f. *renvier* REVIE *v.*] In card-playing, a higher stake ventured by a player against that proposed by an opponent –1680.

†**Revie·**, *v.* 1591. [– (O)Fr. *renvier*, f. *re-* RE- + *envier* raise the stakes :– L. *invitare* INVITE.] **1.** In card-playing: To meet by venturing a larger stake than that proposed by an opponent –1673. **2.** *intr.* To make a revie or revies –1680. **b.** To retort or retaliate –1734.

Review (rĭviū·), *sb.* 1565. [– Fr. †*reveue*, now *revue*, f. *revoir*, f. *re-* RE- + *voir* see; see VIEW *sb.*] **I. 1.** The act of looking over something (again), with a view to correction or improvement; a revision (of a book, etc.). Now *rare.* **2.** *Law.* Revision of a sentence, etc., by some other court or authority 1654. **3.** A formal inspection of military or naval forces by the sovereign or other high personage, or by the general or admiral in command 1683. **4.** An inspection, examination 1611. **5.** A general survey or reconsideration 1604. **b.** Without article, esp. *in* or *under r.* 1729. **6.** A retrospective survey of past actions, etc. 1673. **7. a.** A general account or criticism of a literary work (esp. a new or recent one), usu. published as an article in a periodical or newspaper 1649. **b.** A periodical publication consisting mainly of articles in which current events or questions, or literary works, are discussed or criticized 1705.

1. Some things having passed therein, which..in the r...I wished might be altered 1638. 2. A Bill of R., which is brought to examine and reverse a decree made upon a former Bill, which has been duly enrolled, and thereby become a record of the Court 1838. 3. Phr. *To march* or *pass in r.* 4. *In r.*, under examination. 5. He has taken a r. of the effects of all the schemes which have been successively adopted BURKE. 6. I have lived a life of which I do not like the r. JOHNSON. 7. a. Critical R. of Fox's Book of Martyrs 1824.

II. (rī·viu) A second or repeated view 1665.

Review (rĭviū·), *v.* 1576. [f. RE- and VIEW *v.*, or f. prec., after Fr. *revoir.*] †**1.** *trans.* To see or behold again –1796. **2.** (rī·viū). To view, inspect, or examine a second time or again 1576. †**3. a.** To revise (a book, etc.) –1715. **b.** To re-examine; to reconsider (*rare*) –1672. **4.** *Law.* To submit (a decree, act, etc.) to examination or revision 1621. **5.** To survey; to take a survey of 1600. **b.** To look back upon; to regard or survey in retrospection 1751. **6.** To hold a review of (troops, etc.) 1712. **7.** To write an appreciation or criticism of (a new literary work); also *absol.*, to write reviews; to follow the occupation of a reviewer 1781.

1. Anxious to r. his native shore 1762. 2. How they viewed and reviewed us as we passed over the rivulet! STERNE. 4. The order may be reviewed or may be appealed from 1858. 5. b. The past he calmly hath reviewed WORDSW. 7. I would never r. the work of an anonymous authour JOHNSON. Hence **Review·able** *a.* that may be reviewed. **Review·al**, the or an act of reviewing; a review.

Reviewer (rĭviū·əɹ). 1611. [f. REVIEW *v.* + -ER¹.] †**1.** One who revises –1720. **2.** One who criticizes new publications; a writer of reviews. In early use, the author of a special pamphlet criticizing another work 1651.

†**Revification**, erron. f. REVIVIFICATION.

†**Revi·le**, *sb.* 1579. [f. the vb.] **1.** A reviling speech or remark –1645. **2.** Revilement, reviling –1684.

2. Render them not reviling for r. BUNYAN.

Revile (rĭvəi·l), *v.* ME. [– OFr. *reviler*, f. *re-* RE- + *vil* VILE.] †**1.** *trans.* To degrade, abase. ME. only. **2.** To subject to contumely or abuse; to assail with opprobrious or abusive language ME. **3.** *intr.* To use opprobrious language; to rail *at* a person or thing 1526.

2. The man..with reproachfull tearmes gan them r. SPENSER. 3. When he was reviled, reviled not agayne TINDALE 1 *Pet.* 2:23. Hence **Revi·ler.**

Revilement (rĭvəi·lmĕnt). 1590. [f. REVILE *v.* + -MENT.] **1.** The act, fact, or practice of reviling. **2.** An instance of this; a reviling speech 1637.

Revi·ling, *vbl. sb.* 1535. [f. as prec. + -ING¹.] The action of the vb; a reviling remark or speech.

Their reuilings are grieuous to the eare *Ecclus.* 27:15.

†**Revi·nce**, *v.* 1529. [– L. *revincere*, f. *re-* RE- + *vincere* conquer, subdue.] *trans.* To refute, disprove –1686.

Revirescence (rĭvire·sĕns). *rare.* 1741. [f. next; see -ENCE.] Return to a youthful or flourishing condition.

Revirescent (rĭvire·sĕnt), *a. rare.* 1644. [– L. *revirescens, -ent-*, pr. pple. of *revirescere* grow green again, f. *viridis* green; see -ESCENT.] Flourishing anew.

Revisal (rĭvəi·zăl). 1612. [f. REVISE *v.* + -AL¹ 2.] The act of revising; a revision, re-examination.

He had not submitted his dispatch to official r. 1873.

Revise (rĭvəi·z), *sb.* 1591. [f. the vb.] **1.** The act of revising or reviewing; a revision, a looking over or examining again. **b.** A revised version or form 1894. **2.** *Typog.* A revised or corrected form of proof-sheet; a further proof submitted by the printer after having made the required corrections or additions 1612.

Revise (rĭvəi·z), *v.* 1567. [– (O)Fr. *réviser*, †*reviser* or L. *revisere*, f. *re-* RE- + *visere* examine, desiderative and intensive of *vidēre*, *vis-* see.] †**1.** *intr.* To look again or repeatedly *at*, to look back or meditate *on*, something –1640. †**2.** *trans.* To see or behold, look at, again –1772. **3.** To look or read carefully over, with a view to improving or correcting 1611. **b.** To go over again, re-examine, in order to improve or amend; †to condense by revision 1596.

3. Neither did we disdaine to reuise that which we had done 1611. b. To r. the sentence of the court of delegates BLACKSTONE. Hence **Revi·sable** *a.*

Reviser (rĭvəi·zəɹ). 1698. = REVISOR.

Revision (rĭvi·ʒən). 1611. [– (O)Fr. *révision* or late L. *revisio, -on-*, f. *revisere*; see REVISE *v.*, -ION.] **1.** The action of revising; esp. critical or careful examination or perusal with a view to correcting or improving. **b.** A product of this; a revised version 1845. **2.** The fact of seeing some person or thing again 1796.

1. A very great work, the r. of my Dictionary JOHNSON. Hence **Revi·sional, Revi·sionary** *adjs.*

Revisionist (rĭvi·ʒənist). 1865. [f. prec. + -IST.] **1.** One who advocates revision. **2.** *pl.* The revisers of the Bible 1881.

Revisor (rĭvəi·zǭɹ). 1598. [f. REVISE *v.* + -OR 2 a.] One who revises; a reviser.

Revisory (rĭvəi·zəri), *a.* 1846. [f. REVISE

v. + -ORY[2].] Having power to revise; engaged in, of the nature of, revision.

Revivable (rĭvəi·văb'l), *a.* 1810. [f. REVIVE *v.* + -ABLE.] Capable of being revived. So **Revivabi·lity.**

Revival (rĭvəi·văl). 1651. [f. REVIVE *v.* + -AL[1] 2.] **1.** The act of reviving after decline or discontinuance; restoration to general use, acceptance, etc.; an instance or result of this. **b.** The act of restoring an old play to the stage, or of republishing an old literary work 1664. **c.** *Arch.* The reintroduction of Gothic architecture, towards the middle of the 19th c. 1850. **2. a.** Restoration to vigour or activity 1752. **b.** Restoration or return to life or consciousness 1788. **c.** *Chem.* Revivification 1788. **d.** The fact of renewing or raising again 1885. **3.** A general reawakening *of* or *in* religion in a community, or some part of one 1702. **b.** *ellipt.* freq. in depreciatory use 1818.

1. The happy R. of Masquerading among us SWIFT. *R. of learning, letters,* or *literature,* the Renaissance in its literary aspect. **2. d.** The withdrawal and r. of objections 1885. **3. b.** In the Methodist Chapel..where they are in the thick of a r. 1849.

Revivalism (rĭvəi·văliz'm). 1815. [f. prec. + -ISM.] **1.** The state or form of religion characteristic of revivals. **2.** Tendency or desire to revive what has gone out of use or belongs to the past 1874.

Revivalist (rĭvəi·vălist). 1820. [f. as prec. + -IST.] **1.** One who promotes, produces, or takes part in, a religious revival. **2.** One who revives former conditions, methods, etc. 1856.

1. The Irish Shouters, the Welsh Jumpers, and the Cornish Revivalists 1820. Hence **Revi·valistic** *a.*

†**Revi·ve,** *sb. rare.* 1589. [f. the vb.] **a.** Revival, restoration to life. GREENE. **b.** A revival (of a play) on the stage. PEPYS.

Revive (rĭvəi·v), *v.* late ME. [– (O)Fr. *revivre* or late L. *revivere,* f. *re-* RE- + *vivere* live.] **I.** *intr.* **1.** To return to consciousness; to recover from a swoon or faint. **2.** To return to life; to regain vital activity, after being dead; to live again 1526. **b.** *Chem.* To return to the metallic state 1825. **3.** To assume fresh life or vigour after nearly dying or becoming extinct 1526. **b.** To resume courage or strength; to recover from depression 1530. **4.** Of feelings, dispositions, etc.: To become active or operative again 1494. **b.** To return to a flourishing state; to assume fresh life or vigour after decline or decay; also in *Law,* to become valid again 1565. **c.** To return, come back again, after a period of abeyance 1759.

1. When he had drunke, his spirit came againe, and he reuiued *Judg.* 15:19. **2.** Henry is dead, and neuer shall reuiue SHAKS. **3.** Even as a dying coal revives with wind SHAKS. **b.** I r. At this last sight, assur'd that Man shall live MILT. **4.** Ambitious hopes which had seemed to be extinguished, had revived in his bosom MACAULAY. **b.** The abuses which he had suppressed began to r. MACAULAY. **c.** But the old time is dead also, never, never to r. STEVENSON.

II. *trans.* **1.** To restore to consciousness; to bring back from a swoon or faint, or from a state of suspended animation. late ME. **2.** To restore to life; to resuscitate or reanimate; to bring back *from* death or the grave 1470. **3.** To restore from a languid, depressed, or morbid state; to infuse fresh life or vigour into 1547. **b.** To renew; to restore again from or after decline or decay 1631. **4.** To set going, make active or operative, again 1494. **b.** To re-enact (a law, etc.); to renew or re-validate; to re-open (an election) 1548. **c.** To reawaken (a desire, etc.) 1590. **5.** To bring into existence or use, set up, again 1495. **b.** To bring back into knowledge, notice, or currency 1509. **c.** To put (an old play) upon the stage again 1823. **6.** To bring again before the mind; to renew the memory of (a person or thing); to recall 1638. **b.** To renew or freshen up, to bring back to a person (the memory *of* some person or thing) 1592. **7.** *Chem.* To convert, restore, or reduce (a metal, esp. mercury) to or into its natural condition or form; to restore *from* a mixed to a natural state; to revivify 1677. **8.** To treat (faded clothing, etc.) with a reviver; to renovate (*rare*) 1836. **b.** To restore to clearness 1861.

1. This Water reviv'd his Father more than all the Rum or Spirits I had given him DE FOE. **2.** He Lazarus reuiued from the graue 1603. **3.** He.. with sweete delight Of Musicks skill revives his toyled spright SPENSER. **b.** Two poets in an age are not sufficient to r. the splendour of decaying genius GOLDSM. **4.** To R. an old grudge 1696. **b.** You may wish to r. your will after you have revoked it 1858. **c.** Would'st thou r. the deep Despair GRAY. **5.** The great danger..of reviving Jewish ceremonies 1653. To r. the ancient monarchy 1866. **b.** Prevailed upon to r. that ridiculous old story MISS BURNEY. **6.** The surrounding scene revived..all the impressions of my boyhood TYNDALL. **8. b.** Attempts have been made to r. the faded characters 1875. Hence **Revi·vement** (now *rare*), the (*or* an) act of reviving; a reviving influence.

Reviver (rĭvəi·vəɹ). 1592. [f. prec. + -ER[1].] **1.** That which revives, restores, or invigorates; also *slang,* a stimulating drink. **b.** A preparation for restoring a faded colour, polish, or lustre 1836. **2.** One who revives or restores that which has lapsed, become obsolete, or fallen into disuse 1607.

†**Revivi·ction.** *rare.* 1646. [irreg. f. L. *reviviscere.*] Reviviscence –1652.

Revivification (rĭvi:vifikēⁱ·ʃən). 1638. [f. contemp. †*revivificate* vb. (see next) + -ATION.] **1.** Restoration or return from death to life. **b.** *Nat. Hist.* Recovery or awakening from a state of torpidity 1801. **2.** *Chem.* Reduction or restoration of a metal, etc., after combination, to its original state 1643. **3.** Revival, restoration; renewal of vigour or activity 1756.

Revivify (rĭvi·vifəi), *v.* 1675. [– Fr. *revivifier* (XVI) or late and med.L. *revivificare* (also *-ari* intr.); see RE-, VIVIFY.] **1.** *trans.* To restore to animation or activity; to revive or reinvigorate; to put new life into. **2.** To restore to life, make alive again 1744. **3.** *Chem.* **a.** = REVIVE *v.* II. 7. 1727. **b.** *intr.* = REVIVE *v.* I. 2 b. 1727.

1. *transf.* I have..endeavoured to r. the bygone times and people THACKERAY. **2.** A germ to be revivified LAMB.

Revi·ving, *ppl. a.* 1592. [f. REVIVE *v.* + -ING[2].] **1.** That revives, or regains strength or consciousness. **2.** That refreshes, stimulates, or infuses fresh life 1601. **b.** Renewing an enactment 1769. Hence **Revi·vingly** *adv.*

Reviviscence (revivi·sĕns). 1626. [– late L. *reviviscentia,* f. L. *reviviscent-*; see next, -ENCE.] **1.** Return to life or animation. **2.** Revival; restoration to a flourishing or vigorous condition 1711. So **Revivi·scency.**

Reviviscent (revivi·sĕnt), *a.* 1778. [– L. *reviviscens, -ent-,* pr. pple. of *reviviscere* (*-escere*) come to life again, inceptive f. *revivere*; see REVIVE, -ESCENT.] **1.** Returning to life or animation; reviving. **2.** Causing renewed life 1886.

Revivor (rĭvəi·vǭɹ). 1602. [f. REVIVE *v.* + -OR 2.] †**1.** Renewal, revival (*rare*) –1741. **2.** A proceeding for the revival of a suit or action abated by the death of one of the parties, or by some other circumstance. Chiefly in phr. *bill of r.* 1623.

Revocable (re·vŏkab'l), *a.* 1471. [– OFr. *revocable* (mod. *ré-*) or L. *revocabilis*; see REVOKE *v.*, -ABLE.] Capable of being revoked or recalled.

Your rash, and I hope r. resolution RICHARDSON. Acts..not r. by any subsequent authority BURKE. Hence **Re:vocabi·lity, Re·vocableness. Re·vocably** *adv.*

†**Re·vocate,** *v.* 1540. [– *revocat-,* pa. ppl. stem of L. *revocare*; see REVOKE *v.*, -ATE[3].] **1.** *trans.* To recall, call back –1548. **2.** To revoke, rescind –1595.

Revocation (revŏkēⁱ·ʃən). late ME. [– (O)Fr. *révocation* or L. *revocatio, -on-,* f. as prec.; see -ION.] **1.** The action of recalling; recall (of persons); a call or summons to return. Now *rare* or *Obs.* **b.** *transf.* with ref. to things 1649. **2.** The action of revoking, rescinding, or annulling; withdrawal (of a grant, etc.). late ME. †**3.** Recantation; withdrawal (of statements) –1684.

1. The Envoy delivered his Letters of R., and is preparing to leave..Court 1710. **2.** The r. of the edict of Nantz 1788. A general r. of all..grants 1861.

Revocatory (re·vŏkătəri), *a.* late ME. [– late and med.L. *revocatorius,* f. as prec.; see -ORY[2].] Tending or pertaining to, expressive of, revocation; esp. *r. letters,* after med.L. *litteræ revocatoriæ.*

Revok(e)able (rĭvōᵘ·kăb'l), *a.* 1584. [f. REVOKE *v.* + -ABLE.] = REVOCABLE *a.*

Revoke (rĭvōᵘ·k), *sb.* 1709. [f. the vb.] **1.** *Cards,* esp. *Whist.* An act of revoking; a failure to follow suit when a card of that suit is held. **2.** Revocation, recall 1882.

Revoke (rĭvōᵘ·k), *v.* late ME. [– (O)Fr. *révoquer* or L. *revocare,* f. *re-* RE- + *vocare* call.] **I.** *trans.* †**1.** To recall, bring back *to* a (right) belief, etc., or *from* some belief or practice –1687. †**b.** To restrain or prevent *from* something –1616. †**c.** Without const. To check, restrain (*rare*) –1637. **2.** †**a.** To bring back *into* or *unto* life; to restore to consciousness –1664. **b.** To call back to memory. Now *rare.* 1565. †**c.** To bring back into use; to revive –1644. **3.** To recall; to call or summon back 1521. **4.** To annul, repeal, rescind, cancel. late ME. †**5.** To retract, withdraw, recant –1671. †**6.** To take back to oneself –1600. †**b.** To draw back, withdraw (*rare*) –1644.

2. b. Reuoking to minde the former talke betweene the captaine and him 1565. **3.** Now the English forces were revoked from the marches of Scotland 1709. How readily we wish time spent revok'd COWPER. **4.** Her only son, who stood by, implored her to r. the malediction LOCKHART.

II. *intr.* **1.** To make revocation 1500. **2.** *Cards,* esp. *Whist.* To fail or neglect to follow suit when a card of the required suit is held 1592. Hence †**Revo·kement** (*rare*), revocation. **Revo·ker** (*rare*). **Revo·king** *ppl. a.* (*Cards*) that revokes; so **Revo·kingly** *adv.* by way of revocation.

Revolt (rĭvōᵘ·lt, rĭvǫ·lt), *sb.*[1] 1560. [– Fr. *révolte* – It. *rivolta,* f. *rivoltare*; see REVOLT *v.*] **1.** An instance, on the part of subjects or subordinates, of casting off allegiance or obedience to their rulers or superiors; an insurrection. **b.** An act of this nature on the part of an individual; a movement of strong protest against, or refusal to submit to, some condition, practice, etc. 1599. **c.** An emphatic withdrawal *from* a party, etc. 1596. **2.** The act of revolting; also, language tending to this 1586. **b.** *In r.,* in a state of rebellion 1602. †**c.** Revulsion of appetite. SHAKS.

1. Who first seduc'd them to that fowl r.? Th' infernal Serpent MILT. **2.** They fixed upon the 20th of May as the day of r. 1801.

†**Revo·lt,** *sb.*[2] 1585. [perh. – Fr. *révolté,* pa. pple. of *révolter* (see next).] A revolter, or rebel –1627.

Revolt (rĭvōᵘ·lt, rĭvǫ·lt), *v.* 1548. [– Fr. (*se*) *révolter* – It. *rivoltare* (refl. *-arsi*) – Rom. **revolvitare,* intensive of L. *revolvere* REVOLVE.] **I.** *intr.* **1.** To cast off (†or change) allegiance; to rise against rulers or constituted authority. **b.** To fall away *from* a ruler, obedience, etc.; to rise *against* a person or authority 1560. **c.** To go over *to* a rival power 1560. †**2. a.** To go over *to* another religion; to become a pervert (*from* some faith) –1686. **b.** To draw back *from* a course of action, etc.; to return to one's allegiance –1610. **3.** To feel revulsion or disgust *at* something 1760. **b.** To rise in repugnance *against* something 1775. **c.** To turn in loathing *from* something 1782.

1. The youth revolted, and refused to receive their own fathers JOWETT. **b.** [I] shall soon..rid heav'n of these rebell'd..That from thy just obedience could r. MILT. **3.** Errors, at the grossness of which common sense..revolts 1802. **c.** He knew well that her mind revolted from that means of escape 1863.

II. *trans.* †**1.** To turn back. SPENSER. **2.** To affect with disgust or repugnance; to nauseate 1751. **b.** *absol.* To cause revulsion 1898.

2. Grave churchmen..who were revolted by these achievements in an ecclesiastic 1855. Hence **Revo·lter.**

Revo·lting, *ppl. a.* 1593. [f. prec. + -ING[2].] **1.** Rebelling. **2.** Repulsive 1806. Hence **Revo·ltingly** *adv.*

Revoluble, *a. rare.* 1598. [– L. *revolubilis,* f. *revolvere* REVOLVE.] Revolving; rolling. So **Revolubi·lity.**

Revolute (re·vŏliut), *a.* 1753. [– L. *revolutus,* pa. pple. of *revolvere* REVOLVE.] In scientific use (chiefly *Bot.*): Rolled backwards, downwards, or outwards.

Revolution (revŏl[1]ū·ʃən). late ME. [– (O)Fr. *révolution* or late L. *revolutio, -on-,* f. *revolut-,* pa. ppl. stem of L. *revolvere*; see

REVOLVE, -ION.] I. 1. *Astr.* The action or fact, on the part of celestial bodies, of moving round in an orbit or circular course; the apparent movement of the sun, stars, etc., round the earth. b. The time in which a planet, etc., completes a full circuit or course. late ME. 2. The return or recurrence of a point or period of time; the lapse of a certain time. late ME. †b. A cycle, or recurrent period of time; an epoch –1706. †c. The recurrence or repetition *of* a day, event, occupation, etc. –1784. †3. A turn or twist; a bend or winding –1737. 4. The action, on the part of a thing or person, of turning or whirling round, or of moving round some point 1664. b. *esp.* Movement round an axis or centre; rotation 1710. c. A single act of rotation round a centre 1706.

2. They recur..at long intervals; they depend on the slow revolutions of ages 1842. 4. That fear Comes thundring back with dreadful r. On my defensless head MILT. c. The pinion will make 10 revolutions while the wheel performs one 1825.

†II. The action of turning over in the mind; consideration, reflection –1792.

Answerable to any hourely..change in his mistris reuolution B. JONS.

III. 1. Alteration, change, mutation (*rare*). late ME. b. An instance of a great change in affairs or in some particular thing 1450. 2. A complete overthrow of the established government in any country or state by those who were previously subject to it; a forcible substitution of a new ruler or form of government. Also without article. 1600. 3. *Eng. Hist.* †a. The overthrow of the Rump Parliament in 1660, which resulted in the restoration of the monarchy –1725. b. The expulsion, in 1688, of the Stuart dynasty under James II, and the transfer of sovereignty to William and Mary 1688. 4. *French Hist.* The overthrow of the monarchy, and establishment of republican government, in 1789–95. 1790. 5. *Amer. Hist.* The overthrow of British supremacy by the War of Independence in 1775–81. 1789.

1. Heere's fine Reuolution, if wee had the tricke to see't SHAKS. b. A complete r. in our national industry 1870. 2. Rebellion is the subversion of the laws, and R. is that of tyrants 1796. Hence **Revolu·tionism,** advocacy or spread of revolutionary principles. **Revolu·tionist,** a revolutionary.

Revolutionary (revǒlˡū·ʃənări), *a.* and *sb.* 1774. [f. REVOLUTION + -ARY¹, but in gen. use after Fr. *révolutionnaire* 1794.] A. *adj.* 1. Pertaining to or connected with, characterized by, of the nature of, revolution. 2. Revolving; marked by rotation 1832.

1. A..r. government 1827. The R. war 1838.

B. *sb.* One who instigates or favours revolution; one who takes part in a revolution 1850.

What manner of men they are who become revolutionaries KINGSLEY. Hence **Revolu·tionariness.**

Revolu·tioner. 1695. [f. as prec. + -ER¹.] 1. A supporter or approver of the Revolution of 1688. Now *Hist.* 2. A revolutionary 1803.

Revolutionize (revǒlˡū·ʃənəiz), *v.* 1797. [f. REVOLUTION + -IZE 3, after Fr. *révolutionner* 1795.] 1. *trans.* To bring (a country or state) under a revolutionary form of government. 2. To convert into revolutionary forms; to infect with revolutionary principles or ideas 1797. 3. To change (a thing) completely or fundamentally 1799.

1. To r. Bulgaria 1868. 2. They have not revolutionized..diplomatic forms and ceremonies 1797. 3. The opening of the Indies..revolutionized the channels and the direction of commerce 1861.

Revo·lvable, *a.* 1889. [f. REVOLVE *v.* + -ABLE.] Capable of being revolved.

Revolve (rǐvǫ·lv), *sb.* 1595. [f. the vb.] †1. Meditation, determination. 2. Revolution; rotation 1641.

Revolve (rǐvǫ·lv), *v.* late ME. [– L. *revolvere*, f. *re-* RE- + *volvere* roll, turn.] I. *trans.* †1. To turn (the eyes or sight) back or round –1695. †2. To restore; to turn, bring, or roll back (*into* a place or state, or *upon* a person) –1665. 3. To turn over (something) *in* the mind, thoughts, etc. 1460. b. To consider, think over, meditate upon (something). late ME. 4. To turn over, search through, study, or read (a book, etc.). Now *rare.* 1480. 5. To cause (something) to travel in an orbit around a central point; to rotate (something) upon an axis 1667.

3. Revolving in his mind some subtle feat Of thievish craft SHELLEY. b. While I revolved the case of these unfortunate young ladies 1756. 4. This having heard, strait I again revolv'd The Law and Prophets MILT. 5. Then in the East her turn she shines, Revolvd on Heavns great Axle MILT.

II. *intr.* †1. To return *to* a person or place –1755. †2. To deliberate or consider; to meditate *upon* something –1785. 3. To perform a circular motion; to move in a regular orbit *about* or *round* a fixed point 1713. b. To rotate or move upon an axis or centre 1727. 4. To come round again, to move round, in various senses 1769.

2. If this fall into thy hands, reuolue SHAKS. 3. Those bodies that r. round the sun BERKELEY. b. It was made to r. upon hinges 1849. 4. The year revolves CRABBE. Hence **Revo·lvency,** tendency to r.; capacity for revolution. **Revo·lvingly** *adv.*

Revolver (rǐvǫ·lvəɹ). 1835. [f. prec. + -ER¹.] 1. A pistol provided with mechanism by which a set of loaded barrels, or (more usu.) of cartridge-chambers, is revolved and presented successively before the hammer, so as to admit of the rapid discharge of several shots without reloading. 2. A revolving furnace 1879.

Revue (rǐviū·). 1913. [– Fr. *revue* REVIEW.] A theatrical entertainment purporting to give a review (often satirical) of current fashions, events, plays, etc.; often, an elaborate musical entertainment consisting of numerous unrelated scenes or episodes.

Revu·lsant. 1875. [– Fr. *révulsant*, pres. pple. of *révulser*; see next, -ANT.] *Med.* A revulsive.

†**Revu·lse,** *v. rare.* 1669. [f. *revuls-*, pa. ppl. stem of L. *revellere*; see REVEL *v.*²] *trans.* To drag, draw, or pull back; to tear away –1690.

Revulsion (rǐvɒ·lʃən). 1541. [– Fr. *révulsion* or L. *revulsio*, *-on-*, f. as prec.; see -ION.] 1. *Med.* The action or practice of diminishing a morbid condition in one part of the body by operating upon another. (Cf. DERIVATION 1 c.) 2. The action of drawing, or the fact of being drawn, back or away 1609. 3. A sudden violent change of feeling; a strong reaction in sentiment or taste 1816. 4. A sudden reaction or reverse tendency in trade, fortune, etc. 1812.

2. Thrown out of employment by the r. of capital from other trades ADAM SMITH. 3. A natural r. from the baldness and puerility into which Wordsworth too often fell 1853.

Revulsive (rǐvɒ·lsiv), *a.* and *sb.* 1616. [f. prec. + -IVE.] *Med.* A. *adj.* Capable of producing revulsion; tending to revulsion. B. *sb.* An application used to produce revulsion 1661.

Rew. *Obs.* exc. *dial.* [OE. *rǣw*, var. of *rāw* ROW *sb.*¹] †1. In advb. phrases: a. *By r.*, in order, successively. Also *in r.* –1591. b. *On* or *in a r.*, in a row or line –1615. †2. A row or line of persons or things; a rank or series –1664. b. *dial.* A hedgerow OE.

Reward (rǐwǭ·rd), *sb.* ME. [– AFr., ONFr. *reward* = OFr. *reguard* REGARD *sb.*] †I. Regard, consideration, heed –1475. II. 1. A return or recompense made to, or received by, a person for some service or merit, or for hardship endured. late ME. †b. Remuneration (regular or extra) –1776. c. A sum of money offered for the capture or detection of a malefactor, discovery of a missing person, recovery of lost or stolen property, etc. 1593. 2. Recompense or retribution for evil-doing; requital, punishment. late ME.

1. The most recent r. for military merit is the Victoria Cross 1876. c. Whoever shall discover the said Daniel De Foe..shall have a r. of fifty pounds 1702. 2. Hanging was the r. of treason and desertion 1874. Hence **Rewa·rdful** *a.* yielding or producing r. **Rewa·rdless** *a.* devoid of r.

Reward (rǐwǭ·ɹd), *v.* ME. [– AFr., ONFr. *rewarder* = OFr. *reguarder* REGARD *v.*] †I. *trans.* To regard, heed, consider; to look at or observe –1475. II. †1. *trans.* To assign or give (to a person) as a reward or recompense –1650. 2. To repay, requite, recompense (a person) for some service, merit, etc. ME. 3. To requite, make a return for (a service, merit, exertion, etc.) 1533. 4. a. To requite or repay (a person) for evil-doing; to punish, chastise 1484. b. To pay back (injury or wrong) to a person; to visit *upon* a person (*rare*). late ME. 5. *absol.* To make recompense. late ME.

1. Thou hast rewarded mee good, whereas I haue rewarded thee euill 1 *Sam.* 24:17. 2. Then I will r. those that were faithful to me 1685. A magnificent view rewards the traveller 1872. 3. The discovery, when made, would not at all r. the labour expended in the search 1836. 4. The Lord shall r. the doer of euill, according to his wickednesse 2 *Sam.* 3:39. Hence **Rewa·rdable** *a.*, **-ness. Rewa·rdably** *adv.* **Rewa·rder.**

†**Rex**¹. 1566. [Origin obsc.; see REAKS. In sense 2 assoc. w. L. *rex.*] 1. = REAKS –1642. 2. *To play r.*, to act as lord or master; to domineer –1692.

‖**Rex**². *rare.* 1617. [L.] A king.

Rexine (re·ksīn). 1911. Trade name of a variety of artificial leather used in upholstery.

Reynard (re·năɹd). ME. [– (O)Fr. *renard*, †*-art*, orig. proper name of the fox (*le goupil* in the 'Roman de Renart' XIII) – Frank. *Reginhart*, whence MDu. *Reynaert* (*-d*), on which Caxton modelled his form *reynard.*] A quasi-proper name given to the fox; also occas. used as a common noun.

Rh, a consonantal digraph used in Latin, and hence in English, French, etc., to represent Gr. initial ῥ (with spiritus asper); in English it has the same phonetic value as the simple *r*.

†**Rha.** 1578. [Late L. – Gr. ῥᾶ; see RHUBARB.] Rhubarb –1597.

†**Rha·barb.** 1646. Var. f. RHUBARB –1698.

Rhabarbarate (răbā·ɹbărět), *a.* and *sb.* 1696. [f. med.L. RHABARBARUM + -ATE² (cf. AL. *reubarbaratus* XIII); in mod. use + -ATE⁴.] †A. *adj.* Tinctured with rhubarb (*rare*). B. *sb.* A salt of rhabarbaric acid 1840.

Rhabarbaric (ræbaɹbæ·rik), *a.* 1839. [f. med.L. *rhabarbarum* (see next) + -IC 1 b.] *Chem.* = CHRYSOPHANIC. So **Rhaba·rbarin** [-IN¹], chrysophanic acid.

‖**Rhabarbarum** (răbā·ɹbăɹǒm). 1597. [med.L.; see RHUBARB.] Rhubarb-root.

Rhabdite (ræ·bdəit). 1881. [f. Gr. ῥάβδος rod + -ITE¹ 3.] 1. *Zool.* One of the homogeneous rod-like bodies found in the integument of turbellarian worms 1885. 2. *Ent.* One of the three pairs of organs forming the ovipositor of some insects 1890. 3. *Min.* A phosphide of iron and nickel 1881.

Rhabdo- (ræ·bdo, ræbdǫ·), comb. form of Gr. ῥάβδος rod, occurring in a few technical terms (chiefly zoological): **Rha·bdocœl(e** [Gr. κοῖλος hollow] *a.* having a straight digestive cavity, as turbellarian worms; *sb.* a worm of this kind; one of the *Rhabdocœla.* **Rhabdocœ·lian, -cœ·lous** *adjs.* = prec. *a.* **Rha·bdolith** [Gr. λίθος stone], one of the rod-like bodies forming the armature of a rhabdosphere. **Rha·bdomere** [Gr. μέρος], one of the rod-like constituents of a rhabdom. **Rha:bdomyo·ma,** a myoma involving the striated muscular fibres. **Rha·bdosphere,** a name given to certain spherical bodies found in abundance on the surface of the waters in warm seas.

Rhabdoid (ræ·bdoid), *a.* and *sb.* Also **ra-.** 1858. [– mod.L. *rhabdoides* – Gr. ῥαβδοειδής, f. ῥάβδος rod; see -OID.] A. *adj.* Resembling a rod; rod-like. B. *sb.* A rod-shaped body 1900. So **Rhabdoi·dal** *a.*

Rhabdology (ræbdǫ·lŏdʒi). Also **rabdo-.** 1667. [– mod.L. *rhabdologia* (Napier); see RHABDO-, -LOGY.] The act or art of computing by NAPIER'S BONES (or rods). Now *Hist.*

Rhabdom (ræ·bdǫ̆m). Also **-ome.** 1878. [– late Gr. ῥάβδωμα, f. ῥάβδος rod; see -OME.] *Ent.* One of the rods supporting the crystalline lenses in a faceted eye.

Rhabdomancy (ræ·bdomænsi). Also **ra-.** 1646. [– Gr. ῥαβδομαντεία; see RHABDO-, -MANCY.] Divination by means of a rod or wand; *spec.* the art of discovering ores, springs of water, etc., in the earth by means of a divining-rod. So **Rha·bdomancer,** a dowser.

Rhachi(o)-, etc.: see RACHI-, etc.

Rhadamanthus (rædămæ·nþǒs). 1582. [– L. *Rhadamanthus* – Gr. Ῥαδάμανθος.] In Greek mythology, one of the judges in the lower world, a son of Zeus and Europa. Hence allusively: an inflexible judge; a rigorous or severe master. Hence **Rhadama·nthine** *a.* resembling or characteristic of R.

Rhætian (rī·ʃăn), *a.* and *sb.* Also **Rhe-.** 1779. [f. *Rhætia* (see next) + -IAN.] = RHÆTO-ROMANIC.

Rhætic (rī·tik), *a.* and *sb.* Also **Rhe-.** 1861. [– L. *Rhæticus*, adj. of *Rhætia*, ancient name of a district of the Alps.] **A.** *adj. Geol.* Applied to strata, extensively developed in the Rhætian Alps, regarded as passage beds between the lias and trias; belonging to or characteristic of these. **B.** *sb.* The R. formation; *pl.* R. series of strata.

Rhætizite (rī·tizəit). Also **rhe-**; *erron.* **rhœ-.** 1816. [– G. *rhätizit* (1815), f. *Rhætia*; see prec. and -ITE[1] 2 b.] *Min.* A white variety of cyanite.

Rhæ:to-Roma·nic, *a.* and *sb.* Also **Rhe-.** 1867. [f. *Rhæto-*, comb. f. L. *Rhætus* Rhætian + ROMANIC.] *Philology.* Applied to those dialects of the Romance family which are spoken in south-eastern Switzerland and the Tyrol; sometimes particularly to the Rumansch of the Grisons or the Ladin of the Engadine. Also **Rhæ·to-Roma·nce.**

‖**Rhagades** (ræ·gădīz), *sb. pl.* 1601. [L. – Gr. ῥαγάδες, pl. of ῥαγάς rent, chink. Cf. Fr. *rhagade* (XVII).] *Path.* Chaps or fissures of the skin.

Rhamn (ræm). ME. [– late L. RHAMNUS.] The buckthorn; the buckthorn berry.

‖**Rhamnus** (ræ·mnŏs). 1562. [Late L., earlier *rhamnos* (Pliny) – Gr. ῥάμνος.] Formerly the buckthorn (*R. catharticus*) or Christ's thorn (*Paliurus aculeatus*); now, a genus of shrubs typical of the family *Rhamnaceæ* and comprising the buckthorns. Also *attrib.*

Rhapontic (răpǫ·ntik). 1548. [In XVI *rhaponticke*, also *ru-*, *rew-*, – med.L. **rhaponticum*, *ruponticum* (XIII), the first elements corresp. to those explained under RHUBARB; the second = PONTIC *a.* Cf. Fr. †*reupontic* (XV), now *rhapontic.*] †**1.** Greater Centaury, *Centaurea rhapontica* –1617. **2.** A species of rhubard, *Rheum rhaponticum*, or its root. Also applied to other species. Also *attrib.* 1578. Hence **Rhaponticin** (răpǫ·ntisin) [-IN[1]], *Chem.* a yellow principle extracted from the root of *Rheum rhaponticum.*

Rhapsode (ræ·psoᵘd). 1834. [– Gr. ῥαψῳδός, reciter of epic poems; see RHAPSODY. Cf. Fr. *r(h)apsode* (XVI).] = RHAPSODIST 2. So †**Rhapsoder** = RHAPSODIST 1. (*rare*) –1711.

Rhapsodic (ræpsǫ·dik), *a.* 1782. [– Gr. ῥαψῳδικός, f. ῥαψῳδός or ῥαψῳδία see -IC. Cf. Fr. *r(h)apsodique.*] **1.** = next 2. **2.** Consisting of the recitation of rhapsodies 1846.

Rhapsodical (ræpsǫ·dikăl), *a.* 1659. [f. as prec.; see -ICAL.] †**1.** Of a literary work: Consisting of a medley of narratives, etc.; fragmentary or disconnected in style –1759. **2.** Characteristic of or of the nature of rhapsody (sense 3); exaggeratedly enthusiastic or ecstatic in language or manner 1783. **3.** Of the rhapsodists. SHELLEY. Hence **Rhapso·dically** *adv.*

Rhapsodist (ræ·psŏdist). 1646. [f. RHAPSODY + -IST. Cf. Fr. *r(h)apsodiste.*] †**1.** A collector of literary pieces –1671. **2.** *Antiq.* In Ancient Greece, a reciter of epic poems, *esp.* one of a school of persons whose occupation it was to recite the Homeric poems 1656. **b.** *transf.* and *gen.* A reciter of poems 1765. **3.** One who rhapsodizes or uses rhapsodical language; in early use, with implication of want of argument or fact 1741.

2. b. The same populace sit for hours.., listening to rhapsodists who recite Ariosto CARLYLE.

Rhapsodize (ræ·psŏdəiz), *v.* 1607. [f. as prec. + -IZE. Cf. Fr. *r(h)apsodier.*] †**1.** *trans.* To piece (miscellaneous narratives, etc.) together; to relate disconnectedly –1765. **2.** To recite in rhapsódies. Also *absol.* 1822. **3.** *intr.* To utter rhapsody; to talk rhapsodically 1806.

1. To r. them, as I once intended, into the body of the work STERNE.

Rhapsody (ræ·psŏdi), *sb.* 1542. [– L. *rhapsodia*, applied by Cornelius Nepos to a book of Homer, – Gr ῥαψῳδία, f. ῥαψῳδός rhapsodist, f. ῥάπτειν stitch + ᾠδή song, ODE; see -Y[3].] **1.** An epic poem or part of one, suitable for recitation at one time. †**2.** A miscellaneous collection; a medley or confused mass (*of* things); a 'string' (*of* words, sentences, tales, etc.) –1837. †**b.** A literary work consisting of miscellaneous or disconnected pieces; a written composition having no fixed form or plan –1764. †**c.** A collection (*of* persons, nations) –1701. **3.** An exalted expression of sentiment or feeling; an effusion (e.g. a speech, letter, poem) marked by extravagance of idea and expression, but without connected thought or sound argument. Also without article. 1639. **4.** *Mus.* An instrumental composition enthusiastic in character but of indefinite form 1880.

1. Those [verses] of Homer, which..were at length, by Pisistratus's order, digested into books, called rhapsodies E. CHAMBERS. **2.** Such a deed, As..sweete Religion makes A rapsidie of words SHAKS. **b.** I have lately got A. Wood's R. [sc. *Athenæ Oxonienses*] 1710. **c.** A cento and a r. of uncircumcised nations 1647. **3.** This looks like mere r. GLADSTONE. Hence **Rha·psody** *v. intr.* to rhapsodize.

Rhatany (ræ·tăni). Also **ra(t)any, ratanhy.** 1808. [– mod.L. *rhatania* – Pg. *ratanha*, Sp. *ratania* – Quechua *rataña.*] The S. American shrub *Krameria triandra*; the astringent extract of its root, used in adulterating port-wine, and medicinally.

Rhea[1] (rī·ă). 1801. [mod.L. generic name (Möhring, 1752), a use of the mythological name L. *Rhea*, Gr. Ῥέα.] The South American or three-toed ostrich; the genus to which this bird belongs.

Rhea[2] (rī·ă). Also **rheea.** 1853. [Assamese.] = RAMIE.

Rheic (rī·ik), *a.* 1847. [f. RHEUM[2] + -IC 1 b, after Fr. *rhéique.*] *Chem. R. acid*: = next.

Rhein (rī·in). 1838. [f. RHEUM[2] + -IN[1], after Fr. *rhéine.*] *Chem.* An orange-coloured principle obtained from rhubarb; rheic acid.

†**Rhein-berry.** 1578. [– MDu. *rijnbesie*, f. *Rijn* RHINE[3] + *besie* berry.] The buckthorn berry –1706.

·**Rhematic** (rimæ·tik), *a.* and *sb. rare.* 1830. [– Gr. ῥηματικός, f. ῥῆμα, ῥηματ- word, verb; see -IC.] **A.** *adj.* **a.** Pertaining to the formation of words 1856. **b.** Formed on verbs 1877.

a. This period, during which expressions were coined for the most necessary ideas,..forms the first in the history of man,..and we call it the R. Period 1856.

B. *sb.* The science of sentences or propositions 1830.

Rhemish (rī·miʃ), *a.* 1589. [f. *Rhemes*, former Eng. spelling of *Rheims* + -ISH[1].] Of or pertaining to Rheims in the north-east of France: the specific designation of an English translation of the New Testament by Roman Catholics of the English college at Rheims, published in 1582. So **Rhe·mist,** one of the authors of the R. translation of and commentary on the New Testament.

Rhenish (re·niʃ), *a.* and *sb.* [Late ME. *rynis*, *-isch*, *renys* (assim. XVI to L.) – AFr. *reneis*, OFr. *rinois*, *rainois* – med.L. **Rhenensis*, for L. *Rhenanus*, f. *Rhenus* Rhine; see -ISH[1]. The mod. spelling is due to L.] **A.** *adj.* **1.** Of or belonging to the river Rhine, or the regions bordering upon it 1545. †**b.** Applied to the gulden formerly current in Germany and the Netherlands –1787. **2.** *R. wine*: wine produced in the Rhine region. late ME. **B.** *sb.* Rhenish wine. Now *rare.* 1602.

As he dreines his draughts of Renish downe SHAKS.

Rheo- (rī·ŏ, riˌǫ·), combining form of Gr. ῥέος stream, current, used chiefly in names of electrical apparatus.

Rhe·ochord, -cord, a wire used in measuring the resistance or reducing the strength of an electric current. **Rhe·ogra·ph, Rheo·meter,** instruments for measuring the force of electric and other currents; so **Rheome·tric** *a.* **Rheo·metry,** the measurement of electric currents. **Rhe·omotor,** an apparatus by which an electric current is generated. **Rhe·ophore** [Gr. -φορος bearing], (*a*) Ampère's name for the connecting wire of a voltaic cell; (*b*) one of the poles of a voltaic battery; an electrode; hence **Rheopho·ric** *a.* **Rhe·oscope,** an instrument for ascertaining the existence of an electric current; so **Rheosco·pic** *a.* applied to preparations of certain nerves of a frog for showing the variation of electric currents; so *rheoscopic frog, muscle.* **Rhe·ostat** [Gr. στατός], an instrument used to regulate the circuit so that any constant degree of force may be obtained; so **Rheosta·tic** *a.* **Rhe·otome** [Gr. -τομος cutting], a device for interrupting an electric current; = INTERRUPTER b. **Rhe·otrope** [Gr. -τροπος turning], an instrument for reversing an electric current.

‖**Rhesis** (rī·sis). 1871. [– Gr. ῥῆσις word, speech.] A set speech or discourse.

‖**Rhesus** (rī·sŏs). 1839. [mod.L., arbitrary use of L. *Rhesus*, Gr. Ῥῆσος, a mythical king of Thrace.] In full, *R. monkey*: one of the macaque, *Macacus r.*, an Indian monkey.

Rhetor (rī·tǫɹ). [Late ME. *rethor* (later *rhetor*) – late L. *rethor*, var. of L. *rhetor* – Gr. ῥήτωρ.] **1.** A teacher or professor of rhetoric; a rhetorician. **2.** An orator, esp. a professional one. Occas. in depreciatory use: a mere rhetorician. 1588. So **Rheto·ric** *a.* (*rare*) rhetorical; †eloquent.

Rhetoric (re·tŏrik), *sb.* [Late ME. *ret(h)orique* – OFr. *rethorique* (mod. *rhétorique*) – L. *rhetorica* (med.L. *reth-*) – Gr. ῥητορική, subst. use (sc. τέχνη art) of fem. of ῥητορικός rhetorical; see -IC.] **1.** The art of using language so as to persuade or influence others; the body of rules to be observed by a speaker or writer in order that he may express himself with eloquence. **b.** A treatise on, or 'body' of, rhetoric 1565. **2.** †**a.** Elegance or eloquence of language; eloquent speech or writing. **b.** Speech or writing expressed in terms calculated to persuade; hence, language characterized by artificial or ostentatious expression. Often *ironical* or *joc.* late ME. †**c.** *pl.* Elegant expressions; rhetorical flourishes. Also rhetorical terms –1628. **d.** *transf.* and *fig.*, esp. of the persuasiveness of looks or acts 1569. †**3.** Skill in or faculty of using eloquent and persuasive language –1750.

1. The therde of the vii sciences is called Rethoryque CAXTON. *personified.* Some condemn Rhetorick as the mother of lies 1642. **2.** And the perswasive R. That sleek't his tongue MILT. **d.** The heauenly Rhetoricke of thine eye SHAKS.

Rhetorical (ritǫ·rikăl), *a.* 1476. [– L. *rhetoricus*; see prec., -ICAL.] **1.** †**a.** Eloquent, eloquently expressed. **b.** Expressed in terms calculated to persuade; hence, of the nature of mere rhetoric (as opp. to sober statement or argument). **2.** Of, belonging to, concerned with, or comprised in, the art of rhetoric 1530. **3.** Of persons: Given to the use of rhetoric 1651.

1. The facts..were rather r. than logical 1869. *R. question*, one that does not require an answer, but is only put in the form of a question to produce a more striking effect. Hence **Rheto·rically** *adv.*, **-ness.**

Rhetorician (retŏri·ʃăn). late ME. [OFr. *rethoricien* (mod. *rhétoricien*), f. L. *rhetoricus* RHETORIC; see -IAN.] **1.** A professor or teacher of the art of rhetoric (esp. in Ancient Greece and Rome); a professional rhetor or orator. **2.** †**a.** An eloquent or elegant writer. **b.** One who uses rhetorical language or expression; *esp.* (often in depreciatory use) a public speaker who indulges in rhetoric. late ME.

1. Isocrates was a R. by profession: the framing of sentences, and turning of periods, was the great business of his long life 1838.

Rhe·torize, *v.* Now *rare* or *Obs.* 1608. [app. f. RHETOR + -IZE, perh. after late L. *rhetoricare* in same sense.] *intr.* To use rhetorical language. Hence †**Rhe·torized** *ppl. a.* addressed rhetorically. MILT.

Rheum[1] (rūm). Now *arch.* [XIV *reume* – OFr. *reume* (mod. *rhume*) – late L. *rheuma* – Gr. ῥεῦμα flow, bodily humour or defluxion.] **1.** Watery matter secreted by the mucous glands or membranes, such as collects in or drops from the nose, eyes, and mouth, etc.; hence, an excessive or morbid 'defluxion' of any kind. **b.** *poet.* Used for: Tears 1593. †**c.** *transf.* and *fig.* Applied to pernicious moisture or humour, or something resembling it –1650. **2.** *spec.* A mucous discharge caused by taking cold; hence, a cold in the lungs; catarrh. Chiefly *pl.* (occas. used = Rheumatic pains). late ME.

1. b. The Northeast wind..Awak'd the sleepie rhewme, and so by chance Did grace our hollow parting with a teare SHAKS. Hence **Rheumed** *ppl. a.* full of watery mucous.

‖**Rheum**[2] (rī·ŏm). 1753. [mod.L. – Gr. ῥῆον rhubarb.] *Bot.* The generic name for the Rhubarbs.

Rheumatic (rumæ·tik), *a.* and *sb.* late ME. [– OFr. *reumatique* (mod. *rhu-*) or L. *rheumaticus* (Pliny) – Gr. ῥευματικός, f. ῥεῦμα, ῥευματ- RHEUM[1]; see -IC.] **A.** *adj.* †**1.** Consisting of or of the nature of a watery discharge –1696. †2. Full of or dropping with watery mucus –1630. **3.** Of persons, their bodies: †**a.** Suffering from a 'defluxion of rheum' or catarrh –1661. **b.** Affected with, suffering from, or subject to rheumatism or rheumatic pain 1727. **4.** Of a disease, symptom: †**a.** Characterized by rheumy or catarrhal 'defluxion'. **b.** Of the nature of or characteristic of rheumatism. *R. fever*, an acute non-infectious febrile disease marked by inflammation and pain of the joints. 1563. **5.** Of weather, places: Inducing or having a tendency to produce rheumatism 1565.

5. India is a very r. country 1879.

B. *sb.* **1.** *pl.* Rheumatic pains, rheumatism. *colloq.* 1789. **2.** A rheumatic patient (*rare*) 1884. So **Rheuma·tical** *a.*, **Rheuma·tically** *adv.* by or with rheumatism.

Rheumatism (rū·mătiz'm). 1601. [– Fr. *rhumatisme* or L. *rheumatismus* – Gr. ῥευματισμός; see prec., -ISM.] †**1.** A 'defluxion of rheum'. **2.** A disease of which inflammation and pain of the joints are prominent features. In early use commonly with *a* and *pl.*, an attack of this disease. 1688. **3.** *attrib.* 1798.

2. *Acute* (*articular*) *r.*, rheumatic fever. *Muscular r.*, myalgia. **3.** *R. root*, the root of (1) some species of *Jeffersonia*, (2) *Dioscorea villosa*; the plants themselves. Hence **Rheumati·smal** *a.* rheumatic. **Rheumati·smoid**, *a.* resembling r. So **Rheu·matiz** (*dial.* and *vulgar*), rheumatism.

Rheu·mato-, comb. form of Gr. ῥεῦμα, ῥευματ- RHEUM[1], used in the sense of 'rheumatic', or 'rheumatic and ...'.

Rheumatoid (rū·mătoid), *a.* 1859. [f. RHEUMATISM + -OID.] Having the characters of rheumatism. Also, suffering from rheumatism.

Chiefly in *r. arthritis*, a chronic disease of the joints characterized by changes in the synovial membranes, etc., and resulting in deformity and immobility. So **Rheumatoi·dal** *a.*, **-ly** *adv.*

Rheumy (rū·mi), *a.* 1591. [f. RHEUM[1] + -Y[1].] **1.** = RHEUMATIC *a.* 1, 2. **2.** Moist, damp, wet; *esp.* of the air 1601.

1. The r. soberness of extreme age CARLYLE. **2.** *Jul. C.* II. i. 266.

Rhinal (rəi·năl), *a.* 1864. [f. Gr., ῥίς, ῥιν- nose + -AL[1] 1.] Belonging to or connected with the nose.

Rhine[1] (rīn). *s.-w. dial.* 1698. [app. repr. OE. *ryne.*] A large open ditch or drain.

Rhine[2] (rəin). 1641. [orig. *rine hemp* – G. *reinhanf*, lit. 'clean hemp'.] A fine quality of Russian hemp. Usu. *Riga r.* (*hemp*).

Rhine[3] (rəin). 1843. Name of the chief river of Germany, used *attrib.* to designate wines made from grapes grown in the Rhine valley. So **Rhi·neland**, the country around the river Rhine; also *attrib.* as *Rhineland foot, perch*, etc. **Rhi·nestone**, (*a*) a variety of rock crystal; (*b*) an artificial gem of paste or strass, cut to imitate a diamond.

Rhi·negrave. 1548. [– MDu. *Rijngrave* (mod. *-graaf*), G. *Rheingraf*; see GRAVE *sb.*[3]] A count whose domain borders on the river Rhine.

‖**Rhinencephalon** (rəinense·fălǫn). 1851. [f. Gr. ῥίς, ῥιν- nose + ENCEPHALON.] *Anat.* The olfactory lobe of the brain. Hence **Rhinencepha·lic** *a.* pertaining to or consisting of the r.

Rhino[1] (rəi·no). *slang.* 1688. [Origin unkn.] Money; often *ready r.*

Rhino[2] (rəi·no). 1884. Colloq. abbrev. of RHINOCEROS.

Rhino- (rəi·no, rəinǫ·), comb. form of Gr. ῥίς, ῥιν- nose. **Rhi·nolith**, a nasal calculus. **Rhinolo·gical**, *a.* pertaining to rhinology. **Rhino·logist**, a student of rhinology. **Rhino·logy**, the study of the nose, as a part of pathology. **Rhi·nophor(e**, an external olfactory organ; *spec.* in certain molluscs, the hinder pair of tentacles, which appear to have this function. **Rhinopla·stic** [see PLASTIC *a.*], *a. Surg.* pertaining to the plastic surgery of the nose; connected with rhinoplasty; so **Rhi·noplasty**, the rhinoplastic operation. ‖**Rhi:noscleroma**, a rare disease, characterized by a circumscribed, irregularly shaped, flattened, tubercular growth, having its seat about the region of the nose. **Rhi·noscope**, an instrument for examining the nasal cavity; so **Rhinosco·pic** *a.* pertaining to rhinoscopy; performed by means of the rhinoscope. **Rhino·scopy**, examination of the nasal cavity; use of the rhinoscope.

†**Rhinoce·rical**, *a.* 1688. [f. RHINOCEROS + -ICAL; in sense 2 with ref. to RHINO[1].] **1.** Of a nose: Like a rhinoceros' horn; retroussé –1710. **2.** *slang.* Having plenty of 'the rhino'; rich –1796.

Rhinoceros (rəinǫ·sĕrəs). ME. [– L. *rhinoceros* (Pliny), pl. *-otes*, in med.L. usu. *rino-*, – Gr. ῥινόκερως, f. ῥίς, ῥιν- nose + κέρας horn.] A large, unwieldy quadruped of a genus now found only in Africa and Southern Asia, having a horn (or, in some species, two horns) on the nose, and a very thick skin disposed in plates and folds. **b.** *transf.* A large unwieldy person 1885.

attrib. and *Comb.*: **r. auk,** the bird *Ceratorrhina monocerata*, having a horn at the base of its beak; **r. beetle,** a kind of beetle having a horn; **r. bird,** †(*a*) the Indian bird *Buceros rhinoceros*; (*b*) the African Beef-eater or Ox-pecker, genus *Buphaga*, which rids the rhinoceros' skin of ticks; †**r. nose,** = L. *nasus rhinocerotis*, used as descriptive of a sneer. So **Rhino·cerot,** (now *rare*) rhinoceros. **Rhinocero·tic** *a.* of, belonging to, characteristic of, or resembling the r.

Rhizanth (rəi·zænþ). 1840. [– mod.L. *Rhizantheæ*, f. Gr. ῥίζα root + ἄνθος flower.] *Bot.* A plant of the class *Rhizantheæ*, producing (apparently) only a root and flowers. So **Rhiza·nthous** *a.* flowering (apparently) from the root.

Rhizo- (rəi·zo, rəizǫ·), comb. form of Gr. ῥίζα root, used in the formation of botanical and other terms. **Rhi·zocarp** [Gr. καρπός fruit], a plant of the group *Rhizocarpeæ* (= *Marsiliaceæ*). **Rhizoca·rpous** *a.* having a perennial root but perishing stems. ‖**Rhizoce·phala** [Gr. κεφαλή head], an order of parasitic hermaphrodite crustaceans closely related to the cirripedes; also *sing.* ‖**Rhizoce·phalon,** one of these. **Rhi·zodont** [Gr. ὀδούς, ὀδοντ- tooth] *a.* having teeth with branching fangs anchylosing with the jaw, as a crocodile; *sb.* a rhizodont reptile. **Rhi·zogen,** a plant parasitic on the roots of another plant. **Rhizo·phagous** *a.* feeding on roots. ‖**Rhizo·stoma** [Gr. στόμα mouth], a genus of discomedusan hydrozoans having root-like oval arms; an animal of this genus (also **Rhi·zostome**). ‖**Rhizota·xis, Rhi·zotaxy,** arrangement or disposition of roots.

Rhizoid (rəi·zoid). 1858. [f. Gr. ῥίζα + -OID.] **A.** *adj.* Resembling a root. **B.** *sb.* A root-hair or filament 1875.

‖**Rhizoma** (rəizō^u·mă). Pl. **rhizo·mata.** 1830. [mod.L. – Gr. ῥίζωμα, f. ῥιζοῦσθαι take root, f. ῥίζα root; see -OMA.] *Bot.* A prostrate or subterranean root-like stem emitting roots and usu. producing leaves at its apex; a root-stock. Hence **Rhizo·matous** *a.* consisting of or of the nature of a r.; having rhizomata. So **Rhi·zome,** anglicized and more usual form of r.

‖**Rhizophora** (rəizǫ·fŏră). 1832. [mod.L. (sc. *herba* plant), f. Gr. ῥίζα root + -φορος bearing; see -PHORE, -A 2.] *Bot.* A genus typical of the family *Rhizophoraceæ*; a tree of this genus; a mangrove. So **Rhizo·phorous** *a.* root-bearing.

Rhizopod[1] (rəi·zŏpǫd). 1851. [– mod.L. RHIZOPODA.] *Zool.* An animalcule of the class *Rhizopoda.*

Rhizopod[2] (rəi·zŏpǫd). Also **-pode,** and in L. form. 1858. [– mod.L. *rhizopodium*, f. RHIZO- + Gr. πούς, ποδ- foot.] *Bot.* The mycelium of fungi.

‖**Rhizopoda** (rəizǫ·pŏdă), *sb. pl.* 1859. [mod.L., f. as prec.; see -A 4.] *Zool.* The lowest class of Protozoa comprising animalcules having pseudopodia. Hence **Rhizo·podal, Rhizopo·dic, Rhizo·podous** *adjs.* belonging to or characteristic of the R.

Rhodanate (rō^u·dănĕt). 1867. [irreg. f. Gr. ῥόδον rose + -AN + -ATE[4].] *Chem.* = SULPHOCYANATE. **Rhodanic** (rodæ·nik) *a.* = SULPHOCYANIC *a.*

Rhodeoretin (rō^udī,ǫ·rītin). 1845. [– G. *rhodeoretin*, f. Gr. ῥόδεος roseate + ῥητίνη resin.] *Chem.* = CONVOLVULIN.

Rhodes scholar (rō^u·dz skǫ:ləɹ), the holder of any of the scholarships founded at Oxford in 1902 by Cecil Rhodes and tenable by members of the British Commonwealth, South Africa, and the U.S. (Formerly also Germany.)

Rhodian (rō^u·diăn), *a* and *sb.* 1550. [f. L. *Rhodius*, f. *Rhodos, -us*, = Gr. Ῥόδος Rhodes; see -IAN.] **A.** *adj.* **a.** Of or belonging to the order of the Knights of Rhodes or Hospitallers 1592. **b.** Belonging to or inhabiting the island of Rhodes in the Ægean Sea off the south-west coast of Asia Minor 1697.

b. *R. Law* is the earliest system of marine law known to history, said to be compiled.., about 900 years before the Christian era 1866.

B. *sb.* **a.** A Knight of Rhodes; a Hospitaller 1550. **b.** An inhabitant or native of Rhodes 1593.

Rhodium[1] (rō^u·diŏm). 1661. [mod.L. (sc. *lignum* wood), neut. of *rhodius* rose-like (f. Gr. ῥόδον rose).] **1.** *R.-wood*, the sweet-scented wood of two species of Convolvulus, *C. floridus* and *C. scoparius*, of the Canary Islands. **2.** *Oil of r.* [= mod.L. *oleum rhodii*]: oil obtained from rose-wood; rosewood oil 1678.

Rhodium[2] (rō^u·diŏm). 1804. [f. Gr. ῥόδον rose + -IUM.] *Chem.* A very hard white metal of the platinum group, discovered by Wollaston; so named from the rose-colour of a dilute solution of the salts containing it. Symbol Rh, formerly Ro.

attrib., as *r. salt*; **r. gold, ingot,** native gold containing r.; **r. pen,** a steel pen tipped with r. Hence **Rho·dic** *a.* containing r. in smaller proportions, relatively to oxygen, than the rhodous compounds. **Rho·dous** *a.* containing r. in larger proportions than the rhodic compounds.

Rhodizonic (rō^udizǫ·nik), *a.* 1839. [f. Gr. ῥοδίζειν be red, f. ῥόδον rose, after G. *rhodizonsäure* (Heller, 1837); see -IC.] *Chem.* The name of two acids (so named because their salts are red) obtained from carboxide of potassium. Hence **Rhodizo·nate,** a salt of r. acid.

Rhodo- (rō^u·dŏ), comb. form of Gr. ῥόδον rose, used chiefly in names of mineral and chemical substances. **Rhodochro·site** [Gr. ῥοδόχρως], carbonate of manganese occurring in rose-red crystals. **Rhodocri·nite,** a rose-like encrinite. **Rhodo·psin** [Gr. ὄψις sight], visual purple. **Rho·dosperm** [Gr. σπέρμα seed], a seaweed of the class *Rhodospermeæ* characterized by rose-coloured spores.

‖**Rhododendron** (rō^udŏde·ndrǫn). *Pl.* **Rhododendrons, -dendra.** 1601. [L. *rhododendron* oleander (Pliny) – Gr. ῥοδόδενδρον, f. ῥόδον rose + δένδρον tree.] †**1.** The rose-bay or oleander –1607. **2.** A genus of showy ericaceous shrubs or low trees, akin to the azaleas, much cultivated for their evergreen foliage and profusion of large beautiful flowers; a plant or flower belonging to this genus 1664.

Rhodonite (rō^u·dŏnəit). 1823. [– G. *rhodonit*, f. Gr. ῥόδον rose; see -ITE[1] 2 b.] *Min.* Silicate of manganese, of a rose-pink colour when pure; manganese-spar, rose manganese.

Rhomb (rǫmb, rǫm). 1578. [– Fr. *rhombe* or L. RHOMBUS – Gr. ῥόμβος equilateral parallelogram, lozenge.] **1.** *Geom.* A plane figure having four equal sides and the opposite angles equal (two being acute and two obtuse). Also, a lozenge-shaped object or formation; *Nat. Hist.*, etc., a part, disposition of parts, marking, etc. of this shape. **2.** *Cryst.* A solid figure bounded by six equal and similar rhombic planes; a rhombohedron 1800. †**3.** A circle; a magic circle (*rare*) –1697.

1. See how in warlike muster they appear, In Rhombs and wedges, and half moons, and wings MILT.

attrib. and *Comb.*: **r.-ovate** *a.*, partly rhomboid and partly ovate; **-porphyry,** a porphyry enclosing crystals of orthoclase of a rhombic outline; **-spar,** applied to certain specimens of dolomite.

Rhombic (rǫ·mbik), *a.* 1670. [f. RHOMB + -IC.] **1.** Of the form of a rhomb 1701. **b.** *Zool.* Lozenge- or diamond-shaped, often with the corners somewhat rounded 1815. **c.** *Bot.* Oval, but angular at the sides 1857. **2.** Of solid figures: Having a rhomb for its base or section plane; also, bounded by equal and similar rhombs; *Cryst.* = ORTHORHOMBIC 1670.

Rho·mbo-, comb. form of Gr. ῥόμβος RHOMBUS, used to denote (1) rhombic, as in *r.-dodecahedron*; (2) forming a rhombus (and another figure), as in *r.-quadratic*, etc.

Rhombohedron (rǫmbohī·drǫn). *Pl.* **-hedra.** Also **rhomboedron.** 1836. [f. RHOMBO- + *-hedron* as in *polyhedron, tetrahedron.*] *Cryst.* A solid figure bounded by six equal rhombs; a crystal of this form. So **Rhombohe·dral** (rǫmbohī·drăl) *a.* pertaining to or having the form of a r.; *Cryst.* denoting a system in which all the forms are derivable from the r.; also, belonging to this system. **Rhombohe·dric** *a.*

Rhomboid (rǫ·mboid), *a.* and *sb.* 1570. [– Fr. *rhomboïde* or late L. RHOMBOIDES.] **A.** *adj.* **1.** Having the form of a rhomb; *spec.* in *Bot.*, oval, a little angular at the sides 1693. **2.** *Cryst.* = ORTHORHOMBIC. Now *rare.* 1670. **3.** *Anat.* **a.** *R. muscle* = RHOMBOIDEUS 1834. **b.** *R. ligament*: the costo-clavicular ligament. 1848. **B.** *sb.* **1.** A quadrilateral figure having only its opposite sides and angles equal 1570. **2.** *Cryst.* A solid bounded by six equal and similar rhombic faces parallel two and two 1800. **3.** *Anat.* = *R. muscle* 1835. Hence **Rho·mboidly** *adv.* (*rare*) with a r. form.

Rhomboi·dal, *a.* 1658. [f. prec. + -AL[1] 1.] **1.** = prec. A. 1. **2.** *Cryst.* = ORTHORHOMBIC 1729. Hence **Rhomboi·dally** *adv.* in the form of, or so as to form, a rhomboid.

‖**Rhomboides** (rǫmboi·dīz). Now *rare* or *Obs.* 1570. [In sense 1 late L. *rhomboides* – Gr. ῥομβοειδές (sc. σχῆμα), neut. of ῥομβοειδής, f. ῥόμβος; in sense 2 *rhomboides* masc. (sc. *musculus*).] **1.** *Geom.* = RHOMBOID B. 1. **2.** *Anat.* = RHOMBOIDEUS 1693.

‖**Rhomboideus** (rǫmboi·dĭ,ǫ̆s). *Pl.* **-ei** (ĭ,əi). 1835. [mod.L. (sc. *musculus*), f. *rhomboides*; see prec.] Used *attrib.* (with *muscle*) or *absol.*: Either of two muscles connecting the spinous process of the last cervical and first dorsal vertebræ with the scapula.

‖**Rhombus** (rǫ·mbǒs). *Pl.* **rhombuses; †rhombi.** 1567. [L.; see RHOMB.] **1.** *Geom.* = RHOMB 1. **2.** A rhomb-shaped instrument, pattern, etc. 1614. **3.** A genus of flat fishes comprising the turbot and the brill; a fish of this genus 1753. **4.** *Conch.* A shell of the genus *Oliva* 1776.

‖**Rhonchus** (rǫ·ŋkǒs). Also **ronchus.** *Pl.* **rhonchi** (rǫ·ŋkəi). 1829. [L. – Gr. *ῥόγχος, var. of ῥέγχος snoring.] A dry sound heard by auscultation in the bronchial tubes; usu. identified with RÂLE. Hence **Rho·nchal,** also **ronchal,** *a.* pertaining to or characterized by snoring or (*spec.* in *Path.*) r.

Rhopalic (rouᵘpæ·lik), *a.* 1682. [– late L. *rhopalicus* (servius), f. Gr. ῥόπαλος cudgel thicker towards one end; see -IC.] *Pros.* Applied to verses in which each word contains one syllable more than the one immediately preceding it.

Rhopalocerous (rōᵘpălǫ·sĕrəs), *a.* 1882. [f. mod.L. *Rhopalocera*, n. pl. (f. Gr. ῥόπαλος club + κέρας horn) + -OUS.] *Ent.* Belonging to the sub-order *Rhopalocera*; lepidopterous insects having clubbed antennæ (i.e. butterflies).

Rhotacism (rōᵘ·tăsiz'm). Also **rotacism.** 1834. [– mod.L. *rhotacismus* – Gr. *ῥωτακισμός, f. ῥωτακίζειν make excessive or wrong use of *r*, f. ῥῶ letter R; see -ISM, and cf. LAMBDACISM.] **1.** Excessive use or peculiar pronunciation of *r*; *spec.* the use of the burr or *r grasseyé*. **2.** *Philol.* Conversion of another sound (esp. *s*) into *r* 1844.

Rho·tacize, *v.* [– Gr. ῥωτακίζειν; see prec., -IZE.] *intr.* To be characterized or marked by rhotacism.

Rhubarb (rū·baɹb). [Late ME. *rubarbe* – OFr. *ru-*, *reubarbe* (mod. *rhubarbe*) – Rom. **r(h)eubarbum*, shortening of med.L. *r(h)eubarbarum*, alt. by assoc. with *rheum* RHEUM[2] of RHABARBARUM (whence It. *rabarbaro*, G. *rhabarber*), f. late L. *rhā* – Gr. ῥᾶ, said by Ammianus Marcellinus to be called after the ancient name *Rhā* of the river Volga.] **1.** The medicinal root-stock, purgative and subsequently astringent, of one or more species of *Rheum* grown in China and Tibet and formerly imported into Europe through Russia and the Levant; usu. (*e.g.* in pharmaceutical and domestic use) called *Turkey* or *Russian r.*, but now known commercially as *East Indian* or *Chinese r.* **b.** *fig.* as a type of bitterness or sourness 1526. **2.** Any plant of the genus *Rheum*. late ME. **b.** *English* or *French R.*: any of various species cultivated in England or France. *Common* or *Garden R.*: any of the species having heart-shaped, smooth, deep-green leaves growing on thick fleshy stalks; also the leaf-stalks themselves, which are much used in the spring as a substitute for fruit 1650. **3.** *attrib.* or *adj.*: **†a.** *fig.* Bitter, tart 1586. **b.** Of the colour of medicinal rhubarb, yellowish-brown 1802. Hence **Rhu·barby** *a.* resembling r.

Rhumb (rɒm, rɒmb). 1578. [– Fr. *rumb*, †*rum*, earlier †*ryn* (*de vent* of wind) point of the compass, prob. – Du. *ruim* space, room, altered later by assoc. with L. *rhombus* RHOMBUS; cf. Sp. *rumbo*, Pg. *rumbo*, *rumo*, It. *rombo*, which may be partly the source of the Eng. word.] **†1. a.** The line followed by a vessel sailing on one course or a wind blowing continuously in one direction. **b.** Any one of the set of lines drawn through a point on a map or chart and indicating the course of an object moving always in the same direction. *Obs.* exc. *Hist.* **c.** One of the principal points of the compass 1594. **2.** The angular distance, = 11° 15′, between two successive points of the compass 1625.

attrib.: **r-line,** = 1a, b. **-sailing,** sailing on a r.-line.

‖**Rhus** (rɒs). 1611. [L. – Gr. ῥοῦς.] A genus of shrubs and trees, mostly poisonous, especially abundant at the Cape of Good Hope; a plant of this genus, a sumach. **b.** A drug obtained from the sumach 1878.

Rhyme (rəim), *sb.* 1610. [Graphic var. of RIME *sb.*[1], which arose through etymological association with the ultimate source, L. *rhythmus.*] **1.** A piece of poetry or metrical composition in which the consonance of terminal sounds (see 3) is observed; usu. *pl.*, verses, poetry. **2.** Verse marked by consonance of the terminal sounds (see 3) 1652. **3.** *Pros.* Agreement in the terminal sounds of two or more words or metrical lines, such that (in English prosody) the last stressed vowel and any sounds following it are the same, while the sound or sounds preceding it are different 1663.

Examples: *which, rich*; *peace, increase*; *descended, extended.* (See FEMALE, FEMININE, MALE, MASCULINE, RICH, TAILED.)

Imperfect rhymes are tolerated to a large extent in English, e.g. *phase, race*; *did, seed,*; among these some rhyme only to the eye, as *loved, proved*; etc. The term is sometimes extended to include assonance and even alliteration (*initial* or *head rime*).

b. Coupled with *reason.* Chiefly in neg. phrases used to express lack of good sense or reasonableness. 1664. **c.** An instance of rhyme; a rhyme-word 1656.

1. He knew Himself to sing, and build the lofty r. MILT. **2.** Things unattempted yet in Prose or Rhime MILT. To make old prose in modern r. more sweet KEATS. *R. royal*, that form of verse which consists of stanzas of seven five-stress lines rhyming *ababbcc*. (This name succeeded to the older designation *ballade royal*.) **3. b.** This won't do. There's neither r. nor reason about it 1888. **c.** *Single, double, triple* (or *treble*) *r.*, one involving one, two, or three syllables respectively.

Rhyme (rəim), *v.* 1660. [Graphic var. of RIME *v.*[1]; cf. prec.] **1.** *intr.* To make rhymes or verses; to versify 1697. **2.** *trans.* With obj. and compl.; esp. in *to r. to death*, (*a*) orig. with ref. to the alleged destruction of rats in Ireland by incantation; (*b*) to destroy the reputation of (a person) by writing verses upon him; also, to pester with rhymes 1660. **3. a.** To put (one's thoughts) into rhyming form. **b.** To compose (rhymed verses). 1848. **4.** *intr.* **a.** Of words or metrical lines: To terminate in sounds that form a rhyme. **b.** Of a word: To be a rhyme *to* (another word). Also const. *with.* 1672. **5.** To use rhyme; to find or furnish a rhyme *to* (a word) 1690. **6.** To cause (words) to rhyme; to use as rhymes 1824.

1. I am going to Ashestiel for eight days, to fish and r. SCOTT. **2.** Ratts Rhimed to Death, Or, the Rump-Parliament Hang'd up in the Shambles 1660. **3. a.** I r. my thoughts without an aim 1848. **4. b.** The Couplet where a-Stick rhimes to Ecclesiastick STEELE. **6.** *fig.* Nature never rhymes her children, nor makes two men alike EMERSON. Hence **Rhy·mer, Rhy·mester,** one who makes (poor) rhymes or verses; a mere versifier. **Rhy·mist,** a writer of rhymes or verses; one who uses (good or bad) rhymes.

Rhynchocephalian (riŋkosĭfēⁱ·liăn), *a.* (and *sb.*) 1867. [f. mod.L. *Rhynchocephala* (f. Gr. ῥύγχος snout + κεφαλή head) + -IAN.] Belonging to the order *Rhynchocephala* of reptiles (including *Hatteria*). As *sb.* A rhynchocephalian reptile.

Rhynchocœle (ri·ŋkosīl), *a.* and *sb.* 1877. [– mod.L. *Rhynchocœla*, f. Gr. ῥύγχος snout + κοῖλος hollow.] *Zool.* **A.** *adj.* Belonging to the *Rhynchocœla*, a group of turbellarians comprising the Nemerteans. **B.** *sb.* A rhynchocœle turbellarian. Hence **Rhynchocœ·lous** *a.*

Rhyncholite (ri·ŋkŏləit). 1836. [f. Gr. ῥύγχος beak + λίθος stone, -LITE.] *Geol.* A fossilized beak of a tetrabranchiate cephalopod.

Rhynchophore (ri·ŋkofoᵊɹ). 1826. [– mod.L. *Rhynchophora*, n. pl. of *rhynchophorus*, f. Gr. ῥύγχος snout; see -PHORE, -A 4.] *Ent.* A beetle of the group *Rhynchophora*, having the head prolonged into a beak or snout; a weevil. So **Rhyncho·phorous** (riŋkǫ·fŏrəs) *a.* belonging to the *Rhynchophore.*

Rhynchotous (riŋkōᵘ·təs), *a.* 1890. [f. mod.L. *Rhynchota* (f. Gr. ῥύγχος snout) + -OUS.] *Ent.* Belonging to the order *Rhynchota* (= *Hemiptera*) of insects.

Rhyolite (rəi·ŏləit). 1872. [– G. *rhyolit* (Richthofen), irreg. f. Gr. ῥύαξ stream (of lava) + λίθος stone; see -LITE.] *Geol.* A variety of trachyte found in Hungary, containing quartz; later, a general name for volcanic rocks exhibiting a fluidal texture. Hence **Rhyoli·tic** *a.*

Rhyparographer (ripărǫ·grăfəɹ). 1656. [– L. *rhyparographos* = Gr. ῥυπαρογράφος, f. ῥυπαρός filthy; see -GRAPHER. Cf. Fr. *riparographe.*] A painter of mean or sordid subjects. So **Rhyparo·graphist. Rhyparogra·phic** *a.* characteristic of a r. **Rhyparo·graphy,** the painting of mean and sordid subjects; *spec.* still-life or genre painting.

Rhysimeter (rəisi·mĭtəɹ). 1871. [f. Gr. ῥύσις flowing, stream + -METER.] An instrument for measuring the velocity of fluids or the speed of ships.

Rhythm (ri·ð'm, ri·þ'm). 1557. [In branch I a graphic var. of RIME *sb.*[1] (cf. RHYME *sb.*), assim. to L. *rhythmus* or Fr. *rhythme.* The rhyme-words *time, crime,* etc. attest the pron. (rəim). In branch II – L. *rhythmus* or Fr. *rhythme* – Gr. ῥυθμός, rel. to ῥεῖν flow.] **I. †1.** Rhyming or rhymed verse; a form or variety of this –1695. **†2.** A piece of rhyming verse –1677. **†3.** The fact of lines ending in the same sound; an instance of this –1680.

2. When ye these rythmes doo read, and vew the rest SPENSER. And..build a lofty Rhythm, That shall outlast the insolence of time 1677.

II. 1. *Pros.* The measured recurrence of arsis and thesis determined by vowel-quantity or stress, or both combined; kind of metrical movement, as determined by the relation of long and short, or stressed and unstressed, syllables in a foot or line 1560. **b.** Rhythmical or metrical form 1656. **c.** The measured flow of words or phrases 1832. **2.** *Mus.* **a.** That feature of musical composition which depends on the systematic grouping of notes according to their duration. **b.** Kind of structure as determined by the arrangement of such groups. 1776. **3.** *Art.* Due correlation and interdependence of parts, producing a harmonious whole 1776. **4.** *gen.* Movement marked by the regulated succession of strong and weak elements, or of opposite or different conditions 1855. **b.** *Phys.* and *Path.* of functional movements as the heart, respiration, etc. 1722.

1. All Metre is therefore R., but not all R. Metre 1737. **b.** One began and sang in r., the rest.. hearing with silence 1657. **c.** In every sentence, however uttered, there is a r. 1863. **3.** The r. and symmetry of a stately Italian palace 1867. **4.** So do flux and reflux—the r. of change—alternate and persist in everything under the sky T. HARDY. **c.** The 'r.' of cell-division 1890. Hence **Rhy·thmist,** one versed in r. **Rhy·thmless** *a.*

Rhythmed (ri·ðmd, ri·þmd), *a.* 1695. [f. prec. + -ED².] †**1.** Rhymed. **2.** Marked by rhythm; rhythmical 1863.

Rhythmic (ri·ðmik, ri·þmik), *a.* and *sb.* 1603. [– Fr. *rhythmique* or L. *rhythmicus* – Gr. ῥυθμικός, f. ῥυθμός RHYTHM; see -IC.] **A.** *adj.* = next 3, 4.

Much of it, too,..is r.; a kind of wild chanting song CARLYLE. The r. rattling of the train 1873.

B. *sb.* The science or theory of rhythm 1603. Also **Rhy·thmics** 1864.

Rhythmical (ri·ðmikăl, ri·þmikăl), *a.* 1567. [f. as prec.; see -ICAL.] †**1.** Composing verse; rhyming. †**2.** Written in rhyming verse –1706. **3. a.** Of language, verse: Marked by or composed in rhythm; often, having a good, smooth, or flowing rhythm 1589. **b.** *gen.* Of motion, etc. 1619. **c.** *Phys.* and *Path.* 1840. **d.** *Art.* 1880. **4.** Relating to, concerning, or involving rhythm 1619.

3. The rhapsode recited..a species of musical and r. declamation 1846. **b.** The r. cadence of the oars 1889. **c.** R. actions, such as that of the respiration 1883. **4.** Less through rythmical skill than a musical ear POE. Hence **Rhy·thmically** *adv.*

Rhythmo·meter. 1812. [f. Gr. ῥυθμός RHYTHMUS; see -METER.] A kind of metronome.

‖**Rhythmus** (ri·ðmŏs, ri·þmŏs). *Pl.* **-mi** (-məi). 1531. [L. – Gr. ῥυθμός, related to ῥεῖν flow.] **1.** *Pros.* = RHYTHM *sb.* II. 1, 1 b. **2.** *Mus.* = RHYTHM *sb.* II. 2. 1734.

‖**Rhytina** (ritəi·nă). Also **Rytina.** 1835. [mod.L., f. Gr. ῥυτίς wrinkle; see -INA².] A genus of *Sirenia*, represented by one species, *R. stelleri*, now extinct; an animal of this genus; the Arctic Sea-cow.

Rial (rəi·ăl), *sb.* Now *Hist.* late ME. [f. next after Fr. and (later) Sp. models; cf. REAL *sb.*¹] †**1.** A royal person –1475. †**2.** The second branch of a stag's horn, lying immediately above the brow-antler –1486. **3.** A gold coin formerly current in England, orig. worth ten shillings, first issued by Edward IV in 1465. Now *Hist.* 1473. †**4.** A Spanish coin; = REAL *sb.*¹ 1. –1809. †**b.** *R. of plate* (Sp. *real de plata*), an eighth of a dollar or 6½*d.* –1748. †**c.** *R. of eight*, = REAL *sb.*¹ 2. –1738.

†**Ri·al**, *a.* ME. [– OFr. *rial*, var. of *real* REAL *a.*¹] Royal, regal –1584.

‖**Ria·lto.** 1879. [Name of the quarter in Venice in which the Exchange is situated.] An exchange or mart.

Riant (rəi·ănt, Fr. rian̄), *a.* Also occas. **ri-ante** (rian̄t). 1567. [– Fr. *riant*, pr. pple. of *rire* :– L. *ridēre* laugh; see -ANT.] Smiling, mirthful, cheerful, gay.

A..r. landskip 1792. He was jovial, r., jocose rather than serious 1867. Hence **Ri·antly** *adv.*

‖**Riata** (ri,ā·tă). 1869. [Sp. *reata*, f. *reatar* tie again, f. *re-* RE- + *atar* :– L. *aptare* apply, adjust.] = LARIAT.

Rib, *sb.* [OE. *rib(b*, corresp. (with variations in gender and declension) to OFris. *ribb, rebb*, OS. *ribbi* (Du. *rib(be)*, OHG. *rippi, rippa* (G. *rippe*), ON. *rif* :– Gmc. **rebja, -jō*.] **I. 1.** One of the curved bones articulated in pairs to the spine in men and animals and enclosing or tending to enclose the thoracic or body cavity, whose chief organs they protect. **b.** *Zool.* One of the meridional plates characteristic of the *Ctenophora*; a ctenophore 1890. **2.** One of these bones taken from the carcase of an ox, pig, etc., with the meat adhering to it, as used for food. late ME. **3.** With allusion to the creation of Eve (*Gen.* 2:21): A (person's) wife; a woman 1589. †**b.** So *r. of man(kind)*, *lost r.* –1647.

1. *Asternal, floating ribs*: see those adjs. *False r.* = asternal rib. *Sternal* or *true ribs*, those attached to the breast-bone or sternum. *To smite* (a person) *under the fifth r.*, to strike to the heart. **2.** Dined well on some good ribbs of beef roasted and mince pies PEPYS. **3. b.** Surely if feasting ever be in season it is at the recovery of the lost r. [i.e. marriage] 1647.

II. 1. The central or principal nerve or vein of a leaf, extending from the petiole to the apex = MIDRIB 2; also, one of the smaller or secondary nerves. Now *Bot.* late ME. **b.** The shaft or quill of a feather 1545. **c.** *Ent.* A nervure in an insect's wing 1843. **d.** *Bot.* A more dense or firm part extending along or through an organ or structure 1847. **2.** A hard or rocky portion of a mountain, etc., esp. when in the form of a projecting ridge 1586. **b.** A vein of ore, or the solid part of one; a stratum or dyke of stone or rock. Now esp. *Geol.* 1667. **c.** *Mining.* A wall of coal left standing to support the roof of the workings 1839. **3. a.** A narrow strip of land, as that between furrows; also *dial.*, a furrow. **b.** A narrow ridge separating a roadway from the ditch. 1670. **4.** In techn. use, an artificial ridge raised upon some object: **a.** *Mech.* A raised band or flange, esp. one made upon a metal plate in order to stiffen it 1793. **b.** *Gunmaking.* A bar or ridge of metal made on each barrel of a double-barrelled gun, and serving to connect the two 1815. **c.** A raised ridge in a knitted stocking, cloth, or the like 1829. **d.** *Bookbinding.* One of the raised bands upon the back of a book, serving as a covering for the cords and as an ornament 1875. **5.** *Conch.* A salient ridge upon a shell 1711.

2. b. Soon had his crew Op'nd into the Hill a spacious wound And dig'd out ribs of Gold MILT.

III. 1. *Naut.* One of the curved frame-timbers of a ship, extending from the keel to the top of the hull, upon which the planking of the side is nailed; also, in later use, a piece of strong ironwork serving the same purpose 1553. **2.** *Building.* **a.** A piece of timber forming part of the framework or roof of a house; in mod. *dial.*, a purlin. late ME. **b.** An arch supporting a vault; one or other of the transverse or oblique arches by which a compound vault is sustained; the edge or groin of two intersecting arches in a vault. Also, in later use, a projecting band or moulding on a groin or ceiling (whether vaulted or flat), or on some other architectural feature. 1726. **c.** One of a set of arched wooden trusses used for the centring of a bridge; one of a set of parallel timbers or iron beams (whether arched or flat) serving to carry a bridge 1735. **d.** One of the curved pieces of stone-, timber-, or ironwork which form the framework of a dome 1766. **3.** A bar or rod (of wood or iron) serving to strengthen or support a structure 1547. **b.** A bar of a grate or the like. Now *Sc.* and *n. dial.* 1651. **c.** One of the two horizontal bars of a printing-press upon which or in the grooves of which the carriage supporting the bed slides on its way towards the platen 1683. **4. a.** One of the curved pieces of wood forming the body of a lute or the sides of a violin 1676. **b.** One of the strips of whalebone or stout metal wires composing the framework of an umbrella or sunshade 1716. **c.** One of the hoops which serve to form the folds in organ-bellows 1881.

1. Vailing her high top lower then her ribs SHAKS. *Ribs and Trucks*, used figuratively for fragments 1867. Hence **Ri·bless** *a.* **Ri·blet,** a small r.

Rib, *v.* 1547. [f. RIB *sb.*] **1.** To furnish or strengthen with ribs; to enclose as with ribs. †**b.** To form the ribs of (a ship). COWPER. **2.** To mark with rib-like ridges; to form or shape into ridges 1548. **b.** *Agric.* To plough (land), leaving a space between the furrows; to rafter or half-plough 1735.

1. Your Isle, which stands As Neptunes Parke, ribb'd, and pal'd in With Oakes vnskaleable SHAKS. Hence **Ri·bbing,** the action of the vb.; ribs collectively.

Ribald (ri·băld), *sb.* and *a.* [ME. *ribaud* – OFr. *ribaut, -ault, -auld*, (also mod.) *ribaud*, f. *riber* pursue licentious pleasures, f. Gmc. base repr. by OHG. *hriba* whore.] **A.** *sb.* †**1.** One of an irregular class of retainers who performed the lowest offices in royal or baronial households, and were employed in warfare as irregular troops; hence, a menial or dependent of low birth –1647. †**2.** A low, base, worthless, or good-for-nothing fellow; a varlet, knave, rascal, vagabond –1641. †**3.** A wicked, dissolute, or licentious person –1590. **4.** One who uses offensive, scurrilous, or impious language; one who jests or jeers in an irreverent or blasphemous manner. late ME.

4. What eylythe the, rebawde, on me to raue? 1529.

B. *adj.* Offensively abusive, scurrilous, wantonly irreverent or impious 1500.

The ribbald invectives which occupy the place of argument BURKE. The r. crowd SHELLEY. A r. cuckoo 1890. Hence †**Ri·baldish** *a.* (*rare*) ribald-like. **Ri·baldrous** *a.* of ribald character; ribald (now *Obs.* or *arch.*).

Ribaldry (ri·băldri). ME. [– OFr. *re-, ribau(l)derie*. See prec. and -RY.] †**1.** Debauchery; lasciviousness, vice –1645. **2.** Obscenity or coarseness of language; †a coarse tale; in later use, scurrilous or irreverent jesting ME.

Riband (ri·bănd), *sb.* Now *arch.* [Late ME. *reban, riban, ryban*, later *ryband, ribband* – OFr. *riban* (still dial.), *reuban*, (also mod.) *ruban*, prob. – Gmc. compd. of *band* BAND *sb.*² The *d* is parasitic, as in *astound*.] **1.** = RIBBON *sb.* 1. b. = RIBBON *sb.* 2. 1766. **2.** *Her.* = RIBBON *sb.* 3. 1562. **3.** *pl.* Reins 1840. **4. a.** A narrow strip *of* something; an object resembling a ribbon in form 1801. **b.** *pl.* Torn strips; shreds, tatters 1818.

Comb.: **r. jasper,** a variety of jasper having the colours in broad stripes. So **Ri·band** *v. trans.* (now *arch.*) to adorn with ribands. **Ri·banding,** ribbons; ribbon-work.

Ribband (ri·bănd). 1711. [perh. f. RIB *sb.* + BAND *sb.*², but possibly identical with RIBBON, which was so used from the same date.] **1.** *Shipbuilding*, one of a number of long narrow flexible pieces of timber which are nailed or bolted externally to the ribs of a ship from stem to stern, to keep them temporarily in position. **2.** In launching vessels, a square timber fastened on the outer side of the bilge-ways, to prevent the cradle from slipping outwards 1779. **3.** *Mil.* A wood scantling used in the construction of a gun or mortar platform 1859. **4.** A light spar used in the construction of a pontoon-bridge 1899.

Ribbed (ribd), *ppl. a.* 1523. [f. RIB *sb.* or *v.* + -ED.] **1.** Having ribs of a specified kind or number, or arranged in a certain way; as *five-r., close-r.*, etc. **2.** Having ribs or ridges; marked with ribs 1742. **3.** Furnished with ribs 1814.

2. A waistcoat of r. black satin DICKENS. *R. grass* = RIB-GRASS. **R.-nose baboon,** the mandrill. **3.** Some horses are what is called r. home; there is but little space between the last rib and the hip-bone 1831.

Ribble-rabble (ri·b'l ræ·b'l), *adv.* and *sb.* 1460. [redupl. of RABBLE *sb.*¹] **A.** *adv.* In great confusion (*rare*). **B.** *sb.* **1.** Confused meaningless language; rigmarole, gibble-gabble. *arch.* 1601. **2.** = RABBLE *sb.*¹ 2. 1635.

Ribbon (ri·bən), *sb.* 1527. [Later f. RIBAND.] **1.** A narrow woven band of some fine material, as silk or satin, used to ornament clothing or headgear, or for other purposes. **a.** Without article, as a material. **b.** With *a* and *pl.*: A piece or length of this. Also, a particular kind or make of it. 1611. **2.** The badge of an order of knighthood; also *transf.*, high distinction in anything 1651. **3.** *Her.* A subordinary, in width one eighth of the bend, and one half of the cost, usu. borne couped 1704. **4.** *pl.* Reins 1813. **5.** A long narrow strip of anything, e.g. of metal, sky, etc. 1763. **6. a.** *Anat.* and *Zool.* A tissue or structure having the form of a ribbon. *Lingual r.*, = ODONTOPHORE 1803. **b.** *Bot.* A leaf; branch, or other structure, resembling a ribbon 1855. **7.** *pl.* Torn strips of anything; tatters, shreds 1820. **8.** A ribband; a wale or strip of wood 1711.

1. a. From her lifted hand Dangled a length of r. TENNYSON. **2.** There were one or two stars and ribbons 1879. **7.** The sails hung in ribbons from the yards 1883.

attrib. and *Comb.* **1.** In sense 1, as *r.-weaver, factory*, etc.; **R. Society,** a Roman Catholic secret society formed in the north and north-west of Ireland early in the 19th c. to counteract the Protestant influence, and associated with agrarian disorders; so *R. association, pass-word, system, work.* **2.** In sense resembling a r. or ribbons, 'forming a long narrow strip or strips', as *r. border, lightning*, etc.; **r. building,** the erection of houses, etc. along main roads. **b.** Marked with bands or stripes, as *r. agate, jasper, onyx.* **c.** In names of plants, as **r. fern,** etc. **d.** In names of animals, fishes, etc., as **r. gurnard** (*Lepidosomatida*), **worm.** Hence **Ri·bboner,** a member of the R. Society. **R·ibbonism,** the principles or policy of the R. Society.

Ribbon (ri·bən), *v.* 1716. [f. the sb.] **1.** *trans.* To adorn with ribbon or ribbons; to mark or stripe in a way resembling ribbons. Usu. in *pa. pple.* **b.** To separate into thin narrow strips 1856. **2.** *intr.* Of melted soap, wax, etc.: To form into 'ribbons' 1895.

Ri·bbon-fish. 1793. *Zool.* A fish having a very long, slender, flattened body, as those of the genera *Cepola* and *Regalecus*.

Ri·bbon-grass. 1786. A grass having long slender leaves, esp. a variegated variety of *Phalaris*.

Ribbony (ri·bəni), *a.* 1839. [f. RIBBON *sb.* + -Y¹.] Abounding in, decked with, ribbons; resembling a ribbon or ribbons.

R. gum, a name in N. S. Wales for *Eucalyptus viminalis*.

‖**Ribes** (rəi·bīz). 1562. [med.L. – Arab. *rībās* sorrel.] †**1.** As *pl.* (Red, Black, or White) Currants –1657. **2.** *Bot.* A genus of plants comprising the currants and gooseberry 1731.

Rib-grass (ri·bgrɑs). 1538. [f. RIB *sb.* + GRASS.] **1.** = RIBWORT. **2.** The Native Plantain (*Plantago varia*) of Australia and Tasmania 1898.

†**Ribibe.** late ME. [– OFr. *rebebe* (mod. *rebec* REBECK) – Arab. *rabāb* one-, two-, or three-stringed fiddle.] **1.** = REBECK –1450. **2.** An opprobrious or abusive term for an old woman –1616.

Ri·b-roast, *v.* Now *arch.* 1570. [f. RIB *sb.* + ROAST *v.*] *trans.* To belabour with a cudgel; to beat severely; to thrash.

Ribston (ri·bstən). Also **Ribstone.** 1769. [f. *Ribston* Park, between Knaresborough and Wetherby in Yorks.] **1.** *R. pippin*, a choice variety of dessert apple. **2.** *ellipt.* The (*or* a) R. pippin 1844.

Ribwort (ri·bwɒɹt). late ME. [f. RIB *sb.* + WORT¹.] The Narrow-leaved Plantain (*Plantago lanceolata*); ribgrass; so *R. Plantain.* **b.** A plant belonging to the *Plantaginaceæ* 1846.

Ricardian (rĭkā·ɹdiăn), *a.* and *sb.* 1863. [f. the name *Ricardo*; see -IAN.] **A.** *adj.* Of, pertaining to, or accepting the doctrines of the political economist David Ricardo (1772–1823). **B.** *sb.* A follower of Ricardo 1886.

Rice (rəis). [ME. *rys* – OFr. *ris* (mod. *riz*) – It. *riso* :– Rom. **orizum*, for L. *oryza* – Gr. ὄρυζα (also ὄρυζον), of Eastern origin.] **1.** The seeds of the plant *Oryza sativa*, forming one of the important food-grains of the world **2.** The rice-plant, *Oryza sativa* 1562. **3.** With *pl.* A kind or variety of rice 1681. **4.** *Wild r.*, = Canada or Indian Rice 1814.

1. Wot you forsooth why R. is so generally eaten and so valuable? 1638.

attrib. and *Comb.* as *r.-arrack, -bread, -field*, etc.; **r.-bunting,** the r.-bird or bobolink; **-grains,** *Astr.*, granular markings observed on the surface of the sun; **-rat,** an American rodent feeding upon r.; **-troopial,** = *r.-bunting*; **-weevil,** a small beetle, *Calandra oryzæ*, which is very injurious to r.

Ri·ce-bird. 1704. †**1.** An E. Indian bird which lives among the rice. **2.** The Paddy bird or Java sparrow 1743. **3.** The reed-bird or bobolink 1747.

Ri·ce-paper. 1822. A Chinese paper consisting of thin slices of the pith of *Aralia papyrifera*, a tree of Formosa; so *r. plant* or *tree*, the shrub *Aralia* or *Fatsia papyrifera*.

Ri·ce-water. 1797. **1.** A liquid for drinking or other purposes, prepared from rice boiled in water. **2.** Used *attrib.* to describe the evacuations of cholera-patients 1866.

Rich (ritʃ), *a.*, *adv.*, and *sb.* [OE. *rīce* = OFris. *rīk(e*, OS. *rīki*, OHG. *rīchi* (Du. *rijk*, G. *reich*), ON. *rikr*, Goth. *reiks*, Gmc. – Celtic *rīx* = L. *rēx* king; reinforced in ME. by (O)Fr. *riche* (orig. powerful) – Gmc.] **A.** *adj.* †**1.** Of persons: Powerful, mighty, exalted, noble, great –1535. **2.** Having large possessions or abundant means; wealthy, opulent OE. **b.** Of places, countries, etc.: Abounding in wealth or natural resources ME. **3.** With preps.: Wealthy *in*, amply provided *with*, some form of property or valuable possessions ME. **4.** Valuable; of great worth ME. **5.** Of dress, etc.: Splendid, costly; of expensive or superior material or make ME. **b.** Of buildings, furniture, etc.: Made of, or adorned with, valuable materials; also elaborately ornamented or wrought ME. †**c.** *gen.* Fine, splendid, magnificent –1578. **d.** Of feasts: Sumptuous, luxurious ME. **6.** Of choice or superior quality; esp. of articles of food or drink; also, composed of choice ingredients; containing plenty of fat, butter, eggs, sugar, fruit, etc. ME. **b.** Of colour: Strong, deep, warm ME. **c.** Of musical sounds: Full and mellow in tone 1592. **d.** Of odours: Full of fragrance 1599. **7.** Plentiful, abundant 1450. **b.** Of a full, ample, or unstinted nature; highly developed or cultivated 1561. **c.** Of rhyme (after Fr. *rime riche*): Characterized by exact identity between the syllables involved 1656. **d.** Highly entertaining or amusing; also, preposterous, outrageous 1760. **8.** Of mines or ores: Yielding a large quantity or proportion of the precious metals 1555. **b.** Of soil, lands, etc.: Abounding in the qualities necessary to produce good vegetation or crops 1577.

2. R. sons forget they ever had poor fathers MASSINGER. He was..passing r. with forty pounds a year GOLDSM. **b.** New Spain is by far the richest mineral country in the world 1802. **3.** How r. with regal spoils! DRYDEN. Mines..r. in gold and silver 1802. *fig.* Her ample page, R. with the spoils of time GRAY. **4.** With ribanes of red golde and of riche stones LANGL. **5.** Silks..so r., they'd stand alone CRABBE. **b.** An ancient..knocker..of r. Venetian sculpture 1864. **d.** A. r. repast COWPER. **6.** As leanest land supplies the richest wine COWPER. **b.** Red as the Roses, richest of coloure. late ME. **c.** Instruments of a soft and r. tone 1836. **d.** The moist r. smell of the rotting leaves TENNYSON. **7.** A r. theme for scandal 1867. **d.** O Garrick! what a r. scene of this would thy.. powers make! STERNE. **8. b.** The r. grass-fen 1865.

B. *adv.* with pa. and pres. pples., as *rich-laden* ME. **C.** *absol.* or as *sb.* **1.** Those who are rich; rich persons as a class OE. **2.** One who is rich; a rich person ME.

1. The pore schul be made domysmen Apon the ryche at domysday. late ME. Ring out the feud of r. and poor TENNYSON. **2.** The r. hath many friends *Prov.* 14:20. Hence **Ri·chen** *v. trans.* to make richer or more intense; *intr.* to become richer. **Ri·ch-ly** *adv.* in a r., sumptuous, or splendid manner; so as to be r.; amply, thoroughly; intensely; **-ness.**

Riches (ri·tʃėz). ME. [var. of next, assuming the form of a pl., and finally construed as such.] Abundance of means or of valuable possessions; wealth. Also, the possession of wealth, the condition of being rich. †**a.** Construed as a sing. Also, a particular form of wealth. –1667. **b.** Construed as a pl. late ME.

Here is not forbidden to haue r. TINDALE. *transf.* People are the R. of a Country SWIFT. **a.** *transf.* For that ritches where is my deseruing? SHAKS. **b.** As Salomon saith; R. are as a strong hold BACON.

†**Richesse.** [ME. *richesse, -eise* – OFr. *richeise, -esce* (mod. *-esse*); f. *riche* RICH + *-eise, -esse* -ESS². See prec.] Wealth; opulence –1687. **b.** In pl. form –1677.

2. All the beauties and richesses of the Vniuers 1601.

Rich-weed, *U.S.* 1788. [f. RICH *a.*] **a.** A species of Baneberry (*Actæa racemosa*). **b.** Horse-balm or Stone-root (*Collinsonia canadensis*). **c.** Clearweed (*Pilea pumila*).

‖**Ricinus** (ri·sinɒs). 1694. [L. (Pliny).] *Bot.* A genus of plants, of which the castor-oil plant (*Ricinus communis*) is the type.

Rick (rik), *sb.*¹ [OE. *hrēac* = MDu. *rooc, roke* (Du. *rook*), ON. *hraukr*, of unkn. origin. For the vocalism, cf. dial. *ship* for *sheep* (OE. *scēap*).] A stack of hay, corn, peas, etc., esp. one regularly built and thatched; a mow. **b.** *transf.* A heap or pile 1606.

Rick (rik), *sb.*² 1854. [Related to RICK *v.*²] A sprain or overstrain, *esp.* in the back.

Rick (rik), *v.*¹ 1623. [f. RICK *sb.*¹] *trans.* To form (hay, corn, etc.) into a rick; to stack.

Rick (rik), *v.*² 1798. [prob. var. sp. of ME. *wricke* – MLG. (*vor*)*wricken* (LG. *wrikken*) move here and there, sprain. Both noun and verb belong to the southern dial., so that connection with ON. *rykkr* sb., *rykkja* v., is less likely.] **1.** *trans.* To sprain, twist, or wrench (any limb or joint). **2.** *Coursing.* To cause (a hare) to 'wrench' or turn less than quite about. Also *intr.* of a hare: To 'wrench'. 1839.

Ricker (ri·kəɹ). 1820. [Cf. LG. *rick* (pl. *ricke*) pole.] *Naut.* A spar or pole made out of the stem of a young tree.

Ri·cket, sing. f. RICKETS, used attrib. or in comb.

Rickets (ri·kėts). 1645. [Origin doubtful; taken by Whistler (1645) as a corruption of Gr. ῥαχίτης or ῥαχῖτις, the latter of which he adopted as the scientific name. Perh. of local origin, the disease being first observed in Dorset and Somerset. Cf. RACHITIS.] **1.** A disease particularly incident to children, characterized by softening of the bones, esp. of the spine, and consequent distortion, bow-legs, and emaciation. Technically known as RACHITIS. †**2.** A form of blight in corn –1759.

Rickety (ri·kėti), *a.* Also **ricketty.** 1685. [f. RICKET + -Y¹.] **1.** Affected with, suffering from, rickets; subject to rickets. †**b.** *transf.* Of grain: Weakly, unhealthy –1759. **2.** Weakly, feeble, shaky, tottering; lacking in strength or firmness 1738. **3.** Of the nature of rickets; pertaining to rickets 1801.

1. Bones..not unlike those of ricketty children 1720. *fig.* This benevolence, the ricketty offspring of weakness BURKE. **2.** Crude and r. Notions 1738. An old-fashioned and r. stair 1842. A r. canter 1898. **3.** Ricketty curvature of legs 1879. Hence **Ri·cketily** *adv.*

Rickshaw, ricksha (ri·kʃǭ, ri·kʃă). 1887. Abbrev. of JINRICKSHA.

Ri·ck-yard. 1712. [f. RICK *sb.*¹] A farm-yard or enclosure containing ricks; a stack-yard.

Ricochet (ri·kǒʃē, ri·kǒʃet), *sb.* 1769. [– Fr., the skipping of a shot, etc.] *Mil.* **a.** A method of firing by which the projectile is made to glance or skip along a surface with a rebound or series of rebounds; also, the skipping of a cannon-ball or bullet, intentional or accidental. *By r.* (Fr. *à ricochet*), at a rebound. **b.** The subjection *of* a place to this kind of firing 1828.

a. The shot..buried itself in the soft sand. We had no r. to fear STEVENSON.

Ricochet (ri·kǒʃē, ri·kǒʃet), *v.* 1828. [f. the sb. The suppression of the *t* in pronunciation is also extended to the forms *ricochetted, richochetting.* Stressing on the third syllable is common.] **1.** *intr.* Of a projectile or the like: To glance or skip with a rebound or series of rebounds. **2.** *trans.* To subject to ricochet firing 1841.

‖**Rictus** (ri·ktɒs). 1760. [L., 'open mouth', f. pa. ppl. stem of *ringi* gape.] **1.** *Bot.* The orifice or throat of a bilabiate corolla. **2.** Of persons: The expanse or gape of the mouth. Similarly of birds and fishes. 1827. Hence **Ri·ctal** *a.* of or pertaining to the r.

Rid (rid), *v.* *Pa. t.* **rid, ridded.** *Pa. pple.* **rid, ridded;** *Sc.* **ridden.** [ME. (western) *ruden*, (north. and eastern) *ridde* = ON. *ryðja*.] **I. 1.** *trans.* To clear (a way or space), *esp.* to clear (land) of trees, undergrowth, etc.; to stub. **b.** To free from rubbish or encumbrances; to clean or clear out. Also formerly with *up.* late ME. **c.** To clear (a table); to clear *up* (a room, etc.). Now *dial.* 1599. **2.** To deliver, set free, rescue, save (*from, out of, of*, etc.). Now *rare.* ME. **3.** To make (a person or place) free *of* (or *from*) something; to disencumber *of* 1569.

1. If the Spring be forward, cleanse and r. the Coppices 1669. **c.** When you r. up the Parlour Hearth in a Morning SWIFT. **2.** She..bid me deuise some meanes To r. her from this second Marriage SHAKS. **3.** I am ridding you of a troublesome companion SWIFT. Phr. *To be rid of*, to be freed from (a troublesome or useless thing or person). So *to get rid of.*

II. 1. To remove, to take or clear away. Also const. *from, out of*, etc. 1475. †**b.** To remove by violence; to kill, destroy –1639. **2.** To dispatch, accomplish, get through, clear *off* or *away* (work of any kind). Now *dial.* 1530. †**3.** *To r. ground* (or *space*), *to rid way*, to cover ground, to move ahead, to make progress –1785.

1. I shal sone ryd his soule out of his body 1533. **b.** 2 *Hen. VI*, III. i. 233. **2.** Ridding away all the business that you can WESLEY. **3.** We..Will thither straight, for willingnesse rids way SHAKS. Hence **Ri·dder,** one who rids.

Riddance (ri·dăns). 1535. [f. RID *v.* + -ANCE.] **1.** Removal, clearance; an instance of this; a clearing out, scouring. †**2.** Progress or dispatch in work –1763. †**b.** Progress in moving –1647. **3.** Deliverance *from* something 1591. **4.** A deliverance which consists in getting rid of something. Freq. with *good, happy*, etc. Also *transf.*, something of which one gets rid. 1596.

1. Phr. *To make* (*clean*, etc.) *r.* **2.** The nether milstone is heauie, slow, and of small r. 1608. **3.** R. from the wicked 1886. **4.** The loss of so many captives was treated as a happy r. 1844. A good r. of bad rubbish 1863.

Riddle (ri·d'l), *sb.*[1] [OE. *rǣdels, rǣdelse* opinion, riddle, corresp. to OFris. *riedsel,* OS. *rādisli, rādislo* (Du. *raadsel*), OHG. **rātisli* (G. *rätsel*); f. **rǣdan* READ *v.*, REDE; see -ELS, -LE.] **1.** A question or statement intentionally worded in a dark or puzzling manner, and propounded in order that it may be guessed or answered, esp. as a form of pastime; an enigma; a dark saying. **2.** *transf.* Something which puzzles or perplexes; a difficult or insoluble problem; a mystery. late ME. **3.** *concr.* A person or being whose nature or conduct is enigmatical 1663.

1. As that Theban Monster that propos'd Her r., and him, who solv'd it not, devour'd MILT. **2.** The r. of life is unsolved 1859. Judaism is said to have been a dark r. which tormented Hegel all his life 1879. **3.** I am still a r. they know not what to make of SWIFT.

Riddle (ri·d'l), *sb.*[2] [Late OE. *hriddel,* rel. to synon. *hrīder* and *hrīdrian* sift.] **1.** A coarse-meshed sieve, used for separating chaff from corn, sand from gravel, ashes from cinders, etc. **2.** A board or metal plate set with pins, used in straightening wire 1843.

1. Phr. *A r. of claret,* thirteen bottles; so named because the wine was brought in on a r. *To make a r. of,* to pierce with holes; I was to be made a r. of, if I attempted to escape 1842.

Riddle (ri·d'l), *v.*[1] 1571. [f. RIDDLE *sb.*[1]] **1.** *intr.* To speak in riddles, or enigmatically; to propound riddles. **2.** *trans.* To interpret or solve (a riddle or question) 1588. †**3.** To be a riddle to (a person); to puzzle. SCOTT.

1. Madam, you r. strangely 1660. **2.** Were I as wise a warlock as Michael Scott, I could scarce r. the dream you read me SCOTT. Phr. *R. me a* (or *my*) *riddle; r. me this, that, why,* etc.

Riddle (ri·d'l), *v.*[2] ME. [f. RIDDLE *sb.*[2]] **1.** *trans.* To pass (corn, gravel, etc.) through a riddle; to separate with a riddle; to sift. **2.** To pierce with holes like those of a riddle; to perforate (*with* bullets or the like); to shatter by missiles 1849. **b.** *esp.* in pa. pple. *riddled* (*with* holes, etc.) 1817.

1. As ridiculous as..a Duchess ridling cinders! 1784. **2.** Worms will r. the wood-work of a ship 1886. **b.** *fig.* They are as poor as Job and riddled with debts 1897. Hence **Ri·ddler. Ri·ddlingly** *adv.*

Ri:ddlemeree·, ri:ddle-me-ree·. 1710. **1.** A fanciful variant of the phrases *riddle me a riddle, riddle my riddle,* etc. **2.** Rigmarole, nonsense 1736.

Ride (rəid), *sb.* 1779. [f. RIDE *v.*] **1. a.** An excursion or journey in a conveyance, now esp. a public one; †a drive. **b.** A turn or spell of riding 1815. **c.** One of the divisions into which a country is divided for purposes of excise. *R.-officer,* an exciseman 1858. **2. a.** A road or way for riding on horse-back, esp. through a wood 1805. **b.** *spec.* The riding-course in Hyde Park, London 1814. **3.** A batch of mounted recruits 1833. **4.** A saddle-horse 1787.

1. b. A few hours' bicycle r. in the country 1898. **2. b.** We..reach'd the r. Where gaily flows the human tide M. ARNOLD.

Ride (rəid), *v. Pa. t.* **rode** (rōᵘd), *arch.* **rid.** *Pa. pple.* **ridden,** *arch.* **rid.** [OE. *rīdan* = OFris. *rīda,* OS. *-rīdan* (Du. *rijden*), OHG. *rītan* (G. *reiten*), ON. *ríða.*] **I.** *intr.* **1.** To sit upon, and be carried by, a horse or other animal; to move about or journey upon horseback (or on a cycle). **b.** To serve in a cavalry regiment 1711. **c.** Of persons: To weigh when mounted 1836. **d.** To sit on and manage a horse properly 1881. **2.** *spec.* To go on horseback upon a warlike expedition; to take part in a raid or foray. *arch.* ME. **3.** To mount the female; to copulate. (Now low and indecent.) ME. **4.** To be conveyed, travel or journey *in* a wheeled or other vehicle ME. **b.** To be carried or drawn about (*on* or †*in* a cart, hurdle, etc.) as a punishment 1556. **5.** To sit or be carried *on* or *upon* something after the manner of one on horseback; †to hang *on* the gallows, *in* a rope, etc. OE. **6. a.** Of horses: To admit of being ridden; to carry a rider 1470. **b.** Of land: To be of a specified character for riding upon 1864.

1. We..rode over the place of burial of the Turks 1617. *fig.* A young guardsman who had just rode into her heart 1803. Phrases. *To r. whip and spur*: see WHIP *sb. To r. for a fall,* to ride recklessly so as to be liable to a fall; usu. *fig. To r. off* (e.g. on a side issue). *To r. to hounds,* to hunt. **c.** He rode little under fourteen stone 1857. **d.** He can stick in his saddle somehow,..but he can't r. 1881. **2.** As if a tenant could have helped riding with the Laird SCOTT. **4.** I rid with my sword drawn in the coach PEPYS. **b.** Ah, many a wretch has rid on a hurdle who has done less mischief SHERIDAN. **5.** I saw him beate the surges vnder him, And r. vpon their backes SHAKS. *fig.* Death rides upon the sulphury Siroc BYRON. **6. a.** Commonly Rides with her Tongue out of her Mouth 1714. **b.** Rain..made the ground r. soft 1889.

II. 1. Of vessels: To lie *at* (or †*on*) anchor; freq. *to* (or †*at*) *an anchor.* Also ellipt. OE. **2.** To float or move upon the water; to sail, esp. in a buoyant manner OE. **3.** Of things: To move in any way, to be carried or supported, after the manner of one riding 1586. **b.** Of the heavenly bodies: To appear to float in space 1632. **4.** To rest or turn *on* or *upon* something of the nature of a pivot, axle, or protuberance 1597. **b.** To extend or project *over* something 1601. **c.** *ellipt.* in previous senses 1683. **5.** Of a dress, etc.: To work *up* so as to form folds or creases; to ruck 1854.

1. *fig.* This..snug little road-stead, where I thought to r. at anchor for life SCOTT. **2.** It has been prosperous, and you are riding into port THACKERAY. **3.** *fig.* On whose foolish honestie My practises r. easie SHAKS. **b.** When the Sun with Taurus rides MILT. **4.** Strong as the Axletree In which the Heauens r. SHAKS.

III. *trans.* **1.** To traverse on horseback; to ride over, along, or through ME. **2.** To pursue, proceed upon (one's way, etc.) on horseback ME. **3.** *To r. out.* Of a ship: To sustain (a gale or storm) without great damage or dragging anchor 1529. **b.** *fig.* To endure or sustain successfully, to last to the end of, †to spend, pass 1529.

1. The Lord High Admiral, Riding the streets, was traitorously shot MARLOWE. They could not r. the water, it being great 1670. Phr. *To r. a race, course, circuit, match,* etc. **3.** The ship Lagoda.. rode out the gale in safety 1840. **b.** That our faith may r. out every storm of doubt 1877.

IV. *trans.* **1.** To sit or be carried on, to go or travel upon (a horse, etc.); to manage or control while seated on ME. **b.** *Racing.* To urge (a horse) to excessive speed; to 'squeeze' 1863. **c.** To bring into a certain condition by riding, e.g. *to ride to death* 1440. **2.** To mount or cover (the female) 1500. **3. a.** Of the nightmare, witches, etc.: To sit upon, use as a horse 1597. **b.** To have the mastery of (a person); to manage at will; to oppress or harass; to tyrannize over; to dominate completely 1583. **4.** To sit upon, be carried or borne along upon (something) 1597. **b.** Of things: To rest upon, esp. by projecting or overlapping 1713. **5.** *To r. down*: To exhaust (a horse) by excessive riding; to overtake by pursuit on horseback; to charge, or collide with, so as to overthrow 1670. **6.** To cut (an animal) *off* or *out* from the herd by skilful riding 1843. **7.** To cause (a person) to ride 1711. **b.** To convey in a cart or other vehicle. Chiefly *U.S.* 1687. **c.** To keep (a ship) moored; to secure or maintain at anchor 1726.

1. Grimes rode the donkey in front KINGSLEY. *fig.* There is a set of Bishops..Will r. the Devill off his legs, and break his wind 1647. **3. a.** The Men they commonly laid asleep at the place, whereto they rode them 1693. **b.** The tradesman..is ridden by the routine of his craft EMERSON. **4.** The boys will 'r.' a log down the current 1890. **b.** Of spectacles that rode his nose 1801. **7.** To..r. him on a rail for body-snatching 1876. **c.** Bays to r. our Fleets in NELSON.

Phr. **R. and tie.** Of two (or three) persons: To travel with one horse by alternately riding and walking, each one riding ahead for some distance and tying up the horse for the one who comes behind; also as *sb.* or *adv.* (sometimes hyphened.) Hence **Ri·dden** *ppl. a.* **Ri·deable, ri·dable,** *a.,* capable of being ridden through, over, etc.; capable of being ridden or used for riding.

Rider (rəi·dəɹ). [Late OE. *rīdere*; see prec., -ER¹.] **I.** †**1. a.** A knight; a mounted warrior –1596. **b.** A mounted reaver or raider, a moss-trooper. Now *arch.* 1549. **2.** One who rides a horse or other animal (also, a cycle); a mounted person. See also ROUGH-RIDER. ME. **3.** A gold coin, having a figure of a horseman on the obverse, formerly current in Flanders and Holland; also, a gold coin current in Scotland during the 15–16th centuries. (After Du. and Flem. *rijder.*) 1479. †**4.** A riding-master; a horse-trainer –1678. †**5.** A commercial traveller, a bagman –1837. **6.** *Curling.* A stone driven so as to dislodge other stones blocking the tee 1891.

1. b. The Border riders who had subsisted by depredation SCOTT. **2.** A hard r. across country 1881.

II. 1. *Naut.* **a.** *pl.* An additional set of timbers or iron plates used to strengthen the frame of a ship internally or externally 1627. **b.** *pl.* A second or upper tier of casks in a hold 1846. **c.** A rope, or turn of one, overlying another 1841. **2.** *Mining.* **a.** A contrivance of wood and rope on which the miner rides down and up the shafts 1653. **b.** A thin seam of coal or deposit of ore overlying a principal seam or lode 1875. **3.** An additional clause tacked on to a document after its first drafting; *esp.* a supplementary and amending clause attached to a legislative Bill at its final reading 1669. **b.** A corollary or addition supplementing, or naturally arising from, something said or written 1813. **c.** *Math.* A problem arising either directly or indirectly out of the proposition to which it is appended 1851. **d.** A clause added as a corollary to a verdict 1884. **4.** An object bestriding or surmounting another (in various techn. uses) 1793.

3. Colonel B—h..carried a R. as it is called, being a Clause to be added at the last Reading 1734. **d.** The jury..added a r. condemning the use of paraffin lamps..in the Hospital 1886. Hence **Ri·derless** *a.*

Ridge (ridʒ), *sb.* [OE. *hryćġ* = OFris. *hregg,* OS. *hruggi* (MDu. *ruc,* Du. *rug*), OHG. *hrucki* (G. *rücken*), ON. *hryggr* :– Gmc. **χruʒjaz.*] †**1.** The back or spine in man or animals –1678. **2.** The top, upper part, or crest *of* anything, esp. when long and narrow OE. **3.** The horizontal edge or line in which the two sloping sides of a roof meet at the top; the uppermost part or coping of a roof OE. **b.** *Fortif.* The highest part of the glacis 1853. **4.** A long and narrow stretch of elevated ground; a range or chain of hills or mountains OE. **b.** A line or reef of rocks 1695. **5.** *Agric.* A raised or rounded strip of arable land, usu. one of a series (with intermediate open furrows) into which a field is divided by ploughing in a special manner. late ME. **b.** Used as a measure of land OE. **c.** *Hort.* A raised hot-bed on which cucumbers or melons are planted 1725. **6.** A narrow elevation running along or across a surface 1523. **b.** A raised line, bank, bed, or strip *of* something 1763.

2. Dancing upon the r. of dreadful waves 1665. The line that forms the r. of the nose JOHNSON. **5.** *transf.* Each Warrior..expert, When to..close The ridges of grim Warr MILT.

attrib. and *Comb.*: **r.-band** (now *dial.*) = BACK-BAND; **-piece,** a beam at the apex of a roof, upon which the upper ends of the rafters rest; **-pole,** (*a*) the horizontal pole of a tent; (*b*) = *r. piece*; **-rope,** the centre rope of an awning; any of the ropes along the rigging to which it is stretched; a life-line; **-tree,** = *r.-piece.* Hence **Ri·dgelet,** a small r. **Ri·dgy** *a.* rising in ridges or after the manner of a r.

Ridge (ridʒ), *v.* 1445. [f. RIDGE *sb.*] **1.** *trans.* To provide (a building) with a ridge, or a proper covering for this; to make or renew the ridge of (a house, etc.). **2.** To break or throw up (land, a field, etc.) into ridges. Freq. with *up.* 1523. **3.** To mark with or as with ridges; to raise ridges or ripples upon (a surface) 1671. **4.** To plant (*out*) in ridges or hot-beds 1731. **5.** *intr.* To form ridges; to rise (*up*) in ridges 1864.

3. Bristles..like those that r. the back Of chaf't wild Boars MILT. **5.** The Biscay, roughly ridging eastward, shook..her TENNYSON. Hence **Ridged** *ppl. a.* rising in or marked by a ridge or ridges.

Ri·dge-bone. [OE. *hryćġbān.*] The spine or back-bone. Now *rare* or *Obs.*

Ridgel (ri·dʒĕl). Now *dial.* 1597. [app. f. RIDGE *sb.* 1, the testicle being supposed to remain near the animal's back.] An animal which has been imperfectly castrated, or whose genital organs are not properly developed, *esp.* a male animal (ram, bull, or horse) with only one testicle. So **Ri·dgeling** (now *rare*).

Ri·dge-tile. Also **ridge tile.** 1496. [RIDGE *sb.*] A tile used for roofing the ridge of a building.

Ri·dgeway. [OE. *hryćweǵ*; see RIDGE *sb.* 4 and WAY *sb.*] A way or road along a ridge, esp. one following the ridge of downs or low hill-ranges.

Ridicule (ri·dikiūl), *sb.*¹ 1673. [– Fr. *ridicule* – n. sing. of L. *ridiculus*, f. *ridēre* laugh.] **1.** A ridiculous or absurd thing, feature, characteristic, or habit; an absurdity. Now *rare.* 1677. †**b.** A laughing-stock –1694. **2.** Ridiculous nature or character (*of* something) 1711. **b.** That which is ridiculous 1712. **3.** The act or practice of making persons or things the object of jest or sport; language intended to raise laughter against an object 1690. †**4.** A piece of derisive mirth or light mockery –1774.

1. He marked every fault of taste, every weakness, every r. MACAULAY. **2.** The r. of such a supposition 1824. **3.** Such a proposal is just one of those things which admits of great r. 1875. Phr. *To turn (in) to r.*, to make ridiculous.

Ri·dicule, *sb.*² *Obs.* exc. *dial.* 1805. [– Fr. illiterate perversion of *réticule.*] = RETICULE 2.

†**Ri·dicule,** *a.* 1672. [– Fr. *ridicule* (XV) – L. *ridiculus*, f. *ridēre* laugh.] = RIDICULOUS *a.* 1. –1683.

Ri·dicule, *v.* 1684. [f. prec. or RIDICULE *sb.*¹] †**1.** To render ridiculous (*rare*) –1735. **2.** To treat with ridicule or mockery; to make fun of, deride, laugh at 1700.

1. When he..Preaches, Cants, and ridicules himself 1684. **2.** Humanity and compassion are ridiculed as the fruits of superstition and ignorance BURKE. Hence **Ri·diculer.**

Ridiculous (ridi·kiŭləs), *a.* 1550. [f. L. *ridiculus* + -OUS, or – L. *ridiculosus*. Cf. Fr. †*ridiculeux.*] **1.** Exciting ridicule or derisive laughter; absurd, preposterous, comical, laughable. **b.** Outrageous. *dial.* and *U.S.* 1839. **2.** *absol.* with *the*: That which is ridiculous 1742.

1. Gazelles..with r. magnitude of horns 1848. **2.** One step above the sublime, makes the r. 1795. Hence **Ridi·culous-ly** *adv.*, **-ness.**

Riding (rəi·diŋ), *sb.* [In *Est Treding, Estreding, Nort Treding* (Domesday Book), *Nort Riding*, etc. (XII), alt., by change of *tþ* to *t(t*, of late OE. **þriding*, **þriðing* (*treding, trethine, trithing* XI–XIII) – ON. *þriðjungr* third part, f. *þriði* THIRD; see -ING³.] **1.** One of the three administrative districts into which Yorkshire is divided (East, West, North). **2.** A similar division of other counties or districts in the United Kingdom or its Colonies 1675.

Riding (rəi·diŋ), *vbl. sb.* ME. [f. RIDE *v.* + -ING¹.] **1.** In the senses of RIDE *v.* **2.** A way or road specially intended for persons riding; *esp.* a green track or lane cut through (or skirting) a wood or covert; a ride ME.

attrib. and *Comb.*: **r.-master,** a teacher of horsemanship; esp. *Mil.*, an officer having charge of the instruction of troopers in a cavalry regiment; **-officer,** a mounted revenue officer; **-school,** a school for instruction in horsemanship.

Riding (rəi·diŋ), *ppl. a.* OE. [f. RIDE *v.* + -ING².] **1.** That rides (see RIDE *v.*); mounted. †**2.** *R. knot*, a running knot, a slip-knot –1650. **3.** That 'rides' upon, surmounts, or projects over an object or part of an object 1677.

Ri·ding-coat. 1507. [RIDING *vbl. sb.*] A coat worn in riding, *esp.* an overcoat to protect the rider from wet.

Ri·ding-habit. 1666. [RIDING *vbl. sb.*] A dress or costume used for riding; *spec.* a riding-dress worn by ladies, consisting of a cloth skirt worn with a double-breasted tight-fitting jacket.

Ri·ding-hood. 1459. [RIDING *vbl. sb.*] A large hood originally worn while riding, but in later use forming an article of outdoor costume for women and children. (Now chiefly familiar from the tale of *Little Red Riding Hood.*)

Ri·ding rhyme. 1575. [RIDING *vbl. sb.* or *ppl. a.*, but the precise reason for the name is not clear.] The form of verse (the heroic couplet) used by Chaucer in his Canterbury Tales, and, after him, by Lydgate and others.

Spenser thought he was imitating what wise-acres used to call the riding-rhyme of Chaucer 1875.

‖**Ridotto** (ridǫ·to), *sb. Obs.* exc. *Hist.* 1722. [It., = Fr. *réduit* :– med.L. *reductus*, subst. use of pa. pple. of L. *reducere* REDUCE.] An entertainment or social assembly consisting of music and dancing.

‖**Riem** (rīm). *S. Afr.* 1849. [Du., = OE. *rēoma* (dial. *rim*), OS., OHG. *riomo* (G. *riemen*).] A long strip or thong of undressed leather.

‖**Rifacimento** (rifatʃime·nto). 1773. [It., f. *rifac-*, stem of *rifare* remake.] A new-modelling or recasting of a literary work.

Rife (rəif), *a.* and *adv.* [Once in late OE. *rȳfe* for **rīfe*; prob. – ON. *rífr* good, acceptable = WFris. *rjū*, MLG. *rīve*, MDu. *rīve*, *rijf* abundant; cf. ON. *reifa* enrich, *reifr* glad, cheerful.] **A.** *adj.* **1.** Of common or frequent occurrence; prevalent; widespread; in later use *esp.* of infectious diseases or epidemics. **2. a.** Of rumours, reports, etc.: Common; generally current in popular knowledge or talk ME. **b.** Of words or phrases: Commonly or frequently heard. Now *rare.* 1513. **3.** Abundant, plentiful, ample; large in quantity or number ME. **4.** Characterized by plenty *of*, rich *in*, something. Now *rare.* ME. **b.** Amply provided *with* something 1787. **5.** Disposed or inclined; ready, prompt; quick. Const. *for*, †*of*, †*to.* Now *dial.* late ME.

1. It is r. and catching 1705. The activity and noise of city day were r. in the street DICKENS. **2. a.** A rumour of the queen's arrest was r. in London 1856. **3.** Direfull comets never rifer were 1627. Where the foliage was rifest LYTTON. **4. b.** Language r. With rugged maxims hewn from life TENNYSON.

B. *adv.* **1.** Abundantly, copiously, largely; manifoldly ME. †**2.** Frequently, often –1618. †**3.** Promptly, speedily, readily –1525. Hence †**Ri·fe-ly** *adv.*, †**-ness** (*rare*).

Riffle (ri·f'l), *sb. U.S.* 1796. [Cf. RIFFLE *v.*] **1.** A rocky obstruction in the bed of a river; a piece of broken water produced by this; a rapid. **2.** In gold-washing: A slat, bar, cleat, or block, placed across the bottom of a cradle or sluice in order to break the current and detain the gold 1862. **b.** A groove or channel across the bottom of a cradle or sluice, or the space between two bars, etc., serving to catch the gold; a mercury-bath in a washing-table 1875. **c.** *attrib.*, as *r.-bed, -sluice* 1862.

Riffle (ri·f'l), *v. rare.* 1754. [perh. partly a var. of RUFFLE *v.*, partly – Fr. †*riffler* = (O)Fr. *rifler*, †RIFLE *v.*¹] **1.** *intr.* To form a riffle or rapid. *U.S.* **2.** *trans.* To handle in a hesitating manner, so as to produce a slight rattle 1852. **3.** In card-sharping: To bend up (cards) at the corners in shuffling; to shuffle in this manner 1894.

Ri·ffler. 1797. [– Fr. *rifloir* (XVI), f. *rifler* scrape, file; see RIFLE *v.*¹] A tool with a curved file-surface at each end, used by sculptors, metal-workers, and wood-carvers.

Riff-raff, riffraff (ri·f,raf). 1470. [f. phr. †*riff and raff* (XIV) one and all – OFr. *rif et raf*; cf. MDu. *rijf ande raf.* See RAFF¹.] **1.** Persons of a disreputable character or belonging to the lowest class of a community. **b.** The scum *of* a community, class, etc.; the rabble 1545. **c.** One belonging to the rabble (*rare*) 1602. **2.** Worthless stuff; odds and ends; trash, rubbish. Now chiefly *dial.* 1526. **3.** *attrib.* or as *adj.* **a.** Of persons: Low or disreputable; belonging to the rabble 1612. **b.** Of things: Worthless, trashy 1608.

1. A mere parcel of r.! petty traders and shopkeepers 1811. **b.** All the boys and r. of the towns 1851. **3. b.** The large 4to ed. of Sallust full of r. Notes 1711.

Rifle (rəi·f'l), *sb.*¹ Now *dial.* and *U.S.* 1459. [– OFr. *riffle* stick, billet of wood. In Norman dial. *rifle* is used in the same sense as in English.] **1.** A piece of wood used by mowers for sharpening their scythes. **2.** A bent stick attached to the butt of a scythe for laying the corn in rows 1573.

Rifle (rəi·f'l), *sb.*² 1751. [f. RIFLE *v.*³] **1.** One of a set of spiral grooves cut on the interior surface of a gun-barrel with the object of giving to the projectile a rotatory movement on its own axis. **2.** A fire-arm, *esp.* a musket or carbine, having a spirally grooved bore 1775. **b.** *pl.* Troops armed with rifles; riflemen 1853.

2. Rifles for sporting purposes differ from military pieces in being double-barrelled 1880.

attrib. and *Comb.*, as *r.-ball, -barrel, team*, etc.; **r. brigade,** the title of certain regiments of the British army; **-grenade,** a small explosive shell shot from a r.-barrel; **-green** *a.* of the colour of a rifleman's uniform; *sb.* this shade of green; **-pit,** an excavation made to give cover to a rifleman in firing at an enemy.

Rifle (rəi·f'l), *v.*¹ ME. [– (O)Fr. *rifler*, †*riffler* graze, scratch, plunder, f. early Du. *riffelen.* Cf. AL. *rifflerius* robber.] **1.** *trans.* To despoil, plunder, or rob (a person) in a thorough fashion, *esp.* by searching his pockets or clothes; to search (a person) thoroughly with intent to rob. **b.** To plunder or pillage (a receptacle, place, etc.); to ransack, *esp.* in order to take what is valuable. late ME. **c.** To despoil or strip bare *of* something 1495. **2.** *absol.* To engage in pillage or plunder, or in searching with a view to this. late ME. **3.** *trans.* To carry off as booty; to plunder, steal. late ME. †**4.** To affect strongly or injuriously; to break or strip off –1770.

1. The Gyant was rifling of him, with a purpose after that to pick his Bones BUNYAN. **b.** Is it well done to riffell my cofer whyle I am absent? 1530. **c.** Pure Chastity is rifled of her store SHAKS. **2.** Rob, then, r. if ye will LYTTON. **3.** Shall he r. all thy sweets, at will? SMOLLETT. **4.** That lightning which harms not the skin, and rifles the entrals MILT. Hence **Ri·fler** (now *arch.*), a robber, plunderer, spoiler.

Ri·fle, *v.*² *Obs.* exc. *dial.* 1590. [– Du. *rijfelen*, obscurely rel. to Fr. *rafler* RAFFLE *v.*¹] **1.** *intr.* To play at dice; to gamble or raffle (*for* a stake). **2.** *trans.* To dispose of by raffling; to gamble *away* 1607.

Rifle (rəi·f'l), *v.*³ 1618. [In sense 1 ult. repr. (O)Fr. *rifler* (see RIFLE *v.*¹). In sense 2 f. RIFLE *sb.*² 2.] **1.** *trans.* To form spiral grooves in (the barrel of a gun or the bore of a cannon). **2.** To shoot with a rifle. Also *intr.* with *at.* 1821. Hence **Ri·fled** *ppl. a.* (*a*) of fire-arms: having a spirally grooved bore; (*b*) of balls, shells, etc.: grooved; having projecting studs or ribs which fit into the grooves in the bore. **Ri·fling** *vbl. sb.* the operation of making grooves in the bore of a fire-arm; the grooving itself, or the nature of this.

Ri·fle-bird. 1831. [f. RIFLE *sb.*² The precise reason for the name is unc.] An Australian bird of the genus *Ptilorrhis.*

Rifleite (rəi·f'l,əit). 1891. [f. RIFLE *sb.*² 2 + -ITE¹ 4a.] A special slow-burning powder used in certain kinds of rifles.

Rifleman (rəi·f'lmæ̆n). 1775. [f. RIFLE *sb.*² 2.] **1.** A soldier armed with a rifle; one who shoots with a rifle; as a prefixed designation = private of a rifle regiment. **2.** *Ornith.* = RIFLE-BIRD 1826.

Ri·fle-range. 1850. [f. RIFLE *sb.*² 2 + RANGE *sb.*¹] **1.** The distance that a rifle-ball will carry. **2.** A place for practising rifle-shooting 1885.

Ri·fle-shot, ri·fleshot. 1840. [f. RIFLE *sb.*² 2.] **1.** Such a distance as may be covered by a shot from a rifle. **2.** One skilled in shooting with a rifle 1850. **3.** A shot fired with a rifle 1875.

Rift, *sb.*¹ ME. [Of Scand. origin (cf. Norw., Da. *rift* cleft, chink, Icel. *ript* breach of contract); rel. to RIVE.] †**1.** An act of tearing or rending; a splitting, riving –1440. **2.** A cleft or chasm in the earth, a rock, etc. ME. **b.** An opening or break in clouds or mist. late ME. **c.** A split, crack, rent, or chink in any object or article. Now somewhat *rare.* late ME. †**d.** A chap or crack in the skin –1614.

2. b. The Clouds From many a horrid r. abortive pour'd Fierce rain with lightning mixt MILT. **c.** The little r. within the lute TENNYSON. (The phr. has become proverbial and allusive = incipient dissension or malady.) Hence **Ri·ftless** *a.*

Rift, *sb.*² *U.S.* 1755. [perh. alt. of *riff*, obs. var. of REEF *sb.*²] **1.** A rapid, a cataract. **2.** The wash of the surf on a shore 1869.

Rift, *v.*¹ ME. [Of Scand. origin; cf. ON. *ripta* make void, invalidate, and RIFT *sb.*¹] †**1.** *intr.* To form fissures or clefts; to gape open, split –1664. **2.** *trans.* To rend apart or asunder, split, cleave 1566. **b.** To form or force by cleaving 1849.

1. *Wint. T.* v. i. 66. **2.** At sight of him the people with a shout Rifted the Air MILT.

Rift, *v.*[2] Now *Sc.* and *n. dial.* ME. [– ON. *rypta*, f. a stem **rup-*.] **1.** *trans.* To belch out (wind, etc.). **2.** *intr.* To break wind upwards from the stomach; to belch ME.

Rig, *sb.*[1] ME. [North. and Sc. form of RIDGE *sb.*] = RIDGE *sb.*

Rig, *sb.*[2] Now *dial.* ME. [perh. – ON. *hregg* storm.] A storm, tempest, strong wind.

Rig, *sb.*[3] *slang* or *colloq.* 1725. [f. RIG *v.*[3]] **1.** Sport, banter, ridicule. Chiefly in phr. *to run* (one's) *rig(s upon* (another), to make sport or game of. Now *dial.* **2.** A trick, scheme, or dodge; a method of cheating or swindling 1775. **b.** = CORNER *sb.* 8. 1877. **3.** A frolic or prank; an act of a mischievous or wanton kind; a 'game' 1811.

2. (Thimble-riggers) The r. is practised at fairs, at races, or on public roads 1830. Phr. *R. sale*, a sale by auction under false pretences. **3.** Phr. *To run a* (or *the*) *r.*, *to run* (one's) *r.*, to play pranks, to run riot; He little dreamt, when he set out, Of running such a r.! COWPER.

Rig, *sb.*[4] 1822. [f. RIG *v.*[1]] **1.** *Naut.* The arrangement of masts, sails, etc., on a vessel. **2.** *colloq.* Costume, outfit, style of dress. Also *rig-up* and RIG-OUT. 1857. **3.** *U.S.* **a.** Apparatus for well-sinking 1875. **b.** An equipage; a horse vehicle 1885.

1. The r. suited to very small river boats 1856. **2.** You'll do very well as to r., all but that cap HUGHES.

Rig, *v.*[1] 1489. [perh. of Scand. origin (cf. Norw. *rigga* bind or wrap up, Sw. dial. *rigga på* harness).] **1.** *trans.* To make (a ship) ready for the sea; to fit out with the necessary tackle. **b.** In passive sense: To be rigged; to get rigged (afresh) 1614. **c.** To assemble and adjust the parts of (an aircraft). **2.** To dress, clothe, fit out or provide with clothes. Now *colloq.* or *slang.* 1534. **3.** To furnish or provide, to fit or fix *up*, *with* something. Also, rarely, without const. 1594. **b.** To fit *out* in some way 1679. **4.** To adjust or fix. Chiefly *Naut.* 1627. **b.** *Naut.* To run *out*, draw *in*, a boom or stay. Also *intr.* 1769. **5.** To fit up, esp. as an expedient or makeshift 1823.

1. *fig.* That fatall and perfidious Bark Built in th' eclipse, and rigg'd with curses dark MILT. **b.** Eight of the king's ships are rigging and making ready for sea 1614. **2.** Once in seven years came up Madam in the stage coach, to..r. out herself and her family FIELDING. **4.** We must r. the pumps 1836.

Rig, *v.*[2] Now *dial.* 1570. [Of unkn. origin.] *intr.* To play the wanton; to romp or climb about. So **Rig** *sb.*[5], a wanton girl or woman. **Ri·ggish** *a.* wanton, licentious.

Rig, *v.*[3] *slang* or *colloq.* 1823. [Of unkn. origin; cf. RIG *sb.*[3]] **1.** *trans.* To hoax, play tricks on, befool. **2.** To manage or manipulate in some underhand or fraudulent manner 1851.

2. Phr. *To r. the market*, to cause an artificial rise (or fall) of prices with a view to personal profit; to send *up* prices artificially. Hence **Ri·gger**[2], a thimble-rigger, one who rigs the market, etc.

Riga (rəi·gă, rī·gă). 1765. Name of a seaport of Latvia, used attrib. in names of products exported from there, as *R. deal*, *fir*, *hemp*, *oak*, etc. *R. balsam*, an essential oil (also called *Carpathian balsam*) obtained by distillation from *Pinus cembra*.

Rigadoon (rigădū·n), *sb.* 1691. [– Fr. *rigodon*, *rigaudon*, said by Rousseau ('Dictionnaire de Musique') to have been named after its inventor, Rigaud, stated to have been a celebrated dancing-master at Marseilles.] **1.** A lively and somewhat complicated dance for two persons, formerly in vogue. **2.** The music for such a dance 1731.

1. He..gained a great Reputation, by his Performance in a R. ADDISON. Hence **Rigadoo·n** *v. intr.* to dance a r.

Rigel (rəi·dʒĕl, rəi·gĕl). 1592. [– Arab. *rijl* foot.] The star β in the constellation Orion.

Rigescent (ridʒe·sĕnt), *a.* 1873. [– L. *rigescens*, *-ent-*, pr. pple. of *rigescere*, f. *rigēre* be stiff; see -ESCENT.] *Bot.* Tending to be rigid or stiff. So **Rige·scence,** stiffening 1768.

Rigger[1] (ri·gəɹ). 1611. [f. RIG *v.*[1] + -ER[1].] **1.** *Naut.* One who rigs ships. **2.** *Mech.* A band-wheel 1797. **3.** A long pointed sable brush, used by marine painters to delineate the cordage of ships 1883. **4.** A vessel with a specified rig 1807. **5.** Colloq. abbrev. of OUTRIGGER 3. **6.** One who attends to the rigging of aircraft 1921.

Ri·gging, *vbl. sb.* 1486. [f. RIG *v.*[1] + -ING[1].] **1.** *Naut.* The action of equipping a vessel with the necessary shrouds, stays, braces, etc. **2.** The ropes or chains employed to support the masts (*standing r.*), and to work or set the yards, sails, etc. (*running r.*) 1594. **3.** *transf.* Clothing, dress 1662. **4.** Equipment, outfit 1849.

4. This claim has a splendid hydraulic r. 1877.

Right (rəit), *sb.*[1] [OE. *riht* = OFris. *riuht*, OS., OHG. *reht* (Du., G. *recht*), ON. *réttr*; the sb. corresp. to RIGHT *a.*] **I.** †**1.** The standard of permitted and forbidden action within a certain sphere; law; a rule or canon –1610. **2.** That which is consonant with equity or the light of nature; that which is morally just or due. (Often contrasted with *might* or *wrong.*) OE. **b.** The fact or position of being in the right. Chiefly in phr. *to have r.* Now *rare.* late ME. **c.** Consonance with fact; correctness 1796. **3.** Just or equitable treatment; fairness in decision; justice. Freq. in phr. *to do* (a person) *r.* OE. †**b.** With ref. to drinking, in phr. *to do* (one) *r.* –1624. **4.** In prep. phrases, †*with*, *by* (in mod. use, *by rights*), or †*of r.*, = rightfully; with reason or justice OE. **5.** *The r.*: that which is right; righteousness, justice, truth; *esp.* the cause of truth or justice OE.

2. You must acknowledge a Distinction betwixt R. and Wrong, founded in Nature..by which Actions may be call'd just or unjust 1737. **3.** King Charles, and who'll do him r. now? BROWNING. **b.** 2 *Hen. IV*, v. iii. 76. **4.** I should haue beene a woman by r. SHAKS. **5.** Too fond of the r. to pursue the expedient GOLDSM. Phr. *To be in the r.*, to have justice, reason, or fact upon one's side; Your Sex Was never in the r., y're always false, Or silly OTWAY.

II. 1. Justifiable claim, on legal or moral grounds, to have or obtain something, or to act in a certain way OE. **2.** In prep. phrases, *with*, *of*, *by* (*good*) *r.*, also now *by rights*, denoting justifiable title or claim to something OE. **3.** A legal, equitable, or moral title or claim to the possession of property or authority, the enjoyment of privileges or immunities, etc. OE. **4.** With possessive pron. or genitive: The title or claim to something properly possessed by one or more persons OE. **5.** That which justly accrues or falls to any one; what one may properly claim; one's due OE. †**b.** A territory, estate, dominion –1596. †**c.** (Usu. *pl.*) The last sacrament of the Church –1509. **d.** *pl.* A stag's full complement of antlers, consisting of the brow, bay, and tray. late ME.

1. Nor doth it follow that he hath the best in r., who hath the best in fight 1642. Phr. *In r. of* (a person or thing): so *by r. of.* **2.** May I with r. and conscience make this claim? SHAKS. Estates, which of r. belonged to the poorer classes COBBETT. Any little matters which ought to be ours by rights DICKENS. **3.** *Civil*, *natural*, etc., *rights*: see the adjs. *Declaration* or *Bill of Rights*, 'a Bill declaring the Rights and Liberties of England, and the Succession to the Crown', passed in 1689. *To have a* or *no r. to* (do something); in dial. use also employed with ref. to obligation; I have no r. to maintain idle vagrants SMOLLETT. **4.** Human nature at last asserted its rights MACAULAY. Phr. *In r. of*, *in one's* (*own*) *r.*; She has a little money in her own r. DICKENS. **5.** *fig.* Grief claim'd his r., and tears their course SCOTT.

III. 1. *To rights*: **a.** †In a proper manner; to or into a proper condition or order. In later use chiefly with *bring*, *put*, or *set.* ME. **b.** At once, straightway (now *U.S.*); †completely, altogether. Formerly freq. in phr. †*to sink to rights.* 1663. **2.** (Now *pl.*) The true account or interpretation *of* a matter 1749.

1. a. In my chamber, setting things and papers to rights PEPYS. **b.** The Hulk.., by Reason of many Breaches.., sunk to Rights SWIFT. **2.** I have never heard the rights of that story 1846.

IV. 1. a. = RIGHT HAND 2. ME. **b.** The right wing of an army, etc.; the right-hand extremity of a line of men 1707. **c.** *Politics.* In legislative chambers, the party or parties of conservative principles 1887. **2. a.** A boot or shoe for the right foot; a glove for the right hand 1825. **b.** A blow given with the right hand 1898. †**3.** The direct road or way (*rare*) –1595.

1. a. Far to the r., where Apennine ascends GOLDSM. **b.** The Chief occupied the centre of the middle rank, instead of being on the extreme r. SCOTT. **2. b.** Sharkey put over a straight r. on Corbett's nose 1898. **3.** *John* I. i. 170. Hence **Ri·ghtless** *a.* †wrongful, lawless; devoid or deprived of rights.

Right, *sb.*[2] 1590. Erron. spelling for RITE. No doubt they rose vp early, to obserue The r. of May SHAKS.

Right (rəit), *a.* [OE. *riht* = OFris., etc., as in *sb.*[1], Goth. *raihts* :– Gmc. **rextaz*, rel. to L. *rectus*, f. IE. base **reg-* denoting movement in a straight line, extension.] **I.** †**1.** Straight; not bent, curved, or crooked. Also *r. with*, in a line with. –1704. **2.** *R. line*, a straight line 1551. **3.** Formed by or with reference to a right line or plane perpendicular to another right line or plane ME. **b.** Of solid figures: Having the ends or base at right angles with the axis 1674.

2. The r. lines and measured regularity of an American city 1898. **3.** *R. sphere*, is that where the Equator cuts the horizon at R. angles 1795. *R. circle*, a circle drawn at right angles with the plane of projection 1846. *R. sailing*, running a course on one of the four cardinal points, so as to alter only a ship's latitude, or longitude 1867. *R. horizon*, the celestial horizon of a place on the equator the plane of which is perpendicular to that of the equinoctial. *R. ascension*: see ASCENSION 3.

II. 1. Of persons or disposition: Disposed to do what is just or good; upright, righteous. Now *rare.* OE. **2.** Of actions, conduct, etc.: In accordance with what is just or good; equitable; morally fitting. In later use chiefly predicative. OE. **3.** Agreeing with some standard or principle; correct, proper. Also, agreeing with facts; true. OE. **b.** Of belief: Orthodox, true; that ought to be accepted or followed OE. **c.** With agent-nouns: correct, exact 1568. **d.** Leading in the proper direction or towards the place one wishes to reach 1814. **4.** Fitting, proper, appropriate; exactly answering to what is required or suitable OE. **5.** *R. way.* **a.** The way of moral rightness or spiritual salvation OE. **b.** The correct method, or that most conducive to the end in view 1561. **c.** As *adv.* In the proper direction 1704. **6.** *R. side*: **a.** That side of anything which is regarded as the principal, or is naturally turned towards one; the face or upper side 1511. **b.** The party or principle of which one approves 1649. **c.** (With *on.*) The better aspect of anything 1713. **d.** The safe, advantageous, appropriate, desirable side *of* anything 1700. **7.** Properly pertaining or attached to a person or thing ME. **8.** Of the mind or mental faculties: Normal, natural, sound, whole. Chiefly in phr. *to be in one's r. mind* or *senses.* ME. **9.** Of persons: **a.** Mentally normal or sound; sane. Chiefly with negs. 1662. **b.** In good health and spirits; sound, well, comfortable 1837. **10.** Of persons: Correct in opinion, judgement, or procedure 1597. **11.** In a satisfactory or proper state; in good order 1662.

1. According to the rule of a r. conscience 1576. He is a r. man BURKE. **2.** With some regard to what is just and r. [they] Shall lead thir lives MILT. Phr. *It is r. to* or *that.* **3.** A r. description of our sport, my Lord SHAKS. **d.** The change..was in the r. direction 1861. **4.** God knows if his heart lay in the r. place 1809. Phr. *Mr. R.*, *Miss R.*, the destined husband or wife. **5. b.** [He] took the r. way to be depos'd MILT. **6. c.** At all events,..it's a fault on the r. side 1855. **d.** A widow on the r. side of thirty 1809. **7.** Thou hast frighted the word out of his r. sence SHAKS. **8.** So also Harry Monmouth being in his r. wittes,.. turn'd away the fat Knight SHAKS. **9. a.** Phr. *Not r. in the head.* **b.** Phrases. *To set* or *put* (a person) *r.*, to correct or direct; also, to justify (oneself). *R. as my glove*, *as ninepence*, *as a trivet*, etc. **10.** A fool must now and then be r., by chance COWPER. Phr. *Right!* = You are r.; you say well; also *R. you are.* **11.** Phr. *To get..r.*, to set in order. *To make it r.*, to square or settle matters. *To come* (*all*) *r. All r.*, used to express acquiescence or assent. *R.-ho! R.-o!* (slang), used as an expression of agreement or assent: Very well 1902.

III. 1. Having due title or right; rightful, legitimate, lawful. Now *arch.* OE. **2.** Justly entitled to the name; having the true character of; true; real, genuine, not counterfeit or spurious OE.

1. To the r. heyres of the same Elizabeth 1492. **2.** Behold a r. hisrahelite, in whom is no guile TINDALE *John* 1:47. Half an Ounce of r. Virginia Tobacco STEELE. *R. whale*: A whale-bone whale, esp. of the genus *Balæna*.

IV. 1. The distinctive epithet of the hand (see RIGHT HAND) normally the stronger; by extension also of that side of the body, its limbs, their clothing, etc.; hence *transf.* of corresponding parts of other objects. *R. bank* (of a river), that on the right of a person facing down the stream. **2.** *R. side.* **a.** The right-hand side; the right-hand quarter or region ME. **b.** *To rise,* or *get out of bed, on the* (†*one's*) *r. side,* used with allusion to the supposed luckiness of the practice, or its effect on one's temper 1562.

1. The Virgin Mary crowned, with her Babe in her r. arm 1797. **2. a.** The king. .layd him downe on his r. side MORE. *attrib.* The r. side tool. .is thus named because it cuts from the r. hand towards the left 1846. Hence **Ri·ghten** *v. trans.* to put or set r. in various senses. **Right-si·ded** *a.* (*Path.*) situated in or affecting the r. side of the body; having a tendency to use the limbs on the r. side of the body. **Rightward, -wards** *adv.*

Right (rəit), *v.* [OE. *rihtan*, f. *riht* RIGHT *a.*] †**I.** *trans.* **1.** To make straight (a path, way, etc.); to straighten –ME. **2.** To guide, direct (movements, etc) –1440. **3.** To guide as ruler; to govern, rule, judge –1512. **II. 1.** †To set up, establish; to raise, rear, erect, set upright. Now *dial.* OE. **2. a.** *Naut. To r. the helm,* to bring it into line with the keel 1627. **b.** To bring (a ship) back into a vertical position 1748. **c.** *intr.* Of a ship, etc.: To recover or reassume a vertical position 1745. **d.** *refl.* To recover one's balance or equilibrium; to recover one's footing; to correct a false step 1805. **e.** To restore to the proper position after a fall, overturn, breakdown, etc. 1823. **3.** To do justice or make reparation to (a person); to redress the injuries of; to avenge OE. **b.** To vindicate, set right, justify. Chiefly *refl.* late ME. **4.** To avenge or redress (an injustice or injury). late ME.

2. b. They were forced to cut away the masts to r. her 1834. **c.** The lab'ring ship may bend, ne'er more to r. 1762. **e.** We soon righted the carriage 1841. **3.** He thinks that when he is wronged, it is the business of the ruler. .to r. him at once 1891. *refl. L. L. L.* v. ii. 734.

III. 1. To bring into accordance with truth; to correct or render exact (accounts, etc.); to set right or inform (a person) correctly. Also with *up.* OE. **2.** To set in order, to adjust, to set or put right. Now *rare.* OE. **3.** *refl.* To return to a proper or normal condition 1833.

1. He said he was righting his accounts 1690. **2.** After righting all matters to our satisfaction 1793. **3.** Slowly all things r. themselves 1838. Hence **Ri·ghtable** *a.* capable of being righted. **Ri·ghter,** one who settles or sets right.

Right (rəit), *adv.* [OE. *rihte*, f. *riht* RIGHT *a.*] **I. 1.** Of motion or position: Straight; in a direct course or line. **b.** In the proper course ME. **c.** *R. up,* straight up, upright. Now *dial.* 1440. **2.** In a straight or direct course leading quite up *to* a place, person, or thing; hence, all the way *to, into, round, through,* etc.; also with advs. OE. **b.** Quite or completely *off, out, round,* etc. late ME. **3. a.** Immediately *after* some event ME. **b.** †*R. forth,* at once. So *r. off, r. away,* immediately, without delay (orig. *U.S.*). 1440. **c.** *U.S.* Straight (with temporal connotation) 1849. **4.** *R. out,* = OUTRIGHT *adv.* 3, 4; also *dial.,* completely 1610.

1. We had a constant gale blowing r. upon our stern 1748. **b.** He. .directed them that went r. *Ecclus.* 49:9. **2.** The broad verandah which runs r. round the house 1865. **3. b.** I saw now that 'R. away' and 'Directly' were one and the same thing DICKENS. **4.** *Temp.* IV. i. 101.

II. 1. Precisely, exactly, just, quite. altogether, to the full. Now *dial.* or *arch.* **2.** Qualifying advs. (or advb. phrases) of time, esp. *r. now,* †*then,* etc. Now *arch.* OE. **3.** With preps. or advs. of place, as *r. at, in, on,* etc. OE. **b.** With *here, there.* Now *U.S.* ME. **4.** Qualifying *as* or *so* in various constructions. Now *arch.* OE. **5.** With intensive force: Very. Now *arch.* ME. **b.** In titles or forms of address. late ME. †**6.** With negs.: At all; whatever –1571.

2. Haue you forgotten what you said r. now? 1624. **3.** The Wind is r. in our teeth 1669. **5.** I know r. well how tedious I haue beene 1600. *R. honourable*: see HONOURABLE *a.* 2 b.

III. 1. Righteously, uprightly; in harmony with the moral standard of actions OE. **2.** In a proper or fitting manner; in the required or necessary way; properly; duly, aright OE. **b.** In due or proper order ME. **3.** In accordance with facts or the truth of the case; accurately; correctly OE. **4.** On or towards the right side (*of*). See also RIGHT AND LEFT. ME.

1. Thou satest in the throne iudging r. *Ps.* 9:4. **2.** The first thing should be taught him is to hold his Pen r. LOCKE. Phr. *All r., r. enough.* **b.** When once our grace we haue forgot Nothing goes r. SHAKS. **3.** Yes, you guess r. 1878. **4.** ''Tention eyes r.!' 1816.

-right, *suffix,* repr. OE. *riht* adj. and *rihte* adv., which are employed as suffixes in OE. *forðriht, -rihte* FORTHRIGHT, and *upriht, -rihte* UPRIGHT. See also OUTRIGHT.

Right about, *sb., adv.* (and *a.*) Also **right-about, rightabout.** 1700. [f. RIGHT *sb.*¹ IV. 1 a + ABOUT *adv.* II. 2; orig. as two separate words.] **A.** *sb. Mil.* In phr. *To the right about,* a command to turn towards the right so far as to face the opposite way (now simply *right about*). Hence with vbs., as *turn, face,* etc. Also *gen.*

Their fox took the opportunity to swing to the rightabout 1883. Phr. **To send to the r. a.** To cause (troops) to turn and retreat or flee. **b.** To send packing: to dismiss or turn away unceremoniously.

B. 1. *adv.* = A. 1; usu. as a command with additional word, as *wheel, face, turn* 1796. **b.** Hence *right about face* as a compound vb. or adv. 1815. **2.** *attrib.* or as *adj.* with *face* or *turn.* Also in fig. use, denoting a complete change of front; an entire reversal of principles or policy 1862.

1. b. Southey,. .True turn-coat, can right about face, pliant lad 1815. **2.** The Tory right-about-face 1891.

Right and left, right-and-left, *adv.* (*v.*), *a.,* and *sb.* ME. **A.** *adv.* On or towards the right and the left; on both sides, in both directions. **b.** *transf.* On all hands 1893.

b. He is being robbed right and left 1893.

B. *adj.* Of or pertaining to the right and the left hand side, etc.; turning to the right and the left; fitting the right and left hand or foot respectively 1854.

An excellent right-and-left shot 1863. *Right-and-left screw,* one having the threads at the two ends running opposite ways.

C. *sb.* A right-and-left shot 1856.

Ri·ght a:ngle. ME. [f. RIGHT *a.* I. 3 + ANGLE *sb.*²] *Math.* An angle of 90°.

At right angles, perpendicularly (*to* another line, etc.); so as to form an angle of 90°.

Ri·ght-angled, *a.* 1571. [f. as prec. + ANGLED *a.*] **1.** Containing or forming a right angle or right angles; rectangular. **2.** Characterized by right angles 1833.

Right boys. An irregular association formed in S.W. Ireland in 1785–6, and connected with political or agrarian disorders; named after one of their leaders, Captain Right.

Ri·ght-down, *adv.* and *a.* Also **right down, rightdown.** 1623. [f. RIGHT *adv.* + DOWN *adv.* Cf. DOWNRIGHT] **A.** *adv.* †**1.** With verbs: Positively; without any limitation; right out –1709. **2.** With pples. or adjs.: Thoroughly; out and out 1648. **B.** *adj.* Positive; thorough 1623.

Such fellows. .become r. scamps 1875.

Righteous (rəi·tyəs, rəi·tʃəs), *a.* (*sb.*) and *adv.* [OE. *rihtwīs*, f. *riht* sb. or adj. + *wīs* manner, state (cf. -WISE). The sp. *righteous* (XVI) is f. *rightuous* (XV) by assim. to *beauteous, bounteous, plenteous.*] **1.** Of persons: Just, upright, virtuous; guiltless, sinless; acting rightly or justly. (See also RIGHTEOUSNESS.) Also used *absol.* (in sing. or pl.) with *the.* †**b.** As *sb.* A righteous person –1667. **2.** Of actions, etc.: Characterized by justice or uprightness; morally right or justifiable OE. †**3.** As *adv.* Righteously; rightfully –1470.

1. Let me be recorded by the r. Gods, I am as poore as you SHAKS. In his dayes shall the r. flourish *Ps.* 72:7. **b.** The onely r. in a World perverse MILT. **2.** Instructing men in the way of r. living HOBBES. Hence †**Ri·ghteous** *v. trans.* to set right; to justify; to do justice to; to make r.

Ri·ghteously, *adv.* [OE. *rihtwīslīće*; see prec., -LY².] In a righteous manner.

Ri·ghteousness. [OE. *rihtwīsnisse*; see RIGHTEOUS, -NESS.] **1.** The quality or condition of being righteous; conformity of life or conduct to the requirements of the divine or moral law; *spec.* in *Theol.* applied e.g. to the perfection of the Divine Being, and to the justification of man through the Atonement. †**2.** *pl.* Righteous deeds –1611.

2. All our righteousnesses are as filthy ragges *Isa.* 64:6.

Rightful (rəi·tfŭl), *a.* [OE. *rihtful*; see RIGHT *sb.*¹, -FUL.] **1.** Of persons: Disposed to do right; upright, just. Now *rare* or *Obs.* **2.** Of actions, etc: In conformity with what is right or just; equitable, thoroughly fair ME. **3.** Legal, lawful, legitimate ME. **4.** Proper, fitting, correct. Now *rare.* late ME.

1. *Merch. V.* IV. i. 301. **2.** For we by rightfull doom remediles Were lost in death MILT. **3.** Her vndoubted and rightfull successor CAMDEN. **4.** Danube scarce retains his r. course PRIOR. Hence **Ri·ghtful-ly** *adv.,* **-ness.**

Right hand. Also **righthand, right-hand.** OE. [f. RIGHT *a.* IV. 1.] **1.** That hand which is normally the stronger of the two. (Opp. to LEFT HAND.) **b.** *transf.* (*a*) as a symbol of friendship or alliance (rendering L. *dextræ*); (*b*) a person of usefulness or importance; an efficient or indispensable helper or aid 1528. **2. a.** The right side. **b.** The direction towards the right. ME. †**c.** The position of honour. *To take the right hand of,* to take or assume precedence of. –1704. †**d.** Of errors: *On the right hand,* on the right side, in the right direction –1785.

1. To horse!. .or by this good right hand. .I smite you COWPER. *attrib.* Two right-hand gloves 1884. **b.** For Mrs. Jane is the Right-hand of her Mother STEELE. **2. b.** Turne vpon your right hand at the next turning SHAKS.

attrib. and *Comb.* **right-hand lock,** one enabling a door to swing to the right; **right-hand man,** †a soldier holding a position of responsibility on the right of a troop of horse; an efficient and reliable helper or aid; **right-hand rope,** a rope twisted towards the right; **right-hand screw,** one with the thread turning to the right. Hence **Right-ha·nder,** a blow struck with the r.; a right-handed person.

Right-handed, *a.* (*adv.*) late ME. [f. prec. + -ED².] **1.** Having the right hand or arm stronger or more useful than the left; using the right hand by preference. **2.** On the right side; of the right kind 1656. **3. a.** Pertaining or belonging to the right hand. **b.** Of a blow: Delivered with the right hand. **c.** Of implements, etc.: Fashioned for the right hand. 1700. **4.** *Conchol.* = DEXTRAL *a.* 2. 1838. **5.** Characterized by rotation or direction towards the right. Also as *adv.* **b.** Of rotatory polarization (see quots.) 1827. **c.** Producing right-handed polarization 1827. **6.** In the direction of the right; also as *adv.,* to the right 1900.

1. Some are. .ambidexterous or right handed on both sides SIR T. BROWNE. **5. b.** I shall. .designate the polarization right-handed or left-handed, according as we have to turn the analyzing prism to the right or to the left 1854. Hence **Right-ha·nded-ly** *adv.,* **-ness.**

Ri·ght-ho, right-o, see RIGHT *a.* II. 11.

Right-lined, *a.* 1551. [f. RIGHT *a.* I. 2 + LINE *sb.*² + -ED².] = RECTILINEAR *a.*

Rightly (rəi·tli), *adv.* [OE. *rihtlīće*; see RIGHT *a.,* -LY².] **1.** In accordance with equity or moral rectitude. **2.** In the right or proper manner OE. **3.** Correctly, accurately, †precisely OE. †**4.** Directly, straight –1635.

3. He cannot see r. and shoots. .with help of an opera-glass CARLYLE. **4.** *Rich. II,* II. ii. 18.

Right-minded, *a.* 1585. [f. RIGHT *a.* + MIND *sb.* + -ED².] **1.** Having a mind naturally disposed towards what is right. **2.** *colloq.* Of sound mind 1877. Hence **Right-mi·ndedness.**

Rightness (rəi·tnès). [OE. *rehtnisse, rihtnesse*; see RIGHT *a.* and -NESS.] **1.** Uprightness, integrity, moral rectitude. †**2.**

Straightness; the fact of being straight -1626. **3.** Correctness, accuracy; fitness 1561. **b.** An instance of this 1872.

1. A r. which..hath had everlasting residence in the character of the Godhead 1834. **3.** You are answerable, not for the r., but uprightness of the decision 1787.

Right of way (rəitəvwē·). Also **right-of-way.** 1768. **1.** The legal right, established by usage, of a person or persons to pass and repass through grounds or property belonging to another. **2.** A path or thoroughfare which one may lawfully make use of, *esp.* one traversing the property of another 1855. **3.** *U.S.* = PERMANENT *way.*

-rights, *suffix,* ME. var. of -RIGHT.

Rigid (ri·dʒid), *a.* 1538. [- Fr. *rigide* or L. *rigidus,* f. *rigēre* be stiff; see -ID[1].] **1.** Stiff, unyielding; not pliant or flexible; firm, hard. **2.** Of cold, etc.: Severe, hard, rigorous (*rare*) 1611. **3.** Of conduct, persons, etc.: Harsh, severe, inflexible, strict 1624. **4.** Strict in opinion or observance; scrupulously precise in respect of these 1598. **5.** Exact, precise in procedure; admitting of no deviation from strict accuracy 1646.

1. With upright beams innumerable Of r. Spears MILT. *fig.* The..r. forms of antiquity HAZLITT. **b.** *spec.* Of an airship: Having the gas containers enclosed within compartments of a framework, as of metal, which carries the cabins, motors, etc.; also as *sb.* a r. airship 1909. **3.** O r. gods! 1752. R. justice, untempered by mercy, easily changes into oppression 1868. **4.** R. looks of Chast austerity MILT. R. parsimony 1861. R. Catholics 1874. **5.** True, in the most r. sense 1729. Hence **Ri·gid-ly** *adv.*, **-ness.**

Rigi·dity. 1624. [- L. *rigiditas, -at-,* f. *rigidus;* see prec., -ITY. Cf. Fr. *rigidité* (XVII).] **1.** The state of being rigid: stiffness, hardness. **2.** Strictness, harshness, inflexibility 1653.

Rigmarole (ri·gmărōᵘl), *sb.* (and *a.*). 1736. [app. a colloq. survival and alteration of RAGMAN ROLL (sense 2).] **1.** A succession of incoherent statements; a rambling discourse; a long-winded harangue of little meaning or importance. **b.** Without article: Language of this kind 1809. **2.** *attrib.* or *adj.* Incoherent; having no proper sequence of ideas 1753.

1. That's better than a long r. about nothing 1779. Hence **Ri·gmarolish** *a.*, **-ly** *adv.*

Ri·gol, *sb. Obs.* exc. *dial.* 1593. [- (O)Fr. *rigole* water-course, gutter, groove.] †**1.** A ring or circle -1597. **2.** A small channel, gutter or groove 1879.

‖**Rigor** (rəi·gǫɹ, ri·gǫɹ). late ME. [L., numbness, stiffness; see RIGOUR.] *Path.* **1.** A sudden chill, *esp.* one accompanied with fits of shivering which immediately precedes certain fevers and inflammations. **2.** *R. mortis,* the stiffening of the body following upon death 1839.

Rigorism (ri·gŏriz'm). Also **rigourism.** 1704. [f. RIGOUR (see sense 4) + -ISM, assim. to L. sp.; see -OR 2.] **1.** The principles and practice of a rigorist; austerity, stringency; extreme strictness. **2.** *R. C. Theol.* The doctrine of the rigorist school of moral theology 1882.

Rigorist (ri·gŏrist). Also **rigourist.** 1714. [f. as prec. + -IST.] **1.** One who favours or insists upon the severest or strictest interpretation or enforcement of a law, precept, principle, or standard of any kind. **2.** *R. C. Theol.* One who holds that in doubtful cases of conscience the stricter course is always to be followed 1715.

Rigorous (ri·gŏrəs), *a.* late ME. [- OFr. *rigorous* (mod. *rigoureux*) or late L. *rigorosus,* f. L. RIGOR; see -OUS.] **1.** Characterized by rigour; rigidly severe or unbending; austere, harsh, stern; extremely strict. **2.** Of the weather, etc.: Severe; bitterly cold. **3.** Scrupulous, unswerving, strict (*rare*) 1641. **4.** Severely exact, rigidly accurate 1651.

1. I..hope she will not be too r. with the young ones JOHNSON. The r. conditions of peace and pardon GIBBON. **3.** A life of..r. abstinence 1847. **4.** We have need of a more r. scholastic rule 1838. Hence **Ri·gorous-ly** *adv.*, **-ness.**

Rigour (ri·gəɹ). Also formerly (now U.S.) **rigor.** late ME. [- (O)Fr. *rigour* (mod. *rigueur*) - L. RIGOR, *rigor-*; see -OUR.] **I. 1.** Severity in dealing with a person or persons; extreme strictness; harshness. **b.** An instance of this 1548. **2.** The strict terms, application, or enforcement *of* some law, rule, etc. late ME. **3.** Of weather or climate: Severity; extremity or excess of cold; †violence (of storms) 1548. **b.** Extreme distress or hardship 1769. **4.** Strictness of discipline, etc.; austerity of life; an instance of this 1440. **b.** Puritanic strictness; rigorism; †an instance of this 1597. **5.** Strict accuracy, severe exactitude 1565.

1. If..they haue tempered r. with lenitie HOOKER. **2.** A clear fire, a clean hearth, and the r. of the game LAMB. Phr. *The* (..) *r. of the law.* **3.** From regions of Arctic r. 1878. **b.** The utmost r. of famine 1769. **4.** The r. of the monastic discipline 1833. **b.** R. makes it difficult for sliding virtue to recover RICHARDSON. **5.** The term philosophy..when employed in propriety and r. 1836.

II. 1. = RIGOR 1. 1541. †**2.** Of material objects: Stiffness, hardness -1700.

2. The Stones..Did first the r. of their kind expel, And suppled into softness as they fell DRYDEN.

Ri·g-out. *colloq.* 1823. [f. RIG *v.*[2]] An outfit; a suit of clothes; a costume.

Rig-veda (rig,vē·dă). 1776. [Skr. *ṛigvēda,* f. *ṛic* praise + *vēda* VEDA.] The principal of the Vedas or sacred books of the Hindus.

Rile (rəil), *v.* Chiefly *U.S.* and *colloq.* 1825. [orig. var. (cf. *jint* for *joint,* etc.) of ROIL *v.*[2]] **1.** *trans.* To make (a liquid) thick or turbid by stirring up the sediment; to make muddy 1838. **2.** To excite, disturb; to vex, annoy, make angry 1825. **b.** *absol.* with *up.* To get angry 1844.

2. b. The little fellow riled up at this 1863. Hence **Riled** *ppl. a.*

Rill (ril), *sb.* 1538. [prob. of LDu. origin; cf. LG. *ril(le,* Du., EFris. *ril* (whence G. *rille*). Cf. med.L. (Norman) *rilla* (XII).] **1.** A small stream; a brook, runnel, rivulet. **2.** A small narrow trench; a drill. Now *dial.* 1658. **3.** *Astr.* = RILLE 1888.

1. Shallow rills run trickling through the grass ADDISON. *fig.* Rills of oily eloquence..lubricate the course they take COWPER.

Rill (ril), *v.* 1610. [f. prec.] **1.** *intr.* To flow in a small stream. **2.** *trans.* **a.** To form by flowing. **b.** To utter in liquid notes. 1845. †**3.** To make drills in a garden bed. EVELYN.

1. Time's sand-dry streamlet through its glassy strait Rilled restless 1855.

Rille (ril). 1868. [- G. *rille;* see RILL *sb.*] *Astr.* One of the long narrow trenches or valleys observed on the surface of the moon.

Rillet (ri·lėt). 1538. [f. RILL *sb.* + -ET or -LET.] A small rill or rivulet; a brooklet.

Those rillets that attend proud Tamer and her state DRAYTON.

Rim, *sb.*[1] [OE. *rima* = ON. *rimi* ridge of land, of which no other cognates are known.] **1.** The peripheral portion or outer ring of a wheel, connected with the nave or boss by spokes or by a web. late ME. **b.** The hoop-shaped piece of wood which forms the outer frame of a sieve, etc. Also *dial.* a hoop. 1660. **c.** A circular mark or object 1860. **2.** *Naut.* The surface *of* the water 1602. **3.** The edge, border, or margin *of* an object, *esp.* one which has a more or less circular form 1603. **b.** The verge *of* the horizon, sea, hills, etc. Chiefly *poet.* 1842. **4.** An edge, margin, or border; *esp.* a raised or projecting one upon something having a circular form 1669. **b.** A verge or margin of land, sea, etc.; a narrow strip 1781.

1. b. A wheat-riddle of wood..with an oak r. 1844. **3.** The moon lifting her silver r. Above a cloud KEATS. **b.** The steel-blue r. of the ocean 1858. **4.** One little boy complained..that there was no r. to his plate 1832. **b.** The ragged rims of thunder brooding low TENNYSON.

Comb.: **r.-fire** *a.* of a cartridge, having the detonating substance disposed round the edge (opp. to *centre-fire*); hence, of a gun, adapted for such cartridges; **-lock,** a lock having a metal case which stands out from the face of the door. Hence **Rim** *v. trans.* to furnish with a r.; to border or encircle in some way. **Ri·mmed** *a.* having a r. of a specified form, colour, etc.; having or furnished with a r.

Rim, *sb.*[2] Now *dial.* [OE. *rēoma* = MDu. *rieme* (Du. *riem*); see RIEM.] †**1.** A membrane, pellicle, caul -1601. **2.** *R. of the belly* (*womb, paunch,* etc.), the peritoneum. Now *dial.* Also *ellipt.* 1565.

2. I will fetch thy rymme out at thy Throat, in droppes of Crimson blood SHAKS.

‖**Rima** (rəi·mă). 1835. [L., chink.] *Physiol.* Short for *rima glottidis,* the passage in the glottis between the vocal chords and the arytenoid cartilages. So †**Rime** *sb.*[3] -1657.

Rime (rəim), *sb.*[1] ME. [- (O)Fr. *rime* (:- **ritme*) - med.L. *rithmus, rythmus* (used spec. of accentual verse which was usu. rhymed), for L. *rhythmus* RHYTHM.

About 1560 *rime* (*ryme*) was altered on classical models to *rithme, rythme, rhythm(e.* Soon after 1600, prob. from a desire to distinguish between 'rime' and 'rhythm', the intermediate forms *rhime, rhyme* came into use, and *rhyme* finally became the standard form (see RHYME *sb.*). From about 1870 the use of *rime* has been considerably revived.]

1. = RHYME *sb.* †**2.** = RHYTHM *sb.* 1, 4. -1677.

1. *Much Ado* v. ii. 37. Beautie making beautifull old r., In praise of Ladies dead, and louely Knights SHAKS. The Anglosaxon poets..generally used measures without r. 1774. The R. of the Ancyent Marinere COLERIDGE.

Comb.: **r.-letter,** the distinctive initial letter in a line of alliterative verse. Hence **Ri·meless** *a.* **Ri·mester,** a poetaster.

Rime (rəim), *sb.*[2] [OE. *hrīm* = (M)Du. *rijm,* ON. *hrím.*] Hoar-frost; frozen mist. Also *dial.* a chill mist or fog.

Moonlight splendour of intensest r., With which frost paints the pines in winter time SHELLEY. *fig.* Tales that have the r. of age LONGF. Hence **Ri·me** *v.*[2] *trans.* to cover with hoar-frost. **Ri·my** *a.*

Rime (rəim), *v.*[1] ME. [- OFr. *rimer,* f. *rime* RIME *sb.*[1] For the spelling see RIME *sb.*[1]] **1.** *intr.* To make rhymes or verses; to compose rhyming verse; to versify *on, upon.* Cf. RHYME *v.* 1. **2.** *trans.* To recount or celebrate in verse or rhyme; to turn into, or compose in, rhyming verse ME. **b.** To cause (a word) to rhyme *with* (another); to use as a rhyme 1887. **3.** To bring by rhyming 1584. **4.** *intr.* To form a rhyme. Also *fig.*, to agree. 1450. **b.** To have rhyming endings 1660. **5.** To use rhyme 1602.

1. How vildely doth this Cynicke r.! SHAKS. **2.** He rimed history, ballads and legends 1887. **3.** These fellowes..that can ryme themselues into Ladyes fauours SHAKS. **5.** *Haml.* III. ii. 296. Hence **Ri·mer** *sb.*[1]

†**Ri·me-frost.** ME. [f. RIME *sb.*[2] + FROST *sb.*, corresp. to Icel., OSw. *hrímfrost.*] = RIME *sb.*[2] -1626.

Rimer (rəi·məɹ), *sb.*[2] 1815. = REAMER.

Rimose (rəi·mōᵘs, rəimōᵘ·s), *a.* 1726. [- L. *rimosus,* f. RIMA; see -OSE[1].] Full of, or having, fissures or chinks. Chiefly *Bot.* So **Ri·mous** *a.* 1709.

Rimple (ri·mp'l), *sb.* 1440. Now *dial.* [corresp. in sense to (M)Du. and (M)LG. *rimpel.* See also RUMPLE *sb.*] **1.** A wrinkle. **2.** A ripple 1877. Hence **Ri·mple** *v. trans.* to wrinkle, pucker; to ripple. **Ri·mpled** *a.* (now *dial.* or *U.S.*), wrinkled, puckered; rippled.

Rind (rəind), *sb.*[1] [OE. *rind, rinde,* corresp., with variation, to OS. *rinda,* MDu. *rinde, rende, runde* (Du. *run*), OHG. *rinta, rinda* (G. *rinde*); of unkn. origin.] **1.** The bark of a tree or plant; sometimes, inner as contrasted with outer bark. Also with *a* and in pl. (now *rare*). **b.** *Bot.* False, as contrasted with true, bark 1857. †**2.** Coupled with *root* -1530. **3.** The peel or skin of fruits and vegetables. late ME. **4.** The outer crust, skin, or integument (esp. now of cheese, bacon) OE. †**b.** The verge or rim *of* something; the border *of* a country -1608. **5.** The skin of a person or animal. Now *dial.* 1513. †**b.** A membrane or pellicle; *esp.* the pia mater or the peritoneum -1693. **6.** *fig.* (chiefly from sense 1). The surface or external aspect *of* something OE.

3. Take three or four seville oranges.., and boil the rinds 1764. **5.** The Pilot..With fixed Anchor in his skaly r. Moors by his side MILT. **6.** To inspect beyond the Surface and the R. of Things SWIFT. Hence **Rind** *v. trans.* to strip the r. or bark from (a tree, etc.). **Ri·ndless** *a.* (*rare*), without r. or bark. **Ri·ndy** *a.* having a r. or hard skin.

Rind (rəind), *sb.*[2] ME. [prob. - (M)LG. *rīn,* (M)Du. *rijn,* †*rine,* Flem. *rijne;* the *d* is parasitic.] An iron fitting serving to support an upper millstone on the spindle.

Rinderpest (ri·ndəɹpest). 1865. [G., f. *rinder* cattle, pl. of *rind.*] A virulent, infectious disease affecting ruminant animals, *esp.* oxen, characterized by fever, dysentery, and inflammation of the mucous membranes; cattle-plague.

Rindle (ri·nd'l). [OE. *rinnelle, rynele* fem., *rynel* masc., f. stem *rin-, run-*; see RUN *v.*] A small watercourse or stream; a runnel.

Ring (riŋ), *sb.*[1] [OE. *hring* = OFris. *(h)ring*, OS., OHG. *hring* (Du., G. *ring*), ON. *hringr* :– Gmc. **χreŋgaz* (whence Finnish *rengas*).] **I. 1.** A small circlet of (real or simulated) precious metal, frequently set with precious stones, or imitations of these, for wearing upon the finger either as an ornament or as a token (*esp.* of betrothal, marriage, or investiture), and sometimes for use as a seal. **b.** A metal circlet worn elsewhere than on the finger as an ornament OE. **2.** = MAIL *sb.*[1] 1. OE. **3.** A circle of metal, etc., of any dimension, employed as a means of attachment, suspension, compression, etc. OE. **b.** A circular knocker upon a door. Now *rare.* late ME. **c.** [– LG. *ring.*] A measure of boards (= 240) or staves for casks (= 4 shocks) 1674. **4.** A circlet of metal suspended from a post which each of a number of riders endeavoured to carry off on the point of his lance 1513. **5. a.** One of the raised bands passing round the body of cannon as formerly made. Chiefly in combs., as *cornice-, reinforce-, trunnion-r.* 1610. **b.** A kind of gas-check used in a cannon. In full *Broadwell's ring.* 1868.

1. The manne shall geue vnto the womanne a r. *Bk. Com. Prayer.* As if they had King Gyges his enchanted R., they walk invisible 1679. **b.** They wore rings in their ears 1660. **4.** Phr. *To run or ride at the r.*

II. 1. The border, rim, or outer part of some circular object, *esp.* of a coin or a wheel OE. **2.** An object having the form of a circle; a circular fold, coin, or bend; a piece or part (of something) forming a circle. late ME. **b.** *Anat.* A structure of circular form; *esp.* one of the annular joints of the bodies of caterpillars and insects, or one of the cartilages of the trachea 1580. **c.** One of the concentric circular bands of wood constituting the yearly growth of a tree 1671. **d.** One of the raised circular marks at the base of the horns of oxen or cows, varying in number according to the animal's age 1725. **e.** *Bot.* = ANNULUS 3. 1796. **3. a.** A circular mark; also = FAIRY-RING 1626. **b.** A circle, or circular band, of light or colour 1648. **c.** One of the expanding circular ripples caused by something falling or being cast into still water 1821. **III. 1.** A circle or circular group of persons OE. **b.** A number of things arranged in a circle 1587. **2.** A combination of interested persons to monopolize and control a particular trade or market for their private advantage. Chiefly *U.S.* 1869. **b.** An organization which endeavours to control politics or local affairs in its own interest 1872.

2. The 'r.' is being succeeded by a more elaborate organization, known as the 'trust' G. B. SHAW. **b.** The war was the creation of the Whig 'r.' 1882.

IV. 1. An enclosed circular space within which some sport, performance, or exhibition (*esp.* of riding or racing) takes place ME. †**b.** A circular course in Hyde Park, used for riding and driving –1848. **2. a.** A space, originally defined by a circle of bystanders, for a prize-fight or a wrestling-match; often in phr. *to make a r.* Hence *the r.*, pugilism as an institution or profession; also *collect.* those interested in boxing. 1700. **b.** An enclosed space in a racing-ground frequented by bookmakers; also *collect.* the bookmaking profession 1859. **c.** An enclosed or clear space in an auction-mart, used for the display of livestock, etc. 1890. **3.** A circular or spiral orbit or course 1589.

1. The sawdust r. of a bankrupt circus 1883. **3.** First, wide around,..in airy rings they rove THOMSON.

Comb.: **r.-armour,** armour composed of metal rings, r.-mail; **-bolt** *Naut.*, a bolt with an eye at one end to which a r. is attached; **-boot,** a rubber ring placed on a horse's fetlock to prevent interfering; **-bored** *a.* of a gun-barrel, bored roughly, so as to leave the metal in rings; **-canal,** a circular canal forming part of the structure of cœlenterates and of echinoderms; †**-carrier,** a go-between; **-cartilage,** the cricoid cartilage; **-craft,** skill in pugilism; **r. dropper,** a sharper who pretends to have found a dropped r. and offers to sell it; **-farm,** a farm enclosed by a r.-fence; **-joint,** a pipe-joint formed of circular flanges; **-mail** (see MAIL *sb.*[1] 2); **-master,** the manager of a circus performance; **-road,** a road encircling a town which acts as a by-pass road for traffic; **-shell, -shot,** a projectile in which the body is made of iron rings; a segment-shell; **-stopper** = *cathead-stopper*; **-time,** a time of giving or exchanging rings (*nonce-use*); **-wall,** a wall completely surrounding a certain area; *techn.* the inner lining of a furnace; **-work,** (*a*) a circular entrenchment; (*b*) work executed with rings; (*c*) performance in the boxing-r.

b. In names of birds, reptiles, fishes, etc., as **r.-bill,** the ring-necked duck or moon-bill; **-bird,** the reed-bunting (*local*); **r. blackbird, -ouzel,** a bird (*Turdus torquatus*, closely allied to the blackbird) having a white r. or bar on the breast; **-snake,** (*a*) the common European grass- or ringed snake (*Tropidonotus natrix*); (*b*) *U.S.*, a snake of the genus *Diadophis*, esp. *D. punctatus*; **-thrush** = *r.-ouzel.*

Ring (riŋ), *sb.*[2] 1549. [f. RING *v.*[2]] **1.** A set or peal *of* (church) bells. **2.** A ringing sound or noise 1622. **b.** A ringing tone or quality in the voice, or in a (recited) composition 1859. **c.** The resonance of a coin or glass vessel by which its genuineness or wholeness is tested 1855. **3.** An act of ringing; a pull *at* a bell; the sound thus produced 1727.

1. Here is also a very fine r. of six bells, and they mighty tuneable PEPYS. **2.** He must come to the R. of the Midnight Bell 1706. **b.** There was a r. of scorn in the last words GEO. ELIOT. **c.** *transf.* There does not seem always the right r. about him 1886.

Ring (riŋ), *v.*[1] Pa. t. and pple. **ringed.** late ME. [f. RING *sb.*[1] Cf. OE. *ymbhringan* surround.] **I. 1.** *intr.* To make a circle or ring; to gather in a ring *about* or *round* (a person). Now *rare.* **b.** Of a hawk, etc.: To rise spirally in flight 1879. *c.* Of a stag, fox, or hare: To take a circular course when hunted 1882. **2.** *trans.* To surround, encompass, encircle. Also with *round, about.* 1590. **b.** To hem in (cattle or game) by riding or beating in a circle round them; to beat or stalk round (a stretch of country) for game 1835. **c.** To hem or shut *in* 1871. **3.** To place or fasten round something in the form of a ring 1799.

2. A girdle of mist will r. the slopes 1884. Ringed about with cannon smoke and thunder STEVENSON.

II. 1. To adorn (the fingers or nose) with a ring or rings (*rare*) 1552. **2.** To put a ring in the nose of (swine or cattle) to restrain them from rooting or violence; also, to place a ring round the leg of (fowls, pigeons, etc.) as a means of identification 1519. **3.** To deprive (trees) of a ring of bark, in order to check too luxuriant growth and bring into bearing, or to kill them 1800. **4.** To cut into annular slices or rounds 1839.

1. I will..r. these fingers with thy houshold wormes SHAKS. **4.** The onions, being cut in slices and ringed, are put into the frying-pan 1839.

Ring (riŋ), *v.*[2] Pa. t. **rang, rung.** Pa. pple. **rung.** [OE. *hringan*, corresp. to ON. *hringja.*] **I.** *intr.* **1.** To give out the clear or resonant sound characteristic of certain hard metals when struck with, or striking upon, something hard. Also of a trumpet, etc.: To sound loudly. **b.** *fig.* To impress one as having a certain (genuine or false) character 1611. **2.** Of bells: To give forth a clear metallic note under the impact of the hammer or clapper ME. **b.** To convey a summons *to* service, prayers, church, etc. 1509. **3.** Of places: To resound, re-echo, with some sound or noise ME. **b.** To be filled with talk or report *of*, to resound *with* the report or fame of, a thing, event, or person. Also with *that* and clause. 1608. **4.** Of a sound: To be loud or resonant; to resound, re-echo. Also with *out.* late ME. **5.** Of the ears: To be affected by a sensation similar to that produced by the sound of bells, etc.; to tingle, hum, or be filled *with* a sound. late ME.

1. The harp..Which to the whistling wild responsive rung 1768. **b.** But Crassus, and this Caesar here r. hollow B. JONS. **2.** The great bell rung out for Earle of C. C. Coll., fellow WOOD. **b.** Though the day be never so longe, At last the belles ringeth to evensonge 1509. **3.** The arched cloister..Rang to the warrior's clanking stride SCOTT. **b.** The world should r. of him TENNYSON. **4.** *fig.* Fairfax, whose name in armes through Europe rings MILT. Phr. *To r. in one's ears, fancy, heart*, to haunt the memory. **5.** The ears r. with unusual sounds 1882.

II. *trans.* **1.** To cause (a bell) to give forth sound. Also *absol.* OE. **2.** To summon *to* (divine service, church, etc.) by means of a bell. late ME. **3.** With cogn. obj.: To sound forth (a peal, knell, etc.); to perform upon bells ME. **4.** To announce or proclaim (an hour, time, etc.) by sound of bells OE. **5.** To usher *in* or *out* with the sound of bells; to bring or convey in this manner 1554. **b.** To summon (a person) by ringing a bell. Also with *down, in, up*, etc. **c.** To direct (a theatre-curtain) to be drawn *up* or let *down* by causing a bell to ring. Also *absol.* 1836. **d.** *To r. off*, to give signal by a bell for the severance of communication upon a telephone 1888. **6.** To cause to give out a ringing sound; to make to resound. late ME. **b.** To test (coin, etc.) by making it ring 1702. **7.** To utter sonorously; to proclaim aloud; to re-echo. Also with *out.* late ME. **b.** To cause to resound, din, *in* one's ears 1657.

1. *fig.* Fooles can not holde hir tunge; A fooles belle is sone runge CHAUCER. The ringers rang with a will TENNYSON. *To r. up*, to raise (a bell) directly over the beam and r. it in that position. **2.** Phr. *To r. (all) in*, to give the final peal before the service begins. **3.** Sea-Nimphs hourly r. his knell SHAKS. Phr. *To r. the changes*: see CHANGE *sb.* 7 b. **4.** *transf.* Ere the first Cock his Mattin rings MILT. **5. b.** *To r. up*, to communicate with (a person) by telephone; also *absol.* **c.** The curtain had to be rung down before the play was ended 1887. **6. b.** Debating about the genuineness of a coin without ringing it RUSKIN. **7. b.** Persecution was every day rung in our Ears SWIFT. Hence **Ri·nging** *vbl. sb.* the action of the vb.; *ringing engine*, a form of pile-driver, worked by men pulling at ropes after the manner of bell-ringers. **Ri·ngingly** *adv.*, **-ness.**

Ri·ng-bark, *v.* 1887. [f. RING *v.*[1] II. 3.] **a.** *intr.* To remove rings of bark from trees, in order to kill them. **b.** *trans.* To bark (trees) in this way.

Ri·ng-bone. Also **ringbone, ring bone.** 1523. [f. RING *sb.*[1]] **1.** A deposit of bony matter on the pastern-bones of a horse. **2.** The growth of such bony matter, as a specific disease of horses 1594. Hence **Ri·ng-boned** *a.*

Ri·ng-dove. 1538. [f. RING *sb.*[1]] **1.** The wood-pigeon, cushat, or queest (*Columba palumbus*); also called *ring-pigeon.* **2.** The Collared Turtle, *Columbia risonia* 1841.

Ringed (riŋd), *ppl. a.* OE. [f. RING *sb.*[1] or *v.*[1] + -ED.] **1.** Of armour: made of rings (*rare*). **2.** Of persons: Wearing a ring or rings; also, wedded with a ring. late ME. **b.** Of the fingers, etc.: Provided or adorned with a ring or rings 1599. **3.** Marked or encircled by a ring or rings; surrounded by a circular band or bands, etc. 1513. **b.** Deprived of a ring of bark 1820. **4.** Having, put into, the form of a ring 1593. **b.** *Zool.* Composed of rings; annulated 1840.

2. I was born of a true man and a ring'd wife TENNYSON. **3. R. seal,** *Phoca hispida*; **R. snake** = *ring snake* (see RING *sb.*[1]).

Ringent (ri·ndʒěnt), *a.* 1760. [– L. *ringens, -ent-*, pr. pple. of *ringi* gape. Cf. RICTUS.] Gaping or grinning; esp. *Bot.* applied to a labiate corolla having the lips widely opened.

Ringer[1] (ri·ŋəɹ). 1858. [f. RING *sb.*[1] or *v.*[1] + -ER[1].] **1.** *Quoits.* A quoit so thrown that it encloses the pin; a throw of this kind 1863. **2.** *Mining.* A crow-bar 1858. **3.** An animal which runs in a ring when hunted 1891.

Ringer[2] (ri·ŋəɹ). ME. [f. RING *v.*[2] + -ER[1].] One who rings; *esp.* a bell- or change-ringer.

Ri·ng-fence, *sb.* 1769. [f. RING *sb.*[1]] A fence completely enclosing an estate, farm, or piece of ground. Often in fig. phr. Hence **Ri·ng-fence** *v. trans.* to enclose with a ring-fence.

Ri·ng-fi:nger. OE. [RING *sb.*[1]] The third finger of the hand, *esp.* of the left hand.

Ri·nglea:der. 1503. [f. obs. phr. *to lead the ring* to be foremost or first. See RING *sb.*[1] III.] **1.** One who takes a leading part among a number of persons whose character or conduct is reprehensible; *esp.* a chief instigator or organizer of a mutiny, tumult, etc. †**2.** In good or neutral sense: A leader or head –1668.

1. He had been the r. in everything wicked for years 1867.

Ringlet (ri·ŋlět). 1555. [f. RING *sb.*[1] + -LET.]

1. A small ring. **2.** A circular dance or course; a circle of dancers; a fairy-ring 1590. **b.** An annular appearance, marking, formation, part, or piece 1755. **3.** A curled lock or tress of hair 1667. **4.** *Entom.* One of the satyrid butterflies, *Hyparchia hyperanthus* 1812.

2. Through the mystic ringlets of the vale We flash our faery feet in gamesome prank COLERIDGE. 3. Shee..Her unadorned golden tresses wore Dissheveld, but in wanton ringlets wav'd MILT. Hence **Ri·nglet(t)ed** *a.* (of the hair) curled; wearing the hair in ringlets. **Ri·nglet(t)y** *a.* tending to curl in ringlets.

Ri·ng-man. 1483. [f. RING *sb.*[1]] **1.** The ring-finger. Now *dial.* **2.** A bookmaker 1857.

Ri·ng-neck. 1817. **A.** *adj.* = next. **B.** *sb.* A ring-necked plover or duck 1876.

Ri·ng-necked, *a.* 1852. [RING *sb.*[1]] Having the neck ringed or marked with a band or bands of colour. In various names of birds and animals, as *r. barnacle, duck, loon, pheasant,* etc.

Ri·ngster. *U.S.* 1881. [See -STER.] A member of a RING (*sb.*[1] III. 2, b).

Ri·ng-straked, *a.* 1611. [f. RING *sb.*[1] + STRAKE *sb.*[1] + -ED[2].] Having bands of colour round the body.

Ri·ngtail, ri·ng-tail, *sb.* and *a.* 1538. [f. RING *sb.*[1]] **A.** *sb.* **1. a.** The female of the hen-harrier. (Formerly regarded by many as a distinct species.) **b.** The golden eagle before its third year. Usu. *ring-tail eagle* 1776. **2.** *Naut.* 'A small sail shaped like a jib, set occasionally in light winds; it is hoisted on the outer end of the main or spanker gaff' (Young). Freq. *attrib.* with *boom, sail,* etc. 1769. **B.** as *adj.* = next 2, 3. Also *absol.* 1771.

Ri·ng-tailed, *a.* 1725. [f. as prec. + -ED[2].] **1.** *R. harrier* = prec. 1a. *R. eagle* = prec. 1b. **2.** Having the tail ringed with alternating colours 1729. **3.** Having the tail curled at the end, *spec.* applied to certain phalangers 1835.

Ringworm (ri·ŋwɒɹm). late ME. [prob. of foreign origin; cf. Du. *ringworm,* Norw., Da. *ringorm.*] A skin-disease usu. manifesting itself in circular patches, and frequently affecting the scalp in childhood; tinea.

Tinea sycosis, or r. affecting the beard, and *tinea circinata,* or r. affecting the body 1887. *fig.* I have not inke enough to cure all the..Ring-wormes of the State 1647.

Rink (riŋk), *sb.* late ME. [Only in Sc. use till XIX; perh. later form of *renk – OFr. *renc* (mod. *rang*) RANK *sb.*] †**1.** The space of ground within which a combat, joust, or race takes place; a course marked out for riding or running in –1637. **2.** A stretch of ice measured off or marked out for the game of curling 1787. **b.** One of the sets of players into which the sides in a curling, quoiting, or bowls match are divided 1823. **3.** A sheet of ice for skating, sometimes under cover; also, a smooth floor, usu. of asphalt or wood, for roller-skating 1867. Hence **Rink** *v. intr.* to skate on a r.; **ri·nking** *vbl. sb.* the act or practice of skating on a r.

Rinse (rins), *sb.* Also **rinze, rince.** 1837. [f. RINSE *v.*] A rinsing; a final application of water to remove impurities; *colloq.* a wash. **b.** A wash to cleanse the mouth 1898.

Rinse (rins), *v.* Also **rince.** ME. [– (O)Fr. *rincer,* earlier *raincier, reincier,* of unkn. origin.] **1.** *trans.* To wash out (a cup, etc.) by pouring in water or other liquid and emptying it out again (usu. after swilling or stirring it about). **b.** To clean (the mouth, teeth, etc.) by taking a mouthful of water and emitting it again 1565. **2.** To dip (a thing) into, agitate in, or drench with water in order to remove impurities. late ME. **b.** To treat (clothes or textile fabrics) in this way; *spec.* to put through clean water in order to remove the soap used in washing 1440. **3.** To remove, take *away,* clear *out,* by rinsing 1565.

1. Leave the Dregs of..Liquors in the Bottle: To rince them is but Loss of Time SWIFT. 3. That whole flood could not wash or rinch away that one spot of his atheisme 1607. Hence **Ri·nser** (*rare*). **Ri·nsing** *vbl. sb.* the action of the vb.; *pl.* the liquid or liquor with which anything has been rinsed out.

Riot (rəi·ət), *sb.* ME. [– OFr. *riote, riot* (mod. *riotte*) debate, quarrel, f. OFr. *rihoter, ruihoter.*] **1.** Wanton, loose, or wasteful living; debauchery, dissipation, extravagance. Now *rare.* **b.** Unrestrained revelry, mirth, or noise 1728. **2.** An instance or course of loose living; a noisy feast or wanton revel; a disturbance arising from this ME. **b.** A vivid display *of* (colour) 1894. **3.** *Hunting.* The action, on the part of a hound, of following the scent of some animal other than that which he is intended to hunt. Also in phr. *to hunt* or *run r.* late ME. **4.** Violence, strife, disorder, tumult, *esp.* on the part of the populace. late ME. **b.** A violent disturbance of the peace by an assembly or body of persons; an outbreak of active lawlessness or disorder among the populace. late ME.

1. All now was turn'd to jollitie and game, to luxurie and r., feast and dance MILT. 3. *To run r.* (in fig. use), to act without restraint or control; to disregard all limitations; to grow luxuriantly or wildly, etc. 4. Every species of r. and disorder '*Junius*' *Lett.*

Riot Act, the Act (1 Geo. I, st. 2, c. 5) providing that if twelve or more persons unlawfully or riotously assemble and refuse to disperse within an hour after the reading of a specified portion of it by a competent authority, they shall be considered as felons; also *jocular* in phr. *to read the Riot Act*; **r. call** *U.S.* a message for means to deal with a riot.

Riot (rəi·ət), *v.* late ME. [– OFr. *riot(t)er*; see prec.] **I. 1.** *intr.* To live in a wanton, dissipated, or unrestrained manner; to revel; to indulge to excess *in* something. **b.** To take great delight or pleasure *in* something 1741. **2.** *trans.* To spend or waste (money, etc.) in riotous living; to pass (time) in riot or luxury. Const. *away* or *out.* 1597.

1. *Ant. & Cl.* II. ii. 72. 2. Whilst wee..Ryot away, for nought, whole Prouinces DANIEL.

II. 1. †**a.** To force (a person) *to* do some action by persistence or importunity; so, to prevent (a person) *from* doing something –1781. **b.** Of rioters: To attack (persons or property) 1886. **2.** *intr.* To make a disturbance; to storm 1787.

1. This rattle..Mrs. Thrale most kindly kept up, by way of rioting me from thinking 1781. Hence **Ri·otry,** rioting, riotousness; also riotous persons.

Rioter (rəi·ətəɹ). [In XIV *riot(t)our* – AFr. *riotour* (see RIOT *v.*, -OUR), with later change of suffix; see -ER[2] 3.] **1.** A dissolute person; a reveller. Now *arch.* **2.** One who takes part in a riot or rising against constituted authority 1460.

Riotous (rəi·ətəs), *a.* late ME. [– OFr. *riotous, -eus*; see RIOT *sb.*, -OUS.] **1.** Of persons: Given to wantonness, revelry, or dissolute life; prodigal, extravagant. Now *rare.* **2.** Of life, conduct, etc.: Wanton, dissolute, extravagant; marked by excessive revelry. late ME. **b.** Noisy, tumultuous, unrestrained 1508. **3.** Marked by rioting or disturbance of the peace; taking part in or inciting to a riot or tumult; turbulent. late ME.

1. Drunkards and riotus persons they [Persians] hate 1613. 2. Dancing is always the last act of r. banquets 1755. 3. Such a r. act; to wit when hee came to dragg the five Members out of the House MILT. Hence **Ri·otous-ly** *adv.*, **-ness.**

Rip, *sb.*[1] *dial.* ME. [– ON. *hrip.*] A wicker basket or pannier, esp. for holding fish.

Rip, *sb.*[2] 1711. [f. RIP *v.*] **1.** A rent made by ripping; a laceration, tear. **2.** *ellipt.* A rip-saw 1846.

Rip, *sb.*[3] 1775. [app. related to RIP *v.*] **1.** A disturbed state of the sea, resembling breakers; an overfall. **2.** A stretch of broken water in a river 1857.

Rip, *sb.*[4] 1778. [perh. a later form of REP[2].] **1.** An inferior, worthless, or worn-out horse. **2.** A worthless, dissolute fellow; a rake 1797. **b.** Applied to a woman (*rare*) 1791. **3.** A person or thing of little or no value 1815.

Rip (rip), *v.* 1477. [Of unkn. origin.] **I. 1.** *trans.* To cut, pull, or tear (anything) away from something else in a vigorous manner. **2.** To cut or tear apart in a rough or slashing fashion. Also with compl. as *asunder, open.* 1530. **b.** To split or cleave (timber); to saw in the direction of the grain 1532. **c.** To take out or cut away by quarrying, etc.; to divest or clear of surface-soil 1807. **3.** To slash *up* with a sharp instrument; to tear or open *up* with violence; to open *up* (wounds or sores) again in a harsh manner 1565. **4.** *fig.* **a.** To open up, lay bare, disclose, make known; now chiefly, to open *up,* rake *up,* bring *up* again into notice or discussion (esp. something unpleasant or discreditable) 1549.

1. Macduffe was from his Mothers womb Vntimely ript SHAKS. 2. Sails ript, seams op'ning wide, and compass lost COWPER. 3. He..ripp'd up his Wastcoat to feel if he was not wounded DE FOE. It's little my part to r. up old sores 1830. 4. To r. up old grievances HAZLITT.

II. 1. *intr.* To split, tear, part asunder 1840. **2.** *dial.* To use strong language; to swear 1772. **b.** To break *out* angrily 1856. **c.** *trans.* with *out.* To utter with violence 1828. **3.** To rush along recklessly. Chiefly in phr. *let her r.* Orig. *U.S.* 1859.

2. c. He ripped out a horrid blasphemous curse 1889. 3. Let him r.,..we can turn him out when his time is up 1877.

Riparial (rəipēᵊ·riăl), *a.* 1870. [f. L. *riparius* (f. *ripa* bank) + -AL[1] 1.] **1.** = next A. **2.** *Zool.* Living upon, or frequenting, the banks of streams, ponds, etc. 1891. So **Ripa·rious** *a.* (*rare*) growing or living on the borders of rivers, etc. 1656.

Riparian (rəipēᵊ·riăn), *a.* and *sb.* 1849. [f. as prec. + AN.] **A.** *adj.* Of, pertaining to, or situated on, the banks of a river; riverine. **B.** *sb.* A riparian proprietor 1884.

Ripe (rəip), *sb.* Now *rare.* 1470. [– L. *ripa* bank.] The bank of a river; the sea-shore.

Ripe (rəip), *a.* [OE. *rīpe* = OS. *rīpi* (Du. *rijp*), OHG. *rīfi* (G. *reif*); – WGmc.] **1.** Of grain, fruits, etc.: Ready for reaping or gathering; ready for eating or for use as seed. **b.** Resembling ripe fruit; red and full 1590. **2.** Of birds and animals: Fully fledged or developed; *esp.* come to a fit condition for being killed and used as food ME. **b.** Of persons: Fully developed in body or mind; mature, †marriageable. Now *rare.* late ME. **c.** Ready for birth (*rare*) 1565. **d.** Of fish, etc.: Ready to lay eggs or spawn 1861. **3. a.** Of liquor: Ready for use; fully matured, mellow. late ME. **b.** Of suppurations, etc.: Ready to lance or break; fit for curative treatment. late ME. **c.** Of natural products, etc.: Arrived at a mature or perfect state 1635. **4.** Of persons: Of mature judgement or knowledge; fully informed; thoroughly qualified by study and thought. So of the mind, judgement, etc. ME. **5.** Properly considered or deliberated; matured by reflection or study ME. **6.** Of age: **a.** Characterized by full development of the physical or mental powers. late ME. **b.** Well advanced in years. late ME. **7.** Fully prepared, ready, or able, *to* do or undergo something. late ME. **b.** Ready or fit *for* some end or purpose 1592. **c.** Quite prepared *for* action of some kind, *esp.* mischief, revolt, etc. 1599. **8.** Ready for action, execution, or use; arrived at the fitting stage or time for some purpose 1601. **b.** Of time: Sufficiently advanced 1596.

1. I gathered the ears a little before they were r. 1676. *Provb.* All the glorie of man..is as the flower of the fielde, soone r., soone rotten 1569. b. How r. in show, Thy lips those kissing cherries, tempting grow! SHAKS. 2. b. R. men, or blooming in life's spring,..Stood by their Sire WORDSW. 3. c. With riper beams when Phœbus warms the day POPE. 4. He was a Scholler, and a r., and good one SHAKS. As sound in judgement as r. in experience 1615. 5. So wise and rype wordes hadde she CHAUCER. 6. Some man of rype yeares and counsell 1560. b. The r. age of eighty-five 1873. 7. The cause is then r. to be set down for hearing 1768. c. The mob were only too r. for a tumult 1879. 8. A lie R. at their fingers' ends 1789. Hence **Ri·pe-ly** *adv.*, **-ness.**

Ripe (rəip), *v.* [OE. *rīpian* = OS. *rīpon* (Du. *rijpen*), OHG. *rīfēn* (G. *reifen*); f. prec. Now usu. superseded by RIPEN.] **1.** *intr.* To grow or become ripe. **2.** *trans.* To make ripe. late ME. †**3.** *Med.* To bring to a head; to mature –1614.

Ripen (rəi·p'n), *v.* 1561. [f. RIPE *a.* + -EN[5].] **1.** *intr.* To grow ripe; to come to maturity. **b.** *fig.* To develop *into* (or *towards*) something 1606. **2.** *Med.* To come to a head; to maturate 1704. **3.** Of natural products, etc.: To reach the proper condition or stage for being utilized 1756. **4.** *trans.* To make ripe; to bring to maturity or to the proper condition for being used 1565. **5.** To develop to a mature state or condition; to bring to perfection 1570. **6.** *Med.* To bring to a head 1599.

1. All its allotted length of days, The flower ripens in its place TENNYSON. **b.** The acquaintance had ripened into friendship 1833. **4.** The pleached bower, Where hony-suckles ripened by the sunne, Forbid the sunne to enter SHAKS. **5.** Prosperity ripened the principle of decay GIBBON. Hence **Ri·pener,** one who, or that which, causes ripening; one who, or that which, comes to ripeness.

Ripidolite (rəipi·dǫləit). 1850. [f. Gr. ῥιπίς, ῥιπιδ- fan + -LITE (Kobell 1839).] *Min.* A green mineral resembling chlorite but crystallizing on the monoclinic system.

‖**Ripieno** (ripyē·no), *a.* and *sb.* 1724. [It., f. *ri-* RE- + *pieno* full.] *Mus.* **1.** Supplementary, re-enforcing. **b.** *sb.* A supplementary player or instrument 1753. **2.** *transf.* Serving to fill up; supernumerary 1811.

1. Handel's scores contain few bassoon parts, and those..mostly of a r. character 1879. Hence **Ripie·nist,** a performer who assists in the r. parts.

‖**Riposte** (ripōᵘ·st), *sb.* Also **ripost.** 1707. [Fr. *riposte*, earlier †*risposte* – It. *risposta*, subst. use of fem. pa. pple. of *rispondere* RESPOND.] **1.** *Fencing.* A quick thrust given after parrying a lunge; a return thrust. **2.** *transf.* A counterstroke; an effective reply by word or act 1865.

‖**Riposte** (ripōᵘ·st), *v.* Also **ripost.** 1707. [– Fr. *riposter*, earlier †*risposter*, f. the sb.; see prec.] **1.** *Fencing. intr.* To make a riposte. Also *trans.* with personal obj. **2.** *transf.* To reply or retaliate 1851.

2. The Cardinal riposted by an interdict LANG.

Ripper (ri·pəɹ). 1611. [f. RIP *v.* + -ER¹.] **1.** One who rips. Chiefly in techn. uses. **2.** That which rips; esp. (*a*) a tool used in removing old slates; (*b*) a rip-saw 1793. **3.** *slang.* A 'ripping' person or thing 1851.

Rippier (ri·piəɹ). Now *Hist.* Also **ripier.** late ME. [f. RIP *sb.*¹ + -(I)ER. In old statutes latinized *riparius*, as if f. *ripa* bank.] One who carries fish inland to sell.

Ri·pping, *ppl. a.* 1714. [f. RIP *v.* + -ING².] **1.** That rips or tears; *fig.*, cutting. **2.** *slang.* Excellent, splendid; rattling 1826. Hence **Ri·ppingly** *adv.* splendidly.

Ripple (ri·p'l), *sb.*¹ 1660. [corresp. to Fris. *ripel*, Du. *repel*, (M)LG. *repel*, OHG. *riffila* (G. *riffel*). See RIPPLE *v.*¹] An implement toothed like a comb, used in cleaning flax or hemp from the seeds. Also *attrib.*

Ripple (ri·p'l), *sb.*² 1755. [f. RIPPLE *v.*³] **1. a.** *U.S.* A piece of shallow water in a river where rocks or sand-bars cause an obstruction; a shoal. **2.** A light ruffling of the surface of water, such as is caused by a slight breeze; a wavelet 1798. **b.** *transf.* A mark, appearance, or movement resembling or suggestive of a ripple on water 1843. **c.** *ellipt.* A ripple-mark 1852. **3.** A sound as of rippling water 1859. **4.** = RIFFLE *sb.* 2. 1857.

2. If water be rippled, the side of every r. next to us reflects a piece of the sky RUSKIN. **b.** Her black hair waved..with a natural r. THACKERAY.

attrib. and *Comb.*: **r.-cloth,** a soft woollen material with a rippled surface used for making dressing-gowns, etc.; **-mark** (chiefly *Geol.*), a wavy surface, line, or ridge on sand, mud, or rock formed by the action of waves or the wind or both; so **r.-marked** *a.* Hence **Ri·pplet,** a small r.; a wavelet. **Ri·pply** *a.* marked or characterized by ripples.

Ripple (ri·p'l), *v.*¹ [In XIV *ripele*, corresp. to Fris. *ripelje*, (M)Du., MLG. *repelen*, Du. *repelen*, OHG. *rifilōn* (G. *riffeln*). See RIPPLE *sb.*¹] **1.** *trans.* To draw (flax or hemp) through a kind of comb in order to remove the seeds; to clean from seeds in this manner. **2.** To remove or take *off* (the seeds) by this process 1480. Hence **Ri·ppler,** one who ripples flax; also, an instrument for rippling.

Ri·pple, *v.*² Now *n. dial.* late ME. [Cf. Norw. *ripla* to scratch.] **1.** *trans.* To scratch slightly; to graze or ruffle. **2.** To break up (ground) slightly 1764.

Ri·pple, *v.*³ 1670. [Of unkn. origin.] **1.** *intr.* To have or present a ruffled surface; to form ripples. **b.** To flow in ripples 1769. **c.** Of sound: To flow in a sprightly manner 1879. **2.** *trans.* To form little waves upon (the surface of water); to agitate lightly 1786. **b.** To mark with or as with ripples; to cause to undulate slightly 1860.

1. b. *transf.* Stone walls..fragrant with..violets that r. down their sides 1873. Hence **Ri·pplingly** *adv.*

Ri·pple-grass. *Sc.* and *U.S.* 1824. [f. RIPPLE *sb.*²] Rib-leaved plantain.

Rip-rap (ri·p,ræp), *sb.* 1580. [f. RAP *sb.*¹ or *v.*¹] †**1.** An imitation of the sound caused by a succession of blows; hence, a sharp blow. **2.** *U.S.* Loose stone thrown down in water or on a soft bottom to form a foundation for a breakwater or other work 1847. So **Ri·p-ra:p** *v. trans.* to found upon, or cover with, a deposit of loose stone.

Ri·p-saw, *sb.* 1846. [f. RIP *v.*] A saw used for cutting wood in the direction of the grain. Hence **Ri·p-saw** *v. trans.* to cut with a r.

Ripstone, erron. form of RIBSTON.

Ripuarian (ripiu,ēᵊ·riăn), *a.* and *sb.* 1781. [f. med.L. *Ripuarius*; see -IAN.] **A.** *adj.* **1.** The distinctive epithet of the ancient Franks living on the Rhine between the Moselle and Meuse 1839. **2.** The distinctive epithet of the code of law observed by the Ripuarian Franks 1781. **B.** *sb. pl.* The Ripuarian Franks 1781. So **Ri·puary** *a.* = A 2.

Rise (rəiz), *sb.* late ME. [f. the vb.] **I.** †**1.** The act, on the part of a hare, of finally rising to return to its form. †**2. a.** A spring or bound upwards; *esp.* one made with the help of a run –1681. **b.** A start or aid towards rising in a leap; a place from which to rise or soar –1728. **3.** The coming of the sun (moon, or planets) above the horizon; hence also, the region of sunrise, the east. (Now usu. *rising.*) 1599. **4.** Upward movement; ascent; transference to a higher level 1573. **b.** Capacity for rising 1716. **5.** Elevation in fortune or rank 1632. An occasion or means of rising (in fortune or rank) 1680. **b.** Upward course 1721. **6.** *Angling.* The movement of a fish to the surface of the water to take a fly or bait; an instance of this 1651. **7.** The act of rising from the dead, or *from* some condition 1738.

3. She..Lookt left and right to r. and set of day R. BRIDGES. *fig.* So spake our Morning Star then in his r. MILT. **4.** Beyond Gosforth a steep r. is made 1872. **5.** It was considered a r. in life 1866. **b.** The r. and fall of the Whig party 1888. **6.** Phr. *To get, have,* or *take a r. out of* (a person), to raise a laugh at, by some form of pretence or dissimulation.

II. 1. A piece of rising ground; a hill 1639. **2.** An upward slope or direction, *esp.* of strata, coal-beds, veins of ore, etc. 1698. **b.** *Mining.* An excavation or working on the up side of a shaft 1839. **3.** The vertical height of a step, an arch, an inclined surface or object, etc., measured from the base or springing-line to the highest point 1663. **4. a.** A flight *of* steps 1710. **b.** = RISER II. 1. 1711.

1. Distant cumuli,..hanging on the rises of the moorland RUSKIN. **4. b.** The flat surface of a stair is called the tread, and the upright face is termed the r. 1879.

III. 1. An increase in height of the sea, streams, or water, by tides, floods, etc., or of a liquid in a vessel; the amount of this increase 1626. **2.** *Mus.* An increase of pitch in a tone or voice 1626. **3.** An increase in amount 1699. **b.** *colloq.* An advance in wages or salary 1836. **4.** An increase in the value or price *of* a thing 1691.

1. *transf.* The r. And long roll of the Hexameter TENNYSON. **3.** A small r. in the annual payment 1817. **4.** Phr. *On the r.*, becoming more valuable or dearer.

IV. 1. An origin or source; a beginning; a start. Freq. in phr. *to have* or *take one's r.* 1630. †**2.** An occasion; a ground or basis –1820. **b.** *To give r. to*, to occasion, bring about, cause 1705. **3.** The act of coming into existence or notice 1656.

1. Nor Plague of unknown R. that kills In Darkness WESLEY. **3.** The r. of a poet in their tribe 1777.

Rise (rəiz), *v.* Pa. t. **rose**: pa. pple. **risen.** [OE. *rīsan* = OFris. *rīsa*, OS., OHG. *rīsan* (Du. *rijzen*, G. *reisen*, of the sun), ON. *rísa*, Goth. *ur|reisan* :– Gmc. str. vb. of which no cognates are known.] **I.** *intr.* To get up from sitting, lying, or repose. **1.** To get up from a sitting, kneeling, or lying posture; to get upon one's feet ME. **b.** Of animals, esp. game: To get up, issue, from lair or covert. late ME. **c.** Of a horse, etc.: To assume an erect position *on* the hind legs 1658. **d.** Of hair, etc.: To become erect or stiff. Also of things which have been bent: To resume an upright position. 1500. **2.** To get up, or regain one's feet, after a fall ME. **b.** *fig.* To recover from a spiritual fall, or a state of sin ME. **3.** To get up from sleep or rest ME. **4.** To return to life; to come back from death or out of the grave. Also with *up*. ME. **5.** To fall or set *upon*, to take hostile steps or measures *against* OE. **b.** To take up arms, make insurrection *against* (†*on, upon*); to rebel or revolt OE. **6. a.** *Mil.* To break up camp; to retire or draw off *from* (a siege) 1557. **b.** Of a deliberative assembly, etc.: To adjourn, *esp.* for a vacation or recess 1663. †**7.** *To r. up to*, to show deference to (some authority, etc.) –1699.

1. Then shall the Priest r., the people still reuerently knelyng *Bk. Com. Prayer.* **2.** Pride falls unpitied, never more to r. COWPER. **3.** *Prov.* He that would thrive—must r. by five SCOTT. **4.** Others were raised but He onely rose DONNE. *fig. Haml.* I. ii. 257. **5.** O God the proud against me r. MILT. **b.** How vain Against th'Omnipotent to r. in Arms MILT. **6. b.** There is an idea that Congress will r. about the middle of July 1790.

II. To ascend, mount up. **1.** Of the heavenly bodies: To come above the horizon. Also *transf.* of daylight, darkness, ships, etc. ME. **2. a.** Of smoke, vapour, or the like: To ascend into the air ME. **b.** Of trees, etc.: To grow, in respect of height 1601. **3.** Of the sea, rivers, or water: To increase in height, esp. through the tides or floods; to swell ME. **b.** To attain to a greater height or size; to swell up; to puff out. late ME. **c.** Of dough or paste: To 'work' or swell under leaven; to expand under heat 1548. **d.** Of fluids: To reach a higher level in a containing vessel. Hence of a thermometer or barometer in respect of the mercury in the tube. 1658. **e.** Of liquids: To boil up 1839. **4.** Of the heart or emotions: **a.** To be elated with joy or hope; to become more cheerful. late ME. **b.** To be stirred by excitement, *esp.* by indignation or passion ME. **c.** Of the stomach: To nauseate or keck (*at* something) 1508. **5.** To extend directly upwards or away from the ground; to exhibit successive superposition of parts; to form an elevation from the level ME. **b.** To have an upward slant or curve; to slope or incline upwards 1634. **6.** To move or be carried upwards; to ascend. late ME. **b.** Of birds: To take wing and ascend from the ground 1528. **c.** Of a horse in leaping 1839. **7.** To come up to the surface of the ground or water. Also with *out.* 1530. **b.** Of a fish: To come to the surface of the water to take a fly, bait, etc. 1653.

1. The Moon Rising in clouded Majestie MILT. *fig.* Kings are like stars—they r. and set SHELLEY. **2. a.** As Ev'ning Mist Ris'n from a River o're the marish glides MILT. **3.** The sun was obscured.., and the sea was rising fast 1836. **4. a.** His spirits rising as his toils increase COWPER. **b.** When I cease..to feel my soul r. against oppression, I shall think myself unworthy to be your son MACAULAY. **5.** Along the lawn, where scattered hamlets rose GOLDSM. **6.** 'Tis he, I ken the manner of his gate, He rises on the toe SHAKS. *fig.* Whose Fortunes shall r. higher, Cæsars or mine? SHAKS. **b.** Again their ravening eagle rose In anger TENNYSON. **7.** A large alligator rose within three feet of the boat 1862.

III. To attain to a higher stage or degree. **1.** To ascend to a higher level of action, feeling, thought, or expression; to become more elevated, striking, impressive, or intense. Also const. *to* action of some kind ME. **2.** To advance in consequence, rank, influence, fortune, or social position; to attain *to* distinction or power; to come *into* estimation ME. **3.** To increase in amount, number, or degree; to amount or reach *to* ME. **b.** To become dearer or more valuable; to increase *in* price, value, etc. 1513. **4. a.** Of the wind: To increase in force; to become more vehement 1620. **b.** Of the voice, etc.: To increase in pitch or volume; to ascend in the musical scale 1548. **c.** To become more intense or strong; to increase in strength *to* a certain point 1593.

1. Thoughts and expressions in which he [Plato] rises to the highest level 1875. We do not r. to philanthropy all at once 1850. **2.** Some r. by sinne, and some by vertue fall SHAKS. **3.** His expenses, with his income, r. 1746. **b.** Sugar is ris', my boy THACKERAY. **4. a.** The winds r., and the winter comes on POPE. **b.** His voice rising with his reasoning, so that it was very loud at last DICKENS. **c.** In the presence of danger the courage of the man rose to its full height 1874.

IV. To spring up, come into existence. **1.**

Of persons: To come upon the scene; to appear; to be born; to spring or issue *of* or *from* a person or family. Also with *up*. ME. **2. a.** Of plants or trees: To spring up; to grow ME. **b.** Of blisters, etc.: To become prominent on the skin or surface. late ME. **3.** To originate; to result or issue. Const. *of, from, out of*. ME. **4.** To come to pass, come about, occur, happen, take place ME. **5.** Of wind, etc.: To begin to blow or rage ME. **b.** Of sounds: To strike upon the ear, esp. in a loud manner ME. **c.** Of reports, rumours, etc.: To come into circulation ME. **6.** Of a river: To have its spring or source. late ME. **7.** To be built or reared 1570. **8.** To come into being by growth or creation 1601. **b.** To come before the eye or mind 1712.

1. A holy Prophetesse, new risen vp SHAKS. 2. a. Sweet Plants that r. naturally ADDISON. 3. From study will no comforts r.? CRABBE. 4. Then rose a little feud betwixt the two TENNYSON. 5. a. The winds begin to r. And roar from yonder dropping day TENNYSON. 7. Beside the eternal Nile, The Pyramids have risen SHELLEY.

V. *trans.* **1.** To raise (the dead) to life (*rare*) 1440. **2.** To rouse or stir up; to start; to put up or flush (birds); to cause to rise 1500. **b.** *Angling*. To cause or induce (a fish) to come to the surface of the water 1850. **3.** To increase; to make higher or dearer. Now *rare* exc. *dial.* 1605. **4.** *Naut.* = RAISE *v.* III. 7 b. 1669. **b.** To raise; to lift up; to cause to ascend or mount up 1706. **c.** To promote (a person) in dignity or salary 1801. **5.** To surmount, gain the top of (a hill or slope); to ascend. Chiefly *U.S.* 1808. **6.** *colloq.* To raise or grow; to rear, bring up 1844.

2. b. I killed three salmon and rose many more 1867. 4. Since she had tacked, she had risen her hull out of the water 1842. 5. [We] discovered two horsemen rising the summit of a hill 1808. Hence **Ri·sen** (ri·z'n) *ppl. a.* that has risen, in the senses of the vb.

Riser (rəi·zəɹ). late ME. [f. RISE *v.* + -ER[1].] **I. 1.** One who rises up, *esp.* from bed 1440. **†2.** One who rises in revolt –1655. **3.** A fish that rises to an angler's fly or bait 1867. **II. 1.** The upright part of a step; the vertical piece connecting two treads in a stair 1771. **2.** *Mining*. An upthrow fault 1846. **3.** *Founding*. An opening through a mould, into which metal rises as the mould fills 1875. **4.** An electrical conductor or water-pipe passing from one floor of a building to another 1909.

Risible (ri·zib'l), *a.* and *sb.* 1557. [– late L. *risibilis*, f. *ris-*, pa. ppl. stem of L. *ridēre* laugh; see -IBLE. Cf. (O)Fr. *risible*.] **A.** *adj.* **1.** Having the faculty or power of laughing; inclined or given to laughter. **2.** Pertaining to, or used in, laughter 1747. **3.** Capable of exciting laughter; laughable, ludicrous 1727.

1. He is the most r. misanthrope I ever met with SMOLLETT. 2. The Dutch negroes at Communipaw..are famous for their r. powers 1809. 3. The jokes..are extremely queer and r. 1789.

B. *sb. pl.* The risible faculties or muscles. Chiefly *U.S.* 1785. Hence **Risibi·lity**, the faculty of laughing; laughter; a disposition to laugh; *pl.* the r. faculties (*U.S.*). **Ri·sibly** *adv.*

Rising (rəi·ziŋ), *vbl. sb.* ME. [f. RISE *v.* + -ING[1].] In the senses of RISE *v.*; *esp.* **1.** Resurrection. More fully *r. again, r. from the dead*. **2.** The act of taking up arms or engaging in some hostile action; an insurrection or revolt. late ME.

Rising (rəi·ziŋ), *ppl. a.* 1548. [f. RISE *v.* + -ING[2].] **1.** Having an upward slope or lie; elevated above the surrounding or adjacent level. **2.** That ascends or rises; mounting 1596. **b.** Of tides or water: Mounting, increasing in height 1697. **3.** Of the heavenly bodies: Appearing or emergent above the horizon 1610. **4.** Increasing in degree, force, or intensity 1603. **b.** Advancing in fortune, influence, or dignity 1631. **c.** Increasing in pitch 1674. **5.** Coming into existence; developing, growing 1667.

2. A gradually r. glass foretells improving weather if the thermometer falls 1860. b. *fig.* He would stem the r. tide of revolution 1875. b. Rise-ing winds the face of Ocean sweep GRAY. b. He was looked on at court as a r. man HUME. 5. The hopes of the r. generation JOHNSON.

Comb.: **r. diphthong**, one in which the stress falls on the second element; so *r. stress*; **r. front** (*Photogr.*), a camera front which can be elevated so as to reduce the foreground in a view; **r. main**, the vertical pipe of a pump; **r. rod**, part of the mechanism of a Cornish steam-engine.

Rising (rəi·ziŋ), *pr. pple.* 1610. [f. RISE *v.*] **1.** *Her.* Preparing for flight; taking wing. **2.** Of horses, and *transf.* of persons: Approaching (a given age) 1760. **3.** *U.S.* **a.** In excess *of*, upwards *of* 1817. **b.** Fully as much as; rather more than 1848.

Risk, *sb.* 1661. [– Fr. *risque* – It. †*risco, rischio*, f. *rischiare* run into danger.] **1.** Hazard, danger; exposure to mischance or peril. Freq. const. *of*. **2.** The chance or hazard of commercial loss, *spec.* in the case of insured property or goods 1719. **3.** *Risk-money*, an allowance made to a cashier to cover accidental deficits 1849.

1. To cut my Elder Brother's Throat, without the Risque of being hanged for him 1696. Phr. *To run a* or *the r.* 2. An Insurance made on Risks in Foreign Ships 1755. Hence **Ri·skful** *a* hazardous, uncertain.

Risk, *v.* Also †**risque**. 1687. [– Fr. *risquer*, f. the sb. or – It. †*riscare, rischiare*; see prec.] **1.** *trans.* To hazard, endanger; to expose to the chance of injury or loss. **2.** To venture upon, take the chances of 1705.

1. To risque the certainty of little for the chance of much JOHNSON. 2. Nor had Emana Christos forces enough to r. a battle 1790. Hence **Ri·sker**, one who risks something.

Risky (ri·ski), *a.* 1826. [f. RISK *sb.* + -Y[1].] **1.** Dangerous, hazardous, fraught with risk. **2.** [After Fr. *risqué*.] Involving suggestions of or verging upon what is improper or indelicate 1881.

1. 'Twill be a r. job 1827. 2. 'R.' situation and indelicate suggestion W. S. GILBERT. Hence **Ri·ski-ly** *adv.*, **-ness**.

‖**Risotto** (riso·to). 1884. [It.] A dish of rice cooked in stock, with butter, onions, etc.

‖**Risqué** (ri̇ske), *a.* 1883. [Fr., pa. pple. of *risquer* to RISK.] = RISKY *a.* 2.

Rissole (ri·soul). 1706. [– Fr. *rissole*, later form of OFr. *ruissole*, dial. var. of *roissole, roussole* :– Rom. **russeola* (sc. *pasta* paste), subst. use of fem. of late L. *russeolus* reddish, f. L. *russus* red.] An entrée made of meat or fish, chopped up and mixed with bread-crumbs, egg, etc., rolled into a ball or small thick cake and fried.

‖**Risus** (rəi·sɒ̈s). 1693. [L., f. *ridēre* laugh.] *Path. R. sardonicus*, an involuntary or spasmodic grin consequent on some morbid condition.

Rite (rəit). ME. [– (O)Fr. *rit*, later *rite* or L. *ritus* (religious) usage.] **1.** A formal procedure or act in a religious or other solemn observance. **b.** A custom or practice of a formal kind 1581. **2.** The general or usual custom, habit, or practice of a country, people, class of persons, etc.; now *spec.* in religion or worship, e.g. *the Roman r.* late ME.

1. The rytes and sacramentes and the articles of our faith 1529. b. The rites of hospitality 1865. *transf.* Time goes on crutches, till Loue haue all his rites SHAKS. 2. The English observe the R. of the Church of England, prescribed in the Book of Common Prayer 1728. Hence **Ri·teless** *a.* destitute of r. or ceremony. †**Ri·tely** *adv.* in due form –1675.

‖**Ritornello** (ritǫrne·lo). 1675. [It., dim. of *ritorno* RETURN *sb.*] *Mus.* An instrumental refrain, interlude, or prelude in a vocal work.

A Returnello by Martial Instruments 1675. Also in anglicized form **Ritorne·l**.

†‖**Ritra·tto.** 1722. [It. Cf. RETRAIT *sb.*[2]] A picture, portrait –1771.

‖**Ritter** (ri·təɹ). 1824. [G., var. of *reiter*.] A mounted warrior; a knight.

Ri·ttmaster. *rare.* 1648. [– G. *rittmeister*, f. *ritt* riding.] The captain of a troop of horse.

Ritual (ri·tiuăl), *a.* and *sb.* 1570. [– L. *ritualis*, f. *ritus* RITE; see -AL[1]. Cf. Fr. *rituel*, †*-al* (XVI).] **A.** *adj.* **1.** Pertaining or relating to, connected with, rites. **2.** Of the nature of, forming, a rite or rites 1631.

1. The r. laws restrained the Jews from conversing familiarly with the heathens 1740. Phr. *R. choir*, that part of the church in which the choir-offices are performed. 2. R.-murder as a practice has been learnedly and thoroughly disproved 1896.

B. *sb.* **1.** A prescribed order of performing religious or other devotional service 1649. **b.** A book containing the order, forms, or ceremonies, to be observed in the celebration of religious or other solemn service 1656. **2.** *pl.* Ritual acts or observances 1656. **3.** The performance of ritual acts 1867.

1. There was a..dignity in the Jewish r. 1772. 3. *attrib.* The appointment of the R. Commission 1882. **Ri·tualize** *v. intr.* to practice ritualism; *trans.* to convert into a r.; to bring over to ritualism. **Ri·tually** *adv.*

Ritualism (ri·tiuăliz'm). 1843. [f. RITUAL + -ISM.] The observance, practice, or study of religious rites; ritual observance (cf. next 2).

Ritualist (ri·tiuălist). 1657. [f. as prec. + -IST.] **1.** One versed in ritual; a student of liturgical rites and ceremonies. **2.** One who advocates or practises the observance of religious rites. (In the 19th century applied *spec.* to the extreme High Church party in the Church of England.) 1677.

2. *attrib.* The whole extreme R. party is practically infallibilist PUSEY. Hence **Rituali·stic** *a.* of or pertaining to, characteristic of, ritualists or ritualism; devoted to, or fond of ritual; **-ally** *adv.*

Rivage (rəi·vėdʒ). ME. [– (O)Fr. *rivage*, f. *rive* :– L. *ripa* bank; see -AGE.] **1.** A coast, shore, or bank. Now *poet.* **†2.** Shore or river dues –1706.

1. The River full of Ships,..the r. full of seafaring men 1658.

Rival (rəi·văl), *sb.* and *a.* 1577. [– L. *rivalis* one who uses the same stream with another, f. *rivus* stream; see -AL[1].] **A.** *sb.* **1.** One who is in pursuit of the same object as another; one who strives to equal or outdo another in any respect. **2.** One who, or that which, disputes distinction or renown with some other person or thing 1646.

1. The medical name for a r. is 'colleague' 1899. 2. The Spanish generals stood without rivals in their military skill 1874.

B. *adj.* Holding the position of a rival or rivals 1590.

The R. Chariots in the Race shall strive DRYDEN. Hence **Ri·valess**, a female r. or competitor. **Ri·valless** *a.* without a r.

Rival (rəi·văl), *v.* 1605. [f. RIVAL *sb.*] **1.** *trans.* To enter into competition with; to strive to equal or excel (another) 1609. **2.** *intr.* To act as a rival, be a competitor 1605.

1. These Beauties R. each other on all Occasions STEELE. *transf.* A crash which rivalled thunder 1860. 2. *Lear* I. i. 194.

Rivality (rəivæ·liti). 1582. [– L. *rivalitas*; see RIVAL *sb.*, -ITY. Cf. Fr. *rivalité*.] = RIVALRY.

Rivalry (rəi·vălri). 1598. [f. RIVAL *sb.* + -RY.] The act of rivalling; competition, emulation.

Jealousies, rivalries, envy, intervene to separate others from our side SCOTT.

Rivalship (rəi·vălʃip). 1632. [f. RIVAL *sb.* + -SHIP.] The state or character of a rival; emulation, competition, rivalry.

Rive (rəiv), *v.* Pa. t. **rived**; pa. pple. **rived, riven.** ME. [– ON. *rifa* = OFris. *riva*; of unkn. origin.] **I.** *trans.* **1.** To tear apart or in pieces by pulling or tugging; to rend or lacerate with the hands, claws, etc.; to pull asunder. Also with various advs. and preps. **2.** To sever, cleave, or divide, by means of a knife or weapon; †to pierce or thrust. late ME. **3.** To rend or split by means of shock, violent impact, or pressure, etc.; to strike asunder ME. **b.** To split or cleave (wood, stone, etc.) by appropriate means. Also with *up, off.* 1440. **4.** To rend (the heart, soul, etc.) with painful thoughts or feelings ME.

1. Thy loved one from thee riven BYRON. It went through the land,..riving sects 1863. I would r. the heart out of my breast 1873. 2. She roofe hir selfe to the herte CHAUCER. 3. Yonder blasted boughs by lightening riven 1768. 4. All thoughts to r. the heart are here, and all are vain HOUSMAN.

II. *absol.* **1.** To commit spoliation or robbery; to take away *from*. Now *dial.* 1489. **2.** To tear voraciously; to tug *at* something 1552.

2. Standing..roared and riven at by the wind DICKENS.

III. *intr.* **1.** To part asunder; to cleave, split, crack, open up ME. **b.** Of wood or stone: To admit of splitting or cleaving 1699. **2.** *fig.* **a.** Of the heart: To break or burst with sorrow. late ME. **b.** Denoting the effect of repletion, excessive laughter, etc. 1586.

1. b. The body of the willow tree rives into pales 1772. Hence **Rive** *sb.* a pull, tug, tear, crack.

Rivel (ri·v'l), *v.* Now *rare.* ME. [Cf. next.] **1.** *intr.* To become wrinkled or shrivelled; to form wrinkles or small folds. **2.** *trans.* To cause (the skin) to wrinkle or pucker; to shrivel *up* 1583.

2. A man with a sour rivell'd Face ADDISON. So †**Ri·vel** *sb.* a wrinkle or fold upon the skin (*esp.* of the face) or on the rind of a fruit.

Rivelled (ri·v'ld), *a.* Now *dial.* or *arch.* [OE. *rifelede*, app. f. **rivel*, whence ME. *ryvel* wrinkle (–XVII), of unkn. origin.] **1.** Wrinkled; full of wrinkles or small folds; corrugated, furrowed. **2.** Shrunken, shrivelled, esp. by heat 1629. **3.** Twisted, coiled (*rare*) 1594.

Riven (riv'n), *ppl. a.* ME. [pa. pple. of RIVE *v.*] **1.** Split, cloven, rent, torn asunder. †**2.** Ornamentally slashed (*rare*) –1548.

River (ri·vəɹ), *sb.*[1] ME. [– AFr. *river(e*, (O)Fr. *rivière* †river bank, river :– Rom. **riparia*, fem. used subst. (sc. *terra* land) of L. *riparius* RIPARIAN.] **1.** A copious stream of water flowing in a channel towards the sea, a lake, or another stream. **b.** *transf.* A copious stream or flow *of* (something). late ME. **c.** Used euphemistically for the boundary between life and death 1790. †**2.** A stream, or the banks of a stream, as a place frequented for hawking. Hence, the sport of hawking. –1625. †**3.** The coast or littoral (of Genoa) –1693.

1. 'Tis like a rolling r., That murm'ring flows, and flows for ever! GAY. *fig.* The fruitfull Riuer in the Eye SHAKS. **b.** A Crimson riuer of warme blood SHAKS. **c.** And hast thou crost that unknown r., Life's dreary bound? BURNS.

attrib. and *Comb.* as *r.-bar, -basin, -channel*, etc.; *r.-boy, -rat*, etc.; **r.-bank**, the raised or sloping edge of a r.; the ground adjacent to a r.; **-bed**, the channel in which a r. flows; **-craft**, boats or vessels used in r. traffic. **b.** With the names of fishes and other animals (freq. contrasted with *sea-*), as **r. bass** (*U.S.*), the black bass, *Micropterus*; **r. chub** (*U.S.*), the horny-head or jerker, *Ceratichthys biguttatus*; **r. crab**, any crab which inhabits rivers, freshwater pools, or swamps; also, a crayfish; †**r. dragon**, the crocodile (with allusion to Pharaoh of Egypt); **r. duck**, any duck belonging to the *Anatinæ*; **r. eel**, the common freshwater eel; **r. herring** (*U.S.*), = ALE-WIFE[2]; **r. hog**, (*a*) the capybara or water-hog; (*b*) a S. African hog of the genus *Potamochœrus*; **r. jack (viper)**, a West African viper having a flat head and a somewhat long horn on either side of the snout; **r. limpet**, a pulmonate gasteropod of the genus *Ancylus*, found in rivers; **r. wolf**, †(*a*) the pike; (*b*) a kind of otter (*Lutra brasiliensis*) found in South America. Hence †**Ri·ver** *v. trans.* to wash (wool or sheep) in a r. **Rivered** (ri·vəɹd) *ppl. a.* watered by rivers; furnished with a r. or rivers. **Ri·verling**, a small r., or stream. **Ri·very** *a.* (*rare*), †resembling a r.; abounding in streams or rivers; pertaining to a r.

River (rəi·vəɹ), *sb.*[2] 1483. [f. RIVE *v.* + -ER[1].] **1.** One who rives, rends, or cleaves. †**2.** One who robs; a reaver –1568.

Riverain (ri·vəreⁱn), *a.* and *sb.* 1858. [– Fr. *riverain*, f. *rivière* RIVER *sb.*[1]] **A.** *adj.* **1.** Pertaining to a river or its vicinity. **2.** = RIVERINE *a.* 1. **B.** *sb.* One who dwells on the banks or in the vicinity of a river 1867.

Ri·ver-drift. 1839. [f. RIVER *sb.*[1] + DRIFT *sb.*] *Geol.* Ancient alluvia of rivers in which early palæolithic remains are found.

Riveret (ri·veret). Now *rare* or *Obs.* 1538. [– Fr. †*riveret* (now *riviérette*), dim. of *rivière* RIVER *sb.*[1] See RIVULET.] **1.** A small river or stream; a rivulet or brook. **2.** *transf.* A surface vein 1603.

Ri·ver-fish. late ME. Any fish whose habitat is in a river or stream; a freshwater fish.

Ri·ver-god. 1661. [f. RIVER *sb.*[1] + GOD *sb.* 1.] *Mythol.* A tutelary deity supposed to dwell in and to preside over a river.

Ri·ver-horse. 1601. [f. RIVER *sb.*[1] + HORSE *sb.*] **1.** The hippopotamus. **2.** The water-kelpie; see KELPIE 1851.

Riverine (ri·vərəin), *a.* and *sb.* 1860. [f. RIVER *sb.*[1] + -INE[1].] **A.** *adj.* **1.** Situated or dwelling on the banks of a river; riparian. **2.** Of or pertaining to a river 1871. **B.** *sb.* The banks or vicinity of a river 1895.

Ri·verside. Also **river-side.** ME. [f. RIVER *sb.*[1] + SIDE *sb.*] The side or bank of a river; the ground adjacent to, or stretching along, a river. Also *attrib.*, as *r. inn*, etc.

Ri·ver-wa:ter. Also **river water.** late ME. [f. RIVER *sb.*[1] + WATER *sb.*] Water in, forming, or obtained from, a river or stream.

Rivet (ri·vėt), *sb.*[1] late ME. [– OFr. *rivet*, f. *river* clinch, of unkn. origin. Cf. AL. *rivettus* (XIII).] A short nail or bolt for fastening together metal plates or the like, the headless end of which is beaten out after insertion. **b.** A burr or clinch upon a nail (*rare*) 1634.

The Armourers accomplishing the Knights, With busie Hammers closing Riuets vp SHAKS.

Rivet (ri·vėt), *sb.*[2] 1580. [Of unkn. origin.] Bearded or cone wheat. Also in pl. form *rivets*. Also used *attrib.* with *wheat*.

Rivet (ri·vėt), *v.* late ME. [f. RIVET *sb.*[1] Cf. AL. *rivettare* (XIV).] **1.** *trans.* To secure (a nail or bolt) by hammering or beating out the projecting end of the shank into a head or knob; to clinch. Also with *down*. **2.** To secure or fasten with or as with rivets. Also with *down, in, together*. late ME. **3.** *transf.* To fix, fasten, or secure firmly 1629. **4.** To fix intently (the eye or the mind); to command or engross (the attention) 1602. **b.** To engross the attention of (a person) 1762.

2. Seize him,..R. him to the rock E. B. BROWNING. **3.** I am wholly ignorant in what manner.. his first attachment may have riveted his affections 1788. Things become riveted in the memory 1849. **4.** Giue him needfull note, For I mine eyes will riuet to his Face SHAKS. Hence **Ri·veter**, one who rivets; a machine which rivets.

‖**Rivière** (rivyę̄·r). 1880. [Fr.; see RIVER *sb.*[1]] A necklace of diamonds or other gems, esp. one consisting of more than one string.

†‖**Ri·vo.** 1592. [app. of Sp. origin.] An exclam. used at revels or drinking-bouts –1607.

Rivose (rəi·voᵘs, ri-), *a.* 1826. [– late L. *rivosus*, f. L. *rivus* stream; see -OSE[1].] *Entom.* Applied to somewhat sinuate furrows which do not run in a parallel direction.

Rivulet (ri·viŭlėt). 1587. [alt. of earlier RIVERET, perh. after It. *rivoletto*, dim. of *rivolo*, dim. of *rivo* :– L. *rivus* stream; see -LET.] A small stream or river; a streamlet.

By Fountain or by shadie R. He sought them both MILT. *transf.* The rivulets of intelligence which are continually trickling among us JOHNSON.

Rix-dollar (ri·ksdǫləɹ). Now *Hist.* 1598. [– Du. †*rijksdaler*, f. gen. of *rijk* (see RICH) + *daler* DOLLAR.] A silver coin and money of account, current *c*1600–1850 in various European countries and in their commerce with the East; the value varied from about 4*s*. 6*d*. to 2*s*. 3*d*.

Ri·zzar, *v. Sc.* 1818. [– Fr. †*ressoré* 'parched, etc.', f. *re-* RE- + *sorer* 'to reeke; to drie, or make red' (Cotgr.); see SORE *a.*[2], SORREL *a.*] *trans.* To dry or parch (esp. haddocks) in the sun. So **Ri·zzared** *ppl. a.*

Roach (rōᵘtʃ), *sb.*[1] ME. [– OFr. *roche, roce*, also *roque, rocque*; origin unkn.] A small freshwater fish (*Leuciscus rutilus*) of the Carp family, common in the rivers of northern Europe. *Blue r.* = AZURINE. In *U.S.*, also applied to various small fishes resembling, or mistaken for, the roach. Also *attrib.*, as *r.-backed*, etc.

Phr. *As sound as a r.* = Fr. *sain comme un gardon*.

Roach (rōᵘtʃ), *sb.*[2] 1794. [Of unkn. origin.] *Naut.* 'An upward curve cut in the foot of a square sail'.

Roach, *sb.*[3] 1836. Abbrev. of COCKROACH.

Roach (rōᵘtʃ), *v.* 1848. [f. ROACH *sb.*[2]] **1.** *trans.* To cut (a sail) with a roach 1851. **2.** *U.S.* To clip or trim (a person's hair or horse's mane) so that it stands on end 1833.

Road (rōᵘd), *sb.* [OE. *rād* = OFris. *rēd*, MDu. *red*, ON. *reið*, rel. to *rīdan* RIDE *v.*] †**1.** The act of riding on horseback; also, a spell of riding; a journey on horseback –1613. †**2.** *spec.* A hostile incursion by mounted men; a foray, raid –1665. **3.** A sheltered piece of water near the shore where vessels may lie at anchor in safety; a roadstead. Usually *pl.* ME. **4.** An ordinary line of communication between different places, used by horses, travellers on foot, or vehicles 1596. **b.** *U.S.* A railroad or railway 1837. **5.** Any path, way, or (material) course 1602. **b.** *fig.* A way or course, esp. *to* some end 1599. **6.** A way or direction taken or pursued by a person or thing; a course followed in a journey 1612. **7.** The usual course, way, or practice. In phr. *out of the r. of*. 1608.

1. *Hen. VIII*, IV. ii. 17. **2.** Borderers, whan they make rodes into Scotlande 1523. **3.** The Towne Gravesend is a knowne Roade 1617. Phr. †*At r.*, riding at anchor. **4.** The most villanous house in al London rode SHAKS. Phr. *On, upon, the r.*, travelling, journeying, upon or during a journey, etc.; on tour. *To take the r.*, to set out. *The r.*, the highway; *to go upon, take to, the r.*, to become a highwayman; *gentleman, knight of the r.*, a highwayman (now *arch.*). *To give* (a person) *the r.*, to allow one to pass. *To take the r. of*, to take precedence of. *The rule of the r.*, the fixed custom which regulates the side to be taken by vehicles, etc. (or *transf.* by vessels) in progressing or passing each other. **b.** A prominent station on the Central Pacific r. 1872. **5.** Where Silver Swans sail down the Wat'ry Rode DRYDEN. **b.** Precipitating themselves in the r. to ruin 1783. Phr. *Royal r.*, a smooth or easy way. **6.** Phr. *Out of the* (or *one's*) *r.*, out of the way, in various senses (chiefly *Sc.* and *n. dial.*). *In one's* (or *the*) *r.*, in one's way, so as to cause obstruction or inconvenience.

attrib. and *Comb.*: **r.-agent** (*U.S.*), a highway robber; **R.-Board**, the authority entrusted with the business of making and improving roads, and having the administration of a *r. fund*; **-book**, also **r. book**, a book exhibiting or describing the roads of a district or country; **r. hog**, one who rides or drives recklessly and dangerously on the r. without regard to the comfort of others; esp. a reckless cyclist or motorist; **-metal**, broken stone used in making roads; hence *r.-metalling*; **r. post**, (*a*) a signpost; (*b*) a military post stationed or situated on a r.; **-runner** (*U.S.*), the paisano or chaparral cock; **-sense**, the faculty of perceiving instinctively and promptly the best method of dealing with all kinds of emergencies on the r. Hence **Roa·dless** *a.* destitute of or having no roads.

Road (rōᵘd), *v.* 1856. [Of unkn. origin.] *trans.* Of a dog: To follow up (a game-bird) by the scent. Also with *up*, and *absol.*

Roa·d-maker. 1799. [f. ROAD *sb.*] One who makes roads.

Roa·dside. Also **road-side.** 1712. [ROAD *sb.* 4.] †**1.** The side next to the road. STEELE. **2.** The side, or border, of the road; wayside 1744.

Roadstead (rōᵘ·dsted). 1556. [f. ROAD *sb.* 3.] A place where ships may conveniently or safely lie at anchor near the shore.

Roadster (rōᵘ·dstəɹ). 1744. [f. ROAD *sb.* 3 and 4; see -STER.] **1.** *Naut.* A vessel lying, or able to lie, at anchor in a roadstead; one which lies at anchor in a roadstead when tide or wind is unfavourable. **2.** A horse for riding (or driving) on the road 1818. **b.** A cycle or car for use on the road 1883. **3.** One who is accustomed to the road; a coach-driver or traveller 1841. **4.** *Hunting.* One who keeps to the road 1858.

Roa·dway. 1597. [ROAD *sb.* 4.] **1.** A way used as a road; †a highway. **2.** The main or central portion of a road, esp. that used by vehicular traffic, in contrast to the side-paths 1807. **3.** That portion of a bridge, railway, etc., on which traffic is conducted 1834.

Roa·dworthy, *a.* 1819. [ROAD *sb.* 4 + WORTHY *a.*] Fit for the road; in a suitable condition for using on the road. Hence **Roa·dworthiness.**

Roam (rōᵘm), *v.* ME. [Of unkn. origin.] **1.** *intr.* To wander, rove, or ramble; to walk about aimlessly, esp. over a wide area. **2.** *trans.* To wander over or through (a place) 1603.

1. Shaggy forms o'er ice-built mountains r. GRAY. **2.** False titl'd Sons of God, roaming the Earth MILT. Hence **Roam** *sb.* the act of wandering or roaming; a ramble. **Roa·mer,** one who roams; a wanderer.

Roan (rōᵘn), *a.* and *sb.*[1] 1530. [– OFr. *roan* (mod. *rouan*), of unkn. origin.] **A.** *adj.* Of animals: Having a coat in which the prevailing colour is thickly interspersed with some other; *esp.* bay, sorrel, or chestnut mixed with white or grey. Also *absol.* as the name of a colour. (In the case of horses, the prevailing colour is freq. expressed, as *black, blue, red, silver, strawberry r.*) **B.** *sb.* A roan horse, cow, antelope, etc. 1580.

Roan (rōᵘn), *sb.*[2] late ME. [Of unkn. origin; in sense 1 perh. f. *Roan*, old form of the place-name *Rouen*, but the identity of this with the much later sense 2 is not established.] †**1.** *R. skin*, some kind of skin or leather –1583. **2.** A soft flexible leather made of sheepskin, used in bookbinding as a substitute for morocco 1818.

Roan-tree, var. of ROWAN-TREE.

Roar (rōᵊɹ), *sb.*[1] late ME. [f. ROAR *v.*] **1.** A full, deep, prolonged cry uttered by a lion or other large beast; a loud and deep sound uttered by one or more persons, esp. as an expression of pain or anger. **b.** A boisterous outburst *of* laughter; also *ellipt.* for this 1778. **2.** *transf.* The loud sound of cannon, thunder, a storm, the sea, or other inanimate agents 1548.

1. Sure it was the roare Of a whole heard of Lyons SHAKS. A r. of hired applause KINGSLEY. **b.** A r. of laughter interrupted him KIPLING. **2.** Arm! arm! it is..the cannon's opening r.! BYRON.

†**Roar**, *sb.*[2] late ME. [– MDu. *roer*, LG. *rōr* = OS. *hrōra*, OHG. *ruora* (G. *ruhr*) motion. See UPROAR.] Confusion, tumult, disturbance –1610. **b.** A wild outburst of mirth. (In mod. use assoc. w. prec.)

By your Art..you haue Put the wild waters in this Rore SHAKS. **b.** *Ham.* V. i. 211.

Roar (rōᵊɹ), *v.* [OE. *rārian*, corresp. to MLG. *rāren*, *rēren*, MDu. *reeren*, OHG. *rērēn* (G. *röhren*); WGmc., of imit. origin.] **1.** *intr.* Of persons: To utter a very loud and deep or hoarse cry (or cries), *esp.* under the influence of rage, pain, or great excitement; to vociferate, shout, yell. †**b.** To shout in revelry; to behave in a noisy, riotous manner –1763. **2.** Of animals (*esp.* of lions): To utter a loud deep cry. Also with *out.* ME. **b.** Of horses: To make a loud sound in breathing 1880. **3.** Of cannon, thunder, wind, the sea, etc.: To make a loud noise or din ME. **b.** Of a place: To resound or echo with noise. late ME. **4.** *trans.* To utter or proclaim loudly; to shout (*out*). late ME. **b.** With compl.: To force, call, bring, render, etc., by roaring 1607.

1. You..roared for mercy, and still ranne and roar'd SHAKS. **2.** Whereat his horse did snort, as he Had heard a lion r. COWPER. **b.** The tendency to r. is not a matter of heredity 1889. **3.** The faggot blazed and crackled, and roared up the chimney 1861. **4.** The songs those young fellows were roaring THACKERAY. **b.** We'll r. the rusty rascal out of his tobacco 1617.

Roarer (rōᵊ·rəɹ). late ME. [f. ROAR *v.* + -ER[1].] **1.** One who or that which roars. †**b.** A noisy, riotous bully or reveller –1709. **2.** A horse affected with roaring 1811. **3.** *U.S. slang.* Something superlatively good 1852.

1. What cares these roarers for the name of King? SHAKS.

Roaring (rōᵊ·riŋ), *vbl. sb.* OE. [f. ROAR *v.* + -ING[1].] **1.** The utterance of a loud deep cry. †**2.** Bullying, boisterous, or riotous conduct –1642. **3.** A disease of horses, causing them to make a loud noise when breathing under exertion; the act of making this noise 1823.

Roa·ring, *ppl. a.* late ME. [f. as prec. + -ING[2].] **1.** That roars or bellows; *spec.* of horses (see prec. 3). **2.** Behaving or living in a noisy, riotous manner. Now *arch.* 1611. **3.** Of voice, sound, etc.: Extremely loud 1548. **4.** Characterized by riotous or noisy revelry; full of din or noise 1715. **b.** *The r. forties*: see FORTY *sb.* **5.** Of trade: very brisk, highly successful 1796.

1. They gaped vpon me..as a rauening and a r. Lyon *Ps.* 22:13. **4.** We'll have a r. Night 1759. *The r. game* (or *play*), the game of curling. *R. drunk*, excessively drunk and noisy. Hence **Roa·ringly** *adv.*

Roast (rōᵘst), *sb.* ME. [In sense 1 – OFr. *rost* masc. (mod. *rôt*) or *roste* fem., roasting, roast meat, f. *rostir*. In sense 2 a subst. use of the pa. pple. of ROAST *v.* In other senses mainly from the verbal stem.] **1.** A piece of roast meat, or anything that is roasted for food; a part of an animal prepared or intended for roasting. **2.** Roast meat; roast beef. late ME. **3.** An operation of roasting (metal, coffee, etc.), or the result of this 1582. **4.** The process of bantering unmercifully 1740.

1. I love no rost, but a nut browne toste And a crab layde in the fyre 1575. Phr. *To rule the r.* (or *roost*), to be master; The ladies always rule the r. in this part of the world 1778. **2.** He eateth flesh: he rosteth rost, and is satisfied *Isa.* 44:16.

Roast (rōᵘst), *v.* ME. [– OFr. *rostir* (mod. *rôtir*) – WGmc. **raustjan*, f. **raust*, **rausta* gridiron, grill, whence OS., OHG. *rōst* (OHG. also *rōsta*), *rōstisarn* grill, gridiron.] **1.** *trans.* To make (flesh or other food) ready for eating by prolonged exposure to heat at or before a fire. Also freq. in mod. use, to cook (meat) in an oven (= *bake*). **b.** *techn.* To expose (metallic ores, etc.) to protracted heat in a furnace; to calcine 1582. **c.** To expose (coffee beans) to heat in order to prepare for grinding 1724. **2.** To torture by exposure to flame or heat ME. **3.** To ridicule, banter, jest at, quiz (a person) in a severe or merciless fashion 1726. **4.** *absol.* To perform, carry on, the process of roasting. late ME. **5.** *intr.* To undergo the process of being cooked, tortured, or calcined by exposure to fire or heat ME.

1. That day of an auncient custome there is roosted a whole Oxe 1560. **2.** Blow me about in windes, r. me in Sulphure, Wash me in steepe-downe gulfes of Liquid fire SHAKS. **4.** I have had no difficulty in teaching men how to r. 1877. **5.** Cast thereon smale salt as he rosteth 1450.

Roast (rōᵘst), *ppl. a.* ME. [Old pa. pple. of ROAST *v.*] Roasted.

Roast beef. 1635. [ROAST *ppl. a.* Hence Fr. *rosbif*.] Beef roasted for eating.

Roaster (rōᵘ·stəɹ). 1440. [f. ROAST *v.* + -ER[1].] **1.** One who roasts. **2.** *Min.* A furnace in which metallic ores are calcined 1778. **b.** A kind of oven in which meat, etc., can be cooked by roasting 1799. **c.** An apparatus for roasting coffee-beans 1837. **3.** A pig, or other article of food, fit for roasting 1690.

Roasting (rōᵘ·stiŋ), *vbl. sb.* late ME. [f. ROAST *v.* + -ING[1].] The action of the vb. **b.** *attrib.*, as *r.-ear* (of maize), one suitable for roasting; *r.-jack*, a contrivance for turning meat, etc., while it is being roasted.

Roast meat. Also **roast-meat.** 1530. [f. ROAST *ppl. a.*] Meat cooked by roasting.

Phr. †*To make roast meat of*, to burn (a person); to destroy or finish off. †*To cry roast meat*, to be foolish enough to announce to others a piece of private good luck or good fortune.

Rob (rǫb), *sb.* Now *rare.* 1578. [– med. and mod.L. *rob* or Fr. *rob* – Arab. *rubb*.] The juice of a fruit, reduced by boiling to the consistency of a syrup and preserved with sugar; a conserve of fruit.

Rob (rǫb), *v.* ME. [– OFr. *rob(b)er*, of Gmc. origin; f. base **raub-*, repr. also by REAVE *v.*[1] Cf. ROBE.] **1.** *trans.* To deprive (a person) of something by unlawful force or the exercise of superior power; to despoil by violence. **2.** To plunder or strip (a person) feloniously *of* (something belonging to him); to deprive (a person) *of* (something due) ME. **3.** To plunder, pillage (a place, house, etc.). Freq. const. *of* that which is taken. ME. **4.** *absol.* To commit depredations; to plunder; to take away property by force ME. **5.** To carry off as plunder; to steal. Now *rare.* ME. **6.** *Card-playing.* To exchange the trump-card, if an ace, for any other card in the pack 1611.

1. Se yᵗ thou robbe not yᵉ poore because he is weake COVERDALE *Prov.* 22:22. Phr. *To r. Peter to pay* (*clothe*) *Paul*: see PETER *sb.* 1. **2.** For who would r. a Hermit of his Weeds? MILT. **3.** One that is like to be executed for robbing a Church SHAKS. **4.** I am accurst to r. in that Theefe company SHAKS. **5.** The descendants of the Negroes who were robbed from Africa 1887.

Roband (rōᵘ·bænd), *-end* [ME. *roband* – LDu. *raband*, f. *rā* (pron. *râ*) sailyard + *band* BAND *sb.*[1]] *Naut.* A piece of small rope passed through an eyelet-hole in the head of a sail and used to secure it to the yard above.

Robber (rǫ·bəɹ). ME. [– AFr., OFr. *rob(b)ere*, f. *rob(b)er* ROB *v.*; see -ER[2] 2.] One who practises or commits robbery; a depredator, plunderer, despoiler.

Then Theeues and Robbers raunge abroad vnseene SHAKS.

attrib. and *Comb.*: *r.-gold*, *-inn*, *r. lair*, etc.; **r.-council** or **-synod**, the ecclesiastical council held at Ephesus in 449, the decrees of which were subsequently rescinded; **-crab**, a large tropical crab which feeds on coco-nuts; **-fly**, a fly of the family *Asilidæ*, given to preying upon other insects.

Robbery (rǫ·bəri). ME. [– AFr., OFr. *rob(b)erie*, f. as prec.; see -ERY.] **1.** The action or practice of robbing; spoliation, depredation. **b.** An instance of this; a depredation ME. †**2.** *concr.* Plunder, booty –1535.

1. R. is committed by Force, or Terror, of which neither is in Theft; for Theft is a secret Act HOBBES. **2.** They gather together euell gotten goodes, and laye vp r. in their houses COVERDALE *Amos* 3:10.

Ro·bbin. Now *rare* or *Obs.* 1497. [var. of ROBAND.] *Naut.* = ROBAND.

Robe (rōᵘb), *sb.* ME. [– (O)Fr. *robe* :– Rom. **rauba*, of Gmc. origin, as ROB *v.*, the orig. sense being 'booty', (hence) clothes, regarded as spoil.] **1.** A long loose outer garment reaching to the feet or the ankles, worn by both sexes in the Middle Ages, and still by men of some of the Eastern nations; a gown. Now *rare*, exc. as in 2. **b.** A trade name for a special form of lady's dress; a piece of material, partly shaped for a gown 1878. **2.** A long outer garment of a special form and material worn in virtue of, and betokening, a particular rank, calling, condition, or office. Also *pl.* with the same connotation ME. **3.** *pl.* Outer garments or clothes in general 1575. **b.** *fig.* A covering or vesture compared to a long enveloping garment 1623. **4.** *U.S.* and *Canada.* The dressed skin of a buffalo, musk-ox, etc. used as a garment or rug 1836.

1. Turbans and flowing robes are adapted to hot countries 1796. **2.** *The long r.*, (the dress of) the legal or clerical profession; *the short r.*, (that of) 'all that profess arms, or usually wear swords' (Cotgr.); so *both robes*, *either r. The R.*, the legal profession. Phr. *Coronation*, *parliament robes*, etc. *Master*, *Mistress*, *Yeoman*, *of the Robes*: see these words. **3. b.** Another [cottage] wore A close-set r. of jasmine TENNYSON.

Robe (rōᵘb), *v.* ME. [f. the sb.] **1.** *trans.* To clothe or invest in a robe or robes; to apparel; to dress. **2.** *intr.* To put on robes or vestments 1626.

1. Ulysses rob'd him in the cloak and vest POPE. *fig.* Love robed her in a blush 1850. **2.** Only to Roab, and Feast, and performe Rites BACON.

‖**Robe de chambre** (rob də ʃaṅbr). 1731. [Fr.; see ROBE *sb.* and CHAMBER *sb.*] A dressing-gown or négligé.

Robert (rǫ·bəɹt). ME. [The Fr. name *Robert* – Gmc.] †**1.** = ROBIN (REDBREAST). –late ME. **2.** = HERB ROBERT. Also *robert's bill.* 1847. **3.** A policeman. (Cf. BOBBY 2.) 1870. **4.** A waiter. (From articles in *Punch*, 1881–1882, professedly written by a waiter named Robert.) 1886.

Robin[1] (rǫ·bin). late ME. [– OFr. *Robin*, familiar var. of the masc. name *Robert* (used XV for 'robin').] **I.** The personal name.

Iakke þe iogeloure..And Robyn þe Rybaudoure *Piers Plowman.*

II. 1. = ROBIN REDBREAST 1 a. 1549. **b.** Any bird of the genus *Erithacus* 1855. **2.** *U.S.* The red-breasted thrush, *Turdus migratorius* 1798. **3.** The name given to various colonial birds, as in New Zealand to those of the genus *Miro*, in Australia to species of *Petroica* and other genera, etc. 1880. **b.** Used attrib. or appositively in names of various birds 1555.

1. On the nigh-naked tree the r. piped Disconsolate TENNYSON. **2.** In America I shoot robins and find them thrushes 1888. **3.** *Blue r.*, the blue-bird. *Golden r.*, the Baltimore oriole. **b. R. breast**, = *r. snipe*; **R. dipper** (*U.S.*), the buffle-headed duck; **R. snipe**, (*a*) = KNOT *sb.*[2]; (*b*) the red-breasted snipe.

III. A name given locally or dialectally to various plants, as red campion, ragged robin, herb Robert, etc. 1694. **b.** In genitive combs., as **robin's eye(s, flower**, herb Robert, rose campion, etc.; **robin's plantain** (*U.S.*), a species of fleabane (*Erigeron belledifolium*) 1846. **IV.** The name of various fishes: **a.** *dial.* A small or inferior codfish 1618. **b.** *U.S. Decapterus punctatus*; also, the sea-robin 1876.

†**Robin**[2]. 1748. = ROBING *vbl. sb.* 2 –1789.

Robinet (rǫ·binet). late ME. [– OFr. *Robinet*, dim. of *Robin*; see ROBIN[1], -ET.] †**1.** Some form of hoisting-tackle –1512. †**2.** A kind of small cannon –1611. **3.** = ROBIN[1] II. 1. Now *n. dial.* late ME. **4.** A cock or faucet of a pipe 1867.

Ro·bing, *vbl. sb.* 1470. [f. ROBE *v.* + -ING[1].] **1.** Apparel, array; a costume or gown. **2.** A trimming in the form of bands or stripes upon a gown or robe 1727. **3.** The action of putting on robes 1838.

attrib.: **r.-room**, a room specially appropriated to the putting on of official robes.

Robin Goodfellow (rǫ·bin gu·dfelo"). 1531. [See ROBIN[1] and GOODFELLOW.] A sportive and capricious elf or goblin believed to haunt the English countryside in the 16–17th centuries; also called Hobgoblin or Puck. †**b.** *gen.* A fairy or goblin of this kind –1635.

When Hobgoblin and Robin good Fellow made country wenches keepe their houses cleane ouer-night 1622.

Robin Hood (rǫ·bin hu·d). late ME. [A personal name, perh. fictitious.] **1.** The name of a popular English outlaw traditionally famous from at least the 14th c.; hence allusively, an outlaw or bandit, or a leader of such persons. †2. One who acted the part of Robin Hood in a mummer's play or yearly festival; the play or festival itself. Hence *Robin Hood's days, men.* –1616.

1. †*A tale* (or *gest*) *of Robin Hood*, an extravagant story.

‖**Robinia** (robi·niă). 1759. [mod.L. (Linn.), f. *Robin*, name of the royal gardener at Paris, who introduced these trees to Europe in 1635; see -IA[1].] *Bot.* A genus of N. Amer. trees and shrubs of the bean family, chiefly represented by the locust-tree.

Ro·bin re·dbreast. 1450. [Cf. ROBIN[1] and REDBREAST.] **1. a.** The European redbreast or robin (*Erithacus rubecula*), usu. as a proper name, but also with *a* and *pl.* **b.** *dial.* The red campion, *Lychnis diurna* 1886. **2.** *slang.* A Bow Street runner 1841.

Roborant (rōᵘ·b-, rǫ·bŏrănt), *sb.* and *a.* 1661. [– L. *roborans, -ant-*, pr. pple. of *roborare*; see next, -ANT.] **A.** *sb.* An invigorating or strengthening medicine. **B.** *adj.* Strengthening; restorative 1836.

†**Ro·borate,** *v.* late ME. [– *roborat-*, pa. ppl. stem of L. *roborare* strengthen, f. *robur, robor-* strength; see -ATE[3].] **1.** *trans.* To ratify, confirm (a charter, league, etc.) –1655. **2.** To strengthen, invigorate; to fortify –1710. So †**Robora·tion** 1657.

Robot (rōᵘ·bǫt). 1923. [– Czech, f. *robota* compulsory service, corresp. to Pol., Ukrainian *robota* (whence G. †*robot* forced labour), Russ. *rabota* work.] One of the mechanical men and women in the play *R.U.R.* (*Rossum's Universal Robots*) by Karel Capek; hence, a living being that acts automatically (without volition). **b.** A machine devised to function in place of a living agent; one which acts automatically or with a minimum of external impulse 1925.

Robots..persons all of whose activities were imposed upon them and who were not allowed 'even the luxury of original sin' G. B. SHAW. Hence **Robote·sque, Robo·tian,** *adjs.* **Ro·botism. Ro·botize** *v. trans.* to render mechanical. **Ro·botry.**

Rob Roy (rǫb‚roi·). 1866. [Name (meaning 'Red Robert') of a Highland freebooter (1671–1734) given by John Macgregor (1825–92) to a canoe.] *Rob Roy canoe*, a light canoe for a single person propelled by alternate strokes of a double-bladed paddle.

‖**Robur** (rōᵘ·bŭɹ). *rare.* 1601. [L., oak.] A very hard-wooded variety of oak. Also *robur-oak*.

Roburite (rōᵘ·bərəit). 1887. [f. L. *robur* strength + -ITE[1] 4 a.] A flameless explosive of very high power.

R...consists of chlorinated dinitrobenzene mixed with sufficient ammonium nitrate to completely oxidize it 1891.

Robust (robɒ·st), *a.* 1549. [– (O)Fr. *robuste* or L. *robustus* oaken, firm and hard, solid, f. *robus*, older form of L. *robur* oak, strength.] **1.** Of persons: Strong and hardy in body or constitution; strongly and stoutly built; of a full and healthy habit. **b.** Similarly of the body or the constitution; of plants, animal structures, etc. 1625. **2. a.** Coarse, rough, rude. Now *rare.* 1560. **b.** Pertaining to, or requiring, bodily strength or hardiness; vigorous 1683. **3.** *fig.* Strong, vigorous, healthy 1788. **b.** Vigorous in mind, voice, etc. 1852.

1. Stronge & robuste persons 1563. **b.** Your r. nervous system 1860. **2. a.** He..began a r. flirtation with one of them 1872. **b.** R. exercises 1801. **3.** English is a r. language 1888. **b.** A most r. thinker 1852. Hence **Robu·st-ly** *adv.*, **-ness.**

Robustious (robɒ·stiəs), *a. arch.* 1548. [f. ROBUST + -IOUS.] **1.** Of persons, the body etc.: Robust; stout and strong or healthy-looking. **b.** Of things: Big and strong; massive 1548. **2.** Violent, boisterous, noisy, strongly self-assertive 1548. **b.** Of storms or climate: Violent, severe 1612.

1. This Gunner was a r. Vulcan 1654. **2.** You are so r., you are like to put out my Eye SWIFT. Hence **Robu·stious-ly** *adv.*, **-ness** (now *rare*).

Roc (rǫk). 1579. [In early use *roche, roque, ruc, ruck* – Sp. *rocho, ruc* – Arab. *ruk*.] A mythical bird of Eastern legend, imagined as being of enormous size and strength.

Rocambole (rǫ·kămbōᵘl). 1698. [– Fr. *rocambole* – G. *rockenbolle*.] **1.** A species of leek (*Allium scorodoprasum*) indigenous to Northern Europe, used as a seasoning for dishes; Spanish garlic, sand-leek. **2.** A plant of this, or the edible portion of one 1707.

Roccellic (rǫkse·lik), *a.* 1838. [f. mod.L. *roccella* (*tinctoria*) orchil + -IC.] *Chem.* In *r. acid*, an acid forming white, rectangular crystals, $C_{17}H_{32}O_4$. Hence **Rocce·llate,** a salt formed by the action of r. acid upon a base.

Roccellin (rǫkse·lin). 1852. [f. as prec. + -IN[1].] *Chem.* A coal-tar colour used in dyeing, derived from the orchil lichen.

Roche (rōᵘtʃ), *sb.* Now *dial.* ME. [– (O)Fr. *roche*; see ROCK *sb.*[1]] A rock or cliff; a rocky height.

Roche (rōᵘtʃ), *v.* 1631. [f. prec.] †**a.** *intr.* To form crystals –1673. **b.** *trans.* To recrystallize (alum) in lead-lined casks after previous dissolution by water or steam 1678.

Roche alum (rōᵘtʃ‚æ·ləm). ME. [f. ROCHE *sb.* + ALUM, after Fr. *alun de roche.*] = ROCK alum.

Roche lime. 1756. [f. ROCHE *sb.*] Unslaked lime; lime shells.

Rochelle (roʃe·l). late ME. [Place-name (*La*) *Rochelle*, a seaport of western France.] †**1.** Used *attrib.* or *absol.* to designate the wine exported from this place –1731. **2.** *R. salt*, sodium potassium tartrate. †*R. powder* = Seidlitz powder. 1753.

2. *R. Salt*..is prepared by not quite neutralizing hot solution of carbonate of soda with powdered cream of tartar 1888.

Rochet[1] (rǫ·tʃĕt). late ME. [– (O)Fr. *rochet*, var. of *roquet*, corresp. to med.L. *rochetum*, etc., dim. f. Gmc. base found in OE. *rocc*, OS., (M)Du. *rok*, OHG. *roch* (G. *rock*) coat, ON. *rokkr*; see -ET.] **1.** An outer garment of the nature of a smock-frock, cloak, or mantle. Now *dial.* **2.** *Eccl.* A vestment of linen, of the surplice type, usu. worn by bishops and abbots. late ME. **b.** *transf.* One who wears a rochet; a bishop 1581.

2. The r. is only a modification of the surplice 1849.

Rochet[2] (rǫ·tʃĕt). Now *local.* late ME. [– OFr. *rouget*, f. *rouge* red; see -ET.] The Red Gurnard.

Roching (rōᵘ·tʃiŋ), *vbl. sb.* 1631. [f. ROCHE *v.* + -ING[1].] The action of recrystallizing (alum); chiefly *attrib.* in *r. cask, pan.*

Rock (rǫk), *sb.*[1] late ME. [– OFr. *ro(c)que*, var. of (O)Fr. *roche* (see ROCHE *sb.*), in med.L. *rocca, rocha*; of unkn. origin.] **1.** A large rugged mass of stone forming a cliff, crag, or natural prominence on land or in the sea. **b.** A boulder; also *U.S.* and *Austral.*, a stone of any size 1709. **2. a.** Without article, or in generalized use: Hard and massive stone 1590. **b.** *Agric.* The base on which the subsoil immediately lies 1765. **c.** *Geol.* One of the stratified or igneous mineral constituents of which the earth's crust is composed, including sands, clays, etc. 1789. **3.** *transf.* A hard confection of candied sugar, variously flavoured; *dial.* sweetstuff 1736. **4. a.** = ROCK-FISH 1. 1698. **b.** The rock-dove or rock-pigeon (*Columba livia*). Usu. *blue r.* 1863.

1. A ragged, fearefull, hanging Rocke SHAKS. *fig.* If it dasheth against the rocke of sinne, it is in great ieopardie 1606. Be thou my r., though I poore changeling rove 1633. He that was a r. to all assaults of might and violence 1667. Phr. *Of the old*, or *new r.*, said of precious stones. *On the rocks*, quite destitute of means. *To pile up the rocks* (U.S. slang), to make money.

Comb.: **r. apostle,** St. Peter (Matt. 16:18); **r.-bed,** a floor or under-stratum of r.; **r.-butter,** (*a*) a soft yellowish mixture of alum and iron which exudes from certain aluminiferous rocks; (*b*) a sauce made by beating butter with about twice its weight of sugar, and flavouring; **-cake,** a small cake or bun with a rugged surface; **r. cork,** a light variety of asbestos; pilolite; **-drill,** a r.-boring instrument or machine; **r. English,** the mixed English of Gibraltar; **-flint,** impure flint; chert; **-garden,** a garden consisting of rocks and r.-plants; **-hammer,** a hammer used for r.-breaking; **-meal,** a white cotton-like variety of carbonate of lime, occurring as an efflorescence, which falls into powder when touched; **-oil,** native naphtha; †**-ruby,** a species of garnet or amethyst; **-scorpion,** a nickname applied to a person born at Gibraltar; **r. silk,** a silky variety of asbestos; **-soap,** a kind of bole; mountain soap; **r. tar,** petroleum.

b. In names of beasts, as **r. barnacle,** a cirriped of the genus *Balanus*; **r. cavy,** a Brazilian species of cavy (*Cavia rupestris*); **r. crab,** a crab frequenting rocky coasts, *esp.* the American *Cancer irroratus*; **r. goat,** the ibex; **r. kangaroo** = *r. wallaby*; **r. lobster,** a crustacean of the family *Palinuridæ*, to which the crayfish belongs; **r. rabbit,** a rodent of the genus *Hyrax*, esp. the Syrian and South African species; **r. seal,** the common seal (*Phoca vitulina*); **r. serpent,** (*a*) = *r. snake*; (*b*) a poisonous Indian snake of the genus *Bungarus*; **r. snake,** a python, esp. *P. reticulatus* or *molurus*; **r. wallaby,** a kangaroo of the genus *Petrogale*.

c. In names of birds: **r.-bird,** a bird that haunts rocks; *esp.* a puffin; **-dove,** = ROCK-PIGEON; **r. duck,** the harlequin duck; **-hawk,** the merlin; **-hopper (penguin),** a species of crested penguin (*Eudyptes chrysoscome*); **-ouzel,** the ring-ouzel; **r. parakeet,** an Australian grass parakeet (*Euphema petrophila*); **r. partridge,** (*a*) the white grouse or ptarmigan; (*b*) the Greek or Barbary partridge; **r. pipit,** the sea-lark (*Anthus obscurus*) of the British Islands; **r. plover** (*local U.S.*), the purple sand-piper; **r. ptarmigan,** the Amer. species, *Lagopus rupestris*; **r. sparrow,** a bird of the genus *Petronia*; **-thrush,** a thrush of the genus *Monticola*; **r. warbler,** *Origma rubricata*, also called Cataract Bird; **r. wren,** a brownish grey Amer. bird, speckled with black and white dots.

d. In names of fishes: **r. bass,** any of several Amer. fishes, as the red-eye or goggle-eye (*Ambloplites rupestris*), the striped bass, and black sea-bass; **r. codling,** a N. Amer. species of cod; **r. cook,** a species of wrasse; †**r. ray,** the thorn-back; **r. salmon,** (*a*) the coalfish; (*b*) an Amer. fish of the genus *Seriola*; **r. trout,** (*a*) a New Zealand fish, *Galaxias alepidotus*; (*b*) a N. Amer. fish, *Chirus constellatus*.

e. In names of plants: **r. cress,** (*a*) a plant of the genus *Arabis*; †(*b*) samphire; **r. moss,** (*a*) the orchil lichen; (*b*) cudbear; **r. tripe,** name in N. America for several species of lichens belonging to *Gyrophora* and *Umbilicaria*. Hence **Ro·ckless** *a.* devoid of rocks.

Rock (rǫk), *sb.*[2] ME. [– MLG. *rocken*, MDu. *rocke* (Du. *rok, rokken*) or ON. *rokkr* = OHG. *rocko* (G. *rocken*) :– Gmc. **rukkon*, of unkn. origin.] **1.** A distaff. Now *arch.* or *Hist.* **2.** A distaff together with the wool or flax attached to it; the quantity of wool or flax placed on a distaff for spinning 1550.

1. The three Parcæ,..the one holding the r., the other the spindle, and the third the sheeres B. JONS.

Rock (rǫk), *v.* [Late OE. *roccian*, prob. f. Gmc. **rukk-* move, remove (of which no outside cognates are known), repr. also by MLG., MDu. *rukken, rocken* (Du. *rukken*), OHG. *rucchan* (G. *rücken* move, push), ON. *rykkja* pull, tug.] **1.** *trans.* To move (a child) gently to and fro in a cradle, in order to soothe or send it to sleep. **b.** *transf.* and *fig.* of the wind, sea, earth, sleep, etc. 1597. **2.** To bring into a state of slumber, rest, or peace by gentle motion to and fro. Const. *to, into*, or *asleep*. late ME. **b.** To maintain *in* a lulling state of security, plenty, hope, etc. 1581. **3.** To move or sway (a person) to and fro, esp. in a gentle or soothing manner. late ME. **4.** To make (a cradle) swing to and fro, in order to put a child to sleep. late ME. **b.** *transf.* In gold-washing (see CRADLE *v.* 7.). Hence *absol.* to use a rocker in gold-digging. Also *trans.*, to work *out* with a rocker. 1849. **5.** To cause to sway to and fro or from side to side; to move backwards and forwards. Also *refl.* ME. **6.** *intr.* To sway to and fro under some impact or stress; to oscillate. Also *dial.*, to stagger or reel in walking. late ME. **b.** Of vessels under the effect of waves 1513. **c.** To swing oneself to and fro, esp. while sitting in a rocking-chair 1795.

1. That's not my native place, where I was rockt MARSTON. **b.** Sleepe rocke thy Braine SHAKS. **2.** As the working of a sea Before a calm, that rocks itself to rest COWPER. **4.** All the Graces rockt her cradle being borne SPENSER. **5.** The god whose earthquakes r. the solid ground POPE. **6.** The earth rocked beneath his feet 1797.

Comb.: **r.-staff,** part of the apparatus for working a smith's bellows. Hence **Rock** *sb.*[3] the action of the vb. **Ro·cky** *a.*[2] unsteady, tottering; in early use, tipsy.

Rockaway (rǫ·kăweⁱ). *U.S.* 1846. [prob. f. prec.] A four-wheeled carriage, open at the sides, with two or three seats and a standing top.

Ro·ck-ba:sin. 1754. [ROCK *sb.*[1]] A basin-shaped hollow in a rock, esp. one of natural origin; *spec.* in *Geol.* a large depression in a rocky area, attributed to the action of ice-masses.

Ro·ck-bed. 1839. [ROCK *sb.*[1]] A floor or base of rock; a rocky bottom or under-stratum.

Ro·ck-bo·ttom, *sb.* and *a.* 1884. *colloq.* orig. *U.S.* [f. ROCK *sb.*[1] + BOTTOM *sb.*] **A.** *sb.* The very bottom. **B.** *attrib.* or as *adj.* The lowest possible.

Tools at absolutely r. prices 1922.

Ro·ck cod. 1634. [ROCK *sb.*[1]] **1.** A cod found on rocky sea-bottoms or ledges. Chiefly *Sc.* and *north.* **2.** Applied to various fishes of other genera, as the Californian yellow-tailed rock-fish, the red garrupa, the rock-trout of Puget Sound, etc. 1796. So **Ro·ck co:dfish.**

Ro·ck cry:stal. 1666. [ROCK *sb.*[1]] **1.** Pure silica or quartz in a transparent and colourless form, most usu. occurring in hexagonal prisms with hexagonal pyramid ends. **2.** A piece of this 1839.

Rocker (rǫ·kəɹ). late ME. [f. ROCK *v.* + -ER[1].] **1.** A nurse or attendant charged with the duty of rocking a child in the cradle. Now *arch.* or *Obs.* Also *gen.*, one who rocks a cradle. **2.** One of the pieces of wood with a convex under-surface fixed to each end of a cradle, to the legs of a chair, or to any other thing, in order to enable it to rock 1787. **3.** Something which rocks or is rocked after the manner of a cradle: **a.** A rocking-horse 1846. **b.** *U.S.* A rocking-chair 1857. **c.** A gold-miner's cradle 1858. **d.** A scientific instrument illustrating the effect of heat in producing vibration 1863. **e.** *Engraving* = CRADLE *sb.* 12. 1875. **4.** Chiefly *U.S.* A skate with a curving sole 1869. **b.** = *rocking-turn* 1893.

2. Phr. *Off one's r.*, crazy; distracted; demented (*vulg. slang*). Hence **Ro·ckered** *a.* curved like a r.

Rockery (rǫ·kəri). 1845. [f. ROCK *sb.*[1] + -ERY.] **1.** A heap or pile of rough stones and soil used for the ornamental growing of ferns and other plants. **2.** Natural rockwork 1856.

Rocket (rǫ·kėt), *sb.*[1] 1530. [– Fr. *roquette* (XVI) – It. *rochetta*, var. of *ruchetta*, dim. of *ruca* :– L. *eruca* caterpillar, plant with downy stems.] **1.** A cruciferous annual (*Eruca sativa*) having purple-veined white flowers and acrid leaves, used in Southern Europe as a salad. Also, †wild rocket. **b.** With specific epithets, esp. *Garden r.*, *Roman r.*, and *R. gentle* 1548. **2.** A cruciferous plant of the genus *Hesperis*, esp. *H. matronalis*, a garden-flower which is sweet-scented after dark 1629.

Base r., the wild mignonette (*Reseda luteola*). **Blue r.**, (*a*) one of several kinds of wolf's-bane or aconite; (*b*) applied to several kinds of larkspur (*Delphinium*); (*c*) the blue-bell (*Scilla nutans*). **Wild r.**, hedge mustard. **Yellow r.**, the winter-cress.

Rocket (rǫ·kėt), *sb.*[2] 1611. [– (O)Fr. *roquette* – It. *rocchetto*, dim. of *rocca* ROCK *sb.*[2], so called from the cylindrical form.] An apparatus consisting of a cylindrical case of paper or metal containing an inflammable composition, by the ignition of which it may be projected to a height or distance. Also *attrib.*, as *r. apparatus*, *brigade*, etc.

Congreve r.: see CONGREVE 1.

Rocket (rǫ·kėt), *v.* 1803. [f. ROCKET *sb.*[2]] **1.** *trans.* To discharge rockets at; to bombard with rockets. **2.** *intr.* **a.** Of a horse or rider: To spring or bound up like a rocket; to dart like a rocket 1883. **b.** Of game-birds: To fly up almost vertically when flushed; to fly fast and high overhead 1860.

2. b. Nothing was shot, though some pheasants 'rocketed' over our guns 1860. Hence **Ro·cketer, Ro·cketter,** a game-bird that rockets.

Ro·ck-fish. 1611. [ROCK *sb.*[1]] A fish frequenting rocks or rocky bottoms, *spec.* as the name of many unrelated fishes, such as the black goby or sea-gudgeon, the striped bass, the wrasse, etc. Also, with defining words, applied to a number of Amer. fishes, chiefly of the genera *Sebastichthys* and *Sebastomus.*

Rocking (rǫ·kiŋ), *ppl. a.* late ME. [f. ROCK *v.* + -ING[2].] That rocks; swaying, oscillating; also, causing to rock. **2.** In technical terms, as *r. shaft*, etc. 1805.

attrib. and *Comb.*: **r.-chair,** a chair mounted on rockers; also, a chair having a rocking seat attached to the base by springs; **r.-horse,** a wooden horse mounted on rockers for children to ride upon with a rocking motion; **r.-stone,** a large stone or boulder so poised on a limited base as to be easily swayed to and fro; a logan-stone; **r. turn** *Skating*, a turn in which one edge of the skate only is used, the body being revolved in the same direction as in the corresponding three turns.

Rockling (rǫ·kliŋ). 1602. [f. ROCK *sb.*[1] + -LING[1].] A small gadoid fish of the genera *Onos* or *Rhinonemus* (formerly *Motella*), esp. the sea-loach or whistle-fish (*R. cimbrius*).

Ro·ck-pi:geon. 1611. [ROCK *sb.*[1]] **1.** A species of dove (*Columba livia*) inhabiting rocks and believed to be the source of the domestic pigeon; the rock-dove. **2.** *Anglo-Ind.* A sand-grouse 1885.

Ro·ck-plant. 1691. [ROCK *sb.*[1]] †**1.** A petrified plant –1753. **2.** A plant that grows upon or among rocks 1694.

Ro·ck-rose. 1731. [ROCK *sb.*[1]] A plant of the genus *Helianthemum* or *Cistus* (formerly united in the Linnæan genus *Cistus*), esp. *H. vulgare.*

Ro·ck-salt. 1707. [ROCK *sb.*[1]] Salt found in a free state disposed in strata, and capable of being extracted in large lumps.

Ro·ck-shaft. 1875. [ROCK *v.*] A shaft which merely rocks or oscillates about its axis in place of making complete revolutions; *esp.* one working the levers connected with certain valves in some forms of engines.

Ro·ck-weed. 1626. [ROCK *sb.*[1]] A sea-weed, esp. one of the genera *Fucus* and *Sargassum*, growing on tide-washed rocks.

Ro·ck-work. 1706. [ROCK *sb.*[1]] **1.** A natural mass or group of rocks or stones. **2.** Stones piled together with soil interspersed for growing Alpine and other plants in a garden; also, grotto-work, rough stone-work resembling or imitating natural rocks 1790. **3.** *Arch.* Masonry very roughly or rudely faced. 1842. **4.** Skill in climbing rocks; rock-craft 1898.

Rocky (rǫ·ki), *a.*[1] late ME. [f. ROCK *sb.*[1] + -Y[1].] **1.** Full of, abounding in, rocks; consisting or formed of rock; having the character of rock. **2.** *fig.* **a.** Of the heart or disposition: Flinty, stony, unfeeling 1586. **b.** Firm as a rock; unflinching, steadfast 1622. †**3.** *R. bone*, the petrosal portion of the temporal bone –1683. **4.** Growing upon or among rocks (*rare*) 1640.

1. England.., Whose r. shore beates backe the enuious siedge Of watery Neptune SHAKS. *R. Mountains*, the great mountain-range lying towards the western coast of N. America; called also *The Rockies* (quasi-*sb.*). Hence **Ro·ckiness.**

Rococo (rokō[u]·ko), *a.* and *sb.* 1836. [– Fr. *rococo*, fanciful alt. of *rocaille* pebble- or shell-work, f. *roc* ROCK *sb.*[1]] **A.** *adj.* **1.** Old-fashioned, antiquated. **2.** Of furniture or architecture: Having the characteristics of Louis Quatorze or Louis Quinze workmanship, such as conventional shell- and scroll-work and lavish decoration; florid or ornate 1844.

2. That r. seventeenth-century French imitation of the true Renaissance PATER.

B. *sb.* A style of art, architecture, literature, etc. having rococo features 1840.

Rod (rǫd), *sb.* [Late OE. *rodd*, synon. with continental forms cited s.v. ROOD, but formally distinct; prob. rel. to ON. *rudda* club.] **I. 1.** A straight, slender shoot or wand, growing upon or cut from a tree, bush, etc. **b.** *fig.* An offshoot, a scion; a tribe. (*Biblical*) 1460. **2.** An instrument of punishment, either one straight stick, or a bundle of twigs bound together OE. **b.** *fig.* A means or instrument of punishment; also, punishment, chastisement. late ME. **3.** A wand or stick carried in the hand, such as a walking-stick, shepherd's or herdsman's stick, enchanter's wand, etc. ME. **b.** A stick or switch carried in the hand when riding. late ME. **c.** A divining-rod 1617. **4.** A wand or staff (of wood, ivory, or metal) carried as a symbol of office, authority, or dignity. (See also BLACK ROD.) 1440. **b.** As a symbol of power or tyrannical sway 1526. **5.** An angling-rod; a fishing-rod 1450. **b.** *transf.* An angler 1867.

2. Phr. *To spare the r.*, etc.: see SPARE *v.* **b.** *To make a r. for one's own back. To kiss the r.*: see KISS *v.* 6: *A r. in pickle*, usu. *fig.* a punishment in store. **4.** The sergeantes smote him with their rods of office 1557. **b.** Hands that the r. of empire might have sway'd GRAY.

II. 1. A stick used for measuring with. Also *measuring r.* 1495. **2. a.** A measure of length, equal to 5½ yards or 16½ feet; a PERCH or POLE 1450. **b.** A measure of area: A square perch or pole 1477. **c.** A measure of brickwork 1663. **III. a.** A straight slender bar of metal; a connecting part or shaft which is slender in proportion to its length. See also *connecting-*, *lightning-*, *piston-rod.* 1728. **b.** In scientific use: An animal or vegetable structure having an clongated slender form 1864. **c.** Something resembling a rod in shape 1860. **IV.** *attrib.* in sense 'having the form of a rod', as *r.-bolt*, *-iron*, *-lead*; *r.-body*, *-cell* 1690.

Rode (rō[u]d), *v.* 1768. [Of obscure origin. Sense 2 is evidently rel. in some way to COCK-ROAD, -ROOD.] **1.** *intr.* Of wild-fowl: To fly landward in the evening. **2.** Of woodcock: To perform a regular evening flight during the breeding season 1865.

Rodent (rō[u]·děnt), *a.* and *sb.* 1833. [– L. *rodens*, *-ent-*, pr. pple. of *rodere* gnaw; see -ENT.] **A.** *adj.* **1.** *Zool.* Gnawing; belonging to the order *Rodentia.* **2.** *Path.* Of an ulcer or cancer 1853. **B.** *sb. Zool.* An animal of the order *Rodentia*, characterized by having no canine teeth and strong incisors 1835. Hence **Rode·ntial** *a.* of or pertaining to the *Rodentia* or r. animals.

‖**Rodeo** (rodē·o, *U.S.* rō[u]·dio). 1834. [Sp. *rodeo*, f. *rodear* go round, based on L. *rotare* ROTATE.] **1.** A driving together of cattle in order to separate, count, inspect, or mark them; a round-up. **2.** A place or enclosure where cattle are brought together for any purpose 1847. **3.** An exhibition of skill in rounding up cattle, riding unbroken horses, etc.; *transf.* an exhibition of 'stunting' in the riding of motor-cycles, etc. 19..

3. There will be a..motor-cycle r. in the afternoon 1928.

Rodomont (rǫ·dŏmǫnt). *arch.* 1598. [– Fr. *rodomont* – It. *rodomonte* bragger, boaster, appellative use of *Rodomonte*, name of a boastful Saracen leader in Boiardo's 'Orlando Innamorato' and Ariosto's 'Orlando Furioso'.] A great bragger or boaster.

Rodomontade (rǫdŏmǫntē[i]·d), *sb.* and *a.* †Also **rhod-**. 1612. [– Fr. *rodomontade* – It. †*rodomontada*, *-ata*, f. Fr. *rodomont*, It. *-monte*; see prec., -ADE.] **A.** *sb.* **1. a.** A vain-glorious brag or boast; an extravagantly boastful or arrogant saying or speech; †an arrogant act. **b.** Extravagant boasting or bragging 1648. †**2.** *transf.* = RODOMONT –1697.

1. Challengers cartells, full of Rodomontades DONNE. **b.** We could discern its meaning through a cloud of r. MACAULAY.

B. *adj.* Bragging; boastful; ranting 1754. So **R(h)odomonta·de** *v. intr.* to boast, brag. **R(h)odomonta·der.** †**R(h)odomonta·do** *sb.* and *a.* rodomontade.

Roe[1] (rō[u]). [OE. *rā*, earlier *rāa*, *rāha* (also *rāhdēor*) = OS., OHG. *rēho* (Du. *ree*, G. *reh*), ON. *rá* :– Gmc. **raix-*.] A small species of deer (*Capreolus capræa*, formerly *Cervus capreolus*) inhabiting various parts of Europe and Asia; a deer belonging to this species.

Roe[2] (rō[u]). [Late ME. *row(e*, *rough*, *roof* :– **roʒe* – MLG., MDu. *roge* = OHG. *rogo*; contemp. forms are dial. *rown* (XV), later *roan* (XVII) – MLG. *rogen* or ON. *hrogn* = OHG. *rogan* (G. *rogen*).] The mass of eggs contained in the ovarian membranes of a fish.

Hard r., the spawn of a female fish; *soft r.*, the milt or sperm of a male fish.

Roebuck (rō[u]·bɒk). late ME. [f. ROE[1] + BUCK.] The buck or male of the roe-deer.

Roed (rō[u]d), *a.* 1611. [f. ROE[2] + -ED[2].] Having roe; full of spawn; as *hard-*, *soft-r.*

Roe·-deer. OE. [f. ROE[1] + DEER.] Deer, or a deer, of the roe kind; a roe.

Roentgen, etc.: see RÖNTGEN, etc.

Roe·stone. 1804. [f. ROE[2].] = OOLITE.

Rogation (rogē[i]·ʃən). late ME. [– L. *rogatio*, *-on-*, f. *rogat-*, pa. ppl. stem of *rogare* ask; in med.L. pl. (in sense 1) *Rogationes*; see -ION.] **1.** *Eccl.* (usu. *pl.*) Solemn supplications consisting of the litany of the saints, chanted during procession on the three days before Ascension Day; hence freq. the days on which this is done, the Rogation days. **2.**

Rom. Antiq. The act, on the part of a consul or tribune, of submitting a proposed law to the people for their acceptance; also, a law so submitted and accepted. late ME. †**3.** A formal request –1680.

1. *R. days*, the Monday, Tuesday, and Wednesday preceding Ascension Day. *R. week*, the week in which Ascension Day falls. *R. Sunday*, the fifth Sunday after Easter, being the Sunday before Ascension Day. *R. flower*, the milkwort (*Polygala vulgaris*), formerly made into garlands and carried in processions on Rogation days.

Roger (rǫ·dʒəɹ). 1631. [A personal name of men – OFr. *Roger*, *Rogier*, of Gmc. origin.] **1.** Used as a generic or special name for persons. **2.** *The Jolly R.*, the pirate's flag 1785.

Roger de Coverley (rǫ·dʒəɹ dĭ kʋ·vəɹli). 1685. [In early use *Roger of Coverly*; the later form is due to Addison's use of it in the *Spectator*.] An English country-dance (and tune). Also used with the prefix *Sir*, and abbreviated as *Sir Roger*.

Rogue (rōᵘg), *sb.* 1561. [orig. one of the numerous canting words that are recorded from mid-XVI; perh. based on †*roger* begging vagabond pretending to be a poor scholar from Oxford or Cambridge (XVI, Copland), prob. f. L. *rogare* ask, beg.] **1.** One belonging to a class of idle vagrants or vagabonds. Now *arch.* as a legal term. **2.** A dishonest, unprincipled person; a rascal 1578. †**b.** Applied abusively to servants –1781. **3.** One who is of a mischievous disposition 1597. **4.** *Hort.* An inferior plant among seedlings 1859. **5.** [tr. Cingalese *hora*, *sora* = Skr. *chōra* thief] An elephant, etc., driven away, or living apart, from the herd, and of a savage or destructive disposition 1859. **6.** A horse which is inclined to shirk its work on the racecourse or in the hunting-field 1881.

2. He who is carried by horses must deal with rogues 1858. **b.** My Lord, your R. has me safe here STEELE. **3.** That sly r. Cupid has pierced your heart 1784.

Comb. with genitive: **rogue's gallery**, a collection of the portraits of criminals; **rogue's Latin**, thieves' Latin or cant; **rogue's march**, one played by the trumpeters or fifers of a regiment in drumming out a man from a camp or garrison; **rogue's yarn**, 'a thread of worsted in the strands of rope manufactured for the Royal Navy, introduced for the purpose of detecting theft or embezzlement;..it serves also to trace any bad rope to the precise yard where it was made'. Hence **Ro·gueship**, the state of being a r.; used as a mock-title in *your rogueship*, etc.

Rogue (rōᵘg), *v.* 1570. [f. ROGUE *sb.*] **1.** *intr.* To wander idly about after the manner of rogues; to live like a rogue or vagrant; later, to play the rogue or rascal. †**2.** *trans.* To call (a person) a rogue; to accuse of roguery –1683. †**b.** To cast discredit on (something) –1685. **3.** To swindle 1841. **4.** To free from inferior plants or seedlings 1766.

Roguery (rōᵘ·gəri). 1596. [f. ROGUE *sb.* + -ERY.] **1.** Conduct or practices characteristic of rogues; knavishness, rascality; †idle vagrancy. **2.** A knavish or rascally act 1620. **3.** Playful mischief; waggishness; fun 1664.

1. The unrighteous man..had far better not yield to the illusion that his r. is clever 1875.

Roguish (rōᵘ·giʃ), *a.* 1572. [f. ROGUE *sb.* + -ISH¹ 2.] **1.** Pertaining or appropriate to, characteristic of, rogues (†or vagrants); disreputable. **2.** Acting (†or wandering) like rogues; knavish or rascally in conduct 1596. **3.** Playfully mischievous; arch, waggish 1681. **4.** Of plants: Inferior 1762.

1. Bought an idle rogueish French book PEPYS. **3.** She has twa sparkling rogueish e'en BURNS. So **Roguish-ly** *adv.*, **-ness.** †**Ro·guy** *a.* (in senses 1–3).

Roil, *v.*¹ *Obs.* exc. *dial.* ME. [Of unkn. origin.] †**1.** To roam or rove about; to gad about, wander –1619. **2.** To play or frolic; to romp, rampage 1788.

Roil, *v.*² Now *U.S.* and *dial.* 1590. [perh. – OFr. *ruiler* mix mortar :– late L. *regulare* REGULATE.] **1.** *trans.* To render (water or any liquid) turbid or muddy by stirring up the sediment. **2.** To disturb in temper; to vex, irritate, make angry 1734. Hence **Roil** *sb.* agitation or stirring up (of water).

†**Roin**, *sb.* late ME. [– OFr. *roigne* (mod. *rogne*) – pop. L. **arōnea*, for L. *aranea* spider.] A scab, scurf. CHAUCER. Hence †**Roi·nish**, *a.* covered with scale or scurf; scabby, coarse, mean, paltry, base.

Roister (roi·stəɹ), *sb.* Now *arch.* 1551. [– (O)Fr. *rustre* ruffian, alt. of *ruste* :– *rusticus* RUSTIC; for the repr. of Fr. (ü) by Eng. (oi) cf. †*moil* MULE, †*ois* USE, RECOIL.] A swaggering or blustering bully; a riotous fellow; a rude or noisy reveller. (Now usu. ROISTERER.) **b.** *dial.* A romp 1790. Hence **Roi·ster** *v. intr.* to play the r.; also with *it*. **Roi·sterer**, a swaggering or noisy reveller. **Roi·sterous** *a.* given to noisy revelling; uproarious.

Roke (rōᵘk), *sb.* Now *dial.* ME. [prob. of Scand. origin. Cf. REEK *sb.*¹] Smoke, steam; vapour, mist, fog; drizzling rain. Hence **Roke** *v. intr.* to give off steam or vapour; to steam; to smoke; to be foggy or misty (now *dial.*). **Ro·ky** *a.* misty; foggy; drizzly (chiefly *dial.*).

Roland (rōᵘ·lănd). ME. [OFr. *Roland*, of Gmc. origin.] The legendary nephew of Charlemagne, celebrated in the *Chanson de Roland* (frequently together with his comrade Oliver); hence, one comparable to Roland in respect of courage, warlike deeds, or friendship; one who is a full match for another.

England all Oliuers and Rowlands bred, During the time Edward the third did raigne SHAKS. Phr. (*To give*) *a R. for an Oliver*, (to give) as good as one gets, a quid pro quo or tit for tat.

‖**Rôle** (rōᵘl). Also †**roll.** 1606. [Fr. †*roule*, †*rolle*, *rôle* ROLL *sb.*¹, orig. the 'roll' containing an actor's part.] The part or character which one undertakes, assumes, or has to play. Chiefly *fig.* with ref. to the part played by a person in society or life.

Roll (rōᵘl), *sb.*¹ ME. [– OFr. *rolle*, *roulle* (mod. *rôle*, see prec.) :– L. *rotulus*, var. of *rotula*, dim. of *rota* wheel.] **I. 1.** A piece of parchment, paper, or the like, which is written upon or intended to contain writing, etc., and is rolled up for convenience of handling or carrying; a scroll. **2.** *spec.* Such a piece of parchment, paper, etc., inscribed with some formal or official record; a document or instrument in this form. late ME. **3.** A register, list, or catalogue (of names, deeds, etc.) late ME. **b.** The official list of those qualified to act as solicitors (†or attorneys). Commonly pl. 1840. **4.** A list of names used to ascertain whether each one of a set of persons is present; esp. *Mil.* (= MUSTER-ROLL) or in scholastic use 1597.

1. Atlas bearing Heauen with a roule inscribed in Italian CAMDEN. A r. of music 1888. **2.** *Rolls of Chancery, Court, Parliament*; COURT-, RENT-ROLL, etc. *Master* (also †*Clerk* or *Keeper*) *of the Rolls*, one of the four ex-officio judges of the Court of Appeal and a member of the Judicial Committee, who has charge of the rolls, patents, and grants that pass the great seal, and of all records of the Court of Chancery. *The Rolls*, the former buildings in Chancery Lane in which the records in the custody of the Master of the Rolls were preserved (now represented by the Public Record Office). Also = *Rolls Court*. *attrib.*, as *Rolls-Chapel*, *-Court*. Also **Rolls Series**, a series of 'chronicles and memorials of Great Britain and Ireland published under the direction of the Master of the Rolls': so *Rolls edition*. **3.** *R. of fame*; Happy King, whose name The brightest shines in all the rolls of fame! POPE. *R. of honour*, a list of those who died for their country in war. **b.** Phr. *To be struck off the rolls*, to be debarred from practising as a solicitor in consequence of some delinquency. **4.** Where's the R.?..let them appeare as I call SHAKS.

II. 1. A quantity of material (*esp.* cloth) rolled or wound up in a cylindrical form, sometimes forming a definite measure. Also, a number of papers, etc. rolled together. late ME. **b.** A quantity (usu. small) of some soft substance formed into a cylindrical mass 1547. **c.** A quantity of tobacco leaves rolled up into a cylindrical mass; tobacco in this form 1633. **2.** A small quantity of cloth, wool, straw, etc., rolled up into the form of a band or fillet. Now *spec.* a carding of this form. 1548. **3.** †**a.** A round cushion or pad of hair or other material, forming part of a woman's head-dress –1777. **b.** An annular pad for placing on the head in order to facilitate or ease the carrying of heavy articles on it. Now *dial.* 1681. **4.** A small loaf of bread, properly one which has been rolled or doubled over before baking 1581. **5. a.** *Arch.* A spiral scroll used in Corinthian and Ionic capitals; a cylindrical moulding; a curl, volute 1611. **b.** *Building.* A strip of wood, rounded on the top and fastened on the ridge or the lateral joints of a roof, to raise the edges of sheet-lead or zinc and so prevent the entrance of rain-water 1833. **6.** A part which is rolled or turned over 1671.

3. b. Those rolls our prudent milk-maids make use of to fix their pails upon 1716. **4.** I have sat at home all day, and eaten only a mess of broth and a r. SWIFT. **5. a.** *R. and fillet*, 'a round moulding with a small square fillet on the face of it'.

III. 1. A cylindrical piece of wood or metal used to facilitate the moving of something; a windlass. late ME. **b.** *Bookbinding.* A revolving patterned tool used in impressing and gilding; the pattern produced by this 1656. **2. a.** A roller used for levelling soil or crushing clods 1634. **b.** A roller used to crush, flatten, or draw out something, esp. in metal-working 1656.

Roll, *sb.*² 1688. [f. ROLL *v.*] **1.** The act of rolling; the fact of moving in this manner. Also with *a* and *pl.* **b.** A rolling gait or motion; a swagger 1836. **2.** *Mil.* Of a drum: A rapid, uniform beating, produced by alternate strokes of the sticks, and falling upon the ears as a continuous sound 1688. **3.** Of thunder, etc.: A loud, reverberating peal; a continuous reverberation; a prolonged shout 1818. **4.** A rich sonorous or rhythmical flow of words in verse or prose 1730. **5.** An undulation or swell on the surface of land 1874.

1. The r. of the Atlantic was full, but not violent 1871. *fig.* I hear the r. of the ages TENNYSON. **2.** *Long r.*, a beat of drum by which troops are assembled at any particular spot or rendezvous or parade 1802. **4.** The r. of Ciceronian prose 1870.

Roll (rōᵘl), *v.* late ME. [– OFr. *rol(l)er*, (also mod.) *rouler* :– Rom. **rotulare* (in AL., XII), f. L. *rotulus* ROLL *sb.*¹] **I.** *trans.* **1.** To move or impel forward (an object) on a surface by making it turn over and over; to shift about, to send down to a lower level, etc., in this manner. Also with *up* or *down*, *away*, etc. **b.** To drive or draw on wheels; to wheel (a cycle); to move by means of rollers 1513. **c.** To convey in a wheeled vehicle 1778. **2.** To form into a mass by turning over and over; to pile up in this manner 1547. **3.** To drive or cause to flow onward with a rolling or sweeping motion. Also with *down*. 1667. **b.** To cause (smoke, etc.) to ascend in rolls 1743. **4.** *transf.* **a.** To utter, give forth (words, etc.) with a full, rolling sound or tone. Chiefly with *out*. 1561. **b.** To pronounce or sound with a trill 1846. **5.** To turn round on or as on an axis; to cause to revolve or rotate; to turn over and over *in* something or between the hands; also, to carry *round* in revolving. late ME. **b.** *Naut.* Of vessels: To cast (masts, etc.) overboard, to submerge (tackle, etc.) by rolling 1633. **c.** To cause to swing or sway from side to side 1804. **d.** To cause to fall and turn *over* by means of a blow, shot, etc.; to bowl *over* 1850. **6.** *fig.* To revolve, turn over (a matter) *in* the mind; †to consider, meditate upon (something). late ME. **7.** To turn (the eyes) in different directions with a kind of circular motion 1513. **8.** To coil round and round upon itself or about an axis; to form into a roll or ball; to wind, fold, or curl up. Also with *up*. 1526. **9.** To wrap, envelop, or enfold *in* something; to wrap *about* with something. Also with *up*. late ME. **10.** To spread out (paste) with a rolling-pin; to level or smooth (ground) with a roller; to render compact, smooth, or flat by means of pressure with a cylinder. Also with *out*. late ME. **b.** To reduce (stone or rock) to a smooth, rounded form by propulsion in flowing water and consequent attrition 1811.

1. An Egg that fell from Heaven into Euphrates, and [was] by Fishes rolled on Land 1665. Phr. *R. up* (*Mil.*) to drive the flank of the enemy line back and round so that the line is shortened and surrounded. **2.** Down they fell by thousands, Angel and Arch-Angel rowl'd MILT. **3.** Where.. fringed with roses, Tenglio rolls his stream THOMSON. *fig.* Hearing the holy organ rolling waves Of sound on roof and floor TENNYSON. **5.** He hath..rolled me in the dust COVERDALE *Lam.* 3:16. **6.** I came home rolling resentments in my mind and framing schemes of revenge SWIFT. **8.** *fig.* Housemaid, butler, and footman rolled into one 1887. **9.** Their Kings, whose bodies are..lapped in white skinnes and rowled in mats PURCHAS. **10.** The gold bars are rolled cold to the thickness of the coin 1866.

II. *intr.* **1.** To move by revolving or rotating on (or as on) an axis; to move forward on a surface by turning over and over. Also with advs. late ME. **b.** To advance with an easy, soft, or undulating motion. late ME. **c.** Of vehicles: To move or run on wheels 1721. **2. a.** To wander, roam, travel or move about. late ME. **b.** *To r. up* (slang), to congregate, gather, assemble (orig. *Austral.*) 1887. **3.** To ride or travel in a carriage 1513. **b.** To be carried, or move, upon flowing water 1672. **4.** Of times or seasons: To elapse; to move *on* or *round*; to pass *over* or *away* 1513. **5.** Of the heavenly bodies: To perform a periodical revolution 1604. **b.** With compl. To traverse in revolving 1667. **6.** Of seas, rivers, etc.: To flow with an undulating motion; to move in a full, swelling, or impetuous manner 1565. **b.** To move or sweep along or up with a wave-like motion; to ascend or descend in rolls or curls 1626. **c.** Of land: To undulate; to extend in gentle falls and rises 1847. **7.** Of thunder, etc.: To reverberate; to form a deep continuous sound like the roll of a drum 1598. **b.** Of language, talk, etc.: To flow; to run *on* 1743. **c.** Of sound: To flow in deep or mellow tones 1819. **d.** To trill or warble in song 1886. **8.** To turn over (and over). late ME. **b.** Of the eyes: To move or turn round in the sockets; to rotate partially. late ME. **c.** To turn upon an axis 1646. **d.** †To hinge or depend *on* something; to turn or centre *on* a subject 1707. **9.** To turn oneself over and over *in* something; hence *fig.* to luxuriate or abound *in* riches, luxury, etc. 1535. **10.** Of thoughts, etc.: To revolve in the mind 1547. **11.** Of a ship: To sway to and fro; to swing from side to side. (Opp. to *pitch.*) Also of masts. 1600. **b.** To sail with a rolling motion 1796. **c.** To walk with a rolling gait; to swagger 1843. **12.** To form into a roll; to shrink or fold *together*; to curl *up* 1613.

1. The ball..rolled between his legs DICKENS. **b.** The poor distressed panther rowled after him in humble manner 1607. **c.** The carriages of the nobility and guests r. back to the West THACKERAY. **2. b.** The miners all rolled up to see the fun 1887. **4.** Generations and ages might r. away in silent oblivion GIBBON. **5.** A stone by nature is inclined to descend, and the Sunne to rowle about the world 1604. **b.** Thrice hath Hyperion roll'd his annual race GRAY. **6.** Through midst thereof a little river rold SPENSER. *fig.* Deep woes r. forward like a gentle flood SHAKS. **b.** The fog rolled slowly upward 1858. **c.** Before them rolled the sweep of upland 1894. **7.** The organ rumbled and rolled as if the Church had got the colic DICKENS. **8. b.** Eyes which rowle towards all, weep not but sweat DONNE. **d.** Our conversation rolled chiefly on literary and political subjects BORROW. **9.** Rolling in wealth which you do not want 1782. **11.** The Sloop..rolled and pitched..violently 1748. Hence **Ro·llable** *a.* capable of being rolled. **Ro·llway** *U.S.*, a natural slope on the bank of a river, or an inclined shoot for expediting the descent of logs, etc., to the surface of water or ice; *transf.* the pile of logs on a river-bank awaiting transportation.

Roll-call (rōᵘ·l,kǭl). 1802. [f. ROLL *sb.*¹ + CALL *sb.*] **1.** The act of calling over a list of the names of persons forming a military or other body, in order to ascertain who are present; the marking of such a list at a particular time. **2.** *Mil.* The signal summoning men to be present at the calling of the roll 1890.

Ro·ll-co:llar. 1836. [ROLL *sb.*¹] A turned-over collar on a garment.

Rolled (rōᵘld), *ppl. a.* 1467. [f. ROLL *v.* + -ED¹.] In the senses of ROLL *v.*

R. gold, orig., a thin coating of gold applied to a baser metal by rolling; now, a kind of filled gold rolled or drawn out so that the gold becomes very thin.

Roller (rōᵘ·ləɹ), *sb.*¹ late ME. [f. ROLL *v.* + -ER¹.] **I. 1.** A rolling-pin. Now *dial.* **2.** A cylinder of wood or metal, revolving on pivots or a fixed axis, for lessening the friction of anything passed over it; also, a rounded piece of wood over which an endless towel is passed. late ME. **b.** The revolvable drum, barrel, or axis of a winch or windlass 1659. **3.** One of a number of cylinders of wood, etc., either attached or free, for diminishing friction when rolling or moving a heavy body 1565. **c.** A heavy cylinder of wood, stone, or (now usu.) metal, fitted in a frame with shafts or a handle, for crushing clods, etc., and smoothing the ground by compression 1530. **b.** A rotating cylinder or roll for pressing, stamping, crushing, or rolling; one of a set of rolls for forming metal, etc., into bars or sheets; also, the revolving cylinder of a printing-machine for impressing the paper upon the printing-matter 1728. **c.** *Printing.* A cylinder or roll of thick, elastic composition, mounted on a metal or wooden axis, for inking a form of letter, etc., before printing; also a metal cylinder for distributing ink upon this 1790. **5.** A cylindrical piece of wood, etc.; esp. one on which cloth or other material is rolled up 1567. **6.** *Organ-building.* A rounded slip of wood or piece of metal tube, turning, by the action of the key, on pins inserted into its ends, and having two or more arms at right angles to its length 1632. **b.** The toothed or studded revolvable barrel of a musical box 1875. **7.** A small wheel rotating on an axle or axis; a short cylinder serving as a wheel 1802. **8.** A roller-chain for a cycle (i.e. one in which flexibility is attained by the use of small rollers in each link) 1897. **II.** A long bandage, formed in a roll, for winding firmly round a limb, etc. Now more freq. *r.-bandage.* 1534. **b.** A broad, padded girth for a horse 1688. **III. 1.** *Zool.* A variety of tumbler-pigeon 1867. **2.** A long swelling wave, moving with a steady sweep or roll; a heavy billow 1829. **IV.** One who rolls up or forms into a roll or coil; one who compresses or shapes metal by passing it between cylinders or rolls 1591. **2.** A butterfly or moth which causes leaves to roll up 1832.

attrib. and *Comb.* **r.-bandage,** = sense II; **board,** the board carrying the rollers in an organ; **-bolt,** part of the splinter-bar of a carriage, serving also as a step; **-gin,** a cotton-gin in which the cleaning is effected by rollers; **-mill,** a mill in which the grinding is done by rollers; **-shop,** the part of an iron-works where the metal is rolled; **-towel,** a towel running on a r.

Roller (rōᵘ·ləɹ), *sb.*² 1678. [– G. *roller*, f. *rollen* (cf. ROLL *v.* II. 7) + -ER¹.] **1.** An insessorial coracoid bird (usu. the common r., *Coracias garrulus*), having the form of a crow, and brilliant plumage. **b.** Applied to other birds, as *Eurystomus australis*, *E. azureus*, etc. 1752. **2.** A variety of canary, remarkable for rolling or trilling in song 1884.

Ro·ller-skate. orig. *U.S.* 1874. [ROLLER *sb.*¹ I. 7.] A skate mounted on small wheels or rollers, usually two pairs, for use in skating on smooth flooring, etc. Hence **Ro·ller-skate** *v. intr.* to use or to perform on roller-skates.

Rolley (rǫ·li). Also **rolly.** 1825. [perh. conn. w. ROLL *v.*; in sense 2, also *rulley.*] **1.** *Mining.* A kind of truck without sides, formerly much in use for carrying corves along underground horse-roads or upon rails to the shaft. **2.** A lorry 1857.

Rollick (rǫ·lik), *v.* 1826. [prob. of dial. origin; perh. blending of *romp* and *frolic.*] *intr.* To frolic, sport, or romp, in a joyous, careless fashion; to go off, move along, enter, etc., in this manner. Freq. *transf.* of things or animals.

'Q.' appears as a rollicking humourist. He rollicks..a little too laboriously. 1888. Hence **Ro·llick** *sb.* exuberant gaiety or joviality; a sportive frolic or escapade. **Ro·llicker. Ro·llicking** *ppl. a.* extremely jovial or gay; boisterously sportive.

Rolling (rōᵘ·liŋ), *ppl. a.* ME. [f. ROLL *v.* + -ING².] **1.** That turns over and over, esp. so as to move forward on a surface or down a slope 1500. **b.** That moves or runs upon wheels 1565. **c.** Of a person, his opinions: Changeable, shifting, variable, inconstant. Now *rare* or *Obs.* 1561. **d.** Of time or seasons: Steadily moving onwards; also, moving round, recurring 1695. **2.** Revolving, rotating, turning on, or as on, an axis; moving round a centre 1591. **b.** Of the eyes: Moving to and fro or up and down in the sockets 1576. **c.** Turning round, turned over, in a coil or fold. late ME. **d.** Swinging, swaying; as a *r. gait* 1755. **3.** Heaving, surging, swelling, flowing steadily and strongly onwards 1633. **b.** Ascending or moving in curls or rolls 1664. **4.** Producing a continuous swelling sound; reverberating, resounding 1652. **b.** Continuously sounded or trilled 1863. **5.** Of prairie-land, etc.: Having a succession of gentle undulations. Also *transf.* Orig. *U.S.* 1819.

1. His thoughts are like a r. axeltree *Ecclus.* 33:5. **b.** A R. wagon 1648. **d.** Oft as the r. Years return PRIOR. **2.** The r. world 1848. **c.** The r. scrolls, borrowed from the Romans 1883. **3.** *fig.* Fix'd in the r. flood of endless years COWPER. **b.** A tremulous..Agitation of rowling fumes 1664. **4.** A r. organ-harmony Swells up TENNYSON. **5.** A r., rugged down, flecked with patches of..heath 1890.

attrib. **r.-stock,** the locomotives, wagons, carriages, etc. used on a railway. **Ro·llingly** *adv.*

Ro·lling-mill. 1787. [f. *rolling* vbl. sb. or ppl. a.] A mill or powerful machine in or by which metal, etc., is rolled out or flattened.

Ro·lling-pin. 1589. [f. as prec.] A cylindrical piece of wood or other material for rolling out dough, paste, or, formerly, leather.

Ro·lling-press. 1625. [f. as prec.] **1.** A copperplate-printers' press in which the plate passes in a bed under a revolving cylinder. **2.** A press which flattens, smooths, etc., by means of cylinders or rollers; a rolling-machine 1833.

Rolling stone, ro·lling-stone. 1546. [f. as prec.] **1.** In the provb. *A rolling stone gathers no moss*, or variants of this; see MOSS *sb.* II. 1. **2.** A rambler, wanderer; a good-for-nothing 1611. **3.** A cylindrical stone used for crushing, flattening, etc. 1611.

Ro·ll-top. 1890. [f. ROLL *v.*] The sliding cover of a writing desk, made of parallel slats fastened to a flexible backing; also, = *roll-top desk.*

Roly-poly (rōᵘ·li,pōᵘ·li), *sb.* and *a.* Also **rolypoly.** 1601. [Fanciful formation on ROLL *v.*; the origin of sense 1 is obscure; the second element may contain POLL *sb.*¹] **A.** *sb.* †**1.** A worthless fellow; a rascal –1609. **2.** The name of various games, in most of which the rolling of a ball is the chief feature 1713. **3.** A pudding, consisting of suet pastry covered with jam or preserves, formed into a roll and boiled or steamed 1848. **B.** *aadj.* Short and stout; podgy, dumpy, plump. Chiefly of children. 1820.

‖**Rom** (rǫm). Also *pl.* **Roma(s.** 1841. [Gipsy (Romany) *rom* man, husband; pl. *romá.*] A male Gipsy, a Romany.

Romaic (romēⁱ·ik), *a.* and *sb.* 1809. [– Gr. Ῥωμαϊκός Roman (f. Ῥώμη Rome), used spec. of the Eastern empire.] **A.** *a.* **1.** Forming, composed in, pertaining to, the vernacular language of modern Greece. **2.** *R. dance* = next 2. 1830. **B.** *sb.* The vernacular language of modern Greece or a dialect of it 1810.

Romaika (romēⁱ·ikă). 1625. [– mod. Gr. ῥωμαϊκή; see prec.] †**1.** = prec. B. PURCHAS. **2.** A modern Greek dance 1811.

‖**Romal, rumal** (ro-, rumā·l). 1683. [Urdu (Pers.) *rūmāl*, f. *rū* face + *māl* (base of *mālidan* wipe) wiping.] **1.** A silk or cotton square or handkerchief; a thin silk or cotton fabric with a handkerchief pattern. **2.** The handkerchief or bandage used by Indian Thugs to strangle their victims 1836.

Roman (rōᵘ·măn), *sb.* [ME. *Romein*, *-ain(e* – (O)Fr. *Romain*; see next.] **I. 1.** An inhabitant or native of ancient Rome; a Roman citizen or soldier; one belonging to the Roman state or empire. **b.** An inhabitant or native of mediæval or modern Rome 1547. **2.** *pl.* Those inhabitants of ancient Rome who had accepted the Christian faith. late ME. **b.** *ellipt.* St Paul's Epistle to the Romans: abbrev. *Rom.* late ME. **3.** *Printing.* The style of letters distinguished by this name (see ROMAN *a.* 5.); also *pl.* letters of a Roman fount 1598.

1. *King*, or *Emperor*, *of the Romans*, the sovereign head of the Holy Roman Empire. **2.** Paul commendeth his calling to the Romanes *Rom.* 1.

II. A member or adherent of the Roman Catholic Church; a Roman Catholic. Now *colloq.* 1547.

Roman (rōᵘ·măn), *a.* [ME. *Romein*, *-ain* – (O)Fr. *Romain* – L. *Romanus*, f. *Roma* Rome, capital of Italy; later assim. in sp. to L.;

see -AN.] **I. 1.** Of persons: Inhabiting, belonging to, or originating from the ancient city of Rome or its territory; holding the position of a citizen or member of the ancient republic or empire of Rome. **2.** Of things: Of or pertaining to, connected with, ancient Rome, its inhabitants or dominion; practised or used by, current or usual among, the Romans, etc. ME. **b.** Of language, etc. = LATIN *a.* 2. ME. **3.** Of antiquities, etc.: Belonging to, surviving from, the time of the Romans 1548. **4.** Of a type or kind characteristic of, or exemplified by, the Romans; Roman-like, esp. in respect of honesty, strictness, courage, or frugality 1577. **b.** Of a nose: Having a prominent upper part or bridge 1624. **5.** Of letters: Belonging to the modern type which most directly represents that used in ancient Roman inscriptions and manuscripts, esp. in contrast to *Gothic* (or *black letter*) and *Italic* 1519. **b.** Of handwriting: Round and bold 1601. **6. a.** Of the alphabet or its characters: Employed by the Romans, and (with modifications) by all the modern nations of Western Europe and their colonies 1728. **b.** Of numeral letters: The letters I, V, X, L, C, D, M. (Opp. to *Arabic.*) 1728. **7.** *Arch.* = COMPOSITE *a.* 2. 1624. **8.** Engaged in the study of Roman law, antiquities, history, etc. 1845.

1. The R. Emperors residing in the East 1660. **2.** The northern nations who established themselves upon the ruins of the R. Empire 1776. Tin, used in the R. coinage 1819. *R. Law*, the system or code of law developed by the ancient Romans, and still accepted in principle by many countries. **3.** Ride by the side of the R. road 1774. **4.** He was dispos'd to mirth, but..A Romane thought hath strooke him SHAKS. **5. b.** I thinke we doe know the sweet Romane hand SHAKS. **8.** To the R. lawyer the study of R. antiquities is essential 1845.

II. 1. Pertaining to Rome in its ecclesiastical aspect; belonging to, connected with, the Church of Rome; = ROMAN CATHOLIC *a.* 1535. **2.** (*Holy*) *R. Empire*: the Romano-Germanic Empire which originated with Charlemagne in 800, and continued to exist down to 1806. So *R. Emperor.* 1610. **†3.** = ROMANCE I b. –1804.

1. *R. collar*, a special form of collar worn by Roman Catholic, and some Anglican, clerics.

III. Of or pertaining to mediæval or modern Rome or its inhabitants; printed at Rome, etc. 1608.

R. school, the school of painting of which Raphael is the leading representative. *R. fever*, a form of malarial fever prevalent in Rome.

Special collocations: **R. alum,** a reddish alum found in Italy, or a manufactured imitation of this; **R. balance, beam,** the ordinary form of steelyard; **R. candle,** a cylindrical firework which throws out a succession of stars; **R. cement,** a cement or hydraulic mortar made by the addition of calcareous or argillaceous matter to lime, sand, and water; also as vb.; **R. mosaic,** a mosaic 'formed of short and slender sticks of coloured glass'; **R. steelyard** = *R. balance.*

Ro·man Ca·tholic, *sb.* and *a.* 1605. [Representing the full official designation 'Ecclesia *Romana Catholica* et Apostolica' (see ROMAN *a.* II. 1. and CATHOLIC *a.* II. 2); app. orig. used as a conciliatory term, in place of *Roman*, *Romanist*, or *Romish*, early in XVII. Now the recognized legal and official designation, though in ordinary use *Catholic* alone is common.] = ROMAN *sb.* II, *a.* II. 1. Hence **Ro·man-Catho·lically, -Ca·tholicly** *advs.* **Ro·man Catho·licism.**

Romance (romæ·ns), *sb.* (and *a.*) [ME. *roma(u)nz, -a(u)ns* – OFr. *romanz, -ans*, fem. *-ance* the vernacular tongue, work composed in this – pop. L. **romanice* in the vernacular, adv. of L. *Romanicus*, f. *Romanus* ROMAN + *-icus* -IC.] **I. a.** *orig.* The vernacular language of France, as opp. to Latin. In later use also extended to related forms of speech, as Provençal and Spanish, and now a generic or collective name for the whole group of languages derived from Latin. **b.** *attrib.* or as *adj.* Derived from or representing the old Roman tongue; descended from Latin. Also composed in, using, etc., a vernacular tongue of Latin origin. late ME.

II. 1. A tale in verse, embodying the life and adventures of some hero of chivalry, and belonging in matter and form to the ages of knighthood; also, in later use, a prose tale of a similar character ME. **2.** A fictitious narrative in prose of which the scene and incidents are very remote from those of ordinary life; *esp.* one of the class prevalent in the 16th and 17th centuries, with long disquisitions and digressions. Also occas., a long poem of a similar type. 1638. **b.** A romantic novel or narrative 1831. **3.** A Spanish historical ballad or short poem of a certain form 1605. **b.** *Mus.* A short vocal or instrumental piece of a simple or informal character 1797. **4.** That class of literature which consists of romances; romantic fiction 1667. **b.** Romantic or imaginative character or quality; suggestion of or association with the adventurous and chivalrous 1801. **5.** An extravagant fiction, invention, or story; a wild or wanton exaggeration; a picturesque falsehood. Also without article. 1497. **6.** *attrib.*, as *r.- novel*; also as *adj.* with the sense: Having the character or attributes associated with romance; chivalrous, romantic 1653.

1. The first metrical r...is the famous *chanson de Roland* 1802. **2.** In the Romance you lent me none of the great Heroes were ever false in love GAY. **b.** The r. of the Pirate SCOTT. *transf.* The last romance of Science..is the Story of the Ascent of Man 1894. **4.** And what resounds In Fable or R. of Uthers Son MILT. *fig.* Lady of the Mere, Sole-sitting by the shores of old r. WORDSW. **b.** R. goes out of a man's head when the hair gets grey 1873. **5.** This is r.—I'll not believe a word on't 1667. **6.** The poetical or r. accounts of these last Gaulish invasions 1842. Hence **Roma·nceless** *a.* unromantic. **†Roma·ncial** *a.* (*rare*) 1653. **Roma·ncical** *a.* (*rare*) of the nature of r., composing or inventing romances 1656. **†Roma·ncy** *a.* romantic 1654–82.

Romance (romæ·ns), *v.* 1671. [f. the sb.] **a.** *intr.* To exaggerate or invent after the fashion of romances; to talk hyperbolically. **b.** To have romantic ideas; to use romantic language 1849.

a. Now, when, for the first time, they told the truth, they were supposed to be romancing MACAULAY.

Romancer (romæ·nsəɹ). ME. [f. ROMANCE *v.* + -ER[1]. In XIV – OFr.] **1.** The author of a romance; a writer of romances or romantic fiction. **2.** One who deals in extravagant fictions; an inventor of false history; a fantastic liar 1663.

Romancist (romæ·nsist). 1656. [f. ROMANCE + -IST. In XVII perh. – Sp. *romancista.*] A composer of romances; a romantic novelist.

Romanesque (rō^{u}măne·sk), *a.* (and *sb.*) 1715. [– Fr. *romanesque*, f. *roman* ROMANCE; see -ESQUE.] **1.** = ROMANCE *sb.* I. b. **2.** *Arch.* Prevalent in, or distinctive of, the buildings erected in Romanized Europe between the close of the classical period and the rise of Gothic architecture 1819. **b.** Built in the Romanesque style 1830. **c.** Characterized by the use or prevalence of the Romanesque style 1850. **d.** *absol.* as *sb.* The Romanesque style of art or architecture 1830.

2. b. The three great R. cathedrals 1830. **c.** The later R. period 1850.

Romanic (romæ·nik), *a.* (and *sb.*) 1708. [– L. *Romanicus*, f. *Romanus* ROMAN; see -IC.] **1.** Of languages: Descended from Latin; Romance. **b.** *absol.* as *sb.* = ROMANCE *sb.* I. a. 1708. **2.** Derived or descended from the Romans; belonging to the Romance peoples 1847.

Romanish (rō^{u}·măniʃ), *a.* and *sb.* OE. [In sense 1 f. L. *Romanus* + -ISH[1] 1; in later uses f. ROMAN *sb.* or *a.*] **†1.** = ROMAN *a.* I. 1. –ME. **2.** = ROMISH *a.* 1. 1591. **3.** *absol.* as *sb.* = ROMANSH 1689.

Romanism (rō^{u}·măniz'm). 1674. [f. ROMAN *a.* + -ISM.] **1.** *trans* religion or doctrines, Roman Catholicism. **2.** A feature of Roman architecture 1827. **3.** Roman institutions; the prevailing spirit of the Roman world; Roman sway or influence 1877.

Romanist (rō^{u}·mănist), *sb.* (and *a.*). 1523. [– mod.L. *Romanista* (Luther); see ROMAN *a.*, -IST.] **1.** A member or adherent of the Church of Rome; a Roman Catholic. **b.** *attrib.* or as *adj.* Belonging or adhering to the Church of Rome 1635. **2.** One who is versed in or practises Roman Law; a lawyer of the Roman school 1647. **3.** A student of Roman antiquities 1858. **4.** One who makes a special study of Romance languages or philology 1886.

Romanize (rō^{u}·mănəiz), *v.* 1607. [f. ROMAN *a.* + -IZE, or f. Fr. *romaniser.*] **1.** *trans.* To render Roman in character; to bring under the influence or authority of Rome. **2.** *intr.* To follow Roman custom or practice; to accept the principles of Roman law 1629. **b.** To follow, tend towards, or go over to, the Church of Rome; to become Roman Catholic 1637.

2. b. So apishly Romanizing, that the word of command still was set downe in Latine MILT. Hence **Ro:maniza·tion. Ro·manizer.**

Romano- (romē^{i}·no), used as comb. form of ROMAN *a.*, as *Romano-Celtic*, etc.

Romansh (roma·nʃ), *sb.* and *a.* 1663. [– the native name *Rum-*, *Roman(t)sch*, *-on(t)sch* :– med.L. *romanice* adv.; see ROMANCE.] The language, of Latin origin, spoken in the Grisons or eastern district of Switzerland. Also *attrib.* or as *adj.*

Romantic (romæ·ntik), *a.* and *sb.* 1659. [f. *romant*, early var. of ROMAUNT + -IC.] **A.** *adj.* **1.** Of the nature of or having the qualities of romance in respect of form or content. **b.** *Mus.* Characterized by the subordination of form to theme, and by imagination and passion 1885. **2.** Of a fabulous or fictitious character; having no foundation in fact 1667. **†b.** Imaginary; purely ideal –1711. **3.** Of projects, etc.: Fantastic, extravagant, quixotic; going beyond what is rational or practical 1671. **4.** Having a tendency towards romance; readily influenced by the imagination 1690. **b.** Tending towards or characterized by romance as a basis or principle of literature or art. (Opp. to *classical.*) 1754. **5.** Marked by or invested with romance or imaginative appeal 1666.

1. It was a step in my advance towards r. composition SCOTT. **2.** These things are almost romantique, and yet true PEPYS. **3.** The r. and visionary scheme of building a bridge over the river at Putney 1671. **4.** I am not r.;—I have not the least design of doing good to either of you 1778. **b.** *R. movement*, the movement in literature (and art) originating in a revolt against the formalities and conventions of classicism, and characterized in the 19th c. by conscious preoccupation with the subjective and imaginative aspects of nature and life. **5.** You feel that armour is r., because it is a beautiful dress, and you are not used to it RUSKIN. The grandest and most r. character that Israel ever produced, Elijah the Tishbite 1856. Hence **Roma·ntical** *a.* 1678, **-ly** *adv.* 1668. **Roma·nticize** *v. trans.* to render r. in character; *intr.* to indulge in romance. **Roma·ntic-ly** *adv.* 1681, **-ness.**

B. *sb.* **1.** A feature, characteristic, idea, etc., belonging to, or suggestive of, romance 1679. **2.** A romantic person; *esp.* an adherent of romanticism in literature 1865.

Romanticism (romæ·ntisiz'm). 1803. [f. prec. + -ISM.] **1.** A romantic fancy or idea. **2.** Tendency towards romance or romantic views 1840. **3.** The distinctive qualities or spirit of the romantic school in art, literature, and music 1844.

3. Stein belonged to the class of society which naturally furnished recruits to R. 1878. So **Roma·nticist,** an adherent of r. (sense 3).

Romany (rǫ·măni), *sb.* and *a.* Also **Rommany,** etc. 1812. [Gipsy *Romani*, fem. and pl. of *Romano* adj., f. *Rom* gipsy; see ROM.] **1.** A gipsy; also *collect.* the gipsies. **2.** The language of the gipsies 1812. **3.** *attrib.* or as *adj.* = GIPSY 4. 1841.

Romaunt (romǭ·nt), *sb.* and *a.* *arch.* 1530. [– OFr. *roma(u)nt*, (later *roman*), deduced (as if an oblique case) from *roma(u)nz* ROMANCE.] **1.** A romance; a romantic tale or poem. **2.** A Romance form of speech; also *attrib.*, Romance, Romanic, in respect of language 1530.

1. The Romante of the Rose PALSGR. There are the minstrels, with their romaunts and ballads SCOTT.

Rombowline (rʊmbō^{u}·lin). Also **r(h)um-.** 1841. [Of unkn. origin.] *Naut.* Condemned canvas, rope, etc. used for temporary purposes not requiring strength.

Rome (rō^{u}m), *sb.* Also **†Roome.** OE. [– L. *Roma* and (O)Fr. *Rome.* Pronounced (rūm) by some as late as XIX.] **1.** The city or state of Rome; the Roman empire. Freq. personified. **2.** The city of Rome as the original capital of Western Christendom, and the seat of the Pope; hence, the Roman Catholic Church, its influence or institutions, etc. late ME.

1. Theym that founded roome CAXTON. R... has been the source of law and government 1841. 2. King Iohn hath reconcil'd Himselfe to R. SHAKS.

Romeine (rōᵘ·mein). 1849. [Named after the crystallographer *Romé de L'Isle*; see -INE⁵.] *Min.* A native antimoniate of calcium occurring in yellow crystals. Also **Ro·meite.**

Ro·me-penny. Now *Hist.* OE. [f. ROME *sb.* 2 + PENNY. Cf. AL. *pecunia Romana* (XI).] = PETER('S)-PENNY.

Ro·me-scot. Now *Hist.* OE. [See ROME *sb.* 2 and SCOT *sb.* Cf. AL. *romascot* (XII), *rom(e)scotum* (XIII).] = ROME-PENNY.

Romeward (rōᵘ·mwǫ̆ɹd), *adv.* and *a.* ME. [-WARD.] 1. Towards or in the direction of Rome. 2. Towards the Roman Catholic Church or Roman Catholicism 1864. 3. as *adj.* Directed to or tending towards the Roman Catholic Church 1851.

3. His distinct repudiation of R. doctrine 1887. So **Ro·mewards** *adv.*

Romic (rōᵘ·mik), *a.* and *sb.* 1877. [f. ROMAN *a.* + -IC.] The name of a system of phonetic notation devised by Dr. Henry Sweet.

This system, which I call 'Romic' (because based on the original Roman value of the letters) SWEET.

Romish (rōᵘ·miʃ), *a.* 1531. [f. ROME + -ISH¹, prob. after Du. *Roomsch*, G. *Römisch.*] 1. Belonging, pertaining, or adhering to Rome in respect of religion; Roman Catholic. (Chiefly *hostile.*) †2. = ROMAN *a.* 1. –1797.

1. Upon promise of the Duke to become R. MILT. Hence **Ro·mish-ly** *adv.*, **-ness.**

Romp (rǫmp), *sb.* 1706. [perh. alt. of RAMP *sb.*¹] 1. One who romps; *esp.* a play-loving, lively, merry girl (or woman). 2. A piece of lively, boisterous play; a merry frolic. Freq. in *pl.* 1734.

2. My little rogue soon engaged him in a r. 1797. Hence **Ro·mpish,** *a.* inclined to romp.

Romp (rǫmp), *v.* 1709. [perh. alt. of RAMP *v.*¹, with modification of sense.] 1. *intr.* To play, sport, or frolic in a very lively, merry, or boisterous manner. 2. Chiefly *Racing slang*: **a.** To move, cover the ground, easily and rapidly 1891. **b.** To get *in* (or *home*), to win a race, prize or contest with the greatest ease 1888.

2. b. Eclipse..romped in, the easiest of winners 1888.

†**Rompee.** 1610. [Alteration of Fr. *rompu* (pa. pple. of *rompre*) after heraldic terms in *-ee.*] *Her.* Broken –1728.

Romper (rǫmpəɹ). 1922. [f. ROMP *v.* + -ER¹.] Chiefly *pl.* A washable overall worn by small children to protect their clothes.

Ro·mping, *ppl. a.* 1711. [f. ROMP *v.* + -ING.²] 1. Of persons: That romps; engaged in, or given to, romping. 2. Of actions etc.: Having the character of a romp or romps 1802. Hence **Ro·mpingly** *adv.*

‖**Roncador** (rǫŋkădōᵊɹ). *U.S.* 1882. [Sp., agent-n. f. *roncar* snore, snort.] One or other of several sciænoid fishes of the Pacific coast of N. America.

‖**Rondache** (rǫndæ·ʃ, Fr. rondaʃ). 1604. [Fr. *rondache*, †*rondace*, f. *rond* ROUND *a.*] 1. A small circular shield or buckler. †2. *transf.* A foot-soldier –1646.

Ronde (rǫnd). 1838. [– Fr. *ronde*, fem. of *rond* ROUND *a.*] *Typog.* A form of type imitating handwriting.

‖**Rondeau** (rǫ·ndo, Fr. rondo). 1525. [(O)Fr., later form of *rondel* (see next). Cf. ROUNDEL.] 1. A short poem, consisting of ten, or in stricter sense of thirteen, lines, having only two rhymes throughout, and with the opening words used twice as a refrain; *transf.* a refrain. 2. *Mus.* = RONDO 1773.

Rondel (rǫ·ndĕl). ME. [– OFr. *rondel* (later *rondeau*), f. *rond* ROUND *a.*; see prec., -EL. Cf. ROUNDEL.] 1. A circle; a circular object. Now *arch.* †**b.** *Fortif.* A round tower –1704. 2. A rondeau, or a special form of this. late ME.

2. With Charles d'Orléans, the r. took the distinct shape..of fourteen lines on two rhymes 1887.

‖**Rondeletia** (rǫndĕlī·ʃⁱă). 1771. [mod.L., after the French naturalist *Rondelet*; see -IA¹.] 1. A tropical American genus of *Cinchonaceæ*; a plant or shrub of this genus. 2. A perfume resembling that which is characteristic of this genus of plants 1840.

‖**Rondo** (rǫ·ndo). 1797. [It. – Fr. RONDEAU.] *Mus.* 1. A piece of music having one principal subject, to which a return is twice made after the introduction of other matter. 2. = ROUND *sb.*¹ IV. 1 b.

Rondure (rǫ·ndiŭɹ). 1600. [– Fr. *rondeur*, with ending assim. to -URE.] A circle or round object; roundness.

All things rare, That heauens ayre in this huge r. hems SHAKS.

Röntgen (rö·ntyĕn). 1896. Name of a German scientist (Prof. Conrad W. *Röntgen*), used attrib. in *R. rays* (see RAY *sb.*¹.) Hence **Rö·ntgenism,** morbid condition induced by R. rays. **Rö·ntgenize** *v. trans.* to discharge electricity through gases by means of R. rays. **Rö·ntgenogram,** a photograph taken by R. rays. **Röntgeno·graphy,** photography by R. rays. **Röntgeno·logy,** the study of R. rays. **Röntgeno·scopy,** observation by means of R. rays. **Rö:ntgeno-the·rapy,** healing by means of R. rays.

Rood (rūd), *sb.* [In branch I, OE. *rōd* = OFris. *rōd(e*, OS. *rōda*, OIcel. *róða*, *-i* (perh. from OE.); in branch II the Continental forms are OS. *rōda*, (M)Du. *ro(o)de* (also mod. *roede*), OHG. *ruota* (G. *rute*).] I. †1. = CROSS *sb.* 1. –late ME. 2. The cross upon which Christ suffered; the cross as the symbol of the Christian faith. Now *arch.* OE. **b.** In asseverations, *by the r.!* etc. Now *arch.* ME. 3. A crucifix, *esp.* one stationed above the middle of a rood-screen; also *rarely*, a figure of the cross in wood or metal, as a religious object OE.

2. Good hope I have Of help from Him that died upon the r. MORRIS. **b.** By the r.! they are wise enough 1896. See also HOLY ROOD (DAY).

attrib. and *Comb.*: **r.-beam,** a transverse beam supporting the r., usu. forming the head of a r.-screen; **-cloth,** a cloth used to cover the crucifix over the r.-screen during Lent; **-loft,** a loft or gallery forming the head of a r.-screen; **-screen,** a screen, properly surmounted by a r. crossing the nave of a church beneath the chancel-arch and separating the nave from the choir; **-steeple, -tower,** the tower or steeple built over the intersection of the body and cross-aisles of a church; †**-tree.** = sense 2.

II. 1. As a linear measure: A rod, pole, or perch. Now only *local*, and varying from 6 to 8 yards. OE. 2. A superficial measure of land, properly containing 40 square poles or perches, but varying locally; a plot of land of this size OE. **b.** A measure (of land, paving, building, etc.) corresponding to a square pole or perch, but with local and other variation 1464.

Roo·d day. *Hist.* ME. [ROOD *sb.* 2.] The Exaltation of the Cross (14 Sept.), or the Invention of the Cross (3 May).

Roof (rūf), *sb.* [OE. *hrōf* = OFris. *hrōf*, (M)LG. *rōf*, MDu. *roof* (Du. *roef* cabin, coffin lid), ON. *hróf* boat shed, of which no certain cognates are known.] 1. The outside upper covering of a house or other building; also, the ceiling of a room or other covered part of a house, building, etc. **b.** Used by extension to denote a house or chamber. Chiefly *poet.* 1591. 2. *fig.* **a.** The highest point or summit of something; that which completes or covers in OE. **b.** Something which in form or function is comparable to the covering of a house 1611. **c.** *Mining.* The stratum lying immediately over a bed of coal; the top of a working or gallery 1686. 3. *The roof of the mouth*, the palate. Also *ellipt.* So of other parts of the body, etc. OE. 4. The top of a carriage, coach, etc. 1706.

1. Among the ancients, in those countries where it seldom rained, roofs were made quite flat 1815. For about two years they lived..under the r. of their father's youngest sister 1888. **b.** *A. Y. L.* II. iii. 17. 2. This most excellent Canopy the Ayre ..this Maiesticall Roofe SHAKS. Why should we only toil, the r. and crown of things? TENNYSON. 4. The r. of a crazy coach 1806.

attrib. and *Comb.*: **r.-cat,** an Indian species of cat; **-garden,** a garden or collection of plants in large pots, etc., on the (flat) r. of a house or other building; **-mask,** an outer r. which protects the inner r. from the weather; **-swell,** a variety of organ swell. Hence **Roo·fage,** the material of a r.; roofing. **Roo·fless** *a.* **Roo·fy** *a.* furnished with a r.; abounding in roofs.

Roof (rūf), *v.* 1475. [f. prec.] 1. *trans.* To provide or cover with a roof. Also with *in*, *over.* 2. To be or form, to lie as, a roof over (something). Also with *in.* 1615. **b.** To shelter, house 1820.

1. Ancient Roman buildings..roofed with either vaults or arches ADDISON. 2. As thunder-clouds that..Roof'd the world with doubt and fear TENNYSON. Hence **Roo·fer,** (*a*) one who constructs or repairs roofs; (*b*) a letter of thanks for entertainment sent by a departed visitor.

Roofed (rūft), *ppl. a.* 1500. [f. ROOF *v.* or *sb.* + -ED.] 1. Having a roof; covered with or as with a roof; also with *in, over.* 2. In combs. denoting a particular kind of roof 1600.

1. Here had we now our Countries Honor, roof'd, Were the grac'd person of our Banquo present SHAKS. 2. Their houses are flat-rooffed HAKLUYT.

Roo·fing, (*vbl.*) *sb.* 1440. [f. ROOF *sb.* or *v.* + -ING¹.] 1. The act of covering with a roof; material used or suitable for roofs; that which forms a roof or roofs. 2. *Mining.* The wedging of the top of the loaded skip against the top of an underground passage 1747.

1. The hovel was of mud-walls, without any r. 1760.

Roo·f-tree. 1440. [f. ROOF *sb.* + TREE *sb.* 3.] The main beam or ridge-pole of a roof.

Ye have riven the thack off seven cottar houses —look if your ain r.-tree stand the faster SCOTT.

‖**Rooinek** (rōᵘ·inek). 1897. [S. Afr. Du. (= Du. *rood-e* red + *nek* neck).] A British or European immigrant in S. Africa; in the Boer War, a British soldier.

Rook (ruk), *sb.*¹ [OE. *hrōc* = (M)LG. *rōk*, MDu. *roec* (Du. *roek*), OHG. *hruoh*, ON. *hrókr* :– Gmc. **χrokaz*, prob. of imit. origin.] 1. A black raucous-voiced European and Asiatic bird (*Corvus frugilegus*), nesting in colonies; in the north of Britain usu. called a *crow.* 2. Applied to persons as an abusive or disparaging term 1508. **b.** A cheat, swindler, or sharper, *spec.* in gaming 1577. †**c.** A gull, a simpleton –1637.

1. A blackening train Of clamorous rooks thick urge their weary flight THOMSON. 2. Rakish rooks like Rob Mossgiel BURNS.

Comb.: **r.-pie,** a pie made with (young) rooks; **-rifle,** a rifle of small bore for shooting rooks. Hence **Roo·ky** *a.* full of, abounding in, consisting of, rooks.

Rook (ruk), *sb.*² [ME. *rok, roke* – OFr. *roc(k, rok*, f. (ult.) Arab. *rukk*, of uncertain orig. meaning.] *Chess.* One of four pieces which at the beginning of the game are set in the corner squares, and have the power of moving in a right line backward, forwards, or laterally over any number of unoccupied squares; a castle. Hence **Rook** *v.*² *intr.* to castle.

Rook (ruk), *v.*¹ 1590. [f. ROOK *sb.*¹ 2 b.] 1. *trans.* To cheat; to defraud by cheating, *esp.* in gaming; to charge extortionately. Chiefly *slang* or *colloq.* †2. To take by cheating –1695. †3. *intr.* To practise cheating –1693.

1. Drawn in by guinea-droppers, and rook'd of forty guineas and a watch 1710.

Rookery (ru·kəri). 1725. [f. ROOK *sb.*¹ + -ERY.] 1. A collection of rooks' nests in a clump of trees; a colony of rooks. 2. A breeding-place, common resort, or large colony (of sea-birds, *esp.* penguins, also of seals or other marine mammals) 1838. 3. A cluster of mean tenements densely populated by people of the lowest class 1829.

1. The many-winter'd crow that leads the clanging r. home TENNYSON. 3. Market Street,..a well-known r. of prostitutes 1851.

Room (rūm, rum), *sb.* [OE. *rūm* = OFris. OS., OHG., ON., Goth, *rūm* (Du. *ruim*, G. *raum*), subst. use of Gmc. **rūmaz* spacious (see next), f. **ru-*, which has been connected with L. *rus, ruris* country. For the vocalism cf. *cooper, droop*, etc.] I. 1. Space; dimensional extent. 2. Sufficient space; accommodation. Also const. *for*, or *to* with infin. OE. 3. *To make r.*: †**a.** To clear a space for oneself –1535. **b.** To make way, yield place, draw back or retire, so as to allow a person to enter, etc. So *to give r.*, and with imperative suppressed. late ME. **c.** To provide or obtain space or place for something by the removal of other things 1666. 4. *transf.* and *fig.*

Opportunity or scope *to* do something OE. **b.** Opportunity or scope *for* something, by which it is rendered possible 1692.

1. Both Labour and R. was saved by their repeated Contractions 1699. **2.** Syt nye together, yt I maye haue rowme COVERDALE *Isa.* 49:20. Phrases. *No r. to turn in, no r. to swing a cat*, implying extremely restricted space. **b.** Is there roome in thy fathers house for vs to lodge in? *Gen.* 24:23. **b.** Make roome and let him stand before our face SHAKS. Roome for Antony, most Noble Antony SHAKS. **4.** R. to deny ourselves KEBLE. **b.** As to most of the provisions there was little r. for dispute MACAULAY. Phr. *R. for improvement*, implying a state of affairs not entirely satisfactory.

II. 1. A particular portion of space; a certain space or area ME. †**2.** A particular place or spot, without ref. to its area –1674. **3.** An interior portion of a building divided off by walls or partitions; *esp.* a chamber or apartment in a dwelling-house 1457. **b.** *pl.* Lodgings 1837. **c.** The persons assembled in a room; the company 1712. **4.** In various techn. applications; *esp.* one of the passages or spaces for working left between the pillars of a coal-mine. Chiefly in phr. *pillar and r.* 1789.

1. A journal of the weather..which exhibits in a little r., a great train of different observations JOHNSON. *R. and space* (Shipbuilding) is the distance from the edge of one timber to the corresponding edge of the timber next to it; *space* being the distance between the two timbers and *R.* the width of a timber 1846. **3.** The rooms of the cottage were low 1891. **b.** I trust I shall have the pleasure of seeing you and your friend at my rooms DICKENS.

III. 1. †**a.** A particular place assigned or appropriated to a person or thing –1721. **b.** Contrasted with *company* 1577. †**2.** An office, function, appointment; a post, situation, employment –1644. **3.** An office or post considered as pertaining to a particular person; *esp.* by right or by inheritance. *Obs.* exc. in phrases. 1450.

1. b. I'd rather have his r. than his company 1880. **2.** He..forsooke a right worshipfull roome when it was offered him CAMDEN. **3.** *In one's r.*, in one's place, denoting substitution of one person or thing for another. *In the r. of*, in the place (†or office) *of*, in lieu *of*, instead *of*. Hence **Roo·mage** *U.S.*, space; internal capacity; accommodation. **Roo·mful,** as much or as many as a r. will hold. **Roo·mful** *a.* capacious, roomy. **Roo·mless** *a.* (*rare*).

†**Room,** *a. Obs.* exc. *Sc.* [OE. *rūm* = OFris. *rūm*, MDu. *ruum* (Du. *ruim*), (M)LG. *rūm*, OHG. *rūmi*, ON. *rúmr*, Goth. *rums* :– Gmc. **rūmaz* spacious; see prec.] Spacious, large; wide, extensive –1635.

Ther was no rommer herberwe in the place CHAUCER. Hence †**Roo·msome** *a.* ample, capacious, roomy.

Room (rūm, rum), *v. U.S.* 1828. [f. ROOM *sb.*] **a.** *intr.* To occupy rooms as a lodger; to share a room or rooms *with* another. **b.** *trans.* To accommodate or lodge (guests) 1864.

a. She rooms with me, and is very interesting and agreeable 1828. Hence **Roo·mer** *U.S.*, a lodger who occupies a room or rooms without board.

Roomed (rūmd), *a.* 1548. [f. ROOM *sb.* + -ED².] With defining word prefixed: Having rooms of a specified number or kind, as *one-, double-r*; also *wide-r.*, †spacious.

Roo·m-mate. *U.S.* 1838. One who occupies the same room or rooms with another.

Roomth (rūmþ). Now *dial.* 1504. [f. ROOM *a.* + -TH¹.] **1.** Space; *esp.* ample or unconfined space 1540. †**2.** An office, function, or dignity –1604. †**b.** *In the r. of*, in the place of, instead *of*. Also with possessives. –1625. Hence **Roo·mthy** *a.* (now *dial.*), roomy.

Roomy (rū·mi), *a.* 1627. [f. ROOM *sb.* + -Y¹.] **1.** Of ample dimensions; capacious, large; wide. **2.** Of female animals: Of large proportions internally 1796.

1. This makes a Ship more r. 1627. Hence **Roo·mily** *adv.* **Roo·miness.**

Roop (rūp). 1674. [var. of ROUP *sb.*³] Hoarseness; a hoarse note or sound. Hence **Roo·py** *a.* (chiefly *dial.*), hoarse.

Roorback (rūə·ɹbæk). *U.S.* Also **-bach.** 1864. [A fictitious personal name.] A false report or slander invented for political purposes.

Roosa, rusa (rū·să). 1853. [Hindi *rúsá.*] *R. grass*, an Indian grass (*Andropogon schœnanthus* or *Cymbopogon martini*), from which *r. oil* is distilled.

Roost (rūst), *sb.*¹ [OE. *hrōst* = MDu., Du. *roest*, and perh. OS. *hrōst* spars of a roof; of unkn. origin.] A perch for domestic fowls; also *gen.* a perching- or resting-place of a bird. **b.** A hen-house, or that part of one in which the fowls perch at night 1580. **c.** A collection or number *of* fowls, etc., such as may occupy a roost 1827. **d.** *fig.* A resting-place; a lodging, bed 1858.

Sooner than the matin-bell was rung, He clapp'd his wings upon his r., and sung DRYDEN. Phrases. *To go*, etc., *to r.*; also *fig.* of persons: to retire to rest. *At r.*, roosting, perched. *To take r.*, to perch. *To come home to r.*, to recoil upon the originator.

attrib.: **r.-cock** (now *rare*), a domestic cock. Hence **Roo·ster** (chiefly *U.S.* and *dial.*), a cock; also *transf.* of persons.

Roost (rūst), *sb.*² 1654. [– ON. *rǫst.*] A tumultuous tidal race formed by the meeting of conflicting currents off various parts of the Orkney and Shetland Islands.

Roost (rūst), *v.* 1530. [f. ROOST *sb.*¹] **1.** Of birds: To settle on a perch or the like for sleep or rest; to settle for sleep, go to rest. **b.** Of persons: To seat oneself, to perch. *colloq.* 1816. **2.** To lodge, harbour. In mod. use: To pass the night. 1593. **3.** *trans.* To afford a resting-place to (a person) 1845.

1. On the cliff-side the pigeons R. deep in the rocks M. ARNOLD. Phr. *To rule the r.*: see ROAST *sb.*¹ **2.** Stopped to r. at Terracina 1855.

Root (rūt), *sb.* [Late OE. *rōt* – ON. *rót* :– Scand. **wrōt-*, obscurely rel. to L. *radix* root, *ramus* branch, and OE. *wyrt* (see WORT¹).] **I. 1.** That part of a plant or tree which is normally below the earth's surface; in *Bot.*, the descending axis of a plant, tree, or shoot, developed from the radicle, and serving to attach the plant to and convey nourishment from the soil, with or without subsidiary rootlets or fibres; also applied to the corresponding organ of an epiphyte, and to the rootlets attaching ivy to its support. **2.** The permanent underground stock of a plant from which the stems or leaves are periodically produced; also, by extension, a plant, herb ME. **3.** The underground part of a plant used for eating or in medicine; now *spec.* in *Agric.*, one of a fleshy nature, as the turnip or carrot, and, by extension, any plant of this kind OE. **4. a.** The imbedded or basal portion of the hair, tongue, teeth, fingers, nails, etc. ME. **b.** The more or less 'muddy' base of a crystal or gem. esp. of an emerald 1695. **c.** That part of anything by which it is united to something else 1632. **5.** The bottom or base *of* something material; *esp.* the foot of a hill. late ME.

1. Phr. *By the root(s*, denoting the complete pulling up of a plant or tree. *To take r.*, to settle properly in the ground. **3.** Very few turnips are with us this season; this r. having generally failed 1801.

II. 1. The source or origin *of* some quality, condition, tendency, etc. Also occas. without const. ME. **2.** A source of some quality, etc.; *esp.* a virtue or vice giving rise to some condition or action ME. **3.** A person or family forming the source of a lineage, kindred, or line of descendants ME. **b.** A scion, offshoot. (Chiefly Biblical.) ME. **4.** That upon or by which a person or thing is established or supported; the basis upon which anything rests ME. **5.** The bottom or real basis, the inner or essential part, of anything. late ME. **6.** *To take, strike r.*, to obtain a permanent footing or hold; to settle down *in* a place, etc. 1535.

1. The r. of all this ill is prelacy SHELLEY. **2.** Faith, the r. whence only can arise The graces of a life that wins the skies COWPER. **3.** It was saide.. that my selfe should be the Roote, and Father Of many Kings SHAKS. **b.** In that day there shall bee a roote of Iesse, which shall stand for an ensigne of the people *Isa.* 11:10. **4.** A high wind under a cloudless sky..seems to have no r. in the constitution of things STEVENSON. **5.** His resolute desire to get at the r. of things SWINBURNE. *The r. of the matter*, a literal rendering of Heb. *šōreš dābār* in Job 19:28. **6.** The idea struck r. 1899. Phr. *Root and branch*: see BRANCH *sb.*; in advb. use: Completely, utterly; also in attrib. use of persons and things.

III. 1. *Math.* **a.** A number, quantity, or dimension, which, when multiplied by itself a requisite number of times, produces a given expression. *Cube* (or *third*) *r.*: see CUBE *sb.* 2. *Square* (or *second*) *r.*: see SQUARE *a.* I. 1. **b.** The value or each of the values of an unknown quantity which will satisfy a given equation 1728. **2.** *Philol.* One of those ultimate elements of a language that cannot be further analysed, and form the base of its vocabulary. †**b.** A primary word or form from which others are derived. 1530. **3.** *Mus.* The fundamental note of a chord; the note on which the harmonics are based, and which gives its name to the chord 1811.

2. Sharon, a name of the same r. as that used to designate the table-lands beyond the Jordan STANLEY. **b.** It is a fault only in the declension and the roots of the words continue untouch'd STERNE.

attrib. and *Comb.*: **r.-beer** *U.S.*, a beverage prepared from roots; **-climber,** a plant which climbs by the aid of rootlets developed on the stem; **-form,** (*a*) a basal or primitive form (of something); (*b*) an insect form which infests roots; **-house,** (*a*) an ornamental building made principally of tree-roots, esp. in a garden; (*b*) a house or barn for storing roots; **-leaf,** a radical leaf; **-position** *Mus.*, that position of a chord in which the r. is the lowest note; **-run,** the space over which the roots of a plant extend. Hence **Roo·tery,** a pile formed of tree-roots with interspersed soil for the ornamental growing of garden-plants; cf. ROCKERY. **Roo·tless** *a.* without roots; destitute of roots. **Roo·tling** = ROOTLET 1.

Root (rūt), *v.*¹ ME. [f. ROOT *sb.*] **I. 1.** *trans.* To furnish with roots; to fix or establish firmly; to implant deeply, attach strongly. Const. *in, into, to*, etc. **2.** *intr.* Of plants: To take or strike root 1440. **b.** *fig.* To take root; to settle, establish oneself. Freq. with *in.* ME. **c.** To have a basis *in* something 1882.

1. Amazement roots me to the ground DRYDEN. **2.** A tender plant, that will scarce r. in stiff or rocky ground 1673. **b.** The small continuous vices, which r. under ground and honeycomb the soul 1869.

II. 1. *trans.* To pull, tear, drag, or dig *up* by the roots; to uproot. late ME. **2.** To pull, dig, or take *out* by the roots; hence *fig.*, to extirpate, exterminate, destroy 1450. **3. a.** To clear *away* completely. late ME. **b.** To drag, tear, remove by force, *from* a place 1567. **c.** Without const. To uproot, outroot 1582. **4.** To lop the roots or rootlets from 1844.

1. The Lord..shall r. vp Israel out of this good land, which hee gaue to their fathers 1 *Kings* 14:15. **2.** To r. out popular Errors ADDISON. **3. b.** To see thy brother's seede Ruin'd, and rent, and rooted from the earth 1624.

Root (rūt), *v.*² 1538. [Later var. of *wroot*, OE. *wrōtan* = (M)LG. *wrōten*, (M)Du. *wroeten*, OHG. *ruozzen*, ON. *róta* (partly the immed. source), rel. to OE. *wrōt*, LG. *wrōte* snout, G. (with instr. suffix) *rüssel* snout, and perh. ult. to L. *rodere* gnaw.] **1.** *intr.* Of swine: To turn up the soil by grubbing with the snout; to dig with the snout in search of food. Also *transf.* of certain fishes, worms, etc. **b.** *dial.* To poke about, rummage; to pry or poke *into* a thing, to lounge or idle about 1831. **c.** *U.S. slang.* To be active *for* another by giving support, encouragement, or applause 1895. **2.** *trans.* To turn over, dig up, with the snout. Also *fig.*, to search *out*, hunt *up*. 1592. Hence **Roo·ter**² (*rare*).

1. d. *Root, hog, or die* (U.S.), used of or addressed to persons, implying the necessity of labour or exertion to maintain life or prosperity 1834.

Rooted (rū·tėd), *ppl. a.* late ME. [f. ROOT *v.*¹ and *sb.* + -ED.] **1.** Having roots; furnished with roots 1557. **2.** Planted in the ground; attached or fixed by roots; firmly implanted; having taken root. late ME. **b.** *transf.* Of habits, opinions, etc. 1526. **c.** Of maladies: Deep-seated, chronic 1744. **3.** Torn *up* by the roots 1797.

2. There was nevere r. tre, That stod so faste GOWER. **b.** Can'st thou not..Plucke from the Memory a r. Sorrow? SHAKS. A..r. dislike to the society of women 1883. Hence **Roo·ted-ly** *adv.*, **-ness.**

Rooter¹ (rū·təɹ). 1560. [f. ROOT *v.*¹ or *sb.* + -ER¹.] **1.** An extirpator, eradicator, uprooter (*of* something). Usu. const. *out, up.* **2.** *spec.* A 'root-and-branch' man. Now *Hist.* 1642.

Rootlet (rū·tlėt). 1793. [f. ROOT *sb.* + -LET.] **1.** A branch of the root of a plant; a subsidiary root. **2.** *Malting.* The radicle of a steeped grain. Also *collect.* 1830. **3.** *Anat.* A slender branch or fibre of some structure, such as a vein or nerve 1875.

Roo·t-stock. 1832. [f. ROOT *sb.*] **1.** *Bot.* A rhizome; a stem that grows entirely underground; a creeping stem. **2.** A source from which offshoots have arisen; a primitive form 1877.

Rooty (rū·ti), *a.* 1483. [f. ROOT *sb.* + -Y[1].] Abounding in, full of, or consisting of roots. Hence **Roo·tiness.**

Rope (rōᵘp), *sb.*[1] [OE. *rāp* = OFris. *rāp*, (M)LG. *rēp*, (M)Du. *reep*, (O)HG. *reif*, ON. *reip*, Goth. *raip* (in *skaudaraip* shoe-thong) :- Gmc. **raipaz*, *-am* (adopted in Finnish as *raippa* rod, twig).] **I. 1.** A length of strong and stout line or cordage, usu. made of twisted strands of hemp, flax, or other fibrous material, but also of strips of hide, pliant twigs, metal wire, etc. **b.** Without article, as a material 1769. **2.** In special uses: **a.** A stout line used for measuring; a sounding line; hence, in later use, a certain measure of length, esp. for walling or hedging. Now *local*. Also *r.-length*. OE. **b.** = Tight-rope 1620. **c.** *pl.* The cords marking off a prize-ring or other enclosed space 1854. **3.** A cord for hanging a person; a halter; the hangman's cord ME. †**b.** As an allusive or derisive cry –1663.

1. b. The strength of Manilla r. is less than that of hemp r. 1876. **3. b.** 1 *Hen. VI*, I. iii. 53.

Phrases. *To give a person r.* (*enough*, or *plenty of r.*), to allow him free scope or action, esp. in order that he may commit himself. *To come to the end of one's r.*, to be finally checked in wrong-doing. *To know the ropes*, to understand the way to do something; to know all the dodges; so *to learn, put one up to, the ropes*. *On the high ropes*: see HIGH *a.* II. Phrases. *On the r.* (of mountaineers) roped together.

II. 1. A rope-like structure; a thing having the elongated form of a rope or cord. late ME. **2.** A number *of* onions, etc., strung or plaited together 1469. **b.** A (thick) string *of* pearls. Also *ellipt.* 1630. **3.** A viscid or gelatinous stringy formation in beer, etc. 1747.

1. Phr. *A r. of sand*, something having no coherence or binding power; Like ropes of sand..doe these things hang together 1624. **2. b.** Rubies, sapphires, And ropes of orient pearl MASSINGER.

attrib. and *Comb.*: **r.-drill,** a form of military drill in which a stretched r. is used to represent part of a company; **-ferry,** a ferry worked by a r.; **r. ladder,** a ladder made of two long pieces of r. connected at intervals by pieces of r., wood, or metal; **-pump,** a pump consisting of a r. rapidly revolving over two pulleys, one of which is at the top and the other in the water of the well; **-walk,** a stretch of ground appropriated to the making of ropes; **-walker,** a r.-dancer. Hence **Ro·pish** *a.* somewhat ropy; tending to ropiness.

Rope (rōᵘp), *sb.*[2] Now *dial.* [OE. *rop* (*hrop*), = MDu. *rop*, of uncertain relationship.] A gut, entrail, intestine. Freq. in *pl.*

Rope (rōᵘp), *v.* ME. [f. ROPE *sb.*[1]] **1.** *trans.* To tie, bind, fasten, or secure with a rope. Also with *up*. **b.** In mountaineering, to attach (persons) to each other by means of a rope for greater safety 1862. **c.** To assist with ropes 1890. **2.** To enclose or mark off (a certain space) with a rope. Usu. const. *in, off, out, round*. 1738. **3.** *Naut.* To sew a bolt-rope round the edges of (a sail) 1846. **4. a.** *U.S.* and *Austral.* To catch with a rope; to lasso 1848. **b.** *To r. in*, to draw into some enterprise, to ensnare, lure, or decoy. Orig. *U.S.* 1848. **5.** *Racing.* To pull back or check (a horse) so as to prevent it from winning in a race 1857. **b.** *absol.* To lose a race intentionally by holding back 1887. **6.** *intr.* To be drawn out into a filament or thread; to become viscid or ropy 1565. **b.** *trans.* To pull, draw out, or twist into the shape of a rope 1843.

1. The slain deer roped on to the pony 1873. **2.** The ground is roped out 1866. **4. b.** I won't be roped into this kind of business again 1899.

Ro·pe-band. 1769. Etymologizing form of ROBAND.

Ro·pe-da:ncer. 1648. [ROPE *sb.*[1] I. 2 b.] One who 'dances' or balances on a rope suspended at some height above the ground; a funambulist. So **Ro·pe-da:ncing** *vbl. sb.*

Roper (rōᵘ·pəɹ). ME. [f. ROPE *sb.*[1] + -ER[1].] **1.** One who makes ropes; a rope-maker. **2.** One who secures bales, etc., with a rope 1850. **3.** *Racing.* A jockey who prevents a horse from winning by holding it in; one who intentionally loses any race by similar methods 1870. **4.** *U.S.* One who uses a lasso 1808. **5.** A gambling-house decoy 1859.

Ropery (rōᵘ·pəri). late ME. [f. ROPE *sb.*[1] + -ERY 1.] **1.** A place where ropes are made; a rope-walk. **2.** Trickery, knavery, roguery. Now *arch.* 1530.

2. What sawcie Merchant was this that was so full of his roperie? SHAKS.

Rope's end, *sb.* 1460. [ROPE *sb.*[1]] **1.** The end of a rope; *esp.* a piece from the end of a rope used as an instrument of punishment. **2.** A halter; a hangman's noose 1821.

1. I beat him, and then went up in to fetch my rope's end PEPYS. Hence **Rope's-end** *v. trans.* to flog with a rope's end.

Ro·pe-work. 1797. [ROPE *sb.*[1]] **1.** A place where ropes are made. **2.** An arrangement of ropes 1816.

Ro·pe-yarn. Chiefly *Naut.* 1623. [ROPE *sb.*[1]] **1.** A single yarn forming part of a strand in a rope; a piece of yarn obtained by unpicking an old rope. **b.** Used to denote a small or trifling thing 1801. **2.** Yarn obtained by untwisting an old rope, or such as is used for making ropes 1626.

1. b. If you touch a r. of this ship, I shall board instantly 1879.

Ropy (rōᵘ·pi), *a.* 1480. [f. ROPE *sb.*[1] + -Y[1].] **1.** Forming or developing viscid, glutinous, or slimy threads; sticky and stringy. Also *transf.* of the air. **2.** Having the form or tenacity of a rope; suggestive of a rope 1765.

1. Like Snakes engendring were platted her Tresses, Or like to slimy streaks of R. Ale 1651. My lungs..have been irritated..by the thick r. air 1788. Hence **Ro·pily** *adv.* **Ro·piness.**

‖**Roquefort** (rokfor). 1837. A kind of cheese made with a mixture of goats' and ewes' milk at Roquefort in the S.W. of France.

Roquelaure (rǫ·kĕlōᵊɹ). Now *Hist.* 1716. [– Fr., f. name of Antoine-Gaston, duc de *Roquelaure* (1656–1738), marshal of France.] A cloak reaching to the knee worn by men during the eighteenth and the early part of the nineteenth centuries.

Roquet (rōᵘ·ke), *v.* 1862. [app. an arbitrary variation of CROQUET.] *trans.* In croquet: †**a.** = CROQUET *v.*; also *absol.* **b.** Of a ball: To strike (another ball). **c.** To strike (another player's ball) with one's own; also *absol.* Hence **Ro·quet,** the act of hitting another player's ball with one's own. **Roqueted** (rōᵘ·ked) *ppl. a.* **Roqueting** (rōᵘ·ketiŋ), *vbl. sb.* and *ppl. a.*

Roral (rōᵊ·răl), *a. rare.* 1656. [f. L. *ros, ror-* dew + -AL[1].] Dewy, roscid. So **Rori·ferous** *a.* bringing or bearing dew.

†**Ro·rid,** *a.* 1602. [– L. *roridus*, f. *ros, ror-* dew; see -ID[1].] Dewy; of the nature of dew –1715. So †**Ro·ry** *a.* (*rare*) dewy –1621.

Rorqual (rǫ·ɹkwǫl). 1827. [– Fr. *rorqual* (Cuvier) – Norw. *røyrkval* :- *reyðarhvalr*, f. *reyðr* (specific name) + *hvalr* WHALE.] A whale of the genus *Balænoptera*; the finner.

Rorty (rǫ·ɹti), *a. slang.* Also **raughty.** 1864. [Of unkn. origin.] Fine, splendid, jolly.

Rosace (rōᵘ·zeⁱs, Fr. rozas). 1849. [– Fr. *rosace* – L. *rosaceus* (see next).] **1.** A rose-window. **2.** A design resembling a rose; a rosette 1873.

Rosaceous (rozēⁱ·ʃəs), *a.* 1731. [f. L. *rosaceus* (f. *rosa* ROSE) + -OUS; see -ACEOUS.] **1.** *Bot.* Belonging to or characteristic of the family *Rosaceæ*, of which the rose is the type. **2.** Resembling a rose in form or colour; rose-like 1783. So **Rosa·cean** *Bot.*, a plant of the family *Rosaceæ*, a rosaceous plant.

Ro·sal, *a. rare.* 1566. [f. ROSE + -AL[1]. In sense 1 prob. after OFr. *rosal* (XIV) rosy.] †**1.** Rosy, roseate, ruddy –1641. **2.** *Bot.* Rosaceous (*rare*) 1846.

†**Rosalger.** late ME. [var. of RESALGAR.] Realgar, disulphide of arsenic –1662.

Rosaniline (rōᵘzæ·niləin). 1862. [f. ROSE *sb.* + ANILINE.] *Chem.* A powerful organic base, derived from aniline by treatment with a reagent, yielding crystalline salts much used in dyeing; a dye-colour obtained from this.

Rosarian (rozēᵊ·riăn). 1864. [f. L. *rosarium* (see ROSARY) + -AN I. 1.] **1.** One who cultivates roses; *esp.* an amateur rose-grower. **2.** *R. C. Ch.* A member of a Confraternity of the Rosary 1867.

‖**Rosarium** (rozēᵊ·riŏm). 1841. [L.; see ROSARY.] A rose-garden.

Rosary (rōᵘ·zări). late ME. [– L. *rosarium* rose-garden, AL. (XIII) *rosarius* (sc. *nummus* penny), subst. uses of n. and masc. of adj. f. *rosa* ROSE; see -ARY[1].] **1.** *Hist.* A base or counterfeit coin, of foreign origin, of the value of one penny, declared illegal in England by Edward I. late ME. **2.** A piece of ground set apart for the cultivation of roses; a rose-garden; a ROSERY 1440. †**3.** Used as the title of a book of devotion –1583. **4.** (More fully *R. of Our Lady.*) A form of prayer or set of devotions consisting in the recitation of fifteen decades of Aves, each decade being preceded by a Paternoster and followed by a Gloria; Our Lady's Psalter; a book containing this 1547. **5.** A string of a hundred and sixty-five beads divided into fifteen sets (each having ten small and one large bead), used to assist the memory in the recitation of the Rosary; also, a similar set of fifty-five beads (*the lesser r.*). The small beads represent Aves and the large ones Paternosters and Glorias. 1597. **6.** Any similar devotion or aid thereto 1651.

2. Alas, the Rosaries, how are they broken down! 1657. **6.** Every day propound to your selfe a R. or Chaplet of good Works, to present to God at night 1667.

†‖**Rosa solis** (rōᵘ·ză sōᵘ·lis). Also **rosa-solis.** 1563. [mod.L., lit. 'rose of the sun' (f. *rosa*, and *solis*, gen. of *sol* sun).] **1.** The plant sundew, *Drosera rotundifolia* –1796. **2.** A cordial orig. made from or flavoured with the juice of the plant sundew, but subseq. composed of spirits (esp. brandy) with various essences or spices, sugar, etc. –1818.

Roscian (rǫ·ʃⁱăn), *a.* 1636. [– L. *Roscianus* (Cicero), f. Quintus *Roscius* Gallus (d. 62 B.C.) a famous Roman actor; see -AN.] Characteristic of Roscius as an actor; eminent in respect of acting.

Roscid (rǫ·sid), *a.* Now *rare.* 1626. [– L. *roscidus* dewy, f. *ros* dew.] Dewy, moist, dank; resembling or falling like dew.

Rose (rōᵘz), *sb.* and quasi-*adj.* [OE. *rōse*, corresp. to MDu. *rōse* (Du. *roos*), OHG. *rōsa*, (G. *rose*), ON. *rósa*; Gmc. – L. *rōsa*, rel. obscurely to Gr. ῥόδον, reinforced in ME. from (O)Fr. *rose*.] **A.** *sb.* **I.** The flower or plant. **1.** A beautiful and usu. fragrant flower which grows upon a shrub of the genus *Rosa*, usu. of a red, white, or yellow colour. **2.** A rose-plant, rose-bush, or rose-tree. late ME. **3.** With defining term prefixed (denoting either one of the numerous varieties of the common rose, or some other plant), as *Banksian, blush-, brier-, cabbage-, Christmas-r.*, etc. 1797. **b.** With defining term (genitive phrase) added 1598.

1. As soon Seek roses in December—ice in June BYRON. *Oil of roses*, r.-oil. **2.** I have a green R., evidently a climber 1882. **3.** Eglantine r., or sweet briar 1786. The single Macartney R. 1837. **b.** *R. of Jerusalem*, a species of Amomum. *R. of the Virgin*, the rose of Jericho. Also ROSE OF JERICHO, ROSE OF SHARON.

II. In allusive, emblematic, or fig. uses. **1. a.** The flower as distinguished by its beauty, fragrance, or rich red colour OE. **b.** With ref. to the prickles (commonly called *thorns*) of the rose-bush OE. **c.** In miscellaneous uses. late ME. **2.** *transf.* A peerless or matchless person; a paragon; *esp.* a woman of great beauty, excellence, or virtue. Also const. *of.* late ME. **3.** *Eng. Hist.* The flower, white or red, which was respectively the badge, emblem, or symbol of the rival houses of York and Lancaster. Also *transf.*, the parties thus symbolized. 1509. **b.** As the emblem of England 1629.

1. a. Sweet as a r. her breath and lips GAY. Red as a r. is she COLERIDGE. **b.** As the r. amonge the thornes, so is my loue amonge the daughters COVERDALE *Song Sol.* 2:1. **c.** The Saints are virgins; They love the white r. of virginity TENNYSON. Phr. *Bed of roses*, (*fig.*) a delightful resting place, a position of ease and comfort. **2.** Mystical R., Pray for us 1720. A Saxon heiress..a r. of loveliness SCOTT. **3.** Whose marriages conioyn'd the White-rose and the Red DRAYTON. *Wars of the Roses*, the civil wars in the fifteenth century, between the Yorkists and Lancastrians.

Phr. *Under the r.*, privately, in secret, in strict confidence; SUB ROSA.

III. As a designation of colour. **1.** A delicate red or light crimson colour 1530. **2.** Chiefly *pl.* The fresh pink or ruddy hue of the complexion, esp. in young women 1590. **3.** *The r.*, a popular term for erysipelas or St. Anthony's fire 1599. **4.** A rose-coloured or reddish variety of apple, pear, potato, etc. 1676.

1. One great mountain that soaked up all the r. of sunset 1864. **2.** How now my love? Why is your cheek so pale? How chance the Roses there do fade so fast? SHAKS.

IV. A figure or representation of the flower. **1. a.** *Her.* A conventional design or figure representing this flower, usu. consisting of five lobes or petals ME. **b.** As an emblem of the houses of York and Lancaster, or of England 147.. **2.** A rose-shaped design of metal or other material; an imitation of a rose in metal-work, etc. 1459. **b.** †The card of a mariner's compass, or of a barometer 1527. **c.** A knot or ornamental device inserted in the sound-hole or the table of certain stringed instruments of the guitar type 1676. **d.** *Arch.* = ROSETTE 2. 1728. **3.** An ornamental knot of ribbon, etc., worn upon a shoe-front 1602. **b.** A rosette worn on a cap or hat, *spec.* that of a clergyman 1779. **4.** A perforated metal cap or nozzle attached to the spout of a watering-pot, etc., to distribute water in fine sprays 1706. **5.** *ellipt.* **a.** = ROSE DIAMOND 1678. **b.** A rose-window 1823. **c.** = ROSE-NAIL 1851.

2. *Golden r.*, an ornament of wrought gold, blessed by the pope on the fourth Sunday in Lent, and usu. sent as a mark of favour to some notable Roman Catholic person, city, or church. **3.** Two Prouinciall Roses on my rac'd Shooes SHAKS.

V. *attrib.* and *Comb.* **1.** attrib.: **a.** *gen.*, as *r.-amateur, -bloom*, etc. ME. **b.** In the sense of 'used for cultivating roses', 'overgrown, overspread with roses', 'bordered with roses', as *r.-arbour, -garden, -walk*, etc. OE. **c.** In sense 'made of roses', as *r.-garland, -wreath.* late ME. **d.** In sense 'made from roses', as *r. camphor, -oil, -powder*, etc. 1552. **e.** In sense 'designed or made in the form of a rose', as *r.-knot*, etc. 1510. **2.** attrib., in sense 'having the colour of a rose'; passing into *adj.*, rosy, roseate, rose-coloured 1816.

2. She was ordinarily pale, with a faint r. tinge in her cheeks THACKERAY. The lights, r., amber, emerald, blue TENNYSON.

Comb.: **r.-burner,** a form of gas-burner in which the gas issues from a circle of holes; **-catarrh, -cold, -fever,** *U.S.*, a kind of fever resembling hay-fever; **-nozzle** = sense IV. 4; **-point,** point lace exhibiting the raised pattern of a conventional r.; **-pump,** one having a r. at the shaft-end; **-rash** *Path.*, = ROSEOLA; **-spot** *Path.*, a red spot characteristic of certain fevers; **-sprinkler** = sense IV. 4; **-vinegar,** a preparation made by steeping r. petals in vinegar, and used as a perfume. **b.** In names of plants, flowers, etc.: **r. acacia,** a tree (*Robinia hispida*) having r.-coloured flowers; the Amer. moss-locust; **r. briar,** a r.-tree; **r. geranium,** a r.-scented species of geranium, *Pelargonium capitatum*; **r. laurel,** the oleander; **r. mallow,** (*a*) the hollyhock, *Althæa* (or *Malva*) *rosea*; (*b*) the genus *Hibiscus* of the family *Malvaceæ*; a plant of this genus; **r. vine** *U.S.*, a climbing r., **c.** *Entom.* In the names of insects which frequent and feed upon the r.: **r.-aphis,** the plant-louse *Aphis* (or *Siphonophora*) *rosea*; **-beetle, -bug, -fly,** the ROSE-CHAFER; **r. gall-fly,** an insect which produces galls on r.-leaves; **-grub, -maggot,** a grub or maggot of a r.-infesting insect. **d.** Special collocations in sense V. 2; **r.-aniline,** = ROSANILINE; **-comb,** a flesh-coloured caruncle lying flat upon the head of certain fowls, as in the Sebright cock; also, a Sebright cock; **-ear,** a dog's ear so hanging as to expose the flesh-coloured inner side; **-fish,** a scorpænoid fish, *esp.* the Norway haddock, *Sebastes marinus*, or the red-fish; **-garnet** *Min.*, a r.-red variety of garnet found in Mexico; **r. manganese** *Min.*, rhodonite; **r. quartz** *Min.*, a translucent variety of quartz, of a r.-red colour.

Rose (rōᵘz), *v.* 1610. [f. ROSE *sb.* In sense 3 after Fr. *roser.*] **1.** *trans.* To colour like a rose; to make rosy. Usu. in *pa. pple.* **2.** To perfume with rose-scent 1875. **3.** To treat (wool, etc.) with a chemical mixture in order to impart a rosy tint 1839.

1. Ros'd all in lively crimsin ar thy cheeks 1610.

Roseal (rōᵘ·ziăl), *a.* Now *arch.* 1531. [f. L. *roseus* + -AL[1].] = ROSEATE *a.* 1–3.

Rose-apple. 1626. [f. ROSE *sb.* + APPLE.] †**1.** A kind of apple having rose-coloured flesh –1693. **2. a.** A small tree of the genus *Eugenia* (esp. *E. jambos*), extensively grown in the tropics for its foliage and fruit. **b.** The edible, sweet-scented fruit of this tree, used for making preserves, etc. 1812.

Roseate (rōᵘ·ziĕt), *a.* 1589. [f. L. *roseus* rosy + *-atus* -ATE[2].] **1.** Rose-coloured, rose-red, rosy. **2.** Formed of, consisting of, roses 1607. †**3.** Rose-scented (*rare*) –1720. **4.** *fig.* Rosy; happy 1873. **b.** Rose-coloured, optimistic 1868.

1. The r. whiteness of ridged snow on Alps 1874. **2.** Devise sweet roseat coronets 1607. **4. b.** A.. person who could depict the merits of his scheme with r. but delusive eloquence 1881. Hence **Ro·seately** *adv.*

Ro·se-bay. 1548. [f. ROSE *sb.* + BAY *sb.*[1]] **1.** The oleander or rose-laurel, *Nerium oleander.* Also *rose-bay tree.* **2. a.** The rhododendron and azalea. **b.** A tree or plant of either of these 1760. **3.** The willow-herb, *Epilobium angustifolium* 1671.

Ro·sebud. Also **rose-bud.** 1611. [f. ROSE *sb.*] **1.** The flower of a rose before it opens. **2.** *transf.* A pretty maiden; a girl in the first bloom of womanhood 1790. **b.** *U.S.* A young débutante 1885.

1. Gather ye Rose-buds while ye may HERRICK.

Ro·se-bush. 1587. [f. ROSE *sb.* + BUSH *sb.*[1]] A bush of the rose kind.

Rose-campion. 1530. [f. ROSE *sb.* + CAMPION[2].] A pretty garden-plant of the genus *Lychnis* or *Agrostemma*, having rose-coloured flowers; esp. *L.* or *A. coronaria*; mullein-pink.

Ro·se-cha:fer. 1704. [f. ROSE *sb.* + CHAFER[1].] *Entom.* A beetle of the genus *Cetonia* (esp. *C. aurata*), of a burnished green or copper colour, frequenting roses and in the grub-state very destructive to vegetation; the rose-fly.

Ro·se-co:lour. ME. [f. ROSE *sb.* or *a.*] **1.** The colour of a rose; rosy or crimson tint or hue. **2.** *fig.* A pleasant experience or outlook. (Cf. COULEUR DE ROSE.) 1883.

2. Even a fashionable painter's life is not all r. 1883.

Ro·se-co:loured, *a.* 1526. [f. ROSE *sb.*] **1.** Having the pink or light crimson colour of a rose; roseate, rosy. **2.** *fig.* Characterized by cheerful optimism, or tendency to regard matters in a highly favourable light 1861.

2. He continued..to behold towers, and quadrangles, and chapels,..through r. spectacles 1861.

Ro·se-cut, *a.* and *sb.* Also **rose cut.** 1842. [ROSE *sb.* IV. 5.] Cut as a rose-diamond; as *sb.* = next and ROSE IV. 5 a.

The rose cut consists of triangular facets arranged upon and around a central hexagon 1850.

Rose-diamond. 1698. [f. ROSE *sb.* IV. 5.] A nearly hemispherical flat-bottomed diamond, having the upper surface cut into many triangular facets or planes, a rose-cut diamond.

Ro·se-drop. 1719. [f. ROSE *sb.* + DROP *sb.*] **1.** A hyperæmic form of acne, *acne rosacea*, which marks the skin with red blotches. **2.** A lozenge flavoured with essence of rose 1858.

Ro·se-e:ngine. 1839. [f. ROSE *sb.*] An appendage to a turning-lathe by means of which curvilinear or intricate patterns can be engraved.

Ro·se-leaf. late ME. [f. ROSE *sb.* + LEAF *sb.*] The leaf of a rose; usu., a rose-petal.

Phr. *Crumpled r.*, a slight vexation disturbing general happiness or comfort (with ref. to the fairy story of the princess and the rose-leaf).

Rose-lipped, *a.* Also **-lipt.** 1604. [f. ROSE *sb.* + LIPPED *ppl. a.*] Having lips of a rosy hue.

Roselite (rōᵘ·zĕləit). 1830. [f. Prof. G. *Rose* (1798–1873), a German mineralogist + -LITE.] *Min.* A rare hydrous arsenate of cobalt and calcium, of vitreous lustre, found in rose-red crystals at Schneeberg in Saxony.

Rose·lla[1]. 1847. [app. for *Rose-hiller*, f. *Rose-hill*, Parramatta, near Sydney.] The rose parakeet of Australia, *Platycercus eximius.*

Rose·lla[2], rose·lle. Also **rozelle.** 1857. [perh. corrupt. of Fr. *l'oseille* (sorrel) *de Guinée.*] The red or Indian sorrel, *Hibiscus sabdariffa.*

Rosemary (rōᵘ·zmări). 1440. [alt., by assoc. with ROSE *sb.* and MARY, of ROSMARINE, either immed. – L. *ros marinus*, late L. *rosmarinum*, or through (i) OFr. *rosmarin* (mod. *romarin*), or (ii) MDu. *rosemarine* (Du. *ros(e)marijn*). The L. name means 'sea-dew'.] **1.** An evergreen shrub (*Rosmarinus officinalis*), of the family *Labiatæ*, native to the south of Europe, the leaves of which have an agreeable fragrance, and are used in perfumery and cookery, and to some extent in medicine. **b.** With *pl.* A plant or species of rosemary 1866. **2.** Used as an emblem, or on particular occasions (as funerals and weddings), or for decoration, etc. 1584. **3.** Applied to other plants, usu. with qualifying word prefixed, as *golden, Spanish, wild r.* 1597.

2. Rosemarie is for remembrance 1584. My body to the earth without any ceremony then R. and wine 1682. As trim as a Brides r. 1601.

Ro·se-nail. 1640. [f. ROSE *sb.*] A wrought nail having a round head made with, or cut into, triangular facets.

Rose noble. Now *Hist.* 1473. [f. ROSE *sb.* + NOBLE B. 2.] A gold coin current in the 15th and 16th centuries, having a rose stamped upon it, and of varying value at different times and places.

Ro·seo-, comb. form, repr. L. *roseus* in the sense 'rose-coloured', in names of salts, alkalis, etc., as *r.-chrome, -cobalt, -cobaltia, -rhodium.*

Rose of Jericho. late ME. [Cf. *Ecclus.* 24:14.] A small annual cruciferous plant *Anastatica hierochuntina*), native to the arid deserts of South-west Asia and North-east Africa, the dried fronds of which unfold under the influence of moisture; the resurrection plant, Mary's flower, or rose of the Virgin.

Rose of Sharon (ʃēᵊ·rǫn). 1611. [Heb. *šārôn*, name of a fertile level tract of Palestine between Jaffa and Mount Carmel.] An Eastern flower variously identified with the crocus, polyanthus, narcissus, and cistus.

fig. I am the rose of Sharon, and the lillie of the valleys *Song Sol.* 2:1.

Roseola (rozī·ŏlă). 1818. [A mod. var. of RUBEOLA, f. L. *roseus* rose-coloured + dim. suffix *-ola*. Cf. Fr. *roséole.*] *Path.* A rash of rosy spots or eruptions occurring in measles, etc.; also, false or German measles. Hence **Rose·olar, Rose·olous** *adjs.* of or pertaining to, of the nature of, r.

Rose-pink, *sb.* and *a.* 1735. [f. ROSE *sb.* + PINK *sb.*[5]] **A.** *sb.* **1.** A pigment of a pinkish hue, produced by colouring whiting or chalk with a decoction of Brazil-wood, etc. **2.** A pink tint or hue like that of roses 1864. **B.** *adj.* **1.** Of a pinkish colour resembling that of the rose; rosy pink, roseate 1843. **2.** *fig.* = ROSE-COLOURED *a.* 2. 1837.

2. That rosepink vapour of Sentimentalism CARLYLE.

Rose-red, *a.* and *sb.* ME. [f. ROSE *sb.* + RED *a.* or *sb.*] **A.** *adj.* Red like a rose; rose-coloured. **B.** *sb.* A red like that of a rose. late ME.

Rose rial. *Obs.* exc. *Hist.* 1617. [f. ROSE *sb.* + RIAL *sb.* 3.] A gold coin of the value of thirty shillings, coined by James I, and having the figure of a rose upon one side.

Ro·se-root. 1597. [f. ROSE *sb.* + ROOT *sb.*] *Bot.* One of certain related herbaceous plants, esp. *Sedum rhodiola* or *Rhodiola rosea*, growing in rocky districts or on cliffs, the root of which emits a rose-like fragrance when bruised or dried.

Rosery (rōᵘ·zəri). 1864. [f. ROSE *sb.* + -ERY.] A portion of a garden set apart for growing roses; a rosarium; a plantation of rose-bushes.

Roset (roze·t). 1485. [Based upon ROSE *sb.*] †**1.** A rose-coloured pigment, or the colour produced by this –1688. **2.** = ROSETTE 1807.

Ro·se-tree. Also **rose tree.** ME. [f. ROSE *sb.* + TREE *sb.*] A rose-bush.

Rose·tta-wood. 1843. An East Indian wood, of an orange-red colour.

Rosette (roze·t). 1797. [– Fr. *rosette*, dim. of *rose*; see ROSE *sb.*, -ETTE.] **1.** A bunch or knot of ribbons, leather strips, worsted or the like, concentrically disposed so as to resemble a rose, and worn as an ornament or badge 1802. **b.** *spec.* as a decoration of harness 1858. **2.** *Arch.* An ornament resembling a rose in form, painted, sculptured, or moulded upon, attached to, or incised in a wall or other surface 1806. **b.** A rounded ornamental perforation; a rosace or rose-window 1836. **3.** *Metall.* One of the disc-like plates formed by successive sprinklings of water upon the molten copper in a crucible 1797. **4.** *Biol.* A cluster of organs or parts, a marking or group of markings, resembling a rose in form or arrangement 1834. **5. a.** A circular rose-like pattern; also, one of the pattern-discs of a rose-engine 1843. **b.** Any object, or arrangement of parts, resembling a rose in form 1856.

Comb.: **r. copper** (see sense 3). Hence **Rose·tted** *a.*

Rose-water (rōᵘ·z,wǭ:təɹ). late ME. [f. ROSE *sb.* + WATER *sb.*] **1.** Water distilled from roses, or impregnated with essence of roses, and used as a perfume, etc. Also with *a* and *pl.* (*rare*). **2.** *attrib.* in fig. uses: **a.** Mild, sentimental 1837. **b.** Elegant, superfine 1840.

1. We may yet find a r. that will wash the negro white EMERSON. **2. a.** It is not a Revolt, it is a Revolution; and truly no r. one! CARLYLE. **b.** Not dandy, poetical, r. thieves; but real downright scoundrels THACKERAY.

Rose-window. 1773. [f. ROSE *sb.* + WINDOW *sb.*] *Eccl. Arch.* A circular window, *esp.* one divided into compartments by mullions radiating from a centre, or filled with tracery suggestive of the form of a rose; a Catherine or marigold window.

Rosewood (rōᵘ·zwud). 1660. [f. ROSE *sb.* + WOOD *sb.*] **1.** One of several kinds of valuable, fragrant, close-grained cabinet-wood, chiefly that yielded by tropical leguminous trees of the genera *Dalbergia* (esp. *D. nigra*) and *Machærium*; also, a tree yielding this wood. **2.** The fragrant wood of certain species of Convolvulus, as *C. floridus* and *C. scoparius*, and of the allied genus *Rhodorrhiza*, natives of the Canary Islands 1671. **3.** The West Indian candlewood, *Amyris balsamifera*; also *A. montana* 1756. **4.** Applied to several Australasian trees, esp. *Trichilia glandulosa*, of New South Wales 1779. **5.** With defining terms 1866.

5. African r., the West African tree *Pterocarpus erinaceus*; also, the wood of this. **Jamaica r.**, the sweet-smelling wood of *Amyris balsamifera*, or of *Linociera ligustrina*.

Rosewort (rōᵘ·zwɒɹt). 1578. [f. ROSE *sb.* + WORT^1. In sense 1 prob. – G. *rosenwurz*, Du. *roosenwortel*.] **1.** = ROSEROOT. Now *rare*. †**2.** = ORPINE 2. –1758. **3.** *pl.* Lindley's name for the *Rosaceæ* 1845.

Rosicrucian (rōᵘzikrū·ʃ'ăn), *sb.* and *a.* 1624. [f. mod.L. *rosa crucis* (XVII in Du Cange) or *crux*, as a rendering of G. *Rosenkreuz*. Cf. Fr. *rose-croix* (XVII).] **A.** *sb.* A member of a supposed society or order, reputedly founded by one Christian Rosenkreuz in 1484, but first mentioned in 1614, whose members were said to claim various forms of secret and magic knowledge, as the transmutation of metals, the prolongation of life, and power over the elements. **B.** *adj.* Belonging or pertaining to, connected with, or characteristic of this Society 1662.

Ro·sier. *Obs.* exc. *poet.* 1523. [– (O)Fr. *rosier* :– L. *rosarium* rose-garden, f. *rosa* ROSE.] A rose-tree, rose-bush.

Rosin (rǫ·zin), *sb.* [unexpl. alt. of RESIN.] **1.** = RESIN *sb.*; *spec.*, this substance in a solid state obtained as a residue after the distillation of oil of turpentine from crude turpentine ME. **b.** With *a* and *pl.* A particular kind of rosin 1604.

Comb.: **r.-oil**, 'an oil obtained from the resin of the pine-tree, used by painters for lubricating machinery', etc.; **-weed** *U.S.*, the compass plant (*Silphium laciniatum*).

Rosin (rǫ·zin), *v.* 1497. [f. prec.] **1.** *trans.* To smear over, or seal up, with rosin; to rub (*esp.* a violin bow or string) with rosin. Also *absol.* **2.** *fig.* To supply with liquor; to make drunk; also *intr.*, to indulge in drink. Now *dial.* 1729.

1. Those, who make musick with so harsh an instrument, need to have their bow well rosend before 1642.

Rosinante (rǫzinæ·nti). 1759. [– Sp. *Rocinante* (f. *rocin* horse, jade), the name of the horse ridden by Don Quixote.] A poor, worn-out, or ill-conditioned horse; a hack, jade.

†**Rosmarine.** OE. [Earlier form of ROSEMARY.] **1.** Rosemary –1742. **2.** Sea-dew. B. JONS.

2. That purer brine, And wholsome dew called Rosmarine 1616.

Rosolic (rozǫ·lik), *a.* 1835. [f. L. *rosa* + -OL + -IC 1 b.] *Chem.* In *R. acid* = AURIN.

Rosolio (rozōᵘ·lio). 1819. [– It. var. of *rosoli*; see ROS SOLIS.] A sweet cordial made in Italy and Southern Europe from spirits, raisins, sugar, etc.

Ross (rǫs), *sb.*^{1} 1475. The name of a county in the north of Scotland, used *attrib.* in *Ross herald*, one of the six Scottish heralds.

Ross (rǫs), *sb.*^{2} 1577. [app. of Scand. origin, corresp. to Norw. dial. *ros* (*rus*) scrapings.] †**1.** Rubbish, refuse, dregs –1630. **2.** The scaly outer portion of the bark of trees. Chiefly *U.S.* 1778.

Ross, *v.* *U.S.* 1864. [f. prec.] *trans.* To remove the ross from; to divest a tree of (bark).

†‖**Ros solis.** 1578. [mod.L. use of L. *ros* dew + *solis*, gen. of *sol* sun.] = ROSA SOLIS –1757.

Rostel (rǫ·stĕl). 1793. [Anglicized f. ROSTELLUM.] *Bot.* The radicle of a seed.

‖**Rostellum** (rǫste·lǒm). 1760. [L. *rostellum* small beak or snout (Pliny), dim. of ROSTRUM.] †**1.** *Bot.* **a.** A radicle –1832. **b.** The short beak-shaped process on the stigma of many violets and orchids 1841. **2.** *Zool.* **a.** The tubule and enclosed siphuncle of the various species of louse, replacing the usual mouth apparatus of insects 1826. **b.** The protruding fore-part of the head of tapeworms, armed with hooklets or spines 1849. Hence **Roste·llar, Roste·llate, Roste·lliform,** *adjs.*

Roster (rōᵘ·stəɹ). †Also **rolster, rollster.** 1727. [– Du. *rooster* (i) grating, gridiron, (ii) table, list (from the appearance of a paper ruled with parallel lines), f. *roosten*; see ROAST *v.*, -ER^1.] **1.** *Mil.* A list or plan exhibiting the order of rotation, or turns of duties and service, of officers, men, and bodies of troops. **2.** *transf.* A list or table exhibiting the names of a set of persons, esp. as taking turns of duty 1858.

Rostral (rǫ·străl), *a.* (and *sb.*) late ME. [In sense 1 app. – med.L. **rostralis*, f. ROSTRUM; in sense 2 alt. of (the proper word) ROSTRATE by suffix-substitution, perh. after Fr. *rostral*(*e*; in sense 3 f. ROSTRUM 5 + -AL^1.] †**1.** *R. bone*, the coracoid process. Also *absol.* as *sb.* –1541. **2.** Of columns, pillars, etc.: Adorned with the beaks of galleys or with representations of these 1709. **3.** *Zool.* Of or pertaining to, situated in or upon, the rostrum 1826.

2. *R. crown*, a golden crown, adorned with figures of ships' beaks, awarded to the person who first boarded an enemy's ship.

Rostrate (rǫ·strĕt), *a.* 1601. [Sense 1 repr. L. (*corona*) *rostrata*, f. ROSTRUM + *-ata* -ATE^2; sense 2 is f. ROSTRUM 5 + -ATE^2.] †**1.** = prec. 2. –1674. **2.** *Bot.*, *Zool.*, etc. Having, or furnished with, a rostrum; terminating in a rostrum. 1819. So **Ro·strated** *a.* in sense 2.

Rostri·ferous, *a.* 1852. [f. *rostri-*, as comb. form of L. *rostrum* + -FEROUS.] Having a rostrum (esp. as dist. from a proboscis).

‖**Rostrum** (rǫ·strǒm). Pl. **rostra,** *rarely* **rostrums.** 1579. [L., beak, snout, etc. (cf. sense 1), f. *rodere* gnaw.] **1.** *Rom. Antiq.* The platform or stand for public speakers in the Forum of ancient Rome, adorned with the beaks of ships taken from the Antiates in 338 B.C.; also, that part of the Forum in which this was situated. **a.** In *pl.* 1579. **b.** In *sing.*; also applied to the orators' stand in the Athenian Assembly 1713. **2.** *transf.* A platform, stage, stand, etc., adapted for public speaking 1766. **b.** *spec.* A pulpit 1771. **3.** *Rom. Antiq.* = BEAK 7. 1674. †**4. a.** The beak or nose of an alembic or still –1684. **b.** A pair of forceps of a beak-like form –1722. **5.** *Zool.*, *Bot.*, etc. A beak or snout; an oral apparatus of an elongated form 1753.

2. Mr. Tappertit mounted on an empty cask which stood by way of r. in the room DICKENS.

Rosulate (rǫ·ziulĕt), *a.* 1832. [f. late L. *rosula*, dim. of *rosa* rose + -ATE^2.] *Bot.* Arranged like the petals of a rose, or in the form of a rosette.

Rosy (rōᵘ·zi), *a.* late ME. [f. ROSE *sb.* + -Y^1.] **1.** Having the crimson or pink colour of a rose; rose-red. **b.** Said of persons, their features, etc., esp. as betokening good health 1593. **c.** Blushing 1611. **d.** *ellipt.* as a slang term for 'wine'. DICKENS. **2.** Resembling a rose; *esp.* sweet-smelling as a rose, rose-scented 1586. **3.** Abounding in, decorated with, roses; composed of roses 1508. **4.** Of times, circumstances, etc.: Bringing happiness; bright; promising, hopeful 1775.

1. For see the Morn..begins Her rosie progress smiling MILT. **b.** That sweet Rosie Lad SHAKS. **3.** His rosie Wreath was dropt not long before DRYDEN.

Comb. as *r.-bosomed*, *-cheeked*, etc.; also, **r. cross,** the supposed emblem of the Rosicrucians (also *attrib.*); **r. drop** [tr. medical L. *gutta rosacea*], an inflamed condition of the face of hard drinkers, etc. Hence **Rosy** *v.* (*rare*) *trans.* and *intr.* to make or become r. or rose-red.

Rosy-fingered, *a.* 1590. Having rosy fingers. Chiefly after Homeric ῥοδοδάκτυλος (ἠώς). The rosy fingred Morning faire SPENSER.

Rot (rǫt), *sb.* ME. [orig. perh. – Scand.; cf. Icel., Faer., Norw. *rot*, Sw. dial. *råt*, obs. Da. *rodt*, *rod*, *raad* (XVI).] **1.** The process of rotting or state of being rotten; decay, putrefaction; also, rotten or decayed matter. **2.** A virulent disease affecting the liver of sheep which are fed on moist pasture-lands; inflammation of the liver caused by the fluke-worm, liver-rot. Usu. with *the*. late ME. **b.** A particular form, instance, or epidemic, of this disease 1538. **3.** A putrescent or wasting disease in people. late ME. **4.** Decay in timber or other vegetable products, stone, etc. See also DRY-ROT. 1830. **5.** *slang.* Nonsensical rubbish; trash, bosh 1848. **6.** *Cricket.* A rapid breakdown or fall of wickets during an innings 1884.

2. His cattel must of R. and Murren die MILT. *White r.*, the plant *Hydrocotyle vulgaris*, belonging to the order *Umbelliferæ*; marsh pennywort, sheep-rot; also, rot-grass. **b.** *fig.* Among the muses there's a general r. 1667. **5.** You are just the sort of woman to believe in that kind of r. 1882.

Rot (rǫt), *v.* [OE. *rotian* = OFris. *rotia*, OS. *roton*, MDu. *roten*, OHG. *rōʒʒēn*, rel. to MLG. *röten*, MHG. *rœʒen*; cf. ROTTEN.] **1.** *intr.* Of animal substances: To undergo natural decomposition; to decay, putrefy, through disease, mortification, or death. Also of timber, fruit, vegetable matter, etc. **2.** *fig.* in various contexts, chiefly denoting decay of a moral or abstract kind ME. **3.** Of persons: To become affected with some putrescent or wasting disease, esp. as the result of confinement in jail ME. **b.** Of sheep: To become affected with the rot 1523. **4.** *trans.* To affect with decomposition, putrescence, or decay; to make rotten. late ME. **5.** To affect (sheep) with the rot. Also *absol.* late ME. **6.** Used in imprecations 1588. **7.** *slang.* To chaff severely. Also *absol.*, to talk nonsense. 1890.

1. Corne not reaped, but suffered to rotte 1581. Dead men rotting to nothing MORRIS. **3. b.** The hungry Sheep..R. inwardly, and foul contagion spread MILT. **4.** *fig.* Better that we had rotted out our lives in exile 1848. **6.** The South-Fog r. him SHAKS.

Rota (rōᵘ·tă). 1660. [– L. *rota* wheel.] **1.** A political club, founded in 1659 by J. Harrington, which advocated rotation in the offices of Government; also, a society of this type. **2.** A rotation (of persons, etc.); a round or routine (of duties, etc.); †a rote 1673. **b.** A list of persons acting in rotation; a roster 1856. **3.** *R. C. Ch.* (with cap.) The supreme court for ecclesiastical and secular causes 1679.

2. According to a r. to be agreed on between each other 1868. **3.** The *R.* consists of twelve Doctors chosen out of the four Nations of Italy, France, Spain, and Germany 1728.

Rotal (rōᵘ·tăl), *a.* 1656. [f. L. *rota* and ROTA + -AL^1.] **1.** Pertaining to a wheel or wheels. **2.** Pertaining to rotation or circular motion 1855. **3.** *R. C. Ch.* Connected with the Rota 1907.

Rotalian (rotēⁱ·liăn), *sb.* and *a.* 1862. [f. mod.L. *Rotalia* (Lamarck, 1809), f. L. *rota* wheel, perh. after *mammalia*; see -AN.] **A.** *sb.* A foraminifer of the genus *Rotalia* 1869. **B.** *adj.* Of, belonging to this genus 1862.

Rotarian (rotēᵊ·riăn), *a.* and *sb.* 1912. Of or pertaining to, a member of, a Rotary club.

Rotary (rōᵘ·tări), *a.* and *sb.* 1731. [– med.L. *rotarius*, f. L. *rota* wheel; see -ARY[1].] **A.** *adj.* **1.** Of motion: Circular: taking place round a centre or axis. **2.** Operating by means of rotation; rotative 1799. **3.** (With initial cap.) Epithet of a world-wide society, with many branches, of representatives of trades, businesses, or professions, organized for the purpose of international service to humanity; orig. named from the fact that the first club (formed at Chicago in 1905) met at the premises of each member in turn. **B.** *sb.* A rotary machine or apparatus 1888.

A. 2. All our general storms are cyclonic in their character, that is, r. and progressive 1884.

Rotate (rōᵘ·tĕt), *a.* 1875. [f. L. *rota* wheel + -ATE[2].] *Bot.* Wheel-shaped; *esp.* of a monopetalous corolla with a short tube and spreading limb.

Rotate (rotēⁱ·t), *v.* 1808. [– *rotat-*, pa. ppl. stem of L. *rotare* revolve, f. *rota* wheel, see -ATE[3].] **1.** *intr.* To move round a centre or axis; to perform one or more revolutions. **2.** *trans.* To cause (a thing) to turn round or revolve on a centre or axis 1831. **3.** To change, or take, in rotation 1879.

3. She could mow a field, . . and r. its crops 1879.

Rotation (rotē·ʃən). 1555. [– L. *rotatio*, -*on-*, f. as prec.; see -ION. Cf. (O)Fr. *rotation.*] **1.** The action of moving round a centre, or of turning round (and round) on an axis; also, the action of producing a motion of this kind. **2.** The fact of coming round again in succession; return or recurrence; a recurring series or period 1610. **b.** Regular and recurring succession in office, duties, etc., of a number of persons. Freq. in phr. *by* or *in r.* 1656. **c.** *Agric.* A change or succession of crops in a certain order on a given piece of ground, in order to avoid the exhaustion of the soil 1778.

1. *fig.* The perpetuall R. of fortune 1647. **2.** Medicines . . suffer a r. of fashions like our cloaths 1756. **b.** In America . . the tendency is towards 'rotation' in office 1888. **c.** A regular r. of Crops and Fallow 1778. Hence **Rota·tional** *a.* acting in r.; of or belonging to r.

Rotative (rōᵘ·tătiv), *a.* 1778. [f. ROTATE *v.* + -IVE. Cf. (sense 1) Fr. (*machine*) *rotative.*] **1.** Rotating, turning round like a wheel; acting or operating by circular motion. **b.** Produced by rotation; producing, connected with or of the nature of rotation 1823. **2.** Acting or coming in rotation; recurrent 1813.

1. A r. or wheel engine 1778. **b.** The Earth's r. movement 1868. **2.** Cotton was cultivated . . as a r. . . crop 1864.

Rotativist (rotēⁱ·tivist), *sb.* and *a.* 1909. [f. prec. + -IST.] One who supports an autocratic system of government whereby persons and parties pass in and out of office by mutual arrangement, without reference to the interests or desires of the public. Also freq. *attrib.* or as *adj.*

The collapse of the Portuguese colonial empire must come with the continuance of the struggle between r. Royalism and revolutionary Republicanism 1917. So **Rota·tivism.**

Rotator (rotēⁱ·təɹ). 1676. [orig. (sense 1) – L. *rotator*, f. as ROTATE *v.* + -OR 2; in later use f. ROTATE *v.* + -OR 2. Cf. Fr. *rotateur.*] **1.** *Anat.* A muscle by which a limb or part can be moved circularly. **2.** A thing, apparatus or part which has a rotary motion or action 1772. **3.** One of the *Rotatoria*; a rotifer 1876.

Rotatory (rōᵘ·tătəri), *a.* and *sb.* 1755. [f. ROTATE *v.* + -ORY[2].] **A.** *adj.* **1. a.** Of the nature of rotation; connected with rotation. **b.** Rotating; working by means of rotation 1812. **c.** Causing rotation 1828. **2.** Going round, or coming, in rotation 1824.

1. A r. movement at the hip-joint 1845. **b.** The track of five . . r. storms 1850. **2.** I become . . wearied with the repetition of r. acts 1831.

B. *sb.* A rotifer 1835.

Rotche (rǫtʃ). Also **rotch, roach; rotchie.** 1809. [Later form of Du., Fris. *rotge* (Martens, 1675), of obsc. origin.] The little auk.

Rote (rōᵘt), *sb.*[1] ME. [– OFr. *rote* = Pr. *rota*; cf. MLG., MDu. *rot(t)e*, OHG. *rot(t)a*; the Rom. and Gmc. words are identical with the Celtic word repr. in CROWD *sb.*[1]] A mediæval musical instrument, probably of the violin class. Now *Hist.*

Rote (rōᵘt), *sb.*[2] ME. [Of unkn. origin.] †**1. a.** Custom, habit, practice –1440. **b.** Mechanical practice or performance; regular procedure; mere routine –1768. **2.** *By r.*, in a mechanical manner, by routine, *esp.* by the mere exercise of memory without proper understanding of, or reflection upon, the matter in question; also, †with precision, by heart. late ME.

2. Hee tels you lyes by r. EARLE. To learn to play by r. or ear without Book 1662. Words learn'd by r. a parrot may rehearse COWPER.

Rote (rōᵘt), *sb.*[3] Now *U.S.* 1610. [Of unkn. origin. Cf. contemp. RUT *sb.*[3]] The roaring of the sea or surf.

While the seas r. doth ring their doleful knell 1610.

Rote (rōᵘt), *v.* 1593. [f ROTE *sb.*[2]] **1.** *trans.* To repeat, run *over*, rattle *off*, from memory. Also *absol.* †**2.** To learn or fix by rote (*rare*) –1775.

2. Words That are but roated in your Tongue SHAKS.

Ro·t-gut, ro·tgut. 1633. [f. ROT *v.* + GUT *sb.*] **1.** An adulterated or unwholesome liquor; *spec.* bad small beer, or (in *U.S.*) inferior whiskey. **2.** *attrib.* or as *adj.* Of liquor: Unwholesome, injurious to the system 1706.

Rother (rǫ·ðəɹ). Now *dial.* [OE. *hrīðer*, *hrȳðer* = OFris. *(h)rither*, a deriv. from the stem *hrith*, OHG. *hrind* (G. *rind*).] An ox; an animal of the ox kind; *pl.* oxen. So †**R.-beast** –1698.

Rother, obs. f. RUDDER.

Rothesay (rǫ·psĕ). late ME. Name of an ancient castle in Scotland, used *attrib.* in *R. herald*, one of the six Scottish heralds. Also *ellipt.*

‖**Rotifera** (roti·fĕră). 1830. [mod.L., n. pl. of *rotifer(us*, f. L. *rota* wheel + *-fer* bearing.] A class of minute (usu. microscopic) animalcules, having rotatory organs which are used in swimming. So **Ro·tifer** (rōᵘ·tifəɹ), an animalcule belonging to this class 1793.

Rotograph (rōᵘ·tǒgraf). 1898. [f. *roto-*, used as comb. form of L. *rota* wheel, + -GRAPH.] A photographic print made by exposing the object through a lens and prism, so that its reversed image is thrown upon part of a roll of sensitive paper.

‖**Roto·nda.** Now *rare.* 1670. [It., subst. use (sc. *camera*) of fem. of *rotondo* round :– L. *rotundus*. See ROTUNDA.] **1.** *spec.* The Pantheon. †**2.** A round or circular object. ADDISON. **3.** A rounded part of a coach 1874.

Rotor (rōᵘ·tǫɹ). 1903. [irreg. for ROTATOR.] **1.** The rotating part of a dynamo or motor. **2.** A vertical rotating metal cylinder used as a means of obtaining greater power from wind 1924.

Rottan (rǫ·t'n). 1500. Var. of RATTON.

Rotten (rǫ·t'n), *a.* ME. [– ON. *rotinn*, which has the form of a pa. pple. on the base *raut- *reut- *rut-, repr. by ROT *v.* and RET *v.*] **I. 1.** Of animal matter: In a state of decomposition or putrefaction; decomposed, putrid. **2.** Of vegetable substances, etc.: In a state of thorough decay ME. †**3.** Of air, water: Putrid, corrupted, tainted, foul –1802. **4.** Of ground, soil, etc.: Extremely soft, yielding, or friable by reason of decay 1440. **b.** Of rocks: Partly decomposed 1805. **5.** Of sheep: Affected with the rot 1460. **6.** *local.* Damp, wet, rainy 1599.

1. The sweet War-man is dead and r. SHAKS. **2.** In the r. Trunks of hollow Trees DRYDEN. *fig.* You'l be r. ere you bee halfe ripe SHAKS. **3.** †*R. fever*, putrid fever. **4.** The ice [was] very dangerous, being r. 1806. **6.** A raw r. fog after frost 1844.

II. 1. Morally, socially, or politically corrupt. late ME. **b.** *R. borough*: see BOROUGH 3. **2.** Weak, unsound 1607. **b.** *slang.* In a very poor state, of a very bad quality, quite worthless. Also as a mere expletive. 1881.

1. Root up the r. race of the ungodly 1555. He is R. at the Core, and his Soul is dishonest 1718. **2.** Nor sleepe, nor sanctuary . . shall lift vp Their r. Priuiledge . . 'gainst My hate to Martius SHAKS. **b.** You may imagine how r. I have been feeling STEVENSON. Just like you. Forgot the r. centrebit. 1892. Hence **Ro·tten-ly** *adv.*, **-ness.**

Rotten-hearted, *a.* ME. Of a thoroughly corrupt nature or character.

Þis roten hertid synne of Accidie CHAUCER.

Ro·tten Row·. 1799. [app. f. ROTTEN *a.* + ROW *sb.*[1] Reason for the name unkn.] A road in Hyde Park, extending from Apsley Gate to Kensington Gardens, much used as a fashionable resort for horse or carriage exercise. Now usu. called *The Row.*

Ro·tten-stone, ro·ttenstone. 1677. [f. ROTTEN *a.* + STONE *sb.*] A decomposed siliceous limestone chiefly used as a powder for polishing metals. Hence **Ro·tten-stone** *v. trans.* to polish with r.

Rotter (rǫ·təɹ). *slang.* 1894. [f. ROT *v.* + -ER[1] 1.] In vaguely depreciative use: One who is objectionable on moral or other grounds.

‖**Rotula** (rǫ·tiŭlă). Pl. usu. **-læ** (lī). late ME. [L., dim of *rota* wheel; see -ULE.] **1.** *Anat.* **a.** The knee-cap, patella. **b.** The point of the elbow 1760. **2.** One of five radial pieces forming part of the oral skeleton of sea-urchins 1877. Hence **Ro·tular** *a.*

Rotund (rotɒ·nd), *a.* 1705. [– L. *rotundus*, f. *rotare* ROTATE *v.*] **1.** Round, circular, orbicular. Now *rare* exc. in scientific use. **2.** Of the mouth: Rounded in the act of utterance. Hence *transf.*, sonorous, full-toned. (After L. *ore rotundo.*) 1830. **3.** Of the physique: Rounded 1834.

2. A most r. and glowing negative DICKENS. Hence **Rotund** *sb.* (*rare*), a round object or expanse. **Rotu·nd-ly** *adv.*, **-ness** (*rare*).

‖**Rotunda** (rotɒ·ndă). 1687. [alt., after L. *rotundus*, of ROTONDA. See also ROTUNDO.] **1.** A building round in shape both inside and outside, *esp.* one with a dome 1700. **b.** As the name of the Pantheon at Rome and other buildings of this form 1687. **2.** A circular hall or room within a building 1828.

2. The Reading Room of the British Museum . . that immense r. 1901.

Rotundate (rotɒ·ndĕt), *a.* 1776. [– *rotundat-*, pa. ppl. stem of L. *rotundare*, f. *rotundus* ROTUND; see -ATE[2].] *Bot.* and *Zool.* Rounded off.

Rotu·ndi-, comb. form of L. *rotundus* round, used in **rotundifo·liate, -fo·lious** *adjs.*, having round leaves; etc.

Rotundity (rotɒ·ndĭti). 1589. [– (O)Fr. *rotondité* or L. *rotunditas*, f. *rotundus* ROTUND; see -ITY.] **1.** The condition of being round or spherical; roundness, sphericity 1597. **b.** *concr.* A round or spherical mass; a round building, etc. 1744. **2.** Rounded fullness, *esp.* of language 1589. **3.** Roundness of the body or its parts; fullness of habit. Also *concr.* 1786.

1. They believe the r. of the earth 1660. **2.** He began . . with true legal r. of verbiage 1879. **3.** The faultless rotundities of a lusty country girl HARDY.

Rotu·ndo. Now *rare* or *Obs.* 1625. [Alteration of ROTUNDA.] †**1.** A circular form or figure –1632. **2.** A circular building, chamber, or space 1632. **3.** = ROTONDA 3. 1867.

Rotu·ndo-, used as comb. form of L. *rotundus*, as in **r.-ovate** *a.*, oval but roundish.

‖**Roture** (rotūr). 1682. [(O)Fr. *roture* = OFr. *routure* (orig.) newly broken ground :– med.L. *ruptura* assart; see RUPTURE.] **1.** Plebeian tenure. **2.** Plebeian rank 1795.

‖**Roturier** (rotürye), *sb.* and *a.* Also fem. **-iere** (-yę̄r). 1586. [Fr., f. *roture*; see prec., -IER.] **A.** *sb.* **1.** A plebeian; a person of low rank. **2.** In Canada, one who holds real estate subject to an annual rent 1861. **B.** *adj.* Plebeian 1614.

His manners, though courteous . . , are r. and vulgar 1835.

Rouble (rū·b'l). 1554. [Earliest forms *rubbel, roble, ruble*, later *rouble* (after Fr.); – Russ. *rubl'*.] **1.** The Russian monetary unit, in early times a money of account equal in value to an English mark, or 13*s.* 4*d.*, now a silver coin worth (since 1897) 2*s.* 1½*d.* **2.** A paper money of less value than the silver rouble 1811.

Roucou (rūkū·), *sb.* 1666. [– Fr. *ro(u)cou* – Tupi *rucu, urucú.*] **1.** A dye-yielding tree, *Bixa orellana*, of the West Indies and S. America. Also *r.-tree.* **2.** The dye or dye-stuff obtained from this tree, also called *anatta* or *arnatto* 1666.

‖**Roué** (ru·e). 1800. [Fr., pa. pple. of *rouer* break on the wheel.] One who is given to, or leads, a life of pleasure and sensuality; a debauchee, a rake.

Rouen (ru·aṅ). 1728. Name of a city in Northern France, used *attrib.* in *R. bushel, duck* (a common domestic variety), *lilac*.

Rouge (rūʒ), *a.* and *sb.*[1] 1485. [– (O)Fr. *rouge* :– L. *rubeus* RED.] **A.** *adj.* **1.** *R. Croix* (or †*Cross*), *R. Dragon*, the titles of two of the Pursuivants of the English College of Arms, so called from their badges. **2.** *R. royal*, a Belgian marble of a reddish colour 1858. **B.** *sb.* **1.** A fine red powder prepared from safflower, and used as a cosmetic to give an artificial colour to the cheeks or lips 1753. **2.** A red preparation of oxide of iron, used as a plate powder 1839. **3.** A 'red', republican, etc. 1821. **4.** The red colour in the game of *rouge et noir* 1827.

‖**R. et noir** (rūʒ e nwār), a card game, so called because the table at which it is played has two red and two black diamond-shaped marks, upon which the players place their stakes according to the colour which they favour.

Rouge (rūdʒ), *sb.*[2] 1863. [Eton College term, of unkn. origin.] **a.** A scrimmage. **b.** A point in the wall-game, three of which make a goal.

Rouge (rūʒ), *v.* 1777. [f. ROUGE *sb.*[1]] *trans.* To colour with rouge. Also *absol.* **b.** *fig.* To cause to colour or blush 1815.

Rough (rʋf), *sb.* 1480. [f. next] **I. 1. a.** Rough or broken ground. **b.** A stretch of rough ground; *esp.* a steep bank or slope covered with undergrowth or trees; a coppice. Now *local.* 1600. **c.** The rough ground at the edge of, or between the greens on, a golf-course 1901. **2.** A spike inserted in each heel of a horseshoe in 'roughing' horses to prevent slipping 1884.

1. a. The fiend..through strait, r., dense, or rare,..pursues his way MILT. **c.** Thanks to Vardon having pulled into the r. the Scotsman secured the sixteenth [hole] 1901.

II. 1. The rough disagreeable part, side, or aspect of anything; that which is harsh or unpleasant; rough treatment, hardship 1642. **2.** A rowdy 1837. **III. 1.** Rough or refuse matter in the working of minerals 1677. **2.** The rough state or material of anything 1799.

Phr. *In the r.*, (*a*) in a rough, imperfect, or unfinished state; in a preliminary sketch or design; (*b*) in disorder; without preparation.

Rough (rʋf), *a.* [OE. *rūh* = MLG., MDu. *rūch*, *rū* (Du. *ruig, ruw*), OHG. *rūh* (G. *rauh*) :– WGmc. **rūχ(w)a*.] **I. 1.** Having a surface diversified with small projections, points, bristles, etc.; not even or smooth. **b.** Of cloth: Coarse OE. **2.** Having the skin covered with hair; hairy, shaggy. In later use *spec.* unclipped, unshorn; having a rough coat of hair. OE. **3.** Of ground: Difficult to traverse; uneven, broken; uncultivated, wild OE.

1. The tongue is r., and beset with prickles GOLDSM. **2.** Till new-borne chinnes Be r., and Razor-able SHAKS. **3.** These high wilde hilles, and r. vneeuen waies, Drawes out our miles SHAKS.

II. 1. a. Of the sea, weather, wind, etc.: Stormy, violent ME. **b.** Of a voyage or journey: Attended with, performed in, rough weather 1854. **2.** Of actions, etc.: Violent; marked by violence towards, or harsh treatment of, others ME. **3.** Of persons, their actions, language, appearance, etc.: Inclined to be harsh, violent, rude, or ungentle. late ME. †**b.** Of horses: Not properly broken in (*rare*) –1797. †**4.** Of remedies, medicines, etc.: Violent in effect; strong, powerful –1705. **5.** *colloq.* **a.** Bearing or falling hardly *on* a person 1870. **b.** Severe *on*, 'down' *on*, a person 1870.

1. a. *fig.* A quiet ebb will follow this r. tide 1596. Time, and the Houre, runs through the roughest Day SHAKS. Nor is the wind less r. that blows a good man's barge M. ARNOLD. **2.** R. deeds of Rage, and sterne Impatience SHAKS. Things promised a r. time for the Church at Ephesus 1891. **3.** The..r. frowne of Warre SHAKS. [He] called him..Lyar, Dog, and other r. Appellatives STEELE. White Winter, that r. nurse, Rocks the death-cold Year today SHELLEY. Phr. *To cut up r.*: see CUT *v. The rougher sex*, the male sex. **5. a.** Phr. *R. luck, r. luck on* (a person), worse luck than he deserves. **b.** They're mighty r. on strangers 1870.

III. 1. Of sounds: Discordant, harsh. late ME. **b.** *Gram.* Aspirated 1736. **2.** Sharp or harsh to the taste, *esp.* of wine or cider 1545. **3.** Of persons, diction, style, etc.: Wanting grace or refinement; unpolished, rugged 1535. **4.** Of occupations or exercises: Requiring or associated with rude energy or strength 1717.

1. The r. and woeful music that we have SHAKS. **b.** H still remained as the r. breathing 1880. **3.** A plain, r., honest Man, and wise, tho' not learned ADDISON. A sort of r. eloquence SCOTT. A r. and hearty welcome 1873. **4.** The softness and warmth o the climate forbid..all r. exercises 1717.

IV. 1. Of materials: In a natural or crude state; undressed, unwrought; not brought by working into a finished condition or form. late ME. **2.** Made in a general way without detailed minuteness; having an approximate accuracy or adequacy; rudely sufficient; also, in a preliminary form 1607. **3.** Not very good or perfect 1812. **b.** Lacking in comfort or refinement 1859. **4.** Comprising or requiring only the ruder degrees or processes of workmanship or skill 1680. **b.** Ignoring, or incapable of, fine distinctions; not entering into minutiæ or details 1819.

1. A chair or pulpit of r. timber GIBBON. **2.** The r. Draught of the Marriage Settlement STEELE. I add a r. drawing of the arms SCOTT. The supposed deeds were only r. copies 1888. **4.** We know.. their Pharmacy was R. and Barbarous 1704. **b.** In this r. justice of the world there is a natural distribution of rewards 1873.

Special collocations: **r. coat,** the first coat of plaster on lath; **r. coating,** = ROUGH-CAST *sb.* 2; **r. diamond,** see DIAMOND *sb.*; **r. file,** a file with a deep-cut face; **r. house** *U.S.*, a disturbance, row; hence as *vb.* (*trans.* and *intr.*); **mast,** a spar fit for making a mast; **r. neck** *U.S.*, a rough, 'tough'; **r. rice,** unhusked rice, paddy; **-scuff** *U.S.*, = *r. neck*; **r. strings,** the framed timbers which support the steps of a staircase; **r. stuff,** (*a*) the bottom stuff for boots and shoes; (*b*) coarse paint used before the final coat; **r.-waller,** a builder of rough-stone walls. Hence **Rou·gh-ly** *adv.*, **-ness.**

Rough (rʋf), *adv.* 1560. [f. prec.] In a rough manner; roughly, rudely; without special care or accuracy.

Phr. *To lie* (or *sleep*) *r.*, to sleep at night in one's clothes without bedding, esp. out of doors.

Comb.: **r.-spoken** *a.* blunt or rough in speech; **-wrought** *a.* roughly worked, shaped, or prepared.

Rough (rʋf), *v.* 1483. [f. the adj.] **I. 1.** *trans.* †**a.** To raise a nap on (cloth). **b.** To turn, pull, scrape or rub *up*, so as to make rough 1763. **c.** To make rough; to ruffle 1844. **d.** *spec.* To put large-headed nails into a horse's shoes in order to prevent the horse from slipping 1825. **2. a.** To use rough language to (a person); to ruffle 1861. **b.** To deal roughly with, ill-use 1868. **3.** *intr.* To bristle or ruffle *up* 1904.

1. b. If the hurricane roughs up the straw on all the ricks 1879. **2. a.** [He] lost no chance of roughing him in his replies HUGHES.

II. 1. *To r. it*, to do without ordinary conveniences or luxuries; to live in a rough way 1768. **2.** *trans.* **a.** To break in (a horse) 1802. **b.** To expose (an animal) to rough weather and hard or scanty fare 1858.

1. We were obliged to ruff it the whole passage 1768.

III. 1. With various advs. **a.** To trim or work *off* in a rough fashion 1789. **b.** To shape or cut *out* roughly; to plan or sketch *out* roughly 1793. **c.** To fill or work *in*, to sketch *in*, roughly 1864. **2.** To work or shape in a rough preliminary fashion 1815. **b.** To heckle (flax) roughly 1882.

Roughage (rʋ·fėdʒ). 1883. [f. ROUGH *a.* + -AGE.] The rough or refuse part of grain or crops; in dietetics, the bran of cereals or vegetable fibre, which stimulates the movements of the alimentary canal.

Rough-and-ready, *a.* 1810. **1.** Of things: Not elaborately ordered, contrived or finished; just good enough to serve the purpose. **2.** Of persons: Ready to take things as they come; not finical or particular; working in a rough but prompt and effective manner 1849. **3.** Of manner, etc.: Roughly efficient or effective, without entering into minutiæ or observing a regular procedure 1860.

3. The rough and ready style which belongs to a people of sailors..farmers and mechanics 1860.

Rough-and-tumble, *a.*, *sb.*, and *adv.* 1810. [orig. boxing slang.] **A.** *adj.* **1.** Having the character of a scuffle or scramble 1832. **2.** Of persons: Practising irregular methods of boxing; inclined to be rough or violent 1848. **3.** *transf.* Riotous, disorderly, forming a confused mass or group 1858.

1. That circle of r. political life where the fine fibred men are at a discount 1872.

B. *sb.* **1.** Haphazard or random fighting struggling, or adventure; scuffle, scramble 1810. **2.** With *a.* A random or free fight or set-to 1821. **C.** *adv.* In a rough, informal manner 1818.

Rough-cast, roughcast (rʋ·fkɑst), *ppl. a.* and *sb.* 1519. [f. ROUGH *adv.* and *a.* See CAST *v.* and *sb.*] **A.** *ppl. a.* **1.** Of walls, etc.: Roughly coated with a mixture of lime and gravel. **2.** Roughly or rudely contrived, designed, or made; of a rough, imperfect type 1591. **B.** *sb.* **1.** A composition of lime and gravel, used as a plastering for the outside of walls 1590. **b.** *attrib.* Consisting of rough-cast 1599. †**2.** A rough sketch or outline. (Prop. in two words.) –1644.

A. 2. A half-true and roughcast opinion 1880.

Rough-cast (rʋ·fkɑst), *v.* 1565. [f. ROUGH *adv.* + CAST *v.*] **1.** *trans.* To coat, cover, or fill in, with rough-cast. **2.** To mould or shape roughly; to prepare in a rough form 1586.

2. I have commenced, and have rough-cast several of the chapters W. IRVING. Hence **Rou·gh-ca:ster,** a workman who puts on rough-cast.

†**Rou·gh-draw,** *v.* 1672. [ROUGH *adv.*] *trans.* To draw, draft, or design roughly –1779.

Rou·gh-dry, *v.* 1837. [ROUGH *adv.*] *trans.* To dry (clothes) without smoothing or ironing. So **Rou·gh-dry** *a.*

Roughen (rʋ·f'n), *v.* 1582. [f. ROUGH *a.* + -EN[5].] **1.** *trans.* To render or make rough; to bring into a rough state. Also with *up*. **b.** To rough (a horse) 1864. **c.** *fig.* To irritate, ruffle 1859. **2.** *intr.* To become rough 1730.

2. The wind was rising and the sea roughening 1865.

Rou·gh-footed, *a.* 1495. [ROUGH *a.*] **1.** Having feathered feet, as *r. dove, eagle*, etc. **2.** Wearing shoes of undressed hide with the hair on. Now *Hist.* 1529.

Rou·gh-grind, *v.* 1660. [ROUGH *adv.*] *trans.* To grind roughly or so as to leave an unsmoothed or uneven surface.

Rough-hew (rʋ·fhiū), *v.* 1530. [ROUGH *adv.*] *trans.* To hew (timber) roughly; to shape out roughly; to work or execute in the rough.

fig. There's a Diuinity that shapes our ends, R. them how we will SHAKS. Hence **Rou·gh-hewer.**

Rough-hewn (rʋ·fhiūn), *ppl. a.* 1530. [ROUGH *adv.* Cf. prec.] **1.** Roughly hewn or shaped out, roughly wrought. **2.** Of persons: Lacking in refinement; uncultivated, plain, blunt; †rough-natured, cruel 1600.

2. The r. native of the north SCOTT.

Roughing (rʋ·fiŋ), *vbl. sb.* 1755. [f. ROUGH *v.* + -ING[1].] **1.** The action of making rough. **2.** The action or operation of preparing roughly or treating in a preliminary manner. Also with advs., as *down, in, up*. 1825. **3.** The fact of undergoing hardships, or living under hard conditions 1841.

2. Bastard stucco is of three coats, the first is r. in or rendering 1873.

Roughings (rʋ·fiŋz). *dial.* 1674. [app. a var. of ROWEN, infl. by ROUGH *a.* through the var. ROW *a.*] Aftermath.

Roughish (rʋ·fiʃ), *a.* 1764. [f. ROUGH *a.* + -ISH[1].] Somewhat rough.

Rough leaf. 1733. [ROUGH *a.*] **1.** The first true leaf of a (garden or field) plant, as dist. from the cotyledons; a foliage leaf 1754. **2.** The stage of growth when the true leaves have appeared 1733.

Rough-legged, *a.* 1611. [ROUGH *a.*] Having hairy or feathered legs; *esp.* of birds: having the tarsi feathered.

Rough-rider (rʋ·fˌrəi:dəɹ). 1791. [ROUGH *a.*] **1.** A horse-breaker. **b.** *Mil.* A non-commissioned officer who assists the riding-master 1802. **2.** A horseman of a rough type; one engaged in rough work or who can ride an unbroken horse 1828. **b.** *Mil.* An irregular cavalryman 1884.

Roughshod (rʋ·fʃǫd), *a.* and *pa. pple.* 1688. **A.** *adj.* Of horses: Having shoes with the nail-heads projecting; chiefly *fig.* in phr. *to ride r. over*, to domineer or tyrannize over, to treat without any consideration. **B.** *pa. pple.* Provided with shoes which are roughed to prevent slipping 1826.

Rought, obs. pa. t. of REACH, RECK.

Rough-tree. 1629. [In earlier use a var. of RUFF-TREE and ROOF-TREE 2; later also f. ROUGH *a.*] *Naut.* A mast, yard, or boom, serving as a rail or fence above the ship's side, from the quarter-deck to the forecastle; any unfinished mast or spar.

‖**Roulade** (rulad). 1706. [Fr., f. *rouler* to roll; see -ADE.] *Mus.* A quick succession of notes, prop. as sung to one syllable.

‖**Rouleau** (rulō·). *Pl.* **-eaus, -eaux.** 1693. [Fr. (XVI), deriv. of *rôle*; see RÔLE, -EL².] **1.** A number of gold coins made up into a cylindrical packet. **b.** *transf.*, esp. of blood-corpuscles 1858. **2.** A roll, coil 1795. **3.** A trimming of a rolled form 1827.

‖**Roulette** (rule·t). 1734. [Fr. *roulette* (OFr. *roelette*), dim. of *rouelle* (OFr. *roele*) wheel :- late L. *rotella*, dim. f. *rota* wheel.] †**1.** A small wheel. NORTH. **2.** A game of chance played on a table with a revolving centre, on which a ball is set in motion, which finally drops into one of a set of numbered compartments 1745. **b.** The centre part of a roulette table 1850. **3.** *Geom.* The curve traced by any point in the plane of a given curve when the latter rolls without sliding over another fixed curve. 1867. **4.** A device to keep the hair in curl 1860. **5.** *Engraving.* A small instrument used to produce a series of dotted lines on a plate 1854. **6.** A revolving toothed wheel for perforating postage stamps 1867. Hence **Roule·tted** *pa. pple.* of postage stamps: perforated by means of a r.

Rouman (rū·măn), *sb.* and *a.* 1856. [- Fr. *Roumain* - the native name *Român* :- L. *Romanus* ROMAN.] = next.

Roumanian, Rum- (rumēⁱ·niăn), *a.* and *sb.* 1865. [f. *Roumania* + -AN.] **A.** *adj.* Of, or belonging to, Roumania. **B.** *sb.* A native of Roumania; the language of Roumania 1878.

Roumeliote, Rum- (rumī·liōᵘt). 1838. [- mod.Gr. Ῥυμελιότης; see -OTE.] A native of Roumelia. Also *attrib.* or as *adj.*

Rounce (rauns). 1683. [- Du. *ronds(e*, *ronse* in same sense.] *Typog.* **1.** The handle of the winch by which the spit and wheel are turned so as to run the carriage of a hand-press in and out. **2.** The spit and wheel (or girth-barrel) of a printing-press 1683.

Rouncival (rau·nsivăl). 1573. [perh. f. the place-name *Roncesvalles* (*Roncevaux*).] In full *R. pea*, a large variety of garden or field pea.

Rouncy (rau·nsi). Now *arch.* [ME. *ronsi*, *rouncyn* - OFr. *ronci*, *roncin* = med.L. *roncinus*, *runcinus* (XI); of unkn. origin.] A horse, *esp.* a riding-horse.

Round (raund), *sb.*¹ ME. [f. ROUND *a.*] **I. 1.** A spherical or globular body; a sphere, globe, planet. Somewhat *rare.* **b.** The vault of heaven 1590. **2.** An object of a circular form 1500. **b.** A large round piece *of* beef, usually one cut from the haunch 1821. **c.** *Brewing.* A large vessel or cask employed in the final process of fermenting beer 1806. **3.** A rung or rundle of a ladder 1548. **b.** A tooth or stave of a trundle 1731. **c.** A round cross-bar connecting the stilts of a plough, or the legs of a chair; a stretcher 1875. **4.** †**a.** A piece of sculpture or statuary executed in the round -1700. **b.** *Arch.* A rounded moulding 1673. **c.** A plane with a convex bottom and iron, for working hollows or grooves 1846. **5.** *The r.*: **a.** That form of sculpture in which the figure stands clear of any ground, as dist. from *relief* 1811. **b.** A rounded or convex form 1797. **c.** The natural form of timber, without being squared in any way 1813.

1. *This* (*earthly*, etc.) *r.*, the earth; To the uttermost convex Of this great R. MILT. **b.** Nature that heard such sound Beneath the hollow r. Of Cynthia's seat MILT. **3.** A Ladder of Ten Rounds 1709. *fig.* I may consider myself on the first r. of the ladder 1875. **4. a.** A r. is better to draw by.. than any flat or painting whatsoever 1622. **5. a.** Many early pieces, modelled in high relief and in the r., are probably of this origin 1873.

II. 1. The circumference or outer bounds *of* some circular object; the complete circle *of* something (with or without implication of the included area). late ME. **2.** A circle, ring, or coil; an annular enclosing line or device. late ME. **b.** A single turn of yarn, etc., when wound as on a reel 1753. **3.** A structure, or part of one, a building, enclosing wall, etc., having a circular form 1578. **b.** A circular part, form, or arrangement of natural origin 1602. **c.** A curve or bend, as of a river, bay, etc. 1616. **4.** A circular group or assemblage of persons. Freq. in phr. *in a r.*, in a ring. 1590. **b.** A circular group of things; a number of things set or arranged in a ring 1598.

1. The wide r. of earth..holds nothing that I would call a recompense SCOTT. **2.** What is this, that..weares vpon his Baby-brow, the r. And top of Soueraignty? SHAKS. **4. b.** *fig.* Repeating again and again the same small r. of memories GEO. ELIOT.

III. 1. A dance in which the performers move in a circle or ring, or around a room, etc. 1513. **2.** Movement in a circle, or about an axis; motion round a certain course or track 1604. **b.** A roundabout way or course; one which turns round in a circle 1590. **3.** A recurring or revolving course *of* time 1710. **b.** A recurring or continuous succession or series *of* events, occupations, duties, etc. 1655. **4.** *Mil.* The walk or circuit performed by the watch among the sentinels of a garrison, camp, etc.. esp. during the night. Chiefly in phr. *to go*, *pace*, or *walk the r.* 1598. **b.** A watch under the command of an officer, which goes round a camp, the ramparts of a fortress, etc., to see that the sentinels are vigilant, or which parades the streets of a town to preserve good order; a military patrol 1581. **5.** A customary circuit, walk, or course; the beat or course traversed by a watchman, constable, vendor, etc. Freq. in phr. *to walk, take, go*, etc., *one's round(s)*. 1607. **6.** A turn, walk, or drive round a place or to a series of places, for the purpose of recreation, sight-seeing, purchasing, etc. 1611. **b.** A series *of* visits or calls 1772. **c.** *Golf.* A spell of play in which the player goes right round the course 1879. **7.** The circuit *of* a place, etc. 1609. **b.** *To go the r.*, of communications, news, etc., to be passed or handed on round a whole set of persons. Also const. *of.* 1669. **c.** *pl.* Cf. ROUNDSMAN 1. 1795.

1. *fig.* Where rivulets dance their wayward r. WORDSW. **2.** His kill-joy visage will never again stop the bottle in its r. SCOTT. **b.** Ile leade you about a R...through bush, through brake, through bryer SHAKS. **3.** Shall Error in the r. of time Still father Truth? TENNYSON. **b.** This is the r. of my day JOHNSON. **5.** The watchful Bellman march'd his R. STEELE. **6. c.** A 'round', as it is termed, of the links is very nearly four miles 1879. **7.** You have danc'd the R. of all the Courts ARBUTHNOT. **b.** The following anecdote, that is now going the r. of the papers THACKERAY. **c.** Most labourers are, (as it is termed,) on the Rounds; that is, they go to work from one house to another round the parish 1795.

IV. 1. *Mus.* †**a.** A song sung by two or more persons, each taking up the strain in turn -1683. **b.** 'A species of Canon, for three or more equal voices, in which one voice sings a short complete melody, which is then sung by a second voice, the first voice proceeding to another accompanying melody' 1776. **2.** A quantity of liquor served round a company, or drunk off at one time by each person present 1633. **b.** A piece *of* toast, made from a slice cut right across the loaf 1840. **3.** A single discharge of each piece of artillery or firearm; each of the shots fired by a single piece 1725. **b.** A single charge of ammunition for a firearm 1747. **4. a.** *Card-playing.* A single turn of play by all the players 1735. **b.** *Pugilism.* A single bout in a fight or boxing-match 1812. **c.** *Sport.* A spell of play forming a definite stage in a competition or match 1902. **5. a.** A separate or distinct outburst *of* applause, cheers, etc. 1815. **b.** A single stroke in succession from each bell of a set or peal 1826.

2. Serve out a r. of brandy to all hands 1883. **3.** The great Guns..fired several Rounds 1725. **b.** Wolfe's regiment carried into the field 24 rounds a man 1747. **4. b.** The r. lasted three minutes 1812. **5. a.** The roars of welcome and the rounds of cheers DICKENS.

Round (raund), *sb.*² 1769. [f. ROUND *v.*¹ III. 1 d.] The act of rounding. Chiefly *Naut.* with *aft, down.*

Round (raund), *a.* [ME. *rond*, *round* - OFr. *rond-*, *round-*, inflexional stem of *ront*, *roont*, earlier *reont* (mod. *rond*) :- Rom. **retundus*, for L. *rotundus* ROTUND.] **I. 1.** Having all parts of the surface equidistant from the centre; spherical, globular; resembling a ball. **2.** Cylindrical; circular in respect of section ME. **b.** Of the shoulders: Having a forward bend from the line of the back 1709. **3.** Of persons (or animals): Plump, free from angularity; also, stout, corpulent ME. **b.** Of limbs: Plump, full; well-shaped. late ME. **c.** Of garments: Made so as to envelop the body or limbs in a circular manner; cut circularly at the bottom, so as to have no train or skirts. late ME. **4.** Having all parts of the circumference equidistant from the centre; circular, formed like a circle; also, annular, spiral ME. **b.** Exhibiting a curvilinear form or outline; curved; forming a segment of a circle 1662. **c.** Of vowels: Produced by contracting the lips towards a circular form 1867. **5.** Going round in, tracing out, a circle. *R. dance*, one danced by people in couples and including whirling or revolving steps 1530. **6.** *Boxing.* Of blows: Delivered with a swing of the arm 1808.

1. *R. shot*, spherical balls of cast-iron or steel for firing from smooth-bore cannon. **2.** Hollow Engins long and r. Thick-rammd MILT. **b.** The Butler.. was noted for r. Shoulders, and a Roman Nose 1709. **3.** A little, r., fat, oily man of God THOMSON. **c.** A r. cloth jacket for winter wear 1882. **4. b.** *R. chisel*, an engraver's tool having a rounded belly. *R. plane*, a plane with a round sole for making rounded work. 1875. **c.** R. or Labialised Vowels 1867. **6.** The left elbow must be raised outwards until in a line with the shoulder..The blow is a r. one 1901.

II. 1. Of numbers: Full, complete, entire; esp. *r. dozen.* Also *transf.* expressed roundly. ME. **b.** Of computation, etc.: Approximately exact; roughly correct (*rare*) 1631. **2.** Of a sum of money; Large, considerable in amount 1579. **3.** Brought to a perfect finish or completeness; neatly turned or finished off 1568. †**b.** Thoroughly accomplished (*rare*) -1665. **c.** Of the voice, sounds, etc.: Full and mellow; sonorous, full-sounding 1832.

1. A r. half dozen of pretty girls HAWTHORNE. Phr. *R. number*, a number which is only approximately correct, usu. one expressed in tens, hundreds, etc., without precise enumeration of units; so *r. figures.* **b.** I may form a r. guess SCOTT. **2.** A good r. somme of money 1579. **3.** All his sentences be rownd and trimlie framed ASCHAM.

III. †**1.** Of blows, etc.: Heavy, hard, severe, swingeing -1772. †**b.** Of fighting: Vigorous; general -1654. †**c.** Of measures, etc.: Summary, vigorous; severe, harsh -1715. **2.** Of movement: Quick, brisk, smart. Chiefly in phr. *a* (*good*) *r. pace.* 1548. **3.** Plain, honest, straight-forward 1516. **4.** Of persons: Plain-spoken, uncompromising, severe in speech (†or dealings) *with* another 1524. **b.** Of speech, esp. reproof or chiding. late ME. **5.** Of lies or oaths: Bold, arrant, downright; not toned down in any way 1645. **b.** Of assertions, etc.: Positive, unqualified 1737.

1. c. A good r. Whipping ARBUTHNOT. **2.** He.. proceeded on his way at a r. trot PEACOCK. **3.** I will a r. vn-varnish'd Tale deliuer SHAKS. **4.** He will not heare, till feele; I must be r. with him SHAKS. **b.** Your reproofe is something too r. SHAKS. **5.** To swear a few r. oaths DICKENS.

Special collocations: **r.-back,** a person having a rounded back; **r. coal,** coal from which the small has been separated; large or lumpy coal; **r. game,** any game, esp. at cards, in which each of a number of persons plays on his own account; **r. meal,** coarse oatmeal; **round O,** (*a*) a 'round' lie; (*b*) a circle or number of persons; **r. text,** large r.-hand; **r. tool,** a r.-nosed chisel for making concave mouldings; **-top** *Naut.*, a platform (formerly circular) about a mast-head; **r. towel,** one which has the two ends sewed together; **r. tower** *Archæol.*, one of a number of high circular towers, somewhat tapering from the base to a conical roof-crowned top, which are found in Ireland, etc.; **r. trip,** (*U.S.*) a circular tour or trip; an outward and return journey; **r. turn,** one complete turn of a rope round anything. **b.** In names of fishes, etc., as **r. fish,** fish of a rounded (as opp. to flat) form; **r.-fish:** (*a*) the pilot-fish, *Coregonus quadrilateralis*; (*b*) the common carp.

Comb. **r.-nosed** *a.* having a r. nose; chiefly of tools; **-winged** *a.* (*Ent.*) in the names of moths as *r. winged muslin*, etc.

Round (raund), *adv.* and *prep.* ME. [As adv., f. ROUND *a.*; as prep., perh. aphetic of AROUND.] **A.** *adv.* **I. 1.** Of motion: With a circular course, so as to return again to the point of departure. Also *transf.* of time. **b.**

To each in turn of an assembled company (orig. as seated at table); hence, with (successive) inclusion of all those belonging to a company, body of persons, etc. 1613. †**c.** From all sides; all over (*rare*) –1766. **d.** Throughout; from beginning to end. Chiefly in phr. *all the year r.* (also used *attrib.*). 1753. **e.** So as to include or visit in succession a number of places or persons 1821. **2.** In a ring or circle; so as to encompass, encircle, or enclose something; on each wall or side (of a room, etc.) ME. **3.** In every direction from a centre; on all sides; all about 1440. **b.** By measurement in all directions from a given centre 1656. **c.** In the neighbourhood or vicinity; round about 1785. **4.** By a circuitous, roundabout, or indirect way or course 1668. **b.** Denoting arrival or presence at some point or place reached by an indirect route 1698. **5.** *Cricket.* **a.** In the direction lying behind the batsman; 'to leg' 1857. **b.** = ROUNDARM 1. 1859.

1. Once more the slow dumb years Bring their avenging cycle r. 1863. **b.** A health Gentlemen, Let it goe r. SHAKS. **e.** Employing a number of young men to go r. with samples 1884. **2.** Twice five miles of fertile ground With walls and towers were girdled r. COLERIDGE. **3.** All r. the forest sweeps off, black in shade M. ARNOLD. **b.** All the sheep..for a mile r. 1833. **4.** The horse-way..was five miles r., though the foot-way was but two GOLDSM.

II. 1. With a rotatory or whirling movement 1500. **2.** In a curve, spirally 1611. **3.** In the opposite direction; to or towards the opposite quarter 1765. **b.** To the opposite view; to a different opinion, frame of mind, etc. 1825.

1. He that is giddie thinks the world turns r. SHAKS. **3.** If his horse has stopt and turned r. five thousand times with him 1787. **b.** He had talked him pretty well r. 1855.

†**III. 1.** Roundly; with a full or round utterance; in round terms –1780. **2.** With a free or easy motion; with celerity or freedom –1597. **b.** Openly, straightforwardly (*rare*) –1650.

2. b. I went r. to worke, And (my yong Mistris) thus I did bespeake SHAKS.

B. *prep.* **1.** Of motion: So as to encircle, or make the complete circuit of; so as to go around 1602. **b.** So as to include, traverse, visit, etc., in turn or successively; also, all about (a certain area) 1605. **c.** Throughout, all through; from beginning to end of (a period of time) 1715. **2.** Around; about; on the circuit or outer bounds of; so as to surround or envelop 1662. **b.** Having (some person or thing) as the central figure or subject 1898. **3.** In all (or various) directions from; on all sides of 1729. **4.** So as to revolve about (a centre or axis) 1728. **5.** So as to make a turn or partial circuit about, or reach the other side of 1743.

1. The God, dove-footed, glided silently R. bush and tree KEATS. **b.** R. the Streets the reeling Actors ran DRYDEN. **c.** Verdant olives flourish r. the year POPE. **2.** We sate..r. a temperate repast GOLDSM. **3.** When r. me silent Nature speaks of death 1816. **5.** They..drove him r. the bay 1894. Phr. *To come r.*: see COME *v.* *To get r.* (a person), to cajole, wheedle; to circumvent, get the advantage of.

Round (raund), *v.*[1] late ME. [f. ROUND *a.*, in early use perh. after OFr. *rondir.*] **I.** *trans.* **1.** To make round; to invest with a circular or spherical form. Also *refl.*, to contract into a circle or ball. **b.** To draw together, or expand, into a rounded form. Also *refl.* 1867. **c.** To labialize (a vowel) 1867. **2.** †**a.** To deface (coin) by cutting or paring –1625. †**b.** To cut (the hair) short round the head; to trim, crop (the head, a person) in this way –1781. **c.** To crop (the ears of dogs) 1781. **3.** To make convex or curving in outline; to raise to a relief; to form into a cylinder 1677. **b.** To develop or fill out to a rounded form 1839. **4.** To finish off, bring to completeness or to a perfect form 1610. **b.** To frame or turn (a sentence, etc.) neatly or gracefully; to finish or end (a sentence) *with* something 1732.

1. What rounded the sun and planets? TYNDALL. **2. b.** Ye shall not r. the corners of your heads *Lev.* 19:27. **3.** Getting one [block of wood] as big as I had Strength to stir, I rounded it DE FOE. **4.** We are such stuffe As dreames are made on; and our little life Is rounded with a sleepe SHAKS.

With advs. **R. down** (*Naut.*) = OVERHAUL *v.* 1. **R. in.** **a.** (*Naut.*) To haul in. **b.** = *R. up* c. **R. off.** **a.** To make round, convex, or curved by trimming off edges or angles; to cut off (points, etc.) so as to make round. **b.** To finish off, complete (an estate, etc.) by addition of adjacent lands. **c.** To finish or complete appropriately; to end neatly or elegantly. **R. over,** to turn over so as to close at the end. **R. up.** **a.** To gather up in a round mass or ball. **b.** (*Naut.*) To shorten a tackle. **c.** (orig. *U.S.* and *Austral.*) To collect (cattle, etc.) by riding round the scattered herd and driving it together; also *transf.*

II. 1. To make the complete circuit of, to pass or travel round (the world, a place, etc.) 1592. †**b.** To walk round, make the rounds of (a place, etc.) –1736. **2.** To pass round so as to get to the opposite side of (a place) 1743. **3.** To surround or encircle; to encompass *with* something 1593. **4.** To cause to turn round, or move in a circle; to bring round. Also with *off.* 1728.

1. The low Sun..in thir sight Had rounded stil th' Horizon MILT. **2.** The daring adventurer.. rounded the Cape of Good Hope 1874. **3.** The hollow Crowne That rounds the mortall Temples of a King SHAKS. **4.** The day..slowly rounded to the east The one black shadow from the wall TENNYSON.

III. *intr.* **1.** To walk or go about; *spec.* of a guard, to go the rounds 1532. **b.** To take a circular or winding course; to make a turn, curve, or sweep; to turn around 1674. **d.** *Naut. R. to*, to come to the wind and heave to 1830. **e.** *slang.* To become an informer, peach *on* 1859. **f.** To turn *on* (a person) with reproach or rebuke 1877. **2.** To become round, circular, or spherical; to grow or develop to a full round form 1611. **b.** To have or assume a curved or rounded form; to curve or inflect. Also with *away* or *up.* 1670. **c.** Of a whale: To prepare or make ready to dive by arching the back 1889. **d.** *To r. up*, to collect in a body 1890.

1. b. We tore clear from her, and rounding to the wind shot a-head MARRYAT. **d.** She rounded-to and let go her anchor 1840. **2.** *Wint. T.* II. i. 16. Hence **Rou·nded** *ppl. a.* (*Phonetics*) of a vowel: affected by labialization.

Round (raund), *v.*[2] Now *arch.* [OE. *rūnian*, ME. *rune, roune* = OS. *rūnon*, MLG., MDu. *rūnen*, OHG. *rūnēn*, (G. *raunen*), OSw. *runa*; f. OE. *rūn*, ME. *run, roun* dark saying, counsel, RUNE. For the parasitic *d* cf. BOUND *ppl. a.*[1], SOUND *sb.*[2]] **1.** *intr.* To whisper; †also occas., to mutter or murmur. **2.** *trans.* To whisper (something) OE. **3.** To address (a person) in a whisper; in later use *esp.* to take privately to task. late ME. **b.** To whisper (something) to (a person) 1579.

2. What rowne ye with oure mayde? CHAUCER. Ill Margraf rounded things into the Crown-Prince's ear, in an unmannerly way CARLYLE. **3. b.** He slily rounded the first lady in the ear, that an action might lie against the Crown LAMB.

Round about, *adv.* and *prep.* ME. [See ROUND *adv.* and ABOUT.] **A.** *adv.* **1.** In a ring or circle; all round; on all sides or in all directions. **2.** With a circular or encircling movement; so as to pass or turn right round 1500. **3.** To the opposite direction 1582. **4.** By a circuitous route 1870. **5.** Approximately 1926.

1. From Jerusalem and the costes rounde aboute TINDALE *Rom.* 15:19.

B. *prep.* **1.** So as to move or pass round; so as to encircle by moving round 1484. **2.** In a ring or circle about; on all sides of; in all directions from 1535.

1. Round about the Caldron go SHAKS. **2.** Round about the prow she wrote 'The Lady of Shalott' TENNYSON.

Roundabout (rau·ndăbaut), *sb.* and *a.* Also **round-about.** 1535. [f. prec.] **A.** *sb.* **1.** A circle; a circular course or object; a circular encampment, a surrounding hedge, etc. **b.** A one-way circular system of traffic 1927. **2.** *U.S.* **a.** A short jacket 1818. **b.** An arm-chair with a rounded back 1864. **3.** A circuitous or indirect way; a detour 1755. **b.** An indirect utterance; a circumlocution 1616. **4.** †**a.** A kind of round dance –1815. **b.** A merry-go-round 1763.

4. b. Phr. *To make up on the swings what one loses on the roundabouts*, (with allusion to two prominent features of fairs), to make 'things' balance.

B. *adj.* **1.** Not following a straight course; not straightforward; circuitous, indirect 1608. **2.** Taking a complete survey (*rare*) 1704. **3.** Of garments: Cut circularly round the bottom; without a train or tails; going right round 1710. **4.** Of persons: Plump in figure 1806. **5.** That surrounds or encircles 1860.

1. I would..prepare him by some r. insinuation SMOLLETT. A rogue is a r. fool COLERIDGE. **2.** Large, sound, round about Sense LOCKE.

Rou·nd-arch. 1840. [ROUND *a.*] *Arch. attrib.* Characterized by arches of a semi-circular or rounded form, as in the Romanesque style.

Rou·nd-arm, *a.* (and *adv.*). 1850. [ROUND *a.*] **1.** *Cricket.* Of bowling: Performed with an outward swing of the arm; also *ellipt.* **2.** Of blows: Dealt with a circular sweep of the arm. Also as *adv.* 1886.

Round-eared, *a.* 1704. [ROUND *a.*] Having round ears, or ear-like appendages.

The round-ear'd shining Willow 1704. A gentle, quiet, old-fashioned looking girl, in a white apron and r. cap 1847.

Roundel (rau·ndĕl). ME. [– OFr. *rondel* or *-elle*, f. *rond* ROUND *a.*; see -EL, and cf. RONDEL.] **I. 1.** A circle drawn, marked out, or formed in any way. Now *dial.* **b.** Something forming a ring or circle. Now *rare.* 1486. **2.** A circular wooden trencher 1797. **3.** A small round shield. Now *Hist.* 1538. **4.** A small circular object; a little disc or rounded piece 1542. **5. a.** *Her.* = ROUNDLE 1 b. 1562. **b.** A decorative panel, plate, medallion, etc., of a round form 1859. **c.** A small round pane or window 1865. **6.** †**a.** A sphere or globe –1601. **b.** A ball or bead-moulding 1535. **7.** *Fortif.* A circular bastion 1853. **II. 1.** A rondeau or rondel. late ME. **2.** A round dance 1590.

1. He rode..Humming a r. with a smile MORRIS. **2.** Rousing the mole-cricket with their midnight roundels upon the pearly grass 1863.

Roundelay (rau·ndĕlē[i]). 1573. [– (O)Fr. *rondelet* ROUNDLET, f. *rondel* RONDEL, ROUNDEL, with ending assim. to VIRELAY or LAY *sb.*[2]] **1.** A short simple song with a refrain. **b.** *transf.* A bird's song or carol 1641. **2.** The music of a song of this type 1593. **3.** A kind of round dance 1589.

1. b. The Cuckoe and the Nightingale..with their pleasant roundelayes bid welcome in the Spring WALTON. **2.** The breath of Winter..plays a r. Of death among the bushes and the leaves KEATS.

Rounder (rau·ndəɹ). 1624. [f. ROUND *sb.*[1] and *v.*[1] + -ER[1].] **I. 1.** One who goes round, in special senses: †**a.** One who goes the round of a watch or sentinels; esp. *Mil.* an officer or soldier of the round –1770. **b.** *U.S.* One who makes the round of prisons, workhouses, drinking saloons, etc.; a habitual criminal, loafer, or drunkard 1884. **2.** *pl.* A game played usu. with bat and ball between two sides, in which each player endeavours to hit and send the ball as far away as he can, and to run to a base or right round the course without being struck by the fielded ball 1856. **b.** A complete run at this game 1856.

2. Rounders and marbles were our principal amusements 1894.

II. 1. *slang.* One who rounds on others 1884. **2.** One who rounds any kind of work; *esp.* in shoemaking 1881. **3. a.** A kind of boring-tool 1839. **b.** A tool by which a rounded form is given to something 1846. **4.** *Phonetics.* A sign used to indicate the rounding of a vowel 1888.

Rou·nd-hand. 1682. [f. ROUND *a.* + HAND *sb.*] **1.** A style of handwriting in which the letters are round, bold, and full. **2.** *attrib.* Of bowling: Performed with a horizontal swing of the hand or arm; round-arm 1851.

Roundhead, round-head (rau·ndhed). *sb.* (and *a.*). 1641. [ROUND *a.*] **1.** *Eng. Hist.* A member or adherent of the Parliamentary party in the Civil War of the 17th c., so called from their custom of wearing the hair close cut. (In this sense now usu. with capital and as one word.) †**2.** A kind of weapon –1645. **3. a.** A siluroid fish of S. America. **b.** The weakfish of N. America. 1842. **4.** *attrib.* or as *adj.* Roundheaded 1840.

1. A R. is a man whose braine's compact, Whose Verilies and Trulies are an Act Infallible 1642.

Round-headed, *a.* 1598. [ROUND *a.*] Having a round head, in various senses; *esp.* **1.** Of persons: Wearing the hair closely cut; *spec.* belonging to the Roundhead party. **2.** Of arches, windows, etc., or buildings characterized by these 1758.

Rou·nd-house. 1589. [In sense 1 app. f. ROUND *sb.*[1] III. 4 b; in 2, 3, f. ROUND *a.*] **1.** A lock-up; a place of detention for arrested persons. Now *Hist.* **2.** *Naut.* A cabin or set of cabins on the after-part of the quarter-deck 1626. **3.** *U.S.* A circular shed for locomotives, with a turn-table in the centre 1875.

Rou·nding, *vbl. sb.* 1551. [f. ROUND *v.*[1] + -ING[1].] **1.** The action of ROUND *v.*[1], in various senses. **2.** A rounded edge or surface; a curvature; a curved part or outline 1551. **3.** *Naut.* A service of small rope or cordage, wound round a cable, spar, etc., to prevent chafing 1748. **4.** *pl.* Clippings, parings 1883.

Rou·ndish, *a.* 1545. [-ISH[1] 3.] Somewhat round.

Roundle (rau·nd'l). 1544. [var. of ROUNDEL.] **1.** A ring or circle; an object of circular form; a disc, round plate, etc. Now *rare.* 1559. **b.** *Her.* One of various circular charges distinguished by their tincture 1610. **†2.** A sphere or globe –1674. **†3.** A round of a ladder –1663. **†4.** = ROUNDEL II. 1. –1579.

4. Sike a r. never heard I none SPENSER.

Rou·ndlet. late ME. [– (O)Fr. *rondelet*; see ROUNDELAY.] **†1.** A short roundel –1589. **2.** A small circle or circular object. late ME. **b.** *Her.* = ROUNDLE 1 b. 1688. **†3.** A small cask; a runlet –1730.

Roundly (rau·ndli), *adv.* 1450. [f. ROUND *a.* + -LY[2].] **1.** To the full; completely, thoroughly; in a thoroughgoing manner. **2.** Plainly, outspokenly, bluntly 1528. **b.** Frankly, openly 1593. **3.** Without circumlocution, straight 1534. **b.** Without qualification; absolutely 1596. **4.** Sharply, severely; unsparingly 1570. **†5.** Fluently, glibly; readily –1696. **6.** Rapidly, smartly, briskly, promptly 1548. **7.** In a circular manner; in a circle; rotundly 1565.

1. We are able to produce the most perfectly and r. illdone things that ever came from human hands RUSKIN. 2. Tell him r. of his faults 1682. 4. He takes them vp..very r., calleth them a generation of vipers 1607. 5. *Rich. II,* II. i. 122. 6. I..enforced my commands with a blow, which he returned as r. SCOTT.

Roundness (rau·ndnės). late ME. [f. ROUND *a.* + -NESS.] **1.** The quality of being round; rotundity. **2.** Compass; circumference. Now *rare* or *Obs.* late ME. **3.** A round object or formation; a rounded projection. late ME. **4.** Fullness or careful finish of language or style 1557. **5.** Plainness or severity (of speech) 1610.

1. Righte as the Perl of his owne kynde takethe Roundnesse, righte so the Dyamand..takethe squarenesse MAUNDEV. 4. The r. of periods charms the ear, and affects the mind 1727.

Round Ro·bin. 1546. **†1.** A blasphemous name for the Sacrament –1555. **†2.** Applied to persons –1671. **3.** A document (esp. one embodying a complaint, remonstrance, or request) having the names of the subscribers arranged in a circle so as to disguise the order in which they have signed 1731. **4.** *U.S.* The fish *Decapterus punctatus* 1876.

1. There were at Paules..fixed railing bils against the Sacrament, terming it Jacke of ye boxe, the sacrament of the halter, round Robin, with lyke unseemely termes RIDLEY. 3. [He] so tormented his crew that they signed a round robin, and sent it to the Admiralty 1870.

Round-shouldered, *a.* 1586. [ROUND *a.*] Having round shoulders; round-backed.

Ro·undsman. 1795. [f. ROUND *sb.*[1]] **1.** A labourer in need of parochial relief, who was sent round from one farmer to another for employment, partly at the expense of the farmer, and partly at the cost of the parish. **2.** One who makes rounds of inspection; esp. *U.S.*, a police-officer in charge of a patrol 1883. **3.** A person employed by a tradesman to go the round of his customers for orders and the delivery of goods 1884.

Round Table. Also **Table Round.** ME. [– OFr. *table ronde.*] **1. a.** The table, celebrated in mediæval legend, round which Arthur and his chosen knights were supposed to have sat, and which was made round so that there might be no pre-eminence or rivalry. **b.** The body of knights of the order of the Round Table ME. **†c.** A meeting of Arthur's knights and nobles –1470. **2.** An imitation of Arthur's Round Table as an institution; an assembly of knights for the purpose of holding a tournament and festival. late ME. **3.** A name applied locally to various natural or artificial antiquities, freq. reputed to have associations with King Arthur. late ME. **4.** Used generally (alone or as *attrib.* phrase) to denote a number of persons seated round a circular table, or imagined as forming a gathering of this kind; *esp.* in *round-table conference* 1826.

1. For I shalle gyue hym the table round, the whiche Vtherpendragon gaue me MALORY. In dyuers places of Englond many remembraunces ben yet of hym..At wynchester the rounde table CAXTON. 4. The snug round-table dinner-party 1852. The 'New Round Table' is a symposium on Home Rule 1889.

Rou·nd-up. 1769. [See ROUND *sb.*[2] and *v.*[1]] **1.** *Ship-building.* The upward curvature or convexity to which the transoms and beams of a ship are shaped. **2.** (orig. *U.S.* and *Austral.*). The driving of cattle, etc., together or into an enclosure, usu. for the purpose of registering ownership or counting. 1878. Also *transf.*

Roundure (rau·ndiŭɹ). 1600. [In XVII var. of RONDURE with assim. to ROUND *a.*; later f. ROUND *a.* + -URE.] Roundness; rounded form or space.

Rou·ndwise, *adv.* and *a.* 1577. [f. ROUND *a.* + -WISE.] **A.** *adv.* In a circular form, disposition, or arrangement; circularly. **†B.** *adj.* Circular, round. P. FLETCHER.

Round-worm, round worm. 1565. A parasitic worm of a rounded form infesting the human intestines: **a.** A worm of the genus *Lumbricus* or *Ascaris.* **b.** A nemathelminth or a nematode worm 1836.

Roup (raup), *sb.*[1] *Sc.* and *north.* 1693. [f. ROUP *v.* 2.] An auction; the act of selling or letting by auction.

Roup (rūp), *sb.*[2] 1551. [Of unkn. origin.] A disease in poultry characterized by morbid swellings on the rump.

Roup (rūp), *sb.*[3] 1585. [prob. imit.] **1.** *Sc.* and *north.* Hoarseness, huskiness. **2.** A form of purulent catarrh affecting domestic poultry 1808.

Roup (raup), *v. Sc.* and *north.* ME. [Of Scand. origin; cf. Icel. *raupa* boast, brag.] **1.** *intr.* To cry, shout, roar; to croak. Now *arch.* **†b.** *trans.* To proclaim with a loud voice –1572. **2.** To sell or let by auction 1568. **b.** To sell up (a person) 1817. Hence **Rou·per.**

Rousant (rau·zănt), *a.* 1688. [f. ROUSE *v.* + -ANT.] *Her.* Applied to a bird rising, as if preparing to take wing.

Rouse (rauz), *sb.*[1] 1589. [f. ROUSE *v.*] **†1.** A shake (of the feathers, etc.) –1672. **2.** *Mil.* The signal for arousing; the réveille 1802. **3.** A violent stir 1824.

2. The first notes of the r. are dismal 1863.

Rouse (rauz), *sb.*[2] Now *arch.* 1602. [prob. aphet. f. *carouse,* due to wrong division of the phr. *to drink carouse.*] **1.** A full draught of liquor; a bumper. **2.** A carousal or bout of drinking 1602.

2. She has heard..Your rowses and your wenches 1619. Phr. *To take over one's r., have, give a r.*

Rouse (rauz), *v.* 1486. [orig. a techn. term in hawking and hunting, and so prob. of AFr. origin. Cf. AROUSE.] **I. †1.** *refl.* Of a hawk: To shake the feathers (*rare*) –1825. **2.** *trans.* To cause (game) to rise or issue from cover or lair 1531. **†3. a.** To raise or set up, to ruffle –1604. **b.** To raise or lift up –1650. **4.** To cause to start up from slumber or repose; to awaken from sleep, meditation, etc. Also with *up, out.* 1593. **†b.** To disturb, chase away (sleep). MILT. **5.** *fig.* **a.** To awaken or startle from a state of ease or security 1594. **b.** To stir up, provoke to activity 1586. **6.** To stir up, agitate, put into motion, bring into an active state 1582. **7.** *Naut.* To haul *in, out, up,* with force 1625.

2. Thou mayst..Rouze from their Desart Dens, the bristled Rage of Boars DRYDEN. 3. a. An Eagle, seeing pray appeare, His aery plumes doth rouze SPENSER. b. 2 *Hen. IV,* IV. i. 118. 4. Rouz'd vp with boystrous vntun'd drummes SHAKS. Sweete, r. your selfe SHAKS. 5. a. I mean to r., to alarm the whole nation PITT. b. Emetics..might r. the liver from its state of torpor 1808. 6. He began..to rowze vp his furie 1589. Blustring winds, which all night long Had rous'd the Sea MILT.

II. *intr.* **†1.** Of hawks or other birds and animals: To shake the feathers or body –1678. **2.** Of game: To rise from cover (*rare*) 1575. **†3.** To rise up, stand on end. SHAKS. **4.** To get up from sleep or repose; to waken up 1589. **b.** Of qualities or feelings 1671.

2. A red buck roused, then crossed in view 1826. 4. Whiles Nights black Agents to their Prey's doe rowse SHAKS. *fig.* Be it ours to r. at once To action COWPER. b. His fierie vertue rouz'd From under ashes into sudden flame MILT.

Rouser (rau·zəɹ). 1611. [f. ROUSE *v.* + -ER[1].] **1.** One who or that which rouses or stirs up. **b.** An implement or apparatus used for stirring (*esp.* beer in brewing) 1830. **2.** One who, or that which, is remarkable in some respect; *esp.* an outrageous lie 1825. **3.** A loud noise; a noisy person, song, etc. 1731.

Rousing (rau·ziŋ), *ppl. a.* 1641. [f. ROUSE *v.* + -ING[2].] **1.** That rouses, awakens, or stirs up. **2. a.** Of a lie: Outrageous 1664. **b.** Of a fire: Roaring 1682. **c.** Of trade, etc.: Brisk, lively 1767. **3.** Of the nature of, connected with, awakening or rising 1671.

3. Now lapdogs give themselves the rowsing shake POPE. Hence **Rou·singly** *adv.*

||**Roussette** (ruset). 1774. [Fr. (XVI), fem. of OFr. *rousset* reddish, f. *roux* red; see -ETTE.] **1.** The frugivorous bat, *Pteropus vulgaris.* **2.** A shark of the family *Scylliidæ* 1882.

||**Roussillon** (rusi·lyoṅ). 1768. [See def.] A red wine made in the old province of Roussillon in the south of France.

Roust (raust), *sb.* Now *Sc.* ME. [– ON. *raust.*] Voice, cry; shout, roar. Hence **Roust** *v.*[1] *intr.* to shout, bellow, make a loud noise.

Roust (raust), *v.*[2] *dial.* and *U.S.* 1658. [perh. alteration of ROUSE *v.*] *trans.* To rout *out.*

Roustabout (rau·stăbaut). 1868. [f. ROUST *v.*[2]] **1.** *U.S.* A wharf labourer or deck hand. **2.** *Austral.* A handy man 1883.

Rout (raut), *sb.*[1] [ME. *rute, route* – AFr. *rute,* OFr. *route* :– Rom. **rupta* 'broken or fractional company', subst. use (*sc. turba, turma* band, crowd) of fem. pa. pple. of L. *rumpere* break.] **I. 1.** A company, assemblage, band, or troop of persons. Now chiefly *poet.* **b.** A number of animals going together; a pack, flock, herd. Now *rare.* ME. **c.** A large number or collection of things. late ME. **2.** An attendant company; a suite, retinue, train ME.

1. The r. of rurall folk come thronging in B. JONS. Phr. *In* (†*on*) *a r.,* in a troop, body, etc.

II. 1. A disorderly, tumultuous, or disreputable crowd of persons ME. **b.** *Law.* An assemblage of three or more persons proceeding to commit an unlawful act. late ME. **2.** The whole number of persons constituting a certain (disreputable) class. late ME. **†3.** *The* (*common, vulgar*) *r.,* the common herd, the rabble –1730. **4.** Riot, disturbance, stir, uproar. Now *poet.* or *arch.* late ME. **b.** Fuss, clamour, noise. Now *dial.* 1684. **5.** A fashionable gathering or assembly, a large evening party or reception, much in vogue in the 18th and early 19th centuries 1742.

1. A hireling r. scraped together from the dregs of the people MILT. 3. Did ever God or Man's Lawe preferre the feete before the head, the rowt before the ruler 1593. 4. Then made they revell route and goodly glee SPENSER. b. Phr. *To make a r. about* (something). 5. One rarely heard..of her going to a theatre, or a r., or a cricket-match RUSKIN.

Rout (raut), *sb.*[2] 1598. [– Fr. †*route* (in the sense of *déroute*), prob. – It. *rotta* breakage, discomfiture of an army :– Rom. **rupta* (cf. prec.).] **1.** Disorderly retreat on the part of a defeated army, body of troops, etc. **2.** An instance of this; a complete overthrow and flight 1611. **3.** A defeated and fleeing band or army 1621.

1. Men once disordered..commonly fall to r. 1598. Phr. *To put to* (*the*) *r.*; The Dragon, put to second r., Came furious down MILT. 2. Then beganne..A Rowt, confusion thicke; forthwith they flye SHAKS.

Rout (raut), *v.*[1] Now *dial.* [OE. *hrūtan* = OFris. *hrūta,* OS. *hrūtan,* OHG. *hrūȥȥan,* prob. of imit. origin.] *intr.* To snore.

Rout (raut, *Sc.* rut), *v.*[2] Now *rare.* Chiefly *north.* and *Sc.* ME. [prob. of Scand. origin; cf. Norw. *ruta* in same sense.] *intr.* Of the sea, winds, thunder, etc.: To roar, make a loud noise. Hence **Rout** *sb.*[3] a loud shout or noise.

†**Rout**, *v.*³ ME. [Partly – OFr. *router*, f. *route* ROUT *sb.*¹ and ROUTE *sb.*; sense 2 may have some other origin.] **1.** *intr.* To assemble; to gather or herd *together* –1622. **2.** To stir, move; to make a movement –1553. **3.** To be riotous, behave riotously –1591.

Rout (raut), *v.*⁴ 1547. [irreg. var. of ROOT *v.*²] **1.** *intr.* Of swine: To turn up the soil with the snout in search of food. Now chiefly *dial.* **b.** To poke about, rummage 1711. **2.** *trans.* To turn over, or dig *up*, with the snout 1571. **b.** *transf.* To tear *up*, scoop *out* 1726. **3.** To fetch or turn (a person) out of bed; to cause to get up. Also with *out*. 1787. **b.** To search out, bring to light 1805. **4.** To toss or drive about 1845.

Rout (raut), *v.*⁵ 1600. [f. ROUT *sb.*²] **1.** *trans.* To put (an army, etc.) to rout; to compel to flee in disorder. †**2.** *intr.* To break into rout; to flee in disorder. Also *refl.* in same sense. –1680.

1. Stand..The lane is guarded: Nothing rowts vs, but The villany of our feares SHAKS.

Route (rūt), *sb.* Also †**rout.** ME. [– OFr. *rute*, (also mod.) *route* :– Rom. **rupta*, subst. use (sc. *via* way) of fem. of pa. pple. of L. *rumpere* break (cf. ROUT *sb.*¹,²). In military use and in U.S. still pronounced (raut).] **1.** A way, road, or course; a certain direction taken in travelling from one place to another; a regular line of travel or passage. **2.** Routine, regular course (*rare*) 1725. **3.** *Mil.* The order to march 1784. ‖**4.** See EN ROUTE 1779.

1. They had gone by separate routes to separate ports FROUDE. **3.** Phr. *To get, give, the r.*, to receive, or issue, marching orders. *Column of r.*, the formation assumed by troops when on the march. *R. march*, march of a battalion, etc. for training purposes. **4.** They changed horses twice en route 1872. Hence **Route** *v. trans.* to mark as available, to send or forward, to direct to be sent, by a certain route.

†**Rou·ter**, *sb.*¹ late ME. [– AFr. *routour*, OFr. *routeur*, f. *route* in the sense either of 'band, troop' (ROUT *sb.*¹) or of 'road' (ROUTE *sb.*); in med.L. *ru(p)tarius* marauder. Cf. RUTTER.] **1.** A lawless person; a robber, ruffian –1536. **2.** A swaggering soldier or bully 1557–76.

Router (rau·təɹ), *sb.*² 1846. [f. ROUT *v.*⁴ 2 b.] **1.** A kind of plane used in moulding. **2.** One who routs *out* or draws forth 1890. Hence **Rou·ter** *v. trans.* to cut out with a r.

Routine (rutī·n). 1676. [– Fr. *routine*, †*rotine*, f. *route* ROUTE *sb.*] **1.** A regular course of procedure; a more or less mechanical or unvarying performance of certain acts or duties 1680. **b.** A set form (of speech); a regular set or series (of phrases, etc.) 1676. **2.** Without article: Regular, unvarying, or mechanical procedure or discharge of duties 1789. Hence **Routi·nary** *a.* (*rare*) according to r. **Routinee·r, Routi·nist,** one who acts by, or adheres to, r. **Routi·nism,** prevalence or domination of r.

Routous (rau·təs), *a.* Now *arch.* 1632. [f. ROUT *sb.*¹ + -OUS.] *Law.* Of the nature of, concerned in, constituting, a rout. Hence **Rou·tously** *adv.* in a r. manner (now *arch.*).

Rove (rōᵘv), *sb.*¹ 1440. [– ON. *ró*, in the same sense. The *v* is excrescent.] A small metal plate or ring on which the point of a nail or rivet is clinched or beaten down in the building of boats or small ships; a burr.

†*R. and clinch* (*nails*), nails provided with roves for clinching.

Rove (rōᵘv), *sb.*² 1702. [f. ROVE *v.*¹] **1.** A ramble or wandering 1742. **2.** *dial.* A method of light ploughing 1702.

Rove (rōᵘv), *sb.*³ 1789. [Related to ROVE *v.*³] **1.** A sliver of any fibrous material (esp. cotton or wool) drawn out and very slightly twisted. **2.** *collect.* Textile material in this form 1901.

Rove (rōᵘv), *v.*¹ 1474. [perh. southernized form of (dial.) *rave* stray (XIV), prob. of Scand. origin (cf. Icel. *ráfa* in same sense). In branch II prob. infl. by ROVER¹.] **I.** †**1.** *intr.* To shoot with arrows *at* a mark selected at pleasure or at random, and not of any fixed distance. Also without const. –1674. †**2.** To shoot away *from* a mark; hence, to wander *from* the point; to diverge, or digress –1648. †**3.** To shoot (an arrow, etc.) without fixed aim. Hence, to utter at random. –1607. **4.** *intr. Angling.* To troll with live bait 1661.

2. But from that mark how far they roave we see MILT.

II. 1. *intr.* To wander about with no fixed destination; to move hither and thither at random or in a leisurely fashion; to stray, roam, ramble 1536. **b.** Of the eyes: To look in various directions; to wander 1656. **2.** *trans.* To wander over, traverse 1634.

1. On Sea we rou'd three dayes as darke as night 1627. *fig.* Then roved his spirit to the inland wood CRABBE. **b.** A Boer searchlight..roved like an angry eye from end to end of our line of march 1902. **2.** Roving the trackless realms of Lyonnesse TENNYSON.

†**Rove** *v.*² 1548. [– MLG., MDu. *rōven* rob; see REAVE *v.*¹] *intr.* To practise piracy; to sail as pirates –1698. Hence †**Ro·ving** *vbl. sb.*²

Rove (rōᵘv), *v.*³ 1789. [Of unkn. origin. Cf. ROVE *sb.*³] *trans.* To form (slivers of wool or cotton) into roves or rovings. So **Ro·ver**³ one who makes cotton etc., into roves; an attendant at a roving-frame.

Ro·ve-beetle. 1781. [perh. f. ROVE *v.*¹] A beetle of the family *Staphylinidæ*.

Rover¹ (rōᵘ·vəɹ). 1468. [f. ROVE *v.*¹ + -ER¹.] **1.** *Archery.* A mark selected at will or at random, and not of any fixed distance from the archer. Also, later, a mark for long-distance shooting (contrasted with *butt*). Usu. in phr. (*to shoot*) *at rovers*. †**2.** *At rovers* (rarely *at r.*), without definite aim or object; at random, haphazard –1725. **3.** One who roves or wanders, *esp.* to a great distance; a roving person or animal 1611. †**b.** An inconstant lover; a male flirt –1721. **4.** *Croquet.* **a.** A ball that has gone through all its hoops and is ready to peg out 1863. **b.** A player whose ball is a rover 1874.

1. The god nine days the Greeks at rovers kill'd DRYDEN. *fig.* But Nature shoots not at Rovers 1661. **2.** Phr. *To run, talk, live*, etc., *at rover(s)*. **3. c.** A boy scout over seventeen years of age.

Rover² (rōᵘ·vəɹ). late ME. [– MLG. MDu. *rōver*, f. *rōven* rob; see ROVE *v.*²] **1.** A sea-robber, pirate. †**b.** A pirate-ship; a privateer –1726. †**2.** A marauder, robber –1707.

1. Algier hauing beene of olde, and still continuing a receptacle of Turkish Rouers PURCHAS.

Roving (rōᵘ·viŋ), *vbl. sb.*¹ 1475. [f. ROVE *v.*¹ + -ING¹.] **1.** *Archery.* The action or practice of shooting at a random mark. **2.** The action of wandering or roaming 1611. So **Ro·ving** *ppl. a.* Hence **Ro·vingly** *adv.* †without fixed mark or aim; in a wandering fashion.

Ro·ving, *vbl. sb.*²: see ROVE *v.*²

Roving (rōᵘ·viŋ), *vbl. sb.*³ 1795. [f. ROVE *v.*³ + -ING¹.] **1.** The process of converting cotton, wool, etc., into roves 1825. **2.** *concr.* A rove; roves collectively 1802. **3.** *attrib.*, as *r.-box, -frame*, etc.; *r.-department, -waste* 1795.

Row (rōᵘ), *sb.*¹ [ME. *raw, row* (XIII) points to OE. **rāw* (of doubtful authenticity), var. of *rǣw* (ME. *rew*) :– **raiȝwa*, prob. obscurely rel. to MDu. *rīe* (Du. *rij*), MHG. *rīhe* (G. *reihe*).] **1.** A number of persons or things arranged in a straight line. **b.** A number of persons or things arranged in a circle (*rare*) 1576. **c.** *transf.* A string or series *of* something 1510. **2.** An array of persons (or things) of a certain kind; a class or category. Now *rare.* ME. †**3.** A (written or printed) line –1598. **4.** A number of houses standing in a line; a street (esp. a narrow one) formed by two continuous lines of houses. Chiefly *Sc.* and *north.* 1450. **b.** In Yarmouth, one of a number of narrow lanes connecting the main streets 1599. **c.** In Chester, one of several raised and covered galleries running along the sides of the four main streets 1610. **5.** A line of seats in a theatre, etc. 1710. **6.** A line of plants in a field or garden 1733.

1. He knew to rank his Elms in even Rows DRYDEN. **2.** She has an only daughter..who is.. approaching the old-maid's r. 1787. **3.** He most rede many a Rowe On Virgile or on Claudian CHAUCER. **4.** *The R.*, used *ellipt.* for Goldsmiths' Row(?), Paternoster Row, and Rotten Row, in London. **6.** Phr. *To have a hard* (*long*, etc) *r. to hoe*, to have a difficult task to perform. *To hoe one's own r.*, to do one's own work; to mind one's own business. (Both *U.S.*) Hence **Rowed** *a.* having (a specified number of) rows.

Row (rau), *sb.*² *slang* or *colloq.* 1787. [Of unkn. origin.] **1.** A violent disturbance or commotion; a noisy dispute or quarrel. **2.** Noise, din, clamour 1845.

1. Phrases. *To make, kick up, a r. What's the r.?* What is all the noise about? What is the matter? *To get into a r.*, to be severely reprimanded or rated. **2.** Never was there heard..such a noise, r., hubbub, babel, shindy, hullabaloo KINGSLEY.

Row (rōᵘ), *sb.*³ 1847. [f. ROW *v.*¹] A spell of rowing; a journey on the water in a rowing-boat.

Row (rau), *a.* Now *dial.* or *arch.* OE. [Inflexional var. of ROUGH *a.*] = ROUGH *a.* Hence †**Row** *adv.* roughly; angrily, fiercely –1500.

Row (rōᵘ), *v.*¹ [OE. *rōwan* = OFris. **roia*, MLG. *rojen* (Du. *roeijen*), ON. *róa*, rel. to L. *remus*, Gr. ἐρετμόν oar. Cf. RUDDER.] **I. 1.** *intr.* Of persons: To use oars, sweeps, etc., for the purpose of propelling a boat or other vessel. **b.** With complement denoting the place of the rower in the boat 1856. **2.** Of a boat or other vessel: To move along the surface of water by means of oars. late ME. **b.** *trans.* To be fitted or rowed with, to carry (so many oars) 1769. **3.** Of †persons, waterfowl, fish: To swim, paddle 1631.

1. They pray as they r., backwards 1706. Phr. *To r. over*, to go over the course without a competitor, thus winning a race or heat; in bumping races, to complete the course without bumping or being bumped. *To r. against the flood, stream, wind and tide*, etc., freq. in fig. use, to undertake a difficult or arduous task; to work in adverse circumstances or in the face of opposition. *To r. in the same* or *in one boat*, to be embarked in the same scheme; to be of similar principles. **b.** A companion who will not mind a few splashes..should be put in to 'r. stroke' 1856. **2. b.** A light little yawl..that rowed four oars 1854. **3.** In the pond The finely-checker'd duck before her train Rows garrulous THOMSON.

II. 1. *trans.* To propel (a boat, etc.) by means of oars ME. **b.** To make (a stroke), use (an oar), in the course or exercise of rowing 1866. **c.** With *race, heat*, etc., as compl. 1888. **2.** To convey (a person) on the water in a boat propelled by oars. Also *refl.* late ME. **3.** *transf.* To convey, transport, propel, move in a manner or with a movement similar to rowing 1667. **4.** *U.S. slang.* **a.** *To r.* (a person) *up Salt River*, to rout or defeat in politics; also = b. 1835. **b.** *To r.* (a person) *up*, to treat him to a severe verbal castigation 1845. **5. a.** To have, make use of, in a rowing match 1888. **b.** To row against (another person or crew) 1888. **c.** *To r. down*, to overtake by rowing 1869.

1. Alone he row'd his boat CRABBE. **c.** This is the only dead heat ever rowed in this race 1888. **2.** This Mayer..was rowed thyther by water 1513. **3.** The Swan..Rowes Her state with Oarie feet MILT. **5. a.** Corpus..rowed an untrained man 1900. **b.** Beach..rowed Wallace Ross for the championship 1888. Hence **Row·able** *a.* (*rare*) capable of being rowed or rowed upon. **Row·ing** *vbl. sb.*¹ also *attrib.* as *r.-boat*, a boat propelled by oars.

Row (rau), *v.*² *slang* or *colloq.* 1790. [f. ROW *sb.*²] †**1.** *trans.* To assail (a person) in a rough manner; to rag (a man or his rooms) –1863. **2.** To rate or scold (a person) angrily or severely; to take sharply to task 1809. **3.** *intr.* To make a row or disturbance 1797.

2. She rowed me for writing to Lord Palmerston about her accident GLADSTONE. Hence **Row·ing** *vbl. sb.*² a rating, scolding, or severe talking to.

Rowan (rōᵘ·ăn, *Sc.* rau·ăn). *north.* and *Sc.* 1804. [Of Scand. origin; cf. Norw. *rogn* and *raun*, Icel. *reynir*.] **1.** = next. **2.** The berry of the mountain ash. Also *r.-berry*. 1814.

Row·an-tree. *north.* and *Sc.* 1548. [See prec.] The mountain ash, *Pyrus aucuparia*.

Row-boat (rōᵘ·bōᵘt). 1538. [f. ROW *v.*¹] A boat propelled by oars; a rowing-boat.

Row-de-dow (raudĭdau·). 1848. [imit.] Noise or din, uproar, disturbance.

Row-dow-dow (raudau,dau·). 1814. [imit.] An imitation of the sound of a drum. Cf. *tow-row-row*.

Rowdy (rau·di), *sb.*¹ and *a.* 1819. [orig. American, but the source is unkn.] **A.** *sb.* Orig., a backwoodsman of a rough and lawless type; hence, a rough, disorderly person. **B.** *adj.* **1.** Belonging to the class of rowdies; of a rough, disorderly type 1819. **b.** *transf.* Of animals: Refractory; inclined to give trouble 1872. **2.** Characteristic of rowdies; *esp.* marked by disorderly roughness or noise

1852. Hence **Row·diness. Row·dyish** *a.* **Row·dyism,** r. conduct.

Rowdy-dowdy, *a. slang.* 1882. [Reduplicated f. prec.] Characterized by rowdiness.

Rowel (rau·ĕl), *sb.* late ME. [– OFr. *roel, roele* :– late L. *rotella*, dim. of L. *rota* wheel.] **1.** A small stellar wheel or disc with sharp radial points and capable of rotation, forming the extremity of a spur; also *attrib.*, as *r.-deep* adv., *-head*, etc. **b.** The rowel-head 1844. †**2.** A knob on a horse's bit –1607. **3.** *Farriery.* A circular piece of leather or other material, with a hole in the centre, inserted between the flesh and skin of a horse or other animal to cause discharge of humours; also, any kind of insertion used for this purpose 1580.

1. With sounding whip, and rowels dyed in blood COWPER. **2.** The yron rowels into frothy fome he bitt SPENSER.

Rowel (rau·ĕl), *v.* 1580. [f. prec.] **1.** *trans.* To insert a rowel in (a horse or other animal). **2.** *intr.* To use the spur-rowels 1599.

Rowen (rau·ĕn). Now chiefly *dial.* and *U.S.* [ME. *rewayn*, etc. – ONFr. **rewain* = (O)Fr. *regain*, f. OFr. *regaaignier*, for the second element see GAIN *sb.*[2], *v.*[2] Cf. AL. *rewaynum, regainum* XIII.] **1.** The second growth or crop of grass or hay in a season; aftermath, eddish. Cf. ROUGHINGS. Also *pl.* **2.** *attrib.*, as *r. crop, hay*, etc.; also †**r. (-tailed) partridge**, a partridge frequenting a field of r. grass or hay.

Rower (rōᵘ·əɹ). ME. [f. ROW *v.*[1] + -ER[1].] One who rows; an oarsman.

Rowlock (rɒ·lək). 1750. [alt., by substitution of ROW *v.*[1] for the first syll., of OARLOCK.] A device, usu. consisting of a notch, two thole-pins, or a rounded fork, on the gunwhale of a boat, forming a fulcrum for the oar in rowing.

Row·-port. 1769. [f. ROW *v.*[1] + PORT *sb.*[3] 2.] *Naut.* An opening cut through the sides of a small sailing-vessel so that sweeps may be used during calm weather.

Roxburghe (rǫ·ksbŏrə). 1877. [Named after the 3rd Duke of *Roxburghe* (1740–1804).] A style of bookbinding consisting of plain leather backs with gilt lettering, cloth or paper sides, and leaves with untrimmed edges.

Royal (roi·ăl), *a.* and *sb.* late ME. [– OFr. *roial* (mod. *royal*) :– L. *regalis* REGAL *a.*] **A.** *adj.* **I. 1.** Of blood, etc.: Originating from, connected with, a king or a line of kings. **b.** Of persons: Having the rank of king or queen; belonging to the royal family 1513. **c.** Of parts of the body 1598. **2.** Of rank, etc.: Of or pertaining to a sovereign, or the dignity or office of a sovereign. late ME. **b.** So of insignia or emblems of royalty. late ME. **c.** Of persons: In the service of the king or sovereign. Also *transf.* of pawns in chess. 1648. **3.** Belonging to, occupied or used by, a king or kings. late ME. **4.** Pertaining to the king (or queen) as civil or military head or representative of the state 1593. **5.** *R. Burgh*, A Scottish burgh which derives its charter directly from the Crown 1648. **6.** Founded or established by, under the patronage of, a sovereign or royal person 1509. **7.** Proceeding from, performed by, a (or the) sovereign 1611. **b.** Of the king or sovereign 1821.

1. Of the R. Stock Of David..shall rise A Son MILT. **b.** *R. Highness*: see HIGHNESS 2. **c.** The power of the r. hand that heals in touching RUSKIN. **2.** On a Throne of R. State MILT. **b.** This royall Throne of Kings, this sceptred Isle,..this England SHAKS. **c.** The chief art in the Tacticks of Chess consists in the nice conduct of the r. pawns 1763. **3.** The..town which contained the r. mansion 1835. Phr. *R. fish*, fish in which the crown has special rights: The term 'r. fish' includes the..sturgeon, whale, and porpoise 1883. **4.** *R. Artillery, Engineers, Marines, Naval Reserve*, etc. **6.** *R. Society*, a Society incorporated by Charles II in 1662 for the pursuit and advancement of the physical sciences. *R. Academy*: see ACADEMY 5. **7.** Besides that which Solomon gaue her of his royall bountie 1 *Kings* 10:13. **b.** His innocence..could not save him from the r. vengeance 1845.

II. 1. Befitting, appropriate to, a sovereign; *esp.* stately, magnificent, splendid. late ME. **b.** Finely arrayed; resplendent; grand or imposing. late ME. **c.** Having rank comparable to that of a king. late ME. **d.** *colloq.* Noble, splendid, first-rate 1583. **2.** Of persons: Having the character proper to a king; noble, majestic; generous, munificent; also applied to animals. late ME. **b.** Of character, feelings, etc. 1565. **3.** In various military and related uses, denoting something on a grand scale, or of great size or strength, esp. *battle r.* 1489. **4.** *R. paper*, †*paper r.*, paper of a size measuring 24 by 19 inches as used for writing and 25 by 20 for printing 1497. **5. a.** In names of birds, reptiles, animals, etc., as *r. eagle, r. leopard, r. python, r. stag* (see B. 3 c) 1575. **b.** In plant-names, as *r. bay*, the plant *Laurus indicus*; *r. fern*, osmund royal; *r. palm*, the palm *Oreodoxa regia* found in the West Indies and Florida 1849.

1. Rich, Royall food! Bountyfull Bread! CRASHAW. **b.** A Royall Traine beleeue me SHAKS. **2.** Hee..can..recount, what a royall housekeeper his great grandfather was 1616. **b.** Pitt's bearing in this grand juncture and crisis, is r. CARLYLE. **4.** *R. folio, quarto, octavo.*

Special collocations: **r. antler** (see B. 3 b); **r. arch**, one of the degrees of freemasonry; **r. evil** = KING'S EVIL; **r. flush** *Poker*, the ace, king, queen, knave, and ten of the same suit; **r. mast** (*Naut.*), a smaller mast at the head of the topgallant mast; **-sail** (*Naut.*), a small sail hoisted above the topgallant sail; **r. tine** = B. 3 a.

b. With names of colours, as **r. blue**, a deep bright blue; *r. purple, red.*

B. *sb.* **1.** *colloq.* A member of the royal family; a royal personage 1788. †**2. a.** = RIAL *sb.* 3. –1688. **b.** = REAL *sb.*[1] 1. –1755. **c.** = REAL *sb.*[1] 2. –1634. **3.** †**a.** The second branch or tine of a stag's horn, lying above the brow-antler –1623. †**b.** The antler next above the bez-antler –1627. **c.** A stag having a head of twelve points or more 1857. **4.** *Naut.* A royal sail 1769. **b.** *attrib.* (also for *r. mast*) 1840. **5.** A kind of small mortar 1790. **6.** *pl.* A name for the First Regiment of Foot, also called *Royal Scots* 1762.

2. a. *Rose r.* = ROSE-NOBLE.

Royalet (roi·ălet). Now *rare.* 1650. [f. ROYAL *sb.* + -ET, perh. after Fr. *roitelet.*] A petty king or chieftain; a kinglet, princelet.

Royalist (roi·ălist). 1643. [f. ROYAL *a.* + -IST, perh. modelled on Fr. *royaliste.*] A supporter of the sovereign or the sovereign's rights, esp. in times of civil war, rebellion, or secession; a king's man; a monarchist. So **Ro·yalism,** attachment to the monarchy or to the principle of monarchical government. **Royali·stic, -al** *adjs.*

Royalize (roi·ăləiz), *v.* 1586. [f. ROYAL *a.* + -IZE 2.] **1.** *trans.* To render royal; to invest with a royal character or standing 1590. **b.** To render famous, celebrate 1586. **2.** *intr.* To bear rule as a monarch; to play the king. Also with *it.* 1606. Hence **Royaliza·tion.**

Royally (roi·ăli), *a.* [f. ROYAL *a.* + -LY[2].] In a royal manner; *colloq.* gloriously, splendidly.

Royal oak. 1771. **1.** A sprig of oak worn to commemorate the restoration of Charles II in 1660. Hence *Royal Oak Day*, the 29th of May, Oak Apple Day. (Now *local.*) **2.** The species *Quercus regia* 1841.

Royalty (roi·ălti). late ME. [– OFr. *roialte* (mod. *royauté*); see ROYAL, -TY[1]. Superseded earlier REALTY[1].] **1.** The office or position of a sovereign; royal dignity; royal power, sovereignty. †**b.** The personality of a sovereign; (his or her) majesty –1611. †**c.** The sovereignty or sovereign rule *of* (a state) –1594. †**2.** Magnificence, pomp, splendour –1642. **3.** King-like or majestic character or quality; greatness, lordliness; munificence, generosity 1548. **4.** Royal persons collectively or individually 1480. **b.** *pl.* Royal persons; members of the royal family 1813. **5.** *pl.* Prerogatives, rights, or privileges pertaining to, or enjoyed by, the sovereign. Also rarely in *sing.* late ME. †**b.** *pl.* Emblems or insignia of sovereignty –1769. **6.** A royal prerogative or right, esp. in respect of jurisdiction, granted by the sovereign to an individual or corporation. Also *pl.* (In later use, denoting chiefly rights over minerals.) 1483. **b.** A payment made to the landowner by the lessee of a mine in return for the privilege of working it 1839. **c.** A sum paid to the proprietor of a patented invention for the use of it 1864. **d.** A payment made to an author, editor, or composer for each copy of a book, piece of music, etc., sold by the publisher, or for the representation of a play 1880. †**7.** A domain, manor, etc., in possession of royal rights or privileges –1710. **8.** A royal domain; a kingdom, realm; a monarchical state 1638. **b.** Monarchical government 1878.

1. Heare our English King, For thus his Royaltie doth speake in me SHAKS. *fig.* His striped blanket that hung like r. upon his stately form KINGLAKE. **b.** *Wint. T.* I. ii. 15. **c.** *Rich. III*, III. iv. 42. **3.** Profane thy inborn r. of mind GRAY. **4.** To the succeeding R. he leaues The healing Benediction SHAKS. **5.** Wherefore do I assume These Royalties, and not refuse to Reign? MILT. **6.** The lordship of Man was accounted as a r. and conveyed within the island itself certain sovereign rights STUBBS. **7.** I have bought that little Hovel which borders upon his Royalty STEELE. So †**Roya·lity** (*rare*).

Royston crow (roi·stən). 1611. [f. the place-name *Royston.*] The hooded or grey crow.

Rub (rɒb), *sb.*[1] 1586. [f. RUB *v.*[1]] **1.** An act or spell of rubbing 1615. **2. a.** *Bowls.* An impediment by which a bowl is hindered in, or diverted from, its proper course; also, the fact of a bowl meeting with such impediment 1586. †**b.** *gen.* Any physical obstacle or impediment to movement –1821. **3.** An obstacle, impediment, hindrance, or difficulty, of a non-material nature. Now *rare* or *Obs.* 1590. †**4.** A roughness; an unevenness or inequality –1747. **5. a.** An intentional wound or chafe given to the feelings of another; in later use *esp.* a slight reproof or teasing 1642. **b.** An encounter with something annoying or disagreeable 1645. **6.** *dial.* A mower's whetstone 1823.

1. The feathers all came off with a r. 1891. **2. a.** It is impossible to play at bowls without meeting with rubs 1757. *R. of* (or *on*) *the green*, in golf, an accidental interference with the course or position of a ball. **3.** I have no sense to sorrow for his death, whose life was the only r. to my affection 1607. Phr. *There's* (or *Here lies*) *the r.*; To sleepe, perchance to Dreame; I, there's the r. SHAKS. **4.** To leaue no Rubs nor Botches in the Worke SHAKS. **5. a.** Each felt the r., And in Spain not a Sub.. can stomach a snub 1841. **b.** Let not the rubs of earth Disturb thy peace QUARLES.

Rub (rɒb), *sb.*[2] 1830. Abbrev. of RUBBER *sb.*[2]

Rub (rɒb), *v.*[1] ME. [perh. – LG. *rubben*, of unkn. origin.] **I.** *trans.* **1.** To subject (a surface or substance) to the action of something (as the hand, a cloth, etc.) moving over it, or backwards and forwards upon it, with a certain amount of pressure and friction. late ME. **b.** To make (one's hands) move over and press upon each other, as a sign of satisfaction 1778. **c.** *spec.* (See quot.) 1856 (implied in *brass-rubber*). **2.** To subject to pressure and friction in order to clean, polish, make smooth, or sharpen. Also const. *with.* late ME. **b.** *fig.* To revive, stir up, in respect of memory or recollection. More freq. with *up.* 1580. **3. a.** To affect painfully or disagreeably; to annoy, irritate 1523. **b.** To chafe, abrade, make rough or ragged 1805. **4.** To treat (a surface) *with* some substance applied by means of friction and pressure 1535. **5.** To bring into contact with another body or surface by means of friction accompanied with pressure. Const. *against, on, over,* and *together.* late ME. **b.** To bring (a part of the body) into reciprocal contact; hence *to r. shoulders* (etc.) *with*, to come into contact, to associate, *with* others 1645. **6. a.** To remove, take or clear away, *from, off,* or *out of*, by rubbing 1508. **b.** To reduce *to* powder by rubbing 1726. **c.** To force *into* or *through*, spread *over* a surface by rubbing 1778.

1. The king awoke,..And yawn'd, and rubb'd his face TENNYSON. **b.** [He] rubbed his hands, and was scarce able to contain the fullness of his glee MISS BURNEY. **c.** These brasses are capable of being 'rubbed', that is, of having an impression taken of them..by covering them with paper, and rubbing with some fitting substance upon the paper 1861. **2.** I rubbe thynges with a cloute to make them cleane 1530. **3.** You r. the sore, When you should bring the plaister SHAKS. **4.** A rubs himselfe with Ciuit SHAKS. **5.** He rubs his Sides against a Tree DRYDEN. **b.** She had rubbed shoulders with the great THACKERAY.

With advbs. **R. away**, to remove by rubbing.

R. down. a. To clean (a horse) from dust and sweat by rubbing. **b.** To make smooth, reduce, grind down, etc., by rubbing. **R. in. a.** To apply (dry colours) by rubbing; to draw or sketch in this way. **b.** To apply (an ointment, etc.) by continued rubbing. **c.** *slang.* To emphasize or reiterate (*esp.* something disagreeable). **R. off,** to remove by rubbing. **R. out. a.** To efface, erase, obliterate by rubbing. Also *fig.* (chiefly *U.S.*), to wipe out, kill. **b.** To extract (corn) from the ear by rubbing. **R. over,** to go over (with the hand, a tool, etc.) in the process of rubbing. **R. up. a.** To revive, recall to mind (some recollection, incident, etc.). **b.** To refresh (one's memory, etc.); to make clearer or stronger. **c.** To brush up, revive one's knowledge of (a subject). **d.** To prepare or mix by rubbing. **e.** With *the wrong way* (cf. I. 3 a).

II. *intr.* **1.** To exert friction accompanied by pressure; to move and at the same time press *upon* or *against* something ME. **b.** Of a bowl: To encounter some impediment which retards or diverts its course 1588. **2.** *fig.* To continue in a certain course with more or less difficulty or restraint; to contrive to get *on, through, along,* live or last *out,* pass or go *off* 1469. **3.** To go, run, make *off.* Now *rare* or *Obs.* 1540. **4.** To admit of being rubbed (*off, out*) 1683.

1. Where the fish lye so thick, the ship brushes, and rubbes upon them 1660. **b.** So, so, r. on, and kisse the mistresse SHAKS. **2.** I hope we shall always manage to r. on somehow 1880.

†**Rub,** *v.*² 1597. [var. of ROB *v.* 6.] *intr.* At cards: To take all the cards of one suit –1642.

Rub-a-dub (rʊ·bădʊ:b), *sb.* 1787. [imit.] The sound of a drum; a drumming sound. So **Rub-a-dub** *v. intr.* **Rub-a-dub-dub.**

‖**Rubato** (rubā·to). 1887. Ellipt. for *tempo rubato* (lit. 'robbed time'): see TEMPO.

Rubber (rʊ·bəɹ), *sb.*¹ 1536. [f. RUB *v.*¹ + -ER¹.] **I. 1.** A hard brush, a cloth, or the like, used for rubbing in order to make clean. †**b.** A strigil –1623. **c.** A towel used for rubbing the body after a bath 1577. **2.** A whetstone, RUBSTONE. Now *dial.* 1566. **3.** An implement of metal or stone used for rubbing, esp. in order to smooth or flatten a surface 1664. **b.** A pad or roll used for rubbing and polishing 1837. **4.** A large coarse file. Also *r.-file.* 1677. **5.** A part of some apparatus which operates by rubbing; a machine which acts by rubbing 1771. **II. 1.** A masseur or masseuse 1610. **b.** An attendant who rubs the bathers at a Turkish bath 1680. **2.** One who rubs in any way 1611. **b.** One who takes rubbings of brasses, etc. 1861. **3.** *fig.* A rebuke or irritating remark; a source of annoyance 1706. **III.** Ellipt. for INDIA-RUBBER. **1.** Caoutchouc. Also *colloq.* A piece of this for erasing pencil marks. 1788. **b.** *pl.* Overshoes made of rubber. *U.S.* 1859. **2.** *attrib.*, as *r. tyre, r. plant, r. tree,* etc. 1866.

Hence **Ru·bber** *v.* (*U.S. slang*) = r. neck. *Comb.* **rubber-neck** (orig. *U.S. slang*), one who cranes his neck or gapes in curiosity; *attrib.*, as *r.-n. car,* etc., for tourists to see the sights of a place; also as vb.

Rubber (rʊ·bəɹ), *sb.*² 1599. [perh. spec. application of prec.] In various games of skill or chance, e.g. bowls, whist, cribbage, backgammon, a set of (usu.) three games, the last of which is played to decide between the parties when each has gained one; hence, two games out of three won by the same side. Also, a set of five games, or the winning of three of these by one side.

Ru·bbing, *vbl. sb.* late ME. [-ING¹.] The action of RUB *v.*¹; *concr.* a copy made by rubbing (1845).

Ru·bbing-stone. 1648. [f. prec.] A stone used for rubbing.

Rubbish (rʊ·biʃ), *sb.* (and *a.*). [Late ME. *robous, robys, -ishe, rubbes* – AFr. *rubbous,* perh. for *robous, pl. of *robel RUBBLE; assim. to *-ish* (XV) and *-idge* (XVI). Cf. AL. *rubisum* (XV), *robusum* (XIV).] **1.** Waste or refuse material, in early use, esp. such as results from the decay or repair of buildings; debris, litter; rejected and useless matter of any kind. †Also, a heap of rubbish. **2.** *fig.* Worthless stuff; trash 1601. **b.** Worthless, ridiculous, nonsensical ideas, discourse, or writing 1612. **c.** In interjectional use 1863. **3.** *attrib.* or †as *adj.* 1594.

1. We perceiving from the Walls several Arms and Legs in the Air, mingled with the Smoke and Rubbidge 1684. The r. of mortar from houses 1813. **2.** The body is but meer r. to the soul 1656. **b.** From hence to the end of your Book, I find nothing but R. and Trifles 1692. The jumbled r. of a dream TENNYSON. **c.** 'Oh, r.,..How can a skeleton sit and air himself?' 1888.

Comb.: **r.-price,** a paltry price, such as might properly be paid for r.; **r. pulley,** 'a simple form of tackle-block used with a rope in hoisting materials from a foundation or excavation'. Hence **Ru·bbishy** *a.* abounding in, covered with, r. or litter; paltry, contemptible, worthless.

Rubble (rʊ·b'l). [Late ME. *robyl, rubel* (cf. AL. *rubylla* XIV, *robulla* XV), perh. – AFr. **robel* (see prec.), f. OFr. *robe* spoils; see ROBE, -EL¹, -LE.] **1.** Waste fragments of stone, esp. from decayed or demolished buildings; †also, rubbish in general. **2.** Pieces of undressed stone used in the construction of walls, esp. as a filling-in. Also *r.-stone.* 1565. **b.** *ellipt.* Rubble-work 1815. **3.** *Geol.* Loose angular stones or fragments of broken material forming the upper covering of some rocks, and found beneath alluvium or over-lying soil; also, water-worn stones. Also *r.-stone.* 1796. **b.** Small coal; slack 1883. **4.** *local.* The bran of wheat, before it is sorted into pollard, bran, sharps, etc. 1858.

2. They were equally at home in the use of brick, or flint, or r. 1878. Hence **Ru·bbly** *a.* abounding in, consisting of, r.; having the nature or form of r.

Ru·bble-work, ru·bblework, ru·bble work. 1823. [f. prec.] Masonry composed of rubble or unwrought stones; also, fragments of stone mixed with mortar and used as a filling-in.

Rubefacient (rūbĭfē¹·ʃĕnt), *a.* and *sb.* 1804. [– L. *rubefaciens, -ent-,* pr. pple. of *rubefacere;* see RUBIFY, -FACIENT.] *Med.* **A.** *adj.* Producing redness or slight inflammation; *spec.* of counter-irritants. **B.** *sb.* An application producing redness of the skin; *esp.* a counter-irritant having this effect 1805.

Rubefaction (rūbĭfæ·kʃən). 1658. [See prec. and -FACTION. Cf. Fr. *rubéfaction.*] **1.** *Med.* The action of making (the skin) red; redness of the skin, esp. as produced by some application. **2.** The production of a red colour in water 1860.

‖**Rubella** (rube·lă). 1883. [mod. use of n. pl. of L. *rubellus* reddish.] *Path.* German measles.

Rubellite (rū·bĕləit). 1796. [f. L. *rubellus* reddish + -ITE¹ 2 b.] *Min.* A variety of tourmaline.

‖**Rubeola** (rubī·ŏlă). 1676. [orig. – med.L. **rubeola* (whence Fr. *rougeole* XV), subst. use of dim. of L. *rubeus* red. Cf. ROSEOLA.] *Path.* †**1.** Small red spots, usu. incident to smallpox or measles –1693. **2.** Measles. Now *rare* or *Obs.* 1803. **3.** German measles; rubella 1858.

Ruberythric (rūbĕri·þrik), *a.* 1857. [f. L. *rubia* madder + ERYTHRIC *a.*] *Chem. R. acid,* a yellow crystalline compound contained in madder-root.

Rubescent (rube·sĕnt), *a.* 1731. [– L. *rubescens, -ent-,* pr. pple. of *rubescere,* f. *ruber* red; see -ESCENT.] Tending to redness; reddening, blushing. Hence **Rube·scence** (*rare*), the fact of becoming red.

Rubiaceous (rūbi,ē¹·ʃəs), *a.* 1832. [f. mod. L. *Rubiaceæ* (Jussieu, 1789), f. *Rubia* (L. *rubia*) the genus madder; see -ACEÆ, -ACEOUS.] *Bot.* Pertaining to or characteristic of a family of plants of which madder (*Rubia*) is the typical genus.

Rubiacin (rū·biăsin). 1848. [f. L. *rubia* madder + -(c)IN¹.] *Chem.* A yellow colouring matter obtained from madder-root. So **Rubia·cic** *a.*

Rubian (rū·biăn). 1851. [f. L. *rubia* madder + -AN.] *Chem.* The bitter principle of madder-root. Hence **Rubia·nic** *a.* applied to an acid produced by the oxidation of r. in contact with alkalis.

Rubicelle (rū·bisel). 1671. [– Fr. *rubicelle, rubacelle,* also *rubace* (XVIII), dim. forms based on *rubis* RUBY.] A variety of spinel, of a yellow or orange-red colour.

Rubicon (rū·bikǫn). 1626. [Ancient name of a small stream which formed part of the boundary between Italy and Cisalpine Gaul; the crossing of it by Cæsar marked the beginning of the war with Pompey.] **1.** *To cross* or *pass the R.*, to take a decisive or final step, *esp.* at the outset of some undertaking or enterprise. **2.** A boundary, bounding line, or limit. *lit.* or *fig.* 1690. **3.** *attrib.* Applied to a variety of bezique 1887.

1. The die being cast and R. crossed 1643. **2.** The bancks of the Boyn..,the ould R. of the Pale 1711.

Rubicund (rū·bikənd), *a.* 1503. [– Fr. *rubicond* or L. *rubicundus,* f. *rubēre* be red.] †**1.** Of things: Inclined to redness; red –1671. **2.** Of the face, etc.; Reddish, flushed, highly coloured, esp. as the result of good living 1696. **b.** Of persons: Red-faced (with good living) 1827.

2. A sleepy eye, a r. face, and carbuncled nose SMOLLETT. Hence **Rubicu·ndity,** the state of being r.; redness.

Rubidine (rū·bidəin). 1868. [f. L. *rubidus* red + -INE⁵.] *Chem.* A compound belonging to the pyridine series.

‖**Rubidium** (rubi·diŏm). 1862. [f. L. *rubidus* red, with ref. to the two red lines in its spectrum; see -IUM.] A soft, silvery-coloured metal belonging to the group which includes cæsium, lithium, potassium, and sodium.

†**Rubifica·tion.** 1592. [orig. – med.L. *rubificatio, -ion-,* f. *rubificat-,* pa. ppl. stem of *rubificare;* see next, -ION; in later use var. of RUBEFACTION; see -FICATION.] The process of heating to redness –1645.

Rubify (rū·bifəi), *v.* late ME. [– OFr. *rubifier,* (also mod.) *rubéfier* – med.L. *rubificare,* for L. *rubefacere,* f. *rubeus* red; see -FY.] *trans.* To make red; to redden. Now *rare.*

Rubiginous (rubi·dʒinəs), *a.* 1656. [f. L. *rubigo, rubigin-* rust, blight + -OUS.] **1.** Rusty, rust-coloured, ferruginous 1671. †**2.** Of plants: Affected by rust or blight. BLOUNT. So **Rubi·ginose** *a.* (*Bot.*) applied to a surface whose peculiar colour is due to glandular hairs.

†**Ru·bin(e.** 1511. [var. of RUBY, corresp. to OFr. and Sp. *rubin,* med.L. *rubinus.*] A ruby –1691.

‖**Rubor** (rū·bǫɹ). 1656. [L., related to *ruber* red.] Redness, ruddiness.

Rubric (rū·brik), *sb.* and *a.* late ME. [– OFr. *rubriche, -ice* (XIII), beside *rubrique,* or its source L. *rubrica* red earth, title of a law, law itself (written with red ochre), subst. use (sc. *terra* earth) of adj. f. base of L. *rubeus, ruber* red.] **A.** *sb.* **1.** Red earth, red ochre, ruddle. Now *arch.* **2.** A heading of a chapter, section, etc., of a book, written or printed in red, or otherwise distinguished in lettering; a particular passage or sentence so marked 1450. **b.** *transf.* A descriptive heading or title; a designation or category (*rare*) 1831. **3.** A direction for the conduct of divine service inserted in liturgical books, and properly written or printed in red. late ME. **4.** A red-letter entry (of a saint's name) in the Church calendar; hence, a calendar of saints 1611. **5.** The title or heading of a statute or section of a legal code (orig. written in red) 1604.

2. The event is so unusual that it deserves to be printed as a r. in the official report 1885. **3.** As a Minister, I teach her Doctrines. I use her Offices. I conform to her Rubricks. WESLEY. **5.** It is neither mentioned in the title nor the r. of the Act of Parliament SCOTT.

B. *attrib.* passing into *adj.* **1.** Written or printed in red 1475. †**b.** Inscribed with the titles of books –1755. **2.** Red, ruddy, rubicund. Now *arch.* 1659. **b.** Applied to certain lake-colours 1835.

1. What tho' my Name stood r. on the walls POPE. **b.** Curl's chaste press, and Lintot's r. post POPE. **2.** A rubrick nose, and a canonical belly 1694. Hence **Ru·bric** *v. trans.* to rubricate.

Rubrical (rū·brikăl), *a.* 1641. [f. RUBRIC *sb.* + -AL¹.] †**1.** Pertaining to the colour red. MILT. **2.** Marked by red letters (*rare*) 1666. **3.** Of or pertaining to liturgical rubrics; conforming to, enjoined by, the rubrics 1754.

3. A lifeless r. piety WARBURTON. Hence **Ru·brically** *adv.*

Rubricate (rū·brike¹t), *v.* 1570. [– *rubricat-,* pa. ppl. stem of L. *rubricare,* f. *rubrica;* see RUBRIC, -ATE³.] **1.** *trans.* To mark or colour with red; to write, print, or mark in red letters. **b.** To place in the calendar as a red-letter saint 1570. **c.** To furnish with red-letter headings; to regulate by rubrics 1846. **2.** *intr.* To sign by mark instead of name 1846.

1. c. A formal..religion, according to which the thoughts of men were to be clast and rubricated for ever after 1846. So †**Ru·bricate** *ppl. a.* rubricated. **Rubrica·tion,** the action or result of rubricating. **Ru·bricator,** one charged with the execution of the rubrics in manuscripts, etc.

Rubrician (rubri·ʃăn). 1849. [f. RUBRIC *sb.* + -IAN.] One who studies or adheres to liturgical rubrics. So **Ru·bricist.**

Rubricity (rubri·sĭti). 1800. [f. as prec. + -ITY.] **1.** Assumption of a red colour. **2.** Adherence to liturgical rubrics 1876.

1. The periodical..r. of the Nile GEDDES.

Rubstone (rɒ·bstō^{u}n). late ME. [f. RUB *v.*^{1} + STONE *sb.*] A stone used for rubbing or sharpening; *esp.* a kind of whetstone.

Ruby (rū·bi), *sb.* and *a.* ME. [– OFr. *rubi* (mod. *rubis*) – med.L. *rubinus*, subst. use (sc. *lapis* stone) of adj. f. base of L. *rubeus*, *ruber* red.] **1.** A very rare and valuable precious stone (the *true* or *oriental r.*), of a colour varying from deep crimson or purple to pale rose-red; now classed as a variety of corundum. Also, a less valuable stone (an aluminate of magnesium) dist. as the *spinel* ruby, or a rose-pink variety of this, the *balas* ruby. **b.** The jewel of a watch (in the finest work usu. a variety of ruby) 1875. **2.** A red pimple on the face 1558. **3.** The colour of the ruby; a glowing purple-tinged red. Also †*Her.* = GULES. 1572. **4.** *transf.* Applied to: **a.** *pl.* The lips 1592. **b.** Red wine 1671. **c.** *Pugilistic slang.* The blood 1860. **5.** (See quots.) 1696. **6.** *Printing.* A size of type, intermediate between nonpareil and pearl. (Cf. AGATE *sb.* 4.) 1778. In U.S. = BRILLIANT *sb.* 4.

This line is printed in Ruby type.

7. as *adj.* Having the colour of the ruby 1508.

1. At thee the R. lights its deep'ning glow THOMSON. Phr. *Above rubies*, of inestimable value. **3.** The swinging spider's silver line, The r. of the drop of wine EMERSON. **4. b.** Still the Vine her ancient R. yields FITZGERALD. **5.** What is called r. of arsenic or of sulphur is the realgar; the r. of zinc is the red blend; and the r. of silver is the red silver ore 1797. **7.** *Jul. C.* III. i. 260.

Special collocations: **r. blende,** red silver, proustite; **r. glass,** glass coloured by the oxides of copper, iron, lead, tin, etc.; **r. silver,** proustite; **r. spinel** = *spinel r.*; **r. tail** *a.* having a r.-red hinder part; applied to hymenopterous insects of the genus *Chrysis*, esp. the golden wasp; *sb.* the golden wasp; so also **r.-tailed** *a.*; **r.-throat,** a r.-throated humming-bird or warbler; **r.-throated** *a.* having a r.-red gorget; **r. wood,** 'an E. Indian wood, the produce of *Pterocarpus santalinus*'; **r. zinc,** sphalerite or zincite of a deep-red colour. Hence **Ru·bied** *a.* coloured like a r.; r.-tinged. **Ru·bious** *a.* r.-coloured. **Ru·by** *v. trans.* to dye or tinge with the colour of the r.

Rucervine (rusə̄·ɹvəin), *a.* 1881. [f. mod. L. *Rucervus*; see RUSA and CERVINE *a.*] *Zool.* Of or belonging to a genus (*Rucervus*) of East Indian deer.

‖**Ruche** (ruʃ, Fr. rüʃ), *sb.* 1827. [(O)Fr. *ruche* :– med.L. *rūsca* bark of tree, of Celtic origin.] A frill or quilling of ribbon, gauze, lace, or the like, used to ornament some part of a garment or headdress. Hence **Ruche** *v. trans.* to trim with a r. **Ruching,** a trimming consisting of ruches.

Ruck (rɒk), *sb.*^{1} ME. [app. of Scand. origin, corresp. to Norw. *ruka* with the same meanings.] **1.** A heap or stack of fuel or combustible material. **2.** A rick or stack of hay, corn, etc.; †a shock or stook. *Sc.* and *n. dial.* 1546. **3.** A heap or pile of any material. Freq. in phr. *in a r.* Now *dial.* 1601. **b.** *transf.* A large number or quantity; a multitude, crowd, throng 1581. **4.** *The r.*: **a.** *Racing.* Those horses which are left behind in a body by the fastest goers. **b.** The undistinguished crowd or general run (of persons or things). 1846.

3. b. Finishing with a r. of figures all at once 1847. **4. a.** Who headed the R.? 'I', said Lord George 1846. **b.** Far more honest,..than the r. of their sect 1859.

Ruck (rɒk), *sb.*^{2} 1787. [– ON. *hrukka* (Norw. *hrukka*) :– **hrunka*, rel. to Norw. *rukla*, *rukka*, MSw. *rynkia* (cf. ME. and dial. *runkle*).] A crease, fold, or wrinkle; a ridge.

Ruck (rɒk), *v.*^{1} Now *dial.* ME. [perh. of Scand. origin; cf. Norw. dial. *ruka* crouch.] *intr.* To squat, crouch, cower, huddle together.

Ruck (rɒk), *v.*^{2} 1812. [f. RUCK *sb.*^{2}] **1.** *intr.* To slip *up* or work into creases or ridges; to become creased or wrinkled. **2.** *trans.* To crease; to wrinkle or cause to work *up* into ridges 1828. **b.** To draw or gather into small folds 1896.

2. Mr. Sawyer..rucked his plaid trousers up to his knees 1860.

Ruckle (rɒ·k'l), *v.*^{1} 1839. [f. RUCK *v.*^{2} + -LE 3.] **1.** *intr.* To work (*up*) into folds or wrinkles. **2.** *trans.* To form, draw together, into folds 1889.

Ruckle (rɒ·k'l), *v.*^{2} 1530. [Of Scand. origin; cf. Norw. dial. *rukla* in same sense.] *intr.* To make a rattling or gurgling sound; to rattle in the throat.

Rucksack (rɒ·ksæk). 1895. [– G. *rucksack*, f. *rucken*, dial. var. of *rücken* back + *sack* SACK *sb.*^{1}] A kind of knapsack worn by tourists.

Ruction (rɒ·kʃən). *dial.* or *colloq.* 1825. [Of unkn. origin.] Usu. *pl.* A disturbance, riot, tumult, row.

Rud (rɒd), *sb.* Now *dial.* and *arch.* [OE. *rudu* red colour, rel. to *rēad*, *rēod* RED; cf. RUDDY.] **1.** Red or ruddy colour; redness, ruddiness. **2.** Complexion (of those parts of the face which are naturally reddish) OE. **3.** Chiefly *dial.* Ruddle; †a red cosmetic OE.

Rud, *v.* Now *dial.* ME. [Related to prec. and RUDDY *a.*] †**1.** *trans.* To make red or ruddy –1700. **2.** *dial.* To mark or colour with ruddle 1680.

Rudas (rū·dăs), *sb.* and *a. Sc.* 1725. [Of unkn. origin. Cf. RUDESBY.] **A.** *sb.* A coarse, unmannerly (old) woman; a termagant, virago, hag. **B.** As *adj.* Hag-like; coarse, unmannerly 1802.

Rudd (rɒd). 1606. [app. f. RUD *sb.*] A freshwater cyprinoid fish (*Leuciscus erythrophthalmus*) resembling the roach; the red-eye.

Rudder (rɒ·dəɹ). [OE. *rōþer* = OFris. *rōther*, MLG., MDu. *rōder* (Du. *roer*), OHG. *ruodar* (G. *ruder*) :– WGmc. **rōþra-* (ON. *róðr* denotes the act of rowing), rel. to ROW *v.*^{1}] †**1.** A paddle or oar used for steering or propelling a vessel –1602. **2.** A broad, flat piece or framework of wood or metal, attached vertically to the sternpost of a boat or ship (later, also to an aeroplane or airship) in such a way that it can be employed in steering it ME. **b.** *fig.* One who or that which guides, directs, or controls. late ME. **3.** *Brewing.* A kind of paddle used in stirring malt in the mash-tub 1440. **4.** *Ornith.* = RECTRIX 2. 1884.

2. The Barke abandoned of her Rother, ranne whither the wind carried her 1632. **b.** Rhime the Rudder is of Verses 1663.

attrib. and *Comb.*, as *r.-chain*, etc.; also in specific names of birds and fishes, as **r.-bird, -duck,** a name for *Erismatura rubida*, one of the Spiny-tailed Ducks; **-perch** = next (*a*). Hence **Ru·dderless** *a.* having no r.; *fig.* without guidance or control.

Ru·dder-fish. 1734. [RUDDER *sb.*] The name of several species of fish which follow or accompany vessels; *esp.* (*a*) the rudder-perch, a W. Indian sea-fish; (*b*) the pilot-fish *Naucrates ductor*; (*c*) the log- or barrel-fish (*Lirus* or *Palinurus perciformis*) of America; (*d*) a bluish fish (*Seriola zonata*), native to the Western Atlantic.

Ruddle (rɒ·d'l), *sb.*^{1} 1538. [Related to RUD *sb.* and *v.*; see -LE. Cf. RADDLE *sb.*^{2}, REDDLE *sb.*] A red variety of ochre used for marking sheep and for colouring.

Ru·ddle, *sb.*^{2} 1582. Var. of RIDDLE *sb.*^{2} 1.

Ruddle (rɒ·d'l), *v.* 1718. [f. RUDDLE *sb.*^{1}] *trans.* To mark, smear, or paint with ruddle.

A woman..was ruddling her doorstep 1859.

Ruddock (rɒ·dək). [OE. *rudduc*, related to RUD *sb.*, RUDDY *a.*; see -OCK.] **1.** The red-breast or robin. *Erithacus rubecula.* Now chiefly *dial.* †**2.** *Cant.* A gold coin; hence *pl.*, gold, money –1628. †**3.** A species of toad –1749.

1. The tame rodok & the coward kyte CHAUCER. **2.** If..he haue golden ruddocks in his bagges, he must be wise and honourable LYLY.

Ruddy (rɒ·di), *a.* (*sb.*) [Late OE. *rudiġ*, f. base of *rudu*; see RUD *sb.*, -Y^1.] **1.** Of the face, complexion, etc.: Freshly or healthily red. **b.** Of persons: Having a fresh red complexion ME. **c.** Characterized by, or associated with, healthy redness of feature 1820. **2.** *gen.* Red or reddish. late ME. †**c.** Causing redness in vegetation –1719. **3.** *slang.* Euphemism for BLOODY *a.* 8. 1914. **B.** *absol.* or as *sb.* Ruddy colour. late ME.

1. R. his lips, and fresh and fair his hue DRYDEN. **b.** The Inhabitants comely and tall, rather ruddie then blacke 1613. **c.** A figure..instinct with r. vigorous life 1860. **2.** Faire and whiteish ruddie cloudes sparkeling aboute the skie 1554. As deere to me, as are the r. droppes That visit my sad heart SHAKS. R. duck..with the neck all round and the upper parts brownish-red 1872. R. plover..head, neck and upper parts varied with black, ashy and bright reddish 1872. **B.** The r. of youth had fled his cheek 1823. Hence **Ru·ddily** *adv.* **Ru·ddiness.**

Ruddy (rɒ·di), *v.* 1689. [f. prec.] **1.** *trans.* To render ruddy in hue; to redden. **2.** *intr.* To blush (*rare*) 1845. Hence **Ru·ddied** *ppl. a.* rendered r., reddened.

Rude (rūd), *a.* and *adv.* ME. [– (O)Fr. *rude* – L. *rudis* unwrought, uncultivated, orig. techn. term of handicraft, rel. to *rudus* rubble.] **A.** *adj.* **I. 1.** Uneducated, unlearned; ignorant. late ME. **b.** *absol.* as *pl.* The unlearned or ignorant. late ME. †**c.** Of animals: Irrational. –late ME. **2.** Inexperienced, inexpert, unskilled. Now *arch.* and *rare.* late ME. **b.** Inexact, superficial 1691. **3.** Uncultured, unrefined. late ME. **b.** Uncivilized, barbarous 1483. **4.** Unmannerly, uncivil, impolite; offensively or deliberately discourteous. late ME. **5.** Ungentle, violent, harsh, rugged; marked by unkind or severe treatment of persons, etc. late ME. **b.** Involving hardships or discomfort 1734. **c.** Of persons: Acting in a rough or harsh manner; violent in action 1800. **6.** Turbulent, violent, boisterous, rough. Chiefly of the sea, winds, etc. late ME. **b.** Of health: Robust, vigorous 1792. **7.** Of sounds: Discordant, harsh, unmusical ME.

1. They shall leave their cure not to a r. and unlerned person but to a good, lerned, & experte curate CROMWELL. **c.** The r. asse and the ox also. late ME. **2.** Here the r. chisel's rougher strokes I traced 1746. He was altogether r. in the art of controversy MACAULAY. **b.** He has been but a r. observer of them 1691. **3.** The r. Porter that no manners had Did shut the gate against him in his face SPENSER. The r. state of manners and general ignorance of the clergy 1827. **b.** The r. people he framed to a civilitie HOOKER. **4.** We have done with civility. We are to be as r. as we please. JOHNSON. The profound respect..was..changed into r. familiarity GIBBON. **5.** Let goe that r. unciuill touch SHAKS. Hands more r. than wintry sky BYRON. **b.** Such is our r. mortal lot SHELLEY. **c.** The exasperated r. Titan rives and smites these Girondins CARLYLE. **6.** In Cradle of the r. imperious Surge SHAKS. R. thunders rake the crags 1807. **7.** Peace you vngracious Clamors, peace r. sounds SHAKS. This man's r. and clamorous grief SCOTT.

II. 1. Of language, composition, etc.: Lacking in elegance or polish; deficient in literary merit ME. **b.** Of drawings, etc.: Rough; not very accurate or finished 1679. **c.** Roughly correct 1854. **2.** Coarse, inelegant, rough (*rare*). late ME. **3.** Of natural scenery or objects: Rugged, rough; uncultivated, wild. late ME. **4.** Imperfect, unfinished. Now *rare* or *Obs.* late ME. **b.** Of natural products: Unwrought; unmanufactured, raw 1555. **c.** Left in a natural rough state; undressed 1800. **5.** Of a rough, inelegant, or rugged form; in early use, big and coarse; strong but ill-shaped. late ME. **b.** Roughly made or formed; imperfect 1612. **6.** Of an imperfect, undeveloped, or primitive character 1600.

1. A r. version of the Old Testament 1861. **b.** Some r. design In crayons or in charcoal 1746. A r. school-boy hand 1890. **3.** An open, r. common 1756. The r. rock remains uncovered 1867. **4. b.** Either the r. or manufactured produce ADAM SMITH. The cotton..in its r. state DISRAELI. **c.** Three pillars of r. stone WORDSW. **5.** The Heav'n-born-childe, All meanly wrapt in the r. manger lies MILT. **b.** It is easy to descend into it by a r. path SCOTT. **6.** In the r. idolatry of the Arabs GIBBON.

B. *adv.* In a rude manner; rudely (*rare*) 1475. Hence **Ru·de-ly** *adv.*, **-ness.** **Ru·dish** *a.* somewhat r.

Rudesby (rū·dzbi). Now *arch.* 1566. [f. RUDE *a.*; see -BY 2. Cf. RUDAS.] An insolent, unmannerly, or disorderly fellow.

Rudesheimer (rū·dəshəiməɹ). 1797. [– G. *Rüdesheimer* (sc. *wein*).] A fine white wine produced at Rüdesheim on the Rhine.

Rudiment (rū·diměnt), *sb.* 1548. [– Fr. *rudiment* or L. *rudimentum* (Livy), f. *rudis* RUDE, after *elementum* ELEMENT.] **1.** *pl.* The first principles or elements of a subject; those points which are first taught to, or acquired by, the beginner; also const. *of* (the thing to be learned). **b.** *sing.* A first principle; an initial step or stage 1548. **2.** *pl.* The imperfect beginnings of some (material or immaterial) thing, which are the foundation of later growth or development 1566. **b.** *sing.* A beginning; an initial or imperfect form or stage 1626.

1. From these first Rudiments he grew To nobler Feats 1680. The rudiments of Arithmetick 1638. 2. Rudiments, however, may occur in one sex, of parts normally present in the other sex DARWIN. *Rudiments of the world*; We, as longe as we were children, were in bondage vnder the rudiments of the worlde N.T. (Genev.) *Gal.* 4:3. **b.** Several species have been found..with a r. of a thumb 1880. Hence **Rudime·ntal, Rudime·ntary** *adjs.* pertaining to, connected with, the rudiments of knowledge; of the nature of a r.; undeveloped, immature, imperfect.

Rudolphine (rudǫ·lfəin), *a.* 1656. [f. the name *Rudolph* (see def.) + -INE[1].] *R. tables, numbers*, a series of astronomical calculations published by Kepler in 1627 and named after the Emperor Rudolph II.

Rue (rū), *sb.*[1] Now *dial.* or *arch.* [OE. *hrēow* = MLG., MDu. *rouwe*, Du. *rouw*, OHG. *(h)riuwa* (G. *reue*), rel. to RUE *v.*] **1.** Sorrow, distress; repentance; regret. **2.** Pity, compassion ME.

1. With r. my heart is laden For golden friends I had HOUSMAN.

Rue (rū), *sb.*[2] late ME. [– (O)Fr. *rue* :– L. *ruta* – Gr. ῥυτή, orig. a Peloponnesian word.] **1.** A perennial evergreen shrub of the genus *Ruta*, esp. *R. graveolens*, having bitter, strong-scented leaves formerly much used in medicine. **2.** With qualifying word prefixed applied to various plants 1731. **b.** With *pl.* A species of rue 1731.

1. Then purg'd with Euphrasie and R. The visual Nerve, for he had much to see MILT. *fig.* For one shall..drink life's r., and one its wine 1862. **2. Goat's r.** (see GOAT).

Rue (rū), *v.* [OE. *hrēowan* = OFris. *hriōwa*, OS. *hreuwan* (Du. *rouwen*), OHG. *(h)riuwan* (G. *reuen*); Gmc. str. vb., of which no cognates are known.] †**I.** *trans.* With dat. (or acc.) of the person, and usu. with impersonal subject. **1.** To affect a person with penitence (for sins or offences committed). –late ME. **2.** To affect with regret (for some act); to make (one) wish one had acted otherwise –1440. **3.** To affect with sorrow; to distress or grieve –1548. **4.** To affect with pity or compassion –1590.

2. Me rewith sore I am unto hir teyd CHAUCER. 4. Deare dame, your suddein overthrow Much rueth me SPENSER.

II. *trans.* With personal subject. **1.** To repent of (wrongdoing); to feel penitence (for sin) ME. **2.** To repent of (some act or course of action); to regret and wish undone or altered, on account of the consequences ME. **3.** To regard or think of (an event, fact, etc.) with sorrow or regret; to wish that (something) had never taken place or existed ME. †**4.** To regard with pity or compassion; to feel sorry for (a person, etc.) –1611.

1. Ruing the spoile done by his fatall hand DRAYTON. 2. Rome has had to r. many a too hasty step 1874. Phr. *To r. it, the day, hours*, etc.; Ye shall r. the day ye took it 1782. 3. The world will have cause to r. this iniquitous measure BURKE. Take him away, before I r. the day I saw him 1887. 4. Die is my dew; yet rew my wretched state SPENSER.

III. *intr.* **1.** To be penitent or contrite; to feel repentance or remorse ME. **2.** To be repentant, or full of regret and dissatisfaction, in respect of some act (in mod. *Sc.* use *esp.* of a bargain or promise). late ME. **3.** To feel sorrow or grief, *esp.* by reason of suffering from some fact or event; to lament ME. †**b.** To be sorry, feel reluctant, *to* do something –1630. **4.** To have, take, or feel pity or compassion. With †*of*, *on* or *upon* (arch.); †also without const. ME.

1. Hereafter..honour awakes, causeth a wretch to r. 1871. 2. Avoid green gooseberries, or you will have cause to r. 1830. 4. R. on this realme, whoes ruine is at hand SURREY.

Rueful (rū·fŭl), *a.* ME. [f. RUE *sb.*[1] + -FUL 1.] **1.** Exciting sorrow or compassion; pitiable; doleful, dismal; expressive of sorrow. †**2.** Full of pity or compassion –1440.

1. [The cat] maketh a rufull noise, and a gastefull, when one profereth to fighte with another 1572. *Knight of the R. Countenance*: Don Quixote. Hence **Rue·ful-ly** *adv.*, **-ness.**

‖**Ruelle** (rü,el). late ME. [(O)Fr., lane, dim. of *rue* street.] **1.** The space between a bed and the wall; the part of a bed next the wall. **2.** A bedroom, where ladies of fashion, in the seventeenth and eighteenth centuries, esp. in France, held a morning reception of persons of distinction; hence, a reception of this kind 1676.

Rufescent (rufe·sĕnt), *a.* and *sb.* 1815. [– L. *rufescens, -ent-*, pr. pple. of *rufescere*, f. *rufus* reddish; see -ESCENT.] Of a colour tending to reddish; somewhat rufous. Hence **Rufe·scence,** r. tendency.

Ruff (rʊf), *sb.*[1] late ME. [prob. subst. use of ROUGH; cf. mod.L. *aspredo* (f. *asper* rough) applied to the fish by John Caius. Cf. *ruffle* sea-bream (XVII).] †**1.** A sea-bream or other sparoid fish –1668. **2.** A small freshwater fish (*Acerina cernua*) of the perch family, of olive-brown colour with brown and black spots, and having rough prickly scales 1450.

Ruff (rʊf), *sb.*[2] 1523. [perh. subst. use of *ruff* ROUGH *a.*] †**1.** A circular outstanding frill on the sleeve of a garment; a ruffle –1647. **2.** An article of neckwear, usu. consisting of starched linen or muslin arranged in flutings, and standing out all round the neck, worn esp. in the reigns of Elizabeth I. and James I. 1555. **3.** A collar of projecting or distinctively coloured feathers or hair round the neck of various animals 1698. **b.** An artificial variety of the domestic pigeon resembling the jacobin 1735. **4.** A circular object resembling a ruff 1693.

2. That heath'nish Ruffe of thine, that perks Upon thy stiffe-neckt coller QUARLES. 3. The grouse..wears A sable r. around his mottled neck 1856. 4. Soft on the paper r. its leaves I spread POPE.

Ruff (rʊf), *sb.*[3] 1589. [– OFr. *roffle, rouffle*, earlier *ronfle, romfle*, corresp. to It. *ronfa*, perh. alt. of *trionfo* TRUMP *sb.*[2]] †**1.** A former card-game. Also *r. and honours.* –1688. **2.** The act of trumping at cards, esp. in whist 1856. So **Ruff** *v.*[2] *trans.* to trump 1598.

Ruff (rʊf), *sb.*[4] 1634. [transf. use of RUFF *sb.*[2] 3.] The male of a bird of the sandpiper family (*Tringa* or *Machetes pugnax*), distinguished during the breeding season by a ruff and ear-tufts.

Ruff (rʊf), *sb.*[5] 1688. [perh. imit. Cf. RUFFLE *sb.*[3]] = RUFFLE *sb.*[3]

†**Ruff,** *sb.*[6] 1548. [Cf. Sw. *ruff* spirit, 'go'.] **1.** The highest pitch or fullest degree *of* some exalted or excited condition –1692. **2.** An exalted or elated state; elation, pride; vainglory –1690. **3.** *Her.* Of a ship: *In her r.*, in full course –1688. **4.** Excitement, passion, fury; freq. *in a r.* –1641. Hence †**Ruff** *v.*[4] *intr.* to swagger, bluster, domineer.

Ruff (rʊf), *v.*[1] Now *rare.* 1548. [perh. f. RUFF *sb.*[2] Cf. RUFFLE *v.*[1]] **1.** *trans.* To form into a ruff or ruffs; to provide with a ruff or ruffs. Also with *up.* †**2.** Of a bird: To ruffle (the feathers) –1597. †**3.** *Falconry.* Of a hawk: To strike (the quarry) without securing it –1646.

Ruff (rʊf), *v.*[3] *Sc.* 1826. [f. RUFF *sb.*[5] Cf. *ruffle* vb. in same sense (XVIII).] **1.** *trans.* To beat a ruff or ruffle upon (a drum). Also *intr.* of a drum: To be thus beaten. 1827. **2.** *trans.* and *intr.* To applaud by making a noise with the feet 1826.

†**Ru·ff-coat.** 1653. [prob. f. *ruff*, obs. var. of ROUGH *a.*] The caddis-worm –1833.

Ruffed (rʊft), *ppl. a.* 1586. [f. RUFF *sb.*[2] or *v.*[1] + -ED.] **1.** Ruffled 1591. **2.** Wearing a ruff; provided with ruffs 1586. **b.** In names of animals: Having a ruff-like collar or markings, as *r. grouse, pigeon*; *r. lemur*, etc. 1783.

Ruffian (rʊ·fiăn), *sb.* and *a.* 1531. [– (O)Fr. *ruf(f)ian* (mod. also *rufien*) – It. *ruffiano*, supposed to be f. dial. *rofia* scab, scurf, of Gmc. origin (OHG. *ruf* scurf).] **1.** A man of a low and brutal character; one habitually given to acts of violence or crime; a cut-throat villain. †**2.** One distinguished as a swaggering bully or dissolute person by his dress or appearance –1675. †**3.** A confederate or protector of prostitutes. Cf. BULLY *sb.*[1] 4. 1618. **4.** *attrib.* or as *adj.* **a.** Characteristic of or appropriate to ruffians 1553. **b.** Having the manners, behaviour, or appearance of ruffians 1597.

1. Stab me yourself, nor give me to the knife Of midnight ruffians 1752. 3. The Common sorte lodge with Baudes called Ruffians, to whome in Venice they pay of their gayne the fifth parte 1618. 4. **a.** Some fought from r. thirst of blood SCOTT. Hence **Ruffian** *v. intr.* to play the r.; *esp.* of wind, etc., to rage, bluster. **Ru·ffianage,** ruffianism; ruffians collectively. **Ru·ffianish** *a.* (*rare*) ruffianly. **Ru·ffianism,** conduct or manners befitting a r.; violence, brutality; ruffians collectively. †**Ru·ffianous** *a.* ruffianly.

Ru·ffian-like, *a.* and *adv.* 1580. [f. RUFFIAN *sb.* + -LIKE.] **A.** *adj.* Befitting, appropriate to, a ruffian; resembling, having the qualities or manners of, a ruffian. **B.** *adv.* In the manner of a ruffian (*rare*) 1600.

Ruffianly (rʊ·fiănli), *a.* 1570. [f. RUFFIAN *sb.* + -LY[1].] **1.** Having the character, appearance, or demeanour of a ruffian. **2.** Characteristic of or appropriate to ruffians 1579.

2. Two common soldiers of r. aspect 1874.

†**Ru·ffin.** ME. [Also obs. and dial. †*ruffy* (XVI); of unkn. origin.] **1.** The name of a fiend –1500. **2.** *Cant.* The Devil –1641.

Ruffle (rʊ·f'l), *sb.*[1] 1533. [f. RUFFLE *v.*[1]] **I.** †**1.** Disorder, confusion –1712. **2.** A disturbed state (of the mind); perturbation, excitement 1704. **b.** A disturbing or annoying experience or encounter; annoyance, vexation 1718. **3.** A break or alteration in the evenness or placidity of some surface 1713. **4.** The act of ruffling cards 1872.

2. An administration..calm and without r. 1767. 3. A r. of sourness shot over the features of the earl MEREDITH. Never..a r. on the gently heaving water 1894.

II. †**1.** The loose turned-over portion or flap of a top-boot. B. JONS. **2.** A strip of lace, etc., gathered on one edge and used as an ornamental frill on a garment, esp. at the wrist, breast, or neck 1707. **b.** An object resembling a ruffle; *esp.* the ruff of a bird 1862.

Ru·ffle, *sb.*[2] 1534. [f. RUFFLE *v.*[2]] **1.** A riotous disturbance or tumult; a hostile encounter or skirmish; a contention or dispute. †**2. a.** *Sc.* A check or defeat –1721. **b.** A disturbing cause or event; a commotion –1716. †**3.** Ostentatious bustle or display –1694. †**4.** = RUFF *sb.*[6] –1688.

1. In the r. between two pretenders, the right owner often finds the possession 1710.

Ru·ffle, *sb.*[3] 1802. [Cf. RUFF *sb.*[5]] *Mil.* A vibrating drum-beat, which is less loud than a roll. So **Ruffle** *v.*[3] *intr.* of a drum: to beat a r.

Ru·ffle, *v.*[1] ME. [Of unkn. origin.] **I. 1.** *trans.* To destroy the smoothness or evenness of, to spoil the regular or neat arrangement of (cloth, the skin, etc.). **b.** To roughen, raise, or abrade (the skin, etc.) as by rubbing or grazing upon 1615. **c.** To draw together in a ruffle or ruffles; to trim with ruffles. (Usu. in pa. pple.) 1653. **2.** To disorder, disarrange (hair or feathers); to cause to stick up or out irregularly 1490. **b.** Of a bird: To set *up*, stiffen (the feathers), esp. as a sign of anger 1643. **3.** *gen.* To disorder, render uneven or irregular, in some manner. Also *refl.* 1528. **4.** †**a.** To stir *up* to indignation. SHAKS. **b.** To annoy, irritate, vex, discompose (a person, the mind, etc.) 1658. **c.** To trouble, disturb (a state of mind, etc.) 1701. **5.** To turn over (the leaves of a book) hurriedly; to slip (cards) rapidly through the fingers 1621. **6.** *intr.* To rise unevenly or irregularly; to form small folds or bends; to flutter in this manner 1577. **b.** To stir with anger or impatience 1719.

1. Pray thee looke the gowne be not rufled 1607. A brow..too apt to be ruffled 1833. **c.** The legs ruffled with black riband like a pigeon's leg PEPYS. 2. Not a hair Ruffled upon the scarfskin TENNYSON. **b.** A swan ruffling up its feathers at the presence of an eagle 1870. 3. A hurricane blew.. ruffling the lake 1883. 4. **a.** *Jul. C.* III. ii. 232. **b.** He is sensible of every Passion, but ruffled by none STEELE. 6. [The sea] ruffles to the breeze and swells into the storm 1887.

†**II. 1.** *trans.* To put into disarray or confusion; to tangle, ravel –1638. **b.** To involve in obscurity or perplexity; to bewilder (a person) –1679. **2.** To fold, wrap, heap, rattle *up*, in a rough or careless manner –1658. Hence **Ru·ffler**[1], an attachment to a sewing-machine for making ruffles.

Ruffle (rʊ·f'l), *v.*[2] 1440. [Of unkn. origin.]

1. *intr.* To contend or struggle *with*, to do battle *for*, a person or thing. Now *arch.* **2.** To make a great stir or display; to hector, swagger, bear oneself proudly or arrogantly. Now *arch.* Also const. with *it* and *out* 1484. **3.** Of winds, etc.: To be turbulent, rage, bluster 1579. †**4.** *trans.* To handle roughly; to set upon with violence; to bully –1721. †**b.** To handle (a woman) with rude familiarity –1720. †**5.** To take or snatch rudely –1715.

1. Men of activity that could..r. with the several rude persons in the country 1660. **2.** [He] gets drunk, ruffles, and roysters KINGSLEY. **b.** I.. would willingly r. it out once more in the King's cause SCOTT. **5.** *Lear* III. vii. 41.

Ruffler[2] (rʊ·flǝɹ). Now *arch.* 1535. [f. RUFFLE *v.*[2] + -ER[1].] †**1.** One of a class of vagabonds prevalent in the 16th c. –1818. **2.** A proud, swaggering, or arrogant fellow 1536.

†**Ruff-tree:** see ROOF-TREE and ROUGH-TREE.

Rufi- (rū·fi), comb. form of L. *rufus* red, as in *ruficarpous* having red fruit, *ruficaudate* red-tailed, *rufigallic*, etc.

Rufo- (rū·fo), comb. form (on Gr. types; see -O-) of L. *rufus* red, in some adjs. denoting colour with the sense 'rufous', as *rufo-fulvous*, etc.

Rufous (rū·fǝs), *a.* (*sb.*). 1782. [f. L. *rufus* red, reddish + -OUS.] **1.** Of a brownish-red colour; reddish; ferruginous. **2.** *ellipt.* as *sb.* **a.** A brownish-red colour 1783. **b.** A r.-coloured moth 1832.

Ru·fter-hood. 1575. [Of unkn. origin.] A form of hood used for a newly-taken hawk.

Rug (rʊg), *sb.* 1551. [prob. of Scand. origin (cf. Norw. dial. *rugga* coverlet, Sw. *rugg* ruffled or coarse hair) and rel. to RAG *sb.*[1]] †**1.** A rough woollen material, a sort of coarse frieze, in common use in the 16–17th century –1711. †**b.** With *pl.* A kind of frieze; also, a frieze cloak or mantle –1680. **2.** A large piece of thick woollen stuff (freq. of various colours) used as a coverlet or as a wrap in driving, railway-travelling, etc. 1591. **3.** A square or oblong mat for the floor, usu. of thick or shaggy stuff 1810.

1. December must be..clad in Irish rugge, or coorse freeze 1622. **2.** Mighty hot weather; I lying this night..with only a rugg and a sheet upon me PEPYS.

attrib.: **r.-headed** *a.* shock-headed.

†**Rug,** *a.* 1700. [Gaming slang; origin unkn.] Safe, secure –1797.

Fear nothing, Sir; Rug's the Word, all's safe ROWE.

Rug (rʊg), *v. Sc.* and *n. dial.* ME. [prob. of Scand. origin; cf. Norw. *rugga*, obs. Da. *rugge*, to rock (a cradle), to sway.] **1.** *trans.* To pull forcibly, violently, or roughly; to tear, tug. **2.** *intr.* To pull, tear, or tug (*at* something) ME. †**b.** *R. and reave*, to practise robbery –1596.

‖**Ruga** (rū·gă). Pl. **rugæ** (rū·dʒī). 1775. [L.] *Bot., Zool.*, etc. A wrinkle, fold, or ridge. So **Ru·gate** *a.* having rugæ; wrinkled.

Rugby (rʊ·gbi). Name of the public school at Rugby in Warwickshire, used *attrib.* or *absol.* to designate one of the two leading forms of the game of football 1864. Hence **Rugbeian** (-bī·ăn), a former or present pupil of Rugby school.

Rugged (rʊ·gėd), *a.* (and *adv.*). ME. [prob. of Scand. origin; cf. RUG *sb.*, and Sw. *rugga* roughen.] **A.** †**1.** Rough with hair; hirsute, shaggy; also of horses, rough-coated –1726. †**b.** Of cloth: Hairy, coarse, rough –1826. **2.** Having small rough projections; broken into irregular prominences; rough, uneven 1548. **b.** Of ground: Broken, uneven; full of stones, rocks, abrupt rises or declivities, etc. 1656. **3.** Of features: Wrinkled, furrowed; irregular; strongly marked 1596. **b.** Wrinkled with care or displeasure; frowning 1605. **4.** Of weather, etc.: Rough, stormy, tempestuous. Now *rare.* 1549. **b.** Involving hardships or severe toil 1730. **5.** Rough to the ear; harsh; unpolished 1590. **6.** Austere, harsh, severe, ungentle 1597. **7.** Lacking in culture and refinement; rude, uncultivated; also, rough and hardy 1625. **8.** Of a rough but strong or sturdy character 1827. **9.** *U.S.* Strong, robust, vigorous 1848. **B.** As *adv.* Ruggedly 1661.

1. Approach thou like the r. Russian Beare SHAKS. **2.** Beneath those r. elms GRAY. **b.** The road very r. with stones BERKELEY. **3.** You have a good face now, but 'twill grow r. 1617. **b.** Sleeke o're your r. Lookes, Be bright and Iouiall SHAKS. **4.** He..question'd every gust of r. wings That blows from off each beaked Promontory MILT. **b.** R. hours and fruitless toil KEATS. **b.** But ah! my rymes too rude and r. arre SPENSER. **6.** We..dislike those r. pastors who will make no allowance for the follies of the age 1817. **7.** Force is a r. Way of making Love 1680. Hence **Ru·gged-ly** *adv.*, **-ness.** So **Ru·ggy** *a.* (now *dial.*) rugged; rough; †shaggy; †wild; stormy.

Rugger (rʊ·gǝɹ). orig. *University slang.* 1893. [f. RUGBY; see -ER[6].] RUGBY football.

†**Rug gown.** 1558. [f. RUG *sb.*] **1.** A gown made of rug –1657. **2.** One wearing a rug gown; *spec.* a watchman –1646.

Rugose (rū·gōᵘs), *a.* 1703. [– L. *rugosus*, f. *ruga* wrinkle; see -OSE[1].] Marked by rugæ or wrinkles; wrinkled, corrugated, ridgy.

R. leaf, that whose veins are sunk deep, and between which the membranous and fleshy part of the leaf rises in irregular forms 1753. Hence **Rugo·sely** *adv.* So **Ru·gous** *a.* 1615.

Rugosity (rugǫ·sĭti). 1599. [– Fr. *rugosité* or late L. *rugositas*, f. L. *rugosus*; see prec., -ITY.] **1.** The state of being rugose or wrinkled. **2.** With *a* and *pl.* A corrugation or wrinkle; a slight roughness or inequality 1664.

2. *fig.* History is apt to smooth out these rugosities 1900.

Rugulose (rūgiulōᵘ·s), *a.* 1819. [f. RUGA, after *globulose*, etc., see -ULOSE.] *Entom., Bot.*, etc. Having small wrinkles; slightly rugose.

Ruin (rū·in), *sb.* [In XIV *ruyne, ruine* – (O)Fr. *ruine* – L. *ruina*, f. *ruere* fall.] **I. 1.** The act, on the part of some building or structure, of giving way and falling down. Now *rare.* **2.** A ruinous condition. late ME. **b.** That which remains after decay and fall; ruins (*rare*) 1460. **3.** *pl.* The remains of a decayed and fallen building or town. Freq. *fig.* of persons, features, institutions, states, etc. 1454. **c.** *transf.* Of material things 1597. **4.** A ruined or ruinous building, town, etc. 1592. **5.** *pl.* Damage, injury, done to anything 1592.

1. The death of the Duke of Britaine, slaine by the ruine of a wall 1632. **2.** The old towne fals to r. 1582. Whilst here the Vine o'er hills of ruine climbs ADDISON. **3.** Palestine is a land of ruins 1856. **4.** *fig.* The Noble ruine of her Magicke, Anthony,..Leauing the Fight in heighth SHAKS. **5.** Vain endeavours to repair by Art and Dress the Ruins of time SWIFT.

II. 1. The downfall or decay of a person or society; utter loss of means, position, or rank. late ME. **b.** Dishonour of a woman; degradation resulting from this 1624. **c.** Complete destruction *of* anything 1673. **2.** The condition of being ruined or reduced to an abject or hopeless state. late ME. **3.** That which causes destruction or downfall. late ME. **4.** *gen.* Destruction, complete overthrow or devastation 1586. **5.** *slang.* Gin of a poor quality. Usu. *blue r.* (see BLUE *a.*) 1817.

1. To perfecte their Ruine, there hapned another fatal Mischance to them 1665. **2.** Princely counsel in his face yet shon, Majestick though in r. MILT. Phr. *Rack and r.*: see RACK *sb.*[4] **3.** They were the ruine of him, and of all Israel 2 *Chron.* 28:23. **4.** R. seize thee, Ruthless King! GRAY.

attrib.: **r. agate, jasper, marble** (so called from the markings they exhibit).

Ruin (rū·in), *v.* 1581. [– (O)Fr. *ruiner* or med.L. *ruinare*, f. L. *ruina*; see prec.] **I.** *trans.* **1.** To reduce (a place, etc.) to ruins 1585. **b.** *fig.* To overthrow, destroy (a kingdom, etc.) 1585. †**2.** To destroy, extirpate, eradicate; to do away with by a destructive process –1725. **3.** To inflict or bring great and irretrievable disaster upon (a person or community) 1613. **b.** To bring to financial ruin; to reduce to a state of poverty 1660. **c.** To dishonour (a woman) 1679. **d.** To demoralize completely 1832. **4.** To spoil, damage, injure, in a completely destructive manner 1656. **b.** To involve in disaster or failure; to make entirely abortive 1596. **c.** To invalidate entirely 1665.

1. The wall, which was of tough mud, was imperfectly ruined 1849. **b.** What ruins Kingdoms, and lays Cities flat MILT. **3.** Marke but my Fall, and that that Ruin'd me SHAKS. **b.** Many gentlemen and ladies are ruined by play BERKELEY. **d.** It was universally agreed that college had ruined me DISRAELI. **4.** He rides..till the thorns have ruined his silken surcoat 1889. **b.** People r. their fortunes by extravagance 1736. **c.** It ruines his hypothesis 1693.

II. *intr.* **1.** To fall into ruins; to fall headlong; to go down with a crash. Also with *in.* 1604. **2.** To come to ruin; to be brought to poverty; to be overwhelmed by failure 1596.

1. Hell saw Heav'n ruining from Heav'n MILT. Hence **Ru·inable** *a.* that may be ruined; perishable. **Ru·iner,** one who or that which ruins.

Ruinate (rū·ineᶦt), *ppl. a.* 1538. [– med.L. *ruinatus*, pa. pple. of *ruinare*; see next, -ATE[2].] **1.** Of buildings, etc.: Ruined, ruinous. Now somewhat *rare.* **2.** Involved in ruin or disaster. Now *rare.* 1591.

1. A famous Citie now r. MILT.

Ruinate (rū·ineᶦt), *v.* 1548. [– *ruinat-*, pa. ppl. stem of med.L. *ruinare*; see RUIN *v.*, -ATE[3].] **1.** *trans.* To reduce to ruins. **2.** To bring destruction upon, to overthrow (a kingdom, state, etc.) 1574. **3.** To ruin or impoverish (a person) 1577. †**4.** To demolish or destroy; to lay waste –1740. †**5.** To overthrow, overturn, subvert utterly –1695. **6.** *intr.* To go or fall to ruin 1560.

1. *fig.* You r. the whole tower of Faith 1670. **5.** T' attempt to r. So glorious a Design DANIEL. Hence **Ru·inated** *ppl. a.* **Ruina·tion,** the action of ruining; the fact or state of being ruined.

Ruinous (rū·inǝs), *a.* late ME. [– L. *ruinosus*, f. *ruina*; see RUIN *sb.*, -OUS.] **1.** Falling or fallen into ruin; decayed, dilapidated, broken down. **2.** Brought to, sunk into, ruin or decay (*rare*) 1587. **3.** Bringing or tending to bring ruin; disastrous, destructive, pernicious 1526. †**4.** Pertaining to a fall or crash. MILT.

1. The Town..is very r., nothing left entire 1660. **2.** Is yon'd despis'd and r. man my Lord? SHAKS. **3.** Any attempts to raise its price..would be r. to the wool trade 1842. Hence **Ru·inous-ly** *adv.*, **-ness.**

Rulable (rū·lăb'l), *a.* Also **ruleable.** 1449. [f. RULE *v.* and *sb.* + -ABLE.] †**1.** Capable of being ruled; governable –1680. **2.** *U.S. colloq.* Allowable by rule; permissible 1888.

Rule (rūl), *sb.* [ME. *riule, reule* – OFr. *riule. reule, ruile* :– Rom. **regula*, for L. *rēgula* straight stick, bar, pattern, rel. to *regere* rule, *rex* king.] **I. 1.** A principle, regulation, or maxim governing individual conduct. **b.** *transf.* Applied to a person or thing. late ME. **2.** The code of discipline or body of regulations observed by a religious order or congregation; hence *occas.*, the order or congregation itself ME. **3.** A principle regulating practice or procedure; a fixed and dominating custom or habit. late ME. **b.** A regulation determining the methods or course of a game or the like 1697. **c.** Without article: Rigid system or routine. *Out of r.*, contrary to custom. 1796. **4.** *Law.* **a.** An order made by a judge or court, the application of which is limited to the case in connection with which it is granted. Also called a *particular r.* or *r. of court.* 1447. **b.** A formal order or regulation governing the procedure or decisions of a court of law; an enunciation or doctrine forming part of the common law, or having the force of law. Also called a (*standing*) *r. of court.* 1530. **5.** A regulation framed or adopted by a corporate body, public or private, for governing its conduct and that of its members 1558. **6.** *The rules*, a defined area in the neighbourhood of certain prisons, *esp.* those of the Fleet and King's Bench, within which certain prisoners, esp. debtors, were permitted to live on giving proper security 1662. **b.** The freedom of these bounds or 'rules' 1766.

1. All endeavour to deduce rules of action from balance of expediency is in vain RUSKIN. **2.** There are foure rules, or religious Orders 1631. Their r...obliges them to..a total abstinence from flesh 1738. **3.** Phr. *R. of the road*: see ROAD *sb.* 4. So *Rule(s) of the sea.* **b.** The Rules of fair battle will be punctually observed SCOTT. **4. a.** Phr. *R. absolute*, an order following a rule nisi and changing a conditional direction into a peremptory command. *R. nisi*: see NISI. **5.** *Joint r.*, one observed by both branches of a legislature of two houses. *Standing r.*, a permanent regulation of a corporate body governing its ordinary procedure. **6. b.** *On r.*, allowed to live in the rules; Her lodgers used commonly to be prisoners on r. from that place [*sc.* the Fleet] THACKERAY.

II. 1. A principle regulating the procedure or method necessary to be observed in the pursuit or study of some art or science. (See also RULE OF THUMB.) late ME. **b.** *Grammar.* A general principle formulated concerning the form or position of words in a sentence 1495. **2.** *Math.* A prescribed method or process for finding unknown numbers or values, or solving problems 1542. **3.** Without article in preceding senses, esp. in phr. *by r.* late ME.

1. [This] May prove, though much beside the rules of art, Best for the public COWPER. **2.** *R. of alligation, practice,* etc.: see those words. *R. of three,* a method of finding a fourth number from three given numbers, of which the first is in the same proportion to the second as the third is to the unknown fourth. Also called the *golden r.* (see GOLDEN *a.* 5), *r. of proportion.* **3.** A certain skill in quarrelling by r. 1859.

III. 1. A standard of discrimination or estimation; a criterion, test, canon. late ME. **2.** A fact, or the statement of one, that holds generally good; that which is normally the case ME.

1. There can be no hard and fast r. by which to construe..commercial agreements 1884. **2.** The possession of the gift throughout the Christian community was the r. and not the exception 1862. Phr. *As a* (or *the*) *r.,* normally, usually. (*The*) *exception proves the rule*: see EXCEPTION 1.

IV. †1. *Good* (or *right*) *r.,* good order and discipline. So without adj. –1605. **†2.** Conduct, behaviour, manner of acting –1601. **†b.** Misrule, disorder, stir, riot –1703. **3.** Control, government, sway, dominion. late ME. **4.** The control or government *of* (= exercised by) a person or thing ME. **5.** The control, management, government, etc. *of* (= exercised over or in) something. late ME.

1. *Macb.* V. ii. 16. **3.** The woman's power is for r., not for battle RUSKIN. **4.** Lead forth the Years for Peace and Plenty fam'd, From Saturn's R., and better Metal nam'd PRIOR. **5.** Neptune..Took in by lot..Imperial r. of all the Sea-girt Iles MILT.

V. 1. A graduated strip of metal or wood (marked with feet, inches, etc.) used for measuring length, esp. by carpenters and masons ME. **2.** *poet.* A shaft or beam *of* light 1634. **†3.** A straight line drawn on paper, *esp.* for the writing of music –1662. **3.** = RULER 3 b. 1703. **4.** *Typog.* A thin slip of metal (usu. brass) used for separating headings, columns of type, articles, etc., and in ornamental work; also a dash, short or long, in type-metal, thus – (en rule) or thus — (em rule), used in punctuation, etc. 1683. **b.** Without article (*brass r.*), as a material 1771. **c.** A composing- or setting-rule 1683.

1. Phr. *To run the r. over* (colloq.), to go thoroughly over (a person as in medical examination), to estimate (his qualifications, etc.) or to go through (his pockets as a pickpocket, etc.). **2.** Som gentle taper..visit us With thy long levell'd r. of streaming light MILT.

Rule (rūl), *v.* ME. [– OFr. *reuler* :– late L. *regulare* REGULATE *v.*] **I. 1.** *trans.* To control, guide, direct, exercise sway or influence over (a person, his actions, life, etc.). **2.** To moderate, restrain, curb (one's appetites, etc.) by the exercise of self-control. late ME. **3.** To direct, guide, manage (a thing); to have under one's control. late ME. **4.** To govern, exercise sovereign power over, to control with authority. late ME. **5.** *absol.* To exercise sovereignty, to govern; to hold supreme command or sway 1509. **6.** *Comm.* Of prices: To be at a certain rate; to be current or prevalent 1629. **b.** Of commodities or trade: To bear a (specified) current price or value; to maintain a (given) average or quality 1690. **c.** To go in a certain way; to have a certain character, place, or quality 1676.

1. My blood begins my safer Guides to r. SHAKS. Phr. *To be ruled,* to submit to counsel, guidance, or authority; to listen to reason. **2.** He that ruleth his spirit [is better] then he that taketh a citie *Prov.* 16:32. **4.** She, who ne'er answers till a Husband cools, Or, if she rules him, never shews she rules POPE. The star that ruled his doom was far too fair SHELLEY. 5. What madnesse rules in braine-sicke men SHAKS. A prince that rules by example, more than sway B. JONS. **6.** Sales dragged somewhat, prices ruling about the same as on Monday last 1889. **b.** Trade ruled dull at barely late rates 1881.

II. *trans.* To lay down judicially or authoritatively; to decide, determine, declare formally. In later use const. *that,* or with *out of.* late ME. **b.** To decide, settle; to decree 1843. **c.** To shut or put *out* by formal decision 1890.

Public opinion..rules that every conclusion is absurd..except such as it recognizes itself NEWMAN. **c.** Four instructions were ruled out..as capable of being dealt with in Committee 1893.

III. 1. To mark (paper, etc.) with parallel straight lines drawn with a ruler or by a machine 1440. **2.** To form or mark out (a line) with or as with a ruler 1599.

Rule-joint. 1782. A movable joint such as is used for measuring-rules.

Ruleless (rū·l,lės), *a.* 1443. [f. RULE *sb.* + -LESS.] **1.** Ungoverned; lawless, unrestrained; not subject to rule or order. **2.** Devoid of rules, irregular 1867.

Rule of thumb. Also hyphened. 1692. [RULE *sb.*] A method or procedure derived entirely from practice or experience, without any basis in scientific knowledge; a roughly practical method.

The English..have in all their changes proceeded, to use a familiar expression, by the rule of thumb M. ARNOLD. *attrib.* Beyond this rule of thumb calculation, no experience could bring him to penetrate his mystery 1837.

Ruler (rū·ləɹ). late ME. [f. RULE *v.* + -ER¹.] **1.** One who, or that which, exercises rule, *esp.* of a supreme or sovereign kind. **2.** One who has control, management, or headship within some limited sphere. Now *Obs.* or *arch.* late ME. **3. †a.** = RULE *sb.* V. 1. **b.** A straight-edged strip or cylinder, usu. of wood or ivory, used for guiding a pen, pencil, etc. in forming straight lines upon paper, etc. late ME. **4.** A workman who rules straight lines in account-books, etc. 1858.

1. Stern r. of the sky! Whose sport is man, and human misery 1757. **3.** *Parallel ruler(s)*: see PARALLEL *a.* 1 b. Hence **Ru·lership.**

Ruling (rū·liŋ), *vbl. sb.* ME. [f. RULE *v.* + -ING¹.] **1.** The action of governing; exercise of authority. **2.** A judicial decision; also *gen.* an authoritative pronouncement 1560. **3.** The action of using a ruler. Also *attrib.* as *r.-machine, -pen,* etc. 1611. **b.** *concr.* A ruled line or lines 1890.

Ruling (rū·liŋ), *ppl. a.* 1593. [f. RULE *v.* + -ING².] **1.** Exercising rule or authority; governing, reigning 1648. **b.** *R. Elder,* among Presbyterians, a lay elder. 1593. **2.** Predominating, dominant, prevalent 1732. **3.** Of prices, etc; Current, general; average 1861.

1. He belonged half to the r. and half to the subject caste MACAULAY. **2.** The r. Passion conquers Reason still POPE. Hence **Ru·lingly** *adv.*

Ruly (rū·li), *a.* late ME. [orig. f. RULE *sb.* + -Y¹, but in mod. use prob. a back-formation from UNRULY.] Observing or amenable to rule or good order; law-abiding, disciplined, orderly. Opp. to UNRULY.

Rum (rɒm), *sb.*¹ 1654. [perh. an abbrev. of RUMBULLION or RUMBUSTION.] **1.** A spirit distilled from various products of the sugar-cane (esp. molasses and dunder), and prepared chiefly in the West Indies and Guiana. **b.** *U.S.* Used generically as a hostile name for intoxicating liquors 1858.

Comb.: **r.-bud,** redness caused by excessive drinking, appearing first on the nose, and extending over the face; also, an excessive drinker; **r. punch, shrub, toddy,** beverages in which r. is the principal ingredient.

†Rum, *sb.*² *slang.* 1720. [In sense 2 f. RUM *a.*] **1.** A poor country clergyman in Ireland. SWIFT. **2.** Ellipt. for *rum customer* –1845.

Rum (rɒm), *a. slang.* 1774. [perh. var. of ROM in collocations like *rum cove.*] Odd, strange, queer.

There's rummer things than women in this world though, mind you DICKENS. This was the rummest go he ever saw THACKERAY. Phr. *R. start,* (slang) surprising occurrence. *R. customer,* a person or animal that is dangerous to meddle with. Hence **Ru·mly** *adv.,* **-ness.**

Rumal, var. of ROMAL.

Rumbelow (rɒ·mbĕlōᵘ). Now *rare.* ME. [See sense 1.] **1.** A meaningless combination of syllables serving as a refrain, orig. sung by sailors when rowing. (Cf. HEAVE-HO, HEY-HO.) **2.** A kind of carriage 1881.

1. Heue and how rombelow, rowe the bote, Norman, rowe SKELTON.

Rumble (rɒ·mb'l), *sb.* late ME. [f. RUMBLE *v.*¹] **1.** A low, continuous, murmuring, grumbling, or growling sound as that of thunder, distant cannon, heavy vehicles, etc. **b.** Applied to language or utterance 1680. **†2.** Commotion, bustle, tumult, uproar –1682. **3.** The hind part of a carriage when so arranged as to provide sitting accommodation, or to carry luggage 1808.

1. The r. of a distant Drum FITZGERALD. **2.** A stormy peple..Delitynge euere in rumbul that is newe CHAUCER. **3.** Miss D. and Isabella go in the r., as it is called, behind 1808. Hence **Ru·mbly** *a.* of a rumbling character.

Rumble (rɒ·mb'l), *v.*¹ [prob. – MDu. *rommelen, rummelen* (Du. *rommelen*), of imit. origin.] **1.** *intr.* To make a low, heavy, continuous sound. **2.** To move or travel with a continuous murmuring, or low, rolling sound. late ME. **b.** *transf.* Of persons: To be conveyed in a rumbling vehicle 1832. **3.** To produce a rumbling noise by agitating or moving something (*rare*). late ME. **4.** *trans.* To utter, run *over,* drone *out,* give *forth,* send *down,* with a rumbling sound 15..

1. Romble, romble goe the waters DEKKER. The wind-shaken ropes r. and rustle 1638. **2.** A Spring of water mildely romblying downe SPENSER. **4.** They rumbled and roared..prayers with a zeal that shook the window-panes 1892. Hence **Ru·mbler,** one who or that which rumbles. **Ru·mbling** *vbl. sb.* and *ppl. a.* **Ru·mblingly** *adv.*

Rumble, *v.*² *slang.* 1898. [Of unkn. origin.] *trans.* To discover, detect, fathom.

Ru·mble-tu·mble. 1801. [f. RUMBLE *v.* + TUMBLE *v.*] **†1.** = RUMBLE *sb.* 3. –1858. **2.** A rumbling coach, carriage, or cart 1806. **3.** A rough or tumbling motion. BROWNING.

Rumbo (rɒ·mbo). Now *arch.* 1751. [app. f. RUM *sb.*¹] A variety of strong punch, made chiefly of rum.

Rumbow·ling. *Naut. slang.* 1874. [perh. var. of ROMBOWLINE.] Grog.

†Rumbu·llion. 1651. [Of unkn. origin.] Rum –1672.

†Rumbu·stion. 1652. [Of unkn. origin.] Rum.

Rumbustious (rɒmbɒ·stiəs), *a. colloq.* 1778. [prob. alt. of ROBUSTIOUS.] Boisterous, unruly, uproarious.

Rumen (rū·men). 1728. [– L. *rumen* throat, gullet.] The first stomach of a ruminant animal.

‖**Rumex** (rū·meks). 1771. [L., sorrel.] *Bot.* A genus of plants which includes the sorrel and dock; a plant of this genus.

Rumicin (rū·misin). Also **-ine.** 1864. [f. L. *rumex, rumic-* sorrel + -IN¹.] *Chem.* An acid obtained from the root of *Rumex hydrolapathum*; chrysophanic acid.

Ruminant (rū·minănt), *sb.* and *a.* 1661. [– L. *ruminans, -ant-,* pr. pple. of *ruminari, -are,* f. *rumen, rumin-* throat, gullet; see -ANT.] **A.** *sb.* An animal that chews the cud; one of the *Ruminantia.* **B.** *adj.* **1.** Chewing the cud, ruminating 1691. **2.** Contemplative, meditative 1849.

‖**Ruminantia** (rūminæ·nʃ'ă). 1830. [L., n. pl. of pr. pple. of *ruminari, -are*; see prec., -IA².] The class of ruminant animals.

Ruminate (rū·mineⁱt), *v.* 1533. [– *ruminat-,* pa. ppl. stem of L. *ruminari, -are*; see prec., -ATE³.] **1.** *trans.* To revolve, turn over and over in the mind; to meditate deeply upon. **b.** To meditate, consider (a design, etc.) with a view to subsequent action 1588. **2.** To chew or turn over in the mouth again 1609. **3.** *intr.* To chew the cud 1547. **4.** To muse, meditate, ponder 1575.

1. Conduct me, where from company, I may reuolue and r. my greefe SHAKS. **b.** Ruminating wrath, he scorns repose POPE. **3.** He made various sounds with his mouth; sometimes as if ruminating, or what is called chewing the cud BOSWELL. **4.** My head But ruminates on necromantic skill MARLOWE. The blossom of an idea..came out into full blow as I ruminated upon my pillow MME. D'ARBLAY. Hence **Ru·minated** *ppl. a.* meditated, considered, digested. **Ru·minative** *a.* contemplative, meditative. **Ru·minator,** one who ruminates.

Rumination (rūminēⁱ·ʃən). 1600. [– L. *ruminatio, -on-,* f. as prec.; see -ION. Cf. Fr. *rumination* (XVII).] **1.** Contemplation, meditation. **b.** *pl.* Meditations, reflections 1638. **2.** The action of chewing the cud 1658.

1. In which my often r. wraps me in a most humorous sadnesse SHAKS. **2.** The Voluntary Motion of the Stomach, is that only which accompanies R. 1676.

Ru·mkin¹. Now *arch.* 1636. [f. Du. *roemer* RUMMER + unexpl. -KIN.] A variety of drinking-vessel.

Ru·mkin². 1672. [app. f. RUMP *sb.* +

-KIN.] The Persian rumpless or tailless cock or hen.

Rummage (rɒ·mėdʒ), *sb.* 1526. [– AFr. *rumage (cf. AL. *rumagium* XIII), aphetic f. OFr. *arrumage* (mod. *arrimage*), f. †*arrumer*, var. of OFr. *arimer*, *aruner*, *ariner*, f. *a-* AD- + *run* ship's hold (cf. RUN *sb.* V. 1) – (M)Du. *ruim* space (ROOM); see -AGE.] **1.** †**a.** *Naut.* The arranging of casks, etc., in the hold of a vessel –1688. **b.** Miscellaneous articles, lumber; rubbish 1598. †**c.** Place of storage; storage capacity –1639. **2.** Bustle, commotion, turmoil. *Obs.* exc. *Sc.* 1575. **3.** An overhauling search 1753. **b.** *spec.* A thorough search of a vessel by a Customs examining officer 1867.

2. *Haml.* I. i. 107. **3.** I shall have a r. for it among the old music-book shops 1873.

Comb.: **r. goods**, goods out of date in warehouse; **r. sale** (*a*) a clearance sale of unclaimed goods at the docks, or of odds and ends left in a warehouse; (*b*) a kind of charity bazaar.

Rummage (rɒ·mėdʒ), *v.* 1544. [f. prec.] **I.** *trans.* †**1.** *Naut.* **a.** To arrange, or re-arrange (goods) in the hold of a ship. Also *gen.* –1725. †**b.** To set in order, put straight (a ship, the hold) by re-arranging the cargo –1625. **2.** *Naut.* **a.** To search thoroughly, ransack (the hold of a vessel, etc.) 1628. **b.** *spec.* of Customs officers 1763. **3.** To make a search in or among; to overhaul in order to find something 1616. **4.** To scrutinize, examine minutely, investigate 1704. **5.** To disarrange or disorder; to knock, stir, or drive about; to force or rout out by searching or making a stir. Somewhat *rare.* 1591. **b.** To bring *ou* by searching; to fish *out* or *up* 1715.

2. a. We rummaged our Prize, and found a few Boxes of Marmalade 1697. **3.** We rummaged our pockets in vain for the required passport 1833. **4.** Upon this, they fell again to romage the Will SWIFT. **5. b.** She has also rummaged up a coop that will hold six chickens COWPER.

II. *intr.* **1.** *Naut.* To make search (†arrange or re-arrange cargo, etc.) in a vessel 1595. **2.** To engage in a search, make an investigation, of any kind 1666.

1. Their Business is to r. in the Hold on all Occasions 1728. **2.** He pulled out a pocket-book, and rummaged some time, but to no purpose 1789. A jolly ghost, that..tapt at doors, and rummaged like a rat TENNYSON. Hence **Ru·mmager,** †one who arranges cargo in a ship; one who makes a search or overhaul.

Rummer (rɒ·məɹ). 1654. [Of LDu. origin; cf. Du. *roemer*, LG. (whence G.) *römer*, f. *roemen*, etc., extol, praise, boast.] A large drinking-glass.

Rummy (rɒ·mi), *sb.* 1919. [Of unkn. origin.] A card-game, played with two packs, in which the players aim at making sequences of the same suit and sets of the same denomination, each player in turn taking either an exposed or a revealed card, and in exchange discarding a card from his hand.

Rummy (rɒ·mi), *a. slang* or *colloq.* 1828. [f. RUM *a.* + -Y[1].] Odd, queer, singular. Hence **Ru·mmily** *adv.* **Ru·mminess.**

Rumorous (rū·mŏrəs), *a.* 1550. [f. RUMOUR *sb.* + -OUS.] **1.** Making a loud confused sound; resounding. Now *arch.* **2.** Of the nature of rumour; rumoured (*rare*) 1605. **3.** Full of rumours or reports (*rare*) 1641.

Rumour (rū·məɹ), *sb.* Also (chiefly *U.S.*) **rumor.** [Late ME. *rumur*, *rumo(u)r* – OFr. *rumur*, *-or* (mod. *-eur*) – L. *rumor* noise, din, etc.] **1.** †**a.** A (widespread) report of a favourable or laudatory nature. late ME. only. **b.** Talk or report *of* a person or thing in some way noted or distinguished. Now *arch.* 1440. †**c.** The fact of being generally talked about; reputation, renown. MILT. **2.** General talk, report, or hearsay, not based upon definite knowledge. late ME. **3.** A statement or report circulating in a community, of the truth of which there is no clear evidence. late ME. †**4.** Loud expression of disapproval or protest –1568. **5.** Clamour, outcry; noise, din. Now *arch.* 1440. †**6.** Uproar, tumult, disturbance –1639.

1. b. Great is the r. of this dreadfull Knight SHAKS. **c.** Fame..Nor in the glistering foil Set off to th' world, nor in broad r. lies MILT. **2.** You seem.. Too..companionable a man To act the deeds that r. pins on you SHELLEY. **3.** Does the Rumor hold for true That hee 's so full of Gold? SHAKS. **5.** The r. of the wind among the garden trees 1885.

Rumour (rū·məɹ), *v.* Also *U.S.* **rumor.** late ME. [f. prec.] **1.** *intr.* †**a.** To resound with disapproval. late ME. only. **b.** To invent or circulate rumours 1858. **2.** *trans.* To circulate by way of rumour 1594. **3.** *intr.* To make a murmuring noise 1900.

2. This haue I rumour'd through the peasant-Townes SHAKS. **3.** The sea that rumoured light and soothingly round the rock of Doom 1900. Hence **Ru·mourer** (*rare*), one who disseminates rumours.

Rump (rɒmp). [In XV *rumpe*, prob. of Scand. origin; cf. (M)Da. *rumpe*, (M)Sw. *rumpa*, Icel. *rumpr.*] **1.** That part of the body (of an animal or bird) from which the tail springs; †the tail; hence, the hind-quarters, posteriors, buttocks. **2.** This part of an animal or fowl as cut off and used for food 1486. **3.** *fig.* A small, unimportant, or contemptible remnant or remainder of a body of persons (esp. of a Parliament) 1649. **b.** *Hist.* The remnant of the Long Parliament (restored in May, 1659) which was dissolved by Monk in 1660; also (esp. in later use) the earlier remnant of the same Parliament from the time of Pride's Purge (Dec. 1648) to its dissolution by Cromwell in April, 1653. 1659. **c.** So *R. Parliament* 1670.

3. b. The R. was universally detested and despised MACAULAY.

Comb.: **r.-band,** a leather band passing over the r. of a horse to support the trace-chains; **-bone,** the coccyx (now *rare*); **-fed** *a.* fed on the best joints, pampered; **-strap** = *r.-band.* Hence **Ru·mper,** (*Hist.*) a member or supporter of the R. parliament. **Ru·mpless** *a.* having no r. or tail; tailless.

Rumple (rɒ·mp'l), *sb.* Now *rare.* 1500. [– (M)Du. *rompel*, deriv. of MDu. *rompe*, MLG. *rumpe* wrinkle, or – MDu., MLG. *rumpelen, rompelen.*] A wrinkle, fold, crease. Hence **Ru·mply** *a.* full of rumples (*rare*).

Rumple (rɒ·mp'l), *v.* 1603. [f. prec.] **1.** *trans.* To wrinkle, crease, draw into wrinkles, render uneven or irregular. **2.** To touzle, disorder, crumple. Also with *up.* 1650. †**3.** To squeeze together, distort –1687.

1. Beds of bogbean foliage, rumpling the green floating carpet of lily-leaves 1893. **2.** Girls like to be..rumpled a little..sometimes GOLDSM. Hence **Ru·mpled** *ppl. a.* wrinkled, crumpled, creased; touzled.

Rumpus (rɒ·mpŏs), *sb. colloq.* 1764. [prob. fanciful.] A riot, uproar, disturbance, row. Hence **Ru·mpus** *v. intr.* to make a disturbance.

Run (rɒn), *sb.* 1450. [f. RUN *v.*] **I. 1.** A single spell or act of running. **b.** A distance covered, or taking a certain time to cover, by running 1596. **2. a.** *Cricket.* An act of running successfully from one popping-crease to the other by both batsmen, counting as an addition of one to the score 1746. **b.** *Baseball.* A unit of scoring obtained by running the round of the bases 1875. **3. a.** A spell of riding after hounds or in a race 1812. **b.** A round of running at hare-and-hounds. Also, the course taken by the harriers. 1857. **4. a.** A spell of sailing, esp. between two ports 1712. **b.** An excursion, trip; a rapid journey accompanied by a short stay at a place 1854. **c.** A single journey made by a locomotive engine; the distance thus traversed 1870. **5.** A landing of smuggled goods 1832. **6.** A rapid course; esp. *with a r.*, rapidly, with a rapid fall 1822. **7.** *Golf.* A stroke in which the ball is made to run along the ground; usu. *r.-up* 1901. **8.** With advs., as **run-in**; *spec.* in Rugby football, an act of running over the touch-line of the opposite side with the ball; also, the home stretch in a run at hare and hounds, or in a race; **run-out,** an instance of a batsman being put out while trying to make a run.

1. Phr. *To have a r. for one's money*, to have some kind of return or satisfaction for one's expenditure or exertions. (Orig. racing slang.) **2. a.** We had made our 80 runs in less than two hours 1859. **3. a.** A real Lincolnshire r. at a good hunting pace 1812.

II. 1. A small stream, brook, rivulet, or watercourse; a channel or overflow. Chiefly *U.S.* and *n. dial.* **b.** A strong rush or sweep of the tide, etc. 1814. **c.** A flow of sand; a slip, slide, sudden fall of earth. Chiefly *Mining.* 1854. **2.** *Mus.* A roulade 1835. **III. 1.** A continuous stretch *of* something 1674. **b.** A continued course or spell *of* some condition or state of things 1714. **c.** A course or spell of (good or ill) fortune, *esp.* in games of chance 1697. **d.** *Mining* and *Geol.* A continuous vein of rock or ore 1747. **2.** A continuous series or succession 1709. **b.** A shoal of fish in motion, *esp.* ascending a river from the sea for spawning 1820. **c.** A pair of millstones. *U.S.* 1828. **3.** A series or rush of sudden and pressing demands made upon a bank or treasury for immediate payment 1692. **b.** An extensive or well-sustained demand for something. Const. *on.* 1818. **c.** *Gaming.* A continued spell of chance falling *on* a particular colour, etc. 1826. **d.** A concourse or resort of customers, etc. 1844. †**4.** A persistent set *against*, or attack *upon*, some thing or person –1779. **5.** A success with the public, so as to be extensively bought or run after 1719. **6.** A continuous period of being represented on the stage 1714. **7.** A spell of making or allowing something liquid to run; the amount run off at one time 1710. **b.** A spell of making or allowing machinery to run or continue to work 1875. **8.** *Common, general,* or *ordinary r.*, the usual, or average type or class: the generality or great majority. Also without adj. 1712. **b.** A line or class of goods 1883.

1. A very promising r. of trout and grayling water 1867. **b.** Wicked men have..a continu'd r. of success 1714. **c.** The dice took a r. against him STERNE. **2.** A r. of wet seasons 1774. **3.** When a r. comes upon them, they..endeavour to gain time by paying in sixpences 1776. **5.** It is impossible for detached papers to have a general r...if not diversified with humour ADDISON. **6.** This comedy..had a lengthened r. 1857. **7. b.** An experimental r. to test the machinery 1882. **8.** In the common R. of Mankind, for one that is Wise and Good you find ten of a contrary Character ADDISON. **b.** Makers of the ordinary runs of cloth 1883.

IV. 1. A regular track made by certain animals 1821. **b.** An enclosure for domestic animals or fowls to range or take exercise in 1856. **2.** An extensive range of pasture- or grazing-land. Chiefly *Austral.* 1826. **3.** A slope, track, or support along or on which something may run or move 1834. **4.** A pipe or trough along or down which water may run 1833.

1. Hares have their regular highways or 'runs' 1878. **2.** It is, generally speaking, a good sheep r. 1826. **3. b.** *U.S.* A rent or ladder in a garment 1922.

V. 1. *Naut.* That part of a ship's bottom which rises from the keel and bilge, and narrows toward the stern (†or bows) 1618. **2. a.** The time during which a dramatic work holds the stage continuously 1705. **b.** The progress or prevalence *of* a disease 1717. **3.** The act of running, esp. in rapid retreat or flight. Chiefly in phr. *to* or *on the r.* 1660. **b.** A running pace 1840. **c.** Capacity for, or power of, running 1857. **4.** The rush, flow, or onward movement *of* water, air, etc. 1626. **b.** The flow or melody *of* verse 1725. **c.** *By the r.* = with a run 1800. **5.** The course, direction, or tendency *of* something immaterial 1730. **6. a.** The direction, line, or lie *of* anything 1748. **b.** *Mining.* 'The horizontal distance to which a drift may be carried' 1864. **7. a.** The freedom or range *of* a house, etc.; the privilege of free resort, access, or use 1755. **b.** *The r. of one's teeth*: free board, usu. in return for work done; maintenance, support 1841. **c.** The pasture of an animal for a certain period 1854.

1. A rakish..craft,..with a deep keel and sharp r. 1831. **2. a.** The usage was to engage stars for the r. of the piece 1885. **3. b.** We started at a r., men and dogs, for the solid ice 1856. The r. of luck is against us 1809. **7. a.** I have the r. of two good houses 1809.

Run (rɒn), *v.* Pa. t. **ran.** Pa. pple. **run.** [OE. *rinnan* = OFris. *rinna, renna,* OS., OHG. *rinnan,* ON. *rinna,* Goth. *rinnan*; Gmc. str. vb. of unkn. origin. The common ME. present tense forms *rinne, renne* were prob. due to ON. *rinna, renna.* In finite parts the present form with *-u-* is not current before XVI (*runne*), but the var. *ronne* is earlier. The vowel resulted from levelling through from forms in which it was original.]

I. Intransitive senses. (Occas. conjugated in compound tenses with *be* instead of *have* to the end of the 18th c.) **Of persons and animals.* **1.** To move the legs quickly (the one foot being lifted before the other is set down) so as to go at a faster pace than walking; to cover the ground rapidly in this manner. **b.** Used to denote (hurried) travelling or going about, esp. to distant places ME. **2.** To go about freely, without being restrained or checked in any way. Freq. with *about*; also with predicative adjs., as *wild*. OE. **3.** To hasten *to* some end or object, or *to* do something; to make haste, be active OE. **b.** To go or resort *to* a person, etc., *esp.* for help or guidance ME. **4.** To retire or retreat rapidly; to take to flight; to abscond or desert. Also const. *from* a place, person, etc. ME. **b.** So *to r. for it* 1642. **5.** To rush *at*, *on*, or *upon* a person with hostile intention; to make an attack *on* ME. **†6.** To ride on horseback at a quick pace; *spec.* to ride in a tournament, to tilt or joust –1652. **7.** To compete, or take part, in a race (*for* a prize). Occas. with compl. denoting final position in the race. ME. **b.** To compete, stand as a candidate, *for* a position, seat, etc. Orig. *U.S.* 1861. **8.** *transf.* Of fish: To swim rapidly 1520. **b.** *spec.* To pass to or from the sea; to migrate 1887.

1. She is run upstairs,..this very instant STERNE. The young ones r. about as soon as they are out of the shell GOLDSM. Phr. *That he who runs may read*, an alteration of *Habakkuk* 2:2, 'That he may r. that readeth it'. **b.** I have sometimes been obliged to r. half over London, in order to fix a date correctly BOSWELL. **2.** This meane whyle ranne sir Tristram naked in the forest MALORY. R. about and divert yourself 1782. **3.** The people..r. almost from all places to assist his cause 1654. **b.** That day first I did seem to glimpse why folk in trouble r. to drink so READE. **4.** He.. had been forced to cut and r. 1893. **5.** He ran at me and kicked me 1889. **6.** 1 *Hen. IV*, II. iv. 377. Phr. *To r. (full) tilt at* or *against*: see TILT *sb.* **7.** A Plate of 40 *l.* Value was to be run for 1713. Gosson..had run second to her for the Champagne Stakes 1891. Phr. *Also ran*, said of a horse which is not 'placed' in a race; hence as *sb.*, and *fig.* a failure. **b.** If he..ran for President 1870. **8.** The pike made a splendid fight, often running to weed 1867. **b.** The season when the eels are 'running' 1892.

** *Of inanimate things in rapid motion.* **9.** Of things, esp. the heavenly bodies: To move rapidly through space OE. **b.** Of vehicles, etc.: To move easily or rapidly by reason of being set on wheels ME. **10.** Of a vessel (or those on board): To sail swiftly or easily OE. **b.** To sail or be driven *on* or *upon* the shore, rocks, etc.; to come *aground* or *ashore* ME. **c.** *To r. foul of*, to collide or become entangled with (another vessel, etc.); to foul 1698. **11. a.** To take a (hurried) journey for the purpose of making a short stay at or visit to a place. Chiefly with *down, over, up*. 1798. **b.** Of a conveyance, vessel, etc.: To ply between (two) places 1825. **12. a.** To spread, pass, or move quickly from point to point: usu. with advb. phrases OE. **b.** Of sounds: To spread or pass rapidly *along, down, through* a place, company, etc.; to be caught up or repeated in quick succession. late ME. **c.** Of statements, reports, etc.: To spread abroad rapidly; to be or become widely current. late ME. **d.** Of plants: To creep or climb 1565. **13. a.** Of thoughts: To come suddenly *into*, to course or pass *through*, the mind ME. **b.** Of the eye: To glance, look quickly. Also of persons, to give a rapid glance (*with* the eye). 1611. **c.** To go *back* in retrospect 1702. **14.** Of a weapon, etc.: To pass easily and quickly *through* something, *to* a certain point, etc. ME. **15.** To slip, slide, or move easily or freely: freq. with preps. or advs. ME. **b.** Of the tongue: To wag freely 1553. **c.** Of bark: To peel off easily from a tree 1784. **d.** To unravel, come undone 1878. **e.** To slip, diverge, go awry 1846. **16.** Of a ball, etc.: To roll forward on a surface. Said also of dice when thrown. late ME. **b.** *transf.* Of a player at billiards: To make the ball roll 1875. **17.** To revolve on or as on an axis ME. **b.** Of machinery or mechanical devices: To go; to continue operating 1562. **18.** Of thoughts, etc.: To revolve *in* the mind; to return persistently to the memory 1601. **b.** To form, be present as, an impression 1798.

9. Far ran the naked moon across The..ocean's heaving field TENNYSON. **b.** *fig.* Your tongue so runs on wheels HOBBES. **10.** We were obliged to r. away afore the wind DE FOE. **b.** They had no escape but to r. aground 1877. Phr. *To r. aboard, on board (of)*: see BOARD *sb.* V. 1. **11. a.** I wish you could have run over for a week 1831. **b.** Steamboats r. between London Bridge and Chelsea on weekdays 1886. **12. a.** Squalls Ran black o'er the sea's face M. ARNOLD. **c.** There r. reports that made me shudder CARLYLE. **13. a.** The extravagant analogies which then ran through my brain TYNDALL. **14.** Looke, in this place ran Cassius Dagger through SHAKS. **15.** *fig.* Life ran smoothly in its ordinary grooves 1889. **b.** Though your teeth be gone..Yet your tongue can renne on patins UDALL. **16.** He who blows upon a ball when running makes the stroke foul 1850. **18.** This Thought run long in my Head DE FOE.

*** *Of liquids, sand, etc.* (*or vessels containing these*). **19.** Of milk, etc.: To coagulate, curdle, form a curd. Now *dial.* late ME. **b.** To unite, combine (*into one*), esp. in a moist or melted state 1715. **20.** Of liquids: To flow. OE. **21.** Of the sea, tides, etc.: To course or flow, esp. in an impetuous manner. Also with compl., esp. *to r. high* (see HIGH *adv.*), or *mountain(s high* (see MOUNTAIN I. 1.) ME. **22. a.** To flow as the result of melting; to melt and flow. late ME. **b.** To spread on being applied to, or poured upon, a surface 1612. **c.** Of colours: To spread in a fabric when immersed in water or exposed to moisture 1711. **23. a.** Of the sands of an hour-glass: To pass from one compartment into the other 1557. **b.** Of loose earth: To slip or fall in 1799. **24.** To flow, stream, be wet *with* a liquid. Also with adjs., as *r. red*. ME. **25. a.** To discharge (or carry off) a liquid ME. **b.** Of a vessel: To overflow; to leak ME. **c.** Of an hour-glass: To allow the sand to pass from one compartment to the other. 1500.

19. b. The Church party and the Dissenters were now run into one 1715. **20.** He thrashed his naked back, until the blood ran 1862. *fig.* His Verses r. like the Tap EARLE. **21.** What a devilish Sea there runs? 1694. Evil and good r. strong in me 1887. **c.** Beg her not to wash them too hard, or they may r. 1867. **23. a.** Now our sands are almost run SHAKS. **24.** Her veins r. with water, not blood 1884. **25. a.** Syn that my tappe of lif bigan to renne CHAUCER. **c.** Look on thy glass, see how it runs 1650.

**** *Of time, money, practices, or other things having course, continuance, or extension.* **26.** Of a period of time: To come to an end, be complete, expire. Only in pa. pple. OE. **27.** Of time: To pass or go by; to elapse; also, to be passing or current ME. **b.** To continue, go on, last; to remain existent or operative ME. **c.** Of a play: To be played continuously (for a specified time) 1808. **28. a.** Of money: To have currency; to be in circulation; to pass current ME. **b.** Of a writ, proclamation, etc.: To issue; to have legal course or effect; to operate. late ME. **c.** Of payments, practices, etc.: To be current or generally prevalent. late ME. **29.** To have course or continuance; to go on; to go, proceed, etc., in various fig. uses ME. **b.** Of qualities, etc.: To be persistent or common *in* a family 1777. **30.** To extend or stretch; to form a continuous line or boundary. late ME. **b.** *Law.* Of memory, recollection, etc.: To extend or go back in time 1447.

26. The night was almost run DE FOE. **27. b.** Leases r. in general for nineteen years 1843. **c.** The piece..will r. the season 1828. **28. b.** Countrees where the Kynges Writt renneth noght 1436. **29.** The covenant will not r., that is, it will not bind the assignee, nor pass to him 1837. **b.** Learning that had r. in the family like an heir-loom SHERIDAN. **30.** Tartaria..runneth along without controll by the high looking walls of China 1630. *fig.* His patriotism very often runs far..into the region of prejudice 1890. **b.** The memory of man runneth not to the contrary 1765.

***** *Of things passing into, assuming, or maintaining a certain condition or quality.* **31.** To pass into or out of a certain state. late ME. **b.** With adj. or other compl.: To become, end in being, turn, grow, fall, etc. 1449. **32. a.** To have a given tenor or purport; to be worded or expressed in a specified manner 1586. **b.** To be constituted or conditioned 1724. **33.** To have a specified character, quality, arrangement, form, etc. Const. with preps. and adjs. 1658. **b.** To be of a specified (average or maximum) size, price, etc. 1762. **c.** To be in the (average) proportion of 1849.

31. Many one there be, that renne out of their wyttes..for their wyues sakes COVERDALE 1 *Esdras* 4:26. **b.** *To r. amuck* (see AMUCK 2), *mad* (see MAD *a.* 1), *riot* (see RIOT *sb.* 3). *To r. dry*, to cease to yield water or milk; hence *fig.*, to become exhausted or spent. *To r. low*, to be nearly exhausted, to become scanty. *To r. short*: see SHORT *a.* **32. a.** So runs the Fable POPE. **b.** We must take things rough and smooth as they r. 1764. **33.** German traditions of obedience r. on different lines entirely 1890. **b.** The trout r. to a good size in Portugal 1890. **c.** His oats run 44 lb. to the bushel 1892.

II. Transitive senses.

* *To traverse, accomplish, aim at* or *avoid*, etc., *by running.* **1.** To pursue or follow (a certain way or course) in running, sailing, etc. OE. **b.** *Hunting.* To pursue, follow up (a scent) 1607. **c.** *transf.* Of immaterial things 1864. **2.** To traverse or cover by running, sailing, etc. ME. **b.** To scour, run about in (a place) 1648. **c.** To slip or shoot down (a rope, river, etc.) 1883. **3.** To perform or accomplish by running or riding 1494. **4. a.** To go upon (an errand or message) 1500. **b.** *Billiards.* See COUP *sb.*[3] 3. 1850. **d.** *Croquet.* To play through (a hoop) or up to (a peg) 1874. **5.** To flee or escape from (a place, country, etc.); to desert from (a ship) 1608. **6. †a.** *To r. ..fortune(s)*, in various phrases denoting voluntary sharing of another's lot –1713. **b.** To expose oneself, or be exposed, to (a chance, danger, etc.) 1592. **c.** To incur, meet with, encounter 1624. **7. a.** *To r. it*, or *a voyage*, to sail without convoy in time of war 1787. **b.** *To r. the* (or *a*) *blockade*: see BLOCKADE *sb.* 1. 1869. **8.** To sew slightly and quickly, usu. by taking a number of stitches on the needle at a time 1708. **9.** To pursue, chase, hunt (game, etc.) 1484. **b.** To contend with (a person, etc.) in a race 1786. **c.** To press *hard* or *close*, so as to inconvenience in some way. Also without adv. 1790. **d.** To press (a person or thing) *close* or *hard* in competition or rivalry 1806.

1. Our fox..did not r. the chain of woodlands, but held on southwards 1892. **b.** Hounds are running a high scent through a stiff country 1890. **c.** Affairs ran their fated course 1889. **2.** We..run from forty to fifty leagues a day 1748. **b.** Many.. would sooner let their children r. the streets 1861. **3.** The doom has run its course, the hour is here 1854. The Derby has been run in a snowstorm 1873. Phr. *To r.* (a thing) *fine*, to leave a very slight margin (*esp.* of time). *To r. the gauntlet*: see GAUNTLET[2]. **5.** Some..were..obliged to r. their Country 1727. **6. b.** He who goes to Sea, or to War, runs a Venture 1675. *To r. a risk*: see RISK *sb.* 1. **8. b.** To attach (a ribbon, etc.) to cloth by passing it through a series of holes.

** *To cause to run, move rapidly,* or *extend.* **10.** To cause or force (a horse, etc.) to go rapidly, esp. when riding it OE. **b.** *Racing.* To enter (a horse, etc.) for a race; also *fig.* to pit (lives) against each other 1750. **c.** To allow to run or feed at large, to graze (cattle, sheep, etc.) 1812. **11.** To bring into a certain state, affect in a certain way, by running. Chiefly *refl.* and in phrases. 1548. **b.** To bring, lead, drag, or force (one) *into* some state, action, etc. 1621. **c.** To force, drive (a person or thing) *out of*, or *off*, some place 1727. **12.** To cause (a boat or ship) to move rapidly or easily forwards, esp. towards or against the land 1548. **b.** To bring, convey, transport, in a vessel, down a stream, along rails, etc. 1700. **c.** To land, smuggle (contraband goods) 1706. **d.** To sail (a vessel) in time of war without a convoy 1813. **e.** To get (something) hastily carried through 1891. **13. a.** To drive or cause (one's head, etc.) to strike forcibly *against* (a person or thing) 1589. **b.** To thrust, *esp.* to dash or force (one's head, etc.) *into* or *through* something 1523. **14. a.** To drive (a vehicle, etc.) *into, against*, or *through* something 1663. **15.** To thrust or force (a weapon or the like) *through* or *into* a person, etc. 1480. **b.** To pierce or stab (a person). Usu. with *through* (a specified part). 1533. **16. a.** To cause to roll quickly; *spec.* in *Bowling*, to drive away (the jack) 1593. **b.** To cast or pass (the eye, hand, etc.) rapidly *along, down, over* (etc.) something 1728. **c.** To allow (bills or accounts) to accumulate for some time before paying 1861. **17.** To cause to move, slide, pass, etc., in a quick or easy manner. Usu. with advs. or preps. denoting direction. 1683. **b.** To carry, pass, or suspend (a line or rope) between two points 1769. **18.** To cause (a conveyance, vessel, etc.) to ply from place to place, or between two places 1764. **b.** To keep (a mechanical contrivance, etc.) moving or working 1849. **c.** To direct, conduct, carry on (a business, etc.).

Orig. *U.S.* 1864. **d.** To introduce or push (a person) in society 1897. **19. a.** To put or set up as a candidate. Orig. *U.S.* 1862. **b.** *U.S.* and *Austral.* To tease, nag, or vex 1879. **c.** To prosecute (a person); to bring (a person) in *for* damages 1891. **20. a.** To cut (a mark), draw or trace (a line), on a surface 1641. **b.** To trace or pursue (a parallel, resemblance, etc.); to draw (a distinction) 1716. **c.** To lead, take, extend, carry (a thing) in a certain direction, or to a certain length 1713. **d.** *Plastering.* To form (a cornice, etc.); also, to cover (a space) with plaster 1825.

10. As they that r. their horses for a wager, spur hardest at the races end 1647. **b.** An owner runs his horse ostensibly to win 1892. **11.** He had almost run himself to a standstill 1892. **b.** These wild woods..Will r. me mad FLETCHER. **c.** Arresting a free negro, with a view to r. him out of the State 1822. **12.** Our Palinurus now ran us ashore 1816. **c.** It was a smuggler running a cargo 1887. **13. a.** If we r. our heads against walls we're safe to hurt ourselves 1887. **14. a.** He..pretty nearly ran us into a cart 1872. **15.** If you had run a poniard into him SCOTT. **b.** Ile r. him vp to the hilts, as I am a soldier SHAKS. **16. a.** *Rich. II,* II. i. 123. **c.** At Oxford I ran what accounts with the tradesmen I liked RUSKIN. **17.** R. a red-hot fire-shovel over it, to brown it MRS. GLASSE. **18. b.** The hands we can't employ, the mills we can't r. C. BRONTË. **c.** *transf.* It is often said of the President that he is ruled, or as the Americans express it, 'run' by his secretary 1888. Phr. (*slang*) *To r. the show,* to 'manage' an undertaking. **20. a.** *To r. the line(s,* to determine or mark off a boundary-line (*U.S.*). **b.** One might r. the parallel much farther STERNE.

*** *To cause to flow or come together.* **21.** To give forth, to flow with (a specified kind of liquid) ME. **22. a.** To cause to coagulate, or to unite in a viscid mass. late ME. **b.** To unite or combine 1781. **c.** To convert *into* a certain form 1700. **23. a.** To smelt (metal); to form into sheets, bars, etc., by allowing to flow into moulds 1663. **b.** = CAST *v.* IX. 1690. **c.** To cause (a liquid) to flow *into* a vessel, *through* a strainer, etc. 1728. **24.** To fill up or fasten *together* with molten metal, etc. 1657. **25.** To let water escape through or from (a sluice, pool, etc.); esp. *r. dry.* 1839.

21. Rivers are said to r. blood after an engagement 1835. **22. b.** The events of two days have been run into one 1868. **23. a.** It should be first run into ingots, then melted 1873. **25.** The sluices have been run to night 1839.

Specialized uses, with preps. **Run across—,** to meet or fall in with. **R. after—. a.** To endeavour to gain the companionship or society of; to pursue with admiration or attentions. **b.** To follow or take up with, eagerly. **R. against—. a.** To act, operate, take effect, or be directed, against (one). **b.** To dash rapidly and forcibly against (a person or thing); to encounter suddenly or casually. **R. in—,** to lapse or fall into arrears of (payment, debt, etc.). **R. into—. a.** To incur (blame, displeasure, loss, etc.); to involve oneself in (debt, expenses, etc.). **b.** To rush headlong, fall into (some practice). **c.** To go on, advance, into (something); to mount up or amount to. **d.** To pass by change or transformation, to develop, into (something). **e.** To merge into; to blend or coalesce with. **f.** To fall into; or tend towards; to be displayed in. **g.** To dash into or collide with, esp. by accident. Also of dogs, to close with (an animal). **R. on—. a.** To discourse on; to refer or relate to. **b.** Of the mind: To be engrossed or occupied with (a subject). **c.** To show a marked demand or preference for (some particular thing). **R. out of—,** to come to the end of, to exhaust, one's supply of (something). **R. over—. a.** To take a mental review of; to think over. **b.** To glance over; to survey, scan, peruse, or read, rapidly. **c.** To repeat or recite quickly; to tell over again. **d.** To treat, perform, enjoy, etc., in a slight or hasty manner. **e.** To go over with the hand; to go through (a piece of music) rapidly. **f.** Of a vehicle, rider, or driver: To pass over (a person, etc., knocked down or lying in the way). **R. through—. a.** To examine, inspect, peruse, treat of or deal with, rapidly. **b.** To pass or go through, in the way of trial or experience. **c.** To wear out, consume, spend, waste, in a rapid or reckless manner. **d.** To be or continue present in; to pervade. **R. to—. a.** To come, amount in numbers, extend in size or depth, to (a specified quantity). (*b*) To be able for (*esp.* capable of purchasing). (*c*) To cover the expense of, be sufficient for. **b.** To lapse or fall to (waste, ruin, etc.). **c.** Of land: To produce naturally. **d.** Of plants: To tend to the (undesirable) development of (seed, straw, etc.). **e.** To pass or develop into (some excess). **R. upon—. a.** To have a tendency to, or a favour or fancy for, to seek much after (something). **b.** To dwell upon, be occupied with (a subject) in thought or discourse. **c.** To incur, bring on oneself, fall into. **d.** To make a sudden demand upon (a bank) for the purpose of withdrawing deposits, etc. **e.** To come upon suddenly. **R. with—. a.** To go along with; to accompany; to march with. **b.** To concur, accord, or agree with.

With advs. **R. away. a.** To make off, retreat hurriedly, flee, in the face of danger or opposition. **b.** To abscond; to depart surreptitiously *from* or *to* a person; to elope *with* some one. **c.** *To r. away with:* (*a*) To depart surreptitiously with, to carry off (something). (*b*) To take up with, accept, believe (an idea, etc.) hurriedly, without due reflection. (*c*) To carry off, gain. (*d*) To consume or exhaust. **d.** Of a horse, etc.: To rush off ungovernably, to bolt (*with* a person). **e.** To get away *from,* to outdistance completely, in running or racing. **R. down. a.** *intr.* Of a clock, etc.: To become completely unwound; to cease to go. **b.** To decline, fall off, in vigour or health. **c.** To diminish or decrease. **d.** To deteriorate. **e.** *trans.* To knock down or overthrow (a person); to dash into, collide with, sink (a vessel). **f.** To pursue (game) until caught or killed; to hunt down. **g.** To put down, overwhelm (a person) by superior force, argument, talk, etc. **h.** To disparage or vilify. **R. in. a.** *intr.* To rush in, close with, in attacking or assailing. **b.** *Rugby football.* To run with the ball and touch it down behind the adversary's goal-line. **c.** To pay a short or passing visit *to* a person. **d.** *trans.* To fix, fill in, *with* (melted lead, etc.). **e.** To arrest and take (a person) into custody. **f.** To insert, slip in. **g.** To enter and secure the election of (a person). **R. off. a.** *intr.* To take to flight; to abscond or elope (*with* a person or thing). **b.** Of water, etc.: To flow off or away. **c.** To diminish. **d.** To go off, digress, in talk. **e.** *trans.* To dash or rattle off; to write or recite rapidly. **f.** To allow to flow out; to draw or drain off (a liquid). **g.** *Sport.* To decide (a race) finally. **R. on. a.** *intr.* To continue running or going on. **b.** To continue in operation, effect, etc. Also const. *to* (a certain point). **c.** Of time: To pass or elapse. **d.** To continue speaking; to speak volubly; also, to chatter. **e.** To expand or develop *into.* **f.** *Printing.* To make (two paragraphs, etc.) into one; so in phr. *r. on chapters,* an intimation that the beginning of chapters in a work is not necessarily to start on a fresh page. **g.** *trans.* To continue to narrate (a story). **R. out. a.** *intr.* Of a period of time, etc.: To expire, terminate, come to an end. **b.** Of water, etc.: To escape from the containing vessel, part, etc. (*b*) Of vessels, etc.: To leak. **c.** (*a*) To come to the end of one's resources or stock. (*b*) To become expended or exhausted; to come to an end. **d.** *Cricket.* To move out rapidly from the block to hit the ball. **e.** Of a rope; To pass out in continuous length. **f.** To extend or project; to protrude, jut out. **g.** To shoot out (*into* excrescences, etc); to go on *to* something. **h.** To come out of (a contest) in a specified manner or position. **i.** *trans.* To finish or complete (a race, or period of time). (*b*) *Sport.* To bring (a race, etc.) to a conclusive result; to decide. †**j.** To go through, spend, squander (money or property). (*b*) *Agric.* To impoverish, exhaust (land). **k.** (*a*) To advance (a gun) so that the muzzle projects from the port-hole (or embrasure). (*b*) To expand, extend, or fill out. (*c*) To allow or cause (a line) to be drawn or carried out. **l.** *Cricket.* To put out (a batsman) while he is running between the popping-creases. **m.** *refl.* To exhaust (oneself) by running; to come to an end, exhaust one's means, etc. **R. over. a.** *intr.* Of a vessel, etc.: To overflow. **b.** Of liquid or grain: To flow over the side of a vessel. **c.** (*passing into*) *trans.* To recount, relate, or repeat rapidly or succinctly. **d.** To review rapidly. Usu. *in* the mind, etc. **e.** To glance over, read hurriedly. **f.** To retouch slightly or quickly. **R. through. a.** To pierce or stab through the body with a weapon, etc. **b.** To read over rapidly. **c.** To draw a line through (words). **R. together. a.** To combine, coalesce, unite, *esp.* in a moist or melted state. †**b.** To join in combat, engage in fight; *esp.* to tilt or joust. **R. up a.** *intr.* To shoot up; to grow rapidly. (*b*) To increase, mount up. **b.** To go back in time or memory. **c.** To rise *to* a high price or value. (*b*) To amount *to* a large sum. (*c*) To attain *to* a certain weight, size, etc. **d.** Of cloth, etc: To shrink or or contract after wetting. **e.** *Sporting.* To be runner-up in a race, etc. **f.** *trans.* (*a*) To make up (a sum or number); to augment (one's fortune). (*b*) To accumulate (a bill, debt, etc.) against oneself or another. (*c*) To bid against (a person) at an auction in order to compel him to pay more. (*d*) To cause (prices) to rise; to force (a thing) up to a higher price. **g.** To trace or follow up in some way. **h.** (*a*) To build, erect, set up (a wall, etc.). (*b*) To bring (a gun) up to the firing position. **i.** (*a*) To build or construct rapidly or hurriedly (and unsubstantially). (*b*) To add up (a column of figures, etc.) rapidly. (*c*) To sew quickly (and loosely).

Run (rɒn), *ppl. a.* 1669. [f. RUN *v.*] **I. 1.** Of liquor That has run out or leaked. **2.** *Naut.* That has deserted. *R. man,* a deserter, 1702. *Obs.* or *arch.* **3.** Of a fish: that has made a migration up a freshwater stream from the sea 1828. **4. a.** *Mining.* Of coal: Soft, bituminous 1730. **b.** *dial.* Of milk: Coagulated, clotted 1866. **II. 1.** Of goods: Illicitly landed or imported; smuggled 1714. **2.** Poured in or out in a melted state; caused to flow out. *R. butter:* see BUTTER *sb.*^{1} 1806. **b.** *R. metal, steel,* a form of cast iron 1833. **3.** Carried on, continuous, running 1811. **4.** *R. stitch,* a running stitch. Also as *vb.* 1880.

Ru·n-about, runabout. 1549. **1.** One who runs about from place to place; *dial.* a pedlar. **b.** *attrib.* Given to wandering or roving 1788. **2.** *Austral. pl.* Cattle left to graze at will 1890. **3.** A small light horse-vehicle or motor-car. Also *attrib.* with *car.* 1890.

Runagate (rɒ·năge^{i}t), *sb.* (and *a.*). Now *arch.* 1530. [Alteration of *renna-,* RENEGATE, by association with *ren(ne* RUN *v.* + AGATE *adv.*] †**1.** An apostate –1692. **2.** A deserter, fugitive, runaway 1548. **3.** A vagabond, wanderer; a run-about 1547. **4.** *attrib.* or as *adj.* 1563.

2. Crews of these desperadoes,..the runagates of every country and every clime W. IRVING. **3.** A crew of wild thieves and runnagates 1677. **4.** A r. rogue without property..or influence 1851.

Runaway (rɒ·năwe^i), *sb.* (and *a.*). 1547. [f. RUN *v.* + AWAY *adv.*] **A.** *sb.* **1.** One who runs away; a fugitive, a deserter. †**b.** An apostate, a renegade –1647. **c.** A horse which bolts while being ridden or driven 1607. **2.** An act of running away; *spec.* an elopement, a runaway match 1724.

1. A general Defection ensu'd upon this Runaways Example 1712. **2.** Many of the young people made..a 'r.' 1830.

B. *attrib.* or as *adj.* **1.** Of persons: Having run away; given to running away; fugitive 1548. **b.** Pertaining to, connected with, accompanied by, running away or elopement 1748. **2.** Of horses, etc.: Escaped, or given to escaping, from the control of the rider or driver 1607. **3.** *Sporting.* Easily won; one-sided 1895.

1. Rather more than half were r. rebels and murderers DARWIN. **b.** All the dinners and duels..and run-away matches, were..discussed 1871. *R. knock, ring,* one given at a door as a trick or joke, and followed by the rapid flight of the giver.

Runch (rɒnʃ). *Sc.* and *north.* 1552. [Of unkn. origin.] **a.** Charlock or wild mustard, *Brassica sinapistrum.* **b.** Wild radish, *Raphanus raphanistrum.*

Runcinate (rɒ·nsinĕt), *a.* 1776. [mod.L. *runcinatus* f. L. *runcina* a plane (formerly also taken to mean a saw) + -ATE^2.] *Bot.,* etc. Irregularly saw-toothed, with the lobes or teeth curved toward the base. So **Ru·ncinated** *a.* Also **Ru·ncinato-,** comb. form.

Rundale (rɒ·ndē^{i}l). 1545. [Anglicized f. Sc. *ryndale,* f. *rin,* Sc. var. of RUN *v.* + DALE^2.] **1.** A form of joint occupation of land, each joint holder occupying and cultivating several small strips or patches not contiguous to each other. **2.** Land occupied in this manner, or a share in such land 1819.

Rundle (rɒ·nd'l). ME. [var. of ROUNDLE.] †**1.** A circle; a circular or annular form, appearance, or arrangement; a round –1843. †**2.** An object of a circular or spherical form –1680. **b.** A circular enclosure or field. Now *dial.* 1577. **3.** *Her.* = ROUNDEL 5 b. 1562. †**4.** *Bot.* A whorl, verticil, umbel –1807. **5. a.** A cylinder or roller of wood; *spec.* one of the bars in a lantern-wheel 1565. **b.** A solid wheel or barrel 1611.

Run-down, *ppl. a.* 1683. [RUN *v.*] †**1.** Downtrodden, oppressed (*rare*). **2.** Of watch-plates: Faced with only one coat of enamel 1834. **3.** Completely unwound 1894. **4.** In a low state of health 1901.

Rune (rūn). 1690. [Adopted from Danish writers on Northern antiquities, and repr. ON. **rún,* pl. *rúnar, rúnir* secret or hidden lore, runes, magical signs (Sw. *runa,* Da. *rune*) = OE. *rūn* mystery, runic letter, secret consultation, OS., OHG., Goth. *rūna;* see ROUND *v.*^{2}] **1.** A letter or character of the earliest Teut. alphabet, which was most extensively used by the Scandinavians and Anglo-Saxons. Also, a similar character or mark having mysterious or magical powers attributed to it. **2.** †**a.** An incantation or charm denoted by magic signs (*rare*) –1796. **b.** A Finnish poem or division of a poem, *esp.* one of the separate songs of the Kalevala. Also incorrectly applied to old Scandinavian poems. 1854. **c.** *transf.* Any song, poem, or verse 1847. **3.** *attrib.*, in sense 'inscribed with runes', as *r.-stone*, etc. 1151.

2. c. My heart would sit and sing Shrillest runes of wintry cold 1860.

Rune-staff. 1705. [– Sw. *runstaf*, f. *runa* RUNE + *staf* STAFF.] **a.** A magic wand inscribed with runes. **b.** A runic calendar or clog-almanack.

Rune-stave. Now only *arch.* [OE. *rūnstæf*, f. *rūn* RUNE + *stæf* STAFF, STAVE.] A runic letter or symbol.

Rung (rʊŋ), *sb.* [OE. *hrung* = MLG. *runge* (Du. *rong*), OHG. *runga* (G. *runge* from LG.), Goth. *hrugga* ῥάβδος.] **1.** A stout stick of a rounded form, *esp.* one used as a rail (in a cart, etc.), cross-bar, or spoke. **2.** A round or stave of a ladder ME. **3.** *Shipbuilding.* A floor-timber. Now *rare.* 1625.

2. *fig.* One of the lowest rungs of Memory's ladder 1883. Hence **Runged** *ppl. a.* **Ru·ngless** *a.*

Rung, *ppl. a.* 1630. [f. RING *v.*[1]] **a.** Having a ring inserted in the nose. **b.** Ring-barked.

Runic (rū·nik), *a.* and *sb.* 1662. [– mod.L. *runicus*, f. ON. **rún* RUNE; see -IC.] **A.** *adj.* **1.** Consisting of runes. **b.** Carved or written in runes; expressed by means of runes 1685. **c.** Inscribed with runes 1728. **2.** Of poetry, etc.: Such as might be written in runes; belonging to the peoples or the age which made use of runes: *esp.* ancient Scandinavian or Icelandic. Now *rare.* 1690. **b.** *transf.* Applied to ancient Scottish poetry or poets 1759. **3.** Belonging to ancient Scandinavia or the ancient North 1665. **b.** Of ornament: Of the interlacing type (orig. Celtic) which is characteristic of rune-bearing monuments, metal-work, etc. 1838.

1. Lyons, bears,..&c. wrought on the hardest rocks, together with R. characters EVELYN. **b.** Odin invented Poetry; the music of human speech, as well as that miraculous r. marking of it CARLYLE. **3.** Time, Which settles all things, Roman, Greek, or R. BYRON.

B. *sb.* †**1.** The ancient Scandinavian tongue –1690. **2.** A runic inscription 1866. **3.** *Typog.* A style of display lettering (in the Roman alphabet) having a thickened face, and often of a condensed form 1873.

Runlet[1] (rʊ·nlėt). Now only *arch.* or *Hist.* late ME. [– OFr. *rondelet*, dim. of *rondelle*, f. *ronde* ROUND *a.*; cf. ROUNDEL.] A cask or vessel of varying capacity; the quantity of liquor contained in this.

Large runlets appear usu. to have varied between 12 and 18½ gallons, small ones between a pint or quart and 3 or 4 gallons.

Runlet[2] (rʊ·nlėt). 1755. [f. RUN *sb.* + -LET.] A little run or stream; †a channel. A r. flowing..down the rocky steps 1874.

Runnel (rʊ·n'l). 1577. [Later form (by assim. to RUN) of *rinel*, OE. *rynel*, f. the stem *rin-*, *run-*; see RUN *v.*, -EL.] **1.** A small stream of water; a brooklet, rivulet, rill, or trickle. **2.** A small watercourse or channel; a gutter 1669.

1. A little runnell tumbled neere the place 1600. Herons stand in the little runnels which trickle over the flats 1883.

Runner (rʊ·nəɹ). [ME. *urnare*, *rennere*, etc.; f. RUN *v.* + -ER[1]; anticipated by OE. *fore-iornere* fore-runner.] **I. 1.** One who runs; a racer. †**2.** A fugitive, deserter –1624. **3.** One who carries messages on foot or horseback; a messenger, courier, errand-bearer; a scout ME. †**b.** One employed as spy to a gambling-den, band of thieves, etc. –1776. **c.** One employed or acting as a collector, agent, or intelligencer for a bank, broker, †government, †newspaper, bookmaker, etc. 1768. **d.** A police-officer. Also *Bow-street r.* (see BOW-STREET) and *police-r.* (see POLICE *sb.*). Now *Hist.* 1771. **e.** One who solicits custom for a hotel, tradesman, etc. Orig. *U.S.* 1840. **4.** A horse capable of running well; a good roadster or racer; a horse taking part in a race 1582. **5. a.** The water-rail. *Rallus aquaticus*; also *dial.* the land-rail 1668. **b.** A bird belonging to the order *Cursores* 1870. **c.** *U.S.* A name given to several fishes 1876. **6.** A fast-sailing ship; †*esp.* one for the carrying of dispatches without convoy in time of war 1700. **7. a.** One engaged in running contraband goods; a smuggler; also, a smuggling vessel. Now *dial.* 1721. **b.** A blockade-runner 1867. **8.** A strip of cloth, usu. embroidered, used as a decoration for tables, pianos, etc. **II. 1.** *Founding.* A channel along which molten metal runs from the furnace to the mould 1843. **2. a.** A horizontal millstone capable of revolution, being usu. the upper one of a pair 1533. **b.** A vertical millstone, or a disc of stone, metal, etc., employed in the same manner 1707. **c.** A slab of stone or (rarely) iron, used in polishing stone surfaces 1850. **3.** *Naut.* A stout rope rove through a single block, with one end passed round a tackle-block and the other having a hook attached to it. Often coupled with *tackle*. Also *attrib.*, as *r.-block*, etc. 1625. **4.** A naked creeping stem thrown out from the base of the main stem of the strawberry and certain other plants, and itself taking root 1664. **b.** One of several varieties of beans which twine round stakes for support, esp. the scarlet runner (see SCARLET *a.*). 1786. **5.** A ring or other device capable of sliding along a strap, rod, etc., or through which something may readily be passed or drawn 1688. **6.** A long piece of wood or metal, curved at the ends, supporting the body of a sledge, toboggan, or the like 1765. **b.** The blade of a skate; a skate with a blade curved up at the toe 1860. **7.** A support or groove, along, on, or in which anything slides; a roller 1833. **8.** A wagon or trolley 1853.

Ru:nner-u·p. 1842. **1.** *Coursing.* A dog that takes the second prize, losing only the final course to the winner. **b.** *gen.* A competitor or competing team that comes in second, or takes second place 1886. **2.** One who 'runs up' bids at an auction 1905.

Running (rʊ·niŋ), *vbl. sb.* OE. [f. RUN *v.* + -ING[1].] **1.** The action of RUN *v.*, in various senses. *esp.* **2.** The action, on the part of a horse, of going at (great) speed, *esp.* in a race; racing; †a race OE. **3.** Capacity for or power of running or racing 1842. **4.** The flowing or discharge of blood or humours from the body; a sore which discharges matter OE. **5.** The flow of liquor during the process of wine-making, brewing, or distillation; the liquor obtained at a specified stage of process 1601.

2. Phr. *To make (strong, etc.) r. To make the r.*, to set the pace. *To take up the r.*, to take the lead. *Out of the r.*, having no place among the leading competitors in a race. **3.** He had plenty of r. still in him 1842. **5.** *fig.* From the Dregs of Life, think to receive What the first sprightly r. could not give DRYDEN.

Comb.: **r. board**, orig. *U.S.*, a footboard along the side of a locomotive, motor-car, or the roof of a freight-car; **r. powers**, permission granted to a railway company to run trains over the lines of another company.

Running (rʊ·niŋ), *ppl. a.* ME. [f. RUN *v.* + -ING[2].] **I. 1.** Of water, streams, etc.: Flowing. **2. a.** Fluid, liquid; melting readily. late ME. **b.** Of sand or soil: Having no coherence 1833. **3.** Of sores, etc: Discharging matter; suppurating 1535.

1. *R. water*, water taken straight from a running stream; river-water. **3.** Ne can my r. sore find remedie SPENSER.

II. 1. Passing rapidly from place to place. late ME. **b.** Of diseases, etc.: Passing from one part of the body to another; *esp.* spreading over the skin. late ME. **2.** Employed to run as a messenger, etc. 1604. **b.** Moving rapidly about, esp. in the course of one's business or profession 1611. **3.** Of plants: Creeping, climbing, or spreading rapidly; sending out many runners 1548. **4.** Of metre, music, etc.: Of a smooth, easy, or rapid character 1589. **5.** Of a ship: Sailing in time of war without a convoy 1816.

2. b. He might be a 'R. Lecturer', not tied to one locality CARLYLE.

III. 1. Performed with, or accompanied by, a run; rapid, hasty ME. †**b.** Of a banquet, collation, etc.: Taken hurriedly; slight –1728. **2.** *R. hand*, a cursive form of script 1648.

1. *R. fire*, a rapid successive discharge of firearms by each of the men forming a rank or ranks; a rapid and continuous fire. *R. fight*, a naval engagement carried on during a retreat or flight. **b.** A r. collation to stay his stomach—no set meal to satisfy his hunger FULLER.

IV. 1. Carried on or extending continuously. Used *esp.* of architectural or decorative ornament. late ME. **b.** Of measurements: Linear 1663. **2.** Continuous, sustained; going on, carried on, right through or continuously 1492. **b.** Of accounts, etc.: Allowed to run on for a certain (specified or indefinite) time 1742. **3.** (Placed after the sb.) Following each other; successive, in succession 1719.

1. *R. title, head(line)*, a short title or headline placed at the top of the page. **2.** His face is the r. comment on his acting HAZLITT. *R. commentary* spec., a broadcast report by an eye-witness of a ceremony, sporting event, etc.

V. 1. Current, prevalent, general 1449. **2.** That is in progress, going on, or existing, at the present time 1584. †**b.** Of cash: Available for use –1727. **3.** Temporary 1632.

2. My r. quarter's salary 1861. **b.** The r. Cash of the Nation,..must daily diminish SWIFT.

VI. 1. Moving easily or rapidly by mechanical means or as a piece of mechanism; easily moved, slid along, shifted, etc. late ME. **2.** Of ropes, etc.: Capable of moving when pulled or hauled; *esp.* moving or passing through a block, ring, etc. Chiefly *Naut.* 1625. **3.** Of knots, nooses, etc. Slipping or sliding easily, esp. so as to catch something tightly 1648. **4.** *R. stitch*, a loose open stitch 1850.

1. The r.-gear of a good waggon 1876. **2.** A r. bowline passed around the fish's tail 1885. *R. rigging* see RIGGING *sb.* 2. **3.** Every man speaks under correction of the yard-arm and a r. noose SCOTT. Hence **Ru·nningly** *adv.* †concurrently *with* something; rapidly, readily.

†**Ru·nnion.** [Of unkn. origin.] An abusive term applied to a woman SHAKS.

Runo-, comb. form of mod.L. *runa* RUNE, used in **Runo·logist**, one who studies or is skilled in runes 1866; **Runo·logy**, the study or science of runes.

Runrig (rʊ·nrig). *Sc.* 1437. [f. RUN *v.* + RIG *sb.*[1] Cf. RUNDALE.] **1.** A ridge of land lying among others held by joint tenure. **2.** = RUNDALE 1. 1583. **3.** As *adv.* In separate ridges cultivated by different occupiers 1695. **4.** *attrib.* Held or characterized by this mode of tenure 1751.

Runt (rʊnt). 1501. [Of unkn. origin.] **1.** An old or decayed stump of a tree. Now *dial.* **2.** An ox or cow of a small breed or size 1549. **b.** A small or inferior horse 1725. **c.** A small pig, esp. the smallest in a litter: *dial.* and *U.S.* 1841. **3.** *transf.* **a.** An ignorant, uncouth, or uncultivated person 1614. **b.** An old woman; a hag. Now *Sc.* or *dial.* 1652. **c.** A stunted or undersized person; a dwarf 1700. **d.** A dwarfish or diminutive object 1845. **4.** A domestic pigeon of a breed characterized by size and stoutness of build 1661.

1. Neither yong poles nor old runts are fit for durable building HOLLAND. **3. a.** A pretty pass, when a set of beggarly Welsh runts use threats to their betters 1830. Hence **Ru·ntish** *a.* of animals, stunted, dwarfish. **Ru·nty** *a.* dwarfish, undersized; small and ill-made; of low, thick-set build.

Run-up. 1834. [f. RUN *v.*] The act of running up to a certain point; esp. **a.** *Coursing.* The race between two greyhounds up to the first turn or wrench of the hare. **b.** The act of taking or sending a ball up to the goal or into a position for final play 1897.

b. Vardon, after being short in his run up, missed the hole for a 3. 1901.

Runway (rʊ·nwē[1]). Chiefly *U.S.* 1835. [f. RUN *v.*] **1.** The customary track or run of an animal (*esp.* of deer) or a fish. **2.** Any artificial (sloping or horizontal) track or gangway made for convenience of passage or carriage 1888. **3.** A groove in which anything slides 1890.

Rupee (rupī·). 1612. [– Urdu *rūpiyah* :– Skr. *rūpya* wrought silver.] The monetary unit of India, represented by a silver coin now valued at 1*s.* 6*d.*

Rupert's drop, metal: see DROP *sb.* I. 8. and PRINCE *sb.*

‖**Rupia** (rū·piă). 1815. [mod.L. (Bateman), f. Gr. ῥύπος filth, dirt; see -IA[1].] *Path.* A skin disease characterized by an eruption of broad, flattish, scattered vesicles, succeeded by thick ulcerating scabs. Hence **Ru·pial** *a.* pertaining to, of the nature of, affected with, r.

Ruption (rʊ·pʃən). Now *rare.* 1483. [– Fr. †*ruption* or late L. *ruptio*, *-on-*, f. *rupt-*; see next, -ION.] **1.** Breach of the peace; disturbance (*rare*). **2.** Breaking or rupture of some membrane or tissue of the animal body 1541.

Rupture (rʊ·ptiŭɹ, -tʃəɹ), *sb.* 1481. [–(O)Fr. *rupture* or L. *ruptura*, f. *rupt-*, pa. ppl. stem of *rumpere* break; see -URE.] **1.** †**a.** Breach *of* a covenant, intercourse, or the peace –1645.

b. A breach of harmony or friendly relations between two persons or parties 1583. **2.** *Path.* Abdominal hernia; a case of this 1539. **3.** †**a.** A break in a surface or substance, such as the skin, flesh, etc. –1674. **b.** A break in the surface of the earth; a ravine, chasm, gorge, rift 1555. **4.** The act of breaking or bursting; the fact of being broken or burst 1642.

1. The r. of the Treaties with Spain 1645. **b.** The r. between Church and State was now complete 1862. **4.** The Egg that soon Bursting with kindly r. forth disclos'd Thir callow young MILT.

Rupture (rʊ·ptiŭɹ, -tʃəɹ), *v.* 1739. [f. prec.] **1.** *trans.* **a.** To break, burst (a vessel, membrane, etc.). **b.** To cause a breach of; to sever 1854. **c.** To affect (a person) with hernia 1818. **2.** *intr.* To suffer a break or rupture 1863.

Ru·pturewort. 1597. [f. RUPTURE *sb.* 2.] **1.** A plant of the genus *Herniaria*, esp. *H. glabra*, formerly supposed to cure rupture or hernia. **2.** A West Indian plant, *Alternanthera polygonoides* 1864.

Rural (rū°·răl), *a.* and *sb.* late ME. [– (O)Fr. *rural* or late L. *ruralis*, f. *rus, rur-* the country; see -AL[1].] **A.** *adj.* **1.** Of persons: Living in the country; having the standing, qualities, or manners of country-folk; agricultural or pastoral. **2. a.** *R. dean, deanery*: see DEAN[1] 5. 1450. **b.** Employed or stationed in country districts 1840. **3.** Of or pertaining to, characteristic of, country-folk; rustic 1513. **4.** Of poetry, music, etc.: Natural or appropriate to the country or to country-people; unpolished, simple 1470. **5.** Of, pertaining to, or characteristic of the country or country life as opp. to the town 1590. **6.** Of a rustic form or make (*rare*) 1624.

1. To keep company—odious phrase—with some r. swain 1876. **3.** I see the r. virtues leave the land GOLDSM. **4.** It was a kind of rurall harpe 1610. **5.** On to thir mornings r. work they haste Among sweet dewes and flours MILT.

B. *sb.* An inhabitant of the country; a countryman, rustic. Now *rare.* 1513.

Every r. began to be busie in the fields 1657. Hence **Ru·ralism,** r. quality or character; country life. **Ru·ralist,** a countryman; peasant; one who leaves the town for the country. **Rura·lity,** r. quality or character, rusticity; country life, manners, or scenery; also with *a* and *pl.* **Ru·rally** *adv.*

Ruralize (rū°·rălaiz), *v.* 1805. [f. RURAL *a.* + -IZE 2.] **1.** *trans.* To render rural or rustic in character. **2.** *intr.* To go into the country; to rusticate 1822.

Ruridecanal (rū°ridĭkē·năl, -de·kănăl), *a.* 1861. [f. L. *ruri-*, comb. f. *rus* country + DECANAL *a.*] Of or pertaining to a rural dean or deanery.

Rusa (rū·să). 1827. [mod.L. (C. Hamilton Smith, 1827), – Malay.] **a.** A genus of large East Indian deer, including the sambur and rusa proper. **b.** A deer of this genus, esp. the Javanese *R. hippelaphus.* Hence **Ru·sine** *a. Zool.* of or belonging to, characteristic of, the genus *R.*

Ruse (rūz). late ME. [– (O)Fr. *ruse*, f. *ruser* drive back, perh. :– Rom. **ru(r)sare*, f. L. *rursus* back(wards). Cf. RUSH *v.*[2]] †**1.** *Hunting.* A detour; a doubling or turning of a hunted animal to elude the dogs. late ME. only. **2.** A trick, stratagem, artifice, 'dodge' 1625. **b.** Without article 1815.

2. b. Seizing by r. the game that evaded other snares 1863.

Rush (rʊʃ), *sb.*[1] [OE. *rysc(e*, recorded chiefly in place-designations, corresp. to MLG., MHG. (Du., G.) *rusch.* The development *u* :– *y* before point-consonants is paralleled in *blush, cluster, such, thrush*, etc.] **1.** A plant of the order *Juncaceæ*, having straight naked stems or stalks (properly leaves) and growing in marshy ground, or on the borders of rivers or ponds; a single stem or stalk of this. **b.** Used for burning; also *ellipt.*, a rush-light. late ME. †**c.** Used for making a finger-ring –1601. †**d.** In reference or with allusion to the practice of strewing fresh rushes for visitors –1738. **e.** Without article 1728. **2.** As a type of something of no value or importance, esp. in neg. phrases as *not to care a r., not worth a r.* ME. **3.** With specific epithets. **a.** Denoting various species of *Juncus* 1753. **b.** Applied to many plants of different genera, more or less resembling the rush, as *bog-, sweet, wood-r.*, etc.

1. The Queene..sate alone alowe on the rushes all desolate T. MORE. **b.** Without the glimmer of a farthing r.! HOOD. **c.** *All's Well* II. ii. 24. **d.** Rushes, Ladys, rushes, Rushes as green as Summer for this stranger FLETCHER. **2.** A figge for the whole world. A r. for thee. 1610.

attrib. and *Comb.*: **r.-grass,** a species of grass having a r.-like appearance; **-holder,** a device for holding a rushlight; **-toad,** the natter-jack; **-wheat,** a species of wild wheat (*Triticum junceum*) growing on sandy shores. Hence †**Rusher**[1], one who strews rushes on a floor –1630.

Rush (rʊʃ), *sb.*[2] late ME. [f. RUSH *v.*[2]] **1.** The act, or an act, of rushing; a sudden violent or tumultuous movement; a charge, an onslaught. **2. a.** *Football*, etc. An attempt by one or more players, *esp.* the forwards, to force the ball through the opponents' line and towards their goal. Also, a player who is skilled in this. 1857. **b.** *Croquet.* A roquet played with considerable force 1874. **c.** *Amer.* A scrimmage or struggle between first and second year students 1871. **3.** A sudden migration of numbers of people to a certain place, *esp.* to a new goldfield 1850. **b.** *transf.* The scene of such a migration 1855. **4.** An eager demand *for*, a strong run *on*, something 1856. **5.** Dysentery in cattle 1799.

1. Some mighty current, r., or eddy of the tide 1789. The ceaseless clangour, and the r. of men Inebriate with rage SHELLEY. *fig.* To this hour I have sudden vague rushes of terror DICKENS. **2. a.** The Dark Blues broke away, but the r. was well saved 1897. **4.** There was..a bit of a r. on American rails 1884. Phr. *With a r.*, with a sudden onset; in a rapid or sweeping manner 1859.

attrib. and *Comb.*: **r. hour,** the part of the day in which there is normally a r. on trains, shops, etc.: **r. order,** an order for goods required in a hurry.

Rush (rʊʃ), *v.*[1] late ME. [f. RUSH *sb.*[1]] **1.** *trans.* **a.** To strew with rushes. **b.** To tie up, work or make, with rushes 1848. **2.** *intr.* To gather rushes (*rare*) 1530.

2. Don't y' go a-rushing, maids, in May 1896. Hence **Ru·shed** *ppl. a.* overgrown or strewn with rushes.

Rush (rʊʃ), *v.*[2] late ME. [– AFr. *russher*, var. of OFr. *russer, ruser*; see RUSE. For *-sh* cf. *bushel, push.*] **I.** *trans.* †**1.** To force out of place or position by violent impact; to drive back, down, etc. late ME. only. **2.** To cause to move with great speed and force; to send or impel violently. Chiefly with preps. late ME. **3.** †**a.** *refl.* To move with speed and force; to impel (oneself) heedlessly, violently, or hurriedly *upon* or *on* something –1659. **b.** *trans.* To drag, force, or carry rapidly and violently *into, to, out of*, etc. 1577. **c.** *transf.* To get or bring *out*, carry *through*, push on, etc., in an unusually rapid manner 1830. **4.** To force at an unusual or excessive pace or speed. Also with *on, up.* 1850. **b.** To cheat, 'do'; to extort from; to charge (a person) so much (esp. an exorbitant price); also, *for* so much. *slang.* 1885. **5. a.** *Mil.* To overcome, take, capture, carry by means of a sudden rush 1865. **b.** To cross, penetrate, traverse, negotiate (or endeavour to do so) with a rush 1884. **c.** To occupy by a rush (of gold-miners) 1879. **d.** *Croquet.* To roquet (a ball) with considerable force 1874. **e.** *Football*, etc. To make a rush for (the opposite goal).

2. Into what a sea of misery have I now rushed saile! 1654. **3.** What, stab her, And r. her into blood? YOUNG. **c.** There is no disposition to r. business 1893. **4.** While the country boy is allowed to grow up, the city boy is rushed up 1887. **5. a.** The Arabs 'rushed' the town, putting every man to the sword 1884. **c.** The locality was 'rushed' for gold 1879.

II. *intr.* **1.** Of persons or animals: To run, dash, or charge with violence or impetuous rapidity. Usu. const. with advs. or preps. late ME. **b.** *fig.* To make an attack or descent, *on* or *upon* a person 1535. **c.** *fig.*, denoting rash or precipitate action. Freq. const. *into.* 1560. **d.** To pass or travel rapidly 1852. **2.** Of things: To move, flow, fall, etc., with great speed or impetuosity. late ME. **b.** To come suddenly into view 1798.

1. Then the colt rushed by them..hard held 1862. **c.** So many foolish persons are rushing into print 1872. **2.** Nor slept the winds Within thir stony caves, but rush'd abroad MILT. *fig.* A dreadful rumour rushed through the University THACKERAY. **b.** The Sun's rim dips; the stars rush out COLERIDGE. Hence **Ru·sher**[2], one who or that which rushes; *colloq.* a 'go-ahead' person. **Ru·shingly** *adv.*

Ru·sh-bea:ring. 1617. [RUSH *sb.*[1]] An annual ceremony in northern districts of carrying rushes and garlands to the church and strewing the floor or decorating the walls with them.

Ru·sh-ca:ndle. 1591. [RUSH *sb.*[1]] A candle of feeble power made by dipping the pith of a rush in grease; a rushlight.

Rushen (rʊ·ʃ'n), *a.* [OE. *rysćen*, f. *rysć(e* RUSH *sb.*[1] + -EN[4].] Made of rushes, or of a rush.

Ru·sh-grown, *a.* 1545. [RUSH *sb.*[1]] †**1.** Having the slender tapering form of a rush –1828. **2.** Overgrown with rushes 1777.

Ru·shlight. Also **rush-light.** 1710. [RUSH *sb.*[1]] **a.** = RUSH-CANDLE. **b.** Without article: The light of a rush-candle 1847.

Ru·sh-like, *a.* 1578. [f. RUSH *sb.*[1] + -LIKE.] Resembling a rush or rushes.

Ru·sh-ring. 1579. [RUSH *sb.*[1]] A ring made of a rush or rushes. **b.** Used as a wedding-ring 1668.

b. I'l Crown thee with a Garland of straw then, and I'le Marry thee with a Rush ring DAVENANT.

Rushy (rʊ·ʃi), *a.* late ME. [f. RUSH *sb.*[1] + -Y[1].] **1.** Made or consisting of rushes; rushen. **2.** Producing, full of, covered with, rushes 1586. **3.** Resembling a rush or rushes; rush-like 1597.

1. Then turn tonight, and freely share..My r. couch and frugal fare GOLDSM.

Rusk (rʊsk). 1595. [– Sp., Pg. *rosca* twist, coil, twisted roll of bread, of unkn. origin.] **1.** Bread in the form of small pieces which have been refired so as to render them hard and crisp; formerly much used on board ships. **2.** A piece of bread hardened or browned by re-firing and sometimes sweetened 1759.

Ruskin (rʊ·skin). The surname of John Ruskin (1819–1900), distinguished as a writer on art and social subjects, used *attrib.* in *R. linen*, a kind of hand-woven linen produced near Keswick in Cumberland; *R. ware*, a kind of pottery with leadless glaze produced at Birmingham. Hence **Ruski·nian** *a.*, characteristic of R.; *sb.* a follower of R. (so **Ru·skinite**).

Rusma (rʊ·zmă). 1615. [app. – Turk. *hirisma* – Gr. χρῖσμα ointment (see CHRISM).] A depilatory composed of lime and orpiment, now chiefly used in tanning.

Russ (rʊs), *sb.* and *a.* 1567. [– Russ. *Rus'*, old name for the Russian lands and people before the sixteenth century. Cf. med.L. *Russus* (XII).] **A.** *sb.* **1.** A Russian. Now *rare.* †**b.** An adherent of the Russian Church –1635. **2.** The Russian language 1571. **B.** *adj.* Russian 1574. Hence **Ru·ssify** *v. trans.* to Russianize; hence **Ru·ssifica·tion.**

†**Russel.** 1488. [prob. Flem. *Rijsel* Lille.] A kind of woollen fabric –1703.

Russell (rʊ·sĕl). 1868. [Of unkn. origin.] A ribbed or corded fabric formerly in use. Also *R. cord.*

Russet (rʊ·sĕt), *sb.* and *a.* ME. [– AFr. *russet*, var. of OFr. *rousset, rosset*, dim. of *rous* (mod. *roux*) – Pr. *ros*, It. *rosso* :– L. *russus* red; see -ET.] **A.** *sb.* **1.** A coarse homespun woollen cloth of a reddish-brown, grey, or neutral colour, formerly used for the dress of peasants and country-folk; also with *a* and *pl.*, a kind or make of this. †**b.** *pl.* Garments of such cloth –1645. **2.** A reddish-brown colour; a shade of this 1532. **3. a.** A variety of eating apple, of a reddish or yellowish brown colour, or marked with brownish spots, and having a rough skin; an apple of this kind 1708. †**b.** A variety of pear –1725.

1. I wore r. before I wore motley SCOTT.

B. *adj.* **1.** Of a reddish-brown colour. late ME. **b.** Applied to varieties of apples (†and pears) 1664. **2.** Of garments, etc.: Made of russet cloth 1440. **3.** Clad in russet or homespun cloth 1613. **4.** Rustic, homely, simple 1588. **5.** Of boots or shoes: Tan, brown 1667.

1. R. Lawns, and Fallows Gray, Where the nibling flocks do stray MILT. **2.** The Morne in R. mantle clad SHAKS. **4.** R. yeas, and honest kersie noes SHAKS. Hence **Ru·sset** *v.* to make or become r. in colour. **Ru·ssety** *a.* inclining to a r. colour.

Russet coat. 1552. **1.** A coat of russet cloth or colour, typical of a humble or rustic condition. †**2.** A peasant, rustic –1597. **3.** A russet apple 1602.

Russet-coated, *a.* 1596. [RUSSET *a.*] Wearing a russet coat; rustic, homely.

A plain russet-coated Captain who knows what he fights for CROMWELL.

Russeting (rɒ·sétiŋ). 1588. [f. RUSSET *sb.* or *a.* + -ING³.] †1. Russet clothing. †2. A peasant, rustic; a simple fellow –1632. 3. A russet apple 1607.

Russia (rɒ·ʃă). 1658. [– med.L. *Russia*, f. *Russi* the Russians; see RUSS, -Y³. Russ. *Rossiya* prob. – Gr. Ῥωσία.] The name of the country in the east of Europe which is now the Russian Socialist Federal Soviet Republic (R.S.F.S.R.); used attrib. in specific designations.

R. leather, a very durable leather made of skins impregnated with oil distilled from birch-bark, extensively used in bookbinding. Also simply *russia*. *R.-matting*, 'matting manufactured in Russia from the inner bark of the linden'. *R. sheet-iron*, 'sheet-iron made in Russia, and having a smooth, glossy surface of a purplish colour, sometimes mottled'.

Russian (rɒ·ʃăn), *sb.* and *a.* 1538. [– med.L. *Russianus*, f. *Russia*; see prec., -AN.] **A.** *sb.* **1.** A native of Russia. **2.** The language of Russia; also, a form or dialect of this 1716. **3.** *ellipt.* for *R. hemp, iron, leather, wheat* 1862.

1. My grooms are Arabs;..my housemaids Russians 1716.

B. *adj.* **1.** Of or pertaining to Russia or its people; inhabiting, native to, characteristic of, Russia 1588. **2.** Of or pertaining to, concerned with, the Russian language or literature 1797. Hence **Ru·ssianize** *v. trans.* to render R. in character.

Russniak (rɒ·sniæk), *sb.* and *a.* 1829. [– the native name *Rusnyák*.] Little Russian or Ruthenian.

Russo- (rɒ·so), comb. form (on Gr. analogies) of RUSS, as in *Russo-Turkish*, etc.; also in adjs. or sbs. denoting tendency to admire or favour Russia, Russian methods, policy, etc., as **Ru·ssophil(e, Russophilism** (-ǫ·filiz'm); or morbid dread of these, as **Ru·ssophobe, -pho·bia, -pho·bian, -pho·bism, -pho·bist.**

Rust (rɒst), *sb.* [OE. *rūst* = OS., (O)HG. *rost*, (M)Du. *roest*, based on Gmc. **ruð-* **reuð-* **rauð-* RED.] **1.** A red, orange, or tawny coating formed upon the surface of iron or steel by oxidation, esp. through the action of air or moisture; also, a similar coating formed upon any other metal by oxidation or corrosion. **2.** Moral corrosion or canker; corruption OE. **3.** Any deteriorating or impairing effect or influence upon character, abilities, etc., esp. as the result of inactivity OE. **4.** A disease in plants marked by ferruginous spots and caused by uredinous fungi; also loosely, any plant-disease presenting a similar appearance ME. **b.** One or other of the uredinous fungi producing 'rust' in plants 1813. **5.** A coating or stain resembling rust 1684. **6.** The colour of rust 1716.

1. *fig.* Authors, like coins, grow dear as they grow old; It is the r. we value, not the gold POPE. 2. I hope to Rube A-waye the Ruste, with penaunce, frome my gostely syhte 1440. 3. Sunday clears away the R. of the whole Week ADDISON.

attrib. and *Comb.*: **r.-cement**, a composition for joints which oxidizes on exposure to the air; **-joint** a joint made with r.-cement; **-mite**, a gall-mite producing r.-like excrescences on plants. Hence **Ru·stless** *a.* free from r.; not liable to be rusted.

Rust (rɒst), *v.* ME. [f. prec.] **I.** *intr.* **1.** Of iron or other metals: To contract rust, grow rusty; to undergo oxidation. †**b.** To form a rust. SHAKS. **2.** To deteriorate, degenerate, spoil, *esp.* through inactivity or want of use. Also with *out*. ME. **3.** To become rust-coloured 1541. **4.** Of wheat, etc.: To become affected with rust or blight 1868.

1. Thy needles..Now r. disus'd, and shine no more COWPER. 2. Then must I r. in Ægypt, never more Appear in Arms? DRYDEN. 3. When the bracken rusted on their crags TENNYSON.

II. *trans.* **1.** To affect with rust; to oxidize 1596. **2.** To corrupt or corrode morally or physically 1697. **3.** To affect (corn, etc.) with rust or blight 1759. **4.** To waste *away* by idling 1853.

1. Keepe vp your bright Swords, for the dew will r. them SHAKS. 4. We must not r. away our lives here 1887.

Rustic (rɒ·stik), *a.* and *sb.* 1440. [– L. *rusticus*, f. *rus* country. Cf. (O)Fr. *rustique*.] **A.** *adj.* **1.** Of or pertaining to the country (as opp. to the town); found in the country. **2.** Of persons: Living in the country as opp. to the town; following country occupations; of peasant or agricultural stock or condition 1601. **3.** Of persons: Having the appearance or manners of country people; lacking in elegance, refinement, or education; *occas.*, clownish, boorish 1585. **4.** Characteristic or typical of country-folk or peasants; *esp.* unmannerly, unrefined; rough 1589. **b.** Plain and simple; unsophisticated; having the charm of the country 1600. **5.** Of rude or country workmanship; of a plain or simple form or structure; *spec.* constructed of roughly trimmed branches or roots of trees 1594. **b.** Of letters: Having a free or negligent form; applied *spec.* to one of the styles employed in early Latin manuscripts (in contrast to *square*) 1784. **6.** *Arch.* Characterized by a surface artificially roughened or left rough-hewn, or by having the joints (esp. the horizontal ones) deeply sunk or chamfered; also, †of or pertaining to the Tuscan order 1563. **b.** *R. work*, masonry of this type 1715.

1. Of that kind Our rusticke Garden's barren SHAKS. 2. And many a holy text around she strews, That teach the r. moralist to die GRAY. 3. A Rustick Fellow, one..without cleanliness, and of a slovenly Speech 1688. 4. Unmannerly and rusticke behaviour 1637. b. The r. grace and sweetness of the *May Queen* 1855. 5. Three rustick arches, set off with ivy, moss, icicles and all the rocky appurtenances 1752.

B. *sb.* **1.** A countryman, peasant 1550. **b.** A boorish person (*rare*) 1706. **2.** *Arch.* Rustic work 1731. **b.** A stone (†or joint) of the kind employed in rustic work. Usu. in *pl.* 1728.

1. In how many countrey affairs must the scholar take the r. for his master? 1722. Hence **Ru·sticly** *adv.* in a r. manner; rustically.

Rustical (rɒ·stikăl), *a.* and *sb.* late ME. [– OFr. *rustical* or med.L. *rusticalis*; see prec., -ICAL.] **A.** *adj.* **1.** = RUSTIC *a.* 2. Now *arch.* **2.** = RUSTIC *a.* 3. 1513. †**b.** Physically strong, robust –1693. **3.** = RUSTIC *a.* 1. 1546. **4.** = RUSTIC *a.* 4. 1550. **5.** Of a kind, make, or fashion appropriate to the country; *esp.* plain or simple 1483.

2. b. The others..are more r. and hardy EVELYN.

B. *sb.* A countryman, peasant, rustic. Now *arch.* 1555.

If thou doe not kiss hir.., then thou shalt be taken for a rusticall 1579. Hence **Ru·stical-ly** *adv.*, †**-ness** –1661.

Rusticate (rɒ·stikeˈt), *v.* 1660. [– *rusticat-*, pa. ppl. stem of L. *rusticari* live in the country, f. *rusticus*; see RUSTIC, -ATE³.] **1.** *intr.* To go or retire into the country; to stay or sojourn in the country; to assume rural manners; to live a country life. **2.** *trans.* **a.** To dismiss or 'send down' from a university for a specified time, as a punishment 1714. **b.** To remove or send into, settle (a person) in, the country. Also *refl.* 1733. **3.** To imbue with rural manners; to countrify 1766. **4.** To mark masonry by sunk joints or roughened surfaces 1715.

1. We went to..an old lonely Inn, where was the last place we rusticated 1698. 2. a. I was rusticated for..painting the college pump scarlet 1868.

Rustication (rɒstikēˈʃən). 1623. [– L. *rusticatio, -on-*, f. as prec.; see -ION.] **1.** The action of rusticating; a spell of residence in the country; †a rural pursuit or occupation. **b.** The condition naturally attaching to life in the country 1771. **2.** Temporary dismissal from a university; an instance or period of this 1734. **3.** The action of banishing, or the state of being banished, into the country 1751. **4.** *Arch.* The action or practice of rusticating masonry; the style of masonry produced by this 1815. **b.** A rustic feature or part 1839.

Rusticity (rɒsti·sĭti). 1531. [– Fr. *rusticité* or L. *rusticitas*; see RUSTIC *a.* and -ITY.] **1.** Lack of breeding, culture, or refinement; clownishness. **b.** An instance of this 1803. **2.** Lack of intellectual culture; ignorance 1583. **3.** Of language, composition, etc.: Lack of polish or refinement; uncouthness, inelegance 1565. **b.** A rustic expression 1711. **4.** Rustic or rural life, quality, or character 1638. **b.** A rural feature or characteristic; a rural thing or object 1662.

1. The wisedome of God receives small honour from those vulgar heads that rudely stare about, and with a grosse r. admire his workes SIR T. BROWNE.

Rustle (rɒ·s'l), *sb.* 1759. [f. the vb.] **1.** A continuous succession of light crisp sounds produced by some kind of movement. **2.** *U.S. colloq.* Bustle, hustle 1899.

1. Thou shalt hear..R. of the reaped corn KEATS.

Rustle (rɒ·s'l), *v.* late ME. [Of imit. origin; cf. Fris. *russelje, risselje*, Flem. †*ruysselen, rijsselen*, Du. *ridselen, ritselen*.] **1.** *intr.* Of things: To give forth a continuous succession of light, rapid, crisp sounds, as the result of some kind of movement. **b.** Of persons or animals: To cause sounds of this nature to be produced 1560. **2.** With advs. or preps.: To come, go, move, etc., with a rustling sound 1586. **b.** To go about, be finely dressed, *in* some material which rustles 1598. **3.** *trans.* **a.** To cause to move in some way with a rustling sound 1648. **b.** To shake or stir with a rustling sound 1821. **4.** *U.S. colloq.* **a.** *intr.* To bestir oneself or move about vigorously; to work with strenuous energy; to hustle 1872. **b.** *trans.* To shift, deal with, rapidly; to acquire or get together, by one's own exertions 1882.

1. The dry leaf rustles in the brake SHELLEY. b. Woman rustles, and bustles, and creaks, and fusses 1892. 2. Where the deer r. through the twining brake THOMSON. b. Rustling in unpayd-for Silke SHAKS. 3. a. Many sleeping Saints.. Russled their Dust together, and gat up 1648.

Rustler (rɒ·slǝɹ). 1820. [f. RUSTLE *v.* + -ER¹.] **1.** One who or that which rustles. **2.** *U.S.* **a.** An energetic or bustling man 1872. **b.** A cattle-thief 1882.

Rusty (rɒ·sti), *a.*¹ [OE. *rūstiġ*; see RUST *sb.*, -Y¹.] **I. 1.** Covered or affected with rust or red oxide of iron; rusted. †**2.** Morally foul or corrupt –1586. **3.** Of persons: Presenting an appearance suggesting something old and rusted. late ME. **4. a.** Lacking in polish or refinement; rough, rude; surly, morose, churlish 1500. **b.** Hoarse, raucous, harsh, grating. Now *rare*. 1570. **5. a.** Stiff through want of exercise or old age 1508. **b.** Of knowledge, accomplishments, etc.: Impaired by neglect; requiring to be polished up 1796. **6.** Old, antiquated, obsolete 1551.

1. Bars and bolts Grew r. by disuse COWPER. 3. A little r., musty old fellow, always groping among ruins W. IRVING. 5. a. My body so lusty, Whiche for lacke of exercise is nowe almost rustye 1537. b. For the benefit of those whose Greek is rather r..., I have added a Latin version 1796. 6. That Prayer..has lain by till 'tis almost r. BUNYAN.

II. 1. Of plants: Affected with rust or mildew 1502. **2.** Having the colour of rust; rubiginous, ferruginous; *spec.* in *Path.*, of sputa 1528. **b.** Of (dark) clothes: Showing signs of age or use; shabby, worn, or faded 1709. **c.** Of colours: Inclining towards, modified by, the colour of rust 1791.

1. The wheat was r. 1880. 2. b. His r. old suit of clothes was the cast-off of a waiter 1892.

Rusty (rɒ·sti), *a.*² Now chiefly *dial.* 1515. [var. of REASTY, RESTY *a.*²] Reasty, rancid.

Rusty (rɒ·sti), *a.*³ 1562. [var. of RESTY *a.*¹, perh. infl. by RUSTY *a.*¹] **1.** Of horses: Restive. **b.** In phr. *to ride* or *run r.* Freq. of persons: To become intractable or obstinate; to be angry or annoyed; to take offence. 1709. **2.** *colloq.* Ill-tempered, cross, nasty. Chiefly in phr. *to cut up r., turn r.* 1815.

2. The people got r. about it SCOTT.

Rut (rɒt), *sb.*¹ late ME. [– (O)Fr. *rut*, †*ruit* rutting (-time), †bellowing (of stags) :– Rom. **rūgitus*, for L. *rugītus*, f. *rugire* roar.] **1.** The annually recurring sexual excitement of male deer; also, *transf.* of other animals. †**2.** The company of deer among which a stag goes to rut –1640. Hence **Rut** *v.*¹ *intr.* to be at rut.

Rut (rɒt), *sb.*² 1580. [Early forms also *rote, roote, rupt*; prob. – OFr. *rote*, early form of ROUTE; the shortening of the vowel may be due to lack of stress in the comp. †*cartrote*.] **1.** A (deep) furrow or track made in the ground, esp. in a soft road, by the passage of a wheeled vehicle or vehicles. **b.** *fig.* A settled habit or mode of procedure; a narrow, undeviating course of life or action; a groove 1839. **2.** A track or passage hollowed out, cut, or excavated in the ground (*rare*) 1611. **3.** *transf.* A deep mark or depression on the skin, some part of the body, etc. 1623.

1. b. Parliaments, lumbering along in their deep ruts of commonplace CARLYLE. **2.** The soil lying hollow with the mole's ruts 1787. Hence **Ru·tty** *a.* marked by or full of ruts.

Rut (rɒt), *sb.*[3] Now *U.S.* and *dial.* 1633. [Cf. ROTE *sb.*[3]] The roaring of the sea.

Rut (rɒt), *v.*[2] 1607. [f. RUT *sb.*[2]] *trans.* To mark (a road or the ground) with ruts; to furrow. (Chiefly in *pa. pple.*)

Rutaceous (rutēⁱ·ʃəs), *a.* 1830. [f. mod. L. *Rutaceæ* the rue family, f. L. *ruta* rue; see -ACEOUS.] Of or belonging to the family *Rutaceæ*; resembling rue; rue-like.

Ruth (rūþ). Now *arch.* [Early ME. *reuþe*, f. *rewen* RUE *v.*, prob. after ON. *hrygð*; see -TH[1].] **1.** The quality of being compassionate; pitifulness; compassion, pity. **2.** Contrition, repentance; remorse. Now *rare.* ME. **3.** Sorrow, grief, distress; †lamentation ME. †**4. a.** Matter or occasion of sorrow or regret –1626. **b.** Mischief; calamity; ruin –1647. †**5.** With *a* and *pl.* in senses 3, 4. –1589.

1. Look homeward Angel now, and melt with r. MILT. Phr. *To have r.*, usu. const. †*of*, *on* or *upon*. So *to take r.* **2.** When our Teares doe testifie our r. 1603. **3.** Here lies, to each her Parents r., Mary, the Daughter of their youth B. JONS.

Ruthenate (rū·pĕnĕt). 1879. [f. RUTHENIUM + -ATE[1] 1 c.] *Chem.* A salt formed by the action of ruthenic acid. So **Ruthe·niate.**

Ruthene (ruþī·n), *sb.* and *a.* 1548. [– med.L. *Rut(h)eni* (pl.), related to *Ruzi*, *Russi* Russians; cf. RUSSIAN.] **1.** Of or pertaining to, a member of, the Little Russian race, inhabiting the south of Russia and portions of the north-west of Austria. **2.** The language of the Ruthenes 1891. So **Ruthe·nian** 1850.

Ruthenium (ruþī·niŏm). 1848. [f. med. L. *Ruthenia* Russia (having been first noticed in platinum ores from the Ural Mountains) + -IUM.] A metal of the platinum group, first isolated by Claus in 1845. Chem. symbol Ru. Hence **Ruthenic** (ruþe·nik) *a.* pertaining to or derived from r.; containing r. **Ruthe·nious** *a.*

Ruthful (rū·þful), *a.* Now *arch.* ME. [f. RUTH + -FUL.] **1.** Full of compassion or pity; compassionate. **2.** That excites compassion or pity; lamentable, piteous, rueful ME. **b.** Of sounds, actions, etc.: Expressive of grief or sorrow ME. **c.** Of persons or feelings: Sad, dejected, doleful 1513.

2. Or say a r. chance broke woof and warp BROWNING. Hence **Ru·thful-ly** *adv.*, **-ness.**

Ruthless (rū·þlės), *a.* ME. [f. RUTH *sb.* + -LESS.] Devoid of pity or compassion; pitilessly merciless.

What a ruthlesse thing is this.., to take away the life of a man? SHAKS. Hence **Ru·thless-ly** *adv.*, **-ness.**

Rutic (rū·tik), *a.* 1857. [f. L. *ruta* rue + -IC 1 b.] *Chem. R. acid*, a colouring matter discovered in the common rue; capric acid.

Rutilant (rū·tilănt), *a.* Now *rare.* 1497. [– L. *rutilans*, *-ant-*, pr. pple. of *rutilare*, f. *rutilus* reddish; see -ANT.] Glowing, shining, with either a ruddy or a golden light.

Rutile (rū·til). 1803. [– Fr. *rutile* or G. *rutil* (Werner, 1803), f. L. *rutilus* reddish.] *Min.* An ore of titanium (a form of titanium dioxide). So **Ru·tilite.**

Ru·tin. 1857. [– G. *rutin* (Fr. *rutine*), f. L. *ruta* RUE *sb.*[2]; see -IN[1].] *Chem.* Rutic acid, capric acid.

Rutter (rɒ·təɹ). 1500. [– MDu. *rutter*, var. of *ruter*, *ruyter* (Du. *ruiter*, whence G. *reuter*), – OFr. *routier*, *routeur*; see ROUTER *sb.*[1]] A cavalry soldier (*esp.* a German one), of the kind employed in the wars of the 16th and 17th centuries. Now *arch.* Hence †**b.** A gay cavalier, a dashing gallant –1603.

You are a R. borne in Germanie 1592. Hence †**Ru·tterkin,** a swaggering gallant or bully –1581.

Ru·ttier. Now *arch.* 1500. [– (O)Fr. *routier*, f. *route* ROUTE *sb.*] A set of instructions for finding one's course at sea; a marine guide to the routes, tides, etc.

†**Ru·ttish,** *a. rare.* 1601. [f. RUT *v.*[1] + -ISH[1] 3.] Lewd, lustful, lascivious –1602. Hence **Ru·ttishness** (*rare*).

Ruttle (rɒ·t'l), *v.* Now *dial.* late ME. [= MLG. *rutelen*, prob. imit. cf. RATTLE *v.*] *intr.* To rattle; to make a rattling noise in the throat. Hence **Ru·ttle** *sb.* a noise of this kind.

Rutyl (rū·til). 1868. [f. as RUTIC *a.* + -YL.] *Chem.* = CAPRYL.

Rutylene (rū·tilīn). 1868. [f. prec. + -ENE.] *Chem.* A hydrocarbon polymeric with acetylene.

-ry, *suffix*, a reduced form of -ERY, occurring chiefly after an unstressed syllable ending in *d*, *t*, *l*, *n*, or *sh*, but also after stressed vowels or diphthongs. The older examples sometimes represent OFr. forms in *-rie*, with variants in *-erie*, but the majority are comparatively late English formations. Examples are *ribaldry*; *harlotry*, *devilry*; *yeomanry*; *Irishry*; *avowry*.

Rye (rəi). [OE. *ryġe* = ON. *rugr* :– Gmc. **ruʒiz*, beside **roʒʒan-*, **ruʒʒn-*, repr. by OFris. *rogga*, OS. *roggo* (Du. *rogge*, *rog*), OHG. *rokko* (G. *roggen* is f. LG.).] **1.** A food-grain obtained from the plant *Secale cereale*, extensively used in northern Europe. **2.** The plant itself. Also *collect.*, a number of growing plants of this kind (in a field). 1440. **b.** *Wild r.*: Any of various grasses of the genus *Elymus*; esp. *Elymus virginicus* or Lime Grass 1475.

Comb.: **r.-asthma,** hay-fever; **r.-brome grass,** a variety of brome with rye-like seeds, occurring as a weed in wheat-fields; **-flour,** flour made from r.; **-straw,** (*a*) the dried haulm of r.; (*b*) a single straw of this; *fig.* a weak insignificant person.

Rye-bread. 1579. Bread made from rye.

Rye-grass (rəi·grɑs). 1753. [In sense 1 an alteration of RAY-GRASS. In sense 2 perh. f. RYE.] **1.** One or other of several species of *Lolium*, esp. *L. perenne* (common r.) and *L. italicum* (Italian r.), extensively used as forage and fodder grasses. **2.** = *Wild rye* 1760.

Ryepeck (rəi·pek). Also **rypeck, ripeck.** 1857. [Of unkn. origin.] An iron-shod pole used for mooring a punt, or serving as a mark for competitors in aquatic sports.

Ryot (rəi·ət). 1625. [– Urdu *raᶜīyat*, *raiyat* – Arab. *raᶜīya* RAYAH.] An Indian peasant, husbandman, or cultivating tenant.

‖**Ryotwar** (rəi·ətwāɹ), *a.* 1827. [Urdu *raiyatwar*, f. *raiyat* RYOT + *-wār* pertaining to.] = next A.

‖**Ryotwary** (rəi·ətwări), *a.* and *sb.* 1834. [Urdu *raiyatwārī*, f. *raiyatwār*; see prec.] **A.** *adj.* Of land-tenure in India: Characterized by direct settlement between the government and the cultivators, without the intervention of a zemindar or landlord. **B.** *sb.* The ryotwary system 1858.

‖**Rype** (rū·pə), *Pl.* **ryper.** 1743. [– Norw. *rype*, var. of *rjupe*, *rjupa*, ON. and Icel. *rjúpa*.] The ptarmigan. (The sing. and pl. forms are often confused by English writers.)

S

S (es), the nineteenth letter of the English, and the eighteenth of the ancient Roman, alphabet, derives its form (through the ≶, ⋚, ⋛ of early Latin and Greek inscriptions) from the Phœnician W, which represented a voiceless sibilant: in some of the Semitic langs. (s), in others (ʃ). In Ancient Greek and Latin the value of the letter is believed to have been always (s).

In mod. English the general rule is that *s* is pronounced (s) at the beginning of a word or of the second element of a compound, and when doubled or in contact with a voiceless consonant. Between vowels, and as an inflexional final element, a single *s* is mostly (z). But there are many anomalies and variations, especially in classical derivatives; cf., e.g., *absurd* (æbsɒ̄·ɹd), *observe* (ǫbz-); *dishonour* (dis-, diz-).

The phonetic combinations (sy), (zy), which arose from the collocation of (s), (z) with the first element of such diphthongs as (yu), (yə) have passed into (ʃ), (ʒ), which are consequently symbolized by *s* in combination with certain letters or groups of letters, as in *sure* (ʃūᵊɹ), *sugar* (ʃu·gəɹ), *censure* (se·nʃəɹ), *mission* (mi·ʃən), *Asia* (ēⁱ·ʃă), *treasure* (-ʒŭɹ, -ʒəɹ), *evasion* (-ʒən).

S is silent in some words adopted from Old French, as in *aisle*, *isle*; in the Law French *mesne*, *demesne*, a silent *s* was inserted by false analogy.

1. The letter and its sound. **2.** The shape of the letter; an object having this shape. **b.** *Collar of S, S's, SS.*, or *Esses*: see COLLAR *sb.* 2. **c.** *attrib.* and *Comb.*, as *S-shaped* adj.; *S-curve*, *-piece*, etc. **3.** Used to denote serial order, applied to the nineteenth (or more usu. eighteenth, either I or J being omitted) member of a series.

Abbreviations: **a.** S. = various proper names, as Samuel, Sarah, etc.; = Saint; so SS. = Saints; = Society (L. *societas*), as in F.R.S., Fellow of the Royal Society; F.S.A., Fellow of the Society of Antiquaries; S.J., Society of Jesus; S.P.G., Society for the Propagation of the Gospel (in Foreign Parts); S.P.C.K., Society for the Promotion of Christian Knowledge; *Mus.* = Solo; *Chem.* = Sulphur; *Anat.* and *Zool.* = sacral (vertebra); *Her.* (also *l.c.*) = Sable; = snow (in ship's log-book). S.A. = (*a*) Salvation Army. (*b*) Sex Appeal. (*c*) small-arms. S.B. = smooth bore (gun); simultaneous broadcast. S.M. = Silver Medallist (in shooting competition); = short metre. S.P. = starting price (in betting). S.S. = steam ship. **b.** S. = South; also S.E., SE., South-east, etc. **c.** s. = L. *solidus* and so used for shilling(s); = second (of time). **d.** S.O.S.: See SOS.

'S, a euphemistic shortening of *God's* in certain oaths; written continuously with the following word, as in 'SBLOOD, 'SDEATH. Cf. ZOUNDS.

's, repr. a shortened pronunc. of various monosyllables when unstressed. (Written continuously with the preceding word.) **1.** = *is*; see BE *v.* Now *colloq.* and *poet.* 1584. **2.** = *has*: see HAVE *v. colloq.* 1845. **3.** = US *pron.* Now *dial.* exc. in *let's* = let us (*colloq.*) 1588.

-s, *suffix*, forming advs.; orig. *-es*, identical with the suffix of the genitive sing. of many neut. and masc. sbs. and adjs. See also -WARDS, -WAYS.

Sabæan, Sabean (săbī·ăn), *a.* and *sb.* 1586. [f. L. *Sabæus*, Gr. Σαβαῖος (f. *Saba*, Σάβα, Arabic *sabā*, *saba'*, = Heb. *šᵉbā*, ancient name of the people of Yemen, by Gr. and Roman writers imagined to be the name of the capital city) + -AN.] **A.** *adj.* Of or belonging to the ancient population of Yemen in Arabia. In poetic use, often with allusion to the ancient renown of the spices brought from Yemen. **B.** *sb.* One of the ancient inhabitants of Yemen 1607.

Sabaism (sēⁱ·bĕ,iz'm). Also **Sabeism, Tsabaism, Zabaism.** 1669. [– Fr. *sabaïsme*, f. Heb. *ṣābā* host (of heaven), after the presumed etym. of SABIAN; see -ISM.] The worship of 'the host of heaven'; star-worship. Also sometimes used for SABIANISM. So **Sa·baist** 1662. **Sabai·stic** *a.*

‖**Sabaoth** (sæ·be,ōᵘþ). ME. [– L. *Sabaoth* (Vulg.) – Gr. Σαβαώθ (LXX and N.T.) – Heb. *ṣᵉbāōt*, pl. of *ṣābā* army, host.] A Heb. word (lit. 'armies', 'hosts') retained untranslated in the N.T. and the *Te Deum*, in the designation *The Lord* (*Lord God*) *of Sabaoth.* ¶ **b.** Confused with *sabbath*. SPENSER.

‖**Sabbat** (saba). 1652. [Fr.; a special application of *sabbat* SABBATH.] A 'witches' sabbath'; see SABBATH 3.

Sabbatarian (sæbătēᵊ·riăn), *a.* and *sb.* 1613. [f. late L. *sabbatarius* adj. (Augustine), sb. pl. Jews (Martial), f. L. *sabbatum*; see next, -ARIAN.] **A.** *adj.* †**a.** Of or pertaining to the Sabbath or its observance. **b.** Having relation to the tenets of the Sabbatarians. 1631. **B.** *sb.* **1.** A Jewish observer of the (Saturday) Sabbath 1613. **2.** A

Christian who regards the Lord's Day as a Sabbath, deducing its obligation from the Fourth Commandment. Also, more usu., one whose observance of Sunday is excessively strict. 1620. **3.** A member of a Christian sect which maintained that the Sabbath should be observed on the seventh day of the week; a Seventh-day Baptist 1645.

2. I am not a S., I showed it by travelling on Sunday 1864. Hence **Sabbata·rianism,** S. principles or practice.

Sabbath (sæ·bǎþ). [OE. *sabat*, ME. *sabat* (XIII) – L. *sabbatum* and (O)Fr. *sabbat*, †*sabat* – Gr. σάββατον – Heb. *šabbāṯ*, f. *šāḇaṯ* rest. The sp. with *th* and the consequent pronunc. are due to learned assoc. with the Heb. form.] **1. a.** *orig.* The seventh day of the week (Saturday) considered as the day of religious rest enjoined on the Israelites by the fourth commandment of the Decalogue. **b.** Since the Reformation, often applied to 'the Lord's day', i.e. the first day of the week (Sunday) observed by Christians in commemoration of the resurrection of Christ 1509. **c.** *gen.* Applied occas. to the day of the week set apart for rest or worship by any religious body, e.g. to the Friday as observed by Moslems 1613. **d.** Applied to the sabbatical year of the Israelites. late ME. **2.** *transf.* and *fig.* A time or period of rest; a cessation from labour, trouble, pain, and the like. late ME. **3.** A midnight meeting (*witches' s.*) of demons, sorcerers and witches, presided over by the Devil, supposed in mediæval times to have been held annually as an orgy or festival. Also SABBAT. 1660.

1. a. The Primitive Church kept both the S. and the Lords day JER. TAYLOR. **b.** Severe and sunless remembrances of the Sabbaths of childhood HAWTHORNE. **2.** Why will you break the S. of my days? POPE.

Comb.: **S.-school,** (*a*) = SUNDAY-SCHOOL; (*b*) a Jewish school held on the Saturday for giving religious instruction to children. Hence **Sa·bbathless** *a.* observing no S.

Sa:bbath-day·. ME. **1.** = SABBATH 1 a. **2.** = SABBATH 1 b. 1440. **3.** *gen.* A Sabbath, a day of sacred rest 1755.

1. *Sabbath day's journey*, the distance (2,000 *ammōt* = 1,225 yards) which, according to Rabbinical prescription in the time of Christ, was the utmost limit of permitted travel on the Sabbath.

Sabbatian (sæbeⁱ·ʃiǎn). 1708. [f. *Sabbatius* + -AN.] A member of a sect founded by Sabbatius, who seceded from the Novatianists before A.D. 380.

Sabbatic (sǎbæ·tik), *a.* 1649. [– late L. *sabbaticus* 'seventh', 'of sabbath' – Gr. σαββατικός (Josephus), f. σάββατον SABBATH; see -IC. Cf. Fr. *sabbatique* (XVII).] Of or pertaining to the Sabbath; resembling or appropriate to the Sabbath.

Sabbatical (sǎbæ·tikǎl), *a.* 1599. [– late L. *sabbaticus* (see prec.) + -AL[1]; see -ICAL.] **1.** Pertaining or appropriate to the Sabbath 1645. **b.** *S. river*: an imaginary river celebrated in Jewish legend, which was said to dry up on the Sabbath 1613. **c.** Of the nature of a Sabbath or period of rest 1836. **2. a.** *S. year*: (*a*) the seventh year, prescribed by the Mosaic law to be observed as a 'Sabbath' in which the land was to remain untilled and all debtors and Israelitish slaves were to be released 1599; (*b*) in American universities, a year of absence from duty for the purposes of study and travel, granted to professors at certain intervals 1895. **b.** *S. millenary, millennium*: the last of the seven thousands of years which (on the analogy of the seven days of creation) were supposed to form the destined term of the world's existence 1646. Hence **Sabba·tical-ly** *adv.*, **-ness.**

Sabbatism (sæ·bǎtiz'm). *rare.* 1582. [– late L. *sabbatismus* – Gr. σαββατισμός, f. σαββατίζειν keep the Sabbath, f. σάββατον SABBATH; see -ISM.] **1.** A sabbatical rest: in allusions to Heb. 4:9. **2.** The formal observance of the Sabbath 1611.

Sabbatize (sæ·bǎtəiz), *v.* late ME. [– late L. *sabbatizare* (Tertullian) – Gr. σαββατίζειν, f. σάββατον Sabbath; see -IZE.] **1.** *intr.* To keep the Sabbath; to observe a specified day as a day of rest 1608. **b.** *fig.* To enjoy or undergo a period of rest analogous to a Sabbath. late ME. **2.** *trans.* To observe or keep as a Sabbath; to assimilate to a Sabbath 1609. Hence **Sabbatiza·tion,** the action of sabbatizing.

‖**Sabella** (sǎbe·lǎ). 1851. [mod.L., perh. f. L. *sabulum* sand.] *Zool.* A tubicolous annelid of the family *Sabellidæ*.

Sabellian (sǎbe·liǎn), *a.*[1] and *sb.*[1] late ME. [– eccl.L. *Sabellianus*, f. *Sabellius* (see B); see -AN.] *Theol.* **A.** *adj.* Pertaining to the Sabellians (see B) or their doctrine 1577. **B.** *sb.* One who accepts the view of Sabellius (an African heresiarch of the 3rd c.) that the Father, Son, and Holy Ghost are merely different aspects or modes of manifestation of one Divine person. late ME. Hence **Sabe·llianism,** belief in the S. doctrine of the Trinity.

Sabellian (sǎbe·liǎn), *a.*[2] and *sb.*[2] 1601. [f. L. *Sabellus* + -IAN.] *Hist.* **A.** *adj.* Pertaining to a group of related peoples who inhabited certain parts of ancient Italy, comprising the Sabines, Samnites, and Campanians. **B.** *sb.* A person belonging to any of these peoples.

Sabian (sēⁱ·biǎn), *sb.* and *a.* 1661. [f. Arab. *ṣābi'* + -AN.] **A.** *sb.* **1.** An adherent of a religious sect mentioned in three passages of the Koran (ii. 40, v. 73, xxii. 17), and by later Arabian writers. **2.** In erroneous use: A worshipper of 'the host of heaven'; a star-worshipper 1716.

1. In the Koran the Sabians are classed with Moslems, Jews, and Christians, as believers in the true God. O.E.D.

B. *adj.* Pertaining to the Sabians (in both senses) 1796. Hence **Sa·bianism,** the religion of the Sabians; chiefly in erroneous use, worship of 'the host of heaven', star-worship.

Sabicu (sæbikū·). 1866. [Cuban Sp. *sabicú*.] A timber tree, *Lysiloma sabicu*, native of Cuba, valued for the hardness and durability of its wood; the wood of this tree.

Sabine (sæ·bəin), *a.* and *sb.* late ME. [– L. *Sabinus*, adj. and sb.] *Hist.* **A.** *adj.* Of or pertaining to the Sabines; see B. 1697. **B.** *sb.* One of a race of ancient Italy who inhabited the central region of the Apennines. late ME.

Sable (sēⁱ·b'l), *sb.*[1] late ME. [– OFr. *sable* (XII) sable fur, also in *martre sable* 'sable-marten' (animal and its fur) – med.L. *sabelum* (XII); of Balto-Sl. origin.] **1.** A small carnivorous quadruped, *Mustela zibellina*, nearly allied to the martens, and native of the arctic and sub-arctic regions of Europe and Asia. Also *Russian, Siberian s.* **b.** A pencil made of the sable's hair 1891. **2.** The skin or fur of the sable. late ME. **3.** A superior quality of Russian iron, so called from being orig. stamped with a sable 1815.

Comb.: **s.-mouse** [= G. *zobelmaus*] = LEMMING.

Sable (sēⁱ·b'l), *sb.*[2] and *a.* ME. [– OFr. *sable*, commonly identified with prec., although the fur of the sable is not black but brown.] **A.** *sb.* **1.** *Her.* Black, as one of the heraldic colours; in engraving represented by horizontal and vertical lines crossing each other. Abbrev. *S, Sa.*, †*Sab.* **2.** The colour black; black clothing, also, esp. as a symbol of mourning. *poet.* and *rhet.* late ME. †**b.** Blackness, darkness –1781. **3.** *pl.* Mourning garments; a suit of black worn as an emblem of grief. *poet.* or *rhet.* 1602. **4.** A book-name of several species of pyralid moths, esp. of the genera *Botys* and *Ennychia* 1832. **5.** In full *s. antelope*: A large stout-horned antelope, *Hippotragus* (*Ægocerus*) *niger*, native of South and East Africa, the male of which is black in colour 1850.

2. Now haue ye cause to clothe yow in s. CHAUCER. **3.** The sables she wore were not solely for the dead Earl OUIDA.

B. *adj.* 1. *Her.* Of a black colour; black 1470. **2.** *gen.* Black. Chiefly *poet.* and *rhet.* Now, as applied to Negroes, slightly *joc.* 1485. †**3.** Mournful –1780.

2. Was I deceiv'd, or did a s. cloud Turn forth her silver lining on the night? MILT. The ceremonies were performed by a s. archbishop 1815. Phr. *His s. Majesty*, the devil. **3.** Such a s. state of mind as I labour under COWPER. Hence **Sa·ble** *v.* (chiefly *poet.*) *trans.* to blacken or darken; also, to clothe in sables.

‖**Sabot** (sabo). 1607. [– Fr. *sabot*, OFr. *çabot* (XIII), blending of *çavate* XII (mod. *savate*) with *botte* BOOT *sb.*[3]] **1.** A shoe made of a single piece of wood shaped and hollowed out to fit the foot. **2.** *Mil.* **a.** A wooden disc attached to a spherical projectile by means of a copper rivet for the purpose of keeping it evenly in place in the bore of the piece when discharged. **b.** A metal cup fixed by means of metal straps to a conical projectile, to cause it to 'take' the rifling of the gun. 1855. **3.** *Mech.* A cutting armature at the end of a tubular boring-rod 1884. Hence **Saboted** (sæ·boᵘd) *ppl. a.* shod with sabots.

Sabotage (sæ·bǒtǎdʒ), *sb.* 1910. [– Fr. *sabotage*, f. *saboter* make a noise with sabots, execute badly, destroy wantonly, f. *sabot*; see prec. and -AGE.] The malicious damaging or destruction of an employer's property by workmen during a strike or the like; hence *gen.* any malicious or wanton destruction. Hence **Sa·botage** *v. trans.* to wreck or damage by s.; also *fig.* So **Saboteu·r** [Fr.] one who engages in sabotage.

Sabre (sēⁱ·bəɹ), *sb.* Also *U.S.* **saber.** 1680. [– Fr. *sabre*, unexpl. alt. of *sable* – G. *sabel*, local var. of *säbel*, earlier †*schabel* – Pol. *szabla* or Magyar *száblya*.] **1.** A cavalry sword having a curved blade specially adapted for cutting. **b.** *fig.* Military force 1851. **2.** A cavalry unit; a soldier armed with a sabre 1829.

Comb.: **s.-bill,** a S. Amer. dendrocolaptine bird of the genus *Xiphorhyncus*; **-rattler,** a reckless militarist; so **-rattling**; **-toothed** *a.* in *s.-toothed lion* or *tiger*, a large extinct feline mammal of the genus *Machairodus*, with long s.-shaped upper canines; also **s.-tooth** *a.* and *sb.* Hence **Sa·bre** *v. trans.* to cut, strike, or wound with a s.

Sabretache (sæ·brətaʃ). 1812. [– Fr. *sabretache* – G. *säbeltasche*, f. *säbel* sabre + *tasche* pocket.] A leather satchel suspended on the left side by long straps from the sword-belt of a cavalry officer.

‖**Sabreur** (sabrǒr). 1845. [– Fr. *sabreur*, f. *sabrer* SABRE *v.*] One who fights with a sabre; usu. applied to a cavalry soldier distinguished rather for bravery than for skill in war.

Sabulous (sæ·biŭləs), *a.* 1632. [– L. *sabulosus*, f. *sabulum* sand; see -OUS.] Sandy; consisting of or abounding in sand; arenaceous. **b.** *Med.* Applied to a granular secretion, esp. in the urinary organs 1670.

Sac[1]. [repr. OE. *saca*, accus. and gen. pl. of *sacu* SAKE.] *Old Eng. Law.* Properly only in *sac and soc* (or *soke*), a modernized form of the expression used in charters to denote certain rights of jurisdiction which by custom belonged to the lord of a manor, and which were specified (along with others) as included in the grant of a manor by the crown.

The priviledge called Sake is for a man to have the amerciaments of his tenants in his owne Court 1641.

Sac[2] (sæk). 1741. [– Fr. *sac* or L. *saccus* SACK *sb.*[1] in mod.L. applications.] **1.** *Biol.* Any natural bag-like cavity with its membranous covering, in an animal or vegetable organism. **2.** *Path.* A pouch formed by the morbid dilatation of a part, the membranous envelope of a hernia, cyst, tumour, etc. 1802.

Saccate (sæ·keⁱt), *a.* 1830. [f. SAC[2] + -ATE[2].] **1.** *Bot.* Dilated into the form of a sac. **2.** = ENCYSTED 1846.

Saccharate (sæ·kǎrět), *sb.* 1815. [f. SACCHARIC + -ATE[4].] *Chem.* A salt of saccharic acid.

Saccharated (sæ·kǎreⁱtěd), *a.* 1784. [– mod.L., f. med.L. *saccharum* sugar + -ATE[3] + -ED[1].] Containing or made with sugar; sweetened.

Saccharic (sǎkæ·rik), *a.* 1800. [f. mod.L. *saccharum* sugar + -IC. Cf. Fr. *saccharique*.] *Chem. S. acid*: (*a*) a dibasic acid formed by the action of nitric acid on dextrose; oxalhydric acid; (*b*) a monobasic acid forming crystalline salts prepared by the action of bases on glucoses. *S. ether*, an ether obtained from s. acid.

Sacchariferous (sækări·fĕrəs), *a.* 1757. [f. as prec. + -FEROUS.] Yielding or containing sugar.

Saccharify (săkæ·rifəi, sæ·kărifəi), *v.* 1839. [f. as prec. + -FY.] *trans.* To convert (starch) into sugar. Hence **Sa:ccharifica·tion,** the natural process by which starch and gum become converted into sugar.

Saccharimeter (sækări·mĭtəɹ). 1874. [– Fr. *saccharimètre*, f. as prec. + *-mètre* -METER.] A form of polariscope, an instrument for testing sugars by polarized light. So **Sacchari·metry** = SACCHAROMETRY. **Saccharime·tric, -al** *adjs.*

Saccharin (sæ·kărin). 1880. [– G. *saccharin* (Fahlberg, 1879), f. as prec. + -IN[1].] *Chem.* **1.** The anhydride of saccharic acid. **2.** An intensely sweet substance obtained from coal-tar, used instead of sugar for sweetening food or drink. In non-techn. use commonly called **saccharine** (sæ·kărīn). 1885. Hence **Sacchari·nic** *a.* = SACCHARIC.

Saccharine (sæ·kărəin, -in), *a.* and *sb.* 1674. [f. as prec. + -INE[1].] **A.** *adj.* **1.** Of, pertaining to, or of the nature of, sugar; characteristic of sugar; sugary. **2.** Composed chiefly of sugar; of a plant, containing a large proportion of sugar; also, of urine, containing sugar in excess of what is normal 1710. **3.** Resembling sugar. **a.** *Geol.* Of rocks: Granular in texture 1833. **b.** *Bot.* Covered with shining grains like those of sugar 1891.

1. *S. fermentation* = SACCHARIFICATION. **2.** *S. diabetes*, diabetes characterized by excess of s. matter in the urine.

B. *sb.* Saccharine matter, sugar 1841.

Saccharo- (sæ·kăro), comb. form of Gr. σάκχαρον sugar, forming compounds with the sense 'partly saccharine and partly (something else)'; 'containing sugar and (something else)', as *saccharo-farinaceous*, etc.

Saccharoid (sæ·kăroid), *a.* and *sb.* 1833. [f. mod.L. *saccharum* sugar + -OID.] **A.** *adj. Geol.* Having a granular texture resembling that of loaf-sugar. **B.** *sb. Chem.* A saccharine substance 1882. So **Saccharoi·dal** *a.* = A.

Saccharometer (sækărǫ·mĭtəɹ). 1784. [f. SACCHARO- + -METER.] **1.** A form of hydrometer for estimating the amount of sugar in a solution by specific gravity. **2.** Used for SACCHARIMETER (*rare*) 1852. So **Saccharo·metry,** the process of determining the quantity of sugar in a solution.

‖**Saccharomyces** (sæ:kăromǝi·sīz). 1873. [mod.L., f. Gr. σάκχαρον sugar + μύκης mushroom.] A genus of ascomycetous fungi, including the yeast-fungi; a fungus of this genus, esp. the yeast-plant.

Saccharose (sæ·kărōᵘs). 1876. [f. mod.L. *saccharum* sugar + -OSE[2].] *Chem.* Any one of the group of sugars having the formula $C_{12}H_{22}O_{11}$.

Saccharum (sæ·kărŏm). 1839. [– mod.L. *saccharum* (repl. med.L. *succharum* SUGAR) – Gr. σάκχαρον (whence L. *saccharon* Pliny), see SUGAR.] An invert sugar prepared from cane sugar, used chiefly in brewing.

Sacchulmin (sækʊ·lmin). 1842. [f. mod. L. SACCHARUM + ULMIN.] *Chem.* A brown substance obtained in the decomposition of sugar by dilute acids. So **Sacchu·lmic** *a.* in *s. acid*, an acid obtained by treating s. with alkaline solutions.

Sacciform (sæ·ksifǫɹm), *a.* 1819. [f. L. *saccus* (see SAC[2]) + -FORM.] Having the form of a sac or pouch; sac-shaped.

Saccoon (săkū·n). *Obs.* exc. *Hist.* 1708. [Perversion of Fr. *seconde.*] = SECONDE.

Saccular (sæ·kiŭlăɹ), *a.* 1861. [f. SACCULUS + -AR[1].] Of the nature of or resembling a sac.

Sacculated (sæ·kiŭleᶦtėd), *a.* 1835. [f. SACCULUS + -ATE[2] + -ED[1].] Composed of or divided into saccules. So **Sa·cculate** *a.* **Saccula·tion.**

Saccule (sæ·kiul). 1836. [Anglicized f. next; see -ULE.] A small sac, cyst, or bag; esp. the smaller of the two vesicles in the internal ear.

‖**Sacculus** (sæ·kiŭlŏs). *Pl.* **-li** (-ləi). 1621. [L., dim. of *saccus* SAC[2].] †**1.** A small bag containing medicaments –1693. **2.** *Anat.*, *Biol.* A small sac; a pouch-like dilatation 1728.

‖**Sacellum** (săse·lŏm). *Pl.* **sacella** (săse·lă). 1806. [L., dim. of *sacrum* shrine, n. of *sacer* holy.] **1.** *Eccl. Arch.* A monumental chapel in a church; also, a small chapel in a village. **2.** *Rom. Antiq.* A small roofless temple consecrated to some deity 1832.

Sacerdocy (sæ·səɹdōᵘsi). 1657. [– L. *sacerdotium* priestly office, f. *sacerdos, sacerdot-* priest; see SACERDOTAL *a.*] **a.** The sacerdotal character, spirit, or system. **b.** A priestly function or office.

Sacerdo·tage. *joc.* 1859. [f. L. *sacerdot-* (see next) with allusion to *dotage.*] **a.** The sacerdotal order, or the partisans of sacerdotalism. **b.** Sacerdotalism as characteristic of a religion in its 'dotage'.

Sacerdotal (sæsəɹdōᵘ·tăl), *a.* late ME. [– (O)Fr. *sacerdotal* or L. *sacerdotalis*, f. *sacerdos, -dot-* priest; see -AL[1].] **A.** *adj.* **1.** Of or belonging to the priests or priesthood; of or pertaining to a priest; befitting or characteristic of a priest; priestly. **b.** Holding the office of a priest 1681. **2.** Applied to doctrines that assert the existence in the Christian Church of an order of priests charged with sacrificial functions and invested with supernatural powers transmitted to them in ordination 1871.

1. That's a s. thought, And not a soldier's BYRON. **2.** The sacramental and s. developments of Anglicanism 1871. Hence **Sacerdo·tally** *adv.*

Sacerdotalism (sæsəɹdōᵘ·tăliz'm). 1847. [f. prec. + -ISM.] **1.** The sacerdotal spirit or system; the principles or practice of the priesthood. Chiefly dyslogistic: Undue assumption of authority on the part of the priesthood; pursuit of or excessive devotion to the interests of the priestly order. **2.** The assertion of the existence in the Christian church of a sacerdotal order (see prec. 2) 1856. So **Sacerdo·talist,** one who advocates or defends s. **Sacerdo·talize** *v. trans.* to make subservient to s.

Sachem (sēᶦ·tʃĕm, sæ·tʃĕm). 1622. [– Narraganset *sachem* = Penobscot *sagamo* SAGAMORE.] **1.** The supreme head or chief of some American Indian tribes. **2.** *U.S. Politics.* One of a body of twelve high officials in the Tammany Society of New York 1890.

Grand s., the head of the Tammany Society. Hence **Sa·chem-dom, -ship,** the position or 'realm' of a s.

Sachet (sæ·tʃĕt, Fr. saʃę). 1483. [– (O)Fr. *sachet*, dim. of *sac* SACK *sb.*[1]] †**1.** A small bag, a wallet (*rare*) –1487. **2.** A small perfumed bag or satchel 1838. **3.** A dry perfume made up into a packet for placing among articles of clothing, etc. 1855.

Sack (sæk), *sb.*[1] [OE. *sacc* – L. *saccus* bag, sack, sackcloth, corresp. to Gr. σάκκος, of Semitic origin; cf. MDu. *sak* (Du. *zak*), OHG. *sac* (G. *sack*), ON. *sekkr*, Goth. *sakkus.*] **I. 1.** A large bag oblong in shape and open at one end, usu. made of coarse flax or hemp, used for the storing and conveyance of corn, flour, fruit, wood, coal, etc. **2.** A sack with its contents; also, the amount usu. contained in a sack; hence as a unit of measure or weight for corn, flour, fruit, wool, coal, etc. ME. **3.** slang. *To give* (a person) *the s.*: to dismiss from employment or office; *transf.* to discard, turn off (a lover). So *to get the s.*: to receive one's dismissal. 1825.

1. *The sack*, the punishment (awarded in ancient Rome to a parricide) of being sewn in a sack and drowned.

†**II.** Sackcloth, esp. as the material of penitential or mourning garments. Also, a piece or garment of sackcloth. –1620.

Comb. **s.-coal,** screened coal for delivery in sacks; **s. race,** a race in which each competitor is enveloped in a sack, the mouth of which he holds round his neck.

Sack (sæk), *sb.*[2] 1549. [– Fr. *sac* (in phr. *mettre à sac* 'put to sack') – It. *sacco* SACK *sb.*[1] (in phr. *fare il sacco*, etc., perh. orig. referring to the filling of bags with plunder).] The action of SACK *v.*[2]; sacking, plundering; esp. in phr. *to put to s.*

Those inhabitants who had favoured the insurrection expected s. and massacre MACAULAY.

Sack (sæk), *sb.*[3] *Obs.* exc. *Hist.* 1531. [orig. (*wyne*) *seck* (XVI) – Fr. *vin sec* dry wine.] A general name for a class of white wines formerly imported from Spain and the Canaries. **b.** With qualifying word, as *Canary, Malaga, Sherris* or *Sherry s.* 1597.

If sacke and sugar be a fault, God helpe the wicked SHAKS.

Comb., in the names of beverages, etc., made with s., as **s.-cream, -mead, -posset, -whey.**

Sack (sæk), *sb.*[4] Also **sacque.** 1599. [prob. orig. a use of SACK *sb.*[1], later assoc. with Fr. *sac* (cf. G. *französischer sack*, Du. *zak*).] **1.** †A loose kind of gown worn by ladies. Also, from the 18th c., an appendage of silk attached to the shoulders of such a dress, and forming a train. **2.** A loose-fitting coat the back of which is not shaped to the figure, but hangs more or less straight from the shoulders 1847.

1. My wife this day put on first her French gown, called a Sac PEPYS.

Sack (sæk), *v.*[1] late ME. [f. SACK *sb.*[1]; in sense 1 partly after med.L. *saccare* or MDu. *sacken*, etc.] **1.** *trans.* To put into a sack; to pack or store (goods) in sacks. **b.** To put (a person) in a sack to be drowned. late ME. **2.** *colloq.* To 'pocket' 1807. **3.** *slang.* **a.** To 'give the sack' to, dismiss (a person) from, his employment or office. Chiefly *pass.* 1841. **b.** To beat in a contest 1820. **4.** *intr.* To bulge or 'bag' 1799.

1. It threshes, cleans, and finally sacks the grain 1845. **2.** To s. a reasonable profit 1830. **3. a.** The committee ought to be sacked 1890.

Sack (sæk), *v.*[2] 1547. [f. SACK *sb.*[2]] *trans.* To give over (a city, town, etc.) to plunder by the soldiery of a victorious army; to strip (a person or place) or possessions or goods; to plunder, despoil.

We sack't the Citty after nine Moneths siege 1634. Hence **Sa·cker,** one who sacks or plunders.

Sackage (sæ·kėdʒ), *sb.* Now *rare.* 1577. [– Fr. *saccage*, f. *saccager* – It. *saccheggiare*, f. *sacco* SACK *sb.*[2]] The action, or an act, of sacking (a city, etc.).

Sackbut (sæ·kbʊt). 1509. [– Fr. *saquebute*, earlier *-boute, -bot(t)e* (XV), recorded earlier in the sense of a hooked lance for pulling a man off his horse, f. *saquer*, var. of OFr. *sachier* pull + *bouter* BUTT *v.*[1]] An obsolete musical instrument; a bass trumpet with a slide like that of a trombone for altering the pitch. †**b.** A player on the sackbut –1647.

Sackcloth (sæ·k,klǫþ). ME. [f. SACK *sb.*[1] + CLOTH. Cf. med.L. *pannus sacci* (XV), *pannus saccinus* (XIV).] A coarse textile fabric (now of flax or hemp) used chiefly in the making of bags or sacks and for the wrapping up of bales, etc.; sacking. late ME. **b.** As the material of mourning or penitential garb; also, as the coarsest possible clothing, indicative of extreme poverty or humility ME.

In s. and ashes (Bibl.), clothed in s. and having ashes sprinkled on the head as a sign of lamentation or abject penitence. Hence **Sa·ckclothed** *a.* clad in s.

Sackful (sæ·kful). 1484. [f. SACK *sb.*[1] + -FUL 2.] As much as would fill a sack; hence, a great quantity.

Sacking (sæ·kiŋ). 1707. [f. SACK *sb.*[1] + -ING[1].] A coarse woven material of flax, jute, hemp, etc., used chiefly in the making of sacks and bags. Also, a piece of such material.

Sackless (sæ·klės), *a.* [Late OE. *saclēas* – ON. *saklauss*, f. *sak-*, *sǫk*; see SAC[1], -LESS.] †**1.** Secure from accusation or from dispute; unchallenged, unmolested –1819. **2.** Not guilty, innocent. Now *arch.* OE. **b.** *Sc.* and *n. dial.* Innocent of wrong intent, guileless, simple; also, of a thing, harmless. Hence, feeble-minded; lacking energy, dispirited. 1600.

Sacque: see SACK *sb.*[4]

Sacral (sēᶦ·krăl), *a.*[1] (*sb.*). 1767. [f. SACRUM + -AL[1].] *Anat.* Pertaining to the sacrum. **b.** Belonging to the lower part of the body 1803. **c.** *sb.* = *s. vertebra* 1854.

Sacral (sēᶦ·krăl), *a.*[2] 1882. [f. L. *sacrum* sacred thing, rite, etc. (n. sing. of *sacer*) + -AL[1] 1.] *Anthropology.* Of or pertaining to sacred rites and observances.

Sacrament (sæ·krămĕnt), *sb.* [ME. *sacrement* (also *sa(c)ra-*, by assim. to L.) – (O)Fr. *sacrement* – L. *sacramentum* solemn engagement, etc., f. *sacrare* hallow, f. *sacer* SACRED. In Chr. L. the word was the accepted rendering of Gr. μυστήριον MYSTERY[1].] **1.** *Eccl.* Any one of certain rites of the Christian Church, of which Baptism and the Lord's Supper are held to be generally necessary to salvation.

Those who accept the number seven, and many of those who admit only two, hold that the sacraments differ from other rites in being channels by which supernatural grace is imparted. Others differentiate the two 'sacraments' from other observances by their paramount obligation as having been expressly commanded by Christ Himself, and by the special spiritual benefits arising from their faithful use.

2. *spec.* (with *the*). The Lord's Supper, Eucharist, or Holy Communion. Often called *the S. of the Altar, the Blessed S., the Holy S.* ME. **b.** The consecrated elements, esp. the bread or Host ME. **3.** In widened application: **a.** Something likened to the recognized sacraments, as having a sacred character or function; the pledge of a covenant between God and man ME. **b.** A type, token, sign, or symbol 1534. **c.** [After L. *sacramentum* as a rendering of μυστήριον.] A mystery; something secret or having a secret meaning. late ME. **4.** An oath or solemn engagement, esp. one which is ratified by a rite. (Chiefly as a Latinism.) late ME. **5.** *Rom. Law.* The *sacramentum* or pledge which each of the parties deposited or became bound for before beginning a suit 1880.

1. *Q.* What meanest thou by this word *S.*? *A.* I mean an outward and visible sign of an inward and spiritual grace given unto us [etc.] *Bk. Com. Prayer, Catechism.* **2.** Phr. *To receive, take the s.*, to communicate. *To take* or *receive the s.* (*to do* something, or *upon* a matter), to receive Holy Communion as a confirmation of one's word. He take the S. on't SHAKS. **3. b.** The Temple..was a figure, a S., or a signification of Christe 1563. **c.** This s., or hid trewthe WYCLIF *Dan.* 2:30. **4.** Bound by no s. of military obedience to the state 1832.

attrib.: as **s.-money**, the alms collected at Holy Communion, formerly used as a fund for poor-relief; **S. Sunday**, the Sunday on which the Lord's Supper is celebrated. So **Sa·crament** *v.* (*rare*) *trans.* to bind by an oath or solemn engagement; to make sacred, consecrate.

Sacramental (sækrăme·ntăl), *a.* and *sb.* late ME. [– Fr. *sacramental* (better, *-tel*) XVI or late L. *sacramentalis*, f. L. *sacramentum*; see prec., -AL[1].] **A.** *adj.* **1.** Pertaining to, or of the nature of, a sacrament of the Church. **b.** *spec.* Pertaining to the sacrament of the Lord's Supper 1552. **c.** Of religious doctrine and the like: Based upon the sacraments 1871. **2.** Of the nature of, relating to, or expressed by, an outward sign or symbol 1534. **3.** Of an oath, obligation, etc.: Peculiarly sacred; ratified by a religious sanction 1460. **4.** *Rom. Law.* Belonging to an action in which a *sacramentum* or pledge was deposited by each of the parties beforehand 1861. **5.** *joc.* Of a form of speech: Sacred to the occasion; 'consecrated' 1896.

1. Afterwards it was brought so Sacramentall, that no adultery or desertion could dissolve it MILT. **3.** A s. obligation 1863.

B. *sb. Eccl.* A rite, ceremony, or observance analogous to a sacrament, but not reckoned among the sacraments; e.g. the use of holy water and of holy oil, the sign of the cross 1450. Hence **Sacrame·ntalism** = SACRAMENTARIANISM. **Sacrame·ntalist** (*rare*) = SACRAMENTARIAN B. 1, 3, **Sa:cramenta·lity**, s. character. **Sacrame·ntally** *adv.* in a s. manner.

Sacramentarian (sækrămĕntēə·riăn), *a.* and *sb.* 1535. [f. mod.L. *sacramentarius*, applied like Luther's *sacramentirer*, *sacramenter* to deniers of the Real Presence; see -ARIAN.] **A.** *adj.* **1.** *Hist.* Relating to the views held by the Sacramentarians concerning the Eucharist (see B. 1) 1640. **2.** *gen.* Relating to the sacraments (or to 'high' doctrine in regard to them) 1865. **B.** *sb.* **1.** *Hist.* A name given by Luther to those Protestant theologians (esp. Zwingli and Œcolampadius) who maintained that it is merely in a 'sacramental' or metaphorical sense that the bread and wine of the Eucharist are called the body and blood of Christ. Hence used in the 16th c. as a hostile name for all deniers of the Real Presence 1535. **2.** *Hist.* A nickname given to the early Methodists at Oxford 1733. **3.** One who holds 'high' doctrine as to the sacraments 1651. Hence **Sacramenta·rianism**, 'high' doctrine in regard to the sacraments.

Sacramentary (sækrăme·ntări), *a.* and *sb.* Now *rare.* 1538. [– mod.L. *sacramentarius* (see prec.); in B. 2 – med.L. *sacramentarium* (Du Cange).] **A.** *adj.* = prec. A. 1. Of a person: Holding sacramentarian views. 1563. **B.** *sb.* **1.** *Hist.* = prec. B. 1. 1538. **2.** [med.L. *sacramentarium*.] An early form of office book in the Western Church, containing the rites and prayers belonging to the several sacraments 1624.

1. A few years later, a s. had ceased to be a criminal FROUDE. **2.** The S. comprised the collects and the canon or prayers that never varied 1832.

‖**Sacrarium** (săkrēə·riŏm). *Pl.* **sacraria** (-riă). 1727. [L. *sacrarium*, f. *sacer* SACRED; see -ARIUM. In sense 2 a – late and med.L. use; sense 2 b. XIII.] **1.** *Rom. Antiq.* Any place in which sacred objects were deposited and kept; the adytum of a temple; also, a small apartment in a house where the images of the penates were kept 1746. **2.** *Eccl.* **a.** That part of a church immediately surrounding the altar or communion table; the sanctuary 1727. **b.** In R.C. use: = PISCINA 2. 1848. So †**Sacrary** = sense 1, 2 a. –1727.

†**Sa·cre**, *v.* ME. [– (O)Fr. *sacrer* – L. *sacrare* consecrate, dedicate to a divinity, f. *sacer* consecrated, holy.] **1.** *trans.* To consecrate (the elements, or the body and blood of Christ) in the Mass –1485. **2.** To consecrate (a king or bishop) to office –1648. **3.** To bless, sanctify, make holy –1677. **4.** To dedicate –1641.

Sacred (sē[i]·krĕd), *a.* and *sb.* ME. [orig. pa. pple. of prec.; see -ED[1].] **A.** *adj.* **1. a.** Consecrated *to*; esteemed especially dear or acceptable *to* a deity. **b.** Dedicated, set apart, exclusively appropriated *to* some person or some special purpose 1667. **2.** Of things, places, persons and their offices, etc.: Set apart for or dedicated to some religious purpose; made holy by association with a god or other object of worship; consecrated, hallowed. late ME. **b.** Applied as a specific defining adj. to various animals and plants that are or have been considered sacred to certain deities 1783. **3.** *transf.* and *fig.* Regarded with or entitled to respect or reverence similar to that which attaches to holy things 1560. **b.** *esp.* as an epithet of royalty. Now chiefly *Hist.* or *arch.* 1590. **4.** Secured by religious sentiment, reverence, sense of justice, etc., against violation, infringement, or encroachment 1530. **b.** Of a person or his office: Sacrosanct, inviolable; protected by some sanction *from* injury or incursion 1565. **5.** [After L. *sacer*.] Accurst. Now *rare*. 1588.

1. The dove s. to Venus 1874. **b.** S. to the memory of Samuel Butler 1721. The papyrus, s. to literature 1811. **2.** I trace the village, and the s. spire 1744. The s. boats of the dead 1857. *S. book, writing*, etc., one of those in which the laws and teachings of a religion are embodied. *S. concert*, a concert of s. music. *S. history*, the history contained in the Bible. *S. music*, music which accompanies religious words or which is intended for performance in a church, etc. *S. number*, a number (esp. seven) held peculiarly significant in religious symbolism. *S. poetry*, poetry concerned with religious themes. **b.** The S. Ibis (*I. religiosa*) 1840. The S. Monkey of the Hindoos (*Semnopithecus entellus*) 1870. **3.** S. and sweet was all I saw in her SHAKS. To a feather-brained schoolgirl nothing is s. C. BRONTË. To obtain from Mr. Bentham's executors a s. bone of his great, dissected Master M. ARNOLD. **4.** He assured them that their property would be held s. MACAULAY. **b.** The s. and vnuiolable power of the Tribunes 1565. S. from punishment 1845. **5.** Our Empresse with her s. wit To villainie and vengance consecrate SHAKS.

Special collocations. **S. axe**, a mark on Chinese porcelain, supposed to designate warriors. **S. college**: see COLLEGE *sb.* 1. **S. fire** [L. *sacer ignis*], erysipelas. **S. malady** [L. *sacer morbus*], epilepsy. **S. War**: see WAR.

†**B.** *sb. pl.* [after L. *sacra* n. pl.] Sacred rites or solemnities –1749. Hence **Sa·cred-ly** *adv.*, **-ness.**

†**Sacri·fical**, *a.* 1608. [– L. *sacrificalis*, f. *sacrificus*, f. *sacer* sacred + *-ficus* -FIC; see -AL[1].] Sacrificial.

Sacrificator (sæ·krifikē[i]təɹ). *rare.* 1548. [– late L. *sacrificator*, f. *sacrificat-*, pa. ppl. stem of L. *sacrificare*; see SACRIFY, -OR 2.] One who sacrifices. So †**Sa·crificatory** *a.* belonging to sacrifice.

Sacrifice (sæ·krifəis), *sb.* ME. [– (O)Fr. *sacrifice* – L. *sacrificium*, rel. to *sacrificus*; see SACRIFICAL.] **1.** Primarily, the slaughter of an animal as an offering to God or a deity. Hence, the surrender to God or a deity, for the purpose of propitiation or homage, of some object of possession. Also *fig.* the offering of prayer, thanksgiving, penitence, submission, etc. **2.** That which is offered in sacrifice; a victim immolated on the altar; anything offered to God or a deity as an act of propitiation or homage ME. **3.** *Theol.* The offering by Christ of himself to the Father as a propitiatory victim in his voluntary immolation upon the cross; the Crucifixion in its sacrificial character. late ME. **b.** Applied to the Eucharistic celebration regarded as a propitiatory offering of the body and blood of Christ in perpetual memory of the sacrifice offered by him in his crucifixion 1504. **4.** The destruction or surrender of something valued or desired for the sake of something having a higher or more pressing claim; the loss entailed by devotion to some other interest; also, the thing so devoted or surrendered 1592. **b.** A victim; one sacrificed to the will of another; also, a person or thing that falls into the power of an enemy or destructive agency. Now *rare*. 1697. **5.** A loss incurred in selling something below its value for the sake of getting rid of it 1844.

1. Divines divide Sacrifices into bloody, such as those of the old law; and bloodless, such as those of the new law 1727. **2.** Make of your Prayers one sweet S. SHAKS. **3. b.** He exhorteth the people to flee from the accustomed sacrifices of the masse 1560. **4.** As rich shall Romeo by his Lady ly, Poore sacrifices to our enmity SHAKS. Phr. *The great, last*, or *supreme, s.*, death for one's country in war.

Sacrifice (sæ·krifəis), *v.* ME. [f. prec.; cf. (O)Fr. *sacrifier*, L. *sacrificare*.] **1.** *trans.* To offer as a sacrifice; to make an offering or sacrifice of. **2.** *intr.* To offer up a sacrifice ME. **3.** *trans.* To give up (something) for the attainment of some higher advantage or dearer object 1706. **b.** To permit injury or ruin to the interests of (a person) for the sake of some desired object. Also *refl.* 1751.

1. The Picture of..Abraham sacrificing his son SIR T. BROWNE. **3.** Henry..was never known to s. an inclination to the interest or happiness of another 1837. **b.** He is too much an artist to s. himself to his clothes 1873. Hence **Sa·crificer**, one who sacrifices; *spec.* a sacrificial priest.

Sacrificial (sækrifi·ʃăl), *a.* 1607. [f. L. *sacrificium* SACRIFICE + -AL[1].] **1.** Pertaining to or connected with sacrifice. **2.** *Comm.* Involving 'sacrifice' or loss to the vendor 1895.

1. Raine Sacrificiall whisperings in his eare SHAKS. **2.** Next week's s. sales 1895.

†**Sa·crify**, *v.* ME. [– (O)Fr. *sacrifier* – L. *sacrificare*, f. *sacrificus*; see SACRIFICAL, -FY.] **1.** *trans.* To offer as a sacrifice –1590. **2.** *intr.* To offer sacrifice –1555.

Sacrilege (sæ·krilĕdʒ). ME. [– (O)Fr. *sacrilège* – L. *sacrilegium*, f. *sacrilegus* one who steals sacred things, f. *sacer* sacred + *legere* take possession of.] **1.** The crime or sin of stealing or misappropriating what is consecrated to God's service. In eccl. use, extended to include any kind of outrage on consecrated persons or things, and the violation of any sacred obligation. Also, an instance of this offence. **b.** *spec.* in pop. use as a name for robbery from a church, etc. 1820. **2.** *transf.* and *fig.* The profanation of anything held sacred. late ME.

1. After this adding s. to profanation he carried away the altar of incense 1734. **2.** To kill a herald was, by the law of arms, s. FROUDE. Hence **Sa·crileger** (*arch.*), one who commits s. So **Sacrilegist** (sækri·lidʒist).

Sacrilegious (sækrili·dʒəs, -ī·dʒəs), *a.* 1582. [f. L. *sacrilegium* (see prec.) + -OUS; the pronunc. has been affected by assoc. with *religious.*] **1.** Committing sacrilege; guilty of sacrilege. **2.** Involving sacrilege 1621.

1. The wicked sacrilegous, non-conformists 1696. Hence **Sacrile·gious-ly** *adv.*, **-ness.**

Sacring (sēⁱ·kriŋ), *vbl. sb.* Now *literary.* ME. [f. SACRE *v.* + -ING¹.] **1.** The consecration of the eucharistic elements in the service of the Mass. **2.** The ordination and consecration of persons to certain offices, as those of bishop, king, queen ME.

Sa·cring-bell. late ME. [f. prec.] **1.** A small bell rung at the elevation of the Host. **2.** In post-Reformation times applied to a small bell rung to summon parishioners to morning service, or to mark the point in the Communion Service at which the people should go up to communicate 1598.

Sacrist (sēⁱ·krist). 1577. [– (O)Fr. *sacriste* or med.L. *sacrista*, f. L. *sacer* sacred + *-ista* -IST.] An official charged with the custody of the sacred vessels, relics, vestments, etc., of a religious house or a church.

Sacristan (sæ·kristăn). late ME. [– med.L. *sacristanus*, f. *sacrista*; see prec., -AN. Cf. SEXTON.] **a.** The sexton of a parish church. *Obs.* or *arch.* **b.** = SACRIST.

Sacristy (sæ·kristi). 1656. [– Fr. *sacristie*, It. *sacrestia* or med.L. *sacristia*, f. *sacrista*; see -Y³.] The repository in a church in which are kept the vestments, the sacred vessels, and other valuable property.

Sacro-¹ (sæ·kro, sēⁱ·kro), assumed as comb. form of L. *sacer* sacred, as in **s.-pictorial** *a.*, relating to sacred portraiture; **-secular** *a.*, partly sacred and partly secular.

Sacro-² (sēⁱ·kro), *Anat.*, used as comb. form of L. (*os*) *sacrum* SACRUM, forming compounds with the sense 'pertaining jointly to the sacrum and (some other part indicated by the second element)', as in *s.-coccygeal*, *-iliac* adjs.

Sacrosanct (sæ·krosæŋkt, sēⁱ·kro-), *a.* 1601. [– L. *sacrosanctus*, prop. two words, *sacro* abl. of *sacrum* sacred rite, and *sanctus* pa. pple. of *sancire* render holy or inviolable.] Of persons and things, esp. obligations, laws, etc.: Secured by a religious sanction from violation or encroachment; inviolable, sacred. Hence **Sa:crosa·nctity,** inviolability, sacredness.

Sacrum (sēⁱ·krŏm). *Pl.* **sacrums, sacra.** 1753. [Short for late L. *os sacrum*, tr. Gr. ἱερὸν ὀστέον 'sacred bone'.] *Anat.* A composite, symmetrical, triangular bone which articulates laterally with the ilia, forming the dorsal wall of the pelvis and resulting from the ankylosis of two or more vertebræ between the lumbar and coccygeal regions of the spinal column.

Sad (sæd), *a.* and *adv.* [OE. *sæd* = OS. *sad* (Du. *zat*), OHG. *sat* (G. *satt*), ON. *saðr*, Goth. *saþs* :– Gmc. **saðaz*, rel. to L. *sat, satis* enough.] **A.** *adj.* **I.** †**1.** Having had one's fill; sated, weary, or tired (of something) –1450. †**2.** Settled, firmly established, in purpose or condition; steadfast, firm, constant –1667. †**3.** Orderly and regular in life; of trustworthy character and judgement; grave, serious –1665. **b.** Of thought, consideration: Mature, serious. *Obs.* exc. *arch.* in phr. *in s. earnest.* 1485. **4.** Of persons, their feelings or dispositions: Sorrowful, mournful. late ME. **b.** Of looks, tones, gestures, costume, etc.: Expressive of sorrow. late ME. **c.** Of times, places, actions, etc.: Characterized by sorrow, sorrowful. late ME. †**d.** Morose, dismal-looking. SHAKS. **e.** Causing sorrow; distressing, calamitous, lamentable. late ME. **5.** Deplorably bad; chiefly as an intensive. Often *joc.* 1694.

1. Yet of that Art they kan nat wexen sadde ffor vnto hem it is a bitter sweete CHAUCER. **2.** Settl'd in his face I see S. resolution and secure MILT. **3.** What woman nowe-a-dayes (that is sadde and wyse) will be knowne to haue skill of dauncing, &c.? 1579. **4.** Th' Angelic Guards ascended, mute and s. For Man MILT. A sadder and a wiser man He rose the morrow morn COLERIDGE. I felt a little s. at the thought 1860. **b.** Where the love-lorn Nightingale Nightly to thee her s. Song mourneth well MILT. His s. enquiring eye 1792. **c.** A place.., s., noysom, dark MILT. 'Tis a s. life, for a woman to have no help from her husband in things that are good DE FOE. **e.** S. overthrow and foul defeat MILT. How s. is the condition of a Gentleman without Learning 1688. **5.** *S. dog*: cf. DOG *sb.* 3 b; *Sil.* You are an ignorant,..impudent Coxcomb. *Braz.* Ay, ay, a s. Dog. FARQUHAR.

II. 1. Of material objects. †**a.** Solid, dense, compact; massive, heavy –1641. **b.** Of soil: Stiff, heavy. *Obs.* or *dial.* ME. **c.** Of bread, pastry, etc.: That has not risen properly; heavy; not thoroughly baked. Now *dial.* 1688. **2.** Of colour: Dark, deep. In later use: Not cheerful-looking; neutral-tinted, dull, sober. late ME. †**b.** Dark-coloured, sober-coloured –1711. †**3.** Of blows: Heavy –1578.

1. To those that..tell you..I am but as a feather, I shall be found sadder than lead STRAFFORD. **2.** Colours lyght and s. 1578. She had always.. been dressed in s. colours 1867. **b.** A Man.. between 20 and 30 years of Age, pale Visage and s. Hair 1711.

B. *adv. Obs.* exc. *poet.* = SADLY.

Towards Eden..his grievd look he fixes s. MILT.

Sad (sæd), *v.* late ME. [f. SAD *a.*] **1.** *trans.* To make solid, firm, or stiff; to compress. Now *dial.* †**2.** To make sorrowful; to sadden –1810.

Sadden (sæ·d'n), *v.* 1600. [f. SAD *a.* + -EN⁵.] **1.** *trans.* = SAD *v.* 1. Now *dial.* **2.** To render sad or sorrowful; to depress in spirits. Also, to give a sad appearance to. 1628. **b.** *intr.* To become sad or gloomy 1718. **3.** *Dyeing*, etc. To tone down (colours) by the application of certain chemicals 1791.

1. If Marle s. Land, or make it stiff or binding, you must dung it well 1707. **2.** Her gloomy presence saddens all the scene POPE. **b.** Better be merry with the fruitful Grape Than s. after none, or bitter, Fruit FITZGERALD.

Saddle (sæ·d'l), *sb.* [OE. *sadol, -ul* = MDu. *sadel* (Du. *zadel, zaal*), OHG. *satal, -ul* (G. *sattel*), ON. *sǫðull* :– Gmc. **saðulaz*, perh. ult. rel. to IE. **sed-* SIT, which is repr. by Goth. *sitls*, L. *sella* seat.] **I. 1.** A seat for a rider, to be used on the back of a horse or other animal; esp. a concave seat of leather having side flaps and fitted with girths and stirrups. Also, an analogous kind of seat for use on a cycle. **2.** That part of the harness of a shaft-horse which takes the bearing of the shafts; a cart- or gig-saddle 1837.

1. *For the s.*, for riding purposes. *In the s.*, on horseback; *fig.* in office; also, in readiness for work. †(*I will*) *either win the s. or lose the horse* (or vice versa), said by one engaging in an adventure of which the issue will be either highly profitable or ruinous. *To lay, put*, or *set the s. upon the right horse*, to lay the blame on the right person.

II. Something resembling a saddle in shape or position. **1.** *Physical Geogr.*, *Mining*, etc. **a.** A depression in a hill or line of hills. **b.** A long elevation of land with sloping sides; a ridge, esp. one connecting two hills; also, a similar formation of ice or snow. 1555. **2.** In mechanical uses, e.g. **a.** *Naut.* A block of wood, hollowed out above and below, fastened to a spar to take the bearing of another spar attached to it 1512. **b.** *Bridge-construction.* (*a*) A block on the top of a pier to carry the suspension cables. (*b*) A frame used in the construction of a pontoon-bridge. 1831. **c.** *Telegraphy.* A bracket to support the wire on the top of a pole or ridge 1867. **3.** *Cookery.* In full *s. of mutton*, etc. A joint of mutton, venison, etc., consisting of the two loins and conjoining vertebræ 1747.

attrib. and *Comb.*, as **s.-bar** *Glazing*, each of the small horizontal bars to which the lead panels are secured; **-gall,** a sore produced on the back of a horse by the chafing of the saddle; **-horse,** a horse used for riding; **-oyster,** any of certain anomioid bivalves, the shape of which resembles that of a saddle; **-pin,** the pin of a cycle saddle which fits into a socket on the cycle frame; **-roof,** a saddleback roof; **-room,** a room in which saddlery is kept; **-shaped** *a.* resembling a saddle in shape; *Geol.* anticlinal; **-shell** = *s.-oyster*; **-sore** *a.* chafed with the s.; **s. wire** *Telegr.*, the wire running along the tops of telegraph posts.

Saddle (sæ·d'l), *v.* [OE. *sadolian*, f. *sadol* SADDLE *sb.*] **1.** *trans.* To put a riding-saddle upon (a horse, etc.); freq. *to s. up.* Also *absol.* †**2.** *trans.* To ride, bestride (an animal) –1713. **3.** *intr.* To get into the saddle. In Colonial use, *to s. up.* 1835. **4.** *trans.* To charge or load *with* (a burden); now only *fig.* to load *with* (something) as a burden 1693. **5.** To put (a burden) *upon* (another's back) 1808. **6.** To bend downwards in the middle 1803.

1. He sadled vp his horse, and roade in post away 1587. Phr. *To s. and bridle* fig., to subject to control. **4.** I'll s. him with this scrape SHERIDAN. **5.** I found her only too eager to marry anyone upon whom she could s. her debts 1881. **6.** Walls are cracked and roofs 'saddled' in every direction 1880.

Saddleback (sæ·d'lbæk), *sb.* and *a.* 1545. [f. SADDLE *sb.* + BACK *sb.*] **A.** *sb.* **1.** †**a.** *Archery.* A saddle-backed feather. **b.** A saddle-backed hill. **2.** *Arch.* A roof of a tower, having a gable at two opposite sides connected by a ridge-roof; a pack-saddle roof 1849. **3.** Any of various birds and fishes; *esp.* **a.** The adult of either of the Black-backed Gulls, *Larus marinus* and *L. fuscus*; also *s. gull.* **b.** The male of the Greenland or Harp Seal (*Phoca grœnlandica*) when three years old; in full *s. seal.* **c.** A kind of oyster, considered unfit for human food. 1847. **4.** *Geol.* An anticlinal 1887. **B.** *adj.* **1.** = next 1677. **2.** *Geol.* Anticlinal 1854. **3.** Used for 'horse-back' 1899.

Saddle-backed (sæ·d'lbækt), *a.* 1545. [f. as prec. + -ED².] **1.** Having the back, upper surface, or edge curved like a saddle; having a concavely curved outline. **2.** Of a horse: Having a considerable hollow behind the withers 1650. **3.** *Arch.* **a.** Of coping: Thicker in the middle than at the edges 1842. **b.** Of a tower: Having a saddle-back 1870. **4.** Applied to birds having saddle-like markings on the back, as *s. crow*, the Grey Crow, *Corvus cornix* 1838.

Sa·ddle-bag. 1796. **1.** A bag carried at the saddle; esp. one of a pair laid across the back of a horse, behind the saddle. **2.** *attrib.* Applied to a fine quality of carpeting, made in sizes and designs imitating the saddle-bags carried in the East by camels 1882.

Sa·ddle-bow. Now *arch.* or *poet.* [OE. *sadulboga* = OHG. *satalbogo*; see BOW *sb.*¹] The arched front of a saddle-tree or of a saddle.

Sa·ddle-cloth. 1481. A cloth placed on a horse's back beneath the saddle; †in early use, a foot-cloth, housing-cloth.

Saddled (sæ·d'ld), *ppl. a.* OE. [f. SADDLE *v.* + -ED¹.] **1.** Furnished with a saddle. **2.** Applied to fishes, insects, etc., having saddle-like markings 1803.

Saddler (sæ·dləɹ). late ME. [f. SADDLE *sb.* + -ER¹.] **1.** One who makes or deals in saddles or saddlery. **2.** *Mil.* An official who has charge of the saddlery in a cavalry regiment. Also *s. corporal, sergeant.* 1865. **3.** A saddle-horse. *colloq. U.S.* 1888. **4.** The saddleback seal; see SADDLEBACK 3 b. 1873.

Saddlery (sæ·dləri). 1449. [f. prec. + -Y³; see -ERY.] **1.** The art or occupation of a saddler. **2.** *collect.* Articles made or sold by a saddler; saddles and other articles pertaining to the equipment of a horse 1796. **3.** A place where saddles, etc., are made or kept 1841.

Sa·ddle-tree. late ME. **1.** The framework which forms the foundation of a saddle. **2.** The N. Amer. tulip tree, *Liriodendron tulipifera* 1866.

Sadducaic (sædiŭkēⁱ·ik), *a.* 1840. [f. Gr. Σαδδουκαῖος (see SADDUCEE), after PHARISAIC.] Pertaining to or characteristic of the Sadducees.

Sadducean, -cæan (sædiŭsī·ăn), *a.* and *sb.* 1547. [f. late L. *Sadducæus* SADDUCEE + -AN 1.] **A.** *adj.* Of, belonging to, or resembling, the Sadducees. †**B.** *sb.* = next –1678.

Sadducee (sæ·diŭsī). [OE. *sad(d)ucēas*, ME. *saduceis, saduce(e)s*, later *Sadduces*, pl.; – late L. *Sadducæus* – late Gr. Σαδδουκαῖος, f. post-bibl. *ṣᵉdûḳî*, prob. f. personal name *ṣadôḳ* (2 Sam. 8:17), represented in the LXX as both Σαδδούκ (whence Σαδδουκαῖος) and Σαδώκ Zadok.] **1.** A member of one of the three 'sects' (the others being the Pharisees and Essenes) into which the Jews were divided in the time of Christ. They denied the resurrection of the dead, the existence of angels and spirits, and the obligation of the unwritten law alleged by the Pharisees to have been handed down by tradition from Moses. **2.** A person of Sadducean disposition; a materialist, a denier of the resurrection. Also as *adj.* 1607. Hence **Sa·dduceeism,** the doctrine or tenets of the Sadducees; materialistic unbelief; denial of immortality.

Sade (sēⁱd), *v.* [OE. *sadian* :- WGmc. **saðojan,* f. *saða* SAD *a.*] *intr.* and *trans.* To become or make weary.

Sa·d-iron. 1832. [f. SAD *a.* or *v.*] A smoothing iron, prop. a solid flat-iron, as dist. from a box-iron.

Sadism (sēⁱ·diz'm, sā·diz'm). 1888. [– Fr. *sadisme,* f. the name of the Count (usu. called 'Marquis') de *Sade* (1740–1814; infamous for his crimes and the character of his writings); see -ISM.] A form of sexual perversion marked by a love of cruelty. So **Sa·dist,** one affected with s. **Sadi·stic** *a.*

Sadly (sæ·dli), *adv.* ME. [f. SAD *a.* + -LY².] †**1.** Heavily –1633. †**2.** Firmly, tightly, closely –1485. †**3.** Steadfastly, firmly, fixedly, unchangingly –1622. †**4.** Seriously; in earnest; gravely, soberly –1777. **5.** Sorrowfully, mournfully ME. **6.** In a manner to cause sadness; lamentably, grievously, deplorably, badly 1658. **7.** *predic.*: In bad health, ill, poorly. Now *dial.* 1711.

1. An empty cart runs lightly away: but if it be soundly laden, it goes s. 1633. **4.** This can be no tricke, the conference was s. borne SHAKS. **5.** Musick to heare, why hear'st thou musick s.? SHAKS. **6.** Authors..Are s. prone to quarrel COWPER. So **Sa·dness,** the condition or quality of being sad; †*in* (*sober*) *sadness,* in earnest, not joking.

‖**Safari** (săfā·ri). 1892. [Swahili, f. Arab. *safara* to journey, travel.] In East and Central Africa, an expedition, esp. for hunting; the men, animals, and equipment of such an expedition; a caravan. Also *attrib.*

Safe (sēⁱf), *sb.* 1440. [orig. *save,* f. SAVE *v.*; later assim. to SAFE *a.*] A receptacle for the safe storage of articles; esp. **a.** A ventilated chest or cupboard for provisions; a meat-safe. **b.** A fire-proof and burglar-proof receptacle for valuables 1838.

Safe (sēⁱf), *a.* [ME. *sauf, sāf,* orig. inflected *sauve, save* – (O)Fr. *sauf* (AFr. *saf*) :- L. *salvus* uninjured, entire, healthy. For the vocalism cf. *chafe, mavis, save, wafer.*] **I.** Free from hurt or damage. **1.** Unhurt, uninjured, unharmed; having escaped some real or apprehended danger. Now only with quasi-advb. force after verbs of coming, going, bringing, etc. ME. †**2.** In sound health, well, 'whole'; usu. healed, cured, restored to health –1526. †**3.** *Theol.* [After L. *salvus* in the Vulgate.] Delivered from sin or condemnation, saved; in a state of salvation, spiritually 'whole' –1562. †**4.** Mentally or morally sound or sane –1611.

1. The papers came s. to hand 1737. Phr. *S. and sound,* occas. *s. and sure. To be, arrive,* etc. *s.* (or *s. and sound*): a colloq. or epistolary formula for 'to be duly arrived'. **4.** A Trade Sir, that I hope I may vse with a s. Conscience SHAKS. Are his wits s.? Is he not light of Braine? SHAKS.

II. Free from danger; secure. **1.** Not exposed to danger; not liable to be harmed or lost; secure. late ME. **2.** Of a place or thing: Affording security or immunity; not exposing to danger; not likely to cause harm or injury. late ME. **3.** *transf.* in S.-CONDUCT, SAFE-GUARD; hence with sbs. of similar meaning, as *s. convoy,* etc. 1536. **4.** Of an action, procedure, etc.: Free from risk, not involving danger or mishap, guaranteed against failure. Sometimes = free from risk of error, as in *it is s. to say...*1568. **5.** Secured, kept in custody; unable to escape. Hence, not likely to come out, intervene, or do hurt; placed beyond the power of doing harm, not at present dangerous. 1600. **6. a.** Sure in procedure; not liable to fail, mislead, or disappoint expectation; trustworthy. **b.** Cautious, keeping to 'the safe side'. 1604. **7.** †**a.** With *of*: Sure to obtain –1846. **b.** *To be s.* followed by inf., is predicated of a person or thing to express the certainty of the fact or event involved in the predication. Hence used attrib. in colloq. phrases like '*He is a* **s. first**' = he is s. to take a first class. 1790.

1. I greatly feare my monie is not s. SHAKS. Whil'st thou ly'st warme at home, secure and s. SHAKS. A person once infected with the small-pox is s. from having it a second time 1801. **2.** A Station s. for Ships, when Tempests roar DRYDEN. That part of the world is at a s. distance DICKENS. **4.** 'Tis never s. to despise an enemy DE FOE. *On the s. side*: with a margin of security against error. **5.** *Provb.* S. binde, s. finde 1573. But Banquo's s.? *Mur.* I, my good Lord: s. in a ditch he bides. SHAKS. **6. b.** My blood begins my safer Guides to rule SHAKS. **7. b.** He'll win it, as s. as s.! 1860. Phr. *A s. catch.*

Special collocations. **S. deposit** (orig. *U.S.*), a place in which valuables are stored; also *attrib.* **S. edge,** a smooth edge of a file. **S. load,** a load which leaves a required margin of security against causing breakage or injury to a structure. Hence †**Safe** *v.* (*rare*) *trans.* to render s. or secure; to conduct safely *out of* –1611. **Sa·fe-ly** *adv.,* **-ness.**

Safe-conduct (sēⁱfkǫ·ndǝkt), *sb.* ME. [– (O)Fr. *sauf conduit,* med.L. *salvus conductus*; see SAFE *a.,* CONDUCT *sb.*] **1.** The privilege, granted by a sovereign or other competent authority, of being protected from arrest or molestation while making a particular journey or travelling within a certain region. **2.** A document by which this privilege is conveyed. late ME. **3.** **3.** The action of conducting in safety; safe convoy ME.

1. *In, with s., under, upon* (*a*) *s.*; He had come over under a safe conduct, and he was not detained FROUDE. Hence †**Safe-conduct** *v. trans.* to lead, convoy, or conduct safely –1639.

Safeguard (sēⁱ·fgaɹd), *sb.* [ME. *sauf garde* – AFr. *salve garde,* (O)Fr. *sauve garde* (AL. *salva gardia* XIV); see SAFE *a.,* GUARD *sb.*] **1.** Protection, safety. Now *rare* or *Obs.* **2.** Protection or security afforded by a specified person (or thing). Now *rare* or *Obs.* 1456. †**3.** = SAFE-CONDUCT 1. –1607. **4.** = SAFE-CONDUCT 2. Also, a guard or escort granted for the same purpose. 1633. **5.** A warrant granted by a military commander to protect a place from pillage. Also, a guard or detachment of soldiers sent to protect the place. 1706. **6.** *gen.* Something that offers security from danger; a defence, protection; e.g. a legal proviso or a stipulation serving to prevent some encroachment; a course of action, a habit or sentiment, tending to protect the subject against some temptation 1471. †**7.** An outer skirt or petticoat worn by women to protect their dress when riding –1789.

2. Phr. *In, under* (*the*) *s. of.* **3.** On safegard he came to me SHAKS. **4.** Whosoever shall presume to violate a Save-gard, shall die without mercy 1642. **6.** His owne valour was his s. 1634. The old reticence of the Bench was a grand s. of its dignity 1891.

Safeguard (sēⁱ·fgaɹd), *v.* 1494. [f. prec.] *trans.* To keep secure from danger or attack; to guard, protect, defend. Now chiefly with immaterial obj. (e.g. interests, rights); *spec.* = PROTECT *v.* 2. Hence **Sa·feguarding** *vbl. sb.* = PROTECTION 4.

Safe-hold. 1793. [f. HOLD *sb.*¹; cf. STRONGHOLD.] A place of safety from attack.

Sa·fe-kee·ping, *vbl. sb.* late ME. The action of keeping safe; protection, custody.

Safety (sēⁱ·fti). [ME. *sauvete* (three sylls.) – (O)Fr. *sauveté* :- med.L. *salvitas, -tat-,* f. L. *salvus*; see SAFE *a.,* -TY¹.] **1.** The state of being safe; exemption from hurt or injury; freedom from danger. †**b.** Sometimes *pl.* = the safety of more than one person –1814. †**2.** Close custody or confinement –1595. †**3.** A means or instrument of safety; a protection, safeguard –1793. **4.** The quality of being unlikely to cause hurt or injury; freedom from dangerousness; safeness 1717. **5.** *Engineering. Factor* or *coefficient of s.*: the ratio between the strains put upon any material and the ultimate strength of the material 1858. **6.** In full *s.-bolt.* A contrivance for locking the trigger of a gun, so as to prevent accidental discharge. Also, a gun fitted with this 1881. **7.** In full *s. bicycle.* The type of bicycle now in use, differing from its predecessor in the lower position of the saddle, whereby greater safety is afforded to the rider 1877.

1. It is..his duty..not to hazard the s. of the Community '*Junius*' *Lett. Provb.* There is s. in numbers. Phr. *In s.*: safe(ly). *To play for s.* (Billiards): Of a player, to leave his opponent's ball in such a position as to make his next stroke a very difficult one; hence *gen.* (usu. with derogatory implication) to act with circumspection so as not to be exposed to danger or risk. **2.** *Rom. & Jul.* V. iii. 183. **4.** *S. first*: a maxim or slogan inculcating caution, esp. on the highway.

attrib. Used freely since *c* 1800 as a specific designation for contrivances for ensuring safety, or for implements, machines, etc., constructed with a view to safety in use; as **s. bicycle** (see sense 7); **s. bolt, catch** (see sense 6); **s. cage,** (*a*) the wire guard of a safety lamp; (*b*) a miner's cage fitted with apparatus to prevent its falling if the rope breaks; **s. curtain,** a fire-proof curtain in a theatre cutting off the auditorium from the stage; **s. fuse,** a fuse which can be ignited at a safe distance from the charge; **s. lamp,** a miner's lamp the flame of which is so protected that it will not ignite fire-damp; **s. match,** one which ignites only when rubbed on a prepared surface; **-razor,** a razor provided with guards for the blade.

Sa·fety-pin. 1857. **1.** A pin for fastening clothing, bent back on itself so as to form a spring, and with a guard or sheath to cover the point and prevent its accidental unfastening. **2.** A pin used for fastening, locking, or securing some part of a machine 1878.

Sa·fety-valve. 1797. **1.** A valve in a steam-boiler which automatically opens to permit steam to escape when the pressure is becoming dangerous. Also, a similar valve opening inwards, to admit air when a partial vacuum has been formed. **2.** *fig.* An opening or channel for 'letting off steam', giving vent to excitement, or the like 1818. **3.** Phr. *To sit on the s.,* to follow a policy of repression.

Safflower (sæ·flauᵊɹ). 1562. [– Du. *saffloer* or G. *safflor* – OFr. *saffleur* – It. †*saffiore,* var. of *asfiore, asfrole, zaffrole*; infl. by assoc. with *saffron* and *flower.*] **1.** The dried petals of the *Carthamus tinctorius,* also the red dye produced from these petals. **2.** The thistle-like plant *Carthamus tinctorius,* extensively cultivated for the dye obtained from its flowers; the seeds yield an oil used for lamps 1682.

Saffron (sæ·frǝn), *sb.* and *a.* [ME. *saffran, safron* – (O)Fr. *safran* – Arab. *zaᶜfarān,* of unkn. origin.] **A.** *sb.* **1.** An orange-red product consisting of the dried stigmas of *Crocus sativus* (see 2). Now used chiefly for colouring confectionery, liquors, etc., and for flavouring. **b.** *Indian s.*: any plant of the genus *Curcuma* 1727. **2.** The Autumnal Crocus, *Crocus sativus,* which produces saffron. late ME. **b.** Bastard S. = SAFFLOWER 2; called also American, Dyer's, †Mock S., Meadow or Wild S., *Colchicum autumnale.* 1548. **3.** The orange-yellow colour of saffron (sense 1). late ME.

Comb.: **s. cake,** a cake flavoured with s.; **s. wood,** the timber of a S. African tree, *Elæodendron croceum.*

B. *adj.* Resembling saffron in colour 1567.

There let Hymen oft appear In S. robe MILT.

Collocations: **s. butterfly, moth,** collectors' names for certain lepidoptera having yellow wings; **s. plum,** a W. Indian sapotaceous tree (*Bumelia cuneata*) having a yellow fruit. Hence **Sa·ffron** *v.* (*rare*) *trans.* to season or dye with s.; to give a s.-yellow colour to. **Sa·ffroned** *a.* coloured with, or having the colour of, s.; flavoured with s. **Sa·ffrony** *a.* (*rare*) of a colour somewhat resembling s.

Safranin (sæ·frănin). 1868. [– Fr. *safranine,* f. *safran* SAFFRON + *-ine* -IN¹.] *Chem.* **a.** The yellow colouring matter of saffron. **b.** A coal-tar colour which dyes yellowish-red.

Sag (sæg), *sb.* 1580. [f. next.] The action of sagging. **1.** *Naut.* Movement or tendency to leeward. **2.** In a rope, wire, etc. supported at two points: The dip below the horizontal line, due to its weight 1861. **3.** A sinking or subsidence; quasi-*concr.* a place where the surface has subsided, a depression 1872. **4.** *Comm.* A decline in price 1891.

Sag (sæg), *v.* Infl. **sagged, sagging.** late ME. [– (M)LG. *sacken* = Du. *zakken*, in same sense; for the development or variation of *-g*, *-gg-* from *-k*, *-ck-* see SMUG, TRIGGER, etc.] **1.** *intr.* To sink or subside gradually, by weight or pressure. **b.** Of a part of the body (occas. of a person): To droop; to sink or hang *down* loosely 1526. **c.** Of a garment: To hang unevenly, to slip out of position. Now chiefly *dial.* and *U.S.* 1592. **d.** To bend or curve downwards in the middle, from its own weight or superincumbent pressure. Said, e.g., of a rope supported at two points, of a beam, plank, etc. 1753. **2.** To decline to a lower level, through lack of strength or effort. (Common in U.S.) 1508. **b.** *Comm.* To decline in price 1887. **3.** To drag oneself along wearily or feebly 1573. **4.** *Naut.* Of a ship or boat: To drift, be carried out of the intended course. Chiefly in the phr. *to s. to leeward.* 1633. **5.** *trans.* To cause to bend downwards in the middle 1755.

1. The old pavements have sunk or sagged considerably DARWIN. **b.** The head slowly sagged down on to the cushions 1902. **d.** One..comes to wonder why the whole ceiling does not s. 1886. **2.** The minde I sway by, and the heart I beare, Shall neuer sagge with doubt, nor shake with feare SHAKS. **4.** We're sagging south on the Long Trail KIPLING. **5.** Their bottoms were thus sagged down by the cargoes 1777.

‖**Saga** (sā·gă). 1709. [– ON. (Icel.) *saga* SAW *sb.*²] **1.** Any of the narrative compositions in prose that were written in Iceland or Norway during the Middle Ages; in Eng. use often applied *spec.* to those which embody the traditional history of Icelandic families or of the kings of Norway. Also *transf.*, a story of heroic achievement or marvellous adventure. ¶**2.** (Partly after G. *sage*). A mythical story, which has been handed down by oral tradition; historical or heroic legend 1864.

1. *transf.* Dick delivered himself of the s. of his own doings KIPLING. **2.** The Sagas of Guy of Warwick and Bevis of Hampton 1883. *Comb.* **s.-man** [= ON. *sǫgumaðr*], a writer of sagas.

Sagacious (săgēⁱ·ʃəs), *a.* 1607. [f. L. *sagax*, *sagac-* + -IOUS; see -ACIOUS.] †**1.** Acute in perception, esp. by smell –1732. **2.** Gifted with acuteness of mental discernment; of keen penetration and judgement; shrewd 1650. **b.** Characterized by sagacity 1831. **3.** Of animals: Intelligent 1759.

2. True Charity is s., and will find out hints for beneficence SIR T. BROWNE. **b.** This s. conjecture 1857. Hence **Saga·cious-ly** *adv.*, **-ness.**

Sagacity (săgæ·sĭti). 1548. [– Fr. *sagacité* or L. *sagacitas*, *-tat-*, f. as prec.; see -ITY.] The quality of being sagacious. †**1.** Acute sense of smell –1798. **2.** Acuteness of mental discernment; keenness and soundness of judgement; penetration, shrewdness 1548. **b.** *pl.* Sagacious observations 1866. **3.** Of animals: Exceptional intelligence 1555.

1. Some [animals] show that nice s. of smell COWPER. **2.** Men of skill and s. do sometimes foretel futurities 1693. A man of great s. in money matters DICKENS. **3.** The s. of the beaver in cutting down trees 1837.

Sagamore (sæ·gămōᵊɹ). 1613. [– Penobscot *sagamo*; see SACHEM.] = SACHEM.

‖**Sagan** (sēⁱ·găn). 1625. [Late (Talmudic) use of Heb. *sāḡan* or *seḡen* – Assyrian *šaknu* prefect (of conquered territory). In the Bible the word denotes a civil governor.] *Jewish Antiq.* The deputy of the Jewish high-priest; the second highest functionary of the Temple.

‖**Sagapenum** (sægăpī·nǒm). 1579. [Late L. – Gr. σαγάπηνον a plant, prob. *Ferula persica*; also its gum.] A gum-resin, the concrete juice of *Ferula persica*, formerly used as an anti-spasmodic and emmenagogue, or externally. Also *gum s.*

Sagathy (sæ·găþi). *Obs.* exc. *Hist.* 1707. [In Fr. *sagatis*, Sp. *sagati*; origin unkn.] A light-weight stuff made either of silk and wool or silk and cotton. **b.** *attrib.* or *adj.* Made of s. 1711.

Sage (sēⁱdʒ), *sb.*¹ [ME. *sauge* – (O)Fr. *sauge* :– L. *salvia* 'the healing plant', f. *salvus* safe. For the phonology cf. *chafe*, *gauge*, *safe*, *Ralph* (rēⁱf).] **1.** A plant of the genus *Salvia*, of the *Labiatæ*; esp. *S. officinalis*, an aromatic culinary herb. Hence, the dried leaves of this plant used in cooking. **2.** Cookery. *S. and onions*: a stuffing chiefly composed of those ingredients, used for goose, duck, pork, etc. Also *s.-and-onion stuffing.*

attrib. and *Comb.*, as *s. ale*, *bread*, *wine*, etc.; also **s.-brush, -bush,** a collective name applied to various species of *Artemisia*, esp. *A. tridentata*; **-cheese,** a kind of cheese which is flavoured and mottled by mixing a decoction of sage-leaves with the cheese-curd; **-green,** a dull greyish green resembling that of the foliage of the s.-plant *Salvia officinalis*; **s. tea,** an infusion of s.-leaves, used as a stomachic and slight stimulant; **-willow,** a dwarf grey American willow, *Salix tristis*.

b. In the names of animals, etc. found chiefly in the sage-brush districts of N. America, as **s.-cock, grouse,** the largest grouse found in America, *Centrocercus europhasianus*; **s. hare** = *s. rabbit*; **s. hen,** the female of the sage grouse; **s. rabbit,** a small hare, *Lepus artemisia*; **-sparrow,** a sparrow of the genus *Amphispiza*, esp. *A. belli*; **s. thrasher,** the mountain mocking-bird, *Oreoscoptes montanus*. Hence **Sa·gey, sa·gy** *a.* (*rare*) of the nature of s.

Sage (sēⁱdʒ), *a.* and *sb.*² ME. [– (O)Fr. *sage* :– Gallo-Rom. *sapius (cf. L. *nesapius* ignorant, f. *sapere* be wise.] **A.** *adj.* Now *literary*. **1.** Of a person: Wise, discreet, judicious. In mod. use: Practically wise, rendered prudent or judicious by experience. **b.** Of advice, conduct, etc.: Characterized by profound wisdom; based on sound judgement 1531. **c.** Of the countenance, bearing, etc.: Exhibiting sageness or profound wisdom. Now usu. somewhat *ironical*. 1816. †**2.** Grave, dignified, solemn –1644.

1. S. graue men SHAKS. The wise reasoning of a certain s. magistrate BERKELEY. **b.** Little thought he of this s. caution MILT. **2.** Great Bards beside In s. and solemn tunes have sung, Of Turneys MILT.

B. *sb.* A man of profound wisdom; *esp.* one of those persons of ancient history or legend who were traditionally famous as the wisest of mankind; hence, one entitled to a like degree of veneration with these. Occas. in weaker sense, a wise man. ME. **b.** Used playfully or ironically 1751.

A Starr..proclaims him com, And guides the Eastern Sages, who enquire His place MILT. *The seven sages of Greece*: Thales, Solon, Periander, Cleobulus, Chilon, Bias, and Pittacus, to each of whom some wise maxim is attributed by ancient writers. **b.** The sages of the village 1822. Hence **Sa·ge-ly** *adv.*, **-ness.**

‖**Sagene**¹ (sa·ʒen). 1737. [Russ.] A measure of length used in Russia, equal to seven English feet.

Sagene² (sădʒī·n). *rare*. 1846. [– L. *sagena* – Gr. σαγήνη.] A fishing-net; *fig.* a network (of railways, etc.).

Sagenite (sădʒī·nəit). 1802. [f. Gr. σαγήνη + -ITE¹ 2 b. Named by H. B. de Saussure, 1796.] *Min.* A variety of rutile in which slender crystals are interlaced, forming a network. Hence **Sageni·tic** *a.*

Saggar (sæ·găɹ), **seggar** (se·găɹ), *sb.* 1768. [prob. a contr. of SAFEGUARD *sb.*] **1.** A protecting case of baked fire-proof clay in which the finer ceramic wares are enclosed while baking in the kiln. **2.** The clay of which saggars are made 1839.

Saginate (sæ·dʒineⁱt), *v. rare*. 1623. [– *saginat-*, pa. ppl. stem of L. *saginare*, f. *sagina*, process or means of fattening; see -ATE³.] *trans.* To fatten (animals). So **Sagina·tion** 1607.

‖**Sagitta** (sădʒi·tă). 1594. [L., lit. an arrow.] **1.** *Astr.* A northern constellation lying between *Hercules* and *Delphinus* 1704. **2.** *Geom.* The versed sine of an arc 1594. **3.** *Arch.* The keystone of an arch 1703. **4.** The middle horizontal stroke in the Greek letter ϵ 1864. **5.** *Anat.* The sagittal suture 1891. **6.** *Zool.* **a.** One of the otoliths of a fish's ear 1888. **b.** One of the components of certain sponge-spicules 1898.

Sagittal (sădʒi·tăl), *a.* 1541. [– Fr. *sagittal* – med.L. *sagittalis*, f. *sagitta* arrow; see -AL¹.] **1.** *Anat.* **a.** *S. suture*: the median suture between the parietal bones of the skull. **b.** Pertaining to the sagittal suture; pertaining to or lying in the median longitudinal antero-posterior plane of the body, or to any plane parallel with this 1831. **2.** Pertaining to an arrow; resembling an arrow or an arrow-head in shape (*rare*) 1656. Hence **Sagi·ttally** *adv. Anat.* 'in the direction of the s. plane'.

‖**Sagittarius** (sædʒitēᵊ·riǒs). late ME. [L., archer, subst. use of adj.; see next.] **1.** *Astr.* (With capital S.) The zodiacal constellation of the Archer; hence, the ninth sign of the zodiac, which the sun enters about 22 Nov. **b.** The mythical Centaur who was fabled to have been transformed into this constellation 1590. **2.** *Her.* A bearing representing a centaur with a drawn bow 1619.

Sagittary (sæ·dʒitări). late ME. [– L. *sagittarius*, pertaining to arrows, f. *sagitta* arrow; see -ARY¹.] †**1.** *Astr.* = prec. 1. –1788. **2.** A centaur; *spec.* the centaur who according to mediæval romance fought in the Trojan army against the Greeks 1509. **3.** A representation of a centaur or of a mounted archer; *spec.* in *Her.* = prec. 2. 1610. **4.** An archer 1832.

Sagittate (sæ·dʒiteⁱt), *a.* 1760. [f. L. *sagitta* arrow + -ATE².] *Bot.* and *Zool.* Shaped like an arrow-head. So **Sa·gittated** *a.* 1752.

Sago (sēⁱ·go). 1555. [– (orig. through Pg.) Malay *sāgū*.] **1.** The tree from which sago (see 2) is obtained. **2.** A species of starch prepared from the pith of the trunks of several palms and cycads, esp. *Metroxylon læve* and *M. rumphii*, chiefly used as an article of food 1580.

2. *French s.*, common arrowroot. *Japan s.*, the s. prepared from various species of *Cycas*. *Pearl s.*: see PEARL.

attrib. and *Comb.*: **s.-palm (tree)** = sense 1; **-spleen,** amyloid degeneration of the Malpighian corpuscles of the spleen, resembling boiled sago.

Sagoin (săgoi·n). 1607. [– Fr. *sagouin*, †*sagoin* – Pg. *saguim* – Guarani *sagui*, *çagui*.] A small S. Amer. monkey, *esp.* one of the genus *Callithrix*.

‖**Sagum** (sēⁱ·gǒm). *Pl.* **saga.** 1600. [L.; also *sagus*, = late Gr. σάγος; said to be of Gaulish origin.] *Rom. Antiq.* A Roman military cloak; also, a woollen cloak worn by the ancient Gauls, Germans, and Spaniards.

Sahara (săhā·ră). 1613. [– Arab. *ṣaḥrā'* desert.] The great desert of Libya or northern Africa. (With capital S.) **b.** *transf.* and *fig.* A desert, wilderness 1862. Hence **Saha·ran, Saha·rian, Saha·ric** *adjs.*

‖**Sahib** (sā·ʰib). 1627. [Urdu use of Arab. *ṣāḥib* companion, friend, lord, master.] A respectful title used by the natives of India in addressing an Englishman or European (= 'sir'); also, in native use, an Englishman or European. Also affixed as a title (= 'Mr.' prefixed) to the name or office of a European. (See also MEMSAHIB.)

Sahidic (săhi·dik), *a.* 1825. [f. Arab. *ṣa'īd* upper + -IC.] Belonging to the dialect of Coptic spoken in Thebes and Upper Egypt. Also quasi-*sb.*, the S. language, or the S. version of the Bible.

Sahlite (sā·ləit). 1807. [– G. *sahlit*, f. *Sahla* (*Sala*) in Sweden; see -ITE¹ 2 b.] *Min.* A variety of pyroxene.

‖**Sai** (sā·i). 1774. [– Brazilian *sahy*, *çahy*.] A S. Amer. monkey, *Simia capucina*.

‖**Saic** (seᵢī·k). 1667. [– Fr. *saïque* – Turkish *ṣayka*.] A kind of sailing vessel common in the Levant.

Said (sed), *ppl. a.* ME. [pa. pple. of SAY *v.*¹] **1.** Named or mentioned before. (Also *abovesaid*, *aforesaid*.) †**2.** Spoken, uttered; in phr. *s. saw* –1659.

Saiga (sēⁱ·gă, sai·gă). 1801. [– Russ.] A kind of antelope (*S. tartarica*) of the steppes of Russia. Also *s.-antelope*.

Sail (sēⁱl), *sb.*¹ [OE. *seġ(e)l* = OFris. *seil*, OS. *segel* (Du. *zeil*), OHG. *segal* (G. *segel*), ON. *segl* :– Gmc. *seȝlam, of unkn. origin.] **1.** One of the shaped pieces of canvas or other textile material fastened to the masts, spars, or stays of a vessel, so as to catch the wind and cause the vessel to move through the water. Also occas. a similar apparatus for propelling a wind-driven carriage. **b.** *transf.* Applied to the wing of a bird (*poet.*). Also *techn.* in Falconry, the wing of a hawk. 1590. **2.** Sails collectively. late ME. **3. a.** In collective sing. (also †in pl.) chiefly with numeral: (So many) sailing-vessels. late ME. **b.** A ship or other vessel esp. as descried by its sails 1517. **4.** An apparatus (now usu. an arrangement of boards) attached to each of the arms of a windmill for the purpose of catching the wind. Also (windmill) sails collectively, surface presented by the sails. ME. **5.** *Zool.* **a.** The large dorsal fin of the sail-fish. **b.** One of the two large tentacles of the Nautilus, formerly believed to be used as sails. 1817. **6.** *S. Afr.* A tarpaulin or canvas sheet for covering a wagon 1850.

1. Thy tacklings are loosed..they could not spread the saile *Isa.* 33:23. *fig.* Where Tullie doth set vp his saile of eloquence ASCHAM. **b.** The mountain eagle..Spread her dark sails on the wind SCOTT. **2.** The Admiral..carried all s. 1806. *Full s.*: a sail (or sails collectively) filled by the wind; the condition of a ship with sails so filled. *At*, †*with full sail(s* [= L. *pleno velo, plenis velis*, Fr. *à pleines voiles*], (sailing) with a strong favourable wind, at full speed; so also *full s.* as advb. phr. In mod. use, *in full s.* is applied to describe the condition of a ship with all sails set. *Under s.*, having the sails set. **3.** The Royal navy comprised in all twenty-seven s. 1863. †*Sail of the line*; a squadron of the largest ships of the royal navy. **b.** A S., a S. Where? Fair by us. 1669.

Comb.: **s.-arm**, one of the beams of a windmill: = WHIP *sb.* III. 2; **-axle**, the axle on which the sails of a windmill revolve; **-boat** (*U.S.*), a sailing-boat; **-fish**, any of various fishes, as *Selachus maximus*, having a large dorsal fin; **-fluke**, the whiff, *Rhombus megastoma*; **-hook**, a small hook for holding the seams of a sail while it is being sewn; **-loft**, a place where sails are constructed; **-maker**, one whose business it is to make, repair, or alter sails; **-needle**, a large needle used in sewing canvas; **-room**, a room (in a ship) for storing sails; **-winged** *a. poet.* [after L. *velivolus*], (*a*) of ships, having sails that serve as wings (*b*) *transf.* as an epithet of the sea; (*c*) having wings like sails. Hence **Sai·lless** *a.* having no sails or ships.

Sail (sē[i]l), *sb.*[2] 1602. [f. next.] **1.** An act of sailing; a voyage or excursion on a sailing-vessel 1604. **2.** Only in *nonce-uses.* A number sailing 1608. **3.** Sailing qualities; speed in sailing 1602.

1. Phr. *To take s.*, to embark. **2.** Wee-haue descryed.., a portlie saile of ships SHAKS.

Sail (sē[i]l), *v.* [OE. *seġl(i)an* :– Gmc. **sezljan*, f. **sezlam* SAIL *sb.*[1]] **I.** *intr.* **1.** Of persons: To travel on water in a vessel propelled by the action of wind upon sails; now often, to travel on water in a vessel propelled by any means other than oars; to navigate a vessel in a specified direction. **2.** Of a ship or other vessel: To move or travel on water by means of sails, or (in mod. use) by means of steam or any other mechanical agency ME. **3.** To begin a journey by water; to set sail. late ME. **4.** *transf.* To glide on the surface of water or through the air, either by the impulsion of wind or without any visible effort. late ME. **5.** Of persons, in *transf.* senses. **a.** To move or go in a stately or dignified manner, suggestive of the movement of a ship under sail. (Chiefly of women.) 1841. **b.** *To s. in* (slang): to proceed boldly to action 1889.

1. I loue nat to sayle by see, but when I can nat chose 1530. Phr. *To s. near* (or *close to*) *the wind*: (see WIND *sb.*[1] III. 3); *fig.* to come very near to transgression of a law or a received moral principle; to run the risk of disaster. **2.** Light boates saile swift, though greater hulkes draw deepe SHAKS. Steamships s. from every shore 1886. **3.** The fleet of the prince was already sailed GOLDSM. On the 13th,..I sailed from Plymouth Sound 1777. **4.** Swans that s. along the Silver Flood DRYDEN. Where great whales come sailing by M. ARNOLD. **5. a.** Then all the great people sailed in state from the room C. BRONTË.

II. *trans.* **1.** To sail over or upon, to navigate (the sea, a river, etc.). Now somewhat *arch.* late ME. **2.** With cognate obj.: *To s. through, out*: to continue (a sailing-match, race), to the end 1886. **b.** To sail or glide through (the air) 1725. **3.** To navigate (a ship or other vessel) 1566. **b.** To put (a toy boat) on the water and direct its course 1863.

1. A thousand Ships were man'd to s. the Sea DRYDEN. **2.** The uninjured vessel shall s. out the race 1899. **b.** The buzzard..on broad wings.. slowly sails the sky 1899. **3.** He loved the sea; he liked to s. his own boat 1890. Hence **Sai·lable** *a.* (now *rare* or *Obs.*) of a ship: that is in a condition to sail; of the sea, etc.: that can be sailed on; navigable.

Sailcloth (sē[i]·lklǭþ). ME. [f. SAIL *sb.*[1] + CLOTH *sb.*] †**1.** A piece of cloth forming or designed to form part of a sail of a vessel or a windmill –1598. **2.** Canvas or other textile material such as is used for sails 1615. **b.** A piece of this used as a covering 1778.

Sailer (sē[i]·ləɹ). late ME. [f. SAIL *v.* + -ER[1].] **1.** One who sails. Now *rare.* **2.** A ship or vessel with ref. to her powers of sailing 1582. **b.** A sailing vessel 1871.

2. A very strong light ship, and a..good s. DE FOE.

Sailing (sē[i]·liŋ), *vbl. sb.* OE. [f. SAIL *v.* + -ING[1].] **1.** The action of SAIL *v.* **2.** Progression, style or speed of progression, of a ship or other vessel (orig. of a sailing-vessel) 1687. **3.** Departure (of a ship) from port 1748.

Comb.: **s.-boat**, a (small) boat propelled by a sail; **-line**, the line on a vessel's hull which marks the level of the water when she is ballasted and rigged for sailing, but not laden or armed; **-master**, an officer charged with the navigation of a vessel (in British use chiefly with ref. to yachts; in the U.S. navy, a commissioned officer, usu. a lieutenant, appointed to direct the navigation of a ship of war); **s. orders**, the directions given to a captain of a vessel with regard to time of departure, destination, etc.

Sailor (sē[i]·ləɹ). 1642. [Alteration of SAILER: see -OR 2 d.] **1.** One who is professionally occupied with navigation; a seaman, mariner. Also, a member of a ship's company below the rank of officer. †**2.** = SAILER 2. –1775. **3.** Short for *s. hat* 1898.

1. Phr. *To be a good s.* [= Fr. *être bon marin*]: to be exempt from sea-sickness.

attrib. and *Comb.*: **s.-fish** = *sail-fish*; **s. hat**, a hat such as is worn by sailors; hence, a form of hat (with flat brim of even breadth all round) formerly worn by women, and a different form (with turned-up brim) worn by children; **-man**, in uneducated and joc. use = sense 1; also *occas.* an adult sailor. **b.** with possessive: **sailor's choice**, *U.S.*, a name given locally to various American fishes; **sailors' home**, a home built by subscription, for the accommodation of sailors on moderate terms; **sailor's knot**, any of the kinds of knot used by sailors; also, a kind of knot used in tying a neck-tie. Hence **Sai·lorless** *a.* without sailors. **Sai·lorly** *a.* befitting, or having the characteristics of, a s.

Sailyard (sē[i]·lyāɹd). OE. [f. SAIL *sb.*[1] + YARD *sb.*[2]] *Naut.* One of the yards or spars on which the sails are spread.

‖**Saimiri** (saimī[ə]·ri). 1774. [Brazilian Pg. *saimirim* – Tupi *çahy miri* little monkey (f. *çahy* SAI + *miri* little).] A small S. Amer. squirrel-monkey of the genus *Chrysothrix.*

Sain (sē[i]n), *v.* Now *arch.* and *dial.* [OE. *seġnian* = OS. *segnon* (Du. *zegenen*), OHG. *seganōn* (G. *segnen* bless), ON. *signa*; – L. *signare* sign (in eccl. use to sign with the cross), f. *signum* SIGN *sb.*] **1.** *trans.* To make the sign of the cross on (a thing or person) in token of consecration or blessing; or for the purpose of exorcizing a demon, warding off the evil influences of witches, poison, etc. **b.** *refl.* To cross (oneself) OE. **2.** *trans.* To bless ME. ¶**b.** Associated by some mod. writers with L. *sanare* to heal 1832. **3.** To secure by prayer or enchantment *from* evil influence 1670.

1. Patrick sained the earth and it swallowed up the wizard 1887. **2.** Mary, Mother, s. and save! 1839. **b.** There flowers no balm to s. him HOUSMAN.

Sainfoin (sē[i]·nfoin). 1626. [Fr. †*saintfoin* (mod. *sainfoin*) orig. lucerne – mod.L. *sanctum fœnum* 'holy hay', alt. of *sanum fœnum* 'wholesome hay', which was based on L. *herba medica* 'healing plant', itself erron. alt. of *herba Mēdica*, Gr. Μηδικὴ πόα 'Median grass'.] A perennial herb, *Onobrychis sativa*, much grown as a forage plant. Also, locally, lucerne (*Medicago sativa*).

Saint (sē[i]nt; unstressed sĕnt, snt), *a.* and *sb.* ME. [OE. *sanct*, superseded (XII) by *seint(e, sant, saint* (before a name with initial cons., *sein, sayn*) – OFr. *seint*, (also mod.) *saint*, fem. *seinte, sainte* :– L. *sanctus* sacred, holy, prop. pa. pple. of *sancire*, used subst. in the Vulgate.] **A.** *adj.* = HOLY, in special applications. **1.** Prefixed to the name of a canonized person (see B. 2), also to the names of the archangels; now felt to be the sb. used appositively. Abbrev. S. and St., *pl.* SS. and Sts. **2.** *transf.* †**a.** Of heathen deities, etc. –1588. **b.** allus. or iron. *Obs.* in general use. late ME. †**3.** Prefixed to various common nouns (in collocations taken over from Latin and French), esp. *Charity, Cross, Spirit, Trinity* –1710. **4.** Attributive and possessive collocations of proper names with the prefix 'Saint' ('St.') in sense 1. **a.** Many plants, animals, and other objects have been named after saints of the calendar. For these see the saints' names or the sbs. qualified by them. **b.** Many diseases have been named after saints that are supposed to ward off or relieve them. **c.** Many objects are called after a place-name or a surname beginning with 'Saint' ('St.'); see below.

1. The possessive of names preceded by 'Saint' is often used ellipt. in names of churches, as *St. Paul's, St. Peter's.* Hence various names of towns, villages, etc., as *St. Albans, St. Andrews, St. Bees.* **2. a.** Saint Cupid then, and Souldiers to the field SHAKS. **b.** *St. Monday*: see MONDAY. *St. Lubbock's day*, (joc.) any of the bank holidays instituted by Sir John Lubbock's Act, 1871. **3.** By gis, and by S. Charity SHAKS. **4. b.** *St. Anthony's fire*: see FIRE *sb.* 12. *St. Vitus' dance*: see DANCE *sb.* **c. St. Bernard (dog)**, in full *Great St. Bernard dog*, a dog of a breed kept by the monks of the Hospice of the Great St. Bernard (a dangerous pass in the Alps between Switzerland and Italy) for the rescue of travellers in distress. **St. Germain pear**, a fine dessert pear. **St. Leger**, a horse-race for three-year-olds run at Doncaster; instituted by Colonel St. Leger in 1776. **St. Michael's**, the name of one of the Azores, which produced a fine quality of orange.

B. *sb.* A holy person. **1.** One of the blessed dead in Heaven. Usu. *pl.* ME. **2.** *Eccl.* One of those persons who are formally recognized by the Church as having by their exceptional holiness of life attained an exalted station in heaven, and as being entitled in an eminent degree to the veneration of the faithful; a canonized person ME. **b.** A representation or image of a saint 1563. **3.** In Biblical use, one of God's chosen people; in the N.T., one of the elect under the New Covenant; a member of the Christian church; a Christian. Hence used as their own designation by some puritanical sects in the 16–17 c., and by the Mormons. late ME. **b.** In Biblical use applied to angels. late ME. **4.** A person of extraordinary holiness of life. Sometimes *iron.*, A person making an outward profession of piety. 1563. **5.** A nickname for: **a.** A member of a religious association at Cambridge. Now *Hist.* 1793. **b.** One of the party which promoted the agitation in England against slavery. Now *Hist.* 1830.

1. She, half an angel in her own account, Doubts not hereafter with the saints to mount COWPER. **2.** In a cave To bidde, and rede on holy seyntes lyves CHAUCER. A considerable number of churches are called after the names of the primitive saints of our island 1847. *transf.* The graves of Moslem saints 1876. **3.** The fellowship of his Saincts in this present world HOOKER. **b.** Gabriel..lead forth my armied Saints MILT. **4.** For such an iniurie would vexe a very s. SHAKS.

Comb.: **saint's day**, a day set apart by the Church for observing the memory of a s. Hence **Sai·ntdom**, the condition of a s.; saints collectively. †**S.-errant** [after KNIGHT-ERRANT], a s. who travelled in quest of spiritual adventures (*ironical*). **Sai·ntess**, a female s. **Sai·ntish** *a.* s.-like (chiefly *contempt.*). **Sai·ntling**, a little or petty s.

Saint (sē[i]nt), *v.* ME. [f. prec.] **1.** *pass.* To be or become a saint in Heaven. *Obs.* or *arch.* **2.** *trans.* To call (a person) a saint, give the name of 'saint' to; *spec.* to enrol among the number of saints formally recognized by the Church; to canonize. late ME. **3.** To cause to be regarded, or to appear, as a saint; to represent as a saint (*rare*) 1609. †**4.** To ascribe holy virtues or a sacred character to –1657. **5.** *intr.* To act or live as a saint; to play the saint. In later use chiefly with *it.* 1460.

1. I hold you as a thing en-skied, and sainted SHAKS. **2.** A Shooe-maker that has been Beatify'd, tho' never Sainted ADDISON. **3.** The

Picture..would Martyr him and S. him to befoole the peeople MILT. **5.** Whether the Charmer sinner it or s. it POPE.

Sainted (sēⁱ·ntėd), *ppl. a.* 1598. [f. prec. + -ED¹.] **1.** Enrolled among the saints; canonized; that is a saint in Heaven 1631. **2.** Of sanctified or holy life or character 1605. **3.** Such as belongs to or befits a saint; sacred 1598.

1. The s. Figures on the Casement painted LONGF. **2.** His virtuous and s. wife DISRAELI. **3.** The broad sun Hangs over s. Lebanon MOORE.

Sainthood (sēⁱ·nthud). 1550. [f. SAINT *sb.* + -HOOD.] The condition, status, or dignity of a saint; also, saints collectively.

Sai·ntlike, *a.* 1580. [f. as prec. + -LIKE.] Resembling a saint or that of a saint; of saintly life or character.

Saintly (sēⁱ·ntli), *a.* 1660. [f. SAINT *sb.* + -LY¹.] Of, belonging to, or befitting a saint or saints; of great holiness or sanctity; sainted.

The same weake silly lady as ever, asking such s. questions PEPYS. Hence **Sai·ntliness.**

Saintship (sēⁱ·nt,ʃip). 1606. [f. as prec. + -SHIP.] **1.** The condition or status of a canonized saint 1631. **2.** The condition of being a saint or saintly person; saintliness of life or character 1613. **3.** As a kind of title. Often *ironical.* 1606.

Saint-Simonian (sēⁱ:nt-, sěnt,simōᵘ·niăn), *a.* and *sb.* Also **St.-.** 1831. [f. *Saint-Simon* + -IAN.] **A.** *adj.* Belonging to or characteristic of the socialistic system propounded by the Comte de Saint-Simon (1760–1825), who advocated state control of all property and a distribution of the produce according to individual vocation and capacity. **B.** *sb.* An advocate of this system. Also **Saint-Simonist** (səi·mǒnist). Hence **Saint-Simo·nianism, -Si·monism,** advocacy of or adherence to this system.

Saithe (sēð). *Sc.* 1632. [– ON. *seiðr* 'gadus virens' a kind of fish; cf. Icel. *seiði* fry.] The coal-fish.

‖**Sajou** (saʒū·). 1774. [Fr. (Buffon), shortened from *sajouassu* – Tupi *saiuassu*, f. *sai* SAI + *-uassu* augm. suffix.] One of various small S. Amer. monkeys, varieties of Sapajous, and Capuchin monkeys.

Sake (sēⁱk). [OE. *sacu* = OFris. *sake*, OS. *saka* (Du. *zaak*), OHG. *sahha* (G. *sache*), ON. *sǫk* :– Gmc. **sakō* affair, thing, cause, legal action, accusation, crime, f. **sak-*, rel. to **sōk-* SEEK.] †**I.** As an independent sb. **1.** Contention, strife, dispute; in OE. also, a lawsuit, cause, action –ME. **2.** A charge or accusation (of guilt); a ground of accusation –late ME. **3.** Guilt, sin; a fault, offence, crime –1450. †**4.** *nonce-use.* Regard or consideration for some one. SPENSER.

4. Tho mov'd with wrath, and shame, and Ladies s. SPENSER.

II. Phr. *For the s. of*; *for* (one's, a thing's) *s.* **1.** Out of consideration for; on account of one's interest in, or regard for (a person); on (a person's) account ME. **b.** When the preceding genitive is pl., the pl. *sakes* is often used 1530. **2.** Out of regard or consideration for (a thing); on account of, because of (something regarded as an end, aim, purpose, etc.); often = out of desire for, in order to attain. ME.

1. For my own s. as well as for yours, I will do my very best JOWETT. **b.** For both our sakes I would that word were true SHAKS. **2.** It is doing mischief for mischiefs s. 1770. Flattering of rich men for the s. of a dinner JOWETT. For sweet marriage-s. SWINBURNE. Phr. *For one's name('s) s.*, out of regard for one's name. *For God's s., for goodness', Heaven's s.*; Hold on, for Heaven's s.! 1879. †*For any s.*, in any case, at all events. *For old sake's s.*, for the s. of old friendship. *Sakes alive!* and simply *Sakes!*: a vulgar exclam. of surprise (*dial.* and *U.S.*).

‖**Saké, saki** (sæ·ke). 1687. [Japanese.] A Japanese fermented liquor made from rice.

Saker (sēⁱ·kəɹ). late ME. [– (O)Fr. *sacre* – Arab. *ṣaḳr.*] **1.** A large lanner falcon (*Falco sacer*), used in falconry, esp. the female. **2.** An old form of cannon smaller than a demi-culverin, formerly much employed in sieges and on ships. Now *Hist.* or *arch.* 1521.

Sakeret (sēⁱ·kərėt). *Obs.* or *arch.* late ME. [– Fr. *sacret*, dim. of *sacre* SAKER.] The male of the saker.

Saki (sā·ki). 1774. [– Fr. *saki* (Buffon), irreg. – Tupi *çahy*, corresp. to Guarani *çagui* (see SAGOIN).] A S. Amer. monkey of the family *Cebidæ*, of either of the two genera *Pithecia* or *Brachyurus.*

‖**Sal**¹ (sæl). late ME. [L., = salt.] †**1.** *Chem.*, *Alch.*, and *Pharm.* = SALT *sb.*¹ –1674. **2.** With qualifying word: †*s. marine* [med.L. *sal marinus*], common salt; *s. mirabile* (*-is*) [mod.L., 'wonderful salt'], Glauber's salts, sulphate of soda; *s. soda* [med.L. *sal sodæ*], crystallized sodium carbonate. See also SAL-AMMONIAC, SAL VOLATILE. late ME.

Sal² (sāl). Also **saul.** 1789. [Hindi *sāl* = Skr. *sāla.*] A valuable timber tree of India, *Shorea robusta*, yielding the resin dammar.

‖**Sala** (sā·la). 1611. [It., Sp. = SALLE.] A hall or large apartment; *spec.* a dining-hall.

Salaam (sălā·m), *sb.* 1613. [– Arab. *salām* = Heb. *šālôm* peace.] The Arabic salutation *as-salām 'alaykum*, Peace be upon you. Hence applied to a ceremonious obeisance accompanying this salutation, consisting (in India) of a low bow with the palm of the right hand placed on the forehead. **b.** *transf.* Respectful compliments 1623.

1. The Moor rose instantly, with profound salaams, before her 1867.

Salaam (sălā·m), *v.* 1693. [f. prec.] **1.** *trans.* To make a salaam to; to salute with a salaam; to offer salutations to. **2.** *intr.* To make a salaam or obeisance 1698.

2. Putting their hands to their brow, and salaaming down to the ground 1852.

Salacious (sălēⁱ·ʃəs), *a.* 1645. [f. L. *salax, salac-* (f. *salire* leap) + -OUS; see -IOUS.] **1.** Lustful, lecherous; sexually wanton 1659. **2.** Tending to provoke lust (*rare*) 1645. Hence **Sala·cious-ly** *adv.*, **-ness.**

Salacity (sălæ·sĭti). 1605. [– Fr. *salacité* or L. *salacitas*, f. as prec.; see -ITY.] The quality or condition of being salacious; lustfulness, lecherousness, sexual wantonness.

Salad (sæ·lăd). Also (*dial.* or *arch.*) **sallet.** late ME. [– (O)Fr. *salade* – Pr. *salada* :– Rom. **salata*, subst. use (sc. *herba*) of pa. pple. fem. of **salare*, f. L. *sal* SALT.] **1.** A cold dish of herbs or vegetables (e.g. lettuce, endive), usu. uncooked, to which is often added sliced hard-boiled egg, cold meat, fish, etc., the whole being seasoned with salt, pepper, oil, and vinegar. Also (*fruit s.*) extended to a mixture of fruits served in their syrup. **b.** *fig.* and allus., as a type of something mixed (or †savoury) 1601. **2.** Any vegetable or herb used in a raw state as an article of food, esp. in the dish described in 1; = *s.-herb* 1460.

1. The s. is the glory of every French dinner and the disgrace of most in England 1846. **b.** I remember one said, there was no Sallets in the lines, to make the matter sauoury SHAKS. Our Garrick's a s., for in him we see Oil, vinegar, sugar, and saltness agree GOLDSM.

attrib.: **s. burnet,** the common burnet, *Poterium sanguisorba*; **s. days,** days of youthful inexperience; **s. dressing** (see DRESSING *vbl. sb.* 4 a); †**s.-herb** = sense 2; **-oil,** olive oil of superior quality, such as is used in dressing salads. Hence **Sa·lading,** herbs and vegetables used for salad.

Salal (sæ·lăl). 1838. [Chinook Jargon *sallal.*] An evergreen shrub (*Gaultheria shallon*) of California and Oregon, bearing sweet edible berries.

Salamander (sæ·lămɑndəɹ, sælămɑ·ndəɹ). ME. [– (O)Fr. *salamandre* – L. *salamandra* – Gr. σαλαμάνδρα.] **1. a.** A lizard-like animal supposed to live in, or to be able to endure, fire. Now *allusive.* **b.** Any tailed amphibian of the urodelous family *Salamandridæ*, or some closely allied family 1611. **c.** A figure of the mythical salamander used as an emblem 1688. **2.** *transf.* and *fig.*, applied to persons, etc. with ref. to sense 1 a. 1596. **b.** A spirit supposed to live in fire 1657. **3.** Applied to various articles used in fire or capable of withstanding great heat. †**a.** Asbestos –1700. **b.** An iron or poker used red-hot for lighting a pipe, igniting gunpowder, etc. 1698. **c.** *Cookery.* A circular iron plate which is heated and placed over a pudding, etc., to brown it 1769. **4.** *local U.S.* A pouched rat or gopher, esp. *Geomys pinetis* 1859. **5.** A German form of drinking a toast 1868.

1. a. Like the S., that is ever in the fire and never consumed 1591. **c.** *S.* (*Her.*), an emblem of constancy, is represented in flames 1823. **2.** I haue maintain'd that S. [= fiery-red face] of yours with fire, any time this two and thirtie yeeres SHAKS.

Comb.: **s.-cloth,** an incombustible cloth made from asbestos; **salamander's hair,** a kind of asbestos; †**s. stone** = AMIANTHUS; †**salamander's wool,** asbestos. Hence **Salama·ndrian** *a.* resembling (that of) a s.; *sb.* a salamandrian batrachian.

Salamandrine (sælămæ·ndrin), *a.* and *sb.* 1712. [f. SALAMANDER + -INE¹.] **A.** *adj.* **1.** Resembling or characteristic of the salamander in being able to resist fire, or live in it. **2.** *Zool.* Of or pertaining to the *Salamandrinæ* 1865. **B.** *sb.* A spirit supposed to live in fire; also = SALAMANDER 1 b. 1797.

Salamandroid (sælămæ·ndroid), *a.* and *sb.* 1854. [f. SALAMANDER + -OID.] **A.** *adj.* Resembling a salamander. **B.** *sb.* A urodele of the genus *Salamandra* or allied genera 1863.

‖**Salame** (sălā·me). *Pl.* **salami.** 1852. [It., repr. pop. L. **salamen*, f.**salare* to salt.] A kind of sausage.

Sal-ammoniac (sælămōᵘ·niæk). ME. [– L. *sal ammoniacus* (in med.L. *-acum*); see SAL¹, AMMONIAC A. 1.] Ammonium chloride.

Salamstone (sălæ·m,stōᵘn). 1816. [– G. *salamstein* (Werner).] *Min.* A blue variety of sapphire from Ceylon.

Salangane (sæ·lăŋgēⁱn). 1793. [– Fr. *salangane*, f. *salamga* name of the bird in Luzon.] *Zool.* One of the birds of the genus *Collocalia*, which make edible nests; an esculent swallow.

Salariat (sălēᵊ·riæt). 1918. [– Fr. *salariat*, f. *salaire* SALARY, after *prolétariat.*] The body of people in an industry, trade, or department who receive a salary (as dist. from wage-earners).

Salaried (sæ·lărid), *ppl. a.* 1600. [f. SALARY *sb.* or *v.* + -ED.] **1.** Having or receiving a salary. **2.** Having a salary attached to it 1836.

1. Most of them are his s. schollers, or agents 1600. **2.** The poorly-s. Chair of Civil History 1872.

Salary (sæ·lări), *sb.* late ME. [– AFr. *salarie* = (O)Fr. *salaire* :– L. *salarium* orig. money allowed to Roman soldiers for the purchase of salt, (hence) pay, stipend, subst. use (sc. *argentum* money) of *salarius*, f. *sal* salt; see -ARY¹.] **1.** Fixed payment made periodically to a person as compensation for regular work; now usu. for non-manual or non-mechanical work (as opp. to *wages*). †**2.** Remuneration for services rendered; fee, honorarium –1643. †**b.** *gen.* Reward, recompense –1686.

1. Sir Humphry Winch, Baronet, hath from the Court 500*l.* per annum Sallery 1677. **2. b.** Felicitie, which is the salarie and reward of Vertue 1619.

Salary (sæ·lări), *v.* 1477. [Chiefly f. SALARY *sb.* In early use – Fr. *salarier.*] *trans.* To recompense, reward; to pay for something done (*Obs.* or *arch.*); to pay a regular salary to.

The Chinese system—s. the doctor and stop his pay when you get ill 1893.

Salband (sā·lbænd). Also **sahlband.** 1811. [– G. *salband*, earlier *sahlband.*] *Geol.* A thin crust or coating of mineral, etc.

Sale (sēⁱl), *sb.* (and *a.*) [Late OE. *sala* – ON. *sala* = OHG. *sala*, f. base of Gmc. **saljan* SELL.] **1.** The action or an act of selling; the exchange of a commodity for money or other valuable consideration. Also: (Ready, slow, etc.) disposal of goods for money; opportunity of selling. **b.** *spec.* A putting up of goods to be sold publicly; a public auction 1673. **c.** A special disposal of shop goods at reduced prices in order to get rid of them rapidly, e.g. at the end of a 'season' 1886. **2.** *attrib.* or *adj.* That is made to be sold; that may be purchased (not being needed for home use); hence, ready-made; of inferior quality 1455.

1. b. He should pull down the bills advertising the s. of his effects TROLLOPE.

Phrases. *To s.* = 'for s.' Now only in *to put up to s. On s.* = 'for s.' †*Of s.*, that is to be sold; vendible, venal. *For s.*; used adjectively, = intended to be sold; used advb., = with a view to selling. *At s.*: among booksellers, at 30% discount off the published price. *S. and (or) return*, a contract, by which goods are delivered to a retailer, to be paid for at a certain rate, if sold by him; and if not sold, to be returned to the vendor. *S. of work*, a sale of articles made by members of a congregation or association on behalf of some charitable or religious object.

attrib. and *Comb.*, as *s.-price, -room*, etc.; **s. ring**, the ring of buyers formed round an auctioneer at a s. Also with pl., **sales-book**, a book or record of sales; **sales-room** = *s.-room*.

Saleable (sēi·lăb'l), *a.* 1530. [f. prec. + -ABLE.] **1.** Capable of being sold; fit for sale; commanding a ready sale. **b.** Said of the price which an article will fetch 1778. **2.** Venal, mercenary. Now *rare* or *Obs.* 1579.

1. b. Goods to the s. value of 17*l.* 1778. Hence **Saleabi·lity. Sa·leableness. Sa·leably** *adv.*

Salempore (sæ·lĕmpōᵊɹ). 1598. [prob. f. **Salempur* (*pūr* town), f. Salem in the province of Madras, India.] A blue cotton cloth formerly made at Nellore (Madras) in India, and largely exported to the W. Indies.

Salep (sæ·lĕp). 1736. [– Fr. *salep* – Turk. *sālep* – Arab. (*kuṣa-'l-*)*ṯa'lab*, sometimes pronounced *sa'lab*. See SALOOP.] A nutritive meal, drink, or jelly made from the dried tubers of various orchidaceous plants, chiefly those of the genus *Orchis*; formerly also used as a drug.

Saleratus (sælərēi·tŭs). *U.S.* 1846. [– mod.L. *sal aeratus* 'aerated salt'.] An impure bicarbonate of potash containing more carbon dioxide than pearl-ash does, much used as an ingredient in baking-powders. Now also applied to sodium bicarbonate similarly used.

Salesian (sălī·ʒiăn), *a.* and *sb.* 1884. [– Fr. *salésien*, f. name of S. François de *Sales*; see -IAN.] Of or pertaining to, a member of, an order (*a*) of nuns of the Visitation, founded by S. François de Sales, (*b*) of brothers founded by Dom Bosco for the care of poor and neglected children.

Salesman (sēi·lzmæ̆n). 1523. [f. *sale's*, genitive of SALE + MAN *sb.* Cf. *tradesman*, etc.] A man whose business it is to sell goods or conduct sales; *spec. U.S.*, a commercial traveller. Hence **Sa·lesmanship,** the condition or character of being a (good) s. So **Saleswo·man,** a woman who sells goods (e.g. in a shop).

Salian[1] (sēi·liăn), *a.* and *sb.* 1653. [f. L. *Salii*, referred by the ancients to *salire* leap; see SALIENT, -IAN.] **A.** *adj.* Of or pertaining to the Salii or priests of Mars in ancient Rome. **B.** *sb.* One of the Salii.

Salian[2] (sēi·liăn), *a.* and *sb.* 1614. [f. late L. *Salii* the Salian Franks + -AN I. 1.] **A.** *adj.* Of or belonging to a tribe of Franks who inhabited a region near the Zuyder Zee, and to whom the ancestors of the Merovingian dynasty belonged. (Cf. SALIC.) **B.** *sb.* A Salian Frank.

Salic (sæ·lik, sēi·lik), *a.* 1548. [– Fr. *salique* or med.L. *Salicus*, f. *Salii*; see SALIAN[2], -IC.] **1.** *S. Law*: orig., the alleged fundamental law of the French monarchy, by which females were excluded from succession to the crown; hence *gen.*, a law excluding females from dynastic succession. In this sense often *Salique* (sălī·k). **2.** In the original sense of L. *Salicus*: Pertaining to the Salian Franks. Chiefly in *S. law* or *code* (L. *lex Salica*), a Frankish law-book, written in Latin, and extant in five successive enlarged recensions of Merovingian and Carolingian date. 1781.

Salicaceous (sælikēi·ʃəs), *a.* 1846. [f. mod.L. *salicaceus*, f. L. *salix, salic-* willow; see -ACEOUS.] *Bot.* Belonging to the family *Salicaceæ*, which consists of two genera, *Salix* (willow) and *Populus* (poplar).

Salicin (sæ·lisin). 1830. [– Fr. *salicine* (Leroux), f. L. *salix, salic-* willow; see -IN[1].] A bitter crystalline principle obtained from willow-bark, and much used medicinally.

Salicional (săli·ʃənăl). 1843. [– G. *salicional*, f. L. *salix, salic-* willow, with obscure suffix.] An organ stop of a soft reedy tone resembling that of a willow pipe. So **Sa·licet.**

Salicyl (sæ·lisil). 1839. [– Fr. *salicyle*, f. as prec.; see -YL.] *Chem.* The diatomic radical of salicylic acid. Hence **Sa·licylide,** the anhydride of salicylic acid. **Sa·licylite,** a salt formed by the action of salicylol on oxides and hydrates of metals. **Sa·licylol,** an oil intermediate in composition between salicylic acid and salicylic aldehyde.

Salicylate (săli·silĕt). 1842. [f. next + -ATE[1] 1 c.] *Chem.* A salt of salicylic acid.

Salicylic (sælisi·lik), *a.* 1840. [f. SALICYL + -IC 1 b.] **1.** *Chem.* Belonging to a group of benzene derivatives obtainable from salicin; esp. in *s. acid*, a white crystalline substance, and much used as an antiseptic and in the treatment of rheumatism. **2.** *Therapeutics.* Made from, impregnated with, or involving the use of, s. acid 1876. Hence **Sa·licylism,** a toxic condition produced by the administration of s. acid or salicylates. **Sa·licylize** *v. trans.* to treat with s. acid in order to prevent fermentation.

Salicylous (săli·siləs), *a.* 1840. [f. as prec. + -OUS c.] *Chem.* In *s. acid*: a liquid obtained by distillation of salicin with sulphuric acid and bichromate of potash; salicyl aldehyde.

Salience (sēi·liĕns). 1836. [f. next; see -ENCE.] **†1.** The quality of leaping or springing up. L. HUNT. **2.** The fact, quality, or condition of projecting beyond the general outline 1849. **3.** A salient or projecting feature, part, or object 1837. So **Sa·liency** 1664.

Salient (sēi·liĕnt), *a.* and *sb.* 1562. [– L. *saliens, -ent-*, pr. pple. of *salire* leap; see -ENT.] **A.** *adj.* **1.** Leaping, jumping; *esp.* of animals, saltatorial 1646. **b.** Of water: Jetting forth; leaping upwards 1669. **2.** *Her.* Having the hind legs in the sinister base and the fore-paws elevated near together in the dexter chief, as if in the act of leaping 1562. **3.** *S. point* [= Fr. *point saillant*, mod.L. *punctum saliens*]: in old medical use, the heart as it first appears in an embryo; hence, the first beginning of life or motion; the starting-point of anything. *Obs.* or *arch.* 1672. **4.** Of an angle: Pointing outward, as an ordinary angle of a polygon (opp. to *re-entrant*); chiefly in *Fortif.*, pointing away from the centre of the fortification. So *s. point*, etc. 1687. **5. a.** Of material things: Standing above or beyond the general surface or outline; jutting out; prominent among a number of objects 1789. **b.** Of immaterial things, qualities, etc.: Standing out from the rest; prominent, conspicuous. Often in phr. *s. point*. 1840.

1. b. *fig.* He had in himself a s., living spring, of generous and manly action BURKE. 3. That was the s. point from which all the mischiefs..of the present reign took life '*Junius' Lett.* 5. a. Large s. eyes 1854. b. The s. feature in the picture GROTE.

B. *sb.* A salient angle or part of a fortification or system of trenches 1828. Hence **Sa·liently** *adv.*

Saliferous (săli·fĕrəs), *a.* 1828. [f. L. *sal* salt + -FEROUS.] Containing a large proportion of salt; said chiefly of strata.

Salifiable (sæ·lifəiˌăb'l), *a.* 1790. [– Fr. *salifiable*, f. *salifier* SALIFY.] *Chem.* Capable of combining with an acid to form a salt.

Salification (sæːlifikēi·ʃən). 1684. [– mod.L. *salificatio*, f. *salificare* SALIFY; see -ATION.] Conversion into a salt; the action or condition of being salified.

Salify (sæ·lifəi), *v.* Now *rare.* 1790. [– Fr. *salifier* – mod.L. *salificare*, f. L. *sal* salt; see -FY.] *Chem. intr.* To form a salt.

Saligenin (sæli·dʒĕnin). 1852. [– Fr. *saligénine*, f. *sali*(*cine* SALICIN; see -GEN and -IN[1].] *Chem.* A substance obtained in the decomposition of salicin by dilute acid.

Saligot (sæ·ligǫt). 1578. [– OFr. *saligot*.] The water-chestnut, *Trapa natans*.

Salimeter (săli·mĭtəɹ). 1866. [f. L. *sal* salt + -METER.] An instrument for determining the amount of salt in a solution.

‖**Salina** (sălǝi·nă). 1589. [– Sp. *salina* = med.L. *salina* salt-pit; in L. only as pl. *salinæ* (sc. *fodinæ*).] A salt lake, spring, or marsh; a salt-pan, salt-works.

Saline (sēi·lǝin, sălǝi·n), *a.* and *sb.* 1450. [Branch A f. L. *sal* salt + -INE[1]. Cf. Fr. *salin* XVII. Branch B 1 – med.L. *salina*, *-um* salt-pit (cf. prec.); B 2 from the adj.] **A.** *adj.* **1.** †Composed of salt; of the nature of salt; having salt as a preponderating constituent. **b.** Of springs, lakes, etc.: Impregnated with salt or salts 1805. **2.** Like that of salt; like salt; salty 1651. **3.** Of or pertaining to chemical salts; of the nature of a salt 1771. **4.** Of medicines: Consisting of or based upon salts of the alkaline metals or magnesium 1789. **5.** Of plants, †animals: Growing in or inhabiting salt plains or marshes 1802.

1. The s. contents of sea-water 1832. b. Medicinal springs, s. and sulphurous 1872. 2. The..s. taste of nitre 1857. 4. The use of s. purgatives 1802.

B. *sb.* **1.** = SALINA 1450. **2.** A s. purge (see A. 4) 1875. Hence **Sali·neness** (*rare*).

Salinity (săli·nĭti). 1658. [f. prec. + -ITY.] The quality of being saline; saltness.

Salino- (sălǝi·no), comb. form of SALINE, in the sense 'consisting of salt (and..)', as *s.-sulphureous*, etc.

Salinometer (sælinǫ·mĭtəɹ). 1844. [f. SALINE + -METER.] An apparatus for ascertaining the salinity of water, *esp.* one for indicating the density of brine in marine boilers.

Saliretin (sælirī·tin). 1840. [– Fr. *salirétine* (Piria), f. SALI(CIN + Gr. ῥητίνη resin; see -IN[1].] *Chem.* A resinous substance obtained by the action of dilute acids on saligenin.

Saliva (sălǝi·vă). late ME. [– L. *saliva*.] Spittle; the mixed secretion of the salivary glands and of the mucous glands of the mouth, a colourless liquid, having normally an alkaline reaction, which mixes with the food in mastication. So **Sali·val** *a.* (*rare*) salivary. **Salivant** (sæ·livănt), *a.* promoting salivation; *sb.* a sialagogue.

Salivary (sæ·livări, sălǝi·vări), *a.* 1709. [– L. *salivarius*, f. *saliva*; see prec., -ARY[1].] **1.** Secreting or conveying saliva. **2.** Consisting of saliva 1841. **3.** Pertaining to or existing in the saliva or salivary glands 1807.

1. The s. glands in man are the parotid, submaxillary, and sublingual O.E.D.

Salivate (sæ·livēit), *v.* 1657. [– *salivat-*, pa. ppl. stem of L. *salivare*, f. *saliva*; see -ATE[3].] **1.** *trans.* To produce an unusual secretion of saliva in (a person), generally by the use of mercury; to produce ptyalism in. **2.** *intr.* **a.** To secrete or discharge saliva. **b.** To secrete saliva in excess under the influence of sialagogues. 1681. So **Saliva·tion,** secretion or discharge of saliva; *esp.* the production of an excessive flow of saliva by administering mercury 1598.

†**Sali·vous,** *a.* 1567. [– L. *salivosus*, f. *saliva*; see -OUS.] Pertaining to, of the nature of, saliva –1676.

‖**Salle** (sal). 1762. [Fr.; cf. SALA.] **1.** A hall, room (*rare*) 1819. **2.** The sorting department of a paper factory 1888. **3.** In Fr. combinations. **Salle-à-manger** (salamaṅʒe), a dining-hall, dining-room. **Salle d'attente** (saldatāṅt), a waiting-room (at a station). 1762.

Sallee-man (sæ·lĭmæn). 1637. [f. *Sallee*, a Moroccan seaport formerly of piratical repute.] **1.** A Moorish pirate-ship. *Obs.* exc. *Hist.* **2.** A marine hydrozoan, *Velella vulgaris* 1756.

Sallender (sæ·lĕndəɹ). Now only *pl.* 1523. [Of unkn. origin.] A dry scab affecting the hock of a horse.

Sallet (sæ·lĕt), **salade** (sălā·d). 1440. [– Fr. *salade* – Pr. *salada*, It. *celata*, or Sp. *celada* – Rom. **cælata*, subst. use (sc. *cassis, galea* helmet) of fem. pa. pple. of L. *cælare* engrave, f. *cælum* chisel. The form in *-et* arose from reduction of the final syll. due to initial stress.] *Antiq.* In mediæval armour, a light globular headpiece, either with or without a vizor, and without a crest, the lower part curving outwards behind.

Many a time but for a Sallet, my braine-pan had bene cleft with a brown Bill SHAKS.

Sallet, arch. or dial. f. SALAD.

Sallow (sæ·lou), *sb.* Also **sally.** [OE. (Angl.) *salh* (repr. directly by dial. *saugh*, †*salfe* XIV) :- Gmc. **salχaz*, rel. to OHG. *salaha* and ON. *selja*, and to L. *salix*, Gr. ἑλίκη. The form *sallow* descends from the OE. inflexional *salg-*.] **1.** A plant of the genus *Salix*, a willow; chiefly, as dist. from 'osier' and 'willow', applied to several species of *Salix* of a low-growing or shrubby habit. Also, one of the shoots of a willow. **2.** The wood of the sallow tree. late ME. **3.** Collector's name for certain moths the larvæ of which feed on the willow; esp. a moth of the genus *Xanthia* 1829.

Comb. **sally-fly**, a kind of stone fly; **sallow thorn**, a plant of the genus *Hippophae*.

Sallow (sæ·lou), *a.* [OE. *salo* dusky, dark = MDu. *salu*, *saluwe* discoloured, dirty, OHG. *salo* dark-coloured (G. dial. *sal*), ON. *sǫlr* yellow :- Gmc. **salwa-*. For the vocalism, cf. FALLOW *a.*[1]] Of the skin or complexion: Having a sickly yellow or brownish yellow colour.

Ful salowe was waxen hir colour CHAUCER. *transf.* While s. Autumn fills thy lap with leaves COLLINS. Hence **Sa·llow** *v. trans.* to make s. **Sa·llowish** *a.* somewhat s. in hue. **Sa·llowness.**

Sallowy (sæ·loui), *a.* 1840. [f. SALLOW *sb.* + -Y[1].] Abounding in sallows or willows.

Sally (sæ·li), *sb.*[1] 1542. [- (O)Fr. *saillie*, subst. use of fem. pa. pple. of *saillir*, refash. of OFr. *salir* :- *salire* leap.] **1.** A sudden rush (*out*) from a besieged place upon the enemy; a sortie 1560. †**b.** A sally-port -1598. **2.** A going forth, setting out, excursion, expedition (of one or more persons) 1650. **3.** A sudden start into activity 1605. **4.** A breaking forth from restraint; an outburst or transport (*of* passion, delight, etc.); a flash (*of* wit) 1662. **5.** An escapade. Now *rare*. 1639. **6.** A sprightly or audacious utterance or literary composition; now usu., a brilliant remark, a witticism 1756. **7.** A leaping movement. *Obs.* exc. *Naut.* and *dial.* 1589. **8.** *Arch.* A deviation from the alignment of a surface; a projection 1665.

1. A garrison..which is able..to make successful sallies 1786. **2.** I made my second s. into the world DE FOE. **3.** Fretted by sallies of his mother's kisses WORDSW. **5.** This excursion was esteemed but a S. of youth WOTTON.

Sally (sæ·li), *sb.*[2] 1668. [perh. an application of prec. 7.] *Bell-ringing*. **1.** The first movement of a bell when 'set' for ringing; a 'handstroke', as dist. from the 'backstroke'; also, the position of a bell when 'set'. Now *local*. **2.** The woolly grip for the hands near the lower end of a bell-rope 1809.

Comb. **s.-hole**, a hole through which the bell-rope passes.

†**Sa·lly**, *v.*[1] *rare*. 1440. [irreg. - (O)Fr. *saillir*.] *intr.* To leap, bound, dance -1543.

Sally (sæ·li), *v.*[2] 1560. [f. SALLY *sb.*[1]] **1.** *intr.* Of a warlike force: To issue suddenly from a place of defence or retreat in order to make an attack; *spec.* of a besieged force, to make a sortie. **2.** Of a person or party of persons: To set out boldly, to go forth (from a place of abode); to set out on a journey or expedition 1590. **3.** Of things: To issue forth; *esp.* to issue suddenly, break out, burst or leap forth 1660.

1. And now, all girt in armes; the Ports, set wide, They sallied forth CHAPMAN. **2.** In the morning we all sallied forth to hunt DARWIN. **3.** While yet his warm blood sallied from the wound COWPER.

Sally Lunn (sæ·li lʌ·n). 1798. [Said to be from the name of a young woman in Bath who first made them about 1797.] A kind of sweet light teacake, containing sultanas, currants, etc., and eaten with butter.

Sa·llyport. 1649. [f. SALLY *sb.*[1] + PORT *sb.*[3]] **1.** *Fortif.* An opening in a fortified place for the passage of troops when making a sally; sometimes used for 'postern'. **2.** A landing-place at Portsmouth set apart for the use of men-of-war's boats 1833.

Salmagundi (sælmăgʌ·ndi). 1674. [- Fr. *salmigondis*, †*-gondin* (Rabelais), of unkn. origin.] *Cookery*. A dish composed of chopped meat, anchovies, eggs, and onions, with oil and condiments.

fig. His mind was a sort of s. 1797.

Salmi (sæ·lmi). 1759. [Shortening of Fr. *salmigondis*; see prec.] A ragoût of partly roasted game, stewed with wine, bread, condiments, etc.

Salmiac (sæ·lmiæk). 1799. [- G. *salmiak*, contr. of L. *sal ammoniacum* SAL-AMMONIAC.] *Min.* Native sal-ammoniac.

Salmon (sæ·mən), *sb.* and *a.* ME. [- AFr. *sa(u)moun*, (O)Fr. *saumon* :- L. *salmo*, *salmon-* (Pliny). For the repr. of OFr. *au* by (æ) cf. *savage*, *scabbard*, and the (vulgar) *sassage* for *sausage*.] **A.** *sb.* **1.** A large fish belonging to the genus *Salmo*, family *Salmonidæ*, esp. *Salmo salar*, which has red flesh and a silvery skin marked with large black and red spots, and is highly prized as an article of food. **b.** Applied to fishes belonging to other genera of the same family; e.g. a fish belonging to any of the species of the genus *Oncorhynchus*, called the *Pacific s.* 1884. **c.** Applied to fishes resembling a salmon, but not belonging to the *Salmonidæ*. In U.S., the SQUETEAGUE. In Australia and New Zealand, *Arripis salar*. 1798. **2.** Short for *s. colour* 1892.

Comb.: **s. berry** (*U.S.*), a name for certain species of *Rubus*, esp. *R. nutkanus*, the white flowering raspberry; **-colour**, an orange shade of pink; **s. fishing**, (*a*) the catching of s.; (*b*) a salmon-fishery; **s. ladder**, a fish ladder for s.; **s. leap** (see LEAP *sb.*[2]); **s. pass** = *s. ladder*; **s. weir**, a weir for the taking of s.

B. *adj.* [The sb. used *attrib.*] Of the colour of the flesh of salmon; a kind of orange-pink 1786. Hence **Sa·lmonet**, a samlet. **Salmonoid** (sæ·lmŏnoid) *a.* and *sb.* (a fish) of the family *Salmonidæ*; resembling a fish of this family.

Sa·lmon-trou·t. late ME. **1.** A fish of the species *Salmo trutta*, resembling the salmon. **2.** In U.S. and N.S.W. applied to other fishes; *esp.* the Char, or Red-spotted Trout, and the Gray-spotted or Lake Trout 1882.

Salol (sæ·lǫl). 1887. [f. SAL(ICYL + -OL.] *Chem.* A white, crystalline, aromatic powder, prepared from salicylic and carbolic acids, used as an anti-pyretic and antiseptic.

‖**Salon** (salon̈). 1715. [Fr. see next.] **1.** **a.** A large and lofty reception-room in a palace or other great house. **b.** A drawing-room. (Now only with ref. to France or other continental countries.) **2.** *spec.* The reception-room of a Parisian lady of fashion; hence, a reunion of notabilities at the house of such a lady; also, a similar gathering in other capitals 1810. **3.** *The S.*: the annual exhibition at Paris of painting, sculpture, etc. by living artists 1875.

Saloon (săl**ū**·n). 1728. [- Fr. *salon* - It. *salone*, augm. of SALA; see -OON.] **1.** = prec. 1 a. **b.** = prec. 1 b. Now *U.S.* **2.** = prec. 2. Now *rare*. 1810. **3.** A large room or hall, esp. in a hotel or other place of public resort, adapted for assemblies, entertainments, exhibitions, etc. 1747. **4.** **a.** A large cabin for first-class or for all passengers on a ship (also in a large aeroplane) 1842. **b.** In full *s. car* or *carriage*: A railway carriage without compartments furnished luxuriously as a drawing-room, or for a specific purpose, as *dining*, *sleeping s.* Later, also = *s. car.* 1855. **5.** A public apartment for a specified purpose, as *billiard*, *dancing*, *shaving s.*, etc. 1852. **6.** (orig. *U.S.*) A drinking bar; now, in Eng., a first-class bar in a public house or hotel (a *saloon bar*) 1872.

2. I find saloons and compliments too great bores SHELLEY. **5.** In London..we went to places of entertainment, and low dancing saloons 1852.

Comb.: **s. car**, a coach-built covered-in motor-car; also see 4 b; **s. carriage** (see 4 b); **s. deck**, a deck for the use of s. passengers; **s.-keeper** *U.S.*, one who keeps a drinking s.; **s. pistol**, **rifle**, light firearms for firing at short range.

Saloop (săl**ū**·p). 1712. [Altered f. SALEP.] **1.** = SALEP. **2.** A hot drink consisting of an infusion of powdered salep, or (later) of sassafras, with milk and sugar, formerly sold in the streets of London.

S. bush, an Australian shrub, *Rhagodia hastata*.

Salopian (sălōu·piăn), *a.* and *sb.* 1700. [f. *Salop*, alternative name of Shropshire, evolved from *Salopesberia* (XI) and *Salopescire* (XI), AFr. alt. of ME. forms of OE. *Sćrobbesbyriġ* Shrewsbury and *Sćrobbesbyriġscīr* Shropshire; see -IAN.] **A.** *adj.* Of or belonging to Shropshire 1706. **B.** *sb.* **1.** A native or inhabitant of Shropshire 1700. **2.** A past or present member of Shrewsbury School 1866.

Salp (sælp). 1835. [- Fr. *salpe* - mod.L. *salpa*; see next.] *Zool.* = next.

‖**Salpa** (sæ·lpă). *Pl.* **salpæ**; also **salpas.** 1852. [mod.L. *salpa* (Forskål, *a*1763), but the reason for the selection of this word does not appear.] *Zool.* A genus of tunicates, the sole representative of the family *Salpidæ*; also, a tunicate of this genus. So **Sa·lpian**, an individual of the genus *S.* 1839.

†‖**Salpicon** - (sæ·lpikǫn). 1726. [Fr. - Sp. *salpicon*, f. *salpicar* sprinkle (with salt).] *Cookery.* A kind of stuffing for veal, beef, or mutton -1832.

‖**Salpiglossis** (sælpiglǫ·sis). 1833. [mod. L., irreg. f. Gr. σάλπιγξ trumpet + γλῶσσα tongue, from the shape of the corolla.] A genus of herbaceous plants of the family *Scrophulariaceæ*, natives of Chile, cultivated for their showy blossoms.

Salpingitis (salpindʒəi·tis). 1861. [mod. L., f. Gr. σάλπιγξ, σαλπιγγ- (see next) + -ITIS.] *Path.* Inflammation of the Fallopian or the Eustachian tubes.

Salpingo- (sælpi·ngo), comb. form of Gr. σάλπιγξ, σαλπιγγ-, lit. 'trumpet', but used in mod.L. to denote either the Fallopian or the Eustachian tubes.

‖**Salpinx** (sæ·lpiŋks). 1842. [Gr. σάλπιγξ.] **1.** *Antiq.* An ancient Greek trumpet 1865. **2.** **a.** The Eustachian tube. **b.** The Fallopian tube. 1842.

‖**Sal-prunella** (sæ·lprune·lă). 1677. [mod. L. *sal prunella* or *prunellæ*; see SAL and PRUNELLA[3].] Fused nitre cast into moulds.

Salse (sæls). 1832. [- Fr. *salse* (Humboldt) - It. *salsa*, orig. proper name of a mud volcano at Sassuolo, near Modena.] *Geol.* A mud volcano.

Salsify (sæ·lsifi). 1675. [- Fr. *salsifis* (also †*salsefie*, *-fique*, †*sassefrique*) - It. †*salsefica* (mod. *sassefrica*), earlier †*erba salsifica*; of unkn. origin.] A biennial composite plant, the Purple Goat's-beard, *Tragopogon porrifolius*, producing an esculent root.

Black s., *Scorzonera hispanica.*

‖**Salsola** (sæ·lsŏlă). 1801. [mod.L. - It. †*salsola*, dim. of *salso* salt, *adj.*] A genus of herbaceous plants belonging to the family *Chenopodiaceæ*; esp. *S. soda*, a species yielding soda. Also, a plant of this genus. Hence **Salsola·ceous** *a.* belonging to or resembling the genus *S.*

Salsuginous (sælsi**ū**·dʒinəs), *a.* 1657. [f. L. *salsugo*, *-gin-* saltness (f. *salsus* adj. salt) + -OUS.] †Impregnated with salt; brackish. **b.** Of plants: Growing in salt-impregnated soil.

Salt (sǫlt), *sb.*[1] [OE. *salt*, *sealt* = OS. *salt* (Du. *zout*), (O)HG. *salz*, ON., Goth. *salt* :- Gmc. **saltam*, subst. use of adj. **saltaz* (SALT *a.*), extension of IE. **sal-*, repr. by L. *săl*, *sal-*, Gr. ἅλς.] **1.** A substance, sodium chloride (NaCl), extensively prepared for use as a condiment, a preservative of animal food, and in various industrial processes. Freq. called *common s.* **2.** Taken as a type of a necessary adjunct of food, and hence as a symbol of hospitality. late ME. **b.** With ref. to the bitter saline taste of tears 1595. **c.** With ref. to the saltness of the sea, in phrases denoting inclination for a seafaring life 1886. **3.** *fig.* **a.** *The s. of the earth* (after Matt. 5:13): the excellent of the earth; in recent trivial use, the powerful, aristocratic, or wealthy OE. **b.** That which gives liveliness, freshness, or piquancy to a person's character, life, etc. 1579. **c.** Poignancy of expression; pungent wit; †point 1573. **4.** †**a.** *Old Chem.* A solid soluble non-inflammable substance having a taste -1797. **b.** *Salt* (*salts*) *of lemon(s)*, binoxalate of potash, potash combined with oxalic acid 1815. **c.** *colloq. pl.* (*a*) Smelling salts 1767. (*b*) Short for *Epsom salts* (see EPSOM) 1772. **5.** *Chem.* A compound formed by the union of an acid radical with a basic radical; an acid having the whole or part of its hydrogen replaced by a metal. (In wider theoretical use the term 'salt' includes acids, as salts of hydrogen.) 1790. **6.** = SALT-CELLAR 1493. **7.** *pl.* Salt marshes or saltings 1621. **8.** *pl.* Salt water entering a river from the sea 1658. **9.** *colloq.* A sailor, esp. one of much experience 1840.

1. They threw the s. over their shoulders,.. in propitiation of evil powers, when they spilled it at table 1884. *White s.*, salt refined mainly for household use (as contrasted with rock-salt, which is brownish-red). *In s.*, sprinkled with s. or immersed in brine; in pickle. *To cast, drop a pinch of, put, s. on the tail of*, to capture, in allusion to the joc. advice given to children to catch birds by this means. *With a grain of s.* [= mod.L. *cum grano salis*], (to accept a statement) with some reserve. (*To be*) *worth one's s.*, efficient or capable. **2.** Phr. *To eat s. with* (a person), *to eat* (a person's) *s.*, to enjoy his hospitality; also occas. to be dependent on him. **b.** The s. of most vnrighteous Teares SHAKS. **3. b.** Wee haue some s. of our youth in vs SHAKS. **c.** Humour, the s. of well-bred conversation 1874. *Attic s.*: see ATTIC *a.* 2. **6.** Under every s. there was a bill of fare PEPYS. Phr. *Above* (or *below, beneath, under*) *the s.*, at the upper (or lower) part of the table, *i.e.* among the more honoured (or less honoured) guests (with ref. to the formerly prevailing custom of placing a large s.-cellar in the middle of a dining-table). **9.** If you want to hear about the sea, talk to an 'old s.' 1877.

Comb.: **s. bottom** *U.S.*, a 'bottom' (BOTTOM *sb.* 4) covered with saline efflorescence; **s. bush,** any of the plants of the genus *Atriplex*, which grow extensively on the interior plains of Australia; **-cake,** (*a*) s. in the form of a cake; (*b*) crude sulphate of soda; **s. glaze,** a thin glaze of silicate of soda, produced on some stoneware by throwing common salt into the furnace while the ware is still glowing; **-lick,** a place where cattle collect to lick the earth impregnated with s.; **-looking** *a.* of sailor-like appearance; **-marsh,** marsh overflowed or flooded by the sea; **s. mine,** a mine yielding rock salt; **-pit,** a pit where s. is obtained; **-pond,** a pond into which sea-water is run in order to be evaporated; **-radical** *Chem.*, in the binary theory of salts, any body which forms a s. with a metal or its equivalent; **-stand,** a salt-cellar; **-tax** = GABELLE 1; **-well,** a salt spring or well; now, a bored well from which brine is obtained; **-works,** a s. manufactory. Hence **Sa·ltless** *a.* without s.; unsalted. **Sa·ltly** *adv.* with the taste or smell of s. **Sa·ltness,** the property or state of being s., or impregnated with s.

†**Salt,** *sb.*[2] 1519. [– Fr. *saut* (lit. 'leap') :– L. *saltus*, f. *salire* leap. Cf. ASSAUT *adv.*] Sexual desire or excitement (usu., of a bitch) –1648.

Salt (sǫlt), *a.*[1] [OE. *s(e)alt* = OFris. *salt*, ON. *saltr* :– Gmc. **saltaz* adj. See SALT *sb.*[1]] **1.** Impregnated with or containing salt; hence, having a taste like that of salt; saline. **2.** Cured, preserved, or seasoned with salt; salted OE. **3.** †**a.** Of fishes: Living in the sea; opp. to *freshwater*. **b.** Of plants: Growing in the sea or on salt marshes. ME. **4.** Of speech, wit, etc.: Pungent, stinging. Now *rare*. 1600.

1. He seylith in the salte se CHAUCER. Salte teeres CHAUCER. Sea-mud, salt-sand,..and river-sludge 1838. The keen s. air 1873. **2.** S. cod for Lent 1861. Phrases (*Naut. joc.*): **S. eel,** a rope's end. **S. horse:** salted beef. **S. junk:** see JUNK *sb.*[2] 3. **S. rising** (*U.S.*), salted batter used as a leaven for bread.

†**Salt,** *a.*[2] 1541. [aphet. f. ASSAUT *adv.* in phr. *to go* or *be assaut*. Cf. SALT *sb.*[2]] Of bitches: In heat –1737. **b.** *transf.* Of persons: Lecherous, salacious; hence (of desire), inordinate –1683.

b. Whose s. imagination yet hath wrong'd Your well defended honor SHAKS.

Salt (sǫlt), *v.* [OE. *s(e)altan* = MLG. *solten*, Du. *zouten*, OHG. *salzan*, ON. *salta*, Goth. *saltan*; Gmc. f. **salt-* SALT *sb.*[1]] **1.** *trans.* To cure or preserve with salt, either in solid form or in the form of brine. Also with *down*. **2. a.** In biblical use: To sprinkle salt upon (a sacrifice); to rub (a new-born child) with salt. **b.** To rub salt into (a wound). **c.** To sprinkle (snow) with salt in order to melt it. ME. **3.** To season with salt OE. **4.** To render salt or salty. Also *fig.*, to embitter. 1786. **5.** *fig.* To season; to render poignant or piquant 1576. **6.** *Photogr.* To impregnate (paper, etc.) with a solution of salt or a mixture of salts 1879. **b.** To treat with chemical salts 1904. **7.** *Comm. slang. To s. an invoice, account*, etc.: to put down an extreme price for each article. *To s. books*: to make fictitious entries in books, so as to swell the apparent turn-over, when selling a business, etc. 1882. **8.** *Mining slang.* To make (a mine) appear to be a paying one by fraudulently introducing rich ore, sprinkling gold dust in it, etc. 1864.

1. In Ffraunce the peple salten but lytill mete, except thair bacon 1460. Snails she had salted down in a barrel 1875. Phr. *To s. down, away* (slang), to put by, store away (money, stock). **5. b.** *To s. down* (U.S. colloq.), to 'dress' down 1904. **8.** He purchased some valuable specimens of gold quartz, with which he salted the estate 1892.

Saltant (sæ·ltănt), *a.* 1601. [– L. *saltans, -ant-*, pr. pple. of *saltare* dance, frequent. of *salire* leap; see -ANT.] †**a.** Leaping, dancing –1827. **b.** *Her.* Applied to small animals when salient 1850.

‖**Saltarello** (sæltăre·lo). 1724. [It. *salterello*, Sp. *saltarelo*, rel. to It. *saltare*, Sp. *saltar* leap, dance :– L. *saltare*; see prec.] An Italian and Spanish dance for one couple, in which there are frequent sudden skips or jumps. Also, the music for this.

Saltate (sæ·lteⁱt), *v. rare.* 1623. [– *saltat-*, pa. ppl. stem of L. *saltare*; see SALTANT, -ATE[3].] *intr.* To leap, jump, skip.

Saltation (sæltēⁱ·ʃən). 1623. [– L. *saltatio, -on-*, f. as prec.; see -ION.] **1.** Leaping, bounding, or jumping; a leap 1646. **b.** *spec.* Dancing; a dance 1623. **c.** *fig.* An abrupt movement, change, or transition 1844. †**2.** *spec.* Pulsation or spurting forth of blood –1767.

1. Locusts..being ordained for s., their hinder legs doe far exceed the other SIR T. BROWNE. **c.** We greatly suspect..that she [*sc.* Nature] does make considerable jumps in the way of variation now and then, and that these saltations give rise to some of the gaps which appear to exist in the series of known forms HUXLEY.

Saltatorial (sæltătōᵊ·riăl), *a.* 1789. [f. L. *saltatorius* SALTATORY + -AL[1].] **1.** Of, pertaining to, or characterized by leaping (or *spec.* dancing). **2.** Adapted for leaping; *spec.* belonging to the group *Saltatoria* of insects 1842. So **Saltato·rious** *a.*

Saltatory (sæ·ltătəri), *a.* 1656. [– L. *saltatorius*, f. *saltator*, agent-noun of *saltare*; see SALTANT, -ORY[2].] Of, pertaining to, characterized by, or adapted for leaping or dancing; *spec.* = prec. 2. **b.** *fig.* Proceeding by abrupt movement 1844.

I soon began to avoid exhibiting my s. talents, and I seldom danced EDGEWORTH. The Frog is a small s. Reptile 1874. **b.** Nature hates calculators; her methods are s. and impulsive EMERSON.

Sa·lt-cat. ME. [orig. northern; the second element is unexplained.] A mass of salt, or salt mixed with other matter; *esp.* a mixture of salt, gravel, old mortar or lime, cummin seed, and stale urine, used to attract pigeons and to keep them at home.

Sa·lt-ce:llar. late ME. [f. SALT *sb.*[1] + *saler, sel(l)er* – AFr. **saler(e*, OFr. *sal(l)iere* (mod. *salière*), also *salier* :– med.L. *salarium, salaria*, f. L. *sal* salt; see -ARIUM, -ER[2] 2. Assim. in sp. to CELLAR (XVII).] **1.** A small vessel placed on the table for holding salt. **2.** The depression above the collar-bone, when conspicuous, in a woman's neck, regarded as a disfigurement 1913.

Salted (sǫ·ltėd), *ppl. a.* ME. [f. SALT *sb.*[1] or *v.* + -ED.] **1.** Cured, preserved, or pickled with salt. **2.** Containing or impregnated with salt 1526. **b.** Treated with salt 1824. **3.** *fig.* 'Seasoned' with wit or good sense; sensible 1647. **4.** *slang* or *colloq.* Of horses, etc.: Seasoned; hence of persons: Experienced in some business or occupation 1879. **5.** *slang.* Of a mine, business, etc.: Having its value fraudulently enhanced 1886.

4. A 's.' horse will always command a good price 1879. An old s. trader 1892. **5.** Their bogus companies and their s. gold-mines 1889.

Salter (sǫ·ltəɹ). [OE. *sealtere*, f. *sealtan* SALT *v.*; see -ER[1].] **1.** A manufacturer of or dealer in salt; also *spec.* = DRYSALTER. **2.** A workman at a salt-works 1606. **3.** One who salts meat or fish 1611.

Saltern (sǫ·ltəɹn). [OE. *sealtærn*, f. *sealt* SALT *sb.*[1] + *ærn* building, dwelling, house (cf. BARN, RANSACK).] A building in which salt is made by boiling or evaporation; a salt-works; a plot of land, laid out in pools and walks, in which sea-water is allowed to evaporate naturally.

Saltigrade (sæ·ltigrēⁱd), *a.* and *sb.* 1840. [f. mod.L. *Saltigradæ* pl., f. *saltus* leap + *gradi* to advance, step.] *Zool.* **A.** *adj.* Belonging to the *Saltigradæ*, a group of vagabond spiders having legs adapted for leaping. **B.** *sb.* A spider of this group.

‖**Saltimbanco** (sæltimbæ·ŋko). 1646. [– It. *saltimbanco*, f. *saltare* leap + *in* on + *banco* bench.] A mountebank; a quack.

Saltimbancoes, Quacksalvers, and Charlatans 1646.

Salting (sǫ·ltiŋ), *vbl. sb.* ME. [f. SALT *v.* + -ING[1].] The action of SALT *v.*; *spec.* **1.** The curing of meat, fish, etc., with salt. **2.** Chiefly *pl.* Salt lands 1712.

Saltire (sæ·ltəiᵊɹ). late ME. [Early forms *sawturoure, sawtire*, later *saltier -ire* – OFr. *saut(e)our, -ouer, sau(l)toir*, stirrup cord (perh. forming a deltoid figure when in use), stile with cross-pieces, saltire :– med.L. *saltatorium*, subst. use of n. of L. *saltatorius* SALTATORY.] *Her.* An ordinary in the form of a St. Andrew's cross, formed by a bend and a bend sinister, crossing each other. Hence *In s.*: crossed like the limbs of a St. Andrew's cross. Hence **Sa·ltire-ways, -wise** *advs.* in s.

Saltish (sǫ·ltiʃ), *a.* 1477. [f. SALT *a.*[1] + -ISH[1].] †**a.** Salt, salty. **b.** Somewhat salt. Hence **Sa·ltish-ly** *adv.*, **-ness.**

Sa·lt-pan. 1493. [Cf. Du. *zoutpan*, G. *salzpfanne*).] **a.** (Usu. *pl.*) A shallow depression near the sea, in which sea-water evaporates, leaving a deposit of salt; in Africa, applied (after Du. *zoutpan*) to dried-up salt lakes or marshes. **b.** A shallow vessel in which brine is evaporated in salt-making; *pl.* a salt-works.

Saltpetre (sǫltpī·təɹ). Also (now *U.S.*) **-peter.** 1501. [alt., by assim. to SALT *sb.*[1], of †*salpetre* (XIV) – (O)Fr. *salpètre* – med.L. *salpetra*, prob. for **sal petræ* 'salt of rock.'] A crystalline substance, potassium nitrate, having a saline taste; the chief constituent of gunpowder.

Chili or *cubic s.*, sodium nitrate.

attrib. and *Comb.*: as **s. paper** = TOUCH PAPER; **s. rot,** white efflorescence which forms on new or damp walls, caused by s. working through to the surface. Hence **Saltpe·treing,** the formation of s. rot.

Salt rheum. 1590. [SALT *a.*[1]] †**1.** A running cold. SHAKS. **2.** *U.S.* A popular name for various cutaneous eruptions, particularly for those of eczema 1828.

Salt water, *sb.* and *a.* OE. [SALT *a.*[1]] **A.** *sb.* Water impregnated with salt; sea-water. **b.** Applied *joc.* to tears. late ME. **B.** *attrib.* as *adj.* Of, pertaining to, consisting of, or living in salt water 1528. **b.** In specific names of sea animals, as *salt-water louse*, etc. 1828.

Sa·ltwort. 1568. [prob. after Du. *zoutkruid.*] **1.** Any plant of the genus *Salsola*, spec. *S. kali* (Common or Prickly S.). **2.** Black S., *Glaux maritima.* = MILKWORT 2. 1597. **3.** A plant of the genus *Salicornia*, esp. *S. herbacea*; = GLASSWORT a. 1597.

Salty (sǫ·lti), *a.* 1440. [f. SALT *sb.*[1] + -Y[1].] **1.** = SALT *a.*[1] 1. †**2.** Consisting of salt (*rare*) –1665. Hence **Sa·ltiness.**

Salubrious (săl¹ū·briəs), *a.* 1547. [f. L. *salubris* (f. *salus* health) + -OUS; see -IOUS.] Favourable or conducive to health.

A species of food so very palatable and s. as turtle 1748. In summer the air is remarkably s. 1774. Hence **Salu·brious-ly** *adv.*, **-ness.**

Salubrity (săl¹ū·brĭti). late ME. [– L. *salubritas*, f. *salubris*; see prec., -ITY.] **1.** The quality of being salubrious. ¶**2.** Healthy condition, health 1654.

1. The s. of the air had a surprising effect in strengthening both the appetite and digestion 1767.

†**Salue·,** *v.* ME. [– (O)Fr. *saluer* :– L. *salutare* SALUTE *v.*] *trans.* = SALUTE *v.* –1606.

And he saleweth hire with glad entente CHAUCER.

Saluki (sălū·ki, sălū·gi). 1890. Also **sa-, seluġ(h)i.** [– Arab. *salūḳī.*] The Arabian gazelle-hound.

Salutary (sæ·liŭtări), *a.* 1490. [– (O)Fr. *salutaire* or L. *salutaris*, f. *salus, salut-* health, welfare, greeting, salutation, rel. to *salvus* safe; see -ARY[2].] **1.** Conducive to health; usu., serving to promote recovery from disease, or to counteract a deleterious influence 1649. **2.** Conducive to well-being; beneficial. Often with fig. notion of sense 1. 1490.

1. Abana and Pharphar..were not so s. as the waters of Jordan to cure Naamans leprosie 1649. **2.** The natives having a s. dread of the guns LIVINGSTONE.

Salutation (sæliŭtēⁱ·ʃən). late ME. [– (O)Fr. *salutation* or L. *salutatio, -on-*, f. *salutare*; see SALUTE, -ATION.] **1.** The action, or an act, of saluting; a manner of saluting; an utterance, form of words, gesture, or movement, by which one person salutes another. **b.** *Naut.* The action of saluting by the firing of guns, lowering of flags, etc.; an instance of this. Now *rare.* 1585. **2.** Ellipt. for 'I offer salutation'. *arch.* 1535.

1. In all publick meetings, or private addresses.. use those forms of s. which..[are] usual amongst the most sober persons JER. TAYLOR. He had bowed his head and taken off his hat in s. 1851. *The Angelical S.*, †*the s. of our Lady*, etc., the AVE MARY (see *Luke* 1:29); also, a representation of the Annunciation. **2.** S. and greeting to you all SHAKS.

Salutatorian (săliūtătōᵊ·riăn). *U.S.* 1847. [f. next + -AN[1] 1.] The student who delivers the 'salutatory' (see next A. b) oration at the annual commencement day exercises.

Salutatory (săliū·tătəri), *a.* and *sb.* 1641. [– L. *salutatorius*, f. *salutare* SALUTE; see -ORY[1] and [2].] **A.** *adj.* Pertaining to, or of the nature of, a salutation 1895. **b.** *U.S.* Applied to the address of welcome (usu. in Latin), which introduces the exercises of commencement in American schools and colleges 1702. **B.** *sb.* †**1.** [= med.L. *salutatorium.*] A place of salutation –1656. **2.** *U.S.* The 'salutatory' oration (see A. b) 1851. Hence **Salu·tatorily** *adv.* (*rare*) by way of greeting.

Salute (săl[i]ū·t), *sb.* late ME. [Partly – (O)Fr. *salut* (as sb. to *saluer* SALUE), partly from the Eng. verb.] **1.** An utterance, gesture, or action of any kind by which one person salutes another; a salutation. **2.** A kiss, by way of salutation 1590. **3.** *Mil.* and *Naut.* **a.** A discharge of cannon or small arms, display of flags, dipping of sails, cheering of men, manning the yards, etc., as a mark of respect, or as military, naval, or official honour, for a person, nation, event, etc. 1698. **b.** A raising of the hand to the cap by an inferior when meeting or leaving, addressing, or addressed by a superior, both being in uniform 1832. **c.** The position of the sword, rifle, hand, etc., or the attitude assumed in saluting 1833. **4.** *Fencing.* A formal greeting of swordsmen when about to engage, consisting of a conventional series of guards, thrusts, etc. 1809.

1. O what avails me now..that s. Hale highly favour'd, among women blest MILT. **3. c.** Phr. (*To stand*) *at* (*the*) *s.*

Salute (săl[i]u·t), *v.* late ME. [– L. *salutare*, f. *salus, salut-* health.] **1.** *trans.* To accost or address with some customary formula, or with words expressing good wishes, respect, etc.; to greet in words. **b.** To hail or greet (as king, etc.) 1560. **c.** *poet.* Of birds, etc.: To greet (the sun, the dawn) with song 1682. **2.** To greet with some gesture or visible action conventionally expressive of respect or courteous recognition 1440. **b.** *absol.* and *intr.* To perform a salutation 1589. **c.** *spec.* in *Mil.* and *Naval* use. (*a*) *trans.* To pay respect to (a superior) by a prescribed bodily movement, the presenting of arms, or the like. (*b*) Of a ship, a body of troops, a commander: To honour or ceremoniously recognize by a discharge of artillery or small arms, by lowering of flags, or the like. (*c*) *absol.* and *intr.* To perform a salute. 1582. **d.** *Fencing.* To perform the salute used in fencing 1809. **e.** *trans.* To kiss, or greet with a kiss (*arch.*) 1716. †**3.** To pay one's respects to; to pay a complimentary visit to –1698. **4.** *transf.* and *fig.* Of inanimate things: To appear or come forth as if in welcome of; to approach, come into contact with; †(in Shaks.) to affect or act upon in any way 1440. **b.** Of a sight or sound: To strike (the eye or ear) 1586.

1. Being admitted to his presence they saluted him in the queen's name 1845. Phr. *I s. you*, used as itself a formula of salutation; I s. thee, Mantovano, I that loved thee since my day began TENNYSON. **b.** King Henrie..for the time was saluted Lord of Ireland 1617. **2.** Deere Earth, I doe s. thee with my hand SHAKS. **e.** I had the honour of saluting the far famed Miss Flora Macdonald JOHNSON. **4.** Would I had no being If this s. my blood a iot SHAKS. Hence **Salu·ter,** one who salutes.

Salutiferous (sæliuti·fĕrəs), *a.* 1540. [f. L. *salutifer* (f. as prec.) + *-ous*; see -FEROUS.] Conducive to health, well-being, safety, or salvation.

Safe, wholesome and s. Medecins 1604. The ..s. streames of the waters of life 1629. Hence **Saluti·ferously** *adv.*

Salvability (sælvăbi·lĭti). 1654. [f. as next + -ITY.] *Theol.* Capability of being saved.

Salvable (sæ·lvăb'l), *a.* 1667. [– med.L. **salvabilis* in sense 1 (see SALVE *v.*[2], -ABLE); sense 2 f. SALVE *v.*[3] + -ABLE.] **1.** *Theol.* Capable of being saved, admitting of salvation. **2.** Of a ship, cargo: That can be salvaged 1797.

1. He is not in a s. state WESLEY. Hence **Sa·lvableness.**

Salvage (sæ·lvėdʒ), *sb.* 1645. [– (O)Fr. *salvage* – med.L. *salvagium*, f. L. *salvare* SAVE *v.*; see -AGE.] **1.** A compensation to which those persons are entitled who have by their voluntary efforts saved a ship or its cargo from impending peril or rescued it from actual loss; e.g. from shipwreck (*civil s.*) or from capture by the enemy (*military* or *hostile s.*). **2.** The action of saving a ship or its cargo from wreck, capture, etc. 1713. **b.** *gen.* The salving of property from fire or other danger 1878. **3.** Property salved or saved 1755.

2. S. of life is rewarded at a higher rate than s. of property 1886. Phr. *To make s. of.*

Comb.: **s. corps,** a body of men kept in some towns to save property from fire; a fire brigade; **s. money** = sense 1. Hence **Sa·lvage** *v. trans.* to make s. of; to save from shipwreck, fire, etc.

Salvage: see SAVAGE, *a.* and *sb.*

Salvarsan (sæ·lvăɹsæn). 1910. [– G. (P. Ehrlich), f. L. *salv(are* save + G. *ars(enik.*] *Chem.* Proprietary name of an arsenical compound, dihydrochloride of dioxy-diamino-arseno-benzene, $C_{12}H_{12}O_2N_2$-$As_2(HCl)_2 2H_2O$, used in the treatment of syphilis; also called 606.

Largely superseded by a later invention of Ehrlich, *neo-salvarsan* or 914.

Salvation (sælvēⁱ·ʃən). [ME. *sa(u)vacioun, salv-* – OFr. *sauvacion, salv-* (mod. *salvation*) – eccl. L. *salvatio, -on-* rendering Gr. *σωτηρία*, f. *salvare* SAVE *v.*] **1.** The saving of the soul; the deliverance from sin, and admission to eternal bliss, wrought for man by the atonement of Christ. [eccl. L. *salvatio*, rendering Gr. *σωτηρία*.] **2.** *gen.* Preservation from destruction, loss, or calamity. (In mod. use chiefly with some allusion to sense 1.) late ME. **3.** A source, cause, means of salvation; a person or thing that saves. Now chiefly in phr. *to be the s. of.* late ME.

1. Euen so worke out your awne saluacion with feare and tremblynge COVERDALE *Phil.* 2:12. **2.** Shall Ionathan die, who hath wrought this great saluation in Israel? 1 *Sam.* 14:45. **3.** Sleep is the s. of the nervous system 1878. Hence **Salva·tional** *a.* (*rare*). **Salva·tionalism** = SALVATIONISM b.

Salvation Army. 1878. An organization, on a quasi-military model, founded by the Rev. William Booth for the revival of religion among the masses.

Salva·tionism. 1883. [f. SALVATION + -ISM.] **a.** Religious teaching which lays prime stress on 'salvation', or the saving of the soul. **b.** The principles or methods of the Salvation Army. So **Salva·tionist,** a member of the Salvation Army.

Salvatory (sæ·lvătəri), *sb.* 1549. [– med.L. *salvatorium* place of preservation, f. *salvare* SAVE *v.*; see -ORIUM. Sense 1 is due to assoc. with SALVE *sb.*[1]] †**1.** A box for holding ointment –1715. **2.** *gen.* A repository for safe storage (*rare*) 1677.

Salvatory (sæ·lvătəri), *a.* *rare.* 1830. [f. SALVATION on the model of *preservation/preservatory*, etc.] Saving, imparting safety or salvation (*to*).

Salve (sāv), *sb.*[1] [OE. *salf, sealf(e* = OS. *salba* (Du. *zalf*), OHG. *salba* (G. *salbe*) :– Gmc. **salbō*; cf. SALVE *v.*[1]] **1.** A healing ointment for application to wounds or sores. **b.** A mixture, usu. of tar and grease, for smearing sheep 1523. **2.** *fig.* **a.** A remedy (esp. for spiritual disease, sorrow, etc.). Now *rare.* ME. **b.** *esp.* Something which serves to soothe wounded feelings, honour, or a tender conscience 1736.

2. b. Let us hope that this little s. to self-esteem never lost its efficacy 1874.

†**Salve,** *sb.*[2] 1577. [– Fr. *salve* – It. *salva*; see SALVO *sb.*[2]] = SALVO *sb.*[2] –1693.

†**Salve,** *sb.*[3] 1628. [f. SALVE *v.*[2] Cf. SALVO *sb.*[1]] **a.** A solution of a difficulty; also, a sophistical excuse or evasion. **b.** A salvo or means of salving a person's honour, etc. –1665.

‖**Salve** (sæ·lvi), *sb.*[4] late ME. [L., = 'hail', 'good morning'; 2nd sing. imper. of *salvēre* be well.] **1.** The utterance of the word *s.* or its equivalent; a salutation on meeting 1583. **2.** (More fully *S. Regina.*) In the R. C. Ch., an antiphon, beginning 'Salve, Regina', now recited after the Divine Office from Trinity Sunday to Advent. A musical setting for this. late ME.

Salve (sāv), *v.*[1] [OE. *s(e)alfian* = OFris. *salvia*, OS. *salbon* (Du. *zalven*), OHG. *salbōn* (G. *salben*), Goth. *salbōn*; f. Gmc. **salbō* SALVE *sb.*[1]] **1.** *trans.* To anoint (a wound, etc.) with salve or healing unguent. *Obs.* or *arch.* **b.** *trans.* To smear (sheep) with a mixture of tar and butter, or the like 1523. †**2.** In extended sense: To heal or remedy (a disease). Chiefly *fig.*, to heal (sin, sorrow, etc.). –1624. †**b.** To heal (a person) *of* (sickness, sin, etc.) –1596. †**3.** *fig.* To heal, remedy, make good, make up, smooth over (something amiss, a disgrace, offence, etc.) –1712. **4.** *fig.* (From sense 1.) To soothe (irritated feeling, an uneasy conscience, etc.) 1825.

1. Since plain speech salves the wound it seems to make BROWNING. **3.** But Ebranck salved both their infamies with noble deedes SPENSER. **4.** In the endeavour to s. their wounded pride 1878.

†**Salve,** *v.*[2] 1571. [app. – *salvare* SAVE *v.* in med.L. senses, and infl. by SOLVE *v.*] **1.** *Astr. To s.* (*the appearances, the phenomena*), to frame a hypothesis which will account for all the observed facts of the apparent motions of the heavenly bodies. Hence *gen.*, to account for by hypothesis. –1691. **2.** To clear up, account for (a difficulty, point in dispute, etc.); to overcome (a doubt, objection); to harmonize (a discrepancy) –1744. **3.** To render tenable (an opinion); to vindicate from incredibility (an alleged fact) –1720. **4.** To maintain unhurt (one's honour, credit, etc.). Hence, to make good (one's oath). –1814.

2. What may we do..to s. this seeming inconsistence? MILT. **4.** An afterthought to s. decorum SOUTHEY.

Salve (sælv), *v.*[3] 1706. [In XVIII app. back-formation from SALVAGE.] *trans.* To save (a ship, its cargo) from loss at sea; to save (property) from destruction by fire; to make salvage of.

Salver (sæ·lvəɹ). 1661. [f. Fr. *salve* tray for presenting objects to the king, or its source Sp. *salva* †foretasting or assaying of food or drink, tray on which assayed food was placed, f. *salvar* SAVE, render safe, assay; the ending *-er* is due to assoc. with *platter.*] A tray, used for handing refreshments, presenting letters, etc.

Comb.: **s.-shaped** *a.* (*Bot.*) = HYPOCRATERIFORM *a.*

‖**Salvia** (sæ·lviă). 1844. [mod.L. (Tournefort, 1700) use of L. *salvia* SAGE *sb.*[1]] *Bot.*

A large genus of *Labiatæ*, including the common sage; a plant of this genus.

Salvo (sæ·lvo), *sb.*[1] 1642. [– L., abl. n. sing. of *salvus* SAFE *a.*, as occurring in med.L. law phrases like *salvo jure* 'without prejudice to the right of' (some specified person), etc.] **1.** A saving clause; a reservation. Const. *of* (a right, etc.). **2.** A dishonest mental reservation; a quibbling evasion; a consciously bad excuse 1665. †**3.** A solution (of a difficulty), an answer (to an objection) –1770. **4.** An expedient for saving (a person's reputation) or soothing (offended pride, conscience) 1754.

1. With an express s. of their right to liberty of conscience 1826. **2.** Some new attempt on his part to find a s. for staying in office 1828. **4.** This would be a s. for the disgrace of removing them 1855.

Salvo (sæ·lvo), *sb.*[2] 1591. [repl. earlier SALVE *sb.*[2] (and occas. †*salva*) by substitution of *-o* for *-a* (cf. -ADO); ult. – It. *salva*.] **1.** A salute consisting in the simultaneous discharge of artillery or other firearms 1719. **2.** A simultaneous discharge of artillery or other firearms, whether with hostile intent or otherwise 1591. **b.** *transf.* Chiefly used for a 'volley' of applause 1734.

2. The Russians..were firing salvoes by batteries of eight guns 1879. Hence **Sa·lvo** *v.* to salute (a vessel, etc.) by firing of a s.

Sal volatile (sæ:l vǒlæ·tĭli). 1654. [mod. L., 'volatile salt'; see SAL and VOLATILE *a.*] Ammonium carbonate, *esp.* an aromatic solution of this used as a restorative in fainting fits.

Salvor (sæ·lvəɹ, sæ·lvǫɹ). 1678. [f. SALVE *v.*[3] + -OR 2.] **1.** One who saves or helps to save vessels or cargo from loss at sea. **2.** A vessel used in salvage 1815.

Sam (sæm), *sb. slang*. 1823. [In sense 2 prob. shortening of †*salmon*, †*salomon*, cant term for 'alter or masse', in phr. †*by the salomon*, †*by salmon* (XVIII), presumably a perverted use of L. (Vulg.) *Salomon* Solomon.] **1.** *To stand S.*: to pay expenses, esp. for refreshment or drink. **2.** *Upon my S.*: a jocular asseveration 1879.

†**Sam,** *adv.* ME. [Shortened f. OE. **samen*, *somen*, ME. *samen* together.] Together; mutually –1600.

For what concord han light and darke s.? SPENSER.

‖**Samara** (sæ·mără). 1577. [mod.L. use of L. *samara* seed of the elm.] *Bot.* The indehiscent winged fruit of the elm, ash, etc.

Samaritan (sămæ·rităn), *sb.* and *a.* OE. [– late L. *Samaritanus*, f. Gr. Σαμαρείτης, f. Σαμαρεία; see -ITE[1], -AN.] **A.** *sb.* A native or inhabitant of Samaria, a district of Palestine; *esp.* one who adheres to the religious system which had its origin in Samaria. **b.** *fig.* with ref. to the 'good Samaritan'; see *Luke* 10:33. 1644. **B.** *adj.* Of or pertaining to Samaria or the Samaritans. late ME.

S. Pentateuch, a recension of the Hebrew Pentateuch used by the Samaritans. Hence **Sama·ritanism,** the S. religious system; also, imitation of the 'good S.'

Samarium (sămēº·riŏm). 1883. [f. SAMAR(SKITE + -IUM.] *Chem.* A metallic element (symbol Sm); the bands supposed to indicate it were first found in the spectrum of samarskite.

‖**Samarra** (sămæ·ră). 1688. [= med.L. *samarra* (Du Cange); see CYMAR, SIMAR.] *Hist.* A garment, painted with flames, worn on the way to execution by persons condemned by the Inquisition to be burnt.

Samarskite (sămā·ɹskəit). 1849. [Named after Col. *Samarski*; see -ITE[1] 2 b.] *Min.* A complex columbate of uranium and other bases.

Sambo (sæ·mbo). *Pl.* **-bos, -boes.** 1748. [– Sp. *zambo*, identified with *zambo* bandy-legged; see ZAMBO.] **1.** Applied in America and Asia to persons of various degrees of mixed Negro and Indian or European blood. **2.** (With capital S.) A nickname for a Negro. [perh. a different word.] 1860.

1. A quadroon looks down upon a mulatto, while a mulatto looks down upon a s., that is, half mulatto half negro MARRYAT.

Sam Browne (sæm braun). 1915. In full *Sam Browne belt* (1898): an officers' field belt having a supporting strap over the right shoulder, invented by Gen. Sir *Sam*uel J. *Browne* (1824–1901).

‖**Sambuca** (sæmbiū·kă). late ME. [– L. *sambuca* – Gr. σαμβύκη, cogn. with Aram. *śabbᵉkâ*.] **1.** *Ancient Music.* A triangular stringed instrument having a shrill tone. **2.** *Rom. Antiq.* A military engine for storming walls 1489.

Sambur (sæ·mbəɹ). 1698. [– Hindi *sābar*, *sāmbar*.] The Indian elk, *Rusa aristotelis*.

Same (sēⁱm), *a.*, *pron.*, *adv.* [– ON. *same* masc., *sama* fem., n. = OHG., Goth. *sama* :– Gmc. adj. **samaz* :– IE. **somós*, whence Skr. *samás* level, equal, same, Gr. ὁμός (see HOMO-). Superseded ILK and SELF in general use.] The ordinary adjectival and pronominal designation of identity. Normally preceded by *the*, exc. after a demonstrative; the omission of the article occurs only in dial. or vulgar speech and in certain specially elliptical varieties of diction (e.g. in commercial correspondence). **A.** *adj.* **I. 1.** Identical with what is indicated in the following context. Const. *as*, *with*, or relative clause. **2.** Identical with what has been indicated ME. **3.** Expressing the identity of an object designated by different names, standing in different relations, or related to different subjects or objects 1621. **b.** More explicitly, *one and the s.* 1551. **4.** Coupled for emphasis with a synonymous adj., as in *the very s.* ME. **5.** Appended redundantly to a demonstrative (*this, these, that, those, yon*). Usu. expressing some degree of irritation or contempt, sometimes playful familiarity. Now *arch.* ME.

1. The standard itself was blown down the s. night it had been set up CLARENDON. The Horse and Man on the Medal are in the s. Posture as they are on the Statue ADDISON. The Greeks and Macedonians,..looked on the Egyptian Ammon as the s. god with their own Zeus 1873. He defends it on the s. ground that he would defend the 'Lycidas' of Milton 1876. **2.** Into poudre must I crepe, ffor of that s. kynde I am. late ME. **3.** The s. Person is to be paid twice for the s. thing STEELE. All the planets travel round the Sun in the s. direction 1868. **5.** This s. Truth, is a Naked, and Open day light BACON.

Phrases. *At the s. time*: see TIME *sb.* *By the s. token*: see TOKEN *sb.*

II. In modified senses. **1.** Exactly agreeing *in* (amount, quality, etc.). Of a person: Unchanged in character, condition of health, etc. Chiefly *predic.* 1611. **b.** Corresponding in relative position 1672. **2.** *predic.* Equally acceptable or the contrary; indifferent 1803.

1. What matter where, if I be still the s. MILT. She was always the s. to me DICKENS. His salary was the s. with that of the Lord Lieutenant MACAULAY. **b.** He and I were both shot in the s. leg at Talavera THACKERAY. **2.** It's all the s. to me DICKENS.

B. *absol.* and as *pron.* **1.** The same person or persons ME. **2.** The same thing ME. †**3.** Pleonastically emphasizing a demonstrative, used absol. or with ellipsis of sb. –1611. **4.** *The s.*, †*that* (*this*) *s.*: the aforesaid person or thing. Often merely, he, she, it, they. Still common in legal documents; also (with ref. to things) in commercial language (where *the* is sometimes omitted). late ME. **b.** †As an answer when addressed by name; = 'I am he'; *colloq.* in confirming a conjecture as to the identity of a person mentioned by the speaker 1599.

2. Here that common Proverbe holds true, 'When two do the s. it is not the s.' 1677. **3.** What Letter is this s.? SHAKS. **4.** But he that shall endure vnto the end, the s. shall be saued *Matt.* 24:13. **b.** *Ben.* Count Claudio. *Clau.* Yea, the s. SHAKS.

C. *adv.* **1.** *The s.*: **a.** in the same manner. Const. *as*. (Now rare in literary use.) Also occas. = 'all the same'. 1766. **2.** *All the s.*: nevertheless, notwithstanding 1803. **3.** *Just the s.*: **a.** Exactly in the same manner. Const. *as*. **b.** None the less. 1874.

1. a. *To think the s. of*, to have the same (good) opinion of (a person); You'll never think the s. Of me again GEO. ELIOT. **2.** What you say is well worth attention; but all the s. I feel we are on the eve of a..crisis DISRAELI. **3.** And..Dillingham will continue his visits here just the s.? 1874.

Samel (sæ·mĕl), *a.* 1601. [Origin obsc.; perh. repr. an OE. **samǣled* half-burnt.] Of a brick or tile: Imperfectly burnt.

Samely (sēⁱ·mli), *a.* 1799. [f. SAME *a.* + -LY[1].] Monotonous. Hence **Sa·meliness.**

Sameness (sēⁱ·mnės). 1581. [f. SAME *a.* + -NESS.] **1.** The quality of being the same. **2.** Uniformity, monotony; an instance of this 1743.

Samian (sēⁱ·miăn), *a.* and *sb.* 1580. [f. L. *Samius*, Gr. Σάμιος + -AN.] **A.** *adj.* Of or pertaining to Samos, an island in the Ægean Sea, the birthplace of Pythagoras.

S. letter, the letter *Y*, used by Pythagoras as an emblem of the different roads of virtue and vice. **S. ware,** a fine kind of pottery found extensively on Roman sites.

B. *sb.* A native or inhabitant of Samos 1580.

Samiel (sēⁱ:miĕl). 1687. [– Turk. *samyeli* hot wind, f. Arab. *samm* poison + Turk. *yel* WIND.] The simoom.

‖**Samisen** (sæ·misen). 1864. [Jap. f. Chinese *san-hsien* (*san* three, *hsien* string).] A Japanese guitar of three strings, played with a plectrum.

Samite (sæ·məit). *Obs.* exc. *Hist.* ME. [– OFr. *samit*, ult. – med.L. *examitum* – med.Gr. ἑξάμιτον, f. Gr. ἑξα- HEXA- + μίτος thread.] A rich silk fabric worn in the Middle Ages, sometimes interwoven with gold. Also, †a garment or cushion of this.

In the myddes of the lake Arthur was ware of an arme clothed in whyte samyte MALORY.

Samlet (sæ·mlėt). 1655. [alt. of earlier *samonet* (f. SALMON + -ET) by assoc. with -LET.] A young salmon.

Sammy (sæ·mi), *v.* 1891. [Extended form of *sam* vb., of unkn. origin.] *Leather-dressing. trans.* To dry (leather) partially. So **Sa·mmier,** a machine for expressing water from skins during tanning 1884.

Samnite (sæ·mnəit), *sb.* and *a.* late ME. [– L. *Samnites* (pl.), rel. to *Sabinus* SABINE; see -ITE[1].] **A.** *sb.* One of a people of ancient Italy, believed to be an offshoot of the Sabines; their territory, Samnium, was adjacent to Latium. **B.** *adj.* Of or pertaining to the Samnites; in use among the Samnites 1696.

Samoan (sămōᵘ·ăn), *a.* and *sb.* 1846. [f. *Samoa*, an island in the Pacific, + -AN.] **A.** *adj.* Pertaining to Samoa, or the Samoans. **B.** *sb.* A native of Samoa; the Samoan language 1846.

Samosatenian (sæmosătī·niăn), *sb.* and *a.* 1597. [– late L. *Samosatenus* (Gr. Σαμοσατηνός, f. Σαμόσατα) + -IAN.] Pertaining to, a follower of, Paul of Samosata.

Samothracian (sæmoþrēⁱ·ʃ'ăn), *sb.* and *a.* 1653. [f. L. *Samothrace*, Gr. Σαμοθράκη, an island in the Ægean Sea, + -IAN.] **A.** *sb.* An inhabitant of Samothrace. **B.** *adj.* Of or pertaining to Samothrace; *esp.* with ref. to the Cabiric mysteries which originated there.

‖**Samovar** (sæmovā·ɹ). 1830. [– Russ. *samovár*, f. *samo-* self- + *varit'* boil.] A Russian tea-urn.

Samoyed(e (sæmoye·d, -ī·d), *sb.* and *a.* 1556. [– Russ. *sámoed.*] **A.** *sb.* **1.** One of a Mongolian race inhabiting Siberia. **2.** (usu. *-ede*) A dog of a white Arctic breed 1889. **B.** *adj.* Of or pertaining to the Samoyeds. Also quasi-*sb.*, their language. 1667.

A. 2. Samoyede sledge dog 1889. **B.** From the North Of Norumbega, and the Samoed shoar MILT. Hence **Samoye·dic** *a.* of or pertaining to the Samoyeds; quasi-*sb.* their language.

Samp (sæmp). *U.S.* 1643. [– Algonquin *nasamp*, lit. 'softened by water'.] Coarsely-ground Indian corn; a porridge made from it.

Sampan (sæ·mpæn). 1620. [– Chinese *san-pan* boat (*san* three, *pan* board).] Applied by Europeans in the China seas to any small boat of Chinese pattern.

Samphire (sæ·mfəiᵊɹ). 1545. [In XVI *sampere*, *sampiere* – Fr. (*herbe de*) *Saint Pierre* 'St. Peter's herb'; the later form may be due to assim. to *camphire*, var. of CAMPHOR.] **1.** The plant *Crithmum maritimum* (growing on rocks by the sea), the aromatic, saline, fleshy leaves of which are used in pickles. Also called *Rock s.* **b.** As a name for other maritime plants, esp. the glasswort (*Salicornia*) 1703. **2.** *Cookery.* The leaves of samphire, used chiefly as a pickle 1624.

1. Halfe way downe Hangs one that gathers Sampire: dreadfull Trade SHAKS.

Sample (sɑ·mp'l), *sb.* ME. [Aphetic –

AFr. *assample*, var. of OFr. *essample* EXAMPLE *sb.*] †**1.** A fact, incident, story, or suppositious case, which serves to illustrate, confirm, or render credible some proposition or statement –1529. **2.** A relatively small quantity of material, or an individual object, from which the quality of the mass, group, species, etc., which it represents may be inferred; a specimen; a pattern. Now chiefly *Comm.* late ME. †**3.** = EXAMPLE *sb.* 6. –1611. **4.** *attrib.* Serving as a sample 1820.

2. A s. of his Ingenuity 1706. The collection of samples of air for analysis 1882. **3.** Liu'd in Court.., A s. to the yongest SHAKS. **4.** That..s.-bottle of Hollands THACKERAY.

Comb. **s. card,** a piece of cardboard to which is fastened a s. of cloth, etc.; = *pattern-card.*

Sample (sa·mp'l), *v.* 1592. [f. prec.] †**1.** *trans.* To parallel; to intend as a match *for*. Also, to put in comparison *with*. –1689. †**2.** To illustrate or explain by examples or analogies; to symbolize –1664. **3.** To take a sample or samples of; to judge of the quality of (a thing) by a sample or specimen; to obtain a representative experience of 1767. **b.** To present samples or specimens of 1870.

3. I won't turn my back..on any man in the country at sampling wheat 1858.

Sampler[1] (sa·mplər). ME. [Aphetic – OFr. *essamplaire*, var. of *essemplaire* EXEMPLAR.] †**1.** An example to be imitated; a model, pattern; an archetype –1680. **2.** †**a.** A piece of embroidery serving as a pattern to be copied –1675. **b.** A piece of canvas embroidered by a beginner as a specimen of her skill, usu. containing the alphabet and some mottos, with various decorative devices 1523. **3.** *Forestry.* A young tree left standing when the rest are cut down 1535.

2. b. [To] create upon a s. Beasts that Buffon never knew CALVERLEY. Hence **Sa·mplery,** the making of samplers; s. work.

Sampler[2] (sa·mplər). 1778. [f. SAMPLE *v.* + -ER[1].] One who samples goods.

‖**Samshoo** (sæ·mʃū). 1697. [Pidgin-English; of doubtful etym.] Chinese spirits distilled from rice or sorghum.

Samson (sæ·msən). Also †**Sampson.** 1565. [– L. (Vulg.) *Sam(p)son*, Gr. Σαμψών – Heb. *šimšôn*.] The name of the Hebrew hero whose exploits are recorded in Judges 13–16, applied allus. to persons, with ref. to his enormous strength, to his having been blinded, etc. Hence **Samso·nian** (sæmsōᵘ·niăn) *a.* and *sb.* 1654.

Samson's post. 1577. [prob. named in allusion to Judges 16:29.] †**1.** A kind of mousetrap –1828. **2.** *Naut.* A strong stanchion passing through the hold of a merchant-ship, or between the decks of a man-of-war.

‖**Samurai** (sæ·murai). 1874. [Japanese.] In feudal Japan, one of the class of military retainers of the daimios; sometimes more widely, a member of the military caste. Now applied to any Japanese army officer. (Unchanged in the pl.)

San. 1927. Colloq. abbrev. of SANATORIUM (3).

Sanative (sæ·nătiv), *a.* late ME. [– OFr. *sanatif* or late L. *sanativus*, f. *sanat-*, pa. ppl. stem of L. *sanare* heal; see -IVE.] **1.** Having the power to heal; conducive to health; curative, healing. **2.** Of, pertaining to or concerned with healing 1695.

Sanatorium (sænătōᵊ·riŏm). *Pl.* **-ia.** Also *erron.* **-arium.** 1840. [– mod.L. *sanatorium*, f. *sanat-*; see prec., -ORIUM.] **1.** An establishment for the treatment of invalids, esp. convalescents and consumptives. **2.** A place with good climatic and other conditions, to which invalids resort; *spec.* a hill-station in a hot country, esp. in India, to which residents periodically resort to recuperate 1842. **3.** A room in a school, etc. for the isolation of the sick 1860.

Sanatory (sæ·nătəri), *a.* 1832. [app. a var. of SANATIVE by substitution of -ORY[2].] = SANATIVE.

2. The mechanical parts of the s. art 1870.

Sanbenito (sænbenī·to). 1560. [– Sp. *sambenito*, f. *San Benito* St. Benedict; so called ironically from its resemblance to the Benedictine scapular.] Under the Spanish Inquisition, a yellow penitential garment, resembling a scapular in shape, and having a red St. Andrew's cross before and behind, worn by a confessed and penitent heretic; also, a similar garment of a black colour ornamented with flames, devils, and other devices (occas. called a SAMARRA) worn by an impenitent confessed heretic at an auto-da-fé.

‖**Sancho** (sæ·ŋko). 1817. [Ashanti *osanku*.] A kind of simple guitar used by West African Negroes.

Sanctification (sæ:ŋktifikēⁱ·ʃən). 1526. [– Chr. L. *santificatio, -on-*, f. *sanctificat-*, pa. ppl. stem of *sanctificare*; see SANCTIFY, -ION.] **1.** *Theol.* The action of the Holy Ghost in sanctifying or making holy the believer, by the implanting within him of the Christian graces and the destruction of sinful affections. Also, the condition or process of being so sanctified. **2.** The action of consecrating or setting apart as holy or for a sacred use or purpose; hallowing 1550. **3.** *Eccl.* Canonization as a saint 1855.

1. The only sign of S. is Holiness 1754. **2.** The s. of dayes and times is a token of that thankfulnesse..which we owe to God HOOKER.

Sanctified (sæ·ŋktifəid), *ppl. a.* 1485. [f. SANCTIFY *v.* + -ED[1].] **1.** Of a person: Made holy; *spec.* made holy by the divine grace of the Holy Spirit. **2.** Affecting holiness; sanctimonious 1600. **3.** Of things: Holy or consecrated; rendered spiritually profitable 1632. **b.** Of ground, etc.: Consecrated (*rare*) 1525.

2. I see not why we should give ourselves such s. airs 1860. **3. b.** *All's Well* I. i. 152.

Sanctifier (sæ·ŋktifəiˌəɹ). 1548. [f. next + -ER[1].] **1.** *Theol.* One who sanctifies or makes holy; *spec.* the Holy Ghost. **2.** *occas.* Something that sanctifies 1753.

Sanctify (sæ·ŋktifəi), *v.* [In earliest use *seintifie* – OFr. *saintifier*, later infl. by *sanctifier* – Chr. L. *sanctificare* (Tertullian), f. L. *sanctus* holy; see -FY.] †**1.** *trans.* To set apart religiously for an office or function; to consecrate (a king, etc.) –1660. †**2.** To honour as holy; to ascribe holiness to –1601. **b.** To manifest (God, his might, etc.) as holy 1535. **3.** To consecrate (a thing); to set apart as holy or sacred 1483. **4.** To make (a person) holy; to cause to undergo sanctification 1526. **b.** Chiefly in O.T.: To free from ceremonial impurity 1500. **5.** To render holy, impart sanctity to (a thing, quality, action or condition); to render legitimate or binding by a religious sanction. late ME. **6.** *transf.* To impart real or apparent sacredness to; to give a colour of morality or innocence to; to justify, sanction. Now *rare* or *Obs.* 1606. **7.** To make productive of or conducive to holiness or spiritual blessing 1597.

1. Thus God sanctified Aaron JER. TAYLOR. **3.** And [God] blessed the seuenth daye, & sanctified it COVERDALE *Gen.* 2:3. **5.** That holy Man, amaz'd at what he saw, Made haste to sanctifie the Bliss by Law DRYDEN. **6.** Custom, which sanctifies all absurdities BENTHAM. **7.** Sanctifie, we beseech thee, this thy fatherly correction to him *Bk. Com. Prayer, Visit. Sick.* Hence **Sa·nctifyingly** *adv.*

Sanctimonious (sæŋktimōᵘ·niəs), *a.* 1603. [f. L. *sanctimonia* SANCTIMONY + -OUS; superseding †*sanctimonial* – late L.] †**1.** Possessing sanctity; sacred, holy, consecrated –1801. **2.** Of pretended or assumed sanctity or piety, affecting the appearance of sanctity 1603.

2. *Meas. for M.* I. ii. 7. A set of s. humbugs and thieves 1871. Hence **Sanctimo·nious-ly** *adv.*, **-ness.**

Sanctimony (sæ·ŋktiməni). 1540. [– L. *sanctimonia*, f. *sanctus* holy; see -MONY.] †**1.** Holiness of life and character; the profession of holiness; religiousness, sanctity –1725. †**2.** Sacredness –1683. **3.** Pretended, affected or hypocritical holiness or saintliness; assumed or outward sanctity 1618.

1. *All's Well* IV. iii. 59.

Sanction (sæ·ŋkʃən), *sb.* 1563. [– Fr. *sanction* – L. *sanctio, -on-*, f. *sanct-*, pa. ppl. stem of *sancire* render inviolable, etc., f. var. of base of *sacer* SACRED.] **1.** [So L. *sanctio*.] A law or decree; esp. an eccl. decree. Now *Hist.* **2.** *Law.* The specific penalty enacted in order to enforce obedience to a law 1633. **b.** Hence, The provision of rewards for obedience, along with punishments for disobedience, to a law (*remuneratory* as dist. from *punitive s.*) 1692. **c.** [After L. *sanctio*.] The part or clause of a law which declares the penalty attached to infringement thereof 1651. **3.** *Ethics.* A consideration which operates to enforce obedience to any law or rule of conduct; a recognized motive for conformity to moral or religious law 1681. **4.** Binding force given to an oath; something which makes an oath or engagement binding; a solemn oath or engagement 1611. **5.** The action of rendering legally authoritative or binding; solemn confirmation given to a law, enactment, etc., by a supreme authority 1658. **6.** An express authoritative permission or recognition (e.g. of an action, custom, institution, etc.) 1720. **b.** *fig.* Now more loosely, countenance or encouragement given to an opinion or practice by custom, public sentiment, etc. 1738. **7.** Something which serves to support, authorize, or confirm an action, procedure, etc. 1728. †**b.** A testimonial –1813.

1. *Pragmatic S.*, see PRAGMATIC A. 1. **2.** The fear of death..is the most formidable s. which legislators have been able to devise MACAULAY. **3.** With regard to any supposed moral standard—what is its s.? what are the motives to obey it? MILL. **4.** We swear by thee! and to our oath do thou Give s. SHELLEY. **6. b.** Follies that have the s. of antiquity PENNANT. **7.** The wedded yoke that each had donned, Seeming a s., not a bond PATMORE. Hence **Sa·nctionary** *a.* relating to sanctions (sense 1). **Sa·nctionist** *a.* and *sb.* (sense 2 c). **Sa·nctionless** *a.* having no s. attached.

Sanction (sæ·ŋkʃən), *v.* 1778. [f. prec.] **1.** *trans.* To ratify or confirm by sanction or solemn enactment; to authorize; to countenance. **2.** To enforce (a law, etc.) by attaching a penalty to transgression 1825.

1. These statements are sanctioned by common sense 1836. A covenant sanctioned by all the solemnities of religion 1838. Hence **Sa·nctionative** *a.* (*Law*) pertaining to sanctioning.

Sanctitude (sæ·ŋktitiūd). 1450. [– L. *sanctitudo*, f. *sanctus* holy; see -TUDE.] The quality of being holy or saint-like; holiness, sanctity. Now *rare*.

Sanctity (sæ·ŋktiti). late ME. [Partly (in forms *sauntite, saintite*) – OFr. *sain(c)tité* (mod. *sainteté*); partly immed. – L. *sanctitas*, f. *sanctus* holy; see -ITY.] **1.** Holiness of life, saintliness. **2.** The quality of being sacred or hallowed; claim to religious reverence; inviolability 1601. **b.** *pl.* Sacred obligations, feelings, etc.; also quasi-*concr.*, objects possessing sanctity 1808.

1. For deep discernment prais'd And..fam'd For s. of manners undefil'd COWPER. **2.** His affirmations have the s. of an oath LAMB. **b.** Woman completes her destiny by occupying herself with the industries and sanctities of the home 1894.

Sanctorian (sæŋktōᵊ·riăn), *a.* 1740. [f. mod.L. *Sanctorius* (It. *Santorio*), a Venetian physician (1561–1636); see -AN.] Of or pertaining to Sanctorius, who made experiments and calculations on insensible perspiration.

S. perspiration, insensible perspiration, first discovered by Sanctorius.

Sanctuarize (sæ·ŋktiŭˌărəiz), *v. rare.* 1602. [f. next + -IZE.] *trans.* To afford sanctuary to; to shelter by means of sacred privileges.

Sanctuary (sæ·ŋktiuˌări). ME. [– AFr. *sanctuarie*, (O)Fr. *sanctuaire* – L. *sanctuarium*, f. *sanctus*, after SACRARIUM; see -ARY[1].] **I.** A holy place. **1.** *gen.* A building or place set apart for the worship of God or of one or more divinities; applies, e.g., to a Christian church, the Jewish temple, a heathen temple, etc.; also *fig.* to the church or body of believers. **b.** *fig.* Used for: The priestly office or order. late ME. **c.** Applied to Heaven. late ME. **2.** A specially holy place within a temple or church. **a.** The HOLY PLACE, including the 'Holy of holies'; sometimes the latter only. late ME. **b.** *Eccl.* The sacrarium; also *occas.* the chancel. late ME. **c.** The most sacred part of any temple; the cella, adytum. late ME. **3.** A piece of consecrated ground; the precincts of a church; a churchyard, cemetery. Now *dial.* late ME.

1. *transf.* The famous isle of Iona was once the

seat and s. of western learning 1796. **c.** From santuary hy Let him come downe SIDNEY *Ps.* 20:2.

II. 1. A church or other sacred place in which, by the law of the mediæval church, a fugitive from justice, or a debtor, was immune from arrest. Hence, any place in which by law or custom a similar immunity is secured to fugitives. late ME. **b.** A similar place of refuge in a non-Christian country. late ME. **2.** Immunity from punishment and the ordinary operations of the law secured by taking refuge in a sanctuary; the right or privilege of affording such shelter; shelter, refuge, protection. late ME. **3.** *Hunting.* The 'privilege of forest'; the close season 1603.

1. All the while he by his side her bore, She was as safe as in a S. SPENSER. *transf.* They have made..London..a s. to refugees of every political and religious opinion EMERSON. **2.** Phr. *Privilege of s. To violate* or *break s.*, to violate the privilege or right of a s. *To take* s., to take refuge in a s.

||**Sanctum** (sæ·ŋktŏm). 1577. [L., neut. of *sanctus* holy.] **1.** The 'holy place' of the Jewish tabernacle and temple. Also, a sacred place or shrine in other temples and churches. **2.** = next 2. 1819.

2. He found the banker in his private s. LYTTON.

||**Sanctum sanctorum** (sæ·ŋktŏm sæŋktōᵊrŏm). *Pl.* **sancta sanctorum.** ME. [L., n. sing. and n. gen. pl. of *sanctus*, tr. (= LXX τὸ ἅγιον τῶν ἁγίων) of Heb. *ḳōdeš haḳḳᵒdāšîm* holy of holies.] **1.** The Holy of holies of the Jewish temple and tabernacle. †In early use also pl. **2.** A person's private retreat, where he is free from intrusion 1706.

||**Sanctus** (sæ·ŋktŏs). late ME. [L., = 'Holy', the first word of the hymn.] **1.** The 'angelic hymn' (from Isa. 6:3) beginning with the words *Sanctus, sanctus, sanctus* ('Holy, holy, holy') which forms the conclusion of the Eucharistic preface. Also called TERSANCTUS (thrice holy). Also the music for this. **†2.** *Black s.*, a burlesque hymn; a discord of harsh sounds expressive of contempt –1861.

Sa·nctus bell. 1479. [f. prec. + BELL *sb.*[1]] A bell rung at the Sanctus at Mass; in post-Reformation times often used to summon the people to Church.

Sand (sænd), *sb.* [OE. *sand* = OFris. *sand, sond*, OS. *sand*, OHG. *sant* (Du. *zand*, G. *sand*), ON. *sandr* :– Gmc. **sandam*, **sandaz.*] **1.** A material consisting of comminuted fragments and waterworn particles of rocks (mainly siliceous) finer than those of gravel; often *spec.* as the material of a beach, desert, etc. **b.** With *a* and *pl.* A sand-bank, shoal 1495. **c.** A sandy soil. Chiefly *pl.* 1610. **d.** A grain of sand 1596. **e.** *Geol.* and *Mining.* A stratum of sand or soft sandstone 1851. **2.** Metaphorical and similative uses, with ref. to the innumerability of the grains of sand, to its instability as a foundation, etc., or in phrases implying the exercise of fruitless labour OE. **3.** *pl.* Tracts of sand: **a.** Along a shore, estuary, etc. or composing the bed of a river or sea 1450. **b.** Sandy or desert wastes 1547. **4.** As used for various purposes, e.g. as an adulterant, as an ingredient of mortar, to dry wet ink marks. late ME. **5.** The sand of a sand-glass or hour-glass; also, with *a* and *pl.*, a grain of this 1557. **6.** Chiefly *U.S. slang.* Firmness of purpose, pluck, stamina, 'grit' 1883. **7.** *Anat.* and *Path.* Applied to substances resembling sand, present either normally or as morbid products in certain animal organs or excretions 1577.

1. A shore of hard white s. Met the green herbage MORRIS. **b.** *Henry V*, IV. i. 100. **c.** On bad sands trefoile and ray grass are chosen 1794. **e.** *Oil s.*: see OIL *sb.* **2.** A heart As full of Sorrowes, as the Sea of sands SHAKS. That s. on which thy crumbling power is built SHELLEY. Phr. *Rope of s.*: see ROPE *sb.* II. 1. *To plough the sands*: see PLOUGH *v.* **3. a.** Come vnto these yellow sands SHAKS. **b.** Oceans unknown, inhospitable sands! GRAY. **4.** Everything..was..shining with soft soap and s. DICKENS. The tales we hear about the presence of s. in sugar 1857. His system, as Caius said of his style, was s. without lime 1862. **5.** The Sands are numbred, that makes vp my Life SHAKS. **7.** *Urinary s.*, a substance of finer particles than those of gravel.

Comb.: **†s. ball,** a kind of toilet soap, mixed with fine s.; **-bank,** a bank of s. formed in a river or sea by the action of tides and currents; also = SAND-HILL; **-bath** *Chem.*, a vessel of heated sand used as an equable heater for retorts, etc.; **-bar,** a bank of sand formed at the mouth of a river or harbour by the action of the water; **-bed,** a layer or stratum of s.; *Founding*, a bed of s. into which the iron from a blast-furnace is run; **s. belt,** an arid ridge of sand often extending many miles; **-blast,** a contrivance for depolishing or grinding glass, metal, etc. by means of a jet of s. impelled by compressed air or steam; **-boy,** perh. a boy who hawks s. for sale; in provb. phr. *as jolly as a sandboy*; **-crack,** a disease incident to the hoofs of a horse; **-drift,** (an accumulation of) drifting sand; **-furnace** = *s.-bath*; **-hog** *U.S.* a man who works underground, as in a caisson; **-man,** one who digs s.; in nursery language, a personification of sleep or drowsiness; **-mould,** a mould for a casting, composed of s.; **-pillar** = *s.-spout*; **-pipe,** (*a*) *Geol.* a tubular cavity in chalk, filled with gravel and s.; (*b*) a pipe conducting s. to the rails from the sand-box of a locomotive; **-pit,** a pit from which sand is excavated; **-pump,** a pump for raising wet sand, detritus, etc., from a drill-hole, oil-well or caisson; **-rock,** a sandstone rock; **-shoes,** shoes for wearing on the sands or at the seaside, *spec.* canvas shoes with gutta-percha or hemp soles; **-spout,** a pillar of s. raised by a whirlwind in a desert; **-storm,** a desert storm of wind accompanied with clouds of s.; **s. valve,** the valve by which the escape of s. from the sand-box of a locomotive is regulated.

b. In the names of animals, etc., as **s.-badger,** (*a*) a Javanese badger, *Meles ankuma*; (*b*) the Indian badger, *Arctonyx collaris*, also called **s. bear**; **s. bird,** a bird whose habitat is the sea-shore, esp. the SANDPIPER; **-bug,** (*a*) a member of the family *Galgulidæ*; (*b*) a burrowing crab, *Hippa talpoidea*; **-crab,** (*a*) a crab of the family *Ocypodidæ*; (*b*) the Lady Crab, *Platyonichus ocellatus*; **-cricket** *U.S.*, a cricket belonging to the genus *Stenopelmatus*, esp. *S. fasciatus*; **-eel,** (*a*) a fish of the genus *Ammodytes*, having a body like that of an eel; (*b*) a fish of the genus *Gonorhynchus*; **s. flea,** (*a*) = CHIGOE; (*b*) *U.S.*, a crustacean belonging to the genus *Orchestia*; (*c*) a brine shrimp, *Artemia salina*; **-fly,** a small fly or midge, esp. one belonging to the genus *Simulium*; **-grouse,** any bird of the genus *Pterocloмorphæ*, inhabiting sandy tracts of the old world; **-hopper,** a crustacean, *Talitrus locusta*; also, a s.-flea of the genus *Orchestia*; **-lizard,** a common European lizard, *Lacerta agilis*; **s. martin,** a variety of the martin, *Hirundo* or *Cotile riparia*, which nests in the sides of sand-pits; **-monitor,** the land-crocodile, *Monitor* or *Psammosaurus arenarius*; **-partridge,** a partridge of the genus *Ammoperdix*; **s. rat,** a N. Amer. rat of the genus *Thomomys*, esp. *T. talpoides*; **s. roller,** the trout perch; **s. runner,** a sand-plover or sandpiper; **-saucer,** the egg-mass of the *Nauticas*: **-shark,** (*a*) *U.S.*, a kind of shark *Odontaspis littoralis*; (*b*) *Australia*, a variety of ray-fish, *Rhinobatus granulatus*; **-snipe,** any species of sandpiper; **-sole,** *Solea lascaris*; **-sucker,** the flat-fish *Platessa limandoides*; **-swallow,** *Hirundo riparia*; **-worm,** the lug-worm *Arenicola marina* or *piscatorum*.

c. In the names of plants: **s. elm,** a variety of elm, *Ulmus suberosa*; **s. grass,** any species of grass which grows in s. and serves as a s.-binder; **s. myrtle,** *Leiophyllum* or *Ledum buxifolium*; **-wort,** (*a*) the genus *Arenaria*; (*b*) any of various plants which grow in sandy places.

Sand (sænd), *v.* late ME. [f. prec.] **1.** *trans.* To run (a ship) on a sandbank; also *pass.* of a person, to be run aground 1560. **2.** To sprinkle with or as with sand. late ME. **3.** To overlay with sand, to bury under a sand drift 1624. **b.** To put sand upon (land) as a dressing 1721. **4.** To intermix sand with (sugar, wool, etc.) with fraudulent intent 1848.

4. To s. the sugar, and sloe-leave the tea KINGSLEY.

Sandal (sæ·ndăl), *sb.*[1] late ME. [– L. *sandalium* – Gr. σανδάλιον, dim. of σάνδαλον wooden shoe, prob. of Asiatic origin (cf. Pers. *ṣandal* sandal).] **1.** A protective covering for the sole of the foot fastened by means of fillets or thongs of leather passed over the instep and round the ankle. **2.** A half-shoe of red leather, silk, etc., embroidered and fastened with straps and bands, forming part of the regalia of a sovereign or of the official dress of a bishop or abbot 1485. **b.** Applied to various kinds of low shoes, slippers, etc. 1794. **3.** A strap for fastening a low shoe or slipper, passed over the instep or round the ankle 1829.

1. While the still morn went out with Sandals gray MILT. **2. b.** Dancing sandals..made of pink satin 1900.

attrib.: **s. shoon** (*arch.*), sandals. Hence **Sa·ndaling,** elastic web woven in narrow strips for sandals.

Sandal (sæ·ndăl), *sb.*[2] late ME. [– med.L. *sandalum* (with var. *santalum* SANTAL), ult. – Skr. *čandana*, through Pers. *čandal*, Arab. *ṣandal*, late Gr. σάνδανον, σάνταλον. See SANDERS.] = SANDALWOOD. †An ointment made of powdered sandalwood.

Sandal (sæ·ndăl), *v.* 1713. [f. SANDAL *sb.*[1]] *trans.* To furnish with or as with sandals.

Sa·ndalwoo:d. 1511. [SANDAL *sb.*[2]] **1.** A scented wood obtained from several species of *Santalum*; also, an inodorous dye-wood, *Pterocarpus santalinus*, red sanders. **2.** Applied to trees of other genera, which produce a wood often used as a substitute for the true sandalwood 1846.

1. *White s.* is obtained from *S. album*, a tree resembling the myrtle, found on the Malabar coast. *Citron* or *Yellow s.* is from *S. freycinetianum*, found in the South Sea Islands. *Red s.*: see RED (*Comb.*).

Sandarac (sæ·ndăræk). 1550. [– L. *sandaraca* – Gr. σανδαράκη, -άχη, of Asiatic origin.] **1.** = REALGAR. **2.** In full *gum s.* A resin which exudes from the tree *Callitris quadrivalvis*, native of N.W. Africa; it is used in the preparation of spirit varnish and pounce 1655.

Sa·nd-bag, sa·ndbag, *sb.* 1590. [SAND *sb.*] **1. a.** *Fortif.* A bag filled with sand or earth; used to make the parapet of a trench, etc. **b.** used as ballast; esp. for a boat or balloon 1831. **c.** as a weapon: In recent use (chiefly *U.S.*), a long, cylindrical bag (sometimes an eelskin) filled with sand, by which a heavy blow may be struck without leaving a mark 1594. **d.** A bag or cushion filled with fine sand, used in engraving, as a support for the plate 1658. **e.** A long narrow bag, usu. of flannel, containing fine sand, used to cover a crevice and exclude draught or light 1858. Hence **Sa·ndbag** *v. trans.* to furnish with sandbags; to fell with a blow from a s. **Sa·ndba·gger** *U.S.*, one who uses a sand-bag as a weapon.

Sa·nd-blind. Now *arch.* and *dial.* late ME. [repr. ult. OE. **samblind*, f. *sam-* half- (shortening of WGmc. **sāmi-* :– IE. **sēmi-* SEMI-) + BLIND; assim. to SAND.] Half-blind, dim-sighted, purblind.

Sa·nd-box. 1572. [f. SAND *sb.* + BOX *sb.*[2]] **1.** A box with a perforated top for sprinkling sand as a blotter upon wet ink. *Obs.* exc. *Hist.* **2. a.** A sand-mould. **b.** A box of sand on a locomotive for use when the wheels slip. **c.** *Golf.* A receptacle for the sand used to 'tee' the ball. 1688. **3.** The fruit of the W. Indian forest tree, *Hura crepitans*; the tree itself 1750.

Sanded (sæ·ndėd), *ppl. a.* 1570. [f. SAND *sb.* and *v.* + -ED.] **†1.** Of a sandy colour –1686. **†2.** Composed of or covered with sand –1746. **3.** Sprinkled with sand 1760. **4.** Adulterated with sand 1883.

Sandemanian (sændĭmēⁱ·niăn), *sb.* and *a.* 1792. [See sense 1, -IAN.] **A.** *sb.* One of a religious sect developed by Robert *Sandeman* (1718–71) from the Glassites. **B.** *adj.* Of or belonging to the Sandemanians. Hence **Sandema·nianism.**

Sanderling (sæ·ndəɹliŋ). 1602. [perh. repr. OE. **sandyrðling*, f. SAND *sb.* + *yrðling* ploughman, also the name of some bird.] A small wading bird, *Calidris arenaria*.

Sanders (sɑ·ndəɹz). ME. [– OFr. *sandre*, var. of *sandle*, *sandal* SANDAL *sb.*[2]] **1.** = SANDALWOOD. **†2.** The sandalwood tree; sandalwood trees –1783.

Sa·nd-glass. 1556. [f. SAND *sb.* + GLASS *sb.*] A contrivance for measuring time, consisting of two glass vessels connected by a narrow neck, and containing so much sand as will take a given time to pass from the receptacle placed uppermost into that placed below; an hour-glass, a minute-glass, an egg-boiler, etc.

Sa·nd-hill. OE. [SAND *sb.*] A hill or bank of sand; esp. a dune on the sea-shore. Hence **Sa·nd-hiller,** one of a class of 'poor whites' living in the pine-woods that cover the sandy hills of Georgia and S. Carolina.

Sandiver (sæ·ndivəɹ). late ME. [app. – Fr. *suin de verre* (*suin*, now *suint*, exudation from wool, app. f. *suer* to sweat; *de* of; *verre* glass).] A liquid saline matter found floating over the glass after vitrification; glass-gall.

Sandling (sæ·ndliŋ). 1611. [f. SAND *sb.* + -LING.¹] A small flat-fish; a dab.

Sa·nd-pa:per, sa·ndpa:per, *sb.* 1812. [SAND *sb.*] Paper upon which a layer of sand has been fixed by means of an adhesive, used chiefly for smoothing or polishing woodwork. Hence **Sa·ndpa:per** *v. trans.* to smooth with or as with s.

Sandpiper (sæ·ndpəi:pəɹ). 1674. [f. SAND *sb.* + PIPER.] A small wading bird which runs along the sand and utters a piping note; esp. *Tringoides hypoleucus*, the Common S., and *Actitis macularia*, the N. Amer. S.

Sandstone (sæ·ndstōᵘn). 1668. [f. SAND *sb.* + STONE *sb.*] A rock composed of consolidated sand.

Old and *New Red S.*, two series of British rocks lying respectively below and above the carboniferous.

Sandwich (sæ·ndwitʃ, -widʒ), *sb.* 1762. [Named after John Montagu, 4th Earl of *Sandwich* (1718–1792), who once spent twenty-four hours at the gaming-table without other food than beef sandwiches.] Two slices of bread with a layer of sliced meat, usu. beef or ham (or, later, any comestible) placed between; freq. specified as *ham, egg, watercress s.* Also, a confection of layers of sponge cake with jam or cream between. Also *transf.* and *fig.*

attrib.: **s.-board,** a board carried by a sandwich-man; **-boat,** the boat occupying the last position in a higher, and the first in a lower, division in bumping races at Oxford and Cambridge, and thus rowing twice in the same day; **s. box, case,** a box or case in which to carry sandwiches; **-man,** a man who carries two advertisement boards suspended from the shoulders, one in front and the other behind.

Sandwich (sæ·ndwitʃ, -widʒ), *v.* 1861. [f. prec.] *trans.* To put in or as in a sandwich; chiefly *fig.*, to insert (some person or thing) between two others, freq. of a widely different character; rarely, to enclose like a sandwich.

Sandy (sæ·ndi), *sb.* 1473. A shortened hypocoristic form of Alexander, used chiefly in Scotland. Hence, a nickname for a Scotchman.

Sandy (sæ·ndi), *a.* [OE. *sandiġ*, f. SAND *sb.* + -Y¹.] **1.** Of the nature of sand; containing a large proportion of sand. **b.** Of or containing sand as used for measuring time (*poet.*) 1591. **2.** *fig.* Like sand in lacking cohesion or stability 1590. **3.** Having hair of a yellowish-red colour; of hair, yellowish-red 1523. **4.** Qualifying the names of colours 1819.

1. With s. Ballast Sailors trim the Boat DRYDEN. **b.** 1 *Hen. VI*, IV. ii. 36. **2.** S. sentences without lime NASHE. **3.** A florid young man..with s. hair MARRYAT. Hence **Sa·ndiness.**

‖**Sandyx** (sæ·ndiks). *Hist.* 1601. [– L. *sandyx, -dix* – Gr. σάνδυξ, -δυξ.] A red pigment, mentioned by ancient writers.

Sane (sēⁱn), *a.* 1628. [– L. *sanus* healthy.] **1.** Of the body, its organs or functions: Healthy, sound, not diseased (*rare*) 1755. **2.** Sound in mind; in one's senses; not mad. Also, of the mind: Not diseased. 1721. **3.** Sensible, rational; free from delusive prejudices or fancies 1843.

2. The activity of s. minds in healthful bodies COLERIDGE. *Of s. memory*: see MEMORY 2. Hence **Sa·ne-ly** *adv.*, **-ness.**

Sangaree (sæŋgărī·). 1736. [– Sp. *sangría* (lit. bleeding), 'a drink composed of lemon water and red wine'.] A cold drink composed of wine diluted and spiced, used chiefly in tropical countries.

‖**Sang-de-bœuf** (saṅdəböf). 1886. [Fr.; lit. 'bullock's blood'.] A deep red colour found in old Chinese porcelain.

‖**Sang-froid** (saṅfrwa). 1712. [Fr., lit. 'cold blood'.] Coolness, indifference, absence of excitement or agitation.

†**Sa·nglier.** late ME. [– OFr. *sengler*, (also mod.) *sanglier* :– L. *singularis, -lar-* solitary, used subst. in late L. for a boar separated from the herd, in med.L. *singularis* wild boar.] A full-grown wild boar –1725.

Sangrail (sæŋgrēⁱ·l). 1450. [– OFr. *saint graal*; see SAINT, GRAIL².] = GRAIL².

Sanguiferous (sæŋgwi·fĕrəs), *a.* 1682. [f. L. *sanguis* blood + -FEROUS.] Bearing or conveying blood.

Sanguification (sæ:ŋgwifikēⁱ·ʃən). 1578. [– mod.L. *sanguificatio, -on-*, f. *sanguificare*; see next, -FICATION.] The formation of blood; conversion into blood.

†**Sa·nguify,** *v.* 1620. [– mod.L. *sanguificare*, f. L. *sanguis*; see -FY.] **1.** *intr.* To produce blood –1677. **2.** *trans.* To convert into blood –1707.

‖**Sanguinaria** (saŋgwinēᵊ·riă). 1842. [mod. L. subst. use of fem. of L. adj. *sanguinarius*; see next, -A 2.] The blood-root, *Sanguinaria canadensis*; also the rhizome of this, used in medicine.

Sanguinary (sæ·ŋgwinări), *a.* (and *sb.*) 1550. [– L. *sanguinarius*, f. *sanguis, sanguin-* blood; see -ARY¹. Cf. Fr. *sanguinaire.*] **1.** Attended by bloodshed; characterized by slaughter; bloody. Of laws: Imposing the death-penalty freely. 1625. **2.** Bloodthirsty; delighting in carnage 1623. †**b.** *absol.* as *sb.* A sanguinary person –1632. **3.** Of or pertaining to blood (*rare*) 1684. ¶**4.** Used joc. as a euphemism for BLOODY, in reports of vulgar speech.

1. We may not..propagate Religion, by Warrs, or by S. Persecutions, to force Consciences BACON. **2.** A s. bishop in the reign of Queen Mary 1751. Hence **Sa·nguinarily** *adv.* **Sa·nguinariness.**

Sanguine (sæ·ŋgwin), *a.* and *sb.* late ME. [– (O)Fr. *sanguin*, fem. *-ine* – L. *sanguineus*; see next.] **A.** *adj.* **1.** Blood-red. Also *s. red* (sometimes hyphened). Now *literary.* **b.** *Nat. Hist.* Chiefly in names of animals and plants 1783. **2.** Of or pertaining to blood; consisting of or containing blood. Now *rare.* 1447. **b.** Causing or delighting in bloodshed; bloody, sanguinary. Now *poet.* or *rhet.* 1705. **3.** In mediæval physiology: Belonging to that one of the four 'complexions' in which the blood predominates over the other three humours, and which is indicated by a ruddy countenance and a courageous, hopeful, and amorous disposition. late ME. **b.** Red in the face 1684. **4.** Of persons, etc.: Having the mental attributes characteristic of the sanguine complexion (see sense 3); hopeful, confident 1509.

1. Like to that s. flower inscrib'd with woe MILT. **3.** A prince of haut corage, young lusty and sanguyne of complexion 1548. **4.** That s. temper which overlooks..the obstacles in its way 1855. It far surpassed our most s. expectations 1876.

B. *sb.* †**1.** A blood-red colour –1612. †**2.** The sanguine 'complexion' or temperament –1718. **3.** *Art.* A crayon coloured red with iron oxide; a drawing executed with red chalks 1854.

3. An interesting Greuze sketch in s. 1886. Hence **Sa·nguine-ly** *adv.*, **-ness.**

Sanguineous (sæŋgwi·niəs), *a.* 1520. [f. L. *sanguineus* (f. *sanguis, sanguin-* blood) + -OUS.] **1.** Of or pertaining to blood; of the nature of or containing blood 1646. †**b.** Of animals: Having blood–1667. **2.** Of the colour of blood 1520. **3.** Of or pertaining to bloodshed; giving rise to bloodshed; bloodthirsty, sanguinary. Now *rare.* 1612. **4.** Of persons, etc.: = SANGUINE *a.* 3, 4. In recent use, Full-blooded, plethoric. 1732.

2. His passion, cruel grown, took on a hue Fierce and s. KEATS. Hence **Sangui·neousness.**

Sanguinity (sæŋgwi·nĭti). 1470. [Sense 1 – OFr. *sanguinité* or med.L. *sanguinitas*, f. as prec.; sense 2 f. SANGUINE + -ITY.] †**1.** CONSANGUINITY 1. –1741. **2.** The quality of being sanguine (*rare*) 1737.

Sanguinivorous (sæŋgwini·vərəs), *a.* 1828. [f. L. *sanguis, sanguin-* blood + -VOROUS.] = SANGUIVOROUS.

Sanguinolent (sæŋgwi·nŏlĕnt), *a.* 1577. [– L. *sanguinolentus*, f. as prec.; see -ULENT.] **1.** Of or pertaining to blood; tinged, stained with or containing blood. Now chiefly *Path.* 1597. **2.** Bloodthirsty; cruel; merciless (*rare*) 1577.

Sanguivorous (sæŋgwi·vŏrəs), *a.* 1842. [f. L. *sanguis* blood + -VOROUS.] Feeding on blood.

Sanhedrim, Sanhedrin (sæ·nĭdrim, -in). 1588. [– post-bibl. Heb. *sanhedrīn* – Gr. συνέδριον council, f. σύν together (SYN-) + ἕδρα seat.] *Jewish Antiq.* The highest court of justice and supreme council at Jerusalem; also applied to lower courts of justice. Hence **Sa·nhedrist,** a member of the S.

Sanicle (sæ·nik'l). ME. [– OFr. *sanicle* – med.L. *sanicula, -ulum*, perh. f. L. *sanus* healthy (SANE), with ref. to the plant's reputed healing powers.] **1.** The umbelliferous plant *Sanicula europæa* (more fully *wood s.*). Also, any plant of the genus *Sanicula*, as *S. marilandica*, the black snake-root. **2.** Applied to various plants of other genera, as *Heuchera villosa*, American s. late ME.

Sanidine (sæ·nidīn). 1815. [– G. *sanidin* (K. W. Nose, 1808), f. Gr. σανίς, σανιδ- board; see -INE⁵.] *Min.* A variety of orthoclase, found in flat crystals.

‖**Sanies** (sēⁱni,īz). 1562. [– L. *sanies.*] **1.** *Path.* A thin fetid pus mixed with serum or blood, secreted by a wound or ulcer. †**2.** Any watery fluid of animal origin –1834. So **Sa·nious** *a.* of the nature of s.; consisting of, or containing s.; yielding a discharge of s.

Sanify (sæ·nifəi), *v.* 1836. [f. L. *sanus* healthy (see SANE) + -FY.] **1.** *intr.* To become sane or reasonable. **2.** *trans.* To make healthy; improve the sanitary conditions of 1872.

Sanitarian (sænitēᵊ·riăn), *sb.* and *a.* 1859. [f. SANITARY + -AN; see -ARIAN.] **A.** *sb.* One who studies sanitation or who favours sanitary reform. **B.** *adj.* Pertaining to sanitary matters; advocating sanitary reforms 1884. Hence **Sanita·rianism. Sa·nitari-ly** *adv.* **-ness.** So **Sa·nitarist.**

Sanitarium (sænitēᵊ·riŏm). Chiefly *U.S.* 1851. [quasi-L., f. *sanitas* health; see next and -ARIUM.] = SANATORIUM.

Sanitary (sæ·nitări), *a.* 1842. [– Fr. *sanitaire*, f. L. *sanitas* health, f. *sanus* healthy (SANE); see -ARY¹.] **1.** Of or pertaining to the conditions affecting health, esp. with ref. to cleanliness and precautions against infection, etc.; pertaining to or concerned with sanitation. Also *occas.* free from deleterious influences. **b.** Used as the distinctive epithet of appliances specially contrived with a view to sanitary requirements 1862. **2.** *U.S.* Intended or tending to promote health 1853.

1. *S. cordon*: see CORDON 4.

Sanitation (sænitēⁱ·ʃən). 1848. [irreg. f. prec. + -ATION.] The devising and application of means for the improvement of sanitary conditions. Hence **Sa·nitate** *v. trans.* to put in a sanitary condition; to provide with sanitary appliances. **Sanita·tionist,** one who is skilled in or advocates s.

Sanity (sæ·nĭti). late ME. [– L. *sanitas*, f. *sanus* healthy; see SANE, -ITY.] **1.** Healthy condition, health. *arch.* **2.** The condition of being sane; mental health 1602.

‖**Sanjak** (sæ·n,dʒæk). 1537. [Turk. *sancak*; lit. 'banner'.] **1.** In the Turkish Empire, one of the administrative districts into which a vilayet is divided. †**2.** Misused for ‖**Sa·njakbeg, -bey,** the governor of a s.

Sannup (sæ·nŏp). 1630. [– Narragansett *sannop.*] A married male member of the community; the husband of a squaw.

San(n)yasi, -asin, var. ff. SUNNYASEE.

Sans (sænz), *prep.* ME. [– OFr., *san, sanz* (mod. *sans*), earlier *sen(s* :– Rom. **sene*, for L. *sine*, partly infl. by L. *absentia* (abl.) in the ABSENCE of (whence Pr. *sensa*, It. *senza*).] Without. Now *arch.* (chiefly with reminiscence of Shakespeare) and *Her.*

Second childishnesse, and meere obliuion, S. teeth, s. eyes, s. taste, s. euery thing SHAKS. ‖Fr. phrases and combs. (not naturalized): **sans cérémonie, sans façon,** unceremoniously, without the usual polite form; **sans-gêne** [*gêne* constraint], disregard of the ordinary forms of civility or politeness; **sans peur,** fearless, often in the phr. applied to the Chevalier de Bayard, *s. peur et s. reproche*; **sans phrase** [after *la mort s. phrase*, the alleged words of Sieyès in voting for the death of Louis XVI], without more words, without circumlocution; **sans reproche,** blameless (see *s. peur* above) **sans souci,** lit. without care or concern; as *sb.*, unconcern.

‖**Sansculotte** (sænzkiulǫ·t, Fr. saṅkülot). 1790. [Fr., f. *sans* without (see prec.) + *culotte* knee-breeches; usu. taken to mean 'one who wears trousers (*pantalons*), not knee-breeches'.] **1.** In the French Revolution, a republican of the poorer classes in

Paris. Hence *gen.* an extreme republican or revolutionary. **2.** *transf.* A tatterdemalion; a ragamuffin 1812. Hence ||**Sansculo·tterie,** the principles, spirit or behaviour characteristic of sansculottes; sansculottes collectively. **Sansculo·ttic** *a.* pertaining to the sansculottes or to sansculottism; revolutionary; unbreeched, hence, inadequately clothed. **Sansculo·ttism,** the principles or practice of sansculottes.

Sansculottid (sænskiulǫ·tid). 1813. [– Fr. *sansculottide*, f. prec.] One of the five (in leap-years six) complementary days added at the end of the month Fructidor of the Republican Calendar; *pl.*, the festivities held during these days. Also *attrib.* in *S. days.*

Sanserif (sænse·rif). 1830. [app. f. SANS *prep.* + SERIF.] *Typog.* A form of type without serifs; called also *grotesque.*

Sanskrit, Sanscrit (sæ·nskrit), *sb.* and *a.* 1617. [– Skr. *saṃskṛta* (n. *saṃskṛtam*) put together, well formed, highly wrought, elaborated, perfected, f. *sam* together (rel. to *sama* SAME) + *kṛ* make, do, perform + pa. ppl. ending *-to.*] **A.** *sb.* The ancient and sacred language of India, the oldest known member of the Indo-European family, in which the Hindu literature from the Vedas downwards is composed. In a narrower sense, the classical Sanskrit (opp. to the Epic and Vedic), the grammar of which was fixed by Pāṇini. **B.** *adj.* Of, belonging to, or written in Sanskrit 1773. Hence **Sanskri·tic** *a.* relating to, derived from, based on, or resembling S.; using the S. language. **Sa·nskritist,** a person versed in the S. language or writings.

Santa Claus (sæ·ntă klǭ·z). 1828. [orig. U.S., – Du. dial. *Sante Klaas*, Saint Nicholas; see NICHOLAS.] A legendary character who fills stockings with presents for children during the night of Christmas Eve.

Santal (sæ·ntăl). 1672. [– (O)Fr. *santal* – med.L. *santalum* – late Gr. σάνταλον; see SANDAL *sb.*[2]] **1.** Sandalwood. Also *s.-wood.* **2.** *Chem.* A substance ($C_8H_6O_3$) obtained from sandalwood 1894.

Santalaceous (sæntălē·ʃəs), *a.* 1845. [f. as prec. + -ACEOUS.] Belonging to the family *Santalaceæ*, typified by the genus *Santalum* or sandalwood.

Santalic (sæntæ·lik), *a.* 1849. [f. SANTAL + -IC.] *Chem.* In *s. acid*: = next.

Santalin (sæ·ntălin). 1833. [– Fr. *santaline*, f. *sental*; see SANTAL, -IN[1].] *Chem.* The colouring principle of red sanders.

Santon (sæ·ntǫn). 1599. [– Fr. *santon* – Sp. *santon*, f. *santo* SAINT; see -OON.] A European designation for a monk or hermit among the Moslems; a marabout; also, incorrectly, †a yogi, Hindu ascetic. So ||**Sa·nto.**

Santonate (sæ·ntŏnĕt). 1841. [f. next + -ATE[1] 1 c.] *Chem.* A salt of santonic acid.

Santonic (sæntǫ·nik), *a.* 1836. [f. SANTONIN + -IC; also SANTONINIC.] *Chem.* In *s. acid*: an acid derived from santonin.

Santonin (sæ·ntŏnin). 1838. [f. *santonica*, mod.L. use of L. *santonica* (sc. *herba* plant), subst. use of fem. sing. of *Santonicus*, pertaining to the Santones or Santoni, a people of Aquitania; see -IN[1]. Cf. Fr. *santonine.*] *Chem.* A bitter principle obtained from the dried unexpanded flowers of species of *Artemisia*, and used as a powerful anthelmintic. Hence **Santoni·nic** *a.* in *s. acid*, an acid obtained from s., isomeric with santonic acid.

Sap (sæp), *sb.*[1] [OE. *sæp*, corresp. to (M)LG., (M)Du. *sap*, OHG. *saf* (G. *saft*), prob. repr. Gmc. **sapam*, **sappam*, and rel. to ON. *safi* :– **safon* or **sabon.*] **1.** The vital juice which circulates in plants. †**2.** Juice or fluid of any kind –1613. **3.** = SAP-WOOD 1483.

1. The s. is the life of the tree, as the bloud is to mans body 1615. The s. of youth shrinks from our veins 1832. **2.** *fig. Hen. VIII*, I. i. 148.

attrib. and *Comb.*, as **s.-ball,** a local name for certain fungi of the genus *Polyporus*; **-rot,** a disease of timber, dry-rot; **-sucker,** a name in N. Amer. for many of the smaller woodpeckers, esp. those of the genus *Sphyropicus*; **-tube,** a vessel that conveys s. Hence **Sa·pful** *a.* abounding in s.

Sap (sæp), *sb.*[2] 1591. [Early forms *zappe, sappe* (XVI) – It. *zappa* (Piedmontese *sappa*) and the derived Fr. †*sappe*, †*zappe* (now *sape*) spade, spadework. Cf. late L. *sappa* (VI). Prob. of Arab. origin.] **1.** †The process of undermining a wall or defensive work; the process of constructing covered trenches in order to approach a besieged place. **b.** *fig.* Applied to stealthy or insidious methods of attacking or destroying anything 1748. **2.** A covered trench made for the purpose of approaching a besieged place under the fire of the garrison. In recent use, a narrow communicating trench. 1642.

1. b. Exempt forever from the s. of age COWPER.

Comb.: **s. battery,** a battery at the head of a s.; **-faggot,** a fascine used in sapping, to fill up the spaces between gabions; **-head,** the foremost end of a s.; **-roller,** a large gabion covering the sap-head.

Sap (sæp), *sb.*[3] *School slang.* 1798. [Cf. SAP *v.*[2]] One who studies hard or is absorbed in books.

Sap (sæp), *sb.*[4] 1815. [Short for SAPSKULL.] A simpleton, fool.

Sap (sæp), *v.*[1] 1598. [– Fr. *saper*, †*sapper* – It. *zappare*, f. *zappa*; see SAP *sb.*[2]] **1.** *intr.* To dig a sap; to approach a besieged place by means of a sap. **b.** *fig.* To make way in a stealthy or insidious manner. Also *trans.* in *to s. one's way.* 1732. **2.** *trans.* To dig under the foundations of (a wall, etc.); *transf.* of natural agencies: To undermine 1652. **3.** *fig.* To weaken or destroy insidiously (esp. health, strength, courage, etc.) 1755.

1. b. Lies, while they s. their way and hold their tongues, Are safe enough LANDOR. **2.** We have begun to sappe the Glacis 1689. Sap'd by floods, Their houses fell DRYDEN. *fig.* Not one who did not..s. the foundation of some old opinion 1857.

Sap (sæp), *v.*[2] *School slang.* 1830. [Cf. SAP *sb.*[3]] *intr.* To pore over books; to be studious.

Sapajou (sæ·pădʒū). 1698. [– Fr. *sapajou*, given by d'Abbeville as a Cayenne word.] A S. Amer. monkey of the genus *Cebus.*

Sapan, sappan (sæ·păn). 1598. [– Du. *sapan* – Malay *sapaŋ*, of S. Indian origin.] A dye-wood yielding a red dye, obtained from trees belonging to the genus *Cæsalpinia*, indigenous to tropical Asia and the Indian Archipelago, esp. *C. sappan.* Now *s. wood.*

Sap-green, *sb.* (and *a.*). 1578. [f. SAP *sb.*[1] + GREEN, prob. after Du. *sapgroen.*] A green pigment prepared from the juice of buckthorn berries; the colour of this pigment. Also *attrib.* and *adj.*

Sa·phead. 1828. [f. SAP *sb.*[1] (sense 3). Cf. SAPSKULL.] A fool, simpleton. So **Sap-headed** *a.* 1665.

||**Saphena** (săfī·nă). late ME. [– med.L. *saphena* – Arab. *ṣāfin.*] *Anat.* The distinctive name of two veins in the leg: (1) the *long* or *internal s.*, which extends from near the ankle-joint along the inner surface of the leg, and ends in the femoral vein; (2) the *short, posterior*, or *external s.*, which extends from the foot along the calf of the leg, and finally joins the popliteal vein.

Saphenous (săfī·nəs), *a.* 1840. [f. prec. + -OUS.] Pertaining to or connected with the saphena.

S. vein, the saphena. *S. nerve* = saphena nerve.

Saphie (sæ·fi). *N. Africa.* 1799. [Mandingo *safaye.*] A charm.

Sapid (sæ·pid), *a.* 1634. [– L. *sapidus*, f. *sapere* (cf. SAPIENT); see -ID[1].] **1.** Of food, etc.: Having a decided taste or flavour, *esp.* a pleasant one, savoury, palatable 1646. **2.** In neutral sense: Having taste or flavour 1634. **3.** *fig.* Grateful to the mind or mental taste 1640.

1. Thus Camels to make the water sapide do raise the mud with their feet SIR T. BROWNE.

Sapidity (săpi·dĭti). 1646. [f. SAPID + -ITY.] The quality of being sapid or having taste and flavour.

The body of that element [air] is ingustible, void of all s. SIR T. BROWNE.

Sapience (sē[i]·piĕns). late ME. [– OFr. *sapience* – L. *sapientia*, f. *sapient-*; see next, -ENCE.] **1.** Wisdom, understanding. (Now *rare* in serious use.) †**b.** Correct taste and judgement –1796. **2.** Used depreciatively or ironically: Would-be wisdom. late ME.

1. That Supreme Master of Politicall S. 1659. **2.** This is a piece of s. not worth the brain of a fruit-trencher MILT.

Sapient (sē[i]·piĕnt), *a.* and *sb.* 1471. [– OFr. *sapient* or L. *sapiens, -ent-*, pr. pple. of *sapere* have a taste, be sensible or wise; see -ENT.] **A.** *adj.* Wise. Now usu. *ironical.*

Where the S. King Held dalliance with his faire Egyptian Spouse MILT.

B. *sb.* [= L. *sapiens.*] A wise man, sage. In later use *joc.* 1549. Hence **Sa·piently** *adv.*

Sapiential (sē[i]pie·nʃ[i]ăl), *a.* 1485. [– Fr. *sapiential* or Chr. L. *sapientialis* (Tertullian), f. L. *sapientia*; see SAPIENCE, -AL[1].] **1.** Belonging to or characterized by wisdom; esp. belonging to the wisdom of God. **2.** Epithet of the 'wisdom' books of the Bible (Proverbs, Ecclesiastes, Canticles, Wisdom, Ecclesiasticus); also applied occas. to kindred writings outside the canon 1568. Hence **Sapie·ntially** *adv.*

Sapless (sæ·plĕs), *a.* 1591. [f. SAP *sb.*[1] + -LESS.] **1.** Destitute of sap; dry; withered. **b.** Of soil: Without moisture; barren 1655. **2.** *transf.* and *fig.* **a.** Of persons: Lacking energy or vigour; lacking in character, insipid 1598. **b.** Of immaterial things, ideas, etc.: Destitute of inner worth; insipid, pointless 1602.

2. a. Now s. on the verge of Death he stands DRYDEN. **b.** Old stories and s. anecdotes 1891. Hence **Sa·plessness.**

Sapling (sæ·pliŋ). late ME. [f. SAP *sb.*[1] + -LING[1] 2.] **1.** A young tree. **2.** *transf.* A young or inexperienced person 1588. **3.** A greyhound less than twelve months old 1832. **4.** *appositively* or as *adj.* That is a s. 1700.

Sapodilla (sæpodi·lă). 1697. [– Sp. *zapotillo*, dim. of *zapote* SAPOTA.] **1.** A large evergreen tree, *Achras sapota*, native of tropical America, having a durable wood and an edible fruit. Also called NASEBERRY. **2.** The fruit of this tree 1750.

attrib.: **s.-plum** = sense 2; **-tree** = sense 1.

Sapogenin (săpǫ·dʒĕnin). 1862. [f. SAPO(NIN + -GEN + -IN[1].] *Chem.* A crystalline compound obtained by treating saponin with dilute acids.

Saponaceous (sæponē[i]·ʃəs), *a.* 1710. [– mod.L. *saponaceus* (Fr. *saponacé*), f. L. *sapo, sapon-* SOAP; see -ACEOUS.] **1.** Of the nature of, resembling, consisting of, or containing soap; soapy. **2.** *joc.* Soapy, *lit.* and *fig.*; unctuous in manner; 'slippery', evasive 1824.

2. Among all his pecuniary, s., oleaginous parishioners SYD. SMITH. Hence **Sapona·city** (*joc.*).

Saponification (săpǫ:nifikē[i]·ʃən). 1821. [– Fr. *saponification* or f. SAPONIFY; see -FICATION.] The process of saponifying; the conversion of a fat into soap by the addition of an alkali, the remaining constituent, glycerine, being thereby liberated.

Saponify (săpǫ·nifəi), *v.* 1821. [– Fr. *saponifier*, f. L. *sapo, sapon-* SOAP; see -FY.] **1.** *trans.* To convert (a fat or an oil) into soap by decomposition by an alkali. **2.** *intr.* To become converted into soap 1823. Hence **Sapo·nifiable,** *a.* **Sapo·nifier,** an alkali used in saponification.

Saponin (sæ·pŏnin). 1831. [– Fr. *saponine*, f. L. *sapo, sapon-* soap; see -IN[1].] *Chem.* A glucoside obtained from *Saponaria officinalis, Quillaja saponaria*, and many other plants.

Saponite (sæ·pŏnəit). 1849. [f. L. *sapo, sapon-* SOAP + -ITE[1] 2 b.] *Min.* A hydrous silicate of aluminium and magnesium, occurring in soft, soapy, amorphous masses, filling veins in serpentine, and cavities in trap-rock.

Sapor, sapour (sē[i]·pǫɹ, -pəɹ). 1477. [– L. *sapor*, f. *sapere* have a taste; see SAPIENT and cf. SAVOUR.] A quality such as is perceived by the sense of taste, as sweetness, etc.; a taste, savour; the taste or savour of a substance, esp. of an article of food and drink. Now chiefly in scientific use. **b.** In generalized sense: Quality in relation to the sense of taste 1650.

The exquisite sapor of their French dishes 1826.

Saporous (sē[i]·pŏrəs), *a. rare.* 1670. [In XVII – med.L. *saporosus* (see -OUS) or (as later) f. SAPOR + -OUS.] Of or pertaining to taste; having flavour or taste; yielding some kind of taste. †Also, savoury. So **Saporo·sity,** that property of a body by which it imparts the sensation of taste.

||**Sapota** (săpō[u]·tă). 1560. [In XVI–XVII *sapote* – Sp., Pg. *zapote* – Aztec *tzápotl*; repl. by mod.L. *sapota.*] = SAPODILLA. As mod.L.,

a genus, the type of the *Sapotaceæ*, now referred to *Achras*. Also *attrib.*, as *s. plum, wood*, etc.

Sapotaceous (sæpotē¹·ʃəs), *a.* 1845. [f. mod.L. *Sapotaceæ* (f. prec.); see -ACEOUS.] *Bot.* Of, pertaining to, or characteristic of the *Sapotaceæ*, a family of gamopetalous plants typified by the *Achras* (formerly *Sapota*).

Sapper (sæ·pəɹ). 1626. [f. SAP *v.*¹ + -ER¹, after Fr. *sapeur.*] One who saps, *spec.* a soldier employed in working at saps, the building and repairing of fortifications, etc.; as a prefixed designation = private of the Royal Engineers.

(*Royal*) *Sappers and Miners*, former name of non-commissioned officers and privates of the Engineers, now called Royal Engineers.

Sapphic (sæ·fik), *a.* and *sb.* 1501. [– Fr. *saphique*, †*sapphique* – L. *Sapphicus* – Gr. Σαπφικός.] **A.** *adj.* Of or pertaining to Sappho (Σαπφώ), the poetess of Lesbos (*c*600 B.C); *spec.* epithet of the metres used by her. **B.** *sb.* A metre used by Sappho or named after her. Chiefly *pl.*, verses written in the Sapphic stanza. 1586.

Greater S., a logaœdic distich of which the first line is —◡◡—◡—⏑ and the second (the Greater S. verse) is ⏓—⏑—◡◡—‖—◡◡—◡—⏑. *Lesser S.*, a logaœdic hendecasyllable with a dactyl in the third place (—◡—⏑—◡◡—◡—⏑). The 'S. stanza' consists of three Lesser Sapphics followed by an Adonic (—◡◡—⏑).

Sapphire (sæ·fəiᵊɹ). [ME. *saphir, safir* – OFr. *safir* (mod. *saphir*) – L. *sapphirus*, also *sapp(h)ir* – Gr. σάπφειρος (prob.) lapis lazuli, prob. of Semitic origin (cf. Heb. *sappîr*).] **1.** A precious stone of a beautiful transparent blue. It is a variety of native alumina akin to the ruby. **b.** *Min.* Used as a general name for all the precious transparent varieties of native crystalline alumina, including the ruby. A colourless variety is called *white* or *water s.* 1668. **c.** The deep blue colour of the sapphire 1686. **d.** *Her.* The tincture blue or azure, in blazoning by the names of precious stones 1562. **2.** A name for certain humming-birds 1843. **3.** quasi-*adj.* Sapphire-coloured. late ME.

1. Of Rubies, saphires, and of peerles white Were alle hise clothes brouded vp and down CHAUCER.

Comb. **s.-stone** = sense 1.

Sapphirine (sæ·firəin), *sb.* 1823. [f. prec. + -INE⁵.] *Min.* **a.** A silicate of aluminium and magnesium found in pale blue grains. **b.** A blue variety of spinel.

Sapphirine (sæ·firəin), *a.* late ME. [– L. *sapphirinus* – Gr. σαπφείρινος, f. σάπφειρος SAPPHIRE; see -INE¹.] Consisting of or like sapphire, having the qualities, esp. the colour, of sapphire.

The s. hue of the zenith in spring T. HARDY. *absol.* Thunder from the safe sky's s. BROWNING.

Sapphism (sæ·fiz'm). 1890. [f. the name of *Sappho* (see SAPPHIC), who was accused of this vice; see -ISM 2.] Unnatural sexual relations between women. So **Sa·pphist.**

Sappho (sæ·fo). 1843. [Applications of the name of the poetess (see SAPPHIC).] **1.** *Ornith.* The name of a genus of humming-birds. Hence, a bird of this genus; = COMET *sb.* 3; usu. *S. comet.* **2.** *Astr.* The name of the eightieth asteroid 1875.

Sappy (sæ·pi), *a.* OE. [f. SAP *sb.*¹ + -Y¹.] **1.** Of a plant, tree, etc.: Abounding in sap. **2.** *fig.* Full of vitality, 'goodness' or substance 1558. †**3.** Juicy, succulent –1825. **4.** Fat, plump. Now *dial.* 1694. **5.** Full of moisture; wet; sodden; rainy. Now *dial.* 1470. **b.** Of meat: Putrescent, tainted. *dial.* 1573. **6.** Consisting of or containing sap-wood 1466. **7.** Foolish 1670. Hence †**Sa·ppily** *adv.* –1724. **Sa·ppiness.**

‖**Sapræmia** (sæprī·miă). 1886. [mod.L., f. Gr. σαπρός putrid + αἷμα blood; see -IA¹.] Poisoning by means of septic or putrefactive organisms. Hence **Sapræ·mic** *a.* of, pertaining to or affected with, s.

Saprogenic (sæprodʒe·nik), *a.* 1876. [f. Gr. σαπρός putrid + -GEN + -IC 1.] Causing, or produced by, putrefaction. So **Sapro·genous** *a.*

Saprophagous (sæprǫ·fāgəs), *a.* 1819. [f. Gr. σαπρός putrid + -PHAGOUS.] Living on decomposing matter. So **Sapro·phagan,** belonging to, an insect of, the tribe *Saprophaga.*

Saprophile (sæ·profəil), *sb.* and *a.* 1882. [f. as prec. + -PHILE.] **A.** *sb.* A bacterium inhabiting putrid matter. **B.** *adj.* Of bacteria: Found in putrid matter.

Saprophyte (sæ·profəit). 1875. [f. as prec. + -PHYTE.] Any vegetable organism that lives on decayed organic matter. Hence **Saprophytic** (-fi·tik) *a.* of or pertaining to saprophytes. **Sa·prophytism,** the state of living as a s.

Sapsago (sæpsē¹·go). *U.S.* 1846. [Corruptly – G. *schabzieger*, f. *schaben* scrape, grate + *zieger* kind of cheese.] A kind of hard cheese made in Switzerland, flavoured with melilot.

Sapskull (sæ·pskɒl). Now *dial.* 1735. [f. SAP *sb.*¹ (sense 3) + ·SKULL.] = SAP-HEAD.

‖**Sapucaia** (sapukā·ya). 1613. [Tupi.] **1. a.** A S. Amer. tree of the genus *Lecythis.* **b.** The fruit of the tree, a s.-nut. **2.** *attrib.*, as **s.-nut,** the edible fruit of *Lecythis zabucajo* and *L. ollaria.*

Sa·p-wood. 1791. [SAP *sb.*¹] The softer and more recently formed wood between the bark and heart-wood in exogenous trees.

Sarabaite (særăbē¹·əit). late ME. [– eccl. L. *Sarabaita*; of unkn. origin.] One of a class of monks in the early Church who lived together in small bands without rule or superior.

Saraband (sæ·răbænd). 1616. [– Fr. *sarabande* – Sp., It. *zarabanda*, of disputed origin.] **1.** A slow and stately Spanish dance in triple time. **2.** A piece of music for this dance or in its rhythm, in which the second note of the measure is usu. lengthened 1625.

1. I can dance..Jiggs and Sarabands 1675.

Saracen (sæ·răsĕn), *sb.* and *a.* [– OFr. *Sar(r)azin, -cin* (mod. *Sarrasin*) – late L. *Saracenus* – late Gr. Σαρακηνός, perh. f. Arab. *šarḳī* eastern, f. *šarḳ* sunrise, east.] **A.** *sb.* **1.** Among the later Greeks and Romans, a name for the nomadic peoples of the Syro-Arabian desert; hence, an Arab; by extension, a Moslem, *esp.* with ref. to the Crusades. †**2.** A non-Christian; a heathen or pagan; an infidel –1552. **B.** *adj.* = next. (By Sir C. Wren erroneously applied to Pointed or 'Gothic' architecture.) ME.

Comb. †**Saracen's all-heal, consound,** *Senecio saracenicus*, used by the Saracens in healing wounds; **Saracen's head,** the head of a S., Arab, or Turk, used as a charge in heraldry, as an inn-sign, etc.

Saracenic (særăse·nik), *a.* 1638. [– med. L. *Saracenicus*, f. late L. *Saracenus* SARACEN; see -IC 1.] Of, pertaining to, or characteristic of the Saracens. **b.** Applied to Moslem architecture, or to any features in it 1768. So **Sarace·nical** *a.* 1613.

‖**Sarafan** (sæ·răfæn). 1799. [Russian.] A long mantle, veil, or sleeveless cloak, forming part of the national dress of Russian peasant women.

Saratoga (særătōᵘ·gă). 1893. [prob. f. *Saratoga Springs*, a summer resort in New York State.] In full *S. trunk*: A large kind of trunk much used by ladies.

Sarcasm (sa·ɹkæz'm). Also †**sarcasmus.** 1579. [– Fr. *sarcasme* (Rabelais) or late L. *sarcasmos* – late Gr. σαρκασμός, f. σαρκάζειν tear flesh, gnash the teeth, speak bitterly, f. σάρξ, σαρκ- flesh.] A sharp, bitter, or cutting expression or remark; a bitter gibe or taunt. Now usu. *gen.*: Sarcastic language; sarcastic meaning. Hence †**Sarca·smous** *a.* sarcastic.

Sarcast (sā·ɹkæst). 1654. [f. SARCASM, SARCASTIC, after similar groups, e.g. *enthusiasm|enthusiastic|enthusiast.*] A sarcastic writer or speaker.

Sarcastic (saɹkæ·stik), *a.* 1695. [– Fr. *sarcastique*, f. *sarcasme*, after *enthusiasme, -astique.*] Characterized by or involving sarcasm; given to the use of sarcasm; bitterly cutting or caustic.

Their merriment bluntly sarcastick JOHNSON. So **Sarca·stical** *a.* 1641. **Sarca·stical-ly** *adv.*, **-ness.**

†**Sa·rcel.** 1496. [– OFr. *cercel* (mod. *cerceau*) :– late L. *circellus*, dim. of *circulus*, dim. of *circus* circle; see CIRCUS, -EL, -ULE.] A pinion feather of a hawk's wing –1688.

fig. Vnfledg'd Witt Imp't from that ragged Sarcill Chaucer drop't 1649.

Sarcelle (saɹse·l). [ME. *cercelle* – OFr. *cercelle* (mod. *sarcelle*) = AL. *cercella* (XII) :– pop.L. *cercedula*, for cl.L. *querquedula* (Varro).] A name for the teals and closely allied ducks (*e.g.* the garganey, the long-tailed duck).

Sarcelled (sā·ɹsĕld), *a.* 1688. [Anglicized f. *sarcelle* (+ -ED¹) SARCELLY.] *Her.* = next 2, 3.

Sarcelly (sā·ɹsĕli), *a.* 1500. [– AFr. *sercelé*, *cercelé* = OFr. *cercelé* ringleted, curled, pa. pple. of *cerceler*, f. *cercel* SARCEL; see -Y⁵.] *Her.* **1.** Applied to a variety of the cross moline in which the points are recurved or curled back. **2.** Applied to a cross (esp. a cross moline) voided and open at the ends 1661. **3.** Cut through the middle 1864.

Sarcenet, var. SARSENET.

‖**Sarcina** (sā·ɹsină). *Pl.* **-næ** (nī). 1842. [L., = bundle, f. *sarcire* patch, mend.] *Bot.* A genus of schizomycetous fungi or bacteria, forming masses of cells united in fixed numbers, which are found in various animal fluids.

Sarco- (sā·ɹko, saɹkǫ·), comb. form of Gr. σάρξ, σαρκ- flesh, as in:

‖**Sa·rcobasis** *Bot.*, a very fleshy gynobase. **Sa·rcoblast,** (*a*) one of the minute yellow bodies present in rhizopods; (*b*) a germinal particle of protoplasm. **Sa·rcocarp** *Bot.*, the fleshy part of a drupaceous fruit lying between the epicarp and the endocarp; the part usu. eaten. **Sa·rcocele** (sā·ɹkosīl) *Path.*, hard fleshy enlargement of the testicle. **Sa·rcoderm,** ‖**Sarcode·rma** *Bot.*, the fleshy layer in some seeds, lying between the internal and external integuments. **Sarcola·ctic** *a. Chem.*, in *s. acid*, an acid, isomeric with lactic acid, obtained from muscular tissue. **Sarcole·mma** [LEMMA.²] *Anat.*, the transparent tubular sheath investing muscular fibre. **Sa·rcolite** *Min.*, a silicate of aluminium, sodium, and calcium found in flesh-coloured crystals. **Sarcopside** (saɹkǫ·psid) *Min.*, phosphate of iron and manganese exhibiting a flesh-red colour or fracture.

Sarcocol(l (sā·ɹkŏkǫl). Now *rare.* late ME. [– L. *sarcocolla*; see next.] = next.

‖**Sarcocolla** (sāɹkŏkǫ·lă). 1599. [– L. *sarcocolla* – Gr. σαρκόκολλα, f. σάρξ, σαρκ- flesh + κόλλα glue; so called because of its reputed property of agglutinating wounds.] A sub-viscid gum-resin brought from Arabia and Persia in light yellow or red grains.

Sarcode (sā·ɹkōᵘd), *sb.* and *a.* 1853. [– Fr. *sarcode* (Dujardin, 1835), f. Gr. σάρξ, σαρκ- flesh; see -ODE.] *Biol.* **A.** *sb.* The PROTOPLASM of animals. **B.** *adj.* Sarcodic; protoplasmic 1855. Hence **Sarcodic** (-ǫ·dik) *a.* of, pertaining to, of the nature of s.

Sarcoid (sā·ɹkoid), *a.* and *sb.* 1841. [f. Gr. σάρξ, σαρκ- flesh + -OID.] **A.** *adj.* Resembling flesh; flesh-like; applied to sponges, plants, etc. **B.** *sb.* A sponge particle 1875.

Sarcology (saɹkǫ·lŏdʒi). 1728. [f. SARCO- + -LOGY.] That branch of anatomy which treats of the fleshy parts of the body. Hence **Sarcolo·gic, -al** *adjs.* **Sarco·logist.**

‖**Sarcoma** (saɹkōᵘ·mă). *Pl.* **sarco·mata.** 1657. [– mod.L. *sarcoma* – Gr. σάρκωμα (Galen), f. σαρκοῦν become fleshy, f. σάρξ, σαρκ- flesh; see -OMA.] **1.** *Path.* †**a.** A fleshy excrescence –1752. **b.** A tumour composed of embryonic connective tissue 1804. **2.** *Bot.* The fleshy disc surrounding the ovary 1832. So **Sarco·matous** *a.* pertaining or relating to, of the nature of, s.

‖**Sarcophagus** (saɹkǫ·făgŭs). *Pl.* **-phagi** (-fădʒəi). 1601. [– L. *sarcophagus* – Gr. σαρκοφάγος, subst. use of adj. f. σάρξ, σαρκ- flesh + -φαγος -eating; see -PHAGOUS.] **1.** A kind of stone reputed among the Greeks to have the property of consuming the flesh of dead bodies deposited in it, and consequently used for coffins. Now *Antiq.* **2.** A stone coffin, often embellished with sculptures or bearing inscriptions, etc. 1619. **3.** A flesh-eating person or animal (*rare*) 1617.

2. A s. with ribbed work and mouldings H. WALPOLE.

Sarcophagy (saɹkǫ·fădʒi). *rare.* 1650. [– Gr. σαρκοφαγία, f. σαρκοφάγος; see prec. and -PHAGY.] The practice of eating flesh.

There was no Sarcophagie before the flood SIR T. BROWNE.

‖**Sarcoptes** (saɹkǫ·ptīz). 1874. [mod.L. (Latreille, 1804), irreg. f. Gr. σάρξ, σαρκ-, flesh

+ κόπτειν cut.] *Zool.* A genus of parasites comprising the itch-mite; a mite of this genus. Hence **Sarco·ptic** *a.* caused by itch-mites.

Sarcosin(e (sā·ɹkŏsin). 1848. [– G. *sarkosin* (Liebig, 1847), irreg. f. Gr. σάρξ, σαρκ- + -INE⁵.] *Chem.* A nitrogenous substance, one of the constituents of creatine; methyl glycocoll.

Sarcous (sā·ɹkəs), *a.* 1840. [f. Gr. σάρξ, σαρκ- flesh + -OUS.] Consisting of flesh or muscular tissue.

Sard (sāɹd), *sb.*¹ late ME. [– Fr. *sarde* or L. *sarda*, synon. of SARDIUS.] A variety of CORNELIAN¹, varying in colour from pale yellow to reddish orange.

Sard (sāɹd), *a.* and *sb.*² 1822. [– It. *Sardo*, L. *Sardus*.] = SARDINIAN *a.* and *sb.*

Sardanapalian (sāɹdănăpēⁱ·liăn), *a.* 1555. [f. L. *Sardanapalus*, Gr. Σαρδανάπαλος, name given to the last king of Nineveh, notorious for luxurious effeminacy; see -IAN.] Resembling Sardanapalus; luxuriously effeminate.

Sardelle (sāɹde·l). 1598. [– It. *sardella*, dim. of *sarda* :– L. *sarda* – Gr. σάρδη sardine.] A fish, *Clupea* or *Sardinella aurita*, resembling the sardine and prepared like it in certain Mediterranean ports.

Sardian (sā·ɹdiăn), *a.* and *sb.* 1551. [– L. *Sardianus* – Gr. Σαρδιανός, f. Σάρδεις pl., L. *Sardis, Sardes*, the ancient capital of Lydia.] **A.** *adj.* Of or pertaining to Sardis.

S. stone = SARD *sb.*¹

B. *sb.* **1.** An inhabitant of Sardis 1598. **2.** = SARD *sb.*¹ 1741.

Sardine¹ (sā·ɹdəin). late ME. [– late L. *sardinus* – Gr. σάρδινος, var. reading of σάρδιος SARDIUS.] A precious stone mentioned in Rev. 4:3.

Sardine² (saɹdī·n). late ME. [– (O)Fr. *sardine*, corresp. to It. *sardina* – L. *sardina*; cf. late Gr. σαρδήνη, -ίνη, -ῖνος, and L. *sarda*, Gr. σάρδα; prob. connected with the name of the island Sardinia.] A small fish of the herring family, *Clupea pilchardus*, abundant off the shores of Sardinia and Brittany, or a young Cornish pilchard, when cured, preserved in oil and packed in tins or glass for sale as a table delicacy. **b.** Any of various fishes resembling the sardine, or similarly preserved, e.g. *U.S.* the young of the herring or menhaden 1876.

Sardinian (saɹdi·niăn), *a.* and *sb.* 1598. [f. *Sardinia* (see below) + -AN¹ 1.] **A.** *adj.* **1.** Of or pertaining to either the island, or to the kingdom of Sardinia (1720–1859), which included Piedmont and adjacent territories as well as the island 1748. **†2. a.** Used for SARDONIAN, SARDONIC. **b.** tr. L. *sardonius*, as the epithet of the plant producing 'sardonic' laughter. –1752.

2. a. What the Latins call S. Laughter, a distortion of the face without gladness of heart JOHNSON.

B. *sb.* An inhabitant or native of Sardinia 1598; the language of the Sardinians 1841.

‖**Sardius** (sā·ɹdiŏs). late ME. [– late L. *sardius* – Gr. σάρδιος, prob. f. Σαρδώ Sardinia. See SARDINE¹.] A precious stone mentioned by ancient writers; see SARD *sb.*¹

S., topacius, and iaspis WYCLIF *Ezek.* 28:13.

†Sardo·nian, *a.* 1586. [– Fr. †*sardonien*, f. L. *sardonius* – late Gr. Σαρδόνιος Sardinian, which was substituted for σαρδάνιος (Homer) as the epithet of bitter or scornful laughter.] = SARDONIC *a.* –1794.

And with S. smyle Laughing on her, his false intent to shade SPENSER.

Sardonic (saɹdǫ·nik), *a.* 1638. [– Fr. *sardonique*, alt. of *sardonien*; see prec., -IC.] Of laughter, a smile: Bitter, scornful, mocking. Hence of a person, etc.: Characterized by or exhibiting bitterness, scorn or mockery.

Then smil'd Ulysses a Sardanique smile HOBBES. The s. historian, whose rule it is to exhibit human nature always as an object of mockery 1833. Hence **Sardo·nical** *a.*, **-ly** *adv.*

Sardonyx (sā·ɹdŏniks). late ME. [– L. *sardonyx* – Gr. σαρδόνυξ, presumably f. σάρδιος SARDIUS + ὄνυξ ONYX.] A variety of onyx or stratified chalcedony having white layers alternating with one or more strata of sard.

Our highly valued emeralds and sardonyxes 1875.

‖**Saree, sari** (sā·ri). 1785. [Hindi *sārhī*, *sāṛī*.] A long wrapping garment of cloth or silk, worn by Indian women; also, the material of this.

Sargasso (saɹgæ·so). 1598. [– Pg. *sargaço* of unkn. origin.] = GULF-WEED; a mass or species of this.

S. Sea, a region in the North Atlantic, south of the 35th parallel, where masses of s. are found.

Sargo (sā·ɹgo). 1880. [– Sp. *sargo* :– L. SARGUS.] Any of many species of fishes, several of which occur in the Mediterranean and the neighbouring parts of the Atlantic.

‖**Sargus** (sā·ɹgŏs). 1591. [L. *sargus* = Gr. σάργος.] A fish of the genus *Sargus*, the type of the family *Sparidæ*, the sea-breams.

Sari, var. sp., now usual, of SAREE.

‖**Sarigue** (sarī·g). 1683. [Fr. (Buffon) – Pg. *sarigué*; used erron. for Brazilian *sariguéya*, a deriv. of *Sarigué*, name of a tribe of Indians.] A S. Amer. opossum, *Didelphys opossum*.

Sark (sāɹk), *sb.* *Sc.* and *north.* [ME. (north.) *serk* – ON. *serkr* :– Gmc. **sarkiz*, f. base repr. also by OE. *serće*, *syrće*, *syr(i)ć*.] A garment worn next the skin; a shirt or chemise; occas. a nightshirt; *transf.* a surplice. Hence **Sark** *v. trans.* to furnish with or clothe in a s.

Sarlac (sā·ɹlăk). 1781. [Calmuck *sarluk*.] = YAK.

Sarmatian (saɹmēⁱ·ʃăn), *a.* and *sb.* 1613. [f. L. *Sarmatia* the land of the *Sarmatæ* (Gr. Σαρμάται, also Σαυρομάται); see -AN.] **A.** *adj.* Of or belonging to the ancient Sarmatia, now occupied approximately by the Russians and Poles. **B.** *sb.* One of a nomadic people formerly inhabiting this territory 1613. So **Sarma·tic** *a.* = A.

Sarment (sā·ɹmĕnt). Now *rare.* late ME. [– L. *sarmentum*, chiefly in pl., twigs lopped off, f. *sarpere* prune.] A twig, †a cutting of a tree. So **Sarmenta·ceous, Sarmento·se, Sarme·ntous** *adjs.* (of a stem) producing slender prostrate runners or branches.

‖**Sarong** (sărǫ·ŋ). 1834. [Malay and Javanese *saroeng* (prop.) sheath, quiver.] The Malay national garment, a long strip of cloth, worn tucked round the waist like a skirt.

‖**Saros** (sēᵊ·rǫs). 1613. [Gr. σάρος, σαρός – Assyro-Babylonian *šār(u.)* **1.** *Antiq.* The Babylonian name for the number 3600, and for a period of 3600 years. **2.** *Astr.* Adopted by modern astronomers as the name of the cycle of 18 years and 10⅔ days, in which solar and lunar eclipses repeat themselves 1812.

Sarpo (sā·ɹpo). 1753. [– Sp. *sapo*, lit. 'large toad'.] The toad-fish, *Batrachus tau*, or *B. pardus*.

‖**Sarracenia** (særăsī·niă). 1786. [mod.L., alt. of *Sarracena*; named by Tournefort (1700, after D. *Sarrazin*, of Quebec, who sent him the plant); see -IA¹.] *Bot.* A genus of insectivorous plants, the type of the family *Sarraceniaceæ*, to which belong many of the pitcher-plants.

‖**Sarrasin** (sæ·răzin). 1621. [– Fr. *sarrasin* (XVI), for *blé sarrasin* 'Saracen wheat'.] Buckwheat.

Sarsa (sā·ɹsă). 1625. Short for next.

Sarsaparilla (sāɹsăpări·lă). 1577. [– Sp. *zarzaparilla*, f. *zarza* bramble = Arab. *šaras* thorny plant + (prob.) dim. of Sp. *parra* twining plant.] **1.** A plant belonging to any of the species of the family *Smilaceæ*, indigenous to tropical America from Mexico to Peru; esp. *Smilax officinalis* the Jamaica sarsaparilla. **b.** The dried roots of plants of the various species of *Smilaceæ*; a preparation of the root of *S. officinalis* used as an alterative and tonic 1577. **2.** Applied to plants of other genera, resembling the true sarsaparilla or furnishing a root used as a substitute for it 1840.

Sarsen (sā·ɹs'n). 1644. [app. identical with *Sarsen*, var. of SARACEN.] (In full *s.-stone*, *boulder*.) One of the numerous large boulders or blocks of sandstone found scattered on the surface of the chalk downs, esp. in Wiltshire.

Sarsenet, sarcenet (sā·ɹsnĕt). late ME. [– AFr. *sarzinett*, perh. dim. of *sarzin* SARACEN, suggested by OFr. *drap sarrasinois*, med.L. *pannus saracenicus* 'Saracen cloth'; see -ET.] **1.** A very fine and soft silk material now used chiefly for linings; a dress of this. **2.** *attrib.* or as *adj.* Composed of sarsenet 1521. **†b.** *fig.* Resembling s. in softness –1820.

2. Hange over the eye..a greene sarsenet cloth 1547. **b.** 1 *Hen. IV*, III. i. 256.

Sartor (sā·ɹtǫr). 1656. [– L. *sartor*, f. *sart-*, pa. ppl. stem of *sarcire* patch, botch; see -OR 2.] A tailor (*joc. pedantic*).

Sartorial (saɹtōᵊ·riăl), *a.* 1823. [f. L. *sartor* (see prec.) + -IAL.] Of or belonging to a tailor or his art; characteristic of a tailor.

‖**Sartorius** (saɹtōᵊ·riŏs). 1704. [mod.L. *sartorius* (sc. *musculus* muscle), f. L. SARTOR.] A long narrow muscle which crosses the thigh obliquely in front.

‖**Sarum** (sēᵊ·rŏm). 1570. [med.L. *Sarum*, evolved from a misinterpretation of *Sarȝ*, mediæval abbrev. of *Sarisburia* Salisbury.] Eccl. name of Salisbury, used attrib. in *S. use*, the order of divine service used in Salisbury from the 11th c. to the Reformation; so *S. missal, rubric.*

Sash (sæʃ), *sb.*¹ 1590. [orig. *shash* – Arab. *šāš* muslin, turban; alt. by dissimilation of *sh..sh* to *s..sh*; cf. next.] **†1.** A band of a fine material worn twisted round the head as a turban by Orientals –1718. **2.** A scarf, worn by men, either over one shoulder or round the waist. Also, a similar article worn round the waist by women and children. 1681. Hence **Sash** *v.*¹ *trans.* to dress or adorn with a s.

Sash (sæʃ), *sb.*² late ME. [First recorded in pl. *shashes* (1681), var. of *chasses*, used as pl. of Fr. *châssis* frame, framework; see CHASSIS. For the dissimilation cf. prec.] **1.** A frame, usu. of wood, rebated and fitted with one or more panes of glass forming a window or part of a window; *esp.* a sliding frame or each of the two sliding frames of a SASH-WINDOW. Also (now *U.S.*) applied to a casement. **b.** A glazed light of a glass-house or garden frame; a sash-light 1707. **2.** *U.S.* A rectangular frame in which a saw-blade is stretched to prevent its bending or buckling 1875.

Comb.: **s. cord**, a cord used for hanging window sashes; **s. frame**, (*a*) a frame fixed in the opening of a wall to receive the s. or sashes of a window; also, a s. or sash-light; (*b*) *U.S.* = sense 2; **s. pulley**, a pulley in a window frame over which the s. cord runs; **s. tool**, a glaziers' brush; also, a small brush for painting sashes; **s. weight**, a weight attached to each of the two cords of a s. to counterbalance it at any height. Hence **Sash** *v.*² *trans.* to furnish with s.-windows; to construct as a s.-window.

Sa·sh-wi·ndow. 1686. [f. SASH *sb.*²] A window consisting of a sash or glazed wooden frame; esp. one having a sash or pair of sashes made to slide up and down, as dist. from a casement.

Sasin (sæ·sin). Also **saisin.** 1834. [Nepalese.] The common Indian antelope, *Antilope bezoartica* or *cervicapra*.

Sasine (sēⁱ·sin). 1669. [Sc. var. of SEISIN, after Law Latin *sasina*.] *Sc. Law.* The act of giving possession of feudal property.

Saskatoon (sæskătū·n). 1875. [– Cree *misāskwatomin*, f. *misāskwat* amelanchier + *min* fruit, berry.] The shrub or small tree *Amelanchier canadensis*, and its fruit.

Sassaby (săsēⁱ·bi). 1820. [– Sechwana *tsessébe*, *-ábi*.] A large S. African antelope, *Alcelaphus lunata*, sometimes called the Bastard Hartebeest.

Sassafras (sæ·săfræs). 1577. [– Sp. *sasafrás* or Pg. *sassafraz*, of unkn. origin.] **1.** A small tree, *Sassafras officinale*, with green apetalous flowers and dimorphous leaves, native to N. America. **2.** The dried bark of this tree, used as an alterative; also, an infusion of this 1577.

1. Australian or Tasmanian s. (*Atherosperma moschata*), Brazilian s. (*Nectandra puchury*), Swamp s. (*Magnolia glauca*), trees of other genera having similar medicinal properties to the s.

Sassanian (sæsēⁱ·niăn), *a.* and *sb.* Also **Sasanian.** 1788. [f. *Sasan* (Pers. *Sāsān*) + -IAN.] **A.** *adj.* Of or pertaining to the family of Sasan, rulers of the Persian Empire A.D. 211–651. **B.** *sb.* A member of this family, esp.

one of the Sassanian kings. So **Sassanid,** (sæ·sănid) *sb.* and *a.* 1776.

†**Sasse.** 1642. [– Du. *sas*, of unkn. origin.] = LOCK *sb.*[2] II. 3. –1861.

Sassenach (sæ·sĕnăχ). 1771. [– Gael. *Sasunnoch* = Ir. *Sasanach*, f. *Sasan-* (cf. Gael. *Sasunn*, Ir. *Sasana* England) – L. *Saxones*, OE. *Seaxe, Seaxan* Saxons.] The name given by the Gaelic inhabitants of Great Britain and Ireland to their 'Saxon' or English neighbours.

Sassoline (sæ·sǒlīn). 1807. [– G. *sassolin* (Karsten), f. Lago del *Sasso* in Tuscany + -INE[5], with euphonic *l*.] *Min.* Native boracic acid, found as a crystalline deposit in the hot springs of Tuscany.

‖**Sassy** (sæ·si). 1856. [W. African; believed to represent Eng. SAUCY *a.*] Used *attrib.* in *s.-tree*, the African tree *Erythrophlœum guineense*; also in *s.-bark, -wood*, the bark of this tree, a decoction of which is used in West Africa as an ordeal poison.

Satan (sē̆ⁱ·tăn). OE. [– L. *Satan* (Vulgate) = Gr. Σατάν or Σατᾶν – Heb. *śāṭān* adversary, f. *śaṭan* oppose, plot against.] **1.** The proper name of the supreme evil spirit, the Devil. (Now always with capital S.) †**2.** In wider sense: A devil –1688. **b.** Applied to a person or animal as a term of abhorrence. Now *rare*. 1596.

2. We in all likelihood are to possess the very places from which the Satans by transgression fell BUNYAN.

Satanas (sæ·tănæs). Now *arch.* OE. [– L. (Vulg.) *Satanas* – Gr. Σατανᾶς – Aramaic and Syriac *sāṭānā*, emphatic form of *sāṭān* (– Heb. *śāṭān*); see prec.] = SATAN 1.

Satanic (sătæ·nik), *a.* 1667. [f. SATAN + -IC 1. Cf. Fr. *satanique*.] **1.** Of or pertaining to Satan. **2.** Characteristic of or befitting Satan; diabolical, devilish, infernal 1793. **3.** *S. school*: Southey's designation for Byron, Shelley, and their imitators; subsequently often applied to other writers accused of defiant impiety and delight in the portraiture of lawless passion 1821.

2. A criminal..who with s. wickedness had murdered his benefactor 1793. So **Sata·nical** *a.* 1548. **Sata·nical-ly** *adv.*, †**-ness.**

Satanism (sē̆ⁱ·tăniz'm). 1565. [f. SATAN + -ISM 1 b. Cf. Fr. *satanisme* (sense 3).] **1.** A satanic or diabolical disposition, doctrine, spirit, or contrivance. **2.** The characteristics of the 'Satanic school' 1822. **3.** The worship of Satan; the principles and rites of the Satanists 1896. So **Sa·tanist,** one who is regarded as an adherent of Satan (now *rare*); one who worships Satan 1559.

Satanize (sē̆ⁱ·tănəiz), *v. rare.* 1598. [f. SATAN + -IZE 5.] *trans.* To render like Satan; to make into, or like a devil.

Satanology (sēⁱtănǫ·lŏdʒi). 1862. [f. SATAN + -LOGY.] That part of knowledge which relates to Satan.

Satanophany (sēⁱtănǫ·făni). 1864. [f. SATAN, after *theophany*; see -PHANY.] The appearing, or visible manifestation, of Satan.

Satchel (sæ·tʃĕl). ME. [– OFr. *sachel* :– L. *saccellus*, dim. of *saccus* SACK *sb.*[1]] A small bag; *esp.* a bag for carrying school-books, with or without a strap to hang over the shoulders.

Then, the whining Schoole-boy with his Satchell ..creeping..Vnwillingly to schoole SHAKS. Hence **Sa·tchelled** *a.* having or carrying a s.

Sate (sēⁱt), *v.* 1602. [prob. alt. of dial. *sade* (cf. SADE *v.*), by assoc. with SATIATE *v.*] **1.** *trans.* To fill or satisfy to the full (with food); to gratify to the full any appetite or desire 1613. **b.** To surfeit or cloy by gratification of appetite or desire; to glut, satiate 1602. †**2.** To saturate –1759.

1. Wherefore did Nature powre her bounties forth,..But all to please, and s. the curious taste? MILT. **2.** A spring strongly sated with a kind of salt 1759. Hence **Sa·teless** *a.* insatiable (chiefly *poet.*).

Sate: see SIT *v.*

Sateen (sătī·n). 1878. [Altered f. SATIN, after *velveteen*; see -EEN[1].] A cotton or woollen fabric with a glossy surface like that of satin.

Satellite (sæ·tĕləit). 1548. [– (O)Fr. *satellite* or L. *satelles, satellit-*.] **1.** An attendant upon a person of importance, forming part of his retinue. Often with implication of subservience or unscrupulous service. **2.** A small or secondary heavenly body which revolves round a larger one 1665. **3.** The name of (*a*) a moth; (*b*) a humming-bird 1832. **4.** *S. vein*: a vein that accompanies an artery (mod.L. *vena satelles, vena comes*) 1846.

1. Boswell was..made happy by an introduction to Johnson, of whom he became the obsequious s. 1850. **2. b.** *attrib.* passing into *adj.* Secondary, minor, satellitic 1923. Hence **Satelli·tic** *a.* of, pertaining to, of the nature of, a s. or lesser planet; also *transf.*

Satiable (sēⁱ·ʃiăb'l), *a.* 1570. [f. SATIATE *v.* + -ABLE. Cf. AL. *satiabilis*.] That can be satiated.

Satiate (sēⁱ·ʃiět), *pa. pple.* and *ppl. a.* Now *rare.* 1440. [– L. *satiatus*, pa. pple. of *satiare*; see next, -ATE[2].] †**A.** *pa. pple.* Satiated. **B.** *ppl. a.* Satiated, filled to repletion, glutted.

Satiate (sēⁱ·ʃieⁱt), *v.* 1532. [– *satiat-*, pa. ppl. stem of L. *satiare*, f. *satis* enough, after SATIATE pa. pple.; see -ATE[3].] **1.** *trans.* To fill, satisfy (with food). Hence *gen.*, to gratify to the full (a person or his desires). Now *rare.* **2.** To gratify beyond one's natural desire; to weary or disgust by repletion; to glut, cloy, surfeit 1620. †**3.** To saturate –1791.

1. The idea that satiating the servants of the public with wealth is a secret for rendering them honest 1817. **2.** Quite fatigued and satiated with this dull variety BURKE. Hence **Satia·tion,** the action of satiating or fact of being satiated.

Satiety (sătəi·ěti). 1533. [In XVI *sacietie* – (O)Fr. *sacieté* (mod. *satiété*) – L. *satietas, -tat-*; see -ITY.] **1.** The state of being satiated with food; the feeling of disgust or surfeit caused by excess of food. **b.** *gen.* The condition of having any appetite or desire gratified to excess; hence, weariness or dislike *of* (an object of desire) caused by gratification or attainment 1553. †**c.** The condition of being filled or fully gratified –1722. **2.** A sufficiency or abundance (*rare*) 1635.

1. It is always a case of famine or s. LIVINGSTONE. **b.** Thy words with Grace Divine Imbu'd, bring to thir sweetness no satietie MILT. Phr. *To s.* [= L. *ad satietatem*], to an amount or degree which satisfies or gluts desire.

Satin (sæ·tin), *sb.* (and *a.*) late ME. [– (O)Fr. *satin* – Arab. *zaytūnī*, pertaining to the town Tseutung (Tswan-chu-fu) in China (*aṭlas zaytūnī* satin of Zaitun).] **1.** A silk fabric with a glossy surface on one side, produced by a method of weaving by which the threads of the warp are caught and looped by the weft only at certain intervals. **b.** Applied to fabrics resembling satin, but made of other materials than silk 1517. **2.** The plant Honesty, *Lunaria biennis.* Also *white s.* 1597. **3.** *slang.* Gin. Also *white s.* 1854. **4.** Collector's name for a glossy white moth. Also *white s.* 1766. **5.** *attrib.* or *adj.* Made of, resembling, s. 1521.

1. Cledde In fyne blak satyn de owter mere CHAUCER. **b.** ‖*Satin beauté*, a soft draping dress material of a fine weave, dull crêpe back, and satin face. **5.** His high-crown'd hat and sattin-doublet GRAY.

Comb.: **s. cloth,** a woollen cloth woven like s., chiefly produced at Roubaix in France; **-finish,** a polish for silver produced by means of a metallic brush; also a satin-effect produced on materials; **-paper,** a fine writing paper; **s. sheeting,** a composite material of waste silk and cotton; **s. stitch,** a kind of stitch in embroidery and wool-work, imitating the appearance of s.; **-straw,** soft flexible straw used for hats. **b.** In names of insects, plants, minerals, etc., having a s.-like lustre or smoothness: **s. beauty,** a moth, *Boarmia abietaria*; **-carpet,** a moth, *Ceratopacha fluctuosa*; also = *s. beauty*; **-flower,** (*a*) Honesty; (*b*) the Greater Stitchwort; **s. gypsum,** a fibrous variety of gypsum; **-spar,** a fibrous variety of carbonate of lime; also = *s. gypsum*; **-white,** artificial sulphate of lime; **-wood,** the wood of the Indian tree *Chloroxylon Swietenia* and of several W. Indian trees. Hence **Sa·tin** *v. trans.* to give (to wall-paper) a glossy surface resembling that of s. **Sa·tiny** *a.* resembling s.

Satinette, satinet (sætine·t, sæ·tinět). 1703. [f. SATIN + -ETTE.] **a.** An imitation of satin woven in silk, or silk and cotton. **b.** A fabric woven with a cotton warp and woollen weft, with a satin-like surface 1837.

Satire (sæ·təiᵊɹ). 1509. [– (O)Fr. *satire* or L. *satira*, later form of *satura* (in earliest use) verse composition treating of a variety of subjects, spec. application of the sense 'medley'. Formerly assoc. with SATYR and so spelt.] **I. 1.** A poem, now occas. a prose composition, in which prevailing vices or follies are held up to ridicule. Sometimes, less correctly, a lampoon. **b.** *fig.* A thing, fact, or circumstance that has the effect of making some person or thing ridiculous 1693. **2. a.** Satirical composition 1589. **b.** The employment, in speaking or writing, of sarcasm, irony, ridicule, etc. in denouncing, exposing, or deriding vice, folly, abuses, or evils of any kind 1675.

1. *The Rape of the Lock*, is the best S. extant 1756. **b.** Their very names are a s. upon all government '*Junius*' *Lett.* **2.** My verse is s. YOUNG. I have seen no specimen of Hindú s. 1841.

†**II.** A satirical person, a satirist –1709.

Misacmos is a S., a quipping fellow 1596.

Satiric (săti·rik), *a.* and *sb.* 1509. [– Fr. *satirique* or late L. *satiricus*, f. L. *satira*; see prec., -IC.] **A.** *adj.* **1.** Of, pertaining to, or of the nature of satire; consisting of, or containing satire; that writes or composes satires. †**2.** Addicted to satire, satirical –1763.

1. S. novels, poets bold and free CRABBE. **2.** A lively and satyric People 1763.

B. *sb.* †**1.** A writer of satires; a satirist (*rare*) –1603. **2.** *pl.* Satirical writings (*rare*) 1600.

Satirical (săti·rikăl), *a.* 1529. [f. as prec.; see -ICAL.] **1.** = prec. A. 1. **2.** Given to, indulging in, or characterized by satire 1590. Hence **Sati·rical-ly** *adv.*, **-ness.**

†**Sa·tirism.** *rare.* 1593. [f. SATIRE + -ISM 1.] Indulgence in satire; satirical utterance –1716.

Satirist (sæ·tĭrist). 1589. [f. SATIRE + -IST.] A writer of satires; (const. *of*) one who satirizes some person or thing.

It is for the satyrist to expose the ridiculous BURKE.

Satirize (sæ·tĭrəiz), *v.* 1601. [– Fr. *satiriser*, f. *satire*; see SATIRE, -IZE.] **1.** *intr.* To write satires; to assail some one or something with satire. Now only as absol. use of 2. **2.** *trans.* To assail with satire; to make the object of, or expose to, satire or censure; to describe or ridicule in a satirical manner 1630.

2. It is as hard to s. well a man of distinguished vices, as to praise well a man of distinguished virtues POPE. Hence **Sa·tirizer.**

Satisfaction (sætisfæ·kʃən). ME. [– (O)Fr. *satisfaction* – L. *satisfactio, -on-*, f. *satisfact-*, pa. ppl. stem of *satisfacere*; see SATISFY, -ION.] The action of satisfying; the state or fact of being satisfied. **I.** With ref. to obligations. **1.** The payment in full of a debt, or the fulfilment of an obligation or claim; the atoning *for* an injury, offence, or fault. Also quasi-*concr.*, the pecuniary or other gift or penalty, or the act, by which these are discharged, fulfilled, or atoned for. Now chiefly *Law.* late ME. **b.** An act of compensation or amends; an amount paid in compensation; a penalty. Now *rare.* 1440. **2.** *Eccl.* The performance by a penitent of the penance enjoined by his confessor as payment of the temporal punishment made by Christ for the sins of the world. So *doctrine of s.* late ME. **4.** The opportunity of satisfying one's honour by a duel; the acceptance of a challenge to a duel from the person who deems himself injured. Chiefly in phr., *to give, demand s.* 1602.

1. Unless for him Som other able, and as willing, pay The rigid s., death for death MILT. Phrases. *To make* (or †*do*) *s.*; *in s.* (*of*). *To enter* (*up*) *s.* (Law), to place on the record of a court a statement that the payment ordered by it has been duly made; so *entry of s.* **4.** It is called *Giving a Man S.*, to urge your Offence against him with your Sword STEELE.

II. With ref. to desires or feelings. **1.** The action of gratifying (an appetite or desire) to the full, or of contenting (a person) by the fulfilment of a desire or the supply of a want; the fact of having been thus gratified or contented. late ME. **b.** Satisfied or contented state of mind; now usu., gratification or pleasure occasioned by some fact, event, or state of things 1477. **c.** A particular instance of satisfaction; something which occasions gratification 1687. **2.** Release from suspense; removal of doubt or difficulty; conviction 1586.

1. My guide..did his duty entirely to my s. TYNDALL. **b.** The grettest richesse is satisfacion of the herte 1477. Jones expressed the utmost s. at the account FIELDING. **c.** A quick Relish of the Satisfactions of Life STEELE. **2.** Phr. *to (a person's) s.* Hence **Satisfa·ctionist** (*rare*), one who holds that Christ suffered punishment as s. for the sins of man.

Satisfactive (sætisfæ·ktiv), *a. rare.* 1829. [A var. form of SATISFACTORY (4 a) by substitution of suffix -IVE.] In Bentham's use: Consisting in or concerned with satisfaction or reparation.

Satisfactory (sætisfæ·ktəri), *a.* and *sb.* 1547. [– (O)Fr. *satisfactoire* or med.L. *satisfactorius*, f. *satisfact-*; see SATISFACTION, -ORY[1] and [2].] **1.** *Eccl.* and *Theol.* Serving to make satisfaction or atonement for sin 1547. **2.** Serving to satisfy a debt or obligation (*rare*) 1604. †**3.** Of an explanation or argument: Serving merely to satisfy the inquirer or objector; merely plausible. BACON. **4. a.** Adequate for the needs of the case. Of an argument: Convincing. **b.** That justifies a feeling of satisfaction. 1640.

4. a. A s. reply MACAULAY. **b.** Went home with a triumphant light in his eyes after concluding a s. marriage for his son GEO. ELIOT. Hence **Satisfa·ctori-ly** *adv.*, **-ness.**

Satisfy (sæ·tisfəi), *v.* late ME. [– OFr. *satisfier*, irreg. – L. *satisfacere*, f. *satis* enough; see -FY.] **I.** With ref. to debt or obligation. **1.** *trans.* To pay off or discharge fully (a debt, obligation); to comply with (a demand). Now *rare* exc. in legal use. **b.** To pay (a creditor). Now *rare* exc. in legal use. late ME. †**c.** To remunerate –1771. †**2.** To make compensation or reparation for (a wrong, injury); to atone for (an offence) –1715. **b.** To make atonement or reparation to (a person, his honour, etc.) 1602. **3.** *intr.* To make satisfaction, full payment, reparation, or atonement. Now *Theol.* (said of Christ). 1450.

1. After all my dettes are satisfied 1578. **2.** Thy death shall satisfie thy iniury, & my malice SIDNEY. **3.** So Man..Shall satisfie for Man MILT.

II. With ref. to feelings or needs. **1.** *trans.* To meet or fulfil the wish or desire or expectation of; to be accepted by (a person, his taste, judgement, etc.) as all that could be reasonably desired; to content. Also with obj. a desire, expectation, etc. 1489. **b.** In *pass.*, To be content (*with*); to find it sufficient, desire or demand no more than *to do* something. Also, to be well pleased (*with*, †*at*). 1533. **2.** *absol.* and *intr.* To cause or give satisfaction or contentment 1600. **3.** *trans.* To cause to have enough; to put an end to (an appetite, want) by fully supplying it 1500. **4.** To furnish with sufficient proof or information; to set free from doubt or uncertainty; to convince 1520. **5.** To answer sufficiently (an objection, question); to fulfil or comply with (a request); to solve (a doubt, difficulty) 1581. **6.** To answer the requirements of (a state of things, hypothesis, etc.); to accord with (conditions) 1651. **b.** *Algebra.* Of a known quantity: To fulfil the conditions of, be an admissible solution of (an equation) 1826.

1. It is harde to satisfye all men 1530. I have it in my power to s. your curiosity 1717. Phr. *To s. the examiners*, in English Universities, to be entitled to a 'pass', but not to 'honours'. **b.** We were fain to rest satisfied then, with what we saw of that Monastery from the top of the Mount 1687. **3.** Hee will not be satisfied with blood *Ecclus.* 12:16. **4.** Where I cannot s. my reason, I love to humour my fancy SIR T. BROWNE. No one can..be satisfied of the contrary 1736. **5.** Revelation was not given us to s. doubts, but to make us better men 1834. Hence **Sa·tisfiable** *a.* †satisfactory; able to be or that may be satisfied. **Sa·tisfied-ly** *adv.*, **-ness. Sa·tisfier. Sa·tisfying-ly** *adv.*, **-ness.**

Satispassion (sætispæ·ʃən). 1614. [– med.L. (?AL.) *satispassio* (XIV), f. after *satisfactio*; see SATISFACTION, PASSION.] *Theol.* Atonement by an adequate degree of suffering.

†**Sa·tive,** *a.* 1599. [– L. *sativus*, f. *sat-*, pa. ppl. stem of *serere* sow, plant; see -IVE.] Sown or planted; cultivated, not wild –1725.

Satrap (sæ·træp). late ME. [– (O)Fr. *satrape* or L. *satrapa*, *satrapes* – Gr. σατράπης – OPers. *xšaθra-pāvan* 'protector of the country', f. *xšaθra-* country + *pā-* protect.] **1.** A governor of a province under the ancient Persian monarchy. **2.** *transf.* A subordinate ruler; often with imputation of tyranny or ostentation. late ME. Hence **Sa·trapal** *a.* of or pertaining to a s. or satraps. **Sa·trapess,** a female s. **Satra·pic, -al** *adjs.* pertaining to a s.; *fig.* cruel, tyrannical.

Satrapy (sæ·trăpi). 1603. [– Fr. *satrapie* or L. *satrapia* – Gr. σατραπεία; see prec., -Y[3].] **1.** A province ruled over by a satrap. **2.** The dignity of a satrap 1641. **3.** The period of rule of a satrap 1846.

‖**Satsuma** (sæ·tsŭmă). 1872. [A province in the island of Kiusiu, Japan.] In full *S. ware*, a kind of cream-coloured Japanese pottery.

Saturable (sæ·tiŭrăb'l, sæ·tʃə-), *a.* 1570. [f. SATURATE (sense 3) + -ABLE.] Capable of saturation.

Saturate (sæ·tiŭrĕt, sæ·tʃə-), *a.* 1550. [– L. *saturatus*, pa. pple. of *saturare*; see next, -ATE[2].] †**1.** Satisfied, satiated –1604. **2.** Soaked through, saturated with moisture. Chiefly *poet.* 1784. **3.** Of colours: Intense, deep 1669.

2. The lark is gay, That dries his feathers, s. with dew, Beneath the rosy cloud COWPER. **3.** It would yield a deep s. green tincture 1669.

Saturate (sæ·tiŭre[i]t, sæ·tʃə-), *v.* 1538. [– *saturat-*, pa. ppl. stem of L. *saturare*, f. *satur* full, satiated; see -ATE[3].] †**1.** *trans.* To satisfy, satiate –1816. **2.** To soak thoroughly, imbue *with* 1756. **3.** *Chem.* To cause (a substance) to combine with or dissolve the utmost possible quantity of another substance 1681. **4.** *Physics.* **a.** To charge (air or vapour) with the utmost quantity of moisture that it can hold in suspension 1812. **b.** To magnetize (a piece of metal), charge (a body) with electricity, to the fullest extent of its capacity 1832.

2. Thatch that had got saturated with the smoke 1873. *fig.* A mind not thoroughly saturated with the tolerating maxims of the Gospel BURKE. Hence **Sa·turator,** one who or that which saturates, e.g. a device for supplying air saturated with water-vapour to a room, etc.

Saturated (sæ·tiŭre[i]tĕd, sæ·tʃə-), *ppl. a.* 1668. [f. prec. + -ED[1].] †**1.** Filled to repletion –1820. **2.** Penetrated with moisture, soaked through 1728. **3.** *Physics.* That has combined with or dissolved the largest possible proportion of some other substance 1788. **4.** *Physics.* Charged to the full extent of its capacity 1848. **5.** Of colours: Not diluted with white 1853. **6.** *Phys. Chem.* That has equal and opposite quantities of electricity in each molecule or atom 1888.

2. And s. earth Awaits the morning beam THOMSON. **3.** A s. solution of nitre 1788. **4.** *S. steam*, steam charged with such an amount of heat that less would produce condensation, and more super heat.

Saturation (sætiŭrē[i]·ʃən, sætʃə-). 1554. [– late L. *saturatio*, *-on-*, f. *saturat-*; see SATURATE *v.*, -ION. In later use from the Eng. verb.] †**1.** Satiation –1832. **2.** The action of thoroughly soaking or the condition of being thoroughly soaked with fluid 1846. **3.** The action of charging, or the state of being charged, up to the limit of capacity; *spec.* in *Chem.* the condition of a substance when combined with or holding in solution the largest proportion of another substance that it can take; in *Physics*, the condition of holding as much suspended matter, or being as fully charged with electricity, heat, etc. as possible 1659. **3.** *Chromatics.* Degree of intensity (of a colour); relative freedom from admixture of white 1878.

2. Phr. *Point of s.*, the degree of charge at which a substance becomes saturated.

Saturday (sæ·təɹde[i], -di). [OE. *Sætern(es)dæg*, corresp. to OFris. *saterdei*, MLG. *sater(s)dach*, MDu. *saterdach* (Du. *zaterdag*), tr. of L. *Saturni dies* day of (the planet) Saturn.] The seventh day of the week.

Hospital S.: see HOSPITAL *sb.* *Saturday-to-Monday* often *attrib.* with ref. to railway and other excursion tickets covering this period.

Saturn (sæ·tŏɹn). OE. [– L. *Saturnus*, poss. of Etruscan origin.] **1.** *Mythol.* An Italic god, orig. the god of agriculture, but in classical times identified with the Greek Cronos, the father of Zeus (Jupiter). **2.** *Astr.* A primary planet of the solar system, the most remote known to ancient astronomy OE. **3.** *Alch.* The technical name for lead. late ME. **4.** *Her.* The tincture sable, in blazoning by the names of heavenly bodies 1572.

2. Satourn disposith to malencolye LYDG. Saturne that dull and malevolent planet 1640.

Saturnal (sătŏ·ɹnăl), *a.* and *sb.* 1487. [– L. *Saturnalis*, f. *Saturnus* SATURN; see -AL[1].] †**A.** *adj.* Pertaining to Saturn or his astrological influence –1683. **B.** *sb. pl.* [– Fr. *saturnales* pl.] = next. 1487.

‖**Saturnalia** (sætŏɹnē[i]·liă), *sb. pl.* 1591. [– L. *Saturnalia*, subst. use of n. pl. of *Saturnalis*; see prec.] **1.** *Rom. Antiq.* (Now always with cap.) The festival of Saturn, held in December, observed as a time of general unrestrained merrymaking, extending even to the slaves. **2.** *transf.* and *fig.* (Freq. with small initial.) A period of unrestrained licence and revelry. Occas. as *sing.* 1782.

2. Malignity at least will have its S. H. WALPOLE. Hence **Saturna·lian** *a.* pertaining to the S.; appropriate to S.

Saturnian (sătŏ·ɹniăn), *a.* and *sb.* 1557. [f. L. *Saturnius* (f. *Saturnus* SATURN) + -AN I. 1.] **A.** *adj.* **1.** Pertaining to the god Saturn (chiefly with ref. to the 'golden age' under his reign). **2.** Distinctive epithet of the metre (*versus Saturnius*) used in early Roman poetry, before the introduction of Greek metres 1693. **3.** Of or pertaining to the planet Saturn; †due to the baleful influence of Saturn 1557.

1. Through the fortunate S. land, Into the darkness of the West SHELLEY.

B. *sb.* **1.** One born under the influence of the planet Saturn; a person of saturnine temperament 1591. **2.** An inhabitant of the planet Saturn 1738. **3.** *pl.* Saturnian verses 1899.

Saturnic (sătŏ·ɹnik), *a.* 1879. [f. SATURN + -IC.] Affected with lead-poisoning.

Saturnicentric (sătŏɹnise·ntrik), *a.* 1790. [f. SATURN, after *geocentric*.] Calculated with reference to the centre of Saturn.

Saturnine (sæ·tŏɹnəin), *a.* late ME. [– (O)Fr. *saturnin* or med.L. *Saturninus*, f. *Saturnus* SATURN; see -INE[1].] **1. a.** *Astrol.* Born under or affected by the influence of the planet Saturn. **b.** Hence, sluggish, cold, and gloomy in temperament. **2.** Of or pertaining to lead 1669. **b.** *Path.* Of disorders: Caused by absorption of lead. Of a patient: Suffering from lead-poisoning. 1823.

1. S. heauy headed blunderers NASHE.

Saturnism (sæ·tŏɹniz'm). 1855. [– mod.L. *Saturnismus* (also used), f. L. *Saturnus* SATURN; see -ISM 1 b.] *Path.* Lead-poisoning.

Satyr (sæ·təɹ). late ME. [– (O)Fr. *satyre* or L. *satyrus* – Gr. σάτυρος.] **1.** *Myth.* One of a class of woodland gods or demons, in form partly human and partly bestial, supposed to be the companions of Bacchus; also *fig.*, as the type of lustfulness. **2.** A kind of ape (so Gr. σάτυρος); in mod. use, the orang-utan, *Simia satyrus* (*rare*) late ME. **3.** Any butterfly of the group *Satyridæ* 1871.

1. So excellent a King, that was to this Hiperion to a Satyre SHAKS.

‖**Satyriasis** (sætĭrəi·ăsis). 1657. [– late L. *satyriasis* – Gr. σατυρίασις, f. σάτυρος SATYR; see -ASIS.] *Path.* Excessively great sexual desire in the male. Also = PRIAPISM 1.

Satyric (săti·rik), *a.* and *sb.* 1607. [– L. *satyricus*, Gr. σατυρικός, f. σάτυρος SATYR; see -IC.] **A.** *adj.* Pertaining to satyrs; *esp.* as the epithet of that species of drama in which the chorus was habited to represent satyrs. †**B.** *sb.* A satyric drama. DRYDEN. So **Saty·rical** *a.* 1590.

Satyrion (săti·riŏn). late ME. [– (O)Fr. *satyrion* or L. *satyrion* – Gr. σατύριον, f. σάτυρος SATYR.] Any of various kinds of Orchis.

Sauba (sǫ·bă, ‖sau·ba). 1863. [Tupi *sauba*.] The leaf-cutting ant (*Œcodoma cephalotes*) of tropical S. America.

Sauce (sǫs), *sb.* ME. [– (O)Fr. *sauce* :– Rom. **salsa*, subst. use of fem. of L. *salsus* salted, salt. The etymol. sense is identical with that of *salad*.] **1.** Any preparation, usu. liquid or soft, intended to be eaten with food as a relish. Often with qualifying word denoting the predominant ingredient, as *bread, egg, mint, parsley s.* **2.** *fig.* Something which adds piquancy to a word, idea, thought or action 1500. **3.** Chiefly *U.S.* Vegetables or fruit, fresh or preserved, taken as part of a meal, or as a relish. Often = SALAD. 1629. **4.** A solution of salt and other ingredients used in some manufacturing processes 1839. **5.** †**a.** *vocatively.* An impudent person, a saucebox –1697. **b.** Impertinence. *colloq.* and *dial.* 1835.

1. Of poynaunt s. hir neded neuer a deel CHAUCER. Prov. *What's s. for the goose is s. for the gander.* **2.** What is enticing to other men, must, to interest them, have the piquant s. of extreme danger SCOTT. Phr. *To serve with the same s.*, to subject to the same kind of usage. **3.** *Long s.* (U.S.) = beet, carrots, and parsnips; *short s.* = potatoes, turnips, onions, etc.

Sauce (sǭs), *v.* 1440. [f. SAUCE *sb.*] **1.** *trans.* To season, dress, or prepare (food) with sauces or condiments. *arch.* **2.** *fig.* **a.** To furnish a pleasing accompaniment to; to make pleasant or agreeable, reduce the asperity of 1514. †**b.** To qualify with a mixture of bitterness –1655. **c.** To 'season', make piquant 1555. **3.** *joc.* or *colloq.* †**a.** To charge extortionate prices to. SHAKS. †**b.** To belabour, flog –1726. **c.** To rebuke smartly. Now *dial.* 1600. **d.** To speak impertinently to. *vulgar.* 1864.

2. a. This sad news I shall s. with a little that is more pleasant 1621. **b.** Joy sauced is with payne 1510. **3. c.** Ile s. Her with bitter words SHAKS. **d.** They bully the slavey (but then the slavey sauces them, so perhaps it is only tit for tat) 1885.

Sauce-alone (sǭ·s,ălōᵘn). 1530. [app. f. SAUCE *sb.* + ALONE, implying that the plant is a sufficient sauce by itself.] The plant *Sisymbrium alliaria*, a tall hedge-weed formerly used as a flavouring for sauces and salads.

Sauce-boat (sǭ·sbōᵘt). 1747. [BOAT *sb.* 2.] A small vessel with a lip, used for serving sauce.

Saucebox (sǭ·sbǫks). *colloq.* 1588. [f. SAUCE *sb.* 5 + BOX *sb.*²] A person addicted to making saucy remarks.

Saucepan (sǭ·s,păn). 1686. [f. SAUCE *sb.* + PAN *sb.*¹] A vessel of metal, with a handle projecting from the side, and usu. with a lid; employed for boiling things in cookery.

Saucer (sǭ·səɹ). ME. [– OFr. *saussier*, *saussiere* (mod. only *saucière*) sauce-boat, f. *sauce* SAUCE *sb.*, prob. after late and med.L. *salsarium*.] †**1.** A dish or deep plate in which salt or sauces were placed upon the table –1742. **2.** Any small shallow dish or deep plate of circular shape 1607. **3.** A small round shallow vessel, usu. with concave sides and flat at the bottom, used for supporting a cup, and catching any liquid that may be spilled from it 1753. **4.** Something like a saucer; as *Bot.* any part of a plant resembling a saucer, as the involucre of the *Euphorbiaceæ*, and the tubercle of lichens 1578.

3. Don't pour your tea in your s.—that's vulgar! 1840. There sat the dog with eyes as big as saucers, glaring at him 1876.

Saucer eye. Usu. *pl.* 1664. An eye as large and round as a saucer, generally ascribed to spectres and ghosts. So **Saucer-eyed** *a.* having saucer eyes 1622.

†‖**Sauci·sse.** 1604. [Fr.] *Mil.* = next 3. –1795.

‖**Saucisson** (sosisoṅ). 1634. [Fr. augm. of *saucisse* SAUSAGE.] **1.** A large thick sausage 1760. **2.** A kind of firework, consisting of a tube of paper or canvas packed with gunpowder 1634. **3.** *Mil.* **a.** A large fascine 1702. **b.** A long tube of waterproof canvas, etc., packed with gunpowder and used for firing a mine 1827.

Saucy (sǭ·si), *a.* 1508. [f. SAUCE *sb.* + -Y¹.] †**1.** Flavoured with or pertaining to sauce; resembling sauce; savoury –1630. **2.** Of persons, their dispositions, language, etc.: Insolent towards superiors; presumptuous. Now chiefly *colloq.* with milder sense: Impertinent, 'cheeky'. 1530. **b.** Occas. with the notion: Wanton, lascivious 1603. **c.** Applied to a ship or boat: †(*a*) Presumptuous, rashly-venturing. (*b*) Smart, stylish. 1600. **3.** Scornful, disdainful. Now *dial.* 1716.

2. Sawcy Rascal, to disturb my Meditations DRYDEN. Alençon had a s. tongue 1879. **b.** *Cymb.* I. vi. 151. **c.** S. little crab boats 1873. **3.** In saucy State the griping Broker sits GAY. Hence **Sau·cily** *adv.* **Sau·ciness.**

‖**Sauerkraut, sourcrout** (sau·əɹ-, sauᵊ·ɹ-kraut). 1617. [– G. *sauerkraut* (whence Fr. *choucroute*), f. *sauer* SOUR + *kraut* vegetable, cabbage.] Cabbage which has undergone an acid fermentation, an article of diet in Germany.

Sauger (sǭ·gəɹ). 1882. The smaller Amer. pike-perch, *Stizostedium canadense*.

Saulie (sǭ·li). *Sc.* Now *Hist.* 1621. [Of unkn. origin.] A hired mourner at a funeral.

†**Sault**¹. ME. [– †*sault*, obs. sp. of (O)Fr. *saut* :– L. *saltus*, f. *salire* leap.] A jump; *spec.* of horses –1752.

‖**Sault**² (sō, commonly sū). *N. Amer.* 1600. [Colonial Fr. *sault*, earlier sp. of *saut*; see prec.] A waterfall or rapid.

‖**Saumur** (somür). 1888. [Name of a town in the department of Maine-et-Loire in France.] A French white wine resembling champagne.

Saunter (sǭ·ntəɹ), *sb.* 1712. [f. next.] **1.** The action or habit of sauntering 1728. **2.** A leisurely careless gait 1712. **3.** A leisurely, loitering walk or ramble; a stroll 1828.

2. S. and swagger both united to stamp *prodigal* on the Bond Street Lounger LYTTON. **3.** A quiet s. about a cathedral 1828.

Saunter (sǭ·ntəɹ), *v.* 1475. [Of obscure origin.] †**1.** *intr.* app. To muse, be in a reverie –1589. **2.** †**a.** To wander about aimlessly or unprofitably; to travel as a vagrant. **b.** To walk with a leisurely and careless gait; to stroll. 1667. †**3.** To loiter over one's work, to dawdle –1776.

2. Mr. Harrel sauntered into the breakfast room 1782. Hence **Sau·nterer. Sau·nteringly** *adv.*

Saurel (sǫre·l). 1882. [– Fr. *saurel*, f. late L. *saurus* – Gr. σαῦρος horse-mackerel; see -EL and cf. SAURY.] A fish of the genus *Trachurus*.

‖**Sauria** (sǭ·riă), *sb. pl.* 1834. [mod.L. *Sauria* (Brongniart 1799), f. Gr. σαύρα, σαῦρος lizard; see -IA².] *Zool.* An order of Reptiles, orig. including the Lizards and Crocodiles; subseq. restricted to the Lizards alone. Now commonly repl. by *Lacertilia*.

Saurian (sǭ·riăn), *a.* and *sb.* 1807. [f. prec. + -AN I. 1. Cf. Fr. *saurien*.] *Zool.* **A.** *adj.* **1.** Belonging to the order *Sauria*. **2.** Pertaining to or characteristic of a saurian 1826. **B.** *sb.* A reptile of the order *Sauria*. Now chiefly in pop. use, applied esp. to crocodiles, and to the ichthyosaurus, plesiosaurus, etc. 1807.

Sauro- (sǭ·ro), bef. a vowel **saur-**, comb. form of Gr. σαῦρος lizard; as in **Sauropterygian** (sǫ:roptĕri·dʒiăn) [Gr. πτερύγιον wing, fin.] *Palæont.*, *a.* of or pertaining to the *Sauropterygia* (usu. called *Plesiosauria*), an order of extinct marine reptiles in Owen's classification; *sb.* a reptile of this order; a plesiosaur.

Saurognathous (sǭrǫ·gnăþəs), *a.* 1874. [f. mod.L. *Saurognathæ* pl., f. Gr. σαῦρος lizard + γνάθος jaw; see -OUS.] *Ornith.* Of, pertaining to, or characteristic of the *Saurognathæ* (the woodpeckers and their allies), characterized by an arrangement of the bones of the palate similar to that in lizards. So **Sauro·gnathism**, s. formation of the palate.

Sauroid (sǭ·roid), *a.* and *sb.* 1836. [– Fr. *sauroïde* (Agassiz) – Gr. σαυροειδής, f. σαῦρος lizard; see -OID.] **A.** *adj.* Resembling a saurian or lizard; a distinctive epithet of an order of fishes (*Sauroidei*). **B.** *sb.* **1.** A sauroid fish 1836. **2.** An animal belonging to the *Sauroidea* (later SAUROPSIDA) 1863.

Sauropod (sǭ·ropǫd), *a.* and *sb.* 1891. [f. mod.L. *Sauropoda*; see SAURO-, -POD, -A 4.] **A.** *adj.* = SAUROPODOUS *a.* **B.** *sb.* A member of the order *Sauropoda* of gigantic herbivorous dinosaurs. So **Sauro·podous** *a.* of, pertaining to, or connected with the *Sauropoda*.

‖**Sauropsida** (sǭrǫ·psidă), *sb. pl.* 1864. [mod.L., f. Gr. σαῦρος lizard + ὄψις appearance; see -ID³, -A 4.] *Zool.* The second of the three primary groups of *Vertebrata* in Huxley's classification, comprising reptiles, birds, etc. Hence **Sauro·psidan** *a.* of or pertaining to the *S.*; *sb.* a member of the *S.*

Saury (sǭ·ri). 1771. [perh. f. late L. *saurus*, Fr. *saurel* with different suffix; see SAUREL.] Any of various fishes, esp. the skipper or bill-fish, *Scomberesox saurus*; also *attrib.* as *s. pike*, *salmon*.

Sausage (sǫ·sėdʒ). [In XV *sausige* – ONFr. *saussiche* (var. of Fr. *salsice*, mod. *saucisse*) :– med.L. *salsicia*, subst. use of n. pl. of *salsicius* (sc. *farta*, pa. pple. n. pl. of L. *farcire* stuff), f. *salsus* salted. For the development of (-ėdʒ) cf. CABBAGE.] **1.** Orig. a quantity of finely chopped pork, beef, or other meat, spiced and flavoured, enclosed in a short length of the intestine of some animal so as to form a cylindrical roll; later also *gen.*, meat thus prepared. Now, in its widest use, a preparation of comminuted beef, pork, etc., or a mixture of these, either fresh, salted, pickled, smoked, or cured, with salt, spices, flour, etc. and stuffed into a container made from an intestine or other animal tissue. **2.** *Mil.* **a.** = SAUCISSON 3. 1645. **b.** An observation balloon 1916.

1. *Bologna s.*: see BOLOGNA. *German s.*: see GERMAN *a.*²

attrib. and *Comb.*, as in *s. factory*, *maker*; also in names of appliances for making sausages, as *s.-cutter*, *-machine*, etc.; **s. balloon** = 2 b; **-curl**, a curl resembling a s.; **-meat**, meat minced and spiced to be used in sausages or as a stuffing; **-roll**, a s., or a roll of s.-meat, enclosed in pastry, and cooked.

Saussurite (sǭ·siŭrəit). 1811. [Named after Prof. H. B. de *Saussure* (1740–99); see -ITE¹ 2 b.] *Min.* A very compact variety of zoisite. Hence **Saussuri·tic** *a.*

‖**Sauté** (sote), *a.* and *sb.* 1813. [Fr., pa. pple. of *sauter* leap.] *Cookery.* **A.** *adj.* Of meat, vegetables, etc.: Fried in a pan with a little butter over a quick fire, while being tossed from time to time; (of potatoes) cut into finger-shaped pieces and fried in deep fat; 'chipped' 1869. **B.** *sb.* A dish cooked in this manner 1813. Hence **Sauté** *v. trans.* to cook thus.

‖**Sauterne(s** (sotō·ɹn). 1711. [Named from the district of *Sauternes* near Bordeaux.] A French white wine of the Bordeaux class.

‖**Sauve-qui-peut** (sovkipö). 1815. [Fr., subst. use of a phr. 'save (himself) who can'.] A general stampede or complete rout.

Savable, saveable (sēⁱ·văb'l), *a.* 1450. [f. SAVE *v.* + -ABLE.] Capable of being saved; orig. chiefly *Theol.*

Savage (sæ·vėdʒ), *a.* and *sb.* Also (now *arch.*) **salvage.** [ME. *sa(u)vage* – (O)Fr. *sauvage* (AFr. also *savage*) :– Rom. **salvaticus*, for L. *silvaticus* woodland-, wild, f. *silva* wood, forest.] **A.** *adj.* **I.** That is in a state of nature, wild. **1.** Of animals: Wild; undomesticated; untamed. (Now exclusively with implication of ferocity.) **2.** Of land, country, scenery: †Uncultivated. Hence, Horribly wild and rugged. ME. †**3.** Of a plant, tree, etc.: Uncultivated –1820. **4.** Of movements, noise, manners, etc.: Ungoverned; rude, unpolished. *arch.* late ME. **5.** Uncivilized; existing in the lowest stage of culture 1588. **b.** Pertaining to or characteristic of savages 1614. †**c.** Solitary –1680.

1. To binden leounes sauuage ME. **2.** The moste part of the yle is hilly and sauage 1585. **4.** The sauage strangenesse he puts on SHAKS. **5.** I will take some s. woman, she shall rear my dusky race TENNYSON. *Salvage man* (Her.), the conventional representation of a savage; a human figure naked or enveloped in foliage (*arch.*). **c.** O might I here. .live s. MILT.

II. With ref. to disposition or temper. †**1.** Rude, harsh, ungentle (also *transf.* of the sea, a river) –1655. **2.** Fierce, ferocious, cruel. late ME. **3.** Enraged, furiously angry; rough or unsparing in speech. (Chiefly *colloq.*) 1825.

2. A roaring voice of most sauage wilde beasts *Wisd.* 17:19. Musick has Charms to soothe a s. Breast CONGR. *transf.* Within the direfull grasp Of S. hunger MILT. **3.** I think the Doctor was pretty s. with old Briggs 1899.

B. *sb.* †**1.** A wild beast –1831. **2.** An uncivilized, wild person 1588. **b.** *transf.* A cruel or fierce person. Also, one who is destitute of culture or ignorant or neglectful of the rules of good behaviour. 1606. **3.** = *Salvage man* 1780.

2. I am as free as Nature first made man,.. When wild in woods the noble S. ran DRYDEN. Hence **Sa·vage-ly** *adv.*, **-ness.**

Savage (sæ·vėdʒ), *v.* 1563. [f. SAVAGE *a.*] †**1.** *intr.* To act the savage; to indulge in cruel or barbarous deeds (*rare*) –1646. **2.** *trans.* To render savage, barbarous, or fierce 1611. **3.** Of an animal, esp. a horse: To attack and bite or trample 1880. Also *fig.*

2. Its bloodhounds savaged by a cross of wolf SOUTHEY. **3.** [The horse] galloped about.., savaging every horse or man it could reach 1896.

Savagedom (sæ·vėdʒdəm). 1845. [f. SAVAGE *a.* or *sb.* + -DOM.] The condition of being a savage; savage people collectively.

Savagery (sæ·vėdʒri, sæ·vėdʒəri). 1595. [f. SAVAGE *a.* + -ERY.] **1.** The quality of being fierce or cruel; savage disposition, conduct, or actions; also with *a* and *pl.*, a cruel action or deed. **2.** The condition of being wild or uncivilized; the characteristics of savages; the savage state of human society 1825. **3.** Wildness, as of nature, scenery, etc. 1872. **4.** Wild creatures or savages collectively 1599.

1. This is the bloodiest shame, The wildest Sauagery,..That euer wall-ey'd wrath..Presented to the teares of soft remorse SHAKS. **2.** The s. of the primeval Celt 1904. **4.** *Hen. V*, v. ii. 47. So **Sa·vagism**, = sense 2.

Savannah (săvæ·nă). 1555. [(XVI *zavanna*) – Sp. *zavana*, *çavana* (pronounced with *s-* in S. Amer. Sp.), said by Oviedo (1535) to be a Carib word.] A treeless plain; prop., one of those in parts of tropical America.

attrib.: **s. flower**, a W. Indian name for various species of *Echites*; **s. fox**, *Vulpes cancrivora*; **s. sparrow**, a sparrow of the genus *Passerculus*, esp. *P. savanna*, common throughout the greater part of N. America; **-wattle**, the W. Indian trees *Citharexylum quadrangulare* and *C. cinereum*.

‖**Savant** (savaṅ). 1719. [Fr., subst. use of adj., orig. pr. pple. of *savoir* know.] A man of learning or science; esp. one professionally engaged in learned or scientific research. So ‖**Savante** (savāṅt), a learned (French) woman.

‖**Savate** (savat). 1862. [Fr. *savate* (XII *çavate* kind of shoe); see SABOT.] A method of fighting (commonly used instead of or in conjunction with boxing) in which the feet are used.

Save (sēⁱv), *sb.* 1890. [f. SAVE *v.*] *Football, Hockey*, etc. An act of preventing the opposite side from scoring.

Save (sēⁱv), *v.* [ME. *sauve, salve, save* – AFr. *sa(u)ver*, OFr. *salver*, (also mod.) *sauver* :– late L. *salvare* (*Theol.* rendering Gr. σώζειν) save, f. L. *salvus* SAFE *a.*] **I.** To rescue or protect. **1.** *trans.* To deliver or rescue from peril or hurt; to make safe, put in safety; also *absol.* **2.** *Theol.* To deliver (a person, the soul) from sin and its consequences; to admit to eternal bliss ME. **b.** *transf.* To be the 'salvation' of 1894. **3.** Used in formulas of benediction, greeting, etc.; as *God s. you!* ME. †**4.** To spare instead of killing, allow to live, give (a person) his life –1642. **5.** To deliver *from* some evil which is likely to befall one; to ensure (a person) immunity from hurt or annoyance ME. **6.** To keep, protect, or guard (a thing) from damage, loss, or destruction late ME. **7.** To keep intact or unhurt (honour, credit, chastity, and the like) ME. **8.** With adj. complement: To keep or preserve *whole, unhurt*, etc. ME. †**9.** To store, preserve –1728. **10.** †**a.** Astr. *To s. the appearances, the phenomena* [tr. Gr. σῴζειν τὰ φαινόμενα]: said of a hypothesis which explains all the observed facts –1667. Hence **b.** *To s. appearances*: to contrive to keep up an appearance of propriety, solvency, or the like 1711. **11.** To prevent the loss of (a game, match, wager, etc.) 1611. **12.** To be in time for, manage to catch 1732.

1. One that I sau'd from drowning SHAKS. Could Troy be sav'd by any single hand POPE. A great many lives were saved by the salutary practice of inoculation 1803. Eternal Father, strong to s. 1860. Phr. *To s. one's skin*, to escape unhurt. *To s. one's bacon*: see BACON. **2.** We can not be saued wythout fayeth LATIMER. Phr. *As I hope to be saved*, †*so God* (or *Christ*) *s. me*, etc. **3.** (*God*) *s. the mark*: see MARK *sb.*[1] III. 6. *God s. the king!* **5.** S., s., oh! s. me from the candid friend! CANNING. **6.** Phr. *To s. one's pocket*, to avoid spending one's money. *To s. one's face*, to avoid being disgraced or humiliated (orig. in imitation of Chinese idioms). **7.** The loan saved my credit, and made my fortune LYTTON. Phr. *To s. the situation*, to avert imminent disaster. **8.** If they saue vs aliue, we shall liue 2 *Kings* 7:4. **12.** I have but a moment to s. the post CANNING.

II. To reserve, lay aside. **1.** To keep for a particular purpose or as likely to prove useful; to set apart, lay by, reserve. late ME. **2.** *spec.* To collect and keep (seed) in stock for sowing 1657. **b.** To dry (corn, hay, peat) by exposure to the air; to harvest, stack 1719. **3.** To store up or put by (money, goods, etc.) by dint of economy; also *absol.* and with *up*. late ME. **4.** To avoid spending, giving, or consuming (money, goods, etc.); to keep (a given amount) from being spent, consumed, or lost and so to retain it in one's possession. Also: To enable a person to avoid spending, giving, or losing. late ME. **b.** With immaterial obj., e.g., labour, time, distance to be travelled, etc. 1579. **5.** To use or consume sparingly 1600. **6.** To treat carefully, so as to obviate or reduce fatigue, wear and tear, etc. 1785.

1. I saved the Skins of all the Creatures that I kill'd DE FOE. **3.** He was able to s. money for his son's education 1856. I set myself to s. up for my own old age 1884. **4.** You have already saved several millions to the publick SWIFT. **5.** Phrases. *To s. oneself*, to reduce the amount of one's exertions. *To s. one's breath*, to be silent, refrain from giving advice. *To s. one's pains, trouble*, to refrain from useless exertions.

III. To avoid for one's own part or enable another to avoid (some burden or inconvenience); *occas.* to avoid or obviate the necessity for 1606. †**b.** *To s.* (a woman's) *longing*, to anticipate and so to prevent it –1665. **c.** *Games.* To prevent the opposing side from gaining (a run, goal, etc.). Also *absol.* = to save a goal. 1816.

My letters lie there for me, as it saves their being sent down to Rosebank SCOTT. Hence **Sa·ver.**

Save (sēⁱv), quasi-*prep.* and *conj.* [ME. *sauf* and *sauve* – OFr. *sauf* (masc.) and *sauve* (fem.), orig. varying with the gender of the accompanying sb. (now invariable, *sauf*) :– L. *salvo* and *salva*, abl. sing. of masc. or n. and fem. of *salvus* SAFE *a.*, as used in absolute constr. such as *salvo jure, salva innocentia* without violation of right, of innocence. The later exclusive use of the form *save* is prob. due to the identification of the word with the imper. of SAVE *v.* Cf. SAVING *prep.* and *conj.*] **A.** quasi-*prep.* Except, with the exception of, but. **b.** = but for 1522. **B.** *conj.* **1.** Introducing a sentence which states an exception; now only *s. that* ME. **b.** = 'Were it not' 1600. **c.** = 'Unless', 'if.. not'. late ME. **2.** = EXCEPT C. 3. ME. **b.** *S. for*: but for 1594.

A. Al thinges haue an ende at last by deth, saufe onely deathe LD. BERNERS. I do intreat you, not a man depart, Saue I alone SHAKS. But all saue thee I fell with Curses SHAKS. **b.** She seem'd a splendid angel, newly drest, S. wings, for heaven KEATS. **B. 1.** Naked from the waste vpwards, saue that their heads are couered 1634. **b.** From these would I be gone, Saue that to dye, I leaue my loue alone SHAKS. **2.** S. where the beetle wheels his droning flight GRAY. **b.** S. for the slumbering fire, all was dark within the house 1894.

Save-all (sēⁱ·vǭl). 1645. [f. SAVE *v.* + ALL.] **1.** A means for preventing loss or waste 1655. **2.** A contrivance for holding a candle-end in a candlestick while burning so that it may burn to the end 1645. **3.** A stingy miserly person. Now *dial.* 1785. **4.** *Naut.* A sail set under another sail or between two other sails 1794. **5.** A pinafore, overall. *dial.* 1864. **6.** *attrib.* or *adj.* Parsimonious, stingy 1812.

6. Still pursuing his s. theory of a pin a day is a groat a year 1856.

Saveloy (sæ·vĕloi). 1837. [alt. of Fr. †*cervelat*, (also mod.) *-as* (sɛrvəla) – It. *cervellata*; see CERVELAT.] A highly seasoned cooked and dried sausage.

Savin, savine (sæ·vin). OE. [– OFr. *savine* (mod. *sabine*) :– L. *sabina*, subst. use (sc. *herba* plant) of fem. sing. of *Sabinus* SABINE.] **1.** A small bushy evergreen shrub, *Juniperus sabina*, a native of Europe and Western Asia, with spreading branches covered with short imbricating leaves, and bearing a small, round, bluish-purple berry. Also applied to other trees and shrubs resembling this. **2.** The dried tops of this shrub, used as a drug OE.

Saving (sēⁱ·viŋ), *vbl. sb.* ME. [f. SAVE *v.* + -ING[1].] **1.** The action of SAVE *v.*; an instance of this. **2.** *concr.* A sum of money saved; chiefly *pl.* sums of money saved from time to time and put by 1737. **3.** A reservation, saving clause. Now only in *Law.* 1477.

2. (*War*, 1916), (*national*, 1920) *savings certificate*, a certificate declaring that the holder has invested in a particular form of government funds.

Saving (sēⁱ·viŋ), *ppl. a.* ME. [f. SAVE *v.* + -ING[2].] **1.** That delivers, rescues, or preserves 1535. **2.** *Theol.* That delivers from sin and eternal death by the power of God's grace ME. **3.** *gen.* That delivers from moral or intellectual error; of a quality, 'redeeming' 1599. **4.** Accustomed to save, hoard up, or economize; parsimonious, economical 1581. †**5.** Neither winning nor losing –1832. **6.** Making a reservation; furnishing a proviso 1700.

3. I am not..without a s. sense of humour 1902. **4.** To be sauing in Apparell BACON. Mrs. Crawley was a s. woman and knew the price of port wine THACKERAY. Hence **Sa·ving-ly** *adv.*, **-ness** (*rare*).

Saving (sēⁱ·viŋ), *prep.* and *conj.* late ME. [prob. modification of SAVE *prep.* and *conj.* after TOUCHING *prep.*] **A.** *prep.* **1.** = SAVE *prep.* 1. **2.** Without prejudice or offence to. late ME.

2. Sauing your tale Petruchio, I pray let vs that are poore petitioners speake too? SHAKS. *S.* (one's) *reverence*: see REVERENCE *sb.* 4. *S. correction* [= Fr. *sauf correction*], subject to correction.

B. *conj.* = EXCEPT, SAVE *conjs.* 1535.

S. in the country I seldom go out until after dark DICKENS. S. for her 'plentiful lack' of inborn baby-worship SWINBURNE.

Sa·vings ba:nk. Orig. **saving bank;** also **savings' bank.** 1817. [f. *savings* pl. (see SAVING *vbl. sb.* 2) + BANK *sb.*[3]] An institution for encouraging thrift, by receiving small deposits at interest.

Saviour (sēⁱ·vyəɹ). [ME. *sauve(o)ur* – OFr. *sauvëour* (mod. *sauveur*) :– Chr. L. *salvator*, *-ōr-*, (rendering Gr. σωτήρ, and ult. late Heb. *yēšûᶜa* Jesus), f. *salvare* SAVE *v.*] **1.** One who delivers or rescues from peril. **2.** He who saves mankind from sin and its consequences: as a title of God, and esp. of Christ. (Now always with cap. S.) ME.

2. That Season..Wherein our Sauiours Birth is celebrated SHAKS. Hence **Sa·viouress**, a female s.

‖**Savoir faire** (savwar fɛ̄r). 1815. [Fr.; lit. 'to know how to do'.] Tact, address; instinctive knowledge of the right course of action in any circumstances.

‖**Savoir vivre** (savwar vīvr). 1755. [Fr.; lit. 'to know how to live'.] Ability in the conduct of life, knowledge of the world and of the usages of good society.

The use of red wine with oysters shews great want of sçavoir vivre 1806.

Savorous (sēⁱ·vŏrəs), *a.* late ME. [– OFr. *saverous, savorous* (mod. *savoureux*) :– late L. *saporosus*, f. *sapor*; see SAVOUR, -OUS.] Of good savour, pleasant to the taste 1450. †**b.** *fig.* That is relished or enjoyed, delightful –1657. Hence **Sa·vorously** *adv.*

Savory (sēⁱ·vəri), *sb.* [In XIV *saverey*, perh. repr. (with change of intervocalic ð to v) OE. *sæþerie* – L. *satureia.*] Any plant of the labiate genus *Satureia*; esp. the annual herb *Satureia hortensis* (Garden, Summer S.), or the perennial, *S. montana* (Mountain or Winter S.), used as flavouring in cookery.

Savour, savor (sēⁱ·vəɹ), *sb.* ME. [– OFr. *savour* (mod. *saveur*) :– L. *sapor*, *-ōr-* taste, occas. smell, f. *sapere* taste; see -OUR.] **1.** Quality in relation to the sense of taste; a specific mode of this quality, as sweetness, bitterness; a taste. Now *rare*, exc. as denoting a 'smack'. **b.** Sapidity, tastiness 1440. **2.** A smell, perfume, aroma. *poet.* and *arch.* ME. **b.** *fig.* Repute, estimation. Now *poet.* 1535. **3.** Orig. *fig.* from sense 1: †**a.** Character, style, sort –1639. **b.** Essential virtue or property (with allusion to *Matt.* 5:13). Also, power to excite relish, interest, 1650. **c.** A 'smack', tinge, or admixture 1795.

1. Meats of noblest sort And s. MILT. **b.** I see auld fruit has little s. SCOTT. **2.** The sweet s. of the roasted meat SHELLEY. **b.** A name of evil s. in the land TENNYSON. **3. a.** This admiration Sir, is much o'th's. Of other your new prankes SHAKS. **b.** All the s. of life is departed 1885. Hence **Sa·vourless** *a.* destitute of s.; tasteless or odourless.

Savour, savor (sēi·vəɹ), *v.* ME. [– (O)Fr. *savourer* :– late L. *saporare*, f. *sapor* SAVOUR *sb.*] **I.** To have a savour. **†1.** *intr.* Of food and drink: To taste (well or ill); chiefly, to have an agreeable taste. Often with *dat.*; hence *trans.* to be agreeable to the taste of. –1686. **2.** *intr.* To give forth a (specified) scent or odour; to smell *of* something. *arch.* ME. **3.** *fig.* **†a.** To be agreeable or pleasing. **b.** With qualification: To be *well* or *ill* pleasing. *arch.* ME. **4.** *To s. of*: to show traces of the presence or influence of; to have the appearance of proceeding from. Also *trans.* 1548.

3. What is loathsome to the young Savours well to thee and me TENNYSON. **4.** Wilful barrenness, That..savours onely Rancor and pride MILT. I have written nothing which savours of Immorality DRYDEN.

II. To give a savour to. **1.** To season, flavour; to give tone or character to 1579. **2.** To impart a savour or scent to 1832. **III.** To perceive a savour. **1.** *trans.* To taste, perceive by the sense of taste. In mod. use, to taste with relish, to dwell on the taste of, *fig.*, to give oneself to the enjoyment or appreciation of. late ME. **2.** To be conscious or sensible of (an odour). *Obs.* or *arch.* late ME. **3.** To relish, like, care for. *Obs.* or *arch.* ME. **†4.** To perceive, apprehend; also, to discover traces of, experience 1659.

1. Savoring in advance the long list of dainties for the day 1889. **2.** What vaileth the flower To stand still and wither; If no man it s. It serves only for sight WYATT. **3.** He savoureth only the doctrine of this world BUNYAN. Hence **Sa·vourer. Sa·vouringly** *adv.*

†Sa·vourly, *adv.* late ME. [f. SAVOUR *sb.* + -LY[2].] **1.** With enjoyment; with relish; pleasantly; agreeably; keenly –1690. **b.** Of weeping: Passionately, bitterly –1722. **2.** With understanding; wisely; effectively –1664.

Savoury (sēi·vəri), *a.* and *sb.* [ME. *savure*, later *savori* – OFr. *savouré* sapid, fragrant, f. *savour* SAVOUR *sb.* + *-é* -ATE[2] (see -Y[5]); the ending was assim. to -Y[1].] **A.** *adj.* **1.** Pleasing to the taste; appetizing; agreeable. late ME. **b.** Fragrant. (Now *rare* exc. in neg. context.) 1560. **2.** *fig.* **a.** Pleasant; acceptable ME. **†b.** In religious use. (*a*) Full of spiritual 'savour'; spiritually delightful. (*b*) Having the savour of holiness; of saintly repute or memory. –1855. **3.** Used, in contradistinction to *sweet*, as the epithet of articles of food having a stimulating taste or flavour 1661.

1. All..with keen gust the sav'ry viands share POPE. **2. a.** The..parable, savouriest of all Scripture to rogues RUSKIN. **b.** Practised by the savouriest of people called Quakers 1720. **3.** Omelette, a S. one 1806.

B. *sb.* A savoury dish; *spec.* one served at the beginning or end of dinner as a stimulant to appetite and digestion 1661. Hence **Sa·vouri-ly** *adv.*, **-ness.**

Savoy (săvoi·). 1578. [– Fr. *Savoie*, a region of S.E. France.] **1.** In full, *S. cabbage* (*sprouts*). A rough-leaved hardy variety of the common cabbage, much grown for winter use. **2.** In full, *S. biscuit.* A kind of sponge biscuit, made of finger-shaped pieces of paste covered with sifted sugar which when baked are joined together in pairs; so also *S. drop, ring.* Similarly *S. cake*, a large sponge cake baked in a mould. 1764.

Savoyard (săvoi·aɹd, sævoi,aɹd), *sb.* and *a.* 1687. [– Fr. *Savoyard.* In A 1, B, – Fr., f. *Savoie*; see prec. and -ARD. In A 2, 3, f. *Savoy* in London names.] **A.** *sb.* **1.** A native or inhabitant of Savoy. **2.** An inhabitant of the precinct of the Savoy Palace in London, which formerly possessed the right of sanctuary 1700. **3.** An actor in Gilbert and Sullivan Opera at the Savoy Theatre, London 1908. **B.** *adj.* Belonging to Savoy 1820.

Savvy, savey (sæ·vi), *sb. slang.* 1785. [f. next.] Practical sense, 'nous', gumption.

Savvy, savey (sæ·vi), *v. slang.* 1785. [orig. Negro-Eng. and Pidgin-Eng., after Sp. *sabe usted* you know.] *trans.* To know.

Saw (sǭ), *sb.*[1] [OE. **sagu*, also *saga* = MLG., MDu. *sage* (Du. *zaag*), OHG. *saga*, ON. *sǫg* :– Gmc. **sazō*, **sazon*, of which the gradation-var. **sezō* is repr. by OHG. *sega* (G. *säge*), MDu. *seghe.*] **1.** A cutting tool consisting of a plate (or, in some forms, a band or a tube) of metal (usu. steel), one edge of which is formed into a continuous series of teeth. (Some saws for cutting stone are without teeth.) Freq. with defining words, indicating special varieties of form, structure, mode of operation, or purpose, as *circular s., fretsaw, hand-s., keyhole s.*, etc. **2.** *Zool.* A part or organ with teeth like those of a saw 1664. **3.** [Prop. a distinct word, f. SAW *v.*] **a.** A sawing movement. **b.** *Whist.* = SEE-SAW 1746.

1. *fig.* Faction, hatred, livor, emulation, which.. are, *serræ animæ*, the sawes of the soule BURTON.

attrib. and *Comb.*: **s.-bar,** either of the two bars which hold the s. in a fretwork machine; **-belly** *U.S.*, the glut herring (*Clupea æstivalis*), or the ale-wife (*C. serrata*); **-bench,** a circular s. with a bench to support the material and advance it to the s.; **-buck** *U.S.* [– Du. *zaagbok*], see BUCK *sb.*[6]; **-edge,** a serrated edge; **-file,** a file for sharpening the teeth of saws; **-frame,** (*a*) the frame in which a saw-blade is stretched; (*b*) the sash or gate of a mill s.; **-gate** = GATE *sb.*[1] 6 b; **-gin,** a form of cotton-gin in which the fibres are torn from the seed by revolving toothed discs or circular saws; **-grass** *U.S.*, a sedge of the genus *Cladium*; **-horse,** a saw-buck; **plate,** (*a*) the blade of a s.; (*b*) iron in plates of the thickness of the blade of a s.; **s. palmetto,** a palmetto, *Serenoa serratula*, with prickly leaf-stalks; **-set,** an instrument for setting the teeth of a s.; **-sharpener,** (*a*) one who sharpens saws; (*b*) the Great Titmouse, *Parus major*; **-whet** *U.S.*, a little owl, *Nyctala acadica*; **-whetter,** (*a*) = *s.-whet*; (*b*) the marsh titmouse, *Parus palustris*; **-wort,** any of various species of the genera *Serratula* (esp. *S. tinctoria*), *Saussurea*, and *Carduus arvensis.*

Saw (sǭ), *sb.*[2] [OE. *sagu* = OFris. *sege*, MLG., MDu. *sage*, OHG. *saga* (G. *sage*), ON. *saga* SAGA :– Gmc. **sazō*, f. base of **sazjan* SAY *v.*[1]] **†1.** A saying; discourse; speech –1621. **†2.** A decree, command –1595. **3.** A sententious saying; a traditional maxim, a proverb ME.

1. His felawe That was so ny to herknen al his sawe CHAUCER. **2.** So love is Lord..And rules the creatures by his powrfull s. SPENSER. **3.** Full of wise sawes, and moderne instances SHAKS.

Saw (sǭ), *v.* Pa. t. **sawed**; pa. pple. **sawed, sawn.** ME. [f. SAW *sb.*[1]] **1.** *trans.* To cut with a saw. **b.** To form by cutting with a saw 1530. **c.** *absol.* To use a saw; to cut with a saw ME. **d.** *intr.* with passive force to admit of being sawn 1726. **2.** *transf.* With ref. to the to-and-fro movement used in sawing. **a.** *trans. To s. the air*: to gesticulate with the hands as if sawing something 1602. **b.** To work (the bit) from side to side in a horse's mouth 1850.

1. *Heb.* 11:37. Phr. *To s. wood* (fig.), to work while others deliberate (*U.S. slang*) 1909. **b.** This method of sawing out a pattern 1875. **d.** Beech.. will s. into extreme thin Planks 1726. **2. a.** Do not s. the Ayre too much [with] your hand thus, but vse all gently SHAKS.

Sawbill (sǭ·bil). 1843. [f. SAW *sb.*[1] + BILL *sb.*[2]] Any of various birds having serrated bills; *esp.* the merganser (also *s. diver, duck*). So **Saw·-billed** *a.* having a serrated bill.

Sawbones (sǭ·bōunz). *slang.* 1837. [f. SAW *v.* + BONE *sb.*] A surgeon.

Sawder (sǭ·dəɹ), *sb. colloq.* 1836. [fig. use of *sawder*, var. of SOLDER.] *Soft s.*: flattery, blarney. So **Saw·der** *v. trans.* to flatter, 'butter' 1834.

Sawdust (sǭ·dɒ̆st), *sb.* 1530. [f. SAW *sb.*[1] + DUST *sb.*] **1.** Wood in the state of small particles, produced in the process of sawing. Freq. *transf.* and *fig.* (Sometimes with ref. to the use of s. for stuffing dolls or puppets.) **2.** In wider sense: Dust of any material produced in the process of sawing 1672.

1. *fig.* **b.** I'll knock the saw-dust out of any two men in this hole of a place 1890. Hence **Sawdust** *v. trans.* to cover, sprinkle, or strew with s. **Saw·-dusty** *a.* abounding in, savouring of, or resembling s.

Sawer (sǭ·əɹ). late ME. [f. SAW *v.* + -ER[1].] One who saws. Now *rare*; as a designation of employment repl. by SAWYER.

Sawfish (sǭ·fiʃ). 1664. [SAW *sb.*[1]] A fish of the genus *Pristis*, the snout of which ends in a long flat projection with teeth on each edge. Also applied to fishes of certain allied genera.

Saw·-fly. 1773. [SAW *sb.*[1]] An insect of the family *Tenthredinidæ*, distinguished by the saw-like construction of the ovipositor.

Sawmill (sǭ·mil). 1553. [f. SAW *sb.*[1] + MILL *sb.*] A factory in which wood is sawn into planks or boards by machinery (now usu. propelled by steam or electricity).

Sawney (sǭ·ni), *sb. colloq.* 1700. [Sc. local var. of *Sandy* (XV), pet-form of the proper name *Alexander*; see -Y[6].] **1.** A derisive nickname for a Scotchman 1704. **2.** A simpleton 1700.

Sawney (sǭ·ni), *a.* 1805. [app. f. prec.] Foolish; foolishly sentimental. So **Saw·ney** *v. intr.* to wheedle, cant; to fool.

Saw·-pit. ME. [f. SAW *sb.*[1]] A pit, over the mouth of which a framework is erected on which timber is placed to be sawn with a long two-handled saw by two men, the one standing in the pit and the other on a raised platform.

Sa·w tooth. 1601. [SAW *sb.*[1]] **a.** A tooth of a saw. **b.** A tooth (of an animal or of a machine) shaped like a saw, or forming one of a serrated series.

Sawyer (sǭ·yəɹ). [ME. alt. of SAWER (cf. †*lawer*, LAWYER); see -IER[1].] **1.** A workman whose business it is to saw timber, esp. in a saw-pit. **2. a.** Any wood-boring insect larva, as that of the longicorn beetle of the genus *Monohammus*. **b.** A grasshopper, *Deinacrida megacephala*, native to New Zealand. 1789. **3.** *U.S.* A tree which has fallen into a stream and lies with its branches projecting above and swaying with the motion of the water 1797.

Sax (sæks). [OE. *seax* knife, OFris. *sax*, OS., OHG. *sahs*, ON. *sax* :– Gmc. **saxsam*, f. IE. **sok-* **sek-*, repr. also by L. *secare* cut.] **†1.** A knife; a short sword or dagger –late ME. **2.** A chopping-tool used for trimming slates 1669.

Saxatile (sæ·ksătəil, -til), *a.* 1661. [– Fr. *saxatile* (XVI) or L. *saxatilis*, f. *saxum* rock, stone; see -ATILE.] *Zool.* and *Bot.* Living or growing among rocks.

Saxaul (sæ·ksǫl). 1874. A shrub, *Anabasis* (*Holoxylon*) *ammodendron*, growing on the steppes of Asia.

Sa·xboard. 1857. *Boat-building.* [Cf. ON. *sax* (a use of *sax* = SAX) gunwale near the prow.] The uppermost strake of a boat.

Saxe (sæks). 1864. [– Fr. *Saxe* Saxony – G. *Sachsen.*] Used *attrib.* to designate articles which come from Saxony, as *S. china*; **S. blue** (also ellipt. **Saxe**) = SAXONY *blue.*

Sax-horn, saxhorn (sæ·kshǭɹn). 1845. [f. the name *Sax.*] One of a group of brass musical instruments of the trumpet kind, invented by a Belgian, Charles Joseph Sax (1791–1865), and improved by his son Antoine Joseph, known as Adolphe. Called also **sax-cornet.** So **Sax-tuba,** a brass instrument of this class.

‖Saxicava (sæksi·kăvă). *Pl.* **-æ.** 1826. [mod.L., fem. of *saxicavus*; see next.] A genus of boring bivalve molluscs; a member of this genus.

Saxicavous (sæksi·kăvəs), *a.* 1850. [f. mod.L. *saxicavus* (f. *saxum* rock + *cavare* to hollow) + -OUS.] *Zool.* Hollowing out rock or stone; epithet of certain molluscs.

Saxicoline (sæksi·kŏləin), *a.* 1899. [f. mod.L. *saxicola* (f. *saxum* rock, *colere* inhabit) + -INE; so mod.L. *Saxicolinæ.*] *Zool.* and *Bot.* **a.** Living among or growing on rocks. **b.** *spec.* Pertaining to the subfamily *Saxicolinæ* of passerine birds (the stone-chats).

Saxicolous (sæksi·kŏləs), *a.* 1856. [f. as prec. + -OUS.] *Bot.* Growing on rocks.

Saxifragaceous (sæksifrăgēi·ʃəs), *a.* 1845. [f. as next + -ACEOUS.] *Bot.* Belonging to the family *Saxifragaceæ.*

Saxifrage (sæ·ksifrédʒ). ME. [– (O)Fr. *saxifrage* or late L. *saxifraga* (sc. *herba* plant), f. *saxum* rock + *frag-*, base of *frangere* break.] Any plant of the genus *Saxifraga*, esp. *S. granulata* (White Meadow S.). The species are mostly dwarf herbs with tufted foliage and panicles of white, yellow, or red flowers; many root in the clefts of rocks. Also applied to related plants, as the genus *Chrysosplenium* (Golden S.), *Pimpinella saxifraga* (Burnet or Rough S.), *Silaus pratensis* (Meadow or Pepper S.), the genus *Seseli* (Meadow S.). **b.** (with *pl.*) Any member of the genus *Saxifraga* or of the family *Saxifragaceæ* 1578.

Saxigenous (sæksi·dʒĭnəs), *a.* 1842. [f. L. *saxum* rock + -GEN 'produce, grow' + -OUS.] That produces (coral) rocks or reefs.

Saxon (sæ·ksən), *sb.* and *a.* ME. [– (O)Fr. *Saxon* – L. *Saxo*, *-ōn-*, pl. *Saxōnes* = Gr. Σάξονες – WGmc. *Saxon- (OE. pl. *Seaxan*, *Seaxe*, OS., OHG. *Sahso*, G. *Sachse*), perh. f. *saxsam knife (see SAX). Cf. FRANK *sb.*[1]] **A.** *sb.* **1.** One of a Germanic people which dwelt in a region near the mouth of the Elbe, and of which one portion, dist. as *Anglo-Saxons*, conquered and occupied certain parts of South Britain in the 5th and 6th centuries, while the other, the *Old Saxons*, remained in Germany. **b.** In mod. use *spec.* An Englishman as dist. from a Welshman or Irishman, a Lowland Scot as dist. from a Highlander 1642. **2.** A native or inhabitant of Saxony in its modern German sense 1737. **B.** *adj.* **1.** Of or belonging to the Saxons (see A. 1). Formerly used (like *Anglo-Saxon*) as the distinctive epithet of the Old English language, and of the period of English history preceding the Norman Conquest. 1568. **b.** Applied to the element in the English tongue which is derived from Anglo-Saxon 1589. **c.** Used (primarily by Celtic speakers) for 'English' in contradistinction to Welsh, Irish, or Gaelic. Also like *Anglo-Saxon*, applied to people of the English-speaking communities, chiefly in contradistinction to 'Latin'. 1787. **d.** *Arch.* Designating the variety of Romanesque architecture which preceded the Norman in England 1770. **2.** *absol.* (quasi-*sb.*) The language of the Saxons: **a.** = ANGLO-SAXON. Often used for Modern English speech of Saxon or Anglo-Saxon origin. late ME. **b.** *Old Saxon*: the language of the Old Saxons (see A. 1) 1841. **3.** Of or belonging to Saxony in its modern German sense 1634.

1. *Old S.*, pertaining to the Old Saxons or their language. **3.** *S. blue* = SAXONY *blue*. *S. green*, cobalt green. Hence **Sa·xondom** = ANGLO-SAXONDOM. **Sa·xonist**, a S. scholar; one learned in Anglo-Saxon. **Sa·xonize** *v. trans.* to make S. or Anglo-Saxon.

Saxonic (sæksǫ·nik), *a.* 1550. [– med.L. *Saxonicus*, f. *Saxon-*; see prec., -IC.] **1.** Of or belonging to Saxony 1645. **2.** Belonging to the Anglo-Saxons or their language 1550.

Saxonism (sæ·ksəniz'm). 1676. [f. SAXON + -ISM 3.] **1.** An Anglo-Saxon idiom or expression; Anglo-Saxon characteristics in speech. **2.** The characteristics of the Anglo-Saxon race; attachment to what is Anglo-Saxon 1884.

Saxony (sæ·ksəni). 1843. [– late L. *Saxonia*, the country of the Saxons, f. *Saxon-* SAXON.] The name of a kingdom in Germany (G. *Sachsen*, Fr. *Saxe*), used *attrib.* to designate products of the country: *esp.* **1.** A fine kind of wool, and cloth made from it. Also *absol.* = *S. cloth*. 1844. **2.** *S. blue*: a solution of indigo in concentrated sulphuric acid, much used as a dye. Also called *Saxe*, *Saxon, blue*. 1843.

Saxophone (sæ·ksŏfōᵘn). 1851. [f. the name *Sax* (see SAXHORN) + -PHONE.] A brass wind-instrument with a clarinet mouthpiece, invented by Adolphe Sax. Abbrev. **Sax.**

Say (sēⁱ), *sb.*[1] ME. [– (O)Fr. *saie* :– L. *saga*, collect. pl. (used as sing.) of *sagum* coarse woollen blanket, military cloak, of Gaulish origin according to Polybius.] A cloth of fine texture resembling serge; formerly partly of silk, subseq. entirely of wool.

†Say, *sb.*[2] ME. Aphet. f. ASSAY *sb.* –1817.

Say (sēⁱ), *sb.*[3] 1571. [f. SAY *v.*[1]] **1.** What a person says; words as compared with action; also, a saying, dictum. Now *poet.* **†2.** A proverb, saw –1650. **3.** What one has planned to say; chiefly in phr. *to say (out) one's s.* 1692. **4.** A talk *to* or *with* a person. Now *dial.* 1786.

1. You hearken to the lover's s., And happy is the lover A. E. HOUSMAN. Phr. *To have a s.*, to have a 'voice' in a matter; to have the right to be consulted. *To have the s.* (U.S.) to be in command. **3.** *To have one's s.*, to avail oneself of an opportunity of expressing one's views.

Say (sēⁱ), *v.*[1] 3rd pers. sing. pres. indic. **says** (sez), (*arch.*) **saith** (seþ). Pr. pple. **saying** (sēⁱ·iŋ). Pa. t. and pple. **said** (sed). [OE. *secġan* = OFris. *sega*, *sedza*, OS. *seggian* (Du. *zeggen*), OHG. *sagēn* (G. *sagen*), ON. *segja* :– Gmc. *saȝjan and *saȝǣjan; the IE. base *soq- *seq- is repr. also by OSl. *sočiti*, OL. (imper.) *insece*, *inquam* (:– *insquam) I say, Gr. (imper.) ἔννεπε.] **1.** *trans.* To utter or pronounce (a specified word or words, or an articulate sound). Also used of an author or book, with quoted words as obj. **2.** To declare or state in words (a specified fact, thought, opinion, or intention) OE. **†b.** [After L. *dicere*, Fr. *dire*.] With compl.: To speak of, call (by a specified name or designation); chiefly *pass.* Also *pass.* with adj. or descriptive sb., = 'to be said to be', 'to be called'. –1690. **3.** Absol. uses of 1 and 2. OE. **b.** Used in parenthetic clause indicating the author of a quoted saying. Also in parenthetic expressions like 'shall I say?', 'let us say'. ME. ¶ In this use, the 3rd sing. pres. is often substituted colloq. for the pa. t. *said*. Hence, in vulgar speech, *says I, says you* = 'said I', 'said you'. 1682. **4. †a.** Of words: To mean, signify –1604. **b.** *That is to say* (orig. gerundial inf.): used to introduce a more explicit or intelligible re-statement of what immediately precedes, or a limiting clause necessary to make the statement correct ME. **5.** To declare or make known (*who, what, how, whether*, etc.) OE. **b.** To judge, decide; freq. in expressions like 'it is hard to say', 'I cannot say' 1709. **c.** *absol.* In the imperative, introducing a direct question. Now *poet.* ME. **†6.** To deliver (a speech, discourse); to relate (a story); to express, give (thanks); to tell, speak (truth, lies); to express (one's opinion) –1657. **7.** To recite or repeat (something that has a prescribed form); occas. to recite from memory, in contradistinction to reading ME. **8.** The imperative **say** is idiomatically used: **a.** to introduce a clause, with the sense 'supposing', 'on the assumption *that*'; **b.** parenthetically, to indicate that a preceding sentence expresses a supposition or a selected instance; **c.** prefixed to a designation of number, quantity, date, etc. to mark it as approximate or hypothetical. 1596.

1. Then said they vnto him, S. now, Shibboleth; and he said, Sibboleth *Judg.* 12:6. **2.** What I have said I have said WYCHERLEY. What s. you to that? SWIFT. *It is (has been, will be) said* (with clause, expressed or understood, as real subject): in pres. tense now chiefly = 'it is commonly said', 'people say'. Phrases. *To have something (nothing) to s. to* (or *with*), *fig.* to have (no) dealings with; of things, to have (no) connection with or bearing upon. *To have (something, nothing*, etc.) *to s. for oneself*, to be able to adduce (something, nothing) in defence or extenuation of one's conduct. Also (colloq.), *To have nothing to say for oneself*, to be habitually silent. **3.** Be persuaded by me, and do as I s. 1875. *You don't s. so!* colloq. expression of astonishment at some statement. **b.** Amen, to that faire prayer, say I SHAKS. Says Cary, says he,..I never heard of such a thing SWIFT. **4. b.** Three hours after, that's to s., about eleven a Clock 1687. **5.** How ferful trowly there is no tong can saye 1485. **c.** Say? How is that? SHAKS. **7.** *To s. grace, a lesson, (a) mass, a prayer, (one's prayers)*. **8. c.** Early in the week, or s. Wednesday DICKENS. The wages of my people..average 11*s.* per week...Harvesting, s. £5 more. KINGSLEY.

Phrases, etc. **Not to s..**.: used (*a*) to imply that the speaker is content with a more moderate statement than that which he might have made; (*b*) *colloq.* = 'not what one may call..', 'not.., properly speaking'. **I say: a.** introducing a word, phrase, or statement repeated from the preceding sentence (now somewhat *rare*); **b.** *colloq.* quasi-*int.* (In U.S. *say.*) used to call attention to what is about to be said; also as a mere exclam. *When all is said and done*, after all. **S. on.** In the imper. = 'say what you wish to say'. Now only *intr.* **S. out.** *trans.* (*a*) To say openly. †(*b*) To say to the end. **S. over.** *trans.* To repeat from memory. Hence **Say·able** *a.* capable of being said. **Say·er**[1], one who says.

†Say, *v.*[2] late ME. = ASSAY *v.* –1813. So **†Say·er**[2] –1835.

Saying (sēⁱ·iŋ), *vbl. sb.* ME. [f. SAY *v.*[1] + -ING[1].] **1.** The action of SAY *v.*[1]; utterance, enunciation; recitation. **2.** Something that is said; a dictum; a proverb; *occas.* †a current form of speech ME.

1. Saying and doyng, are twoo thinges, we say HEYWOOD. **2.** I can see into a mill-stone as far as another (as the S. is) STEELE.

Say-so (sēⁱ·sōᵘ), *sb.* Now *dial.* and *U.S.* 1637. [f. SAY *v.*[1] + SO *adv.*] (A person's) mere word or dictum; an ipse dixit. Phr. *To have the s.*, to be the authority.

‖**Sayyid** (sēⁱ·yid). Also **seyd, syed.** 1615. [– Arab. *sayyid* lord, prince; cf. CID, SIDI.] In Moslem countries, a descendant of the Prophet, through his elder grandson Husain.

‖**Sbirro** (sbi·rro). *Pl.* **sbirri** (sbi·rri). 1668. [It.] An Italian police officer.

'Sblood (zblɒd). *Obs.* exc. *arch.* 1598. Euphemistic shortening of *God's blood*, used as an oath or asseveration.

'Sbo·dikins. *Obs.* exc. *arch.* 1676. Euphemistic shortening of *God's bodikins* (BODIKIN 2).

Sc., abbrev. of SCILICET.

Scab (skæb), *sb.* ME. [– ON. *skabbr (OSw. *skabber*, Sw. *skabb*, (O)Da. *skab*) = OE. *sċeabb* (see SHABBY). The application to persons may have been due partly to MDu. *schabbe* slut, scold.] **†1.** Disease of the skin in which pustules or scales are formed; a general term for skin diseases, but sometimes *spec.* = itch or scabies, ringworm or tinea, syphilis; *wet s.*, eczema –1791. **2.** A cutaneous disease in animals, esp. sheep, resembling the itch and the mange. late ME. **b.** A disease of cultivated plants, causing a scab-like roughness 1750. **3.** The crust which forms over a wound or sore during cicatrization. late ME. **b.** *Iron-founding.* A blister on the surface of a casting 1881. **4.** *slang.* **a.** A mean, low 'scurvy' fellow; a scoundrel 1590. **b.** (orig. *U.S.*) A workman who refuses to join an organized movement on behalf of his trade 1811.

Scab (skæb), *v.* 1683. [f. prec.] **1.** *intr.* and *pass.* To become encrusted with a scab or scabs. Also with *over*. **b.** *Iron-founding.* To form 'scabs' 1881. **3.** *slang.* To behave as a 'scab' or 'blackleg' 1905.

Scabbard (skæ·bəɹd), *sb.*[1] [ME. *sca(u)berc*, etc., aphetic – AFr. *escauberc (only in pl. *escaubers, -erz*), *escauberge* (cf. AL. *eschauberca*, *scarbergium* XIII), prob. – comp. of Frankish *skār, *skāra (see SHEAR *sb.*[1]) + *berg- protect (as in HAUBERK).] **1.** The case or sheath which protects the blade of a sword, dagger, or bayonet when not in use. **†2.** *transf.* Applied to various kinds of sheath or integument; a cocoon, etc. –1753.

1. Whiles the sworde of iustice, slept in his scaberd NASHE. *To throw away the s.* (fig.), to abandon all thought of making peace.

Comb.: **s.-fish**, *Lepidopus caudatus*, a fish of long, compressed s.-like form and silvery-white colour; **s. razor-shell**, a razor-shell, *Solen vagina*.

Scabbard (skæ·bāɹd), *sb.*[2] 1635. [– MLG. *schalbort*, f. *schale* shell, rind, etc. (see SCALE *sb.*[1], SHELL *sb.*) + *bort* board.] Thin board used in making splints, scabbards of swords, veneer, etc., and by printers in making register (now called *scale-board*). **b. s.-plane** = SCALEBOARD-*plane* 1846.

Sca·bbard, *v.* 1579. [f. SCABBARD *sb.*[1]] *trans.* To furnish with a scabbard; to sheathe.

Scabbed (skæbd, skæ·bėd), *a.* Now *rare*. ME. [f. SCAB *sb.* + -ED[2].] **1.** Having the scab or a similar skin-disease; covered with scab or scabs. **†2.** 'Scurvy', mean, contemptible –1786. Hence **†Sca·bbed-ly** *adv.*, **-ness.**

Scabble (skæ·b'l), *v.* 1620. [Later var. of SCAPPLE.] **1.** *trans.* To rough-dress (stone). **2.** *Iron-manuf.* = CABBLE *v.* 1849.

Scabby (skæ·bi), *a.* 1526. [f. SCAB *sb.* + -Y[1].] **1.** = SCABBED *a.* 1. **2.** *fig.* Contemptible, mean, vile; stingy, shabby. Now *vulgar*. Hence **Sca·bbiness,** the condition or quality of being s.

‖**Scabies** (skēⁱ·biˌīz). late ME. [L. *scabies* roughness, itch, f. *scabere* scratch, scrape.] *Path.* **†1.** A general term for skin-diseases characterized by scabby or scaly eruption –1742. **2.** A contagious skin-disease, due to a parasite, *Sarcoptes scabiei*; the itch 1814.

Scabious (skēⁱ·biəs), *sb.* late ME. [– med.L. *scabiosa* (sc. *herba* plant), subst. use of fem. sing. of L. *scabiosus*; see next. Cf. (O)Fr. *scabieuse*.] Any of the herbaceous plants of the dipsacaceous genus *Scabiosa*, formerly believed to be efficacious for the cure of certain skin-diseases. **b.** *U.S.* Applied to some species of *Erigeron* 1830.

Blue S., *S. succisa*. **Purple** or **Sweet S.**, *S. atropurpurea*. **Devil's bit S.**: see DEVIL'S BIT.

Scabious (skē·biəs), *a.* Now *rare*. 1603. [– Fr. *scabieux* or L. *scabiosus*, f. *scabies*; see SCABIES, -OUS.] Of the nature of or pertaining to scabies or itch; in early use = SCABBED *a.* 1.

Scabrid (skē·brid), *a.* 1866. [– late L. *scabridus*, f. *scaber*; see next, -ID[1].] *Bot.* Somewhat scabrous.

Scabrous (skē·brəs), *a.* 1549. [– Fr. *scabreux* or late L. *scabrosus*, f. *scaber* (rel. to L. *scabere*, SCABIES); see -OUS.] **1.** Rough with minute points or knobs, as dist. from unevenness of surface; esp. *Nat. Hist.* and *Phys.* **2.** Of an author, his style, etc.: Harsh, unmusical, unpolished 1585. **3.** Full of obstacles, difficult, 'thorny' 1646. **4.** Risky, bordering upon the indelicate 1881.

2. His verse is s., and hobbling DRYDEN. Hence **Sca·brous-ly** *adv.*, **-ness.**

Scad (skæd). Also **skad.** 1602. [Origin unkn.; app. first used in Cornwall.] The fish *Caranx trachurus* (*Trachurus saurus*), found abundantly on the British coasts, and characterized by having its lateral line armed with bony plates; also applied to other fishes of the genus *Caranx* and related genera; the horse-mackerel.

Scaffold (skæ·fǒld), *sb.* [ME. *scaffot*, *scaffald* – AFr. **scaffaut*, OFr. (*e*)*schaffaut*, mod. *échafaud*, earlier *escadafaut* = Pr. *escadafalc* :– Rom. **excatafalcum*, f. *ex-* EX-[1] + **catafalcum*; see CATAFALQUE.] **1.** A temporary platform, usu. supported on poles, designed to hold the workmen and materials employed in the erection, repairing, or decoration of a building. Also *pl.*, but now usu. *sing.* = SCAFFOLDING. **†2.** A raised platform, seat, or stand, used for exhibiting persons or actions to the public view, making proclamations, or the like –1687. **3.** *spec.* A (temporary) platform or stage on which theatrical performance or exhibition takes place. Now *Hist.* late ME. **†4.** A raised platform or stand for holding the spectators of a tournament, play, etc. Also, a gallery in a theatre or church. –1770. **5.** An elevated platform on which a criminal is executed; *the s.*, execution, capital punishment 1557. **6.** A raised framework of wood used for other purposes; among the N. Amer. Indians, for the disposal of the dead 1534. **7.** *Iron-founding.* An obstruction in a blast furnace caused by an accumulation of unreduced materials adhering to the lining 1861.

1. The building's set up, let the scaffolds be pulld down 1646. Every bricklayer who falls from a s. MACAULAY. **2.** An heraud on a s. made an ho CHAUCER. **4.** The other side was op'n, where the throng On banks and scaffolds under Skie might stand MILT. **5.** Phr. *To go to the s.*, to be executed. *To bring or send to the s.*, etc.; Paths which naturally conduct a minister to the s. '*Junius' Lett.*

Scaffold (skæ·fǒld), *v.* 1548. [f. prec. Cf. (O)Fr. *échafauder*.] **†1.** *trans.* To furnish with a platform, stand, or gallery –1704. **2.** To put scaffolding up to (a building) 1662. **3.** To place (food) on a raised framework of wood, for the purpose of drying it or protecting it from animals; among N. Amer. Indians, to expose corpses on a scaffold 1775. **4.** *Iron-founding. intr.* To form a 'scaffold' 1880.

Hence **Sca·ffoldage** (*rare*) = next 1.

Scaffolding (skæ·fǒldiŋ), *vbl. sb.* ME. [f. SCAFFOLD *sb.* + -ING[1].] **1.** The temporary framework of platforms and poles constructed to accommodate workmen and their materials during the erection, repairing, etc. of a building. **2.** The action of SCAFFOLD *v.* 1862.

1. *fig.* Sickness, contributing..to the shaking down this S. of the Body POPE.

‖**Scaglia** (skā·lyă). 1774. [It. = scale, chip of marble; see SCALE *sb.*[2]] *Geol.* A local name in the Italian Alps for limestone of various colours.

Scagliola (skælyǭ·lă). 1582. [– It. *scagliuola*, dim. of *scaglia* (see prec.).] **†1.** = prec. –1774. **2.** Plaster-work of Italian origin, designed to imitate kinds of stone 1747.

Scalable (skē·lăb'l), *a.* 1579. [f. SCALE *v.*[3] + -ABLE.] Capable of being scaled or climbed.

Scalade (skălā·d). Now *rare* or *Obs.* 1591. [– It. *scalada*, now *scalata*, f. *scalare* scale; see ESCALADE.] **1.** = ESCALADE *sb.* **2.** A scaling ladder 1632. So **†Scala·do** –1847.

Scalar (skē·lăɹ), *a.* and *sb.* 1656. [– L. *scalaris*, f. *scala* ladder; see SCALE *sb.*[3], -AR[1].] **A.** *adj.* **1.** Resembling a ladder; *Bot.* = SCALARIFORM. **2.** *Math.* Of the nature of a scalar 1853. **B.** *sb. Math.* In quaternions, a real number 1853.

Scalarian (skălēə·riăn), *a.* and *sb.* 1841. [f. mod. L. *Scalaria*; see prec., -IA[2], -AN.] (A gasteropod) belonging to the genus *Scalaria*.

Scalariform (skălæ·rifǭɹm), *a.* 1836. [f. SCALAR (*Bot.*) + -FORM.] *Bot.*, etc. Of the form of, resembling, a ladder; characterized by ladder-like formation, as cells or vessels of plants having the walls thickened so that they form transverse ridges.

Scalawag, variant of SCALLYWAG.

†Scald, *sb.*[1] 1561. [Altered f. SCALL *sb.*, after SCALD *a.*] = SCALL *sb.* –1693.

Scald (skǭld), *sb.*[2] 1601. [f. SCALD *v.*] **1.** An injury to the skin and flesh caused by hot fluid or steam. **b.** *transf.* Inflammation caused by heat; an inflamed part. Also applied to diseases which produce a similar effect. 1882. **2.** The action or an act of scalding food, utensils, etc. 1661. **3.** A hot liquor or solution used for scalding 1684.

Scald, *sb.*[3]: see SKALD.

Scald (skǭld), *a.*[1] Now *arch.* and *dial.* 1500. [Later spelling of SCALLED.] **1.** Affected with the 'scall'; scabby 1529. **2.** *fig.* 'Scurvy', mean, paltry, contemptible 1500.

2. S. Rimers SHAKS. *Comb.* **s.-pate** = SCALD-HEAD.

Scald (skǭld). *a.*[2] 1791. [pa. pple. of SCALD *v.*] Scalded.

S. cream, clotted or clouted cream.

Scald (skǭld), *v.* [ME. *scalde*, *schalde*, aphetic – AFr., ONFr. *escalder*, OFr. *eschalder* (mod. *échauder*) :– late L. *excaldare* wash in hot water, f. *ex-* EX-[1] + L. *cal*(*i*)*dus* hot, f. *calēre* be warm.] **I.** 'To burn with hot liquor' (J.). **1.** *trans.* To affect painfully and injure with very hot liquid or steam. **b.** *absol.* or *intr.* To be scalding hot ME. **c.** *intr.* for *pass.* To become injured by hot liquid or steam 1590. **2.** *trans.* To produce an injurious effect upon (something) similar to that produced by boiling water ME. **3.** To wash and cleanse with boiling water ME. **4.** *Cookery.* **a.** To heat liquid to a point just short of boiling point. Also *intr.* for *pass.* 1483. **b.** To subject to the action of hot water; to pour hot liquid over. late ME.

1. They all drink it sipping, for fear of scalding themselves 1687. **c.** Now scalds his soul in the Tartarian streams MARLOWE. **2.** I am bound Vpon a wheele of fire, that mine owne teares Do scal'd, like molten Lead SHAKS. **3.** Gut and s. your Pig MRS. GLASSE. Preparing to s. out the frying-pan 1869.

II. To burn. **1.** *trans.* Of the sun, fire, etc.; To scorch, burn. Also said of certain soils. Now *dial.* ME. **b.** *intr.* for *pass.* 1513. **†2.** *trans.* Of desire, thoughts, etc.; To 'burn', inflame, irritate –1667.

2. I am scalded with my violent motion..to see your Maiesty SHAKS. Would not a secret..S. you to keep it? MASSINGER.

Sca·ld-fish. 1812. [app. f. SCALD *a.*[1]] The smooth sole, *Pleuronectes arnoglossus*.

Scald head, sca·ld-head. 1546. [SCALD *a.*[1]] **1.** A person's head diseased with ringworm, etc. **2.** A popular term for tinea or similar scalp affections 1675. So **Scald-headed** *a.*

Scalding hot, *a.* late ME. [f. *scalding*, vbl. sb. f. SCALD *v.* + HOT *a.*] Hot enough to scald.

Scale (skēl), *sb.*[1] ME. [– ON. *skál* bowl, pl. weighing-scales = OHG. *scāla* (G. *schale*) :– Gmc. **skǣlō*, rel. to **skalō*, whence OE. *sćealu* shell, husk, drinking-cup, weighing-scale, OS. *skala* cup (Du. *schaal*), OHG. *scala* SHELL, husk (G. *schale*).] **†I.** A drinking-bowl or cup –1800. **II.** Apparatus for weighing. **1.** The pan, or each of the pans, of a balance. late ME. **2.** *pl.* A weighing instrument; *esp.* one (often called *a pair of scales*) consisting of a beam which is pivoted at its middle and at either end of which a dish, pan, board, or slab is suspended 1480. **3.** *sing.* = sense 2. Often *fig.*, esp. in *to turn the s.*; said of an excess of weight on one side or the other. 1440. **4.** *Astr.* (*pl.* and †*sing.*) The sign of Libra. Chiefly *poet.* 1631.

1. Your vowes to her, and me, (put in two scales) Will euen weigh, and both as light as tales SHAKS. **2.** Their Scales were false, their Weights were light 1719. Phr. *To hold the scales even* or *equally*, to judge impartially. **3.** When the s. was trembling between life and death 1861. Phr. *Equal, even s.* (poet.), a just balance; a condition of equilibrium or indecision; Long time in eeven s. The Battel hung MILT. *Clerk of the Scales* (Racing), the official who weighs the jockeys. *To ride, go to s.*, (of a jockey) to go to the weighing-room before or after the race.

Scale (skēl), *sb.*[2] ME. [Aphetic – OFr. *escale* (mod. *écale* husk, chip of stone) – Gmc. **skalō* (see SCALE *sb.*[1]).] **1.** One of the small thin membranous or horny modifications of the skin in many fishes and reptiles, and some mammals, usu. overlapping, and forming a complete covering for the body; also *collect. sing.* **2.** One of the small laminæ of epidermis which become detached from the tissue beneath in certain diseases of the skin. late ME. **3.** A part (e.g. a husk) that may be peeled off or detached in flakes; a thin plate, lamina, or flake of any kind 1450. **b.** The tartar that collects on the teeth 1594. **c.** *Bot.* A flattened, membranous, more or less circular plate of cellular tissue, usu. a rudimentary or degenerate leaf, as the covering of leaf-buds of deciduous trees, the bracts of catkins, etc. 1578. **d.** The protective covering of insects of the family *Coccidæ*, which remains when they die and protects the eggs and afterwards the young beneath it; hence, = *scale-insect*; also, the diseased condition of plants caused thereby 1822. **4.** Taken (after *Acts* 9:18) as a type of that which causes blindness (physical or moral) ME. **5.** Now usu. *collect. sing.* The film of oxide which forms on iron or other metal when heated and hammered or rolled 1526. **b.** *Salt-making.* An incrustation of dirt or lime on the pan bottoms. **c.** The hard deposit or 'fur' which gathers in boilers, etc. in which water is habitually heated (rarely *pl.*). 1848. **6.** Any of the thin pieces of metal composing scale-armour. Also *collect. sing.* 1809. **7.** *Cutlery.* **a.** Each of the two plates of bone, horn, ivory, or wood which form the outside of the handle of a knife or razor 1834. **b.** Each of the metal sides of the handle of a pocket-knife on which such plates are riveted 1834. **8.** [Fr. *écaille*.] A plate of metal worn instead of an epaulette by soldiers, sailors, and firemen 1846.

1. Leviathan..Turns to the stroke his adamantine scales COWPER. Fishes which were isles of living s. SHELLEY. **3. c.** The glandular scales of the Hop 1884. **4.** The skailes of darknesse which our eyes benight 1629. **6.** Armour of impenetrable s. SHELLEY.

attrib. and *Comb.*: **s.-armour**, armour consisting of small overlapping plates of metal, leather, or horn; **-beetle**, a tiger-beetle (family *Cicindelidæ*); **-blue**, the groundwork of royal blue with a s.-pattern characteristic of some Worcester china; **s. carp**, the common carp, *Cyprinus carpio*: **-fern** = CETERACH; **-insect**, any of the insects of the genus *Coccus* or family *Coccidæ*, having the appearance of scales, which infest and injure certain plants; **-pattern**, an imbricated pattern; **-wing**, a lepidopter; **-winged** *a.* lepidopterous; **-work**, work of an imbricated pattern.

Scale (skēl), *sb.*[3] late ME. [– L. *scala* usu. pl. steps, staircase, (sg., late) ladder :– **scandsla*, f. base of *scandere* climb.] **†I. 1.** A ladder; in early use, a scaling-ladder –1682. **b.** *fig.* and *allus.*, freq. with ref. to Jacob's ladder (*Gen.* 28:12) –1820. **2.** A rung or step of a ladder –1682. **3.** A flight (of stairs); a staircase –1705.

1. b. In th' ascending S. of Heav'n the Starrs that usher Evening rose MILT.

II. 1. *Mus.* **a.** A definite series of sounds ascending or descending by fixed intervals, *esp.* such a series beginning on a certain note selected for the purposes of musical composition. **b.** Any of the graduated series of sounds into which the octave is divided, the sounds varying according to the system of graduation adopted. 1597. **c.** (chiefly *pl.*) Any scale taken as a subject of instruction or practice 1865. **2.** A succession or series of steps or degrees; a graduated series, succession, or progression 1605. **b.** A regular series of tones or shades of colour produced by mixing with different proportions of white or black 1854. **3.** *Math.* **a.** A number of terms included between two points in a progression or series 1695. **b.** *Arith.* Any system of notation based on a number chosen as 'radix' or constant multiplier 1797. **4.** A graduated table (of prices, charges, etc.) 1788.

1. CHROMATIC, DIATONIC, HARMONIC, MAJOR, MINOR, etc. *s.*: see those words. **c.** I do wish she would forget to play her scales some morning 1888. **2.** Plants low in the s. of organisation DARWIN. **3. b** When the radix is 2, the s. is called Binary; when 3, Ternary; when 10, Denary or Decimal 1861. **4.** Reduction in S. of Charges for Advertisements 1865.

III. 1. A set or series of graduations (marked along a straight line or a curve) used for measuring distances, etc.; a graduated line, arc, etc.; *spec.* the equally divided line on a map, chart, or plan which indicates its scale, and is used for finding the distance between two points. late ME. **2.** A strip or blade of wood, ivory, metal, or cardboard having graduated and numbered spaces upon it, used for measuring or laying down distances 1607. **3.** The proportion which the representation of an object bears to the object itself; a system of representing or reproducing objects in a smaller or larger size proportionately in every part 1662. **4.** Relative or proportionate size or extent; degree, proportion 1607. **5.** *fig.* A standard of measurement, calculation, or estimation 1626.

2. *Diagonal, Gunter's, Marquois scales*: see the qualifying words. **3.** Phr. *To s.*, with exactly proportional representation of each part of the model. **5.** The Degrees of Crime are taken on divers Scales HOBBES. Phr. *On* or *upon a* (*large, small, liberal*, etc.) *s.*; Were education. .Conducted on a manageable s. COWPER.

attrib. and *Comb.*, as *s. drawing, plan*; **s.-micrometer,** a graduated scale in the field of a telescope for measuring the distance between objects; **-paper,** paper having printed upon it divisions in eighths, tenths, etc. of an inch for drawing in proportion.

†**Scale** (skēˈl), *sb.*⁴ 1577. [f. SCALE *v.*³] = ESCALADE –1667.

Scale (skēˈl), *v.*¹ 1603. [f. SCALE *sb.*¹] **1.** *trans.* To weigh in scales, find the weight of 1691. †**2.** *fig.* To weigh as in scales; hence, to compare, estimate. SHAKS. **3.** To weigh (so much) 1862. **b.** *Racing.* intr. To be weighed 1859.

2. Skaling his present bearing with his past SHAKS. **3. b.** Phr. *To s. in*, to be weighed after the race.

Scale (skēˈl), *v.*² 1440. [f. SCALE *sb.*²] **1.** *trans.* To remove the scales from (fish). **b.** *techn.*, esp. (*a*) To clean the bore of (a gun or cannon) by firing off a charge of powder; (*b*) To remove tartar from (the teeth) 1784. **2.** To remove as scale, to take *off* or *away* in scales; to separate *into* layers 1552. **3.** *intr.* To come *off* (or *away*) in scales, flakes, or thin pieces; to flake or peel *off*. Of skin eruptions: To shed scales. 1529.

2. Phr. *To be scaled*, to have the surface removed in scales; The stones being. .scaled by frost 1843.

Scale (skēˈl), *v.*³ late ME. [– OFr. *escaler* or med.L. *scalare*, f. L. *scala* SCALA *sb.*³] **I. 1. a.** *trans.* To attack with scaling ladders; to take by escalade. **b.** To climb, get to or reach the top of (a wall, mountain, etc.) 1579. **2.** To 'mount' (the skies); to ascend or climb up into (heaven). late ME. **3.** *intr.* To climb (*over*), ascend, mount 1547. **b.** Of steps, etc.; To ascend, mount 1667.

1. b. How often have I scaled the craggie Oke, All to dislodge the Raven of her nest? SPENSER. **3. b.** The lower stair That scal'd by steps of Gold to Heav'n Gate MILT.

II. To measure or regulate by a scale. **1.** *trans.* To fix the exact amount of. *U.S.* 1798. **b.** With *down*: To reduce in amount according to a fixed scale or standard 1887. **2.** *Lumber-trade.* **a.** To measure (logs), or estimate the amount of (standing timber) 1867. **b.** Of timber: To produce or furnish (so much) 1853. **3.** To estimate the proportions of 1877.

Sca·le-board. 1771. [f. SCALE *sb.*² + BOARD *sb.*² See SCABBARD *sb.*²] Thin board used for hat-boxes, silk hats, etc., and by printers for justifying.

S.-plane, a plane for cutting from a board thin pieces for use as s.

Scaled (skēˈld), *ppl. a.* late ME. [f. SCALE *sb.*² + -ED².] **1.** Having, or furnished with scales, as a fish or a serpent; scaly. Now *rare* exc. in comb. and *Her.* **2. a.** Of armour 1555. **b.** = IMBRICATED 2, 3. 1776. **c.** Covered with tiles in imitation of scales 1862.

2. c. The earlier house and its little gables and grey s. roofs W. MORRIS.

Scaleless (skēˈ·l,lės), *a.* 1611. [f. SCALE *sb.*² + -LESS.] Having no scales.

Scalene (skeˈlī·n), *a.* and *sb.* 1642. [– late L. *scalēnus* – Gr. σκαληνός uneven, unequal, scalene.] **A.** *adj.* **1.** *Geom.* **a.** Of a triangle: Having three unequal sides 1734. **b.** *S. cone, cylinder*: one of which the axis is not perpendicular to the base 1684. **2.** *Anat.* *S. muscle* = SCALENUS 1827. **B.** *sb.* **1.** A scalene triangle 1642. **2.** *Anat.* = SCALENUS 1891.

Scalenohedron (skeˈlīno,hī·drǫn). 1854. [f. Gr. σκαληνός SCALENE + -HEDRON.] *Cryst.* A hemihedral form of the rhombohedral system in which the faces are similar scalene triangles. So **Scalenohe·dral** *a.* pertaining to, having the form of, a s.

Scalenous (skeˈlī·nəs), *a.* Now *rare.* 1656. [f. late L. *scalenus* SCALENE + -OUS.] = SCALENE A. 1 a, b.

‖**Scalenus** (skeˈlī·nǒs). *Pl.* **-i** (-əi). 1704. [mod. subst. use of late L. *scalenus* (sc. *musculus* muscle); see SCALENE.] *Anat.* One of a set of muscles of triangular form situated in the lower lateral region of the neck.

Scaler (skēˈ·ləɹ). 1611. [f. SCALE *v.*² + -ER¹.] **1.** One who removes scales or scale from fish, boilers, etc. **2.** An instrument for removing scales or scale 1881.

Scaliness (skēˈ·linės). 1611. [f. SCALY + -NESS 1.] The condition or character of being scaly.

Scaling (skēˈ·liŋ), *vbl. sb.*¹ 1591. [f. SCALE *v.*² or *sb.*² + -ING.] **1.** The action of SCALE *v.*²; the removal or peeling off of scales or scale. **b.** *concr.* That which scales off; scale, scales 1651. **2.** Arrangement of scales 1721.

Scaling (skēˈ·liŋ), *vbl. sb.*² 1513. [f. SCALE *v.*³ + -ING¹.] **1.** Climbing, mounting; escalade. **2.** Measurement or estimation of quantities; the construction of a scale 1710.

Sca·ling-ladder. late ME. [f. prec.] A ladder used in the assault of fortified places. **b.** A fireman's ladder used for scaling buildings 1868.

Scall (skǭl), *sb.* and *a.* Now *Sc.* and *n. dial.* ME. [– ON. *skalli* bald head, f. Gmc. *skal-; see SCALE *sb.*¹ and ², SHALE *sb.*¹, SHELL *sb.*] **A.** *sb.* A scaly or scabby disease of the skin, esp. of the scalp.

Dry s., psoriasis. *Humid* or *moist s.*, eczema.

B. *attrib.* or *adj.* = SCALD *a.* 1598.

Hence **Scalled** *a.* (now *rare*) = SCALD *a.*

Scallion (skæ·liən). ME. [– AFr. *scal(o)un* = OFr. *escalo(i)gne* :– Rom. **escalonia*, for L. *Ascalonia* (sc. *cæpa* onion) shallot, f. *Ascalo* (Gr. Ἀσκάλων) Ascalon, a port in S. Palestine.] **a.** The shallot. Now *dial.* **b.** The Welsh onion or 'chibol'. **c.** An onion which fails to bulb but forms a long neck and strong blade; *pl.* shoots of old onions planted a second year.

Scallop, scollop (skǫ·ləp, skæ·ləp), *sb.* ME. [Aphetic – OFr. *escalope* ESCALLOP. Usu. pron. (skǫ·ləp), but spelt *scallop.*] **1.** A shell-fish of the genus *Pecten* 1440. **b.** A scallop-shell; a vessel resembling one, used in baptism, etc. late ME. **c.** A pilgrim's cockleshell worn as a sign that he had visited the shrine of St. James at Compostella ME. **2.** Anything resembling a scallop-shell 1609. **b.** *esp.* One of a series of convex rounded projections forming the scalloped edge of a garment, etc. Also, a scalloped form, a scalloping. 1612. †**c.** A scalloped lace band or collar –1661.

Sca·llop, sco·llop, *v.* 1737. [f. prec.] **1.** *trans.* To shape or cut (*out*) in the form of a scallop-shell; to ornament or trim with scallops 1749. **2.** *Cookery.* To bake (oysters, etc.) in a scallop-shell or similar-shaped utensil with bread crumbs, cream, butter, etc. 1737.

Scalloped, scolloped (skǫ·ləpt, skæ·ləpt), *ppl. a.* 1682. [f. SCALLOP *sb.* or *v.* + -ED.] **1.** Having the border, edge, or outline cut into a series of segments of circles like a scallop-shell. **2.** *Cookery.* (See SCALLOP *v.* 2.) 1737.

Scalloper (skǫ·ləpəɹ). 1881. [f. SCALLOP *v.* and *sb.* + -ER¹.] **a.** One who makes scalloped edging, etc. **b.** One who gathers scallops.

Sca·llop-shell. 1530. The shell of the scallop, or, more usu. one valve of it: freq. with ref. to its being a pilgrim's badge.

Scallywag, scallawag (skæ·liwæg, -ăwæg). *slang* or *colloq.* (orig. *U.S.*) 1848. [Of unkn. origin.] **1.** A disreputable fellow; a good-for-nothing, scapegrace, blackguard; formerly in *Trade Union slang*, a man who will not work. **2.** An imposter or intriguer, *esp.* in politics 1864. **3.** *U.S.* A name for undersized or ill-conditioned cattle 1854.

Scalp (skælp), *sb.*¹ [north. ME. *scalp*, prob. of Scand. origin, but the Eng. senses are not found in any Scand. or other Gmc. language.] **1.** The top or crown of the head; the skull, cranium. Now only *Sc.* and *n. dial.* **2.** The integument of the upper part of the head, usu. covered with hair and moving freely over the underlying bones 1616. **b.** *Her.* The skin of the head of an animal 1688. **3.** The scalp with the hair belonging to it cut or torn from a man's head; prized by Amer. Indians as a battle trophy 1601. **4.** A wig made to cover a part of the scalp 1801. **5.** Anything resembling a scalp; e.g. a bare piece of rock or stone, the cap of a mountain 1721.

attrib. and *Comb.*: **s.-dance,** a war-dance of N. Amer. Indians, in which scalps were carried in celebration of a victory; **-lock,** a lock of hair left on the head (the rest being shaved) by N. Amer. Indians as a challenge to their enemies; **-money,** money paid as a reward for 'bringing in' scalps of men or animals.

Scalp (skælp), *sb.*² Chiefly *Sc.* and *north.* 1521. [Cf. *shelp* (XV–XVII) sandbank in a river or sea (Essex).] A bank providing a bed for shellfish, *esp.* oysters and mussels; an oyster or mussel bed or colony.

†**Scalp,** *v.*¹ 1552. [– L. *scalpere*; see SCALPEL.] *trans.* To carve, engrave; to scrape, scratch –1802.

Scalp, *v.*² 1676. [f. SCALP *sb.*¹] **1.** *trans.* To cut off the scalp of (a person): chiefly said of the N. Amer. Indians. **2.** *dial.* To strip off (the turf or upper soil) 1806. **3.** *Milling.* To separate the 'hair' or 'fuzz' from (wheat, etc.), also, to separate the different sizes of grain from one another by attrition and screening 1883. **4.** *Stock Exch.*, etc. To buy at very low rates so as to be able to sell at less than official rates 1888.

Scalpel (skæ·lpəl), *sb.* 1742. [– Fr. *scalpel* or L. *scalpellum, -us*, dim. of *scalprum, scalper* cutting tool, chisel, knife, f. base of *scalpere* scratch, carve; see -EL.] A small light knife used in surgical and anatomical operations.

Scalper¹, **scauper** (skæ·lpəɹ, skǭ·pəɹ). 1688. [Partly – L. *scalper* (see prec.), partly f. SCALP *v.*¹ + -ER¹.] *Engraving.* A kind of graver used for hollowing out the bottom of sunken designs.

Scalper² (skæ·lpəɹ). 1795. [f. SCALP *v.*² + -ER¹.] **1.** One (esp. an Amer. Indian) who removes scalps. **2.** *U.S. slang.* One who buys and sells at a profit, but at a price lower than the official one, *esp.* unused portions of long-distance railway tickets 1882.

Sca·lping-knife. 1759. [f. *scalping*, vbl. sb. f. SCALP *v.*²] A knife such as is used by the N. Amer. Indians in scalping their enemies.

Scalpriform (skæ·lprifǭɹm), *a.* 1828. [f. L. *scalprum* (see next) + -FORM.] Chisel-shaped: applied to the incisors of rodents.

Scalprum (skæ·lprǒm). 1688. [– L. *scalprum*; see SCALPEL.] **1.** *Surg.* A rasping instrument; a raspatory. **2.** *Anat.* The cutting edge of an incisor. Also, a scalpriform incisor. 1842.

Scaly (skē^{i}·li), *a.* 1528. [f. SCALE *sb.*^{2} + -Y^{1}.] **1.** Abounding in, covered with, or consisting of scales; having a surface that peels off in thin plates or layers 1538. **2.** Of fishes, serpents, etc.; freq. in poetry = pertaining to or consisting of fish 1528. **3.** Of plants and their parts: Covered with scales or consisting of scale-like elements 1597. **4.** *slang.* Poor, shabby, despicable; *esp.* (of persons) mean, stingy; occas. 'seedy' 1793.

2. So hear the s. herd when Proteus blows DRYDEN. *S. ant-eater, lizard,* the pangolin. **4.** They had proved themselves so very scaley, by forgetting to remember the waiter 1823.

Scamble (skæ·mb'l), *v.* 1539. [app. related to SHAMBLE and SCRAMBLE *vbs.*] **†1.** *intr.* = SCRAMBLE *v.* 2. –1687. **2.** *trans.* To scatter (money, food) for a crowd to scramble for. Now *dial.* 1573. **3.** *intr.* To make one's way as best one can; to stumble along. Now *dial.* 1571. **4.** To throw out the limbs in a loose and awkward manner in walking; to shamble. Now *dial.* 1633. **5.** *trans.* To 'scrape' *together, up.* Now *dial.* 1577. **6.** To remove piecemeal 1707.

1. *John* IV. iii. 146. **2.** A largesse of money skambled amongst the tribes HOLLAND. **5.** We have scambled vp More wealth by farre then those that brag of faith MARLOWE.

Scammony (skæ·mŏni). OE. [– OFr. *escamonie, scamonee* (mod. *scammonée*) or L. *scammonea, -ia* (also *-eum, -ium*) – Gr. *σκαμμωνία, -ώνιον.*] **1.** A gum-resin obtained from the tuberous roots of *Convolvulus scammonia*, used in medicine as a strong purgative; also, the dried tuberous root from which the drug is prepared. **2.** The plant *Convolvulus scammonia*, native in Syria and Asia Minor, having a fleshy root which furnishes the scammony of commerce 1567.

Scamp (skæmp), *sb.* 1782. [f. SCAMP *v.*^{1}] **1.** A highway robber. *arch.* **2.** A good-for-nothing, worthless person, a 'waster'; a rascal. Also *playfully* as a mild term of reproof 1808.

Scamp (skæmp), *v.*^{1} 1753. [prob. – MDu. *schampen* slip away, decamp – OFr. *escamper, eschamper* :– Rom. **excampare*, f. *ex-* EX-^{1} + *campus* field.] *intr.* **†a.** *cant.* To rob on the highway. **b.** *Sc.* To wander *about* idly 1867.

Scamp (skæmp), *v.*^{2} 1837. [perh. identical with prec., but allied in sense to SKIMP.] **1.** *trans.* To do (work, a task, etc.) negligently or hurriedly. **2.** *U.S. intr.* To be stingy or excessively economical 1894.

‖**Scampavia** (skampavī·a). 1723. [It., f. *scampare* :– Rom. **excampare* (see SCAMP *v.*^{1}) + *via* way, away.] A swift sailing vessel used in the Mediterranean.

Scamper (skæ·mpəɹ), *sb.* 1697. [f. next.] The action of scampering; an instance of this.

Scamper (skæ·mpəɹ), *v.* 1687. [prob. frequent. of SCAMP *v.*^{1}; see -ER^{5}.] **†1.** *intr.* To run away, decamp, 'bolt' –1833. **2.** To run or caper about nimbly; to go or journey hastily from place to place 1691.

2. Barefooted children were scampering up and down these stairs at play 1833. Hence **Sca·mperer.**

Scampish (skæ·mpiʃ), *a.* 1847. [f. SCAMP *sb.* + -ISH^{1}.] Having the character or disposition of a scamp; characteristic of a scamp. Hence **Sca·mpish-ly** *adv.*, **-ness.**

Scan (skæn), *sb.* 1706. [f. next.] The action of scanning; close scrutiny; perception, discernment; a scanning look.

Scan (skæn), *v.* late ME. [– L. *scandere* climb, (late) 'measure' (verses), with allusion to raising and lowering the foot to mark rhythm.] **1.** *trans.* To analyse (verse) by determining the nature and number of the feet or the number and prosodic value of the syllables; to indicate the structure or test the correctness of (a verse) by reciting it with metrical emphasis and pauses, or by counting the feet on the fingers. Also *occas.* to describe prosodically (a word or sequence of words); to find (a particular kind of foot) in a given portion of a verse. Also *absol.* **b.** *intr.* (for *pass.*). To admit of being scanned, to be found metrically correct 1857. **†2.** *trans.* To criticize; to judge *by* a certain rule or standard –1817. **†b.** *intr.* To pass judgement *on, upon*; to form an opinion *of* –1610. **3.** *trans.* To examine, consider, or discuss minutely 1550. **†4.** To interpret, assign a meaning to –1641. **5.** To perceive, discern. Now *rare.* 1558. **6.** To look searchingly at, examine with the eyes 1798. **7.** *Television.* To resolve (a picture) into its elements of light and shade for purposes of transmission 1928.

1. *absol.* An eare that could measure a just cadence, and s. without articulating MILT. **2.** Know then thyself, presume not God to s. POPE. **3.** Careless their merits or their faults to s. GOLDSM. **4.** Hence men came to s. the Scriptures by the Letter MILT.

Scandal (skæ·ndăl), *sb.* ME. [– (O)Fr. *scandale* – Chr. L. *scandalum* (Vulg.) cause of offence – Hellenistic Gr. *σκάνδαλον* snare for an enemy, cause of moral stumbling, orig. trap.] **1.** In religious use. **a.** Discredit to religion occasioned by the conduct of a religious person. Also, perplexity of conscience occasioned by the conduct of one who is looked up to as an example. **b.** An occasion of unbelief or moral lapse; a stumbling-block 1582. **2.** Damage to reputation; rumour or general comment injurious to reputation 1590. **†b.** A disgraceful imputation; in later use, a slander –1814. **3.** A grossly discreditable circumstance, event, or condition of things 1591. **b.** *concr.* A person whose conduct is a gross disgrace to his class, country, position, etc. 1634. **4.** Offence to moral feeling or sense of decency 1622. **5.** The utterance of disgraceful imputations; defamatory talk. Now often in milder sense, malicious gossip. 1596. **6.** *Law.* Any injurious report published concerning another which may be the foundation of legal action 1838. **b.** An irrelevancy or indecency introduced into a pleading to the derogation of the dignity of the court 1750.

1. Catholics. . could not appear in Protestant assemblies without causing s. to the weaker brethen FROUDE. **b.** Heresies and Schismes, are of all others, the greatest Scandals BACON. **2.** Get drunk like a Gentleman, with no S. 1706. **3.** Fleet marriages. . one of the strangest scandals of English life 1878. **4.** To the great s. of the county 1848. **5.** No s. about Queen Elizabeth, I hope? SHERIDAN.

Scandal (skæ·ndăl), *v.* 1592. [f. prec.] **†1.** *trans.* To disgrace, bring into ill repute or obloquy –1684. **2. a.** To spread scandal concerning (a person); to defame. Now *arch.* and *dial.* **†b.** To vituperate, revile. 1601. **†3.** To shock the feelings of; to scandalize –1701.

2. Charms and Sigils, for Defence Against ill Tongues that s. Innocence DRYDEN. Hence **†Sca·ndalled** *ppl. a.* shameful; slandered –1660.

Scandalize (skæ·ndăləiz), *v.*^{1} 1489. [– (O)Fr. *scandaliser* or Chr. L. *scandalizare* – eccl. Gr. *σκανδαλίζειν*, f. *σκάνδαλον*; see SCANDAL *sb.*, -IZE.] **†1.** To make a public scandal of (a discreditable secret). CAXTON. **†2.** To injure spiritually by one's example –1609. **3.** To utter false or malicious reports of (a person's) conduct; to slander. Now *rare.* 1566. **b.** *absol.* and *intr.* To talk scandal 1745. **4.** *trans.* To bring shame or discredit upon; to disgrace. Now *poet.* 1583. **5.** To horrify or shock by some supposed violation of morality or propriety 1647.

Sca·ndalize, *v.*^{2} 1862. [alt. of †*scantelize* shorten (XVII), f. SCANTLE *v.*] *Naut. trans.* To reduce the area of (a sail) by lowering the peak and tricing up the tack.

Scandalous (skæ·ndăləs), *a.* 1592. [– Fr. *scandaleux* or med.L. *scandalosus*, f. Chr. L. *scandalum*; see SCANDAL *sb.*, -OUS.] **†1.** Of the nature of or causing an occasion of offence; also, bringing discredit on one's class or position –1670. **2.** Of the nature of a scandal; grossly disgraceful. Also (now *rarely*) of a person: Infamous. 1595. **3.** Of words and writing: Defamatory, libellous 1603. **4.** Of a statement, etc.: Not pertinent to the case, irrelevant 1750.

1. The debate concerning. . the punishing of s. Clergymen MARVELL. **2.** The most s. Election that ever was in Oxford 1720. **3.** The most s. tongues have never dared censure my reputation FIELDING. Hence **Sca·ndalous-ly** *adv.*, **-ness.**

‖**Sca·ndalum magna·tum.** *Pl.* **scandala magnatum.** Now *Hist.* 1607. [med.L. 'scandal of magnates'.] *Law.* The utterance or publication of a malicious report against any person holding a position of dignity. Also *transf.* in joc. use, something scandalous.

Scandent (skæ·ndĕnt), *a.* 1682. [– L. *scandens, -ent*, pr. pple. of *scandere* climb; see -ENT.] *Zool.* and *Bot.* Climbing; ascending.

Scandinavian (skæ:ndinē^{i}·viăn), *a.* 1765. [f. L. *Scandinavia* (Pliny) + -AN.] Of or pertaining to Scandinavia, a geographical term including the three countries Norway, Sweden, and Denmark. Also as *sb.*, one connected ethnographically with one of these three countries.

Scandium (skæ·ndiŏm). 1879. [f. L. *Scandia*, contr. f. *Scandinavia* + -IUM.] *Chem.* A metal discovered by Nilson in the Scandinavian mineral euxenite.

Scanmag (skæ·nmæ·g). *slang.* 1779. Abbrev. (*scan. mag.*) of SCANDALUM MAGNATUM, used joc. as = 'scandal'.

Scansion (skæ·nʃən). 1671. [– L. *scansio, -ōn-*, f. *scans-*, pa. ppl. stem of *scandere*; see SCAN, -ION.] *Pros.* The action or art of scanning verse; the division of verse into metrical feet; an instance of this. Hence **Sca·nsionist,** one versed in the art of s.

‖**Scansores** (skænsō^{ə}·rīz), *pl.* 1835. [mod. L., f. as next; see -OR 2.] *Ornith.* Illiger's first order of birds, comprising the climbers.

Scansorial (skænsō^{ə}·riăl), *a.* 1806. [f. L. *scansorius*, f. *scans-*, pa. ppl. stem of *scandere* climb; see -ORIAL.] **1.** Of or pertaining to climbing; *spec.* of the feet of birds and animals, adapted for climbing. **2.** That climbs or is given to climbing; *spec.* of a bird, belonging to the Order SCANSORES 1835.

Scant (skænt), *sb. Obs.* exc. *dial.* ME. [– ON. *skamt* (n. adj. used absol.); see next.] Scanty supply; dearth, scarcity.

Scant (skænt), *a.* and *adv.* Now chiefly *literary.* late ME. [– ON. *skamt*, n. of *skammr* short, brief = OHG. *scam.* Superseded largely by SCANTY.] **A.** *adj.* **1.** Existing or available in inadequate or barely sufficient amount, quantity, or degree; stinted in measure, not abundant. **b.** Preceding a sb. without article or other qualifying word: Very little, less than enough 1852. **2.** Of a quantity or amount of anything: Limited, stinted; not full, large, or copious 1556. **b.** Hardly reaching (a specified number or amount). Chiefly *U.S.* 1856. **3.** Limited in extent; not wide or spacious 1533. **4.** Poorly furnished. Const. *of.* 1577. **5.** Deficient or lacking in quality; poor, meagre, not full or rich. Chiefly of immaterial things. Const. *in.* 1631. **†6.** Sparing, not liberal. Also in good sense: Chary, not lavish. Const. *of.* –1651. **7.** *Naut.* Of wind: Too much ahead, so that the ship has to sail very close. (Opp. to *large* or *free.*) 1600.

1. In the country money is rather s. BORROW. **b.** You do s. justice to Dover DICKENS. **2.** In such a s. allowance of Star-light MILT. **b.** A s. two day's allowance of meat 1856. **3.** Though the realme of Italy was s., their hertes were grette 1533. **4.** He's fat, and s. of breath SHAKS. **6.** For this time, Daughter, Be somewhat scanter of your Maiden presence SHAKS.

B. *adv.* **1.** Hardly, scarcely; barely. Now *dial.* 1450. **†2.** Scantily (*rare*) –1620.

1. Some who could s. brook the name of Bishop were content to give. . him a good Report FULLER. Hence **Sca·nt-ly** *adv.*, **-ness.**

Scant (skænt), *v.* late ME. [f. SCANT *a.*] **I.** *intr.* **†1.** To become scant or scarce –1624. **†2.** *Naut.* Of the wind: To become unfavourable, to draw too much ahead. Const. *upon, with.* –1823. **II.** *trans.* **†1.** To furnish (a person, etc.) with an inadequate supply; to stint; to put or keep on short allowance. In *pass.*, to be straitened (*for*). –1719. **b.** To put or keep on short allowance *of*; to keep (a person) short *of.* In *pass.*, to be badly off for. Now *rare.* 1565. **†c.** To limit or restrict *in* (a supply, etc.) –1836. **2.** To make scant or small; to reduce in size or amount, cut down. *obsol.* 1590. **3.** To stint the supply of; to refrain from giving, withhold; to be niggardly of. Now *rare.* 1573. **†4.** *gen.* To confine within narrow bounds; to limit, restrict, hedge in –1631. **5.** To treat slightingly or inadequately; to neglect, do less than justice to. Now *rare.* 1604.

1. He..scants vs with a single famisht kisse SHAKS. **b.** A man, whose fortune scants him of meanes to do you service 1597. **2.** S. not my Cups SHAKS. **3.** Doth like a Miser spoyle his Coat, with scanting A little Cloth SHAKS.

Sca·ntity. *rare.* late ME. [irreg. f. SCANT *a.* + -ITY, perh. after *quantity.*] Scantiness.

Sca·ntle, *sb.* 1596. [perh. f. next.] **1.** A small piece or portion, a scantling. **2.** *Slate-making.* A gauge for measuring slates 1850.

1. 1 *Hen. IV*, III. i. 100 (1st Qo.).

†Sca·ntle, *v.* 1581. [perh. dim. of SCANT *v.*; see -LE 3. In sense 3 perh. a back-formation f. SCANTLING.] **1.** *trans.* = SCANT *v.* II. 1. –1630. **2.** To make scant or small; to cut down, limit, restrict –1641. **3.** To make proportionate *to* –1711.

Scantling (skæ·ntliŋ). 1476. [alt., by assoc. with -LING[1], of †*scantlon* gauge (XIII) dimension (XIV), sample (XV), aphetic – OFr. *escantillon* (mod. *échantillon* sample).] **†1.** A builder's or carpenter's measuring-rod –1678. **2.** Measured or prescribed size, dimensions, or calibre; now *techn.* with ref. to the measurement of timber, stone, etc. 1526. **†3.** Limited measure, space, amount, etc.; a limit –1691. **†b.** *spec.* in *Archery*, applied to the distance from the mark, within which a shot was not regarded as a miss –1661. **4.** A portion, allotted quantity, allowance. *arch.* 1659. **5.** A small or scanty portion or amount, a modicum 1476. **†6.** A sample, pattern, specimen. Hence, a sketch outline, rough draft. –1838. **7.** *concr.* in techn. use. **a.** A small beam or piece of wood; *spec.* one less than five inches square 1663. **b.** *collect. sing.* Timber in the form of scantlings 1794. **c.** A block or slice of stone of a fixed size; also *collect. sing.* stone cut into scantlings 1726.

2. A fine twin screw steamship, built of steel to the same scantlings as if of iron 1888. Phr. †*Of one* (or *a*) *s.*, of the same size; hence, much alike. †*To take a s. of*, to measure or estimate the size or amount of; hence, to judge of, estimate. **3.** Such as exceede not this s. to bee sollace to the Soueraigne and harmelesse to the people BACON. **5.** I am really ashamed to send this s. of paper by the post H. WALPOLE.

Scanty (skæ·nti), *a.* 1660. [f. SCANT *sb.* or *a.* + -Y[1].] **1.** Meagre, slender, not ample or copious. **2.** Deficient in extent, compass, or size 1701. **3.** Existing or present in small or insufficient quantity; not abundant 1674. **†4.** Parsimonious. Of soil: Yielding little. –1796.

1. Me, in no s. measure, thou excell'st COWPER. **2.** S. trousers..and a forward set of the hat 1874. **3.** My paper is s. and time more so 1705. **4.** With.. daily toil Soliciting for food my s. soil COLERIDGE. Hence **Sca·nti-ly** *adv.*, **-ness.**

Scape (skēⁱp), *sb.*[1] ME. [Aphetic var. of ESCAPE *sb.*[1]] **1.** = ESCAPE *sb.*[1] 1. *arch.* (Often written *'scape.*) **†2.** A transgression due to thoughtlessness –1681.

1. *Oth.* I. iii. 136. **2.** Slight scapes are whipt, but damned deeds are praised MARSTON.

Comb.: **s.-spring,** a spring that is automatically liberated; **-wheel,** = *escape-wheel.*

Scape (skēⁱp), *sb.*[2] 1601. [– L. *scapus*, – Gr. σκᾶπος, cogn. w. σκῆπτρον SCEPTRE.] **1.** *Arch.* The shaft of a column 1663. **2.** *Bot.* A long flower-stalk rising directly from the root or rhizome; †*gen.*, a stem or stalk 1601. **4.** *Ent.* The first joint of the antenna of an insect 1826. Hence **Sca·peless** *a.*[1] (*Bot.*)

Scape (skēⁱp), *sb.*[3] 1773. [Abstracted from LANDSCAPE.] A view of scenery of any kind. Also as the second element of combs., as SEA-SCAPE, *cloud-scape*, etc.

Scape (skēⁱp), *v.* ME. [Aphetic var. of ESCAPE *v.* Now *arch.* and *poet.*, and often written *'scape.*] = ESCAPE *v.*

Comb.: **s.-gallows,** one who has escaped the gallows though deserving of capital punishment.

Scape (skēⁱp), *int.* 1862. Conventional imitation of the cry of the snipe when flushed. Hence as *sb.* a nickname for the snipe.

Scapegoat (skēⁱ·pgōᵘt). 1530. [f. SCAPE *sb.*[1] or *v.* + GOAT. App. invented by Tindale as tr. Heb. ᶜᵃzāzēl, (Vulgate *caper emissarius*), represented in the R. V. by 'Azazel' (as a proper name), and 'dismissal' in the margin.] **1.** In the Mosaic ritual of the Day of Atonement (Lev. 16), that one of two goats that was chosen by lot to be sent alive into the wilderness, the sins of the people having been symbolically laid upon it, while the other was sacrificed. **2.** One who is blamed or punished for the sins of others. (So Fr. *bouc émissaire.*) 1824.

Scapegrace (skēⁱ·pgrēⁱs), *sb.* and *a.* 1809. [f. SCAPE *v.* + GRACE *sb.*, as if 'one who escapes the grace of God'.] **A.** *sb.* A man or child of reckless and disorderly habits; an incorrigible scamp. Often used playfully. **B.** *adj.* That is a s.; characteristic of a s. 1830.

Scapeless (skēⁱ·plės), *a.*[2] 1850. [f. SCAPE *sb.*[1] or *v.* + -LESS.] Inevitable.

The s. net spread in thy sight around thee R. BRIDGES.

Scapement (skēⁱ·pměnt). 1755. Aphetic f. ESCAPEMENT.

Scaphander (skæfæ·ndəɹ). 1825. [– Fr. *scaphandre* (so named by La Chapelle, the inventor, 1775), f. Gr. σκάφη boat + ἀνήρ, ἀνδρ- man.] A cork belt used as a support in swimming.

Scaphite (skæ·fəit). 1822. [– mod.L. *scaphites* (Parkinson 1804–11), f. Gr. σκάφη boat + -ITE[1] 3.] *Palæont.* A cephalopod of the genus *Scaphites.*

Scapho- (skæ·fo, skăfǫ·), comb. form of Gr. σκάφη boat, as in **Scapho·cerite** [Gr. κέρας horn], the third section of the antenna of an insect. **Scapho·gnathite** [Gr. γνάθος jaw], a flat oval plate in the gill chamber of fishes, which by movement promotes a constant flow of water through the gill. **Scapholu·nar** *a.*, the epithet of a small bone in the carpus of some animals; also *ellipt.* as *sb.*

‖**Scaphocephalus** (skæ:fose·făləs). 1863. [mod.L., f. Gr. σκάφη boat + κεφαλή head; after *hydrocephalus.*] *Path.* 'Boat-shaped head'; a condition of the skull (caused by premature ossification of the sagittal suture preventing transverse development) in which the length greatly exceeds the breadth. Hence **Sca:phocepha·lic, Scaphoce·phalous** *adjs.* **Scaphoce·phalism, Scapho-ce·phaly.**

Scaphoid (skæ·foid), *a.* and *sb.* 1741. [– mod.L. *scaphoides* – Gr. σκαφοειδής, f. σκάφη boat; see -OID.] **A.** *adj.* Shaped like a boat. Chiefly *Anat.* and *Zool. S. bone* – B. **B.** *sb.* [Short for *s. bone.*] The first proximal carpal bone in Mammalia, or the corresponding bone in the foot 1846.

Scapiform (skēⁱ·pifǭɹm), *a.* 1796. [f. L. *scapus* SCAPE *sb.*[2] + -FORM.] Having the form of a SCAPE.

Scapolite (skæ·pŏləit). 1802. [– G. *skapolith* (D'Andrada 1800), f. Gr. σκᾶπος rod (see SCAPE *sb.*[2]) + λίθος stone; see -LITE.] *Min.* One of a group of minerals (including dipyre, ekebergite, marialite, etc.) composed of silicates of aluminium, calcium, and sodium.

Scapple (skæ·p'l), *v.* 1443. [Aphetic – OFr. *escapeler, eschapeler* dress timber. Cf. AL. *scapulare, escapulare* XIII.] *trans.* To reduce the faces of (a block of stone, †timber) to a plane surface without working them smooth.

‖**Scapula** (skæ·piŭlă). *Pl.* **-æ.** 1578. [Late L., in class. L. only pl. *scapulæ.*] **1.** *Anat.* The shoulder-blade, blade-bone, or omoplate (in man or other animals). **2.** *Ent.* Applied to various analogous parts of insects 1826.

Scapular (skæ·piŭlăɹ), *sb.* 1483. [– late L. *scapulare*, f. *scapula* shoulder (earlier pl. *-æ*); see -AR[1].] **1.** *Eccl.* **a.** A short cloak covering the shoulders; adopted by certain religious orders as a part of their ordinary costume. **b.** An article of devotion composed of two small squares of woollen cloth, fastened together by strings passing over the shoulders, and worn as a badge of affiliation to the religious order which presents it 1870. **†2.** *Surg.* A bandage passing over and around the shoulders to support other bandages, etc. –1758. **3.** *Ornith.* [Ellipt. for *scapular feather.*] Any feather which grows from the *pterylæ humerales* or scapular region 1688.

Scapular (skæ·piŭlăɹ), *a.* 1688. [f. SCAPULA + -AR[1]. Hence in later use mod.L. *scapularis.*] **1.** Of or pertaining to the scapula 1713. **2.** *Ornith.* Applied to any feather which grows upon the *pterylæ humerales* 1688.

Scapulary (skæ·piŭlări), *sb.* ME. [– AFr. **scapelorie*, var. of OFr. *eschapeloyre* (XII) – med.L. *scapelorium, scapularium*; assim. to -ARY[1].] **1.** *Eccl.* = SCAPULAR *sb.* 1 a, b. **2.** = SCAPULAR *sb.* 3. 1854.

Scapulary (skæ·piŭlări), *a.* 1548. [Sense 1 – OFr. *eschapulaire*; sense 2 f. SCAPULA + -ARY[1]; so Fr. *scapulaire* (XIX).] **†1.** *S. mantle*: a cloak covering the shoulders. **2.** = SCAPULAR *a.* 1. 1785.

Scapulette (skæ·piŭlet). Also **scapulet.** 1887. [– G. *scapulette* (Haeckel); see SCAPULA, -ETTE.] *Zool.* A leaf-like appendage of the manubrium of certain *Cnidaria.*

Scapulo- (skæ·piŭlo), comb. form of L. *scapula* SCAPULA, as in **S.-clavi·cular** *a.*, of or belonging to the scapula and the clavicle; also *sb.*, the scapulo-clavicular joint.

‖**Scapus** (skēⁱ·pŏs). *Pl.* **scapi** (skēⁱ·pəi). 1563. [L.; see SCAPE *sb.*[2]] **†1.** *Arch.* = SCAPE *sb.*[2] 1. –1728. **2.** *Ornith.* The shaft of a feather 1882.

Scar (skāɹ), *sb.*[1] [ME. *skerre, skarre* – ON. *sker* low reef. See SCAUR, SKERRY *sb.*[2]] **†1.** A rock, crag –1535. **2.** A lofty steep face of rock upon a mountain-side; a precipice, cliff 1673. **3.** A low or sunken rock in the sea; a rocky tract at the bottom of the sea 1712.

2. O sweet and far from cliff and s. The horns of Elfland faintly blowing! TENNYSON.

attrib.: **s.-limestone,** a carboniferous rock occurring in the Pennine Range.

Scar (skāɹ), *sb.*[2] late ME. [Aphetic – OFr. *escharre* (later *escarre, eschare*) – late L. *eschara* (also *scara*) scar, scab – Gr. ἐσχάρα hearth, brazier, scab. Cf. ESCHAR.] **1.** The trace of a healed wound, sore, or burn. **b.** *fig.* A fault or blemish remaining as a trace of some former condition or resulting from some particular cause 1583. **2.** *Nat. Hist.* A mark or trace indicating the point of attachment of some structure that has been removed; *Bot.* = CICATRIX 2. 1793.

1. A scarre nobly got, Or a noble scarre, is a good liu'rie of honor SHAKS. **b.** The leprous scars of callous Infamy SHELLEY.

Scar (skāɹ), *sb.*[3] 1748. [– L. SCARUS.] = SCARUS. Also *s.-fish.*

Scar (skāɹ), *v.* 1555. [f. SCAR *sb.*[2]] **1.** *trans.* To mark with a scar; to disfigure by inflicting a wound. **2. a.** *trans.* with *up.* To heal, cover with a scar. **b.** *intr.* with *over.* To heal; to become covered with a scar as a sign of healing. 1609.

1. Yet Ile not shed her blood, Nor scarre that whiter skin of hers then Snow SHAKS. *transf.* Durham has been scarred and blackened by.. industrialism 1908.

Scarab (skæ·răb). 1579. [– L. SCARABÆUS.] **1.** In early use, a beetle of any kind. Now *rare* exc. as applied to the scarabæid beetle, *Ateuchus sacer*, reverenced by the ancient Egyptians. **2.** *Antiq.* A gem (of cornelian, emerald, etc.) cut in the form of a beetle (*scarabæus*), having on the flat under-side a design in intaglio 1871.

Scarabæid (skærăbī·id), *a.* and *sb.* 1891. [– mod.L. *Scarabæidæ* (Leach 1817), f. L. *scarabæus*; see next, -ID[3].] *Ent.* **A.** *adj.* Of or belonging to the *Scarabeidæ*, a large family of lamellicorn beetles, including cockchafers, stag-beetles, dung-beetles, etc. **B.** *sb.* A s. beetle.

‖**Scarabæus** (skærăbī·ŏs). *Pl.* **-bæi** (-bī·əi). 1664. [L. *scarabæus*, Gr. σκαράβειος, presumably rel. to κάραβος stag beetle.] **1.** *Ent.* A beetle of the genus *Scarabæus*, an Old World genus of lamellicorn beetles typical of the *Scarabæidæ.* **2.** *Antiq.* = SCARAB 2. 1775.

Scarabee (skæ·răbī). *arch.* 1591. [Anglicized f. prec.] = SCARAB 1.

Scaraboid (skæ·răboid), *sb.* and *a.* 1879. [f. SCARAB + -OID.] **A.** *sb.* **1.** *Antiq.* A scarab only vaguely resembling the insect in shape. **2.** A scarabæid 1891. **B.** *adj.* Resembling a scarab or scaraboid 1888.

Scaramouch (skæ·rămautʃ), *sb.* 1662. [Early forms *Scaramuzza, -moucha, -muchio* – It. *Scaramuccia*, joc. use of *scaramuccia* SKIRMISH; hence Fr. *Scaramouche* (Molière), source of the later and present form.] **1.** (As proper name, with capital S.) A stock character in Italian farce, a boastful poltroon, who is constantly being cudgelled by Harlequin. **b.** A puppet representing Scaramouch 1816. **2.** *transf.* and *fig.* A rascal, scamp 1676.

1. Stout Scaramoucha with Rush Lance rode in, And ran a Tilt at Centaure Arlequin DRYDEN. **2.** He swore no s. of an Italian robber would dare to meddle with an Englishman W. IRVING.

Scarborough (skā·ɹbrə). 1546. The name of a town on the coast of Yorkshire, used *attrib.*, in **S. warning,** very short notice, or no notice at all; a surprise. **S. lily,** *Vallota purpurea.*

Scarce (skēᵊɹs), *a.* and *adv.* [– AFr., ONFr. *scars*, aphetic of *escars*, OFr. *eschars*, mod. *échars* (of coin) below standard value, (of wind) slight :– Rom. **excarpsus* plucked out, pa. pple. of **excarpere*, for L. *excerpere* select out, EXCERPT.] **A.** *adj.* †**1.** Restricted in quantity, size, or amount; scanty –1732. †**2.** Of persons, etc.: Stingy, sparing, parsimonious, penurious. Also with *of.* –1639. **3.** Of food, etc.: Existing or accessible in deficient quantity. late ME. **4.** Existing in limited number; rare. Said chiefly of things sought after by collectors. late ME. **5.** *Scarce of*: poorly or scantily supplied with; deficient in; short of. Now *rare* or *Obs.* 1541.

2. They knewe him to be of nature scarse, and not liberal 1562. **3.** In þat tyme money was skarse 1450. **4.** A scarse Book 1710. Knowledge is s., wisdom is scarcer 1884. **5.** We are s. of provisions MARRYAT.

Phr. *To make oneself s.*, (colloq.) to absent oneself.

B. *adv.* †**1.** Scantily, sparsely –1450. **2.** Barely, only just; not quite. Now *literary.* late ME. †**3.** Seldom, rarely –1663. **4.** Used (after L. *vix*) for: With dfficulty (*rare*) 1667.

2. With worldly cares he was so toste, that scarse he tooke his reste 1577. There he her met, Scarse from the Tree returning MILT. A s. heard Whisper FITZGERALD. **4.** Scarse from his mould Behemoth biggest born of Earth upheav'd His vastness MILT.

Scarcely (skēᵊ·ɹsli), *adv.* ME. [f. SCARCE *a.* + -LY^2.] †**1.** Scantily, in small quantities; inadequately, sparingly, parsimoniously –1669. **2.** Orig. = 'barely', 'only just'; hence also, = 'barely, or not quite', 'only just, if at all'. In sentences relating to belief, expectation, etc., the word now serves as a restricted negative (= 'not quite'). Often, however, it qualifies the degree of the speaker's belief; thus 'You will s. maintain, etc.' = 'I cannot quite believe that you will maintain, etc.' ME. **b.** With ref. to time: Barely, only just. Chiefly with pluperfect tense, before a clause introduced by *when* or *before.* 1542.

1. It was verie s. inhabited PURCHAS. **2.** The genius of Petrarch was s. of the first order MACAULAY. My partner..could s. believe his ears 1885. **b.** In old-fashioned days,..when you were s. born THACKERAY.

Scarcement (skēᵊ·ɹsměnt). *Sc.* and *north.* 1501. [app. f. †*scarce* vb. become or make less (f. SCARCE *a.*) + -MENT.] **a.** *Building.* A flat set-off or rebate in a wall, or in a foundation or bank of earth. Also *transf.* a flat ledge projecting from the face of a rock. **b.** *Mining.* A ledge left projecting into a mine-shaft 1839.

Scarceness (skēᵊ·ɹsnės). Now *rare.* ME. [f. SCARCE *a.* + -NESS.] †**1.** Niggardliness, stinginess. Of soil: Infertility. –1678. **2.** Deficient supply, scarcity; †*absol.* scarcity of food or provisions. late ME. †**3.** Want, poverty –1650. **4.** Uncommonness, rarity 1672.

4. The folly of man rateth things by their s. 1744.

Scarcity (skēᵊ·ɹsĭti). ME. [– ONFr. *escarceté*, OFr. *eschar-* (mod. *écharseté*); see SCARCE *a.*, -ITY.] †**1.** Frugality, parsimony; niggardliness, meanness –1531. **2.** Insufficiency of supply ME. **3.** *absol.* Insufficiency of supply, in a community, of the necessaries of life, dearth. Also, a period of scarcity, a dearth. 1450. †**4.** Deficiency, shortcoming –1450. †**5.** The condition of being slenderly or inadequately provided (const. *of*). Also *absol.*, penury, hardship. –1610.

2. A great s. of rain 1881. *attrib.*: **s. value,** an enhanced value due to s.; so *s. price, rent.* **3.** After such a famine there followed a Scarsitie in South Wales 1584. **5.** S. and want shall shun you SHAKS.

Scare (skēᵊɹ), *sb.*^{1} late ME. [f. SCARE *v.*] †**1.** Fear, dread –1616. **2.** An act of scaring or a state of being scared; *esp.* a state of general or public alarm occasioned by baseless or exaggerated rumours; *occas.* in generalized use, panic 1548. †**3.** Something that scares; *spec.* a scarecrow –1828.

2. He was seiz'd upon the S. of the Popish Plot HEARNE.

Comb.: **s.-head, -heading,** a heading to a column of newspaper matter written in language so extravagant as to produce a scare; **-line,** a sensational announcement upon a newspaper poster.

Scare (skēᵊɹ), *sb.*^{2} 1881. [orig. Sc. dial., joint or splice – ON. *skǫr.*] *Golf.* The part of a golf club where the head joins the shaft.

Scare (skēᵊɹ), *v.* Pa. t. and pple. **scared** (skēᵊɹd). [ME. *skerre*, etc. – ON. *skirra* frighten, (also) avoid, prevent, refl. shrink from, f. *skjarr* shy, timid.] **1.** *trans.* To frighten, terrify. **b.** To frighten away, drive off. Now chiefly with adv., except with ref. to keeping off birds from corn, etc. late ME. †**2.** *intr.* To take fright; to be scared (at) –1721.

1. Who scared me with that Gorgon face? 1839. *S. up, out* (U.S.), to frighten (game) out of cover; hence *fig.*, to bring to light, discover.

Scarecrow (skēᵊ·ɹkrōᵘ). 1553. [f. SCARE *v.* + CROW *sb.*^{1}] **1.** A person employed in scaring birds (*rare*). **2.** A device for frightening birds away from growing crops, usu. a figure of a man dressed in old ragged clothes 1592. **b.** *fig.* Something (not really formidable) that frightens or is intended to frighten 1589. **3.** One who resembles a scarecrow in his dress or whose appearance is ridiculous; †a gaunt figure 1590.

2. b. That idle s.,—the Bribery Act 1812. **3.** Half a dozen scarecrows out at knees and elbows DICKENS.

†**Sca·re-fire.** 1572. [alt. of SCATHEFIRE, after SCARE *sb.*^{1}] A sudden conflagration –1684.

Scaremonger (skēᵊ·ɹmɒ:ŋgəɹ). 1888. [f. SCARE *sb.*^{1} + MONGER.] One who busies himself in spreading alarming reports.

Scarf (skāɹf), *sb.*^{1} *Pl.* **scarfs, scarves.** 1555. [prob. alt. (by assoc. with next) of SCARP *sb.*^{1}] **1.** A broad band of silk or other material, worn (chiefly by soldiers or officials) either diagonally across the body from one shoulder to the opposite hip, or round the waist. **2.** *Eccl.* A band of silk or other material worn round the neck with the two ends pendent from the shoulders in front, as a part of clerical costume. In the 18th c. *spec.* the scarf worn by a nobleman's chaplain; hence, a chaplaincy. 1555. **3.** A broad strip of silk, gauze, etc., worn hung loosely over the shoulders or otherwise as an ornamental accessory to the costume 1562. **b.** *spec.* The scarf of black crape or silk worn over the shoulder by mourners at a funeral 1739. **c.** A band of warm and soft material worn round the neck in cold weather 1844. **d.** A necktie or cravat that more or less covers the bosom of the shirt 1865. †**4.** A sling for an ailing limb –1828. **5.** *Her.* = SCARP *sb.*^{1} 1688.

3. Trickt in skarffe and feather HEYWOOD.

Comb.: **s.-loom,** a loom for weaving figured fabrics of moderate breadth; **-pin,** a pin for fastening a s., or worn for ornament in a s.; **-ring,** a ring for holding a s. in position.

Scarf (skāɹf), *sb.*^{2} 1497. [prob. – OFr. **escarf* (mod. *écart*), f. **escarver* (mod. *écarver*), perh. f. an ON. base repr. by Sw. *skarf*, Norw. *skarv* piece to lengthen a board or a garment, joint or seam effecting this, Sw. *skarfva*, Norw. *skarva* lengthen in this way.] **1.** *Carpentry* and *Ship-building.* A joint by which two timbers are connected longitudinally into a continuous piece, the ends being halved, notched, or cut away so as to fit into each other with mutual overlapping. †**b.** *Shipbuilding.* The overlapping of adjacent timbers in a ship's frame, in order to secure continuity of strength at the joints –1850. **2.** *Metal-working.* The chamfered edges of iron prepared for welding 1875.

Comb.: **s.-joint** = senses 1 and 2; hence **-jointing,** the process of joining timbers by means of a s.

Scarf (skāɹf), *sb.*^{3} *Orkn.* and *Shetl. dial.* 1668. [– ON. *skarfr*, Norw., Sw. *skarf.*] A cormorant or shag.

Scarf (skāɹf), *sb.*^{4} 1851. [Cf. SCARF *v.*^{3}] *Whaling.* A longitudinal cut made in a whale's body.

Scarf (skāɹf), *v.*^{1} 1598. [f. SCARF *sb.*^{1}] **1.** *trans.* To cover or wrap with or as with a scarf or scarves; to invest with a scarf. **2.** To wrap (a garment) *about* or *around* a person in the manner of a scarf (*rare*) 1602. †**3.** To bind up (wounds) with, or as with a scarf –1643.

1. *transf.* Come, seeling Night, Skarfe vp the tender Eye of pittifull Day SHAKS. **2.** Vp from my cabin My sea-gowne scarft about me in the darke, Grop'd I to find out them SHAKS.

Scarf (skāɹf), *v.*^{2} 1532. [f. SCARF *sb.*^{2}] **1.** *trans.* To join by a scarf-joint. **2.** *Metal-working.* To bevel or flatten (the ends or edges of the pieces to be welded) 1831. **3.** *intr.* To be joined with a scarf 1794.

Scarf (skāɹf), *v.*^{3} 1851. [Goes with SCARF *sb.*^{4}] *Whaling. trans.* To make a 'scarf' in the blubber of (a whale). Also *absol.*

Sca·rf-skin. 1615. [SCARF *sb.*^{1}, in sense 'light outer covering'.] The outer layer of the skin; the epidermis, cuticle.

Not a hair Ruffled upon the s. TENNYSON.

Scarification (skæ:rifikēⁱ·ʃən). late ME. [– (O)Fr. *scarification* or late L. *scarificatio, -ōn-*, f. *scarificat-*, pa. ppl. stem of *scarificare*; see SCARIFY, -ION.] **1.** The action of scarifying; an instance of this. **2.** *concr.* A slight incision or a number of these made by scarifying 1541.

Scarificator (skæ·rifikēⁱ:təɹ). 1611. [Latinized form of Fr. *scarificateur* (Paré), f. as prec. + *-eur*; see -ATOR.] *Surg.* An instrument used in scarification, for making several incisions simultaneously.

Scarifier (skæ·rifəiəɹ). 1566. [f. SCARIFY + -ER^1.] **1.** One who or something which scarifies. *lit.* and *fig.* **2.** = SCARIFICATOR 1611. **3.** *Agric.* An implement for loosening the soil 1797. **4.** *Road-making.* A machine used for breaking up a road 1892.

Scarify (skæ·rifəi), *v.* 1440. [– (O)Fr. *scarifier* – late L. *scarificare*, alt. of L. *scarifare* – Gr. σκαριφᾶσθαι scratch an outline, sketch lightly, f. σκάριφος pencil, stilus; see -FY.] **1.** *trans.* (chiefly *Surg.*). To make a number of scratches or slight incisions in (a portion of the body, a wound). Hence *gen.* to cover with scratches. 1541. **b.** *fig.* To make sore, wound. Also, in mod. use, to subject to merciless criticism. 1582. **c.** *transf.* To cover with scars, to scar 1687. **2.** To make incisions in the bark of (a tree) 1440. **3.** *Agric.*, etc. To break up or loosen (ground, a road) with a scarifier 1805.

Scariose (skēᵊ·riōᵘs), *a.* 1785. [– mod.L. *scariosus*; see next, -OSE^1.] *Bot.* = next.

Scarious (skēᵊ·riəs), *a.* 1806. [– Fr. *scarieux* or mod.L. *scariosus.*] **1.** *Bot.* Having a dry and shrivelled appearance. **2.** *Zool.* Dry, not fleshy 1861.

Scarlatina (skāɹlătī·nă). 1803. [– mod.L. (Sydenham, 1676) – It. *scarlattina* (Lancelotti, 1537), fem. (sc. *febbre* fever, after med.L. *febris scarlatina*) of *scarlattino*, dim. of *scarlatto* SCARLET.] *Path.* = SCARLET FEVER. (Pop. often misapprehended as denoting a mild form of the disease.) Hence **Scarlati·nal** *a.* belonging to, resulting from, s. **Scarlati·nous** *a.* affected with s.

Scarless (skā·ɹlės), *a.* 1630. [f. SCAR *sb.*^{1} + -LESS.] **1.** Showing no scar; lacking blemish. **2.** Leaving no scar 1823.

Scarlet (skā·ɹlėt), *sb.* and *a.* ME. [Aphetic – OFr. *escarlate* fem. (mod. *écarlate*); ult. origin unknown.] **A.** *sb.* **1.** †**a.** In early use, some rich cloth, often of a bright red colour. **b.** Later, cloth or clothing of the colour described in 2. **2.** A brilliant vivid red colour, inclining to orange 1440. **b.** A pigment or dye of this colour. Now also *spec.*, any one of a certain group of coal-tar colouring matters used in scarlet pigments and dyes. 1653. **3.** Official or ceremonial costume of scarlet; also, the scarlet coat worn in the hunting field. Hence *occas.* the rank, dignity, or office signified by a scarlet robe. 1496.

1. b. An Ambassador, whose robes are lined with a s. dyed in the blood of Judges BURKE. **2.** His

Friend demanding what S. was? the blind Man answered, It was like the sound of a Trumpet LOCKE. **3.** After this he made little account of his S., or degree of Cardinal 1685.

B. *adj.* (orig. the sb. used attrib.) **1.** Having, or pertaining to, the colour scarlet. late ME. **b.** Clothed in scarlet, wearing a scarlet uniform, etc. 1591. **c.** Red with shame or indignation 1593. **2.** *fig.* Of an offence (after Isa. 1:18): Heinous, deep-dyed 1603.

1. The poppies show their s. coats KEATS. **c.** She flushed s. 1881.

Special collocations: **s.-day,** an occasion in university or civic life marked by the public wearing of state or official robes of s.; **s. lady, whore, woman,** abusive epithets applied to the Church of Rome in allusion to Rev. 17:1–5. **b.** In names of birds, insects, etc.: **s. ibis,** *Eudocimus ruber*, a bird congeneric with the typical Ibis, native in tropical America; **s. mite,** *Trombidium holosericeum*; **s. tanager,** the RED BIRD, *Pyranga rubra*; **s. tiger (moth),** *Hypercampa dominula*. **c.** In names of plants and fruits: **s.-bean** = *s. runner*; **s. geranium,** a pelargonium with s. blossoms, largely used as a bedding-plant; **s. maple,** *Acer rubrum*; **s. oak,** *Quercus coccinea*; also, †the Holm Oak, *Quercus ilex*; **s. pimpernel,** *Anagallis arvensis*; **s. runner (bean),** *Phaseolus multiflorus*. Hence †**Sca·rlet** *v. trans.* to clothe in s.; to colour s. –1688.

Sca·rlet fe·ver. 1676. A contagious febrile disease, distinguished by a scarlet efflorescence of the skin and of the mucous membrane of the mouth and pharynx. Cf. SCARLATINA. **b.** *joc. slang.* A passion for soldiers (red-coats) 1889.

Scarp (skāɹp), *sb.*[1] 1562. [Aphetic – ONFr. *escarpe* = OFr. *escherpe* (mod. *écharpe*), prob. identical with OFr. *escarpe, escharpe* pilgrim's scrip suspended from the neck (cf. ON. *skreppa* SCRIP *sb.*[1]) See SCARF *sb.*[1]] *Her.* A diminutive of the bend sinister, one-half its width, crossing the shield diagonally from the sinister chief to the dexter base.

Scarp (skāɹp), *sb.*[2] 1589. [– It. *scarpa*, whence Fr. *escarpe* ESCARP.] **1.** *Fortif.* = ESCARP *sb.* **2.** The steep face of a hill 1802.

Scarp (skāɹp), *v.* 1596. [f. prec.] *trans.* = ESCARP *v.* Hence **Scarped** *ppl. a.* reduced to a steep face, laid bare, cut away, steep.

Scarred (skāɹd), *ppl. a.* 1440. [f. SCAR *v.* + -ED[1].] **1.** Of the body or its parts: Bearing scars or traces of wounds or sores. **2.** *transf.* Of inanimate objects: Bearing traces of injury, weathering, or the like. Often of rocks: Broken as by a convulsion of nature. 1600. **3.** *Bot.* Marked with cicatrices or traces of leaves that have fallen off 1793.

Scarry (skā·ɹi), *a.* late ME. [f. SCAR *sb.*[1] + -Y[1].] Precipitous, rocky.

‖**Scarus** (skēᵊ·rǒs). *Pl.* **scari** (skēᵊ·rəi). 1601. [L. *scarus* – Gr. σκάρος. Cf. SCAR *sb.*[3]] A fish described by ancient writers; in mod. use, the typical genus of the family *Scaridæ*; a fish of this genus, a PARROT-FISH.

Scary (skēᵊ·ri), *a.* Also *vulgar* **skeery.** 1582. [f. SCARE *sb.*[1] + -Y[1].] **1.** Terrifying, frightful. **2.** Frightened, timorous 1827.

2. Women are skeery critters 1873.

Scat (skæt), *sb.* late ME. [– ON. *skattr* = OE. *sċeat*, OFris. *skett* money, cattle, OS. *skat* (Du. *schat*), OHG. *scaz* (G. *schatz*) treasure, Goth. *skatts* piece of money, money :– Gmc. **skattaz*.] **a.** *gen.* A tax, tribute. Now *Hist.* **b.** In Orkney and Shetland, the land-tax paid to the Crown by a udal tenant 1577.

Scat (skæt), *int. colloq.* 1869. [perh. short for SCATTER *v.*] Begone! Hence joc. used as verb (*intr.*).

Scathe (skēⁱð), *sb.* Now *arch.* and *dial.* OE. [– ON. *skaði* = OE. *sċeaþa* malefactor, (rarely) injury, OFris. *skatha* injury, OS. *skaðo* malefactor, OHG. *scado* (G. *schade*) injury, harm :– Gmc. **skaþon*, f. **skaþ-*, whence also Goth. *skaþis* harm, *skaþjan* injure.] †**1.** One who works harm; a malefactor –ME. **2.** Harm, damage OE. **b.** Something which works harm 1579. **3.** Matter for sorrow or regret. [Cf. G. *schade.*] ME.

2. To the great hurt and skaith of the king's lieges 1670. Phr. *To do s.*, to do harm; And wherein Rome hath done you any s., Let him make treble satisfaction SHAKS. Hence †**Sca·the-fire,** a destructive fire or conflagration –1796.

Scathe (skēⁱð), *v.* ME. [– ON. *skaða* = OE. *sċeaþian*, OFris. *skathia*, OS. *scaðon*, OHG. *skadōn* (Du., G. *schaden*) :– Gmc. **skaþōjan*.] **1.** *trans.* To injure, hurt, damage. Now *arch.* and *Sc.* †**b.** *spec.* To subject to pecuniary loss –1602. **2.** To injure or destroy by fire, lightning, or the like; to blast, scorch, sear. *poet.* and *rhet.* 1667. **3.** *fig.* To 'wither' with fierce invective or satire 1852.

1. As when Heavens Fire Hath scath'd the Forrest Oaks,..With singed top their stately growth though bare Stands on the blasted Heath MILT. **3.** His satire..scathing..his old enemies the monks 1867.

Scatheful (skēⁱ·ðfŭl), *a. arch.* OE. [f. SCATHE *sb.* + -FUL[1].] Harmful, injurious.

Scatheless (skēⁱ·ðlės), *a.* ME. [f. SCATHE *sb.* + -LESS.] Without scathe; unharmed. Hence **Sca·thelessly** *adv.*

Scathing (skēⁱ·ðiŋ), *ppl. a.* 1794. [f. SCATHE *v.* + -ING[2].] **1.** That scathes or blasts. **2.** Of invective, etc.: Very sharp and damaging; searing, 'withering', cutting 1865.

2. He launched from the pulpit the most s. invectives 1865. Hence **Sca·thingly** *adv.*

Scatology (skătǫ·lŏdʒi). 1876. [f. Gr. σκῶρ, σκατ- dung (cf. SCORIA) + -LOGY.] **1.** That branch of medical science which deals with diagnosis by means of the fæces 1897. **2.** *Palæont.* The study of fossil excrement or coprolites 1889. **3.** Filthy literature (*rare*) 1876. So **Scatolo·gical** *a.*

Scatophagous (skătǫ·făgəs), *a.* 1891. [f. Gr. σκατοφάγος, f. as prec.; see -PHAGOUS.] Feeding upon dung.

Scatter (skæ·təɹ), *sb.* 1642. [f. next.] **1.** The action or an act of scattering; wide or irregular distribution. Now chiefly with ref. to shot. **2.** A scattering, sprinkling (*rare*) 1859.

Scatter (skæ·təɹ), *v.* [prob. var. of SHATTER, with (sk) substituted for (ʃ) under Scand. influence.] **1.** *trans.* To dissipate, squander (goods or possessions). *Obs.* or *arch.* **2.** To separate and drive in various directions; to disperse, dissipate; to dispel (clouds, mists) ME. **b.** *intr.* for *refl.* To separate and disperse; to go dispersedly or stragglingly. late ME. **3.** *trans.* To throw about in disorder in various places ME. **4.** To distribute to various positions; to place here and there at irregular intervals. late ME. **5.** To throw or send forth so that the particles are distributed or spread about; to sow or throw broadcast; to sprinkle; to diffuse (fragrance) 1450. **b.** *intr.* for *refl.* 1576. **c.** *trans.* Of a gun: To distribute (the shot). Chiefly *absol.* 1741. **d.** *Physics.* Of a surface, semi-opaque substance: To throw back (light) brokenly in all directions 1833. **6.** To sprinkle or strew *with* something 1590.

1. I leave the rest of all my goods to my first-born Edward, to be consum'd or scatterd (for I never hoped better) 1645. **2.** Buckingham's Armie is dispers'd and scatter'd SHAKS. **b.** The fugitives scattered for miles 1909. **4.** Many tributes to his memory are scattered over his friend's other works LOCKHART. **5.** He..scatereth yᵉ horefrost like ashes COVERDALE *Ps.* 147:16. **b.** The small shot..scattered among them DE FOE. **c.** The gun scatters well 1823. **6.** The ground was scattered with elephant's teeth DE FOE. Hence **Sca·tteredly, Sca·tteringly** *advs.* **Sca·tterer.**

Sca·tter-brain. 1790. [f. prec. + BRAIN *sb.* Cf. the earlier SHATTERBRAIN.] One who is incapable of serious connected thought; a thoughtless, giddy person. So **Sca·tter-brained** *a.*

Scattergood (skæ·təɹgud). 1577. [f. SCATTER *v.* + GOOD *sb.*] One who squanders goods or possessions; a spendthrift.

Scattering (skæ·təriŋ), *vbl. sb.* ME. [f. SCATTER *v.* + -ING[1].] **1.** The action of SCATTER *v.*; an instance of this. late ME. **2.** *concr.* That which is scattered ME. **b.** A sparse number or amount; a small proportion interspersed 1628.

Scatterling (skæ·təɹliŋ). Now *arch.* 1590. [f. SCATTER *v.* + -LING[1].] A wandering or vagabond person; a vagrant.

Neighbour Scots, and forrein Scatterlings SPENSER.

Scattery (skæ·təri), *a.* 1816. [f. SCATTER *v.* + -Y[1].] Scattered; sparse; straggling.

Scaturient (skătiūᵊ·riĕnt), *a.* 1684. [– L. *scaturiens, -ent-*, pr. pple. of *scaturire*, f. *scatēre* flow out; see -ENT.] That flows out or gushes forth.

Scaup (skǭp). 1797. Short for next.

Scaup-duck (skǭ·pˌdɒk). 1672. [f. *scaup*, Sc. var. of SCALP *sb.*[2]] A duck of the genus *Fuligula*, esp. *F. marila*, inhabiting the northern seas.

Scaur (skǭɹ). Var. (chiefly *Sc.*) of SCAR *sb.*[1]

Scavage (skæ·vėdʒ). 1474. [– AFr. *scawage* (whence AL. *scawagium* XIII) = ONFr. *escauwage*, f. *escauwer* inspect – Flem. *scauwen* = OE. *sċēawian* see (SHOW *v.*).] A toll formerly levied on merchant strangers by the mayors, sheriffs, or corporations of various towns, on goods offered for sale within their precincts. Now *Hist.* So †**Sca·vager** = SCAVENGER 1.

Scavenge (skæ·vėndʒ), *v.* 1644. [Back-formation from next.] **1.** *trans.* To clean *out* (dirt, etc.). **2.** To scrape dirt from (the streets); also, to cleanse (the surface of a river) 1851. **3.** *absol.* or *intr.* 1883. **4.** Of an internal-combustion engine: To expel exhaust gases, etc. from the cylinder 1894. Also as *sb.*

Scavenger (skæ·vėndʒəɹ), *sb.* 1503. [alt. of SCAVAGER – AFr. *scawager*, f. *scawage*; see SCAVAGE and -ER[1]. For the *n* cf. *harbinger, messenger, passenger, wharfinger.*] **1.** An officer whose duty it was to take 'scavage', and, later, to keep the streets clean. Now *Hist.* **2.** A person whose employment is to clean streets, by scraping or sweeping together and removing dirt 1530. **b.** *transf.* One who or something which removes dirt or putrid matter. Applied to animals that feed on decaying matter, esp. the s. beetle. 1596. **c.** *fig.* One who collects filth; one who does 'dirty work'. Also, in favourable sense: One who labours for the removal of public evils. 1562. **3.** A child employed in a spinning-mill to collect loose cotton lying about the floor or machinery. Also, a roller used to collect the loose fibres or fluff; also called *s.-roll.* 1833.

Comb.: **s.-beetle,** a necrophagous beetle, esp. one of the family *Scaphidiidæ*; **-crab,** any crab which feeds on dead animal matter; **-vulture,** *Neophron percnopterus*. Hence **Sca·venger** *v. trans.* (*rare*) to remove dirt from, chiefly *fig.*; also, to make dirty with scavenging.

Scavenger's daughter. Also **Skevington's, Skeffington's daughter.** 1564. [joc. perversion of *Skevington, Skeffington* (see below).] An instrument of torture (invented in the reign of Hen. VIII by Leonard Skevington, Lieutenant of the Tower), which (bringing the head to the knees) so compressed the body as to force the blood from the nose and ears.

Scavengery (skæ·vėndʒəri). 1656. [f. SCAVENGER *sb.* + -Y[3].] The municipal or state arrangements for cleaning and removing dirt, refuse, etc.; the action of collecting and removing dirt from the streets.

‖**Scazon** (skēⁱ·zǫn). *Pl.* **scazons,** also **scazontes** (skăzǫ·ntīz). 1651. [– L. *scazon* – Gr. σκάζων, subst. use of pr. pple. masc. of σκάζειν limp, halt.] *Prosody.* = CHOLIAMB. Also *s. iambic*. Hence **Scazo·ntic** *a.* written in scazons; *sb.* = SCAZON.

Scelerate (se·lĕrĕt), *a.* and *sb.* 1513. [– L. *sceleratus*, pa. pple. of *scelerare*, f. *scelus, sceler-* wickedness; see -ATE[2] and [1].] †**A.** *adj.* Atrociously wicked –1734. **B.** *sb.* An atrociously wicked person, a villain, wretch. *Obs.* exc. *arch.* 1715.

Scelidosaur (se·lidosǭɹ). 1861. [– mod. L. *scelidosaurus*, f. *scelido-* used for stem of Gr. σκέλος leg + Gr. σαύρα, σαῦρος lizard.] *Palæont.* A member of the genus *Scelidosaurus* of stegosaurian herbivorous dinosaurs.

‖**Scelidotherium** (se:lidoþīᵊ·riŏm). 1840. [mod.L., f. *scelido-* (see prec.) + Gr. θηρίον wild animal (Owen, 1840).] *Palæont.* A genus of megatherioid edentate mammals.

‖**Scena** (ʃē·nă). 1819. [It. – L. *scena* SCENE.] **a.** A scene in an Italian opera; the words and music of the scene. **b.** A composition consisting largely of recitative of a dramatic and impassioned character, for one or more voices with accompaniment.

‖**Scenario** (ʃenā·rio). 1880. [It. f. *scena* SCENE.] **a.** A sketch of the plot of a play;

giving particulars of the scenes, situations, etc. **b.** The detailed directions for a cinema film.

†**Sce·nary.** 1695. [– It. *scenario*; see prec. and -ARY¹ B. 2.] **1.** = prec. a. –1736. **2.** 'The representation of the place in which an action is performed' (J.) –1808. **3.** = SCENERY 3. –1808.

Scend, var. SEND *sb.* and *v.*²

Scene (sīn). 1540. [– L. *scēna, scæna* stage, scene – Gr. σκηνή tent, booth, stage, scene. Cf. (O)Fr. *scène.*] **I.** With ref. to the theatre. **1.** *Antiq.* The stage of a Greek or Roman theatre, including the platform on which the actors stood, and the structure which formed the background 1638. **2.** The stage or theatre as standing for either the dramatic art or the histrionic profession. Now *arch.* 1682. **3.** A stage performance; a play in representation. *Obs.* exc. in phr. 1592. **4.** The place in which the action of a play, or part of a play, is supposed to occur. Also, the setting of a dialogue, novel, etc. 1592. **5.** A subdivision of an act of a play, or of a short play not divided into acts, marked by the entrance or departure of one or more actors (and often by a change of locale). Hence, the action and dialogue comprised in any one of these subdivisions; a situation *between* certain actors. 1540. **6.** The painted hangings, slides, etc., set at the back and sides of the stage, and intended to give the illusion of a real view of the locale in which the action of a play takes place, or to symbolize it; the view thus presented to the spectators. Also, any one of these painted hangings, slides, etc. 1540. **b.** *transf.* A curtain or veil; also, a decorative hanging on a wall 1638. **7.** *Behind the scenes*: amidst the actors and stage-machinery, where ordinary spectators are not admitted. Freq. *fig.* 1668.

2. Giddy with praise,..She quits the tragic s. CHURCHILL. **3.** *The s. opens* or *is opened*, the action of a play (an act or scene) begins; S. opens, Muly Labas appears bound in Chains 1673. **4.** Phr. *To lay the s.* (see LAY *v.* III. 4 b.); In faire Verona, where we lay our S. SHAKS. **5.** Does not this poisoning s. The sacred right of Tragedy profane 1756. **6.** Back fly the scenes, and enter foot and horse POPE. **7.** *fig.* I, who have been behind the scenes, both of pleasure and business CHESTERF.

II. 1. The place where an action is carried on and people play their parts as in a drama 1594. **b.** The world in which man is an actor; the theatre of this life 1662. **2.** A view or picture presented to the eye (or to the mind) of a place, concourse, incident, series of actions or events, assemblage of objects, etc. 1653. **3.** An action, episode, complication of events, or situation, in real life 1679. **b.** An episode, situation, etc., forming a subject of narration or description 1630. **4.** An exhibition of excited or strong feeling between two or more persons; a stormy encounter or interview (cf. Fr. *faire une scène à quelqu'un*) 1761.

1. Phr. *To enter* or *appear on the s., to quit the s. The s. of action*, the place where events are happening or business being done. **b.** This universal living s. of things is after all as little a logical world as it is a poetical J. H. NEWMAN. Phr. *To quit the s.*, to die. **2.** The smiling S. wide opens to the Sight POPE. **3.** You were not made for scenes of danger 1766. **b.** Scenes of Clerical Life GEO. ELIOT. **4.** The folly of making a s. 1831.

Comb.: **s.-painter,** one who paints scenes or scenery for the theatre; **-painting,** the art of painting scenes according to the rules of stage-perspective; **-shifter,** one who shifts and arranges the scenes during the performance of a play.

Scenery (sī·nĕri). 1748. [Alteration of SCENARY, as if f. SCENE + -ERY.] †**1.** Dramatic action; a moving exhibition of feeling –1808. **2.** The decoration of a theatre-stage, consisting of painted hangings, slides, etc., representing the scene of the action; theatre-scenes collectively 1770. **3.** The general appearance of a place and its natural features, regarded from the picturesque point of view; the aggregate of picturesque features in a landscape 1784. **4.** (With *a* and *pl.*) A landscape or view; a picturesque scene. Now *rare.* 1777.

3. A..passion for s. and natural beauty..has.. gained an extraordinary power over people's minds 1871.

Scenic (sī·nik, se·nik), *a.* 1623. [– L. *scenicus* – Gr. σκηνικός belonging to the stage; see SCENE, -IC. Cf. (O)Fr. *scénique.*] **1.** Of or belonging to the stage, dramatic, theatrical. **b.** Represented on the stage 1747. **c.** Of or belonging to stage-scenery or stage effect 1868. **2.** *fig.* Dramatic or theatrical in style 1857. **3.** With ref. to painting or sculpture: Representing a 'scene' or incident in which several persons are concerned 1848.

Scenic railway, a miniature railway running through artificial picturesque scenery, forming an attraction at fairs. So **Sce·nical** *a.* scenic; theatrical; †fictitious, imaginary. late ME. **Sce·nically** *adv.* in a s. or scenical manner.

Scenograph (sī·nograf). 1842. [– Gr. σκηνογράφος scene-painter; see SCENE, -GRAPH.] = next.

Scenographer (sīnǫ·grăfəɹ). 1598. [f. as prec.; see -GRAPHER.] A scene-painter; one who draws buildings, etc. in perspective.

Scenography (sīnǫ·grăfi). 1645. [– Fr. *scénographie* or L. *scenographia* – Gr. σκηνογραφία scene-painting; see SCENE, -GRAPHY.] †**1.** The representation of a building or other object in perspective; a perspective elevation –1843. **2.** Scene-painting (in ancient Greece) 1738. So **Scenogra·phic, -al** *adjs.*; **-ally** *adv.*

Scent (sent), *sb.* [In XV *sent*, f. the verb. Orig. a term of hunting.] **1.** The faculty or sense of smell. Now only with ref. to animals (esp. dogs) which find their prey or recognize objects by this sense 1470. **2.** The odour of an animal or man as a means of pursuit by a hound; hence a track or trail as indicated by this odour. late ME. **3.** In wider sense: Distinctive odour. Now almost exclusively applied to agreeable odours, e.g. those of flowers. 1471. **4.** An odoriferous liquid prepared by distillation from flowers, etc.; a perfume 1750.

1. The perfect Hound, in S. and Speed Unrivall'd 1735. *fig.* A s. for heresy 1857. **2.** He [*sc.* a hound]..twice to day pick'd out the dullest sent SHAKS. *fig.* Trim found he was upon a wrong s. STERNE. *transf.* To find s. (i.e. fragments of paper for scattering on the ground) for..Hare-and-Hounds HUGHES. *Cold s.*: see COLD *a.* II. 7. *Hot s.*: see HOT *a.* 7. *To lay, put* (hounds) *on* or *upon the s.*; hence fig. *to put* (a person) *on* or *off the s.*, also *on a false, wrong s. To lose, recover the s.*, lit. (of hounds) and fig.; also, *to lose the s.*, (of the game) to baffle the hounds by passing through water. *To carry a* (or *the*) *s.*, (of ground) to retain the scent of the game; also (of fox-hounds) to follow the scent. **3.** A spicy s. Of cinnamon and sandal blent LONGF. *fig.* Perhaps some s. of the coming danger reached him 1868.

Comb.: **s.-bag,** (*a*) a pouch, sac, or gland found in some animals, containing a secreted odoriferous substance; (*b*) a bag containing a strong-smelling substance, drawn over ground to make an artificial scent for hounds; (*c*) = SACHET 3; **-bottle; -gland,** a gland which secretes an odoriferous substance; **-organ** *Ent.* and *Zool.*, an organ that secretes scent, a scent-bag, scent-gland; **-spray,** an ornamental s.-bottle with apparatus for distributing the s. in a fine spray. Hence **Sce·ntful** *a.* full of s., fragrant.

Scent (sent), *v.* [In XIV *sent(e* – (O)Fr. *sentir* feel, perceive, smell :– L. *sentire* feel, perceive. The unexpl. sp. *scent* does not appear till XVII.] **1.** *trans.* To find or track (game, prey, etc.) by the smell; also, *to s. out.* In later use: To become aware of by the sense of smell. **b.** *fig.* To perceive as if by smell; to find out instinctively; to detect 1553. **2.** *intr.* Of a hound or other animal: †**a.** To perceive the smell *of* (the quarry). **b.** To hunt by the sense of smell; also, to sniff the air for a scent. late ME. **3.** To exhale an odour; to smell. Now *rare* or *Obs.* late ME. **4.** *trans.* To impregnate with an odour; to perfume 1697.

1. But soft, me thinkes I sent the Mornings Ayre SHAKS. Like vultures scenting their prey afar 1878. **b.** Perhaps not senting the Design of the Clowns 1658. **2. b.** So sented the grim Feature, and upturn'd His Nostril wide into the mirky Air MILT. **3.** *fig.* The very air scents of knavery 1831. **4.** With Smoak of burning Cedar s. thy Walls DRYDEN.

Scented (se·ntėd), *ppl. a.* 1579. [f. SCENT *v.* and *sb.* + -ED.] †**1.** With prefixed adv.: Endowed with the power of tracking by sense of smell –1656. **2.** Impregnated with perfume 1740. **3.** That has a scent; exhaling a scent 1666.

2. *S. caper*: see CAPER *sb.*¹ 3. **3.** The scentless and the s. rose COWPER.

Scentless (se·ntlės), *a.* 1605. [f. SCENT *sb.* + -LESS.] †**1.** Without the faculty of smell. **2.** Without odour or perfume 1618.

Scepsis (ske·psis). 1876. [– Gr. σκέψις inquiry, doubt, f. σκέπτεσθαι; see SCEPTIC.] Sceptical attitude in philosophy.

Sceptic, *U.S.* **skeptic** (ske·ptik), *a.* and *sb.* 1575. [– Fr. *sceptique* or L. *scepticus*, in sb. pl. *sceptici* followers of the Greek philosopher Pyrrho of Elis (Quintilian) – Gr. σκεπτικός, sb. pl. σκεπτικοί, f. σκέπτεσθαι look about, consider, observe, rel. to σκοπ- in σκοπεῖν, σκοπός; see SCOPE *sb.* The spelling with *sk-* is rare in Eng., usual in U.S. The pron. with (sk) is due to reversion to Gr.] **A.** *adj.* = SCEPTICAL *a.* Now *rare* exc. as the epithet of a school of philosophers. **B.** *sb.* **1.** *Philos.* One who, like Pyrrho and his followers, doubts the possibility of real knowledge of any kind; one who holds that there are no adequate grounds for certainty as to the truth of any proposition whatever. Also, less correctly, applied to those who deny the competence of reason outside the limits of experience. 1587. **2.** One who doubts the validity of what claims to be knowledge in some particular department of inquiry (e.g. metaphysics, theology, natural science, etc.); *pop.*, one who maintains a doubting attitude with reference to some particular question or statement. Also, a person of sceptical temper. 1615. **3.** *spec.* One who doubts, without absolutely denying, the truth of the Christian religion or important parts of it; often *loosely*, an unbeliever in Christianity 1638. **4.** occas., A seeker after truth; an inquirer who has not yet arrived at definite convictions 1618.

1. Hee is a Scepticke, and dare hardly giue credit to his senses 1608. **2.** The Sceptick will not take Pains to search Things to the Bottom, but when he sees Difficulties on both Sides resolves to believe neither of them WATTS. **3.** In listening to the arguments of a s. you are breathing a poisonous atmosphere 1863. **4.** The Sceptick doth neither affirm, neither denie any Position: but doubteth of it RALEGH.

Sceptical, *U.S.* **skeptical** (ske·ptikăl), *a.* 1639. [f. as prec.; see -ICAL.] **a.** Of persons: Inclined to or imbued with scepticism; in mod. use often, dubious or incredulous. **b.** Of doctrines, opinions, etc.: Characteristic of a sceptic; of the nature of scepticism. Hence **Sce·ptically,** *U.S.* **ske·ptically** *adv.*

Scepticism, *U.S.* **skepticism** (ske·ptisiz'm). 1646. [f. SCEPTIC + -ISM. Cf. Fr. *scepticisme.*] **1.** *Philos.* The doctrine of the Sceptics; the opinion that real knowledge of any kind is unattainable 1661. **2.** Sceptical attitude in relation to some particular branch of science; doubt as to the truth of some assertion or supposed fact. Also, sceptical temper in general. 1646. **3.** Doubt of the Christian religion, unbelief 1800.

1. Consistent rationalism always in the end collapses into s. 1908. **2.** A state of s. and suspense may amuse a few inquisitive minds GIBBON.

Scepticize (ske·ptisəiz), *v.* 1698. [f. SCEPTIC + -IZE 3.] *intr.* To play the sceptic; to take up the position of a philosophical doubter.

He hath a great mind to S., and to maintain Paradoxes 1698.

Sceptre (se·ptəɹ), *sb.* [ME. *ceptre, septre* (with later assim. to L. and Gr.) – OFr. *ceptre*, (also mod.) *sceptre* – L. *sceptrum* – Gr. σκῆπτρον, f. σκήπτειν prop. σκήπτεσθαι prop oneself, lean (on).] **1.** An ornamental rod or wand (often of gold and jewelled) borne in the hand as a symbol of regal or imperial authority. **b.** *Her.* A representation of this 1610. **2.** *fig.* Taken as the power or authority symbolized by a sceptre; hence, royal or imperial dignity, sovereignty, supremacy. late ME. †**3.** A constellation in the southern hemisphere –1850.

1. His Scepter shewes the force of temporall power, The attribute to awe and Maiestie SHAKS. **2.** The septre fro Juda shal not be takun awey WYCLIF *Gen.* 49:10. Hence **Sce·ptral** *a.* pertaining to, serving as, a s. **Sce·ptreless** *a.* obeying no s.; wielding no s.

Sceptre (se·ptəɹ), *v.* late ME. [f. prec.] **1.** *trans.* To furnish with a sceptre. **2.** To touch (with a sceptre) as a sign of royal assent or ratification (bills passed by Parliament) 1851.

1. Crown'd with sharp Thorns, and scepter'd with a Reed 1711.

Sch. In mod. Eng. (sk) is the normal pronunciation of *sch* in words of classical derivation, where it represents L. *sch*, Gr. σχ. (The only exceptions are *schist*, etc. *schedule*, and *schism*, etc.) *Sch* is also pronounced (sk) in Italian words, e.g. *scherzo*. The only words in which *sch* represents (s) are *schism* and its derivatives, the pronunciation of the ME. form *cisme* (from OFr. *cisme*) having survived although the spelling has been refashioned. The pronunciation of *sch* as (stʃ) occurs only medially in *escheat*, *eschew*, *discharge*, etc. where the *s* and the *ch* belong to different syllables. In a few alien words from German (e.g. *schnapps*), in *schist*, and in *schedule sch* has the value (ʃ).

‖**Schadenfreude** (ʃā·dənfroidə). 1922. [G., lit. 'harm-joy'.] Malicious joy in the misfortunes of others.

‖**Schanse, schanze, schantze** (skans). *S. Afr.* 1880. [Du. *schans* (S. Afr. Du. *skans*) = G. *schanze*. See SCONCE *sb.*[3]] A heap or breastwork of stones used as a protection against rifle fire.

Schappe (ʃæp). 1885. [G., = 'silk-waste'.] A strong dull-surfaced silk fabric.

Schedule (ʃe·diūl, *U.S.* ske·diūl), *sb.* [Late ME. *cedule*, *sedule* – (O)Fr. *cédule* – late L. *schedula* small slip of paper, dim. of *scheda* (– Gr. σχέδη) leaf of papyrus; see -ULE.] †**1.** A slip or scroll of parchment or paper containing writing; a ticket, label, placard; a short note –1650. **2.** †**a.** Orig., an explanatory or supplementary paper or slip of parchment accompanying or appended to a document; in 16–17th c. occas. used for a codicil to a will. **b.** Hence, an appendix to an Act of Parliament or a legal instrument containing a statement of details. **c.** In wider sense, any tabular or classified statement, as, e.g. an insolvent's statement of assets and liabilities, a return of particulars liable to income-tax, etc. Occas. a blank form to be filled up by the insertion of particulars under the several headings. late ME. **3.** A time-table. Chiefly *U.S.* 1873.

3. *transf.* Halting was not in [his] s. for that afternoon 1873. *On s.* (*time*), to schedule time (orig. *U.S.*).

Schedule (ʃe·diūl, *U.S.* ske·diūl), *v.* 1862. [f. prec.] **1.** *trans.* To enter in a schedule or list. In railway use: To enter (a train) in the time-table. Often in *ppl. a.* **2.** To affix as a schedule (*to* an Act of Parliament) 1885.

1. The train got in at the scheduled time (*mod.*).

Scheelite (ʃī·ləit). 1837. [f. name of K. W. *Scheele*, the discoverer of tungstic acid + -ITE[1] 2 b.] *Min.* Tungstate of calcium, found in brilliant crystals of various colours.

‖**Schelling** (ske·liŋ, Du. sχe·liŋ). *Obs.* exc. *Hist.* 1535. [Du. See SCHILLING, SHILLING, SKILLING.] A silver coin formerly current in the Low Countries, of the value of 6 stivers or from 5*d.* to 7½*d.* sterling.

‖**Schelm** (ʃelm). *arch.* 1584. [G. *schelm*; see SKELLUM.] A rascal.

Schema (skī·mă). *Pl.* **schemata** (skī·mătă). 1839. [– Gr. σχῆμα SCHEME *sb.*[1]] *Philos.* In Kant: Any one of certain forms or rules of the 'productive imagination' through which the understanding is able to apply its 'categories' to the manifold of sense-perception in the process of realizing knowledge or experience.

Schematic (skimæ·tik), *a.* 1701. [f. Gr. σχῆμα, σχηματ- SCHEME + -IC.] **1.** Pertaining to a scheme or schema; †corresponding (to something else) according to a scheme. **2.** Pertaining to logical 'figure' 1838. **3.** Suggested or modified by a preconceived system 1894. **4.** *Fine Art.* Following a conventional type 1868.

4. Their art symbolised these in grand s. forms 1868.

Schematism (skī·mătiz'm). 1617. [– mod.L. *schematismus* (Bacon) – Gr. σχηματισμός the assumption of a certain form or appearance, f. σχηματίζειν; see next, -ISM.] †**1.** The use of a 'scheme' or rhetorical figure. COLLINS. **2.** Mode of arrangement of parts or particles; inner structure. Now *rare.* 1660. **3.** A schematic arrangement; a set form for classification or exposition. Also, the schematic method of presentation. 1701. **4.** *Philos.* 'Schematizing' action (of the intellect). In Kant: The application of the categories, by means of schemata, to the data of sense-perception. 1839.

Schematist (skī·mătist). 1693. [– mod.L. **schematista*, f. as prec.; see -IST.] **1.** The framer of a 'scheme' or system of doctrine. †**2.** One who expounds a scheme; a projector –1730.

Schematize (skī·mătəiz), *v.* 1828. [orig. – Gr. σχηματίζειν assume a certain form, figure, etc.; in later use f. Gr. σχῆμα, σχηματ- SCHEME + -IZE.] **1.** *trans.* To reduce to a scheme or formula. **2.** *Kantian Philos.* To apply the categories, by means of schemata, to the data of sense-perception 1839.

Scheme (skīm), *sb.*[1] 1550. [– L. *schema* – Gr. σχῆμα form, figure.] †**1.** *Rhet.* = FIGURE *sb.* V. 1. –1684. †**2.** A diagram showing the relative positions, either real or apparent, of the heavenly bodies; *esp.* in *Astrol.*, a horoscope –1824. †**3.** In wider sense: A diagram; a figure drawn to illustrate a mathematical proposition, etc.; a map or plan of a town; an architect's designs for a building; and the like –1826. **4.** An analytical or tabular statement. **a.** An epitome exhibiting the structure of a book, passage, argument, etc.; also, an outline draft of a projected literary work 1647. **b.** A table; a prearranged system of classification 1677. **5. a.** A plan, design; a programme of action 1647. **b.** Hence, A plan of action devised in order to attain some end; a project, enterprise. Often with unfavourable notion, a self-seeking or an underhand project, a plot, or a visionary or foolish project. 1718. **c.** An escapade of a humorous character, a 'spree'. Now *dial.* 1758. **6.** †**a.** A theory –1725. **b.** A body of related doctrines, a speculative system 1685. **7.** A system of correlated things, institutions, arrangements, etc.; the manner in which such a system is organized 1736. **b.** Painting. *S. of colour*: the system of selection and arrangement of colours characteristic of a particular painter or school, or adopted in a particular picture. Also *c. scheme*, often used gen. for any arrangement of colours. 1884. †**8.** Form, aspect, appearance –1743.

2. To make a small velvet bag, for the scheme of nativity SCOTT. **3.** A s. of the city of Lepanto 1682. **4. a.** I intend this but for a S. of a larger Design 1695. **b.** In Chapter ix. is given his S. of Sciences 1868. **5. a.** That is the whole s. and intention of all marriage-articles GAY. **b.** But this deep-laid s. was in a moment disconcerted 1759. The great irrigation schemes of the North-West Provinces 1888. Phr. *To lay a s.* **6. b.** His comprehensive s. of theology 1858. **7.** Ah Love! could thou and I with Fate conspire To grasp this sorry S. of Things entire, Would not we shatter it to bits FITZGERALD. **8.** For they had the s. of truth not the substance 1677.

Scheme (skīm), *sb.*[2] 1690 (**skeen**). [Origin unkn.] In full **s.-arch**: The arch of larger radius in the middle of a three-centre arch or elliptical arch. **b.** quasi-*adj.* Constructed with a 'scheme' 1703.

Scheme (skīm), *v.* 1716. [f. SCHEME *sb.*[1]] **1.** *trans.* To devise as a scheme; to lay schemes for; to effect by contrivance or intrigue 1767. **b.** *intr.* To use ingenuity, resort to contrivance; to devise plans, esp. underhand or with sinister motive 1842. **2.** *trans.* To reduce to a scheme or formula (*rare*) 1716.

1. To . s. a mode of escape 1868. Hence **Sche·mer**, one who devises or enters into schemes; one who plots. **Sche·mingly** *adv.*

Schemist (skī·mist). 1724. [f. SCHEME *sb.*[1] + -IST.] †**1.** An intriguing plotter –1825. **2.** One who forms a scheme; a projector 1753.

‖**Scherm** (skerm). *S. Afr.* 1861. [Du., = G. *schirm* screen.] A screen or barrier of brushwood or the like which serves as a protection for troops, as an ambuscade from which to shoot game, or to prevent cattle from straying.

‖**Scherzando** (skertsa·ndo), *adv.* 1811. [It., gerund of *scherzare* play, sport, f. *scherzo* sport, jest, (*Mus.*) lively movement.] *Mus.* A direction: Playfully, sportively. Also *attrib.* (quasi-*adj.*), and *ellipt.* as *sb.*, a s. movement.

‖**Scherzo** (ske·rtso). 1862. [It., lit. sport, jest.] *Mus.* A lively movement, occupying the second or third place in a symphony or sonata.

‖**Schiedam** (skī·dæm, skidæ·m). 1821. A variety of gin, so called from the town in Holland where it is distilled.

‖**Schiller** (ʃi·ləɹ). 1804. [G., play of colours, etc.] *Min.* **1.** In terms adapted from G., denoting minerals or rocks having a shining surface, as *s. asbestos*, *rock*, *-stone*. **2.** A peculiar lustre characteristic of certain minerals, as hypersthene. Also *attrib.* 1835.

Schillerize (ʃi·lərəiz), *v.* 1885. [f. prec. + -IZE.] *trans.* To subject (a crystal) to schillerization. Hence **Schi:lleriza·tion**, a process of change in crystals, giving rise to a 'schiller' appearing when the crystal is turned in various directions.

Schiller spar (ʃi·ləɹ,spāɹ). 1796. [– G. *schillerspath*; see SCHILLER 1 and SPAR *sb.*, and cf. FELDSPAR.] *Min.* = BASTITE.

‖**Schilling** (ʃi·liŋ). 1693. [G.; see SHILLING. Cf. SCHELLING, SKILLING *sb.*[2]] A silver coin and money of account formerly in use in North Germany. **b.** A modern Austrian coin (par about 7*d.*), 100 groschen.

‖**Schindylesis** (skindilī·sis). 1830. [mod. L. – Gr. σχινδύλησις.] *Anat.* An articulation formed by the reception of a thin plate of one bone into a fissure or groove in another.

‖**Schipperke** (ʃi·pəɹkī, ski·p-, Du. ‖sχi·pərkə). 1887. [Du. dial., lit. 'little boatman'.] A kind of lapdog.

Schism (si·z'm). [Late ME. *scisme*, *sisme* – OFr. *scisme*, *sisme* (mod. *schisme*) – eccl. L. *schisma* – Gr. σχίσμα rent, cleft, in N.T. division in the Church, f. *σχιδ-, base of σχίζειν split, cleave. The sp. was assim. (XVI), as in Fr., to the L. form.] **1.** In the versions of the N.T.: A (metaphorical) rent or cleft. **2.** *Eccl.* A breach of the unity of the visible Church; the division of the Church, or of some portion of it, into separate and mutually hostile organizations; the condition of being so divided, or an instance of this. late ME. **b.** *spec.* A state of divided spiritual allegiance in Western Christendom caused by a disputed election to the Papacy; esp. *The Great* (*Western*) *S.* (1378–1417) 1460. **c.** The offence of causing or promoting divisions in the Church. late ME. **d.** A sect or body formed by division within the Church; a schismatic sect 1511. **3.** *gen.* In early use, a state of disunion, dissension, or mutual hostility. Now, a division into mutually opposing parties of a body of persons that have previously acted in concert. Also, in recent use, a discord, breach (between persons or things). late ME.

1. 1 *Cor.* 12:25. **2. c.** From all false doctrine, heresy, and s. *Bk. Com. Prayer, Litany.* **3.** The eternal and inevitable s. between the Romanticists and the Classicists 1839.

Comb.: **S. Act**, the statute 13 Anne c. 7 (1714; repealed in 1719 by 5 Geo. I, c. 4), requiring all teachers to conform to the Established Church.

‖**Schisma** (ski·zmă). *Pl.* **schismata**. 1653. [Late L. *schisma* 'dimidium commatis', spec. use of Gr. σχίσμα division.] *Acoustics.* †**a.** In ancient Gr. use, the half of a comma. **b.** The difference between a diaschisma and a syntonic comma, represented by the ratio 32.805:32.768.

Schismatic (sizmæ·tik), *a.* and *sb.* [In XIV *scismatik*, etc. – OFr. *scismatique* (mod. *schismatique*) – eccl. L. *schismaticus* – eccl. Gr. σχισματικός, f. Gr. σχίσμα, σχισματ-; see SCHISM *sb.*, -IC.] **A.** *adj.* Of or pertaining to schism or schismatics; of the nature of schism; guilty of the offence of schism 1440.

Though the s. Swede, Gustavus, is Gone home BYRON.

B. *sb.* One who promotes or countenances schism in the Church; one who is guilty of the sin of schism; a member or adherent of a schismatical body. late ME. **b.** *spec.* In R.C. use, one of those Roman Catholics who in the reign of Elizabeth conformed by occasionally attending the services of the Church of England, in order to avoid the penalties denounced against recusants 1584. So **Schisma·tical** *a.*, **-ly** *adv.*, **-ness**.

Schismatize (si·zmătəiz), *v.* 1601. [– Fr. †*scismatiser* or med.L. *schismatizare* cause a schism, f. eccl. Gr. σχίσμα, -ματ-; see -IZE.] **1.** *intr.* To behave as a schismatic; to favour or advocate schismatic principles; to lead or belong to a schismatic body. **2.** *trans.* **a.** To lead into schism. **b.** To divide into parties. *rare.* 1645.

Schist (ʃist). 1793. [– Fr. *schiste* – L. *schistos* (*lapis s.* 'fissile stone', Pliny) – Gr. σχιστός (σ. λίθος perh. talc), pa. ppl. adj. f. **skhid*-; see SCHISM.] *Geol.* A crystalline rock whose component minerals are arranged in a more or less parallel manner.

Schistose (ʃi·stōᵘs), *a.* 1794. [f. SCHIST + -OSE¹.] *Geol.* Laminated; having a formation resembling a schist. Hence **Schisto·sity** *Geol.*, the direction or line of cleavage in a rock of crystalline formation. So **Schi·stous** *a.* 1802.

Schizanthus (skəizæ·nþŏs, ski-). 1829. [mod.L., f. SCHIZO- + Gr. ἄνθος flower.] Any plant of the solanaceous genus so-called, having finely divided leaves and showy flowers.

Schizo- (skəi·zo, skəizǫ·), comb. form irreg. repr. Gr. σχίζειν to split.

Schi·zocarp [Gr. καρπός fruit] *Bot.*, a term applied to dry fruits which break up into two or more one-seeded mericarps without dehiscing. **Schi·zocœle** (-sīl) [Gr. κοῖλον hollow] *Zool.*, a perivisceral cavity formed by a splitting of the mesoblast. ‖**Schizoge·nesis** *Biol.*, fissiparous generation. **Schizognathism** (-ǫ·gnăþiz'm) [Gr. γνάθος jaw] *Ornith.* a condition in which the bony palate is cleft from the posterior nares to the end of the beak; hence **Schizo·gnathous** *a.*, having a cleft palate. **Schizogony** (-ǫ·gŏni) [Gr. -γονία reproduction] *Zool.*, = *schizogenesis*; hence **Schizogo·nic** *a.*, pertaining to schizogony; spec. *s. cycle*, the second of the two stages in the life-history of a Coccidian. ‖**Schizomycetes** (-məisī·tīz) *sb. pl.* [MYCETES], a group of microscopic, rod-like, unicellular organisms, multiplying by fission, variously known as *Bacteria*, *Microbes*, etc.; *rarely* in sing. **schizomycete.** **Schi·zophyte** (-fəit) [-PHYTE] *Biol.*, a microscopic organism multiplying by fission, akin to *Schizomycetes*. **Schi·zopod** (-pǫd) *Zool.*, a member of the ‖**Schizo·poda** *sb. pl.* [Gr. ποδ- foot], a sub-order of crustaceans, named from the apparent splitting of the thoracic limbs produced by the great development of the exopodites; hence **Schizo·podous** *a.* **Schizorhi·nal** *a.* [Gr. ῥίς, ῥιν- nose] *Ornith.* having each nasal bone deeply cleft or forked.

Schizophrenia (skəizofrī·niă, skidzo-, -ts-). 1912. [mod.L. (P. E. Bleuler, of Zurich), after Fr. *schizophrénie*; f. Gr. φρήν mind; see prec., -IA¹.] A form of mental disease in which the personality is disintegrated and detached from its environment; 'split-mind'. So **Schi·zophrene** (-frīn), one so affected; **-phrenic** (-fre·nik) *a.*

‖**Schloss** (ʃlǫs). 1838. [G.] A (German) castle.

‖**Schmelz** (ʃmelts), **Schmelze** (ʃme·ltsə). 1851. Also **schmelz glass.** [G. *schmelz(glas*, f. *schmelz* enamel, fusion of colours.] Applied to various kinds of Bohemian glass prepared to receive colour.

‖**Schnapps** (ʃnæps). 1818. [– G. *schnap(p)s* dram of drink, liquor (esp. gin) – LG., Du. *snaps* gulp, mouthful, f. *snappen* seize, snatch (see SNAP *v.*).] An ardent spirit resembling Hollands gin.

Schnebelite (ʃnē¹·bĕləit). 1893. [f. the name *Schnebelin* + -ITE¹ 4 a.] An explosive principally composed of specially treated chlorate of potash, invented by the brothers Schnebelin.

Schneiderian (ʃnəidīᵊ·riăn), *a.* 1803. [f. name of C. V. *Schneider* of Würtemberg (1610–80); see -IAN.] *S. membrane*, the mucous membrane of the nose.

‖**Schnorrer** (ʃnǫ·rəɹ). *Jewish.* 1892. [Yiddish var. of G. *schnurrer*, f. *schnurren* (slang) go begging.] A Jewish beggar.

Scholar (skǫ·lăɹ). [ME. *scoler*, aphetic – OFr. *escoler*, *-ier* (mod. *écolier*) – late L. *scholaris*, f. L. *schola* SCHOOL; see -AR¹. The L. word was adopted in late OE. *scol(i)ere* pupil, learner.] **1.** One who is taught in a school; now *esp.* a boy or girl attending an elementary school. **b.** A pupil (*of* a particular master). Now *arch.* or *rhet.* OE. **c.** *transf.* One who acknowledges another as his master; a disciple 1577. **d.** With qualifying adj.: One who is quick (slow, etc.) at learning 1605. **2.** One who studies in the 'schools' at a university; a member of a university, esp. a junior or undergraduate member. Now *Hist.* and in official use. ME. **3.** A learned or erudite person; esp. one who is learned in the classical languages and their literature. late ME. **b.** In illiterate use, one whom the speaker regards as exceptionally learned. Often merely, one who is able to read and write. 1644. **4.** A student who receives emoluments, during a fixed period, from the funds of a school, college, or university, towards defraying the cost of his education or studies, and as a reward of merit 1511.

1. I am no breeching scholler in the schooles SHAKS. **c.** The Romans confessed themselves the scholars of the Greeks JOHNSON. **3.** As becommed a Gentleman and a Scholer 1621. **b.** Nay, faith, sir, I am not so good a schollard to say much 1667.

Scholarch (skōᵘ·laɹk). 1863. [– Gr. σχολάρχης, f. σχολή SCHOOL; see -ARCH.] *Hist.* The head of a school: *spec.* **a.** The head of an Athenian school of philosophy. **b.** In some Continental countries, an official formerly charged with the inspection of schools.

Scho·larism. Now *rare.* 1588. [f. SCHOLAR + -ISM 1 b.] The learning of the 'schools'; scholarship. Occas. used disparagingly.

†**Schola·rity.** *rare.* 1599. [– OFr. *sc(h)olarité* or med.L. *scholaritas*, f. late L. *scholaris*; see SCHOLAR, -ITY.] The status of a scholar –1895.

Scho·larlike, *a.* and *adv.* 1551. [f. SCHOLAR + -LIKE.] **A.** *adj.* †**1.** Pertaining to scholars or 'the schools'; scholastic –1592. **2.** Resembling or befitting a learned man; scholarly 1589. †**B.** *adv.* Like a scholar or learned man; in a manner befitting a scholar –1627.

A. 2. Truewit was a S. kind of man DRYDEN.

Scholarly (skǫ·lăɹli), *a.* 1638. [f. SCHOLAR + -LY¹.] Pertaining to, or characterizing, a scholar; befitting, or natural to, a scholar; learned, erudite.

A slight s. stoop R. BRIDGES.

Scholarly (skǫ·lăɹli), *adv. rare.* 1598. [f. SCHOLAR + -LY².] As befits a scholar.

Speake schollerly, and wisely SHAKS.

Scholarship (skǫ·lăɹʃip). 1535. [f. SCHOLAR + -SHIP.] **1.** The attainments of a scholar; learning, erudition; esp. proficiency in the Greek and Latin languages and their literature. Also, the collective attainments of scholars; the sphere of polite learning. 1589. **b.** Applied, by unlearned speakers, etc., to more modest educational attainments 1620. **2.** The status or emoluments of a scholar (see SCHOLAR 4) at a school, college, or university 1535.

1. b. Then for my schollership a gentleman, Both reade and write, and cast a count I can 1620. **2.** I'd sooner win two School-house matches running than get the Balliol scholarship any day HUGHES.

Scholastic (skŏlæ·stik), *a.* and *sb.* 1596. [– L. *scholasticus* – Gr. σχολαστικός studious, learning, sb. scholar, f. σχολάζειν be at leisure, devote one's leisure to learning, f. σχολή; see SCHOOL, -IC. Cf. (O)Fr. *scolastique.*] **A.** *adj.* †**1.** Of persons: Having the characteristics of the scholar or student. MILT. **2.** Of or pertaining to the teaching or methods of the Schoolmen 1596. **3.** Pertaining to schools or school education 1647. **4.** Following the methods of the 'schools'; befitting the school; in bad sense, 'pedantic, needlessly subtle' (J.) 1779.

2. The absurdities of s. philosophy GOLDSM. **3.** It is too common for those who have been bred to the scholastick profession..to disregard every other qualification JOHNSON.

B. *sb.* **1.** A Schoolman or a disciple of the Schoolmen 1644. †**2.** A scholar, man of learning; *occas.* a mere scholar, as opp. to a man of the world –1748. **3.** *R. C. Ch.* A member of the third grade in the organization of the Society of Jesus 1853.

1. The shallow commenting of Scholasticks MILT. So †**Schola·stical** *a.* 1531–1793; **-ly** *adv.* 1559.

Scholasticism (skŏlæ·stisiz'm). 1756. [f. prec. + -ISM.] **1.** The doctrines of the Schoolmen; the predominant theological and philosophical teaching of the period A.D. 1000–1500, based upon the authority of the Christian Fathers and of Aristotle and his commentators 1756. **2.** Servile adherence to the methods and teaching of the schools; narrow or unenlightened insistence on traditional doctrines and forms of exposition 1861.

Scholiast (skōᵘ·liæst). 1583. [– late Gr. σχολιαστής, f. σχολιάζειν, f. σχόλιον; see next.] One who writes explanatory notes upon an author; esp. an ancient commentator upon a classical writer. Hence **Scholia·stic** *a.* of or pertaining to a s.

‖**Scholion** (skōᵘ·liǫn). Now *rare.* 1579. [Gr.; see next.] = next 1.

A..Glosse, or s., for thexposition of old wordes 1579.

‖**Scholium** (skōᵘ·liŏm). *Pl.* **scholia** (skōᵘ·liă). 1535. [mod.L. *scholium* – Gr. σχόλιον, f. σχολή learned discussion; see SCHOOL.] An explanatory note or comment; *spec.* an ancient exegetical note or comment upon a passage in a Greek or Latin author. **b.** In certain mathematical works: A note added by the author illustrating or further developing some point treated in the text 1704. So †**Scho·ly** *sb.* scholium –1697; *v. trans.* to write scholia upon; *intr.* to comment –1641.

School (skūl), *sb.*¹ [OE. *scōl*, *scolu*, corresp. to MLG., MDu. *schōle* (Du. *school*), OHG. *scuola* (G. *schule*), Gmc. – med.L. *schōla*, for L. *schola* – Gr. σχολή leisure, employment of leisure in disputation, lecture, (later) school; reinforced in ME. by aphetic – OFr. *escole* (mod. *école*) – Rom. *scola.*] **I. 1.** An establishment in which boys or girls, or both, receive instruction. **b.** Used, without article, to mean: Instruction in, attendance at, a school OE. **c.** Used, without article, for: A session of school; the set time of attendance at school 1598. **d.** Those who are present in, or are attending, a school ME. **e.** Applied (as in *upper*, *lower s.*) to a division of a large school, comprising several forms or classes. Also, in Jesuit schools, a form or class. 1629. **f.** The building in which a school is carried on. At Rugby, a school-house; also, the large class-room of a school-house. 1843. **g. High School.** A designation applied to certain classes of schools for secondary education in the British Islands and the U.S. 1531. **2.** The place in which an ancient Greek or Roman philosopher taught his hearers. late ME. **3.** *gen.* An institution in which instruction of any kind is given (whether to children or adults). In recent use, after French example, employed as the official title of various institutions for superior technical or scientific instruction, e.g. *The S. of Mines*, *The S. of Economics*, etc. 1440. **b.** *spec.* = *riding-s.* 1850. **4.** *fig.* A place, environment, etc., where one gains instruction in virtue, accomplishments, or the like; a person or thing regarded as a source of instruction or training OE. **5.** The body of persons that are or have been taught by a particular master (in philosophy, science, art, etc.); hence, a body or succession of persons who are disciples of the same master, or who are united by a general similarity of principles and methods 1612; also, a type or brand of doctrine or practice 1892. **b.** *fig.* A set of persons who agree in certain opinions, etc. 1798.

1. BOARD-, CHARITY-, GRAMMAR-, INFANT-, PUBLIC, SUNDAY-SCHOOL: see those words; also *Free school* (FREE *a.* IV. 7). **b.** Phr. *To be at s.*, *to go to s.*, *to put*, *send to s.*: She was a vixen when she went to schoole SHAKS. *To go to s.* (*to*), fig., to submit to be taught (by). *To put to s.*, fig., to subject to teaching; often, to presume to correct (one's superior). *To keep* (*a*) *s.*, to be the master or mistress of a s. *To tell tales out of s.*, said *lit.* of children (now *rare* or *obs.*); hence *fig.* to betray damaging secrets. **c.** How now Sir Hugh, no Schoole to day? SHAKS. Keeping me in after s. to study 1893. **3.** *Dancing*, *music*, *riding s. fig.* The S. for Scandal SHERIDAN (*title*). **4.** Empires, and Monarchs, and thir radiant Courts, Best s. of best experience MILT. **5.** The Roman, the Florentine, the Bolognese schools..These are the three great schools of the world in the epick stile. SIR J. REYNOLDS. **b.** *Of the old s.*, old-fashioned.

II. Senses of mediæval academic origin. **1.** An organized body of teachers and scholars in one of the higher branches of study cultivated in the Middle Ages; *esp.* a faculty of a university. Now *Hist.* OE. **b.** *collect. pl.* (In later use always *the schools.*) The faculties composing a university; universities in general; the sphere or domain of academic discussion or traditional academic doctrines and methods. late ME. **2.** *The S.*, *the Schools*: the Schoolmen, the scholastic philosophers and theologians collectively. Now *rare* or *Obs.* 1614. **3. a.** *sing.* The building or room set apart for the lectures or exercises of a particular 'school' (in a university). **b.** *pl.* A building belonging to a university, containing rooms orig. for lectures in the several faculties, later for the disputations and exercises for degrees, etc. Hence, in mod. Oxford use: The building in which most of the university examinations are held. 1590. **4.** In mod. Oxford use. **a.** *pl.* The periodical examinations for the degree of B.A. 1828. **b.** Each of the several courses of study, in any of which an 'honours' degree in Arts may be taken; corresponding to the Cambridge 'Tripos' 1873.

1. Siche doutes we shulden sende to þe scole of Oxenforde WYCLIF. **b.** This whole mystery of Genera and Species, which make such a noise in the Schools LOCKE. **3. b.** There is no more characteristic spot in Oxford than the quadrangle of the schools HUGHES.

†**III.** A particular method or discipline taught –1529.

Frenssh she spak ful faire and fetisly, After the scole of Stratford atte Bowe CHAUCER.

IV. Repr. L. *schola*, Gr. σχολή, in late senses. †**1.** A public building, gallery, or the like –1601. **2.** *Hist.* One of the cohorts or companies into which the Imperial guard was divided 1776.

Comb.: **s.-book,** a book of instruction used at s.; **-craft** (*arch.*), knowledge taught in schools; **-dame,** an old woman who keeps a small s. for young children; **-day,** (*a*) *pl.* the days or period (of one's life) in which one is at s.; (*b*) a day on which there is ordinary instruction in a day-s.; **-divine** = SCHOOLMAN 1; **-divinity,** the religious principles and doctrines taught in the mediæval 'Schools'; **-doctor,** †(*a*) = SCHOOLMAN 1; (*b*) the medical attendant of a s.; **-inspector** (cf. INSPECTOR 1); **-learning,** †(*a*) the learning of 'the schools'; (*b*) education at s.; **-ma'am, -marm,** a schoolmistress; **-mate,** a companion at s.; **-ship,** a ship for training boys in practical seamanship; **-time,** (*a*) the time at which s. commences, or during which s. continues; (*b*) that period of life which is passed at s. Hence **Schoo·lery** (*rare*), that which is taught in a s., or as in a s.

School (skūl), *sb.*[2] late ME. [– MLG., MDu. *schōle* (Du. *school*) troop, multitude, spec. 'school' of whales = OS. *scola*, OE. *scolu* troop :– WGmc. **skula*, perh. orig. division, f. **skul-* **skel-* **skal-* divide (see SHELL *sb.*, SKILL).] **1.** A shoal or large number of fish, porpoises, whales, etc. swimming together whilst feeding or migrating. **2.** *transf.* †**a.** A troop, crowd (of persons); a large number, mass (of inanimate things). **b.** A flock, company (of animals). 1555.

1. A Scool of Pilchards, came swimming..into the Harbour DE FOE.

School (skūl), *v.*[1] 1573. [f. SCHOOL *sb.*[1]] **1.** *trans.* To put or send to school; to educate at school 1577. **2.** 'To teach with superiority, to tutor' (J.) 1573. †**b.** To chastise –1628. **3.** To educate, train (a person, his mind, tastes, powers, etc.); to render wise, skilful, or tractable by training or discipline. Often *transf.*, said of God, the experiences of life, surrounding influences, etc. 1591. **b.** To discipline, bring under control, correct (oneself, one's thoughts, feelings, etc.) 1579. **c.** *pass.* To be educated *in* (certain beliefs, sentiments, habits). Also const. *inf.* 1841. **4.** To instruct (a person) how to act; to teach (a person) his part 1579. **5.** To train or exercise (a horse) in movements 1869. **b.** *intr.* To ride straight across country 1885.

1. Yet hee's gentle, neuer school'd, and yet learned SHAKS. **2.** He schooleth and lessoneth the Pope plainly 1624. **3.** They were too well schooled in the tricks of reservation 1856. **b.** I pray you schoole your selfe SHAKS. **4.** Herodias schooled Salome in the part she was to play 1874.

School (skūl), *v.*[2] 1597. [f. SCHOOL *sb.*[2]] *intr.* To collect or swim together in 'schools'. *To s. up*: to collect at or near the surface of the water, said of fishes.

Schoo·l board. 1870. [BOARD *sb.* II. 4 b.] In England and Wales from 1870–1902, and in Scotland since 1872, a body of persons elected by the ratepayers of a 'school district' to provide sufficient accommodation in public elementary schools for all the children of the district.

Schoolboy (skū·lboi). 1588. [f. SCHOOL *sb.*[1] + BOY.] **1.** A boy attending or belonging to a school. **2.** *attrib.* or *adj.* 1687.

1. Every Schole-boy knows it JER. TAYLOR.

Schoolfellow (skū·lfe:lou). 1440. [f. SCHOOL *sb.*[1] + FELLOW *sb.*] One who is or formerly was at the same school at the same time with another.

Schoolgirl (skū·lgɔ̄ɹl). 1809. [f. SCHOOL *sb.*[1] + GIRL.] A girl attending school. Hence **Schoo·lgi:rlish** *a.*

School-house. late ME. **1.** A building appropriated for the use of a school; also, the dwelling-house provided for the use of the schoolmaster or schoolmistress, usu. adjoining a school. **2.** At some public schools, the name given to the headmaster's house. Also, the boys belonging to this house. 1857.

Schooling (skū·liŋ), *vbl. sb.* 1449. [f. SCHOOL *v.*[1] + -ING[1].] **1.** The action of teaching, or the state or fact of being taught, in a school; scholastic education. **b.** The maintenance of a child at school; cost of school education 1563. †**2.** Disciplinary correction, chastisement; admonition, reproof –1818. **3.** The exercising of horse and rider in the riding-school, or of horses in the hunting-field 1753.

2. I confess I thought the s. as severe as the case merited SCOTT.

Schoolman (skū·lmăn). 1540. [SCHOOL *sb.*[1]] **1.** One of the writers, from about the 9th to the 14th c., who treat of logic, metaphysics, and theology as taught in the mediæval 'schools' or universities; a mediæval scholastic. †**2.** One who is versed in the learning of the 'schools', *esp.* one who is expert in formal logic or school-divinity –1732. **3.** One engaged in scholastic pursuits; a professional teacher or student 1712.

1. He would stand, like the Schoolman's Ass, irresolute..betwixt equal Motives HUME.

Schoolmaster (skū·lmɑ:stəɹ). ME. [f. SCHOOL *sb.*[1] + MASTER *sb.*[1]] **1.** The master of a school, or one of the masters in a school. †**b.** Applied to a private tutor –1654. **2.** Used as a name for certain species of fishes 1734.

1. *The s. is abroad*, a saying of Ld. Brougham, orig. expressing exulting confidence in the results of the spread of popular education, but later used chiefly in derision. **b.** *Tam. Shr.* I. i. 94. Hence **Schoo·lmaster** *v.* (*rare*) *trans.* to govern, regulate, or command in the manner of a s. **Schoo·lmastering** *vbl. sb.* the occupation or profession of a s.; also, an education in school. **Schoo·lmasterish** *a.*

Schoolmistress (skū·lmi:strės). 1500. [f. SCHOOL *sb.*[1] + MISTRESS.] A woman who teaches in a school; the mistress of a school. †In early use, a female teacher, governess.

Schoolroom (skū·lrum). 1775. [f. SCHOOL *sb.*[1] + ROOM *sb.*] A room in which a school is held. Also, a room in a private house, in which the children of the family receive instruction or prepare their lessons.

Schoolward (skū·lwǫ̈ɹd), *adv.* and *a.* 1801. [f. SCHOOL *sb.*[1] + -WARD.] **A.** *adv.* Towards, in the direction of, school. **B.** *adj.* Directed or going toward school 1888. So **Schoo·lwards** *adv.*

Schooner (skū·nəɹ), *sb.*[1] 1716. [Said to be agent-noun (-ER[1]) f. New England vb. **scoon* or **scun* skim along water, for which there is no evidence.] **1.** A small sea-going fore-and-aft rigged vessel, orig. with only two masts, but now often with three or four, and carrying one or more topsails. **2.** *Prairie s.*, a large wagon with a canvas hood, used esp. by settlers crossing the prairies. *U.S.* 1858.

Schooner (skū·nəɹ), *sb.*[2] 1886. [Of unkn. origin. Perh. a fanciful use of prec.] **a.** *U.S.* A tall beer-glass containing about double the quantity of an ordinary tumbler. **b.** Hence, in local British use, a retail measure of about 14 fluid ounces for beer.

Schorl (ʃǭɹl). 1779. [– G. *schörl*, of unkn. origin.] *Min.* Tourmaline, esp. the black variety. Hence **Schorla·ceous** *a.*

‖**Schottische** (ʃǫtī·ʃ, ʃǫ·tiʃ), *sb.* 1859. [– G. (*der*) *schottische* (*tanz*) the Scottish dance.] A dance of foreign origin resembling the polka, first introduced in England in 1848. Also, the music for this. Hence **Schotti·sche** *v. intr.* to dance a s.

Schout (skaut, Du. sχaut). *Hist.* 1481. [– Du. *schout*, rel. to G. *schulze*.] An administrative or municipal officer in the Low Countries and the Dutch Colonies.

Schreibersite (ʃrəi·bəɹzəit). 1846. [f. name of von *Schreibers*, of Vienna; see -ITE[1] 2 b.] *Min.* A phosphide of iron and nickel occurring in meteoric iron.

‖**Schuit** (skoit, Du. sχöit). Also **schuyt.** 1617. [Du., see SCOUT *sb.*[1]] A Dutch flat-bottomed river-boat.

Schultze (ʃu·ltsə). 1881. [Name of E. *Schultze*, the inventor, used attrib.] *S.* (also *Schultze's*) *gunpowder, powder*: an explosive having nitrolignin as its chief constituent; hence *S. cartridge*, one charged with this powder.

Schwa: see SHEVA 2.

‖**Schwärmerei** (ʃvē·rmərai). 1886. Enthusiastic devotion; schoolgirlish attachment.

Schwenkfeldian (ʃweŋkfe·ldiăn), *sb.* and *a.* Also †**Swen(c)k-.** 1562. [f. the name *Schwenkfeld* + -IAN.] **A.** *sb.* One of a sect founded by Caspar Schwenkfeld, a Silesian Protestant mystic (1490–1561). **B.** *adj.* Belonging to this sect.

Sciænoid (səi,ī·noid), *a.* and *sb.* 1840. [f. mod. use of L. *sciæna* – Gr. σκίαινα; see -OID.] **A.** *adj.* Belonging to, characteristic of, or resembling a sciænoid or the sciænoids. **B.** *sb.* A fish of the family *Sciænidæ* (type *Sciæna*).

Sciagraphic (səi,ăgræ·fik), *a.* 1815. [f. SCIAGRAPHY + -IC; see -GRAPHIC.] Of or pertaining to sciagraphy. So **Sciagra·phical** *a.* 1690, **-ly** *adv.* 1727.

Sciagraphy (səiæ·grăfi). 1598. [– Fr. *scia-*, *sciographie* – L. *scia-*, *sciographia* – Gr. σκια-, σκιογραφία, f. σκια-, σκιογράφος, f. σκιά shadow + -γραφος -GRAPH; see -GRAPHY.] **1.** That branch of perspective which deals with the projection of shadows; also, the delineation of an object in perspective with its gradations of light and shade. †**2.** A sciagraphic delineation or picture –1648. †**3.** An outline, draught, rough sketch. Chiefly *fig.* –1738. †**4.** The art or practice of finding the hour of the day or night by observation of the shadow of the sun, moon, or stars upon a dial –1721.

Sciamachy (səi,æ·măki), **skiamachy** (skəi-). 1623. [– Gr. σκιαμαχία, f. σκιά shadow + μαχ-, μάχεσθαι to fight.] A sham fight for exercise or practice; also, the action of fighting with a shadow.

Scian (səi·an), *a.* 1820. [f. *Scio*, It. name of *Chios*, reputed birthplace of Homer.] Chian.

†**Sciathe·rical,** *a.* 1614. [f. late Gr. σκιαθηρικός, f. σκιαθήρας sun-dial, lit. 'shadow-catcher', f. σκιά shadow + θηρᾶν catch; see -ICAL.] Concerned with the recording of the shadows cast by the planets, esp. that of the sun as a means of finding out the hour of the day –1755. So †**Sciathe·ric** *a.* –1755.

Sciatic (səi,æ·tik), *a.* and *sb.* 1541. [– (O)Fr. *sciatique* – late L. *sciaticus*, alt. of *ischiaticus*, for L. *ischiadicus* (after *-aticus* -ATIC) – Gr. ἰσχιαδικός, f. ἰσχίον hip-joint, pl. ἰσχία haunches, hams (cf. med.L. *scia* hip). Cf. ISCHIADIC, ISCHIATIC.] **A.** *adj.* **1.** Affecting the hip or the sciatic nerves 1547. **2.** Of or belonging to the ischium or hip 1597.

1. S. pains GIBBON. *S. passion*, sciatica. **2.** *S. artery*, the larger of the two terminal branches of the internal iliac. *S. nerve*, each of the two divisions of the sacral plexus, esp. the *great s. nerve*, which is the largest nerve in the human body.

B. *sb.* †**1.** The ischium or hip –1565. †**2.** = SCIATICA –1801. **3.** Short for *s. nerve* 1541.

Sciatica (səi,æ·tikă). 1444. [– late L. *sciatica* (sc. *passio* morbid affection, illness), fem. of *sciaticus*; see prec., -A 2.] A disease characterized by pain in the great sciatic nerve and its branches 1450. **b.** An attack of this disease 1444. Hence **Scia·tical** *a.* (now *rare*) pertaining to or of the nature of s.; (of a person) affected with s.

Science (səi·ěns). ME. [– OFr. *science* – L. *scientia* knowledge, f. *scient-*, pr. ppl. stem of *scire* know; see -ENCE.] **1.** The state or fact of knowing; knowledge or cognizance *of* something specified or implied; also, knowledge (more or less extensive) as a personal attribute. Now *Theol.*, and occas. *Philos.* **2.** Knowledge acquired by study; acquaintance with or mastery of any department of learning. late ME. **b.** Trained skill. Now *esp.* (somewhat joc.) with ref. to pugilism. 1785. **3.** A particular branch of knowledge or study; a recognized department of learning: often opp. to *art* (ART *sb.* II. 2) ME. †**b.** A craft, trade, or occupation requiring trained skill –1660. **4.** A branch of study which is concerned either with a connected body of demonstrated truths or with observed facts systematically classified and more or less colligated by being brought under general laws, and which includes trustworthy methods for the discovery of new truth within its own domain 1725. **5.** The kind of knowledge or intellectual activity of which the 'sciences' are examples. In early use, with ref. to sense 3: What is taught in the Schools, or may be learned by study. In mod. use chiefly: The sciences (in sense 4) as dist. from other departments of learning; scientific doctrine or investigation. late ME. **b.** In mod. use, often = 'Natural and Physical Science'. Also *attrib.*, as in *s.-master, -teaching*, etc. 1867. †**c.** *Oxford Univ.* Formerly applied to the portions of ancient and modern philosophy, logic, etc., included in the course of study for a degree in the School of Literæ Humaniores –1903.

1. Life is not the object of S.; we see a little, very little; and what is beyond we can only conjecture JOHNSON. **2.** Be love my youth's pursuit, and s. crown my Age GRAY. **b.** Phr. *The noble s.* (*of defence*), boxing or fencing (now *joc.*) **3.** In the Middle Ages, 'the seven (liberal) sciences' was often used synonymously with 'the seven liberal arts', for the group of studies comprised by the *Trivium* (Grammar, Logic, Rhetoric) and the *Quadrivium* (Arithmetic, Music, Geometry, Astronomy). O.E.D. **4.** Those truths which are the objects of particular sciences 1794. *Exact, experimental, natural, physical sciences*: see the adjs. **5.** This species is new to s. 1864. **c.** He had none of his brother's love for the Greek philosophy, then known as 'science' 1903.

Man of science. †**a.** A man who possesses knowledge in any department of learning, or trained skill in any art or craft. **b.** In mod. use, a man who has expert knowledge of some branch of science (usu., of physical or natural science), and devotes himself to its investigation.

Scient (səi·ĕnt), *a.* late ME. [OFr. *scient* – L. *sciens, scient-*; see prec., -ENT.] Having science, knowledge, or skill. Now *rare*.

‖**Scienter** (səi,e·ntəɹ), *adv.* 1824. [L. *scienter*, f. as prec. with adverbial suffix.] *Law.* Knowingly. Often as *sb.* in the phrase *to prove* (*a*) *s.*, etc., to prove that the act complained of was done knowingly; *law of s.*, the law with regard to the necessity of 'proving a s.' in order to obtain damages.

Sciential (səi,e·nʃăl), *a.* 1456. [– late and med.L. *scientialis*, f. *scientia*; see SCIENCE, -AL[1].] **1.** Of or pertaining to knowledge or science. **2.** Endowed with knowledge 1477.

Scientific (səi,ĕnti·fik), *a.* and *sb.* 1589. [– (O)Fr. *scientifique* or late L. *scientificus*, equiv. to *scientiam faciens* producing knowledge, tr. ἐπιστημονικός (Aristotle); see SCIENCE, -FIC.] **A.** *adj.* †**1.** Of a syllogism, a proof: Producing knowledge, demonstrative –1667. **2.** Of persons, books, institutions, etc.: Occupied in or concerned with science or the sciences 1589. **3.** Of or pertaining to science or the sciences; of the nature of science 1722. **4.** Of an art, practice, operation, or method: Based upon or regulated by science, as opp. to mere traditional rules or empirical dexterity. Of a worker or agent: Guided by a knowledge of science, acting according to scientific principles 1678. **b.** Devised on scientific principles 1794. **c.** Characterized by 'science' or trained skill 1862.

2. The opinion of the s. world 1815. S. periodicals 1888. **3.** Analogy confirmed by experiment becomes S. truth 1812. To study religions in a s. spirit 1902. **4.** The one is profitless taxation, the other s. taxation CHAMBERLAIN. **c.** A batsman.. steady and s. 1862.

B. *sb.* A man of science. *colloq.* 1830.

Scientifical (səi,ĕnti·fikăl), *a.* 1588. [f. as prec.; see -ICAL.] †**1.** = prec. *a.* 1. –1732. †**2.** Designed for the furthering of knowledge –1642. **3.** Expert in science; occupied in or concerned with science. Now *rare*. 1645. **4.** Of or pertaining to science (*rare*) 1777. Hence **Scienti·fical-ly** *adv.*, **-ness.**

Scientist (səi·ĕntist). 1840. [f. *scient-* in L. *scientia* SCIENCE, and in SCIENTIFIC.] A man of science.

‖**Scilicet** (səi·liset), *adv.* (*sb.*) late ME. [L., = *scire licet*, prop. 'you may understand or know'. Cf. VIDELICET.] **A.** *adv.* To wit; that is to say; namely. Abbrev. **scil.** or **sc. B.** as *sb.* The word 'scilicet' or its equivalent, introducing a specifying clause 1650.

‖**Scilla** (si·lă). 1824. [L., = Gr. σκίλλα. Cf. SQUILL.] **a.** *Bot.* A genus of liliaceous plants; a plant of this genus, a squill. **b.** *Pharmacy.* The bulb of *Urginea scilla* (formerly *Scilla maritima*).

Scillitin (si·litin). 1819. [– Fr. *scillitine*, f. *scillitique* – L. *scilliticus* – Gr. σκιλλιτικός, f. σκίλλα SCILLA; see -ITE[1] 1 and -IN[1].] *Chem.* A bitter extract from the squill.

Scillonian (silōᵘ·niăn), *a.* and *sb.* 1750. [f. *Scilly* + *-onian* (perh. after *Devonian*).] **A.** *adj.* Pertaining to the Scilly Isles or their inhabitants. **B.** *sb.* An inhabitant of these.

Scimitar (si·mităɹ). 1548. [Introduced in various forms repr. Fr. *cimeterre, cimiterre*, It. *scimitarra*, †*cimitara*, etc.; of unkn. origin.] A short, curved, single-edged sword, used among Orientals, esp. Turks and Persians.

Comb.: **s.-pod,** the legume of the tropical climber *Entada scandens*; **s. razor-shell,** the *Solen ensis*.

Scincoid (si·ŋkoid), *a.* and *sb.* 1790. [– mod.L. *scincoides*, f. L. *scincus* SKINK *sb.*[1]; see -OID.] **A.** *adj.* Resembling a skink; belonging to the group *Scincoidea* or the family *Scincidæ* of skink-like lizards. **B.** *sb.* A skink-like lizard. So **Scincoi·dian** *a.* and *sb.*

‖**Scintilla** (sinti·lă). 1692. [L. = spark.] A minute particle, an atom.

Scintillant (si·ntilănt), *a.* 1610. [– L. *scintillans, -ant-*, pr. pple. of *scintillare*, f. SCINTILLA; see -ANT.] Scintillating 1737. **b.** *Her.* Emitting sparks 1610.

Scintillate (si·ntileᶦt), *v.* 1623. [– *scintillat-*, pa. ppl. stem of L. *scintillare*; see prec., -ATE[3].] **1.** *intr.* To send forth sparks or little flashes of light; to sparkle, twinkle. **2.** *trans.* To emit as a spark or sparks; to send forth (sparkles of light); to flash forth 1809. **3.** *pass.* To be ornamented with bright specks 1851.

1. *fig.* A work scintillating throughout with wit and humour 1864. **2.** Too much given to s. bitter epigram 1866. So **Scintilla·tion,** the action of scintillating; a flash, spark; a flash, a brilliant display (of wit, etc.); *occas.* misused for SCINTILLA.

Sciolism (səi·ŏliz'm). 1816. [f. next; see -ISM.] The character or qualities of a sciolist; pretentious superficiality of knowledge.

Sciolist (səi·ŏlist). 1615. [f. late L. *sciolus* (see next) + -IST.] A superficial pretender to knowledge; a conceited smatterer. So **Sciolı·stic** *a.*

Sciolous (səi·ŏləs), *a.* Now *rare*. 1639. [f. late L. *sciolus* smatterer (dim. of *scius* knowing, f. *scire* know + -OUS.] Having a smattering of knowledge.

Sciomancy (səi·ŏmænsi). 1623. [– mod.L. *sciomantia*, f. Gr. σκιά shadow; see -MANCY.] Divination by communication with the shades of the dead.

Scion (səi·ən). [ME. *sioun* – OFr. *ciun, cion, sion* (mod. *scion*) shoot or twig; of unkn. origin.] **1. a.** *gen.* A shoot or twig; also, a sucker. Now only *fig.* **b.** *spec.* A slip for grafting, a graft. **2.** An heir, a descendant 1814.

1. a. *fig.* An humble and secular s. of that old stock of religious constancy LAMB. **2.** A s. of the imperial Hapsburg line 1871.

Scioptic (səi,ǫ·ptik), *a.* and *sb.* 1738. [f. Gr. σκιά shadow + ὀπτικός pertaining to vision; see OPTIC *a.*] = SCIOPTRIC.

Sciopticon (səi,ǫ·ptikǫn). 1876. [f. as prec. with Gr. neuter ending.] A magic lantern for the exhibition of photographed objects.

Scioptric (səi,ǫ·ptrik), *a.* and *sb.* Now *rare* or *Obs.* 1704. [f. Gr. σκιά shadow, after *catoptric*, etc.] **A.** *adj. S. ball*: a ball of wood with a hole made through it in which a lens is placed, used in the camera obscura 1764. **B.** *sb.* = *s. ball.* 1704.

‖**Scire facias** (səiᵊ·ri fēᶦ·ʃiæs). 1445. [Law Latin phr. *scire facias* 'do (him) to wit' used subst.] *Law.* A judicial writ, requiring the sheriff to do the party concerned to wit that he should come before the Court to 'show cause' why execution should not be taken against him, or why letters patent, such as a charter, should not be revoked. Often abbrev. *sci. fa.*

Scirrhoid (si·roid, sk-), *a.* 1855. [f. SCIRRHUS + -OID.] Resembling scirrhus.

Scirrhosity (sirǫ·sīti, sk-). 1599. [– mod.L. *scirrhositas* – mod.L. *scirrhosus*; see next, -ITY.] A morbid hardness or scirrhous condition of an organ or a part; the quality or state of being scirrhous.

Scirrhous (si·rəs, sk-), *a.* 1563. [– Fr. *scirr(h)eux* (now *squirreux*) – mod.L. *scirrhosus*, f. L. *scirrhus* SCIRRHUS; see -OUS.] Proceeding from, of the nature of, or resembling a scirrhus. **b.** *transf.* Indurated; covered with hard excrescences 1658.

S. cancer 1878. **b.** Shining, s. skin 1845.

‖**Scirrhus** (si·rŏs, sk-). *Pl.* **scirrhi,** also **scirrhusses.** 1605. [mod.L. – Gr. σκίρρος, prop. σκῖρος a hard coat or covering, a hardened swelling or tumour, related to σκιρός hard.] *Path.* **1.** A hard, firm, and almost painless swelling or tumour; now *spec.* a hard cancer 1615. **2.** The disease of having a scirrhus; an instance or attack of this disease 1605.

Scissel (si·sĕl). 1622. [– (O)Fr. *cisaille* in same sense, f. *cisailler* clip with shears.] Metal clippings; *spec.* the scrap metal from which coin blanks have been cut.

Scissile (si·səil, -il), *a.* 1621. [– L. *scissilis*, f. *sciss-*; see next, -ILE. Cf. Fr. *scissile* (XVII).] Capable of being cut or divided; *spec.* in *Min.*, that splits into laminæ, esp. of alum.

Scission (si·ʃən). 1443. [– (O)Fr. *scission* or late L. *scissio, -ōn-*, f. *sciss-*, pa. ppl. stem of *scindere* cut, cleave; see -ION.] **1.** The action or an act of cutting or dividing, as with a sharp instrument 1676. **2.** *fig.* Division, separation; in early use = SCHISM 1443.

Scissiparity (sisīpæ·rĭti). 1877. [f. L. *sciss-* (see prec.) + *parere* bring forth + -ITY.] *Biol.* Reproduction by fission, schizogenesis.

Scissor (si·zəɹ), *v.* 1612. [f. next.] **1.** *trans.* To cut with scissors, to cut *up, off,* or *into* pieces with scissors. **2.** To clip out (extracts) from newspapers or the like 1865.

Scissors (si·zəɹz), *sb. pl.* [Late ME. *sisoures* – (O)Fr. *cisoires* (now only 'large shears', the sense 'scissors' being appropriated to *ciseaux*, pl. of †*cisel* CHISEL), repr. med.L. **cisoria*, pl. of late L. *cisorium* cutting instrument, f. *-cis-*, *-cidere*, var. in comp. of *cæs-*, *cædere* cut. For the ending *-or(s* see MIRROR. The sp. with *sc-*, dating from XVI, is due to assoc. with L. *scindere* cut, cleave.] **1.** A cutting instrument consisting of a pair of handled blades, so pivoted on a pin in the centre that the instrument can be opened to a shape resembling that of the letter X, and the handles then brought together again so as to cause the edges of the blades to close on the object to be cut. **a.** in *pl.* form with pl. construction, either in sing. or pl. sense. When qualification by a numeral or an indef. article is required, *pair of s.* is used. late ME. ¶**b.** in *pl.* form construed as *sing.* (*rare*) 1843. **2.** *Wrestling.* A grip with the wrists crossed like a pair of scissors 1904. Also in *Rugby Football* and *Swimming*.

1. The s. of Destiny CARLYLE. Phr. *S. and paste* (†*paste and s.*), referred to as the instruments used by the newspaper sub-editor or the mere compiler. **b.** Which is easily removed with a s. 1906.

attrib. and *Comb.* (chiefly in form *scissor-*), as **scissor-bill,** a skimmer or shearwater. esp. *Rhynchops nigra*; **scissor(s)-grinder,** (*a*) a man who grinds scissors; (*b*) *dial.* the nightjar, *Caprimulgus europæus*; **scissor-tail,** either of two American birds of the family *Tyrannidæ*, *Milvulus forficatus* and *M. tyrannus*.

Scissure (si·ʃūɹ). Now *rare* or *Obs.* late ME. [– Fr. *scissure* or L. *scissura*, f. *sciss-*, pa. ppl. stem of *scindere* cut, cleave; see -URE.] **1.** A longitudinal cleft or opening made by cutting or separation of parts; a rent, fissure 1511. **b.** *fig.* A split, division, schism 1643. **2.** *Anat.*, etc. A natural cleft or opening in an organ or part. late ME.

Sciurine (səi·iŭrəin, -in), *a.* and *sb.* 1842. [f. L. *sciurus* – Gr. σκίουρος squirrel (f. σκιά shadow + οὐρά tail) + -INE[1].] **A.** *adj.* Of or pertaining to the genus *Sciurus* or subfamily *Sciurinæ* of squirrels. **B.** *sb.* A sciurine rodent; a squirrel. So **Sciuroid** (səi,iūᵊ·-

roid) *a.* *Zool.* of or pertaining to the *Sciuridæ*, or squirrel-family; *Bot.* bushy, like a squirrel's tail.

Sciuromorph (səi,iū°·romǫɹf), *a.* 1882. [– mod.L. *Sciuromorpha*, f. Gr. σκίουρος (see prec.) + μορφή form.] A rodent of the super-family *Sciuromorpha*, comprising the *Sciuridæ*, *Anomaluridæ*, etc. Hence **Sciuromo·rphic, -mo·rphine** *adjs.*

Sclaff (sklæf), *v.* 1893. [spec. use of Sc. *sclaff* strike with a flat surface, shuffle along, perh. of imit. origin.] *Golf.* **a.** *intr.* To scrape the surface of the ground with the sole of the club before striking the ball. **b.** *trans.* To scrape (the ground) behind the ball in striking; also, to hit (a ball) after having scraped the ground with the club.

‖**Sclera** (sklī°·ră). 1888. [mod.L., f. Gr. σκληρός hard; see -A 2.] The sclerotic coat of the eyeball. Hence **Scle·ral** *a.* of or pertaining to the s. or sclerotic.

‖**Sclerema** (skliº·rī·mă). 1858. [mod.L. form of Fr. *sclérème*, f. Gr. σκληρός hard, after *œdème* ŒDEMA.] A hardening of the cellular tissue.

Sclerenchyma (sklī°re·ŋkimă). 1861. [mod.L., f. Gr. σκληρός hard + ἔγχυμα an infusion, after *parenchyma*.] **1.** *Zool.* The hard substance of the calcareous skeleton of sclerodermic corals. **2.** *Bot.* The tissue of cells with thickened or lignified walls 1875. Hence **Sclerenchy·matous** *a.*

‖**Scleriasis** (skli°rəi·ăsis). 1684. [mod.L., f. Gr. σκληρός hard, after *elephantiasis*.] *Path.* A hard tumour or induration; a scirrhus.

Sclerite (sklī°·rəit). 1861. [f. Gr. σκληρός + -ITE[1] 3.] *Zool.* In the anatomy of invertebrates, each of the definite component portions into which the hard portion of the substance of certain animals is divided. Hence **Scleri·tic** *a.*

Scleritis (sklī°rəi·tis). 1861. [f. SCLERA + -ITIS.] Sclerotitis.

Sclero- (sklī°·ro), occurring in scientific terms.

1. As comb. form of Gr. σκληρός hard: **Scle·robase** [Gr. βάσις BASE], *Zool.* the axis or stem of a compound actinozoan when forming a horny or calcareous skeleton; hence **Scleroba·sic** *a.* pertaining to or consisting of a sclerobase. **Scle·roblast** [-BLAST], *Bot.* a stone-cell; *Zool.* the tissue from which sponge-spicules are produced. **Scle·roderm** [Gr. δέρμα skin], (*a*) a fish of the group *Sclerodermi*, which have the skin covered with hard scales; (*b*) a polyp of the division *Sclerodermata*. ‖**Sclerode·rma**, *Path.* a chronic hardened condition of the skin, resulting from hypertrophy of connective tissue; so **Sclerode·rmia. Sclerode·rmatous, Sclerode·rmic** *adjs.*, (*a*) *Zool.* belonging to the division *Sclerodermata* of zoantharian polyps; (*b*) *Path.* pertaining to the scleroderma. **Sclerode·rmite,** one of the hard bodies of which the skeleton of Crustacea is composed; also, one of the hard skeletal parts in certain Actinozoans. **Scle·rogen** [-GEN], *Bot.* the hard lignified matter on the sides of some cells, which gives hardness to wood, fruit-stones, etc. **Scleroge·nic** *a.*, *Phys.* and *Path.* tending to produce hardening (of animal tissues). **Sclero·genous** *a.*, (*a*) sclerogenic; (*b*) consisting of sclerogen. **Sclero·meter** [-METER], an instrument for measuring the hardness of crystals.

2. As comb. form of SCLERA: **Scle:ro-iri·tis,** inflammation of the sclerotic coat and the iris.

3. Used (after SCLEROTIUM, etc.) to form the names of a number of substances obtained from ergot, as **Scleromu·cin,** a gummy nitrogenous substance.

Scleroid (sklī°·roid), *a.* 1856. [f. Gr. σκληρός + -OID.] *Bot.* and *Zool.* Hard; having a hard texture.

‖**Scleroma** (skli°rōᵘ·mă). 1684. [mod.L. – Gr. σκλήρωμα, f. σκληροῦν harden, f. σκληρός; see -OMA.] *Path.* = SCLERIASIS.

Sclerosed (skli°rōᵘ·st), *ppl. a.* 1878. [f. next + -ED[1].] **a.** *Path.* Affected with sclerosis; rendered abnormally hard. **b.** *Bot.* Hardened; lignified 1881.

Sclerosis (skli°rōᵘ·sis). late ME. [– med.L. *sclerosis, sclir-* – Gr. σκλήρωσις, f. σκληροῦν harden; see -OSIS.] **1.** *Path.* †**a.** A hard external tumour. **b.** A morbid hardening of any tissue or structure. **2.** *Bot.* Induration of a tissue or a cell-wall by lignification 1884.

Sclerotal (skli°rōᵘ·tăl). 1854. [f. mod.L. *sclerotis* SCLEROTICA + -AL[1].] *Anat.* Any of the component plates of the bony ring which protects the sclerotic coat of the eyeball in certain birds and reptiles.

Sclerotic (skli°rǫ·tik), *a.*[1] and *sb.* 1543. [– med.L. (*tēla*) *sclerotica, sclir-*, f. as SCLEROSIS; see -OTIC.] **A.** *adj.* **1.** *Anat.* In *s. coat, membrane, tunic* = B. 1. **b.** Of or pertaining to, connected with, the sclerotic coat of the eye 1822. **2.** Of medicines: Adapted to harden the tissues 1696. **3.** *Path.* Of or pertaining to sclerosis; affected with sclerosis 1543. **4.** *Bot.* Hardened, stony in texture 1884.

1. b. *S. bone, plate* = SCLEROTAL; *s. ring*, the ring formed by the s. bones of the eyeball. **4.** *S. cells*, grit-cells; *s. parenchyma*, stone-cells in pears, etc.

B. *sb.* **1.** The hard outer coat of the posterior portion of the eyeball, forming the white of the eye 1690. **2.** A medicine for hardening the flesh, etc. 1728.

Sclerotic (skli°rǫ·tik), *a.*[2] 1876. [f. SCLEROTIUM + -IC 1 b.] *Chem.* In *s. acid*, one of the two most active constituents of ergot.

‖**Sclerotica** (skli°rǫ·tikă). 1541. [med.L., subst. use of *sclerotica* (sc. *tēla* membrane); see SCLEROTIC *a.*[1]] = SCLEROTIC *sb.* 1.

‖**Sclerotitis** (sklī°rotəi·tis). 1822. [mod.L., f. SCLEROTIC, SCLEROTICA + -ITIS.] *Path.* Inflammation of the sclerotica.

‖**Sclerotium** (skli°rōᵘ·tiŏm). *Pl.* **-tia.** 1790. [mod.L. (Tode, 1790), f. Gr. σκληρός hard; see -IUM.] †**1.** A former genus of *Cryptogamia*, comprising hard black bodies producing smut in wheat and ergot in rye; now known to be a particular stage of growth of the mycelium of certain fungi –1845. **2.** A tuberous body forming on the mycelium of a fungus, from which it becomes detached when its growth is complete 1871. **3.** *Zool.* In *Mycetozoa*, a cyst-like growth enclosing a portion of the plasmodium in its dormant stage 1885.

Sclerotome (sklī°·rotōᵘm). 1857. [f. SCLERO- + -TOME[1] and [2].] *Anat.* **1.** A sclerous element intervening between successive myotomes. **2.** A knife used in incising the sclerotic 1885. So **Sclero·tomy,** incision into the sclera.

Sclerous (sklī°·rŏs), *a.* 1845. [f. Gr. σκληρός + -OUS.] **a.** *Phys.* Of animal tissues: Hard, bony. **b.** *Path.* Indurated, affected by sclerosis.

Scobiform (skōᵘ·bifǫɹm), *a.* 1760. [f. L. *scobis* sawdust, filings + -FORM.] *Bot.* Like sawdust or filings in appearance.

Scoff (skǫf), *sb.*[1] [perh. of Scand. origin; cf. early mod. Da. *skof, skuf* jest, mockery, *skuffe* jest, mock, also (as now) deceive, disappoint, rel. to OFris. *skof* mockery, OHG. *skof, skopf* poet; cf. SCOP.] **1. a.** 'Contemptuous ridicule; expression of scorn; contumelious language' (J.); mockery. Now *rare* or *Obs.* **b.** A derisive jest; an expression of mockery 1573. **2.** An object of contempt or scorn; a mark for derision or scoffing 1640.

1. b. The scoffs and sarcasms of Swift 1751. **2.** Is not he the common s. of all beholders? 1660.

Scoff (skǫf), *sb.*[2] *S. Afr.* 1879. [– S. Afr. Du. *schoff*, repr. Du. *schoft* (prop.) quarter of a day, (hence) any of the four meals of the day.] Food; a meal.

Scoff (skǫf), *v.*[1] late ME. [f. SCOFF *sb.*[1]] **1.** *intr.* To speak derisively, mock, jeer. Chiefly implying unworthy derision, as of something deserving reverence or consideration. **2.** *trans.* To scoff at, deride, ridicule irreverently. *Obs.* exc. *U.S.* 1579.

1. Harvey's grand discovery. .was scoffed at for nearly a whole generation 1886. **2.** I would not scoffe you, nor with taunts torment ye 1624. Hence **Sco·ffer**, one who scoffs; often *spec.* one who scoffs at religion or morality 1470. **Sco·ffingly** *adv.*

Scoff (skǫf), *v.*[2] *slang* and *dial.* 1849. [orig. var. of synon. (dial.) *scaff* (XVIII), rel. to contemp. *scaff* food; later assoc. with SCOFF *sb.*[2]] **1.** *trans.* To eat voraciously, devour; also *gen.* to eat. **b.** *intr.* To eat or feed 1899. **2.** *trans.* To seize, plunder 1893.

Scoinson (skoi·nsən). 1842. [Refashioned f. SCUNCHEON, after its source, OFr. *escoinçon*.] *Arch.* Used *attrib.* in *s. arch* = REAR-ARCH.

Scoke (skōᵘk). *U.S.* 1794. [Of unkn. origin.] The poke-weed, *Phytolacca decandra*.

Scold (skōᵘld), *sb.* ME. [prob. – ON. *skáld* poet, SKALD, in combs. also with dyslogistic implication (e.g. *skáldskapr*, prop. poetry, which has in the Icel. law-books the spec. sense of libel in verse), hence (perh. by a spec. Eng. development), libellous, scurrilous, or ribald persons.] **1.** In early use, a person (esp. a woman) of ribald speech; later, a woman (rarely a man) addicted to abusive language. **2.** [from the vb.] A scolding. *dial.* or *colloq.* 1706.

1. I know she is an irkesome brawling s. SHAKS. *Common s.*, a woman who disturbs the peace of the neighbourhood by her constant scolding.

Comb.: **scold's bit, bridle** = BRANKS 1.

Scold (skōᵘld), *v.* late ME. [f. prec.] **1.** *intr.* †**a.** Orig., to behave as a scold; to quarrel noisily, brawl; to use unseemly language in vituperation: said chiefly of women. **b.** Now: To use undignified vehemence or persistence in reproof or fault-finding; *colloq.* freq. = to utter continuous reproof. **2.** *trans.* To address (esp. an inferior or a child) with continuous and more or less angry reproach; to chide 1715.

1. Mark'd you not how hir sister Began to s., and raise vp such a storme, That mortal eares might hardly indure the din SHAKS. **2.** She scolds the servants from morning till night THACKERAY. Hence **Sco·lder**[1], one who scolds; †a common scold.

Scolder[2] (skōᵘ·ldəɹ). *Orkneys.* 1795. The oyster-catcher, *Hæmatopus ostrilegus*.

Scolecid (skolī·sid). 1864. [– mod.L. *Scolecida*, f. Gr. σκώληξ SCOLEX; see -ID[3].] An animal of the class *Scolecida* of *Annuloida*.

Scolecite (skǫ·lĭsəit). 1823. [f. next + -ITE[1] 2 b.] **1.** *Min.* Hydrous silicate of aluminium and calcium, found in needle-shaped crystals and fibrous or radiated masses. **2.** *Bot.* The vermiform carpogonium of certain fungi 1875.

‖**Scolex** (skōᵘ·leks). *Pl.* **scoleces** (skolī·sīz), also *erron.* **scolices** (skōᵘ·lisīz). 1855. [mod.L. – Gr. σκώληξ, σκωληκ- worm.] The larva or embryo produced directly from the egg in metagenesis; esp. the larva or head of a tapeworm or other parasitic worm.

Scolion (skǫ·liŏn). 1603. [Gr. σκόλιον.] *Gr. Antiq.* A song sung in turn by the guests at a banquet.

‖**Scoliosis** (skǫliōᵘ·sis). 1706. [mod.L. – Gr. σκολίωσις, f. σκολιός bent, curved; see -OSIS.] *Path.* Lateral curvature of the spine. Hence **Scolio·tic** *a.*

Scollop, *sb.* and *v.*: see SCALLOP.

Scolopaceous (skǫlopēⁱ·ʃəs), *a.* 1785. [f. mod.L. *scolopaceus*, f. L. *scolopax, -pac-* snipe, woodcock – Gr. σκολόπαξ; see -ACEOUS.] *Ornith.* Resembling a snipe; *spec.* used as an epithet of a species of courlan, *Aramus scolopaceus*. Also = next.

Scolopacine (skǫ·lopăsəin, -in), *a.* and *sb.* 1889. [– mod.L. *scolopacinus*, f. L. *scolopax*; see prec., -INE[1].] **A.** *adj.* Belonging to the sub-family *Scolopacinæ* or the family *Scolopacidæ*; typified by the genus *Scolopax*, and including the woodcock, redshank, etc. **B.** *sb.* A scolopacine bird.

‖**Scolopendra** (skǫlŏpe·ndră). 1520. [L. – Gr. σκολόπενδρα.] †**1.** A fabulous sea-fish –1635. **2.** A centipede or millipede. Also, a Linnæan genus of myriapods, including the largest and most formidable of the centipedes 1608. So **Scolope·nder** 1562. **Scolope·ndrine** *a.* resembling or related to the centipedes.

‖**Scolopendrium** (skǫlope·ndriŏm). Also †**-ia.** 1520. [mod.L. = late L. *-ion* – Gr. σκολοπένδριον, so called from a fancied resemblance to the scolopendra; see -IUM.] = HART'S-TONGUE.

Scolytid (skǫ·litid). 1899. [– mod.L. *Scolytidæ*, f. *Scolytus*; see -ID[3].] A member of the family *Scolytidæ* of small wood-boring beetles.

‖**Scomber** (skǫ·mbəɹ). *Pl.* **scombri** (skǫ·mbrəi). 1623. [L. – Gr. σκόμβρος tunny or mackerel.] A mackerel. In mod. use only as the L. name of the genus.

Scombroid (skǫ·mbroid), *a.* and *sb.* 1841. [f. Gr. σκόμβρος SCOMBER + -OID.] **A.** *adj.* Resembling the mackerel; belonging to the family *Scombridæ*. **B.** *sb.* A s. fish 1842.

†**Scomm.** 1619. [– late L. *scomma* – Gr. σκῶμμα, f. σκώπτειν jeer, scoff.] A flout or scoff –1711.

Sconce (skǫns), *sb.*[1] late ME. [Aphetic – OFr. *esconse* (i) hiding-place, (ii) lantern or – med.L. *sconsa*, aphetic f. *absconsa* (sc. *laterna*) dark lantern, subst. use of fem. pa. pple. of *abscondere* hide (see ABSCOND).] †**1.** A lantern or candlestick with a screen to protect the light from the wind, and a handle to carry it by –1747. **b.** A flat candlestick with a handle for carrying 1834. **2.** A bracket-candlestick to fasten against a wall. Also, a candle-bracket for a piano, etc. 1450. **3.** The tube in an ordinary candlestick in which the candle is inserted 1850.

2. Candles, arranged upon the walls on sconces 1881.

Sconce (skǫns), *sb.*[2] *arch.* 1567. [perh. joc. use of prec.] Used *joc.* for: The head; esp. the crown or top of the head; hence, ability, sense, wit.

He had received a crack on the s. 1888.

Sconce (skǫns), *sb.*[3] 1571. [– Du. *schans*, †*schantze* brushwood, screen of brushwood for soldiers, earthwork of gabions – (M)HG. *schanze* of unkn. origin.] **1.** *Fortif.* A small fort or earthwork; esp. one built to defend a ford, pass, castle-gate, etc., or erected as a counter-fort. **2.** *transf.* A protective screen or shelter (from fire or the elements) 1591. **3.** *dial.* **a.** A screen, partition 1695. **b.** [perh. a different word.] A seat at one side of the fire-place in an open chimney 1781. **4.** (Also *s.-piece.*) A low water-washed iceberg 1856.

1. *fig. Com. Err.* II. ii. 37. Phr. †*To build a S.*, to run a Score at an Ale-house, Tavern, &c. so as to be afraid to go there, for fear of being dunn'd BAILEY.

Sconce (skǫns), *sb.*[4] 1650. [f. SCONCE *v.*[2]] At Oxford: †**a.** A fine imposed for a breach of university or college discipline. **b.** A fine of a tankard of ale or the like, imposed by undergraduates on one of their number for some breach of customary rule when dining in hall.

†**Sconce,** *v.*[1] 1598. [f. SCONCE *sb.*[3]] **1.** *trans.* To fortify, entrench; in later use, to shelter, protect –1746. **2.** To hide, screen from view –1663.

Sconce (skǫns), *v.*[2] 1617. [Early exx. have allusions to head-money and being 'taxt by the poul', suggesting that the term arose from a joc. ref. to SCONCE *sb.*[2]] *trans.* At Oxford: To fine, mulct; often with the penalty as second object. Now said only of undergraduates when dining in hall: To fine (one of their number) a tankard of ale or the like, as a penalty for breach of good manners or conventional usage.

Scone (skōᵘn, skǫn). 1513. [orig. Sc., perh. shortening of MLG. *schonbrot*, MDu. *schoonbroot* (sχōnbrōt) 'fine bread'.] A large round cake made of wheat or barley-meal baked on a griddle; one of the four quadrant-shaped pieces into which such a cake is often cut, or a cake of this shape separately baked.

Drop, dropped s., one made of a small portion of batter dropped on to a griddle or tin and baked.

Scoop (skūp), *sb.*[1] ME. [– MLG., MDu. *schōpe* (Du. *schoep*) vessel for bailing, bucket of a water-wheel = MHG. *schuofe* (G. †*schufe*); WGmc. f. **skōp-* **scap-*, whence **skappjan* draw water. See SHAPE *v.*] **1.** A utensil for bailing out, ladling, or skimming liquids; usu. in the form of a ladle or a concave shovel with a straight handle. Now chiefly *Naut.* and *dial.* **b.** The bucket of a water-wheel or of a dredging or draining machine 1591. **2.** A kind of shovel used for dipping out or shovelling up and carrying materials of a loose nature; usu. an implement of iron, tin, etc. with a short handle and a broad, concave, or curved blade, the part of which next the handle is often covered over to form a receptacle for the material scooped up 1487. **3.** An instrument with a spoon-shaped or gouge-shaped blade, used for cutting out a piece from some soft material, or for removing a core or an embedded substance 1739. **b.** Applied to certain tools used in excavation of soil; hence, the quantity taken up at once by a scoop 1706. **4.** A variety of coal-box, somewhat resembling a flour-scoop in shape 1850.

Comb. **s.-wheel,** [cf. 1 b], a wheel driven by wind or steam for lifting water.

Scoop (skūp), *sb.*[2] 1742. [f. SCOOP *v.*] **1.** The action or an act of scooping. **2.** *concr.* A place scooped or hollowed out; also, a natural hollow resembling this; *rarely*, an artificial basin for water 1762. **3.** *slang.* **a.** orig. *U.S.* An exclusive piece of information for a newspaper 1886. **b.** A lucky stroke of business, a 'haul' 1893.

3. b. Her engagement..at the Palace is a big 's.' 1909.

Scoop (skūp), *v.* ME. [f. SCOOP *sb.*[1]] **1.** *trans.* To ladle or bail out (water) with or as with a scoop. Now *rare.* **2.** To remove or detach (a portion of friable or soft material, etc.) with a scoop, so as to leave a rounded hollow; to rake in as with a scoop. Also, to take *out* (a core, etc.) with or as with a scoop. Also *absol.* 1622. **3.** To hollow *out* with or as with a scoop; to form a concavity or depression in 1708. **4.** To form by scooping or as by scooping. Also with *out.* 1730. **5.** *slang.* **a.** To take or take up in large quantities; to appropriate (something) in advance of or to the exclusion of other competitors 1882. **b.** In journalistic use (orig. *U.S.*). To 'cut out' a rival reporter or editor, or his paper, by obtaining and publishing exclusive or earlier news 1884.

Hence **Scoo·per,** (*a*) one who or that which scoops; (*b*) the avocet, from the shape of its beak.

Scoo·p-net. 1792. [f. SCOOP *sb.*[1] or *v.*] A small long-handled net; a dip-net.

Scoot (skūt), *v. slang* or *colloq.* 1758. [orig. *scout*, which became obs. in early XIX; the present form seems to have been imported later from the U.S.A.; of unkn. origin.] *intr.* To go suddenly and swiftly, to dart; to go away hurriedly.

Scooter (skū·təɹ). 1825. [f. prec. + -ER[1].] **1.** One who 'scoots' or goes hurriedly. **2.** *U.S.* A boat, propelled by sails, capable of being used both on ice and in water 1903. **b.** A fast motor-boat, used in the war of 1914–18. **3.** A child's toy consisting of a narrow flat piece of wood on low wheels, with a steering-handle, propelled by pushing with one foot on the ground; also, a similar machine propelled by a motor 1917.

Scop (skǫp). *Hist.* Often erron. **scóp, scôp.** [Antiquarian revival (with sp.-pronunc.) of OE. *scop*, *sćeop* = OHG. *scof*, *scopf* poet, ON. *skop* mocking, railing. Cf. SCOFF *sb.*[1]] An Old English poet or minstrel.

‖**Scopa** (skōᵘ·pă). 1802. [L., in class. use only in pl. *scopæ* twigs, shoots, a broom or brush.] *Ent.* A bundle or tuft of bristly hairs on the legs of bees, used for collecting pollen; a pollen-brush. Hence **Sco·pate,** having a s.

Scoparin (skōᵘ·părin). 1850. [f. next + -IN[1].] A diuretic principle found in the broom.

‖**Scoparium** (skopēᵊ·riŏm), **Scoparius** (skopēᵊ·riŏs). 1871. [Use of mod.L. specific name.] Pharmacopœial names for the tops of the common broom, *Spartium scoparium* or *Cytisus* (*Sarothamnus*) *scoparius.*

Scope (skōᵘp). 1534. [– It. *scopo* aim, purpose – Gr. σκοπός mark for shooting at, f. σκοπ-, σκεπ-, as in σκοπεῖν observe, aim at, examine, σκέπτεσθαι (see SCEPTIC).] †**1.** A mark for shooting or aiming at –1683. **2.** Something aimed at or desired; an end in view; an object, purpose, aim. Now *rare.* 1555. †**b.** *To s.*: to the purpose. SHAKS. **3.** The main purpose, intention, or drift of a writer, speaker, book, etc. Now *rare.* 1536. **b.** The intention or tendency of a law; the drift or meaning of a proposal 1647. **4.** The range of a missile weapon 1548. **5.** The distance to which the mind reaches in its workings or purpose; reach or range of mental activity; extent of view, outlook, or survey 1600. **b.** The sphere or area over which any activity operates or is effective; the field covered by a branch of knowledge, an inquiry, concept, etc. 1830. **6.** Room for exercise, opportunity or liberty to act; free course or play 1534. †**b.** An instance of liberty or licence. SHAKS. **7.** (With more ref. to *literal* space or motion.) Space or range for free movement or activity 1555. **8.** Extent in space, spaciousness; a (large) space, extent, tract, or area 1590. **9.** *Naut.* The length of cable at which a ship rides when at anchor. Also *riding-s.* 1697.

2. Alas, poor Dean! his only S. Was to be held a Misanthrope SWIFT. **3.** This is the s. of all I say: That by this course the good become best, the bad prove worst 1617. **5.** Desiring this mans art, and that mans skope SHAKS. **b.** Art, if it lost much in purity and propriety, gained in s. 1874. Phr. *Within, beyond* (one's) *s.* **6.** Phr. *To give s.* (*to* a person or thing); *to have, take, s.*; I gave full s. to my imagination STERNE. **7.** Publick virtue.. requires abundant s. and room, and cannot spread and grow under confinement BURKE. **9.** We'll..ride to a short s. 1893. Hence **Sco·peless** *a.* not affording s.

-scope, an ending repr. mod.L. *-scopium* (f. Gr. σκοπεῖν look at, examine) in MICROSCOPE and TELESCOPE. Hence used to form words denoting scientific instruments or contrivances for enabling the eye to view or examine or make observations, as *baroscope*, *gyroscope*, *laryngoscope*, *stethoscope*, etc.

Scopelid (skǫ·pĭlid). 1882. [– mod.L. *Scopelidæ*, f. SCOPELUS; see -ID[3].] A fish of the family *Scopelidæ.*

Scopeloid (skǫ·pĭloid), *sb.* and *a.* 1880. [f. next + -OID.] *Zool.* **A.** *sb.* A fish of the family *Scopelidæ.* **B.** *adj.* Like or pertaining to the *Scopelidæ.*

‖**Scopelus** (skǫ·pĭlŏs). 1840. [mod.L.; introduced by Cuvier in 1817, who gives the etymon as 'σκόπελος, Greek name of an unknown fish'. The Gr. word, however, means a rock.] *Zool.* The typical genus of the family *Scopelidæ.*

Scopiform (skōᵘ·pifǭɹm), *a.* 1794. [f. L. *scopa* SCOPA + -FORM.] *Nat. Hist.* Arranged in bundles; broom-shaped, fascicular.

Scopol- (skopǫ·l), used *Chem.* and *Pharm.* to form names of certain extractive principles obtained from *Scopolia japonica* (Japanese belladonna), as *scopolamine.*

Scopoline (skǫ·pŏlin). 1887. [f. prec. + -INE[5].] *Chem.* A base; $C_8H_{13}O_2N$, obtained from scopolamine and used as a mydriatic.

Scops (skǫps). 1706. [– mod.L. *Scops* (generic name) – Gr. σκώψ the little horned owl.] A genus of *Strigidæ* containing nearly forty species distinguished by plumicorns upon the head; now usu. *s. owl.* Also, a member of this genus, a horn-owl.

†**Sco·ptical,** *a.* 1611. [f. Gr. σκωπτικός, f. σκώπτειν mock, jeer; see -ICAL.] Mocking, satirical –1684. Hence †**Sco·ptically** –1686.

‖**Scopula** (skǫ·piŭlă). 1802. [L. *scopula*, dim. of *scopa* broom, besom; see -ULE.] *Ent.* A small brush-like group of hairs upon the tarsus of bees and spiders. Hence **Sco·pulate** *a.* furnished with or having a s. So **Sco·pulipede** *a.* (of certain bees) having the feet furnished with scopulæ.

Scorbutic (skǫɹbiū·tik), *a.* and *sb.* 1655. [– mod.L. *scorbuticus*, f. med.L. *scorbutus* scurvy, perh. for **scorbucus* – MLG. *schorbūk*, Du. *scheurbuik*, f. MLG., MDu. *schoren* break, lacerate + *būk* (*buik*) belly; cf. Du. †*scheurmond* scurvy of the gums, *scheurbeen* scorbutic affection of the bones.] *Path.* **A.** *adj.* **1.** Of or pertaining to scurvy; symptomatic of or proceeding from scurvy; of the nature of scurvy. Of a patient: Affected with scurvy. †**2.** Of articles of diet, remedies, etc.: Good against scurvy, antiscorbutic –1789. **B.** *sb.* †**1.** An antiscorbutic –1774. **2.** A person affected with scurvy 1855. Hence †**Scorbu·tical** *a.* –1753. †**-ly** *adv.* –1676.

‖**Scorbutus** (skǫɹbiū·tŏs). 1866. [med.L.; see prec.] *Path.* Scurvy.

Scorch (skǭɹtʃ), *sb.* 1611. [f. next.] **1.** A mark or impression produced by scorching. **2.** Scorching effect (of the sun or fire) 1646. **3.** An act of 'scorching'; a rapid run on a cycle or motor-car 1885.

Scorch (skǭɹtʃ), *v.*[1] late ME. [rel. obscurely to †*skorkle* (Chaucer), frequent. of **skorke* (cf. *scorrcnenn* in 'Ormulum', which may be – ON. *skorpna* be shrivelled).] **1.** *trans.* To heat to such a degree as to shrivel, parch, or dry up, or to char or discolour the surface; to burn superficially. **b.** *transf.* To shrivel up as if by heat 1600. **c.** *intr.* for *pass.* To be parched, etc. with heat 1707. **2.** *intr.* To cycle or motor at excessive speed. [Cf. Fr. *brûler le pavé.*] 1885.

1. Power was giuen vnto him to s. men with fire *Rev.* 16:8. Summer drouth, or singed air Never s.

thy tresses fair MILT. Hence **Sco·rching** *ppl. a.* that scorches; **-ly** *adv.*

†**Scorch,** *v.*[2] 1550. [alt. f. SCORE *v.*, perh. after *scratch.* Cf. SCOTCH *v.*[1]] *trans.* To slash as with a knife –1656.

We have scorch'd the snake, not kill'd it SHAKS.

Scorched (skǭɹtʃt), *ppl. a.* 1593. [f. SCORCH *v.*[1] + -ED[1].] **1.** Burnt and discoloured by heat, touched by fire 1595. **2.** Parched by the sun 1593. **3.** *Nat. Hist.* Having colouring resembling a scorch 1832.

2. Like to a Lyon of scortcht desart Affricke MARLOWE.

Scorcher (skǭ·ɹtʃəɹ). 1874. [f. as prec. + -ER[1].] One who or that which scorches; *esp.* (*colloq.* or *slang*) a very hot day, one who cycles or motors furiously, a scathing rebuke or attack.

‖**Scordatura** (skordatū·ra). 1876. [It., f. *scordare* be out of tune.] *Mus.* An alteration in the manner of tuning some stringed instruments in order to produce particular effects.

Score (skōᵊɹ), *sb.* [Late OE. **scoru*, pl. *scora, -e* – ON. *skor* notch, tally, twenty :– **skurō*, f. **skur-* **sker-* cut, SHEAR.] **I.** A cut, notch, mark. **1.** †A crack, crevice; a cut, notch, or scratch; a line drawn with a sharp instrument. late ME. **b.** *Naut.* and *Mech.* (*a*) The groove of a block or dead-eye round which the rope passes; (*b*) a notch or groove made in a piece of timber or metal to allow another piece to be neatly fitted into it 1794. **2.** A line drawn; a stroke, mark; a line drawn as a boundary. Now *rare.* ME. **3.** *spec.* The 'scratch' or line at which a marksman stands when shooting at a target, or on which the competitors stand before beginning a race 1513. **4.** *Mus.* A written or printed piece of concerted music, in which all the vocal or instrumental parts are noted on a series of staves one under the other 1701. **b.** A musical composition with its distribution of parts 1881.

2. Draw a s. through the tops of your t's SCOTT. **3.** Phr. *To go off* (*set off, start*) *at s.*, of a horse, etc., to make a sudden dash at full speed; *fig.* of a person, to break out suddenly into impetuous speech or action; so *to go off full s.*

II. Notch cut for record, tally, reckoning. †**1.** A notch cut in a stick or tally, used to mark numbers in keeping accounts; also the tally itself –1593. †**b.** *Games.* A mark made for the purpose of recording a point or the like –1801. **2.** A record or account (of items of uniform amount to be charged or credited) kept by means of tallies, or (in later use) by means of marks made on a board (with chalk), on a slate, or the like. Hence occas. *transf.*, a customer's account for goods obtained on credit. late ME. **3.** The sum recorded to a customer's debit in a 'score'; the amount of an innkeeper's bill or reckoning 1600. **4.** [Orig. a fig. use of sense II. 2.] Account, reason, ground, sake, motive. In phrases *on, upon the s.* (*of*). 1651. †**5.** A list, enumeration; number as counted –1596. **6.** *Games.* The record or register of points made by both sides during the progress of a game or match; also the number of points made by a side or individual 1742. **7.** *colloq.* [from the vb.] **a.** *lit.* in games: An act of 'scoring' or gaining a point or points. **b.** *fig.* A successful 'hit' in debate or argument. 1844.

1. 2 *Hen. VI*, IV. vii. 38. **2.** There shall bee no mony, all shall eate and drinke on my s. SHAKS. **3.** After he scores, he neuer payes the s. SHAKS. Phr. *To clear, pay, quit a s.*, or *scores*, to requite an obligation; sometimes, to revenge an injury. **4.** Men..began to be over-easie upon that S. DE FOE. **6.** Phr. *To make a s. off one's own bat*, with ref. to a s. made by a player's own hits; *fig.* solely by his own exertions, by himself.

III. A group of twenty. [app. from the practice, in counting sheep, etc., of counting orally from 1 to 20, and making a 'score' or notch on a stick, before proceeding to count the next twenty.] **1.** A group or set of twenty. Primarily a sb., const. *of* (in OE. *gen. pl.*), but often serving as a numeral adj. OE. **2.** A weight of twenty or twenty-one pounds, esp. used in weighing pigs or oxen 1460. †**3.** A distance of twenty paces –1672.

1. Shee may perhaps call him halfe a s. knaues, or so SHAKS. There were a s. of generals now round Becky's chair THACKERAY. **3.** As easie, as a Canon will shoot point-blanke twelue s. SHAKS.

attrib. and *Comb.*: **s.-board,** (*a*) a blackboard in a public-house, on which debts are chalked up; (*b*) in *Cricket*, a large board erected so as to be seen by the onlookers, on which the s. of the game is kept; **-book,** a book for preserving the scores of games; **-card,** a printed card with a blank form on which to enter the s. in a game of cricket, etc.; **-game** *Golf*, a game decided by strokes (opp. to *match-game*, which is decided by holes); also in *Lawn Tennis.*

Score (skōᵊɹ), *v.* late ME. [Partly – ON. *skora* make an incision, count by tallies, f. *skor* (see prec.); partly f. the Eng. sb.] **I.** To cut, mark with incisions. **1.** *trans.* To cut superficially; to make scores or cuts in; to mark with incisions, notches, or abrasions of the skin. **b.** *spec.* in *Cookery.* To make long parallel cuts upon (meat, etc.) 1460. †**c.** To mark by cuts of a whip. Also *absol.* –1806. **d.** *Geol.* To mark with scratches or furrows; said esp. with ref. to glacial action 1862. **2.** To produce (marks, figures, etc.) by cutting. Also, to record or express by cuts or notches. 1590. **3.** *Naut.* To make a 'score' or groove in; to fix by means of a 'score' 1779. **4.** *U.S.* To rate, scold severely 1891.

1. Trees..scored by the axe 1824. **c.** Let vs s. their backes SHAKS. **d.** All around the rocks are carved, and fluted, and polished, and scored TYNDALL.

II. 1. To mark with a line or lines. late ME. †**b.** To mark *out* (a path, boundary) –1712. **2.** To draw a line through (writing, etc.) in order to cancel. Often with *out.* 1687. **3.** *Mus.* **a.** To write down in score. **b.** To compose or arrange for orchestral performance. 1839.

1. Passages had been scored in his favourite books THACKERAY.

III. To record by scores. **1.** To record (debts) by means of notches on a tally; hence, to write down as a debt. Also with *up.* late ME. †**2.** *intr.* To run up a score; to obtain drink, goods, etc. on credit –1779. **b.** *trans.* To add (an item) to one's score 1681. **3.** To enter as a debtor. Also with *up.* 1592. †**b.** To placard as an offender –1596. **4.** To record the number of (anything) by notches or marks; to count and set down the number of (e.g. sheep). Also with *up.* late ME. **5.** In a game or contest: To set down in the score. Chiefly in *pass.* 1742. **b.** *absol.* or *intr.* To record the points in a game or contest, to act as scorer 1846. **6.** *trans.* Of a player or competitor: To add (so many points) to one's score. Also said of an incident in the game: To count for (so many points) in a player's score. 1742. **b.** *intr.* To make points in a game or contest: said of a player or competitor; also, of a card or an incident in the game 1844. **c.** To be reckoned in a score 1885. **7.** *transf.* and *fig.* (chiefly *colloq.*) **a.** *trans.* To gain, win (a success, etc.) 1883. **b.** *intr.* To achieve a success; to make a hit. *To s. off* (a person): to make a point at the expense of. 1882.

1. *fig.* Nor need I tallies thy dear love to s. SHAKS. **3. b.** *Tam. Shr.* Induct. ii. 25. **5. b.** Mr. Whittaker ..accompanied Mr. Mynn, and scored for him 1846. **6.** My first stroke scored three 1856. *To s. a miss*: see MISS *sb.*[1] III. 1. **c.** The hazard scores to the striker 1885. **7.** She felt that she had scored the first success in the encounter 1883.

IV. *intr.* To 'go off at score' (see SCORE *sb.* I. 3) 1858.

Scorer (skōᵊ·reɹ). late ME. [f. prec. + -ER[1].] One who or that which scores; *esp.* one who records the score in a game or contest.

‖**Scoria** (skōᵊ·riă). *Pl.* **scoriæ** (skōᵊ·riˌī) and (occas.) **sco·rias.** late ME. [L. – Gr. σκωρία, f. σκῶρ dung.] **1.** The slag or dross remaining after the smelting out of a metal from its ore. **2.** Rough clinker-like masses formed by the cooling of the surface of molten lava upon exposure to the air, and distended by the expansion of imprisoned gases 1792. Hence **Sco·riac, Scoria·ceous** *adjs.*

Scorification (skōᵊ:rifikēˈ·ʃən). 1754. [f. SCORIFY; see -FICATION.] The process of reducing to scoria, formation of scoria or slag; *spec.* as a method of refining or assay.

Scorifier (skōᵊ·rifəiəɹ). 1758. [f. SCORIFY + -ER[1].] A vessel of fire-clay used in the process of purifying metals in assaying.

Scoriform (skōᵊ·rifǭɹm), *a.* 1794. [f. SCORIA + -FORM.] Having the form of, resembling, scoria.

Scorify (skōᵊ·rifəi), *v.* 1754. [f. SCORIA + -FY.] **1.** *trans.* To reduce to scoria or slag. **2.** To convert (lava) into scoria 1852.

Scoring (skōᵊ·riŋ), *vbl. sb.* 1546. [f. SCORE *v.* + -ING[1].] **1.** The action of SCORE *v.*; an instance of this. **2.** *concr.* Lines or figures scored 1688.

attrib. **s.-board** = SCORE-*board* (*b*); **-book** = SCORE-*book*; etc.

Scorious (skōᵊ·riəs), *a.* 1646. [f. SCORIA + -OUS.] Of the nature of scoria; abounding in scoria.

Scorn (skǭ·ɹn), *sb.* ME. [– OFr. *escarn*, corresp. to Pr. *esquern*, etc., f. the verbs (see next).] **1.** Mockery, derision, contempt; in mod. use, indignant or passionate contempt. **2.** A manifestation of contempt; a derisive utterance or gesture; a taunt, an insult. *arch.* ME. **3.** †**a.** Matter for scorn, something contemptible. **b.** An object of mockery or contempt. ME.

1. Disdaine and Scorne ride sparkling in her eyes, Mis-prizing what they looke on SHAKS. A Briton's s. of arbitrary chains COWPER. **2.** Do but..marke the Fleeres, the Gybes, and notable Scornes That dwell in euery Region of his face SHAKS. **3.** Made of my enemies the s. and gaze MILT.

Phrases. *To laugh to s.*: see LAUGH *v.* 3. *To speak s. of*, to revile. *To think s. of*, to despise. *To think* (*it*) *s.* (now *arch.* and *literary*), to disdain (const. *that* or *inf.*).

Scorn (skǭɹn), *v.* [ME. *scarne, scorne*, aphetic – OFr. *escharnir, eschernir* :– Rom. **escarnire*, **eskernire* – Gmc. **skarnjan*, **skernjan*, f. base of OS. *skern*, etc., jest, mockery.] †**1.** *intr.* To speak or behave contemptuously; to use derisive language, jeer –1816. †**2.** *trans.* To treat with ridicule, to show extreme contempt for, to mock, deride –1631. **3.** To hold in disdain, to contemn, despise ME. **4.** With *inf.* as obj. To feel it beneath one, disdain indignantly *to* do something 1605.

1. She gecked and scorned at my northern speech and habit SCOTT. **3.** Heav'n has no Rage, like Love to Hatred turn'd, Nor Hell a Fury, like a Woman scorn'd CONGREVE. *fig.* Where lawns extend that s. Arcadian pride GOLDSM. **4.** The congress scorned to receive them BURKE. Hence **Sco·rner,** one who scorns; esp. one who scoffs at religion; *seat* (*chair, stool*) *of the scorner*, the position of a mocker (cf. Ps. 1:1).

Scornful (skǭ·ɹnfŭl), *a.* late ME. [f. SCORN *sb.* + -FUL 1.] **1.** Full of scorn, contemptuous, derisive. Also *absol.* †**2.** Regarded with scorn, contemptible –1624.

1. Blessed is yᵉ man, yᵗ..sytteth not in yᵉ seate of the scornefull COVERDALE *Ps.* 1:1. And dart not scornefull glances from those eies SHAKS. The English Muse..S. of Earth and Clouds, should reach the Skies PRIOR. **2.** The scornefull marke of euerie open eye SHAKS. Hence **Sco·rnful-ly** *adv.*, **-ness.**

Scorodite (skǫ·rŏdəit). 1823. [– G. *skorodit*, f. Gr. σκόροδον garlic (so called from its odour when heated); see -ITE[1] 2 b.] *Min.* Hydrous phosphate of iron, found in pale-green or brown crystals and crusts.

‖**Scorpæna** (skǫɹpī·nă). 1706. [L. – Gr. σκόρπαινα a kind of fish; app. irreg. fem. f. σκορπίος SCORPION.] In early use, applied vaguely to various prickly fishes, chiefly of the families *Scorpænidæ* and *Cottidæ*. Now only as the name of a genus of acanthopterygian fishes; the typical genus of the family *Scorpænidæ*. Hence **Scorpæ·nid,** a fish of the family *Scorpænidæ*. **Scorpæ·noid** *a.* of or pertaining to the *Scorpænidæ*; *sb.* a scorpænoid fish.

Scorpene (skǫ·ɹpīn). 1777. [Anglicized f. prec.] = prec.; now only *U.S.*, the species *Scorpæna guttata.*

Scorper (skǫ·ɹpəɹ). 1843. [A misspelling of *scauper*; see SCALPER[1].] *Wood-* and *Metal-work.* A gouging tool for working in a depression. Also = SCALPER[2] 2.

‖**Scorpio** (skǫ·ɹpio). late ME. [L.; see SCORPION.] *Astr.* A zodiacal constellation, the Scorpion. Also, the eighth sign of the zodiac, named from this; situated between Libra and Sagittarius, and entered by the sun about 23 October.

Scorpioid (skǫ·ɹpioid), *a.* and *sb.* 1839. [– Gr. σκορπιοειδής, f. σκορπίος SCORPION; see -OID.] **A.** *adj.* **1.** *Bot. S. cyme*, a unilateral cyme the undeveloped portion of which is circinate. **2.** *Zool.* **a.** Resembling a scorpion; belonging to the scorpion family. **b.** Resembling the tail of a scorpion. 1864. **B.** *sb.* **1.** *Bot.* A circinate inflorescence 1855. **2.** *Zool.* A scorpion or scorpion-like animal 1887. So **Scorpioi·dal** *a.* = SCORPIOID *a.* 1. 1835.

Scorpion (skǭ·ɹpiən). ME. [– (O)Fr. *scorpion* :– L. *scorpio, -ōn-*, extension of *scorpius* :– Gr. σκορπίος.] **1.** An arachnid of any of the genera (*Scorpio, Buthus, Androctonus*, etc.) forming the group *Scorpionidæ*, having a pair of large nippers and a general resemblance to a miniature lobster; they inhabit tropical and warm temperate countries in both hemispheres. The intense pain caused by the sting of the scorpion (situated at the point of the tail) is proverbial. **b.** *Her.* A representation of a scorpion as an armorial bearing 1780. **c.** Applied to other animals resembling or popularly confounded with the scorpion; e.g. in the U.S., to tarantulas, centipedes, various lizards, etc. 1709. **2.** *Astr.* The constellation and (now somewhat rarely) the zodiacal sign SCORPIO. late ME. **3.** In Australia and America, the local name for certain species of *Scorpænidæ* 1874. **4.** A kind of whip made of knotted cords, or armed with plummets of lead or steel spikes, so as to inflict excessive pain (cf. 1 Kings 12:11 and 2 Chron. 10:11). late ME. **b.** Hence quasi-*Hist.* as the name of a supposed ancient instrument of torture. Also *Antiq.* as the name of a mediæval weapon. 1541. **5.** (tr. Gr. σκορπίος, L. *scorpio, scorpius.*) An ancient military engine for hurling missiles, used chiefly in the defence of the walls of a town. late ME.

1. *fig.* O, full of Scorpions is my Minde SHAKS. **4.** My fader beet ȝou with scourgis, I forsothe schal beten ȝou with scorpiouns WYCLIF 2 *Chron.* 10:11. Back to thy punishment, False fugitive, and to thy speed add wings, Least with a whip of Scorpions I pursue Thy lingring MILT.

attrib. and *Comb.*: **s.-bug** *U.S.*, the water-scorpion; **s. fish,** any spiny fish of the genus *Scorpæna* or family *Scorpænidæ*; **-fly,** an insect of the family *Panorpidæ*, the slender abdomen of which is armed with forceps, and curls like the tail of a s.: **s. senna,** the *Coronilla emerus*, a common plant of Southern Europe, with bright-yellow flowers; **-shell,** a gastropod of the Indian seas and Pacific, of the genus *Pteroceras*, having a development of long tubular spines from the outer lip of the aperture; **-spider,** any arachnidan of the order *Pedipalpi*; **scorpion's tail,** any plant of the genus *Scorpiurus*; **scorpion('s thorn,** a plant of South-western Europe, *Genista scorpius*; **-wort** (*a*) = SCORPION GRASS; (*b*) *Ornithopus scorpioides*, native of Southern Europe.

Scorpion grass. 1578. A plant of the genus *Myosotis*, the forget-me-not or mouse-ear.

Scorpionid (skǭ·ɹpionid), *a.* 1895. [f. mod.L. *Scorpionidæ*, f. L. *scorpio, -ōn-*; see -ID[3].] Of or pertaining to the group *Scorpionidæ* of arachnidans, typified by the genus *Scorpio.*

Scorse (skǭɹs), *v.* Now *dial.* 1509. [Early XVI *scose, scorse*, related to COSS, CORSE *vbs.*] *trans.* and *intr.* To barter or exchange. Hence **Sco·rser.**

Scortation (skǫɹtēⁱ·ʃən). *rare.* 1556. [– late and med.L. *scortatio*, f. *scortat-*, pa. ppl. stem of L. *scortari* associate with harlots, f. *scortum* harlot; see -ION.] Fornication. So **Sco·rtatory** *a.* (*rare*).

Scorzonera (skǭɹzonīᵊ·ră). 1629. [– It. *scorzonera*, f. *scorzone* :– Rom. **scurtione*, alt. of med.L. *curtio, -ōn-* poisonous snake, for whose venom the plant may have been an antidote.] A plant of the modern genus *Scorzonera*, esp. *S. hispanica* or black salsify, much cultivated in Europe for its root which somewhat resembles the parsnip.

Scot[1] (skǫt). [OE. **Scot*, only in pl. *Scottas* – late L. *Scottus* (c400), whence also OHG. *Scotto* (G. *Schotte*). The regular med.L. form was *Scōtus*. Ult. origin unknown.] **1.** *Hist.* One of an ancient Gaelic-speaking people, first known to history as inhabitants of Ireland, who in the 6th century A.D. settled in the north-west of Great Britain, and from whom the northern part of the island ultimately received its name. **2.** A native of Scotland, a Scotchman ME.

Scot[2] (skǫt). ME. [In ME. partly – ON. *skot* (= OE. *scot* SHOT *sb.*[1]), partly aphetic – OFr. *escot* (mod. *écot*), of Gmc. origin; in later use to some extent an antiquarian revival of the OE. form (cf. SCOP).] **1.** A payment, contribution, 'reckoning'; esp. payment for entertainment; a or one's share of such payment; chiefly in the phr. *to pay (for) one's s. lit.* and *fig.* †**2.** A custom paid to the use of a sheriff or bailiff; a local or municipal tax –1646. **3.** *spec.* A tax levied on the inhabitants of the marshes and levels of Kent and Sussex 1793.

Phr. *S. and lot* (earlier *lot and s.*), a tax levied by a municipal corporation in proportionate shares upon its members for the defraying of municipal expenses. *To pay* (a person *off*) *lot and s.*, (fig.) to pay out thoroughly, to settle with.

Sco·tale, sco·t-ale. *Obs.* exc. *Hist.* ME. [f. SCOT[2] + ALE.] An 'ale' or festival at which ale was drunk at the invitation of the lord of the manor or a forester or other bailiff, for which ale a forced contribution was levied.

Scotch (skǫtʃ), *sb.*[1] 1450. [f. SCOTCH *v.*[1]] **1.** An incision, cut, score or gash. **2.** *spec.* A line scored or marked upon the ground, in the game of HOPSCOTCH 1677.

Scotch (skǫtʃ), *sb.*[2] 1601. [occas. *skatch*, which may indicate identity with *scatch*, (XVI) stilt – OFr. *escache*, whence Du. *schaats* SKATE *sb.*[2]] A block placed under a wheel, a cask, or the like, to prevent moving or slipping.

Scotch (skǫtʃ), *a.* and *sb.*[3] 1591. [contr. var. of SCOTTISH.] **A.** *adj.* **1.** Of persons: Of, belonging to, or native to, Scotland 1606. **b.** Characteristic of Scotland or its people 1815. **2.** Of things: Of or pertaining to Scotland or its inhabitants 1591. **b.** As the epithet of various weights and measures, etc. (differing from the English standard) used formerly in Scotland 1774. **3.** As the designation of the variety of northern English which is vernacular in Scotland. Hence of words, idioms, etc., belonging to this, and of works composed in it. 1730.

1. He had no S. blood in him that I know of 1894. *S. cousin*, a distant relative (in allusion to the practice in Scotland of tracing kinship to remote degrees). **2. b.** *S. acre*, 6,084 square yards. *S. ell*, 37·0958 inches. **3.** To secure the adherence of stout, able-bodied, and, as the S. phrase then went, *pretty* men SCOTT.

Special collocations. **S. bonnet** (see BONNET *sb.* 1); **S. collops** (see COLLOP[1] 2); **S. fir** (see FIR 1); **S. marriage** (see MARRIAGE 2); **S. mist** (see MIST *sb.*[1] 1); **S. pebble** (see PEBBLE *sb.* 2 b); **S. spur** *Her.*, a bearing representing a prick spur; **S. terrier** (see TERRIER[2]); **S. woodcock** (see WOODCOCK 3 c).

b. In names of plants: **S. broom,** *U.S.*, the common broom; **S. kale,** a variety of borecole with less wrinkled leaves, of a purplish colour; **S. pine** (see PINE *sb.*[2] 2); **S. thistle,** a species of thistle (*Onopordon acanthium*), regarded as the national emblem of the Scotch.

B. *sb.* [The adj. used ellipt.] **1.** *The S.* (pl.): The inhabitants of Scotland or their immediate descendants in other countries 1781. **2.** The Scotch language: see A. 3. 1700. **3.** Often *ellipt.*, e.g. for *S. whisky*; also = a glass of S. whisky. Also formerly for *S. snuff.* 1823.

2. I can read French as well as I can English, but it is impossible for me to comprehend S. 1896. **3.** Two bitters and a small S. 1893.

Scotch (skǫtʃ), *v.*[1] late ME. [Of unkn. origin.] †**1.** *trans.* To make an incision or incisions in; to cut, score, gash –1747. **2.** [From Theobald's emendation of *scorch'd* in Shaks. *Macb.* III. ii. 13.] To inflict such hurt upon (something regarded as dangerous) that it is rendered temporarily harmless 1798. **b.** To crush, stamp upon, stamp out (something dangerous) 1825.

1. S. with your knife the back of the Carp 1675. **2.** The snake must be killed not scotched 1798. Hence **Scotched** *ppl. a.* cut, scarred; also in *scotched collops*, etymologizing perversion of SCOTCH *collops.*

Scotch (skǫtʃ), *v.*[2] 1601. [f. SCOTCH *sb.*[2]] **1.** *trans.* To block or wedge (a wheel, log, gate, etc.) so as to keep from moving or slipping 1642. **2.** *intr.* (Chiefly w. neg.) To hesitate, scruple, boggle, or stick *at*; to hesitate *to do* something. *Obs.* exc. *dial.* 1601.

1. *fig.* I scotched the project of retreat for this council, at any rate 1897.

Scotch cap. 1591. A man's head-dress made of thick firm woollen cloth, without a brim, and decorated with two tails or streamers.

Scotch-Irish, *a.* 1876. Belonging to that part of the population of northern Ireland which is descended from Scotch settlers. Also *absol.* in pl. sense.

Scotchman (skǫ·tʃmæ̆n). 1570. [f. SCOTCH *a.* + MAN.] **1.** A man of Scottish nationality. (The usual English form. Cf. SCOTSMAN.) **b.** (Also *Flying S.*, (*Flying*) *Scotsman.*) A familiar name for the Scotch express (London to Edinburgh) on the London and North Eastern Railway 1874. **2.** *Naut.* A piece of hide, wood, or iron, etc. placed over a rope to prevent its being chafed 1841. **3.** *S. Afr.* A florin 1879. So **Sco·tchwo:man,** a woman who is a native of Scotland or of Scotch descent.

Scoter (skōᵘ·təɹ). 1674. [Of unkn. origin.] A duck of the genus *Œdemia*, esp. *Œ. nigra*, a native of the Arctic regions and common in the seas of northern Europe and America. Also *s.-duck.*

Scot-free, *a.* ME. [f. SCOT *sb.*[2] + FREE *a.*] Free from payment of 'scot', tavern score, fine, etc.; exempt from injury, punishment, etc.; scatheless. Almost always *predic.*

Oxford escaped scot fre of the plague WOOD.

‖**Scotia** (skōᵘ·ʃiă). 1563. [L. – Gr. σκοτία, f. σκότος darkness (so called from the dark shadow within the cavity).] *Arch.* = CASEMENT 1.

Scotic (skǫ·tik), *a.* 1645. [– late and med.L. *Scoticus*; see SCOT[1], -IC.] †**1.** *absol.* The Scottish dialect. **2.** Pertaining to the ancient Scots 1796.

Scotist (skōᵘ·tist), *sb.* and *a.* 1530. [– med.L. *Scotista*, f. *Scotus*, proper name; see -IST.] *Eccl.* **A.** *sb.* A follower of John Duns Scotus (known as 'the Subtle Doctor'), a scholastic philosopher and theologian of the 13th c., whose system in many respects was opposed to that of Thomas Aquinas. **B.** *adj.* Belonging to the Scotists. So **Sco·tism,** the teaching of Scotus or the Scotists.

Scotland Yard (skǫ·tlănd yā·ɹd). Name of a short street off Whitehall, London, until 1890 the head-quarters of the Metropolitan Police Force, now at New Scotland Yard on the Thames Embankment; hence, the force itself, *esp.* the detective department.

Scoto- (skǫ·to, skōᵘ·to), comb. form of late L. *Scotus* SCOT *sb.*[1], as in *S.-Britannic, -Irish, -Scandinavian*, adjs.

Scotography (skotǫ·grăfi). *rare.* 1896. [f. Gr. σκότος darkness; see -GRAPHY.] = RADIOGRAPHY. Hence **Scotogra·phic** *a.*

‖**Scotoma** (skotōᵘ·mă). *Pl.* **scotomata** (skotōᵘ·mătă). 1543. [late L. – Gr. σκότωμα dizziness, f. σκοτοῦν darken, f. σκότος darkness.] *Path.* †**1.** Dizziness accompanied by dimness of sight –1829. **2.** An obscuration of part of the visual field, due to lesion of the retina or of the ophthalmic centres in the brain 1875. So †**Sco·tomy** = sense 1. –1710.

†**Sco·toscope.** 1664. [f. Gr. σκότος darkness + -SCOPE.] An instrument which enables the user to see in the dark –1670.

Scots (skǫts), *a.* (*sb.*) ME. [orig. *Scottis*, northern var. of SCOTTISH.] **1.** Of or belonging to Scotland or its inhabitants, Scottish, Scotch. **b.** Qualifying the name of a coin or money of account (in contradistinction to *sterling*), as *pound S., shilling S.* Also in names of weights and measures denoting a particular variation from the English standard. *arch.* or *Hist.* 1520. **c.** With ref. to law 1766. **d.** In the names of trees and plants (more commonly SCOTCH) 1710. **2.** Of language: The distinguishing epithet of the dialect of English spoken by the inhabitants of the Lowlands of Scotland. Also *absol.* as *sb.*, the Scottish dialect. 1542. **3.** *Mil.* In names of regiments in the British army, as *S. Fusiliers, S. Guards* 1637.

2. Kilted loons that dinna ken the name o' a single herb..in braid S., let abee in the Latin tongue SCOTT. **3.** *S. Greys*: see GREY *sb.* 8.

Scotsman (skǫ·tsmæ̆n). late ME. [f. SCOTS *a.* + MAN *sb.*] = SCOTCHMAN. (The prevalent form used now by Scotch people.) So **Sco·tswoman** = SCOTCHWOMAN.

‖**Scotticè, Scoticè** (skǫ·tisi), *adv.* 1818. [med.L.] In Scotch.

Scotticism, Scoticism (skǫ·tisiz'm). 1717. [f. late L. *Scoticus* (*Scotticus*) + -ISM 3.] **1.** An idiom or mode of expression characteristic of Scots; esp. as used by a writer of English. **2.** Scottish sympathies 1807.

2. He seems to me a remarkably good critic, where his Scoticism doesn't come in his way 1862.

Scotticize (skǫ·tisəiz), *v.* 1763. [f. as prec. + -IZE.] **1.** *trans.* To imbue with Scottish ideas or characteristics. **2.** To give a Scottish form to (a foreign word); to turn (a work) into Scottish dialect 1874.

Scottish (skǫ·tiʃ), *a.* and *sb.* ME. [repl. OE. *Scyttisc*, after SCOT[1]; see -ISH[1].] **A.** *adj.* **1.** Of or belonging to Scotland or to the people of Scotland; of Scotch nationality, birth, or descent. **b.** With ref. to law 1726. †**2.** *transf.* Marked by Scottish characteristics –1620. **3.** Applied to the language (see SCOTS *a.* 2) 1718.

1. The King's Own S. Borderers 1888.

B. *sb.* (the adj. used absol.) **1.** The Scottish language 1708. **2.** *The S.* (with pl. sense): the Scots (*rare*) 1632.

Scoundrel (skau·ndrəl), *sb.* and *a.* 1589. [Of unkn. origin.] **A.** *sb.* 'A mean rascal, a low petty villain' (J.). Now usu., an audacious rascal, one destitute of all moral scruple. Also *attrib.* and *appositive*.

If your ancient, but ignoble blood Has crept thro' scoundrels ever since the flood POPE.

B. *adj.* Now *rare.* **1.** Of a person: That is a scoundrel; scoundrelly. Of a company: Composed of scoundrels. 1643. **2.** Pertaining to or characteristic of a scoundrel. Of conduct: Mean, unprincipled. 1681.

2. 'A penny savèd is a penny got'—Firm to this s. maxim keepeth he THOMSON. Hence **Scou·ndreldom,** the world of scoundrels, scoundrels collectively; also = *scoundrelism.* **Scou·ndrelism,** the character, conduct, or practices of a s.; also, a piece of scoundrelism. **Scou·ndrelly** *a.* having the character of a s.; of, belonging to, or characteristic of a s.; characterized by scoundrelism.

Scour (skauᵊɹ), *sb.* 1619. [f. SCOUR *v.*[2]] **1.** An apparatus for washing auriferous soil. **2.** The action of a current or flow of water in clearing away mud or other deposit; in *Civil Engineering*, an artificial current or flow produced for this purpose; also, an engineering work constructed for the purpose of producing such a current 1729. **3.** A place in a river where the bottom is scoured by the stream; a river-shallow with a gravel bottom 1681. **4.** A kind of diarrhœa in cattle 1764. **5.** An act of scouring, cleansing, or polishing 1825.

Scour (skauᵊɹ), *v.*[1] ME. [Of unkn. origin.] **1.** *intr.* To move *about* hastily or energetically; *esp.* to range about in search of something, or in movements against a foe. **b.** To move rapidly, go in haste, run ME. **2.** *trans.* To pass rapidly over or along (a tract of land or water); *esp.* to traverse in quest of something, or in order to capture or drive away a foe. late ME. †**3.** *spec.* in 17th–18th c. slang (cf. SCOURER[1] 2). **a.** *intr.* To roam about at night uproariously, breaking windows, beating the watch, and molesting wayfarers –1756. **b.** *trans.* To ill-treat or 'maul' (the watch, wayfarers, etc.) while roistering in the streets –1723.

1. Sirra go you and scoure about the hill HEYWOOD. **b.** I..scoured on my way with more speed than before BORROW. **2.** Patrols..s. the streets, all that night CARLYLE. **3. b.** Scowring the Watch grows out of fashion wit DRYDEN.

Scour (skauᵊɹ), *v.*[2] late ME. [– MLG., MDu. *schūren* – Fr. *escurer* (mod. *écurer* clean, scour) :– late L. *excurare* (med.L. (*e*)*scurare*), f. L. *ex* EX-[1] + *curare* take care of, med.L. clean, f. *cura* CURE.] **1.** *trans.* To cleanse or polish (metal, earthenware, wood, etc.) by hard rubbing with some detergent substance. Sometimes with compl. adj., as *bright, clean*, etc. Also const. *of, from* (rust, etc.). Also *absol.* or *intr.* **b.** To clean the inside of (a gun) after firing 1611. **2.** To remove grease or dirt from (cloth, wool, silk, etc.) by some detergent process. Also *absol.* 1467. **3.** To wash vigorously (the hands, face, teeth); to 'scrub'. Now only *joc.* 1589. **4.** To cleanse (a wound, ulcer, the entrails of an animal) by treating with some medicament. late ME. **5.** To clear out (a channel, ditch, drain, etc.) by removing dirt, weeds, etc. late ME. **6.** To clear out or cleanse by flushing with water 1587. **7.** To purge (an animal, a person, the body, etc.); to evacuate (the stomach or bowels). Also, to cleanse (worms, fish, etc.) by purging. late ME. **b.** *intr.* (for *refl.*) To be purged. Of cattle: To have diarrhœa. 1592. **8.** *fig.* To rid, clear (a place, the sea, etc.) *of* or *from* an enemy or other undesirable occupants ME. †**9.** *fig.* To beat, scourge. Hence, to punish, treat severely. –1730. **10.** To sweep or rake (a place, position, etc.) with gun-shot. Also, to command (a position) with one's guns. 1563. **11.** To remove, get rid of. Chiefly with advs., as *away, off, out.* late ME.

1. *absol.* Item, she can wash and scoure SHAKS. **2.** *absol.* Warme Water scoureth better than Cold BACON. **4.** Take your eel and s. it well with salt MRS. GLASSE. **5.** Working hard to s. their moats DE FOE. **9.** But I will pay the dog, I will s. him FIELDING. **11.** The stains will not easily (if at all) be scoured off again 1631. The tide enters far up each channel, scouring out mud and sand 1849. Hence **Scoured** (skauᵊɹd) *ppl. a.* in various senses; also *sb.* (*Austral.*) = scoured wool.

Scourer[1] (skauᵊ·rəɹ). late ME. [In sense 1 *scoverour* (XV), aphetic f. *descoverour* – OFr. *descouvreor*, f. *descouvrir* DISCOVER; afterwards as agent-n. f. SCOUR *v.*[1] + -ER[1].] †**1.** One sent out to reconnoitre; a scout or avant-courier –1826. **2.** In the 17th–18th c.: One who made a practice of roistering through the streets at night, beating the watch, breaking windows, etc. 1672.

Scourer[2] (skauᵊ·rəɹ). late ME. [f. SCOUR *v.*[2] + -ER[1].] **1.** One who cleanses by rubbing; esp. as the designation of certain servants in the Royal Household 1576. **2.** A person or thing which cleans or scours; *spec.* †a contrivance for cleaning out the bore of a gun. late ME.

Scourge (skɔ̄ɹdʒ), *sb.* ME. [Aphetic f. OFr. *escurge, escorge*, f. *escorgier*; see next.] **1.** A whip, lash. Now only *rhet.* **2.** *fig.* and in fig. context; chiefly, a thing or person that is an instrument of divine chastisement. late ME. **3. a.** A cause of (usu., widespread) calamity. **b.** One who 'lashes' vice or folly. 1535. †**4.** [After L. *flagellum.*] An offshoot of a vine or other tree, a sucker –1578.

1. Mortify Your flesh, like me, with scourges and with thorns TENNYSON. **2.** *The S. of God* (= L. *flagellum Dei*): a title given by historians to Attila, the leader of the Huns in the 5th century. **3. a.** Raleigh, the s. of Spain! THOMSON. **b.** Swift, that severe s. of the vices and follies of his time 1756.

Scourge (skɔ̄ɹdʒ), *v.* ME. [– OFr. *escorgier* :– Rom. *excorrigiare, f. *ex* EX-[1] + L. *corrigia* thong, whip.] **1.** *trans.* To beat with a scourge; to whip severely, flog. Now *rhet.* **b.** To drive or force by or as by blows of a whip 1667. **c.** In fig. context 1591. **2.** *fig.* To punish, chastise, correct (often said of God, with ref. to Heb. 12:6); to 'lash' with satire or invective; to afflict, torment; to devastate (a country) with war or pestilence. late ME. **3.** *Sc.* To exhaust the fertility of (land) 1799.

1. Therfore Pilat took thanne Jhesu and scourgide WYCLIF *John* 19:1. **b.** Scourged from the council with a storm of blows 1870. **c.** The waves..Scourged by the wind's invisible tyranny SHELLEY. **2.** Forsoth he scourgith euery sone that he receyeuth WYCLIF *Heb.* 12:6. **3.** Flax..is a crop which scourges the ground 1888. Hence **Scou·rger,** one who scourges or flogs (*lit.* and *fig.*).

Scouse (skaus). 1840. [Shortened f. LOBSCOUSE.] = LOBSCOUSE.

Scout (skaut), *sb.*[1] late ME. [– MDu. *schūte* (Du. *schuit*), adopted earlier as *schoute* (XIV), rel. to ON. *skúta* (Da. *skude*) light fast vessel; perh. to be referred to the base of SHOOT in the sense 'move rapidly'.] A flat-bottomed boat; 'a Dutch vessel, galliot rigged, used in the river trade of Holland'.

Scout (skaut), *sb.*[2] 1553. [– OFr. *escoute*, f. *escouter*; see SCOUT *v.*[1]] **1.** The action of spying out or watching in order to gain information; chiefly in *on* or *in* (*the*) *s.*, *to the s.* **2.** *Mil.* One sent out ahead of the main force in order to reconnoitre the position and movements of the enemy. Hence occas.: One sent out to obtain information. 1555. **b. Boy s.:** a member of an organization consisting of boys who meet periodically to practise exercises and to undergo training in the duties belonging to a scout 1908. †**3.** A body of men sent out to gain information –1775. **4.** One who keeps watch upon the actions of another; a watchman. †Formerly often: A mean spy, a sneak. 1584. **5.** A type of war-vessel adapted for the purposes of reconnoitring; also, an air-vessel similarly used 1706. †**6.** *Cricket.* = FIELDSMAN a. Also in *Baseball.* **b.** A boy who is employed to run after the balls at 'practice'. 1824.

1. I set my self upon the S. as often as possible DE FOE. **2.** Scouts each Coast light-armed scoure, Each quarter, to descrie the distant foe MILT.

Scout (skaut), *sb.*[3] 1596. [Of unkn. origin.] A local name for various sea-birds native to Great Britain; as the Guillemot, Razor-bill, and Puffin.

Scout (skaut), *sb.*[4] 1708. [Of unkn. origin; perh. spec. use of SCOUT *sb.*[2]] At Oxford (also at Yale and Harvard): A (male) college servant.

Scout (skaut), *v.*[1] late ME. [Aphetic – OFr. *escouter* (mod. *écouter*) listen, alt. of *ascolter* :– Rom. *ascultare, for L. *auscultare* listen.] **1.** *intr.* To act as a scout, to play the spy; to travel about (in search of information). **2.** *trans.* To reconnoitre, to examine with a view to obtaining information 1704.

1. S. mee for him at the corner of the Orchard like a bum-Baylie SHAKS. **2.** To s. the country 1900. Hence **Scou·ting** *vbl. sb.* the action of the vb.; the exercises practised by 'boy scouts'.

Scout (skaut), *v.*[2] 1605. [prob. of Scand. origin (cf. ON. *skúta, skúti* a taunt, *skútyrði, skotyrði* abusive language), prob. f. base of *skjóta* SHOOT.] †**1.** *trans.* To mock at, deride. Also *absol.* –1768. **2.** To reject with scorn (a proposition); to treat as absurd (an idea); to dismiss scornfully the pretensions of (a person, a work, etc.) 1710.

1. Flout 'em, and cout 'em: and skowt 'em, and flout 'em SHAKS.

Scou·tma:ster, scou·t-ma:ster. 1579. [f. SCOUT *sb.*[2] + MASTER *sb.*[1]] A leader or captain of a band of scouts. Now also, the officer who has charge of a 'troop' of boy scouts.

S. General (Hist.), the chief of the intelligence department of the Parliamentary army.

Scow (skau), *sb.* *U.S., Scotland,* and *Ireland.* 1775. [– Du. *schouw*, earlier *schouwe, schoude* = LG. *schalde*, rel. to OS. *skaldan* push (a boat) from the shore.] A large flat-bottomed lighter or punt. Hence **Scow** *v. intr.* to cross *over* (a river) by means of a s.; *trans.* to transport in a s.

Scowl (skaul), *sb.* 1500. [f. next.] A louring or malevolent look. **b.** *transf.* Of clouds, the elements, etc. 1648.

Received with scowls and curses 1909. **b.** Sky—what a s. of cloud BROWNING.

Scowl (skaul), *v.* ME. [prob. of Scand. origin (cf. Da. *skule* cast down one's eyes, give a sidelong look); perh. ult. rel. to late OE. *scūlēġede* squint-eyed.] **1.** *intr.* To look with louring brows and a malignant or threatening expression; to look angry or sullen. Const. *at, on, upon.* **b.** To be exhibited or expressed frowningly or with a scowl. *poet.* or *rhet.* 1719. **2.** *transf.* and *fig.* Of inanimate things (sometimes personified): To assume a gloomy, forbidding, or threatening aspect 1587. **3.** *trans.* in *nonce-uses.* To send forth or express with a scowl 1667.

1. Myne enemy skouleth vpon me with his eyes COVERDALE *Job* 16:9. **b.** A menace scowled upon the brow W. IRVING. **2.** When winter scowls COWPER. Hence **Scow·ler. Scow·lingly** *adv.*

Scr- may represent OE. *scr-* (variously in mod. dialects as ʃr-, ʃər-, sr-) or ON *skr-*, as in SCRAPE *v.*; cf. *shred* and *screed* from OE. *scrēade*, and *shrew*, dial. *screw*, from OE. *scrēawa.* **2.** There are many instances of initial *scr-* varying with *cr-*, e.g. *scrag, crag; scrunch, crunch.*

Scrabble (skræ·b'l), *sb.* 1842. [f. next.] A scrawling character in writing; hence, a document composed of such characters. Also, a picture composed of or characterized by careless or hastily-executed line-work.

Scrabble (skræ·b'l), *v.* 1537. [– MDu. *shrabbelen*, frequent. of *shrabben* scratch, scrape; cf. synon. MDu. *schrāven* and SCRAPE *v.*] **1.** *intr.* To make marks at random; to scrawl, scribble. **b.** *trans.* To write or depict (something) in a scrawling manner; also, to scrawl upon (something) 1856. **2.** *intr.* Of an animal: To scratch about hurriedly with the claws or paws; hence, of a person, to scratch or scrape about with the hands or feet 1600. **3.** Of a person: To scramble on hands and feet; to stumble or struggle along; also *occas.* of an animal. Now somewhat *rare.* 1638.

1. And he..scrabled on the dores of the gate BIBLE (1537) 1 *Sam.* 21:13. **2.** Gangs of the prying gull That shriek and s. on the river hatches KIPLING. **3.** Little-faith came to himself, and getting up made shift to s. on his way BUNYAN.

Scrabe (skrēⁱb). *Sc.* and *n. dial.* 1676. [– Da. *scrabe* – Færoëse *skrápur*; cf. next.] The Manx Shearwater, *Puffinus anglorum.*

Scraber (skrēⁱ·bəɹ). *Sc.* 1698. [Of obscure origin; in Gaelic *sgrabair.* Cf. prec.] A name for the Manx Shearwater, and the Black Guillemot, *Uria grylle.*

Scrag (skræg), *sb.*[1] 1542. [perh. alt. of CRAG *sb.*[2]; see SCR-.] **1.** A lean person or animal. (In depreciatory use.) **2.** The lean and inferior end of a neck of mutton (or veal). Also (earlier) *s.-end.* 1644. **3.** *slang.* The neck (of a human being) 1756. **4. S. whale,** a finner-whale of the sub-family *Agaphelinæ*, esp. *Agaphelus gibbosus*, common in the North Atlantic 1701.

2. Lady Mac-Screw..serves up a s.-of-mutton on silver THACKERAY. Hence **Scragged** (skrægd) *a.*[2] scraggy.

Scrag (skræg), *sb.*[2] Now chiefly *dial.* 1567. [Parallel to SCROG *sb.*, SHRAG *sb.*, *shrog* bush, pl. underwood (XV).] **1.** A stump of a tree; also, a rough projection (on a pole, trunk, or stump of a tree, rock, etc.). **2.** Rough, rocky and barren ground 1858.

Scrag (skræg), *v. slang.* 1756. [f. SCRAG *sb.*[1]] *trans.* To hang (on the gallows). **b.** To wring the neck of; also, to garotte 1823. Hence **Scra·gger,** the hangman.

†**Scragged,** *a.*[1] 1519. [app. alteration of CRAGGED *a.*[1]; see SCR-]. Rough and irregular in outline; of ground, rugged and barren –1725.

Scraggy (skræ·gi), *a.*[1] 1611. [f. SCRAG *sb.*[1] + -Y[1].] **1.** Lean, thin, bony. (Chiefly *depreciatory.*) **b.** *transf.* and *fig.* Meagre, thin, scanty 1837. **2.** Of meat: Lean 1725.

1. A bevy of dowagers, stout or s. THACKERAY. **b.** The scraggiest of prophetic discourses CARLYLE. Hence **Scra·ggily** *adv.*[1] **Scra·gginess**[1].

Scraggy (skræ·gi), *a.*[2] 1574. [f. SCRAG *sb.*[2] + -Y[1].] Rough, irregular or broken in outline or contour; esp. of rocks, rugged. Hence **Scra·ggily,** *adv.*[2] **Scra·gginess**[2].

Scramble (skræ·mb'l), *sb.* 1674. [f. next.] **1.** A struggle with others for something or a share of something; hence, an indecorous struggle, a confused or disorderly proceeding. **2.** An act of scrambling; a scrambling journey 1755.

1. But the s. for new lands..will become less acute as there is less territory to be absorbed 1907. **2.** A brisk s. to the top 1873.

Scramble (skræ·mb'l), *v.* 1586. [Of symbolic form, combining SCAMBLE *v.* and CRAMBLE *v.* (XVI), of allied meaning.] **1.** *intr.* To raise oneself to an erect posture, to get through or into a place or position, by the struggling use of the hands and feet; hence, to make one's way by clambering, crawling, jumping, etc. over difficult ground or through obstructions. **b.** *trans.* To collect or gather *up* hastily or in disorder 1822. **2.** *intr.* To strive or struggle with others for mastery; to contend with a crowd for a share of food, coin, wealth, etc. 1590. **b.** *trans.* To contend or struggle with others for (a share of something distributed) 1647. **3.** To cook (eggs) in the manner called 'scrambled' 1850.

1. We..then scrambled up a very high and steep hill 1687. *fig.* I had not even scrambled into my clothes 1900. **b.** He hastily scrambled up the papers 1833. **2.** Of other care they little reck'ning make, Then how to s. at the shearers feast, And shove away the worthy bidden guest MILT. Hence **Scra·mbler.**

Scrambled (skræ·mb'ld), *ppl. a.* 1609. [f. prec. + -ED[1].] In senses of the verb.

S. eggs, a dish of eggs broken into the pan and cooked with milk, butter, salt, and pepper.

Scrambling (skræ·mbliŋ), *ppl. a.* 1607. [f. as prec. + -ING[2].] **1.** Of persons: That scramble or contend one with another. **2.** Irregular or rambling in form or habit. Of a plant: Of straggling growth. 1688. **b.** Of a person: Shambling, uncouth 1765. **3.** Irregular, unmethodical 1778.

2. A huge old s. bed-room SCOTT. Hence **Scra·mblingly** *adv.*

Scran (skræn). *slang* and *dial.* 1724. [Of unkn. origin.] †A reckoning at a tavern; eatables, provisions; broken victuals. *Bad s. to* (Irish): bad luck to.

Scranch (skrǫnʃ), *v. Obs.* exc. *dial.* 1620. [perh. var. form of contemp. CRANCH, CRAUNCH; see SCR-.] *trans.* = CRUNCH *v.* 1, 2.

Scrannel (skræ·nĕl), *a.* 1637. [Obscurely rel. to synon. dial. *scrank* (XVII), Sc. *scranky* (Ramsay, XVIII), *scranny*; all prob. ult. from a base repr. by Norw. *skran* shrivelled, *skrank* lean large-boned figure.] Thin, meagre. Now chiefly, after Milton: Harsh, unmelodious.

Their lean and flashy songs Grate on their s. Pipes of wretched straw MILT.

Scranny (skræ·ni), *a.*[1] Chiefly *dial.* 1820. [See prec., and cf. SCRAWNY.] Lean, thin. Of diet: Poor, meagre.

Scranny (skræ·ni), *a.*[2] orig. *dial.* 1858. [Of unkn. origin.] Crazy.

Scrap (skræp), *sb.*[1] late ME. [– ON. *skrap* scraps, trifles, f. base of *scrapa* SCRAPE *v.*] **1.** *pl.* The remains of a meal; fragments (of food); broken meat. *rare* in *sing.* **2.** A remnant; a fragmentary portion 1583. **b.** A small picture, cutting, etc. to be put in a SCRAP-BOOK or used for ornamenting a screen, box, or the like 1880. **3.** *pl.* The pieces of blubber, fish, etc. remaining after the oil has been extracted. Also *collect. sing.* 1631. **4.** *Founding.* **a.** *pl.* Remnants of metal produced in cutting up or casting 1736. **b.** = SCRAP-IRON 1846. **5.** *attrib.* quasi-*adj.* Consisting of scraps 1815.

1. 'Twas but for scraps he ask'd POPE. **2.** Forced to get what Scraps of Learning I could by my own Industry STEELE. There is not a s. of evidence in support of it 1868. *S. of paper* (with allusion to an alleged reference (Aug. 1914) by the German Chancellor to the treaty securing the neutrality of Belgium), any agreement that can be lightly set aside or disregarded.

Scrap (skræp), *sb.*[2] *slang.* 1874. [perh. f. SCRAPE *sb.* II. Cf. next.] A struggle, scrimmage, tussle; a boxing-match. **b.** A row, quarrel, heated discussion 1889.

Scrap (skræp), *v.*[1] *slang.* 1874.. [f. prec.] **a.** *intr.* To fight, box. Also, to scrimmage. **b.** *trans.* To box with (an opponent) 1893. **c.** *intr.* To quarrel, engage in angry dispute 1909.

Scrap (skræp), *v.*[2] 1891. [f. SCRAP *sb.*[1]] **1.** *trans.* To break up into scrap-iron (machinery, etc.); to consign to the scrap-heap 1902. Also *fig.* **2.** To make scrap or refuse of (menhaden or blubber) 1891.

Scra·p-book. 1825. [f. SCRAP *sb.*[1]] A blank book in which pictures, newspaper cuttings, and the like are pasted for preservation.

Scrape (skrēⁱp), *sb.* 1440. [f. next.] **I. 1.** A scraper. **2.** An act of scraping 1483. **b.** An awkward bow or salutation in which the foot is drawn backwards on the ground 1628. **c.** A drawing of the bow over the violin 1831. **d.** A sound of scraping 1886. **3.** A place scraped bare on a hillside. *dial.* 1781. **4.** A layer (of butter) scraped thin; chiefly in *bread and s.* (*colloq.*) 1847.

2. *S. of a pen* (Sc.), a hasty scribble, a small scrap of writing. **b.** I..made him abundance of bows and scrapes DE FOE.

II. An embarrassing or awkward predicament or situation, usu. one into which a person is brought by his own imprudence and thoughtlessness 1709.

I was generally the leader of the boys and sometimes led them into scrapes 1771.

Scrape (skrēⁱp), *v.* Pa. t. and pple. **scraped** (skrēⁱpt). ME. [– ON. *skrapa* or (M)Du. *schrapen* = OE. *scrapian* scratch, ME. †*shrape.*] **1.** *trans.* To remove (an outer layer, etc.) by drawing across the surface the edge of some instrument held nearly perpendicularly. Chiefly with advs. late ME. †**b.** *spec.* To erase (writing, etc.) with a knife –1688. **2.** To deprive of an outer layer or to free from excrescent or adhering matter by drawing the edge of some instrument over the surface; to abrade, clean, or render smooth, or to obtain scrapings from, by this process. late ME. **b.** To inscribe or portray on stone by scraping away the surface 1532. **c.** To produce (a mezzotint engraving) by scraping the prepared copper plate 1747. †**3.** Of a beast or bird: To remove (soil, etc.) by scratching with the feet or claws; to make (a hole) thus –1662. **b.** *trans.* with adv. or phr. 1530. †**4.** To scratch with the finger-nails or claws; also *intr.* –1607. **5.** (*fig.* of sense 3.) 'To gather by great efforts, or penurious or trifling diligence' (J.); to amass, collect, or bring together with difficulty. Now only with *together* or *up.* 1549. **b.** *To s.* (*an*) *acquaintance*: to get on terms of acquaintance *with* by careful effort and insinuation 1600. **c.** *absol.* and *intr.* To hoard up penuriously; to gather together money, etc. with labour and difficulty. Now chiefly *dial.* 1552. **6.** Used disparagingly for: To play (a fiddle); occas. *to s. catgut*; to play (a tune, etc.) on the fiddle 1599. **7.** To rub harshly on (a surface) in passing along or over it; to draw (something) roughly over a surface 1731. **b.** *intr.* To graze *against* or *on* 1774. **c.** To draw one's feet noisily over the floor 1561. **8.** *intr.* To make obeisance, to bow awkwardly, drawing the foot back 1645.

1. Like dry colours scraped off a picture 1877. **b.** *Meas. for M.* I. ii. 9. **2.** An ironclad's..bottom is always foul when she cannot be periodically docked and scraped 1884. **b.** The family arms were just new scraped in stone THACKERAY. **5.** The first money he was able to s. together by strict frugality 1888. **b.** To slave..and s. to get a house over your head 1881. **7. c.** Another [orator] was coughed and scraped down MACAULAY. **8.** Bowing and scraping and rubbing his hands together TROLLOPE.

Phrases. *To s. along*, to manage or 'get along' with difficulty. *To s. through*, to get through a trial, an examination, so as just to escape failure.

Comb.: **s.-gut,** a fiddler; †**-penny,** a miser. Hence **Scra·ping** *ppl. a.* that scrapes; *esp.* money-grubbing, miserly.

Scraper (skrēⁱ·pəɹ). 1552. [f. SCRAPE *v.* + -ER[1].] **I.** One who scrapes. **1.** One who 'scrapes together'; *esp.* a money-grubber. Now *rare.* 1561. **2.** One who scrapes (something specified or implied); *esp.* a fiddler 1591. **II.** An instrument for scraping with. **1.** A scraping instrument held in the hand. **a.** *gen.* 1552. **b.** = STRIGIL 1667. **c.** An instrument used for scraping off paint, tar, adhesive labels, etc. from wooden surfaces 1691. **d.** *Engraving.* A three-sided tool used to remove burrs left by the graver, etc., or to obliterate lines. Also the similar instrument used in 'scraping' mezzotint. 1747. **2.** An appliance fixed outside the door of a house for persons to scrape off upon it the dirt from the soles of their boots or shoes before entering 1729. **3.** A machine (or scoop) drawn by horses or oxen for excavating ditches, canals, etc., for levelling and making roads, or for raising and removing soil, dirt, weeds, etc. a short distance 1840. **b.** An instrument for scraping dirt, mud, etc. from roads, etc. Also *road-s.* 1831.

Scra·pe-tre:ncher. *Obs.* exc. *Hist.* 1603. [f. SCRAPE *v.* + TRENCHER.] A servant whose office was to scrape the trenchers after use.

Scra·p-heap, *sb.* 1838. [f. SCRAP *sb.*[1]] A heap of SCRAP IRON. Hence *fig.* in phrases, as *to consign to the s.*, to cast aside as worn out or superseded. Hence **Scra·p-heap** *v. trans.* to consign to the s.

Scraping (skrēⁱ·piŋ), *vbl. sb.* 1440. [-ING[1].] **1.** The action of SCRAPE *v.* **b.** The noise produced by drawing something roughly over a surface 1561. **2.** *pl. concr.* That which is scraped off, up, or together. Rarely *sing.* 1511.

2. The dust and scrapings from roads 1790.

Scrap iron. 1823. [f. SCRAP *sb.*[1]] Iron which has already been cast or wrought and broken up or cast aside for re-casting or re-working; broken pieces and small articles of old and disused ironwork. Also *attrib.*

Scrappy (skræ·pi), *a.* 1837. [f. SCRAP *sb.*[1] + -Y[1].] Consisting of scraps; made up of odds and ends; disjointed, unconnected.

A dreadfully s. dinner THACKERAY. Hence **Scra·ppily** *adv.* **Scra·ppiness.**

Scrat, *sb. Obs.* or *dial.* [Late ME. *scrate* (XV) – ON. *skrat(t)i* wizard, goblin, monster, rel. to OHG. *scrato* (G. *schrat*) satyr, sprite. See SCRATCH *sb.*²] A hermaphrodite.

Scrat, *v. Obs.* exc. *dial.* [See SCRATCH *v.*] **1.** *intr.* To use the nails or claws for attack; to scratch (*at* a person). **2.** *trans.* and *intr.* = SCRATCH *v.* 1, 4, 5. ME.

Scratch (skrætʃ), *sb.*¹ 1586. [f. SCRATCH *v.*] **I.** Result of scratching. **1.** A slight tearing or incision of the skin produced by a sharp instrument. (Sometimes applied slightingly to a trifling flesh-wound.) **2.** *pl.* A disease of horses, in which the pastern appears as if scratched 1591. **3.** A mark or furrow produced by the grinding contact of two substances; a shallow linear incision 1662. **4.** A rough or irregular mark made by a pencil, paint-brush, etc.; hence, a slight sketch, a hasty scrawl 1646. **5.** *Sporting.* A line or mark drawn as an indication of a boundary or starting-point; in *Pugilism*, the line drawn across the ring, to which boxers are brought for an encounter 1778. **b.** The starting-point in a handicap of a competitor who receives no odds 1867. **6.** The sound produced by the friction of two more or less rough surfaces 1787; *spec.* during the reproduction of a sound film or record 1930.

1. A little s., rather then a wound SIDNEY. **4.** Every s. of his pen was accounted a treasure COWPER. **5.** Phr. (often fig.) *To come up to* (*the*) *s.*, *to bring to the s.*, *to toe the s.*

II. An act of scratching (*rare*) 1765. **III.** Ellipt. for *scratch periwig* 1755.

Comb.: (in sense 5b) as **s.-line, -player; s.-cat,** (joc.) a spiteful person; **-grass,** a dial. name for cleavers, and, in U.S., the arrow-leaved tear-thumb; **-periwig, -wig,** a small, short wig.

Scratch (skrætʃ), *sb.*² *colloq.* (now chiefly *dial.*) 1740. [alt. of SCRAT *sb.*] A name for the devil, usu. *Old S.*

Scratch (skrætʃ), *a.* 1853. [orig. SCRATCH *sb.*¹ used attrib.] **1.** Hastily sketched. **2.** Hastily assembled or put together 1859.

2. *S. vote, division, majority*, one which, owing to accident or stratagem, does not represent the actual state of opinion in a deliberative body, etc.

Scratch (skrætʃ), *v.* 1474. [prob. blending of synon. SCRAT *v.* and CRATCH *v.*; the origin of these forms is obscure, but their meaning associates them with the similar MLG., MDu. *kratsen*, OHG. *krazzōn* (G. *kratzen*), OSw. *kratta* scratch.] **1.** *trans.* To wound superficially by dragging the claws or finger-nails over the skin. Also, in wider sense: To wound superficially with anything pointed and hard dragged over the skin or in contact with its moving surface, so as to produce a slight linear tearing or abrasion. **b.** With adv.: To tear *out* (e.g. the skin, a pimple, etc.) with the claws or nails 1591. **c.** *absol.* or *intr.* To use the claws or nails as weapons of offence. Also occas. of inanimate things, to produce a scratch. 1589. **2.** *trans.* To rub or scrape lightly (a part of the body) with the finger-nails or claws (e.g. to relieve itching). So *to s. one's head*, as a gesture indicating perplexity. Also *intr.* for *refl.* 1530. **3.** To make slight linear abrasions on (a surface of any kind) 1669. **b.** *hyperbolically.* To furrow (the soil) very lightly for the purpose of cultivation 1697. **c.** To produce (marks) or portray (an object) by light incisions on a surface 1644. **4.** *intr.* Of a bird or animal: To remove earth, etc. with the claws 1520. **5.** *fig.* **a.** To struggle to make money, to 'scrape'. Also *trans.* to scrape up (money). Now *dial.* 1509. **b.** *intr.* with adv. To get *along, on, through* with difficulty 1838. †**6.** *trans.* To seize rapaciously, as a bird with its claws; to get possession of by effort or with difficulty –1680. **7. a.** trans. *To s. out*: to erase (writing) with a penknife; also, to delete by crossing through with a pen 1711. **b.** To erase the name of (a person) from a list; hence, to expunge from a list of candidates or competitors; *Sporting*, to withdraw (a horse, etc.) from the list of entries for a race, etc. 1685. **c.** *U.S. Politics.* Of a voter: To erase the name of (a candidate) from the party ticket 1888. **d.** *intr.* for *refl.* To withdraw from a competition; *joc.* to withdraw one's acceptance of an invitation 1866. **8.** To drag the nails or claws over a surface so as to make a faint grating noise. Also, of a pen, to move over the paper with a slight noise. 1703. **b.** *trans.* To rub gratingly on a rough surface 1864. **9.** To scribble, write hurriedly or carelessly 1789.

1. He scracchid hym in the visage CAXTON. **c.** How the long brambles do s. HOOD. **2.** If my haire do but tickle me, I must s. SHAKS. The homely adage, 'S. my back and I'll s. yours' 1885. **3.** Marble is soft, and can be scratched with a knife 1794. *To s. the surface* (fig.), to be superficial. **4.** Phr. *To s. out*, to extricate or disinter with the claws. *To s. up*, to heap up by scratching. **8. b.** A match being scratched on a box 1875.

Comb.: **s.-back,** an instrument for scratching the back to allay itching, usu. in the form of a small hand of ivory or metal fixed to a long handle; formerly, a toy which produces a sound of tearing cloth when rubbed upon a person's back.

Scratch-brush (skræ·tʃ,brʌʃ), *sb.* 1797. [f. SCRATCH *sb*¹. or *v.*] A brush of fine wire used in gilding, electroplating, etc. to polish or clean articles of metal. Hence **Scra·tch-brush** *v. trans.* to polish by means of a s.

Scratcher (skræ·tʃəɹ). 1517. [f. SCRATCH *v.* + -ER¹.] One who scratches. **b.** *Ornith.* Used in *pl.* to render mod.L. *Rasores* (Illiger), an order of birds that scratch for their food 1831. **c.** A tool used in plastering to roughen the surface of the preliminary coating 1812.

Scratchy (skræ·tʃi), *a.* 1817. [f. SCRATCH *sb.*¹ + -Y¹.] **1.** Of work executed with the pen or brush: Composed of scratches, as opposed to bold, firm lines. **2.** Apt to scratch 1866. **3.** *Sporting.* Of action: Ill-sustained, uneven, 'ragged' 1881.

2. Written with a s. pen 1866.

Scraw (skrǭ). *dial.* (Anglo-Irish, Sc., Manx.) 1725. [– Irish and Gael. *sgrath*, pronounced (skrā).] **1.** A turf. †**2.** A thin covering of grass-grown soil formed upon the surface of a bog –1820.

Scrawl (skrǭl), *sb.*¹ 1693. [f. SCRAWL *v.*²] **1.** Something scrawled; a hastily and badly written letter, a careless sketch. †**b.** *pl.* Scrawled or illegible characters –1807. **2.** A careless illegible style of handwriting 1710.

1. A s. from his pencil brings an enormous price 1840. **2.** Her hand-writing..a miserable s. 1775.

Scrawl (skrǭl), *sb.*² *dial.* 1847. [perh. f. SCRAWL *v.*¹] The young of the dog-crab (*Cancer caninus*).

Scrawl, *v.*¹ *Obs.* exc. *dial.* late ME. [app. alt. f. CRAWL *v.*, perh. suggested by SPRAWL *v.* of cognate meaning; see SCR-.] †**1.** *intr.* To spread the limbs abroad in a sprawling manner; to gesticulate –1582. **2.** = CRAWL *v.* 1. 1530.

Scrawl (skrǭl), *v.*² 1611. [perh. transf. use of prec.] **1.** *trans.* To write or draw in a sprawling, untidy manner 1612. **b.** To cover (a surface) with scrawling inscriptions or marks. Also with *over.* 1647. **2.** *intr.* To scribble, to write carelessly or awkwardly 1611.

1. b. The windows of all the inns are scrawled with doggrel rhimes SMOLLETT. Hence **Scraw·ler,** one who writes carelessly. **Scraw·ly** *a.* badly or untidily written; irregularly designed.

Scrawny (skrǭ·ni), *a. U.S.* 1833. [var. of SCRANNY.] Lean, scraggy.

Scray (skrēⁱ). 1668. [Of unkn. origin.] The common tern, *Sterna hirundo.*

Scraze (skrēⁱz), *v. dial.* 1662. [Blending of SCRATCH, GRAZE *vbs.*] *trans.* To graze.

Screak (skrīk), *v.* Now chiefly *dial.* 1500. [Of Scand. origin; cf. ON. *skrækja*, Norw. *skrika.* See SCREECH, SHRIEK.] *intr.* To utter a shrill harsh cry; to screech or scream. Also with *out.* **b.** Of an ungreased hinge or axle, etc.: To make a shrill grating sound 1565. Hence **Screak** *sb.* a shrill cry; a shrill grating sound.

Scream (skrīm), *sb.* 1513. [f. next.] A shrill piercing cry, usu. expressive of pain, alarm, mirth, or other sudden emotion. **b.** *slang.* Something which causes one to 'scream' with laughter; a supremely ridiculous person or thing. (Cf. the earlier SCREAMER 4 b.) 1915.

She dropped them with a s. of terror THACKERAY. *transf.* The eagles answer'd with their s. SCOTT.

Scream (skrīm), *v.* [Either aberrant repr. (see SCR-) of late OE. **scrǣman*, ME. *shreame* (XIII) or – the rel. MDu. **schreemen* (so WFlem.; cf. MDu. *schreem* sb.) = OFris. **skrēma* (WFris. *skrieme* weep).] **1.** *intr.* To utter a shrill piercing cry, normally expressive of pain, alarm, mirth, or other sudden emotion. Also, to produce unpleasantly loud and shrill upper notes in singing. **b.** Of certain birds and beasts: To emit their characteristic shrill cry ME. **c.** To make a noise like a scream 1784. **2.** *trans.* To utter with a scream 1710.

1. She screamed for help MACAULAY. quasi-*trans.* She would s. the house down 1862. **b.** I heard the Owle schreame, and the Crickets cry SHAKS. **c.** The fiddle screams Plaintive and piteous COWPER.

Screamer (skrī·məɹ). 1712. [f. prec. + -ER¹.] **1.** One who screams; one who sings in shrill piercing tones. **2.** An animal that utters a cry like a scream 1801. **3.** *spec.* **a.** Any bird of the S. Amer. family *Palamedeidæ*; esp. the KAMICHI or Horned S., and *Chauna chavaria*, the Crested S. 1773. **b.** The swift (*local*) 1813. **4.** *slang.* **a.** A person, animal, or thing of exceptional size, attractiveness, etc.; a splendid specimen 1837. **b.** A composition of a startling or exaggerated character; e.g. a thrilling or funny story, a 'screaming' farce 1844.

4. a. I..lost one s. just up the back ditch there. He must have been a four-pounder. 1861.

Screaming (skrī·miŋ), *ppl. a.* 1602. [f. SCREAM *v.* + -ING².] **1.** That screams; sounding shrilly. **2.** *transf.* and *fig.* **a.** Tending to excite screams of laughter; said esp. of a farce 1854. **b.** Violent or startling in effect; glaring 1848. **c.** *slang.* First-rate, splendid 1864.

1. Like so many s. grasse-hoppers B. JONSON. **2. c.** A s. success 1879. Hence **Screa·mingly** *adv.*

Scree (skrī). 1781. [prob. back-formation from *screes*, for **screethes* pl. – ON. *skriða* land-slip, rel. to *skríða* slide, glide = OE. *scrīþan*, OHG. *skrītan* (G. *schreiten*).] A mass of loose detritus, forming a precipitous, stony slope upon a mountain-side. Also, the material composing such a slope.

Screech (skrītʃ), *sb.* 1560. [See next and SCRITCH *sb.*] **A.** A loud shrill cry, usu. one expressive of violent and uncontrollable pain or alarm. **2.** *transf.* A harsh, squeaking sound made by some inanimate object 1832.

Comb.: in dial. names of birds with ref. to their harsh discordant cry, as **s.-bird, -thrush,** the Fieldfare (*Turdus pilaris*); **-hawk,** the Nightjar (*Caprimulgus europæus*); **-thrush,** the Missel-thrush (*Turdus viscivorus*).

Screech (skrītʃ), *v.* 1577. [alt. (with expressive lengthening of the vowel) of SCRITCH *v.*] **1.** *intr.* To utter a sharp, piercing cry, as of pain or alarm; to call out shrilly; also occas. used *transf.* of inanimate things. **2.** *trans.* To utter (a word or sentence) with a loud, shrill, piercing sound 1844.

1. A draggled fishwife screeches at the gates 1888. Hence **Scree·cher,** one who screeches; *dial.* any of several birds having a harsh screaming cry, e.g. the Swift, the Gull-billed Tern, the Missel-thrush.

Scree·ch-owl. 1593. [alt., after prec., of earlier SCRITCH-OWL.] **1.** The Barn Owl, from its discordant cry, supposed to be of evil omen. **2.** *transf.* Applied to a bearer of evil tidings, or one who presages misfortune 1606.

1. The time when Screech-owles cry, and Bandogs howle SHAKS. **2.** *Tr. & Cr.* V. x. 16.

Screechy (skrī·tʃi), *a.* 1830. [f. SCREECH *sb.* + -Y¹.] Of a voice: Given to screech; loud, shrill, and discordant.

Screed (skrīd). ME. [prob. var. repr. (see SCR-) of OE. *scrēade* SHRED *sb.*] **1.** A fragment cut, torn, or broken from a main piece; in later use, a torn strip of some textile material. *Obs.* exc. *dial.* **b.** A strip of land; a parcel of ground 1615. **2.** *fig.* A long roll or list; a lengthy discourse or harangue; a gossiping letter or piece of writing 1789. **3.** *Plastering.* An accurately levelled strip of plaster formed upon a wall or ceiling, as a guide in running a cornice or in obtaining a perfectly even surface in plastering; a strip of wood used for the same purpose 1812.

2. Richardson's reply is a s. of malevolence 1902.

Screen (skrīn), *sb.* late ME. [Aphetic – ONFr. *escren*, var. of *escran* (mod. *écran*) –

OFrankish *skrank = OHG. *skrank* (G. *schrank* cupboard) bar, barrier, fence.] **1.** A contrivance for warding off the heat of a fire or a draught of air. **a.** An upright board, or a frame hung with leather, canvas, etc., or two or more such boards or frames hinged together. **b.** A frame covered with paper or cloth, or a disc of thin wood, etc., with a handle by which a person may hold it between his face and the fire 1548. **c.** A wooden seat or settle with a high back to keep away draughts 1826. **d.** A flat vertical surface prepared for the reception of images from a magic lantern or the like; a contrivance in the form of a screen for affording an upright surface for the display of objects of exhibition 1815. **2.** *Arch.* A partition of wood or stone, pierced by one or more doors, dividing a room or building (e.g. a church) into two parts; *spec.* = *chancel-s.*, *rood-s.* 1460. **b.** A wall thrown out in front of a building and masking the façade 1842. **3.** *transf.* **a.** Applied to any object that affords shelter from heat or wind 1538. **b.** Something so interposed as to conceal from view 1605. **c.** *Mil.* A small body of men detached to cover the movements of an army 1892. **d.** A line or belt of trees planted to give protection from the wind 1644. **4.** *fig.* A means of securing from attack, punishment, or censure 1610. **5.** An apparatus used in the sifting of grain, coal, etc. 1573. **6.** Applied to various parts of optical, electrical, and other instruments, serving to intercept light, heat, electricity, etc. 1819. **b.** *Electr.* A device which protects an electrical apparatus from external electric or magnetic influences 1915. **c.** *Photogr.* A transparent plate or sheet of glass, ruled with fine lines, used in photographing for half-tone reproduction 1897.

1. d. *Silver s.*, the s. on which cinematograph pictures are projected; hence, cinematography. **e.** *Cricket.* An erection of white canvas or wood placed near the boundary to enable a batsman to see the ball better 1895. **3. b.** *Macb.* v. vi. 1. **4.** There be so many Skreenes betweene him, and Envy BACON.

Comb.: **s.-craft,** the cinematographic art; **-struck** *a.* (after *stage-struck*); **-wiper,** a device for keeping the wind-screen of a motor vehicle clear.

Screen (skrīn), *v.* 1485. [f. prec.] **1.** *trans.* To shelter or protect with or as with a screen, *from* heat, wind, light, missiles, or the like 1632. **b.** To shut *off* by something interposed 1700. **2.** To hide from view as with a screen; to shelter from observation or recognition 1686. **b.** *Mil.* To employ a body of men to cover (an army's movements). Also *absol.* 1881. **3.** To shield or protect from hostility or impending danger; *esp.* to save (an offender) *from* punishment or exposure; to conceal (a person's offence) 1485. **4.** *trans.* To sift by passing through a 'screen' 1664. **5.** In the Inns of Court: To post upon a screen or notice-board 1870. **6.** To project (a lantern-slide, cinematograph picture, etc.) upon a screen; hence, to make a cinema film of 1915.

Hence **Scree·ning** *vbl. sb.* (*concr.* cf. sense 4).

Screeve (skrīv), *v. slang.* 1851. [perh. – It. *scrivere* :– L. *scribere* write.] *intr.* To be a 'pavement artist'. Hence **Scree·ver,** a pavement artist.

Screw (skrū), *sb.* late ME. [– OFr. *escroue* fem. (mod. *écrou* masc.) either (i) – WGmc. *scrūva = MHG. *schrūbe* (G. *schraube*), corresp. to MDu. *schrūve*, or (ii) :– (the source of the Gmc. forms) L. *scrofa* sow, med.L. female screw (for the sense development cf. Sp. *puerca* sow, screw.] **I.** The general name for that kind of mechanical appliance of which the operative portion is a helical groove or ridge cut either on the exterior surface of a cylinder (*male s.*) or on the interior surface of a cylindrical cavity (*female s.*). **1.** A male screw (see above) with a correspondingly grooved or ridged socket; used for the purpose of converting a motion of rotation into a motion of translation bearing a fixed proportion to it. **a.** As an apparatus for raising weights or applying pressure or strain. **b.** Considered as one of the mechanical powers; in mechanical theory treated as a modification of the inclined plane 1570. **c.** Used for regulating or measuring longitudinal movement 1612. **2.** *fig.* A means of 'pressure' or coercion 1648. **3.** A metal pin or bolt (cylindrical or slightly tapering) with a spiral ridge upon its shank, used in joining articles of wood or metal, fastening fittings to woodwork, etc. (It is turned and driven in by means of a screwdriver or spanner.) 1622. **4.** Each of the component parts of a screw-fastening or screw-joint 1648. **5.** The worm or boring part of a gimlet 1577. **6.** An instrument terminating in a 'worm' for screwing into something in order to pull it out; esp. a corkscrew; also, the 'worm' itself 1657. **7.** A screw-propeller (see PROPELLER 3) 1838. **8.** A ship driven by a screw-propeller 1867. **9.** Something having a spiral course or form 1649. **b.** = *s.-stone* 1729.

1. *Bench s.*, a joiner's vice. *Double s.*, one with a pair of screws to carry the vice-cheek with a parallel motion. *Endless s.*, see ENDLESS *a.* *Perpetual s.* = *endless s.* *S. of Archimedes, water s.* = ARCHIMEDEAN screw. *The screws* (rarely *the s.*), an instrument of torture designed to compress the thumbs of a prisoner; *dial.* or *colloq.*, rheumatism. **2.** Phr. *To put on, apply, turn the s.*, or *screws*, etc.: (*a*) to apply moral pressure; (*b*) to force the payment of a debt or loan; also *rarely*, to limit the giving of credit. **3.** Phr. *A s. loose*, fig. something wrong in the condition of things; a dangerous weakness in some arrangement; *to have a s. loose*, to be 'dotty'. **6.** *S. or kettle* = cork-screw (*i.e.* wine) or hot water (*i.e.* grog).

II. From SCREW *v.* **1.** An act of screwing up; a turn of the screw 1709. **b.** *Billiards.* A stroke by which a twist is given to the cue-ball by striking it below its centre; also, the twist resulting from this stroke, esp. in the phr. *to put on s.* 1849. **c.** *Cricket.* A twist imparted to the ball in its delivery 1867. **2.** The state of being twisted awry; a contortion 1708. **3.** A small portion (of a commodity) wrapped up in a twist or cornet of paper; esp. a penny packet (of tobacco); also, a wrapper of this kind 1836. **4.** One who forces down (prices) by haggling; a stingy, miserly person 1835.

3. A knife, some butter, a s. of salt DICKENS. **4.** They both agreed in calling him an old s. THACKERAY.

III. Senses of obsc. origin. **1.** A horse not perfectly sound 1821. **2.** *slang.* Salary, wages 1864.

attrib. and *Comb.*: **s. battery,** a battery composed of s.-guns; **-blank,** the piece of metal on which a thread or worm is to be cut to form a s.; **-bolt,** a bolt with a thread or worm at the end to be secured by means of a s.-nut; hence **-bolt** *v. trans.*, to fasten with a s.-bolt; **-box,** a tool for cutting the thread on a wooden s.; **-dock** *U.S.*, a dock in which the cradle is raised by screws; **s. engine,** (*a*) a machine for raising water by means of a s., a water-s.; (*b*) a steam-engine adapted to drive a screw-propeller; **-gear,** gear consisting of an endless s. and a toothed wheel; **-joint** (*a*) *Mech.*, a joint formed by screwing together the ends of piping, etc.; (*b*) *Anat.*, a joint in which there is a slight lateral sliding of one bone upon the other; **-key,** (*a*) = *s.-wrench*; (*b*) a key furnished with a thread or worm; **-machine,** (*a*) a machine operated by a s.; (*b*) a machine for making screws; **s. nut** (see NUT *sb.* II. 3); **-plate,** a hardened steel plate for cutting the threads of small screws by means of a series of drilled and tapped holes of various diameters; **-press,** a machine in which pressure is applied by means of a s.; **s. propeller** (see I. 7); **-pump,** an ARCHIMEDEAN S.; **s. spanner** = *s.-wrench*; **-stone,** a stone containing the hollow cast of an encrinite; **-thread,** the spiral ridge of a s.; also, one complete turn of its thread as a portion of a unit of length of the axis of the s.; **s. tool,** a lathe-tool for cutting screws; **-wheel,** the toothed wheel associated with the endless s. in s.-gearing; **-worm,** the larva of certain American flesh-flies; **-wrench,** a wrench or spanner adapted to fit over or grasp the heads of s.-bolts, nuts, etc., and turn them. **b.** In names of plants, as **s.-bean, -mezquit,** *Prosopis pubescens*, so called from the s.-like form of its pods; **-palm, -pine,** any of the plants belonging to the family *Pandanaceæ*.

Screw (skrū), *v.* 1599. [f. prec.] **I.** *trans.* To attach with an inserted screw or screws; hence *fig.*, to fix firmly 1611.

To s. down, up, to close and secure with screws; Think of being screwed down in a coffin, and put into the cold ground 1862.

II. 1. To press, strain, or force with or as with a screw; to compress or hold fast in or as in a vice 1612. **2.** To stretch tight by turning a screw; *esp.* to increase the tension or pitch (of a musical string) by winding *up* the screws or keys 1652. **b.** With immaterial obj.; *esp.* to stretch, strain the meaning of (words) 1628. **3.** To operate or adjust (an instrument) by turning its screw 1708. **4.** To extort by pressure 1622. **5.** To put compulsion upon, to constrain, oppress 1658. **b.** To examine rigorously. *Obs.* exc. in *U.S.* college slang. Also *absol.* 1626. **6.** To produce, attain, or elicit with an effort 1679. **7.** *intr.* To be parsimonious 1849.

1. Phr. *To s. up*, to tighten by turning a screw. *To s. in, up*, to compress the waist of (a person) by tight-lacing. **2.** They break the strings by scruing them up too high 1656. *fig.* But s. your courage to the sticking place, And wee'le not fayle SHAKS. **b.** *To s. up*, to raise (a payment, rent, etc.) to an exacting or extortionate figure. **4.** I screwed out of him these particulars SCOTT. The rate of taxation is simply the maximum that can be screwed out of the people 1882. **5.** They are so screwed by taxes..that they never have a farthing in hand 1838. **7.** I must s. and save in order to pay off the money THACKERAY.

III. To turn a screw. **1.** *trans.* To work (a screw or something fashioned as a screw) by turning 1635. **2.** To insert or fix one thing *in*, *into*, *on*, *to*, or *upon* another or two things *together* by a turning or twisting movement, one or both having the surface or part of it cut into a screw for the purpose 1611. **b.** *intr.* in passive sense. To be adapted for joining or taking apart by means of component screws 1680. **3.** *intr.* To penetrate as a screw; to penetrate with a winding course; *fig.* to worm one's way 1614.

2. *fig. To have one's head screwed on the right way* (colloq.), to be able to use one's brains to advantage, to 'know what one is about'. **b.** Rods..in three pieces..which screwed together 1776.

IV. To move in a twisting direction. **1.** *trans.* To twist round, esp. to twist with violence so as to alter the shape 1711. **2.** To twist awry, contort (the features, body, mouth); to twist (one's head, oneself) *round* in order to look at something 1599. **3.** To propel by a spiral movement; to force or squeeze (one's body) *into*, *through*, etc. (a comparatively small space) 1635. **4.** *Sporting.* **a.** *intr. Rowing.* To swing the body from one side to the other during the stroke 1875. **b.** *trans. Rugby Football.* To cause (the scrummage or one's opponents in a scrummage) to twist round by pushing in a body to the right or left. Also *absol.* 1887. **c.** *Cricket*, etc. To impart a screw or twist to (the ball); to cause to swerve. Also *absol.* 1839. **d.** *intr.* (for *refl.*) *Racing.* Of a horse: To force his way *through*. Also *trans.* To force (a horse) *over* (an obstacle); *to s. in*, to force to the front at the finish of a race. 1840. **5.** Of ice-floes: To ram together 1901.

1. Phr. *To s.* (a person's) *neck*, to kill by wringing the neck. *To s. up*, to twist (e.g. a piece of paper) into a spiral form. **2.** *To s. up*, to contract the surrounding parts of (the mouth, eyes); Jo screws up his mouth into a whistle DICKENS.

V. 1. *trans.* To furnish with a helical groove or ridge; to furnish (a screw-blank, pin, etc.) with a thread or worm; to cut a screw-thread *upon* 1635. **2.** *intr.* To travel on the water by means of a screw-propeller; also *trans.* in *to s. its way* 1860.

Comb.: **s. back** *Billiards*, a rotary motion causing the ball to run backwards after striking another ball; **s. cannon** (also **screw-back cannon**) *Billiards*, a cannon made by striking the ball very low down and so causing it to recoil from the object ball; **s. kick, shot, stroke** (in various games), one that causes the ball to swerve. Hence **Screw·er. Screw·ing** *vbl. sb.* freq. in combs. in the sense 'cutting screw threads', as *screwing machine*.

Screwdriver (skrū·drəi:vəɹ). 1812. A tool for turning screws into or out of their places. It is shaped like a chisel, with a blunt end which fits into the nick in the head of the screw.

Screwed (skrūd), *ppl. a.* 1646. [f. SCREW *v.* + -ED[1].] **1.** In the senses of SCREW *v.* **2.** Partly intoxicated; 'tight' 1838.

Screw·-pin. 1614. [SCREW *sb.*] A pin with a screw cut upon it: **a.** the screw of a vice; **b.** an adjusting screw, finger screw; **c.** the pin which forms the foundation of a screw.

Screwy (skrū·i), *a.* 1820. [f. SCREW *sb.* and *v.* + -Y[1].] **1.** Slightly tipsy. **2.** Of a person: Given to screwing, mean, stingy

1851. **3.** Of a horse (see SCREW *sb.* III. 1). Unsound 1852.

Scribable (skrəi·băb'l), *a. Obs.* exc. *arch.* late ME. [– med.L. *scribabilis*, f. L. *scribere* write; see -ABLE. Cf. AL. *paperus scrivabilis* (XIV).] Suitable for being written on.

Scribal (skrəi·băl), *a.* 1857. [f. SCRIBE *sb.*[1] + -AL[1] 1.] **1.** Of, pertaining to, or characteristic of a scribe or copyist, or his work. **2.** Of or pertaining to the Jewish scribes 1863.

Scribble (skri·b'l), *sb.* 1577. [f. next.] **1.** Something hastily or carelessly written, esp. a depreciatory term for a letter (usu. one's own); also, a worthless or trivial composition. **2.** Hurried or negligent and irregular writing; an example of this. Also, a number of irregular and unmeaning marks made with a pen, pencil, or the like. 1709.

1. He made a shift to get a livelyhood by his mendicant scribbles WOOD. **2.** The s. of men who think good writing a thing for clerks and shopmen 1881.

Scribble (skri·b'l), *v.*[1] 1465. [– med.L. *scribillare* (cf. rare L. *conscribillare*), dim. formed on L. *scribere* write; see -LE.] **1.** *trans.* To write hastily or carelessly. **a.** To write in an irregular, slovenly, or illegible hand through haste or carelessness. **b.** To write hurriedly or thoughtlessly. **c.** To cover with scribblings. Chiefly with *over*. 1540. **2.** *intr.* To write something hastily or carelessly, either as to handwriting or composition; to produce abundance of worthless writing 1534.

1. b. Writers who s. bosh 1884. **c.** *2 Hen. VI*, IV. ii. 88. **2.** If a man scribbles for a Newspaper, or writes a magazine article 1880. Hence **Scri·bblement,** something scribbled. **Scri·bblingly** *adv.*

Scribble (skri·b'l), *v.*[2] 1682. [prob. f. LG.; cf. the synon. G. *schrubbeln, schrobbeln*, frequent. f. LG. *schrubben, schrobben*; see SCRUB *v.*] *trans.* To card or tease (wool) coarsely, to pass through a 'scribbler'.

Scribbler[1] (skri·bləɹ). 1553. [f. SCRIBBLE *v.*[1] + -ER[1].] One who scribbles; hence 'a petty author, a writer without worth' (J.).

Scribbler[2]. 1682. [f. SCRIBBLE *v.*[2] + -ER[1].] **1.** A person who scribbles wool, or who tends a scribbling-machine. **2.** A machine for scribbling (wool) 1805.

Scribbling (skri·bliŋ), *vbl. sb.*[1] 1532. [f. SCRIBBLE *v.*[1] + -ING[1].] **1.** The action of SCRIBBLE *v.*[1] **2.** Something scribbled; a scrawl or scribble 1705.

attrib., as *s.-block, book*, etc.; **s. itch**, tr. L. *cacoethes scribendi*.

Scri·bbling, *vbl. sb.*[2] 1682. [f. SCRIBBLE *v.*[2] + -ING[1].] The action of SCRIBBLE *v.*[2]; the first process in carding wool. Also *attrib.*, as *s.-machine, -mill*, etc.

Scribe (skrəib), *sb.*[1] late ME. [– L. *scriba* official or public writer (in Vulg. tr. Gr. γραμματεύς, Heb. *sōpēr*), f. *scribere* trace characters, write.] A writer; one whose business is writing. **1.** *Jewish Hist.* A member of the class of professional interpreters of the Law after the return from the Captivity; in the Gospels often coupled with the Pharisees as upholders of ceremonial tradition. **2.** *Anc. Hist.* A general designation for any public official concerned with writing or the keeping of accounts; a secretary, clerk. late ME. **†3.** One who writes at another's dictation; an amanuensis –1838. **4.** A copyist or transcriber of manuscripts; now esp. the writer of a particular MS. copy of a classical or mediæval work 1535. **5.** A penman, one (more or less) skilled in penmanship. Now somewhat *arch.* 1588. **6.** One who writes or is in the habit of writing; an author; the writer (of a letter, etc.) 1585. **b.** Applied to a political pamphleteer or journalist; a party hack 1826.

1. And so may sarasenes be saued, scribes and iewes LANGL. **6.** As I am often writing..he commonly calls me the s. MME. D'ARBLAY.

Scribe (skrəib), *sb.*[2] 1812. [f. next.] A tool for scribing in *Carpentry, Building*, etc. *attrib.* **s.-mark,** a mark made with a scribing-iron on a log, etc.

Scribe (skrəib), *v.* 1678. [Of obscure development; varying with *scrive*; perh. orig. for DESCRIBE, DESCRIVE.] **1.** In techn. uses. **a.** *trans.* Orig., in *Carpentry*, to mark the intended outline of (a piece of timber) with one point of a pair of compasses, moved parallel with the other point which is drawn along the edge of the piece to which the 'scribed' piece is to be fitted. Now more widely: To mark or score (wood, metal, bricks) with a pointed instrument in order to indicate the outline to which the piece is to be cut or shaped; to draw (a line, etc.) in this way. **b.** Hence, to shape the edge of (a piece of timber, metal, etc.) so that it will fit into the irregular edge of another piece or to an uneven surface 1679. **c.** To mark (timber, a cask, etc.) with a scribing-iron 1859. **2. a.** *intr.* To act as a scribe, to write. **b.** *trans.* To write down. *rare* exc. *dial.* 1742. Hence **Scri·bing** *vbl. sb.* the action of the vb.; *concr.* the identifying mark on a cask, etc.; *pl.* incised markings on stone, etc.; also *attrib.*, in *scribing-block, -iron*, etc.

Scriber (skrəi·bəɹ). 1834. [f. prec. + -ER[1].] A tool or appliance for scribing.

Scribism (skrəi·biz'm). 1657. [f. SCRIBE *sb.*[1] + -ISM 2 b.] The teaching and literature of the ancient Jewish scribes; also, their qualities.

Scriggle (skri·g'l), *v.* Chiefly *dial.* 1806. [app. a blending of WRIGGLE and STRUGGLE; cf. †*scruggle* (XVI).] *intr.* To wriggle or struggle. Hence **Scri·ggle** *sb.* a wriggle; a scrawly piece of writing.

Scrim (skrim). 1792. [Of unkn. origin.] A kind of thin canvas for lining in upholstery, etc. Also *attrib.*

Scrimmage (skri·midʒ), **scrummage** (skrɒ·midʒ), *sb.* 1470. [alt. of †*scrimish*, var. of SKIRMISH *sb.*, with assim. of the ending to -AGE; for the change of (iʃ) to (idʒ) cf. dial. *rubbidge* for *rubbish*.] **†1.** = SKIRMISH *sb.* Also, a fencing bout. –1643. **2.** *colloq.* A noisy contention or tussle; also, a confused struggle between persons, a scuffle 1780. **3.** *Rugby Football.* (Now usu. abbrev. SCRUM.) Orig., a confused struggle in which each side endeavours to force its opponents and the ball towards the opposite goal; now, an ordered formation in which the two sets of forwards pack themselves together with their heads down and endeavour by pushing to work their opponents off the ball and break away with it or heel it out 1857. **b.** A tussle for the ball among players (in various games) 1883.

3. Phr. *To carry the s.*, to gain ground in a s. *To hold the s.*, to prevent one's opponents from gaining ground.

Scri·mmage, scru·mmage, *v.* 1833. [f. prec.] **1.** To bustle about. **2.** *Rugby Football.* To put (the ball) in a scrummage as a means of re-starting the game when and where it has been temporarily stopped, as for some breach of the rules; also, to propel or take along in a scrimmage 1881.

Scrimp (skrimp), *a.* and *adv.* 1718. [In early use Sc.; of unkn. origin; for possible cogns. see SHRIMP and for similar expressive structure cf. SKIMP *a.*] **A.** *adj.* Scant, scanty, meagre. **†B.** *adv.* Scarcely, barely –1834.

Scrimp (skrimp), *v.* 1774. [Goes with prec.] **1.** *trans.* To keep on short allowance, *esp.* of food. **2.** To cut short in amount, be sparing of 1834. **3.** *intr.* To economize, be niggardly 1848.

3. While we are saving and scrimping at the spigot, the government is drawing off at the bung 1848.

Scrimpy (skri·mpi), *a.* 1825. [f. SCRIMP *a.* + -Y[1].] Of meagre dimensions, scanty. Hence **Scri·mpiness.**

Scrimshank (skri·mʃæŋk), *v.* 1890. [Of unkn. origin; for the form cf. next.] *Mil. slang. intr.* To shirk duty. Hence **Scri·mshanker,** a shirker.

Scrimshaw (skri·mʃǭ), *sb.* 1851. [Also *scrimshander, -shandy*; of unkn. origin; perh. f. the surname *Scrimshaw*; for the form cf. prec.] *Naut.* A general name (also *s. work*) for the handicrafts practised by sailors by way of pastime during long whaling and other voyages, and for the products of these, as carvings on bone, ivory, shells, and the like. Also **Scri·mshaw** *v. trans.* to decorate or produce as s. work; *absol.* to employ oneself in s. work.

Scringe, *v. Obs.* exc. *dial.* 1608. [alt. f. CRINGE; see SCR-.] **1.** *trans.* To screw up (one's face); to shrug (the back or shoulders) from cold. **2.** *intr.* To flinch, cower 1825.

Scriniary (skri·niări). 1866. [– late L. *scriniarius*, f. L. *scrinium* book-box, letter-case; see -ARY[1].] A keeper of archives.

Scrip (skrip), *sb.*[1] ME. [Aphetic – OFr. *escrep(p)e* purse, bag for alms, var. of *escherpe* (mod. *écharpe*) or – ON. *skreppa*, which may itself be – OFr.] A small bag, wallet, or satchel; *esp.* one carried by a pilgrim, shepherd, or beggar.

A staffe and scryppe of Seynt James 1524.

Scrip (skrip), *sb.*[2] *Obs.* exc. *dial.* 1617. [perh. alt. of SCRIPT by assoc. with SCRAP *sb.*[1]] **1.** A small piece or scrap (of paper, etc.). **2.** *S. (of a pen)*: a small scrap of writing 1710. **3.** *U.S.* Fractional paper currency 1889.

Scrip (skrip), *sb.*[3] 1762. [Short for SUBSCRIPTION.] **1.** (Short for †*subscription receipt*.) Orig., a receipt for a portion of a loan subscribed. Now, a provisional document entitling the holder to a share or shares in a joint-stock undertaking, and exchangeable for a formal certificate when the necessary payments have been completed; often *collect. sing.* Hence, loosely, share certificates in general. Also *attrib.* **2.** *Book-selling.* (Short for *subscription price*.) A trade price 25 per cent. below the published price 1884.

Scripee (skripī·). *U.S.* 1909. [f. SCRIP *sb.*[3] + -EE[1].] One to whom land is allotted by scrip.

Scrippage (skri·pédʒ). 1600. [f. SCRIP *sb.*[1] + -AGE.] In Shakespearian phr. *scrip and s.*, modelled on *bag and baggage*; rarely used independently.

Script (skript). late ME. [In late ME. aphetic – OFr. *escript*, for *escrit* (now *écrit*):– L. *scriptum*, subst. use of n. pa. pple. of *scribere* write.] **1.** Something written; a piece of writing. Now *rare*. **2.** Handwriting; the characters used in handwriting. Also *attrib.*, as in *s. hand, letter*. 1860. **b.** *Typog.* (In full *s. type*.) Type resembling handwriting 1838.

This line is in Script Type

c. Used *attrib.* of systems of shorthand which resemble longhand in general appearance and in the movements of the hand that are required 1888. **3.** A kind of writing, a system of written characters 1883. **4.** *Law.* The original or principal instrument, where there is also a counterpart 1856. **5.** *Theatr.* Short (*'script*) for MANUSCRIPT 1897.

Scription (skri·pʃən). 1597. [– L. *scriptio, -ōn-*, f. *script-*, pa. ppl. stem of *scribere* write; see -ION.] **†1.** A writing, document, inscription –1693. **2.** Handwriting; a kind of handwriting (*rare*) 1846.

‖**Scriptorium** (skriptōᵊ·riŏm). *Pl.* **-ia, -iums.** 1774. [med.L., f. as prec.; see -ORIUM.] A writing-room; *spec.* the room in a religious house set apart for the copying of manuscripts.

Scriptory (skri·ptəri), *a.* and *sb. rare.* 1483. [In A. – L. *scriptorius*, f. as prec.; see -ORY[2]; in B. – med.L. SCRIPTORIUM; see -ORY[1].] **A.** *adj.* **1.** Pertaining to or used in writing 1682. **2.** Expressed in writing, written 1704. **B.** *sb.* A scriptorium 1483.

A. 2. Of Wills, *duo sunt genera*, Nuncupatory and S. SWIFT.

Scriptural (skri·ptiŭrăl, -tʃər-), *a.* 1641. [– late and med.L. *scripturalis*, f. L. *scriptura*; see SCRIPTURE, -AL[1].] **1.** Based upon, derived from, or depending upon Holy Scripture. **2.** Of or pertaining to writing 1802. Hence **Scri·ptural-ly** *adv.*, **-ness.**

Scripturalism (skri·ptiŭrăliz'm, -tʃər-). 1858. [f. prec. + -ISM.] Close adherence to or dependence upon the letter of Holy Scripture. So **Scri·pturalist,** an advocate of s. 1857.

Scripture (skri·ptiŭɹ, -tʃər). ME. [– L. *scriptura*, f. *script-*, pa. ppl. stem of *scribere* write; see -URE.] **1.** (Usu. with initial cap.) The sacred writings of the Old or New Testament, or (more usu.) of both together; Holy Writ; the Bible. Often with *holy* prefixed. **b.** A particular passage or text of the Bible. Now *rare* (after biblical use). late ME. **c.** *pl.* or (now rarely) *sing.* Sacred writings 1581. **2.** The action or art of writing; handwriting, penmanship. Also *concr.* written characters. Now *rare.* late ME. **3.** An inscription or superscription; a motto, legend, or posy. Also *gen.*, inscribed words. *Obs.* exc. *arch.* late ME. **4.** A written record or composition; *pl.* writings. *Obs.* exc. *arch.* late ME. †**b.** Written composition –1595. **5.** *attrib.* **a.** With the sense 'of or pertaining to Holy Scripture', as in *s.-lesson*, etc.; 'recorded in Holy Scripture', as in *s. history, miracle*, etc. 1627. **b.** With the sense 'used in or adopted from Holy Scripture', as in *s. expression*, etc.; 'derived from, prescribed by, or conformable to Holy Scripture, scriptural', as in *s. doctrine*, etc. 1594.

1. The diuell can cite S. for his purpose SHAKS. That there is a God; or, That the S. is his Word 1676. I would teach the knowledge of the scriptures only 1782. **c.** Most men do not know that any nation but the Hebrews have had a s. 1854. **2.** The handwriting was of that form of s. which attracts; refined yet energetic; full of character DISRAELI. **4.** What is heere, The Scriptures of the Loyall Leonatus, All turn'd to Heresie? SHAKS. Hence **Scriptu·rian** (*rare*), a scripturist. **Scri·pturism,** reliance on the Scriptures alone; devotion to S.

Scripturist (skri·ptiŭrist, -tʃər-). 1624. [f. SCRIPTURE *sb.* + -IST.] **1.** One who is versed in the Scriptures 1661. **2.** One who bases his religious belief or opinions upon Scripture alone 1624.

Scritch (skritʃ), *sb. arch.* 1513. [See next.] A screech, shriek, loud cry.

Sudden scritches of the jay TENNYSON.

Scritch (skritʃ), *v. arch.* ME. [*Scriche* XIII, f. imit. base in OE. *scriććettan*; cf. SKREAK *v.*, dial. *skrike*, of Scand. origin (cf. ON. *skrækja*, Norw. *skrika*).] *intr.* To utter a loud cry; to screech or shriek.

Scri·tch-owl. Now *arch.* 1530. [f. SCRITCH *sb.* + OWL.] = SCREECH-OWL.

Scrivener (skri·v'nəɹ). late ME. [f. ME. *scrivein* (XIII), aphetic – OFr. *escrivein* (mod. *écrivain*) :– Rom. **scribano*; f. L. *scriba* SCRIBE, with *-anus* -AN; see -ER[1].] **1.** A professional penman; a scribe, copyist; a clerk, secretary, amanuensis. **2.** A notary 1477. **3.** One who 'received money to place out at interest, and who supplied those who wanted to raise money on security' (Tomlins). Also *money s. Obs.* exc. *Hist.* 1607.

1. *Scrivener's cramp, palsy*, writer's cramp. **3.** The Scriueners and Broakers doe valew vnsound Men BACON.

Scrobicular (skrobi·kiŭlăɹ), *a.* 1888. [f. SCROBICULE + -AR[1].] Pertaining to or surrounded by scrobicules.

Scrobiculate (skrobi·kiŭlĕt), *a.* 1806. [f. next + -ATE[2].] *Bot.* and *Zool.* Having many small depressions; furrowed or pitted; *Ent.* foveate. So **Scrobi·culated** *a.*

Scrobicule (skrōᵘ·bikiŭl). 1880. [– L. *scrobiculus*, dim. of *scrobis* trench; see -CULE.] *Biol.* A small pit or depression; *spec.* the smooth area around the tubercles of a sea-urchin.

Scrod (skrǫd). *U.S.* Also **scrode.** 1873. [Of unkn. origin.] A young cod weighing less than three pounds, *esp.* one that is split and fried or boiled.

Scrofula (skrǫ·fiŭlă). late ME. [In early use pl. after late L. *scrofulæ* swelling of the glands, dim. of *scrofa* breeding sow (supposed to be subject to the disease). Later sing. after med.L. *scrofula.*] A constitutional disease characterized mainly by chronic enlargement and degeneration of the lymphatic glands. Also called KING'S EVIL and STRUMA. So **Scro·fulide** (skrǫ·fiŭlid) *Path.*, [Fr. *scrofulide*] a scrofulous or strumous skin-disease.

Scrofulous (skrǫ·fiŭləs), *a.* 1612. [f. prec. + -OUS.] **1.** Caused by, or of the nature of, scrofula. **2.** Affected with, or suffering from, scrofula 1708. **3.** *fig.* Of literature, etc.: Morally corrupt 1842.

1. He had inherited..a s. taint MACAULAY. **3.** My s. French novel On grey paper with blunt type! BROWNING. Hence **Scro·fulous-ly** *adv.*, **-ness.**

Scrog (skrǫg), *sb.* Chiefly *Sc.* and *n. dial.* late ME. [Parallel to SCRAG *sb.*[2]] A stunted bush; usu. *pl.*, brushwood, underwood. **b.** *Her.* A branch of a tree; a blazon sometimes used by Scottish heralds 1780. Hence **Scro·ggy** *a.* abounding in s. Also, of trees, stunted.

Scroll (skrōᵘl), *sb.* [Late ME. *scrowle*, alt., after *rowle* ROLL *sb.*[1], of SCROW.] **1.** A roll of paper or parchment, usu. one with writing upon it. **b.** A roll or bundle of any material 1852. **2.** A piece of writing, *esp.* a letter 1534. **b.** A list, roll, or schedule (of names) 1546. **3.** A strip or ribbon-shaped slip of paper with a legend inscribed; a graphic or plastic representation of this 1600. **b.** *Her.* The ribbon-like appendage to a coat of arms, on which the motto is inscribed. Also *transf.*, the words inscribed upon the scroll. 1610. **4.** An ornament resembling a scroll of paper partly unrolled. **a.** A convoluted or spiral ornament; *spec.* the volute of the Ionic and Corinthian capitals 1611. **b.** *Shipbuilding.* A curved piece of timber bolted to the knee of the head 1797. **c.** The curved head of instruments of the violin kind 1836. **d.** *U.S.* A flourish (or sometimes a circle) added to a person's signature to represent a seal, and having the same value 1856. **5.** Applied variously in techn. use to scroll-shaped or spiral parts, figures, etc. 1868. **b.** *Geom.* A skew ruled surface 1862.

1. And heven vanysshed awaye as a s. when hit is rolled togedder TINDALE *Rev.* 6:14. **2.** Do not exceede The Prescript of this Scroule SHAKS. **b.** Now good Peter Quince, call forth your Actors by the scrowle SHAKS.

attrib. and *Comb.*, as **s.-bone,** a turbinal bone; **s. chuck,** a lathe-chuck with a spiral arrangement for operating the jaws; **-gear,** a spiral gear-wheel; **-head** = sense 4 b; **-saw,** a saw for cutting scrolls; **-wheel,** a wheel actuated by scroll-gear.

Scroll (skrōᵘl), *v.* 1606. [f. prec.] **1.** *trans.* To write down in a scroll (*rare*). **2.** *intr.* for *refl.* To roll or curl up 1868.

Scrolled (skrōᵘld), *ppl. a.* 1603. [f. SCROLL *sb.* or *v.* + -ED.] **1.** In the form of, or decorated with, scrolls; *transf.* curled. **2.** Inscribed with mottoes 1875.

1. *transf.* An envoy with a s. mustache GEO. ELIOT.

Scroop (skrūp), *v.* 1787. [imit.] *intr.* To make a strident, grating, or scraping sound; to grate, creak, squeak. So **Scroop** *sb.* a harsh, strident, or scraping noise.

‖**Scrophularia** (skrǫfiŭlēᵊ·riă). 1663. [– med.L. *scrofularia* (sc. *herba*), f. *scrofula, scrophula*; see SCROFULA, -ARY[1] 3.] *Bot.* A genus of monopetalous plants (the fig-worts), typical of the family *Scrophulariaceæ*; a plant of this genus. Hence **Scrophularia·ceous** *a.* belonging to the family *Scrophulariaceæ.*

Scrotal (skrōᵘ·tăl), *a.* 1800. [f. SCROTUM + -AL[1].] Of or pertaining to the scrotum.

Scrotiform (skrōᵘ·tifǫɹm), *a.* 1775. [f. SCROTUM + -FORM.] *Bot.* and *Biol.* Pouch-shaped.

Scrotocele (skrōᵘ·tosīl). 1693. [f. *scroto-*, comb. f. SCROTUM + Gr. κήλη tumour; see -O-, CELE.] *Path.* A scrotal hernia.

‖**Scrotum** (skrōᵘ·tǒm). 1597. [L.] *Anat.* The tegument enclosing the testicles.

Scrouge (skrūdʒ, skraudʒ), *v. colloq.* and *vulgar.* 1755. [alt. of SCRUZE.] *trans.* To incommode by pressing against (a person); to encroach on (a person's) space in sitting or standing; to crowd. Also *intr.*

Scrounge (skraundʒ), *v. slang.* 1919. [var. of dial. *scrunge* steal.] *trans.* To hunt about for; to take without permission, steal. Hence **Scrou·nger.**

Scrow (skrōᵘ), *sb.* ME. [Aphetic – AFr. *escrowe*, OFr. *escroe* strip, esp. parchment; see ESCROW.] †**1.** = SCROLL *sb.* 1. –1615. †**b.** *pl.* Writings –1646. **2.** *pl.* or *collect. sing.* Strips or clippings of hide or leather used for making glue ME.

†**Scroyle.** 1595. [Of unkn. origin.] A scoundrel –1821.

Scrub (skrɒb), *sb.*[1] late ME. [var. of SHRUB (see SCR-).] **I. 1.** A low stunted tree. **2.** *collect.* Brushwood; also, a tract of country overgrown with this 1809.

1. *Mallee s.* (*Eucalyptus oleosa*), *Horizontal s.* (*Anodopetalum biglandulosum*), Australian trees, common in thickets and undergrowth.

II. 1. A breed of cattle distinguished by their small size 1555. **2.** *transf.* A mean insignificant fellow 1589.

2. He is an arrant s., I assure you FIELDING.

attrib. and *Comb.*: as **s.-itch,** a skin-disease peculiar to the jungles of New Guinea; **-oak,** *Villaresia moorei* and *Casuarina cunninghamii.*

Scrub (skrɒb), *sb.*[2] 1621. [f. SCRUB *v.*] **1.** The action or an act of scrubbing. **2.** A broom or brush with short hard bristles 1687. **3.** One who scrubs; a drudge 1709. **b.** *U.S.* A player not belonging to the regular team; a second or weaker team 1903.

attrib. **s.-race, -game,** *U.S.* an impromptu race or game between untrained competitors.

Scrub (skrɒb), *a.* 1710. [SCRUB *sb.*[1] used attrib.] Chiefly *U.S.* = SCRUBBY *a.* 3.

Scrub (skrɒb), *v.* 1595. [ME. *scrobbe*, beside *shrubbe*, prob. – MLG., MDu. *schrobben, schrubben* (cf. SCR-).] †**1.** *trans.* To scratch, rub (a part of one's body) –1725. **2.** To clean (esp. a floor, wood, etc.) by rubbing with a hard brush and water 1595. **3.** *techn.* To cleanse (coal-gas) by means of a scrubber 1885. **4.** *Comb.*, as *s.-brush, -woman* (U.S.).

†**Scru·bbed,** *a.* 1596. [f. SCRUB *sb.*[1] + -ED[2].] Stunted, dwarfed –1835.

Scrubber (skrɒ·bəɹ). 1839. [f. SCRUB *v.* + -ER[1].] **1.** One who or something which scrubs. **2.** An apparatus for cleansing coal-gas from impurities 1853.

Scrubbing-brush (skrɒ·biŋbrɒʃ). 1681. A brush with hard bristles for scrubbing.

Scrubby (skrɒ·bi), *a.* 1591. [f. SCRUB *sb.*[1] + -Y[1].] **1.** Stunted, under-developed. **2.** Covered with brushwood 1676. **3.** Insignificant, shabby, paltry, of poor appearance 1782.

1. S. lichens 1860. **2.** S. Pasture 1676. **3.** To be treated like a little s. apprentice? 1782.

Scruff (skrɒf), *sb.*[1] 1526. [Metathetic var. of SCURF *sb.*[1]] **1.** SCURF *sb.*[1] 2. **2.** A thin crust or coating 1591. **3.** Refuse, litter; †*spec.* base money; also used (like 'muck') as a contemptuous term for money 1559. Hence **Scru·ffy** *a.* scaly, covered with scurf.

Scruff (skrɒf), *sb.*[2] 1790. [orig. alt. of SCUFF *sb.*, of which there is a synon. var. CUFF *sb.*[3]; perh. based ult. on ON. *skoft* (= OHG. *scuft*, Goth. *skuft*) hair of the head; cf. (M)HG. *schopf.*] The nape of the neck.

Scrum (skrɒm). 1888. [abbrev. f. SCRUMMAGE.] = SCRIMMAGE *sb.* 3. Comb. **s.-half.**

Scrummage: see SCRIMMAGE *sb.* and *v.*

Scrumptious (skrɒ·mpʃəs), *a. colloq.* or *vulgar.* 1836. [Of unkn. origin.] **1.** Fastidious, hard to please. ? *U.S.* only. 1845. **2. a.** *U.S.* Stylish, handsome. **b.** First rate, 'glorious'. 1836. **Scru·mptious-ly** *adv.*, **-ness.**

Scrunch (skrɒnʃ), *sb.* 1854. [f. next.] The noise made by, or an act of, scrunching.

Scrunch (skrɒnʃ), *v.* 1825. [Expressive alt. of CRUNCH; see SCR-.] **1.** *trans.* = CRUNCH *v.* 1, 2. **2.** *intr.* To produce a sound of being scrunched 1844. Hence **Scru·nchy** *a.*, that emits a crunching sound when crushed.

Scruple (skrū·p'l), *sb.*[1] 1564. [– Fr. *scrupule* or L. *scrupulus, -um* small sharp or pointed stone, smallest division of weight, hence fig., dim. of *scrupus* rough or sharp pebble, anxiety (Cicero).] **1.** A unit of weight = 20 grains, $\frac{1}{3}$ drachm, $\frac{1}{24}$ oz. Apothecaries' weight. Denoted by the character ℈. **2.** One sixtieth of a degree; a minute of arc 1610. †**3.** As a unit of time. *S. of an hour*: the sixtieth part of an hour, a minute 1603. **4.** *fig.* A very small quantity or amount; a very small part or portion 1574.

4. Look into Italy and Spain, whether those places be one s. the better MILT.

Scruple (skrū·p'l), *sb.*[2] 1526. [Identical with prec.] **1.** A thought or circumstance that troubles the mind or conscience; a doubt, uncertainty, or hesitation in regard to right and wrong, duty, propriety, etc.; esp. one which is regarded as over-refined or over-nice. Also in generalized sense. †**2.** An intellectual difficulty, perplexity, or objection –1741. †**b.** Disbelief or doubt *of* –1672.

1. Some crauen s. Of thinking too precisely on th'euent SHAKS. Phr. *S. of conscience. Without s. To have scruples*; *to have little, no s.*, etc., *about* (a matter), *in* (doing something). *To make s.* (also *a, no*, etc. *s.*) to entertain or raise a scruple or doubt; to hesitate, be reluctant, esp. on conscientious grounds. **2. b.** Phr. †*To have* or *make s. of*, to hesitate to believe or admit; Whereat, I..Made s. of his praise SHAKS.

Scruple (skrū·p'l), *v.* 1627. [f. the sb. or – Fr. *scrupuler*.] †**1.** *trans.* To have or make scruples about; to demur to, take exception to; to hesitate or stick at (doing something) –1837. †**2.** To doubt, question, hesitate to believe (a fact, allegation, etc.) –1846. †**3.** To cause (a person) to feel scruples –1689. **4.** *intr.* To entertain or raise scruples; to hesitate, demur, †doubt. Chiefly *to s. at*. Now *rare*. 1639. **5.** Const. *inf.*: To hesitate or be reluctant (*to do* something), esp. on grounds of conscience or propriety 1660.

1. He scrupled no means to obtain his ends CHESTERF. **3.** The dangerous tentations of the devil..do mainly..s. the consciences of the weaker amongst us 1657. **4.** The sovereigns..who scrupled at no means for securing themselves on the throne SOUTHEY. **5.** He scrupl'd not to eat Against his better knowledge MILT. Hence **Scru·pler**, one who scruples, one who has scruples. So **Scru·pulist**, one who has scruples or raises difficulties.

Scrupulosity (skrūpiulǫ·sĭti). 1526. [– (O)Fr. *scrupulosité* or L. *scrupulositas*, f. *scrupulosus*; see next, -ITY.] **1.** The state or quality of being scrupulous; an instance of this; †a scruple. †**2.** *Astr.* Minute determination (of time) 1633.

1. Avoid a needless S. of Conscience, as a thing which keeps our Minds always uneasie 1690.

Scrupulous (skrū·piŭləs), *a.* 1450. [– (O)Fr. *scrupuleux* or L. *scrupulosus*, f. *scrupulus*; see SCRUPLE *sb.*, -OUS.] **1.** Troubled with doubts or scruples of conscience; over-nice or meticulous in matters of right and wrong. Also (of things, actions, etc.), characterized by such scruples. †**b.** Prone to hesitate or doubt; cautious or meticulous in acting, deciding, etc. Also (of actions, etc.), characterized by doubt or distrust; (of objections) cavilling. –1695. †**2.** Of a thing: Causing or raising scruples; liable to give offence; dubious, doubtful –1685. **3.** Careful to follow the dictates of conscience; strict in matters of right and wrong 1545. †**b.** With inf.: Careful (to do something) in obedience to one's conscience 1729. **4.** Of actions, etc.: Characterized by a strict and minute regard for what is right 1756. **5.** Minutely exact or careful (in non-moral matters); strictly attentive even to the smallest details 1638.

1. 3 *Hen. VI*, IV. vii. 61. **2.** As the Cause of a Warre ought to be Iust; so the Iustice of that Cause ought to be Euident; Not Obscure, not S. BACON. Phr. †*To make it s.*, to scruple, hesitate (*to do* something). **3. b.** We should be religiously s. and exact to say nothing..but what is true 1729. **4.** He gave to business the most s. attention 1779. **5.** Great men are seldom over s. in the arrangement of their attire DICKENS. Hence **Scru·pulous-ly** *adv.*, **-ness.**

Scrutable (skrū·tăb'l), *a.* 1600. [prob. extracted from INSCRUTABLE. Cf. late and med.L. *scrutabilis* searchable.] That can be understood by scrutiny.

Scrutation (skrutēⁱ·ʃən). 1593. [– L. *scrutatio*, *-ōn-*, f. *scrutat-*, pa. ppl. stem of *scrutari*; see next, -ION.] Minute search or examination.

Scrutator (skrutēⁱ·təɹ). 1580. [– L. *scrutator*, *-ōr-*, f. *scrutari* search, examine, f. *scruta* trash, rubbish, the orig. application being to the rummaging of rag-pickers or the searching of persons; see -ATOR.] **1.** One who examines or investigates 1593. **2.** *spec.* One whose office it is to examine or investigate closely; *esp.* one who acts as an examiner of votes at an election 1680. **b.** As the title of a university official. Now *Hist.* 1580.

Scrutineer (skrūtinīᵊ·ɹ). 1557. [f. SCRUTINY + -EER¹ (repl. †*scrutiner* XVI).] One whose duty it is to scrutinize or examine, esp. one who examines votes at an election, etc.

Scrutinize (skrū·tinəiz), *v.* 1671. [f. next + -IZE.] **1.** *trans.* To subject to scrutiny. **b.** *spec.* with ref. to votes 1750. †**2.** *intr.* To make scrutiny. Const. *into*. –1788.

1. She began..to s. her heart, with an uncommon degree of severity 1800. **b.** The Westminster election, which is still scrutinising, produced us a parliamentary event this week H. WALPOLE. Hence **Scru·tinizer.** So **Scru·tinous** *a.* [– Fr. †*scrutineux*] (now *rare*), closely examining; searching 1599; **Scru·tinously** *adv.* 1649.

Scrutiny (skrū·tini). 1450. [– L. *scrutinium*, f. *scrutari*; see SCRUTATOR, -Y⁴.] **1.** The formal taking of individual votes, as a method of electing to an office or dignity, or of deciding some question; an instance of this procedure. Now chiefly in *Canon Law*. **2.** Investigation, critical inquiry; an instance of this 1604. **b.** An official examination of the votes cast at an election, in order to eliminate any votes that are invalid, and to rectify or confirm the numbers stated in the return 1728. **3.** The action of looking searchingly at something; a searching gaze 1796.

1. We have at last a new Pope, after many scrutinies 1623. **2.** An accurate scrutinie of all my actions past EVELYN. **3.** A careful s. of her countenance DICKENS.

Scrutoire (skrutwā·ɹ, -twǭ·ɹ). 1626. [Aphetic f. *escrutoire*, unexpl. var. of ESCRITOIRE.] = ESCRITOIRE.

Scruze (skrūz), *v.* Now *dial.* 1590. [perh. blending of SCREW *v.* and SQUEEZE. Cf. SCROUGE.] *trans.* To squeeze.

†**Scry**, *sb.* late ME. [Aphetic f. ASCRY *sb.* or ESCRY *sb.* Cf. next.] **1.** Crying out, exclamation, clamour –1819. **2.** An attack; a reconnoitre –1587.

Scry (skrəi), *v.* 1528. [aphet. f. DESCRY *v.*] **1.** *trans.* To descry, see, perceive. *Obs.* exc. *dial.* 1555. **2.** *intr.* To see images in a crystal, etc. which reveal the future or secrets of the past or present; to act as a crystal-gazer. (Revived recently as a techn. term.) 1528. Hence **Scry·er**, a crystal-gazer.

Scud (skɒd), *sb.* 1609. [f. next.] **1.** The action of scudding; hurried movement. **2. a.** Light clouds driven rapidly before the wind 1669. **b.** A driving shower (of rain or snow) 1687. **c.** A sudden gust of wind 1694. **d.** Ocean foam or spray driven by the wind 1850. **3.** *School slang.* A swift runner 1857.

2. a. The S. comes against the Wind, 'twill blow hard 1669. **d.** The air was drenched with spume and flying s. 1894.

Scud (skɒd), *v.* 1532. [poss. alt. of SCUT, as if to race like a hare.] **1.** *intr.* To run or move briskly or hurriedly; to dart nimbly from place to place. **b.** In the imper.: Be off! Make haste! 1602. **2.** To sail or move swiftly on the water. Now chiefly (in techn. nautical use), to run before a gale with little or no sail. 1582. **3.** Of clouds, foam, etc.: To be driven by the wind 1699. **4.** *trans.* To pass, travel, or sail quickly over 1632.

1. The Trout within the weeds did s. 1013. **2.** There was too much wind to s. 1884. **3.** Crisp foam-flakes s. along the level sand TENNYSON.

Scuddle (skɒ·d'l), *v.* Now *dial.* 1577. [frequent. of prec. Cf. SCUTTLE *v.*¹] *intr.* To run away hastily, to scuttle.

‖**Scudo** (skū·do). *Pl.* **scudi** (skū·di). 1644. [It. *scudo* :– L. *scutum* shield. Cf. ÉCU.] A silver coin and money of account formerly current in various Italian states, usu. worth about four shillings.

Scuff (skɒf), *sb.* 1787. [See SCRUFF *sb.*²] The nape of the neck (only in references to seizing by the 'scuff (of the neck)'.

Scuff (skɒf), *v.* 1768. [perh. partly imit.; perh. conn. w. SCURF *v.* With sense 3 cf. CUFF *v.*¹] **1.** *trans.* To touch lightly in passing 1824. **b.** To scrape (the ground, boards, etc.) with the feet; to wear off by treading 1897. **2.** *intr.* To walk (through dust, snow, etc.) so as to brush it aside or throw it up; hence *trans.*, to throw *up* (dust by this manner of walking) 1768. **b.** To shuffle with the feet 1847. **3.** *trans.* To buffet (a person) 1841.

Scuffle (skɒ·f'l), *sb.*¹ 1606. [f. SCUFFLE *v.*¹] **1.** A scrambling fight; an encounter with much hustling and random exchange of blows; a tussle. **2.** The action of scuffling; confused utterance (of speech); shuffling (of feet) 1899.

1. There had been a s. among them in which one of their canoes had been overset DE FOE. *transf.* A s. for places BURKE.

Scuffle (skɒ·f'l), *sb.*² 1798. [– Du. *schoffel* weeding-hoe. See SHOVEL.] **1.** = SCUFFLER². **2.** A gardener's thrust-hoe. *local* and *U.S.* 1841.

Scuffle (skɒ·f'l), *v.*¹ 1579. [prob. f. Scand. base (cf. Sw. *skuff*, *skuffa* push) to be referred to Gmc. **skuf-* SHOVE.] **1.** *intr.* To struggle confusedly *together* or *with* another; to fight at close quarters in a disorderly manner 1590. **2.** *trans.* To put *on*, *out*, *up*, etc. in a scrambling or confused manner 1579. **3.** *intr.* To struggle *through*, *on*, *along*; hence, to go hurriedly or superficially (*through* or *over* some operation) 1784. **4.** To go in hurried confusion; to move with much effort and fuss; also *trans.* (causatively) 1838. **5.** To move with a shuffling gait; also, to shuffle (with the feet) 1825.

1. I..haue seene in former dayes The best Knights of the world, and scuffled in some frayes DRAYTON. *transf.* Both at Sea and Land we Tug and S. for Dominion and Wealth 1678. Hence **Scu·ffler**¹, one who scuffles. **Scu·fflingly** *adv.*

Scuffle (skɒ·f'l), *v.*² 1766. [f. SCUFFLE *sb.*²] *trans.* To scarify or stir the surface of (land) with a thrust-hoe or horse-hoe; to hoe (a crop), cut up (weeds), turn in (seed) by means of a scuffle or scuffler. Hence **Scu·ffler**², an implement for scarifying and stirring the surface of the ground, esp. between the rows of crops; a horse-hoe.

Scull (skɒl), *sb.*¹ ME. [Of unkn. origin.] **1.** A kind of oar. **a.** An oar used to propel a boat by working it from side to side over the stern of the boat, reversing the blade at each turn. **b.** One of a pair of short and light oars, which can be operated at once by one person, who sits midway between the sides of the boat. †**2.** A sculling-boat –1661. †**3.** A sculler (*rare*) –1719. **4.** *pl.* A sculling-race 1878. **5.** An act of sculling 1886.

Scull (skɒl), *sb.*² 1813. A local name for various species of gulls.

Scull (skɒl), *v.* 1624. [f. SCULL *sb.*¹] **1.** *intr.* or *absol.* To proceed by means of a boat propelled with a scull or a pair of sculls; to use a scull or a pair of sculls in propelling a boat. **b.** *trans.* To make (a particular stroke) in sculling 1875. **2.** To propel (a boat) by means of a scull or a pair of sculls 1665. **b.** *intr.* Of a boat: To admit of being sculled (well, easily, etc.) 1891. **3.** *trans.* To convey (a person) by water in a sculling-boat or by sculling 1827. Hence **Scu·ller**, one who sculls; a boat propelled by sculling, a sculling-boat.

Scullery (skɒ·ləri). 1440. [– AFr. *squillerie*, for OFr. *escuelerie*, f. *escuelier* maker or seller of dishes, f. *escuele* :– Rom. **scūtella* (by assoc. with L. *scutum* shield), for L. *scutella* salver, waiter, dim. of *scutra* wooden dish or platter; see -ERY.] **1.** The department of a household concerned with the care of the plates, dishes, and kitchen utensils. Also the room or rooms devoted to this. *Obs.* exc. *Hist.* **2.** In mod. use: A small room attached to a kitchen, in which the washing of dishes and other dirty work is done 1753.

attrib., as *s. maid*, etc.

Scullion (skɒ·lyən). 1483. [Of unkn. origin.] A domestic servant of the lowest rank in a household, who performed the menial offices of the kitchen; hence, a person of the lowest order, esp. as an abusive epithet. Now *arch.* **b.** quasi-*adj.* Base, mean 1658.

Haveloke..having been first a skullen in the King's Kitchin HOLLAND. Hence **Scu·llionship.**

†**Sculp**, *sb.* 1696. [f. next.] An engraving used as an illustration in a book –1706.

Sculp (skɒlp), *v.* 1535. [f. L. *sculpere* carve.] †**1.** *trans.* To carve or engrave (upon something) –1695. **2.** To sculpture. Now chiefly *colloq.* or *joc.* Also *intr.* or *absol.* 1784.

2. Men who write, and paint, and s. KIPLING.

Sculpin (skɒ·lpin), *sb.* 1672. [perh. alt. of SCORPENE.] **1.** A name for various small worthless fish having a spiny appearance; **a.** A fish of the genus *Callionymus*, e.g. *C. draco*; **b.** A fish of the genus *Cottus*, e.g. *C. virginianus*; **c.** *Hemitripterus hispidus* or *americanus*; **d.** *Scorpæna guttata* (see SCORPENE). **2.** *transf.* A mean, worthless person or animal 1833.

Sculpt (skɒlpt), *v.* *rare* exc. *joc.* 1864. [– Fr. *sculpter*, f. *sculpteur* SCULPTOR, but now apprehended as a jocular back-formation from SCULPTOR.] *trans.* To sculpture; *absol.* to practise the art of sculpture.

†**Scu·lptile**, *a.* and *sb.* ME. [– L. *sculptilis*, also (late L.) sb. *sculptile* graven image, f. *sculpt-*; see next, -ILE.] **A.** *adj.* Sculptured,

graven –1842. **B.** *sb. pl.* Graven images –1609.

Sculptor (skɒ·lptəɹ). 1634. [– L. *sculptor*, f. *sculpt-*; see next, -OR 2. Cf. Fr. *sculpteur*.] **1.** One who practises the art of sculpture; chiefly, an artist who produces works of statuary in marble or bronze. †**2.** An engraver –1658. So **Scu·lptress,** a female s.

Sculpture (skɒ·lptiŭɹ, -tʃəɹ), *sb.* late ME. [(occas. †*sculture* XVI – It. *scultura*); – L. *sculptura*, f. *sculpt-*, pa. ppl. stem of *sculpere*, var. of *scalpere*; see SCALP *v.*¹, -URE.] **1.** Orig., the process or art of carving or engraving a hard material so as to produce designs or figures in relief, in intaglio, or in the round. In mod. use, that branch of fine art which is concerned with producing figures in the round or in relief, either by carving, by fashioning some plastic substance, or by making a mould for casting in metal; the practice of this art. (Now chiefly used with ref. to work in stone or bronze, and to the production of figures of considerable size.) **2.** *concr.* **a.** The product of the sculptor's art; sculptured figures in general. late ME. **b.** A work of sculpture; a sculptured figure or design 1616. †**3.** An engraving; engravings collectively –1781. **4.** *Nat. Hist.* Marking of the skin, shell, or surface of any animal or plant resembling that produced by a carving tool 1826.

2. Some frail memorial still erected nigh, with uncouth rhimes and shapeless s. deck'd GRAY. **4.** But in some of these plants the seeds also differ in shape and s. DARWIN. Hence **Scu·lptural** *a.* of or pertaining to s.; having the qualities of a piece of s.; **-ly** *adv.* **Sculpture·sque** *a.* like s., having the qualities of s.

Sculpture (skɒ·lptiŭɹ, -tʃəɹ), *v.* 1645. [f. prec.] **1.** *trans.* To represent in sculpture, to carve (a design or figure) from the solid. **2.** To decorate with sculpture. Also *pass.* (*Nat. Hist.*), to bear marks resembling sculpture. 1645.

1. They who sculptured loveliness in stone 1852. *transf.* The edges are soon sculptured off by the action of the sun TYNDALL.

Scum (skɒm), *sb.* ME. [– MLG., MDu. *schūm* (Du. *schuim*) = OHG. *scūm* (G. *schaum*; cf. MEERSCHAUM); Gmc. **skūma-*, f. **skū-* cover.] †**1.** Foam, froth; *pl.* bubbles –1694. **2.** †**a.** Dross which rises to the surface in the purifying of a metal; refuse, slag –1811. **b.** A film or layer of floating matter formed upon the surface of a liquid in a state of fermentation, ebullition, etc.; hence, a film formed upon stagnant or foul water 1440. **3.** *transf.* Applied to persons: The off-scourings of humanity; the lowest class of the population of a place or country 1586. †**b.** An assemblage or body of 'scum' –1829. †**c.** A worthless wretch –1818.

1. *fig.* The s. & froth of my letters 1637. **2. b.** Spawn, weeds, and filth, a leprous s., Made the running rivulet thick and dumb SHELLEY. **3.** Scoundrels! Dogs.! the S. of the Earth! 1712. **b.** A s. of Brittaines, and base Lackey Pezants SHAKS. Hence **Scu·mmy** *a.* having the appearance of s.; abounding in s.

Scum (skɒm), *v.* late ME. [f. the sb.] †**1.** *trans.* To clear (the surface of a liquid) of impurities or floating matter; to SKIM. Also, to skim *off*. –1817. †**2.** To scour (the sea or land) –1690. **3.** *intr.* †**a.** To rise to the surface as scum –1525. **b.** To throw up foul matter as a scum; to become covered with a scum 1661.

1. Some scumd the drosse that from the metall came SPENSER. **2.** Without certain seat, they liv'd by scumming those Seas and shoars as Pyrats MILT.

Scu·mber, *sb. Obs.* exc. *dial.* 1647. [f. next.] The dung of a dog or fox. Hence *dial.*, filth, dirt.

Scu·mber, *v. Obs.* exc. *dial.* late ME. [app. aphetic – OFr. *descombrer* relieve of a load (mod. *décombrer* clear of rubbish). Cf. DISCUMBER, of equivalent formation.] **1.** *intr.* Of a dog or fox: To evacuate the fæces. Also *joc.* of a person. **2.** *trans.* To void (ordure); *fig.* to produce (something foul) 1596.

Scumble (skɒ·mb'l), *sb.* 1834. [f. next.] A thin coat (of colour) put on by scumbling; a softened effect produced by scumbling.

Scumble (skɒ·mb'l), *v.* 1675. [poss. f. SCUM *v.* + -LE.] *trans.* In *Oil Painting.* To soften (the colours in a portion of a picture) by overlaying with a thin coat of opaque or semi-opaque colour; to spread or 'drive' (a colour) thinly over a portion of a picture in order to soften hard lines or blend the tints; to produce (an effect) by this process. Also *absol.* So in *Pencil, Chalk,* or *Monochrome drawing,* to soften the lines by rubbing with a stump, etc.

†**Scu·mmer.** ME. [f. SCUM *v.* + -ER¹; in sense 1 after OFr. *escumoir* (mod. *écumoire*), in sense 2 after OFr. *escumeor* (mod. *écumeur*), respectively instrumental noun and agent-noun to *escumer* skim, f. *escume* SCUM *sb.*] **1.** A shallow ladle or sieve for removing scum or floating matter from the surface of a liquid –1825. **2.** One who scours the sea; a rover, pirate –1585.

Scumming (skɒ·miŋ), *vbl. sb.* 1530. [f. SCUM *v.* + -ING¹.] **1.** The action of removing scum from the surface of a liquid 1611. **2.** *concr.* in *sing.* and *pl.* The matter removed in the form of scum. †Also, the matter rising to the surface as scum. 1530.

Scuncheon (skɒ·nʃən). late ME. [Aphetic – OFr. *escoinson* (mod. *écoinçon*), f. *es-* EX-¹ + *coin* corner (cf. COIGN).] *Arch.* The bevelled inner edge of the side or jamb of a window, door, etc.

Scunner (skɒ·nəɹ), *sb. Sc.* and *n. dial.* 1500. [f. next.] A loathing disgust; esp. in the phr. *to take a s. at, against.*

Scunner (skɒ·nəɹ), *v. Sc.* and *n. dial.* late ME. [Of unkn. origin.] **1.** *intr.* †**a.** To shrink back with fear, to flinch. **b.** To be affected with violent disgust, to feel sick. **2.** *trans.* To disgust, sicken 1871.

Scup (skɒp). *U.S.* 1848. [Shortened – Narragansett *mishcup* 'thick-scaled', f. *mishe* large + *cuppi* scale.] The fish *Pagrus argyrops.*

Scuppaug (skɒ·pǫg). *U.S.* 1873. [Shortened – Narragansett *mischcuppâuog*, pl. of *mishcup*; see prec.] = prec.

Scupper (skɒ·pəɹ), *sb.* 1485. [perh. – AFr. aphetic deriv. of Fr. *escopir* (mod. *écopir*) :- Rom. **skuppire* to spit, of imit. origin; cf. G. *speigatt* scupper, f. *speien* spit (SPEW *v.*) + *gat(t)* hole (GATE *sb.*¹).] An opening in a ship's side on a level with the deck to allow water to run away.

Scupper (skɒ·pəɹ), *v. Mil. slang.* 1885. [Of unkn. origin; app. first used in the Sudan.] *trans.* To annihilate, 'do for'. Often *pass.* to be 'done for', killed.

Scuppernong (skɒ·pəɹnǫŋ). *U.S.* 1854. [Name of a river in North Carolina.] *S.* (*grape*), a variety of the Fox-grape (*Vitis vulpina*) indigenous to the basin of the Scuppernong River.

Scurf (skɒɹf), *sb.*¹ [Late OE. *scurf*, prob. alt. of *sćeorf* by the influence of ON. **skurfr*, implicit in *skurfóttr* scurfy, f. base allied to that of OE. *sćeorfan* gnaw, *sćeorfian* cut into shreds; cf. (M)HG., (M)LG. *schorf* scab, scurf.] †**1.** A morbid condition of the skin, esp. of the head, characterized by the separation of branny scales, without inflammation –1661. †**b.** A similar condition in animals –1607. **2.** The scales or small laminæ of epidermis that are continually being detached from the skin; esp. such scales detached in abnormally large quantity, as a consequence of disease, or forming accumulations at the roots of the hair. †Formerly also, a single scale or lamina of this kind. OE. **b.** *transf.* in *Bot.* Minute scales found on the leaves of certain plants 1839. **3.** Any incrustation upon the surface of a body; rust, †a scab; a saline or sulphurous deposit, mould, or the like. Now *rare.* 1440. **b.** *spec.* A deposit of coke on the inner surface of a gas retort 1884. †**4.** A thin layer of turf –1726. **5.** The 'scum' of the population (*rare*) 1688.

3. *fig.* By length of time The S. is worn away, of each committed Crime DRYDEN.

Scurf (skɒ̆ɹf), *sb.*² 1483. [perh. identical w. prec.] The Sea-trout, *Salmo eriox* or *S. trutta.*

Scurf (skɒ̆ɹf), *v.* 1599. [f. SCURF *sb.*¹] †**1.** *trans.* To cover with a scurf or incrustation –1699. **2.** To remove by scraping; to chip off (hard deposits) from the surface of a boiler or retort 1839.

Scurfy (skɒ̆·ɹfi), *a.* 1483. [f. SCURF *sb.*¹ + -Y¹.] **1.** Covered with scurf; suffering from cutaneous disease. Also, of the nature of scurf. **2.** *transf.* Covered as with scurf incrusted; like scurf 1731. Hence **Scu·rfi-ly** *adv.*, **-ness.**

Scurrile, scurril (skɒ·ril), *a.* Now somewhat *arch.* 1567. [– Fr. *scurrile* or L. *scurrilis*, f. *scurra* buffoon; see -ILE.] = SCURRILOUS.

That it containe not base, filthy or s. matter 1586.

Scurrility (skɒri·lĭti). 1508. [– Fr. *scurrilité* or L. *scurrilitas*, f. *scurrilis*; see prec., -ITY.] The quality of being scurrilous; buffoon-like jocularity; coarseness or indecency of language, esp. in invective and jesting. **b.** Something scurrilous 1589. †**c.** Buffoon-like behaviour –1624.

Your reasons..haue beene..pleasant without scurrillity SHAKS. **b.** Several dull and dead scurrilities in the..London Journals POPE.

Scurrilous (skɒ·riləs), *a.* 1576. [f. SCURRILE *a.* + -OUS.] 'Using such language as only the licence of a buffoon can warrant' (J.); characterized by coarseness of language, esp. in jesting and invective.

They are grown s. upon the Royal family ADDISON. Hence **Scu·rrilous-ly** *adv.*, **-ness.**

Scurry (skɒ·ri), *sb.* 1823. [f. next.] **1.** The act of scurrying; a hurried movement, a rush; hurry, haste, bustle. **2.** *Sporting.* A short quick run or race on horseback 1824. **3.** A fluttering assemblage (e.g. of birds, snow, foam) moving or driven rapidly through the air. †Also, a confused tangle of material. 1839.

1. The s. and the scramble..of London life 1910.

Scurry (skɒ·ri), *v.* 1810. [Second element of HURRY-SCURRY used independently.] **1.** To go rapidly, move hurriedly. **2.** *trans.* To cause to go hastily or move rapidly 1850.

1. They s. away like rabbits when they see her coming 1872.

Scurvy (skɒ̆·ɹvi), *sb.* 1565. [f. next, partly ellipt. for †*s. disease* XVI, the spec. application being determined by assoc. with the like-sounding Fr. *scorbut*, LG. *schorbŭk*; see SCORBUTUS.] A disease characterized by general debility of the body, extreme tenderness of the gums, foul breath, subcutaneous eruptions, and pains in the limbs, resulting from a deficiency in the diet of vitamin C, which occurs in fresh foods, esp. fruits and vegetables. †**b.** *pl.* Attacks of this disease –1764.

Comb.: **s.-grass,** a cruciferous plant, *Cochlearia officinalis,* believed to possess anti-scorbutic properties.

Scurvy (skɒ̆·ɹvi), *a.* 1515. [f. SCURF *sb.*¹ + -Y¹.] †**1.** Covered with scurf; suffering from, or of the nature of, skin disease; scurfy, scabby –1758. **b.** *transf.* Of vegetable growths: Resembling scurf, scurfy 1763. **2.** *fig.* Sorry, worthless, contemptible. Of treatment, etc.: Shabby, discourteous. 1579.

1. Whether he be blynde,..or is gleyd, or is skyrvye or scaulde COVERDALE *Lev.* 21:20. *S. disease* = SCURVY *sb.* **2.** Steele and I sat among some s. company over a bowl of punch SWIFT. Hence **Scu·rvi-ly** *adv.* (now *arch.*), †**-ness** –1727.

Scuse, 'scuse (skiŭz), *v.* 1476. Aphetic f. EXCUSE *v.* Now careless or jocular *colloq.*

Scut (skɒt). 1440. [rel. to †*scut* adj. short (XV), †*scut* vb. cut short, dock (XVI); of unkn. origin.] **1.** A short erect tail, esp. that of a hare, rabbit, or deer 1530. **2.** A hare. **3.** A contemptible fellow (*colloq.* or *dial.*) 1895.

1. My Doe, with the blacke S.? SHAKS. **2.** Masid as a marche hare, he ran lyke a s. SKELTON.

Scutage (skiŭ·tėdʒ). *Obs.* exc. *Hist.* 1460. [– med.L. *scutagium*, f. L. *scutum* shield, after OFr. *escuage*; see ESCUAGE.] A tax levied on knight's fees: chiefly, such a tax paid in lieu of military service.

Scutal (skiŭ·tăl), *a.* 1857. [f. SCUTUM + -AL¹.] **1.** *Zool.* Of the nature of or pertaining to a scutum. **2.** Of or pertaining to a (heraldic) shield. *Extra-scutal* adj., (*Her.*) placed outside the shield. 1868.

Scutate (skiŭ·teⁱt), *a.* 1826. [f. SCUTUM + -ATE².; hence mod.L. *scutatus*.] **1.** *Zool.* Covered with scuta or large flat scales. **2.** *Bot.* Buckler-shaped 1836. Hence **Scu·tated**

a. = sense 1. **Scuta·tion** *Zool.*, arrangement of scuta.

Scutch (skɒtʃ), *sb.*[1] 1688. [– OFr. *escouche* (mod. *écouche*), f. *escoucher*; see SCUTCH *v.*[2]] = SCUTCHER 1. Also *s.-rod.*

Scutch (skɒtʃ), *sb.*[2] *dial.* 1685. [var. of SQUITCH.] = QUITCH *sb.*

Scutch (skɒtʃ), *v.*[1] Now chiefly *dial.* 1611. [prob. imit.] *trans.* To strike with a stick or whip, to slash, switch. Also *intr.* to strike *at.*

Scutch (skɒtʃ), *v.*[2] 1733. [– OFr. *escoucher*, dial. var. of *escousser* (mod. *écoucher*) :– Rom. **excussare*, f. pa. ppl. stem *excuss-* of L. *excutere*, f. *ex* EX-[1] + *quatere* shake.] **1.** *trans.* To dress (fibrous material, flax, hemp, cotton, silk, wool) by beating. **2.** To strike the grain from (ears of corn) 1844.

Comb.: **s.-mill**, a mill for preparing flax.

Scutcheon (skɒ·tʃən). Sometimes written **'scutcheon.** late ME. [Aphetic var. of ESCUTCHEON.] **1.** = ESCUTCHEON 1, 2. †**2.** A badge –1598. **3.** Anything shaped like an escutcheon; *esp.* a keyhole plate, name-plate, etc. 1483.

1. The burial..was a most vile thing...No plumes,..led horses, scutcheons, or open chariots. H. WALPOLE. *fig.* Carefully avoiding a sort of blot in their s. which they think would degrade them for ever BURKE. Hence **Scu·tcheoned** *ppl. a.* furnished or decorated with scutcheons.

Scutcher (skɒ·tʃəɹ). 1766. [f. SCUTCH *v.*[2] + -ER[1].] **1.** An implement or apparatus for scutching. **2.** The part of a thrashing machine which strikes off the grain 1797. **3.** A person employed in scutching 1847.

Scute (skiūt). late ME. [– L. *scutum* shield; see ÉCU.] = ÉCU. *Obs.* exc. *Hist.* **b.** Used vaguely for a coin of small value 1594. **2.** *Zool.* A large scale or bony plate, forming part of the integument of certain animals, as the tortoise, armadillo, echinoderms, various fishes, etc. 1848.

Scutella (skiute·lă). *Pl.* **-æ.** 1771. [mod. L.; orig. a use of L. *scutella* platter, but mistaken for a dim. of L. *scutum* shield.] = SCUTELLUM.

Scutellate (skiū·teleˈt), *a.* 1785. [f. SCUTELLUM + -ATE[2].] **1.** Saucer- or platter-shaped; esp. *Bot.* **2.** *Zool.* Having a scutellum; covered with scutella 1826. So **Scu·tellated** *a.* 1729.

Scutellation (skiūtělēˈ·ʃən). 1872. [f. prec.; see -ATION.] *Zool.* **a.** Scutellate formation (of the feet of birds). **b.** Arrangement of scutes or scales (in lizards, serpents, etc.).

Scutelliform (skiute·lifǭɹm), *a.* 1826. [f. next + -FORM.] Having the form of a scutellum.

Scutellum (skiute·lŏm). *Pl.* **-a.** 1760. [mod.L.; app. intended as a correction of SCUTELLA, as if a dim. of L. *scutum* shield.] **1.** *Bot.* **a.** An orbicular concave fructification. **b.** An anterior cotyledon in certain grasses 1832. **2.** *Zool.* **a.** *Ent.* The third of the four sclerites composing any segment of the tergum of an insect 1819. **b.** *Ornith.* One of the horny plates which cover the feet of certain birds 1840.

Scutibranchiate (skiūtibræ·ŋkiĕt), *a.* and *sb.* 1836. [f. mod.L. *Scutibranchiata*, f. *scutum* shield + *branchiæ* gills; see -ATE[2].] **A.** *adj.* Pertaining to the *Scutibranchiata*, a group of gasteropods comprising the sea-ears and limpets. **B.** *sb.* A member of this group. So, in the same senses, **Scutibra·nchian** *a.* and *sb.*; **Scutibranch** (skiū·tibræŋk) *a.* and *sb.*

Scutiform (skiū·tifǭɹm), *a.* 1656. [f. L. *scutum* shield + -FORM.] Chiefly *Anat.* Shield-shaped.

‖**Scutiger** (skiū·tidʒəɹ). 1842. [mod.L., f. L. *scutum* + *-ger*; see -GEROUS.] *Zool.* A centipede of the genus *Scutigera*; any member of the family *Scutigeridæ*.

Scutter (skɒ·təɹ), *sb.* Chiefly *dial.* 1826. [f. next.] An act of 'scuttering'; a hasty, scrambling, noisy rush.

Scutter (skɒ·təɹ), *v.* *colloq.* and *dial.* 1781. [perh. alt. of SCUTTLE *v.*[1], with substitution of -ER[5].] *intr.* To go hastily with much fuss and bustle, as from excitement or timidity.

Scuttle (skɒ·t'l), *sb.*[1] [ME. *scutel* first in northern use – ON. *skutill*, corresp. to OS. *skutala* = MLG. *schötele*, MDu. *schotele* (Du. *schotel*), OHG. *scuzzila* (G. *schüssel*); all – L. *scutula* or *scutella*, rel. to *scutra* dish, platter.] †**1.** A dish, trencher, platter –1701. **2. a.** A basket for sifting or winnowing corn; hence, a large shovel to cast grain in winnowing, a casting-shovel. Now *dial.* late ME. **b.** A large open basket wide at the mouth and narrow at the bottom, usu. of wicker-work, used for carrying corn, earth, vegetables, etc. late ME. **c.** More fully COAL-SCUTTLE: A scoop-shaped receptacle with a handle for holding coals for a fire 1849. **Scu·ttleful,** as much as will fill a s.

Scuttle (skɒ·t'l), *sb.*[2] 1497. [perh. – Fr. †*escoutille* (mod. *écoutille*) hatchway – Sp. *escotilla*, dim. of *escota* cutting out of cloth, f. *escotar* cut out, f. L. *ex* EX-[1] + Gmc. **skaut-* (see SHEET *sb.*[1]).] **1.** *Naut.* A square or rectangular hole or opening in a ship's deck smaller than a hatchway, furnished with a movable cover or lid, used as a means of communication between deck and deck; also a similar hole in the deck or side of a ship for purposes of lighting, ventilation, etc. **b.** The lid of a scuttle-hole or hatchway 1688. **2.** An opening in the roof, floor, wall, etc. of a building closed with a shutter or lid; a trap-door; also the shutter of such an opening. Now *U.S.* 1707. **3.** The section of an automobile connecting the bonnet and body; the 'cowl' 1914.

Comb.: **s.-butt, -cask,** a butt or cask with a square hole cut in it, kept on deck to hold water ready for use; **-hole** = sense 1.

Scuttle (skɒ·t'l), *sb.*[3] 1530. Altered f. CUTTLE *sb.*[1] Also *s. fish.*

Scuttle (skɒ·t'l), *v.*[1] 1450. [Parallel with synon. SCUDDLE *v.*] *intr.* To run with quick hurried steps. Chiefly with *away, off.* **b.** *transf.* in *Political slang.* To withdraw in a precipitate and undignified manner from the occupation or control of a country 1883. Hence **Scu·ttle** *sb.*[4] the action or an act of scuttling.

Scuttle (skɒ·t'l), *v.*[2] 1642. [f. SCUTTLE *sb.*[2]] **1.** *trans.* To cut or bore a hole or holes in the sides or bottom of (a vessel, for the purpose of sinking her). **2.** To cut a hole in (the deck of a vessel), esp. for the purpose of salving the cargo 1789.

1. The mildest manner'd man That ever scuttled ship or cut a throat BYRON.

‖**Scutulum** (skiū·tiŭlŏm). *Pl.* **-a.** 1888. [mod.L. use of L. dim. of *scutum* shield.] *Path.* A shield-shaped crust or disc developed in the skin-disease favus. **b.** *Zool.* A scutellum 1902.

‖**Scutum** (skiū·tŏm). *Pl.* **scuta** (skiū·tă). 1771. [techn. use of L. *scutum* oblong shield.] **1.** *Bot.* 'The broad dilated stigma in some asclepiads' 1832. **2.** *Ent.* The second segment of each of the three divisions of the tergum in insects 1830. **3.** *Zool.* A shield-like dermal plate; a scute 1771.

‖**Scybalum** (si·bălŏm). Usu. pl. **scybala.** 1684. [– late and med.L. *scybalum* dung – Gr. σκύβαλον.] *Path.* One of a collection of round masses of constipated fæces formed in the bowels in certain diseases.

Scye (səi). 1830. [Sc. and Ulster dial. word of unkn. origin.] *Tailor's term.* The opening in a coat in which a sleeve is inserted.

Scylla (si·lă). 1520. [– L. *Scylla* – Gr. Σκύλλα.] A rock upon the Italian side of the Straits of Messina facing CHARYBDIS (q.v. for phr. *between S. and Charybdis*, etc.); also personified as a dangerous sea-monster.

‖**Scypha** (səi·fă). 1832. [mod.L. – Gr. σκύφη var. of σκύφος drinking-cup.] *Bot.* = SCYPHUS.

Scyphi- (səifi), comb. form of L. *scyphus* SCYPHUS. **Scy·phiform** *a. Bot.*, cup-shaped; *Zool.*, boat-shaped, scaphoid. ‖**Scyphisto·ma** *Zool.*, = SCYPHOSTOMA.

Scypho- (səi·fo, səifǫ·), repr. Gr. σκυφο-, comb. form of σκύφος SCYPHUS. **Scy·phomancy** [-MANCY], divination by means of a cup. ‖**Scy:phomedu·sa** [mod.L.] *Zool.*, a group of Hydrozoa. **Scy·phophore** (-fōᵊɹ) [– mod.L. *scyphophorus*] *Zool.*, a member of the *Scyphophori*, an order of physostomous fishes. **Scypho·stoma** [Gr. στόμα mouth] *Zool.*, a non-sexual hydroid form of the Hydrozoan Acraspeda.

‖**Scyphus** (səi·fŏs). *Pl.* **scyphi** (səi·fəi). 1777. [mod.L. use of L. *scyphus* – Gr. σκύφος a large drinking vessel without a foot.] **a.** The corona of certain plants when forming a cup or funnel-shaped appendage. **b.** A dilatation of the podetium in lichens bearing shields on its margin.

Scythe (səið), *sb.* [OE. *siþe*, earlier **siğði* (written *sigdi*) = MLG. *segede, sigde* (LG. *seged, seid, sichte*), ON. *sigðr* :– Gmc. **seȝiþō*, f. **seȝ-* (:– **sek-* cut), whence also synon. OS. *segisna*, MDu. *seisene* (Du. *zeis*), OHG. *segansa* (G. *sense*). The sp. with *sc-* (XVII) is prob. due to assoc. with SCISSORS.] **1.** An implement for mowing grass or other crops, having a long thin curving blade fastened at an angle with the handle and wielded with both hands with a long sweeping stroke. **2.** *transf.* and *fig.*, esp. as the attribute of Time or Death. late ME. **3.** A weapon having a long curving blade resembling a reaping hook. *Obs.* exc. *Hist.* with ref. to scythed chariots. ME.

1. Thy valleys.., Where now the sharp-edg'd Sithe sheeres vp the spyring grasse DRAYTON. **2.** And nothing gainst Times sieth can make defence SHAKS.

Comb.: **s.-stone,** a whetstone for scythes.

Scythe (səið), *v.* 1597. [f. prec.] *trans.* To cut or mow with a scythe.

Time had not sithed all that youth begun SHAKS.

Scythed (səiðd), *ppl. a.* late ME. [f. SCYTHE *sb.* and *v.* + -ED.] **1.** Furnished with a scythe; esp. *Hist.* (= Gr. δρεπανηφόρος, L. *falcatus*) of war-chariots provided with scythes fastened to a revolving shaft projecting from the axle-trees; attributed by classical writers to the Persians and the Britons. **2.** Cut down with a scythe 1865.

Scytheman (səi·ðmăn). 1577. [f. SCYTHE *sb.* + MAN *sb.*] **1.** One who uses a scythe. **2.** One of an irregular body of troops armed with a scythe as a weapon 1849. **2.** *fig.* Applied to Time and to Death 1818.

Scythian (si·ðiăn, si·þiăn), *a.* and *sb.* 1543. [f. L. *Scythia* – Gr. Σκυθία (f. Σκύθης) + -AN.] **A.** *adj.* Pertaining to Scythia, an ancient region extending over a large part of European and Asiatic Russia, or to the nomadic people who inhabited it 1567. **B.** *sb.* **1.** A person belonging to the race by which Scythia was inhabited 1543. **2.** The language of Scythia 1668. So **Scy·thic** *a.* Scythian.

'Sdeath (zdeþ), *int.* *Obs.* exc. *arch.* 1606. A euphemistic abbrev. of *God's death*, used in oaths and asseverations.

†**Sdeign,** *sb.* *rare.* 1590. [– It. *sdegno*, f. *sdegnare.*] Disdain –1819. So †**Sdeign,** *v.* 1590. [– It. *sdegnare*, aphet. for *disdegnare* to DISDAIN.] –1667.

As if he..sdeign'd the low degree SPENSER.

Se-, *prefix*, occurring only in L. derivs., represents the L. *se-*, = OLatin *se* (also *sed*) prep. and adv., without, apart, in *secede, seclude, secure* adj., *sedition*, etc.

Sea (sī). [OE. *sǣ* = OFris. *sē*, OS. *sēo, sēu*, dat. *sēwa*, OHG. *sēo, sē*, dat. *sēwe* (Du. *zee*, G. *see*), ON. *sær, sjár, sjór*, Goth. *saiws* :– Gmc. **saiwiz*, of unkn. origin (there being no common IE. word).] **1.** The continuous body of salt water that covers the greater part of the earth's surface. Often *poet.* with epithet as *broad, deep, salt*, etc. **b.** Often coupled with *land*, to express the idea of the whole surface of the earth OE. **c.** *pl.* Different parts or tracts of the ocean OE. **d.** In pregnant use, with ref. to naval operations, the shipping trade, etc. ME. **2.** A part of the general body of salt water, having certain land-limits or washing a particular coast, and having a proper name, as *Red, Black, Adriatic S.* OE. **3.** A large lake or landlocked sheet of water, whether salt or fresh. *Obs.* exc. in *inland s.* and in proper names, as the S. of Galilee, etc. OE. **4.** The volume of water in the sea considered in regard to the ebb and flow of the tide OE. **5.** With an epithet indicating the roughness or smoothness of the waves. Hence without qualification = a heavy swell, rough water. OE. **b.** The direction of the waves or swell 1769. **c.** A large heavy wave 1582. **6.** *fig.* With ref. to metaphorical sailing, drowning, waves, etc.; also, a copious or overwhelming mass (*of* something) ME. **7.** *transf.* **a.** A large level tract (*of* some material substance or aggregate of objects) 1585. **b.** Hyperbolically, a great quantity of liquid, esp. (in fig. context) of blood 1598. **8.** *Antiq.* The great brazen laver in the Jewish Temple. [Literalism from Heb.] late ME.

1. This precious stone, set in the siluer s. SHAKS. **b.** The light that never was, on sea or land WORDSW. **c.** Magic casements, opening on the foam of perilous seas KEATS. **d.** The Command of the Seas BACON. *To keep the sea*, to prevent the enemy from occupying it, to keep it clear for one's own ships and traffic. **High s.** (Now usu. *pl.*) The deep or open sea; the main sea or main. *spec.* in *Law.* (*sing.* and *pl.*): (*a*) The main sea, as far as it is regarded as being within the jurisdiction of the courts of admiralty; (*b*) The area of the sea not within the jurisdiction of any nation, but the free highway of all nations. **2.** *The four seas*, the seas bounding Great Britain on the four sides. *Within the four seas* = in Great Britain. *The Severn S.* (arch.), the Bristol Channel. **4.** †*Full s.*, high tide (also *fig.*). **5.** It was pitch-dark, a good deal of s. on 1837. Phr. *Salt* or *bitter s.*, sea-water (*poet.*). **c.** A s. struck us on the weather side 1861. **6.** To take Armes against a S. of troubles SHAKS. **7.** So on this windie S. of Land, the Fiend Walk'd up and down alone MILT. **b.** These wars, which have spilled such seas of blood BURKE.

Phrases. **At sea. a.** Out on the sea, on shipboard; in employment as a sailor. **b.** *fig.* In a state of uncertainty or perplexity, at a loss. Also *all at s.* **Beyond (the) s.** or **seas.** Out of the country, abroad. **By s.** †**a.** At the sea-side. (Now *by the s.*) **b.** By way of the sea, on or over the sea (as a mode of transit or conveyance). **c.** In the region of the sea, at sea. †**By long s.** Short for *by long sea passage*. Also *by the long seas.* **On** or **upon the s. a.** On the sea's surface, afloat, at sea, on shipboard. **b.** Of a dwelling, etc.: At the sea's edge, on the sea-coast. **Over the s. a.** Of motion: Across the sea, to the other side of the sea. **b.** Of position: On the other side of the sea; abroad. **To s.** Out on the water, on a voyage, or on shipboard. *To go to s.*, to go on a voyage; to enter upon, or follow, the profession of a sailor. *To put, put off, put out, to s.*: see PUT *v.*[1] *To stand out to s.*: see STAND *v.* **To take the s.** To go on board ship, embark; to start on a sea-voyage, launch forth, put out to sea (said also of the ship). Cf. Fr. *prendre la mer.*

Comb.: **s.-anchor** = *drift-anchor* (see DRIFT *sb.*); **-bathing,** bathing in the s.; **-beach** = BEACH *sb.* 2; †**borderer,** one who inhabits the land adjacent to the sea; **-bordering,** *a.* (*rare*), bordering on the s.; **-bound,** *a.*[1] bound or confined by the s.; **-bound,** *a.*[2] bound for or on the way to the s.; **-change,** a change wrought by the sea; **-chest,** a seaman's chest or box for his own clothing, etc.; **-cloth,** a painted cloth spread over the stage and moved so as to represent waves; **-cook,** a cook on board ship; esp. in *son of a s.-cook*, used as a term of abuse; **-crust,** the incrustation formed on an iron ship during a s.-voyage; **-dike,** an embankment against the s., a s.-wall; **-fencible,** an old coast-guard; **-fire,** phosphorescence at sea; **-froth,** (*a*) s.-foam; (*b*) meerschaum; †**-ground,** the bottom of the s.; **-horizon,** the line where sky and sea seem to meet; in *Navigation*, 'the small circle which bounds the portion of the surface visible to a spectator in the open sea'; **-ivory,** ivory from the tusks and horns of marine mammalia; **-law,** a law relating to the duties and rights of persons on the seas; **-league,** three nautical miles; **-light,** a beacon, lighthouse, or harbour-light to guide ships at s.; **-log,** an official record of a ship's voyage; **-lord,** a naval lord (of the Admiralty); **-mile,** a geographical or nautical mile (see MILE *sb.*[1]); †**-ox,** the hippopotamus; **-pass,** a document carried in time of war by neutral merchant vessels to show their nationality; **-purple** = PURPLE *sb.* 3, also the dye derived from it; **-rim,** the s. horizon; **S. Scouts,** a maritime auxiliary of the Boy Scouts; **-song,** a song such as is sung by sailors; **-speed,** the ordinary speed of a vessel when at sea, as dist. from *full speed*; **-thief,** a pirate, s.-rover; **-valve,** any one of several valves in the bottom or side of a steamship communicating with the sea below the water-line; **-view,** (*a*) a s.-scape; (*b*) a view or prospect of the s., or at s.

b. In names of marine mammalia, as **s.-bear,** the ursine or fur-seal, *Callorhinus ursinus*, of the N. Pacific; also applied to the smaller otaries of the southern seas; **-canary,** a sailor's name for the white whale, *Delphinapterus leucas*; **-leopard,** any one of various seals of the antarctic and southern seas, esp. of the genus *Ogmorhinus*; **-morse,** = MORSE *sb.*[2]; **-pig,** applied to the porpoise, the dolphin, the dugong, etc.

c. In names of birds: **s.-coot,** †(*a*) the cormorant; (*b*) the guillemot; (*c*) the American coot; **-crow,** local name for various birds as the cormorant, chough, razor-billed auk, etc.; **-dotterel,** the turnstone, *Strepsilas interpres*; also *local*, the ring-plover; **-drake,** a cormorant or s.-crow; also *U.S.*, the male eider-duck; **-duck,** any duck of the subfamily *Fuligulinæ*, as the common scoter, the eider-duck, etc.; **-goose** *U.S.*, a phalarope; **-hawk,** one of various gull-like birds, as one of the skuas, and the frigate-bird; **-lark,** local name for various small birds frequenting the sea-shore, as the ringed plover, various sandpipers, etc.; **-mall, -maw** = SEA-MEW; **-pigeon,** local name for various birds, as the rock-dove, *Columba livia*, the black guillemot, grey kittiwake, etc.; **-quail** *U.S.*, the turnstone; **-turtle**[1], the black guillemot; **-widgeon,** (*a*) the pintail duck; (*b*) the scaup duck.

d. In names of fishes, jelly-fishes, molluscs, shells, etc., as **s.-acorn** = ACORN-SHELL; **-adder,** the pipe-fish; **-anemone,** (see ANEMONE 2); **-angel,** the angel-fish, *Squatina squatina*; **-bass,** *U.S.* (*a*) a serranoid fish, *Centropristis furvus* (black s.-bass); (*b*) a sciænoid fish, *Cynoscion nobilis* (white s.-bass); (*c*) *Sciæna ocellata*; **-bat,** (*a*) a flying-fish, esp. the flying gurnard, *Dactylopterus volitans*; (*b*) *Malthe vespertilio*; (*c*) a fish of the genus *Platax*; **-blubber** = BLUBBER *sb.* 3; **-bream,** any of several sparoid fishes, esp. *Pagellus centrodontus*; **-cat,** (*a*) the wolf-fish, *Anarrhichas lupus*; (*b*) the great weever, *Trachinus draco*; (*c*) a shark, *Scyllium catulus*; (*d*) *Chimæra monstrosa*; (*d*) any s.-catfish; **-catfish,** any of various marine siluroid fishes; **-crab,** a marine crab, as dist. from a river- or land-crab; **-ear,** a univalve mollusc of the genus *Haliotis*; **-eel,** a salt-water eel, a conger; **-egg,** a s.-urchin; **-fan,** an alcyonarian polyp of the suborder *Gorgoniacea*, esp. *Rhipidogorgia flabellum*; **-feather,** a coral or polyp of the family *Pennatulidæ*; **-fox,** the thrasher-shark, *Alopias vulpes*; **-gherkin,** one of several holothurians, akin to the s.-cucumber; **-hare,** a mollusc, *Aplysia depilans* (and other species), having an oval body with four tentacles; **-hog,** the porpoise (now *rare*); **-hound,** a dog-fish; **-jelly,** a jelly-fish; **-lemon,** (*a*) a nudibranchiate gastropod of the family *Dorididæ*; (*b*) *Austral.*, a holothurian of the genus *Cuvieria*; **-lungs,** an acaleph of the *Ctenophora* (said to be so called from the alternate contraction and expansion, as if breathing); **-melon,** a holothurian of the family *Pentactidæ*; **-needle,** the garfish, *Belone vulgaris*; **-nettle,** any of certain radiate marine animals of the class *Acalephæ*, having the property of stinging when touched; **-orange,** a large holothurian (*Lophothuria fabricii*) of a globose shape and orange-coloured; **-orb,** a swell, globe, or orb-fish; **-owl,** the lump-fish, *Cyclopterus lumpus*; **-pad,** a star-fish; **-pear,** an ascidian or sea-squirt of the genus *Boltenia*; **-pen,** a polyp of the genus *Pennatula* or family *Pennatulidæ*; **-pheasant,** the turbot; **-porcupine,** the porcupine-fish, *Diodon hystrix*; **-scorpion,** (*a*) a scorpion-fish; (*b*) a sculpin, *Cottus scorpius*; **-sleeve,** a cuttle-fish or calamary; **-squirt,** any ascidian or tunicate; **-strawberry,** a polyp, *Alcyonium rubiforme*; **-sunflower,** a sea-anemone; **-toad,** (*a*) the fishing-frog, *Lophius piscatorius*; (*b*) *U.S.* the sculpin; (*c*) the toad-fish; **-turtle**[2], a turtle; **-unicorn,** the narwhal; **-wife,** a kind of wrasse, *Acantholabrus yarrelli*; **-wing,** a wing-shell.

e. In names of seaweeds: **s.-belt,** *Laminaria saccharina*; **-colander** U.S. *Agarum turneri*; **-girdle,** *Laminaria digitata*; **-lace,** *Chorda filum*; **-lentil,** the gulf-weed; **-lettuce,** *Ulva lactuca* and *U. latissima*; **-moss** = CORALLINE *sb.*[1]; **-thong,** any of several cord-like seaweeds, as *Chorda filum*, etc.; **-trumpet,** a large seaweed, *Ecklonia buccinalis* (so called because the hollow upper stem is used as a trumpet at the Cape of Good Hope); **-turnip,** a seaweed of the genus *Nereocystis*.

f. In names of plants growing on the sea-shore: **s.-beet,** (*a*) a variety of the common beet, *Beta vulgaris*, often called *Beta maritima*; (*b*) = *s.-lavender*; **-bent,** *Psamma* or *Ammophila arenaria*; **-blite,** *Suæda fruticosa*; **-cabbage, -cole** = SEA-KALE; **s. campion,** *Silene maritima*; **-fennel,** samphire; **-gilliflower** = SEA-PINK; **-heath,** a 'heath' of the genus *Frankenia*; **-laurel,** the seaside laurel; **-lavender,** *Statice limonium*; **s. matgrass, matweed,** *Psamma arenaria*; **-plantain,** *Plantago maritima*; **-radish,** a variety of the wild radish, sometimes regarded as a species (*Raphanus maritimus*); **-rush,** a species of *Juncus*; **-starwort,** *Aster tripolium*; **-thistle** = SEA-HOLLY; **-thrift** = SEA-PINK; **-willow,** the papyrus or paper-reed, BIBLUS.

Sea air. 1685. The air above or in the neighbourhood of the sea; air containing saline or gaseous matter derived from sea-water.

Sea-bank. ME. [BANK *sb.*[1]] **1.** †**a.** The sea-coast or sea-shore –1794. **b.** A dune or sand-hill 1848. **2.** An embankment built for protection against the sea, a sea-wall 1647.

Sea·-bean. 1607. †**1.** A small stone or pebble –1847. **2.** A name given to the seeds of the tropical leguminous plant *Entada scandens*, carried by sea to the British coasts, and often made into trinkets 1696. **3.** A small univalve shell of the family *Triviidæ*; also, the operculum of any shell of the family *Turbinidæ* 1885.

Sea·-beast. 1450. A beast living in the sea.

Sea·-bird. 1589. A bird frequenting the sea, or the land near the sea. Also *attrib.*

Seaboard (sī·bōᵊɹd), *sb.* and *a.* 1490. [f. SEA + BOARD *sb.*] **A.** *sb.* †**1.** With preps. *a, at, on, to s.*, on or to the seaward side (of a ship, etc.) –1635. †**2.** *By* (*be*) *s.*: by sea. *On s.*: at sea, on board ship. –1597. **3.** The line where land and sea meet, the coast-line; the sea-shore or the land near the sea 1825.

3. On the seabord of this wild land is a rim of grassy country, where cattle can subsist CARLYLE.

B. *adj.* Bordering on or adjoining the sea (*rare*) 1590.

Sea·-boat. OE. **1.** †**a.** A boat for the sea. **b.** A vessel considered in ref. to her behaviour at sea. **2.** A *Chiton* or coat-of-mail shell 1884.

Sea·-born, *a.* 1593. Born in or of the sea. **a.** Of persons, chiefly mythological, esp. of Venus. **b.** Produced by or having its origin in the sea 1646. **c.** Of an island, etc. rising from the sea 1726.

a. Like Neptune and his Sea-borne Neece 1645.

Sea·-borne, *a.* 1823. [BORNE *ppl. a.*] **1.** Conveyed by sea. (Said usu. of articles of commerce.) **2.** Of a ship, etc.: Carried or floating on the sea 1840. **3.** *ellipt.* quasi-*sb.* Sea-borne coal 1892.

Sea·-breeze. 1697. [BREEZE *sb.*[2]] A breeze blowing from the sea.

Sea·-calf. late ME. [CALF[1].] The seal, esp. the common seal, *Phoca vitulina.*

Sea·-captain. 1612. The captain or commander of a ship, usu. of a merchant vessel.

†**Sea·-card.** 1555. [CARD *sb.*[2] Cf. Du. *zeekaart.*] **1.** A chart of the sea –1745. **2.** The card of the mariner's compass –1710.

Sea·-cliff. OE. A cliff on the sea-shore. In *Geol.* occas. a rock which is now inland, but was on the shore of a former sea.

Sea-coal (sī·kōᵘl). OE. [Cf. AL. *carbo maris, c. marinus* XIII.] †**1.** In OE: Jet (which was washed up by the sea). **2. a.** Mineral coal (prob. so called locally because brought by sea). Now *Hist.* ME. **b.** Very small coal cast up by the sea 1645.

Sea-coast. ME. **1.** The land adjacent to the sea. **2.** *attrib.* or *adj.* 1622.

Sea·-cock. 1684. [COCK *sb.*[1]] **1.** *local.* Any of various birds, as the grey plover, *Squatarola helvetica.* **2.** A name for species of gurnard, *Trigla cuculus* and *T. hirax* 1704. **3.** *joc.* A bold sea-rover 1865. **4.** In a marine steam-engine: A cock on the pipe which runs from the boiler into the sea 1855.

Sea·-cow. 1613. [COW *sb.*[1]] **1.** The manatee; also the dugong and other sirenians. †**2.** The morse or walrus –1837. **3.** [S. Afr. Du. *zeekoe.*] The hippopotamus 1731.

Sea cucumber. 1601. [= Fr. *concombre de mer.*] Any holothurian; sometimes restricted to the *Psolidæ.*

Sea·-de:vil. 1594. **1.** A devil supposed to inhabit the sea. **2.** Any of various ugly fish, as the fishing-frog, various large rays, etc. 1611.

Sea·-dog. 1598. [Cf. Du. *zeehond*, G. *seehund.*] **1.** The common or harbour seal, *Calocephalus vitulinus.* †**2.** A dog-fish or small shark –1802. **3.** A privateer or pirate, esp. of the time of Queen Elizabeth 1659. **4.** A sailor, usually one long used to the sea, an 'old salt' 1840. **5.** A luminous appearance near the horizon, regarded by mariners as a prognostic of bad weather 1825.

Sea·-dra:gon. 1551. **1.** Various fishes, as the weever; the bullhead; a dragonet; a flying sea-horse, etc. **2.** A mythical marine monster resembling a dragon 1749.

Sea·-ea:gle. 1668. **1.** An eagle of the genus *Haliaëtus*, esp. the White-tailed Eagle, *H. albicilla.* Also, the frigate-bird and the skua-gull. **2.** The eagle ray 1722.

Sea·-e:lephant. 1601. The elephant seal, *Macrorhinus elephantinus* or *proboscideus.* Formerly applied to the morse or walrus.

Seafarer (sī·fēᵊrəɹ). 1513. [f. SEA + FARER.] A traveller by sea, esp. one whose life is spent in voyaging, a sailor.

Seafaring (sī·ˌfēᵊ:riŋ), *sb.* 1592. [f. SEA *sb.* + *faring*, vbl. sb. f. FARE *v.*] Travelling by sea; the business or calling of a sailor.

Sea·-fa:ring, *a.* ME. [f. SEA + *faring*, ppl. a. of FARE *v.*] Travelling on the sea; following the sea as a calling.

Sea·-fern. 1688. **1.** Any alcyonarian polyp or coral resembling a fern. **2.** A fern, the sea-spleenwort 1855.

Sea·-fight. 1600. A naval battle.

Sea·-fish. OE. [Cf. ON. *sæfiskr.*] A fish of the sea as dist. from a freshwater fish. So **Sea·-fishery, -fishing,** the business or occupation, etc. of catching fish in the sea.

Sea·-flower. 1805. A flower growing in or by the sea. Also, an actinia or sea-anemone.

Sea·-foam. ME. **1.** Foam of the sea. **2.** [tr. G. *meerschaum.*] = MEERSCHAUM 1837.

Sea·-food. *U.S.* 1836. Food obtained from the sea; fish or shell-fish, etc. used as food.

Sea·-fowl. ME. [Cf. OE. *sǣfugol* only as proper name.] A sea-bird.

Sea·-front. 1879. **1.** That portion or side of a building, etc. which faces the sea. **2.** The land on the side of a town, etc. facing the sea.

Sea·-gate[1]. 1583. [GATE *sb.*[2]] A long rolling swell; also, the condition in which two vessels are when thrown aboard one another by such a swell.

Sea·-gate[2]. 1861. [GATE *sb.*[1]] **1.** A gate towards, or giving access to, the sea; or a convenient approach to the sea. **2.** A place of access to the sea 1883.

Sea·-girt, *a.* 1621. Girt or surrounded by the sea. (Sometimes said of a peninsula.)

Sea·-god. 1565. A god of the sea, a marine deity. So **Sea·-go:ddess,** a goddess of the sea.

Sea·-go:ing, *a.* 1829. **1.** Going on the sea, applied to a vessel which makes distant journeys, as opp. to a coasting, harbour, or river vessel. **2.** Going to the sea, esp. of a fish, catadromous 1842. **3.** Seafaring 1855.

Sea·-grape. 1578. **1.** The glassworts *Salicornea herbacea* and *Salsola kali.* **2.** In W. Indies, the grape-tree or seaside grape, *Coccoloba uvifera* 1806. **3.** *pl.* The clustered egg-cases of the cuttle-fish and other cephalopods 1835. **4.** The gulf-weed, which has large bladders in clusters resembling grapes 1825.

Sea·-grass. 1578. [With sense 2 cf. Du. *zeegras* seaweed.] **1.** A grass which grows by the sea. **2.** One of various plants and seaweeds growing in the sea; *esp.* the eel-grass or grass-wrack, *Zostera marina* 1591.

Sea·-green, *a.* and *sb.* 1598. [Cf. Fr. *vert de mer.*] **A.** *adj.* Pale bluish-green 1603. **B.** *sb.* A sea-green colour 1598.

Sea·-gull. 1542. = GULL *sb.*[1]

‖**Seah** (sī·ă). 1705. [Heb. *sᵉāh*, in the Eng. Bible translated 'measure' (e.g. 2 Kings 7:1).] A Hebrew dry measure – six times the cab, and one-third of the ephah.

Sea·-he:dgehog. 1602. **1.** An echinus or sea-urchin. **2.** The globe-fish or other diodont fish; so called from having erectile spines.

Sea·-hen. 1611. [Cf. Du. *zeehaan* gurnard, gurnet, grunter.] **1.** The piper-gurnard, *Trigla lyra*, and the lump-fish, *Cyclopterus lumpus.* **2.** A local name for the common guillemot and the great skua 1672.

Sea·-ho:lly. 1548. Eryngo.

Sea·-holm. 1550. [HOLM[2].] = prec.

Sea·-horse. 1475. **1.** The walrus. **2.** A fabulous horse-like marine animal, represented as having the fore-parts of a horse and the tail of a fish 1587. **3.** = HIPPOCAMPUS 2. 1589. †**4.** The hippopotamus –1759.

4. Sea-Horses floundring in the slimy mud DRYDEN.

Sea·-i:sland, *a.* 1807. Applied to a fine variety of cotton grown on the islands off the coast of Georgia and South Carolina, now also acclimatized in other countries. Also *absol.*

Sea·-kale. 1699. A cruciferous plant, *Crambe maritima*, found wild on the shores of western Europe, and often cultivated for its young shoots.

Sea·-king. 1582. [In sense 1 after ON. *sækonungr*; = OE. *sǣcyning.*] **1.** One of the piratical Scandinavian chiefs, who in the ninth and succeeding centuries ravaged the coasts of Europe 1819. **2.** Applied to the god of the sea 1582.

Seal (sīl), *sb.*[1] [OE. *seŏl-*, inflexional form of *seolh* (whence Sc. *selch*) = NFris. *selich*, MLG. *sēl*, MDu. *seel, zēle*, OHG. *selah*, ON. *selr* :– Gmc. **selχaz*, of unkn. origin. The sp. *seal* occurs XV.] **1.** A member of the family *Phocidæ*, sub-order *Pinnipedia*, of aquatic carnivorous mammals, with limbs developed into flippers and adapted for swimming, and having an elongated body covered with thick fur or bristles and terminated by a short tail; *spec.* the Common Seal, *Phoca vitulina.* Also with defining word. **2.** Short for SEALSKIN 1886.

1. *Elephant, Fur, Hair*, etc. *s.* (see these words). **Bottle-nosed S.,** *Phoca leonina.* **Great S.,** *Phoca barbata.* **Marbled S.,** *Calocephalus discolor.*

Comb.: **s. calf,** the young of the seal; **-fur,** the skin of the hair-seal (*Otaria*) used as a material for garments; **-grain,** a preparation of seal-leather used in ornamental work; **-plush,** a fabric made to imitate sealskin.

Seal (sīl), *sb.*[2] ME. [– AFr. *seal*, OFr. *seel* (mod. *sceau*) :– L. *sigillum* small picture, statuette, seal, dim. of *signum* SIGN *sb.*[1]] **1.** A device impressed on a piece of wax or other plastic material adhering or attached to a document as evidence of authenticity or attestation; also, the piece of wax, etc. bearing this impressed device. **b.** *fig.* A token or symbol of a covenant; something that authenticates or confirms; a final addition which completes and secures ME. **c.** The impression of one's signet placed upon an article as evidence of a claim to possession; *fig.* a mark of ownership 1782. **d.** *transf.* An impressed mark serving as visible evidence of something 1592. **e.** An impression left by the foot of an animal in soft ground or mud, esp. that of the otter 1686. **2.** A piece of wax or some other plastic or adhesive substance fixed on a folded letter or document, or on a closed door or receptacle of any kind, in such a way that an opening cannot be effected without breaking it ME. **b.** *fig.* That which 'seals a persons lips'; an obligation to silence, a vow of secrecy; *esp. the s. of confession* or *the confessional.* Also (often with allusion to Rev. 5 and 6) that which prevents the understanding of Holy Scripture or some other book. ME. **3.** An engraved stamp of metal or other hard material used to make an impression upon wax, etc. affixed as a 'seal' (in sense 1 or 2) ME. **b.** As a mark or sign of office. Chiefly *the seals*, as the symbol of the position of Lord Chancellor or of Secretary of State. 1480. **c.** A device or inscription engraved on a seal 1609. **d.** A trinket, containing either an engraved stone for sealing letters, or a flat stone, etc., simulating this, formerly often worn as an appendage to a watch-guard. Hence *pl.* applied to the bunch of such trinkets worn in this manner. 1837. **4. Great Seal.** The seal (in sense 3) used for the authentication of documents of the highest importance issued in the name of the sovereign or (in the case of a republic) of the highest executive authority; also, the impression of this on wax. Formerly also BROAD SEAL. late ME. †**b.** *ellipt.* The custodian of the Great Seal, the Lord High Chancellor or Lord Keeper –1641. †**5.** An assembly for the purpose of witnessing the affixing of the Great Seal to documents; a sealing by the Chancellor or the Commissioners having the custody of the Great Seal –1705. **6.** *techn.* (transf. use of 2.) **a.** = DIP-*pipe.* **b.** The quantity of water or tar left in the dip-pipe for preventing the escape of gas. **c.** A small quantity of water left in a trap to prevent the escape of foul air from a sewer or drain. 1853.

1. Till thou canst raile the seale from off my bond Thou but offend'st thy Lungs to speake so loud SHAKS. Phr. *To set one's s.*, to affix one's seal *to* a document; *fig.* to express one's assent *to. Under (one's) s.*, in a document attested by one's seal. **b.** *Mids. N.* III. ii. 144. **c.** The haughty..passions that..set their s. upon her brow DICKENS. **d.** But my kisses bring againe, bring againe, Seales of loue, but seal'd in vaine, seal'd in vaine SHAKS. **2.** What Letter is this same?..Ile be so bold to breake the seale for once. SHAKS. **3. b.** Sunderland..was suffered to retain his seals MACAULAY. **c.** The s. a sunflower; *'Elle vous suit partout'* BYRON.

attrib. and *Comb.*, **s.-lock,** a lock fitted with a 'seal' (often a small square of glass) which must be broken before the lock can be opened; **-pipe** = DIP-*pipe*; **-ring,** a finger ring bearing a s.; **-top** *a.* (of a spoon) having the handle finished with a s. (also ellipt.)

Seal, *sb.*[3] Now *dial.* 1579. [– ON. *selja*, and partly repr. the normal flexional form of the stem in OE. *sealh* gen. sing., *sealas* pl.; see SALLOW *sb.*[1]] A willow. In Spenser: Willow twigs.

Seal (sīl), *v.*[1] ME. [– OFr. *seeler* (mod. *sceller*), f. *seel* SEAL *sb.*[2]] **I.** To attest by a seal. **1.** *trans.* To place a seal upon (a document) as evidence of genuineness, or as a mark of authoritative ratification or approval. Also *absol.* **b.** *fig.* To authenticate or attest solemnly by some act compared to the affixing of a seal 1600. **c.** To conclude (an agreement, etc.) by affixing the seals of the parties to the instrument. Also *fig.*, to ratify or clinch (a bargain) by some ceremonial act. 1470. **d.** To grant (a charter) under one's seal; †also *fig.* 1625. **e.** To impose (an obligation, a penalty) *on* a person in a binding manner 1622. **f.** *fig.* Of a thing or act: To attest or ratify as a seal does; to be a 'seal' of 1648. **g.** To decide irrevocably (the fate of a person or thing); to complete and place beyond dispute or reversal (a victory, defeat, etc.) 1810. **2.** To mark by a seal as reserved for a particular destination. Chiefly *fig.*: To designate, set apart, assign *to* another person or bind *together*, by an inviolable token or pledge. ME. **b.** In allusions to Rev. 7:5–8. 1637. **c.** Among the Mormons: To set apart (a woman) *to* a man as one of his 'spiritual wives' 1857. **3.** To impress a seal upon (weights or measures) to indicate that their correctness has been tested by lawful authority. Also, to place an official stamp on (merchandise) to certify that it is of standard measure or quality. 1467. †**4.** *intr.* To set one's seal (*to* a document). Also *spec.* to set one's seal to or execute a promissory note; to become security *for* a person. –1683.

1. Goe with me to a Notarie, seale me there Your single bond SHAKS. *Signed, sealed, and delivered*, a legal phrase indicating the complete execution of a deed. **c.** Peace was concluded, and sealed by a marriage 1836. **f.** Then with his sable Brow he gave the Nod, That seals his Word POPE. **g.** Tomorrow would s. his triumph DISRAELI. **2.** Hath some wound,..seal'd him for The grave 1630. **b.** An Epistle, answering to one that asked to be Sealed of the Tribe of Ben B. JONS.

II. To fasten with or as with a seal. **1.** *trans.* To fasten (a folded letter or other document) with melted wax or some other plastic material and impress a seal upon this, so that opening is impossible unless the seal is broken ME. **b.** To stamp the wax fastening (a letter) *with* something substituted for a seal 1718. **c.** To fasten up (a letter, parcel) with sealing-wax, a wafer, gum, or the like 1818. **2.** To place a seal upon the opening of (a door, a chest, etc.) for security. Also with *up.* ME. **3.** To close (a vessel, an aperture, etc.) securely by placing a coating of wax, cement, or lead, over the orifice, or by any kind of fastening that must be broken before access can be obtained. Also *absol.* 1661. **b.** *Surg.* To close up (a wound) with a covering that is not to be removed until healing has taken place 1862. **4.** To fasten *on* or *down* with wax or cement 1665. **b.** *fig.* To fasten, fix immovably 1661. **5.** *transf.* (*trans.*) To enclose, shut *up* within impenetrable barriers 1667.

1. I will s. my letter early SWIFT. **c.** This letter, sealed with a wafer 1848. **2.** Phr. (fig.) *To s.* (a person's) *lips*, to bind to silence or secrecy. *To s.* (a person's) *eyes* or *ears*, to render blind or deaf, also to restrain from looking or listening. **4. b.** But, ah, she gave me never a look, For her eyes were sealed to the holy book M. ARNOLD. **5.** In case we should lose our vessels or become sealed up in permanent ice 1853.

Seal (sīl), *v.*[2] 1828. [f. SEAL *sb.*[1]] *intr.* To hunt for seals.

Sea·-law:yer. 1811. **1.** A shark, the tiger-shark. Also the grey or mangrove snapper. **2.** An argumentative sailor 1848.

Sealed (sīld), *ppl. a.* ME. [f. SEAL *v.*[1] + -ED[1].] **1.** Bearing the impression of a signet in wax, etc., as evidence or guarantee of authenticity. **b.** *Nat. Hist.* In specific names: Bearing a mark resembling a seal 1803. **2.** Fastened with a seal; so closed that access (to the contents) is impossible without breaking the fastening. Also *fig.* late ME.

1. Sealed Book: any of the printed copies of the authentic Book of Common Prayer of 1662 certified under the Great Seal and deposited as a standard in cathedrals and collegiate churches. **S. pattern,** in British military and naval use, a pattern (e.g. of a weapon, etc.) accepted by the War Office or the Admiralty. **2.** *S. orders,* written directions given to the commander of a vessel concerning the destination of a voyage, which are not to be opened until the vessel has left port. *S. verdict,* a verdict delivered in a sealed packet in the absence of a judge. *A s. book,* often used predic. of something involved in obscurity, or beyond a person's comprehension.

Sea·-legs, *pl. joc.* 1712. [Cf. Fr. *avoir le pied marin*; Du. *zeebenen.*] In phrases, *To have* or *get one's sea legs (on), to find one's sea legs,* to have or acquire the power of walking steadily on the deck of a ship in motion.

Sealer (sī·ləɹ), *sb.*[1] late ME. [f. SEAL *v.*[1] + -ER[1].] **1.** One who affixes a seal to a document. **2.** †**a.** One who attaches the official mark or seal to leather or other material as evidence of quality, etc. **b.** An inspector of weights and measures. 1467.

Sealer (sī·ləɹ), *sb.*[2] 1820. [f. SEAL *v.*[2] + -ER[1].] **1.** A vessel engaged in sealing. **2.** One who hunts the seal 1842.

Sea·-le:vel. 1806. The mean level of the surface of the sea, the mean level between high and low tide.

Sea·-line. 1687. [LINE *sb.*[2]] **1.** The coast-line or sea-board. **2.** The horizon, the line where sea and sky appear to meet 1880. **3.** A line used at sea; (*a*) a sounding-line; (*b*) a long line used in sea-fishing in deep water 1828.

Sea·ling-wax. ME. [f. *sealing,* vbl. sb. of SEAL *v.*[1]] In early use, beeswax or a composition containing this, later, a composition consisting of shellac, rosin, and turpentine, prepared for the purpose of receiving the impression of seals.

Sea·-lion. 1601. †**1.** A kind of lobster or crab. HOLLAND. **2.** A fabulous animal 1661. **3.** One of several large eared seals: (*a*) the largest otary of the North Pacific, *Otaria (Eumetopias) stelleri,* Steller's or the Northern s.; (*b*) the Southern or Patagonian s., *Otaria jubata*; (*c*) the *Zalophus lobatus* of the Australian seas, also the distinct species *Z. californianus* of the North Pacific.

Sea·-louse. 1601. [= L. *pediculus marinus* (Pliny).] **1.** A parasitic isopod crustacean of *Cymothoa* and allied genera; a fish-louse. **2.** The Molucca crab, *Limulus moluccensis* 1681.

Sealskin (sī·lskin), *sb.* and *a.* ME. [f. SEAL *sb.*[1] + SKIN *sb.*] **A.** *sb.* **1.** The skin of any of the fur seals, prepared for use as a garment, for the covering of a box, etc. **b.** Applied to textile fabrics imitating the appearance of sealskin 1860. **2.** A garment made of sealskin 1873. **B.** *adj.* Made of sealskin 1769.

Sealyham (sī·liăm, sī·lihæm). 1894. [Name of the seat of the Edwardes family in Pembrokeshire.] A breed of wire-haired terrier.

Seam (sīm), *sb.*[1] [OE. *sēam* = OFris. *sām,* MDu. *sōm* (Du. *zoom*), OHG. *soum* (G. *saum*), ON. *saumr* – Gmc. **saumaz,* f. **sau-* **su-* SEW.] **I.** Suture, junction. **1.** The junction made by sewing together the edges of two pieces of cloth, leather, etc.; the ridge or the furrow in the surface which indicates the course of such a junction; occas. the protruding edges of the joined pieces on the wrong side of the cloth. **b.** An embellished seaming used in joining costly fabrics; an ornamental strip of material inserted in or laid over a seam; also, material for this purpose. late ME. †**2.** *Anat.* A suture –1668. **3.** An interstice formed by the abutting edges of planks; a narrow crevice between the edges and ends of the planks or plates of a ship. Chiefly *pl.* OE. **4.** A line, groove, furrow, or the like, formed by the abutting edges of two parts of a thing; an indentation or mark resembling this; *esp.* the scar of a healed wound ME. **5.** *Geol.* A thin layer or stratum separating two strata of greater magnitude 1592. **6.** A joint used in uniting the edges of sheet metal; also, the line produced by this process 1825. **7.** *Knitting.* [transf. use of 1.] A line of purled stitches down the leg of a stocking, simulating the appearance of a joining. Also = *s.-stitch* 1825.

1. *fig.* Chidynge and reproche..vnsowen the seemes of freendshipe in mannes herte CHAUCER. *French s.,* a seam formed by stitching once on the right side of the material, then paring close and turning, so as to re-seam on the wrong side. **3.** The ship..let in the water at every s. 1748. **4.** A deep gash, now healed into an ugly s. DICKENS.

II. Sewing, needlework. *White s.,* plain needlework. *Obs.* exc. *dial.* late ME.

Comb.: **s.-lace,** lace used for insertion in or for covering and ornamenting seams; also *seaming-lace*; **s. set,** a set for smoothing or closing the seams (of boots and shoes, thin metals, etc.); **-stitch** (see I. 7 above) = *purl-stitch.*

Seam (sīm), *sb.*[2] [OE. *sēam,* OHG. *soum* (G. *saum*), a WGmc. adoption of med.L. *sauma, salma,* for late L. *sagma* – Gr. σάγμα baggage, pack-saddle, f. σάττειν, σαγ- pack, load. Cf. SUMPTER.] **1.** A pack-horse load. Now *dial.* **b.** The amount of a horse-load ME. **2.** A cart-load; esp. a definite amount of 3 cwt. (of hay or manure) or 2 cwt. (of straw). *west. dial.* 1726.

Seam (sīm), *sb.*[3] ME. [– OFr. *saïm,* later *sain* (mod. only *saindoux* lard) :– Rom. **sagimen* (whence med.L. *sagimen*), for L. *sagina* fattening, fatness.] †**1.** Fat, grease –1697. **2.** Hogs' lard 1530.

1. Part scour the rusty Sheilds with S. DRYDEN.

Seam (sīm), *v.* 1582. [f. SEAM *sb.*[1]] **1.** *trans.* To sew the seam or seams of; to fasten or join *on, together, up* with a seam or seams. †**b.** To furnish or ornament with an inserted seam; also, of a material, to serve as a seam for –1740. **c.** *Knitting. trans.* and *intr.* To form a seam-stitch; to make a seam or seam-stitch in (a piece of knitting) 1842. **2.** *trans.* To mark (a surface) with lines or indentations; to furrow 1596. **3.** *trans.* To join (sheets of lead or metal) by means of a seam 1703.

2. A most beautifull and sweet countrey..seamed throughout with many goodly rivers SPENSER. Scars of Honour seam'd his manly Face 1695. Her..meagre face Seam'd with the shallow cares of fifty years TENNYSON.

Sea·-maid. *poet.* 1590. = MERMAID 1. Also, a goddess or nymph of the sea.

Certaine starres shot madly from their Spheares, To heare the Sea maids musicke SHAKS. So **Sea-maiden.**

Seaman (sī·mæn). *Pl.* **-men.** [OE. *sǣman(n,* with Gmc. parallels.] **1. a.** *gen.* One whose occupation is on the sea; a sailor as opp. to a landsman. Now *poet.* or *rhet.* Also, with qualifying word: One skilled in navigation. **b.** *spec.* A sailor below the rank of officer. †**2.** = MERMAN –1753.

1. *Leading, able, ordinary s.,* the three grades (beginning with the highest) of seamen in the R. N. *Merchant s.,* a seaman in the merchant service.

Seamanlike (sī·mænləik), *a.* and *adv.* 1796. [f. prec. + -LIKE.] **A.** *adj.* Characteristic of or befitting a (good) seaman. **B.** *adv.* In a seamanlike manner. So **Sea·manly** *a.* and *adv.*

Seamanship (sī·mænʃip). 1766. [f. SEAMAN + -SHIP.] The art or practice of managing a ship at sea; the skill of a good seaman.

Sea·-mark. 1485. **1.** The boundary or limit of the flow of the sea. **2.** A conspicuous object distinguishable at sea which serves to guide or warn sailors in navigation 1566.

Seamew (sī·miū). late ME. [f. SEA *sb.* + MEW *sb.*[1]] The common gull, *Larus canus.*

Seaming (sī·miŋ), *vbl. sb.* 1450. [-ING[1].] The action of SEAM *v.*; *concr.* a seam or seams.

attrib., as **s. lace** = *seam-lace*; **s. machine,** a machine for forming the joints at the edges of sheet-metal plates.

Seamless (sī·mlės), *a.* 1483. [f. SEAM *sb.*[1] + -LESS.] Without a seam; of a garment, woven without a seam.

Sea·-monk. 1611. †**1.** The monk-fish –1666. **2.** The monk-seal 1891.

Sea·-mo:nster. 1586. A monster of the sea. **1.** A huge fish, cetacean, or the like. **2.** A fabulous marine animal of terrifying proportions and shape 1596.

2. Dagon his Name, Sea Monster, upward Man And downward Fish MILT.

Sea·-mouse. 1520. **1.** A marine dorsibranchiate annelid of the family *Aphroditidæ,* esp. *Aphrodite aculeata.* **2.** *local.* The dunlin and other small shore-birds 1885.

Seamster, sempster (sī·mstəɹ, se·mᵖstəɹ). [OE. *sēamestre,* fem. corresp. to *sēamere* tailor, f. *sēam* SEAM *sb.*[1] + -ER[1]; see -STER.] One who sews; one whose occupation is sewing; a tailor, seamstress. (Now only applied to one of the male sex.)

Seamstress, sempstress (sī·mstrės, se·mᵖstrės). 1613. [See prec. and -ESS[1].] A woman who seams or sews; a needlewoman whose occupation is plain sewing.

Seamy (sī·mi), *a.* 1604. [f. SEAM *sb.*[1] + -Y[1].] **1.** Having a seam or suture, characterized by seams. **2.** Of the nature of or resembling, marked with, a seam or seams 1776.

1. *S. side,* lit. the under side of a garment, etc. on which the rough edges of the seams are visible; *fig.* (after Shaks.) the worst, most degraded, or roughest side (of life, etc.). **2.** A one-eyed woman, with a scarred and s. face 1857.

‖**Séance** (sē·aṅs). 1803. [Fr., f. OFr. *seoir* :– L. *sedēre* sit.] **1.** *gen.* A sitting of a deliberative or other body or society, or of a number of persons assembled for discussion, instruction, etc. **2.** *spec.* A meeting for the study of spiritualistic phenomena 1845. **3.** A 'sitting' for medical treatment 1875.

Sea·-nymph. 1565. **1.** *Myth.* A nymph (NYMPH 1) supposed to inhabit the sea; a Nereid. **2.** An antarctic petrel, *Procellaria nereis* 1875.

Sea·-o:tter. 1664. A marine otter of the shores of the North Pacific, *Enhydris marina* or *lutris.*

Sea-otter's cabbage, the large seaweed *Nereocystis lütkeana* of the North Pacific, the fronds of which are a favourite resort of sea-otters.

Sea·-pa:rrot. 1664. **1.** The puffin. **2.** One of several fishes (see PARROT-FISH) 1666.

Sea·-pie[1]. 1531. [PIE *sb.*[1]] The oyster-catcher, *Hæmatopus ostralegus.*

Sea·-pie[2]. 1751. [PIE *sb.*[2]] A dish of meat and vegetables, etc. boiled together, with a crust of paste.

Sea·-piece. 1656. [PIECE *sb.* 8.] A picture representing a scene at sea.

Sea·-pike. [PIKE *sb.*[4]] Any of several sea-fishes resembling the pike in their elongate form and voracity, as the garfish, hake, barracuda.

Sea·-pink. 1731. [PINK *sb.*[4]] The plant Thrift, *Armeria maritima.*

Sea-plane, seaplane (sī·plēⁱn). 1913. [PLANE *sb.*[3] 1 e (*b*).] An aeroplane adapted for rising from and landing on water.

Seaport (sī·poᵊɹt). 1596. [PORT *sb.*[1]] = PORT *sb.*[1] 1 and 2. Also *attrib.*

Sea-purse. 1806. **1.** A zoophyte of the genus *Alcyonium.* **2.** The horny egg-case of a skate, ray, or shark; a mermaid's purse 1856. **3.** *U.S., Atlantic coast.* A swirl of the undertow or a double undertow formed by two waves meeting at an angle, making a small whirlpool on the surface of the water, dangerous to bathers 1891.

Sea·-quake, sea·quake. 1680. [After EARTHQUAKE.] A convulsion or sudden agitation of the sea from a submarine eruption or earthquake.

Sear (sīᵊɹ), *sb.* 1560. [prob. – OFr. *serre* grasp, lock, bolt, (now) foot of a bird of prey, f. *serrer* grasp, hold fast :– Rom. **serrare,* for late L. *serare* bar, bolt, f. *sera* bar for a door. Cf. SERE *sb.,* SERRY *v.*] The catch in a gun-lock which keeps the hammer at full or half-cock, and which is released (at full cock) by pressure upon the trigger.

Tickle or *light of the s.,* (fig.) easily made to 'go off'.

Comb. **s.-spring,** a spring which keeps the s. in position, also, in some gun-locks, a spring which throws the hammer back to half-cock after a discharge.

Sear (sīᵊɹ), *v.* [OE. *sēarian* = OHG. *sōrēn* :– Gmc. **saurōjan,* f. **sauraz* SERE *a.*] **1.** *intr.* To dry up, wither away; to become sere. Now *rare.* **2.** *trans.* To cause to wither, to blight. late ME. **3.** To burn or char (animal tissues) by the application of a hot iron; to cauterize (a wound, etc.) in order to destroy virus or prevent the flow of blood 1530. **b.** *fig.* Chiefly after 1 Tim. 4:2, to render (the conscience) incapable of feeling 1582. **c.** *To s. up,* to close (a wound, vein, etc.) by actual cautery 1600. †**d.** To brand, stigmatize –1644. †**4.** To burn, scorch –1810.

2. When summer sears the plains COWPER. **3. b.** Sear'd in heart, and lone, and blighted BYRON. **d.** Calumnie will seare Vertue it selfe SHAKS.

Sea·-ra:ven. 1611. **1.** The cormorant. **2.**

A large N. Amer. fish, *Hemitripterus americanus* 1672.

†**Searce,** *sb.* [ME. *saarce* – (with unexpl. *r*) OFr. *saas* (mod. *sas*) – pop. L. **sætacius* (*pannus*) lit. (cloth) made of bristles, f. L. *sæta* bristle.] A sieve or strainer –1844.

†**Searce,** *v.* late ME. [f. prec.] *trans.* To sift through a searce –1831. Hence **Sea·rcer,** a searce or sieve.

Search (sɔ̄ɹtʃ), *sb.* late ME. [– AFr. *serche*, OFr. *cerche* (†*cherche*), if not from the vb.]

1. The action or an act of searching; examination or scrutiny for the purpose of finding a person or thing. Const. *after, for,* †*of* (the object sought). †Also, effort to ascertain something. **2.** *spec.* **a.** An examination of a ship's cargo, etc. for the purpose of enforcing customs duties 1462. **b.** An examination of a register or of documents in public custody, for the discovery of information which is believed to be contained therein 1465. †**3.** Range to which search extends –1792. **4.** Searching effect (of cold or wind) 1609. **5.** *concr.* Applied to persons: †**a.** A searcher, examiner –1652. †**b.** A search-party. SHAKS.

1. Robin Oig absconded, and escaped all s. SCOTT. A s. after knowledge JOWETT. Phr. *In s. of*, in quest of, in order to find; also, *predic.*, occupied in searching for. *To make (a) s.*, to search (*for* some lost, concealed, or desired object). **2.** Phr. *Right of s.*, the right, recognized by the law of nations, by which a duly commissioned ship of war is empowered, outside neutral waters, to stop and examine a merchant vessel for contraband.

attrib. and *Comb.*: **s.-party,** a company of people organized to make search for a person, etc.; **-room,** the room in the Public Record Office provided for members of the public who wish to search documents there preserved; **-warrant,** a warrant authorizing the searching of the dwelling of a person suspected of crime. Hence **Sea·rchful** *a.* diligent in search.

Search (sɔ̄ɹtʃ), *v.* ME. [– AFr. *sercher*, OFr. *cerchier* (mod. *chercher*) :– late L. *circare* go round, f. L. *circus* CIRCLE.] **I.** To explore, examine thoroughly. **1.** *trans.* To go about (a country or place) in order to find, or to ascertain the presence or absence of, some person or thing; to explore in quest of some object. **2.** To look through (a building, an apartment, a receptacle) in quest of some object concealed or lost. late ME. **3.** To examine (a person) by handling, removal of garments, and the like, to ascertain whether any article (usu. something stolen or contraband) is concealed in his clothing. late ME. **4.** To look through, examine (writings, records) in order to discover whether certain things are contained there. late ME. **5.** With immaterial object: To investigate; to examine rigorously (one's own heart, thoughts, etc.); to examine, penetrate the secrets of (another's mind or thoughts). Also with *out.* late ME. **b.** Of an impersonal agency: To test, reveal the nature of 1586. **6.** To look scrutinizingly at 1811. †**7.** To probe (a wound) –1687. **8.** Of wind, cold, fire-arms, etc.: To penetrate, reach the weak places of. late ME.

1. Send thou men, that they may s. the lande of Canaan *Num.* 13:2. **2.** Even now they s. the tower, and find the body SHELLEY. **4.** I have been at the trouble to s. the Journals in the period between the two last wars BURKE. **5.** O Lorde, thou searchest me out, and knowest me COVERDALE *Ps.* 139:1.

II. To look for or seek diligently; to try to find. Now only with *out* exc. (*rarely*) *poet.* ME. †**b.** To seek to discover. Also with *out.* –1644.

He hath bin search'd among the dead & liuing; But no trace of him SHAKS. His primary object is to s. out the truth 1887.

III. *absol.* and *intr.* **1.** To make a search. Const. *after, for, into* ME. †**2.** To devise means (*to do* something) –1567.

1. S. even as thou wilt, But thou shalt never find what I can hide SHELLEY. Hence **Sea·rchable** *a.* capable of being searched. **Sea·rchableness.**

Searcher (sɔ̄·ɹtʃəɹ). late ME. [Two formations, which do not admit of being distinguished: (1) – AFr. *cerchour*, OFr. *cerchere*, *cercheor*, f. *cerchier* SEARCH *v.*; (2) f. SEARCH *v.* + -ER[1].] **1.** One who searches. Also *s.-out.* **2.** One whose office is to search; *esp.* **a.** An officer of the custom-house appointed to search ships, baggage, or goods for dutiable or contraband articles. late ME. †**b.** One appointed to observe and report on any offences against discipline or good order in a religious house, a community, body of workmen, etc. –1845. †**c.** As the designation of various municipal and government officials; e.g. a sanitary inspector; an inspector of markets; an examiner of certain articles of manufacture; etc. –1835. †**d.** A person appointed to view dead bodies and to make report upon the cause of death –1759. **e.** An official appointed to search the clothing and person of any one arrested and detained by the police 1726. **3.** An instrument used in making a search. **a.** *Surg.* A probe or sound 1597. †**b.** An instrument for testing the soundness of cannon after discharge –1859. **c.** In microscopical work: An objective of low power used to obtain a general view of the object 1870.

Searching (sɔ̄·ɹtʃiŋ), *ppl. a.* 1580. [-ING[2].] That searches. **1.** Of observation or examination: Minute, rigorous. Of a look: Penetrating, keenly observant. **b.** Of liquids, wind, rain, etc., or of bodily diseases: That finds out weak points, keen, sharp, piercing 1593. **2.** Engaged in or given to searching 1626.

1. b. A maruellous s. Wine SHAKS. Hence **Sea·rching-ly** *adv.*, **-ness.**

†**Sea·rchless,** *a.* 1605. [f. SEARCH *sb.* + -LESS.] Inscrutable, impenetrable –1834.

Sea·rchlight. 1883. [f. SEARCH *sb.* + LIGHT *sb.*] An electric arc-lamp or acetylene light fitted with a reflector and suspended in a frame so that it may throw a beam of light in any desired direction; used in naval, military and air defence and for signalling, etc. **b.** The beam of light thrown by such a lamp.

Searing (sīᵊ·riŋ), *vbl. sb.* late ME. [f. SEAR *v.* + -ING[1].] The action of SEAR *v.*

Comb.: **s.-iron,** an iron used for cauterizing, branding, etc.

Sea·-ro:bin. 1844. [ROBIN[1].] **1.** *U.S.* A gurnard or trigloid fish, esp. of the genus *Prionotus.* **2.** *local.* **a.** *U.S.* The red-breasted merganser, *Mergus serrator* 1891. **b.** The spotted fly-catcher, *Muscicapa grisola* 1899.

Sea·-room. 1554. Space at sea free from obstruction in which a ship can be manœuvred easily. Esp. in phr. *to have, give,* or *take s.*

Sea·-ro:ver. 1579. [orig. – Du. *zeerover* pirate; see SEA, ROVER[2].] **1.** A pirate. (Now often apprehended as meaning one who 'roves' over the sea.) **2.** A pirate-ship 1828. Hence **Sea-roving** *vbl. sb.* and *ppl. a.*

Sea·-salt, *sb.* 1601. Common salt obtained by the evaporation of sea-water. So **Sea·-salt** *a.* (*rare*) salt like the sea; impregnated with or containing s.

Sea-sand. ME. **1.** Sand of the sea or seashore. **2.** *pl.* Tracts of sea-sand. late ME.

Sea-scape, seascape (sī·skeⁱp). 1799. [After LANDSCAPE; see SCAPE *sb.*[3]] **1.** A picture of the sea, a sea-piece; sea-pieces collectively. **2.** A picturesque view or prospect of the sea 1806.

Sea·-se:rpent. 1646. **1. a.** Any ophidian inhabiting the sea; esp. any of the venomous snakes of the order *Hydrophidæ*, inhabiting the tropical Indo-Pacific Ocean 1671. **b.** *The (great) s.*: a sea-monster of serpentine form and great length, frequently reported to have been seen at sea 1774. **2.** Applied to various fishes. †**a.** A kind of eel or muræna found in the Mediterranean. †**b.** = ELLOPS 2. **c.** The king of the herrings, *Regalecus glesne.* 1646.

Sea·-se:rvice. 1610. Service at sea; the condition or function of serving in the navy; naval as opp. to land service. Also, service or employment (of a person, ship, etc.) on the high seas, as dist. from shore or harbour duty.

Sea·-shell. OE. A marine shell, the shell of any salt-water mollusc. **b.** Material consisting of sea-shells 1837.

Sea-shore. 1526. The coast of the sea, or the land lying adjacent to the sea; also, the ground actually washed by the sea at high tides (usu. covered with sand or shingle).

Sea·-sick, *a.* 1566. **1.** Suffering from sea-sickness. Chiefly *predic.* †**2.** Weary of travelling by sea. SHAKS. So **Sea-sickness,** nausea and vomiting induced by the motion of a ship.

Sea-side, seaside. ME. [SIDE *sb.*[1] III. 5 b.] **1.** (sī:səi·d) The margin or brink of the sea. Now *rare* or *Obs.* **2.** (sī·səid) Now chiefly: The sea-coast as resorted to for health or pleasure 1797. **3.** (sī·səid) The side towards or facing the sea 1867. **4.** *attrib.* or quasi-*adj.* (sī·səid) Belonging to, situated or taking place at the sea-side 1784.

Sea·-slug. 1779. **1.** = TREPANG. **2.** Any marine gasteropod of the order *Opisthobranchiata* 1845.

Sea·-snail. OE. **1.** Any of various marine gasteropods. **2.** A fish of the family *Liparididæ*, esp. the *Liparis vulgaris*, or unctuous sucker 1672.

Sea·-snake. 1755. = SEA-SERPENT 1 a, b.

Sea·-snipe. 1767. **1.** Local name for the dunlin, the knot, and other sandpipers. **2.** †**a.** A kind of gar-fish. **b.** The trumpet-fish or snipe-fish, *Centriscus scolopax*, so called from its long tubular snout 1826.

Season (sī·z'n), *sb.* [ME. *seson* – OFr. *seson* (mod. *saison*) :– L. *satio, -ōn-* sowing, in Rom. time of sowing, seed-time, f. **sə-*, as in L. *satus* sown.] **I.** A period of the year. **1.** Any one of the periods into which the year is naturally divided by the earth's changing position in regard to the sun, and which are marked by varying length of day and night, by particular conditions of temperature, weather, etc. More specifically, each of the four equal periods—Spring, Summer, Autumn, Winter—into which the year is divided by the passage of the sun from equinox to solstice and from solstice to equinox; also, each of the two periods—the rainy and the dry—into which the year is divided in tropical climates. **b.** A day or period of the year marked by some special festivity, as Christmas and New Year 1791. **c.** In reckoning time or age: A year (*rare* or *poet.*) 1827. **2.** A period or time of year mentioned with ref. to the conditions of weather, etc. that characterize it in a particular year. late ME. **3.** The time of year assigned to some particular operation of agriculture ME. **4.** The time of year when a plant flourishes, when it blooms or bears fruit, etc. ME. **5.** The time of year when an animal is in heat, pairs, breeds, migrates, is killed for food or hunted, etc. (Also *pairing, breeding, close,* etc. *s.*). late ME. **6.** A period of time astronomically fixed or recurring 1535. **7.** The portion of a year regularly devoted to a particular business, sport, or amusement, or when the greatest activity prevails therein 1656. **8.** The period of the year during which a particular place is most frequented for business, fashion, or amusement; esp. the time (now May to July) when the fashionable world is assembled in London 1705. **9.** *transf.* (from 2). †**a.** A spell of (bad or inclement) weather –1667. **b.** *spec.* The 'rains' or spells of wet weather in tropical countries. In the southern U.S., a shower of rain or period of damp weather suitable for setting out tobacco plants, etc. 1707.

1. Now had the s. returned, when the nights grow colder and longer LONGF. **b.** The compliments of the s. to my worthy masters LAMB. **2.** A most extraordinary wet and cold s. EVELYN. **4.** Like a tre.., yᵗ bringeth forth his frute in due s. COVERDALE *Ps.* 1:3. **6.** He in whose hand all times and seasons roul MILT. **7.** *The fishing, hunting, publishing, racing, theatrical, holiday s. Dead, dull,* or *off s.*, the period when such pursuits are inactive. *Silly s.*: see SILLY *a.* 5 b. **8.** You cannot figure a duller s.: the weather bitter, no party, little money H. WALPOLE. *Dead s.*, the period when 'society' has departed from a place of resort. **9. a.** *Lear* III. iv. 32.

II. *gen.* A time, period, occasion. **1.** A particular time or period during which something happens, or which is defined by some characteristic feature or circumstance ME. **2.** A time at which, or an occasion when, something happens. Now *rare.* ME. **3.** The right, proper, due or appointed time; a fit or favourable occasion, an opportunity ME.

1. Phr. *For a s.*, for an indefinite period, for some time; This..beautiful human soul; who walked with me for a s. in this world CARLYLE. **2.** He knew the proper s. to shew the violence of his Revenge 1686. **3.** When my s. comes to sit On David's Throne MILT.

†**III.** [f. the vb.] Seasoning, relish, flavour –1664. **IV.** Short for *s.-ticket* 1896.

Phrases. **In season. a.** At the right and proper time, opportunely. **b.** Of game, etc.; At the time for hunting, catching, etc. *To be in s.* (of a plant or animal) to flourish, be in the best condition for eating; also, (of an animal) to be in heat. So *to come in* or *into s.* **Out of s. a.** Unseasonably, inopportunely; *predic.* unseasonable, inopportune. **b.** Not in season; not at the time for hunting, catching, eating, etc. **c.** Not in fashion. **In s. and out of s.** At all times, without regard to what is considered opportune.

Comb.: **s.-ticket,** a ticket which admits the holder to travel on a boat or on a line of railway, to enter an exhibition, place of amusement, etc., an unlimited number of times during a season or specified period, at a reduced rate of payment; hence *s.-ticket holder.* Hence **Sea·sonless** *a.* having or knowing no change of s.

Season (sī·z'n), *v.* late ME. [— OFr. *saisonner*, f. *saison* SEASON *sb.*] **1.** *trans.* To render (a dish) more palatable by the addition of some savoury ingredient. **b.** *fig.* To mix, intersperse, or imbue with something that imparts relish; to adapt or accommodate *to* a particular taste 1520. †**c.** To moderate, alleviate, temper. SHAKS. †**2.** *transf.* To imbue with a taste or scent –1591. †**b.** To imbue (a person, his mind) *with* opinions, ideas, etc.; in later use only in a good sense –1791. †**3.** *trans.* To embalm –1638. **4.** To mature, ripen; to render fit for use by prolonged exposure, or by gradual subjection to conditions of the kind to be undergone in actual working; often, to dry and harden (timber) by keeping. Also *intr.* for *refl.* 1545. **b.** *trans.* To fortify (a person) by habit against conditions that might otherwise be deleterious; to acclimatize 1601. †**c.** To prepare or fit (a person); also, to discipline, train –1658. †**5.** To impregnate, to copulate with –1601.

1. All s. their food with a great quantity of spices 1769. **b.** You s. still with sports your serious hours DRYDEN. **c.** S. your admiration for a while With an attent eare SHAKS. **2. b.** Garrick, who I can attest..had his mind seasoned with pious reverence BOSWELL. **3.** *Twel. N.* I. i. 30. **4.** Knowledge and timber shouldn't be much used till they are seasoned O.W. HOLMES. **b.** In war well season'd, and with labours tann'd BYRON. **c.** Am I then reueng'd, To take him in the purging of his Soule When he is fit and season'd for his passage? SHAKS.

Seasonable (sī·z'năb'l), *a.* late ME. [f. SEASON *v.* and *sb.* + -ABLE.] Opportune. **b.** Of weather, etc.: Suitable to the time of year. late ME. **c.** = SEASONAL *a.* 2. 1923.

His Caution was so s., and his Advice so good DE FOE. Hence **Sea·sonableness. Sea·sonably** *adv.*

Seasonal (sī·z'năl), *a.* 1838. [f. SEASON *sb.* + -AL¹.] **1.** Pertaining to or characteristic of the seasons of the year, or some one of them. **b.** *transf.* Pertaining to the seasons or periods of human life 1843. **2.** Of certain trades: Dependent on the seasons. Of workers, servants: Employed only during a particular season. 1904. **3.** Periodical, (regularly) recurrent 1880.

1. *S. dimorphism*, a variation in the appearance of different broods of the same insect according to the time of year at which they are produced. **2.** The problem of the casual and s. worker 1904. Hence **Sea·sonally** *adv.*

Seasoner (sī·z'nəɹ). 1598. [f. SEASON *v.* + -ER¹.] One who or something which seasons.

Seasoning (sī·z'niŋ), *vbl. sb.* 1511. [-ING¹.] **1.** The action of SEASON *v.* **2.** *concr.* Something added to a dish which gives it a distinctive or appetizing flavour 1580.

2. *fig.* His favourite clown..whose jests..served for a sort of s. to his evening meal SCOTT.

Sea· spi:der. 1666. **a.** A spider-crab or maioid. **b.** A marine arthropod of the group *Pycnogonida* 1855. **c.** An octopus 1858.

Sea·-star. OE. [In sense 1, esp. tr. med.L. *stella maris*, title of the B.V.M.; in sense 2, cf. L. *stella* (later *s. marina*) starfish.] †**1.** A star which guides mariners at sea –1817. **2.** A starfish 1569.

Sea·-swa:llow. 1598. **1.** = FLYING FISH. **2. a.** Any one of the terns (from their general resemblance to swallows). **b.** The stormy petrel, *Procellaria pelagica.* 1647. **3.** The trepang or bêche-de-mer (see SWALLO) 1802.

Seat (sīt), *sb.* ME. [— ON. *sæti* = OE. *ġesete*, MDu. *gesæte* (Du. *gezeet*), OHG. *gasāzi* (G. *gesäss* †seat, posteriors) :— Gmc. **ʒasǣtjam*, f. **sǣt- *set-* SIT.] **I.** Action or manner of sitting. †**1.** *gen.* The action of sitting –1420. **2.** Manner of sitting (on horseback). Also *predic.*, one who has a (good, etc.) seat, a (good, etc.) horseman. 1577.

2. A firm and graceful S. on Horseback LOCKE.

II. Place or thing to sit upon. **1.** The place on which a person is sitting, or is accustomed to sit; a place to seat one person at a table, in a conveyance, etc. ME. **b.** Hence, the use of, or right to use, a seat (in a church, theatre, conveyance, etc.) 1520. **c.** A right to sit as a member, or the position of being a member, of a deliberative or administrative body, *esp.* of Parliament or other legislative assembly; a place (whether occupied or temporarily vacant) in the membership of the House of Commons, Congress, or the like 1774. **2.** Something adapted or used for sitting upon, as a chair, stool, sofa, etc. Also *spec.* a bench to seat one or more persons; a horizontal board or framework in a boat, etc. late ME. **b.** That part (of a chair, saddle, etc.) upon which its occupant sits 1778. **3.** Contextually applied to the throne of a king or a bishop, or the like, the throne of God or of an angel. Hence *fig.* the authority or dignity symbolized by sitting in a particular chair or throne. ME. **b.** *spec.* The throne *of* a particular kingdom 1599. **4.** The sitting part of the body; the posteriors. Also joc., *s. of honour*, etc. 1607. **b.** That part (of a garment) which covers the posteriors 1835. **5.** The 'form' of a hare. *rare.* 1735. **6.** *Boot-trade.* An engagement to work at making boots of a specified kind 1791.

1. She ordered me a s. at her right hand 1716. **c.** A s. in the cabinet 1849. By the..Reform Act of 1867..twenty-six seats were taken from boroughs 1885. **2.** They came To a stone s. beside a spring SHELLEY. **b.** Chairs without any seats 1809. **3.** I, for myself, th' Imperial S. will gain DRYDEN. Phr. †*Apostolic s.*, *Holy s.*, *Peter's s.*, the papal chair, its occupant, or his office; = SEE *sb.* 2 c. **b.** We neuer valew'd this poore seate of England SHAKS.

III. Residence, abode, situation. **1.** Applied *spec.* (after L. *sedes*) to: The abiding place or resting place (of departed souls); a position in this place. Now *arch.* or *poet.* ME. **2.** A city in which a throne, court, government is established or set up; a capital. late ME. **b.** = SEE *sb.* 2 d. Now only *s. of a bishop.* late ME. **3.** The thing (esp. the organ or part of the body) in which a particular power, faculty, function or quality 'resides'; the locality of a disease, sensation, or the like. late ME. **b.** Similarly, of the soul or its parts 1579. **4.** A place where something takes place, or where some particular condition of things prevails 1560. **b.** A city or locality in which (a branch of trade, learning, etc.) is established 1585. **5.** A place of habitation or settlement (of a tribe, people, etc.). Also *transf.* (of birds). 1535. **b.** = COUNTRY-*seat* 1607. †**6.** Local position or situation –1695. **7.** Position as regards surroundings, climate, etc.; situation, site 1549. †**8.** A definite place (on a surface, in a body or organ, in a series) –1775.

1. Mount, mount my soule, thy seate is vp on high SHAKS. **2.** Peking, the Royal S. of the Chinese Emperor DE FOE. **3.** The heede is pryncypall place and seete of wyttes TREVISA. **b.** Sin has its s. in the soul 1847. **4.** Phr. *S. of war* [= L. *sedes belli*], the region in which warfare is going on. **b.** Blackfriars was..the s. of fashion 1865. **5.** The s. of the old Irish..was the province of Ulster CLARENDON. **6.** †*S. of living*, habitat (of an animal). **7.** This Castle hath a pleasant s. SHAKS.

IV. Basis, foundation, support. †**1.** A place prepared for something to be erected or set up upon it; a building site –1662. **2.** The part upon which a thing rests or appears to rest 1661. **3.** *Mech.* A part or surface upon which the base of something rests 1805. **4.** *Shoe-making.* A piece of leather pegged or sewn to the boot as a foundation for the heel 1882.

Phrases. *To hold, keep a* or *one's s.*, to remain seated, to keep from falling; also, to retain one's position as a Member of Parliament; so, *to lose one's s. To take a s.*, to sit down. *To take one's s.*, to take the sitting-place assigned to one; to assume one's official position, to be formally admitted to Parliament or Congress. *To take a* or *the back s.*, orig. *U.S.*, *fig.* to occupy a subordinate place.

Comb. **s.-bone** *Anat.*, the innominate bone or hip-bone; more strictly the ISCHIUM; **-stick,** a walking-stick which may be adapted to form a seat. Hence **Sea·tless** *a.* having no seat or seats.

Seat (sīt), *v.* 1577. [f. prec.] **1.** *trans.* To place on a seat or seats; to cause to sit down 1613. **b.** *refl.* To take one's seat, sit down 1589. †**c.** *intr.* for *refl.* To sit down. Of a hare: To sit in its form. –1772. **d.** *trans.* To cause or enable to sit *in* or *on* a throne, chair of state or office, etc. Hence, to establish (a person) in a position of authority or dignity. 1593. **e.** To put into a seat in a deliberative assembly 1797. **f.** To find seats for; to assign seats to. Of a building, room, etc.: To afford sitting accommodation for. 1828. **2.** *pass.* To be sitting 1608. **3.** *trans.* To settle or establish in a particular locality. Now *rare.* 1589. †**b.** *refl.* To settle (in a place). Also *intr.* for *refl.* –1797. **4.** *trans.* With a thing as object: To place in a 'seat' or situation. (*rare* exc. *pass.* as in 5.) 1603. **5.** *pass.* To have its seat, be situated 1577. **b.** Of a disease: To have its seat *in* a certain part of the body. Also *to be deeply seated*: lit. to be situated far below the surface; hence (often *fig.*) to be beyond the reach of superficial remedies. 1619. †**6.** *trans.* To 'plant' with inhabitants, settle (a country) –1784. **7.** To fix a seat on (a chair); to repair (trousers, a chair) by renewing or mending the seat 1762. **8.** To furnish (a building, room, etc.) with seats 1818.

1. So now y'are fairely seated SHAKS. **d.** To inshrine Belus or Serapis thir Gods, or s. Thir Kings MILT. **2.** While Shepherds watched their flocks by night All seated on the ground TATE. **5.** *Merch. V.* I. ii. 8. The Garden, seated on the level Floor DRYDEN. **8.** A portion of which was seated with pews, and used as a church SCOTT.

-seater (sī·təɹ). 1906. [f. SEAT *sb.* and *v.* + -ER¹.] Freq. in comb., as *two-s.*, *four-s.*, etc., a motor car, etc. having seats for two, four, etc. in the body.

Seating (sī·tiŋ), *vbl. sb.* 1596. [f. SEAT *sb.* and *v.* + -ING¹.] †**1.** The action of providing with a residence, or of settling in a country; quasi-*concr.* opportunity for settling, footing –1699. **2.** The action of providing with seats; the manner in which a building, etc. is seated; *concr.* the seats with which a building, etc. is provided 1880. **3.** Material for upholstering the seats of chairs, etc. 1833. **4.** *Mech.* A fitted support for a part of a structure or machine, usu. *pl.* or *collect. sing.* 1844. **5.** That part of a structure, etc. which rests on some other part 1805.

2. The s. of the church is but little altered 1880. *attrib.*, as *s. accommodation, capacity.*

Sea·-trout. 1745. **1.** The *Salmo trutta* = SALMON-TROUT 1; also the bull or grey trout, *S. eriox.* **2.** In U.S. and Australia applied to other fishes 1859.

Sea·-urchin. 1591. An animal of the genus *Echinus* or the other *Echinoidea.*

Seave (sīv). *north.* late ME. [— ON. *sef* (Sw. *säf*, Da. *siv*).] A rush; also, a rushlight. Hence **Sea·vy** *a.* containing or overgrown with rushes; composed of rushes.

Sea-wall. OE. **1.** A wall or embankment to prevent the encroachment of the sea, etc. **2.** The sea as a wall or barrier of defence (*rare*) 1879. So **Sea-walled** (wǭld) *a.* surrounded or protected by the sea as a wall of defence.

‖**Seawan(e, seawant** (sī·wēⁱn, -wǫnt). *Amer. Ind.* 1701. [Narragansett *seawohn* scattered, loose (in opposition to the strung beads, called *peag*).] Wampum.

Seaward (sī·wǫɹd), *adv.* (and quasi-*sb.*) and *a.* late ME. [f. SEA *sb.* + -WARD.] **A.** advb. phrases and *adv.* **1.** Phrases. **a.** *To (the) s.*: towards, in the direction of, the sea; away from the land. *To the s. of*: to or at a place nearer the sea (or, at sea, farther from the land) than. **b.** *From (the) s.*: from the direction in which the sea lies 1719. **2.** *adv.* Towards the sea or the open sea (away from the land) 1610. **B.** *adj.* **1.** Going out to sea, going to seaward 1621. **2.** Directed or looking towards the sea; situated on the side or portion (of a thing) which is nearest the sea 1725. **b.** Of a wind: Blowing from the sea 1810.

2. Your cannons moulder on the s. wall TENNYSON. Hence **Sea·wardly** *a.* habituated to looking s.; *adv.* towards the sea (*rare*).

Seawards (sī·wǫɹdz), *adv.* 1517. [f. SEA *sb.* + -WARDS.] = prec. adv.

Sea·-ware. [OE. *sǣwār*; see SEA, WARE *sb.*¹] Seaweed; esp. coarse large seaweed thrown up on the shore by the sea, and used as manure, etc.

Sea·-wa:ter. OE. The water of the sea, or water taken from the sea.

Sea·-way, sea·way. OE. **1.** A way over the sea; the sea as a means of communication; the open sea. **2.** The progress of a ship through the sea 1787. **3.** A rough sea 1840.

3. The coracle..was a very safe boat..both buoyant and clever in a s. STEVENSON.

Seaweed (sī·wīd). 1577. [f. SEA *sb.* + WEED *sb.*[1]] **1.** *collect.* Any marine plants of the class *Algæ* (see ALGA). **2.** A particular marine alga 1700.

Sea·-wolf. ME. †**1.** A fabulous amphibious beast of prey –1607. **2.** A voracious sea-fish; esp. the bass, *Labrax lupus*, and the wolf-fish, *Anarrhichas lupus*. late ME. †**3.** A seal; a sea-elephant or sea-lion –1839. **4.** quasi-*arch.* A pirate, sea-robber; also, a privateer vessel 1849.

Seaworthy (sī·wɒ̄ːɹði), *a.* 1807. [f. SEA *sb.* + WORTHY *a.*] Of a ship: In a fit condition to undergo a voyage, and to encounter stormy weather. Hence **Sea·wo:rthiness,** s. condition.

Sea·-wrack. 1548. [WRACK *sb.*[2]] †**1.** *pl.* Property cast ashore by the sea. **2. a.** *collect.* Seaweed, esp. any of the large coarse kinds cast up on the shore, as *Fucus, Laminaria*, etc. 1551. **b.** A particular kind of seaweed 1611.

Sebaceous (sĭbēⁱ·ʃəs), *a.* 1728. [f. L. *sebaceus*, f. *sebum* tallow; see -ACEOUS.] **1.** Pertaining to, of the nature of, or resembling tallow or fat; oily, greasy 1783. **2.** *Phys.* **a.** Having the nature or characteristics of SEBUM; as *s. humour*, etc. 1747. **b.** Connected with the secretion of sebum; as *s. follicle, gland*, etc. 1728. **3.** *Path.* Of a cyst, tumour: Formed upon a sebaceous gland 1872.

Sebacic (sĭbæ·sik), *a.* 1790. [f. L. *sebaceus* + -IC 1 b.] *Chem. S. acid*: an acid obtained by the distillation of oleic acid.

Sebastine (sĭbæ·stin). 1884. [Patented in Sweden in 1872.] An explosive composed of nitroglycerine, charcoal, and saltpetre.

‖**Sebat** (sī·bæt), **Shebat** (ʃī·bæt). late ME. [Heb. *šᵉbaṭ.*] The eleventh month of the Jewish ecclesiastical and fifth of the civil year.

Sebate (sī·bĕt). 1794. [f. L. *sebum* tallow + -ATE[4].] *Chem.* A combination of sebacic acid with a base.

Sebesten (sĭbe·stĕn). late ME. [– med.L. *sebestĕn* – Arab. *sabastān* – Pers. *sapistān.*] *Bot.* The plum-like fruit of a tree of the genus *Cordia* (formerly *Sebestena*); a preparation of this used as a medicine. Also the tree itself.

Sebiparous (sĭbi·părəs), *a.* 1855. [f. SEBUM + -PAROUS.] Producing sebum.

Seborrhœa (seborī·ă). 1876. [f. *sebo-* as comb. form of SEBUM, after *gonorrhœa*, etc.] *Path.* An excessive discharge from the sebaceous glands forming a greasy or scaly coating upon the skin.

‖**Sebum** (sī·bɒm). 1876. [mod.L. use of L. *sebum* suet, grease.] *Phys.* The fatty secretion which lubricates the hair and the skin.

‖**Sec** (sęk). 1889. [Fr.] Of wines = DRY *a.* 8.

Sec., abbreviation of SECANT, SECOND (for which it is used colloq. as a word, e.g. 'half a sec'), SECRETARY, SECTION.

Secant (sī·kănt), *a.* and *sb.* 1593. [– Fr. *sécant* adj., *sécante* sb. (sc. *ligne*) – mod.L. use of L. *secans, secant-*, pr. pple. of *secare* cut; see -ANT.] **A.** *adj. Geom.* Of a line or surface in relation to another line or surface: Cutting, intersecting. **B.** *sb.* (Ellipt. for *s. line.*) **a.** *Trig.* orig. The length of a straight line drawn from the centre of a circular arc through one end of the arc, and terminated by the tangent or line touching the arc at the other end; in mod. use, the ratio of this line to the radius, or (equivalently, as a function of an angle) the ratio of the hypotenuse of a right-angled triangle to that of one side, the given angle (or, if obtuse, its supplement) being that contained between them. (Abbrev. *sec*) 1593. **b.** *Geom.* A line that cuts another; esp. a straight line that cuts a curve in two or more parts 1684. Hence **Se·cancy,** the fact of being s.

‖**Sécateur** (sekatŏr). 1881. [Fr. *sécateur*, irreg. f. L. *secare* cut + *-ateur* -ATOR.] A kind of pruning shears with crossed blades. (Usu. *pl.*)

‖**Secco** (se·kko), *a.* and *sb.* 1852. [It. :– L. *siccus* dry.] **A.** *adj. Mus.* Performed without accompaniment 1876. **B.** *sb. Painting.* Ellipt. for It. *fresco secco* 'dry fresco', a process of painting on dry plaster with colours mixed with water 1852.

Seccotine (se·kŏtīn), *sb.* 1894. [app. arbitrarily f. It. *secco* dry.] Maker's name for a composition serving as a strong adhesive. Hence **Se·ccotine** *v. trans.* to cement with s.

Secede (sĭsī·d), *v.* 1702. [– L. *secedere*, f. *se-* SE- + *cedere* go, CEDE.] †**1.** *intr.* To go away from one's companions, go into retirement. **2.** To withdraw formally from an alliance, an association, a federal union, a political or religious organization 1755. Hence **Sece·der,** one who secedes; *spec.* a member of the Secession Church.

Secern (sĭsɔ̄·ɹn), *v.* 1656. [– L. *secernere*, f. *se-* SE- + *cernere* separate, distinguish, secrete, in sense 2 (in med.L.) rendering Gr. ἀποκρίνειν.] **1.** *trans.* To separate; now only, to separate in thought; to distinguish, discriminate. **2.** *Phys.* To separate from the blood; to SECRETE. Now *rare.* 1657.

1. Whereby the good from ill they might s. 1855. **2.** An unusual proportion of bile is secerned 1822. Hence **Sece·rnment,** the action of secreting.

Secernent (sĭsɔ̄·ɹnĕnt), *a.* and *sb.* 1808. [– L. *secernens, -ent-*, pr. pple. of *secernere*; see prec., -ENT.] **A.** *adj.* That secretes 1822. **B.** *sb. Phys.* A secreting organ 1808.

†**Sece·ss.** 1563. [– L. *secessus*, f. *secedere*; see next.] Withdrawing, retirement; a secession –1675.

Secession (sĭse·ʃən). 1533. [– Fr. *sécession* or L. *secessio*, f. *secess-*; see SE-, CESSION.] †**1.** The action or an act of going away from one's accustomed neighbourhood, or of retiring from public view; the condition of being retired –1847. **2.** *Rom. Hist.* Used as tr. L. *secessio (plebis)*, the temporary migration of the plebeians to a place outside the city, in order to compel the patricians to grant redress of their grievances 1533. **3.** The action of seceding or formally withdrawing from an alliance, a federation, a political or religious organization, etc. Hence, a body of seceders. 1600. **b.** *spec.* The separation from the Established Church of Scotland in 1733; the religious body (more fully *the S. Church*) which originated from this separation 1733.

3. *War of S.*, the American Civil War (1861–5), which arose out of the attempt of eleven of the Southern States to secede from the United States of North America.

attrib., as *S. church, movement*, etc.; also as *adj.* = secessionist. Hence **Sece·ssional** *a.* of or pertaining to s. **Sece·ssionism** *U.S. Hist.*, the principles of those in favour of s.; *Scottish Ch. Hist.*, the principles and doctrines of the S. Church. **Sece·ssionist,** one who favours s.; one who joins in a s.; *spec.* in *U.S. Hist.*; also *attrib.* or as *adj.*

Seckel (se·kĕl). Also **Seckle.** 1817. [f. name *Seckle*, the originator, of Philadelphia.] A kind of pear. Also *S. pear.*

Seclude (sĭklū·d), *v.* 1451. [– L. *secludere*, f. *se-* SE- + *claudere* shut.] †**1.** To shut off (a thing) –1548. **2.** †**a.** To shut up apart –1746. **b.** To remove or guard from public view; to withdraw from opportunities of social intercourse. Often *refl.*, to live in retirement or solitude. 1628. **c.** To shut off or screen *from* some external influence 1601. †**3.** To shut or keep out *from* a place, society, etc.; to debar *from* a privilege, dignity, etc. –1775. †**4.** To exclude from consideration –1725. **5.** *Textual criticism.* To exclude as spurious 1893. †**6.** To separate, keep apart, select –1876.

2. a. The women were secluded from the men, being seated above in galleries EVELYN. **b.** Great Allowances should be given to a King who lives wholly secluded from the rest of the World SWIFT. **6.** No plunder taken in war was used by the captor until the Druids determined what part they should s. for themselves GOLDSM.

Secluded (sĭklū·dĕd), *ppl. a.* 1604. [f. prec. + -ED[1].] **1.** Shut up; withheld from view or from society. Now *rare.* **2.** Of localities: Remote from observation or access; seldom visited or seen on account of inaccessibility 1798.

Secluse (sĭklū·z), *a.* Now *rare.* 1597. [– L. *seclusus*, pa. pple. of *secludere*, f. as next.] Secluded.

Seclusion (sĭklū·ʒən). 1623. [– med.L. *seclusio, -ōn-*, f. *seclus-*, pa. ppl. stem of L. *secludere*; see SECLUDE, -ION.] **1.** The action of secluding; †exclusion. **2.** The condition or state of being secluded; an instance of this 1784. **3.** A place or abode in which one is secluded 1791.

2. Oh, blest s. from a jarring world, Which he, thus occupied, enjoys! COWPER. *In s.*, apart from society. Hence **Seclu·sionist,** one who advocates s.; applied e.g. to a supporter of monasticism, and to a Chinese or Japanese who is averse to the admission of foreigners to his country.

Seclusive (sĭklū·siv), *a.* 1834. [f. SECLUDE, after *include/inclusive*, etc.] Serving or tending to seclude; affecting seclusion.

Second (se·kənd), *sb.*[1] late ME. [– OFr. *seconde* – med.L. *secunda*, fem. of L. *secundus* SECOND *a.*, used ellipt. for *secunda minuta*, lit. 'second minute', i.e. the result of the second operation of sexagesimal division; the result of the first such operation (now called 'minute' simply), being the 'first' or 'prime minute' or 'prime' (see PRIME *sb.*[2] 2).] *Math.* **1.** *Geom.* (*Astr., Geog.*, etc.) A sixtieth part of a minute, $\frac{1}{3600}$th part of a degree. **2.** In measurement of time: The sixtieth part of a minute $\frac{1}{3600}$th of an hour 1588. **b.** Used vaguely for an extremely short time, an 'instant' 1825.

2. The pendulum which vibrates seconds at London, has been commonly esteemed 39,2 English inches 1762. **b.** There was a second's panic in the crowd 1897.

attrib. and *Comb.*: **s.-(seconds-)hand,** a hand or pointer of a timepiece indicating seconds; **s.-(seconds-)mark** *Math.*, the character ″, denoting a second or seconds (either of angle or of time).

Second (se·kənd), *a.* and *sb.*[2] ME. [– (O)Fr. *second*, fem. *-onde* – L. *secundus* following, favourable, second, f. base of *sequi* follow.] **A.** *adj.* **1.** Coming next after the first: the ordinal corresponding to the cardinal two. Often with ellipsis of sb. understood from the context. **2.** Next in rank, quality, importance, or degree of any attribute, *to* (a person or thing regarded as first). Hence, in neg. and limiting contexts, Inferior (*to none, only to*..). late ME. **b.** In designations of office, denoting the lower of two, or the next to the highest of several persons holding the same office; e.g. *s. lieutenant* (in the army), *s. lord* (of the Admiralty), *s. master* (in a school), etc. 1702. **c.** *Mus.* Used to distinguish the next to the highest part in a piece of concerted music. Hence of a voice or instrument: Rendering such a part. 1724. **3.** Having the degree of quality, fineness, etc. next to the best; of the second grade or class. Now only *Comm.* in stereotyped uses. 1440. **4.** Other, another; additional to that which has already taken place, been mentioned, etc. late ME. **5.** quasi-*adv.* Secondly (*rare*); as the second in succession. late ME.

1. The second day of Maii 1507. S. Nuptials DRYDEN. I liked her at first sight, and better at s. RICHARDSON. *The s.*, appended to a personal name to designate the second bearer of the name in a succession of persons (chiefly sovereigns); hence after the names of ships, horses, etc. **2.** S. to none that liues heere in the Citie SHAKS. Phr. *S. in command* (Mil.), holding a position only subordinate to the chief commander of an army or one of its subdivisions; often *absol.* (quasi-*sb.*). **c.** Assuming the disguise of a S. Trombone, I joined the band W. S. GILBERT. **3.** My coat..made of good s. cloth 1799. S. butter 1856. **4.** Could any one bear the story of a s. city being taken by a wooden horse? SCOTT. *S. self* [after L. *alter idem*, Gr. ἄλλος or ἕτερος αὐτός], a friend who agrees absolutely with one's tastes and opinions, or for whose welfare one cares as much as for one's own. *S. nature* (in allusion to the Latin provb. *consuetudo est altera* (or *secunda*) *natura*).

Comb., as *s. childhood, cousin, fiddle; intention, order, thought(s), wind*, etc. (see these words); **s. Adam, Man** *Theol.*, titles given to Christ with ref. to 1 Cor. 15:45, 47; **S. Advent** *Theol.*, the expected s. coming of Christ as judge; hence **S. Adventist,** one who believes that the S. Advent will precede the millennium; **s. ballot,** an electoral system whereby, if the winner on the first ballot has not polled more than half the votes cast, a second ballot is taken between him and the candidate with the next highest number of votes; **s. birth,** (*a*) *Theol.* = REGENERATION 2; †(*b*) = SECUNDINE 1; †(*c*) the entrance upon a new life after death; **s. chamber,** in a bicameral legislature, the chamber which has chiefly the function of revising the measures prepared and passed by the other; **s. division** (*a*) *Civil Service*, the lower grade of government clerks; (*b*) prison treatment prescribed by the judge which is intermediate between hard labour and first division; **s. floor,** the floor or story of a building next but one above the ground-floor; also *attrib.*; **S. Person (of the Trinity)** *Theol.*, the Son; **s. string**, a person or thing held in reserve as a resource if the one preferred should fail.

B. *sb.*[2] **I.** One who or something which is second. **1. a.** *Gram.* Used ellipt. for *second person* (usually before *singular* or *plural*) 1530. **b.** A place in the second class in an examination; one who takes such a place. Also, the competitor who comes next to the winner in contest. 1852. **2.** One next to the first in rank, quality, etc. Also, †a second instance, a match *to* something. 1594. **b.** = *Second in command* 1604. **3.** *Mus.* **a.** A note one diatonic degree above or below any given note; the interval between two such notes; a tone (*major s.*) or diatonic semitone (*minor s.*); the harmonic combination of two such notes 1597. **b.** The next to the highest part in a piece of concerted music. Hence, a voice suitable to such a part. 1774. **4.** *pl. Comm.* A quality (of bricks, flour, stockings, etc.) second and inferior to the best 1600. **5.** In the duodecimal system of mensuration: The twelfth part of a 'prime' or inch 1703.

1. b. Miss Jones has a first-class and Miss Smith a s. 1907. **2.** And see if Time..Can shew a S. to so pure a Love DRAYTON. **3. a.** *Augmented s.*: the interval equivalent to three semitones, a minor third.

II. One who or something which renders aid or support to another. †**a.** *gen.* –1740. **b.** *spec.* One who acts as representative of a principal in a duel, carrying the challenge, loading weapons, etc. Similarly in a pugilistic contest. 1613. †**c.** Assistance. Also pl. *rare.* –1640.

a. Ile be thy S. SHAKS. **b.** It was usual to have more seconds even to the number of five or six SCOTT.

Second (se·kənd), *v.*[1] 1586. [– Fr. *seconder* – L. *secundare* favour, further, f. *secundus* SECOND *a.*] **1.** *trans.* To support, back up, assist, encourage. †**b.** To follow, attend, accompany. In *pass.*, to be accompanied (*with*). –1632. **2.** *esp.* To support (a combatant, a body of troops) in attack or defence. Also, to act as second to (a pugilist). 1588. †**b.** To take the place of, succeed (a combatant who is *hors de combat*) –1614. **3.** To support (a speaker, or proposition) in a debate or conference by speaking in the same sense; *spec.* to rise to support (a mover or motion) as a necessary preliminary to further discussion or to the adoption of the motion 1597. †**b.** To support, back (a statement, opinion, a person *in* his opinion); to confirm (a report) –1741. **4.** To further, reinforce (a thing, activity, etc.) 1586. †**5.** To follow up or accompany *with* (or *by*) some second thing –1774. †**b.** To repeat (an action, esp. a blow) –1831. †**6.** To match with a second instance –1632.

1. His family had imbibed all his views, and seconded them DISRAELI. **2.** Let him feele your Sword, Which we will s. SHAKS. **b.** 2 *Hen. IV*, IV. ii. 45, 46. **3.** It is a good precept generally in seconding another: yet to adde somewhat of ones owne BACON. **4.** Deeds must s. words 1858.

Second (sĭkǫ·nd), *v.*[2] 1802. [f. Fr. phr. *en second* in the second rank (said of officers; cf. the use of SECOND *lieutenant*).] *trans.* To remove (an officer) temporarily from his regiment or corps, for employment on the staff, or in some other extra-regimental appointment. Also *transf.*

Secondary (se·kəndări), *a.* and *sb.* late ME. [– L. *secundarius* of the second class or quality, f. *secundus* SECOND *a.*; see -ARY[1]. Cf. (O)Fr. *secondaire.*] **A.** *adj.* **1.** Belonging to the second class in respect of dignity or importance; entitled to consideration only in the second place. Also, and usu.: Not in the first class; of minor importance, subordinate. †**b.** Second best –1601. **c.** Of a lower kind. late ME. †**d.** Of an official: Second in rank or status. Of a judge: = PUISNE *a.* 1 b. –1630. **e.** Of persons: Second-rate (*rare*) 1827. **f.** Subsidiary, auxiliary 1751. **2.** Derived from, based on, or dependent on something else which is primary; not original, derivative. late ME. **b.** Having only a derived authority; subordinate 1667. **c.** *Philos.* (*a*) Applied to those qualities of bodies that were supposed to be derived from the four 'primary' qualities recognized by Aristotle, hot, cold, wet, dry. *Obs.* exc. *Hist.* 1656. (*b*) Applied to those properties or qualities of matter (as colour, smell, taste, etc.) which are distinguished as not existing, like 'primary' qualities, in the bodies themselves independently of perception, but depending upon the action of the primary qualities on the percipient. Cf. PRIMARY *a.* 3. 1656. **d.** *Cryst.* Of crystalline forms: Derivative, not primitive 1805. **e.** *Electr.* Of a current: Induced. Hence of apparatus, etc.: Pertaining to an induced current. Also *s. battery*, a storage battery as dist. from one in which a current is produced. 1843. **f.** *Chem.* Applied to certain types of organic compounds which are formed from others by certain definite processes of replacement 1862. **g.** *Meteorology.* Said of a subsidiary depression taking place on the border of a primary cyclone 1876. **3. a.** Belonging to the second order in a series of subdivisions or ramifications. Chiefly *Biol.* 1796. **b.** Belonging to the second stage in a process of compounding or combination; consisting of two primary elements 1807. **4.** With ref. to temporal sequence: Pertaining to a second period or condition of things; adventitious, not primitive. Chiefly scientific and techn. **a.** *Geol.* = MESOZOIC 1813. **b.** *Biol.* Belonging to the second stage of development or growth 1857. **c.** *Surg.* Performed or occurring after a definite time or occurrence 1837. **d.** *Path.* Characteristic of or pertaining to the second stage or period of a disease, esp. of syphilis 1722. **e.** *S. education* or *instruction*: that between the primary or elementary education and the higher or university education. *S. school*, one in which such education is given. 1861. **5.** Connected with what is second in local position 1768.

1. Things..purely Ornimental, are no more than of s. Consideration 1735. **2.** A s. and derivative Virtue 1738. *S. cause*, a proximate or instrumental cause, a cause produced by a primary cause (also used in sense 1). *S. planet*, a satellite which revolves round a primary planet. *S. circle* (Geom. and Astr.), a great circle passing through the poles of another great circle perpendicular to its plane. *S. bow* or *rainbow*, an outer and fainter bow parallel with the primary bow. **c.** (*b*) Among the s. qualities [of matter] are classed heat and cold, colour and sound, taste and odour 1856. **3. b.** *S. colours*: see COLOUR *sb.* I. 2. **4. c.** *S. amputation*, amputation performed after suppuration has set in. **5.** *S. feather, quill*, a feather growing from the second joint of a bird's wing. *S. wing*, one of the hind wings of an insect.

B. *sb.* [the adj. used ellipt. Mostly in *pl.*] **1.** *gen.* One who acts in subordination to another; a delegate or deputy; also, a thing which comes second in importance. Now *rare.* 1595. **b.** A cathedral dignitary of second rank. late ME. **c.** An officer of the corporation of the City of London. †Also, an official in certain government offices and law courts. 1461. **2.** Short for *s. planet* 1721. **3.** Short for *s. circle* 1715. **4.** *Path.* in *pl.* Secondary symptoms (of syphilis) 1843. **5.** *Geol.* The secondary series of rocks, or any of the secondary formations 1890. **6.** *Ornith.* Short for *s. feather* 1768. **7.** *Electr.* Short for *s. coil* or *wire* 1869. **8.** *Meteorology.* Short for *s. depression* 1887. Hence **Se·condari-ly** *adv.*, **-ness.**

Second best, second-best, *a.* late ME. **1.** Next in quality to the first. **2.** *absol.* Something inferior to the best 1708. **3.** quasi-*adv.* In phr. *to come off second best*, to be defeated in a contest 1777.

Second-class, *a.* 1837. **1.** Of or belonging to the class next to the first. **b.** *S. matter* (U.S.): postal matter consisting of periodicals sent from the office of publication 1883. **2.** quasi-*adv.* By a second-class conveyance 1906.

‖**Seconde** (səgō·nd). 1707. [Fr., fem. of *second* SECOND *a.*] The second of the eight parries recognized in sword-play.

Seconder (se·kəndəɹ). 1598. [f. SECOND *a.* and *v.* + -ER[1].] **I.** [f. the adj.] **1.** One who comes second, or in the second rank. Now *local*, a second hand on a farm. **2.** A student of the second grade in social rank at the Universities of Glasgow and St. Andrews. *Obs.* exc. *Hist.* 1655. **II.** [f. the vb.] **a.** One who supports (what is proposed by another); one who furthers the designs of another 1607. **b.** *spec.* One who seconds a motion; one who seconds a nomination or candidature 1678.

Second hand, second-hand. 1474. [Cf. HAND *sb.* II. 4, Fr. *de seconde main*, and FIRST HAND.] **A.** *phrase.* (*Second hand.*) †**1.** In sb. use: An intermediary, middleman –1727. **2.** In advb. phrases 1474.

2. *At second hand*, (to buy, receive, learn, etc.) from another than the maker, or original vendor (of goods), or the primary source (of information, etc.). †*By second hand*, through another person as agent.

B. *adj.* (*Second-hand.*) **1.** Not original or obtained from the original source; borrowed; imitative, derivative 1654. **2.** Not new, having been previously worn or used by another, as *s. clothes, books*, etc. 1673. **3.** quasi-*adv.* = at second hand 1849.

1. Even of this s. knowledge there was very little 1868. **2.** The warehouse of some second hand Bookseller 1656. So **Second-ha·nded** *a.* (now *dial.*).

Secondly (se·kəndli), *adv.* late ME. [f. SECOND *a.* + -LY[2].] †**1.** For a second time –1771. **2.** In the second place. late ME. **3.** quasi-*sb.* The word *secondly* used in making subdivisions of a subject 1759.

2. Man, consider first the nature of the thing that thou intendest, and s. thine owne nature 1610.

Second-rate, *a.* and *sb.* 1669. [See RATE *sb.*[1] III. 1.] **A.** *adj.* Of the second 'rate' (said of ships). Hence, Of the second class in quality or excellence; usu.: Not first-rate, of only moderate quality.

Any of the s. theatres in London 1748.

B. *sb.* **1.** *Naut.* A war-vessel of the second 'rate' 1679. **2.** *transf.* A person or thing of inferior class 1799. Hence **Second-rater.**

Second sight. 1616. **1.** A supposed power by which occurrences in the future or things at a distance are perceived as though they were actually present. **2.** The image or vision produced by this faculty 1763.

1. Their Faith and firm Belief In Second Sight, and Mother Shipton 1763. Hence **Second-sighted** *a.* having the gift of second sight.

Secrecy (sī·krĕsi). late ME. [repl. †*secretie* (XV), f. *secre* or SECRET + -TY[1] or -Y[3], prob. after *private/privacy.*] **1.** The quality of being secret or of not revealing secrets; the action, habit, or practice of keeping things secret. **2.** The condition or fact of being secret or concealed 1563. †**b.** Retirement, seclusion –1667. **3.** Something which is or has been kept secret; a secret; the secret nature or condition of something. Often *collect. sing.* or *pl.*, secret matters, mysteries, *Obs.* or *arch.* 1450. †**4.** Intimate acquaintance, confidence –1671.

1. Constant you are..and for secrecie, No Lady closer SHAKS. **2.** *In s.*, secretly; The Lady Anne, Whom the King hath in secrecie long married SHAKS. **3.** Leaving secrecies to conscience MILT.

Secret (sī·krĕt), *a.* and *sb.* late ME. [– (O)Fr. *secret* – L. *secretus* adj. (neut. *secretum* used sb., a secret), orig. pa. pple. of *secernere* SECERN.] **A.** *adj.* **1. a.** *predic.* Kept from public knowledge, or from the knowledge of persons specified. **b.** Of a place: Retired, remote, secluded; hence, affording privacy or seclusion. Chiefly *arch.* 1500. †**c.** Of a person, etc.: Secluded from observation –1667. **d.** Of actions, etc.: Done with the intention of being concealed; clandestine 1548. **e.** Of doctrines, ceremonies: Kept from the knowledge of the uninitiated 1526. **f.** Of feelings, thoughts: Not openly avowed or expressed; concealed, disguised 1500. †**g.** Abstruse, recondite –1775. **h.** Of a committee, etc.: Conducted with secrecy 1667. **i.** Hidden from sight; unseen, invisible 1559. **j.** Of a door, drawer, etc.: Designed to escape observation or detection 1591. **k.** Of an agent: That works in secret. Of a person: That is secretly (what is expressed by the sb.). 1600. **l.** quasi-*adv.* Apart; secretly, in secret 1539. **2.** Of a person: †Reticent or reserved in conduct or conversation; not given to indiscreet talking or the revelation of secrets; uncommunicative, close. Also *fig.* of silence, night, etc. 1440. †**3.** That is a confidant; intimate *with* –1648.

1. a. The Renegados..kept his death s. 1600. **b.** Put them in s. holds SHAKS. **c.** In this Citty will I stay, And liue alone as s. as I may SHAKS. **d.** Hide me from the s. counsel of the wicked *Ps.* 64:2. **f.** I haue vnclasp'd To thee the booke euen of my s. soule SHAKS. I had a s. joy at the news DE FOE. **g.** *Macb.* IV. i. 48. **i.** *S. parts, members*, the external organs of sex. **j.** *S. ink*, 'invisible' or 'sympathetic' ink. **k.** Others, who were my s. Enemies

SWIFT. 1. She had devised How she might s. to the forest hie KEATS. 2. I can be s. as a dumbe man SHAKS. 3. He was s. with yᵉ Duke 1533.

Special collocations.: **S. service**: services rendered to a government, the nature of which cannot be disclosed to the public, but which are paid for from a fund set apart for the purpose; also *attrib.*, as *s. service agent, fund*, etc. **S. society**, an organization formed to promote some cause by secret methods, its members being sworn to observe secrecy.

B. *sb.* Something kept secret. **1.** Something unknown or unrevealed or that is known only by initiation or revelation; chiefly *pl.*, the hidden affairs or workings (of God, Nature, Science, etc.). late ME. **2.** In Liturgical use: A prayer or prayers said by the celebrant in a low voice after the Offertory and before the Preface. See SECRETA¹. late ME. **3.** Some fact, affair, design, action, etc., known only to oneself or shared only with a limited number 1450. **4.** A method or process (of an art, etc.) hidden from all except the initiated 1486. **b.** (Const. *of.*) That which accounts for something surprising or extraordinary; the essential thing to be observed in order to secure some end 1738. †**5.** A place of concealment or retreat –1635. †**6.** *pl.* = *s. parts* (see A. 1 i). Also *sing.* –1758. **7.** *Antiq.* A coat of mail or piece of armour concealed under one's usual dress 1578.

1. Jealous Nature hath lock'd her secrets in a Cabinet DAVENANT. **3.** Sir Thurio, giue vs leaue (I pray) a while, We haue some secrets to confer about SHAKS. Phr. *An open s.*, something which is ostensibly a s., but which requires little effort or penetration to discover. **4.** A pretended s. of multiplying gold EVELYN. **b.** The..s. of success KINGSLEY.

Phrases. *In s.* [= L. *in secreto*, Fr. *en secret*], in private; secretly. *To be in the s.*, to be one of the participants in a s. *To let* (a person) *into the s.*, to confide to him the s. (*of* an affair, trade). *To make a s. of* (something), to make it a matter of concealment; to keep it to oneself. Hence †**Se·cret** *v. trans.* to keep s., conceal –1734. **Se·cret-ly** *adv.*, **-ness.**

‖**Secreta¹** (sĭkrī·tă). *Pl.* **-tæ.** 1740. [eccl. L. *secreta* (sc. *oratio*), fem. of L. *secretus.*] *Eccl.* = SECRET *sb.* 2.

‖**Secre·ta²**, *pl.* 1877. [L.; n. pl. of pa. pple. of *secernere* SECRETE *v.*¹] The products of secretion.

Secretage (sī·krĭtèdʒ). 1791. [– Fr. *secrétage*, f. *secréter* SECRETE *v.*³ and -AGE.] A process of preparing furs for felting by the application of nitrate of mercury.

‖**Secretaire** (sekrĭtēᵊ·ɹ, Fr. səkretɛ̄r). 1818. [– Fr. *secrétaire*; see SECRETARY 5.] A piece of furniture in which private papers can be kept, with a shelf for writing on, and drawers and pigeon-holes; a bureau.

Secretarial (sekrĭtēᵊ·riăl), *a.* 1801. [f. SECRETARY *sb.* + -AL¹.] Of or pertaining to a secretary or secretaries. So †**Secreta·rian** *a.* (*rare*) 1734–1801.

Secretariat(e (sekrĭtēᵊ·riăt, -ĕt). 1811. [– Fr. *secrétariat* – med.L. *secretariatus*, f. *secretarius* SECRETARY; see -ATE¹.] The office of a secretary; the body or department of secretaries; the place where a secretary transacts business, preserves records, etc.

Secretary (se·krĭtări), *sb.* (and *a.*). late ME. [– late L. *secretarius* confidential officer, subst. use of adj. f. *secretum* SECRET *sb.*; see -ARY¹.] **A.** *sb.* †**1.** A confidant; one privy *to* a secret. Also *fig.* of things personified. –1815. **2.** One whose office is to write for another; esp. one who is employed to conduct correspondence, to keep records, and (usu.) to transact other business, for another person or for a society, corporation, or public body. late ME. †**b.** In the titles of books on the art of letter-writing –1715. **3.** In the official designations of certain ministers presiding over executive departments of state 1599. **b.** *Mr. Secretary*: used before the name of a secretary of state or as a title instead of his name. Now only *official* and *Hist.* 1529. **4.** Short for *s. hand, type* 1771. **5.** A secretaire 1833. **6.** The secretary-bird 1781.

1. Reueale it she durst not, as daring in such matters to make none her secretarie LODGE. *fig.* The night, sad s. to my mones KYD. **2.** *Private s.*, a s. employed by a minister of state, etc. for the personal correspondence connected with his official position; also applied to a s. employed in purely personal service. *S. of embassy, legation*, an official ranking next to the ambassador or envoy, and empowered to some extent to supply his place in his absence. **3.** In peacetime. the duties of the Colonial S., in his character as S. of War, were very slight KINGLAKE. **b.** A letter from Mr. S. Pitt 1760.

Comb.: **s.-bird**, a raptorial bird of southern Africa, *Serpentarius secretarius*: so called from a tuft of feathers at the back of the head which have a fanciful resemblance to pens stuck behind the ear.

B. *adj.* As the distinctive epithet of a style of handwriting used chiefly in legal documents from the 15th to the 17th c. Hence applied to a kind of black-letter type imitating this. 1571. Hence **Se·cretaryship,** the office of a s.

Secrete (sĭkrī·t), *v.*¹ 1707. [f. *secret-*, pa. ppl. stem of L. *secernere* (see SECERN), partly as a back-formation on SECRETION.] **1.** *trans.* To produce by means of secretion. **2.** *intr.* To perform the act of secretion 1872.

Secrete (sĭkrī·t), *v.*² 1741. [alt., after L. *secretus* SECRET, of SECRET *v.*] **1.** *trans.* To place in concealment, to keep secret. **2.** To remove secretly, to appropriate (the possessions of another) in a secret manner 1749.

1. How had Sibyll dared to s. from him this hoard LYTTON. A..French lady..had secreted herself on board the vessel 1893. **2.** The secreting of the 500 l. was a matter of very little hazard FIELDING.

Secre·te, *v.*³ 1839. [– Fr. *secréter*, f. *secret* SECRET *sb.* (in the sense of 'secret process').] *trans.* To subject to the process of SECRETAGE.

Secretin (sĭkrī·tin). 1902. [app. irreg. f. SECRETION + -IN¹.] *Chem.* A substance produced by the action of the acid of the gastric juice on the intestinal mucous membrane and acting as a stimulus to pancreatic secretion.

Secretion (sĭkrī·ʃən). 1646. [– Fr. *sécrétion* (XVII) or med.L. use of L. *secretio* separation. Cf. SECERN.] **1.** *Phys.* In an animal or vegetable body, the action of a gland or some analogous organ in extracting certain matters from the blood or sap and elaborating from them a particular substance, either to fulfil some function within the body or to undergo excretion as waste. **2.** *concr.* That which is produced by the action of a secreting organ 1732. †**3.** In etym. sense: **a.** Separation. **b.** *Philos.* (= Gr. ἀπόκρισις.) Giving off of particles. –1678

Secretive (sĭkrī·tiv), *a.* 1853. [Back-formation from next; but apprehended as f. SECRETE *v.*² + -IVE.] Addicted or inclined to secrecy; reticent; not frank or open. **b.** *transf.* of things. Also of looks, etc.: Indicating secretiveness. 1865.

She was a shy, s. maid 1884. **b.** A s. smile 1865.

Secretiveness (sĭkrī·tivnės). 1815. [Formed after Fr. *secrétivité* (Gall, 1808), f. *secret* SECRET; see -IVE and -NESS.] The quality of being secretive; disposition to secrecy.

Secretory (sĭkrī·təri), *a.* and *sb.* 1692. [f. SECRETE *v.*¹ + -ORY¹ and ².] **A.** *adj.* Having the function of secreting; pertaining to or concerned with secretion. **B.** *sb.* A secreting vessel or duct 1768.

‖**Secretum** (sĭkrī·tŏm). *Pl.* **-ta.** 1864. [L., n. of *secretus* SECRET *a.*; in med.L. ellipt. for *sigillum secretum* privy seal.] *Antiq.* A private seal.

Sect (sekt). late ME. [– (O)Fr. *secte* or L. *secta* (used as cogn. obj. in *sectam sequi* follow a certain course of conduct, follow a person's guidance), party faction, school of philosophy, f. older pa. ppl. stem *sect-* of *sequi* follow.] †**1.** A class or kind (of persons) –1628. †**b.** A religious order –1814. **c.** Sex. Now only in illiterate or joc. use. late ME. †**2.** Body of followers or adherents –1667. **3.** A religious following; adherence to a particular religious teacher or faith. *esp.* **a.** A body of persons who unite in holding certain views differing from those of others who are accounted to be of the same religion; a party or school among the professors of a religion; sometimes applied *spec.* to parties that are regarded as heretical. late ME. **b.** In mod. use, commonly applied to a separately organized religious body having its distinctive name and its own places of worship; a 'denomination'. Also, less widely, one of the bodies separated from the Church. 1577. **4.** The system or body of adherents of a particular school of philosophy. late ME. **5.** *transf.* A school of opinion in politics, science, etc. 1605.

1. c. 'Tis the easiest Art and cunning for our s. to counterfeit sicke MIDDLETON. **3.** Kynge Salamon louyd ouermoche..straunge wymen of other sectes CAXTON. **a.** *The Clapham S.*, a derisive name applied early in the 19th c. to a coterie of persons of Evangelical opinions and conspicuous philanthropic activity, some of whom lived at Clapham; among the chief members were Wilberforce, Zachary Macaulay, and Henry Thornton. **b.** *The sects*, applied by Anglicans to the various bodies of Dissenters, by Roman Catholics to all forms of Protestantism. **4.** The S. Epicurean MILT. **5.** Socialism is rather a s. than a party 1899.

Sectarial (sektēᵊ·riăl), *a.* 1816. [f. SECTARY + -AL¹.] Pertaining to or distinctive of sect. Chiefly with ref. to Indian religions.

Sectarian (sektēᵊ·riăn), *a.* and *sb.* 1649. [f. SECTARY + -AN; see -ARIAN.] **A.** *adj.* **1.** Pertaining to a sectary or sectaries; 'belonging to a schismatical sect' (Phillips). *Obs.* exc. *Hist.* **2.** Pertaining to a sect or sects; confined to a particular sect; bigotedly attached to a particular sect. In recent use, often a pejorative synonym of *denominational*, esp. with ref. to education. 1796.

2. A Christian, and yet not s. University 1836.

B. *sb.* **1.** Orig., an adherent of the 'sectarian party' (i.e. the Independents as designated by the Presbyterians); subsequently, a schismatic. Now chiefly *Hist.* 1654. **2.** An adherent of a specified sect; a sectary of a particular teacher. Now *rare.* 1819. **3.** A bigoted adherent of a sect; a person of sectarian views or sympathies 1827. Hence **Secta·rianism,** adherence or excessive attachment to a particular sect or party, esp. in religion; undue favouring of a particular denomination. **Secta·rianize** *v. intr.* to act in a s. manner; *trans.* to render s.

Sectary (se·ktări), *sb.* and *a.* 1556. [– mod. L. use (XVI) in sense 'schismatic' of med.L. *sectarius* adherent, partisan (XIII), f. *secta*; see SECT, -ARY¹. So Fr. *sectaire* (XVI).] **A.** *sb.* **1.** A member of a sect; one who is zealous in the cause of a sect 1558. **2.** An adherent of a schismatical or heretical sect. In the 17–18th c. commonly applied to the English Protestant Dissenters. Now chiefly *Hist.* 1556. **3.** A follower *of* a particular leader, teacher, party, or school. Now *rare* (with mixture of sense 1). 1589.

1. It is not as religious sectaries they [school inspectors] have to discharge their duties, but as civil servants M. ARNOLD. **2.** Many sectaries experienced much inhuman treatment 1860.

B. *adj.* Of or pertaining to a sect; sectarian 1590.

A kind of S. passion 1638. Hence **Se·ctarism,** sectarianism. †**Se·ctarist** = A. 1. –1833.

Sectator (sektēⁱ·təɹ). Now *rare.* 1541. [– L. *sectator* follower, f. *sectari*, frequent. of *sequi* follow. Cf. Fr. *sectateur* (XVI).] A follower, disciple; one who follows a particular school, teacher, or leader; a partisan, sectary.

Sectile (se·ktil, -əil), *a.* 1716. [– L. *sectilis*, f. *sect-*; see next, -ILE.] Capable of or suited for being cut. Hence **Secti·lity.**

Section (se·kʃən), *sb.* 1559. [– Fr. *section* or L. *sectio, -ōn-*, f. *sect-*, pa. ppl. stem of *secare* cut; see -ION.] **1.** The action, or an act, of cutting or dividing. Now *rare* exc. with ref. to surgery or anatomical operations. **2.** A part separated or divided off from the remainder; one of the portions into which a thing is cut or divided. *esp.* **a.** A subdivision of a written or printed work, a statute, or the like. Often represented by the symbol § (preceding a numeral figure); also abbrev. *sect.* (rarely *sec.*). 1576. **b.** *Nat. Hist.* Used variously for a subdivision of a classificatory group, e.g. of a class, order, family, or genus. In *Bot.* now chiefly = *sub-genus.* 1720. **c.** A separable portion of any collection or aggregate of persons, e.g. of the population of a country; a group forming part of a political or religious party, etc. 1832. **d.** (*a*) *U.S.* An area of one square mile into which undeveloped lands are divided; (*b*) *Colonial.* A division of undeveloped land; (*c*) Chiefly *U.S.* A district or portion of a town or country exhibiting uniform characteristics or considered as divided from the rest on account of such characteristics 1816. **e.** *Mil.* A fourth part of a company (now of a platoon) 1805. **f.** *U.S. Railways.* (*a*) A portion of a sleeping-car containing two berths 1874; (*b*) The smallest administrative subdivision of a railway 1890. **g.** One of the component parts of something which is built up of a number of similar portions so as to admit of enlargement when necessary, or which is constructed to be taken to pieces for facility or transport 1875. **3.** *Math.* †**a.** A segment of a circle –1715. **b.** The curve of intersection of two superficies 1704. **c.** The cutting of a solid by a plane; the plane figure resulting from such a cutting; the area of this. Hence, of a material object, the figure which would be produced by cutting through it in a certain plane. 1704. **d.** The action of dividing a line into parts 1820. **4.** A drawing representing an object as it would appear if cut through in a plane at right angles to the line of sight 1669. **b.** *Geol.* A surface exposed by a cutting or by some natural agency, showing the succession of strata 1858. **5.** A thin slice of a vegetable or animal structure, or of an inorganic body, cut off for microscopic examination 1870. **6.** *Printing.* The sign §, orig. used to introduce the number of a 'section'; subseq. used also as a mark of reference to notes in the margin or at the foot of a page. Also called *s.-mark*. 1728.

2. a. In the printed editions..we see each statute divided into sections, and each s. numbered BENTHAM. **c.** The Church had at this time..sunk into a mere s. of the landed aristocracy 1874. **g.** There is always a steamer in sections in every story of a good expedition 1897.

Comb.: **s. line,** †(*a*) the boundary of a s.; (*b*) a line drawn to indicate the manner of making a s.; **-liner,** a device for ruling parallel lines; **-mark** (see sense 6). Hence **Se·ction** *v. trans.* to divide into sections. **Se·ctionary** *a.* †of or pertaining to a s. or sections (*rare*); *sb.* a member of a s. (of a party, etc.) opposed to the remainder.

Sectional (se·kʃənăl), *a.* 1816. [f. prec. + -AL¹.] **1.** Pertaining to a section or division of a larger part, e.g. of a country, society, or population; sometimes (of interests, etc.) with implied opposition to *general*. **2.** Of or pertaining to a section (sense 4), relating to the view of the structure of a body in section 1825. **3.** Composed of several sections or parts fitting into one another 1875.

1. The further embitterment of s. and sectarian strife [in Ireland] 1886. Hence **Se·ctionalism,** confinement of interest to a narrow sphere, undue accentuation of minor local, political, or social distinctions. **Se·ctionalize** *v. trans.* to divide into sections. **Se·ctionally** *adv.* from a s. point of view.

Sectionize (se·kʃənəiz), *v.* 1828. [f. SECTION *sb.* + -IZE.] *trans.* **a.** To divide into sections or parts. **b.** To delineate in section 1876. **c.** To cut sections or thin slices from 1896.

Sectism (se·ktiz'm). 1864. [f. SECT + -ISM 2 b.] Devotion to a sect; sectarian spirit. So †**Se·ctist,** a sectary –1654.

Sector (se·ktəɹ), *sb.* 1570. [– late L. techn. use (Boethius) of L. *sector* (agent-n. of *secare* cut), tr. Gr. τομεύς cutter; see SECTION, -OR 2.] **I. 1.** *Geom.* **a.** A plane figure contained by two radii and the arc of a circle, ellipse, or other central curve intercepted by them. **b.** *S. of a sphere*: a solid generated by the revolution of a plane sector about one of its radii 1656. **c.** *Mil.* A section of a front corresponding to the sector of a circle of which a headquarters is the centre 1916. **2.** A body or figure having the shape of a sector 1715. **II. 1.** A mathematical instrument, invented by Thomas Hood and improved by Edmund Gunter, used for the mechanical solution of various problems. (In its present form it consists of two flat rules stiffly hinged together, inscribed with various kinds of scales.) 1598. **2.** An astronomical instrument consisting of a telescope turning about the centre of a graduated arc. See DIP-*s.*, ZENITH-*s.* 1711. Hence **Se·ctor** *v. trans.* to divide into sectors; to provide with sectors.

Sectorial (sektō^ə·riăl), *a.*¹ 1803. [f. prec. + -AL¹.] Of or pertaining to a sector.

Sectorial (sektō^ə·riăl), *a.*² 1840. [f. mod. L. *sectorius* (f. L. *sector* cutter) + -AL¹.] Having the function of cutting; the distinctive epithet of the premolar teeth.

Secular (se·kiŭlăɹ), *a.* and *sb.* ME. [In I – OFr. *seculer* (mod. *séculier*) – L. *sæcularis*, f. *sæculum* generation, age, in Chr. L. the World (esp. opp. to the Church); in II immed. – L. *sæcularis*; see -AR¹.] **A.** *adj.* **I.** Of or pertaining to the world. **1.** *Eccl.* Of members of the clergy: Living 'in the world', and not subject to a religious rule: dist. from 'regular' and 'religious'. **b.** Of or pertaining to secular clergy 1570. **2.** Belonging to the world and its affairs as dist. from the church and religion; civil, lay, temporal. Chiefly as a neg. term, with the meaning non-ecclesiastical, non-religious, or non-sacred. ME. †**b.** *transf.* Of or belonging to the 'common' or 'unlearned' people –1629. **c.** Of literature, history, art (esp. music), hence of writers, artists: Not concerned with or devoted to the service of religion; not sacred; profane. Also of buildings, etc.: Not dedicated to religious uses. 1450. **d.** Of education, instruction: Relating to non-religious subjects. Of a school: That gives secular education. 1526. **3.** Of or belonging to the present or visible world; temporal, worldly 1597. **b.** Unspiritual (*rare*). late ME.

1. *S. abbot*, a person not a monk, who had the title and part of the revenues, but not the functions of an abbot. **2.** *S. arm* (= med.L. *brachium seculare*, Fr. *le bras séculier*), the civil power as 'invoked' by the church to punish offenders; Truth never fears the encounter; she scorns the aid of the s. arm FRANKLIN. **b.** Hang him poore snip, a s. shop-wit! B. JONS. **3.** I do not believe that s. motives are adequate either to propel or to restrain the children of our race GLADSTONE.

II. Of or belonging to an age or long period. **1.** Occurring or celebrated once in an age, century, or very long period 1599. **2.** Living or lasting for an age or ages. Also (of trees, etc., after Fr. *séculaire*), centuries old. 1629. **3.** In scientific use, of processes of change: Having a period of enormous length; continuing through long ages 1801.

1. *S. games, plays, shows* [L. *ludi sæculares*], in ancient Rome, games continuing three days and three nights, celebrated once in an 'age' or period of 120 years. *S. poem* [L. *carmen sæculare*], a hymn composed to be sung at the secular games. **2.** The s. leisures of Methusaleh 1870. A forest of s. trees 1876. **3.** The contraction of the globe due to s. cooling 1880.

B. *sb.* **1.** One of the secular clergy, as dist. from a 'regular' or monk ME. †**2.** One who is engaged in the affairs of the world as dist. from the church; a layman –1829. Hence **Se·cular-ly** *adv.*, **-ness.**

Secularism (se·kiŭlăriz'm). 1846. [f. SECULAR *a.* + -ISM 2 b.] **1.** The doctrine that morality should be based solely on regard to the well-being of mankind in the present life, to the exclusion of all considerations drawn from belief in God or in a future state. **2.** The view that national education should be purely secular 1872.

Secularist (se·kiŭlărist), *sb.* (and *a.*). 1851. [f. SECULAR + -IST.] **1.** An adherent of secularism. **2.** An advocate of exclusively secular education 1872. **3.** *attrib.* and *appos.* (quasi-*adj.*) 1890. Hence **Se:culari·stic** *a.* of or pertaining to secularism.

Secularity (sekiŭlæ·rĭti). late ME. [– Fr. *sécularité*, or – med.L. *sæcularitas*, f. L. *sæcularis*; see -ITY.] †**1.** Secular jurisdiction or power –1535. **2.** The condition or quality of being secular; *esp.* occupation with secular affairs (on the part of clergymen); also occas., worldliness, absence of religious principle or feeling. late ME. **3.** A secular matter. Chiefly *pl.* Secular affairs; worldly possessions or pursuits. 1511. **4.** The character of having long periods 1844.

2. The s. of the clergy in complying with the.. vanities..of the age 1711.

Secularization (se:kiŭlărəizē^ı·ʃən). 1706. [f. next + -ATION. Cf. Fr. *sécularisation* (XVI–XVII).] **1.** The conversion of an ecclesiastical or religious institution or its property to secular possession and use; the conversion of an ecclesiastical state or sovereignty to a lay one. **2.** The giving of a secular or non-sacred character or direction to (art, studies, etc.); the placing (of morals) on a secular basis; the restricting (of education) to secular subjects 1863.

Secularize (se·kiŭlărəiz), *v.* 1611. [– Fr. *séculariser*, f. L. *sæcularis* SECULAR; see -IZE.] **1.** *trans.* To make secular; to convert from ecclesiastical to civil possession or use. **b.** To laicize 1846. **2.** To make (a monk or monastic order) secular 1683. **3.** To convert from religious or spiritual to material and temporal purposes; to turn (a person, his mind, etc.) from a spiritual state to worldliness 1711.

1. To surprize the possessions of the Church, and to S. her patrimony 1657.

Secund (sĭ·kɒnd), *a.* 1777. [– L. *secundus* following, SECOND.] *Bot.* and *Zool.* Arranged on or directed towards one side only; esp. *Bot.* of the flowers, leaves, or other organs of a plant.

Secundine (se·kɒndəin, -in). late ME. [– late L. *secundinæ*, fem. pl. (for which earlier L. had *secundæ*), f. L. *secundus* following; see SECOND *a.*, -INE¹.] **1.** *Obstetrics.* The placenta and other adjuncts of a fœtus extruded from the womb after the expulsion of the fœtus in parturition; the afterbirth. Freq. *pl.* **2.** *Bot.* The second of two coats or integuments of an ovule, orig. the inner one, later applied to the outer covering: see PRIMINE 1671.

Secu:ndoge·niture. 1855. [f. L. *secundo*, advb. form of *secundus* SECOND *a.*, after *primogeniture*.] The right of succession or inheritance belonging to a second son; the possession so inherited.

The kingdom of Naples..was constituted a s. of Spain 1876.

Secundum (sĭkɒ·ndŏm). 1563. [L., 'according to'.] Used in various med.L. phrases, sometimes occurring in Eng. contexts.

S. artem: in accordance with the rules of the art (chiefly of medicine). *S. magis et minus*: 'according to more and less'; in a quantitative manner or respect; in various degrees. *S. naturam*: naturally. *S. quid*: 'according to something', in some particular respect only (opp. to *simpliciter*).

‖**Secundus** (sĭkɒ·ndŏs), *a.* 1826. [L. *secundus* SECOND *a.*] Added to a personal name: The second of that name.

Securance (sĭkiū^ə·răns). *rare.* 1642. [f. SECURE *v.* + -ANCE.] The action or means of securing; assurance, security.

Secure (sĭkiū^ə·ɹ), *sb.* 1802. [f. SECURE *v.*] The position in which a rifle or musket is held when it is 'secured'; see SECURE *v.* 2 c.

Secure (sĭkiū^ə·ɹ), *a.* 1533. [– L. *securus*, f. *se-* SE- + *cura* care.] **I.** (Often in predic. use, esp. *poet.*) **1.** Without care, careless; free from care, apprehension, anxiety, or alarm; over-confident. Now *arch.* **b.** Said of times, places, actions: In which one is free from fear or anxiety 1602. †**2.** Free from doubt or distrust; feeling sure or certain –1794. †**b.** Confident in expectation –1732.

1. The way to be safe, is never to bee s. 1641. Lie still, dry dust, s. of change TENNYSON. **b.** Vpon my s. hower thy Vncle stole With iuyce of cursed Hebenon in a Violl SHAKS. **2.** *John* IV. i. 130. **b.** S. to be as blest, as thou canst bear POPE.

II. 1. Rightly free from apprehension; protected from or not exposed to danger; safe 1582. **b.** Of actions or conditions: Involving no danger; safe 1617. **c.** Of an argument, means, agent, etc.: Not liable to fail, trustworthy, safe 1729. **d.** Of a material thing, a support or fastening: Not liable to be displaced or to yield under strain; firmly fixed, safe 1841. **2.** Of a place, also of means of protection or guardianship: Affording safety 1610. **3.** *predic.* In safe custody; safely in one's possession or power 1591. **4.** Free from risk as to the continued or future possession *of* something; having a safe prospect *of* some acquisition or desirable event 1664. **5.** Of a possession, acquisition, desirable event, etc.: That may be counted on with certainty; sure to continue or to be attained 1713.

1. Your grace may sit s., if none but wee Doe wot of your abode MARLOWE. The divell..would perswade him he might be s. if hee cast himselfe from the pinacle SIR T. BROWNE. From the contagion of the world's slow stain, He is s. SHELLEY. **b.** A seeming-secure and supine sleep 1643. **2.** I could pity thee exil'd From this s. retreat COWPER. **3.** In Iron Walls they deem'd me not s. SHAKS. **4.** When they seemed most s. of victory SCOTT. **5.** If the worst comes to the worst..my retreat is s. THACKERAY. Hence **Secu·re-ly** *adv.*, **-ness.**

Secure (sĭkiū^ə·ɹ), *v.* 1593. [f. SECURE *a.*] †**1.** *trans.* To make free from care or apprehension; also, to make careless or over-confident (*rare*) –1655. †**b.** To satisfy, convince. Also, to make (a person) feel secure *of* or *against* some contingency. –1668. **2.** To make secure or safe. Also †*refl.* 1593. **b.** *Mil.* To render secure from attack or molestation by the enemy; to take defensive means for the safe execution of (a movement); to guard efficiently (a pass, a defile) 1617. **c.** *To s. arms*: 'to hold a rifle or musket with the muzzle down, and lock well up under the arm, the object being to guard the weapon from the wet' 1802. **3.** To make secure or certain; 'to place beyond hazard' (J.), to ensure 1610. **b.** To make (a creditor) certain of receiving payment, by means of a mortgage, bond, pledge or the like 1677. **c.** To make the payment of (a debt, pension, etc.) certain by a mortgage or charge *upon* certain property 1818. **4.** To seize and confine; to keep or hold in custody; to imprison. Now somewhat *rare.* 1645. **5.** To make fast or firm 1663. **b.** *Surg.* To close (a vein or artery) by ligature or otherwise, in order to prevent loss of blood 1662. **6.** To get hold or possession of (something desirable) as the result of effort or contrivance 1743.

1. *Oth.* I. iii. 10. **2.** A pass..securing me through Brabant and Flanders EVELYN. The hedge-hog, so well secured against all assaults by his prickly hide BURKE. **b.** The out workes, which secured the suburbs 1645. **3.** For he who sings thy Praise, secures his own DRYDEN. **4.** Wilson and Robertson,..each secured betwixt two soldiers of the city guard SCOTT. **5.** A girdle..secured by a large buckle of gold SCOTT. **6.** We took Care to s. some Powder, Ball, and a little Bread 1743. Hence **Secu·rable** *a.* (*rare*) capable of being secured.

Securement (sĭkiū³·ɹmĕnt). *rare.* 1622. [f. SECURE *v.* + -MENT.] The action or an act of securing; ensuring or making sure.

Securi- (sĭkiū³·ri, se:kiŭri·), comb. form of L. *securis* axe, f. *secare* to cut, as in ‖**Secu·rifer** [L.], *Ent.* one of the *Securifera* or phyllophagous hymenoptera.

Securiform (sĭkiū³·rifǭɹm), *a.* 1760. [f. SECURI- + -FORM.] Axe-shaped, having the form of an axe or hatchet.

Security (sĭkiū³·rĭti). late ME. [– (O)Fr. *sécurité* or L. *securitas*, f. *securus* SECURE *a.*; see -ITY.] **I.** The condition of being secure. **1.** The condition of being protected from or not exposed to danger; safety. **2.** Freedom from doubt. Now chiefly, well-founded confidence, certainty. 1597. **3.** Freedom from care, anxiety or apprehension; a feeling of safety. *arch.* Formerly often *spec.* culpable absence of anxiety, carelessness. 1555.

1. The emperor and his court enjoyed..the s. of the marshes and fortifications of Ravenna GIBBON. **2.** She told Mr. Hall they might count on her with s. C. BRONTË. **3.** S. Is Mortals cheefest Enemie SHAKS.

II. A means of being secure. **1.** Something which makes safe; a protection, guard, defence 1586. **2.** Ground for regarding something as secure, safe, or certain; an assurance, guarantee 1623. **3.** Property deposited or made over, or bonds, recognizances, or the like entered into, by or on behalf of a person in order to secure his fulfilment of an obligation, and forfeitable in the event of non-fulfilment 1450. **4.** One who pledges himself (or is pledged) for another, a surety 1597. **5.** A document held by a creditor as guarantee of his right to payment. Hence, any form of investment guaranteed by such documents. Chiefly *pl.* 1690.

1. Concealment was his only s. 1791. A good fire ..was always a perfect s. against..wild beasts 1832. **2.** When love is an unerring light, And joy its own s. WORDSW. **3.** Phr. *To enter* (*in* or *into*), *find, give* (*in*), *go,* †*put in, take s.*; Being this day summoned..to give in s. for his good behaviour PEPYS. *transf.* The word of a Gracchus..was his bond; and a bond which was a first-rate s. 1878. **5.** Liquid Securities, or in other words, those easily convertible into cash when necessity arises 1879.

Sedan (sĭdæ·n). 1635. [perh. based on a S. Ital. dial. var. with *-dd-* of a Rom. deriv. of L. *sella* SADDLE.] **a.** A closed vehicle to seat one person, borne on two poles by two bearers, one in front and one behind. **b.** *transf.* A litter, palanquin, or the like 1646. **c.** A motor car having a single compartment for four or more persons including the driver (*U.S.*) 1915.

Sedan chair. *Hist.* 1615. = prec. a, b.

Sedate (sĭdē¹·t), *a.* 1663. [– L. *sedatus*, pa. pple. of *sedare* settle, assuage, calm, f. **sēd-* **sed-*, as in *sedēre* sit; see -ATE².] **1.** Calm, quiet, composed; cool, sober, collected; undisturbed by passion or excitement. †**2.** Of physical objects: Quiet; motionless, or smooth and steady in motion –1728.

1. He was..of a s. look, something approaching to gravity STERNE. That s. and clerical bird, the rook DICKENS. Hence **Seda·te-ly,** *adv.*, **-ness.**

Sedation (sĭdē¹·ʃən). 1543. [– Fr. *sédation* or L. *sedatio, -ōn-*, f. as prec.; see -ION.] The action of allaying, assuaging, or making calm.

Sedative (se·dătiv), *a.* and *sb.* late ME. [– (O)Fr. *sédatif, -ive* or med.L. *sedativus*, f. as prec.; see -IVE.] *Med.* **A.** *adj.* That has the property of allaying, assuaging, or soothing. **B.** *sb.* A sedative medicine 1785.

‖**Se defendendo** (sī dĭfende·ndo). 1548. [Law Latin.] *Law.* 'In self-defence': a plea which if established is held to remove legal guilt from a homicide.

Sedent (sī·dĕnt), *a.* 1682. [– L. *sedens, -ent-*, pr. pple. of *sedēre* sit; see -ENT.] Of a figure: Sitting.

Sedentary (se·dĕntări), *a.* and *sb.* 1598. [– Fr. *sédentaire* or L. *sedentarius*, f. *sedent-*; see prec., -ARY¹.] **A.** *adj.* **1.** Of habits, occupations, etc.: Requiring continuance in a sitting posture 1603. **2.** Of persons: Accustomed or addicted to sitting still: engaged in sedentary pursuits; not in the habit of taking physical exercise 1662. †**b.** Slothful, inactive –1707. **3.** Remaining in one place of abode; not migratory. Of a tribunal, assembly, judge, etc.: Established in one place; not ambulatory. Now *rare.* 1598. †**b.** Of a material thing: Motionless –1787. **c.** *Zool.* Inhabiting the same region through life; not migratory. Also of mollusca, etc.: Confined to one spot, not locomotory. Of spiders: see B. 1834. †**4.** Deliberate –1673.

1. If thy life be s., exercise thy body FULLER. **2.** S. victims of unhealthy toil 1816. **3. b.** While the sedentarie Earth..attaines Her end without least motion MILT. **4.** S. sinnes FULLER.

B. *sb. Zool.* One of a group of spiders (*Sedentariæ*) which take their prey by means of a web in or near which they remain watching 1815. Hence **Se·dentari-ly** *adv.*, **-ness.**

‖**Sederunt** (sĭdī³·rŏnt). *Sc.* 1628. [L., 'there were sitting' (*sc.* the following persons), 3rd pers. pl. perf. ind. of *sedēre* sit, used subst.] **1.** A sitting of a deliberative or judicial body; now chiefly of an eccl. assembly. **b.** *transf.* A sitting for discussion or talk. Also, loosely, a sitting (of a person) at some occupation, over the bottle, or the like. 1825. **2.** The list of persons present at a sitting 1701.

1. Phr. *Act of S.* (Sc. Law), an ordinance for regulating the forms of procedure before the Court of Session.

Sede vacante (sī·di văkæ·nti). 1535. [L., 'the seat being vacant'.] ‖**1.** *Eccl.* As advb. phr.: During the vacancy of an episcopal see. **2.** As *sb.*: The vacancy of a see or seat 1589.

Sedge (sedʒ). [OE. *secg*, masc., n. :– Gmc. **saʒjaz*, f. **saʒ-* **seʒ-* :– IE. **sek-*, repr. by L. *secare* cut.] **1.** Any of various coarse, grassy, rush-like or flag-like plants growing in wet places; also variously applied *spec.*, e.g. to the cyperaceous genera *Carex* and *Cladium*, to the Sweet Flag (*Acorus*) and the Wild Iris (*Iris pseudacorus*). **b.** An individual plant or stalk of sedge (*rare*) 1450. **c.** *Bot.* Formerly, a plant of the genus *Carex*; now usu. in wider sense, a plant of the family *Cyperaceæ* 1785. **2.** Short for *s.-fly.* Chiefly *silver s.* 1889.

attrib. and *Comb.*: **s.-fly,** a caddis or may-fly; also, an imitation of this used in fly-fishing; **-warbler,** a small bird, *Acrocephalus schœnobænus*, of the family *Sylviidæ*, common in marshy districts.

Sedged (sedʒd), *a.* 1610. [f. prec. + -ED².] †**1.** Woven with sedge. SHAKS. **2.** *Agric.* Of oats: Affected with SEDGING 1844. **3.** Bordered with sedge 1866.

3. And what s. brooks are Thames's tributaries M. ARNOLD.

Sedging (se·dʒiŋ). 1820. [f. SEDGE + -ING¹.] *Agric.* A disease incident to oats, characterized by a thickening of the stem near the ground, said to be caused by a grub.

Sedgy (se·dʒi), *a.* 1566. [f. SEDGE + -Y¹.] **1.** Covered or bordered with sedge or sedges. **2.** Having the nature or properties of sedge 1625. †**3.** Made of or thatched with sedge –1835.

1. On the gentle Seuernes siedgie banke SHAKS.

‖**Sedile** (sĭdəi·li). *Pl.* **sedilia** (sĭdi·liă). 1793. [L., f. *sedēre* sit; see -ILE.] *pl.* A series of seats in a church, usu. three in number, either movable or recessed in the wall and crowned with canopies, pinnacles, etc., usu. placed on the south side of the choir near the altar for the use of the clergy. Rarely *sing.* one of the sedilia.

Sediment (se·dimĕnt), *sb.* 1547. [– Fr. *sédiment* or L. *sedimentum* settling, f. *sedēre* sit, settle; see -MENT.] **1.** Matter composed of particles which fall by gravitation to the bottom of a liquid. **2.** *spec.* (in *Geol.*, etc.). Earthy or detrital matter deposited by aqueous agency 1684.

2. The snow gradually wasted, but it left its s. behind TYNDALL. Hence **Se·diment** *v. trans.* to deposit as s. **Sedime·ntal** *a.* of the nature of s. (*rare*).

Sedimentary (sedime·ntări), *a.* and *sb.* 1830. [f. prec. + -ARY¹. Cf. Fr. *sédimentaire.*] **A.** *adj.* **1.** Of, pertaining to, or of the nature of sediment 1846. **2.** *Geol.* Of rocks, etc.: Formed by the deposition of sediment 1830. **B.** *sb.* A s. formation or deposit 1878.

Sedimentation (se:dimĕntē¹·ʃən). 1874. [f. SEDIMENT *sb.* + -ATION.] Deposition of sediment; *spec.* in *Geol.* (see SEDIMENT *sb.* 2).

Sedition (sĭdi·ʃən). late ME. [– (O)Fr. *sédition* or L. *seditio, -ōn-*, f. *sed-* SE- + *itio* going, f. *it-*, pa. ppl. stem of *ire* go; see -ION.] †**1.** Violent party strife; an instance of this –1628. **2. a.** A concerted movement to overthrow an established government; a revolt, rebellion, mutiny. Now *rare.* 1585. **b.** Conduct or language inciting to rebellion against the constituted authority in a state 1838.

1. But there would be thoughts of s. in one towards another in the city HOBBES. **2. a.** The matter of seditions is of two kindes, Much povertye and much discontent BACON. **b.** As for s. itself I do not think that any such offence is known to English law 1883. Hence **Sedi·tionary** *sb.* = SEDITIONIST (now *rare*); *adj.* seditious.

Seditionist (sĭdi·ʃənist). 1786. [f. prec. + -IST.] One who practises sedition or incites others to sedition.

Seditious (sĭdi·ʃəs), *a.* 1447. [– (O)Fr. *séditieux* or L. *seditiosus*, f. *seditio*; see SEDITION, -OUS.] **1.** Given to or guilty of sedition; in early use, factious, turbulent; now chiefly, engaged in promoting disaffection or inciting to revolt against constituted authority. **b.** *absol.* Seditious persons 1535. **2.** Of, pertaining to, or of the nature of sedition; tending to incite to or provoke sedition 1455.

1. That sedicious and wicked cite COVERDALE. 1 *Esd.* 4:12. An illegal or possibly s. club 1908. **2.** He had made sedicious sermons 1560. S. words, s. libels, and s. conspiracies 1883. Hece **Sedi·tious-ly** *adv.*, **-ness.**

Seduce (sĭdiū·s), *v.* 1477. [– L. *seducere*, f. *se-* SE- + *ducere* lead.] **1.** *trans.* To persuade (a vassal, servant, soldier, etc.) to desert his allegiance or service. **2.** To lead (a person) astray in conduct or belief; to tempt, entice, or beguile *to do* something wrong, foolish, or unintended 1519. **3.** To induce (a woman) to surrender her chastity 1560. **4.** To decoy (*from* or *to* a place); to lead astray (*into*). *Obs.* exc. with notion of sense 2. 1668.

1. Suttle he needs must be, who could s. Angels MILT. **2.** For me, the Gold of France did not s. SHAKS. He is seduced into a life of pleasure 1875. Hence **Sedu·ceable, Sedu·cible** *a.*

Seducement (sĭdiū·smĕnt). *Obs.* or *rare.* 1586. [f. prec. + -MENT.] **1.** The action of seducing. **2.** Something which seduces; an insidious temptation 1644. **3.** The fact or condition of being seduced 1605.

Seducer (sĭdiū·səɹ). 1545. [f. as prec. + -ER¹.] One who or something which seduces; *esp.* one who seduces a woman.

He, whose firm faith no reason could remove, Will melt before that soft s., love DRYDEN.

Seducing (sĭdiū·siŋ), *ppl. a.* 1575. [f. SEDUCE *v.* + -ING².] That seduces. **1.** Tempting to evil. **2.** Alluring, attractive, 'bewitching'. (Cf. Fr. *séduisant.*) Now *rare.* 1748.

2. Well, it is very s. to be pitied, after all SCOTT. Hence **Sedu·cingly** *adv.*

Seduction (sĭdɒ·kʃən). 1526. [– Fr. *séduction* or L. *seductio, -ōn-*, f. *seduct-*, pa. ppl. stem of *seducere* SEDUCE; see -ION.] **1.** The action or an act of seducing (a person) to err in conduct or belief. †**b.** The condition of being led astray –1653. **2.** The action of inducing (a woman) to surrender her chastity 1785. **3.** Something which seduces; a cause of error; an allurement 1554.

3. Surrounded by all the seductions most dazzling to youth 1838.

Seductive (sĭdʊ·ktiv), *a.* 1771. [f. SEDUCTION, after *induction/inductive*, etc.] †**1.** Tending to lead astray –1782. **2.** Alluring, enticing, winning 1771.

2. The s. pleasures of opium-eating 1871. Hence **Sedu·ctive-ly** *adv.*, **-ness.**

Seductress (sĭdʊ·ktrės). 1803. [f. †*seductor* (XV) + -ESS[1].] A female seducer.

Sedulity (sĭdiū·lĭti). 1542. [– L. *sedulitas*, f. *sedulous* SEDULOUS; see -ITY.] The quality of being sedulous; painstaking attention to duty, diligent application, industry. †**b.** *pl.* Assiduities, attentions –1707.

I stood amazed at his s. and memory EVELYN.

Sedulous (se·diŭləs), *a.* 1540. [f. L. *sedulus* eager, zealous + -OUS.] **1.** Diligent, active, constant in application to the matter in hand; assiduous, persistent 1593. **2.** Of actions: Constant, persistent 1540.

1. He was s. in paying court to the people 1836. 2. He paid s. attention to the interests of his borough 1833. Hence **Se·dulous-ly** *adv.*, **-ness.**

‖**Sedum** (sī·dŏm). 1440. [L., houseleek.] †**a.** Any of certain crassulaceous plants, houseleek, stonecrop, orpine, etc. **b.** *Bot.* A genus of plants (family *Crassulaceæ*), the British species of which are known as stonecrop.

See (sī), *sb.* ME. [– AFr. *se, sed*, OFr. *sie, sied* :– Rom. *s*ĕde*, repr. L. *sēdes* seat, f. **sēd-* **sed-* SIT.] **1.** A seat, place of sitting. †**a.** A seat of dignity or authority; esp. a royal seat, throne. Hence the rank or position symbolized by a throne. –1590. †**b.** *transf.* and *fig.* (One's) place of abode –1596. **2. a.** The seat, chair, or throne of a bishop in his church. Now only *arch.* ME. **b.** The office or position indicated by sitting in a particular episcopal chair; the position of being bishop of a particular diocese 1450. **c.** *spec.* (Chiefly with defining word, e.g. *Apostolic, Holy.*) The office or position of Pope; the Papacy: the authority or jurisdiction belonging to the Pope; occas. the Pope in his official capacity ME. †**d.** A city in which the authority symbolized by the throne (of a bishop, etc.) is considered to reside –1757.

1. a. Ioue laught on Venus from his soueraigne s. SPENSER.

See (sī), *v.* Pa. t. **saw** (sǭ); pa. pple. **seen** (sīn). [OE. *sēon* = OFris. *sīa*, OS., OHG. *sehan* (Du. *zien*, G. *sehen*), ON. *séa, sía, siá*, Goth. *saihwan* :– Gmc. str. vb. **saixwan*, – IE. **seqʷ-*, by some identified with the base of L. *sequi* follow, the etymol. sense being 'follow with the eyes'.] **1.** *trans.* To perceive (light, colour, external objects and their movements) with the eyes, or by the sense of which the eye is the specific organ. **b.** Predicated of the eye ME. **c.** To behold (visual objects) in imagination, or in a dream or vision ME. **d.** With sb. or pron. and inf. or compl. as obj. OE. **2.** *absol.* and *intr.* To perceive objects by sight. Formerly often, to have the faculty of sight, not to be blind. ME. **3.** (*fig.*) *trans.* To perceive mentally; to apprehend by thought (a truth, etc.), to recognize the force of (a demonstration). Often with ref. to metaphorical light or eyes. ME. **b.** In literary use, expressions like 'we have seen', 'we shall s.', etc. are common with ref. to what has been or is to be narrated or proved in the book. late ME. **c.** *absol.* Often with virtual ellipsis of obj.-clause, esp. in parenthetic use, or preceded by *as* or *so* ME. **d.** *trans.* To perceive, apprehend, or appreciate in a particular manner. Also *absol.* esp. in *to s. with* = to agree in opinion with another person. 1586. **4.** *trans.* With mixed literal and fig. sense: To perceive by visual tokens ME. **b.** To learn by reading. late ME. **5.** To direct the sight (literal or metaphorical) intentionally to; to look at, contemplate, examine, inspect, or scrutinize; to visit (a place); to attend (a play, etc.) as a spectator ME. **b.** To look at, read (a book, document, etc.). Now chiefly in certain formulæ (see below). ME. **c.** The imper. *see* is used in books to refer to a passage elsewhere in which information will be found 1608. **d.** The imper. is often employed exclamatorily: = Behold! OE. **6.** With indirect question as obj.: To ascertain by inspection, inquiry, experiment, or consideration. Also *absol.* late ME. **b.** To make sure by inspection *that* certain conditions exist 1440. **7.** With adv. or phrase: To escort (a person) *home, to the door*, etc. 1607. **8.** To ensure by supervision or vigilance that something shall be done or not done ME. **b.** Coupled by *and* with another verb: To be careful to (do something) *colloq.* 1766. **9.** To view or regard as, to judge, deem ME. **10.** To know by observation (ocular and other), to witness; to meet with in the course of one's experience; to have personal knowledge of; to be living at (a certain period of time) OE. **b.** With clause, obj. and inf., or obj. and complement: To observe, find. Also (chiefly in the future tense), to find, to come to know in the course of events. Often *absol.* late ME. **c.** Willingness (or unwillingness) *to s.* an event is often predicated as equivalent to willingness (or unwillingness) that the event should occur. Hence, occas. = to allow (something to happen). late ME. **d.** *transf.* Of things, places, etc.: To be contemporary with and in the neighbourhood of, to be the scene of (an event); to be in existence during (a period of time). Also of a period of time: To be marked by (an event). 1739. **11.** To experience in one's own person; to undergo, enjoy, or suffer. Now *rare.* OE. **12.** To be in the company of, to meet and converse with (a person) ME. **b.** To obtain an interview with, call upon, or meet in order to consult or confer with, give directions to or receive directions from. In U.S. *colloq.* 'To interview or consult in order to influence, esp. improperly, as in order to bribe'. 1782. **c.** To receive as a visitor; to admit to an interview 1500. †**d.** absol. *To s.* (*together*): to meet one another –1613. **13.** *Gaming.* To meet (a bet), or meet the bet of (another player), by staking an equal sum. Now chiefly in *Poker.* 1599. **14.** *Mil.* Of a fortification, artillery, etc.: To command or dominate (a position) 1829.

1. The other Comet could be seen with the naked eye 1665. Phr. *To s. double*, to s. two objects where only one exists, esp. as a sign of drunkenness. *To s. the red light*, to see danger ahead; to take fright. *To s. the back of*, to be rid of (an unwelcome visitor, etc.); so *to s. the last of. To s. things* (colloq.), to have hallucinations. *To s. the light, red, one's way*: see the associated words. *To s. daylight* or *light*, to have a clear perception of things. **c.** Phr. *To s. a vision.* **d.** I saw the tears start from his eyes 1779. I say what I saw done SWINBURNE. **2.** I write and read till I can't s., and then I walk 1712. So drunk that he could not s. FIELDING. There are no ears to hear, or eyes to s. KEATS. **3.** She saw nothing before her but distress and misery 1825. I see that you are speaking your mind 1875. Why didn't you tell Geoffrey you didn't s. the good of sending so many? 1888. **b.** What..the English did will be seen later on KIPLING. **c.** Look'ee Serjeant, no Coaxing, no Wheedling, d'ye s. FARQUHAR. *I s.*, often used *colloq.* in assenting to an explanation or argument. *You s.*, sometimes appended parenthetically to a statement of a fact known to the hearer, which explains or excuses something that provokes surprise or blame. **d.** Thou..dost neuer s. me as I am SIDNEY. Phr. *To s. eye to eye*: see EYE *sb.*[1] I. 4. **4.** Don't you s. I am tired to death? 1765. She was never seen angry but twice or thrice in her life THACKERAY. **b.** Did you s. her death in the paper? THACKERAY. **5.** The finish was one worth going miles to s. 1878. We have trotted about,.. and seen the sights 1881. **b.** No man would advance money upon an estate without seeing the title deeds 1818. *Seen and allowed, seen and approved*, etc., a formula used in certifying the official inspection of a document. **d.** But s., the evening star comes forth! WORDSW. **6.** I am just going to ride out to s. if air and exercise will get me a stomach 1766. *absol.* Ah, something terrible has happened! I must run and s.! HAWTHORNE. **7.** We saw the ladies into the brougham 1888. *To s.* (a person) *off*, to be present at (his) starting for a journey; used *imper.* to a dog to urge him to scare a person away. *To s.* (a book) *through the press.* **8.** It behoves us to s. that we are not outstripped by our rivals abroad 1884. **b.** If you get your letters ready..,I will s. and get them franked 1825. **9.** Others may doe as they s. good 1663. **10.** I never saw his equal for pluck and daring THACKERAY. Phr. *To s. life, the world*, to acquire experience of the activities or pleasures of human existence. *To have seen better days*, to have been formerly better off than now. *To have seen one's day, one's best days*, to be no longer in one's prime. **b.** At length he came to a resolution..to 'wait and s.' what would turn up for the best 1825. See also WAIT *v.* **c.** Phr. *I'll s. him hanged* (*damned, further*, etc.) *first* (colloq.). **d.** Eighteen rivers have seen their navigation improved 1849. **11.** Remember, my sonne, that shee saw many dangers for thee *Tobit* 4:4. They s. A happy youth, and their old age Is beautiful and free WORDSW. *To have seen service*: see SERVICE[1] II. 6 b. **12.** Phr. *To go* or *come to* (or *and*) *s.*, to visit, call upon. *To s. much* or *little of* (a person), to be often or seldom in his society; He saw little of any Whigs MACAULAY. **b.** I want him to come and s. a physician about the illness of which he spoke to me 1875. **c.** My master is just going to dinner, and can't s. anybody now 1802. **d.** *Cymb.* I. i. 124.

Phr. *Let me s., let us s.*, indicating that the speaker is trying to recall something to memory, or finds it necessary to reflect before answering a question. (*Fair*, etc.) *to see*, in visible aspect.

Phraseological combs. with preps. **See about —.** To attend to; to take steps with reference to; also, to see what can be done with regard to. *I'll s. about it*, often used *colloq.* to evade giving an immediate decision. **S. into —.** To perceive (by physical or mental sight) what is below the surface of. †**S. on, upon —.** To look on, look at. **S. through —.** To s. objects on the other side of (an aperture, or something transparent). Hence *fig.*, to penetrate (a disguise, fallacious appearance), to detect (an imposture), to perceive the real character or aims of (a person). Phr. *To s. through a brick wall*, to have abnormal acuteness. **S. to —. a.** To attend to, do what is needful for; to provide for the wants of; to charge oneself with (a duty, a business). **b.** To take special care about (a matter). **with advs. **S. out. a.** To survive. **b.** In a drinking contest, to outlast. **c.** To go through with to the end. **S. through.** To continue to watch or take part in (a matter) until the end; to take care that (a person) comes successfully through his difficulties.

See-bright (sī·brəit). 1863. [f. SEE *v.* + BRIGHT *a.* A rendering of *clear-eye*, perversion of *clary.*] = CLARY *sb.*[2]

Seed (sīd), *sb.* [OE. *sǣd*, Anglian *sēd*, corresp. to OFris *sēd*, OS. *sād* (Du. *zaad*), OHG. *sāt* (G. *saat*), ON. *sáð*, Goth. *-seþs* in *manaseþs* :– Gmc. **sǣðiz*, **sǣðam*, f. **sǣ-* SOW *v.*] **1. a.** That which is or may be sown; the (ripe) ovules of a plant or plants, esp. as collected for the purpose of being sown. Also, *Agric.* and *Hort.*, applied to other parts of plants (e.g. tubers, bulbs) when preserved for the purpose of propagating a new crop. In *pl.*, kinds of seed. **b.** An individual grain of seed. In *Bot.*, restricted to the fertilized ovule of a phanerogam, but pop. applied also to the 'spore' of a cryptogam, etc. OE. **c.** *pl.* (*a*) Land sown with corn. (*b*) Clover and 'artificial' grasses raised from seed. 1794. **d.** *collect. sing.* and *pl.* Various kinds of grain suitable as the food of a cage-bird 1897. **2.** *fig.* The germ or latent beginning of some growth or development. Also, with ref. to the Parable of the Sower, applied to religious or other teaching, viewed with regard to its degree of fruitfulness. OE. **3.** = SEMEN. Now *rare.* ME. **4.** Offspring, progeny. Now *rare* exc. in Biblical phraseology. OE. **5. a.** *sing.* and *pl.* The ova of the lobster and of the silkworm moth 1620. **b.** Oyster-spat 1721.

1. Every herb bearing s. *Gen.* 1:29. Phr. *To run to s.* (see RUN *v.*[2]); also †*to grow to s., be in s.*; Oh fie, fie, 'tis an vnweeded Garden That growes to S. SHAKS. **b.** Like the dry remnant of a garden flower Whose seeds are shed WORDSW. **2.** Yet then likewise the wicked seede of vice Began to spring SPENSER. The seeds of knowledge may be planted in solitude, but must be cultivated in publick JOHNSON. **4.** His s. shal bycome faderles in straunge lond CAXTON.

attrib. and *Comb.*: **s.-bed,** a bed for sowing seeds; the seedlings growing there; **-box,** (*a*) the receptacle for the s. in a grain-sowing-machine; (*b*) *U.S.* a plant of the genus *Ludwigia* (from its cubical pod); **-bud,** *Bot.* the lower part of the pistil; the rudiment of the s.-vessel or the embryo fruit; **-coat,** *Bot.* = TESTA; **-cotton,** cotton in its native state, with the seed not separated; **-eater, -feeder,** any granivorous bird, *spec.* the Grass-quit, *Phonifara bicolor*; **-field,** a field where s. is sown; **-lac,** resin broken off the twigs of trees and triturated with water; **-leaf, -lobe** = COTYLEDON 3; **-pan,** a pan of red earthenware used for the raising of plants from seed; **-plant,** (*a*) a plant grown from seed, a seedling; (*b*) a plant grown for its seed; **-plot** = *s.-bed* (now only *transf.* and *fig.*); **-snipe,** a bird of the S. Amer. genus *Thinocorys*; **-tick,** a mite of the family *Ixodidæ*; **-vessel** = PERICARP; **-weed,** a weed that propagates itself by seeding. Hence **See·dless** *a.* devoid of s. or seeds.

Seed (sīd), *v.* late ME. [f. prec.] **I.** *intr.* To produce seed; to run to seed. †Also occas.

pass. **b.** To develop *into* something undesirable 1898.

First doe we bud, then blow; next s., last fall 1600.

II. *trans.* **1.** To sow (land) with seed 1440. **2.** To sow (a particular kind of seed) upon land 1560. †**3.** To sprinkle or cover a surface lightly with; so, to decorate the material of a garment with powdering of small ornament –1678. **4.** To remove the seeds from (fruit), to 'stone 1904. **5.** *Lawn Tennis*, etc. To place the names of selected players in a tournament in certain places in an order of names otherwise decided by lot, so as to ensure that those players shall not meet in an early stage of the tournament (orig. *U.S.*) 1911.

1. He giues them also Wheat to s. their land 1598. Phr. *To s. down*, to sow grass or clover seeds amongst (a crop of oats, wheat, etc.). **3.** Theosophia..all in white, a blue mantle seeded with starres B. JONS.

See·d-cake. 1573. A sweet cake flavoured with caraway seeds.

See·d-corn. 1592. Grain (*occas.* a grain of corn) for sowing in order to produce a new crop.

Seeder (sī·dəɹ). [OE. *sǣdere*, f. *sǣd* SEED *sb.*; see -ER¹.] †**1.** One who sows seed; a sower –1500. **2.** A mechanical contrivance for sowing seed 1875.

Seedling (sī·dliŋ), *sb.* and *a.* 1660. [f. SEED *sb.* + -LING¹.] **A.** *sb.* **1.** A young plant developed from a seed, esp. one raised from seed as dist. from a slip, cutting, etc. **2.** A small seed 1809.

2. Not so much as the shadow, hint, or merest s. of a kiss HARDY.

B. *adj.* **1.** Developed or raised from seed 1683. **2.** Of the nature of a small seed; existing in a rudimentary state 1886. **3.** Of oysters: Hatched from 'seed' 1862.

2. He saw that I..had some s. brains which would come up in time RUSKIN.

Seed-lip (sī·dlip). [OE. *sǣdlēap*; see SEED *sb.*, LEAP *sb.*²] A basket in which seed is carried in the process of sowing by hand.

†**See·dness.** 1440. [f. SEED *v.* + -NESS.] The action of sowing or state of being sown –1710.

Seed-pearl (sī·dpɔ̄ɹl). 1551. [f. SEED *sb.*] A minute pearl having the appearance of a seed, usu. drilled and fastened to some material to be worn as an ornament.

Bracelets of braided Hair, Pomander, and Seed-Pearl STEELE.

Seedsman (sī·dzmæ̆n). 1592. [f. genitive of SEED *sb.* + MAN *sb.*] **1.** A sower of seed. **2.** A dealer in seed 1691.

Seed-time (sī·d,təim). late ME. [f. SEED *sb.* + TIME *sb.*] The season of sowing seed.

While the earth remaineth, seed-time and haruest..shall not cease *Gen.* 8:22.

Seedy (sī·di), *a.* 1574. [f. SEED *sb.* + -Y¹.] **1.** Abounding in seed; full of seed. **2.** Shabby, ill-looking (like a flowering plant that has run to seed) 1739. **b.** Unwell, poorly, 'not up to the mark' 1858. **3.** *Glass-making.* Containing minute bubbles 1856.

2. A s. (poor) half-pay Captain 1739. **b.** This morning I was very dull and s. DICKENS.

Comb. **s.-toe**, a diseased condition of a horse's foot. Hence **See·di-ly** *adv.*, **-ness.**

Seeing (sī·iŋ), quasi-*conj.* 1503. [orig. pres. pple. of SEE *v.*] *S.* (*that*): Considering the fact that; inasmuch as; since, because.

As towching the house of the Charterhouse I pray..that it may be turned into a better use (s. it is in the face of the world) CRANMER.

Seek, *sb.* 1500. [f. next.] A series of notes upon a horn calling out hounds to begin a chase. Usu. *to blow a s.* –1826.

Seek (sīk), *v.* Pa. t. and pa. pple. **sought** (sǭt). [OE. *sēċan*, (cf. BESEECH) = OFris. *sēka*, *sēza*, OS. *sokian* (Du. *zoeken*), OHG. *suohhan* (G. *suchen*), ON. *sœkja*, Goth. *sōkjan* :– Gmc. **sōkjan*, f. base **sōk-* :– Western IE. **sāg-* **səg-*, repr. also by L. *sagire* perceive by scent, etc.] **I.** *trans.* **1.** To go in search or quest of; to try to find, look for. **2.** To try to discover or find out. Also with *out*, *up*. Now *rare* or *Obs.* OE. **3.** To go to, visit, resort to (a place). *arch.* OE. **4.**†To come or go to (a person) in order to see or visit him; to resort to (for help, or the like) –1538. **b.** *spec.* To approach, draw near to (God), in prayer, etc. [A Hebraism.] OE. †**5.** To pursue with hostile intention; to go to attack, advance against; to persecute, harass, afflict –1606. **6.** To try to obtain; to try to bring about or effect. Also with *out.* OE. **7.** To ask for, demand, request (*from* a person); to inquire OE. **b.** *pass.* To be courted, to be 'in request' as a companion. Of a woman: To be wooed or asked in marriage. 1671. **8.** To search, explore (a place) in order to find something ME. †**b.** With immaterial obj.: To examine, investigate, scrutinize; to try, test –1611. **9.** To make it one's aim, to try or attempt *to* (do something) OE.

1. I will go seeke Some Ditch, wherein to dye SHAKS. Other persons should be sought who can do the necessary business with more skill BURKE. Phr. *To s. dead*, chiefly in the imper., as an order given to a dog to seek and retrieve killed game. **2.** Now let vs on, my Lords,..And seeke how we may preiudice the Foe SHAKS. Its cause must be sought in the state..of the atmosphere 1803. **3.** †*To s. a saint*, etc., to visit his shrine; To Cauntурbury they wende The hooly blisful martir for to seke CHAUCER. **4. b.** O God..early wil I seke the COVERDALE *Ps.* 62[3]. **5.** *Ant. & Cl.* II. ii. 161. **6.** She sought consolation in district visiting 1908. **7.** I will seeke satisfaction of you SHAKS. **b.** His daughter, sought by many Prowest Knights MILT. **8. b.** *Cymb.* IV. ii. 160. **9.** He sought to drown his sorrow for the defeat in floods of beer THACKERAY.

II. *intr.* **1.** *absol.* To make search OE. **2.** To go, resort, pay a visit (*to*, *unto* a person, *to*, *into* a place). *Obs.* exc. *arch.* ME. **b.** To apply, have recourse *to* or *unto* (a person, *for* something); to pay court, make request or petition *to*. *Obs.* exc. *arch.* late ME. †**c.** To resort to (a remedy, means of help) –1819.

1. Yf ȝe wyll haue hym, goo, & syke, syke, syke! 1450. *To have far to s.*; cf. III. 1. **2.** Wisdoms self Oft seeks to sweet retired Solitude MILT. **b.** You have been sought to by some of the first Families in the Nation, for your Alliance RICHARDSON. **c.** S. to prayer and penance SCOTT.

Phr. **S. after** —. To go in quest of, look for; to try to find, reach, or obtain. Now chiefly in passive: To be desired or in demand; to be courted, to have one's presence desired. **S. for** —. (= I. 1, 2, 5.) †**S. on, upon** —. **a.** To set on, attack, assail. **b.** To approach, (a person) in order to obtain something.

III. Uses of the infinitive *to seek*. **1.** Not to be found or not yet found, not at hand, absent, missing, lacking. *Far to s.*, far out of reach, a long way off. late ME. **b.** With neg.: Not hard to find, not absent or wanting. Also *not far to s.* late ME. **2.** Of a person, his faculties, etc.: **a.** At a loss or at fault; unable to act, understand, etc.; puzzled to know or decide. *Obs.* or *arch.* late ME. **b.** Wanting or deficient *in*; without skill or learning *in*. With *for*: At a loss for, unable to find. *arch.* 1522.

Comb.: **s.-no-farther, -further,** a kind of apple.

Seeker (sī·kəɹ). ME. [f. SEEK *v.* + -ER¹.] **1.** One who seeks. **b.** *Eccl. Hist.* (With capital S.) As the designation assumed by a class of sectaries in the 16–17th c., who professed to be seeking the true church, etc. 1645. **2.** An instrument used in seeking or searching 1658.

†**Seel,** *v.*¹ 1618. [Of unkn. origin.] *Naut.* *intr.* Of a ship: To make a sudden lurch to one side –1753. Hence †**Seel** *sb.* –1753.

Seel (sīl), *v.*² 1500. [Later form of †*sile* (XVI) – OFr. *ciller*, *siller* or med.L. *ciliare*, f. L. *cilium* eyelid.] **1.** *trans.* To close the eyes of (a hawk or other bird) by stitching up the eyelids with a thread tied behind the head; chiefly used as part of the taming process in falconry. Also, to stitch *up* (the eyes of a bird). **2.** *transf.* To close (a person's eyes). Also *fig.* to make blind, hoodwink. 1591.

2. Shee that so young could giue out such a Seeming To seele her Fathers eyes vp SHAKS.

Seely (sī·li), *a.* *Obs.* exc. *dial.* [ME. *seli(e* :– OE. **sǣliġ*; see SILLY.] **1.** Happy, blissful; fortunate, lucky, well-omened, auspicious. **2.** Spiritually blessed; pious, holy, good ME. **3.** Innocent, harmless ME. **4.** Deserving of pity or sympathy; miserable; helpless, defenceless ME. **5.** Insignificant; mean, poor; feeble ME. **7.** Foolish, simple, silly 1529.

Seem (sīm), *v.* [ME. *seme* – ON. *sœma* honour (MSw. befit), f. *sœmr* fitting, seemly.] †**I.** quasi-*trans.* with obj. orig. dative. To be suitable to, befit, beseem. Also *absol.* –1615.

For it seemeth much in a King, if..he can take hold of any superficiall Ornaments and shewes of learning BACON.

II. *intr.* To have a semblance or appearance. **As personal verb.* **1.** To appear to be, to be apparently (what is expressed by the complement) ME. **2.** With *inf.*: To appear *to be* or *to do* something ME. **b.** In mod. use, the combination of *seems* with an inf. often = the finite verb qualified by 'probably', 'if the evidence may be trusted' 1841. **c.** To appear to oneself; to imagine oneself, or think one perceives oneself, *to do* something 1638. **3.** To appear to exist or to be present. Chiefly in *there seems* (followed by the subject); otherwise *poet.* or *rhet.* Also, *there seems to be.* late ME.

1. As the mone lyght, Ageyn whom all the sterres semen But smale candels CHAUCER. A silly rogue, but one that would seem a gentleman PEPYS. **2.** The Parian Marble, there, shall s. to move, In breathing Statues DRYDEN. Young women are not the angels they s. to be 1756. **b.** Sicily seems to contain no iron 1841. **c.** I s. again to share thy smile, I s. to hang upon thy tone SHELLEY. **3.** There seemed a general consensus of opinion that inventors were a nuisance 1883.

***Impersonal uses.* **1.** *It seems.* **a.** It appears, it is apparently true (*that*); it is seen (*that*). Also followed by *as if*, *as though.* ME. **b.** Used parenthetically. Often = 'So I am informed', or 'As it appears from rumour or report'. late ME. **c.** *It should s.*, *it would s.*: expressing more of hesitation or uncertainty than *it seems.* late ME. **2.** The *it* of the impersonal verb is sometimes omitted ME.

1. It seemes to mee, That yet we sleepe, we dreame SHAKS. It seems I must remit seeing you 1687. Phr. *It seems so, so it seems* = 'it seems that it is so'. **b.** There is still, however, it seems, a hope for mankind MACAULAY. **c.** From all this it would s. that he could not have been much under fifty when he was compelled to abjure 1902. **2.** Her seemed she scarce had been a day One of God's choristers D. G. ROSSETTI. If he did so, as seems likely enough, it was excusable 1912.

†**III.** *trans.* To think, deem. *To s. good* = to think good. –1627. **b.** To think fit –1610.

It was a Fairye, as al the peple semed CHAUCER. Hence **See·mer**, one who seems, or makes a pretence or show.

Seeming (sī·miŋ), *vbl. sb.* late ME. [-ING¹.] The action of SEEM *v.* **1.** The action or fact of appearing to be. **2.** The form in which a person or thing seems or appears; look, aspect. late ME. **3.** External appearance considered as deceptive, or as distinguished from reality; an illusion, a semblance 1576.

1. The events which are the most threatening in their s., speak to us of hope 1845. Phr. *In s.*, *in all s.*, to all appearance. †*To* (*my*) *s.*, as (I) think. **2.** Your behaviour is above your s. H. WALPOLE.

Seeming (sī·miŋ), *ppl. a.* ME. [-ING².] That seems. †**1.** Suitable, beseeming; according –1687. **2.** Apparent to the senses or to the mind, as distinct from what *is* ME. **3.** Used advb. (often hyphened) with other adjs. = next 2. 1590.

2. A s. Widow, and a secret Bride DRYDEN. **3.** With chaunge of cheare the s. simple maid Let fall her eyen SPENSER. Hence **See·mingness,** unreal pretence, plausibility; s. existence or presence.

Seemingly (sī·miŋli), *adv.* 1483. [f. prec. + -LY².] **1.** Fittingly, becomingly. Now *rare.* **2.** To external appearance, apparently 1598. **3.** So far as it appears from the evidence; so far as one can judge from circumstances 1715. **b.** *parenthetically.* As it seems 1702.

2. Now the City-Dame was so well bred, as s. to take All in Good Part 1692.

See·mless, *a.* *Obs.* exc. *arch.* 1596. [f. SEEM *v.* (assumed to be the source of SEEMLY *a.*) + -LESS.] Unseemly; shameful; unfitting.

Seemly (sī·mli), *a.* [ME. *semeliche* – ON. *sœmiligr*, f. *sœmr*; see SEEM *v.*, -LY¹.] **1.** Of a pleasing or goodly appearance, fair, well-formed, handsome. *Obs.* exc. *dial.* **2.** Of things: Pleasant (*esp.* to the sight); handsome in appearance; of fine or stately proportion ME. **3.** Of conduct, speech, appearance: Conformable to propriety or good taste; becoming, decorous ME. †**4.** Appropriate –1634.

1. She is nothing so Fayre as she hathe bene reportyd, howbeit she is well and semelye CROMWELL. **2.** Their gownes..white or of other seemlie colour 1585. **3.** That our liues be honest and semely, not dissolute and lawlesse 1579. **4.** Delight is not seemely for a foole *Prov.* 19:10. Hence **See·mlihead,** (*arch.*) seemliness. †**See·mli-ly** *adv.*, **-ness.**

Seemly (sī·mli), *adv.* ME. [– ON. *sœmiliga*, f. *sœmr*; see prec., -LY².] **1.** In a pleasing manner; so as to present a fair, handsome, or stately appearance. Now *arch.* **2.** Fittingly, appropriately; becomingly ME.

1. A man before him stood, Not rustic as before, but seemlier clad MILT.

Seen (sīn), *ppl. a.* late ME. [pa. pple. of SEE *v.*] **1.** In senses of the verb. Now *rare* exc. in antithesis with *unseen*. **2.** *To be* (*well, ill*, etc.) *s.*: to be (well, ill, etc.) versed *in* some art or science. Now *arch.* 1528. (See also WELL-SEEN.)

2. A schoole-master Well seene in Musicke SHAKS. Men of mature yeares, and seene in the warres 1620.

Seep (sīp), *v. dial.* and *U.S.* 1790. [perh. dial. development of OE. *sipian*; see SIPE *v.*] *intr.* = SIPE *v.* So **Seep** *sb.* moisture that seeps out; a small spring; *U.S.* a place where petroleum oozes out slowly. **See·py** *a. U.S.* badly drained.

Seepage (sī·pėdʒ). *dial.* and *U.S.* 1825. [f. prec. + -AGE.] Percolation or oozing of water or fluid; leakage; also, that which oozes.

Seer¹ (sīᵊɹ, in sense 1 also sī·əɹ). late ME. [f. SEE *v.* + -ER¹.] **1.** *gen.* One who sees (*rare*). **2.** One to whom divine revelations are made in visions. In mod. use occas. *transf.*, one gifted with profound spiritual insight. late ME. **3.** A magician; one who has the power of second sight. Also a crystal-gazer, a scryer. 1661.

1. Strangers & seldome seers feel the beauty of them more than you who dwell with them JER. TAYLOR. Hence **See·ress**, a female s. **See·rship**, the office or function of a s.

‖**Seer²** (sīᵊɹ). *Anglo-Ind. Pl.* **seer, seers.** 1618. [Hindi *ser*.] A denomination of weight varying in different parts of India from over 3 lb to 8 ounces (usu. = 2 lb.). As a measure of capacity = a litre, or 1·76 pints.

Seer-fish: see SEIR-FISH.

Seersucker (sīᵊ·ɹsʊkəɹ). 1757. [E. Indian alt. of Pers. *šīr o šakar* lit. 'milk and sugar', transf. 'a striped linen garment'.] A thin linen, occas. cotton, fabric of Indian manufacture, striped and having a crapy surface. Now chiefly applied to imitations made in the U.S.

See-saw, *int.*, *sb.*, and *a.* 1640. [A reduplicating formation symbolic of alternating movement.] **A.** *int.* (sī·sǭ·) Used as part of a rhythmical jingle, app. sung by sawyers, or by children imitating them at their work. Hence in nursery songs. **B.** *sb.* (sī·sǭ) **1.** The motion of going up one moment and down the next, or of swaying backwards and forwards. Also, a child's amusement in which children sit one or more at each end of a board or piece of timber balanced so that the ends move alternately up and down. 1704. **b.** *Whist.* = CROSS-RUFF 2. 1746. **2.** A plank arranged for playing see-saw 1824. **C.** *adj.* (sī·sǭ) Moving up and down, or backwards and forwards, in the manner of a see-saw. Also *fig.* 1735.

His wit all s., between *that* and *this*, Now high, now low, now master up, now miss POPE.

See·-saw:, *v.* 1712. [f. SEE-SAW *sb.*] **1.** *intr.* **a.** To move up and down, or backwards and forwards; to undergo a see-saw motion; also to play see-saw. **2.** *trans.* To cause to move in a see-saw motion 1801.

2. He ponders, he see-saws himself to and fro LYTTON.

Seethe (sīð), *v.* Pa. t. **seethed, †sod.** Pa. pple. **seethed, †sodden.** [OE. *sēoþan* = OFris. *siātha*, OS. **sioðan*, OHG. *siodan* (Du. *zieden, sieden*), ON. *sjóða*, f. Gmc. **seuþ-* **sauþ-* **suð-*.] **1.** *trans.* To boil; to make or keep boiling hot; to subject to the action of boiling liquid; *esp.* to cook (food) by boiling or stewing; also, to make an infusion or decoction of (a substance) by boiling or stewing. *Obs.* or *arch.* **2.** *intr.* (for passive). To be boiled; to be subjected to boiling or stewing; to become boiling hot. ME. **3.** *trans.* To reduce to a condition resembling that of food which has lost its flavour or crispness by boiling or stewing; to soak or steep in a liquid; to dissipate the vitality or freshness of (the brain, blood, spirits, etc.) by excessive heat or by intoxicating liquor. Chiefly *pass.* 1599. **4.** *intr.* (transf. from 2). Of a liquid, vapour, etc.: To rise, surge or foam up, as if boiling; to form bubbles or foam 1535. **5.** *fig.* To be in a state of inward agitation, turmoil, or 'ferment' 1606.

1. Cold meat, seethed, Italian fashion, in nauseous oil 1835. **2.** The water begins to seeth 1801. **3.** They drown their wits, seeth their brains in ale BURTON. **5.** The city had all through the interval been seething with discontent 1874. Hence **Seethe** *sb.* seething, ebullition; intense commotion or heat. **See·thingly** *adv.*

Sefton (se·ftən). 1885. [From the title of the Earl of *Sefton*.] A form of landau.

Segment (se·gmĕnt), *sb.* 1570. [– L. *segmentum*, f. *sec-*, stem of *secare* cut; see -MENT.] **1.** A piece cut or broken off; a fragment (*rare*) 1586. **2.** *Geom.* A plane figure contained by a right line and a portion of the circumference of a circle. In full *s. of a circle*. 1570. **b.** A segmental portion of anything having a circular or spherical form 1646. **3.** *Geom.* The finite part of a line between two points; a division of a line 1617. **b.** *Acoustics.* Each of the portions into which the length of a vibrating string, wire, etc. is divided by the nodes 1863. **4.** Each of the parts into which a thing is or may be divided; a division, section 1762. **5.** *Bot.* Each of the portions into which a leaf or other plant-organ is divided by long clefts or incisions 1713. **6.** *Biol.* and *Embryol.* **a.** Each of the longitudinal divisions composing the body in some animals, esp. in the Articulata; a somite, metamere 1826. **b.** A cell formed by segmentation 1862. **7.** *Anat.* Each complete series of bones forming a vertebra of the spinal column; also, each of the three annular divisions of the cranium proper 1844. **b.** A division of the spinal cord and nerves 1855. **8.** = *s.* (or SEGMENTAL) *arch.* 1836.

2. *S. of a sphere*, a solid figure bounded by a portion of the surface of a sphere and an intersecting plane. **4.** Being unable to divide the orange into its segments, he ventures upon a great liquid bite 1847.

attrib. and *Comb.*, with the meaning SEGMENTAL (sense 1), esp. in the names of mechanical appliances, parts of machinery, etc., indicating the shape of the essential or working part, as *s.-arch, -roof, vault*; *s.-gear, -valve, -wheel*, etc.

Segment (se·gmĕnt), *v.* 1859. [f. prec.] **1.** *trans.* To subject to the process of segmentation or division and multiplication of cells; to produce (new cells) by this process. **2.** *intr.* Of a cell or ovum: To divide or split up and give origin to one or more new cells by segmentation 1888. **3.** *trans.* To divide into segments 1872. Hence **Se·gmented** *ppl. a. Anat., Bot.*, etc. consisting of, divided into, segments; divided or split up by segmentation into cells.

Segmental (segme·ntăl), *a.* 1816. [f. SEGMENT *sb.* + -AL¹.] **1.** Having the form of a segment (or, loosely, of an arc) of a circle; *esp. Arch.* of an arch, a pediment, window-head, etc. 1816. **2.** Of, pertaining to, or composed of segments or divisions 1854. **b.** *Path.* Characterized by segmentation or division into segments 1896. Hence **Segme·ntally** *adv.*

Segmentary (segme·ntări), *a.* 1853. [f. as prec. + -ARY. Cf. Fr. *segmentaire*.] **1.** Segmental. **2.** Pertaining to segments or divisions; composed of segments 1898.

Segmentation (se:gmĕntēⁱ·ʃən). 1851. [f. SEGMENT *v.* + -ATION.] The process of division into segments, chiefly in biological applications; *spec.* in *Embryol.*, the process by which, in the Metazoa, the germinal cell or protoplasmic mass is converted by division into a multitude of cells, which become metamorphosed into the tissue of the body.

attrib.: **s. cavity** = BLASTOCELE.

Segregate (se·grĭgĕt), *a.* and *sb.* late ME. [– L. *segregatus*, pa. pple. of *segregare*; see next, -ATE¹ and ².] **A.** *adj.* **1.** Separated, set apart, isolated. Now *rare*. **2.** *spec.* (*Zool., Bot.*, etc.) Separated (wholly or partially) from the parent or from one another; not aggregated 1793. **B.** *sb. Math.* One of a smallest select aggregate of products of irreducible covariants which suffices to provide by linear combination all covariants of every degree and order 1878.

Segregate (se·grĭgeⁱt), *v.* 1542. [– *segregat-* pa. ppl. stem of L. *segregare* separate from the flock, etc., f. *se-* SE- + *grex, greg-*, flock; see -ATE³.] **1.** *trans.* To separate (a person, a body or class of persons) from the general body, or from some particular class; to set apart, isolate, seclude. **2.** To separate or isolate (one thing from others); *esp. Chem., Geol.*, etc. (of natural agencies) to separate out and collect (certain particular constituents of a compound or mixture). In scientific classification: To remove (certain species) etc. from a group and place them apart. 1579. **3.** *intr.* for *refl.* To separate from a main body or mass and collect in one place 1863.

1. So the Anabaptistes in our time. .segregated themselues from the companye of other men LATIMER.

Segregation (segrĭgēⁱ·ʃən). 1555. [– late L. *segregatio, -ōn-*, f. as prec.; see -ION.] **1.** The action of segregating 1615. **b.** The separation of a portion or portions of a collective or complex unity from the rest; the isolation of particular constituents of a compound or mixture 1612. **†c.** *spec.* Separation from a church or ecclesiastical organization –1683. **2.** The condition of being segregated 1668. **3.** *concr.* Something segregated 1563.

Segregative (se·grĭgeⁱtiv), *a.* 1588. [– med.L. *segregativus*, f. as prec.; see -IVE.] **1.** Having the power or effect of separating. **†a.** *Gram.* and *Logic.* Applied to adversative and disjunctive conjunctions. Hence of a proposition, Consisting of members joined by a segregative conjunction. –1626. **b.** Having the property of separating the elements or constituent parts of matter 1674. **2.** Of persons: Given to separation or disunion. Of an individual: Unsociable. 1685.

Segregator (se·grĭgēⁱtəɹ). 1903. [f. SEGREGATE *v.* + -OR 2.] An instrument for obtaining the urine from each kidney separately.

‖**Seguidilla** (segidi·lʸa). 1763. [Sp., f. *seguida* following, sequence, f. *seguir* follow.] A Spanish dance in ¾ or ⅜ time; also, the music for this.

‖**Seicento** (seiˌtʃe·nto). 1866. [It.; short for *mil seicento* one thousand six hundred.] The 17th c. considered as a period of Italian art.

Seidlitz (se·dlits). 1784. Name of a village in Bohemia, where there is a spring impregnated with magnesium sulphate and carbonic acid. Used *attrib.* in **†S. salt**, magnesium sulphate; **†S. water**, an artificial aperient water of the same composition as the water of the S. spring. Hence in **S. powder** (arbitrarily named), a dose consisting of two powders, one of tartaric acid and the other of a mixture of potassium tartrate and sodium bicarbonate, which are mixed in water and drunk while effervescing.

‖**Seigneur** (sęnʸör). 1592. [– (O)Fr. *seigneur* :– L. *senior, -ōr-*; see SEIGNOR.] **a.** *Fr. Hist.*, A feudal lord; a noble taking his designation from the name of his estate. **b.** In Canada, the holder of a SEIGNEURY; one of the landed gentry.

Grand s., a person of high rank or whose deportment or behaviour suggests this.

Seigneurial (sēⁱniūᵊ·riăl), *a.* 1656. [– Fr. *seigneurial*, f. *seigneur*, infl. by *seigneurie*; see prec., -AL¹.] Pertaining to a seigneur (in France or Canada). Also occas. = SEIGNORIAL.

Seigneury (sēⁱ·niŭri), ‖**Seigneurie** (sęnʸöri). 1620. [– Fr. *seigneurie* (OFr. *seignorie*); see SEIGNEUR, -Y³, and cf. SEIGNIORY.] **1. a.** *Fr. Hist.* A territory under the government of a seigneur. **b.** In Canada, a landed estate, held (until 1854) by feudal tenure. **2.** In Canada, the mansion of a seigneur 1895.

Seignior (sēⁱ·niŏɹ). ME. [– AFr. *segnour*, OFr. *seignor* (mod. *seigneur*) :– L. *senior, -ōr-*; see SEIGNEUR, -OR 4.] **1.** Orig., synonymous with LORD; a person high in rank or authority, a ruler, a feudal superior; the lord of a manor. Now *rare*. **†2.** Used to represent It. SIGNOR or Fr. SEIGNEUR in designations of Italians or Frenchmen –1718.

Seigniorage, seignorage (sēⁱ·nyŏrėdʒ). 1444. [– OFr. *seignorage, -eurage* (mod. *-euriage*), f. *seignor*; see prec., -AGE.] **†1.** Lordship, dominion –1820. **2.** A duty levied on the coining of money for the purpose of covering the expenses of minting, and as a source of revenue to the crown, claimed by the sovereign by virtue of his prerogative 1444. **3.** A duty claimed by the over-lord upon the output of certain minerals, a royalty 1859.

3. The seignorage levied on tin in the Duchy of Cornwall MACAULAY.

Seigniory, seignory (sē¹·nyŏri). ME. [– OFr. *seignorie* (later *seigneurie*); see SEIGNEUR, -Y³, and cf. SEIGNEURY.] †**1.** Lordship, domination, sovereignty –1684. **2.** *spec.* Feudal lordship or dominion; the authority, rights, and privileges of a feudal lord 1464. **b.** A particular feudal lordship; in *Eng. Law* chiefly, the relation of the lord to the tenants of a manor 1466. **3.** The territory under the dominion of a lord; *esp.* a feudal domain. Sometimes used for SEIGNEURY with ref. to France or Canada. ME. **4.** A body of 'seigniors' or lords. Often with ref. to Italy, = SIGNORIA. 1485.

1. If hee would. . do homage to him, he should re-accept his seniory 1638. **2. b.** A s. appendant passes with the grant of the manor; a s. in gross —that is a s. which has been severed from the demesne lands of the manor to which it was originally appendant—must be specially conveyed by deed of grant 1886.

Seignoral (sē¹·nyŏrăl), *a. Hist.* 1627 [app. f. SEIGN(I)OR + -AL¹.] = next.

Seignorial (sē¹nyō³·riăl), *a.* 1818. [f. as prec. + -IAL.] Pertaining to a seignior or seigniors.

Seine (sē¹n), *sb.* [OE. *segne* = OS., OHG. *segina* :- WGmc. **sa·gina* – L. *sagēna* (whence OFr. *saïne*, mod. *seine*) – Gr. σαγήνη; reinforced in ME. from OFr.] A fishing net designed to hang vertically in the water, the ends being drawn together to enclose the fish.

To shoot a s. (or *s.-net*), to throw it out into position.

Comb.: **s.-boat**, a boat adapted for carrying and throwing out a s.; **-net**, a s. Hence **Sei·ner**, a fisherman who uses a s., or one employed to haul in a s.; also, a s.-boat.

Seine (sē¹n), *v.* 1836. [f. prec.] **a.** *intr.* To fish or catch fish with a seine. **b.** *trans.* To catch or fish with a seine.

Seir-fish, seer-fish (sī³·ɹfiʃ). 1727. [The first element repr. Pg. *serra*, name of the fish.] An East Indian scombroid fish, *Cybium guttatum*.

Seise, *v. Law.* The usual spelling of SEIZE *v.* in the sense: To put in possession, invest with the fee simple *of*.

Seisin (sī·zin). [ME. *sesin(e, seisin(e* – AFr. *sesine*, OFr. *seisine*, (also mod.) *saisine*, f. *seisir* SEIZE; see -INE⁴.] **1.** In early use, Possession. Now only in *Law*, Possession as of freehold. **b.** In pop. language occas., applied loosely to the object (e.g. a turf, key, staff) handed over in 'livery of s.' (see LIVERY *sb.* 5a) as a token of possession 1523. **2.** *Sc. Law.* The act of giving possession of feudal property by the delivery of symbols; also, the instrument by which such possession is proved. late ME.

1. Phrases. *To have, take s.* (*in, of*). *Primer* (also *premier*) *s.*: see PRIMER *a.* 3 b.

Seismic (sai·zmik), *a.* 1858. [f. Gr. σεισμός earthquake (f. σείειν shake) + -IC.] Pertaining to, relating to, characteristic of, connected with, or produced by an earthquake, earthquakes, or earth vibration. So **Sei·smical** *a.*, **-ly** *adv.* **Seismi·city,** the frequency per unit area of earthquakes of a particular country; the number representing this.

Seismism (sai·zmiz'm). 1902. [f. Gr. σεισμός + -ISM.] The phenomena of earthquake movements collectively.

Seismograph (sai·zmograf). 1858. [f. *seismo-*, comb. form of Gr. σεισμός + -GRAPH.] An instrument for recording automatically the phenomena of earthquakes. Hence **Seismogra·phic, -al** *adjs.* connected with, furnished by, or relating to a s.; of or pertaining to seismography. **Seismo·graphy,** the descriptive science of earthquakes; also, the use of the s.

Seismology (saizmǫ·lŏdʒi). 1858. [f. as prec. + -LOGY.] The science and study of earthquakes, and their causes, effects, and attendant phenomena. Hence **Seismolo·gic, -al** *adjs.* of or pertaining to s. **Seismo·logist,** an investigator of s.

Seismometer (saizmǫ·mĭtəɹ). 1841. [f. as prec. + -METER.] An instrument for measuring the intensity, direction, and duration of earthquakes. Hence **Seismome·tric, -al** *adjs.* of or pertaining to seismometry, or to a s. **Seismo·metry,** the scientific study, determination and recording of earthquake phenomena, esp. by means of the s.; the scientific study, theory, and application of the s.

Seismoscope (sai·zmoskō³p). 1851. [f. as prec. + -SCOPE.] A simple form of seismometer; a contrivance for detecting or indicating the occurrence of an earthquake shock.

Seity (sī·ĭti). *rare.* 1709. [– med.L. *seitas*, f. L. *se* oneself; see -ITY.] That which constitutes the self, selfhood.

Seizable (sī·zăb'l), *a.* 1461. [f. next + -ABLE.] Capable of being seized. Chiefly of property, that may lawfully be seized.

Seize (sīz), *v.* ME. [– OFr. *seizir*, (also mod.) *saisir* :- Gallo-Rom., Frankish L. *sacīre* (as in phr. *ad proprium s.*, claim as one's own), Gmc. **sakjan*, f. **sak-* process, procedure (see SAKE), which may have been partly conflated with Gmc. **satjan* place, settle, SET *v.*] **I.** To put in possession. **1.** *Law.* (In techn. use written **seise.**) *trans.* To put (a person) in legal possession *of* a feudal holding; to invest or endow *with* property; to establish *in* a holding or an office or dignity. **b.** *To be seised of* or *in*: to be the legal possessor of. late ME. **2.** *transf. To be seized* (*seised*) *of* or †*with*: to be in possession of. Now only *arch.* and with allusion to the legal use. 1477. †**3.** To settle, establish in a place; to place, seat, fix –1633. †**b.** Of a beast of prey: To fasten (its claws) upon. SPENSER.

1. b. Phr. *To be seised in fee, to be seised of* (a manor, etc.) *in his demesne as of fee*, to be the holder of the fee simple. **2.** If any that sell Goose Eggs do chance to be taken siesed with Hens eggs. . they are presently punished with thirty lashes 1653.

II. To take possession. **1.** Of a feudal superior or a sovereign: To take possession of, confiscate (the property of a vassal or subject). Also, to annex (a country) to one's own dominions. ME. **b.** To take possession of (goods) in pursuance of a judicial order 1482. **2.** To take possession of by force; to capture (a city); to take as plunder ME. **b.** To take prisoner, to catch. late ME. **3.** To take hold of with the hands, claws, teeth, etc.; in mod. use, to take hold of suddenly or eagerly, to clutch ME. **b.** *To s. hold of*: to take hold of suddenly and roughly 1839. **4.** *fig.* **a.** With impersonal subject, e.g. death, calamity: To oppress or attack suddenly. Also of a fear, belief, etc.: To take sudden possession of (a person, his mind). late ME. **b.** Of an object of perception, a fact, etc., hence of a speaker, writer, or artist: To arrest (the attention), to impress irresistibly (the mind, etc.) 1772. **c.** To avail oneself eagerly or dexterously of, take advantage of (an opportunity) 1618. **d.** To grasp with the mind or perceptive faculties 1855. **5.** *intr.* **a.** *To s. on* or *upon* = to seize (in senses II. 2–4). late ME. †**b.** Of a weapon: To penetrate deeply *in* –1600.

1. Phr. *To s. into one's hands*; The said Citie. . was seised into the saide King Edward's hondes 1447. **b.** Being quite moneyless, and in danger of having my goods seized for rent 1733. **2.** Robbers, who seized church goods without remorse 1883. **3.** Lothaire abruptly seized him by the arm 1797. **4.** Ruin s. thee, ruthless King! GRAY. The young prince. .was seized by the small pox MACAULAY. **d.** A beauty which a foreigner cannot perfectly s. M. ARNOLD. **5. a.** A morbid melancholy seized upon the Irishman BORROW.

III. Techn. **1.** *trans.* (*Naut.*). †**a.** To reach, arrive at. Also with *in*. –1635. **b.** To fasten (two ropes or parts of a rope) together, or to attach (a rope) to something else, by binding with marline, yarn, or the like 1644. **2.** *intr.* Of a part of a machine, etc. To become stuck owing to excessive heat or pressure 1878.

b. *To s. up*, to fasten (a man) by the wrists to the shrouds, in preparation for a flogging. Hence **Sei·zer,** one who or that which seizes.

Seizing (sī·ziŋ), *vbl. sb.* ME. [f. SEIZE *v.* + -ING¹.] **1.** The action of SEIZE *v.* late ME. **2.** *concr. Naut.* †**a.** A rope for attaching a boat to a ship. **b.** A small cord for 'seizing' two ropes together, or a rope to something else. **c.** Cordage or yarn, used for 'seizing'. ME.

Seizure (sī·ʒ¹ŭɹ). 1482. [f. SEIZE *v.* + -URE.] **1.** The action or an act of seizing, or the fact of being seized; confiscation or forcible taking possession (of land or goods); a sudden and forcible taking hold. †**b.** Grasp, hold; a fastening –1621. **c.** A sudden attack of illness, esp. a fit of apoplexy or epilepsy. Also, a sudden visitation (of calamity). 1779. †**2.** Possession, seisin –1658. **3.** The action of SEIZE *v.* III. 2. 1903.

1. The s. of the estates of the church BURKE. **c.** The s. was, I think, not apoplectical JOHNSON. **2.** When chillie age had seasure of this earth LODGE.

Sejant (sī·dʒănt), *a.* 1500. [prop. *seiant* – OFr. **seiant*, var. of (also mod.) *séant*, pr. pple. of *seoir* sit :– L. *sedēre*; see -ANT.] *Her.* In a sitting posture; *esp.* of a quadruped: Sitting with the fore-legs upright.

Sejoin (sĭ͵dʒoi·n), *v. rare.* 1568. [f. SE- + JOIN *v.*, after L. *sejungere.*] *trans.* To separate, disjoin. So **Seju·nction** 1530.

‖**Séjour** (seʒūr). 1755. [Fr., f. *séjourner* SOJOURN.] **1.** The act of staying or sojourning in a place (for a longer or shorter period). **2.** A place of sojourn or residence 1769.

Selachian (sĭlē¹·kiăn), *a.* and *sb.* 1835. [f. mod.L. *Selache* (– Gr. σελάχη, pl. of σέλαχος shark) or its deriv. *Selachii* + -IAN, after Fr. *sélacien* (Cuvier).] **A.** *adj.* Of or belonging to the genus *Selache* of sharks, or to the group *Selachii*, the sharks and their allies. **B.** *sb.* A shark or allied fish.

‖**Seladang** (sĕlā·dæŋ). Also **saladang.** 1884. [Native name.] **1.** The large wild ox or gaur of the Malay countries. **2.** The Malayan tapir 1909.

‖**Selaginella** (sĭlæ¹dʒ-, sĭlædʒine·lă). 1865. [mod.L., dim. of SELAGO.] *Bot.* A genus of cryptogams; (with *pl.*) a plant of this genus.

‖**Selago** (sĭlē¹·go). 1627. [L.] †**a.** The club-moss *Lycopodium selago*. **b.** A Linnæan genus of S. African herbs or undershrubs.

‖**Selah** (sī·lă). 1530. [Heb. *se·lāh.*] A Hebrew word, occurring frequently at the end of a verse in the Psalter, etc., by the LXX rendered διάψαλμα; supposed to be a musical or liturgical direction, perhaps indicating pause or rest. Hence *allus.*

†**Se·lcouth,** *a.* OE. [f. OE. *seldan* SELDOM + *cūð* COUTH *a.*] Unfamiliar, unusual; strange, marvellous, wonderful –1815.

†**Seld,** *adv.*, and *a.* [Early ME. *selde*, formed as positive to (OE.) *seldor, seldost*, compar. and superl. of *seldan* SELDOM.] = next –1652.

Seldom (se·ldəm), *adv.* and *a.* [OE. *seldan*, corresp. to OFris. *sielden*, MLG., MDu. *selden* (Du. *zelden*), OHG. *seltan* (G. *selten*), ON. *sjaldan*, dat. f. on Gmc. **selda-*, repr. also in OE. *seldlić* strange, wonderful, Goth. *sildaleiks* wonderful.] **A.** *adv.* On few occasions, in few cases or instances, not often; rarely, infrequently.

Listners seldome hear good of themselves 1678.

B. *adj.* Rare, infrequent. *Obs.* exc. occas. with agent-n. or noun of action. 1483.

Blunting the fine point of seldome pleasure SHAKS. Seldom-readers are slow readers LAMB.

Hence †**Se·ldom-ly** *adv.* –1620, **-ness.**

†**Se·ldseen,** *a.* [OE. *seldsīene*, f. *seldan* (prec.) + *ġesīene, ġesēne*, pa. pple. of SEE *v.*] Seldom to be seen or met with; rare –1616.

Select (sĭle·kt), *a.* (and *sb.*). 1565. [– L. *selectus*, pa. pple. of *seligere*; see next.] **A.** *adj.* **1.** Selected, chosen out of a larger number, on account of excellence or fitness; picked. **2.** Choice; composed of or containing the best, choicest or most desirable; superior 1590. **b.** Of persons, company, etc. Now often: Unexceptionable with regard to social standing or estimation. 1602. **3.** Careful in selection. Hence, (of a society, etc.) exclusive; (of a place or resort) frequented only by persons of good position. 1842.

1. To the smaller plot. .only a few s. traitors

were privy MACAULAY. *S. committee* (of the House of Commons, etc.), one consisting of a small number of members, selected to investigate a special matter. *S. meeting*, (amongst Quakers) a meeting of ministers and elders. **2.** Most s. Remedies for every Disease 1656. **b.** Company at first aristocratic and s. CARLYLE. **3.** Such a sweet, s. watering-place. All the best people go there. 1888.

†**B.** *sb.* **a.** A selected person or thing. **b.** A selected class or group, a selection. –1805. Hence **Sele·ct-ly** *adv.*, **-ness.**

Select (sĭle·kt), *v.* 1567. [– *select-*, pa. ppl. stem of L. *seligere* choose out, f. *se-* SE- + *legere* collect, choose.] **1.** *trans.* To choose or pick out in preference to another or others. **2.** *intr.* To make a selection 1833.

1. You desire me to s...some Things from the first Volume of your Miscellanies POPE. Hence **Sele·ctor,** one who or that which selects; also, as a name for various appliances in metallurgy, telegraphy, etc.

Selection (sĭle·kʃən). 1646. [– L. *selectio, -ōn-*, f. as prec.; see -ION.] **1.** The action of selecting or choosing out; also the fact of being selected or chosen. **2.** A particular choice; choice of a particular individual or individuals; *concr.* the (†person or) thing selected; a number of selected (†persons or) things 1805. **b.** *Sporting.* The horse or horses selected by a racing prophet as likely to win or obtain a place 1901. **3. a.** Applied *spec.* to the action of a breeder in selecting individuals from which to breed, in order to obtain some desired quality or characteristic in the descendants 1813. **b.** Hence *Biol.*, used to designate any process, whether artificial or natural, which brings about a particular modification of an animal or vegetable type by ensuring that in successive generations the individuals that reproduce their kind shall be those that have transmissible variations from the ancestral form in the direction of this modification 1857.

1. It should seem, then,..that the essence of right conduct lay in s. and rejection 1744. **2.** The English public..does not pretend to care for poetry except in 'selections' 1887. **3.** *Natural s.*, the operation of natural causes by which those individuals of a species that are best adapated to the environment tend to be preserved and to transmit their characters, while those less adapted die out, so that in the course of generations the degree of adaptation to the environment tends progressively to increase. *Sexual s.*, that kind of natural s. which arises through the preference by one sex of those individuals of the other sex that have some special characteristic, in consequence of which that characteristic tends to be transmitted, with progressive enhancement in succeeding generations.

Selective (sĭle·ktiv), *a.* 1625. [f. SELECT *v.* + -IVE.] Having the quality or faculty of selecting; characterized by choice or selection. **b.** *Wireless Telegr.* Having the power to select a particular wave-length or frequency and to exclude others 1903. Hence **Selecti·vity,** the quality of being s.

Sele·ctman. *U.S.* 1646. [f. SELECT *a.* + MAN *sb.*] One of a board of officers elected annually to manage various local concerns in a 'town' or 'township' in New England.

Selenate (se·lĭnĕt). 1818. [f. SELENIC + -ATE[4].] *Chem.* A salt of selenic acid.

Selenic (sĭle·nik), *a.* 1818. [f. SELENIUM + -IC.] *Chem. S. acid*, a dibasic acid, H_2SeO_4, forming salts called *selenates*.

Selenide (se·lĭnəid). 1849. [f. as prec. + -IDE.] *Chem.* A combination of selenium with an electro-positive element or with a radical.

Seleniferous (selĭni·fĕrəs), *a.* 1823. [f. SELENIUM + -FEROUS.] Containing or yielding selenium.

Sele·nio-, sele·no-. 1831. Used as comb. forms of SELENIUM, as in *selenocyanide*, etc.

Selenious (sĭlī·niəs), *a.* 1834. [f. SELENIUM; see -OUS.] *Chem. S. acid.* a dibasic acid, H_2SeO_3, forming salts called *selenites.*

Selenite[1] (se·lĭnəit). 1567. [– L. SELENITES.] **1.** A stone described by ancient writers; app. to be identified with the mineral now so called (see 2). **2.** *Min.* Sulphate of lime (gypsum) in a crystalline or foliated form. Also, a slip or film of this mineral used for the polarization of light. 1668. †**b.** *Chem.* Sulphate of lime without regard to structure –1823.

Selenite[2] (sĭlī·nəit). 1645. [f. Gr. σεληνίτης (pl. Σεληνῖται men in the moon), f. σελήνη moon. See -ITE[1] 1.] A supposed inhabitant of the moon.

Selenite[3] (se·lĭnəit). 1831. [f. SELENIUM + -ITE[1] 4 b.] *Chem.* A salt of selenious acid.

†‖**Selenites** (selĭnəi·tīz). late ME. [L. *selenites* – Gr. σεληνίτης (sc. λίθος) 'moon-(stone)', so called because supposed to wax and wane with the moon, f. σελήνη moon.] = SELENITE[1] –1820.

Selenitic (selĭni·tik), *a.* 1756. [f. SELENITE[1] + -IC.] Of, pertaining to, resembling or containing selenite. †Of water: Impregnated with sulphate of lime. So †**Seleni·tical** *a.* 1755–1799.

Selenium (sĭlī·niŏm). 1818. [mod.L., f. Gr. σελήνη moon (Berzelius, 1818); see -IUM.] *Chem.* One of the rarer elements, closely resembling tellurium in properties, formerly classed among the metals, but now regarded as non-metallic. Symbol Se; atomic weight 70.

Selenocentric (sĭlīnose·ntrik), *a.* 1852. [f. Gr. σελήνη moon + CENTRIC *a.*] Having relation to the centre of the moon or to the moon as a centre; as seen or estimated from the centre of the moon.

Selenodont (sĭlī·nodǫnt), *a.* and *sb.* 1883. [f. Gr. σελήνη moon + ὀδούς, ὀδοντ- tooth; for the second element cf. *mastodont* = *mastodon.*] **A.** *adj.* Of molar teeth: Having crescentic ridges on the crowns. Also, having such teeth, of or pertaining to the *Selenodonta.* **B.** *sb.* A s. animal.

Selenograph (sĭlī·nograf). 1868. [f. as prec. + -GRAPH.] A map or chart of a part of the surface of the moon.

Selenography (selinǫ·grăfi). 1650. [– mod.L. *selenographia* (Bacon), f. Gr. σελήνη moon; see -GRAPHY.] **a.** A description of the moon's surface. **b.** The description and delineation of the moon's surface; the descriptive science relating to the moon, 'lunar geography' 1784. Hence **Seleno·grapher,** one engaged in s. **Selenographic, -al** (sĭlīnogræ·fik, -ăl) *adjs.* belonging to s. **Seleno·graphist,** a selenographer.

Selenology (selinǫ·lŏdʒi). 1821. [f. Gr. σελήνη moon + -LOGY.] The science relating to the moon; chiefly, the science of the movements and astronomical relations of the moon (or, occas., the science of the formation of the moon's crust, lunar 'geology'), in contradistinction to *selenography.* Hence **Selenolo·gical** *a.*, **-ly,** *adv.* **Seleno·logist,** one versed in s.

Selenotropic (sĭlīnotrǫ·pik), *a.* 1883. [f. Gr. σελήνη moon + -τροπος turning + -IC, after Fr. *sélénétropique* (sic: Ch. Musset, 1883).] *Bot.* Bending or turning under the influence of moonlight. So **Seleno·tropism. Seleno·tropy.**

Self (self), *pron., a.,* and *sb. Pl.* **selves.** [OE. *self* str., *selfa* wk. = OFris. *self, selva,* OS. *self, selbo,* OHG. *selb, selbo* (Du. *zelv, -zelve, -zelfde,* G. *selb-, selbe*), ON. (only str.) *sjálfr,* Goth. (only weak) *silba* :– Gmc. **selba-*, **selbon-*, of unkn. origin.] **A.** *pron.* and *pronominal adj.* In the sense of the Latin *ipse.* In concord with a sb. or pron., to indicate emphatically that the reference is to the person or thing mentioned and not, or not merely, to some other. **1.** With sb. *Obs.* exc. *arch.*; superseded by the use of the 'emphatic pronouns', *himself, herself,* etc., or, after a def. art. or demonstrative, by (*the, this, that*) *very.* †**2.** With pers. pron. in the nominative (*rare* after OE.) –1633. **3.** Following a pron. in oblique case. *Obs.* exc. in HIMSELF, HERSELF, THEMSELVES. OE. †**b.** Used in 16–17th c. for: Own, peculiar –1654. †**4.** Used *absol.* as independent pron. (= he himself, I myself, etc.) –1616. **5.** In commercial use (hence *joc.* or *colloq.*) substituted for *myself,* or occas. for *himself* 1758.

1. Thys is the thing selfe that is in debate 1532. I confess to a satisfaction in the s. act of preaching LOWELL. **2.** S. did I see a swain not long ago P. FLETCHER. **3. b.** *Macb.* v. viii. 70. They Gormandize at their selfe pleasures 1632. **5.** I am, dear Sirs, for s. and partners, Yours most faithfully, Samuel Jackson THACKERAY. S. and friend took train..for Leatherhead 1863.

B. *adj.* **I.** = SAME (and in derived senses). †**1.** = SAME *a.* I. 1–3. –1632. **2.** Of a colour: The same throughout, uniform. Often prefixed to adjs. denoting colour (sometimes hyphened), as *s.-black, s. russet.* 1601. **b.** Of a carnation: Self-coloured 1852. **3.** Of whisky: Not blended 1904.

1. Two gentlemen, subiect to the selfe and same lawes 1606. I neuer saw any of that selfe Nation, to begge bread 1632. Phr. †*One s.*, one and the same. **2.** A peece of selfe russet cloth HOLLAND. **b.** A new variety of s. carnation 1902.

II. Senses related to the pronominal use. **1. a.** Of a portion of an instrument: Of one piece with the instrument itself 1888. **b.** Of a trimming: Of the same material as the garment itself 1904. **2.** Of a bow: Made all of one piece 1801. †**3.** *Mining.* Of a rock, etc.: Detached, of material different from its surroundings –1855.

C. *sb.* **I.** From the pronoun. **1.** (The pronominal notion expressed subst.) **a.** Preceded by a possessive pron., with which it forms a comb. serving as a reflexive or an emphatic personal pronoun. Often qualified by an adj., as *my own s., your dear s., our two selves,* etc. ME. **b.** Preceded by a sb. in the possessive = the sb. + *himself, herself, itself,* etc. ME. **2.** *transf.* in various uses, *esp.* a person whom one loves as oneself or who is a counterpart of oneself (*obs.* exc. in *other s., second s.*) 1605. **3.** Chiefly *Philos.* That which in a person is really and intrinsically *he* (in contradistinction to what is adventitious); the ego (often identified with the soul or mind as opp. to the body); a permanent subject of successive and varying states of consciousness 1674. **4. a.** What one is at a particular time or in a particular aspect or relation; one's nature, character, or (sometimes) physical constitution or appearance, considered as different at different times. Chiefly with qualifying adj., (*one's*) *old, former,* etc. *s.* 1697. **b.** An assemblage of characteristics and dispositions which may be conceived as constituting one of various conflicting personalities within a human being 1595. **5.** One's personal welfare and interests as an object of concern; chiefly in bad sense, self-interested motives, selfishness 1680.

1. a. Their hideous wives, their horrid selves and dresses BYRON. **b.** She..Delia's s...surpass'd MILT. **2.** My dear heart and s. and son Charles H. WALPOLE. **3.** A secret s. I had enclos'd within TRAHERNE. I, one and the same s., perceive both colours and sounds BERKELEY. **4. a.** In vain he burns..And in himself his former s. requires DRYDEN. **b.** *Better s.*, the better part of one's nature. **5.** S. is their god and Selfishness their religion 1906.

II. From the adj. **1.** A 'self-coloured' flower, esp. a carnation 1852. **2.** A self bow 1856.

D. -self in compound pronouns. **1.** *To be —self.* **a.** *colloq.* To be in (one's) normal condition of body or mind; to be in (its) accustomed state 1849. **b.** To act according to one's true character, without hypocrisy or constraint 1864. **2.** The refl. pron. assumes in certain contexts the sense: The normal condition (of the person or thing) 1450. **3.** *By —self*: alone, without society; unaided; separately OE.

1. *To feel like —self.* **b.** For..a girl to dare to be herself 1896. **2.** Phr. *Out of —self* (now *rare*), *beside —self*, out of (one's) mind or senses, deranged. **3.** Mr. C. dines all by himself at present, I merely looking on MRS. CARLYLE.

Self, *v.* 1905. [f. prec.] *pass.* To be fertilized by self-pollination.

Self-, the word SELF used as a prefix [OE. *self-, sylf-*] with refl. meaning = 'oneself', 'itself'.

The basis of compounds falling under headings 1 and 2 (below) is normally a reflexive verbal phrase; thus, from 'to accuse oneself', is formed a series of formally related words, *self-accusation, -accusatory, -accusing, -accused,* any of which may arise independently of the others.

1. Compounds in which *self-* is in the objective relation to the second element: **a.** With nouns of action; as *self-abandonment,* abandonment by oneself of oneself, one's power, rights, desires, or the like; *-accusation,, -advancement, -criticism,* and many more. **b.** With vbl. sbs.; as *s.-abominating* = self-abomination, *-advertising, -schooling,* etc. **c.** With agent-nouns; as *s.-advertiser,* one who advertises himself, etc. **d.** With nouns of state or condition; as *s.-awareness*, the condition of being aware of oneself; *-mastery*, mastery of oneself, self-command; *-reverence*, etc. **e.** With adjs.; as *s.-adaptive*, capable of adapting oneself or itself, (hence, by extension) pertaining to, involving, or characterized by self-adaptation; *-communicative*, *-laudatory*, etc. **f.** With ppl. adjs. in *-ing*; as *s.-abandoning*, abandoning oneself, (hence, by extension), pertaining to, involving, or characterized by self-abandonment; *-betraying*, *-mastering*, etc. **g.** With †vbs. and pres. pples.; as *s.-blind*, *-vaunting*, etc. **h.** With advs. related to actual or possible formations in e and f (above); as *s.-consolingly*, *-vindicatingly*, etc.

2. Compounds with pa. pples. and ppl. adjs. in which *self-* denotes the agent or what is conceived as the agent; = by oneself or itself, by one's own (unaided) efforts or action, without help from others.

Such compounds may qualify the designation of: (*a*) a person or thing that is the subject and object of the action, as *s.-appointed censors* = censors appointed by themselves; (*b*) a thing that is operated upon, performed, produced, etc. by oneself, as *s.-appointed duties* = duties appointed by the person himself; (*c*) a thing conceived as operated upon by itself, as *s.-arched rocks* = rocks formed into arches of themselves without human or mechanical agency; *s.-balanced* = balanced without external support. **b.** Rarely, with adjs. in *-able*; as *s.-impairable* = liable to be impaired by one's own action.

3. Compounds in which *self-* is adverbial: **a.** With sbs., adjs., vbs., advs. = for, in, into, on or upon, to or towards, with oneself or itself, the prep. to be supplied being that required in the construction of the word which forms the second element; e.g. *s.-absorbed*, *-absorption* = absorbed, absorption in oneself; *s.-acquaintance* = acquaintance with oneself; *s.-addressed* = addressed to oneself; *s.-compassion* = compassion for oneself. **b.** With adjs. and related sbs., vbs., pples. = of or in oneself or itself, of or in one's or its own nature or power; e.g. *s.-apparent* = apparent of itself. **c.** With pples. = from or out of oneself or itself (as a source or point of origin); e.g. *s.-arising*, arising from or out of oneself.

4. In techn. use, forming compounds to designate machines, appliances, or processes, by or in which certain operations are performed without human or animal agency or special manipulation or adjustment for the purpose; usu. = automatic, automatically; as in *s.-adjusting*, *-feeding*, *-starter*, *-winding*, etc.

5. Compounds in which *self-* is in the adjective relation: †**a.** = relating to oneself, one's own, personal, individual, private, intimate; as *s.-affairs*, *-disgrace*, etc. **b.** = inherent in, depending upon, or proceeding from oneself (itself), one's nature, etc.; belonging to oneself (itself) as an independent creature; in 17th c. often *spec.*, dependent or relying upon one's own efforts or merits apart from the grace of God; as *s.-ability*, *-excellency*, *-insufficiency*, etc. *Obs.* or *arch.* **c.** = having an independent existence, position, or authority; †pristine, original; as *s.-agency*, *-sovereignty*, etc. **d.** = having self as the object or aim; as *s.-desire*, *-profit*, etc. **e.** = caused or brought about by oneself; e.g. *s.-captivity*, *-portrait*.

Self-aba·sement. 1656. [SELF- 1 a.] Humiliation of oneself. So **Self-aba·sed** *ppl. a.* **Self-aba·sing** *ppl. a.*

Self-abu·se. 1605. [SELF- 1 a.] †**1.** Self-deception. SHAKS. **2.** Abuse or revilement of oneself 1795. **3.** Self-pollution 1728.

Self-a·cting, *ppl. a.* 1740. [SELF- 3 b, 4.] **1.** Acting independently, without external impulse or influence. Also applied to motion characterized by such action. **2.** *Mech.* Acting automatically without the manipulation (or mechanism) which would otherwise be required. Also said of the operation. 1824. So **Self-a·ction,** action uninfluenced by external impulse. †**Self-a·ctive** *a.* acting of itself without external impulse 1642–92. **Self-a·ctor** *Mech.*, a s. mule in a spinning-machine.

Self-applau·se. 1678. [SELF- 1 a.] Approval or commendation of oneself. So **Self-applau·ding** *ppl. a.* given to s. 1654.

Self-asse·rtion. 1806. [SELF- 1 a.] The action of asserting one's individuality, or insisting upon one's claims or supremacy. So **Self-asse·rting, -asse·rtive** *adjs.* full of or characterized by s.

Self-assu·rance. 1594. [SELF- 1 d.] Feeling of security as to oneself; self-confidence. So **Self-assu·red** *a.* self-confident.

Self-bego·tten, *pa. pple.* and *ppl. a.* 1671. [SELF- 2.] Begotten of oneself by one's own power.

Self-bi·nder. orig. *U.S.* 1882. [SELF- 4.] A reaping-machine which has an apparatus for binding the corn into sheaves automatically. So **Self-bi·nding** *ppl. a.*

Self-born, *ppl. a.* 1587. [SELF- 3 b.] Born of or originating from oneself or itself. From himself the Phœnix only springs: S. DRYDEN.

Self-ce·ntred, *ppl. a.* 1676. [SELF 3 a.] **1.** Fixed or stationary, as a centre round which other things move. **2.** Of persons, their activities, etc.: Centred in oneself (or itself); independent of external action or influence 1764. **b.** Engrossed in self, selfishly independent 1783.

1. There hangs the ball of Earth and Water mixt, Self-Center'd, and unmov'd DRYDEN. **2. b.** That s. satisfaction which makes life tolerable 1884. So **Self-ce·ntring** *ppl. a.* †(*a*) = prec. 1; (*b*) *Mech.* applied to chucks, etc., which hold the object in a central position without the necessity of tentative adjustments.

Self-colle·cted, *ppl. a.* 1711. [SELF- 3 a.] = COLLECTED 2.

Self-co·lour. 1665. [SELF B. 2.] **1.** One uniform colour; orig. used of flowers. Also, a colour belonging to the same series as another. **2.** The natural colour 1851. So **Self-co·loured** *ppl. a.* of one colour; of the natural colour.

Self-comma·nd. 1699. [SELF- 1 a.] Control of one's actions or feelings, self-control.

Self-compla·cence, -co·mplaisance. 1748. [SELF- 3 a.] = COMPLACENCE 1. So **Self-compla·cency** 1687. **Self-compla·cent** *a.* = COMPLACENT *a.* 2. 1763.

Self-concei·t. 1588. [SELF- 1 a.] One's opinion or estimate of oneself; *esp.* exaggerated opinion of oneself, one's talents, attainments, etc. So **Self-concei·ted** *ppl. a.* (now somewhat *rare*) full of or marked by s.; **-ly** *adv.*, **-ness.**

Self-co·nfidence. 1653. [SELF- 3 a.] Confidence in oneself; often, arrogant or impudent reliance on one's own powers.

Self-confidence is the first requisite to great undertakings JOHNSON. So **Self-co·nfident** *a.*, **-ly** *adv.*

Self-congratula·tion. 1712. [SELF- 1 a.] Congratulation of oneself.

Self-co·njugate, *a.* 1866. [SELF- 3 a.] *Math.* Applied to a figure each side of which is, relatively to some conic, the polar of the opposite vertex.

Self-co·nscious, *a.* 1697. [SELF- 1 e.] **1.** *Philos.* Having consciousness of one's identity, actions, sensations, etc.; reflectively aware of one's actions. Also said of action, thought, etc. †**b.** Of which one is conscious in oneself –1824. **2.** Marked by undue or morbid preoccupation with one's own personality; so far self-centred as to suppose one is the object of observation by others 1837.

1. b. My s. Worth DRYDEN. **2.** S., conscious of a world looking on CARLYLE. Hence **Self-co·nsciously** *adv.*

Self-co·nsciousness. 1690. [SELF- 1 d.] **1.** *Philos.* Consciousness of one's own identity, acts, thoughts, etc. **2.** Internal knowledge or conviction *of* a thing 1751. **3.** The condition of being self-conscious (sense 2) 1851.

Self-co·nsequence. 1778. [SELF- 5 a.] Self-importance. So **Self-co·nsequent** *a.*

Self-consi·stency. 1692. [SELF- 3 a.] The quality of being self-consistent. So **Self-consi·stent** *a.* marked by consistency; constantly adhering to the same principles of thought or action.

Self-contai·ned, *ppl. a.* 1591. [SELF- 3 a.] Having all that one (it) needs in oneself (itself); independent of external means or relations; esp. (of persons) not dependent upon, or communicating oneself to, others; reserved or restrained in behaviour. **b.** Of a house, etc.: Of which the apartments and approaches are restricted to the use of one household 1827. **c.** Of a machine or device: Complete in itself 1828.

Se:lf-contradi·ction. 1658. [SELF- 1 a.] The act or fact of contradicting oneself (or itself); also, a statement which contains elements that contradict one another. So **Self-contradi·cting** *ppl. a.* 1655. **Self-contradi·ctory** *a.*

Self-contro·l. 1711. [SELF- 1 a.] Control of oneself, one's desires, etc.

Self-convi·cted, *ppl. a.* 1729. [SELF- 2.] Convicted by one's own words or action. So **Self-convi·ction** 1640.

Self-crea·ted, *ppl. a.* 1677. [SELF- 2.] Created, brought into existence, or constituted by oneself.

Self-cu·lture. 1847. [SELF- 1 a.] The cultivation or development by one's own efforts of one's mind, faculties, manners, etc.

Self-dece·ption. 1677. [SELF- 1 a.] The action or fact of deceiving oneself; self-delusion. So **Self-decei·t. Self-decei·ved** *ppl. a.* 1671.

Self-defe·nce. 1651. [SELF- 1 a.] The act of defending oneself, one's rights or position.

Homicide in s., or *se defendendo*, upon a sudden affray, is..excusable rather than justifiable, by the English law BLACKSTONE. Phr. *The* (*noble, manly*) *art of self-defence*, †(*a*) fencing: (*b*) pugilism, boxing. So **Self-defe·nsive** *a.* of, pertaining to, or involving the principle of, s.

Self-deli·very. 1864. [SELF- 4.] Automatic delivery: **a.** by a reaping-machine of the corn in swaths or sheaves; **b.** of a pattern from the mould in founding.

Self-delu·sion. 1634. [SELF- 1 a.] The act of deluding oneself; an instance of this. So **Self-delu·ded** *ppl. a.*

Self-deni·al. 1642. [SELF- 1 a.] Abnegation of oneself; sacrifice of one's personal desires.

Self-deny·ing, *ppl. a.* 1632. [SELF- 1 e.] That denies himself; characterized by or involving self-denial.

Self-denying ordinance (Eng. Hist.), 'an Ordinance appointing, That no Member of either House, during the Time of this War, shall have or execute any Office or Command, Military or Civil' (Jrnl. Ho. Commons, Dec. 11, 1644); also *transf.* (*colloq.*) applied to any course of action by which a person deprives himself of some advantage or benefit. Hence **Self-deny·ingly** *adv.*

Self-depe·ndent, *a.* 1677. [SELF- 3 a.] Possessing or characterized by self-dependence. So **Self-depe·ndence, -depe·ndency,** dependence entirely upon oneself, one's own efforts, etc. **Self-depe·ndently** *adv.* **Self-depe·nding** *ppl. a.*

Self-destroy·er. 1654. [SELF- 1 c.] One who is the cause of his own destruction 1657. **b.** A suicide 1654. So **Self-destroy·ing** *vbl. sb.* and *ppl. a.* 1612.

Self-destru·ction. 1586. [SELF- 1 a.] Destruction of oneself, one's life; *esp.* self-murder, suicide. So **Self-destru·ctive** *a.* 1654.

Se:lf-determina·tion. 1683. [SELF- 1 a.] Determination of one's mind or will by oneself or itself. **b.** The independent determination by a state or community of its own polity 1918. So **Self-dete·rmining** *ppl. a.* determining one's own acts; possessing s. 1662.

Self-distru·st. 1789. [SELF- 1 d.] Distrust of oneself, one's powers, etc.

Selfdom (se·lfdəm). *rare.* 1863. [f. SELF *sb.* + -DOM.] The realm or domain of self.

Self-effa·cement. 1866. [SELF- 1 a.] The keeping of oneself out of sight or in the background.

Self-ele·cted, *a.* 1818. [SELF- 2.] Elected by oneself, (of a body) elected by its members; *transf.* of an office to which a person has appointed himself. So **Self-ele·ction,** election of oneself by oneself 1790. **Self-ele·ctive** *a.* having the right of electing oneself 1787.

Self-estee·m. 1657. [SELF- 1 a.] Favourable appreciation or opinion of oneself. **b.** *Phrenology.* One of the mental faculties to which a 'bump' is assigned; the 'bump' itself 1815.

Self-e·vidence. 1682. [SELF- 1 d.] **a.** Evidence of its own truth. **b.** The quality or condition of being self-evident.

Self-e·vident, *a.* 1690. [SELF- 3 b.] Evident of itself without proof; axiomatic. Hence **Self-e·vidently** *adv.*

Se:lf-examina·tion. 1647. [SELF- 1 a.] Examination of oneself with regard to one's conduct, motives, etc., esp. as a religious duty.

Self-exci·ting, *ppl. a.* 1884. [SELF- 1 f.] *Electr.* Designating a dynamo-electric machine that excites its own field. So **Self-excita·tion.**

Self-exi·stence. 1697. [SELF- 5 c.] Existence of a being by virtue of his inherent nature independently of any other being.

Self-exi·stent, *a.* 1701. [SELF- 3 b.] **1.** Having the property of self-existence; existing of or by oneself (itself). **2.** Having a primary or independent existence 1779.

Self-explai·ned, *ppl. a.* 1725. [SELF- 2.] Explained by itself, understood without specific explanation. So **Self-explai·ning** *ppl. a.*, **-expla·natory** *a.*

Self-expre·ssion. 1892. [SELF- 1.] The expression (often esp. artistic or literary) of one's personality.

Self-fee·ling. 1879. [SELF- 1 d, 5 d. Cf. G. *selbstgefühl.*] **1.** Feeling centred in oneself. **2.** The sense of one's individual identity 1908.

Self-fe·rtile, *a.* 1859. [SELF- 3 b.] *Bot.* Of a flower: Having the property of fertilizing itself by the action of its pollen on its pistil. Of a plant: Fertilized by the pollen of its own flowers alone. Also applied to hermaphrodite animals. So **Self-fertiliza·tion. Self-fe·rtilized** *ppl. a.*

Self-forge·tful, *a.* 1864. [SELF- 1 e.] Forgetful of one's self or one's own individuality; having or characterized by no thought of self. So **Self-forge·tfulness** 1832.

Self-glo·rious, *a.* 1599. [SELF- 3 a.] Marked by vain-glory or boasting.

Self-go·vernment. 1734. [SELF- 1 a.] **1.** Self-control. Now *rare.* **2.** Administration by a people or state of its own affairs without external direction or interference 1798.

2. The residuary rights are reserved to their (the American States) own s. JEFFERSON. So **Self-go·verned** *ppl. a.* acting or living according to one's own desires uninfluenced by others; marked by self-control; having s.

Self-heal (se·lfhīl). late ME. [f. SELF- 1 + HEAL *v.*] Any of various plants believed to have great healing properties, esp. *Prunella vulgaris* (Common S.), *Sanicula europæa*, and formerly *Pimpinella saxifraga.*

Self-he·lp. 1831. [SELF- 1 a.] **1.** The action or faculty of providing for oneself without assistance from others. **2.** *Law.* Redress of one's wrongs by one's own action, without recourse to legal process 1875.

Selfhood (se·lfhud). 1649. [f. SELF *sb.* + -HOOD; orig. repr. G. *selbheit.*] **1.** The quality by virtue of which one is oneself; personal individuality; ipseity; that which constitutes one's own self or individuality; (one's) self. **2.** Oneself as the centre of one's life and action; hence, self-centredness; devotion to self, selfish life or conduct 1649. **3.** One's personality, one's personal interests or character 1854.

Self-ide·ntity. 1866. [SELF- 3 a.] The identity of a thing with itself. So **Self-ide·ntical** *a.*

Self-impo·rtance. 1775. [SELF- 5 a.] The sense of one's own importance; bearing or conduct arising from this. So **Self-impo·rtant** *a.* marked by self-importance, having an exaggerated opinion of one's own importance.

Self-impo·sed, *ppl. a.* 1781. [SELF- 2.] Imposed on one by oneself.

Self-indu·ction. 1873. [SELF- 3 b.] *Electr.* The production of an induced current in a circuit by means of a variation in the current of that circuit. So **Self-indu·ctance,** in same sense; also, the coefficient of s. **Self-indu·ced, -indu·ctive** (1834) *adjs.* produced by s.

Self-indu·lgence. 1753. [SELF- 1 a.] Indulgence of one's desires. So **Self-indu·lgent** *a.*

Self-infli·cted, *ppl. a.* 1784. [SELF- 2.] Inflicted by oneself or one's own hand.

Self-i·nterest. 1649. [SELF- 5 a.] **1.** One's personal profit, benefit, or advantage. Now *rare* or *Obs.* 1658. †**b.** A private or personal end –1867. **2.** Regard to, or pursuit of, one's own advantage or welfare, *esp.* to the exclusion of regard for others 1649. Hence **Self-i·nterested** *a.* actuated solely by regard for one's personal advantage or welfare.

Self-invo·lved, *ppl. a.* 1842. [SELF- 3 a.] Wrapped up in oneself or one's own thoughts. So **Self-involu·tion** 1817.

Selfish (se·lfiʃ), *a.* 1640. [f. SELF *sb.* + -ISH[1] 2.] Devoted to or concerned with one's own advantage or welfare to the exclusion of regard for others. **b.** Used (by adversaries) as a designation of those ethical theories which regard self-love as the real motive of all human action 1847.

Want makes almost every man s. JOHNSON. 'Well, but what's to become of me?' urged the s. man DICKENS. **b.** The Epicurean, or S., System 1868. Hence **Se·lfish-ly** *adv.*, **-ness.**

Selfism (se·lfiz'm). 1791. [f. SELF *sb.* + -ISM.] Devotion to or concentration upon one's own interests; self-centredness. Also, the 'selfish theory' of morals.

Selfist (se·lfist). *rare.* 1649. [f. SELF *sb.* + -IST.] A self-centred or selfish person.

Self-ju·dgement. 1745. [SELF- 1 a.] Judgement passed upon oneself.

Self-ju·stified, *ppl. a.* 1897. [SELF- 2.] *Printing.* Arranged by means of automatic justifying mechanism. So **Self-ju·stifying** *ppl. a.* 1895.

Self-know·ing, *ppl. a.* 1667. [SELF- 1 f, 3 b.] **1.** Knowing oneself; having self-knowledge. **2.** Knowing of oneself, without help from another 1828.

Self-know·ledge. 1613. [SELF- 1 a, d.] Knowledge of oneself, one's character, capabilities, etc.

Selfless (se·lf,lės), *a.* 1825. [f. SELF *sb.* + -LESS.] Having no regard for or thought of self; not self-centred; unselfish. Hence **Se·lfless-ly** *adv.*, **-ness.**

Se·lf-life. 1613. **1.** [SELF- 5 c.] = SELF-EXISTENCE. **2.** [SELF- 5 d.] Life lived for oneself; life devoted to selfish ends 1848.

Self-lo·ve. 1563. [SELF- 1 a, d.] **1.** Love of oneself; in early use most freq. = AMOUR-PROPRE; later, usu. = regard for one's interests or well-being; chiefly *opprobrious*, self-centredness, selfishness. **2.** *Philos.* Regard for one's own well-being or happiness, considered as a natural and proper relation of a man to himself 1683.

2. That..sort of Benevolence which we call s. 1688.

Self-made, *ppl. a.* 1615. [SELF- 2.] Made by oneself, one's own action or efforts; of one's own making.

S. man, one who has risen from obscurity or poverty by his own exertions (orig. *U.S.*)

Se·lf-mate, *sb.* 1888. [SELF- 1 a.] *Chess.* Checkmate produced by the side that is mated. Also as *vb.*

Self-mo·tion. 1619. [SELF- 5 c.] Motion produced by inherent power apart from external impulse; voluntary or spontaneous motion.

Self-mu·rder. 1563. [SELF- 1 a.] The taking of one's own life; self-destruction; suicide. So **Self-mu·rderer.**

Se·lfness. 1586. [f. SELF *sb.* + -NESS.] **1.** Self-centredness; egoism; selfishness; †occas. *pl.* selfish acts or manifestations. Also, due regard for oneself (*rare*). †**2.** Individuality, essence (*rare*) –1651.

Self-opi·nion. Now *rare.* 1579. [SELF- 1 d.] High opinion of oneself, self-esteem; esp. self-conceit; obstinacy in one's own opinion. So **Self-opi·nioned** *ppl. a.* 1624.

Self-opi·nionated, *ppl. a.* 1671. [f. prec.] **1.** Having an exaggerated opinion of oneself; self-conceited. **2.** Obstinate in one's opinion 1770.

Self-pi·ty. 1621. [SELF- 1 d.] Pity or tender feeling for oneself.

Self-pollu·tion. 1626. [SELF- 1 a.] Masturbation, self-abuse.

Self-po·rtrait. 1840. [After G. *selbstbildnis.*] A portrait made by a person of himself.

Self-posse·ssed, *ppl. a.* 1838. [Formed after next; see SELF- 2.] Characterized by self-possession.

Self-posse·ssion. 1745. [SELF- 1 d.] Command of one's faculties or feelings; self-command, composure.

Self-prai·se. 1549. [SELF- 1 a.] Praise or commendation of oneself.

S. is no commendation 1826.

Se:lf-preserva·tion. 1614. [SELF- 1 a.] The preservation of one's existence; *esp.* applied to the natural law or instinct which impels living creatures to take measures to prolong life and avoid injury.

S. is the first of laws DRYDEN.

Self-pri·de. 1586. [SELF- 3 a.] Pride in oneself, one's achievements, one's position; personal pride.

Self-ra·ising, *ppl. a.* 1854. [SELF- 3 b.] Applied to a kind of flour which causes dough or paste to rise without the addition of baking-powder, etc.

Se:lf-realiza·tion. 1876. [SELF- 1 a.] The fulfilment by one's own efforts of the possibilities of development of the self.

Self-rega·rd. 1595. [SELF- 1 a, 3 a.] **1.** Regard of or consideration for onself. **2.** = SELF-RESPECT 2. 1811.

Self-reli·ance. 1837. [SELF- 3 a.] Reliance upon oneself, one's own powers, etc. So **Self-reli·ant** *a.* **Self-rely·ing** *ppl. a.*

Self-repre·ssion. 1870. [SELF- 1 a.] Repression of oneself, one's desires or opinions.

Self-reproa·ch. 1779. [SELF- 1 a.] Reproach of oneself.

Self-repu·gnance. Now *rare.* 1649. [SELF- 1 d.] Self-contradictory quality or character. So **Self-repu·gnant** *a.* self-contradictory.

Self-respe·ct. 1613. [In 1, SELF- 5 a, d; in 2, SELF 1 d.] †**1.** A private, personal, or selfish end. (Chiefly *pl.*) –1675. **2.** Proper regard for the dignity of one's person or one's position 1795.

Self-restrai·nt. 1775. [SELF- 1 a.] Restraint imposed by oneself upon one's actions, etc. So **Self-restrai·ned** *a.* marked by or involving self-restraint 1700.

Self-ri·ght, *v.* 1881. [Back-formation from SELF-RIGHTING.] *intr.* To right itself. So **Self-ri·ghter,** a self-righting boat.

Self-ri·ghteous, *a.* 1680. [SELF- 3 b.] Righteous in one's own esteem. So **Self-ri·ghteously** *adv.* **Self-ri·ghteousness,** the condition of being s. 1656.

Self-ri·ghting, *vbl. sb.* 1855. [SELF- 1 b.] Of a boat: The action of righting itself after being upset. So **Self-ri·ghting** *ppl. a.*

Self-sa·crifice. 1805. [SELF- 1 a.] Sacrifice of oneself; the giving up of one's own interests, happiness, and desires, for the sake of duty or the welfare of others. So **Self-sa·crificing** *ppl. a.*

Give unto me, made lowly wise, The spirit of S. WORDSW.

Selfsame (se·lfsēⁱm), *a.* (*sb.*) Now *literary.* late ME. [orig. two words (see SELF A. 1 b, B. 1 c, and SAME A. 4); later, written as a compound with a hyphen, now as one word.] **A.** *adj.* (The) very same, very identical. †**B.** *absol.* or *sb.* The selfsame person or thing; rarely as *sb. pl.* identical things –1701.

We were nurst upon the self-same hill MILT.

Se:lf-satisfa·ction. 1793. [Formed after next.] The condition or quality of being self-satisfied.

Self-sa·tisfied, *ppl. a.* 1734. [SELF- 3 a.] Satisfied with oneself, one's achievements, etc.; marked by self-satisfaction. So **Self-sa·tisfying** *ppl. a.* that satisfies oneself; affording self-satisfaction 1671.

The s. smirk of flash Toby Crackit DICKENS.

Self-see·ker. 1632. [Formed after next.] One who selfishly seeks his own welfare.

Self-see·king, *vbl. sb.* 1586. [SELF- 1 b.] The seeking after one's own welfare before that of others. So **Self-see·king** *ppl. a.*

Self-slau·ghter. 1602. [SELF- 1a.] = SELF-MURDER.

Self-sown, *ppl. a.* 1608. [SELF- 2.] Sown by itself without human or animal agency.

Self-sta·rter. 1887. [SELF- 4.] A mechanism for starting an internal-combustion engine without the use of a crank-handle, etc. So **Self-starting** *ppl. a.*

†**Self-substa·ntial,** *a.* *rare.* [SELF- 3 b.] Derived from one's own substance. SHAKS.

Self-suffi·ciency. 1623. [f. next (see -ENCY), rendering Gr. αὐτάρκεια.] The quality or condition of being self-sufficient; *esp.* as an attribute of God. So **Self-suffi·cience.**

Self-suffi·cient, *a.* 1589. [SELF- 3 b; in 1, tr. Gr. αὐτάρκης.] **1.** Sufficient in or for oneself (itself) without external aid or support; able to supply one's needs oneself. Not now of persons. **2.** Having excessive confidence in oneself, one's powers, etc.; characterized by overweening behaviour 1734.

1. A compleat s. Country, where there is rather a Superfluity than Defect of anything 1645. 2. A s. jackanapes 1842. So **Self-suffi·cing** *ppl. a.*

Self-sugge·stion. 1899. [SELF- 3 b.] Suggestion to oneself; the voluntary fixing in one's mind some idea in order that it may afterwards operate subconsciously or automatically. So **Self-sugge·stive** *a.* 1848.

Self-suppo·rt. 1774. [SELF- 1 a.] The act of supporting oneself (itself) without external assistance; the fact of being self-supporting. So **Self-suppo·rting** *ppl. a.*, supporting oneself (itself) without external aid, (of a physical object) not requiring the usual support, (of an enterprise) paying its way.

Self-surre·nder. 1702. [SELF- 1 a.] The surrender or giving up of oneself to an influence, emotion, or the like.

Self-taught, *ppl. a.* 1725. [SELF- 2.] Taught by oneself without direct aid from others; self-educated. **b.** Of what is learnt: Acquired by one's own unaided efforts 1774.

†**Self-vi·olence.** 1671. [SELF- 3 a.] The laying of violent hands upon oneself: a euphemism for SELF-MURDER –1787.

Self-wi·ll. [OE. *selfwill* = MLG. *sulfwille*, OHG. *selbwillo* (G. *selbstwille*), ON. *sjálfvili*; see SELF-, WILL *sb.*] †**1.** One's own will or desire –1456. **2.** Wilful or obstinate persistence in following one's own desires or opinions. late ME. So †**Self-wi·lly** *a.*, self-willed –1631.

Self-willed, *a.* 1470. [f. prec. + -ED².] Wilful or obstinate in the pursuit of one's own desires or opinions; characterized by self-will. Hence **Sèlfwi·lledness.**

Self-wise, *a.* 1561. [SELF- 3 b.] Wise in one's own conceit, relying on one's own wisdom. So **Self-wi·sdom,** the condition of being s.

Selion (se·li̯ǫn). *Hist.* and *local.* 1450. [– AFr. *seilon* (whence AL. *selio*, etc. XII), OFr. *seillon* measure of land (mod. *sillon* furrow).] A portion of land of indeterminate area comprising a ridge or narrow strip lying between two furrows formed in dividing an open field, a 'narrow-land'.

Seljuk (se·lˌdʒuk), *a.* and *sb.* 1834. [f. Turk. *seljūq*, name of the reputed ancestor of the Seljuk dynasties.] **A.** *adj.* The distinctive epithet of certain Turkish dynasties which ruled over large parts of Asia from the 11th to the 13th c. **B.** *sb.* A member of the Seljuk tribe or dynasty 1841. So **Seljukian** (seldʒū·kiăn) *a.* (1603) and *sb.* (1638).

Sell (sel), *sb.*¹ Now *arch.* late ME. [– (O)Fr. *selle* †stool, saddle :– L. *sella* seat, chair, (later) saddle (:– **sedla*; see SADDLE).] †**1.** A seat, a low stool; a seat of dignity –1627. **2.** A saddle. late ME.

Sell (sel), *sb.*² 1838. [f. SELL *v.*] **1.** An act of betraying or giving up to justice. **2.** *slang.* A contrivance, fiction, etc., by which a person is 'sold'; a hoax, take-in. Also, something that utterly disappoints high expectations. 1853. **3.** *U.S.* **Sell-out.** An agreement or contract corruptly made by a public body, involving sacrifice of public to private interest 1890.

Sell (sel), *v.* Pa. t. and pple. **sold** (sōᵘld). [OE. *sellan* = OFris. *sella*, OS. *sellian*, OHG. *sellen*, ON. *selja* give up, sell, Goth. *saljan* offer sacrifice.] †**1.** *trans.* To give, in various senses; esp. to hand over (something, esp. food, a gift) voluntarily or in response to a demand or request; to deliver up (a person, esp. a hostage) to the keeping of another; to grant (forgiveness, etc.) –ME. **2.** To give up (a person) treacherously to his enemies; to betray (a person, cause, country, etc.) OE. **3.** To give up or hand over (something) to another person for money (or something that is reckoned as money); esp. to dispose of (merchandise, possessions, etc.) to a buyer for a price; to vend. Also, in habitual sense, of a shopkeeper, etc.: To deal in, keep for sale (a particular commodity). OE. **b.** To dispose of (one's commission in the army) by sale under the purchase system. Now *Hist.* Also *absol.* 1713. **c.** *causatively.* To promote the sale of 1709. **d.** To hand over (a person, a people) into slavery or bondage for a sum of money. In Biblical use (after Heb.) often, To hand over to the dominion of another, to enslave. OE. **4.** *absol.* and *intr.* ME. **5.** *To s.* (gerundial inf. used predic.): on sale, offered for sale. Now *rare.* ME. **6.** *intr.* in passive sense. Of a commodity: To find purchasers. *To s. for, at* = to fetch (a price). 1606. **7.** *trans.* In various fig. uses. ME. **8.** *slang.* To cheat, trick, deceive, take in 1607.

2. Brougham, it is said, grossly, has sold the Queen 1820. **3.** Yet s. your face for fiue pence and 'tis deere SHAKS. **d.** 2 *Kings* 17:17. **e.** *U.S.* To advertise or publish the merits of (a book, etc.) to encourage sales 1925. **f.** *U.S.* To give (a person) information *on* the value of something; to inspire with desire to possess something 1926. **4.** *Merch. V.* I. iii. 36. **6.** Prior's *Journey* sells still SWIFT. **7.** 2 *Hen. VI*, IV. i. 41. [They] Have..sold my Reputation for a Song FITZGERALD. Phr. *To s. one's life dear, dearly*, etc., to destroy many of one's adversaries before giving up one's life in an encounter. *To s. oneself*, to dispose of one's services for money; to enslave oneself. *To s. a match, game*, to lose it for a bribe. *To sell the pass, a pup*: see PASS *sb.*¹ II. 1 b, PUP *sb.*¹

With advs. **S. off.** *trans.* To dispose of by sale (esp. at reduced prices); to sell the whole of (one's stock, possessions, etc.). Also *absol.* **S. out. a.** *trans.* To distribute by sale. **b.** To dispose of (stocks, shares, etc.) by sale. Also *absol.* **c.** *intr.* To dispose of one's commission in the army by sale. Now *Hist.* **d.** *trans.* To dispose of the whole of (one's stock, property, etc.) by sale. Also *absol.* **S. up. a.** *trans.* To dispose of the whole of (a person's stock, goods, etc.) by sale. Also *absol.* **b.** To dispose of the whole or a portion of the goods of (an insolvent or bankrupt person) for the benefit of his creditors. Also with the goods as obj.

‖**Sella** (se·lă). 1693. [L. *sella* seat, (later) saddle.] *Anat.* A saddle-shaped portion of the sphenoid, more fully *sella equina, sphenoidalis* or *turcica.*

Sellenger's round. 1567. [*Sellenger* represents the pronunciation of the surname *St. Leger.*] An old country dance; also, the music for this.

Seller (se·ləɹ). ME. [f. SELL *v.* + -ER¹.] **1.** One who sells. **2.** A book, later, any article or type of article with a (wide, poor, etc.) sale; also, without qualification, a book, etc. that sells well 1900. Now esp. in *best-s.* (1912). **3.** *colloq.* = SELLING-*race* 1922.

Selling (se·liŋ), *vbl. sb.* ME. [f. SELL *v.* + -ING¹.] The action of SELL *v.*; an instance of this.

attrib. and *Comb.*: **s. price,** the price at which an article is sold; **s. race,** a race for horses which are to be sold after the race; so *s. handicap, plate* (hence *s. plater*).

S'elp. Also **swelp.** ME. Contr. of 'So help', in the oath 'So help me God'. Now *vulgar.*

Seltzer (se·ltzəɹ). 1741. [Alteration of G. *Selterser*, f. *Selters*, a village in Hesse-Nassau, Prussia.] (In full *s.-water.*) An effervescent mineral water obtained near Nieder-Selters, containing sodium chloride and small quantities of sodium, calcium, and magnesium carbonates. Also, an artificial mineral water of similar composition.

Seltzogene (se·ltsŏdʒīn). 1860. [– Fr. *sel(t)zogène*, f. *seltz, selz* seltzer water + *-gène* -GEN.] An apparatus for the production of artificial seltzer and other mineral and aerated waters.

Selvage, selvedge (se·lvėdʒ), *sb.* 1460. [f. SELF + EDGE, after early mod. Du. *selfegghe* (now *zelfegge*), LG. *sülfegge*; cf. synon. Du. *zelfkant* (*kant* border), *zelfeinde* (*einde* end).] **1.** The edge of a piece of woven material finished in such a manner as to prevent the ravelling out of the weft. Also, a narrow strip or list at the edge of a web of cloth, which is intended to be cut off or covered by the seam when the material is made up. **b.** *transf.* A marginal tract, border, edge 1650. **2.** *Naut.* and *Mil.* = SELVAGEE 1711. **3.** *Mining.* A thin layer of clayey or earthy matter surrounding a metalliferous vein 1757.

Selvage, selvedge (se·lvėdʒ), *v.* 1611. [f. prec.] *trans.* To form a boundary or edging to.

Selvagee (se·lvădʒī). 1750. [app. f. SELVAGE *sb.* (sense 2). Cf. -EE².] A hank or skein of rope-yarn marled together, and used as a strap to fasten round a shroud or stay, or as slings, etc.

Semantic (sĭmæ·ntik), *a.* and *sb.* 1895. [– Fr. *sémantique* – Gr. σημαντικός significant, f. σημαίνειν show, signify, f. σῆμα sign; see -IC.] **A.** *adj.* Relating to signification or meaning. **B.** *sb. pl.* = SEMASIOLOGY 1894.

Semaphore (se·măfōᵊɹ), *sb.* 1816. [– Fr. *sémaphore* (1812), irreg. f. Gr. σῆμα sign, signal + -φορος -PHORE.] An apparatus for making signals, consisting of an upright post with one or more arms moving in a vertical plane. **b.** *attrib.*, as *s. house, lamp.* Also, in recent use, applied to a special form of flag-signalling. 1821. Hence **Se·maphore** *v. trans.* and *intr.* to signal by s. **Semapho·ric, -al** *adjs.* relating to, of the nature of, a s.; **-ly** *adv.*

Semasiology (sĭmēˈsiˌǫ·lŏdʒi). 1877. [– G. *semasiologie* (1839), f. Gr. σημασία signification, f. σημαίνειν signify; see -LOGY.] That branch of philology which deals with the meanings of words and their sense-development. Hence **Semasiolo·gical** *a.*, **-ly** *adv.*, **-o·logist.**

Sematic (sĭmæ·tik), *a.* 1890. [f. Gr. σῆμα, σηματ- sign + -IC.] *Biol.* Of mimetic colours: Serving for signal or warning.

Sematography (sīmătǫ·grăfi). 1902. [f. as prec. + -GRAPHY.] The use of signs or symbols (instead of letters) in writing. So **Sematogra·phic** *a.* of or pertaining to s.

Sematology (sī-, semătǫ·lŏdʒi). 1831. [f. as prec. + -LOGY.] **1.** The doctrine of the use of 'signs' (esp. words) in relation to thought and knowledge. **2.** = SEMASIOLOGY 1880.

Semblable (se·mblăb'l), *a.* (and *sb.*). late ME. [– (O)Fr. *semblable*, f. *sembler*; see SEMBLE *v.*¹, -ABLE.] **A.** *adj.* †**1.** Like, similar. Const. *to.* –1840. †**b.** The like, such-like –1653. †**2.** Corresponding, proportional, suitable –1817. **3.** Apparent, seeming, not real. †Of treason: Presumptive, constructive (*rare*). 1627.

1. It is a wonderfull thing to see the s. Coherence of his mens spirits, and his SHAKS. **3.** What is gained..by supposing..the miracle was only s., not real? 1874.

†**B.** *sb.* **1.** *absol.* and quasi-*sb.* (occas. pl. *semblables*): Something that is like or similar –1627. **2.** With qualifying possessive: (One's) like, (one's) fellow –1607.

2. To make true dixion of him, his s. is his mirrour SHAKS. Hence †**Se·mblableness** (*rare*) –1638. **Se·mblably** *adv.*

Semblance (se·mblăns). late ME. [– (O)Fr. *semblance*, f. *sembler*; see SEMBLE *v.*¹, -ANCE. Superseded next.] **1.** The appearance or outward aspect of a person or thing. **b.** The form, likeness or image *of* a person or thing, considered in regard to another that is similar. late ME. **2.** A person's appearance or demeanour, expressive of his thoughts, feelings, etc., or feigned in order to hide them. late ME. **3.** An appearance or outward seeming *of* (something which is not actually there or of which the reality is different from its appearance) 1489. **4.** A person or thing that resembles another; an image or copy *of* 1513. **5.** The fact or quality of being like something 1576.

1. A timely-parted Ghost, Of ashy s. SHAKS. **b.** And now the lake narrowed to the s. of a tranquil river 1867. **2.** A dissembling friend with faire and false words and semblances draweth his neighbour into some dangerous inconvenience 1633. **3.** To reach down a well-bound s. of a volume LAMB. The fall of Strafford had put an end to all s. of rule 1874.

Phr. *In s.*, in seeming, in appearance (only). *To make s.*, to make an appearance or pretence.

†**Se·mblant,** *sb.* ME. [– (O)Fr. *semblant*, subst. use of the pr. pple; see next.] **1.** A person's outward aspect or appearance; esp. demeanour, look, expression –1651. **2.** Appearance, seeming, outward aspect; also an appearance or show (whether true or false) *of* some quality, etc. Also, something that exists only in appearance or pretence. –1624. **3.** A likeness or resemblance, an image or portrait (*of*) –1617.

1. A minde which could cast a carelesse s. vppon the greatest conflictes of Fortune SIDNEY.

Phr. **To make s.** [= Fr. *faire semblant*]. **a.** To have or assume a (specified) expression, look, or demeanour. **b.** To make a show, appearance, or pretence *of*; to seem likely, threaten *to do.* **c.**

With neg.: Not to let one's thoughts, feelings, etc., appear; to show no sign (*of*); not to seem (or not to seem likely) *to be* or *do* something.

Semblant (se·mblănt), *a.* 1485. [– (O)Fr. *semblant*, pr. pple. of *sembler*; see next, -ANT.] †**1.** Like, similar –1729. **2.** Seeming, counterfeit 1840.

†**Se·mble,** *v.*[1] ME. [– (O)Fr. *sembler* :– L. *similare, simulare*, f. *similis* like.] **1.** *trans.* To be like, resemble –1713. **2.** *intr.* To seem, appear –1526. **3.** *trans.* To simulate, feign; *absol.* to practise simulation –1590. **4.** To represent, picture –1706.

‖**Semble** (se·mb'l), *v.*[2] *impers.* 1817. [Fr. 3rd pers. sing. pr. ind. of *sembler* seem.] *Law.* = 'It seems'; used in judicial utterances to introduce the incidental statement of an opinion on a point which it is not necessary to decide authoritatively. Abbrev. *sem., semb.*

‖**Semée** (se·mi, Fr. səme), *a.* 1562. [– Fr. fem. of *semé*, pa. pple. of *semer* sow.] *Her.* = POWDERED *ppl. a.* 2. Also **Se·méed** *a.*

Semeiology (sīməi,ǫ·lŏdʒi). 1694. [f. *semeio-* comb. form of Gr. σημεῖον sign, f. σῆμα signal, + -LOGY.] **1.** Sign language. **2.** The branch of medical science which is concerned with symptoms 1839. Hence **Semeiolo·gic, -al** *adjs.* pertaining to s. **Semeio·logist,** one skilled in sign-language.

Semeiotic (sīməi,ǫ·tik), *a.* 1625. [– Gr. σημειωτικός significant; cf. prec., -OTIC.] Relating to symptoms. So **Semeio·tical** *a.* 1588.

Semeiotics (sīməi,ǫ·tiks). 1670. [f. as prec.; see -IC 2.] The branch of medical science relating to the interpretation of symptoms.

Semen (sī·men). late ME. [– L. *semen*, f. base of *serere* Sow *v.*] The impregnating fluid of male animals; the seed or sperm.

Semester (sǐme·stəɹ). 1827. [– G. *semester* – mod. L. *semestris* (XVI in academic use), – L. *semestris* of six months, f. *se-*, comb. form of *sex* SIX + *mensis* MONTH.] A period or term of six months, esp. in German universities and some U.S. colleges, the college half-year. So **Seme·strial, seme·stral** *a.* half-yearly; taking place every six months; lasting for six months, (of persons) holding office for six months; exercising office every six months.

Semi (se·mi). *Sc.* 1661. [app. short for *semi bejanus* (see BEJAN).] In some Scottish universities, a student in his second year; also called *s.-bachelor, s.-bejan.*

Semi- (se·mi), *prefix.* [repr. L. *semi-* (partly through Fr., It., etc. *semi-*), corresp. to Gr. ἡμι-, Skr. *sāmi*, and OS. *sām-*, OHG. *sāmi-*, OE. *sām-* (see SAND-BLIND).] = HALF-; cf. DEMI-, HEMI-.

I. In general use. **1.** Compounded with adjs. and pples., with the meaning 'half, partly, partially, to some extent'; as **s.-animate, -animous,** half-alive; **-attached,** partially or loosely attached; **-divine,** half-divine; that is a demigod; **-feral,** half-wild; **-formed,** half-formed; **-nude,** half-naked; **-occasional,** *U.S.*, occurring once in a while; **-opaque,** partly opaque; only partially transparent; **-perfect** (*rare*), imperfect, incomplete; **-skilled;** etc. **b.** Compounded with a sb. to form an adj. phrase, as **s.-state,** etc. **2.** Compounded with sbs.: **a.** with nouns of action or condition, as **s.-allegiance,** partial, imperfect, or incomplete allegiance; **-opacity,** the condition or quality of being s.-opaque; **b.** with descriptive sbs., as **s.-acquaintance,** one with whom one is partially acquainted; **-barbarian,** one who is half-barbarian; **-deity, -god,** a demigod; **-savage** = *s.-barbarian.* **3.** Compounded with vbs., as **s.-castrate,** to castrate partially; **-flex,** to bend into a position half-way between that of extension and that of complete flexure. **4.** With advs., as **s.-consciously,** half-consciously; **-occasionally** *U.S.*, every now and then.

II. In special and technical use. **1. a.** With designations of quantity, extent of space or time and the like, as *s.-arc, -century*, etc. **b.** With adjs., advbs., and sbs. expressing periodical recurrence or duration, *semi-* denotes that the period is halved (after SEMI-ANNUAL); **s.-centennial** *a.*, of or pertaining to a period of 50 years; **-daily** *a.* and *adv.*, (occurring) twice daily; **-horal** *a.*, half-hourly; **-mensual** *a.*, recurring twice a month; **-millenary** *a.*, lasting 500 years; **-monthly** *a.* and *adv.*, (occurring, issued, etc.) twice a month; also *sb.* a fortnightly periodical; so **-weekly.** **c.** *Mus.* Designating a note, etc. of half the length, as SEMIBREVE, SEMIQUAVER. **d.** *Astr.* †**s.-quadrate,** †**-quartile, -quintile, -sextile,** denoting aspects of planets when they are 45°, 36°, 30°, respectively, distant from one another; **-square** = *s.-quadrate.*

2. a. Designating a (geometrical) form derived from another by bisection (usu.) in a vertical or longitudinal direction, as *s.-canal, -cone, -cylinder, -dome, -ellipse, -globe, -hexagon; -hexagonal, -oval, -ovate, -rotund* adjs.; *-spheroid* adj., etc. **b.** *Math.* Designating a bisected line, arc, area, segment, etc., or the half of a definite quantity, as *s.-angle, -circumference, -diameter, -segment*, etc.; (in conic sections) *-ordinate, -parameter, -transverse*; also, **s.-axis,** the half of the axis of an ellipse, etc.; **-difference,** half the difference between two quantities; **-infinite** *a.*, limited in one direction, and extending to infinity in the other; **-quadrantally** *adv.*, from 0° to 45°; **-sum,** half the sum of two or more quantities; **-tangent,** the tangent of half an arc. **c.** *Nat. Hist.* With adjs. and sbs. descriptive of shape in the contour or marking of natural objects; **s.-annular,** of the form of a half-ring; **-collar, -coronet, -fascia, -ring,** a band, etc., roughly semicircular or extending half-way round a part or an organ; **-coronated** *a.*, having a semicircle of spikes, bristles, etc.; **-floret,** a floret having a ligulate corolla, as in the dandelion. **d.** *Nat. Hist.* Denoting that a part has a certain form or character (*a*) for half the extent, or along half the length, etc. of an organ, 'half-way', as *s.-adherent, -bifid, -erect*, etc.; (*b*) on one side only, or so as to exhibit the half of a particular figure, as *s.-cordate(d, -lanceolate, -terete*, etc. **e.** In *Building*, designating structural forms of half the full width, breadth, or girth, resulting from (usu.) vertical or longitudinal bisection, as *s.-arch, -column, -shaft*, etc.; **s.-beam** = CANTILEVER 2; **-engaged** *a.*, (of a column) attached to a wall so that half its diameter projects; etc. **f.** *Cryst.* **s.-prismated,** applied to a crystal in which 'only half of the edges on the common basis are obliterated by lateral planes'; etc. **g.** *Her.* = DEMI- B. 1; as *s.-chevron*, etc. **h.** *Printing.* **s.-quotes** *colloq.*, single quotation-marks (' ').

3. = to the extent of (only) a half, imperfect(ly), incomplete(ly). **a.** With adjs. and sbs. expressing kinds or degrees of composition, consistency, texture, colour, as *s.-cartilaginous, -coagulated, -crystalline, -diaphanous, -pasty, -resinous, -solid, -transparent, -vitreous*, etc. **b.** In designations of heresies, sects, and schools of thought, expressing partial adherence to the tenets or theories connoted by the second element of the compound, as *s.-Augustinian, -Darwinian, -infidel*, etc. **c.** *Gram.*, as *s.-nasal* adj.; **s.-consonant** = SEMI-VOWEL; **-deponent,** a verb in Latin in which the tenses of the present group have active forms and those of the perfect group passive forms, as *gaudeo, gavisus sum*; etc. **d.** *Nat. Hist.* = imperfectly, incompletely, partly (of a certain habit, form, texture, etc.), as *s.-aquatic, -articulate, -osseous, -palmate*, etc. **e.** Designating an animal or vegetable form, class, species, etc., which has only some of the characteristics of that denoted by the second element, or is intermediate between that and another, as *s.-ape* (= HALF-APE, lemur), *-lichen, -rapacious* adj.; **s.-nymph,** a nymph of such insects as undergo only a slight change in passing to the imago stage. **f.** In *Anatomy*, chiefly in names of muscles (*a*) situated partly in a certain region, as *s.-spinalis*, or (*b*) being partly of a certain texture or shape, as *s.-membranosus, -orbicularis*, etc.; **s.-bulb,** the bulbous vestibuli, either of two vascular bodies on either side of the entrance of the vagina. **g.** In *Pathology* and *Therapeutics*, as *s.-albinism, -coma, -prone*, etc. **h.** In *Chemistry*, as *s.-acid, -oxygenated*, etc.; **s.-combined** *a.*, partially or loosely combined. **i.** In *Geology, Mineralogy*, and *Geography*, as *s.-calcareous, -extinct, -volcanic* adjs. **j.** In names of articles or processes of manufacture: **s.-china, -porcelain,** ware resembling china, etc., but having an inferior glaze and finish; **-steel,** puddled steel. **k.** Denoting styles of architecture having only some of the features connoted by the second element, as *s.-classic, -Gothic*, etc. **l.** In names of mechanical contrivances, as **s.-automatic,** having only some of the movements automatic; **-rotary,** partly rotary; etc.

4. Miscellaneous: **s.-bull** *R. C. Ch.*, a bull issued by a pope before his coronation; **-final,** in football and other contests, the match or round immediately preceding the final one; **-precious** *a.*, (of stones) not of sufficient value to rank as gems; **-rigid** *a.*, (of an airship) having a stiffened keel attached to a flexible gas container.

Semi-a·nnual, *a.* (and *sb.*) 1794. [SEMI- II. 1 b.] **1.** Recurring every half-year; half-yearly. **2.** Lasting for half a year (only); esp. of plants. Also *sb.* = s. plant. 1882.

Semi-A·rian, *a.* and *sb.* 1616. [– eccl. L. *Semiariani* (pl., IV exeunt.); see SEMI- II. 3 b and ARIAN.] **A.** *adj.* Partially Arian; used chiefly with ref. to a sect which arose in the 4th c. A.D., holding that the Son is of like substance (ὁμοιούσιος) but not of the same substance (ὁμοούσιος) with the Father. **B.** *sb.* One who holds S. views.

Semibreve (se·mibrīv). 1591. [f. SEMI- II. 1 c + BREVE *sb.* 2, after obs. Fr. *semibrève.*] *Mus.* A note having half (†in 'perfect time', one third) the length of a breve; in mod. music the longest note in ordinary use. (Its figure is now an open oval ○.) Also *attrib.*, as *s. rest.*

Semi-cho·rus. 1797. [f. SEMI- + CHORUS, tr. Gr. ἡμιχόριον.] **a.** One of two parts into which the main body of a chorus is divided; chiefly *Mus.* **b.** A piece of music to be performed by a company of singers selected from a chorus. Hence **Semi-cho·ric** *a.*

Semicircle (se·misəɹk'l). 1526. [– L. *semicirculus*; see SEMI- II. 2 b and CIRCLE *sb.*] **1.** The half of a circle divided by a diameter, or the half of its circumference. **2.** A set of objects or an arrangement in the form of a half-circle 1597. **3.** = GRAPHOMETER 1712. Hence **Se·micircle** *v. trans.* to surround with a s.; *intr.* to form a s. **Se·micircled** *ppl. a.* (chiefly *poet.*) of the form of a s.; arranged in a s.

Semicircular (semisə̄·ɹkiŭlăɹ), *a.* late ME. [– late L. *semicircularis*, f. as prec. + *-aris* -AR[1].] Of the form of a semicircle. **b.** *Anat.* Designating †(*a*) the orbicular muscle of the eyelid; (*b*) the three canals of the internal ear 1706. Hence **Semi-ci·rcularly** *adv.* in a s. form; in a half-circle.

Semicirque (se·misə̄ɹk). *poet.* 1795. [f. SEMI - II. 2 a + CIRQUE.] A semicircle.

Semicolon (semikōu·lŏn). 1644. [f. SEMI- + COLON[2].] A punctuation-mark consisting of a dot placed above a comma (;). In its present use it is the chief stop intermediate in value between the comma and the full stop.

Semi-cu·bical, *a.* 1677. [SEMI- II. 2 b.] *Math.* Applied to the curve of the third degree with a cusp referred to rectangular axes, the equation to which can always be reduced to the form $ay^2 = x^3$.

The exponent of the power of the abscissa which is proportional to the ordinate is 3/2, whence the name.

Semi-demi-. 1836. Used (1) = half-half, i.e., quarter, in **semidemisemiquaver,** a note the 64th part of a semibreve; (2) vaguely in a diminutive sense, as in *semi-demi-dinner.* Cf. DEMI-SEMI.

Se:mi-deta·ched, *a.* 1859. [SEMI- I. 1.] Partially detached. **b.** *spec.* Designating either of a pair of houses joined together and forming a block by themselves 1859.

Se:mi-diu·rnal, *a.* 1594. [SEMI- II. 1 b.] **1.** *Astr.* Pertaining to, consisting of, or performed in, half the time between the rising and setting of a celestial body. Chiefly in *s. arc.* **2.** Occurring every twelve hours. Chiefly of the tides. 1794. **3.** *Ent.* Partly diurnal, flying at twilight 1890.

Semi-dou·ble, *a.* (*sb.*) 1720. [SEMI- I. 1.] **1.** *Liturg.* Also *sb.* = s. feast, a feast of less solemnity than a double, only the first half of the antiphon being recited before the psalms. 1728. **2.** Of flowers: Having the innermost stamens perfect, while the outermost have become petaloid 1720.

1. Sundays and Days within an Octave are Semi-doubles 1850.

Semiflu·id, *a.* and *sb.* 1731. [SEMI- II. 3 a.] **A.** *adj.* Of a consistency midway between fluid and solid 1775. **B.** *sb.* A semi-fluid substance 1731.

Se·mi-form. 1836. [SEMI- I. 2, II. 2 f.] An imperfect form; *Cryst.*, a hemihedral form.

Semilunar (semil[1]ū·năɹ), *a.* (*sb.*) 1597. [f. SEMI- II. 2. a + LUNAR *a.* 3.] **A.** *adj.* Half-moon-shaped; crescentic; *spec.* in *Zool., Bot.*, and *Anat.*

S. Valves..are little Valves or Membranes of a S. Figure, placed in the Orifice of the Pulmonary Artery, to prevent the Relapse of the Blood into the Heart at the time of its Dilatation 1728. In man..[the third eyelid] exists..as a mere rudiment, called the s. fold DARWIN.

B. *sb.* A semilunar bone, valve, etc. 1893. So **Semilu·nary** *a.* (now *rare* or *Obs.*) = A. **Semilu·nate** *a.* = LUNATE.

Se·mi-lune. 1858. [f. SEMI- II. 2 a, after DEMI-LUNE.] A semilunar or crescent-shaped form, structure, etc.; *Fortif.* = DEMI-LUNE 2.

Semi-me·tal. 1661. [f. SEMI- I. 2 + METAL.] *Old Chem.* A non-malleable metal. Hence **Se:mi-meta·llic** *a.* partly metallic; *spec.* of the nature of a s.

Seminal (se·minăl), *a.* (and *sb.*) late ME. [– (O)Fr. *séminal* or L. *seminalis*, f. *semen*, *semin-* seed; see SEMEN, -AL[1].] **A.** *adj.* **1.** Of or pertaining to the seed or semen of men and animals; of the nature of semen. **2.** With ref. to plants: Pertaining to or of the nature of seed. *Bot.* Of organs or structures: Serving to contain the seed. 1658. †**b.** Produced from seed –1796. **3.** *gen.* Of or pertaining to the seed or reproductive elements existing in organic bodies, or attributed in pre-scientific belief to inorganic substances. Formerly often in *s. power, virtue*, the power of producing offspring. 1605. **4.** *fig.* Having the properties of seed; containing the possibility of future development 1639.

1. Animals, of spontaneous and s. generation 1673. **2.** The s. spike of Mercurie weld SIR T. BROWNE. **4.** It is pleasant to see great works in their s. state, pregnant with latent possibilities of excellence JOHNSON.

†**B.** *sb.* A seminal particle; a seed, germ –1682. Hence †**Semina·lity**, s. quality, principle, or condition; *pl.* s. properties; s. particles, germs. **Se·minally** *adv.* in a s. state or manner; as regards germination or reproduction.

‖**Seminar** (se·mināɹ). 1889. [G. – L. *seminarium* SEMINARY *sb.*[1]] In German universities (hence in certain British and American universities), a select group of advanced students associated for advanced study and original research under the guidance of a professor. Also *transf.*, a class that meets for systematic study under the direction of a teacher.

Seminarist (se·minăriˌst). 1583. [f. next + -IST.] **1.** A Roman Catholic priest educated in a foreign seminary in the 16th and 17th c., esp. at Douay for the English mission. Now *Hist.* **2.** A student in a seminary; chiefly, one in a seminary for the training of Roman Catholic priests 1835. **b.** *pl.* The teaching staff in a seminary 1668. **3.** A member of a seminar 1865.

Seminary (se·minări), *sb.*[1] 1440. [– L. *seminarium* seed-plot, subst. use of n. of adj. *seminarius*, f. *semen*, *semin-*; see SEMEN, -ARY[1].] †**1.** A piece of ground in which plants are sown (or raised from cuttings, etc.) to be afterwards transplanted; a seed-plot –1829. †**2.** *transf.* A place where animals are bred; a region which supplies (some kind of animal). Also, a stock or breed (of animal). –1665. **3.** *fig.* **a.** A place or thing in which something (e.g. an art or science, a virtue or vice) is developed or cultivated 1592. **b.** A place, country, society, condition of things, or the like, in which some particular class of persons is produced or trained 1604. **4.** A place of education, a school, college, university, or the like (often with qualifying word, as *s. of science, theological s.*) 1585. **5.** *R. C. Ch.* A school or college for training persons for the priesthood. Also *attrib.*, as *s. priest.* 1581. **6.** = SEMINAR 1889. †**7.** Short for *s. priest* –1685.

1. Then taking your grafted trees out of the s., you shall transplant them into this nursery EVELYN. **3. a.** The bloud of this noble Army of Martyrs became the fruitful s. thereof 1656. **4.** Westminster School a most famous seminarie of learning FULLER. To place his daughter in a s. for female education SCOTT. Hence **Semina·rian**, †a seminary priest; a seminarist.

†**Se·minary**, *a.* and *sb.*[2] 1583. [– L. *seminarius* pertaining to seed; see prec.] **A.** *adj.* **1.** = SEMINAL *a.* –1742. **2.** Occupied in sowing seed. *fig.* with allusion to prec. 7. –1640. **B.** *sb.* **1. a.** A germ, embryo, seminal particle –1671. **b.** *spec.* The morbific matter or principle (of a disease); *pl.* germs (of infection) –1694. **2.** A sower of seed –1680.

Seminate (se·mineɪt), *v.* Now *arch.* 1535. [– *seminat-*, pa. ppl. stem of L. *seminare* sow, f. *semen*, *semin-*; see SEMEN, -ATE[3].] *trans.* To sow; chiefly *fig.* to disseminate. So **Se·minative** *a.* (*rare*) having the function of sowing or propagating. late ME.

Semination (seminēɪ·ʃən). 1531. [– L. *seminatio*, *-ōn-*, f. as prec.; see -ION.] **1.** The action or process of sowing. Chiefly *fig.* **2.** The production of seed or semen 1658. **3.** The natural dispersion of seeds 1765.

Seminiferous (semini·fĕrəs), *a.* 1692. [f. L. *semen*, *semin-*; see SEMEN, -FEROUS.] **1.** *Bot.* Bearing or producing seed. **2.** *Anat.* Containing or conveying the seminal fluid; bearing or producing semen 1831.

1. *S. scale*, in *Coniferæ* the scale above the bract-scale bearing the ovules, and ultimately the seeds.

‖**Seminium** (sĭmi·niŏm). *rare.* *Pl.* **-ia.** 1676. [L. *seminium* procreation, also race, stock, breed, f. as prec.; see -IUM.] The first principle (of anything), the germ, etc.

Se:mi-noctu·rnal, *a.* 1594. [SEMI- II. 1 b.] *Astr.* Pertaining to, or accomplished in, half a night.

Semi-o·pal. 1794. [tr. G. *halbopal* (Werner, 1788).] An inferior variety of opal harder and more opaque than common opal.

Se:mipara·bola. 1656. [SEMI- II. 2 b.] *Math.* **1.** Half of a parabola. **2.** 'A curve of such a nature that the powers of its ordinates are to each other as the next lower powers of its abscissas' 1728. Hence **Se:mi-parabo·lical** *a.* comprising half a parabola.

Se·mi-ped(e. 1756. [– L. *semipes*, *-ped-*, f. *semi-* SEMI- + *pes*, *ped-* foot.] *Pros.* A half-foot.

Se:mi-Pela·gian, *a.* and *sb.* 1600. [– eccl. L. *Semipelagianus*; see SEMI- II. 3 b, PELAGIAN.] **A.** *adj.* Pertaining to the semi-Pelagians or semi-Pelagianism 1626. **B.** *sb.* An adherent of semi-Pelagianism 1600. Hence **Se:mi-Pela·gianism**, a doctrine intermediate between Augustinianism and Pelagianism, taught by Cassian of Marseilles in the 5th c.

Semiquaver (se·mikwēɪvəɹ). 1576. [SEMI- II. 1 c.] *Mus.* A note half the length of a quaver, the sixteenth part of a semibreve. †**b.** *allus.* A very short space of time –1635.

Semi-Sa·xon, *a.* and *sb.* 1735. [SEMI- I. 1, 2.] **A.** *adj.* Intermediate between 'Saxon' and 'English'; formerly used by philologists to designate the first period of Middle English, from *c*1100–50 to *c*1250. **B.** *sb.* The 'Semi-Saxon' language; Early Middle English.

Se·misphere. Now *rare.* 1659. [f. SEMI + SPHERE, orig. after It. *semisfera*. Cf. also med.L. *semisphera* XII, OFr. *semispere*.] A hemisphere. Hence **Semisphe·ric, -al** *adjs.*

‖**Semita** (se·mită). 1877. [mod.L. use of L., narrow path.] *Zool.* A band of minute close-set tubercles which bear ciliated clubbed spines, characteristic of the spatangoid sea-urchins.

Semite (sī·-, se·məit). 1875. [– mod.L. *Semita*, f. (Vulg.) *Sēm* – Gr. Σήμ Shem; see -ITE[1] 1.] A person belonging to the race of mankind which includes most of the peoples mentioned in Gen. 10 as descended from Shem son of Noah, as the Hebrews, Arabs, Assyrians, and Aramæans. Also, a person speaking a Semitic language as his native tongue.

Semitertian (semitə̄·ɹʃăn), *a.* (*sb.*) 1611. [f. SEMI- + TERTIAN, rendering Gr. ἡμιτριταία.] *Old Path.* Applied to an intermittent fever combining the symptoms of a quotidian and a tertian, consisting of a paroxysm occurring every day with a second stronger one every other day.

Semitic (sĭmi·tik), *a.* and *sb.* 1813. [– mod.L. *Semiticus*, f. *Semita* SEMITE.] **A.** *adj.* Of or pertaining to the Semites. (In recent use often *spec.* = Jewish.) 1826. **b.** The distinctive epithet of that family of languages of which Hebrew, Aramæan, Ethiopic, and ancient Assyrian, are the principal members. Hence, (in *S. scholar, studies*, etc.) concerned with the S. languages. 1813. **B.** *sb.* **a.** A Semite (*rare*). **b.** The Semitic family of languages; *occas.* the Semitic language of Babylon in opposition to Sumerian. **c.** *pl.* *U.S.* The scientific study of the language, religion, etc. of Semitic peoples. 1875.

Semitism (sī·-, se·mitiz'm). 1851. [f. SEMITE + -ISM 3.] **1.** The attributes characteristic of the Semitic peoples. Also, the fact of being Semitic. **b.** Jewish ideas or influence in politics and society 1885. **2.** A Semitic word or idiom 1880. So **Se·mitist**, a Semitic scholar. **Se·mitize**, *v. trans.* to render Semitic in character, language or religion.

Semitone (se·mitoᵘn). 1609. [– (O)Fr. *semiton* or med.L. *semitonus* (XIII); cf. late L. *semitonium*, Gr. ἡμιτόνιον HEMITONE. Senses 2 and 3 (usu. written *semi-tone*) are new formations distinct from 1.] **1.** *Mus.* An interval approximately equal to half a tone, the smallest interval in the ordinary scales. **2.** *Art.* An intermediate tone or tint in a picture; a half-tone 1782. **3.** A soft or gentle tone of voice; an undertone 1837. Hence **Se·mitonal, Semito·nic** *adjs.* pertaining to or consisting of a s. or semitones; (of a scale) chromatic.

Semi-u·ncial, *a.* (*sb.*) 1734. [SEMI- II. 1 a.] *Palæogr.* Applied to a style of writing intermediate between uncial and minuscule.

Semivowel (se·mivauˌĕl). 1530. [f. SEMI- II. 3 c + VOWEL, after L. *semivocalis*.] A vocal sound that partakes of the nature of a vowel and of a consonant; a letter representing such a sound.

As a technical term the word now most commonly denotes only *w* and *y*, but sometimes it includes these together with the liquids and nasals, chiefly in their non-syllabic values.

Semmit (se·mit). *Sc.* An undershirt or vest.

Semolina (semŏlī·nă). 1797. [alt. of It. *semolino*, dim. of *semola* bran, based on L. *simila* flour.] An article of food consisting of those hard portions of 'flinty' wheat which resist the action of the millstones, and are collected in the form of rounded grains. Also *attrib.*, as *s. pudding.*

‖**Semper-** (se·mpəɹ), the L. adv. *semper* always, used in various combs., as **s.-green,** an evergreen; **sempervirent** (-vəiᵊ·rĕnt) *a.* [L. *virent-*, *virere* to be green] evergreen.

‖**Sempervivum** (sempəɹvəi·vŏm). 1591. [L., 'ever-living'.] **a.** The houseleek. **b.** A genus of crassulaceous plants containing the houseleek, *S. tectorum*, and about 50 other species; a plant of this genus.

Sempitern (se·mpitəɹn), *a. arch.* late ME. [– OFr. *sempiterne* – L. *sempiternus*, f. *semper* always; see ETERNE *a.*] = next.

Sempiternal (sempitə̄·ɹnăl), *a.* late ME. [– (O)Fr. *sempiternel* – late L. *sempiternalis*, f. L. *sempiternus*; see prec., -AL[1].] Enduring constantly and continually; everlasting, eternal. Hence **Sempite·rnally** *adv.*

Sempstress: see SEAMSTRESS.

‖**Semsem** (se·msem). 1841. [Arab. *simsim*; see SESAME.] = SESAME.

‖**Semuncia** (simɒ·nʃˈiă). *Pl.* **-iæ** (-iˌī). 1656. [L., f. *semi-* SEMI- + *-uncia* OUNCE *sb.*[1]] *Rom. Antiq.* A half-ounce, the twenty-fourth part of an *as*. Hence **Semu·ncial** *a.*

‖**Sen** (sen). 1802. [Japanese.] A Japanese copper or bronze coin of small value. Usu. *collect.* as *pl.*

‖**Senarius** (sĭnēᵊ·riŏs). *Pl.* **-ii.** 1540. [L. *senarius* (sc. *versus* verse, line), subst. use of adj., f. *seni* six each, f. *sex* six.] *Prosody.* A (Greek or Latin) verse consisting of six feet, each of which is either an iambus or some foot which the law of the verse permits to be substituted; an iambic trimeter. (More fully *iambic s.*) So **Sena·rian** = s.

Senary (sī·nări, se·nări), *a.* 1661. [– L. SENARIUS.] Pertaining to the number six.

S. scale, the scale of arithmetical notation of which the radix is six. *S. division*, division into six parts.

Senate (se·năt). ME. [– (O)Fr. *sénat* – L. *senatus*, f. *senex*, *sen-* old (man); see -ATE[1].] **1.** An assembly or council of citizens charged with the highest deliberative functions in the government of a state. **a.** In ancient Rome: A legislative and administrative body, consisting orig. of representatives elected by the patricians, and later, partly of appointed members, and partly of the actual and former holders of certain high offices of state. **b.** Used as the equivalent of Gr. γερουσία (lit. 'body of elders') and βουλή (lit. 'council') 1586. **c.** *gen.* The governing or legislative assembly of a nation. Often applied to the British parliament. 1560. **d.**

In the 18th and 19th c. adopted as the official name for the upper and smaller branch of the legislature in various countries, as the United States (and each of the separate states of the Union), France, Italy, etc. 1780. **2.** In the Univ. of Cambridge, and in some other British universities, the official title of the governing body. (Cf. SENATUS.) 1736. **b.** *U.S.* In some American colleges, a council composed of members of the faculty and elected students, having the control of the discipline, etc., of the students 1891.

1. a. The S. was..a body composed of men of any order who had secured the suffrages of the people FROUDE. **c.** He says there is no place in the bar or the s. that Georgy may not aspire to THACKERAY.

Se·nate-house. 1550. [HOUSE *sb.*[1]] **1.** A house or building in which a senate meets. **2.** *spec.* The building which serves for the meeting of the senate of a university, esp. of Cambridge 1748.

attrib.: **S. examination,** examination for degrees in Cambridge University; so **S. examiner; S. problem,** a mathematical problem proposed in a S. examination.

Senator (se·nătəɹ). ME. [– (O)Fr. *sénateur* – L. *senator*, *-ōr-*, a parallel formation with *senatus* SENATE; see -OR 2.] **1.** A member of a senate. **b.** In vaguer sense: A counsellor, statesman; †a leader in Church or State. late ME. **2.** In papal Rome, the title given at various periods from the 12th c. onwards to the civil head of the city government, appointed by the Pope ME. **3.** *S. of the College of Justice*: in Scotland, the official designation of a Lord of Session 1540.

1. The Senators of Athens, greet thee Timon SHAKS. **b.** *fig.* Those green-rob'd senators of mighty woods, Tall oaks KEATS. Hence **Se·natorship,** the office or dignity of a s.

Senatorial (senătōᵊ·riăl), *a.* 1740. [f. L. *senatorius* (f. *senator* SENATOR) + -AL[1]. Cf. Fr. *sénatorial.*] **1.** Of or pertaining to a senator or senators; characteristic of or befitting a senator; consisting of senators. **2.** Of a Roman province under the Empire: Administered by the senate (not by the emperor) 1841. **3.** *U.S.* Entitled to elect a Senator, as a s. district 1891.

1. *S. order*, the highest of the three ranks of citizens in the later Roman republic. Hence **Senato·rially** *adv.*

Senatorian (senătōᵊ·riăn), *a.* 1614. [f. as prec. + -AN. Cf. (O)Fr. *sénatorien.*] = prec. 1, 2.

Senatory (se·nătəri). 1804. [f. SENATOR + -Y[3] (cf. -ORY[1]), perh. after Fr. *sénatorerie.*] *Fr. Hist.* The landed estate granted to a senator under the consulate and the First Empire.

‖**Senatus** (sĭnēⁱ·tŏs). 1835. [L.; see SENATE.] The title given to the governing body in certain universities. More fully *s. academicus.*

‖**Sena·tus consu·ltum.** *Pl.* **consulta.** Also anglicized **senatus consult.** 1696. [L. 'decree of the senate'.] **a.** A decree of the ancient Roman senate. **b.** A decree of the 'senate' in certain modern states, e.g. France under Napoleon I and Napoleon III 1813.

Send (send), *sb.* Also **scend.** 1726. [Belongs to SEND *v.*[2]] *Naut.* **1.** The carrying or driving impulse of a sea or wave; more fully *s. of a* or *the sea.* **2.** A sudden plunge (of a boat) *aft, forward*, etc. 1836.

Send (send), *v.*[1] Pa. t. and pa. pple. **sent** (sent). [OE. *sendan* = OFris. *senda*, *sēnda*, OS. *sendian*, OHG. *sendan*, *senten* (Du. *zenden*, G. *senden*), ON. *senda*, Goth. *sandjan* :– Gmc.* *sandjan*, f. **sanð-* :– **sanþ*, causative of **senþ*, repr. by OE., OS. *sīþ* SITHE *sb.*[1]] **I.** To order or direct to go or be conveyed. **1.** *trans.* To commission, order, or request (a person) to go *to* or *into* a place or *to* a person. Chiefly, to dispatch as a messenger or on an errand. **b.** With specified destination considered as a place of residence, or connoting a sphere of employment; e.g. *to s.* (one or more members) *to Parliament* (said of a constituency) 1531. **c.** To occasion or induce to go to a place or in a particular direction; to recommend or advise to go to a place or a person; *fig.* to refer (a reader) to some author or authority 1449. **d.** Without the notion of destination or errand; To cause or order to depart *from* one; to dismiss. Chiefly with *away, off.* 1533. **2.** To compel or force to go; to drive, impel. Also *transf.* of a circumstance, impulse, etc. OE. **b.** To drive (a person) *into* some state or condition; to cause to go *to* sleep; also with adj. complement 1831. **3.** To cause (a person) to be carried or conducted to a destination OE. **4.** To cause (a thing) to be conveyed or transmitted by an intermediary to another person or place OE. **b.** To serve up (food, a course, meal); only with *in, up*, and in phr. *to s. to table* 1662. **c.** *transf.* and *fig.* Also with *up.* ME. **5.** To dispatch (a boat, carriage, etc.) OE. **6.** To dispatch (a message, letter, telegram, etc.) by messenger, post, etc. So *To s.* (*out*) *cards* (of invitation). OE. **7.** Of God, fate, chance: 'To grant as from a distant place' (J.); to cause to happen or come into existence; to ordain as a blessing or a punishment OE. **8.** *absol.* To send a message or messenger. Const. *after, to.* OE. **9. S. for—a.** To send a messenger or message for; to send (a person) to fetch ME. **b.** With adv. qualifying 'to come' or 'be brought' understood 1592. **c.** Of a sovereign: To command the attendance of; *esp.* to summon a prominent member of a political party, for the purpose of offering him the office of prime minister 1744.

1. If he was sent of an errand he would forget half of it DE FOE. **b.** He was sent to sea to be got rid of MARRYAT. *To s. to school, college*, etc. (sometimes with the notion of defraying the expenses of the person's education). *To be sent* (*into the world*), said of a child as born for some divine purpose, or as a gift to the parents. **d.** And the rich hee hath sent emptie away *Luke* 1:53. *To s. flying, packing*: to dismiss summarily. **2.** Such a volley of musketry as sent the rebel horse flying in all directions MACAULAY. **b.** He..sent the Colonel to sleep, with a long, learned, and refreshing sermon THACKERAY. **3.** Thus was I.. sent to my account With all my imperfections on my head SHAKS. Ere they could strangle him, he sent three of them to the Deuill 1634. Rascals; men fit to s. to the hulks THACKERAY. **4. c.** We from the West will send destruction Into this Cities bosome SHAKS. **6.** Ile s. to him to meet The Prince and me KYD. *To s.* (a person) *word*, to transmit a message (to a person); to inform, notify. *To s.* (one's) *compliments, love, respects*, etc. **7.** God s. him well SHAKS. The Nymphs.. have..sent a Plague among thy thriving Bees DRYDEN. Lord s. us safe to Old England, say I! 1776. **8.** S. to me in the morning SHAKS. I have sent every half hour to know how she does RICHARDSON. **9. a.** The guard..sent for drink CLARENDON. **b.** S. for him up SWIFT. **c.** The King could do no better than to s. for Lord Grenville 1806.

II. To cause to go, by physical means or by direct volition. **1.** *trans.* To discharge and direct (a missile); to throw or propel in a particular direction; occas. †to thrust (a dagger). Also said of a missile weapon. OE. **b.** To deliver (a blow) 1626. **c.** To drive (a ball) 1782. **2.** To emit, give forth as a source OE. **3.** To direct (a thought, look, glance). late ME. **4.** To cause (sound, one's voice) to 'carry' or travel. Chiefly *poet.* 1593. **5.** To drive by pulsation, impulse, etc. 1767. **6.** Of a blow, etc., also of the agent, a weapon: To cause to go or fall violently. Also with *down.* 1822. **7.** To cause (a thing, prices, one's spirits, etc.) to go *down, up*, etc. 1657. **8.** To cause to move or travel; to cause to work 1864.

1. In his right hand Grasping ten thousand Thunders, which he sent Before him MILT. **2.** Doth a fountayne sende forth at one place swete water and bytter also? COVERDALE *Jas.* 3:11. When ev'ry star..Sent forth a voice COWPER. It sends out several stems from the root 1812. **4.** The cry of a gull sent seaward HENLEY. **6.** In an instant it was sent flying to the other side of the road 1887. **7.** Marriage sends a doctor's income up DOYLE. **8.** To s. the engines full speed astern 1885.

In idiomatic combination with advs. **S. along.** *trans.* To cause to travel rapidly; *fig.* to accelerate the progress or growth of. **S. down. a.** *trans.* To dispatch from the King or the Lords to the Commons, from the capital, a city, etc. into the country. **b.** To compel (an undergraduate) to leave the University (permanently or for a specified time) as a punishment. **S. in. a.** *trans.* To give (one's name), hand (one's card) to a servant when making a call. **b.** To cause (a thing) to be delivered at its destination; esp. to render (an account, a bill). **c.** *Cricket.* To s. (a batsman) into the field to bat. **S. round. a.** *trans.* To circulate. **b.** *To s. round the hat*: see HAT *sb.* **c.** *colloq.* To s. (something; also *absol.* to send a message) to some one in the neighbourhood. **S. up. a.** *trans.* Of things: To emit, give off, shoot out (something that rises or travels upwards). **b.** To cause (a person) to go or (a thing) to be taken 'upstairs'; esp. to serve up (a meal), to s. in (one's name or card as a visitor). **c.** *Public Schools.* To s. (a boy) to the headmaster (*a*) for reward, (*b*) for punishment. **d.** *slang.* To put in prison.

Send (send), *v.*[2] Pa. t. **sended.** Also **scend.** 1625. [Often written *'scend*, as if aphetic of DESCEND, which may in fact be the source.] *Naut. intr.* Of a ship: To pitch deeply with head or stern into the trough of a wave.

Sendal (se·ndăl). Now *Hist.* ME. [– OFr. *cendal*, (also Pr.) *sendal*, obscurely derived from Gr. σινδών SINDON.] **1.** A thin rich silken material; also a covering or garment of this. †**2.** As tr. L. *sindon*: Fine linen, lawn; a piece of this –1606.

1. There was pyght vp a pauilyon of crymasyn sendall, right noble and riche 1523.

Sender (se·ndəɹ). ME. [f. SEND *v.*[1] + -ER[1].] One who or something which sends. **b.** One who signals a message 1904. **c.** The transmitting instrument of a telephone or telegraphic apparatus = TRANSMITTER b. 1879.

Se·nd-off. *colloq.*, orig. *U.S.* 1872. A friendly demonstration on the occasion of a person's starting on a journey or undertaking.

Seneca (se·nĭkă). *U.S.* 1826. [app. identical with *Seneca*, the name given by white men to one of the 'Six Nations' of the Iroquois confederacy, living near Lake Seneca (N.Y.).] *attrib.* in **S. grass,** Northern holy-grass (*Hierochloa borealis*); †**S. oil,** crude petroleum.

Senectitude (sĭne·ktitiūd). 1796. [– med. L. *senectitudo*, irreg. f. L. *senectus* old age.] Old age. So **Sene·ctude** 1756.

Senega (se·nĭgă). 1738. [app. a variant form of SENECA.] The N. Amer. plant *Polygala senega.* Also, a drug obtained from the root of this plant, formerly used as an antidote for snake-bite.

Senegal (se·nĭgǫl). 1781. The name of a French colony, and river, of western Africa used *attrib.* **a.** In many names of beasts, birds, and plants native to this district. **b.** *S. gum* = GUMS. 1887.

Senegin (se·nĭgin). 1830. [f. SENEGA + -IN[1].] An amorphous glucoside, consisting of sapogenin and sugar, obtained from senega.

Senescence (sĭne·sĕns). 1695. [f. next; see -ENCE.] The process or condition of growing old.

Senescent (sĭne·sĕnt), *a.* 1656. [– L. *senescens*, *-ent-*, pr. pple. of *senescere* grow old; see -ENT.] Growing old, elderly.

Seneschal (se·nĭʃăl). late ME. [– OFr. *seneschal* (mod. *sénéchal*) :– med.L. *seni-*, *siniscalcus* (Frankish and Alemannic Laws) – Gmc. **siniskalkaz*, f. **seni-* old + **skalkaz* servant (OE. *scealc*, etc., Goth. *skalks*); cf. MARSHAL.] **1.** An official in the household of a sovereign or great noble, to whom the administration of justice and entire control of domestic arrangements were entrusted. In wider use: a steward, 'major-domo'. **2.** As the title of a governor of a city or province, and of various judicial officers. Now *Hist.* exc. with ref. to the Channel Islands. late ME.

1. Then marshal'd Feast Serv'd up in Hall with Sewers, and Seneshals MILT. Hence **Se·neschalship** *Hist.*, the office and functions of a s.

Sengreen (se·ngrīn). Now *dial.* [OE. *singrēne*, subst. use of *singrēne* adj. evergreen, f. Gmc. **sen-* :– IE. *sem-* one, always, repr. in L. *semel* once, *semper* always; see GREEN.] **1.** The houseleek, *Sempervivum tectorum.* **2.** Applied to other plants, *esp.* **a.** the sedums; **b.** varieties of saxifrage; **c.** the periwinkle, *Vinca minor*; **d. Water s.,** *Stratiotes aloides.* OE.

‖**Senhor** (senʸō·r). 1795. [Pg. :– L. *senior*, *-ōr-*; cf. SEIGNEUR, SEIGNOR.] In Pg. use, or with ref. to Portuguese: A term of respect placed before the name of a man in addressing him or speaking of him = 'Mr.' Also used without the name as a form of address, = 'sir'. Hence, a Portuguese gentleman. So ‖**Senhora** (senʸō·ra), a term of respect applied to Portuguese ladies; hence, a Portuguese lady. ‖**Senhorita** (senʸorī·ta), applied to young Portuguese ladies.

Senile (sī·nəil), *a.* 1661. [– Fr. *sénile* or L. *senilis*, f. *senex* old (man); see -ILE.] **1.** Belonging to, suited for, or incident to old age. Now only of diseases, etc.: Peculiar to the aged. **2.** Exhibiting the weakness of old age 1848. **3.** *Phys. Geog.* Approaching the end of a cycle of erosion 1902.

1. S. gangrene 1875. **2.** S. anger 1848. Hence **Se·nilely** *adv.* **Senility** (sĭni·lĭti), the condition of being s.; old age or the infirmity due to old age 1628.

Senior (sī·niəɹ), *a.* and *sb.* late ME. [– L. *senior*, compar. of *senex* old, rel. to Gr. ἕνος old (in ἕνη last day of the moon), Goth. *sineigs* old, *sinista* elder.] **A.** *adj.* **1.** Older, elder; esp. used after a person's name to denote the elder of two bearing the same name in a family. Abbrev. *sen.* (U.S. *sr.*). **2.** That ranks before others in virtue of longer service or tenure of a position; superior *to* others in standing 1513. **b.** In school and college use. Applied in the U.S. to a student in his last year or term. 1651. **c.** In commercial use, applied to the partner in a firm who has precedence of the rest in the formal enumeration of the members 1864.

1. Tho. Crabb, Sen. and Tho. Crabb, Jun. of Malborrow 1708. **2.** Phr. *The s. service*, the navy as dist. from the army. **b.** *S. student* (Christ Church, Oxford): see STUDENT 3 a. *S. fellow*, applied at Cambridge and Dublin to a select number of the fellows of longest standing in a college, in whom the greater part of its government was formerly vested.

Special collocations: **S. wrangler,** the head of the 'wranglers', i.e. of the first class of those who are successful in the Mathematical Tripos at Cambridge; similarly **S. classic, S. moralist,** the student who takes the first place in the Classical and the Moral Sciences Tripos respectively. (The status indicated by these titles has ceased to exist, the class-lists being now arranged alphabetically.) **S. optime,** one placed in the second class in the Mathematical Tripos.

B. *sb.* An elder person. **1.** One superior or worthy of deference by reason of age; one having pre-eminence in dignity by priority of election, appointment, etc. late ME. **2.** In school and college use: (*a*) one of the more advanced students; (*b*) one no longer a freshman; (*c*) a graduate, as dist. from a non-graduate, member of a college or university. In *U.S.* a student in his fourth year. 1612. **b.** A senior fellow of a college 1645.

1. His s. at the bar SCOTT. She was a year or two my s. 1862.

Seniority (sīniǫ·rĭti). 1450. [– med.L. *senioritas*, f. L. *senior*: see prec., -ITY.] **1.** The state or quality of being senior; priority by reason of birth, superior age 1533. **2.** Priority or precedence in office or service; esp. *Mil.* Superiority in standing to another of equal rank by reason of earlier entrance into the service or an earlier appointment 1450. **3.** The body of seniors or senior fellows of a college 1678.

Senna (se·nă). 1543. [Earlier *sena* – med.L. *sena* – Arab. *sanā*. Repl. †*sene* (XV–XVII) – (O)Fr. *séné*, med.L. *sene*.] **1.** *Bot.* A shrub of the genus *Cassia*, native in tropical regions, bearing yellow flowers and flat greenish pods. **b.** Applied to shrubs of other genera having similar medicinal properties; as **Bladder s.,** *Colutea arborescens*; **Wild s.,** *Poinciana pulcherrima* or *Globularia alypum*. **2.** *Pharm.* The dried leaflets of various species of *Cassia*, used as a cathartic and emetic 1571.

attrib.: **s.-tea,** an infusion of the drug taken as a purgative.

Sennachie (se·năχi). 1534. [– Gael. *seanachaidh* (= OIr. *senchaid*), f. *sean* old (OIr. *sen*).] In Ireland and the Scottish Highlands, one professionally occupied in the study and transmission of traditional history, genealogy, and legend; now chiefly *Sc.* a Gaelic teller of legendary romances.

†**Se·nnet**[1]. 1590. [perh. var. of SIGNET.] A set of notes on the trumpet or cornet, ordered in the stage-directions of Elizabethan plays, apparently as the signal for the ceremonial entrance or exit of a body of players –1619.

Sennet[2] (se·nėt). 1671. [perh. from some W.-Indian language.] *Nat. Hist.* A West-Indian fish; = BARRACUDA.

Sennight (se·nəit). *arch.* [OE. *seofon nihta* seven nights, ME. *seouenihte*, later *sennyȝt* (XV); see SEVEN, NIGHT, and cf. FORTNIGHT.] A week.

The bold Iago, Whose footing heere anticipates our thoughts, A Senights speed SHAKS. Newes.. That Waller was at Abingdon on Tuesday last was sevenight 1644.

Sennit (se·nit). 1625. [var. of SINNET.] *Naut.* **a.** = SINNET. **b.** Plaited grass, palm leaves, etc., used for making hats.

Senocular (sĭnǫ·kiŭlăɹ), *a.* 1713. [f. L. *seni* six each + *oculi* eyes + -AR[1].] Having six eyes. So **Seno·culate** *a.*

Senonian (sĭnōᵘ·niăn), *a.* (*sb.*) 1850. [– Fr. *sénonien*, f. L. *Senones*, a people of central Gaul.] *Geol.* Designating a subdivision of the Cretaceous system in France and Belgium corresponding to the 'Upper Chalk with flints' of British geologists.

‖**Señor** (senʸō·r). *Pl.* **señores** (senʸō·res). 1622. [Sp. :– L. *senior*, *-ōr-*; cf. SENHOR.] In Spanish use or with ref. to a Spaniard: A title of respect placed before the name of a man, = 'Mr.' **b.** Used without the name as a form of address 1832. **c.** A Spanish gentleman 1868.

‖**Señora** (senʸō·ra). 1579. [Sp., fem. of prec.] A title of respect prefixed to the name of a Spanish lady, or used without the name in addressing her; hence, a Spanish lady.

‖**Señorita** (senʸorī·ta). 1845. [Sp., dim. of SEÑORA.] A Spanish title of respect prefixed to the name of a young lady, or used without the name in addressing her 1850. **b.** A young Spanish lady 1845.

Sensate (se·nsėt), *a.* 1500. [– late L. *sensatus* gifted with sense, f. *sensus*; see -ATE[2] 2.] **1.** Endowed with physical sensation. **2.** Perceived by the senses 1847.

Sensate (sensēⁱ·t), *v.* 1652. [f. L. *sensus* SENSE *sb.* + -ATE[3], after SENSATION.] **1.** *trans.* To perceive by sense; to have a sensation of. †**2.** *intr.* To have sensation –1687.

Sensation (sensēⁱ·ʃən). 1615. [– med.L. *sensatio*, *-ōn-*, f. L. *sensus* sense, after late L. *sensatus* SENSATE *a.*; see -ATION and cf. (O)Fr. *sensation.*] **1.** An operation of any of the senses; a psychical affection or state of consciousness consequent on and related to a particular condition of some portion of the bodily organism, or a particular impression received by one of the organs of sense. Now commonly, in more precise use, restricted to the subjective element in any operation of one of the senses, a physical 'feeling' considered apart from the resulting 'perception' of an object. **b.** In generalized use: The operation or function of the senses; 'perception by means of the senses' (J.). Now commonly the subjective element in the operation of the senses; physical 'feeling'. 1642. **c.** Faculty of perceiving by the senses, physical sensibility 1799. **2.** A mental feeling, an emotion. Now chiefly, the characteristic feeling arising in some particular circumstances. 1755. **b.** Mental apprehension, sense, or 'realization' *of* something 1639. **3.** An excited or violent feeling. **a.** An exciting experience; a strong emotion aroused by some particular occurrence or situation. Also, the production of violent emotion as an aim in works of literature or art. 1808. **b.** A condition of excited feeling produced in a community by some occurrence 1779. **c.** An event or a person that 'creates a sensation' 1864.

1. When I grasp an ivory ball in my hand, I feel a certain sensation of touch 1785. **b.** O sunken souls, slaves of s. 1642. **2.** A s. of distress 1755. **b.** So to represent familiar objects as to awaken..freshness of s. COLERIDGE. **3. a.** The cheap publications which supply s. for the million in penny and halfpenny numbers 1863. **b.** His death created a profound s. 1879. **c.** The greatest s. of the day: grand Incantation Scene from Der Freischütz 1864.

Comb. as *s.-monger, -seeking.*

Sensational (sensēⁱ·ʃənăl), *a.* 1840. [f. prec. + -AL[1].] **1.** Of, pertaining to, or dependent upon, sensation or the senses. **2.** Of philosophical theories: Regarding sensation as the sole source of knowledge 1855. **3.** Of works of literature or art, hence, of writers: Dealing in sensation (see SENSATION 3 a), aiming at violently exciting effects. Also of incidents: Calculated to produce a startling impression. 1863.

1. No experience of external things is purely s. 1840. Hence **Sensa·tionally** *adv.*

Sensationalism (sensēⁱ·ʃənăliz'm). 1865. [f. prec. + -ISM.] **1.** *Philos.* The theory that sensation is the only source of knowledge 1867. **2.** Addiction to what is sensational in literature or art 1865.

Sensationalist (sensēⁱ·ʃənălist). 1855. [f. as prec. + -IST.] **1.** *Philos.* One who regards the senses as the ultimate source of all knowledge. **2.** One whose aim is to make a sensation; a sensational writer 1868.

Sensationalize (sensēⁱ·ʃənăləiz), *v.* 1863. [f. as prec. + -IZE.] *trans.* **a.** To subject to the influence of 'sensation' or factitious emotion. **b.** To exaggerate in a sensational manner.

Sensationism (sensēⁱ·ʃəniz'm). 1863. [f. SENSATION + -ISM.] = SENSATIONALISM 2. So **Sensa·tionist,** one who deals in sensation; a sensational novelist, journalist, etc. 1861.

Sense (sens), *sb.* late ME. [– L. *sensus* faculty of feeling, sensibility, mode of feeling, thought, meaning, f. *sens-*, pa. ppl. stem of *sentire* feel. Cf. (O)Fr. *sens.*] **I.** Faculty of perception or sensation. **1.** Each of the special faculties, connected with a bodily organ, by which man and other animals perceive external objects and changes in the condition of their own bodies. Usu. reckoned as five—sight, hearing, smell, taste, touch. Also called *outward* or *external s.* 1526. †**b.** Used for: An organ of sense –1604. **c.** *pl.* The faculties of physical perception or sensation as opp. to the higher faculties of intellect, spirit, etc. 1841. **d.** Applied to similar faculties of perception, not scientifically delimited, or only conjectured to exist 1690. **2.** *transf.* An instinctive or acquired faculty of perception or accurate estimation. Now chiefly const. *of* (locality, distance, etc.). 1567. **3.** *gen.* The senses viewed as forming a single faculty in contradistinction to intellect, will, etc.; the exercise or function of this faculty, sensation 1538. **4.** *pl.* The faculties of corporeal sensation considered as channels for gratifying the desire for pleasure and the lusts of the flesh. Also *sing.*, any one of such faculties so regarded. 1597. **b.** *collect. sing.* 1586. †**5.** Capability of feeling, as a quality of the body and its parts; liability to feel pain, irritation, etc. –1771. **6.** *pl.* A general term for the faculties of perception (including the 'five senses'), which are in abeyance when their owner is asleep or otherwise unconscious. Also *sing.*, any one of these faculties. 1597. **b.** *collect. sing.* The perceptive faculty of a conscious animate being 1585. **7.** Applied to faculties of the mind or soul compared or contrasted with the bodily senses; usu. with defining word, as *inner*, *interior*, *s.* 1566. **8.** Capacity for perception and appreciation *of* (beauty, humour, some quality, etc.) 1604. **9.** *pl.* The mental faculties in their normal condition of sanity; one's 'reason' or 'wits' 1568. †**b.** *sing.* (with the same meaning) –1694. **10.** Natural understanding, intelligence, esp. as bearing on action or behaviour; practical soundness of judgement 1684.

1. I must have the evidence of more senses than one to confirm me of its truth FARQUHAR. My s. of hearing is painfully acute BECKFORD. **b.** Mine Eyes, mine Eares, or any Sence SHAKS. **d.** *Muscular s.*: see MUSCULAR *a.* 1. *Sixth s.*, a faculty of perception supposed not to depend upon any 'outward sense'; instinct, intuition. **2.** Take from them now The sence of reckning SHAKS. **3.** Thus wee adore vertue, though to the eyes of s. shee bee invisible SIR T. BROWNE. **4. b.** This bastard Loue..vtterly subuerts the course of nature, in making reason giue place to s. SIDNEY. **7.** *Moral s.*: see MORAL *a.* 1 c. **8.** A strong s. of humour 1885. **9.** Phr. *In one's (right) senses*, in one's right mind. *To bring* (a person) *to his senses*, to cure of his folly (one who is behaving 'madly'). (*To frighten*, etc.) *out of one's* (*seven*) *senses*, out of one's wits. **b.** *Lear* IV. iv. 9. **10.** You speak, ma'am, like a lady of s. MISS BURNEY. Phr. *To have the s.*, to be wise enough *to do* something. So *to have too much s. to, to have more s. than to* do something. **b.** Knowledge of how to act under given conditions; usu. with defining word, as *court s., road s., stage s.*

II. Actual perception or feeling. **1.** A feeling or perception *of* (something external) through the channels of touch, taste, etc.; the feeling or consciousness *of* some bodily affection as pain, fatigue, comfort, etc. 1586. **2.** A more or less vague perception or impression *of* (an outward object, as present or imagined) 1596. **3.** A more or less indefinite consciousness or impression *of* (a fact, state of things, etc.) as present or impending 1604. **4.** Mental apprehension, appreciation, or realization *of* (some truth, fact, state of things) 1540. **b.** The recognition *of* (a duty, virtue, etc.) as incumbent upon one, or as a motive or standard for one's own conduct 1604. **5.** Emotional consciousness of something; a glad or sorrowful, grateful or resentful recognition *of* (another person's conduct, an event, a fact or a condition of things) 1604. **6.** A consciousness or recognition *of* (some quality, condition, etc.) as attaching to oneself 1614. **7.** An opinion, view, or judgement held or formed †**a.** by an individual –1761. **b.** by an assemblage of persons (or by a majority of their number). Now *arch.* 1654.

1. An idle craving without s. of flavours GEO. ELIOT. **2.** And the darkening air Thrills with a s. of the triumphing night HENLEY. **3.** There was a general s. of security MACAULAY. **4.** He seemed visited by a s. of the vanity of all things J. H. NEWMAN. **b.** These fellows have no s. of gratitude DE FOE. **5.** No better way of showing our s. of his hospitality..has occurred to us HAWTHORNE. **6.** To confess herself mistaken was..opposed to her s. of personal dignity 1908. **7. a.** Phr. †*To speak* or *give one's s.*, to express one's opinion. †*In one's s.*, in one's opinion. †*To abound in one's own s.*: see ABOUND *v.*[1] 4. **b.** Phr. *To take the s. of*, to ascertain the general feeling or opinion of.

III. Meaning, signification. **1.** The meaning or signification of a word or phrase; also, any one of the different meanings of a word 1530. **b.** A meaning recorded in a dictionary 1755. **2.** The meaning of words in connected or continuous speech; the meaning of a passage or context. Also, one of two or more meanings which the words naturally bear. 1513. †**b.** The meaning or interpretation of a dream, or of anything cryptic or symbolical –1650. **c.** The gist of words spoken or written 1596. **3.** Any of the various meanings or interpretations (*literal, mystic, moral*, etc.) of which a word or passage of Holy Scripture was considered to be susceptible. Hence *transf.* late ME. †**4.** The meaning of a speaker or writer –1735. **5.** The substance of a passage 1568. **6.** Discourse that has a satisfactory and intelligible meaning 1598. **7.** What is wise or reasonable 1600. **8.** [After Fr. *sens.*] A direction in which motion takes place (*rare*) 1797.

1. There bee some wordes that bee not of the same s. euery where 1611. **2.** He had barely enough Greek to make out the s. of the epigram GEO. ELIOT. **c.** This is the general s. of his remark 1777. **3.** These Greekes,..follow the literall s. of the Scriptures 1617. **4.** Let no Court Sycophant pervert my s. POPE. **6.** Phr. *To talk, speak, write* (*good*) *s. To make s. of*, to find a meaning in. *To give, have, make s.*, to be intelligible. **7.** Phr. *There is not much s. in this.*

Phrases. *In a* (specified) *s.*, according to a particular acceptation or interpretation (of a word, phrase, etc.); often *in a s., in any s., in no s.* (which sometimes come to mean 'in some degree', 'in no respect', etc.).

Sense (sens), *v.* 1598. [f. the sb.] †**1.** *trans.* To perceive (an outward object) by the senses; also, to feel (pain) –1873. †**b.** To test, make trial of. BUNYAN. †**2.** To expound the sense or meaning of; to ascribe a meaning to; to take in a particular sense –1726. **3.** To perceive, become aware of, 'feel' (a fact, state of things, etc.) more or less vaguely or instinctively 1872. **4.** To comprehend, 'take in'. Chiefly *U.S.* and *dial.* 1860. **5.** *Philos.* To have a sense-perception of. Also *absol.*, to experience sensations. 1661.

3. He 'senses' the least coldness towards himself 1872. **5.** Is he sure, that objects are not otherwise sensed by others, then they are by him? 1661.

Senseful (se·nsfŭl), *a.* 1591. [f. SENSE *sb.* + -FUL 1.] **1.** Full of sense or meaning; significant. †**2.** Intelligent –1700.

1. Sensefull speach SPENSER. **2.** Men, otherwise s. and ingenious, quote such things..as would never pass in conversation 1700.

Senseless (se·nslės), *a.* 1557. [f. SENSE *sb.* + -LESS.] **1.** Destitute or deprived of sensation; physically insentient. **b.** That is in a state of unconsciousness 1585. **c.** Of things: Incapable of sensation or perception 1577. **2.** Destitute of mental sensibility, incapable of feeling or perception. Also const. *of.* Now *rare* or *Obs.* 1561. **3.** Of a person, etc.: Devoid of sense or intelligence, stupid, silly, foolish 1565. †**b.** quasi-*adv.* Unreasonably. SHAKS. **4.** Of actions, words, etc.: Proceeding from lack of sense or intelligence, foolish. Also, without sense or meaning; unmeaning meaningless, purposeless. 1579.

1. I would I were senselesse sir, that I might not feele your blowes SHAKS. **b.** I was almost s. with terror MISS BURNEY. **c.** I stand, immoveable, like s. marble! 1720. **2.** I am senselesse of your Wrath SHAKS. **3.** An honest senselesse dolt, A good poore foole MARSTON. **4.** The horrid and s. Custom of Duels STEELE. Hence **Se·nseless-ly** *adv.*, **-ness.**

Sensibility (sensibi·lĭti). late ME. [– late and med.L. *sensibilitas, -tat-*, f. *sensibilis*; see next, -ITY; partly f. SENSIBLE. Cf. (O)Fr. *sensibilité.*] **1.** Power of sensation or perception; †the specific function of the organs of sense. Now often, the (greater or less) readiness of an organ or tissue to respond to sensory stimuli; sensitiveness. **b.** *Philos.* Power or faculty of feeling, capacity of sensation and emotion as dist. from cognition and will 1838. **2.** Emotional consciousness; glad or sorrowful, grateful or resentful, recognition of a person's conduct, or of a fact or a condition of things 1751. **3.** Quickness and acuteness of apprehension or feeling; sensitiveness. Also, with const., sensitiveness *to*, keen sense *of* something. 1711. **b.** *pl.* Emotional capacities 1634. **c.** *sing.* and *pl.* Liability to feel offended or hurt by unkindness, or lack of respect; susceptibilities 1769. **4.** In the 18th and early 19th c. (subseq. somewhat *rarely*): Capacity for refined emotion; delicate sensitiveness of taste; also, readiness to feel compassion for suffering, and to be moved by the pathetic in literature or art 1756. **5.** Of plants and their organs, also of instruments or other inorganic objects: Aptness to be affected by external influences; sensitiveness. Const. *to*, (rarely *of*). 1662.

1. S. resides in the nervous system 1834. Common sensation or tactile s. 1875. **b.** Even though these pleasures are much diminished by..decay of his passive sensibilities MILL. **2.** A s. of our own weakness 1790. **3.** A man's s. to pecuniary influence BENTHAM. A s. to colour..being very different from a s. to form RUSKIN. **b.** Doubtless this feeling was due to his unusually acute sensibilities—his keen sense of the beautiful 1892. **4.** Where Affectation holds her seat, And sickly S. BYRON.

Sensible (se·nsĭb'l), *a.* (and *sb.*). late ME. [– (O)Fr. *sensible* or L. *sensibilis*, f. *sens-*; see SENSE *sb.*, -IBLE.] **A.** *adj.* **I. 1.** Perceptible by the senses. (In *Philos.*, opp. to INTELLIGIBLE 3; in this use, now *rare.*) †**b.** Of or pertaining to the senses or sensation –1793. **2.** Perceptible by the mind or the inward feelings 1597. **3.** Easy to perceive, evident 1586. **4.** Large enough to be perceived or to be worth considering; appreciable. Now only of immaterial things (as quantities, magnitudes, etc.). late ME. †**5.** Of discourse, etc.: Easily understood; striking, effective –1744. †**6.** Such as is acutely felt; markedly painful or pleasurable –1819.

1. Taste and other s. Qualities 1732. Phr. *S. horizon*: see HORIZON 1. *S. heat*: used in contradistinction to *latent heat* (HEAT *sb.* 2 c). *S. perspiration*, sweat, as dist. from the emission of vapour through the pores. **b.** *Haml.* I. i. 57. **2.** The visible and s. connexion of sacred and profane history 1734. **3.** A very s. odor of garlic 1816. **4.** We could discover no s. difference in weight SIR T. BROWNE. **6.** Scorpions..whose stinging is most s., and deadly 1655.

II. Capable of feeling or perceiving. **1.** Endowed with the faculty of sensation. late ME. †**2.** Having (more or less) acute power of sensation; sensitive –1831. †**b.** Sensitive *to* or *of* –1829. **3.** Capable of or liable to mental emotion; *esp.* sensitive *to* some specified emotional influence. Also const. *of.* Now *rare.* 1675. **4.** *transf.* Of material things or substances, esp. of instruments of measurement, as a balance, a thermometer: Readily affected by physical impressions or influences, sensitive. Now *rare.* 1661.

1. It is the Understanding that sets Man above the rest of s. Beings LOCKE. Outside of the s. skin 1850. **2.** These Gentlemen, who are of such s. and nimble Lungs, that they alwayes vse to laugh at nothing SHAKS. **b.** Albinoes..are painfully s. to light 1829. **3.** Johnson had, from his early youth, been s. to the influence of female charms BOSWELL. **4.** A very s. hygrometer LOCKE.

III. Actually perceiving or feeling. **1.** Cognizant, conscious, aware of something (often as a ground for pleasure or regret). Now somewhat *rare.* late ME. **2.** Emotionally conscious; having a pleasurable, painful, grateful, or resentful sense *of* something. Now usu., gratefully conscious *of* (kindness, etc.). 1634. **3.** Conscious, free from physical insensibility or delirium 1732.

1. Which shows how little we are s. of the weight of the business upon us PEPYS. Looking s. Of having play'd the fool BYRON. **2.** Lady Carlisle..is..very s. of your goodness to us all 1775.

IV. Endowed with good sense; intelligent, reasonable, judicious 1584. **b.** Of action, behaviour, discourse, etc.: Marked by, exhibiting, or proceeding from good sense 1653.

A moral, s., and well-bred man Will not affront me, and no other can COWPER. It was tame,..s., and not near so noisy or dirty as a Chimpanzee 1860. **b.** A s. and penetrating countenance MME. D'ARBLAY.

B. *absol.* and *sb.* **1.** That which produces sensation; that which is perceptible; an object of sense, or of any one of the senses 1589. †**2.** The element (in a spiritual being) that is capable of feeling. MILT.

1. A blind man conceives not colours, but under the notion of some other s. 1665. Hence **Se·nsibleness**, the quality or state of being s.

Sensibly (se·nsĭbli), *adv.* late ME. [f. SENSIBLE *a.* + -LY[2].] **1.** In a manner perceptible to the senses; so far as can be perceived; appreciably. †**2. a.** With self-consciousness, consciously. **b.** Of feeling: Acutely, intensely. –1806. †**3.** Clearly, strikingly –1700. **4.** With good sense, intelligently; judiciously, reasonably 1755.

1. The sea is said to be s. decreasing in size 1880. **2. a.** As each thing to more perfection grows, It feels more s. both good and pain CARY. **3.** He behaved s. under the circumstances 1911.

Sensifacient (sensifēi·ʃiĕnt), *a.* 1879. [f. L. *sensus* SENSE + -FACIENT.] Producing sensation.

Sensiferous (sensi·fĕrəs), *a.* 1656. [f. as prec. + -FEROUS.] Conveying sensation.

Sensific (sensi·fik), *a.* 1822. [f. as prec. + -FIC. Cf. late L. *sensificus.*] Of nerves: Producing sensation.

Sensify (se·nsifəi), *v.* 1678. [In XVII – late and med.L. *sensificare*; later f. as prec. + -FY.] *trans.* To transform (physical changes) into sensation.

Sensile (se·nsil, -əil), *a.* 1813. [– L. *sensilis*, f. *sens-*; see SENSE *sb.*, -ILE.] Capable of perception, sentient.

Sensist (se·nsist). 1874. [f. SENSE *sb.* + -IST.] = SENSATIONALIST 1.

Sensitive (se·nsitiv), *a.* and *sb.* late ME. [– (O)Fr. *sensitif, -ive* or med.L. *sensitivus*, irreg. f. *sens-*; see SENSE *sb.*, -IVE.] **A.** *adj.* **1.** Having the function of sensation or sensuous perception. **b.** Of life, knowledge, perception (also formerly †of desires, feelings): Connected with the senses, sensuous. †Of objects: Perceptible by the senses. 1530. **2.** Of living beings: Endowed with the faculty of sensation. Formerly often: †'Having sense or perception, but not reason' (J.). 1509. **3.** Of plants and their organs: Capable of responding to stimulation 1633. **4.** That feels quickly and acutely. **a.** In physical sense, of a living being, an animal organ or tissue: Having quick or intense perception or sensation; readily and acutely affected with pain or pleasure by some particular influence 1849. **b.** With ref. to mental feelings: Impressionable; easily wounded by unkindness; *occas.*, ready to take offence, 'touchy' 1816. **5.** *transf.* Readily altered or affected by some influence specified or implied 1828. **b.** *Photogr.* Of paper, chemical substances, etc.: Susceptible to actinic influence 1839. **c.** Of a scientific instrument: Indicating readily slight changes of condition, easily moved or affected 1857. **d.** Of market prices, stock, etc.: Having a tendency to fluctuate rapidly upon the publication of outside reports 1866. **6.** Mus. *S. note*: the leading note of a scale 1867.

1. *S. soul* [med.L. *anima sensitiva*], in scholastic philosophy, that one of the three kinds of 'soul' or of constituent parts of the soul which is concerned with sensation, and which is characteristic of animals; dist. from the *vegetative soul*, which is common to animals and plants, and from the *intellective soul* which in rational animals (men) is superadded to the two others. Similarly *s. virtue* [*virtus sensitiva*], the faculty of sensation. **b.** Our s. perception of objects 1877. **3. S. plant**, a shrub (*Mimosa pudica*, or *M. sensitiva*) possessing a high degree of irritability, causing the leaflets of the bipinnate leaves to fold together at the slightest touch; also applied with defining word to various plants having a similar quality; e.g. **American S. plant** (*Cassia nictitans*), also called *Wild S. plant* and *S. pea*. **S. Brier,** *Schrankia uncinata*. **S. Fern,** *Onoclea sensibilis*. **4. a.** The tongue is one of the most sensitive of organs JOWETT. **b.** The scenes of blood which followed shocked his s. nature 1824. **5.** Plants.. s. of drought 1828. **b.** The paper is..very s. to all white light 1893. **c.** Balances are made s. to the fraction of a grain 1872.

B. *sb.* †**1.** A being that is capable of sensation –1727. †**2.** The faculty of sensation –1627. **3.** The Sensitive plant 1707. **4.** One sensitive to spiritualist or other occult influences, a medium 1850. **5.** One in whom the sensitive faculty is highly developed. Also = SENSITIVIST. 1884. Hence **Se·nsitive-ly** *adv.*, **-ness.**

Sensitivist (se·nsitivist). 1891. [f. SENSITIVE *a.* + -IST.] One of a school of novelists in Holland, who aim at combining in their methods the valuable qualities of impressionism and realism.

Sensitivity (sensiti·vĭti). 1803. [f. as prec. + -ITY.] **1.** The quality of being sensitive. **2.** The experience of the senses 1889.

Sensitize (se·nsitəiz), *v.* 1856. [f. as prec. + -IZE.] **1.** *trans.* (*Photogr.*) To render (a plate, film, or paper) sensitive to the influence of light. **2.** To make (a person) sensitive 1880.

1. Nitrate of silver..is the salt usually employed to sensitise the paper 1865. Hence **Se:nsitiza·tion,** the act or process of sensitizing. **Se·nsitizer,** a substance or preparation used for sensitizing.

Sensitometer (sensitǫ·mĭtəɹ). 1880. [f. SENSITIVE; see -METER.] *Photogr.* An instrument for ascertaining the degree of sensitiveness of photographic plates, films, etc.

†**Se·nsive,** *a.* 1553. [– OFr. *sensif, -ive* or med.L. *sensivus*, f. *sens-*; see SENSE *sb.*, -IVE.] Having the function of sensation or sensuous perception –1865.

Sensor (se·nsǫɹ), *a.* 1865. [irreg. shortened f. SENSORY, after *motor.*] = SENSORY *a.*

Sensori- (se·nsŏri), comb. form of SENSOR or SENSORY, chiefly in **sensori-motor** *a.*, applied to nerves which are both sensory and motor; also to reflex actions which arise from stimulation of the organs of sense. Similarly *s.-reflex, volitional* adjs., etc.

Sensorial (sensōᵊ·riăl), *a.* 1768. [f. SENSORIUM or SENSORY + -AL¹.] Of or relating to the sensorium. Also, relating to sensation or sensory impressions. †**b.** Pertaining to the brain as the centre of nervous energy; esp. in *s. power*, vital energy proceeding from the brain to the rest of the system –1833.

‖**Sensorium** (sensōᵊ·riŏm). 1647. [– late L. *sensorium* (Boethius), f. *sens-*, pa. ppl. stem of L. *sentire* feel; see -ORIUM.] The seat of sensation in the brain of man and other animals; the percipient centre to which sense-impressions are transmitted by the nerves. Also *common s.* (L. *sensorium commune*). Formerly used in a wider sense, for the brain as the organ of mind and the centre of nervous energy. **b.** Used playfully (sometimes for 'brain' or 'mind') 1759.

Sensory (se·nsŏri), *sb.* 1626. [– L. *sensorium*; see prec. and -ORY¹.] †**1.** An organ of sense –1714. **2.** = prec. 1653.

Sensory (se·nsŏri), *a.* 1749. [f. L. *sens-* or its derivative SENSE *sb.* + -ORY².] Belonging to sensation; carrying or transmitting sensation.

Sensual (se·nsiuăl, -ʃuăl), *a.* and *sb.* 1450. [– late L. *sensualis*, f. L. *sensus* SENSE *sb.*; *see* -AL¹. Cf. Fr. *sensuel.*] **A.** *adj.* **1.** Of or pertaining to the senses or physical sensation; sensory. Now *rare*. **b.** Perceptible by the senses (*rare*) 1529. †**2.** Endowed with the faculty of sensation (but not with reason) –1696. **3.** Of appetites and pleasures: Connected with the gratification of the senses. **a.** In neutral use: Sensuous, physical. Now *rare*. 1542. **b.** In pejorative use, now often, lewd, unchaste 1477. **4.** Of persons, their conduct, etc. **a.** Absorbed in the life of the senses; indifferent to intellectual and moral interests. In religious use: Destitute of spiritual life, worldly, irreligious. Now *rare* or *obs.* 1557. **b.** Excessively inclined to the gratification of the senses, voluptuous; often *spec.*, lewd, unchaste. Of physiognomy, etc.: Indicative of a sensual disposition. 1530. **5.** Of opinions or ideas: Materialistic 1656.

1. Ye soft pipes, play on; Not to the s. ear, but.. Pipe to the spirit ditties of no tone KEATS. **3. a.** No gratification, however s., can, of itself, be esteemed vicious HUME. **b.** To roule with pleasure in a s. stie MILT. The s. pleasure of the glutton 1850. **4. a.** These are they which segregate themselues, s., hauing not the Spirit *N.T.* (Rhem.) *Jude* 19. S. Men are not willing to believe any thing whereby they have not a sufficient Evidence, as they think, to their Sense 1676. **b.** By nature coarse and s. in his habits 1881. The full mouth, with the s. lips 1905. **5.** The common s. idea of heaven 1871.

†**B.** *sb. pl.* **1. a.** The sensual faculties and appetites. **b.** The objects of sense. –1676. **2.** Beings capable only of sensation, brutes –1644. Hence **Se·nsually** *adv.*

Sensualism (se·nsiu-, -ʃuăliz'm). 1803. [f. SENSUAL *a.* + -ISM. Cf. Fr. *sensualisme* (1812 in sense 1).] **1.** *Philos.* The doctrine that the senses are the sole source of knowledge; sensationalism. **2.** Addiction to sensual indulgence 1813.

2. A face coarsened by s. 1906.

Sensualist (se·nsiu-, -ʃuălist). 1662. [f. as prec. + -IST. Cf. Fr. *sensualiste* (1812 in sense 2).] **1.** One whose disposition and conduct are sensual; chiefly, one who is devoted to sensual pleasure, or given to vicious indulgence of the animal passions. **2.** = SENSATIONALIST 1852. Hence **Se:nsuali·stic** *a.* pertaining to sensualism in philosophy or art.

Sensuality (sensiu-, -ʃuæ·lĭti). ME. [– (O)Fr. *sensualité* – late L. *sensualitas*, f. *sensualis*; see SENSUAL *a.*, -ITY.] †**1.** The part of the nature of man that is concerned with the senses; chiefly, the animal instincts and appetites; the lower nature as dist. from the reason; also *occas.* the faculty of sensation –1828. †**2.** The lower or animal nature regarded as a source of evil; the lusts of the flesh. Also *pl.* –1621. **3.** Excessive fondness for, or vicious indulgence in, the pleasures of the senses 1450. **4.** *spec.* Lasciviousness, unchastity 1463.

3. Those pampred animalls, That rage in sauage sensualitie SHAKS. *pl.* The pleasures and sensualities of a luxuriant table 1893. **4.** Judging the s. of a nation by its statistics of illegitimate births 1869.

Sensualize (se·nsiu-, -ʃuăləiz), *v.* 1612. [f. SENSUAL *a.* + -IZE.] **1.** *trans.* To render sensual; to explain by reference to sensation; *esp.* to imbue with sensual habits or dispositions; to inure to vicious indulgence 1687. **2.** *intr.* **a.** To live sensually 1612. **b.** To entertain sensual notions 1846.

1. Not to suffer ones self to be sensualiz'd by pleasures 1725. Locke sensualized the conception of the understanding 1877. Hence **Se:nsualiza·tion,** the action of sensualizing.

Sensuism (se·nsiu-, -ʃuˌiz'm). 1829. [f. L. *sensus* SENSE *sb.* + -ISM.] *Philos.* = SENSUALISM 1.

Sensuous (se·nsiuˌəs, -ʃuˌəs), *a.* 1641. [app. first used by Milton, to avoid certain associations of the existing word *sensual.*] **1.** Of or pertaining to the senses; derived from, perceived by, or affecting the senses; concerned with sensation or sense-perception. **b.** Of words, etc.: Relating to sensible objects. Of opinions, etc.: Based on representations of sense, material. 1864. **c.** Of pleasure: Received through the senses 1856. **2.** Readily affected by the senses; keenly alive to the pleasures of sensation. Also of physiognomy, etc., indicating a sensuous temperament. 1870.

1. To which Poetry would be made subsequent or indeed rather precedent, as being lesse suttle and fine, but more simple, s., and passionate MILT. **b.** Their religion..was of a s. character 1864. **2.** Keats as a poet is abundantly and enchantingly s. M. ARNOLD. Hence **Se·nsuous-ly** *adv.*, **-ness.**

Sent (sent), *ppl. a.* 1483. [pa. pple. of SEND *v.*] In senses of the vb. *rare* exc. in comb. as *heaven-sent.*

Sent, obs. form of SCENT.

Sentence (se·ntĕns), *sb.* ME. [– (O)Fr. *sentence* – L. *sententia* mental feeling, opinion, judgement (philos.) tr. Gr. δόξα and γνώμη, f. *sentire* feel; see -ENCE.] †**1.** Way of thinking, opinion –1609. †**2.** The opinion pronounced by a person on some particular question –1725. **3.** An authoritative decision; a judgement pronounced by a tribunal. †**a.** *spec.* = s. of excommunication –1523. **b.** *gen.* The judgement or decision of a court in any civil or criminal cause. Now *rare* in pop. use; still techn. applied to the decisions of the eccl. and admiralty courts. late ME. **c.** The judicial determination of the punishment to be inflicted on a convicted criminal. Hence, the punishment to which a criminal is sentenced. ME. †**4.** A quoted saying of some eminent person, an apophthegm. Also, a pithy or pointed saying, an aphorism, maxim. –1823. †**b.** Aphoristic speech, sententiousness –1649. **5.** An indefinite portion of a discourse or writing; a 'passage'. Now only, a short passage of Scripture in liturgical use. late ME. **6.** A series of words in connected speech or writing, forming the grammatically complete expression of a single thought; in pop. use often, such a portion of a composition or utterance as extends from one full stop to another. In *Grammar*, the verbal expression of a proposition, question, command, or request, containing normally a subject and a predicate. 1447. **b.** *Mus.* A complete idea, usu. consisting of two or four phrases 1891. †**7.** Sense, substance, or gist –1561. †**b.** *gen.* Significance –1589.

1. Touching the s. of antiquitie in this cause HOOKER. **2.** My s. is for open Warr MILT. *The four books* (or *the Book*) *of the Sentence*(*s*, the *Sententiarum libri quatuor*, a compilation of the opinions of the Fathers on questions of Christian doctrine, by Peter Lombard (12th c.), thence called *The Master of the Sentences.* **3. b.** A S. of Judicial Separation 1857. **c.** When s. of death, ..is pronounced BLACKSTONE. *fig.* We are all under a s. of death for the first Man's sin DE FOE. **4.** Sentences have great weight in discourse for two reasons 1823. **b.** A discourse full of s. MILT. **5.** After which he reads a short S. of Scripture 1753. **6.** I would not lose a s. that I could gain from lips so instructive RICHARDSON. English grammarians usually recognize three classes: simple sentences, complex sentences (which contain one or more subordinate clauses), and compound sentences (which have more than one subject or predicate). O.E.D. **7.** *Mulier est hominis confusio*: Madame, the s. of this latyn is, Womman is mannes Ioye and al his blis CHAUCER.

Sentence (se·ntĕns), *v.* late ME. [– (O)Fr. *sentencier*, f. *sentence* SENTENCE *sb.* Cf. med.L. *sententiare* pronounce sentence (XII).] †**1.** *intr.* To pass judgement –1710. †**2.** *trans.* To decree or order judicially; to decide judicially; to declare judicially or authoritatively –1681. †3. To pass judgement on (a person or his actions, the merit of anything) –1809. 4. To pronounce sentence upon; to condemn *to* a punishment 1592.

3. After this cold considerance, s. me SHAKS. 4. The offender was sentenc'd and repriev'd EVELYN. *transf.* The man sentenced to a living tomb 1895. Hence **Se·ntencer,** one who sentences.

Sentential (sente·nʃ'ăl), *a.* Now *rare.* 1475. [– late L. *sententialis*, f. L. *sententia* SENTENCE *sb.*; see -AL¹.] †1. Containing, or of the nature of 'sentences' or maxims –1645. 2. Pertaining to a sentence or series of words in syntactical connection 1646. †3. Of the nature of a 'sentence' or final judicial decision –1701. Hence **Sente·ntially** *adv.* (*Obs.* or *rare*) by way of (judicial) sentence.

Sententiary (sente·nʃ'ări). *Hist.* 1603. [– med.L. *sententiarius*, f. L. *sententia* SENTENCE *sb.*; see -ARY¹.] a. One who writes or utters sentences or aphorisms. b. A compiler of 'sentences' or opinions of doctors of the Church on theological questions. c. A commentator or lecturer on the Book of Sentences.

Sententiosity (sentenʃiǫ·sĭti). *rare.* 1646. [f. SENTENTIOUS + -ITY.] Sententiousness; also, a sententious remark.

Sententious (sente·nʃəs), *a.* 1440. [– L. *sententiosus* (Cicero), f. *sententia* SENTENCE *sb.*; see -OUS.] †1. Full of meaning; of persons, full of intelligence or wisdom –1648. 2. Of the nature of a 'sentence' or aphoristic saying 1542. 3. Of discourse, style, etc.: Abounding in pointed maxims, aphoristic. Now often in bad sense, affectedly or pompously formal. 1509. 4. Of persons: Given to the utterance of maxims or pointed sayings. Now often in bad sense, addicted to pompous moralizing. 1598.

1. Your reasons at dinner haue been sharpe & s. SHAKS. 2. Brief s. precepts MILT. 3. His grace.. in speaking..was pleasant and yet graue:.. s., and yet familiar 1579. A long s. letter, full of Latin quotations KINGSLEY. 4. Sallust was a s. pedant BERKELEY. Hence **Sente·ntious-ly** *adv.*, **-ness.**

Sentience (se·nʃ'ĕns). 1839. [f. SENTIENT *a.*; see -ENCE.] The condition or quality of being sentient, consciousness, susceptibility to sensation. So **Se·ntiency.**

Sentient (se·nʃ'ĕnt), *a.* and *sb.* 1603. [– L. *sentiens*, *-ent-*, pr. pple. of *sentire* feel.] A. *adj.* 1. That feels or is capable of feeling; having the power or function of sensation or of perception by the senses 1632. 2. *Phys.* Of organs or tissues: Responsive to sensory stimuli 1822. 3. Characterized by the exercise of the senses 1906.

1. [The legend] ascribes to the ship s. powers GROTE. 3. S. experience..is reality 1906.

B. *absol.* and *sb.* a. That which has sensation or feeling. b. One who or something which has sensation. 1603. Hence **Se·ntiently** *adv.*

Sentiment (se·ntimĕnt). late ME. [In XIV *sentement* – OFr. *sentement* (mod. *senti-*) – med.L. *sentimentum*, f. L. *sentire* feel; see -MENT. Refash. after Fr. and L. XVII.] †1. Personal experience, one's own feeling. late ME. only. †2. Sensation, physical feeling. In later use, a knowledge due to vague sensation. –1829. 3. What one feels with regard to something; mental attitude (of approval or disapproval, etc.); an opinion or view of what is right or agreeable. Often *pl.* with collective sense. 1639. †b. In wider sense: An opinion, view (e.g. on a question of fact or scientific truth) –1838. 4. A mental feeling, an emotion. Now chiefly applied to those feelings which involve an intellectual element or are concerned with ideal objects. 1652. b. *Phrenology.* In *pl.*, used as the name for the class of 'faculties' (including Veneration, Self-esteem, Wonder, etc.) which are concerned with emotion, and to which 'organs' are assigned at the top of the brain 1815. 5. A thought coloured by or proceeding from emotion 1762. b. *esp.* An emotional thought expressed in literature or art 1709. c. An epigrammatical expression of some striking or agreeable thought or wish announced in the manner of a toast 1777. 6. *gen.* a. Refined and tender emotion; emotional reflection or meditation; appeal to the tender emotions in literature or art. Now chiefly as conveying an imputation of insincerity or mawkishness. 1768. b. Emotional regard to ideal considerations, as a principle of action or judgement 1851.

2. She cold was and withouten sentement CHAUCER. 3. In one s., indeed, you are pretty well agreed—that the Bible is to be discarded 1852. 4. My uncle assured him he..spoke from a s. of friendly regard to his interest SMOLLETT. 5. b. The sentiments and language are the poet's own COLERIDGE. c. Come, Mr. Premium, I'll give you a s.; here's *Success to usury!* SHERIDAN. 6. a. The tear of elegant s. permanently in his eye STEVENSON. b. Family s. is not everything 1908.

Sentimental (sentime·ntăl), *a.* 1749. [f. prec. + -AL¹.] 1. Characterized by sentiment. orig., Characterized by or exhibiting refined and elevated feeling. In later use: Addicted to indulgence in superficial emotion; apt to be swayed by sentiment. Also *absol.* (with *the*). 2. Pertaining to sentiment. a. Arising from or determined by feeling rather than reason 1752. b. That is a matter of sentiment and not of material interest 1891. 3. Of literary compositions, etc.: Appealing to sentiment; expressive of the tender emotions, esp. those of love 1762.

1. A soft s. whisper DISRAELI. You have no s. nonsense, no silly infatuation..to fear from me 1862. Hence **Sentime·ntalism,** the s. habit of mind; an idea or expression indicative of sentimentality. **Sentime·ntalist,** one who cultivates or affects sentimentality; one who holds s. doctrines. **Sentimenta·lity,** the quality of being s.; affectation of sensibility, exaggerated insistence upon the claims of sentiment; *pl.* s. notions. **Sentime·ntally** *adv.*

Sentimentalize (sentime·ntăləiz), *v.* 1764. [f. prec. + -IZE.] 1. *intr.* To indulge in sentimental thoughts or expressions. 2. *trans.* To make (a person, etc.) sentimental; to imbue (a person, work of art, etc.) with sentiment or sentimental qualities 1821.

1. Here the historian of the conspiracy sentimentalizes SOUTHEY. Hence **Sentime·ntaliza·tion, Sentime·ntalizer.**

Sentinel (se·ntinĕl), *sb.* 1579. [– Fr. *sentinelle* – It. *sentinella*, of unkn. origin; for the fem. gender cf. the originals of *guard, scout*, SPY, *vedette*.] 1. = SENTRY *sb.*¹ 2. Also *transf.* and *fig.* One who or something which keeps guard like a military sentinel. †2. The occupation, duty, or service of a sentinel; chiefly in *to keep s.* –1703. †3. A military watch-tower for the defence of a camp or the walls of a city –1643. †4. (*Private*) *centinel*: a private soldier –1894.

1. They went all to sleep,..without so much as a centinel placed for their guard DE FOE. Phr. *To stand s.* The grim cliff on which the castle stands s. over the North Sea 1908.

attrib.: **s. crab,** a crab of the Indian Ocean, *Podophthalmus vigil.* Hence **Se·ntinelship.**

Sentinel (se·ntinĕl), *v.* 1593. [f. prec.] 1. *trans.* To stand guard over, to watch as a sentinel. †2. *intr.* To act as sentinel, stand sentinel, keep guard (*rare*) –1610. 3. *trans.* To furnish with or as with a sentinel or with sentinels 1656. 4. To post as a sentinel 1827.

1. And mountains, that like giants stand, To s. enchanted land SCOTT. 4. A statue of the builder sentinelled high up in an airy niche 1870.

Sentry (se·ntri), *sb.*¹ 1611. [perh. shortening of †*centrinel*, *-onel* (XVI), vars. of SENTINEL, with assim. to -RY.] †1. = SENTINEL *sb.* 3. –1653. 2. *Mil.* and *Naval.* An armed soldier or marine posted at a specified point to keep guard and to prevent the passing of an unauthorized person; spec. *Mil.*, each of the men of a military guard posted at regular intervals round an army in garrison or in the field to watch the enemy, prevent a surprise attack, and to challenge all comers 1632. b. *transf.* and *fig.* One who or something which keeps guard like a military sentry 1650. 3. The occupation, duty, or service of a sentry; also, the watch kept by a sentry, esp. in *to keep s.* 1639. 4. *Naut.* An apparatus in the form of an inverted kite (towed from the stern of a vessel at a set depth), which is automatically released from its slings on striking the bottom and thus gives warning of the shoaling of the water by sounding a gong on board the vessel 1894.

2. On the approach of any person, the S. will port Arms and call out, Halt! 1877. Phr. *To stand s.* b. Wild geese..when on the feed throw out sentries which keep a strict look out 1901. 3. Here Toils, and Death, and Death's half-brother, Sleep, Forms terrible to view, their Centry keep DRYDEN.

Sentry (se·ntri), *sb.*² *Obs.* exc. *Comb.* in proper names. 1590. [contr. form of *sentuarie*, var. of SANCTUARY infl. by Fr. *saintuaire*.] = SANCTUARY.

Sentry (se·ntri), *v. rare.* 1873. [f. SENTRY *sb.*¹] a. *trans.* To guard as a sentry. b. *intr.* To perform the office of a sentry.

Se·ntry-box. 1728. [f. SENTRY *sb.*¹ + BOX *sb.*² III. 1.] A small wooden structure in which a sentry may stand at his post in bad weather.

Se·ntry-go. 1852. [orig. a phr. of command; SENTRY (used vocatively) + GO *v.* (imper.).] †a. An order to a new sentry to proceed to the relief of the previous one. b. The patrol of a sentry; also, the duties of a sentry.

Sepal (se·păl). 1829. [– Fr. *sépale*, mod.L. *sepalum* (originated by N. J. de Necker, 1790), formed after *pétale* by substitution of the first syllable of *séparé*, L. *separatus* SEPARATE *a.*] *Bot.* Each of the divisions or leaves of the calyx of a flower. Hence **Se·pal(l)ed** *a.* only in comb., as *gamo-, two-sepalled*, etc. having united, two sepals, etc.

Sepaline (se·pălin), *a.* 1857. [f. SEPAL + -INE¹.] Of or belonging to the sepal of a flower.

Sepalody (se·păloᵘdi). 1887. [f. mod.L. *sepalum* + -ODE + -Y³, after *phyllody*.] *Bot.* The reversion of the petals of a flower into sepals by inverse metamorphosis.

Sepaloid (se·păloid), *a.* 1830. [f. SEPAL + -OID.] *Bot.* Of the nature of or resembling a sepal.

Separable (se·părăb'l), *a.* late ME. [– Fr. *séparable* or L. *separabilis*, f. *separare*; see SEPARATE *v.*, -ABLE.] Capable of being separated.

That the Magistrate is s. from the man is evident 1643. *S. accident, quality*, one which can be separated from its subject. *S. prefix* (Gram.), a prefix which can be used as an independent word. Hence **Se:parabi·lity, Se·parableness. Se·parably** *adv.*

Separate (se·părĕt), *pa. pple.*, *a.*, and *sb.* late ME. [– L. *separatus*, pa. pple. of *separare*; see next, -ATE².] †A. *pa. pple.* Separated –1692. B. *adj.* 1. Parted, divided, or withdrawn *from* others; disconnected, detached, set or kept apart 1667. b. Of persons, a dwelling, etc.: Withdrawn from society or intercourse; shut off from access 1600. 2. Withdrawn or divided from something else so as to have independent existence by itself 1700. b. Belonging or peculiar to one, not common to or shared with the other or the others 1673. c. Considered or reckoned by itself; single, individual 1840.

1. He sought them both, but wish'd his hap might find Eve s. MILT. b. Phr. *S. confinement, s. system*, the system of confining prisoners in s. cells. 2. An Essay on the s. existence of Matter 1861. Phr. *S. establishment*, often used to indicate that a married man maintains a paramour. b. A married woman, although having s. estate, and living apart from her husband 1858. *S. maintenance*: see MAINTENANCE 2.

C. *sb.* (the adj. used absol. or ellipt.) 1. One who withdraws from the Church; a separatist 1612. 2. *U.S.* An article or document issued separately; esp. a copy of an article reprinted from a magazine, volume of transactions, etc., for separate distribution 1886. Hence **Se·parate-ly** *adv.*, **-ness.**

Separate (se·părēᶦt), *v.* late ME. [– *separat-*, pa. ppl. stem of L. *separare*, f. *se-* SE- + *parare* make ready; partly after prec.; see -ATE³.] I. *trans.* 1. To put apart, set asunder (two or more persons or things, or one *from* another); to disunite, disconnect, make a division between. b. To put asunder in thought; to distinguish, treat as distinct 1651. 2. To remove from conjugal cohabitation, esp. by a judicial decree 1540. 3.

To keep apart or divide by an intervening space or barrier. Of the intervening medium: To part by lying between; to occupy the interval between. 1553. **4.** To segregate for a special purpose. Const. *for, to, unto*. (Chiefly in Biblical language.) 1526. **5.** To remove or part (a substance) *from* another with which it is combined or mixed. Also with *out*. 1617.

1. Life and these lips haue long bene seperated SHAKS. Being thus separated from my attendants, I lost my way 1839. **b.** Men had not yet learned to satisfy their consciences by separating the person from the office 1864. **3.** The goulph of Ponthus..separateth Asia from Europe 1585. **4.** Separat me Barnabas and Saul for the worke where vnto I have called them TINDALE *Acts* 13:2. **5.** It is in the furnace that the dross is separated 1850. Hence **Separated** *ppl. a.*, often *spec.* of married people living apart.

II. *intr.* **1.** To go away, secede, or withdraw *from* (esp. a church) 1684. **b.** Of two or more persons: To quit each other's society or company; (of a company) to break up 1690. **c.** To withdraw from conjugal cohabitation 1686. **2.** Of a thing: To part (*from* something else); to be disunited or disjoined, to become detached; to draw apart or asunder 1638. **b.** Of a mineral or chemical substance: To be parted or disengaged from a mass or compound; to be drawn *out* from a solution in the form of crystals or as a precipitate 1863.

2. The roof of the nave has separated in one place from the wall 1832.

Separation (sepărē^i·ʃən). late ME. [– (O)Fr. *séparation* – L. *separatio, -ōn-*, f. as prec.; see -ION.] **1.** The action of separating; the state of being separated or parted. **2.** The action of separating oneself, withdrawing, or parting company 1450. **3.** Cessation of conjugal cohabitation, either by mutual consent of the parties or imposed by a judicial decree granted at the suit of one of them 1600. **4.** The place where two or more objects separate or are divided from one another; a parting, line of division 1615. **5.** Something that separates; an interval or break between two objects; a cause of separating (*rare*) 1715. †**6.** *Alchemy* and *Old Chem.* A process of analysis, extraction, or the like –1728. **7.** *Med.* The process by which dead tissue becomes detached from the sound flesh 1612.

1. After the age of six years, the time has arrived for the separation of the sexes JOWETT. **3.** The usual Causes of S. is assign'd as the Fault of the Wife 1700. *Judicial s.*, the name now given to the 'divorce *a mensa et thoro*'; see DIVORCE *sb.* 1.

attrib.: **s. allowance,** an allowance paid to the wife of a soldier in war-time; **-order,** an order of court for judicial separation.

Separatism (se·părătiz'm). 1628. [f. SEPARATE *a.* + -ISM.] The disposition to separate or to be separate; advocacy of separation (esp. in regard to Church or State); the principles and practices of separatists.

Separatist (se·părătist), *sb.* and *a.* 1608. [f. SEPARATE *a.* or *sb.* + -IST.] **A.** *sb.* **1.** One who advocates ecclesiastical separation; one who belongs to a religious community separated from the Church or from a particular church. **b.** *gen.* A schismatic, sectarian; also, a member of a congregation not belonging to any recognized denomination 1641. **2.** Often interpreted to mean: One who holds himself apart from others on the ground of superior piety. Hence as tr. *Pharisee*. 1620. **3.** One who advocates political separation; applied, e.g. (by opponents) to the advocates of Home Rule for Ireland 1871.

1. They [*sc.* Wesleyan Methodists] ought more properly, perhaps, to be called separatists than dissenters 1846. **2.** The Separatists, or Sanctified, as they terme themselves 1620.

B. *attrib.* or as *adj.* That is a separatist; pertaining to, consisting of, or characteristic of separatists 1830. Hence **Se:parati·stic** *a.* pertaining to or of the nature of separation.

Separative (se·părĕtiv), *a.* 1592. [– Fr. *séparatif* or late L. *separativus*, f. L. *separat-*; see SEPARATE *v.*, -IVE.] **1.** Tending to separate or to cause separation. **2.** *Gram.* Of conjunctions: Alternative, disjunctive 1888. Hence **Se·parative-ly** *adv.*, **-ness.**

Separator (se·pără^i·təɹ). 1607. [– eccl. L. *separator* schismatic (Tertullian), f. as prec.; see -OR 2. Later f. SEPARATE *v.* + -OR 2.] **1.** One who or something which separates; *spec.* †one who separates from the Church, a separatist; a critic who ascribes the Iliad and Odyssey to different authors (tr. Gr. χωρίζων). **2.** An instrument or appliance for separating, in various arts and crafts; often short for *cream-s.* 1830.

Se·paratory, *a.* 1715. [f. SEPARATE *v.* + -ORY².] Having the function of separating.

‖**Separatrix** (se·pără^i·triks). 1660. [mod. use of late L. *separatrix*, fem. of SEPARATOR; see -TRIX.] †**1.** The mark (orig. L, later |), formerly used to separate the figures representing decimals from those representing integers; now superseded by the decimal point. **2.** The slanting stroke used in proof correction to mark and separate alterations 1892. **3.** The line separating light and shade on a partly illuminated surface 1891.

‖**Sephardi** (sīfā·ɹdi). *Pl.* **Sephardim** (-dim), **-din** (-din). 1851. [post-bibl. Heb. *s^epardî*, f. *s^epārad*, the name of a country mentioned only *Obad.* 20, and identified by the Rabbis with Spain.] A Spanish or Portuguese Jew, a Jew of Spanish or Portuguese descent. Hence **Sepha·rdic** *a.* pertaining to the Sephardim.

Sephen (se·fen). 1854. [– mod.L. *sephen* (specific name) – Arab. *safan* rough skin.] A kind of sting-ray.

‖**Sephiroth** (se·firoþ), *pl.* Rarely in *sing.* **sephira.** 1569. [Heb., f. *sāpar* to number.] In the philosophy of the Cabbala, the ten hypostatized attributes or emanations by means of which the Infinite enters into relation with the finite.

Sepia (sī·piă). 1569. [– L. *sepia* – Gr. σηπία. In sense 2 prob. (as Fr. *sépia*) immed. – It. *seppia.*] **1.** The cuttle-fish; now *rare* exc. *Zool.* a cuttle of the genus *Sepia* or family *Sepiidæ*; also, the genus itself. **2.** A pigment of a rich brown colour (used in monochrome water-colour painting) prepared from the inky secretion of the cuttle-fish; the colour of this pigment. Also called *Roman s.* Often *attrib.* as in *s. drawing, tone.* 1821. **3.** In full *s. bone*: Cuttle-bone, *esp.* as used in pharmacy, etc. 1840. Hence **Se·pioid,** a cuttle-fish of the genus *S.*

Sepiacean (sīpi,ē^i·ʃăn), *a.* and *sb.* 1842. [f. mod.L. *Sepiaceus*, f. SEPIA; see -ACEAN.] *Zool.* Pertaining to, or a member of, the group *Sepiacea* of cuttle-fishes. So **Sepia·ceous** *a.*

‖**Sepiola** (sīpəi·ŏlă). 1797. [mod. use of L. *sepiola*, dim. of SEPIA. Cf. Fr. *sépiole* (Cuvier).] *Zool.* A cuttle-fish of the genus so named.

Sepiolite (sī·piŏləit). 1854. [– G. *sepiolith* (Glocker, 1847), f. Gr. σήπιον SEPIUM; see -LITE.] *Geol.* Meerschaum.

Sepiostaire (sīpiŏstē^ə·ɹ). 1836. [– Fr. *sépiostaire*, f. Gr. σηπία SEPIA + ὀστοῦν bone + *-aire* (cf. -ARY¹).] *Zool.* Cuttle-bone.

‖**Sepium** (sī·piŏm). 1835. [mod.L. – Gr. σήπιον.] *Zool.* Cuttle-bone.

†**Sepo·se,** *v.* 1593. [Based on L. *seponere* (whence †*sepone* vb.), after POSE *v.*¹; cf. DEPONE, DEPOSE, etc.] **1.** *trans.* To set aside –1664. **2.** To set apart or reserve –1641. So †**Seposi·tion,** setting aside –1656.

Sepoy (sī·poi, sīpoi·), **sipahi** (sipā·i). *Anglo-Ind.* 1717. [– (prob. through Pg. *sipae*) Urdu-Pers. *sipāhī* horseman, soldier, f. *sipāh* army. Cf. SPAHI.] A native of India employed as a soldier under European, esp. British, discipline.

attrib.: **s.-crab,** a species of crab found in the Indian and Pacific Oceans; **S. Mutiny** or **Rebellion,** a revolt against British rule in India in 1857–8, commonly called *the Indian Mutiny*.

Seps (seps). 1562. [– L. *seps* – Gr. σήψ, f. base of σήπειν make rotten.] **1.** A very venomous serpent described by classical writers. **2.** A lizard of the scincoid genus *Seps*, having a serpentlike body; a serpent-lizard 1802.

Sepsine (se·psin). 1880. [f. next + -INE⁵.] **a.** A poisonous crystalline substance obtained from decomposing yeast. **b.** A ptomaine causing septic poison.

‖**Sepsis** (se·psis). 1876. [– mod.L. – Gr. σῆψις, f. σήπειν make rotten.] Septic poisoning.

Sept (sept), *sb.*¹ 1548. [– L. *septum* SEPTUM.] **1.** An enclosure; an area marked off for a special purpose; a fold (*fig.*). **2.** *Arch.* A dividing screen, railing, etc. 1821.

Sept (sept), *sb.*² 1517. [poss. alt. of SECT (also so used XVI); cf. AL. *septus* (XVI), and med.L. *septa*, repr. OFr. *sette* sect, It. *setta.*] A division of a nation or tribe; a clan; orig. in ref. to Ireland. **b.** *transf.* A 'tribe' or class 1610.

ThErle of Desmonde, and the Geraldines of his kyn and septe 1536. Hence **Se·ptal** *a.*²

‖**Septæmia** (septī·miă). Also *U.S.* **septemia.** 1887. [mod.L., f. Gr. σηπτός putrefying, putrefactive (f. σήπειν rot, make putrid) + αἷμα blood.] = SEPTICÆMIA.

Septal (se·ptăl), *a.*¹ 1839. [f. SEPTUM + -AL¹.] Pertaining to, consisting of, or forming a septum or septa.

†**Septangle.** 1551. [f. L. *septem* seven + ANGLE *sb.*², after *triangle*, etc.] A heptagon –1656.

Septangular (septæ·ŋgiŭlăɹ), *a.* 1656. [f. L. *septem* seven + ANGULAR, after *triangular*, etc.] Having seven angles, heptagonal.

‖**Septarium** (septē^ə·riŏm). *Pl.* **-aria** (-ē^ə·riă). 1785. [mod.L., f. L. *septum*; see SEPTUM and -ARIUM.] *Geol.* **1.** A septal arrangement. **2.** A nodule of argillaceous limestone, ironstone, or the like, of which the parts near the centre are cracked, the spaces between being filled with some mineral: formerly much used for cement 1791. Hence **Septa·rian** *a.* of the form or character of septaria.

Septate (se·pte^it), *a.* 1846. [f. SEPTUM + -ATE², after *dentate, foliate*, etc.] *Nat. Hist.* Containing or divided by a septum or septa. So **Se·ptated** *a.* **Septa·tion,** division by a septum or septa.

Septem-, L. *septem* seven, = SEPTI-¹ (which is more frequent): as in **Septe·mfluous** [L. *septemfluus*] *a.* flowing in seven streams. **Septemfo·liate** *a. Bot.* having seven leaflets. **Septempa·rtite** *a. Bot.* divided nearly to the base into seven parts.

September (septe·mbəɹ). Abbrev. **Sep., Sept.**, in 17th c. also 7^br. OE. [– L. *September*, f. *septem* seven, or (in ME.) Fr. *septembre*, this month being the seventh of the old Roman year.] The ninth month of the year (according to the modern reckoning).

Septembrist (septe·mbrist). 1840. [f. prec. + -IST.] **a.** In Portugal, a supporter of the (successful) insurrection of September 1836 in favour of the restoration of the constitution of 1822. **b.** = SEPTEMBRIZER 1.

Septembrize (se·ptembrəiz), *v.* Also **-ber-.** 1793. [– Fr. *septembriser*, f. *septembre* SEPTEMBER; see -IZE.] *trans.* and *intr.* (orig. *Fr. Hist.*) To assassinate like the Septembrizers.

Septembrizer (se·ptembrəizəɹ). Also **-ber-.** 1794. [– Fr. *septembriseur*, f. *septembriser* (see prec.).] **1.** *Fr. Hist.* One who took part in or advocated the massacre of the political prisoners in Paris on September 2nd–5th, 1792. Also *transf.*, a bloodthirsty revolutionary. **2.** = SEPTEMBRIST a. 1840. **3.** One who shoots partridges (in September): with allusion to sense 1. 1824.

Septemvir (septe·mvəɹ). *Pl.* **-viri** (-virəi). 1760. [L., sing. of *septemviri*, f. *septem* seven + *viri* men.] One of a body of seven men associated in an office or commission.

Septemvirate (septe·mvirĕt). 1640. [– L. *septemviratus*, f. *septemvir*; see -ATE¹.] **1.** The office or dignity of a septemvir, government by septemviri. **2.** A group or set of seven men 1750.

‖**Septenarius** (septĭnē^ə·riŏs). *Pl.* **-arii** (-ē^ə·ri,əi). 1819. [L., f. *septeni* seven each.] *Pros.* A line of seven feet, esp. the trochaic or iambic tetrameter catalectic.

Septenary (se·ptĭnări, septī·nări), *a.* and *sb.* 1577. [– L. *septenarius*, f. *septeni*; see prec. and -ARY¹.] **A.** *adj.* Pertaining or relating to the number seven; forming a group of seven 1601. **b.** With ref. to the division of time into periods based on the number seven, e.g. a week 1646.

S. number, the number seven. **b.** That s. notation of days which we call the week 1848.

B. *sb.* †**1.** The number seven –1690. **2.** A group or set of seven 1594. **3.** A period of seven years (*occas.* weeks, days) 1577. **4.** *Mus.* The seven notes of the diatonic scale 1662. **5.** *Pros.* = SEPTENARIUS 1887.

3. The dayes of men are usually cast up by septenaries SIR T. BROWNE.

Septenate (se·ptĭnĕt), *a.* 1830. [f. L. *septeni* seven each + -ATE².] *Bot.* Growing in sevens, having seven divisions, heptamerous.

Septennary (septe·nări), *a.* 1644. [– L. *septennis* (f. *septem* seven + *annus* year) + -ARY¹.] Septennial.

Septennate (septe·nĕt). 1874. [– Fr. *septennat*, f. L. *septennis* (see prec.) + *-at* -ATE¹.] A period of seven years during which office is held, etc.

Septennial (septe·niăl), *a.* 1640. [– late L. *septennis, septennium* (see prec.) + -AL¹.] **1.** Consisting of, or lasting, seven years 1656. **2.** Recurring every seven years 1640.

1. A s. parliament 1772. **2.** S. revaluations 1886. Hence **Septe·nnially** *adv.* every seven years.

‖**Septennium** (septe·niŏm). 1855. [Late L. (for *septuennium*), f. *septem* seven + *annus* year; see -IUM.] A period of seven years.

†**Septentrial**, *a.* 1549. [irreg. f. L. *septentrio* (see next) + -AL¹.] = SEPTENTRIONAL –1631.

Septentrion (septe·ntriŏn), *sb.* and *a.* *Obs.* exc. *arch.* late ME. [– L. *septentrio*, sing. of *septentriones*, orig. *septem triones*, the seven stars of the Great Bear, f. *septem* + *triones*, pl. of *trio* plough-ox.] **A.** *sb.* **1.** *pl.* (chiefly as Latin.) The constellation of the Great Bear, *occas.* the Little Bear 1532. **2.** The north; the northern region(s) of the earth or the heavens. late ME. **3.** A northerner (*rare*) 1607. **B.** *adj.* Northern; = next 1632.

A. 2. Thou art as opposite to euery good, As.. the South to the S. SHAKS. **B.** Cold S. blasts MILT.

Septentrional (septe·ntriŏnăl), *a.* Now *rare*. late ME. [– L. *septentrionalis*, f. *septentrio, -ōn-*; see prec., -AL¹.] Belonging to the north, northern; formerly (of learning, etc.), pertaining to northern countries.

Dr. Marshall the..reviver of S. Learning in the University of Oxford 1718.

Septet(t, -ette (septe·t). 1837. [– G. *septet*, f. L. *septem* seven; see -ET, -ETTE.] *Mus.* A composition for seven voices or instruments. **b.** *transf.* A set of seven 1886.

Septfoil (se·tfoil). 1578. [– late L. *septifolium*, after CINQFOIL, TREFOIL.] **1.** The plant tormentil. Now *rare*. **2.** *Arch.* An ornament with seven cusps or points 1849.

Septi-¹, comb. form of L. *septem* seven, in Eng. forming adj. compounds for the most part adapted from or modelled on L. compounds.

Se·ptico:loured *a.* of seven colours. **Septifo·lious** [L. *folium* leaf], *a.* having seven leaves. **Se·ptiform** *a.*¹ sevenfold. **Septila·teral** *a.* seven-sided. **Se·ptipartite** *a.* = SEPTEMPARTITE. **Septi·valent** *a.* *Chem.* combining with seven atoms of hydrogen or other univalent element or radical.

Septi-², comb. form of SEPTUM, as in **Se·pticidal** [L. *-cidere*, comb. f. *cædere* cut] *a.* *Bot.* applied to the form of dehiscence in which the pod splits through the dissepiments. **Septi·ferous,** *a.* having a septum or septa. **Se·ptiform,** *a.*² of the form or nature of a septum. **Septi·fragal** [L. *frag-, frangere* break] *a.* *Bot.* applied to the form of dehiscence in which the septa are separated from the valves.

Septic (se·ptik), *a.* and *sb.* 1605. [– L. *septicus* – Gr. σηπτικός, f. σήπειν make rotten; see -IC.] **A.** *adj.* Putrefactive, putrefying; in mod. use, of disease, caused by the absorption of the products of putrefaction. †**B.** *sb.* A septic or putrefactive substance –1771.

‖**Septicæmia** (septisī·miă). Also *U.S.* **septicemia.** 1866. [mod.L., f. Gr. σηπτικός SEPTIC + αἷμα blood; see -IA¹.] Septic poisoning. Hence **Septicæ·mic** *a.*

Se·ptical, *a.* Now *rare* or *Obs.* 1646. [f. as SEPTIC; see -ICAL.] = SEPTIC *a.* Hence **Se·ptically** *adv.* so as to produce putrefaction.

Septicity (septi·sĭti). 1828. [f. SEPTIC + -ITY, after Fr. *septicité*.] The quality or condition of being septic.

Septillion (septi·lyən). 1690. [– Fr. *septillion* (XVI), f. *sept* (or L. *septem*), after *billion*, etc.; cf. BILLION.] *Arith.* The seventh power of a million, denoted by 1 followed by 42 ciphers. In American (following the later Fr.) use, the eighth power of a thousand, denoted by 1 followed by 24 ciphers.

Septimal (se·ptimăl), *a.* 1855. [f. L. *septimus* seventh + -AL¹, after *decimal*.] **1.** Of a numerical system: Based on the number 7. **2.** *Mus.* Pertaining to a seventh 1867.

Septime (se·ptim). 1889. [– L. *septimus*, ordinal of *septem* seventh.] *Fencing.* A parry.

Septimole (se·ptimōᵘl). 1854. [Arbitrarily f. L. *septimus* seventh; cf. QUINTOLE.] *Mus.* A group of seven notes to be played in the time of four or six.

Septinsular (septi·nsiŭlăɹ), *a.* (*sb.*) 1809. [f. L. *septem* (see SEPTI-) + *insula* island + -AR¹.] *S. Republic*, etc.: the Ionian Islands. Also as *sb. pl.*, the people of the Ionian Islands.

Septo-¹, comb. form of Gr. σηπτός, vbl. adj. f. σήπειν rot, as in **Septoge·nic,** *a.* producing sepsis; etc.

Septo-², used as comb. form of SEPTUM, as in **Se:pto-maxi·llary** *a.* applied to a small bone lying above the vomer in some birds and fishes.

Septuagenarian (se:ptiŭădʒĭnēᵊ·riăn), *a.* and *sb.* 1715. [f. L. *septuagenarius*, f. *septuageni* seventy each; see -ARIAN.] **A.** *adj.* **1.** Pertaining to the number seventy (*rare*). **2.** Seventy years old; characteristic of that age 1793. **B.** *sb.* A person seventy years old 1805.

Septuagenary (se:ptiŭădʒī·nări), *a.* and *sb.* Now *rare*. 1605. [– L. *septuagenarius* (see prec.). Cf. Fr. *septuagénaire*.] = prec.

Septuagesima (se:ptiŭădʒe·simă). late ME. [– L. *septuagesima* (sc. *dies*), fem. of *septuagesimus* seventieth, f. *septuaginta* seventy.] **1.** In full *S. Sunday*: the third Sunday before Lent. †**2.** The seventy days beginning with the third Sunday before Lent and ending with the Saturday in Easter week –1483.

Septuagint (se·ptiŭădʒint). 1577. [– L. *septuaginta* seventy.] †**1.** The 'seventy translators' of the Old Testament into Greek (see 2); = L. *septuaginta* (*interpretes*), Gr. οἱ Ο'. Also *pl.* in the same sense. –1684. **2.** The Greek version of the Old Testament, which derives its name from the story that it was made by seventy-two Palestinian Jews at the request of Ptolemy Philadelphus (284–247 B.C.) and completed by them, in seclusion on the island of Pharos, in seventy-two days. (Denoted by LXX.) 1633. **3.** A group of seventy 1864. Hence **Se:ptuagi·ntal** *a.* of or pertaining to the S.

‖**Septulum** (se·ptiŭlŏm). 1826. [mod.L., dim. of next; see -ULE.] *Nat. Hist.* A small or thin septum. Hence **Se·ptulate** *a.* having a s.

‖**Septum** (se·ptŏm). *Pl.* **septa** (se·ptă). 1720. [– L. *septum, sæptum*, f. *sepire, sæpire* enclose, f. *sepes, sæpes* hedge.] A partition; a dividing wall, membrane, layer, etc.; a dissepiment 1728. **b.** *Anat.* e.g. the partition between the nostrils (*septum nasi*), the membrane separating the ventricles of the heart (*septum cordis*) 1726. **c.** *Bot.* e.g. the division-wall of a cell, a partition in a compound ovary or spore 1720. **d.** *Zool.* e.g. one of the radiated plates of the cell of corals, one of the partitions of a chambered shell 1815.

Septuor (se·ptiŭǫɹ). 1850. [– Fr. *septuor*, f. L. *septem* seven, after *quatuor* quartet. Cf. SEXTUOR.] *Mus.* = SEPTET.

Septuple (se·ptiup'l), *a.* and *sb.* 1692. [– late L. *septuplus* (also *-plum* sb.), f. L. *septem* seven. Cf. Fr. *septuple*.] **A.** *adj.* **1.** Sevenfold 1834. **2.** *Mus.* Having seven beats in a bar 1884. **B.** *sb.* The seventh multiple 1692. So **Se·ptuple** *v. trans.* to multiply by seven, increase seven times 1615.

Septuplet (se·ptiŭplet). 1891. [f. late L. *septuplus* (see prec.) after *triplet*, etc.] *Mus.* = SEPTIMOLE.

Sepulchral (sĭpʊ·lkrăl), *a.* 1615. [– Fr. *sépulchral* or L. *sepulchralis*, f. *sepulchrum*; see next, -AL¹.] **1.** Of or pertaining to burial or a place of burial. **a.** Pertaining to or serving as a sepulchre or tomb; forming part of a sepulchre, or its furniture; monumental 1631. **b.** Pertaining to burial rites and customs 1615. **2.** *transf.* Appropriate to a tomb; dismal, gloomy, melancholy 1711.

1. a. Old s. urns COWPER. **b.** S. libations 1729. **2.** A deep sepulcral sound the cave Return'd SOUTHEY. Hence **Sepu·lchrally** *adv.*

Sepulchre (se·pŏlkəɹ), *sb.* [ME. *sepulcre* – (O)Fr. *sépulchre* – L. *sepulcrum*, erron. *-chrum*, f. stem of *sepultus*, pa. pple. of *sepelire* bury.] **1.** A tomb or burial-place. Now only *rhet.* or *Hist.* Also *transf.* and *fig.* **2.** *The Holy S.*: The cave in which Jesus Christ was buried outside the walls of Jerusalem; hence, the buildings erected over the traditional site of this cave. Also in the title of churches erected in memory of this. **3.** *Antiq.* A permanent or temporary structure prepared in a church for the symbolic burial of the reserved Sacrament (sometimes also the Cross) on Maundy Thursday. late ME. **b.** The altar of repose (REPOSE *sb.* 1) 1753. **4.** Interment, burial (*rare*). late ME.

1. *Whited* (†*painted*) *s.*, in biblical language, used for a hypocrite, or one whose fair outward semblance conceals inward corruption. *fig.* The whole earth is the s. of famous men JOWETT. **2.** *Knight of the* (*Holy*) *S.*, a member of a secular confraternity of those knighted in the crusades, esp. at the Holy S. itself; since 1342, a religious organization, having the Latin Patriarch of Jerusalem as its Grand-master.

Sepulchre (se·pŏlkəɹ), *v.* 1591. [f. prec.] **1.** *trans.* To place in a sepulchre; to bury. **2.** To receive as in a sepulchre, to serve as a burial-place for 1605.

1. My bones s. not from thine apart COWPER. *fig.* Where merit is not sepulcher'd aliue B. JONS. **2.** When Ocean shrouds and sepulchres our dead BYRON.

Sepulture (se·pŏltiŭɹ, -tʃəɹ), *sb.* ME. [– (O)Fr. *sépulture* – L. *sepultura*, f. *sepultus*; see SEPULCHRE *sb.*, -URE.] **1.** Interment, burial. **2.** A burial-place, grave, tomb. Now *arch.* late ME.

1. Even the honours of s. were long withheld from his remains MACAULAY. *fig.* For dronkenesse is verray s. Of mannes wit and his discrecion CHAUCER. Hence **Sepu·ltural** *a.* of or pertaining to s. **Se·pulture** *v. trans.* to bury, inter.

Seq. *Pl.* **seqq.** Also **sq.** *Pl.* **sqq.** 1726. Abbrev. forms in *sing.* of L. *sequens* the following, *sequente* and in what follows, *sequitur* it follows; in *pl.* of *sequentes, -tia* the following, *sequentibus* in the following places. Also, *et seq.*

Sequacious (sĭkwēⁱ·ʃəs), *a.* 1640. [f. L. *sequax, sequac-*, f. *sequi* follow; see -IOUS, -ACIOUS.] **1.** Given to following another or others, esp. a leader. †Const. *to, of*. 1643. **b.** Given to slavish or unreasoning following of others (esp. in matters of thought or opinion) 1653. †**2.** Of things: Readily yielding to traction; easily moulded; ductile, pliable, flexible –1752. **3.** Of musical notes, metrical feet: Following one another with unvarying regularity of order 1795.

1. Trees unrooted left their Place, S. of the Lyre DRYDEN. **2.** Of all Fire there is none so ductile, so s. and obsequious as this of Wrath 1640. **3.** The long s. notes Over..surges sink and rise COLERIDGE. Hence **Sequa·cious-ly** *adv.*, **-ness.**

Sequacity (sĭkwæ·sĭti). 1626. [– late L. *sequacitas*, f. *sequac-* (see prec.) + -ITY.] †**1.** Ductility, pliability (of matter). BACON. **2.** Disposition or readiness to follow; lack of independence 1654.

Sequel (sī·kwĕl), *sb.* late ME. [– (O)Fr. *séquelle* or L. *sequela* (*-ella*), f. *sequi* follow.] †**1.** A train of followers, following, suite; *rarely*, a follower. In *Feudal Law*, the offspring, retinue, chattels, and appurtenances of a villein. –1640. †**2.** Descendants, posterity; successors in inheritance –1572. **3.** That which follows as a result of an event or course of action; an after-consequence 1477. †**4.** That which follows or is thought to follow as a logical consequence; an inference –1689. †**5.** Sequence, order of succession; also, a series –1771. **6.** What happened or will happen afterwards; the ensuing course of affairs; issue, result, upshot 1524. **b.** An age or period as following and influenced by (a former period) 1837. **7.** The ensuing narrative, discourse, etc.; the remaining part of a narrative, etc.; that which follows as a continuation; esp. a literary work that, although complete in itself, forms a continuation of a preceding one 1513.

3. That every phenomenon in the moral or material world was the s. of a natural cause 1883. **4.** 'Tis a false s.. to suppose that, 'cause it is now ill, 'twill ere be so LOVELACE. **5.** Homer.. wrote a s. of Songs and Rhapsodies BENTLEY. **6.** O plague right well preuented! so will you say, when you haue seene the sequele SHAKS. The October-Club..proved in the S. to be the chief Support of those who suspected them SWIFT. **7.** In *Love's Last Shift*, and in the S. of it, the *Relapse* CIBBER. We shall meet with it again.. in the s. of this history 1884.

‖**Sequela** (sĭkwī·lă). *Pl.* **-læ** (-lī). 1793. [L.; see prec.] *Path.* A morbid affection occurring as the result of a previous disease. Chiefly *pl.* **b.** *transf.* A consequence 1883.

Sequence (sī·kwĕns). late ME. [– late L. *sequentia*, f. *sequens*, *-ent-*, pr. pple. of *sequi* follow; see -ENCE.] **1.** The fact of following after or succeeding; the following of one thing after another in succession; an instance of this 1593. **2.** Order of succession 1586. **b.** *Gram.* Chiefly in *s. of tenses*, the manner in which the tense of a subordinate clause depends on that of the principal clause 1848. **3.** A continuous or connected series 1575. **b.** *Mus.* The repetition of a melodic or harmonic progression at a different pitch 1752. **4.** *Cards.* A group of three or more cards of the same suit following in numerical order; a 'run' 1575. **5.** Something that follows. **a.** A logical consequence; also †an inference, conclusion 1613. **b.** A subsequent event; sometimes contextually, a consequent event, a result 1853. **6.** The quality of being sequent; the fact of following as a logical inference or as a necessary result; continuity, consecutiveness 1828. **7.** *Eccl.* A composition in rhythmical prose or accentual metre said or sung, in the Western Church, between the Gradual and the Gospel. Also called *prose*; see PROSE *sb.* 2. late ME.

1. For how art thou a King But by faire s. and succession? SHAKS. There are fixed in his.. memory certain sequences as always occurring 1884. *Phr. In s.*, one after another. **2.** Works.. arranged in chronological s. 1862. **3.** Then came a long s. of reflections SCOTT. **4.** A S. of King, Queen, and Knave 1746. **5. b.** Maritime commerce was the natural s. to that along the courses of rivers 1872. **6.** In this remarkable Volume,..of true logical method and s. there is too little CARLYLE. So **Se·quency,** the quality of being sequent.

Sequent (sī·kwĕnt), *a.* and *sb.* 1560. [– OFr. *sequent* or late L. *sequens*, *-ent-*; see prec., -ENT.] **A.** *adj.* **1.** That follows or comes after. †**a.** That one is about to say or mention; (the) following –1821. **b.** That succeeds in time or serial order 1601. That follows another (*rare*) 1612. **2.** That follows as a result or logical conclusion. Const. *to, on, upon.* 1601. **3.** Following one another or in a series; successive 1604. **b.** Characterized by continuous succession; consecutive 1600.

1. b. The Rector..enjoyed his s. glass of port 1873. **2.** Indeed your O Lord sir, is very s. to your whipping SHAKS. **3.** The Gallies Haue sent a dozen s. Messengers..at one anothers heeles SHAKS.

B. *sb.* †**1.** A follower, attendant. SHAKS. †**2.** A unit of a sequence; esp. of playing-cards –1734. **3.** That which follows in order 1833. **4.** That which follows naturally as a result; the consequent of an antecedent 1838.

Sequential (sĭkwe·nʃăl), *a.* 1822. [f. SEQUENCE, SEQUENT, after *consequence, consequent, consequential.*] **1.** That follows as a sequel or a sequela. **2.** That is characterized by the regular sequence of its parts; continuous 1844. **3.** *Mus.* Of the nature of a sequence 1889. Hence **Seque·ntially** *adv.*

†**Seque·ster,** *sb.*[1] ME. [– L. *sequester* depositary of a thing in dispute.] In *Civil Law*, a person with whom the parties in a suit deposit the thing contested until the case has been decided. Also, a mediator. –1633.

†**Seque·ster,** *sb.*[2] 1568. [– (O)Fr. *séquestre* – L. *sequestrum*, orig. n. of *sequester* adj.; see prec.] **1.** Sequestration, seclusion, isolation. SHAKS. **2.** The office or court to which goods sequestered are taken 1568.

Sequester (sĭkwe·stəɹ), *v.* late ME. [– (O)Fr. *séquestrer* or late L. *sequestrare*, f. *sequester*; see SEQUESTER *sb.*[1]] **1.** *trans.* To set aside, separate; †to separate and reject. †**b.** *Eccl.* To excommunicate –1642. †**c.** To set apart, consecrate to a particular service –1697. †**d.** To remove from membership of a body, or from a public office or station –1827. **e.** To seclude (a person, thing, or place) from general access or intercourse. Now *rare* or *Obs.* exc. in SEQUESTERED *ppl. a.* late ME. **2.** To confiscate, appropriate, take forcible possession of 1513. **3.** *Law.* **a.** To remove (property, etc.) from the possession of the owner temporarily; to seize and hold the effects of a debtor until the claims of creditors be satisfied; *Eccl.* to divert the income of a benefice to the payment of debts due from the incumbent, or for the purpose of making good the dilapidations; to hold the income of a benefice during a vacancy for the benefit of the next incumbent 1530. **b.** To apply the process of sequestration to (a person); to sequestrate the estate or benefice of 1681. †**4.** *intr.* To withdraw into seclusion, to retire, keep apart –1838.

1. e. I had wholly sequestred my thoughts from ciuill affaires BACON. He sequestered himself from his subjects in the recesses of his palace DE QUINCEY. **2.** He is in rebellion and his estate sequestered 1644. **4.** To s. out of the world into Atlantick and Eutopian polities..will not mend our condition MILT.

Sequestered (sĭkwe·stəɹd), *ppl. a.* 1600. [f. prec. + -ED[1].] †**1.** Separated; cut off from congenial surroundings –1782. **b.** Under sentence of sequestration; esp. *Eccl. Hist.* of the dispossessed clergy under the Commonwealth: Deprived of a benefice 1661. **2.** Sheltered, retired, secluded 1658. **b.** Of persons: Retired, living a secluded life or in a quiet, unfrequented place 1643.

1. *A.Y.L.* II. i. 33. **b.** He is a poor sequestred Parson 1673. **2.** Along the cool sequester'd vale of life They kept the noiseless tenor of their way GRAY. **b.** Eremites, (the most s. of begging Fryers) FULLER.

†**Seque·strable,** *a.* 1652. [f. as prec. + -ABLE.] Capable of being sequestered, liable to sequestration –1807.

Sequestral (sĭkwe·străl), *a.* 1887. [f. SEQUESTRUM + -AL[1].] Of or pertaining to a sequestrum.

Sequestrate (sĭkwe·streɪt, sī·kwĕstrēɪt), *v.* 1513. [– *sequestrat-*, pa. ppl. stem of late L. *sequestrare*; see SEQUESTER *v.*, -ATE[3].] **1.** *trans.* To remove, put away; to seclude, keep away from general access or intercourse; to put in a place of concealment or confinement. Now *rare.* **2.** *Law.* To divert the income of an estate or benefice, temporarily or permanently, from its owner into other hands (cf. SEQUESTER *v.* 3 a) 1609. **b.** *Sc. Law.* To place (lands) in the control of a judicial factor or trustee; now, to take the property of a bankrupt into judicial possession 1726. **3.** *gen.* To confiscate 1640.

Sequestration (sīkwestrēɪ·ʃən). late ME. [– (O)Fr. *séquestration* or late L. *sequestratio*, *-ōn-*, f. as prec.; see -ION.] **1.** An act or the action of sequestering, banishment, exile; esp. *Eccl.*, excommunication. **b.** *transf.* Separation, disjunction 1567. **2.** A state of being sequestered, separation, seclusion, retirement 1565. **3.** *Law.* **a.** The appropriation of the income of a property in order to satisfy claims against the owner; esp. *Eccl.*, the diversion of the income of a benefice to the advantage of the creditors of the incumbent; a writ for this 1565. **b.** An order of court appointing the goods of a deceased person whose executor or executors have renounced probate to be secured and administered; also, a writ of Chancery empowering commissioners or a sheriff to seize the property of the person against whom it is directed 1591. **c.** Seizure of the possessions of a subject by the state; esp. the act of a belligerent power in seizing debts owing from its own subjects to the opposing power 1568. **d.** *Sc. Law* (see prec. 2 b) 1765. **4.** *gen.* Seizure, confiscation 1640.

2. It is no other, but a place of retyring, and s. from the World 1628. **3. c.** His former delinquencies..were severely punished by fine and s. SCOTT.

Sequestrator (sī·kwestrēɪtəɹ). 1644. [– AL. *sequestrator* collector, receiver, f. as prec.; see -OR 2.] One who sequestrates; a trustee or bailiff having control of property upon which there are claims by creditors. Also, a person named in a writ of sequestration as authorized to collect and administer the income of a sequestrated estate. So †**Sequestree·**, sequestrator 1611–1845.

‖**Sequestrum** (sĭkwe·strŏm). *Pl.* **sequestra.** 1831. [mod.L. use of L. *sequestrum* something separated, orig. n. of *sequester* adj.; cf. SEQUESTER *sb.*[2]] *Path.* A detached piece of bone lying within a cavity formed by necrosis. Also applied to a portion of skin separated by disease from the surrounding parts.

Sequin (sī·kwin), *sb.* 1617. [– Fr. *sequin* – It. *zecchino*, f. *zecca* the mint – Arab. *sikka* die for coining, coin. Cf. SICCA.] **1.** An Italian gold coin (orig. Venetian), worth about 9 shillings. Now *Hist.* **2.** A small spangle used to ornament dresses, etc. 1882. Hence **Se·quin** *v. trans.* to ornament with sequins.

‖**Sequitur** (se·kwitŭɹ). 1836. [L., 'it follows'.] An inference or conclusion following from the premisses. Cf. NON SEQUITUR.

Sequoia (sĭkwoi·ă). 1866. [– mod.L. (Endlicher, 1847), from *Sequoiah*, name of a Cherokee who invented a syllabary for his native language.] A genus of large American coniferous trees belonging to the *Abietinæ*; a tree of this genus. Pop. often called *Wellingtonia*.

Serac (sĕræ·k). 1860. [– Swiss Fr. *sérac*, orig. name of a compact white cheese, prob. deriv. of L. *serum* whey.] An irregular-shaped pinnacle of ice on a glacier, formed by the intersection of crevasses.

Seraglio (sĕrā·lyo, sĕ-). 1581. [– It. *serraglio* – Turk. – Pers. *sarāy* palace. See next, SERAIL.] **I.** Enclosure, place of confinement. **1.** The part of a Moslem dwelling-house (esp. of the palace of a sovereign or great noble) in which the women are secluded; the apartments reserved for wives and concubines; a harem. **b.** The inmates of the harem; a polygamous household 1634. †**2.** *gen.* An enclosure; a place of confinement –1700.

1. b. *transf.* Woman was his mistress; and the whole Sex his S. 1709. **2.** The Jewes dwell as in a suburbe by themselues..I passed by the Piazza Judea, where their S. begins EVELYN.

II. = SERAI †1, 2. 1599.

‖**Serai** (sərai·). 1609. [Turk. – Pers.; see prec.] **1.** In Eastern countries, A building for the accommodation of travellers; a caravanserai. **2.** A Turkish palace; esp. the palace of the Sultan at Constantinople 1617.

Serail (sərēɪ·l). Now *rare.* 1585. [– Fr. *sérail* – It. *serraglio* SERAGLIO.] **1.** = SERAGLIO I. 1. †**2.** = SERAI 2. –1782.

Seralbumen, -in (sīəræ·lbiū·men, -in). 1835. [f. SERUM + ALBUMEN.] *Chem.* The albumen of the blood.

‖**Serang** (səræ·ŋ). *Anglo-Ind.* 1799. [Hind. and Hindi, vulgar form of (Pers.) *sarhang*

-commander.] A native boatswain or captain of a Lascar crew.

‖**Serape** (serā·pe). 1847. [Mexican Sp. *serape, sarape.*] A shawl or plaid worn by Spanish-Americans.

Seraph (se·răf). 1667. [Back-formation from SERAPHIM, SERAPHIN (on the analogy of *cherubim, -in, cherub*).] One of the SERAPHIM. **b.** *fig.* A seraphic person, an 'angel' 1853.

Brightest S. tell In which of all these shining Orbes hath Man His fixed seat MILT.

Seraphic (sĕræ·fik), *a.* 1632. [– med.L. *seraphicus*, f. *seraph, -im*; see -IC. Cf. Fr. *séraphique.*] **1.** Of or pertaining to the seraphim. **2.** Of attributes: Resembling what pertains to the seraphim; worthy of a seraph; ecstatically adoring 1659. **3.** Resembling a seraph; characterized by ecstatic fervour of devotion 1762. **b.** Of discourse, actions, appearance: Showing ecstasy of devout contemplation 1668.

1. S. choirs 1755. **2.** Seraphick Ardour dwelling in each Vein KEN. On the thick Hyperborean, cherubic reasoning, s. eloquence were lost CARLYLE. **3.** S. saints, and gorgeous scenes by Tintoret 1870.

Special collocations: **S. Doctor,** St. Bonaventura; **S. Father,** St. Francis; **S. friar,** a Franciscan, hence *s. habit, order*; **S. hymn,** the Sanctus (see Isa. 6:3). So **Sera·phical** *a.* 1540, **-ly** *adv.*

Seraphim (se·răfim), †**se·raphin.** [OE., ME. *seraphin*, later *seraphim* (XVI) – biblical L. *seraphim, -in* (= Gr. σεραφίμ, -φείμ) – Heb. *śᵉrāpîm.*] **1.** In Biblical use: The living creatures with six wings, hands and feet, and a (presumably) human voice, seen in Isaiah's vision as hovering above the throne of God. late ME. **2.** By Christian interpreters the seraphim were from an early period supposed to be a class of angels, the highest of the nine orders. The presumed derivation of the word from a Heb. root *śārap̱* to burn, led to the view that the seraphim are specially distinguished by fervour of love, and to the symbolic use of red as the colour appropriate to them in artistic representations. OE. **3.** A Swedish order of knighthood 1784. **4.** *Geol. sing.* and *collect.* A fossil crustacean of the genus *Pterygotus* 1839. **5.** A moth of the genus *Lobophora* 1832.

2. Where the bright S. in burning row Their loud up-lifted Angel trumpets blow MILT.

Seraphine (se·răfīn). Also **seraphina.** 1839. [f. SERAPH + -INE⁴.] A musical instrument of the reed kind.

‖**Seraskier** (serǣskīᵊ·ɹ). 1684. [repr. Turk. pronunciation of Pers. *sarʿaskar*, f. *sar* head + Arab. *ʿaskar* army.] The title of the Turkish minister of war, who is also commander in chief of the army. Hence ‖**Seraskie·rat(e,** the war office at Constantinople.

Serb (sɔ̄ɹb), *sb.* and *a.* 1813. [– Serbian *Srb.*] **A.** *sb.* **1.** †**a.** A Wend of Lusatia. **b.** A native of Serbia, a Serbian. **2.** The Serbian language 1886. **B.** *adj.* Serbian 1876.

Serbian (sɔ̄·ɹbiăn), *a.* and *sb.* Formerly SERVIAN. 1862. [f. prec. + -IAN.] **A.** *adj.* Of or pertaining to Serbia, a country of south-eastern Europe occupied by a Slavonic people and now, with Slavonia and Croatia, forming Yugoslavia 1876. **B.** *sb.* A native or inhabitant of Serbia; the language of Serbia 1862.

Serbo-, used as comb. form of SERBIAN.

Serbonian (sɔɹbōᵘ·niăn), *a.* 1667. [f. Gr. Σερβωνίς (λίμνη) + -AN¹.] *S. bog*: Milton's name for Lake Serbonis in Lower Egypt, a marshy tract (now dry) covered with shifting sand. Hence *allus.*

A gulf profound as that S. Bog,..where Armies whole have sunk MILT.

†**Sere,** *sb.* 1606. [– OFr. *serre* foot of a bird of prey, f. *serrer*; see SEAR *sb.*] A claw, talon –1864.

Sere, sear (sīᵊɹ), *a.* [OE. *sēar* = MLG. *sōr* (LG. *soor*, Du. *zoor*) :- Gmc. (of the LG. area, but cf. OHG. *sōrēn* become dry) **sauzaz.*] **1.** Dry, withered. Now *poet.* or *rhet.* †**2.** Of textile fabrics: Thin, worn –1798.

1. He is..crooked, old, and s. SHAKS. I haue liu'd long enough, my way of life Is falne into the Seare, the yellow Leafe SHAKS. **2.** A roaring wind..shook the sails That were so thin and s. COLERIDGE.

‖**Serein** (sərǣn). 1870. [Fr.; see SERENE *sb.*¹] *Meteorol.* A fine rain falling from a cloudless sky after sunset.

Serenade (serĭnēⁱ·d, serə-), *sb.* 1649. [– Fr. *sérénade* – It. SERENATA.] **1.** A performance of vocal or instrumental music given at night in the open air, esp. such a performance given by a lover under the window of his lady. **2.** *Mus.* A piece of music suitable or specially composed for singing or playing in the open air as a complimentary performance 1728.

1. Serenate, which the starv'd Lover sings To his proud fair MILT.

Serenade (serĭnēⁱ·d, serə-), *v.* 1668. [f. the sb.] **1.** *trans.* To entertain (a person) with a serenade 1672. **2.** *intr.* (or *absol.*) To perform a serenade 1668. Hence **Serena·der.**

‖**Serenata** (serenā·ta). 1743. [It. *serenata* (formerly also, purity, serenity), f. *sereno* SERENE, in the current sense infl. by *sera* evening.] **1.** A song or form of cantata suitable for performance in the open air. **2.** A piece of instrumental music, developed from the orchestral suite, and usu. composed of a march, and a minuet interposed between two movements of another kind 1883.

Serendipity (serendi·pĭti). 1754. [f. *Serendip(-b)*, former name of Ceylon + -ITY; formed by Horace Walpole upon the title of the fairy-tale *The Three Princes of Serendip*, the heroes of which 'were always making discoveries, by accidents and sagacity, of things they were not in quest of'.] The faculty of making happy and unexpected discoveries by accident.

†**Serene,** *sb.*¹ 1591. [– Fr. *serein*, OFr. *serain* :- Gallo-Rom. **seranum*, f. L. *serum* evening, subst. use of n. of *serus* late.] A light fall of moisture or fine rain after sunset in hot countries (see SEREIN), regarded as a noxious dew or mist –1682.

Serene (sĭrī·n, sĕ-), *a.* and *sb.*² 1508. [– L. *serenus* clear, fair, calm (of weather, etc.).] **A.** *adj.* **1.** Of the weather, air, sky: Clear, fine, and calm (without cloud or rain or wind). **b.** Of the heavenly bodies: Shining with a clear and tranquil light 1704. **c.** Hence *poet.* of colour: Pure, clear, bright. Also, quiet, sober. 1750. **2.** Of other natural phenomena (e.g. the sea): Calm, tranquil 1812. **3.** Of a person, his mind, etc.: Calm, tranquil, untroubled, unperturbed. Of the countenance: Expressive of inward calm, unruffled. 1635. **4.** An honorific epithet given to a reigning prince (esp. of Germany), formerly also to a royal house, etc. **5.** *Drop s.*: Milton's rendering of L. *gutta serena* amaurosis. Hence *allus.* 1667.

1. Regions milde of calm and s. Ayr MILT. **b.** The moon, s. in glory, mounts the sky POPE. **c.** Full many a gem of purest ray s. GRAY. **2.** A brighter Hellas rears its mountains From waves serener far SHELLEY. **3.** He who resigns the World..is in constant Possession of a s. Mind STEELE. *All s.* (slang), 'all's well', 'all right' 1856.

B. *sb.* (the adj. used absol.). Now *rare* or *Obs.* **a.** A condition of fine quiet weather 1644. **b.** The serene expanse of clear sky, air, or calm sea 1769. **c.** Calm brightness 1821. **d.** Serenity, tranquility (of mind or conditions) 1742.

b. The bark that plows the deep s. COWPER. Yet did I never breathe its pure s. KEATS. **c.** With moonlight patches..Or fragments of the day's intense s. SHELLEY. Hence **Sere·ne-ly** *adv.*, **-ness.**

Serene (sĭrī·n, sĕ-), *v.* Now *rare* or *Obs.* 1613. [– L. *serenare*, f. *serenus* SERENE *a.*] *trans.* To make serene.

Hope, like a cordial,..Man's heart, at once, inspirits, and serenes YOUNG.

Serenity (sĭre·nĭti). 1450. [– (O)Fr. *sérénité* or L. *serenitas*, f. as prec.; see -ITY.] **1.** Clear, fair and calm weather; clearness and stillness of air and sky 1538. **2.** Tranquillity, peacefulness (of conditions, etc.) 1635. **3.** Cheerful tranquillity (of mind, temper, countenance, etc.) 1599. **4.** A title of honour given to reigning princes and other dignitaries 1450.

1. There is never no Rain, Dew, Hail, Snow, or Wind but still a clear s. 1669. **3.** His countenance had recovered its usual s. 1794.

‖**Seres** (sīᵊ·rez), *pl.* late ME. [L. *Seres* (Gr. Σῆρες), whence *sericum* silk.] A people anciently inhabiting some part of Eastern Asia (prob. China), whose country was believed to be the original home of silk.

Serf (sɔ̄ɹf). 1483. [– (O)Fr. *serf* :- L. *servus* slave.] †**1.** A slave, bondman –1484. **2.** A person in a condition of servitude or modified slavery, dist. from what is properly called 'slavery' in that the services due to the master, and his power of disposal of his 'serf', are more or less limited by law or custom 1611.

2. In most of the typical examples of serfdom, the serf was 'attached to the soil' (*adscriptus glebæ*), i.e. he could not be removed (except by manumission) from the lord's land, and was transferred with it when it passed to another owner. O.E.D. Hence **Se·rfage, Se·rfdom,** the state or condition of a s.; bondage. **Se·rfhood,** the collective body of serfs.

Serge (sɔ̄ɹdʒ). [In XIV *sarge*, later *serge* (XVI) – OFr. *sarge*, later *serge* (XVI) :- Rom. **sarica*, for L. *serica*, fem. (sc. *lana* wool) of *sericus* – Gr. σηρικός of silk; see SERES, SILK.] **1.** A woollen fabric; now a very durable twilled cloth of worsted, or with the warp of worsted and the woof of wool, extensively used for clothing. **b.** A garment made of serge 1583. **2.** *Silk s.*: a silk fabric twilled in the manner of serge, used for linings of coats, and formerly for mantles *Hist.* 1844. **3.** *attrib.* or *adj.* Made of serge 1608.

Sergeancy, serjeancy (sā·ɹdʒənsi). *Hist.* ME. [– AFr. *sergeancie*, graphic var. of *sergeantie* SERGEANTY. In later use, f. SERGEANT + -CY.] †**1.** The body of sergeants in a country, the sergeant-class. ME only. †**2.** = SERGEANTY 1. –1630. **3.** The office of a sergeant or serjeant in various senses; also the commission of sergeant in the army 1670.

Sergeant, serjeant (sā·ɹdʒənt). ME. [– OFr. *sergent, serjant* (mod. *sergent*) :- L. *serviens, -ent-* (see -ANT), pr. pple. of *servire* SERVE.] †**1.** A serving-man, attendant, servant –1450. †**b.** *transf.* A servant (of God, of Satan) –1570. †**2.** A common soldier –1490. †**3.** A tenant by military service under the rank of a knight; esp. one of this class attending on a knight in the field –1425. †**4.** An officer who is charged with the arrest of offenders or the summoning of persons to appear before the court –1680. **5.** **Sergeant** (or **Serjeant)-at-Arms.** †**a.** In early use *gen.*, an armed officer in the service of a lord; *spec.* one of a body of men of knightly rank, who were required to be in immediate attendance on the king's person, to arrest traitors and other offenders. **b.** An officer of each of the two Houses of Parliament, who is charged with the duty of enforcing the commands of the House, the arrest of offenders, etc. Hence, an officer having corresponding duties under the U.S. Senate and House of Representatives, etc. late ME. **6.** As a title borne by a lawyer. (Now always written **serjeant.**) **a.** A member of a superior order of barristers (abolished in 1880), from which, until 1873, the Common Law judges were always chosen (hence a serjeant was always called by a judge 'my brother So-and-so'). More explicitly **Sergeant at law** ME. **b.** *The King's* (or *Queen's*) *Serjeant*: a title given to a limited number of the serjeants at law, appointed by patent. late ME. **c.** *Prime serjeant*: the first in rank of the three (earlier two) serjeants at law in Ireland. (Since 1805 called *first s.*) 1666. **d. Common Serjeant (at law).** A judicial officer appointed by the Corporation of London as an assistant to the Recorder 1556. **7.** (Now usu. written **sergeant.**) In the titles of certain officers of the Royal Household. **a.** The head of a specified department, as *s. of the cellar*, etc. 1450. **b.** Prefixed to certain designations of office, as *s.-cater, -surgeon, -trumpeter*, etc. 1614. **8.** In the titles of certain inferior officers employed by the Corporation of the City of London, and by other municipal bodies. late ME. **9.** *Mil.*

(Now always written **sergeant.**) In mod. use, a non-commissioned officer of the grade above that of corporal. See also COLOUR-*s.*, DRILL-*s.*, SERGEANT-MAJOR, etc. 1548. **b.** Prefixed to various designations of offices in which sergeants are employed, as *s. armourer, farrier, instructor*, etc. 1810. **10.** (Now always written **sergeant.**) A police-officer of higher rank than a simple constable; in Great Britain ranking next below an inspector 1839.

4. Saul sente sergeauntis that schulden rauysche Dauid WYCLIF 1 *Sam.* 19:14. *fig.* Had I but time (as this fell Sergeant death Is strick'd in his arrest) oh I could tell you SHAKS. **9.** Serjeants, Corporals, Drummers, and private Men 2d per diem each, besides Bread 1690. Hence **Se·rgeantship, Se·rjeantship,** the office of a s., in various senses.

Se·rgeant-ma·jor. 1573. [f. prec. + MAJOR *a.*] †**1.** In the 16–17th c.: **a.** A field officer, one in each regiment, next in rank to the lieutenant-colonel, and corresponding partly to the 'major', partly to the 'adjutant' of the modern army –1704. †**b.** A general officer, corresponding to the modern major-general –1647. **2.** A non-commissioned officer of the highest grade 1802. **3.** An Amer. fish, the cow-pilot 1876. **4. s.-m.'s tea** *slang*, tea with rum in it.

†**Se·rgeantry, se·rjeantry.** late ME. [– OFr. *sergenterie* (AL. *sergenteria*, etc., XII), f. *sergent*; see SERGEANT, -ERY.] = next –1830.

Sergeanty, serjeanty (sā·ɹdʒənti). 1449. [– OFr. *serjantie, sergentie* (AL. *serjantia*, etc. XII), f. as prec.; see -Y³.] *Hist.* A form of feudal tenure on condition of rendering some specified personal service to the king 1467. **b.** Dist. as *grand* and *petit* (or *petty*) *s.* 1449.

According to *Britton*, *grand s.* obliges the tenant to a service 'touching the defence of the country', such as acting as marshal, putting an army in the field,..while *petit s.* binds him to a service 'amounting to half a mark or less', such as carrying to the king a bag, a brooch, an arrow, or a bow without string, etc. O.E.D.

Serial (sīᵊ·riăl), *a.* and *sb.* 1841. [f. SERIES + -AL¹, perh. after Fr. *sérial*. Cf. med. L. *serialis* continuous.] **A.** *adj.* Belonging to, forming part of, or consisting of a series; taking place in a regular succession 1854. **b.** *spec.* of the publication of a literary work, *esp.* a story, in successive instalments 1841. **c.** In scientific use; *esp.* applied to the disposition of the parts of an organism in a straight line or longitudinal succession 1855.

b. *S. rights*, rights attaching to the publication of a story in serial form. **c.** *S. temperatures*, temperatures taken at different successive depths between the bottom and the surface of water.

B. *sb.* A serial or periodical publication, *esp.* a novel published in serial (as opp. to *book*) form 1846. Hence **Seria·lity** (sīᵊriæ·lĭti), s. arrangement. **Se:rializa·tion,** publication in s. form. **Se·rialize** *v. trans.* to publish in s. form. **Se·rially** *adv.*

Seriate (sīᵊ·riet), *a.* 1846. [f. SERIES + -ATE².] Chiefly *Zool.* and *Bot.* Arranged or occurring in one or more series or rows. So **Se·riated** *a.* **Se·riately** *adv.*

Seriatim (sīᵊriēⁱ·tim), *adv.* (and *a.*) 1680. [– med.L. *seriatim*, after GRADATIM, LITERATIM, etc.] One after another, one by one in succession.

Seriation (sīᵊriēⁱ·ʃən). 1658. [f. SERIES + -ATION. Cf. contemp. MATERIATION (XVII).] Serial succession; formation of or into a series.

Seric (se·rik), *a. rare.* 1842. [– L. *sericus*; see SILK, SERES.] **1.** Chinese. **2.** Silken 1886.

Sericeous (sĭri·ʃiəs), *a.* 1777. [f. L. *sericus* SERIC; see -EOUS. For XVIII, cf. med.L. *sericeus* silken (XII).] *Zool.* and *Bot.* Silky, covered with silky down.

Sericin (se·risin). 1841. [f. late L. *sericum* (see SILK) + -IN¹.] **1.** = MYRISTIN. **2.** The gelatinous constituent of silk 1868.

Sericite (se·risəit). 1854. [– G. *sericit* (1852), f. late L. *sericum*; see SILK, -ITE¹ 2 b.] *Min.* A fibrous variety of muscovite. **b.** *attrib.* Sericitic 1879. Hence **Sericitic** (serisi·tik) *a.* containing or having the character of s.

‖**Sericterium** (seriktīᵊ·riŏm). *Pl.* **-eria** (-īᵊ·riă). 1826. [mod.L., irreg. f. Gr. σηρικόν SILK + -τηριον, after *sialisterium* (σιαλιστήριον) salivary gland of insects.] *Entom.* A glandular apparatus in silkworms for the production of silk; a silk or spinning gland.

Sericulture (se·rikɒltiūɹ, -tʃəɹ). 1851. [Shortened – Fr. *sériciculture*, f. late L. *sericum*; see SILK, CULTURE.] The production of raw silk and the rearing of silkworms for the purpose. Hence **Sericu·ltural** *a.* **Sericu·lturist.**

Seriema (seri,ī·mă), **çariama, cariama** (sæ-, kæriā·mă). [mod.L. *seriema, cariama*, – Tupi *siriema, sariama, çariama*, explained as = crested.] A large long-legged crested bird, *Cariama cristata*, inhabiting parts of Brazil; the crested screamer.

Series (sīᵊ·rīz, -iz, sīᵊ·ri,īz). *Pl.* **series.** 1611. [– L. *series* row, chain, series, f. *serere* join, connect.] **I.** General senses. **1.** A number or set *of* material things of one kind ranged in a line, either contiguously or at more or less regular intervals. **2.** A number *of* things of one kind (chiefly immaterial) following one another in temporal succession, or in the order of discourse or reasoning 1618. **b.** A number *of* persons in succession holding the same office or having some characteristic in common 1625. †**3.** A succession, sequence, or continued course (*of* action or conduct, *of* time, life, etc.) –1816. †**4.** The connected sequence (*of* discourse, writing, thought) –1712. †**5.** Order of succession; sequence –1779. **6.** A number of magnitudes, degrees of some attribute, or the like, viewed as capable of being enumerated in a progressive order. Also, a set of objects of one kind, differing progressively in size, composition, etc., or having a recognized order of enumeration. 1786.

1. The s. of squares called Belgravia EMERSON. **2.** That the repayment of the money to be borrowed should be spread over a s. of years 1886. **3.** A more decent..and prudent s. of proceeding BURKE. **5.** The s. of his works I am not able to deduce JOHNSON.

II. Technical senses. **1.** *Math.* A set of terms in succession (finite or infinite in number) the value of each of which is determined by its ordinal position according to a definite rule known as the *law* of the series 1671. **2.** A set of coins, medals, etc. belonging to a particular epoch, locality, dynasty, or government. Also, a set of postage stamps, bank notes, etc., of a particular issue. 1697. **3.** A set of literary compositions having certain features in common, published successively or intended to be read in sequence; a succession of volumes or fascicules forming a set by itself. Also, in recent use, a succession of books issued by one publisher in a common form and having some similarity of subject or purpose. 1711. **4.** *Nat. Sci.* A group of individuals exhibiting similar characteristics or a constant relation between successive members 1823. **5.** *Geol.* A set of successive deposits or group of successive formations having certain common fossil or mineral features 1822. **6.** *Electr.* and *Magn.* A number of cells or conductors so placed that the current passes through each in succession. (Such cells or conductors are said to be *in s.*) 1873. **b.** *attrib.* or as *adj.* = (*a*) arranged or connected in series; (*b*) Short for *s.-wound*, i.e. wound in series, or so that the coils on the field-magnets are placed in series with the outer circuit. 1884. **7.** *Philol.* (tr. G. *reihe.*) In the Indo-European languages, a set of vowels, or of diphthongs and vowels or sonants, which are mutually related by ablaut 1888. **8.** A parcel of rough diamonds 1909.

Serif (se·rif). Also †**ceriph,** †**seriph.** 1831. [perh. – Du. *schreef* (sχrēf) dash, line, earlier *schrēve* line, mark, prob. f. Gmc. **skreb-*, repr. by OHG. *screvōn* scratch in. Cf. SANSERIF.] *Typogr.* One of the fine cross-strokes at the top and bottom of a letter.

Serin¹ (se·rin). 1530. [– Fr. *serin* canary, of disputed origin.] **1.** A bird of the genus *Serĭnus*. **2.** In full, *S. finch*: the finch *S. serinus* (*S. hortulanus*), a native of central Europe 1672.

Serin² (se·rin). 1876. [f. SERUM + -IN¹.] *Chem.* **a.** Serum albumin. **b.** Amido-glycerol.

Seringa (sĕri·ŋgă, sĕ-). 1740. [– Fr. *seringa* – L. SYRINGA.] **1.** = SYRINGA. ‖**2.** The Pg. name for Brazilian plants of the genus *Hevea* (*Siphonia*), yielding india-rubber 1853.

Serio- (sīᵊ·rio), used as comb. form (see -O-) of SERIOUS, = partly serious, and partly...

Se:rio-co·mic, *a.* (*sb.*) 1783. [f. SERIO- + COMIC *a.*] Partly serious and partly comic; (of an actor, vocalist, etc., or his performance) presenting a comic plot, situation, etc. under a serious form. **b.** as *sb.* A s. actor, vocalist, etc. 1907. So **Se:rio-co·mi·cal** *a.* 1749, **-ly** *adv.*

Serious (sīᵊ·riəs), *a.* 1440. [– (O)Fr. *sérieux* or late L. *seriosus*, f. *serius* (used only of things in classical times); see -OUS.] **1.** Of persons, their actions, etc.: Having, involving, expressing, or arising from earnest purpose or thought; of grave or solemn disposition or intention; not light or superficial; now often, concerned with the grave and earnest sides of life. †**b.** Earnestly bent or applied; keen –1671. **2.** Earnest about the things of religion; religious 1796. **3.** Dealing with or regarding a matter on its grave side; not jesting, trifling, or playful; in earnest. Hence, of theatrical compositions or actors, not jocular or comic. 1590. **4.** Requiring earnest thought, consideration, or application; performed with earnestness of purpose 1531. **5.** Of grave demeanour or aspect 1613. **6.** Weighty, important, grave; (of quantity or degree) considerable 1584. **b.** Attended with danger; giving cause for anxiety 1800.

1. He was too s. to smile; indeed, I cannot remember him ever smiling, except sadly 1882. **b.** All my mind was set S. to learn and know MILT. **2.** Pleasant Place, Finsbury. Wages, twelve guineas. No tea, no sugar. S. family. DICKENS. **3.** The gentlemen are not s., but are only playing with you 1875. **4.** He makes Cards and Dice his s. Entertainment 1706. **5.** A weighty and a s. brow SHAKS. **6.** The damage is not thought to be s. 1884. **b.** It is feared that his condition is s. 1891. Hence **Se·rious-ly** *adv.*² in a s. manner; **-ness.**

†**Se·riously,** *adv.*¹ late ME. [tr. med.L. *seriose*, used as adv. of *series* SERIES.] From beginning to end; seriatim –1611.

Serjeant, etc.: see SERGEANT, etc.

†**Sermocina·tion.** 1514. [– L. *sermocinatio, -ōn-*, f. *sermocinari* talk; see -ATION.] Talk; a discourse, sermon –1674. So †**Sermocinator.**

Sermon (sə̄·ɹmən), *sb.* ME. [– AFr. *sermun*, (O)Fr. *sermon* :– L. *sermo, sermōn-* talk, discourse.] †**1.** Something that is said; talk, discourse –1594. †**b.** *pl.* The satires (*sermones*) of Horace –1671. **2.** A discourse, usu. delivered from a pulpit and based upon a text of Scripture, for the purpose of religious instruction or exhortation ME. **b.** as a written or published work. late ME. **c.** Applied to the discourses of our Lord and the Apostles ME. **3.** *transf.* and *fig.* **a.** A discourse (spoken or written) on a serious subject, and containing instruction or exhortation. Also *contempt.* a long or tedious discourse or harangue. 1596. **b.** Something that affords instruction or example 1600.

2. Which is worse, to stay from a S., or sleep at a S.? 1692. Phr. *At, after s.* = at, after church. **b.** And Sermons are less read than Tales PRIOR. *S. on the Mount*, the discourse recorded in Matt. 5–7 and introduced by the words 'he went up into a mountain..and taught them, saying'. **3. a.** Making a s. of continencie to her SHAKS. **b.** Bookes in the running brookes, Sermons in stones SHAKS.

attrib. and *Comb.*: **s. paper,** writing paper of foolscap 4to size. Hence **Sermone·tte,** a short sermon. **Sermo·nic** *a.* of the form or nature of a s.; resembling (that of) a s. (somewhat *depreciatory*). **Se·rmonish** *a.* sermonic.

Sermon (sə̄·ɹmən), *v.* Now *rare.* [– AFr. *sarmuner*, OFr. *sermouner* (mod. *sermonner*), f. *sermon*; see prec. In mod. use a new formation on SERMON *sb.*] **1.** *trans.* To preach to (a person). **2.** To preach (*at* a person). KEATS. †3. *intr.* To speak (*of* a thing) –1606.

Sermoner (sɔ̄·ɹmənəɹ). *rare.* ME. [f. SERMON *sb.* + -ER¹; in ME. after AFr. *sarmuner.*] A preacher of sermons.

†**Se·rmoning,** *vbl. sb.* ME. [f. SERMON *v.* + -ING¹.] **1.** Preaching; also, a sermon –1657. **2.** Talk, discourse, conversation –1535.

Sermonist (sɔ̄·ɹmənist). 1630. [f. SERMON *sb.* + -IST.] A preacher, sermonizer.

Sermonize (sɔ̄·ɹmənəiz), *v.* 1635. [f. as prec. + -IZE.] **1.** *intr.* = PREACH *v.* 1. Chiefly *depreciatory.* **b.** To talk seriously. Also with *it.* 1753. **2.** *trans.* To preach a sermon to (*rare*); to talk seriously or earnestly to, 'preach' to, 'lecture' 1802. **3.** To bring into a specified condition by preaching 1768.

Sero- (sīᵊ·ro), used as comb. form of SERUM in the senses: (*a*) of or pertaining to serum, as *serothe·rapy*, treatment of disease or infection by serums, serum-therapy; (*b*) pertaining to, consisting of, or involving serum (and something else), as *sero-pus*, serous pus; (*c*) characterized by serous effusion or infiltration, or involving a serous membrane, as *s.-dermatosis.*

Serolin (sīᵊ·rǒlin). 1835. [– Fr. *séroline*, f. *sérum* SERUM, L. *oleum* oil + *-ine* -IN¹.] A fatty substance found in blood serum.

Serology (sīᵊrǫ·lǒdʒi). 1913. [f. SERO- + -LOGY.] The scientific study of serums and their action. Hence **Sero·logist.**

Seron (sīᵊ·rǫn, sīrū·n). 1545. [– Sp. *seron* hamper, crate (f. *sera* large basket), partly through Fr. *serron.*] A bale or package (of exotic products, e.g. almonds, medicinal bark, cocoa) made up in an animal's hide.

Serosity (sīrǫ·sīti). 1601. [– med.L. *serositas* (XIII), f. *serosus*; see SEROUS, -ITY. Cf. Fr. *sérosité*, (XVII).] **1.** Watery fluid in an animal body; the serous or watery part of blood or milk, serum; freq. *pl.* in 17–18th c. = watery humours. **b.** A yellowish alkaline liquid produced when serum is heated 1807. **2.** The condition of being serous (*rare*) 1743.

Serotine (se·rǒtəin), *sb.* 1771. [– Fr. *sérotine* (Buffon) – fem. of L. *serotinus* late flowering, also (late and med.L.) of the evening, f. *sero*, adv. of *serus* late.] A small European bat flying late in the evening, *Vespertilio serotinus.*

Serotinous (sīrǫ·tinəs), *a.* 1656. [f. L. *serotinus* late flowering (see prec.) + -OUS.] Late in occurrence or development; chiefly of plants, late-flowering.

Serous (sīᵊ·rəs), *a.* 1594. [– Fr. *séreux* or med.L. *serosus*, f. *serum*; see SERUM, -OUS.] **1.** Of or pertaining to serum; consisting of or containing serum; of the nature of serum. **b.** *Path.* Involving or characterized by an effusion of serum 1779. **2.** *Anat.* Secreting or moistened with serum, as a membrane 1732.

Serow (se·roᵘ). Also **surow, saraw.** 1847. [Native name.] Any of the Asiatic antelopes of the genus *Nemorhædus*, esp. *N. thar* (*N. bubalinus*), the THAR.

Serpent (sɔ̄·ɹpĕnt), *sb.* ME. [– (O)Fr. *serpent* :– L. *serpens, -ent-*, subst. use of pr. pple. of *serpere* creep; see -ENT.] **1.** Any of the scaly limbless reptiles regarded as having the properties of hissing and 'stinging'; *Zool.* a reptile of the genus OPHIDIA; a snake; now applied chiefly to the larger and more venomous species. †**b.** A creeping thing or reptile, *esp.* one of a noxious kind –1691. **c.** Applied to serpent-like animals inhabiting the sea 1608. **d.** In proverbs, etc. referring to the serpent's guile, treachery, or malignancy. late ME. **2.** The serpent that tempted Eve (Gen. 3:1–5); the Tempter, the Devil, Satan. Also, *the Old S.* (after Rev. 12:9). ME. **3.** *fig.* as a symbol of envy, jealousy, malice, or wiliness. late ME. **b.** A treacherous, deceitful, or malicious person 1590. **4.** A representation of a serpent, esp. as a symbol or an ornament ME. **5.** *Astron.* The northern constellation *Serpens* 1565. **6.** A kind of firework which burns with a serpentine motion or flame 1634. **7.** An obsolete bass wind instrument of deep tone, about 8 feet long, made of wood covered with leather and formed with three U-shaped turns 1730. **8.** *transf.* A candle of spiral form; a 'rope' of hair; the crank-shaft in a weaving-machine. *Pharaoh's s.*: see PHARAOH. 1802. **9.** quasi-*adj.* Resembling a serpent or that of a serpent 1592.

1. The green s. from his dark abode,..At noon forth-issuing THOMSON. **d.** †*The serpent's tongue*, vulgarly supposed to be the 'sting'; *allus.* 'venomous speech'. **3. b.** With doubler tongue Then thine (thou s.) neuer Adder stung SHAKS.

Comb.: **s.-bearer** = OPHIUCHUS; **s. cucumber,** a cucumber of the genus *Trichosanthes*, having long serpent-like fruit, esp. *T. colubrina*; **s. eagle,** a bird of prey of the genus *Spilornis*; **-eater,** (*a*) the secretary-bird; (*b*) the markhor; **-fish,** the red snake-fish, *Cepola rubescens*; **-star,** an ophiuran; **-wand,** the caduceus; **-withe,** *Aristolochia odoratissima.* **b.** with *serpent's*: **serpent's head, skull,** species of cowry; **serpent's tongue,** †(*a*) ADDER'S-TONGUE; (*b*) the fossil tooth of a shark.

Se·rpent, *v.* Now *rare.* 1606. [– (O)Fr. *serpenter*, f. *serpent*; see prec.] *intr.* To move in a serpentine manner; to follow a tortuous course; to wind.

‖**Serpentaria** (sɔ̄ɹpĕntēᵊ·riă). 1803. [– late and med.L. *serpentaria* (sc. *planta*), f. L. *serpens* (see SERPENT) + *-aria* as in *fritillaria, lunaria*; see -ARY¹ 3.] = SERPENTARY 2. **b.** *Chem.* An alkaloid obtained from serpentary 1831.

Serpentarius (sɔ̄ɹpĕntēᵊ·riŏs). 1728. [mod.L. (see next).] *Astron.* = OPHIUCHUS.

Serpentary (sɔ̄·ɹpĕntări), *sb.* 1450. [Sense 2 – late and med.L. SERPENTARIA; transf. in sense 1.] †**1.** A kind of retort or still –1615. **2.** Virginian Snake-root, *Aristolochia serpentaria*; its root, used medicinally 1658.

Serpentiform (sɔɹpe·ntifǭɹm). 1777. [– late L. *serpentiformis*, f. L. *serpens*; see SERPENT, -FORM.] Having the form of a serpent; serpentine in shape.

Serpentine (sɔ̄·ɹpĕntəin), *sb.* late ME. [– med.L. *serpentina, serpentinum*, subst. uses of the fem. and n. of *serpentinus*; see next. Cf. Fr. *serpentine, serpentin.*] **1.** A name for certain plants reputed to contain an antidote to the poison of serpents; e.g. dragonwort, fenugreek. **2.** A kind of cannon. Now only *Hist.* 1450. **3.** A rock or mineral, consisting mainly of hydrous magnesium silicate, of a dull green colour with markings resembling those of a serpent's skin. Also, an ornamental stone made of this. late ME. **4.** The coiled pipe or worm of a distilling apparatus. *Obs.* exc. as repr. Fr. *serpentin.* 1519. **5.** A winding path or line 1885.

Serpentine (sɔ̄·ɹpĕntəin), *a.* late ME. [– (O)Fr. *serpentin* – late (eccl.) L. *serpentinus*, f. *serpens, -ent-*; see SERPENT, -INE¹.] **1.** Of or pertaining to a serpent or serpents; of the form of or resembling a serpent, or that of a serpent. **2.** Having the evil qualities of a serpent; pertaining to the Serpent as the tempter of mankind; diabolical, Satanic; devilishly wily or cunning. late ME. **3.** Following a course resembling that of a serpent in motion; tortuous, winding 1615.

1. *S. verse*, a metrical line beginning and ending with the same word. **2.** A s. generation,..made of fraud, of policies and practises 1599. **3.** The branching and serpentin cours of the River Seine 1645. *S. temple* (Antiq.), one having the supposed symbolical form of a serpent. Hence **Se·rpentinely** *adv.*

Serpentine (sɔ̄·ɹpĕntəin), *v.* 1774. [f. prec.] **1.** *intr.* To move in a serpentine manner; to pursue a serpentine or tortuous path; to wind. **2.** *trans.* To cause to take a serpentine direction; to wind 1850.

Serpentine marble. 1601. [– med.L. *marmor serpentinum.* Cf. Fr. *marbre serpentin.*] The mineral serpentine in massive form.

Serpentinize (sə·ɹpĕntinəiz), *v.* 1791. [f. SERPENTINE *sb.* or *a.* + -IZE.] **1.** *intr.* = SERPENTINE *v.* 1. **2.** *trans.* (*Geol.*) To convert into serpentine 1889.

Serpentinous (sɔ̄·ɹpĕntəinəs), *a.* 1833. [f. SERPENTINE *sb.* or *a.* + -OUS.] **1.** Of the nature of or consisting of serpentine. **2.** Serpentine, winding 1882.

Serpentize (sɔ̄·ɹpĕntəiz), *v.* Now *rare.* 1629. [f. SERPENT *sb.* + -IZE.] **1.** *intr.* = SERPENTINE *v.* 1. **2.** *trans.* To cause to take a serpentine shape, motion, or course 1762.

1. The Euphrates serpentizes among wonderful plants 1718.

Serpentry (sɔ̄·ɹpĕntri). 1818. [f. SERPENT *sb.* + -RY.] **1.** Serpents or serpentine creatures collectively. **2.** A place where serpents are kept and reared 1846. **3.** A winding like that of a serpent 1848.

Se·rpent-stone. 1681. **1.** = AMMONITE 1. Now *Obs.* or *local.* **2.** An artificial 'stone' used as a remedy for the poison of serpents. Also = BEZOAR 2 a. 1681.

‖**Serpigo** (səɹpəi·go). *Pl.* **serpigines** (səɹpi·dʒinīz), **serpigoes.** late ME. [– med.L. *serpigo*, f. L. *serpere* creep.] A general term for creeping or spreading skin diseases; *spec.* ringworm. Hence **Serpiginous** (səɹpi·dʒinəs) *a.*, **-ly** *adv.*

‖**Serpula** (sɔ̄·ɹpiŭlă). *Pl.* **-læ.** 1767. [mod. L. use of late L. *serpula* small serpent.] *Zool.* A marine annelid which inhabits a tortuous calcareous tube. Hence **Ser·pu·lean, Serpu·lidan,** an annelid belonging to a group or family of which *Serpula* is a typical genus. **Se·rpulite** *Geol.*, a fossil s.

‖**Serra**¹ (se·ră). *Pl.* **serræ.** 1450. [L., = saw, saw-fish.] **1. a.** A fabulous marine monster. **b.** A saw-fish 1854. **2.** Dentation resembling the teeth of a saw, as of the edge of a leaf, the sutures of the skull; *pl.* the 'teeth' of a serrated edge 1800.

‖**Serra**² (se·ra). 1830. [Pg. :– L. *serra* saw. Cf. SIERRA.] A ridge of mountains or hills (in Portuguese territory).

Serran (se·răn). 1803. [– mod.L. *serranus*, f. L. *serra* saw; see SERRA¹, -AN.] *Ichth.* A fish of the genus *Serranus* or the family *Serranidæ*, which includes many food-fishes, as the black sea-bass. Hence **Se·rranoid** *a.* and *sb.* belonging to, a fish of, the family *Serranidæ.*

Serrate (se·rĕⁱt), *a.* 1668. [– L. *serratus*, f. *serra* saw + *-atus* -ATE².] Chiefly *Nat. Hist.* Having or forming a row of small projections resembling the teeth of a saw; jagged or notched like a saw.

Serrate (se·reⁱt), *v.* 1750. [– *serrat-*, pa. ppl. stem of late L. *serrare*, f. L. *serra* saw; see -ATE³.] *trans.* To make serrated or saw-toothed; to impress in a serrated form. So **Se·rrated** *a.* = prec. 1703.

Serration (serēⁱ·ʃən). 1842. [f. SERRATE *v.* + -ION.] The condition of being serrated, indentation like that of a saw; chiefly *concr.* and *pl.* saw-like indentations.

Serra·to-, comb. form (see -O-) of L. *serratus* SERRATE *a.*, in the senses 'serrate and..', 'in a serrate manner, with serrate indentation', as *s.-dentate*, etc.

Serrature (se·ratiŭɹ, -tʃəɹ). 1541. [– late L. *serratura*, f. *serratus* SERRATE *a.*; see -URE.] = SERRATION.

Serrefile (se·rəfəil). 1796. [– Fr. *serrefile*, f. *serrer* + *file* FILE *sb.*²] *Mil. pl.* The line of supernumerary and non-commissioned officers placed in the rear of a squadron or troop; *sing.* one of these.

Serri-, comb. f. SERRA¹ with sense 'serrated', as in *se·rricorn, serriro·strate.*

Serried (se·rid), *ppl. a.* 1667. [Either (i) f. SERRY *v.* + -ED¹, or (ii) sp. of †*serred* (disyll.), pa. pple. of †*serr* (XVI) – (O)Fr. *serrer* SERRY *v.*] Of files or ranks of armed men: Pressed close together, shoulder to shoulder, in close order.

transf. The dark ranks of the s. clouds 1834.

Serrulate (se·riŭlĕⁱt), *a.* 1793. [– mod.L. *serrulatus*, f. L. *serrula*, dim. of *serra* saw; see -ATE².] *Nat. Hist.* Finely or minutely serrated; having small serrations. So **Se·rrulated** *a.* Hence **Serrula·tion,** the condition of being s.

Serry (se·ri), *v.* 1581. [prob. f. (O)Fr. *serré*, pa. pple. of *serrer* :– Rom. **serrare* press close, alt. of L. (in comps.) *serare*, f. *sera* lock, bolt. Cf. SERRIED.] **1.** *intr.* To press close *together* in the ranks; to stand or move in close or serried order. **2.** *trans.* To cause to stand in close order, to close up (the ranks) 1635.

‖**Sertularia** (sɔ̄ɹtiŭlēᵊ·riă). *Pl.* **-iæ, -ias.**

1767. [mod.L., f. L. *sertula*, dim. of *serta* (n. pl.) garlands; see -ARY[1] 3.] *Zool.* One of a genus of branching hydroids having small sessile hydrothecæ; the genus itself. Hence **Sertula·rian** *a.* of or belonging to the genus *S.* or the family *Sertularidæ* of hydroids; *sb.* a sertularian hydroid.

‖**Sertulum** (sə̄·ɹtiŭlə̆m). Also **se·rtule.** 1831. [mod.L., dim. of *sertum*, assumed sing. of *serta* n. pl., garlands. See prec.] *Bot.* A simple umbel.

Serum (sīə·rə̆m). *Pl.* **sera** (sīə·ră), **serums.** 1672. [L., = whey, watery fluid. So Fr. *sérum* (Paré).] Watery animal fluid, normal or morbid; *spec.* blood-serum, the greenish yellow liquid which separates from the clot when blood coagulates. **b.** *Therapeutics.* The blood serum of an animal used as a therapeutic or diagnostic agent 1895.

Servable (sə̄·ɹvăb'l), *a.* 1855. [f. SERVE *v.* + -ABLE.] That may be served, worthy to be served.

Servage (sə̄·ɹvėdʒ). ME. [– (O)Fr. *servage*, f. *serf*; see SERF, -AGE.] †**1.** Servitude, bondage, slavery –1586. †**2.** A service, or its equivalent in money, due from a serf to his lord –1587. **3.** Serfdom (*rare*) 1848.

Serval (sə̄·ɹvăl). 1771. [– mod.L., Fr. *serval* (Buffon, 1765) – Pg. (*lobo*) *cerval* 'deer-like wolf' (cf. Fr. *loup-cervier*), f. *cervo* :– L. *cervus* deer.] †**a.** Some Asiatic wild cat or lynx; also, an American animal resembling this. **b.** A carnivorous quadruped, *Felis s.*, native of S. Africa, having a tawny coat spotted with black, a short tail, and large ears. So **Se·rvaline** *a.* resembling the s.

Servant (sə̄·ɹvănt), *sb.* ME. [– OFr. *servant* masc. and fem. (now only fem. *-ante*), subst. use of pr. pple. of *servir* SERVE; see -ANT.] A person of either sex who is in the service of a master or mistress; one who is under obligation to work for the benefit of a superior, and to obey his (or her) commands. **1.** A personal or domestic attendant. (Sometimes with defining word, as *domestic s.*). **2.** One who is under the obligation to render certain services to, and to obey the orders of, a person or a body of persons, esp. in return for wages or salary. late ME. **b.** *fig.* Applied to things ME. **c.** Applied occas. to any state official, as expressing his relation to the sovereign. So *s. of the state, public s.*, etc. 1570. **3.** In the N. Amer. colonies in the 17–18th c., and subseq. in U.S., *servant* was the usual designation for a slave 1643. **4.** *transf.* †**a.** A professed lover; one who is devoted to the service of a lady. Also, a paramour, gallant. –1700. **b.** With religious signification ME. **c.** *Your* (*humble, obedient*) *s.*: one of the customary modes of subscribing a letter, or of addressing a patron in the dedication of a book. †(*Your*) *s.*: a mode of expressing submission to another's opinion; a form of greeting or leave-taking. 1474.

1. *Upper s.*, a domestic s. of superior grade of employment, as a butler or a housekeeper. *General s., s. of all work*, a female servant who does all kinds of housework. *Servants' hall*, a room for use as a common room by the servants in a large house; The ethics of the kitchen and servants'-hall 1813. **2. b.** Fire and water be good servants, but bad masters 1639. **c.** Public Servants voting at Elections 1845. **4. a.** Pegg, and her s., Mr. Lowther PEPYS. **b.** *S. of the servants of God* tr. *servus servorum Dei*, a title assumed by the Popes (first by Gregory the Great). *attrib.*, as *s.-girl, -maid.* Hence **Se·rvantless** *a.* having no s. **Se·rvantry** (*rare*), servants collectively. **Se·rvantship,** the condition of being a s.

†**Se·rvant,** *v. rare.* 1607. [f. prec.] *trans.* To put in subjection *to.* SHAKS.

Serve (sə̄ɹv), *sb.* 1688. [f. next.] *Tennis.* An act of serving, a service.

Serve (sə̄ɹv), *v.* ME. [– (O)Fr. *servir* or L. *servire*, f. *servus* slave.] **I. 1.** *intr.* To be a servant; to perform the duties of a servant. †**b.** To be a slave or bondman; to labour as a bondman. Also with cogn. obj. (A latinism.) –1671. **2.** To go through a term of service under a master. Usu. with advb. accus. denoting the period, as *to s. one's time*, etc. 1553. **b.** *trans.* To go through, work out (a term of imprisonment, a penal sentence). Also ellipt. *to s. time* and simply *to s.* 1873. **3.** To be a servant to; to work for (a master or mistress) ME. **b.** To work for (a body of persons, a company) as a paid servant 1844. **4.** To attend upon (as a servant does); to wait upon, minister to the comfort of ME. **5.** To assist (a priest) *at* mass as server. Also *absol.*, to act as server. Also *to s. mass* (= Fr. *servir la messe*). late ME. **6.** (In the earliest use, with obj. in dative.) To be (officially) a servant of (God, a heathen deity); to take official part in the worship of ME. **7.** †**a.** *trans.* To worship (God, a deity) with religious rites; to offer praise and prayer to, give divine honour to –1702. **b.** To render habitual obedience to (God, a heathen deity, Satan) ME. **8.** To render obedience and service to, to fulfil one's duty to (a feudal superior, a sovereign) ME. **b.** To be the 'servant' or lover of (a lady). late ME. †**9.** To obey (a person's will); to execute (a command, etc.) –1822. **b.** To gratify (desire); to minister to, satisfy (one's need). late ME. **10.** *To s. the time* [L. *tempori servire*]: to shape one's conduct in self-interested conformity to the views that are in favour at the time 1560. **11.** To render active service to (a king or commander) as a soldier or sailor; to fight for, 'to obey in military actions' (J.) 1518. **12.** *intr.* To take one's part in war under a sovereign or commander; to be a soldier or man-of-war's-man. Said also of a ship. 1518. **13.** *trans.* To perform the duties of (an office, cure of souls, etc.). late ME. **b.** To work for, assist at, take part in (a function); to take part in the service of (an institution); esp. to minister in (a church) or at (an altar) 1477. **14.** *intr.* To perform official duties, hold office (e.g. as sheriff or M.P., or on a jury) 1477. **15.** *trans.* To render useful service to (a person); to work for or assist *in* any matter 1638. **b.** To labour for (a cause) 1847.

1. Better to reign in Hell, then s. in Heav'n MILT. **b.** The Egyptians made the children of Israel to serue with rigour *Exod.* 1:13. **3.** A young Fellow who had served my Aunt 1740. **4.** S. yourself, would you be well served, is an excellent adage LONGF. **6.** A priest who has forsworn the God he serves SHELLEY. **7.** The costome of the primitive Saints in serving God with Hymns EVELYN. **b.** Who best beare his milde yoak, they s. him best MILT. **8. b.** That gentle Lady, whom I loue and serue SPENSER. **10.** Who never sold the truth to s. the hour TENNYSON. **12.** The 84th Regiment, in which I formerly served 1869. **15.** In all his calamities, they never discovered the least inclination to s. him SMOLLETT.

II. 1. Of a thing: To be subordinate or subsidiary to (another) ME. **2.** To be useful or advantageous to; to answer the requirements of; to be used by. Const. inf. of purpose. With neg.: To avail or profit (a person) nothing. ME. **b.** To be used in common by (a number of persons). late ME. **c.** Of a bodily faculty or organ: To render its normal service to (the owner) ME. **d.** Of a thing: To supply the need or contribute to the working of (another thing) 1580. **3.** *intr.* To have a definite use or function, answer a purpose, effect or conduce to an end; to admit of being used for some end. With neg. = to be of no use, not to avail. ME. **b.** To be usable or available *for* 1528. **4.** *trans.* To help to fulfil or bring about (an end, purpose, etc.); to be a means to, conduce to 1568. **5.** *trans.* and *intr.* To discharge a specified function; to take the place of some specified agency. late ME. †**6.** *trans.* Of one's courage, conscience, inclination, etc.: To prompt (one) *to do* something; (with neg.) to permit, suffer. Also *intr.* –1597. **7.** *trans.* and *intr.* Of time, occasion, wind, weather, etc.: To be opportune or favourable (*to*); to afford (one) opportunity. late ME. **8.** *trans.* and *intr.* Of the memory: To assist or prompt its owner, be at his call 1634. **9.** *trans.* To suffice (a person) in regard to some need or requirement. Also, to last (a person) *for* a specified time. 1450. **b.** To furnish what is requisite for (a thing) 1566. **10.** *intr.* To meet the needs of the case; be adequate or sufficient. Also, to last for a given period. 1496. †**11.** To hold good; to be available *for*; to be satisfactory. Of coin: To pass current. –1726. **12.** *trans.* To suit, fit. (Chiefly of clothes.) *Obs.* exc. *Sc.* 1540.

2. That scuse serues many men to saue their gifts SHAKS. **c.** Her eyes serving her as well as ever EVELYN. **3.** This little Brand will s. to light your Fire DRYDEN. The manganese that has been once used..will s. again 1815. The nerve of vision..can never serve for hearing 1844. **4.** It would s. no useful purpose 1893. **5.** One turfe shall serue as pillow for vs both SHAKS. My Stomach serves me instead of a Clock SWIFT. **6.** *Merch. V.* II. ii. 1. **7.** If fortune serue me, Ile requite this kindnesse SHAKS. When opportunity serves 1879. **8.** Or perhaps your memory don't s. you as well as it did 1861. **9.** It will serue you to mend your shooes SHAKS. Phr. *To s. one's turn*, see TURN *sb.* V. 3. **10.** Tis not so deepe as a well, nor so wide as a Church doore, but 'tis inough, 'twill serue SHAKS. **12.** *Two Gent.* IV. iv. 167.

III. 1. To wait upon (a person) at table; hence, to set food before, help (a person) to food ME. **b.** To supply (a person) *with* food at a meal, to help (a person) to food ME. **2.** *absol.* To wait at table ME. **3.** *trans.* To set food on (the table), to spread *with* food. late ME. **4.** To set food before, feed (animals) 1523. **5.** To attend to the request of (a customer in a shop). Hence, to supply (a customer) *with* a commodity. late ME. **b.** *intr.* To attend to customers in a shop 1825. **6.** *trans.* To supply or furnish with something necessary or requisite. Also, to furnish (a person, town, etc.) with a regular or continuous supply. ME. **b.** To supply with means of transit and conveyance: esp. of railways 1866. †**7.** *refl.* To make use *of*, avail oneself *of*. Also const. *with.* [After Fr. *se servir de.*] –1846.

1. Let your Betters be serv'd before you SWIFT. **b.** S. him with ven'son, and he chooses fish COWPER. Prov. *First come, first served.* **2.** For whether is greater, he that sitteth at meate: or he that serveth? TINDALE *Luke* 22:27. **3.** *To s. tables* (cf. Acts 6:2), now sometimes used with ref. to the secular functions of the clergy, viewed as encroaching on the time available for their more spiritual work. **5.** Phr. *To s. the shop*, to attend to customers. **6.** A Conduit of water which serves all the Towne 1617. A woman who ..used to s. my family with butter 1726.

IV. 1. To set (meat or drink) on the table or before a person; to bring in or dish up (a meal). late ME. **b.** To dish up or send to the table in a specified manner. late ME. **2.** *To s. out*, to distribute or deal out (food, ammunition, etc.) in portions 1802. †**3.** To supply, furnish (a commodity); to yield a regular or continuous supply of –1700. **4.** †To play (a person) a *trick*; to do (a person) a *good* or *bad turn* 1591.

1. It was getting on for two before supper was served 1885. **b.** Boil these gently together and s. on toast 1864. **2.** I served out some kegs of gunpowder 1827. **3.** The pump..that serves water to his garden EVELYN.

V. 1. To treat in a specified (usu. unpleasant or unfair) manner. Now chiefly *colloq.* ME. **2.** *To s. out*: To punish, take revenge on; to retaliate on (a person) *for* something objectionable. *colloq.* (orig. pugilists' slang) 1817.

1. Phr. *To s.* (a person) *right*, to treat (an offender) as he deserves; now chiefly *it serves* (me, you, etc.) *right*; also colloq. *serves* (you, etc.) *right*, (*and*) *s.* (you, etc.) *right*, an exclamation of satisfaction at seeing a person punished for his folly or wrongdoing.

VI. Techn. senses. **1.** *Law.* To make legal delivery of (a process or writ). Const. *on* or *upon* (a person). 1442. **b.** To present (a person) *with* a writ 1575. **2.** *Tennis* (and similar games). **a.** *intr.* To start play by striking the ball into the opposite court 1585. **b.** *trans.* To put (the ball) in play 1696. **c.** To strike the ball to (one's opponent) 1647. **3.** Of a male animal: To cover (the female); esp. of stallions, etc. kept and hired out for the purpose. Also *absol.* 1577. **4.** *Falconry* and *Coursing.* To provide quarry for 1576. **5.** Chiefly *Naut.* **a.** To bind (a rope, rod, etc.) with small cord or the like, so as to protect or strengthen 1627. **b.** To wrap (a rope, bandage) round an object 1586. **6.** *Mil.* To operate, keep in play or action (a gun, battery, etc.) 1706.

Serventism (serve·ntiz'm). 1833. [f. It. *servente* (in *cavaliere servente*; see CAVALIER *sb.*) + -ISM.] The system which countenances the devotion of a man to a married woman; cicisbeism.

Server (sə̄·ɹvəɹ). late ME. [f. SERVE *v.* + -ER¹.] **1.** One who serves, in various senses. **b.** *Eccl.* One who attends and assists a celebrant at the altar (cf. SERVE *v.* I. 5) 1853. **2.** Something which is used for serving. **a.** = SALVER² 1686. **b.** *pl.* A spoon and fork for serving salad or other foods 1884.

Servian (sə̄·ɹviăn), *a.* and *sb.* 1555. [f. mod.L. *Servia*; see -IAN.] Older form of SERBIAN.

Service¹ (sē·ɹvis). [– OFr. *servise*, (also mod.) *service*, or – L. *servitium* slavery, f. *servus*; see SERF, -ICE.] **I. 1.** The condition, status, or occupation of a servant. (In mod. use almost exclusively *spec.* = *domestic s.*) **2.** Const. *of* or possessive: The condition of being a servant of a particular master ME. **b.** The condition or fact of being a servant (of God); †the condition of being the 'servant' (of one's lady). late ME. **3.** †**a.** A place as servant. **b.** A particular employ; the serving of a certain master or household. 1469. **4.** The condition or employment of a public servant (of a sovereign or state) ME. **5.** A branch of public employment, or a body of public servants, concerned with some particular work or the supply of some particular need 1685. **b.** *The s.*: the Army, the Navy, or the Air Force (as implied in the context) considered as a sphere of duty or occupation, or as a profession. So *the (fighting) services*, the Army, the Navy, and the Air Force 1706.

1. *In, out of s.; to be in s.; to go, get, put into s.*; He had put two of his daughters into s. THACKERAY. **2.** To leaue a rich Iewes service SHAKS. **b.** O God..whose seruice is perfect fredome *Bk. Com. Prayer, Morn. Prayer.* **4.** *In the British, French,* etc. *s.*: (chiefly of a soldier or sailor). *To take s.*, to join a fighting force. **5.** *The consular s., the diplomatic s., the* CIVIL SERVICE, etc. **b.** The S. is going to the dogs 1872. *The United Services*, the Army and the Navy. *The senior s.*, the Navy.

II. 1. Performance of the duties of a servant; attendance of servants; work done in obedience to and for the benefit of a master ME. **b.** An act of serving; a duty or piece of work done for a master or superior ME. **2.** In feudal use: †**a.** Feudal allegiance, fealty; homage –1595. **b.** A duty which a tenant is bound to render periodically to his lord ME. **3.** *transf.* In complimentary expressions: Respect, 'duty'. Now *rare* or *Obs.* 1601. †**b.** *pl.* in the same sense –1723. **c.** *At* (a person's) *s.*: ready to obey his commands 1554. **4.** The devotion or suit of a lover; professed love. *arch.* late ME. **5.** The serving the sovereign or the state in an official capacity; the duties or work of public servants. late ME. **6.** The duty of a soldier or sailor; the performance of this duty. Often, actual participation in warfare; more fully *active s.* 1590. **b.** A military or naval operation in which a soldier or a regiment serves (often *pl.*) 1590.

1. He was allowed the s. of a boy 1845. **b.** *Temp.* IV. i. 35. **2. a.** Vpon your oath of seruice to the Pope SHAKS. **3.** Phr. *My s. to you*, a phrase accompanying the drinking to a person. *Give my s. to* (in letters) = remember me respectfully to (a third person). **c.** †*At your s.* used *ellipt.* as a phr. of politeness. **5.** *On His* (or *Her*) *Majesty's S.*, a formula (often abbrev. O.H.M.S.) printed on the cover of a letter to indicate that it is official (and therefore exempt from postage). *Secret s.*: see SECRET *a.* **6.** Phr. *To see s.*, (of a soldier) to have experience of warfare; hence (in perfect tense) of a thing, to have been much used or worn.

III. In religious uses. **1.** The serving (God) by obedience, piety, and good works ME. **2.** Worship; esp. public worship according to form and order. Now *rare* or *Obs.* exc. in *divine s.* ME. **3.** A celebration of public worship. (Often without the article.) late ME. **4.** A ritual or series of words and ceremonies prescribed for public worship, or for some particular occasion or ministration. Often with defining word, as *baptismal, burial, communion, marriage s.* (The earliest recorded sense.) **b.** In full *divine s.* †(*a*) The daily office or hours of the breviary –1583; (*b*) Morning and Evening Prayer (Matins and Evensong) 1549. **5.** A musical setting of those portions of the church-offices which are sung; esp. the music for the canticles at Morning and Evening Prayer 1691. **6.** A service-book. Now only *Church S.*, a volume containing the Book of Common Prayer together with the daily lessons. 1700.

1. Our voluntarie s. he requires MILT. **2.** A drear and dying sound Affrights the Flamins at their s. quaint MILT. **3.** I looked into the church, where s. was going on 1859.

IV. 1. The action of serving, helping, or benefiting; conduct tending to the welfare or advantage of another. Chiefly in *to do, render s.* 1582. **b.** An act of helping or benefiting; an instance of beneficial or friendly action 1533. **c.** *collect. pl.* Friendly or professional assistance 1832. †**2.** With *of* or possessive: A person's interest or advantage –1774. **3.** The work which an animal or thing is made to do 1470. **4.** Supply of the needs *of* (persons, occas. of things) ME. **5.** Serviceableness, utility. Now *rare.* 1595. †**6.** *At one's s.*, at one's disposal, ready or available for one to use 1669.

1. He also rendered good s. to our old ally the Porte 1853. **c.** We..shall have no need of Mr. Bowls's kind services THACKERAY. **3.** Phr. *To do s.*; I passed the rod to X——, in whose hands it did better s. 1882. **4.** A great fountain for the common seruice of the house 1585. **5.** *Of s.* (predic.): of use or assistance; useful, helpful.

V. 1. The act of waiting at table or dishing up food; the manner in which this is done. late ME. **b.** That which is served up or placed on the table for a meal. Now *rare.* ME. †**c.** A course –1765. **2.** The furniture of the table. Often with defining word, as *dinner, dessert, breakfast, tea s.* 1468. **b.** A set of vessels for †the altar, the toilet, etc. 1700. **3.** The supply or laying-on of gas, water, etc., through pipes from a reservoir; the apparatus of pipes, etc., by which this is done 1879. **4.** Provision (of labour, material appliances, etc.) for the carrying out of some work for which there is a constant public demand 1853. **5.** Accommodation for conveyance or transit afforded by vehicles plying regularly on a route 1854.

1. Phr. *The s. of the table* (now *arch.*). **c.** His dinner—four services 1765. **4.** [The hospital] has a s. of 710 beds 1886. **b.** Expert advice or assistance given to customers after sale by manufacturers or vendors 1925. **5.** The ordinary s. of trains 1885.

VI. Action of serving, in technical senses. **1.** *Law.* The action or an act of serving (a writ, notice, etc.) upon a person. late ME. **b.** *Sc. Law.* The procedure for ascertaining and declaring the heir of a person deceased 1597. **2.** *Tennis*, etc. The act of 'serving' the ball; a particular player's manner of doing this; the ball served 1611. **3.** *Naut.* Small cord, or the like, wound about a rope to protect it 1729. **4.** The action of covering a female animal 1844.

1. Phr. *To accept s.* (of a writ): see ACCEPT *v.* 3. *Comb.*: **s.-book**, a book containing one or more forms of divine service, (in the 17th c. often applied to the Book of Common Prayer); **s. flat**, one of a number of flats having the cooking and serving of meals, cleaning, etc. performed by a common staff of servants; **s. measure, metre**, the 14-syllable line which is the equivalent of a couplet of common metre; also used = common metre (see COMMON *a.* 19); **-time**, the time of divine service.

Service² (sə̄·ɹvis). 1530. [Early forms *sarves, servyse*, pl. of †*serve*, OE. *syrfe* :– **surbjōn* – pop. L. **sorbea*, f. L. *sorbus* service tree.] **1.** A tree, *Pyrus* (*Sorbus*) *domestica*, bearing small pear-shaped or round fruit edible when in an over-ripe condition. †**2.** The fruit of this tree –1796. **3.** *Wild S.*: a bush or low tree (*Pyrus torminalis*) bearing bitter fruit 1741.

attrib. and *Comb.*: **s.-berry**, †(*a*) the fruit of the S.; (*b*) a N. Amer. shrub, *Amelanchier canadensis*, the Shad-bush; (*c*) the fruit of the white-beam, *Pyrus aria*; **-tree**, (*a*) = sense 1; (*b*) the wood of this tree; (*c*) *wild s.-tree* = sense 3; (*d*) = *s.-berry* b.

Serviceable (sə̄·ɹvisăb'l), *a.* ME. [– OFr. *serviceable, -isable* (with suffix in active sense), f. *service*; see SERVICE¹, -ABLE.] **1.** Ready to do service; willing to be of service; active or diligent in service. Now *rare.* †**b.** Of actions or conditions: Involving or expressing readiness to serve –1629. **2. a.** Of persons: Profitable, useful 1660. **b.** Of things: Capable of being applied to an appropriate purpose, or to the performance of a proper function. late ME.

1. A seruiceable Villaine, As duteous to the vices of thy Mistris, As badnesse would desire SHAKS. **b.** And all about the Courtly Stable, Bright-harnest Angels sit in order s. MILT. **2. b.** The barometer..is also s. in measuring the heights of mountains GOLDSM. Hence **Se·rviceableness. Se·rviceably** *adv.*

Servient (sə̄·ɹviĕnt), *a.* 1615. [– L. *serviens, -ent-*, pr. pple. of *servire* SERVE *v.*; see -ENT.] **1.** Subordinate, subject to rule. †Also *absol.* **2.** Law. *S. land, tenement*: a land or tenement over which a servitude has been granted or acquired in favour of a dominant land or tenement. *S. proprietor*: the tenant of a servient land or tenement. 1681.

Serviette (sə̄ɹvie·t). Latterly considered *vulgar.* 1489. [– (O)Fr. *serviette* towel, napkin, f. *servir*; see -ETTE and cf. OUBLIETTE.] A table-napkin.

Servile (sə̄·ɹvəil, *U.S.* -il), *a.* and *sb.* late ME. [– L. *servilis*, f. *servus* slave; see -ILE. Cf. (O)Fr. *servile.*] **A.** *adj.* **1.** Of, belonging to or proper to a slave or slaves 1450. **b.** Of arts, employments, labour: Befitting a slave; unworthy of a free man; hence, 'mechanical' as opp. to *liberal* 1514. **2.** Of a person: Subject as a slave or serf to a master or owner; living in servitude. Of a class, etc.: Composed of slaves or serfs. 1565. †**b.** Belonging to the serving class or to the lower orders –1727. **3.** Of a person: That behaves like a slave; meanly submissive, 'cringing, fawning' (J.); destitute of independence in thought and action 1605. **b.** Befitting, or characteristic of a slave or a state of servitude; slavish, ignoble 1526. **4.** Of a people, state, its condition, etc.: Politically enslaved; subject to despotic or oppressive government or to foreign dominion. Now *rare* or *Obs.* 1547. †**5.** Of immaterial things: Subject *to* the control of something else; not free –1805. **6.** Of imitation, translation, etc.: Unintelligently close to the exemplar or original; slavish. Hence of a person as agent. 1605. **7.** *Philol.* **a.** Of words: Expressing mere grammatical relations, auxiliary 1668. **b.** *Semitic Gram.* Of a letter: Not belonging to the root of the word in which it occurs; serving to express a derivative or flexional element. Opp. to *radical.* 1653.

1. This lad of s. birth PATER. †*S. habit*, formerly sometimes applied *transf.* to the dress of a labourer or a poor man. *S. war, insurrection*, one raised by slaves against their masters. **b.** Phr. *S. work* [after L. *opus servile*], in religious use applied *spec.* to laborious or mechanical work forbidden on the Sabbath and hence on the major festivals of the Church. **2. b.** *Tit. A.* V. ii. 55. **3.** Be courteous to all men, s. to none LYTTON. **b.** The..S. Fears usual in those of a mean depending Condition 1705. **4.** His Subjects..shall s. be to Turks and Infidels 1661. **5.** Reason thus with life..a breath thou art, Seruile to all the skyie-influences SHAKS.

B. *sb.* (the adj. used ellipt. or absol.) **1.** A servile person 1830. **2.** *Heb. Gram.* A servile letter 1738. Hence **Se·rvile-ly** *adv.*, **-ness.**

Servilism (sə̄·ɹviliz'm). 1831. [f. SERVILE *a.* + -ISM. Cf. Fr. *servilisme.*] **1.** Systematic servility. **2.** The doctrine which advocates political 'slavery' (a hostile term for anti-Liberal opinions) 1831.

Servility (səɹvi·lĭti). 1573. [f. SERVILE *a.* + -ITY.] †**1.** Servile condition; the quality or status of being a slave –1667. **2.** Servile disposition or conduct; *esp.* mean submissiveness, cringing 1573.

2. This unhappy s. to custome 1674. The domestics..had an air of s. and constraint 1797.

Serving (sə̄·ɹviŋ), *vbl. sb.* ME. [f. SERVE *v.* + -ING¹.] The action of SERVE *v.* in various senses; an instance of this. **b.** *concr.* A helping (of food, etc.) 1769.

Serving (sə̄·ɹviŋ), *ppl. a.* ME. [f. SERVE *v.* + -ING².] **1.** That serves, or does service to, another; that acts as a servant. Often hyphened, as in *serving-maid*, etc. **2.** Of a soldier, etc. That is on service 1570.

S.-man (now *arch.*), a man who serves; a male servant or attendant; so **s.-wo:man.**

Servite (sə̄·ɹvəit), *sb.* and *a.* 1550. [– med.L. *Servitæ* pl., f. L. *servus* servant (in *Servi Beatæ Mariæ*, the formal name of the order); see -ITE¹.] **A.** *sb.* A friar or nun of the order of 'Servants of Blessed Mary', founded in 1233. **B.** *adj.* Of or pertaining to this order 1756.

Servitor (sə̄·ɹvitəɹ). ME. [– OFr. *servitor* (mod. *-teur*) – late L. *servitor*, *-ōr-*, f. *servit-*, pa. ppl. stem of. L. *servire* SERVE *v.*] **1.** A (male) personal or domestic attendant; a man-servant. Now *arch.* **b.** *gen.* A servant 1450. †**2.** Used in expressions of humility or politeness –1645. **3.** One who serves in war; *spec.* one of a class of persons to whom lands were assigned in Ulster under James I, as having served in a military or civil office in Ireland. *Obs.* exc. *Hist.* 1561. **4.** *Oxford Univ.* Formerly, in certain colleges, one of a class of undergraduate members who received their lodging and most of their board free, and were excused lecture fees. (Orig. the servitors acted as servants to the fellows.) 1642. **5.** *Glass-making.* †A master workman's assistant; *spec.* the second man of a 'chair' 1662.

3. A valiant servitour in sundry wars beyond sea 1640. Hence **Se·rvitorship,** the position, state, or duties of a s. at an Oxford college (*Obs.* exc. *Hist.*).

Servitude (sə̄·ɹvitiūd). 1471. [– (O)Fr. *servitude* – L. *servitudo*, f. *servus* slave; see -TUDE.] **1.** The condition of being a slave or serf; absence of personal freedom. Often, and now usu., with additional notion of subjection to the necessity of excessive labour. Also, a (more or less rigorous) state of slavery or serfdom. **b.** With ref. to animals: Subjection to mankind. Now *rare* or *Obs.* 1697. **c.** Subjection to a foreign power or to oppressive rule 1471. **d.** *transf.* and *fig.* A state of degrading or burdensome subjection 1474. †**e.** *concr.* Slaves or servants collectively. MILT. **2.** The condition of being a servant, service; esp. domestic service. Now *rare* or *Obs.* 1651. †**3.** Apprenticeship –1835. **4.** Compulsory labour as a punishment for criminals. Chiefly *penal s.* 1828. **5.** *Civil* (and *Scots*) *Law.* (= L. *servitus*). A subjection or subserviency of property either: (1) to some definite person other than its owner (*personal s.*), or (2) to some definite property other than that of its owner for the benefit of the dominant property (*prædial s.*) 1652.

1. The greatest part of the nation was gradually reduced into a state of s. GIBBON. **c.** A disturbed Liberty is better than a quiet s. ADDISON. **d.** This is s., To serve th' unwise MILT.

Servo- (sə̄·ɹvo), = SERBO-.

Servo-motor. 1889. [– Fr. *servo-moteur* (1873), f. L. *servus* slave + Fr. *moteur* MOTOR.] An auxiliary motor, e.g. one used for directing the rudders of a Whitehead torpedo, or the reversing gear of a large marine engine.

Sesame, †sesam (se·sămi, †se·săm, sĭ·săm). 1440. [– L. *sesamum*, *sis-*, *sesama*, *-ima* – Gr. σήσαμον, σησάμη, of Oriental origin.] A widely cultivated E. Indian plant, *Sesamum indicum.* Also the seeds of this plant from which an oil is expressed. **b.** = OPEN SESAME 1785.

attrib.: **s. grass** = GAMA GRASS.

Sesamoid (se·sămoid), *a.* and *sb.* 1696. [f. SESAME + -OID, perh. after Gr. σησαμοειδής.] **A.** *adj.* Shaped like a sesame-seed; applied in *Anat.* to certain small bones and cartilages formed in tendinous structures. **B.** *sb.* A sesamoid bone or cartilage 1854. So **Sesamoi·dal, Sesamoi·deal** *adjs.*

‖**Sesamum** (se·sămŏm). 1577. = SESAME.

Sesban (se·sbæn). 1860. [– Fr. *sesban*, ult. – Arabo-Pers. *saysabān.*] Any leguminous plant of the genus *Sesbania*, esp. *S. ægyptiaca* and *aculeata.*

Sescuple (se·skiup'l), *a.* Now *rare.* 1694. [– L. *sescuplus* or *sescuplex*, var. *sesquiplus* or *sesquiplex*, f. *sesqui-* SESQUI- + *-plus*, *-plex* -FOLD.] = SESQUIALTER *a.*

Sesqui- (se·skwi), – L. prefix [*sesqui-*, contr. of **semis-que* a half in addition], expressing a superparticular ratio.

1. With designations of measure or amount, denoting one and a half times the unit; as **se·squipes,** a foot and a half (see SESQUIPEDALIAN); †**se·squitone** *Mus.*, an interval consisting of a tone and a semitone, a minor third. **b.** *Chem.* In the names of salts, expressing a proportion of 3 to 2 between the constituents, *viz.* a combination of 3 atoms or equivalents of the substance denoted by the word to which it is prefixed with 2 atoms of another element or radical; e.g. **sesquibro·mide,** a bromide containing 3 atoms of bromine for 2 of another substance; so **sesquio·xide; sesquiba·sic** [see BASIC *a.*], having 3 equivalents of the base for 2 of the acid. **c.** In *Astrol.*, **sesquiqua·drate, -qua·rtile,** denoting an aspect of planets when 135° from one another; so **sesqui-squa·re.** †**d.** Prefixed to words descriptive of forms of religious belief, = extreme(ly), excessive(ly), ultra-; e.g. *sesqui-conformist*, *-deist.*

2. With an ordinal numeral adjective, denoting the proportion $1 + \frac{1}{n}: 1$, *i.e.* n. + 1: n, where n is the corresponding cardinal number, as *sesquioctavus*, bearing the ratio of $1\frac{1}{8}$:1, *i.e.* 9:8; so SESQUIALTER, -ALTERA, etc. **b.** *Mus.*, after SESQUIALTERA, etc.; **sesquiqua·rta, -qui·nta,** etc., applied (*a*) to harmonic intervals producible by sounding four-fifths, five-sixths, etc. of a given string; (*b*) to rhythmic combinations of four notes against five, five against six, etc.

‖**Sesquialter** (seskwiæ·ltəɹ), *a.* (*sb.*) 1570. [L., f. *sesqui-* SESQUI- + *alter* second.] **1.** Of a proportion: That is as $1\frac{1}{2}$ is to 1. Of an object: Proportionate *to* another object as $1\frac{1}{2}$ is to 1; that is such a multiple *of.* **2.** = next 2. 1841.

‖**Sesquialtera** (seskwiæ·ltĕră), *a.* (*sb.*) 1501. [L., fem. (sc. *ratio*) of *sesquialter* (see prec.).] †**1.** = prec. Also as *sb.*, a sesquialteral proportion. –1650. **b.** *Mus.* (See quot.) Also, a perfect fifth. 1501. **2.** An organ stop, consisting of several ranks of pipes, of a brilliant tone. Usu. *absol.* as *sb.* 1688.

1. b. In rhythmic combinations, S. is used as the general symbol of Triple Time. The term S. is also applied to passages of three notes sung against two 1883.

Sesquialteral (seskwi,æ·ltĕrăl), *a.* 1603. [f. L. *sesquialter* + -AL¹.] = SESQUIALTER 1. So **Sesquia·lterate, -a·lterous** *adjs.*

Sesquiduple (se·skwidiū:p'l), *a.* 1850. [f. SESQUI- + DUPLE, to express the meaning 'two and a half' (on a false analogy), after *sesquialteral.*] Involving a ratio of $2\frac{1}{2}$ to 1. So **Sesquidu·plicate** *a.* 1775.

Sesquipedal (sĕskwi·pĭdăl, se·skwipedăl), *a.* 1611. [– L. *sesquipedalis*, f. SESQUI- + *pes*, *ped-* foot + *-alis* -AL¹.] = next.

Sesquipedalian (se:skwipĭdēⁱ·liăn), *a.* and *sb.* 1615. [f. L. *sesquipedalis*; see prec. and -IAN.] **A.** *adj.* Of words, etc. (after Horace, *A.P.* 97): Of many syllables 1656. **b.** *transf.* Given to using long words 1853.

Finding one of his s. words hang fire BOSWELL.

B. *sb.* **1.** A person or thing that is a foot and a half in height or length 1615. **2.** A sesquipedalian word 1830. Hence **Se:squipeda·lianism,** style characterized by the use of long words; lengthiness; so **Sesquipe·dalism; Sesquipeda·lity,** *s.* quality; *transf.* lengthiness.

Sesquiplicate (seskwi·plikĕt), *a.* 1714. [– mod.L. *sesquiplicatus*, f. SESQUI- + *plicatus* folded, PLICATE, to express 'sub-duplicate of the triplicate'. (L. *sesquiplex* = taken once and a half.)] Bearing or involving the ratio of the square roots of the cubes of the terms of a certain ratio.

Thus, *a* is to *a'* in the s. ratio of *b* to *b'*, when $a{:}a'::\sqrt{b^3}:\sqrt{b'^3}$.

‖**Sesquitertia** (seskwitə̄·ɹʃă). 1597. [L., fem. (sc. *ratio*) of *sesquitertius*, f. SESQUI- + *tertius* third.] Denoting a ratio of $1\frac{1}{3}$ to 1, *i.e.* 4 to 3; chiefly *Mus.* denoting (*a*) an interval having this ratio, viz. the perfect fourth; (*b*) a rhythm of three notes against four. Hence †**Sesquite·rtial** *a.* –1696. †**Sesquite·rtian** *a.* expressing a ratio of 4:3. –1774.

†**Sess,** *v.* 1465. [aphet. f. ASSESS *v.*] = CESS *v.*¹, 1, 2, 4. –1764.

†**Se·ssa,** *int.* [perh. var. of *sa-sa.*] An exclam. of uncertain meaning. SHAKS.

Sessile (se·səil, se·sil), *a.* 1753. [– L. *sessilis*, f. *sess-*, pa. ppl. stem of *sedēre* SIT; see -ILE.] **1.** Having no footstalk. **a.** *Bot.* Of leaves, fruits, flowers, etc.: Immediately attached by the base; not having a peduncle, pedicel, or the like. **b.** *Zool.* Of limbs or organs: Having no connecting neck or footstalk. Also of certain animals. 1777. **c.** *Path.* Of morbid growths, warts, etc.: Adhering close to the surface 1725. **2.** Of certain animals: Sedentary, fixed to one spot; not ambulatory. Of cells: Immobile. 1860.

Session (se·ʃən). late ME. [– (O)Fr. *session* or L. *sessiō(n-*, f. as prec.; see -ION.] **1.** The action or an act of sitting; the state or posture of being seated; also a manner of sitting. Now *rare.* 1615. **b.** *spec.* The 'sitting' of Christ at the right hand of God 1557. **2.** The sitting together of a number of persons (esp. of a court, a legislative, adminstrative, or deliberative body) for conference or the transaction of business. Also (now somewhat *rarely*), a single continuous sitting of persons assembled for conference or business. 1444. **3.** A continuous series of sittings or meetings of a court, a legislative, administrative, or deliberative body, held daily or at short intervals; the period or term during which the sittings continue to be held; opp. to *recess* or *vacation* 1553. **b.** *spec.* The period between the opening of Parliament and its prorogation 1577. **c.** In some universities and colleges, an academical year 1775. **4.** A judicial sitting. **a.** *gen.* A sitting of a judge or judges to determine causes; a judicial trial or investigation. *sing.* and *collect. pl.* (often const. as *sing.*) *Obs.* exc. *arch.* late ME. **b. Sessions of the peace** (in ordinary language simply **sessions**): the periodical sittings of justices of the peace (or, in some instances, of a stipendiary magistrate or a recorder). Often const. as *sing.* late ME.

1. Vivien. .Leapt from her s. on his lap TENNYSON. **2.** A Prayer for the High Court of Parliament, to be read during their S. *Bk. Com. Prayer.* The British geologists. .here in solemn annual s. assembled HUXLEY. **3. b.** I doubt the s. will not be over till the end of April SWIFT. *Autumn s.*, the exceptional resumption of the sittings of the Houses, after an adjournment, in what is normally the autumn recess; a use condemned by parliamentary authorities as incorrect. **c.** Also of a school, and in U.S., the teaching period of a day. **4. b.** *Petty* (†*petit*) *sessions*, a court held by two or more justices or a stipendiary magistrate, exercising summary jurisdiction in minor offences within a particular district. *Brewster* or *licensing sessions*, a periodical meeting of the justices of a division for the hearing of applications for licences to sell alcoholic drinks. *General* or *quarter sessions*, a court held four times a year (in a county, riding, etc. by the justices of the peace, and in certain boroughs by the recorder), having a limited civil and criminal jurisdiction and certain administrative functions. (*The sessions*, without qualification usu. = the quarter sessions.) Hence **Se·ssional** *a.* pertaining to a s. or sessions. **Se·ssionally** *adv.*

Sesterce (se·stəɹs). *Pl.* **sesterces** (se·stəɹsiz). 1598. [– L. *sestertius* (sc. *nummus* coin) that is two and a half, f. *semis* half + *tertius* third; see SEMI-, SESQUI-.] A Roman coin, orig. = $2\frac{1}{2}$ asses, later 4 asses; the fourth part of a denarius.

‖**Sestertium** (sestə̄·ɹʃiŏm). *Pl.* **sestertia** (-ʃiă). 1540. [L., usu. explained as the gen. pl. *sestertium* of *sestertius* SESTERCE (with ellipsis of *mille* a thousand), taken as n. sing.] A sum of a thousand sesterces.

‖**Sestertius** (sestə̄·ɹʃiŏs). *Pl.* **sestertii** (-ʃi,əi). 1567. [L.; see SESTERCE.] = SESTERCE.

Sestet(t, sestette (seste·t). 1801. [– It. *sestetto*; see next and -ET, -ETTE, and cf. SEXTET.] **1.** *Mus.* A composition for six voices or instruments. **2.** *Pros.* The last six lines of a sonnet 1859.

‖**Sestetto** (seste·to). 1801. [It., f. *sesto* sixth (:– L. *sextus*) + dim. suffix *-etto.*] = prec. 1.

‖**Sestina** (sestī·nă). 1838. [– It. *sestina*, f. *sesto* sixth; see prec.] *Pros.* A poem of six-line stanzas (with an envoy) in which the line-endings of the first stanza are repeated, but in different order, in the other five. So **Sesti·ne** 1586.

Set (set), *sb.*[1] Also **sett** (now prevalent in many techn. senses). late ME. [Mainly f. SET *v.*, but sense I. 1 may be in part due to ON. *-setr, -seta* (as in *sólarsetr, -seta* sunset).] **I.** The action of setting or condition of being set. **1.** The act of setting (of a luminary); the apparent descent of the heavenly bodies towards the horizon at the close of their diurnal period. Now only *poet.* exc. in SUNSET. †**2.** The condition of being stopped or checked; a check –1768. **3.** The act of a dog in setting game 1727. **4.** = *dead set*, a, b. 1829. **5.** (Usu. *sett.*) A form of power used by shipwrights 1794. **6.** The action of setting or hardening, or the condition of being set 1837. **7. Dead set,** often in phr. *to make a dead s. at.* **a.** A pointed attack; a determined onslaught; const. *at, against.* Also, an attitude or position of hostility. 1835. **b.** Of a woman: A determined attempt to gain a man's affections. Also *occas.* conversely of a man. 1823. **c.** A complete check; phr. *at a dead s.* 1806. **d.** *Sporting.* An abrupt stop made by an animal with its muzzle in the direction of the prey; *esp.* the position taken up by a dog in pointing game 1819.

1. That will be ere the s. of Sunne SHAKS. *S. of day*, (*a*) the time at which the sun sets; (*b*) the west. **4.** No one could say that Miss N. was making a s. at him 1887. **7. a.** The disaffected sections of the Irish population made a dead s. against him 1885.

II. The manner or position in which a thing is set. **1.** Tendency, inclination; determination in a certain direction; often = settled direction, fixed habit 1567. **2.** The direction in which a current flows or a wind blows; also, the action of the water, etc. in taking a particular direction 1719. **3.** *Weaving.* (Usu. *sett.*) The adjustment of the reeds (of a loom) necessary for the making of a fabric of a particular texture; hence, the make of a fabric as determined by this 1780. **b.** (Usu. *sett.*) Each or any of the squares in the pattern of a tartan; the pattern itself 1721. **4.** The form which a body assumes as the result of strain or pressure or in the process of solidification, etc.; *esp.* the permanent deflexion of a bar or plate of metal or wood 1812. **5.** The way in which an article of dress is arranged or 'hangs'; similarly of a ship's sails 1822. **6.** The position or attitude given to a limb or a part of the body 1855. **7. a.** The dip of the arm of an axle-tree; the elevation of a gun 1844. **b.** The slight lateral deflexion in opposite directions of the alternate teeth of a saw; the amount of this deflexion 1837. **c.** *Typogr.* The position of the letters with ref. to the amount of space between them 1892.

1. According to..the S. of the Time DANIEL. **2.** A straw will prove the s. of a current 1876. **6.** The s. of her head and neck GEO. ELIOT.

III. Something which is set. **1.** (Usu. *sett.*) The area of ground worked by a particular mining company. Chiefly *Cornwall.* 1778. **2.** 'Any thing not sown, but put in a state of some growth into the ground' (J.); a twig, slip, or sucker, used for planting or grafting; also, a young plant, *esp.* a bedding-out plant 1513. **b.** A potato, or a portion of a potato, used as seed 1767. †**3.** The stake put down at dice, etc. –1611. †**4.** A game at dice or cards; hence, the number of points to be made in order to be 'up' –1687. †**b.** *fig.* Match, contest –1687. **5.** *Tennis.* (Occas. spelt *sett.*) A certain series of games: see quot. 1578. †**6.** One of the pleats of a ruff; also, the arrangement of a ruff in pleats –1651. **7.** (Usu. *sett.*) A squared stone (chiefly granite) used for paving 1871. **8. a.** *Plastering.* The finishing coat on walls prepared for painting 1823. **b.** A young oyster when first attached; the crop of young oysters in a locality 1881.

IV. A place where something is set. **1.** A place where stationary fishing nets are fixed 1745. **2.** The earth or burrow of a badger 1898.

V. (Often *sett.*) A tool or device used for 'setting' in various techn. senses 1750.

5. Six Games make a S. of Tennis, but if what is called an Advantage S. is played, two successive Games above five Games must be won to decide; or, in Case it should be six Games all, two successive Games must still be won on one Side to conclude the S. 1769.

Set (set), *sb.*[2] Also **sett.** late ME. [– OFr. *sette* :– L. *secta* SECT; but in later developments infl. by SET *v.* and apprehended as 'number set together' (cf. SET *sb.*[1]); the application to things may be partly due to MLG. *gesette* set or suite of things (cf. Da. *sæt* set of china, suit of clothes, G. *satz*).] **I.** A number or group of persons. †**1.** A religious body, sect –1538. **2.** A number, company, or group (*of* persons) associated by community of status, habits, occupations, or interests. Often *depreciatory.* Also *absol.* 1682. **3.** A group of persons in society having its own peculiar interests, fashions, and conventions; a social group of a select or exclusive character 1777. **4.** The number of couples required to perform a country dance or square dance 1766.

2. A s. of smugglers, gipsies, and other desperadoes SCOTT. **3.** They will move in the first s. in Bath JANE AUSTEN.

II. A collection or number of things. **1.** A collection of instruments, tools, or machines customarily used together in a particular operation; a complete apparatus employed for some specific purpose 1561. **2.** †**a.** A number of musical instruments arranged to play together; a band; also *s. of music.* **b.** A suite *of* bells to be rung together. 1561. †**3.** A 'pair' of beads –1634. **4.** A collection of volumes by one author, dealing with one subject, belonging to one department of literature, or issued in a series 1596. **b.** A number of musical compositions forming a whole, as a church 'service' 1590. **c.** A complete series of the parts of a periodical publication 1701. **d.** A series of prints by the same engraver 1768. **e.** A definite number of copies of a bill of lading or of exchange 1818. **5.** A number of things connected in temporal or spatial succession or by natural production or formation 1604. **b.** The complement *of* teeth (natural or artificial) with which a person (or animal) is furnished 1654. **6.** A number of things grouped together according to a system of classification or conceived as forming a whole 1690. **7.** The complete collection of the 'pieces' composing a suite of furniture, a service of china, a clothing outfit, etc. 1687. **8.** A series of buildings or apartments associated in use; *esp.* a suite of apartments let as lodgings 1722. **b.** *Mining.* In full *s. of timber(s*: A frame for supporting the side of a level or shaft, or the roof of a gallery 1830. **9.** A team of (usu. six) horses 1687. **10.** The series of movements or figures that make up a square dance or country dance, *esp.* the quadrille; the music adapted to this 1834.

1. A Sett of Mathematical Instruments 1773. **b.** *Wireless.* A receiving apparatus. **5.** A new s. of words to the old tune of 'Over the Water to Charlie' SCOTT. **6.** The s. of notions which he had acquired from his education 1802. **7.** A s. of Irish diamonds and cairngorms THACKERAY. **8.** First we went into lodgings,—into three sets in three weeks THACKERAY.

Set (set), *v.* Pa. t. and pple. **set.** [OE. *settan* = OFris. *setta*, OS. *settian* (Du. *zetten*), OHG. *sezzan* (G. *setzen*), ON. *setja*, Goth. *satjan* :– Gmc. **satjan*, causative of **setjan* SIT.] **I.** To cause to sit, seat; to be seated, sit. **1.** *trans.* To place in a sitting posture; to cause to occupy a seat; to seat. **b.** To put (a hen) to sit on eggs 1440. **2.** *pass.* To be seated ME. **b.** To be seated to partake of a meal (*to meat, at* or *to dinner*, etc.). *Obs.* or *arch.* ME. **3.** *intr.* To sit, be seated. Now *dial.* or *vulgar.* ME. **b.** Of a hen: To sit *upon* eggs 1586. **c.** To have a certain 'set'; to sit (well or ill, tightly or loosely, etc.) 1804. **4.** *trans.* To become, befit, suit. Chiefly *Sc.* (in mod. use often ironical). 1480.

1. Setting us upon Camels 1735. Provb. *To s. a beggar on horseback*, to give an undeserving person an advantage he will misuse. **2.** Most of the party were set to cards THACKERAY. **3. c.** Sleeves lined with stiff or harsh linings never s. well 1887.

II. To sink, descend. Of the sun or other luminary: To go down; to make an apparent descent towards and below the horizon ME. **b.** Of the day: To come to its close. *poet.* 1604. **c.** *fig.* To decline, wane 1607.

The sun setting red SCOTT. **c.** The glory of Egypt seemed to have set 1892.

III. To put (more or less permanently) in a definite place. **1.** *trans.* To put (a shoot, young plant, tuber, or bulb) into the ground to grow; to plant (a tree, also by extension, a vineyard, a crop). Also, less usu., to plant (seed) by hand, as opp. to *sowing.* OE. **2.** †To deposit (a security); to put down as a stake; to stake, wager. *Obs.* or *arch.* OE. **b.** *absol.* or *intr.* To put down a stake, lay money *on* (or *at*). Also *fig.* to give a challenge *to.* *Obs.* or *arch.* 1553. **c.** *Dominoes.* To play first 1897. **3.** *trans.* To put (a thing) in a place allotted or adapted to receive it; (contextually) to fit, fix ME. †**b.** To fit or attach (one thing) to another –1595. **c.** To put (eggs) *under* a hen to be hatched 1726. **4.** *pass.* To have a certain position or arrangement by nature ME. **5.** *trans.* To put or place, cause to be, lie, rest, or stand, in a locality specified by an advb. expression OE. **b.** *pass.* To be situated, lie (in a certain locality); to be placed (at a certain height, interval, etc.) OE. **6.** *trans.* To place (a part of the body) upon a surface or an object OE. **7.** To put down in a record, catalogue, etc.; to mention or treat of in writing: now *s. down* ME. **8.** To put (one's signature), affix (a seal) *to* (†*on*) a document ME.

1. The seed is to be set by hand 1830. **2.** He is nettled, and sets me twenty: I win them too DRYDEN. **3.** While the Creator Great His constellations set MILT. **b.** *John* IV. ii. 174. **5.** S. him brest deepe in earth, and famish him SHAKS. Phr. *To s. before*, orig. = to place so as to be seen by; hence, to put before one for use, consideration, imitation, etc. **b.** Betwixt them and you will be a great gulf set 1650. **6.** *To s. (one's) hand to*, to lay hold of, take into one's hand; *fig.* to set about, engage upon. **7.** All his faults obseru'd, Set in a Note-Booke SHAKS. **8.** In witness whereof I have hereunto set my Hand and Seal 1736.

IV. To place or cause to be in a certain position (other than merely local), condition, relation, or connection. **1.** *trans.* To place in a state or sphere specified by an advb. expression. (Now less freq. than *place* or *put.*) ME. **2.** To cause to be or become (so-and-so) OE. †**3.** To place (a person) in some sphere of activity or occupation; esp. *to s. to school* –1697. **b.** orig. *to s. upon the muzzle*: To muzzle (a horse) so as to prevent him feeding improperly 1834. **4.** To place (a person or thing) in one's possession or control, or in a condition to be used, dealt with, or occupied ME. **5.** To cause (a thing) to assume a certain physical position expressed by a complementary adj. or advb. phr.; chiefly *to s. open, s. on end, s. upright* ME. **6.** To place (a person, his body, or limbs) in a certain posture. Also *refl.* late ME. **7.** *To s. fire to* (†*in*): to kindle, ignite. late ME. **8.** To stake the welfare or existence of (something) *upon*; also *pass.* to be dependent for its destiny *upon* 1594. **9.** To put (one thing) in the balance *against* another; to compare (one thing) *by* or *to* another 1589. **10.** To place (one's hope or trust) *in* (†*on*); to cause (one's thoughts or affections) to dwell *upon* or be centred *in* something. Phr. *to s. one's heart on.* OE. **11.** To rest (one's eye, one's look) *upon* ME. **12.** To put (a mark, impression) *upon*; to place as a distinguishing mark, token, or imprint. Now *rhet.* OE. **13.** To lay or spread (a surface of a certain kind) *on* an object; hence, to put (a favourable or specious appearance) *upon* a thing 1540. **14.** To put (an edge or point) *on, to* 1600. **15.** To fix (a certain price) *upon* a thing; now chiefly in *to s.* a *price upon one's head*, and the like 1530. **b.** *fig.* To put (a certain value) *upon*, have (a certain estimate) *of* 1611. †**16.** To lay (something burdensome) *upon*; to impose or inflict (a penalty, etc.) *upon* –1761.

1. Everything remains in the course and order wherein it was set at the Creation 1662. **2.** Phr. *To s. at ease, at rest, to rest, at peace; to s. at odds, at* *one, at variance, at war, by the ears; to s. agog, astray; to s. aglow, afire, on fire, aflame, in flame(s,* etc.; *to s. in array, in order, in readiness, to rights; to s. at large, at leisure, at liberty; to s. on edge; to s. in or on a roar; to s. in action, motion, operation; to s. at bay, at fault; to s. at contempt, at defiance;* etc. **4.** Phr. *To s. in hand*: †(*a*) to take in hand, undertake; also *intr.* with *with*, in the same sense; (*b*) to put out to be done. *To s. to* (*for, on*) *sale*: see SALE *sb.* **6.** Phr. *To s. on one's feet, legs*: see FOOT *sb.*, LEG *sb.* I. 1 c. **8.** To s. Vpon one Battell all our Liberties SHAKS. **9.** Against his professed theory may be s. his actual practice SPENCER. **10.** He had set his heart on seeing his son a clergyman 1870. **11.** The first time I s. eyes on captain Wilkins..I accost him 1765. **12.** In womens waxen hearts to s. their formes SHAKS. **13.** Phr. *To s. a good face upon*: cf. FACE *sb.* II. 3; Kick'd out, we set the best face on't we cou'd DRYDEN. **14.** This did but s. an edge to her wanton appetite 1620.

V. To appoint, institute (a person); to prescribe, ordain, establish (a thing). **1.** To post or station (a person) in a certain place *to* perform certain duties OE. **2.** To place in a position of superiority or control *over* another (e.g. as a ruler, protector, guard) OE. **3.** To appoint (a boundary, limit) OE. **4.** To ordain or establish (a regulation); to lay down (a law); to prescribe (a form or order). *Obs.* or *arch.* OE. **5.** To fix or appoint (a time) for the transaction of an affair, or as the term of a period. Also, to fix a time for. OE. **6.** To present (an example or pattern) for others to follow; to introduce (a fashion) ME. **b.** To put before a person (a specimen of work) to be followed; to mark out (the lines) on which he is to work or proceed 1593. **7.** To allot or enjoin (a task) ME. **b.** *Mining.* To appoint the amount of (work to be done) 1742. **c.** To propound (a question or set of questions) to be solved or answered; to prescribe (a book) for an examination or a course of study 1711. **8.** To let on lease, lease, let. Now *local.* late ME. †**9.** *trans.* To establish by agreement or authority (a settled condition, an alliance, etc.) –1652.

1. Loke that ye set good watche at euery gate 1533. **2.** Us his prime Creatures,..Set over all his Works MILT. **3.** Ambitious fellows, who set no bounds to their desires SMOLLETT. **5.** The club's opening day..is set for April 22. 1893. **6.** A fashion, as the phrase goes, has to be 'set' 1895. Phr. *To s. the pace*, to proceed at a rate of speed to be followed by another (freq. *fig.*); so *to s. the stroke* (in rowing). **b.** I could turn writing-master..and s. copies to children POPE. **7.** The Club were set 64 runs to win 1892.

VI. To put in position, arrange, fix, adjust. **1.** *trans.* To spread (a net) to catch animals, lay (a trap) OE. **2.** To put (a thing) in place; to fix up in the proper or required manner; in early use often = *s. up* i. late ME. **b.** = *s. going* 1500. **3.** To insert (a stitch). Phr. *to s. a stitch*, to sew. 1683. **4.** *Baking, Glass-making*, etc. To put into the oven or furnace 1483. **5.** To fix (a stone or gem) in a surface of metal as an ornament 1500. **b.** *transf.* and *fig.* To place (a thing) *in* a certain setting 1530. **c.** To fix (artificial teeth) on the plate 1844. **6.** To put (a sail) up in position to catch the wind. Also said of a ship carrying (so much canvas). ME. **b.** Phr. *To s. sail*: to start on a sea voyage 1513. **7.** To put (a movable part of an instrument or piece of mechanism) in a certain position. late ME. **8.** *Bell-ringing.* To ring (a bell) up till it stands still in an inverted position, either balanced or held by the stay and the slider. Also *intr.* of the bell. 1671. **9. a.** To put (liquid) in a vessel, at a certain temperature, strength, etc., ready to undergo a process; *spec.* in *Cheese-making* 1736. **b.** *Baking* and *Brewing.* To add barm or yeast to. *To s. the sponge*: to leaven a mass of flour. 1743. **10. a.** To make (a table) ready for a meal, spread (a table) *with* food, etc. **b.** To lay (a meal). late ME. **c.** To arrange the colours in the desired order on (a palette) 1847. **11.** *Printing.* To compose, set up (type); hence, to put (manuscript) into type 1530. **12.** To put (words) *to* music; to write (a musical composition) *for* certain voices or instruments 1502. **13.** *Theatr.* To make up (a scene) on the stage; to arrange (an item of the scenery) in a particular way. Also *to s. the stage.* 1779. **14.** To put an edge on (a cutting instrument, *esp.* a razor) 1461. **b.** fig. phr. *To be sharp* or *keen set*: to be hungry or keen 1540. **15.** To adjust (the teeth of a saw) by deflecting them alternately in opposite directions so as to produce a kerf of the required width. Also *to s. a saw.* 1678. **16.** To stretch (leather) 1884. **17.** To put (a broken or dislocated bone) in a position adapted to the restoration of the normal condition. Also *intr.* said of the bone. 1572. **18.** To adjust, settle (†the attire, the hair) ME. **19.** *Weaving.* To fix the texture of (a fabric) 1839. **20.** To give the requisite adjustment, alinement, or shape to (a mechanical contrivance, an instrument, etc.) 1879. **21.** To regulate, adjust *by* a standard; *esp.* to put (a clock, etc.) right. late ME. **22.** To fix the amount of (a fine or other payment), put down *at* a certain amount. *Obs.* or *arch.* late ME.

1. The snare was set..outside the field 1890. **5.** Vertue is like a rich stone, best plaine sett BACON. **d.** To fix (the hair) when damp so that it dries in waves 1926. **10. a.** She gan the hous to dighte, And tables for to sette CHAUCER. **18.** Combing his Peruke and setting his Cravat DRYDEN.

VII. To place mentally; to suppose, estimate. †**1.** *trans.* To posit, assume, suppose. Phr. *s. the case* = suppose, supposing. ME. **2.** To place mentally or conceptually in some category; †to regard as being (so-and-so); to consider (a thing) to reside *in* or to depend *on* another. late ME. **b.** To place (a person or thing) *before* or *after* another in estimation. Now *poet.* late ME. **3.** To fix the value of (a thing), to assess (a person), *at* so much. *Obs.* or *arch.* 1460. **b.** To estimate the amount of *at* so much 1863. **4.** To assess (a person) *at* so much. *Obs.* or *arch.* 1521. **5.** To have (a certain estimate) of a person or thing: in idiomatic phrases ME.

1. S. the case that there be two men who make a covenant BUNYAN. **2.** Tradition sets Wiklif's birth in the year 1324 ROGERS. **3.** *fig.* There shall no figure at that Rate be set, As that of true and faithful Juliet SHAKS. Phr. *To s. at naught* or *nought* (see NOUGHT *sb.* 2), *at little, at nothing; to s. at a pin's fee.* **b.** The yearly increase..is set at about 8*s.* per acre 1863. **5.** Phr. *To s. little, much, more*, etc. *by* (*Obs.* exc. *arch.* or *dial.*). *To s.* (*no, more*, etc.) *store by*; see STORE *sb.* *To s. a* (*great, little*) *price upon.*

VIII. To put or come into a settled or rigid position or state. **1.** *pass.* To be resolved or determined; to have a settled purpose. Now *dial.* ME. **2.** To have one's mind or will fixed *upon* something. late ME. **3.** *trans.* *To s. one's* or *the face* (*countenance*): to give a fixed or settled expression to the countenance 1560. **b.** *pass.* and *intr.* (and *refl.*). Of the eyes, the features, the countenance: To have or assume a fixed look or expression 1601. **4.** *trans.* To press (the teeth, lips) together into a rigid position; to clench (the teeth), compress (the lips, mouth). Also *refl.* and *intr.* 1602. **b.** *pass.* and *intr.* Of muscles, or the like: To have or assume a rigid attitude or state 1851. **c.** *intr.* To become bent or twisted as a result of strain 1798. **5.** *Dyeing.* (*trans.*) To make (a colour) fast or permanent 1601. **6.** To cause to become firm, hard, or rigid in consistency; to curdle, coagulate (milk, etc.). Also *intr.* 1736. **b.** Of cream: To collect and settle on the top of the milk 1859. **7.** To cause (fruit) to form on a tree by the process of fertilization; to cause (a flower) to develop into fruit: said of bees, etc. and (also *absol.*) of the tree bearing the fruit 1693. **b.** *intr.* Of blossom or fruit: To develop as the result of fertilization. Also said of hemp fibre. 1718. **8.** *Plastering.* To put a finishing coat on 1693. **9. a.** *Sheep-breeding.* To settle or establish (a particular stock) 1782. **b.** *intr.* Of a period of time or weather: To become settled 1800. **c.** *Cricket.* (*pass.*) To have become accustomed to the bowling 1865. **10.** *trans.* To check; to puzzle, nonplus, 'stump'; to tax the resources of. Now *n. dial.* 1586. **11.** *Dancing.* (*intr.*) To take up a position and perform a number of steps with one's face *to* one's partner or *to* the dancer on one's right or left. Chiefly in *s. to partners, to corners.* 1652.

2. When I perceiv'd all set on enmity MILT. **3.** *To s. one's face as a flint*, after Isa. 50:7. **b.** His face set and sulky 1898. **4.** The old woman set her lips firmly, and drew her dagger KINGSLEY. Phr. *To s. one's teeth*; see TOOTH. **10.** Learning was pos'd, Philosophie was set G. HERBERT.

IX. To put in the way of following a certain course, cause to take a particular direction. **1.** *intr.* To proceed in a specified direction; to begin to move, start off, put out, set out. Now only in *s. forth, forward, off, on*, etc. OE. **2.** Of a current, wind: To take or have a (certain) direction or course. late ME. **3.** *trans.* To cause to pass into a certain place or from one place to another; to convey, transport. Now *rare.* late ME. **b.** To accompany or escort (a person) for part or all of the way he has to go. Chiefly *n. dial.* 1737. **4.** Of a current, wind, etc.: To cause to move, carry along in a (certain) direction 1450. **5.** To propel (a boat or other craft) with a pole; to punt. Also *absol.*, to use a punt pole or setting pole; now *esp.* in punt-shooting, to move up *to* the fowl, to get within shooting distance 1566. **6.** To direct or point (one's face, foot, etc.) *to, towards, for* a place 1611. **b.** To put (a person) *on the way* leading to a destination 1678. **7.** To put (a person) *to* a piece of work or a task. Also const. inf. ME. **8.** To direct (one's mind, intention, or will) *to* the consideration or performance of something ME. **b.** *refl.* To apply oneself *to* a piece of work, a task, or employment. Now always const. inf. Also *intr.* in the same sense. ME. **9.** trans. *To s.* (a person) *upon*: to cause to be occupied with (something); often with implication of urging or impelling. Also const. gerund (esp. *to set (a-)going*). late ME. **10.** To cause to be busy *about*. Also *refl.* and *pass.* 1622. **11.** To incite (a dog or other animal, also a person) to make an attack or pursuit: chiefly with preps. *at, on* 1440. **b.** To encourage (an animal) to perform some evolution or feat; to pit (fighting cocks) 1586. **12.** To place in a position of hostility or opposition; to cause to be hostile or antagonistic; to pit (one) *against* (another). Also *refl.* and *pass.* ME. **b.** *intr.* To make an attack ME.

1. The King is set from London SHAKS. **2.** The prevalent winds s. from the west 1890. *fig.* The public opinion..is setting against the practice 1885. **3.** After being set across [the ferry].., we drove back to Melrose HAWTHORNE. **6.** I, with my wife, &c. set our faces towards home EVELYN. **b.** Your host comes out with you to set you upon your way 1883. **7.** We set the children to their regular lessons 1836. Provb. *S. a thief to catch a thief.* *transf.* By setting one evil thing to counteract another 1841. **8.** All my mind was set Serious to learnan d know MILT. **b.** She set herself to study it 1880. **9.** Phr. *To set afoot* or *on foot*, to originate or start; to set going. This rude shock..set Usher upon a more careful examination 1879. **11.** They set dogs on us as though we were rats 1889. **b.** She would s. her horse at anything 1890. **12.** Will you s. your wit to a Fooles? SHAKS. Phr. *To s.* (a person) *against*, to cause him to have an antipathy for. *To s. one's face against*, to take up an attitude of determined hostility towards.

X. Senses which appear to have arisen by reversal of construction or by an ellipsis. †**1.** *trans.* To beset (a place) for the purpose of intercepting or capturing a person –1593. **2.** To plant (ground) *with* 'sets' or (young) trees. *To be s. with* = to have growing upon it. ME. **3.** To ornament (metal or other surface) by inlaying or encrusting it with stones or gems. late ME. **b.** To surround (a large stone) *with* a mount of small stones; to mount (an object) *in* a particular metal 1506. **4.** *pass.* To be studded, dotted, lined, etc. *with* a number of objects. *To be set about* (arch.) or *round with*, to be surrounded or encircled with, to have a circle of. late ME. **5.** *trans.* †**a.** To beset or besiege (a place or a person) –1530. **b.** *fig.* esp. in *to be hard set*, to be in great straits or hard put to it. late ME. **6.** Of a hunting dog: To mark the position of (game) by stopping dead and pointing the muzzle towards it. Also *intr.* 1621. **7.** *Naut.* To take the bearings of (an object) 1626. **8.** To mark down as prey, fix on as a victim; to watch for the purpose of apprehending or robbing. *slang.* 1670.

3. A superb watch, set with brilliants 1795. 4. How thick the City was set with Churches ADDISON. 5. b. They were ill set to liue 1673. 7. We set the Tower of Arabia near the port of Alexandria 1769.

Comb. 1. With preps. in specialized senses (intr.). **S. about—.** a. To begin working at, take in hand, begin upon. b. To set upon, attack (*colloq.*). **S. against—.** †a. To make an attack upon, be hostile to. b. To move in a direction opposed to. **S. at—.** To assail, attack. **S. on—.** = *s. upon.* **S. upon—.** a. To attack, assail, fall violently upon. b. To urge strongly (*rare*). †c. = *s. about* a.

2. With advs. in specialized senses (trans. or intr.). **S. about.** To circulate (a statement, report). Chiefly *n. dial.* **S. abroach.** *arch.* a. To broach (a cask, liquor). b. To set on foot, give publicity to. **S. afloat.** *arch.* a. To launch, float. b. To bring to the surface (as the dregs of a liquid); hence *fig.* to set (*esp.* something bad) in motion, set agog, stir up, make active. **S. apart.** To separate for a special purpose; to devote to some use. **S. aside.** a. To put on one side. †b. To discontinue the performance or practice of. c. To dismiss from one's mind, abandon the consideration of. d. To reject or throw over as being of no value, cogency, or pertinence; to over-rule. e. To discard or reject from use or service, in favour of another. f. To annul, quash, render void or nugatory. Chiefly *Law.* g. To separate out for a particular purpose. **S. back.** a. To hinder the progress of, give a check to. b. To put (a clock, its hands) to an earlier time. c. *intr.* To flow in the reverse direction. **S. by.** To lay up or lay by for future use. **S. down.** a. See simple trans. senses and DOWN *adv.* b. To place so as to rest upon a surface; to put down, as upon the ground. Also *absol.* (*b*) To cause or allow to alight from a vehicle; to 'drop' (a person at a place). Also *absol.* c. To put down in writing or in print; to put on paper; to enter in a catalogue or account; to write out, compose; to put on record; to relate. (*b*) To put down, as in a schedule or table, *to be* performed at a certain time; †to appoint a time for the performance of (something). d. To estimate, reckon; now only, to regard (a person) *as*, take (him) *for*, consider (him) *to be* (so-and-so). e. *refl.* To begin to devote oneself *to*. †f. *intr.* To be encamped; to 'sit down' *before* (a town) to besiege it. **S. forth.** a. To promulgate, publish, issue (a regulation, proclamation, etc.). b. To publish (a literary work). c. To express in words, give an account of, present a statement of, *esp.* in order, distinctly, or in detail; to declare, expand, relate, narrate, state, describe. d. To adorn, decorate. Now *rare.* e. *intr.* To set out *on* a journey, *against* an enemy, *in* pursuit, etc. **S. forward** (**†forwards**). a. To carry, send, or thrust forward. *To s. one's* (*best*) *foot forward*: see FOOT *sb.* b. To assist (a person) in the way of progress; to help on (a matter, plan, etc.); to advance, promote. c. To put forward, promulgate; to advance (an opinion). d. *intr.* To go forward, set out, start. **S. in** a. See simple trans. senses and IN *adv.* b. *intr.* To set to work, begin (upon something); *esp.* followed by *to*, *for*. *Obs.* exc. *dial.* c. To begin, become prevalent: chiefly of the weather entering upon a particular state. d. Of a current or wind: To flow or blow towards the shore. **S. off.** a. See simple trans. senses and OFF *adv.* b. To start off, give (a person or thing) a start; to send off *into* a fit of laughter, etc. c. To apportion or assign to a particular purpose; to portion off. d. To mark or measure off (a certain distance) on a surface; to lay off (the lines of a ship). e. To set in relief, make prominent or conspicuous by contrast. f. To show to advantage, enhance, embellish. g. To give a flattering description of, commend, praise. h. To take into account by way of compensation or equivalent; to put in the balance (*against* something); *spec.* in *Law*, to allow or recognize as a counter-claim. Also *absol.* i. *intr.* To start on a journey or course; *transf.* to start (doing something). j. *Printing.* To soil the next leaf or sheet; said of the ink or of the printed page. **S. on.** a. See simple senses and ON *adv.* †b. To set on foot, instigate, promote. c. (*a*) To urge (an animal, *esp.* a dog) to attack. (*b*) To instigate, urge on (a person) *to do* something. d. To set in motion, set going. e. To start (a person) doing something. f. To set or appoint (a person) to do something. g. *intr.* To advance, go forward. h. To make an attack. Now *dial.* in *s. on at* or *to*. **S. out.** a. See simple senses and OUT *adv.* †b. To fit out (a ship, fleet) for a voyage; to equip for an expedition; to send out (forces), fit out (an expedition). †c. To issue, promulgate. d. To display (wares) for sale. †e. To extol, 'crack up'. †f. To embellish, adorn, deck out, trick out. g. To put down on paper in express or detailed form; to describe or enumerate expressly; to detail. h. To delimit, define, mark out. i. (*a*) To arrange (a table, a room, etc.) for a meal or other purpose; to spread (a table, etc.) *with* ornaments, etc.; to dress (a window). (*b*) To put out or arrange (things necessary for a meal, game, etc.), *esp.* on a table; to lay (a meal). (*c*) To arrange (objects) at proper intervals or with a due amount of display; *spec.* to plant out; to leave (plants) at a distance apart, by thinning. j. *intr.* To begin or start on a journey; to start on one's way. (*b*) const. *inf.* To begin one's career or start off with the object of doing something; to lay oneself out (*to do*). k. To start on a certain course; to begin or start *off* (*with* or *by doing* something). **S. over.** †a. To convey to the other side of (a piece of water). Also *absol.* or *intr.* b. To make over, transfer. **S. to.** †a. To affix (one's seal or signature). b. *intr.* To make a beginning; *esp.* to begin seriously or energetically. (*b*) *Pugilism.* To begin fighting (*with*). **S. up.** a. To place in a high or lofty position; to raise to an elevated situation. †b. To hoist (sail, a flag). c. To raise (a cry); to utter (vocal sound). †d. To put up for sale or auction. e. To post up (a paper or notice); to give notice of, advertise. f. *Naut.* To take in the 'slack' of (shrouds, stays), make taut. g. To place in an exalted, eminent, or superior position; to raise to power or authority; sometimes *spec.* to put on the throne. Also *absol.* (*b*) To appoint (an officer or functionary). (*c*) To appoint to or nominate for a position. h. To make (a person) elated, proud, or vain; *esp.* in *pass.* to be elated; to be 'stuck-up'. i. To place in an erect position; to set or stand upright; to erect (an image, statue); to raise (a standard). (*b*) *To s. up one's bristles*: to be irate. *To s. one's back up*: see BACK *sb.*[1] j. To erect and make ready for use; to pitch (a tent); †to erect (a building). k. To put together the parts of (a machine) and erect it in position. (*b*) To start (a piece of work) on a loom, etc. l. *Typogr.* To put (types) into the composing-stick; to arrange (type) in words or blocks of words; to put (a book, etc.) into type. Also *absol.* m. To place (the dead body of an animal stuffed or otherwise treated for preservation) in an erect or lifelike position. n. *To be well* (*straight*) *set up*: to have a stalwart, well-knit frame. o. To make erect and soldierly by drill. p. To put into operation; to bring into use or vogue; to establish a course or series of. Now *rare.* (*b*) To cause (a certain condition, *esp.* of disease) to arise. Often *pass.* q. To establish (a state of things, a custom, a form of government, a society, etc.). r. To set on foot, establish (a business, profession); to begin (housekeeping, life). (*b*) To begin the use or practice of; to adopt as part of one's establishment, etc. s. To provide (a person) with means; to place in a position of prosperity or in the way of retrieving one's fortune; to set 'on one's legs' *again*. t. To establish or start (a person) in a business or profession; *transf.* said of the money, stock, or outfit sufficient to equip a person. u. To bring to a proper state of health and strength; to restore to health. v. To put into an attitude of hostility or opposition; to incite, instigate. w. To put forward (a claim, defence, a case in law). x. To advance, propose, put forward (a theory, idea, plan). y. (orig. *absol.* of r.) To start in business, begin the exercise of a trade or profession. z. **To s. up for.** (*a*) *To s. up for oneself*, to start on a career on one's own account. (*b*) To lay claim to being (so-and-so). (*c*) To lay claim to (a quality, virtue, etc.). aa. (*absol.* of w.) To lay claim or pretend *to be*. †bb. To put up *at* an inn or other lodging. cc. To punt, esp. so as to get close *to* water-fowl to shoot them. dd. Of a soft-nosed bullet: To expand on impact.

Set (set), *ppl. a.* OE. [pa. pple. of SET *v.*] 1. In various strictly ppl. uses, with ref. to the corresponding senses of the vb.; *esp.* a. Of a task, a subject of discourse or study: Imposed or prescribed. Now *rare* exc. in *s. book.* ME. b. Of the teeth: Clenched 1810. c. Of types: That have been 'set up' 1837. 2. Appointed or prescribed beforehand. Hence, Fixed, definite, not subject to uncertainty or alteration. OE. 3. Deliberate, intentional 1456. 4. (In *s. battle, field*) = PITCHED *ppl. a.* 2. Now *rare.* late ME. 5. Formal, ceremonious, regular 1513. 6. That has assumed a permanent form or condition; immovable, persistent 1605. 7. With prefixed adv.: Having a specified position, arrangement, build, adjustment, disposition, etc. ME.

1. When you are to talk on a S. Subject 1709. 2. Which a sett rent can no wise affoord 1587. The Indians have no s. time of eating 1769. No s. form of liturgy 1883. 3. *Of s. purpose. In good s. terms* (after Shaks.), 'roundly', with outspoken severity. 5. *S. speech*, public speech more or less elaborate; an oration, as dist. from extemporaneous or informal utterances. 6. Those even, s. tones, so common among readers 1760. He is very s. in his ways 1848. *S. fair*, (of weather) usu. marked on English barometers at the point indicating that the height of the mercury is 30½ inches.

Comb.: **s. changes** *Bellringing*, = *s. peal*; **s. dance**, a quadrille, country-dance, or the like; **s. iron** *Shipbuilding*, a bar of soft iron, admitting of being bent so as to be used for transferring curves from the scrive-board to the bending plate; **s. line**, a fishing-line with baited hooks, pegged or anchored; **s. net**, a fishing net fastened across a stream or channel, into which the fish are driven; †**s. peal** *Bellringing*, a ringing of a peal of bells in one position for a considerable length of time before a change is given; **s. piece**, (*a*) a painting or a sculptured group of figures; (*b*) a picture or design composed of fireworks; **s. scene**, an apparatus built up and placed in position upon a theatrical stage before the rise of the curtain; a collection of side scenes, 'skies', etc. depending upon one another for a particular effect; so *s. scenery*; **s. square**, (*a*) a plate of wood, metal, etc. in the form of a right-angled triangle, the acute angles being either 60° and 30° or both 45°, used by draughtsmen as a guide for drawing lines at one of these angles; (*b*) a form of T-square with an additional arm turning on a pivot, for drawing lines at fixed angles to the head; (*c*) a joiner's square.

Set-, the stem of SET *v.* in comb., chiefly in sbs. derived from phrases with advs.

s.-in, the beginning of a period of time, a spell of weather, or the like; **-up**, (*a*) an object set up or upright; (*b*) the manner or position in which a thing is set up; *U.S.*, personal bearing or carriage; also *fig.*

‖**Seta** (sī·tă). *Pl.* **setæ** (sī·tī). 1793. [L. *seta, sæta* bristle.] 1. *Bot.* A stiff hair or bristle-like body. Also, the stalk which supports the theca or capsule of mosses. 2. *Zool.* A bristle; a bristle-like appendage 1820.

Setaceous (sĭtēi·ʃəs), *a.* 1664. [f. mod.L. *setaceus*, f. L. *seta* bristle; see -ACEOUS.] 1. Having the form or character of a bristle. Chiefly in scientific use, of the nature of a seta or setæ. 2. Bristly 1787. Hence **-ly** *adv.*

Se·t-back. 1674. [f. vbl. phr. *set back*.] 1. *fig.* A check to progress, a retardation or retrograde movement, a relapse, reverse. 2. *Arch.* A plain, flat set-off in a wall 1864. 3. A setting back or backward 1900. 4. *U.S.* = BACK-SET *sb.* 2. 1888.

Set-down. (Stress variable.) 1761. [f. vbl. phr. *set down.*] 1. a. A single drive (ending where the passenger first alights) in a vehicle plying for hire; the distance covered by such a drive. b. A 'lift' 1792. 2. An unexpected and humiliating rebuff. Also, a severe scolding. 1786.

Seti-, used as comb. form of L. *seta* SETA, as in: **Seti·ferous,** *a.* having setæ or bristles. **Se·tiform,** *a.* having the form of a seta or bristle; bristle-shaped. **Setiger** (sī·tidʒəɹ), a setigerous worm. **Seti·gerous** *a.* furnished with or having setæ. **Seti·parous** *a.* producing setæ.

Setness (se·tnės). 1642. [f. SET *ppl. a.* + -NESS.] The quality, state, or character of being set; also, an instance of this.

Se·t-off. *Pl.* **set-offs.** 1621. [f. vbl. phr. *set off.*] 1. Something used to set off or adorn; an adornment, decoration, or ornament. 2. The act of setting off on a journey, etc.; a start 1759. 3. *Comm.* and *Law.* An act of 'setting off' one item of an account against another; an item or amount which is or should be set off against another in the settlement of accounts; a counter-claim, or a counterbalancing debt, pleaded by the defendant in an action to recover money due; also, this mode of defence 1766. b. More widely: A taking into account of something as a counterbalance to, or a partial compensation for, something else; a counterbalancing or compensating circumstance or consideration 1773. 4. a. *Arch.* (Also *sett-off.*) = OFFSET *sb.* 6. 1717. b. A similar reduction in a metal bar, etc. 1830. 5. *Printing*, etc. The transference of ink from one page to another 1842. b. An impression transferred 1839.

3. b. Something is required from you as a set off against the sin of your retirement 1799.

Seton (sī·tən), *sb.* late ME. [– med.L. *setō(n-*, app. f. L. *seta* bristle, in med.L. also silk. Cf. (O)Fr. *séton.*] *Surg.* 1. A thread, piece of tape, etc. drawn through a fold of skin so as to maintain an issue or opening for discharges, or drawn through a sinus or cavity to keep this from healing up. 2. The issue so formed 1597.

1. *S.-needle*, a needle used for passing a s. through the skin.

Setose (sī·tōᵘs), *a.* 1661. [– L. *setosus*, f. *seta* bristle; see -OSE¹.] **1.** *Anat.* and *Zool.* Set or covered with bristles or stiff hairs, bristly. Also, of a bristly nature. **2.** *Bot.* Having setæ or bristles 1760.

Set-out. (Stress variable.) Chiefly *colloq.* and *dial. Pl.* **set-outs.** 1806. [f. vbl. phr. *set out.*] **1.** A display, e.g. of plate, china, food, etc.; a 'turn-out', i.e. a carriage with its horses, etc.; a person's 'get-up'; a show or public performance. **2.** A beginning or start 1821. **3.** Outfit, equipment 1831.

Sett: see SET *sb.*¹ and ².

Settee¹ (setī·). Now *Hist.* 1587. [– It. *saettia*, held to be f. *saetta* arrow :– L. *sagitta.*] A decked vessel, with a long sharp prow, carrying two or three masts with a kind of lateen sails, in use in the Mediterranean.

Settee² (setī·). 1716. [perh. a fanciful variation of SETTLE *sb*; see -EE².] A seat (for indoors) holding two or more persons, with a back and (usu.) arms.

Setter (se·təɹ). late ME. [f. SET *v.* + -ER¹.] **I.** One who or something which sets. **1.** *gen.* One who sets something specified or contextually implied. Often as the second element of a compound, as in BONE-SETTER, TYPE-SETTER, etc. **b.** With advb. extension or complement, as *s.-forth*, †*-on*, *-up*, etc. 1548. **2.** A workman employed to 'set' something, e.g. jewels, saws, razors, etc. late ME. **3.** In *Dice-play.* The player who stakes on the throw of the 'caster' 1726. **4.** In quarrying and mining work: The foreman by whom the contracts are made with the workmen 1884. **5. a.** A confederate of sharpers or swindlers, employed as a decoy 1592. **b.** A police spy or informer 1630. **6.** A dog trained to 'set' game; *esp.* as the name of a special breed 1576.

5. **a.** O 'tis our S., I know his voyce: Bardolfe, what newes? SHAKS. **6.** Of the breed now so called, there are three varieties, the *English*, the *Irish*, and the *Gordon setters*. The name was formerly applied to a kind of spaniel. O.E.D.

II. An instrument or tool used in setting; *esp.* in *Gunnery*, a wooden instrument used, with the aid of a mallet, to set the fuse into a shell 1526.

Setterwort (se·təɹwɔ̄ɹt). 1551. [– MLG. *siterwort*; the first element is of unkn. origin. See WORT.¹] The plant Bear's-foot or Fetid Hellebore, *Helleborus fœtidus*; also, the Green Hellebore, *H. viridis*.

Setting (se·tiŋ), *vbl. sb.* late ME. [f. SET *v.* + -ING¹.] **I. 1.** The action of SET *v.* in various trans. senses. Also, the fact of being set. **b.** *Sport.* (*a*) The action of a dog in indicating game 1621. (*b*) The sport of 'putting up' game with a setter 1661. **2.** The manner or position in which anything is set, fixed, or placed. late ME. **3.** The manner in which a jewel is 'set' or mounted; *concr.* the frame or bed (of precious metal or the like) in which a jewel is set 1815. **b.** *transf.* and *fig.* A person's or thing's environment; literary or historical background, or the like 1841. **4.** The manner in which a poem or form of words is set to music; a piece of music composed for a particular poem, etc. 1879. **5.** *Plastering.* The finishing coat of plaster, the *s. coat* 1823.

3. **b.** The s. of the piece is charming 1885.

II. Senses related to intr. uses of SET *v.* **1.** The sinking of a heavenly body towards and below the horizon; the quarter or direction in which a heavenly body sets. Also, the fall of night or darkness. late ME. **2.** The process or fact of becoming set, hard, or stiff; coagulation 1791. **3.** The flowing of a current in a particular direction; the direction of flow 1595.

1. *fig.* The Soul that rises with us, our life's Star, Hath had elsewhere its s. WORDSW. **3.** *fig.* The powerful s. of the current of human motive and inclination 1875.

Comb.: **s. coat,** a finishing coat of fine plastering, **-pole,** a pole, esp. one used by wild-fowlers for propelling a boat or punt on mud-banks, securing wounded birds, etc.; **-rule,** a composing-rule.

†**Setting dog.** 1611. = SETTER I. 6. –1835.

Settle (se·t'l), *sb.* [OE. *setl*, corresp. to MLG., MDu. *setel*, OHG. *sezzal* (G. *sessel*), Goth. *sitls* :– Gmc. **setlaz*, **setlam*, rel. to L. *sella*; see SADDLE.] †**1.** Something to sit upon; a chair, bench, stool, etc. –1483. **2.** *spec.* A long wooden bench, usu. with arms and a high back, and having a locker or box under the seat 1553. **3.** A ledge, raised platform 1611.

Settle (se·t'l), *v.* [OE. *setlan* (once) place, implied also in *setlung* sitting down, setting of the sun, f. *setl* SETTLE *sb.*] **I.** To seat, place. †**1.** *trans.* To seat; to put in a seat or place of rest; also, to cause to sit down –1692. **2.** To place (material things) in order, or in a convenient or desired position; to adjust (e.g. one's clothing) 1515. **3.** To place (a person) in an attitude of repose, so as to be undisturbed for a time. Chiefly *refl.* 1515. **b.** *pass.* To be installed in a residence, to have completed one's arrangements for residing 1643. **4.** To cause to take up one's residence in a place; *esp.* to establish (a body of persons) as residents in a town or country; to plant (a colony) 1573. **b.** To fix or establish permanently (one's abode, residence, etc.) 1562. **c.** To assign to (a person) a legal domicile in a particular parish. Chiefly *pass.* 1572. **d.** To furnish (a place) with inhabitants or settlers 1702. †**5.** To fix (something) *in* (a person's heart, mind, etc.) –1690. †**6.** To set firmly on a foundation; to fix (a foundation) securely –1666.

2. He adjusted the cock of his hat a-new, settled his sword-knot STEELE. **3.** The man.. settled her comfortably in the stern-sheets 1893. **b.** We were soon settled in barracks 1837. **4.** Maryland..was first settled by Roman Catholics 1830. **6.** Before the mountaines were setled.. was I begotten BIBLE (Geneva) *Prov.* 8:25.

II. To come to rest after flight or wandering. **1.** *intr.* Of a bird, flying insect: To take up a position of rest *from* flight; to alight *on* something ME. **b.** Of things, esp. flying or floating objects, also *transf.* and *fig.* of darkness, silence, etc.: To come down and remain. late ME. **2.** To come together from dispersion or wandering; esp. *Hunting*, (of hounds) to keep steadily to the scent. late ME. **3.** Of things: To lodge, come to rest, in a definite place after wandering 1622. **b.** Of pain or disease: To establish itself *in* or *on* a definite part of the body 1594. **c.** Of the wind: To become 'set' *in* (*at*, *into*) a specified quarter 1626. **d.** Of affections, etc.: To come after wandering *to*, become fixed *on*, an object 1628. **4.** Of persons: To cease from migration and adopt a fixed abode; to establish a permanent residence, become domiciled. Also with *down*, *in*. 1627. **b.** Of a people: To take up its abode in a foreign country. Also, to establish a colony. 1682. **5.** = *to s. oneself* (sense I. 3). *To s. in*: (*a*) to dispose oneself for remaining indoors; (*b*) now, to establish oneself in new quarters. 1818.

1. The common blue fly which settles on meat 1875. **b.** A deep gloom settled on his spirits 1779. **3. b.** A cough settled on her chest 1856. **4.** My Father being a Foreigner of Bremen, who settled first at Hull DE FOE. **5.** Like a clamour of the rooks..ere they s. for the night TENNYSON.

III. To descend, sink down; to lower. [From sense II. 1.] **1.** To sink down gradually by or as by its own weight. Of the ground: To subside. Of a structure: To sink downwards from its proper level. ME. **2.** *Naut.* **a.** Of a ship: To sink gradually; also with *down* 1819. **b.** *trans.* To diminish the height of, to reduce to a lower level (a deck, topsail) 1625. **3.** *intr.* Of soil, loosely compacted materials: To subside into a solid mass. Of new masonry or brickwork: To become consolidated by its own weight and drying of the mortar. 1560. **b.** *trans.* To cause to subside into a solid mass; to consolidate. Also with *down*, *home.* 1611.

1. The..Pier..was observed to s. 1751. **2. a.** The ship was evidently settling now Fast by the head BYRON. **3.** Roads s. in spring after frost and rain 1828. **b.** Then give the whole a good watering to s. the soil 1845.

IV. To come or bring to rest after agitation. **1.** *intr.* Of a liquid: To become still after agitation or fermentation, so that the suspended particles or impurities are separated as scum or sediment. late ME. **b.** *trans.* To cause (liquor) to deposit dregs or work off impurities; to clarify 1599. **2.** *intr.* Of suspended particles or impurities in a liquid: To come to rest after agitation or disturbance; now chiefly, to sink to the bottom as sediment. Also *to s. out.* late ME. **3.** To subside, calm down; to become composed 1578. **4.** *trans.* To quiet, tranquillize, compose (a person, his mind, nerves, etc.); to allay (passion) 1530. **b.** *To s. the stomach*: to check vomiting or nausea 1662. **5.** To quiet with a blow; to knock down dead or stunned; to 'do for' 1611. **6.** *intr.* To come to an end of a series of changes or fluctuations and assume a definite form or condition. Also *to s. down* (*to*). 1684. **b.** Of the weather: To become steadily fine. Also, *to s.* (*in*) *for*: to come gradually to a steady condition of (rain, frost, etc.). 1719.

3. Then till the fury of his Highnesse s. Come not before him SHAKS. Maurice Blake was too excited..to s. at once to sleep 1896. **4.** Hoping that sleep might s. his brains, with all haste they got him to bed BUNYAN. **5.** There's nothing will s. me but a Bullet SWIFT. Phr. *To s.* (a person's) *hash*: see HASH *sb.* 2. **6.** This smile should not s. into a simper 1859.

V. To render or become stable or permanent; to fix or become fixed in a certain condition. **1.** *trans.* To ensure the stability or permanence of (a condition of things, a quality, power, etc.). late ME. **2.** To fix, make steadfast or constant (a wavering, irresolute or doubting person, heart, mind, etc.). late ME. **3.** *refl.* To fix one's attention *upon* an object; to make up one's mind *to do* something; to set oneself steadily *to* some employment. Now usu., to compose oneself after excitement or restlessness and apply oneself quietly to work. (Often with *down.*) Also *intr.* in the same senses. 1530. **4.** *trans.* To secure or confirm (a person) *in* a position of authority, an office; to establish *in* an office, an employment 1548. **b.** (Chiefly *Sc.* and *U.S.*) To appoint (a minister) to the charge of a parish; also, to appoint a minister to (a parish) 1719. **5.** To establish (a person) in the matrimonial state. Now chiefly *refl.* and *pass.* 1566. **b.** *intr.* 'To establish a domestic state' (J.) 1718. **6.** *trans.* To secure (payment, property, title) *to*, *on*, or *upon* (a person) by decree, ordinance, or enactment 1625. **b.** Of a private individual: To secure (property, succession) *to*, *on*, or *upon* (a person) by means of a deed of settlement 1661. **7.** To subject to permanent regulations, to set permanently in order, place on a permanent footing (institutions, government); to bring (a language) into a permanent form 1597. **b.** *To s. one's estate, one's affairs*: to arrange for the disposal of one's property, the payment of one's debts, etc., esp. with a view to one's death, retirement from business, etc. 1652.

1. 'Tis hard to s. order once again TENNYSON. **3.** When I s. myself down to my pursuits 1833. She went down into the drawing-room, and could not s. to anything 1865. **5.** Phr. *To s. in the world* or *in life.* **b.** Why don't you marry, and s.? SWIFT. **6.** The statute settling the present title to the Crown 1863. **b.** I..have settled upon him a good Annuity for Life ADDISON. **7.** To s. the Government on a Parliamentary basis 1874. Tyndale, Coverdale, and Cranmer had done so much to s. our language 1886. **b.** I..made my Will, settled my estate, and took leave of my friends STEELE.

VI. To fix (what is uncertain), to decide (a question). **1.** To appoint or fix definitely beforehand, to decide upon (a time, place, plan of action, price, conditions, etc.) 1596. **b.** To fix by mutual agreement 1620. **c.** *intr.* To come to a decision; to decide *to do* something; to decide *upon* (a plan of action, an object of choice) 1782. **2.** *trans.* To decide (a question, a matter of doubt or discussion); to bring to an end (a dispute) 1651. **b.** *Law.* To decide (a case) by arrangement between the contesting parties. More fully, *to s. out of court.* 1900. **c.** To put beyond dispute (a principle, fact) by authority or argument 1733. **3.** *intr.* To come to terms or agreement *with* a person 1527. **b.** To make an arrangement to compound *with* a creditor 1838. **4.** *trans.* To close (an account) by a money payment; to pay (an account, bill, score) 1687. **b.** *absol.* or *intr.* To settle accounts by payment. Chiefly const. *with.* 1788.

1. Then it's as good as settled 1891. **b.** We have at last settled that Business 1687. **c.** But settling upon new clothes is so trying HARDY. **2.** In settling the value of a copyhold fine 1883. The dispute at Llandulas quarries has been settled 1886. **4. b.** The 'settling' days occur twice in each month, when the transactions of the preceding fortnight are settled for in cash 1873.

Settled (se·t'ld), *ppl. a.* 1556. [f. prec. + -ED[1].] In various senses of the vb.; firmly fixed, established, determined, etc.; **b.** *spec.* (Of weather of a specified kind.) Established and maintaining itself without change 1628; (of weather without specification) calm and fine 1717. Hence †**Se·ttledly** *adv.*, **-ness.**

Settlement (se·t'lmĕnt). 1626. [f. SETTLE *v.* + -MENT.] **I. 1.** The act of fixing (a person or thing) in a secure or steady position; the state of being so fixed. **b.** Establishment in life, in marriage, in an office or employment, in a permanent abode, (in Presbyterian churches) in a pastoral charge 1651. **c.** Legal residence or establishment in a particular parish, entitling a person to relief from the poor rates; the right to relief acquired by such residence 1662. **2.** The act of settling as colonists or new-comers; the act of peopling or colonizing a new country, or of planting a colony 1675.

1. b. Every Man. .Applies himself. .toward the Attaining of his End; whether it be Honour, Wealth, Power, or any other sort of Advantage, or S. in the World 1692.

II. 1. The act or process of regulating or putting on a permanent footing; the act of establishing (public affairs, etc.) in security or tranquillity; a settled arrangement, an established order of things 1645. **b.** Decision of a question, dispute, etc.; the establishing of an opinion, the text of a document, etc. 1777. **2.** *Law.* The act of settling property upon a person or persons; the particular terms of such an arrangement; the deed or instrument by which it is effected. Often *spec.* = *marriage s.* 1677. **b.** *U.S.* A sum of money or other property granted to a minister on his ordination, in addition to his salary 1828. **3.** The settling or payment of an account; the act of coming to terms (*with* a person) 1729. **b.** *spec.* The fortnightly (or, for government securities, monthly) settling of accounts on the Stock Exchange 1772. **4.** In India: The process of assessing the government land-tax over a specific area 1789.

1. The s. that should be made after the war 1900. **2.** Your wife. .may. .claim a s. out of it for herself and her children 1858.

III. 1. The act of settling and clarifying after agitation or fermentation 1626. **2.** A sinking down or subsidence (of a structure, loose earth, etc.) 1793. **3.** The process of becoming calm or tranquil 1837.

IV. An assemblage of persons settled in a locality. **1.** A community of the subjects of a state settled in a new country; a tract of country so settled, a colony, esp. one in its earlier stages 1697. **2.** In the outlying districts of America and the Colonies: A small village or collection of houses. Also, the huts forming the living quarters of the slaves on a plantation. 1827. **3.** An establishment in the poorer quarters of a large city where educated men or women live in daily personal contact with the working class for co-operation in social reform 1884.

1. *Back s.*: see BACK *a.* 1. *Straits Settlements*, the British possessions in the Malay Peninsula.

Settler (se·tləɹ). 1598. [f. SETTLE *v.* + -ER[1].] **1.** One who or a thing which settles, fixes, decides, etc. **b.** *colloq.* Something that settles or 'does for' a person, a finisher; a crushing or finishing blow, shot, speech, etc. 1744. **2.** One who settles in a new country; a colonist 1695. **b.** *gen.* One who settles in a place as a resident 1815. **3.** *Law.* = SETTLOR 1800. **4.** A pan or vat into which a liquor is run off to 'settle' or deposit a sediment 1674.

1. b. This was a s.; I could make no answer to that HOGG. **2.** The half-pay provincial officers are valuable settlers 1786.

Settling (se·tliŋ), *vbl. sb.* 1440. [f. SETTLE *v.* + -ING[1].] The action of SETTLE *v.* **1.** The action of fixing, establishing, arranging permanently, deciding, coming to rest, etc. 1553. **2.** The adjusting or liquidating of accounts; also *s. up* 1761. **b. Settling day,** a day appointed for settling accounts; *spec.* the fortnightly pay-day on the Stock Exchange 1806. **3.** The action of sinking down, subsiding, forming a deposit or sediment, etc.; also, the result of this 1440. **b.** *concr.* Sediment, lees, dregs. Chiefly *pl.* 1594.

Settlor (se·tlǭɹ). 1818. [Altered f. SETTLER; see -OR 2 d.] *Law.* One who makes a settlement of property.

Set-to (set,tū·). *Pl.* **set-tos** (-tū·z). 1743. [f. vbl. phr. *set to.*] **a.** orig. *Pugilism.* The action of 'setting to'; hence, a bout or round; a pugilistic encounter or boxing match. **b.** *gen.* and *fig.* A fight, contest (often, a verbal dispute, sharp argument) 1794. **c.** An attack or 'go' (*at*) 1801. **d.** *Racing.* The struggle at the end of a race between two horses that are nearly equal 1842.

Setule (sī·tiul, se·tiul). 1826. [– mod.L. *setula* (also used), dim. of *seta* SETA.] A small seta or bristle. Hence **Se·tulose, Se·tulous** *adjs.* covered with setules.

Setwall (se·twǭl). [ME. *zedewal, zeduale, cetewale* – AFr. *zedewale,* OFr. *citoual* – med. L. *zedoale* (cf. AL. *zituale, cytowalla,* etc. XIII), var. of *zedoarium* ZEDOARY.] †**1.** = ZEDOARY –1640. **2.** The plant valerian, *Valeriana pyrenaica* 1548.

‖**Sève** (sę̄v). 1742. [Fr., = sap.] The fineness and strength of flavour proper to a wine.

Seven (se·v'n), *a.* and *sb.* [OE. *seofon* = OFris. *soven,* etc., OS. *sibun,* OHG. *sibun* (Du. *zeven,* G. *sieben*), ON. *sjau,* Goth. *sibun* :– Gmc. **sebun* :– IE. **septṃ́,* repr. by Skr. *saptá,* Gr. ἑπτά, L. *septem,* OSl. *sedmĭ.*] The cardinal number next after six, represented by the symbols 7, VII, vii. **A.** *adj.* **1.** In concord with a sb. expressed. **b.** Used predic. 1622. **c.** Used (*a*) symbolically, often denoting completion or perfection (esp. in echoes of the Bible), or (*b*) typically, in expressions of time, etc. for a large number or quantity OE. **2.** With ellipsis of sb. OE. **3. a.** Multiplying another numeral OE. **b.** Coupled with a higher (cardinal or ordinal) numeral, so as to form a compound (cardinal or ordinal) numeral OE. **c.** Forming fractional numerals 1726.

1. When s. girls succeed each other in one family 1865. *S. days.* a week; the period of the Creation; in England a common term of imprisonment. *S. months' child,* one born at the seventh month; a type of weakliness. **b.** The stars in her hair were s. ROSSETTI. **c.** Add thy Spear, A Weavers beam, and s.-times-folded shield MILT. †*This s. year(s,* etc. (= a long period). **2.** Sure it is no sinne, Or of the deadly seuen it is the least SHAKS. *S.* (i.e. hours) *o'* (†*of the,* †*a*) *clock*; also simply *s.*; *half-past s., s. fifteen,* etc. *To be more than s.,* to 'know one's way about'. *The S.,* (*a*) the seven deacons of Acts 6:5; †(*b*) the Seven Sages of Greece (see SAGE *sb.*[2] B); (*c*) the seven Argive heroes that made war against Thebes. **3.** Tomorrow I may be Myself with Yesterday's Sev'n Thousand Years FITZGERALD. **b.** The seuen and sixtieth Chapter 1579. Slashed by s.-and-twenty wounds CARLYLE.

Special collocations: **S. bishops,** those who protested against James II's Declaration of Indulgence in 1688. **S. champions,** the national saints of England, Scotland, Wales, Ireland, France, Spain, and Italy, viz. George, Andrew, David, Patrick, Denys, James, and Anthony. **S. Seas,** the Arctic, Antarctic, North and South Pacific, North and South Atlantic, and Indian Oceans.

B. *sb.* **1.** The abstract number seven OE. **2.** A set of seven persons or things 1590. **b.** A playing card marked with seven pips 1656. †**3.** In the game of hazard, with ref. to the throwing of a main –1839. **4.** A person or thing numbered seven in a set or series, e.g. in an eight-oared boat, the rower occupying the seat behind stroke. Also *number s.* 1830.

1. *At sixes and sevens*: see SIX *sb.* 2. **2.** Of euery cleane beast thou shalt take to thee by seuens *Gen.* 7:2. **b.** With the s. and eight of diamonds 1783. **3.** *Seven's the main*: see MAIN *sb.*[2]; A gambling-house, whence many a bout of seven's-the-main. .has been had THACKERAY.

Comb.: **s.-bore,** a shot-gun with calibre seven; **-gills,** a shark of the genus *Heptanchus* or *Notidanus.*

Seven-day(s, -days', *attrib. phr.* 1797. **1.** Consisting of or extending over seven days or a week 1823. **2.** *Seven-day(s disease,* a form of tetanus 1797.

Sevenfold (se·v'nfōuld), *a.* and *adv.* [OE. *seofonfeald*; see SEVEN and -FOLD.] **A.** *adj.* **1.** Consisting of seven together or seven in one; having seven parts, divisions, elements, or units. **b.** *Theol.* [tr. eccl. L. *septiformis.*] Applied to seven gifts of the Holy Ghost enumerated in Isaiah 11:2; see also Rev. 1:4. OE. **2.** Seven times as great or numerous; seven times increased or repeated. Hence, typically = very great, strong, etc. OE. **3.** Seven in number. *poet.* 1614.

1. From seuenfold Nilus to Taprobany GREENE. **b.** Thou the anointing Spirit art, Who dost thy s. gifts impart 1627. **2.** A s. night of superstitition and unbelief 1872. **3.** Thebes of the gates s. MORRIS.

B. *adv.* In a sevenfold manner or degree; seven times. Hence, exceedingly, greatly. ME.

The population. .has multiplied s. MACAULAY.

Se·ven-hilled, *a.* 1608. Standing on seven hills; epithet of the city of Rome.

Se·ven-league(d, *a.* 1799. *Seven-league(d boots* [Fr. *bottes de sept lieues*], the boots in the fairy story of Hop o' my Thumb, which enabled the wearer to cover seven leagues at each step. Hence allus. = of enormous size or speed.

Sevenpence (se·v'npĕns). 1671. [f. SEVEN + PENCE.] A sum equal to seven pennies.

Sevenpenny (se·v'npĕni), *a.* late ME. [See PENNY *sb.* III.] Costing or valued at sevenpence; hence †trifling, contemptible.

Seven sisters. ME. **1.** The Pleiades. **2.** *Hist.* Seven cannon, resembling each other in size and make, cast by Robert Borthwick and used at the battle of Flodden 1513.

Seven sleepers. OE. [tr. L. *septem dormientes.*] Seven youths of Ephesus said to have hidden in a cave during the Decian persecution and to have slept there for several hundred years. Also occas. *transf.* in *sing.*

†**Seven stars.** [OE. *seofon steorran.*] **a.** The Pleiades. **b.** The Great Bear. –1860.

Seventeen (sev'ntī·n, se·v'ntīn; see -TEEN), *a.* and *sb.* [OE. *seofontiene* = OFris. *soventene,* OHG. **sibunzehan* (G. *siebzehn*), ON. *sjautján*; see -TEEN.] The cardinal number next after sixteen, composed of ten and seven, represented by the symbols 17, XVII, xvii. **A.** *adj.* **1.** In concord with a sb. expressed. Also, qualifying a higher numeral. **2.** With various ellipses, esp. of *years* ME.

1. There was an old woman toss'd in a blanket, S. times as high as the moon 17. . **2.** From seuentene to seuen and twentie (the most dangerous tyme of all a mans life) ASCHAM. *Sweet s.,* used typically for the most attractive period of a girl's life.

B. *sb.* The abstract number seventeen; the symbol representing this 1594.

Seventeenth (sev'ntī·nþ, se·vtīnþ), *a.* and *sb.* [OE. *seofontēoþa*; see prec. and -TEENTH.] **A.** *adj.* The ordinal number corresponding to the cardinal seventeen; qualifying a sb. expressed or implied. **B.** *sb.* **1.** A seventeenth part 1728. **2.** *Mus.* A note seventeen degrees above or below a given note (both notes being counted); the interval between, or consonance of, two notes seventeen degrees apart; a chord containing this interval 1597.

Seventh (se·v'nþ), *a.* and *sb.* [New formation, directly f. SEVEN + -TH[2], repl. (i) OE. (Anglian) *seofunda,* ME. *sevende,* (ii) OE. *seofoþa,* ME. *seveþe.*] The ordinal number corresponding to the cardinal SEVEN. **A.** *adj.* **1.** In concord with a sb. expressed or understood. **b.** With various ellipses 1598. **2.** *S. heaven*: see HEAVEN *sb.* 1818. **3.** = SEVENTHLY (*rare*) 1576.

1. b. He ordered me to picket two squadrons of the s. 1841.

B. *sb.* **1.** = Seventh part 1557. **2.** *Mus.* **a.** A note seven degrees above or below a given note (both notes being counted); the note immediately below the octave in a scale = *leading note.* **b.** The interval between two notes seven degrees apart. **c.** (In full, *chord of the s.*) A chord consisting of a note together with its third, fifth, and seventh; denominated from that note of the scale which forms the root, as *dominant s., tonic s.* 1591.

Se·venth-day. 1684. The seventh day of the week, Saturday; the (Jewish) Sabbath; *transf.* Sunday 1692. **b.** In the designations of bodies of Christians who observe the seventh day of the week (Saturday) as the principal day of rest and religious observance 1684.

b. *S. adventists*, a millenarian sect holding sabbatarian principles. *S. Baptist*: see SABBATARIAN *sb.* 3.

Seventhly (se·v'nþli), *adv.* 1532. [f. SEVENTH *a.* + -LY².] In the seventh place (in an enumeration). **b.** as *sb.* with ref. to the heads of a sermon 1815.

Seventieth (se·v'ntiėþ), *a.* ME. [f. next + *-eth*, -TH².] The ordinal numeral corresponding to the cardinal SEVENTY.

Seventy (se·v'nti), *a.* and *sb.* [OE. *(hund)-seofontiġ* = OS. *sivuntig*, OHG. *sibunzug*, ON. *sjautigr*; ; see SEVEN, -TY².] **A.** *adj.* **1.** The cardinal number equal to seven tens, represented by 70. LXX, or lxx; **a.** with sb. expressed or implied. **b.** With various ellipses. late ME. **2.** In comb. with numbers below ten (ordinal and cardinal), as *seventy-one, one and s., s. and one, seventy-first*; often with ellipsis (e.g. of *years*) ME.

1. A ship..that carried s. guns CLARENDON. **b.** My first friendship at sixteen, was contracted with a man of s. POPE. *The S.*, *(a)* the s. disciples of our Lord whose mission is recorded in Luke 10:1; *(b)* = SEPTUAGINT. **2.** *S.-five* (= Fr. *soixante-quinze*), a French rapid firing 75 mm. field gun. *S.-four*, a ship carrying s.-four guns (now *Hist.*). *S. twos, s.-twomo* [= 72mo], the size of the page of a book in which each leaf is one s.-second part of a whole sheet.

B. *sb.* **1.** A set of seventy persons or things 1590. **2.** *The seventies*: the decade 70 to 79 in a century or in a person's life 1865.

Seven year(s, -years', *attrib. phr.* 1593. Consisting of or lasting for seven years; having a period of seven years.

†*These (this) seven years day*, this long time. *Seven Years' War*, the third Silesian war (1756–63), in which Austria, France, Russia, Saxony, and Sweden were allied against Frederick II of Prussia.

Sever (se·vəɹ), *v.* late ME. [– AFr. *severer*, OFr. *sevrer* (now, wean) :– Rom. **seperare*, for L. *separare* SEPARATE *v.*] **I.** *trans.* **1.** To put apart, set asunder (two or more persons or things, or one *from* another). †**b.** To part or remove by some technical process (a substance) *from* another with which it is combined or mixed –1796. †**c.** (In Biblical language.) To set apart or segregate for a special purpose. Also with *out*. –1718. **2.** To separate in thought or idea; to distinguish, treat as distinct; to mark off *from*. late ME. **3.** To keep distinct or apart by an intervening barrier or space. Of the intervening medium: To occupy the space or interval between. late ME. **4.** To divide into (two or more) parts. Now *rare* or *Obs.* exc. as in 5. late ME. **5.** To part or divide suddenly or forcibly; to cut in two, cleave or rend asunder. late ME. **b.** To break up, scatter, disperse (an assemblage or company of individuals). Now *rare*. late ME. **6.** 'To part by violence from the rest' (J.); to separate suddenly and forcibly; to cut, tear, or pull off 1626. **7.** *Law.* **a.** To divide (a joint estate) into independent parts 1544. **b.** To detach (growing fruit or trees, minerals, fixtures, etc.) from the soil 1602. **c.** To separate and remove (one of the plaintiffs in a joint action, when he is nonsuited) 1602. **d.** To part (two or more defendants) in their trial 1660. **8.** *absol.* To make a separation or division (*between*). *rare*. 1611.

1. Least harm Befall thee sever'd from me MILT. Her lips are sever'd as to speak TENNYSON. A revolution which severed England from the papacy 1856. **2.** He is a poor Divine that cannot s. the good from the bad 1654. **3.** Immense The space that severed us! WORDSW. **5.** Thus it was that this great tie was severed 1861. **6.** I struck, and with a single blow The tangled root I severed WORDSW.

II. *intr.* **1.** Of a person: To go away, part, be sundered *from*. Of two or more: To be separated, quit each other, go asunder, part. late ME. **b.** Of things 1545. **c.** Of a whole or aggregate: To part, become divided, be separated into parts. late ME. **2.** *Law.* **a.** Of two or more defendants: To plead independently 1625. **b.** Of joint tenants: To divide their jointure 1895.

1. Ae fond kiss, and then we s. BURNS. **2. a.** The defendants had severed in their defence to the action 1884. Hence **Se·verable** *a.* capable of being severed.

Several (se·vĕrăl), *a.*, *adv.*, and *sb.* late ME. [– AFr. *several* (whence AL. *severalis*) – AL. *separalis*, f. L. *separ* separate.] **A.** *adj.* **I.** Existing apart, separate. †**1.** Having a position, existence, or status apart; separate, distinct –1707. **2.** Qualifying a pl. sb.; Individually separate, different 1445. **b.** In legal use: More than one 1531. **3.** Being one of a number of individuals of the same class 1543. **4.** As a vague numeral: Of an indefinite (but not large) number exceeding two or three; more than two or three but not very many. (The chief current sense.) 1661. †**b.** A good many –1753. **c.** *ellipt.* and *absol.*, esp. followed by *of* 1685. †**5.** Of diverse origin or composition –1674.

1. The Reeve, the Miller, and the Cook, are s. Men DRYDEN. **2.** It seems to have been built at s. times, and by different Persons 1710. Three s. pillars, each a rough-hewn stone WORDSW. Now combine These s. propositions 1866. **b.** S. counts on the same cause of action shall not be allowed 1853. **3.** *Every* or *each s.*: every or each individual or single; Ile kisse each seuerall paper, for amends SHAKS. **4.** Some of the men..remembered..to have seen s. strangers on the road STEVENSON. **c.** There are still s. of these Topicks that are far from being exhausted ADDISON.

II. Pertaining to an individual person or thing. **1.** Chiefly *Law.* (Opp. to *common.*) Private; privately owned or occupied. late ME. **2.** Belonging, attributed, or assigned distributively to certain individuals referred to; different for each respectively 1457. **3.** *Law.* (Opp. to *joint.*) Pertaining separately to each of the tenants of an estate, parties to a bond or suit, etc. Of inheritance, tail: By which land is conveyed or entailed to two persons separately by moieties. Of an obligation to which several are parties: Enforceable against each of the parties independently of the others 1532.

1. The commons..are inclosed, made seueral 1583. *S. fishery*, a right to fish derived through or on account of ownership of the soil. **2.** Bid each kinde their severall places fill P. FLETCHER. While each pursues his s. road WORDSW. **3.** The.. rule of law is, that a contract of s. persons is joint and not s. 1863.

†**B.** *adv.* = SEVERALLY *adv.* –1777. **C.** *sb.* **1. In several** [AFr. *en several*]: †**a.** Of land, pasture: As private property; in private hands, under separate ownership, not common –1707. **b.** Separately, individually; apart from others or the rest; as a separate member, unit, etc. Now *rare.* 1586. **2.** Land in private ownership or over which a person has a particular right; chiefly, a plot of such land; *esp.* enclosed pasture land, as opp. to common. *Obs.* exc. *dial.* 1460. †**b.** *gen.* Private property or possession –1642. **3.** *pl.* †**a.** Particular or individual points, parts, or qualities; particulars, details –1703. †**b.** Individual persons or things –1650. **c.** Several persons or things. *Sc.*, *Ir.*, and *U.S.* 1654.

1. a. Good store of Pasture, either in s. or common 1707. **b.** They all, will fight in seuerall then CHAPMAN. **3. a.** All our abilities, gifts, natures, shapes, Seuerals and generals of grace SHAKS. **b.** *Wint. T.* I. ii. 226.

Se·veral-fold, *a.*, *adv.*, and *sb. rare.* 1738. [f. SEVERAL *a.* + -FOLD.] Used like MANIFOLD, but with the implication of not very many.

Severality (sevĕræ·liti). *rare.* 1562. [alt. of SEVERALTY by substitution of -ITY.] *pl.* Individual or particular points, matters, or objects.

Se·veralize, *v. rare.* 1645. [f. SEVERAL *a.* + -IZE.] *trans.* To separate or distinguish (*from*).

Severally (se·vĕrăli), *adv.* late ME. [f. as prec. + -LY².] **1.** Separately, individually; each of a number of persons or things by himself or itself; each successively or in turn. **b.** In legal language, opp. to *jointly* 1447. **2.** Apart from others or from the rest; not together or in a company; independently. *arch.* 1530. **3.** Respectively 1585. †**4.** Differently, variously –1644.

1. He turned s. to each for their opinion GOLDSM. **2.** Abraham, Isaac, and Jacob..to whom the Promise of the Blessed Seed was s. made 1709. **3.** The parts which I and they have s. taken 1827.

Severalty (se·vĕrălti). 1449. [– AFr. *severalte, -aute*, whence AL. *separalitas* (XIV); see SEVERAL, -TY¹.] **1.** The condition of being separate or distinct; separateness, distinctness, independence. **2.** Land held by an individual not joined with other owners. The condition of land so held; a state of being owned by individuals. 1570.

2. Till land is placed in a state of s.,..inclosures are seldom erected in any country 1814.

Phr. **In severalty** [AFr. *en severalte*]. **a.** *Law.* Of land: (Held) in a person's own right without being joined in interest with another (opp. to joint-tenancy, coparcenary, and tenancy-in-common); (held) as private enclosed property (opp. to common). **b.** Separately, apart from others, particularly. **c.** In or into several divisions or parts.

Severance (se·vĕrăns). late ME. [– AFr. *severance*, OFr. *sevrance*, f. *severer, sevrer*; see SEVER *v.*, -ANCE.] **1.** The act or fact of severing; the state of being severed; separation. **2.** *Law.* **a.** The division of a joint estate into independent parts; the destruction of the unity of interest in a joint estate 1539. **b.** The detaching of fruit, minerals, fixtures, etc. from the soil 1602. **c.** The separation of two or more parties joined in a writ 1607.

1. Our s. from the British empire 1787. To draw..lines of s. between truth and falsehood GLADSTONE.

Severe (sĭvīᵊɹ), *a.* 1548. [– (O)Fr. *sévère* or L. *severus.*] **I.** Rigorous in condemnation or punishment. **1.** Of persons, their disposition, etc.: Rigorous in one's treatment of, or attitude towards, offenders; unsparing in the exaction of penalty; not inclined to leniency. Also *absol.* **b.** Of a person's looks, demeanour, etc.: Betokening a severe mood or disposition 1565. **2.** Of law, judgement, punishment, discipline, and the like: Involving strict and rigorous treatment; carried out with rigour; not leaning to tenderness or laxity; unsparing 1562. **b.** Of a compact: Stringent. Of an account: Unsparingly exacted. 1591. **3.** Unsparing in censure, criticism, or reproof 1561.

1. His seuere wrath shall he sharpen for a sword *Wisd.* 5:20. Men of s. tempers 1715. Justice, to herself s. GRAY. **b.** The Iustice,..With eyes seuere, and beard of formall cut SHAKS. **2.** Severer penalties awaited drunkenness, dissipation, or dicing 1861. **b.** Strict and seuere Couenants SHAKS. **3.** Her very appearance was sufficient to silence the severest satirist of the sex GOLDSM. Phr. *To be s. on* (or *upon*): to pass harsh judgement upon, 'to be hard upon'.

II. Conforming to a rigorous standard. **1.** Extremely strict in matters of conduct or behaviour; austere with oneself 1565. **2.** Of intellectual operations, thought, etc.: Conforming to an exacting standard of mental effort; rigidly exact or accurate; not shrinking from what is toilsome or difficult 1605. **3.** Of style, etc.: Shunning redundance or unessential ornament; sober, restrained, austerely simple 1665.

1. Come, you are too seuere a Moraller SHAKS. The Spartan manners were rough, simple, and s. 1828. **2.** Truth s., by Fairy Fiction drest GRAY. *absol.* Happily to steer From grave to gay, from lively to s. POPE. **3.** Even Brummel..was marked by the severest simplicity in dress 1856.

III. Of impersonal agencies: Pressing hardly, rigorous. **1.** Of the weather, etc.: Causing great discomfort or injury to living things; very cold, wet or stormy 1676. **b.** Of fire or light: Painfully or searchingly intense (*rare*) 1652. **c.** Of an attack of illness or disease: Attended with a maximum of pain or distress, violent 1725. **2.** Of pain, suffering, loss, or the like: Grievous, extreme 1742. **3.** Of events or circumstances, labour or exercise, a struggle, test, trial, etc.: Hard to sustain or endure; arduous 1774. **4.** *colloq.* (chiefly *U.S.*) A vague epithet denoting superlative quality; very big or powerful; hard to beat 1834. **5.** quasi-*adv.* Severely 1599.

1. This had been the severest winter that any man alive had known in England EVELYN. **c.** I finally caught a s. cold 1823. **2.** The loss inflicted on the infantry was also s. 1838. **3.** The pace was too s. 1867. **5.** The Lord shall scoff them, then s. Speak to them in his wrath MILT. Hence **Seve·reness.**

Severely (sĭvīᵊ·ɹli), *adv.* [f. prec. + -LY².] In a severe manner, in various senses; phr. *to leave* or *let s. alone*, to avoid, ignore, or isolate deliberately or of set purpose.

Severity (sĭve·rĭti). 1481. [– (O)Fr. *sévérité* or L. *severitas*, f. *severus*; see SEVERE, -ITY.] **1.** Strictness or sternness in dealing with others; stern or rigorous disposition or behaviour; rigour in treatment, discipline, punishment, or the like 1530. **b.** An act or instance of severity 1538. **c.** Harshness of judgement, criticism, or rebuke. Also *pl.* severe rebukes or criticisms. 1660. **d.** Sternness of aspect or countenance; a severe look or expression 1711. **2.** Strictness or austerity of life, morals, etc. 1481. **3.** Strictness in matters of thought or intellect; rigid accuracy or exactness; undeviating conformity to truth or fact. Also *pl.* instances of this. 1638. **4.** Austere purity or simplicity of style, taste, etc. 1709. **5.** Rigour or inclemency (of weather or climate); esp. extremity of cold 1676. **6.** Violence or acuteness (of illness) 1808. **7.** Grievousness (of affliction, penalties, etc.) 1849.

1. Excessive s. in the laws HUME. **c.** Bacon has been judged with merciless s. 1884. **2.** He affected the s. of the Stoic 1741. **3.** The process of reasoning called *deductio ad absurdum*, which even the s. of geometry does not reject BURKE. **4.** The s. of French taste GOLDSM. **7.** The tax falls with excessive and undue s. upon one class 1893.

Severy (se·vĕri). late ME. [– AFr. *civorie, OFr. *civoire* CIBORIUM.] *Arch.* A bay or compartment of a vaulted roof. Also, a compartment or section of scaffolding.

Seville (se·vil), *a.* late ME. [Name (Sp. *Sevilla*) of a city and province of Andalusia, used attrib.] †**1.** *S. oil*: olive oil brought from S. –1618. **2.** *S. orange*: the bitter orange, *Citrus bigaradia*, used for making marmalade 1593.

‖**Sèvres** (sęvr), *a.* 1764. [Name of a town in France, near Paris.] The designation of a costly porcelain made at Sèvres. Also *absol.*

‖**Sevum** (sī·vŏm). 1440. [L. *sevum, sebum.* Cf. SEBUM.] Suet, as used in pharmacy.

Sew (sōᵘ), *v.*¹ Pa. t. **sewed** (sōᵘd). Pa. pple. **sewed, sewn** (sōᵘn). [OE. *siwan, siowan* = OFris. *sīa*, OHG. *siuwen*, ON. *sýja*, Goth. *siujan* :– Gmc. **siwjan*, f. IE. **siw-* **sju-*, repr. also by L. *suere* Gr. (κασ)σύειν.] **1.** *trans.* To fasten, attach, or join (pieces of textile material, leather, etc.) by passing a thread in alternate directions through a series of punctures made either with a needle carrying the thread, or with an awl; to make the seams of (a garment, etc.). **b.** *Surgery.* = *s. up*: see 4 a 1502. **c.** *Bookbinding.* To fasten together the sheets of (a book) by passing a thread or wire backwards and forwards through the back fold of each sheet, so as to attach it to the bands: dist. from *stitch* 1637. **2.** *absol.* and *intr.* To work with a needle and thread 1450. **3.** *trans.* = *s. up*: see 4 b ME. **4. S. up. a.** To close (an orifice, a wound, also anything that envelops) by stitching the edges together 1490. **b.** To enclose *in* a cover or receptacle and secure it by sewing 1611. **c.** *slang.* (*a*) To tire out (a horse) 1826. (*b*) To tire out, exhaust (a person); to nonplus, bring to a standstill; to put *hors de combat*; to outwit, cheat, swindle 1837. (*c*) To make hopelessly drunk 1829.

1. Shoes, That are wel sowed 1576. To S. on a Button 1855. **3.** The diamonds were sewed into her habit THACKERAY. **4. c.** (*b*) 'Busy!' replied Pell; 'I'm completely sewn up' DICKENS. Hence **Sewed** (sōᵘd) *ppl. a.* joined, etc. by stitching (esp. of books). **Sewer** (sōᵘ·əɹ) *sb.*³ one who sews.

†**Sew,** *v.*² 1440. [Back-formation from SEWER *sb.*²] *trans.* To place (food) on the table as a sewer does; *intr.* to act as a sewer –1609.

Sew (siū), *v.*³ 1513. [– OFr. **sewer*, aphetic var. of OFr. *essever, essewer* drain off :– Rom. **exaquare*, f. L. *ex* EX-¹ + *aqua* water. Cf. med.L. *seware*, etc.] **1.** *trans.* To drain, draw off the water from. Now *dial.* **2.** *intr.* Of a liquid: To ooze out. (Said also of the containing vessel.) Now *dial.* 1565. **3.** *Naut.* Of a ship: To be grounded or high and dry; to have its water-line (so much) above the water 1588.

3. If the water has left her two feet, she has sued two feet 1882.

Sewage (siū·ėdʒ), *sb.* 1834. [Formed after SEWER *sb.*¹ by substitution of suffix; see -AGE.] **1.** Refuse matter conveyed in sewers. **2.** = SEWERAGE 1, 2. *rare.* 1834.

1. *fig.* The literary s. which is pouring forth from the Paris press 1884.

attrib. and *Comb.*: **s. farm,** a farm on which s. irrigation is practised; so **s. farming; s. grass,** grass grown on land fertilized by s.; **s. irrigation,** the system of disposing of liquid s. by turning it on to land. Hence **Sew·age** *v. trans.* to irrigate or fertilize with s.; to drain with sewers.

Sewellel (sĭwe·lĕl). 1814. [Columbia River Indian.] A small rodent, *Haplodon rufus*, of the Western coast of the U.S. Called also *mountain-beaver.*

Sewer (siū·əɹ), *sb.*¹ late ME. [– AFr. *sever(e*, ONFr. *se(u)wiere* channel to carry off overflow from a fishpond (whence med.L. *seweria*) :– Rom. **exaquaria*, f. **exaquare* SEW *v.*³] **1.** An artificial watercourse for draining marshy land and carrying off surface water into a river or the sea. Also *water-s.* **2.** An artificial channel or conduit, now usu. covered and underground, for carrying off and discharging waste water and the refuse from houses and towns 1606.

2. *Common s.*, a drain through which all or a large part of the sewage of a town passes, a main drain collecting and discharging the contents of auxiliary drains: *fig.* London! the needy villain's general home. The common s. of Paris, and of Rome JOHNSON.

Comb.: **s.-air, gas,** atmospheric air mixed with gas formed by the decomposition of sewage; **-rat,** the brown rat (*Mus decumanus*) common in sewers and drains. Hence **Sew·er** *v. trans.* to furnish (a town, road, etc.) with a system of sewers.

Sewer (siū·əɹ), *sb.*² Now *Hist.* late ME. [Aphetic f. AFr. *asseour*, f. (O)Fr. *asseoir* place a seat for :– L. *assidēre*, f. *ad* AD- + *sedēre* SIT; see -ER² 3.] An attendant at a meal who superintended the arrangement of the table, the seating of the guests, and the tasting and serving of the dishes. Formerly an officer of the Royal Household.

The s. with savoury meats Dish after dish, served them COWPER.

Sewerage (siū·ərėdʒ). 1834. [f. SEWER *sb.*¹ + -AGE.] **1.** Drainage by means of sewers; a system of draining by sewers. **2.** *concr.* Sewers collectively; the system of sewers draining a particular locality 1834. **3.** Sewage 1851.

Sewin (siū·in). 1532. [Of unkn. origin.] A fish of the salmon tribe (*Salmo cambricus* or *eriox*), the bull-trout, found in Welsh rivers.

Sewing (sōᵘ·iŋ), *vbl. sb.* ME. [f. SEW *v.*¹ + -ING¹.] **1.** The action of SEW *v.*¹; the use of a needle and thread; the uniting of pieces of material, etc. by this means. **2.** *concr.* Work sewn; materials to be sewn; the stitches or seams of anything. late ME. **3.** *pl.* Sewing thread or silk 1844.

attrib. and *Comb.* as *s.-class, -cotton, -maid*, etc.; **s.-machine,** a machine which performs the operation of sewing.

Sewn (sōᵘn), *ppl. a.* 1866. [pa. pple. of SEW *v.*¹] Stitched, fastened by means of sewing. Chiefly with prefix, as *hand-s.*, *machine-s.*

Sex (seks), *sb.* late ME. [– (O)Fr. *sexe* or L. *sexus.*] **1.** Either of the two divisions of organic beings distinguished as male and female respectively; the males or the females (esp. of the human race) viewed collectively. **2.** Quality in respect of being male or female 1526. **3.** The distinction between male and female in general. In recent use: The sum of those differences in the structure and function of the reproductive organs on the ground of which beings are distinguished as male and female, and of the other physiological differences consequent on these; the class of phenomena with which these differences are concerned 1631. ¶**4.** Used, by confusion, in senses of SECT 1575.

1. *The fair(er), gentle(r), soft(er), weak(er) s., the devout s., the second s.*, the female sex, women. *The sterner s.*, men. *The s.*, the female sex (now *rare*). Cf. Fr. *le (beau) sexe.* **3.** *Organs of s.*, the reproductive organs in sexed animals or plants.

Comb. **s.-cell,** a reproductive cell, with either male or female function; a sperm-cell or an egg-cell. **b.** Characterized by excessive or morbid consciousness of sex; pertaining to the reactions of a member of one sex to a member of the other; as *sex appeal, instinct, urge.*

Sex (seks), *v.* 1884. [f. prec.] *trans.* To determine the sex of, by anatomical examination; to label as male or female.

Sex- (seks), repr. L. *sex* six in comb. (as in *sexennis* SEXENNIAL), occurs in many mod. formations, chiefly scientific or technical.

1. Forming parasynthetic compounds, as *sexlocular, sexradiate*, adjs.; **sexdi·gital, -di·gitate(d)** *adjs.*, having six digits (fingers or toes); **sexdi·gitism,** the condition of having six digits; **sexdi·gitist,** one who has six digits. **b.** *Chem.* In the name of classes of compounds, denoting the presence of six atoms, molecules, or combining proportions of the substance indicated by the second part of the compound, as *sexdecyl*, etc. Also in **sexva·lent** *a.*, having an equivalence of six, combining with or replacing six hydrogen atoms. **2.** Combined with a numerical element: **sexde·cimo** = SEXTO-DECIMO; **sexmille·nary, -mille·nnial** *adjs.*, of 6,000 years.

Sexagenarian (se·ksădʒĭnēᵊ·riăn), *a.* and *sb.* 1738. [f. L. *sexagenarius*; see next and -IAN.] **A.** *adj.* Of the age of sixty years. Also, characteristic of one sixty years old. 1862. **B.** *sb.* A person sixty years old 1738. Hence **Sexagena·rianism,** the state of being sixty years old.

Sexagenary (seksæ·dʒĭnări), *a.* and *sb.* 1594. [– L. *sexagenarius*, f. *sexageni* sixty each, distributive of *sexaginta* sixty; see -ARY¹.] **A.** *adj.* **1.** *Math.* Of or belonging to the number 60; composed of or proceeding by sixties; pertaining to a scale of numbers of which the modulus is 60. **2.** = prec. A. 1638.

1. *S. arithmetic* = SEXAGESIMAL *arithmetic. S. table*, a table of proportional parts which shows at sight the product or quotient of any two sexagenary numbers.

B. *sb.* †**1.** *Math., Astr.* = SEXAGESIMAL B. –1728. **2.** = prec. B. Now *rare* or *Obs.* 1814.

Se·xagene. Also in L. form. 1570. [mod.L. use of fem. of late L. *sexagenus* containing 60, or med.L. *sexagena* 60 pieces, f. L. *sexageni* sixty each; see prec.] *Math.* A quantity or number multiplied by sixty or a power of sixty; an arc of sixty degrees.

Sexagesima (seksădʒe·simă). late ME. [eccl. L., fem. (sc. *dies*) of L. *sexagesimus* sixtieth, f. *sexaginta* sixty.] In full *S. Sunday*: the second Sunday before Lent.

Sexagesimal (seksădʒe·simăl), *a.* and *sb.* 1685. [f. L. *sexagesimus* sixtieth + -AL¹.] **A.** *adj.* Proceeding by sixties; *esp.* pertaining to, involving, or based upon division into sixty equal parts (as seconds and minutes). **b.** *S. fraction*: a fraction whose denomination is 60 or a power of 60 1685.

S. arithmetic, a method of computation based upon the number 60. *S. table* = SEXAGENARY *table.*

B. *sb. pl.* Sexagesimal fractions; also, the system of sexagesimal fractions 1685. Hence **Sexage·simally** *adv.* into sixtieths.

Sexcentenary (seks,se·ntĭnări), *a.* and *sb.* 1779. [In A. 1, f. L. *sexcenteni* 600 each; in A. 2 and B, f. SEX- + CENTENARY.] **A.** *adj.* **1.** Pertaining to the number 600. **2.** Relating to a period of 600 years 1864. **B.** *sb.* The six-hundredth anniversary (of an event) 1885.

Sexed (sekst), *a.* 1598. [f. SEX *sb.* + -ED².] **1.** Pertaining to one or both of the sexes (specified by a prefixed word). **2.** Of an animal or plant: Having sex; not neuter or asexual. 1891. Also with prefixed adv., as *highly s., over-s.*

Sexennial (sekse·niăl), *a.* 1646. [f. L. *sexennis* or *sexennium* + -AL¹.] Continuing for a period of six years; occurring every six years. Hence **Sexe·nnially** *adv.*

Sexfoil (se·ksfoil), *a.* and *sb.* 1688. [f. SEX-, after *trefoil*, etc.] **A.** *adj.* Having six foliations 1848. **B.** *sb. Arch.* and *Her.* = SIXFOIL 1688. So **Se·xfoiled** *a.* = A.

Sexi-, occas. used as comb. form of L. *sex* six: **Se·xifid** = *sexfid* (see SEX- 1). **Sexisylla·bic** *a.*, of six syllables; so **Sexisy·llable.**

Sexless (se·kslės), *a.* 1598. [f. SEX *sb.* + -LESS.] Without sex; lacking the characteristics of sex; asexual. **b.** *Nat. Hist.* = NEUTER *a.* 4. 1827. Hence **Se·xless-ly** *adv.*, **-ness.**

Sexpartite (sekspā·ɹtəit), *a.* 1760. [f. SEX-, after *bipartite*, *tripartite*, etc. Cf. PARTITE (Bot.).] Divided into or consisting of six parts.

Sext (sekst). late ME. [In 1 – L. *sexta* (sc. *hora* hour), fem. of *sextus* sixth. (Cf. PRIME *sb.*[1] I.). In 2 – L. *sextus* (sc. *liber* book). In 3 – L. *sexta* (sc. *pars* part).] **1.** *Eccl.* The third of the lesser canonical hours; so called because belonging orig. to the sixth hour of the day (midday). Also *pl.* **2.** *Eccl.* The sixth book added to the Decretals by Pope Boniface VIII. 1656. **3.** *Mus.* **a.** An interval of a sixth. **b.** An organ stop of two ranks of pipes having an interval of a sixth between them 1876.

Sextan (se·kstăn), *a.* 1657. [– med.L. *sextana* (sc. *febris*) XIII; cf. QUARTAN, QUINTAN.] Designating a fever of which the paroxysms recur every fifth (according to old reckoning, every sixth) day.

Sextant (se·kstănt). 1596. [– mod.L. use (by Tycho Brahe, 1602) of L. *sextans*, *sextant-* sixth part (of an as, etc.), f. *sextus* sixth.] †**1.** The sixth part of the Roman as –1656. †**2.** The sixth part of a circle –1730. **3.** An astronomical instrument resembling a quadrant, furnished with a graduated arc equal to a sixth part of a circle, used for measuring angular distances between objects, esp. for observing altitudes of celestial objects in ascertaining latitude at sea 1628. **4.** *Bot.* Each of a group of six segment-cells 1875. **5.** *Astr.* The constellation *Sextans* 1795.

Sextary (se·kstări). late ME. [– L. *sextarius* (also used), f. *sextus* sixth; see -ARY[1].] **1.** An ancient Roman liquid measure containing the sixth part of a CONGIUS. **2.** A dry measure containing the sixteenth part of a MODIUS. late ME.

Sextet (sekste·t). Also **-ett.** 1841. [Alteration of SESTET after L. *sex* six.] **1.** *Mus.* = SESTET 1. **2.** A stanza of six lines 1850. **3.** A group or set of six persons or things 1873.

Sextic (se·kstik), *a.* and *sb.* 1853. [f. L. *sextus* sixth + -IC; cf. contemp. QUANTIC, QUARTIC, QUINTIC.] *Math.* **A.** *adj.* Of the sixth degree or order. **B.** *sb.* A quantic, or equation, of the sixth degree; a curve of the sixth order 1872.

Sextile (se·kstəil, -il), *a.* and *sb.* 1557. [– L. *sextilis*, f. *sextus* sixth; see -ILE. Cf. QUINTILE, QUARTILE.] *Astrol.* **A.** *adj. S. aspect*, the aspect of two heavenly bodies which are 60° or one sixth part of the zodiac distant from each other. **B.** *sb.* A sextile aspect. Phr. *in (a) s.* 1592.

Sextillion (seksti·lyən). 1690. [– Fr. *sextillion*, f. L. *sex* six, after *septillion*, etc.] *Arith.* The sixth power of a million, denoted by 1 followed by 36 ciphers. In American (and later Fr.) use, the seventh power of a thousand, denoted by 1 followed by 21 ciphers.

Sexto (se·ksto). 1847. [– L. *sexto*, abl. case of *sextus* sixth; cf. QUARTO, etc.] The designation of the size of a book, or of the page of a book, in which each leaf is one-sixth of a sheet.

Sexto-decimo (sekstoˌde·simo). 1688. [– L. *sexto decimo*, abl. case of *sextus decimus* sixteenth.] = DECIMO-SEXTO, SIXTEENMO.

Sextole (se·kstoᵘl). 1854. [– G. *sextole*, arbitrarily f. L. *sextus* sixth. Cf. QUINTOLE.] *Mus.* A group of six notes to be played in the time of four. So **Se·xtolet.**

Sexton (se·kstən). [Late ME. *segerstane*, *secristeyn*, *sexteyn* – AFr., OFr. *segerstein*, *secrestein* – med.L. *sacristanus* SACRISTAN.] **1.** A church officer having the care of the fabric of a church and its contents, and the duties of ringing the bells and digging graves. (In pop. use from the 16th c. usu. = bell-ringer and grave-digger.) **2.** A sexton beetle 1885.

1. I haue bin sixeteene heere, man and Boy thirty yeares SHAKS.

Comb.: **s. beetle,** a beetle of the genus *Necrophorus*; a burying beetle. Hence **Sex·toness,** *a* female s. (or sacristan). **Se·xtonship,** the office or position of a s.

Sextry (se·kstri). late ME. [perh. f. SEXTON after *vestry*, or alt. of OFr. *sacrestie* (mod. *sacristie*), med.L. *sacristia*.] †**1.** = SACRISTY –1691. **2.** The residence of a sacrist or sacristan 1585.

Sextuor (se·kstiuǫɹ). 1824. [– Fr. *sextuor*, f. L. *sex* six, after *quatuor* quartet. Cf. SEPTUOR.] *Mus.* = SESTET 1.

Sextuple (se·kstiup'l), *a.* and *sb.* 1626. [– med.L. *sextuplus*, irreg. f. L. *sex* six, after late L. *quintuplus* QUINTUPLE, etc.] **A.** *adj.* Sixfold; six times as great or numerous; consisting of six parts or things. **B.** *sb.* The number which is six times a specified number 1657. Hence **Se·xtuple** *v. trans.* to multiply by six; *intr.* to increase sixfold.

Sextuplet (se·kstiuplet). 1852. [f. SEXTUPLE *a.* after *triplet*.] A group, set, combination, etc. of six things; esp. *Mus.* = SEXTOLE.

Sextuplex (se·kstiupleks), *a.* 1668. [– med.L. *sextuplex*, irreg. f. *sex* six, after L. QUADRUPLEX. Cf. SEXTUPLE.] Sixfold. **b.** *Electric Telegr.* Applied to a system by which six messages may be transmitted simultaneously by the same wire 1889.

Sexual (se·ksiuăl, -kʃu-), *a.* 1651. [– late L. *sexualis*, f. L. *sexus* SEX.] **1.** Of or pertaining to sex or the attribute of being either male or female; existing or predicated with regard to sex. **2.** Pertaining to sex as concerned in generation or in the processes connected with this 1799. **b.** Of or pertaining to the organs of sex 1836. **3.** Relative to the physical intercourse between the sexes or the gratification of sexual appetites, as *s. morality*, *excess*, etc. 1878. **4.** Of animals and plants: Having sex; sexed; separated into two sexes; having sexual organs; producing offspring by means of sexual congress. (Opp. to *asexual*.) 1830. **b.** Of reproduction in animals or plants: Taking place by means of the congress of the two sexes. (Opp. to *asexual* or *agamic*.) 1872. **5.** Characteristic of or peculiar to the one sex or the other 1815.

1. The stage of s. differentiation HUXLEY. **2.** *S. intercourse*, copulation (of human beings). *S. organs*, the organs of s. generation in animals or plants. *S. system* (or *method*), the Linnæan classification of plants, based on the differences in their s. organization. **b.** *S. diseases*, diseases of the s. organs 1898. **2.** *S. cell*, a male or a female reproductive cell; a sperm-cell or an egg-cell. **5.** *Secondary s. characters*, those marks of sex (e.g. the beard in man, the distinctive plumage in birds) which are not immediately connected with the reproductive structure. Hence **Se·xualist** (*rare*), one who attributes sexuality to certain organisms; an adherent of the 's. system' of botanical classification. **Se·xualize** *v. trans.* to make s., endow with sex, attribute sex to. **Se·xually** *adv.* in a s. manner; with respect to sex.

Sexuality (seksiuæ·lĭti, -kʃu-). 1800. [See SEXUAL *a.* and -ITY.] **1.** The quality of being sexual or having sex. **2.** Possession of sexual powers, or capability of sexual feelings 1879. **3.** Recognition of or preoccupation with what is sexual 1848.

†**'Sfoot,** *int.* 1602. Shortening of *God's foot*; see 'S. –1662.

‖**Sforzando** (sfǫɹtsa·ndo). 1801. [It., gerund of *sforzare* use force.] *Mus.* A direction indicating that the note so marked is to be specially emphasized or rendered louder than the rest. Abbrev. *sf.*, *sfz.*

‖**Sforzato** (sfǫɹtsā·to). 1801. [It., pa. pple. of *sforzare*.] = prec.

‖**Sgraffito** (sgrafˌfī·to). *Pl.* **sgraffiti** (sgrafˌfī·tī). 1730. [Earlier (XVIII) equiv. of GRAFFITO, *s-* repr. L. *ex* EX-[1].] = GRAFFITO.

Sh, a consonantal digraph representing the simple sound (ʃ). From the time of Caxton it has been the established notation for (ʃ) in all words except those in which (as *machine*, *schedule*, *Asia*, the derivs. in -*tion*, etc.) it is otherwise represented on etymological grounds.

Sh (ʃ), *int.* Also written **'sh** (as if an abbrev. of *hush*). 1847. = HUSH *int.*

†**Sh.** Abbrev. of SHILLING.

Shab (ʃæb), *sb.* [OE. *sćeabb* = ON. **skabbr* SCAB *sb.*] **1.** = SCAB *sb.* 1–3. Now *dial.*, a cutaneous disease in sheep. †**2.** *slang.* A low fellow –1851. Hence **Shabbed** *a.*, †scabby; shabby (*Obs.* exc. *dial.*).

Shab (ʃæb), *v. Obs.* exc. *dial.* 1677. [Of obscure origin; sense 2 suggests connection with SHAB *sb.* 2.] **1.** *trans.* with *off*: **a.** To get rid of; get (a person) out of the way. **b.** To put (a person) off *with* (something unsatisfactory) 1840. **2.** *intr.* with *off* or *away*: To slink away, sneak off 1700.

Shabby (ʃæ·bi), *a.* 1669. [f. SHAB *sb.* + -Y[1].] **1.** That has lost its newness or freshness of appearance; dingy and faded from wear or exposure 1685. **b.** Of persons, their appearance, etc.: Poorly-dressed, 'seedy' 1669. **c.** *transf.* Discreditably inferior in quality, making a poor appearance 1820. **2.** Of persons, their actions, etc.: Contemptibly mean, ungenerous, or dishonourable. Often applied to conduct which is less friendly or generous than one had hoped for. 1679. **b.** Of a gift or the like: Small or poor as estimated by the giver's means 1753.

1. A s. house DICKENS. An old book in a very s. binding 1866. A poacher In s. velveteen 1884. **b.** A s. old half-pay father 1882. **c.** My Lord Duke's entertainments were both seldom and s. THACKERAY. **2.** A s. excuse THACKERAY. **b.** This s. present was an insult to us 1857. Hence **Sha·bbi-ly** *adv.*, **-ness.**

Sha·bby-gentee·l, *a.* 1754. Attempting to look genteel and to keep up appearances in spite of shabbiness.

‖**Shabracque, shabrack** (ʃæ·bræk). 1667. [– G. *schabracke*, Fr. *schabraque*, of East European origin (Russ. *shabrak*, Turk. *çaprak*).] A saddle-cloth used in European armies.

†‖**Shabunder** (ʃăbʊ·ndəɹ). 1599. [– Pers. *šāh-bandar*, lit. 'king of the port'.] The title of an officer at native ports in the Indian seas, often also head of the customs –1797.

Shack (ʃæk), *sb.*[1] Now *dial.* 1536. [f. *shack*, dial var. of SHAKE *v.*] **1.** Grain fallen from the ear, and available for the feeding of pigs, poultry, etc., after the harvest; a supply of fallen grain for this purpose. Also, fallen beech-mast or acorns. **2. a.** In phr. *to be, go, run at s.*, said of pigs, poultry, etc., when turned into the stubble to feed on the 'shack'. Hence **b.** The right of sending pigs or poultry to 'run at s.' on another's land after the harvest; also, the right of pasturing cattle in winter on another's land. 1629. **3.** An animal or animals 'at s.' 1842.

Shack, *sb.*[2] *dial.* and *U.S.* 1682. [perh. short for †*shack-rag* (XVII); cf. dial. *shake*, and SHAKE-RAG, in same sense.] **1.** An idle disreputable fellow, a vagabond. **2.** A worthless horse (*U.S.*) 1911.

1. A fellow . . having much the appearance of a town s. BORROW.

Shack, *sb.*[3] *U.S.* and *Canadian.* 1881. [perh. shortened – Mex. *jacal*, Aztec *xacalli* wooden hut, which are more closely repr. by occas. U.S. *shackle*.] A roughly built cabin or shanty of logs, mud, etc.

Shack (ʃæk), *v.*[1] *dial.* 1658. [f. SHACK *sb.*[1]] *trans.* To turn (pigs or poultry, etc.) into stubble-fields; also, of animals, to feed on (stubble). Also *intr.* to feed *upon* stubble.

Shack, *v.*[2] *dial.* 1787. [f. SHACK *sb.*[2]] *intr.* To idle away one's time; to loaf *about*.

Shackbolt (ʃæ·kbōᵘlt). 1610. [perh. shortened f. *shackle-bolt*; see next.] *Her.* A shackle or fetter used as a charge.

Shackle (ʃæ·k'l), *sb.* [OE. *sć(e)acul*, corresp. to LG. *shäkel* link of a chain, shackle, hobble, Du. *schakel*, ON. *skǫkull* waggon-pole, f. Gmc. **skak-*, repr. also by OE. *sćeac*, LG. *schake*; see -LE.] **I.** A kind of fetter. **1.** A fetter for the ankle or wrist of a prisoner, usu. one of a pair connected together by a chain, which is fastened to a ring-bolt in the floor or wall of the cell. In OE., a ring or collar for the neck of a prisoner. †**2.** A fetter-like bond, esp. one used as an ornament, an armlet or anklet (*rare*) –1697. †**3.** A hobble for a horse –1814.

1. They resolved rather to dye fighting then to live in schackells 1641. *fig.* To knock off the Shackles of Ignorance and Prejudice 1738.

II. In techn. senses. **1.** A ring, clevis, or similar device, used for attaching or coupling, so as to leave some degree of freedom of movement; often a U-shaped piece of iron, closed by a movable bar passing through holes in the ends; as, a fastening for a port-hole, a coupling for lengths of chain cable, the hinged and curved bar of a padlock which passes through the staple, etc. ME. **2.** *Telegr.* A form of insulator used in overhead lines for supporting the wire where a sharp angle occurs 1855.

Comb.: **s.-bar,** (*a*) the swingle-tree of a coach, etc.; (*b*) *U.S.* the coupling between a locomotive and its tender; **-bolt,** the bolt which passes through the eyes of a s.; (*Her.*) this used as a bearing; **-bone** (*Sc.* and *dial.*) the wrist; **-joint,** (*a*) a joint in the form of a s. (sense II. 1.), esp. one for adjusting the tension of rods, wires, etc.; (*b*) a peculiar kind of articulation in the vertebræ of some fishes.

Shackle (ʃæ·k'l), *v.* 1440. [f. prec.] **1.** *trans.* To confine with shackles; to put a shackle or shackles on. **2.** To join, couple, or fix by means of a shackle. Also *intr.* for *refl.* 1834. **3.** *Telegr.* To attach to or furnish with a shackle (SHACKLE *sb.* II. 2) 1852.

1. Edmond Mortimer..whome..Owen Glendor kepte in filthy prison shakeled with yrons 1548. *fig.* The views of Paul were..less shackled by associations 1879.

Shackly (ʃæ·kli), *a.* *U.S.* and *dial.* 1848. [f. *shackle*, freq. of SHAKE *v.*; see -Y¹.] Shaky, rickety; ramshackle.

Shad (ʃæd). [Late OE. *sćeadd*, of unkn. origin.] **1.** Any clupeoid fish of the genus *Alosa*; the British species are the allice, *A. communis* or *vulgaris*, and the twaite (or herring-s.), *A. finta*; the common or white s. of America is *A. sapidissima*, and the Chinese s. is *A. reevesi*. **2.** *U.S.* Applied to other fishes, as **gizzard s.,** the genus *Dorosoma*; **green-tailed, hard-head(ed, yellow tailed s.,** the menhaden; **Ohio s.,** *Pomolobus chrysochloris* 1884.

Comb. (U.S. names of plants which are in flower or fruit when the s. are found in the rivers, and of birds, insects, etc. that appear about that time); **s.-berry,** the s.-bush or its fruit; **-bush,** the genus *Amelanchier*, esp. *A. canadensis*, also called *June-berry* or *service-berry*; **-fly,** a fly which appears when s. are running; **-frog,** *Rana halecina* or *virescens*; **-trout,** the squeteague; **-waiter,** the Menomonee whitefish, *Coregonus quadrilateralis*.

Sha·d-be:lly. *U.S.* 1842. [f. prec. + BELLY *sb.*] In full, *s. coat*, a Quaker coat, so called from its shape; hence a Quaker.

Shaddock (ʃæ·dǫk). 1696. [After a Captain *Shaddock*.] The fruit of *Citrus decumana* (also called POMPELMOOSE) resembling an orange, but very much larger. In stricter use, applied to the large pear-shaped varieties of the species, the smaller and rounder varieties being called *grape-fruit*. **b.** The tree bearing this fruit 1785.

Shade (ʃēⁱd), *sb.* [OE. *sć(e)adu* fem. (obl. cases repr. by SHADOW), and obl. cases *sćeade*, *sćeadu*, etc. of *sćead* n.] **I.** Comparative darkness. **1.** Partial or comparative darkness; absence of complete illumination; esp. the comparative darkness caused by a more or less opaque object intercepting the direct rays of the sun or other luminary. **b.** *fig.* Comparative obscurity 1650. **c.** *transf.* A fleeting look of displeasure, a 'cloud' on a person's brow or countenance 1818. **2.** *pl.* **a.** *The shades* (*of night, of evening*, etc.): the darkness of night; the growing darkness after sunset 1582. **b.** *The shades*: the darkness of the nether world; the abode of the dead, Hades 1594. **3.** *Drawing* and *Painting.* Absence of complete illumination as represented pictorially; the part or parts of a picture representing this; the darker colour expressing absence of illumination. Often in *light and s.* 1662. **4.** Degree of darkness or depth of colour; hence, any of the slightly differing varieties of quality that may exist in what is broadly considered as one and the same colour 1690. **b.** *transf.* and *fig.* A minutely-differentiated degree or variety (of a quality, a condition, meaning, etc.). Often advb. with comparatives, *a s. better, less*, etc. 1749. **c.** A tinge, a minute qualifying infusion (of some quality); *colloq.*, a minute quantity or portion added or removed 1791.

1. The pensive s. of twilight was pleasing to her MRS. RADCLIFFE. **b.** Phr. *To be in the s.*, to be in retirement, to be little known. *To cast, throw into the s., put into the s.*, to obscure by contrast of superior brilliancy, to surpass so as to render insignificant. **c.** A s. of annoyance crosses his face 1879. **2. b.** Then let our swords..Dismiss him to the shades 1749. **3.** *fig.* The shades which were in his private conduct, are to be forgotten BOSWELL. *Light and s.*, in a literary work, a musical performance, or the like, the contrast necessary to artistic effect, of passages of lighter and graver tone, or of greater and less brilliancy. **4. b.** Men of all shades of opinion..combined against him 1888. **c.** There was now in his conduct a s. of lunacy SCOTT.

II. 1. A dark figure thrown upon a surface by a body intercepting light; a shadow. Now *dial.* and *poet.* OE. **b.** *fig.* An unsubstantial image of something real; something that has only a fleeting existence, or that has become reduced almost to nothing. Now *poet.* or *rhet.* ME. **2.** The visible but impalpable form of a dead person, a ghost. Also, a disembodied spirit, an inhabitant of Hades (= L. *umbra*). Often collect. pl., *the shades*: the world of disembodied spirits, Hades. 1616. †**b.** A spectre, phantom. SHAKS. **c.** In humorous invocation of the spirit of a deceased person, as likely to be horrified or amazed by some action or occurrence 1818. †**3.** = SILHOUETTE *sb.* 1. –1842.

1. After a few hours, we see the shades lengthen JOHNSON. **b.** They are but shades, not true things where we live SIDNEY. **2.** Where grateful Science still adores her Henry's holy S. GRAY.

III. Protection from glare and heat. **1.** Cover afforded by the interposition of some opaque or semi-opaque body between an object and light, heat, etc.; esp. the shelter from the sun afforded by trees; quasi-*concr.* (*sing.* and *pl.*) overshadowing foliage OE. **2.** A place sheltered from the sun; chiefly, a piece of ground overshadowed by trees. Now *rare* exc. in *collect. pl.*, with poetical colouring. OE. **b.** *transf.* A retired spot. Hence, a quiet habitation. Chiefly *pl.* Now *poet.* or *rhet.* 1605. **3.** Something which affords protection from light, heat, etc.; as a covering worn to protect the eye from light; a globe or cylinder of some semi-transparent substance placed over the flame of a candle, lamp, etc. to soften or diffuse the light; *U.S.* a window-blind; etc. 1624.

1. Vnder the s. of melancholly boughes SHAKS. Phr. *In the s.*, in a position screened from the direct action of the sun's rays; opp. to *in the sun*. **2. b.** In the depth of college shades..the poor student shrunk from observation LAMB. **3.** One shot broke the mirror over the chimney piece, another the s. of the clock KINGLAKE. The two customary candles were burning under their green shades HARDY. Hence **Sha·deful** *a.* (*rare*) abounding in s.; umbrageous.

Shade (ʃēⁱd), *v.* late ME. [f. prec.] **1.** *trans.* To screen from light or heat, to protect from the glare or heat of the sun's rays. †**b.** *transf.* To overshadow protectingly; to protect –1701. **c.** To cover with a screen, to protect (a light) from draughts 1827. **2.** To conceal from view; to hide partially, as by a shadow; to veil, obscure; to disguise 1530. **3.** To cover with shadow, to darken 1599. **b.** To appear like a shadow upon 1704. **4.** *Painting* and *Drawing.* To represent the shade or shadow on (an object); to furnish (a picture) with the indications of shade. In black-and-white or monochrome work: To furnish (a drawing) with the gradated dark markings indicating shade and colour of the object. Hence *occas.* to darken (parts of a diagram, etc.) in a similar manner. 1786. **5. a.** *intr.* Of a colour, hence *gen.*: To pass by imperceptible degrees *to* or *into* something else; also with *away, off* 1819. **b.** *trans.* To change or make to pass by imperceptible degrees *into* something else; also with *away, off* 1818. **c.** To modify the pitch of (an organ pipe) 1890.

1. The overhanging rock That shades the pool SHELLEY. **b.** Now good Angels..s. thy person Vnder their blessed wings SHAKS. **2.** A Seraph wing'd; six wings he wore, to s. His lineaments Divine MILT. **5. d.** *Commerce.* To make a slight or gradual reduction in (prices) 1898.

Shadeless (ʃēⁱ·dlės), *a.* 1814. [f. SHADE *sb.* + -LESS.] **1.** Lacking shade, without shelter (from heat, etc.). **2.** Affording no shade 1890. **3.** Not marked by shadows, unrelieved by shade 1835. Hence **Sha·delessness.**

Shading (ʃēⁱ·diŋ), *vbl. sb.* 1611. [f. SHADE *v.* + -ING¹.] The action of SHADE *v.* **1.** Protection from light or heat. **2.** Delineation of shade; a marking or colouring resembling this 1663. **3.** A minute variation or difference (of a colour, hence of a quality, species, etc.) 1775. **b.** *S.-off*: decrease in the intensity of a colour, or its passage *into* some other, by imperceptible gradations; also *fig.* of a quality, species, or the like 1858.

Shadoof (ʃădū·f). 1836. [Egyptian Arabic *šādūf*.] A contrivance used in the East for raising water for irrigation purposes, consisting of a rod or pole working upon a pivot, at one end of which is fastened a bucket and at the other a weight to serve as a counterpoise.

Shadow (ʃæ·doᵘ), *sb.* [ME. *sceadewe, shadewe*, repr. obl. forms, *scead(u)we*, of OE. *sćeadu* SHADE, corresp. to OS. *scado* (Du. *schaduw*), OHG. *scato* (G. *schatte*, later *schatten*), Goth. *skadus* :– Gmc. **skaðwaz*, **skaðwō* :– IE. **skotwós, -wā́* or **skatwós, -wā́*; cf. Gr. σκότος darkness.] **I. 1.** Comparative darkness, esp. that caused by interception of light; a tract of partial darkness produced by a body intercepting the direct rays of the sun or other luminary. **b.** *fig.* Gloom, unhappiness; a temporary interruption of friendship; something that obscures the lustre of a reputation; etc. 1855. **2.** *pl.* The darkness of night; the growing darkness after sunset. late ME. **3.** *Painting* and *Drawing.* = SHADE *sb.* I. 3 (now more usual) 1486.

1. The fronts of the ridges..remain in s. all the day TYNDALL. Phr. *S. of death*, a Biblical expression; in the O.T. = 'intense darkness'; and used chiefly to denote the gloom and horror of approaching dissolution. *The valley of the s. of death* (Ps. 23:4), often applied to the experience of being brought by illness apparently near to the grave. **b.** There never was a s. between us until this accursed affair began 1894.

II. Image cast by a body intercepting light. **1.** The dark figure which a body 'casts' or 'throws' upon a surface by intercepting the direct rays of the sun or other luminary; the image which this figure presents of the form of the intercepting body ME. **b.** As a type of what is fleeting or ephemeral ME. **2.** A reflected image ME. **3.** *fig.* **a.** An unreal appearance; a delusive semblance or image; a vain and unsubstantial object of pursuit. Often contrasted with *substance.* ME. †**b.** Applied rhet. to a portrait as contrasted with the original –1679. **c.** An obscure indication; a symbol, type; a prefiguration, foreshadowing. late ME. **d.** Something of opposite character that necessarily accompanies or follows something else, as shadow does light 1830. **e.** An imitation, copy; a counterpart 1693. **f.** Used to designate a person extremely emaciated or feeble 1588. **g.** An attenuated remnant 1450. **h.** A slight or faint appearance, a trace 1586. **4.** A spectral form, phantom. late ME. **5.** One that constantly accompanies or follows another like a shadow. **a.** A parasite, toady; also (= L. *umbra*) a companion whom a guest brings without invitation 1579. **b.** A spy or detective who follows a person in order to keep watch upon his movements 1859.

1. *fig.* Coming events cast their shadows before CAMPBELL. Phr. *To be afraid of one's own s.*, to be unreasonably timorous. *May your s. never grow (be) less!* may you keep on increasing (in prosperity)! [A Persian phrase.] **b.** Man..passes away Als a shadu on the somers day HAMPOLE. **2.** Such Mirrors..That you might see your s. SHAKS. **3.** What shadows we are, and what shadows we pursue BURKE. **b.** To your s., will I make true loue SHAKS. **c.** But all these were but fygures and shadowes of thynges to come 1526. **e.** The Roman Empire was the s. of the Popedom 1864. **f.** He appeared to wither into the s. of himself SCOTT. **g.** The prerogative of the Crown was reduced to a s. BROUGHAM. Phr. *S. of a name* = L. *nominis umbra*, a shadowy renown.

III. Shelter from light and heat. **1.** Protection from the sun; shade. Now *rare.* ME.

2. Overshadowing (of wings, etc.) as affording security; protection or shelter from danger or observation ME. †3. a. A handscreen; also, a parasol, sunshade –1623. b. A woman's headdress, or a portion of a headdress, projecting forward, so as to shade the face –1641. *Comb.*: **s.-boxing,** boxing against an imaginary opponent as a form of training; **s. cabinet,** a cabinet formed by Opposition leaders; **-land,** a place conceived as the abode of phantoms and ghosts, an imaginary land of spirits; **-photograph,** a picture taken by means of the Röntgen rays; hence **-photography; s.-test,** (*a*) a method of finding out by refraction whether an eye is myopic or hypermetropic; (*b*) a method of examining the outer side of an eye affected with cataract in its second stage. Hence **Sha·dowless** *a.* casting no s.; having no shadows on its surface; unsheltered from the sun.

Shadow (ʃæ·dou), *v.* [OE. *sćeadwian*, f. *sćeadu* SHADOW *sb.*] 1. *trans.* To protect or shelter (a person or thing) from the sun; to shade. Now *rare* or *Obs.* 2. = OVERSHADOW *v.* 2. Chiefly in Biblical use. *Obs.* exc. *poet.* with *over.* OE. †3. To screen, protect from attack; to be a security or protection to; to screen from blame or punishment, or from wrong –1704. 4. To cast a shadow upon, to cover or obscure with a shadow. late ME. b. *intr.* To cast a shadow. Now *rare.* late ME. †5. *trans.* To screen from view or knowledge; to keep dark, conceal –1608. 6. To represent by a shadow or imperfect image; to symbolize, typify, prefigure. Now chiefly with *forth, out.* 1575. †7. To paint the likeness of; to draw or paint (a picture) –1669. †8. To depict the shadows in (an object, a scene); to place the shadows in (a picture); to shade –1821. 9. *intr.* (Also *pass.*) To pass by degrees, shade off *to* or *into* a certain hue 1839. 10. To follow (a person) like a shadow; in mod. journalistic language said of a detective who dogs the steps of a person under surveillance 1602.

2. Let Thy dove S. me over, and my sins Be unremember'd TENNYSON. 3. This tree, So faire and great, that shadowed all the ground SPENSER. 5. *Macb.* v. iv. 5. 6. Augustus is still shadow'd in the Person of Æneas DRYDEN. 10. A Spanish Steamer shadowed by a British Cruiser 1899. Hence **Sha·dowed** *ppl. a.* furnished with or lying in shade; indicated obscurely, disguised. Hence **Sha·dower.**

Shadowgraph (ʃæ·dougrɑf), *sb.* 1888. [f. SHADOW *sb.* + -GRAPH.] 1. A picture formed by a shadow (usu., of the operator's hands) thrown upon a screen or other lighted surface. 2. A photograph taken by means of X-rays, a radiograph 1896. Hence **Shadowgraph** *v.*

Shadowing (ʃæ·douiŋ), *vbl. sb.* OE. [-ING¹.] The action of SHADOW *v.*: *esp.* 1. The position or distribution of shadow, in a visible object or scene; the placing of the shadows in a picture 1603. 2. An imperfect or obscure representation; a prefiguring or adumbration. Also with *forth.* 1642.

Shadowy (ʃæ·doui), *a.* late ME. [f. SHADOW *sb.* + -Y¹.] 1. Resembling or of the nature of a shadow; unsubstantial; fleeting; spectral; vague. †b. Symbolic, typical –1726. 2. a. Protected from the sun, shaded. late ME. b. Enveloped in shadow 1840. †c. Retired; hence, remote, inaccessible –1613. 3. Casting a shadow, affording shade 1607.

1. Thise shadewy transitorie dignitees CHAUCER. A silken robe of white, That s. in the moonlight shone COLERIDGE. A s. sail, silent and gray, Stole like a ghost across the bay HENLEY. b. Indeed the description is. . typicall and shadowie MILT. 2. a. S. lanes 1824. b. From the s. archway came a shining lantern 1876. 3. The s. palm 1796. Hence **Sha·dowi-ly** *adv.*, **-ness.**

Shady (ʃēⁱ·di), *a.* 1579. [f. SHADE *sb.* + -Y¹.] 1. Affording shade. 2. Shaded, protected by shade 1589. 3. †Opaque; also (now *poet.*), not luminous, dark 1605. 4. *colloq.* a. Of questionable merit or prospects of success; uncertain, unreliable 1848. b. Of a nature or character unable to bear the light; disreputable 1862.

1. The s. trees couer him with their shaddow *Job* 40:22. 2. Her angels face. . made a sunshine in the s. place SPENSER. Phr. (fig.) *On the s. side of,* older than (a specified age). 3. From dawning Day till s. Night 1746. 4. a. What looks very well one way may look very s. the other 1858. b. A rather s. attorney 1882. Hence **Sha·diness.**

Shafiite (ʃæ·fi,əit). 1838. [f. Arab. *šāfiʿī* + -ITE¹.] A member of one of the four sects or schools of the Sunnites or orthodox Moslems, named from the cognomen (*aš-šāfiʿī*) of their founder, Abu Abdullah Muhammad ibn Idris, 767–819.

Shaft (ʃɑft), *sb.*¹ [OE. *sćæft, sćeaft* = OFris. *sceft*, OS., OHG. *scaft* (Du., G. *schaft*), ON. *skaft*, :- Gmc. **skaftaz, -am, -iz*, perh. rel. to L. *scapus* shaft, Gr. σκᾶπτον staff, σκῆπτρον SCEPTRE.] 1. The long slender rod forming the body of a lance or spear, or of an arrow. Also of a staff, harpoon, etc. b. A spear or lance. Now *arch.* OE. 2. An arrow. *Cloth-yard s.*: see CLOTH-YARD. late ME. b. *loosely.* A missile. *rhet.* 1786. c. *transf.* A beam or ray (of light, etc.), a streak of lightning, etc. Chiefly *poet.* late ME. 3. A pole, flagstaff; *spec.* †a maypole. *rare.* OE. 4. A stem, a columnar or straight portion of something. a. The stem or trunk of a tree. Now *rare.* late ME. b. In scientific uses. (*a*) The main stem or scape of a feather 1748. (*b*) The part of a hair between the root and the point 1851. (*c*) *Anat.* The middle portion of a long bone 1835. (*d*) *Ent.* The scape of an antenna or of a halter. c. The part of a candlestick which supports the branches. late ME. d. The part of a chimney between the base and the cornice 1450. e. *Arch.* The body of a column or pillar between the base and the capital 1483. f. The upright part of a cross; *esp.* the part between the arms and the base 1781. g. The long straight handle of a tool, etc.; the shank of an anchor; the stem of a pipe; †the stalk or foot of a goblet or wine-glass 1530. 5. a. *Arch.* A slender column, *esp.* one of the small columns which are clustered round pillars, or used in the jambs of doors or windows, in arcades and the like 1835. b. *U.S.* An obelisk or column erected as a memorial 1847. 6. a. One of the long bars, between a pair of which a horse is harnessed to a vehicle; a thill 1613. b. Either of the two side-pieces of a ladder 1888. 7. *Mech.* A long cylindrical rotating rod upon which are fixed the parts for the transmission of motive power in a machine; also, a separable portion of a line of shafting 1688. 8. *Weaving.* Each of a pair of long laths between which the heddles are stretched; also applied to the pair taken together 1801.

1. b. Hyperion's march they spy, and glitt'ring shafts of war GRAY. 2. The air was darkened by the shafts from the hosts of English archers 1854. *fig.* Shafts Of gentle satire. ., That harm'd not TENNYSON. 5. b. The gray s. that commemorated the Morristown dead of the last civil war 1873.

Shaft (ʃɑft), *sb.*² late ME. [– MLG. (whence (M)HG.) *schacht*, prob. spec. application of SHAFT *sb.*¹, as if the vertical channel were compared to the leg (*schaft*) of a boot.] 1. A vertical or slightly inclined well-like excavation made in mining, tunnelling, etc., as a means of access to underground workings, for hoisting out materials, testing the subsoil, ventilation, etc. 2. *transf.* Applied to other well-like excavations, or passages 1820. Hence **Sha·fting**², the sinking of a s.; the shafts of a mine collectively.

Shaft (ʃɑft), *v.* 1611. [f. SHAFT *sb.*¹] 1. *trans.* To fit (an arrow-head, a weapon or tool) with a shaft. 2. To propel (a barge, etc.) with a pole 1869.

Shafted (ʃɑ·ftėd), *a.* 1586. [f. SHAFT *sb.*¹ + -ED².] Having or furnished with a shaft or shafts. a. *Her.* Of a spear, arrow, etc.: Having the shaft of a specified tincture. b. Furnished with a shaft or handle 1641. c. *Arch.* Ornamented with or resting upon shafts 1801.

c. Hence proceeded the pointed arches, the s. columns 1801.

Shafting¹ (ʃɑ·ftiŋ). 1825. [f. SHAFT *sb.*¹ + -ING¹.] 1. A system of connected shafts for communicating motion from the prime mover to the machinery. Also, material from which to cut lengths of shafts. 2. Shafts or ornamental columns 1868.

Sha·ftment. *Obs.* exc. *dial.* [OE. *sćeaftmund*, f. *sćeaft* SHAFT *sb.*¹ + *mund* hand, hand-breadth.] The distance from the end of the extended thumb to the opposite side of the hand, used as a measure, = about 6 inches.

Shafty (ʃɑ·fti), *a.* 1891. [f. SHAFT *sb.*¹ (sense 8) + -Y¹.] Of wool: Having a long, close, strong staple.

Shag (ʃæg), *sb.*¹ [Late OE. *sćeacga* (once), rel. to ON. *skegg* beard (:- **skaȝjam*), OE. *sćeaga* coppice, SHAW.] 1. Rough matted hair, wool, etc. *rare* or *arch.* b. A mass of matted hair; also shreds (of bark) 1607. c. The nap (esp. long and coarse) of cloth 1661. d. A (tangled) mass of shrubs, trees, foliage, etc. 1836. e. *fig.* Roughness, brutality of manner 1784. 2. A cloth having a velvet nap on one side, usu. of worsted, but sometimes of silk. Also, a kind or variety of this. 1592. †3. A garment, rug, or mat of shaggy material –1854. 4. (In full *s. tobacco.*) A strong tobacco cut into fine shreds 1789.

1. d. Dark shags of ling BLACKMORE. e. Ability to smooth The s. of savage nature COWPER.

Shag (ʃæg), *sb.*² 1566. [perh. a use of prec., with ref. to the 'shaggy' crest.] A cormorant, esp. the crested cormorant, *Phalacrocorax graculus*, which in the breeding season has a crest of long curly plumes.

Shag (ʃæg), *a.* Now *rare* or *arch.* 1592. [From attrib. use of SHAG *sb.*¹] 1. Having shaggy hair. †2. Of hair, a mane, etc.; Long and rough, shaggy –1647.

1. Round hooft, short ioynted, fetlocks s., and long SHAKS. So **Shag-haired** *a.* (*arch.*) having shaggy hair 1577.

Shag (ʃæg), *v.* 1596. [f. SHAG *sb.*¹] †1. *intr.* To be shaggy; to hang down in a shaggy manner (*rare*) –1801. 2. *trans.* To render rough or shaggy, *esp.* the surface of the earth, a rock, etc. (*with* a growth of trees, etc.) 1612.

2. Caverns shag'd with horrid shades MILT.

Shagbark (ʃæ·gbāɪk). *W. Ind.* and *U.S.* 1691. [f. SHAG *a.* + BARK *sb.*¹] 1. *W. Ind.* A W. Indian tree *Pithecolobium micradenium.* 2. *U.S.* A variety of HICKORY; also the wood or the nut of this tree 1751.

Shagged (ʃægd, ʃæ·gėd), *a.* Now *rare.* [Late OE. *sćeacgede* (twice); superseded by next. See SHAG *sb.*¹, -ED².] 1. Having or covered with shaggy hair, rough with hair. Chiefly said of animals. †2. Of textile fabrics, garments: Having a rough or long nap –1691. b. *transf.* Of a hill-side, etc.: Covered with scrub, trees, or some rough or shaggy growth 1820. c. Jagged; having a rough, uneven surface 1589. 3. Of hair, etc.: Long and rough; shaggy 1587.

Shaggy (ʃæ·gi), *a.* 1590. [f. SHAG *sb.*¹ + -Y¹.] 1. Covered with or having long coarse or bushy hair. Of persons: Unkempt. b. *Phys., Path.*, etc. Bristling with hair-like processes 1799. c. *transf.* = prec. 2 b. 1591. d. Having a rough surface 1693. 2. Of hair, etc.: Rough, coarse, tangled 1638. b. *transf.* Of a wood, trees, etc.: Resembling a rough growth of hair 1789.

1. A mounted shepherd on his wild and s. horse 1882. 2. b. Land of brown heath and s. wood SCOTT. Hence **Sha·ggi-ly** *adv.*, **-ness.**

Sha·g-rag, *a.* and *sb.* 1590. [Jingling alteration of SHAKE-RAG.] A. *adj.* Ragged, rascally; shaggy, unkempt. B. *sb.* A ragged, disreputable person; a rascally fellow 1611.

Shagreen (ʃăgrī·n). 1677. [var. of CHAGRIN *sb.*] A species of untanned leather with a rough granular surface, prepared from the skin of the horse, ass, etc., or of the shark, seal, etc., and frequently dyed green. Also, an imitation of this. b. The skin of various sharks, rays, etc., which is covered with close-set calcified papillæ, forming a hard rough surface; used for polishing, etc. 1870. Hence **Shagree·ned** *a.* having a roughened surface or appearance like s.; covered with s.

Shah (ʃā). 1564. [– Pers. *šāh*, shortened from OPers. *ḵšāyṯiya* king, allied to Skr. *kšatra* dominion, Gr. κτάομαι acquire, get.] A Persian title equivalent to 'king'; in Europe the usual designation of the monarch of Persia, the PADISHAH.

‖**Shaheen** (ʃahī·n). 1839. [Urdu, – Pers. *šāhīn*, lit. royal (bird), f. prec.] An Indian falcon, *Falco peregrinator* and other species.

‖**Shahi** (ʃā·i). 1566. [Pers. *šāhī* royal, f. SHAH.] Formerly a small silver, now a small copper, coin of Persia.

‖**Shahzadah** (ʃāzā·dā). 1662. [Pers., f. *šāh* king + *zādeh* child.] The son of the Shah; a king's son.

‖**Shaitan** (ʃēⁱtā·n). 1638. [– Arab. *šayṭān* –

Heb. *śāṭān* SATAN.] **1.** The Devil, Satan; an evil spirit. **2.** *transf.* An evil-disposed or vicious person or animal 1834. **3.** A dust-storm 1900.

Shake (ʃēik), *sb.* 1565. [f. next.] **I.** The action or an act of shaking. **1.** An act of shaking a person or thing 1581. **b.** (Usu. in full *a s. of the hand.*) An act of shaking hands or a person's hand, a handshake 1712. **c.** *S. of the head*: see SHAKE *v.* III. 2. 1713. **d.** An act of shaking oneself 1712. **e.** *colloq.* or *slang.* As the type of instantaneous action, esp. in the phr. *in a s.*, *in a brace* or *couple of shakes* 1816. **2.** Irregular vibratory or tremulous movement, esp. as the result of impact or disturbance of equilibrium; irregular lateral movement (of something revolving or moving in a line). *Naut.* A fluttering or shivering (of a sail). 1665. **b.** The shock of an earthquake. Now only *U.S.* 1622. **3.** A shivering or trembling of the body or limbs; also, a state of tremor. *The shakes*, nervous agitation caused by fear or horror. 1624. **b.** An attack of a shaking disease 1782. **c.** A tremor (in the voice) 1859. **4.** *Mus.* A regular and rapid alternation of a note with the note above 1659. **5.** A concussion or blow which impairs the stability of something; often *fig.* a damaging blow (e.g. to an institution, a person's health); a shock (to the mind or nerves) 1565.

1. b. Our Salutations..consisting of many kind Shakes of the Hand ADDISON. **e.** He'll be up at the church in a couple of shakes BARHAM. **3. b.** The Dismal Swamp is a first-rate place for concealment, if you are not afraid of shakes and agues 1867. Phr. *To be no great shakes*, to be nothing extraordinary in ability or importance. *S. out* (Stock Exchange), a crisis in which the weaker speculators are driven out of the market. *S. up*, a rousing up to activity.

II. Something produced by shaking. **1.** A natural cleft or fissure produced during growth or formation 1651. **2.** *U.S.* pl. **a.** A set of barrel staves 1820. **b.** Pieces of split timber, a kind of shingles 1845. **3.** *Printing.* A slur 1888.

1. *Water s.*, a cleft in a rock into which a stream empties itself.

Shake (ʃēik), *v.* Pa. t. **shook** (ʃuk); pa. pple. **shaken** (ʃēi·k'n). [OE. *sć(e)acan* = OS. *skakan*, ON. *skaka* :- Gmc. **skakan.*] †**I.** *intr.* A poet. word for: To go, pass, move, journey; to flee, depart –1500.

II. To vibrate irregularly. **1.** Of things having freedom of movement: To move irregularly and quickly to and fro, up and down, or from side to side; to quiver, quake, vibrate, waver OE. **2.** Of a thing normally stable or still: To vibrate irregularly, tremble, either as a whole or in its parts, as the result of impact or disturbance of equilibrium. Hence, to totter, lose stability, become weakened. ME. **b.** Of a band of persons: To become unsteady, to reel, give way. late ME. **3.** Of a person, his body, limbs, etc.: To quake or tremble with physical infirmity or disease; to quiver with emotion; to shiver with cold, to quake with fear ME. **b.** To be convulsed with laughter 1728.

1. The mighty pine-forests which s. In the wind 1872. **2.** We felt the good ship s. and reel TENNYSON. **3.** Her small frame shook with weeping 1909. Phr. *To s. in one's shoes*, to tremble with fear.

III. To cause to vibrate, agitate. **1.** *trans.* To brandish or flourish threateningly (a weapon or something used as a weapon); †to wield. Also, to flourish, wave (something) in ostentation or triumph. OE. **2.** To move to and fro irregularly or tremulously, agitate (some part of the body); (of a bird) to flap, flutter (its wings) esp. as preparing to fly. Also said of a thing personified. late ME. **b.** *refl.* Of a person or animal: To give a shake to his or its body (e.g. in order to throw off wet, snow, dust, etc., or to remove the stiffness caused by repose); *fig.* to bestir oneself. late ME. **3.** *trans.* To cause to move irregularly to and fro by external force; to make to flutter or quiver; to agitate. *Naut.* To cause (a sail) to flutter in the wind. OE. **b.** With additional notion of a purpose of dislodging or discharging something adhering or contained. late ME. **4.** To grasp or seize and move (a person) roughly to and fro ME. **b.** Of an animal: To worry (its antagonist or prey) 1565. **5.** To clasp and move to and fro (another person's hand) as a customary salutation or an expression of friendly feeling 1535. **b.** *absol. To s.* = to shake hands. In mod. use *U.S. slang* (chiefly *imper.*). 1601. **6.** To put into a quaking, quivering, or vibrating motion (a thing normally firm or fixed); to cause (a structure) to totter; hence, to impair the stability of. *To s. down*, to cause to totter and fall. OE. **7.** Of physical infirmity, emotion, etc.: To cause (a person, his frame, etc.) to quiver or tremble; to agitate, convulse. late ME. **b.** To disturb, upset 1567. **c.** To cause (a person, his sides) to quiver with laughter or mirth. Also, *to s. one's sides*, to be convulsed with laughter. 1593. **8.** With adv. or phr.: To reduce by shaking to a specified condition. late ME. **9.** To dislodge or get rid of (something, a person's hold, etc.) by shaking one's body, limbs, clothes, etc. Const. *from*, *off*; also with adv. ME. **10.** To dislodge or eject by shaking the receptacle or support 1500. **11.** To distribute with a shake, to scatter, sprinkle. Also with *forth*, *down*. late ME. **b.** To cast (dice) usu. with a preliminary shake; also with personal object, to 'throw' against (a person) *for* whatever is staked 1570. **12. a.** *refl.* and *intr.* Of timber: To split or crack 1679. **b.** *trans.* To separate the staves of (a cask) 1867. **13.** *Mus.* To accompany or execute with a shake; also *absol.* or *intr.* to execute a shake 1611.

1. And over them triumphant Death his Dart Shook, but delaid to strike MILT. **2.** Rattlesnakes ..swiftly vibrating and shaking their tailes EVELYN. Shaking wide thy yellow hair SHELLEY. Phr. *To s. one's head*, to turn the head slightly to one side and the other in sorrow or scorn, or to express disapproval, dissent, or doubt. *To s. one's ears* (fig.), to bestir oneself; also, to show indifference or dislike, pleasure in freedom, mirth, etc. *To s. one's elbow*, to gamble with dice. *To s. a foot, leg, toe, one's bones*, etc. = to dance. **b.** Just s. yourself sober and listen, will you? GEO. ELIOT. **3.** Went ye out to se a rede shaken with the wynde? TINDALE *Matt.* 11:7. **b.** S. the table clothe or you laye it on agayne 1530. Ere our comming see thou s. the bags Of hoording Abbots SHAKS. **4.** He hath also taken me by my necke, and shaken me to pieces *Job* 16:12. Though he s. thee something roughly by the shoulders, to awake thee SCOTT. **5.** *To s. hands* (said of two persons mutually saluting thus); We shoke handes, and parted 1546. Now we have shaken hands on the bargain 1908. *To s. hands with* (another); I have long since shook hands with the world WESLEY. **6.** Age shakes Athena's tower, but spares gray Marathon BYRON. *fig.* That no compunctious visitings of Nature S. my fell purpose SHAKS. Too much shaken in mind and body to compose a letter THACKERAY. An attempt was made to s. the dominion which he had established over Wessex 1871. **7.** A sudden fit of ague shook him GRAY. **8.** *To s. down*, to cause to settle or subside by shaking. *To s. together*, to shake so as to ensure intimate mixture or subsidence into smaller compass. *To s. down* (intr. for refl.), to find temporary accommodation, esp. with ref. to sleeping, to occupy a 'shakedown'. *To s. down into*, to accommodate oneself to (circumstances, a condition, position, etc.). *To s. together*, (of a company of persons) to mix, get on friendly terms with each other. **9.** Vile thing let loose, Or I will s. thee from me like a serpent SHAKS. Phr. *To s. the dust from* or *off one's feet*, lit. in Gospel passages hence *allus.* to take one's departure from an uncongenial place. **10.** Macbeth Is ripe for shaking SHAKS. **11.** S. down plenty of straw in the great barn SCOTT.

With advs. **S. off. a.** To cast off or get rid of with a shake or an effort. **b.** To get rid of (a person); to draw away from (a competitor in a race). **c.** *Naut.* To unfasten (a sail). **S. out. a.** To cast out or remove with a shake. **b.** To unfasten or unfurl and let out with a shake (a flag, sail); to straighten out by shaking (something crumpled or folded). **S. up. a.** To shake together for the purpose of combining or mixing; to shake (a liquid) so as to stir up the sediment. **b.** To rouse up with or as with a shake. **c.** To loosen (bedding, etc.) by shaking. †**d.** To rate soundly. Also, to harass, afflict. Also as *sb.*

Sha·ke-down. 1730. **1.** A bed made upon straw loosely disposed upon the floor; hence, any makeshift bed, esp. one on the floor. **2.** An act of shaking down 1878. **b.** *U.S.* A forced contribution; an exaction 1903.

Sha·kefork. Now *dial.* ME. [f. SHAKE *v.*] A wooden fork with two tines or prongs used by threshers to shake and remove the straw from the grain; also, a pitchfork.

Shaken (ʃēi·k'n), *ppl. a.* 1523. [pa. pple. of SHAKE *v.*] **1.** Put into a quick or violent alternating motion; (of seed, etc.) sprinkled 1725. **2.** Moved abruptly or violently with a blow or shock: hence, weakened in structure 1614. **3.** Of a cask: Taken to pieces and bound up in a compact form for transport 1557. **4.** Of timber: Cracked or split defectively 1523.

2. *transf.* This our s. Monarchy, that now lies labouring under her throwes MILT.

Shaker (ʃēi·kəɹ). 1440. [f. SHAKE *v.* + -ER[1].] **1.** One who or something which shakes. **2.** †**a.** In the 17th c. applied to various sectaries whose devotional exercises were accompanied by 'shaking' or convulsions; often used as = 'Quaker' –1694. **b.** One of an American religious sect (calling itself 'The Society of Believers in Christ's Second Appearing'), which exists in the form of mixed communities of men and women living in celibacy 1784. **3.** In full, *s. pigeon*: The fantail pigeon 1668. **4.** An implement, machine, etc. used for shaking 1791. Hence **Sha·keress**, a female S. **Sha·kerism**, the principles and practice of the Shakers.

Sha·ke-rag. 1571. [f. SHAKE *v.* + RAG; see SHACK *sb.*[2]] A ragged disreputable person; also *attrib.* or *adj.*, beggarly.

Shakespearian (ʃēikspīə·riăn), *a.* (and *sb.*) Also **Shaksperian, -ean.** [f. *Shakespeare* + -IAN.] **A.** *adj* Of or pertaining to, or having the characteristics of William Shakespeare (1564–1616) or his dramatic and poetical productions. **B.** *sb.* An authority on or student of the writings of Shakespeare; a Shakespearian scholar 1837.

Hence **Shakespea·rianism,** (*a*) a form of expression peculiar to or imitated from Shakespeare; (*b*) the imitation of Shakespeare or the effects of his influence.

Shaking (ʃēi·kiŋ), *vbl. sb.* late ME. [-ING[1].] **1.** The action of SHAKE *v.* **2.** A disease in sheep and swine. Also the ague. Chiefly in *pl.* 1642. **3.** *concr.* That which is shaken off, out, down, etc.; esp. *Naut. pl.*, refuse of cordage, canvas, etc. late ME.

Shako (ʃæ·kou). 1815. [– Fr. *schako* – Magyar *csákó*, short for *csákó(s) süveg* peaked cap (*csákos*, f. *csák* peak – G. *zacken* point, spike).] A military cap in the shape of a truncated cone, with a peak and either a plume or a ball or 'pompom'.

Shaky (ʃēi·ki), *a.* Also **shakey.** 1703. [f. SHAKE *v.* or *sb.* + -Y[1].] **1.** Of timber: Fissured. **2.** Of a structure: Given to shaking by the looseness of its parts; liable to break down or give way; unsound. Of ground: Not firm or solid. 1850. **3.** Of a person or his limbs: Trembling with age, infirmity, apprehension, or fear 1850. **b.** Of writing: Tremulous 1848. **4.** In immaterial sense. **a.** Of a person's credit, position, securities, etc.: Insecure, unreliable 1841. **b.** Uncertain, not to be depended on 1860. **c.** Not completely sound in health 1844. **d.** Unsettled in allegiance or belief 1853.

1. Some of the pines..were s. 1868. **2.** The bridge was so frail and s. 1860. **3. b.** A s., clerk-like hand THACKERAY. **4. a.** His seat in Parliament was s. 1908. **b.** He is s. in his spelling 1889. **c.** I am rather s. just now DICKENS. Hence **Sha·ki-ly** *adv.*, **-ness.**

Shale (ʃēil), *sb.*[1] *Obs.* exc. *dial.* [OE. *scealu* shell, husk, rel. to ON. *skál* SCALE *sb.*[1]] †**1.** A shell, husk, esp. the shell of a nut –1668. **2.** A scale (of a fish, of metal, of a scaly disease, etc.). late ME.

Shale (ʃēil), *sb.*[2] 1747. [prob. – G. *schale* (not used in this sense, but cf. *schalstein* laminated limestone, *schal-gebirge* mountain system of thin strata) = OE. *sć(e)alu*; see prec., SCALE *sb.*[1]] An argillaceous fissile rock, the laminæ of which are usu. fragile and uneven, and mostly parallel to the bedding; often overlying a coal formation. **b.** A variety or specimen of this rock 1830.

Comb.: **s.-naptha, -oil,** naphtha and oil obtained by the destructive distillation of bituminous shale; **-tar,** tar derived from bituminous shale.

Shale (ʃēil), *v. Obs.* exc. *dial.* late ME. [f. SHALE *sb.*[1]] †**1.** *trans.* To free from the shell or husk; to remove, take *off* (the shell or husk) from a nut, bean, fruit, etc.; to decorticate (hemp) –1693. **2.** *intr.* Of grain, seed, etc.: To drop out 1578.

Shall (ʃæl), *sb.* 1553. [f. next.] **1.** An utterance of the word 'shall'; a command, promise, or determination. **2.** The word 'shall' as idiomatically used in contradistinction to 'will' 1837.

1. The external *shalls* and *shall nots* of the law M. ARNOLD. 2. Perhaps no Scot ever yet mastered his 'shalls' and 'wills' 1891.

Shall (ʃæl, *unstressed* ʃəl, ʃ'l), *v.* Pa. t. **should** (ʃud, ʃəd). [Gmc. perfect-present verb, orig. meaning †I owe, (hence) †I ought, must, am to, passing thence into a tense-sign of the future and a mark of contingency. OE. pr. tense *sćeal* (pl. *sćulon*, pa. t. *sćeolde* should) = OFris. *skel*, OS. *skal*, OHG. *scal* (Du. *zal*, G. *soll*), ON., Goth. *skal*; f. Gmc. (**skel-*) **skal-* **skul-* owe :– IE. **skel-* **skol-* **skl̥-*.] †**I.** *trans.* To owe (money, allegiance). –late ME.

And by that feyth I shal to god and yow CHAUCER.

II. Followed by an infinitive (without *to*). **The present tense* **shall.** †**1.** In general statements of what is right or becoming: = 'ought' –1562. †**2.** In OE. and ME. = 'must', 'must needs'; later, in stating a necessary condition: = 'will have to', 'must' (if something else is to happen) –1818. †**3.** Indicating what is appointed or settled to take place = the mod. 'is to', 'am to', etc. –1625. **4.** In commands or instructions, equiv. to imper. OE. **5.** In the second and third persons, expressing the speaker's determination to bring about (or, with neg., to prevent) some action, event, or state of things in the future, or (occas.) to refrain from hindering what is otherwise certain to take place, or is intended by another person OE. **6.** In special interrogative uses related to the senses 4 and 5. **a.** In the first person, used in questions to which the expected answer is a command, direction, or counsel, or a resolve on the speaker's own part OE. **b.** Similarly in the third person, where the subject represents or includes the speaker 1610. **c.** In the second and third person, where the expected answer is a decision on the part of the speaker or of some person other than the subject ME. **d.** In indirect question OE. **7.** As a mere auxiliary, forming (with present infinitive) the future, and (with perfect infinitive) the future perfect tense. **a.** Used, in all persons, for prophetic or oracular announcements of the future, and for solemn assertions of the certainty of a future event OE. **b.** In the first person, used as the normal auxiliary for expressing mere futurity. (*a*) Of events conceived as independent of the speaker's volition. (To use *will* in these cases is now a mark of Scottish, Irish, provincial, or extra-British idiom.) ME. (*b*) Of voluntary action or its intended result. Here *I* (*we*) *shall* is always admissible exc. where the notion of a present (as dist. from a previous) decision or consent is to be expressed (in which case *will* must be used). Further, *I shall* often expresses a determination insisted on in spite of opposition, and *I shall not* (colloq. *I shan't*) a peremptory refusal. ME. **c.** In the second person, *shall* as a mere future auxiliary is normal only in categorical questions; e.g. '*Shall* you miss your train? I am afraid you will.' **d.** In the third person. *Obs.* (repl. by *will*) exc. when another's statement or expectation respecting himself is reported in the third person, e.g. 'He says he shall not have time to write' (though here also *will* is probably more frequent) ME. †**e.** In neg. (or virtually neg.) and interrog. use, *shall* often = 'will be able to' –1773. **f.** Used in statements of a result to be expected from some action or occurrence. Now usu. (exc. in the first person) repl. by *will*; but *shall* survives in literary use. ME. **g.** In clause expressing the object of a promise, or of an expectation accompanied by hope or fear. Now only where *shall* is the ordinary future auxiliary. 1475. **8.** In the idiomatic use of the future to denote what ordinarily or occasionally occurs under specified conditions, *shall* was formerly the usual auxiliary. In the second and third persons, ordinary language now substitutes *will* or *may*. OE. **9.** In hypothetical, relative, and temporal clauses denoting a future contingency, the future auxiliary is *shall* for all persons alike ME. **10.** In clauses expressing the purposed result of some action, or the object of a desire, intention, command, or request. (Often replaceable by *may*.) ME.

2. You s. seeke all day ere you finde them SHAKS. 3. Arte thou he that s. come? TINDALE *Luke* 7:19. 4. Thow shalt not tak the name of the Lord thi God in veyn WYCLIF *Exod.* 20:7. Your Grace s. pardon me, I will not backe SHAKS. Scandalous persons shal be kept from the Sacrament 1645. 5. And syker assuraunce and borowes ye shal haue MALORY. Verona s. not hold thee SHAKS. 6. a. O Cuckoo! s. I call thee Bird, Or but a wandering Voice? WORDSW. 'It's rather slow work', said he, 'down here; what s. we do?' THACKERAY. b. O where now s. a man trust? 1871. c. What s. he haue that kild the Deare? SHAKS. d. Let her say what shall be done with it 1865. 7. a. Now do I Prophesie..A Curse s. light vpon the limbes of men SHAKS. b. (*a*) When s. we three meet againe? SHAKS. (*b*) I..s. let my wife and daughters know, that I will be master of my own house 1779. e. If I draw forward, and others draw backwards, what s. it avail? 1565. f. ȝif ony thing falle in to that Lake, it schalle nevere comen up aȝen MANDEV. g. I hope his visits shall not be intruded upon me FIELDING. 8. He was as handsome a man, as you s. see on a summer's day 1760. One man s. approve..the same thing that another man s. condemn 1793. 9. If you s. fail to understand What England is..On you will come the curse of all the land TENNYSON. We extend our sympathies..to the unborn generations which..s. follow us on this earth 1874. When War's loud shuttle shall have woven peace 1896. 10. I'll take you five children from London, who shall cuff five Highland children JOHNSON. Mr. Mill recommends that all males of mature age..s. have votes MACAULAY.

***The past tense* **should** *with temporal function.* †**11.** Expressing a former obligation or necessity: = 'was bound to', 'had to' –late ME. †**12.** = 'was to', or (contextually) 'was about to' –1622. **13.** Used in indirect reported utterances, or other statements relating to past time, where *shall* would be used if the time referred to were present OE. **14.** Forming with the inf. a substitute for the pa. t. indic. (or, with perf. inf., for the pluperf.) in the oblique report of another's statement in order to imply that the speaker does not commit himself to the truth of the alleged fact. *Obs.* exc. *dial.* OE. **15.** In indirect question relating to a past matter of fact. (The pa. t. or perf. is now preferred.) *Obs.* exc. *arch.* ME. **16.** In questions introduced by *who, whom, what*, and followed by *but*, serving to express the unexpectedness of some past occurrence 1626.

13. 'Tis commanded I should do so SHAKS. I thought I never should have got out 1846. Clancarty was pardoned on condition that he should leave the kingdom MACAULAY. He had wished that the doctor should inquire into the cause of his trouble 1861. 15. The Assembly were wondering what should be the meaning of it 1704. 16. Just as he said this, what should hap At the chamber door but a gentle tap? BROWNING.

****The past tense* **should** *with modal function.* **17.** In statements of duty, obligation, or propriety (orig., as applicable to hypothetical conditions not regarded as real) OE. **b.** *Should be*: ought according to appearances to be, presumably is 1605. **c.** *You should hear, see* = I wish you could hear, etc. 1842. **18.** In the apodosis of a hypothetical proposition (expressed or implied), indicating that the supposition, and therefore its consequence, is unreal. **a.** Where *shall* (in senses II. 4, 5, 6, 7, or 8) would be used if the hypothesis were accepted OE. **b.** When the pres. tense of the principal verb would be used if the hypothesis were accepted. late ME. **c.** With vbs. of liking, preference, etc., *should* in the first person (and interrogatively in the second) is regarded as more correct than *would* 1779. **d.** The original conditional notion is obscured in the phr. *It should seem.* So *I should think*, (*suppose*, etc.) = 'I am inclined to think (suppose, etc.)'; also *colloq.* as a strong affirmation. late ME. **e.** *I should* (*do* so and so): orig. with expressed or understood protasis 'if I were you', but now often used loosely = 'I would advise you to (do, etc.)' 1908. **19.** In a hypothetical clause expressing a rejected supposition ME. **20.** In a hypothetical clause relating to the future, *should* takes the place of *shall*, or of the equivalent use of the present tense, when the supposition, though entertained as possible, is viewed as less likely or less welcome than some alternative. (With future, future perf., or imper. in the apodosis.) 1675. **21.** In a noun-clause (normally introduced by *that*). **a.** In dependence on expressions of will, desire, etc. ME. **b.** In statements relating to the necessity, propriety, etc. of something contemplated as future, or as an abstract supposition 1527. **c.** In expressions of surprise or its absence, approval or disapproval, of some present or past fact ME. **d.** In clause dependent on sentence expressing possibility, probability, or expectation 1600. **e.** In clause expressing the object of fear or precaution. late ME. **22.** In special interrogative uses. **a.** In questions introduced by *why* (or equivalent word), implying the speaker's inability to conceive any reason for something actual or contemplated, or any ground for believing something to be fact OE. **b.** In questions introduced by *how*, implying that the speaker regards something as impossible or inadmissible ME.

17. Some men should have been women, and he, I think, is one 1756. *Prov. phr.* That same Lord Stewkly is no better than he should be 1764. 18. a. I often think we should all be better without it THACKERAY. b. I shouldn't know how to begin 1882. c. I should like to have stayed longer at Noyon 1869. d. I should rather think he has a mind to finger its finances 1775. 19. Pope writing dialogue resembled..a wolf, which, instead of biting, should take to kicking MACAULAY. Phr. *As who should say* [cf. Fr. *comme qui dirait*] = as much as to say (*arch.*). 20. Should any soluble salt remain it will be soda 1846. 21. a. Chantrey..wishes I should sit to Bartolini 1819. b. It is time..That old hysterical mock-disease should die TENNYSON. e. However, lest conversation should lag, I'll give it you BORROW. 22. a. Men have one common original, and why should relations quarrel? 1779. b. How *should* you understand what is so little intelligible? MISS BURNEY.

III. Elliptical and quasi-elliptical uses. **23.** = 'shall go'. *arch.* OE. **24.** With ellipsis of active infinitive to be supplied from the context OE. **25.** The place of the inf. is sometimes supplied by *that* or *so* placed at the beginning of the sentence ME. †**26.** With ellipsis of *be* or passive inf., or with *so* in place of this (where the preceding context has *is, was*, etc.] –1749.

23. If the bottome were as deepe as hell, I shold down SHAKS. Thou shalt with me to Iona SCOTT. 24. This would vex me, but it s. not SWIFT. I knew..That she was uttering what she shouldn't 1872. 25. That s. I not said sir Dynadan MALORY. 26. He is not yet executed, nor I hear not when he s. 1615.

Shalloon (ʃălū·n). 1678. [– (O)Fr. *chalon*: see CHALON.] **1.** A closely woven woollen material chiefly used for linings. **b.** A wig-tie made of shalloon 1845. **2.** *attrib.* or *adj.* Made of s. 1665.

Shallop (ʃæ·ləp), †**shalloop.** 1578. [– Fr. *chaloupe* – Du. *sloep* SLOOP.] **1.** A large heavy boat fitted with one or more masts and carrying fore-and-aft or lug sails and sometimes furnished with guns; a sloop. **2.** A dinghy 1590.

1. A double S., well mann'd, with two guns 1666.

Shallot, shalot (ʃălǫ·t). 1664. [aphet. f. ESCHALOT. The spelling *shallot* is now usual.] A small onion, *Allium ascalonicum*, native to Syria and cultivated for use in flavouring salads, sauces, etc.

Shallow (ʃæ·lo^u), *a.* and *sb.* late ME. [Obscurely rel. to synon. OE. *sćeald*, ME. *schald*; see SHOAL *a.*] **A.** *adj.* **1.** Not deep; having little extension in a downward direction: said e.g. of water, of a dish, of a depression in the ground. **b.** Of the soil of agricultural land: Forming only a thin stratum over rock 1733. **2.** Extending only a short distance inward from the surface or from the front towards the back. Of a lens: Having slight convexity or concavity. 1545. **3.** *fig.* Of thought, reasoning, observation, knowledge, or feeling: Lacking depth, superficial 1586. **b.** Qualifying an agent-noun, or said of a person with ref. to knowledge, etc. 1601. **c.** Of persons and their attributes: Wanting in depth of mind, feeling, or character 1593. **4.** quasi-*adv.* To or at a slight depth 1662.

1. The River in Summer time is very ebbe and s.

1610. **b.** Poor light s. land 1760. **2.** A s. bow-window 1886. **3.** That were but s. policy SMOLLETT. **b.** O how hard it is to be s. enough for a polite audience! WESLEY. **c.** Out, idle words, servants to s. fools! SHAKS.

B. *sb.* **1.** A shallow part of a piece of water, of the sea, of a lake or river; shallow water; a shallow place (often *pl.*) 1571. **2.** A costermonger's barrow 1859.

1. By whose cunning guide We found the shalow of this Riuer Some 1596. *fig.* All the voyage of their life Is bound in Shallowes, and in Miseries SHAKS. Hence **Sha·llow-ly** *adv.*, **-ness.**

Shallow (ʃæ·lo^u), *v.* 1510. [f. SHALLOW *a.*] To make or become shallow.

†**Shallow-brained,** *a.* 1592. [f. SHALLOW *a.*] Having no depth of intellect –1810.

Shaly (ʃē^i·li), *a.* 1681. [f. SHALE *sb.*² + -Y¹.] Composed of, or resembling shale.

Sham (ʃæm), *sb.*¹ and *a.* 1677. [poss. north. dial. var. of SHAME *sb.* and *v.*] **A.** *sb.* †**1.** A trick, hoax, fraud, imposture; a 'sell' –1821. **2.** Something that is intended to be mistaken for something else; spurious imitation, a counterfeit 1728. **3.** *spec.* A removable covering to give a specious appearance to an article, as *pillow-sham* 1721.

1. Phr. †*To put a s. upon*, to hoax, defraud. **2.** For the pain of my thirst is no s. CAMPBELL. The greatest s.,..is he that would destroy shams CARLYLE. It's all s.—he's only afraid 1857.

B. *attrib.* and *adj.* (Sometimes with hyphen.) **1.** Pretended, feigned, false, counterfeit; not genuine or true 1681. **2.** Of a person: That pretends or is falsely represented to be (what is denoted by the sb.) 1683. **3.** Made in imitation of something else; made to appear to be what it is not; made of inferior or base materials 1699. †**4.** False, deceptive –1727.

1. *S. fight*, a mimic battle between two divisions of a military or naval force, either for exercise or display. **2.** The s.-admirer is always more affected, than he that praises with sincerity 1756. **3.** The s. coat of arms which Osborne had assumed 1848. Not one of the girls dared to wear a bit of s. jewellery 1876.

Sham (ʃæm), *sb.*² *slang.* 1849. Short for CHAMPAGNE.

Sham (ʃæm), *v.* 1677. [See SHAM *sb.*¹] †**1.** *trans.* To cheat, trick, deceive, delude with false pretences; to impose upon, take in, hoax –1821. †**b.** To put off, 'fob off' with something deceptive or worthless; to get rid of (a person) by some paltry excuse –1749. †**2.** To impose or attempt to pass off (something) *upon* (a person) by deceit; to palm *off* –1751. †**3.** *intr.* To practise deception or deceit –1689. **4.** *trans.* **a.** To be or to produce a deceptive imitation of 1698. **b.** To assume the appearance of, counterfeit (a specified condition, action, etc.) 1775. **5.** *intr.* To make false pretences; to pretend to be, do, etc. what one is not, does not, etc.; to feign 1787. **6.** *To s. Abra(ha)m* (orig. *Naut. slang*), to feign sickness (see ABRAHAM-MAN) 1752. **b.** Hence *sham-Abra(ha)m* quasi-*sb.* malingering, deception. Also quasi-*adj.* hypocritical. 1828.

1. When they find themselves Fool'd and Shamm'd (as we say) into a Conviction 1692. **2.** Don't go to s. your Stories off upon me DE FOE. **4. a.** Phr. †*To s. one's glass*: to make a pretence of drinking; He keeps up his spirits bravely, and never shams his glass CHESTERF. **b.** Persons shamming an epileptic fit 1869. **5.** What did you s. dead for? 1834. Wondering..whether those who lectured him were such fools as they professed to be, or were only shamming MACAULAY. Hence **Sha·mmer,** one who shams.

‖**Shama(h** (ʃā·mă). 1839. [Hindi *çāmā.*] An Indian song-bird, *Cittocincla tricolor.*

Shaman (ʃā·măn, ʃæ·măn), *sb.* (and *a.*). 1698. [– G. *schamane*, Russ. *shaman* – Tungusian *samán*. Cf. Fr. *chaman.*] **A.** *sb.* A priest or priest-doctor among various northern tribes of Asia. Hence applied to similar personages in other parts, esp. a medicine-man of some of the north-west American Indians. **B.** *adj.* (or *attrib.*) Of or pertaining to a s. or to Shamanism 1780. Hence **Shama·nic** *a.* akin to Shamanism.

Shamanism (ʃā·măniz'm, ʃæ·măniz'm). 1780. [f. prec. + -ISM.] The primitive religion of the Ural-Altaic peoples of Siberia, in which all the good and evil of life are thought to be brought about by spirits which can be influenced only by Shamans; hence applied to similar religions, esp. of north-west American Indians. Hence **Sha·manist, Sha·manite,** a believer in S. **Shamani·stic** *a.* pertaining to S. **Sha·manize** *v. intr.* to perform the incantations of a Shaman; *trans.* to imbue with Shamanistic beliefs.

Shamble (ʃæ·mb'l), *sb.*¹ [OE. *sc̣(e)amul* stool, table = OS. *fōt|skamel*, OHG. *fuoz|-scamil* footstool (also MDu., MHG. *schamel, schemel*, G. *schemel*); WGmc. – L. *scamellum*, dim. of *scamnum* bench.] †**1.** A stool, footstool –1483. **2.** *spec.* A table or stall for the sale of meat ME. **3.** *pl.* A place where meat (or occas. fish) is sold, a flesh- or meat-market. Now *local.* late ME. **4.** *pl.* A slaughter-house 1548. **5.** *transf.* and *fig.* A place of carnage or wholesale slaughter; a scene of blood. Chiefly *pl.* construed as *sing.*; rarely in sing. form. 1593.

3. Raw Meat is bought in the Shambles 1725. **4.** He was felled like an ox in the butcher's shambles DICKENS. **5.** I've fear'd him, since his iron heart endured To make of Lyons one vast human shambles COLERIDGE. Hence **Sha·mble** *v.*¹ *trans.* to cut up or slaughter as in the shambles (*rare*).

Shamble (ʃæ·mb'l), *sb.*² 1828. [f. SHAMBLE *v.*²] A shambling gait.

Shamble, *a. dial.* 1607. [perh. orig. in *shamble legs*, which may have orig. meant 'legs straddling like those of the trestles of a meat-table' (SCAMBLE *sb.*¹ 2); cf. WFris. *skammels* (pl. of *skammel* board on trestles) legs, esp. when badly formed, *skammelje* walk clumsily.] Shambling, ungainly, awkward.

Shamble (ʃæ·mb'l), *v.* 1681. [prob. f. SHAMBLE *a.*] *intr.* To go with an awkward ungainly gait, to walk awkwardly or unsteadily; usu. with adv. as *to s. along.*

Shambling (ʃæ·mbliŋ), *vbl. sb. rare.* 1681. [f. prec. + -ING¹.] An awkward motion in walking or progression.

Shambling (ʃæ·mbliŋ), *ppl. a.* 1690. [f. SHAMBLE *v.* + -ING².] That shambles or is characterized by an awkward, irregular gait or motion. **b.** *transf.* and *fig.* Often of metre and style, etc. 1802.

A s. pot-boy DICKENS.

Shame (ʃē^i m), *sb.* [OE. *sc̣(e)amu* = OFris. *skame, skome*, OS., OHG. *skama* (Du. *schaamin* comp., G. *scham*), ON. *skǫmm* :- Gmc. **skamō.*] **1.** The painful emotion arising from the consciousness of something dishonouring, ridiculous, or indecorous in one's own conduct or circumstances (or in those of others whose honour or disgrace one regards as one's own), or of being in a situation which offends one's sense of modesty or decency. **2.** Fear of offence against propriety or decency, operating as a restraint on behaviour; modesty, shamefastness. late ME. **3.** Disgrace, ignominy, loss of esteem or reputation OE. **b.** An instance of disgrace ME. **c.** *spec.* Violation of a woman's honour, loss of chastity ME. †**4.** What is morally disgraceful or dishonourable; baseness in conduct or behaviour –1682. **5.** Used predic. (without article) for: A fact or circumstance which brings disgrace or discredit (*to* a person, etc.); matter for severe reproach or reprobation. Now *poet.* OE. **b.** Similarly *a s., a great s.* Now common in colloq. use. late ME. **c.** Occas. in non-predic. use: A disgraceful thing, something to be ashamed of. *poet.* 1600. **6.** A person or thing that is a cause or source of disgrace 1586. **b.** *colloq.* A thing which is shockingly ugly or indecent, or of disgracefully bad quality 1764. †**7.** *concr.* The privy members –1611.

1. But for my part (in all humility And with no little s.) I ask your pardons 1623. *Sense of s.* guilty feeling; also, the right perception of what is improper or disgraceful. *Past s., dead to s.*, no longer capable of feeling s., grown callous to s. **2.** Haue you no modesty, no maiden s., No touch of bashfulnesse? SHAKS. **3.** Therfore beare thine owne s. COVERDALE *Ezek.* 16:52. **b.** Let his shames quickely Driue him to Rome SHAKS. **c.** *Child, son of s.*, a child born out of wedlock. **5.** It were s. to our profession were we to suffer it SCOTT. **b.** They..pay fifteen or twenty sometimes per cent. for their money which is a most horrid s. PEPYS. **c.** A peace that was full of wrongs and shames TENNYSON. **6.** Erasmus, that great injured name, (The glory of the Priesthood, and the s. !) POPE.

Phrases. *To think s.*, to be ashamed. *To take s.* †**a.** To be disgraced, to incur disgrace. **b.** To feel ashamed, to acknowledge that one is in fault. More fully *to take s. to* (*unto, upon*) *oneself.* †*To do* (a person) *s.*: to inflict injury or dishonour, offer reproach or obloquy. *To put to s.*: to bring into disgrace, bring disgrace upon; also *fig.* to outshine, eclipse. *For s.*: from a sense of s., because one feels s.; also, for fear of s. **b.** esp. in adjuration or remonstrance; often as *int.* Also in ejaculatory formulæ of imprecation or indignant disapproval, as *Shame! Fie for s.!* etc. *To one's s.*, so as to cause one s. Also, parenthetically, with ellipsis of 'be it spoken'. *To cry s. on, upon*: to express vigorous reprobation of.

Shame (ʃē^i m), *v.* Pa. t. and pple. **shamed** (ʃē^i md). [OE. *sc̣(e)amian* intr. and impers., corresp. immed. to OS. *skamon*, OHG. *skamōn*, and rel. to OHG. *skamēn*, Goth. *skaman*, and MHG. *schemen* (G. *schämen*), ON. *skemma.*] **1.** *intr.* To feel or conceive shame; to become or be ashamed. *Obs.* exc. *dial.* **2.** *trans. impers.*, as in (*it*) *shames me* = I am ashamed. In later use only with *it.* Now *rare.* OE. **3.** To feel shame in regard to (a person or thing); to hold in awe or reverence; to dread or shun through shame. *Obs.* or *arch.* late ME. **4.** To make ashamed, fill with shame, cause to feel shame 1530. **b.** *pass.* To be ashamed. Now *poet.* ME. **5.** To inflict or bring disgrace upon, be a cause of disgrace to, dishonour ME. **6.** To put to shame by superior excellence; to outrival. late ME.

4. Nay, father,..s. me not Before this noble Knight TENNYSON. Phr. *To tell* (*say, speak*) *the truth and s. the devil*, to tell the truth boldly in defiance of strong temptation to the contrary. **5.** This John..shamed the Churche of Rome wonderfully w^t his lyuing 1556. **6.** She'll s. 'em with her good looks, yet DICKENS.

Shamefaced (ʃē^i·mfe^i st), *a.* 1555. [f. SHAME *sb.* + FACE *sb.* + -ED²; orig. an etymological misinterpretation of SHAMEFAST.] **1.** Modest, bashful, shy. **2.** Ashamed, abashed 1873.

1. He felt s. as a schoolboy before the great world 1873. Hence **Sha·mefaced-ly** *adv.*, **-ness.**

Shamefast (ʃē^i·mfɑst), *a. arch.* [OE. *sc̣(e)amfæst*, f. *sc̣(e)amu* SHAME *sb.* + *fæst* FAST *a.*] **1.** Bashful, modest. In a depreciatory sense: 'Sheepish'. **b.** Of actions, behaviour, appearance: Characterized by or indicating modesty or bashfulness ME. †**2.** Ashamed, abashed –1634.

1. Yf thy daughter be not s., holde her straitly COVERDALE *Ecclus.* 26:10. **b.** Hir schamefast.. smyles 1611. Hence **Sha·mefast-ly** *adv.*, **-ness.**

Shameful (ʃē^i·mfŭl), *a.* [OE. *sc̣(e)amful*; see SHAME *sb.*, -FUL 1.] †**1.** Modest, shamefaced –1625. †**2.** Ashamed –1772. **3.** That brings to shame; that causes or ought to cause shame; disgraceful, scandalous, degrading ME.

3. The s. close of all his mispent years COWPER. S.! Three against one! CARLYLE. Hence **Sha·meful-ly** *adv.*, **-ness.**

Shameless (ʃē^i·mlės), *a.* [OE. *sc̣(e)amlēas*; see SHAME *sb.*, -LESS.] **1.** Lacking shame; impudent, audacious, immodest; insensible to disgrace. **2.** Indicating or characterized by absence of shame or modesty. Of actions: Indicating absence of shame on the part of the agent, impudent. OE.

1. Though these men are so s. as to deny it 1683. **2.** He..degraded the nobility by a s. sale of peerages 1874. Hence **Sha·meless-ly** *adv.*, **-ness.**

Shammy (ʃæ·mi). 1651. [repr. perverted pronunc. of CHAMOIS 2.] **1.** In full **s.-leather:** a kind of soft, pliable leather. Also a piece of this, a wash-leather. 1714. **2.** *attrib.* or *adj.* Made of 'shammy' or chamois leather 1651.

2. I have got my cravat and s. shoes H. WALPOLE.

Shamoy (ʃæ·moi), *v.* 1837. [repr. perverted pronunc. of CHAMOIS *v.*] *trans.* To prepare (leather) by working oil or grease into the skin.

Shampoo (ʃæmpū·), *sb.* 1838. [f. next.] The act of shampooing; also, a 'wash' (or powder, *dry s.*) used for shampooing.

Shampoo (ʃæmpū·), *v.* 1762. [– Hind. *chhāmpo*, imper. of *chhāmpnā* press.] **1.** *trans.* To subject (a person, his limbs) to massage. Now *rare* or *Obs.* exc. as designating a part of the process of a Turkish bath. **2.** To subject (the scalp, the hair) to washing and rubbing with some cleansing agent, as soap and water, shampoo powder, etc. 1860. Hence **Shampoo·er,** one who shampoos.

Shamrock (ʃæ·mrǫk). 1571. [– Irish *seamróg* (= Gael. *seamrag*), dim. of *seamar* clover.] **1.** A plant with trifoliate leaves, used (according to a late tradition) by St. Patrick to illustrate the doctrine of the Trinity, and hence adopted as the national emblem of Ireland; a spray or leaf of this plant. (The name is now commonly applied to the lesser yellow trefoil, *Trifolium minus*, the plant worn as an emblem on St. Patrick's Day.)

Shandean (ʃæ·ndiăn, ʃændī·ăn), *a.* 1762. [f. (*Tristram*) *Shandy*, the title of a novel (1759–67) by Sterne + -AN.] Pertaining to *Tristram Shandy*, or the Shandy family there portrayed.

Shandrydan (ʃæ·ndridæn). 1820. [Of unkn. origin.] A kind of chaise with a hood. In later use, a joc. name for any rickety old-fashioned vehicle.

Shandygaff (ʃæ·ndigæf). Also **shandy.** 1853. [Of unkn. origin.] A drink composed of a mixture of beer and ginger-beer or lemonade.

Shanghai (ʃæŋhəi·), *sb.* 1853. [f. *Shanghai* or *Shanghae*, one of the chief seaports of China.] **1.** A long-legged, large breed of domestic fowls, with feathered shanks, reputed to have been introduced from Shanghai; now developed into the brahmas and cochins. **2.** *Austral.* A catapult 1863.

Shanghai (ʃæŋhəi·), *v.* 1871. [f. as prec.] **1.** *trans. Naut. slang.* (orig. *U.S.*) To drug or otherwise render insensible, and ship on board a vessel wanting hands. **2.** *Austral.* To shoot with a 'shanghai' or catapult 1902.

Shank (ʃæŋk), *sb.* [OE. *sceanca*, LG. *schanke*, Flem. *schank* :– WGmc. **skaŋka*, rel. to MLG. *schenke*, Du. *schenk* leg bone, LG., (M)HG. *schenkel*.] **1.** That part of the leg which extends from the knee to the ankle; the tibia or shin-bone. Also (now *joc.*) the leg as a whole; chiefly *pl.*, one's legs. **b.** The lower part of the foreleg of some animals; *spec.* of a horse, the part between the so-called knee and the fetlock. Also, the tarsus of a bird; the tibia or fourth joint of the leg of an insect OE. **c.** As part of a joint of meat, e.g. in a ham, a leg of mutton, etc. 1806. **2.** *transf.* **a.** Each of the two portions of a pair of scissors between the bow and the joint 1833. **b.** *Arch. pl.* The plane spaces between the grooves of the Doric triglyph 1823. **c.** Each of the two cheeks or side-pieces of a spur 1891. **3.** The stem or straight part of anything. **a.** The stem of a goblet, glass, etc. 1553. **b.** The straight part of a nail or pin, between the head and the taper of the point. Also of a drill or borer. 1483. **c.** The stem of a plant; the pedicel or footstalk of a flower; the footstalk or connecting part of any organ in a plant 1513. **d.** The shaft or stem of an anchor, connecting the arms and the stock 1549. **e.** The straight part of a fish-hook, to which the line is attached 1613. **f.** *Typog.* The body of a type, as dist. from the shoulder, face, and foot 1683. **g.** The stem of a tobacco-pipe 1688. **h.** The blank part of a screw, or screw-bolt, between the thread and the head 1677. **i.** The tapering part of an oar between the handle and the blade 1857. **4.** A part or appendage by which something is attached; e.g. the wire loop by which some kinds of buttons are attached, that part of a ring which encircles the finger 1677. **5.** *Founding.* A clay-lined ladle having long handles, one of them T-shaped, in which to carry molten metal from the furnace to the mould 1843. **6.** *dial.* and *U.S.* The latter end or part of anything 1828.

1. Sundry flowring bankes, To sit and rest the walkers wearie shankes SPENSER. *Shanks'* (or *Shanks's*) *mare, pony*, etc., one's own legs as a means of conveyance.

Comb. **s.-bone**, the tibia of an animal. Hence **Shank** *v. intr.* of a plant or fruit: to decay at the stem or footstalk; usu. *to shank off*; *trans.* (*Golf*) to strike (the ball) with the heel of the club. **Shanked** (ʃæŋkt) *a.* furnished with or having a s. or shanks.

Sha·nk-pai:nter. 1495. [PAINTER².] The rope or chain with which the shank and flukes of the anchor, when carried at the cathead, are confined to the ship's side.

Shanny (ʃæ·ni). 1836. [Of unkn. origin; rel. to earlier *shan* (1713).] The smooth blenny. Also applied to several fishes of the genus *Chasmodes* of Eastern North America.

Shan't, sha'n't (ʃānt). 1664. A colloq. contraction of *shall not*. Also used *subst.*

Shantung (ʃæntʊ·ŋ). 1882. [f. name of a province of North-east China where it is manufactured.] A soft undressed Chinese silk (formerly always undyed).

Shanty (ʃæ·nti), *sb.*¹ 1820. [orig. in N. Amer. use; perh. – Ir. *sean tig* (*toig*) 'old house'.] **1.** Chiefly *U.S.* and *Canada*. A small, mean, roughly constructed dwelling; a cabin, hut. **2.** *Austral.* A public-house, esp. unlicensed 1864. Hence **Sha·nty** *v. intr.* to live in a s.; *Austral.* to frequent 'shanties' or public-houses.

Shanty (ʃæ·nti), *sb.*² Also **chant(e)y.** 1869. [app. repr. Fr. *chantez*, imper. of *chanter* sing.] A sailor's song, esp. one sung during heavy work.

Shape (ʃēⁱp), *sb.* [orig. repr. OE. *ġe|sċeap* creation, etc., corresp. to OS. *giskapu* pl. creatures, ON. *skap* condition, pl. fate; f. **skap-* base of the vb., of which the sb. came to be later apprehended as a derivative.] **1.** External form or contour; that quality of a material object (or geometrical figure) which depends on constant relations of position and proportionate distance among all the points composing its outline or its external surface; a particular variety of this quality. **b.** The contour or outlines of the trunk of the body. late ME. **c.** Impressed or represented form; a picture, image. *Obs.* exc. *dial.* late ME. †**2.** The appearance of a human or animal body or its parts, (often, of the general form as dist. from the face) considered as beautiful or the contrary –1734. **3.** The visible form or appearance characteristic of a particular person or thing, or of a particular species of animate or supernatural beings OE. **4.** A person's body considered with regard to its appearance 1601. **b.** An imaginary, spectral, or ethereal form; a phantom. Now *rare*. 1591. **c.** A figure dimly or uncertainly perceived 1834. **5.** Assumed appearance, guise, disguise 1594. **6.** *Theatr.* †**a.** A part, a character impersonated; the make-up and costume suited to a particular part. **b.** A stage dress or suit of clothes. 1603. **7.** One of the forms or diversities of appearance, structure, or properties, in which a thing may exist 1667. **8.** *In the s. of*: **a.** Represented by, embodied in (a person or thing) 1750. **b.** Of the nature of 1754. **c.** In the form of, existing or presenting itself as 1823. **9.** Definite, regular or proper form; orderly arrangement 1633. †**10.** An attitude (in dancing, etc.) –1634. **11.** orig. *Sport.* Condition with respect to efficiency, 'form' 1901. **12.** *concr.* in techn. uses. **a.** *Cookery.* A mould for forming jelly, blanc-mange, etc., into a particular shape; a portion of jelly, blanc-mange, etc. moulded into an ornamental shape 1769. **b.** *Millinery.* The body of a straw bonnet or woman's hat or cap previous to trimming 1881. **c.** A portion of material cut or moulded so as to have a particular shape; *spec.* a piece of rolled or hammered iron of cross-section differing from that of merchant bar 1845. **d.** *Naut.* A cone, ball, or drum of metal or canvas used in signalling 1879.

1. I know the s. of 's Legge SHAKS. By pressure ice can be moulded to any s. TYNDALL. *To keep in s.*, to secure from change of s. *Out of s.*, changed from its proper s. **2.** Hither come the Country Gentlemen to shew their Shapes 1700. **3.** Thou com'st in such a questionable s. That I will speake to thee SHAKS. **4. b.** Before the Gates there sat On either side a formidable s. MILT. **5.** The brute Serpent in whose s. I Man deceav'd MILT. **7.** Phr. *In any* (*no*) *s.* (*or form*), used loosely for: in any (no) manner, (not) at all. **8. b.** I had nothing in the s. of food 1863. **c.** Recognition of his services in the s. of a small pension 1880. **9.** Phr. *To take s.*; *to put into s.*

Shape (ʃēⁱp), *v.* Pa. t. **shaped** (ʃēⁱpt); pa. pple. **shaped** (ʃēⁱpt), *arch.* **shapen** (ʃēⁱp'n). [Early ME. new formation on the pa. pple., repl. orig. OE. **sċieppan, sċeppan*, (pa. t. *sċōp*, pa. pple. *sċapen*), corresp. to OFris. *skeppa*, OS. **giskeppian*, Goth. *gaskapjan*; f. **skap-* create, fashion; first established as a wk. vb. XVI; the OE. pa. pple. survives chiefly in *misshapen*.] **I.** To create, fashion, form. †**1.** *trans.* To create; in later use, to form, fashion (said of God or Nature) –1557. **2.** To make, fashion out of pre-existing materials. In later use, to make by alteration of shape (as by moulding or carving) *out of* something else; to make in a definite shape. OE. **b.** To frame, fashion (an immaterial thing) ME. **3.** *pass.* To have a certain shape OE. †**4.** *trans.* To cut out or fashion (clothing) –1828. †**5.** *intr.* To attain maturity of form and proportions. BACON. **6.** *trans.* To trim, cut, or mould to a particular shape; to adapt in shape *to* 1457. **7.** To give definite form to; to put *into* a certain form, to embody in words; also *refl.* 1589. **b.** Of events, etc.: To show a specified tendency 1865. **8.** To give a direction and character to (one's life, conduct, etc.) 1823.

1. I was shapen in wickedness BIBLE (Great) *Ps.* 51:5. **2.** Come to the Forge with it, then s. it SHAKS. **3.** The head was well shapen 1884. **5.** Young men, when they knit and s. perfectly, doe seldome grow to a further stature BACON. **6.** Some [sleeves] are shaped to the elbow and have cuffs 1861. **7.** And there I shaped The city's ancient legend into this TENNYSON. The valleys.. shaped themselves..into a succession of graceful curves 1869. Phr. *To shape an answer* (*to*).

II. To devise, plan, prepare. **1.** To devise (a plan, a remedy). late ME. **2.** *To s. one's course*: Naut., to steer *for*, *to* a place 1593. **3.** To appear promising (chiefly *Sc.* and *dial.*). Often with ref. to physical exercises, as drill, rowing, etc.: To show signs of becoming efficient. 1865. **b.** Of a batsman: To get into the proper attitude and position for dealing with the bowling 1884. **c.** Of a horse: To exhibit capabilities; to develop *into* 1887.

2. *transf.* Minding now to s. my course so as I might winter in Italy EVELYN. Hence **Sha·p(e)-able** *a.* capable of being shaped, plastic; shapely.

Shapeless (ʃēⁱ·plės), *a.* ME. [f. SHAPE *sb.* + -LESS.] **1.** Without shape or form; having no definite or regular shape. **2.** Unshapely 1588. **3.** Without guidance or direction, aimless (*rare*) 1591.

1. Sunk are thy bowers in s. ruin all GOLDSM. **3.** To..Weare out thy youth with shapelesse idlenesse SHAKS. Hence **Sha·pelessness.**

Shapely (ʃēⁱ·pli), *a.* late ME. [f. SHAPE *sb.* + -LY¹.] †**1.** Fit, likely, suitable; also, like (*to* something). late ME. only. **2.** Of good or elegant shape, well-formed. late ME. **b.** Having definite form (*rare*) 1827.

1. Euerich..Was shaply for to been an Alderman CHAUCER. **2.** Where the s. column stood COWPER. Hence **Sha·peliness.**

Shapen (ʃēⁱ·p'n), *ppl. a.* ME. [Strong pa. pple. of SHAPE *v.*] **1.** Having a (specified) shape. *Obs.* exc. in *well s.* (arch.). **2.** Furnished with a definite shape; fashioned 1483.

Shapen (ʃēⁱ·p'n), *v. rare.* 1535. [f. SHAPE *sb.* + -EN⁵.] *trans.* To shape, impart a shape to.

Shaper (ʃēⁱ·pəɹ). ME. [f. SHAPE *v.* + -ER¹.] †**1.** The Creator or Maker (of the universe) –1496. **2.** One who or something which makes (a thing) in the required shape; one who fashions (material). late ME. **b.** *spec.* in various trades as the designation of an operative 1881. **3.** A machine or tool for shaping material; *spec.* a machine for shaping metal pieces and parts of machinery 1853.

‖**Shapoo** (ʃā·pu). 1858. [Tibetan *sha-pho* wild sheep.] A kind of sheep (*Ovis vignei*) found in Ládák (Kashmir) and Tibet.

Shard, sherd (ʃāɹd, ʃɔ̄ɹd), *sb.*¹ [OE. *sċeard*, corresp. to OFris. *skerd* cut, notch, MLG. *skart* crack, chink, MDu. *scarde, schart* flaw, fragment (Du. *schaard*), (M)HG. *scharte*, ON. *skarðr* notch, gap, subst. uses of the adj. repr. by OE. *sċeard* :– Gmc. **skarðaz* cut, notched, diminished, pa. ppl. formation on **skar-* **sker-* SHEAR *v.*] **I.** A gap in an enclosure, esp. in a hedge or bank. Now chiefly *dial.* **II.** A fragment of broken earthenware, POTSHERD OE.

Phr. *To break*, etc. *into sherds*, to reduce to fragments, break beyond repair. Hence **Shard** *v. trans.* to break into fragments (*rare*).

Shard (ʃāɹd), *sb.*² *Obs.* exc. *dial.* 1545. [app. cogn. w. dial. and Sc. *sharn* dung.] A patch of cow-dung.

Comb. **s.-beetle,** a beetle of the family *Geotrupidæ*, found under dung, a dor-beetle. Hence †**Sha·rded** *a.* of a beetle: living in dung. SHAKS.

Shard (ʃāɹd), *sb.*³ 1755. [Evolved from a misunderstanding of SHARD-BORN in Shaks.]

The elytron or wing-case of a coleopterous insect.

Sha·rd-born, -borne, *a.* 1605. [f. SHARD *sb.*[2] + BORN *a.*] **a.** Of a beetle: Born in dung; *spec.* applied to the SHARD-BEETLE. **b.** Used with the meaning (due to misinterpretation of Shaks.): Borne on shards (SHARD *sb.*[3]).

Ere..The shard-borne Beetle, with his drowsie hums, Hath rung Nightes yawning Peale SHAKS.

Share (ʃēᵊɹ), *sb.*[1] [OE. *sćær, sćear*, corresp. to OFris. *sker*, MLG. *schar(e*, OHG. *scar, scaro* (G. *schar*); WGmc. deriv. of Gmc. **skar-* **sker-* SHEAR *v.* Cf. next.] The iron blade in a plough which cuts the ground at the bottom of the furrow; a ploughshare. **b.** The analogous part of a seed-drill, or similar implement 1731.

Share (ʃēᵊɹ), *sb.*[2] [repr. spec. development, earliest in AFr. and AL. documents, of OE. *sćearu*, lit. 'cutting, division', corresp. to OS. *scara* feudal service, troop, MLG. *schare* troop, share, OHG. *scara* troop, share of forced labour (Du. *schaar*, G. *schar* troop, multitude), ON. *skari* :– Gmc. deriv. of **skar-* **sker-* SHEAR *v.* Cf. prec.] **1.** The part or portion (*of* something) which is allotted or belongs to an individual, when distribution is made among a number; also, the portion or quota which is contributed by an individual. **b.** In pregnant sense = One's due, proper, or fair share; one's full share (of something enjoyed or suffered in common with others) 1645. **c.** The measure or degree *of* a quality, condition, etc. which is allotted to an individual by nature or Providence 1722. **2.** *Comm.* A definite portion of a property owned by a number in common; *spec.* each of the equal parts into which the capital of a joint-stock company or corporation is divided 1601. **3.** A part taken in (an action, experience, etc.). Chiefly in phr. *to have, take, bear a* (*one's*, etc.) *s. in*, to have or take part in, participate in. 1592. †**4.** *gen.* A part, piece, or portion (*of* anything) –1772. †**b.** With etymol. ref. to *shear*: A piece hewn out, or cut or torn away –1776.

1. Taking our turns to row, of which..my share came to little less than 20 leagues EVELYN. There is gold here, my friend, and we must get our s. of it 1888. **c.** That amiable pity, of which your really superior woman always has such a s. to give away THACKERAY. **2.** The ship, wherein my Father had halfe s. 1660. *Deferred, preference shares*: see DEFERRED, PREFERENCE. *Ordinary shares*, the shares which form the common stock and are without 'preference'.

Phrases. *S. and s. alike*, with equal shares, having each a like s. Also *to go s. and s. alike*. *To fall to one's s.*, to be assigned as one's portion; hence, to fall to one's lot (*to do*, etc.) *To go shares with* (another or others) *in* (a possession, enterprise, etc.) to enjoy a part in, participate in, contribute towards.

†**Share,** *v.*[1] 1553. [var. of SHEAR *v.*] *trans.* To cut into parts; to cut off –1735.

The sword..deep entring shar'd All his right side MILT.

Share (ʃēᵊɹ), *v.*[2] 1586. [f. SHARE *sb.*[2]] **1.** *trans.* To divide and apportion in shares between two or more recipients. Now chiefly with *out*. 1590. **b.** To apportion to an individual as his share. Also with *out. arch.* 1586. **c.** To divide (what one has or receives) into portions, and give shares to others as well as one's self. Const. *with*. 1592. **2.** Of two or more persons: To divide into shares and take each a portion. Also *absol.* 1594. **3.** To grant or give another or others a share in. Also const. *with*. 1662. **4.** To receive, possess, or occupy together with others 1592. †**b.** To take or receive as one's share. *poet.* –1618. †**c.** *To s. from*, to gain at the expense of. SHAKS. **5.** To perform, enjoy, or suffer in common with others; to possess (a quality) which other persons or things also have. Const. *with*. 1590. **6.** *intr.* To have a share (*in* something); to participate *in*, take part *in* 1598. **b.** To participate *with* (a person) *in* something (*rare*) 1594. **c.** Used in reduplicated form *s. and s.* (*alike*, etc.): the phrase in SHARE *sb.*[2] being misapprehended grammatically 1821.

1. Suppose I s. my Fortune equally between my own Children and a Stranger SWIFT. **b.** He part of his small feast to her would s. SPENSER. **2.** *Rich. III*, I. iii. 159. **3.** Well may he then to you his Cares impart And s. his Burden where he shares his Heart DRYDEN. **4.** He shares the frugal meal with those he loves 1804. *fig.* In vain doth Valour bleed While Avarice, and Rapine s. the land MILT. **b.** *Rich. III*, V. iii. 268. **c.** What glory our Achilles shares from Hector SHAKS. **5.** A man that all his time Hath..Shar'd dangers with you SHAKS. **6. b.** MILT. *P.L.* IX. 831. **d.** We all s. and s. alike in camp 1906. Hence **Shared** (ʃēᵊɹd) *ppl. a.*, spec. in *Physics* of electrons (1923).

Shareholder (ʃēᵊ·ɹhoᵘːldəɹ). 1828. [f. SHARE *sb.*[2] + HOLDER[1].] One who owns or holds a share or shares in a joint-stock company, or other joint fund or property. Hence **Sha·re-holding** *vbl. sb.* the possession of shares; *pl.*, shares held in various undertakings.

Sharer (ʃēᵊ·rəɹ). 1589. [f. SHARE *v.*[2] + -ER[1].] **1.** One who shares something (const. *of*) or shares *in* something 1603. †**2.** *spec.* A member of a company of players, who paid the expenses, and received the profits, and employed the 'journeymen' members of the company –1704. †**b.** A shareholder –1812.

Shark (ʃāɹk), *sb.*[1] 1569. [Of unkn. origin.] **1.** A selachian fish of the sub-order *Squali* of the order *Plagiostomi*; in popular language chiefly applied to the large voracious fishes of this sub-order, as the genera *Carcharodon, Carcharias*, etc. **b.** With defining word 1655. **c.** *transf.* **Freshwater s.,** (joc.) the pike, alluding to its voracity 1799. **2.** *fig.* (Cf. SHARK *sb.*[2]) One who enriches himself by taking advantage of the necessities of others; a rapacious usurer, an extortionate landlord, a financial swindler, etc. 1713. **b.** A customs officer; also *pl.* the press-gang 1785. **c.** *U.S.* An exceptionally capable person 1909. **3.** *Ent.* Any moth of the genus *Cucullia* (*Noctua*) 1819.

1. The S. hath not this name for nothing, for he will make a morsell of any thing he can catch, master, and devour 1655. **b. Angel-s.,** the monk-fish, *Squatina angelus*; **Gangetic s.,** *Carcharias gangeticus*, inhabiting some rivers; **Greenland s.,** the North Atlantic s., *Laemargus borealis*; **Grey s.,** the sand-s., *Carcharinus americanus*; **Hammer-headed s.,** *Zygaena malleus*; **Sea-s.,** a s. of the high seas, esp. 'a large s. of the family *Lamnidæ*'; **Spine s.,** the Picked Dogfish, *Acanthias*; **Spinous s.,** a s. of the genus *Echinorhinus*, as *E. spinosus*; **White s.,** a man-eating s., *Carcharodon rondeleti*. **2.** The slop-sellers, and other sharks, at this port 1804.

Comb. **s.-fin,** the fin of a s., considered a delicacy by the Chinese; **-moth** = sense 3; **-ray,** the angel-fish, also a rhinobatid or beaked ray; **-toothed** *a.* applied to ornamentation suggesting shark's teeth. Hence **Sharking** *vbl. sb.*, fishing for sharks.

†**Shark,** *sb.*[2] 1599. [Connection with prec. cannot be made out.] A worthless and impecunious person who gains a precarious living by sponging on others, by executing disreputable commissions, cheating and petty swindling; a sharper –1700.

Shark (ʃāɹk), *v.* 1596. [See prec.] **1.** *intr.* †**a.** *To s. on* or *upon*: to prey like a shark upon; to victimize, sponge upon, swindle; to oppress by extortion. **b.** To depend on or practise fraud or the arts of a 'shark', or sharper; to live by shifts and stratagems. Often *to s. for* (something). 1608. **2.** *trans.* **a.** *To s. up*: to collect hastily (a body of persons, etc.) without regard to selection. Now *arch.*, as an echo of *Haml.* I. i. 98. 1602. **b.** To steal, pilfer, or obtain by underhand or cheating means. *arch.* 1612.

1. b. To shift and sharke in every bie-corner for comfort 1641.

Sharp (ʃāɹp), *a.* and *sb.* [OE. *sć(e)arp* = OFris. *skarp, skerp*, OS. *skarp* (Du. *scherp*), OHG. *skarf, scarpf* (G. *scharf*), ON. *skarpr* :– Gmc. **skarpaz*.] **A.** *adj.* **1.** Well adapted for cutting or piercing; having a keen edge or point; opp. to *blunt*. **b.** Of sand, gravel, etc.: Composed of materials having sharp points; hard, angular, gritty. Now *techn.* 1618. †**2.** Rough, rugged (chiefly as tr. L. *asper*) –1596. **3.** Acute or penetrating in intellect or perception. **a.** †(*a*) Keen-witted, sagacious. (*b*) Quick-witted, clever (said esp. of children). OE. **b.** Of reasoning or discourse: †Acute, sagacious. In later use, of remarks: Pointed, apt, witty. 1580. **c.** Of sight, hearing, the eyes or ears: Acute, keen OE. **d.** Hence of observation, an observer: Vigilant 1535. **e.** Businesslike, smart; often, quick to take unfair advantage of others 1697. **4.** Eager, impetuous, violent OE. **b.** (*a*) Of a hawk: Eager for prey, hungry. (*b*) Of the appetite: Keen. Of the stomach: Craving for food. 1486. **c.** Quick or active in bodily movement. Of movements: Brisk, energetic. 1440. **d.** Of a stream: Rapid. Now *rare*. 1655. **e.** Of winter, wintry weather, frost, wind, air: Cuttingly cold, keen. late ME. **5.** Severe, strict, harsh OE. **b.** Of pain, suffering, grief, etc.: Keen, acute, intense. Of experiences: Intensely painful. OE. †**c.** Of a mode of life: Austere –1611. **6.** Pungent in taste; also, having strong acid, alkaline, or caustic properties OE. **7.** Of sound: Penetrating, shrill, high-pitched. late ME. **b.** *Phonetics.* (*a*) Expressing the acoustic quality of high-front vowels 1532. (*b*) An antiquated designation for unvoiced consonants 1841. **8.** *Mus.* **a.** Of a note: Relatively high in pitch. **b.** Of a note, singing, an instrument: Above the regular or true pitch. **c.** *A, C, D*, etc. *s.*: the sound which is a semitone higher than A, C, D, etc. Also, the key or other contrivance in a musical instrument for producing such a note. **d.** Of an interval, †key, †scale: = MAJOR *a.* I. 2. **e.** Of a key: Having sharps in the signature. 1597. **9.** With ref. to form only (without implication of cutting or piercing). **a.** Tapering to a (relatively) fine point ME. **b.** Of an angle: †(*a*) = ACUTE *a.* 1 –1688. (*b*) Abrupt; involving sudden change of direction; so *s. turn* 1825. **c.** Of an ascent or descent, a rise or fall: Abrupt 1725. **d.** *Naut.* Of the shape of a vessel: Having a narrow and wedge-shaped bottom 1709. **e.** Of features: Emaciated, peaked, thin 1561. **10.** Having the angles or edges not rounded off or flattened; hence, clear or distinct in outline. Often of contrasts, distinctions, etc.: Abrupt, strongly marked. 1675.

1. A busshe full of s. thornes CAXTON. I know, his Sword Hath a sharpe edge SHAKS. *fig.* The s. edge..of public curiosity 1807. Phr. *S. as a razor, as a needle*, etc. **b.** Clean but coarse s. sand 1859. **3. a.** (*b*) A very s. lad 1870. **b.** He..alleadged Many sharpe reasons to defeat the Law SHAKS. **c.** The grey eye..is sharpest of sight 1630. **d.** Phr. *To keep a s. look-out*. **e.** They got a s. Newcastle attorney SCOTT. See also SHARP PRACTICE. Similarly, *s. work*. **4.** The contest between good and evil becomes s. and deadly 1845. **c.** A s. gallop 1842. Provb. phr. *Sharp's the word* (used as an injunction to promptitude). **e.** Though the air was s., he had been carrying his cloak over his arm 1894. **5.** Skelton a sharpe Satirist 1589. A rigorous and s. penance 1663. Phr. *To be s. upon*, to be hard or severe upon (now only by way of censure or criticism). **b.** Sharpe miserie had worne him to the bones SHAKS. S., lancinating pains 1843. **c.** *Cymb.* III. iii. 31. **6.** Wo was his cook, but if his sauce were Poynaunt and s. CHAUCER. **7.** S. Violins proclaim Their jealous Pangs DRYDEN. **9. a.** Hys nese at þe poynt es s. and smalle HAMPOLE. **c.** A very s. rise leads from the Pacific to the range of the Andes HUXLEY. **10.** The sharpest geographical contrast 1856.

B. *sb.* **1.** A sharp weapon; *spec.* a small sword; a rapier used for duelling as opp. to a 'blunt' or buttoned weapon. *Obs.* or *arch.* late ME. †**2.** A sharp edge; *spec.* the edge of a sword –1734. **3.** *Mus.* **a.** A high-pitched note (*rare*). **b.** A note raised half a tone above the natural pitch. **c.** In musical notation, the sign ♯ which indicates this raising of the note. *Double s.*: the sign x indicating that a note must be raised two semitones. **4. a.** = SHARPER 2 1797. **b.** *colloq.* An expert, connoisseur, a wise man or one professing to be so 1865. **5.** *pl.* The 'middlings' between bran and flour 1801. **6.** *pl.* One of the three grades of needles, including those of greatest length and most acutely pointed 1849.

1. Phr. †*To fight, play*, etc. *at the s., at sharp(s*, to fight with unbated swords, to fight in earnest, in contradistinction to fencing; A combate of fensers (called *Gladiatores*) fighting at the sharpe NORTH. **2.** Phr. *The s. of the hand*, the edge of the hand. **3.** I chatter over stony ways, In little sharps and trebles TENNYSON. **4. a.** The sharps have queered me 1797.

Comb.: **s.-eyed** *a.*, keen of sight; *transf.* observant, penetrating; **-fanged** *a.*, having a s. tooth; *fig.* biting (in speech), caustic, sarcastic; **-featured** *a.*, peaked, thin; **-nosed** *a.*, having a pointed nose; *fig.* quick at fault-finding, captious; **-sighted** *a.*, having acute or quick sight; having acuteness of mental vision; **-tailed** *a.*, having a tapering tail or pointed tail-feathers, *spec.* in names of birds; **-tongued** *a.*, bitter of speech; **-toothed** *a.*, keen of tooth; *transf.* rending, tearing; **-witted** *a.*, sagacious, intelligent.

Sharp (ʃāɹp), *adv.* [OE. *sćearpe*, f. *sćearp* SHARP *a.*] **1.** In a sharp manner; †shrilly; †niggardly, stingily. **b.** Abruptly, suddenly 1836. **c.** In an invitation or appointment: Punctually, precisely (at the hour specified) 1840. **d.** *Look s.*: see LOOK *v.* I. 5. **2.** *Naut.* As near fore and aft as possible, trimmed as near as possible to the wind 1669.

1. If Flies and small Gnats bite sharpe and sore 1635. **b.** The horse..turns s. round and stands stock still 1860. **c.** They should dine that day at three o'clock s. THACKERAY. Hence **Sha·rp-ly** *adv.*, **-ness.**

Sharp (ʃāɹp), *v.* [OE. **sćierpan*, *sćerpan* :– Gmc. **skarpjan.* Later prob. blending with a new formation on the adj.] **1.** *trans.* = SHARPEN *v.* 1. Now only *dial.* ME. †**2.** = SHARPEN *v.* 2. –1633. †**3.** *intr.* To play the sharper –1785. **4.** *trans.* **a.** To cheat, swindle, trick (a person) 1700. **b.** To obtain by swindling, to steal 1706.

Sharp-edged, *a.* (Stress variable.) OE. Having a sharp edge or sharp edges.

fig. S. words have sharp edges to wound DICKENS.

Sharpen (ʃā·ɹp'n), *v.* 1450. [f. SHARP *a.* + -EN[5].] **1.** *trans.* To put a sharp edge or point upon; to furnish (a weapon, implement, etc.) with a cutting edge or fine point 1530. **2.** To make sharp or sharper. **a.** To render more acute (a person's wit, sight, appetite, etc.); to intensify (hostile feeling) 1450. **b.** To give an acid flavour or quality to, to make (a liquid) sour or bitter 1675. **c.** To increase the severity of (a law, punishment) 1709. †**d.** To exacerbate (persons, their temper) –1792. **e.** To aggravate (pain or suffering) 1768. **f.** To make (the features) sharp or thin 1835. **3.** *Mus.* To raise the pitch of a note sounded upon a musical instrument 1824. **4.** *Naut.* To brace sharp up 1841. †**5.** *intr.* To become sharp, to taper to a point; to grow thin –1851.

1. Flints sharpened by chipping 1890. **2. a.** My hearing..has been sharpened by my blindness SCOTT. **c.** A Law..for sharpening Laws against Papists 1709. **e.** An injury sharpened by an insult STERNE. **5.** His face..sharpened like the face of a sick man 1851. Hence **Sha·rpener,** one who or something which sharpens

Sharper (ʃā·ɹpəɹ). 1567. [f. SHARP *v.* + -ER[1].] **1.** One who or something which 'sharps' or sharpens. **2.** A cheat, swindler, rogue; one who lives by his wits and by taking advantage of others; esp. a fraudulent gamester 1681.

Sharpie (ʃā·ɹpi). *U.S.* 1864. [app. f. SHARP *a.*; see -Y[6].] A long, sharp, flat-bottomed fishing-boat.

Sharp-pointed, *a.* (Stress variable.) 1530. **1.** Tapered or tapering to a point. **b.** *Bot.* Acuminate, mucronate 1565. **2.** Having a fine point adapted for piercing or stabbing 1594. **3.** Having irregular, sharp projections 1748.

Sharp practice. 1847. **1.** Work that demands brisk activity (*rare*). **2. a.** Hard bargaining; relentless pursuit of advantage. **b.** Dishonourable taking of advantage, trickery. 1847.

Sharp-set, *a.* (Stress variable.) 1540. [f. SHARP *a.* (as compl.) + SET *ppl. a.*] **1.** Eager or keen for food, very hungry. Also said of the stomach. **2.** *transf.* Keen, eager; having desire fixed *upon*, craving *after* 1580. †**b.** Having a craving for sexual indulgence –1794.

2. The town is s. on new plays 1711.

Sharpshooter (ʃā·ɹpˌʃūtəɹ). 1802. [f. SHARP *a.* + SHOOTER.] A marksman of accurate aim; *spec.* in naval and military use, a member of a division engaged in skirmishing and outpost work. Hence **Sha·rpshooting** *vbl. sb.*

Shaster (ʃæ·stəɹ), ‖**Shastra** (ʃā·stră). 1630. [– Hindi *çāstr*, Skr. *çastra.*] Any one of the sacred writings of the Hindus.

‖**Shastri** (ʃā·strī). 1645. [Hindi *çāstrī*, Skr. *çāstrin*, f. *çāstra* SHASTER.] One who is earned in, or teaches, the shasters.

Shatter (ʃæ·təɹ), *sb.* 1640. [f. next.] **1.** *pl.* Fragments into which a thing is broken, rent, or torn. *Obs.* exc. *dial.* **2.** A shattered state of nerves (*rare*) 1777.

1. Phr. (*To break*, etc.) *into* or *to shatters*, (*to be*) *in shatters*; For the Ministry, it is all in shatters H. WALPOLE.

Shatter (ʃæ·təɹ), *v.* ME. [Origin and relation to SCATTER obscure.] **1.** *trans.* To scatter, disperse; to cause (seed, leaves, etc.) to fall or to be shed. *Obs.* exc. *dial.* **2.** To break in pieces by a sudden blow or concussion; to dash into fragments, disrupt into parts 1450. **b.** To damage ruinously (a structure, a living organism, etc.) by battery or violent concussion; to damage or destroy by fracture of the parts 1513. **c.** *fig.*, or with immaterial object. Also, to damage or destroy the fortunes of (a person or body of persons). 1683. **d.** To wreck (a person's constitution, nerves, etc.) by sickness, hardship, or the like. Also, to wreck the health, strength, or spirits of (a person). 1785. **3.** *intr.* To become scattered or dispersed; to be shed or strewn about. Of grain, etc.: To drop out of the husk from over-ripeness. Of a flower: To drop its petals. Now *dial.* 1577. **4.** To become broken suddenly or violently into fragments or separate parts; to fly in pieces or asunder 1567. **b.** Of earth: To fall or crumble in pieces. *dial.* 1733. **5.** To dash or strike noisily against some hard object; to clatter, rattle (*rare*). late ME.

1. S. your leaves before the mellowing year MILT. **2.** The bottles twain behind his back Were shatter'd at a blow COWPER. **b.** Cossack and Russian Reel'd from the sabre-stroke Shatter'd and sunder'd TENNYSON. **c.** The war or revolution..that shatters a rotten system EMERSON. **d.** Shattered in mind, and perilously sick in body DICKENS. **4.** Some Fragile Bodies breake but where the Force is; Some s. and fly in many Peeces BACON. **5.** The casements s., tatter and clatter 1623.

Comb.: **s.-brain, -pate, -wit,** a person of 'cracked' brain or wandering wits; a giddy, thoughtless person; so **s.-brained, -pated, -witted,** *adjs.*, crazy, light-witted; giddy, thoughtless.

Sha·ttering, *ppl. a.* 1567. [f. prec. + -ING[2].] **1.** That is broken up suddenly or forcibly; falling in pieces or asunder. **2.** Ruinously destructive; that breaks or destroys by a sudden blow or concussion 1577. **b.** Of sound: Rending the air, ear-splitting 1842.

2. *fig.* Her answer to this was as s. as it was rapid DE QUINCEY. **b.** The s. trumpet shrilleth high TENNYSON. Hence **Sha·tteringly** *adv.*

Shattery (ʃæ·təri), *a.* 1728. [f. SHATTER *v.* + -Y[1].] Of rock, stone, or soil: Apt to break in pieces or crumble; friable.

Shave (ʃēⁱv), *sb.*[1] [OE. *sćeafa* = MDu. *schave* (Du. *schaaf*), OHG. *scaba* (G. *schabe*), ON. *skafa* :– Gmc. **skabōn, -on,* f. **skab* SHAVE *v.*] Any of various tools adapted for scraping, paring, or removing the surface of material in very thin slices; a drawing or paring knife; also, short for SPOKESHAVE, etc.

Shave (ʃēⁱv), *sb.*[2] 1604. [f. next.] **1.** Something shaved off; a shaving, paring, thin slice. **2.** An act of shaving the beard 1838. **3.** An act of swindling or extortion 1863. **b.** A premium paid for an extension of the time of delivery or payment, or for the right to vary a contract. 1864. **4.** *Mil. slang.* An unauthenticated report 1813. **5.** A slight or grazing touch; hence, a narrow escape from touching, more emphatically *a close, near s.* and the like 1834.

3. *Clean s.*, a complete swindle. **5.** We passed clear; but it was a close s. 1856.

Shave (ʃēⁱv), *v.* Pa. t. **shaved;** pa. pple. **shaven, shaved.** [OE. *sć(e)afan* = OS. **scaban*, OHG. *scaban* (Du. *schaven*, G. *schaben*), ON. *skafa*, Goth. *skaban* :– Gmc. **skaban.* Str. vb. became weak XIV, with the literary survival str. pa. pple. SHAVEN.] **1.** *trans.* To scrape, to scrape away the surface of, to cut down or pare away with a sharp tool, thereby removing very thin portions of the surface. Also with *off.* **b.** To scrape or pare (a skin, hide, etc.) 1467. **2.** To remove by scraping and paring; to cut off in thin slices or shavings; also *to s. off.* late ME. **3.** To cut off (hair, esp. the beard) close to the skin with or as with a razor. Also with *away, off.* ME. **4.** To cut off the beard, whiskers, or moustache from (a person, his chin, upper lip, etc.) with a razor ME. **5.** To remove the hair from (the head, crown, etc.) with a razor. Also (now *rarely*) with the person as object (= to s. the head of) ME. **b.** *esp.* To tonsure (a cleric). late ME. **6. a.** *absol.* Of a barber. late ME. **b.** *intr.* for *refl.* To shave oneself 1715. **7.** *trans.* †To strip (a person) clean of money or possessions; to practise exaction or extortion upon; to fleece. Also *absol.* Now *colloq.* or *slang.* late ME. **8.** To cut off cleanly or closely 1598. **b.** To cut off closely the growth of (ground, a lawn, etc.); also *transf.* of artillery fire 1764. **9.** To touch lightly in passing, to graze; hence, barely to escape touching 1513. **b.** *intr. To s. through*: to get through only by grazing (that which has to be passed); *fig.* to scrape *through* (an examination) 1860. **10.** trans. *U.S. slang.* To discount (a promissory note) at an exorbitant rate of interest; also *to s. paper* 1832.

3. With crowne and berde all fressh and newe y-shaue CHAUCER. Take my counsel, and s. off them mustachios, or they'll bring you into mischief THACKERAY. **4.** Stepping into a barber's shop to be shaved SMOLLETT. **5.** *Prov.* Enuy.. will offer to shaue an eg 1626. He shaved, however, only the fore part of his head 1770. **6. a.** A poor Barber who shaves for Two-pence 1718. **7.** We should never travel without—a case of good razors..But no matter, I believe we shall be pretty well shaved by the way GOLDSM. **9.** Three hansoms shaved him by an inch BARRIE.

Comb.: **s.-hook,** a plumbers' tool consisting of a blade, commonly triangular, set transversely in a handle, used for scraping metal before soldering.

Shavegrass (ʃēⁱ·vgrɑs). 1450. [f. prec. + GRASS *sb.*] A plant of the genus *Equisetum*; esp. *E. hyemale.*

Shaveling (ʃēⁱ·vliŋ), *sb.* (and *a.*). 1529. [f. as prec. + -LING[1].] **A.** *sb.* **1.** A contemptuous epithet for a tonsured ecclesiastic. **2.** A youth, young 'shaver' (*rare*) 1854. **B.** *adj.* Of, pertaining to, or characteristic of a tonsured ecclesiastic 1577.

A. 1. Counting up the number of shavelings still in France 1911.

Shaven (ʃēⁱv'n), *ppl. a.* ME. [Strong pa. pple. of SHAVE *v.*] **1.** Shaved. Chiefly of the head, crown, or of a person; often = tonsured. **2.** Of turf, grass: Closely cut 1632. **3.** Trimmed or polished by shaving 1660.

Shaver (ʃēⁱ·vəɹ). late ME. [f. SHAVE *v.* + -ER[1].] **1.** One who shaves with a razor. **2.** †**a.** One who pillages or plunders; an extortioner –1823. **b.** *U.S.* One who 'shaves' (SHAVE *v.* 10) 1813. **3.** = 'Fellow', 'chap'; also, a humorous fellow, joker, wag. Now commonly of a youth or boy, with the epithet *young, little.* 1592. †**4.** A shaving instrument or tool –1648.

2. a. *Cunning s.*, a swindler, sharper; The Devil is a cunning s. DE FOE. **3.** Forty-five years ago I was just such a little s. as this 1887.

Shavian (ʃēⁱ·viăn), *a.* 1920. [f. *Shavius*, latinized f. proper name *Shaw*: see -IAN.] Of, pertaining to, or characteristic of George Bernard Shaw (1856–1950) or his plays or other writings.

Shaving (ʃēⁱ·viŋ), *vbl. sb.* ME. [f. SHAVE *v.* + -ING[1].] **1.** The action of removing the hair from the head or face with a razor; an instance of this. **2.** *concr.* A thin slice taken off the surface of anything with a sharp tool; esp. a thin slice of wood cut off with a plane. Chiefly *pl.* late ME. **3.** *slang.* The action or process of defrauding 1606. **b.** *U.S.* The discounting of bills at an exorbitant rate of interest 1834.

2. All shavings of horns . . is good manure for land 1760.

Comb.: **s.-brush,** a brush used to put on the lather before shaving.

Shaw (ʃǭ). *arch.* and *dial.* [OE. *sćeaga*, corresp. to OFris. *skage* farthest edge of cultivated land, ON. *skagi* promontory, rel. to OE. *sćeacga* (see SHAG *sb.*[1]).] **1.** A thicket, a small wood, copse or grove. **2.** *spec.* A strip of wood or underwood forming the border of a field 1577.

1. Gaillard he was as Goldfynch in the shawe CHAUCER. A new-blawn plumrose in a hazle s. BURNS.

Shawl (ʃǭl), *sb.* 1662. [– Urdu, etc. – Pers. *šāl*, prob. f. *Shāliāt*, a town in India.] **1.** An article of dress worn by Orientals (commonly as a scarf, turban, or girdle), consisting of an oblong piece of material manufactured in Kashmir from the hair of the Tibetan 'shawl-goat'. **2.** An oblong or square piece of any textile or netted fabric, whether of wool, cotton, silk, or mixtures of these; worn in Europe and the West, chiefly by women as a covering for the shoulders or the head 1767.

Comb.: **s.-dance,** an Eastern dance, in which a s. or scarf is waved; **-goat,** a goat of Tibet (*Capra *lanigera*) which furnishes the wool for making the Indian shawls; **-wool,** the wool of the s.-goat.

Shawl (ʃǭl), *v.* 1812. [f. prec.] *trans.* To cover with a shawl, put a shawl on.

Shawm (ʃǭm), *sb.* [ME. (i) *schallemele*, (ii) pl. *chalm(e)yes*, *schalmes*, later (sing.) (iii) *schalmus*, *schawme* (XVI). – (i) OFr. *chalemel* (mod. *chalumeau*) :- Rom. **calamellus*, dim. of L. *calamus* reed – Gr. κάλαμος; (ii) OFr. (unexpl.) *chalemie*; (iii) OFr. *chalemeaus*, pl. of *chalemel*.] A mediæval musical instrument of the oboe class, having a double reed enclosed in a globular mouthpiece.

With shaumes, and trompets, and with clarions sweet SPENSER. Hence **Shawm** *v. intr.* to play on the s. (*rare*).

Shawnee (ʃǭ·nī). 1909. Name of a tribe of Algonquin Indians, used *attrib.* in **S.-haw,** the larger withe-rod, *Viburnum nudum*; **S.-wood,** the western catalpa or catawba-tree, *Catalpha speciosa*.

Shay (ʃēⁱ). 1717. [A back-formation from CHAISE (ʃēⁱz) mistaken for a pl.] = CHAISE.

It is n't everybody that can ride to heaven in a C-spring s. O. W. HOLMES.

She (ʃī, ʃi), *pers. pron.*, *3rd sing. fem. nom.* ME. [This form repr. east midl. ME. *scæ*, *sʒe*, *sse*, *sche*, parallel with which there was ME. *scho*, *sho*, north. *sco*, surviving in n.w. dial. *shoo* (see HEO). These two types appear to descend from divergent developments of OE. fem. demons. pron.-adj. *sīo*, *sēo*, acc. *sīe* (see THE), resulting from the conversion of the falling diphthongs *īo*, *īe* into rising diphthongs *jō*, *jē*, viz. *sjō*, *sjē* passing into ʃō, ʃē; cf. the development of OE. *hēo* to ME. *ʒho*, mod. dial. *hoo*, *oo*; see HEO.] **I.** As proper feminine pronoun of the third person nominative case. **1.** The female being in question, or last mentioned. **b.** Used of animals of the female sex. Also (esp. in rustic use) of certain animals (e.g. the cat, the hare), the names of which have a quasi-grammatical feminine gender exc. when a male is specifically referred to. late ME. ¶**c.** Misused for *I* (also for *you* and *he*) in literary representations of Highland English 1450. **2.** Used (instead of *it*) of things to which female sex is conventionally attributed. late ME. **3.** Used pleonastically. Now only *arch.* and in uneducated use. 1440. **4.** Used for *her*, as obj. or governed by a prep. Now *rare* exc. *vulg.* 1530.

1. S. shalbe called woman, because shee was taken out of man *Gen.* 2:23. **2.** The Moone cannot shine except shee receiue light from the Sunne 1614. S...was a fine roomy ship 1748. Nature must not be hurried, and s. avenges herself of every attempt to do so SCOTT. **3.** The Liner she's a lady by the paint upon 'er face KIPLING. **4.** I neuer saw a woman But onely Sycorax my Dam, and s. SHAKS. I have got rid of s. 1762.

II. As antecedent pronoun, followed by relative, etc. The or that woman, or person of the female sex (*that* or *who*..). ME.

Him that got thee, s. that gaue thee sucke SHAKS.

III. As demonstrative pronoun. late ME.

The Venus of the Medici?—s. of the diminutive head and the gilded hair? POE.

IV. As *sb.* (not changing in the objective). **1.** A female; a woman or girl; a lady-love 1538. **b.** A female animal 1556. **2.** Opp. to *he*: Female 1500.

1. Who ere she be, That not impossible s. That shall command my heart and me CRASHAW. Those are not shes – they're both men 1894.

V. *attrib.* passing into *adj.* Female. late ME.

‖**Shea** (ʃi, ʃī·ă). 1799. [Mandingo *si*, *se*, *sye*.] A sapotaceous tree of tropical Africa, *Bassia parkii*, from the kernels of which is obtained *s. butter*, a substance used as food by the natives and in Europe for the manufacture of soap, etc.

Sheading (ʃī·diŋ). 1577. [var. f. *shedding* vbl. sb.] Each of six administrative subdivisions (three to each 'district') of the Isle of Man.

Sheaf (ʃīf), *sb.* [OE. *scēaf* = OS. *skōf* (Du. *schoof*), OHG. *scoub* sheaf, bundle, or wisp of straw (G. *schaub*), ON. *skauf* fox's brush :- Gmc. **skauƀaz*, (-*am*), f. **skauƀ*- **skeuƀ*- **skuƀ*-; see SHOVE.] **1.** One of the large bundles in which it is usual to bind cereal plants after reaping. Also, a similar bundle of the stalks or blooms of other plants. **2.** A bundle or quiverful of 24 arrows ME. **3.** A representation of a sheaf (of corn, arrows, etc.). late ME. **4.** *gen.* A cluster or bundle of things tied up together; a quantity of things set thick together 1728. **b.** Emphatically in pl.: A large number, mass, or quantity 1865. **5.** *Physics* and *Math.* A bundle of rays, lines, etc. all passing through a given point 1863.

1. Corn reaped and standing in sheaves 1717. †*Tenth, ninth, third*, etc. *s.*, a specified proportionate part of the annual crop paid to the lord or to the church. **2.** Half a shef of arwes LANGL.

Comb. **s.-binder,** one who binds sheaves, a machine which does this. Hence **Shea·fy** *a.* consisting of or resembling a sheaf or sheaves.

Sheaf (ʃīf), *v.* 1506. [f. prec.] *trans.* To bind into a sheaf or sheaves; also with *up*.

absol. They that reap must sheafe and binde SHAKS.

Shealing, var. of SHIELING.

Shear (ʃīᵊɹ), *sb.*[1] [OE. (i) *scērero* pl. :- **skǣrizō*, (ii) *scēara*, pl. of *scēar* fem., corresp. to MLG. *schēre*, MDu. *scāre*, *scēre* (Du. *schaer*), OHG. *skar*, pl. *skari* (whence G. *scheere*), ON. *skæri* n. pl.; f. **skǣr*-; see SHEAR *v.*] **1.** orig. (and still *Sc.* and *dial.*) = SCISSORS. In later use commonly applied to scissors of large size and to other cutting instruments which operate similarly. **a.** in pl. form, with pl. construction, either in sing. or pl. sense. When qualification by a numeral or an indef. article is required, *pair of shears* is used. OE. **b.** in sing. form, = a pair of shears. Now *rare*. ME. **c.** *fig.*, esp. as attributed to the Fates 1590. **d.** *Mech.* Applied to various machines for cutting metals, more or less analogous to shears in manner of operation 1834. **e.** *Cloth-manuf.* The cutting apparatus of a cloth-cropping machine composed of a series of spiral blades on a revolving cylinder 1839. **2.** *pl.* (Often construed as sing.) A device used upon ships, and in dockyards and mines, for raising and fixing masts, boilers and other heavy gear, consisting of two (or occas. more) poles steadied (in a sloping position) by guys and fastened together at the top, from which the hoisting tackle depends, and with their lower ends separated as a base and secured to the deck or platform. Often spelt **sheers.** 1625.

1. a. For cutting thin sheet metal and wire, a pair of hand-shears 1902. *Prov.* †*There goes but a pair of shears between them*, they match each other as if cut from the same cloth; they are 'of a piece'. **c.** Comes the blind Fury with th'abhorred shears, And slits the thin spun life MILT.

Comb.: **s.-tail,** (*a*) *dial.* the Common Tern (*Sterna fluviatilis*); (*b*) a Peruvian bird (*Thaumastura cora*).

Shear (ʃīᵊɹ), *sb.*[2] Now chiefly *dial.* 1614. [f. SHEAR *v.*] **I.** Action or result of shearing. **a.** A mowing of grass or corn, a crop 1794. **b.** Used in stating the age of sheep with ref. to the number of times the fleece has been shorn. *One s.*, *two s.*, one, two years old. 1614. **II.** In scientific uses. **1. a.** *Physics* and *Mech.* (*a*) A kind of strain consisting in a movement of planes of a body that are parallel to a particular plane in a direction parallel to a line in that plane through distances proportional to their distances from that plane. (*b*) The stress called into play in a body which undergoes this kind of strain. 1850. **b.** *Geom.* The transformation produced in a plane figure by motion in which all the points of the figure describe paths parallel to a fixed axis and proportional in length to their distance from it 1885. **2.** *Geol.* Applied to the operation of transverse compression on a mass of rock, resulting in alteration of structure or breach of continuity 1888.

Shear (ʃīᵊɹ), *sb.*[3] Also **sheer.** 1812. [Of unkn. origin.] The bar, or one of the two parallel bars, forming the bed of a lathe on which the poppets slide.

Shear (ʃīᵊɹ), *v.* Pa. t. **sheared** (ʃīᵊɹd), **shore** (ʃōᵊɹ); pa. pple. **sheared, shorn** (ʃǭɹn). [OE. *scēran* = OFris. *skera*, OS. *bi*|*sceran* (Du. *scheren*), OHG. *sceran* (G. *scheren*), ON. *skera* :- Gmc. **sker*- **skar*- **skǣr*- **skur*- cut, divide, shear, shave.] **1.** *trans.* To cut (something) with a sharp instrument. *Obs.* exc. *arch.* **b.** *absol.* or *intr.* Now chiefly, To cut *through* (an obstacle) with the aid of a weapon. ME. **c.** To cut (glass, tin-plate, etc.) with shears. Also, to cut (iron or steel bars, etc.) with shears. 1837. **2.** To remove (a part) from a body by cutting with a sharp instrument ME. **3.** To remove (the hair or beard) by means of some sharp instrument (also with *off*, *away*); to shave (the head or face); to cut (the hair) close or short; to cut or shave the hair or beard of (a person). Now *rare* exc. in pa. pple. *shorn*. OE. †**b.** To give the tonsure *to*. Usu. *pass.* –1653. **4.** pass. *To be shorn*: to be deprived *of* some part or appurtenance by or as by cutting. Chiefly *transf.* and *fig.* 1740. **5.** To cut the fleece from (an animal); also, to cut off (the fleece, wool, etc.) OE. **6.** To cut off (the superfluous nap of woollen cloth) in the process of manufacture; also, in hat-making, to remove (nap) by singeing or scouring ME. **7.** To cut down, to reap (grass, crops, etc.) with a sickle (†formerly also, with a scythe). Now *dial.* ME. **b.** *absol.* or *intr.* To cut standing crops; to use a sickle ME. **c.** To clip, cut, or trim (a tree or bush, a lawn) ME. **8.** To cleave, divide; said esp. of birds, ships, etc. ME. **b.** *intr.* for *refl.* *Where wind and weather* (or *water*) *shears*: on the ridge of a hill 1556. **9.** *Mech.*, *Geol.*, etc. *trans.* To subject to a shearing stress; to distort or fracture by shear 1850.

1. As bright as if shorn by a file SMEATON. **b.** By a back stroke of his own cimeter shore through the cuirass LYTTON. **2.** The plume was partly shorn away SCOTT. **3.** They have shorn their bright curls off to cast on Adonis E.B. BROWNING. **4.** Sadly I know I am shorn of my strength POE. *fig.* He cannot bear the thought of..appearing among the gentlemen of the neighbourhood shorn of his beams JOHNSON. **8.** Like a plough that shears the heavy Land R. BRIDGES. Hence **Shea·rer,** a reaper of standing crops; one who or that which shears the fleece from an animal.

Shear-grass (ʃīᵊ·ɹgrɑs). 1483. [f. prec.] Popular name of several kinds of sharp-edged grass or sedge, as the saw-grass.

Shearing (ʃīᵊ·riŋ), *vbl. sb.* ME. [f. SHEAR *v.* + -ING[1].] **1.** The action or an act of cutting, clipping, or shaving with shears or some other sharp instrument. **2.** Something which is cut off with shears, etc. Now only *pl.* 1536. **3.** *dial.* A sheep after the first shearing, a shearling 1641. **4.** *Mining.* The vertical cutting or the ends of a portion of an undercut seam of coal 1875. **5.** *Physics*, etc. See SHEAR *v.* 9; the causing of a shear 1850.

2. It was like the s. of the Hogs, all Bristles 1673. *Comb.*: **s. strain,** a strain of the nature of a shear; **s. strength,** power of resistance to s.; **s. stress,** a stress tending to produce or resist a shear.

Shear-legs. 1860. [SHEAR *sb.*[1]] A device consisting of three poles of wood or iron bolted together at their upper ends and extended below, carrying tackle for raising heavy weights for machinery.

Shearling (ʃīᵊ·ɹliŋ). late ME. [f. SHEAR *v.* + -LING[1].] **1.** A sheep that has been once shorn. †**2.** The fleece of such a sheep –1680.

Shearman (ʃīᵊ·ɹmăn). ME. [f. SHEAR *v.* + MAN *sb.*] **1.** One who shears woollen cloth. Now *Hist.* **2.** One who conducts the process of shearing metal 1881.

Shears *pl.*: see SHEAR *sb.*[1]

Shear steel. 1815. [f. SHEAR *sb.*[1]] Blister steel improved in quality by heating, rolling, and tilting; formerly used for shear-blades.

†**'Sheart.** 1596. A euphemistic shortening of *God's heart*, used as an oath or asseveration –1706.

Shearwater (ʃīᵊ·ɹwǭ:təɹ). 1671. [f. SHEAR *v.* + WATER *sb.*] **1.** A bird of the genus *Puffinus*, esp. *P. anglorum*, the Manx Shearwater, and *P. major*, the Greater Shearwater. **2.** *U.S.* The Black Skimmer, *Rhynchops nigra* 1794.

Sheath (ʃīþ), *sb.* [OE. *scǣþ*, *scēaþ* = OS. *skēðia* (Du. *scheede*, *schee*), OHG. *sceida* (G. *scheide*), ON. *skeiðir* pl. scabbard :- Gmc. **skaiþiz*, **skaiþjo*, prob. f. **skaiþ*- divide (see SHED *v.*[1], SHIDE).] **1.** A case or covering into which a blade is thrust when not in use; usu. close-fitting and conforming to the shape of the blade, esp. of a sword, dagger, knife, etc. **2.** A sheath-like covering. *esp.* **a.** *Zool.* The tubular fold of skin into which the penis is retracted 1555. **b.** *Bot.* A tubular or enrolled part or organ that is rolled round a stem or other body, as the spathe of a flower, the lower part of the leaves of grasses, etc. 1671.

c. *Bot.* 'A limiting layer of surrounding cellular tissue' 1884. **d.** *Anat.* The connective tissue covering which closely invests a part or elongated organ, and binds it together and holds it in place 1805. **e.** The elytron or outer hard wing-case of a coleopterous insect 1826. **f.** The fold of skin into which the claws of a feline animal are retracted 1774. **3.** A structure or banking of loose stones to prevent the overflow of a river 1850.

1. Handles, Scabbards, Sheaths for Knives 1669.
Comb.: **s. bill,** a sea-bird of the genus *Chionis*, having the basal part of the bill ensheathed in a horny case; **-knife,** a dagger-like knife encased in a sheath; **-winged** *a.*, having the wings encased in elytra, coleopterous, vaginipennate. Hence **Sheathed** (ʃīþt) *a. Nat. Hist.* having or surrounded by a s.; put in or capable of being withdrawn into a s. **Sheaˑthless** *a.* not encased in a s., having no s.

Sheathe (ʃīð), *v.* Also *techn.* **sheath** (ʃīþ). late ME. [f. prec.] †**1.** *trans.* To fit or furnish (a sword, etc.) with a sheath –1596. **2.** To put (a sword, dagger, etc.) into a sheath or scabbard. late ME. **b.** *transf.* To bury (a sword) as in a sheath (e.g. *in* an enemy's body). Also with obj. an animal's tusk, claw, etc. 1584. **c.** *fig.* To lay aside, cause to be laid aside (hostility, malice). Now *rare* or *Obs.* 1598. **d.** To retract or draw in (the claws) 1681. **3.** To cover or encase (esp. a person or part of the body) *in* (something, usu. protective) 1632. **4.** †**a.** *Med.* To mitigate the acridity or pungency of (a drug) by the use of an emollient vehicle –1811. **b.** *gen.* To mitigate the painfulness of 1820. **5.** (Often *sheath.*) **a.** To cover (a ship, door, roof, etc.) with a sheathing of metal 1615. **b.** To cover a telegraph cable with a protective envelope 1884. **6.** *Nat. Hist.* To surround with a 'sheath' or covering 1664.

1. Walters dagger was not come from sheathing SHAKS. **2.** Phr. *To s. the sword* (fig.), to cease hostilities, to put an end to war or enmity; The sword should not be sheathed till he had been brought to..punishment MACAULAY. **b.** 'Tis in my breast she sheaths her Dagger now DRYDEN. **d.** The Leopard..always keeps the Claws of his fore-feet turned up from the ground, and sheath'd as it were in the Skin of his Toes 1681. **3.** Warriors sheathed in complete steel SCOTT. Hence **Sheathed** (ʃīðd; *techn.* ʃīþt) *ppl. a.*, of a sword, etc., put into or encased in a sheath; of a ship, having the bottom covered with sheathing. **Sheather** (ʃīˑðəɹ), one who or that which sheathes.

Sheath-fish (ʃīˑþfiʃ), **sheat-fish** (ʃīˑt). 1589. [f. SHEATH + FISH, prob. after G. *scheide, scheiden*. The var. *sheat-fish* is recorded somewhat later.] A large freshwater fish, *Silurus glanis*, common in the Danube and other rivers of eastern Europe. **b.** In extended use, as a name for the order *Siluridæ* or for a subdivision of it which includes the genus *Silurus* 1851.

Sheathing (ʃīˑþiŋ, ʃīˑðiŋ), *vbl. sb.* 1499. [f. SHEATHE *v.* + -ING¹.] **1. a.** The action of putting into a sheath. **b.** The action of putting on a protective layer to a ship's bottom 1623. **2.** A protective layer or covering laid on the outside of the bottom of a wooden ship. Formerly of boards, etc., now usu. of thin plates of metal (copper). 1587. **b.** *gen.* A covering or envelope in which something is encased for protection or ornament; material prepared for use as an envelope or casing. Chiefly in techn. applications: e.g. a covering of boards, plates of metal, etc., fitted to the surface of a wall, roof, a piece of machinery, or the like 1859. **3.** A banking of loose stones to prevent the overflowing of a river 1867.

Sheave (ʃīv), *sb.* ME. [repr. OE. **scīfe*, rel. to *scīfe* = OFris. *skīve*, OS. *scība*, (M)LG., MDu. *schīve* (Du. *schijf*), OHG. *scība* (G. *scheibe*), f. base (**skīb*) meaning variously disc, quoit, wheel, pulley, pane of glass, slice of bread; see SHIVE¹.] **1.** A slice of bread. late ME. **2.** A wheel having a groove in the circumference to receive a cord passing over it, a pulley; esp. one of the pulleys connected in a block. Also, a wheel having a groove in the circumference to enable it to run on a rail or bar. ME. **b.** An eccentric or its disc 1887.

Sheave (ʃīv), *v.*¹ 1579. [f. SHEAF *sb.*] *trans.* To bring together, gather or put up (corn, etc.) into a sheaf or sheaves. Hence **Sheaved** *ppl. a.* put up or gathered into a sheaf or sheaves.

Sheave (ʃīv), *v.*² [perh. repr. ME. *schēve*, OE. *scēofan*, var. of *scūfan* SHOVE *v.*] *intr.* To back a boat.

Shebang (ʃībæˑŋ). *U.S. slang.* 1867. [Of unkn. origin.] **1.** A hut, shed; one's dwelling, quarters. **2.** Any matter of present concern; thing; business 1895.

Shebeen (ʃībīˑn). 1787. [Anglo-Ir. *sibin*, *séibín*, f. *séibe* liquid measure, mug + *-in* -EEN².] Chiefly in Ireland and Scotland: A shop or house where excisable liquors are sold without a licence; any low wayside public-house.

Shed (ʃed), *sb.*¹ [OE. (*ġe*)*scēad*, alt. of (*ġe*)*scēād* f. base of SHED *v.* Cf. OHG. *sceitil* division, G. *scheitel* parting of the hair.] †**1.** Distinction, discrimination, separation (of one thing from another) –1703. **2.** The parting made in the hair by combing along the top of the head; also, the part of the head thus indicated, the top of the crown. *Obs.* exc. *dial.* ME. **b.** A parting made in the wool of sheep in order to grease or anoint the skin 1523. **3.** A ridge of high ground dividing two valleys or tracts of lower country; a 'divide' 1530. **4.** *Weaving.* The opening made between the threads of the warp by the motion of the heddles for the shuttle to pass through 1792.

Shed (ʃed), *sb.*² 1481. [prob. specialized use of *shad(de, shed(de*, by-forms of SHADE *sb.*, which itself survives dialectically in this sense.] **1.** A slight structure built for shelter or storage, or for use as a workshop, either attached as a lean-to to a permanent building or separate; often with open front or sides. **b.** A similar structure, but large and strongly built; often consisting of a roof supported by columns. Also *Austral.*, short for WOOLSHED. 1840. **2. a.** *poet.* A hut, cottage, poor dwelling 1600. **b.** *gen.* A structure that affords shelter or covering; the hiding-place, lair, or nest of an animal 1616. **3.** In a telegraph-line insulator, a covering in the form of an inverted cup, a 'petticoat' 1859.

1. In such a season born when scarce a S. Could be obtain'd to shelter him or me From the bleak air MILT. **2. a.** At last an hospitable House they found, A homely S. DRYDEN.
Comb.: **s.-roof,** a roof with only one slope (as in a lean-to s.). Hence **Sheˑdding,** sheds collectively.

Shed (ʃed), *sb.*³ *rare.* 1648. [f. SHED *v.*¹] Something that is or has been shed; e.g. a silkworm's cocoon; a light fall of snow; the cast shell of a crab.

Shed (ʃed), *v.*¹ Pa. t. and pa. pple. **shed.** [OE. *sć(e)ādan*, corresp. directly or with cons.-variation to OFris. *skēda, skētha* wk., OS. *skēdan, skēthan* (Du. *scheiden*), OHG. *sceidan* (G. *scheiden*), Goth. *skaidan* :– Gmc. **skaiðan*, **skaiþan*. Cf. SHEATH, SHIDE.] **1.** *trans.* To separate, divide. Now only *dial.*, chiefly in farming uses: To separate (lambs) from the ewes, or (calves) from the cows; to separate (cattle, sheep) from the herd or flock. †**b.** *intr.* for *refl.* To part company, separate –1696. **2.** *trans.* **a.** To part (the hair; also, the hair or wool of an animal). Now *Sc.* and *dial.* **b.** *Weaving.* To divide (the warp-threads), to make a 'shed' in (a web) 1839. †**3.** To scatter, sprinkle; in later use only, to sow (seed) –1770. **b.** To throw off, repel (rain, sunlight, etc.). Now chiefly *dial.* late ME. †**c.** *refl.* and *intr.* To be dispersed, scatter –1650. **4.** *trans.* To pour, pour out; to emit, give forth ME. **5.** To cause (blood) to flow from the body by cutting or wounding; to let fall (a person's blood) on the ground, etc. ME. **b.** With pregnant sense ME. **6.** To emit and let fall in drops (tears, rain, dew, etc.) ME. **7.** To send forth as an emanation. **a.** To throw (light) *upon* something ME. **b.** To give forth, diffuse (fragrance, sound, heat, etc.); to pour out, impart (influence, blessings, qualities, etc.). Also with *abroad*, †*forth*, etc. ME. **8.** To cast off by natural process. **a.** To cast off as exuviæ; to undergo the falling of (hair, etc.) 1510. **b.** Of trees, plants: To lose, cast off (leaves, flowers, bark, etc.) 1598. **c.** Of plants: To let fall, cast (seed) out of the receptacle 1523. **d.** *colloq.* To drop, let go; to take off (a garment); to give away (something of no particular value) 1855. **9.** *intr.* for *refl.* †**a.** Of the hair: To fall out –1755. **b.** Of grain: To fall from the ear. Also of leaves or flowers: To drop off. 1557.

3. He..shede the seed into the erthe WYCLIF *Gen.* 38:9. **b.** As a shaggy dog sheds water from his coat 1885. **c.** Sike prayse is smoke, that sheddeth in the skye SPENSER. **4.** Roaches do then s. their Spawn 1630. As when a fountain sheds Dark waters streaming down a precipice 1870. **5. b.** *To s. the blood of* (another person or persons), to kill in a manner involving the effusion of blood; often *loosely*, to kill by violent means. So *to s. blood*, to destroy human life by violent means. *To s.* (one's own) *blood*, to undergo wounds or violent death in battle, martyrdom, or the like (*for* some person or cause, one's country, etc.). **6.** He could only s. childish tears of despair and terror 1862. **7. a.** The statement.. sheds little light upon a situation still enveloped in mystery 1912. **8. a.** When hens are shedding their feathers they don't lay eggs 1845. *fig.* He sheds his bad reputation as a snake its skin 1910. Hence **Sheˑdding** *vbl. sb.* the action of the verb; *concr.* (*pl.*) shed leaves, etc.

Shed (ʃed), *v.*² 1850. [f. SHED *sb.*²] *trans.* To place in a shed.

Shedder (ʃeˑdəɹ). late ME. [f. SHED *v.*¹ + -ER¹.] **1.** One who sheds. **2.** *spec.* **a.** A female fish of the *Salmonidæ* after spawning 1588. **b.** A crab during the period when it is casting its covering integument or shell 1872.

Sheel (ʃīl), *v.* Now *dial.* 1440. [Related to SHALE *sb.*¹] *trans.* To shell; to take off the husk or outer covering of. Hence **Sheeˑling** *vbl. sb.* the grain removed from the husk; the husks of oats, etc.

Sheen (ʃīn), *sb.* 1602. [f. next; apprehended as abstr. noun of SHINE *v.*] Shining, brightness. In recent use chiefly, gleaming, lustre, radiance as of a body reflecting light; a gleam. *rare* before 19th c. **b.** Gorgeous or bright attire 1802.

The azurn s. of Turkis blew MILT. **b.** In costly s. and gaudy cloak array'd BYRON.

Sheen (ʃīn), *a.* Now *poet.* [OE. *scēne*, WS. *sćiene* = OFris. *skēne*, OS., OHG. *scōni* (Du. *schoon*, G. *schön*), Goth. *skauns* :– Gmc. **skauniz*, **skaunjaz*, f. **skau-* behold; see SHOW *v.*] **1.** Beautiful. **2.** Bright, shining, resplendent OE.

1. Hayle be thou Mary, maydyn shen 1536. Narcissus will I twine, and lilies s. 1873. **2.** By fountaine cleere, or spangled star light sheene SHAKS.

Sheen (ʃīn), *v.* late ME. [f. prec.] *intr.* **a.** = SHINE *v.* Now only *Sc.* and *dial.* **b.** *poet.* To cast a gleam, glisten 1812.

b. This town, That, sheening far, celestial seems to be BYRON.

Sheeny (ʃīˑni), *sb. slang.* 1824. [Of unkn. origin.] Opprobrious term for: A Jew.

Sheeny (ʃīˑni), *a.* 1625. [f. SHEEN *sb.* + -Y¹.] Covered with sheen, full of sheen; having a bright shiny surface.

Sheep (ʃīp). *Pl.* **sheep.** [OE. (Anglian) *scēp*, (WS.) *scǣp*, *scēap* = OFris. *skēp*, OS. *scāp* (Du. *schaap*), OHG. *scāf* (G. *schaf*) :– WGmc. **skǣpa*, of which no cogns. are known.] **1.** Any animal of the ruminant genus *Ovis* (sometimes horned), closely allied to the goats; esp. of the widely domesticated species *Ovis aries*, of which there are many varieties, and which is reared for its flesh, fleece, and skin. **b.** With qualifying word denoting the species 1604. **2.** Similative (often passing into fig.) uses OE. **b.** *Lost s.*: one who has strayed from the right way 1611. **c.** *Black s.*: a bad character 1792. **3.** *fig.* In biblical and religious language, applied (as collective plural) to persons, in expressed or implied correlation with *shepherd*. Said, e.g. of Israel, the Church, or mankind generally, viewed as under the protection of God; also of those who are led by Christ as the Good Shepherd (John 10:1–16); etc. OE. **4.** A person who is as stupid, timid, or poor-spirited as a sheep 1542. **5.** *ellipt.* (For *s. leather.*) Leather made from the skin of the sheep; used in bookbinding 1705.

1. b. The Rocky Mountain s...is closely related to the chamois of Europe 1875. **2.** We have erred and strayed from thy wayes, lyke lost shepe *Bk. Com. Prayer.* Thou Wolfe in Sheepes array SHAKS. I will not..be flayed like a s. for the benefit of some pettifogging..attorney SCOTT. **c.** Provb. *There is a black s. in every flock.* Phr. *To return to our s.*: see MUTTON. **3.** In thy book record their groanes Who were thy S. MILT. **4.** I know he would not be a Wolfe, But that he sees the Romans are but Sheepe SHAKS.

attrib. and *Comb.*: as **s.-back** = *roche moutonnée* (see MOUTONNÉE); **-bot (fly)**, the bot-fly *Œstrus ovis*; †**-counter**, a counter or token used in counting s.; **-dip**, (*a*) a preparation or solution used for washing sheep; (*b*) a place where sheep are washed; **-dog**, a dog that tends sheep; applied *spec.* to the Scotch collie and the bob-tailed English s.-dog; **-farm**, a tract of land devoted to sheep-rearing; so **-farm** *v.*, **-farmer, -farming**; **-gate**, (*a*) pasturage, or the right of pasturage for sheep (or a s.); (*b*) a gate for the passage of sheep; a hurdle for enclosing sheep; **-hook** (now *rare*), a shepherd's crook; **-kill, -laurel**, a N. Amer. shrub, *Kalmia angustifolia*, supposed to be very poisonous to sheep; **-louse**, a louse, *Trichodectes sphærocephalus*, which infests the wool of sheep; **-mark**, the mark used by a sheep-owner to distinguish his sheep, and app. formerly by illiterate persons as a substitute for their signature; **-pest**, (*a*) a common Australian weed, *Acæna ovina*, the hooked spines of which catch in the wool of sheep; (*b*) = S.-TICK; **-pock, -pox**, a form of smallpox to which sheep are subject; **-rot**, (*a*) the rot in s., caused by the presence of flukes in the liver; (*b*) a name for plants supposed to cause disease in sheep, as butterwort and marsh pennywort; **-scab**, a skin-disease of sheep, due to an acarus; **-sorrel** = *sheep's sorrel*; **-walk**, a tract of grass-land used for pasturing sheep; **-wash**, the washing of sheep before shearing, the place where this is done; also, = *s.-dip* (a); **-weed**, soapwort; **-wool** = *sheep's wool*.

b. Combs. with genitive *sheep's*: **sheep's bit (scabious)** = *sheep's scabious*; **sheep's fescue (grass)**, see FESCUE *sb.* 4; **sheep's gut(s** = CATGUT; **sheep's scabious**, *Jasione montana*; **sheep's sorrel**, *Rumex acetosella*; **sheep's wool** (*a*) wool from the fleece of a s.; (*b*) a W. Indian sponge, *Spongia equina*, var. *gossypina*; (*c*) *sheep's-wool fat*, lanoline. Hence **Shee·p-like** *a.* resembling a s. or that of a s.; *adv.* meekly, submissively, pusillanimously. **Shee·py** *a.* (*rare*).

Shee·p-bi:ter. 1548. **1.** A dog that bites or worries sheep. Now *rare.* †**2.** *fig.* A shifty, sneaking, or thievish fellow –1778. †**3.** One who runs after 'mutton'; a woman-hunter, whoremonger –1719.

2. There are Political Sheep-biters as well as Pastoral 1692.

Sheepcote (ʃī·pkōᵘt). late ME. [f. SHEEP + COTE *sb.*[1]] A slight building for sheltering sheep; a sheep-house. So **Shee·pcot.**

Sheepfold (ʃī·pfōᵘld). late ME. [f. SHEEP + FOLD *sb.*[1]] A pen or enclosure for sheep.

fig. The Prince of all Shepheards whose sheepefold is the world 1635.

Sheepish (ʃī·piʃ), *a.* (*adv.*). ME. [f. SHEEP + -ISH[1].] **1.** †**a.** Of, pertaining to, or concerned with sheep. **b.** Resembling sheep or their characteristics. Now *rare.* †**2.** Simple, silly –1692. †**b.** Excessively meek or submissive; mean-spirited –1711. **3.** Bashful or awkward in the presence of others; esp. in society to which one is unaccustomed; embarrassed or out of countenance from an excess of shyness or diffidence 1693.

Hence **Shee·pish-ly** *adv.*, **-ness.**

Shee·pman. 1591. †**1.** A shepherd –1641. **2.** *U.S.* A sheep-breeder, -owner, or -tender 1883.

Sheep's eye(s. 1529. **1.** Phr. *To cast* (or *throw*) *a sheep's eye at* or *upon*, now usu. *to cast sheep's eyes at*: to look lovingly, amorously, or longingly at. **2.** An amorous glance 1604.

1. I have often see him cast a Sheep's Eye out of a Calf's Head at you SWIFT.

Sheepshank (ʃī·pʃæŋk), *sb.* 1627. **1.** The shank or leg of a sheep 1675. **2.** *Naut.* In full †*sheepshank(s) knot*: A knot cast on a rope for temporarily shortening it without cutting it or unfastening the ends. Hence **Shee·p-shank** *v. trans.* to shorten (a rope) by means of a s.

Sheep's head. ME. **1.** The head of a sheep; a dish consisting of this. **2.** A fool, simpleton. †Also as *adj.*, stupid. 1542. **3.** A large and much esteemed food fish, *Archosargus* or *Diplodus probatocephalus* (*Sargus ovis*), abundant on the coasts of the U.S. 1676. **b.** A freshwater fish resembling the drumfish of the Mississippi and the Great Lakes; also locally in N. America applied to various other fishes 1836.

Shee·p-shea:rer. 1539. One who shears sheep. **b.** A machine for shearing sheep 1908.

Shee·p-shea:ring, *vbl. sb.* 1586. **1.** The act or practice of shearing sheep. **2.** The season for shearing sheep 1688. **3.** The feast held at the shearing-season 1611.

Shee·pskin. Also **sheep's skin.** ME. **1.** The skin of a sheep; *esp.* one used as a garment or in the making of a garment. **2.** The skin of sheep used for parchment, for the making of drumheads, in bookbinding, etc. ME. **b.** *U.S. slang.* A parchment diploma received on taking a degree; the holder of such a diploma 1843. **3.** *attrib.* or *adj.* Made or consisting of s. or parchment; written on parchment 1602.

3. So doth a sheepe-skin Bond make money breed 1624.

Shee·p-tick, †**sheep's tick.** late ME. [See TICK *sb.*[1]] A horny bristly wingless fly, *Melophagus ovinus*, which infests sheep, embedding its head in the skin and extracting the blood.

Sheer (ʃīᵊɹ), *sb.*[1] 1670. [f. SHEER *v.*[1]] *Naut.* **1.** An abrupt divergence or deviation of a vessel from the line of her course; a swerve. **2.** An oblique position given to or taken by a vessel when under way or when riding at single anchor 1794.

2. Phr. *To break her s.*, of a vessel at anchor, to be forced by change of wind or current out of the position of s. in which she was placed.

Comb.: **s.-boom** *Lumbering*, a boom to catch floating logs and turn them in the desired direction; **-line**, in military bridges, the stretched hawser of a flying bridge along which the boat passes.

Sheer (ʃīᵊɹ), *sb.*[2] 1691. [prob. f. SHEAR *sb.*[2]; cf. synon. Fr. *tonture* 'shearing' (XVII).] *Naut.* **1.** The fore-and-aft upward curvature or rise of the deck or bulwarks of a vessel; the curve of the upper line of a vessel as shown in vertical section. **2.** = *s.-strake* 1841.

Comb.: **s.-draught (-draft)**, the s.-plan; **-line**, the line of elevation of a ship's deck; **-plan**, the section of a ship which would be made by a vertical plane passing through the keel; **-strake, -wale**, the uppermost strake of the side planking or plating of a vessel.

Sheer (ʃīᵊɹ), *a.* and *adv.* ME. [prob. alt. of (dial.) *shire* clear, pure, mere, thin, weak, OE. *scīr* = OFris. *skīre*, OS. *skīr*(*i*, ON. *skírr*, Goth. *skeirs* :– Gmc. **skīraz*, *skīrjaz*, f. **skī*- SHINE. There is no proof of continuity with ME. *schere* free, clear, fine. Cf. SHEER THURSDAY.] **A.** *adj.* †**1.** Exempt, free (from service or fealty). –late ME. †**2.** Of light: Bright, shining. Of water, crystal, etc.: Clear and pure; translucent. –1871. **3.** Of textile fabrics, etc.: Thin, fine, diaphanous 1565. **4.** Of a material substance: Unmixed or unaccompanied with other matter. Esp. of strong drink: (*a*) Undiluted with water; (*b*) taken alone without solid food. 1596. **b.** Of an immaterial thing: Taken or existing by itself,.. alone. Now *rare* or *Obs.* 1622. **5.** Neither more nor less than (what is expressed by the sb.); that and nothing else; unmitigated, unqualified; downright, absolute, pure 1583. **6.** Of a descent or ascent, the face of a wall, cliff, etc.: Continued perpendicularly or very steeply down or up without break or halting-place 1800.

2. Afterward they began to yeeld sheere and cleere water in great aboundance HOLLAND. **3.** Shear muslins fit for head dresses and neckcloths 1706. **4.** If she say I am not xiiii. d. on the score for sheere Ale SHAKS. **5.** Out of s. love and kindness to Lord Chatham '*Junius*' *Lett.* **6.** This lake,.. whose barriers drear Are precipices sharp and s. SCOTT.

B. *adv.* **1.** Completely, absolutely, altogether, quite 1600. **2.** Perpendicularly or very steeply up or down; straight up or down without break or halting-place 1829.

1. Thrown by angry Jove S. o're the Chrystal Battlements MILT. **2.** It rose s. up above the contiguous roofs CARLYLE. Hence **Shee·r-ly** *adv.* **-ness.**

Sheer (ʃīᵊɹ), *v.*[1] 1626. [perh. – (M)LG. (whence G.) *scheren*; identical with SHEAR *v.*] *Naut.* **1.** *intr.* Of a ship: To turn aside, alter its direction, swerve, in obedience to the helm. **b.** To swerve to either side irregularly or unsteadily, not in obedience to the helm. Also with *round.* 1635. **c.** *transf.* and *fig.* Chiefly with *off*: To change one's course; to depart, go away; to go off in a new direction or on another 'tack' 1704. **2.** *trans.* To cause (a vessel) to sheer; to direct (a vessel) obliquely towards a given point 1633.

1. Phr. *To s. alongside, to, up*, to bear up obliquely towards a vessel or other point.

Sheer (ʃīᵊɹ), *v.*[2] *rare.* 1851. [f. SHEER *a.*] *intr.* Of a rock-face: To rise or descend vertically or very steeply.

Sheer-hulk, shear-hulk. 1768. [f. *sheer* SHEAR *sb.*[1] 2 + HULK *sb.* 3.] The hulk or body of an old or disused ship fitted with shears, etc. for hoisting purposes; also, a vessel specially built and fitted with shears. (In the pop. fig. use of the word the first element is often misunderstood as *sheer* adj., and the compound written as two words.)

fig. Here, a sheer hulk, lies poor Tom Bowling DIBDIN. She had been built for a sheer-hulk 1799.

Sheer Thursday. *Hist.* [ME. *shere-*, *shire* (cf. SHEER *a.*), corresp. to ON. *skærr*, *skírr* clean, pure, which were used in the same way and were adopted XII–XIII with *sk-*.] Maundy Thursday.

Sheet (ʃīt), *sb.*[1] [OE. (Anglian) *sċēte*, (WS.) *sċīete* :– **skautjōn*, f. **skaut-* **skeut-* **skut-* (see SHOOT *v.*, SHOT *sb.*[1]), one meaning of which is 'project'. The unmutated stem is repr. by OE. *sċēat* lap, skirt, cloth, and the forms s.v. SHEET *sb.*[2]] **1.** †**a.** A napkin, cloth, or towel. **b.** A broad piece of linen or cotton stuff, canvas, or the like, for covering, swathing, protecting from injury, etc. (Now felt as a transf. use of 3.) **2.** = WINDING-SHEET OE. **3.** A large oblong piece of linen, cotton (or, formerly, hempen) cloth, used as an article of bedding, one being placed immediately above and one below the person ME. **b.** *pl.* in phrases with ref. to sexual intercourse 1604. **4.** A sail. Chiefly *poet.* late ME. **5.** An oblong or square piece of paper or parchment, *esp.* for writing or printing; *spec.* one of the pieces of definite size (varying according to the kind) in which paper is made, 24 (formerly also 25) going to a quire 1510. **b.** A piece of paper which is divided by means of perforations or the like into sections which may be torn or cut away as required 1776. **6.** In printing and bookbinding, such a piece of paper printed and folded so as to form pages of a required size (folio, quarto, etc.). Also, a quantity of printed matter equal to that contained in a sheet. 1589. **c.** *pl.* Pages or leaves of a book; esp. *these sheets, the following sheets* = the book now before the reader. Now *rare.* 1591. **d.** A newspaper. Now *rare.* 1749. **7.** A continuous extent or 'sweep' of something conceived as hanging, falling, or moving in a certain direction 1605. **8.** A broad expanse or stretch of something lying out flat, presenting a white or glistening surface, or forming a relatively thin covering or layer; *spec.* in *Geol.*, *Anat.*, *Path.* 1593. **9.** A relatively thin piece of considerable breadth *of* a malleable, ductile, or pliable substance 1675. **b.** A flat piece of tin, used for baking cakes, etc. 1747. **c.** Sheet iron or steel; a length of this 1884. **10.** quasi-*adj.* Rolled out in a sheet; esp. of metals, as *s. iron, lead, steel.* Also = printed on a single sheet or broadside, esp. *s.-almanac.* 1582.

1. She should..cover up every article of furniture..with large dusting-sheets 1888. **2.** Tybalt, ly'st thou there in thy bloudy s.? SHAKS. **3.** *The sheets*, the pair of sheets belonging to a bed. *Between the sheets* (colloq.) in bed. **b.** My Daughters got 'tweene the lawfull sheets SHAKS. **4.** The Boat was push'd off, the S. was spread 1712. **5.** He had..managed to fill two sides of a s. of letter-paper 1857. *In sheets*, lying flat or expanded, not folded. **6.** A Magazine s. is sixteen pages DICKENS. *In sheets*, (of books) not bound 1693. **7.** A broad s. of lightning 1847. A heavy squall with sheets of rain 1894. **8.** Sheets o' daisies white BURNS. **9.** A s. of plate glass 1893.

attrib. and *Comb.*: **s. glass** (*a*) cylinder glass; (*b*) a vessel made of this glass; **-lightning**, lightning in a sheet-like form due to reflection by the clouds; **s. music**, music published in sheet form as opposed to book form. Hence **Shee·tful**, as much as a s. will contain. **Shee·ty** *a.* spreading in a broad s.: chiefly of water.

Sheet (ʃīt), *sb.*[2] ME. [repr. OE. *sċēata* 'pes veli', but used for *sċēatlīne* (see LINE *sb.*[2]) = MLG. *schōtlīne* (cf. ON. *skautreip*), prob. after ON. *skaut* or MLG., MDu. *schōte*; both in this sense. OE. *sċēata* corresp. to (M)LG. *schōte*, OHG. *scōza* skirt, ON. *skauti* kerchief; cf. SHEET *sb.*[1]] **1.** A rope (or chain) attached to either of the lower corners of a square sail (or the after lower corner of a fore-and-aft sail), and used to extend the sail or to alter its direction. **2.** See quot. 1644.

1. A wet s. and a flowing sea CUNNINGHAM. *Three sheets in the wind*, very drunk; A thought tipsy..a s. or so in the wind, as folks say TROLLOPE. **2.** *Sheets*, the spaces in a rowing boat forward and abaft the thwarts, and named respectively *fore-sheets* and *stern-sheets* 1891.

Sheet (ʃīt), *v.*[1] 1606. [f. SHEET *sb.*[1]] **1.** *trans.* To wrap or fold in or as in a sheet; now *spec.* to cover with a protecting sheet of canvas, tarpaulin, etc. 1621. **2.** To spread a sheet or layer of some substance upon (a surface); to cover with a sheet (e.g. of snow or ice) 1606.

1. [A racehorse] sheeted to the tail 1860. **2.** When Snow the Pasture sheets SHAKS. Its roof was sheeted, like St. Peter's, with copper 1845.

Sheet (ʃīt), *v.*[2] 1797. [f. SHEET *sb.*[2]] trans. *To s. home*: to extend the sheets of (the topsails) to the outer extremities of the yards so that the clews are close to the sheet-blocks. Also *absol.*

Sheet-anchor (ʃī·t,æ:ŋkəɹ). 1495. [The earliest forms (*shute anker* XV) point to deriv. from †*shoot* sheet of a sail (XV–XVII) – (M)LG. *schōte* (SHEET *sb.*[2]), (M)Du. *schoot*; the connection in sense is not obvious, but the correspondence seems to be confirmed by the substitution of SHEET *sb.*[2] in XVII.] A large anchor, formerly always the largest of a ship's anchors, used only in an emergency. **b.** *fig.* That on which one places one's reliance when all else has failed 1524.

b. It is Foreign Trade that is the main Sheet-Anchor of us Islanders 1676. Hence **Shee·t-cable** *Naut.*, the cable belonging to the s.

Sheeted (ʃī·tèd), *ppl. a.* 1604. [f. SHEET *sb.*[1] or *v.*[1] + -ED.] **1.** Wrapped in a sheet, *esp.* a winding-sheet; applied to the dead and ghosts. **b.** Enveloped in a sheet or sheets for protection against injury, etc. 1766. **2.** In the form of a sheet; expanded or spread out like a sheet: chiefly of rain, snow, lightning 1796. **3.** Of cattle: Having a broad band of white round the body 1834.

1. The s. dead Did squeake and gibber in the Roman streets SHAKS.

Sheeting (ʃī·tiŋ), *vbl. sb.* 1711. [f. SHEET *sb.*[1] + -ING[1].] **1.** Stout cloth of linen or cotton, such as is used for bed linen. **2.** A lining or covering of timber or metal, laid on a surface as a protection 1776. **3.** The action or process of making (lead) into sheets: the action of covering with sheets or laying in sheets 1778.

Sheffield (ʃe·fīld). late ME. Name of a manufacturing city of Yorkshire, famous for cutlery, used *attrib.* as *S. ware*; **S. plate,** plate made of copper coated with silver by a special process perfected in Sheffield (but now disused).

‖**Sheikh** (ʃēik, ʃīk). 1577. [ult. – Arab. *šayḵ* (prop.) old man, f. *šāḵa* be or grow old. Cf. Fr. *cheik, scheik, †seic*, Sp. *jeque*.] **1.** The chief of an Arab family or tribe; the headman of an Arabian village; an Arab chief; †an Eastern governor, prince, king. Now also, among Arabs, a general title of respect. **2.** The head of a religious order or community; a great religious doctor or preacher; now *esp.* a saint having a local cultus 1613. **3.** In India, one of a dissenting sect of Moslems; now, a general term for Hindu converts to Islam. (Usu. *shekh, shaikh.*) 1883.

2. *S.-ul-Islam* (properly *šayḵu-'l-'islām*): the supreme authority in matters relating to religion and sacred law; in Turkey, the mufti; hence *Sheikh-ul-Islamate.*

Shekel (ʃe·kĕl). 1560. [– Heb. *šeḳel*, f. *šāḳal* weigh.] **1. a.** An ancient unit of weight of the Babylonians, and hence of the Phœnicians, Hebrews, and others, equal to one-sixtieth of a mina. **b.** A coin of this weight; *esp.* the chief silver coin of the Hebrews. **2.** *fig.* (*pl.*) Coin, money. *colloq.* 1883.

Shekinah, shechinah (ʃĭkəi·nă). 1663. [– late Heb. *šᵉḵīnāh*, f. *šāḵan*, rest, dwell.] The visible manifestation of the Divine Majesty, esp. when resting between the cherubim over the mercy-seat or in the temple of Solomon; a glory or refulgent light symbolizing the Divine Presence. **b.** *transf.* spec. applied to Jesus Christ 1682.

b. Truth indeed is veiled, But with a Schekinah of dazzling light 1834.

Sheld (ʃeld), *a. dial.* 1507. [rel. to MDu. *schillede* variegated, f. *schillen* (mod. Du. *verschillen* differ) diversify.] Particoloured, pied, piebald.

Sheld-duck, shell-duck (ʃe·ldɒk). 1707. [f. next, by substitution of *duck* for *drake*.] = next. So **Sche·ld-fowl.**

Sheldrake (ʃe·ldrēik). ME. [prob. f. SHELD *a.* + DRAKE[2].] A bird of the genus *Tadorna* of the duck tribe, frequenting sandy coasts in Europe, North Africa, and Asia and remarkable for its variegated colouring.

Shelf (ʃelf) *sb.*[1] *Pl.* **shelves** (ʃelvz). late ME. [– (M)LG. *schelf* shelf, set of shelves, with accommodation to Eng. words in *sh-*, more normally repr. by (dial.) *skelf* (XIV); rel. to OE. *sċylfe* partition, compartment, *sċylf* rugged rock, crag, pinnacle; cf. Gmc. **skelf*-split.] **I. 1.** A slab of wood, etc. fixed in a horizontal position to a wall, or in a frame, to hold books, vessels, ornaments, etc.; one of the transverse boards in a bookcase, cabinet, or the like. **b.** *transf.* A shelf with ref. to its contents; the contents of a shelf (*esp.* of books) 1732. **2.** *Shipbuilding.* A timber on the inner side of the frame to support the deck-beams 1834.

1. Phr. (fig.) *On the s.*, (*a*) on one side, out of the way, in a position of inactivity or uselessness; esp. *to lay* (*put*, etc.) *on the s.*; (*b*) of women, without prospects of marrying. **b.** You may confute a whole s. of schoolmen BERKELEY.

II. Senses influenced by SHELF *sb.*[2] **1.** A ledge, platform, or terrace of land, rock, etc. 1809. **2.** *Mining* and *Geol.* Bed-rock 1671.

1. *Continental s.*, the relatively shallow belt of sea-bottom bordering a continental mass, the outer edge of which sinks rapidly to the deep ocean-floor.

attrib.: **s.-catalogue, -list,** a short-title catalogue of books in a library giving their shelf positions; **s.-mark** = PRESS-MARK. Hence **Shelf** *v. trans.* to lay on the s., shelve. **She·lf-ful,** a quantity sufficient to fill a s.; the contents of a s.

Shelf (ʃelf), *sb.*[2] 1545. [prob. alt., by assoc. with prec., of synon. †*shelp* (XV), repr. OE. *sċylp* 'scopulus, murex', of unkn. origin.] A sandbank in the sea or river rendering the water shallow and dangerous. Also loosely applied to a submerged ledge of rock. Hence **She·lfy** *a.*[1] abounding in sandbanks lying near the surface of the water.

Shelfy, *a.*[2] *dial.* (Devon and Cornwall.) 1602. [f. dial. *shelf, shilf* broken slate.] Full of slaty rock.

Shell (ʃel), *sb.* [OE. (Anglian) *sċell*, (WS.) *sċiell* = (M)LG., MDu. *schelle, schille*, Du. *schel, schil* pod, rind, scale, shell, ON. *skel* sea-shell, Goth. *skalja* tile :– Gmc. **skaljō*, f. *skal-*; see SCALE *sb.*[1], SHALE *sb.*[1] and [2].] **I.** The hard outside covering of an animal, a fruit, etc. **1.** The calcareous or chitinous outer covering of crustaceans, molluscs, and other invertebrates. Freq. used allusively. **2.** A shell of this kind (or a vessel resembling one) used for a specific purpose. late ME. **3.** As tr. Gr. ὄστρακον, the potsherd or tile used in the OSTRACISM of the ancient Greeks 1565. **4.** *pl.* Burnt limestone before it is slaked 1743. **5.** Used as the second element of the name of a particular shellfish, as *razor-s.*; hence (chiefly *pl.*) = shellfish 1751. **6.** The hard calcareous envelope of a bird's egg. Also, the similar integument of the eggs of other creatures. OE. **7.** = NUTSHELL ME. **b.** The fibre-covered envelope of a coco-nut 1638. **8.** The outer covering of a seed, etc.; a husk, pod. (e.g. *pea-s.*); putamen, pericarp 1561. **9.** The hard covering or 'house' of a snail. late ME. **b.** In fig. phrases, referring to avoidance of society or extreme reserve 1853. **10.** The hard covering of a tortoise or turtle; the material of which this is composed; cf. TORTOISESHELL 1545. †**b.** *poet.* A lyre (according to legend orig. a tortoise shell stringed); occas. 'lyric poetry' –1821. **11.** The integument of an armadillo, glyptodon, ostraciont, etc.; the elytron of an insect; the cast skin of a pupa 1774.

1. They used to gather up Shells on the Sea-Shore STEELE. **2.** By scaly Tritons winding s. MILT. Whiskey was served round in a s., according to the ancient Highland custom BOSWELL. **6.** *fig.* My young nouice..not yet crept out of the s. 1593. Phr. *In the s.*, (of an egg or a bird, etc.) unhatched; also *fig.* in embryo. **9. b.** Under the soothing influence of coffee and tobacco, he came out of his s. 1889. **10. b.** 'Twas Milton struck the deep-toned s. GRAY.

II. A shell-shaped object; something concave or hollow. **1.** *gen.* A hollow spherical, hemispherical, or dome-shaped object 1599. **2.** The semicircular guard of a sword 1685. **3.** The apsidal end of the school-room at Westminster School, so called from its conch-like shape. Hence, the name of the form (intermediate between the fifth and sixth) which orig. tenanted the 'shell' at this school, and *transf.* of forms (intermediate between forms designated by numbers) in other public schools. 1736. **4.** The outer ear 1847. **5.** *U.S.* A light narrow racing-boat 1873. **b.** The floating part of a racing boat 1895. **c.** In various techn. uses, e.g. a concave grinding tool, the outer wall of a mould in casting 1819. **III.** An exterior or enclosing cover or case. **1. a.** A covering (of earth, stone, etc.) 1667. **b.** The crust of the earth 1704. **2.** A case of metal, etc. in which powder and shot is made up, esp. for use as a hand-grenade 1644. **b.** Hence, an explosive projectile or bomb for use in a cannon or mortar. Also *collect. sing.* 1651. **c.** A cartridge case of paper or metal 1799. **3.** A wooden coffin, esp. a rough or temporary one. Also a thin coffin of lead or other material to be enclosed in a more substantial one. 1788.

2. b. The bomb-ship..plied the French with her shells 1767.

IV. A mere exterior or framework. **1.** The external part, exterior, or outward aspect, the externals (of something immaterial) 1652. **2.** An empty or hollow thing; mere externality without substance 1791. **3. a.** The outer part of an edifice or fabric, the interior of which has been removed or destroyed 1657. **b.** The skeleton or carcass of a building or a ship 1705. **c.** *U.S.* A rough, wooden structure, without decoration or furniture 1852.

1. The outward form and s. of religion 1774. **2.** Mere effigies and shells of men CARLYLE. **3. b.** I preached..in the s. of the new house WESLEY.

V. A scale or scale-like object. **1.** A scale of a fish or reptile; a hard epidermal excrescence (*rare*) OE. **2.** A scale or lamina (of stone, †bone, etc.) ME. **3.** Any of the thin pieces of metal composing scale-armour 1585. **4.** An epaulette 1848.

Comb.: **s.-back,** (*a*) *joc.* (a hardened or experienced) sailor; (*b*) a marine turtle; **-breaker,** an instrument used in lithotomy; **-fire,** (*a*) *dial.* phosphorescence or lambent fire seen enveloping or issuing from bodies; (*b*) the firing of shells from guns; **-flower,** *Molucella lævis*, the genus *Chelone*, and some species of *Alpinia*; **-game** (*U.S.*), a swindling game resembling THIMBLE-RIG; **-gland,** (*a*) an excretory organ beneath the shell in the lower crustaceans; (*b*) the shell-secreting gland of a mollusc; **-gold,** gold for painting or writing, laid in a mussel-shell; **-heap,** a mound of domestic remains consisting chiefly of refuse shells accumulated by aborigines who subsisted on shell-fish; **-jacket,** an undress tight-fitting military jacket, short in the back; **-lime,** lime made by burning sea-shells; **-money** = WAMPUM; **-mound** = *s.-heap*; **-plate,** one of the plates forming the outer shell of a vessel, boiler, etc.; **-pump** = *sand-pump* (see SAND *sb.*); **-sac** = *s.-gland*; **-shock,** derangement of the nervous system resulting primarily from exposure to shell-explosion at close quarters; so **-shocked** *a.*; **-work,** arrangement of shells in patterns for ornamentation; shells lining the walls of an artificial grotto. Hence **She·ll-less** *a.* without a s. or shells.

Shell (ʃel), *v.* 1562. [f. prec.] **1.** *trans.* To remove (a seed) from its shell, husk, or pod. Also with *out*. **b.** *intr.* Of grain, seed, etc.: To drop out of the shell or husk 1828. **2.** *trans.* To remove the shell, husk, etc. of 1694. **3.** *intr.* To come away or fall off as a shell, crust, or outer coat; to come *off* in thin pieces, peel or scale *off* 1676. **4.** *trans.* To enclose in, or as in, a shell; to encase 1637. **5.** To bombard with shells (also *absol.*); to drive *out of* a place by shelling 1827.

1. S. your pease just before you want them 1796. Phr. (colloq.) *S. out*, *trans.* to disburse, pay up, hand over; *intr.* to pay up. **2.** Some shrimps shelled 1806. **4.** S. thee with steel or brass.. Death from the casque will pull thy cautious head 1685. Hence **She·ller,** one who or that which shells.

Shellac (ʃĕlæ·k, ʃe·læk). 1713. [f. SHELL *sb.* + LAC[1], tr. Fr. *laque en écailles* lac in thin plates.] Lac melted and run into thin plates.

Shelled (ʃeld), *a.* 1577. [f. SHELL *sb.* +

-ED².] **1.** Having a shell. **2.** Of ammunition: Contained in shells 1900.

Shelleyan (ʃe·li,ăn), *a.* (and *sb.*) 1849. [f. the name *Shelley* + -AN¹.] Pertaining, relating to, or characteristic of Percy Bysshe Shelley (1792–1822), his poetry, or the ideas expressed in his works. As *sb.*, an admirer of Shelley. So **She·lleyism** 1822. **She·lleyite.**

Shell-fish (ʃe·lfiʃ). [OE. *sćilfisć* = ON. *skelfiskr.*] Any animal living in water whose outer covering is a shell, whether testaceous, as an oyster, or crustaceous, as a crab.

Shelling (ʃe·liŋ), *vbl. sb.* 1598. [f. SHELL *v.* + -ING¹.] **1.** The action of SHELL *v.* 1725. **2.** *concr.* (chiefly *pl.*) **a.** Husks or chaff 1598. **b.** Grain, etc. from which the husk has been removed 1705. **3.** The firing of shells, bombardment with shells 1860. **4.** The collecting of sea-shells 1861.

Shelly (ʃe·li), *a.* 1555. [f. SHELL *sb.* + -Y¹.] **1.** Abounding in (sea)shells; of a geological formation, consisting wholly or mainly of shells. **2.** Consisting of or of the nature of a shell; forming a covering resembling a shell; shell-like 1592. **3.** Of an animal: Having a shell; shell- 1593. **4.** Formed of a (sea)shell; consisting of (sea)shells or shell-fish 1716.

1. The s. shore POPE. Marle of the s. kind 1824. **2.** The shellie skin of the sea Vrchin HOLLAND. **3.** Animals of the s. tribe GOLDSM. **4.** S. Hautboys 1721.

S'help. 1904. = S'ELP.

Shelta (ʃe·ltă). 1876. [Of unkn. origin.] A cryptic jargon used by tinkers, gipsies, etc., composed partly of Irish or Gaelic words disguised by inversion or by arbitrary alteration of initial consonants.

The tinkers protect themselves by the use of a secret language,..known as S.,..Shelter,..'Bog Latin',..or 'the Ould Thing' 1891.

Shelter (ʃe·ltəɹ), *sb.* 1585. [poss. alt. of †*sheltron* phalanx :- OE. *sćieldtruma*, f. *sćield* SHIELD + *truma* troop.] **1.** A structure affording protection from rain, wind, or sun; any screen or place of refuge from the weather. **b.** Something which affords a refuge from danger, attack, pursuit, or observation; a place of safety; *Mil.* a wall or bank behind which persons can obtain safety from gunshot 1605. **c.** Protection from the weather; trees, walls, or the like, which afford this 1613. **d.** A covering to protect an object from injury 1700. **e.** A place of temporary lodging for the homeless poor 1895. **2.** The state of being sheltered; protection from the elements; security from attack 1593.

1. Their tent was a sufficient s. from the rain DE FOE. *fig.* And thou shalt proue a s. to thy friends SHAKS. **e.** A Salvation Army s. 1895. **2.** Where..a ship might find good s. 1726. Phr. *To seek, find, take*, etc. *s. Under the s. of* = protected by.

Comb.: **s.-deck,** in a passenger vessel, a light deck more or less closed at the sides but open at the ends; **-pit** *Mil.*, a small pit for one man only; **-tent,** a small ridged tent; a dog-tent. Hence **She·ltery** *a.*

Shelter (ʃe·ltəɹ), *v.* 1551. [f. prec.] **1.** *trans.* To be or provide a shelter for. **b.** *fig.* To screen from punishment, censure, etc. 1594. **c.** 'To succour with refuge, to harbour' (J.); to take under one's protection. Of a place: To be a secure home or refuge for. 1663. **2.** *refl.* To take shelter; to take refuge from pursuit or attack 1611. **b.** *fig.* Chiefly, to protect oneself from punishment or censure 1598. **3.** *intr.* for *refl.* To take shelter; to find a refuge 1602.

1. A wall of rock..sheltered us from the north wind TYNDALL. Harbours and ports, which may s. the navy in the operations of war 1862. **b.** In vain I strove to..s. Passion under Friendship's Name PRIOR. **c.** These Ruines sheltered once His Sacred Head DRYDEN. **2. b.** Phr. *To s. oneself under, behind* —, to use the protection afforded by (what is specified). **3.** A company of buccaniers.. s. here 1727. Hence **She·lterer,** one who takes shelter; one who shelters another.

Shelterless (ʃe·ltəɹlės), *a.* 1714. [f. SHELTER *sb.* + -LESS.] **1.** Without a shelter or covering; unprotected from the elements. **2.** That affords no shelter 1760.

1. Now sad and s., perhaps, she lyes, Where piercing Winds blow sharp 1714.

Sheltie, shelty (ʃe·lti). *Sc.* 1654. [prob. repr. the Orkney pronunc. of ON. *Hjalti* Shetlander.] A Shetland pony; now, any small pony.

Shelve (ʃelv), *sb.*¹ 1582. A new sing. evolved from *shelves*, pl. of SHELF *sb.*², q.v.

Shelve (ʃelv), *sb.*² 1701. [f. SHELVE *v.*¹ 1.] A ledge or shelf of rock, or mountain.

Shelve (ʃelv), *v.*¹ 1591. [f. *shelves* pl. of SHELF *sb.*¹] †**1.** *intr.* To project like a shelf, overhang SHAKS. **2.** *trans.* To provide with shelves, *esp.* with bookshelves 1598. **3.** To place on a shelf or shelves; *esp.* to place or arrange (books) upon shelves 1650. **4.** *fig.* To lay aside as on a shelf, to put away or up as done with 1812.

4. Some of the present Government..will be shelved 1850. The Circumlocution Office.. shelved the business DICKENS. Hence **She·lving** *vbl. sb.*¹ the action of the verb; shelves collectively.

Shelve (ʃelv), *v.*² 1587. [perh. back-formation from SHELVY *a.*¹] **1.** *intr.* Of a surface: To slope gradually 1614. †**2.** To have an inclined position –1763. **3.** *trans.* To tilt or tip up (a cart). *dial.* 1587.

1. The bank shelves away very fast from the Northern shore 1726. Hence **She·lving** *vbl. sb.*² the fact or condition of sloping; the degree of sloping; a sloping surface; a shelve. **She·lving** *ppl. a.* that shelves or slopes.

Shelvy (ʃe·lvi), *a.*¹ 1598. [f. SHELVE *sb.*¹ + -Y¹.] Of a shore: Having shelves or dangerous sand-banks; also †of a brook.

I had beene drown'd, but that the shore was sheluy and shallow SHAKS.

Shelvy (ʃe·lvi), *a.*² 1831. [f. SHELVE *sb.*² + -Y¹.] Projecting like a shelf; overhanging.

Shemite (ʃe·məit), *sb.* and *a.* 1659. [f. *Shem*, name of the eldest son of Noah (cf. Gen. 6:10) + -ITE¹ 1.] = SEMITE *a.* and *sb.* **Shemi·tic** *a.* and *sb.* **Shemi·tish** *a.* **She·mitism.**

Shemozzle (ʃemǫ·z'l). orig. *East End slang.* Also **schle-.** 1899. [Of Yiddish origin, and based on post-bibl. Heb. *šel-lō'-mazzāl* of-no-luck (planet or planetary influence).] A muddle or complication; a quarrel, 'row', mêlée.

Shend (ʃend), *v.* Now *dial.* and *arch.* Pa. t. and pa. pple. **shent** (ʃent). [OE. *sćendan* put to shame or reproach, ruin, discomfit = OLG. *scendian* (Du. *schenden*), OHG. *scentan* (G. *schänden*) :- WGmc. **skandjan*, f. **skand-* ashamed :- **skamđa-*, pa. pple. formation on **skam-* SHAME.] **1.** *trans.* To put to shame or confusion; to confound, disgrace. **2.** To blame, reproach, reprove; to revile, scold. In later use the passive often = to suffer for one's deeds, be punished. OE. **3.** To destroy, ruin. Also, in milder sense, to injure, damage, spoil. OE. †**b.** To disfigure, spoil; to defile, soil –1876. †**4.** To discomfit (in battle or dispute) –1829.

1. Debatefull strife, and cruell enmitie, The famous name of knighthood fowly s. SPENSER. **2.** Yet was his Loyalty shent, but not sham'd FULLER.

Shent (ʃent), *ppl. a. arch.* [ME. *schent* :- OE. *ġesćend*, pa. pple. of *sćendan* SHEND *v.*] Disgraced, lost, ruined.

She-oak. *Austral.* 1792. [See SHE V; cf. *he-oak.*] **1.** A tree of the genus *Casuarina.* **2.** *slang.* Colonial beer 1888.

‖**Sheol** (ʃī·oᵘl, ʃī·ǫl). 1599. [Heb. *še'ōl.*] The underworld; the abode of the dead or departed spirits, conceived by the Hebrews as a subterranean region clothed in thick darkness, return from which is impossible.

Shepherd (ʃe·pəɹd), *sb.* [OE. *sćēaphierde*; see SHEEP, HERD *sb.*²] **1.** A man who guards, tends, and herds a flock of sheep (grazing at large); usu. one so employed for hire; or one of a pastoral people who herds (his own) sheep, goats, etc. **b.** Applied to the rustic personages of pastoral poetry. Hence in pastoral poetry formerly often used to designate the writer and his friends or fellow-poets. 1591. **c.** Fr. Hist. *The Shepherds* [= Fr. *les Pastoureaux*]: those who took part in the peasant insurrections of 1251 ff. and 1320. 1759. **2.** *fig.* **a.** = A spiritual guardian or pastor of a 'flock' ME. **b.** In Biblical use, applied to God in relation to Israel or the Church; also to Christ (esp. with ref. to John 10:12). late ME. **c.** Applied to temporal rulers 1577. **3.** (With initial capital.) = SHEPHERD KING 1. 1813. **4.** *Austral.* A miner who holds a claim but does not work it 1864.

1. b. If that the World and Loue were young, And truth in euery shepheards toung RALEGH. **2. b.** Heare o thou shepherde of Israel, thou yᵗ ledest Iacob like a flocke of shepe COVERDALE *Ps.* 79:1.

attrib. and *Comb.*: **s.-bird** = PASTOR *sb.* 4; **-dog** = *shepherd's dog*; **s. spider,** the harvest-spider; **s. tartan** = *shepherd's tartan.* **b.** Combs. with *shepherd's*: **shepherd's calendar,** a calendar containing weather predictions and seasonable instructions for shepherds (app. proverbially referred to as unreliable); hence adopted as the title of certain pastoral poems; **shepherd's check, plaid, tartan,** a woollen cloth with a black-and-white check pattern; **shepherd's dog,** a large variety of dog employed by shepherds to control and protect flocks of sheep; **shepherd's pie,** a pie made of mashed potatoes and minced meat, with a crust of mashed potatoes browned; **shepherd's pipe,** the pastoral oboe or musette; **shepherd's spider** = *s. spider.* **c.** In names of plants (chiefly *dial.*): **shepherd's calendar,** the scarlet pimpernel; **shepherd's club,** the common mullein, *Verbascum thapsus*; **shepherd's needle,** †(*a*) crane's bill, (*b*) lady's comb; **shepherd's rod,** *Dipsacus pilosus*; **shepherd's staff,** (*a*) = *shepherd's rod*; (*b*) the common mullein. Hence †**She·pherdish** *a.* pastoral. **She·pherdize** *v.* (*rare*) *intr.* to pretend to lead the pastoral life. **She·pherdless** *a.* without a s.

Shepherd (ʃe·pəɹd), *v.* 1790. [f. prec.] **1.** *trans.* To tend, guard, and watch (sheep) as a shepherd. Also *absol.* **2.** *transf.* and *fig.* To tend, watch over, or guide as a shepherd does his sheep 1820. **3.** *Austral.* To watch over or guard (a mining claim) by working on it superficially (esp. by digging small pits) so as to retain legal rights. Also *intr.* 1861. **4.** *colloq.* or *slang.* To watch over, to follow closely and watchfully 1885. **b.** *Mil.* To force (a body of the enemy) into an unfavourable position 1900.

2. Arethusa arose From her couch of snows.. Shepherding her bright fountains SHELLEY. **4.** Admiral Dowell is reported to be closely shepherding the Russian vessels in these seas 1885.

Shepherdess (ʃe·pəɹdės). late ME. [f. SHEPHERD *sb.* + -ESS¹.] A female shepherd; a woman or girl who tends sheep; also in pastoral poetry (see SHEPHERD 1 b). **b.** A representation (in painting, etc.; esp. in china or earthenware) of a shepherdess 1771.

Shepherd king. 1587. **1.** *pl.* [tr. Gr. βασιλεῖς ποιμένες, Manetho's rendering of the Egyptian designation which he transliterates as Ὑκσως (Hyksos).] The designation of a succession of kings of Egypt (the 15th and 16th dynasties of Manetho), belonging to some foreign people. (By historians often called *Hyksos.*) **2.** *gen.* A king who is a shepherd 1727.

Shepherdly (ʃe·pəɹdli), *a.* Now *rare.* 1559. [f. SHEPHERD *sb.* + -LY¹.] Pertaining to or befitting a shepherd (*lit.* and *fig.*); that has the characteristics of a shepherd; †that is a shepherd. †**b.** Pastoral, rural, rustic –1743.

b. I hate the country: I am past the s. age of groves and streams H. WALPOLE.

Shepherd's purse. late ME. [After med. L. *bursa pastoris* (XIII); cf. Fr. *bourse-à-pasteur*, G. *hirtentasche.*] **1.** A common cruciferous weed, *Capsella bursa-pastoris*, bearing pouch-like pods. **2.** *dial.* The fossil echinus found in the chalk 1893.

Sherardize (ʃe·răɹdəiz), *v.* 1904. [f. name of *Sherard* Cowper-Coles; see -IZE.] *trans.* To coat (iron articles) with zinc by a particular process.

Sheraton (ʃe·rătən), *a.* 1883. [Name of Thomas *Sheraton* (1751–1806), furniture-maker and designer.] Designating a severe style of furniture developed in England towards the end of the 18th c., chiefly by Thomas Sheraton.

Sherbet (ʃə̄·ɹbət). 1603. [– Turk., Pers. *šerbet* – Arab. *šarba*, f. *šariba* vb. drink. Cf. SHRUB², SYRUP.] **1. a.** A cooling drink of the East, made of fruit juice and water sweetened, often cooled with snow. **b.** A European imitation of this; now esp. an effervescing drink made of sherbet powder (see 2). **2.** In full *s. powder*: A preparation of bicarbonate of soda, tartaric acid, sugar, etc., variously flavoured, for making an effervescing drink 1856. **b.** *U.S.* A variety of water ice.

1. b. To bring in s., ginger-pop, lemonade 1845.

‖**Shereef** (ʃərī·f). 1560. [– Arab. *šarīf* noble, high-born, f. *šarafa* be noble, exalted.] **1.** A descendant of Mohammed through his daughter Fatima. †Occas. *spec.* a Moslem priest. **2.** Hence used as the title of certain Arab princes, esp. the sovereign of Morocco; also, the chief magistrate, or local governor of Mecca 1600. ‖**Sheree·fa,** the wife of a

Moroccan s., **-ee·fian** *a.* pertaining to the s. of Morocco.

Sheriff (ʃe·rif). [OE. *scīrġerēfa*, f. *scīr* SHIRE *sb.* + *ġerēfa* REEVE *sb.*[1]] **1. a.** *England* (and *Wales*). In England before the Norman Conquest, a high officer, the representative of the royal authority in a shire, who presided in the shire-moot, and was responsible for the administration of the royal demesne and the execution of the law. At the present time the sheriff of a county (more fully called *high s.*), appointed for one year by royal patent, is nominally responsible for the keeping of prisoners in safe custody, preparing the panel of jurors for the assizes, the execution of writs, and of the sentence of death. In addition to these duties, which are discharged by the under-sheriff, the high sheriff acts as presiding officer at parliamentary elections for the county, and is required to attend on the judges at assizes. In *Ireland* (1542) and *U.S.* (1662) applied to similar officers (in U.S. usu. elective). Those boroughs and cities that are counties of themselves, and also the City of Oxford, have a sheriff (or in some instances two) chosen annually by the Corporation, the specific duties attached to the office varying in different towns. The City of London elects annually two sheriffs, who are also sheriffs of Middlesex. **b.** *Scotland.* In early times, a high officer of a county with functions analogous to those of the English sheriff of the same period, together with a civil and criminal jurisdiction of very wide extent. The judicial duties of the office were performed by the *sheriff-depute*, who was necessarily a lawyer. Since the act 20 Geo. II, c. 43 (1747) the title of sheriff is given to the sheriff-depute, who is the chief local judge in a Scottish county, and popularly to the sheriff-substitute, who usu. hears cases in the first instance, subject to an appeal to the sheriff-depute. Both offices are now held for life, and the appointment rests with the crown. late ME.

Comb.: **sheriff's clerk**, *Sc.* **s. clerk**, the clerk of the sheriff's court; **sheriff's officer**, an official employed to execute the sheriff's writs, to distrain and arrest, etc. Hence **She·riffalty** (ʃe·rifălti) = SHRIEVALTY. †**She·riffhood**, the office of s. –1629. **She·riffwick** = next.

Sheriffdom (ʃe·rifdəm). late ME. [-DOM.] **1.** *Sc.* A district or territory under the jurisdiction of a sheriff. **2.** The office of sheriff 1596.

Sherris (ʃe·ris). *arch.* 1597. [= *Sherries*, repr. old pronunc. of *Xeres* (now *Jerez*).] = next.

Comb.: **s.-sack**, 'sack' imported from Xeres.

Sherry (ʃe·ri). 1608. [alt. of SHERRIS apprehended as a pl. or derived from *sherris sack* (see SACK *sb.*[3]).] Orig., the still white wine made near Xeres (now Jeres de la Frontera, near Cadiz); in mod. use, extended to a class of Spanish white wines of similar character, and to wines made elsewhere in imitation of Spanish sherry.

Comb.: **s.-cobbler**; see COBBLER 3.

Sherryvallies (ʃerivæ·liz), *sb. pl. U.S.* 1778. [prob. immed. – Pol. *szarawary* (General C. Lee), corresp. to Russ. *sharovárў*, wide trousers, LXX σαράβαρα, rendering Aram. *sarbalā*, Arab. *sirbāl* cloak, mantle. Cf. late and med.L. *sarabara*, *saraballa*, etc.] Overalls made of thick velvet or leather, buttoned on the outside of each leg, and worn over the trousers as a protection from mud, etc.

Sheth (ʃeþ). *local* and *techn.* 1431. [cogn. with WFlem. *schet*, *schette* rail, etc.] A bar, lath, esp. one of a series; *Mining* and *Agric.* one of a series of rows or workings.

Shetland (ʃe·tlănd). 1790. [Name of a group of islands to the north-north-east of the mainland of Scotland.] Used *attrib.*

S. pony, *horse*, etc., one of a breed (orig. from the Shetlands) of small hardy ponies having a rough coat and a long mane and tail. *S. wool*, a variety of wool spun in the Shetlands; hence applied to things made of this wool. Hence **She·tlander**, an inhabitant of the Shetland Isles; a S. pony.

Sheva (ʃəvā·). 1582. [Rabbinic Heb. *šᵉwā*, app. arbitrary alt. of *šaw'* emptiness, vanity.] **1.** *Heb. Gram.* The sign ְ under a consonant letter to indicate (what Jewish grammarians regard as) the absence of a vowel. *Movable s.*: the neutral vowel (ə). **2.** *Phonetics.* (sometimes in G. form **schwa.**) The neutral vowel-sound, *esp.* in comparative grammar 1888.

Shew, var. of SHOW *sb.* and *v.*

Shewbread (ʃōᵘ·bred). 1530. [f. *shew* SHOW *sb.*, after G. *schaubrot* (Luther), repr. Heb. *leḥem pānīm*, LXX ἄρτοι ἐνώπιοι, Vulg. *panes propositionis.*] *Jewish Antiq.* The twelve loaves that were placed every Sabbath 'before the Lord' on a table beside the altar of incense, and at the end of the week were eaten by the priests alone.

Shewel (ʃū·əl). *Obs.* exc. *dial.* [ME. *scheules* cogn. with MLG. *schūwelse* (= G. *scheusal*), deriv. of the verb which appears as OHG. *sciuhen* (G. *scheuen*). Cf. SHY *a.*] A scarecrow. Also *Hunting*, something set up to keep a deer from entering a particular place, or from going in a particular direction.

‖**Shiah** (ʃī·ă). 1626. [Arab. *šī'a* faction, party, f. root *šā'a* spread news, publicize.] **a.** Properly, a collective name for the Moslem sect which maintains that Ali (Mohammed's cousin and son-in-law) was the true successor of the prophet, and regards the three first caliphs of the Sunnites as usurpers. **b.** Commonly, an adherent of this sect, a Shiite.

Shibboleth (ʃi·bŏleþ). ME. [– Heb. *šibbōlet* ear of corn.] **1.** The Hebrew word used by Jephthah as a test-word by which to distinguish the fleeing Ephraimites (who could not pronounce the *sh*) from his own men the Gileadites (Judges 12:4–6). **2.** *transf.* **a.** A word used as a test for detecting foreigners, or persons from another district, by their pronunciation 1658. **b.** *loosely.* A custom, habit, mode of dress, or the like, which distinguishes a particular class or set of persons 1806. **3.** *fig.* A catchword or formula adopted by a party or sect, by which their adherents or followers may be discerned, or those not their followers may be excluded 1638.

1. In that sore battel when so many dy'd Without Reprieve adjudg'd to death, For want of well pronouncing S. MILT. **3.** The fetters of party shibboleths 1862.

Shide (ʃəid). *Obs.* exc. *dial.* [OE. *scīd* = OFris. *skīd*, OHG. *scīt* (G. *scheit*), ON. *skíð* :– Gmc. **skīđam*, f. **skīđ-* divide; see SHEATH, SHED *v.*[1]] A piece of wood split off from timber, a block, billet; a board, plank, beam. As a quantity; Half a cubic foot of timber.

Shiel (ʃīl). *Sc.* and *north.* [ME. *shāle*, *shēle*, of unkn. origin.] **1.** A temporary building, usu. of boards; a SHIELING. **2.** A small house, cottage, hovel ME.

Shield (ʃīld), *sb.* [OE. *sćeld*, *sćield* = OFris. *skeld*, OS., OHG. *scild* (Du., G. *schild*), ON. *skjǫldr*, Goth. *skildus* – Gmc. **skelduz*, prob. orig. 'board' and so f. base **skel-* **skal-* **skæl-* divide, separate; cf. SCALE *sb.*[1]] **I. 1.** An article of defensive armour carried in the hand or attached by a strap to the left arm of a soldier, as a protection from the weapons of the enemy. Sometimes *spec.* an article of this kind larger than the BUCKLER, and smaller than the PAVIS. **2.** *transf.* and *fig.* Something serving as a defence against attack or injury ME. **b.** Applied (as a Biblical Hebraism; see, e.g. Ps. 23:20), to a personal protector or defender (esp. to God) OE. **3.** *Her.* = ESCUTCHEON 1 ME. **4.** An ornamental piece of plate, more or less in the form of a shield, freq. offered for competition in an athletic or other contest 1868.

2. b. Thow be my sheld for þy benignite CHAUCER. **3.** *S.-of-arms*, an escutcheon with armorial bearings. *S. of pretence* = ESCUTCHEON *of pretence.*

II. A protective covering or shelter. **1.** Applied to certain parts of animal bodies. **a.** The thick tough skin upon the sides and flanks of the boar; *spec.* an article of food (in full, *s. of brawn*), made by placing a piece of this skin round the inside of a mould and filling up with meat, and cooking until soft and tender. late ME. **b.** *Zool.* A protective plate covering a part; a scute, a carapace, a plastron, or the like 1704. **2.** A framework erected for the protection of workmen engaged in boring or tunnelling and pushed forward as the work progresses; also, a watertight case used in submarine tunnelling to keep back quicksands and inrushes of water 1837. **3.** A protective device attached to a field-gun in order to shelter the gunners from rifle-fire 1898. **b.** A protective plate or screen in machinery generally 1888. **c.** Any protective device in clothing. **III.** Applied to things shaped like a shield. **1.** *Bot.* The apothecium of lichens 1796. **2.** *Cutlery.* A small metal plate fixed on the handle of a penknife or pocket-knife, for ornament or to be engraved with the owner's name 1876. **3.** *gen.* A flat or slightly convex surface more or less resembling a shield in shape 1849. **4.** A breed of pigeons of various colours 1855. **5.** *U.S.* A policeman's badge 1903.

Comb.; **s.-arm**, the left arm; **-bearer**, an attendant who carries the s. of a warrior; **-bud**, a bud and a portion of the bark surrounding it, used in grafting; **-fern**, various forms of the genus *Aspidium.* Hence **Shie·ldless** *a.*, having no s.; unprotected by a s.

Shield (ʃīld), *v.* [OE. *sćeldan*, *sćildan*, f. the sb.] **1.** *trans.* To protect (a person or object) by the interposition of some means of defence; to protect (an accused person, etc.) by authority or influence. **2.** *absol.* To offer a defence, to act as a shield OE. †**3.** To ward off, to keep away. Also with *off.* –1822. †**4.** In deprecatory phr. *God s.*, usu. with a clause or sentence as direct obj.; also *absol.* as an exclam.: = God forbid –1674.

1. Thow shalt bee shielded with my protection alway 1582. **2.** A desire to s. and save BYRON. **4.** God shilde that it sholde so bifalle CHAUCER.

Shielded (ʃī·ldėd), *ppl. a.* OE. [f. SHIELD *sb.* and *v.* + -ED.] **1.** Bearing a shield. **b.** *Nat. Hist.* In names of various animals characterized by a hard shield-like carapace or scute 1662. **2.** Furnished or hung with shields 1805. **3.** *techn.* Protected by a 'shield' 1855.

1. b. The s. tortoise 1662. **2.** The s. hall of Valhalla 1892.

Shieling, shealing (ʃī·liŋ). *Sc.* 1568. [f. SHIEL + -ING[1].] **1.** A piece of pasture to which cattle may be driven for grazing. **2.** A hut of rough construction erected on or near such a piece of pasture 1585.

Shift (ʃift), *sb.* ME. [f. next.] †**I.** A movement to do something, a beginning. ME. only. **II. 1.** An expedient, an ingenious device for effecting some purpose 1530. **b.** Faculty of contrivance, resourcefulness (*rare*). Cf. SHIFTLESS *a.* 1542. **2.** A fraudulent or evasive device, a stratagem; a piece of sophistry, an evasion, subterfuge 1545. **3.** An expedient necessitated by stress of circumstances 1647. **4.** *To make (a) shift.* **a.** To make efforts, bestir oneself. Now *dial.* 1460. **b.** To attain one's end by contrivance or effort; to succeed; to manage *to do* something 1504. **c.** To succeed with difficulty, to manage with effort *to do* something 1538. **d.** To do one's best *with* (inferior means), to be content *with*, put up *with* 1577.

1. Ile finde a thousand shifts to get away SHAKS. **b.** Hang them, say I, that has no S. SWIFT. **2.** Their whole life is a succession of shifts, excuses, and expedients HAZLITT. **3.** It were endless to recount the shifts to which I have been reduced JOHNSON. Phr. *One's* (or *the*) *last s.*, the last resource. *To be at one's last shift(s*, to be at the last extremity; so to *put*, *drive*, *reduce*, etc. *to the last shifts.* **4. d.** I cannot make s. nor bear fatigue as I used to do SWIFT. We..have to make a s. with cheap labour 1885.

III. Change, substitution, succession. †**1.** Change or substitution of one thing for another of the same kind –1625. **2.** Change (of clothing); *concr.* one of several suits of clothing, or garments of the same kind belonging to one person. *Obs.* exc. *dial.* 1570. **3.** A body-garment of linen, cotton, or the like; usu. a woman's 'smock' or chemise. Now *rare.* 1598. **4.** Each of the successive crops in a course of rotation 1787. **5.** A relay or change of workmen 1812. **b.** The length of time during which such a set of men work 1809. **6.** A change (of wind) 1594.

1. My going to Oxford was not merely for s. of air WOTTON. **5.** The night shifts receive so much higher pay for their labour 1912.

IV. Change of position, removal. **1.** A shifting, removal; a change of position or attitude; *dial.* a change of residence or employment 1826. **2.** *Mus.* In violin-playing, a change of the position of the hand on the finger-board 1771. **3.** *Building.* The arrangement of timbers, stones, etc. so that the joints of adjacent rows do not coincide 1805. **4.** *Mining.* A slight 'fault' or dislocation in a seam or stratum 1802.

Shift (ʃift), *v.* [OE. *sćiftan* = OFris. *skifta*, MLG. *schiften, schichten* (G. *schichten*), ON. *skipta* divide, separate, change, f. base **skip-* as in ON. *skipa* arrange, assign.] **I.** To put in order, arrange. **†1.** *trans.* To appoint, assign, dispose in order. late ME. **2.** To apportion, distribute; to separate into shares, divide OE. **†3.** *intr.* To manage matters; to deal, bargain, make arrangements *with*; to make provision *for* ME. **4.** To manage to effect one's purposes; to succeed, get on (well or ill); to make shift 1532. **5.** To employ shifts or evasions; to practise or use indirect methods; to practise or live by fraud, or temporary expedients 1579. **6.** *To s. for oneself*, to provide for one's own safety, interests, or livelihood (implying either absence of aid, or, occas., want of concern for others); to depend on one's own efforts 1513.

3. Phr. †*To let* (persons) *s.* [= Fr. *laisser faire*] to let (them) take their own course, not to interfere. **4.** She that hath wit, may s. any-where MIDDLETON. Might not the colonists s. for the present with the southern island? 1865.

II. To change. **†1.** *trans.* To change, to replace by another of the kind. With pl. object: To quit one and take another of (the things indicated) –1864. **b.** *intr.* To undergo transmutation; to change 1605. **2.** To change (one's own or another's clothing). Also *refl.* and *intr.* for *refl.* Now chiefly *dial.* late ME. **3.** *trans.* To change (the scene) 1599. **b.** *intr.* Of a scene: To change 1828. **†4.** *trans.* To cause (a set of workmen) to change places with another set. Also said of a gang of workmen: To replace (another gang or set) as a relief; also *intr.* for *refl.* –1791.

1. There staid..till he shifted his horses PEPYS. Phr. †*To s. hands* = 'to change hands'; also, to change one's ground in argument; so *to s.* one's *ground.* **2.** I went immediately to s. my clothes DE FOE. **3.** The scene shifts to the latter place 1861.

III. To change the place of, to remove. **1.** *trans.* To transfer from one place to another; to remove; to alter the position of. late ME. **2.** *Naut.* **a.** To change or alter the position of (a sail, spar, the helm, etc.) 1667. **b.** Of a ship or a navigator: To undergo displacement of (cargo or ballast) 1854. **c.** *intr.* Of cargo, ballast: To move from its proper position, so as to disturb the equilibrium of the vessel 1797. **3.** *trans.* To alter the direction of 1698. **b.** *intr.* Of the wind: To change its direction 1645. **4.** *trans.* To change or alter (one's or its position, place); to change (one's lodging, abode, etc.) 1563. **5.** To get (a person) out of the way. Now *slang* or *colloq.*, to dislodge (a body of the enemy); of a horse, to throw (the rider); also *euphem.*, to 'put out of the way', murder. 1604. **†6.** To avoid, escape, elude –1816. **7. S. off. †a.** To put off, remove (a covering, a garment); *fig.* to remove from oneself or another (a burden) –1805. **b.** To evade, turn aside (an argument); to evade fulfilment of (a duty, a promise) 1577. **c.** To put (a person) off with an excuse or a subterfuge; to get rid of (a person) 1585. **8.** *intr.* To move from one place to another; esp. to change one's lodging 1530. **9.** To move about, to move from one position to another, to move slightly 1595. **10.** To move away, withdraw, depart; esp. to slip off unobserved. Now only with *away.* 1590.

1. Every man shifting the fault from himself CLARENDON. Cæsar had shifted his camp continually 1879. **3. b.** The wind has shifted round to due west 1885. **5.** Cassio came hither. I shifted him away. SHAKS. **10.** Oh Mistris, Mistris, s. and saue your selfe SHAKS. Hence **Shi·ftable** *a.*

Shifter (ʃi·ftəɹ). 1555. [f. prec. + -ER[1].] **1.** One who shifts something; *spec.* a scene-shifter. †2. One who resorts to petty shifts, or who practises artifice; an idle, thriftless fellow; a trickster, cozener, etc. –1670. **b.** One who uses evasive reasoning 1567. **3.** *Naut.* One who assists the ship's cook 1704. **4.** *Mech.* A contrivance used for shifting, e.g. a kind of clutch serving to transfer a belt from one pulley to another 1869.

1. He is no great s.; once a yeare his Apparel is ready to reuolt B. JONS. **2.** In worldly matters, practis'd and cunning Shifters MILT.

Shifting (ʃi·ftiŋ), *ppl. a.* 1479. [f. as prec. + -ING[2].] **1.** That shifts or changes position or direction. **2.** That uses shifts, tricks, deceit, expedients, subterfuges, or evasions 1581.

1. A whole parish was swallowed up by the s. sands SCOTT. Special collocations: **s. ballast**, ballast capable of being moved to trim the vessel; **s. centre** = METACENTRE; **s. use** *Law*, a use properly created for the benefit of one person, but so as to pass from him upon a specified contingency and vest wholly or in part in another. Hence **Shi·fting-ly** *adv.*, **-ness.**

Shiftless (ʃi·ftlės), *a.* 1562. [f. SHIFT *sb.* + -LESS.] **†1.** Helpless for self-defence; void of cunning or artifice –1698. **2.** Lacking in resource; incapable of shifting for oneself; hence, lazy, inefficient 1584. **b.** Of actions: Indicating shiftlessness; ineffective, futile 1613. **3.** Without a shift or shirt (*rare*) 1680.

2. Going to hunt up her s. husband at the inn HARDY. Hence **Shi·ftless-ly** *adv.*, **-ness.**

Shifty (ʃi·fti), *a.* 1570. [f. as prec. + -Y[1].] **1.** Full of shifts or expedients; well able to shift for oneself. **2.** Fond of indirect or dishonest methods; addicted to evasion or artifice; not straightforward, not to be depended on 1837. **3.** Changeable or changeful; wavering (*rare*) 1882.

1. The canny, s., far-seeing Scot, with that mingled daring and caution of his KINGSLEY. **2.** A most s. old fox he is 1841. I scorn your s. evasions DICKENS. Hence **Shi·fti-ly** *adv.*, **-ness.**

Shiite (ʃi·əit). 1728. [f. SHI(AH + -ITE[1] 1.] A member of the Shiah sect. Also *attrib.* or *adj.* Hence **Shii·tic** *a.*

Shikar (ʃikā·ɹ), *sb. Anglo-Ind.* 1613. [– Urdu – Pers. *šikār*.] Hunting; sport (shooting and hunting); game. Hence **Shika·r** *v. trans.* and *intr.* to hunt.

Shikari, -ee (ʃikā·rī). *Anglo-Indian.* 1827. [– Urdu – Pers. *šikārī*, f. *šikār*; see prec.] A hunter or sportsman; esp. a native who brings in game on his own account, or accompanies European sportsmen as a guide.

Shillelagh (ʃilē[i]·lă, -ē[i]·li). 1772. [Name of a barony and village in Co. Wicklow.] An Irish cudgel of blackthorn or oak.

Shilling (ʃi·liŋ). [OE. *sćilling* = OFris., OS., OHG. *scilling* (MDu., Du. *schelling*, G. *schilling*), ON. *skillingr*, Goth. *skilliggs* :- Gmc. **skilliŋgaz*, of much disputed origin. Cf. SCHELLING, SCHILLING, SKILLING *sb.*[2]] **1.** An English money of account, of the value of 12 pence or $\frac{1}{20}$ of a pound sterling. Abbrev. s. (= L. *solidus*; see SOLIDUS), formerly also sh., shil.; otherwise denoted by the sign /- after the numeral. **b.** Used in emphatic or rhetorical statements, where one wishes to be understood as deliberately reckoning every item, however small, of a given sum or expense 1737. **2.** A silver coin of the value of 12 pence. First issued in 1503, by Henry VII 1513. **b.** With defining word indicating a particular coinage 1699. **†3.** Used to render or represent the names of various foreign moneys –1776. **4.** With prefixed numerals, forming adjs. of price or value. Also in phr. denoting rate of payment. 1578.

1. Afterwards to ninepins, where I won a s. PEPYS. **b.** I will not engage to pay one s. more than the expenses really incurred by Hanover WELLINGTON. **3.** *Double s.*, a Dutch florin or guilder. **4.** Sold..in five s. and ten s. bottles SCOTT.

Phrases. *To cut off with a s.*, to disinherit deliberately. *To take the s., the King's* (or *Queen's*) *s.*, to enlist as a soldier by accepting a s. from a recruiting officer (a practice now disused).

Shillingsworth (ʃi·liŋzwəɹþ). Formerly **shillingworth** (now *rare*). ME. [WORTH *sb.*] The amount or quantity which may be bought for a shilling; as much as is worth a shilling or a (specified) number of shillings.

Shilly-shally (ʃi·liʃæ:li), *adv. phr., a., sb.* 1700. [orig. *shill I, shall I*, altered form of *shall I, shall I.* Cf. WISHY-WASHY.] **A.** *To stand shill I, shall I*: to vacillate, to be irresolute or undecided.

I'm for marrying her at once—Why should I stand s., like a Country Bumpkin? STEELE.

B. *adj.* Vacillating, irresolute 1734.

I am s. about it in my own mind 1743.

C. *sb.* Vacillation, irresolution 1755.

There can be no s. now GEO. ELIOT.

Shi·lly-shally, *v.* 1782. [f. prec. adv. phr.] *intr.* To vacillate, be irresolute or undecided. Hence **Shi·lly-sha:llyer,** one who shilly-shallies.

Shim (ʃim), *sb. local.* 1723. [Of unkn. origin.] **1.** A piece of iron attached to an agricultural implement for scraping the surface of the soil. **2.** In full *s.-plough*: A kind of horse-hoe or shallow plough, used in Kent and elsewhere, for hoeing up weeds between rows of beans, hops, etc. 1736. **3.** A thin slip, usu. of metal, used to fill up a space between parts subject to wear, to aline or adjust the level of rails, etc. 1864. Hence **Shim** *v. intr.* to use the s. for hoeing; *trans.* to hoe (crops) with a s.

Shimmer (ʃi·məɹ), *sb.* 1821. [f. next.] A shimmering light or glow; a subdued tremulous light.

Two silver lamps..diffused..a trembling..s. through the quiet apartment SCOTT.

Shimmer (ʃi·məɹ), *v.* [Late OE. *sćymrian*, **sćimerian* = (M)LG., (M)Du. *schēmeren* be shaded or shadowy, glimmer, glitter, G. *schimmern*, iterative (see -ER[5]) f. Gmc. **skim-*, extension of **ski-* SHINE *v.*] *intr.* To shine with a tremulous or flickering light; to gleam faintly. In early use also, to shine brightly, glisten.

Shimmy[1] (ʃi·mi). 1839. *dial.* and *U.S.* popular reduction of CHEMISE.

Shi·mmy.[2] 1919. *U.S.* [Short for *shimmy-shake*; of unkn. origin.] A kind of fox-trot accompanied by tremulous motions of the body. Also as *vb.*

Shin (ʃin), *sb.* [OE. *sćinu* = (M)LG., MDu. *schēne* (Du. *scheen*), OHG. *scina* shin, needle (G. *schiene* thin plate, *schienbein* shin-bone); the basic meaning is prob. 'thin or narrow piece'.] **1.** The front part of the human leg between the knee and the ankle; the front or sharp edge of the shank-bone. **b.** The lower part of a leg (of beef), the meat of which is lean and streaked 1736. **2.** Used, after G. *schiene*, for an iron plate or band 1747.

attrib. and *Comb.*, as *s.-guard, pad*, etc.; **s.-leaf,** the N. Amer. ericaceous plant *Pyrola elliptica* (also *P. rotundifolia*); **-plaster** *U.S. slang*, a piece of paper money, esp. one of a low denomination, depreciated in value.

Shin (ʃin), *v.* 1829. [f. prec.] **1.** *intr.* (orig. *Naut.*) To climb by using the arms and legs without the help of steps, irons, etc. **b.** *trans.* To climb up 1891. **2.** *US. intr.* To 'use one's legs'; to move quickly; to run *round* 1845. **3.** *trans.* To kick (a person) on the shins 1845.

1. We had to..s. up and down single ropes caked with ice 1840.

Shin-bone (ʃi·nbō[u]n). [OE. *sćinbān* = MLG. *schēnebein* (Du. *scheenbeen*), MHG. *schinebein* (G. *schienbein*); see SHIN *sb.*, BONE *sb.*] = TIBIA 1.

Shindy (ʃi·ndi). 1821. [unexpl. alt. of SHINTY.] **1.** = SHINTY 1. *local.* 1846. **2.** A spree, merrymaking 1821. **3.** A row, commotion, 'shine' 1845.

3. Phr. *To kick up a s.*

Shine (ʃəin), *sb.*[1] 1529. [f. SHINE *v.*] **1.** Brightness or radiance shed by a luminary or an illuminant. **†b.** A beam or ray; a halo –1654. **2.** Lustre or sheen of an object reflecting light, as metal, water, silk 1599. **b.** *Painting* and *Photogr.* Shininess; a shiny patch 1880. **c.** The polish given to a pair of boots by a bootblack; *transf.* a job of boot-blacking 1871. **3.** Sunshine, *esp.* as opp. to *rain*; hence, fine weather 1622. **4.** *fig.* Brilliance, radiance, splendour, lustre. †Also [after G. *schein*], a specious appearance, a 'show'. 1530. **b.** A brilliant display, a 'dash' 1819.

1. And mooned Ashtaroth..Now sits not girt with Tapers holy s. MILT. **2.** Dazled with the glittering s. of Gold 1667. **3.** Come storm, come s., whatever befall HENLEY. **4.** The bright s., and worthines of his auncestors 1586. **b.** Colloq. phrases. *To cut a s. To take the s. out of*, to deprive (a person or thing) of his or its brilliance or pre-eminence; to surpass.

Shine (ʃəin), *sb.*[2] 1830. [perh. uses of prec. sb., but the senses are notably like those of SHINDY.] **1.** A party, convivial gathering;

usu. *tea-s.*, a 'tea-fight'. *dial.* 1838. **2.** A disturbance, row, fuss. *colloq.* 1832. **3.** *pl.* Capers, tricks. *U.S.* 1830. **4.** *To take a s. to* (*U.S.*): to take a fancy for 1848.

Shine (ʃəin), *v.* Pa. t. and pple. **shone** (ʃɒn). [OE. *scīnan* = OFris. *skīna*, OS. *skīnan*, OHG. *scīnan* (Du. *schijnen*, G. *scheinen*), ON. *skína*, Goth. *skeinan* :– Gmc. **skīnan*, f. **skī-* with present-stem formative *-n-* carried through into the pa. t. and pa. pple. Cogns. are SHEER *a.*, SHIMMER *v.*] **1.** *intr.* Of a heavenly body or an object that is alight: To shed beams of bright light; to give out light so as to illuminate; to be radiant. Also with *forth*, *out*. **b.** Of the day: To be sunny or bright; also, to dawn. Chiefly *poet.* late ME. **2.** Of a metallic, polished, smooth, or glassy object: To be bright or resplendent; to gleam, glisten, or glitter with reflected light OE. **b.** To be bright *with* 1606. **3.** To be radiant or brilliant with bright colouring; to be effulgent with splendour or beauty; to make a brave show OE. **4.** Of persons: To be conspicuous or brilliant in ability, character, achievement, or position; to be eminent or distinguished, to excel OE. **5.** Of something immaterial: To appear with conspicuous clearness; to be brilliantly evident or visible; to stand out clearly ME. **b.** To be clearly evident *through* an outward appearance 1590. **6.** *trans.* To cause (light) to shine, to emit (rays) 1588. **7.** *To s. down*: to surpass in brilliance 1613. **8.** To cause to shine, put a polish on; *U.S.* (inflected *shined*) to black (boots) 1613. **9.** *U.S.* (*Hunting.*) To throw the light of a lantern, etc. on (the eyes of an animal); to locate the position of (an animal) in this way 1845.

1. The fog became thin, and the sun shone through it TYNDALL. *To s. upon*, to look favourably upon, be favourable to, said of a star, or of the face of God. *fig.* As for them that dwel in the londe of the shadowe of death, vpon them shal the lyght s. COVERDALE. *Isa.* 9:2. **b.** We can.. dismiss thee ere the Morning s. MILT. †*It shines*, it is sunny. **2.** The huge hall-table's oaken face, Scrubb'd till it shone SCOTT. **3.** Her light foot Shone rosy-white TENNYSON. **4.** He..never shone as an orator 1836. **5.** Princely counsel in his face yet shon MILT. **6.** She approached, shining smiles upon Esmond THACKERAY.

Shiner (ʃəi·nəɹ). ME. [f. SHINE *v.* + -ER[1].] **1.** An object that shines. **b.** *pl.* Coin, money, *esp.* sovereigns or guineas; occas. *sing.* a silver or gold coin. *slang.* 1760. **c.** A mirror; *spec.* one used by cheaters at cards. *slang.* 1812. **2.** One who shines (See SHINE *v.* 4.) 1810. **b.** A bootblack 1912. **3.** Applied to various small silvery fishes; the young of the mackerel; *U.S.* any of various small fresh-water fishes, chiefly cyprinoids, as the dace 1836.

Shingle (ʃi·ŋg'l), *sb.*[1] [ME. *scincle*, *scingle*, *singel* (whence AL. *cingulum* XIII, *cingula*, *shingula* XIV), repr., with unexpl. modification, L. *scindula*, later form of *scandula* after Gr. σχίδαξ, σχινδαλμός.] **1.** A thin piece of wood having parallel sides and one end thicker than the other, used as a house-tile. **b.** *gen.* A piece of board 1825. **c.** *U.S.* A small sign-board 1847. **d.** 'Shingled' hair; this manner of cutting the hair 1924. **2.** *attrib.* or *adj.* 1810.

1. Your house..covered with cedar shingles COBBETT. **2.** When the s. roof rang sharp with the rains E. B. BROWNING. *Comb.* **s.-oak,** (*a*) the laurel-oak, *Quercus imbricaria*; (*b*) the she-oak.

Shingle (ʃi·ŋg'l), *sb.*[2] 1513. [Of obscure origin and history.] **1.** Small, roundish stones; loose, waterworn pebbles such as are found collected upon the sea-shore; *collect. sing.* and *pl.* 1574. **2.** A beach or other tract covered with loose roundish pebbles 1513.

Shingle (ʃi·ŋg'l), *v.*[1] 1562. [f. SHINGLE *sb.*[1]] **1.** *trans.* To cover, roof (a house, etc.) with shingles 1562. **2.** orig. *U.S.* To cut (hair), properly so as to give the effect of overlapping shingles, by exposing the ends of hair all over the head; to cut (women's hair) in a style in which it is made to taper from the back of the head to the nape of the neck; also *absol.* 1857.

1. *transf.* The..walls and..roof are shingled with slate 1885. Hence **Shi·ngler**[1], one who shingles houses, etc.; also *U.S.* a machine which cuts and prepares shingles.

Shingle, *v.*[2] 1674. [– Fr. *cingler* – G. *zängeln*, f. *zange* tongs, pincers.] *Iron-manuf. trans.* To subject (the puddled ball) to pressure and blows from a hammer so as to expel impurities. Hence **Shi·ngler**[2], one who or a machine which shingles puddled iron.

Shingles (ʃi·ŋg'lz), *sb. pl.* late ME. [repr. med.L. *cingulus*, var. of *cingulum* girdle, used to render Gr. ζώνη or ζωστήρ in the medical sense.] An eruptive disease (*Herpes zoster*) often extending round the middle of the body like a girdle (whence the name); usu. accompanied by violent neuralgic pain.

Shingly (ʃi·ŋgli), *a.* 1775. [f. SHINGLE *sb.*[2] + -Y[1].] Consisting of or covered with shingle; of the nature of shingle.

Shining (ʃəi·niŋ), *ppl. a.* OE. [f. SHINE *v.* + -ING[2].] **1.** That shines; luminous, lustrous, gleaming; also, of bright or brilliant aspect or exterior; resplendent. **2.** With ref. to intellectual or moral qualities: Eminent, distinguished, brilliant. Now *rare.* OE. **3.** Of looks: Radiant, beaming 1821.

1. Fish..with thir Finns & s. Scales MILT. Phr. *S. light* (after John 5:35), a person conspicuous for some excellence. *To improve the s. hour* (after Watts), to make good use of time. **2.** Men of the greatest and the most s. Parts 1711. **3.** A..s. sanguine face LAMB. Hence **Shi·ning-ly** *adv.*, **-ness**.

Shinny (ʃi·ni). 1672. [*Shinny* (XVII) and SHINTY (XVIII) appear to be derived from cries used in the game, *shin ye*, *shin you*, and *shin t'ye* 'shin to you'; other dial. names are *shinnins*, *shinnack*, *shinnup*.] A (north-country and American) game similar to hockey, played with a ball and sticks curved at one end; also, the stick and the ball used.

Shinto (ʃi·nto). 1727. [– Jap. *shinto* – Chinese *shin tao* way of the gods.] **1.** The native religious system of Japan, the central belief of which is that the mikado is the direct descendant of the sun-goddess and that implicit obedience is due to him. **2.** An adherent of Shinto beliefs 1829. Hence **Shi·nto,ism** = sense 1. **Shi·nto,ist** = sense 2. **Shinto,i·stic,** *a.* belonging to or characteristic of S.

Shinty (ʃi·nti). 1771. [See SHINNY.] = SHINNY.

Shiny (ʃəi·ni), *a.* (and *sb.*) 1590. [f. SHINE *sb.*[1] + -Y[1].] Full of light or brightness; luminous; having a bright or glistening surface.

Vpon a Sommers shynie day SPENSER. S. boots, tall hat, go-to-meeting coat 1868. Hence **Shi·niness.**

B. *sb.* A shiny or bright object. *The s.* (slang), money. 1856.

Ship (ʃip), *sb.*[1] [OE. *scip* = OFris., OS. *skip* (Du. *schip*), OHG. *skif* (G. *schiff*), ON., Goth. *skip* :– Gmc. **skipam*, of unkn. origin.] **1.** A large sea-going vessel (opp. to a *boat*); *spec.* (in modern times) a vessel having a bowsprit and three masts, each of which consists of a lower, top, and topgallant mast. **b.** In rowing parlance, applied to the racing eight-oar boat; also used playfully of other craft 1878. **c.** *fig.* Applied to the state 1675. **2.** With qualifying word or phrase indicating the kind or use. late ME. **3.** In fig. and allusive phrases, *esp.* where *ship* typifies the fortunes or affairs of a person, etc. or the person himself in regard to them 1500. **4.** *transf.* Applied to various objects that are, or are conceived to be, navigated. late ME. **5.** A vessel, utensil, ornament, etc. shaped like a ship. late ME. **6.** A ship's company or crew ME.

1. A stately S. Of Tarsus, bound for th' Isles Of Javan or Gadier MILT. Phr. *To take s.* (see TAKE *v.* IV. 2c). **b.** The..steadiness of their s...helped the Oxford men very much 1901. **2. King's s.** (now *Hist.*), one of the fleet of ships provided and maintained out of the royal revenue; a ship of the royal navy; later, a ship-of-war equipped at the public expense (opp. to *privateer*). For *flagship*, *steamship*, *warship*, etc., see these words. *When one's s. comes home* (or *in*), when one comes into one's fortune. **4.** An aeroplane or other form of aircraft. *S. of the desert*, *desert-s.*, the camel. *S. of Guinea*, *Guinea s.*, sailor's name for a floating medusa. **5.** A s. of silver for the almes disshe 1525. Two thuribles, with a s. for incense 1843.

attrib. and *Comb.*, as *s.-bell*, *-canal*, etc.; **ship('s) biscuit,** hard biscuit prepared for use on board ship, hard tack; formerly called **ship('s) bread; ship('s) boy,** a boy who serves on board ship; **-breaker,** a person who buys old vessels to break them up for sale; **s.-broker,** a mercantile agent who transacts the business of a ship when it is in port, or is engaged in buying and selling ships, or in procuring insurance on them; **-brokerage,** the business of a ship-broker; **ship('s) carpenter,** a carpenter employed in the building or repairing of ships; hence **-carpentry; ship('s) company,** the crew of a ship; **-fever,** a form of typhus fever, called also *gaol fever* and *hospital fever*; **-ladder,** a ladder used in boarding or leaving a ship; **-letter,** a letter carried by a private vessel and not by the ordinary mail boat; **-mate,** one who serves with another in the same ship; **-owner,** one who owns, or has a share in, a s. or ships; **-papers,** now usu. **ship's papers,** the documents (passport, muster-roll, charter-party, log-book, etc.) with which a ship is required by law to be provided; **-plate,** an inferior grade of wrought iron plate; **-railway,** an inclined railway running into the water over which a ship may be drawn out on land for repairs, etc.; **-rigged** *a.* carrying square sails on all three masts; **ship('s) stores,** provisions and supplies for use on board ship; **-timber,** timber for shipbuilding; **ship('s) time,** the local mean time of the meridian where the ship is; **shipway,** (*a*) a way or bed on which ships are built or laid for examination; (*b*) a ship-canal. **b.** In the names of animals: **s.-borer** = *s.-worm*; **-rat,** a variety of rat found on board ship; **-worm,** any of the worm-shaped molluscs of the genus *Teredo* and allied genera, esp. *T. navalis*. **c.** Combs. with *ship's*: **ship's articles,** the terms according to which seamen take service on board ship; **ship's days,** the days allowed for loading and unloading a ship; **ship's husband** (see HUSBAND *sb.*). Hence **Shi·pful,** as much or as many as a s. will hold. **Shi·pless** *a.* unoccupied by ships; possessing no ships; deprived of one's ship or ships. **Shi·plet,** a small ship.

Ship, *sb.*[2] 1875. *Printing.* A colloq. abbrev. of COMPANIONSHIP[2].

Ship (ʃip), *v.* [Late OE. *scipian*, f. *scip* SHIP *sb.*[1] Later, directly from SHIP *sb.*[1]] †**1.** *pass.* To be furnished with a ship or ships –1647. **2.** To put or take (persons or things) on board ship ME. **b.** Said of the ship 1800. †**3. a.** *pass.* Of a person: To have gone on board, to be embarked –1621. **b.** *refl.* To go on board ship, embark. *Obs.* or *arch.* late ME. **4.** *intr.* To go on board ship, embark. Now *rare.* ME. †**5.** To go by ship *to*, *into*, or *from* a place –1654. **6.** *trans.* To send or transport by ship. late ME. **b.** *transf.* To transport (goods) by rail or other means of conveyance. *U.S.* 1881. **c.** *fig.* To send off, send packing 1588. **7.** Of a vessel: To take in (water) over the side; to be submerged or flooded with (water) by waves breaking over it; esp. *to s. a sea.* Said also of the occupants of the vessel. 1698. **8.** To take or draw (an object) into the ship or boat to which it belongs 1630. **b.** To lift (an oar or scull) out of its rowlock, and (now, in sculling) to bring it into the boat. Also *absol.* as a command = 'ship oars!' 1700. **9.** orig. and esp. *Naut.* To put (an object) in position for performing its proper function; *spec.* to fix (an oar) in the rowlock, in readiness to row; hence, to put in position for any purpose 1616. **10.** To put on (clothing, etc.); also, to shoulder (a burden) 1829. **11.** To engage for service on a ship 1643. **b.** *intr.* To engage to serve on a ship 1829.

1. Is he well ship'd? SHAKS. **2.** King Henry the fifth, was shipping his men for France 1640. **b.** A little vessel was shipping grain 1882. **3. a.** Twenty to one then, he is ship'd already SHAKS. **b.** The Puritans..shipped themselves off for America 1761. **4.** I shipped at Rye, in Sussex 1517. **6.** The third [son] was a Roué, and was shipped to the Colonies DISRAELI. **7.** We shipt Seas over our Poop 1734. **8. b.** The stranger came to the bank, shipped his sculls, and jumped out 1861. **9.** A new rudder.., which was immediately shipped 1798.

-ship *suffix*, in OE. *-*sciepe*, *-scipe*, *-scype* :– OTeut. **skapiz*, f. **skap-* to create, ordain, appoint (see SHAPE *v.*).

1. Added to adjs. and pa. pples. to denote the state or condition of being so-and-so. The only survivals of this formation now in common use are HARDSHIP and WORSHIP.

2. Added to sbs. to denote the state or condition of being what is expressed by the sb., e.g. *authorship*, *fellowship*, *suretyship*. **b.** By extension, when the sb. is the designation of a class of human being, such compounds assume the sense of the qualities or character associated with, or the skill or power of accomplishment of, the person denoted by the sb.; e.g. *craftsmanship*, *kingship*, *workmanship*.

3. Added to sbs. designating an official or person

of rank to denote the office, position, dignity, or rank of the person designated, as *ambassadorship, professorship*, etc. In the case of *fellowship, scholarship, postmastership* and the like, the connotation has come to include the emoluments, etc., pertaining to the office or position. **b.** With poss. pron. prefixed, the compounds *ladyship, lordship, worship*, have passed into honorific designations of the persons who are entitled to the style of 'Lady', 'Lord', 'the Worshipful'. Hence the suffix has been freely employed to form mock titles or humorous styles of address.

4. Added to sbs. to denote a state of life, occupation, or behaviour, relating to or connected with what is denoted by the sb. These compounds are now rare; COURTSHIP (first in Shaks.) is the chief instance.

5. Added to sbs. forming compounds having a collective sense. TOWNSHIP (OE. *tūnsċipe* the inhabitants of a *tūn*) is the one survival from the OE. period.

Shipboard (ʃi·pbōəɹd). ME. [f. SHIP *sb.*[1] + BOARD *sb.*] †**1.** The side of a ship (see BOARD *sb.* V.) –1848. **b.** *On s.*, on board ship 1470. †**2.** A plank of a ship –1560.

Shi·pbui:lder. 1700. One whose occupation is to design and construct ships; a naval architect. So **Shi·pbuilding** *vbl. sb.* the business or art of building ships; naval architecture.

Shi·p-cha:ndler. 1642. [See CHANDLER.] A dealer who supplies ships with necessary stores. Hence **Shi·p-cha:ndlery,** the business of, or goods dealt in by, a s.

Shi·p-load. 1706. A load (of persons or things) carried or capable of being carried by a ship.

Shipman (ʃi·pmæ̆n). *Pl.* **-men.** OE. [f. SHIP *sb.*[1] + MAN *sb.*] **1.** A seaman or sailor. Now *arch.* **2.** A master mariner; the master of a ship; a skipper. Also, a pilot. late ME.

Shi·pma:ster. late ME. [f. SHIP *sb.*[1] + MASTER *sb.*] **1.** The master, captain, or commander of a ship; formerly also, a pilot, steersman. **2.** A man who owns the ship which he commands 1562.

Shipment (ʃi·pmĕnt). 1802. [f. SHIP *v.* + -MENT.] **1.** The act of shipping (goods, etc.) for transportation. **2.** That which is shipped; a consignment for transportation 1861.

Shi·p-mo:ney. Now *Hist.* 1636. An ancient tax levied in time of war on the ports and maritime towns, cities, and counties of England to provide ships for the king's service. It was revived by Charles I (with an extended application to inland counties), but was finally abolished by statute in 1640.

Shi:p-of-wa·r. Now *rare.* 1479. A ship equipped for warfare; a man-of-war, warship.

Shipper (ʃi·pəɹ). [Late OE. *sċipere*, f. SHIP *sb.*[1] + -ER[1].] †**1.** A seaman –1728. †**2.** A skipper –1634. **3.** One who ships goods for transportation 1755. **b.** *U.S.* One who transports goods by rail or other means of conveyance 1903. **c.** A commodity that is shipped or is suitable for shipping 1883. **4.** *Mech.* A device for shifting a belt from one pulley to another 1869.

Shipping (ʃi·piŋ), *vbl. sb.* ME. [f. SHIP *v.* + -ING[1].] **1.** A ship or ships for the use or accommodation of a person or thing. **2.** Ships collectively; the body of ships that belong to a person's or country's fleet, that frequent a particular port or harbour, or that are used for a certain purpose 1591. †**3.** Navigation –1700. †**b.** A voyage, a sailing –1688. **4.** The action of putting persons or things on board ship or transporting them by ship 1483.

1. Phr. *To take s.* (now *arch.*), to embark; occas. pregnantly, to go abroad. **2.** A river very commodious for s. DE FOE. **3. b.** Phr. *God send you good s.!* used proverbially in the 16th and 17th c. as a wish for success in any venture. **4.** A licence for the s. of his stores and provisions 1748.

Comb.: **s.-agent,** a licensed agent who transacts a ship's business for the owner; **-articles** = *ship's articles* (see SHIP *sb.*[1]); **-master,** an official who superintends the signing-on and discharging of seamen; **-office,** (*a*) an office where seamen sign on for a voyage; (*b*) an office where a s.-agent receives goods for shipment; **-papers** = *ship's papers.*

Shippon, -en (ʃi·pən). Now *dial.* [OE. *sċypen* fem. :– Gmc. **skupīnī*, f. **skup-*, repr. also in MLG. *schoppen, schuppen* (whence G. *schuppen*) shed; see -EN[2]. Cf. SHOP *sb.*] A cattle-shed, a cowhouse.

Shippound (ʃi·pˌpaund). 1545. [– MLG. *schippunt*, MDu. *schippond*; see POUND *sb.*[1]] A unit of weight used in the Baltic trade, varying from 300 to 400 pounds; = 20 lispounds.

Ship-shape (ʃi·pʃēⁱp), *a.* (*adv.*). 1644. [f. SHIP *sb.*[1] + SHAPEN (later reduced to *shape*).] Arranged neatly and compactly, as things on board ship should be; trim, orderly; orig. *Naut.* Occas. as *adv.*, in a seamanlike manner, in trim fashion.

It would have been more s. to lower the bight of a rope 1823. Neat s. fixings and contrivances BROWNING.

Shipwreck (ʃi·prek), *sb.* ME. Also †**shipwrack.** [f. SHIP *sb.*[1] + WRECK *sb.* (WRACK *sb.*[2])] **1.** What is cast up from a wreck; the remains of a wrecked vessel; wreckage. In later use chiefly *fig.* **2.** Destruction or loss of a ship by its being sunk or broken up by the violence of the sea, or by its striking or stranding upon a rock, etc. 1450. **b.** An instance of this 1548. **3.** *fig.* Destruction, total loss or ruin 1526.

2. †*To make s.*: see MAKE *v.* IX. 7. **b.** All in a shipwrack shift their severall way 1633. **3.** A generall shipwrake of the Popes uniuersall power 1566. The S. of our Fortunes DE FOE.

Phr. *To make s. of* (arch.), to suffer the loss of, as in *to make s. of a good conscience* (cf. 1 Tim. 1:19); to bring to destruction or total ruin.

Shipwreck (ʃi·prek), *v.* 1589. [f. prec.] **1.** *trans.* To cause (a person) to suffer shipwreck; chiefly *pass.* to suffer shipwreck; also, to cause the loss of (goods) by shipwreck. **b.** To wreck (a vessel). Now *rare.* 1624. **c.** *transf.* and *fig.* 1599. **2.** *intr.* To suffer shipwreck. *Obs.* or *arch.* 1607.

1. Shipwrack'd I floated on a driving Mast 1703. **b.** I..Who like a foolish Pilot have shipwrack't My Vessel MILT. **c.** Men, who have ship-wreck'd their fortunes as well as their reputations upon this rock 1721.

Shipwright (ʃi·prəit). OE. [f. SHIP *sb.*[1] + WRIGHT *sb.*] A man employed in the construction or repair of ships.

Shipyard (ʃi·pyāɹd). 1700. [f. SHIP *sb.*[1] + YARD *sb.*[1]] An enclosure, adjoining the sea or a river, in which ships are built or repaired.

‖**Shiraz** (ʃīᵊ·ræz). 1634. Name of a city in Persia (formerly the capital); used *attrib.* as the designation of a wine made in the district; also *absol.* = Shiraz wine.

Shire (ʃəiᵊɹ), *sb.* [OE. *sċīr* = OHG. *scīra* (in two glosses) care, official charge. Cf. AL. *schira* (*scir-*) 1086, *shira* 1156 shire.] †**1.** (OE. only.) Official charge; administrative office. †**2.** A province or district under the rule of a governor; the see of a bishop, the province of an archbishop, or the like; in wider sense, a country, region, district –1824. **3.** *spec.* In Old English times, an administrative district, consisting of a group of hundreds or wapentakes, ruled jointly by an ealdorman and a sheriff, who presided in the SHIRE-MOOT. Under Norman rule, the AFr. *counté*, Anglo-Latin *comitatus*, was adopted as the equivalent of the English term. At the present day *shire* is current mainly as a literary synonym for *county* (chiefly restricted to those counties that have names ending in *-shire*). OE. **4.** As the terminal element in names of counties (as Berkshire, Derbyshire) and of certain other districts (as Hallamshire, Bedlingtonshire, etc.) which have from early times been regarded as separate unities. Pronounced (-ʃəɹ); in dialects often (-ʃiᵊɹ). OE. **5. The Shires. a.** A term applied to other parts of England by the inhabitants of East Anglia, Kent, Sussex, Essex, and Surrey; also *gen.* applied to those counties the names of which end in *-shire.* Usu. pron. (ʃīᵊɹz). 1796. **b.** *Foxhunting.* As the name of a hunting 'country' 1860. **6.** Short for next 1877.

3. How many suffer injurie, when one hundred of a Shiere is spoiled? 1549. **5. a.** The Inhabitants of Kent, to express a person's coming from a great distance..will say, he comes a great way off, out of the shires 1796.

Comb.: †**s.-court** = COUNTY-COURT; **-hall** = *county-hall*; **-member,** a representative of a s. in parliament; **-oak,** an oak tree marking the boundary of a s., or a meeting place for a s.-court; **-reeve,** etymologizing form of SHERIFF; **-town,** a town which is the capital of a shire or county.

Shire, *a.* *Obs.* exc. *dial.* [OE. *sċīr*; see SHEER *a.*] = SHEER *a.* 2, 4, 5; also, thin, sparse.

Shire horse. Also **shires horse.** 1875. A horse of a heavy powerful breed, used for draught, chiefly bred in the Midlands.

Shi·re-moot. 1614. [f. SHIRE *sb.* + MOOT *sb.*, after OE. *sċīrġemōt*.] *Hist.* The judicial assembly of the shire in Old English times.

†**Shirk,** *sb.*[1] 1639. [perh. – G. *schurke* scoundrel. Connection with synon. SHARK *sb.*[2] cannot be made out.] A needy, disreputable parasite –1730.

Shirk (ʃɔ̄ɹk), *sb.*[2] 1818. [f. next.] **1.** One who shirks (work, obligations). **2.** An act or the practice of shirking (*rare*) 1877.

Shirk (ʃɔ̄ɹk), *v.* 1633. [rel. to SHIRK *sb.*[1]] †**1.** *intr.* To practise fraud or trickery, esp. instead of working as a means of living; to prey or sponge upon others –1850. **2.** To go evasively or slyly; to slink; to sneak *away, out*, etc. 1681. **3.** *trans.* To evade (a person, his conversation, acquaintance, etc.). Now *rare* or *Obs.* 1787. **b.** At Eton: To avoid meeting (a master, a sixth-form boy) when out of bounds. Also *absol.* 1821. **4.** To evade (one's duty, work, obligations, etc.) 1785. **b.** *U.S.* To shift (responsibility, etc.) *on to* or *upon* (another person). Also with *off.* 1845. **c.** *absol.* To practise evasion of work, one's duties, responsibilities, etc. 1853.

2. He and his comrades had been obliged to s. on board at night, to escape from their wives THACKERAY. One of the cities shirked from the league BYRON. **4.** This trick..was intended..to s. responsibility 1880. **c.** The disposition to s. seems to be constitutional with the human race 1865. Hence **Shi·rker,** one who shirks (duty, work, etc.).

Shirley (ʃɔ̄·ɹli). 1886. [The name of *Shirley* Vicarage, Croydon, where the Rev. W. Wilks first cultivated the flower.] In full *S. poppy*: Any of certain varieties, grown in a great range of colours, of the single garden poppy.

Shirr (ʃɔ̄ɹ), *sb.* *U.S.* 1858. [Of unkn. origin.] **1.** Rubber thread woven into a fabric to make it elastic. **2.** A series of parallel gatherings 1891.

Shirr (ʃɔ̄ɹ), *v.* *U.S.* 1892. [app. back-formation from next.] *trans.* = GAUGE *v.* 8. Hence **Shirring** *vbl. sb.* (*a*) gathering in the form of shirrs; (*b*) elastic webbing made with shirrs.

Shirred (ʃɔ̄ɹd), *a.* *U.S.* 1847. [In senses 1 and 2 f. SHIRR *sb.* + -ED[2].] **1.** Having elastic threads woven into the texture. **2.** Gathered 1860. **3.** *Cookery.* Of eggs: Poached (in cream) 1883.

Shirt (ʃɔ̄ɹt), *sb.* [OE. *sċyrte* (once, as an obscure gloss on 'prætexta'), corresp. formally to (M)LG. *schört(e, schorte*, MDu. *schorte* (Du. *schort*), G. *schürze* apron, ON. *skyrta* shirt (whence SKIRT), based on Gmc. **skurt-* SHORT.] **1.** An undergarment for the upper part of the body, made of linen, flannel, silk, or other washable material; orig. worn next to the skin, now often over an undershirt or 'vest'. Formerly a garment common to both sexes, but now an article of male attire with long sleeves. Also, an infant's undergarment with short body and sleeves. **b.** Applied to a loose garment resembling a shirt 1553. **2.** A woman's blouse made in a severe style, with a collar, front, and cuffs, and so somewhat resembling a man's shirt 1896. **3.** *transf.* An inner casing or covering 1611.

1. *Boiled s.* (U.S.), a white linen s. as dist. from a coloured or flannel s.; now, a dress shirt with starched fronts. *Bloody s.*, a blood-stained s. exhibited as a symbol of murder or outrage. *S. of mail* [= Fr. *chemise de maille*]. *In one's s.*, in one's night attire; without one's coat and waistcoat. (To have) *not a s.* (*to one's back*), no goods or possessions, not even the necessaries of life. (To give away) *the s. off one's back*, i.e. all one's possessions. †*Not to tell one's s.*: to keep a matter strictly secret. *Near is my s. but nearer is my skin* = one's own interests come before one's nearest friend's. *To get* (a person's) *s. out*, to cause him to lose his temper. *To put one's s. on* (a horse), to bet all one's money on (*slang*). **3.** The internal lining or s. of the furnace 1868.

Comb.: **s.-band** = BAND *sb.*[2] 4; also *dial.* the wrist-band of a s.; **-blouse** = sense 2; **-button,** a small-sized button usu. of linen or mother of pearl pierced with thread holes and used on shirt fastenings; **-frill,** a frill formerly worn on the front and wrist-bands of a s.; **s. front** = FRONT *sb.* 5b; also *transf.* a white patch on the chest (of a dog); **-pin,** an ornamental pin used to fasten the s. at the throat. Hence **Shirt** *v. trans.* to clothe with or as with a s. **Shi·rtless** *a.* without a s.

Shirting (ʃə·ɹtiŋ). 1604. [f. SHIRT *sb.* + -ING^{1}.] Material for shirts; *spec.* a kind of piece-goods of stout cotton cloth suitable for shirts which are to be subjected to hard wear.

Shirt-sleeve. 1566. A sleeve of a shirt. Chiefly *pl.*

Phr. *In one's shirt-sleeves,* with one's coat off.

Shirty (ʃə·ɹti), *a. slang.* 1859. [f. SHIRT *sb.* + -Y^{1}.] Ill-tempered. Hence **Shi·rtiness.**

Shit (ʃit), **shite** (ʃəit), *sb.* Not now in decent use. OE. [Gmc. root **skīt-*.] **1.** Excrement from the bowels, dung 1585. **b.** A contemptuous epithet applied to a man 1508. †**2.** Diarrhœa, esp. in cattle –late ME. Also vb. *trans.* and *intr.*

‖**Shittah** (ʃi·tă). 1611. [Heb. *šiṭṭāh*.] *S. tree*: a tree belonging to some species of Acacia, from which SHITTIM wood was obtained.

Shittim (ʃi·tim). late ME. [– Heb. *šiṭṭīm*, pl. of *šiṭṭāh*; see prec.] (More fully *S. wood.*) The wood of the shittah tree, acacia wood.

Shive^{1} (ʃəiv). Chiefly *dial.* [ME. *schive*, prob. – MLG., MDu. *schive*, with assim. to Eng. phonetic conditions (see SH-); cf. SHEAVE *sb.*] **1.** A slice (of bread; rarely of other edible). **2.** A thin flat cork for stopping a wide-mouthed bottle; also, a thin bung for a cask 1869. †**3.** A piece (of wood) split off, a billet –1786.

Shive^{2} (ʃiv). *Obs.* exc. *dial.* 1483. [= WFlem. *schif*, f. Gmc. base **skīf-* split, whence also SHEAVE *sb.*, SHIVE^{1}, and next.] A particle of husk; a splinter; a piece of thread or fluff on the surface of cloth, etc.; *pl.* the refuse of hemp or flax.

Shiver (ʃi·vəɹ), *sb.*^{1} [Early ME. *scifre, scivre*, corresp. to OHG. *scivaro* splinter (G. *schiefer* slate, for *schieferstein*), f. Gmc. **skīf-*. See prec.] **1.** A fragment, chip, splinter. Now *rare* exc. in phrases. **b.** *spec.* A flake or splinter of stone. Now *Sc.* and *dial.* 1600. **2.** [perh. – G. *schiefer.*] Any kind of stone of a slaty or schistous character 1729.

1. Phr. *In shivers*, broken, in small fragments (so *to break, burst*, etc. *in* or *into shivers*); (*all*) *to shivers*, into small fragments.

Shiver (ʃi·vəɹ), *sb.*^{2} [ME. *schivere*, f. Gmc. base **skiƀ-*; see SHEAVE *sb.*] †**1.** = SHIVE^{1} 1. –1753. **2.** SHEAVE *sb.*^{1} 2. 1485.

Shiver (ʃi·vəɹ), *sb.*^{3} 1727. [f. SHIVER *v.*^{2}] **1.** An act or condition of shivering; a quivering or trembling, esp. of the body from cold, emotion, etc. **2.** (*The*) *shivers*: an attack of shivering; often *spec.* the ague; also *transf.*, a feeling of horror or nervous fear 1861.

2. It gives me the cold shivers when I think what might have become of me 1888.

Shiver (ʃi·vəɹ), *v.*^{1} ME. [f. SHIVER *sb.*^{1}] **1.** *trans.* To break or split into small fragments or splinters. **2.** *intr.* To fly into pieces; to split ME. **3.** [perh. after G. *schiefern.*] To split along the natural line of cleavage 1728.

1. Looking-Glasses had been..shivered into ten thousand Splinters STEELE. *S. my timbers*, a mock oath attributed in comic fiction to sailors. **2.** As he crossed the hall, his statue fell, and shivered on the stones 1879.

Shiver (ʃi·vəɹ), *v.*^{2} [Early ME. *chivere*, superseded by *shiver* XV, prob. by assoc. with *shake* (cf. *chivere and shake* XIV); perh. orig. referring to chattering of the teeth (cf. *chevere with the chin* XV) and so an alt., by substitution of -ER^{5}, of ME. *chavele, chefle* wag the jaws, chatter, and *chevele, chivele* shiver (Piers Plowman), f. OE. *ċeafl* jaw, JOWL *sb.*^{1}] **1.** *intr.* To tremble, quake, quiver; esp. to tremble with cold or fear. **2.** *trans.* To pour out or give forth with a trembling motion 1821. **3.** *Naut.* **a.** *intr.* Of a sail: To flutter or shake (in the wind) 1769. **b.** *trans.* To cause (a sail) to flutter or shake in the wind; to bring a sail edge-on to the wind 1769. **4.** *intr.* To quiver, to tremble with a shrinking movement 1869.

1. Why stand we longer shivering under feares That show no end but Death? MILT. The dry rushes s. in the sand 1878. **3. b.** S. the mizen topsail or brail up the spanker 1875. Hence **Shi·vering** *ppl. a.*

Shivery (ʃi·vəri), *a.*^{1} 1683. [f. SHIVER *sb.*^{1} + -Y^{1}.] Apt to split into flakes, brittle, flaky.

Shivery (ʃi·vəri), *a.*^{2} 1747. [f. SHIVER *v.*^{2} + -Y^{1}.] **1.** Characterized by a shaking, quivering motion, or appearance of motion. **2.** Inclined to shiver 1837. **3.** Causing a shivering feeling, chilly 1839.

Shlemozzle, variant of SHEMOZZLE.

Shoad, shode (ʃō^{u}d). *local.* 1602. [prob. – OE. *sċ(e)ādan* divide; see SHED *v.*^{1}] Loose fragments of tin, lead, or copper ore mixed with earth, lying on or near the surface and indicating the proximity of a lode. Also, one of these fragments. Hence **Shoa·ding,** the process of searching for shoad-ore by digging small pits.

Shoal (ʃō^{u}l), *sb.*^{1} ME. [absol. use of SHOAL *a.*] A place where the water is of little depth; a shallow; a sand-bank or bar.

Among the shoals and eddies with which the Sutlej abounds 1853. *fig.* Wolsey, that once.. sounded all the Depths, and Shoales of Honor SHAKS.

Comb.: **s.-mark,** a buoy or other mark set to indicate a s.

Shoal (ʃō^{u}l), *sb.*^{2} 1579. [prob. – MLG., MDu. *schōle* (adopted earlier as SCHOOL *sb.*^{2}), with English sound-substitution (ʃ for Du. sχ).] **1.** = SCHOOL *sb.*^{2} 1. Phr. *in a s., in* or *by shoals*. **b.** Hence occas. used of a number of aquatic animals or floating objects 1593. †**2.** A flock of birds –1801. **3.** *transf.* A large number; a troop, crowd 1579.

1. Herrings offer themselves in shoals 1774. **b.** A s. of boats 1839. **3.** Wherewith whole showls of martyrs once did burn 1610. Never-ending shoals of small troubles CARLYLE.

Shoal (ʃō^{u}l), *a.* (and *adv.*). [alt. of late ME. *schoold, schold*, Sc. *schald* (XIV), repr. OE. *sċ(e)ald* (only in local names, *æt sċealdan fleote* Shalfleet, etc.) :– **skaldaz*, rel. to SHALLOW.] **A.** *adj.* Of water: Not deep; shallow. **B.** *adv.* [ME. *schealde.*] To or at a slight depth ME.

A. Our shipps running all a-ground, it being so s. water PEPYS.

Shoal (ʃō^{u}l), *v.*^{1} 1574. [f. SHOAL *a.*] **I.** *intr.* Of water, a watercourse, harbour, sounding, etc.: To become shallow or more shallow.

It shoals suddenly from ten to two fathoms 1779. *To s. out*, to become gradually more shallow until no water is to be seen.

II. *trans.* **1.** *Naut.* To find (one's soundings) gradually more shallow; to pass from a greater into a less depth of (water), as shown by sounding 1670. **2.** To cause (a piece of water) to become shallow; also, to obstruct by shoals 1864. **3.** *Otter-hunting.* To drive (the otter) to the shallows 1897. Hence **Shoa·ler,** a vessel or a sailor in the coasting trade.

Shoal (ʃō^{u}l), *v.*^{2} 1610. [f. SHOAL *sb.*^{2}] **1.** *intr.* Of fish: To collect or swim together in a shoal or shoals. **2.** *transf.* To crowd together, assemble in swarms 1618.

1. The mackerel shoaling in each bay 1901.

Shoaling (ʃō^{u}·liŋ), *vbl. sb.* 1574. [f. SHOAL *v.*^{1} + -ING^{1}.] **1.** The process of becoming shallow or more shallow; an instance of this 1633. **2.** *concr.* A place where the water becomes shallow 1574.

1. A sudden s. up of the port of discharge 1886.

Shoaly (ʃō^{u}·li), *a.* 1612. [f. SHOAL *sb.*^{1} + -Y^{1}.] Full of shoals or shallows.

[The river] hasting to his fall, his sholy grauell scowr's DRAYTON. Hence **Shoa·liness** (*rare*).

Shoat (ʃō^{u}t). *dial.* and *U.S.* late ME. [Cf. WFlem. *schote, schoteling* a pig under one year old.] **1.** A young weaned pig. **2.** *transf.* An idle worthless person 1800.

Shock (ʃǫk), *sb.*^{1} ME. [XIV, but implied earlier in AL. *socca* (XII), *scoka* (XIII), either repr. OE. **sċ(e)oc* or – (M)LG., (M)Du. *schok* shock of corn, group of 60 units (with assim. of sχ to ʃ), in OS. *scok* = MHG. *schoc* heap, also (as in G. *schock*) sixty; of unkn. origin.] **1.** A group of sheaves of corn placed upright and supporting each other in order to permit the drying and ripening of the grain before carrying. **2.** *transf.* A crowd (of persons); a heap, bunch, bundle (of things). late ME.

1. He found Three hundred S. of Corn in the Fields 1746.

Shock (ʃǫk), *sb.*^{2} Now *Hist.* 1583. [– G. *schock*, Du. *schok*; prob. a special use of prec.] *Comm.* A lot of sixty pieces. (Used with ref. to certain articles of merchandise orig. imported from abroad.)

Shock (ʃǫk), *sb.*^{3} 1565. [– Fr. *choc*, f. (O)Fr. *choquer* SHOCK *v.*^{1}] **1.** *Mil.* The encounter of an armed force with the enemy in a charge or onset; also, the encounter of two mounted warriors or jousters charging one another. **2.** A sudden and violent blow, impact, or collision, tending to overthrow or to produce internal oscillation in a body subjected to it; also, the disturbance of equilibrium or the internal oscillation resulting from this 1614. **b.** *spec.* (= *earthquake s.*) A sudden and more or less violent shake of a part of the earth's surface; a single movement of the series of movements constituting an earthquake 1692. **3.** *transf.* and *fig.* A sudden and violent effect tending to impair the stability or permanence of something; a damaging blow (to a condition of things, a belief, etc.) 1654. **4.** A sudden and disturbing impression on the mind or feelings; usu., one produced by some unwelcome occurrence or perception, or by violent emotion, and tending to occasion lasting depression or loss of composure; in weaker sense, a thrill or start of surprise, or of suddenly excited feeling of any kind 1705. **b.** Used for: An occurrence, discovery, etc. that occasions a shock 1841. **c.** A feeling of being shocked; a pained sense of something offensive to morality or decorum 1876. **5.** *Med.* A sudden debilitating effect produced by over-stimulation of nerves, intense pain, violent emotion, or the like; the condition of nervous exhaustion resulting from this 1804. **6.** A momentary stimulation of a nerve. Also, a stimulation of nerves with resulting contraction of muscles and feeling of concussion; *spec.* = *electric s.* 1818.

1. This doubtfull shocke of Armes SHAKS. *transf.* The s. and encounter of thought 1879. **2.** With twelve great shocks of sound, the shameless noon Was clash'd and hammer'd from a hundred towers TENNYSON. **3.** The s. given to commercial credit 1833.

Comb.: **s.-absorber,** a device fitted to mechanically-propelled vehicles in order to absorb vibration; a device on an aeroplane to relieve strain when landing; **-action** *Mil.*, a method of attack esp. by a charge of cavalry, in which the force of the impact is principally relied upon; **-tactics** *Mil.*, tactics in which shock-action forms a principal part; **s. troops,** [tr. G. *stosstruppen*], units of men reserved for forlorn-hope service; in the British army, units specially formed for storming positions. **b.** In the U.S.S.R. applied to workers used for a specially arduous task, as *s.-brigade, -worker*.

†**Shock,** *sb.*^{4} 1638. [Also *shock-dog* poodle (XVII), presumably var. of †*shough* (XVI); of unkn. origin.] A dog having long shaggy hair, *spec.* a poodle –1800.

Shock (ʃǫk), *sb.*^{5} 1819. [prob. for *shock head*: see SHOCK *a.*] A thick mass (of hair).

Shock (ʃǫk), *a.* 1681. [Based on *shock, shock-dog*; see SHOCK *sb.*^{4}] Having rough thick hair. Of hair: Rough and thick, shaggy.

Shock (ʃǫk), *v.*^{1} 1568. [– (O)Fr. *choquer* = Sp. *chocar*, of unkn. origin.] **1.** *intr.* To come into violent contact, to collide, class *together*; esp. to encounter in the shock of battle. Now only *arch.* or as a Gallicism. 1576. †**2.** To assail with a sudden and violent attack, to charge (an enemy) with troops, etc. –1767. †**3.** To throw (troops) into confusion by an onset or charge; to damage or weaken by impact or collision; to destroy the stability of –1770. **4.** In early use, to wound the feelings of, offend, displease. Later: To affect with a painful feeling of intense aversion or disapproval; to outrage (a person's sentiments, prejudices, etc.). Often *pass.*, to be scandalized or horrified *at*. Also *absol.* 1656. **5.** To impart a physical shock to, to cause (a person or a part of the body) to suffer a nervous shock 1733. **b.** To give (a person) an electric shock 1746.

1. All at fiery speed the two Shock'd on the central bridge TENNYSON. **4.** They are no more shocked at Vice and Folly, than Men of slower Capacities STEELE. Pope..was terriby shocked when he found himself accused of heterodoxy 1880. Hence **Sho·ckable** *a.* easily shocked.

Shocked (ʃǫkt) *ppl. a.* scandalized, horrified 1861.

Shock (ʃǫk), *v.*[2] Now *dial.* late ME. [f. SHOCK *sb.*[1] In AL. *soccare* XIV.] **1.** *trans.* To arrange (sheaves) in a shock. Also with *up.* 1440. †**2.** *refl.* and *intr.* To crowd together –1622. Hence **Sho·cker,** a person or machine for piling sheaves in shocks.

†**Shock-dog.** 1673. [See SHOCK *sb.*[4]] = SHOCK *sb.*[4] –1845.

Shocker (ʃǫ·kəɹ). 1824. [f. SHOCK *v.*[1] + -ER[1].] Something which shocks or excites; esp. a work of fiction of a sensational character.

Sho·ck-head. 1818. [f. SHOCK *a.*; see SHOCK *sb.*[5]] A head covered with a thick crop of hair.

A. s. of red hair SCOTT. *attrib.* The s. willows TENNYSON. So **Shock-headed** *a.*

Shocking (ʃo·kiŋ), *ppl. a.* 1691. [f. SHOCK *v.*[1] + -ING[2].] That shocks. *esp.* **1.** That gives offence; offensive. Also, causing unpleasant surprise. Now *rare* or *Obs.* **2.** Revolting to the feelings; exciting intense horror or repugnance 1704. **3.** 'Shockingly' bad, 'execrable' 1798. **b.** quasi-*adv.* Shockingly. *colloq.* 1831.

1. There is such a s. familiarity both in his railleries and civilities ADDISON. **2.** It is s. enough to see noble beasts ruthlessly mangled 1891. *hyperbolically.* S. To think we buy gowns lined with ermine For dolts BROWNING. **3.** The s. way those boys spell 1872. **b.** A s. bad road 1857. Hence **Sho·cking-ly** *adv.*, **-ness.**

Shod (ʃǫd), *ppl. a.* late ME. [pa. pple. of SHOE *v.*] **1.** Wearing shoes. Chiefly with qualifying adv., *well, neatly,* etc. **2.** Of things: Furnished with a shoe of metal, etc.; tipped, edged, or sheathed with metal 1565. **b.** Of cart wheels: Furnished with tyres. Hence of a cart: Having shod wheels. 1481.

Shoddy (ʃǫdi), *sb.* 1832. [Of dial. but obscure origin.] **1.** Woollen yarn obtained by tearing to shreds refuse woollen rags, which, with the addition of some new wool, is made into a kind of cloth. **2.** A cloth composed of shoddy wool; more fully *s. cloth* 1847. **3.** *transf.* and *fig.* Worthless material made to look like material of superior quality; that which is worthless and pretentious in art, manufactures, ideas, etc.; the class of persons characterized by the endeavour to pass for something superior to what they really are 1862.

3. Theological s.,—old fragments of decaying systems woven into a web of the usual polish and flimsiness 1873.

Comb.: **s.-hole,** a place in which rubbish is deposited. Hence **Sho·ddyism,** pretentious vulgarity.

Shoddy (ʃǫ·di), *a.* 1862. [attrib. use of prec. 3.] **1.** Of a person: That pretends to a superiority to which he has no just claim. **2.** Of a thing: Having a delusive appearance of superior quality 1882. **3.** Of, pertaining to, or dealing in shoddy goods 1864.

1. That s. saviour of society, called L. Cornelius Cinna 1896. **2.** S. cottages..mere traps to catch rent 1891. **3.** Felting..made by some s. contractor 1874. Hence **Sho·ddily** *adv.*, **-ness.**

Shode, var. of SHOAD.

Shoder (ʃōᵘ·dəɹ). 1763. [– Fr. *chauderet, chaudret.*] *Gold-beating.* The packet of skins into which the gold taken from the 'cutch' is placed and beaten out before its final beating in the 'mould'.

Shoe (ʃū), *sb. Pl.* **shoes** (ʃūz); *dial., poet.,* and *arch.* **shoon** (ʃūn). [OE. *scō(h)* = OFris. *scōh,* OS. *scōh* (Du. *schoen*), OHG. *scuoh* (G. *schuh*), ON. *skór,* Goth. *skōhs* :– Gmc. **skōχaz* or **skōχwaz,* with no known cogns.] **1.** An outer covering for the human foot, normally made of leather (but often of other materials) and consisting of a more or less stiff sole and a lighter upper part. Chiefly in more specific sense (distinguished from *boot*), a 'low shoe', which does not reach above the ankle. **2.** A plate of metal, usually iron, nailed to the under-side of the hoof of a horse as a protection from injury; a horseshoe. late ME. **3.** Something resembling a shoe (sense 1 or 2) in shape, position, or function. **a.** A metal rim, ferrule, casing, or sheath, esp. for the end of a pile, pole, rod, or the like 1495. **b.** The receptacle beneath the hopper of a mill 1688. **c.** The short section which turns out the water at the foot of a water pipe 1769. **d.** A kind of drag or skid for the wheel of a vehicle; also, the concave part of a brake, which acts upon the wheel 1837. **e.** A strip of iron, steel, etc. fastened upon that part of a vehicle, machine, etc. which is liable to be worn out by friction 1837. **f.** A socket for the reception of a bolt, pin, or the like 1858. **g.** *Naut.* A block of wood for an anchor fluke 1750. **h.** A block, plate, etc. which serves as a socket or bearing for the foot of a pole, the legs of sheers, etc. to prevent slipping or sinking 1843. **i.** An iron plate shaped to receive the end of one or more pieces of timber in roof-construction 1842. **j.** An ingot of precious metal, somewhat in the form of a Chinese shoe, current in silver in China 1702. **k.** *Electr. traction.* A block attached to an electric car in such a position that it slides upon a conductor-wire or rail and collects the current for the propulsion of the car 1891.

1. The dull swayn Treads on it daily with his clouted shoon MILT. [She] felt..her heart sink to her shoes 1887. *High shoes,* boots with high uppers. *Shoes of swiftness,* the magic shoes of the giant in the story of Jack the Giant-killer; occas. used allus. *Old s.,* a type of something discarded as worn out, useless, or worthless. *Another pair of shoes* (predic.), quite a different matter or state of things. *To shake in one's shoes*: see SHAKE *v.* II. 3. *Over (the) shoes,* deeply immersed or sunk (*in* something). *To know best where the s. pinches*: see PINCH *v.* I. 1 b. *To be in* (another person's) *shoes,* to be in his position or place. *To step into the shoes of* (another person), to occupy the position vacated by him. *To wait for dead men's shoes,* to wait for the death of a person with the expectancy of succeeding to his possessions or office.

Comb.: **s.-beak, bill, bird,** a bird, *Balæniceps rex,* found in Central Africa; **s. buckle,** a fastening for a s., in the form of a buckle; also, an ornamental buckle worn on the front of a s.; **-lace** = *s.-string*; **s. pack** *U.S.,* a s. of tanned leather made without a separate sole after the manner of a moccasin; **-string,** a string or tie used to fasten or lace a s.; **-valve,** a valve at the foot of a pump-stock, or at the bottom of a reservoir. Hence **Shoe·less** *a.* without shoes.

Shoe (ʃū), *v.* Pa. t. and pa. pple. **shod** (ʃǫd), *rarely* **shoed** (ʃūd). [OE. *scōg(e)an* = MLG. *schoi(g)en* (Du. *schoeien*), OHG. *scuohōn* (G. *schuhen*), ON. *skúa.*] **1.** *trans.* To put shoes on (one's feet); to put on (one's) shoes; to clothe or protect the feet with shoes; to provide (a person, oneself) with boots or shoes. **2.** To provide (a horse, etc.) with a shoe or shoes ME. **3.** To protect (the point, edge, or face of a thing, esp. something made of timber) with a plate, rim, ferrule, or sheath of metal, etc. ME. **4.** *transf.* To cover or protect as with a shoe or shoes 1639.

1. Shod with snow-shoes LONGF. **3.** Bootes.. shodde vnderneath with yron 1585.

Shoeblack (ʃū·blæk). 1778. [f. SHOE *sb.* + BLACK *v.*] One who cleans boots and shoes for a living.

Shoe-horn (ʃū·hǫɹn). 1589. **1.** A curved instrument of horn, metal, etc. used to facilitate the slipping of one's heel into a shoe by placing it between shoe and heel. **2.** *fig.* = next 2. 1630.

Shoe·ing-horn. 1440. [f. *shoeing,* vbl. sb. f. SHOE *v.*] **1.** = prec. 1. **2.** *fig.* **a.** An appetizer for food or drink 1536. **b.** Something serving to facilitate a transaction, to bring on a condition, or to procure acceptance for something else 1584. **c.** A person used as a tool by another; esp. one employed as a decoy 1602.

Shoe·-leather. 1576. Leather for the making of shoes; the leather of which (one's) shoes are made 1660. **b.** Used for the wear of shoes in walking 1576.

As good a lad as ever stepped in s. 1818.

Shoemaker (ʃū·mēⁱ:kəɹ). late ME. **1.** One whose trade it is to make shoes. **2.** In the names of fishes; as the Threadfish, *Blepharis crinitus,* the Runner, *Elagatis pinnulatus* 1688. So **Shoe·making** *vbl. sb.* the making of shoes.

Shoer (ʃū·əɹ). [OE. *scōere*; see SHOE *v.* and -ER[1].] One who shoes. In OE. a shoemaker; later usu., one who shoes horses, etc.

Shog (ʃǫg), *sb.* Now *dial.* and *arch.* 1611. [f. next.] A shake, jerk.

Shog (ʃǫg), *v.* Now chiefly *dial.* [Late ME. *s(c)hogge,* parallel to contemp. *schokke* move swiftly, MLG., MHG. *schocken* swing, sway. Cf. JOG.] **1.** *trans.* To shake or roll (something heavy) from side to side; to rock (a cradle); to shake, agitate (a liquid or the vessel containing it); to jolt or jar (some one or something). †**b.** To shake or jog (a person) –1651. **2.** To walk, ride or move with a succession of bumps or jerks; to jog along. Now usu., to travel steadily on. late ME. **b.** To go away. Also with *off. Obs.* exc. *dial.* 1599.

‖**Shogun** (ʃōᵘ·gun). 1615. [Jap. *shōgun,* a sound-substitution for Chinese *chiang chiin* (*chiang* to lead, *chiin* army).] The hereditary commander-in-chief of the Japanese army, until 1867 the virtual ruler of Japan. Hence **Sho·gunal** *a.* **Sho·gunate,** the office or dignity of a s. or the shoguns.

‖**Shola** (ʃōᵘ·lă). 1836. [Hindi *sholā* = Bengali *solā.*] = SOLA.

Shone, pa. t. and pa. pple. of SHINE *v.*

Shoo (ʃū), *v.* 1622. [f. next.] **1.** *trans.* To scare or drive away (fowls, etc.) by calling out 'shoo'. **2.** *intr.* To cry out 'shoo' in order to frighten or drive away fowls, etc. 1746.

Shoo (ʃū), *int.*[1] 1483. [Of instinctive origin; cf. LG. *schu,* (M)HG. *schū,* Fr. *shou,* It. *scio.*] An exclam. used to frighten or drive away fowls or other intruders. Also as *sb.*

Shoo (ʃū, ʃu), **sho** (ʃō), *int.*[2] *dial.* and *U.S.* 1845. [Instinctive; cf. prec.] An exclam. indicating impatient or contemptuous rejection of a statement. Cf. PSHAW.

Shook (ʃuk), *sb.* Now chiefly *U.S.* 1768. [Of unkn. origin.] A set of staves and headings sufficient for one hogshead, barrel, cask, or the like, prepared for use and bound up compactly for convenience of transport. Also boxes similarly packed and prepared. Hence **Shook** *v. trans.* to pack in shooks.

Shook (ʃuk), *ppl. a.* In educated use only *arch.* 1695. [pa. pple. of SHAKE *v.*] = SHAKEN.

Shoon, *arch.* and *dial.* pl. f. SHOE.

Shoot (ʃūt), *sb.* 1450. [f. next.] **1.** An act of shooting; a discharge of arrows, bullets, etc. Now only *arch.* 1534. †**b.** Range, distance or reach of a shot; shooting distance –1719. **c.** A game-shooting expedition 1852. **d.** A shooting party 1885. **e.** The right to shoot game in a given area; also the area itself 1861. **f.** A shooting match or contest; a round of shots in such a contest 1892. **2.** The action of shooting, sprouting, or growing; the amount of growth (also *concr.* the new wood, etc. produced) in a certain period 1572. **b.** A young branch which shoots out from the main stock of a tree, plant, etc. 1450. **c.** *gen.* An offshoot; a growth or sprout from a main stock 1610. **3.** A motion or movement (of a thing) as though shooting or being shot in a particular direction; also, the space or distance covered by such a motion or by a push 1596. **b.** Of an immaterial thing: A sudden advance 1752. **c.** A short sharp twinge (of pain) 1756. **4.** *Weaving.* One movement or throw of the shuttle between the threads of the warp; the length of thread thus placed; also, the weft 1717. **5.** A heavy and sudden rush of water down a steep channel; a place in a river where this occurs, a rapid. (Confused with CHUTE 1.) 1613. **b.** An artificial channel for conveying water by gravity to a low level; or for the escape of overflow water from a reservoir, etc.; also for forcing water into a railway engine in rapid motion 1707. **6. a.** A sloping channel or conduit for letting down coal, ore, wheat, etc. into a lower receptacle 1844. **b.** A place where rubbish may be 'shot' 1851. **7.** *Mining.* A considerable and somewhat regular body or mass of ore in a vein, usu. elongated and vertical or inclined in position 1850.

1. How many a rogue would give his two crop ears to have a s. at either of us! STEVENSON. **c.** A big s. in the jungle 1895. **f.** Second-rate pigeon shoots 1892. **2.** *transf.* Ridges of barren land, that seemed like shoots of the adjacent Andes 1847. **b.** The French in Canada eat the tender shoots in spring as Asparagus 1812. **3.** Both [yachts] had a long s. up in the eye of the wind 1894. **5.** A single s. carried a considerable stream over the face of a black rock SCOTT.

Shoot (ʃūt), *v.* Pa. t. and pa. pple. **shot**

(ʃūt). [OE. *scēotan*, pa. t. *scēat*, *scuton*, pa. pple. *scoten* (cf. SHOTTEN) = OFris. *skiata*, OS. *skietan*, OHG. *sciozzan* (Du. *schieten*, G. *schiessen*), ON. *skjóta* :– Gmc. str. vb. **skeutan*, f. **skeut-* **skaut-* **skut-*, whence also OE. *scēat*, *scīete* SHEET *sb.*[1] and [2], *scot* SHOT, *scotian* shoot with arrows, *scyttan* SHUT *v.* The phonetic development of *shoot* is as in CHOOSE.] **I.** To go swiftly and suddenly. **1.** *intr.* To go or pass with a sudden swift movement through space; to be precipitated; to fly as an arrow from a bow. **b.** Of a 'star' or meteor: To dart across the sky ME. **c.** Of light, etc.: To be emitted in rays, to dart. Of a glance: To dart. 1693. **d.** *fig.* Of thoughts, etc.: To pass suddenly *into*, *across*, etc. a person's mind 1542. **e.** Of a person's feet: To slip suddenly *from under one*. late ME. **f.** *Naut.* Of ballast: = SHIFT *v.* III. 2 c. 1678. **g.** Of a ball: To move with accelerated speed after its first impingement; esp. in *Cricket*, of a bowled ball: To move rapidly close to the ground after pitching 1833. **2.** To pass swiftly and suddenly from one place to another; to precipitate oneself, rush, dart OE. **3.** Of a vessel (hence of its commander or crew): To move swiftly in a certain direction. late ME. **4.** *trans.* With obj. denoting what is passed through, over, or under by 'shooting', e.g. a bridge, a rapid or cataract 1570. **b.** *Naut.* To succeed in sailing through (a dangerous strait, passage, gulf, etc.). Hence *to s. the gulf*, *Niagara* (fig.), provb. for any daring enterprise. 1622. **c.** *Racing.* To dash past (another competitor) 1868. **5.** *intr.* Of a pain: To pass in a sudden paroxysm along the nerves; to dart. Hence of a part of the body, a wound, etc.: To have darting pains. OE. **6.** Of a plant, bud, etc.: To emerge from the soil (also with *up*) or from the stem, etc.; to sprout, grow 1483. **b.** Of parts of animal bodies, teeth, hair, morbid growths 1607. **7.** To put forth buds or shoots, as a plant; to germinate 1560. **8.** To increase rapidly in growth (sometimes, to sprout and grow rapidly); to advance to maturity. Now only with *up*, etc.: To grow quickly tall, 'spring up' to a height (said of plants, young persons, buildings, etc.; also of immaterial things). 1530. **9.** Of a solution: To produce crystals. Also said of the crystals. Of a salt: To crystallize from solution or evaporation. 1626. **b.** *trans.* To form (crystals); of a solution, to deposit in the form of crystals. Also *refl.* and *pass.*, to crystallize; of a substance, to assume some definite form by internal movement. 1662. **10.** *intr.* To project, jut out; to extend in a particular direction OE.

1. The lambent lightnings s. Across the sky THOMSON. **b.** Certaine starres shot madly from their Spheares SHAKS. **c.** A gleam of anger shot along his features SCOTT. **2.** A lively young fellow in a fustian jacket shot by me STEELE. **3.** 'Tis.. the boat, shooting round by the trees! M. ARNOLD. Phr. *To s. ahead*, of a vessel, to increase speed suddenly, so as to pass accompanying or competing vessels; hence *fig.* **4.** In half an hour I had shot Putney Bridge MARRYAT. *To s. the moon*, to remove household goods by night in order to avoid seizure for rent. **5.** *fig.* A pang of homesickness shot through him 1895. **6.** *fig.* Delightful task! to rear the tender thought, To teach the young idea how to s. THOMSON. **7.** The Cypress Tree..when cut down, never shoots again 1710. **8.** Great D'Ambois (Fortunes proud mushrome shot vp in a night) CHAPMAN. She had shot up into a woman all in a minute 1880. **10.** That Region [Cornwall]..shooteth out farthest into the West HOLLAND.

II. To send forth, esp. swiftly or by sudden impulse. **1.** *trans.* To throw suddenly or with violence. *Obs.* exc. as *transf.* from sense III. 1. OE. **b.** To empty out (gold, grain, earth, etc.) by overturning or tilting the receptacle; to dump (rubbish); to send (goods, debris, etc.) down a 'shoot'. late ME. **c.** *refl.* To throw or precipitate oneself; to rush. Now *rare.* 1587. **d.** To throw (rain, or running water) *from*, *off* the surface 1573. **e.** To put hurriedly and carelessly 1833. **2.** To launch (a vessel); to cast forth or let down (an anchor); to lower and place in position (a fishing net). Also *absol.* late ME. **b.** To cause (a vessel) to move forward suddenly or swiftly. late ME. **3.** To push or slide (a bar or bolt of a door or the like) into or out of its fastenings. Also, to force (a lock). OE. **b.** *intr.* Of a bolt: To slide *into* its fastenings; to admit of being shot 1886. **4.** *trans.* **a.** *Weaving.* To pass (the shuttle, the weft) between the threads of the warp 1603. **b.** To variegate by admixture of different coloured threads in the woof. Hence, to variegate (an expanse of colour) by interspersing streaks or flecks of some other colour. 1532. **5.** To emit swiftly and forcibly (rays, flames, etc.). late ME. **b.** To put forth, utter (words, sounds); chiefly with adv., *out*, *forth*. ME. **c.** To cause (a pain, an emotion, etc.) to pass rapidly *through* 1842. **6.** To thrust (one's hand, a limb, a weapon, etc.) *into* something. Also to thrust *out*, *forth*, *up*, etc. ME. **b.** *To s. out*: To protrude (the tongue, the lips), usu. as an expression of mockery 1535. †**7.** To eject from the body; *esp.* to discharge (excreta) –1775. **b.** Of a fish: To discharge (spawn). 1609. **8.** Of a plant: To put forth (buds, leaves, branches, etc.). Chiefly with *forth* or *out*. 1526. **9.** With ref. to stationary position: To throw out as a projection or protuberance; *refl.* to stand out, protuberate in a particular direction ME.

1. A more fractious horse..had finally shot him over his head 1858. **b.** A tract of suburban Sahara, where..rubbish was shot DICKENS. **d.** A great Cap for my Head, with the Hair on the Outside to s. off the Rain DE FOE. **e.** He..shot his instrument into its case 1833. **2.** The nets were shot over the starboard 1894. **b.** Phr. *To s.* (a vessel) *to*, to bring it by 'shooting' to a required position. **4. b.** One couerlyt shot wyth blew and red 1566. His stiff, black hair a little shot with gray 1860. **5.** My sweet guide, who, smiling shot forth beams From her celestial eyes CARY. **6. b.** They shute out their lippes COVERDALE *Ps.* 22:7. **8.** Apt to make the wheat s. fresh ears 1766. **9.** Where Hibernia shoots Her wondrous causeway far into the main COWPER.

III. To send missiles from an engine. **1.** *trans.* To send forth, let fly (arrows, bolts, etc.) from a bow or other engine, or (bullets or shot) from a firearm OE. **b.** *transf.* To discharge, send forth like an arrow or a shot. Also *fig.* with obj. a glance, question, etc. 1612. **2.** *absol.* and *intr.* To send forth missiles from a bow, firearm, etc. OE. **b.** *transf. intr.* Formerly, to take a snapshot with a camera; now to take cinematic photographs. Also *trans.* to take a snapshot of; to photograph cinematically. 1890. **3.** *fig.* and in fig. context OE. **4.** Of a bow, engine, or firearm: **a.** *trans.* To send forth (a missile). late ME. **b.** *intr.* To send forth missiles; to 'carry' a certain distance. Also, of a gun, to be discharged, go off (e.g. in a salute). 1575. **5.** *trans.* To discharge (a bow, catapult, etc.), to fire (a gun or other firearm); also with *off*, *out*. 1482. **6.** To propel (a marble, pellet, etc.) as from the thumb and forefinger 1820. **7.** *Football.* To kick (the ball) at goal. In *Hockey*, *Lacrosse*, etc.: to hit or drive (the ball) at goal. 1882. **b.** *intr.* To kick or drive the ball at goal 1874.

1. A third [cannon ball]..said to have been shot into the wall at the siege of Padua 1756. *Phr. To have shot one's bolt* (fig.) to have done all that one can do. Provb. *A fool's bolt is soon shot*: see BOLT *sb.*[1] 1. **b.** The sullen and indignant glances which they shot at them SCOTT. **2.** Whose there?.. speake quickly, or I shoote SHAKS. *Well shot!* an applauding exclam. when a shooter hits the mark. quasi-*trans. To s. a match*, to engage in a shooting-match. *To s. off a tie*, to decide a tie in a shooting-match by a supplementary contest. *To s. up*, to terrorize (a locality) by shooting (*U.S.*). **3.** If it is a Pleasure to be envyed and shot at, to be maligned standing,..then it is a Pleasure to be great 1660. Phr. *To s. at*, (*a*) to aim at, to seek to have or accomplish; to aspire to, strive after (now *arch.*); †(*b*) to 'drive at', mean, have reference to; †(*c*) to aim at imitating. *To s. off one's mouth*, to talk indiscreetly or abusively (*U.S. slang*).

IV. To assail, wound, or kill with a shot. **1.** *trans.* To wound or kill with a missile from a bow or firearm (in early use, occas. with a spear or javelin). OE. **b.** To hit or wound with a shot *in* or *through* a part of the body ME. **2.** *intr.* To engage in or practise the sport of killing game with a gun (formerly with a bow or the like) ME. **3.** *trans.* With advs. and advb. phrases ME. **4.** slang or vulgar. *I'll be shot if—*, used as a strong expression of denial or refusal 1826. **5.** *transf.* fig. Of Cupid, love, etc. 1471. **6.** *intr. To s. over* or *to* (a dog), to train by use on a shooting expedition. *To s. over* (a cover, a tract of country), to kill game upon. 1868. **b.** *trans.* To go over (a piece of country) shooting game 1833. **7.** *Mining.* To blast 1830.

1. My Lord himselfe had his horse shot under him 1617. I shot him dead 1863. **b.** Hambden.. being shot into the shoulder with a brace of bullets CLARENDON. Phr. *To s. flying*, to shoot (birds) on the wing: now usu. *absol.*, as denoting a sportsmanlike accomplishment. **2.** Cadogan and Thomond are gone into the country to s. 1766. **3.** We shot away their middle mast 1632. His.. equerry had his head shot off by a cannon ball 1859. *To s.* (a person) *down*, to kill by a shot (usu. with suggestion of merciless cruelty or determination). *To be shot by the board* (Naut.), of masts, etc., to be broken by the enemy's shot in a fight. *To be shot between wind and water*, of a vessel, to receive a shot causing a dangerous leak.

V. †**1.** *Sc.* To avoid, escape –1685. **b.** *dial. pass.* To be rid *of* 1802. **2.** *Carpentry* and *Joinery.* To plane accurately (the edge of a board), esp. with the aid of a shooting-board 1530.

1. b. Are you not glad to be fairly shot of him! SCOTT.

Comb. **s.-off**, the subsequent competition between tied contestants in a shooting-match.

Shooter (ʃū·təɹ). ME. [f. SHOOT *v.* + -ER[1].] **1.** One who shoots; now chiefly applied to a sportsman who shoots game. **2.** Something that shoots or is used for shooting, esp. *colloq.* or *slang.* A shooting instrument, *esp.* a revolver. 1812. **b.** *Cricket.* A ball which on touching the ground keeps very close to the turf, often with an increase of pace 1856.

Shooting (ʃū·tiŋ), *vbl. sb.* [f. SHOOT *v.* + -ING[1].] **1.** The action or practice of discharging missiles from a bow or gun. **b.** The sport of killing game with the gun 1642. **c.** An exclusive right to shoot game on a particular estate or tract of country. Hence also, a tract of country on which a person has such an exclusive right. Often *collect. pl.* 1848. **2.** The feeling of a sudden pain; a thrill or dart of pain 1528. **3.** In various senses of the verb 1464.

1. He daily practised s. at a mark 1727. **b.** But there's no s. (save grouse) till September BYRON. **c.** He rented..the s. of Mixbury 1896. **2.** The s. of my Corn 1710. **3.** I have known the s. of a Star spoil a Night's Rest ADDISON.

Comb.: **s.-block, -board**, an appliance to facilitate the accurate planing of the edge of a board or stereotype plate; **s.-box**, a small country house in or adjacent to a shooting locality used as a residence while shooting; **-gallery**, a long room, or a booth at a fair, fitted up for the practice of shooting; **-ground**, (*a*) that part of a gun-factory where rifles, etc., are tested; (*b*) a place where rubbish is shot; **-iron**, a firearm, esp. a revolver; **-lodge** = *s.-box*; **-range**, a ground with butts for rifle practice; **-seat, -stick** = SEAT-*stick*; **-tool** *Mining*, a tool used in blasting.

Shooting star. 1593. [See SHOOT *v.* I.] **1.** A meteor, resembling a star, that darts across the sky. **2.** *U.S.* A Western name for the American Cowslip, *Dodecathcon meadia* 1856.

1. *attrib.* The periodic shooting star shower known as the Leonids 1886.

Shop (ʃǫp), *sb.* [Aphetic – AFr., OFr. *eschoppe* (mod. *échoppe*) lean-to booth, cobbler's stall – MLG. *schoppe*, corresp. to OE. *sc(e)oppa* (once, rend. Vulg. 'gazophylacium'), OHG. *scopf* porch, vestibule (G. *schopf* porch, lean-to, cartshed, barn), rel. to OE. *scypen* SHIPPON.] **1.** A house or building where goods are made or prepared for sale and sold. †**b.** *Banker's shop*: a bank. (Orig. the shop of a goldsmith or other tradesman who practised banking.) –1796. **2.** A building or room set apart for the sale of merchandise. late ME. **3.** A building or room set apart and fitted up for the carrying on of some particular kind of handiwork or mechanical industry; a workshop. Now often, a building or room in a factory, appropriated to some particular department or stage of the work carried on there. late ME. †**b.** *fig.* (Chiefly after L. *officina.*) A place where something is produced or elaborated, or where some operation is performed. Often said of the heart, liver, or other internal organs. –1737. **4.** *colloq.* or *slang.* A place of business; the place where one's ordinary occupation is carried on. Also used joc. for 'place'. *The S.* (Army slang): the Royal Military Academy, Woolwich. 1841. **b.** *Stage slang.* An engagement, a 'berth' 1888. **5.** Matters pertaining to one's trade or profession; discourse on matters of this kind, esp. as introduced unseasonably into general conversation; chiefly in phr. *to talk s.* 1814. **6.** *Stock Exch.* The inside influences affecting or controlling a company by the exercise of special knowledge; also a name for the S. African gold market 1889.

1. You are a gouldsmith and haue a lytle plate in your shoppe 1592. **2.** Phr. *To keep s.*: to exercise the calling of a shopkeeper; to take charge of a s. temporarily. *Shop!* an exclam. used to summon an attendant or shopkeeper. **3.** Engineering and repairing shops 1869. Phr. *The s.*, the workshop of a factory as dist. from the offices, etc. **b.** The sanctuary was now become..a s. of tyranny 1737. **4.** Senior Wrangler, indeed; that's at the other s. THACKERAY.

Phrases. *To set up s.*, to start a business. *To shut up s.*, to close business premises; hence, to bring any business to a close. *To smell of the s.*, (*a*) to indicate the spirit characteristic of a shopkeeper; (*b*) of expressions, to savour unduly of the speaker's calling. *To come to the right* (or *wrong s.*, to apply to the right or wrong person in order to obtain something. *All over the s.*, scattered about the place; following an erratic and undefined course.

Comb.: **s.-book,** a shopkeeper's or mechanic's account book; **-breaker,** a burglar who breaks into a s.; so **-breaking**; **-mark,** a private mark placed by a dealer upon his goods; **-soiled** *a.*, depreciated in value and appearance by being exposed for sale in a s.; **-walker,** an assistant exercising general supervision over a department of a s.; an attendant who directs customers to that part of the premises where the goods they require are to be found; **-worn** *a.* = *s.-soiled.* Hence **Sho·ppish** *a.* characteristic of persons connected with a s.

Shop (ʃǫp), *v.* 1583. [f. prec.] **1.** *trans.* To shut up (a person), to imprison. Of an informer, evidence, etc.: To 'get (a person) into trouble'. Now only *slang* or *dial.* **2.** To bring or take (an article) to a shop; to expose for sale in a shop 1688. **3.** *intr.* To visit a shop or shops for the purpose of making purchases or examining the contents 1764.

3. I thought..that you would be shopping 1845.

Sho·p-board. 1524. [f. BOARD *sb.*] **1.** A counter or table upon which a tradesman's business is transacted or upon which his goods are exposed for sale. **2.** A table or raised platform upon which tailors sit when sewing 1589.

Sho·pkeeper. 1530. [f. SHOP *sb.* + KEEPER.] One who carries on business in a shop. *A nation of shopkeepers*, applied disparagingly to a nation whose chief interest and concern lies in commerce (esp. to England). So **Sho·pkeeping** *sb.* and *a.*

Sho·plifter. 1680. [f. SHOP *sb.* + LIFTER.] A person who steals from a shop, a shop-thief. So **Sho·plifting** *vbl. sb.* the action of stealing from a shop.

Shopman (ʃǫ·pmǣn). 1591. [f. SHOP *sb.* + MAN *sb.*] **1.** The owner of a shop. Now *rare.* **2.** An assistant in a shop 1758. **3.** A workshop hand 1926. So **Sho·p-woman** 1753.

Shopper (ʃǫ·pəɹ). 1862. [f. SHOP *v.* + -ER¹.] One who frequents a shop or shops for the purpose of inspecting or buying goods.

Shopping (ʃǫ·piŋ), *vbl. sb.* 1764. [f. SHOP *v.* + -ING¹.] The action of visiting a shop or shops for the purpose of inspecting or buying goods.

Shoppy (ʃǫ·pi), *a.* 1840. [f. SHOP *sb.* + -Y¹.] **1.** Of the nature of 'shop' or professional concerns or conversation. **2.** Characterized by having a number of shops, forming a centre for business 1851. **3.** Belonging to retail trade 1854.

1. A novel of clerical life written by a clergyman is apt to be..s. 1900. **3.** I don't like s. people MRS. GASKELL. Hence **Sho·ppiness.**

Shop-window. 1447. **1.** A window of a shop, in which goods are displayed for sale. **2.** *transf.* and *fig.* A display of anything, resembling the display of goods by a tradesman, intended to catch the attention 1905.

Shore (ʃōᵊɹ), *sb.*¹ [– (with assim. to Eng. phonetics as in next) MLG., MDu. *schōre*, perh. f. the base of SHEAR *v.*] The land bordering on the sea or a large lake or river. **b.** In *Law*, usu. the tract lying between ordinary high and low water mark 1622. **c.** In vague or rhet. use (*sing.* or *pl.*): A seacoast or the country which it bounds 1611. **d.** *transf.* and *fig.* 1599.

Canute..caus'd his Royal Seat to be set on the shoar, while the Tide was coming in MILT. **c.** You have since accompanied our Royal Master to other Shores 1691. **d.** Deposited upon the silent s. Of memory WORDSW.

Phrases. *On s.*, on the s., ashore, on land; *in s.*, near or nearer to the shore (from the water).

Comb.: **s.-anchor,** that which lies between the s. and the ship when moored; **-boat,** a small boat plying near the s. or between the s. and large vessels farther out; **-gun,** a gun for s.-shooting; **-gunner, -gunning** = *s.-shooter, -shooting*; **-line** (*a*) the line where s. and water meet; (*b*) = *s.-rope*; **-rope,** a rope connecting a net with the s.; **-shooter,** one who shoots birds on the s.; **-shooting,** the sport of shooting birds on the s. (as dist. from punt-shooting); **-side,** the edge of the s.; the part of the land or sea adjacent to the s.; **-weed,** a weed growing on the s., spec. *Littorella lacustris.*

b. With names of animals: **s.-bird,** a bird that frequents the sea-s. or estuaries; *spec.* the sand-martin, *Cotile riparia*; **-crab,** the common small crab, *Carcinus mænas*; **s.-fish,** a general name for fish whose habitat is near the s.; **s. lark,** *Otocorys* (formerly *Alauda*) *alpestris*; **s. pipit,** the rock pipit, *Anthus obscurus*; **s. sandpiper,** the ruff, *Machetes pugnax*; **s. snipe,** (*a*) the common sandpiper, *Totanus hypoleucus*; (*b*) *U.S.* the grey plover, *Squatarola helvetica.*

Shore (ʃōᵊɹ), *sb.*² [– (with LDu. *sx* assim. to ʃ) MLG., MDu. *schōre* (Du. *schoor*) prop, stay.] **1.** A piece of timber or iron set obliquely against the side of a building, of a ship in dock, etc., as a support when it is in danger of falling or when undergoing alteration or repair; a prop or strut. **2.** A prop or stake used for various purposes 1601.

1. *fig.* The true shoares of the unstable wheele of fortune 1603.

Shore (ʃōᵊɹ), *sb.*³ 1598. [orig. in *common shore*, perh. an application of this phr. (SHORE *sb.*¹) in the sense 'no-man's-land at the water-side, where filth was deposited for the tide to wash away'. Not a var. of SEWER *sb.*¹ (*common sewer* is later).] = SEWER *sb.*¹ 2. Orig. in *common s.* = common sewer.

Olde receptacles, or common-shores of filthe SHAKS.

Shore (ʃōᵊɹ), *v.*¹ ME. [– (M)LG., (M)Du. *schōren*, f. *schōre* SHORE *sb.*²] **1.** *trans.* To prop, support with a prop. Often with *up.* †**2.** To lift up, raise (the eyes) –1617. †**3.** *intr.* To lean, slope, shelve –1621.

1. The old inn, long shored and trussed and buttressed STEVENSON. Hence **Sho·rer,** a thing (rarely a person) that shores up. **Sho·ring** *vbl. sb.* the action of the verb; *concr.* shores or props.

Shore (ʃōᵊɹ), *v.*² 1600. [f. SHORE *sb.*¹] **1.** *intr.* To go ashore. **2.** *trans.* To put ashore; to land (passengers or goods); to beach (a vessel) 1611. **3.** To border as a shore 1832. **4.** *intr.* To sail *along* (a coast) 1632.

4. They had been *shoring*..to see if they could find anything worth their labour DE FOE.

Shore, pa. t. of SHEAR *v.*

Sho·re-going, *vbl. sb.* and *a.* 1895. Going ashore (from the sea); going, living, on shore.

Shoreless (ʃōᵊ·ɹlės), *a.* 1628. [f. SHORE *sb.*¹ + -LESS.] Having no shore. Of a sea, or what is compared to a sea: Boundless.

Lost upon that shorelesse Sea 1643. The s. tides of delirium KIPLING.

Shoreman (ʃōᵊ·ɹmǣn). Also *U.S.* (sense 2) **shoresman.** 1643. [f. SHORE *sb.*¹ + MAN *sb.*] **1.** A dweller on the seashore. **2.** One who is employed on shore in the business of a fishery 1690. **3.** One who makes his living by shooting on the shore; a shore-shooter 1882.

Shoreward (ʃōᵊ·ɹwǫ̈ɹd), *adv.* and *a.* 1582. [f. SHORE *sb.*¹ + -WARD.] **A. 1.** *advb. phr. To* (*the*) *s.*: in the direction of the shore. **2.** *adv.* In the direction of or towards the shore 1691. **B.** Situated or directed towards the shore 1804. So **Sho·rewards** *adv.* = A. 2.

Shorn, pa. pple. and ppl. a. of SHEAR *v.*

Short (ʃǭɹt), *a.*, *sb.*, and *adv.* [OE. *sćeort* = OHG. *scurz* :– Gmc. *skurtaz; cf. SHIRT, SKIRT.] **I.** With ref. to spatial measurement. **1.** Having small longitudinal extent; measuring little along its greatest dimension, or from end to end. Opp. to *long.* **b.** Const. *in*: Having a specified part short 1800. **c.** Of distance: Not great. Of a journey, flight, etc.: Extending over a short distance. 1597. **d.** *fig.* In Biblical expressions, said of a person's 'hand' or 'arm', implying inadequacy or limited range of power 1549. **e.** Of action, vision, etc.: Reaching but a little way. Hence *fig.* of mental powers, ideas, etc.: Contracted in range. late ME. **f.** Abbreviated in form (*for*)... **2.** Of persons: Low in stature; opp. to tall OE. **3.** *S. dung, manure*: manure containing short straw and in an advanced state of fermentation 1618. **4.** Of the sea, etc.: Having short waves; choppy 1834.

1. Thay beir verie schorte tailis 1596. The s. woolly hair of the Africans 1823. I see no reason why a governess..should not wear s. petticoats if she has good legs 1892. *To cut, trim s.*, to make s. by cutting, trimming, etc. **b.** My coat was..s. in the sleeves 1841. **c.** The way..to the..Inne is ..s. 1597. **d.** Is the Lords hand waxed s.? *Num.* 11:23. **e.** Our s. views 1736. **2.** A man.. somewhat s. of stature 1891. **4.** The shallow Baltic where the seas are steep and s. KIPLING.

II. With ref. to duration or serial extent. **1.** Having little extent in duration, lasting but little time, brief. *At s. intervals*: at times separated by brief intervals. OE. **b.** Occas. applied to conditions, qualities, etc. not usu. described in terms of duration: Not lasting a long time, soon over, short-lived. Somewhat *arch.* OE. **c.** Qualifying a sb. denoting a period of time, to indicate a pleased or regretful sense of its brevity 1715. **d.** Of a person's memory: Not long retaining anything ME. **2.** Of an appointed date in the future: Allowing but a short time, early, near at hand. late ME. **b.** Of notice: Given not long beforehand 1811. †**3.** Quick, speedy, immediate –1780. **4.** Of a speech, sentence, book, word, etc.: Having a small extent from beginning to end; brief OE. **b.** Of a speaker: Brief, occupying little time. Now *rare.* 1515. **5.** Of a style of writing or speaking, hence of a writer or speaker: concise, succinct 1487. **6.** Of utterances (occas. of gestures, etc.): Rudely, angrily, or sternly brief or curt. Of persons (chiefly *predic.*): Rudely or angrily curt in expression; returning short answers; snappish (const. *with* a person). late ME. **b.** Hasty in temper, easily provoked, irascible. Said also of the temper. 1599. **7.** Of breath, breathing: Coming in hurried gasps, impeded. Of a cough: Abrupt, checked; recurring abruptly at frequent intervals; dry, fast. Of a pulse: Making short beats, quick. late ME. **8.** Of a series or succession: Of small extent, having few members or terms. *Obs.* exc. in phrases. **9.** *Phonetics* and *Prosody.* Applied to a vowel (less freq. to a consonant) when its utterance has the less of the two measures of duration recognized in the ordinary classification of speech-sounds. Also, in *Prosody*, of a syllable: Belonging to that one of the two classes which is supposed to be distinguished from the other by occupying a shorter time in utterance. OE. **10.** colloq. *Something s.*: undiluted spirits 1823.

1. The lyf so s., the craft so long to lerne CHAUCER. So s. an acquaintance 1885. Phr. *To make s. work of* (occas. *with*), to dispose of quickly. **c.** Seven s. weeks of quiet CARLYLE. **d.** Great men are apt to have s. memories 1839. **2.** Phr. *A s. day* (Law), (a bill) *at s. date* or *sight* (Comm.). **3.** There is no s. remedy for our disease BURKE. **4.** The s. and simple annals of the poor GRAY. Phr. *To make* (*cut*) *a long story s. S. story*, a prose work of fiction, shorter and less elaborate than a novel. *S. and sweet*, brief and pleasant; now usu. more or less *iron.* **5.** †*To be s.*: in short. **6.** No other answer but only a s. *yes* 1686. **b.** Prince Bismarck's s. temper 1885. **8.** Phr. *S. hour*, an hour indicated by a few strokes of the clock. *A s. purse*, a purse soon exhausted; scanty resources. *A s. kennel*, a small pack of hounds. **9.** *S.* †*accent, mark*, the mark(˘) placed over a vowel letter to indicate short quantity. **10.** A drop of summut s. HOOD.

III. Not reaching to some standard. **1.** Of things: Inadequate in quantity. late ME. **b.** Qualifying a sb. denoting a period of time, distance, number, quantity, etc., to indicate an extent less than that expressed by the sb. 1702. **c.** Qualifying a noun of action 1884. **2.** Of a throw, a missile, etc.: Travelling too short a distance, not reaching the mark 1545. **3.** *S. of*: Not fully attaining or amounting to (some condition or degree); not equalling (some other person or thing); inferior to; less than (a specified number or quantity)

1560. **4.** *predic.*, used chiefly of persons: **a.** Defaulting in payments 1586. †**b.** Lacking in performance –1662. **c.** Having an insufficient supply of money, food, or something else implied by the context; *spec.* not having the means to meet one's engagements 1762. **d.** *S. of*: having an insufficient quantity of. Also, not possessing, lacking (something necessary or desirable); in want of (something to complete the desired number) 1697. **5.** *To run s.* **a.** Of persons: To 'run out' *of* (something). Also without const. 1752. **b.** Of supplies: To prove insufficient 1850.

1. *S. measure, weight*, defective quantity by measure or weight; also, a measuring rod, vessel, etc., or a scale-weight which defrauds the purchaser. *S. commons*: see COMMONS; so *s. allowance, rations*, etc. **b.** A s. league distant BORROW. **c.** *S. delivery, shipment* (Comm.), delivery or shipment of goods less in quantity than agreed on or invoiced. **3.** Cheese little s. of the best Parmeggiano EVELYN. And such a Constitution, little s. of miraculous CARLYLE. Nothing s. of that will do 1892. **4. b.** Very large in Pretence and Promise, but s. in Performance 1697. **c.** Phr. *To go s.*, to suffer privation, have less than enough. **d.** Allow me to take your hat—we are rather s. of pegs DICKENS.

IV. Not tenacious in substance, friable, brittle. (Prob. conn. w. branch I through the notion 'having little length of fibre'.) **1.** Of edible substances: Friable, easily crumbled. late ME. **2.** *gen.* Wanting in tenacity; friable, brittle. Of metals: cf. COLD-SHORT, RED-SHORT. 1607.

1. To make s. paste in Lent 1594. Phr. *To eat s.*, to break up or crumble in the mouth. **2.** Phr. *To work s.*, to break or crumble when being worked.

Comb.: **s.-coat**, a person wearing a s. coat; *pl.* the garments in which an infant is clothed when the long clothes are discarded; so as *v. trans.* to dress (an infant) in s. clothes; **s. division** (*Arith.*): see DIVISION 5; **-frock**, a s. garment, usu. worn in childhood; hence *fig.* in *pl.* habits, etc., associated with childhood; **-grained** *a.*, of wood: having a s. fibre rendering it liable to snap easily; **-head**, *Anthropology*, a brachycephalic person; *Racing*, a distance less than the length of a horse's head; **s. heeled** *a.*, having a s. heel; *fig.* wanton; **s. metre**, a form of stanza used in hymn-writing, consisting of four lines, of which the first, second, and fourth are of six syllables and the third of eight, abbrev. S.M.; **S. Parliament** (see PARLIAMENT); **s. rib**, any of the lower ribs which do not attach to the sternum; also a piece of butcher's meat, esp. of pork, containing one or more of such ribs; **s. shrift** (see SHRIFT *sb.*); **s. staple** *a.* having a short fibre; a commercial term applied to cotton of an inferior grade; also *absol.*; **s. suit** *Cards*, a suit of which one has less than four cards; **-sword**, a sword with a s. blade (*Hist.*); **-timer** (cf. TIMER 3); **s. title**, the abbreviated title by which an Act of Parliament is officially designated; **-waisted** *a.*, (of a person or garment) short in the waist; **s. wave**, spec. in *Wireless*, a wave having a wavelength of less than 100 metres. **b.** In names of animals, as **s.-hair**, one of a breed of short-haired cats; **-head**, a name given by sailors to the young of the whale; **-wing**, a diving-bird of the group *Brachypteri*. **c.** In *Cricket*: **s. ball**, a ball which pitches short of a length (see LENGTH *sb.*); **s. leg** (see LEG *sb.*); **s. pitch**, the pitch of a s. ball; **s. run**, (*a*) a run made when the ball does not travel far enough to give time for an easy run; (*b*) a run which does not count by reason of a batsman not having technically completed it; **s. slip** (see SLIP *sb.*[3]). **d.** *Comm.*, as **s. bill**, a bill having less than ten days to run; **-exchange**, exchange having a s. time (commonly thirty days or less) to run; **s. loan**, a loan repayable at an early date; **-money**, money to borrow or to lend upon s.-time loans; **-paper**, s. bills; **-payment**, payment at an early date after the completion of the transaction; **s. price**, a low price (in *Betting*, low odds).

B. quasi-*sb.* and *sb.* **I.** The neuter adj. used *absol.* **1.** With preps., forming advb. phrases. late ME. **2.** *The s.*: the total, the result, upshot; a brief summing up of something previously explained in full. Now *dial.* 1586.

1. *In s.*, briefly, concisely (now only parenthetically); These were, in s., the Orleans mob 1833. *For s.*, as an abbreviation; Father Dick—so they called him for s. 1845. **2.** The s. of the matter is this WESLEY.

II. *sb.* **1.** Something that is short. **a.** *Prosody.* A short syllable 1795. **b.** *Electr.* = SHORT CIRCUIT 1906. **c.** Neat spirits: = 'something short' 1823. **2.** *Comm.* A broker who sells more stock than he has in his hands at the time of sale, intending to take advantage of a possible drop in prices to obtain the remainder 1881. **3.** *pl.* **a.** A mixture of the bran and coarse part of meal 1765. **b.** Knee-breeches, small-clothes. *Rowing-shorts*: short drawers worn by oarsmen; similarly *football, running*, etc. *shorts.* 1826. **c.** The refuse clippings or trimmings in certain manufactures, e.g. cuttings of tobacco 1840. **d.** What is 'short' or lacking; *esp.* that amount of stock which a broker who 'sells short' needs to cover his deficiency 1901. **4.** *colloq.* A short extract, piece, film, etc.

C. *adv.* **1.** Of a manner of speaking: Briefly, concisely, curtly. Now *rare* in educated prose use. ME. **2.** In various uses relating to size or distance: With short garments, appendages, etc.; to a short distance 1706. **3.** Abruptly, suddenly; esp. in phr. *to turn s.* (*round*) 1579. **b.** *To take* (a person) *s.* (*a*) To take by surprise, at a disadvantage; to come suddenly upon; *rarely* with *up*. Often *Naut.* of wind or bad weather. 1553. (*b*) To interrupt with a reply; not to allow to complete his speech or offer explanations. Often with *up*. 1565. **4.** On the hither side of the point aimed at or contemplated. Const. *of*. 1588.

1. Now to speak s. and plain 1681. **2.** A..girl.. big enough to be sixteen, and dressed s. enough to be eleven 1887. Phr. *To break, snap* (etc.) *s.* (*off*); to break straight across, so as to leave nothing beyond the plane of fracture; to break *off* close to the point of attachment. **4.** He met me..in a Garden s. of the Town 1698. Phr. *To fall s.* (*of*): see FALL *v.* *To stop s. of*, not to go the length of (some extreme action).

Phrases: *To come s.*, to be imperfect or inadequate. *To come s. of*, to fail to reach (a standard); not to equal *in* some quality; to be something less than. †*To come s. home*, to return from an expedition in reduced numbers: hence, to fail to return. *To cut s.* [= Fr. *couper court*], to put a sudden end to (a person's life or career, a course of events, an action, speech, etc.); hence, to stop (a person) abruptly in a course of action or speech. *To sell s.* to effect a sale of stock or goods which the seller does not at the time possess, but hopes to buy at a lower price before the time fixed for delivery.

†**Short,** *v.*[1] [OE. *sċ(e)ortian*, f. *sċeort* SHORT *a.*] To grow or make short or shorter; to shorten –1641.

Short, *v.*[2] *trans.* and *intr.* 1907. = SHORT-CIRCUIT *v.* (cf. SHORT *sb.* II. 1 b.)

Shortage (ʃǭ·ɹtėdʒ). orig. *U.S.* 1868. [f. SHORT *sb.* + -AGE.] Deficiency in quantity; the amount by which a sum of money, a supply of goods, or the like, is deficient.

Sho·rt-bread. 1801. [SHORT *a.* IV. 1.] A hard flat (often round) cake, the essential ingredients of which are flour, butter, sugar, mixed in such proportions as to make the cake 'short' when baked. Also *attrib.* as *s.-biscuit*.

Short-breathed (brep̄t), *a.* 1470. [f. SHORT *a.* + BREATH *sb.* + -ED[2].] Short of breath; suffering from difficulty of breathing, dyspnœic.

Sho·rt-cake. 1594. [SHORT *a.* IV. 1.] A thin flat cake made 'short' with butter or lard (the application varying locally).

Short circuit, *sb.* 1876. *Electr.* A circuit made through a small resistance, esp. one that acts as a shunt to a circuit of comparatively large resistance.

Short-circuit, *v.* 1873. [f. prec.] *trans.* **1.** *Electr.* **a.** To connect by a short circuit; to establish a short circuit in (an electric system). **b.** Of a conducting body: To be traversed by (a current) by way of short circuit. Also *refl.* of a current: To make a short circuit. 1882. **c.** To cut off the current from (part of an apparatus) by establishing a short circuit 1882. Also *fig.* **2.** *Surg.* To form a direct communication between two portions of an intestine above and below an obstruction; to make a direct passage from (an organ) *into* some other part when the normal passage is obstructed; to avoid (an obstruction) by this means 1897.

Sho·rtco·ming, *vbl. sb.* 1680. [f. phr. *to come short*; see SHORT *adv.*] The condition or fact of coming short; an instance of this. **a.** Failure to come up to a standard or to fulfil a duty; a defect. (Chiefly in *pl.*) **b.** Failure to reach an amount; a deficiency.

Short cut, *sb.*[1] 1568. [CUT *sb.*[2]] †**1.** A short passage or journey –1673. **2.** A path or a course which is shorter than the ordinary road taken between two places. Now often hyphened. 1618. **b.** *fig.* A compendious method of attaining some object 1589.

Short cut, *a.* and *sb.*[2] 1596. [f. *cut* pa. pple. of CUT *v.*] **A.** *adj.* Cut to a short length. **B.** *sb.* A kind of tobacco 1789.

Short-dated, *a.* 1815. [f. SHORT *a.* + DATE *sb.* + -ED[2].] Of bills, notes of hand, etc.: Falling due at an early date. So **Sho·rt-date** *a.* **Sho·rt-da:ter,** a short-dated bill, etc.

Shorten (ʃǭ·ɹt'n), *v.* 1513. [f. SHORT *a.* + -EN[5].] **1.** *trans.* To make shorter, to diminish the length of, to abridge, curtail. **b.** *fig.* In Biblical phrase, *To s. the arm* or *hand of*: to limit the power of 1535. **c.** To diminish in working length; to tighten (a rein); to hold (a weapon) nearer to the middle, in order to deal a more effective blow 1597. **d.** With reference to phonetic quantity 1589. **2.** *intr.* To grow shorter 1568. **b.** Of a price, odds: To be lowered or lessened 1884. **3.** *trans.* †**a.** To hold in check, restrain –1700. **b.** To keep from the attainment *of* 1837. **4.** *Naut.* **a.** *To s. sail(s*, to take in some of the sails of a vessel in order to slacken speed 1627. **b.** *To s. in*: to heave in (the cable) so that a shorter length remains overboard. Also *absol.* 1854. **5.** To make 'short' or friable. Also (of manure) *intr.* for *refl.* 1733. **6.** To put (a child) into short clothes 1871.

1. When Autumn..adds to Nights, and shortens Days DRYDEN. To s. my Story, she was married to another STEELE. **2.** I am glad to see my labour s. MARVELL. **3. a.** Here, where the Subject is so fruitful..I am shorten'd by my Chain DRYDEN. **6.** The blue sash he wore the day he was shortened 1871. Hence **Sho·rtener,** one who or something which shortens.

Shortening (ʃǭ·ɹt'niŋ), *vbl. sb.* 1542. [-ING[1].] **1.** The action or an act of the verb SHORTEN. **2.** *concr.* Fat used for 'shortening' pastry, cakes, etc. 1823.

Shorthand (ʃǭ·ɹthænd). 1636. [f. SHORT *a.* + HAND *sb.*] A method of speedy writing by means of the substitution of contractions or arbitrary signs or symbols for letters, words, etc.; brachygraphy, stenography. **b.** quasi-*adj.* Of the nature of shorthand; compendious 1822.

b. Every new short-hand mode of doing things 1822.

attrib. as in *s. clerk, reports*; *s. typist*, a s. clerk who types.

Short-handed, *a.* (Stress variable.) 1794. Lacking a full complement of 'hands'; undermanned, understaffed.

Shorthorn (ʃǭ·ɹt,hǭɹn). 1847. [f. SHORT *a.* + HORN *sb.*] One of a breed of cattle having short horns, orig. bred in the north-eastern counties and now widely distributed over Great Britain and exported to other countries.

Shortish (ʃǭ·ɹtiʃ), *a.* 1800. [f. SHORT *a.* + -ISH[1].] Rather short.

Short-lived (ʃǭɹt,livd, -ləivd; stress variable), *a.* 1588. [f. SHORT *a.* + *live* LIFE + -ED[2]. Often apprehended as f. *lived* pa. pple. of LIVE *v.*] **1.** Having a short life. **2.** *transf.* Lasting only a short time, brief, ephemeral 1588.

1. The short lif'd days of flesh and blood 1645. **2.** O short liu'd pride SHAKS.

Shortly (ʃǭ·ɹtli), *adv.* OE. [f. SHORT *a.* + -LY[2].] **1.** Briefly, concisely, in few words. **b.** Abruptly, curtly, sharply 1815. **2.** In a short time; soon OE. **3.** At a short time *after, before* 1548. **4.** For a short time (*rare*) 1809.

1. The Attorney General was heard s. in reply 1805. **b.** 'I think very differently', answered Elizabeth s. JANE AUSTEN. **2.** A French ship.. s. bound for Alexandria 1632. **3.** On a given morning..shortly after noon 1886. **4.** He's been but s. in office SCOTT.

Shortness (ʃǭ·ɹtnės). OE. [f. SHORT *a.* + -NESS.] **1.** The quality or fact of being 'short', in various senses. **2.** Defective reach (of vision, memory, etc.) 1635. **3.** The condition of being 'short *of*' something; deficiency, want (esp. of money, food, etc.); also, scantiness (of a supply, a crop, etc.) 1669.

1. Such as the shortnesse of the time can shape SHAKS. *S. of breath*, breathlessness. **2.** Their fatal s. of vision CARLYLE. **3.** There was no s. of money 1882.

Short sight. 1822. [SHORT *a.* I. 1 e.] The

defect of sight by which only near objects are seen distinctly; myopia.

Short-sighted, *a.* (Stress variable.) 1622. [Cf. prec. and SIGHTED *a.*] **1.** Having short sight; having the focus of the eye at less than the normal distance; unable to distinguish objects clearly at a distance; myopic. **2.** *fig.* Lacking in foresight or in extent of intellectual outlook 1622. **3.** Characterized by or proceeding from want of foresight or limited mental vision 1736.

2. So s. are politicians in power D'ISRAELI. A s. and suicidal policy KINGSLEY. Hence **Short-si·ghted-ly** *adv.*, **-ness.**

Short-tongued, *a.* (Stress variable.) 1575. Having a short tongue; hence (now *dial.*) inarticulate, stammering, lisping. Also *occas.* taciturn, unready in speech.

Short-winded, *a.* (Stress variable.) 1450. [f. SHORT *a.* + WIND *sb.* + -ED[2].] Short of breath; suffering from or liable to difficulty of breathing; that soon becomes out of breath with any exertion.

Short wool. 1728. **1.** Wool having a short staple or fibre. **2.** (Hyphened.) A sheep producing such wool 1837. **Short-woolled** *a.*

Shot (ʃǫt), *sb.*[1] [OE. *sć(e)ot, ġesć(e)ot* = OFris. *skot*, OS. *sil|scot* 'balista', MLG. *(ge)scot*, OHG. *scoz* and *giscoz* (G. *schoss, geschoss*), ON. *skot* :- Gmc. **skutaz*, **gaskutam*, f. **skut-* **skeut-* SHOOT *v.*] **I.** The action of shooting. **1.** A rapid movement or motion (*rare*). **2.** A discharge, flux, or issue 1500. **3.** *Fisheries.* The spread or cast of a net; the throw and haul-in of a fishing-net 1859. **4.** The action of shooting with the bow, catapult, or firearms; the mechanical discharge of arrows or other projectiles as a means of attack; shots or discharges of missiles collectively. Now *arch.* late ME. **b.** An act of shooting OE. **c.** *Mining.* An explosion of a blasting charge 1881. **d.** The film record of a scene in cinematography 1923. **5.** The range of a shot, or distance to which a shot will go 1455. **6.** An attempt to hit with a projectile discharged from a gun 1653. **b.** *fig.* A remark aimed at some one, esp. in order to wound 1841. **7.** A random guess attempting to 'hit' the right answer 1840. **b.** An attempt or try 1756. **8.** An aim or stroke, esp. in a game, as tennis, golf, billiards, etc. 1868. **b.** A throw of a ball, stone, etc. 1852. **c.** In *Football, Hockey, Lacrosse*, an attempt to drive the ball into goal 1868. **d.** In *Boat-racing*, an attempt to 'bump' the boat in front 1868.

3. A second s. of the net produced eleven more [mullet] 1859. **4.** Their admiral lost an eye by the s. of an arrow HUME. **b.** Phr. *To fire*, also (now *arch.*) *to make, shoot a s.* *A s. between wind and water* (cf. SHOOT *v.* IV. 3.). *Like a s.* (colloq.) at once, with rapidity; also, most willingly. *A s. in the eye* (colloq.), an ill turn. **5.** Phr. *In, within, out of s.*: in, within, out of shooting distance. *transf. Haml.* I. iii. 35. **6.** Phr. *To exchange shots*, said with ref. to a skirmish or a duel. *Not..by a long s.*, hopelessly out of reckoning. **7.** Phr. *To make a s.*, to attempt an answer by guessing. **b.** Pinks is going to have a s. at the Wingfield Sculls 1912.

II. That which is discharged in shooting. †**1.** That which is discharged from a bow, an arrow or arrows; also, in early use, projectiles thrown by a catapult or other engine; ammunition for such an engine –1664. **2.** Projectiles (esp. balls or bullets, as dist. from explosive 'shells') designed to be discharged from a firearm or cannon by the force of an explosive 1474. **b.** A cannon-ball. Also (with numerals) as *collect. sing.* or uninflected pl. 1622. **c.** Hence, an iron globe like a cannon ball, used in the sport of 'putting the shot' (or 'weight'): see PUT *v.*[1] I. 2. 1881. **3.** Lead in small pellets, of which a quantity is used for a single charge of a sporting gun. Also (less frequently), a single pellet, a shot-corn (pl. *shot*, esp. with numerals; sometimes *shots*). 1770. **4.** *Mining.* The charge of powder sufficient for a blast in a mine (esp. a coal-mine); also the bored hole into which the charge is put 1851.

1. The Law of Arms doth bar The use of venom'd s. in War 1664. **2.** *Bar-, chain-, grape-shot*, etc.: see the first words. **b.** Phr. *(Not) a s. in the locker*: see LOCKER *sb.* 3b. *Small s.*, small pellets of lead, as dist. from bullets. **3.** A strong silk-worm gut, with a s. or two on it 1833.

III. That which shoots. †**1.** Firearms –1727. †**2. a.** *collect. sing.* Soldiers armed with muskets or other firearms (rarely with bows) –1706. **3.** One who shoots; an expert in shooting 1780.

3. No, I am no s. DISRAELI. *Dead s.*: see DEAD *a.* V. 3.

IV. [Cf. OE. *scēotan* to pay, contribute.] Payment, share. The reckoning, amount due or to be paid, esp. at a tavern or for entertainment; a or one's share in such payment. Phr. *To stand s.*, to pay the bill (for all). Now *colloq.* 1475. **V. 1.** A division of land 1490. **2.** A corpse disinterred by body-snatchers 1828.

attrib. and *Comb.*: **s.-corn**, a small s., a grain of s.; **-hole**, a hole made by the passage of a s.; *arch.* a small hole in a fortified wall through which to shoot; *Mining*, a hole for the insertion of a blasting-charge; **-plug, -prop**, a tapered cone of wood to stop a s.-hole in a vessel's side, to prevent leakage; **-pouch**, a sportsman's pouch or bag, usu. of leather, for carrying s.; **-proof** *a.* impenetrable by s.; **-putter**, one who puts the s. in athletic sports; **-star**, (*a*) a shooting star; (*b*) the alga *Nostoc commune*; **-tower**, a tall round tower in which small s. are made by dropping molten lead from the top into water; **-window**, a window that can be opened and shut by turning on its hinges; a casement; a shutter with a few panes of glass at the top.

Shot (ʃǫt), *sb.*[2] 1883. [SHOT *ppl. a.*, used ellipt.] A 'shot' silken or other fabric.

Shot (ʃǫt), *v.* 1681. [f. SHOT *sb.*[1]] **1.** *trans.* To load (a fire-arm) with shot. **2.** To weight by attaching a shot or shots, so as to cause to sink in water 1857.

1. *fig.* Their every word was shotted with an oath 1884. Hence **Sho·tted** *ppl. a.* loaded with shot or ball as well as powder; weighted with shot, having a shot attached.

Shot (ʃǫt), *ppl. a.* late ME. [pa. pple. of SHOOT *v.*] **1.** Of a fish: Having discharged its spawn. **2.** Of a stalk, blade, etc.: That has grown or sprouted 1629. **3.** Of a bullet, arrow, etc.: That is discharged. Also of a bolt that has been pushed into or out of the lock. 1863. **4.** Hit, wounded or killed by a projectile discharged from a gun or bow 1837. **5.** Of a textile fabric: Woven with warp-threads of one colour and weft-threads of another, so that the fabric changes in tint when viewed from different points 1763. **b.** Of a colour, etc.: Changeable, variable 1824.

Shot-free, *a.* 1586. [f. SHOT *sb.*[1] + FREE *a.* Cf. G. *schussfrei* (sense 1).] †**1.** Safe from shot, shot-proof –1778. **2.** = SCOT-FREE. Now *rare.* 1596.

Sho·t-gun, sho·tgun. orig. *U.S.* 1828. A smooth-bore gun (fowling-piece) used for firing small-shot, as dist. from a rifle for firing a bullet.

Shotten (ʃǫ·t'n), *ppl. a.* 1451. [pa. pple. of SHOOT *v.*] **1.** Of a fish (esp. a herring): That has spawned. **b.** *transf.* and *fig.* In *s. herring*, applied to a person who is exhausted by sickness or destitute of strength or resources. (*arch.*) Hence *gen.* †Thin, emaciated; worthless, good-for-nothing. 1596.

Should, pa. t. of SHALL, *v.*

Shoulder (ʃōᵘ·ldəɹ), *sb.* [OE. *sćuldor*, corresp. to OFris. *skuldere*, MLG. *schuldere*, (M)Du. *schouder*, OHG. *sculter(r)a* (G. *schulter*) :- WGmc. **skuldr-*, of unkn. origin.] **1.** Each of the two corresponding portions (right and left) of the human body, including the upper joint of the arm with its integuments and the portion of the trunk between this and the base of the neck; esp. the curved upper surface of this (*spec.*, as a military position in which the rifle is shouldered); in *pl.* often including the part of the back between the two. In quadrupeds, the upper part of the fore-limb and the adjacent part of the back. **b.** In fishes (*sing.* and *pl.*), the upper part of the trunk, adjoining the head 1820. **c.** The upper part of the wing or wing-case of a bird, beetle, butterfly, etc. adjoining the point of articulation 1735. **d.** = *s.-joint*: chiefly in *to put one's s. out.* 1611. **2.** As the part of the body on which burdens are carried; also, as the seat of muscular strength employed in carrying, pushing, etc. OE. **3.** The fore-leg and adjacent parts cut from the carcass of a deer, sheep or other animal; a joint consisting of this prepared for the table ME. **4.** That part of a garment which covers the wearer's shoulder 1473. **5.** A projection or protuberance resembling the human shoulder in shape, position or function 1545. **b.** A sudden inward curvature in the outline of something, from which it tapers to a point 1618. **c.** A rebate which serves as an abutment; a projection which serves as a support 1669. **d.** A comparatively gentle slope on the side of a hill and near the top 1817. **6.** An arched piece of wood or metal, or a frame of metal rods, placed inside the shoulders of a garment to be hung up in a wardrobe, etc. 1899.

1. Phr. *To put an old head on young shoulders*, to make a young person as staid or experienced as an elderly one. *To have a head upon one's shoulders*, to have good sense. *S. to s.*, lit. of soldiers, so as to shoulder one another, in close conflict; also, in close formation; hence *fig.* of persons, with united effort. (*Straight*) *from the s.*, (of a blow) with the fist brought to the shoulder and then swiftly sent forward; made with the arm straight. *To rub shoulders with*: see RUB *v.* 5b. See also COLD SHOULDER. **2.** Make broad thy shoulders to receive my weight, And bear me to the margin TENNYSON. *fig.* All the debts are put upon my shoulders, on account of my known wealth THACKERAY. Phr. *His shoulders are broad (enough)*, he is able to bear great burdens or responsibility. Phr. *To put (lay, set) one's s. to the wheel*, (lit.) so as to extricate the vehicle from the mire; hence *fig.* to set to work vigorously. *To open the shoulders*, to give free play to the muscles of the shoulders in making a stroke. **3.** *S. of mutton fist*, a large, heavy, fleshy fist. *S. of mutton sail*, a triangular sail attached to a mast. **5.** The neck [of the amphora] is not cylindrical, but slopes upon the shoulders 1857.

Comb.: **s.-belt** = BANDOLEER; **-brace**, a contrivance for flattening rounded shoulders; **-butt**, a pistol butt shaped for firing from the s.; **-clapper**, an officer charged with the arrest of an offender, a bailiff, sheriff's officer; **-girdle** *Anat.* (see GIRDLE *sb.*[1] 4 a); **-high** *a.* and *adv.*, as high as one's s.; **-joint**, the joint of the s.; the articulation by which the arm or fore-leg is connected with the trunk; **-shot, -shotten** *adjs.*, (of an animal) having a strained or dislocated s. (*arch.*); **s. slip**, a strain or dislocation of the s. joint; **-yoke**, a yoke for carrying pails.

Shoulder (ʃōᵘ·ldəɹ), *v.* ME. [f. prec.] **1.** *trans.* To push against (a person or thing) with the shoulder; (of a crowd) to push shoulder against shoulder; hence, to push roughly, unceremoniously, or insolently; to thrust aside with the shoulder; to hustle, jostle. Now *rare* or *Obs.* exc. with adv. or advb. phr. **2.** *transf.* Of inanimate things 1590. **3.** *absol.* and *intr.* To push with the shoulder; to use the shoulders (in a struggle or contest). Const. *against, at.* 1440. **b.** To make one's way by pushing with the shoulders; more fully *to s. one's way*; also *refl.* 1581. †**4. a.** *trans.* To put (soldiers) shoulder to shoulder in close rank. **b.** *intr.* To stand shoulder to shoulder –1781. **5.** *trans.* To support with, bear up or carry on the shoulder or shoulders; to take or place on one's shoulder to be carried 1611. **b.** *fig.* To take upon oneself as a burden (expense, responsibility, etc.) 1900. **6.** *Mil.* To place (a weapon, etc.) upon the shoulder 1595. **7.** To furnish (a thing) with a shoulder; to cut shoulders or a shoulder on; to fit *into* with a shoulder. Also with *down, up.* late ME. **8.** Of inanimate things: To form a shoulder, project as a shoulder, or spread out into a shoulder; also with *up* 1611.

1. Around her, numberless, the rabble flowed, Shouldering each other, crowding for a view 1713. *fig.* Custom and prejudice. should'ring aside The meek and modest truth COWPER. **2.** Walls of rock ..shouldering back the billows COLERIDGE. **3.** All tramped, kicked, plunged, shouldered, and jostled SCOTT. **5.** We shouldered our knapsacks, and started for the Lizard 1851. **6.** Phr. *To s. one's* or *a rifle*, etc., often used for: to join the ranks, enlist as a soldier. *To s. arms*, to hold one's rifle in a vertical position, supported by the right hand at the lock, hence *at s. arms*, at the position directed by this word of command. **8.** The hill shoulders up very steeply for three-fourths its height 1870. Hence **Shou·ldering** *vbl. sb.* the action of the vb.; *concr.* something which projects or supports as a shoulder.

Shou·lder-blade. ME. Each of the two flat triangular bones articulated with the humerus, and lying over the ribs in the upper part of the back in all mammals; the scapula.

Shou·lder-bone. ME. = prec.

Shouldered (ʃō^{u}·ldəɹd), *ppl. a.* ME. [f. SHOULDER *sb.* and *v.* + -ED.] **1.** Having shoulders. Chiefly with qualifying adv. or advb. phr. Also ROUND-S. **2.** Having a shoulder or projection; made with a shoulder or with shoulders 1671. **3.** Placed and carried at, on, or over the shoulder; spec. *Mil. To stand s.*: to stand with shouldered arms 1760.

Shou·lder-knot. 1676. A knot of ribbon or lace worn on the shoulder by men of fashion in the 17th and 18th c.; also, a knot, formerly of ribbons of the family colours, now of lace, worn on the shoulder by some livery servants; a knot or bow of ribbon worn on the shoulder by a woman or child; also *Mil.* = AGLET 2.

Shou·lder-piece. 1580. **1. a.** *Antiq.* A piece of armour covering the shoulder. **b.** A piece or each of the pieces of material forming the shoulders of a garment 1611. **2.** The piece forming the shoulder (of a tool, etc.) 1811.

Shou·lder-strap. 1688. **1.** Each of the two short straps which go over the shoulders, connecting and supporting the fore and back parts of a garment. **2.** Each of the narrow straps fastened upon the shoulders of a military tunic; esp. an ornamental strap distinguishing the corps and grade of an officer 1840.

Shout (ʃaut), *sb.* [Late ME. *schoute*, poss. repr. a deriv. of *skūt- *skut- *skeut- send forth forcibly, SHOOT *v.* Cf. ON. *skúta, skúti* SCOUT *v.*^{2}] **1.** A loud, vehement cry expressing joy, grief or pain, fear, triumph, warning, encouragement, etc.; a loud cry to attract attention at a distance; a tumultuous uproar made by a large body of people. **b.** *transf.* Applied to any loud noise or cry forcing itself upon the attention 1503. **2.** *Colonial slang.* A call to a waiter to replenish the glasses of the company; hence, a turn in paying for a round of drinks. Also, a free drink given to all present by one of the company; a drinking party. 1863.

1. This generall applause, and chearefull showt SHAKS. An involuntary s. of laughter 1809. **b.** Great was the s. of guns from the castles PEPYS.

Shout (ʃaut), *v.* late ME. [See prec.] **1.** *intr.* To utter a loud call, to make a loud outcry expressive of joy, exultation, etc. or to raise an alarm, to incite to action, etc. **b.** Of a place: To resound with shouts. Of an inanimate thing: To make a loud uproar. *rare.* 1513. **c.** *U.S.* To be loud in support of (a candidate) 1907. **2.** *trans.* To utter (something) with a loud voice 1500. **3.** *Austral. slang.* **a.** *intr.* To stand drinks 1859. **b.** *trans.* To call for (drinks, etc.) in order to treat the bystanders 1867.

1. The word of Peace is render'd: hearke how they showt SHAKS. *To s. at* (a person), to assail with shouts, *esp.* of derision or anger. *To s. down*, to reduce to silence by shouts of disapproval; to howl down. Hence **Shou·ter**, one who shouts.

Shove (ʃɒv), *sb.* ME. [f. next.] An act of shoving; a strong thrust or push to move a body away from the agent. Often *fig.*

fig. It would be such a fine thing for all the family: I could give all the boys such a s. 1873.

Shove (ʃɒv), *v.* Pa. t. and pa. pple. **shoved** (ʃɒvd). [OE. *scūfan* = OFris. *skūva*, MLG., MDu. *schūven* (Du. *schuiven*), OHG. *sciuban* (G. *schieben*), Goth. *af|skiuban* push away :– Gmc. str. vb. **skeuban*, **skaub-*, **skub-*.] (Generally equivalent to *thrust, push*; but now less dignified in use.) **1.** *trans.* To thrust away with violence; to precipitate; to 'cast' (into prison, etc.). *Obs.* exc. *arch.* **2.** To move (a heavy or resisting object) forward by the application of muscular strength from behind; to push along with effort ME. **b.** To force (a person, etc.) onwards by pushing. Also, to cause to fall *over* (a cliff, etc.) or *out of* (a place) by a push. late ME. †**c.** Of winds, etc.: To drive, propel, impel –1705. **3.** *spec.* To propel (a boat, etc.) either by pushing at the stern or with a pole worked from the inside. Also *absol.* 1513. **b.** With *out, off,* or const. *from.* (*a*) *trans.* To launch (a boat) by means of a steady push applied at the stern OE. (*b*) *absol.* To push one's vessel away from the bank. Also *transf.* of the boat. 1513. **4.** *trans.* Without the notion of difficulty. To push (something) so as to make it slide along a surface or in a groove or channel; also to move *up* or *down* by pushing 1633. †**b.** To put surreptitiously or improperly *in, on, under* –1773. **c.** (Chiefly *colloq.*) To put or thrust (carelessly or hastily) into a place or receptacle; also to thrust *aside, away* 1827. **d.** To push *out of* a position, *away*, by gradual encroachment 1629. **5.** *absol.* and *intr.* To push, to apply force against an object in order to move it from its position OE. **6.** *intr.* To push about or jostle in a crowd; to make one's way by jostling or elbowing ME. **b.** *refl.* To make one's way by shoving 1489. **7.** *trans.* To push (a person) with one's body or elbows; to knock against, jostle 1530.

2. He was the first to s. the gangway on to the vessel 1873. **c.** The Seas..s. the loaden Vessels into Port ADDISON. **3.** The seamen towed, and I shoved SWIFT. **b.** The boats were shoved off MARRYAT. **4. b.** To shorten man's duty..by shoving a commandment out of Moses's tables 1773. **5.** Phr. *To s. at*, to push against (an object) in order to displace or overthrow. **7.** Laughing and shoving each other about KINGSLEY.

Comb.: **s.-halfpenny**, *slang*, a gambling game similar to shovel-board.

Shove-groat. *Obs.* exc. *Hist.* 1488. [f. SHOVE *v.* + GROAT *sb.*] = SHOVEL-BOARD.

Shovel (ʃɒ·v'l), *sb.* [OE. *sċofl*, corresp. to (M)LG. *schuffel*, MDu. *schof(f)el* (Du. *schoffel*) shovel, hoe; with rel. forms showing a long vowel, as in OHG. *scūvala* (G. *schaufel*); f. Gmc. **skŭf- skŭb-* SHOVE; see -EL^{1}.] **1.** A spade-like implement, consisting of a broad blade of metal or other material (more or less hollow and with upturned sides), attached to a handle and used for raising and removing quantities of earth, grain, coal or other loose material. (In some dialects applied to a spade.) **2.** = SHOVEL HAT 1841. **3.** *Mil.* A contrivance fitted to a field-gun to act as a brake to lessen the recoil 1899.

attrib. and *Comb.*: **s.-bill** = SHOVELLER^{2}; **s. head**, the bonnet-headed shark, *Reniceps tiburo*; **-nose**, a nose having the shape and fulfilling the functions of a s., also *attrib.* in the names of certain animals and fishes having this characteristic; hence **-nosed** *a.*; **-penny** = SHOVEL-BOARD; **-stirrup**, a stirrup with a broad rest for the foot, extending beyond the heel.

Shovel (ʃɒ·v'l), *v.*^{1} 1440. [f. prec.] **1.** *trans.* To take up and remove with a shovel. **b.** *transf.* (With adv.) To remove as rubbish; to move about roughly and without consideration 1816. **2.** To excavate, dig up (the ground, etc.), dig (a hole, etc.) with a shovel 1470. **3.** To throw (quantities of some material) *into* a receptacle, to cast (earth, dust, etc.) *on* or *upon* something or somebody 1611. **4.** To gather (something) *up* in quantities as with a shovel 1685. **5.** *intr.* To use a shovel 1685. **6.** *trans.* To turn (something) over with a shovel 1775.

1. The men that s. the dirt out of the road 1791. **3.** One of them..was shovelling tipsy-cake into his ample mouth 1913. **4.** Store-keepers..are simply shovelling up money 1879. **5.** In relays, 3,000 of the Militia-men dig and s. night and day CARLYLE. Hence **Sho·veller**^{1}, one who shovels.

Shovel (ʃɒ·v'l), *v.*^{2} Now *rare.* late ME. [app. frequent. of SHOVE *v.* Cf. SHUFFLE *v.*] *intr.* To make movements *with* the feet, without raising them from the ground; to walk languidly or lazily.

In walking he does not tread, but s. and slide CARLYLE.

†**Sho·velard.** 1440. [f. SHOVEL *sb.* + -ARD; perh. after MALLARD.] The spoonbill, *Platalea leucorodia* –1646.

Shovel-board (ʃɒ·v'l,bō^{ə}ɹd), **shu·ffle-board.** 1532. [Unexplained alteration of †*shove-board.*] **1.** A game in which a coin or other disc is driven by a blow with the hand along a highly polished board, floor, or table marked with transverse lines. **b.** The table on which the game is played 1603. **2.** *transf.* A game played on shipboard by pushing wooden or iron discs with a cue (called a *shovel*) so that they may rest on one of nine squares of a diagram chalked on the deck 1877.

Comb.: †**s.-shilling**, a shilling (sometimes of Edw. VI) used in the game of s.

Shovelful (ʃɒ·v'lful). 1533. [-FUL 2.] A quantity that fills a shovel; as much as a shovel can hold or take up at one time.

Shovel hat. 1829. A stiff broad-brimmed hat, turned up at the sides with a shovel-like curve in front and behind, worn by some ecclesiastics. Hence **Shovel-hatted** *a.*

Shoveller^{2} (ʃɒ·v'ləɹ). 1460. [Alteration of SHOVELARD.] †**1.** = SHOVELARD –1796. **2.** Applied to the Spoonbill Duck, *Spatula clypeata*, a bird with a broad shovel-like beak. Also *s. duck.* 1674.

Shover (ʃɒ·vəɹ). 1500. [f. SHOVE *v.* + -ER^{1}.] **1.** One who or that which shoves. **2.** Jocular substitute for CHAUFFEUR 1908.

Show (ʃō^{u}) *sb.* Also †**shew.** ME. [f. next.] **I. 1.** The action or an act of exhibiting to view or notice. Now *rare* exc. in specific use or phrase. **b.** A demonstration or display of military strength or of intention to take severe measures. Chiefly in phr. *to make a s.* 1548. **2.** The external aspect (of a person or thing). Now *rhet.* or *poet.* in gen. sense. 1555. **b.** *Theol.* and *Philos.* Used occas. as an equivalent for 'accident', 'phenomenon', 'species' 1560. **3.** With qualifying word: A (fine, striking, etc.) appearance. Also without qualification, a fine or striking appearance, imposing display. 1550. **b.** (Now *U.S.* and *Austral.*) An opportunity for displaying or exerting oneself; a chance, 'opening' 1579. **4.** In generalized sense: Ostentatious display 1713. **5.** An appearance or display (*of* something, a quality, activity, sentiment, etc.) to which there is at least some degree of reality to correspond. Chiefly in negative contexts, or with a limiting word. **b.** An indication, sign, or token *of* something; a trace or vestige *of*. Now only in neg. contexts. 1563. **c.** *U.S.* and *Austral.* An indication of the presence of metal in a mining ground, of oil in a well, etc. 1600. **6.** An unreal or illusory appearance (*of* something) 1547. **b.** In generalized sense: Empty appearance without reality 1583. **7.** An appearance (*of* some quality, feeling, activity, etc.) assumed with more or less intention to deceive; a simulation or pretence. Also, a half-hearted or inchoate attempt or 'offer' (*of* doing something). Formerly often *pl.* 1526.

1. Phr. *On s.*, in process of being shown or exhibited; on view. *S. of hands*, the holding up the hand above the head, as a means of indicating a vote or judgement on a proposition. **2.** But I haue that Within, which passeth s.; These, but the Trappings, and the Suites of woe SHAKS. Phr. *In s.*, in appearance; often, in appearance only, ostensibly, seemingly. *To have a* (or *the*) *s. of*, to appear to be, appear to partake of; to look like, resemble. **3.** Their names made a famous s. in the bills THACKERAY. **b.** Phr. *To give* (a person) *a s. To have* or *stand a* (or *no*) *s.* **4.** A True Spaniard: Nothing but S. and Beggary ADDISON. **7.** His refusal was cloked under a s. of feudal loyalty 1867. Phr. *To make* (*a*) *s.*, to make a pretence or feint; to pretend; Two little men, who did nothing, made a s. of doing it all DICKENS.

II. *concr.* Something shown or presented to view. **1.** A person or thing exhibited or gazed at as an object of admiration, curiosity, mockery, or the like 1535. **2.** *gen.* A sight, spectacle. Usu. with qualifying word. 1577. **3.** A phantasmal appearance; an apparition 1611. **4.** A display on a large scale of objects for public inspection 1837. **5.** A spectacle elaborately prepared or arranged; a pageant, masque, procession, or similar display on a large scale 1561. **b.** *gen.* Pageantry 1912. **6.** An exhibition of strange objects, wild beasts, dancers, acrobats, etc., held usu. in a booth or portable building, with a small charge for admission. Cf. PEEPSHOW, SIDESHOW. 1760. **b.** The booth or building (with its contents) 1840. **7.** Applied *colloq.* or *joc.* to any kind of public display; e.g. an exhibition of pictures, a theatrical performance, a fashionable gathering, a speech-making, etc. 1863. **8.** *slang.* A matter or affair, a concern. Also, a body or collection of persons. 1889.

1. [Venice] Perchance even dearer in her day of woe, Than when she was..a marvel, and a s. BYRON. **3.** What you saw, was all a Fairy S. DRYDEN. **4.** S. of Horses at the Agricultural Hall 1864. **5.** A shew of gladiators 1770. *Lord Mayor's S.*: see LORD MAYOR. **6.** The travelling menageries, or..'Wild-beast shows' DICKENS. **8.** Phr. *To boss* or *run the s.*, to assume control. *To give the s. away*, to blab; to betray the deficiencies, pretentiousness, etc. of an affair.

III. Techn. uses. **1.** *Med.* A sanguinoserous discharge from the vagina prior to labour. Also the first appearance of a menstrual flow. 1753. **2.** *Mining.* A lambent blue flame appearing above the ordinary flame of a candle or lamp when fire-damp is present 1851.

attrib. and *Comb.*, as *s.-bench, -keeper, -monster, -piece*, etc.; **s.-bill,** a bill or placard announcing a s., public sale, etc.; **-boat** (orig. *U.S.*), a steam-boat in which theatrical performances are given; **-bottle,** a large glass bottle containing coloured liquid, to make a show in a druggist's window; **-box,** a box in which objects of curiosity are exhibited; **-card,** a card containing a tradesman's advertisement of goods, etc.; **-case,** a glass case for exhibiting articles in a shop or museum; **-glass,** a glass case for exhibiting valuable or delicate goods; **S.-Sunday,** (*a*) the Sunday before the Oxford Commemoration, on the evening of which a kind of University parade used to be held in the Broad Walk of Christ Church; (*b*) among artists, the Sunday before 'sending-in day'; **-yard,** an enclosure in which live-stock, machinery, and other large objects are exhibited.

Show, shew (ʃōu), *v.* Pa. t. **showed, shewed** (ʃōud). Pa. pple. **shown, shewn** (ʃōun). [OE. *scēawian* = OFris. *skawia, skowia, schoia*, OS. *skawon* (Du. *schouwen*), OHG. *scouwōn* (G. *schauen*) :- WGmc. wk. vb. **skauwōjan*, f. **skau-* see, look.] †**I.** *trans.* To look at, gaze upon, behold, view; to inspect, review; to look at mentally; to 'see', read, find (in a book) –ME. **II.** To cause or allow to be seen or looked at. **1.** *trans.* To bring forward or display (an object) in order that it may be looked at; to expose or exhibit to view ME. **b.** To display in a (specified) condition or with a (specified) appearance ME. **c.** To hold up or place (a light) where it can be seen (as a signal, to point out the way in the dark, etc.) ME. **d.** To exhibit (a sign, token). Hence, in Biblical language, to exhibit (a 'sign' or marvel), to work (a miracle). ME. **e.** To display (goods, wares, for sale or in an exhibition) ME. **f.** To display, hang out, unfurl (a banner, ensign, etc.) 1470. **g.** To exhibit (a spectacle, some interesting object) for the amusement of the public; to make a show of 1500. **h.** To exhibit threateningly. Hence *joc.*, to make the slightest possible application of. 1833. **2.** To produce or submit for inspection. **a.** To produce (a legal document, etc.) for official inspection; to exhibit (something) in proof that one possesses it ME. †**b.** To muster (soldiers); to make an array of (fighting cocks). **c.** *fig.* To (be able to) present to (physical or mental) view 1611. **3.** To let (a person) read or examine (a book, writing); to bring (it) to his notice 1677. **4.** To represent in sculpture or graphic art 1660. **5.** To display deliberately or ostentatiously in order to attract notice or win admiration 1509. **6.** To allow (a part of the body) to be seen ME. **7.** *refl.* To appear, allow oneself to be seen ME. **8. a.** Of plants, the seasons, etc.: To bring forth to view (fruit, flowers, etc.) ME. **b.** Of animals or plants: To display (their colours, beauties, etc.) 1667. **c.** Of a luminous body: To display (its light). late ME. **9.** To be the means of displaying, revealing to sight, or allowing to be seen. late ME. **b.** To be in such a state or position as to allow (something) to be seen 1848. **10.** To have visibly (some external feature or mark); to have (a part of itself) in a position exposed to view 1585. **b.** Of a list, a recording instrument, etc.: To be found to indicate 1866.

1. S. me your tongue—let me feel your pulse 1833. Phr. *To s. one's hand*, to display one's cards face upwards; *fig.* to allow one's plans or intentions to be known. **c.** 'Light him down,' said Sikes,..'s. him a light' DICKENS. **f.** The chase then shewed Hamburgh colours, and returned the fire SCOTT. **h.** To press the horse too suddenly up to the snaffle by showing the whip 1833. **2. a.** A call by the guard to 'shew tickets' 1866. *To have* (something) *to s. for* (one's labour, expenditure, etc.), to be able to exhibit as a result. *To s. up*, to hand up (a school-exercise, etc.), for inspection. **b.** Earth has not anything to s. more fair WORDSW. **3.** I showed Lord Steyne your pamphlet on Malt THACKERAY. **5.** Fools,..walking up and down to shew their new Cloaths 1693. Phr. *To s. off*, to display ostentatiously. **6.** Phr. *To s. one's face, head*, etc., joc. *to s. one's nose*, to allow oneself to be seen, make an appearance. *To s.* (a person) *one's heels, a clean* or *fair pair of heels*, to flee (from him). *To s. the cloven foot* (*hoof*), to betray something diabolic or sinister in one's character or motives. *To s. one's teeth*, to exhibit signs of resistance or attack. **8. c.** The sun..showed its broad disk above the eastern sea SCOTT. **9.** Very short petticoats, only not showing the knees 1859. *To s. off, out*, to display in relief or by contrast; to set off, enhance in appearance (*rare*). **b.** *To s. daylight*, to have holes or openings through which light can be seen. **10.** Her planks s. signs of age 1883. **b.** His watch showed 7.30 p.m. 1910.

III. To guide another person's sight to (an object). **1.** To enable a person to discover or identify (a visible object) by pointing to it, or by conducting him to a place where it can be seen. Also, to direct a person's observation to the various parts or features of (a country, town, building, or any complex object). ME. **b.** To point out or indicate a place *where* (etc.) 1450. **2.** (With inverted const.) To guide or conduct (a person) *to, into* a particular place, room in a house, etc., *over* or *through* the rooms of a house. late ME.

1. I pray you shew my youth old Shylockes house SHAKS. *fig.* S. me a cavalry chief like him now that Murat is gone THACKERAY. *To s.* (a person) *the way*, to guide him in a required direction, by leading or accompanying him, or by giving him instructions. *To s.* (a person) *the door*, to order him to leave the room or house; to turn out of doors. **2.** The grim janitor..shewed me into a parlour SMOLLETT. Phr. *To s. up, upstairs*, to conduct (a person) upstairs. *To s. out*, to take (a person) to the exit door; to insist upon the departure of (a person) from the house. *To s. in*, to bring (a person) into a house or room. *To s. round*, to s. (a person) over a place, s. the 'sights'.

IV. To exhibit or manifest by outward signs. **1.** To exhibit, allow to be seen (some inward quality, feeling, condition, etc.) by one's outward appearance; occas. said of the appearance. Also with obj. cl. ME. **2.** To display (a quality, condition, feeling, etc.) by one's action or behaviour ME. **b.** With obj. cl.: To make it plain in regard to oneself (*that*) ME. **3.** *refl.* **a.** With compl. or inf.: To exhibit oneself in a (specified) light or character; to manifest or exemplify a (specified) quality, etc., in one's behaviour ME. **b.** Of a quality, condition, etc.: To manifest itself; to become evident by signs or tokens ME. **4.** To display (kindness, mercy, courtesy, malice, neglect, etc.) *to* a person by one's acts or behaviour; to accord or grant (favour, honour; a courtesy, etc.) ME. †**5.** To put forth, exert (one's power, strength). Also of things. –1595. **b.** To offer, attempt (resistance) 1634.

1. He showed all the outward signs of a mind at ease GEO. ELIOT. **2. b.** In both transactions he showed he was no fool (*mod.*). **3.** He shewed hym selfe a fermer frend to Zanzaber..then to me 1615. **4.** He is troubled that my wife shows my sister no countenance PEPYS. **5. b.** *To s. fight*, to display pugnacity or readiness to fight.

V. To make known by statement or argument. **1.** To point out, reveal, make known; to make evident or clear, explain, expound ME. **b.** With indirect obj.: To inform, instruct, teach (a person) *how to* (do something). Also with ellipsis of the inf. 1567. **2.** To communicate, announce, declare, narrate, state, tell (a fact, story, news, etc.); to describe, give an account of. Now *arch.* ME. **b.** To set forth, allege (in a legal document). Often in petitionary formulæ. late ME. **c.** To state, allege, plead (a cause, reason, etc.). Now chiefly in *Law.* ME. **3.** To prove, demonstrate (a fact, statement) by argument, reasoning, allegation of evidence or instances, experiment, etc. ME. **b.** With complementary obj.: To prove, make out (a person or thing) to be (something). Also with accus. and inf. 1563. **4.** Of a thing: To be a proof, evidence, sign or indication of ME. **5. S. up. a.** In school language: To report (a scholar) for punishment 1845. **b.** To disgrace or discredit by a thorough exposure; to expose (a person's faults, ignorance,.misdeeds, etc.) 1826.

1. O let me liue, And all the secrets of our campe Ile shew SHAKS. The consequences of which a little time will shew EVELYN. **b.** Ile shew you how t'obserue a strange euent SHAKS. Phr. †*To s. one's mind*, to reveal one's thought or intention; to express one's opinion or judgement. **2.** My mouthe shall shewe forth thy prayse *Bk. Com. Prayer.* **3.** Many arguments are used to s., that motion is the source of life 1875. **4.** Nothing showing worse taste than to load your plate 1859. **5. b.** That mathematical mysticism, so mercilessly shown up by Berkeley MILL.

VI. *intr.* To be seen, be visible, appear. **1.** To be or become visible; to make an appearance ME. **b.** Of a thing: To be seen (*through, over, under*, etc.) something that partly covers or conceals it. Also, to be visible as a fault or defect. 1842. **2.** To appear in public, make a display in public. In mod. use chiefly *colloq.*: To appear in company or society; to make an appearance in an assembly, among guests, etc. 1625. **3.** With complement (*adj.* or †*sb.*): To look, seem, appear. *arch.* ME. **b.** With adv. or advb. phr. To present a (specified) appearance; to make a (good, bad, etc.) show. late ME. **c.** To look *like. arch.* 1578.

1. The fire i'th' Flint Shewes not, till it be strooke SHAKS. **b.** Cut underneath, where it won't s. 1852. The type shows through the page 1886. He meant more by the words than showed upon the face of them STEVENSON. **2.** I believe he never shews till just before dinner TROLLOPE. **3.** The wood when cut showed sound as a bell 1893. **b.** Becket never showed to more advantage than in moments of personal danger 1877.

With advs.: **S. off:** to act or talk for show; to make a deliberate or ostentatious display of one's abilities or accomplishments (*colloq.*). **S. up. a.** To appear conspicuously or in relief. **b.** To become prominent, catch the eye. **c.** To put in an appearance; to be present or 'turn up' (*colloq.*).

Comb.: **s.-down,** in *Card-playing*, the act of laying down one's cards with their faces up; *fig.* an open disclosure of plans, means, etc. (chiefly *U.S.*); also, an exhibition of achievements or possibilities.

Shower (ʃauəɹ, ʃau·əɹ), *sb.*[1] [OE. *scūr* = OFris. *skūr* fit of illness, OS. *skūr* (MDu. *schuur*, Du. *schoer*), OHG. *scūr* (G. *schauer*), ON. *skúr*, Goth. *skūra* storm :- Gmc. **skūraz*, **skurō*.] **1.** A fall of rain, of short duration and (usu.) comparatively light. Also, a similar fall of sleet or hail, rarely of snow. **b.** In extended use: A copious down-fall of anything coming or supposed to come from the clouds or sky; in recent use often of meteors. late ME. **2.** *transf.* A copious fall or discharge of water or other liquid in drops. Often of tears. late ME. **b.** *poet.* Of light, sound, etc. 1781. **c.** Short for SHOWER-BATH 1889. **d.** *Pyrotechny.* A device for producing a shower of small slow-burning 'stars', which fall from a rocket 1839. **3.** *fig.* A copious or liberal supply bestowed ME. **b.** *U.S. colloq.* A large number of gifts, usu. of a specified nature, given e.g. to a bride; an occasion when these are bestowed (a *s.-party*) 1926. Also N.Z. **4.** A copious fall or flight of objects, esp. of missiles. Also of blows. OE.

1. A light s. drifted down the valley 1907. **b.** Meteoric showers 1835. **2.** This brought only another s. of tears 1846. **b.** What showers of gold the sunbeams rain! 1840. **3.** Sweet Highland Girl, a very s. Of beauty is thy earthly dower! WORDSW. A s. of..letters of hearty congratulation 1888. **4.** They were received with a s. of stones MACAULAY.

Comb.: **s.-cloud,** a cumulo-nimbus cloud.

Shower (ʃōu·əɹ), *sb.*[2] [OE. *scēawere* scout, watchman, f. *scēawian* to SHOW. Later, f. SHOW *v.* + -ER[1].] **1.** One who shows, points out, or exhibits ME. †**2.** Something which shows; an indicator –1668.

1. The breeders of Herefords have always been keen showers 1868. **2.** The second [finger] is cal'd..the shewer, or pointer 1668.

Shower (ʃauər, ʃau·əɹ), *v.* 1573. [f. SHOWER *sb.*[1]] **1.** *intr.* To rain in a shower, or in showers. Chiefly *impers.* **2.** To fall down in a shower or showers, or as a shower of rain 1582. **3.** *trans.* To pour down or discharge in a shower or showers; to send down or pour out in abundance and rapidly 1582. **4.** To water with or as with a shower; to wet copiously with rain or with water in drops or spray; *transf.* to cover or strew as with rain 1667.

1. It showered all afternoon and poured..all night STEVENSON. **2.** Teares from her eies did s. 1601. *fig.* It rain'd downe Fortune showring on your head SHAKS. **3.** They showered him with special honours (*U.S.*). **4.** When God hath showrd the earth MILT. Ladies..bright In silks, with spangles shower'd KEATS.

Show·er-bath. 1803. A bath in which water from above is poured in a shower upon the person. Also an apparatus for producing such a bath.

Showery (ʃauᵊ·ri), *a.* 1591. [f. SHOWER *sb.*[1] + -Y[1].] **1.** Raining in showers; characterized by frequent showers of rain. **2.** Causing or producing showers; bringing showers 1607. **3.** Pertaining to, produced by, or resembling a shower or showers 1667.

2. 'Tis not s. south, nor airy wester 1871. **3.** Colours of the showrie Arch MILT. Hence **Show·eriness.**

Showing (ʃōᵘ·iŋ), *vbl. sb.* OE. [f. SHOW *v.* + -ING[1].] **1.** The action of SHOW *v.*; with *pl.*, an instance of this. **2.** Manner of putting a case; in phrases *on this s.*, *on one's own s.*, etc. 1857. **3.** A statement or presentation of figures, accounts, or the like. Chiefly *U.S.* 1868. **4.** *U.S.* An appearance or display of a specified kind 1890. **5.** Outward appearance (*arch.* or *Obs.*) ME.

4. Phr. *To make a* (good or bad) *s.*

†**Show·ish,** *a.* Common in the 18th c. 1671. [f. SHOW *sb.* + -ISH[1].] = SHOWY *a.* –1768.

Showman (ʃōᵘ·mæ̆n). 1734. [SHOW *sb.*] One who exhibits or is proprietor of a show.

Show·manship. 1859. [f. prec. + -SHIP.] The art of being a showman; *transf.* the capacity for exhibiting one's wares, capabilities, etc.

Show·-place. 1579. †**1.** A place for public shows or spectacles; a theatre. (Used as tr. *θέατρον*, *circus*, etc.) –1647. **2.** A place (e.g. a large mansion or estate) which is regularly exhibited to visitors 1817.

Show·room. 1616. [f. SHOW *sb.*] **1.** A room used for the display of goods or merchandise. **2.** *pl.* The rooms in a large mansion which are regularly shown to visitors 1863.

Showy (ʃōᵘ·i), *a.* 1712. [f. SHOW *sb.* + -Y[1].] Characterized by show. **a.** Of visible objects: Presenting an imposing or striking appearance; making a good display. **b.** Of immaterial things, qualities, etc.: Brilliant, striking, 'effective'. Of persons: Displaying brilliant talents, etc. 1728.

a. Inferior but s. watches 1832. **b.** Forming friendships with every shewy adventurer that comes in your way 1782. Hence **Show·i-ly** *adv.*, **-ness.**

Shrag (ʃræg), *sb.* *Obs.* exc. *dial.* 1552. [Parallel form to SCRAG *sb.*[2] See SCR-.] A twig; a branch lopped off. So **Shrag** *v. trans.* to lop, prune 1440.

Shrapnel (ʃræ·pnĕl), *sb.* 1804. [f. name of General Henry *Shrapnel* (1761–1842), who invented this shell during the Peninsular War.] A hollow projectile containing bullets and a small bursting charge which, when fired by the time fuse, bursts the shell and scatters the bullets in a shower. Also *s. shell.*

Shred (ʃred), *sb.* [OE. **scrēad* (pl. *scrēada*), *scrēade*, corresp. to OFris. *skrēd* hair-cutting, clipping of coin, OS. *skrōd*, MLG. *schrōt*, *schrāt* cut-off piece, OHG. *scrōt* (G. *schrot*); f. WGmc. **skraud-* **skreud-* **skrŭd-* cut; see SHROUD *sb.*[1], SCREED.] **1.** A fragment cut or broken off; a strip; a scrap. **2.** In OE., *pl.* Parings (of fruit, etc.); in mod. use, a narrow strip (of peel, vegetable, root, etc.) shaved so thin that it curls OE. **3.** A fragment or strip of textile material cut or torn off; a small piece of cloth, a fragment of clothing; *pl.* scanty or ragged garments. late ME. **b.** *transf.* (of cloud, mist, etc.) 1834. **4.** A length or end of gold or silver thread or lace. *arch.* 1450. **5.** A fragment, small piece, scrap (of something immaterial). late ME.

3. Her clothes became ragged, and she mended them with shreds of any colour 1850. Phr. *Of shreds* (*and patches*), made up of rags or scraps; hence *allus.*; A King of shreds and patches SHAKS. *In, into shreds*, in or into small fragments. *To tear to shreds*, to rend into small pieces; also *fig.* to destroy.

Shred (ʃred), *v.* Pa. t. **shredded,** pa. pple. **shredded, shred.** [OE. *scrēadian*, f. **scrēad*; see prec.] †**1.** *trans.* To rid (a tree, vine, vineyard) of superfluous growth; to prune –1762. †**2.** To lop *off* (branches), esp. in pruning –1725. †**b.** To cut or strip *off*; to cut (a piece) *from* or *out of* –1823. **3.** To cut or tear into shreds or small thin strips or slices. late ME. **4.** To divide *into* small portions 1660. **b.** *intr.* To be reduced to shreds 1646. **5.** *trans.* To cut in two, sever, as with scissors; chiefly with ref. to severing the thread of life. Now *rare.* 1565.

3. S. very fine a pound of suet 1756. Machinery for washing and shredding rags 1890. **4.** Indivisibles, such as can't be shread 1674. **5.** When ye s. with fatall knife His line SPENSER. So **Shre·dding** *vbl. sb.* [OE. *scrēadung*], †pruning or lopping of trees; *concr.* a fragment; a shred (now *rare*); †*pl.* or *collect. sing.* prunings or loppings of trees.

Shred-pie. *Hist.* 1580. [prob. f. *shred*, ppl. a. of SHRED *v.*; cf. MINCED-PIE.] A mince-pie.

Shrew (ʃrū), *sb.*[1] [OE. *scrēawa*, *scrǣwa* shrewmouse, rel. to OHG. *scrawaz* dwarf, MHG. *schrawaz*, *schrat*, *schröuwel* devil, Icel. *skrǫggr* old man, Norw. *skrogg* wolf, *skrugg* dwarf, Sw. dial. *skrugge* devil, *skragga*.] Any of the small insectivorous mammals belonging to the genus *Sorex* or the family *Soricidæ*, much resembling mice but having a long sharp snout; a SHREWMOUSE.

Shrew (ʃrū), *sb.*[2] and *a.* ME. [perh. transf. use of prec., but poss. spec. application of a word meaning ill-disposed being.] †**1.** A wicked, evil-disposed, or malignant man; a mischievous or vexatious person; a rascal, villain. *spec.* the Devil. –1650. †**2.** A thing of evil nature or influence; something troublesome or vexatious –1620. **3.** A person, *esp.* (now only) a woman given to railing or scolding or other perverse or malignant behaviour; freq. a scolding or turbulent wife ME.

1. Such as were shrewes to their wiues DEKKER. **2.** Enmitie, hatred, and ill will is a s. 1620. **3.** To be a shrewe in the kitchin, a saint in the Church 1589.

†**B.** *adj.* = SHREWD (in various senses); wicked, evil-disposed; shrewish –1638.

†**Shrew,** *v.* Also **'shrew.** ME. [app. f. prec.; cf. BESHREW *v.*] *trans.* To curse; = BESHREW 2. –1668.

O vile proude cherl I shrewe his face CHAUCER.

Shrewd (ʃrūd), *a.* [ME. *schrewed*(*e*, f. SHREW *sb.*[2] + -ED[2], as in *crabbed, dogged, wicked, wretched*; but some of the senses suggest that the formation is a pa. pple. (-ED[1]) of SHREW *v.*] **1.** Depraved, wicked; evil-disposed, malignant. Also, malicious, mischievous. *dial.* †**b.** Of children: Naughty –1645. †**c.** Of animals: Bad-tempered; vicious, fierce –1630. †**2.** Of material things (*esp.* animals): Mischievous, hurtful; dangerous, injurious –1621. †**3.** Of things: Of evil nature, character, or influence –1678. †**b.** Of reputation, opinion, meaning: Evil, bad, unfavourable –1664. †**c.** Poor, unsatisfactory –1616. †**4.** Of events, affairs, conditions: Fraught or attended with evil or misfortune; having injurious or dangerous consequences; vexatious, irksome, hard; (of a task) difficult, dangerous –1821. †**5.** As an intensive, qualifying a word denoting something in itself bad, irksome, or undesirable: Grievous, serious, 'sore' –1819. †**6.** Of persons and their actions: Severe, harsh, stern –1654. **7.** Of a blow, etc.: Severe, hard. *arch.* 1481. **8.** Of a weapon, pain, etc.: Sharp, piercing, keen. *arch.* 1642. †**9.** Of a sign, token, etc.: Of ill omen; hence, strongly indicative (of something unfavourable) –1732. **10.** Of a piece of evidence: Hard to get over, 'awkward'. *arch.* 1606. †**11.** Given to railing or scolding; shrewish. Also of language. –1661. **12.** †Cunning, artful. Now only: Clever or keen-witted in practical affairs; astute, penetrating, or sagacious in action or speech 1520. **b.** Of action, speech, etc.: †Cunning, artful; characterized by penetration or practical sagacity 1589. **13.** Of a suspicion or guess: Coming 'dangerously' near to the truth of the matter 1588.

1. That shrew'd and knauish spirit Cal'd Robin Good-fellow SHAKS. Phr. *S. turn*, a mischievous or malicious act (*arch.*); †a piece of misfortune, an accident. **b.** *L. L. L.* v. ii. 12. **2.** An Ant. .is a s. thing, in an Orchard, or a garden BACON. **4.** Ah fowle, shrew'd newes SHAKS. **5.** That is a s. loss SCOTT. **7.** Me thought hee made a s. thrust at your Belly SHAKS. **8.** *advb.* The ayre bites s.; it is an eager and An nipping winde SHAKS. **9.** When a man is against reason, it is a s. sign reason is against him BERKELEY. **11.** His curst and s. wife COVERDALE. S. words are sometimes improved into smart blows betwixt them FULLER. **12.** A s. observer 1867. A woman of s. intellect and masculine character 1880. **13.** I have a s. idea that it is a humbug THACKERAY. Hence **Shrew·d-ly** *adv.*, **-ness.**

Shrewish (ʃrū·iʃ), *a.* late ME. [f. SHREW *sb.*[2] + -ISH[1].] †**1.** Wicked, malignant –1481. **2.** Of a woman: Having the character or disposition of a shrew; given to or characterized by scolding 1565. **b.** In wider sense: Ill-natured, ill-tempered; cross-grained 1596.

2. Shee was a s. snappish bawd, that wold bite off a mans nose with an answere NASHE. Hence **Shrew·ish-ly** *adv.*, **-ness.**

Shrewmouse (ʃrū·maus). *Pl.* **-mice.** Also hyphened and as two words. 1572. = SHREW *sb.*[1] (See MOUSE *sb.* I. 1 b.)

Shrewsbury (ʃrū·z-, ʃrōᵘ·zbəri). The name of the county town of Shropshire, used *attrib.*

S. cake, a flat round crisp biscuit-like cake.

Shriek (ʃrīk), *sb.* 1590. [f. next. Cf. SHRIKE *sb.*[1]] An act of shrieking; a shrill, piercing, or wild cry expressive of terror or pain. Also, an utterance of loud high-pitched laughter. **b.** Applied to the wild cry of birds, etc. 1765. **c.** The loud high-pitched piercing sound produced by an instrument of music, the whistle of a locomotive, etc. 1599. **d.** *fig.* A hysterical exclamation 1853.

Whose mournfull cryes and shreekes to heaven ascend KYD. **d.** Virtuous shrieks of 'flattery', 'meanness',. .and so forth KINGSLEY.

Shriek (ʃrīk), *v.* 1567. [Also †*shreak*, †*shrick*; parallel to (dial.) SCREAK *v.* (XV) – ON. *skrækja*; other *shr-* forms are (dial.) SHRIKE *v.* (XII) and *shritch* (XIII), repr. the base of OE. *scrićettan*. Cf. SCREECH.] **1.** *intr.* To utter a loud sharp shrill cry. **a.** of a human being in terror or pain; also, said of loud high-pitched laughter 1577. **b.** of the characteristic cry of certain animals 1567. **c.** of inanimate things 1596. **2.** *trans.* To utter (a shriek); to utter (words) with a shriek or shrieks 1592. **3.** To bring (oneself) into a certain condition by shrieking 1642.

1. Ghosts did shrieke and squeale about the streets SHAKS. **b.** The Owle shriek'd at thy birth SHAKS. **c.** The winter wind, which shrieks through the bare branches RUSKIN. **3.** I. .shriekt my self awake 1642. Hence **Shrie·ker,** one who shrieks or utters a shriek.

Shrie·k-owl. Now *rare.* 1567. [f. prec. + OWL *sb.*] The screech-owl.

Shrieval (ʃrī·văl), *a.* 1681. [f. *shrieve*, obs. var. SHERIFF + -AL[1].] Of or belonging to a sheriff.

Shrievalty (ʃrī·vălti). 1502. [f. as prec. + *-alty*, repr. OFr. *-alté* (mod. *-auté*), as in *mayoralty*, etc.] The office or dignity of sheriff; a sheriff's jurisdiction or term of office.

Shrift (ʃrift), *sb.* Now *arch.* or *Hist.* [OE. *scrift*, corresp. to OFris. *skrift*, (M)Du. *schrift*, OHG. *scrift* (G. *schrift*), ON. *skript*, *skrift*, f. SHRIVE; see -T[1].] †**1.** Penance imposed by the priest after confession. –late ME. **2.** In certain contexts = absolution OE. †**3.** A confessor –1638. **4.** Confession to a priest; auricular confession; also, the sacrament of penance OE. **5.** An instance of this; a confession on a particular occasion ME. **6.** Confession (*of* sin or wrong); admission (*of* guilt); revelation (*of* something private or secret) ME.

2. I need no other s. Than mine owne conscience 1635. **4.** *To come, go to s.*, to resort to confession, seek the ministry of a priest in the sacrament of penance. **5.** Phr. *To make one's s.*, *to hear a s.* *Short s.*, orig. a brief space of time allowed for a criminal to make his confession before execution; hence, a brief respite; *to give short s. to*, to make short work of. Hence **Shrift** *v. trans.* to shrive (*rare*).

Shri·ft-fa:ther. *Obs.* exc. *arch.* ME. [f. SHRIFT *sb.* + FATHER *sb.*] A confessor.

Shrike (ʃrəik), *sb.*[1] *Obs.* or *dial.* late ME. [f. SHRIKE *v.*] = SHRIEK *sb.*

Shrike (ʃrəik), *sb.*[2] 1544. [Of obscure origin; phonetically corresp. formations are OE. *scric* thrush, MLG. *schrik* corncrake, ON. *sól|skrikja* snow-bunting, Sw. *shrika* jay, rel. to vbs. cited under SHRIEK.] Any of the birds of the numerous species of the family *Laniidæ*, characterized by a strong hooked and toothed beak; the majority of them are insectivorous, but several species, as the (Great or European) Grey Shrike, *Lanius* *excubitor*, prey upon mice and small birds. **b.** Applied to similar birds of other families (e.g. *Prionopidæ*), e.g. CUCKOO, DRONGO, SWALLOW s.

Shrike (ʃrəik), *v. Obs.* exc. *dial.* ME. [See SHRIEK *v.*] = SHRIEK *v.* †Of birds: To pipe.

Shrill (ʃril), *sb.* 1591. [f. SHRILL *v.*] A shrill sound, cry, whistle, etc.

Shrill (ʃril), *a.* and *adv.* [contemp. with SHRILL *v.*: superseding (dial.) *shille* adj. and vb., OE. **sciell, scyl*, and **sciellan, scyllan*; cf. LG. *schrell*, G. *schrill*, rel. to OE. *scrallettan*, Du. *schrallen*, Icel. *skrölta*; f. Gmc. **skral-* **skrel-*.] **A.** *adj.* **1.** Of voice, sound: Of a sharp high-pitched piercing tone. late ME. **2.** Emitting or producing a sound of this kind 1508. **3.** Characterized or accompanied by sharp high-pitched sounds 1725. **4.** *transf.* Keen, sharp, pungent; poignant 1608.

1. The s. Matin Song Of Birds MILT. **2.** The first larum of the cock's s. throat COWPER. Churl and noble, fair lady and s. fish-wife 1866. The blast of a s. bugle SCOTT. **3.** Let winds be s., let waves roll high BYRON.

B. *adv.* With a shrill voice or tone; shrilly. Now *rare*. ME. **b.** Qualifying a ppl. adj. used attrib. (usu. with hyphen) 1562.

Through the high wood echoing s. MILT. **b.** The ..s.-piping reed MORRIS. Hence **Shri·llish** *a.* **Shri·lly**, *a.* (*poet.*) and *adv.* **Shri·llness.**

Shrill (ʃril), *v.* ME. [See SCHRILL *a.*] **1.** *intr.* Of a voice, cry: To sound shrilly. Hence of noises, the wind, or the like, or a place echoing with sound. **2.** To speak, cry, or sing with a shrill voice; to make a shrill noise 1440. **3.** *trans.* To utter, give forth (a sound, cry, words) in shrill tones; to exclaim or proclaim with a shrill voice 1595.

1. A wind, that shrills All night in a waste land TENNYSON. Breake we our pypes, that shrild as lowde as Larke SPENSER. The Ouzell shrills, the Ruddock warbles soft SPENSER. **3.** Harke..How poor Andromache shrils her dolour forth SHAKS.

Shrimp (ʃrimp). ME. [Obscurely related to MLG. *schrempen* contract, wrinkle, *schrimpen* wrinkle the nose, *schrumpen* wrinkle, fold (whence G. *schrumpfen*), MHG. *schrimpfen* contract, ON. *skreppa* slip away, and SCRIMP *v.* Cf. CRIMP *v.*[1]] **1.** Any of the slender, long-tailed, long-legged (chiefly marine) crustaceans of the genus *Crangon* and allied genera, closely related to the prawns; esp. *C. vulgaris*, the common s., which inhabits the sand on the coasts of Great Britain and is an article of food. **2.** A diminutive or puny person (*rarely* thing). Chiefly *contempt.* late ME.

2. When he was a babe, a childe, a shrimpe, Thus did he strangle Serpents SHAKS. Hence **Shri·mper**, one who catches shrimps; also, a vessel engaged in shrimping. **Shri·mping** *gerund* and *vbl. sb.* catching shrimps. **Shri·mpish** *a.* diminutive, puny, insignificant.

Shrine (ʃrəin), *sb.* [OE. *scrīn* = OFris. *skīn*, MLG. *schrīn*, MDu. *schrīne* (Du. *schrijn*), OHG. *scrīni* (G. *schrein*), ON. *skrín*; Gmc. – L. *scrinium* case or chest for books or papers.] †**1.** A box, coffer; a cabinet, chest –1658. **2.** The box, casket, or other repository in which the relics of a saint are preserved. Also, a tomb-like erection of rich workmanship, enclosing the relics of a saint. OE. **b.** A receptacle containing an object of religious veneration; occas. a niche for sacred images 1526. **3.** A case or casket for a dead body; also, a tomb or cenotaph of an elaborate kind. late ME. **4.** *transf.* That which encloses, enshrines, or screens, or in which something dwells. late ME. **5.** A place where worship is offered or devotions are paid to a saint or deity; a temple, church 1629. **b.** *fig.* in contexts referring to the veneration or idolizing of some person or thing 1575.

2. The Miracles at the Shrines and Sepulchres of the holy Martyrs 1638. **4.** You living powres enclosed in stately s. Of growing trees SIDNEY. **5.** Apollo from his s. Can no more divine MILT. **b.** Worshippers at the s. of Mammon! 1853.

Shrine (ʃrəin), *v.* ME. [f. prec.] **1.** *trans.* To enclose (relics) in a shrine; to provide (a saint or deity) with a shrine or sanctuary. Now *rare*. **2.** To enclose, envelop, engird, as a shrine or sanctuary does the body or the image of a saint 1577. **3.** To enshrine in one's heart or thoughts 1579.

1. Believe a Goddess shrin'd in ev'ry tree POPE. **2.** Th' Almightie Father where he sits Shrin'd in his Sanctuarie of Heav'n secure MILT. In painting her I shrined her face Mid mystic trees ROSSETTI. **3.** The man of real genius..has the feeling of truth already shrined in his own breast HAZLITT.

Shrink (ʃriŋk), *v.* Pa. t. **shrank** (ʃræŋk), pa. pple. **shrunk** (ʃrɒŋk). [OE. *scrincan*, corresp. to Sw. *skrynka* wrinkle (OSw. *skrunkin* pa. pple. shrivelled, wrinkled), Norw. *skrekka, skrøkka*.] **I.** *intr.* †**1.** To wither or shrivel through withdrawal of vital fluid or failure of strength –1611. **2.** To become reduced in size, volume, or extent; *esp.* to contract through heat, cold, or moisture. Also with *up, away*. ME. **b.** Of a textile fabric: To contract when wetted 1483. **3.** To draw the limbs together, bring the body into a small compass; to cower, huddle *together*; (of the body) to contract as with pain, fear, or cold; (of a plant) to shrivel or curl *up* OE. **4.** In immaterial sense: To be contracted or reduced in extent; to be drawn together *into* certain limits 1449. **5.** To move *backward*, retire, or retreat *into* a cavity, shelter, or place of refuge; to draw oneself or itself *in*. late ME. **6.** To withdraw *from* a place or position, esp. in a secret or furtive manner; to turn *aside, away, back*, etc. furtively or nimbly; to slip or slink *away*. Now *rare*. late ME. **7.** To draw *back* or give way so as to avoid physical contact or conflict; to recoil through physical weakness or lack of courage or with abhorrence *from* 1513. †**b.** To give way; to collapse –1616. **8.** To refuse or hesitate to act in the face of anything irksome, grievous, horrible, or distasteful; to recoil mentally or morally 1470. †**9.** To be a deserter or rebel; to fall *away from* duty or allegiance, or *from* a person –1594.

1. His synewis shronke and withdrewe them CAXTON. **2.** When a body of water is cooled, it shrinks in bulk HUXLEY. **b.** Patent flannel, which does not s. in washing 1879. **3.** Isaac shrunk together, and was silent SCOTT. **4.** Are all thy Conquests, Glories, Triumphes, Spoiles, Shrunke to this little Measure? SHAKS. **5.** Jorian..shrunk in and became impenetrable as a hedgehog READE. **7.** She shrunk back from his grasp SCOTT. **b.** *Cor.* V. iv. 20. **8.** His herte is stablished, he will not shrencke COVERDALE *Ps.* 112:8. Opinions which he never shrunk from expressing 1891. **9.** *Rich. III*, V. iii. 222.

II. *trans.* **1.** To cause to contract or be reduced in size, volume, or extent; to cause to contract by moisture, heat, or cold; to cause (a limb, sinew, plant) to wither or (the skin) to wrinkle. Also with *up*. late ME. **b.** *spec.* To treat (a textile material) with water so that it may not shrink after it is made up 1856. **c.** *Mech.* To cause (a piece, e.g. the tyre of a wheel) to be fixed tightly *on* (*to*) another (which it is intended to fit) by heating it, slipping it into place when sufficiently expanded, and then rapidly cooling it 1839. **2.** To draw (the body, the limbs, oneself) into a smaller compass. late ME. **3.** In immaterial sense: To reduce to smaller limits or compass 1628. †**4.** To cause to withdraw or disappear; to draw *in* (the horns, the claws); also with *back, up*. Hence *allus.* –1713. **5.** To draw (the head, hand, etc.) *aside, back*, or *away* in a furtive, ashamed, or retiring manner. Now *rare*. 1489. †**b.** = SHRUG *v.* 3 –1720.

1. To shrinke mine Arme vp like a wither'd Shrub SHAKS. Return Alpheus, the dread voice is past, That shrunk thy streams MILT. **2.** Her body huge she shrank MORRIS. **3.** Logical cobwebbery shrinks itself together CARLYLE. **4.** The Libyc Hammon shrinks his horn MILT. **5. b.** Phr. *To s. up one's shoulders*: to shrug one's shoulders; *fig.* (with *at*) to regard with displeasure, aversion, or indifference. Hence **Shrink** *sb.* an act of shrinking or flinching. **Shri·nker,** one who shrinks or recoils from duty, danger, or the like. **Shri·nking-ly** *adv.*

Shrinkage (ʃri·ŋkėdʒ). 1800. [f. SHRINK *v.* + -AGE.] **1.** The act or fact of shrinking; reduction in the size or volume of a substance or material due to contraction such as is caused by heat, cold, or wet. **2.** The amount of such contraction or loss in bulk, volume, or measurement 1862. **b.** *Gun-making.* In shrinking on hoops or tubes, the difference between the inner diameter of the outer cylinder and the outer diameter of the inner cylinder 1891. **3.** Of immaterial things: Diminution or reduction in quantity, amount, or size; depreciation or decrease in value; the amount of this 1879.

3. The failure is attributed to bad debts, s. in the value of goods, and the withdrawal of capital 1879.

Shrive (ʃrəiv), *v. arch.* Pa. t. **shrove** (ʃrōᵘv), pa. pple. **shriven** (ʃri·v'n). [OE. *scrīfan* impose as a penance = OFris. *skrīva* write, impose penance, OS. *skrīban*, OHG. *scrīban* write, prescribe (Du. *schrijven*, G. *schreiben* write, spell); WGmc. str. vb. – L. *scrībere* write.] **1.** *trans.* In OE. (const. dat.) To impose penance upon (a person); hence, to administer absolution to; to hear the confession of. **b.** *absol.* or *intr.* To perform the office of a confessor; to exercise the ministry of absolution; to hear confessions (*rare*) OE. **2.** *pass.* To 'take shrift'; to be confessed; to make one's confession and receive absolution and penance OE. **3.** *refl.* To make one's confession, go to confession, confess ME. **4.** *intr.* To confess one's sins, go to confession ME. †**5.** *trans.* To reveal, disclose –1818. **6.** To relieve (one) *of* a burden 1604.

1. Giue me leaue To shriue her; lest shee should dye vn-absolu'd 1633. **2.** You ought first to bee shriven of one of the Monkes 1570. **3.** Let me s. me clean, and die TENNYSON. **4.** And who art thou, thou Gray Brother, That I should s. to thee? SCOTT. **6.** A..tomb: Such as to look on shrives The heart of half its care R. BRIDGES. Hence **Shri·ver**, one who shrives, a confessor. **Shri·ving** *vbl. sb.* shrift.

Shrivel (ʃri·v'l), *v.* 1588. [poss. of ON. origin (cf. Sw. dial. *skryvla* wrinkle).] **1.** *intr.* To become contracted and wrinkled or curled up, as from great heat or cold. Also with *up. away*. **b.** *transf.* and *fig.* To be reduced to an inanimate or inefficient condition; (of a person) to shrink physically or mentally 1680. **2.** *trans.* To cause to be shrunk into wrinkles. Often with *up*. 1608.

1. That his nose might be shrivelled with cold 1798. **b.** Undeveloped faculties that s. for want of using 1887. **2.** A fire from heaven came and shrivell'd up Their bodies SHAKS. Hence **Shri·vel** *sb.* something shrivelled up.

Shriven (ʃri·v'n), *ppl. a.* 1846. [pa. pple. of SHRIVE *v.*] Confessed, absolved.

Shroff (ʃrǫf), *sb.* 1618. [Anglo-Ind. alt. of the source of *saraf*, ult. Arab. *ṣarrāf*, f. *ṣarafa* exchange.] A banker or money-changer in the East; in the Far East, a native expert employed to detect bad coin. Hence **Shroff** *v. trans.* to examine (coin) in order to separate the genuine from the base. **Shro·ffage,** the commission charged for shroffing coin.

Shroud (ʃraud), *sb.*[1] [OE. *scrūd*, corresp. to ON. *skrúð* and *skrúði* fittings, gear, textile fabric, etc., f. Gmc. **skrūð-* **skreuð-* cut; see SHRED *sb.*] †**1.** A garment; an article of clothing; *sing.* and *pl.* (one's) clothes, clothing –1638. **2.** The white cloth or sheet in which a corpse is laid out for burial; a winding-sheet 1570. ¶By association with the black of mourning, *shroud* has received the epithet *sable* 1637. †**3.** A place or dwelling which affords shelter; a shelter, esp. one of a slight or temporary kind –1657. **4.** *pl.* (rarely *sing.*) A crypt, vault. Now *Hist.* 1549. †**5.** Shadow, shade; *fig.* protection –1611. **6.** A thing serving as a covering or protection; a covering, screen, veil, 'cloak', disguise. Now somewhat *rhet.* 1558. **7.** *techn.* **a.** Either of the two annular plates at the periphery of a water-wheel, forming the ends of the buckets 1759. **b.** A rim or flange cast on the ends of the teeth of a gear-wheel 1797.

2. Bid fair peace be to my sable srowd MILT. Soon the grave must be your home And your only suit a s. COWPER. **3.** Run to your shrouds, within these Brakes and Trees MILT. **4.** A church vnder the ground, like to the shrouds in Pauls HAKLUYT. **5.** *Ant. & Cl.* III. xiii. 71. **6.** A grey s. of rain sweeping up from the westward 1850.

Comb.: **s.-brass,** a memorial brass in which the deceased is represented in his s.; **-plate** = 7 a.

Shroud (ʃraud), *sb.*[2] late ME. [prob. a use of prec.] *pl.* A set of ropes, usu. in pairs, leading from the head of a mast and serving to relieve the latter of lateral strain; they form part of the standing rigging of a ship. Also *collect. sing.* **b.** *sing.* Any one of these 1748.

Shroud (ʃraud), *sb.*[3] Now *dial.* 1475. [Formally identical with SHROUD *sb.*[1], but in sense derived from the sense 'to cut' of the root.] **a.** *collect. sing.* and *pl.* Loppings of a tree. **b.** (chiefly *pl.*) A branch or bough.

Shroud (ʃraud), *v.*[1] ME. [f. SHROUD *sb.*[1]] †**1.** *trans.* To clothe; to adorn, deck –1520. **2.** To give shelter or housing to; to shelter. *arch.* 1450. **b.** *intr.* To take shelter or refuge. *arch.* 1579. †**3.** To cover so as to protect; to screen from injury or attack; to afford protection to –1810. †**4.** To conceal in a secret place or in a secret manner –1642. **5.** To hide from view, as by a veil, darkness, cloud; to cover so as to conceal; to screen, veil. late ME. **6.** In immaterial sense: To screen from observation; to veil under an appearance or 'show'; occas. with implication of disguise or concealment for an evil purpose. late ME. **7.** To put a shroud on (a corpse), lay in a shroud; hence, to prepare for burial, bury 1577. **8.** *Mech.* To furnish (a water-wheel, cogs) with shrouds 1834.

2. Ill wast thou shrouded then, O patient Son of God MILT. **b.** I will here shrowd till the dregges of the storme be past SHAKS. **4.** I'll shrowde my selfe behinde the Arras SHAKS. **5.** The hills, shrouded in grey mist 1902. **6.** Its proceedings were impenetrably shrouded from the public eye 1838. **7.** He has been showded—full three hundred Years 1718. Hence **Shrou·ding** *vbl. sb.* the action of the vb.; *Mech.* the shrouds of a water-wheel.

Shroud (ʃraud), *v.*[2] *local.* 1577. [f. SHROUD *sb.*[3]] *trans.* To lop (a tree or its branches); occas. *absol.*

Shrove Monday. 1450. [See SHROVE-TIDE.] The Monday before Shrove Tuesday.

†**Shrove Sunday.** 1463. [See next.] Quinquagesima Sunday –1843.

Shro·ve-tide. late ME. [Abnormally f. pa. t. stem *shrōv-* of SHRIVE *v.* + TIDE *sb.*] The period comprising Quinquagesima Sunday and the two following days, 'Shrove' Monday and Tuesday.

Shrove Tuesday. 1500. [f. as prec.] The Tuesday immediately preceding Ash Wednesday; often called *pancake day.* †**b.** *allus.* A time of merriment –1621.

Shro·ving, *vbl. sb. Obs.* exc. *dial.* 1537. [f. *shrove-* in SHROVE-TIDE + -ING[1].] The keeping of Shrove-tide; the merrymaking characteristic of this season; festive rejoicing.

Shrub[1] (ʃrɒb). late ME. [OE. *śċrubb* and *śċrybb* shrubbery, underwood, app. rel. to NFris. *skrobb* broom, brushwood, WFlem. *schrobbe* climbing wild pea or vetch, Norw. *skrubba* dwarf cornel, Da. dial. *skrub* brushwood. Cf. SCRUB *sb.*[1]] **1.** A woody plant smaller than a tree; *spec.* in *Bot.* a perennial plant having several woody stems growing from the same root. †**2.** = SCRUB *sb.*[1] II. 2. –1690.

2. The Gyants in grace, as well as the weak and shrubs BUNYAN.

Shrub[2] (ʃrɒb). 1747. [– Arab. *šurb, šarāb,* f. *šariba* to drink; cf. SHERBET, SYRUP.] **1.** A prepared drink made with the juice of orange or lemon (or other acid fruit), sugar, and rum (or other spirit). **2.** *U.S.* A cordial or syrup made from the juice of the raspberry, with vinegar and sugar 1860.

Shrubbery (ʃrɒ·bəri). 1748. [f. SHRUB[1] + -ERY.] **1.** A plantation of shrubs; a plot planted with shrubs. **2.** Shrubs collectively or in a mass 1777.

Shrubby (ʃrɒ·bi), *a.* 1540. [f. SHRUB[1] + -Y[1].] **1.** Having the habit, growth, or size of a shrub 1581. **b.** In specific names of plants, often rendering L. *fruticosus* 1597. **2.** Of the nature of or consisting of shrubs 1540. **3.** Covered, planted, or overgrown with shrubs 1598. **4.** Characteristic of a shrub 1776.

2. A lowe shrubbie boggie wood 1633. **3.** Due west it rises from this s. point MILT.

†**Shruff.** 1541. [perh. – G. *schroff* fragment of mineral.] Old brass (or copper) –1825.

Shrug (ʃrɒg), *sb.* 1460. [f. SHRUG *v.*] †**1.** A tug, pull, shake. **2.** A raising and contraction of the shoulders to express dislike, disdain, indifference, or the like 1594.

2. He is a lively man, full of chat, and foreign shrugs and gestures MME. D'ARBLAY.

Shrug (ʃrɒg), *v.* late ME. [Of unkn. origin.] **1.** *intr.* To shiver; to shudder for cold or fear. Now *rare* or *Obs.* **2.** To raise (and contract) the shoulders, esp. as an expression of disdain, indifference, disclaiming responsibility, etc. 1450. **3.** *trans.* To raise and contract (the shoulders) in this way 1547. †**4.** *intr.* (and *refl.*) To move the body from side to side as with uneasiness, or as a gesture of joy or self-satisfaction; to fidget about –1652. **5.** To jerk, pull or tug *up. U.S.* 1807.

1. He will be chill, and s. for cold 1580. **2.** I was quite shocked for her, and could only s. in dismay MME. D'ARBLAY. **3.** He..shrugs his shoulder when you talk of Securities STEELE.

Shrunk (ʃrɒŋk), *ppl. a.* 1530. [pa. pple. of SHRINK *v.*] Contracted or reduced in size; drawn together into a smaller compass. (Now *rare* in attrib. use.) So **Shru·nken** *ppl. a.* OE.

‖**Shuba** (ʃū·bă). 1591. [Russ.] A fur gown or greatcoat.

Shuck (ʃɒk), *sb.* Chiefly *dial.* and *U.S.* 1674. [Of unkn. origin.] **1.** A husk, pod, or shell; *esp.* the outer coverings or strippings of Indian corn, chestnuts, hickory nuts, etc. **b.** The shell of an oyster or clam 1881. **2.** As a type of something valueless 1847. **3.** *pl.* As an interj. of contempt or indifference 1885.

Shuck, *v. U.S.* 1819. [f. SHUCK *sb.*] *trans.* To remove the shucks from (corn, etc.). **Shu·cker,** one who shucks oysters or clams.

Shudder (ʃɒ·dəɹ), *sb.* 1607. [f. next.] An act of shuddering; a convulsive tremor of the body occasioned by fear, repugnance, or chill.

Phr. *To give one the shudders.*

Shudder (ʃɒ·dəɹ), *v.* [ME. *shod(d)er* – MLG. *schōderen,* MDu. *schūderen,* frequent. (see -ER[5]) f. Gmc. **skŭd-* shake, repr. also in OFris. *schedda,* OS. *skuddian,* OHG. *scutten* (G. *schütten*).] **1.** *intr.* To have a convulsive tremor of the body caused by fear, abhorrence, or cold; hence, to tremble with horror or dread. **2.** To move tremulously, vibrate, quiver 1849.

1. I shuddered, and drew involuntarily back, when..I saw Mr. Burke MME. D'ARBLAY. My mind shudders when I think of her awful, awful situation THACKERAY. Hence **Shu·dderingly** *adv.*

Shuffle (ʃɒ·f'l), *sb.* 1628. [f. next.] †**1.** A shifting from one place to another; an interchange of positions –1692. **2.** A tricky exchange or alternation (of arguments, expedients, etc.) 1641. **3.** An evasive trick, evasion, subterfuge 1628. **4.** Movement of the feet along the ground without lifting them; a gait characterized by such movement 1847. **5.** A dance of a rude kind, in which the feet are shuffled along the floor 1659. **6.** The act of shuffling playing-cards; also *ellipt.* (a player's) turn to shuffle 1651.

1. The unguided agitation and rude shuffles of Matter BENTLEY. **2.** Life becomes a mere s. of expedients 1860. **3.** You'll answer it now, yes or no, plain word and no s. 1893. **4.** The bear.. dancing him from side to side in its heavy s. L. HUNT. **5.** *Double s.*: one in which two movements of the same kind are made by each foot alternately; also *fig.*

Shuffle (ʃɒ·f'l), *v.* 1532. [– or cogn. with LG. *schuffeln* walk clumsily or with dragging feet, based on Gmc. **skuf-*; see SHOVE *v.*, -LE, and cf. SCUFFLE *v.*[1]] **1.** *intr.* To move the feet along the ground without lifting them, so as to make a scraping noise; to walk with such a motion of the feet; to go with clumsy steps or a shambling gait. Also said of the feet. 1598. **b.** To move restlessly or fidget in one's seat 1881. **c.** *trans.* To move (the feet) along the ground or floor without raising them 1576. **d.** To perform (a dance or a dance-step) with a shuffle. Also *absol.* or *intr.* 1818. **2.** To manipulate (the cards in a pack) so as to change their relative position. Formerly freq. in allusive use, *to s. the cards* = to manipulate matters. Also *absol.* and *intr.* 1570. **3.** To push along, about, or together in a disorderly mass or heap, or in a manner suggesting the shuffling of feet 1567. **4.** To huddle or jumble *together* indiscriminately, incongruously, or without order 1570. **5.** To smuggle (a thing) *in* or *into* (something else); to thrust *in* somehow or other 1565. †**b.** To remove, put *aside* or *away* in a hurried, secret, or underhand manner –1754. **c.** To bring, put, or thrust *into* or *out of* a position or condition in a haphazard, underhand, or shirking manner, or by rough-and-ready means 1628. **d.** *To s. off*: to get rid of evasively; to shirk (a duty or obligation) 1601. **6.** *intr.* or *refl.* To get *in, into,* or *out of* a position or condition, by some means or other, in an underhand, shifty, or evasive manner 1565. **b.** *To s.* †*over, through*: to perform hurriedly or perfunctorily, get through somehow 1656. †**c.** To make scrambling efforts, scuffle –1625. **7.** To act in a shifting or evasive manner; to shift one's ground in argument, etc.; to make use of deceitful pretences or shifty answers 1598. †**8.** *To s. up,* to get or put together hastily or in a perfunctory manner –1659. **9.** To put (a thing) *off from* one *to* another, or *upon* a person 1612. **10.** To shift from one place to another; to move *about* this way and that 1694. **11.** To put (a thing) *into* a receptacle, put or take (a thing) *on, off,* etc. in a clumsy or fumbling manner 1694. **b.** *intr.* To get *into* an article of clothing in a clumsy or fumbling manner 1865.

1. The Bear..shuffling along at a strange Rate DE FOE. **2.** [They] had shuffled their cards so cunningly as to be out of the reach of law 1643. They draw, they sit, they s., cut and deal CRABBE. **4.** When Lots are shuffled in a Lap, Urn, or Pitcher 1685. Good Days, bad Days so shuffled together LAMB. **5. b.** Her Mother..hath appointed That he shall likewise s. her away SHAKS. **c.** Thus was he shuffled into your father's Employment 1729. **d.** When we have shuffel'd off this mortall coile SHAKS. **6.** He shuffles out of the consequences by vague..charges of undue influence 1887. **b.** The service..was shuffled through..coldly and unfeelingly W. IRVING. **c.** Your life, good Master, Must s. for it selfe SHAKS. **7.** I..am faine to s.: to hedge, and to lurch SHAKS. **9.** Is he trying to s. off guilt from his own shoulders? 1875. **11.** He shuffled off his slippers at the threshold DISRAELI. Hence **Shu·ffler,** one who acts in a shifty or evasive manner; one who shuffles cards. **Shu·ffling** *vbl. sb.* (in various senses).

Shuffle-board: see SHOVEL-BOARD.

Shu·ffling, *ppl. a.* 1596. [f. SHUFFLE *v.* + -ING[2].] **1.** That shuffles in walking. Hence, of a walk, pace, gait: Consisting of or characterized by a shuffle. **2.** Of persons: Given to shifty or evasive action or behaviour 1616. **b.** Of action, conduct, speech: Evasive, shifty 1644.

Hence **Shu·fflingly** *adv.*

Shun (ʃɒn), *v.* Pa. t. and pa. pple. **shunned** (ʃɒnd). [OE. *śċunian* (chiefly in *ā-, onsċunian*); a peculiarly Eng. vb. of unkn. origin.] †**1.** *trans.* To abhor, detest, loathe –ME. †**2.** To seek safety by concealment or flight from (an enemy, his pursuit, etc.) –1638. †**b.** To evade (a blow, missile) –1667. **3.** To avoid (now always to avoid persistently or habitually) from repugnance, fear, or caution; to keep away from; to eschew, abstain carefully from ME. **4.** To escape (a threatened evil, an unwelcome task). Now *rare* or *Obs.* ME. †**5.** *intr.* To shrink back physically; to move or go aside (so as to escape or evade some person or thing); to fly (from an enemy, etc.); also with *aside, away* –1600.

2. b. I forewarn thee, s. His deadly arrow MILT. **3.** I would say, s. late hours BERKELEY. The tim'rous hare..Scarce shuns me COWPER. They rode on all day, shunning towns and villages MACAULAY. *transf.* Scarcity and want shall s. you SHAKS. **4.** No man of woman born Coward or brave, can s. his destiny 1870. Hence **Shu·nless** *a.* that cannot be shunned.

'Shun! Abbrev. of *attention!* as a word of command.

Shunt (ʃɒnt), *sb.* 1842. [f. next.] **1.** An act of shunting 1884. **2.** *Electr.* A derived circuit introduced to diminish the current flowing through the main circuit; esp. a resistance coil connected in parallel with a dynamo, etc.; more fully *s. circuit, coil* 1863. **b.** *Telegr.* A device for diverting the current from one line to another; a switch 1878. **3.** *Railways.* A switch 1842. **4.** *Ordnance.* Short for *s. rifled gun,* also, a curve in the rifling of a shunt rifled gun 1864.

2. *In s.,* connected so as to form a multiple current.

attrib. and *Comb.*: **s. dynamo,** a s.-wound dynamo; **s. line, road,** a railway siding; **-rifling,** a method of rifling cannon so that the projectile undergoes a s. or lateral change of position in the process of loading; so *s. (rifled) gun,* etc.; **-wound** *a.* having the s. circuit wound in parallel with the main circuit.

Shunt (ʃɒnt), *v.* [ME. *schunte*, perh. a deriv. of SHUN *v.*] †**1.** *intr.* To start or go aside (so as to avoid some person or thing); to shy; to hang back –1550. **2.** *trans.* To shove or push aside or out of the way. Also *intr.* of a thing, to move from its proper position, to give way. Chiefly *dial.* 1706. **3.** To move (a train or some portion of it) from the main line to a side-track or from one line of rails to another; also to move *back* 1849. **b.** *fig.* To side-track; also, to get rid of 1858. **4.** *intr.* To move off the main line; to move from one line of rails to another 1851. **5.** *Electr.* To divert (a portion of an electric current) by means of a shunt; also, to divert current from (a galvanometer) 1873.

3. b. Practically, General Peel is not shunted, but shelved 1858. Hence **Shu·nter**, a railwayman who shunts trains; a mechanical device to facilitate shunting; (*slang*) an able organizer.

Shush, redupl. var. of SH *int.*; also (by contact with *hush*) as vb., to hush, be silent.

Shut (ʃɒt), *sb.* 1460. [f. next.] **1.** Something which shuts off or closes up; *esp.* a hinged or sliding door or plate for closing an aperture. **2.** The action, time, or place of shutting. Chiefly *poet.*, the close (of day), the closing in (of evening). 1667. **3.** A join, mend, splice; a weld, the line of junction of two pieces of welded metal 1721.

2. When the chill rain begins at s. of eve KEATS. **3.** *Cold s.*, an imperfect weld due to chill; an imperfection in a casting, caused by the flow of liquid metal on a chilled surface.

Shut (ʃɒt), *v.* Pa. t. and pa. pple. **shut.** [OE. *sćyttan* = OFris. *sketta*, (M)LG., (M)Du. *schutten* shut up, obstruct :– WGmc. **skuttjan*, f. **skut-* **skeut-* SHOOT.] †**1.** *trans.* To put (a lock, bar, bolt, etc.) in position so as to fasten a door, etc. –1633. †**2.** To fasten (a door or aperture) with a lock or bar –1825. **3.** To bring (a door, gate, window, lid, etc.) into the position in which it closes the aperture ME. **b.** *intr.* for *refl.* Of a door, etc.: To close of its own accord, or by some unseen agency. Also, to admit of being shut, or of being shut in a specified manner 1470. **4.** *trans.* To close (the eyes, mouth) by bringing together the outward covering parts. ME. **5.** To close by folding up or bringing together of parts (e.g. a book, a clasp-knife, one's hand). Also *intr.* for *refl.* late ME. **6.** *trans.* To weld (cf. SHUT *sb.* 3) 1490. **7.** To close (an aperture) by placing something upon it or by drawing something across it; to stop up (a road) with obstacles or barriers. late ME. **8.** To prevent access to or egress from (a place, building, etc.) by closing the doors or apertures. Now *rare* exc. in *to s. a shop.* ME. **9.** To enclose, secure, or confine (a person or thing) *in* or *within* a place, building, or receptacle; to put *in* a place and shut the door. Also *refl.* ME. †**10. a.** To bar or exclude (a person) *from* some possession or enjoyment; to restrain *from* doing something –1719. **b.** To separate (one thing) *from* another; to cut off from view. Now *rare.* 1697. **11.** To set free *from*, relieve *of* (something troublesome). *Obs.* exc. *pass.* (*dial.* and *colloq.*). 1500.

3. The Gate used to be kept shut 1737. She.. shut her own door briskly on herself THACKERAY. *transf.* Resistance to power, has shut the door of the House of Commons to one man BURKE. **4.** fig. *To s. (one's) eyes to, against, on*, to ignore, refuse to recognize or consider; That man is to be pitied who can s. his eyes to facts KINGSLEY. *To s.* (one's) *mouth*, to cease from speaking, to hold one's tongue; so (vulgar) *to shut* (one's) *head, face*, *To s.* (another's) *mouth*, to render unable to speak, reply, find fault, disclose secrets, etc. **5.** The Scene Shuts DRYDEN. She..shut the piano 1863. I can't s. the clasp of my journal 1905. **7.** They would..for ever s. the Passage into Abyssinia JOHNSON. **8.** Bank-Holiday with the shops of London shut 1886. *To s. one's purse*, etc., *against*, to refuse help to. **9.** You s. yourselves within your park walls and garden gates RUSKIN. **10. b.** A turn in the road shut them from his sight 1831. **11.** Phr. *To be, get shut of, to s. one's hands of*: to be rid of, free from.

With advs. **S. down. a.** *intr.* To be closed with a lid; to come close down like a lid. Of fog, night; To come down and blot out the view. **b.** *trans.* To close by lowering, etc. **c.** To close (a manufactory). **d.** *absol.* To stop working. **S. in. a.** *trans.* To prevent access to or confine (a person or thing) by shutting a door, etc. or closing a receptacle. Also *refl.* **b.** To enclose with a barrier, hem in. †**c.** *intr.* Of the day, evening, etc.: To close in, grow dusk. **d.** To be closed in (to the view). **S. off. a.** *trans.* To prevent the passage of; to cut off (steam, etc.) by the closing of a valve or tap. **b.** To cut off, separate *from.* **S. out. a.** *trans.* To exclude (persons, also commodities, light, air) from a place, situation, circumstances, etc.; to deny (a person) right of entry to a place, etc. **b.** To screen from view. **S. to.** *trans.* To close (a door); †to shoot (a bolt); also *intr.* for *refl.* **S. up. a.** *trans.* To place or store away in a closed box or other receptacle; to keep from view or use; to confine within bounds. **b.** (*a*) To confine (a person or animal) in prison or some kind of restraint; to keep in seclusion; to hem (a person) round in order to prevent his escape. Also, (chiefly *refl.*) to shut the door on (a person within a place, room, etc.) to prevent access; *pass.* to be closeted with. (*b*) In some games of skill: To surround (the pieces of an opponent) so that a move becomes impossible without capture. **c.** To close (an entrance, aperture, etc.); to pull (a door, window, etc.) to. Also *occas.* to shut permanently (the eyes, mouth). Now *rare.* **d.** To close, prevent access to or exit from (a place, house, shop, room, etc.); *Agric.* to close (a meadow) to pasture, in preparation for a hay crop; to close (a box or other receptacle); *Naut.* to stop the leaks in (a ship). *To s. up shop*, see SHOP *sb.* **e.** To close (something) by folding together; to fold (something) up. Also *intr.* for *refl.* **f.** *intr.* Of a person: To bring one's remarks to a close (now *rare*). **g.** *trans.* To cause (a person) to stop talking, to reduce to silence. **h.** *intr.* To shut one's mouth, to stop talking (*colloq.* or *slang*).

Shute (ʃūt). *dial.* 1790. [Partly a dial. form of SHOOT *sb.*, partly a variant spelling of CHUTE.] **1.** A channel or open trough for conveying water, esp. to a lower level; a gutter fixed beneath the eaves of a building. **2.** A steep (artificial) channel or enclosed passage, down which ore, coal, grain, etc. is 'shot' to reach a receptacle below 1847.

Shut-eye (ʃɒ·təi). *slang.* 1919. [f. SHUT *v.*] Sleep.

Shutter (ʃɒ·təɹ), *sb.* 1542. [f. SHUT *v.* + -ER¹.] **1.** *gen.* One who or something which shuts. **2.** *spec.* **a.** A movable wooden or iron screen, applied to the outside or the inside of a window, to shut out the light or to ensure privacy or safety 1683. **b.** A folding cover hinged to a picture-frame in order to protect the picture from light, dust, etc. 1700. **c.** *Photogr.* A device for opening and closing the aperture of a lens in order to regulate the duration of the exposure 1862. **d.** *Founding.* A gate or movable partition designed to cut off the passage to a mould from the channel in which the molten metal flows 1856. **e.** *pl. Organ-building.* The louvre boards forming one or more sides of the swell-box, which regulate the volume of sound from the swell-organ 1881. **f.** A lid or slide for obscuring the light of a lamp or lantern 1910.

2. a. *To put up the shutters*, to bring one's business to a close for the day or permanently. Hence **Shu·tter** *v. trans.* to close with a s.; *refl.* to close oneself *in*, shut oneself *off*, with shutters. **Shu·ttered** (ʃɒ·təɹd) *ppl. a.* closed or provided with shutters.

Shuttle (ʃɒ·t'l), *sb.*¹ [repr. OE. *sćytel* dart, arrow, corresp. to ON. *skutill* harpoon, bolt :– Gmc. **skutilaz*, f. **skut-* SHOOT; see -LE.] †**1.** A dart, missile, arrow. OE. only. **2.** An instrument used in weaving for passing the thread of the weft to and fro from one edge of the cloth to the other between the threads of the warp ME. **3.** *transf.* **a.** A thread-carrying device in the form of a weaver's shuttle, used for knotting, tatting, and embroidery 1767. **b.** A reciprocating thread-holder in a sewing-machine, which carries the lower thread through the loop of the upper one to make a lock-stitch 1846. **c.** A curved type-bar (in some typewriters) guided into position by a race 1911. **4.** A shuttlecock. Also the game. *Obs.* exc. in *Badminton.* 1440. **5.** †**a.** A trochoid shell. **b.** In full *weaver's s.*, a shuttle-shell, esp. *Radius volva*; also, the shell of this gastropod. 1750.

Comb.: **s. armature** *Electr.* an armature shaped like an elongated shuttle, the wires being run longitudinally in grooves; **-box**, †(*a*) the cavity in the side of a s. to hold the spindle; (*b*) a tray or case at the end of the s.-race to receive the s.; **-race**, the ledge or track along which the s. passes; **-shell**, a gastropod of the genus *Radius*; **-train**, a train running a short distance to and fro, as on a short branch-line.

Shuttle (ʃɒ·t'l), *sb.*² 1440. [f. SHUT *v.* + -LE.] **1.** A floodgate which opens to allow the flow and regulate the supply of water in a mill-stream. Also, a similar gate in a drain. **2.** A small gate through which metal is allowed to pass from the trough to the mould 1858.

Shuttle (ʃɒ·t'l), *v. Obs.* exc. *dial.* 1550. [f. SHUTTLE *sb.*¹] **1.** *trans.* To move (a thing) briskly to and fro like a shuttle. Also, to throw swiftly. **2.** *intr.* To go or move backwards and forwards like a shuttle; to travel quickly to and fro 1823.

1. A face of most extreme mobility, which he shuttles about..in a very singular manner while speaking CARLYLE.

Shuttlecock (ʃɒ·t'lkǫk), *sb.* 1522. [f. SHUTTLE *sb.*¹ + COCK *sb.*¹] **1.** A small piece of cork, or similar light material, fitted with a crown or circle of feathers, used in the game of 'battledore and shuttlecock', and also in badminton. **2.** The game (more fully *battledore and s.*) in which the shuttlecock is hit backwards and forwards between two players using the battledore, or by one player into the air as many times as possible without dropping it 1599. **3.** quasi-*adj.* Light, tossed hither and thither 1660.

1. *fig.* This Reform question ought not to be made the s. of party 1858. Hence **Shu·ttlecock** *v. trans.* to throw, send backwards and forwards or to toss like a s.; *intr.* to move or go backwards and forwards.

Shy (ʃəi), *sb.*¹ *Pl.* **shies.** 1791. [f. SHY *v.*¹] A sudden start aside made by a horse, etc. when it sees an object that frightens it.

Shy (ʃəi), *sb.*² *colloq. Pl.* **shies.** 1791. [f. SHY *v.*²] **1.** A quick, jerking (or careless) throw, as of a stone, etc. **b.** *Coco-nut s.*: a form of amusement (with the attendant paraphernalia), which consists in throwing balls at coconuts 1903. **2.** *fig.* **a.** A 'fling' *at* a person or thing 1840. **b.** A trial, an experiment; a 'shot' 1848.

1. Jack-in-the-box—three shies a penny DICKENS. **2. b.** Have a s. at putting the case plainly to me 1881.

Shy (ʃəi), *a.* [OE. *sćēoh* = OHG. **scīoh*, MHG. *schiech* (G. *scheu* is a new formation) :– Gmc. **skeux(w)az*, whence also OHG. *sciuhen* (G. *scheuen* shun, *scheuchen* scare). Cf. ESCHEW. For the phonology cf. THIGH.] †**1.** Easily frightened or startled –1648. **b.** *dial.* Of a horse: Skittish; high-mettled 1787. **2.** Easily frightened away; difficult of approach owing to timidity, caution, or distrust; timidly or cautiously averse to encountering or having to do with some specified person or thing 1600. **3.** Fearful of committing oneself to a particular course of action; chary, unwilling, reluctant 1628. **b.** Averse from admitting (a principle), or from considering (a subject). Const. *of.* 1641. †**4.** Cautiously reserved; wary in speech –1691. **5.** Shrinking from self-assertion; sensitively timid; retiring or reserved from diffidence; bashful 1672. **6.** *transf.* **a.** Of plants, trees, etc.: Not bearing well 1823. **b.** *U.S.* Short (*of*), lacking 1895. **7.** *colloq.* or *slang* (now *rare* or *Obs.*) **a.** Of questionable character, disreputable, 'shady' 1849. **b.** Doubtful in amount or quality 1850.

2. Princes..are (by wisdome of State) somewhat shye of their Successors WOTTON. The cattle.. were not s. of us 1748. Phr. *To be* or *look s. on* or *at*, to regard with distrust or suspicion. **3.** Be s. of loving frankly THACKERAY. Phr. *To fight s.*: see FIGHT *v.* **4.** *Meas. for M.* III. ii. 138. **5.** People too s. or too stupid to talk 1859. *transf.* S. recesses of the lake DE QUINCEY. **6.** The plant ..seems to be a s. blossomer 1836. **7.** Gambling hells and s. saloons 1908. **b.** The dinner, I own, is s., unless I come and dine with my friends THACKERAY. **Shy·-ly** *adv.*, **-ness.**

Shy (ʃəi), *v.*¹ 1650. [f. prec.] **1.** *intr.* To take a sudden fright or aversion; to make a difficulty, 'boggle' about doing something; to recoil, shrink. Now usu. felt as *transf.* from 2. **2.** Of a horse: To shrink or start back or aside through sudden fear 1796. **3.** *To s. off*: to slip away in order to avoid a person or thing; *fig.* to find a means of evasion 1792. **4.** *trans.* To shun or avoid 1802. **5.** To render timid or shy; to frighten *off* 1845.

1. Finding I shied, he left me alone MME. D'ARBLAY. **2.** The horse shyed from the boar SCOTT.

Shy (ʃəi), *v.*[2] Chiefly *colloq.* 1787. [Origin obscure.] **1.** *intr.* To throw a missile, esp. carelessly or by a jerk. Const. *at.* **2.** *trans.* To fling, throw, jerk, toss 1828.

1. To s. at a cow within six feet DE QUINCEY.

Shylock (ʃəi·lǫk). 1894. The name of the Jewish money-lender in Shaks. *Merchant of Venice*; hence *allus.*, an extortionate usurer.

Shyster (ʃəi·stəɹ). *U.S. slang.* 1856. [Origin obscure.] A lawyer who practises in an unprofessional or tricky manner; esp., one who preys on petty criminals; hence, any one who conducts his business in a tricky manner.

Si (sī). 1728. [– Fr. *si* – It. *si*, supposed to be made from the initials of *Sancte Iohannes*, for which see UT.] *Mus.* In solmization, the seventh note of the scale.

Sial (səi·ăl). 1924. [f. SI(LICON + AL(UMINIUM.] *Geol.* That part of the crust of the earth (lithosphere) represented by the continental blocks.

Sialagogue (səi·ălăgǫg), *sb.* and *a.* Also **sialogogue.** 1783. [– Fr. *sialagogue*, f. Gr. σίαλον saliva + ἀγωγός leading, drawing forth.] *Med.* **A.** *sb.* A medicine which produces a flow of saliva. **B.** *adj.* Inducing a flow of saliva 1855.

Siamang (səi·ămæŋ). 1822. [Malay, *si-(y)āmang*, f. *āmang* black.] A species of large ape (*Hylobates syndactylus*), with long black hair, found in Sumatra and the Malay Peninsula.

Siamese (səiămī·z), *a.* and *sb.* 1693. [f. *Siam* + -ESE.] **A.** *adj.* **1.** Of or pertaining to Siam or its inhabitants. **2.** *S. twins*, two male natives of Siam, Chang and Eng (1814–1874), who were united by a tubular band in the region of the waist 1829. **b.** Twin; closely connected or similar 1833. **B.** *sb.* **1.** A native of Siam 1693. **2.** The language of Siam 1808. Hence **Siame·se** *v. trans.* to join, unite, or couple, after the manner of the Siamese twins.

Sib (sib), *sb.*[1] Now *rare.* [OE. *sibb* = OFris. *sibbe*, OS., OHG. *sibbia* ((M)HG. *sippe*), ON. **sif* (pl. *sifjar* kinship), Goth. *sibja*; related to next.] **1.** Kinship, relationship. †**2.** Peace, amity, concord –ME.

Sib (sib), *a.* and *sb.*[2] [OE. *sib(b* = OFris. *sibbe*, MDu. *sib(b)e*, OHG. *sibbi, sippi*, ON. pl. fem. *sifjar*, Goth. *un|sibjis*; of unkn. origin.] **A.** *adj.* **1.** Related by blood or descent. Now chiefly *Sc.* or *arch.* **b.** *transf.* Closely related in some way 1500. **2.** Related by blood or kinship *to* (or †*with*) a person ME. **B.** *absol.* as *sb.* **a.** As *pl.* Kinsfolk, relatives OE. **b.** A kinsman or kinswoman OE.

A. 1. The deuyll and she be syb SKELTON. **B. b.** From goody, gossip, cater-cousin and s. BROWNING.

Si·bbens (also **-ans, -ins**). 1792. Variant of SIVVENS.

Siberian (səibīᵊ·riăn), *a.* and *sb.* 1719. [f. *Siberia* + -AN.] **A.** *adj.* **1.** Of or belonging to, characteristic of, Siberia. **2.** In spec. applications, as *S. crab* (apple), *dog, pine*, etc. 1763. **B.** *sb.* **1.** A native of Siberia 1719. **2.** *pl.* Shares in Siberian gold-mines 1906.

Sibilant (si·bilănt), *a.* and *sb.* 1669. [– L. *sibilans, -ant-*, pr. pple. of *sibilare* hiss, whistle; see -ANT.] **A.** *adj.* **1.** Having a hissing sound; of the nature of, characterized by, hissing. *spec.* in *Path.* **2.** Making a hissing or whistling sound 1802.

1. The dry bronchial rhonchus..includes two varieties, the s. and sonorous rhonchus 1833.

B. *sb.* A speech-sound having a hissing effect; a sound of the nature of *s.* 1822. Hence **Si·bilance** (*rare*), a hissing sound.

Sibilate (si·bileⁱt), *v.* Also †**sibillate.** 1656. [– *sibilat-*, pa. ppl. stem of L. *sibilare*; see prec., -ATE[3].] *intr.* To hiss; to utter a hissing sound. Hence **Si·bilatory** (si·bilătəri) *a.* of the nature of, marked or expressed by, hissing.

Sibilation (sibilēⁱ·ʃən). Also †**sibill-.** 1626. [– late L. *sibilatio(n-*, f. as prec.; see -ION.] The action of hissing or whistling; a hissing or whistling sound.

The sharp fitful sibilations of the dry wiry grasses on the barren places 1892.

Sibilous (si·biləs), *a.* 1768. [f. L. *sibilus* adj. + -OUS.] Hissing, sibilant.

Sibling (si·bliŋ). 1897. [Modern use of OE. *sibling* relative; see SIB *sb.*[2] + -LING[1].] *pl.* Children having one or both parents in common.

Sibyl (si·bil). ME. [– OFr. *Sibile* (mod. *Sibylle*) or med.L. *Sibilla*, L. *Sibylla, Sibulla* – Gr. Σίβυλλα, explained in the Doric form, Σιοβόλλα, by Jerome, as for θεοβουλη 'divinely wise'.] **1.** One of various women of antiquity who were reputed to possess powers of prophecy and divination. (usu. with initial cap.) **2.** A prophetess; a fortune-teller, witch. (Now usu. with a small s.) 1589.

1. The spirit of deepe Prophecie she hath, Exceeding the nine Sibyls of old Rome SHAKS. **2.** Thou art no Sibill, but from fury speak'st, Not inspiration; we reguard thee not 1632.

‖**Sibylla** (sibi·lă). ME. [L.] = prec. 1.

Sibylline (si·biləin), *a.* and *sb.* 1579. [– L. *Sibyllinus*, f. *Sibylla* SIBYL.] **A.** *adj.* **1.** Pertaining to, uttered or written by, one or more of the Sibyls. (usu. with initial cap.) **2.** Oracular, occult, mysterious 1817. **3.** Excessive, exorbitant. (In allusion to the Sibyl who sold three books to Tarquinius Superbus at the price of the original nine.) 1859. **4.** Resembling a Sibyl 1837.

3. My terms are Sybilline 1859.

B. *sb. pl.* The Sibylline books or oracles 1875.

Sibyllist (si·bilist). 1605. [– late Gr. Σιβυλλιστής; see SIBYL and -IST.] One who believes in the Sibylline prophecies; esp. applied to the early Christians who accepted the Sibylline writings as genuine.

Sic (sik), *a. Sc.* and *north.* late ME. [Reduced form of *swik, swilk*; see SUCH *a.*] = SUCH *a.*

‖**Sic** (sik), *adv.* 1887. [L. *sīc* so, thus.] A parenthetical insertion used in printing quotations or reported utterances to call attention to something anomalous or erroneous in the original, or to guard against the supposition of misquotation.

‖**Sicca** (si·kă). *Anglo-Ind.* 1619. [– Hind. *sikka* – Arab. (Pers.) *sikka* die for coining, impression on money. See SEQUIN.] *S. rupee*, orig. a newly-coined rupee, and therefore of full standard weight; latterly, a rupee coined under the Government of Bengal from 1793, and legally current till 1836, of a greater weight than the East India Company's rupee. Also *ellipt.*

Siccative (si·kătiv), *a.* and *sb.* 1547. [– late L. *siccativus*, f. *siccare* to dry; see -ATIVE.] **A.** *adj.* Having the property of absorbing moisture. **B.** *sb.* A substance that dries up moisture, esp. as used in oil-painting; a dryer 1825. So †**Si·ccate** *v. trans.* to make dry. †**Sicca·tion**, the action or process of drying.

†**Si·ccity.** 1477. [– L. *siccitas*, f. *siccus* dry; see -ITY.] Dryness –1849.

The s. and drines of its flesh SIR T. BROWNE.

Sice (səis), **size** (səiz). late ME. [– OFr. *sis* (mod. *six*) :– L. *sex* six.] **1.** The number six marked upon dice; a throw in which the die turns up six. **2.** *Sice point.* In backgammon, the sixth point from the inner end of each table 1552. †**3.** *slang.* Sixpence –1709.

1. *Sice cinque*, a throw with two dice turning up six and five. Similarly *s. quatre, trey, deuce. Size-ace, sice-ace*, a throw with two dice turning up six and one; also, †a variety of backgammon.

†**Sicer.** ME. [– eccl. L. *sicera*; see CIDER.] Intoxicating liquor, strong drink –1623.

Sich(e, obs. or dial. ff. SUCH.

Sicilian (sisi·liăn), *a.* and *sb.* 1513. [f. L. *Sicilia* + -AN.] **A.** *adj.* Of or pertaining to Sicily or its inhabitants; characteristic of Sicily or the Sicilians 1611.

Sicilian Vespers,..a general Massacre of all the French in Sicily, in the Year 1282; to which the first Toll that call'd to Vespers was the Signal 1728.

B. *sb.* **1.** A native of Sicily 1513. †**2.** = SICILIANA (*rare*) –1728.

‖**Siciliana** (sisiliā·nă). Also pl. **-ane.** 1724. [It., fem. of *Siciliano* Sicilian.] A dance of the Sicilian peasantry, resembling a jig; the music for this.

‖**Sicilienne** (sisilie·n). 1881. [Fr., fem. of *sicilien* Sicilian.] **1.** A fine poplin made of silk and wool. **2.** A mohair fabric 1908.

Sick (sik), *a.* and *sb.* [OE. *sēoc* = OFris. *siāk*, OS. *siok*, OHG. *sioh* (Du. *ziek*, G. *siech*), ON. *sjúkr*, Goth. *siuks* :– Gmc. **seukaz*, of unkn. origin.] **A.** *adj.* **I. 1.** Suffering from illness of any kind; ill, unwell. Now chiefly literary, official (e.g. in the services), and *U.S.* †**b.** Of parts of the body: Not in a sound or healthy state –1821. **2.** Having an inclination to vomit, or actually vomiting 1614.

1. In this meane while, king Henry waxed sicker and sicker GRAFTON. *fig.* Thou lyest in reputation sicke SHAKS. Phr. *S. man*, a term frequently applied, during the latter part of the 19th c., to the Sultan of Turkey. **b.** At last his Third Finger was s. 1700. **2.** O lend me a bason, I am sicke, I am sicke B. JONSON. *fig.* The noon of summer made The valleys s. with heat 1856.

II. †**1.** Spiritually or morally ailing; corrupt through sin or wrong-doing –1738. **2.** Deeply affected by some strong feeling, as sorrow, longing, envy, repugnance or loathing, producing effects similar or comparable to those of physical ailments OE. **b.** *slang.* Disgusted, mortified, chagrined 1853. **3.** Thoroughly tired or weary *of* a thing 1597.

1. *Hen. VIII*, II. iv. 204. **2.** Hope deferred maketh the heart sicke *Prov.* 13:12. The sad heart of Ruth, when s. for home She stood in tears amid the alien corn KEATS. **b.** How s. he was when the jury..gave five hundred pounds damages against him 1853. **3.** The world is s. of such societies 1842.

III. 1. Mentally affected or weak. Now *rare.* ME. **2.** Of things: Out of condition in some respect; corrupted or spoiled. late ME. **3.** Of a sickly hue; pale, wan 1592. **4.** Accompanied by illness or sickness; denoting sickness 1593. **5. a.** Appropriated or given up to, occupied by, one or more persons in a state of illness, as *s.-bay, -berth*, etc. 1748. **b.** Of or pertaining to, connected with, persons suffering from illness, as *s.-allowance, -club, -cookery*, etc. 1595.

2. Renish [wine]..commonly goes s. in June, if not rack'd 1703. *fig.* The enterprize is sicke SHAKS. **3.** *Rom. & Jul.* II. ii. 8. **4.** Now comes the sicke houre that his surfet made SHAKS. **5. a.** *S.-bay*, a place set apart in a ship for invalids or wounded men 1846.

B. *absol.* or as *sb.* **1.** *absol.* as pl. Those who, such as, are suffering from illness OE. †**2.** A person suffering from illness –1799. **3.** †A disease or illness; a fit of sickness; a sickening (*rare*). ME.

1. Ther is phisique for the seke GOWER. **2.** Then sayd he vnto the sicke of the palsey TINDALE *Matt.* 9:6. Hence **Si·ckless** *a.* free from sickness or ill-health.

†**Sick,** *v.*[1] ME. [f. SICK *a.*] **1.** *intr.* To suffer illness; to fall ill, sicken –1597. **2.** *trans.* To cause to sicken; to make ill –1645.

Sick (sik), *v.*[2] Also **sic.** 1885. [dial. var. of SEEK *v.*] **1.** *trans.* Of a dog: To set upon, attack. Chiefly in imperative. 1890. **2.** To incite or encourage (a person) to attack. Const. with *on* adv. or prep. 1885.

Si·ck-bed. late ME. [SICK *a.*] A bed upon which a person lies ill.

Sicken (sik'n), *v.* ME. [f. SICK *a.* + -EN[5].] **1.** *intr.* To become affected with illness, to fall ill or sick. Also const. *of* or *with.* **2. a.** To feel faint with horror or nausea; to revolt or experience revulsion *at* something 1601. **b.** To grow weary or tired *of* a thing 1782. **c.** To pine with yearning; to long eagerly 1802. **3.** *trans.* To affect with illness; to make sick 1613. **4. a.** To give (one) a sickener; to make (a person) sick or tired *of* a thing 1797. **b.** To affect with nausea, loathing, or disgust 1825. **c.** To render faint with fear or horror 1821.

1. We s. to shun sicknesse when we purge SHAKS. *fig.* Speckl'd vanity Will s. soon and die MILT. **2. a.** I hate, abhor, spit, sicken at him TENNYSON. **c.** His strong heart..sickened with excess of love SHELLEY. **3.** His fetid breath sickened me 1902. *transf.* The pool was still; around its brim The alders sickened all the air 1876. **4. a.** The Blenheim,..gave us a respite, and sickened the Dons NELSON. Hence **Si·ckener,** something which nauseates or disgusts; an overdose or excess of anything; a sickening experience.

Sickening (si·k'niŋ), *ppl. a.* 1725. [f. prec. vb. + -ING[2].] **1.** Falling or turning sick. **2.** That causes sickness, nausea, or faintness;

that disgusts or revolts; repulsive, loathsome 1789. Hence **Si·ckeningly** *adv.*

Sicker (si·kəɹ), *a.* and *adv.* Now *Sc.* and *n. dial.* [OE. *sicor* = OFris., OS. *sikor* (MDu. *seker*, Du. *zeker*), OHG. *sihhur* (G. *sicher*); early WGmc. – late form **sicurus* of L. *securus* SECURE.] **A.** *adj.* **I. 1.** Free from danger or harm; secure, safe. **2.** That may be depended on; certain OE. **3.** Firm, unshaken, fast; stable ME. **4.** Indubitable; absolutely certain. late ME. **5.** Certain of its effect; effective ME. **II.** †**1.** Having assured possession or prospect *of* something. –1719. **2.** Fully assured or convinced ME. **B.** *adv.* †**1.** With security; safely; confidently –1440. **2.** Assuredly, certainly, without doubt ME. **3.** Effectively, strongly, firmly 1450. **4.** Securely; without risk of falling or shifting 1586. Hence **Si·ckerness**, the quality or state of being s. (*Obs.* exc. *Sc.*)

Si·ckerly, *adv.* Now *Sc.* and *n. dial.* [Late OE. *sicerlīce*; see prec., -LY².] †**1.** With certainty –1586. **2.** Without doubt; certainly ME. **3.** With assurance; confidently ME. **4.** Securely ME. **5.** In a stable or steady manner. late ME. **6.** With certainty of result ME. **7.** Sharply, severely, smartly 1596.

2. And sikurly sche was of gret disport CHAUCER.

Si·ckish (si·kiʃ), *a.* 1581. [f. SICK *a.* + -ISH¹.] **1.** Somewhat ill or sick; indisposed. **2.** Somewhat nauseating 1817.

2. A sweet, s. effluvium 1817. Hence **Si·ckish-ly** *adv.*, **-ness.**

Sickle (si·k'l). [OE. *sicol, sicel* = MLG., MDu. *sekele, sikele* (Du. *zikkel*), OHG. *sichila* (G. *sichel*) – var. **sicila* of (Campanian) L. *secula* (cf. It. *segolo* pruning-hook), f. *secare* cut.] **1.** An implement resembling a reaping-hook, but with a serrated cutting-edge. **2.** Something having the curved or crescent form of a sickle; e.g. a form of spur or gaff for a fighting-cock 1459. **b.** Applied to the crescent moon, etc. 1657. **c.** A group of stars in the constellation Leo 1882.

1. Oft did the harvest to their s. yield GRAY. **2. b.** Ere the silver s. of that month Became her golden shield TENNYSON.

Comb.: **s.-bill,** any of various birds having a highly curved bill, e.g. a curlew; **-moon,** the crescent-moon; **-pod,** an Amer. species of rock-cress. Hence **Sickled** (sik'ld) *ppl. a.* provided with a s.; cut by means of a s. **Si·ckler,** a reaper.

†**Si·cklewort.** 1450. [f.p rec. + WORT¹.] **a.** The scarlet pimpernel. **b.** = SELF-HEAL. –1863.

Si·ck-list. 1794. [SICK *a.*] An official list of sick persons, esp. soldiers or sailors. Colloq. phr. *On the s.*, ill.

Sickly (si·kli), *a.* ME. [prob. after ON. *sjukligr*; see SICK *a.*, -LY¹.] **1.** In a poor state of health; not robust or strong. **b.** Of the mind: Weak, disordered 1741. **2.** Of conditions, etc.: Connected with, arising from, characterized by, ill-health. late ME. †**3.** Pertaining to sickness or the sick –1814. **4.** Marked by the occurrence or prevalence of sickness; unhealthy 1602. **5.** Causing sickness or ill-health; producing discomfort or nausea 1604. **6.** Of light, colour, etc.: Faint, feeble 1695. **7.** Of feelings, etc.: Weak, mawkish 1766.

1. Feeble and s. children 1894. **2.** A s. Complaining Life they lead 1704. **3.** She at your s. Couch will wait SWIFT. **4.** This Physicke but prolongs thy s. dayes SHAKS. **5.** Dense gray mists ..enshrouding the pretty village in their s. vapours 1882. **6.** The s. winter sun was feebly trying to shine 1888. **7.** The fastidiousness of s. taste 1805. Hence **Si·cklied** *a.* rendered s. or mawkish. **Si·ckli-ly** *adv.*, **-ness.**

Sickly (si·kli), *v.* 1602. [f. SICKLY *a.*] *trans.* **a.** To cover *over* with a sickly hue. Chiefly *fig.* and in direct echoes of Shaks. **b.** To render sickly or pale 1763.

1. a. The Natiue hew of Resolution Is sicklied o're, with the pale cast of Thought SHAKS. **b.** Sicklied with age, and sour'd with self-disgrace 1807.

Sickness (si·knės). OE. [f. SICK *a.* + -NESS.] **1.** The state of being sick or ill; the condition of suffering from some malady; illness, ill-health. **2.** A particular disease or malady OE. **b.** A defect in wines 1674. **3.** A disturbance of the stomach manifesting itself in retching and vomiting 1604. **4.** *fig.* Utter disgust or weariness 1779.

1. Noble Anthony, not sickenesse should detaine me SHAKS. **2.** The Causes..of ev'ry S, that infects the Fold DRYDEN. **4.** When the spirit is sore fretted, even tired to s. of the janglings..of the world LAMB.

Si·ck-nurse, *sb.* 1821. [SICK *a.*] A nurse who attends upon the sick. Hence **Si·ck-nurse** *v. intr.* to act as a s.

†**Sicle.** ME. [– OFr. *sicle* – late L. *siclus* – Gr. σίκλος, σίγλος – Heb.; see SHEKEL.] A shekel –1649.

‖**Sida** (səi·dă). 1753. [mod.L. – Gr. σίδη some water-plant.] *Bot.* A genus of malvaceous plants of a woolly or downy character, indigenous to warm climates; a plant of this genus, esp. *S. rhombifolia* or Queensland hemp. Also *S.-weed.*

Si·ddow, si·dder, *a.* Now *dial.* 1602. [Of unkn. origin.] Soft, tender, mellow. Chiefly of peas, grain, or other vegetables.

Side (səid), *sb.*¹ [OE. *sīde* = OFris., OS. *sīde*, OHG. *sīta* (Du. *zijde, zij*, G. *seite*), ON. *síða* :– Gmc. **sīđō*, prob. f. **sīđaz* adj. extending lengthways, long, deep, low (see SIDE *a.*); rel. to OE. *sīþ* late, etc. (see SINCE).] **I. 1.** Either of the two lateral surfaces or parts of the trunk in persons or animals, extending between the shoulders and the hips; the corresponding parts in fishes, reptiles, etc. **b.** Used with reference to generation or birth. (Cf. LOIN *sb.* 2 b.) *arch.* OE. **c.** In phrases denoting the effect of exertion in speaking (after L. *latera*), or boisterous mirth 1604. **2.** In phrases denoting close proximity to a person (properly to one hand or the other), as *by one's s.* OE. **3.** One of the lateral halves of the body of an animal, or the part about the ribs, used for cooking. Now chiefly in *s. of bacon.* ME.

1. His brawny sides, with hairy bristles arm'd SHAKS. *fig.* I haue no Spurre To pricke the sides of my intent SHAKS. **c.** Laughter holding both his sides MILT. **2.** Let us forth, I never from thy s. henceforth to stray MILT. Phr. *S. by s.*, close together and abreast of each other; in later use also of things. **3.** A great dish of s. of lamb PEPYS.

II. 1. One or other of the two longer (usually vertical) surfaces or aspects of an object, in contrast to the ends, or of the two receding surfaces or aspects, in contrast to the front and back OE. **b.** One or other of the bounding lines or surfaces of any right-lined figure or object. late ME. **c.** In a rounded, cylindrical, or spherical object, a part of the surface having a particular aspect OE. **2.** That part of the framework of a ship or boat extending from stem to stern between the gun-wale and the main-wale or the water-line OE. **3. a.** The slope of a hill or bank, esp. one extending for a considerable distance ME. †**b.** The outskirts of a wood, town, etc. –1750. **4. a.** The bank or shore of a river or water; also, the land or district bordering on a river ME. **b.** A surface serving to enclose or bound a space or hollow 1474. **5.** One or other of the two surfaces of a thing having little or no appreciable thickness; also, the inner or outer surface or aspect of a thing. late ME. **6. a.** A page of a book or writing. *Obs.* or *arch.* 1530. **b.** *Tanning.* Either half of a hide which has been cut down the middle of the back 1763. **7.** An aspect or view of something immaterial 1449.

1. I trow there are but two sides of a long table, and two ends 1628. **b.** The sides of each triangle 1863. **c.** Woodpeckers explore the sides Of rugged oaks for worms COWPER. **3. a.** The shatter'd s. Of thundring Ætna MILT. **4. a.** By the Silver s. Of some cool Stream DRYDEN. RIVER-, SEA-, WATER-*side*: see these words. **b.** Dauid and his men remained in the sides of the caue 1 *Sam.* 24:3. **5.** I knowe on whiche syde my breade is buttred 1546. **7.** The ridiculous s. of everyone CARLYLE. **b.** *On the* (so-and-so) *side*, rather so-and-so.

III. 1. Place or direction with ref. to some central point; a point of the compass OE. **2.** One or other direction to either hand of an object, space, or imaginary line; the position, space, or area implied in this OE. **3.** The space lying to either hand *of*, or in any direction from, a specified place, point, etc. late ME. **4. a.** In phrases denoting position, movement, or inclination away from a central line or point, e.g. *on* or *to one s.*, ASIDE 1586. **b.** *Billiards.* Direction given to a ball by striking it at a point not directly in the middle 1873. **5.** A part *of* a place or thing lying in one or other direction from a centre or median line. late ME. **b.** A region or district, or the inhabitants of this. (Cf. *country-side.*) late ME. **c.** A portion of a building set apart for particular persons or purposes ME. **6.** The line or limit, on either side, up to which something extends ME.

1. *fig.* On that s. he multiplied his precautions, and set double watch MACAULAY. Phr. *On each* or *every s.*, *on all sides.* **2.** Suppose the beam should dip on the wrong s. COWPER. Phr. *On either* or *each s.*, *on both sides.* **3.** On the East s. of the Groue SHAKS. *fig.* On the windy s. of Care SHAKS. *This s.*, used by Europeans and Americans for the side of the Atlantic on which they happen to be. Similarly, *the other s.* **4.** Phr. *On the s.* (orig. *U.S.*), as a subordinate occupation. **5.** The other s. a'th City is risen: why stay we prating heere? SHAKS. **c.** The female 'side' of a prison gives more trouble..than the male 1904.

IV. 1. Used to denote the action, attitude, etc., of one person, or a set of persons, in relation to another or others ME. **b.** One of the two alternative views which may be taken of a question, problem, argument, etc. 1597. **c.** A division of a school devoted to a particular class of studies 1884. **2.** The position or interests of one person, party, etc., in contrast to that of an opposing one ME. **3.** Kinship or descent through father or mother. late ME. **4.** One of the parties in a transaction, battle, or debate; a political party; a faction. late ME. **b.** One of the parties in an athletic or sporting contest or game of skill. *No s.*, the announcement of the conclusion of a game of football. 1545. **5. a.** One of the two divisions of a choir 1519. **b.** At Cambridge, a body of students under the supervision of a college tutor 1852.

1. I was sorry on my s. for the occasion I had given him STERNE. **b.** There are two sides to the question 1884. **c.** The Classical s. 1884. **2.** To be ever of the loosing s. 1668. Phr. *On* (*one's*) *s.* *To take a* (or *one's*) *s.*, *take sides.* **3.** Distantly related to the Rochesters by the mother's s. C. BRONTË. **4.** 5000 of each s. killed on the place 1676.

attrib. and *Comb.* **1.** General: as *s.-aisle, -altar*, etc., *s. armour, -band, -comb*, etc.; *s.-bough, -branch, -shoot*, etc.; *s.-blow, -jump*, etc.; *s.-elevation, -front*, etc.; *s.-effect, -issue*, etc. **2.** Special: as **s.-arms** *Mil.*, weapons worn at the s., as dagger, sword, or bayonet; **-axe,** an axe with a handle slightly bent to one s.; **-bet,** a bet of one s. against another; **-car,** (*a*) a conveyance in which the seats face to the sides; a jaunting-car; (*b*) a car for passengers, attachable to the s. of a motor-cycle; (*c*) a kind of cocktail; **-dish,** a dish which is accessory to the principal one in a course; **-drawn** *a.*, sketched from the s.; **-drum,** a drum which is slung at the s. of the performer; **-face,** the human face in profile; a view or representation of this; **-hill** (now *U.S.*) a hillside, an acclivity; **-land,** a strip of land lying along the s. of a ploughed field; also *attrib.*, sloping; **-look,** an oblique look, a s.-glance; **-note,** a note made or placed at the s. of a page; **-pocket,** a pocket in the s. portion of a garment (esp. a coat or jacket); **-rail,** a rail placed or fixed at the s. of something; **-seat,** (*a*) the mode of sitting on horseback which accompanies a s.-saddle; (*b*) in a vehicle, etc. a seat in which the occupant has his back against the s. of the vehicle; **-splitter,** a very funny story, farce, etc.; **-splitting** *a.*, that convulses with merriment, extremely funny; also as *vbl.' sb.*; **-stroke,** (*a*) a stroke used in swimming on the s., the arm remaining always in the water; (*b*) an incidental or subsidiary operation of an act; **-tackle** *U.S.*, in football one or other of two players stationed at each end of the rush-line; **-tool,** a tool cutting on the s., used in wood-turning; **-view,** a view of anything obtained or taken from the s.; **-wheel** *attrib.*, of steamers, having paddle-wheels at the sides; hence *-wheeler*; **-work,** (*a*) in fortification, a lateral work; (*b*) the action of bounding sidewards, on the part of a horse.

Side (səid), *sb.*² *slang.* 1878. [perh. identical with prec. Cf. next 3.] Assumption of superiority, swaggering conduct or attitude. Freq. *to put on s.*, to give oneself airs.

Side (səid), *a.* Now *Sc.* and *n. dial.* [OE. *sīd*, MDu. *sīde, zīde*, ON. *síðr*, f. **sīđaz* SIDE *a.*] †**1.** Large, ample, spacious, extensive –late ME. **2.** Extending lengthways; long OE. **3.** Haughty, proud 1508.

2. A street so 'syde-and-wyde' that there was elbow-room for everyone in Boulder in it 1876. **3.** The haire of their head long, their beards s. and overgrowne HOLLAND. †*Side-robe* = LONG ROBE.

Comb.: **s.-coat** (now *dial.*), a long coat, a great-coat.

†**Side**, *adv.* [OE. *síde*, MLG., MDu. *sīde*; f. *sīd* SIDE *a.*] **1.** To a great distance or length; far. Chiefly in *wide and s.*, far and wide. –1621. **2.** Low down; towards or on the ground –1538.

1. For the Grecian Colonies were diffused farre and neere, wide and s. 1621.

Side (səid), *v.* 1470. [f. SIDE *sb.*[1]] **I.** *trans.* †**1.** To cut or carve (a pig or haddock) into sides –1854. **2.** To walk or stand by the side of; to be side by side with 1613. **b.** *fig.* To equal, match 1603. †**3.** To support or countenance (a person) –1618. **4.** *refl.* To take a side or party 1591. †**5.** To assign to one of two sides or parties. SHAKS. **6.** *dial.* To put in order, arrange; to clear or tidy *up* 1825. **b.** To clear *away* 1848. **7.** *Naut.* To draw (a rope) *over* or *out* 1834. **8.** To make of certain dimensions on the side; to square the sides of (timber) 1794. **9.** To furnish (a structure) with sides 1868.

2. The old benchers..might not be sided or jostled LAMB. **b.** He had sure read more..than any Man I ever knew, my Lord Falkland only excepted, who I think sided him CLARENDON.

II. *intr.* **1.** To take a side; to join or form sides or parties. Usu. const. *with.* 1600. **2.** To move or turn sideways 1668.

Hence **Si·der**, one who sides *with* a person or cause; a partisan, adherent.

Si·deband. 1926. [f. SIDE *sb.*[1] + BAND *sb.*[2]] *Wireless.* The band of frequencies on either side of the carrier frequency.

Si·de-bar. 1686. [SIDE *sb.*[1]] **1.** *Law.* **a.** A former bar in the Outer Parliament House in Edinburgh. **b.** A former bar in Westminster Hall 1795. **2.** A lateral bar or longitudinal side-piece, as in a saddle, carriage, etc. 1875.

1. b. Phr. *S. rule*, a rule granted without formal application to the court; so called because moved for by the attorneys at the s. of the court.

Sideboard (səi·dbōᵊɹd). ME. [SIDE *sb.*[1]] **1.** †**a.** A table (*esp.* for taking meals at) placed towards the side of a room, hall, etc. –1726. **b.** A piece of dining-room furniture for holding side-dishes, wine, plate, etc., and often having cupboards and drawers 1671. **2.** A board forming the side, or a part of the side, of any structure 1611.

Si·de-bone. 1819. [SIDE *sb.*[1]] **1.** That part of the pelvis on either side of a bird or fowl which is easily separated from the backbone in carving; also sometimes, the scapula or shoulder-blade. **2.** Ossification of the side cartilages in a horse's foot 1886.

Si·de-box, *sb.* 1678. [SIDE *sb.*[1]] A box or enclosed seat at the side of a theatre. †**b.** The occupants of a side-box –1732. Hence †**Side-box** *v. trans.* to gaze at from a side-box.

Sided (səi·dėd), *ppl. a.* late ME. [f. SIDE *sb.*[1] and *v.* + -ED.] **1.** Having sides; (esp. compounded with a numeral) furnished with (a specified number of) sides. **2.** *Naut.* Having a (specified) dimension in the direction contrary to that of the moulding 1794. **3.** Of timber: Dressed on one or more sides 1865.

1. A Pentagon, or five-sided Figure 1731. Hence **Si·dedness** (chiefly in combs.).

Side-door. (Stress var.) 1535. [SIDE *sb.*[1]] A door in the side of a building, garden, etc.; a door on one side of, or subsidiary to, the main door. Also *fig.* applied to indirect, oblique, or illegitimate action.

Si·de-glance, *sb.* 1611. [SIDE *sb.*[1]] A glance directed sideways. **b.** *fig.* An indirect or slight reference 1831. So **Si·de-glance** *v.*

Si·de-light. Also **side light, sidelight.** 1610. [SIDE *sb.*[1]] **1. a.** Light coming from the side. **b.** *fig.* Incidental light or information on a subject 1871. **2.** A window, or opening for light, in the side of a building, ship, lamp, etc. 1827. **b.** A side-portion of a large window; a window by the side of a door or other window 1851. **3.** *Naut.* A light carried on either side of a ship under way in the night 1887. **b.** The lamp on either side of a motor vehicle 1912.

1. b. The reader needs all the side-lights which can be thrown upon its translated forms 1871.

Si·de-line, *sb.* 1768. [SIDE *sb.*[1]] **1.** A line extending along or towards one side of a thing or space; *spec.* in *Football, Tennis*, etc. either of two lines bounding the pitch, court, etc., at the sides. **b.** A railway or tramway extending away from the main line 1898. **2.** A line used for securing an animal by tying together the fore and hind leg on one side 1831. **3.** An auxiliary line of goods, trade, or occupation 1890. **b.** *fig.* Something subsidiary to the main subject, line of action, etc. 1927. Hence **Si·de-line** *v. trans.* to secure (cattle, etc.) with a s.

Sideling (səi·dliŋ), *sb.* late ME. [f. SIDE *sb.*[1] + -LING[1].] †**1.** A strip or piece of land lying by the side of a larger portion or by a stream –1726. **2.** A slope, *esp.* one along the side of which a track or road runs. *local.* 1808.

Sideling (səi·dliŋ), *adv.* and *a.* ME. [f. SIDE *sb.*[1] + -LING[2].] **A.** *adv.* **1.** With a sideward movement; in a side-long direction; sideways; obliquely. †**2.** On a side-saddle; facing to the side –1698.

1. Hee hath the witte yet to enter s., like a gentlewoman with an huge farthingall 1609. Crabs move s. SIR T. BROWNE. **2.** Queen Anne.. being the first that taught women to ride s. on horseback 1612.

B. *adj.* **1.** Directed or moving sideways; oblique 1611. **b.** *fig.* Of speech, etc.: Indirect 1789. **2.** Having an inclination; sloping, steep 1611.

2. It is a good plan to plough sidling ground in a circle 1854. So **Si·delings** *adv.* = A.

Si·delong, *adv.* and *a.* Also **side-long.** 1523. [alt. of SIDELING *adv.*; see -LONG.] **A.** *adv.* **1.** Towards the side; sideways, obliquely 1580. **2.** To the side *of*; side by side; presenting the side *to* something 1643. **3.** On the side; with the side to the ground 1667. **4.** As *prep.* By or along the side of 1523.

3. Side-long the plough beside the field-gate lay MORRIS.

B. *adj.* **1.** In a slanting direction; in a sloping position; inclining to one side; lying on the side 1597. **b.** *spec.* Of ground: Sloping 1792. **2.** Directed to one side or sideways 1608. **b.** Glancing, moving, or extending sideways 1818. **3.** Indirect; not straightforward or open 1654.

2. He gives a dreadful s. glance of suspicion THACKERAY. **3.** Their s. Answers, and silly Excuses will not do 1697.

Si·de-post. 1535. [SIDE *sb.*[1]] **1.** One of the posts at either side of a doorway; a door-post. (Chiefly in echoes of the Bible.) **2.** A post supporting a roof at or towards one side 1625.

1. Strike the lintel and the two side postes with the blood that is in the bason *Exod.* 12:22.

-sider. 1841. Forming the second element in a comb. as *near-s.*, a horse standing on the near side; *hillsider*, one living on a hillside.

Sideral (səi-, si·dĕrăl), *a.* 1594. [– L. *sideralis*, f. *sidus, sider-* constellation, star; see -AL[1].] **1.** Of or pertaining to the stars; sidereal, starry. **2.** Coming from, caused by, the stars. Chiefly of malign influences. 1611.

2. S. blast, Vapour, and Mist, and Exhalation hot MILT.

†**Si·derate**, *v.* 1623. [– *siderat-*, pa. ppl. stem of L. *siderari* be planet-struck, f. *sidus, sider-* star, etc.; see -ATE[3].] *trans.* To strike with malign (sidereal) influence, to blast. Chiefly *pass.*, to be blasted, struck by lightning; *fig.* to be thunderstruck. –1679.

Sidera·tion. Now *rare.* 1612. [– L. *sideratiō(n-*, f. as prec.; see -ION.] **1.** Blasting of trees or plants 1623. **2.** Sudden paralysis; complete mortification of any part of the body 1612. **3.** *Path.* Erysipelas of the face or scalp 1828.

Sidereal (səidɪə·rĭăl), *a.* 1634. [f. L. *sidereus* (f. *sidus, sider-* star) + -AL[1].] **1.** Of or pertaining to the stars 1647. **2.** Star-like, lustrous, bright (*rare*) 1634. **3.** Of periods of time: Determined or measured by means of the stars. 1681. **4.** Of planetary or lunar motion: Relative to the stars 1815. **5.** Concerned with the stars 1833.

1. That general Astronomy which includes our whole s. system SPENCER. **3.** The Sydereal year is the space of time, in which the Sun returns to the same star from whence he departed 1681. The s. month is the interval between two successive conjunctions of the moon with the same fixed star 1868. Hence **Side·realize** *v. trans.* **Side·really** *adv.*

Siderite (si·dĕrəit, səidɪə·rəit). 1579. [In early use – Fr. *sidérite* or L. *siderites, -itis* – Gr. σιδηρίτης, -ῖτις, f. σίδηρος iron; in later use f. Gr. σίδηρος + -ITE[1] 2 b.] *Min.* †**1.** Load-stone –1694. **2.** A steel-coloured stone, prob. sapphire 1623. †**3.** A phosphate of iron; pharmacosiderite, cube-ore –1805. **4.** A blue variety of quartz 1823. **5.** Rhombohedral carbonate of iron, native ferrous carbonate, spathic iron-ore 1850. **6.** A meteorite consisting mainly of iron 1875. So †**Sideri·tes** (in senses 1–3). **Sideri·tic** *a.* of the nature of s. (in sense 3).

Sidero- (si·dĕro, səidɪə·ro), comb. form of Gr. σίδηρος iron.

1. In various names of minerals, as *s.-calcite, -graphite*, etc. **2.** In miscellaneous combs., as **Si·derograph**, an engraving produced by siderography. **Siderogra·phic, -al**, *adjs.* pertaining to siderography. **Sidero·graphist**, 'one who engraves steel plates,, or performs work by means of such plates'. **Sidero·graphy**, a method of engraving on steel, employed especially for bank-notes. **Si·deroscope**, an instrument used to detect minute quantities of iron by means of a combination of magnetic needles.

Siderolite (si·dĕrələit, səidɪə·roləit). 1863. [f. prec. + -LITE.] A meteorite composed of a mixed mass of iron and stone. Hence **Sideroli·thic** *a.* of the nature of a s.

‖**Siderosis** (sidĕrōᵘ·sis). 1880. [f. Gr. σίδηρος iron + -OSIS.] *Path.* Accumulation of oxide of iron in the lungs.

Siderostat (si·dĕrostæt). 1877. [f. L. *sidus, sider-* star, after *heliostat.*] *Astr.* An astronomical instrument by which a star under observation may be kept in the same part of the field of a telescope. Hence **Sidero-sta·tic** *a.*

Si·de-sa:ddle, *sb.* (and *adv.*). 1493. [SIDE *sb.*[1]] A saddle so contrived as to enable a woman to sit with both feet on one (usually the left or near) side of a horse; in mod. use *spec.* one with horns or crutches to support and give a hold to the knees of the rider, who sits facing forward with the right knee raised. **b.** as *adv.* On a side-saddle; sideways 1885.

attrib.: **s. flower** (or **plant**), (*a*) an Amer. swamp-plant of the genus *Sarracenia*, the leaves of which retain a considerable quantity of water; (*b*) the plant *Darlingtonia californica.* Hence **Si·de-saddle** *v.*

Si·de-show. 1855. [SIDE *sb.*[1]] A 'show' which is subsidiary to a larger one; a minor attraction in an exhibition or entertainment; hence, a minor issue, a subordinate matter.

Si·de-slip, *sb.* 1872. [f. SIDE *sb.*[1] + SLIP *sb.* and *v.*] **1.** An illegitimate child. GEO. ELIOT. **2.** The action or fact of slipping sideways, *esp.* on the part of a cycle, motor-car, or aeroplane 1896. So **Si·de-slip** *v. intr.* to slip sideways; (of an aeroplane) to fall as the result of an excessive bank or roll 1887.

Sidesman (səi·dzmĕn). 1632. [alt. of †*sideman* (XVI–XVII) 'a man who stands at the side of a churchwarden'.] One of the persons elected as assistants to the churchwardens of a parish.

Si·de-step, *sb.* 1847. [SIDE *sb.*[1] or *adv.*] **1.** A step to one side. **2.** A step fixed to the side of a ship, vehicle, etc. 1867.

Hence **Si·de-step** *v. intr.*, to step to one side; *trans.*, to avoid by stepping sideways (*spec.* in *Football*).

Si·de-stick. 1683. [SIDE *sb.*[1]] *Printing.* One of a pair of wedge-shaped sticks, usu. of wood, with one side slanting, used in locking up a form.

Si·de-table. late ME. [SIDE *sb.*[1]] A table placed beside the wall of a room (*esp.* a dining-room), or to the side of a main or high table.

Si·de-track, *sb.* orig. *U.S.* 1881. [SIDE *sb.*[1]] A railway siding. Also *fig.*

Si·de-track, *v.* orig. *U.S.* 1881. [f. prec.] **1.** *trans.* To run or shunt (a train, etc.) into a siding. **2.** *intr.* To run into a siding 1888. **3.** *fig.* (*trans.* and *intr.*) To divert (be diverted) from the main course, line, object, etc. 1889.

Si·de-walk. 1667. [SIDE *sb.*[1]] **1.** A walk or path running parallel to a main or central one (*rare*). **2.** A (raised) path for foot-passengers along the side of a street, road, etc.; a footway or pavement. Now *U.S.* 1739.

Si·de-wall. late ME. A wall forming the side of a structure or an enclosure.

Sideward (səi·dwǒɹd), *adv.* and *a.* late

ME. [f. SIDE *sb.*[1]] **A.** *adv.* Towards one side or the other. **B.** *adj.* Directed, moving, or tending towards one side 1831. So **Si·dewards.**

Si·deway, *sb.* Also **side-way.** 1552. [SIDE *sb.*[1]] **1.** A path or way diverging from, or lying to the side of, a main road; a byway. **2.** A (raised) path along the side of a road; a footway. Now *U.S.* 1738.

Si·deway, *adv.* and *a.* 1612. [f. SIDE *sb.*[1] + -WAY.] **A.** *adv.* = next *adv.* **B.** *adj.* (Directed or moving) towards or from one side; indirect 1800.

Sideways (səi·dwēⁱz), *adv.* and *a.* 1577. [f. SIDE *sb.*[1] + -WAYS.] **A.** *adv.* **1.** From one side. **2.** Presenting the side instead of the face, front, or end; in the direction of the side; facing to the side, etc. 1598. **3.** In a lateral or sideward direction; towards one side; obliquely 1611. **4.** So as to incline to one side 1631. **5.** By an indirect way or route; indirectly 1723. **B.** *adj.* = SIDEWAY *a.* 1868.

A. 1. If the Wind be side-ways, it may do well enough 1725. **2.** Some side-ways, some head first, some stern first DICKENS. **3.** We listened and looked s. up! COLERIDGE.

Si·de-wind. Also **side wind, sidewind.** late ME. [SIDE *sb.*[1]] **1.** A wind blowing from one side, or on the side of a vessel, etc. **2.** *fig.* An indirect means, method, or manner. Chiefly in phr. *by a s.* 1648. **3.** *attrib.* as *adj.* Indirect, oblique; illegitimate 1680.

1. *fig.* Some sail to the port of their own praise by a s. 1642. **2.** Some Expressions, which by a S. reflected on me SWIFT.

Side-winder[1] (səi·dˌwiːndəɹ). *U.S.* and *dial.* 1859. [f. SIDE *sb.*[1] + *winder* a blow.] A heavy blow with the fist delivered from or on the side.

Side-winder[2] (səi·dˌwəiːndəɹ). *U.S.* 1888. [f. SIDE *sb.*[1] + WIND *v.*] A species of rattle-snake, *Crotalus cerastes*.

Sidewise (səi·dwəiz), *adv.* and *a.* 1571. [f. SIDE *sb.*[1] + -WISE.] **A.** *adv.* **1.** In a lateral direction; to one side; sidewards. **2.** = SIDEWAYS A. 2. 1608. **3.** On or from the side 1613. **4.** = SIDEWAYS A. 4. 1828. **B.** *adj.* Directed towards one side; sideward 1853.

1. Joltings, backwards, forwards, and s. 1854.

‖**Sidi** (sī·di). 1615. [– Urdu *sīdī* – Arab. *sayyidī* 'my lord', SAYYID.] Orig., a title of honour given in Western India to African Moslems holding high positions under the kings of the Deccan; in later use, an African, a Negro. Now chiefly in comb. *s.-boy*.

Siding (səi·diŋ), *vbl. sb.* 1603. [f. SIDE *v.* or *sb.*[1] + -ING[1].] **I. 1.** The action of taking sides; party spirit, partisanship, factiousness; an instance of this. **2.** The action of tending or moving to a side 1646. **3.** *U.S.* The action of dressing or trimming the sides of timber 1875. **II. 1.** *U.S.* The boarding forming the sides of a timber building; weather-boarding; also (with *a* and *pl.*), a piece of this 1858. **2.** *Ship-building.* 'The size or dimensions of timber the contrary way to the moulding, or moulded side' 1797. **3.** A short piece of additional track parallel to the main line of a railway or tramway, and connected with it by switches, for enabling trains, trucks, etc., to pass each other or to lie by 1825.

Sidle (səi·d'l), *v.* 1697. [Back-formation from SIDELING *adv.*, SIDELONG *adv.*, after verbs in -LE 3.] **1.** *intr.* To move or go sideways or obliquely; to edge along, esp. in a furtive or unobtrusive manner, or while looking in another direction; to make advances in this manner. **2.** *trans.* To move, turn, or direct sideways 1779.

1. Sir Harry..sidled to the door,..and then slipped out RICHARDSON. Hence **Si·dle** *sb.* an act of sidling, a sidelong or oblique movement. **Si·dlingly** *adv.*

Sidonian (səidōᵘ·niăn), *sb.* and *a.* 1535. [f. L. *Sidonius* – Gr. Σιδώνιος, f. Σιδών, the Phœnician city of that name; see -AN.] **A.** *sb.* A native or inhabitant of Sidon. **B.** *adj.* Of or pertaining to Sidon 1594.

A. They were farre from the Zidonians *Judges* 18:7.

Siege (sīdʒ), *sb.* [ME. *sege* – OFr. *sege* (mod. *siège*), f. *assegier* (mod. *assiéger*) ASSIEGE.] **I.** †**1.** A seat, *esp.* one used by a person of rank or distinction –1616. †**b.** An ecclesiastical see –1579. †**2.** A place in which a person has his seat or residence; a seat of rule, empire, etc. –1630. **b.** The station of a heron on the watch for prey 1452. †**3.** A privy –1555. †**b.** Evacuation –1700. †**c.** Excrement, ordure –1662. †**4.** The anus or rectum –1670. **5.** *techn.* **a.** The floor of a glass-furnace 1839. **b.** A hewer's table or bench 1854.

1. *fig.* I fetch my life and being, From Men of Royall Seige SHAKS. **2.** He [Constantine] made his s. Bizantium, that retaines his name ere since 1592.

II. 1. The action, on the part of an army, of investing a town, castle, etc., in order to cut off all outside communication and in the end to reduce or take it; an investment, beleaguering ME. **b.** Without article. late ME. **2.** *attrib.*, as *s.-artillery, -gun, -operations*, etc. 1450.

1. *fig.* Love stood the s., and would not yield his breast DRYDEN. **b.** *To lay s. to*: see LAY *v.* III. 3 c.

Siege (sīdʒ), *v.* ME. [f. prec., or aphetic f. ASSIEGE *v.*] **1.** *trans.* To besiege, beleaguer, lay siege to. †**2.** To place; to seat (oneself) –1594.

1. They sieg'd him a whole summer night SCOTT.

Sienese (sīĕnī·z) *sb.* and *a.* Also **Siennese.** 1756. [f. *Siena, Sienna* + -ESE.] **A.** *sb.* An inhabitant or native of Siena, a city in Tuscany. **B.** *adj.* Of or pertaining to Siena 1830.

Sienna (siˌe·nă). 1787. [Earlier *terra-sienna* for It. *terra di Sienna* 'earth of *Sien(n)a* (see prec.).] **a.** A ferruginous earth used as a pigment in oil and water-colour painting (called *burnt s.* when it has been exposed to a red heat). **b.** The colour of this pigment, a rich reddish brown.

‖**Sierra** (siˌe·ră). 1613. [– Sp. *sierra* :– L. *serra* saw.] **1.** A range of hills or mountains, rising in peaks which suggest the teeth of a saw. **b.** *gen.* A mountain-range of this description 1850. **2.** *Astr.* = CHROMOSPHERE 1851.

1. The bleak winds of the s. gave an austerity to the climate 1843. Hence **Sie·rran** *a.*

‖**Siesta** (siˌe·stă). 1655. [– Sp. *siesta* :– L. *sexta* (*hora*) sixth hour of the day. Cf. SEXT.] An afternoon rest or nap; *esp.* that commonly taken during the hottest hours of the day in tropical countries.

Sieve (siv), *sb.* [OE. *sife* = MLG., MDu. *seve* (Du. *zeef*), OHG. *sib, sip* (G. *sieb*) :– WGmc. **sibi*.] **1.** A utensil consisting of a circular frame with a finely meshed or perforated bottom, used to separate the coarser from the finer particles of any loose material, or as a strainer for liquids. **b.** In phr. denoting something that cannot be done, or that is waste of labour. late ME. **c.** *fig.* Of persons; *esp.* one who cannot keep a secret 1601. **2.** Used locally as a measure for various kinds of produce. 1440.

1. Sieves..to sift the Lime and Sand withal 1703. (Formerly often with ref. to its use for divination, and by witches for sailing in.) **b.** As he that fetcheth Water in a Sive 1477. **c.** Here's none but wee, I am no Sive? I prithee, Swain, be free QUARLES.

Comb.: **s.-cell, -disc, -pore, -tissue, -tube, -vessel,** botanical terms having reference to sieve-like openings in the walls or ends of plant-cells; **-plate,** (*a*) *Bot.* a sieve-like plate on the wall of a plant-cell; (*b*) in paper-making, a plate through which pulp is strained.

Sieve, *v.* 1499. [f. prec.] = SIFT *v.* 1, 4, 7.

‖**Siffleur** (siflǿr). 1703. [Fr., f. *siffler* whistle.] **a.** An animal that makes a whistling noise, *spec.* the whistling marmot. **b.** (with fem. *-euse*). A whistling artiste 1923.

Sift (sift), *v.* [OE. *siftan* = MLG., MDu. *siften, sichten* (Du. *ziften*); f. **sib-* (see SIEVE *sb.*).] **1.** *trans.* To pass (something) through a sieve, in order to separate the coarse from the fine particles, or to strain. **2.** *fig.* **a.** To make trial of (a person) ME. **b.** To subject to close questioning 1566. **3.** *fig.* To examine closely into, to scrutinize narrowly, so as to find out the truth 1573. **4.** To separate, to take or get *out*, by the use of a sieve. late ME. **b.** *fig.* To find *out*, get to know, by a process of elimination or close inquiry. 1586. **5.** To let fall through, scatter from or by means of, a sieve 1664. **6.** *intr.* To use a sieve; to do sifting. Chiefly *fig.*, esp. to pry *into*, make inquiry. 1535. **7.** To pass or fall as through a sieve 1599.

1. Two of the Fair Sex who are usually employed in sifting Cinders STEELE. *fig.* To s. the nations with the sieue of vanitie *Isa.* 30:28. **2. a.** Satan hath desired to haue you, that he may s. you as wheat *Luke* 22:31. **b.** You must speak with this wench,..you must s. her a wee bit SCOTT. **4.** I have sifted out..the flower of my fancye 1602. **b.** I endeavour'd to s. the Secret from him 1726. **5.** *fig.* From leaden skies the snow flakes were sifted over the land 1869. **6.** I will not s. into them too minutely 1699. **7.** Golden leaves were sifting down on the..floor 1867. Hence **Sift** *sb.* (*rare*) the act of sifting; the fact of falling as from a sieve; sifted material.

Sifter (si·ftəɹ). 1579. [f. SIFT *v.* + -ER[1].] **1.** One who sifts. **2.** A sieve; also *dial.*, a fire-shovel, kitchen shovel 1611.

Sig. *dial.* and *U.S.* 1691. [Of unkn. origin.] Urine.

Sig., in printing, abbrev. of SIGNATURE.

Sigh (səi), *sb.* ME. [f. the vb.] **1.** A sudden, prolonged, deep and more or less audible respiration, following on a deep-drawn breath, esp. indicating or expressing dejection, weariness, longing, pain, or relief. **2.** *transf.* A sound made by the wind, suggestive of a sigh 1810.

1. Stopping the Cariere Of Laughter, with a s. SHAKS. **2.** Autumn's hollow sighs in the sere wood SHELLEY.

Sigh (səi), *v.* Pa. t. and pple. **sighed** (səid). [ME. *sihen, siȝen, sighen*, prob. a back-formation on *sihte, siȝte*, pa. t. of *sīhen* (:– OE. *sīcan*), with a var. SIKE *v.*; of unkn. origin.] **1.** *intr.* To emit, give, or heave a sigh. **b.** Of the wind, trees, etc.: To make or give out a sound suggestive of a sigh 1757. **2. a.** To express desire or longing by the utterance of sighs; hence, to wish or long ardently. Const. *for* (†*after*), or *to* with inf. 1549. †**b.** To be sorry. Const. *that, to*. –1734. **3.** *trans.* To speak or utter (words, etc.) with a sigh 1553. **b.** To emit, give out, impart, etc., by sighing 1593. **4. a.** To spend, consume, or while away (time) by sighing 1599. **b.** To bring into a certain state or condition by sighing 1603. **5.** To lament (an event, circumstance, etc.) with sighing 1600.

1. To s., and to wincke as thoughe he were a slepe 1560. Nature from her seat Sighing through all her Works gave signs of woe MILT. **b.** Yon neglected shrub..That..sighs at every blast GOLDSM. **2. a.** Long have I sigh'd for a calm TENNYSON. **3. a.** Bvt wretch'd Iob, sigh't forth these words, and said, Ah me! QUARLES. **b.** Sapores..sighed out his affrighted ghost, at the age..of seventy one 1638. **4. a.** Wearied I am with sighing out my dayes MILT. **b.** *refl.* The gale had sigh'd itself to rest SCOTT. **5.** I s. the lacke of many a thing I sought SHAKS. Hence **Si·gher,** one who sighs. **Si·ghing** *vbl. sb.*

Sighing (səi·iŋ), *ppl. a.* 1440. [f. SIGH *v.* + -ING[2].] **1.** Accompanied by, uttered with, a sigh. **2.** Of persons, etc.: That sigh(s) 1593.

1. With dew all turned to tears; odour, to s. ruth SHELLEY. Hence **Si·ghingly** *adv.*

Sight (səit), *sb.* [OE. *sihþ*, more usu. *ġesihþ*, corresp. to OS. *gisicht*, MLG. *sichte*, MDu. *sicht* (Du. *zicht*), OHG., MHG. (*ge*)*sicht* (G. *gesicht*; *sicht* XIX – LG.) sight, vision, face, appearance; WGmc. deriv. of **seχ*(*w*)- SEE *v.*; see -T[1].] **I. 1.** A thing seen, esp. of a striking or remarkable nature; a spectacle. †**b.** A vision. *Book of sights*, the Apocalypse. –1825. **c.** *pl.* Those features or objects in a particular place or town which are considered to be specially worth seeing 1632. **2.** A show or display *of* something; hence, a great number or quantity; a 'deal' or 'lot'. Also advb. Now *colloq.* or *slang*. late ME. †**3.** Aspect, appearance –1680.

1. White teeth is a good s. in a woman 1561. Phr. *To be a s.*, to be an object of ridicule, horror, etc. *A s. for sore eyes*, a welcome person or thing; esp. a welcome visitor. *S. unseen* (*U.S.* and *dial.*), without previous inspection. **2.** O ye Gods, what a s. of things do not I want? BURTON. You're a s. too clever for me 1889.

II. 1. The perception or apprehension *of* something by means of the eyes; the presentation *of* a thing to the sense of vision ME. **b.** Without article, chiefly in phrases as *to catch, have, lose s. of* ME. **c.** The first perception or view *of* something. Usu. in phr. *at* or *upon* (*the*) *s. of*. 1471. **d.** A position or point commanding or giving a view *of* something. Chiefly *in* or *within s. of*. 1533.

2. A view, look, or glimpse *of* something ME. **3.** With omission of the dependent genitive, in phrases related to 1 c. ME. **4.** A look or glance (at something, or in a certain direction). Now *rare*. ME. **b.** An observation with a surveying or other similar instrument; an aim with a gun, etc. 1835.

1. Therefore he never inform'd the Captain of the S. of Land 1743. **b.** As if he dreaded losing s. of her 1898. *To lose s. of* (fig.): not to bear in mind. **2.** You should have had a s. of the Copy 1692. **3.** *At first s. At* or *on s.*, as soon as the person or thing is seen. *At* (formerly also *on* or *upon*) *s.*, used spec. with ref. to the payment of bills; also *after s. At* (so many) *days'* (etc.) *s.*, of bills. **4. b.** Some sights obtained for the chronometer gave the longitude 94° 40′ 1835.

III. 1. The faculty or power of seeing, as naturally inherent in the eye; eyesight ME. **b.** *fig.* Mental or spiritual vision. See also SECOND SIGHT. ME. **2.** The sense or power of vision in relation to the individual possessing or exercising it; freq. approaching to a concrete use, = eye or eyes ME. **3.** The range or field of one's vision; chiefly in phr. *out of one's s.* Also *spec.*, the focal distance of a lens. ME. **b.** Without article, in the phrases *in s.*, *out of s.* ME. **4.** The exercise of the faculty of vision; the act of seeing or looking; esp. *by s.*, freq. denoting merely visual knowledge ME. **b.** Examination, inspection, scrutiny 1452. **5. a.** Opinion, estimate, judgement; respect, regard, view. Now *rare*. ME. †**b.** Knowledge, skill insight. Const. *in*. –1600.

1. Most Eyes have perfect S., tho' some be blind 1599. **b.** To thee, O Lord most just, I lift my inward s. 1586. **2.** Nor farther word she spoke, but closed her s. DRYDEN. Phr. *In one's s.*, before one's eyes. *To s.*, to the eye; so as to be seen. **3.** The two armies lay in s. of each other HUME. Phr. *Out of (all) s.*, immeasurably, beyond comparison. **4.** Lord Conway is barely known to me by s. 1831. Phr. *Line of s.*, (*a*) an imaginary line between the sights of a gun and the object at which it is aimed; (*b*) an imaginary line drawn between the fovea of the eye and the point fixated by the two eyes in normal vision.

IV. 1. a. The pupil of the eye. Now *dial.* late ME. †**b.** A visor –1666. **c.** *pl.* Spectacles. Now *dial.* 1619. **2.** An appendage to a surveying or observing instrument, serving to guide the eye 1559. **b.** A device, of the nature of a projection or notch, on a fire-arm or piece of ordnance, etc., to assist in taking aim 1588. **3.** The opening in a picture-frame; that part of the picture which shows in this 1850.

1. b. Their eyes of fire, sparkling through sights of Steele SHAKS. **2.** An accurate land-surveyor, with his chain, s., and theodolite BURKE.

attrib. and *Comb.*: **s.-chase,** a chase in which the dogs hunt by s.; **-reader,** one who is able to read music at sight; †**-shot,** the range of vision; **-singing,** the practice or art of singing at sight; **-worthy** *a.*, worth seeing or visiting.

Sight (səit), *v.* 1556. [f. prec.] **1.** *trans.* †**a.** *Sc.* To look at, view, inspect, examine, scrutinize –1706. **b.** To examine by taking a sight 1884. **2.** To get or catch sight of, to see, to get or go within sight of (anything) 1602. **3.** *intr.* To take a sight, *esp.* in shooting 1842.

2. We sighted her one morning at daybreak 1887. **3.** Together they sighted, and together they fired 1842.

Sighted (səi·tėd), *ppl. a.* 1552. [f. SIGHT *sb.* + -ED².] **1.** Having sight of a specified kind, as *dim-*, *long-*, *short-s.*, etc. **2.** Endowed with sight; able to see. Also *absol.* 1836. **3.** Furnished or fitted with a sight or sights 1859.

Sighter (səi·təɹ). 1897. [f. SIGHT *v.* + -ER¹.] A sighting shot in rifle or artillery shooting.

†**Si·ghtful,** *a.* late ME. [-FUL 1.] **1.** Visible –1545. **2.** Endowed with sight; seeing –1613. **3.** Sightly –1571. Hence †**Si·ghtfulness.**

Si·ght-hole. 1559. [SIGHT *sb.*] A hole to see through, *esp.* in a surveying or other instrument.

Wee..Must..stop all sight-holes SHAKS.

Sighting (səi·tiŋ), *vbl. sb.* 1752. [f. SIGHT *v.* + -ING¹.] **1.** The action of SIGHT *v.*; *esp.* the action of giving to a gun the proper elevation and direction to hit the object aimed at. **2.** *attrib.*, esp. *s.-shot*, a preliminary shot allowed to each competitor in a shooting-match 1861.

Sightless (səi·tlės), *a.* ME. [f. SIGHT *sb.* + -LESS]. **1.** Unable to see; without the power of sight; blind. **2.** Invisible, unseen, dark; impenetrable by vision 1589. †**3.** Unsightly –1632. †**4.** Out of sight –1816.

1. A cruel mockery of his [Samson's] s. woe LONGF. **2.** The lark becomes a s. song TENNYSON. **3.** Vnpleasing blots, and sightlesse staines SHAKS. Hence **Si·ghtless-ly** *adv.*, **-ness.**

Sightly (səi·tli), *a.* (and *adv.*). 1532. [f. SIGHT *sb.* + -LY¹.] **A.** *adj.* †**1.** Visible; conspicuous –1579. **b.** *U.S.* Of places: Open to the view; that may be seen from a distance; commanding a wide prospect 1828. **2.** Pleasing to the sight; handsome, beautiful 1562. **B.** as *adv.* Handsomely, finely 1591.

2. The s. constellation of the southern cross 1850. Hence **Si·ghtliness.**

Si·ght-see:ing, *vbl. sb.* 1847. [f. SIGHT *sb.* I. 1 c.] The action or occupation of seeing sights. So **Si·ght-seer,** one who goes about to see the sights of a place or places.

Sightsman (səi·tsmǣn). 1700. [f. pl. or gen. sing. of SIGHT *sb.*] **1.** A local guide, a cicerone. **2.** One who reads or performs music at sight 1776.

Sigil (si·dʒil). 1610. [– late L. *sigillum* sign, trace, impress, in med.L. seal (cl. L. *sigilla* n. pl. little images, seal), dim. of L. *signum* SIGN *sb.*] **1.** A seal or signet. **2.** *Astrol.* An occult sign or device supposed to have mysterious powers 1659. **3.** *Rom. Antiq.* A small image 1738.

2. Sign and s. well doth he know SCOTT.

‖**Sigillaria** (sidʒilēᵊ·riă). 1831. [mod.L., f. *sigillum* seal; see prec., -ARIA.] *Geol.* A fossil tree, the leaf-scars of which resemble the impressions of a seal, found chiefly in coal-deposits. Hence **Sigilla·rid.**

Sigillate (si·dʒileⁱt), *v.* 1471. [– *sigillat-*, pa. ppl. stem of *sigillare* in med.L. senses, f. late L. *sigillum* SIGIL.] *trans.* To seal; to seal up. Hence **Si·gillated** *ppl. a.* impressed with a seal; esp. *sigillated earth*, Lemnian earth, sphragide. **Sigilla·tion.**

‖**Sigla** (si·glă). 1706. [Late L. *sigla* n. pl., perh. for *singula*, n. pl. of *singulus* SINGLE; cf. *singulæ litteræ*, so used.] Letters (esp. initials) or other characters used to denote words; abbreviations or marks of abbreviation. Also in sing., **siglum.**

Sigma (si·gmă). 1607. [– L. *sigma*, Gr. σίγμα, the 18th letter of the Greek alphabet]. **1.** The name of the Greek letter Σ, σ, ς, the equivalent of the English S, s, in its uncial form having the shape of C. **2.** Something having the form of S or C 1788. Hence **Si·gmate** *v. trans.* to add a s. or *s* to (a word, stem, etc.). **Sigmatic** (sigmæ·tik) *a.* characterized by the addition of s. or *s* to the stem. **Si·gmatism,** the marked use or repetition of *s*; an instance of this.

Sigmodont (si·gmŏdǫnt), *a.* and *sb.* 1877. [– mod.L. *Sigmodontes*, f. Gr. σίγμα SIGMA + ὀδούς, ὀδοντ- tooth; cf. MASTODONT.] *Zool.* **A.** *adj.* Belonging to the *Sigmodontes*, a class of murine animals in which the molars exhibit sigmoid patterns. **B.** *sb.* An animal belonging to this class.

Si·gmoid (si·gmoid), *a.* and *sb.* 1670. [– Gr. σιγμοειδής; see SIGMA and -OID.] Chiefly *Anat.* **A.** *adj.* **1.** Having the shape of the uncial sigma C; crescent-shaped, semicircular. Chiefly in *s. cavity, notch, valve.* **2.** Having a double curve like the letter S 1786.

2. *S. flexure*, the last curving portion of the colon before terminating in the rectum.

B. *sb.* The sigmoid flexure of the colon 1891. So **Sigmoi·dal** *a.* = A. 1666; **-ly** *adv.*

Sign (səin), *sb.* ME. [– (O)Fr. *signe* – L. *signum* mark, token.] **I. 1.** A gesture or motion of the hand, head, etc., serving to convey an intimation or to communicate some idea. **b.** A signal 1601. **2.** A mark or device having some special meaning or import attached to it, or serving to distinguish the thing on which it is put ME. **b.** A conventional mark, device, or symbol, used techn. (as in music, mathematics, botany) in place of words or names written in ordinary letters 1557. †**3.** A mark of attestation (or ownership) written or stamped upon a document, seal, etc. –1609. †**4. a.** A device borne on a banner, shield, etc.; a cognizance or badge –1562. **b.** Something displayed as an emblem or token; *esp.* an ensign, banner, standard –1667. **5.** A characteristic device attached to, or placed in front of an inn (†house) or shop, as a means of distinguishing it from others or directing attention to it; in later use commonly a board bearing a name or other inscription, with or without some ornament or picture 1467.

1. Then Hudibras, with face and hand, Made signs for Silence BUTLER. **b.** Mark Antony, shall we giue signe of Battaile? SHAKS. **2.** *S. of the Cross*: cf. CROSS *sb.* 3. **b.** Two minus signs in arithmetic or algebra make a plus 1875. **4. b.** The great Ensign of Messiah blaz'd Aloft by Angels born, his S. in Heav'n MILT. **5.** Putting up their pictures as signs for their taverns and ale-houses 1780. Phr. *At the s. of* (*the Bell, Sun*, etc.). †*At the s. of the moon*, in the open air by night (after Fr. *à l'enseigne de la lune*).

II. 1. A token or indication (visible or otherwise) *of* some fact, quality, etc.; also *spec.* in *Med.* (= symptom), etc. ME. **b.** *U.S.* The trail or trace of wild animals, etc. (occas. in pl., but the sing. is the technical use) 1847. **2.** A trace or indication *of* something; a vestige. Chiefly in neg. phrases. ME. †**b.** A mere semblance *of* something –1693. **3.** An indication of some coming event; *spec.* an omen or portent ME. **4.** An act of a miraculous nature, serving to demonstrate divine power or authority. (In biblical use, after L. *signum*, Gr. σημεῖον) ME. **5.** *Astr.* One or other of the twelve equal divisions of the Zodiac, each distinguished by the name of a constellation and freq. denoted by a special symbol ME.

1. What meanest thou by this word Sacrament? I meane an outward and visible signe, of an inward and spirituall grace. *Bk. Com. Prayer, Catechism* 1604. [It was] no s. of grace, For folks in fear are apt to pray GRAY. Phr. *In s. of* (or *that*); In signe of truth, I kisse your Highnesse Hand SHAKS. **b.** We had noticed bear 'sign' in a thick patch of rose-bushes 1890. **2.** There is no s. of life in this wild place 1872. **b.** If it be but to punish that s. of a Husband there DRYDEN. **3.** These signs the coming mischief did foretell SHELLEY. **4.** Many wonders and signes were done by the Apostles *Acts* 2:43. **5.** I was looking..on that S. in the Heavens which is called by the Name of the Ballance STEELE.

Sign (səin), *v.*¹ ME. [– (O)Fr. *signer* – L. *signare*, f. *signum* SIGN *sb.*] **I. 1.** *trans.* To mark, protect, consecrate, etc., *with* the sign of the cross. **b.** To cross (*esp.* oneself). late ME. **c.** To make the sign of (the cross) by a movement of the hand 1810. **2.** To place some distinguishing mark upon (a thing or person); to mark with a sign. late ME. †**3.** To put a seal upon (something). Also *intr.*, to use seals. –1638. **4.** To attest or confirm by adding one's signature; to affix one's name to (a document, etc.) 1477. **b.** To fix *down*, make *over*, give *away*, by signing 1589. **5.** *intr.* To affix one's signature (*to*) 1617. **6.** *trans.* To write or inscribe (one's name) as a signature 1817. **b.** *refl.* To denominate or designate (oneself) in a signature or signatures 1885. **c.** To engage by the signing of an agreement. Also with *on*. 1889.

1. He kissed the ground and signed himself with the cross 1878. **b.** Then, s. thyself, and peaceful go thy ways 1861. **2.** *fig.* Earth, Air, and Seas, with Prodigies were sign'd DRYDEN. **4.** I am not well, send the deed after me, And I will signe it SHAKS. *fig.* Turner always signs a locality with some given incident RUSKIN. **b.** Signing away vague and enormous sums of money DICKENS. **6.** Then you should s. your name in their presence 1858. **c.** The men can only be 'signed on' in the presence of the Board of Trade officer 1894. *To s. up* (U.S.), to enlist.

II. 1. a. To indicate, signify, betoken. late ME. †**b.** *intr.* To prognosticate, bode –1606. **2. a.** To make a sign or signs by some movement of the hand, etc. 1700. **b.** *trans.* To intimate, convey, by a sign 1719.

1. b. Musicke i' th' Ayre..It signes well, do's it not? SHAKS. **2. b.** Upon this he sign'd to me, that he should bury them with Sand DE FOE. Hence **Si·gnable** *a.* **Signer** (səi·nəɹ), a signatory; *spec.* (*U.S.*), one of the signatories to the Declaration of Independence.

†**Sign,** *v.*² ME. [aphet. f. ASSIGN *v.*] *trans.* To assign, appoint –1582.

Signal (si·gnăl), *sb.* late ME. [– (O)Fr. *signal*, alt. of earlier *seignal* :– Rom. (med.L.) *signale*, subst. use of n. of late L. *signalis*, f. *signum* SIGN; see -AL¹.] †**1. a.** A visible sign; a badge or symbol –1601. †**b.** A mark of distinction or honour –1685. **2.** A sign, token, or indication (*of* something) 1591. **3.** A sign agreed upon or understood as the occasion of concerted action, *esp.* one ordering the movement of troops or ships; also *fig.* an exciting cause 1593. **4.** A sign or notice, perceptible by sight or hearing, given esp. for the purpose of conveying warning, direction, or information 1598. **b.** An object serving to convey an intimation 1687. **c.** *Electr.* The intelligence, message, etc. conveyed in telegraphy or telephony.

2. The wearie sonne..Giues signall of a goodlie day to-morrow SHAKS. **3.** The s. of battle being given with two cannon shot we marched in order of battalia DE FOE. **4.** A bell rang which was a s...that a train was coming 1896. **b.** *Railway s.*, an apparatus by which engine drivers ascertain whether the line is clear.

attrib. and *Comb.*, as *s. apparatus, beacon, fire,* etc.; *s. box, cabin,* etc.; *s. corps, lieutenant,* etc.; **s. strength,** the strength of reception of wireless signals. Hence **Si·gnalist,** one who makes signals; one specially employed in signalling; a signaller.

Signal (si·gnăl), *a.* 1641. [– Fr. *signalé*, earlier †*segnalé* – It. *segnalato*, pa. pple. of *segnalare* make illustrious, f. *segnale* SIGNAL *sb.* For the loss of final syll. cf. ASSIGN *sb.*[2], COSTIVE, DEFILE *sb.*] **1.** Distinguished from the ordinary as by some sign or mark; notable. **2.** Constituting or serving as a sign 1655.

Hence **Si·gnally** *adv.*

Signal (si·gnăl), *v.* 1805. [f. the sb.] **1.** *trans.* To make signals to (a person, ship, etc.); to summon, direct, or invite by signal. **2. a.** To communicate or make known by signalling; to notify or announce by signal(s) 1871. **b.** To mark out clearly 1869. **3.** To work (a railway) in respect of signals; to furnish with signalling apparatus 1888. **4.** *intr.* To give notice, warning, or information, or make any other communication, by signal 1864.

1. We were all signalled to be present at the Ferry Depôt 1892. **2. a.** Soon as..thine eyes shall s. a welcome 1871. **4.** They are signalling night and day..by flag and fire 1864.

Signa·lity. Now *rare.* 1646. [f. SIGNAL *sb.* or *a.* + -ITY.] †**1.** The quality of a sign or indication. SIR T. BROWNE. †**2.** Signification; significance –1693. **3.** Notability 1650.

Signalize (si·gnăləiz), *v.* 1654. [f. SIGNAL *a.* + -IZE.] **1.** *trans.* To make signal; to distinguish; to render conspicuous, remarkable, or noteworthy. **b.** To display in a striking manner 1702. **2.** To characterize or mark conspicuously 1698. **3.** To point out, note or mention specially, draw attention to 1711. **4.** To make signals to; to communicate with by means of a signal 1824. **b.** *intr.* To make or send signals 1853.

1. She named Whitgift.., who had already signalised his pen in controversy HUME. **b.** Has he ever signalised his courage? 1702. **2.** The cheers which signalised the success of the Minister's speech 1882. **4.** They were signalising their consort with lights BYRON. Hence **Si·gnaller,** *U.S.* **signaler,** one who or that which signals.

Si·gnalman. 1737. [f. SIGNAL *sb.*] **1.** (Chiefly *Naval.*) A man employed to make, convey, display, or give signals. **2.** A railway employee who attends to the signals which show whether the line is clear or not 1840.

Signate (si·gnĕt), *a.* 1649. [– L. *signatus*, pa. pple. of *signare* SIGN *v.*] Marked or distinguished in some way.

Signation (signēi·ʃən). Now *rare.* 1607. [– late and med.L. *signatiō(n-* signing (of the cross), f. as prec.; see -ION.] **1.** The action of signing with the cross, or of marking with a seal. †**2.** A distinctive mark –1653.

Signatory (si·gnătəri), *a.* and *sb.* 1647. [– L. *signatorius*, f. as prec.; see -ORY.] **A.** *adj.* †**1.** Used in sealing (*rare*) –1656. **2.** Forming one of those (persons or states) whose signatures are attached to a document 1870.

2. An understanding with the s. Powers 1870.

B. *sb.* One of those whose signatures are attached to a document of any kind 1866.

Signature (si·gnătiŭɹ, -tʃəɹ), *sb.* 1580. [– med.L. *signatura* sign manual (in late L. marking of sheep), f. as prec.; see -URE.] **1.** The name (†or special mark) of a person written with his or her own hand as an authentication of some document or writing. **b.** The action of signing one's name, or of authenticating a document by doing so 1621. †**2.** The action of impressing or stamping. BACON. **3.** A distinctive mark, a peculiarity in form or colouring, etc., on a plant or other natural object, formerly supposed to be an indication of its qualities, esp. for medicinal purposes. Now *Hist.* 1613. **b.** A distinguishing mark of any kind 1626. **c.** A stamp, impression 1649. **4.** An image; a figure; an imitative mark. Now *rare* or *Obs.* 1658. **5.** *Printing.* A letter or figure, a set or combination of letters or figures, etc., placed by the printer at the foot of the first page (and frequently on one or more of the succeeding pages) of every sheet in a book, for the purpose of showing the order in which these are to be placed or bound. Abbrev. *sig.* 1656. **b.** A sheet, as distinguished by its signature 1712. **6.** *Mus.* A sign, or set of signs, placed at the beginning of a piece of music, immediately after the clef, to indicate its key or time 1806.

1. I wish I had Miss MacWhirter's s. to a cheque for five thousand pounds THACKERAY. **3.** Whether men, as they say of plants, have signatures to discover their nature by, is hard to determine 1697.

Comb. **s.-tune,** a special tune used in broadcasting to announce a particular band, etc. Hence **Si·gnaturist** (*rare*), one who maintains the theory of signatures in plants.

Signature (si·gnătiŭɹ, -tʃəɹ), *v.* 1653. [f. the sb.] †**1.** *trans.* To indicate symbolically; to mark out, designate –1740. **2.** *Printing.* To put a signature on (a sheet) 1889. **3.** To put one's signature to; to authenticate or confirm by one's signature 1900.

Sign-board (səi·nbōᵊɹd). 1632. [SIGN *sb.* I. 5.] A board on which the sign of a shop, inn, or other place of business is painted or otherwise displayed.

Signet (si·gnėt), *sb.* ME. [– (O)Fr. *signet* or med.L. *signetum*, dim. of *signe, signum* seal; see SIGN *sb.*, -ET.] **1.** A small seal, usu. one fixed in a finger-ring. **2.** A small seal of this kind in formal or official use. late ME. **3.** *spec.* The smaller seal orig. used by the sovereigns of England and Scotland for private purposes and for certain documents of an official character. Also called *privy* or *King's* (*Queen's*) *s.* Hence *Clerk of* (or *to*), *Keeper of, the s.* late ME. **4.** An impressed seal or stamp; *esp.* the stamp or impression of a signet. late ME. **b.** *fig.* A mark, sign, stamp 1662.

1. Taking his s. from his finger 1770. **2.** She wrote a letter vnder Achabs name, and sealed it with his s. COVERDALE 1 *Kings* 21:8. *Writer to the s.* (Sc.): see WRITER. Hence **Si·gnet** *v. trans.* (*Sc.*), to stamp with a signet.

Si·gnet-ri:ng. 1681. [SIGNET *sb.*] A finger-ring containing a signet.

†**Si·gneur,** obs. var. of SENIOR *sb.* SHAKS.

Signifer (si·gnifəɹ). Now *rare.* late ME. [– L. *signifer*, f. *signum* SIGN *sb.* + *-fer* bearing.] †**1.** The zodiac –1601. **2.** A standard-bearer, leader (*rare*) 1450.

1. And S. his kandles sheweth brighte CHAUCER.

Significance (signi·fikăns). 1450. [– OFr. *significance* or L. *significantia*, f..*significant-*; see SIGNIFICANT, -ANCE.] **1.** The meaning or import *of* something. **b.** Without const.: Meaning; suggestiveness 1814. **2.** Importance, consequence 1725.

1. Empty sentences, that have..the s. of nothing pertinent MILT. **b.** A parting smile and nod of s. SCOTT. **2.** The omission is not of any real s. 1875.

Significancy (signi·fikănsi). 1595. [See prec. and -ANCY.] **1.** The quality of being highly significant. **2.** The quality of being significant, of having a meaning or import 1631. **b.** = prec. 1. 1641. **3.** = prec. 2. 1679.

1. Antiquated words..are never to be reviv'd, but when Sound or S. is wanting in the present Language DRYDEN.

Significant (signi·fikănt), *a.* and *sb.* 1579. [– *significant-*, pr. ppl. stem of L. *significare*; see SIGNIFY *v.*, -ANT.] **A.** *adj.* **1.** Full of meaning or import. **b.** Important, notable 1761. **2.** Signifying something 1597. **3.** Expressive or indicative *of* something 1793.

1. His words few, but s. and weighty 1668. A s. act followed these emphatic words 1874. **b.** A little man may be a very s. man 1857. **2.** Math. *To* (so many) *s. figures*: with the degree of accuracy indicated by the figures given, sequences of 0's at the end (of an integral number) or at the beginning (of a decimal fraction) not being counted.

B. *sb.* Something which conveys or expresses a meaning; a sign, symbol, indication 1588.

Since you are tongue-ty'd, and so loth to speake, In dumbe significants proclayme your thoughts SHAKS. So **Signi·ficantly** *adv.* in a s. manner 1577.

Significate (signi·fikĕt), *sb.* 1449. [– late L. *significatum*, subst. use of n. pa. pple. of L. *significare*; see SIGNIFY *v.*, -ATE[1]. Cf. Fr. †*significat.*] That which is signified or symbolized.

Signification (si:gnifikēi·ʃən). ME. [– (O)Fr. *signification* – L. *significatiō(n-*, f. *significat-*, pa. ppl. stem of *significare*; see SIGNIFY *v.*, -ION.] **1.** The fact or property of being significant or expressive of something. **b.** Importance, consequence, significance. Now *rare* or *dial.* 1670. **2.** That which is signified by something; meaning, import, implication. Freq. const. *of.* late ME. **3.** A thing, event, etc., which is significant or expressive of something ME. **4.** An indication or intimation of something. late ME. **b.** *spec.* Notification in proper legal form 1533.

1. The Rainbow hath in it two contrary significations, *viz.* of rain, and fair-weather 1643. **2.** Shewe me the dreame and the significacion of it COVERDALE *Dan.* 2:6. **4.** Feeling myself inspired with courage by the s. of your noble desire..I stoutly fell to my taske 1638.

Significative (signi·fikătiv), *a.* and *sb.* late ME. [– (O)Fr. *significatif, -ive*, or late L. *significativus*, f. as prec.; see -IVE.] **A.** *adj.* **1.** Serving to signify something; having a signification or meaning. **b.** Serving as a sign or indication *of* something 1637. **2.** Highly significant or suggestive 1677.

1. It does not appear that, like the bees, they emit any s. sounds 1816. **2.** A most s. and mysterious warning 1855.

B. *sb.* A thing or word serving to signify or indicate something 1641.

Hence **Signi·ficative-ly** *adv.*, **-ness.**

Significator (si·gnifikeitəɹ). 1584. [– late L. *significator*, in med.L. astrol. use, f. as prec.; see -OR 2.] **1.** *Astrol.* The planet by which the querent or the quesited is specially signified. **2.** That which signifies or indicates (*rare*) 1649.

1. The position of the S., or lord of the Ascendant, in the fixed sign Taurus 1895.

Significatory (signi·fikătəri), *a.* Now *rare.* 1579. [– late L. *significatorius* (in med.L. *litteræ significatoriæ*), f. as prec.; see -ORY[2].] Serving to signify or intimate.

‖**Significavit** (signifikēi·vit). late ME. [L., 3rd sing. perf. indic. of *significare* SIGNIFY.] *Eccl. Law.* A form of writ employed in ecclesiastical cases; *spec.* one formerly issued by Chancery for the arrest of an excommunicated person; also, the bishop's certificate on which such a writ is based.

Signify (si·gnifəi), *v.* ME. [– (O)Fr. *signifier* – L. *significare*, f. *signum* SIGN *sb.*; see -FY.] **1.** *trans.* To be a sign or symbol of; to represent, betoken, mean. Also *absol.* **b.** To foreshow, indicate as something that is to take place ME. **2.** Of words, etc.: To have the import or meaning of; to mean, denote. Also *absol.* ME. **3.** To make known, intimate, announce, declare ME. †**4.** To notify or inform (a person) –1690. **5.** *intr.* To be of importance or consequence; to have significance; to avail or matter 1661.

1. The secret grace which they [the sacraments] signifie and exhibit 1597. **b.** A gret sterre,.. whiche synified gret sorw, & myschef þat fylle aftyrward 1475. **2.** We now employ the term *Energy* to s. the power of doing work 1876. **3.** Scott's wish as signified in the letter last quoted LOCKHART. **5.** But it signify'd little 1686. His eye is still bloodshot, but nothing to s. 1817.

Sign-manual. late ME. [– AL. *signum manuale* (*c*1204; earlier *signum manus* 676); see SIGN *sb.*, MANUAL *a.*] **1.** An autograph signature (*esp.* that of the sovereign) serving to authenticate a document. **2.** A sign made with the hand or hands 1841.

‖**Signor** (sī·nyǫɹ). 1577. [– It. *signor* clipped form of *signore* :– L. *senior, seniōr-*; see SENIOR, SIRE, and cf. SEIGNEUR, SEÑOR, SENHOR.] **1.** The Italian term of respect placed before the name of a man in addressing him or speaking of him, now = English 'Mr.' 1584. **b.** Used without the name = 'sir' in English 1590. **c.** An Italian gentleman, *esp.* a singer 1779. **2.** A person of note or distinction; one having rank or authority; a gentleman or nobleman; an overlord. See also GRAND SIGNIOR. 1577.

1. A thousand thankes signior Gremio SHAKS. **b.** The stranger..said, 'S., your steps are watched' 1797.

‖**Signora** (sinyǭ·ră). 1636. [It., fem. of next. Cf. SEÑORA, SENHORA.] The Italian term of respect applied to ladies, corresponding to 'Mrs.' and 'Madam' in English; hence (with *a, the,* etc.), a lady of Italian nationality.

‖**Signore** (sinyǭ·re). 1594. [It.; see SIGNOR.] = SIGNOR.

‖**Signoria** (sinyorī·a). 1549. [It.; cf. SIGNORY.] The governing body of some of the old Italian republics, *esp.* that of Venice.

‖**Signorina** (sinyorī·nă). 1820. [It., dim. of SIGNORA.] The Italian term of respect applicable to a young unmarried lady.

†**Si·gnorize,** *v.* 1588. [f. SIGNOR + -IZE, or – *signoriss-*, extended stem of Fr. *seign-, signorir,* f. *seigneur* SEIGNEUR, assim. to vbs. in -IZE. Cf. †*seignorize* (XVII).] **1.** *intr.* To rule, reign, have or exercise dominion (*in, over*) –1658. **2.** *trans.* To govern, control, exercise dominion or rule over –1602.

Signory (sī·nyŏri). late ME. [orig. – OFr. *signerie, signorie,* etc., vars. of *seignorie,* subseq. infl. by It. *signoria.*] **1.** Lordship, domination, rule. **2.** A lordship, domain, territory 1533. **3.** A governing body, *esp.* that of Venice or other mediæval Italian republic 1604.

2. His Sons..won them Lands and Signories in Germany MILT. Hence **Signo·rial** *a.*

Si·gn-post. 1620. [SIGN *sb.*] **1.** A post supporting a sign, usu. that of an inn or shop. **2.** A guide- or direction-post, set up to indicate the proper road to a place; a finger-post 1863.

1. When did the Lamb and Dolphin ever meet, except upon a Sign-Post? ADDISON.

Sike, syke (səik), *sb.*[1] *north.* and *Sc.* ME. [The northern form repr. OE. *sīc,* ME. *siche,* dial. *sitch.* Cf. ON. *sík.* Thus DIKE, DITCH.] A small stream of water, a rill or streamlet, esp. one flowing through flat or marshy ground, and often dry in summer; a ditch or channel through which a tiny stream flows.

Sike (səik), *v.* Now *dial.* ME. [var. of ME. *sīhen*; see SIGH *v.*] **1.** *intr.* To sigh. †**2.** *trans.* To emit (a sigh). ME. only. So **Sike** *sb.*[2] a sigh.

Sikh (sik, sīk). 1781. [– Hindi *sikh* :– Skr. *sishya* disciple.] **1.** A member of a military community belonging to the Punjab, where it was originally established as a religious sect by Nanak Shah in the early part of the 16th c. **2.** *attrib.* or *adj.* Of or pertaining to the Sikhs 1845. Hence **Si·khism,** the tenets of the Sikhs.

Silage (səi·lédʒ). 1884. [Alteration of ENSILAGE, after SILO.] = ENSILAGE 2.

Sile (səil), *sb.*[1] *north.* and *Sc.* 1459. [– ON. **síl* (Norw. and Sw. *sil*); cf. SILE *v.*[2]] A strainer or sieve, esp. one for milk.

Sile (səil), *sb.*[2] *north.* and *Sc.* 1769. [Of Scand. origin; cf. ON. and Icel. *síld,* etc.] Young herring.

Sile, *v.*[1] *Obs.* exc. *n. dial.* ME. [prob. of Scand. origin.] **1.** *intr.* To go, pass, move; to glide. **2.** To fall or sink (*down*). late ME. **3.** †**a.** Of tears, etc.: To flow –1878. **b.** *dial.* Of rain: To pour (*down*) 1703.

Sile, *v.*[2] Now *dial.* late ME. [Of Scand. origin; cf. MSw. *siila, sila,* Sw. and Norw. *sila* in the same sense.] *trans.* To strain; *esp.* to pass (milk) through a sieve or strainer.

Silence (səi·lĕns), *sb.* ME. [– (O)Fr. *silence* – L. *silentium,* f. *silens, -ent-,* pr. pple. of *silēre* be silent; see -ENCE.] **1.** The fact of abstaining or forbearing from speech or utterance; the state or condition resulting from this; muteness, reticence, taciturnity. Occas. with *a* or in pl. **b.** Used imperatively, = Be silent; make no noise 1590. **2.** The state or condition when nothing is audible; complete quietness or stillness; noiselessness. Also const. *of* (the night, etc.). late ME. **b.** Used allusively to denote the state beyond this life. Chiefly in pl. and with initial capital. 1803. **3.** Omission of mention, remark, or notice in narration 1513. **b.** Neglect or omission to write (about something); failure to communicate or reply 1617. **4.** *Mus.* A rest 1752.

1. Nor dream that I will..with my s. sanction tyranny SHELLEY. Phr. *To keep s., to break s., in s. To put to s.,* to silence by argument or prohibition; †to put to death. *S. gives consent*: see CONSENT *sb.* 1. **b.** S., ye troubl'd waves, and thou Deep, peace MILT. **2.** Through the soft s. of the list'ning night MILT. **b.** Power to make Our noisy years seem moments in the being Of the eternal S. WORDSW. **3.** Phr. *To pass with, pass over in, s.*

Silence (səi·lĕns), *v.* 1560. [f. prec.] **1.** *trans.* To cause or compel (a person) to cease speaking on a particular occasion; also, to overcome in argument 1603. **b.** To cause (an animal or thing) to cease from giving out its natural sound; to still, quieten; (*colloq.*) to put to death 1604. **2.** To reduce (a person, etc.) to silence by restraint or prohibition, esp. in order to prevent the free expression of opinions 1597. **b.** To put down, repress (any expression of feeling, etc.) 1647. **3.** *Mil.* and *Naval.* To compel (a gun, battery, or ship) to cease firing; to disable by superior fire; to stop (the fire of a gun) 1748. **4.** *intr.* To cease speaking; to become silent or still (*rare*) 1560.

1. This learned priest has silenc'd the parson 1733. **b.** S. that dreadfull Bell, it frights the Isle, From her propriety SHAKS. **2. b.** A threat of excommunication silenced the murmurs of the clergy 1874. **3.** We silenced three of her lower deck guns 1755.

Silencer (səi·lĕnsəɹ). 1635. [f. SILENCE *v.* + -ER[1].] **1.** One who, or that which, silences; a conclusive argument or retort. **2.** A piece of mechanism used to silence or reduce the sound caused by the working of a piece of machinery, as a motor vehicle, a maxim gun or rifle, a water cistern, etc. 1898.

Silene (səilī·ni). 1785. [mod.L. – L. *Silenus* – Gr. Σειληνός species of satyr.] *Bot.* A genus of caryophyllaceous plants typifying the family *Silenaceæ*; a plant belonging to this genus; catchfly.

Silent (səi·lĕnt), *a.* and *sb.* 1565. [– L. *silens, -ent-,* pr. pple. of *silēre* be silent; see -ENT.] **A.** *adj.* **1.** Keeping silence; refraining from speech or utterance; mute, dumb. Also, taciturn, reserved. **2.** Of writers, books, etc.: Omitting mention of or reference to something in narration; containing no account or record 1601. **3.** Characterized by silence or absence of speech; performed, made, suffered, etc., in silence or without speaking 1592. **b.** Of letters: Not sounded; mute 1605. **4.** Characterized by the absence of sound or noise; quiet, noiseless, still 1588. **b.** Making or giving out little or no noise 1753. **5.** †**a.** Of the moon: Not shining –1727. **b.** Inactive, not operative 1745. **c.** Of distilled spirit: Possessing no flavour 1839.

1. He is as s. as a Stone 1580. The s. sow sups all the broth 1828. *fig.* My duty cannot be s., when I thinke your Highnesse wrong'd SHAKS. **2.** As to the other shire..history is equally s. 1871. **3.** *The s. system,* a method of discipline enforced in a prison, penitentiary, etc., which imposes complete silence on all occasions. **b.** The final *e* seems to have become s. 1869. **4.** Three mountain-tops, Three s. pinnacles of aged snow TENNYSON. *Mod.* A s. film (opp. to *talkie*). **5. b.** A volcano, after being s. for ages, may suddenly start forth into fresh life 1878. Hence **Si·lent-ly** *adv.*, **-ness.**

B. *sb.* †**1.** The time of silence. SHAKS. **2.** A device by which a clock or alarm may be prevented from striking or acting 1834. **3.** A s. film 1929.

1. Deepe Night, darke Night, the s. of the Night SHAKS.

Silentiary (səile·nʃ[i]ări). 1611. [– L. *silentiarius,* a confidential domestic servant; in later Empire, a privy counsellor, f. *silentium*; see SILENCE, -ARY[1]. Cf. Fr. *silenciaire* (XVII).] **1.** One who observes or recommends silence, *esp.* from religious motives. **2.** An officer of the Byzantine court, whose duty orig. was to obtain silence, but who frequently acted as a confidential adviser or agent. Now *Hist.* 1677. **b.** An official whose duty it is to command silence 1838.

‖**Silenus** (səilī·nŏs). *Pl.* **Sileni** (səilī·nəi). 1710. [L.; see SILENE.] **1.** *Gr. Myth.* The foster-father of Bacchus, and leader of the satyrs; also, a wood-god, a satyr. **2.** *Zool.* A species of macaque 1871.

Silesia (səilī·ʃ[i]ă). 1674. [Latinized form of G. *Schlesien,* a province in the east of Germany.] **1.** Used *attrib.* with *cloth, lawn,* etc. = SILESIAN. **b.** A fine linen or cotton fabric orig. manufactured in Silesia 1727. **2.** A variety of lettuce 1731. So **Sile·sian** *a.* of or pertaining to S.; *sb.* a native of S. 1645.

Silex (səi·leks). 1592. [L.] Flint, silica.

Silhouette (silu,e·t), *sb.* 1798. [f. Étienne de *Silhouette* (1709–1767), a French author and politician.] **1.** A portrait obtained by tracing the outline of a profile, head, or figure, and filling in the whole with black; an outline portrait cut out of black paper; a figure or picture drawn or printed in solid black. **b.** *fig.* A slight verbal sketch in outline of a person, etc. 1819. **2.** A dark outline, a shadow in profile, thrown up against a lighter background 1847.

1. Phr. *En* (or *in*) *s.*, in outline, in profile.

Silhoue·tte, *v.* 1876. [f. prec.] **1.** *trans.* To represent in silhouette. **2.** *intr.* To show like a silhouette 1884.

1. I have seen it silhouetted hard against tornado-clouds 1897. Hence **Silhoue·ttist.**

Silica (si·likă). 1801. [f. L. *silex, silic-* flint, after *alumina,* etc.] An important mineral substance (the dioxide of silicon), which in the form of quartz enters into the composition of many rocks, and is contained in sponges and certain plants. Hence **Si·licide** *Chem.*, a compound of silicon with another element. **Silici·ferous** *a.* yielding or producing silex or s.

Silicate (si·likĕt). 1811. [f. prec. + -ATE[4].] A salt produced by the action of silicic acid. *Comb.*: **s. board,** a board made incombustible by being saturated with s.; **s. cotton,** slag-wool. So **Si·licated** *a.* coated or impregnated with silex or silica. **Silica·tion,** combination with silica; silicification. **Silicatiza·tion,** silicification.

Sili·ceo-, comb. form of SILICEOUS, as in *s.-calcareous,* etc.

Siliceous (sili·ʃəs), *a.* 1656. [f. L. *siliceus,* f. *silex, silic-* flint, + -OUS.] Containing or consisting of silica; of the nature of silica.

Silici- (si·lisəi), comb. form of SILEX or SILICA, as in *silicicalcareous,* etc.

Silicic (sili·sik), *a.* 1817. [f. SILICA + -IC.] *Chem.* Pertaining to, consisting of, or formed from silica. Chiefly in *s. acid* (H_4SiO_4).

Silicify (sili·sifəi), *v.* 1828. [f. *silica* (see SILICI-) + -FY.] **1.** *trans.* To convert into, impregnate with, silica 1830. **2.** *intr.* To undergo silicification 1828.

1. Fossil wood which has been 'silicified' 1872. So **Sili·cified** *ppl. a.* converted into silica; chiefly in *silicified wood* 1822. **Sili:cifica·tion,** the process of becoming silicified, conversion into silica.

Silicious (sili·ʃ[i]əs), *a.* 1721. [var. of *siliceous*; see -IOUS.] = SILICEOUS *a.*

Silicium (sili·ʃ[i]ŏm). 1808. [f. L. *silex, silic-* flint + -IUM; repl. by SILICON.] = SILICON q.v.

Siliciuret (sili·siŭret). 1827. [f. prec.; see -URET.] *Chem.* = SILICIDE. Hence **Sili·ciure:tted** *a.* combined or impregnated with silicon.

Silicle (si·lik'l). 1785. [– Fr. *silicule* or L. *silicula,* dim. of SILIQUE; see -ULE.] *Bot.* A small short seed-pod.

Silico- (si·liko), comb. form of SILICA or SILICON. **a.** With adjs., as *s.-alkaline, -fluoric,* etc. **b.** With nouns, as *s.-aluminate, -borate, -fluoride,* etc.

Silicon (si·likŏn). 1817. [f. L. *silex, silic-* flint. Named by T. Thomson (1817), in place of Sir H. Davy's SILICIUM (1808).] A non-metallic element, which in respect of its abundance in nature ranks next to oxygen, and is usu. found combined with this as *silica*; it may be obtained in the form of powder, scales, or crystals. Chemical symbol Si.

Silicosis (silikō[u]·sis). 1891. [f. L. *silex, silic-* flint + -OSIS.] *Path.* A lung disease induced by inhaling flinty or siliceous particles.

Siliculose (sili·kiŭlō[u]s), *a.* 1731. [f.

L. *silicula* (see SILICLE) + -OSE[1].] *Bot.* Bearing small short pods.

‖**Siliqua** (si·likwă). *Pl.* **-æ.** 1704. [L., pod or husk of leguminous plants.] *Bot.* A long pod-like seed-vessel. So **Silique** (silī·k). Hence **Sili·quiform** *a. Bot.* having the form of a s.

Siliquose (si·likwōus), *a.* 1693. [– mod.L. *siliquosus*, f. *siliqua*; see prec., -OSE[1]. Cf. Fr. *siliqueux* (XVI).] **1.** *Bot.* Bearing pods or siliques. **2.** Having the form of a silique 1821. **Si·liquous** *a.* (*rare*) 1668. = 1.

Silk (silk), *sb.* (and *a.*) [OE. *sioloc, seol(e)c*, for **siluc*, corresp. to ON. *silki* and OSl. (Russ.) *shelku*, Lith. †*zilkaĩ*, OPruss. (gen.) *silkas* – **sericum*, for late L. *sēricum*, n. of L. *sēricus*, f. *sēres* – Gr. Σῆρες (see SERGE), oriental people from whom silk was first obtained and passed through Slavonic countries into the Baltic trade.] **1.** The strong, soft, lustrous fibre produced by the larvæ of certain bombycine moths which feed upon mulberry leaves, etc., and by certain spiders; silken thread or filament. **2.** The cloth or textile fabric woven or made from this OE. **b.** Used allus. to indicate the rank of a King's (or Queen's) Counsel, marked by the right to wear a silk gown. Also collectively, denoting the persons wearing such gowns. 1810. **c.** As the material of a jockey's jacket 1891. **3.** With *a* and *pl.* A particular make of silk cloth or fabric 1538. **b.** *pl.* Garments made of silk; silk stockings 1508. **c.** A lady's silk dress 1861. **d.** A King's (or Queen's) Counsel; a 'silk gown' 1884. **4.** *U.S.* The silk-like filiform styles of unripe maize 1817. **5.** *attrib.* or as *adj.* Made of silk; silken ME. **b.** Clad in silk (*rare*) 1603. †**c.** Silky SHAKS.

1. *Artificial s.* [Fr. *soie artificielle*], thread or yarn manufactured from collodion or wood pulp; also, a fabric resembling silk made from this (abbrev. *art silk, artsilk*). **2. b.** Phr. *To receive, obtain,* or *take s.*

Comb.: **s.-coal,** a variety of coal found in Shropshire; **-glue,** sericin; **s. gown** = sense 3 d; **-gut,** the gut in the silkworm from which the s. is produced; **s. hat,** a cylindrical hat having a light stiff body covered with s. plush or shag; **s. paper,** a kind of tissue-paper; **-shag,** a local name for young herring; **s. snapper,** a Bermudan fish; **s. stocking,** a stocking made of s.; *U.S. politics*, a member of a section of the Whig party in the early 19th c.; **-thrower, -throwster,** one who converts raw s. into s. thread. **b. s.-oak,** *Grevillea robusta*; **-tree,** a low-headed spreading Amer. tree (*Albizzia julibrissin*), with very graceful foliage. **c.** In the names of various s.-producing insects: †**s.-fly,** the silkworm moth; **s. moth,** *Bombyx mori*; **-spider,** one or other of various species of s.-spinning spiders. **d.** In the names of birds: **s.-bunting** *U.S.*, one or other of the buntings of the genus *Spiza*, esp. *S. americana*; **s. cock,** a species of domestic fowl, esp. *Phasianus gallus* or *Gallus lanatus*, native to eastern Asia; **s. fowl,** a s. cock or hen; **-hen,** the female of the s. cock; **s. starling,** a species of starling (*Sturnus sericeus*), native to China. Hence **Silk** *v. trans.* to clothe in or cover with s. **Si·lker,** one who works in or with s.

Silk-cotton. 1697. [f. SILK *sb.* + COTTON *sb.*[1]] **1.** The silky, elastic down or fibre obtained from various bombaceous and other tropical trees, and chiefly used for packing, stuffing pillows and cushions, making paper, etc. **2.** *S. tree*, any of various species of tropical trees belonging to the genera *Bombax, Eriodendron, Ochroma*, and *Pachira*, producing s. 1712.

Silken (si·lk'n), *a.* OE. [f. SILK *sb.* + -EN[4].] **I. 1.** Made or consisting of silk. †**2.** Worked in silk (*rare*) –1597. †**3.** Producing silk; characterized by the prevalence of silk –1820. **4.** Clad in silk 1640.

1. They would not suffer a man to were a Ring, or a woman a s. gown 1645.

II. 1. Silky, silk-like; soft, glossy, shining, lustrous 1513. **2.** Of words, etc.: Elegant; ingratiating, soft, flattering. So of persons, their looks, voice, etc. 1588. **3.** Effeminate, luxurious 1599. **4.** Soft, sweet, balmy; gentle 1599. **b.** Of sounds: Soft, low 1784.

1. All day..in silence The s. butterflies glide 1871. **2.** Taffata phrases, s. tearmes precise SHAKS. **3.** The s. son of dalliance GRAY. **4. b.** The gray owl's s. flight. 1800. Hence **Si·lken** *v. trans.* to invest with a silky lustre.

Silk grass. Also **silk-grass.** 1620. [f. SILK *sb.* + GRASS *sb.*] **1. a.** One or other of various species of lustrous grasses native to America and the West Indies, esp. *Bromelia* or *Nidularium karatas*; also, the fibrous leaves produced by these. **b.** Applied to various species of aloe, agave, or yucca, or the fibre derived from these 1753. **2.** The grass *Oryzopsis cuspidata* of the western U.S., the glumes of which bear long silky hairs; also *Stipa comata* of the same region 1891.

Silkman (si·lkmǣn). 1553. [f. SILK *sb.* + MAN *sb.*] One who makes or deals in silks. So **Si·lkwo:man** 1440.

Si·lkstone. 1867. A variety of coal obtained at *Silkstone*, near Barnsley in Yorkshire.

Si·lk-tail. 1685. [tr. G. *seidenschwanz*, f. *seide* silk + *schwanz* tail.] The waxwing or Bohemian chatterer, *Garrulus bohemicus*.

Si·lkweed. Also **silk-weed.** 1846. [f. SILK *sb.* + WEED *sb.*[1]] *Bot.* **1.** *U.S.* A plant of the N. Amer. genus *Asclepias*. **2.** A plant of the genus *Conferva* 1857.

Si·lk-wi:nder. 1611. [f. SILK *sb.* + WINDER[1].] **1.** One who winds or coils silk filament or thread preparatory to weaving. **2. a.** A silk-reel. **b.** A machine by which silk thread in the hank is transferred to the bobbin before spinning. 1858.

Silkworm (si·lkwɒ̄ɹm). [OE. *seolcwyrm*; see SILK *sb.*, WORM *sb.*] **1.** The caterpillar of the mulberry-feeding moth *Bombyx* (or *Sericaria*) *mori*, orig. a native of northern China, which on changing into the pupa state spins a cocoon made of silken filament; also, the caterpillar of any bombycid or other moth which thus yields silken cocoons of commercial value. **2.** *contempt.* One who wears a silken dress 1613.

attrib. and *Comb.*: **s. gut,** a fine, strong, light gut, made of the drawn-out glands of the s.; **s. moth,** any of the various bombycid moths, whose larvæ produce cocoons; **s. rot,** a fungous plant, *Botrytis bassiana*, which kills silkworms in great numbers.

Silky (si·lki), *a.* 1611. [f. SILK *sb.* + -Y[1].] **1.** Silken; made or consisting of silk. **2.** Having the delicate softness of silk 1666. **b.** Of liquor: Having a soft delicate taste 1743. **3.** Of speech, manners, etc.: = SILKEN II. 2. 1778. **4. a.** Having the gloss of silk 1730. **b.** Having a texture like that of silk 1757. **5.** *Bot.* Covered with fine, soft, close-set hairs having a silk-like gloss; sericeous 1776. **6.** *Nat. Hist.* Having silk-like hair, plumage, etc. 1781. Hence **Si·lkily** *adv.* **Silkiness.**

Sill[1] (sil). [OE. *syll, sylle* = MLG. *sulle, sul*, MDu. *sulle*, rel. to MLG., MDu. *sille*, ON. *svill, syll*, and OHG. *swelli, swella* (G. *schwelle* threshold).] **1.** A strong, horizontal timber (occas. a stone or iron substitute for this) serving as the foundation of a wall or other structure; hence, †a large beam or piece of squared timber. **b.** *dial.* and *U.S.* One of the lower framing-timbers of a cart or railway-car 1875. **2.** The piece of wood- or stone-work forming the lower horizontal part of a window-opening. late ME. **b.** *Naut.* A port-sill 1815. **c.** *Fortif.* The inner edge of the bottom of an embrasure 1859. **3.** The threshold of a door or gateway; the lower horizontal part of a door-case 1591. **b.** *Mining.* The floor of a gallery in a mine 1747. **c.** A horizontal timber (or structure) at the bottom of the entrance to a dock or canal-lock, against which the gates close 1789. **4. a.** A kind of clay found in coal-measures 1774. **b.** *Geol.* A bed, layer, or stratum of rock 1794. **5.** The foot or lower part *of* a title-page or title 1834.

Sill[2]. 1787. Dial. var. of THILL.

Sillabub, syllabub (si·lăbʊb). 1537. [Of unkn. origin. Cf. SILLIBOUK.] **1.** A drink or dish made of milk or cream, curdled by the admixture of wine, cider, or other acid, and often sweetened and flavoured. **2.** *fig.* Something unsubstantial and frothy; *esp.* floridly vapid discourse or writing 1706.

Sillery (si·ləri). 1680. [f. *Sillery*, in the department of the Marne, Champagne.] A high-class wine produced in and around the village of Sillery in Champagne.

Sillibouk. *dial.* 1573. [var. of SILLABUB.] A sillabub.

Sillimanite (si·limănəit). 1830. [f. Benjamin *Silliman*, an American chemist (1779–1864); see -ITE[1] 2 b. Named by G. T. Bowen in 1824.] *Min.* A silicate of alumina, occurring in slender rhombic prisms or in fibrous masses.

Sillock (si·lək). *Sc.* 1654. [Orkney and Shetland dial.] A young coal-fish (saithe), at a certain stage of its first year.

Silly (si·li), *a.*, *sb.*, and *adv.* [Later form of ME. *sely* SEELY *a.*] **A.** *adj.* **1.** Deserving of pity, 'poor'. Now *north.* and *Sc.* **b.** Helpless, defenceless 1500. **2.** Feeble, frail; insignificant 1567. **b.** Weakly, ailing. *Sc.* and *north.* 1585. †**c.** Scanty, sorry, poor –1767. **3.** Unsophisticated, simple, ignorant. *Obs.* or *arch.* 1547. †**b.** Of humble rank; lowly –1647. **c.** Of things: Plain, simple, homely 1570. **4.** Feeble-minded, imbecile 1550. **5.** Foolish, empty-headed 1576. **b.** Of words, actions, etc.: Evincing or associated with foolishness 1588. **c.** *Cricket.* Applied to (the position of) point, mid-on, and mid-off, when they stand dangerously near the wicket 1900. **6.** Stunned, stupefied, dazed, as by a blow 1886.

1. Good wife, for your courtesie, Will ye lodge a s. poor man? 1724. **b.** His s. sheep, what wonder if they stray? COWPER. **2.** Thou onely art The mightie God, but I a sillie worm HERBERT. **b.** She was but of a s. constitution 1821. **c.** 3 *Hen. VI*, III, iii. 93. **3. c.** Perhaps their loves, or els their sheep, Was all that did their s. thoughts so busie keep MILT. **4.** The King's uncle, being rather weak in intellect, was called S. Billy 1881. **5.** Of this sort are they which creep into houses, and leade captiue s. women 2 *Tim.* 3:6. **b.** This is the silliest stuffe that ere I heard SHAKS. Phr. *S. season*, the months of August and September, when newspapers supply the lack of real news by articles or discussions on trivial topics. **6.** I..got knocked s. for my pains 1889. Hence **Si·llily** *adv.* **Si·lliness.**

B. *sb.* A silly or foolish person. *colloq.* 1858. You are not to be a s. 1896.

C. *adv.* In a foolish or silly manner. Now *dial.* or *colloq.* 1704.

Silly-how. Now *Sc.* and *north.* 1574. [f. *sely* SEELY *a.* + *how* HOUVE.] A child's caul.

Silo (səi·lou), *sb.* 1835. [– Sp. *silo* (whence also Fr. *silo*) :– L. *sirus* – Gr. σιρός pit to keep corn in. Cf. ENSILE *v.*] **1.** A pit or underground chamber used for the storage of grain, roots, etc. **2.** *spec.* A pit, or an air- and water-tight chamber, in which green food is preserved for fodder by ensilage 1881. Hence **Si·lo** *v. trans.* to put (green food) into a s.; to turn into ensilage.

‖**Silphium** (si·lfiɒm). 1753. [L. – Gr. σίλφιον.] A plant of the Mediterranean region, yielding a gum-resin or juice much valued by the ancients as a condiment or medicine; the juice obtained from this plant, also called LASER.

Silt (silt), *sb.* 1440. [prob. denoting orig. a salty deposit, and so perh. – a Scand. word repr. by Norw., Da. *sylt*, Norw. and Sw. dial. *sylta* salt marsh, sea beach, corresp. to OLG. *sulta* (LG. *sulte, sülte*; Du. *zult*), OHG. *sulza* (G. *sülze*) salt marsh, salt pan, brine, f. Gmc. **sult- *salt-* SALT.] Fine sand, clay, or other soil, carried by moving or running water and deposited as a sediment on the bottom or beach; sometimes occurring as a stratum in soil.

Comb.: **s.-snapper,** a Jamaican fish. Hence **Si·lty** *a.* of the nature of or resembling s.; composed of or containing s.

Silt, *v.* 1799. [f. the sb.] **1.** *intr.* Of a channel, river-bed, etc.: To become filled or choked *up* with silt or sediment. **b.** To flow or drift *in* after the manner of silt. Also *transf.* to pass gradually *away*. 1863. **2.** *trans.* Of silt: To fill, block, or choke *up* (a channel, etc.) by gradual accumulation. Chiefly in pa. pple. 1825. **b.** To cover *up* or *over* with silt 1830.

Silure (siliūᵊ·ɹ). 1802. [– Fr. *silure* – L. SILURUS.] *Ichth.* A siluroid fish, esp. the sheath-fish (*Silurus glanis*).

Silurian (siliūᵊ·riăn), *a.* and *sb.*[1] 1708. [f. L. *Silures*, an ancient British tribe which inhabited the south-eastern part of Wales.] **1.** Of or belonging to the ancient Silures, or to the district inhabited by them. **2.** *Geol.* The name given to the system or series of Palæozoic rocks lying immediately below the Devonian or Old Red Sandstone; of or belonging to this formation, or to the period when it was deposited 1835. **b.** As *sb.* in *pl.* Silurian strata 1842. So **Si·lurist,** a native of the district formerly inhabited by the Silures 1650.

Silu·rian, *sb.*[2] 1842. [f. SILURUS + -IAN.] A siluroid fish. So **Silu·rid, Silu·ridan,** *a.* and *sb.* = SILUROID.

Siluro- (siliū°·ro), used as a comb. form of SILURIAN *a.*, as *S.-Cambrian* adj.

Siluroid (siliū°·roid), *a.* and *sb.* 1849. [f. SILURUS + -OID.] *Ichth.* **A.** *adj.* Belonging to the family *Siluridæ*, of the order *Physostomi*; characterized by the want of true scales; having only a naked skin or large bony plates. **B.** *sb.* A siluroid fish 1851.

Silurus (siliū°·rǒs). *Pl.* **Siluri.** 1601. [– L. *silurus* – Gr. σίλουρος.] *Ichth.* A genus of fish typical of the family *Siluridæ*; a fish belonging to this genus, esp. the sly s. (*S. glanis*), or sheath-fish.

Silva, etc.: see SYLVA, etc.

Silver (si·lvəɹ), *sb.* and *a.* Also *Sc.* **siller.** [OE. *siolfor, seolfor* = OFris. *sel(o)ver*, OS. *silubar, silobar*, OHG. *sil(a)bar, silbir* (Du. *zilver*, G. *silber*), ON. *silfr*, Goth. *silubr*, Gmc. **silubr-*, rel. indeterminately to various Balto-Sl. forms, perh. all ult. of Oriental origin.] **A.** *sb.* **1.** One of the precious metals (in general use ranking next to gold), characterized in a pure state by its lustrous white colour and great malleability and ductility. Chem. symbol Ag. (Also applied to several natural or artificial substances resembling or imitating the real metal as *German, inflammable, mock s.*) **2.** The metal regarded as a valuable possession or medium of exchange; hence, silver coin; also (chiefly *Sc.*), money in general OE. **3.** Articles made of silver; silverware, silver plate ME. **4.** The metal as used for the ornamentation of textile fabrics; silver thread. late ME. **5.** As a tincture in heraldry, more commonly called ARGENT 1450. **6.** A silvery colour or lustre 1481. **7. a.** A variety of insect, fish, bird, etc., having silvery colouring or markings 1832. **b.** *Photogr.* A salt of silver, *esp.* nitrate of silver 1891.

3. For cups and s. on the burnish'd board Sparkled and shone TENNYSON.

B. *attrib.* passing into *adj.* **1.** Made or consisting of silver OE. **b.** Containing threads of silver, or some imitation of this 1728. **2.** Producing or yielding silver 1475. **3.** Of or pertaining to, connected with, characteristic of, silver or silver articles 1610. **b.** Denoting compounds of which silver forms a part 1797. **c.** Advocating, relating to, etc., the adoption of silver as a currency or standard 1890. **4.** Having the whiteness or lustre of silver; silvery. Chiefly *poet.* late ME. **5.** Of sounds: Having a clear gentle resonance like that of silver; soft-toned, melodious 1526. **b.** Eloquent, persuasive, sweet-spoken 1594. **6.** Of or pertaining to the silver age of Latin (SILVER AGE b.) 1889.

1. The British s. coinage 1858. **b.** *S.-lace*, wire coated with s. and woven into lace 1858. **2.** A rich s. mine 1789. **3.** Our gold and s. standards 1860. **b.** Gold of 20 carats with 4 carats of silver alloy 1879. **4.** Auncient men, upon whose siluer heads the Almond-tree hath blossomde NASHE. Faire Galatea, with thy silver Feet, O, whiter than the Swan DRYDEN. Provb. phr. *S. lining*; Don't let's be down-hearted! There's a s. lining to every cloud W. S. GILBERT. **5.** A Swaine..Marrying his sweet Noates with their siluer sound 1613.

attrib. and *Comb.*: **s.-bath,** a solution, esp. of s. nitrate, used for sensitizing photographic plates and printing-paper; a dish to contain this; **s. bronze,** a metallic powder used in s. printing; **-glance,** a variety of s. ore; argentite; **-grain,** the lines of the medullary rays in longitudinal sections of some woods as elm, oak, etc.; **s. lustre,** a composition used for silvering potter's ware; **-point,** the process of making a drawing with a s. pencil on specially prepared paper; a drawing made in this way; **s. print,** a photograph produced by **s.-printing,** the process of producing a photograph on paper sensitized by a s. salt; **s. sand,** a fine white sand used in horticulture, etc.; **s. screen** (see SCREEN *sb.*); **-side,** the upper part of a round of beef; **s. steel,** a fine steel containing a small amount of s.; **-stick,** 'the name given to a field-officer of the Life Guards when on palace duty'; **s. streak,** the English Channel; **s. thaw,** the phenomenon of rain freezing as it falls and forming a glassy coating on the ground, trees, etc.; **s. wedding,** the twenty-fifth anniversary of a wedding; **s. weight,** (*a*) the weight used for s.; (*b*) the equivalent weight in s. **b.** In names of beasts, insects, etc.; **s. fox,** a North Amer. variety of the red fox with black s.-tipped hairs, the black fox; **-line(s),** a species of moth. **c.** In names of birds, as **s.-bill,** (*a*) one of several birds of the genus *Munia*; (*b*) a South Amer. tyrant bird of the genus *Lichenops*; **-dun,** a particular breed of domestic pigeon; **s. pheasant,** any pheasant of the species *Euplocamus nycthemerus*; also, a local name for the S.-spangled Hamburgh; **s. plover,** the gray plover, *Squatarola helvetica*, etc. **d.** In names of fishes, as **s.-belly, -bream,** a small fish, *Gerres ovatus*; **s. eel,** the Broad-nosed Eel, *Anguilla latirostris*. **e.** In names of plants or trees, as **s. bell (tree),** *Halesia tetraptera* of the southern U.S.; **-bush,** the plant Jupiter's beard; **s. chain,** the white laburnum; **-tree,** a tree with silvery lanceolate leaves (*Leucadendron argenteum*), native to Cape Colony. Hence **Si·lveriness,** silvery quality or character. **Si·lverize** *v. trans.* to silver; to treat with a preparation of s.; to render silvery in colour. **Si·lverless** *a.* without money; having no money.

Silver (si·lvəɹ), *v.* 1440. [f. the sb.] **1.** *trans.* To cover or plate with silver; to coat with silver-leaf. Freq. with *over.* **b.** To coat (glass) at the back with a mixture of tinfoil and quicksilver, esp. for use as a mirror 1635. **2.** To invest or suffuse with a silvery hue or lustre 1594. **b.** To turn (the hair, beard, etc.) white or silvery 1602. **3.** *intr.* **a.** To flow with a silvery gleam 1807. **b.** To take on a silvery lustre 1878.

1. My coach..is silvered over, but no varnish yet laid on PEPYS. **b.** The amalgam of tin is largely used in what is called silvering mirrors 1833. **2.** The moon..silvered the wood on one side 1797. **b.** His Beard was..A Sable Siluer'd SHAKS. **3. b.** The darkness silvers away, the morn doth break BRIDGES.

Silver age. 1565. The second age of the world, according to the Greek and Latin poets, inferior in simplicity and happiness to the first or golden age. **b.** The period of Latin literature from the death of Augustus to that of Hadrian 1736.

Silver-coloured, *a.* 1594. [SILVER *sb.*] Having the colour of silver; of a greyish white hue with a metallic lustre.

Silver fir. 1707. [SILVER *sb.*] **1.** A tall species of fir (*Abies* or *Picea pectinata*) native to southern and central Europe and to some parts of Asia, introduced into Britain in the 17th c. and extensively used for planting. **b.** A tree belonging to this species 1789. **2.** Applied to various other species of fir 1831.

Si·lver(-)fish. 1703. **1.** One of the various silver-coloured fishes found in different parts of the world. **2.** An insect of the genus *Lepisma*, esp. *L. saccharina* or *domestica*; a bristletail or springtail 1855.

Silver(-)foil. late ME. [SILVER *sb.*] Silver beaten out thin; silver-leaf.

Silver(-)gilt. late ME. **1.** Gilt silver or silverware. **b.** *attrib.* or as *adj.* 1705. **2.** An imitation of gilding, consisting of silver-foil varnished with a yellow lacquer 1891.

Si·lver grass. Also **silver-grass.** 1600. **a.** The striped or ribbon-grass. **b.** The Australasian grasses *Danthonia pallida* and *Poa cæspitosa*. **c.** *dial.* The silverweed.

Silver-grey, *a.* and *sb.* 1607. [SILVER *sb.*] **A.** *adj.* Of a silvery or silver-flecked grey colour; also, having silvery grey hair. **B.** *sb.* A silvery grey colour 1712.

Silver-haired, *a.* 1665. [SILVER *sb.*] **1.** Having hair silvered with age. **2.** Having hair naturally of a silver colour 1678.

2. Mounted upon a brown s. Gelding 1678. So **Silver-headed** *a.* (in sense 1) 1643.

Si·lvering, *vbl. sb.* 1710. [f. SILVER *v.* + -ING[1].] **1.** The action of SILVER *v.* 1738. **2.** *concr.* Silver plating; a coating of silver, silver nitrate, or quicksilver 1710.

Silver(-)lead. 1601. †**1.** A composition of lead and tin. **2.** Silver in combination with lead, esp. in the form of ore. Chiefly *attrib.* 1860.

Silver(-)leaf. 1728. [SILVER *sb.*] Silver-foil; a piece of this. **b.** (In full *s. l. disease*) A disease incident to trees, esp. plum-trees, which causes the leaves to assume an unhealthy silvery colour 1890.

Si·lverling. Now *arch.* 1526. [– G. *silberling.*] A shekel.

Silverly (si·lvəɹli), *adv.* 1595. [f. SILVER *sb.* + -LY[2].] **1.** With a silvery appearance or colour. **2.** With a silvery sound 1752.

1. Let me wipe off this honourable dewe, That siluerly doth progresse on thy cheekes SHAKS.

Silvern (si·lvəɹn), *a.* Now *poet.* and *arch.* [OE. *seolfren, silfren*; see SILVER *sb.* and -EN[4].] **1.** Made of silver; consisting of silver. **2.** Silver-coloured (*rare*) 1885.

1. *fig.* Speech is a s., Silence is golden CARLYLE.

Silver(-)ore. ME. An ore containing silver.

Silver paper. Also **silver-paper.** 1817. †**1.** A fine white tissue-paper –1873. **2.** Paper covered with silver-foil or an imitation of it 1875; also, loosely, tinfoil used as a wrapping 1911. **3.** *Photogr.* Paper sensitized with a silver solution 1898.

Silver plate. Also **silver-plate.** 1526. **1.** A thin flat piece of silver. **b.** A silver dish in the form of a plate 1710. **2.** *collect.* Vessels or utensils made of silver 1610.

Silversmith (si·lvəɹsmiþ). OE. [SILVER *sb.*] A worker in silver; one who makes silverware.

Silver-tongued, *a.* 1592. [f. SILVER *sb.*] Having a pleasant or melodious utterance; sweet-spoken; eloquent.

Si·lverware. 1860. [SILVER *sb.*] Articles, esp. tableware, made of silver.

Si·lverweed. Also **silver-weed, silver weed.** 1578. [SILVER *sb.*] **a.** A common wayside plant of the genus *Potentilla*, with prostrate rooting stems and silvery leaves; goose-grass. **b.** Any East Indian shrub of the genus *Argyreia* 1829.

Si·lver-work. 1535. [SILVER *sb.*] **1.** Articles made of silver; silver vessels or ornaments; silverware. **2.** A place where silver is smelted 1674.

Silvery (si·lvəri), *a.* 1600. [f. SILVER *sb.* + -Y[1].] **1.** Having the hue or lustre of silver 1611. **2.** Having a clear gentle metallic resonance; silver-toned, melodious 1600. **3.** Producing silver; containing silver 1870.

1. One small bright s. likeness of a cloud RUSKIN. *S. iron*, an inferior kind of pig-iron, more commonly called *white iron.* **2.** In his ears one s. voice was ringing KINGSLEY.

Silvi-: see SYLVI-.

Sima (səi·mă). 1909. [f. SI(LICA + MA(GNESIA.] *Geol.* That portion of the earth's crust which forms the substratum of the ocean bed.

Simar (simā·ɹ). 1641. [– Fr. *simarre* – It. *cimarra, zimarra.* Cf. CHIMER[1].] **1.** = CYMAR 1. **2.** = CHIMER[1]. 1840.

Simaruba (simărū·bă). 1753. [Native name in Guyana.] **1.** A tree of the genus *Simaruba*, esp. *S. amara* or *officinalis*, a native of northern Brazil, Guyana, etc. **2.** The bark of the root of *S. amara*, which contains quassine and is employed as a tonic or astringent 1778.

Simeonite (si·mīənəit). 1823. [f. name of the Rev. Charles *Simeon* (1759–1836) + -ITE[1] 1.] A follower or adherent of Simeon or a supporter of his theological doctrines; a Low Churchman or Evangelical.

‖**Simia** (si·miă). *Pl.* **simiæ** (si·mi,ī). 1753. [L., perh. f. *simus*, Gr. σιμός snub-nosed, flat-nosed.] The class of animals consisting of the apes and monkeys, and more specifically of the tailless apes only, or of certain kinds of these, as the orang-outang; also, an animal of this kind. Hence **Si·mial** *a.* (now *rare*). **Si·mious** *a.* belonging to the S.; having ape-like characteristics; typical of apes.

Simian (si·miăn), *a.* and *sb.* 1607. [f. prec. + -AN.] **A.** *adj.* **1.** Characteristic of apes; resembling that of apes; ape-like. **2.** Of or belonging to, comprising or consisting of, the apes or *Simiæ* 1863. **B.** *sb.* An ape or monkey 1880.

Similar (si·milăɹ), *a.* and *sb.* 1611. [– Fr. *similaire* or med.L. *similaris*, f. L. *similis* like; see -AR[1].] **A.** *adj.* †**1.** Of the same substance or structure throughout; homogeneous –1704. **2.** Having a marked resemblance or likeness; of a like nature or kind (*to*, †*with*) 1611. **3.** *Geom.* Applied to figures which may become congruous by adjusting their linear dimensions without changing their angles 1704. **b.** *Mus.* (See quot.) 1801.

3. *S. segments* of a Circle are such as contain equal Angles...*S. Triangles* are such as have all their

three Angles respectively equal to one another. 1704. S. Products are those whose Corresponding Factors are Proportional 1706. **b.** *S. motion*, that in which two or more parts..ascend or descend at the same time 1861. Hence **Si·milarly** *adv.*

B. *sb.* A thing or person similar to or resembling another; a counterpart (*of*) 1654.

Similarity (similæ·rĭti). 1664. [f. SIMILAR *a.* + -ITY, or – Fr. *similarité.*] **1.** The state or fact of being similar; likeness, resemblance. **2.** *pl.* Points of resemblance 1838.

1. Certain insects escape danger by their s. to plants 1879.

†**Si·milary,** *a.* 1564. [See SIMILAR *a.* and -ARY².] = SIMILAR *a.* 1, 2. –1692.

Fat is a s. Body void of Life 1668.

Similative (si·milĕⁱtiv), *a.* 1883. [f. L. *similis* like, SIMILAR + -ATIVE.] Expressing likeness, applied e.g. to such compounds as *crystal-clear.*

Simile (si·milĭ). Also †**simily** (*pl.* **-ies**). late ME. [– L. *simile*, n. of *similis* like.] A comparison of one thing with another, esp. as an ornament in poetry or rhetoric.

1. A s., to be perfect, must both illustrate and ennoble the subject JOHNSON.

Similitude (simi·litiūd). late ME. [– (O)Fr. *similitude* or L. *similitudo*, f. *similis* like; see -TUDE.] **1.** A person or thing resembling, or having the likeness *of*, some other person or thing; a counterpart or equal; †a similarity. **2.** The form, likeness, or image *of* some person or thing. late ME. **3.** †**a.** A sign or symbol; the symbolic representation of something –1558. **b.** A comparison drawn between two things or facts; the expression of such a comparison; †a simile. late ME. **c.** A parable; an allegory. (Chiefly in Biblical use.) late ME. **4.** The quality or state of being like; resemblance, similarity. Now *rare.* late ME. †**b.** Likelihood –1548.

1. The shadow stood, s. exact Of Nestor COWPER. 2. Let us make now Man in our image, Man In our s. MILT. 3. b. London is often likened to Babylon; but the s. is a very unjust one 1875. 4. The s. of Passions, which are the same in all men HOBBES. b. Phr. †*By* or *of* (*all, any, some*) *s.*

Similize (si·miləiz), *v.* Now *rare.* 1620. [f. L. *similis* or SIMILE; see -IZE.] †**1.** *trans.* To compare, liken –1670. **2.** To symbolize; to express or describe in similes 1668. **b.** *intr.* To use a simile or comparison 1686.

1. Similizing the Braine to a Garden 1653.

Similor (si·milǭɹ). 1783. [– Fr. *similor* (1742), f. L. *similis* like + *or* gold.] A very yellow kind of brass used in making cheap jewellery.

Si·mkin. *Anglo-Ind.* 1853. [Urdu corruption of *champagne.*] Champagne.

Simmer (si·məɹ), *sb.* 1809. [f. the vb.] The state or condition of simmering. Chiefly in phr. *on the* (or *at a*) *s.*

Simmer (si·məɹ), *v.* 1653. [Later form of SIMPER *v.*¹] **1.** *intr.* Of liquids: To make a subdued murmuring sound under the influence of continued heat; to be at a heat just below boiling-point. Also *transf.* of the containing vessel, etc. **b.** Of feelings, tendencies, etc.: To be in a state of gentle activity; to be on the verge of becoming active or breaking out 1764. **c.** Of persons, etc.: To be in a state of suppressed excitement or agitation 1840. **2.** *trans.* To keep in a heated condition just below boiling-point 1823.

1. The water in the singing brass Simmer'd COWPER. b. The disaffection was already simmering in Devonshire FROUDE.

Simnel (si·mnĕl). Now *arch.* or *local.* ME. [– OFr. *simenel* (mod. dial. *simnel*), derived ult. f. L. *simila, similago*, or Gr. σεμίδαλις fine flour. Cf. SEMOLINA.] **1.** A kind of bread or bun made of fine flour and prepared by boiling, sometimes with subsequent baking. Now *Hist.* **b.** A rich currant cake, usu. eaten on Mid-Lent Sunday in certain districts 1648. **c.** *attrib.*, as *s.-cake*, **-Sunday,** Mid-Lent or Mothering Sunday 1674. **2.** *U.S.* A variety of squash 1648.

Simoniac (simō̆ᵘ·niæ̆k), *sb.* and *a.* ME. [– (O)Fr. *simoniaque* or med.L. *simoniacus*, f. *simonia*; see SIMONY, -AC.] **A.** *sb.* One who practises simony; a buyer or seller of benefices, ecclesiastical preferments, or other spiritual things. Freq. with initial capital. **B.** *adj.* = next 1632. So †**Simo·nian**¹ *a.* and *sb.* (*rare*).

Simoniacal (simŏnəi·ăkăl), *a.* 1567. [f. prec. + -AL¹; see -ACAL.] **1.** Of the nature of, pertaining to, or involving simony. **2.** Of persons: Guilty of or practising simony 1569. †**3.** Tainted or marked by simony –1641.

2. Away with such young mercenary striplings and their Simoniacall fathers MILT. Hence **Simoni·acally** *adv.*

Simonian² (səimō̆ᵘ·niăn), *sb.* and *a.* 1607. [– med.L. *simonianus* simoniac, f. *Simon* (see def.).] **A.** *sb.* A member of an early Christian sect named after Simon Magus and regarded as heretical. **B.** *adj.* Pertaining to, characteristic of, the sect of the Simonians 1883.

Simon Pure (səi·mən piūᵊɹ). *colloq.* 1815. [Name of a Quaker in *A bold stroke for a wife* (1717), who is impersonated by another character during part of the play.] *The* (*real*) *Simon Pure*, the real, genuine, or authentic person or thing. **b.** *attrib.* or as *adj.* Real, genuine, authentic 1889.

Simony (si·mŏni, səi·mŏni). ME. [– (O)Fr. *simonie* – late L. *simonia*, f. name of *Simon* Magus in allusion to his offer of money to the Apostles Peter and John for the gift of conferring the Holy Ghost (Acts 8:18, 19); see -Y³.] **1.** Traffic in sacred things; *spec.* the act or practice of buying or selling ecclesiastical preferments, benefices or emoluments. †**2.** The money paid in simony. Also *transf.* a tip (to a verger). –1707. Hence **Simo·nious** *a.* = SIMONIACAL (now *rare* or *Obs.*). **Si·monist,** one who practices or upholds s.

‖**Simoom** (simū·m). Also **simoon.** 1790. [– Arab. *samūm*, f. *samma* to poison. Cf. Fr. *simoun*, G. *samum.*] A hot, dry, suffocating sand-wind which sweeps across the African and Asiatic deserts at intervals during the spring and summer.

Simous (səi·məs), *a.* 1634. [f. L. *simus* flat-nosed, snub-nosed – Gr. σιμός; see -OUS.] †**1.** Bending or curving inward; concave –1697. **2.** Having a flat nose; snub-nosed (*rare*) 1656.

Simper (si·mpəɹ), *sb.* 1599. [f. SIMPER *v.*²] An affected and self-conscious smile; a silly smiling look; a smirk.

Si·mper, *v.*¹ *Obs.* exc. *dial.* 1477. [perh. of imit. origin; see -ER⁵.] *intr.* To simmer.

Simper (si·mpəɹ), *v.*² 1563. [With sense 1 cf. Da., Norw., and Sw. dial. *semper, simper*, G. *zimper, zimpfer* elegant, delicate.] **1.** *intr.* To smile in a silly, self-conscious, or affected manner; to smirk. **2.** *trans.* To say or utter with a simper 1801.

1. She..lisps affectedly, simpers designedly, and looks conceitedly MME. D'ARBLAY. Hence **Si·mperer,** one who simpers. **Si·mperingly** *adv.*

Simple (si·mp'l), *a.* and *sb.* ME. [– (O)Fr. *simple* – L. *simplus.*] **A.** *adj.* **I. 1.** Free from duplicity, dissimulation, or guile; innocent and harmless; undesigning, honest, open, straightforward. **2.** Free from, devoid of, pride, ostentation, or display; humble, unpretentious ME. **3.** Free from elaboration or artificiality; artless, unaffected; plain, unadorned ME. **b.** Of persons: Unsophisticated, unspoiled 1794.

1. Here wily Jesuits s. Quakers meet CRABBE. A s. innocent boy SHELLEY. 2. Lowly and symple is he, he rydeth vpon an asse COVERDALE. 3. The short and s. annals of the poor GRAY. b. Pastoral people.., S. and spirited; innocent and bold SHELLEY.

II. 1. Of persons, or their origin: Poor or humble in condition; of low rank or position; undistinguished, mean, common ME. **2.** With designations or titles: Ordinary; not further distinguished in office or rank ME. **3.** Of persons or their attire: Not marked by any elegance or grandeur; very plain or homely. late ME. **b.** So of living, diet, abode, etc. ME. **4.** Small, insignificant, slight; of little account or value; also, weak or feeble. late ME. **5.** Deficient in knowledge or learning; characterized by a certain lack of acuteness or quick apprehension ME. **6.** Lacking in ordinary sense or intelligence; more or less foolish, silly, or stupid; also, half-witted (now *dial.*) 1604.

1. His place of birth a solemn Angel tells To s. Shepherds MILT. †Phr. *As s. as*, or *s. though, I stand here.* 2. This change affected however only the s. barons 1875. 3. b. Blest be those feasts, with s. plenty crown'd GOLDSM. *The s. life*, a mode of life in which anything of the nature of luxury is intentionally avoided. 4. I am a s. woman, much too weake T' oppose your cunning SHAKS. 5. The s. and unletter'd poor COWPER. 6. The good old Gentlewoman was not so s..; she began to smell a Rat 1713. *S. Simon*, a silly fellow (with ref. to nursery rhymes).

III. 1. With nothing added; considered or taken by itself; mere, pure, bare ME. **2. a.** *Med.* Of wounds, diseases, etc.: Unaccompanied by complications. late ME. **b.** *Law.* Not specially confirmed 1546. **3.** Consisting or composed of one substance, ingredient, or element; uncompounded, unmixed (or nearly so). late ME. **4.** Not composite or complex in respect of parts or structure. late ME. **5.** Not complicated or involved; presenting little or no complexity or difficulty 1555.

1. Yet s. Nature to his hope has giv'n.. an humbler heav'n POPE. Phr. *Pure and s.* (often following the sb.): orig. a term of jurisprudence (e.g. 'a pure and simple obligation'); hence *gen.* unconditioned, mere (e.g. 'pure and s. robbery', 'robbery pure and s.'). 2. a. The Suppuration proceeding kindly, the Wound became a s. Wound 1758. b. *S. contract*, one made by word of mouth or not under seal. 3. A Needle is a s. Body, being made only of Steel; but a Sword or a Knife is a Compound 1724. 4. Those tenses are called s. tenses, which are formed of the principal, without an auxiliary verb 1824. The s. microscope may consist of one..or of two or three lenses; but these latter are so arranged as to have the effect only of a single lens 1867. Leaves ..which are not divided into separate leaflets are termed s. 1872. *S. feast*, a feast which is not a double or a semi-double. *S. interest*: see INTEREST *sb.* II. 2. *S. machine*, any of the six or more elementary mechanical devices, e.g. the lever, wedge, etc. *S. sentence*, a sentence containing only one member having a subject and predicate of its own. *S. tense*, a tense formed with a single word. 5. *S. Quantities* in Algebra, are such as have but one Sign, whether Positive or Negative 1704. A S. Equation, is that which contains only one power of the unknown quantity, without including different powers 1798. A s. proposition is that in which one predicate is affirmed or denied of one subject MILL. We must prefer the simpler hypothesis to the more complicated 1884.

B. *absol.* as *sb.* **1.** As *pl.* Persons in a humble or ordinary condition of life. Also as *sing.* a person of this class. ME. **2.** As *pl.* Those who are unlearned, ignorant, easily misled, unsuspecting; also as *sing.* an ignorant or foolish person 1560. **3.** A simple word; a verb in its simple form or without prefix 1530. **4.** †A medicine or medicament composed or concocted of only one constituent, *esp.* of one herb or plant; hence, a plant or herb employed for medical purposes. Now *arch.* 1539. **5.** A single uncompounded or unmixed thing; a substance free from foreign elements, *esp.* one serving as an ingredient in a composition or mixture 1560. **b.** A simple proposition, quantity, idea, etc. 1654. **6.** *Weaving.* One of a number of lines or cords attached to the warp in a draw-loom 1731. **b.** A draw-loom 1875.

1. Gentle or semple shall not darken my doors the day my bairn's been carried out a corpse SCOTT. 2. A snare to the s. of heart 1853. 4. From the knowledge of Simples, she had a Receipt to make white hair black SIR T. BROWNE. Hence **Simple** *v. intr.* to seek for or gather simples. **Si·mpler** (now *arch.*), one who collects or studies simples; a herbalist.

Simple-hearted, *a.* late ME. [f. SIMPLE *a.* + HEART *sb.* + -ED².] Possessed of, or characterized by, a simple heart or spirit; ingenuous, sincere, unsophisticated; †ignorant, simple-minded.

Simple-minded, *a.* 1744. [f. SIMPLE *a.* + MIND *sb.* + -ED².] Having a simple mind; possessing little or no subtlety of intellect; also, feeble- or weak-minded. Hence **Simple-mi·ndedness.**

Simpleness (si·mp'lnės). ME. [f. SIMPLE *a.* + -NESS.] The quality or state of being SIMPLE, in various senses.

Si·mplesse. *Obs.* exc. *arch.* ME. [– (O)Fr. *simplesse*, f. *simple*; see SIMPLE, -ESS².] = SIMPLENESS.

Simpleton (si·m'pltən). 1650. [f. SIMPLE + -TON (q.v.), as in many surnames derived from place-names; cf. *idleton* idle fellow (XVIII), †*sillyton* (XVIII), and the use of *-by* as in RUDESBY, etc.; see -BY 2.] One who is deficient in sense or intelligence; a silly or foolish person; a fool.

Simplex (si·mpleks), *a.* and *sb.* 1594. [– L. *simplex* single, var. of *simplus* SIMPLE with second element as in *duplex*, *multiplex*, etc.] **A.** *adj.* Consisting, or composed of, characterized by, a single part, structure, etc. **B.** *sb.* A single uncompounded word 1892.

‖**Simpliciter** (simpli·sitəɹ), *adv.* 1545. [L.] Absolutely, unconditionally; without any condition or consideration. Chiefly in *Sc. Law.*

Simplicity (simpli·sĭti). late ME. [– (O)Fr. *simplicité* or L. *simplicitas*, *-tat-*, f. *simplex*, *simplic-*; see SIMPLEX, -ITY.] **1.** The state or quality of being simple in form, structure, etc.; absence of compositeness, complexity, or intricacy. **2.** Want of ordinary knowledge or judgement; ignorance; rusticity 1514. **b.** A simple person; a simpleton (*rare*) 1633. **3.** Freedom from artifice, deceit, or duplicity; sincerity, straightforwardness; also, absence of affectation or artificiality; plainness, naturalness 1526. **b.** Simple, unsophisticated ways or manners; plainness of life. Also (in *pl.*), an instance of this. 1585. **4.** Of language or style: Absence or lack of elegance or polish; in later use, freedom from over-elaboration; plainness or directness of an attractive kind 1553. **5.** Absence of ornament or decoration; freedom from useless accessories 1609.

1. In contriving machines, s. of parts should always be studied 1815. **2.** That other s. which is only a euphemism for folly 1875. **3.** Nathanael was. .full of holy s., a true Israelite without guile 1649. **b.** The simplicities of cottage life WORDSW. **4.** S. is become a very rare quality in a writer COWPER. **5.** Give me a face, That makes s. a grace B. JONSON.

Simplification (simplifikēⁱ·ʃən). 1688. [– Fr. *simplification*, f. *simplifier*; see next, -ATION.] The action or process of simplifying; the result of this.

Simplify (si·mplifəi), *v.* 1642. [– Fr. *simplifier* – med.L. *simplificare* f. L. *simplus*; see SIMPLE, -FY.] *trans.* To make simple; to render less complex, elaborate, or involved; to reduce to a clearer or more intelligible form; to make easy. Also *absol.*

The laws of commerce. .are simplified and expanded SYD. SMITH. In a state of nature man. . does not s. and fix his motives J. H. NEWMAN.

Simplist (si·mplist). 1597. [f. SIMPLE B. 4 + -IST.] One who studies simples; a herbalist. Now *rare.* So **Simpli·stic** *a.* of the nature of, or characterized by, (extreme) simplicity.

Simply (si·mpli), *adv.* ME. [f. SIMPLE *a.* + -LY², with later contraction as in *gently*, *nobly*.] **1.** With simplicity (of mind) or sincerity; in an honest or straightforward manner; also, in later use, unaffectedly, artlessly. **2.** Humbly in respect of dress or surroundings. late ME. **3.** In simple language; also, plainly, clearly. late ME. **b.** Without elaboration or complication 1746. †**4.** Poorly, badly, indifferently; meanly, inadequately; weakly –1754. **5.** In a foolish, silly, or stupid manner; without common sense or sagacity. Also *s. disposed*, of a simple disposition. 1466. **6.** Without addition or qualification. late ME. **b.** Without exception; absolutely. (Frequently used as an intensive.) 1590. Also, *simply and solely.*

1. By things deemd weak Subverting worldly strong, and worldly wise By s. meek MILT. **3. b.** A fine massive piece of architecture, s. grand 1816. **5.** If an elephant chance to meet with a man wandering s. out of his way HOLLAND. **6.** If he take her, let him take her s. SHAKS. It is s. a question of degrees 1836. **b.** The plates are s. magnificent 1888.

Simulacre (si·miŭlēⁱkəɹ). *arch.* late ME. [– L. SIMULACRUM; cf. (O)Fr. *simulacre*.] **1.** An image (of a god, etc.) to which honour or worship is rendered. **2.** An image, a material or mental representation, *of* a person or thing 1483.

2. A knight, in whom Sir Osborne might easily distinguish the s. of himself 1830.

‖**Simulacrum** (simiŭlēⁱ·krŏm). *Pl.* **simulacra** and **-acrums.** 1599. [L., f. *simulare* make like, SIMULATE.] **1.** A material image, made as a representation of some deity, person, or thing. **2.** Something having merely the form or appearance of a certain thing 1805. **b.** A mere image, a specious imitation or likeness, *of* something 1833.

Simular (si·miŭlăɹ), *sb.* and *a.* 1520. [irreg. f. L. *simulare* + -AR¹, perh. after SIMILAR *a.*] **A.** *sb.* One who, or that which, simulates, or puts on a false appearance (*of* something). **B.** *adj.* Simulated, pretended, counterfeited. Also, simulative *of* something. 1611.

I return'd with s. proofe enough, To make the Noble Leonatus mad SHAKS.

Simulate (si·miŭlĕt), *ppl. a. arch.* late ME. [– L. *simulatus*, pa. pple. of *simulare*; see next, -ATE².] Simulated.

Simulate (si·miŭleⁱt), *v.* 1652. [– *simulat-*, pa. ppl. stem of L. *simulare*, f. *similis* like; see -ATE³.] **1.** *trans.* To assume falsely the appearance or signs of (anything); to feign, pretend, counterfeit, imitate; to profess or suggest (anything) falsely. **b.** To have the external features of 1661. **c.** *Biol.* = MIMIC *v.* 5. 1876. **2.** *intr.* To pretend or feign 1823.

1. A government. .in word and action simulating reform ARNOLD. **b.** If purely artificial it [a vault] doth most lively s. nature 1661.

Simulation (simiŭlēⁱ·ʃən). ME. [– OFr. *simulation* or L. *simulatiō(n-*, f. as prec.; see -ION.] **1.** The action or practice of simulating, with intent to deceive; false pretence, deceitful profession ME. **b.** Unconscious imitation 1870. **2.** A false assumption or display, a surface resemblance or imitation, *of* something. late ME.

1. S. is a Pretence of what is not, and Dissimulation a Concealment of what is STEELE.

Simulative (si·miŭlĕtiv), *a.* 1490. [f. SIMULATE *ppl. a.* and *v.* + -IVE.] Characterized by simulation or pretence.

Simulator (si·miŭleⁱtəɹ). 1835. [f. SIMULATE *v.* + -OR 2.] One who practises simulation.

Simultaneous (simŏltēⁱ·niəs), *a.* 1660. [f. med.L. *simultaneus* in same sense (XIV), f. *simul* at the same time, prob. after *instantaneus*, *momentaneus*; see -OUS.] **1.** Existing, happening, occurring, operating, etc., at the same time; coincident in time. **2.** *spec.* in *Math.* as *s. equation* (see quot.), *function*, etc. 1816.

1. The s. use of both eyes 1879. **2.** Pairs or sets of equations in which the same unknown symbols appear, which are assumed to possess the same values throughout, are called s. equations 1842. Hence **Simultaneity** (simŏltănī·iti), the quality or fact of being s.; occurrence at the same time. **Simulta·neous-ly** *adv.*, **-ness.**

‖**Simurgh** (simū·ɹg). 1786. [– Pers. *simurġ*, f. Pahlavi *sīn* eagle + *murġ* bird.] A monstrous bird of Persian legend, imagined as rational and of great age.

Sin (sin), *sb.* [OE. *syn(n* (:– *sunjo), rel. to other Continental forms with dental, as OFr. *sende*, OS. *sundea*, OHG. *sunt(e)a*, *sund(e)a* (G. *sünde*), ON. *synd*; taken to be cogn. with L. *sons*, *sont-* guilty.] **1.** A transgression of the divine law and an offence against God; a violation (esp. wilful or deliberate) of some religious or moral principle. **b.** *transf.* A violation of some standard of taste or propriety 1780. **2.** Without article or pl. Violation of divine law; action or conduct characterized by this; a state of transgression against God or His commands OE. (See also DEADLY *a.* 5, MORTAL *a.* 5, VENIAL *a.* 1 a.)

1. Plenary remission of their synnes 1524. At present, for my sins, I live in a village of the plain BORROW. *The seven deadly sins*; The Seven curs'd deadly Sins. .Pride, Envy, Sloth, Intemp'rance, Av'rice, Ire, And Lust 1711. *For my sins*: phr. often used trivially = as a judgement. *Like s.* (slang), vehemently, furiously. **b.** The many literary sins I know I must have committed 1907. **2.** 'Tis s. to misemploy an hour DRYDEN. Phr. *Child*, or *man, of s.*; *as black*, or *ugly, as s. In s.*, in a state of free sexual union or adultery.

Comb.: **s.-eater,** one hired to take upon himself the sins of a deceased person by means of food eaten beside the dead body; **-flood** [after G. *sündflut*, an alteration of OHG. *sinvluot* general flood], the Deluge; †**-money,** money brought as an offering in expiation of s.

Sin (sin), *v.* [OE. *syngian* (:– *sunnīʒō jan), ME. *süngen*, *singen*, etc.; repl. by *sinne*, based on the sb.] **1.** *intr.* To commit sin; to do a sinful act. **b.** *spec.* To commit fornication or adultery *with* (or †*on*) ME. **c.** To offend *against* some principle, standard, etc.; to be faulty or wrong 1704. **2.** *trans.* To do, perform, or perpetrate sinfully; to commit (a sin) ME.

1. The Tempter, or the Tempted, who sins most? SHAKS. I am a man, More sinn'd against, then sinning SHAKS. **c.** Faces sinning Against proportion BYRON. **2.** There remains so much to be sinned and suffered in the world 1859. Phr. *To s. one's mercies*, to be ungrateful for one's blessings or good fortune.

Sin (sin), *adv.*, *prep.*, and *conj.* Now *Sc.* and *north. dial.* ME. [contr. f. SITHEN. (Cf. SYNE.) In later use freq. written *sin'*, as if short for *since*.] **A.** *adv.* **1.** Then, thereupon; thereafter, subsequently. **2.** From that time onwards. late ME. **3.** Ago; before now 1490. **B.** *prep.* From, after; subsequent to ME. **C.** *conj.* **1.** From or since the time that ME. **2.** Seeing or considering that ME.

Sinæan (səinī·ăn), *a. rare.* 1667. [irreg. f. late L. *Sinæ* – Gr. Σῖναι (Ptolemy), prob. – Arab. *ṣīn*, the empire of China.] Chinese.

Sinaic (səinēⁱ·ik), *a.* 1769. [f. *Sinai* (Heb. *sinay*) + -IC.] = next.

Sinaitic (səinĕ,i·tik), *a.* 1786. [var., with euphonic *t*, of prec.; cf. Fr. *sinaïtique*.] Of, or pertaining to, Mount Sinai or the peninsula in which it is situated; given or promulgated at Mount Sinai.

The actual subdivision of the pages of the S. manuscript 1883.

Sinalbin (sinæ·lbin). 1875. [f. L. *sinapis* mustard + *alba* white + -IN¹.] *Chem.* A glucoside contained in white mustard-seed.

Sinamine (si·năməin). 1850. [f. L. *sinapis* mustard + AMINE.] *Chem.* A basic compound obtained from thiosinamine.

Sinapate (si·năpeⁱt). 1857. [f. SINAPIC + -ATE¹ c.] *Chem.* A salt formed by the action of sinapic acid on an alkali.

Sinapic (sinæ·pik), *a.* 1857. [f. next + -IC.] *Chem.* Of, pertaining to, or derived from sinapine.

S. acid, an acid derived from sinapine by the action of potash and soda.

Sinapine (si·năpin). 1838. [f. L. *sinapis* mustard + -INE⁵.] *Chem.* An unstable compound, existing as a sulphocyanate in white mustard-seed.

Sinapisine (sinæ·pisin). 1840. [irreg. f. L. *sinapis* mustard + -INE⁵.] *Chem.* A white, scaly, crystalline substance obtained from black mustard-seed by extraction with alcohol and ether.

Sinapism (si·năpiz'm). 1601. [– Fr. *sinapisme* or late L. *sinapismus* – Gr. σιναπισμός use of a mustard plaster (σινάπισμα), f. σίναπι mustard, of Egyptian origin; see -ISM.] *Med.* A plaster or poultice consisting wholly or partly of mustard flour; a mustard plaster.

Sinapoline (sinæ·polin). 1850. [f. L. *sinapis* mustard + -OL + -INE⁵.] *Chem.* An organic base obtained from cyanate of allyl.

Since (sins), *adv.*, *prep.*, and *conj.* (also *a.*). 1450. [Late ME. *synnes*, *syns*; either (i) reduced form of SITHENCE, or (ii) directly f. SIN *adv.* + -S.] **A.** *adv.* †**1.** Then, thereupon; immediately afterwards –1568. **2.** From that time till now. Often with *ever.* 1470. **3.** At some or any time between then and now; subsequently, later 1549. **b.** As *adj.* That has been since (*rare*) 1598. **4.** Ago; before now. With time specified, or preceded by *long.* 1489.

2. You know s. Pentecost the sum is due, And s. I haue not much importun'd you SHAKS. **3.** It was written and s. is lost PURCHAS. **b.** My s. experience of Sunday evenings FROUDE. **4.** He went out a little while s. 1862.

B. *prep.* **1.** Ever or continuously from (a specified time, etc.) till now 1530. **2.** During the period between (a specified time) and now; at some time subsequent to 1515.

1. He sleeps s. thirty years THACKERAY. **2.** They seem to have changed s. Spenser's time 1880.

C. *conj.* **1.** From the time that. late ME. †**b.** With vbs. of recollection: When; the time when –1690. **2.** Because; seeing that; inasmuch as 1450. †**b.** So *s. that* –1682.

1. 'Tis an age since I saw you 1753. I have known him ever s. he was in petticoats 1877. **b.** *Mids. N.* II. i. 149. **2.** But s. no reason can confute ye, I'll try to force you to your Duty 1664.

Sincere (sinsīᵊ·ɹ), *a.* 1533. [– L. *sincerus* clean, pure, sound. Cf. Fr. *sincère* (XVI).] **1.** Not falsified or perverted in any way; genuine, pure; veracious; exact 1536. **2.** Pure, unmixed; free from any foreign element or ingredient 1538. **b.** *spec.* Unadulterated; genuine. *Obs.* or *arch.* 1557. **3.** Containing no element of dissimulation or deception; not feigned or pretended; real, true 1539. **4.** Characterized by the absence of all dissimulation or pretence; honest, straightforward 1533.

1. The syncere and pure doctrine of Goddes worde 1536. **2.** Their enjoyments are s., unallayed with fears or suspitions 1676. Scarce any s. gall issued forth on incision 1763. **3.** Weak grace, if s., shall always find acceptance with Christ 1703. **4.** Master Wickliffe was noted..to be a man..of a very s. life 1533. She had not one s. friend left 1837. Hence **Since·re-ly** *adv.* (*Yours sincerely* a stereotyped formula used in concluding a letter), **-ness.**

Sincerity (sinse·rĭti). 1546. [– L. *sinceritas*, f. *sincerus*; see -ITY. Cf. Fr. *sincérité* (XVI).] The character, quality, or state of being sincere. †**1.** Freedom from falsification, adulteration, or alloy; purity, correctness –1653. **2.** Freedom from dissimulation or duplicity; honesty, straightforwardness 1557. **b.** Of feelings: Genuineness 1611. **c.** *pl.* Sincere feelings or actions 1840.

2. There is nothing so pitilessly..cruel as s. formulated into dogma 1870. **b.** The s. of his friendship has been suspected GIBBON.

Sinciput (si·nsipɒt). 1578. [– L. *sinciput*, for **senciput*, f. *semi-* half, SEMI- + *caput* head.] Chiefly *Anat.* The front part of the head or skull. Hence **Sinci·pital** *a.* of or pertaining to the s.

Sindon (si·ndən). Now *Hist.* 1450. [– L. *sindon* – Gr. σινδών, prob. of Oriental origin.] **1.** A fine thin fabric of linen; a kind of cambric or muslin. **2.** A piece of this fabric used: **a.** As a shroud, *spec.* that in which the body of Christ was wrapped 1500. **b.** As a wrapper 1577. **c.** As a surgical appliance, being made up into a small roll or pledget, usu. with some medicament, and used to fill up an open wound 1657. **3.** *attrib.* Made or consisting of sindon 1500.

2. b. There were found in it a Book, and a Letter; Both..wrapped in Sindons of Linnen BACON.

Sine (səin). 1591. [– med.L. use of L. *sinus* bend, bay, fold of toga, bosom (see SINUS), used to translate Arab. *jayb* bosom in sense 2.] †**1.** A gulf or bay. SYLVESTER. **2.** *Trig.* One of the three fundamental trigonometrical functions (cf. TANGENT, SECANT): Orig., the length of a straight line drawn from one end of a circular arc parallel to the tangent at the other end, and terminated by the radius; in mod. use, the ratio of this line to the radius, or (equivalently, as the function of an angle), the ratio of the side of a right-angled triangle opposite the given angle to the hypotenuse (the sine of an obtuse angle being numerically equal to that of its supplement). (Abbrev. *sin*) 1593. **b.** Const. *of* an angle 1728.

2. *Coversed, logarithmic, versed s.*: see the adjs.

Sinecure (səi·nĭkiūᵊɪ, si·n-), *sb.* and *a.* 1662. [– L. *sine cura* in the phr. *beneficium sine cura* (see def.), from *sine* without, *cura* abl. sing. of *cura* care.] **1.** An ecclesiastical benefice without cure of souls. **2.** Any office or position which has no work or duties attached to it, esp. one which yields some stipend or emolument 1676. **3.** *attrib.* or as *adj.* Of the nature of a sinecure; involving no duties or work 1761.

2. Many of the best institutions moulder into Sinecures 1800. **3.** I never could myself understand the difference between a Pension and a S. Place 1761. Hence **Si·necurism,** the practice of holding or permitting sinecures; the prevalence of sinecures in the church or any other sphere of work. **Si·necurist,** one who has or seeks a s.

‖**Sine die** (səi·nĭ dəi·ī). 1631. [L., *sine* without + *die*, abl. sing. of *dies* day.] Without any day being specified (for reassembling, resumption of business, etc.); indefinitely.

The *fête* was postponed *sine die* 1842.

‖**Sine qua non** (səi·nĭ kwēⁱ nǫn). 1602. [L., *sine* without + *qua*, abl. sing. fem. of *qui* which (agreeing with *causa*) + *non* not.] **1.** With adjectival force: Indispensable, absolutely necessary or essential 1615. **2.** Somebody or something indispensable 1602.

1. The Preliminary Article *sine quâ non*, was that ..he should surrender his place of Recorder 1734. A ghost or a witch is a *sine qua non* ingredient in all the dishes of..my hobgoblin repast 1798. **2.** It was a *sine qua non* that the Indians should be included in the pacification 1814. Also (*Sc. Law*) **Sine quo non.**

Sinesian (səinī·ʃⁱăn), *a.* 1899. [f. late L. *Sinæ* (see SINÆAN) + -ESE + -IAN.] Of or pertaining to the Chinese and kindred races or to those parts of Asia inhabited by them.

Sinew (si·niu), *sb.* [OE. *sin(e)we, sionwe, seonew-*, obl. forms of *sinu, seonu* = OFris. *sini, sin(e,* (M)LG., MDu., MHG. *sene* (Du. *zeen*, G. *sehne*), ON. *sin* :– Gmc. **senawō* (whence OS., OHG. *senawa*).] **1.** *Anat.* A strong fibrous cord serving to connect a muscle with a bone or other part; a tendon. **b.** A tendon taken out of an animal body and used for some purpose, esp. for binding or tying with; hence, a string in a musical instrument ME. **c.** Sinewy substance or material 1825. †**2.** A nerve –1621. **3.** Chiefly *pl.* Strength, energy, force 1560. **4.** The main strength, mainstay, or chief supporting force, *of* something. (More freq. in pl.) 1579.

1. c. The tassels had been fastened by split s. DARWIN. **3.** His authoritie hath no sinews 1617. **4.** *sing.* Achilles..The s., and the forehand of our Hoste SHAKS. *pl.* The discipline of the masses has hitherto knit the sinews of battle RUSKIN. Phr. *The sinews of war* [after L. *nervi belli pecunia* (Cicero)], i.e. money. Hence †**Si·newish** *a.* (*rare*) sinewy –1597.

Sinew (si·niu), *v.* 1592. [f. prec.] **1.** *trans.* To run through, tie together, cover over with, or as with, sinews (*rare*). **2.** To supply with sinews; to strengthen as by sinews; to nerve, harden 1614.

2. Christianity needs something to nerve and s. it 1852.

Sinewed (si·niūd), *ppl. a.* 1588. [f. SINEW *sb.* or *v.* + -ED.] **1.** Having sinews of a specified kind. **2.** Strengthened with sinews; strong, firm, vigorous, powerful, sinewy 1604.

1. Strong sinew'd was the youth, and big of bone DRYDEN. **2.** The great Eagle..Whose s. wings.. Beat the thin air DRAYTON.

Si·newless, *a.* 1552. [f. SINEW *sb.* + -LESS.] Destitute of sinews; *fig.* lacking vigour; feeble, weak, powerless.

Sinewous (si·niuəs), *a.* 1495. [f. SINEW *sb.* + -OUS.] Sinewy; also *fig.*, strenuous, vigorous.

Sinewy (si·niui), *a.* late ME. [f. SINEW *sb.* + -Y¹.] **1.** Furnished with, full of, sinews. **2.** Having strong, well-developed, or prominent sinews. (Usu. implying strength, but occas. leanness.) late ME. **3.** Of the nature of sinews; tough, stringy 1578.

1. An awfully s. leg of beef 1885. **2.** Fainting as he touch'd the shore, He dropt his s. arms POPE. *transf.* The sinnowy vigour of the trauailer SHAKS. Nervous and s. Arguments 1641.

Sinful (si·nfŭl), *a.* and *sb.* OE. [f. SIN *sb.* + -FUL.] **1.** Of persons, etc.: Full of sin; wicked, corrupt. Also *absol.* **2.** Of acts, etc.: Involving sin; characterized or marked by sin ME. **b.** Highly reprehensible 1863.

1. What is man? Sinful and weak, in ev'ry sense a wretch. COWPER. **2.** Like that bad prophet at Bethel..while he sat at his s. meat J. H. NEWMAN. Hence **Si·nful-ly** *adv.*, **-ness.**

Sing (siŋ), *v.* Pa. t. **sang** (sæŋ), **sung** (sɒŋ). Pa. pple. **sung.** [OE. *singan* = OFris. *siunga, sionga*, OS., OHG. *singan* (Du. *zingen*, G. *singen*), ON. *syngva*, Goth. *siggwan* :– Gmc. **seŋgwan.*] **I.** *intr.* **1.** To articulate or utter words or sounds in succession with musical inflexions or modulations of the voice, so as to produce an effect entirely different from that of ordinary speech; *spec.* to do this in a skilled manner, as the result of training and practice. **b.** *transf.* and *fig.* To cry *out*; to make a noise, to boast *about* something. late ME. **2.** To tell *of* in song or verse OE. **b.** To compose in verse; to make poetry 1637. †**3.** To chant or intone, in the performance of divine service; to say mass –1599. **4.** Of birds: To produce tuneful or musical sounds; to warble OE. **b.** Of cocks: to crow (*out*) OE. **c.** Said of the raven, sea-mew, toad, etc., and of the cricket OE. **5.** Of things: To give out a ringing, murmuring, or other sound having the quality of a musical note OE. **b.** Of missiles, etc.: To sound in this way by reason of rapid motion through the air 1565. **6.** Of the ears: To ring, be filled with a humming sound 1621. **7.** To admit of being sung; to be usually sung 1728.

1. I sange by the morowe And now at eue I wepe 1400. When to the lute She sung SHAKS. **b.** They sholde singen, if that they were hent CHAUCER. S. out when we head right! SCORESBY. **2.** Minstrels, who sung of war and ladies love SCOTT. **b.** Who would not s. for Lycidas? he knew Himself to s., and build the lofty rhyme MILT. **3.** *Hen. V*, IV. i. 319. **4.** Hearke, hearke, the Larke at Heauens gate sings SHAKS. **b.** The Bird of Dawning singeth all night long SHAKS. **5.** When the bagpipe sings i' the nose SHAKS. **b.** Whose bullet through the night-air sang? BYRON.

II. *trans.* **1.** To utter (a song, etc.) with musical modulations of the voice OE. **b.** With obj. denoting the key, voice, note, etc. late ME. **2.** To chant or intone (a lesson, mass, etc.) OE. **3.** To declare, relate, recount, or celebrate, in song or verse OE. **b.** To proclaim in a musical or resonant manner; to announce clearly or distinctly 1605. **c.** To call *out* 1833. **4. a.** To bring into a certain state, or to a certain place, by or with singing 1500. **b.** To drive, take, force, etc., by or with singing 1604. **c.** To make (one's way) with singing 1890.

1. The harper had songe his songe to the ende MALORY. **b.** A Frenchman who sung an admirable basse EVELYN. Phr. *To s. another song* or *a different tune*, to speak or act in a very different manner. *To s. the same* (or *one*) *song*, to harp on the same strain. *To hear a bird s.*, etc., denoting the receipt of private information. **3.** He sang the creation of the world, and the origin of man 1850. Phr. *To s. one's praises*, to be loud in laudation of (a person, etc.). **b.** I hear a tempest coming That sings mine and my kingdom's ruin FLETCHER. **c.** Moon and stars shining overhead, and the bell singing out the watch THACKERAY. **4.** This..swan, who..sings His soule and body to their lasting rest SHAKS. **b.** Oh she will s. the Sauagenesse out of a Beare SHAKS. Hence **Sing** *sb.*, an act of singing, a singing noise; **Si·ngable** *a.*

Singe (sinᵈʒ), *sb.* 1658. [f. the vb.] The act or effect of singeing; a slight surface burn; a scorch.

Singe (sinᵈʒ), *v.* [OE. *senćgan*, usu. *besenćgan*, = OFris. *senga, sendza*, OS. *bisengian* (Du. *zengen*), (M)HG. *sengen* :– WGmc. **saŋgjan*, f. **saŋg-* **seŋg-* **suŋg-*.] **1.** *trans.* **a.** Of persons: To burn (something) superficially or lightly, to burn the ends or edges of (hair, wings, etc.); *esp.* to subject (the carcase of a pig, fowl, etc.) to flame or fire in order to remove the bristles or hair. **b.** *techn.* To pass (a woven fabric) over a heated plate or roller or through gas flame, in order to remove superfluous fibres, or to dress the nap 1728. **2.** Of fire or flame: To burn (something) slightly or superficially. Also *techn.* ME. **3.** To take *off*, remove, by superficial burning 1590.

1. No man blameth the candle..though butter flyes sindge theyr winges in it 1626. *fig.* I go..to s. the King of Spain's beard KINGSLEY. **2.** *transf.* The scorching sky Doth s. the sandy wilds of spiceful Barbary DRAYTON. Hence **Singed** (sinᵈʒd) *ppl. a.* **Singer**² (si·nᵈʒər).

Singer¹ (si·ŋəɹ). ME. [f. SING *v.* + -ER¹.] **1.** One who sings; a trained vocalist. **b.** Of song-birds. (More freq. *songster.*) 1626. **2.** A composer of poetry or verse; a poet 1560.

2. Dauid.., the swete s. of Israel BIBLE (Geneva) 2 *Sam.* 23:1. Hence †**Si·ngeress,** a female singer.

Singhalese, var. of SINHALESE.

Singing (si·ŋiŋ), *vbl. sb.* ME. [f. SING *v.* + -ING¹.] **1.** The action of the verb; an instance of this. **2.** A sound as of musical notes *in* the ears or head 1605. **3.** *attrib.*, as *s.-master, -school*, etc. late ME.

Singing, *ppl. a.* ME. [-ING².] **1.** That sings; giving forth song. **2.** That makes or gives out a sound of a musical character 1565. **3.** Of the nature of singing; having the musical qualities of song. late ME.

1. *S. man*, a man engaged to sing in an ecclesiastical choir. *S. bird*, a bird that sings; a songster (usu. applied to cage-birds; the pl. is also occas. used as a rendering of OSCINES 2). **2.** *S.-buoy*, a buoy having something attached which gives out a s. sound. Hence **Si·ngingly** *adv.* in a s. manner or tone.

†**Singing bread.** late ME. [Cf. SING *v.* I. 3 and II. 2.] The wafer used in the celebration of the mass –1616.

Single (si·ŋg'l), *sb.* 1486. [SINGLE *a.* used subst.] **1. a.** *Falconry.* The middle or outer claw on the foot of a hawk or falcon. Now *arch.* **b.** *Hunting.* The tail of a deer 1576. **2.** *Sc.* and *n. dial.* A handful or small bundle of gleanings 1508. **3.** In various spec. or techn. senses.

a. A simple uncompounded word 1589. **b.** A form of change in bell-ringing 1684. **c.** A single (as opp. to a double) flower 1796. **d.** A silk thread consisting of a single strand 1831. **e.** *Cards.* Scoring the game after the other side has scored three or four up 1850. **f.** *Cricket,* etc. A hit for which one run is scored; a single point 1858. **g.** *Tennis,* etc. A game or match in which only one person on each side plays at one time 1884.

4. A single thing, person, etc. *In singles,* each one separately, singly. 1646.

Single (si·ŋg'l), *a.* [ME. *sengle* – OFr. *sengle, single* :– L. *singulus,* f. *sim-* as in *simplus* SIMPLE.] **I. 1.** In predic. use: Unaccompanied or unsupported by others; alone, solitary. **2.** Individual, as contrasted with larger bodies or numbers of persons or things. late ME. **b.** Of, pertaining to, or connected with, one person only. Freq. with possessive pronoun 1592. **3.** Separate; distinct from each other or from others; not combined or taken together. late ME. **4.** Undivided, unbroken, absolute (*rare*) 1590. **5.** One only; one and no more. Occas. strengthened by *one.* 1538. **6.** Sole, only, solitary; †mere 1639. †**7.** Standing alone in comparison with other persons or things; unique –1817.

1. Misfortunes never come S. ADDISON. He is left alone, s. and unsupported 1780. **2.** Nor do those Ills on s. Bodies prey; But oft'ner bring the Nation to decay DRYDEN. **b.** With my s. fist Ile combat thee KYD. **3.** Dropped by s. pieces into the copper while in full boil 1826. **4.** Yet nought but s. darknes do I find MILT. **5.** Thus all will judge, and with one s. aim 1728. France had not possessed a s. man who dared to think for himself 1857. **6.** Heroes who carry victory with their s. presence SOUTHEY. **7.** I . .am almost s. in not having been to see him 1750.

II. 1. Unmarried, celibate. Also *absol.* as pl. ME. **b.** Of, pertaining to, or involving celibacy, *esp.* in *s. life* 1549. †**2.** Of cloth, garments, etc.: Of one thickness of material; unlined –1670. **3.** Composed or consisting of only one part, feature, etc.; not double, compound, or complex; also, of the ordinary or small size, as dist. from DOUBLE A. 4. late ME. **b.** Of flowers: Having only one whorl or set of petals; also, of plants: Bearing such flowers; opp. to DOUBLE A. 1 d. 1551. **c.** Intended for or accommodating one person 1859. †**4. a.** Simple; plain; without further qualification or addition –1736. †**b.** Slight, poor, trivial –1638. **5.** Of beer, ale, etc.: Weak, poor; small. Now *arch.* 1485. **6.** Simple, honest, sincere, single-minded; free from duplicity or deceit 1519. **b.** Of the eye, after Biblical use 1526. **7.** Of a combat or fight: Between two persons; man to man 1592. **8.** In quasi-advb. use 1450.

1. Who that is s. and wyll have a wyfe, Right out of joy he shall be brought in stryfe 1509. *A s. man,* a bachelor. *A. s. woman,* a spinster. **b.** *S. blessedness:* see BLESSEDNESS. **3.** A s. line furnished with sidings to enable the laden waggons to pass the empty ones 1862. **c.** A strip of faded carpet stretched in front of a small s. bedstead 1867. **4. b.** 2 *Hen. IV,* I. ii. 207. **6.** S. Truth and simple Honestie Do wander up and downe, despys'd of al SPENSER. **b.** When thine eye is s.; then is all thy body full of light TINDALE *Luke* 11:34. **7.** The two kings shall decide the matter by s. combat FREEMAN.

Comb., etc.: **s. court,** a court laid out for two players only; **-cut,** (of files) having but a single rank of teeth; **s. entry,** a method of book-keeping by which each item is entered to the debit or credit of a single account; **s. file,** a line of men, etc. one behind the other; **s. Gloucester;** see GLOUCESTER.

Single (si·ŋg'l), *v.* 1570. [f. the adj.] **1.** *trans.* To separate or part from each other; to take asunder. Now *rare.* **2.** *Hunting.* To separate (one deer, etc.) from the herd; to pick out and chase separately. Also with *forth* or *out.* 1575. **3.** To separate (one person or thing) from others; to draw or take aside or apart. Also const. *from,* †*forth.* 1582. **4.** To pick out or distinguish from others. Also with *out.* 1588. **5.** To thin (seedling plants), so as to leave each plant separate; to pick *off* (shoots). Also const. *out.* 1731. **6.** To render single, reduce to one, concentrate 1824. **7.** *intr.* **a.** To go singly; to separate from others. Also with *out* and *off.* 1616. **b.** *U.S.* Of a horse: To be SINGLE-FOOTED 1864.

2. The hound had at length singled out a particular deer 1873. **3.** Now Clifford, I haue singled thee alone SHAKS. **4.** He, whom my jealousy. . Hath singled for destruction! SMOLLETT. **7. a.** Let. .all go on At once. To s. is to weaken you. HOBBES.

Single-acting, *ppl. a.* 1825. [f. SINGLE *a.*] Acting in one direction or by one method, *spec.* of a steam-engine. Opp. to *double-acting.*

S. engine, an engine in which steam is admitted to one side only of the piston 1875.

Single-breasted, *a.* 1796. [f. SINGLE *a.*] Of a coat, waistcoat, etc.: Having only one thickness over the breast; not doubled by overlapping. Opp. to DOUBLE-BREASTED.

Single-eyed, *a.* 1705. [f. SINGLE *a.*] **1.** *fig.* Having the eye single or sound; sincere, honest, straightforward. **2.** *lit.* Having one eye or eye-like mark; monoculous 1839.

Si·ngle-foot. *U.S.* 1882. [f. SINGLE *v.* 7 b.] A particular gait of a horse, variously identified with the amble and the rack.

S. is an irregular pace,. .distinguished by the posterior extremities, moving in the order of a fast walk and the anterior ones in that of a slow trot 1882. So **Single-footed** *a.* 1864.

Single-handed, *a.* 1709. [f. SINGLE *a.*] **1. a.** Of actions: Carried on or performed by one person, ship, etc., alone or unaided, or by one person on each side. **b.** Adapted for using with one hand 1834. **2.** Working alone or unassisted; by one's self; unaided 1768. So **Single-hand** *a.* Hence **Single-ha·nded-ly** *adv.,* **-ness.**

Single-hearted, *a.* 1577. [f. SINGLE *a.*] **1.** Possessed of a single or sincere heart; straightforward, honest; simple-hearted. **2.** Of actions, etc.: Proceeding from or characterized by sincerity of heart or purpose 1804. Hence **Single-hea·rted-ly** *adv.,* **-ness.**

Si·ngle-line, *a.* 1868. [f. SINGLE *a.*] **1.** Consisting of or having only a single line of plants, rails, etc. **2.** Occupying one line in writing or printing 1892.

Single-minded, *a.* 1577. [f. SINGLE *a.*] **1.** Sincere in mind or spirit; honest; ingenuous. **2.** Proceeding from or characterized by sincerity or honesty of mind 1836. **3.** Having but one aim or purpose 1860.

Si·ngleness. 1526. [f. SINGLE *a.* + -NESS.] **1.** Sincerity, straightforwardness, honesty, integrity; freedom from deceit, duplicity, or guile. **2.** The condition of being unmarried, or of not marrying again; celibacy 1560. **3.** The quality of being single; the fact of consisting of one in number or kind; oneness 1592. **4.** The fact of standing alone; solitude, solitariness, isolation (*poet.*) 1805. **5.** The quality or fact of having (one single aim or purpose) 1806.

5. His failure seems. .due to a want of s. of aim 1886.

Si·ngle-stick, *sb.* Also **singlestick.** 1771. [f. SINGLE *a.* + STICK *sb.*] Fighting, fencing, or exercise with a stick provided with a guard or basket and requiring only one hand. **b.** A stick used for this 1837. Hence **Single-stick** *v. intr.* to fight or fence with a single-stick.

Singlet (si·ŋglĕt). 1746. [f. SINGLE *a.* + -ET, after DOUBLET.] An unlined woollen garment (knitted or woven), now usu. close-fitting and worn as an undershirt or jersey.

Singleton (si·ŋg'ltən). 1876. [f. SINGLE *a.* + -TON. Cf. SIMPLETON.] **1.** *Cards.* In whist or bridge: The only card of a suit in a hand. **2.** A single thing, as dist. from a pair 1887.

Si·ngle-tree. *U.S.* and *Austral.* 1847. = SWINGLE-TREE.

Si·ngle-wi·cket. 1736. [f. SINGLE *a.* I. 5.] A form of cricket in which there is only one wicket and consequently only one batsman at a time.

Singly (si·ŋgli), *adv.* ME. [f. SINGLE *a.* + -LY[2], with later contraction as in *simply,* etc.] **1.** As a single person or thing; by oneself or itself; separately. **b.** Unassisted, single-handed 1608. **2.** Solely, only; merely. Now *rare* or *Obs.* 1654. †**3.** Truly, honestly –1637.

1. He is greater then his subjects s. and apart 1673. **b.** Singlie of my selfe I will oppose all danger 1633. **2.** People do not improve, s., by travelling, but by the observations they make CHESTERF.

Sing-sing. 1854. [Native name.] An African antelope, *Kobus sing-sing.*

Si·ng-song, *sb.* 1609. [f. SING *v.* + SONG *sb.*] **1.** A ballad or a piece of verse of a monotonous or jingling character. **2.** Verse or rhyme of this type 1693. **b.** Tone of voice marked by a monotonous rise and fall, with a kind of singing effect 1822. **3.** An amateur concert of an informal nature; a convivial meeting where each person is expected to contribute a song 1769. **4.** *attrib.* **a.** Of persons: Making mere jingling rhyme or monotonous verse 1687. **b.** Characterized by a jingling triviality or monotonous rise and fall 1734. **c.** Monotonous in cadence 1825.

2. b. The fine old Norfolk words, and twang, and squeaky s. have gone 1887. Hence **Sing-song** *v. trans.* to utter or express in a monotonous chant; *intr.* to sing, make verses, utter words, etc., in a s. manner.

Singular (si·ŋgiŭlăɹ), *a., adv.,* and *sb.* [ME. *singuler* – OFr. *singuler* (mod. *-ier*) – L. *singularis,* f. *singuli* SINGLE *a.* The form in *-er* was not finally displaced by the latinized *-ar* till XVII; see -AR[1], -ER[2] 1.] **A.** *adj.* **I.** †**1.** Alone; away from others; solitary –1787. **2.** One only; one and no more; single. late ME. **b.** Unique, solitary, single. Also (with *the*), sole, only. 1555. **3. a.** *Gram.* Denoting or expressing one person or thing. Chiefly in *s. number.* Opp. to PLURAL *a.* and DUAL *a.* late ME. **b.** *Logic.* Considered alone or as a single instance 1654. **c.** *Math.* Having properties not shared by other things of the same class 1845. †**4.** Of a combat: = SINGLE *a.* II. 7. –1826.

1. His way of living was s. and retired 1278. **2. b.** He was the s. instance in Scotland 1715. **3. b.** The proposition is s. when the subject is an individual name MILL. **4.** Those in his high place fight no s. combats SCOTT.

†**II. 1.** Separate, individual, single –1719. **2.** Of or pertaining to, connected with or affecting, the individual, in contrast to what is common or general; personal, private, one's own –1692. **b.** Special; peculiar *to* one –1710.

1. Every singuler persoone of the same chirche 1450. Phr. *All and s.,* every one. Also *each and s.* (rare, now *arch.*). **2.** One that preferred the dignitee. .of the commenweale, before his owne singulare avauntage 1542.

III. †**1.** Separate from others by reason of superiority or pre-eminence –1635. †**b.** Of persons: Eminent, distinguished, notable –1691. †**c.** Used in forms of address, esp. to a person of title 1638. **2.** Above the ordinary in amount, extent, worth, or value; especially good or great; special, particular. Now *rare.* ME. †**b.** Of remedies, medicines, etc.: Excellent; highly efficacious or beneficial –1694. **3.** Remarkable; extraordinary, unusual, uncommon. Hence, rare, precious. late ME. †**4.** Differing *from* others in opinion; standing alone; peculiar in this respect –1791. **5.** Different from or not complying with that which is customary, usual, or general; strange, odd, peculiar 1684. †**6.** Quasi-*adv.* Singularly, especially, particularly –1693.

1. b. A s. Grecian, and an exact Philologer 1691. **c.** The Countesse of Arundell and Surrey, my s. good Ladie and Mistresse 1638. **2.** Offices, or any other s. marke of the Soveraigns favour HOBBES. **3.** A s. gift of Providence 1862. **4.** Sir, he must be very s. in his opinion, if he thinks himself one of the best of men BOSWELL. **5.** He was called strange and s. long before he was acknowledged to be great LANDOR. **6.** A s. good principle CONGREVE.

B. *sb.* **1. a.** An individual. Now *rare.* **b.** A single thing; a single point or detail 1615. **c.** (in *pl.*) Contrasted with a class or with universals 1640. **2.** *Gram.* The singular number; a word in its singular form. late ME.

1. a. Eloquence would be but a poor thing, if we should only converse with singulars; speak with man and man together B. JONS.

Si·ngularist. 1593. [f. SINGULAR *a.* + -IST. In sense 2 after PLURALIST; cf. DUALIST.] †**1.** One who affects singularity –1677. **2.** *Eccl.* One who holds a single benefice, as contrasted with a PLURALIST (*rare*) 1799.

1. A clownish s., or non-conformist to ordinary usage, a stiff opiniatre 1677.

Singularity (singiulæ·rĭti). late ME. [– (O)Fr. *singularité* – late L. *singularitas, -tat-,* f. L. *singularis;* see SINGULAR, -ITY.] **I.** †**1.** A single or separate thing or entity; a unit –1708. **2.** The quality or fact of being one in number or kind; singleness, oneness. Now *rare*. 1583.

1. 'Wee' importeth a multitude and not a singularitee 1548. 2. The s. in the number of God's Being 1850.

II. 1. A solitary instance 1814. †**2.** Distinction due to, or involving, some superior quality; special excellence or goodness –1632. **3.** The fact or quality of differing or dissenting from others or from what is generally accepted, esp. in thought or religion; personal, individual, or independent action, judgement, etc. 1502. **4. a.** Individuality; distinctiveness 1583. **b.** Peculiarity, eccentricity, oddity, strangeness 1768. **5.** With *a* and *pl.* **a.** An instance of individual departure from common ideas or practice 1570. **b.** A distinctive, noteworthy, or curious thing; esp. *pl.*, notable features or objects 1570. **c.** A peculiar, exceptional, or unusual feature or characteristic 1663.

1. A friendship of forty years, I have found a rarity, though not a s. 1814. 3. So much the restless eagerness to shine, And love of s., prevail 1814. Avoid s. of opinion as well as of every thing else HAZLITT. 4. b. The s. of his manners had attracted as much notice as his eminence at the bar D'ISRAELI. 5. a. I pardon our religious Men the sad Singularitie of eating nothing but Herbs DRYDEN. b. Many haue wrote of the singularities of old Rome 1632.

Singularize (si·ŋgiŭlăraiz), *v.* 1589. [f. SINGULAR *a.* + -IZE. Cf. Fr. *singulariser* (XVI).] **1.** *trans.* To mark conspicuously; to make distinct or conspicuous. **2.** To make singular or one; to individualize; to convert into the singular number (*rare*) 1663.

Singularly (si·ŋgiŭlăɹli), *adv.* ME. [f. SINGULAR *a.* + -LY².] **1.** Singly; by oneself or itself; one by one, separately, individually. Now *rare*. †**b.** After one's own fashion; independently –1671. **2.** In the singular number; so as to denote one. late ME. **3.** Specially, particularly, unusually. late ME. †**4.** Excellently –1617. **5.** Oddly (*rare*) 1752.

1. b. His lot who dares be s. good MILT. 3. A man of s. clear judgement and s. lofty spirit MACAULAY.

Si·ngult. *arch.* 1590. [– L. SINGULTUS.] = next –1661.

‖**Singultus** (siŋgʊ·ltɒ̆s). 1754. [L., sob.] **1.** *Path.* Hiccups, hiccuping. †**2.** A sob. BYRON.

Sinh (ʃin). *Math.* 1880. Abbrev. used for *hyperbolic sine*.

Sinhalese (sinhălī·z), *sb.* and *a.* Also **Singhalese, Singalese.** 1797. [f. Skr. *siṅhalam* Ceylon + -ESE. Cf. CINGALESE.] **A.** *sb.* **1.** As *pl.* The native inhabitants of Ceylon 1802. **2.** The language spoken in Ceylon 1802. **B.** *adj.* Pertaining to Ceylon or its natives 1797.

Sinical (si·nikăl), *a.* 1593. [f. SINE + -ICAL.] *Math.* Of or relating to a sine or sines; employing or founded upon sines.

†*S. quadrant*, a former nautical instrument having intersecting sines drawn from each side.

Si·nigrin. 1876. [irreg. f. L. *sinapis* mustard + *nigra* black + -IN¹.] *Chem.* Myronate of potassium.

Sinister (si·nistəɹ), *a.* late ME. [– (O)Fr. *sinistre* or L. *sinister* left, left-hand. Down to the time of Pope stressed *sini·ster*.] **I.** †**1.** Of information, advice, etc.: Given with intent to deceive or mislead; prompted by malice or ill-will –1601. †**2.** Of opinions, etc.: Prejudicial, unfavourable, darkly suspicious –1795. **3.** Of actions, practices, etc.: Dishonest, unfair; underhand; dark 1455. **4.** Corrupt, evil, bad, base 1474. **5.** Of omens, etc.: Portending or indicating misfortune or disaster; inauspicious, unfavourable 1579. **b.** Of looks, places, etc.: Suggestive of evil or mischief 1797. **6.** Attended with mishap, misfortune, or disaster; unlucky; adverse 1576. **7.** Unfavourable, harmful, or prejudicial *to* a person, his interests, etc. 1725.

3. Nimble and s. trickes and shiftes BACON. 4. All the evils came from the s. interests of the nobles 1871. 5. Guided by some s. starre 1600. b. The typical Irish immigrant, with his s. animal features 1864. 6. A trauailer that hath sustained harm by s. fortune LYLY.

II. 1. Situated on the left side of the body 1475. **b.** Lying on or towards the left hand 1483. **2.** *Her.* Forming, or situated on, the left half of a shield (regarded from the bearer's point of view). Also *absol.* See also BAR-, BEND-*sinister*. 1562. **3.** Directed to the left; characterized by moving or turning towards the left (*rare*) 1615.

1. My Mothers bloud Runs on the dexter cheeke, and this s. Bounds in my fathers SHAKS. b. The s. winge of the vantguard 1600. 2. *S. bend* = BEND-*sinister*. Hence **Si·nister-ly** *adv.*, **-ness.**

Si·nistrad, *adv. rare.* 1803. [f. L. *sinistra* left hand + -AD II (see DEXTRAD).] To or towards the left side; sinistrally. Also with *of*.

Sinistral (si·nistrăl), *a.* 1475. [f. SINISTER + -AL¹. Not dependent on OFr. *senestral* or med.L. *sinistralis*, which repr. only the literal senses of II (XIX).] †**I. 1.** Adverse; unlucky (*rare*). **2.** Likely, or designed, to cause mischief –1561. **3.** Darkly suspicious; very unfavourable –1572. **4.** Heterodox; unsound –1547. **II. 1.** Situated on the left side of the body; of or pertaining to the left hand or side 1803. **2.** *Conch.* Characterized by turning spirally from right to left; reversed, left-handed 1833. **3.** Of persons: Left-handed 1904.

3. Two per cent. of mankind are naturally s. 1904. Hence **Sinistra·lity,** s. state or quality. **Si·nistrally** *adv.* in a s. manner; towards the left.

Sinistro- (si·nistro), used as comb. form of SINISTER, in the sense 'on, situated in, directed or turning towards the left', as *s.-gyrate* adj.

Sinistrorse (si·nistrǭɹs), *a.* 1856. [– L. *sinistrorsus*, contr. f. **sinistrovorsus*, f. *sinister* left + *vertere* to turn.] **1.** *Bot.* Twining or turning spirally from right to left. **2.** Moving or going towards the left 1891. So **Sinistro·rsal** *a.* 1828, **-ly** *adv.*

The word has been used in two opposite senses, owing to a difference in the supposed position of the observer. Cf. DEXTRORSE.

Sinistrous (si·nistrəs, sini·strəs), *a.* 1560. [f. SINISTER + -OUS.] **I.** †**1.** Erroneous, perverse, heretical –1632. †**2.** Malicious, unfair, prejudiced –1751. †**3.** Underhand; dishonest; corrupt –1717. **4.** Betokening or attended with misfortune or disaster; ill-omened, unlucky; baleful, malign 1575.

4. Which to my soule s. signes impart 1607.

†**II. 1.** Pertaining to or situated on the left hand or side –1678. **2.** *fig.* Left-handed; slow SIR T. BROWNE. Hence **Si·nistrously** *adv.*

Sink (siŋk), *sb.* 1440. [f. SINK *v.*] **I. 1. a.** A pool or pit formed in the ground for the reception of waste water, sewage, etc.; a cesspool. **b.** A conduit, drain, or pipe for carrying away dirty water or sewage; a sewer. Now *rare*. 1499. **c.** A basin or receptacle made of stone, metal, etc. and having a pipe attached for the escape of water to a drain, etc.; *esp.* such a basin fitted in a kitchen or scullery 1566. **2.** *transf.* and *fig.* as in quots.

2. Hell is the Worlds s., and the receptacle of all the Filth in this Great Frame 1684. The Man..was the very s. of Fraud and Deceit 1707. Rome, that s. of sinks 1874. †*The sink(s of the body*, the organs of digestion and excretion.

II. †**1.** The well of a ship. (= L. *sentina*.) –1711. **2.** *Mining.* A pit-shaft. Now *rare*. 1576. **3.** A flat, low-lying area, basin, etc., where waters collect and form a bog, marsh, or pool, or disappear by sinking or evaporation. Now *U.S.* 1596. **b.** = SINK-HOLE 2. Chiefly *U.S.* 1791. **III. 1. a.** *U.S.* An oblong boat used in wild-fowl shooting, which becomes submerged to the water-level and serves to conceal the sportsman 1857. **b.** = SINKER II. 2. 1865. **c.** *Theatr.* A part of the stage constructed to sink and rise by machinery 1859. **2.** A depression or hollow, esp. one in a flat surface 1875.

Sink (siŋk), *v.* Pa. t. **sank** (sæŋk), **sunk** (sʊŋk). Pa. pple. **sunk** (sʊŋk), **sunken** (sʊ·ŋk'n). [OE. *sincan* = OFris. *sinka*, OS., OHG. *sinkan*, MLG., MDu. *sinken* (Du. *zinken*, G. *sinken*), ON. *sǫkkva*, Goth. *siggqan*; Gmc. str. vb., of unkn. origin.] (The perf. and pluperf. tenses were formerly freq. conjugated with the vb. *to be* instead of *have*.)

Intr. uses. **I. 1.** To become submerged in water; to go under or to the bottom; (of ships) to founder. **b.** To become partly or completely submerged in quicksand, marshy ground, snow, etc. ME. **2.** To subside or go down into, to be swallowed up by, the earth, etc. ME. **3.** To descend to a lower plane or level; to slip, drop, or fall *down*; to pass *in* by falling OE. **b.** To subside; to give way and go *down*, to fall *away*; to be beaten *in* 1530. **c.** Of the sun or moon: To descend in the sky; to move toward or pass beneath the horizon 1601. **d.** To pass out of sight; to disappear 1521. **e.** Of land, etc.: To have a downward lie or slope; to dip 1726. **4. a.** Of water, etc.: To go down; to fall to a lower level; to subside OE. **b.** Of flames, etc.: To die down; to go out 1611. **5.** To drop or fall gradually down to the ground, on a seat, etc., from want of power to remain erect; †to faint *away*. late ME. **b.** To fall down, fall *in* ruin; to give way through weakness or fatigue. Also of soil: To be soft or yielding. 1535. **c.** To drop down in a slow or easy manner into a lying or sitting posture 1825. **6.** Of water, etc.: To pass into or penetrate a substance, to be soaked up or absorbed ME. †**b.** Of paper: To absorb ink –1797. **7.** Of a weapon or blow: To make way *into* or *through* ME. **b.** To recede *into* 1530.

1. The boot was full of water and sanck CAXTON. b. They s. up to the Belly in the looser snow 1686. 2. Her gates are sunke into the ground *Lam.* 2:9. 3. With that her head sunk down upon her brest MARSTON. c. So sinks the day-star in the Ocean bed MILT. 5. He was sinking with hardship, fatigue, and hunger 1879. b. Sunk are thy bowers in shapeless ruin all GOLDSM. 6. Nilus shal synke awaye, & be dronke up COVERDALE *Isa.* 19:4. 7. The stone sunke into his forehead 1 *Sam.* 17:49.

II. 1. a. To penetrate *into* (†*to, unto, through*), enter or be impressed *in*, the mind, heart, etc. ME. **b.** To press or weigh *on* one 1764. **c.** To descend or fall (*up*)*on* a person or place; to settle down (*over*) a district 1808. **2.** To be immersed or plunged deeply *in* something; to dip deep *in*. Chiefly in *pa. pple.* ME. **3.** Contrasted with *swim*, to denote success, prosperity, etc., or (in later use) determination to do something without regard to consequences. late ME. **4.** To fall, lapse, or degenerate *into* some inferior or unsatisfactory state or condition. Also const. *from* (a better state). ME. **b.** To pass *into* oblivion, insignificance, etc., or *from* (notice) 1704. **c.** To change, be transformed *into* some lower form 1770. **5.** To pass or fall gently *into* (or *to*) sleep, rest, peace, etc. 1718. **b.** To lapse or fall *into* reverie, contemplation, etc. 1794. **6.** To give way *under* (or *beneath*) misfortune, affliction, etc.; to be weighed down or crushed 1592. **b.** To become depressed or dejected; to droop or languish 1605. **c.** To decline rapidly; to fail in health or strength; †also, to die. Freq. const. *under* (some trouble, etc.). 1718. **7.** To go downwards in the scale of fortune, success, or relative position 1599. **b.** To degenerate 1678. **c.** To fall in estimation; to decline in value or appreciation 1685. **8.** To fall low; to diminish or decrease; also, to disappear, to vanish 1655. **b.** Of sounds: To die away 1794.

1. These things s. into my heart 1852. c. Night sinks on the sea SWINBURNE. 2. They..were both sunk in the deepest sleep 1850. 3. I will be just and honest, s. or swim 1668. 4. The Republick sunk into those two Vices.., Luxury and Avarice ADDISON. b. Treatises..which are already sunk into..oblivion SWIFT. c. It is, indeed, possible.. for men to s. into machines RUSKIN. 5. She at length sunk to repose 1794. 6. Vnder loues heauy burthen doe I sinke SHAKS. b. My heart as well as pursse being quite sunck 1655. c. His health began to s. under the vexations of his mind 1780. 7. It was his heauie fortune to sinke B. JONS. c. He had sunk by this time to the very worst reputation THACKERAY. 8. Towards the beginning of Harvest, prices sunk much 1801.

Trans. uses. **III. 1.** To cause (a vessel, etc.) to plunge or go down beneath the water; to submerge by rendering incapable of floating; to destroy in this way ME. **b.** To submerge; to put or thrust under water ME. **2.** To cause (a thing) to descend or fall to a lower plane or level; to force, press, or weigh down in any way ME. **b.** To allow (the hand, etc.) to fall lower 1680. **3.** To excavate (a well, pit-shaft, etc.) by digging vertically downwards; to lower (ground, etc.) by excavation. Also *absol.* ME. **4. a.** To excise or cut out; to form (a cavity, etc.) in this way, or by heavy pressure 1632. **b.** To lower by cutting away; to cut patterns or designs in (a die, etc.) 1679. **c.** To let in or insert into the substance of a thing by scooping, hollowing, or cutting 1825. **5.** To lower the level of (ground, water, etc.) 1627. **b.** To lose sight of (an object on the horizon) by sailing away 1762. **c.** To descend, move down (a slope, etc.) 1862.

1. If I take any of you vpon the Sea, I will sinke you 1623. **b.** The line is shotted so as just to s. it 1856. **2.** Doth it not then our eyelids sinke? SHAKS. **b.** Each sentinel sunk his weapon SCOTT. **4.** Any Place in the Ouze,..where a Ship may..s. herself a Place to lie in CHAMBERS. **c.** The holes for sinking the heads of..screws 1825. **5.** You sunk the river with repeated draughts ADDISON. **b.** This island was sunk from the deck 1810.

IV. 1. To reduce or bring to ruin or a low estate; to overwhelm, destroy; to weigh down 1599. **b.** Used as an imprecation. *arch.* 1630. **c.** To swear. Now *dial.* or *arch.* 1663. **2.** To lower; to make of less repute or estimation 1601. **b.** To debase or degrade (a person) 1706. **c.** To reduce *to*, lose *in*, something lower 1751. **3.** To cause (a person, the mind, spirits, etc.) to become dejected or depressed 1630. **4.** To reduce in amount, value, or price 1700. **b.** To drop or lower (the voice) in speaking 1821. **5. a.** To abandon or cease to use; to give up; to allow to be merged *in* something else 1705. **b.** To avoid mentioning or alluding to (a person or matter). Also const. *upon* the person or persons spoken to. 1749. **c.** To suppress in pronouncing 1742. **d.** To set aside; to leave out of consideration 1860. **6.** To make away with; to appropriate (money, etc.) for one's own use 1713. **7.** To pay up or wipe out (a debt, etc.) 1727. **8.** To invest 1727. **9.** To invest or spend unprofitably; to lose (money) in unfortunate investment, etc. 1777.

1. If I haue a Conscience, let it sincke me,..if I be not faithfull SHAKS. **b.** S. them all for parsons TROLLOPE. **c.** We swear like Gentlemen of Rank, Curse, Damn, S. 1663. **2.** I cannot say how it has sunk him in my opinion J. AUSTEN. **b.** Again I might..exalt the brute and s. the man BURNS. **5. a.** I..have not sunk the lover in the husband 1809. **b.** Mr. Allworthy,..out of modesty, sunk everything that related particularly to himself FIELDING. **d.** A happy knack of sinking individual opinion 1884. **7.** This windfall should properly go to s. the unfunded debt 1895. **9.** The ..amounts of cash, that had been sunk in that unhappy speculation! DE QUINCEY. Hence **Si·nkable** *a.* **Si·nkage,** the act of sinking; an instance of this; also, that which sinks or has sunk.

Sinker (si·ŋkəɹ). 1526. [f. SINK *v.* + -ER¹.] **I. 1.** One who engraves figures or designs on dies. Chiefly *Sc.* (Cf. *die-sinker.*) **2.** One who sinks a pit-shaft, well, or the like 1708. **3.** One who causes (something) to sink 1632. **II. 1.** In a stocking-frame or knitting-machine, a jack-sinker or a lead-sinker 1779. **2.** A weight of lead, stone, etc. for sinking a fishing-line or -net in the water 1844. **b.** A weight of lead or other metal for sinking a sounding-line, buoy, or mine in water 1882. **c.** *U.S.* A (heavy) dough-nut 1903. **3.** *attrib.* as *s.-bar, -wheel* (in a knitting-machine), *-bar, -rod* (in boring apparatus) 1834.

Sink-hole (si·ŋkhōᵘl). 1456. [f. SINK *sb.* + HOLE *sb.*] **1.** A hole or hollow into which foul matter runs or is thrown; †a sink, or a hole by which a sink is emptied. **2.** A hole, cavern, or funnel-shaped cavity in the earth, freq. forming the course of an underground stream; a swallow-hole. Chiefly *U.S.* 1791.

Sinking (si·ŋkiŋ), *vbl. sb.* late ME. [f. SINK *v.* + -ING¹.] **1.** The action of the vb. in intr. senses. **b.** A lowering or drooping of the spirits, etc. 1663. **c.** Decline of vital power 1730. **2.** The action of the vb. in trans. senses 1605. **3.** A depression, or the amount of this; a recess or worked hollow 1712.

1. **c.** That kind of sensation which patients describe by a s. 1776.

Si·nking fund. 1724. [See SINK *v.* IV. 7 and FUND *sb.*] A fund formed by periodically setting aside revenue to accumulate at interest, usu. for the purpose of reducing the principal of a national, municipal, or company's debt.

Sink-stone (si·ŋkstōᵘn). Also **sinkstone.** 1865. [f. SINK *sb.* or *v.* + STONE *sb.*] A stone sinker for submerging a fishing-line or -net.

Sinless (si·nlės), *a.* OE. [f. SIN *sb.* + -LESS.] Free from, devoid of, without sin. Also const. *of.* Hence **Si·nless-ly** *adv.*, **-ness.**

Sinner (si·nəɹ). ME. [f. SIN *v.* + -ER¹.] **1.** One who sins; a transgressor against the divine law. **2.** In trivial use: A reprobate, rogue; an offender against some rule or custom 1809.

1. Phr. *As I am a s.*; As I am a s. My eager stomach crokes, and calls for Dinner! 1682.

Sinnet (si·nėt). 1611. [Of unkn. origin.] *Naut.* A kind of flat braided cordage formed by pleating together several strands of rope-yarn, coarse hemp, grass, etc.

Sinn Fein (ʃin fēⁱ·n). 1907. [Ir., = 'we ourselves'.] A political society, party, or movement having as its object the political independence of Ireland, the revival of the Irish language, etc. Hence **Sinn Fei·ner.**

Sino- (si·no), comb. form of Gr. Σίναι, L. *Sinæ* (see SINÆAN) the Chinese, as in **Sino·lo·gical** *a.* relating to the Chinese language or literature; **Sino·logist, Sinologue** (si·nolǫg), one versed in the Chinese language, or in the customs and history of China; **Sino·logy,** the study of things Chinese. **b.** Combined with another adj. = 'Chinese and', as **Sino-Japanese.**

Si·n-o:ffering. 1535. [f. SIN *sb.*, prob. after G. *sündopfer*, used by Luther as tr. Heb. *ḥaṭṭāṯ*, f. *ḥāṭā'* to sin.] In the older Jewish religion, an offering (of an animal for sacrifice) made as an atonement for sin.

Sinon (səi·nǫ̆n). 1581. [Name of the Greek who induced the Trojans to bring the wooden horse into Troy.] One who misleads by false tales; a perfidious person; a betrayer.

†Sinoper. late ME. [– OFr. *sinopre*, var. of *sinople* SINOPLE. Cf. AL. *cinoprum* (XIV).] **1.** A colour of some shade of red –1688. **2. a.** A kind of red earth used as a pigment (orig. one brought to Greece from Sinope). **b.** Cinnabar. –1726.

Sinopic (sinǫ·pik), *a.* 1748. [– L. *Sinopicus* – Gr. Σινωπικός, f. Σινώπη, a Greek colony in Paphlagonia.] Obtained from Sinope or its neighbourhood.

Sinopite (si·nopəit). 1868. [– G. *sinopit*, f. L. *Sinopis* or *Sinope* (see next) + -ITE¹ 2 b. (Hausmann, 1847).] *Min.* A ferruginous clayey earth of a brick-red colour used by ancient races as a paint.

†Sinople. 1450. [– (O)Fr. *sinople* – L. *sinopis* (sc. *terra* earth) – Gr. Σινωπίς, f. Σινώπη Sinope. Cf. SINOPER.] **1.** = SINOPER 1. –1509. **2.** = SINOPER 2. –1683. **3.** The colour green; *spec.* in *Her.*, vert –1728. **b.** *attrib.* or as *adj.* Of a green colour –1698. **4.** *Min.* A variety of ferruginous quartz –1836.

Sinter (si·ntəɹ). 1757. [– G. *sinter* = Eng. *sinder* CINDER.] A hard incrustation or deposit formed upon rocks, etc., by precipitation from mineral waters; esp. *siliceous s.*, geyserite.

‖Sintoc (si·ntǫk). Also **sindoc.** 1842. [Malay *sintoq.*] The bark of *Cinnamomum sintoc.*

Sinuate (si·niu,ĕt), *a.* 1688. [– L. *sinuatus*, pa. pple. of *sinuare* bend, wind, curve, f. SINUS; see -ATE².] *Bot.* Of leaves: Having a margin made wavy or uneven by alternate rounded and somewhat large sinuses and lobes; sinuous. Similarly in *Ent.* of wing-cases, etc.

Sinuated (si·niu,eⁱtėd), *ppl. a.* 1578. [f. as prec. + -ED¹.] **1.** *Bot.* = prec. **2.** Sinuous 1859.

Sinuation (siniu,ēⁱ·ʃən). 1653. [– late L. *sinuatiō, -on* f. L. *sinuare*; see prec., -ION.] **1.** The act or fact of winding about, or pursuing a winding course. **2.** A sinuosity 1676.

Sinuato- (si·niu,eⁱto), comb. form of SINUATE, with the sense 'sinuately', 'sinuate and', as *s.-dentate(d, -undulate*, etc.

Sinuose (si·niu,ōᵘs), *a.* 1829. [– L. *sinuosus*, f. SINUS; see -OSE¹.] Full of or characterized by bends or windings; sinuous.

Sinuosity (siniu,ǫ·sĭti). 1598. [– Fr. *sinuosité* or med.L. *sinuositas*, f. L. *sinuosus*; see prec., -ITY.] **1.** The character, condition, or quality of being sinuous. **2.** (Chiefly *pl.*) A curve or bend, *esp.* one of a series 1720. **b.** *fig.* A complexity or intricacy 1827. **3.** A sinuous movement 1892.

1. Meander is a river..famous for the s. and often returning thereof DRAYTON. **2.** Winding by a narrow path along the sinuosities of the valley SCOTT. **b.** The sinuosities of the discussion 1864.

Sinuoso- (siniu,ōᵘ·so), comb. form of L. *sinuosus*, with the sense 'sinuately', 'sinuate and', as *s.-lobate*, etc.

Sinuous (si·niuəs), *a.* 1578. [– L. *sinuosus* or Fr. *sinueux*; see SINUS, -OUS.] **1.** Characterized by or abounding in turns, curves, or sinuosities; sinuate, curving. **b.** *transf.* Intricate, complex; roundabout 1853. **c.** *fig.* Deviating from the right; morally crooked 1850. **2.** Of movements: Taking place in curves 1877.

1. Insect or Worme,..Streaking the ground with s. trace MILT. A s. band of highlands stretches almost continuously 1878. **c.** A man..who has acquired high station by no s. path 1850. Hence **Si·nuous-ly** *adv.*, **-ness.**

Sinupa·llial, -pa·lliate (siniu-), *adjs.* 1863. [f. *sinu-*, stem of SINUS + PALLIAL *a.*, PALLIATE *a.*] *Conch.* Of certain lamellibranchs: Having the pallial line deeply incurved or inflected beneath the impression of the posterior adductor muscles, for the retraction or expansion of the pallial siphons.

Sinus (səi·nŏs). *Pl.* **sinuses.** 1597. [– L. *sinus* semicircular fold, bosom, bay, etc.] **1.** *Path.* An imposthume, abscess, or sore, forming a narrow suppurating tract and having a small orifice; the cavity or hollow caused by this. **2.** A curvature, flexure, or bend; *spec.* in *Zool.*, a curved recess in a shell 1615. **b.** *Bot.* One of a series of small rounded depressions on the margin of a leaf 1753. **3.** *Anat.* **a.** Any of various venous cavities or reservoirs in different organs or parts of the body 1672. **b.** A natural hole, cell, or cavity in the substance of a bone or other tissue, and either closed or having a relatively small opening 1704. **†4.** A cavity or hole in the earth –1784. **†5.** A bay, gulf, or arm of the sea –1789.

Sinusoid (səi·nŏsoid). 1823. [– Fr. *sinusoïde*, f. L. SINUS + -OID.] **1.** *Math.* A curve of sines (CURVE *sb.* 1). **2.** *Anat.* Venous meshwork in the tissues of an organ 1900. Hence **Sinusoi·dal** *a.* resembling, pursuing, flowing in, the wave-like course of a s.

-sion (ʃən, ʒən), repr. (often through Fr.) L. *-sio, -sion-*, f. pa. ppl. stems ending in *s* + *-io, -ion-* -ION, as in *ascension, mansion, tension*, and *fusion, lesion, occasion.*

Sip, *sb.* 1633. [f. next.] An act of sipping; a small quantity *of* some liquid taken in this way. **b.** *fig.* A mere taste *of* something 1728.

b. A s. is all that the public..ever care to take from reservoirs of abstract philosophy DE QUINCEY.

Sip, *v.* late ME. [prob. symbolic modification of SUP *v.*¹ to express less vigorous action; but cf. LG. *sippen*, which, if early enough, might be the immed. source.] **1.** *intr.* To take up liquid in small quantities with the lips; to drink by a sip or sips; freq. with *of* (a specified liquid). **2.** *trans.* To drink (liquid, etc.) in a very small draughts; to imbibe, or partake of, by sipping. Said also of bees, etc. 1602. **b.** *fig.* To take a mere taste of (something) 1618. **3.** To take honey from (a flower) by sipping 1697.

1. Yee doe here but sippe of this cuppe, but then ye shall drinke up the dreggs of it for ever 1628. **2.** *fig.* Weele drinke a health, while they two sip a kisse MARSTON. **b.** Pleasures he rather sipped than drank off 1639. **3.** The Wingèd Nation.. skim the Floods, and s. the purple Flow'rs DRYDEN.

Sipe (səip), *sb.* Chiefly *Sc.* and *U.S.* OE. [Goes with next.] **1.** The act of percolating or soaking through, on the part of water or other liquid; the water, etc., which percolates. **2.** A small spring or pool of water 1825.

Sipe (səip), *v.* Chiefly *Sc.* and *n. dial.* [repr. OE. *sīpian*, corresp. to OFris. *sīpa*, MLG. *sīpen*, of unkn. origin. Cf. SEEP.] *intr.* Of water, etc.: To percolate or ooze through; to drip or trickle slowly. Hence **Si·page,** leakage or oozing of water.

Siphon (səi·fən), *sb.* Also **syphon.** 1659. [– Fr. *siphon* or L. *sipho, -ōn-* – Gr. σίφων pipe, tube.] **1.** A pipe or tube, bent so that one leg is longer than the other, and used for drawing off liquids. The head of liquid in the longer leg draws the liquid over the bend in the pipe, the column of liquid being sustained by atmospheric pressure. **b.** *transf.* A channel or tube through which water passes on this principle 1744. **c.** *ellipt.* A siphon-bottle, *esp.* one containing aerated water 1875. **2.** *Zool.* **a.** = SIPHUNCLE 1. 1822. **b.** A tube-like organ serving as a canal for the passage of water or other fluid; also, a breathing-tube or suctorial organ 1826. **c.** In certain echinoids and annelids, a tube arising from the posterior extremity of the œsophagus and lying close to the inner margin of the intestine 1888. **3.** *Bot.* One or other of a number of elongated cells which surround the large monosiphonous cell in the frond of certain florideous red algæ 1899. **4.** *attrib.* In names of apparatus, etc., of which a s. forms a part, or which involve the principle or use of the s., as *s. barometer, bottle, condenser, cup, gauge, pump, trap*, etc. Also *s. pipe, tube*, = sense 1; **s.-shell,** a gasteropod having a s. Hence **Si·phonal** *a.* having the form or character of a s.; of or pertaining to a s. (Chiefly *Zool.*) **Si:pho·nic** *a.* of or pertaining to a s.; siphonal (*Zool.*); working by means of, or on the principle of, a s. **Siphoni·gerous** *a. Zool.* having a s.; siphonate.

Siphon (səi·fən), *v.* Also **syphon.** 1859. [f. prec.] **1.** *trans.* To draw off or bring up (liquid, etc.) by means of a siphon 1892. **2.** To empty after the manner of a siphon 1892.

Siphonage (səi·fŏnėdʒ). Also **sy-.** 1855. [f. SIPHON *sb.* + -AGE.] The action of drawing off liquid by means of a siphon; also *spec.* the accidental emptying of a siphon-trap.

‖**Siphonaria** (səifŏnēᵊ·riă). 1861. [mod.L.; see SYPHON *sb.*] A pulmonate gasteropod of the genus *Siphonaria*, distinguished by a siphon passing from the apex to the margin.

Siphonate (səi·fŏnĕt), *a.* and *sb.* 1870. [f. SIPHON *sb.* + -ATE² 2.] **A.** *adj.* Of molluscs: Furnished with, or characterized by having, a siphon. **B.** *sb.* A mollusc furnished with a siphon 1877. So **Si·phonated** *a.* = A. 1851.

Siphonet (səi·fənet). 1826. [f. SIPHON *sb.* + -ET.] *Entom.* A small siphon or tube by which an aphis emits a sweet, honey-like fluid.

Siphono- (səi·fŏno), – Gr. σιφωνο-, comb. form of σίφων SIPHON, used in various terms of *Zool.* and *Bot.*, as **Si:phonobra·nchiate,** *sb.* one of the *Siphonobranchiata*, a former order of gastropods, including those in which the branchial cavity terminates in a prolonged tube or siphon, by which the respiratory current of water is received and expelled; *adj.* having such a tube or siphon; belonging to the order *Siphonobranchiata*. **Siphono·phoran,** *sb.* **Si·phonophore** (-fōᵊɹ) *sb.* a member of the *Siphonophora*, a group of colonial hydrozoans; *adj.* of or belonging to these. **Si:phonosto·matous** *a.*, of the shells of certain crustaceans: having the aperture of the shell notched in front. **Si·phonostome,** one of a family of crustaceans, having a siphon-shaped mouth for suction; also, applied to those gastropods which have the opening of the shell prolonged into a siphon.

Siphuncle (səi·fɒŋk'l). 1822. [– L. *siphunculus*; see next.] **1.** *Zool.* A small canal or tube traversing and connecting the shell-chambers in certain cephalopods. **2.** *Ent.* A small siphon or suctorial organ 1826. Hence **Si·phuncled** *a.* possessing or furnished with a s. **Siphu·ncular** *a.* of or pertaining to, acting or serving as a s. **Siphu·nculated** *a.* possessing or furnished with a s.

‖**Siphunculus** (səifɒ·ŋkiŭlɒs). *Pl.* **-li.** 1752. [L., dim. of *sipho* SIPHON.] *Zool.* = prec. 1.

Sipper (si·pəɹ). 1611. [f. SIP *v.* + -ER¹.] One who sips; hence, a drinker, toper.

Sippet (si·pėt). 1530. [Intended as a dim. of SOP *sb.*; see -ET.] A small piece of toasted or fried bread, usu. served in soup or broth, or with meat, or used for dipping into gravy, etc. **b.** *fig.* A fragment.

Sipple (si·p'l), *v.* + 1566. [f. SIP *v.* + -LE 3.] **1.** *trans.* To drink (liquor, etc.) slowly or by sips; to sip *up*. **2.** *intr.* To sip liquor, etc. leisurely 1606.

Sipu·nculoid, *sb.* and *a.* 1857. [See next and -OID.] *Zool.* **A.** *sb.* A member of the group *Sipunculoidea* of gephyrean worms. **B.** *adj.* Of or belonging to the *Sipunculoidea* 1881.

‖**Sipunculus** (səipɒ·ŋkiŭlɒs). *Pl.* **-li.** 1841. [L., var. of SIPHUNCULUS.] *Zool.* A gephyrean annelid with a retractile proboscis, belonging to the typical genus of the family *Sipunculidæ*.

‖**Si quis** (səi kwis). Also **si-quis, siquis.** 1597. [L. *si* if, *quis* any one (sc. *invenerit* shall have found, etc.), the opening words of the notice or bill (see def.), when written in Latin.] A public notice, freq. one exhibited on a post, door, etc., requesting information, advertising something lost, etc.; later only *Eccl.*, a notice, required in certain cases, intimating that a candidate seeks ordination, and asking if any one knows of any impediment.

Sir (sɔ̄ɹ), *sb.* [ME. *sir, ser, sur*, Sc. *scher*, denoting unstressed vars. of SIRE *sb.*] **I. 1.** The distinctive title of honour of a knight or a baronet, placed before the Christian name. **2.** Applied retrospectively to notable personages of ancient, esp. sacred or classical history. Now *arch.* ME. **3.** Used fancifully, or as a mock title. late ME. †**4.** Placed before the Christian name of ordinary priests (also that of a pope) –1635. †**5.** Used (as tr. L. *dominus*), with the surname of the person, to designate a Bachelor of Arts in some Universities –1822.

1. Sir Nich. Kemys was governour 1645. 2. Shall I Sir Pandarus of Troy become? SHAKS. 3. I am Sir Oracle, And when I ope my lips let no dog barke SHAKS. 5. Sir Wilkinson of Queen's 1714.

II. 1. Placed before a common noun, and forming with it a term of address, as *Sir clerk, knight*, etc. Now *arch.* ME. **b.** With contemptuous, ironic, or irate force. late ME. **2.** Used as a respectful term of address to a superior, or, in later use, an equal (sometimes with additions, as *dear, good*, etc.); also formally in addressing the Speaker of a legislative assembly ME. **b.** Used in beginning or subscribing letters. late ME. **3.** Used with scornful, contemptuous, indignant, or defiant force 1592. **4.** Applied to women. Now *dial.* 1578. **5.** A person of rank or importance; one who might be addressed as 'sir' ME.

1. I am one, that had rather go with sir Priest, then sir knight SHAKS. **b.** *Much Ado* v. i. 83. 2. 'Sir to you', said Mr. Foker politely THACKERAY. 5. A Lady to the worthiest Sir, that euer Country call'd his SHAKS.

Sir (sɔ̄ɹ), *v.* 1576. [f. prec.] **1.** *trans.* To address (a person) as 'sir'. **2.** *intr.* To use the term 'sir' in addressing a person 1798.

1. Don't *Sir* me! don't you know my name? 1890.

‖**Sirdar** (sɔ̄·ɹdāɹ, səɹdā·ɹ). 1615. [– Urdu *sardār*, f. Pers. *sar* head + *dār* possessor.] In India and other Eastern countries, a military chief, a leader or general of a force or army; also *spec.* in recent use, the British commander-in-chief of the Egyptian army. Hence **Sirdarship.**

Sire (səiᵊr), *sb.* ME. [– (O)Fr. *sire* :– Rom. **seior*, for L. *senior* SENIOR.] †**I. 1.** = SIR *sb.* I. 1, 2, and 4. –1492. †**2.** = SIR *sb.* II. 1. –1500. **3.** In early use = SIR *sb.* II. 2. Now only *arch.* (= 'your majesty') or as an echo of French usage. ME.

3. 'S.', said he, 'there has been a battle before Pavia' 1845.

II. 1. One who exercises dominion or rule; a lord, master, or sovereign. Now *rare* or *Obs.* ME. **2.** A person of some note or importance; an aged or elderly man. Also *gen.* man, fellow. late ME. **3.** A father; a male parent; also a forefather. Now chiefly *poet.* ME. **4.** A male parent of a quadruped; *esp.* a stallion: correl. to *dam* 1523.

2. At length a Reverend S. among them came MILT. 3. The sceptre of his sires he took COWPER. *fig.* S. of Insects, mighty Sol PRIOR. 4. So Kids and Whelps their Sires and Dams express DRYDEN. Hence **Si·reless** *a.*

Sire (səiᵊɹ), *v.* 1611. [f. SIRE *sb.*] *trans.* To beget or procreate; to become the sire of. **b.** *spec.* Of animals, esp. horses 1828.

Cowards father Cowards, & Base things Syre Bace SHAKS.

Siredon (səirī·dən). 1842. [– late L. *Siredon* – Gr. Σειρηδών, late form of Σειρήν SIREN.] The axolotl.

Siren (səiᵊ·rən). Also **syren.** [ME. *sereyn, sirene* – OFr. *sereine, sirene* – late L. *Sirena*, fem. form (cf. -A 2) of L. *Siren* (to which the Eng. word was finally assim.) – Gr. Σειρήν (pl. Σειρῆνες).] †**1.** An imaginary species of serpent –1520. **2.** *Greek* and *Latin Myth.* One of several fabulous monsters, part woman, part bird, who were supposed to lure sailors to destruction by their enchanting singing. late ME. **3.** One who, or that which, sings sweetly, charms, allures, or deceives, like the Sirens 1590. **4.** One or other of the eel-like gradient and tailed amphibians belonging to the family *Sirenidæ*, native to N. America; esp. the mud-iguana, *Siren lacertina* 1791. **5.** An acoustical instrument (invented by Cagniard de la Tour in 1819) for producing musical tones and used in numbering the vibrations in any note 1820. **b.** An instrument, made on a similar principle but of larger size, used on steamships, motor-vehicles, etc. for giving fog-signals, etc. 1879.

2. They hauing Sirens tongues and Crocodiles teares, thereby entic'd him to intangle him 1598. 3. Blest pair of Sirens,..Sphear-born harmonious Sisters, Voice and Vers MILT.

attrib., esp. in sense 'characteristic of, resembling that of, a Siren', as *s. air, beauty, note*, etc.; also *s. daughter, enemy*, etc.; *s.-voiced*, etc. Hence **Si·renize** *v. trans.* to delight or charm; to allure or enchant (now *rare*).

Sirenian (səirī·niăn), *sb.* and *a.* 1883. [f. mod.L. *Sirenia*, f. L. SIREN + -IA²; see -IAN.] *Zool.* **A.** *sb.* Any member of the order *Sirenia* of fish-like aquatic mammals. **B.** *adj.* Pertaining to or having the characteristics of this order 1891.

Sirenic (səire·nik), *a. rare.* 1704. [f. SIREN *sb.* + -IC.] **1.** Melodious; charming, fascinating, alluring. **2.** Of persons: Sweet-singing 1797.

1. Spell-caught by their Syrenick Voice 1704. So **Sire·nical** *a.* 1599.

Sirian (si·riăn), *a.* 1591. [f. SIRIUS + -AN.] *Astr.* **1.** Of or belonging to Sirius. **2.** Having a spectrum like that of Sirius 1892.

‖**Siriasis** (sirəi·ăsis). 1601. [– L. *siriasis* – Gr. σειρίασις, f. σειριᾶν be hot and scorching.] *Path.* A disease affecting children, characterized by inflammation of the brain and membranes, and burning fever. **b.** Sunstroke.

‖**Sirius** (si·riɒs). late ME. [L. *Sirius* – Gr. Σείριος.] *Astr.* A fixed star of the first magnitude, the chief of the constellation Canis Major or Great Dog, and the brightest in the heavens; the dog-star.

‖**Sirkar** (sɔ̄·ɹkāɹ). *Anglo-Ind.* 1619. [– Urdu – Pers. *sarkār*, f. *sar* head + *kār* agent, doer.] †**1.** The court or palace of a native king or prince –1626. **2.** A province; a revenue division 1627. **3.** The State or Government 1798. **4.** A house-steward (usu. native) 1772. **5.** A native clerk, accountant, or agent 1828.

Sirloin (sɔ̄·ɹloin). Also **surloin.** late ME. [– OFr. **surloigne*, var. of med. and mod. Fr. *surlonge*, f. *sur* over, above (see SUR-) + *longe* LOIN.] The upper and choicer part of a loin of beef, used for roasting. Also const. *of*. **b.** *transf.* Of persons 1648.

Sirmark (sɔ̄·ɹmaɹk). Also **surmark.** 1664. [perh. f. *sur-* over + MARK *sb.*¹] *Shipbuilding.* One or other of several marks made upon a mould to indicate where the respective bevellings are to be applied to the frame-timbers of a vessel.

Siroc (səi·rǫk, sirǫ·k). 1775. [– Fr. †*siroc(h*; see next.] = SIROCCO 1.

Sirocco (sirǫ·ko). 1617. [– Fr. *sirocco*, earlier †*siroc(h* – It. *scirocco*, ult. – Arab. *šurūķ* rising of the sun, east.] **1.** An oppressively hot and blighting wind, blowing from the north coast of Africa over the Mediterranean and affecting parts of Southern Europe (where it is also moist and depressing). Usu. with *the*. **b.** With *a* and *pl.* 1820. **2.** A sirocco drying-machine 1890.

attrib., as *s. blast, wind*, etc.; also **s. drying-closet, drying-machine, oven,** a closet, machine, or oven for drying hops or tea-leaves by means of a hot, moist current of air.

Sirrah (si·ră). Now *arch.* 1526. [Early forms *syrra, sirah*, etc., prob. repr. late ME. *sirĕ* SIRE with the last syll. finally assim. to AH.] **1.** A term of address used to men or boys, expressing contempt, reprimand, or assumption of authority on the part of the speaker. †2. Applied to women (seriously or in jest) –1711.

1. S., I'll break your bones! MME. D'ARBLAY. Give me a glass of brandy, s. host 1860. 2. You lose all your money at cards, s. Stella SWIFT.

Sir-re·verence. *Obs.* exc. *dial.* 1575. [Alteration of *save* (abbrev. *sa'*) *reverence.*] †1. *S. of*, with all respect for, with apologies to. Also without const. –1687. 2. Human excrement 1592. b. With *a*. A lump or piece of this 1592.

1. A very reuerent body: I such a one, as a man may not speake of, without he say sir reuerence SHAKS.

Sirup, obs. and U.S. var. SYRUP.

‖**Sirvente** (sɪrvɑ̃nt). 1819. [– Fr. *sirvente* – Pr. *sirventes*, the final *s* of which was misapprehended as a pl. ending; of unkn. origin.] A form of poem or lay, usu. satirical, employed by the troubadours of the Middle Ages.

Sisal (sisā·l sai·sǎ). 1843. Name of a port in Yucatan, used attrib. to designate the prepared fibre of several species of *Agave* and *Fourcroya*, used in rope-making. Also *S. plant*, the aloe or other plant from which the fibre is obtained. Also *ellipt.*, chiefly *attrib.* 1883.

Siscowet (si·skoˌet). 1849. [Ojibwa, lit. = 'cooks itself'.] A variety of the great lake trout of N. America, found in Lake Superior.

Sisel (si·sěl). 1880. [– G. *ziesel*; cf. earlier ZIZEL.] A kind of ground-squirrel, *Spermophilus citillus.*

Siserary (sisěrēᵊ·ri). Now *dial.* Also **siserara**, etc. 1481. [Popular corruption of CERTIORARI.] †1. A writ of Certiorari –1761. 2. *With a s.*, with a vengeance; suddenly, promptly 1607. 3. A severe scolding; a sharp blow; a torrent *of* (language) 1771.

Siskin (si·skin). 1562. [– MDu. *siseken*, early Flem. *sijsken* (Du. *sijsje*), dim. based on MLG. *sisek*, *czītze*, MHG. *zīsec*, *zīse* (G. *zeisig*), of Slav. origin.] 1. A small song-bird, in some respects closely allied to the goldfinch; also called ABERDEVINE. 2. Applied with defining words to other small birds related to or resembling the siskin 1783.

2. *Chrysomitris pinus*, . .American S. 1884.
attrib.: **s.-green,** a light green inclining to yellow.

Siss, *sb.*[1] *U.S.* Also **sis.** 1859. Abbrev. of *sister*, used in addressing girls and young women. So **Si·ssy** [-Y[6]] orig. and chiefly *U.S.*; also an effeminate or inefficient man or boy.

Siss, *sb.*[2] 1870. [Cf. next.] A hissing sound.

Siss (sis), *v.* Now *dial.* and *U.S.* [ME. *cissen*, *sissen*, = MDu. *cissen*, Du. and LG. *sissen*; of imit. origin.] To hiss.

‖**Sissoo** (si·sū). 1810. [Urdu (Hindi) *sīsū*.] 1. A valuable Indian timber-tree *Dalbergia sissoo*. 2. The timber of this tree 1810.

Sist, *sb.* 1693. [f. next.] *Sc. Law.* A stay or suspension of some proceeding; *spec.* an 'order or injunction of the Lord Ordinary prohibiting diligence to proceed' (Bell).

Sist, *v. Sc.* 1652. [– L. *sistere* cause to stand.] 1. *trans.* To stop, stay, or suspend (some proceeding, etc.), *esp.* by judicial decree. 2. To cause or order (a person) to appear *before* a court; to summon or cite 1721.

1. The whole business of metaphysic. .is summarily sisted 1881.

Sister (si·stəɹ), *sb.* [– ON. *systir*, superseding native forms (*suster*, *soster*) repr. cogn. OE. *sweoster*, *swuster*, *swyster*, *suster* = OFris. *swester*, *suster*, *sister*, OS. *swestar*, MLG., MDu. *suster* (Du. *zuster*), OHG. *swester* (G. *schwester*), Goth. *swistar* :– Gmc. **swestr* :– IE. **swesr-*, **swesŏr*, repr. in L. *soror* (:– **swesor*).] 1. A female in relationship to another person or persons having the same parents. (Also applied to animals.)

Sometimes loosely used in the sense of HALF-SISTER, and in that of SISTER-IN-LAW.

2. *fig.* One who is reckoned as, or fills the place of, a sister OE. 3. a. A female member of a religious order, society, or guild; *spec.* a nun OE. b. A female fellow-member of the Christian Church as a whole; or of some body or association within this 1449. c. A member of a body of nurses; now *spec.* a head-nurse having charge of a ward in an infirmary or hospital 1552. 4. a. Used to designate qualities, conditions, etc., in relation to each other or to some kindred thing ME. b. Applied to mythological or imaginary beings; esp. *the* (*fatal* or *three*) *sisters*, the Fates or Parcæ. late ME. 5. A thing having close kinship or relationship to another 1613.

1. Daughter, s., wife, And mother of their Cæsars GRAY. 2. Sey to wisdam, My s. thou art WYCLIF *Prov.* 7:4. 3. a. One Isabell, a S. SHAKS. *Sister(s) of Charity*, *of Mercy*, etc. 4. Thou with Eternal wisdom didst converse, Wisdom thy S. MILT. b. Begin then, Sisters of the sacred well MILT. 5. Sparta. .in laws and institutions is the s. of Crete 1875.

attrib. and *Comb.* †a. The old uninflected genitive remained in common use down to the 16th c. in terms of relationship, esp. *sister son*. b. *spec.*: **s.-block,** one of two blocks made of ash, and turned out of a solid piece, one above the other; **-hook,** a double hook in which the shanks of the respective portions form mousings for the fellow portions.

Si·ster, *v.* 1608. [f. prec.] 1. *trans.* To stand to (a person or thing) in the relationship of a sister or sisters. 2. To call (a person) sister; to address as a sister 1663.

Sister-german. late ME. [f. SISTER *sb.* + GERMAN *a.*[1]] A sister through both parents; a full sister.

Sisterhood (si·stəɹhud). late ME. [f. SISTER *sb.* + -HOOD.] 1. The state or condition of being a sister; sisterly status or relationship. 2. A society of sisters; *esp.* a society of women bound by certain vows and living together under conventual rule, or otherwise devoted to religious or charitable work as a vocation 1592. b. Used loosely to denote a number of females having some common characteristic or calling. Often in depreciatory sense. 1609.

1. She. .left to doo the part Of s., to doo that of a wife 1609. 2. Ile dispose of thee, Among a S. of holy Nunnes SHAKS. b. Have the whole S. of Canting Females banished 1718. *fig.* A s. of churches 1883.

Sistering (si·stəriŋ), *ppl. a.* 1597. [f. SISTER *v.* + -ING[2].] Having a relationship comparable in some way to that of a sister or sisters.

Si·ster-in-law. 1440. [See -IN-LAW.] a. The sister of one's husband or wife. b. The wife of one's brother. c. The wife of one's husband's or wife's brother.

Sisterly (si·stəɹli), *a.* 1570. [f. SISTER *sb.* + -LY[1].] 1. Of or pertaining to a sister; befitting or like a sister. 2. Of or pertaining to a sisterhood 1883.

1. They. .exchanged a s. kiss, and a s. good-night SCOTT. Hence **Si·sterliness.**

‖**Sistrum** (si·strǒm). *Pl.* **sistra** (**sistrums**). late ME. [L. – Gr. σεῖστρον, f. σείειν shake.] A musical instrument consisting of a thin oval metal frame furnished with transverse metal rods loosely fixed in it and a handle by which it was shaken.

Orig. peculiar to Egypt and the worship of Isis, but subseq. used in other Oriental countries.

Sisyphean (sisifī·ăn), *a.* 1635. [f. L. *Sisypheius* – Gr. Σισύφειος, f. Σίσυφος Sisyphus, name of a king of Corinth, whose punishment in Hades was to roll a heavy stone up a hill; as he reached the top, the stone rolled down again.] Of or pertaining to Sisyphus; like (that of) Sisyphus; resembling the fruitless toil of Sisyphus; endless and ineffective. So **Sisyphian** (sisi·fiăn) *a.* 1599.

Sit (sit), *sb.* 1776. [f. the vb.] 1. The manner in which an article of dress, or some part of one, is disposed or fits the person. 2. A spell of sitting 1832. 3. A sinking or settling down (of a wall, the roof of a mine, etc.) 1808.

1. Long lectures about the s. of a cap 1776.

Sit (sit), *v.* Pa. t. and pa. pple. **sat** (sæt). [OE. *sittan* = OFris. *sitta*, OS. *sittian*, OHG. *sizzen* (Du. *zitten*, G. *sitzen*), ON. *sitja* :– Gmc. (Goth. has *sitan*) **sitjan*, **setjan*, f. **set-* :– IE. **sed-* **sod-* **sd-*, repr. also in L. *sedēre*, Gr. ἕζεσθαι.] I. *intr.* 1. Of persons: To be or remain in that posture in which the weight of the body rests upon the posteriors; to be seated. b. *spec.* Used of persons seated (usu. at a table) for the purpose of, or while engaged in, eating, drinking, gaming, etc. ME. 2. To occupy a seat in the capacity of a judge or with some administrative function OE. b. To occupy an episcopal, or the papal, see. late ME. c. To have a seat in, be a member of, a council or legislative assembly. Also const. *for* (a constituency). late ME. 3. Of a legislative or other assembly: To hold a session; to be engaged in the transaction of business 1518. 4. a. To place oneself in a position for having one's portrait painted or for being photographed. Also const. *for* (one's portrait), *to* (a painter, etc.). 1538. b. To serve as a model *for* a painting or a character in a novel 1673. c. To present oneself *for* examination; *Camb. Univ.* to be a candidate *for* a fellowship 1830. 5. To be, to continue or remain, *in* a certain condition. Now *rare* or *Obs.* OE. 6. To have one's seat, quarters, or place; to abide, dwell, remain (in a place) OE. b. To be tenant of, to occupy, a house, farm, etc.; to remain during a lease; to continue a tenancy. Usu. const. *at* (a certain rent), or with compl. 1598. 7. To remain at a siege OE. 8. Of birds: To perch or roost; also, to rest the body on the ground or other surface OE. b. To take up or continue in the posture necessary for the hatching of eggs. Also const. *on.* 1483. 9. Of animals: To rest the body in a manner analogous to that of a seated person ME. 10. To support the body *on the knees*. *Obs.* exc. *dial.* OE.

1. Like silly Beggars. .sitting in the Stockes SHAKS. I sha'n't dare to sit cross-legg'd for you without offence 1754. I see them s., they linger yet GRAY. I had sat on pins during the inquisition 1885. *fig.* Thy rapt soul sitting in thine eyes MILT. *To s. on the* or *one's throne*, to reign. 2. The summons was heard by the registrar, sitting as Deputy Chancellor 1896. Phr. *To s. in judgement*: see JUDGEMENT 1. c. You used to s. for Silverbridge TROLLOPE. 3. In the House of Lords the presence of three members is sufficient to enable the House to s. 1863. 4. b. *fig.* Airy dreams Sat for the picture COWPER. 5. While Virtue, Valour, Wisdom s. in want MILT. Conscience sat mistress over the whole earth 1833. 6. *fig.* The lady. .who sits, indeed, very near my heart FIELDING. b. S. wha like, I'll flitt 1844. 8. b. *fig.* Thou. .Dove-like satst brooding on the vast Abyss And mad'st it pregnant MILT. 10. While he sat on his knees before me, mopping and mowing SCOTT.

II. 1. Of things: To have place or location; to rest or lie *on* OE. b. Of the wind: To blow from, be in, a particular quarter. c. In fig. phr. said of the effect of emotion, etc. *on* the mind, food *on* the stomach. late ME. 2. Of clothes: a. With dative: To fit or suit (a person, etc.). *rare.* ME. b. To fit (well, tightly, etc.). late ME. †3. Usu. *impers.* To suit; to be fitting or proper –1579.

1. The Ship sat upright DE FOE. The village of Cocurès, sitting among vineyards and meadows STEVENSON. *fig.* Truth sits upon the lips of dying men M. ARNOLD. b. Sits the winde in that corner? SHAKS. 2. A close dress of scarlet which sate tight to his body SCOTT. *fig.* A light stoicism sits gracefully on him CARLYLE.

III. 1. To seat oneself; to take a seat; to sit down OE. 2. To rise *upright*, *on end*, move or lean *back*, in a sitting posture ME.

1. This said, he sat HOBBES.

With advs. **S. down.** a. To seat oneself; to take a seat. b. To establish oneself in some position or place; to settle, take up one's abode. Now chiefly *U.S.* (*b*) To encamp *before* a town, etc., in order to besiege it. (*c*) *fig.* Of persons or things, to settle down in some way. c. To put up, rest content, *with*, †to acquiesce *in*, something. **S. on.** To continue to sit, to remain, stay on. **S. out.** a. To sit apart from others, or to remain seated, so as to take no part in a game, dance, etc. b. To sit in the open air. **S. up.** a. To raise the body to (an upright) sitting posture. b. To defer the hour for retiring to bed until late; to wait up *for*; to watch through the night (or some part of it) *with* one. c. To be in a sitting posture, in contrast to lying in bed. *To s. up and take notice*: said orig. of a person beginning to recover from an illness; hence, to become aware of the state of things. d. *To make* (a person) *s. up* (*slang*), to astonish, startle, have a powerful effect on him. With preps. **S. on** or **upon.** a. To sit in judgement or council, to deliberate, on (a person or matter). b. To have a seat on (a jury, commission, etc.). c. *slang.* To squash, check, snub. **S. over.** a. To be occupied with (a matter etc.), while sitting; to pore over (a book). b. *Bridge.* To be on the left hand of, and so in an advantageous position over. **S. under,** to listen to, be a hearer of, attend the church of (a minister or preacher).

IV. 1. *refl.* To seat oneself OE.; esp. with *down* 1450. 2. *trans.* To sit, or keep one's seat, on 1542. b. To sit on (eggs) 1600. c. To sit in (a boat) with proper poise 1866. 3. To cause to sit *down, up*; seat in a certain place 1470. **4.** To resist, endure, put up with (*rare* or *Obs.*) late ME.

S. thee by our side SHAKS. I s. me down a pensive hour to spend GOLDSM. **2.** It was difficult to s. our horses WESLEY. **4.** I don't know how to sit it sometimes NEWMAN.

S. out. a. To remain seated and take no part in (a game, etc.). **b.** To remain sitting throughout the course of. **c.** To sit longer than (another) at a meeting, etc. **S.-down,** applied to a strike in which workmen occupy their place of employment while refusing to work or to allow others to do so.

Sitar (si·tāɹ). *Anglo-Ind.* 1845. [– Urdu *sitār.*] An ancient Indian long-necked lute-like musical instrument with seven strings.

Site (səit), *sb.* late ME. [– AFr. *site* (XIV) or L. *situs* local position, perh. f. *sit-*, pa. ppl. stem of *sinere* leave, allow to remain.] †**1.** The place or position occupied by some specified thing. Freq. implying original or fixed position. –1691. †**b.** With *a* and *pl.* –1716. †**c.** Without article: Place, position, situation –1697. †**d.** Attitude, position, or posture (of the body, etc.) –1746. **2.** The situation or position of a place, town, building, etc. Occas. without article. 1567. **3.** The ground or area upon which a building, town, etc., has been built, or which is set apart for some purpose. Also, a plot, or number of plots, of land intended or suitable for building. 1461. **b.** *transf.* The seat *of* (an industry); the scene *of* (some condition, etc.) 1637.

1. Of the providence and wisdome of God in the s. and motion of the Sun SIR T. BROWNE. **d.** The attitude of a lover, fix'd In melancholy s. THOMSON. **2.** The sublime s. of the Castle 1781. **3.** In rude and unsettled times, these insular sites afforded safe retreats 1863. *Plane of s.*, in *Fortif.*, a plane coinciding approximately with that of the ground occupied by a work.

Site (səit), *v.* 1598. [f. the sb.] **1.** *trans.* To locate, to place. **2.** *intr.* To be situated or placed; to lie 1630.

Sited (səi·tėd), *ppl. a.* 1455. [f. SITE *sb.* + -ED² or L. *situs* + -ED¹.] **1.** Of buildings, countries, etc.: Having a (certain) site or situation; situated. (Re-formed in the 20th c.) †**2.** Of things, persons, etc.: Having a particular place or position; placed, seated –1660.

1. A little howse..s. in midst of a small wood 1619.

Si·t-fast, sitfast, *sb.* and *a.* 1611. [f. SIT *v.* + FAST *adv.*] **A.** *sb. Farriery.* A hard excrescence, induration, or tumour, tending to ulceration, produced on the back of a horse by the uneven pressure or chafing of the saddle. **B.** *adj.* Marked or characterized by sitting firmly; fixed, firm 1807.

Which the cultivators of the soil have not yet been able to dig up from its sitfast hold 1807.

Sith, *adv., prep.*, and *conj.* Now *dial.* or *arch.* [OE. *siþþa*, ME. *siþþe, siþ(e*, clipped form of *siþþan* SITHEN.] **A.** *adv.* †**1.** Then, thereupon; afterwards –1450. †**b.** Next in succession, order, or place. – late ME. †**2.** Continuously or ever from or since that time –1621. †**3.** = SINCE *adv.* 3, 4. –1549. †**B.** *prep.* = SINCE *prep.* –1593. **C.** *conj.* †**1.** From, subsequent to, or since the time that –1581. **2.** = SINCE *conj.* 2. Now *arch.* or *poet.* late ME. †**b.** So *s. that* –1678.

2. For s. the day is come þat I shal dye, I make pleynly my confession CHAUCER.

†**Sithe,** *sb.*¹ [OE. *siþ* = OS. *sīþ*, OHG. *sind, sint*, ON. *sinn*, Goth. *sinþs* journey; see SEND *v.*¹] Journey; time, occasion –1630.

Sithe (səið), *v.* Now *dial.* ME. [var. of SIGH *v.*] *intr.* To sigh. Also *trans.*, to say with a sigh. So **Sithe** *sb.*² a sigh.

†**Si·then,** *adv., conj.*, and *prep.* [OE. *siþþon, -an*, for earlier **sīð þon* (*þan*) 'subsequently to that', with shortening of the first vowel.] = SITH *adv.* (–1669), *conj.* (–1572), *prep.* (–1604).

Si·thence, *adv., conj.*, and *prep. Obs.* exc. *arch.* Also **sithens** (*arch.*). late ME. [f. prec. + -S; cf. SINCE.] = prec., in all uses.

Sitio- (sitio), comb. form of Gr. σιτίον food made from grain, bread, as **Sitio·logy,** dietetics. **Sitioma·nia, Sitiopho·bia,** morbid repugnance or aversion to food.

Sito- (səito), comb. form of Gr. σῖτος food made from grain, bread, as **Sito·logy,** = SITIOLOGY. **Sitoma·nia, Sitopho·bia,** = SITIOPHOBIA; hence **Sitopho·bic** *a.*

‖**Sitringee** (sitri·ndʒī). *Anglo-Ind.* 1621. [– Urdu *shaṭranjī*, f. Pers. *šaṭranj* chess, with ref. to the original chequered pattern.] A carpet or floor-rug made of coloured cotton, now usually with a striped pattern.

Sitter (si·təɹ). ME. [f. SIT *v.* + -ER¹.] **1.** One who sits or occupies a seat; *esp.* one who sits to an artist, photographer, or sculptor, for a portrait, etc., or as a model. **b.** A passenger in a boat as dist. from the rowers or steersman; *spec.* at Eton 1653. **c.** One who has a séance with a medium or the like 1909. **2.** A female bird, *esp.* a domestic hen, which sits on eggs for the purpose of hatching them 1614. **3.** *slang* or *colloq.* An easy mark or shot (as at a sitting bird); a thing easily done, a certainty 1908.

Sittine (si·təin), *sb.* and *a.* 1829. [f. mod.L. *Sittinæ*.] *Ornith.* **A.** *sb.* A member of the *Sittinæ*, a sub-family of the Linnæan genus *Sitta*. **B.** *adj.* Of or pertaining to this family.

Sitting (si·tiŋ), *vbl. sb.* ME. [f. SIT *v.* + -ING¹.] **1.** The action of SIT *v.*; the fact of being seated; an instance of this. **2.** The action on the part of hen-birds of sitting on and hatching eggs; incubation. late ME. **b.** A number of eggs placed under a sitting bird for incubation; a clutch 1854. **3.** The fact of being engaged in the exercise of judicial, legislative, or deliberative functions; an instance or occasion of this; a meeting of a legislative or other body; the period of time occupied by this. late ME. **b.** A séance 1880. **4.** A thing or place on which one sits; a seat, *esp.* in later use, a seat for one person in a church, etc. late ME. **5.** A spell of sitting or of remaining seated 1596. **6.** With advs., as *down, out, up* 1535.

1. Why should a student indulge so much in the lazy and unhealthy habit of s.? 1874. **2.** The Male ..amuses and diverts her with his Songs during the whole Time of her S. ADDISON. **3.** The speaker was twenty hours in the chair, which was the longest s.,..that is remembered 1764. **5.** I am going to give Kneller my last s. 1829. Phr. *At a* or *one s.*, at one time or spell of continuous action, work, or study.

Comb.: **s.-room,** a room or apartment used for sitting in, esp. in contrast to a bedroom or kitchen; also, room or space in which to sit or available for sitting.

Situate (si·tiu,ėt), *ppl. a.* 1523. [– late L. *situatus*, f. L. *situs* SITE *sb.*; see -ATE².] Situated.

Situate (si·tiu,eⁱt), *v.* Now *rare.* 1532. [f. *situat-*, f. med. L. *situare*; see -ATE³.] *trans.* To give a site to; to place, locate. **b.** To place in a certain situation 1896.

Situated (si·tiu,eⁱtėd), *ppl. a.* 1560. [f. SITUATE *ppl. a.* + -ED¹.] **1.** Of places or things: Placed, located. **2.** Of persons: Placed in relation to, or in respect of, circumstances 1702.

1. *Oxford*, a city..s. on a gentle eminence 1808. **2.** It was impossible for me to be thus s., and not feel..the demon of my race at work within me 1857.

Situation (sitiu,ēⁱ·ʃən). 1490. [– (O)Fr. *situation* or med.L. *situatiō, -on* f. *situat-*, pa. ppl. stem of *situare* place, set up, etc., f. L. *situs* SITE *sb.*; see -ION.] **I. 1.** The place, position, or location *of* a city, country, etc., in relation to its surroundings. **2.** †**a.** The place occupied by something; the site *of* a building, etc. –1730. **b.** A place, locality 1610. **3. a.** Place or position of things in relation to surroundings or to each other 1600. †**b.** A place or locality in which a person resides, or happens to be for the time –1825.

1. The s. of the cytie of Saba in Ethiopia vnder Egipt 1553. **2. b.** The pleasant scituation called Beaulieu 1610. **3. b.** Educated in a remote s. SCOTT.

II. 1. The position in life, or in relation to others, held or occupied by a person 1710. **b.** A post of employment; a position in which one works for wages 1813. **2.** Condition or state (*of* anything). *Obs.* or *arch.* 1710. **b.** Physical condition; state of health. In later use only *spec.* of women. 1749. **3.** Position of a person with regard to circumstances 1728. **4.** Position of affairs; combination of circumstances 1750. **b.** A particular conjunction of circumstances under which the characters are presented in the course of a novel or play 1779.

1. My s., as a soldier under command SCOTT. **b.** The s. of army-agent 1813. **2. b.** Mrs. Bunny's in an interesting s...and has given the Lieutenant seven already THACKERAY. **3.** The difficulties of his s. increased 1860. **4.** The financial s. is perceptibly clearer 1884. **b.** There's s. for you! there's an heroic group! SHERIDAN.

‖**Situs** (səi·tŏs). *rare.* 1701. [L.; see SITE *sb.*] Situation, position.

Sitz bath (si·ts,bɑþ). Also **sitz-bath.** 1849. [– G. *sitzbad*, f. *sitzen* sit + *bad* bath.] **1.** A bath in which one sits; a hip-bath. **2.** A bath taken by means of this 1852.

Sivaism (sī·vă,iz'm). 1875. [f. Skr. *Siva* 'the auspicious one' (see def.) + -ISM.] The special worship of Siva, the third deity of the Hindu triad, to whom are attributed the powers of reproduction and dissolution.

‖**Sivatherium** (sīvăþīᵊ·riŏm). 1835. [mod. L., f. *Siva* the Hindu god + Gr. θηρίον wild beast.] *Palæont.* A fossil ruminant of great size, with four horns, discovered in the Siwalik or Sub-Himalayan hills in Northern India.

Si·vvens. *Obs.* exc. *Hist.* See also SIBBENS. 1762. [– local Gael. *suibhean* raspberry.] An infectious skin disease formerly prevalent in Scotland.

A loathsome and very infectious disease of the venereal kind, called the *Sivvens*.. Sometimes a fungus appears in various parts of the body, resembling a raspberry, in the Erse language called *Sivven*. 1776.

Six (siks), *a.* and *sb.* [OE. *siex, syx, seox, sex* = OFris. *sex*, OS., OHG. *sehs* (Du. *zes*, G. *sechs*), ON. *sex*, Goth. *saihs* :– Gmc. **seks*, varying in IE. with **sweks*, and repr. by L. *sex*, Gr. ἕξ.] The cardinal number next after five, represented by the symbols 6, VI, or vi. **A.** *adj.* **1.** In concord with a sb. expressed. **b.** Followed by *hundred* or *thousand*, or the ordinals of these. Also, *six-sevenths, -tenths*, etc. six (parts, etc.) out of seven, ten, etc. OE. **c.** Coupled with a higher cardinal or ordinal numeral following, so as to form a compound number OE. **2.** With ellipsis of sb., which may usu. be supplied from the context OE.

1. The Creation of the world in the s. daies work 1662. *S. Nations* (of Amer. Indians), the Mohawks, the Oneidas, the Onondegas, the Cayugas, the Senecas, and the Tuscaroras. **b.** Into the valley of Death Rode the s. hundred TENNYSON. **c.** The sixe and thirtieth Chapter 1579. S.-and-twenty years of travel KINGSLEY. **2.** At s...he was a charming child BYRON. The rule..was to rise and sup at s. 1834. A coach and s. 1849. Phr. *S. of one and half-a-dozen of the other*, denoting that there is no difference of choice between two (sets of) persons or things.

B. *sb.* **1.** The abstract number six, or the symbol denoting this. late ME. **2.** Chiefly *pl.* **a.** A set of six spots or pips on a die, domino, or card; also, a card, etc., having six pips or spots 1599. **b.** A set of six persons 1796. **3.** *pl.* In various elliptic uses. **a.** Lines of six syllables 1586. **b.** Gloves, shoes, etc., of the sixth size 1796. **c.** Six-pounder guns 1804. **d.** Candles weighing six to the pound 1825. **e.** Six-inch flower-pots 1851. **f.** Bonds bearing interest at six per cent. 1867.

2. a. 'Tis a hundred to one, if a man fling two Sixes COWLEY. **3. g.** A six-cylinder motor car 1920.

Phr. *S. and seven, sixes and sevens*, etc., originally denoting the hazard of one's whole fortune, a carelessness as to the consequences of one's actions, and in later use the creation or existence of, or neglect to remove, confusion, disorder, or disagreement.

C. *Comb.* **1.** Combining (usually hyphened) with a sb. and forming an attrib. compound, as *six-bar* (gate), *six-bottle* (man) 1614. **b.** In phr. *six-year(s)-old* used attrib. or absol. 1630. **2.** In comb. with sbs. ending in *-er*, as *six-footer, -wheeler* 1844. **3.** In advb. sense, = 'in six parts', as *six-partite*, etc. **4.** Miscellaneous, as **s.-chamber,** a six-chambered revolver; **-oar,** a six-oared boat; **-shot, stroke,** a stroke in billiards counting six points; etc.

Sixain (sī·zeⁱn). 1575. [– Fr. *sixain* (OFr. *sisain*), f. *six* six.] A six-lined stanza.

Sixer (si·ksəɹ). *colloq.* 1870. [f. SIX *a.* + -ER¹.] Anything that counts as six (as a hit for six runs at cricket).

Si·xfoil. 1849. [f. SIX *a.*, after *cinquefoil*, etc.] *Arch.* and *Her.* An ornamental design (or opening) having the form of six leaflets or petals radiating from a common centre.

Sixfold (si·ksfōᵘld), *a.* OE. [f. SIX *a.* + -FOLD.] Consisting of six together; comprising six things, kinds, etc.; also, six times as great or as numerous; sextuple.

Si·x-foot, *a.* 1683. [See SIX C. 1.] **1.** Measuring six feet in length, breadth, or height. **2.** Containing six (metrical) feet 1891.

1. *Six-foot way*, the space between two parallel railway lines; also with ellipsis of *way*.

Sixpence (si·kspĕns). late ME. [f. SIX *a.* + PENCE.] **1.** A sum of money equal in value to six pennies. **2.** A British silver coin worth six pennies 1598.

Sixpenny (si·kspĕni), *a.* (and *sb.*) late ME. [SIX *a.*] **1.** *S. nail*, a nail orig. costing sixpence per hundred. **2.** Of persons: That may be hired for sixpence; earning no more than sixpence; worth only sixpence; paltry, petty 1561. **3.** Costing, or priced at, sixpence 1591. **b.** As *sb.* A book (*esp.* a novel) or magazine published at sixpence 1894. **4.** Amounting to, having the value of, sixpence 1592.

2. 1 *Hen. IV*, II. i. 82. **3.** Bring him a s. bottle of ale B. JONSON. **4.** *S. bit* or *piece* = SIXPENCE 2.

Six-pounder (si:kspau·ndəɹ). 1684. [f. SIX *a.* + POUNDER² II. 1.] **1.** A cannon throwing shot six pounds in weight. **2.** A thing, e.g. a shot, weighing six pounds 1855.

Si·xscore, *a.* Now *arch.* ME. [f. SIX *a.* + SCORE *sb.*] One hundred and twenty.

Si·x-shoo·ter. 1856. [f. SIX C. 2.] A revolver capable of firing six shots without reloading; a six-chambered revolver.

Sixteen (sikstī·n, si·kstīn), *a.* and *sb.* [OE. *siextiene*, etc.; see SIX *a.*, -TEEN.] The cardinal number composed of ten and six, represented by the symbols 16, XVI, or xvi. **A.** *adj.* **1.** In concord with a sb. expressed. **2.** With ellipsis of sb. (esp. *years*), which may usu. be supplied from the context ME.

1. Some sixteene moneths SHAKS. **2.** When I—was s. 1891.

B. *sb.* **1.** The abstract number sixteen OE. **2.** A sheet of sixteen leaves; a book in sixteenmo 1606. **3.** A girl of sixteen 1840.

Sixtee·nmo. 1847. [English reading of the symbol 16mo.] = SEXTO-DECIMO.

Sixteenth (sikstī·nþ, si·kstīnþ), *a.* and *sb.* ME. [f. SIXTEEN + -TH², repl. OE. *syxtēoþa*, etc.] The ordinal numeral belonging to the cardinal sixteen. **A.** *adj.* **1.** In concord with a sb. expressed or implied. **2.** *S. note*, the sixteenth part of a semibreve; a semiquaver 1861. **B.** *sb.* **1.** A sixteenth part 1611. **2.** *Mus.* **a.** The interval of two octaves and a second. **b.** A sixteenth note. 1876.

Sixth (siksþ), *a.* and *sb.* [f. SIX *a.* + -TH², repl. OE. *siexta*, ME. *sixt(e.*] The ordinal numeral belonging to the cardinal six. **A.** *adj.* **1.** In concord with a sb. expressed or implied. **b.** Following on the names of kings, popes, etc. late ME. **2.** *ellipt.* 1573.

1. And the euening and the morning were the s. day. *Gen.* 1:31. **b.** King James the S. 1857. **2.** The sixt of May 1631.

B. *sb.* **1.** A sixth part 1577. **2.** *Mus.* A tone on the sixth degree above or below another, both tones being counted; the harmonic combination of two such tones; an interval comprising six degrees of the scale 1597. **3.** The sixth form in a school 1857. Hence **Si·xthly** *adv.* in the s. place.

Sixtieth (si·kstiĕþ), *a.* and *sb.* [f. SIXTY + *-eth* -TH², repl. OE. *siextigoþa*.] **A.** *adj.* The ordinal numeral belonging to the cardinal sixty. **B.** *sb.* A sixtieth part 1800.

Sixty (si·ksti), *a.* and *sb.* [OE. *siextiġ*; see SIX *a.*, -TY².] The cardinal number equal to six times ten, represented by the symbols 60, LX, or lx. **A.** *adj.* **1.** In concord with a sb. expressed or implied. **2.** Followed immediately by a lesser numeral, as *sixty-one*, etc. 1597. **3.** Forming part of an ordinal number 1647. **b.** With *part*, or used absol. in this sense, esp. *sixty-fourth* 1768. **B.** *sb.* **1.** The abstract number sixty ME. **2.** Sixty years of age. Also *sixty-one*, etc. 1717. **3.** *pl.* The years from 60 to 69 in a century, or in a person's life; the period 1860–1869. 1886.

Comb.: *Sixty-fourmo*, the size of the page of a book in which each leaf is $\frac{1}{64}$ of a full sheet; abbrev. 64mo. *Sixty-fours*, a sheet in 64mo.

Sixtyfold (si·kstifōᵘld), *a.* (and *sb.*) OE. [-FOLD.] Sixty times as great or as much.

Sizar (səi·zăɹ). Also †**sizer.** 1588. [f. SIZE *sb.*¹ I. 4 + -AR³, -ER².] In the University of Cambridge, and at Trinity College, Dublin, an undergraduate member admitted under this designation, and receiving an allowance from the college to enable him to study.

The name probably indicates that the person so admitted received his 'sizes' free. Formerly the sizar performed certain duties now discharged by the college servants. Hence **Si·zarship,** the position or status of being a s.

Size (səiz), *sb.*¹ ME. [– OFr. *sise*, *size*, aphetic of *assise* ASSIZE, or aphetic var. of the Eng. word.] **I. 1.** = ASSIZE *sb.* 7, 8, 9. Now *dial.* †**2.** An ordinance fixing the amount of a payment or tax –1733. †**3.** = ASSIZE *sb.* 5. –1688. †**4.** A quantity or portion *of* bread, ale, etc.; *spec.* in Cambridge use (see quots.) –1785.

1. I will never . . bring you to the sizes or sessions 1760. **4.** 'Tis not in thee . . to cut off my Traine, . . to scant my sizes SHAKS. A s. is a portion of bread and drinke: it is a farthing which schollers in Cambridge have at the buttery: it is noted with the letter S as in Oxford with the letter Q for halfe a farthing 1617. *transf. Ant. & Cl.* IV. xv. 4.

II. 1. The magnitude, bulk, bigness, or dimensions *of* anything. late ME. **b.** In abstract use: Magnitude 1667. **2.** A particular magnitude or set of dimensions, *esp.* one of a series in manufactured articles, as boots, gloves, etc. 1591. **3.** Magnitude, extent, rate, amount, etc., as a standard of immaterial things 1530. **b.** Of persons in respect of mental or moral qualities, rank or position, etc.; †hence, class, kind, degree, order 1679. **c.** *pl.* As *adv.* Many times, far 1861.

1. *Of a* (or *one*) *s.*, of the same magnitude or dimensions. **b.** The books precisely matched as to s. DICKENS. **2.** *fig.* He was 'between sizes in politics' 1879. *ellipt.* A large s. plate 1889. **3.** He understood well the s. of their understandings BURNET. That seems to be about the s. of it 1860.

Comb.: **s.-roll** (*a*) a military roll showing the s. of each man; (*b*) a piece of parchment added to a roll; **-stick,** a shoemaker's measuring-stick to determine the length of feet.

Size (səiz), *sb.*² 1440. [perh. identical with SIZE *sb.*¹, but the history is obscure.] †**1.** A glutinous or viscid wash applied to paper, parchment, etc., to provide a suitable ground for gilding, painting, or other work –1763. **2.** A semi-solid glutinous substance, prepared from materials similar to those which furnish glue, and used to mix with colours, to dress cloth or paper, etc. 1530. **3.** *attrib.*, as *s.-gelatin*, etc. 1603.

Size (səiz), *v.*¹ late ME. [f. SIZE *sb.*¹, or, in early use, aphetic for ASSIZE *v.*] †**1.** *trans.* To regulate or control, *esp.* in relation to a fixed standard –1771. **2.** In University use (at Cambridge, Harvard, and Yale): To enter as a 'size' upon the buttery or kitchen books; to score (an amount) against oneself in this manner 1598. **b.** *intr.* To order 'sizes', or have them entered against one 1598. **3.** To make of a certain size; to give size to; to adjust in respect of size. Also with *out*. 1609. **4.** To classify or arrange according to size. Also *transf.* to class or rank (*with* others). 1635. **b.** *Mil.* To arrange or draw up (men) in ranks according to stature 1802. **5.** *colloq.* (orig. *U.S.*) Usu. with *up*: To take the size or measure of; to regard so as to form an opinion of; to make an estimate of 1884.

4. The said broken products were then sized and separated 1886. **5.** The grey-haired . . man who met us mentally sized me up at once 1896. Hence **Si·zer,** a device for testing the size of articles or for separating them according to size.

Size (səiz), *v.*² 1667. [f. SIZE *sb.*²] *trans.* To cover, smear, prepare, treat, or stiffen with size. Hence **Sized** *ppl. a.*² treated or prepared in some way with size.

Sizeable, sizable (səi·zăb'l), *a.* 1613. [f. SIZE *v.*¹ + -ABLE.] Of a fair (†proper or convenient) size; fairly large.

The people are fond of purchasing sizeable trees for building 1789. Halifax is a sizable place 1855.

Sized (səizd), *ppl. a.*¹ 1582. [f. SIZE *sb.*¹ or *v.*¹ + -ED.] **1.** Having a specified or indicated size. †**2.** Matched in size. DRYDEN. **3.** Of a fair, proper, or standard size 1728.

1. *Fair-*, *large-*, *middle-s.*, *moderately s.* With *the*, = the size of; The s. type most suitable 1824.

Sizing (səi·ziŋ) *vbl. sb.*¹ 1596. [f. SIZE *v.*¹ + -ING¹.] **1.** In Univ. use: The action or practice of procuring 'sizes' from the buttery or kitchen; a portion or quantity so obtained; a size. **b.** *transf.* A share or allowance 1822. **2.** The action of separating and arranging according to size; also, singling of plants 1660.

Sizing (səi·ziŋ), *vbl. sb.*² 1635. [f. SIZE *v.*² + -ING¹.] **1.** The action of applying size, or of preparing in some way with size. **2.** Size prepared for use; also, the materials from which size is prepared 1825.

Sizy (səi·zi), *a.* 1687. [f. SIZE *sb.*² + -Y¹.] Resembling size; having the consistency of size; thick and viscous; glutinous. Hence **Si·ziness, †sizyness.**

Sizzle (si·z'l), *sb.* 1823. [f. the vb.] A hissing sound, *esp.* one produced by the action of frying or roasting; also, broiling heat.

Sizzle (si·z'l), *v.* 1603. [Imitative; cf. *sizz*, SISS, FIZZLE.] **1.** *trans.* To burn or scorch so as to produce a hissing sound; to burn *up* with intense heat. **2.** *intr.* To make a kind of hissing sound, esp. in the process of frying, roasting, or burning 1825.

‖**Sjambok** (ʃæ·mbǫk), *sb.* 1804. [S. Afr. Du. *sam-*, *tjam-*, *sjambok* – Malay *samboq*, *chamboq* – Urdu *chābuk*; see CHABOUK.] A strong and heavy whip made of rhinoceros or hippopotamus hide, used in S. Africa for driving cattle and sometimes for administering chastisement. Hence **Sjambok** *v. trans.* to strike with a s.

Skail, *v. north.* ME. [Of unkn. origin.] To scatter, *trans.* and *intr.*

Skald, scald (skǭld, skæld). ME. (Orm), 1763 (Percy). [– ON. *skald*, of unkn. origin.] An ancient Scandinavian poet.

Before taking the field of battle, it was the office of the S. to compose a poem suited to the occasion 1818. Hence **Ska·ldic, sc-,** *a.* of or pertaining to the skalds or their poetry.

‖**Skat** (skāt). 1864. [– G. *skat* – It. *scarto* (= Fr. *écart*) cards laid aside, f. *scartare* (see ÉCARTÉ).] A card-game.

Skate (skēⁱt), *sb.*¹ ME. [– ON. *skata*.] A fish of the genus *Raia*; esp. the common species *Raia batis*, a very large, flat, cartilaginous fish much used for food.

Comb.: **s.-leech, -sucker,** a leech which infests the s.

Skate (skēⁱt), *sb.*² 1656. [orig. in pl. *scates*, occas. *scatses* – Du. *schaats* (pl. *schaatsen*), in MDu. *schaetse* – ONFr. (with unexpl. development of sense) *eschasse* (mod. *échasse*) stilt. The final *s* of the Du. word was from the first apprehended as a pl. ending.] **1.** A steel blade mounted in a wooden sole, and fixed to the boot by means of a screw and straps, used for the purpose of gliding over ice; in later use a similar device made entirely of steel and clamped or strapped to the boot. Also = ROLLER-SKATE. Chiefly in *pl.* **b.** *pl.* = SKI *sb.* 1698. **2.** [from the vb.] An act or spell of skating 1853.

1. Over the Parke (where I first in my life . . did see people sliding with their skeates, which is a very pretty art) PEPYS.

Skate (skēⁱt), *v.* 1696. [f. SKATE *sb.*²] **1.** *intr.* To glide over ice upon skates; to use skates as a means of exercise or pastime. Also with *over*. **b.** *transf.* To slide or glide along; to move lightly and rapidly 1775. **2.** *trans.* To contest (a match), to compete with (some one) by skating 1847.

1. b. Other insects merely dive into the water . . or s. upon the surface 1891. Hence **Ska·ter.**

Skatol (skæ·tǫl). 1879. [f. Gr. σκατός, gen. of σκῶρ dung + -OL.] *Chem.* An aromatic substance produced by the decomposition of albumen in the intestinal canal.

†**Skayles.** 1566. [app. var. of KAYLES.] A form of the game of skittles or ninepins; also, one of the pins –1647.

Skedaddle (skĭdæ·d'l), *sb. colloq.* 1870. [f. the vb.] A hasty or precipitate flight; a scurry.

Skedaddle (skĭdæ·d'l), *v. colloq.* 1862. [Of unkn. origin; prob. fanciful.] **1.** *intr.*

Of soldiers, troops, etc.: To retreat or retire hastily or precipitately; to flee. (Orig. U.S. military slang.) **2.** *gen.* To run away, 'clear out' 1862. **b.** Of animals: To run off, stampede 1879.

Skeeball (skī·bǫl). 1923. [f. SKI + BALL *sb.*] A game consisting in throwing a ball along an alley in the centre of which is a bump which causes the ball to leap high in the air and enter a target.

Skeel (skīl). Now *dial.* ME. [– ON. (now Icel.) *skjól* pail, bucket.] A wooden bucket, pail, tub, or similar vessel, used for holding milk or water.

Skee·ling. *Orkney dial.* 1578. [prob. of Scand. origin.] *S.-goose*, the sheldrake.

Skeet (skīt), *sb.* 1440. [Of unkn. origin.] A long-handled scoop or shovel; in later use *Naut.*, a scoop for throwing water over the planks of a ship's sides, etc. **Skeet** *v. trans.* to throw (water) over (sails) etc. with a s.

Skeg[1]. 1598. [– ON. *skegg* beard. Sense 2 perh. – Du. *scheg, schegge* f. the same source.] **1.** *local.* A species of bearded oat, of inferior quality. **2.** *Shipbuilding.* The after part of the keel in a screw steamer; the triangular piece taking the place of the after part of the keel in a flat-bottomed boat 1625.

Skeg[2]. Now *dial.* 1601. [Of unkn. origin.] A species of wild plum, esp. the bullace (*Prunus insititia*) or the sloe (*P. spinosa*).

Skegger (ske·gəɹ). 1653. [Of unkn. origin.] A young salmon, a samlet; salmon fry.

Skein[1] (skēⁱn). ME. [Aphetic – OFr. *escaigne* (mod. *écagne*), of unkn. origin.] **1.** A quantity of thread or yarn, wound to a certain length upon a reel, and usually put up in a kind of loose knot.

A skein of cotton consists of eighty turns of the thread upon a reel fifty-four inches in circumference.

2. *transf.* **a.** A small cluster or arrangement resembling a skein 1687. **b.** A flight of wild fowl 1851. **3.** *attrib.*, as *s.-silk*, etc. 1764.

1. *fig.* They disentangle from the puzzled s... The threads of politic and shrewd design COWPER. **2.** The mazy skeins of her shadowy hair T. HARDY.

Skein[2]. Also **skain.** 1837. [– Du. *scheen*; see SHIN *sb.*] **1.** A split of osier after being dressed for use in fine basket-work. **2.** *U.S.* A metal head or thimble protecting the spindle of a wooden axle 1862.

Ske·lder, *v. Obs.* exc. *arch.* 1599. [Cant term of unkn. origin.] **1.** *intr.* To beg; to live by begging. **2.** *trans.* To swindle, cheat, defraud (a person); also, to obtain (money) by cheating 1601.

Skeldraik, -drake, *var.* SHELDRAKE.

Ske·let. *Obs.* exc. *dial.* 1565. [– older Fr. (XVI) *sc-, sk-, squelete* (mod. *squelette*), or Gr. *σκελετός, -όν*; see SKELETON.] = SKELETON.

Skeletal (ske·lĭtăl), *a.* 1854. [f. SKELETON *sb.* + -AL[1].] Of or belonging to, forming or formed by, forming part of, or resembling, a skeleton.

Ske·leto-, comb. form of Gr. *σκελετός, -όν*, as in **skeleto·genous** *a.*, producing, or helping to form, a skeleton; **skeleto·graphy,** a description of the skeleton; **skeleto·logy,** a treatise on the solid parts of the body.

Skeleton (ske·lĭtǫn). 1578. [– mod.L. *sceleton, skeleton* – Gr. *σκελετόν*, subst. use (sc. *σῶμα* body) of n. of *σκελετός* dried up. f. *σκέλλειν* dry up.] **1.** The bones or bony framework of an animal body considered as a whole; also, more generally, the harder (supporting or covering) constituent part of an animal organism. **2.** *transf.* A very thin, lean, or emaciated person or animal 1629. **b.** *fig.* A mere outline; a thing having a bare, meagre, unattractive character 1607. **3.** The supporting framework of anything, as of buildings, etc. 1658. **4.** The bare outlines or main features, the most necessary elements, *of* something 1647. **b.** The outlines, plan, or scheme of a sermon 1724. **5.** *Mil.* The small number of men (and officers) representing a regiment which is far short of its full strength 1802. **6.** *attrib.* That is, or has the character of, a skeleton 1778.

1. Phr. *A s. in the closet, cupboard*, etc., a secret source of shame or pain to a family or person. *A s. at the feast* (or *banquet*), a reminder of serious or saddening things in the midst of enjoyment; a source of gloom or depression (in allusion to a practice of the ancient Egyptians). **2.** We are become an army of mere skellitons 1715. **3.** The s. or frame of a skin canoe 1817. **6.** A patched and much-soiled s. suit; one of those straight blue cloth cases in which small boys used to be confined DICKENS. *S. hand*; *s. map, plan, sermon*, etc.; *s. battalion, company, crew, regiment, staff*, etc.; **s. key,** a thin light key having a large part of the bits filed away so that it may open a number of locks as a master key; **s. shrimp,** a crustacean of the genus *Caprella.* **s. type,** a face of type with thin light lines.

This line is in Skeleton type.

Skeletonize (ske·lĭtŏnəiz), *v.* 1644. [f. SKELETON *sb.* + -IZE] **1.** *trans.* To reduce to a skeleton. **2.** To draw up in outline; to sketch out 1865. **3.** *intr.* To become a skeleton 1831. Hence **Ske·letonizer,** an insect which reduces leaves to a skeleton.

Skellum (ske·lŏm). 1611. [– Du. *schelm* (sχe·ləm) – G. *schelm* rascal.] **1.** A rascal, scamp, scoundrel villain. Now *arch.* (exc. in S. Africa). **2.** In S. African use applied to animals 1850.

Skelly (ske·li), *v. Sc.* and *n. dial.* 1776. [– ON. **skjelga* (refl. *skjelgask*), also *skalgja* make squint, f. *skjálgr* wry, oblique.] *intr.* To squint.

Skelp, *sb.*[1] Chiefly *north.* and *Sc.* 1440. [Related to SKELP *v.*] A blow, *esp.* one given with the flat of the hand, or with something having a flat surface; a slap or smack; also, the noise made by such a blow.

Skelp, *sb.*[2] Also **scelp.** 1811. [Of unkn. origin.] A thin narrow plate or flat strip of iron or steel, which by twisting and welding is converted into the barrel of a gun.

Skelp, *v.* Chiefly *north.* and *Sc.* late ME. [prob. imitative.] **1.** *trans.* To strike, beat, slap, smack, in later use *spec.* on the breech. **2.** *intr.* To skip, trip, walk, or run rapidly; to hurry. Also with *it.* 1721.

Skelter (ske·ltəɹ), *v.* 1852. [f. the second element in HELTER-SKELTER.] *intr.* To dash along, hurry, rush, scurry.

Sken, *v. dial.* 1611. [perh. rel. to the stem of ASKANCE.] *intr.* To squint; to give a side look; to glance.

Skene (skīn). Now *Hist.* or *arch.* Also **skean,** etc. 1527. [– Ir. and Sc. Gael. *sgian* (genitive *sceine, scine*); cf. W. *ysgien.*] **1.** A form of knife or dagger, in former times one of the chief weapons of the Irish kerns, and also in use among the Scottish Highlanders. **2. a.** *Skene-dhu* [Gael. *sgian dubh* black knife], a small dagger carried by Highlanders (now only as an ornament), frequently thrust into the stocking 1819. **b.** *Skene-ochles, ochil, -occle* [Gael. *achlais* arm-pit], a knife carried in the sleeve near the arm-pit 1754.

1. The good claymores, the dirks, skeans, and pistols 1879.

Skep. Also **skip.** [– ON. *skeppa* basket, bushel (whence late OE. *sćeppe*) in AL. *sceppa, skeppa* XII, *skippa* XIII; obscurely rel. to OS. *scepil*, OHG. *sceffil* (G. *scheffel*) of the same meaning.] **1.** A specific quantity *of* grain, malt, charcoal, etc.; a skepful. **2.** A basket or hamper ME. **b.** *Mining* = SKIP *sb.*[2] 1860. **3.** A beehive 1494.

Skeptic, -al, etc.: see SCEPTIC, etc.

†**Skerry,** *sb.*[1] 1540. [Of unkn. origin.] A small punt or boat designed to carry two persons and used chiefly in fenny districts –1861.

Skerry (ske·ri), *sb.*[2] 1612. [Orkney dial., f. ON. *sker* (whence Gael. *sgeir*); see SCAR *sb.*[1]] A rugged insulated sea-rock or stretch of rocks covered by the sea at high water or in stormy weather; a reef.

Skerry (ske·ri), *a.* and *sb.*[3] 1800. [Of unkn. origin.] **A.** *adj.* Of the nature of shale; shaly, slaty. **B.** *sb.* Earth or stone of a shaly nature 1844.

Sketch (sketʃ), *sb.* 1668. [– Du. *schets* or G. *skizze* – It. *schizzo*, f. *schizzare* make a sketch :– Rom. **schediare*, f. L. *schedius* – Gr. *σχέδιος* done extempore.] **1.** A rough drawing or delineation of something, giving the outlines or prominent features without the detail, esp. one intended to serve as the basis of a more finished picture, or to be used in its composition; a rough draught or design. Also, in later use, a drawing or painting of an unpretentious nature. **2.** A brief account, description, or narrative, not going into details; a short or superficial essay or study 1668. **b.** The general plan or outline, the main features, of anything (*rare*) 1697. **3.** *Mus.* **a.** A short piece, usu. for the pianoforte, either slight in construction or vividly descriptive 1840. **b.** A preliminary study for a finished work or composition 1883. **4.** A short play or performance of slight dramatic construction; also, a musical performance by one person in which playing, singing, and talking are combined 1861.

1. b. Something odd, ludicrous, or the like; a 'sight'. **2.** Sketches by Boz DICKENS (*title*). *attrib. s.-block, -map*, etc.

Sketch (sketʃ), *v.* 1694. [f. prec.] **1.** *trans.* To describe briefly, generally, or in outline; to give the essential facts or points of without going into details; to outline. Also with *out.* **2.** To draw the outline or prominent features of (a picture, figure, etc.), esp. as preliminary to further development; to make a sketch or rough draught of (something); to draw or paint in this manner 1725. **3.** *intr.* or *absol.* To practise sketching 1874.

2. The method of Rubens was to s. his compositions in colours REYNOLDS. Hence **Ske·tcher. Ske·tching** *vbl. sb.* (attrib. in *s. block.*)

Ske·tch-book. 1820. [f. SKETCH *sb.*] **1.** A book having leaves of drawing-paper specially reserved or adapted for making sketches on. **b.** As the title of a book containing literary sketches 1820. **2.** A note-book containing a composer's preliminary studies 1883.

1. b. The Irish Sketch-Book THACKERAY (*title*).

Sketchy (ske·tʃi), *a.* 1805. [f. SKETCH *sb.* + -Y[1].] **1.** Giving only a slight or rough outline of the main features, facts, or circumstances without going into details. **2.** Of pictures, etc.: Of the nature of, or resembling, a sketch; consisting or composed of outline without much detail 1817. **3.** *colloq.* Light, flimsy, unsubstantial, fragmentary 1878.

1. Sketches of society,—very s. indeed 1828. **2.** Landseer's very s. lions 1884. **3.** A house with.. only very s. wooden window-shutters 1897. Hence **Ske·tchily** *adv.* **Ske·tchiness.**

Skew (skiū), *sb.*[1] ME. [– OFr. *escu* (mod. *écu*) :– L. *scutum* shield.] †**a.** A stone specially intended or adapted for being placed with other similar ones to form the sloping head or coping of a gable, rising slightly above the level of the roof –1533. **b.** The line of coping on a gable. Chiefly *Sc.* 1789.

Skew (skiū), *sb.*[2] 1688. [f. SKEW *a.* or *v.*] A slant; a deviation from the straight line; an angle, esp. that at which a bridge spans a road or river; a sideward movement. **b.** *transf.* A slip, an error 1869.

On the (or *a*) *s.*, on the slant, slantwise.

Skew (skiū), *a.* and *adv.* 1609. [f. SKEW *v.* or aphetic f. ASKEW.] **A.** *adj.* **1.** Having an oblique direction or position; turned to one side, slanting, squint. **2.** In special collocations, denoting that the thing in question deviates from a straight line, or has some part not at right angles with the rest, as *s. arch, bridge, girder*, etc., or *s. bevel, chisel, facet, iron*, etc. 1678. **B.** *adv.* Obliquely, askew (*rare*) 1706. Also **Skew-whiff** *dial.* or *colloq.* 1754.

Skew (skiū), *v.* 1470. [Aphetic – ONFr. *eskiu(w)er, eskuer*, var. of OFr. *eschuer* ESCHEW *v.*] **1.** To take an oblique course or direction; to turn *aside*, move sideways. **b.** To shy (as a horse), to swerve 1679. **2.** To squint *at*, to look *at* (or *upon*) sideways, esp. in a suspicious or slighting manner; hence, to make side-hits *at*, reflect *upon*, something 1570. **3.** To cut *off*, set *back*, insert, etc., obliquely 1611.

2. The cows stood round her..Skewing at her 1827.

Skew-back. 1703. [f. SKEW *sb.*[2] or *v.* + BACK *adv.*] **1.** *Arch.* The springing-line of an arch; the sloping surface on which either extremity of an arch rests; a course of stone or brickwork, an iron plate, etc., immediately supporting the foot of an arch. **2.** *Mech.* A cap or other casting made to receive the end of a diagonal rod or brace 1884.

Skewbald (skiū·bǫld), *a.* and *sb.* 1654. [f. synon. †*skued* (XV), of uncertain origin, perh. f. OFr. *escu* (mod. *écu*) shield :– L.

scutum (cf. L. *scutulatus* as the colour of a horse, f. dim. of *scutum*); modelled on PIEBALD.] **A.** *adj.* Of animals, esp. horses: Irregularly marked with white and brown or red, or some other colour. **B.** *sb.* A skewbald horse 1863. So **Skewed** (skiūd) *a.* 1440.

Skewer (skiū·əɹ), *sb.* 1679. [var. of SKIVER *sb.*[1], of unkn. origin, but perh. the more original form.] A long wooden or metal pin, used especially to fasten meat or the like together, to keep it in form while being cooked. **b.** Applied contemptuously to a weapon 1838.

Send up your Meat well stuck with Scewers, to make it look round and plump SWIFT.

Skewer (skiū·əɹ), *v.* 1701. [f. prec.] **1.** *trans.* To fasten (meat, etc.) with a skewer or skewers. **b.** To run through, transfix, with a sword or other weapon 1837. **2.** To fix, fasten, or secure to or into something else with, or as with, a skewer or skewers; to truss 1777. **3.** To fix or thrust (*into* or *through* something) like a skewer or skewers 1869.

1. b. Perhaps *not* to part, but to fall mutually skewered through with iron CARLYLE. **3.** He skewered his great eyes into mine 1869

Ski (ʃī, skī), *sb. Pl.* **ski, skis.** 1885. [– Norw. *ski* ʃī (*skji, sjii, skid*) – ON. *skíð* billet of cleft wood, snow-shoe = OE. *scid* SHIDE.] One of a pair of long slender pieces of wood fastened to the foot and used as a snow-shoe, enabling the wearer to slide down hill with great rapidity. *Comb.* **ski-joring,** being drawn over snow or ice wearing skis. Hence **Ski** *v. intr.* to travel on s.

Skiagram (skəi·ăgræm). Also **scia-, skio-.** 1801. [f. Gr. σκιά shadow + -GRAM.] **1.** An outline of the shadow of an object filled in with black; a picture painted or produced in this style. **2.** A skiagraph, radiograph 1896.

Skiagraph (skəi·ăgrɑf), *sb.* Also **scia-, skio-.** 1896. [f. as prec. + -GRAPH.] A picture obtained by means of the Röntgen rays; a radiograph. Hence **Ski·agraph** *v. trans.* to photograph by this means. **Skia·graphy.**

Skid (skid), *sb.* 1609. [Of unkn. origin, but in form and sense resembling ON. *skíð* (see SHIDE, SKI).] **1.** A beam, plank, or piece of timber, *esp.* one of a number upon which something rests or is supported, or by which a thing is held in position. **b.** One of a number of beams, or pieces of stone, on which a vessel is built, or placed during repair 1856. **2. a.** *Naut.* A wooden fender hung on the outside of a ship to protect it when hoisting in cargo, boats, etc. 1743. **b.** A plank or roller on which a heavy thing may be slid or pushed along 1846. **c.** *Lumbering.* One of a number of peeled logs, partially sunk into the ground, and forming a roadway down which logs are drawn or slid. *U.S.* 1851. **d.** Each of two runners attached to an aeroplane to facilitate landing or taxiing 1909. **3.** A device for locking the wheel of a vehicle or for retarding its motion in descending a hill; *esp.* an iron shoe (a *s.-pan*) chained to the vehicle and placed in front of the wheel so as to be caught between it and the ground 1766. **4.** [f. the vb.] An act of skidding; also, a side-slip 1909.

Skid (skid), *v.*[1] 1674. [f. SKID *sb.*] **1.** *trans.* To apply or fasten a skid or brake to (a wheel) in order to retard its motion; to lock (a wheel) in this way. **2.** *intr.* Of a wheel: To be retarded by a skid 1838. **b.** To slide forwards or backwards or sideways, esp. owing to the state of the road 1884. **c.** Of an aeroplane: To slip sideways from the centre of curvature while turning (cf. SIDE-SLIP *v.*) 1916.

Skid (skid), *v.*[2] *rare.* 1815. [var. of SCUD *v.*] *intr.* To run or go quickly, to scud.

Skidding (ski·diŋ), *vbl. sb.* 1859. [f. SKID *sb.* or *v.*[1] + -ING[1].] **1.** *concr.* Timber or planks used as a support for a gun, etc., or to facilitate its removal. **2.** The action of SKID *v.*[1] 1889.

Skied (skəid), *ppl. a.* 1730. [f. SKY *sb.* or *v.* + -ED.] †**1.** Seeming to touch the sky; lofty. THOMSON. **2.** In combs.: Having a sky of a specified kind 1839. **3.** *Cricket.* Of a ball: Hit or sent up high in the air. Also *transf.* of a stroke. 1868.

Skiey, var. of SKYEY *a.*

Skiff (skif), *sb.* 1575. [– Fr. *esquif* – It. *schifo* – Lombardic **skif* (= OHG. *schif* SHIP).] **1.** A small sea-going boat, adapted for rowing and sailing; esp. one attached to a ship. Hence, a small light boat of any kind. **2.** *spec.* A kind of clinker-built sculling- or pleasure-boat. Also, a long narrow racing-boat for one oarsman, outrigged, usually fitted with a sliding-seat, and covered in fore and after with canvas. 1793.

Skiff (skif), *v.* 1625. [f. prec.] †**1.** *trans.* To cross, row or sail over (a river) in a skiff. **2.** *intr.* To row or scull in a skiff; to go on a river in a pleasure-skiff 1869.

Skilful (ski·lfŭl), *a.* ME. [f. SKILL *sb.* + -FUL.] †**1.** Endowed with reason; rational –1440. †**2.** Reasonable, just, proper –1460. **3.** Having practical ability; possessing skill; expert, dexterous, clever. Also const. *to.* ME. †**b.** Having a good knowledge *of* a subject –1631. **4.** Displaying or requiring skill 1586.

3. A Captaine of the Sea, moste skylfull 1560. Skilfull in Astronomye 1555. **4.** Irony..is one of those edged tools which require s. handling 1895. Hence **Ski·lful-ly** *adv.*, **-ness.**

Skill (skil), *sb.* ME. [– ON. *skil* distinction, discernment, etc., rel. to *skila* (see next) and MLG. *schēle,* (M)Du. *geschil, verschil* difference.] †**1.** Reason as a faculty of the mind; the power of discrimination –1500. †**2.** That which is reasonable, proper, right, or just –1460. †**3.** Cause, reason, or ground. Also with *a* and *pl.* –1642. †**4.** In the phr. *can* (or *could*) *s.,* to have discrimination or knowledge, esp. in a specified matter. Usu. const. *of, in,* or *to* with inf. –1869. **5.** Practical knowledge in combination with ability; cleverness, expertness ME. †**b.** An art or science –1667. **c.** A craft, an accomplishment (now *U.S.*). **6.** Knowledge or understanding *of* something. Now *arch.* 1587.

2. It is reason and skyll, We your pleasure fulfyll SKELTON. **3.** I thinke you haue As little s. to feare, as I haue purpose To put you to 't SHAKS. **4.** Let them iudge that can s. 1581. Many such men as you are, can s. to giue good words 1601. **5.** Utterly destititute of the s. necessary to the conduct of great affairs MACAULAY. No s. of speech have I SWINBURNE. **b.** Richard..quickly got money, the sinewes of warre, by a thousand princely skills 1647. Hence **Ski·lless, Ski·lless** *a.*

Skill (skil), *v.* Now *arch.* ME. [– ON. *skila* give reason for, expound, decide, *skilja* divide, distinguish, decide, etc., rel. to MLG., MDu. *schillen, schēlen* differ, make a difference.] **1. a.** *impers.* In negative or interrogative clauses: To make a difference, to be of importance, to matter 1460. **b.** *impers.* To avail, help 1528. **2.** To understand, comprehend. Now *dial.* 1500. †**b.** *intr.* To have knowledge *of,* or skill *in,* something –1691. **c.** With inf.: To know how *to* do something. Also with *how.* 1586.

1. a. What skilleth you though that he dye this nyght? 1509. **b.** But what skills talking? 1880. **2.** The speaker little skilleth the use of speech, or the rule of conversation 1677. **c.** They now skild not how from him to wend SIDNEY.

Skilled (skild), *ppl. a.* 1533. [f. SKILL *sb.* + -ED[2].] **1.** Of persons: Possessed of skill or knowledge; properly trained or experienced. **2.** Of work: Requiring or showing skill 1776.

1. To be well s. in the law 1552. Every physician and every s. artist does all things for the sake of the whole 1875. **2.** Every branch of public administration is a s. business MILL.

Skillet (ski·lĕt). late ME. [Earliest form *skelet* (XV), in AL. *skeletta, schiletta* (XIV); perh. aphetic – OFr. *escuelete* small platter, dim. of *escuele* (mod. *écuelle*) :– pop. L. *scūtella,* alt. of L. *scutella* SCUTTLE *sb.*[1]; see -ET.] A cooking utensil of brass, copper, or other metal, usu. having three or four feet and a long handle, used for boiling liquids, stewing meat, etc.; a saucepan, stew-pan.

Skilligalee (ski:ligălī·). *slang.* 1819. [prob. fanciful.] **1.** = SKILLY. **2.** With neg.: A single coin of the smallest value 1833.

Skilling (ski·liŋ), *sb.*[1] late ME. [Of unkn. origin.] A shed or outhouse, *esp.* a lean-to, a penthouse.

‖**Ski·lling,** *sb.*[2] 1700. [In sense 1 – Du. *schelling*; in sense 2 – Da., Sw., or Norw. *skilling.*] †**1.** = SCHELLING. **2.** A small copper coin and money of account formerly in use in Scandinavia 1793.

Skilly (ski·li). 1839. [abbrev. of SKILLIGALEE.] A kind of thin, watery porridge, gruel, or soup, commonly made from oatmeal, and formerly used esp. in prisons and workhouses.

Skim, *sb.* 1539. [f. SKIM *v.*; in earlier use taking the place of SCUM *sb.*] †**1.** = SCUM *sb.* 2 b. –1764. **2.** An addition to the coulter of a plough by which the surface of the ground is pared off 1799. **3.** *ellipt.* = SKIM-MILK 1. 1885. **4.** The act of skimming or moving lightly 1851.

Skim, *v.* late ME. [Back-formation from SKIMMER.] **I. 1.** *trans.* To clear (a liquid or a liquid mass) from matter floating upon the surface, usually by means of a special utensil; to deprive (milk) of cream by this method; to deal with (a pot, etc.) in this way. Also *absol.* (Cf. SCUM *v.* 1.) late ME. **b.** *Agric.* To plough (land) very lightly 1799. **2.** To remove or collect by skimming 1651. **3.** To cover with a thin layer, as with scum 1666. **b.** *intr.* To put on a thin layer 1865.

1. Are you not hee That..Skim milke? SHAKS. **2.** We forget that the newspaper skims the scum of life 1894. **3.** The Fountain of Trevi skimmed almost across with a glassy surface HAWTHORNE.

II. 1. *trans.* To deal with, treat, or study, in a cursory and superficial manner 1586. **b.** *esp.* To read rapidly or carelessly; to glance over without close attention 1799. **2.** To move, glide, fly or float, lightly and rapidly over (the ground, etc.) 1697. **3.** To cause to fly lightly; to throw (a thing, esp. one having a flat surface) so that it maintains an evenness of balance or poise in its flight 1611. **4.** *intr.* To sail, glide, float, fly, run, etc., with a light and easy motion, on or close to some surface, or through the air 1591. **b.** To glance *over,* without reading closely 1738. **c.** To pass *over* lightly, without dwelling upon 1741. †**5.** To glance *round* the horizon. KEATS.

1. Such as love only to s. things, and have not the patience to keep their minds to a deep and close attention 1665. **2.** Smooth as Swallows s. The new-shorn Mead 1735. **3.** He skimmed his cocked-hat in the air SCOTT. **4. c.** He skims over rather than dives into the subjects of which he treats 1824. Hence **Ski·mming** *ppl. a.* moving lightly along the surface; *fig.* not deep or thorough; **-ly** *adv.*

Ski·mble-ska:mble, *a., sb.,* and *adv.* 1596. [f. SCAMBLE *v.,* with usual variation of vowel in the first element; cf. *clitter-clatter, tittle-tattle,* etc.] **A.** *adj.* Confused, incoherent, nonsensical, rubbishy. (Now after Shaks.) **B.** *sb.* Confused or worthless discourse 1619. **C.** *adv.* Confusedly; in confusion 1775.

A. Such a deale of skimble-scamble Stuff SHAKS.

Ski·m-cou:lter. 1778. [f. SKIM *v.*] *Agric.* A coulter fitted with a plate of iron or steel which shaves off the top-layer of the ground and turns it into the furrow.

Skimmed (skimd), *ppl. a.* [f. SKIM *v.* + -ED[1].] In senses of SKIM *v.*; *s. milk* = SKIM-MILK 1623; so *s. cheese.*

Skimmer (ski·məɹ). late ME. [Earliest forms *skemour, skymour* (later with assim. to -ER[1]) – OFr. *escumoir* (mod. *écumoire*), f. *escumer,* f. *escume* SCUM *sb.*] **1.** A shallow utensil, usually perforated, employed in skimming liquids; also, any utensil used for an analogous process. **b.** *U.S.* A clam or scallop, the shell of which may be used for skimming milk, etc. 1881. **2.** One who skims, e.g. in reading 1611. **3.** A bird of the N. American genus *Rhynchops,* esp. the black skimmer (*R. nigra*) 1785.

Ski·m-milk. 1596. [f. SKIM *v.* + MILK *sb.*] Milk with the cream skimmed off or otherwise removed. Also *attrib.,* as *s. cheese.*

Ski·mming, *vbl. sb.* 1450. [f. SKIM *v.* + -ING[1].] **1.** That which is removed or obtained by skimming. Usu. *pl.* **2.** The action of SKIM *v.* in various senses 1611.

Ski·mming-dish. 1641. [SKIMMING *vbl. sb.*] A dish used for skimming with; *esp.* one used in skimming milk or in cheese-making.

Skimmington (ski·miŋtən). 1609. [Possibly from *skimming* + -TON as in *simpleton,* with the object of simulating a personal name.] †**1.** The man or woman personating the ill-used husband or the offending wife in the procession (see 2) intended to ridicule the one or the other. Also *transf.* a husband whose wife is unfaithful to him, a shrewish woman. –1813. **2.** A ludicrous procession, formerly common in villages and country districts, usu. intended to bring ridicule or odium upon a woman or her husband where the one was unfaithful to, or ill-treated, the other 1634.

2. *To ride* (*the*) *s.*, to hold a procession of this kind.

Skimp, *a.* 1775. [poss. related to SCRIMP *a.*] Scanty. So **Skimp** *v.* = SCRIMP *v.*

Skimpy (ski·mpi), *a.* 1847. [f. SKIMP *a.* + -Y¹. Cf. SCRIMPY.] Of a scrimp, meagre, scanty, or spare character; stinted or stunted in some respect. Hence **Ski·mpily** *adv.* **Ski·mpiness.**

Skin, *sb.* [Late OE. *scin(n* – ON. *skinn* :– **skinþ-*, rel. to MLG. *schinden* (Du. *schinden*) flay, peel, OHG. *scinden* (G. *schinden*).] **I. 1.** The integument of an animal stripped from the body, and usu. dressed or tanned (with or without the hair), or intended for this purpose; a hide, pelt, or fur; also occas., an article made of this. **2.** A complete hide of a sheep, calf, etc., or a part of one, specially prepared as parchment or vellum and used for writing or painting upon ME. **3.** A vessel made of the hide of a small animal, such as a sheep or goat, and used for holding liquids, etc. 1547.

1. Skins of Beasts, the rude Barbarians wear DRYDEN. I do not like to divide the s. before we have caught the bear 1899. **2.** The ponderous deed of eight skins of parchment 1870. **3.** The best Xeres that ever smacked of the s. 1846.

II. 1. The continuous flexible integument forming the usual external covering of an animal body; also, one or other of the separate layers of which this is composed, the derma or epidermis ME. **2.** A membrane covering any internal part of an animal body. late ME. **3.** Anything which resembles skin in nature or use; an outer coat or covering of anything. late ME. **b.** *Arch.* The facing of a wall in contrast to the material in the heart of it 1884. **4.** *Naut.* **a.** The planking, or iron plating, covering the ribs or frame of a vessel 1769. **b.** That part of a sail which is used as a cover for it when furled 1841.

1. Phr. *S. and bone(s*, denoting extreme emaciation or leanness. *To sleep in a whole s.*, etc., to escape being wounded, to remain uninjured. *To the s.*, through all one's garments; hence, thoroughly, completely. *To jump*, etc., *out of one's s.* (with joy, etc.). *By* (or *with*) *the s. of one's teeth*, with difficulty, narrowly, barely. *To save one's* (*own*) *s.*, to save oneself from loss or injury. **2.** See GOLD-BEATER'S *s.*

attrib. and *Comb.*: as *s.-disease*, etc.; *s.-boat*, *-bottle*, *-canoe*, etc.; also, **s.-bound** *a.*, having the s. tightly drawn; hide-bound; **s. effect** *Electr.*, the tendency of a high-frequency alternating current to be greater at the surface of the conductor than in its interior; **s. friction,** the friction developed between a solid and a fluid or gaseous body; the friction of the air with the roughnesses of an aeroplane's surface; **-graft** *v.*, to subject to the process of skin-grafting (see GRAFT *v.*¹ 6); **-plating,** metal plating forming the s. of a vessel; **-wool,** wool taken from the s. of a dead sheep.

Skin, *v.* 1547. [f. SKIN *sb.* Cf. Norw. *skinna* cover with skin.] **I. 1.** *trans.* To furnish or cover (*over*) with skin; to cause skin to form or grow on; to heal by the formation of skin. **b.** *fig.* To cover (*over*) in some slight or superficial manner 1603. **2.** *intr.* To form skin; to become covered with skin; to grow a new skin; to heal *over* in this way 1579.

1. It will but s. and filme the Vlcerous place SHAKS. **b.** Your Amsterdam affaires are rather skinned than cured 1650. **2.** Her excoriated carkasse began to s. again 1654.

II. 1. *trans.* To strip or deprive of the skin; to flay; to peel 1591. **b.** To rub the skin off (a surface); to bark 1855. **c.** In phrases denoting excessive meanness or desire for gain, esp. *to s. a flint* 1694. **2.** To strip or pull *off* (a skin, etc.); to remove by drawing off inside out 1658. **3.** *intr.* To shed or cast the skin; to lose the skin by rubbing 1772. **4.** *slang.* **a.** *trans.* To clean out (a person) at play 1812. **b.** To strip (*of* clothing or money); to fleece 1851. **c.** *To keep one's eyes skinned* (orig. U.S.): to keep a sharp look-out 1852. **5.** *U.S. slang.* To copy or crib. *trans.* and *intr.* 1849.

1. A fishmonger who was skinning an eel alive BOSWELL. **4. b.** Some new device is invented for enmeshing and skinning the investor 1898.

Skin-deep, *a.* and *adv.* 1613. [f. SKIN *sb.* + DEEP *a.* and *adv.*] **A.** *adj.* Penetrating no deeper than the skin; superficial, shallow.

Beauty that's only skin deep Must fade like the gowans of May 1725. *fig.* The s. joy of ungodly men 1730.

B. *adv.* Superficially, slightly 1633.

When I know her further than S. I'll tell you more of my mind STEELE.

Ski·nflint. 1700. [f. SKIN *v.* + FLINT *sb.*] One who would skin a flint to save or gain something; an avaricious, penurious, mean or niggardly person; a miser.

Ski·nful. 1650. [f. SKIN *sb.* + -FUL.] As much as a skin can or does hold; *transf.* a full allowance. *To have a s.* (slang): to be drunk.

Skink (skiŋk), *sb.*¹ 1590. [– Fr. †*scinc* (now *scinque*) or L. *scincus* – Gr. σκίγκος.] *Zool.* A small lizard (*Scincus officinalis*) common in northern Africa and Arabia, formerly regarded as of great value in medicine for its stimulative qualities; also, any lizard belonging to the same family (the *Scincidæ*).

Skink, *v.* Now *dial.* or *arch.* late ME. [– MLG., MDu. *schenken*, rel. to OFris. *skenka*, OS. *skenkian*, OHG. *skenken* (G. *schenken*), corresp. to OE. *sćencan*.] **1.** *trans.* To pour out or draw (liquor); to offer, present, serve (drink, etc.). **2.** *absol.* To draw, pour out, or serve drink 1575. Hence **Skink** *sb.*² drink. **Ski·nker,** one who draws, pours out or serves liquor, a tapster.

Skinless (ski·nlės), *a.* ME. [f. SKIN *sb.* + -LESS.] Destitute or deprived of skin; having only a very thin skin.

Skinned (skind), *a.* late ME. [f. SKIN *sb.* or *v.* + -ED.] **1.** Having or covered with skin. **2.** Stripped of skin 1673.

Skinner (ski·nəɹ). ME. [f. SKIN *sb.* or *v.* + -ER¹.] **1.** One whose work or business is concerned with the preparation of skins for commercial purposes. **2.** One who skins 1699.

1. The Principal Companies..are the Mercers,.. Skinners 1675.

Ski·nnery. 1480. [f. SKIN *sb.* + -ERY.] A skinner's factory.

Skinny (ski·ni), *a.* 1573. [f. SKIN *sb.* + -Y¹.] **1.** Consisting or formed of skin; resembling skin or film; cutaneous, membranous. **2.** Having the skin prominently shown; lacking flesh; thin, lean, emaciated 1605. **3.** Mean, miserly, niggardly, stingy 1833.

2. *Macb.* I. iii. 45. Hence **Ski·nniness.**

Skin-tight (ski·n,təit), *a.* 1885. [SKIN *sb.*] Fitting tightly to the skin; close-fitting.

Skip (skip), *sb.*¹ 1440. [f. SKIP *v.*¹] **1.** An act of skipping; a slight bound or spring. **2.** An act of passing from one thing or point to another with omission or disregard of what intervenes 1656. **b.** *Mus.* A passing from one note to another at a greater interval than one degree 1730. **c.** Matter in a book which may be skipped in reading 1833. **3.** [prob. short for SKIP-KENNEL.] A footman, lackey, or manservant. Later *spec.* at Trinity College, Dublin, a college-servant, a scout. 1698.

1. *Hop, s., and jump* (see HOP *sb.*²). **2. d.** *Wireless.* A silent belt between the point where the direct ray from a transmitting station becomes inaudible and the point where the reflected or indirect ray becomes audible. Also *attrib.*

Skip, *sb.*² 1815. [var. of SKEP *sb.* (q.v. for *skip* in other senses).] In mining or quarrying, a bucket, box, basket, cage, or wagon, in which materials or men are drawn up or let down. Also *attrib.*, as *s.-road*, *-shaft.*

Skip, *sb.*³ 1858. [f. SKIP *v.*²] 'In sugar-making in the West Indies, a charge or strike of syrup from the coppers' (Simmonds).

Skip, *sb.*⁴, abbrev. of SKIPPER *sb.*² 1830.

Skip, *v.*¹ ME. [prob. of Scand. origin, but the synon. MSw. *skuppa*, *skoppa* does not formally agree.] **I.** *intr.* **1.** To raise oneself off the ground by a light and graceful movement; to spring or leap lightly and easily, *spec.* in the exercise of skipping with a rope. **2.** To move or advance by a skip or skips ME. **b.** To hasten, hurry, move lightly and rapidly; to make off, abscond. Now *U.S. colloq.* ME. **3.** To pass from one point, matter, etc., to another with omission of what intervenes; in mod. use *spec.* to do this in reading. late ME. **b.** So with *over*. Also occas., to pass *over* with very slight or superficial treatment. late ME. **4.** Of things, in lit. or fig. senses. late ME. **b.** *Mus.* To pass from one note to another at an interval of more than one degree 1868.

2. They s. up stairs two at a time 1898. **b.** By Jove, you'd better s. for it MARRYAT. **3.** The art of reading is to s. judiciously 1873. **4.** In this wise skippeth venial in-to deedly synne CHAUCER.

II. *trans.* **1.** To pass over in reading, etc. Also with *over*, and in fig. context. 1526. **b.** To pass over without mentioning, dealing with, taking into account, etc.; to omit 1531. **c.** To pass over, pass by, without touching or affecting in any way. Also with *over.* 1599. **2. a.** To jump or leap lightly over (something); to go off, leave (rails) 1732. **b.** *U.S. colloq.* To flee (the country) 1884. **3.** To cause to skip, bound, or jump 1683.

1. I do not think that I skipped a word of it [*sc.* a book] LAMB. **b.** Two virtues remain; shall we s. one and go to the other? JOWETT. **c.** Let not thy sword s. one: Pitty not honour'd Age for his white Beard SHAKS. **3.** He had skipped pebbles on it 1894.

Comb.: **s. mackerel** *U.S.*, the blue-fish or skipjack. Hence **Ski·pping** *vbl. sb.* (attrib. in *s.-rope* 1836), **-ly** *adv.*

Skip, *v.*² 1818. [– Du. *scheppen* ladle, bale, dip, draw (water), etc.] *trans.* To transfer (sugar) from one vessel to another in the process of manufacture.

Skipjack (ski·p,dʒæk), *sb.* and *a.* 1554. [f. SKIP *v.*¹ + JACK *sb.*¹] **A.** *sb.* **1.** A pert shallow-brained fellow; a puppy; a conceited fop. Now *arch.* †**2.** A horse-dealer's boy; a jockey –1700. **3.** A toy made of the merry-thought of a fowl and so contrived that it can be made to skip; the merrythought itself 1797. **4.** Any of various fishes which have a habit of leaping out of the water, *esp.* the blue-fish (*Temnodon* or *Pomatomus saltator*) of tropical and subtropical seas 1703. **5.** A beetle belonging to the family *Elateridæ*; a click-beetle or spring-beetle 1817. **B.** *adj.* **1.** Having the qualities of a skipjack; foppish. Also *transf.* of things. 1597. **2.** Hopping, jumping, skipping 1605.

†**Skip-kennel.** 1668. [f. SKIP *v.*¹ + KENNEL *sb.*²] One who has to jump over the kennels or gutters; a lackey, footman –1828.

Skipper (ski·pəɹ), *sb.*¹ 1440. [f. SKIP *v.*¹ + -ER¹.] **1.** One who or that which skips or jumps. †**b.** Applied contempt. to a youth. SHAKS. **2.** *spec.* **a.** A skipjack or spring-beetle 1796. **b.** A butterfly of the family *Hesperiidæ* 1817. **c.** *dial.* and *U.S.* A cheese-maggot, or other small maggot, etc., of similar habits 1828. **3.** *spec.* The saury pike 1674. **4.** One who omits passages in reading 1824.

Skipper (ski·pəɹ), *sb.*² late ME. [– MLG., MDu. *schipper*, f. *schip* SHIP *sb.*¹; see -ER¹.] **1.** The captain or master of a ship, esp. of a small trading, merchant, or fishing vessel; †a shipman, seaman. **b.** *Skipper's daughters*, high white-crested waves 1888. **2.** The captain or director of a sporting team or side 1830. Hence **Ski·pper** *v. trans.* to act as s. of.

Skirl (skɔ̈ɹl), *sb. Sc.* and *n. dial.* 1513. [f. the vb.] **1.** A shrill cry, a shriek; shrill talk. **2.** A shrill sound, *esp.* that characteristic of the bagpipe 1860.

Skirl (skɔ̈ɹl), *v. Sc.* and *n. dial.* late ME. [prob. of Scand. origin; early forms *scrille*, *skrille*, corresp. to Norw. dial. *skrylla*; ult. imit.] **1.** *intr.* To scream, shriek, cry out shrilly. **b.** Of the bagpipe (or its music): To produce the shrill sounds by which it is characterized; to sound shrilly 1665. **2.** To play the bagpipe 1828. **3.** *trans.* To sing, utter, play, etc., in loud and shrill tones 1786. Hence **Ski·rling** *vbl. sb.* shrill crying, shrieking, etc.

Ski·rling, *sb. local.* 1776. [Of unkn. origin.] A young salmon; a samlet, sparling.

Ski·rmish (skɔ̄·ɹmiʃ), *sb.* [Late ME. (i) *skarmuch*, aphetic – OFr. *escar(a)muche* – It. *scaramuccia*, of unkn. origin; superseded by (ii) *skarmich*, *skyrmish*, which were based on OFr. *eskermiss-*, *eskirmiss-*; see next. Cf. SCRIMMAGE.] **1.** An irregular engagement between two small bodies of troops, esp. detached or outlying portions of opposing armies; a petty fight or encounter. Also occas. without article, as a mode of fighting. **2.** *transf.* **a.** Any contest or encounter 1576. **b.** An action or proceeding of a slight character; a slight display *of* something 1651.

2. a. They neuer meet, but there's a s. of wit between them SHAKS.

Skirmish (skə̄·ɹmiʃ), *v.* late ME. [– *eskermiss-*, *eskirmiss-*, lengthened stem of OFr. *eskermir*, *eskirmir*, also *escremir*, *escrimir* (mod. Fr. *escrimer* fence) – Frankish **skirmjan* (= OHG. *skirmen*, G. *schirmen*) defend; see -ISH[2].] **1.** *intr.* To engage in a skirmish or irregular encounter; to fight in small parties. Freq. const. *with*. †**2.** To fence; to make flourishes with a weapon –1763. †**3.** *trans.* To engage or attack (an enemy) in or with a skirmish –1679.

Skirmisher (skə̄·ɹmiʃəɹ). ME. [f. prec. + -ER[1].] One of a number of soldiers taking part in a skirmish or acting in loose order. Also *transf.* and *fig.*

Skirr (skə̄ɹ), *v.* 1548. [synon. with SCOUR *v.*[1], but identity with this is not favoured by the forms *skyr*, *sker*.] **1.** *intr.* To run hastily (*away*); to flee, make off. **2.** To move, run, fly, sail, etc., rapidly or with great impetus. Sometimes implying a whirring sound accompanying the movement. 1567. **3.** *trans.* To pass or go rapidly over, esp. in search of something or some one 1605. **4.** To throw with a rapid skimming motion 1652.

3. Send out moe Horses, skirre the Country round SHAKS. Hence **Skirr** *sb.* a sound of a grating, rasping, or whirring character.

Skirret[1] (ski·rit). [ME. *skirwhit(e*, perh. f. †*skire* clear, bright (– ON. *skírr* SHEER *a.*) + WHITE.] A perennial umbelliferous plant, *Sium sisarum*, a species of water parsnip, formerly much cultivated in Europe for its esculent tubers; the root of this plant.

Skirret[2] (ski·rit). 1853. [Of unkn. origin.] An instrument for measuring land, aligning trenches, etc., working on a revolving centre-pin.

Skirt (skə̄ɹt), *sb.* ME. [– ON. *skyrta* shirt = OE. *scyrte* SHIRT *sb.* The change of meaning is not accounted for; but the corresp. LG. *schört* means 'woman's gown' locally.] **I. 1.** The lower part of a woman's dress or gown, covering the person from the waist downwards; also, a separate garment serving this purpose. **b.** A woman. Now *vulgar slang*. 1560. **2.** The lower part of a man's gown or robe. Now chiefly *Hist.*, or with ref. to Eastern countries. ME. **b.** The bottom, lower portion, or tail of a coat or similar garment. Chiefly *pl.* 1598.

1. *Divided s.*, a form of s. divided in the middle and presenting the appearance of full knicker-bockers; also, a s. made in two widths and open back and front, used in riding or cycling. **2. b.** †*To sit* (*stick*) *in* or *upon* (a person's) *skirts*, to press hard upon, punish severely; A..gentleman ..determined to stick in my skirts, and either ruin or marry me 1809.

II. 1. a. One of the flaps or lower portions of a saddle. Also *saddle s.* late ME. **b.** The rim or base of a bell or bee-hive 1555. **c.** The border, rim, outer portion, extremity, or tail-end of anything 1566. **d.** *Naut.* A side or leech of a sail 1627. †**2.** A rim or border; an edging (*rare*) –1713. **3.** The diaphragm or midriff of an animal, *esp.* as used for food 1725.

1. a. This letter was sowen up in the s. of a saddle 1736. **2.** This consists of a narrow lace, or a small s. of fine ruffled linnen, which runs along the upper part of the stays before ADDISON.

III. 1. The border, boundary, or outlying part *of* a territory, country, kingdom, etc. Chiefly in *pl.* 1470. **b.** *pl.* The suburbs *of* a town or city. Also rarely *sing.* 1598. **c.** *pl.* The parts *of* an army farthest distant from the centre or main body; the edge, border, or fringe *of* a crowd, etc. 1533. **2.** The edge, margin, verge *of* a wood, lake, cloud, etc.; the foot or lower slopes *of* a mountain or hill 1598. **3.** A number of trees, etc., surrounding or bordering a place 1617.

1. Upon the s. and fringe of our fair land TENNYSON. **2.** I came to the S. of the Wood DE FOE. *fig.* I am a shadow now,..Upon the skirts of human-nature dwelling KEATS. **3.** A s. of thickets hid the approach of the..enemy 1835.

attrib. and *Comb.*: **s.-board,** (*a*) a shaped board on which skirts, dresses, etc. are ironed or pressed; (*b*) = SKIRTING-BOARD; **-dancing,** a form of ballet dancing in which the steps are accompanied by the manipulation of long flowing skirts or drapery; so **s.-dance.**

Skirt (skə̄ɹt), *v.* 1602. [f. the sb.] **I.** *trans.* **1.** To form the skirt or edge of; to lie along-side of; to bound or border. **2.** To surround, edge, or border, *with* something 1667. **3.** Of persons, ships, etc.: To go or pass along the border, edge, or side of (a country, district, etc.); to go round, in place of crossing 1735. **b.** To scour or search the outskirts of (a wood, etc.). *rare.* 1724.

1. Those vast and trackless forests that skirted the settlements W. IRVING. *fig.* So is man's narrow path By strength and terror skirted EMERSON. **3.** We skirted a large reedy swamp 1865.

II. *intr.* **1. a.** Of persons: To travel, move, hang about, etc., on the outskirts or confines of something, or in a casual manner 1623. **b.** Of hunting-dogs: To leave the pack when following the scent or in a chase 1781. **2.** Of roads, rivers, etc.: To lie or run *along* or *round* the edge or border of a place, etc. 1776.

1. a. Then I set off up the valley, skirting along one side of it BLACKMORE. **2.** A sandy desert.. skirts along the doubtful confine of Syria GIBBON.

Skirter (skə̄·ɹtəɹ). 1781. [f. SKIRT *v.* + -ER[1].] One who skirts, esp., *Hunting*, a hound which leaves the pack while following scent.

Skirting (skə̄·ɹtiŋ), *vbl. sb.* 1764. [f. SKIRT + -ING[1].] **1.** A border, edge, edging, or margin. **2.** Material for skirts 1852. **3.** *Carpentry.* The narrow boarding, edging of slate or cement, etc., placed vertically along the base of the wall of a room, or other place in a building, next to the floor. Also *collect.*, material suitable for this. 1825.

Ski·rting-board. 1759. [Cf. prec. 3.] The narrow board placed round the wall of a room, etc., close to the floor.

Skit, *sb.* 1572. [Related to SKIT *v.*] **1.** A vain, frivolous, or wanton girl. Chiefly *Sc.* **2.** A quizzing or satirical reflection *upon*, or hit *at*, a person or thing; a remark of this nature 1727. **b.** A piece of light satire, parody, or caricature 1820. **3.** A slight shower 1847.

2. I know you mean all that as a s. upon my edication 1779.

Skit (skit), *v.* 1611. [perh. based (as prec. and next) ult. on ON. **skyt-*, mutation of **skut-* **skeut-* SHOOT *v.*; cf. dial. *skite* move rapidly, dart, prob. f. ON. **skýt-* mutated stem of *skjóta* SHOOT *v.*] **1.** *intr.* To shy or be skittish; to move lightly and rapidly; to caper, leap, or spring. **2. a.** *trans.* To cast indirect reflections or light satire upon (a person, etc.); to ridicule or caricature by means of a skit 1781. **b.** *intr.* To make satirical hits *at* a person or thing 1821.

Skittish (ski·tiʃ), *a.* late ME. [See prec., and -ISH[1].] **1.** Of disposition, etc.: Characterized by levity, frivolity, or excessive liveliness. **2.** Of horses, etc.: Disposed or apt to start or be unruly without sufficient cause; unduly lively or spirited 1510. **3.** Fickle, inconstant; tricky, difficult to deal with or manage 1601. **4.** Spirited, active, lively; frolicsome 1592. **5.** Inclined to show coyness or reserve 1648.

1. T 'address The s. fancy with facetious tales COWPER. **2.** Balancing our s. bark upon the green waters 1841. **3.** Som men creepe in s. fortunes hall SHAKS. **4.** She is like a frog in a parsley-bed, As s. as an eel 1592. Hence **Ski·ttish-ly** *adv.*, **-ness.**

Skittle (ski·t'l). 1634. [Parallel with *kittle pins* (somewhat later in XVII); cf. SKAYLES and KAYLES; of unkn. origin, but the base may be the same as in SKIT *v.* (cf. Sw., Da. *skyttel* shuttle, marble, gate-bar).] **1.** *pl.* = NINE-PINS 1. **b.** *colloq.* Nonsense, rubbish. Also as *int.* 1904. **c.** Chess not played seriously (*colloq.*) 1856. **2.** One of the pins with which the game of skittles is played 1680.

1. Phr. (*Not*) *all beer and skittles*, etc., used to denote that something is (not) unmixed enjoyment. Hence **Ski·ttle** *v.* **Ski·ttler. Ski·ttling** *vbl. sb.* (esp in chess).

Skive (skəiv), *sb.*[1] Also **skieve.** 1843. [– Du. *schijf* (sxəif), MDu. *schîve*; see SHIVE[1].] A diamond-wheel.

Skive (skəiv), *sb.*[2] 1875. [f. the vb.] The surface part of a sheet of leather cut off by a skiving-machine; a skiver.

Skive (skəiv), *v.* 1825. [– ON. *skífa*, related to ME. *schive* SHIVE[1].] *trans.* To split or cut (leather, rubber, etc.) into slices or strips; to pare or shave (hides). Also with *off*.

Skiver (ski·vəɹ), *sb.*[1] Chiefly *dial.* 1664. [Of unkn. origin; see SKEWER.] A skewer.

Skiver (skəi·vəɹ), *sb.*[2] Also **skyver.** 1800. [f. SKIVE *v.* + -ER[1].] **1.** A thin kind of dressed leather split from the grain side of a sheep-skin and tanned in sumach, used for book-binding, lining hats, etc. **2.** One who or that which skives; *esp.* a workman who pares or splits leather 1875. Hence **Skiver** *v.*[2] *trans.* to cut or pare (leather).

Skiver (ski·vəɹ), *v.*[1] 1832. [f. SKIVER *sb.*[1]] *trans.* To pierce or stab with or as with a skewer; to fasten with a skewer.

Skiving (skəi·viŋ), *vbl. sb.* 1825. [f. SKIVE *v.* + -ING[1].] **1.** The parings of hides; the piece or sheet of split leather from the inner, or flesh, side. **2.** The action of splitting leather, etc. 1884.

Skivvy (ski·vi). 1922. *colloq.* [perh. alt. of *slavvy* SLAVEY.] Depreciatory term for a female domestic servant, esp. a rough 'general'.

Skua (skiū·ă). 1678. [– mod.L. – Færoese *skúgvur* = ON. *skúfr*, of unkn. origin.] A predatory gull belonging to the genus *Stercorarius*, esp. the largest European species, *S. catarrhactes*, which breeds in Shetland, the Færoes, and Iceland. Also *s.-gull*.

Skulk (skɒlk), *sb.* ME. [f. the vb.] **1.** One who skulks or hides himself; a shirker. †**2.** A number, company, or gathering (of persons or animals given to skulking) –1883.

2. We say a flight of doves.., a s. of foxes W. IRVING.

Skulk (skɒlk), *v.* Also **sculk.** ME. [Of Scand. origin; cf. Norw. *skulka* lurk, lie watching, Sw. *skolka*, Da. *skulke* shirk, play truant.] **1.** *intr.* To move in a stealthy or sneaking fashion, so as to escape notice. Usu. with *about*, *away*, *into*, or the like. **2.** To hide or conceal oneself, to avoid observation, esp. with some sinister motive or in fear of being discovered; to lurk ME. **b.** To hide, to withdraw or shelter oneself, in a cowardly manner 1621. **c.** To shirk duty; *spec.* to malinger 1781.

1. It is a poor thing for a fellow to get drunk at night, and sculk to bed JOHNSON. **2.** Man is a yong Lyon,..lurking and sculking to doe mischiefe 1641. **b.** Ah! s. behind the women, do! 1877. Hence **Sku·lker,** one who skulks. **Sku·lk-ingly** *adv.*

Skull (skɒ̄l). [ME. *scolle*, *schulle*, of unkn. origin, but remarkably similar to synon. ON. *skoltr* (Norw. *skolt*, *skult*, Sw. *skult*, dial. *skulle*).] **1.** The bony case or frame containing or enclosing the brain of man or other vertebrate animals; also, the whole bony framework or skeleton of the head. **b.** The head as the proper seat of thought or intelligence. Commonly with allusion to dullness of intellect. 1523. **c.** A representation of a human skull, as an emblem or reminder of death or mortality 1826. †**2.** A skull-cap of metal or other hard material; a close-fitting head-piece –1674.

1. b. Your Sexe, Whose empty Sculles..your selues peruersely vexe 1632. **c.** She was a perpetual *memento mori*; a s. and cross-bones would hardly have been more efficacious 1826.

Comb.: **s.-fish,** a whalebone whale above two years of age.

Skull, var. or obs. f. SCULL *sb.* and *v.*

Skull-cap (skɒ·lkæp). 1682. [CAP *sb.*[1]] **1.** A light, close-fitting cap, usu. of silk, velvet, or other soft material, for covering the head or the crown of it. **2.** *Hist.* A steel or iron cap, a form of casque or helmet fitting closely to the head 1820. **3.** *Bot.* One or other of various species of plants belonging to the genus *Scutellaria*, in which the calyx finally assumes the appearance of a helmet 1760. **4.** *Anat.* The bony structure covering the brain; the top or roof of the head 1855.

2. There was a ferocious tyrant in a skullcap like an inverted porringer, and a dress of red baize 1824.

Skunk (skɒŋk), *sb.* 1634. [– Amer. Indian (Abenaki) *seganku* or *segongw*.] **1.** A N. American animal of the weasel kind, *Mephi-*

tis mephitica, noted for emitting a very offensive odour when attacked or killed. **b.** *ellipt.* The fur of the skunk 1862. **2.** *colloq.* A thoroughly mean or contemptible person. Also in playful use. 1841.

attrib. and *Comb.*, *as s.-fur*, etc.; also, **s.-bird, -blackbird** *U.S.*, the bobolink, so called from a resemblance in the colours of the male bird to those of the s.; **-cabbage** *N. Amer.*, a perennial stemless plant of the arum family, *Symplocarpus fœtidus*, giving out an offensive odour, esp. when bruised; **-head** *U.S. local*, the Labrador duck; **-weed** *U.S.*, = *s.-cabbage*. Hence **Sku·nkish** *a.* resembling a s.; contemptible.

Skunk (skɒŋk), *v. U.S. slang.* 1848. [f. prec.] *trans.* To defeat an opponent so completely in a game of chance that he makes no score.

‖**Skupshtina** (sku·pʃtină). 1862. [Serb., = assembly.] **a.** The national assembly of Serbia and of Montenegro. **b.** Now, the parliament of Yugoslavia.

Sky (skəi), *sb.* ME. [– ON. *ský* cloud (:– **skiuja*), rel. to OE. *scēo*, OS. *scio* (:– **skeuw-*) and (more remotely) OE. *scūwa*, OHG. *scuwo*, ON. *skuggi* shade, shadow, Goth. *skuggwa* mirror :– **skuwwon*.] †**1.** A cloud –1550. **2.** *The skies*, the clouds (*obs.*); the upper region of the air; the heavens. Chiefly *poet.* ME. **b.** Used without *the*, in limited sense 1503. **3.** *The s.*, the apparent arch or vault of heaven; the firmament ME. **4.** *poet.* or *rhet.* **a.** The celestial regions; heaven; the heavenly power, the deity 1590. **b.** The sky (sense 3) of a particular region; hence, climate, clime 1701. **5. a.** The colour of the sky; sky-blue 1667. **b.** The representation of a sky in a painting, etc. 1747.

1. A certeyn wynde..blewe so hydously and hye, That hyt ne left a skye In alle the welkene CHAUCER. **2.** The skyes rang for schoutyng of the larkis DUNBAR. **b.** It was a dismal day with leaden skies overhead 1907. **3.** Lead itself can fly, And pond'rous slugs cut swiftly thro' the s. POPE. *fig.* I, in the cleare Skie of Fame, o're-shine you SHAKS. *To the s.* or *skies*, to the highest possible degree, enthusiastically, extravagantly. *In the skies*, in an ecstasy, in the realms of fancy. **4. a.** Now am I dead, now am I fled, my soule is in the s. SHAKS. **5. b.** The s. is unusually careless RUSKIN.

Comb.: **s.-blink**, = ICE-BLINK 1; **-flyer**, an ambitious person; **-pilot** *slang* (*a*) a clergyman, *esp.* one who has a spiritual charge among seamen; (*b*) a licensed aviator; **-scape**, a view or painting of the sky; **-stone**, a meteorite; **-writing**, legible smoke-trails made by aeroplanes for advertising or in displays. Hence **Sky·ish**, *a.* lofty, approaching the s.; resembling that of the s.

Sky (skəi), *v.* Pa. t. and pa. pple. **skied.** 1802. [f. prec.] **1.** *trans.* **a.** *slang.* To throw or toss up (a coin). **b.** *Cricket*, etc.: To strike (a ball) into the air 1873. **2.** To hang (a picture, etc.) high up on the wall or near the ceiling, *esp.* at an exhibition 1865. **3.** To cover like the sky; to overshadow 1844.

3. Napoleon!..that great word..skied us overhead E. B. BROWNING.

Sky-blue, *sb.* and *a.* 1728. [SKY *sb.*] **A.** *sb.* **1.** A pure blue colour like that of the sky in daylight; a fabric of this colour 1738. **2.** Thin or watery milk, having a bluish tint 1798. †**3.** *slang.* Gin –1796. **B.** *adj.* Of the blue colour of the sky; azure 1728.

'Twas there gay Phylla..Glanc'd the soft passion from her s. eye 1773.

Skye (skəi). 1851. [Gael. *Sgith* (skī).] The name of the largest island of the Inner Hebrides used attrib., esp. in *S. terrier*, a small breed of dog, long-haired, long-bodied, and short-legged 1856. **b.** *ellipt.* A Skye terrier 1851.

Skyey (skəi·i), *a.* 1603. Also **skiey.** [f. SKY *sb.* + -Y[1].] **1.** Of or pertaining to the sky; emanating from the sky. Also, lofty. **2.** Resembling the sky in colour; azure 1816.

1. A breath thou art, Seruile to all the skyie-influences SHAKS. The mountains..are of s. height COLERIDGE.

Sky-high, *adv.* and *a. colloq.* 1818. [SKY *sb.*] **A.** *adv.* As high as the sky; very high. **B.** *adj.* Reaching to the sky 1840.

Skylark (skəi·lāɹk), *sb.* 1686. [SKY *sb.*] **1.** The common lark of Europe, *Alauda arvensis*, so called from its habit of soaring towards the sky while singing. **2.** *U.S.* The Missouri pipit, *Anthus spraguei*; the prairie lark 1872.

Skylark (skəi·lāɹk), *v.* 1809. [f. prec.] *intr.* To frolic or play; to play tricks; to indulge in rough sport or horse-play. In early use chiefly *Naut.*

Skylarking, a term used by seamen, to denote wanton play about the rigging, and tops, or in any part of the ship 1815.

Skylight (skəi·ləit). Also **sky-light.** 1679. **1.** Light from the sky; light coming into a room, etc., from above. †**b.** = DAYLIGHT 3. –1824. **2.** A small opening in a roof, or in the ceiling of a room, filled in with glass, for admitting daylight; the framework and glass fitted to such an opening 1690.

Sky·-line. 1860. [SKY *sb.*] The line where earth and sky meet; the horizon. **b.** The outline of a building, etc. seen against the sky 1903.

Sky·-ro:cket. 1688. [SKY *sb.*] A rocket which ascends high into the sky before exploding.

Sky·-sail. Also **skysail.** 1829. [SKY *sb.*] *Naut.* In square-rigged vessels, a light sail set above the royal.

Sky·-scra:per. 1794. [SKY *sb.*] **1.** *Naut.* A triangular sky-sail. **2.** A high building of many storeys, *esp.* one of those characteristic of American cities 1891.

Sky·-sign. 1880. [SKY *sb.*] **1.** *poet.* A celestial sign or portent. BROWNING. **2.** A sign of the nature of an advertisement, so constructed and placed that the letters, etc., usu. illuminated at night, stand out against the sky 1890.

Skyward (skəi·wǒɹd), *adv.* and *adj.* 1582. [SKY *sb.*] **A.** *adv.* Towards, in the direction of, the sky. **B.** *adj.* Leading to the sky; going towards the sky; heavenward 1838. So **Sky·wards** *adv.*

Slab (slæb), *sb.*[1] ME. [Of unkn. origin.] **1.** A flat, broad, and comparatively thick piece or mass of anything solid. **2.** A rough outside plank of timber cut from a log or tree-trunk preparatory to squaring the main portion, or sawing it into planks 1573. **3.** A flat piece of wood or stone used as a table, counter, etc.; a small table hinged to the wall in the passage or hall of a house 1739. Hence **Sla·bbing,** slabs collectively, slab-work. **Sla·bby** *a.*[2] of the nature of a s.; covered with slabs.

Slab (slæb), *sb.*[2] 1610. [prob. of Scand. origin (cf. ODa. *slab* mud, Icel., Norw., Sw. *slabb* wet filth).] **1.** A muddy place; a puddle. Now *dial.* **2.** Wet and slimy matter; ooze, sludge 1622.

Slab (slæb), *a.* 1605. [Related to SLAB *sb.*[2]] Semi-solid; viscid. (In mod. use entirely as an echo of Shakespeare.)

Make the Grewell thicke, and s. SHAKS.

Slab (slæb), *v.* 1703. [f. SLAB *sb.*[1]] **1.** *trans.* To dress (timber) by removing the outside slabs; to clear of bark-wood. **2.** To convert into a slab or slabs 1868. **3.** To lay or pave with slabs 1832.

Slabber (slæ·bəɹ), *sb.*[1] 1718. [Related to SLABBER *v.*] **1.** Slaver; excessive saliva. **2.** Slobbering talk 1840.

Slabber (slæ·bəɹ), *sb.*[2] 1875. [f. SLAB *v.* + -ER[1].] **a.** A saw or machine for removing the outside slabs from timber, or dressing the outer portion of logs. **b.** A machine for dressing nuts or bolts.

Slabber (slæ·bəɹ), *v.* Now chiefly *dial.* 1573. [rel. to SLAB *sb.*[2]; see -ER[5]. Cf. SLAVER *v.*, SLOBBER *v.*] **1.** *trans.* To wet or befoul with saliva; to beslaver or beslobber 1579. **2.** To wet in a dirty or disagreeable manner 1573. **3.** To gobble *up*, swallow *down*, in a hurried or unrefined manner 1573. **4.** *intr.* To let saliva flow or fall from the mouth; to slaver, dribble; to disgorge water 1648.

1. He..slabber'd me all over from Cheek to Cheek, with his great Tongue 1712. **2.** Her milke pan and creame pot, so slabbered and sost 1573. **4.** Slabbering, whining, crying 1793. Hence **Sla·bbery** *a.* sloppy, slabby, slushy.

Slabby (slæ·bi), *a.*[1] 1542. [f. SLAB *sb.*[2] + -Y[1].] **1.** Wet, miry, muddy, slushy, sloppy. Now *dial.* **2.** Of liquids: Thick, ropy 1654.

2. They present you with a Cup, and you must drink of a s. stuff 1654. Hence **Sla·bbiness.**

Slabline (slæ·bˌləin). 1647. [prob. – Du. *slaplijn*, f. *slap* slack.] *Naut.* A small cord passing up behind the main-sail or fore-sail of a vessel and used to truss up the sail.

Slab-sided (slæ·bˌsəidėd), *a. U.S.* 1825. [f. SLAB *sb.*[1]] Having sides like slabs; flat-sided; long and lank.

Slack (slæk), *sb.*[1] *north.* and *Sc.* late ME. [– ON. *slakki* in sense 1.] **1.** A small shallow dell or valley; a hollow or dip in the ground; a depression in a hill-side or between two stretches of rising ground. **2.** A boggy hollow; a morass 1719.

Slack (slæk), *sb.*[2] 1440. [Late ME. and dial. *sleck*, prob. of LDu. origin (cf. LG. *slakk*, Du. *slak*, G. *schlacke* dross).] Small or refuse coal.

Slack (slæk), *sb.*[3] 1756. [f. SLACK *a.* or *v.*] **1.** A cessation in the strong flow of a current or of the tide. **2.** An interval of comparative inactivity; a lull in business or in action of any kind 1851. **3.** That part *of* a rope, sail, etc., which is not fully strained, or which hangs loose; a loose part or end 1794. **4.** *dial.* and *U.S. colloq.* Impertinence, cheek 1842. **5.** *pl.* Trousers (*dial.*); *spec.* trousers worn as part of military uniform instead of breeches and puttees 1822.

1. The tide was low water s., and the weather was fine and clear 1892. **4.** Let's have none of your s. 1876.

Slack (slæk), *a.* and *adv.* [OE. *slæc* = OS., (M)Du. *slak*, OHG. *slah*, ON. *slakr* :– Gmc. **slakaz*, cogn. with L. *laxus* LAX, *languēre* LANGUISH.] **A.** *adj.* **I. 1.** Of persons: Lacking in energy or diligence; inclined to be lazy or idle; remiss, careless; negligent or lax in regard to one's duties. **2.** Not busy; having little work 1834.

1. For in very dede he wil come, and not be slacke COVERDALE *Hab.* 2:3.

II. 1. Of conduct, actions, etc.: Characterized by remissness or lack of energy OE. **2.** Of pace: Slow; not smart or hurried OE. **3.** Comparatively weak or slow in operation; deficient in strength or activity; dull. late ME. **b.** Of heat, etc.: Gentle, moderate 1495. **c.** Of wind, or tide: Blowing, or running, with very little strength or speed 1670. **4.** Of work, etc.: Not brisk or active; also *transf.* of time 1813.

1. He becommeth poor that dealeth with a slacke hand *Prov.* 10:4. **2.** Their pace was formal, grave, and s. DRYDEN. **3.** By Study worn, and s. with Age PRIOR. **b.** Set them in a s. Oven till they are tender 1741. **4.** When betting became s. 1813.

III. 1. Not drawn or held tightly or tensely; relaxed, loose ME. **b.** *Phonetics.* Of a vowel: Pronounced with relaxed muscles 1906. **2.** Lacking cohesiveness or solidity; not compact or firm; crumbling, loose; soft 1440. **3.** Of the hand: Not holding or grasping firmly 1667. **b.** Similarly of one's hold of anything 1836.

1. In the morning wee bore a s. saile 1621. **3.** A s. hand had..been held upon them DE FOE.

Special collocations: **s. barrel, cask,** one made to hold dry goods; **s. jaw, s. lip,** tiresome or impertinent talk; **s. wire,** a wire not drawn tight, on which an acrobat performs. Hence **Sla·ck-ly** *adv.*, **-ness.**

B. *adv.* In a slack manner; slackly 1641.

Slack (slæk), *v.* 1520. [f. SLACK *a.*, in some senses replacing the earlier SLAKE *v.*] **I.** *trans.* **1.** To be slack or remiss in respect of (some business, duty, etc.); to leave undone or not properly attended to 1530. †**b.** To neglect or let slip (an opportunity, etc.) –1697. †**c.** To lose or waste (time) –1633. **2.** To cease to go on with, or prosecute, in a vigorous and energetic manner; to allow to fall off or decline 1520. **b.** To allow to mitigate or abate (*rare*) 1560. **3. a.** To reduce the force or strength of; to make less active, vigorous, or violent 1589. **b.** To slake (one's thirst) 1631. **4.** To make lax, neglectful, or remiss 1597. **5.** To delay or retard; to render slower in respect of motion or progress. Also with *up*. Now *rare*. 1577. **6.** To make slack or loose; to relax. Also *absol.* 1530. **7.** To cause (lime) to disintegrate by the action of water or moisture; to slake 1703.

1. Whye slacke you your busynesse thus? PALSGR. **b.** Time calls you now,..S. not the good Presage DRYDEN. **2.** I do not s. my labour. I can preach and write still. WESLEY. **3.** I slack'd my Fire gradually DE FOE. **4.** Love slack'd my Muse, and made my numbers soft MARLOWE. **5.** I am nothing slow to s. his hast SHAKS. **6.** Tak the ..horse to the stable, and slack his girths SCOTT.

II. *intr.* †**1.** To delay, tarry (*rare*) –1611. **2.**

To be inactive or idle; to fail to exert oneself in a due manner. In mod. use *colloq.* 1543. **b.** To be backward or dilatory *to* do something. Now *rare.* 1560. **3.** Of persons (or animals): To become less energetic, active, or diligent. Also with *off.* 1560. **4.** To diminish in strength or speed; to moderate in some respect 1580. **b.** Of affairs, business, etc.: To fall off; to go more slowly; to be less brisk 1606. **5.** To become less tense, rigid, or firm 1577. **6.** Of lime, etc.: To become disintegrated under the action of moisture 1703.

2. b. Slack not my woords to remember 1582. **4.** The breeze slacked, and we slowly worked up to the north 1865.

Slack-baked, *a.* 1823. [SLACK *adv.*] Of bread: Imperfectly or insufficiently baked.

Slacken (slæ·k'n), *v.* 1580. [f. SLACK *a.* + -EN[5].] **I.** *trans.* **1.** = SLACK *v.* I. 5. **2.** To render less vigorous or eager; to cause or allow to fall off or decline 1631. **3.** To relax in point of strictness or severity; to render less severe or stern 1605. **4.** To give relaxation to (one's thoughts, etc.) 1643. **5.** = SLACK *v.* I. 3 a. 1685. **6.** To render, to allow to become, less tense, taut, or firm; to reduce the tension of 1611. **7.** To make loose; to loosen 1815.

1. As the river approaches its mouth, the flow becomes slackened 1878. **2.** Thy freeborn sons.. Nor sloth can s., nor a tyrant bind 1807. **5.** That consideration should..s. the fierce rages of grief 1685. **6.** *fig.* In Spain, directly government slackened its hold, the nation fell to pieces 1861.

II. *intr.* **1.** = SLACK *v.* II. 3. 1641. **2.** = SLACK *v.* II. 4, 4 b. 1651. **3.** To diminish in speed; to become slower 1721. **4.** Of lime: To become slaked 1703. **5.** = SLACK *v.* II. 5. 1850.

1. When the people s., and fall to loosenes and riot MILT. **2.** Our exertions must not s. NELSON. When the demand for iron slackens 1832. **3.** His pace slackened SCOTT. **5.** The line for an instant slacken'd 1850.

Sla·cker. 1797. [f. SLACK *v.* + -ER[1].] **1.** A drawgate to hinder the passage of water in a sluice. **2.** *colloq.* A person who shirks work, or avoids exertion, exercise, etc. 1898.

Sla·ck-rope. 1749. [f. SLACK *a.*] A rope, loosely stretched, on which an acrobat performs. (Contrasted with TIGHT-ROPE.)

Slack-water. Also **slackwater, slack water.** 1769. [f. SLACK *a.*] **1.** The time at high or low water when the tide is not flowing visibly in either direction. **2.** A stretch of comparatively still water in the sea, due to the absence of currents 1853. **3.** A part of a river lying outside of the current, or one in which the flow is lessened by a lock or dam 1867.

attrib.: **s. navigation,** navigation carried on by the use of locks or dams on a river.

Sladang, variant of SELADANG.

Slade (slē[i]d), *sb.*[1] [OE. *slæd* = OS. *slada*, LG. *slade*, Icel. *slǫðr*, Da., Norw. *slad(e*. The present form descends from OE. obl. cases.] A valley, dell, or dingle; an open space between banks or woods; a forest glade; a strip of greensward or of boggy land.

Slade (slē[i]d), *sb.*[2] 1867. [perh. related to SLIDE *v.*] The sole of a plough.

Slag (slæg), *sb.* 1552. [– MLG. *slagge*, perh. f. *slagen* strike, with ref. to fragments resulting from hammering.] **1.** A piece of refuse matter (see 2) separated from a metal in the process of smelting. **2.** A vitreous substance, composed of earthy or refuse matter, which is separated from metals in the process of smelting; any similar product resulting from the fusion or distillation of other substances 1620. **3.** *Geol.* A rough clinker-like lump of lava; lava in this form 1777. Hence **Sla·ggy** *a.* of the nature of s.; pertaining to or resembling s.

Sla·g-hearth. 1778. [SLAG *sb.*] A furnace for treating the slag-products of lead-smelting.

Sla·g-lead. 1668. [SLAG *sb.*] Lead obtained by re-smelting *grey slag*, i.e. slag from the Flintshire lead furnace, which is rich in lead.

Slake (slē[i]k), *sb.* ME. [f. SLAKE *v.*] The act of slacking or slackening in some respect; an instance of this.

Slake (slē[i]k), *v.* [OE. *slacian*, f. *slæc* SLACK *a.*; corresp. to (M)Du. *slaken* relax, diminish.] **I.** *intr.* †**1.** Of persons: To diminish the intensity of one's efforts; also, to undergo or manifest a weakening in some respect –1596. **2.** †**a.** To become relaxed, slack, or loose –1599. **b.** Of lime: To become hydrated or slacked 1766. **3.** To decrease in force or intensity; to become less violent, oppressive, or painful; to abate, moderate. Now *rare.* ME. **b.** Of fire: To burn less strongly; to die down, die away, go out ME. †**4.** To lessen, fall off –1614. †**5.** To become or grow less in number, quantity, or volume; to fall or subside –1613. **II.** *trans.* †**1.** To make slack or loose; to lessen the tension of; to allow to become slack or relaxed –1581. **b.** To disintegrate or slack (lime) 1662. †**2.** To reduce, diminish, lessen –1612. **3.** To render less acute or painful; to abate, mitigate, or assuage. Now *rare.* ME. †**4.** To make less vehement, violent, or intense –1664. **b.** To allow to diminish in vehemence or vigour; to moderate (one's anger, etc.). Now *rare.* ME. **5.** To appease, allay, or satisfy (desire, thirst, †hunger) ME. **6.** To quench or extinguish (fire); to cause to burn less strongly 1566. **7.** To cool or refresh by means of water or other fluid. late ME. **b.** To moisten, soak (*rare*) 1810. †**8.** To render less active or vigorous –1608.

1. b. The Lyonese builders..s. the lime by aspersion 1837. **4. b.** He shall s. that loue which he now voweth to Cynthia LYLY. **5.** His rage of lust, by gazing qualified; Slakt, not supprest SHAKS. **7.** I reached a little patch of snow, and managed to s. my parched lips 1871. **b.** Oatmeal slaked with cold water SCOTT. **8.** Now sleep yslaked hath the rout SHAKS. Hence **Sla·keless** *a.* incapable of being slaked, quenched, or mitigated; insatiable.

Slalom (slā·lǫm). 1921. In ski-ing, a race down a course defined by artificial obstacles, esp. flags.

Slam (slæm), *sb.*[1] 1672. [Related to SLAM *v.*[1]] **1.** A severe blow; a violent impact. **2.** A violent closing of a door, etc., producing a resounding noise; the noise so made, or a noise of this nature 1837.

2. Closing his prayer-book with an angry s. 1871.

Slam (slæm), *sb.*[2] Also **slamm.** 1621. [perh. shortening of †*slampant, -am, -aine*, in phr. *give* (one) *the slampant* trick, hoodwink.] †**1.** The card-game ruff and honours –1674. **2.** The fact of losing or winning all the tricks in a game of cards, esp. in whist 1660. **b.** With the qualifying terms *grand* and *little*, chiefly in bridge 1892.

2. b. 'Grand s.', *i.e.* taking every trick, or 'minor s.', every trick but one 1899.

Slam (slæm), *v.*[1] 1691. [prob. of Scand. origin (cf. ON. *slam(b)ra*, Sw. *slämma*, Norw. *slemma*).] **1.** *trans.* To beat or slap vigorously. *dial.* **2.** To shut (a door, window, etc.) with violence and noise; to bang; to close with unnecessary force 1775. **b.** To dash, throw, push, etc., with some degree of violence or force 1899. **3.** *intr.* Of doors, etc.: To shut, or strike against anything, with violence and resounding noise 1823. **4.** Used with advb. force: With a slam or heavy blow; suddenly and violently 1726.

2. He would s. the door to again 1873. **b.** Slamming every available man into the firing line 1899. **3.** The huge Drawbridge slams down CARLYLE.

Slam (slæm), *v.*[2] 1746. [f. SLAM *sb.*[2]] **1.** *trans.* To beat by winning a slam; also *dial.*, to trump. Hence *transf.* to beat completely. **2.** *intr.* To win a slam 1833.

Slam-bang, *adv., a.*, and *v.* Also **slam bang.** 1837. [f. SLAM *v.*[1] + BANG *v.*[1]] **A.** *adv.* With a slam and a bang; with noisy violence 1847. **B.** *adj.* Noisy, violent 1889. **C.** *vb. intr.* and *trans.* To slam and bang 1837.

Sla·mmakin, Sla·mmerkin, *sb.* and *a.* Chiefly *dial.* 1756. [Of unkn. origin.] **A.** *sb.* †**1.** A loose gown. **2.** A slovenly female, a slattern 1785. **B.** *adj.* Untidy, slovenly 1794.

Slander (slɑ·ndəɹ), *sb.* [ME. *sclaundre*, aphetic – AFr. *esclaundre*, OFr. *esclandre*, alt. of *escandle* SCANDAL *sb.*] **1.** The utterance or dissemination of false statements or reports concerning a person, or malicious misrepresentation of his actions, in order to defame or injure him; calumny, defamation. **2.** A false or malicious statement or utterance intended to injure, defame, or cast detraction on the person about whom it is made ME. †**3.** Discredit, disgrace, or shame, incurred by or falling upon a person or persons; evil name, ill repute, opprobrium –1678. †**b.** A source of shame or dishonour; a discreditable act; a disgrace; a wrong –1540. †**c.** A person who is a discredit, disgrace, or scandal to some body or set of persons –1596. †**4.** = SCANDAL *sb.* 1 b, OFFENCE *sb.* 2. –1586.

1. Shall S...Spit her cold venom in a dead man's ear? COLERIDGE. **2.** His slanders were monstrous: but they were well timed MACAULAY. **3. c.** That shamefull Hag, the slaunder of her sexe SPENSER.

Slander (slɑ·ndəɹ), *v.* ME. [– OFr. *esclandrer*, f. *esclandre*; see prec.] †**1.** *trans.* In or after Biblical use: To be a stumbling-block to; to offend; to cause to lapse –1563. †**2.** To bring into discredit, disgrace, or disrepute –1603. **3.** To defame or calumniate; to assail with slander; to speak evil of, traduce (a person, etc.) ME. †**b.** To accuse *of* something discreditable –1607. †**4.** To misrepresent or vilify (a thing) –1623. **5.** *intr.* or *absol.* To speak or utter slanders. late ME.

1. If thyn eye sclaunder or shame thy self put hit fro the CAXTON. **3.** Full ten years slander'd, did he once reply? POPE. **b.** *Two Gent.* III. ii. 38. **5.** Let them rail, then, scoff, and s. BURTON. Hence **Sla·nderer,** one who slanders; a defamer, a calumniator.

Slanderous (slɑ·ndərəs), *a.* late ME. [– OFr. *esclandreux*, f. *esclandre* SLANDER *sb.*; see -OUS.] †**1. a.** Of bad repute; discreditable, disgraceful, shameful –1589. **b.** Forming a source of shame or disgrace *to* some one (*rare*) –1595. **c.** Giving occasion for slander. SHAKS. **2.** Of words, reports, language, etc.: Of the nature of, characterized by, or containing slander or calumny; calumnious, defamatory. late ME. **3.** Of persons: Given to the use of slander or calumny; employing slander as a means of defaming or injuring others. Also *absol.* 1521.

1. b. If thou..wert grim, Vgly, and slandrous to thy Mothers wombe SHAKS. **c.** *Jul. C.* IV. i. 20. **2.** The highest judge in the land is answerable..for s. language 1883. **3.** Zealous..and pious, but.. fierce and s. 1838. Hence **Sla·nderous-ly** *adv.*, **-ness.**

Slang (slæŋ), *sb.*[1] *dial.* 1610. [Of unkn. origin.] A long narrow strip of land.

Slang (slæŋ), *sb.*[2] 1756. [A word of cant origin; ult. source unkn.] **1.** The special vocabulary used by any set of persons of a low or disreputable character; language of a low and vulgar type. (Now merged in c.) **b.** The cant or jargon of a certain class or period 1802. **c.** Language of a highly colloquial type, considered as below the level of standard educated speech, and consisting either of new words or of current words employed in some special sense 1818. **2.** A travelling show 1859. **b.** *attrib.*, as **s. cove, cull,** a showman 1789.

1. Such grossness of speech, and horrid oaths, as showed them not to be unskilled in the s...of the lowest blackguards in the nation 1809. **b.** Correct English is the s. of prigs 1872. **c.** If I had ever talked s., I might have said that we chummed together famously 1887.

Slang (slæŋ), *sb.*[3] *Cant.* 1812. [app. – Du. *slang* snake, etc.] **1.** A watch-chain; a chain of any kind. **2.** *pl.* Fetters, leg-irons 1812.

Slang (slæŋ), *a.* (and *adv.*). 1758. [Related to SLANG *sb.*[2]] **1.** Of language, etc.: Having the character of, belonging to, expressed in, slang. †**2.** Given to the use of slang; of a fast or rakish character; impertinent –1864. †**b.** Of dress: Loud, extravagant –1858. **c.** Of tone, etc.: Slangy, rakish 1834. **3.** *Coster's slang.* Of weights and measures: Short, defective 1812. **b.** *adv.* So as to give short measure 1851.

1. The cant language, commonly called the s. patter 1758. **2.** Daring, saucy girls, s. and fast 1864.

Slang (slæŋ), *v. colloq.* or *slang.* 1812. [f. SLANG *sb.*[2] or *a.*] **1. a.** *trans.* To defraud, cheat. **b.** *intr.* (also with *it*). To employ cheating; to give short measure. **2.** To utter or use slang; to rail in abusive or vulgar language 1828. **3.** *trans.* To abuse or scold violently 1844.

2. Mr. Carlyle slangs like a blaspheming pagan 1868. **3.** He could..s. coal-heavers..better than anyone else in London 1844.

Slangwhang (slæ·ŋ,hwæŋ), *v.* Chiefly *U.S.* 1829. [f. SLANG *sb.*[2] 1 + WHANG *v.*]

trans. and *intr.* To assail with, to make use of, violent language or abuse. So **Sla·ng-wha:nger,** a noisy or abusive talker or writer 1807.

Slangy (slæ·ŋi), *a.* 1850. [f. SLANG *sb.*[2] 1 + -Y[1].] **1.** Of persons: **a.** Of a flashy or pretentious type. **b.** Given to the use of slang. **2. a.** Of dress: Somewhat loud or vulgar 1861. **b.** Of language, etc.: Pertaining to, of the nature of, slang 1864. Hence **Sla·ngily** *adv.* **Sla·nginess.**

Slant (slɑnt), *sb.*[1] 1655. [f. earlier SLANT *adv.* and *v.*, obscurely related to SLENT *sb.* and *v.*] **1.** The slope *of* a hill, piece of ground, etc.; a sloping stretch of ground; an inclined plane or surface. **b.** A small surface, a short line, having an oblique position or direction 1711. **c.** A sloping beam or ray *of* light 1855. **d.** *Mining.* A heading driven diagonally between the dip and the strike of a coal-seam 1881. **e.** A vessel or surface having a sloping bottom or depression for paint-brushes or colours 1875. **f.** A bacteriological culture in a test-tube laid in a slanting position 1901. **2.** Slope, inclination, obliquity. *On the s.*, aslant, obliquely. 1817. **3.** *dial.* and *U.S.* **a.** A sly hit or sarcasm 1825. **b.** An opportunity, occasion 1837. **c.** A way of regarding a thing, point of view (*U.S.*) 1905.

Slant (slɑnt), *sb.*[2] 1596. [Later form of *slent*, in same sense – ON. **slent* (Norw. *slett*), f. **slenta* (ON. *sletta*) dash, throw, etc.] *Naut.* A slight breeze or spell *of* wind, etc.

Slant (slɑnt), *adv.* and *a.* 1495. [Aphetic for ME. *a-slonte*, *o-slante*, etc.; see ASLANT *adv.*] **A.** *adv.* In a slanting, sloping, or oblique manner or direction; slantingly, aslant. **B.** *adj.* **1.** Of wind, etc.: Blowing or coming from the side; moving obliquely 1618. **2.** Having an oblique or sloping position or direction; inclined from the perpendicular or horizontal; falling, lying, placed, etc. slantwise 1776. **b.** Of direction: Oblique 1793.

1. The s. Lightning, whose thwart flame driv'n down Kindles the gummie bark of Firr or Pine MILT. Hence **Sla·ntly** *adv.*

Slant (slɑnt), *v.* 1521. [Later var. of SLENT *v.*, prob. infl. by ASLANT *adv.*] **1.** *intr.* To strike obliquely *on*, *upon*, or *against* something. **2.** To be in, to have or take, an oblique direction or position; to slope 1698. **b.** Of light or shadow: To fall obliquely 1795. **3.** Of persons: To travel, move, sail, etc. in an oblique direction; to diverge from a direct course. Also *U.S.*, to move off. 1692. **b.** Of things: To take an oblique course 1849. **4.** *trans.* To give an oblique or sloping direction to (something); to cause to slope 1805.

2. That deep romantic chasm which slanted Down the green hill COLERIDGE. **b.** The shadows of the convent-towers S. down the snowy sward TENNYSON. **4.** The rain came down in torrents, slanted by the wind 1891. Hence **Sla·nting** *ppl. a.* that slants or slopes; *adv.* obliquely. **Sla·ntingly** *adv.*

Slantindicular (slɑntindi·kiŭlăɹ), *a.* Also **slanting-, slanten-.** 1840. [f. *slanting*, after *perpendicular*; orig. U.S., and colloq. or humorous.] Slanting, sloping, oblique. So **Slantindi·cularly** *adv.* 1834.

Slantways (slɑ·ntwēⁱz), *adv.* 1826. [f. SLANT *a.* + -WAYS.] = next A.

Slantwise (slɑ·ntwəiz), *adv.* and *a.* 1573. [f. SLANT *a.* + -WISE.] **A.** *adv.* In a slanting or sloping direction or position; slantingly, obliquely. **B.** *adj.* Slanting, oblique 1856.

Slap (slæp), *sb.* 1648. [– LG. *slapp*, of imitative origin.] **1.** A smart blow, esp. one given with the open hand, or with something having a flat surface; a smack; an impact of this nature. **b.** A gust *of* wind 1890. **2.** *transf.* **a.** A reprimand, reproof; a side-hit 1736. **b.** An attempt, venture, go, *at* something 1855.

2. b. Come, lads!..take another s. at them; we must get on deck somehow 1884.

Slap (slæp), *v.* 1632. [f. SLAP *adv.* or *sb.*] **1.** *trans.* To strike or smack (a person or thing) smartly, esp. with the open hand or with something having a flat surface; to hit (a person) *on*, *upon*, or *over* (a certain part) in this way. **b.** *Pottery.* To work (clay) by flinging masses of it violently down 1786. **2.** To strike, bring down (one's hand, etc.) *on* or *upon* something with a slap; to clap (the hands) *together* 1717. **3.** To shut (a door, gate, etc.) sharply or with a slap. Also with *to.* 1708. **4.** *intr.* Of a door, etc.: To slam (*rare*) 1796. **5.** Of waves, water, etc.: To beat or strike *on* or *against* something with a slapping sound 1840.

1. He slapped his forehead as if he had hit upon something material GOLDSM.

Comb.: **s.-stick,** orig. and chiefly *U.S.*, the wand used by the harlequin in a pantomime; used *attrib.* to define knockabout comedy or the like, or slapdash methods.

Slap (slæp), *adv. colloq.* 1672. [– LG. *slapp*, of imitative origin.] **1.** With, or as with, a slap or smart quick blow; suddenly, without warning or notice. **2.** Directly, straight 1829.

1. Let us be serious and finish this comedy s. off 1852. **2.** A turnstile leading s. away into the meadows DICKENS.

Slap-bang, *adv.*, *a.*, and *sb.* Also **slap bang.** 1785. [f. SLAP *adv.* + BANG *v.*] **A.** *adv.* With, or as with, a slap and a bang; without delay, immediately; without due consideration. **B.** *adj.* †**1.** *S. shop*, an eating-house or cook-shop where there is no credit given –1835. **2.** Characterized by carelessness, heedlessness, or haste 1815.

1. Cow-heel or hot alamode from the s. shop 1838.

C. *sb.* **1.** A slap-bang shop 1836. **2.** Some kind of liquor. DISRAELI.

Slap-dash, *adv.*, *a.*, and *sb.* Also **slap dash, slapdash.** 1679. [f. SLAP *adv.* + DASH *adv.*] **A.** *adv.* With, or as with, a slap and a dash; in a hasty, sudden, or precipitate manner; *esp.* without much consideration, thought, ceremony, or care. **B.** *adj.* **1.** Marked or characterized by haste, carelessness, or want of due preparation or consideration; done, performed, etc. in a dashing and haphazard manner or style 1792. **2.** Of persons: Given to acting in this way 1833. **C.** *sb.* **1.** Roughcast 1796. **2.** Carelessness, roughness, or want of finish in style or workmanship; writing or work done in this style 1826. Hence **Sla·p-dash** *v. intr.* to write, work, etc. in a s. manner or style; *trans.* to roughcast.

Slape (slēⁱp), *a. n. dial.* 1460. [– ON. *sleipr* slippery.] Slippery; smooth. Also *fig.* crafty, cunning, deceitful.

S.-ale, plain ale as opp. to medicated or mixed ale (Ray); rich, soft, or smooth ale (Grose).

Slapjack (slæ·pˌdʒæk). Also **slap-jack, slap jack.** 1820. [f. SLAP *v.* + JACK *sb.*[1] Cf. FLAPJACK.] *U.S.* A griddle-cake.

Slapper (slæ·pəɹ). 1781. [f. SLAP *v.* + -ER[1].] **1.** *dial.* A large person or object; a 'whopper'. **2.** One who slaps; *spec.* in *Pottery* 1860. **3.** An implement used for slapping with 1886.

Sla·pping, *ppl. a.* 1812. [f. SLAP *v.* + -ING[2].] **1.** Of pace, etc.: Extremely fast; rapid, rattling. **2.** Of horses: Big, powerfully built 1828. **b.** Of persons or things: Unusually large or fine; very good; strapping 1825. **3.** That slaps 1898.

1. The first run was at a s. pace 1812.

Sla·p-up, *a. slang* and *colloq.* 1827. [SLAP *adv.*] Very or unmistakably good or fine; first-rate, first-class, grand.

Slash (slæʃ), *sb.*[1] 1576. [f. SLASH *v.*] **1.** A cutting stroke delivered with an edged weapon or instrument, or with a whip. **b.** The debris of felled trees 1905. **2.** A long and deep or severe cut; a gash; a wound of this character 1580. **3.** A vertical slit made in a garment in order to expose to view a lining or under-garment of a different colour 1615.

1. *transf.* Rough slashes of sarcasm CARLYLE.

Slash (slæʃ), *sb.*[2] *U.S.* 1799. [Of unkn. origin.] A piece of wet or swampy ground overgrown with bushes. **b. s.-pine,** a loblolly or Cuban pine 1882.

Slash (slæʃ), *v.* late ME. [perh. aphetic – OFr. **esclaschier*, var. of *esclachier* break, obscurely rel. to *esclater*, mod. *éclater* (see SLAT *v.*[3]); prob. reinforced by symbolical assoc. with *slit*, *lash*.] **1.** *trans.* To cut or wound with a sweep or stroke of a sharp weapon or instrument; to gash, †hew. **2.** *intr.* To deliver or aim cutting blows (also const. *at*); to make gashes or deep wounds 1548. **b.** To strike violently or at random; to lay about one with heavy blows; to move rapidly and violently, etc. 1654. **3.** *trans.* To cut slits in (a garment) and so expose to view an under-garment or a lining of a contrasting colour; to vary *with* another material or colour in this way 1698. **4.** To cut with a scourge or whip; to lash, thrash severely 1614. **5.** To rebuke or assail cuttingly; to criticize severely. Also *absol.* 1653. **6.** To crack (a whip); to bring down in a slashing manner 1660. **7.** Used advb. to denote action or sound 1654.

1. b. *U.S.* To cut down or reduce severely 1906. **5.** History must not cauterise, and s. with Malice, those Noble Parts 1653. Hence **Sla·shy** *a.* of a slashing nature (*rare*).

Slashed (slæʃt), *ppl. a.* 1633. [f. prec. + -ED[1].] **1.** Of garments: Having vertical slits to show a contrasting lining; in mod. use, having a piece of a different colour inserted. **2.** Gashed, cut; deeply wounded 1835. **3.** *Bot.* Deeply cut; laciniate 1839.

1. Charles I. with ruff, ribband, and s. habit H. WALPOLE.

Slasher (slæ·ʃəɹ). 1559. [f. SLASH *v.* + -ER[1].] **1.** One who slashes; a fighter, a bully; a slashing fellow. **2.** A sword; a weapon for slashing 1815. **b.** A billhook 1882. **3.** A severe criticism or review 1849. **4.** A form of sizing-machine for yarn, so called on account of its rapid working 1862.

Slashing (slæ·ʃiŋ), *ppl. a.* 1735. [f. SLASH *v.* + -ING[2].] Severely critical; spirited, dashing.

Slat (slæt), *sb.*[1] late ME. [Aphetic – OFr. *esclat* (mod. *éclat*) splinter, piece broken off, f. *esclater*; see SLAT *v.*[3], and cf. SLATE *sb.*] **1.** A roofing-slate; a thin slab of stone used for roofing. Now *dial.* **2.** Slate used for roofing buildings. Now *dial.* late ME. **3.** A long narrow strip of wood or metal, used for various purposes 1764.

3. Arranged in transverse rows, like slats on a blind 1885.

Slat (slæt), *sb.*[2] 1611. [f. SLAT *v.*[2]] **1.** A slap; a slapping blow. Now *dial.* **2.** A sudden gust or blast *of* wind 1840.

Slat (slæt), *sb.*[3] 1870. [perh. Irish.] A salmon out of season; a spent salmon.

Slat (slæt), *v.*[1] 1475. [f. SLAT *sb.*[1]] **1.** *trans.* To cover with slates. Now *dial.* **2.** To furnish, or make, with slats 1886.

Slat (slæt), *v.*[2] *local.* ME. [Of unkn. origin.] **1.** *trans.* To cast, dash, impel quickly and with some force. **2.** To strike, beat; to knock *out* 1577. **3.** *intr.* To flap violently 1840.

2. *Men.* How did you kill him? *Mal.* Slatted his braines out. MARSTON.

Slat (slæt), *v.*[3] Now *dial.* 1607. [– OFr. *esclater* (mod. *éclater*; cf. SLAT *sb.*[1]) split, splinter, shatter, repr. Rom. **exclatare*, f. *ex* EX-[1] + imit. base **clat-*.] *intr.* and *trans.* To split.

†**Slatch.** 1625. [var. of SLACK *sb.*[3]] *Naut.* **a.** The slack of a rope –1627. **b.** A brief respite or interval; a short period or spell (*of* some kind of weather, etc.) –1719.

Slate (slēⁱt), *sb.* Also (chiefly *north.* and *Sc.*) **sclate.** ME. [– OFr. *esclate*, fem. corresp. to masc. *esclat* SLAT *sb.*[1]] **1.** A thin, usu. rectangular, piece of certain varieties of stone which split readily into laminæ (see 4), used especially for covering the roofs of buildings. **b.** A slab of slate; a laminated rock 1601. **2.** A tablet of slate, usually framed in wood, used for writing on. late ME. **b.** *fig.* A record of any kind concerning or against a person; esp. in phr. *a clean s.* 1868. **c.** *U.S.* A draft list of candidates to be proposed for nomination or for election 1877. **3.** Roofing-slates collectively, or the material from which these are made ME. **4.** An argillaceous rock of sedimentary origin, the different varieties of which have the common property of splitting readily into thin plates 1653.

Many varieties are distinguished, esp. in *Geol.*, by special terms, as *clay, hornblende, mica, talc s.*

b. With *a* and *pl.* A kind of variety of slaty rock 1704. **5.** A bluish-grey colour like that of slate 1882.

1. Phr. *To have a s. loose* or *off*, to be weak in intellect. *slang* or *colloq.* **2.** Take alle the signes,.. & wryte hem in þy s. CHAUCER.

Comb.: **s.-axe,** an axe for shaping slates for

roofing; **s. clay,** shale; **s. club,** a sharing-out club, whose accounts are nominally kept on a s.; **-galiot,** a vessel carrying slates; **-knife,** a knife used for splitting slates; **-nail, -peg, -pin,** a nail, peg, or pin used to fix a s. on a roof; **-saw,** a machine for trimming the edges of slate-slabs to shape.

Slate (slē^{i}t), *v.*^{1} 1530. [f. prec.] **1.** *trans.* To cover or roof with slates. **2.** To put down (a name, etc.) on a writing-slate; to set down, book, *for* something 1883. **3.** To remove hair from (hides) 1897.

Slate (slē^{i}t), *v.*^{2} *colloq.*, orig. *slang.* 1825. [Of dial. origin, presumably f. SLATE *sb.*] †**1.** *trans.* To knock the hat over the eyes of (a person). †**2.** To beat or thrash severely 1825. **b.** *Mil.* To punish (an enemy) severely 1854. **3.** To assail with reproof or abuse; to rate or reprimand; to scold severely 1840. **b.** To criticize (a book or author) severely; to castigate 1848.

Slate (slē^{i}t), *v.*^{3} *north.* and *Sc.* ME. [– ON. **sleita*, corresp. to OE. *slǣtan*.] **1.** *trans.* To incite or set on (a dog). **2.** To bait, assail, or drive, with dogs ME.

Sla·te-colour. 1826. [SLATE *sb.*] The bluish-grey colour of slate. So **Sla·te-coloured** *a.* of the colour of slate, usu. bluish-grey 1801.

Slate-pencil. 1759. [SLATE *sb.*] **1.** A pencil, usu. made of soft slate, used for writing on a slate. **2.** The material of which slate-pencils are made 1801.

Slater (slē^i·təɹ). ME. [f. SLATE *sb.* or *v.*^{1} + -ER^1.] **1.** One whose work consists in laying slates. **2.** A wood-louse. Chiefly *Sc.* and *n. dial.* 1684.

Slating (slē^i·tiŋ), *vbl. sb.*^{1} 1579. [f. SLATE *v.*^{1} + -ING^1.] **1.** The fixing of slates (on a roof or elsewhere); the business of fixing slates. **2.** *collect.* The slates covering a roof 1816.

Slating (slē^i·tiŋ), *vbl. sb.*^{2} 1870. [f. SLATE *v.*^{2} + -ING^1.] **1.** A severe punishment; a beating 1872. **2.** A severe reprimand or scolding 1881. **3.** A severe criticism or literary castigation 1870.

Slatter (slæ·təɹ). Now *dial.* late ME. [f. SLAT *sb.*^{1} or *v.*^{1}, -ER^1.] = SLATER.

Sla·ttering, *ppl. a. dial.* 1674. [pr. pple. of dial. *slatter* spill or splash awkwardly, slop, frequent. (see -ER^5) of SLAT *v.*^{2}] Careless, slovenly.

Slattern (slæ·təɹn), *sb.* and *a.* 1639. [prob. alt. of prec.] **A.** *sb.* A woman or girl untidy and slovenly in person, habits, or surroundings; a slut.

Butterflies one day, and slatterns the next 1766.

B. *adj.* Slovenly, untidy, slatternly. Said of appearance, etc., or of persons. 1716.

A certain degree of s. elegance 1822.

Slattern (slæ·təɹn), *v.* 1747. [f. prec.] *trans.* To fritter or throw *away* (time, opportunity, etc.) by carelessness or slovenliness.

Slatternly (slæ·təɹnli), *a.* 1680. [f. SLATTERN *sb.* + -LY^1.] **1.** Of persons: Having the condition or habits of a slattern; slovenly; untidy. **2.** Of appearance, etc.: Appropriate to, characteristic of, a slattern 1776. Hence **Sla·tterntiness.**

Slaty (slē^i·ti), *a.* 1529. [f. SLATE *sb.* + -Y^1.] **1.** Composed of slate; resembling slate; having the nature or properties of slate. Also of land: Lying upon slate. **2.** Characteristic or typical of slate 1796. **3.** Slate-coloured 1822.

2. The principal fracture is straight, s. 1854.

Slaughter (slǭ·təɹ), *sb.* ME. [– ON. **slahtr* (ON. *slátr*, mod. Icel. *slátur* butcher's meat), f. **slaχ-* SLAY *v.*; repl. ME. *slaȝt*, †*slaught* (–XVII).] **1.** The killing of cattle, sheep, or other animals for food. **2.** The killing or slaying of a person; murder, homicide, esp. of a brutal kind ME. **3.** The killing of large numbers of persons in war, battle, etc.; massacre, carnage ME. **b.** Persons slain in battle, etc. (*rare*) 1757. **4.** An instance of slaying or massacre 1483.

3. S. grows murder when it goes too far, And makes a Massacre what was a War DRYDEN. **b.** His body being found amidst a heap of s. GOLDSM.

Phr. *To* or *for the s.*; Wee are counted as sheepe for the s. *Ps.* 44:22. Hence **Slau·ghtery,** slaughter; a slaughter-house.

Slaughter (slǭ·təɹ), *v.* 1535. [f. prec.] **1.** *trans.* To kill (cattle, sheep, or other animals), *spec.* for food. **2.** To kill, slay, murder (a person), esp. in a bloody or brutal manner 1582. **b.** *U.S. colloq.* To defeat or demolish completely 1903. **3.** To kill or slay (persons) in large numbers; to massacre 1589.

3. What do these Worthies, But rob.., s., and enslave Peaceable Nations MILT. fig. *Wint. T.* I. ii. 93. Hence **Slau·ghterer,** one who slaughters.

Slau·ghter-house. late ME. [SLAUGHTER *sb.*] **1.** A house or place where animals are killed for food. **2.** *transf.* A place or scene in which persons are killed or slaughtered 1578.

Slau·ghterman. ME. [f. SLAUGHTER *sb.*] **1.** One who kills or slays; an executioner. **2.** One employed in killing cattle, etc. for food.

Slaughterous (slǭ·tərəs), *a.* 1582. [f. SLAUGHTER *sb.* + -OUS.] Murderous, destructive. Hence **Slau·ghterously** *adv.*

Slav (slāv, slæv), *sb.* and *a.* late ME. [In earliest use – med.L. *Sclavus*, corresp. to med. Gr. Σκλάβος; later after med.L. *Slavus*, Fr., G. *Slave*.] **A.** *sb.* A person belonging by race to a large group of peoples inhabiting eastern Europe and comprising the Russians, Bulgarians, Serbo-Croats, Poles, Czechs, Moravians, and Wends or Slovenes. **B.** *adj.* Belonging to, characteristic of, or originating with the Slavs; Slavic; Slavonian 1876. Hence **Sla·vdom,** the Slavonic race generally. **Sla·vism,** the collective qualities or racial character of the S. peoples.

Slave (slē^{i}v), *sb.* [ME. *sclave*, aphetic – (O)Fr. *esclave*, prop. fem. of *esclaf* = med.L. *sclavus*, *sclava*, identical with the ethnic name *Sclavus* SLAV, the Slavonic races having been reduced to a servile state by conquest.] **1.** One who is the property of, and entirely subject to, another person, whether by capture, purchase, or birth; a servant completely divested of freedom and personal rights. **b.** Used as a term of contempt. Now *arch.* 1537. †**c.** Rascal; fellow –1607. **2.** *transf.* One who submits in a servile manner to the authority or dictation of another or others; a submissive or devoted servant 1521. **b.** *fig.* One who is completely under the domination *of*, or subject *to*, a specified influence 1559. **3.** One whose condition in respect of toil is comparable to that of a slave 1774. **4.** *Ent.* An ant captured by, and made to serve, ants of another species 1817.

1. Wee'll visit Caliban, my slaue, who neuer Yeelds vs kinde answere SHAKS. **b.** Thou pawnbroking s. SCOTT. *transf.* This yellow Slaue [*sc.* gold] Will knit and breake Religions SHAKS. **2.** The head of a party, and consequently..the s. of a party MACAULAY. **b.** Giue me that man That is not Passions Slaue SHAKS. **3.** The women..of these countries, are the greatest slaves upon earth GOLDSM.

Comb.: **s.-bangle,** a bangle of gold, silver, glass, etc., worn by women above the elbow; **-born** *a.*, born of a s. parent or parents; born in the condition of a s.; **-captain,** the captain of a s.-ship; **S. Coast,** a part of the west coast of Africa, from which slaves were exported; **-holder,** one who owns slaves; **-power,** a power based upon, or recognizing, slavery as an institution; **-ship** = SLAVER *sb.*^{2} 1; **s. state,** one or other of the southern United States of America, in which s.-holding was legal. Hence **Sla·vedom,** (*a*) slavery, (*b*) the position of a s.

Slave (slē^{i}v), *v.* 1559. [f. prec.] **1.** *trans.* To enslave; to bring into subjection. **2.** To treat as a slave; to employ in servile labour 1699. **3.** *intr.* To toil or work hard like a slave 1719. **b.** *trans.* To wear *out*, etc., by severe toil 1864. †**4.** To traffic in slaves (*rare*) 1726.

3. b. I may s. my life out, and there isn't one of you will..help me 1864.

Sla·ve-me:rchant. 1747. [SLAVE *sb.*] One who traffics or deals in slaves; a slave-dealer.

Slaver (slæ·vəɹ), *sb.*^{1} ME. [Related to SLAVER *v.*] Saliva issuing or falling from the mouth. **b.** *fig.* Drivel, nonsense; also, gross flattery 1825.

Of all mad creatures..It is the s. kills, and not the bite POPE.

Slaver (slē^i·vəɹ), *sb.*^{2} 1830. [f. SLAVE *sb.* + -ER^1.] **1.** A vessel engaged in slave-traffic. **2.** One who deals or traffics in, or owns, slaves 1842.

2. The Slaver's thumb was on the latch LONGF.

Slaver (slæ·vəɹ), *v.* ME. [prob. of symbolic origin like synon. SLABBER (– Scand.); prob. of LDu. origin, like SLOBBER; see -ER^5.] **1.** *intr.* To let the saliva run from the mouth; to slabber. **b.** *fig.* To drivel; to fawn 1730. **2.** *trans.* To wet with saliva; to slobber 1591. **b.** *fig.* To fondle or flatter, in a disgusting or sycophantic manner 1794. Hence **Sla·verer,** one who slavers; also *fig.* a servile flatterer.

Slavering (slæ·vəriŋ), *ppl. a.* 1576. [f. prec. + -ING^2.] **1.** Characterized or accompanied by the emission of slaver. **2.** That slavers; allowing saliva to fall. Hence **Sla·veringly** *adv.*

Slavery (slē^i·vəri), *sb.* 1551. [f. SLAVE *sb.* + -ERY.] **1.** Severe toil like that of a slave; heavy labour, hard work, drudgery. **2.** The condition of a slave; the fact of being a slave; servitude; bondage 1604. **b.** The condition of being entirely subject to, or dominated by, some power or influence 1577. **c.** A state of subjection or subordination comparable to that of a slave; also with *pl.*, an instance of this 1586. **3.** The fact of slaves existing as a class in a community; the keeping of slaves as a practice or institution 1728.

2. Being taken..And sold to slauery SHAKS. **b.** Instilling their barren hearts with a conscientious s. MILT. **c.** The extream s. and subjection that courtiers live in EVELYN. **3.** On this abstract question of s. there can..be but one opinion MRS. STOWE.

Slavery (slæ·vəri), *a.* late ME. [f. SLAVER *sb.*^{1} + -Y^1.] Like slaver; befouled with slaver; characterized by, given to, slavering.

Sla·ve-trade. 1734. [SLAVE *sb.*] Traffic in slaves; *spec.* the former transportation of African Negroes to America. So **Sla·ve-tra:der** = SLAVER *sb.*^{2}

Slavey (slē^i·vi, slæ·vi). *colloq.* 1812. [f. SLAVE *sb.* + -Y^6.] †**1.** A male servant or attendant –1855. **2.** A female domestic servant, *esp.* one who is hard-worked 1821.

Slavic (slā·vik, slæ·vik), *a.* and *sb.* Also **Sclavic.** 1813. [f. SLAV *sb.* + -IC.] **A.** *adj.* Slavonian, Slavonic. **B.** *sb.* = SLAVONIC *sb.* 1866.

Slavish (slē^i·viʃ), *a.*^{1} 1565. [f. SLAVE *sb.* + -ISH^1.] **1.** Of, belonging to, or characteristic of, a slave; befitting a slave; servile, abject. **2.** Having the character of slaves; of a submissive, unmanly disposition 1565. **3.** Vile, mean, ignoble 1593. **4.** Implying or involving slavery 1593. **5.** Servilely imitative 1753.

1. See how he lies..In s. habit, ill-fitted weeds MILT. **2.** Scourge of thy people,..Sent in Jove's anger on a s. race POPE. **3.** To lye is a s. Vice 1700. **4.** *Rich. II*, II. i. 291. **5.** There was no s. adherence to the old law 1861. Hence **Sla·vish-ly** *adv.*, **-ness.**

Slavish (slā·viʃ, slæ·viʃ), *a.*^{2} and *sb.* 1834. [f. SLAV *sb.* + -ISH^1.] **A.** *adj.* Pertaining to or characteristic of the Slavs. **B.** *sb.* The Slavonic language.

Slavo- (slā·vo, slæ·vo), comb. form. of SLAV, as in *S.-Germanic*, *-Lithuanian*, etc.; also **Sla·vophil(e,** one who admires or favours the Slavs, Slavonic ideals, etc.; **Sla·vophobe,** one who has a morbid dread of these.

Slav(e)ocracy (slē^{i}vǫ·krăsi). 1848. [f. SLAVE *sb.* + -CRACY, but with erroneous application.] The domination of slave-holders; slave-holders collectively as a dominant or powerful class.

Slavonian (slăvō^u·niăn), *sb.* and *a.* †Also **Scl-.** 1577. [f. med.L. *S(c)lavonia* the country of the Slavs, f. *S(c)lavus* SLAV; see -IAN.] **A.** *sb.* **1.** The language of the Slavs; Slavic; Slavonic. **2.** A person of Slavonic origin; a Slav 1601. **B.** *adj.* **1.** Of or pertaining to the Slavs 1605. **2.** Of or pertaining to Slavonic countries, as *S. falcon, grebe* 1809. **3.** Coming from Slavonic regions 1812.

3. As snow..piled by rough Sclavonian blasts CARY.

Slavonic (slăvǫ·nik), *a.* and *sb.* 1614. [– med.L. *S(c)lavonicus*, f. *Slavonia*; see prec., -IC.] **A.** *adj.* Slavic; Slavonian. **B.** *sb.* A generic term for the languages of the Slavs 1668.

Old or *Church S.*, Old Bulgarian.

Slaw (slǭ). *U.S.* Also **slaugh.** 1864. [– Du. *sla*, syncopated form of *salade* SALAD.] A salad made of sliced cabbage, etc.

Slay, sley (slē^i), *sb.* [OE. *sleġe* = OS. *slegi*; f. base of next.] An instrument used in weaving to beat up the weft; a reed.

Slay (slē^i), *v.* Pa. t. **slew** (slū). Pa. pple. **slain** (slē^{i}n). Now mainly *literary* and *rhet.*

[OE. *slēan* = OFris. *slā*, OS., OHG., *slahan* (Du. *slagen*, G. *schlagen*), ON. *slá*, Goth. *slahan*; the Gmc. base **slax-* **slaȝ-* **slōȝ-* has no recognizable cogns.] †**I. 1.** *trans.* To smite, strike, or beat –ME. **2.** To strike (a spark, fire) from flint or other hard substance –1513. **II. 1.** To strike or smite so as to kill; to put to death by means of a weapon; also *gen.*, to deprive of life by violence OE. **2.** *absol.* To commit slaughter or murder OE. **3. a.** Of the Deity: To deprive (man, etc.) of life; to bring death upon, to destroy OE. **b.** Of natural forces, accidents, etc. Now *dial.* OE. †**4.** To put to death as a criminal; to execute –1667. **5.** To kill (a domestic animal or beast of game), *esp.* for food or as a sacrifice; to slaughter OE. †**b.** To destroy (vermin, etc.) by some means –1578.

1. The nombre of them that were slaine..was accompted a thousand 1560. *fig.* Sad souls are slain in merry company SHAKS. **2.** The Parthian turn'd his Steed,..and as He fled, He slew PRIOR. **3. a.** Lest I..set her like a drie land, and s. her with thirst *Hosea* 2:3. **b.** There was above thirty Persons..slain by a Blast 1708. **4.** Naild to the Cross By his own Nation, slaine for bringing Life MILT.

III. †**1.** To bring to spiritual death; to destroy with sin –1611. †**2.** To overcome with affliction or distress –1568. **3.** To destroy, put an end to, suppress completely (*esp.* something bad) ME. **4.** *intr.* Of grain: To become affected by smut, blight, or the like 1641.

1. *absol.* The lettre sleith, forsoth the spirit quykeneth WYCLIF 2 *Cor.* 3:6. **3.** With this swerd shal I slen envie CHAUCER. In the very act of slaying the Bill 1884. Hence **Slay·er**[1], one who slays or kills. **Slay·ing** *vbl. sb.*[1] the action of the vb.; killing, slaughter.

Slaying, sleying (slē[i]·iŋ), *vbl. sb.*[2] 1613. [f. SLAY *sb.* + -ING[1].] The separating and arranging of the counts of warps to the different sets of slay, so as to preserve a uniformity of fabric in similar species of cloth. Hence **Sla·yer**[2], one who separates the threads and arranges them in a slay.

Sleave (slīv), *sb.* 1591. [f. next; cf. SLEAVE-SILK.] †**1.** A slender filament of silk obtained by separating a thicker thread; silk in the form of such filaments; floss-silk –1635. **2.** *transf.* and *fig.* 1605.

2. Sleepe that knits vp the rauel'd Sleeue of Care SHAKS.

Sleave (slīv), *v.* Now *dial.* 1628. [OE. *slǣfan* (in comp. *tōslǣfan*), causative f. **slāf-*, rel. to **slīfan* SLIVE *v.*[1]] **1.** *trans.* To divide (silk) by separation into filaments. **2.** To cleave, split, rend, tear apart 1828. So **Sleaved** *ppl. a.*, in *sleaved silk* 1577.

†**Sleave-silk.** 1588. [f. SLEAVE *v.* 1.] Silk thread capable of being separated into smaller filaments for use in embroidery, etc. –1703.

Sleazy, sleezy (slī·zi), *a.* 1644. [Of unkn. origin.] Thin or flimsy in texture; having little substance or body. **b.** *transf.* and *fig.* Slight, flimsy, unsubstantial 1645.

'Sleezy' silks, wispy surahs, or cottony velvets 1893. Hence **Slea·ziness** (*rare*), the fact or quality of being s.

Sled (sled), *sb.* Now chiefly *dial.* and *U.S.* late ME. [– MLG. *sledde*, corresp. to MHG. *slitte* (G. *schlitten*), and rel. to MLG., MDu. *slēde*, Du. *slede*, *slee* (see SLEIGH), OHG. *slito*, *slita*, ON. *sleði*, f. **slid-* **slīd-* SLIDE *v.* Cf. SLEDGE *sb.*[2]] **1.** = SLEDGE *sb.*[2] 2. **2.** A sledge or sleigh used as a vehicle in travelling or for recreation 1586.

Sled, *v.* Chiefly *U.S.* 1718. [f. prec.] **1.** *intr.* To travel in a sledge 1780. **2.** *trans.* To convey on a sled or sleds 1718.

Sle·dded, *a. rare.* 1602. [f. SLED *sb.* + -ED[2].] **a.** Mounted on sleds. **b.** Made like a sled.

a. So frown'd he once, when in an angry parle He smot the s. Pollax on the Ice SHAKS.

Sle·dding, *vbl. sb. U.S.* 1755. [f. SLED *v.* + -ING[1].] The action of using a sled; conditions favourable for this. **b.** *fig.* Work or progress in any sphere of action 1839.

Sledge (sledʒ), *sb.*[1] [OE. *sleċġ* = (M)Du. *slegge*, ON. *sleggja* :– **slaȝj-* f. **slax-* strike; see SLAY *v.*] A large heavy hammer usu. wielded with both hands, esp. the large hammer used by a blacksmith; a sledge-hammer.

Sledge (sledʒ), *sb.*[2] 1617. [– MDu. *sleedse* (Du. dial. *sleeds*), rel. to *slēde* SLED *sb.*] **1.** A carriage mounted upon runners instead of wheels, and gen. used for travelling over snow or ice; a sleigh. **2.** A simple form of conveyance, having runners instead of wheels, employed in the transport of goods over ice or snow or in heavy traffic unsuited to wheeled vehicles. Rarely, a similar vehicle with low wheels; a trolley. 1684. **b.** Formerly used for conveying condemned persons to execution 1651. **3.** *Rope-making.* A travelling structure of considerable weight to which the rope-yarns are attached at one end 1794. Hence **Sledge** *v. intr.* to travel in a s.; *trans.* to carry or convey on a s.

Sle·dge-ha:mmer. 1495. [f. SLEDGE *sb.*[1]] A large heavy hammer used by blacksmiths. *fig.* Johnson's s. smashes his flimsy platitudes to pieces 1874.

Sleech (slītʃ). *dial.* 1587. [app. later form of dial. *slitch*, repr. OE. **slīċ.*] Mud deposited by the sea or a river; soil composed of this.

Sleek (slīk), *a.* and *adv.* 1589. [Later var. of ME. *slike* SLICK *a.*] **A.** *adj.* **1.** Of animals, their limbs, etc.: Having, or covered with, hair or fur which lies close and smooth, usually a sign of good condition or careful attention 1590. **b.** Of hair, etc., in this condition 1829. **2.** Of surfaces: Perfectly smooth and polished 1589. **b.** Of the sea or sky: Unruffled, tranquil (*rare*) 1603. **3.** Oily, fawning, plausible, specious 1599. **4.** Of persons: Having a smooth skin, esp. as the result of being in good condition; plump 1637. **B.** *adv.* In a smooth or sleek manner 1602.

A. 1. While I..sticke muske roses in thy s. smoothe head SHAKS. **2. b.** On the sleeke waters waft her sayles along DRAYTON. **3.** The smoothest and sleekest knaves in a country 1605. **4.** S. well-fed blue-coat boys LAMB. Hence **Slee·k-ly** *adv.*, **-ness.** **Slee·ky** *a.* marked by s. condition; *Sc.* artful, plausible.

Sleek (slīk), *v.* 1440. [Later var. of ME. *slike* SLICK *v.*] **1.** *trans.* To make sleek or smooth by rubbing or polishing. **b.** To reduce to smoothness 1513. **2.** To make (the skin, hair, etc.) smooth and glossy 1508.

1. b. S. eu'ry little Dimple of the Lake: Sweet Syrens DRAYTON. **2.** He smooth'd his chin, and sleek'd his hair TENNYSON. *transf.* and *fig.* Gentle my Lord, sleeke o're Your rugged Lookes SHAKS. The perswasive Rhetoric That sleek't his tongue MILT. Musing how to smooth And s. his marriage over to the Queen TENNYSON.

Sleep (slīp), *sb.* [OE. *slēp*, *slǣp* = OFris. *slēp*, OS. *slāp* (Du. *slaap*), OHG. *slāf* (G. *schlaf*), Goth. *slēps* :– Gmc. **slǣpaz*, rel. to corresp. vb. **slǣpan*, whence OE. *slǣpan*, OS. *slāpan*, etc.] **1.** The unconscious state or condition regularly and naturally assumed by man and animals, during which the activity of the nervous system is almost or entirely suspended, and recuperation of its powers takes place; slumber, repose. **b.** Personified (after L. *Somnus*, Gr. Ὕπνος). late ME. **2.** A period or occasion of slumber ME. **b.** As an indication or division of time ME. **3.** *fig.* **a.** The repose of death OE. **b.** A state of inactivity or sluggishness (in persons or things) OE. **c.** The condition of being quiet and peaceful; complete absence of noise or stir 1807. **4. a.** *Bot.* A condition assumed by many plants, esp. during the night, marked by the closing of petals or leaves 1757. **b.** A state of numbness in a limb, produced by prolonged pressure upon it 1882.

1. S. comes as a medicine to weariness, as a repairer of decay 1658. Damn that boy, he's gone to s. again DICKENS. *Dead s.*, s. so profound as to suggest death. **b.** The golden slepe me wrapt vndir his wyng 1460. **2.** They are euen as a slepe and fade awaye sodenly like the grasse COVERDALE *Ps.* 89:5. **b.** Their division of time is by sleeps, and moons, and winters 1702. **3. b.** He had put his doubts to s. 1889. **c.** The s. that is among the lonely hills WORDSW. Hence †**Slee·pish** *a.* somewhat sleepy.

Sleep (slīp), *v.* Pa. t. and pa. pple. **slept.** [OE. *slēpan*, *slǣpan* = OFris. *slepa*, OS. *slāpan* (Du. *slapen*), OHG. *slāfan* (G. *schlafen*), Goth. *slēpan*; see prec.] **I.** *intr.* **1.** To take repose by the natural suspension of consciousness; to be in the state of sleep; to slumber. Also occas., to fall asleep. **b.** With *upon* or *on* (a matter), denoting the postponement of a decision till the following day 1519. **c.** With *in*: (*a*) To sleep in the house, or on the premises, where one is employed; (*b*) to oversleep (*Sc.* and *north.*) 1888. (*c*) To sleep late (*dial.* and *U.S.*) 1931. **2.** *fig.* To lie in the grave OE. **3.** *transf.* **a.** Of limbs: To be numb, esp. as the result of pressure OE. **b.** Of plants: To be in a quiescent or drooping condition 1797. **c.** Of a top: To spin so rapidly that the motion is imperceptible 1854. **4.** *fig.* To be dormant, inert, inactive, inoperative, or quiescent OE. **b.** To rest peacefully and quietly; to remain calm or motionless 1596. **5.** To be careless, remiss, or idle. late ME.

1. He that slepeth well thynketh no harme 1530. Phr. *To s. like a log, top*; Juan slept like a top, or like the dead BYRON. **2.** Beneath those rugged elms..The rude Forefathers of the hamlet s. GRAY. **4.** The restless enmity of the Angevin never slept 1869. **b.** How sweet the moonelight sleepes vpon this banke SHAKS.

II. *trans.* **1.** With cogn. obj.: To take rest in, continue in (sleep) OE. †**2.** To put off or delay; to disregard, pay no attention to –1792. **3. a.** With *off* or †*out*: To get rid of, remove the effects of, by sleeping 1552. **b.** With *away*: To remove, get rid of, lose, or waste by sleeping 1565. **c.** *refl.* To make (oneself) *sober* by sleeping. Also simply, to sleep. 1565. **4.** With *out* or *away*: To pass or spend (a certain time) in sleep 1565. **5.** To provide with sleeping accommodation 1884.

1. Phr. *To s. the sleep of the just.* (joc.), to s. soundly. *Not to s. a wink*: see WINK *sb.* **3. a.** In the morning, after he had slept his wine off, he was very gay THACKERAY. **b.** To s. away Sorrow 1687. **5.** The parents, owing to poverty, had to s. their children in the same bed as themselves 1895.

Sleep-at-noon. 1661. The goat's-beard, so called because its flowers close at midday.

Sleeper (slī·pəɹ). ME. [f. SLEEP *v.* + -ER[1].] **I. 1.** One who is inclined to sleep, or spends much time in sleep; one who sleeps (well or ill, etc.); also *fig.*, an indolent or inactive person. **2.** One who is asleep. Also *fig.*, a dead person. 1590. **b.** *spec.* in *pl.* (see SEVEN SLEEPERS) 1827. **3.** *Zool.* **a.** A dormouse. Now chiefly *dial.* 1693. **b.** As the name of various fishes 1668. **4.** A thing in a dormant or dead state 1625. **5.** A railway sleeping-car 1882.

1. b. A sleeping partner 1892. **3. b.** *E*[*leotris*]*dormatrix*, the S., is a large fish 1854. **4.** Let Penall Lawes, if they haue beene Sleepers of long..be by Wise Iudges confined in the Execution BACON.

II. 1. A strong horizontal beam or balk supporting a wall, joist, floor, or other main part of a building 1607. **2.** *Shipbuilding.* A strong internal timber in a ship 1626. **3. a.** *Mil.* A piece of timber forming one of the rests of a wooden platform for artillery 1688. **b.** A piece of timber or other material used to form a support (usually transverse) for the rails of a tramway or railway 1789. **c.** A strong longitudinal beam in a wooden bridge, supporting the transverse planks or logs 1823. **d.** *gen.* A horizontal beam, plank, etc., used to support any weighty body 1848.

2. *Sleepers*, pieces of compass timber fayed and bolted upon the transoms and timbers adjoining, ..to strengthen the buttock of the ship 1850.

Sleepful (slī·pfŭl), *a.* late ME. [f. SLEEP *sb.* + -FUL 1.] **1.** Sleepy (*rare*). **2.** Marked by sleep; restful through sleep 1827. Hence **Slee·pfulness,** sleepiness.

Sleeping (slī·piŋ), *vbl. sb.* ME. [f. SLEEP *v.* + -ING[1].] The fact, state, or condition of being asleep; an instance or occasion of this. *transf.* and *fig.* You euer Haue wish'd the s. of this business SHAKS.

attrib., as *s. apartment*, *car*, etc.; *s.-bag*, *-sack*, etc.; in sense 'inducing sleep' (cf. SLEEPING *ppl. a.* 2), as *s. draught*; also **s. sickness,** now *spec.*, a fatal disease prevalent in some parts of Africa.

Sleeping (slī·piŋ), *ppl. a.* ME. [f. SLEEP *v.* + -ING[2].] **1.** That is asleep; slumbering. Also *absol.* **b.** Seen in sleep 1781. †**2.** Inducing sleep, soporific (*rare*) –1597. **3.** Numb; devoid of sensation 1562. **4.** Inactive, torpid, quiescent 1538. **5.** Quiet, silent; motionless 1784.

1. A s. boy the Mother held the while CRABBE. **4.** *S. table*, an immovable apparatus on which ore is washed. *S. rent*, a dead rent (see DEAD *a.* V. 2). *S. partner*, a partner in a business who takes no share in the actual working of it. **5.** The moonbeam, sliding softly in between The s. leaves COWPER.

Sleepless (slī·plės), *a.* late ME. [f. SLEEP *sb.* + -LESS.] **1.** Deprived of sleep; unable to sleep. **2.** Yielding no sleep; marked by the absence or want of sleep 1633. **3.** Continually active or operative 1792. **b.** Unceasing in motion; ever-moving 1795.

3. b. Winds are rude in Biscay's s. bay BYRON. Hence **Slee·pless-ly** *adv.*, **-ness.**

Slee·p-wa:lker. 1747. [SLEEP *sb.*] One who walks while asleep; a somnambulist. So **Slee·p-wa:lking** *vbl. sb.* and *ppl. a.*

Sleepy (slī·pi), *a.* ME. [f. SLEEP *sb.* + -Y^1.] **1.** Inclined to sleep; having a difficulty in keeping awake; drowsy, somnolent. **b.** Given to sleep; lethargic, heavy. late ME. **2.** Characterized by, appropriate or belonging to, suggestive of, sleep or repose ME. **3.** Inducing sleep; soporific. Now *rare.* late ME.

1. Let a man sleep when he is s. 1874. **b.** There slepeth ay this god vnmerie, With his slepy thousande sones CHAUCER. *transf.* and *fig.* Love.. oft..Awakes the s. Vigour of the Soul DRYDEN. An apple or pear beginning to rot is said to be s. 1790. **2.** Surely It is a s. Language; and thou speak'st Out of thy sleepe SHAKS. Down the s. roadway..pipes a chaffinch MEREDITH. *S. sickness, (a)* misused for 'sleeping sickness' (SLEEPING *vbl. sb.*); *(b) Encephalitis lethargica.* **3.** S. Poppies harmful Harvests yield DRYDEN.

Comb.: **s.-head,** a s. or lethargic person. Hence **Slee·pi-ly** *adv.*, **-ness.**

Sleet (slīt), *sb.* ME. [repr. OE. **slēte*, **slīete* :- **slautjan-*, rel. to MLG. *slōten* pl. hail, MHG. *slōze*, *slōz* (G. *schlosse*) hail(stone) :- Gmc. **slautan-*.] Snow which has been partially thawed by falling through an atmosphere of a temperature a little above freezing-point, usu. accompanied by rain or snow. **b.** A storm or shower of sleet (*rare*) 1728.

transf. Shot Sharp s. of arrowie showers MILT.

Sleet (slīt), *v.* ME. [f. SLEET *sb.*] **1.** *intr.* **a.** *It sleets,* sleet falls. **b.** To fall as, or like, sleet 1566. **2.** *trans.* To pour or cast like sleet 1786.

Sleety (slī·ti), *a.* 1725. [f. SLEET *sb.* + -Y^1.] **1.** Of storms, wind, etc.: Laden with, accompanied by, sleet. **b.** Sleet-like 1804. **2.** Of weather or time: Characterized by the presence or prevalence of sleet 1826.

1. A cold s. wind 1884. **b.** The flakes were..small and s. 1892. **2.** It was mid-winter; snowy, foggy, s., wet 1826. Hence **Slee·tiness** (*rare*).

Sleeve (slīv), *sb.* [OE. (Anglian) *slēfe*, (WS.) *slīefe*, and *slief*, *slȳf*, corresp. to EFris. *slēwe*, NFris. *slēv*, *slīv* sleeve, and ult. rel. to MDu. *sloove*, *sloof* covering.] **1.** That part of a garment which covers the arm. In early use freq. a separate article of dress which could be worn at will with any body-garment. **b.** A piece of armour for covering and protecting the arm. *Obs.* exc. *Hist.* 1465. **2.** [After Fr. *La Manche*.] The English Channel. *Obs.* exc. as *nonce-use.* 1574. †**b.** A channel or strait –1655. †**3.** *Mil.* A body *of* troops placed on the flanks of an army, battalion, etc.; a wing or flank –1604. **4.** *techn.* A tube, or hollow shaft, fitting over or enclosing a rod, spindle, etc., and designed to protect or strengthen it, or to connect one part with another. Also *attrib.* as *s.-axle*, *-coupling*, *-nut.* 1864.

1. Short was his gowne, with sleues longe and wyde CHAUCER. That Sleeue is mine, that heele beare in his Helme SHAKS. *Hippocrates' s.*, = HIPPOCRAS 2. Phrases. *To have in* or *up one's s.*, to have in reserve, at one's disposal, or ready for some need or emergency. †*To hang on, upon* (another's) *s.*, to depend or rely upon for support or assistance. *To laugh* or *smile in one's s.*: see LAUGH *v.* 1. *To pin..on, upon,* or *to one's s.*: see PIN *v.* 3.

Comb.: **s.-board,** a shaped board on which sleeves are ironed or pressed; **-button,** a button for fastening a wristband or cuff; a s.-link; **-fish,** a fish of the family *Loligo*; esp. the squid, *L. vulgaris*; **-link,** two bars, buttons, or the like, linked together, for fastening a cuff or wristband; **-valve,** a valve in the form of a cylinder with sliding movement.

Sleeve (slīv), *v.* 1440. [f. SLEEVE *sb.*] **1.** *trans.* To provide with a sleeve or sleeves. †**2.** To provide (a body or troops) with a wing or wings –1613. †**b.** *intr.* To draw or line *up* on the flanks or wings –1635. **3.** To fix or fasten *on*, to couple, by means of a sleeve or tube 1875.

3. The motors are sleeved on the axles 1902.

Sleeved (slīvd), *ppl. a.* 1500. [f. SLEEVE *v.* or *sb.* + -ED.] Fitted or provided with sleeves; having sleeves of a certain kind, as *long-*, *short-s.*

Sleeveless (slī·vlės), *a.* OE. [f. SLEEVE *sb.* + -LESS.] **1.** Of a garment: Having no sleeves; made without sleeves. **2.** †**a.** Of words, tales, answers, etc.: Futile, feeble; giving no information or satisfaction; irrelevant, trifling –1700. **b.** Of errands: Ending in, or leading to, nothing; having no adequate result or cause. Now *rare.* 1546. **c.** *gen.* Paltry, petty, frivolous; vain or unprofitable. *Obs.* exc. *arch.* or *dial.* 1550.

2. a. With no more but No, a sleevless reason,.. to be sent home frustrat and remediless MILT. **b.** Shee..had of purpose sent them forth on sleeue-lesse arrands DEKKER. **c.** The s. quarrel fixed on him SCOTT.

Sleezy, variant of SLEAZY.

Sleigh (slēⁱ), *sb.* Chiefly *U.S.* and *Canada.* 1703. [orig. U.S. – Du. *slee*; see SLED *sb.*] **1.** A sledge constructed or used as a vehicle for passengers, usually drawn by one or more horses. **2.** A sledge or sled employed for the transport of goods over ice or snow 1748. **b.** *Mil.* A sledge or sled used for the transport of artillery 1797.

attrib. and *Comb.*: **s.-bell,** one of a number of small bells attached to a s. or to the harness of a horse drawing it. Hence **Sleigh** *v. intr.* to travel or ride in a sleigh.

Sleighing (slēⁱ·iŋ), *vbl. sb.* 1775. [f. SLEIGH *sb.* or *v.* + -ING^1.] Riding in or driving a sleigh, esp. as a pastime; also, the state of the ground when this is possible.

When the s. arrives, it will be an affair of two days up and two days down 1780.

Sleight (slait), *sb.* [ME. *sleȝþ* – ON. *slægð* (OSw. *slögdh*, Sw. *slöjd* SLOYD, etc.), f. *slægr* SLY. For the final *-t* cf. *height*, and see -T^2.] **1.** Craft or cunning employed so as to deceive; deceitful, subtle, or wily dealing or policy; artifice, strategy, trickery. Now *rare* or *Obs.* †**2.** Prudence; wisdom, knowledge. –late ME. **3.** Skill, skilfulness, cleverness, or dexterity in doing or making something, in handling a tool or weapon, etc. Now *rare.* late ME. **4.** The precise art or method, the special knack or trick, *of* (doing) something. Now *dial.* ME. **b.** *spec.* Skill in jugglery or conjuring; sleight of hand 1664. **5.** Adroitness, activity, smartness, nimbleness *of* mind, body, etc. late ME. **6.** A cunning trick; an artifice, ruse, stratagem, or wile. Now *rare.* ME. **b.** A feat of jugglery or legerdemain 1596. †**c.** A design or pattern. SPENSER.

1. Every interest did by right, or might, or s., get represented EMERSON. **4. b.** The juggler's s., That with facility of motion cheats The eye 1850. **5.** A new s. of tongue to make fools clap MACAULAY. **6.** Unpractised in the sleights and artifices of controversy FRANKLIN. Hence †**Sleight** *a.* artful, crafty, wily; of juggling, etc., expert, deceptive. †**Slei·ghtful** *a.* (*rare*) characterized by craft or artifice; crafty, cunning. †**Slei·ghtness,** craftiness, subtlety.

Sleight of hand. Also **sleight-of-hand.** late ME. **1.** Dexterity or skill in using the hand or hands for any purpose; expertness in manipulation or manual action. **b.** In ref. to jugglery, conjuring, or the like 1622. **2.** With *a* and *pl.* A dexterous trick or feat; a piece of nimble juggling or conjuring 1605.

Sleighty (slai·ti), *a.* Now *rare.* late ME. [f. SLEIGHT *sb.* + -Y^1.] **1.** Possessed of or making use of sleight or craft. **2.** Crafty, subtle. late ME. Hence †**Slei·ghtily** *adv.*

Slender (sle·ndəɹ), *a.* ME. [Of unkn. origin.] **I. 1.** Not stout or fleshy; slim, spare. (Freq. implying gracefulness of form.) **b.** Denoting absence of robustness. †Also *transf.* of age, etc.: Tender, immature. 1500. **2.** Of things: Small in diameter or width in proportion to length; long and thin; attenuated 1513. **3. a.** Slight or slim in size or structure 1444. †**b.** Of vowels: Narrow, close 1755. **4.** Of small extent, size, or capacity 1610.

1. These yer s. gals will bear half killin' to get their own way! 1852. **2.** The s. line, nearly four miles long, which your army must make 1788. **3. a.** A very s. book 1875. **b.** The s. *a*, or that heard in *lane* 1828.

II. †**1.** Moderate in power or strength; lax –1657. **2. a.** Of arguments, etc.: Lacking in cogency; unconvincing 1533. **b.** Having but slight foundation 1562. **3.** Slight, small, insignificant, trifling 1530. **4.** Small or limited in amount, number, range, etc. 1564. **b.** Of sounds: Weak, lacking in fullness 1784.

1. The s. and negligent execution of the Forest Lawes 1598. **2. a.** The proofs were as s. as the crimes gross FULLER. **b.** Some claim (generally of the slenderest kind) 1886. **3.** But what a s. answer is this 1641. He has but s. Parts 1687. **4.** Her s. earnings were the sole support of the family LAMB. **b.** It gave one little s. squeak HAWTHORNE. Hence **Sle·nderize** *v.* to perform or subject to 'slimming' operations 1923. **Sle·nder-ly** *adv.*, **-ness.**

Slent, *sb.* Now *dial.* ME. [– ON. **slent* (Norw. *slent* side-slip, Sw. *slänt* slope, slant) rel. to **slenta* SLENT *v.* See SLANT *sb.*^{1}] **1.** = SLANT *sb.*^{1} 1. †**2.** = SLANT *sb.*^{1} 3a. –1612.

Slent, *v.* Now *dial.* ME. [– ON. **slenta* (ON. *sletta*) dash, throw, etc.; see SLANT *v.*] **1.** *intr.* To slip, fall, or glide obliquely; to strike or lie aslant. †**2.** To make sly hits or gibes –1579.

†**Sleuth,** *sb.*^{1} [OE. *slǣwþ*, ME. *sleuþ(e*, f. *slāw* SLOW *a.*; see -TH^1. Superseded by SLOTH *sb.*] Sloth; laziness –1629.

†**Sleuth,** *sb.*^{2} ME. [– ON. *slóð* track, trail. Cf. SLOT *sb.*^{3}] The track or trail of a person or animal; a definite track or path –1470.

Sleuth, *sb.*^{3} orig. *U.S.* 1876. Short for next. Hence **Sleuth** *v. trans.* to track (a person); *intr.* to play the detective.

Sleuth-hound (slū·þ,haund). orig. *north.* and *Sc.* late ME. [f. SLEUTH *sb.*^{2}] **1.** A species of bloodhound, formerly employed in Scotland. *Hist.* or *arch.* **2.** *transf.* A keen investigator; a tracker; *U.S.* a detective 1856.

Slew (slū), *sb.*^{1} Also **slue, sleugh.** 1708. [var. spellings of *sloo*, ME. *slō*; see SLOUGH *sb.*^{1}] **1.** *N. Amer.* A marshy or reedy pool, pond, small lake, backwater, or inlet. **2.** *Coal-mining.* A natural swamp in a coal seam 1883.

Slew (slū), *sb.*^{2} Also **slue.** 1860. [f. SLEW *v.*] The act of turning, or causing to turn, without change of place; a turn, a twist; the position to which a thing has been turned.

Slew (slū), *v.* Also **slue.** 1769. [orig. naut.; of unkn. origin.] **1.** *trans.* To turn (a thing) round upon its own axis, or without shifting it from its place; also loosely, to swing round. **b.** *fig.* To intoxicate; also in *pa. pple.*, beaten, 'done' 1888. **2.** *intr.* To turn about; to swing *round* 1823.

1. Slue the mast round 1882. A roller caught us and slued the boat round 1884. **2.** The floe..began to 'slue' or revolve 1823.

Slewed (slūd), *ppl. a. slang.* 1834. [f. prec. + -ED^1.] Intoxicated.

Sley, variant of SLAY, *sb.*

†**Slibber-sauce.** 1573. [perh. f. Flem. *slibber* (Kilian) slime, ooze, – MDu. *slibbe*, Du. *slib*, LG. *slibbe*.] **1.** A compound or concoction of a messy, repulsive, or nauseous character, used esp. for medicinal purposes –1656. **2.** A preparation of this kind used as a cosmetic –1633.

Slice (slais), *sb.*^{1} [ME. *s(c)lice*, aphetic – OFr. *esclice*, (mod. *éclisse*) small piece of wood, etc., f. *esclicier*; see SLICE *v.*] **I.** †**1.** A fragment, a splinter –1596. **2.** A relatively thin, flat, broad piece cut from anything. late ME. **3.** *transf.* A portion, share, piece, etc. 1550.

3. A fellow..who has spent a good s. of his life here 1857.

II. †**1.** A spatula used for stirring and mixing compounds –1686. **2.** One or other of several flattish utensils (sometimes perforated) used for various purposes in cookery, etc., as a *fish-s.* 1459. **3.** A form of fire-shovel; also, an instrument for clearing the bars of a furnace when choked with clinkers 1465. **4.** A flattish instrument, implement, etc., of various kinds 1483. **5.** *Printing.* **a.** An ink-knife 1683. **b.** The sliding bottom of a s.-galley 1683. **6.** *Ship-building.* One of the tapered pieces of wood driven between the bilgeways, etc., in preparation for launching a vessel 1791.

attrib. and *Comb.*: **s.-bar,** a hooked poker for removing slag and cinders from the grate-bars of furnaces; **-galley,** a galley having a movable false bottom or s.

Slice (slais), *sb.*^{2} 1611. [f. SLICE *v.*] †**1.** A sharp cut, a slash. COTGR. **2.** *Golf.* A slicing stroke 1886.

Slice (slais), *v.* late ME. [– OFr. *esclicier* splinter, shatter – Frankish *slītjan* (= OHG. *slīzan*, G. *schleissen*, OE. *slītan* SLIT *v.*).] **1.** *trans.* To cut into slices; to cut into or through with a sharp instrument. **2.** To cut *out* or *off* in the form of a slice or slices; to remove with a clean cut 1550. **3.** *intr.* To cut cleanly or easily 1605. **b.** To use a slice or fire-shovel 1893. **4.** *trans.* To make (a way) by slicing 1872. **5.** *Golf.* To hit (the ball) a glancing blow so that it curves off to the right 1890. Hence **Sliced** *ppl. a.*, **Sli·cer.**

Slick (slik), *sb.* 1849. [f. SLICK *a.* or *v.*] **1.** *Carpentry.* A wide-bitted paring chisel 1875. **2. a.** *U.S.* A smooth place or streak on the surface of water, usually caused by the presence of some oily or greasy substance 1849. **b.** *Mining.* A smooth parting or plane of division in strata 1883.

Slick (slik), *a.* Now chiefly *dial.* and *U.S.* [ME. *slike*, prob. repr. OE. **slice*, rel. to **slician* (as in *niġ|slicod* 'newly polished', glossy) and Icel. *slikja*, Norw. *slikja* be or make smooth. Cf. SLEEK *a.*] **1.** Of skin, hair, etc.: Smooth, glossy, sleek. **2.** Of animals, etc.: Sleek in hair or skin; plump; well-conditioned. Now *rare.* 1440. **3.** = SLEEK *a.* 3. 1599. **4.** Adroit, deft, quick, smart; skilful in action or execution 1818. **b.** Smartly or cleverly done 1838. **5.** First-class, excellent 1866.

1. Bent browis, smothe and slyke CHAUCER. **3.** S. flattery and she Are twin-born sisters B. JONS. **4.** I ain't..s. at the gruelling of sick folks 1830. Hence **Slick** *adv.* smartly, easily, quickly, completely 1825.

Slick (slik), *v.* [OE. **slician*; see SLICK *a.* and cf. SLEEK *v.*] **1.** *trans.* To render smooth or glossy; to polish; to smooth with a slicker. **b.** *transf.* To polish up, make elegant or fine ME. **2.** To make (the skin, hair, etc.) sleek or glossy, esp. by some special treatment ME.

1. c. *intr.* with *up.* (U.S.) To make oneself or a place neat and tidy; also *fig.* 1841.

Slickens (sli·kens). *U.S.* 1882. [perh. f. *slick* (– G. *schlich*) finely pounded ore.] The pulverized matter from a quartz-mill; the fine soil of a hydraulic mill.

Slickenside (sli·k'nsəid). Also **-sides.** 1768. [f. dial. *slicken*, var. of SLICK *a.*, + SIDE *sb.*[1]] **1.** *Min.* A specular variety of galena found in Derbyshire. **2.** *Geol.* A polished (and occas. striated) surface on the wall of a mineral lode, or on a line of fracture in a rock-mass; a smooth glistening surface produced by pressure and friction 1822.

Slicker (sli·kəɹ). 1851. [f. SLICK *a.* or *v.* + -ER[1].] **1. a.** A tool used for scraping or smoothing leather. **b.** A tool used for smoothing the surfaces of moulds in founding 1875. **2.** *U.S.* A waterproof coat 1884.

Slicking (sli·kiŋ), *vbl. sb.* 1495. [f. SLICK *v.* + -ING[1].] **1.** The action of making sleek or smooth. **2.** *Mining.* In *pl.* Narrow veins of ore 1843.

Sli·ckstone. *dial.* ME. Also **sleek-.** [SLICK *v.*] A stone for smoothing.

'Slid, *int. Obs.* exc. *arch.* 1598. Abbrev. of *God's lid*, used as a petty oath or exclam.

Sli·dder, *sb. dial.* 1793. [Cf. SLIDDER *a.* and *v.*] A trench or hollow running down a slope; a steep slope.

†Sli·dder, *a.* [OE. *slidor*, f. *slid-*, wk. grade of *slīdan* SLIDE *v.*] **1.** Slippery –1578. **2.** Inclined to slip or fall (*rare*) –1500. **3.** Of a smooth or slippery nature –1686. So **Sli·ddery** *a.* (now *dial.*) slippery, uncertain, unstable.

Slidder (sli·dəɹ), *v.* Now *dial.* [OE. *slid(e)rian* = MLG., MDu. *slid(d)eren*, G. dial. *schlittern*, frequent. (see -ER[5]) f. *slid-*, the weak grade of *slīdan* SLIDE *v.* See SLITHER *v.*] **1.** *intr.* To slide, slip. **2.** *trans.* To make slippery or smooth. late ME.

1. With that he dragg'd the trembling Sire, Slidd'ring through clotter'd Blood, and holy Mire DRYDEN.

Slide (sləid), *sb.* 1570. [f. SLIDE *v.*] **I. 1.** The act or fact of sliding; an instance of this; also, the manner in which a thing slides. **b.** *Mus.* A grace consisting of two notes diatonically ascending or descending to a principal note; also = PORTAMENTO 1818. **2.** An earthslip, a landslip, an avalanche; a place on a hill-side, etc., where this has happened 1664. **3.** *Mining.* **a.** A fracture in a lode resulting in the dislocation or displacement of a portion of it; a vein of clay, etc., marking such dislocation 1778. **b.** Matter dislodged by an earth-slip 1841. **4. a.** A kind of sledge 1685. **b.** A runner on which a gun is mounted 1830.

1. My third Lieutenant broke his leg by a s. on the deck 1726. **4. b.** Their guns..were fixed on slides..to enable them to be fired over the bows MARRYAT.

II. 1. A sliding part of some mechanism; a part of an instrument or machine designed to be pulled in and out; a device which slides or may be slid 1608. **2.** A kind of tongueless buckle or ring used as a fastener, clasp, or brooch; a small perforated object sliding on a cord, etc. 1779. **3. a.** A slip of glass, etc., on which an object is mounted or placed to facilitate its examination by a microscope 1837. **b.** A picture prepared for use in a magic lantern or stereoscope 1846. **c.** *Photogr.* A flat case or receptacle within which plates are placed for the purpose of being inserted in a camera. Freq. *dark s.* 1856. **4.** *Rowing.* A sliding seat 1875. **III. 1.** A smooth surface, esp. of ice, for sliding on, or formed by being slid on; a slippery place 1687. **2. a.** An inclined plane for the transit of heavy goods, esp. timber. Chiefly *Amer.* 1832. **b.** *Amer.* A sloping channel constructed to facilitate the passage of logs down stream; a chute 1858. **3.** A device of the nature of a bed, rail, groove, etc., on or in which a thing may slide 1846. **4.** The track of an otter 1894.

Slide (sləid), *v.* Pa. t. **slid.** Pa. pple. **slid (slided, slidden).** [OE. *slīdan* = LG. *slīden*, MHG. *slīten*; rel. to OE. *slidor* slippery, and the forms s.v. SLIDDER *v.*, SLED *sb.*] **I.** *intr.* **1.** To pass from one place or point to another with a smooth and continuous movement, *esp.* through the air or water or along a surface. **b.** To move in this manner while standing more or less erect upon a surface, *esp.* that of ice ME. **2.** Of streams, etc.: To glide, flow. Now *rare.* late ME. **3.** Of reptiles, etc.: To glide, crawl. Now *rare.* ME. **4.** To move, go; to proceed unperceived, quietly, or stealthily; to steal, creep, slink or slip *away*, *into*, or *out of* a place, etc. late ME. **b.** *colloq.* To make off. orig. *U.S.* 1859.

1. Fishes which through the flood..did softly slyde And swim away SPENSER. **b.** I had been sliding in Christ-Church meadow JOHNSON. **2.** Where Thames and Isis heire By lowly Æton slides 1633. **4.** Slouching my hat, I slid out of doors 1760.

II. 1. To pass away, pass by, so as to disappear, be forgotten or neglected, etc. Now *rare.* ME. **b.** With *let* (or *allow*). In later use freq., to let (something) take its own course. late ME. **c.** Of time: To pass, slip *away*, go *by*, imperceptibly or without being profitably employed. late ME. **2.** To pass easily or gradually *into* some condition, practice, etc. late ME. **b.** To pass by easy or gradual change or transformation into some other form or character 1500. **3.** To move, pass, make way, etc., in an easy or unobtrusive manner. late ME. **b.** *Mus.* To pass from one note to another without any cessation of sound or distinction between the intervals 1864. **c.** Of the eye or sight: To pass quickly from one object to another 1756.

1. Alack, how good men, and the good turns they do us, s. out of memory LAMB. **b.** Therefore..let the world s. SHAKS. **c.** So sholdestow endure, and laten slyde The tyme CHAUCER. **2.** When an honourable man..slides into some dishonourable action 1847. **b.** Parts answ'ring parts shall s. into a whole POPE. **3.** So desirous..of sliding through life to the end of it unnoted 1748.

III. 1. To slip; to lose one's foothold ME. **b.** Of the foot: To slip ME. **2.** *fig.* To lapse morally; to commit some fault; to err or go wrong OE.

1. So sure, they walk on ice, and never s. CHURCHILL. **b.** Thou hast enlarged my goinge vnder me, and myne ankles haue not slyded COVERDALE 2 *Sam.* 22:37. **2.** I find myself a learner yet, Unskilful, weak, and apt to s. COWPER.

IV. *trans.* **1.** To cause to move with a smooth, gliding motion; to push over a level surface 1537. **2.** With *in* or *into*: To introduce quietly or dexterously; to slip (something) *into* one's hand, etc. 1627. **3.** To move over, traverse, descend, etc., in a sliding manner 1621.

1. *fig.* Madly sliding his splendid army, like a weaver's shuttle from his right hand to his left KINGLAKE. **2.** He was..to s. the Letter into her Hand, but let no Body see STEELE. Hence **Sli·dden** *ppl. a.* that has slipped or slid down.

Slide-, the vbl. stem or the sb. in combs. (sometimes not hyphened): **a.** With names of apparatus, implements, parts of machines, etc., characterized by a sliding action, as *s.-bar*, *-bolt*, *-car*, *-lathe*, etc. 1763. **b.** Denoting something along which objects may slide or be slid, as *s.-ladder*, *-way* 1793. **c.** Misc., as *s.-centerer*; *s.-movement*, *-principle*; etc. 1846.

†Slide-groat. 1552. [f. SLIDE *v.* + GROAT.] Shove-groat, shovelboard –1635.

Slider (sləi·dəɹ). 1530. [f. SLIDE *v.* + -ER[1].] **1.** One who slides. **b.** *U.S.* The red-bellied terrapin 1883. **2.** A beam or plank on which something heavy may be slid; also *dial.*, a sledge 1582. **3.** A thing or part which slides or may be slid; *esp.* a sliding part or device in some mechanical apparatus 1681.

Sli·de-rest. Also **slide rest.** 1839. [f. SLIDE *v.*] An appliance for holding tools in turning, enabling the tools to be variously held in relation to the material worked on.

Sli·de-rule. 1663. [f. SLIDE *v.*] A sliding rule (see SLIDING *ppl. a.* II. 4).

Sli·de-valve. Also **slide valve.** 1802. [f. SLIDE *v.*] A valve having a sliding plate for opening and closing an orifice; *spec.* one which does this alternately and regularly.

Sliding (sləi·diŋ), *vbl. sb.* ME. [f. SLIDE *v.* + -ING[1].] **1.** The action of SLIDE *v.* **2.** *attrib.*, as *s.-place*; *s. contact*, *motion*, *principle* 1611.

Sliding (sləi·diŋ), *ppl. a.* OE. [f. SLIDE *v.* + -ING[2].] **I. 1.** *fig.* That slides or slips away; transitory; unstable, inconstant; passing. **2.** Slippery ME. **3.** That moves by sliding or slipping; flowing, gliding, etc. late ME. **b.** Accompanied by a sliding movement 1796. **4.** Of language or music: Flowing easily 1627.

1. The Seasons of the s. Year DRYDEN. **3.** Safelye slips away the slyding shippe 1562. Seuerall s. rills B. JONS. **b.** Craigengelt..made a s. bow to the Marquis SCOTT.

II. In special uses. **1.** Of a knot: Made so as to slip along a cord; running 1591. **2.** Designating parts of apparatus or machinery which slide, or are characterized by some sliding device, as *s.-bar*, *-collar*, *-joint*, etc. 1778. **b.** Designating doors, lids, panels, etc., which are opened or shut by sliding 1715. **3.** *Naut.*, etc. **a.** *S. keel*, an extra deep keel which slides vertically through the bottom of a vessel. Also *attrib.* 1797. **b.** *S. seat*, a seat in an outrigger which moves backwards and forwards with the action of the rower 1874. **4.** *S. rule*, a mathematical gauging or measuring instrument consisting of two graduated parts, one of which slides upon the other, and so arranged that when brought into proper juxtaposition the required result may be obtained by inspection 1663. **5.** *S. scale*: **a.** A sliding rule 1706. **b.** A scale or standard (of payments, etc.) which rises or falls in proportion to, or conversely to, the rise or fall of some other standard 1843.

'Slife (sləif), *int. Obs.* exc. *arch.* 1634. Abbrev. of *God's life*, used as a petty oath or exclam.

Slight, obs. f. SLEIGHT.

Slight (sləit), *sb.* 1549. [f. SLIGHT *a.* and *v.*] **†1.** A very small amount or weight; a trifle –1678. **2.** Display of contemptuous indifference or disregard; small respect *for* one 1701. **3.** An instance of slighting or being slighted 1719.

Slight (sləit), *a.* and *adv.* [ME. (orig. north.) *sleght*, *slyȝt* – ON. **slehtr*, *sléttr* level, smooth, soft = OFris. *sliuht*, OS. *sliht*, MLG., MDu. *slecht*, *slicht* simple, defective (Du. *slecht* bad, *slechts* merely), OHG. *sleht* level (G. *schlecht* bad, *schlicht* simple), Goth. *slaihts* level :– Gmc. **slextaz.*] **A.** *adj.* **1.** Smooth, glossy, sleek. *Obs.* exc. *dial.* **2.** Of a small and slender form or build. late ME. **3.** Of light, thin, or poor texture or material; rather unsubstantial. late ME. **b.** Lacking in solid or substantial qualities 1585. **†4.** Of persons: Of little worth or account; mean, low; humble in position –1700. **5.** Small in amount, quantity, degree, etc. 1530. **b.** Unimportant, trifling 1548. **c.** Wanting in fullness or heartiness 1660. **d.** Performed with little exertion 1667.

2. E'en the s. hare-bell raised its head SCOTT. **3.** For which price, but very s. work hath been furnished 1663. **b.** A good but rather s. story 1886. **5.** Sleighte feares make women shrike 1601. **b.** Are we furious upon every sleight occasion? 1656.

d. He..in contempt, At one s. bound high overleap'd all bound Of Hill or highest Wall MILT.

B. *adv.* †**1.** Poorly; slightly; contemptuously –1716. **2.** Slimly, slenderly 1667. †**3.** Slightly; to a small extent –1746.

1. Think not so s. of glory MILT. **2.** A s. made people 1800. **3.** Come nearer, part not hence so s. inform'd MILT. Hence **Sli·ghtness.**

Slight (sləit), *v.* ME. [Sense 1 – ON. **slehta, slétta,* f. *sléttr* (see prec.); sense 2 – Du. *slechten*, LG. *slichten*; sense 3 f. the adj.] †**1.** *trans.* To make smooth or level –1620. †**2.** To level with the ground –1098. **3.** To treat with indifference or disrespect; to disregard, disdain, ignore 1597. †**b.** To throw contemptuously. SHAKS. †**4.** To gloss or pass *over* carelessly or with indifference –1824.

2. *fig.* Christ our Lord..slighted and dismantled that mighty Garrison 1676. **3.** He delighted in the conversation of men of science,..but the men of letters he slighted EMERSON. †*To s. off,* to put *off* disdainfully. Hence **Slighted** *ppl. a.*, **Sli·ghter.**

†**'Slight,** *int.* 1598. Abbrev. of *God's light*, used as a petty oath or exclam. –1668.

†**Sli·ghten,** *v.* 1605. [f. SLIGHT *a.* or *v.* + -EN[5].] = SLIGHT *v.* 3. –1646.

Sli·ghting, *ppl. a.* 1632. [f. SLIGHT *v.* + -ING[2].] **1.** Conveying or implying a slight; of a contemptuous or disdainful character. **2.** Acting contemptuously or disdainfully 1684. Hence **Sli·ghtingly** *adv.*

Slightly (sləi·tli), *adv.* 1521. [f. SLIGHT *a.* + -LY[2].] In various senses corresp. to those of the adj.; unsubstantially; carelessly, lightly; †easily; †slightingly; to a slight degree (1592).

Slighty (sləi·ti), *a. Obs.* exc. *dial.* 1619. [f. SLIGHT *a.* + -Y[1].] †**1.** Superficial –1671. †**b.** Of persons: Negligent, careless –1661. †**2.** Slighting; light –1674. **3.** Slight, trivial; also, unsubstantial, slender, weak. Now *dial.* 1669.

†**Slik(e,** *a. north.* ME. [– ON. *slík-r*, for earlier **swa-líkr* 'so like'; see SUCH *a.*] Such.

Slily, variant of SLYLY.

Slim (slim), *a.* 1657. [– LG., Du. *slim*, repr. MLG. *slim(m*, MDu. *slim(p* slanting, cross, bad = MHG. *slimp (-b)* slanting, oblique, G. *schlimm* grievous, bad :– Gmc. **slimbaz.*] **1.** Slender, (gracefully) thin. **b.** Small, slight; of little substance; poor 1677. **c.** Meagre, scanty, sparse 1852. **2.** Of persons, their actions, etc.: Sly, cunning, crafty, wily, artful 1674.

1. A s. young Girl of..Seventeen STEELE. **b.** The chances of your getting this [letter] are s. 1862. **c.** A very s. audience, not more than a dozen 1852. **2.** The issue of the proclamation by the Boers..is regarded..as a 'slim' (crafty) move on the enemy's part 1899. Hence **Slim** *v. trans.* to make s.; see also SLIMMING. **Sli·m-ly** *adv.*, **-ness.**

Slime (sləim), *sb.* [OE. *slīm* = OFris., MLG., MDu., MHG. *slīm* (Du. *slijm*, G. *schleim* phlegm, slime, mucus), ON. *slím*; Gmc. sb. rel. to L. *limus* mud, slime, Gr. λίμνη marsh.] **1.** Soft glutinous mud; alluvial ooze; viscous matter deposited or collected on stones, etc. **b.** Applied to bitumen 1530. **2.** A viscous substance or fluid of animal or vegetable origin; mucus, semen, etc. ME. **b.** Applied to star-jelly (see JELLY *sb.* 2 b.) 1471. **3.** *fig.* Applied to the human body, mankind, etc., or anything disgusting or repulsive ME. **4.** *Mining.* Finely crushed metallic ore in the form of mud 1758.

1. The teeming Tide..Makes green the Soil with S., and black prolific Sands DRYDEN. *fig.* Lerne, thou erth & slyme, to humble the 1504. **b.** COVERDALE *Gen.* 11:3. *Comb.*: **s.-eel,** *Myxine glutinosa*, which resembles the lamprey.

Slime (sləim), *v.* 1628. [f. SLIME *sb.*] **1.** *trans.* To smear or cover with slime. **2. a.** To make (one's way) in a slimy fashion. **b.** *intr.* To crawl slimily; to become slimy. 1842.

Sli·me(-)pit. 1530. **1.** In or after Biblical use: A pit or hole yielding asphalt or bitumen. **2.** *techn.* A pit or reservoir in which metallic slimes are collected 1778.

Slimming (sli·miŋ), *gerund* and *vbl. sb.* 1927. [f. SLIM *v.* + -ING[1].] The practice of using special means such as dieting and exercises to reduce one's figure; often *attrib.*

Slimsy (sli·mzi, -si), *a. U.S.* 1845. [f. SLIM *a.* + -SY, perh. after *flimsy.*] Flimsy, frail.

Slimy (sləi·mi), *a.* late ME. [f. SLIME *sb.* + -Y[1].] **1.** Of the nature or consistency of slime; viscous. **b.** *techn.* Of ore: In the form of slime 1778. **2.** Characterized by the presence of slime; covered with slime. late ME. **3.** *transf.* and *fig.* Morally defiled or objectionable; vile, disgusting 1575.

1. b. Moving the s. Tin to and fro with a light hand 1778. **2.** A pit of standing water greene, slimie, and stinking 1613. Yea, s. things did crawl with legs Upon the s. sea COLERIDGE. Hence **Sli·mily** *adv.* **Sli·miness.**

Sling (sliŋ), *sb.*[1] ME. [prob. – LDu. (cf. MLG. *slinge*, G. *schlinge* noose), of symbolic origin.] An implement or weapon for hurling stones, etc. by hand with great force or to a distance, consisting of a strap attached to two cords or strings, or to a stick or staff; the impulse is given by rapid whirling of the sling before discharging it. Also locally, a boy's catapult. **b.** A ballista. Now *Hist.* 1535.

Dauid orthrewe hym sone with his stone and his slyng 1450. *fig.* The Slings and Arrowes of outragious Fortune SHAKS.

Comb.: **s.-stone,** a stone or pebble used as a missile to be cast by a s.

Sling (sliŋ), *sb.*[2] ME. [The immed. source is doubtful; poss. identical with prec., the senses of LG. *sling(e*, G. *schlinge* noose, snare, arm-sling to some extent corresp.] **1.** A device for securing or grasping bulky or heavy articles while being hoisted or lowered, usually a belt, rope, or chain formed into a loop and fitted with hooks and tackle; a loop of this kind by which heavy articles are lifted, carried, or suspended. **2.** *Naut.* The middle part of a yard 1670. **3.** A leather strap attached to a rifle, etc., enabling it to be carried slung over the shoulder, or on the arm 1711. **b.** A strap, band, wire, etc., forming a kind of loop by which something is suspended or hung 1771. **c.** A piece of cloth or other material, formed into a loop and suspended from the neck so as to support an injured limb 1720.

1. *Shot s.*, a sling for carrying heavy shot or shell 1876. **2.** *Slings*, that part of a yard encircled by the s.-hoop, which suspends it from the mast, or by which it is hoisted and lowered 1846. **3. c.** He came..with his arm in a s. 1860.

Comb.: **s.-cart** *Mil.*, a two-wheeled cart to which a cannon is slung in order to be transported; **-dog,** an iron hook with an eye at one end, through which a rope may be passed; **-hoop,** a ring which suspends the yard from the mast and by which it is hoisted or lowered.

Sling (sliŋ), *sb.*[3] 1530. [f. SLING *v.*[1]] **1.** The act of slinging, throwing, etc.; a cast, fling, or throw. **2.** *slang.* A drink or draught; a 'pull' (*rare*) 1788.

†**Sling,** *sb.*[4] 1566. [var. of earlier †*slang* (XVI) – MLG., MDu. *slange* (Du. *slang*, G. *schlange*) serpent, cannon, etc.; perh. infl. by SLING *sb.*[1]] A serpentine or culverin –1736.

Sling (sliŋ), *sb.*[5] 1807. [Of unkn. origin.] **1.** An American drink composed of brandy, rum, etc., and water, sweetened and flavoured. (Cf. GIN-SLING.) **2.** The juice of the sugar-cane, as obtained in the manufacture of sugar 1826.

Sling (sliŋ), *v.*[1] Pa. t. and pa. pple. **slung** (slʌŋ). ME. [prob. – ON. *slyngva* str. vb.] **I.** *trans.* **1.** To strike, to bring or knock *down*, by means of a sling (*rare*). **b.** To throw or cast (stones, etc.) by means of a sling ME. **c.** *absol.* To cast or discharge missiles by means of a sling; to use a sling 1440. **2.** To throw, cast, hurl, or fling (a person or thing) in some direction or to some point. Now chiefly *dial.* or *colloq.* ME. **b.** Of sheep: To cast (a lamb) 1750. **c.** *absol.* To strike or launch *out* in boxing 1812. **3.** In colloq. or slang uses, e.g. to hand round, distribute, dispense; to use or relate to a person. late ME.

1. b. All these colde s. stones at an heere breadth, and not faile BIBLE (Geneva) *Judges* 20:16. **2.** Brass Pieces that slung their Shot an incredible way 1698. **3.** *To s. ink*, to write articles, etc. *To s. one's hook*, to make off, clear out; to pick pockets.

II. *intr.* **1.** To move with some force or speed; to fly as if thrown by a sling; to fling oneself ME. **2.** To advance, walk, etc., with long or swinging strides. Chiefly *Sc.* or *north.* and *Austral.* 1808.

Sling (sliŋ), *v.*[2] 1522. [f. SLING *sb.*[2]] **1.** *trans.* To place in, or secure with, a sling or slings for hoisting or lowering; to raise up or let down by means of a sling or slings. **2.** *Naut.* To pass chains or lashings round (a sail or yard) to secure it to the mast 1626. **3.** To hang or suspend, to fix or fasten (something) about the person in a sling or in a loose manner so as to be carried easily 1688. **4.** To hang up or suspend, esp. from one point to another; to put up (a hammock) 1697.

1. The horses were slung down into the stalls 1833. **3.** The lance is slung on the left arm 1833. **4.** *To s. the monkey*, a game played by sailors.

Sling, *v.*[3] *U.S.* 1836. [f. SLING *sb.*[5] 1.] *intr.* To drink or take sling.

Sling-, stem of SLING *v.*[1], used in combs., as **s.-shot** *U.S.*, a catapult; **-trot,** a loose swinging trot or pace.

Sli·nger. late ME. [f. SLING *v.*[1] + -ER[1].] One who slings, *esp.* a soldier armed with a sling. Now *rare.*

Sli·ng(s)man. 1579. [SLING *sb.*[2]] = prec.

Slink (sliŋk), *sb.* 1607. [Related to SLINK *v.*] **I.** An abortive or premature calf or other animal. Chiefly *dial.* **b.** The skin or flesh of a premature calf or other animal 1741. **II. 1.** A sneaking, shirking, cowardly fellow; a skulk. *dial.* or *colloq.* 1824. **2.** A slinking, sneaking, or stealthy pace or tread 1853.

2. Those who went forth with the dog's trot might return with the cat's s. 1896.

Slink (sliŋk), *a. dial.* 1673. [perh. rel. to SLINK *sb.* and *v.*] Lank, lean, poor, ill-conditioned.

Slink (sliŋk), *v.* Pa. t. and pa. pple. **slunk** (slʌŋk); †**slank;** †**slinked.** [repr. OE. *slincan* creep, crawl, corresp. to (M)LG. *slinken* subside, and (dial.) *slench* (XIV) slink, sneak, repr. OE. **slenćan.*] **1.** *intr.* Of persons or animals: To move or walk in a quiet, stealthy, or sneaking manner. late ME. **2.** *trans.* Of animals, esp. cows: To bring forth (young) prematurely or abortively 1640. (Cf. SLING *v.*[1] 2 b.)

1. The wily Fox..slinks behind And slily creeps thro' the same beaten Track 1735. There were some few who slank obliquely from them as they passed LANDOR. *fig.* Seeing the sun quietly s. behind a mass of black clouds 1806. *transf.* Lady Castlemayne, who he believes has lately slunk a great belly away PEPYS. **Sli·nky** *a.*, gracefully slender and flowing.

Slip (slip), *sb.*[1] [OE. *slipa*; *slyppe* slime (so *slipiġ* slimy); cf. Norw. *slip, slipa* slime on fish, and SLOP *sb.*[2] See COWSLIP, OXLIP.] †**1.** A soft semi-liquid mass. OE. only. **2.** Curdled milk. Now *U.S.* late ME. **3.** *techn.* A semi-liquid material, made of finely-ground clay or flint, etc., mixed with water to about the consistency of cream, and used for making, cementing, coating, or decorating pottery, etc.; also, clay suitable for making this 1640.

Comb.: **s.-cheese,** soft cheese made without pressing out the whey; **-coat,** a soft cream cheese; chiefly in *s.-coat cheese.*

Slip (slip), *sb.*[2] 1440. [prob. – MLG., MDu. *slippe* (Du. *slip*) cut, slit, strip (but the earliest Eng. sense is not recorded in these languages.] **I. 1.** A twig, sprig, or small shoot taken from a plant, tree, etc., for the purpose of grafting or planting; a scion, cutting 1495. **b.** A scion or descendant 1588. **2.** A young person of either sex, esp. one of small or slender build 1582. **b.** A thin or slender person 1703. **3.** A sole of intermediate size 1881.

1. The Lab'rer cuts Young Slips, and in the Soil securely puts DRYDEN. **b.** He talk'd of bastard slips, and cursed his bed CRABBE. **2.** Shusey Dogherty was a good-looking s. 1841. There was his wife, and the s. of a girl 1861. **b.** My Lady Shapely has by that thin S. eight Children STEELE.

II. †**1.** The edge, skirt, or flap of a robe or garment –1648. **2.** A spoon-handle having the top cut off obliquely; a spoon with a handle or stem of this form. Now *Hist.* 1530. **3.** A long and relatively thin and narrow piece or strip of some material 1555. **4.** A strip, a narrow piece or stretch, *of* land, ground, etc. 1591. **5.** An example or specimen *of* something having an elongated or slender form 1730. **6.** A window, apartment, passage, etc., of an elongated form 1730. **b.** *U.S.* A narrow, doorless church-pew 1828. **c.** *pl.* The sides of the gallery in a theatre 1805. **7.** A (narrow) piece of paper or parchment 1687. †**b.** A newspaper (or part of one) printed in the form of a long slip of paper –1727. **c.** *Typog.* A proof pulled on a long slip of paper, for revision before the type is made up into pages 1818. **8.** A certain quantity *of* yarn, etc. Now *dial.* 1647.

5. A neat sanded s. of a coffee-room 1825.

Slip (slip), *sb.*[3] 1467. [f. SLIP *v.*[1]] **I. 1.** An artificial slope of stone, etc., built or made beside a navigable water to serve as a landing-place. **b.** *Shipbuilding.* An inclined plane, sloping gradually down to the water, on which ships or other vessels are built or repaired 1769. **c.** A contrivance (patented in 1818) for hauling vessels out of the water in order to repair them 1830. **2.** *local.* A narrow roadway or passage 1739.

1. b. The largest of the available building slips is being prepared for the reception of the new vessel 1894.

II. 1. A leash for a dog, etc., so contrived that the animal can readily be released; esp. one used for a couple of greyhounds in coursing, by which they can be let go simultaneously 1578. **b.** *Bookbinding.* A cord used in fastening the back of a book 1875. **2. a.** A child's pinafore or frock (cf. *gym-slip*) 1690. **b.** An article of women's attire, formerly an outer garment, now worn under a gown of lace or other thin material. Also *transf.*, an infant's garment of this nature. 1761. **c.** A pillow-case 1800. **d.** *Upholstery.* A shot-hem in which a wire or the like may be inserted 1891. **3.** *pl.* The sidings of a theatrical stage, from which the scenery is slipped on, and where the actors stand before entering 1812. **4.** A cylindrical iron case, in which wood for making gunpowder is charred 1876.

2. e. *pl.* In full *bathing slips*: bathing-drawers.

III. 1. *To give* (a person) *the s.*: To evade or escape from (him); to elude, steal off, or slip away from unperceived 1567. †**b.** With punning allusion to SLIP *sb.*[4] –1613. †**c.** An act of evading or escaping (*rare*) –1669. **2.** An act of slipping, sliding, or falling down 1596. **b.** *Naut.* The difference between the pitch of a propelling screw, and the actual advance of the vessel which it drives 1844. **3.** An error in conduct, procedure, argument, etc. 1579. **b.** A slight unintentional error or blunder in writing, speaking, etc. 1620. **4. a.** *Geol.* A slight fault or dislocation caused by the sinking of one section of the strata 1789. **b.** = LANDSLIP 1838. **5.** *Cricket.* A fielder who stands to the right of the wicket-keeper at a short distance behind the wicket; called esp. *short* or *first s.* to distinguish him from *long* or *second s.* 1833. **b.** The ground or position occupied or guarded by these players 1833.

1. b. You have given me a ninepence here, and I'll give you the s. for 't 1613. **2.** By..some S. of my Foot..I fell down DE FOE. *Prov.* There's many a s. between the cup and the lip. **c.** The loss of distance travelled by aircraft arising from the nature of the medium in which its propeller revolves 1897. **d.** *Electr.* The ratio of the difference between the operating and synchronous speed of an induction motor. **3. b.** Phr. *A s. of the tongue, pen*, etc.

†**Slip**, *sb.*[4] 1592. [perh. a spec. use of prec. or SLIP *sb.*[2]] A counterfeit coin –1634.

Phr. *To nail up for a s.*, with reference to the exposure of spurious coin.

Slip (slip), *v.*[1] ME. [prob. – MLG., Du. *slippen* = MHG. *slipfen*; see SLIPPER *a.*, SLIPPERY.] **Intr. senses.* **I. 1.** To escape, get away, make off (*rare*). **2.** To pass or go lightly or quietly; to move quickly and softly, without attracting notice; to glide or steal. Used with various advs. and preps. late ME. **3. a.** To enter gradually or inadvertently *into* a theme, digression, opinion, etc. 1641. **b.** To pass *into* a certain state 1864. **4.** To pass *out of*, escape *from*, the mind, memory, etc. Also without const. ME. **5.** To break or escape *from* a person, the tongue, lips, etc. late ME. **b.** To leak *out* 1848. **6.** Of time: To go by quickly or imperceptibly; to pass unmarked; to run. Chiefly with advs., as *along*, *away*, *by*. 1564. **7. a.** To pass *over* (a subject or matter) without adequate attention or notice; to neglect, overlook 1577. **b.** To progress or travel *across*, *down*, *over*, a stretch of ground, etc., quickly 1864.

2. When slipping from thy Mothers eye thou went'st Alone into the Temple MILT. If the voters are apathetic and let a bad man s. in BRYCE. *fig.* Her memory..Went slipping back upon the golden days TENNYSON. **4.** The experiments..were quite slipt out of my memory 1676. **5.** The reply..slipp'd..glibly from my Tongue 1773. **6.** As time was slipping by,..he felt that he must act DICKENS.

II. 1. Of the foot: To slide; to lose its hold ME. **b.** = SLIDE *v.* III. 1. 1530. **c.** To fall into mistake, fault, or error; to err, †to sin. Also with *into* (error, etc.) ME. **d.** *U.S.* With *up*: To fail; to make a mistake 1856. **2.** To move out of place with an easy sliding motion; to fail to hold or stick; to slide. late ME. **b.** To enter or fall *into* by slipping or losing hold 1679. **3.** To glide or pass easily *out of* (or *from*) *one's hand* or *grasp*, *through* (or *between*) *one's fingers*, etc., so as to escape or be lost. late ME. **4.** To allow oneself to drop or fall with an easy, gliding motion; to slide *down* 1470. **b.** *fig.* (*colloq.*) usu. in *pres. pple.* To be failing in strength, etc.; to 'go downhill'. **5.** Of rivers, etc.: To run smoothly or gently; to flow, glide; to pass *into* the sea 1570. **6. a.** To get *out of* or *into* a garment, etc., in an easy or hurried manner 1500. **b.** To slide *in* or *into* a socket, etc. 1815. **7.** To move easily and smoothly 1680. **b.** To admit of being taken *off*, or put *on*, by a slipping process 1669. **c.** Of bark: To peel off 1788.

1. Better the foot s. then the tongue trip 1611. **c.** Great Masters..s. sometimes unawares 1638. **2.** My axe slipped out of my hand, and slid..away from me TYNDALL. *To s. off the hooks*: see HOOK *sb.* **3.** Hold her fast, She'll s. thorow your fingers like an Eel else 1622. **4.** *To s. by the board*, to slip down by the ship's side 1867. **5.** Where the grown-up river slips Into the sea STEVENSON. **6. a.** He's slipping into a clean shirt 1893. **7. b.** I am grown somewhat fatter,..and my leathern coat slips not on so soon as it was wont SCOTT.

***Trans. senses.* **III. 1.** To cause to move with a sliding motion; to draw or pull in this manner 1513. **2. a.** To strip or take off (a garment, etc.); to cast (the skin, etc.). Occas. with advs., as *down*, *off*. 1535. **b.** To put *on* (an article of apparel) hastily or carelessly 1590. **3.** To withdraw (one's head or neck) *out of* or *from* a collar, etc. 1583. **4.** To insert or introduce gently or surreptitiously. Const. *in*, *into*. 1688. **b.** *Cards.* To palm (a card) 1807. **c.** To give quietly or slyly 1841. **5.** To cause to slip or lose hold; *esp.* to undo (a knot) in this way 1606. **b.** To dislocate (a joint) 1727. **c.** To suffer an accidental slipping or sliding of (one's foot) 1769.

1. A Cinnamon-Tree..bears none but its Bark, which Slips itself off every Year 1707. **2. a.** The snake slips off his skinne DEKKER. **b.** S. on your slippers and trip down the stairs 1660. **3.** *Rich. III*, IV. iv. 112. **4.** He had tried to s. a powder into her drink 1713. **5.** The bonds of heauen are slipt, dissolu'd, and loos'd SHAKS. **b.** My horse, I fear, has slipped his shoulder 1842. **c.** He slipped his foot and fell 1874.

IV. 1. †**a.** To waste or lose (time) –1687. **b.** To allow (an occasion, opportunity, etc.) to slip or pass by; to neglect or fail to take advantage of 1592. †**c.** To fail in keeping (a prescribed time) –1707. **2.** To pass over, omit in speaking; to avoid mention or consideration of 1605. **b.** To neglect; to omit or fail to prosecute, perform, etc.; to skip, to miss 1592.

1. b. S. not thine oportunity MARLOWE. **c.** *Macb.* II. iii. 52. **2.** I do slippe No action of my life, thus, but I quote it JONSON. **b.** To s. a lecture or so 1871.

V. 1. To elude or evade, esp. in a stealthy manner; to escape from; to give the slip to 1513. **b.** To get in front of; to outdistance 1856. **2.** To disengage oneself or get loose from (a collar, halter, etc.) 1579. **3.** To escape from (one's memory); to elude (one's notice, knowledge, etc.) 1652. **4.** To pass or escape inadvertently from (the pen, tongue, etc.) 1751.

1. He sees me; 'tis too late to s. him 1702. **2.** Rascality has slipped its muzzle CARLYLE. **3.** Reasons..which have slipt my memory 1652.

VI. 1. To allow to escape (from one's hand, etc.); to loosen one's hold or grasp of, let go 1586. **b.** To allow to occur; to utter inadvertently. Also with *out*. 1591. †**c.** *To s. one's breath* or *wind*, to expire, die. *colloq.* or *dial.* 1819. **d.** *Knitting.* To pass (a stitch) from one needle to the other without knitting it 1880. **e.** To detach (the end carriage or coach) from an express or non-stopping train while running, in order to allow passengers to get out at a certain station 1866. **2.** To release (a greyhound, etc., or a hawk) from a leash or slip 1596. **3.** *Naut.* To allow (an anchor-cable, etc.) to run out, freq. with a buoy attached, when quitting an anchorage in haste; to drop or disengage (an anchor) in this way. Also *absol.* 1681. **b.** *To s. one's cable*, to die 1751. **4.** Of animals: To miscarry with; to drop prematurely 1665.

1. b. They..mortified us..by slipping out an oath GOLDSM. **2.** When they grow ripe for marriage They must be slipt like Hawkes 1625. **3.** *absol.* Vessels are obliged to s. and run for their lives on the first sign of a gale 1840. **4.** The cheese may swell, or the cows may s. their calf GEO. ELIOT.

Slip (slip), *v.*[2] 1498. [– (M)LG., MDu. *slippen* cut, incise, cleave, etc.] †**1.** *trans.* To cut (a spoon-handle) obliquely at the end –1549. **2.** To part (a slip or cutting) from a stock, stalk, or branch, esp. for propagation; to divide (a plant, root, etc.) *into* slips 1530.

1. ij spones of sylver slipped at the endes 1538. **2.** *absol.* I would I were a Gardiner, and had skill To digge and rake, and plant, and sowe, and slippe 1614.

Slip-, the stem of SLIP *v.*[1] in comb., as **s.-buoy**, a buoy attached to a cable when slipping an anchor; **-carriage, -coach**, a railway carriage detached at a station from a moving train; **-noose**, a noose which tightens and slackens by means of a slip-knot; **-rail** *Austral.* a fence-rail, forming one of a set which can be slipped out so as to leave an opening; chiefly *pl.*; **-stitch**, one slipped over the following stitch without being knitted. **2.** In comb. with advs., as **s.-on**, something that may be slipped on readily, *esp.* a great-coat or overall; so **-over**.

Slipe (sləip), *sb. Sc.* and *north.* 1470. [app. – LG. *slīpe*, var. of the usual *slēpe*, = MHG. *sleife* (G. *schleife*) sledge, train, loop, knot, etc., rel. to LG. *slīpen* whet, and *slēpen* to drag.] A sledge or drag. **b.** *Mining. pl.* Sledge-runners, upon which a skip is dragged from the working breast to the tramway 1860.

Slip-knot (sli·pˌnǫt). Also **slip knot.** 1659. [f. SLIP *v.*[1]] **a.** A knot which may readily be slipped or untied. **b.** A knot so constructed as to slip along the cord or line round which it is made; a running knot; also, a noose.

Slippage (sli·pėdʒ). 1850. [f. SLIP *v.*[1] + -AGE.] **a.** The act of slipping or subsiding. **b.** Amount or extent of slip.

Slipped (slipt), *ppl. a.* 1610. [f. SLIP *v.*[2] + -ED[1].] *Her.* Represented as torn from the stem.

Slipper (sli·pəɹ), *sb.* 1478. [f. SLIP *v.*[1] + -ER[1]; for the use of -ER[1] in I. 1 cf. *drawers.*] **I. 1.** A light and sometimes heelless covering for the foot, capable of being easily slipped on, and worn chiefly indoors. **b.** *transf.* The lip or labellum of an orchid 1902. **2. a.** A form of skid used to retard the speed of a vehicle in descending a hill 1827. **b.** A device for conveying electricity from a conductor rail to a tram or train 1900. **II.** *Coursing.* The person appointed to slip the hounds at the proper moment 1825.

I. 1. If 'twere a kybe 'Twould put me to my s. SHAKS. A s. of his of red velvet, with a very low heel 1756. *Hunt the s.*: see HUNT *v. Comb.*: **s. animalcule**, a common infusorian of the genus *Paramecium*; **-bath**, a partially covered bath shaped somewhat like a s.; **s.-brake, -drag,** = sense I. 2 a; **s. limpet,** a limpet of the family *Acmæidæ*; **s. shell,** a shell of the genus *Crepidula*; **slipperwort,** the calceolaria or campanula.

Slipper (sli·pəɹ), *a. Obs.* exc. *dial.* [OE. *slipor* slippery, morally unstable, = MLG. *slipper*, f. **slip-*; see SLIP *sb.*[1] and *v.*[1]] = SLIPPERY *a.*

As on a s. grounde, oft man doth fall or slide 1510. A s., and subtle knaue, a finder of occasion SHAKS.

Slippered (sli·pəɹd), *ppl. a.* 1600. [f. SLIPPER *sb.* + -ED[2].] **1.** Wearing or shod with slippers. **2.** Characterized by the wearing of slippers 1817. **3.** Retarded by means of a slipper-brake 1905.

1. The leane and slipper'd Pantaloone SHAKS. **2.** He leaned back...enjoying s. ease 1856.

Slippery (sli·pəri), *a.* 1535. [First recorded from Coverdale's tr. of the Bible (Ps. 35:6), who prob. modelled it on Luther's *schlipfferig*, MHG. *slipferig*, f. *slipfern*, extension of *slipfen*, f. Gmc. **slip-*, as repr. in OE. *slipor* (cf. SLIPPER *a.*, SLIP *sb.*[1]); partly alt. of

SLIPPER *a.*] **1.** Having a smooth, polished, or slimy surface, which renders foothold insecure. **2.** Of a soft oily or greasy consistency; having a smooth surface, so as to slip or slide easily; slipping readily from any hold or grasp 1551. **b.** Of persons: Difficult to catch or hold 1573. **3.** Of conditions, affairs, etc.: Unstable, uncertain, insecure; that cannot be relied upon as lasting or assured 1548. **4.** Of persons: Not to be depended on; shifty, deceitful 1555. **b.** Of actions, etc.: Characterized by shiftiness, deceitfulness, or want of sincerity 1579. **5.** Licentious, unchaste; of doubtful morality. *Obs.* or *arch.* 1586. **6.** Liable or prone to slip; readily giving way. Also of the memory, forgetful. 1548.

1. The rocks were steep and s. 1871. **2.** The chiefest that is marked in the Ele is that it is slipperie 1567. *S. elm*, the N. Amer. red elm, *Ulmus fulva*, or the inner bark of this, used medicinally; also, a Californian shrub, *Fremontia californica*, with similar bark. **b.** The slipp'ry God will try to loose his hold DRYDEN. **3.** O slipp'ry State Of human pleasures 1704. **4.** The s. politicians in the capital FROUDE. **b.** He exercised a s. perseverance and a vindictive resolution THACKERAY. **5.** He shall cause hir. . to become slipperie & lascivious 1586. Hence **Sli·pperily** *adv.* **Sli·pperiness.**

Slippy (sli·pi), *a.* 1548. *dial.* or *colloq.* [f. SLIP *v.*[1] + -Y[1].] **1.** = SLIPPERY *a.*, in various senses. **2.** Of persons: Nimble, spry; sharp, quick; *esp.* in phr. *to be* or *look s.* 1847. Hence **Sli·ppiness.**

Slipshod (sli·pʃǫd), *a.* 1580. [f. SLIP *v.*[1] + SHOD *ppl. a.*, after SLIP-SHOE.] **1.** Wearing slippers or very loose shoes, in later use esp. such as are down at the heel. **b.** Of shoes: Loose or untidy; in bad condition; down at the heel 1687. **c.** In shabby condition 1818. **2.** *fig.* Slovenly, careless 1815.

1. With each foot in a cod's decapitated head and looking very slip-shod 1851. **b.** Old slip-shod shoes SCOTT. **c.** Half-bound and slip-shod volumes SCOTT. **2.** She reigned supreme in a slip-shod household 1880.

Sli·p-shoe. *Obs.* exc. *dial.* 1555. [f. SLIP *v.*[1] + SHOE *sb.*] A light or loose shoe; a slipper.

Slip-slop (sli·pˌslǫp), *sb.* 1675. [Reduplication of SLOP *sb.*[2] with vowel variation. In sense 2 with allusion to Mrs. Slipslop's blunders in *Joseph Andrews* (1742).] **1.** A sloppy compound used as a food, beverage, or medicine. †**2.** A blunder in the use of words, esp. the ludicrous misuse of one word for another; the habit of making such blunders –1837. **3.** Twaddle; loose or trifling talk or writing 1811.

2. One of the party (amongst other slipslops) saying instead of *Pasticcios*, he liked *Pistachios* 1826. Hence **Sli·p-slop** *a.* given to the use of slip-slops; of the nature of s. **Sli·p-slop** *v. intr.* to make blunders in the use of words; also, to move about in a sloppy manner or with a flapping sound.

Sli·p-string. Now *dial.* 1546. [f. SLIP *v.*[1] + STRING *sb.*] One who deserves to be hanged; a rogue or rascal, a shifty person.

Slip-way (sli·pweⁱ). Also **slipway.** 1840. [f. SLIP- + WAY *sb.*] A sloping way leading down to the water; a slip.

Slit (slit), *sb.* ME. [f. SLIT *v.*] **1.** A straight and narrow cut or incision; an aperture resembling a cut of this description. **b.** A long narrow aperture in a wall; a window of this form 1607. **2.** *Coal-mining.* A short heading which connects two other headings 1860.

1. c. *spec.* A narrow opening in an optical instrument through which the light is admitted 1832. *attrib.* and *Comb.*: **s.-eyed** *a.*, having long and narrow eyes; **-planting, -setting,** a mode of planting in which mere slits are made in the ground; **-pocket,** a side-pocket made with a vertical opening.

Slit (slit), *v.* Pa. t. and pa. pple. **slit.** [ME. *slitte*, repr. OE. **slittan*, rel. to *slītan* = OFris. *slita*, OS. *slītan*, OHG. *slīzan* (Du. *slijten*, G. *schleissen*), ON. *slíta*, f. Gmc. base having no known cogns.] **1.** *trans.* To cut into, or cut open, by means of a sharp instrument or weapon; to divide or sever by making a long straight cut or fissure; also, to take *off* or *out* in this way. **b.** *fig.* To divide, separate, sever ME. **2.** *techn.* To cut (iron) into rods or (wood) into thin deals 1522.

1. He s. the villaines nose that would haue sent me to the Iaile SHAKS. **b.** Comes the blind Fury with th' abhorred shears, And slits the thin spun life MILT. Hence **Sli·tter,** one who or that which slits; *spec.* as the name of various instruments.

Slit, *ppl. a.* late ME. [f. prec.] **1.** Of garments: Rent, torn; slashed. **2.** Naturally divided or cloven 1607. **3.** Cut with a sharp instrument; divided by slitting 1611.

Slither (sli·ðəɹ), *v.* ME. [alt. of SLIDDER *v.*; for the change of d to ð cf. *hither, together*, etc.] **1.** *intr.* To slip, slide, glide, esp. on a loose or broken slope or with a clattering noise. **b.** *trans.* To make or cause to slide 1892. **2.** *intr.* To walk in a sliding manner; to slip along or away 1848. **3.** Of reptiles: To creep, crawl, glide 1839. Hence **Sli·ther** *sb.* a slipping or sliding.

Sli·tless, *a.* 1881. [f. SLIT *sb.* + -LESS.] Of a spectroscope: Made without the usual slit for admitting light.

Slitting (sli·tiŋ), *vbl. sb.* ME. [f. SLIT *v.* + -ING[1].] The action of making a slit or slits, or of cutting in this manner.

Comb.: **s.-mill** *Metall.*, a mill or machine by which iron bars or plates are slit into nail-rods, etc.; also, a saw-mill for slitting deals.

Slive (sləiv), *v.*[1] Now *dial.* [OE. **slīfan*, occurring in pa. t. *tō|slāf*, but without any known cognates. Cf. SLEAVE *v.*] **1.** *trans.* To cleave, split, divide ME. **2.** To remove, to take *off*, by cutting or slicing. late ME. Hence **Slive** *sb.* a slice (now *dial.*).

Slive (slǝiv), *v.*[2] Now *dial.* late ME. [app. var. of †*sleve*, vb., repr. OE. *slēfan*.] **1.** *trans.* To cause to slip *down, over*, etc.; to slip *on* (a garment). **b.** To convey furtively or quietly 1821. **2.** *intr.* To slide; to slip 1440. **b.** To slip *off* or away; to sneak or hang about; to loiter, idle 1707.

Sliver (sli·vəɹ, ˈslәi·vəɹ), *sb.* late ME. [Of obscure formation on the base of SLIVE *v.*[1]] **1.** A piece cut or split off; a splinter, shiver, slice. **b.** *U.S.* The side of a small fish sliced off in one piece for use as bait 1880. **2.** A continuous ribbon or band of loose, untwisted, parallelized fibres of wool, cotton, flax, etc., ready for drawing, roving, or slubbing 1703. **3.** A slashing cut or stroke 1806.

1. An enuious sliuer broke, When downe the weedy Trophies, and her selfe, Fell in the weeping Brooke SHAKS.

Sliver (sli·ver, slǝi·vəɹ), *v.* 1605. [f. SLIVER *sb.*] **1.** *trans.* To separate or remove as a sliver; to cut, split, or tear into slivers. **b.** *intr.* To split, or split off 1880. **2.** *trans.* To convert (textile fibres) into slivers 1796.

1. Slippes of Yew, Sliuer'd in the Moones Ecclipse SHAKS.

Slob (slǫb), *sb.* 1780. [Mainly – Ir. *slab* (slǫb) mud – Eng. SLAB *sb.*[2] Chiefly with ref. to Ireland.] **1.** Mud, esp. soft mud on the sea-shore; ooze; muddy land. **b.** A stretch of mud or ooze 1842. *Comb.*: **s.-land,** muddy ground; *esp.* alluvial land reclaimed from water. **2.** A large soft worm, used in angling 1815. **3.** A dull, slow, untidy person; a careless workman 1861.

Slobber (slǫ·bəɹ), *sb.* late ME. [Related to next. Cf. SLABBER *sb.*[1] and SLUBBER *v.*] **1.** Mud or slime; slush, sleety rain; a sloppy mess or mixture. **2.** Slaver, slabber. Also *pl.*, a disease in rabbits marked by excessive salivation. 1755. **3.** A jelly-fish 1863.

Slobber (slǫ·bəɹ), *v.* late ME. [Earlier in ME. *byslober, beslobber* (cf. prec.), and corresp. to Du. *slobberen*, with parallel and synon. contemp. formations in SLABBER *v.* (– Scand.) and SLUBBER *v.*, Du. *slabberen*, MLG., MDu. *slubberen*; of imit. or symbolic origin.] **1.** *intr.* **a.** To feed in a slabbering manner. Now *dial.* **b.** To slaver 1733. **2.** *trans.* To wet in a dirty or disagreeable manner; to beslaver, befoul 1709. **3.** To utter thickly and indistinctly 1860. **4.** To execute carelessly or in a slovenly way. Usu. with *over.* 1694. Hence **Slo·bberer.**

Slo·bber-chops. 1667. [f. prec.] One who slobbers in eating, etc.

Slobbery (slǫ·bəri), *a.* late ME. [f. SLOBBER *sb.* or *v.* + -Y[1].] **1.** Characterized by slobber or slobbering; disagreeably wet, slimy, or dirty. **2.** Slovenly, careless 1858.

1. I will sell my Dukedome, To buy a slobbry and a durtie Farme SHAKS.

Slock (slǫk), *v.* Chiefly *Sc.* ME. [f. ON. *slokinn* pa. pple., extinguished; the stem is related to that of SLACK *a.*] *trans.* To extinguish, quench (fire, thirst, etc.). †**b.** To slake (lime) –1655. So **Slo·cken** *v.* [– ON. *slokna*.] *north.* and *Sc.*

Sloe (slōᵘ). [OE. *slā(h* = MLG., MDu. *slē*, *sleuuwe* (LG. *slē, slī*, Du. *slee*), OHG. *slēha, slēwa* (G. *schlehe*) :– Gmc. **slaixwōn*, which has been connected with L. *livēre* be blue, OSl. (Russ.) *sliva* plum.] **1.** The fruit of the blackthorn (*Prunus spinosa*), a small ovate or globose drupe of a black or dark-purple colour and sharp sour taste. **2.** The blackthorn, *Prunus spinosa* 1753.

Comb: **s.-thorn, -tree,** the blackthorn.

Slog (slǫg), *sb. colloq.* 1888. [f. the vb.] **1.** Hard, steady work; a spell of this. **2.** A vigorous blow; a hard hit at cricket 1895.

Slog (slǫg), *v. colloq.* 1824. [Of unkn. origin. Cf. SLUG *v.*[3]] **1.** *trans.* To hit or strike hard; to drive with blows; *fig.* to assail violently. **b.** *intr. Cricket* and *Boxing.* To hit hard and wildly 1880. **2.** To walk heavily or doggedly 1872. **3.** To deal heavy blows, to work hard (*at* something), to labour *away*, etc. 1888.

2. We 'slogged' on. . for a mile or more 1907.

Slogan (slōᵘ·gǎn). 1513. [– Gael. *sluagh-ghairm*, f. *sluagh* host + *gairm* cry, shout.] A Highland or native Irish war-cry or battle-cry. **b.** *transf.* The distinctive note, phrase, cry, etc. of any person or body of persons 1704.

The Name of Hume have for their Slughorn (or S., as our Southern Shires terme it) a *Hume, a Hume* 1689. **b.** 'Duty, God, immortality',—the very s. of the pulpit 1880. **c.** Also in extended use.

Slogger (slǫ·gəɹ), *sb. colloq.* 1857. [f. SLOG *v.* + -ER[1].] One who slogs or delivers heavy blows. Also *fig.* an indefatigable worker.

Sloom (slūm), *sb.* *n. dial.* and *Sc.* [OE. *slūma*; see SLUMBER *v.*] A gentle sleep or slumber; a light doze. So **Sloom** *v. intr.*

Sloo·my, *a. dial.* 1641. [f. dial. *sloom* vb., app. of Scand. origin; see -Y[1].] **1. a.** Of grain: Not properly filled. **b.** Of corn, etc.: Laid through being soft and heavy; beginning to rot 1825. **2.** Sluggish, dull, spiritless. Also as *adv.* 1820.

Sloop (slūp). 1629. [– Du. *sloep*, †*sloepe* (whence also Fr. *chaloupe*, whence Eng. SHALLOP); of unkn. origin.] **1.** A small, one-masted, fore-and-aft rigged vessel, differing from a cutter in having a jib-stay and standing bowsprit. **b.** A relatively small ship-of-war, carrying guns on the upper deck only. Also *s.-of-war.* 1676. †**2.** A long-boat –1719.

Slop (slǫp), *sb.*[1] late ME. [OE. *slop*, in *oferslop* surplice, corresp. to MDu. *(over)slop*, ON. *(yfir)sloppr*, f. Gmc. **slup-*, rel. to **slūp-* in OE. *slūpan*, etc., glide.] **1.** An outer garment, as a loose jacket, tunic, cassock, mantle, gown, or smock-frock. **2.** *pl.* Wide baggy breeches or hose; loose trousers, esp. those worn by sailors. Now chiefly *dial.* 1481. †**b.** *sing.* in the same sense, or denoting only one leg of the garment –1652. **3.** *pl.* Ready-made clothing and other furnishings supplied to seamen from the ship's stores; hence, ready-made, cheap, or inferior garments generally 1663.

2. He would give an occasional hitch, Sailor-like, to his 'slops' 1842. **b.** Signior Romeo, *Bon iour*, there's a French salutation to your French s. SHAKS.

Comb.: **s.-builder,** a jerry-builder; **s.-built** *a.*, jerry-built, *fig.* loosely built or made.

Slop (slǫp), *sb.*[2] late ME. [prob. repr. OE. **sloppe* as in *cūsloppe* COWSLIP, OXLIP, rel. to *slyppe* SLIP *sb.*[2]] †**1.** A muddy place; a mud-hole. late ME. only. **b.** Slush 1796. **2.** An act of spilling or splashing; a quantity of liquid spilled or splashed 1727. **3.** Liquid or semi-liquid food of a weak, unappetizing kind; applied contemptuously to invalids' spoon-food, tea, etc. Now. usu. *pl.* 1657. **b.** *fig.* Weak or sickly sentiment 1924. **4.** Refuse liquid of any kind; rinsings of tea, coffee, etc.; the dirty water, etc., of a household. Usu. *pl.* 1815.

Comb.: **s.-basin,** a basin for holding slops; **-moulding,** a process in which the mould is dipped into water before it receives the clay.

Slop (slǫp), *sb.*[3] 1859. [For *ecilop*, back-slang for *police*.] A policeman.

Slop (slǫp), *v.* 1557. [f. SLOP *sb.*[2]] **1.** *trans.* To spill or splash (liquid); to dash or lay *on* carelessly. Also with *over*. **2.** To gobble *up*. Now *dial.* 1575. **3.** To make wet with spilled liquid 1721. **4.** To walk or travel *through* a place in mud or slush. Also with *along* or *on*. 1834. **5.** To run or flow *over*; to flow or dash *up* 1853. **b.** *fig.* With *over*. To overflow with expressions of weak sentiment, speak or act without restraint, gush (orig. *U.S.*) 1859.

Slope (slōᵘp), *sb.*[1] 1611. [Aphetic f. ASLOPE *adv.*] **1.** A stretch of rising or falling ground; a portion of the earth's surface marked by a gradual ascent or descent, whether natural or artificial 1626. **b.** An inclined surface of the nature of a bank, *esp.* one artificially constructed, as in fortification or engineering 1702. **c.** *Mining.* An inclined roadway 1874. **2.** Upward or downward inclination; deviation from the horizontal or perpendicular 1611. **b.** *Mil.* A position against the shoulder between perpendicular and horizontal (in the case of the rifle, with the hand under the butt) 1868. **3.** A slant; an inclined surface of any kind 1707.

1. A s. of country. . very well wooded 1799. **3. b.** *Bacteriol.* = SLANT *sb.*[1] 1 f. 1925. **c.** *Radio.* Mutual conductance 1918. Hence **Slo·py** *a.* sloping.

Slope (slōᵘp), *sb.*[2] *colloq.* 1859. [f. SLOPE *v.*[2]] An act of making off, running, or slinking away, etc.

Slope (slōᵘp), *a.* Now *poet.* 1502. [f. as SLOPE *sb.*[1]] Sloping, slanting.

There the Water Rowleth, and Moveth, . . with a Sloper Rise, and Fall BACON. Hence †**Slo·peness,** the condition of having a s.; sloping form or position –1624. **Slo·peways** *adv.* in a sloping manner or position; so **Slo·pewise** *adv.*

Slope (slōᵘp), *v.*[1] 1591. [f. as SLOPE *sb.*[1]] **1.** *intr.* To take, to move or proceed in, an oblique direction. **2.** To assume, to have or be in, a sloping or slanting position or direction 1707. **3.** *trans.* To bring into, to place or put in, a sloping or slanting position; to bend down; to direct downwards or obliquely 1605. **b.** *spec.* To bring (a weapon) into, or hold (it) in, a sloping position; now, to carry (a rifle) at the slope 1625. **4.** To cut, form, or make with a slope or slant 1611.

1. The sun was sloping down the sky COLERIDGE. **2.** The corner where the mountain slopes down to the river 1877. **3.** Though Pallaces and Pyramids do s. Their heads to their Foundations SHAKS.

Slope (slōᵘp), *v.*[2] *colloq.* 1839. [orig. U.S.; cf. SLOPE *v.*[1] 1.] **1.** *intr.* To make off, depart, decamp. **b.** To go loiteringly or saunteringly 1851. **2.** *trans.* To leave (lodgings) without paying 1908.

1. If it is dull, they s. off 1861.

Slope (slōᵘp), *adv.* 1470. [Aphetic f. ASLOPE *adv.*] In a sloping or slanting manner or position. (In later use only *poet.*)

Hyperion. . Came s. upon the threshold of the west KEATS.

Slope- in combs., repr. SLOPE *v.*[1] or *sb.*[1], with sbs., as *slope-desk, s. line*, and in parasynthetic compounds, as *slope-roofed* adj.

Sloping (slōᵘ·piŋ), *ppl. a.* 1610. [f. SLOPE *v.*[1] + -ING[2].] That slopes.

With sloping masts and dipping prow. . The ship drove fast COLERIDGE. Hence **Slo·pingly** *adv.*

Sloppy (slǫ·pi), *a.* 1727. [f. SLOP *sb.*[2] + -Y[1].] **1.** Of ground, etc.: Very wet and splashy; covered with water or thin mud. **2.** Of a semi-liquid consistency; watery and disagreeable 1794. **3.** Splashed or soiled with liquid; wet from slopping; covered with slops; messy 1838. **4.** Weak, feeble; lacking in firmness or precision; slovenly; feebly sentimental 1825. **5.** Of dress: Loose, slack, ill-fitting 1825.

1. A wet, s., windy, October day 1890. **2.** The rain began to fall, the ice to get s. 1846. **3.** Idlers, playing cards or dominoes on the s., beery tables 1848. Hence **Slo·ppily** *adv.* **Slo·ppiness.**

Slo·p-seller. 1665. [SLOP *sb.*[1]] A dealer in slop-clothing.

The slop-sellers, and other sharks, at this port 1804.

Slo·p-shop. 1723. [SLOP *sb.*[1]] A shop where slop-clothing is sold.

Slo·p-work. 1849. [f. SLOP *sb.*[1]] **1.** The making of slop-garments; the articles thus made. **2.** Work cheaply and badly done 1861. So **Slo·p-wo:rker.**

Slosh (slǫʃ), *sb.* 1814. [var. of SLUSH *sb.*[1]] **1.** Slush, sludge. **2.** Watery, weak, or unappetizing drink 1819. Hence **Slo·shy** *a.* slushy.

Slosh (slǫʃ), *v.* 1844. [f. prec. or imitative.] **1.** *intr.* To splash about in mud or wet. **2.** *U.S.* To move aimlessly; to loaf about 1854. **3.** To make a splashing sound 1888.

Slot (slǫt), *sb.*[1] Chiefly *north.* and *Sc.* ME. [– (M)LG., (M)Du. *slot* = OHG. *sloʒ* (G. *schloss*) door-bolt, lock, castle, f. WGmc. **slut-* (**slūt-*) **sleut-*, whence also OS. *slutil*, OHG. *sluʒʒil* (G. *schlüssel*) key, OFris. *slūta*, MLG., MDu. *slūten* (Du. *sluiten*), OHG. *sliozan* (G. *schliessen*) close, lock.] **1.** A bar or bolt used to secure a door, window, etc., when closed. Now *dial.* **2.** A metal rod; a flat wooden bar, esp. one forming a cross-piece. late ME.

Slot (slǫt), *sb.*[2] late ME. [– OFr. *esclot* in sense 1, of unkn. origin.] **1.** The slight depression or hollow running down the middle of the breast. Now *Sc.* and *rare*. **2.** An elongated narrow depression or perforation made in the thickness of a piece of timber, etc., usually for the reception of some other part or piece, whether fixed or movable 1523. **b.** The opening in a slot-machine for the reception of a coin 1888. **3.** *dial.* The open hem in which the strings of a purse, work-bag, night-cap, etc. run 1796.

attrib.: **s.-machine, -meter,** a machine or meter which is operated by inserting a coin in a s.

Slot (slǫt), *sb.*[3] 1575. [– OFr. *esclot* horse's hoof-print, prob. – ON. *slóð* track; see SLEUTH *sb.*[2]] **1.** The track or trail of an animal, esp. a deer, as shown by the marks of the foot; occas. misapplied to the scent of an animal; hence *gen.*, track, trace, trail. **2.** A deer's foot 1876.

1. The s. of the bear is quite like that of a human being 1865.

Comb.: **s.-hound,** a sleuth-hound. Hence **Slot** *v.*[3] *trans.* to trace by the s.; to follow the track of (a stag, etc.).

Slot (slǫt), *v.*[1] Now *dial.* 1563. [f. SLOT *sb.*[1] 1.] **1.** *trans.* To bolt (a door). **2.** To secure (a lock) by shooting a bolt 1904.

Slot (slǫt), *v.*[2] late ME. [f. SLOT *sb.*[2]] †**1.** *trans.* To pierce through the 'slot'. late ME. only. **2.** To cut a slot or slots in; to furnish with a slot. Also with *out*. 1747. **b.** *Coal-mining.* To hole 1883. **3.** To drop (a coin) through a slot in a slot-machine 1888. Hence **Slo·tted** *ppl. a.* having a slot or slots.

Sloth (slōᵘþ), *sb.* [ME. *slauþe, slouhþe*, later †*sloath, sloth* (XVI), f. *slāw, slōw*; see SLOW *a.*, -TH[1]; replacing OE. *slǣwþ* SLEUTH *sb.*[1]] **1.** Physical or mental inactivity; disinclination to action, exertion, or labour; sluggishness, indolence: as one of the seven deadly sins = L. *accidia*. **2.** Slowness; tardiness. late ME. **3.** A company *of* bears 1452. **4.** An edentate arboreal mammal of a sluggish nature, inhabiting tropical parts of Central and South America 1613. **b.** Applied to other animals, as the sloth-bear, the koala or koolah, the slow lori or lemur, and the mylodon or megatherium 1790.

Combs.: **s.-animalcule,** a tardigrade; **-bear,** an Indian species of bear (*Melursus labiatus* or *ursinus*); **-monkey,** the slow lori or lemur.

Sloth (slōᵘþ), *v.* Now *rare.* late ME. [f. SLOTH *sb.*] †**1.** *trans.* To allow to slip through slothfulness or delay; to neglect –1708. †**b.** To pass *away* (time) in idleness –1676. **2.** *intr.* To be or become indolent or lazy. late ME.

Slothful (slōᵘ·þfŭl), *a.* late ME. [f. SLOTH *sb.* + -FUL.] **1.** Of persons, etc.: Full of sloth; indisposed to exertion; inactive, indolent, lazy, sluggish. **2.** Of habits, etc.: Characterized by sloth or disinclination to exertion. late ME.

1. Hee is the true Slothfull man that does no good DEKKER. Hence **Slo·thful-ly** *adv.*, **-ness.**

Slotting (slǫ·tiŋ), *vbl. sb.* 1841. [f. SLOT *v.*[2] + -ING[1].] **1.** The action of making or cutting a slot or slots 1844. **b.** *attrib.*, as *s.-machine(ry* 1841. **2.** *Coal-mining. pl.* Coal cut away in the process of holing 1883.

Slouch (slautʃ), *sb.* 1515. [Of unkn. origin; sense 3 is from the vb.] **1.** An awkward, slovenly, or ungainly man; a lubber, lout, clown; also, a lazy, idle fellow. **b.** *U.S. slang.* A poor, indifferent, or inefficient place, thing, person, etc. 1869. **2.** *ellipt.* A slouch hat or bonnet 1714. **3.** A stooping, or bending forward of the head and shoulders, in walking; a loose, ungainly carriage or bearing; a walk or gait characterized by this 1725. Hence **Slou·chy** *a.* slouching, slovenly, untidy.

Slouch, *a. rare.* 1688. [From the *sb.* or *v.*, or back-formation from Combs. like *slouch-eared*.] †**1.** Drooping or hanging loosely; slouching –1829. **2.** *dial.* Clownish, loutish; slovenly 1837. **3.** Slouched 1837.

Slouch (slautʃ), *v.* 1754. [Back-formation from the earlier SLOUCHING *ppl. a.*] **1.** *intr.* To move or walk with a slouch or in a loose and stooping attitude. **b.** To carry oneself with a slouch or stoop; to droop the head and shoulders 1755. **c.** Of a hat: To hang down, droop 1818. **2.** *trans.* To put on, or pull down, (one's hat) in such a way that it partly conceals the face (cf. SLOUCH HAT and SLOUCHING *ppl. a.* 3) 1760.

1. b. He slouched over his oar very badly at the finish 1884. **2.** His hat was unlooped and slouched SCOTT.

Slouched (slautʃt), *a.* 1779. [f. SLOUCH *sb.* or *v.* + -ED.] *S. hat* = next.

Slouch hat. 1837. [For *slouched hat*.] A hat of soft or unstiffened felt or other material, esp. one having a broad brim which hangs or lops down over the face.

Slouching (slau·tʃiŋ), *ppl. a.* 1611. [f. SLOUCH *sb.* + -ING[2].] **1.** Hanging down, drooping (*rare*). **2.** Having an awkward, stooping, slip-shod carriage or gait; moving with a slouch 1668. **3.** Of a hat: Having a brim which hangs over the face 1691. **4.** Characterized by a slouch 1773.

3. They wear the sombrero, or broad s. hat of Spain BORROW. Hence **Slou·chingly** *adv.*

Slough (slau), *sb.*[1] [OE. *slōh, slō(g*, of unkn. origin.] **1.** A piece of soft, miry, or muddy ground; *esp.* a place or hole in a road or way filled with wet mud or mire and impassable by heavy vehicles, horses, etc. **b.** *fig.* A state or condition (esp. of moral degradation) in which a person, etc., sinks or has sunk ME. †**2.** The matter of which a slough is composed; soft mud or mire –1776. †**3.** A ditch, dike, or drain –1685. **4.** *U.S.* (slū). A marsh or reedy pool, pond, small lake, backwater or inlet 1817.

1. Many a time enclos'd in the midst of sloughs and quagmires MILT. **b.** *S. of Despond*, after Bunyan's use: a state of despair or despondency.

attrib.: **s. grass,** a name in the Mississippi valley for *Muhlenbergia glomerata* and *M. mexicana*.

Slough (slɒf), *sb.*[2] [ME. *sloh, sloȝ*, poss. rel. to LG. *sluwe, slu* husk, peel, shell.] **1.** The outer or scarf skin periodically cast or shed by a snake, adder, etc.; also generally, the skin of a serpent, eel, etc. **b.** The skin of a caterpillar, locust, etc. cast in the course of transformation, as from the nymphal to the imago stage 1681. **c.** *fig.* A feature, quality, etc. which is thrown off 1583. **2.** A skin, caul, or membrane, enclosing or covering the body or some part of it ME. **b.** An enclosing or covering layer, coat, or sheath of some kind 1610. **c.** *dial.* The outer skin of certain fruits; a husk 1660. **3.** *Path.* A layer or mass of dead tissue or flesh formed on the surface of a wound, sore, or inflammation; a sphacelus 1513.

1. c. Are we to give them. . the s. of slavery, which we are not able to work off, to serve them for their freedom? BURKE.

Slough (slɒf), *v.* 1720. [f. SLOUGH *sb.*[2]] **1.** *intr.* Of diseased tissue, etc.: To come *away* or *off*, to be shed, as a slough. **b.** To become covered with a slough; to form or develop necrosed tissue 1787. **2.** *trans.* To eat *away*, to throw *off*, by the formation of a slough or sloughs 1762. **3.** Of a serpent, etc.: To cast or shed (the skin) as a slough; to exuviate 1845. **b.** *fig.* To cast *off*, drop, discard, give up, get rid of (something) 1845. **4.** To take *off* in grinding 1844.

1. The diseased part. . sloughs away, and new and healthy skin is reproduced 1847. **3. b.** She could s. off a sadness and replace it by a hope T. HARDY.

Sloughing (slɒ·fiŋ), *vbl. sb.* 1800. [f. SLOUGH *v.* + -ING[1].] **1.** *Path.* The process of forming a slough. **2.** The action or process of casting a slough; exuviation 1835.

Sloughy (slau·i), *a.*[1] 1724. [f. SLOUGH *sb.*[1] + -Y[1].] Of the nature of or resembling slough; abounding in or full of slough; miry, muddy.

Sloughy (slʌ·fi), *a.*² 1483. [f. SLOUGH *sb.*² + -Y¹.] **1.** Consisting or formed of slough or cast skin (*rare*). **2.** *Path.* Of the nature of, resembling, a slough; marked or characterized by the presence of a slough or sloughs 1720.

Slovak (slo̜væ·k, slōᵘ·væk), *sb.* and *a.* Also **Slovac(k.** 1829. [– Slovak, Czech, Russ. *Slovák*, f. the stem *slov-*; see SLOVENE.] **A.** *sb.* **1.** A person belonging to a Slavonic race dwelling in the north-western part of Hungary. **2.** The language or dialect spoken by this people 1862. **B.** *adj.* Of or belonging to the Slovaks, or their language 1887. Hence **Slova·kian** *a.* and *sb.*

Sloven (slʌ·v'n), *sb.* and *a.* 1450. [perh. based on Flem. *sloef* dirty, squalid, Du. *slof* negligent.] **A.** *sb.* †**1.** A knave, rascal –1680. **2.** An untidy or dirty person 1530. **3.** One who works, etc. in a careless, perfunctory or slipshod manner; a writer who is careless in style or composition 1771.

2. Marriage..often melts down a Beau into an errant S. 1700. **3.** It must be conceded that we moderns are but slovens in composition LANDOR.

B. *adj.* Slovenly. Also *U.S.*, uncultivated, untrained. 1815. Hence **Slo·venry,** slovenliness (now *rare*) 1542.

Slovene (slovī·n), *sb.* and *a.* 1883. [– G. *Slowene* – Styrian, etc. *Slovenec* (pl. *-enci*), f. OSl. *Slov-* (as also in SLOVAK), held by some to be f. stem of *slovo* word, *sloviti* speak.] **A.** *sb.* A member of the Serbo-Croatian group of Slavonic peoples, dwelling in Styria, Carinthia, Carniola, and adjacent parts; a Wend. **B.** *adj.* Slovenian 1902.

Slovenian (slovī·niăn), *a.* and *sb.* 1844. [f. prec. + -IAN.] **A.** *adj.* Belonging or pertaining to the Slovenes. **B.** *sb.* The language of the Slovenes. So **Slove·nish** *a.* and *sb.*

Slovenly (slʌ·v'nli), *a.* 1515. [f. SLOVEN *sb.* + -LY¹.] †**1.** Low, base, rascally; lewd (*rare*) –1579. **2.** Of persons: **a.** Careless in dress or appearance; untidy 1583. **b.** Careless or negligent in work of any kind 1781. **3.** Of dress, appearance, habits, etc.: Marked or characterized by untidiness or want of attention to neatness and cleanliness 1568. **4.** Marked or characterized by want of neatness, care, precision, or thoroughness 1621.

2. a. A thin, elderly man, rather threadbare and s. W. IRVING. **b.** Churchill..,Surly and s., and bold and coarse COWPER. **4.** You must suppose it spoke in a very slow and s. voice MME. D'ARBLAY. Hence **Slo·venliness,** the state or quality of being s.

Slo·venly, *adv.* 1576. [f. SLOVEN *sb.* + -LY².] In a careless, negligent, or untidy manner. Now *rare*. So †**Slo·venness,** slovenliness.

Slow (slōᵘ), *sb.* OE. [f. SLOW *a.* or *v.*] **1.** A slow or slow-going person; a sluggard. **2.** A slow-paced horse 1826. **3.** *Cricket.* **a.** A slowly-bowled ball. **b.** A slow bowler. 1862. **4.** [f. the vb.] *Slow-down, slow-up*, an act or instance of slowing a train, etc. 1891.

1. Hou longe, slowe, thou slepist? WYCLIF *Prov.* 24:33.

Slow (slōᵘ), *a.* [OE. *slāw* = OFris. *slēwich*, WFris. *sleau*, OS. *slēu*, MDu. *sleeuw, slee*, OHG. *slēo* (G. dial. *schleh*), ON. *slær, sljár, sljór* :– Gmc. **slǣwaz* :– IE. **slēwos*, of unkn. origin.] **I. 1.** Not quick or clever in apprehending or understanding a thing; obtuse, dull. **2.** Constitutionally inert or sluggish; lacking in promptness or energy OE. **b.** *Med.* Torpid, sluggish 1896. **3.** Not quick, ready, prompt, or willing *to* do something ME. **4.** Tardy or dilatory in action; displaying a lack of promptitude or energy under particular circumstances; doing something in a slow or deliberate manner ME. **5.** Not readily stirred or moved *to* something (esp. anger, revenge, etc.); not too ready, willing, or susceptible. Also with infin. late ME. †**b.** Inattentive *to* something –1746. **6.** Of things, actions, etc.: Marked or characterized by slowness or tardiness ME. **b.** *Med.* Of the pulse: Below the average rapidity 1728. **7.** Of a fire: That burns gently or slowly. Also *transf.* of heat. 1604. **8.** *colloq.* Slow-going; behind the times; out of fashion; not smart or up-to-date 1827. **b.** Dull or tedious; tiresome; apt to bore one 1841. **c.** Of persons: Dull, lifeless, insipid; humdrum 1841.

1. Such reasoning had no effect on the s. understanding and imperious temper of James MACAULAY. **2.** Is not Lead a mettall heauie, dull, and s.? SHAKS. **3.** Freedom..came at length, tho' s. to come DRYDEN. **4.** Seldom-readers are s. readers LAMB. He was a s. bowler 1833. **5.** Vnmooued, could, and to temptation s. SHAKS. **6.** With s. deliberation he unties His glitt'ring purse COWPER. **7.** Let it stew on a s. fire 1769. **b.** Of an oven: That cooks slowly 1846.

II. 1. Taking or requiring a comparatively long time; very gradual ME. **2. a.** Of fevers, etc.: Not rapidly developing into a serious form; not acute ME. **b.** Not rapid in operation or effect 1611. **c.** *Photogr.* Of a plate, etc.: That takes or receives impressions with comparative slowness; not quickly affected by light, and therefore requiring a longer exposure 1889. **3.** Of time: Passing slowly or heavily. Also *transf.* of a dial. 1565. **b.** *S. time*, a rate of marching in which only 75 paces, of 30 inches each, are taken in a minute 1802. **4.** Of clocks, etc.: Behind in time. Also of the sun: Behind mean time. 1696. **b.** Of local time: Less advanced than the standard to which it is referred 1894.

1. Sweet Flowres are s., and Weeds make hast SHAKS. Intellectual education is always s. 1876. **2. c.** Also, of a lens. **3.** When the s. dial gave a pause to care ROGERS. **4.** From the 25th December to the 15th April the sun is always s. 1855.

III. 1. Moving, flowing, etc., in a slow or sluggish manner; having a relatively low speed or velocity. late ME. **2. a.** Of pace, movement, etc.: Leisurely; not quick, fast, or hurried. late ME. **b.** Characterized by slowness of motion, progress, etc. 1709. **c.** Retarding, heavy 1873. **d.** Of a railway track: Utilized for traffic of low speed 1898.

1. The s. canal, the yellow-blossom'd vale GOLDSM. *N[ycticebus] tardigradus*, the common s. lemur or loris 1882. **2. a.** With wandring steps and s. MILT. **b.** A needless Alexandrine..That, like a wounded snake, drags its s. length along POPE.

Comb.: as *s.-blooded, -hearted, -witted*, adjs.; **s.-hound,** a sleuth-hound; **-match,** a rope-match made so as to burn very slowly; **s.-motion,** applied to cinema films which exhibit action at a pace slower than the natural. Hence **Slow·-ly** *adv.*, **-ness.**

Slow (slōᵘ), *adv.* 1500. [f. SLOW *a.*] In a slow or tardy manner; slowly. Now chiefly comb. as *slow-burning, -going, -running* adjs. How s. This old Moon wanes SHAKS.

Slow (slōᵘ), *v.* 1522. [f. SLOW *a.*; not continuous with OE. *slāwian* (*forslāwian*).] **I.** *trans.* †**1.** To lose (time) by delay; to put off (*rare*). **2.** To delay, check, retard; to make slower in some respect 1557. **b.** To reduce the working rate or speed of (an engine); to ease. Also with *down*. 1839. **c.** To cause (a vessel, vehicle, or train) gradually to slacken in speed. Also with *down* or *up*. 1864.

2. b. By slowing her engines, she can stop and take soundings 1859.

II. *intr.* **1.** To slacken in speed; to move or go more slowly. Also with *down, up*. 1594. **b.** Of a railway train: To move with slackening speed *into* a station, etc. 1877. **2.** To become slower, less active or vigorous, etc. Also with *down*. 1879.

1. Slowing up, the..Cunarder..drew towards us 1881. **b.** He caught sight of her just as the train was slowing into the station 1877.

†**Slow·back.** 1577. [f. SLOW *a.* + BACK *sb.*¹] **1.** A slothful person; a sluggard –1639. **2.** *attrib.* or as *adj.* Sluggish –1619.

Slow·-be:lly. 1607. [f. SLOW *a.*, after Gr. γαστέρες ἀργαί (Ep. Tit., in quot. from Epimenides).] A lazy, idle, or indolent person; a sluggard, laggard. Chiefly *pl.*

Slow·-coach. Also **slowcoach, slow coach.** 1837. [f. SLOW *a.*] One who acts, works, or moves slowly; a slow, idle, or indolent person.

Slow·-foot, *a.* 1642. [f. SLOW *a.*] Slow-footed; slow-paced.

The s. hope of the poor MORRIS. So **Slow-footed** *a.* slow of foot; that walks or goes slowly 1642.

Slow-paced, *a.* 1594. [SLOW *a.*] **1.** Having a slow pace, gait, or motion. **2.** Of time, etc.: Slow in coming or passing; tardy, lingering 1629.

2. Each slow-pac'd Minute seems to be a Year 1700.

Slow-worm (slōᵘ·wɒ̈ɹm). [OE. *slāwyrm* 'regulus', 'stellio'; the first element, which has been assim. to SLOW, is of doubtful origin; it appears, with and without the corresp. forms for WORM, in OSw. *slā* (Sw. *orm|slå*), Norw. *ormslo*.] A small harmless scincoid lizard, *Anguis fragilis*, native to most parts of Europe; the blindworm.

My supporters shall be two sloths, my crest a s. BURNS.

Sloyd (sloid). Also **slöjd.** 1885. [– Sw. *slöjd* :– ON. *slœyð* SLEIGHT *sb.*] A system of manual instruction or training in elementary woodwork, etc., orig. developed and taught in Sweden.

Slub (slʌb), *sb.*¹ Now chiefly *dial.* 1577. [perh. – MDu. *slubbe* in the same sense.] Thick sludgy mud; mire, ooze. Hence **Slub** *v.*¹ *trans.* to cover or plaster with mud.

Slub (slʌb), *v.*² Also **slubb.** 1774. [Of unkn. origin.] *trans.* To draw out and twist (wool, cotton, etc.) after carding, so as to prepare it for spinning. Hence **Slub** *sb.*², a slubbing of cotton or wool; a roving.

Slubber (slʌ·bəɹ), *sb.* 1825. [f. prec. + -ER¹.] **1.** One who manipulates a slubbing-machine 1835. **2.** A slubbing-machine 1825.

Slubber (slʌ·bəɹ), *v.* Now chiefly *dial.* 1530. [See SLOBBER *v.*] **1.** *trans.* To stain, smear, daub, soil. **b.** *fig.* To sully (renown, etc.) 1600. **2.** To perform, make, deal with, etc., in a hurried and careless manner 1550. **3.** To run or skim *over* hurriedly and in a careless or slovenly manner 1592. **4.** *intr.* To be lubberly; to slabber or slobber 1820.

1. b. If it be an honest end, That end 's the full reward and thanks but slubbers it 1625. **3.** Sometimes I..s. over my Prayers 1716. Hence **Slu·bbering** *ppl. a.* **-ly** *adv.*

Slubberdegullion (slʌ:bəɹdigʌ·lyən). 1616. *arch.* [f. prec., with fanciful addition.] A slobbering or dirty fellow; a worthless sloven.

Slu·bbing, *vbl. sb.* 1779. [f. SLUB *v.*² + -ING¹.] **1.** A process of drawing and twisting by which cotton or wool slivers are prepared for spinning. **2.** One of the loosely-compacted threads obtained by this process 1786. **3.** *collect.* Cotton or wool which has been slubbed 1836. **4.** *attrib.*, in names of apparatus for s. as *s.-billy, -machine*, etc. 1795.

Sludge (slʌdʒ). 1649. [Cf. more or less synon. SLUTCH and SLUSH; but pa. pple. *sluchched* is much earlier (XIV); prob. all symbolically expressive formations.] **1.** Mud, mire, or ooze, covering the ground or forming a deposit at the bottom of rivers, etc. **b.** *Naut.* Ice imperfectly formed, or broken up into minute pieces 1817. **2.** Any earthy or slimy matter or deposit 1702. **b.** *Metall.* Finely crushed ore mixed with water; metalliferous slime 1757. **c.** The precipitate in sewage tanks 1877.

attrib.: **s.-hole,** the hand-hole, or manhole, in a steam boiler, through which sediment can be removed. Hence **Slu·dger,** an appliance for removing the s. from a bore-hole, or for boring in quicksand.

Sludgy (slʌ·dʒi), *a.* 1782. [f. as prec. + -Y¹.] **1.** Muddy, oozy. **2.** Consisting of newly formed particles of ice; full of sludge-ice 1853.

Slue, variant of SLEW.

Slug (slʌg), *sb.*¹ late ME. [Based on a stem *slug-*; see SLUG *v.*¹] **1.** A slow, lazy fellow; a sluggard. Also, †slothfulness. †**2.** A slow-sailing vessel –1734. **3.** An animal, vehicle, etc., of a slow-moving or sluggish character 1618. **4.** A slow-moving slimy gasteropod or land-snail (of the type represented by the families *Limacidæ* and *Arionidæ*), in which the shell is rudimentary or entirely absent 1704. **5. a.** A slug-worm 1799. **b.** A sea-slug 1855.

2. [The Rose,] being a s., will never make a good man-of-war 1624.

Comb.: **s.-caterpillar,** a caterpillar of the genus *Limacodes*; **-fly,** the fly of the s.-worm; **-snail** = sense 4.

Slug (slʌg), *sb.*² 1622. [perh. identical with prec.] **1.** A piece of lead or other metal for firing from a gun; a roughly-formed bullet. **b.** *slang.* Some kind of strong drink (*obs.*); a dram; a drink. Now *U.S.* 1756. **2.** A heavy piece of crude metal, usually rounded in form; a nugget (of gold) 1891. **3.** *Printing.* A metal bar used as a division, or one produced by a linotype machine for printing from (orig. *U.S.*) 1871. **4.** *U.S.* †**a.** A fifty-dollar gold coin issued in 1849 and 1915. **b.** A piece of metal worth five cents. **5.** A rudimentary horn of an ox or cow 1842.

Slug (slɒg), *v.*[1] Now somewhat *rare.* late ME. [Preceded by much earlier †*sluggy* sluggish (XIII) and †*forslug* neglect through indolence (XIV); prob. of Scand. origin (cf. Sw. dial. *slogga* be sluggish, Norw. dial. *slugg* large heavy body, *sluggjen* slow, backward.] **1.** *intr.* To be lazy, slow, or inert; to lie idly or lazily. Also with *it.* **2.** To move slowly; to loiter or delay 1565. **3.** *trans.* To pass (time) in inactivity or idleness. Also with *out.* 1548. **4.** To relax or slacken; to make inert or sluggish 1600. **5.** To hinder, retard, delay 1605.

2. Their destruction sluggeth not 1565. **5.** To.. slugge the Shippe from furder sayling BACON.

Slug (slɒg), *v.*[2] 1831. [f. SLUG *sb.*[2]] **1.** *trans.* To load (a gun) with slugs. **2.** *pass.* and *intr.* Of a bullet: To adapt its shape to that of the bore in the act of firing 1875.

Slug (slɒg), *v.*[3] Chiefly *north.* and *U.S.* 1862. [Parallel to synon. SLOG *v.*; no further cogns. are found.] *trans.* To strike, drive, throw, etc. heavily or violently; to slog.

Slug-a-bed (slɒ·găbed). Also **slug-abed.** 1592. [f. SLUG *v.*[1] 1 + ABED *adv.*] One who lies long in bed through laziness.

Get up, sweet S., and see The Dew-bespangling Herbe and Tree HERRICK.

Sluggard (slɒ·găɹd), *sb.* and *a.* late ME. [f. SLUG *v.*[1] + -ARD.] **A.** *sb.* One who is naturally or habitually slow, lazy, or idle; a slothful or indolent person. **B.** *adj.* Sluggish, slothful, lazy 1593. Hence **Slu·ggard-ly** *a.*, **-ness.** †**Slu·ggardy,** slothfulness, indolence, laziness.

Sluggardize (slɒ·găɹdəiz), *v.* 1591. [f. SLUGGARD *sb.* + -IZE.] **1.** *trans.* To make idle or lazy. **2.** *intr.* To play the sluggard 1837.

Slugger (slɒ·gəɹ). *U.S.* 1884. [f. SLUG *v.*[3]] **1.** = SLOGGER. **2.** A flat-surfaced boss, knob, or projection on a roll for crushing ore 1903.

Sluggish (slɒ·giʃ), *a.* 1440. [f. SLUG *sb.*[1] or *v.*[1] + -ISH[1].] **1.** Of persons: Indisposed to action or exertion; inclined to be slow or slothful; not easily moved to activity. **2.** Of the mind, disposition, etc.: Characterized by or exhibiting lack of vigour, alertness, or energy; slow in apprehension or decision; dull 1450. **3.** Of conditions, etc.: Characterized by want of, or disinclination to, action or exertion 1561. **4.** Of things: Not readily stirring or moving; slow to stir, act, or make progress in any way 1640. **5.** Moving, flowing, etc., very slowly or tardily; slow in movement 1611. **b.** Of motion, etc.: Very slow or tardy 1648.

1. The Turke, and the Irish-man, are..the most s. liuers vnder the Sunne 1632. **2.** Beating the track of the alphabet with s. resolution JOHNSON. S. imaginations require strong stimulants 1871. **3.** A life of s. inaction 1838. **4.** Matter is of it self a dull and s. thing 1640. A symptom of 's. liver' 1897. **5. b.** His wry looks and s. pace..proclaimed his ill will to the task 1796. So **Slu·ggish-ly** *adv.*, **-ness.** †**Slu·ggy** *a.* (early ME.) sluggish, indolent –1608.

Slu·g-horn. 1770 (Chatterton). [erron. use of *slughorn* SLOGAN.] A trumpet.

Slu·g-worm. 1799. [f. SLUG *sb.*[1] 4, 5a.] One or other of the slug-like and slimy larvæ of certain saw-flies (esp. those formerly classed in the genus *Selandria*).

Sluice (slūs), *sb.* ME. [– OFr. *escluse* (mod. *écluse*) :- Gallo-Rom. **exclusa*, subst. use (sc. *aqua* water) of fem. pa. pple. of L. *excludere* EXCLUDE.] **1.** A structure for impounding the water of a river, canal, etc., provided with an adjustable gate or gates by which the volume of water is regulated or controlled. Also, rarely, the body of water so impounded or controlled. **b.** A paddle or slide in a gate or barrier by which water is held back 1616. **c.** A device by which the flow of water, esp. into or out of some receptacle, is regulated 1617. **2.** A channel, drain, or small stream, *esp.* one carrying off overflow or surplus water 1538. †**3.** A gap, breach, opening, or hole; a gash or wound –1752. **4.** In gold-washing: An artificial channel or flume, into which a current of water is directed in order to separate the particles of gold from the auriferous earth 1862.

1. *fig.* So from the sluices of Ulysses' eyes Fast fell the tears POPE. The ball which opened in his breast the crimson s. of life 1800.

Comb.: **s.-box,** one of the long troughs of which a gold-washing s. is composed; a riffle-box; **-gate,** the gate of a s., the part which can be opened or shut to let out or retain the water; the upper gate of a lock; **-way,** a channel or water-way fed or controlled by means of a s. or sluices.

Sluice (slūs), *v.* 1593. [f. the sb.] **1.** *trans.* To let *out*, to cause to flow *out*, by the opening of a sluice. **b.** To let out or draw *from* some source or place in this manner. Usu. in pa. pple. 1593. **c.** To lead or draw *off* by, or as by, a sluice 1753. **2.** To draw off or let out water from (a pond, lake, etc.) by means of a sluice or sluices 1594. **3.** To cast, fling, or pour (something) as if through a sluice 1610. **4.** To throw or pour water over (a person or thing); to swill with water esp. in order to clean or wash 1755. **b.** *U.S.* and *Austral.* To wash (auriferous ore) in a gold-miner's sluice. Also with *out.* 1859. **5.** *intr.* To flow or pour *out* or down as through a sluice 1593.

1. b. A broad canal From the main river sluiced TENNYSON. **2.** My veins have been sluiced so often that they give me pain in writing SCOTT. **4.** His neck and face, which he had been sluicing with cold water 1861.

Sluicy (slū·si), *a.* Chiefly *poet.* 1697. [f. SLUICE *sb.* + -Y[1].] Of rain, etc.: Falling or pouring copiously or in streams, as if from a sluice; streaming, drenching. Also *transf.* and *fig.*

Oft whole sheets descend of slucy Rain DRYDEN.

Slum (slɒm), *sb.* 1812. [Of cant origin.] †**1.** A room –1824. **2.** A street, alley, court, etc., situated in a crowded district of a town or city and inhabited by people of a low class or by the very poor; a number of these streets or courts forming a thickly populated neighbourhood or district of a squalid and wretched character. Chiefly *pl.*, and freq. in the phr. *back slum(s.* 1825. †**3.** Nonsensical talk or writing; gammon, blarney. Also, gipsy jargon or cant. –1823. Hence **Slu·mmy** *a.*

Slum (slɒm), *v.* 1860. [f. prec.] **1. a.** *intr.* To go into, or frequent, slums for discreditable purposes; to keep to back streets to avoid observation. **2.** To visit slums for charitable or philanthropic purposes, or out of curiosity, esp. as a fashionable pursuit 1884.

Slumber (slɒ·mbəɹ), *sb.* late ME. [f. SLUMBER *v.*] **1.** Sleep, repose. Chiefly *poet.* **2.** A period or occasion of sleep or repose; freq. a light or short sleep. late ME. **3.** *fig.* A state or condition of repose, inactivity, or quiescence 1552.

1. Ere theise eyes of mine take themselues to slomber SHAKS. **2.** Nor sleepe nor wake. But in a s. troublesome to both. 1611. **3.** The human mind awoke from a s. GODWIN. *attrib.* **s. cap,** a net cap worn when the wearer is in bed to keep the hair in order. Hence **Slu·mberless** *a.* obtaining or yielding no s.; sleepless. **Slu·mbery** *a.* slumberous, sleepy.

Slumber (slɒ·mbəɹ), *v.* [ME. *slūmere*, *slūme*, OE. *slūma* (see SLOOM *sb.*) or vb. *slūmen*, corresp. to MLG., MDu. *slūmen*, MLG. *slummen*, with parallel formations in MLG., MDu. *slūmeren* (Du. *sluimeren*), MHG. *slumeren*, G. *schlummern*. For the intrusive *b* cf. *bramble*, *limber*.] **1.** *intr.* To sleep, *esp.* to sleep lightly; to doze or drowse. **b.** *fig.* To lie at rest in death or the grave 1588. **2.** *fig.* To live in a state of inactivity or negligence; to remain or be sunk *in* sin, sloth, etc.; to be dilatory or tardy *in* doing something. late ME. **3.** Of things, faculties, etc.: To be dormant, inoperative, or quiescent 1582. **b.** To be calm, peaceful, or still 1764. †**4.** *trans.* To cause to sleep; to render inactive or inoperative; to dull or deaden –1642. **5.** To pass, spend, or waste (time) in sleep or slumber. Const. *away, out, through*, etc. 1749.

1. He neyther slombrethe nor slepethe, but alwayes watchethe 1599. **3.** The might that slumbers in a peasant's arm 1799. **5.** She had slumbered away the day in order to sit up all night FIELDING. Hence **Slu·mberer,** one who sleeps or slumbers. **Slu·mbering** *vbl. sb.* and *ppl. a.* (whence **Slu·mberingly** *adv.*).

Slumberous, slumbrous (slɒ·mb(ə)rəs), *a.* 1495. [f. SLUMBER *sb.* + -OUS.] **1.** Inclined to slumber or sleep; unduly given to slumber; indolent, lethargic. **b.** Of the eyes or eyelids: Heavy or drooping with slumber or sleep 1828. **2.** Inducing sleep; soporific 1667. **3.** Calm, still, peaceful 1765. **4.** Appropriate to, characterized by, or suggestive of slumber 1818. **b.** Of places, etc.: Quiet, sleepy, tranquil 1863.

2. The slumbrous light is rich and warm TENNYSON. **3.** Faint heaves the s. wave 1765. *transf.* The slumbrous reign..became intolerable to the commonalty 1885. **b.** A sleepy town in a s. land 1883. Hence **Slu·mberous-ly** *adv.*, **-ness.**

Slumming (slɒ·miŋ), *vbl. sb.* 1884. [f. SLUM *v.* + -ING[1].] The visitation of slums, esp. for charitable or philanthropic purposes.

Slump (slɒmp), *sb.*[1] *Sc.* 1718. [– LG. *slump* heap, mass, quantity = Du. *slomp*, Fris. *slompe.*] **1.** A large quantity or number; chiefly in phrases *by* or *in* (*the*) *s.*, as a whole; in the lump 1795. **2.** *attrib.*, as **s. sum,** a lump sum 1718.

Slump (slɒmp), *sb.*[2] 1888. [f. SLUMP *v.*[2]] **1.** *Stock Exch.* A heavy fall or sudden decline in the price or value of commodities or securities. **2.** *transf.* A sudden or heavy decline or falling off; a collapse 1888.

2. There is..no 's.' in the matrimonial market 1896.

Slump (slɒmp), *v.*[1] Chiefly *Sc.* 1822. [f. SLUMP *sb.*[1]] *trans.* To lump; to put, place, regard, deal with, etc., as one quantity, mass, or group. Freq. *to s. together.*

Slump (slɒmp), *v.*[2] Chiefly *dial.* and *U.S.* 1677. [Of symbolic origin, like *clump, lump, plump.*] **1.** *intr.* To fall or sink *in* or *into* a bog, swamp, muddy place, etc.; to fall *in* water with a dull splashing sound. **2. a.** Of the wind: To fall, drop 1855. **b.** Of stocks, values, etc.: To fall heavily or suddenly 1896. **3.** To move or walk in a clumsy, heavy, or laborious manner 1854. **4.** *trans.* To throw *down* heavily; to slam 1836. **b.** To cause to depreciate suddenly 1899.

1. Being in this swamp that was miry, I slumpt in and fell down 1684. **2. b.** Prices slumped from 2 to 5 points 1898.

Slumpy (slɒ·mpi), *a.* 1823. [f. dial. *slump* a marshy or muddy place; cf. LG. *schlump.* See -Y[1].] Marshy, swampy, muddy, boggy.

Slung (slɒŋ), *ppl. a.* 1773. [f. SLING *v.*[2]] Placed in, hung or suspended by, a sling or slings.

Comb.: **s.-shot** *U.S.*, a shot, piece of metal, stone, etc., fastened to a strap or thong, and used as a weapon.

Slunk (slɒŋk), *ppl. a.* 1837. [f. SLINK *v.*] Of calves: Cast prematurely.

Slur (slɒ̄ɹ), *sb.*[1] 1598. [f. SLUR *v.*[2]] †**1.** A gliding movement in dancing –1673. †**2.** A method of cheating at dice (see SLUR *v.*[2] 1) –1680. **3.** A sliding piece of mechanism in a knitting-machine, serving to depress the sinkers 1796.

Slur (slɒ̄ɹ), *sb.*[2] 1609. [Goes with SLUR *v.*[1]] **1. a.** A deliberate slight; an expression or suggestion of disparagement or reproof. **b.** A mark, stain, or blot; a discredit (incurred by or cast upon a person, etc.); †a blunder 1654. **2.** *Printing.* A faulty or smeared impression 1771. **3.** *Mus.* A curved line placed over or under two or more notes of different degrees to show that they are to be played or sung smoothly and connectedly 1801. **4.** A slurred utterance or sound 1861.

1. My Lord Generall..hath received several slurs from the King PEPYS. Phr. *To cast, put, throw* (etc.) *a s. on* or *upon* (a person or thing).

Slur (slɒ̄ɹ), *v.*[1] 1602. [Goes with SLUR *sb.*[2]] **1.** *trans.* To smear, stain, smirch, sully. Now *dial.* **b.** *Printing.* To smudge or blur 1683. **c.** *U.S.* To cover (a wall) with plaster or rough-cast 1885. **2.** To disparage, calumniate, asperse 1660. **3.** To pass over lightly, without proper mention or consideration 1660. **b.** Freq. with *over.* Also with ref. to utterance. 1725. **4.** *Mus.* To sing or play (notes) in a smooth and connected manner; to mark with a slur 1746. **5.** To blur 1782. **6.** To go through hurriedly and carelessly. Also *intr.* with *through.* 1857.

2. To s. the descent of the house of York SCOTT. **3.** To silence a doubt, or s. a difference 1871. **b.** The little word, as, which is always slurred over SHERIDAN. **6.** They only slurred through their fagging 1857. Hence **Slurred** (slɒ̄ɹd) *ppl. a.* run together, rendered indistinct, blurred.

Slur (slɒ̄ɹ), *v.*[2] 1594. [perh. rel. to LG. *slurren* shuffle, (M)LG. *slūren*, MDu. *sloren*, Du. *sleuren* drag, trail.] †**1.** *trans.* To slip or slide (a die) out of the box so that it does not turn –1700. †2. To cheat or cozen –1731. 3. *intr.* To slide, slide about. Now *dial.* 1617.

Slush (slʋʃ), *sb.*[1] 1641. [See SLUDGE.] **1. a.** The watery substance resulting from the partial melting of snow or ice. **b.** Liquid mud or mire 1772. **2.** *Naut.* The refuse fat or grease obtained from meat boiled on board ship 1756. **3. a.** A mixture of grease and other materials used for lubricating 1847. **b.** A mixture of white lead and lime, used for painting parts of machinery to preserve them from oxidation 1864. **4.** Rubbishy discourse or literature; also, sentimental stuff, gush 1896. **5.** *U.S. slang.* (*a*) Illicit commission, bribery, corruption. (*b*) Forged paper money. 1924. **6.** *attrib.*, as *s. funds, melodrama.*

Slush (slʋʃ), *sb.*[2] 1880. [imit., or f. next.] A heavy splashing sound.

Slush (slʋʃ), *v.* 1807. [Partly f. SLUSH *sb.*[1] and partly imit.] **I.** *trans.* **1.** To splash or soak with slush or mud. **2. a.** *Naut.* To grease (a mast) with slush. Also with *down.* 1823. **b.** To paint (machinery) with a mixture of white lead and lime 1864. **c.** To fill *up* or cover by dashing on mortar and cement 1875. **3.** To wash with a copious supply, or with dashing on, of water; to sluice. *dial.* 1854. **b.** To dash (water) *over* a person 1889. **II.** *intr.* **1.** Of pigs: To eat greedily and noisily 1833. **2.** To go or walk through mud, etc., with a dull splashing sound 1855. **3.** To rush (*down*) with a splashing sound 1883.

3. The filthy gutter slushes STEVENSON.

Slushy (slʋ·ʃi), *a.* 1791. [f. SLUSH *sb.*[1] + -Y[1].] **1.** Covered with, consisting of, having the character of slush (in senses 1a and b). **b.** Marked by the prevalence of slush 1848. **2.** Weak, washy 1839. **b.** *fig.* of emotion or the like 1869. **3.** Thick, indistinct 1861.

1. Mud under foot, alternating with s. snow 1857. **b.** S. splashy raw comfortless mornings in . . winter 1871. **2. b.** A sloppy and s. sentimentalism 1894. **3.** He spoke in a s. voice DICKENS. Hence **Slu·shiness.**

Slut (slʋt). late ME. [Of unkn. origin.] **1.** A woman of dirty, slovenly, or untidy habits or appearance; a foul slattern. **b.** A kitchenmaid, drudge (*rare*) 1450. **2.** A woman of a low or loose character; a bold or impudent girl; a hussy, jade 1450. **b.** In more or less playful use 1664. **3.** A female dog, a bitch 1845.

1. She's ugly, she's old, . . And a s., and a scold SHENSTONE. **2. b.** You're a wheedling s., you be so SWIFT.

Slutch (slʋtʃ). Now *dial.* 1669. [See SLUDGE.] Mud, mire, slush. Hence **Slu·tchy** *a.* muddy, slushy.

†Sluttery. 1586. [f. SLUT *sb.* + -ERY.] Sluttishness –1818.

Sluttish (slʋ·tiʃ), *a.* late ME. [f. SLUT *sb.* + -ISH[1].] **1.** Of persons: Dirty and untidy in dress and habits. Now *spec.* of women. **†b.** Of a low or lewd character –1606. **2.** Of things: Unclean, dirty; untidy 1549. **3.** Appropriate to, characteristic of, a slut or sluts 1561.

1. Why is thy lord so sluttissh, I the preye? CHAUCER. The . . maid . . is as lazy and s. as her mistress JOHNSON. **b.** *Tr. & Cr.* IV. v. 62. **2.** Suche hongrye doggs will slabbe vp sluttishe puddinges 1553. **3.** S. plenty deck'd her table PRIOR. Hence **Slu·ttish-ly** *adv.*, **-ness.**

Sly (slǝi), *a.*, *adv.*, and *sb.* [ME. *sleh, sley, sli(ȝ* – ON. *slœgr* clever, cunning, etymol. 'able to strike', f. *slóg-*, pa. t. stem of *slá* strike; cf. SLEIGHT *sb.* For the vocalism cf. DIE *v.*[1], THIGH, etc.] **A.** *adj.* **1.** Of persons: Skilful, clever, dexterous, or expert in doing something; skilled, knowing, wise. (Also occas. of animals.) *Obs.* exc. *n. dial.* **†2.** Showing skilfulness or ingenuity; cleverly or finely made –1721. **3.** Of persons: Adept or skilful in artifice or craft; deceitful, guileful, wily, underhand ME. **b.** Of animals, etc. 1640. **c.** Of looks: Expressive of slyness 1821. **4.** Of actions, things, etc.: Marked by, displaying or indicating, artifice, craft, or cunning; of an insidious or wily nature. late ME. **†b.** Of words, etc.: Full of duplicity or wile; subtle; disingenuous –1829. **5.** Characterized by secrecy or stealth; working, moving, etc., in an underhand manner. Also of places: Quiet, secret. 1440. **6.** Playfully mischievous or malicious; roguish; waggish 1764.

1. You . . (whom grauer age And long experience hath made wise and slie) 1600. **3.** He was, indeed, a little inquisitive; but I was s., sir; devilish s.! SHERIDAN. **b.** A s. old fish, too cunning for the hook CRABBE. **4.** Envy . . works in a s. and imperceptible manner 1755. **5.** The slye slow houres shall not determinate The datelesse limit of thy deere exile SHAKS. **6.** The s., delicate and . . elegant pleasantry of La Fontaine 1805.

†B. *adv.* In a sly, skilful, or cunning manner; slyly –1802. **C.** *absol.* or as *sb.* in phr. *On* (*upon*, *†under*, or *†by*) *the s.*, in a secret or covert manner; without publicity or openness; stealthily 1812.

A certain farmer's man, who wired hares upon the s. 1866.

Sly-boots (slǝi·būts). *colloq.* 1700. [f. SLY *a.* + BOOTS 3.] A sly, cunning, or crafty person; one who does things on the sly. Freq. in mild or joc. use, and usu. in pl. form.

Sly-goose. *Orkney.* Also **slygoose.** 1776. [f. SLY *a.* + GOOSE *sb.*] The sheldrake, *Tadorna cornuta* or *T. vulpanser.*

Slyly, slily (slǝi·li), *adv.* ME. [f. SLY *a.* + -LY[2].] In a sly manner.

While we pursu'd the Horsmen of ye North, He slyly stole away SHAKS. The clerk winked slily at Mr. Pickwick DICKENS. So **Sly·ness.**

Slype (slǝip). 1861. [perh. a use of *slipe* long narrow piece (as of ground XVI–XVII), varying with SLIP *sb.*[2] II. 4.; of unkn. origin.] *Arch.* A covered way or passage, esp. one leading from the cloisters and running between the transept and chapter-house of a cathedral or monastic church.

Smack (smæk), *sb.*[1] [OE. *smæc* = OFris. *smek*, MLG., MDu. *smak* (Du. *smaak*), OHG. *gi|smac* (G. *ge|schmack*). Cf. SMATCH *sb.*] **1.** A taste or flavour; the distinctive or peculiar taste of something, or a special flavour distinguishable from this. **2.** *transf.* A trace, tinge, or suggestion *of* something specified 1539. **†b.** A smattering –1791. **c.** A small quantity *of* liquor; a mouthful 1693. **d.** A touch or suggestion *of* something having a characteristic odour or taste 1848. **†3.** *fig.* Delight or enjoyment; inclination, relish –1620.

1. Midling Ale . . that hath no burnt, musty, or otherwise ill s. 1710. **2.** A s. of real earnestness in his tone 1874. **d.** A rough s. of resin was in the air STEVENSON. **3.** She hath a very great s. of Courtship, and plays with everyone 1620.

Smack (smæk), *sb.*[2] 1570. [rel. to SMACK *v.*[2] Cf. MDu. *smack*, LG. *smacke*, G. dial. *schmacke.*] **1.** A sharp noise or sound made by separating the lips quickly, esp. in kissing, and in tasting or anticipating food or liquor. **b.** A loud or sounding kiss 1604. **2.** The crack *of* a whip, lash, etc. 1781. **3.** A sounding blow delivered with the flat of the hand or something having a flat surface; a slap 1746. **b.** *colloq.* A slap or go *at* something 1889.

1. Tasting the Wine with a judicious S. STEELE. **3.** *A s. in the face* (fig.), a sharp rebuff.

Smack (smæk), *sb.*[3] 1611. [– LG., Du. *smacke*, mod. *smak*, of unkn. origin.] A single-masted sailing-vessel, fore-and-aft rigged like a sloop or cutter, and usually of light burden, chiefly employed as a coaster or for fishing, and formerly as a tender to a ship of war. **b.** *U.S.* A fishing-vessel having a well in which fish may be kept alive 1891.

Comb.: **sma·cksman**, one of the crew of a s., esp. of a fishing-s.; the owner of a s.

Smack (smæk), *v.*[1] ME. [f. SMACK *sb.*[1], superseding SMATCH *v.*] **1.** *trans.* Of persons: To perceive by the sense of taste. †Also *fig.* To experience, to suspect. **2.** *intr.* Of food, liquor, etc.: To taste (well or ill); to have a (specified) taste or flavour; to taste or savour *of* something. late ME. **b.** *fig.* To partake or savour *of*, to be strongly suggestive or reminiscent *of*, something 1595.

1. He soon smacked the taste of physic hidden in this sweetness CARLYLE. **2.** *fig.* Indeede my Father did something s., something grow too; he had a kinde of taste SHAKS. **b.** All Sects, all Ages s. of this vice SHAKS.

Smack (smæk), *v.*[2] 1530. [– MLG., MDu. *smacken* (LG., Du. *smakken*); cf. OE. *ġe|smacian* pat, caress, G. *schmatzen* eat or kiss noisily; of imit. origin.] **1.** *trans.* To open or separate (the lips) in such a way as to produce a sharp sound; to do this in connection with eating or drinking, esp. as a sign of keen relish or anticipation. Also *intr.* or *absol.* **b.** *trans.* To taste (wine or liquor) with keen relish or satisfaction 1822. **2.** To kiss noisily or loudly. Now *Obs.* or *dial.* 1570. **3.** To crack (a whip, thong, etc.) 1700. **4.** To bring, put, or throw *down* with a smack or slap; to clap (the hands) *together*; to slam (a door) *to* 1801. **5.** To strike (a person, part of the body, etc.) with the open hand or with something having a flat surface; to slap 1840. **6.** Used *advb.* **a.** With, or as with, a smack; suddenly and violently; slap 1782. **b.** Completely, entirely; directly 1828.

1. Tom . . smacked his lips over the long-necked glass 1861. **b.** George, . . filling himself a glass of wine, smacked it THACKERAY. **2.** Phr. *To s. calf-skin* (slang), to kiss the Bible in taking an oath. **5.** He smacked his leg with his hand, and burst out laughing 1881. **6. a.** He . . tumbled . . s. on his face 1799.

Smacker (smæ·kəɹ). 1775. [f. prec. + -ER[1].] A smacking blow; a resounding kiss.

Smacking (smæ·kiŋ), *vbl. sb.* 1628. [f. SMACK *v.*[2] + -ING[1].] The action of SMACK *v.*[2]; kissing, or the sound made by this.

Like the faint smackings of an after-Kiss DRYDEN.

Sma·cking, *ppl. a.* 1592. [f. as prec. + -ING[2].] **1.** That smacks, in senses of the vb. **2.** Of a breeze: Blowing vigorously; spanking 1820.

Small (smǭl), *a.* and *sb.* [OE. *smæl* = OFris. *smel*, OS., OHG. *smal* (Du. *smal*, G. *schmal*), ON. *smalr*, Goth. *smals* :– Gmc. **smalaz.*] **A.** *adj.* **I. 1.** Of relatively little girth or circumference in comparison with length; slender, thin. Now *dial.* exc. of the waist. **b.** *spec.* Applied to the more slender portions of the intestines; esp. *s. gut(s)* OE. **2.** Having little breadth or width in proportion to length; narrow. Now *rare.* OE.

1. My sister . . is as white as a lilly, and as s. as a wand SHAKS. He wor soa s. he luk'd like a walkin' clooas prop 1870.

II. 1. Of deficient or comparatively little size; not large (usu. without the emotional implications of *little*) OE. **b.** Of children, etc.: Not fully grown or developed; young ME. **c.** Of a family: Consisting of young children 1829. **2.** Used with collective nouns, denoting the limited size of the individual things, pieces, etc. late ME. **b.** Of money: Of little size and low value. *S. change*: coins of low denomination; hence *transf.* of little value. 1561. **3.** Little in amount or quantity ME. **b.** Of low numerical value or ordinal rank; low. late ME. **4.** Only a little or slight amount or degree of; not much; hardly any. late ME. **b.** *No s.*, great, considerable, marked; much, a good deal of 1548. **c.** Used in the superl. for emphasis: The least, the slightest 1596. **d.** *In the smallest*, in the least (*rare*) 1603. **5.** Of no great length; short, brief. late ME. **6.** Composed or consisting of, containing, few individual members; numerically little or weak 1470. **7. a.** Constituting a lower standard (of weight, size, etc.) than another having the same designation. **b.** Falling somewhat short of the proper or usual standard. 1554.

1. Herbes grete and smale CHAUCER. Rutland, the smallest of the English counties 1846. **b.** To the great delight of various s. boys 1896. **2.** The quaking-asps . . are in s. leaf 1902. **b.** Thou hast shewed vs none but s. money 1561. **c.** Her large s. family 1895. **3.** My wages been ful streite and ful smale CHAUCER. I had gotten a s. cold SWIFT. **4.** I kan but smal grammeere CHAUCER. They had indeed s. Hope of their Lives DE FOE. **b.** A matter of no s. momente 1548. **c.** He risked . . life, if he betrayed the smallest suspicion 1797. **d.** Not molesting Prince Karl in the smallest CARLYLE. **5.** For a s. moment haue I forsaken thee *Isaiah* 54:7. **6.** A s. but faithful Band Of Worthies DRYDEN. **7. b.** After an ascent of a s. half hour we came to a . . fountain of cold water 1753.

III. 1. Composed of fine or minute particles, drops, etc. In later use chiefly of rain. OE. **b.** Fine, as opp. to coarse OE. **2.** Of cloth, yarn, garments, etc.: Fine in texture or structure. *Obs.* exc. *dial.* OE. **3.** Of low alcoholic strength; light, weak 1440. **4.** Of sound or the voice: Gentle, low, soft; of little power or strength; not loud, harsh, or rough ME. **†b.** Of vowels: Narrow, close –1830. **5.** Of wind: Light, gentle 1542. **6.** Of the pulse: Beating weakly 1755.

1. Thick Fogs with s. Rain 1676. **3.** Let me haue sacke for vs old men: For these girles and knaues s. wines are best 1605. **4.** After the fire, a still s.

voice 1 *Kings* 19:12. **5.** A smal and softe wynde 1542.

IV. 1. Of persons: Low or inferior in rank or position; common, ordinary. Now *rare*. ME. **b.** Having but little land, capital, etc.; dealing, doing business, etc., on a small scale 1746. **2.** Of minor rank, note, or importance, in respect of some specified office, function, etc. ME. **b.** That is (such) to a small or limited extent, degree, etc. 1523. **c.** With negative, as in II. 4 b above 1551. **3.** Of things, etc.: Of little or minor consequence, interest, or importance; trifling, trivial ME. **4.** Not prominent or notable; humble, modest; unpretentious. In later use, chiefly in the phr. *in a s. way*. late ME. **5.a.** Base, low; mean, ungenerous 1824. **b.** Incapable of large views or great actions; small-minded, mean-souled 1837. **c.** With *feel*: Humiliated, mortified, injured in self-respect 1840.

1. Your Enemies are many, and not s. SHAKS. **2.** A s. author, and smaller wit DISRAELI. **3.** The fact..accounts..for certain s. recurrent defects 1893. **4.** A composer in a s. way T. HARDY. **5. c.** I should feel a little s. at being seen in such a place 1840.

Special collocations: **s. body,** in Printing, any size of type smaller than Long Primer; **s. capitals,** in Printing, capital letters differing little in size from the lower-case letters of the same fount; **s. cattle,** cattle below the size of oxen, as calves or sheep; **s. holding,** a holding smaller than an ordinary farm; also *spec.* land acquired by a council which exceeds one acre and either does not exceed fifty acres, or is of an annual value not exceeding fifty pounds; so **s. holder; s. people,** in local use, the fairies; **s. stuff** *Naut.*, applied to thin kinds of rope.

B. *absol.* or as *sb.* **1.** Persons or animals of small size or stature; little ones, children. (Now only with *the*.) ME. **2.** Persons of low or inferior rank or position, or of little ability or attainment. Chiefly in phr. *great and s.* ME. **†3.** Little, not much *of* –1640. **4.** *In s.* (rarely *the s.*), on a small scale; in little. In early use in ref. to painting, etc.: In miniature. 1611. **5.** The small, slender, or narrow part *of* something; *esp.* **a.** Of the leg 1489. **b.** Of the back 1536. **6.** Small coal; slack. In recent use also *pl.*, varieties of small coal. 1851. **7.** *pl.* Small clothes: breeches 1837. **b.** Small articles of laundry (*colloq.*). **8.** *pl.* At Oxford: The colloquial term for Responsions 1852. **9.** *S. and early*, a small evening party not intended to continue to a late hour. *colloq.* 1880.

3. Hauing s., yet doe I not complaine Of want SPENSER. **5. a.** *L.L.L.* v. ii. 645. **7.** Her footman, in large plush smalls and waistcoat THACKERAY. **8.** He had been 'ploughed' for 'smalls' 1880. Hence **Sma·llness,** the fact, quality, or state of being s.

Small (smǭl), *adv.* OE. [f. SMALL *a.*] **1.** Into small pieces or morsels. **†2.** Not much; slightly –1637. **3.** Quietly, gently; in a small or low voice ME. **4.** In a fine or small manner; on a small scale, etc. 1637.

1. Geese will..fatten well on carrots cut s. 1759. **2.** If thou dost weep.., it s. avails my mood SHAKS. **3.** She..speakes s. like a woman SHAKS. Phr. *To sing s.*, to adopt a humble tone or manner; to use less assertive language; to say nothing.

Small (smǭl), *v. rare.* late ME. [f. SMALL *a.*] To †make, or become, small.

Smallage (smǭ·lėdʒ). ME. [f. SMALL *a.* + ACHE *sb.*[2] For the change of final tʃ to dʒ cf. *borage, partridge, spinach*, etc.] One or other of several varieties of celery or parsley; *esp.* wild celery or water parsley, *Apium graveolens*. Now *rare*.

Sma·ll-arm. 1805. [Back-formation from next, at first in attrib. use.] **1.** *attrib.* **a.** Using or provided with small-arms. **b.** Intended or adapted for small-arms 1807. **2.** A fire-arm which may be carried in the hand 1875.

Sma·ll-arms. 1710. [f. SMALL *a.* + ARM *sb.*[2] 2.] Fire-arms capable of being carried in the hand, as contrasted with ordnance.

Small beer. 1568. [SMALL *a.* III. 3.] **1.** Beer of a weak, poor, or inferior quality. **2.** *transf.* **a.** Trivial occupations, affairs, etc.; matter(s or person(s of little or no consequence; nothing of importance 1777. **b.** *To think small beer of*, etc.: To have a poor or low opinion of. Chiefly with negs. *colloq.* 1825.

2. [To suckle Fooles, and chronicle small Beere SHAKS.]

Sma·ll-clothes. Also **smallclothes.** 1796. [SMALL *a.*] Breeches; knee-breeches.

Sma·ll coal. Also **small-coal.** 1638. [SMALL *a.* II. 2.] **1.** Charcoal. *Obs.* exc. *Hist.* **2.** Coal of small size; slack 1665.

Smallish (smǭ·liʃ), *a.* late ME. [f. SMALL *a.* + -ISH[1].] Somewhat small; rather little.

Smallpox (smǭ·lpǫks), *sb.* 1518. [orig. *small pokkes* pl. of *small pokke* (in late ME. *pokke smal*); see SMALL *a.* and POCK *sb.* 2. Long written as two words; the adj. distinguishes the disease from the pox proper, or *great pox.*] The pox or pustules on the skin which characterize the acute contagious disease sometimes called variola; hence commonly, the disease itself. (In later use, when denoting the disease, the word is construed as a singular.) **b.** *attrib.*, as *small-pox epidemic*, etc. 1775.

I am..expecting the doctor to give your little godson the s. They are rife in the country. BURNS. Hence **Sma·llpox** *v. trans.* **Sma·ll-poxed** *a.* marked by or suffering from s.

Sma·ll-sword. 1687. [SMALL *a.* I. 2.] A light sword, tapering gradually from the hilt to the point, and used esp. in fencing.

Sma·ll talk, *sb.* 1751. [SMALL *a.* IV. 3.] Light talk or conversation; chit-chat, gossip.

Sma·ll-ware(s. 1617. [SMALL *a.* II. 1.] Small textile articles of the tape kind; narrow bindings of cotton, linen, silk, or woollen fabric; plaited sash cord, braid, etc.; also, buttons, hooks and eyes, etc.

†Sma·lly, *adv.* ME. [f. SMALL *a.* + -LY[2].] **1.** In or into small or minute pieces, fragments, etc.; finely –1662. **2.** Sparsely, scantily –1604. **3.** Not much, very little –1670. **†4.** Slightly, slenderly –1630.

Smalm, variant of SMARM.

Smalt (smǭlt), *sb.* and *a.* 1558. [– Fr. *smalt* – It. *smalto* – Gmc. **small*, rel. to SMELT *v.*] **1.** A species of glass, usually coloured a deep blue by oxide of cobalt, etc., and after cooling finely pulverized for use as a pigment or colouring matter. **2.** A deep blue colour like that of smalt 1881. **3.** A piece of coloured glass. Cf. SMALTO. 1864. **4.** *attrib. s.-glass, -works*, etc.; **-blue,** powder blue 1681. **b.** As *adj.* Deep blue 1880. **Sma·ltite** = next.

Smaltine (smǭ·ltəin). 1837. [f. SMALT *sb.* + -INE[5].] *Min.* Tin-white cobalt.

‖**Smalto** (sma·lto). Also *pl.* **smalti.** 1705. [It.; see SMALT.] Coloured glass or enamel used for mosaic work, etc.; a small cube or piece of this.

Smalts (smǭlts). 1610. [app. the pl. of SMALT taken as a sing.] = SMALT *sb.* 1.

Smaragd (smæ·rægd). Now *rare*. ME. [– OFr. *smaragde* or L. SMARAGDUS.] An emerald.

Smaragdine (smăræ·gdin, -əin), *sb.* and *a.* late ME. [– L. *smaragdinus* of emerald – Gr. σμαράγδινος, f. σμάραγδος SMARAGDUS.] **A.** *sb.* = prec. **B.** *adj.* **1.** Of or belonging to, consisting of, a smaragd; resembling that of a smaragd; of an emerald green 1591. **2.** *S. Table*, a mediæval Latin work on alchemy, *Tabula Smaragdina*, attributed to the Egyptian Hermes Trismegistus 1597.

Smaragdite (smăræ·gdəit). 1804. [– Fr. *smaragdite* (Saussure, 1796), f. Gr. σμάραγδος (see next) + -ITE[1] 2 b.] *Min.* A brilliant grass-green or emerald-green variety of amphibole or hornblende.

‖**Smaragdus** (smăræ·gdŏs). Now *rare*. late ME. [L. – Gr. σμάραγδος, var. of μάραγδος – Prakrit *maragada-* (cf. Skr. *marakata*) – Heb. *bāreḳet* emerald, f. *bāraḳ* flash, sparkle.] = SMARAGD.

Smarm, smalm (smāɹm, smām), *v. colloq.* 1847. [Of unkn. origin.] **1.** *trans.* To smooth *down* (as hair with pomade). **2.** *intr.* To behave in a fulsomely flattering or toadying manner. Hence **Sma·rmy** *a.* inclined to do this.

Smart (smāɹt), *sb.*[1] [ME. *smierte, smerte*, app. :– OE. **smiertu*, f. *smeart* SMART *a.* Cf. MLG., MDu. *smerte, smarte*, OHG. *smerza, smerzo* (G. *schmerz*).] **1.** Sharp physical pain, esp. such as is caused by a stroke, sting, or wound. Also with *a* and *pl.* **2.** Mental pain or suffering; grief, sorrow, affliction; sometimes, suffering of the nature of punishment or retribution ME. **3.** *ellipt.* = SMART-MONEY 1802.

1. He..inflicted both corporall s. and pecuniary mulcts upon them 1641. **2.** The very Eye betrays our inward s. COWLEY.

Smart (smāɹt), *sb.*[2] 1712. [f. SMART *a.*] **1.** One who affects smartness in dress, manners, or talk. Now *Hist.* **2.** Smartness in talk or writing 1845.

Smart (smāɹt), *a.* [Late OE. *smeart*, rel. to *smeortan* SMART *v.*; not repr. in the cognate languages.] **I. †1.** Of a whip, rod, etc.: Inflicting or causing pain; sharp, biting, stinging –1671. **†b.** Severe or hard *on* or *upon* one –1648. **2.** Of blows, strokes, etc.: Sufficiently hard or severe to cause pain ME. **†3.** Of pain, sorrow, wounds, etc.: Sharp, keen, painful, severe –1688. **4.** Of words, etc.: Sharp, severe; cutting, acrimonious. Now *rare*. ME. **5.** Brisk or vigorous; having a certain degree of intensity, force, strength, or quickness ME. **†6.** Sharp, abrupt, clearly outlined –1784. **7.** Considerable (in number, amount, extent, etc.). Chiefly *dial.* and *U.S.* 1839.

2. How s. a lash that speech doth giue my Conscience? SHAKS. **3.** The gospel..threateneth them with the heaviest and smartest judgments BUNYAN. **4.** A Book written..against the Marriage in a s. and stinging Style 1625. **5.** A s. and continued Rain 1692. Whisky,..very s. stuff it is KEATS. **6.** A s. passage at arms 1885. **7.** Madame..left a s. legacy to the..children THACKERAY.

II. †1. Pert, forward, impudent (*rare*) –1607. **2.** Of persons: Quick, active; prompt ME. **3.** Clever, capable, adept; quick at devising, learning, looking after oneself, etc. In later use chiefly *U.S.* 1628. **4.** Clever in talk or argument; good at repartee 1639. **b.** Of sayings, etc.: Clever, pointed; witty 1656. **5.** Alert and brisk; combining briskness with neatness or trimness of appearance 1602. **b.** Neatly and trimly dressed 1789. **c.** Of dress, etc.: Neat and trim; stylish 1716. **6.** Fashionable, elegant, esp. in a very high degree 1718.

2. We were mighty s. getting under way 1899. **3.** In America every s. man is expected to be able to do anything he turns his hand to 1888. A..s. catch at mid-on 1895. **4. b.** He mistakes the question, that he may return a s. answer JOHNSON. **5.** The s. lads of the city march'd downe the streets 1683. **c.** A collection of s..boots and shoes 1859. **6.** I have seen plenty of s. society 1881. Hence **Smart, Sma·rt-ly** *advs.*, **-ness.**

Smart (smāɹt), *v.* [OE. *smeortan* = MDu. *smerten*, (also mod.) *smarten*, OHG. *smerzan* (G. *schmerzen*), based on WGmc. **smert- *smart- *smurt-*, perh. rel. to L. *mordēre* bite, Gr. σμερδνός, σμερδαλέος terrible.] **1.** *intr.* Of wounds, etc.: To be a source of sharp pain; to be acutely painful. **2.** †With dative: To cause pain, be painful, to (a person, etc.) –ME. **b.** With sbs., passing into *trans.*: To affect with pain or smarting ME. **3.** *intr.* To feel sharp pain or distress; to suffer acutely or severely ME. **b.** To bear the penalty, to suffer severely, *for* some offence, etc. 1548.

1. Here woundis sore did smerte 1400. **2. b.** The smoke..smarted the nose 1884. **3.** Countreys that yet smarted with the last years War 1670. **b.** He has done us a wrong, and should be made to s. for it 1884.

Smarten (smā·ɹt'n), *v.* 1815. [f. SMART *a.* + -EN[5].] **1.** *trans.* To make smart or spruce. Usu. with *up*. Also *absol.* **2.** To brighten *up* 1864.

Sma·rt-mo:ney. 1693. [f. SMART *sb.*[1]] **1.** A sum of money paid to sailors, soldiers, workmen, etc., as compensation for disablement or injuries received while on duty or at work. **b.** Any compensation made for injury or the like 1749. **2.** Money paid to obtain the discharge of a recruit who has enlisted in the army 1760. **b.** Money paid on account of cancelling or not fulfilling a bargain or agreement, or in order to free oneself from some disadvantage, recover some lapsed privilege, etc. 1818.

1. b. (*U.S. law.*) *Smart-Money*...Damages beyond the value of a thing sued for, given by a jury in case of gross misconduct or cruelty on the part of a defendant 1851. So **Sma·rt-ti·cket,** a certificate given to wounded seamen entitling them to a pension or gratuity.

Sma·rtweed. Chiefly *dial.* and *U.S.* 1787. [f. SMART *sb.*[1] or *a.*] A name given to species of *Polygonum*, esp. the arsesmart or water-pepper, *P. hydropiper*.

Smarty (smā·ɹti). *U.S.* 1880. [f. SMART *a.* II. 4 + -Y[6].] A would-be smart or witty person.

Smash (smæʃ), *sb.*[1] 1779. [f. SMASH *v.*[1]] **1.** *dial.* or *colloq.* A hard or heavy blow. **b.** *Lawn-tennis.* A hard and fast overhand volley 1882. **2.** A shivered or broken-up condition 1798. Also *fig.* **3.** A loud sound of breaking or crushing; a severe or extensive crushing, shivering, or breaking of anything, esp. accompanied by a crashing sound; a violent collision or impact 1808. **b.** *S.-up* [f. verbal phr.], a complete smash 1858. **4.** Commercial failure; stoppage through insolvency; bankruptcy 1839. **b.** A crushing defeat or overthrow 1854. **5.** An American beverage made of spirit, ice, water, sugar, and flavoured with mint 1859.

2. He determined..to go to s. like a hero 1807. Phr. *to break, knock*, etc. *to s.* **4. b.** It was a final s. to the enemy in the north BADEN-POWELL.

Smash, *sb.*[2] *Cant.* 1795. [Cant, of unkn. origin.] Counterfeit coin.

Smash (smæʃ), *v.*[1] 1778. [prob. imit., combining *sm-* of *smack* and *smite* with *-ash* of earlier *bash, mash*, etc.] **I. 1.** *trans.* To break (a thing) in pieces violently; to dash to pieces; to crush, shatter, or shiver. **b.** *Bookbinding.* To flatten or compress (the sheets of a book) before binding 1875. **2.** To dash or fling (a thing) with noise and violence; to batter; to cause to strike hard 1800. **b.** *Lawn-Tennis.* To strike (the ball) violently and swiftly in an overhand volley. Also *absol.* 1882. **3.** To defeat utterly; to crush completely 1813. **b.** To render insolvent or bankrupt 1857.

1. The bottle is smashed, smashed to atoms! 1851. *absol.* in phr. *S.-and-grab*, applied to robbery consisting of smashing shop windows and grabbing the goods; also, of the thief. **2.** I'll s. your face in 1852. It is asked that their grinders may be smashed in, broken off, or dashed out 1872. **3.** A British expedition to 's.' the Mahdi 1884.

II. *intr.* **1.** To move rapidly with shattering effect, dash violently, crash 1835. **2.** *colloq.* To fail financially; to be ruined. Also with *up.* 1839. **3.** To break or fly in pieces 1904.

2. A Glazier?—what if he should smash! HOOD. Phr. *To go s.*

Smash, *v.*[2] *Cant.* 1811. [Goes with SMASH *sb.*[2]] *trans.* To pass (counterfeit money). Hence **Sma·sher**[2], one who passes or utters counterfeit coin or forged notes.

Smasher[1] (smæ·ʃəɹ). 1794. [f. SMASH *v.*[1] + -ER[1].] **1.** *slang.* Anything uncommon, extraordinary, or unusual, *esp.* unusually large or excellent. **2.** *colloq.* A severe or crushing reply, article, review, etc. 1828. **3.** An appliance or machine which smashes or crushes; *spec.* a bookbinder's compressing-machine; a form of embossing-press 1822. **4.** One who smashes 1884.

Smatch (smætʃ), *sb.* [ME. *smech, smach*, app. an alt. of OE. *smæc* SMACK *sb.*[1] under the infl. of SMATCH *v.* (OE. *smæććan*).] = SMACK *sb.*[1] So **Smatch** *v.* = SMACK *v.*[1]

Smatter (smæ·təɹ), *v.* ME. [Of unkn. origin.] †**1.** *trans.* To dirty, smirch, pollute, defile –1600. †**2.** *intr.* To talk ignorantly or superficially, to prate or chatter, *of* something –1733. †**b.** Without const. –1691. **3.** To have a slight or superficial knowledge or practice *of*; to dabble, to be a smatterer (*in* or *at* something) 1530. **4.** *trans.* To talk or utter without proper knowledge or proficiency 1609.

2. b. Good Prudence, s. with your gossip, go SHAKS. **3.** A man can but s. in six or seven languages 1573. **4.** The barber smatters Latin, I remember B. JONS. Hence **Sma·tter** *sb.* superficial knowledge; a smattering. In *pl.*, scraps, trifles.

Smatterer (smæ·tərəɹ). 1519. [f. SMATTER *v.* + -ER[1].] One who has only a slight or superficial knowledge *of* (now rare) or *in* a matter; a dabbler. Also used without const.

Sma·ttering, *vbl. sb.* 1538. [f. SMATTER *v.* + -ING[1].] **1.** A slight or superficial knowledge *in* or *of* something. †**2.** The action of discoursing or studying superficially (*rare*) –1692.

1. A s. of 'scholarship' 1874. **2.** I would advise them to leave off this dabbling and s. in Philosophy 1692.

Smear (smī³ɹ), *sb.* [In sense 1 OE. *smeoru* = OFris. *smere*, OS., OHG. *smero* (Du. *smeer*, G. *schmer*), ON. *smjǫr*, Goth. *smairþr*; cogn. with Gr. *μύρον* ointment, *σμύρις* EMERY. In later senses from the vb.] †**1.** Fat, grease, lard; ointment –1048. **2.** A mark, smudge, or stain made by smearing, or suggestive of this; a layer or patch of some substance applied by smearing 1611. **b.** A small quantity of some substance smeared upon a slide for microscopical investigation 1903. **3. a.** An application for smearing sheep 1802. **b.** *Pottery.* A mixture used for glazing 1875.

2. Roof, and walls..abounding in old smears of..red-lead, and damp DICKENS.

Smear (smī³ɹ), *v.* [OE. *smierwan*, corresp. to MLG. *smeren*, OHG. *smirwen* (G. *schmieren*), ON. *smyrva, smyrja* :– Gmc. **smerwjan*; see prec.] **1.** *trans.* To anoint with oil, chrism, etc., as a symbolic ceremony. In later use only contemptuous. **2.** To anoint, to rub or daub (a part of the body) with oil, grease, etc. Said also of the oil, etc. OE. **3.** To anoint medicinally; to treat (a wound, etc.) with a copious application of some thick or greasy medicament OE. **b.** To SALVE (sheep). late ME. **4.** To spread, daub, cover thickly or in patches *with* some unctuous, greasy, sticky, or dirty substance. Occas. said of the substance. Also without const. OE. **b.** *techn.* To glaze (pottery) by a process of evaporation 1839. **5.** To lay *on* in a thick or greasy layer ME. **6.** To rub *out* with a smear or smudge; to rub or draw in a smeary manner 1840.

2. The Groom..stript for Wrestling, smears his Limbs with Oyl DRYDEN. **4.** Slugs, pinched with hunger, smear'd the slimy wall 1763. *fig.* People smearing each other over with stupid flattery 1847.

Smear-dab. 1769. [perh. f. SMEAR *sb.* or *v.*] A variety of dab, also called lemon or smooth dab.

S., due to its being frequently covered with slime 1882.

Smeared (smī³ɹd), *ppl. a.* 1584. [f. SMEAR *v.* + -ED[1].] Dirtied or soiled by smearing; bedaubed. **b.** *S. dagger*, a species of moth, *Apatella oblinita* 1883.

Smeary (smī³·ri), *a.* 1529. [f. SMEAR *sb.* or *v.* + -Y[1].] **1.** Marked or characterized by smears; bedaubed, begrimed. **2.** Tending to smear or soil; of a greasy or unctuous nature 1582. Hence **Smea·riness.**

Smeath (smīþ). *local.* 1622. [Obscurely rel. to SMEE, SMEW.] The smee. Also *s. duck.*

Smectite (sme·ktəit). 1811. [f. Gr. *σμηκτίς* + -ITE[1] 2 b.] *Min.* A kind of fuller's earth.

Smectymnuan (smekti·mniuăn), *sb.* and *a.* 1646. [f. *Smectymnuus*, a fictitious name made out of the initials of the five authors of *An Answer to a Book*, etc. (1641).] **A.** *sb.* One or other of the authors of the work published under the name of Smectymnuus; also, one who accepted the views of these writers. **B.** *adj.* Pertaining to, connected with, or characteristic of, the Smectymnuans 1673.

Smeddum, variant of SMITHAM.

Smee (smī). *dial.* and *U.S.* 1668. [Obscurely rel. to SMEATH, SMEW.] A name for the smew, widgeon, pochard, and scaup-duck.

Smeek (smīk), *v.* Latterly *Sc.* and †*north.* [OE. *smēocan* str. vb. = MDu. *smieken*, grade var. of OE. *smocian* SMOKE *v.*] †**1.** *intr.* To emit smoke –1440. **2.** *trans.* To fumigate; to suffocate OE.

Smeeth (smīþ, smīð), *a.* and *sb.* *Obs.* exc. *dial.* [OE. *smǣþe, smēþe* (:– *smōþi-*) rel. to *smōþ* SMOOTH *a.*] **A.** *adj.* Smooth; free from roughness. **B.** *sb.* A level space. *E. Anglian dial.* 1440. Hence **Smeeth** *v. trans.* to make smooth.

‖**Smegma** (sme·gmă). 1819. [L. (Pliny) – Gr. *σμῆγμα* detergent, f. base of *σμήχειν* rub, cleanse.] *Phys.* A sebaceous secretion, *esp.* that found under the prepuce.

Smell (smel), *sb.* ME. [f. SMELL *v.*] **1.** The sense of which the nose is the organ; the faculty of smelling. Now usu. in *sense, organ*, etc., *of s.* **2.** That property of things which affects the olfactory organ; odour, perfume, aroma; stench, stink ME. **3.** *fig.* A trace, suggestion, or tinge *of* something. Also without article, or with adj. 1475. **4.** An act of smelling; a sniff 1560.

1. I have no s. yet, but my cold something better SWIFT. **2.** There was such a rich s. of pines 1847. There was a nasty s. about the premises 1885. **3.** Without the least s. or tang of imperfection BUNYAN.

Smell (smel), *v.* [ME. *smelle*, also *smülle, smille*, pointing to OE. **smiellan*, **smyllan*, of which no cognates are known.] **I.** *trans.* **1.** To have perception of (an object, odour, etc.) by means of the olfactory sense. **b.** To inhale the odour or scent of (a thing); to sniff at; to examine in this way 1830. **2.** To perceive as if by smell; to suspect, to have an inkling of; to divine. late ME. **3.** To search or find *out* by, or as by, the sense of smell 1538. **4.** To distinguish (one thing *from* another) by the smell 1582. **5.** To find or make (one's way) by the sense of smell 1605.

1. Paris may be smelt five miles before you arrive at it 1779. *To s. powder*, to have actual experience of fighting. *To s. a rat*: see RAT *sb.* 1. **2.** The people never smelt the cheat 1798. *To s. the ground*, of ships, to slacken speed as the water becomes shallower. **3.** The Scots folks have an excellent nose to s. out their Countryfolks 1756. **5.** Go thrust him out at gates, and let him s. His way to Douer SHAKS.

II. *intr.* **1.** To exercise, employ, make use of, the sense of smell in relation to a specified object. Const. *at, of* (now *U.S.*), or *to.* ME. **2.** Without const. To possess or exercise the sense of smell; to be able to perceive odours, or to be engaged in doing this ME.

1. She smelt at her salts, and soon recovered that weakness READE. **2.** It will be the object of this Committee..to go smelling in Shoreditch 1898.

III. 1. *intr.* To give out, send forth, or exhale an odour; to have a smell, scent, etc. ME. **b.** *spec.* To give out an offensive odour; to stink. late ME. **2.** To exhale or emit the odour *of*, to smell *of*, something. Also rarely *on* (now *dial.*). 1526. **b.** To have a touch, tinge, or suggestion *of* something 1526. **3.** *trans.* To have or emit a smell of (something) 1586.

1. Hee smels like a fish SHAKS. **b.** If he reach old Age..his Breath smells 1684. *fig.* Oh my offence is ranke, it smels to heauen SHAKS. **2.** One of the..men already smells of sherry DICKENS. **b.** Praises in an enemy are superfluous, or s. of craft MILT. Phr. *To s. of the candle, lamp, oil*, etc., of literary work, to show signs of being laboured and artificial. **3.** He smels April and May SHAKS.

Smeller (sme·ləɹ). 1519. [f. SMELL *v.* + -ER[1].] **1.** One who has or exercises the sense of smell; one who smells *out.* **2.** A feeler; a slender tactile organ, hair, etc.; *esp.* one of the whiskers of a cat 1665. **3.** *slang.* **a.** The nose; *pl.* the nostrils 1700. **b.** A blow on the nose; hence, a hard blow of any kind 1824.

Sme·ll-feast. 1519. [f. SMELL *v.* (or *sb.*) + FEAST *sb.*] **1.** One who scents out where feasting is to be had; one who comes uninvited to share in a feast; a parasite, a greedy sponger. Now *arch.* **b.** *attrib.* Parasitic, sponging 1566. **2.** 'A feast at which the guests are supposed to feed upon the odors only of the viands' 1864.

1. The Smell-feasts rouse them at the hint There's cookery in a certain dwelling-place BROWNING.

Smellfungus (sme·lˌfɒ·ŋgŏs). *Pl.* **-fungi.** 1807. [Sterne's name for Smollett, with reference to the captious tone of Smollett's *Travels through France and Italy* (1766).] A discontented person; a grumbler, faultfinder.

Smelling (sme·liŋ), *vbl. sb.* ME. [f. SMELL *v.* + -ING[1].] **1.** The sense of smell. **b.** The act or fact of smelling. Also with *out.* 1509. †**2.** Odour, scent, smell –1611.

attrib.: **s.-bottle,** a phial or small bottle for containing smelling-salts or perfume ready for use; **-salts,** a preparation of carbonate of ammonia and scent for smelling, used as a restorative in cases of faintness or headache. So **Smelling** *ppl. a.* (chiefly in SWEET-SMELLING).

Smell-less (sme·lˌlĕs), *a.* 1612. [f. SMELL *sb.* + -LESS.] **1.** Giving out no smell; scentless. **2.** Having no sense of smell 1873.

Sme·ll-smock. 1550. [f. SMELL *v.* + SMOCK *sb.*] †**1.** A licentious man –1673. **2.** Dial. name for various plants 1876.

Smelly (sme·li), *a.* 1862. [f. SMELL *sb.* or *v.* + -Y[1].] Emitting a bad smell or smells; stinking.

Smelt (smelt), *sb.* [OE. *smelt, smylt* (in AL. *smeltus* XIII, *smyltus* XIV), obscurely rel. to similar Continental names for species of fish; cf. SMOLT.] **1.** A small fish, *Osmerus eparlanus*, allied to the salmon, and emitting a peculiar odour; the sparling or spirling. **b.** A fish of a related species, esp. *O. mordax* of the American coast 1836. **c.** Applied to the atherine or sand-smelt and other small fishes 1776. †**2.** *transf.* A simpleton –1625.

Smelt (smelt), *v.* 1543. [– MLG., MDu. *smelten* = OHG. *smelzan* (G. *schmelzen*), wk. trans. vb. corresp. to str. intr., f. **smelt-*, var. of the base of MELT *v.*] *trans.* To fuse or melt (ore, etc.) in order to extract the metal; to obtain or produce (metal) by this means. Hence **Sme·ltery**, a place where ores are smelted.

Smelt-, the stem of SMELT *v.* in comb., as **s.-furnace, -house, -mill,** places where smelting is carried on.

Smelter (sme·ltəɹ), *sb.* 1455. [f. SMELT *v.* + -ER[1].] **1.** One who smelts; a workman engaged in smelting; an owner of smelting-works. **2.** Smelting-works; a smeltery. orig. *U.S.* 1877.

Smelting (sme·ltiŋ), *vbl. sb.* 1531. [f. SMELT *v.* + -ING[1].] The action of SMELT *v.* Also *attrib.*, as *s.-furnace, works*, etc.

Smew (smiū). 1674. [Obscurely rel. to SMEE and SMEATH, Du. *smient*, †*smeente*, LG. *smēnt* widgeon, G. *schmi-*, *schmü-*, *schmeiente* small wild duck (*ente* duck).] A saw-billed duck (*Mergus* or *Mergellus albellus*) belonging to the merganser group; the white nun. The female is the *red-headed s.*

†**Smi·cker,** *a.* [OE. *smicer*; cf. OHG. *smehhar*, *smechar*.] Beautiful, handsome –1639. Hence **Smi·cker** *v. Sc. intr.* to look amorously or wantonly; to smile or smirk.

Smicket (smi·kėt). Now *dial.* 1685. [app. dim. of SMOCK *sb.*] A woman's smock or chemise; a small smock.

Smift. 1839. [Of unkn. origin.] *Mining.* A kind of fuse or slow match used in blasting.

Smilacin (smǝi·lăsin). 1836. [– Fr. *smilacin*, f. *smilac-*, stem of SMILAX + -IN[1].] *Chem.* Parillin.

Smilax (smǝi·læks). 1601. [– L. *smilax* (Pliny) – Gr. σμῖλαξ bindweed.] *Bot.* **1.** A large genus of liliaceous plants typical of the order *Smilaceæ*, or a species of this genus, the tuberous rootstocks of which constitute the sarsaparilla of commerce. **2.** A climbing species of asparagus, *Myrsiphyllum asparagoides*, much used for decorative purposes 1870.

Smile (smǝil), *sb.* 1562. [f. SMILE *v.*] **1.** An act of smiling; a slight and more or less involuntary movement of the countenance expressive of pleasure, amusement, affection, etc., or of amused contempt, disdain, incredulity, etc. (the characteristic features are a brightening of the eyes and an upward curving of the corners of the mouth). **2.** *colloq.* A drink, *esp.* of whisky. orig. *U.S.* 1859.

1. This sweet intercourse Of looks and smiles MILT. *transf.* and *fig.* Methought I stood not in the s. of Heauen SHAKS. Turn, Fortune, turn thy wheel with s. or frown TENNYSON. Hence **Smi·let** (*rare*) a little or slight s.

Smile (smǝil), *v.* ME. [perh. of Scand. origin (cf. Sw. *smila*, Da. *smile*); a parallel form is OHG. **smīlan* (in pr. pple. *smilenter*), MHG. *smielen*; f. (with *l*-suffix) the base repr. by forms cited s.v. SMIRK.] **I.** *intr.* **1.** Of persons: To give to the features or face a look expressive of pleasure or amusement, or of amused disdain, scorn, etc. (see prec.). **2. a.** To look *on*, *upon*, *at*, or *to* a person with a smile or pleasant expression. late ME. **b.** To look *on* or *upon* one with favour, approval, or encouragement ME. **c.** To show by the features one's amusement (or pleasure) *at* something. late ME. **3.** Of physical features, things, etc.: To have or present an agreeable or pleasing aspect 1594. **4.** (*U.S.*) *slang.* To have or take a drink 1858.

1. Some that s., haue in their hearts I feare Millions of Mischeefes SHAKS. *transf.* and *fig.* Then let me not pass Occasion which now smiles MILT. The flower that smiles today Tomorrow dies SHELLEY. **2. a.** His mother on him smil'd HOBBES. **b.** Circumstances..seemed to s. on the project 1878. **3.** Cheard with the grateful smell old Ocean smiles MILT.

II. 1. a. To bring or convert into a specified condition by smiling. Const. *in, into, out of,* etc. 1588. **b.** To dismiss, get rid of, drive *away* (something) with a smile or smiles; to while *away* (time), dry *up* (tears), in or by smiling 1760. †**2.** To deride, laugh at. SHAKS. **3. a.** To exhibit, indicate, or express by smiling; to grant, bestow, etc., with a smile 1646. **b.** With cogn. obj.: To give (a smile, esp. one of a specified kind) 1837.

1. a. He does s. his face into more lynes, then is in the new Mappe SHAKS. **b.** A woman's reputation must not be smiled away 1885. **3. a.** She smiled disbelief 1880. **b.** Mr. Weller junior smiled a filial smile DICKENS. Hence **Smi·ling-ly** *adv.*, **-ness.**

Smileless (smǝi·l,lės), *a.* 1719. [f. SMILE *sb.* + -LESS.] **1.** Of persons, etc.: Exhibiting no smile; never smiling; grave, severe. **b.** Of words: Uttered without a smile 1810. **2.** Devoid of brightness or cheerfulness; dark, dull, cheerless 1858.

Smiler (smǝi·ləɹ). late ME. [f. SMILE *v.* + -ER[1].] **1.** One who smiles. **2.** *slang.* A kind of shandy-gaff 1892.

Smirch (smǝ̄ɹtʃ), *v.* 1495. [Of unkn. origin.] **1.** *trans.* Of things: To make dirty, soil, sully, or discolour (something) by contact or touch. **2.** Of persons (or animals): To stain or befoul (the face, person, reputation, etc.) *with* or by means of something dirty, foul, or defamatory 1600.

1. *fig.* Lower thoughts as well as lower passions ..s. the human soul TROLLOPE. **2.** Ile put my selfe in poore and meane attire, And with a kinde of vmber s. my face SHAKS. Hence **Smirch** *sb.* a dirty mark or smear, a stain; that which smirches or dirties.

Smirk (smǝ̄ɹk), *sb.* 1560. [f. SMIRK *v.*] An affected or simpering smile; a silly, conceited, smiling look.

He has the canonical s., and the filthy clammy palm of a chaplain WYCHERLEY. Hence **Smi·rky** *a. Sc.* and *U.S.* smart, neat, smiling; of the nature of a s.

Smirk (smǝ̄ɹk), *a.* and *adv.* 1530. [app. f. SMIRK *v.*, but perh. partly suggested by SMICKER *a.*] **A.** *adj.* Neat, trim, spruce in dress or appearance; pleasant, agreeable. Also *U.S.*, smug. Now chiefly *dial.*

Seest, how brag yond Bullocke beares, So smirke, so smoothe, his pricked eares? SPENSER.

†**B.** *adv.* Smirkingly. HEYWOOD.

Smirk (smǝ̄ɹk), *v.* [OE. *smearcian*, *smercian*, (with *k*-formative) f. **smar-* **smer-* (**smir-*), repr. by OE. *smerian* laugh at, *bi|smer*, *bi|smerian* scorn, **smǣre* in *gāl|smǣre* given to frivolous laughter, OHG. *smierōn* (G. †*schmieren*) smile. Cf. SMILE *v.*] **1.** *intr.* To smile; in later use, to smile in an affected, self-satisfied, or silly manner; to simper. **2.** *trans.* To utter with a smirk. BROWNING.

1. The young perfumer came, smirking and scraping, into the room MME. D'ARBLAY. Hence **Smi·rker. Smi·rkingly** *adv.* in a smirking manner.

Smite (smǝit), *sb.* ME. [f. next.] A stroke or heavy blow with a weapon, the hand, etc., or the sound made by this. Now chiefly *rhet.*

Smite (smǝit), *v.* Pa. t. **smote** (smǒ[u]t), †**smit.** Pa. pple. **smitten** (smi·t'n), **smit** (*arch.*), †**smote.** [OE. *smītan* smear, pollute = OFris. *smīta*, OS. *bismītan*, MLG., MDu. *smīten* (Du. *smijten*), OHG. *smīzan* smear (G. *schmeissen* throw, fling), Goth. *bi|smeitan*, *ga|smeitan* smear :– Gmc. **smītan*.] **I.** *trans.* **1.** To administer a blow to (a person, etc.) with the hand, a stick, or the like; to strike or hit; to beat or buffet; to slap or smack. Now *rhet.* and *rare.* **b.** To strike with the foot (†or spur). Also said of the foot. Now *rhet.* or *poet.* ME. **c.** To strike or touch (a harp, etc.) so as to produce musical sounds. Now *poet.* late ME. **2.** Of the Deity, in or after biblical use: To visit with death, destruction, or overthrow; to afflict or punish in some signal manner OE. **3.** To strike with a weapon, etc., so as to inflict serious injury or death ME. **b.** In or after Biblical use: To strike, or strike down, in battle; to kill, slay ME. **4. a.** Of hail, lightning, flame, etc.: To strike and injure; to destroy, blast. late ME. **b.** To beat or dash against (something) 1440. **c.** Of sunlight, etc.: To beat or shine strongly upon 1588. **5.** Of diseases, distempers, etc.: To attack or affect suddenly or grievously. Freq. in pa. pple., and const. *by* or *with* (a malady, etc.). ME. **6.** To infect, imbue, impress, strike suddenly or strongly *with* some feeling or sentiment. Chiefly in pa. pple. ME. **7.** Of the heart, conscience, etc.: To discompose or disquiet (one); to affect painfully. late ME. **b.** To distress or perturb (a person, the mind, conscience, etc.) 1470. **8.** To strike or impress (the mind, etc.) favourably or attractively. Chiefly in pa. pple. and const. *with.* 1663. **b.** To inspire or inflame with love; to enamour. Chiefly in pa. pple. (*smitten*, also joc. *smit*) and const. *with* or *by.* 1663.

1. The Case was the same with Asa in his Anger, when he smote the Prophet 1675. **c.** Then smyte your tabur, and cry huff, huff, huff and make the fowle to spryng 1486. **2.** The Lorde smote him, so y[t] he dyed COVERDALE 1 *Sam.* 25:38. **3.** I am so deeply smitten thro' the helm That without help I cannot last till morn TENNYSON. Phr. *To s... hip and thigh*: see HIP *sb.*[1] **4. b.** With the din Smitten, the precipices rang aloud WORDSW. **c.** As thy eye beames, when their fresh rayse haue smot The night of dew SHAKS. **6.** Wit strang dred he smiton was ME. **7.** Dauids heart smote him, because he had cut off Sauls skirt 1 *Sam.* 24:5. **8.** Smit with the beauty of so fair a scene COWPER. **b.** Phillis one Day..smote the Heart of a gay West-Indian STEELE.

II. *trans.* **1.** To strike or cut *off* (the head, a limb, etc.) with a slashing blow ME. **b.** To strike or knock, to drive or force with a blow or stroke, *away, back, from, off, out, over,* etc. ME. **2.** To knock, beat, or strike *down, to the earth* or *ground* ME. **3. a.** To hew, cut, chop, or break in pieces, fragments, etc. ME. **b.** To bring *into* a certain condition by, or as by, striking (*rare*) ME. **4.** To strike, deal, or give (a blow, stroke, etc.) ME. **5.** To drive, hammer, knock, strike (a thing) with some degree of force *against, into, on*, etc. something else ME. **b.** To strike, dash, or clap *together* or *against* each other ME. †**6. a.** To make or contract (an agreement, etc.) –1596. †**b.** To strike or coin (money) –1535.

2. Surely they are smitten downe before vs *Judges* 20:39. **3. b.** If we look not wisely on the Sun it self, it smites us into darknes MILT. **5.** Then Iael..went softly vnto him, and smote the naile into his temples *Judges* 4:21.

III. *absol.* or *intr.* **1.** To deal or give a blow or blows; to strike, deliver strokes. Also with advs. as *on, out.* ME. **b.** To strike *with* a hammer in doing smith-work; now *spec.* to strike with the sledge. late ME. †**2.** To come *together* in conflict –1590. **b.** To come *together* with some degree of force; to strike or dash *on* or *against* something ME. **3.** To strike, to pass or penetrate, *in, into*, or *through* something ME.

1. Satan..Saw where the Sword of Michael smote MILT. **2. b.** The heart melteth, and the knees s. together *Nahum* 2:10. **3.** But Arthur..Felt the light of her eyes into his life S. on the sudden TENNYSON. Hence **Smi·tten** *ppl. a.* that has been beaten or struck.

Smiter (smǝi·təɹ). ME. [f. prec. + -ER[1].] **1.** One who smites; a beater, striker. †**2.** A weapon with which one smites; a sword, a scimitar. (Partly suggested by *simiter* 'scimitar'.) –1648. **3.** A variety of fancy pigeon 1668.

Smith (smiþ), *sb.* [OE. *smiþ* = OFris. *smith*, MDu. *smit*, (also mod.) *smid*, OHG. *smid* (G. *schmied*, †*schmid*), ON. *smiðr* :– Gmc. **smiþaz* (in Goth. *aiza|smiþa* coppersmith).] One who works in iron or other metals; *esp.* a blacksmith or farrier; a forger, hammerman. Freq. in combs., as *black-, copper-, silver-, whitesmith.*

Smith (smiþ), *v.* [OE. *smiþian* = OS., OHG. *smiþōn*, ON. *smiða*, Goth. *ga|smiþōn*, f. the sb.] **1.** *trans.* To make, construct, or fashion (a weapon, iron implement, etc.) by forging; to forge or smithy. **b.** To deal with by heating and hammering; to hammer or beat (a blade, etc.) on an anvil. late ME. **2.** *intr.* To work at the forge; to practise smith-work ME.

1. b. After forging, the blade is smithed, or beaten on an anvil 1851. Hence **Smi·ther** (*rare*) a s.; a hammerman.

Smitham (smi·ðăm), **smeddum** (sme·dǝ̆m). [OE. *smed(e)ma* fine flour, meal, of unkn. origin; later assim. to SMITH *sb.* or *v.*] **1.** A fine powder. **2.** *Mining.* The finest lead ore, usu. passed through a sieve, and afterwards ground to powder 1653. **3.** *Sc.* Spirit, energy, go 1790.

Smi·thcraft. 1755. [f. SMITH *sb.* + CRAFT *sb.*] The work, craft, or art of a smith.

Smithereens (smiðərī·nz), *sb. pl. colloq.* and *dial.* 1841. [f. next, with Irish dim. suffix -EEN².] Small fragments; atoms. Usu. in phrases *to knock* (etc.) *to* or *into, to go to, s.*

Smithers (smi·ðəɹz), *sb. pl.* Also sing. *colloq.* and *dial.* 1847. [Of unkn. origin.] = prec.

Smithery (smi·þəri). 1625. [f. SMITH *sb.* + -ERY.] **1.** The trade, occupation, or art of a smith; smithcraft, smith-work. **2.** The forge or workshop of a smith; a smithy; *esp.* in British Admiralty dockyards, the building in which smith-work is done 1755.

1. *fig.* From..this sonorous s. of harsh words.. nothing adequate emerged DE QUINCEY.

Smithfield (smi·þfīld). 1599. [Name of a locality in London (orig. *Smethefeld*, f. SMEETH *a.*), long celebrated as a market for cattle, etc., and now the central meat-market.] **1.** A cattle- or meat-market (*rare*). **†2.** *S. bargain*, a sharp or roguish bargain, or one in which the purchaser is deceived; also *transf.*, a mercenary marriage –1775.

2. To find myselfe made a mere S. bargain of at last! SHERIDAN.

Smithing (smi·þiŋ), *vbl. sb.* ME. [f. SMITH *v.* + -ING¹.] The action of SMITH *v.*; the art or process of fashioning or forging metals; forging.

Smithsonite (smi·þsənəit). 1835. [Named after James *Smithson* (1765–1829), who distinguished it from calamine; see -ITE¹ 2 b.] *Min.* **1.** Silicate of zinc. **2.** *U.S.* Carbonate of zinc 1856.

Smithy (smi·ði), *sb.* Also *Sc.* and *n. dial.* **smiddy.** ME. [– ON. *smiðja*, corresp. to OE. *smiþþe* (surviving in early ME. *smiþ(þ)e*), OFris. *smithe*, MLG. *smede* (*smee*), MDu. *smisse* (Du. *smidse*), OHG. *smidda, smitta* (G. *schmiede*).] **1.** The workshop of a smith; a blacksmith's shop. Also occas., a portable forge. **2.** Smithcraft (*rare*) 1804.

1. His blazing Locks..hiss'd, like red hot Iron within the S. drown'd DRYDEN. Hence **Smithy** *v. trans.* to forge or smith; *intr.* to practise smithing.

Smi·ttle, *a. n. dial.* and *Sc.* 1583. [f. dial. *smit* (f. the weak grade of OE. *smītan* SMITE *v.*) + -LE 1.] Infectious; contagious. So **Smi·ttle** *v. trans.* to infect.

Smock (smǫk), *sb.* [OE. *smoc* = OHG. *smoccho*, ON. *smokkr* (perh. f. Eng.); rel. to MHG. *gesmuc* (G. *schmuck* ornament); parallel to forms based on **smŭʒ-*, viz. OE. *smūgan* creep, MHG. *smiegen*, ON. *smjúga* creep into, put on a garment, OE. *æ|smogu* snake's skin, *smygel*(s burrow. Cf. SMUGGLE.] **1.** A woman's undergarment; a shift or chemise. Now *arch.* or *dial.* **†b.** Used allusively to denote a woman or womankind –1693. **2.** = SMOCK-FROCK 1831.

1. Neare is my petticoat but nearer is my s. 1639. The colonel gave a s. for the young wenches to run for 1722.

attrib. and *Comb.*: **s.-face,** a pale and smooth or effeminate face; a person having a face of this description; so **-faced** *a.*; **-race,** a race in which a s. was offered as a prize to be run for by women or girls. Hence **Smo·ckless** *a.* having no s. or chemise.

Smock (smǫk), *v.* 1614. [f. the sb.] **†1.** *trans.* To render effeminate or womanish. SYLVESTER. **†2.** *intr.* To consort with women –1738. **3.** *trans.* To dress in a smock 1847. **4.** *Needlework.* To gather by means of sewing done in lines crossing each other diagonally at regular intervals after a honeycomb pattern common on smock-frocks 1888. Freq. in *vbl. sb.* (concr. the pattern so formed). Hence **Smo·cker,** one who smocks blouses, etc.

Smock-frock. 1800. [SMOCK *sb.*] A loose-fitting garment of coarse linen or the like, worn by farm-labourers over or instead of a coat and usu. reaching to mid-leg or lower. Hence **Smo·ck-frocked** (frǫkt) *a.* wearing a s.

Smokable (smōᵘ·kăb'l), *a.* and *sb.* Also **smokeable.** 1839. [f. SMOKE *v.* + -ABLE.] **A.** *adj.* That may be smoked; fit or suitable for smoking. **B.** *sb. pl.* Things which may be smoked 1849.

Smoke (smōᵘk), *sb.* [OE. *smoca*, f. the wk. grade of the base repr. by OE. *smēocan* SMEEK *v.* To a different grade (**smauk-*) belong MDu. *smoock* (Du. *smook*), (M)LG. *smōk*, MHG. *smouch* (G. *schmauch*) and OE. *smēoc*, etc.] **1.** The visible volatile product given off by burning or smouldering substances. **b.** *transf.* The pollen of the yew when scattered in a cloud 1868. **2.** With *a* and *pl.* A volume, cloud, or column of smoke. In Amer. and Austr. use *spec.* one serving as a signal, sign of an encampment, etc. late ME. **b.** The smoke arising from a particular hearth or fireplace; hence, a hearth, fire-place, house. Now *rare.* 1591. **3.** Fume or vapour caused by the action of heat on moisture. late ME. **b.** A mist, fog, or miasma 1648. **4. a.** Tobacco. Now *rare* or *Obs.* 1612. **b.** A cigar or cigarette 1882. **5.** [f. the vb.] A spell of smoking tobacco, etc. 1837. **6.** *Cape s.*, a cheap kind of brandy drunk in South Africa 1849.

2. We..leave them a sign to know where we are by making one or more great Smoaks 1697. **5.** Eager for a s. and a talk 1837.

Phrases. *There is no fire without s.* and *no s. without fire* (see FIRE *sb.* I b). †*Out of the s. into the fire, smother*, etc., out of a small danger into a great one. *To sell s.* (after L. *fumum vendere*), to swindle. *To come to, end in, vanish into, s.*, to come to nothing, be without result. *Like s.*, very quickly, rapidly.

attrib. and *Comb.*, as *s.-cloud, -ring, -wreath,*; *s. flue, funnel; s.-blue, -grey* (used as sbs. or adjs.); *s. quartz*, smoky quartz; *s.-consumer, -consuming; s.-proof, -tight* adjs.

Special combs.: **s.-arch** *U.S.*, the s.-box of a locomotive; **-bomb** = S.-BALL; **-box** *techn.* a chamber in a steam boiler between the flues and the chimney-stack; in a locomotive placed at the base of the funnel; **-farthing** *Hist.* an offering made at Whitsuntide by the householders of a diocese to the cathedral church; also, a hearth-tax; **-glass,** an eyepiece of smoked glass; **s. helmet,** a helmet used by firemen, enabling the wearer to see and breathe freely in the midst of smoke; **-house,** a room in a tannery, heated by smouldering spent tan, where hides are unhaired; a house or room used for curing meat, fish, etc., by means of s.; **-sail** (*Naut.*), a small sail put up to prevent the s. of the galley from being blown aft; **-screen** *Mil.*, s. diffused to hide operations; **-test,** a method of testing the state of drains and pipes by means of s.; **-tree,** the Venetian sumach, *Rhus cotinus*, which has a feathery inflorescence suggestive of s.; also, the American species *Rhus cotinoides.*

Smoke (smōᵘk), *v.* [OE. *smocian*, f. *smoca* SMOKE *sb.* To a different grade (**smauk-*) of the base belong (M)Du., (M)LG. *smoken*, LG. *smöken*, G. *schmauchen, schmäuchen.* See prec. and SMEEK *v.*] **I. 1.** *intr.* To produce or give forth smoke. **b.** Of a room, chimney, lamp, etc.: To be smoky, to emit smoke, as the result of imperfect draught or improper burning 1663. **2.** To give off or send up vapour, dust, spray, etc.; *esp.* to steam. late ME. **b.** To rise, spread, or move, like smoke 1595. **c.** To ride, drive, sail, etc., at a rapid pace or great speed. Const. *along* (prep. or adv.). 1697. **†3.** To smart, to suffer severely –1773.

1. The houses fired and smoking farre of 1591. *fig.* Where hertes still burne and malice continually smoketh 1548. **2.** Which made his horse's flanks to s. COWPER. **c.** Proud of his Steeds he smoaks along the Field DRYDEN. **3.** Now I am resolv'd I will go see 'em, or some-body shall smoak for't DRYDEN.

II. 1. *trans.* To fumigate (a person, place, etc.), esp. as a means of disinfecting OE. **b.** To expose or subject to smoke, so as to suffocate, stupefy, or make uncomfortable OE. **c.** To fill with, expose to, smoke, esp. so as to blacken, discolour, or render obscure 1611. **d.** To cure or preserve (bacon, fish, etc.) by exposure to smoke; to smoke-dry 1757. **2.** To drive *out* or *away* by means of smoke 1593. **3.** To get an inkling of, to smell or suspect (a plot, design, etc.). Also *absol.* Now *arch.* 1608. **4.** To make fun of, to jest at; to ridicule, banter, or quiz (a person). Now *arch.* 1700. **5.** To observe, take note of, 'twig'. Now *arch.* 1715.

1. I was smoaking a musty roome SHAKS. **b.** They then s. the bees until they are stupid 1900. **c.** I copy pictures and he smokes them and sells them as old masters 1883. **2.** Till we s. out of his earths the old fox Louis SCOTT. **4.** We hated her and smoked her and baited her and..drove her away KEATS. **5.** Kit, s. his eyes, how they glare 1826.

III. 1. *intr.* To inhale (and expel again) the fumes of tobacco, etc., from a pipe, cigar, or cigarette 1617. **2.** *trans.* To use (tobacco, etc.) as material for smoking 1687. **b.** To use (a pipe, cigar, etc.) in the act of smoking; to take (so many whiffs) 1706. **3.** To wear *out*, waste (*away*), bring *into* a certain state, etc., by smoking tobacco or some similar substance 1604. **4.** *intr.* Of a pipe: To admit of being smoked 1883.

1. Smoking vehemently on his black stump of a pipe CARLYLE. **2.** The bandits' custom of smoking banghi (wild hemp) 1878. **b.** See, I have smoked out your cigar 1842. **3.** Sweet youth, Smoake not thy time 1617.

Smo·ke-ball. 1753. [SMOKE *sb.*] **1.** *Mil.* A projectile filled with a preparation which, when ignited, sends out clouds of smoke, used to conceal military operations, etc. **2.** A ball used in trap-shooting, which, when struck by a shot, emits a puff of smoke 1881.

Smo·ke-black, *sb.* 1712. [BLACK *sb.* 2.] A form of lamp-black obtained by the combustion of resinous materials.

Smo·ke-dry, *v.* 1704. [SMOKE *sb.*] **1.** *trans.* To dry or cure (meat, fish, etc.) by exposure to smoke. **2.** *intr.* To become dried by the action of smoke 1855. So **Smo·ke-dried** *ppl. a.* 1653.

Smo·ke-hole. ME. [SMOKE *sb.*] The vent or external orifice of a flue; a hole in the roof of a hut through which the smoke of the fire escapes. **b.** = FUMAROLE 1899.

Smo·ke-jack. 1675. [JACK *sb.* II. 1.] An apparatus for turning a roasting-spit, fixed in a chimney and set in motion by the current of air passing up this.

Smokeless (smōᵘ·klės), *a.* 1582. [f. SMOKE *sb.* + -LESS.] **1.** Emitting or producing no smoke. **2.** Free from, clear of, smoke 1631.

1. Tenants with sighs the smoakless tow'rs survey POPE. **2.** The sun shines..in s. mackerel-sky CARLYLE. Hence **Smo·keless-ly** *adv.*, **-ness.**

Smoker (smōᵘ·kəɹ). 1599. [f. SMOKE *v.* + -ER¹.] **1.** One who cures fish, bacon, etc., by means of smoke. **2.** Something which emits smoke; e.g. a chimney, locomotive, etc. 1700. **3.** One who smokes tobacco, opium, or the like 1617. **4. a.** A railway carriage or compartment assigned for the use of those travellers who wish to smoke 1883. **b.** A concert at which smoking is permitted 1891.

Smo·ke-stack. 1862. [STACK *sb.* 4 b.] **1.** *U.S.* **a.** The funnel of a steamboat. **b.** The chimney of a locomotive 1875. **2.** The chimney of a stove; a chimney-stack 1871.

Smoking (smōᵘ·kiŋ), *vbl. sb.* 1530. [f. SMOKE *v.* + -ING¹.] The action of the vb. **b.** *attrib.*, as *s.-carriage, -concert*; **s.-bean** *U.S.*, the catalpa bean, the pods of which are smoked by boys; **-room,** a room in a house, hotel, etc. set apart in which to smoke.

Smoking (smōᵘ·kiŋ), *ppl. a.* ME. [f. SMOKE *v.* + -ING².] In the senses of the vb. **b.** quasi-*adv.* in *s.-hot* 1816. Hence **Smo·kingly** *adv.* smokily.

Smoky (smōᵘ·ki), *a.* and *sb.* ME. [f. SMOKE *sb.* + -Y¹.] **A.** *adj.* **1.** Emitting smoke in considerable volume. **b.** Of a chimney: Inclined to send out smoke into the room 1639. **2.** Of vapour, mist, etc.: Having the character or appearance of smoke; smoke-like. late ME. **3.** Full of, or charged with, smoke; rendered offensive or disagreeable by the presence of smoke. late ME. **b.** Blackened or begrimed by smoke 1552. **†4.** *fig.* Having the obscuring, objectionable, or unsubstantial qualities of smoke –1633. **5.** Having the flavour or odour of smoke; tasting or smelling of smoke 1542. **6.** Of the colour of smoke; dark, dusky; *spec.* of a brownish or bluish shade of grey 1555. **7.** Steaming, reeking; rising in fine spray 1590. **8.** Addicted to, associated with, the smoking of tobacco 1596. **†9.** Shrewd, sharp, suspicious –1784. **10.** *U.S.* Foggy, misty 1768.

1. In Sympathizing Night he rowls his smoaky Fires 1663. **2.** The light and s. mist COWPER. **3.** O, he is..Worse then a smoakie House SHAKS. **b.** In lowly sheds With s. rafters MILT. **6.** S. quartz is a transparent..variety, having a s. color 1837. **8.** A s. man must write s. farces LAMB.

B. *sb.* **1.** *dial.* The hedge-sparrow 1889. **2.** *Sc.* A smoked haddock 1891. **3.** A smoke-blue cat 1898. Hence **Smo·kily** *adv.* **Smo·kiness.**

Smolt (smōᵘlt). orig. *Sc.* and *north.* 1469. [In earliest use Sc. (AL. *smoltus* XIV); of unkn. origin. Cf. SMELT *sb.*] **1.** A young salmon in the stage intermediate between the parr and the grilse, when it becomes covered with silvery scales and migrates to the sea for the first time. **2.** *transf.* A small person or thing 1808.

Smooch (smūtʃ), *v.* Latterly *U.S.* 1631. [See SMUDGE *v.*[1]] *trans.* To sully, dirty.

Smoot (smūt). *Printers' slang.* 1683. [Of unkn. origin.] *intr.* To do casual work in a house where one is not regularly employed.

Smooth (smūð), *sb.* 1440. [f. the adj.] **1.** †**a.** = SMEETH *sb.* **b.** *Naut.* A stretch of comparatively smooth or calm water in a rough sea 1840. **2.** The smooth part or surface *of* something; smoothness 1551. **b.** Smooth water or ground 1667. **c.** The agreeable or pleasant part, side, or aspect of anything. (Opp. to *rough.*) 1612. **3.** An act of smoothing 1848. **4.** A smoother; a smooth file 1879.

2. Like the silver-wing'd dove was the s. of her hair 1805.

Smooth (smūð), *a.* [OE. *smōþ* (rare, the usual form being *smēþe* SMEETH, which was gen. superseded); without certain cognates.] **1.** Having a surface free from projections, irregularities, or inequalities; presenting no roughness or unevenness to the sight or touch. **b.** Free from hairs or bristles. late ME. **c.** *Bot.* Of leaves: Free from hairs or any sort of roughness 1688. **2.** Of ground, ways, etc.: Not rugged, rough, or broken; free from obstructions; easy to traverse. late ME. **3.** Of water, the sea, etc.: Not broken or turbulent; free from big waves or roughness; running or flowing evenly, calmly, or gently. Hence, of a passage, etc.: Accompanied by or performed in good weather. late ME. **4.** Of wind or weather: Not rough or stormy; agreeable, pleasant. Now *rare.* late ME. **5.** Of liquids, etc.: Having a uniform or even consistency; free from lumps or knots 1450. **b.** Of liquor: Soft to the taste; free from sharpness or acidity 1743. **6.** Of looks, words, etc.: Pleasant, affable, polite; seemingly amiable or friendly; having a show of sincerity. late ME. **b.** Of the tongue, or of persons: Speaking fair or smoothly; using specious or attractive language; plausible, bland, insinuating, flattering. (Usu. in an unfavourable sense.) 1450. **7.** Of style or diction: Flowing gently or easily; nicely modulated; not harsh or rugged; polished 1589. **b.** Of writers: Having an easy, polished style 1670. **8.** Free from disturbance or excitement 1756. **9.** Free from, unaccompanied by, obstruction, interruption, impediment, or difficulty. Also in phr. *to make s.* 1792. **10.** Of sounds: Soft; not harsh or grating 1775. **b.** *S. breathing*: see BREATHING *vbl. sb.* 9.

1. Brows as pale and s. As those that mourn. . In deathless marble TENNYSON. **b.** Beholde, my brother Esau is rough, and I am s. COVERDALE *Gen.* 27:11. **2.** The road to wickedness is s. and very short 1875. **3.** *S. chance* or *spell*, a stretch of calm water in a rough sea; Watching for 's. chance' 1840. **5. b.** More tuns of marsh water. . than combs of s. ale 1896. **6.** Colour'd with a s. pretence Of specious love and duty DRYDEN. **b.** A s. Preacher, and a rank Whigg 1708. **7.** Their style is clear, masculine, and s., but not florid SWIFT. **8.** Hence have I S. passions, s. discourse, and joyous thought WORDSW. **9.** Consider too whether he had s. times of it CARLYLE.

Comb. Forming parasynthetic adjs., as *s.-bellied, -browed, -chinned*, etc.; **s.-spoken** *a.*, smooth-tongued. Hence **Smoo·th-ly** *adv.*, **-ness.**

Smooth(e (smūð), *v.* ME. [f. SMOOTH *a.*, repl. ME. *smethe* SMEETH *v.*] **1.** *trans.* To make (a surface or substance) smooth, even, or level; to remove or reduce the roughness, irregularity, inequality, or unevenness of 1440. **b.** To iron (linen, etc.). Now *dial.* 1617. **c.** To cause (feathers, hair, etc.) to lie smooth and even 1634. **2.** To make (a way) easy or plain; to free from obstruction, difficulty, or impediment 1582. **b.** To diminish or clear away (an obstruction, difficulty, etc.) 1599. **3.** To render (the brow) free from wrinkles, lines, frowns, etc., by natural effort; to invest with, replace by, a calm or placid expression 1593. **4. a.** To make smooth, plausible, or specious ME. †**b.** To refine (a person or his manners) –1749. **c.** To render smooth to the ear; to polish 1667. †**5.** To use smooth, flattering, or complimentary language to (a person). Also *absol.* –1718. **6. a.** To allay, assuage, mitigate the force of (passion, trouble, etc.) 1589. **b.** To render (the mind, etc.) calm or tranquil; to soothe 1604. **7.** To hush up, gloss over, make less conspicuous or offensive 1592. **8.** *intr.* To become smooth, calm, or tranquil 1837. **9.** With advs. and preps. 1584.

1. To s. the yce, or adde another hew Vnto the Raine-bow SHAKS. **c.** Smoothing the Raven doune Of darknes till it smil'd MILT. **2.** Useful for smoothing a man's way through the world 1779. **3.** Grim-visag'd Warre, hath smooth'd his wrinkled Front SHAKS. **4. a.** An open grave their throat, their tongue they s. MILT. **c.** Great Spencer first. . Smoothed our old Metre, and refined our Lays 1724. **5.** Because I cannot flatter,. . Smile in men's faces, s., deceiue, and cogge SHAKS. **6. a.** Whereof hee soon aware, Each perturbation smooth'd with outward calme, Artificer of fraud MILT. **b.** What could the world afford. . Which did not s. my soule 1604. **7.** Oh had't beene a stranger. . To s. his fault I should haue beene more milde SHAKS. **8.** I trust that things are smoothing now 1864. **9.** *To s. over* (fig.) to gloss over. This he smoothed over to his conscience SCOTT. Hence **Smoo·ther,** one who or that which smooths; a refiner, pacifier; an ironer; a smoothing-iron, etc.

Smoo·th(-)bore. 1848. [f. SMOOTH *a.* + BORE *sb.*[1]] **1.** A cannon or gun of which the barrel is made with a smooth or unrifled bore. **2.** *attrib.* **a.** Having a smooth or unrifled bore 1859. **b.** Adapted for guns having a smooth bore 1859.

Smoothen (smū·ð'n), *v.* 1635. [f. SMOOTH *a.* + -EN[5].] = SMOOTH *v.*

Smooth-faced, *a.* 1580. [SMOOTH *a.*] **1.** Of persons: Having a face free from hair, wrinkles, etc.; clean-shaven, beardless. **b.** *fig.* Having or assuming a bland, ingratiating, or insinuating expression; plausible in manner 1595. **2.** *fig.* Of words, etc.: Specious, plausible 1620. **3.** Of things: Having a smooth face or surface 1647.

1. *transf.* Let thy Heires. . Enrich the time to come, with Smooth-fac'd Peace, With smiling Plenty SHAKS.

Smoothing (smū·ðiŋ), *vbl. sb.* 1577. [f. SMOOTH *v.* + -ING[1].] The action of the verb; an instance of this. **b.** *Phonology.* The reduction of a diphthong to a monophthong 1888. **c.** *Wireless.* Levelling out of fluctuation in the supply of current.

attrib.: **s.-iron,** a flat-iron; an iron slicker used for smoothing leather; **-plane,** a small fine-set plane used in finishing; **-trowel,** a trowel used in plastering.

Smooth-tongued, *a.* 1592. [f. SMOOTH *a.*] **1.** Smooth or plausible in speech; using fair or flattering words; smooth-spoken. **2.** Marked or characterized by, of the nature of, plausibility or speciousness 1761.

1. Those Jesuits are so s. to women 1829.

Smore (smōᵊɹ), *v.* Now *Sc.* and *n. dial.* [OE. *smorian* suffocate, corresp. to (M)LG., (M)Du. *smoren*, of unkn. origin. See SMOTHER *v.*] = SMOTHER *v.*

Smored and styfled, theyr breath failing, thei gaue vp to God their innocent soules 1513.

Smother (smʋ·ðəɹ), *sb.* [Early ME. *smorðer*, later (with loss of the first *r*) *smoþer*; f. base of OE. *smorian* SMORE.] **1.** Dense, suffocating, or stifling smoke, such as is produced by combustion without flame. (Freq. coupled with *smoke.*) **b.** A smouldering state or condition; a smouldering or slow-burning fire 1597. **2.** Dense or suffocating dust, fog, etc., filling the air 1697. **b.** A confused turmoil or welter of foam or water 1840.

1. Thus must I from the smoake into the s. SHAKS. **b.** Men should remedy Suspicion, by procuring to know more, and not to keep their Suspicions in S. BACON.

Comb.: **s.-kiln,** a kiln in which pottery in process of firing is blackened by smoke. Hence **Smo·thery** *a.* tending to smother.

Smother (smʋ·ðəɹ), *v.* [Early ME. *smorðren*, f. prec.] **I.** *trans.* **1. a.** To suffocate with smoke. **b.** To suffocate by the prevention of breathing; to deprive of life by suffocation 1548. **c.** Used hyperbolically to denote an effusive welcome, etc., or the gaining of a complete or overwhelming victory 1676. **2.** †**a.** To conceal by keeping silent about; to hush up (a matter, etc.). (Cf. 6 below.) –1752. **b.** To cover up, so as to conceal or cause to be forgotten 1585. **c.** To repress (feeling, etc.) by the exercise of self-control 1591. **3.** To cover up so as to prevent from having free play or development; to suppress or check in this way 1590. **b.** To prevent (words, etc.) from having full utterance; to render indistinct or silent 1601. **4. a.** To deaden or extinguish (fire, etc.) by covering so as to exclude the air; to cause to smoulder 1591. †**b.** To cook in a close vessel 1809. **5.** To cover up, cover over, densely or thickly by some thing or substance 1598. **6.** With *up.* **a.** = sense 2 a. 1589. **b.** To cover up in a close, dense, or suffocating manner, etc. 1590.

1. b. The helpless traveller. . smother'd in the dusty whirlwind dies ADDISON. **2. c.** She smothered her own grief 1891. **3.** Ability. . smothered by pomposity and vulgar pride 1882. **4. a.** S. the fire with wet cloathes CAPT. SMITH. **5.** The small stations we passed were smothered in green foliage 1872.

II. *intr.* **1.** To be suffocated or stifled; to be prevented by smoke or other means from breathing freely 1520. **2.** To smoulder; to burn slowly. Now *dial.* 1600.

Smouch (smautʃ), *sb.*[1] Now *dial.* 1578. [Of imit. origin, like SMACK *sb.*[2]] A kiss. Hence **Smouch** *v.*[1]

Smouch (smautʃ), *sb.*[2] 1873. [perh. var. of SMUTCH *sb.* Cf. also SMOOCH *v.*] A smudge, a dirty mark.

Smouch (smautʃ), *v.*[2] Now *U.S.* 1826. [perh. f. SMOUCH, var. of SMOUSE.] **1.** *trans.* To acquire dishonestly; to pilfer. **2.** *intr.* To deal unfairly or dishonestly 1848.

Smoulder (smōᵘ·ldəɹ), *sb.* ME. [Goes with next.] **1.** Smother; smoky vapour; the result of smouldering or slow combustion. **2.** A slow-burning fire or the ashes of this 1548.

Smoulder (smōᵘ·ldəɹ), *v.* 1481. [rel. obscurely to LG. *smöln*, MDu. *smölen* (Du. *smeulen* smoulder), Flem. *smoel* sultry.] †**1.** *trans.* To smother, suffocate –1586. **2.** *intr.* To burn and smoke without flame 1529.

2. The floor was smouldering in several places 1859. *fig.* The Civil War. . had continued during some time to s. MACAULAY. Hence **Smou·lderingly** *adv.*

Smouse (smauz), **smouch** (smautʃ). 1705. [– Du. *smous* Jew, usurer, corresp. to G. *schmus* talk, patter – Yiddish *schmuess*, Heb. *šᵉmûʻôṯ* tales, news, the reference being to the persuasive talk of Jewish pedlars.] **1.** *slang.* A Jew. **2.** *S. Afr.* An itinerant trader 1849.

Smudge (smʋdʒ), *sb.*[1] 1768. [f. SMUDGE *v.*[1]] **1.** A dirty mark or stain, esp. such as is caused by a smear or by trying to rub out a previous mark. **b.** *transf.* A blurred indistinct mass or area 1871. **2.** A smeary condition, substance, etc.; the result of smearing or dirtying 1830. **b.** *techn.* The scum of paint 1823. **3.** Very small coal; fine slack 1883.

Smudge (smʋdʒ), *sb.*[2] 1767. [Related to SMUDGE *v.*[2]] **1.** A suffocating smoke. Now *U.S.* **2.** A heap of combustibles ignited and emitting dense smoke, usually made with the object of repelling mosquitoes, etc. Chiefly *U.S.* and *Canada.* 1842.

Smudge (smʋdʒ), *v.*[1] late ME. [Of unkn. origin, but parallel to synon. SMUTCH *sb.* and *v.*, SMOOCH *v.*; cf. the formally corresp. pair *sludge* and *slush*, and forms cited s.v. SMUT *v.*] **1.** *trans.* To soil, stain, blacken, smirch; to mark with dirty stains or smears. **b.** To rub out or in, to paint or lay on, etc., in a smearing or daubing manner 1865. **2.** To bungle, make a mess of (something) 1864.

Smudge (smʋdʒ), *v.*[2] Now *dial.* and *U.S.* 1599. [Of unkn. origin.] **1.** *trans.* †**a.** To cure (herring) by smoking. NASHE. **b.** *U.S.* To make a smoky fire in (a tent, etc.); to fill with smoke from a smudge 1891. **2.** *intr.* To smoulder 1825.

Smudgy (smʋ·dʒi), *a.* 1859. [f. SMUDGE *sb.*[1] or *v.*[1] + -Y[1].] **1.** Grimy, dirty; marked with smudges. **2.** Smeared, smeary; blurred, indistinct 1865. Hence **Smu·dgi-ly** *adv.*, **-ness.**

Smug (smʋg), *a.* 1551. [– LG. *smuk* pretty (as in *smucke deern* = Greene's *smugge lasse*), with *g* (*gg*) for orig. *k* (*ck*) as in *trigger* (for *tricker* – Du. *trecker*), *sag* (– Du. *sacken*), etc. See also SMUGGLE.] **1.** Of persons: Trim, neat, spruce, smart; in later use, having a self-satisfied, conceited, or consciously respectable air. **2.** Of the face (person, etc.): Smooth, sleek; also, in later use = sense 4. 1582. **3.** Of things: Smooth, clean, neat, trim, or tidy; in later use, having an appearance suggestive of complacency or respectability 1596. **4.** Indicative of, characterized by, complacency or conscious respectability 1851.

1. A s. officer of the United States Government THACKERAY. **2.** Sleek their heads And s. their countenances COWPER. **3.** The s. and scanty draperies of his style DE QUINCEY. **4.** Addressing the audience. . in the most s. and self-satisfied tone 1859. Hence †**Smug** *sb.* a quiet hardworking student (*slang*); a s. or self-satisfied person. **Smu·g-ly** *adv.*, **-ness.**

Smug (smɒg), *v.* 1588. [f. prec.] **1.** *trans.* To smarten *up* (oneself or another, one's appearance, etc.); to make trim or gay. Also *absol.* †**2.** To smarten up (a thing); to fit *up* (a room, etc.) neatly or nicely (*rare*) –1751.

1. Your. . master. . has been smugging up his pretty face 1750.

Smuggle (smɒ·g'l), *v.* 1687. [Earlier *smuckle*, as in *smuckellor* (1661) – LG. *smukkelen*, with var. *smuggelen* (whence G. and Scand. forms), Du. *smokkelen*, of unkn. origin.] **1.** *trans.* To convey (goods) clandestinely into (or out of) a country or district, in order to avoid payment of legal duties, or in contravention of some enactment; to bring *in*, *over*, etc. in this way. **b.** *intr.* To practise smuggling 1697. **2.** *transf.* **a.** *trans.* To get possession of by stealth 1766. **b.** To convey, etc., in a stealthy or clandestine manner. Const. with *away, in, into, off, out of*, etc. 1783. **c.** *intr.* To make *off* stealthily 1865.

1. To *S. Goods*, to run them ashore, or bring them in by stealth, without paying the Custom 1706. **b.** The temptation to s. was diminished 1845. **2. b.** A single Plebeian could not be smuggled in 1783.

Smuggler (smɒ·gləɹ). 1661. [Earliest *smuckellor* – LG. *smukkeler*, also *smugg(e)ler*; see prec., -ER¹.] **1.** One who smuggles commodities; *esp.* one who makes a trade or practise of smuggling. **2.** A vessel employed in smuggling 1799.

Smut (smɒt), *sb.* 1664. [See SMUT *v.*] **1.** A fungous disease affecting cereals, etc., which are spoiled by the grain being wholly or partly converted into a blackish powder; also, one or other of the fungi (species of *Ustilagineæ*) causing the disease 1665. **2.** A black mark or stain; a smudge 1664. **3.** *Coal-mining.* Bad, soft, earthy coal 1686. **4.** Soot or sooty matter 1693. **b.** A particle of sooty matter 1806. **c.** A very minute insect 1899. **5.** Indecent or obscene language 1698.

5. The gentlemen talked s., the ladies laughed GOLDSM.

Phr. *Ditto, brother s.*, a tu quoque retort to criticism.

attrib.: **s.-ball,** a single grain of wheat or other cereal affected by smut or bunt; a cohesive body of smut.

Smut (smɒt), *v.* 1587. [Parallel with obs. synon. formations having the cons.-frame *sm . . . t* (with var. *sm . . . d*), as OE. *smitt* smear, *smittian* pollute, *smītan* SMITE, *besmotered* (Ch.), *smotry* (Lydg.) defiled, sullied, *smad* (XV), *smod* stain (XIV), *bismudded* XIII, and forms cited s.v. SMUDGE *v.*¹; cogn. further with Continental Gmc. formations such as LG. *smutt*, MHG. *smutz, smutzen* (G. *schmutz, -en*), LG. *smadden*, Du. *smodderen*.] **1.** *trans.* To mark with some black or dirty substance; to blacken, smudge. **2.** To affect (grain) with smut 1626. **b.** *intr.* Of grain: To be affected by smut 1657. **3.** *trans.* To make obscene 1722. **4.** *intr.* Of fish: To rise at, or feed on, smuts 1889.

1. *fig.* What is the cause why some one sinne doth so blot and s. the most excellent men? 1601.

Smutch (smɒtʃ), *sb.* 1530. [See SMUDGE *sb.*¹] **1.** A black or dirty mark; a stain; a smudge. **b.** *fig.* A moral stain 1648. **c.** A slight mark or indication; semblance; also, a slight or light touch 1776. **2.** Soot, smut, grime, dirt 1790.

1. c. Without a shadow, a relish, a s., a tinge,. . of anger BURKE.

Smutch (smɒtʃ), *v.* 1611. [See SMUDGE *v.*¹] *trans.* To blacken, make dirty, smut, smudge. **b.** *fig.* To stain, sully, besmirch, etc., morally or otherwise 1640.

b. The passion. . is never smutched by sensuality 1865.

Smutty (smɒ·ti), *a.* 1597. [f. SMUT *sb.* or *v.* + -Y¹.] **1.** Of grain: Affected by smut. **2.** Soiled with, full of, characterized by, smut, dirty; blackened 1645. **3.** Of the colour of smut; dusky; dark 1648. **4.** Having the appearance or form of smut 1667. **5.** Indecent, obscene, 'dirty' 1668.

5. He is s., and vulgar and low 1851. Hence **Smu·ttily** *adv.* **Smu·ttiness.**

Smyrna (smə̄·ɹnă). 1735. [L. *Smyrna*, Gr. Σμύρνα.] Name of the chief port of Asia Minor, situated at the head of the gulf of the same name, used *attrib.* in: *S. cotton*, an Indian cotton cultivated in the Levant; *S. wheat*, a kind of wheat with an extremely large ear. **b.** *ellipt.* (*pl.*) Smyrna raisins 1845.

Smyrnæ·an [L. *Smyrnæus*, Gr. Σμυρναῖος] = next 1598.

Smyrniote (smə̄·ɹniout), *sb.* and *a.* 1670. [f. SMYRNA + -OTE, after *Candiote, Cypriote*.] **A.** *sb.* An inhabitant or native of Smyrna. **B.** *adj.* Of or pertaining to Smyrna 1869.

Snack (snæk), *sb.* late ME. [– MDu. *snac(k* in sense 1, rel. to *snacken* (see next).] **1.** A snap or bite, esp. that of a dog. Now *dial.* **2.** A share, portion, part 1683. **3. a.** A mere taste of liquor 1685. **b.** A mere bite or morsel of food, as contrasted with a regular meal; a light or incidental repast 1737. **4.** Comb. *s.-bar, -basket.*

2. *To go snacks* (†or *s.*), to have a share *in* (something), to divide profits; 'Tis about a thousand pounds; we go snacks 1701.

Snack (snæk), *v.* ME. [– MDu. *snacken* snap (of a dog), var. of *snappen* SNAP *v.* Cf. SNATCH *v.*] **1.** *intr.* To bite or snap (at). *north.* and *Sc.* **2.** *trans.* To share, divide 1707. **3.** *intr.* To lunch, take a snack 1807.

Snaffle (snæ·f'l), *sb.* 1533. [prob. of LDu. origin.; cf. OFris. *snavel* mouth, (M)LG., (M)LDu. *snavel*, corresp. to OHG. *snabul* (G. *schnabel*) beak, bill, spout, nose; see -LE.] A simple form of bridle-bit, having less controlling power than one provided with a curb.

Phr. *To ride* (a person) *in, on,* or *with the s.*, to rule easily, to guide with a light hand.

Snaffle (snæ·f'l), *v.* 1559. [f. prec.] **1.** *trans.* To put a snaffle on (a horse, etc.); to control or guide with a snaffle. **2.** *slang.* To arrest; to seize; to acquire by means or machinations not strictly lawful, purloin 1725.

Snag (snæg), *sb.* 1577. [prob. of Scand. origin (cf. ON. *snaghyrndr* sharp-pointed (axe), Norw. dial. *snag, snage* sharp point, spike, Icel. *snagi* peg).] **1.** A short stump standing out from the trunk, or from a stout branch, of a tree or shrub, esp. one left after cutting or pruning. **b.** A trunk or large branch of a tree imbedded in the bottom of a river, lake, etc., with one end directed upwards (forming an impediment or danger to navigation). Orig. *U.S.* 1807. **c.** *fig.* An impediment or obstacle (now usu. unexpected) 1830. **2.** A sharp, angular, or jagged projection 1586. **b.** A broken piece or stump of a tooth; a large or unshapely tooth 1612. **c.** A tine or branch of a deer's horn, *spec.* one which is short or imperfectly developed 1673.

1. c. He's a s. in the Devil's way 1830.

Comb.: **s.-boat,** 'a steamboat fitted with an apparatus for removing snags, or obstructions to navigation in rivers'; **-tooth,** = 2 b.

Snag (snæg), *v.* 1807. [f. prec.] **1.** *trans.* **a.** In passive: To be caught, pierced, or damaged by a snag. Chiefly *U.S.*, and esp. of river-steamers. **b.** *fig.* To occupy or block as with a snag 1863. **2.** To cut roughly, or so as to leave snags 1811. **b.** To tear on or by a sharp projection. *dial.* 1854. **3.** To clear (a river, etc.) from snags 1882.

2. Blazing the trees and snagging the bushes with our tomahawks 1812.

Snagged (snæ·gd), *ppl. a.* 1658. [f. SNAG *sb.* or *v.* + -ED.] **1.** Having projecting points or jagged protuberances; jagged, ragged. **2.** Caught or impaled upon a snag 1872.

Snaggy (snæ·gi), *a.* 1566. [f. SNAG *sb.* + -Y¹.] **1.** Having snags or sharp protuberances; jagged, knotty; snag-like. **2.** Resembling or full of snags 1703.

1. His stalking steps are stayde Vpon a s. Oke SPENSER.

Snail (snēil), *sb.* [OE. *snæġ(e)l, sneġ(e)l* = OS. *snegil*, MLG. *sneil*, OHG. *snegil* (LG. *snagel*), ON. *snigill*, f. **snaʒ-* **sneʒ-*, rel. to MLG. *snigge*, OHG. *snecko* (G. *schnecke*); see -LE.] **1.** One or other of the terrestrial or freshwater gasteropods having a well-developed spiral or whorled shell capable of housing the whole body; also formerly, a slug.

The common types of the true snail belong to the genus *Helix* (esp. *H. aspersa* or *hortensis*, the common garden snail, and *H. pomatia*, the edible snail).

b. Applied to various animals allied to, or resembling, the snails or slugs 1541. **2.** Used with ref. to the exceptionally slow motion of the snail OE. **b.** A slow or indolent person; a sluggard 1590. †**3. a.** A structure or formation resembling a snail-shell; a testudo –1610. †**b.** *Mil.* = LIMAÇON 1. –1591. **4.** *pl.* A species of medick (usu. *Medicago scutellata*) having snail-shaped seed-pods 1629. **5.** *Mech.* A flat, spirally-curved piece of metal; *esp.* a toothed disc of this shape forming part of the striking mechanism of a clock; a spiral cam 1696.

2. Phr. *Snail's gallop, pace*, an excessively slow pace, rate of progress or motion etc. **b.** Dromio, thou Dromio, thou snaile, thou slug SHAKS.

Comb.: **s.-bore** *U.S.*, a shell-fish (*Urosalpinx cinerea*) which injures oysters by boring; **-fish,** a fish related to the lumpsucker; **-flower,** *Phaseolus caracalla*; **-plant,** = sense 4; **-slow** *a.* that is as slow as a s., very sluggish or tardy in motion. Hence **Snai·lery,** a place where (edible) snails are bred or reared.

Snail (snēil), *v.* 1548. [f. SNAIL *sb.*] †**1.** *intr.* Of soldiers: To form into a 'snail' or 'snails'. HALL. **2.** To move, walk, or travel lazily or sluggishly; to go very slowly. Also with *on*. 1582. **3.** *trans.* To make or construct after the spiral form of a snail-shell. Now *spec.* in clockmaking 1591. **b.** To finish off with curved eccentric lines 1884. **4.** To clear of, keep free from, slugs or snails 1661.

Snai·l-like, *a.* and *adv.* 1607. [f. SNAIL *sb.* + -LIKE.] **A.** *adj.* **1.** Like or resembling a snail in appearance, habits, etc. **2.** Slow, tardy 1639.

2. The s. siege of Ptolemais 1639.

B. *adv.* With the slow motion characteristic of a snail; tardily, sluggishly 1825.

Snai·l-paced, *a.* 1594. [SNAIL *sb.*] **1.** Slow, sluggish, or tardy in pace, progress, or motion; slothful, slow-moving. **2.** Marked by tardiness, slowness, or sluggishness 1601.

1. Goe. . bid the snaile-pac'd Aiax arme SHAKS.

†**'Snails,** *int.* 1590. An abbrev. of *God's nails*, used as an oath –1828.

Snai·l-shell. 1530. = COCHLEA 3.

Snake (snēik), *sb.* [OE. *snaca* = MLG. *snake*, ON. *snákr, snókr*.] **1.** One or other of the limbless vertebrates constituting the reptilian order *Ophidia* (characterized by a greatly elongated body, tapering tail, and smooth scaly integument), some species of which are noted for their venomous properties; an ophidian, a serpent. Also, in pop. use, applied to some species of *Lacerta*, and to certain snake-like amphibians. **b.** A representation, figure, or image of a snake 1579. **2.** In fig. or allus. uses 1593. **3.** Applied to persons, esp. with opprobrious force 1590. **4.** Applied to objects resembling a s. 1676. **5.** A species of mediæval war vessel 1864.

1. *Great snakes!* used as an exclam. **2.** Phr. *A s. in the grass* (after Virgil *Ecl.* iii. 93. *Latet anguis in herba*): used to denote some lurking danger, suspicious circumstance or persons, etc. *To see snakes*, to have delirium tremens (*U.S. slang*). **3.** *Poor s.*, a poor, needy, or humble person; a drudge.

Comb.: *s.-charmer*; **s.-bird,** a bird belonging to the genus *Plotus*, esp. the Amer. species *P. anhinga*, characterized by its long s.-like neck; *dial.* the wry-neck; **-boat,** a canoe of great length used in the East; **-fence** *U.S.*, a fence made of roughly-split rails laid zigzag; **-fish,** one or other of certain fishes having some resemblance to a s.; **s. juice** *Austral. slang*, whisky; **-poison** *U.S.*, whisky; **s.-story,** an incredible tale about a s. in regard to its great length or size. Also in collocations with **snake's,** chiefly in plant names as *snake's tail, tongue.*

Snake (snēik), *v.* 1815. [f. SNAKE *sb.*] **I. 1.** *trans.* **a.** *Naut.* (See quot.) 1815. **b.** To move, stretch out, (the head, etc.) after the manner of a snake. Also *refl.* 1887. **2.** *intr.* To move in a creeping, crawling, or stealthy manner suggestive of the movements of a snake 1848. **3.** To wind, twist, curve, etc., in a snake-like manner 1875. **4.** *trans.* To make (one's way) in a sinuous or creeping manner 1879.

1. a. *S.*, to pass small stuff across a seizing at the outer turns by way of finish. To attach lengths of rope between two stays or backstays. 1846.

II. *U.S.* To drag, pull, or draw; *spec.* in *Lumbering*, to haul (logs) along the ground lengthwise by means of chains or ropes 1833. **b.** *transf.* To drag or pull forcibly or quickly 1897.

Sna·ke(-)head. 1845. [SNAKE *sb.*] **1. a.** The N. Amer. plant *Chelone glabra.* **b.** The snake's head or common fritillary 1884. **2.** *U.S.* The loose bent-up end of one of the thin iron rails formerly used on railroads 1848. **3.** A representation of a snake's head 1865. **4.** A fish (*Ophiocephalus*) or turtle having a snake-like head 1891.

Sna·ke-like, *a.* 1612. [f. SNAKE *sb.* + -LIKE.] Like or resembling a snake or that of a snake; having the characteristic form of a snake; long and slender.

fig. This is a snakelike world, And always hath its tail within its mouth 1839.

Sna·ke(-)root. 1635. [f. SNAKE *sb.*] **1.** The root or rhizome of one or other of several Amer. plants reputed to possess properties antidotal to snake-poison, *esp.* the dried root of *Polygala senega* and *Aristolochia serpentaria* used largely in medicine; the medicinal preparation obtained from this. **b.** One or other of these plants 1712. **2.** One or other of several plants so called from a fancied resemblance to a snake in some respect; e.g. *Polygonum bistorta* 1856.

Snake's(-)head. Also **snakeshead.** 1739. [f. SNAKE *sb.*] **1.** *attrib.* **a.** *S. iris*, an iris of the Mediterranean region, *Hermodactylus tuberosus.* **b.** *S. fritillary, lily* (see 2 b) 1899. **2. a.** *U.S.* = SNAKE-HEAD 1 a. **b.** The common fritillary, *Fritillaria meleagris*; so called from the fancied resemblance of the bud to the head of a snake 1859. **3.** *U.S.* = SNAKE-HEAD 2. 1848.

Sna·ke(-)stone. 1661. [f. SNAKE *sb.*] **1.** An ammonite. Now *dial.* **2.** A porous or absorbent substance regarded as efficacious in curing snake-bite or as a remedy against poison; a serpent-stone 1694. **3.** A small perforated stone (cf. *adder-stone*, ADDER *sb.*[2]) 1700. **4.** A kind of hone slate or whetstone, obtained in Scotland; also known as Ayr stone 1850.

Sna·ke-weed. Also **snakeweed.** 1597. [SNAKE *sb.*] **1.** The plant bistort, *Polygonum bistorta.* **2.** = SNAKE-ROOT 1. 1631.

Sna·ke-wood. 1598. [SNAKE *sb.*] **1. a.** A tree or shrub belonging to the genus *Strychnos*, esp. *S. colubrina* of the East Indies; the wood of one or other of these trees used as a remedy for snake-poison. **b.** The East Indian plant *Ophioxylon serpentinum.* **2.** One or other of various trees formerly classed under the genus *Colubrina*, or the West Indian trees *Cecropia peltata*, the trumpet tree, and *Plumieria rubra*, the red jasmine 1832. **3.** The wood of the S. American timber-tree *Brosimum aubletii*, so called from its snake-like markings; letter-wood; also, the tree producing this wood 1843.

Snakish (snē^i·kiʃ), *a.* 1532. [f. SNAKE *sb.* + -ISH[1].] Snake-like, snaky.

Snaky (snē^i·ki), *a.* 1567. [f. SNAKE *sb.* + -Y[1].] **1.** Formed or composed of snakes. **2.** Entwined with snakes. Said of the caduceus. 1591. **3.** Of or pertaining to a snake; freq. in allusive use, venomous, guileful, deceitful, treacherous 1586. **4.** Resembling the form of a snake; long and winding or twisting; sinuous, tortuous 1596. **5.** Of places: Infested with snakes 1856. **6.** Relating to snakes 1882.

1. The Furies fell Theyr s. heads doe combe SPENSER. **2.** In his Hand He holds the Virtue of the S. Wand DRYDEN. **3.** So to the Coast of Jordan he directs His easie steps; girded with s. wiles MILT. **4.** Huge woolly camels..thrust out their shaggy s. necks 1887. Hence **Sna·kily** *adv.* **Sna·kiness.**

Snap (snæp), *sb.* 1495. [Related to SNAP *v.* Cf. LG., Du. *snap* (etc.), in the same or related senses.] **I. 1.** A quick or sudden closing of the jaws or teeth in biting, or of scissors in cutting; a bite or cut made in this way. **2.** *slang.* A share (cf. SNACK *sb.* 2.); something worth securing or getting hold of; an odd chance; a good place or job 1561. **3.** A small piece or portion; a scrap, fragment, or morsel. Now *dial.* 1610. **4.** A slight or hasty meal or mouthful; a snack. Now *dial.* 1642. **5.** A sudden snatch or catch at something; a quick movement or effort 1631. **b.** A method of fishing for pike 1651. **c.** A card-game, in which the call of 'snap' under certain conditions gives one player the right to take cards from another. (Cf. SNIP-SNAP-SNORUM.) 1882. **6.** A curt or sharp speech or manner of speaking; an angry dispute 1648. **7.** A brief and sudden spell *of* cold, winter, etc. orig. *U.S.* 1740. **b.** A sharp and sudden frost; a short spell of cold weather. Chiefly in *cold s.* 1829. **8.** = SNAP-SHOT 1, 2. 1851. **9.** Alertness, energy, vigour, 'go'. orig. *U.S.* 1872.

1. He had the scent of a slow-hound..and the s. of a bull-dog SCOTT. **2.** Also = *soft s.*, an easy pleasant job; a profitable business or undertaking (*U.S.*) 1909. **6.** The moment I ventured to speak I was at once contradicted with a s. GOLDSM.

II. 1. a. An instrument or implement that snaps 1611. **b.** A snap-hook 1839. **c.** A device or implement used for rounding the head of a rivet 1869. **2.** A spring-catch, clasp, or fastening, or one closing with a snapping or clicking sound 1815. **III. 1.** A quick, sharp sound or report 1611. **2.** The act of snapping or breaking suddenly 1755. **3.** *Sc.* and *n. dial.* A small, usu. round, cake or biscuit of crisp gingerbread; a ginger-snap (cf. *brandy-s.*) 1818. **4.** *pl.* (*U.S.*) Also *s.-beans*, French beans 1842.

Snap (snæp), *v.* 1530. [prob. – (M)LG., (M)Du. *snappen* seize (= MHG. *snappen*, G. *schnappen*), but partly imit. See SNACK *v.*, and cf. SNATCH *v.*] **I. 1.** *intr.* Of animals: To make a quick or sudden bite *at* something; to feed *on* in this way. Also without const. **2.** To utter sharp, tart, or cutting words or remarks; to speak irritably or abruptly. Usu. with *at.* 1579. **b.** *trans.* To utter (words) in an angry, sharp, or peevish manner or tone. Also with *out.* 1683. **3.** To snatch, to make a quick or eager catch, *at* a thing 1673. †**b.** *To s. short*, to fail to get or obtain –1738.

1. A little Lap-Dog, that barked and snapped at every one ADDISON. **2. b.** To s. out a refusal 1888. **3.** His resignation was eagerly snapped at SCOTT.

II. 1. (freq. with *up*) *trans.* To catch, capture, or seize quickly, suddenly, or by surprise. Now chiefly *dial.* 1568. **b.** To snatch for one's own use; to take to oneself with a quick movement; to steal or purloin in this manner 1624. **c.** To catch or seize with a quick bite or snap. Also *fig.* 1687. **d.** To secure the passing or giving of (decisions, legislation, etc.) without allowing due time for consideration or discussion 1883. **2.** With *off.* To bite off (a limb, etc.) sharply and quickly. Also *transf.*, to drink off quickly. 1590. **3.** To catch or take (a person) *up* with an abrupt or sharp remark. Also with *short.* 1647. **b.** To interrupt or snub, to cut *short*, in an abrupt or peevish manner. Also with *off.* 1687. **4. a.** To take (an instantaneous photograph); to snap-shot 1890. **b.** *intr.* To take instantaneous photographs 1891.

1. c. The Ægyptian dogs, when they drink at the Nile, are said to run all the while, for fear of being snapped by the Crocodiles 1760. **2.** Phr. *To s.* (a person's) *nose* or *head off*, to speak to a person in a curt, sharp, or angry manner; Old G. snapped my nose off for saying I had sent for him 1742. **3. b.** Your ladyship did s. and snub her confoundedly 1796.

III. 1. *trans.* To close (the jaws, mouth, etc.) suddenly or with a snap 1573. **2.** To pull the trigger of or fire (a pistol); to strike (a flint, etc.) 1673. **3.** To cause (something) to make or give out a sharp sound of the nature of a click or crack; to close or fasten, to open or shut, etc., with this sound; to crack (a whip); to jerk *out* with a snap 1714. **b.** To cause (the fingers) to make a sharp noise by striking the ball of the thumb, esp. as a sign of delight or contempt 1742. **4.** *intr.* Of things: To make or emit a sharp cracking sound or report; to crack, crackle 1673. **b.** To move or slide *into* place, to close or shut, to fit *home*, with a snap 1793. **5. a.** Of the eyelids or eyes: To open and close quickly in an angry manner 1870. **b.** Of jaws, etc.: To close with a snap 1899.

2. He snapped a pocket-pistol at him, which missed him 1798. **3.** Tyranny..Slips the slave's collar on, and snaps the lock COWPER. **b.** Phr. *To s. one's fingers at*, to treat with indifference or contempt; to disregard or ignore. **4.** Cedar..makes a brisk fire, but is..subject to s. and fly 1768.

IV. 1. *intr.* To break suddenly and (usually) with a sharp noise or report; to give way or part suddenly owing to strain or tension 1602. **b.** To be broken *off* with a snap 1806. **2.** *trans.* To break (something) suddenly and cleanly; to break in two; to cause (a rope, etc.) to part or give way 1679. **b.** To break *off* with a snap 1808.

1. *fig.* When the so-called Bonds of Society s. asunder CARLYLE. **2.** From the roof the sleeper fell, And snapped the spinal joint and waked in hell POPE. *fig.* And now this spell was snapt COLERIDGE.

V. *advb.* With, or as with, a snap; quickly, smartly. Freq. in phr. *to go s.* 1583.

Snap-, the stem of SNAP *v.* used in comb., as **snap-action gun,** a gun which, as the hinged barrel closes, is fastened by a spring catch; **s.-beetle, bug,** a click-beetle; **-sound** *Path.*, a snapping sound heard in auscultation; **-weed,** *Impatiens fulva.* **b.** In the names of things or appliances operating, closing, fastening, fitting, etc., with a snap or by means of a catch, as *s.-bolt, -catch, -flask, -gun, -lock.* **c.** In combs. relating to or connected with the use of a snap-hook in fishing, as *s.-angling; s.-bait, -tackle.* **d.** Formed, taken, performed, etc., hastily or rapidly, as *s. exposure, -firing, -judgement*, SNAP-SHOT, etc. **e.** In parliamentary usage, as *s. dissolution, division, vote*, one obtained or taken unexpectedly or without notice, often when comparatively few members are present.

Snapdragon (snæ·pdrægən). 1573. [f. SNAP *v.* + DRAGON.] **1.** A popular name for one or other of the plants belonging to the genus *Antirrhinum*, esp. *A. majus*, a hardy plant bearing showy flowers, freq. grown in gardens. **b.** Applied to various other plants having personate flowers 1753. **2.** A figure or representation of a dragon, esp. one so constructed as to open and shut the mouth, used in mayoral or civic shows or processions. *Obs.* exc. *Hist.* 1611. **3.** A game (usually played at Christmas) in which the players try to snatch raisins out of a bowl or dish of burning brandy or other spirit and to eat them while alight; a bowl or quantity of the liquor, etc., used in this game 1704.

1. The flowers..fashioned like..a dragon's mouth; from whence the women haue taken the name S. 1597.

Snape (snē^ip), *v. techn.* 1794. [perh. identical with dial. *snape* rebuke, restrain, ON. *sneypa* dishonour. See SNEAP.] **1.** *trans.* To cause or make to taper; *spec.* in *Shipbuilding*, to bevel the end of. **2.** *intr.* To taper (*off*) 1794. Hence **Snape** *sb.* (*rare*) a tapering, a bevel, an act of snaping.

Snapha(u)nce (snæ·phɑns). Now *Hist.* 1538. [repr. Du., Flem. *snaphaan*, f. *snappen* SNAP *v.* + *haan* cock. It is not clear whether the sense is 'snapping cock' or 'cock-snapper' (i.e. cock-stealer).] †**1.** An armed robber or marauder; a freebooter or highwayman; a desperate fellow or thief –1609. **2.** An early form of flint-lock used in muskets and pistols; also, the hammer of this 1588. **3.** A musket, gun, etc., fitted with a lock of this kind, in use in the 16–17th centuries 1580.

3. [He] had borne a snap-hance on his shoulder as a volunteer 1860.

Snap(-)head. 1869. [f. SNAP *sb.*] **1.** A round head to a rivet, bolt, etc. **2.** A tool used to shape the head of a rivet 1875.

Snap-hook. 1688. [f. SNAP-.] **1.** *Angling.* A device consisting of three or four hooks connected in a special manner. **2.** A hook with a spring snap by which it is prevented from accidental unhooking 1875.

Snapper (snæ·pəɹ). 1577. [f. SNAP *v.* + -ER[1].] **1.** A thing which snaps or produces a sharp cracking sound: **a.** A pistol (*rare*). †**b.** *pl.* Bones; castanets 1605. **c.** *U.S.* A word, sentence, verse, etc., used as a finishing touch or wind-up 1857. **d.** *U.S.* A cracker on the end of a whip-lash. Also *fig.*, a sharp or caustic remark. 1882. **3.** One who snaps *up* or seizes upon a thing quickly 1611. **4.** A snappish person; one who speaks or answers snappishly or roughly 1648. **5. a.** One or other of various fishes, esp. the West Indian *Lutjanus blackfordii* or *L. vivanus* or other fish of this group, the N. American rose-fish, *Sebastes marinus*, and the Australian *Pagrus unicolor* 1697. **b.** With distinctive epithets, as *alligator, bastard, black s.* 1775. **c.** A snapping-turtle 1872. **d.** A woodpecker 1847. **e.** *U.S.* A flysnapper 1891.

3. My Father..was likewise a snapper-vp of vnconsidered trifles SHAKS.

Sna·pping, *ppl. a.* 1642. [f. SNAP *v.* + -ING².] **1.** Sharp, curt, snappish; peevish, petulant. **2.** That snaps or breaks suddenly 1823. **3.** That snaps with the jaws or beak 1873.

3. *S.-turtle*, one or other of the N. American freshwater tortoises of the family *Chelydridæ*, esp. *Chelydra serpentina*, the alligator terrapin. *S. beetle* (or *bug*) any beetle of the family *Elateridæ*; the skip-jack (*U.S.*). So **Sna·ppingly** *adv.* 1567.

Snappish (snæ·piʃ), *a.* 1542. [f. SNAP *v.* + -ISH¹.] **1.** Of persons: Using, or apt to use, sharp, harsh, or uncivil language; peevish, testy, or ill-natured in speech or reply. **b.** Of manner, etc.: Marked or characterized by sharpness or curtness of speech 1836. **c.** Of the sea: Somewhat choppy or rough 1867. **2.** Of words, language, etc.: Sharp, curt, peevish, ungracious 1551. **3.** Of a dog, etc.: Inclined or prone to snap 1700.

1. I found him morose and s. BORROW. **b.** A..s. tone of voice 1885. **2.** Vexed at a s. answer Madame Williams did give me PEPYS. Hence **Sna·ppish-ly** *adv.*, **-ness**.

Snappy (snæ·pi), *a.* 1834. [f. SNAP *v.* + -Y¹.] **1.** = SNAPPISH *a.* **2.** Of the nature of, producing or emitting, a snap or crack; crackling 1878. **3.** *colloq.* Cleverly smart, bright, or pointed; full of 'go'; brisk 1873. **b.** Neat and elegant; smart, 'natty' 1881. **4.** Quick, sudden, instantaneous; jerky 1872.

1. S. and disagreeable..in their replies 1858. **2.** The birch..makes a hot, s., cheerful fire 1894. **3.** **b.** A s. team of grays 1897. Hence **Sna·ppily** *adv.*

Snap-shot (snæ·pˌʃɒt), *sb.* Also **snap shot, snapshot.** 1808. [f. SNAP-.] **1.** A quick or hurried shot taken without deliberate aim, esp. one at a rising bird or quickly moving animal. **b.** One who fires such a shot 1887. **2.** An instantaneous photograph, esp. one taken with a hand-camera 1890.

2. *transf.* Your Yankee interviewer is a s. incarnate 1897. Hence **Sna·p-shot** *v. intr.* or *absol.* to take snap-shots with a camera; *trans.* to take a s. of or at (a person or thing).

Snare (snēᵊɹ), *sb.* [Late OE. *sneare* – ON. *snara* = OS. *snari* (Du. *snaar*) string, OHG. *snarahha* snare; rel. to MLG. *snare* harp-string, OHG. *snerhan* bind, knot, ON. *snara* wind, twist. Sense 2 is prob. – MLG. or MDu. *snare.*] **1.** A device for capturing small wild beasts or birds, usu. consisting of a string with a running noose in which a foot or the head may be caught. **b.** *Surg.* A device, on the principle of a snare, for removing morbid growths 1884. **2.** One of the strings of gut or rawhide which are stretched across the lower head of a side-drum 1688.

1. The..time..For stalking Cranes to set the guileful S. DRYDEN. *fig.* The snares of deep play 1779. Hence **Sna·ry** *a.* of the nature of, resembling, a s.; ensnaring.

Snare (snēᵊɹ), *v.* late ME. [f. SNARE *sb.*] **1.** *trans.* To capture (small wild beasts or birds) in a snare; to catch by entangling. **b.** *fig.* To entangle, entrap. late ME. **2.** *Surg.* and *Path.* To catch in a loop, *esp.* in order to remove; to cut off with a snare 1884.

1. I..will..instruct thee how to s. the nimble Marmazet SHAKS. **b.** Be thow not snairde in Venus snair 1567. Hence **Sna·rer,** one who snares or traps.

Snark (snāɹk). 1879. [Invented by 'Lewis Carroll' (C. L. Dodgson) in *The Hunting of the Snark* (1876).] An imaginary animal.

Snarl (snāɹl), *sb.*¹ late ME. [f. SNARE *sb.* or *v.*; see -LE.] **1.** A snare, gin; a noose. *Obs.* exc. *dial.* **2.** A tangle, knot, ravel 1609. **3.** A knot in wood (*dial.*) 1881.

Snarl (snāɹl), *sb.*² 1613. [f. SNARL *v.*²] An act of snarling; a display of the teeth accompanied by an angry sound.

Snarl (snāɹl), *v.*¹ late ME. [Cf. SNARL *sb.*¹] **1.** *trans.* To catch in a snare or noose; to entangle or secure with a cord, rope, etc.; to strangle. Now *dial.* **b.** *fig.* To ensnare, entangle, entrap. late ME. **2.** To tangle; to twist together confusedly; to make a tangle of. Now chiefly *dial.* and *U.S.* 1440. **3.** *intr.* To become twisted or entangled; to get into, or form, tangles or knots 1600.

2. The Daughter had..her Hair snarled and matted together 1687. **3.** The yarn tends to 's.' and curl, and cannot be drawn out straight 1884.

Snarl (snāɹl), *v.*² 1589. [Extension of synon. †*snar* (XVI) – (M)LG. *snarren* = MHG. *snarren* (G. *schnarren*); see -LE.] **1.** *intr.* Of dogs, etc.: To make an angry sound accompanied by showing the teeth. **2.** Of persons: To quarrel; to grumble viciously; to show strong resentment or ill-feeling 1594. **3.** *trans.* To utter in a harsh, rude, or ill-natured manner 1693.

1. A dog snarls at a stone, but looks not at the hand that cast it 1732. *fig.* I hear the angry trumpet snarling 1866. Hence **Sna·rler¹.**

Snarl (snāɹl), *v.*³ *techn.* 1688. [perh. f. SNARL *sb.*¹ 3.] *trans.* To raise, or force *up*, into bosses or projections by the use of the snarling-iron. Hence **Sna·rler²,** one who works with a snarling-iron; a snarling-iron. **Sna·rling** *vbl. sb.* a method of producing raised work in metal by means of indirect percussion; chiefly *attrib.* in *s.-iron, tool.*

Snatch (snætʃ), *sb.* ME. [f. SNATCH *v.*, q.v.] †**1.** A hasp or fastening (*rare*) –1528. †**2.** A trap, snare, entanglement –1655. **3.** A hasty catch or grasp; a sudden grab or snap *at* something 1577. †**b.** A catch, check, or hesitancy. SHAKS. **4.** A brief period, short space (*of* time, etc.) 1563. **5.** A hasty meal or morsel; a snack 1573. **6.** A small amount or portion (†taken hurriedly); a mere fragment or disconnected piece 1592. **7.** A short passage, a few words, *of* a song, etc.; a small portion, a few bars, *of* a melody or tune 1602. **b.** *ellipt.* in the same senses 1823. †**8.** A quibble, a captious argument –1687. **9.** *ellipt.* Any open lead for a rope. (See SNATCH-*block.*) 1850.

3. Here and there he made guesses and snatches at the truth M. ARNOLD. Phr. *By* or *in snatches*, by hasty, unsustained efforts; hurriedly, by fits and starts; intermittently, interruptedly. **4.** Then after a shower to weeding a s. 1573. **6.** Snatches of reading..will not make a Bentley or a Clarke JOHNSON. **7.** She chaunted snatches of old tunes SHAKS.

Snatch (snætʃ), *v.* ME. [Obscurely rel. to SNACK *v.*, and north. dial. SNECK *sb.*; these imply a base *snak-, repr. by (M)Du. *snakken* gasp, perh. orig. open the jaws suddenly; cf. SNAP *v.*] **1.** *intr.* **a.** To make a sudden snap or bite (*at* something). **b.** To make a sudden catch *at* a thing, in order to secure possession or hold of it 1530. **2.** *trans.* To seize, to take or lay hold of, suddenly, smartly, or unexpectedly ME. **b.** With immaterial object: To take, obtain, acquire, etc., in a hasty or improper manner, or so as to take advantage of a momentary chance 1563. **3.** To seize, take, or remove hastily 1555. **b.** To remove quickly *from* sight, etc.; to remove suddenly from this world or life; to save or rescue *from* or *out of* danger, etc., by prompt and vigorous action 1582. **4.** *Naut.* To place (a line) in a snatch-block 1769.

1. **b.** This looke of thine will hurle my Soule from Heauen, And Fiends will s. at it SHAKS. **2.** The Sarazin..Snatcheth his sword, and fiercely to him flies SPENSER. **b.** Let us s. what happiness is yet in our power LYTTON. **3.** The Moones an arrant theefe, And her pale fire, she snatches from the Sunne SHAKS. I snatched his Hat off his Head STEELE. **b.** This youth that you see heere, I snatch'd one halfe out of the iawes of death SHAKS. Several who are snatched away by untimely death BERKELEY. Hence **Sna·tchy** *a.* consisting of, characterized by, snatches; irregular; spasmodic; *spec.* of rowing.

Snatch-, the stem of SNATCH *v.* used in comb.: **a.** *Naut.* Denoting devices capable of rapid attachment, or to which a rope can be quickly attached, as *s.-cheek, -hook, sheave*; **s.-block,** a block having a hole in one side to receive the bight of a rope. **b.** In objective combs., as *s.-grace.* **c.** = SNAP- e.

Snatcher (snæ·tʃəɹ). 1575. [f. SNATCH *v.* + -ER¹.] One who or that which snatches; a thief, a robber. **b.** A body-snatcher 1831.

Sna·tchingly, *adv.* 1552. [f. *snatching*, pr. pple. of SNATCH *v.*] In a snatching manner; hurriedly; by snatches.

Snath (snæþ). Chiefly *dial.* and *U.S.* Also **snathe, sneath** 1574. [var. of next.] = next.

Snead (snīd), **sned** (sned). Now *dial.* [OE. *snǣd*, of unkn. origin.] The shaft or pole of a scythe.

Sneak (snīk), *sb.* 1643. [app. f. SNEAK *v.*] **1.** **a.** A sneaking, mean-spirited, paltry, or despicable person; one who acts in a shifty, shabby, or underhand manner. **b.** One who robs or steals in a sneaking manner, or who enters places clandestinely for that purpose 1785. **2.** *Cricket.* A ball bowled so as to roll along the ground; a daisy-cutter 1862.

1. **a.** We call him tuft-hunter, lickspittle, s. THACKERAY. Hence **Snea·ky** *a.* of persons: like or resembling a s.; mean, paltry, sneaking; characterized by, partaking of sneaking. **Snea·kiness.**

Sneak (snīk), *v.* 1590. [prob. of dial. origin; rel. obscurely to early ME. *snike*, OE. *snīcan* creep, crawl, ON. *snikja.*] **I.** *intr.* **1.** To move, go, walk, etc., in a stealthy or slinking manner; to creep or steal furtively, as if ashamed or afraid to be seen; to slink, skulk. **b.** Freq. used to denote want of courage, independence or straightforwardness, without ref. to place or movement 1633. **2.** To cringe or be servile *to* (a person, etc.) 1660. **3.** *School slang.* To peach, inform, tell tales 1897.

1. I hope he will not sneake away with all the money DEKKER. **b.** He sneak'd like a Cock, that hangs down his wings when he's beaten 1699. **2.** We s. to the regicides, but we boldly trample on our poor fellow-citizens BURKE.

II. *trans.* **1.** To turn or draw *aside*, to put or thrust *in* or *into*, to move or slide *to*, etc., in a stealthy manner 1648. **b.** To pass *through* in an underhand or stealthy manner 1891. **2.** *colloq.* To steal in a sneaking or stealthy manner; to filch 1883.

1. I lay stirless, softly sneaking my right hand to the pistol 1889. **2.** Those who sneaked umbrellas 1883.

Sneak-, the sb. or vb.-stem used in comb., as **s.-boat** *U.S.*, a boat by which one may readily move or approach unobserved; *esp.* a sneak-box; **-box** *U.S.*, a small, flat, shallow boat used in wild-fowl shooting, and when in use masked with brush or weeds; **-current** *Electr.*, current which escapes or strays owing to leakage or imperfect insulation; **-thief** (orig. *U.S.*), one who thieves by sneaking into houses through open or unfastened doors, etc.

Sneak-cup. 1596. app. error for SNEAK-UP.

Sneaker (snī·kəɹ). 1598. [f. SNEAK *v.* + -ER¹.] **1.** A person or animal that sneaks; a sneak. **2.** †**a.** A small bowl (*of* punch) –1775. **b.** A glass *of* brandy 1805.

Sneaking (snī·kiŋ), *ppl. a.* 1582. [f. SNEAK *v.* + -ING².] **1.** That sneaks; moving, walking, acting, etc., in a furtive or slinking manner 1590. †**b.** *S.-budge*, one who steals or robs alone –1751. †**c.** Niggardly, mean, near –1773. **2.** Mean, contemptible 1582. **3.** Of feelings, affection, etc.: Unavowedly cherished or entertained; undemonstrative 1748.

1. Lurking footpads and s. pickpockets 1824. **3.** I can't help having a s. regard for him 1842. Hence **Snea·king-ly** *adv.*, **-ness** (*rare*).

Snea·ksby. Now *rare.* 1580. [f. SNEAK *sb.* 1 a or synon. †*sneaks* (XVII) + -BY 2.] A mean-spirited person; a paltry fellow.

Sneak-up (snī·kˌʊp). 1596. [f. SNEAK *v.*] A mean, servile, or cringing person; a sneak; a shirk.

Sneap (snīp), *v.* Now *dial.* and *arch.* 1588. [Later form of dial. *snape*; see SNAPE *v.*] **1.** *trans.* To nip or pinch. **2.** To check, repress; to snub, reprove, chide 1611.

2. My lord Archbishop sneaps us for our sloth 1865. Hence **Sneap** *sb.* a snub, check; a rebuke, reproof.

Sneb, *v.* Now *dial.* 1440. [var. of SNIB *v.*] *trans.* To reprimand, reprove; to snub. Also *absol.*

Thou heardst euen now a yong man s. me sore SIDNEY.

Sneck (snek), *sb.* Chiefly *Sc.* and *n. dial.* ME. [See SNATCH *v.*] The latch of a door or gate; the lever which raises the bar of a latch; †a catch. Hence **Sneck** *v. trans.* to latch (a door or gate); to close or fasten by means of a s.; *intr.* of a door or gate: to latch. **Sne·cket,** a s.; *transf.* a noose, halter.

Sne·ck-draw:er. Now *Sc.* and *north.* late ME. [f. SNECK *sb.* + DRAWER *sb.*¹ Cf. DRAW-LATCH 2.] One who draws or lifts a sneck or latch (in order to enter stealthily); a crafty, flattering, or sly fellow. So **Sne·ck-draw.**

Sned, *v.* In later use *Sc.* and *n. dial.* [OE. *snǣdan*, rel. to *sniþan* cut.] **1.** *trans.* To cut or lop off (a branch). Also with *off.* **b.** To prune (a tree); to divest of branches 1595. **2.** To cut; to form, or sever, by cutting 1789.

Snee (to cut): see SNICKERSNEE.

Sneer (snīᵊɹ), *sb.* 1707. [f. the vb.] An act of sneering; a look or expression implying derision, contempt, or scorn; a disdainful or scornful remark or utterance, esp. one of a covert or indirect nature.

A s. at my understanding GOLDSM. Hence **Snee·rful** *a.* of persons, given to sneering; of words, etc., of the nature of a s.; scornful.

Sneer (snīᵊɹ), *v.* 1553. [perh. of LDu. origin (cf. NFris. *sneer* scornful remark, *sneere* scorn).] **1.** *intr.* Of a horse: To snort. Now *dial.* **2.** To smile scornfully or contemptuously; to express scorn, derision, or disparagement in this way; to speak or write in a manner suggestive of contempt or disparagement 1680. **†3.** To laugh foolishly or smirkingly; to grin –1719. **4.** *trans.* To utter with a sneer or in a sneering tone 1693. **5.** To deride or decry (a person or thing). *Obs.* exc. *dial.* 1707. **6.** To affect in a certain way by sneering; to force by means of sneers or scornful speech or manner 1737.

2. Walpole sheltered himself behind..a pension to s. at the tragi-comedy of life 1874. **4.** He sneered some contemptuous word 1904. **6.** Nor sneer'd nor brib'd from Virtue into Shame 1737. Circles which s. down Voltaire LYTTON. Hence **Snee·rer,** one who sneers. **Snee·ringly** *adv.* in a sneering or scornful manner; with a s.

Sneeshing (snī·ʃiŋ). *Sc.* (*Ir.*) and *n. dial.* 1686. [Alteration of SNEERING *vbl. sb.*] Snuff; a pinch of snuff.

Sneeze (snīz), *sb.* 1632. [f. the vb.] **1.** A powder or preparation for inducing sneezing. Also *attrib.*, as *s.-box, -horn,* etc. *Obs.* exc. *n. dial.* **2.** An act of sneezing; a sudden and involuntary expiration of breath through the nose and mouth, accompanied by a characteristic sound 1646. Hence **Snee·zy** *a.* characterized by sneezing, causing one to sneeze.

Sneeze (snīz), *v.* 1493. [Appears first (XV) in the form *snese* as a substitute in printed texts for an original *fnese* (see FNESE), which had become obs. soon after 1400, being superseded by *nese* (see NEEZE), for which *snese, sneeze* was prob. substituted as more expressive.] **1.** *intr.* To drive or emit air or breath suddenly through the nose and mouth by an involuntary and convulsive or spasmodic action, accompanied by a characteristic sound. **2.** *colloq.* With *at.* To regard as of little value, worth, or consideration; to despise, disregard, underrate. Chiefly in the neg. phrase *not to be sneezed at.* 1806. **3.** *trans.* To utter with a sneeze. Also with *out.* 1851.

1. Being unused to Snuff, some Grains from off her upper Lip made him s. aloud STEELE. **2.** A thousand pounds..was not..to be sneezed at 1891. Hence **Snee·zer,** one who sneezes; (*slang*) something exceptionally good, great, strong, violent, etc., in some respect.

Snee·ze(-)weed. 1856. [f. SNEEZE *v.*] *U.S.* The plant *Helenium autumnale,* or other species of the same genus.

Snee·ze(-)wood. 1834. [f. as prec., after Cape Du. *nieshout.*] A South African timber tree, *Ptæroxylon utile*; also, the wood of this tree; *attrib.* as *s. tree.*

Snee·ze(-)wort. 1597. [f. SNEEZE *v.*] The plant *Achillea ptarmica,* bastard or wild pellitory, the dried leaves of which are powdered and used as a sternutatory.

Sneezing (snī·ziŋ), *vbl. sb.* 1495. [f. SNEEZE *v.*] **1.** The action of the vb.; an instance of this. **†2.** A preparation or powder inducing sternutation; an errhine or sternutatory –1653. **†b.** = SNEESHING –1812.

Snell (snel), *sb. U.S.* 1859. [Of unkn. origin.] A short line of gut or horsehair by which a fish-hook is attached to a longer line. Hence **Snell** *v.* (*U.S.*) *trans.* to tie or fasten (a hook) to a line.

Snell (snel), *a.* and *adv.* In later use *Sc.* and *north.* [OE. *snel, snell* = OS., OHG. *snel* (G. *schnell*) swift, active, etc., ON. *snjallr.*] **A.** *adj.* **1.** Quick in movement or action; prompt, smart, active, strenuous; †good. **2.** Keen-witted, clever, sharp, acute, smart. late ME. **3.** Severe, sharp, unsparing. late ME. **4.** Of weather: Keen, bitter, severe ME. **5.** Grievous, heavy, stinging; rigorous; painful ME.

1. That horny-handed, s., peremptory little man 1859. **4.** The wintry air is s. and keen 1822. **5.** That was a s. law SCOTT.

B. *adv.* **1.** Quickly, promptly, swiftly ME. **2.** Vigorously, strongly, keenly ME.

†Snew, *v.* [OE. *sniwan* = MLG. *snīghen,* MDu. *sniwen, snien,* OHG. *sniwan* (G. *schneien*) :– WGmc. **snizwan,* rel. by gradation to **snaiw-* SNOW *sb.*[1]] *intr.* To snow –1746.

1. *fig.* It snewed in his hous of mete and drynke CHAUCER.

Snib (snib), *v.* Now *dial.* and *Sc.* ME. [– MDa. *snibbe,* MSw. *snybba*; see SNUB *v.*] **1.** *trans.* To reprove, reprimand, rebuke, check sharply or severely. **2.** To check by some repressive action 1500.

1. Hym wolde he snybben sharply for the nonys CHAUCER. Hence **Snib** *sb.* (latterly *Sc.*) a check, sharp rebuke, or snub.

Snick (snik), *sb.*[1] 1775. [f. SNICK *v.*[2]] **1.** A small cut; a nick, notch. **b.** An act of snipping or light cutting 1898. **2.** *Cricket.* A light, glancing blow given to the ball by the batsman, sending it in the direction of the slips or to leg; a ball so hit 1879.

Snick (snik), *v.*[1] *Obs.* exc. *dial.* 1599. [Origin unkn.] Used with *go,* or imperatively, and always followed by *up,* in the sense of 'go hang'.

We did keepe time sir in our Catches. Snecke vp! SHAKS.

Snick (snik), *v.*[2] 1700. [Deduced from *snick and snee,* etc.; see SNICKERSNEE.] **1.** *trans.* To cut, snip, clip, nick. Also *intr.* **2.** To strike or hit sharply 1880. **b.** *Cricket.* To strike (the ball) lightly so that it glances off in the slips or to leg; to obtain (so many runs) in this way 1880. **3.** *colloq.* To cut or slip across or along (a road) quickly or sharply 1883.

Snick (snik), *v.*[3] 1828. [imit.] **1.** *trans.* To cause to click or sound sharply. **2.** *intr.* To make a sharp, clicking noise 1892.

2. Ye may hear a breech-bolt s. where never a man is seen KIPLING. Hence **Snick** *sb.*[2] a sharp noise, a click.

Snick and snee, Snick-a-snee: see SNICKERSNEE.

Snicker (sni·kəɹ), *sb.* 1857. [f. SNICKER *v.*] A smothered laugh; a snigger.

Snicker (sni·kəɹ), *v.* 1694. [Of imit. formation; see -ER[5]. Cf. SNIGGER *v.*] **1.** *intr.* To laugh in a half-suppressed or smothered manner; to snigger. **2.** Of horses: To neigh, nicker 1824. Hence **Sni·ckeringly** *adv.*

Snickersnee (snikəɹsnī·), *v.* and *sb. Obs.* or *arch.* 1613. Also **†snick or snee, †snick and snee, †snick-a-snee.** [alt. of *†snick or snee,* repl. earlier *†stick or snee* (XVII) – Du. *steken* thrust, STICK *v.*[1], and *snee,* dial. var. of *snijen, snijden* cut, repr. Gmc. **snīþan* (OE. *snīþan,* whence dial. *snithe*).] **†A.** As *vb.* To thrust or cut in fighting with a knife; to use a knife in this manner, to fight with knives –1802. **B.** *sb.* **1.** The practice of fighting or a combat with cut-and-thrust knives 1670. **†2.** *transf.* Used to denote one or other of two possible alternatives or courses –1680. **3.** A cut-and-thrust knife (in forms *snick-a-snee, snickersnee*) 1760.

Snide (snəid), *a.* and *sb. Cant.* 1862. [Of unkn. origin.] **A.** *adj.* Counterfeit, sham, bogus. **B.** *sb.* Counterfeit jewellery; base coin 1885.

A. [To] get ready for the trial, and look up the 'snyde witnesses' 1862.

Snider (snəi·dəɹ). 1868. [See def.] *S. rifle,* a form of breech-loading rifle invented by Jacob Snider. Also *ellipt.* for this.

Sniff (snif), *sb.* 1767. [f. the vb.] **1.** An act of sniffing; the sound made in doing this. **2.** An act of sniffing in order to express or show contempt, disdain, incredulity, etc. 1837. **3.** An act (or habit) of clearing the nose by a short inhalation 1860.

2. Miss Miggs gave a great s. to the same effect DICKENS.

Sniff (snif), *v.* ME. [Imitative.] **1.** *intr.* To draw air through the nose with short or sharp audible inhalations; to clear the nose in this way, esp. when under the influence of emotion. **2.** To do this in smelling; to smell with a sniff or sniffs. Said esp. of animals. 1788. **3.** To show or express contempt, disdain, disparagement, incredulity, etc., by sniffing 1729. **4.** *trans.* To take *up,* draw *in* (air, etc.) by inhaling through the nostrils 1796. **5. a.** To smell (a thing) 1845. **b.** *fig.* To perceive as if by smell; to smell or smell out (a plot, etc.); to suspect 1864. **6.** To utter with a (scornful) sniff; to express by means of a sniff 1859.

2. A curious old ewe came to s. at him 1883. **5. b.** It is not only Rome that sniffs heresy in independent thought or action 1873. **6.** Fastidious Edinburgh sniffs disdain 1865. Hence **Sni·ffing** *vbl. sb.* the action of the vb.; an instance of this, a sniff.

Sniffle (sni·f'l), *sb.* 1825. [f. next.] **1.** *The sniffles,* the snuffles. Also *U.S. slang,* a fit of low spirits. **2.** An act of sniffling; a slight snivel or snuffle 1880.

Sniffle (sni·f'l), *v.* 1819. [imit.; cf. SNIVEL *v.*] *intr.* To snivel or snuffle slightly; to sniff. Also *transf.* of a breeze.

Sniffy (sni·fi), *a. dial.* and *colloq.* 1871. [f. SNIFF *v.* + -Y[1].] Prone or inclined to sniff; contemptuous, disdainful; disagreeable. Hence **Sni·ffily** *adv.* **Sni·ffiness.**

Snift (snift), *v.* Now chiefly *dial.* 1703. [perh. – MSw. *snypta,* or MDa. *snyfte,* of imit. origin.] **1.** *intr.* To sniff, in various senses. **b.** Of an engine, etc.: To blow out air or steam 1865. **2.** *trans.* To draw *up* by sniffing; to sniff the smell of (*rare*) 1736.

1. More steamers came along snorting and snifting at the buoys KIPLING. Hence **Snift** *sb. techn.* the waste in bottling aerated waters.

Snifter (sni·ftəɹ). Chiefly *Sc.* and *n. dial.* 1789. [f. prec. + -ER[1].] **1.** A strong or rough breeze or wind. **2.** *pl.* A bad cold in the head, or the stoppage in the nostrils caused by this; the snuffles. Also, a disease of poultry. *Sc.* 1808.

Sni·fting, *ppl. a.* 1744. [f. SNIFT *v.* + -ING[2].] *S. valve,* a valve through which air may be expelled from the cylinder of a condensing steam-engine.

Sni·fty, *a.* 1889. [f. SNIFT *v.* + -Y[1].] Sniffy.

Snig (snig). 1483. [Of unkn. origin.] A young or small eel; a grig.

Snigger (sni·gəɹ), *v.* 1706. [Later var. of SNICKER *v.*] **1.** *intr.* To laugh in a half-suppressed, light or covert manner; to snicker. **2.** *trans.* To utter with a snigger 1857. Hence **Snigger** *sb.* a slight or half-suppressed laugh. **Sni·ggeringly** *adv.*

Sniggle (sni·g'l), *v.*[1] 1671. [f. SNIG, prob. through SNIGGLING *vbl. sb.*] **1. a.** *intr.* To fish *for* eels by the method known as sniggling. **b.** *trans.* To fish for, catch, pull out (an eel or eels) in this way 1844. **2.** To catch (fish) by means of striking a hook into them 1834. Hence **Sni·ggle** *sb.* a baited hook or other device used in sniggling for eels, etc.

Sniggle (sni·g'l), *v.*[2] 1815. [Imitative.] *intr.* To snigger or snicker. Hence **Sni·ggle** *sb.*

Sniggling (sni·gliŋ), *vbl. sb.* 1661. [f. SNIG (cf. *cockling* gather cockles); see -ING[1].] The action or practice of fishing for eels by means of a baited hook or needle thrust into their holes or haunts.

Snip (snip), *sb.* 1558. [f. next, or – LDu. forms.] **I. 1.** A small piece or slip, esp. of cloth, cut off or out; a shred. **2.** A white or light mark, patch, or spot on a horse, esp. on the nose or lip 1562. **3.** A small amount, piece, or portion, a little bit (*of* something) 1588. **b.** Applied to persons in depreciation or contempt. In later use: A young, slight, or diminutive person. 1625. **†4.** A share or portion; a snack –1702.

3. b. This s. of an attorney MASSINGER.

II. 1. A small cut or incision made by, or such as that made by, a pair of scissors; a wound of this nature 1596. **2.** An act of snipping; a single cut or clip *of* scissors, etc. 1676. **3.** *slang* or *colloq.* A tailor. Also as an allusive personal name for a tailor. 1599. **4.** *pl.* Hand shears, as contrasted with bench shears 1846.

3. Sir, here's S. the Taylor Charg'd with a riot 1634.

Snip (snip), *v.* 1586. [– LG., Du. *snippen* (cf. G. dial. *schnippen*), of imit. origin (cf. SNAP *v.*).] **†1.** *trans.* To take (something) quickly or suddenly; to snap or snatch. Also *absol.* –1720. **2.** To cut, to cut up or off, by or as by scissors or the like. Also *absol.* 1593. **3.** To snub, check, repress. Now *dial.* 1601.

1. The captain seldom ordered anything..but I snipped some of it for my own share DE FOE. **2.** He has snipt off as much as he could pinch from every author of reputation LANDOR.

Snipe (snəip), *sb.* ME. [prob. of Scand. origin (cf. Icel. *mýrisnipa*, Norw. *myr-, strand|snipa*). The occas. var. †*snippe* (XIV–XVII) corresp. to obscurely rel. (M)LG., MDu. *snippe* (Du. *snip*), also *sneppe*, and OHG. *snepfa* (G. *schnepfe*). See SNITE *sb.*] **1.** One or other of the limicoline birds of the genus *Gallinago* (formerly included in the Linnæan genus *Scolopax*), characterized by having a long straight bill, and by frequenting marshy places; esp. *G. cælestis* or *media*, the common English species. **b.** Applied to species of birds resembling the snipe 1785. **c.** Without article, in collective sense 1842. **2.** As an opprobrious or abusive term 1604.

1. The s. flies screaming from the marshy verge 1794. See also GUTTER-, HALF-, JACK-, WOOD-SNIPE. **c.** I have..seen flocks of s. crossing the bay 1845.

Comb.: **s.-fish,** any fish of the genus *Centriscus*; esp. the trumpet-fish, bellows-fish or sea-s.

Snipe (snəip), *v.* 1782. [f. SNIPE *sb.*] **1.** *trans.* To shoot or fire at (men, etc.), one at a time, usu. from cover and at long range; to pick off (a person) in this manner. **2.** *intr.* To fire as in snipe-shooting; to shoot at an enemy in this manner. Also with *at* and *away*. 1832.

2. Three hundred Boers hung on the rearguard, sniping but refusing battle 1901.

Sni·pe-bill. Also **snipe's bill.** 1678. [SNIPE *sb.*] **1.** A narrow moulding-plane with a sharp arris, for forming or cutting quirks. **2.** *U.S.* The bolt connecting the body of a cart with the axle. (Also written *snibel.*) 1860.

Sniper (snəi·pəɹ). 1824. [f. SNIPE *v.* + -ER[1].] **1.** One who snipes, or shoots from concealment, etc.; a sharp-shooter. **2.** A snipe-shooter 1840. **3.** *U.S.* A prospector for gold or the like 1902.

Sniping (snəi·piŋ), *ppl. a.* 1821. [f. SNIPE *v.* + -ING[2].] That snipes, or shoots from cover. *S. fire*, individual and irregular shooting from a concealed position.

Snipped (snipt), *ppl. a.* 1578. [f. SNIP *v.* + -ED[1].] **1.** *Bot.* Irregularly notched or serrated; incised. **2.** That has been subjected to snipping; jagged or irregularly cut 1601.

Sni·pper. 1593. [f. SNIP *v.* + -ER[1].] **1.** *pl.* Scissors. **2.** One who snips or clips; *spec.* a tailor 1611.

Sni·pper-sna:pper. Now *dial.* 1590. [Cf. contemp. SNIP-SNAP *v.*] A whipper-snapper.

Sni·ppet. 1664. [f. SNIP *v.* + -ET.] A small piece cut off; a small fragment or portion. **b.** *spec.* A short passage taken from a literary work; a short scrap of literary matter 1864.

fig. That is a poor s. of malicious gossip STEVENSON. Hence **Sni·ppety, -etty** *a.* of the nature of, composed of, a s. or snippets.

Snip-snap (sni·pˌsnæp), *sb.* 1597. [f. SNIP *sb.* + SNAP *sb.*, used with imitative effect.] †**1.** The action of snipping or clipping with a pair of scissors or the like; an instance of this –1638. **2.** Smart remark or reply; sharp repartee 1727.

Snip-snap (sni·pˌsnæp), *a.* 1600. [Attributive use of prec.] †**1.** Making a snipping sound; working or acting by snipping or clipping –1643. **2.** Of the nature of snip-snap; characterized by snip-snap or smart repartee 1673.

2. With volleys of small shot, or s. wit 1702.

Sni·p-snap, *v.* 1593. [f. SNIP-SNAP *sb.*] **1.** *intr.* To indulge in snip-snap or smart repartee; to speak in a snappy manner. **2.** To snip; to clip with a snipping sound 1906. So †**Snip-snap** *adv.* (and *int.*) with snip and snap; with a snipping, snapping sound 1588.

Snip-snap-sno·rum. 1755. [– LG. *snipp-snapp-snorum*, of fanciful coinage.] A round game of cards, in which the players on turning up the requisite cards respectively call 'snip', 'snap', and 'snorum'.

Snipy (snəi·pi), *a.* 1825. [f. SNIPE *sb.* + -Y[1].] **1.** Characterized by having a long pointed nose or muzzle suggestive of a snipe's bill. **2.** Snipe-like 1888. **3.** Frequented by snipe 1903.

Snitch (snitʃ), *sb. slang.* 1676. [Of unkn. origin.] †**1.** A fillip (on the nose) –1700. **2.** The nose 1700. **3.** An informer 1785. So **Snitch** *v. intr.* to inform *upon* a person; to peach (1801); *trans.* to catch in a noose or loop (1900). **Sni·tcher.**

Snite (snəit), *sb.* [OE. *snīte* (also *wudu|snīte*), of unkn. origin.] = SNIPE *sb.* 1.

Snite (snəit), *v.* Now *dial.* and *Sc.* [Late OE. *snȳtan* = (M)LG. *snūten*, OHG. *snūzen* (G. *schneuzen* snuff a candle, blow the nose), ON. *snýta* :– **snūtjan*, f. **snūt-*; see SNOUT *sb.*, and cf. SNOT *sb.*] **1. a.** *intr.* To clean or wipe the nose; to cast away mucus. **b.** *trans.* To remove by wiping, etc. **2.** *trans.* To clean or clear (the nose) from mucus, esp. by means of the thumb and finger only; to blow. Also *fig.*, to tweak or pull. ME.

Snivel (sni·v'l), *sb.* late ME. [f. SNIVEL *v.*] **1.** Mucus collected in, or issuing from, the nose. **2.** A slight sniff indicating, or intended to suggest, suppressed emotion 1848. **b.** A show or pretence of emotion; hypocritical expression of feeling 1878.

Snivel (sni·v'l), *v.* ME. [repr. OE. **snyflan*, implied in late *snyflung* mucus of the nose, f. synon. *snofl*. Cf. LG., Du. *snuffelen* smell out, *snuiven* sniff, Sw. *snövla*, Norw. *snuvla*, Da. *snøvle*, †*snevle*; cf. -LE 3.] **1.** *intr.* To run at the nose; to emit mucus from the nose; also, to draw up mucus audibly. **2.** To make a sniffing or snuffling sound expressive of real or assumed emotion; to be in, or affect, a tearful state 1690. **3.** *trans.* **a.** To affect in some way by snivelling; to address in a snivelling manner (*rare*) 1668. **b.** To utter with a snivelling or sniffing sound, to shed (tears) snufflingly 1780.

2. Every woman in the house was snivelling at the time THACKERAY. Hence **Sni·veller,** one who snivels or whines; a cold breeze (causing one to snivel).

Snob (snǫb), *sb.* 1781. [Of unkn. origin.] **1.** *dial.* or *colloq.* A shoemaker or cobbler; a cobbler's apprentice. †**2.** *Cambridge slang.* Any one not a gownsman; a townsman –1865. †**3.** A person belonging to the lower classes of society; one having no pretensions to rank or gentility –1852. †**b.** A vulgar or ostentatious person –1859. **c.** One whose ideas and conduct are prompted by a vulgar admiration for wealth or social position. Also *transf.* of intellectual superiority. 1848. †**4.** = BLACK-LEG 3. 1859.

3. c. He was..such a s., he felt pleased his clerks should hear a butler ask for a situation 1882. **4.** Those who work for lower wages during a strike are called snobs, the men who stand out being 'nobs' DE QUINCEY. Hence **Sno·bbism** [whence Fr. *snobisme*], the characteristic qualities of a s.; snobbishness. **Sno·bby** *a.* snobbish. **Sno·bling,** a little, young, or petty s. **Snobo·cracy,** the class of snobs as having some power or exerting some influence. **Snobo·grapher,** a writer on, a describer of, snobs.

Snobbery (snǫ·bəri). 1833. [f. SNOB *sb.* 3 + -ERY.] **1.** The class of snobs. †**2.** Snobbishness; vulgar ostentation; an instance of this 1843.

Snobbish (snǫ·biʃ), *a.* 1840. [f. SNOB *sb.* 3 + -ISH[1].] **1.** Of, pertaining to, or characteristic of a snob. **2.** Having the character of a snob 1849. Hence **Sno·bbish-ly** *adv.*, **-ness.**

Snod (snǫd), *a. Sc.* and *north. dial.* 1480. [Of unkn. origin.] **1.** Smooth, sleek; even. **2.** Neat, tidy, trim 1691. **3.** Snug, cosy 1695. Hence **Snod** *v. trans.* to make smooth, trim, or neat; to tidy, put in order.

Snood (snūd), *sb.* [OE. *snōd*, of doubtful origin.] **1.** A fillet, band, or ribbon, for confining the hair; latterly, in Scotland, etc., the distinctive hair-band worn by young unmarried women. **2. a.** In sea-fishing: One of a number of short lines, each carrying a baited hook, attached at regular distances along the main line 1682. **b.** *Angling.* A hair or catgut line attaching the hook to the rod line 1823.

1. Yet ne'er again to braid her hair The virgin s. did Alice wear SCOTT.

Snood (snūd), *v.* 1725. [f. prec.] **1.** *trans.* To bind *up*, fasten *back*, or secure (the hair) with a snood. **2.** *Angling.* To attach (a hook) to a snood 1840. Hence **Snoo·ded** *ppl. a.* wearing a snood; bound by a snood.

Snook (snūk), *sb.* 1697. [– Du. *snoek* = (M)LG. *snōk*, prob. rel. to the base of SNACK.] A name given to various fishes, esp. the sergeant-fish, *Elacate canada*, and the robalo, *Centropomus undecimalis*.

Snooker (snū·kəɹ). 1889. [Of unkn. origin.] A game, played with balls on a billiard table, combining pool and pyramids. Also *snooker('s) pool.*

Snooks (snūks). Also **snook.** 1879. [Of unkn. origin.] A derisive gesture consisting in placing the thumb against the nose and extending the fingers.

Snoop (snūp), *v.* orig. *U.S.* 1848. [– Du. *snoepen* eat (on the sly).] **1.** *trans.* To appropriate. **2.** *intr.* To go round in a prying manner 1864.

Snooze (snūz), *v. colloq.* 1789. [Cant word of unkn. origin.] *intr.* To sleep; to slumber, to doze. Hence **Snooze** *sb.* a sleep, nap, doze; *slang*, a lodging, bed.

Snore (snōᵊɹ), *sb.* ME. [f. the verb.] †**1.** A snort; snorting (*rare*) –1513. **2.** The snuffles 1585. **3.** An act of snoring; a harsh or noisy respiration through the mouth, or through the mouth and nose, during sleep 1605. **4.** *transf.* A sound resembling that of a snore; a loud roaring or droning noise 1709.

3. Thou do'st s. distinctly, There's meaning in thy snores SHAKS.

Snore (snōᵊɹ), *v.* late ME. [f. imit. base **snor-*, repr. (with expressive additions) by (M)LG., (M)Du. *snorken* (whence dial. *snork* XVI, Tindale), Du. *snorken*, and SNORT *v.*] **1.** *intr.* Of animals, *esp.* horses: To snort. Now *dial.* **2.** To make harsh or noisy sounds in sleep by breathing through the open mouth or through the mouth and nose; to breathe in this manner during sleep. Also *poet.* and *rhet.*, to sleep heavily. 1440. **3.** *trans.* With *out* or *away*: To spend or pass (time) in snoring 1597. **4.** To utter with a snore or with a sound resembling this. Also with cogn. obj. 1790.

3. He dranke the Night away..then snor'd out all the Day 1746. Hence **Sno·rer,** one who snores. **Sno·ring** *vbl. sb.* the action of the vb.

Snort (snǭɹt), *sb.* 1619. [f. the vb.] †**1.** A snore –1622. **2.** An act of snorting; a loud sound made by a horse or other animal in driving breath through the nostrils with some force 1808. **b.** A similar sound made by persons in order to express contempt, disdain, or other feeling 1865.

Snort (snǭɹt), *v.* late ME. [ult. imit.; prob. partly alt. of †*fnort* (in some MSS. of Chaucer); cf. the history of SNEEZE *v.*] †**1.** *intr.* Of the nose: To turn *up*, as in sniffing. CHAUCER. †**2.** To snore; to sleep heavily or sluggishly –1680. **3.** Of a horse: To make a characteristic loud or harsh sound by violently driving the breath through the nostrils, esp. when excited or frightened. Also said of other animals. late ME. **4.** *transf.* Of things, esp. in later use of a railway engine: To make or emit a sound resembling or suggestive of a snort 1582. **5.** Of persons: **a.** To express contempt or indignation by a snorting sound 1818. **b.** *dial.* and *U.S.* To laugh loudly or roughly 1825. **6.** *trans.* **a.** To utter with a snort 1634. **b.** To eject or discharge through the nostrils with a snort; to spout *out* in this way 1818.

4. The little circular railway puffed and snorted 1879. **5. a.** Duncan..snorted thrice, and prepared himself to be in a passion SCOTT. **6. a.** 'Dat is gut! haw! haw!' snorted the Baron THACKERAY.

Snorter (snǭ·ɹtəɹ). 1601. [f. SNORT *v.* + -ER[1].] **1.** One who or that which snorts (†or snores); a person who utters a snort in scorn, indignation, etc.; also, a pig. **b.** *dial.* The wheatear 1802. **2.** *slang* or *colloq.* **a.** A stiff or strong wind; a gale 1855. **b.** Anything exceptionally remarkable for size, strength, severity, etc. 1859. So **Sno·rting** *ppl. a.* used *advb.* = remarkably.

Snot (snǫt), *sb.* [prob. – (M)LG., MDu. *snotte*, Du. *snot*, corresp. to OE. *ġe|snot*, OFris. *snotta*, MHG. *snuz* (G. dial. *schnutz*), f. Gmc. **snūt-*; cf. SNITE *v.*, SNOUT *sb.*] **1.** The snuff of a candle; the burnt part of a candle-wick. Now *n. dial.* **2.** The mucus of the nose. Now *dial.* or *vulgar.* late ME. **3.** *dial.* and *slang.* Applied to persons as a term of contempt or opprobrium 1809. Hence **Sno·tter**[1], s. or nasal mucus.

Snot (snǫt), *v.* Now *n. dial.* and *Sc.* late ME. [f. prec.] **1.** *trans.* To snuff (a candle). **2.** To blow or clear (the nose) 1576. **3.** *intr.* To sniff or snivel; to snort 1662.

Sno·tter[2]. 1769. [Of unkn. origin.] **1.** A rope secured to a yard-arm with an eye forming a becket to which a tripping-line is bent, used in sending down topgallant and royal yards 1846. **2.** A loop or ring of rope in which the lower end of the sprit rests 1769.

Sno·tty, *sb. slang.* 1903. [perh. spec. application of next.] A midshipman.

Snotty (snǫ·ti), *a.* 1570. [f. SNOT *sb.* + -Y[1].] **1.** Foul with snot or nasal mucus. **b.** Dirty, mean, paltry, contemptible. etc. Now *dial.* or *slang.* 1681. **c.** *dial.* or *slang.* Angry, curt, short-tempered; pert, impudent; proud, conceited 1870. **2.** Consisting of snot; mucous; of the nature of, or resembling snot; viscous, slimy. 1656. Hence **Sno·ttily** *adv.* **Sno·ttiness; Sno·tty-nosed** *a.* having a s. nose; *fig.* contemptible.

Snout (snaut), *sb.* [ME. *snūte* – MLG., MDu. *snūt(e* (Du. *snuit*), whence MSw. *snuta*, Da. *snude*, G. *schnauze*; ult. f. Gmc. **snūt-*, repr. also by SNITE *v.*, SNOT *sb.*] **1. a.** The trunk of an elephant. **b.** = MUZZLE *sb.* I. 1; the proboscis or rostrum of an insect; etc. ME. **2.** Contemptuously: The nose in man, esp. when large or badly shaped ME. **3.** The end of a ship's prow; the beak or rostrum of a vessel. late ME. **4.** A structure, formation, projecting part, etc., resembling or suggestive of a snout; a nozzle or the like. late ME. **b.** A projecting point of land, rock, etc. 1536. **c.** The front portion or termination of a glacier 1841. **5.** One or other of various species of moths characterized by having abnormally long palpi projecting in front of the head; esp. the snout-moth, *Hypena proboscidalis* 1819.

Comb.: **s.-beetle,** one or other of several species of beetles characterized by having the head prolonged into a rostrum or proboscis. Hence **Snou·ty** *a.* resembling a s. or muzzle; having a pronounced or prominent s.; *colloq.* overbearing, insolent.

Snout (snaut), *v.* 1753. [f. SNOUT *sb.*] **1.** *trans.* To finish *off* with a snout. **2.** *trans.* and *intr.* To root, dig up, or grub, with or as with the snout 1857.

Snouted (snau·tėd), *ppl. a.* late ME. [f. SNOUT *sb.* + -ED[2].] **1.** Of things: Furnished with a snout or distinct terminal part. **2.** Of persons or animals: Provided or furnished with a snout, muzzle, or rostrum 1536. **3.** Shaped or fashioned like a snout; snout-like 1866.

Snow (snō͞u), *sb.*[1] [OE. *snāw* = OFris. *snē*, OS., OHG. *snēo* (Du. *sneeuw*, G. *schnee*), ON. *snær*, *snjár*, *snjór*, Goth. *snaiws* :– Gmc. **snaiwaz*; rel. to L. *nix, niv-*, Gr. *νίφα* (acc.).] **I. 1.** The congealed vapour of the atmosphere falling in flakes characterized by their whiteness and lightness; the fall of these flakes, or the layer formed by them on the surface of the ground. **b.** Taken as a type of whiteness or brightness OE. **c.** With adjs. of colour, denoting snow tinged by various foreign substances, or the alga, etc., to which the colouring is due 1678. **2.** A fall of snow; a snowstorm. Now *rare.* OE. **b.** As marking a period of time; a winter 1825. **3.** *pl.* An accumulation, expanse, or field, of snow. late ME. **b.** *pl.* The arctic regions EMERSON.

1. Chaste as the Isicle That's curdied by the Frost, from purest S. SHAKS. S. is white and opaque in consequence of the air entangled among its crystals 1878. **b.** So is my sweet, much paler than the snowe 1593. **c.** The green s. (*Protococcus viridis*) and the red (*P. nivalis*) are..the same plant 1842. A..fall of..black s. 1898. **2.** Next come the snows, and rain, And frosts, and storms SHELLEY. *transf.* A fragrant s. of blossoms KINGSLEY. **b.** Through four sweet years.., from s. to s. TENNYSON. **3.** Yonder, where the far snows blanch Mute Mont Blanc BROWNING.

II. 1. Applied to various things or substances having the colour or appearance of snow 1597. **2. a.** The white hair of age. Also *pl.* 1638. **b.** White bloom or blossom; spray or foam 1859. **3.** The pure white colour of snow; snow-white. Chiefly *poet.* 1745. **4.** Cocaine (*slang*) 1921.

1. Argentine s., or flowers of antimony 1815. Whip the whites of six eggs to a hard s. 1864. **2.** If my passions be cooled by the s. of my head, I have then never a white hair 1638. The May rain still on their petalled s. 1900. **3.** Her eye sae bright..—Her breast o' mountain snaw 1843.

attrib. and *Comb.*: **1.** General: as *s.-bed, -berg, -blast, -crystals,* etc.; *s.-boot, -fence, -spectacles,* etc.; *s. cake,* etc.; *s.-bound, -capped, -crested* adjs. **2.** Special: **s.-blink,** the reflection from s. or ice-fields in polar regions; **-break,** (*a*) a rush of loose or melting s.; (*b*) a narrow strip of forest serving as a protection against s.; (*c*) the breaking of trees by the weight of s.; an area over which this happens; **-broth,** melted s.; water produced or obtained by the melting of s., esp. from natural causes; **-bucking** *U.S.*, the action of forcing a railway-train through a s.-drift; **-clad** *a.*, clad or covered with s.; **-cold** *a.*, as cold as s.; **-craft,** the art of traversing or dealing with s. in mountaineering; **-field,** an extensive stretch or expanse of s.; **-hole,** a hole or opening in the burner of a pyrites kiln; **-limit,** the limit (towards the equator) for the fall of s. at sea-level; **-scape,** a snow scene; **-sheen,** = *s.-blink*; **-sleep,** a somnolent condition induced by walking in s.; **-wreath,** a heap of s. blown together by the wind; a s.-drift. **b.** In names of animals, insects, etc., as **s.-flea, -fly, -gnat, -insect,** one or other of several species of small insects frequenting s.; **-leopard,** the ounce; **-mouse,** *Arvicola nivalis*; also, *Cuniculus torquatus*, a lemming of Arctic America which turns white in winter; **-panther,** = *s.-leopard*; **-worm,** a worm frequenting or living among s. **c.** In names of birds, as **s.-bunting,** a fringilline bird, *Plectrophanes nivalis*, widely distributed in Arctic regions; **-cock,** a s.-partridge, s.-pheasant, *Tetraogallus*; **-finch,** a species of mountain-finch; **-fleck,** the s.-bunting or Lapland bunting; **-goose,** a northern (American) goose of the genus *Chen*, esp. *C. hyperboreus*, characterized by its pure white plumage; **-grouse,** †**hen,** the ptarmigan; **-owl,** the snowy owl; **-partridge,** (*a*) the s.-pheasant; (*b*) a Himalayan gallinaceous bird, *Lerwa nivicola*; **-pheasant,** one or other of several species of the genus *Tetraogallus*, esp. *T. himalayensis*; also, several species of the genus *Crossoptilum*; **-pigeon,** a pigeon of Northern India and Tibet, *Colomba leuconota*; **-quail** *U.S.*, the white-tailed ptarmigan, *Lagopus leucurus*. **d.** In names of plants or fruits, as **s.-flower,** (*a*) = SNOWDROP 1; (*b*) = SNOWDROP-TREE 1; **-glory,** a hardy garden-plant of the genus *Chionodoxa*; **s.-pear,** a variety of pear, esp. *Pyrus nivalis*, which comes into season after snow has fallen; **-plant,** (*a*) a s.-alga; (*b*) a plant of the Sierra Nevada in California (*Sarcodes sanguinea*), with a dense spike of flowers of a blood-red colour. Hence **Snow·less** *a.* free from s.; characterized by the absence of s.

Snow (snō͞u), *sb.*[2] 1676. [– Du. *sna(a)uw* or LG. *snau*, of unkn. origin.] A small sailing-vessel resembling a brig, carrying a main and fore mast and a supplementary trysail mast close behind the main-mast; formerly employed as a warship.

Snow (snō͞u), *v.* Pa. t. and pa. pple. **snowed** (snō͞ud). ME. [f. SNOW *v.*[1], repl. OE. *snīwan* SNEW *v.*] **1.** *intr.* *It snows*, snow falls. Also occas. with *snow* as subject. **2.** To fall, descend, etc., in the manner of snow ME. **3.** *trans.* To let fall as snow; to cause to descend in the manner of snow; to shower down. late ME. **4.** To strew or cover with or as with snow. late ME. **5.** To cause (the hair, etc.) to turn white like snow; to invest with white hair 1598. **6. a.** With *up.* To block, obstruct, incommode, imprison, etc., with snow. Usu. in pa. pple. 1815. **b.** With *under.* To bury in snow; *fig.* to submerge, overwhelm, overpower, etc. *Orig. U.S.* 1880.

1. When it snoweth, it is good syttynge by a good fyre 1530. **2.** Away shot the cards..snowing upon the audience in the front rows 1894. **3.** *fig.* 'Till age s. white hairs on thee DONNE. **6. a.** News came from the country of trains snowed-up 1862.

Snowball (snō͞u·bǭl), *sb.* late ME. [f. SNOW *sb.*[1] + BALL *sb.*[1]] **1.** A ball of snow, esp. one made for throwing by hand. **2.** *Cookery.* One or other of various dishes or confections intended to resemble a ball of snow in appearance 1769. **3.** The Guelder rose, *Viburnum opulus*, or one of its clusters of white flowers 1799. **4.** = *s.-contribution, letter* (= CHAIN *letter*), etc.

1. My bellies as cold as if I had swallow'd snowbals SHAKS. The Caravan like a snow-ball, increases in bulk as it rolls on 1845.

attrib.: **s.-contribution, -system,** one which increases by a kind of geometrical progression; **-tree,** the Guelder rose.

Snowball (snō͞u·bǭl), *v.* 1684. [f. prec.] **1.** *intr.* To form balls or masses of snow. **b.** *fig.* To accumulate by degrees like a rolling snowball 1929. **2.** *trans.* and *intr.* To pelt or have a pelting-match with snowballs 1855. So **Snow·balling** *vbl. sb.*

Snowberry (snō͞u·be:ri). 1760. [f. SNOW *sb.*[1]] A name given to various plants or shrubs bearing white berries, as *Chiococca racemosa*, a rubiaceous shrub of the West Indies and Florida, and *Symphoricarpus racemosus*, a caprifoliaceous shrub native to N. America and Mexico. **b.** The fruit of these shrubs 1837.

Creeping s., U.S., a trailing evergreen plant (*Chiogenes hispidula*) common in bogs and woods.

Snow·-bird. Also **snow bird, snowbird.** 1688. [f. SNOW *sb.*[1]] **1.** One or other of various small European or American birds, *esp.* the snow-bunting, snow-finch, or snow-sparrow (*Junco hiemalis*). **2.** The ivory gull, *Pagophila eburnea* 1831.

Snow·-blind, *a.* Also **snowblind.** 1748. [f. SNOW *sb.*[1]] Having the eyes or sight affected by exposure to the glare of snow. So **Snow·-blindness,** blindness or defective vision caused by exposure of the eyes to the glare of snow.

Snowdon (snō͞u·dən). 1450. [See note.] *S. herald*, one of the six Scottish heralds.

Snowdon was occas. used as a name for Stirling, but Jamieson cites statements that the designation of the herald was derived from 'Snowdoune castle of the county of Rosse'. O.E.D.

Snow·(-)drift. ME. [f. SNOW *sb.*[1] + DRIFT *sb.* II. 2 b. Cf. ON. *snjódrif.*] **1.** A heap or mass of snow driven together, or piled up, by the action of the wind. **2.** A driving mass or cloud of snow; snow driven before the wind 1836.

Snowdrop (snō͞u·drǫp). 1664. [f. SNOW *sb.*[1]; cf. DROP *sb.* I. 8 c.] **1.** An early-flowering bulbous plant (*Galanthus nivalis*), having a white pendent flower; also, a flower, bulb, or single plant of this. **2.** Used as a name for a variety of wheat or potato 1844.

Snow·drop tree. 1731. [f. prec.] **1.** The Virginian fringe-tree, *Chionanthus virginica*. **2.** A N. Amer. styraceous tree or shrub, *Halesia tetraptera* 1823.

Snow(-)fall (snō͞u·fǭl). 1821. [f. SNOW *sb.*[1]] **1.** A fall of snow; a quantity of snow falling during a certain time. **2.** The amount of snow falling at a particular place 1875.

Snow(-)flake (snō͞u·flēⁱk). 1734. [f. SNOW *sb.*[1] + FLAKE *sb.*[2]] **1.** One of the small masses in which snow commonly falls. **2.** The snow-bunting 1770. **3.** One or other species of *Leucojum* 1798. **4.** A method of weaving woollen cloth, by which small knots are formed upon the 'right' side 1882.

Snow·-line. 1835. [f. SNOW *sb.*[1]] The general level on mountains, etc., above which the snow never completely disappears; the lower limit of perpetual snow, or (more rarely) of snow at a particular season.

Snow·-man. 1827. [f. SNOW *sb.*[1]] A mass of snow made into the figure of a man.

Snow·-plough. 1792. [f. SNOW *sb.*[1]] An implement or machine for clearing away snow from a road, railway track, etc.

Snow·(-)shoe, *sb.* 1674. [f. SNOW *sb.*[1]] **a.** A kind of foot-gear enabling the wearer to walk on the surface of snow, *esp.* one of a pair of racket-shaped frames of light wood, strung and netted with narrow strips of raw hide, used by the Indians and others in North America. **b.** One of a pair of ski 1864. Hence **Snow·-shoe** *v. intr.* to travel on snow-shoes or ski. **Snow·-shoer,** one who uses, or travels on, snow-shoes. **Snow·-shoeing** *vbl. sb.* the action or practice of travelling on snow-shoes, esp. as an exercise or sport.

Snow·(-)storm. 1800. [f. SNOW *sb.*[1]] A storm accompanied by a heavy fall of snow.

Snow-white (stress var.), *a.* and *sb.* OE. [f. SNOW *sb.*[1] + WHITE *a.*] **A.** *adj.* White as snow; pure white. **B.** *sb.* Pure white; a kind of wool of this colour 1890.

A. Two s. and waxen hyacinths 1877.

Snowy (snō͞u·i), *a.* OE. [f. SNOW *sb.*[1] + -Y[1].] **1.** Of weather, time, etc.: Characterized by the presence or prevalence of snow. **2.** Composed of melted snow; consisting, formed, or made of snow ME. **3.** Covered with snow;

abounding in snow 1548. **4.** Resembling the colour of snow; snow-white 1590. **b.** Used to qualify *white* or *whiteness* 1785. **5.** In the specific names of birds or animals 1777.

1. A cold, s., uncomfortable month 1748. **3.** His slanting ray Slides ineffectual down the s. vale COWPER. **4.** So shewes a S. Doue trooping with Crowes SHAKS. *transf.* There did he loose his s. Innocence 1646. **5.** S. plover, *Ægialites nivosus*, a small ring-plover of the Pacific and Mexican Gulf coasts of the United States 1891. *S. egret* or *heron*, an entirely white egret (*Ardea candidissima*) ranging from New York to Chile 1895. The..s. owl (*Nyctea scandiaca*) 1895. Hence **Snow·ily** *adv.* **Snow·iness.**

Snub (snɒb), *sb.*[1] 1537. [f. SNUB *v.*] **1.** An act or instance of snubbing; a remark or action intended to repress or rebuke a person. †**2.** A check, stay or hindrance –1672.

Snub (snɒb), *sb.*[2] and *a.* 1830. [A. short for SNUB-NOSE; B. deduced from SNUB-NOSE.] **A.** *sb.* A snub nose. **B.** *adj.* **1.** Of the nose: Short and turned up 1844. **2.** Snub-nosed 1883. Hence **Snu·bby** *a.* somewhat s.; short, stumpy.

Snub (snɒb), *v.* ME. [– ON. *snubba* (cf. Norw. and Sw. dial. *snubba*, Da. *snubbe* cut short, make stumpy), rel. to MSw. *snybba*, MDa. *snibbe*; see SNIB *v.*] **1.** *trans.* To check, reprove, or rebuke in a sharp or cutting manner; in later use, to treat or receive (a person, suggestion, etc.) in a way calculated to repress or mortify. Also *absol.* †**b.** To take *up* sharply or severely; to order *about* in a sharp fashion –1797. **2.** †**a.** To check or restrain (a thing); to prevent from having free course or development –1688. **b.** *Naut.* and *U.S.* To check or stop (a rope or cable) suddenly while running out; to stop or bring *up* (a boat, etc.) sharply or suddenly, esp. by passing a rope round a post; to fasten or tie (*up*) 1841. **3.** To check the growth of; to shorten; to cut, nip, or break *off*, the end of (a thing). Now *rare.* 1615. **Snu·bbing** *vbl. sb.*

Snub-, the stem of SNUB *v.* used in comb., in †**s.-devil** (*slang*), a clergyman; **s.-line, -post** *U.S.*, a snubbing-line or -post, etc.

Snu·bber. 1925. [f. SNUB *v.* + -ER[1].] A shock-absorber.

Snub(-)nose. 1724. [f. SNUB *v.* 3. Cf. Norw. dial. *snubbnos.*] A short stumpy nose turned up and flattened at the tip. **Snu·b-nosed** *a.* having a snub nose.

Snudge (snɒdʒ), *sb.* Now *dial.* 1545. [Also †*snowge*, †*snuch* (XVI); prob. f. an unrecorded LDu. source. Cf. next.] A miser, a niggard; a sneaking or sponging fellow.

Snudge (snɒdʒ), *v.* 1540. [See SNUDGE *sb.*] †**1.** *intr.* To be miserly, stingy, or saving. Also with *it.* –1611. **2.** To walk in a stooping or meditative attitude. Now *dial.* 1677.

Snuff (snɒf), *sb.*[1] late ME. [Of unkn. origin.] **I. 1.** That portion of a wick, etc., which is partly consumed in the course of burning and requires to be removed at intervals; †a candle-end. **b.** In comparisons, used to describe what is faint, feeble, or on the point of extinction 1534. †**2.** A heel-tap –1738.

1. *fig.* Let me not liue..After my flame lackes oyle, to be the snuffe Of yonger spirits SHAKS. **b.** Thy soul, which..Scarce glimmers like a dying s. SWIFT.

II. 1. †**a.** *To take..in* (*the*) *s.* (or *to snuff*), to take (a matter) amiss, to take offence at, to resent –1716. **b.** *To take s.*, to take offence or umbrage (*at* a thing). *Obs.* exc. *arch.* 1565. **2.** A fit of indignation; a huff, rage or passion. Now *Sc.* 1592.

1. a. This matter the Justice tooke sore to snuffe, and was very angry 1570. **b.** Jupiter took S. at the Contempt, and Punish'd him for't 1692. **2.** He went away in snuffe, and I followed him B. JONS.

Snuff (snɒf), *sb.*[2] 1570. [f. SNUFF *v.*[2]] **1.** An (*or* the) act of snuffing, esp. as an expression of contempt or disdain. **2.** Smell, odour, scent 1763. **3.** A sniff *of* something 1822.

A derisive and defiant s. C. BRONTË.

Snuff (snɒf), *sb.*[3] 1683. [– Du. *snuf*, prob. short for *snuftabak* (so LG. *snuv-*, G. *schnupftabak*), f. MDu. *snuffen* SNUFF *v.*[2]] **1.** A preparation of powdered tobacco for inhaling through the nostrils. **b.** Any powder used like snuff, esp. for medicinal purposes; a sternutatory or errhine. (*rare.*) 1861. **2.** A pinch of snuff 1724. **b.** Used to denote something of small value 1809.

1. He took s. with everybody DICKENS. Phrases. *Up to s.*, knowing, sharp, not easily deceived. *In high s.*, in high feather; elated. *To give* (one) *s.*, to deal sharply or severely with; to punish.

attrib. and *Comb.*: **s.-coloured** *a.* of the colour of s.; brown, brownish; **-dipper**, *U.S.*, one who habitually takes s.

Snuff (snɒf), *v.*[1] 1450. [f. SNUFF *sb.*[1]] **1.** *trans.* To free (a candle, wick, etc.) from the snuff, by pinching or cutting this off, or removing it with a special instrument. **b.** *fig.* To make clearer or brighter; to purge 1574. **2.** With *out*: **a.** To extinguish, put out; to cause to go out or disappear from sight 1687. **b.** To eclipse, efface, wipe out 1852. **3.** *intr.* To die, *slang* or *colloq.* 1865.

1. b. By exact definitions first snuffed, and purged from ambiguity HOBBES. **2. a.** 'Tis strange the mind..Should let itself be snuff'd out by an article BYRON.

Snuff (snɒf), *v.*[2] 1527. [f. MDu. *snuffen* snuffle. In sense II. 3 perh. directly f. SNUFF *sb.*[3]] **I.** *trans.* **1.** To draw *up* or *in* through the nostrils by the action of inhalation. **2.** To inhale, draw up, into or through the nostrils 1547. **3.** To detect, perceive or anticipate, by inhaling the odour of 1697. **4.** To smell at, examine by smelling 1859.

2. The leading Highlander snuffed the wind like a setting spaniel SCOTT. Phr. †*To s. pepper*; see PEPPER *sb.* 4. **3.** The old bull snuffed danger in the wind 1863. **4.** He [a dog]..snuffed him all over 1859.

II. *intr.* **1.** To draw air, etc., into the nostrils by an effort of inhalation; to do this in order to smell something 1530. **b.** Const. *up* one's nose 1714. **2.** To express scorn, disdain, or contempt by snuffing; to sniff. Freq. const. *at* a thing or person. Now *rare* or *Obs.* 1544. **3.** To inhale powdered tobacco; to take snuff 1725.

1. Like a wild Asse..that snoffeth and bloweth COVERDALE *Jer.* 2:23. **b.** Tricks such as snuffing up his nose CHESTERF. Hence **Snu·ffer**[2], one who takes s.; *U.S. local*, a porpoise.

Snu·ff-box. 1687. [SNUFF *sb.*[3] 1.] **1.** A box for holding snuff, usu. small enough to be carried in the pocket. **2.** *slang.* The nose 1853.

1. *Musical s.*, one fitted with mechanism capable of playing tunes.

Snuffer[1] (snɒ·fəɹ). 1465. [f. SNUFF *v.*[1] + -ER[1].] **1.** An instrument for snuffing, or snuffing out, candles, etc. In later use only in pl. form (also *a pair of snuffers*). **2.** One who snuffs candles 1611.

Snuffle (snɒ·f'l), *sb.* 1764. [f. the vb.] †**1.** An (*or* the) act of snuffling. **2.** *pl.* A stopped condition of the nose, through a cold in the head, etc., causing a snuffling sound in the act of respiration 1770. **3.** A nasal tone in the voice 1820.

2. She has at present a little London cold, but her Grace says it is 'only the snuffles' 1770. **3.** With a hypocritical s., and a sly twinkle of his eye SCOTT.

Snuffle (snɒ·f'l), *v.* 1583. [prob. – LG., Du. *snuffelen*, f. imit. base **snuf-*, repr. also by SNUFF *sb.*[3], OE. *snoffa* nausea, *snofl* catarrh; see -LE 3 and cf. SNIVEL *v.*] **I.** *intr.* †**1.** To show dislike or disdain by snuffing; to sniff *at* a thing in contempt –1662. **2.** To draw air into the nostrils in order to smell something; to snuff or smell *at* a thing 1600. **3.** To speak through the nose; to have a nasal twang. (Occas. taken as indicating hypocrisy or canting.) 1600. **4.** To draw up air or mucus through the nostrils in an audible or noisy manner 1600. †**5.** Of the wind: To blow in fitful gusts –1781.

3. Snuffling through the nose with an harmonious twang 1756.

II. 1. *trans.* To inhale, to clear, to search out or examine, by snuffing 1599. **2.** To utter, say, declare, etc., in a snuffling or nasal tone 1641.

2. Even the old Marquis snuffles approval CARLYLE. Hence **Snu·ffler,** one who snuffles or speaks through the nose; one who speaks cantingly. **Snu·fflingly** *adv.*

Snuffy (snɒ·fi), *a.*[1] 1678. [f. SNUFF *sb.*[1] or *v.*[2] + -Y[1].] Annoyed, displeased; ready to take offence.

Snuffy (snɒ·fi), *a.*[2] 1789. [f. SNUFF *sb.*[3] + -Y[1].] **1.** Like, or resembling snuff or powdered tobacco in colour or substance. **2. a.** Of persons: Given to taking snuff; bearing marks of this habit 1790. **b.** Of things: Soiled with snuff 1840.

2. a. A little odd-looking s. old man, with a brown scratch wig DISRAELI. Hence **Snu·ffiness.**

Snug (snɒg), *sb.*[1] 1665. [perh. var. of SNAG *sb.*] **1.** A snag (*rare*). **2.** *techn.* A projection or ridge cast on a plate, bolt, etc., in order to keep something in position, prevent rotation, or for some similar purpose 1843.

Snug (snɒg), *sb.*[2] 1768. [f. SNUG *a.*] **1.** *The s.*, that which is comfortable, quiet, or private (*rare*). **2.** *dial.* or *slang.* = SNUGGERY 1 b. 1864.

Snug (snɒg), *a.* and *adv.* 1595. [First in naut. use and prob. of LDu. origin (cf. LG. *snügger*, *snögger* slender, smooth, dainty, smart, Du. *snuggher*, *snoggher* slender, slim, active (mod. *snugger* lively, sprightly), but the meanings are not close.] **A.** *adj.* **1.** *Naut.* Of a ship or her parts: Trim, neat, compact; properly prepared for, or protected from, bad weather. **b.** *transf.* Of persons: Neat, trim. Now *Obs.* or *dial.* 1714. **2.** In a state of ease, comfort, or quiet enjoyment 1630. **3.** Of places, buildings, etc.: Comfortable and warm, cosy: esp. combining comfort with neatness and compactness 1718. **4. a.** Enabling one to live in comfort and comparative ease 1735. **b.** Moderately well-to-do; comfortably off; 'warm'. Chiefly *Irish dial.* 1802. **c.** Fairly large or substantial 1833. **5.** Comfortable, cosy 1766. **6.** In concealment or hiding; out of sight or observation. Chiefly with *lie* vb. 1687. †**b.** Secret –1766. **7.** Used as an interjection asking for or commanding secrecy, esp. in phr. *snug 's the word* 1700.

1. She will be..s. for any gale 1883. **2.** On southern banks the..sheep Lay s. and warm COWPER. You might sit as s. as a bug in a rug 1833. **3.** Your s. warm bed 1806. **4. a.** A good s. business they've got 1867. **c.** Having a s. legacy from Miss Crawley THACKERAY. **5.** He liked s. dinners of all things in the world THACKERAY. **6.** Be sure..[To] Lie s., and hear what critics say SWIFT.

B. *adv.* Snugly 1674.

He eyes the centre, where his friends sit s. GOLDSM. Hence **Snu·g-ly** *adv.* in a s. manner; **-ness.**

Snug (snɒg), *v.* 1583. [Of obscure origin; in later use assoc. with, and partly f., SNUG *a.*] **1.** *intr.* Of persons (or animals): To lie or nestle closely or comfortably, esp. in bed; to snuggle. Now *rare* or *dial.* **2.** *trans.* To place or put snugly, neatly, or comfortably 1754. **3.** To make snug, comfortable, or tidy; to set nicely in order 1787. **b.** To put or stow *away* snugly 1859. **4.** *Naut.* To make (a ship, etc.) snug or trim, esp. by lashing or stowing movables, furling or reducing sails, lowering topmasts, etc., in preparation for bad weather; to furl (a sail) 1881.

1. The loving couple lay snugging together 1692. **3.** The tent was shut, and everything snugged up 1888. **4.** The men were employed in snugging the decks 1881.

Snuggery (snɒ·gəri). 1815. [f. SNUG *a.* + -ERY.] **1.** A cosy or comfortable room, esp. one of small size, into which a person retires for seclusion or quiet; a bachelor's den. **b.** *spec.* The bar-parlour of an inn or public-house 1837. **2.** A snug, comfortable, or cosy house or dwelling 1833. **b.** A snug place, position, feature, etc. 1850. **3.** A sinecure (*rare*) 1839.

Snuggle (snɒ·g'l), *v.* 1687. [f. SNUG *a.* + -LE 3.] **1.** *intr.* Of persons, esp. children: To lie snug or close, esp. for warmth or comfort; to settle down cosily or comfortably; to get or press close to a person, esp. as a mark of affection; to nestle. **2.** *transf.* Of buildings, etc.: To lie in a sheltered or snug situation; to nestle 1862. **3.** *trans.* To hug or cuddle (a person, etc.) 1775.

So (sō[u]), *adv.* and *conj.* [OE. *swa*, lengthened *swā* (also *swǣ*, *swē*, *se*), corresp., with variations, to OFris. *sa*, *so*, OS. *sō*, OHG. *sō* (Du. *zoo*, G. *so*), ON. *svá*, Goth. *swa* (also *swē*). Cf. ALSO, AS, SUCH.] **I. 1.** In the way or manner described, indicated, or suggested; in that style or fashion. **2.** With the verbs *do*, *say*, *think*, etc., latterly assuming the function of an object and passing into the sense of 'that' OE. **b.** With auxiliary verbs in elliptic use (requiring the addition of *do* or *to do*) OE. **c.** In this way; thus; as follows ME. **3.** Used as predicate with the verb *be* OE. **b.** With auxiliary verbs in elliptic use (requiring the addition of (*to*) *be*, (*to*) *have it*, etc.) OE. **c.** Followed by a clause introduced by *that* ME. **d.** In clauses of supposition (sometimes with omission of *that*) ME. **4.** Representing a word or phrase already employed: Of that nature or description; of or in that condition, etc. OE. **b.** With verbs of thinking, considering, etc.: To be such, as such ME. **c.** With *call, name*, etc.: By that name or designation 1608. **5.** In various elliptic uses: **a.** After adverbs and conjunctions, as *how so? not so, if so*, etc. ME. **b.** As an introductory particle. Also *so, so.* 1593. **c.** As an expression of approval, or a direction to do something in a particular manner. Also in phr. *so best.* 1598. **†d.** = Let it be so; it is well. SHAKS. **e.** With ellipse of 'says' or 'writes' 1613.

1. There was the woman at Pau; and that girl.. at Vienna. He went on just so about them all. THACKERAY. **2.** I cannot doubt that they think so COLERIDGE. Some State legislatures have affected so to do 1888. **b.** *Brut*[*us*]. Repaire to th' Capitoll. *All.* We will so. SHAKS. **c.** For so the Lord sayd vnto me; I will take my rest *Isa.* 18:4. **3.** You argue from fact to necessity; 'Tis so, therefore it must be so 1697. No! Is that so? 1880. **b.** You are a welcome guest, if so you please 1594. **c.** Yet so it is, that People can bear any Quality in the World better than Beauty STEELE. **d.** Thus love I thee, so be thou loue me 1638. **4.** To make men happy, and to keep them so POPE. **b.** Her Attractions would indeed be irresistible, but that she thinks them so STEELE. **c.** My son Johnny, named so after his uncle SWIFT. **5. a.** 'I know China as well as any living Englishman.' 'Quite so.' 1896. **b.** So, let me see: my apron 1602. So, so, ma'am! I..beg pardon SHERIDAN. **c.** So, thus, keep her thus 1669. **d.** If it please you, so: if not: why so SHAKS. **e.** So he; doubting..the truth of his witnesses 1613.

II. Placed at the beginning of a clause with continuative force, and freq. preceded by *and*. **1.** Used to confirm or strengthen a previous statement OE. **2.** Denoting similarity, parallelism, or identity in some respect between two facts, actions, etc. OE. **3.** For that reason, on that account, accordingly, consequently, therefore ME. **b.** As an introductory particle, without a preceding statement (but freq. implying one) 1710. **4.** Denoting sequence, freq. without implication of manner, and hence passing into: Then, thereupon, thereafter, subsequently ME.

1. My father's birthday? Why, so it is! 1898. **2.** The Mayor looked blue; So did the Corporation too BROWNING. **3.** A shelter..is all I seek for. So name your rent. SCOTT. **b.** So one of my nephews is a wild rogue, hey? SHERIDAN. **4.** Then we marched out..to the drum, and so to bed 1892.

III. To that extent; in that degree. **1.** With adjs. or advs. (or equivalent phrases) in neg. and interrog. clauses OE. **2.** In affirmative clauses, with adj. followed by *a*, etc., and with verbs. Freq. as mere intensive. ME.

1. A voice so thrilling ne'er was heard WORDSW. What am I to say in answer to conduct so preposterous? NEWMAN. **2.** The bones of so dogged Contentions 1626. So barefaced a blunder 1845. I held back because I loved you so 1884.

IV. Introducing one or both of two clauses expressing comparison or correspondence. **†1.** After relative pronouns or advs.: So ever –1593. **†2.** *So..so* = As..so –1667. **3.** In adjurations or asseverations: In that way; to that extent OE. **4.** *So..as, so as*, in such or the same way, manner, etc., as ME. **5.** *So..as*, to the same extent, in the same degree, as: **a.** In neg. or interrog. clauses ME. **b.** In affirmative clauses: As..as. Now *arch.* or *dial.* late ME. **c.** With *as* taking the place of an object to the following verb 1555. **6.** *As..so*: **a.** Denoting more or less exact correspondence, similarity, or proportion ME. **b.** Denoting a simple parallelism between two different acts, concepts, etc., and sometimes approaching the sense of 'not only.. but (also)' ME.

1. Commaund What so thy mind affectes MARLOWE. **2.** So high as heav'd the tumid Hills, so low Down sunk a hollow bottom MILT. **3.** This seat..I claim as my right—so prosper me God and St. Barr! SCOTT. *So help*: see HELP *v.* 1. **4.** Do euen so as thou hast spoken COVERDALE *Gen.* 18:5. **5. a.** Women were never soe usefull as now 1646. **b.** The one is become so old as the other 1621. **c.** Is our Perfection of so frail a Make, As ev'ry Plot can undermine or shake? DRYDEN. **6. a.** For as he thinketh in his heart, so is he *Prov.* 23:7. **b.** As we rose with the sun, so we never pursued our labours after it was gone down GOLDSM. As in the arts, so also in politics, the new must always prevail over the old 1881.

V. 1. *So that*, denoting result or logical consequence; also sometimes = 'in order that' OE. **2.** *So..that*, in such a way, to such an extent, that: **a.** With adjs. and advs., and vbs. OE. **b.** With *but* (= that..not) 1842. **3.** With omission of *that*, = prec. sense ME. **b.** With the *so*-clause placed after that stating the consequence or result ME. **4.** *So* (*that*), in limiting sense: On condition that, provided that, so long as, if only OE. **b.** In the event that, in case that (*rare*) OE.

2. So frownd the mighty Combatants, that Hell Grew darker MILT. So ill that she could hardly speak 1802. **b.** There was no heart so bold, But sore it ached MACAULAY. **3.** He..treads so light, he scarcely prints the Plains DRYDEN. **b.** Friends he has few, so high the madness grows DRYDEN. **4.** I'll swiftly go..Nor care what land thou bear'st me to, So not again to mine BYRON.

VI. 1. *So..*, or *so..as, so as*, followed by an infinitive denoting result or consequence. late ME. **2.** *So as*, in such a way that, so that. Now *dial.* 1523. **b.** *So..as*, in similar use 1548. **c.** *So..as that, so as that*, = b. 1583. **3.** *So as*, provided that, etc. 1585.

1. Be so good to continue to favour me with your letters 1767. To repair the drain so as to abate the nuisance 1896. **2. b.** So posted, as they were not to be surprized 1738. **c.** When both flames have approached so near as that they join GOLDSM.

Phrases. **1.** *So to speak*: see SPEAK *v.* I. 3. **And so on**, an abbreviating phrase to avoid further description or enumeration of details. *And so forth*: see FORTH *adv.* **Or so**, or the like; or thereabout. **2.** With various adjs. and advs. of quantity, number, etc. **So far**: see FAR *adv.* 5, FAR-FORTH *adv.* *In so far as* (see IN *prep.* Phr.). *To be so far from..that*, and, by illogical ellipsis, simply *so far from*, are used to distinguish a contrasted statement or supposition. *So far, so good*, used to express satisfaction with matters up to a certain point. **So long**: see LONG *adv.* 1. **So much. a.** *adj.* So great, extensive, or abundant; so large a quantity or number of, etc.; an equal sum or amount of (something). **b.** *adv.* Followed by *the* and a comparative (and sometimes with *by* preceding): To that extent, in that degree. Also, To such an extent; in such a degree. **c.** *sb.* An equal amount; as much; a certain unspecified amount, sum, etc.; thus much, thus far (used to sum up or dismiss a matter); such an amount, quantity, etc. **So much (so)..as** or **that. a.** With *as* in ordinary comparative use. **b.** Used to emphasize a negation (e.g. *not so much as a penny*). **c.** With *that* denoting result or consequence.

Soak (sōᵘk), *sb.* 1598. [f. the vb.] **1. a.** The condition or process of being or becoming soaked; a spell of soaking. Chiefly in the phr. *in s.* **b.** A liquid used for maceration; a steep 1850. **c.** A vat in which hides are macerated 1876. **2.** A percolation of water; water which has oozed through or out of the ground, strata, etc. 1707. **3.** A heavy drinker; a tippler 1820. **4.** A prolonged draught or drinking-bout 1851.

Soak (sōᵘk), *v.* Pa. pple. **soaked, †soaken.** [OE. *socian*, rel. to OE. *soc* sucking at the breast, f. **suk-*, wk. grade of OE. *sūcan* SUCK *v.*] **I.** *intr.* **1.** To lie immersed in a liquid for a considerable time, so as to be saturated or permeated with it; to become thoroughly wet or soft in this manner. **2.** To percolate; to penetrate by saturation or infiltration; to ooze. Also with *in, through*, etc. 1440. **b.** With cogn. object: To make (way) by percolation 1815. **3.** To drink immoderately; to saturate oneself with liquor 1687.

1. As soon as the goose was killed, the liver was put to s. in milk and honey 1853. *fig.* Now, put these little hints 'to s.', as they say out here 1874. **2.** The water..soaked under the wall and wetted the mud below it 1884. **b.** The rivulet..soaked its way obscurely through wreaths of snow SCOTT.

II. *trans.* **1.** Of liquid or moisture: To permeate thoroughly; to saturate with wet ME. **2.** To lay or place in, to wet with, a liquid so as to produce thorough saturation; to steep. late ME. **b.** *refl.* with ref. to excessive drinking 1818. **3.** To bake (bread, etc.) thoroughly 1686.

2. Phr. *To s. one's clay* (colloq. or slang), to drink (heavily). **c.** Phr. *U.S. slang.* To strike hard, pummel; also *fig.* to 'slate'. *To s. it*, to 'give it hot', administer punishment to 1896. **d.** To impose upon (a person) by an extortionate charge or price (*slang*) 1899.

III. 1. To draw *out*, cause to ooze *out*, by means of soaking. late ME. **b.** To draw or suck *out* 1577. **†c.** To drain, exhaust, impoverish. Also *to s. dry* or *up*. –1687. **2.** To allow to sink in; to absorb; to take in by absorption. Also with *up*. 1553. **b.** To drink, imbibe, esp. to excess 1697.

1. Put half the Planks into Water..to s. out their Sap 1733. **c.** A Woman that sokes up a Man 1687. **2. b.** The quantity of port soaked there 1865.

Soakage (sōᵘ·kėdʒ). 1766. [f. prec. + -AGE.] **1.** Liquid which has filtered or oozed out. **2.** Liquid or moisture absorbed 1830. **3.** The process of percolating or soaking through 1867. **4.** The fact of lying in soak 1855.

Soaker (sōᵘ·kəɹ). 1577. [f. SOAK *v.* + -ER[1].] **†1.** A drainer, exhauster –1641. **2.** A drunkard 1593. **3.** *Old s.*, an old hand at anything; *spec.* at drinking 1589. **4.** One who soaks something 1611. **b.** A drenching rain 1839. **5.** A sheet of lead used in roofing to keep out heavy rains 1895.

Soaking (sōᵘ·kiŋ), *vbl. sb.* 1440. [f. SOAK *v.* + -ING[1].] **1.** The action of the vb. **b.** *pl.* Liquid which has soaked through 1846. **2.** In iron-working: A special process by which the heat of an ingot is equally distributed through the mass, in order to fit it for rolling 1884.

Soaking (sōᵘ·kiŋ), *ppl. a.* 1440. [f. SOAK *v.* + -ING[2].] **†1.** Taking in moisture, absorbent; *fig.* drawing to oneself, tending to drain or exhaust –1611. **2.** *Printing. S. pull*, a long and easy pull over of the bar-handle of a printing press 1683. **†3.** Percolating; sinking in; flowing slowly –1699. **4.** Drenching; wetting thoroughly 1641. **5.** Saturated, drenched 1864. **6.** Quasi-*adv.*, in *s. wet* 1847.

1. Conceit is s., will draw in More then the common Blocks SHAKS. **4.** The rain was coming down in a s. drizzle 1894. **5.** The suns of August sucked up the venom from the emerald s. swamp 1882. Hence **Soa·kingly** *adv.*

Soam (sōᵘm). *Sc.* and *north.* late ME. [prob. – OFr. *some* pack-saddle, horse-load, but the difference in the sense is unexplained.] **1.** A rope or chain, attaching a draught-horse, etc., to a wagon, plough, etc.; a trace-rope. **2.** *Coal-mining. pl.* Traces for drawing coal in tubs along the roads 1789.

So-and-so, *sb.*, *a.*, and *adv.* 1596. **A.** *sb.* An indefinite phrase (= 'such a thing, person, number, etc.') used in place of a more lengthy statement, or as a substitute for an expression or name not exactly remembered or stated.

Number s. in such-and-such a street 1861.

B. *adj.* Paltry, worthless; indifferent; poor in health or circumstances; so-so. Now *dial.* 1655. **C.** *adv.* **1.** To a certain number or degree 1631. **2.** In a certain manner or way 1653. **3.** With only moderate prosperity, success, etc. 1844.

2. Vertue and Vice are nothing else but the Soul so and so affected or modified 1678.

Soap (sōᵘp), *sb.* [OE. *sāpe* = (M)LG. *sēpe*, MDu. *seepe* (Du. *zeep*), OHG. *seif(f)a* (G. *seife*) :– WGmc. **saipo* (ON. *sápa* is prob. from OE.), whence Finnish *saip(p)io, saip(p)ua*, Lappish *saipo*, and L. *sāpō, -ōn-*, credited to Gaul by Pliny.] **1.** A substance formed by the combination of certain oils and fats with alkaline bases, and used for washing or cleansing purposes. **b.** *slang.* Flattery (cf. SOFT SOAP *sb.* 2) 1859. **c.** *U.S.* Money; now esp. that used in bribery 1860. **2.** With distinguishing terms, denoting a particular kind or make of soap, as CASTILE s., *hard s.*, SOFT S.; also *s. of soda*, etc. late ME. **3.** With *a* and *pl.* A kind of soap 1562.

1. c. If thy father hath 'the s.', Do not wash your hands of me 1860. **2.** Fixed oil, in combination with soda, forms the finest kind of hard s. 1813.

Comb.: **s.-box**, a box in which soap is packed; used, esp. in U.S., as a makeshift stand for a street orator; *attrib.* characteristic of s.-b. oratory; hence as *vb.*; also **soapboxer**; **s. cerate**, a cerate composed of lead, soap, and the acetates of lead and soda, used to allay inflammation; **†-earth**, soap-stone; **-fat**, the refuse of kitchens, used in making s.; **-fish**, either *Rhypticus saponaceus* or *Promicropterus maculatus*; **-liniment**, a liniment composed of s., camphor, and spirits of rosemary; **s. plaster**, a healing plaster chiefly composed of s.; **-saver**, a wire receptacle with a handle in which remnants of soap are utilized for producing a lather. **b.** Forming names of plants or trees, or their products: **s.-bark**, a vegetable principle obtained from certain trees, as the *Quillaja saponaria* of Chile, the common Soapwort, *Saponaria officinalis*, and allied species, and used as a substitute for s.; saponin; **-fruit**, = SOAPBERRY 1; **-nut**, = SOAPBERRY; **-plant** *U.S.*, an American liliaceous plant, *Chlorogalum pomeridianum*, used as a detersive; also, the soapberry; **-root**, either of two plants, the Egyptian Soap-root (*Gypsophila struthium*), and the Spanish Soap-root (*G. hispanica*), both used for washing; **-tree**, one or other of various trees or plants of which the roots, leaves, or fruits yield a substitute for s.

Soap (sōᵘp), *v.* 1585. [f. SOAP *sb.*] **1.** *trans.* To rub, smear, lather, or treat with soap. Also with *up*. **2.** *slang.* To address with smooth or flattering words; to flatter 1853.

Soapberry (sōᵘ·pbe:ri). Also **soap-berry, soap berry.** 1629. [SOAP *sb.*] **1.** The fruit or nut of various species of *Sapindus* (esp. *S. saponaria*), or of *Acacia concinna*, used in certain countries as a substitute for soap; a soap-nut. **2.** Any of the trees bearing this fruit 1716.

Soa·p-boi:ler. 1594. [SOAP *sb.*] **1.** One who boils (the ingredients of) soap; a soap-maker. **2.** A pot used for boiling soap; a soap-pan 1863. So **Soa·p-boi:ling** *vbl. sb.* the business, occupation, or process of boiling soap.

Soa·p-bu·bble. 1815. [SOAP *sb.*] An iridescent bubble composed of a thin film of soap and water.

fig. The talk has been mere soap-bubbles EMERSON.

Soapery (sōᵘ·pəri). 1674. [f. †*soaper*: see -ERY.] A soap-factory.

Soa·p-ma:ker. 1483. [SOAP *sb.*] One who makes soap; a soap-boiler.

Soap(-)stone (sōᵘ·pˌstōᵘn). 1681. [SOAP *sb.*] *Min.* A massive variety of talc, of which various kinds are found in several countries, having a smooth greasy feel, and used for various economical or ornamental purposes (occas. as a soap); steatite; also loosely applied to certain soft clays, etc.

Soap(-)suds. 1611. [SOAP *sb.*] Water impregnated with dissolved soap, *esp.* water in which clothes have been washed; in attrib. use freq. *soap-sud*.

Soapwort (sōᵘ·pwɒɹt). 1548. [f. SOAP *sb.* + WORT¹, perh. after Du. *zeepkruid*.] **1.** One or other of the herbaceous plants belonging to the genus *Saponaria*, which yield a saponaceous principle; esp. the common species, *S. officinalis*; also, the genus itself. **2.** Any plant of the order *Sapindaceæ* 1846.

Soapy (sōᵘ·pi), *a.* 1610. [f. SOAP *sb.* + -Y¹.] **1.** Smeared with soap; covered with soap-suds or lather. **2.** Impregnated with soap; containing soap in solution 1721. **3.** Of the nature of soap; having the soft or greasy feel of soap; soap-like 1722. **4.** Of appearance, feel, etc.: Resembling that of soap; suggestive of soap 1732. **b.** Having a taste of soap 1892. **5.** *slang.* Ingratiating, suave, unctuous 1865. Hence **Soa·pily** *adv.* **Soa·piness.**

Soar (sōᵊɹ), *sb.* 1596. [f. SOAR *v.*, perh. partly after (O)Fr. *essor*, f. *essorer* (see next).] **1.** The altitude attained in soaring; range of flight upwards. **2.** The act of soaring or rising high 1817.

1. Within soare Of Towring Eagles MILT. **2.** It is ill whistling for a hawk when she is once on the s. SCOTT.

Soar (sōᵊɹ), *v.* late ME. [Aphetic – (O)Fr. *essorer* (used refl.) :– Rom. *exaurare, f. L. *ex* EX-¹ + *aura* air in motion.] **I.** *intr.* **1.** Of birds: To fly or mount upwards; to ascend to a towering height; also loosely, to sail or skim at a great height. Occas. with *up*. **2.** *fig.* To mount, ascend, or rise to a higher or more exalted level in some respect 1593. **3.** Of inanimate objects: To ascend, rise up to a height 1697. **b.** Of a mountain, building, etc.: To rise majestically or imposingly to a great altitude. Also with *up*. 1812.

1. A flight of Condors soaring in circles in a particular spot 1830. *transf.* O, in what orbe thy mightie spirit soares 1602. **b.** *Aeronautics.* To fly without motor power and without loss of altitude 1897. **2.** How high a pitch his resolution soares! SHAKS. When men of infamy to grandeur s. YOUNG.

II. *trans.* **1.** To perform or accomplish (a flight) by rising high 1659. **2.** To attain or reach (a height) by upward flight; to fly up through (the air, etc.) 1667.

2. They summ'd thir Penns, and soaring th' air sublime, With clang despis'd the ground MILT. Hence **Soa·rer. Soa·ring** *ppl. a.*, **-ly** *adv.*

Sob (sǫb), *sb.* late ME. [f. SOB *v.*¹] **1.** An act of sobbing, a convulsive catching of the breath under the influence of grief. **b.** A similar act or sound expressive of pain or exertion 1480. †**c.** An act, on the part of a horse, of recovering its wind after exertion; an opportunity allowed to it of doing this; hence *fig.*, a rest or respite. Chiefly in the phr. *to give. . a s.* –1658. **2.** *transf.* A sound resembling that of a sob 1765.

1. The syghes, the sobbes, the diepe and deadly groane SACKVILLE. **b.** The tremulous s. of the complaining owl WORDSW. **c.** *Com. Err.* IV. iii. 25. **2.** With sea-sobs warning of the awakened wind 1897.

attrib.: **s.-stuff**, *orig. U.S. slang*, exaggerated pathos; sentimental talk or writing. So **s.-story.**

Sob (sǫb), *v.*¹ ME. [First evidenced in easterly texts and perh. of LDu. origin (cf. WFris. *sobje*, Du. dial. *sabben* suck).] **1.** *intr.* To catch the breath in a convulsive manner as the result of violent emotion, esp. grief; to weep in this fashion. **b.** To make a sound resembling sobbing 1676. **2.** *refl.* To bring (oneself) *into* a certain state (e.g. *to sleep*), with sobbing 1658. **3.** *trans.* **a.** To send *out*, bring *up*, etc., by sobbing or with sobs 1718. **b.** To utter with sobs. Usu. with *out*. 1782.

1. See how my wretched sister sobs and weeps SHAKS. **3. b.** Sobbing out their entreaties on their knees FROUDE. Hence **So·bbing** *vbl. sb.* the action of giving vent to sobs; the sound produced by this; freq. in *pl.* **So·bbingly** *adv.*

Sob, *v.*² Now *dial.* and *U.S.* 1625. [app. dial. var. of SOP *v.* 1 b.] *trans.* To soak, saturate, sop. (Usu. in pa. pple.) So **So·bby** *a.* soaked 1611.

The high lands are sobbed and boggy 1859.

Sobeit (sōᵘˌbī·it), *conj.* 1583. [So *adv.* I. 3 d.] Provided *that*; if only.

Sober (sōᵘ·bəɹ), *a.* ME. [– (O)Fr. *sobre* – L. *sobrius*, opp. *ebrius* (see EBRIETY).] **I. 1.** Moderate, temperate, avoiding excess, in matters of appetite, diet, conduct, etc. **2.** Not addicted to the use of strong drink; abstemious. late ME. **3.** Free from the influence of intoxicating liquor; not intoxicated; not drunk. late ME.

1. Of Arthure men say. .he was. .sobre & honest 1338. The Vintage of the Sabine Grape,. .in s. Cups shall crown the Feast 1743. **2.** Men moste enquere. .Wher she be wys, or sobre, or dronkelewe CHAUCER. **3.** Very vildely. .when hee is s., and most vildely. .when hee is drunke SHAKS.

II. 1. Of demeanour, speech, etc.: Grave, serious, solemn; indicating a serious mind or purpose. late ME. **2.** Quiet or sedate in demeanour; of grave, dignified, or discreet deportment; serious or staid. late ME. **3.** Of natural forces, etc.: Quiet, gentle, peaceful. late ME. **4.** Of living, etc.: Characterized by temperance, moderation, or seriousness 1552. **5.** Not readily excited or carried away; of a calm, dispassionate judgement 1564. **6.** Of colour, dress, etc.: Subdued in tone; not glaring, gay, or showy; neutral-tinted 1596. **b.** Unexciting; dull 1838. **7.** Free from extravagance or excess 1607. **b.** Moderate, sensible; not fanciful or imaginative 1619. **8.** Guided by sound reason; sane, rational 1638.

1. Phr. *In s. earnest* or †*sadness*. **2.** What damned error, but some s. brow Will blesse it? SHAKS. **4.** Men. .Live to no s. purpose and contend That their Creator had no serious end COWPER. **5.** Far from the madding crowd's ignoble strife, Their s. wishes never learn'd to stray GRAY. The s. and patient spirit of the English intellect 1862. **6.** Twilight gray Had in her s. Liverie all things clad MILT. **7.** With such s. and vnnoted passion He did behooue his anger ere 'twas spent SHAKS. **8.** Mad all his life, at least not s. BOSWELL. Hence **So·berize** *v.* = SOBER *v.* **So·ber-ly** *adv.*, **-ness.**

Sober (sōᵘ·bəɹ), *v.* late ME. [f. SOBER *a.*] *trans.* and *intr.* To make or become sober, in various senses. Also with *down*.

Shallow draughts intoxicate the brain, And drinking largely sobers us again POPE. When. . solemn speeches s. down a dinner 1877.

Sober-minded, *a.* 1534. [SOBER *a.*] **1.** Of a sober mind; temperate; self-controlled; rational; sensible. Also *absol.* with *the*. **2.** Characterized by soberness of mind 1815. Hence **So:ber-mi·ndedness.**

Sobersides (sōᵘ·bəɹsəidz). 1705. [f. SOBER *a.*] A sedate, serious-minded person.

‖**Soboles** (sǫ·bolīz). Also as pl. 1722. [L., f. *sub* under + **olere* grow.] *Bot.* †**1.** A shoot, a sprout. LISLE. **2.** A creeping underground stem 1832. So **Soboli·ferous** *a. Bot.* bearing shoots.

Sobriety (sǒbrəi·ěti). late ME. [– (O)Fr. *sobriété* or L. *sobrietas*, f. *sobrius* SOBER *a.*; see -ITY.] **1.** The quality of being sober or moderate in the indulgence of appetite; *spec.* moderation in the use of strong drink. **2.** Moderation in any respect; avoidance of excess or extravagance 1582. **3.** Staidness, gravity, seriousness; soundness or saneness of judgement, etc. 1548.

1. Let the sad consequences of Noah his intemperance give caution for s. unto all ancient persons 1655. **2.** S. of dress must be enforced 1884. **3.** Delicacy of feeling and s. of judgement 1841.

‖**Sobriquet** (sōᵘ·brikēⁱ, ‖sobrike). See also SOUBRIQUET. 1646. [– Fr. *sobriquet*, earlier *soubriquet* (XV); identical with *soubriquet* (XIV) tap under the chin, perh. for **souzbequet*, f. *souz* (:– L. *subtus*) under + *bec* beak.] An epithet, a nickname.

Soc (sǫk). Now *Hist.* ME. [var. of SOKE.] **1.** A right of local jurisdiction (see SAC¹). **2.** = SOKE 2 (*rare*) 1728.

Socage (sǫ·kědʒ). Now *Hist.* ME. [– AFr. *socage* (AL. *socagium* 1088), f. *soc*; see SOKE, -AGE.] The tenure of land by certain determinate services other than knight-service. **b.** An estate held in socage (*rare*) 1464. **c.** A payment made to the superior by one holding land in socage 1859. **d.** *attrib.*, as *s. freehold*, tenure 1467.

Free or *common* (also *free and common*) *s.*, the ordinary form of this tenure. Hence **So·cager,** one holding land by s. tenure.

So-called, so called, *ppl. a.* 1657. **1.** In predic. use (prop. without hyphen): Called or designated by that name. **2.** In attrib. use (hyphened): Called or designated by this name or term, but not properly entitled to it or correctly described by it 1837.

Soccer (sǫ·kəɹ). Also **socker.** orig. *University slang.* 1891. [f. *Assoc.* (short for *Association*) + -ER⁶.] Association football.

Sociability (sōᵘʃăbi·lĭti). 1475. [f. next + -ITY.] The character or quality of being sociable; friendly disposition or intercourse.

Sociable (sōᵘ·ʃăb'l), *a.* and *sb.* 1553. [– Fr. *sociable* or L. *sociabilis*, f. *sociare* unite, ASSOCIATE, f. *socius* companion, ally, fellow; see -ABLE.] **A.** *adj.* **1.** Naturally disposed to be in company with others of the same species. **2.** Inclined to seek and enjoy the company of others; disposed to be friendly or affable in company; willing to converse in a pleasant manner 1573. **3.** Characterized by, pertaining to, contact, intercourse, or companionship with others, esp. in a pleasant or friendly manner 1573. †**4.** Capable of being combined or joined together –1679.

1. Man is said to be a S. Animal ADDISON. **2.** We had a s. company in the cabin 1771. **3.** The harvesting of potatoes was s. toil 1898. †*S. coach*; see B. 1 a. **4.** Another Law there is, which toucheth them as they are s. parts united into one body HOOKER.

B. *sb.* **1. a.** An open, four-wheeled carriage having two seats facing each other and a box-seat for the driver 1794. **b.** A tricycle or aeroplane having two seats side by side 1882. **2.** *U.S.* An informal evening party; *esp.* a social church meeting 1826. Hence **So·ciableness,** sociability. **So·ciably** *adv.*

Social (sōᵘ·ʃăl), *a.* and *sb.* 1562. [– (O)Fr. *social* or L. *socialis* allied, confederate, etc., f. *socius* (prec.); see -AL¹.] **A.** *adj.* †**1.** Capable of being associated or united *to* others (*rare*). †**2.** Associated, allied, combined –1686. **3.** Of war: Occurring between allies or confederates; *spec.* (with *the*), in Roman Hist., the war between Rome and the Italian allies, 90–89 B.C.; in Gr. Hist., the war between the Athenians and their confederates, 357–355 B.C. 1665. **4.** Marked or characterized by mutual intercourse, friendliness, or geniality;

enjoyed, taken, spent, etc., in company with others, esp. with those of a similar class or kindred interests 1667. †**b.** Sympathetic –1745. **5.** †**a.** United by some common tie. POPE. **b.** Sociable 1729. **c.** Consisting or composed of persons associated together in, or for the purpose of, friendly intercourse 1849. **6.** Living, or disposed to live, in companies or communities desirous of enjoying the society or companionship of others 1722. **b.** *Zool.* Living together in more or less organized communities; belonging to a community of this kind 1831. **c.** *Bot.* Of plants: Growing in a wild state in patches or masses with other members of the same species, esp. so as to cover a large area 1834. **d.** Of ascidians, etc.: Compound 1860. **7.** Pertaining, relating, or due to, connected with, etc., society as a natural or ordinary condition of human life 1729. **8.** Concerned with, interested in, the constitution of society and the problems presented by this 1841.

4. Thou..Best with thy self accompanied, seek'st not S. communication MILT. *S. evening*, an evening meeting of a society, etc. of the nature of an entertainment; an evening on which such a meeting is held. **5. a.** The s. shades the same dark journey go POPE. **b.** His own friendly and s. disposition JANE AUSTEN. **c.** The club is strictly a 's.' one 1892. **6.** Man not being..accidentally gregarious, but essentially s. 1853. **7.** Forgetfulness of s. duties JOHNSON. Enjoying..an equality of s. rank 1849. *S. contract*, the mutual agreement which, according to Rousseau's *Contrat social* (1762), forms the basis of human society. *S. evil*, prostitution. *S. service*, any activity designed to promote social welfare. **8.** *S. Democrat*, a member of a political party having socialistic views.

B. *sb.* A social gathering or party, esp. one held by members of a club or association 1876. Hence **So·cialness** = SOCIALITY 1.

Socialism (sōᵘ·ʃăliz'm). 1827. [– Fr. *socialisme* (1832); cf. It. *antisocialismo* (Giacomo Giuliana, 1803); see prec., -ISM.] A theory or policy of social organization which advocates the ownership and control of the means of production, capital, land, property, etc. by the community as a whole, and their administration or distribution in the interests of all.

Christian s., a doctrine advocating a form of s. on a Christian basis. *State s.*: see STATE *sb.*

Socialist (sōᵘ·ʃălist). 1833. [f. as prec. + -IST (R. Owen, 1827). Cf. Fr. *socialiste* (Reybaud, 1835).] One who advocates or believes in the theory of socialism; an adherent or supporter of this.

attrib. The worst of all S. plans..is that all have within them..a damning desire to shirk work 1848. Hence **Sociali·stic** *a.* of, pertaining to, characteristic of, or based on socialism; favouring socialism.

Sociality (sōᵘʃiæ·lĭti). 1649. [– L. *socialitas*, f. *socialis*; see SOCIAL, -ITY.] **1.** The state or quality of being social. **b.** With *pl.* A social act or function 1825. **2.** The action or fact on the part of individuals of forming a society or of associating together; the disposition to do this 1775. **3.** Companionship or fellowship *in* or *with* a thing or person 1806.

Socialize (sōᵘ·ʃăləiz), *v.* 1828. [f. SOCIAL *a.* + -IZE.] **1.** *trans.* To render social. **2.** To render socialistic in nature; to establish or develop according to the theories or principles of socialism 1846. Hence **So:cializa·tion.**

Socially (sōᵘ·ʃăli), *adv.* 1642. [f. SOCIAL *a.* + -LY².] †**1.** As a member of a body or society. (Opp. to *severally.*) *rare.* –1647. **2.** In a social manner; sociably 1763. **3.** In respect of or with regard to society 1871.

†**So·ciate**, *sb.* 1450. [Aphetic f. ASSOCIATE *sb.*] An associate or colleague; a companion or comrade –1788.

So·ciate, *pa. pple.* and *ppl. a. arch.* 1501. [– L. *sociatus*, pa. pple. of *sociare*; see next, -ATE².] **1.** *pa. pple.* Associated *with* or *to* some thing or person; joined or united *together.* †**2.** *ppl. a.* Associated, joint. DE FOE.

†**So·ciate**, *v.* 1578. [– *sociat-*, pa. ppl. stem of L. *sociare* unite, associate, f. *socius* companion, etc.; see -ATE³.] **1.** *trans.* To associate, join, or unite together; to form into a society or association –1654. **2.** *intr.* To associate *with* others –1719.

Sociative (sōᵘ·ʃ¹ĕtiv), *a.* 1871. [– Fr. *sociatif, -ive*; see SOCIATE *v.* and -IVE.] *Gram.* Denoting or expressing association.

Societarian (sosəi,ĕtēᵊ·riăn), *a.* and *sb.* 1822. [f. SOCIETY, after words in -ARIAN. Cf. Fr. *sociétaire.*] **A.** *adj.* Societary; socialistic. The all-sweeping besom of s. reformation LAMB.

B. *sb.* **1.** A socialist 1842. **2.** One who moves in or is a member of fashionable society 1891.

Societary (sosəi·ĕtări), *a.* 1847. [f. SOCIETY + -ARY¹.] Of, pertaining to, concerned or dealing with, society or social conditions; social.

Society (sŏsəi·ĕti). 1531. [– (O)Fr. *société* – L. *societas, -tat-*, f. *socius* companion, etc.; see -ITY.] **I. 1.** Association with one's fellow men, esp. in a friendly or intimate manner; companionship or fellowship. Also rarely of animals. †**b.** With *a* and *pl.* An instance of association or companionship with others (*rare*) –1780. **c.** *concr.* Persons with whom one has, or may have, companionship or intercourse. Also *transf.* of plants. 1605. **2.** The state or condition of living in association, company, or intercourse with others of the same species; the system or mode of life adopted by a body of individuals for the purpose of harmonious co-existence or for mutual benefit, defence, etc. 1553. **3.** The aggregate of persons living together in a more or less ordered community 1639. **b.** The aggregate of leisured, cultured, or fashionable persons regarded as forming a distinct class or body in a community; *esp.* those persons collectively who are recognized as taking part in fashionable life, social functions, entertainments, etc. Also with *a* and *the.* 1823. **c.** Personified 1784.

1. S., without which man's life is unpleasant 1531. **b.** *Merry W.* III. iv. 9. **c.** For all s. he had two friends RUSKIN. **2.** In the earliest stages of s. there are many arts, but no sciences 1862. **3.** S. has only one law, and that is custom 1873. **b.** Who *is* Mr. Gascoyne and who *is* Mr. Thistleton? ..Are they in s.? 1893. **c.** S. shrugged its shoulders 1877.

†**II. 1.** Participation in some thing or action –1758. **2.** The fact or condition of being connected or related –1771. **3.** The state or condition of being politically confederated or allied; confederation –1665. **4.** Partnership or combination in or with respect to business or some commercial transaction –1650. **III. 1.** A number of persons associated together by some common interest or purpose, united by a common vow, holding the same belief or opinion, following the same trade or profession, etc.; an association 1548. **b.** A corporate body of persons having a definite place of residence 1588. **2.** A collection of individuals composing a community or living under the same organization or government 1577. **b.** Less widely: A company; a small party. Now *rare* or *Obs.* 1590. **3.** A number of persons united for the promotion of a common purpose by means of meetings, publications, etc. 1665. **b.** *U.S.* = CONGREGATION *sb.* 6. 1828.

1. An old lady of the S. of Friends SCOTT. **b.** The S. of the Inner Temple CLARENDON. **2. b.** Therefore be abhorr'd, All Feasts, Societies, and Throngs of men SHAKS. **3.** He always runs to a disputing s. JOHNSON. The English Historical S. was just being formed 1844.

attrib. and *Comb.*, as *s. meeting*, etc.; *s. journal, man*, etc.; also, **s. hand,** a workman belonging to a trade s.; **s. house,** an establishment conforming to the rules of a trade s.

Socinian (sosi·niăn), *sb.* and *a.* 1645. [– mod.L. *Socinianus*, f. *Socinus*, latinization of the Italian surname *Soz(z)ini.*] **A.** *sb.* One of a sect founded by Lælius and Faustus Socinus, two Italian theologians of the 16th c., who denied the divinity of Christ. **B.** *adj.* Pertaining to the Socinians or their creed 1694. Hence **Soci·nianism,** the doctrines or special views of the Socinians 1643. **Soci·nianize** *v.* to make or become S.

Socio- (sōᵘ·sio), comb. form (on Greek analogies) of L. *socius* fellow, in sense 'society'.

Sociologic (sōᵘsiolǫ·dʒik), *a.* 1861. [– Fr. *sociologique*; see next, -IC.] Of or pertaining to sociology; concerned or connected with the organization, condition, or study of society. So **Sociolo·gical** *a.*, **-ly** *adv.* **Socio·logist,** a student of sociology.

Sociology (sōᵘsiǫ·lŏdʒi). 1843. [– Fr. *sociologie* (Auguste Comte, 1830); see SOCIO-, -LOGY.] The science or study of the origin, history, and constitution of human society; social science.

Sock (sǫk), *sb.*¹ [OE. *socc*, corresp. to MLG., MDu. *socke* (Du. *zok*), OHG. *soc* (G. *socke*), ON. *sokkr*; Gmc. – L. *soccus* light low-heeled shoe or slipper – Gr. σύκχος, συκχάς.] **1.** A covering for the foot, of the nature of a light shoe, slipper, or pump. Now *rare* or *Obs.* **2.** A short stocking covering the foot and usually reaching to the calf of the leg; half-hose ME. **3.** *spec.* A light shoe worn by comic actors on the ancient Greek and Roman stage; hence *allus.* comedy or the comic muse 1597. **4.** *techn.* A loose inner sole for a shoe 1851.

2. Phr. *To pull up one's socks*: to brace oneself for an effort. **3.** Great Fletcher never treads in buskins here, Nor greater Jonson dares in socks appear DRYDEN. *S. and buskin*, comedy and tragedy, the drama or theatrical profession as a whole. Hence **Sock** *v.*² *trans.* to provide with socks; to put socks on. **So·ckless** *a.* without socks; wearing no socks.

Sock, *sb.*² *north.* and *Sc.* late ME. [– (O)Fr. *soc* ploughshare, thought to be of Celtic origin. See SOCKET *sb.*] A ploughshare. Phr. *S. and scythe*, ploughing and mowing.

Sock, *sb.*³ *Eton slang.* 1825. [Of unkn. origin.] Eatables, esp. dainties.

Sock, *sb.*⁴ *slang.* 1700. [Of cant (perh. imit.) origin; see next.] A blow, beating; esp. *pl.* in *to give* (a person) *socks.*

Sock, *v.*¹ *slang.* 1700. [Of cant origin; goes with SOCK *sb.*⁴] **1.** *trans.* To beat, strike hard, hit. **b.** To drive or strike *into* something; to 'give it' *to* a person 1892. **2.** *intr.* To strike out, deliver blows; to pitch *into* a person 1856.

1. We socks 'im with a stretcher-pole KIPLING.

Sockdolager (sǫkdǫ·lădʒəɹ). *U.S. slang.* 1836. [prob. fanciful.] **1.** A heavy or knockdown blow; a finisher. **2.** 'A patent fish-hook, having two hooks which close upon each other by means of a spring as soon as the fish bites' (Bartlett) 1848. **3.** Something exceptional in any respect; esp. a large fish 1869.

Socker, var. SOCCER.

Socket (sǫ·kĕt), *sb.* ME. [– AFr. *soket* (AL. *sokettus* spear-head XIV), dim. of (O)Fr. *soc* ploughshare (SOCK *sb.*²), after AL. *vomerulus* (Matthew Paris XIII), dim. of L. *vomer* ploughshare; see -ET.] †**1.** A lance- or spear-head having a form resembling that of a ploughshare –1535. **2.** A hollow part or piece, usually of a cylindrical form, constructed to receive some part or thing fitting into it 1448. **3.** The part of a candlestick or chandelier in which the candle is placed 1440. **4.** *Anat.* A cavity in which some part or articulation (as a tooth, eye, bone, etc.) is inserted 1601.

attrib. and *Comb.*, as *s.-bar, -bit, -chisel, -pole*, etc. Hence **So·cket** *v. trans.* to place in, or fit with, a s.; *Golf*, to strike (the ball) with the heel of the club. **So·cketed** *ppl. a.* **So·cketless** *a.*

Socle (sǫ·k'l, ‖sokl'). 1704. [– Fr. *socle* – It. *zoccolo* prop. wooden shoe, repr. L. *socculus*, dim. of *soccus* SOCK *sb.*¹] A low plain block or plinth serving as a pedestal to a statue, column, vase, etc.; also, a plain plinth forming a foundation for a wall.

Socman (sǫ·kmæ̆n). 1579. [– AL. *socamannus*, var. of *sokemannus* SOKEMAN.] One who holds lands in socage. Hence **So·cmanry,** = SOKEMANRY.

Socotrine (sǫ·kŏtrin, sōᵘ·k-, -əin), *a.* late ME. [f. *Socotra* or *Socotora*, name of an island in the Indian Ocean.] **1.** *S. aloes*, a drug prepared from the juice of the *Aloe socotrina* (or *perryi*), and orig. obtained from the island of Socotra. **2.** *S. aloe*, the plant yielding the drug 1778.

Socratic (sŏkræ·tik), *a.* and *sb.* 1637. [– L. *Socraticus* – Gr. Σωκρατικός, f. Σωκράτης.] **A.** *adj.* Of or pertaining to, characteristic of, Socrates the Athenian philosopher, or his philosophy, methods, character, etc.

By questions aptly proposed in the S. method 1741.

B. *sb.* A follower of Socrates 1678.

Plato and Aristotle, the two Socratics 1886. So **Socra·tical** *a.* 1581, **-ly** *adv.* **Socra·ticism,**

So·cratism, the philosophy of Socrates or some aspect of this. **Socratize** (sǫ·krătəiz) *v. intr.* to philosophize or live after the manner of Socrates.

Sod (sǫd), *sb.*[1] late ME. [– (M)LG. *sode*, MDu. *sode* (Du. *zode*) = OFris. *sātha*, *sāda*, of unkn. origin.] **1.** A piece or slice of earth together with the grass growing on it, cut out or pared off from the surface of grass land; a turf. Also const. *of* (grass, turf, etc.). **2.** A pair of these used as a saddle. *Sc.* and *north.* 1586. **3.** The surface of the ground, esp. when turfy; the sward. Freq. *poet.* or *rhet.* 1729.

1. For a monument they only raysed a turffe or greene Sodd of the earth 1618. **3.** Tender bluebells, at whose birth The s. scarce heaved SHELLEY.

Comb.: **s.-worm,** the larva of certain moths, as *Crambus exsiccatus*, which destroys the roots of grass and corn. Hence **Sod** *v. trans.* to cover or build up, to provide or lay, with sods or turfs; to turf.

Sod, *sb.*[2] *vulgar.* 1880. Abbrev. of SODOMITE, used as a term of abuse or joc.

Sod (sǫd), *pa. pple.* and *ppl. a.* ME. [pa. pple. of SEETHE *v.* Cf. SODDEN.] †**1.** Of food, liquor, etc.: Boiled –1658. †**b.** *Twice s.* [after L. *crambe repetita*], stale, unpalatable –1641. **2.** *S. oil*, a greasy matter extracted in the treatment of sheepskins 1883.

Soda (sōu·dă). 1558. [– med.L. *soda*, perh. back-formation f. *sodanum*, glasswort, f. *soda* headache, based on Arab. *ṣudā*ᶜ headache (for which the plant, containing soda, was used as a remedy), f. *ṣada*ᶜ*a* split.] **1.** An alkaline substance, now manufactured artificially from common salt, or occurring in a mineral state as a deposit, esp. in certain lakes, or in solution in the water of such lakes (natron); soda-ash; sodium carbonate (Na_2CO_3). **b.** Sodium bicarbonate, used largely for domestic purposes; baking or cooking soda 1851. **2.** *Chem.* Sodium oxide (Na_2O) 1826. **3.** Soda-water 1842.

1. *Caustic s.*, sodium hydroxide or hydrate (NaOH).

attrib. and *Comb.*: in *Photogr.* for hyposulphite of soda, as *s. developer, -pyro, -solution, etc.*; **s.-ash,** the sodium carbonate of commerce; = SODA 1; **-lye,** a solution of hydrate of s., employed in the manufacture of hard soap; **s. waste,** the insoluble oxisulphide of calcium, left as a useless residue, when the soda salts have been dissolved out by water. **b.** Connected or dealing with sodium carbonate or its manufacture, as *s.-apparatus, -furnace, -manufacture*, etc. **c.** Used for, or containing, soda-water, as *s.-bottle, -fountain* (orig. U.S.), *-tumbler*, etc. **d.** Made with or containing sodium bicarbonate, as *s.-biscuit, -cake.* Hence **Sodaic** (sodē·ik) *a.* containing s. or sodium bicarbonate.

Sodalite (sōu·dăləit). 1810. [f. SODA + -LITE.] *Min.* A vitreous, transparent or translucent silicate of aluminium and sodium containing sodium chloride, usually of a greenish blue colour and occurring in certain igneous rocks.

Sodality (sodæ·liti). 1600. [– Fr. *sodalité* or L. *sodalitas*, f. *sodalis* member of a brotherhood or corporation; see -ITY.] **1.** Association or confederation *with* others; brotherhood, companionship, fellowship. **2.** *R.C.Ch.* A religious guild or brotherhood established for purposes of devotion or mutual help or action; the body of persons forming such a society 1600. **b.** A chapel used by a religious sodality 1667. **3.** A society, association, or fraternity of any kind 1633.

Sodamide (sōu·dămaid). 1838. [f. SODA + AMIDE.] *Chem.* A white solid formed by treating sodium with gaseous ammonia.

Soda(-)water. 1802. [f. SODA + WATER *sb.*] **1.** Water containing a solution of sodium bicarbonate, or, more generally, charged under pressure with carbon dioxide (carbonic acid gas), strongly effervescent, and used as beverage or stimulant. **2.** Water containing a solution of sodium carbonate for cooling or wetting metal-working tools 1891.

Sodden (sǫ·d'n), *pa. pple.* and *ppl. a.* ME. [Strong pa. pple. of SEETHE *v.*] **1.** Boiled. Now *rare* or *Obs.* **2.** Of persons, their features, etc.: Having the appearance of that which has been steeped or soaked in water; rendered dull, stupid, or expressionless, esp. owing to indulgence in intoxicants; pale and flaccid 1599. **b.** Characterized by heaviness, dullness, or want of vivacity 1851. **3.** Of food: Heavy, doughy; spoiled through overboiling or imperfect baking 1800. **4.** Saturated or soaked with water or moisture 1820.

2. His complexion was pale and s. 1841. **4.** Don't work the ground when it is s., muddy, or rendered sticky by a recent frost 1856.

Sodden (sǫ·d'n), *v.* 1812. [f. prec. See SOD *pr. pple.* and *ppl. a.*] **1.** *trans.* To make sodden; to soak in, or saturate with, water. **b.** To render (the faculties) dull or stupid 1863. **2.** *intr.* To become soaked or saturated with water or moisture; to grow soft or rotten in this way 1820.

Soddy (sǫ·di), *a.* and *sb.* 1611. [f. SOD *sb.*[1] + -Y[1].] **A.** *adj.* Abounding in sods; consisting or composed of sods; of the nature of a sod. **B.** *sb.* A house made of sods. *U.S.* 1893.

Sodio- (sōu·dio), comb. form of SODIUM, denoting the presence of that substance or its salts, as *s.-aluminic* adj.; *s.-salicylate*.

Sodium (sōu·diŏm). 1807. [f. SODA + -IUM.] *Chem.* An elementary alkaline metal (isolated by Davy in 1807), forming the basis of SODA, closely resembling potassium in its appearance and properties, and occurring most commonly in the chloride (common salt). Symbol Na (for Natrium).

attrib. **a.** In the names of chemical compounds or groupings, as *s.alcohol, -amyl, bicarbonate, bromide, carbonate* 1857. **b.** Misc., as *s.-compound, -flame, -light*; **s.-amalgam,** a compound of mercury and sodium; **s. soap,** soda soap. Hence **So·dic** *a.* of, containing, or composed of s.

Sodom (sǫ·dəm). 1605. [f. L. *Sodoma* (Gr. Σόδομα, Heb. *sᵉdōm*), the name of the early city beside the Dead Sea, the destruction of which is recorded in Gen. 18–19.] An extremely wicked or corrupt place.

S. apple, Apple of Sodom (see APPLE *sb.* 3.) 1615.

Sodomite (sǫ·dəməit). ME. [– (O)Fr. *sodomite* – late L. *Sodomita*, Gr. Σοδομίτης, f. SODOM; see -ITE[1] 1.] †**1.** Sodomy. ME. only. **2.** One who practises or commits sodomy. late ME. **3.** An inhabitant of Sodom 1474.

Sodomitical (sǫdəmi·tikăl), *a.* 1546. [– late L. *Sodomiticus* (f. L. *Sodomita*); see prec. -ICAL.] **1.** Of persons: Guilty of, committing, or practising sodomy. †**b.** With whom sodomy is committed –1634. **2.** Of the nature of, characterized by, consisting in, or involving sodomy 1550. †**3.** Of places, etc.: Polluted or infected by sodomy –1632. So **Sodomi·tic** *a.* (*rare*) 1630. **Sodomi·tical-ly** *adv.*, **-ness.**

Sodomy (sǫ·dəmi). ME. [– med.L. *sodomia*, for Chr. L. *peccatum Sodomiticum* (Jerome), *Sodomita libido* (Prudentius) sin, lust of Sodom; see SODOM, -Y[3].] An unnatural form of sexual intercourse, esp. that of one male with another.

Soe (sōu). Now *dial.* late ME. [– ON. *sár*; also as dial. *say, sey.*] A large tub.

Soever (soˌe·vəɹ), *adv.* Also *poet.* **soe'er** (soˌēᵊ·ɹ). 1557. [See SO *adv.* and EVER *adv.*] Used with generalizing or emphatic force after words or phrases preceded by *how, what, which, whose*, etc.

Whose tongue so ere speakes false SHAKS. To all who are perplexed in any way s. 1835.

Sofa (sōu·fă). 1625. [ult. – Arab. *ṣuffa* through Eur. langs., Fr. *sofa*, †*sopha*, etc.] **1.** In Eastern countries, a part of the floor raised a foot or two, covered with rich carpets and cushions, and used for sitting upon. **2.** A long, stuffed seat with a back and ends or one end, on which to recline or sit; a form of lounge or couch 1717.

2. Convenience next suggested elbow-chairs, And luxury th' accomplish'd S. last COWPER.

Comb.: **s.-bed, -bedstead,** a piece of furniture so constructed as to form a s. or bedstead as required.

Soffit (sǫ·fit). 1613. [Earliest forms *soffita, -ito*, later *sof(f)ite, soffit* – Fr. *soffite* or It. *soffitto, -itta* :– **suffictus, -icta*, for L. *suffixus* (see SUFFIX).] *Arch.* The under horizontal face of an architrave or overhanging cornice; the under surface of a lintel, vault, or arch; a ceiling.

†**So-forth.** 1611. [See FORTH *adv.*] Such and such a thing.

They're here with me already; whisp'ring, rounding: Silicia is a s. SHAKS.

Soft (sǫ̇ft), *sb.* ME. [f. the adj.] †**1.** That which is agreeable, pleasant, or easy; comfort, ease (*rare*) –1677. **2.** That which is soft or yielding; the soft part *of* something; softness 1593. **b.** *pl.* Soft coal; also, soft woollen rags 1883. **3.** *Phonetics.* A 'soft' consonant (see next, 3 b) 1846. **4.** *U.S.* **a.** A member of a local party which advocated a 'soft money' or paper currency. **b.** A member of one or other party holding moderate views. Cf. SOFT-SHELL. 1847. **5.** A soft, simple, or foolish person; a 'softy'. Chiefly *dial.* or *colloq.* 1854.

Soft (sǫ̇ft), *a.* [Late OE. *sōfte* agreeable, comfortable, luxurious, repl. earlier mutated *sēfte* = OFris. *sēfte*, OS. *sāfti*, OHG. *semfti* (obs. G. †*senft*) :– WGmc. **samfti*; the unmutated form, due to infl. from the adv. (OE. *sōfte*, etc.) is paralleled in Continental forms, e.g. (M)HG. *sanft* (:– WGmc. **samft-*).] **I. 1.** Producing agreeable or pleasant sensations; characterized by ease and quiet enjoyment; of a calm or placid nature. †**b.** Pleasing *in* taste; free from acidity or sharpness. Also of odour: Not pungent, strong, or heavy. –1826. **c.** Pleasing to the eye; free from ruggedness or asperity. Also of colour, or with reference to this: Not crude or glaring; quiet, subdued 1702. **2.** Involving little or no discomfort, hardship, or suffering; easily endured or borne ME. **b.** Involving little or no exertion or effort. Now chiefly *colloq.*, easy, lazy, idle. 1639. **3.** Of a sound, the voice, etc.: Low, quiet, subdued. Also, melodious, pleasing to the ear, sweet. ME. **b.** *spec.* in *Phonetics*, voiced (opp. to HARD *a.* III. 4). Now disused. 1636. **c.** Of musical instruments: Making or emitting a soft sound 1561. **4.** Of weather, seasons, etc.: Free from storms or rough winds; genial, mild, balmy ME. **b.** Of the sun, rain, wind, etc.: Shining, falling, or blowing gently; not strong, violent, or boisterous. late ME. **c.** Of the sea, streams, etc.: Smooth, calm; running calmly or gently 1450. **5.** Of pace, progression, or movement: Leisurely, easy; slow; not hasty or hurried. Now *arch.* ME. †**6.** Of a fire: Burning slowly or gently; moderate in heat or intensity; slow –1738. †**7.** Of a slope, ascent, etc.: Gentle, gradual –1819.

1. Where young Adonis oft reposes,. .In slumber s. MILT. Many a joy could he from Night's s. presence glean BYRON. **c.** S. scenes of solitude no more can please POPE. **2.** After ten years' s. durance in all plenty,. .He dyed 1661. **b.** A s. and easy life these ladies lead! BROWNING. The. .idea that romance is 'a s. job' 1894. You wanted a s. time of it 1905. **3.** Her voice was euer s., Gentle, and low, an excellent thing in woman SHAKS. The s. rustle of a maiden's gown KEATS. **c.** Anon they move. .to the Dorian mood Of Flutes and s. Recorders MILT. **4.** In a s. Air and a delicious Situation ADDISON. **b.** In a somer sesun whon softe was þe sonne LANGL. **c.** In thee fresh brooks, and s. streams glance MILT. **5.** A s. pace goes far 1663. **7.** S. declivities with tufted hills COWPER.

II. 1. Of persons: Gentle or mild in nature or character; inclined to be merciful, lenient, or considerate in dealing with others; compassionate, kind, tender-hearted ME. **b.** Of animals: Gentle, docile; lacking in spirit ME. **c.** Not rigid or severe; lax, yielding 1715. **2.** Of disposition, look, qualities, feelings, etc.: Gentle, mild ME. **3.** Of words, language, etc.: **a.** Ingratiating, soothing, bland; tender, sentimental. late ME. **b.** Free from roughness or harshness; tending to tone down or minimize something unpleasant. late ME. **c.** Expressive of what is tender or peaceful 1704. **4.** Of actions, means, etc.: Gentle or moderate in character; carried on, performed, etc., without harshness, severity, or violence 1495. **5.** Of the hand, etc.: Touching lightly or gently 1650. **6.** Of drink: Non-alcoholic. orig. *dial.* and *U.S.* 1880.

1. At the first impulse of passion be silent, till you can be s. CHESTERF. He. .was very s. and gentle with the children THACKERAY. **2.** Sadde of his semblaunt and of s. chiere LANGL. S. pity enters at an iron gate SHAKS. **3. a.** The lippes of an harlot are a droppinge hony combe, and hir throte is softer then oyle COVERDALE *Prov.* 5:3. **b.** You have s. words for hard meanings RICHARDSON. **4.** They are disposed to try s. means at first 1888. **5.** Through the temple. .He went with s. light feet SHELLEY.

III. 1. Yielding readily to emotions of a tender nature; impressionable. Also *absol.* of persons. ME. **2.** Easily influenced or swayed; facile, compliant. Also *absol.* of persons. ME. **b.** Weak, effeminate, unmanly 1593. **c.** Refined, delicate (*rare*) 1601. **3.** Of a weakly or delicate constitution; incapable of much physical endurance or exertion 1661. **4.** *The soft(er sex*, the female sex 1648. **5.** More or less foolish, silly, or simple; lacking ordinary intelligence or common-sense; easily imposed upon or deceived. Also *dial.* or *colloq.*, mentally deficient, half-witted. 1621. **b.** *colloq.* Foolishly kind, benevolent, etc. 1890.

1. Loues feeling is more s. and sensible, Then are the tender hornes of..Snayles SHAKS. Phr. *To be s. on* or *upon* (a person), to be in love with; to regard amorously or sentimentally. **2.** A heart too s. from early life To hold with fortune needful strife SCOTT. **c.** An absolute gentleman,..of very s. society, and great showing SHAKS. **5.** Your greatest Students are commonly..silly, s. fellows 1621.

IV. 1. Presenting a yielding surface to the touch; not offering absolute resistance to pressure ME. **2.** Of cloth, hair, etc.: Of a yielding texture, pleasant to the feel or touch; also, capable of being easily folded, or put into a different form; flexible ME. **b.** *U.S.* Of paper money. (Cf. HARD *a.* I. 2.) 1831. **3.** Of a bed, pillow, etc.: Readily yielding to the weight of the body; into or upon which one sinks or settles down comfortably ME. **4.** Of ground: **a.** Insufficiently hard; allowing a vehicle, etc., to sink in, esp. through excess of wet 1523. **b.** Of a fall: Made on a soft substance, or in such a way as to escape injury 1587. **5.** Of a yielding consistency. late ME. **b.** Of a semi-fluid consistency 1703. **6.** Relatively inferior or deficient in hardness 1599. **7.** Applied to water, such as rain or river water, which is more or less free from calcium and magnesium salts 1755. **8.** Rainy, wet. Chiefly *Sc.* and *n. dial.* 1812.

1. Softer to the touch, than down of Swans DRYDEN. **2.** Satin smooth, Or velvet s. COWPER. *S. wares*, or *goods*, woollen or cotton fabrics, such as cretonne, chintz, lace, muslin, velvet, etc., or articles made of these. **3.** A good s. Pillow for that good white Head SHAKS. *transf.* Good cheer and s. lodging SCOTT. **4. a.** The match was played on a s. wicket (*mod.*). **5. c.** Of rays: Of a low penetrating power 1902. **6.** A head and face rudely carved in a s. stone 1847. *S. coal*, bituminous coal.

attrib. and *Comb.*: *s.-billed*, *-finned* adjs.; **s.-eyed** *a.*, having s. or gentle eyes; **-footed** *a.*, having feet which tread softly; **s. grass**, velvet-grass; **s. pedal**: see PEDAL *sb.* 1 b (*b*); hence as *vb. intr.* to play with the soft pedal; *trans.* to 'tone down'; **-spoken** *a.*, having, speaking with, a s. or gentle voice; plausible, affable; **-wood**, wood which is relatively s. or easily cut; sap-wood, alburnum. **b.** In names of animals: **s. crab**, a soft-shelled crab; **s. tortoise**, any tortoise of the genus *Trionyx*. Hence **So·ftish** *a.* somewhat s.; rather tender.

Soft (sǫft), *adv.* [OE. *sōfte*, adv. of *sēfte*; see prec.] **1.** Softly; gently; without harshness or roughness; quietly; not hastily or hurriedly. †**2.** *S. and fair(ly)*, softly, gently, leisurely –1736. **3.** Used as an exclam. with imperative force, either to enjoin silence or deprecate haste. Now *arch.* 1550.

1. I will..sleepe as s. As Captaine shall SHAKS. How s. the poplars sigh 1896. **2.** S. and Fair goes far 1700. **3.** Not too fast: s., s. SHAKS. S.—who is that stands by the dying fire? M. ARNOLD.

†**Soft**, *v.* ME. [f. the adj.] **1.** *trans.* To render soft, in various senses –1594. **2.** *intr.* To become or grow soft. ME. only.

1. Yet cannot all these flames..her hart more harde then yron s. awhit SPENSER.

‖**Softa** (sǫ·ftă). Also **sophta.** 1613. [Turk. *softa* – Pers. *sūkta* burnt, parched, scorched.] In Turkey, a Moslem theological student; also *gen.*, a pupil engaged in professional studies at a secondary school.

Soften (sǫ·f'n), *v.* late ME. [f. SOFT *a.* + -EN[5]. Cf. SOFT *v.*] **1.** *trans.* **1.** To mitigate, assuage, or diminish; to render less painful or more easy to bear. **2. a.** To render more impressionable or tender. late ME. **b.** To enervate, weaken, render effeminate 1581. **c.** To make more gentle, delicate, or refined. Also with *into*. 1709. **3.** To mollify or appease; to render less harsh or severe 1450. **4.** To make physically soft or softer; to lessen the hardness of (a substance) 1530. **5.** To modify or tone down; to render less pronounced or prominent 1670. **6.** To make softer in sound 1736.

1. That blisful sight softneth al my sorwe CHAUCER. **2.** Misfortune, adversity, s. the human heart 1874. **b.** Troops softened by luxury 1828. **c.** Though some divine thought softened all her face MORRIS. **3.** To s. the anger of an offended deity 1835. **4.** With Fire he..softens iron 1796. **5.** Other proposed to send a deputation to s. the harshness of his removal 1879. **6.** He spoke to her in accents somewhat softened from their usual harshness 1794.

II. *intr.* **1.** To become soft or softer in various non-physical senses; *esp.* to become more gentle, tender, or emotional; to grow fainter or less pronounced 1611. **2.** To become physically soft 1626. Hence **So·ftener**, one who or that which softens; a mollifier; *spec.* a painting-brush of soft hair.

So·ftening, *vbl. sb.* 1568. [f. prec. + -ING[1].] **1.** The action of making soft. Also with *a* and *pl.* **b.** *Path.*, esp. in *s. of the brain* (encephalomalacia) 1830. **2.** *spec.* In Painting, the mixing and diluting of colours with the brush or pencil 1728.

1. b. *S. of the brain*, pop. name for progressive dementia with general paresis; When s. of the brain is accompanied by an increase of bulk 1835.

So·ft-head. 1650. [f. SOFT *a.* + HEAD *sb.*] One who has a soft head; hence, a simpleton. So **So·ft-headed** *a.*

Soft-hearted, *a.* 1593. [SOFT *a.*] Having a soft or susceptible heart; tender-hearted. Hence **Soft-heartedness** 1580.

Softling (sǫ·ftliŋ). 1547. [f. SOFT *a.* + -LING[1] 2.] **1.** An effeminate or unmanly person; a weakling. **2.** A small soft object 1817. **3.** *attrib.* Of a soft nature 1732.

2. Each s. of a wee white mouse BROWNING.

Softly (sǫ·ftli), *adv.* ME. [f. SOFT *a.* + -LY[2].] **1.** In a soft manner, in various senses. **2.** Used imperatively: = SOFT *adv.* 3. 1596.

Phr. *Fair and s.*: see SOFT *adv.* 2. So **So·ftness.** late OE.

Soft-sawder (sǫftˌsǫ·dəɹ), *v. colloq.* 1843. [f. *soft sawder*; see SAWDER *sb.*] *trans.* and *absol.* To flatter; = SAWDER *v.*

Soft-shell. 1853. [f. SOFT *a.*] **1.** *attrib* In the specific names of animals: Having a soft shell 1860. **2.** *attrib.* That adopts or advocates a moderate or temperate course or policy. *U.S.* 1859. **3.** *U.S. ellipt.* **a.** = SOFT *sb.* 4 b. 1853. **b.** A soft-shelled lobster 1884. So **Soft-shelled** *a.* (freq. of a shell-less egg) 1611.

Soft(-)soap, *sb.* 1634. [f. SOFT *a.*] **1.** A smeary, semi-liquid soap, made with potash lye; potash soap. **b.** With pl. A make or kind of this 1783. **2.** *slang.* Flattery; blarney; 'soft sawder' 1848. Hence **Soft(-)soap** *v. trans.* to flatter, 'soft-sawder' (*slang*).

Softy (sǫ·fti). *dial.* or *colloq.* 1863. [f. SOFT *a.* + -Y[6].] A weak-minded or silly person; a simpleton, noodle.

Soggy (sǫ·gi), *a.* Chiefly *dial.* and *U.S.* 1722. [f. dial. *sog* marsh + -Y[1].] **1.** Of land: Soaked with moisture; boggy, swampy, marshy. **2.** Of things: Saturated with wet; soppy, soaked 1863. **3.** Of bread: Sodden, heavy 1868. **4.** Of persons: Dull, spiritless 1896. **5.** Moist, close, sultry 1896.

5. We rattled along through the bush..all the time in deep, s. heat 1896. Hence **So·gginess.**

Soh = SOL[2], in tonic-sol-fa notation.

Soh (sōu), *int. Obs.* or *arch.* 1814. [var. of SO *adv.* 5, or simply of exclamatory origin.] **1.** An exclam. denoting anger, scorn, reproof, surprise, etc., on the part of the speaker. **2.** Used in soothing a restive horse, = Gently! Softly! Easy! 1820.

Soho (souhōu·), *int.* and *sb.* ME. [An AFr. hunting call, prob. of exclamatory origin. In earliest use varying with *howe, he howe, here howe, howe here.*] **1.** A call used by huntsmen to direct attention to a hare which has been discovered or started, or to encourage the dogs; hence used as a call to draw the attention of any person, announce a discovery, or the like. **b.** As *sb.* 1572. **2.** = prec. 1825.

1. b. Such sohoes, whoopes and hallowes 1589. Hence **Soho·** *v. intr.* to shout s.; *trans.* to announce the starting of (a hare) by this shout.

‖**Soi-disant** (swadizań), *a.* 1752. [Fr., f. *soi* oneself + *disant*, pr. pple. of *dire* say.] **1.** Of persons: Calling oneself; self-styled, would-be. (Usually with implication of pretence or deception.) **2.** Of things: Said to be such, without really being so; pretended 1845.

2. The modern s. science of political economy RUSKIN.

Soil (soil), *sb.*[1] late ME. [– AFr. *soil* land, perh. repr. L. *solium* seat (whence Fr. *seuil* threshold), by assoc. with *solum* (Fr. *sol*) ground.] **I. 1.** The earth or ground; the face or surface of the earth. **2.** A piece or stretch of ground; a place or site. Now *rare* or *Obs.* late ME. **3.** A land or country; a region, province, or district. Now *Obs.* or *arch.* late ME. **4. a.** The place of one's nativity; one's (native) land or country. late ME. †**b.** One's domicile or place of residence –1643.

1. The precise spot where his foot first touched the s. 1838. **3.** Is this the Region, this the S., the Clime,..That we must change for Heav'n? MILT. **4. a.** You..To shun my sight, your Native S. forego DRYDEN. **b.** Phr. *To change one's s.*

Phrases. *Lord of the s.*, the owner of an estate or domain. *Child* (*son*, etc.) *of the s.*, a native of a place or country; also, one closely connected with the cultivation of the ground.

II. 1. The ground with respect to its composition, quality, etc., or as the source of vegetation. late ME. **2.** Without article: Mould; earth 1440. **3.** With *a* and *pl.* A particular kind of mould or earth 1560.

1. Most subject is the fattest Soyle to Weedes SHAKS. **3.** *fig.* No s. like poverty for growth divine COWPER.

Comb.: **s.-bound** *a.*, (*a*) 'clagged', clodded; (*b*) bound or attached to the s.; **-cap** *Geol.*, a layer of s. and detritus covering strata or bedrock. Hence **Soi·lless** *a.* destitute of, devoid of, s. or mould.

Soil (soil), *sb.*[2] late ME. [– OFr. **soille*, *souille* (mod. *souille* muddy place, (dial.) *souil* pond, ordure), f. *souiller* SOIL *v.*[1]] **I.** †**1.** A miry or muddy place used by a wild boar for wallowing in –1611. **2.** A pool or stretch of water, used as a refuge by a hunted deer or other animal. Freq. in the phr. *to take s.* late ME.

2. He..Then takes the S., and plunges in the Flood Precipitant 1735. *fig.* The King..singles out the Archbishop, and hunts him to s. at Rome 1647.

II. 1. Staining or soiling; the fact of being stained or soiled; a stain or discolouring mark 1501. **2.** *fig.* Moral stain or tarnish 1597.

2. For all the soyle of the Atchieuement goes With me, into the Earth SHAKS.

III. 1. Filth; dirty or refuse matter 1608. **2.** Filth usually carried off by drains; sewage 1601. **3.** Ordure, excrement; the dung of animals used as a compost; manure. Cf. also NIGHT-SOIL. 1607.

Comb.: **s.-pipe**, a sewage or waste-water pipe.

Soil (soil), *v.*[1] ME. [– OFr. *soill(i)er*, *suill(i)er* (mod. *souiller*) :– Rom. **suculare*, f. L. *suculus, -ula*, dim. of *sus* pig, SOW *sb.*] **I.** *trans.* **1.** To defile or pollute with sin or other moral stain. Also *absol.* **2.** To make foul or dirty, esp. on the surface; to begrime, stain, tarnish ME. **3.** *fig.* To sully or tarnish; to bring disgrace or discredit upon (a person or thing) 1593. **4.** *intr.* To become dirty or stained; to take on a stain or tarnish 1530.

1. My soule was soyld with foule iniquitie SPENSER. **2.** Much handling soileth things 1638. Phr. *To s. one's hands* (fig.). **3.** Black falsehood has ineffaceably soiled her name CARLYLE. **4.** Silver soils sooner than gold 1882.

II. 1. *intr.* and †*refl.* Of a wild boar or deer: To roll or wallow in mud or water. late ME. **2.** Of a hunted stag: To take to water or marshy ground; †to swim *down*. late ME. Hence **Soiled** (soild), *ppl. a.* ME.

†**Soil**, *v.*[2] ME. [– OFr. *soille*, pres. subj., or *soil*, pres. ind. of *soldre, soudre* :– L. *solvere* release, loosen; see ASSOIL *v.*] **1.** *trans.* = ASSOIL *v.* 1. –1530. **2.** To set free *of*, release from, an obligation, etc. late ME. only. **3.** To resolve, clear up, expound, or explain; to answer (a question) –1611. **4.** To refute (an argument or objection); to overcome by argument –1567.

†**Soil**, *v.*[3] 1593. [f. SOIL *sb.*[2]] *trans.* To supply or treat (land) with dung, etc.; to manure –1692.

Just as they Soyl their Ground, not that they love the Dirt, but that they expect a Crop 1692.

Soil (soil), *v.*[4] 1605. [perh. a use of SOIL *v.*[1]] *trans.* To feed (horses, cattle, etc.) on fresh-cut green fodder, orig. for the purpose of purging; †to feed up or fatten (fowls).

Soilure (soi·liŭı). ME. [– OFr. *soilleure* (mod.Fr. *souillure*), f. *soillier* SOIL *v.*[1]; see -URE.] **1.** Soiling, sullying, staining. **2.** A stain, blot, or blemish 1829.

1. *fig.* He merits well to haue her, that doth seeke her, Not making any scruple of her soylure, With such a hell of paine SHAKS.

Soily (soi·li), *a.* Now *rare.* 1575. [f. SOIL *sb.*[2] or *v.*[1] + -Y[1].] †**1.** Apt to soil or stain –1605. **2.** Soiled, stained, dirty 1631. Hence **Soi·liness.**

‖**Soirée** (swa·re). 1820. [Fr., f. *soir* evening.] An evening party, gathering, or social meeting.

‖**Soixante-quinze** (swasant kæ̃nz). [Fr. = 75.] = *seventy-five* (see SEVENTY A. 2).

Sojourn (sǫ·dʒɒɹn, -əɹn, sɒ·-), *sb.* ME. [– AFr. *su(r)jurn*, OFr. *sojor*, etc. (mod. *séjour*), f. the verb; see next.] **1.** A temporary stay at a place. **2.** A place of temporary stay ME.

2. Thee I re-visit now.., Escap't the Stygian Pool, though long detain'd In that obscure s. MILT.

Sojourn (sǫ·dʒɒɹn, -əɹn, sɒ·-), *v.* ME. [– OFr. *sor-*, *sojorner* (mod. *séjourner*) :– Rom. **subdiurnare* 'spend the day', f. L. *sub-* SUB- + late L. *diurnum* day (cf. JOURNAL).] **1.** *intr.* To make a temporary stay in a place; to remain or reside for a time. †**2.** To make stay; to tarry, delay –1594. †**3.** *trans.* To lodge; to rest or quarter (horses); to have as a lodger –1690.

1. They soiourned there a vij nyghte MALORY. *fig.* Mirth is farre away, Nor may it soiourne with sad discontent DRAYTON. **3.** [They] are sojourned there by one Thomson 1690. Hence **So·journment.**

Sojourner (sǫ·-, sɒ·dʒəɹnəɹ). late ME. [f. prec. + -ER[1].] **1.** One who sojourns; a temporary resident. †**2.** A guest or lodger; a visitor –1660. †**b.** A boarder living in a house, school, or college, for the purpose of receiving instruction –1785.

2. b. [Grocyn] became a Sojourner in Exeter Coll. 1691.

Soke (sōᵘk). Now chiefly *Hist.* ME. [– AL. *sōca* – OE. *sōcn* attack, prosecution, right of prosecution or jurisdiction, administrative district = ON. *sókn* attack, etc., Goth. *sōkns* search, inquiry :– Gmc. **sōkniz*, f. **sōk-* SEEK *v.*] **1.** A right of local jurisdiction; = SOKEN 3. 1598. **2.** A district under a particular jurisdiction; a local division of a minor character ME. **3.** = SOKEN 2 b. 1609. **4.** *attrib.*, as *s.-mill* ME.

Sokeman (sōᵘ·kmæ̆n). *Hist.* 1603. [– AFr. *sokeman* or AL. *sokemannus* (XI), f. OE. word repr. by SOKE + MAN *sb.*] A tenant holding land in socage; a socman. So **So·kemanry,** the tenure of land by a s.; also, the sokemen collectively.

Soken (sōᵘ·k'n). Now *Hist.* [repr. OE. *sōcn*; see SOKE.] †**1.** An attack or assault. OE. only. †**2.** Resort to, or visiting of, a place; habitual going or haunting –1440. †**b.** *spec.* Resort of tenants or others to a particular mill to have their corn ground; the right of the mill to such custom –1591. †**3.** Right of prosecution, legal investigation, or jurisdiction. OE. only. **4.** = SOKE 2. OE.

2. b. Gret s. hath this meller.., With whete and malt, of al the lond aboute CHAUCER.

‖**Soko** (sōᵘ·kōᵘ). 1870. [Native Afr. name.] A species of anthropoid ape discovered by Livingstone near Lake Tanganyika.

Sol[1] (sǫl). late ME. [– L. *sol* sun.] **1.** The sun (personified) 1450. †**2. a.** *Alch.* Gold –1758. **b.** *Her.* = OR *sb.* –1709.

Sol[2] (sǫl, sōᵘl). ME. [First syllable of L. *solve*; see UT.] *Mus.* The fifth note of Guido's hexachords, and of the octave in modern solmization; the note G in the natural scale of C major.

‖**Sol**[3] (sǫl). Now *Hist.* 1583. [– Earlier Fr. *sol* (mod. *sou*); see SOU.] A former coin and money of account in France, etc., equal to the twentieth part of a livre, but of varying actual value.

‖**Sól**[4] (sōᵘl). *Pl.* **soles.** 1884. [Sp. *sol* sun; see SOL *sb.*[1]] A Spanish American (now Peruvian) silver coin worth about two shillings.

Sol[5] (sǫl). 1899. [Short for *solution*; cf. GEL.] *Phys. Chem.* A liquid solution or suspension of a colloid.

‖**Sola** (sōᵘ·lă). Also **solah.** 1845. [Urdu and Bengali *solā* = Hindi *sholā*; see SHOLA.] A tall leguminous swamp-plant (*Æschynomena aspera* or *paludosa*) of India; the pith of this used in making light hats. Also *attrib.*

‖**Sola** (sōᵘ·lă), *a.* 1660. [L., fem. of *solus* SOLUS, and It. *sola*, fem. of *solo* SOLO.] **1.** Of females: Sole, solitary, alone. **2.** *Comm.* A single bill, as dist. from one of a 'set' 1866.

†**Sola,** *int.* [Cf. SOHO *int.* and *hola* HOLLA.] A call or cry to attract attention. SHAKS.

Solace (sǫ·lĕs), *sb.* ME. [– OFr. *solas*, *-atz* (mod. dial. *soulas*) :– L. *solatium*, f. *solari* relieve, console.] **1.** Comfort, consolation; alleviation of sorrow, distress, or discomfort. †**2.** Pleasure, enjoyment, delight; entertainment, recreation, amusement –1667. **3.** That which gives comfort, †brings pleasure or enjoyment, etc. ME. **4.** *Printing.* A penalty imposed by the chapel for any breach of its rules 1683.

1. Sorrow would [have] sollace, and mine Age would ease SHAKS. **2.** Great joy he promis'd to his thoughts, and new S. in her return MILT. **3.** To have thee by my side..an individual s. dear MILT. Hence **So·lacement,** solace, solacing, consolation.

Solace (sǫ·lĕs), *v.* ME. [– OFr. *solacier* (mod. dial. *soulasser*), f. *solas* (prec.); so late L. *solaciari.*] **1.** *trans.* To cheer, comfort, console; †to entertain or recreate. Also *refl.* **b.** To make (a place) cheerful or pleasant 1667. **c.** To allay, alleviate, assuage, soothe 1667. †**2.** *intr.* To take comfort or consolation, recreation or enjoyment –1728. **3.** *trans.* Of printers: To punish (a person) corporally for non-payment of a 'solace' 1683.

1. We will with some strange pastime s. them SHAKS. **b.** The smaller Birds with song Solac'd the Woods MILT. **c.** A little hint to s. woe TENNYSON.

†**Sola·cious,** *a.* late ME. [– OFr. *solacieus*, f. *solas*; see SOLACE *sb.*, -IOUS.] Affording solace –1675.

Old Friends to trust, old Gold to keep, old Wine To drink; are a s. good old Trine 1675.

Solan (sōᵘ·lăn). Also **soland.** 1450. [prob. f. ON. *súla* gannet + *and-*, nom. *ǫnd* duck.] The gannet (*Sula bassana*), a large sea-fowl resembling a goose, which frequents a few rocks and small islands of Britain, the Færöes, Iceland, and Canada. Also *attrib.*, *solan goose.*

Solanaceous (sǫlănē̆ⁱ·ʃəs), *a.* 1804. [f. mod.L. *Solanaceæ*, f. L. *solanus* nightshade; see -ACEOUS.] *Bot.* Belonging to the *Solanaceæ*, a family of gamopetalous plants which includes the genera *Solanum, Capsicum, Atropa, Hyoscyamus*, etc.

Solander (sŏlæ·ndəɹ). 1788. [f. D. C. *Solander*, the Swedish botanist (1736–1782).] A box made in the form of a book, used for holding botanical specimens, papers, maps, etc.

Solania (sŏlē̆ⁱ·niă). 1830. [f. SOLANUM + -IA[1].] *Chem.* An alkaloid found in the woody nightshade.

Solanicine (sŏlæ·nisin). 1868. [f. as prec. + -IC + -INE[5].] *Chem.* A base produced by the action of hydrochloric acid on solanine. So **Sola·nidine** *Chem.*, a base produced by the action of acids on solanine.

Solanine (sǫ·lănin). Also **solanina, solanin.** 1838. [– Fr. *solanine* (Desfosses, 1821), f. SOLANUM, -INE[5].] *Chem.* A poisonous alkaloidal glucoside found in various plants of the genus *Solanum.*

‖**Solano** (solā·no). 1792. [Sp. :– L. *solanus*, f. *sol* sun.] In Spain, a hot south-easterly wind.

Solanoid (sǫ·lănoid), *a.* 1851. [f. SOLANUM + -OID.] *Path.* Resembling a raw potato: applied to a form of cancer.

‖**Solanum** (sŏlē̆ⁱ·nŏ̆m). 1578. [L. *solanum* nightshade, f. *sol* sun.] A plant of the nightshade family, or the genus of gamopetalous plants of which this is the type; some amount or preparation of the plant used for medicinal purposes.

attrib. Solanaceæ.—The S. or Potato Order 1861.

Solar (sōᵘ·lăɹ), *a.* and *sb.* 1450. [– L. *solaris*, f. *sol* SOL[1]; see -AR[1].] **A.** *adj.* **1.** Of or pertaining to the sun, its course, light, heat, etc. **b.** Of time: Determined by the course of the sun; fixed by observation of the sun 1594. **c.** Indicating time in relation to, or by means of, the sun 1728. **d.** Of mechanism, etc.: Operating by means of, or with the aid of, the light or heat of the sun 1740. **2. a.** *Astrol.* Subject to the influence of the sun; having a nature or character determined by the sun 1626. **b.** Sacred to the sun; connected or associated with the worship of the sun 1774. **c.** Representing or symbolizing the sun 1807. **d.** Sprung or descended from the sun 1788. †**3.** *S. earth, metal*, gold. **b.** *S. metal*, a coloured metal. –1800. **4.** Of light, heat, etc.: Proceeding or emanating from the sun 1698. **5.** Resembling that of the sun; comparable to the sun 1754.

1. In climes beyond the s. road GRAY. The spots were..s. phenomena 1878. **b.** The mean interval of time between the sun's passing the meridian one day, and his passing it the next, is called a mean s. day 1816. **d.** The s. microscope is..a magic lantern, the light of the sun being used instead of..a lamp 1831. **2. a.** They haue denominated some Herbs S. and some Lunar BACON. **b.** The assumption of Stonehenge having been a s. temple 1906. **4.** A means of filtering the s. beam 1871. **5.** He was in this respect a s. man: he drew after him his own firmament of planets 1861.

Special collocations: **s. apex,** the point in space, situated in the constellation Lyra, towards which the sun is moving; the apex of the s. way; **s. compass,** (*a*) a magnetic instrument turning under the influence of the sun's rays; (*b*) an instrument used in surveying for easy determination of the meridian; **s. eye-piece,** a device used in observations of the sun to diminish its light and heat; **s. ganglion,** = *s. plexus*; **s. lamp,** (*a*) an argand lamp; (*b*) a grade of electric lamp; **s. myth,** a myth resulting from a personification of the sun and describing its course or attributes as those of some god or hero; **s. oil,** commercial name for the heavier portions of petroleum and shale-oil; **s. phosphorus,** a substance which emits light as the result of exposure to sunlight; **s. plexus,** a complex of nerves situated at the pit of the stomach; the epigastric plexus; **s. print,** a photograph made by sunlight; **s. spot,** a sunspot; **s. system,** the sun together with all the planets and other bodies connected with it; **s. tables,** tables by which the position of the sun may be ascertained.

B. *sb. Photogr.* A solar print 1889.

Solari- (solēᵊ·ri), comb. form of L. *solaris* SOLAR *a.*

Solarism (sōᵘ·lăriz'm). 1885. [f. SOLAR *a.* + -ISM.] The theory of solar myths; excessive use of, or adherence to, this theory. So **So·larist,** one who holds this theory, esp. to an excessive degree.

‖**Solarium** (sŏlēᵊ·riŏ̆m). *Pl.* **solaria.** 1842. [L., f. *sol* sun; see -ARIUM.] **1.** A sun-dial. **2.** A terrace, balcony, or room exposed to the rays of the sun, *spec.* one used for treating illness by means of sun-baths 1891.

Solarization (sōᵘ·lărəizē̆ⁱ·ʃən). 1853. [f. next + -ATION.] *Photogr.* The injurious effect produced by over-exposing a negative to the action of light, resulting in the reversal of the image; a similar effect produced by over-printing sensitized paper, etc.

Solarize (sōᵘ·lărəiz), *v.* 1855. [f. SOLAR *a.* + -IZE.] **1.** *trans.* To affect or modify by the influence of the sun or the action of its rays; *spec.* in *Photogr.*, to injure by over-exposure to light. **2.** *intr.* To be affected by solarization. 1868.

†**So·lary,** *a.* 1588. [– med.L. *solarius* (XIII), f. L. *sol* SOL[1]; see -ARY[2].] **1.** Of or belonging to, pertaining to, or connected with, the sun –1716. **b.** Of time: = SOLAR *a.* 1 b. –1697. **2.** *Alch.* and *Astrol.* Of the nature of the sun; subject to the influence of the sun –1671.

‖**Solatium** (sŏlē̆ⁱ·ʃiŏ̆m). 1817. [L.; see SOLACE *sb.*] **1.** A sum of money, or other compensation, given to a person to make up for loss or inconvenience. **2.** *spec.* in *Law.* A sum of money paid, over and above the actual damages, as a solace for injured feelings 1832.

‖**Solazzi** (sola·tsi). 1861. [Italian maker's name.] *S. juice*, a kind of liquorice.

†**Sold,** *sb.* [ME. *soude* – OFr. *sou(l)de* :– L. *solidus* (sc. *nummus* coin), orig. a gold coin. See SOL *sb.*[3], SOU.] Pay (esp. of soldiers); wages, salary –1630. Hence †**Sold** *v. trans.*

to pay; to enlist or retain for service by payment.

Sold (sǭᵘld), *ppl. a.* 1535. [pa. pple. of SELL *v.*] **1.** Disposed of by sale. **2.** Denoting a sale effected 1862.

2. Those pictures which have 's.' tickets 1862.

‖**Soldado** (soldā·do). 1586. [Sp. (and Pg.) = It. *soldato*, f. *soldo* military pay; see SOLD *sb.* and -ADO.] **1.** A soldier. **2.** The S. American heron 1852. **3.** The squirrel-fish (*Holocentrus ascensionis*) of the West Indies, etc. 1902.

Soldan (sǫ·ldăn). Now *arch.* or *Hist.* [ME. *soudan, soldan* – OFr. *soudan, soldan* (med.L. *soldanus*); see SULTAN.] **1.** The supreme ruler of one or other of the great Moslem powers or countries of the Middle Ages; *spec.* the Sultan of Egypt.

The *S.* is sometimes contrasted with the (*Great*) *Turk* and with the *Sophy* of Persia.

2. With *a* and *pl.* A Moslem ruler; one having the rank of sultan ME.

1. Where Champions bold..at the Soldans Chair Defi'd the best of Panim chivalry To mortal combat MILT.

‖**Soldanella** (sǫldăne·lă). 1579. [mod.L. – It. *soldanella* of obscure origin.] *Bot.* †**1.** A species of convolvulus or bindweed, *Convolvulus soldanella* –1712. **2.** A primulaceous plant of the genus *Soldanella*, native in Alpine districts 1629.

Solder (sǫ·ldəɹ, sǭᵘ·dəɹ, sǫ·dəɹ), *sb.* ME. [Early forms *sawdere* (cf. SAWDER), *soudur*, etc. – (O)Fr. *soudure*, f. *souder*, †*solder* :– L. *solidare* fasten together, f. *solidus* SOLID.] **1.** A fusible metallic alloy used for uniting metal surfaces or parts. †**2.** *transf.* Any binding or uniting substance (*rare*) –1610. **3.** *fig.* A quality, principle, etc., which unites in any way; a bond or means of union 1599. **4.** *Soft s.*: **a.** A common kind of solder, usually made from tin and lead 1594. **b.** = SOFT SAWDER 1848.

Solder (sǫ·ldəɹ, sǭᵘ·dəɹ, sǫ·dəɹ), *v.* late ME. [f. prec.] **1.** *trans.* To unite or fasten by means of a metallic solder. **b.** *transf.* To unite firmly or closely, to cause to adhere strongly, by means of some substance or device 1601. †**2.** *Med.* To cause (wounds) to close up and become whole; to reunite (tissues or bones) –1788. **3.** *fig.* To unite, to cause to adhere, in a close, firm, or intimate manner 1597. **4.** *fig.* To bring or restore to a sound or unimpaired condition; to repair, patch up again 1607. **5.** *absol.* To perform the operation of uniting with solder 1588. **6.** *intr.* To adhere, unite, grow together 1470.

3. Friendship..of equalls is ever best soldered 1646. **6.** The Tripple Crown could never s. with the English, nor it with that 1647. Hence **So·lderer.**

So·ldering, *vbl. sb.* 1466. [f. SOLDER *v.* + -ING¹.] **1.** The action of the vb. **2.** Solder; material used for soldering 1648. **3.** *attrib.*, chiefly in the names of tools or apparatus used for soldering, as *s. iron* 1675.

Soldier (sǭᵘ·ldʒəɹ), *sb.* ME. [– OFr. *soud(i)er, so(l)dier* (med.L. *sol(i)darius*), f. *sou(l)de*; see SOLD *sb.*, -IER 1.] **1.** One who serves in an army for pay; one who takes part in military service or warfare; *spec.* one of the ordinary rank and file of an army; a private. **b.** A man of military skill and experience 1603. **2.** *fig.* (usu. with ref. to spiritual service or warfare) ME. **b.** *To come the old s. over*, to impose upon 1824. **3.** *transf.* Used as a name for various animals. **4.** A disease of swine characterized by red patches on the skin 1882.

1. As he is a Gentleman and a Soldiour SHAKS. *Common s.*: see COMMON *a.* II. 3. *Private s.*: see PRIVATE *a.* 1 b. *Foot-soldier*, a s. in an infantry regiment. *S. of Fortune*: see FORTUNE *sb.* 1. **b.** So great a s. taught us there, What long-enduring hearts could do TENNYSON. **2.** To make them Soldiers of Christ 1737. **3. a.** The soldier-crab or hermit-crab 1666. **b.** A fighting ant or termite; also *Austral.*, a species of large red ant 1781. **c.** The red gurnard 1846. **d.** *slang.* A red herring 1811. **e.** A red spider; a small red beetle; a lady-bird 1848.

attrib. and *Comb.*: **s.-fish** *U.S.*, *Pœcilechthys cæruleus*, called also Blue Darter, Rainbow Darter; **-fly** *U.S.*, a name given to flies of the family *Stratiomydæ*; **-moth,** *Euschema militaris*; **-orchis,** an orchis (*Orchis militaris*), having a fancied resemblance to a s. Hence **So·ldieress,** a female s. **So·ldierize** *v. intr.* to serve as a s.; *trans.* to make into a s. **So·ldiership,** the state or condition of being a s.; the qualities of a s.; military experience or skill.

Soldier (sǭᵘ·ldʒəɹ), *v.* 1647. [f. the sb.] *intr.* To act or serve as a soldier. Also with *it*. **b.** To feign illness, to malinger; to make a mere show of working; to shirk (*slang*) 1840. **c.** *Mil. slang.* To furbish up accoutrements, etc. 1885.

b. Finding fault with some fellow for 'sogering', as it is called 1890.

So·ldier-crab. 1668. [Cf. SOLDIER *sb.* 3.] The hermit-crab.

Soldiering (sǭᵘ·ldʒəriŋ), *vbl. sb.* 1643. [f. SOLDIER *v.* + -ING¹.] **1.** The action of serving as a soldier; the state of being a soldier; military service. **2.** Malingering, shirking 1894.

So·ldierlike, *a.* and *adv.* 1542. [f. SOLDIER *sb.* + -LIKE.] **A.** *adj.* **1.** Having the character or bearing of a soldier. **2.** Appropriate to, worthy of, becoming or befitting, a soldier 1553.

1. You are also to be vastly careful..to make them appear always neat and clean, and soldier-like WASHINGTON.

B. *adv.* In a manner befitting a soldier 1571.

Soldierly (sǭᵘ·ldʒəɹli), *a.* and *adv.* 1577. [f. SOLDIER *sb.* + -LY.] **A.** *adj.* **1.** Becoming or appropriate to a soldier or soldiers. **2.** Having the qualities of a soldier 1610.

1. They had fought rather with beastlie furie, then with any souldierly discipline SIDNEY.

B. *adv.* = SOLDIERLIKE *adv.* 1585.

Soldiery (sǭᵘ·ldʒəri). 1570. [f. SOLDIER *sb.* + -Y³; see -ERY.] **1.** Soldiers collectively; the military; a military class or body. **2.** Military training; knowledge or science of military matters 1579.

1. The Souldiery..all flockt unto him 1635.

‖**Soldo** (sǫ·ldo). *Pl.* **soldi.** 1599. [It. :– L. *solidus*; see SOLD *sb.*] An Italian coin and money of account, the twentieth part of a lira, now equal in value to an English half-penny.

Sole (sǭᵘl), *sb.*¹ [Late OE. *solu or *sole (in miswritten pl. *solen*), corresp. to OS., OHG. *sola* (Du. *zool*, G. *sohle*) – pop. L. *sola, for L. *solea* sandal, sill (see also next), f. *solum* bottom, pavement, sole of the foot.] **I. 1.** The under surface of the foot; †the mark made by this upon the ground. **b.** *Farriery.* The concave plate of horn which surrounds the frog 1610. **2.** The bottom of a boot, shoe, etc.; that part of it upon which the wearer treads (freq. exclusive of the heel); one or other of the pieces of leather, etc., of which this is composed. (See also *stocking-sole.*) Also, a properly shaped piece of felt, etc. placed in the bottom of a boot, shoe, etc. 1440. **b.** With punning allusion to SOUL *sb.* 1603.

1. We've but naked soles to run with 1871. **2.** *Haml.* II. ii. 234. **b.** Not on thy s., but on thy soul, harsh Jew, Thou mak'st thy knife keen SHAKS.

II. 1. †**a.** The foundation of a building; the site of a city, etc. (*rare*) –1634. **b.** The bottom, floor, or hearth of an oven or furnace 1615. **c.** *Naut.* A protective lining attached to the rudder, bilgeways, etc. to prevent them from being worn away 1850. **2. a.** = SILL *sb.*¹ 1 and 2. Now *rare.* late ME. **b.** *Naut.* and *Fortif.* The bottom of an embrasure 1769. **c.** *Mining.* A horizontal piece of timber set underneath a prop as a support 1839. **d.** A flat tile used as a rest or support for a draining-tile or drain-pipe 1843. **3.** The inner circle of a water-wheel 1673. **4.** The lower part, bottom, or under surface of anything 1615. **b.** *esp.* The under part or surface of a plane-stock, plough, rudder, electrical instrument, etc. 1607. **5. a.** *Mining.* The bottom or floor of a vein, level, or working 1653. **b.** The bottom or lowest part *of* a valley, etc. 1880. Hence **So·leless** *a.* of boots, shoes, etc. having no soles; without soles.

Sole (sǭᵘl), *sb.*² ME. [– (O)Fr. *sole* – Pr. *sola* :– Rom. *sola for L. *solea*, identical with prec., the fish being so named because of its shape.] **1.** A common British and European flat-fish (*Solea vulgaris* or *solea*), highly esteemed as food; one or other of the various fishes of the genus *Solea*. **b.** In collect. sing. 1661. **2.** With distinguishing terms, as *common s.*, *spotted s.*, see also LEMON². 1668. **3.** In American and Australasian use: One or other of various fishes belonging to related genera (esp. *Achirus*) or to the family *Pleuronectidæ* 1882.

Sole (sǭᵘl), *a.* [Late ME. *soul(e* – OFr. *soule* (mod. *seule*) :– L. *sola*, fem. of *solus* alone, sole.] **1.** Having no husband or wife; single, unmarried; †celibate. Chiefly in legal use and freq. of women. Now *rare* or *Obs.* †**b.** Of life: Pertaining to or involving celibacy –1598. **2.** Without companions; alone, solitary. Usually predicative. late ME. **b.** Of places: Solitary, lonely; secluded 1598. **3.** Being, or consisting of, one person only. late ME. †**4.** In predicative or quasi-advb. use: With no other person or persons; without participation, etc., in something –1671. **5.** One and only 1497. **b.** Singular, unique, unrivalled. late ME. †**6.** Of things, qualities, etc.: Standing alone –1622. **7.** Of things, rights, duties, etc.: Pertaining or due to, possessed or exercised by, vested in, etc., one person or corporate body to the exclusion of all others; exclusive 1597. **8.** Uniform or unvaried (*local*) 1845. **9.** quasi-*advb.* Solely 1562.

1. *Woman s.* = *feme-sole* s. v. FEME. If a woman s. shall doe homage COKE. **b.** Some [men] like a s. life, others thinke it no life without a companion 1598. **2.** I am oft times s., but seldom solitary 1650. **3.** *Corporation s.*: see CORPORATION 3. **4.** I, when no other durst, s. undertook The dismal expedition MILT. **5.** I believe my s. crime was candour LYTTON. The s. manager of these estates 1839. **7.** The right of s. succession 1766. *Comb.* **s.-coloured** *a.* of a single uniform colour; self-coloured.

Sole (sǭᵘl), *v.* 1570. [f. SOLE *sb.*¹] **1.** *trans.* To provide (a boot, shoe, stocking, etc.) with a sole. **b.** To fit the head of a golf-club with a sole 1905. **2.** *Golf.* To place the sole of (a club) on the ground in preparing for a stroke. Also *absol.* 1909.

‖**Solea** (sǭᵘ·liă). 1858. [Byzantine Gr. σολέα.] *Eccl.* A raised floor before the entrance of a chancel or chapel.

Solecism (sǫ·lĭsiz'm). 1577. [– Fr. *solécisme* or L. *solœcismus* – Gr. σολοικισμός, f. σόλοικος using incorrect syntax, guilty of grammatical impropriety, said by ancient writers to refer to the corruption of the Attic dialect by Athenian colonists at Σόλοι in Cilicia; see -ISM.] **1.** An impropriety or irregularity in speech or diction; a violation of the rules of grammar or syntax; properly, a faulty concord. **b.** Without article 1583. **2.** A breach or violation of good manners or etiquette; an impropriety *in* manners, etc. 1599. **3.** An error, incongruity, inconsistency, or impropriety of any kind 1599. **b.** Without article (*rare*) 1649.

1. The last part of the Sentence not agreeing nor answering to the first; which is the proper definition of a Solœcism 1699. **b.** A wary man he is in grammar, very nice as to s. or barbarism DRYDEN. **2.** In those days smoking in the streets was an unpardonable s. 1884. **3.** Where a fat jovial Franciscan would be a s. 1850. So **So·lecist** (*rare*), one who uses solecisms. **Soleci·stic** *a.* of the nature of or involving solecism. **Soleci·stical** *a.*, **-ly** *adv.*

Solecize (sǫ·lĭsəiz), *v.* Now *rare* or *Obs.* 1627. [– Gr. σολοικίζειν, f. σόλοικος; see SOLECISM.] *intr.* To make use of, or commit, solecisms in language, behaviour, conduct, etc.

Soled (sǭᵘld), *ppl. a.* 1480. [SOLE *sb.*¹, *v.* + -ED.] Having a sole or soles (of a specified kind).

So·le-lea:ther. late ME. [f. SOLE *sb.*¹ 2 + LEATHER *sb.*] Leather of a thick or strong kind used or suitable for the soles of boots, shoes, etc.

Solely (sǭᵘ·l,li), *adv.* 1495. [f. SOLE *a.* + -LY².] **1.** As a single person (or thing); without any other as an associate, partner, etc.; alone; occas. without aid or assistance. **2.** Only, merely, exclusively; also (contextually), entirely, altogether 1588.

1. Who meanes to sit solie on Olympus, must suffer no climers LODGE. **2.** Hote furious spirits.. who delight soly in fights and vproares 1628.

Solemn (sǫ·ləm), *a.* [ME. *solem(p)ne* – OFr. *solem(p)ne* – L. *sollemnis*, *-ennis*, *-empnis* celebrated ceremonially and at a fixed date, festive, customary, f. *sollus* whole, entire; the terminal element is unexpl.] **1.** Associated or connected with religious rites or observances; performed with due ceremony and reverence; having a religious character; sacred; *spec.* of church rites performed with full ceremonial. **2.** Of days or seasons: Marked by the celebration of special observances or rites (esp. of a religious character); distinguished by, or set apart for, special ceremonies ME. **3.** Performed with, accompanied by, due formality or ceremony; of a formal or ceremonious character. late ME. †**b.** Formal; regular, uniform –1704. †**c.** Customary; carefully observed. B. JONS. †**4. a.** Grand; imposing; sumptuous –1589. †**b.** Of great dignity or importance –1596. **5.** Of a formal and serious or deliberate character ME. **6.** Of a grave or earnest character 1449. **7.** Impressive, awe-inspiring. late ME. †**b.** Gloomy, dark, sombre –1625.

1. [They] with cursed things His holy Rites, and s. Feasts profan'd MILT. **2.** Þat feyris nor markets had no place in þe kirk in solempne tymis 1400. **3.** Being the King's birth day, there was a solemne ball at Court EVELYN. **4. a.** In solempne robes they glad shall goe 1586. **b.** There was..A limitour, a ful solempne man CHAUCER. **5.** Makyng a grete & a solempne oath CAXTON. *S. League and Covenant*: see COVENANT *sb.* 8. **6.** The sad and solemne Priests SHAKS. What Virgins these.. That bend to earth their s. brow GRAY. **7.** In solem silency this vapour rose From this drad Dale 1642. **b.** Customary suites of solemne Blacke SHAKS. Hence **So·lemn-ly** *adv.*, **-ness**; also (more usu.) **So·lemness.**

Solemnity (sǫle·mnĭti). [ME. *solempnete, -ite* – OFr. *solem(p)nité* (mod. *solennité*) – L. *sollem(p)nitas*; see prec., -ITY.] **1.** Observance of ceremony or special formality on important occasions. **2.** An occasion of ceremony; an observance of special importance; a festival or other similar occasion ME. **3.** *Law.* Necessary formality, such as is requisite to make an act or document valid 1588. **4.** The state or character of being solemn or serious; impressiveness; gravity; a solemn utterance or statement 1712.

1. If a female child be borne, there is small solemnitie PURCHAS. Phr. *With* or *in* (*great*, etc.) *s.* (now *rare*); Wee'll hold a feast in great solemnitie SHAKS. **2.** Among other solemnities, they roasted an Oxe in the middest of the field for the people 1617. **3.** Not being sealled be the seall of the partie, quilk was ane essentiall solemnitie of contracts 1665. **4.** That S. of Phrase, which may be drawn from the Sacred Writings ADDISON.

Solemnization (sǫ:lәmnәizēⁱ·ʃәn). 1447. [– OFr. *solem(p)nisation*, *-ization*, or med.L. *solempnizatio, -on-*; see next, -ION.] The action of solemnizing or celebrating in a ceremonial manner. **b.** *spec.* The celebration or performance *of* a marriage 1497.

Solemnize (sǫ·lәmnәiz), *v.* Also **solemnise.** late ME. [– OFr. *solem(p)niser* – med.L. *solem(p)nizare*, f. L. *solem(p)nis*; see SOLEMN, -IZE.] **1.** *trans.* To dignify or honour by ceremonies; to celebrate with special formality. **2.** To celebrate (a marriage) with proper ceremonies and in due form; also, to perform the ceremony of (marriage). late ME. **3.** To hold, observe, perform, †proclaim, etc., with some amount of ceremony or formality 1483. †**4.** To laud or glorify –1687. **5.** To make solemn; to render serious or grave 1726.

1. These two enraged Princes solemniz'd their mutuall fury by the death of so many thousands 1652. **2.** The mariage whiche was solempnised betwene his maiestie, and..the lady Catherine 1533. **3.** The..peasantry were compelled to s. the obsequies of every Bacchiad 1835. **4.** My hart is bent..God's name to s. 1586. **5.** Holy horrors s. the shade POPE.

Solen (sōᵘ·lĕn). 1661. [– L. *solen* – Gr. σωλήν channel, pipe, syringe, shell-fish.] **1.** *Zool.* The razor-fish, *Solen ensis* or *siliqua*. **2.** *Surg.* A framework to prevent the bedclothes from touching an injured limb 1693. Hence (from sense 1) **Solena·cean** *sb.* and *a.* **Solena·ceous** *a.*

Soleness (sōᵘ·lnės). Now *rare.* 1449. [f. SOLE *a.* + -NESS.] †**1.** Solitude; solitariness –1618. **2.** The state or condition of being sole, alone, or apart 1587.

Solenette (sōᵘlne·t, sǫlĕne·t). 1839. [irreg. f. SOLE *sb.*² + -(*n*)ETTE.] The little sole, *Monochirus linguatulus* or *Solea minuta*.

So·lenite. 1828. [– Fr. *solénite*; see SOLEN, -ITE¹ 2 a.] A fossil razor-fish or solen.

Soleno- (solī·no), comb. form of Gr. σωλήν channel, pipe, etc., as **Sole·nocyte,** one of the cells found in the nephridia of certain polychætan worms; **Sole·nodon(t,** one or other of certain insectivorous mammalian rodents native to the West Indies and America, as the agouta or the almiqui; **Solenosto·matous** *a.*, of, belonging to, or resembling the genus *Solenostomus* of lophobranchiate fishes.

Solenoid (solī·noid, sōᵘ·lĕnoid). 1832. [– Fr. *solénoïde*, f. Gr. σωλήν; see SOLEN, -OID.] **1.** *Electr.* An electro-dynamical spiral, formed of a wire with the ends returned parallel to the axis; a series of elementary circuits arranged on this principle. **2.** *Med.* A cage to enclose a patient during medical treatment 1901.

‖**Solera** (solē·ra). 1851. [Sp.] **1.** A blend of sherry wine. **2.** A wine-cask, usu. containing a double butt 1863.

‖**Soleus** (solī·ŏs, sōᵘ·lĭ,ŏs). 1676. [mod.L., f. L. *solea* SOLE *sb.*¹] *Anat.* A muscle of the calf of the leg, situated between the gastrocnemius and the bone.

Sol-fa (sǫlfā·, sǫ·lfā·), *sb.* 1548. [From the syllables *sol* (SOL *sb.*²) and *fa* (FA) of the scale; see UT.] *Mus.* The set of syllables 'do (or ut), re, mi, fa, sol, la, si', sung to the respective notes of the major scale; the system of singing notes to these syllables; a musical scale or exercise thus sung. †Occas. in the phr. *to sing s. Tonic s.*: see TONIC *a.*

Sol-fa (sǫlfā·, sǫ·lfā·), *v.* 1568. [See prec.] **1.** *trans.* To sing (a tune, air, etc.) to the sol-fa syllables. **2.** *intr.* To sing in this manner; to use the sol-fa syllables in singing 1584.

1. You shall not find a musicion..able to *sol fa* it right 1597. So **Solfaing** *vbl. sb.* 1549.

‖**Solfatara** (sǫlfătā·ră). 1777. [Name of a sulphurous volcano near Naples, f. It. *solfo* sulphur.] A volcanic vent, from which only sulphurous exhalations and aqueous vapours are emitted, incrusting the edge with sulphur and other minerals.

‖**Solfeggio** (sǫlfe·dʒio). *Pl.* **solfeggi** (-ed,dʒi), **solfeggios.** 1774. [It., f. *sol-fa* SOL-FA.] An exercise for the voice, in which the sol-fa syllables are employed; †also *transf.*, an exercise for a musical instrument.

Solferino (sǫlfĕrī·no). 1865. [f. the place-name *Solferino* in Italy, because discovered shortly after the battle fought there in 1859. For the circumstances of origin, cf. MAGENTA, STEENKIRK.] The bright crimson dye-colour rosaniline.

Solicit (sŏli·sit), *v.* 1450. [– (O)Fr. *solliciter* – L. *sollicitare* stir, agitate, etc., (med.L.) look after, f. *sollicitus* agitated, f. *sollus* whole, entire + *citus* put in motion, pa. pple. of *ciēre* (see CITE).] **I.** *trans.* †**1.** To disturb, disquiet, trouble; to make anxious, fill with concern –1788. **2.** To entreat or petition (a person) for, or to do, something; to urge, importune 1530. **3.** To incite or move to some act of lawlessness or insubordination 1565. **4.** To incite, draw on, allure, by some specious representation or argument 1591. **b.** To court or beg the favour of (a woman), *esp.* with immoral intention 1591. **c.** Of women: To accost and importune (men) for immoral purposes 1710. **5.** Of things: **a.** To affect (a person or thing) by some form of physical influence or attraction. Now *rare.* 1601. **b.** To tempt, allure; to attract or draw by enticement, etc. 1663. †**6.** To endeavour to draw out (a dart, etc.) by the use of gentle force –1784. **7.** *Med.* To seek to draw, to induce or bring on, esp. by gentle means 1732.

1. Hath any ill solicited thine ears Befall'n my Myrmidons? CHAPMAN. **2.** The charge of sollliciting the Government for the moneys 1719. **3.** Boadicea..sollicited the Britains..to a Revolt 1683. **3.** Solicite Henry with her wonderous praise. Bethinke thee on her Vertues. SHAKS. **b.** *Much Ado* II. i. 70. **5. a.** Then gently sleep sollicited each eye HOBBES. **b.** That Fruit, which with desire ..Sollicited her longing eye MILT. **6.** But good Agenor gently from the wound The spear sollicits POPE.

II. †**1.** To push forward or prosecute (business, affairs, etc.) –1789. **b.** To conduct (a lawsuit, etc.) as a solicitor; to transact or negotiate in the capacity of a law-agent. 1606. †**2. a.** To urge or plead (one's suit, cause, etc.) –1769. **b.** To urge or press (a matter) –1704. **3.** To request, petition, or sue for (some thing, favour, etc.); to desire or seek by petition 1595. **b.** To seek after 1717. **4.** Of things: To call or ask for, to demand (action, attention, etc.) 1592.

1. b. The attorney-at-law who solicited the suits 1839. **3.** How could he s. her hand? 1797. **b.** I.. Repent old pleasures and s. new POPE. **4.** The formation of a new government solicited his attention 1817.

III. *intr.* **1.** To make request or petition; to beg or entreat 1509. **2.** To act or practise as a solicitor 1596. †**3.** To petition *against*, to make intercession *for*, a person or thing –1741.

1. If you bethinke your selfe of..Grace, Solicite for it straight SHAKS. **2.** We are at a great distance from the King's Court, and have no body there to s. for us SWIFT. Hence **Soli·cit** *sb.* an entreaty or solicitation.

Solicitant (sŏli·sitănt), *sb.* and *a.* 1802. [f. prec. + -ANT.] **A.** *sb.* One who solicits or requests earnestly. **B.** *adj.* That solicits; making petition or request 1886.

Solicitation (sŏlisitēⁱ·ʃәn). 1492. [– Fr. *sollicitation* – L. *sollicitatio, -on-*; see SOLICIT *v.*, -ATION.] †**1.** Management, transaction, or pursuit of business, legal affairs, etc. –1722. **2.** The action of soliciting, or seeking to obtain by earnest request; entreaty, petition, diligent or importunate asking. Also, an instance of this. 1500. **b.** The action of soliciting a person of the other sex 1604. **3.** The exertion or operation of a physically attracting influence or force 1626. **4.** The action of some attractive, enticing, or alluring influence 1676. †**5.** Anxiety; solicitude –1725.

2. At her s. the trustee lent the fund to the husband and it was lost 1883. **b.** *Oth.* IV. ii. 202. **3.** The solicitations of Jupiter's attractive force are..urgent on a swiftly rushing body 1884. **4.** Vicious sollicitations of appetite, if not checked, will grow more importunate JOHNSON.

Solicitor (sŏli·sitәɹ). late ME. [– (O)Fr. *solliciteur* †one who takes charge of business, etc., f. *solliciter*; see SOLICIT, -OR 2. Cf. late L. *sollicitator*.] †**1.** One who urges, prompts, or instigates –1722. †**b.** A thing serving to instigate, etc. –1751. †**2.** One who conducts, negotiates, or transacts matters on behalf of another or others; a representative, agent, or deputy –1741. **3.** One properly qualified and formally admitted to practise as a law-agent in any court; formerly, one practising in a court of equity, as dist. from an *attorney* 1577. **b. Solicitor-General,** a law-officer (in England ranking next to the Attorney-General, in Scotland to the Lord-Advocate), who takes the part of the state or crown in suits affecting the public interest 1533. **4.** One who entreats, requests, or petitions; one who solicits or begs favours; a pleader, intercessor, advocate 1551. **b.** *transf.* of things 1579. †**5.** One who, or that which, draws on or entices –1655. **6.** *U.S.* One who solicits business, contributions, or help of any kind 1903.

So †**Soli·citer** (in senses 3, 4). Hence **Soli·citorship.** †**Soli·citress,** †**Soli·citrix,** a female solicitor.

Solicitous (sŏli·sitәs), *a.* 1563. [f. L. *sollicitus* (see SOLICIT) + -OUS.] †**1.** Anxious, apprehensive –1741. **2.** Troubled, anxious, or deeply concerned, on some specified account 1570. **3.** Extremely or particularly careful or attentive 1609. **4.** Anxious, eager, desirous 1628. **5.** Marked or characterized by anxiety, care, or concern 1563. **6.** Of features: Suggestive of solicitude or anxiety 1868.

2. Much s. how best He may compensate for a day of sloth COWPER. Sollicitous chiefly for the peace of my own country BURKE. **4.** The Prince.. was..most impatiently sollicitous to bring it to pass CLARENDON. **5.** An attentive, s., perhaps painful exercise of their understanding about it BUTLER. Hence **Soli·citous-ly** *adv.*, **-ness.**

Solicitude (sŏli·sitiūd). late ME. [– (O)Fr. *sollicitude* – L. *sollicitudo*, f. as prec.; see -TUDE.] **1.** The state of being solicitous or uneasy in mind; disquietude, anxiety; care, concern. **2.** Anxious, special, or particular care or attention 1535. **3.** *pl.* Cares, troubles, anxieties 1490.

1. Free from s., because free from wants 1833. **2.** Never had such s. been lavished on human being

DISRAELI. **3.** Wearied with perpetual sollicitudes and labours 1750.

Solicitudinous (sǒlisitiū·dinəs), *a.* 1682. [f. L. *sollicitudo, -in-* (see prec.) + -OUS.] †**1.** Filled with anxiety, care, or concern. SIR T. BROWNE. **2.** Characterized by solicitude or anxiety 1829.

Solid (sǫ·lid), *sb.* 1495. [After Fr. *solide*, L. *solidum*, subst. use of n. adj. (see next).] **1.** *Geom.* A body or magnitude of three dimensions; one having length, breadth, and thickness. **2.** A solid substance or body 1698. **b.** *Physiol.* A solid part or constituent of the body. Used in pl. Now *Obs.* or *rare.* 1704. **c.** *Building.* A solid mass of masonry or other construction, esp. that between windows or doors; a pier of a bridge 1736. **3.** *The s.*, the unbroken mass, the main part or body, of something 1776.

1. *S. of revolution*, one formed by the revolution of a plane figure. **3.** Actuated by cams turned from the s. 1908.

Solid (sǫ·lid), *a.* late ME. [– (O)Fr. *solide* or L. *solidus*, rel. to *salvus* SAFE, *sollus* whole (see SOLICIT).] **I. 1.** Free from empty spaces, cavities, interstices, etc.; having the interior completely filled in or up. Opp. to *hollow.* **b.** *spec.* in *Bot.* Fleshy and uniform; not hollow or furnished with internal cavities of any kind 1753. **c.** *Typog.* Having no leads between the lines; unleaded 1808. **d.** Of a wall, etc.: Having no opening or window; unbroken, blank 1865. **2.** *Math.* Of a body or figure: Having three dimensions. late ME. †**b.** Of number or measure: = CUBIC *a.* –1705. **c.** Of, relating or pertaining to, a geometrical solid or solids (†or to cubic numbers) 1570. **3.** Of material substances: Of a dense or massive consistency; composed of particles which are firmly and continuously coherent; hard and compact 1532. **b.** Solidified; frozen 1697. **c.** Of clouds, the atmosphere, etc.: Having the appearance of a solid or unbroken mass; dense, thick, compact. Chiefly *poet.* 1807. **4.** Of states, conditions, etc.: Characterized by solidity or compactness 1597. **5.** Of rain, etc.: Steady, drenching; continuous. Also, of a day: Characterized by rain of this kind. 1621. **6.** Having the property of occupying a certain amount of space (cf. SOLIDITY 4) 1690.

1. This was hollow, the other s. PURCHAS. **2.** *S. Angle*, the angle made by the meeting of three or more planes which join in a point. **b.** There are in a s. Foot 1728 s. Inches 1705. **3.** Oh that this too too s. Flesh would melt, Thaw, and resolue it selfe into a Dew SHAKS. *transf.* Asses..in Judgement sit In s. Deafness, on the Works of Wit 1746. **b.** O'er s. seas, where Winter reigns 1786. **c.** Yonder gap in the s. gray Of the eastern cloud BROWNING. **5.** A sad and sollid shewer without intermission 1621. **6.** Even a particle of water is s. 1794.

II. 1. Of a strong, firm, or substantial nature or quality; not slight or flimsy 1586. **2. a.** Combined; consolidated; united (*rare*) 1596. **b.** Unanimous, undivided. Orig. *U.S.* 1884. **c.** Of persons: Regular or steady in attendance, politics, voting, etc. Chiefly *U.S.* 1883. **3.** Of a day, hour, etc.: Whole, entire, complete. Now *colloq.* 1718. **4.** Entirely of the same substance or material (as that specified); of (gold, etc.) and nothing else 1710. **5.** Of persons, their constitution, etc.: Strong, healthy, sturdy 1741.

1. A Bottle or two of good s. Edifying Port STEELE. Faith is gone, having no s. support 1770. The s. cities of the Greeks and Romans 1870. **2. b.** The vote of the s. South 1884. **c.** I'm s. for Mr. Peck every time 1888. **3.** I walked him up and down,..for a s. hour 1890. **4.** The..statues.. were of s. gold 1844. **5.** He walks there, with s. step CARLYLE.

III. 1. Of persons: **a.** Of sound scholarship or sober judgement in matters of learning or speculation 1600. **b.** Sober-minded, of reliable judgement, in practical matters; steady, sedate, staid 1632. **2.** Of qualities: Well founded or established; of real value or importance; substantial 1601. **3.** Of arguments, reasons, writings, etc.: Having a sound or substantial foundation; based upon sound principles or indisputable facts 1615. **4.** Marked by, or involving, serious study or intention; not light, frivolous, or merely amusing 1647. **5.** Of judgement, etc.: Of a sober, sound, or practical character 1662. **6.** Characterized by a high degree of religious fervour or seriousness –1769. **7.** Thorough, downright, vigorous, etc. Used with intensive force and freq. strengthened by *good, right*, etc. 1830.

1. A s. and well-read man 1709. **b.** The s., and sad man, is not troubled with the floods and ebbes of Fortune 1632. **2.** Having a very s. Respect for humane Nature STEELE. A man of s. learning 1882. **3.** If there were no s. defence to the claim the plaintiff would..obtain his order 1894. **4.** Romances debauch the taste for s. reading 1845. **5.** He who is..cold in affection may have solider judgement, and steadier resolution 1805. **7.** Swear your innocency with a good s. oath STEVENSON.

IV. Quasi-*adv.* In a body or as a whole; unanimously. In phrases with ref. to voting, esp. *to go s.* (*for* or *against* some thing or person). 1884.

The fleet seems to have gone..s. against him 1891. Hence **So·lid-ly** *adv.*, **-ness.**

Solidago (sǫlidē·go). 1771. [– med.L. *solidago*, alt. of late L. *consolida* CONSOUND.] **a.** A large composite genus of perennial plants; golden-rod. **b.** A plant of this genus, esp. *S. virgaurea*, a European and British species, formerly in repute for its medicinal properties.

Solidarity (sǫlidæ·rǐti). 1848. [– Fr. *solidarité*, f. *solidaire* solid; see SOLIDARY *a.*] **1.** The fact or quality, on the part of communities, etc., of being perfectly united or at one in some respect, esp. in interests, sympathies, or aspirations. **2.** Community or perfect coincidence *of* (or *between*) interests 1874. **3.** *Civil Law.* A form of obligation involving joint and several responsibilities or rights 1875.

1. They have s., or responsibleness, and trust in each other EMERSON. Each is responsible to the Czar, but they have no sort of s. 1877.

Solidary (sǫ·lidări), *a.* 1818. [– Fr. *solidaire*; see SOLID *a.*, -ARY¹.] **1.** *Civil Law.* Joint and several. **2.** Characterized by or having solidarity or community of interests 1848.

2. Regarding as s., or indissolubly connected together, all the members of the great human family 1848.

Solidate (sǫ·lideⁱt), *sb. Hist.* 1610. [– med.L. *solidatus, -ata* shilling's worth (e.g. in *solidatus terræ*), f. SOLIDUS; see -ATE¹.] A piece of land of the annual value of a solidus or shilling.

So·lidate, *v.* Now *rare.* 1640. [– *solidat-*, pa. ppl. stem of L. *solidare* make solid, f. *solidus* SOLID *a.*; see -ATE³.] **1.** *trans.* To make solid or firm; to consolidate. †**2.** = CONSOLIDATE *v.* 4. –1684.

Solid-hoofed, -hooved, *a.* 1842. [f. SOLID *a.*] Having the hoof whole or undivided; solidungulate, soliped; *spec.* as the designation of certain swine.

Solidify (sǒli·difəi), *v.* 1799. [– Fr. *solidifier*, f. *solide*; see SOLID *a.*, -FY.] **1.** *trans.* To render solid; to make firm, hard, or compact. **2.** *intr.* To become solid; to change from a liquid or gaseous to a solid state 1837.

1. We cannot as yet s. alcohol 1871. *transf.* Disraeli..sought to s. them into a party 1885. Hence **Soli·difi:able** *a.* capable of solidification. **Soli:difica·tion,** the action or process of solidifying; consolidation, concentration. **Soli·difier.**

Solidism (sǫ·lidiz'm). 1832. [f. SOLID *sb.* + -ISM.] *Med.* The doctrine or theory which refers all diseases to the state of, or to morbid changes in, the solid parts of the body. So **So·lidist,** one who believes in s.

Solidity (sǒli·dǐti). 1532. [– L. *soliditas*, f. *solidus* SOLID *a.*; see -ITY. Cf. Fr. *solidité.*] **1.** The quality of being solid or substantial, in various fig. or transf. senses. **2.** The quality or condition of being materially solid; compactness and firmness of texture, structure, etc. 1603. **3. a.** *Geom.* The amount of space occupied by a solid body; volume, cubic or solid content 1570. **b.** Relative density or mass 1698. **4. a.** The property of occupying a certain amount of space 1690. **b.** Extension in the three dimensions of space 1855. **5.** A solid thing or body 1602. **6.** = SOLIDARITY 3. 1706.

1. Establishing their assertions with great s. SIR T. BROWNE. Assure me of the s. of your recovery 1788. The Persians are unthinking, perpetually joking, and deficient in s. 1821. **2.** They have the s. of the hardest bone GOLDSM. The château.. strikes the spectator by its s. and magnificence 1833. **4. a.** The s. of matter..expresses that property which every body possesses of not permitting any other body to occupy the same place with it at the same time 1815. **5.** Heauens face doth glow, Yea this s. and compound masse.. Is thought-sicke SHAKS.

Solidungulate (sǫlidʊ·ŋgiŭlět), *a.* and *sb.* 1839. [f. L. *solidus* SOLID *a.* + *ungulatus* UNGULATE.] = SOLIPED *sb.* and *a.* So **Solid-u·ngular** *a. rare.* **Solidu·ngulous** *a.* 1650.

||**Solidus** (sǫ·lidʊs). *Pl.* **solidi** (sǫ·lidəi). late ME. [L. *solidus* (sc. *nummus*) SOLID *a.*, used subst.] **1. a.** A gold coin of the Roman empire, orig. worth about 25 denarii. †**b.** A shilling. **2.** A sloping line used to separate shillings from pence, as 12/6; a shilling-mark; used also in writing fractions and for other separations of figures and letters 1891.

Solifidian (sōᵘlifi·diăn), *sb.* and *a.* 1596. [– mod.L. *solifidius*, f. *soli-*, comb. form of L. *solus* SOLE *a.* + *fides* FAITH; see -IAN.] **A.** *sb.* One who holds that faith alone, without works, is sufficient for justification.

The doctrine is based on *Rom.* 3:28, where Luther rendered πίστει by 'allein durch den Glauben' (only by faith).

B. *adj.* **1.** Consisting of, pertaining to, the doctrine of justification by faith alone 1605. **2.** Of persons, etc.: Accepting or maintaining this doctrine 1628. Hence **Solifi·dianism,** the doctrine or tenet of justification by faith alone.

Soliform (sōᵘ·lifǫɹm), *a.* 1678. [f. L. *sol* or SOL¹ + -FORM.] Resembling the sun; sun-like. Also *absol.*

Eye never yet beheld the sun, that was not s. 1806.

||**Soliloquium** (sǫlilōᵘ·kwiŏm). Now *rare.* 1597. [late L.; see SOLILOQUY.] = SOLILOQUY.

Soliloquize (sǒli·lǒkwəiz), *v.* 1759. [f. SOLILOQUY + -IZE.] **1.** *intr.* To engage in soliloquy; to talk to oneself. **2.** *trans.* To utter, address or apostrophize in, soliloquy 1805. Hence **Soli·loquizer.**

Soliloquy (sǒli·lǒkwi). 1604. [– late L. *soliloquium* (Augustine), f. L. *solus, soli-* SOLE *a.* + *loqui* speak.] **1.** An instance of talking to or conversing with oneself, or of uttering one's thoughts aloud without addressing any person. **b.** A literary production representing or imitating a discourse of this nature 1641. **2.** Without article: The act of talking to oneself; soliloquizing 1668.

1. b. The soliloquies of Hamlet..must have been lost upon the groundlings 1873. **2.** He confounds s. and colloquy 1839. So **So·liloque** (*rare*).

Soliped (sǫ·liped), **-pede** (-pīd), *sb.* and *a.* 1646. [– Fr. *solipède* or mod.L. *solipes, -ped-*, for L. *solidipes*, f. *solidus* SOLID *a.* + *pes, -ped-* foot.] **A.** *sb.* An animal having a whole or uncloven hoof. **B.** *adj.* Having a whole hoof; solid-hoofed 1656. So **Soli·pedal, Soli·pedous** *adjs.*

Solipsism (sǫ·lipsiz'm). 1881. [f. L. *solus* SOLE *a.* + *ipse* self + -ISM.] *Metaph.* The view or theory that self is the only object of real knowledge or the only thing really existent. So **So·lipsist,** one who accepts this theory.

Solitaire (sǫ·litēᵊɹ, sǫlitēᵊ·ɹ). 1716. [– (O)Fr. *solitaire* – L. *solitarius*; see SOLITARY *a.*] **1.** A person who lives in seclusion; a recluse. **2.** A precious stone, usually a diamond, set by itself. Also *ellipt.*, a solitaire ring. 1727. **3.** A game which can be played by one person: **a.** One of various card-games. **b.** A game played on a board with marbles or pegs, which have to be removed by jumping as in draughts. 1746. **4.** A loose neck-tie of black silk or broad ribbon worn by men in the 18th c. 1731. **5.** *Ornith.* **a.** A large flightless bird (*Pezophaps solitarius*) formerly existing in the island of Rodriguez 1797. **b.** A Jamaican bird (*Myiodectes solitarius*) 1847. **6.** *attrib.* Intended for one person only 1885.

2. I saw the evening star hanging like a s. from the..western firmament 1886. **4.** He ties a vast s. around his neck 1882. **6.** A variety of..s. breakfast sets 1885.

Solitary (sǫ·litări), *sb.* late ME. [subst. use of next.] **1. a.** One who retires into, or lives in, solitude from religious motives; a hermit or recluse. **b.** One who lives by himself in seclusion or retirement; one who avoids, or is deprived of, the society of others 1763. †2. = SOLITAIRE *sb.* 3. –1806.

1. b. Hardy pioneers, solitaries who had lived on far-off creeks 1898.

Solitary (sǫ·litări), *a.* ME. [– L. *solitarius*, f. *solus* SOLE *a.*; see -ARY¹.] **1.** Quite alone or unaccompanied; destitute or deprived of the society of others. **b.** Keeping apart from society; living alone. late ME. **c.** Standing alone or by itself; not accompanied or paralleled in any way 1633. **d.** With *a*, *one*, etc.: Single, sole 1742. **2.** Of places: Marked by solitude; remote, unfrequented, secluded, lonely. late ME. **3.** Characterized by the absence of all companionship or society. late ME. **4.** *Zool.* In names of various insects, birds, etc., which live alone or in pairs only 1600. **5.** *Bot.* Of parts or of plants: Growing singly or separately; not forming clusters or masses 1796.

1. I am made as sparow s. in þe hous HAMPOLE. He travels on, a s. Man: His age has no companion WORDSW. **b.** Those rare and solitarie, these in flocks Pasturing at once MILT. **d.** Poor moralist! and what art thou? A s. fly. GRAY. **2.** He sodaynly turned into a s. wood next adioyning 1548. **3.** Satan..toward the Gates of Hell Explores his s. flight MILT. **4.** S. Sandpiper, *Tringa solitaria* 1813. *Scolopax major*. S. Snipe 1843. **5.** Bearing.. flowers in a peculiar spike, which is either s. or double 1807. Hence **So·litari-ly** *adv.*, **-ness.**

Solitude (sǫ·litiūd). late ME. [– (O)Fr. *solitude* or L. *solitudo*, f. *solus* SOLE *a.*; see -TUDE.] **1.** The state of being or living alone; loneliness, seclusion, solitariness (of persons). †**b.** The fact of being sole or unique –1646. **2.** Loneliness (of places); remoteness from habitations; absence of life or stir 1585. **3.** A lonely, unfrequented, or uninhabited place 1570. **4.** A complete absence or lack (*rare*) 1605.

1. For sollitude best fits my cheereles mood KYD. **b.** Nor will the s. of the Phœnix allow this denomination, for many there are of that species SIR T. BROWNE. **2.** The s. of the infinite sea 1873. **3.** That busy scene was converted into a silent s. GIBBON. **4.** Thomas Coventry.., who made a s. of children wherever he came LAMB. So **Solitudina·rian**, a recluse.

Solivagant (soli·văgănt), *a.* and *sb.* 1621. [f. L. *solivagus*, f. *solus* SOLE *a.* + *vagari* wander; see -ANT.] **A.** *adj.* Wandering about alone; characterized by going alone 1641. **B.** *sb.* One who wanders about alone 1621. So **Soli·vagous** *a.* (*rare*).

Sollar (sǫ·lăɹ), *sb.* Also **solar.** ME. [– AFr. *soler*, OFr. *solier* :– L. *solarium* sundial, gallery, terrace, f. *sol* SOL¹; not continuous with OE. *solor*, f. WGmc. adoption of the L. word; see -AR².] **1.** An upper room or apartment in a house or other dwelling; in later use, a loft, attic, or garret (orig. one open to the sun). Now *arch.* or *dial.* **b.** An elevated chamber or loft in a church, in later use *spec.* in a steeple or belfry ME. **2.** *Cornish mining.* **a.** A platform in a mine, *esp.* one supporting a ladder 1778. **b.** A raised floor under which air is admitted to a working 1778. Hence **So·llar** *v. trans.* to furnish with a s.

Solleret (sǫ·ləret). Also **soleret(te.** 1826. [– OFr. *sol(l)eret*, dim. of *sol(l)er* (mod. *soulier*) :– med.L. *subtelaris* (sc. *calceus* shoe), f. late L. *subtel* arch of the sole; see -ET.] *Archæol.* A shoe composed of steel plates or scales, forming part of a knight's armour in the 14th and 15th centuries.

Solmization (sǫlmizēⁱ·ʃən). Also **solmisation.** 1730. [– Fr. *solmisation*, f. *solmiser*, f. *sol* SOL² + *mi* MI; see -IZE, -ATION.] The action or practice of solfaing. So **So·lmizate** *v.* to express by, or employ, s.

Solo (sōᵘ·lo), *sb.* and *a.* *Pl.* **solos** (also, as a musical direction, **soli**). 1695. [– It. *solo* :– L. *solus* SOLE *a.*] **A.** *sb.* **I. 1.** *Mus.* An instance of a song, melody, or other piece of music being rendered or performed by one singer or player; a piece of vocal or instrumental music performed, or intended for performance, by a single person. **2.** Performance by one singer or player 1779. **3.** A dance by one person 1794. **b.** *Aviation.* A solo flight 1920. **II.** *Cards.* Any of various games in which one player plays without a partner against the others; esp. in *s. whist*, in which a player undertakes to make five out of the thirteen tricks; also, the call made by such a player 1878.

Comb. **s. organ**, one of the divisions of a larger organ, for producing solo effects; so **s. stop.**

B. *adj.* **1.** Alone; without a companion or partner 1712. **2.** Made to accommodate one person 1774. **3.** Of musical instruments, or the players of these: Playing or taking the solo part 1880. **4.** *Aviation.* Alone, i.e. without an instructor or a mechanic 1914.

3. [He] was..s. euphonium 1901.

So·lo *v.*, to perform by oneself; to fly or climb solo. **Soloist** (sōᵘ·loˌist), one who performs a solo; one who flies solo.

Solomon (sǫ·lŏmǫn). Also †**Salomon.** 1554. [The name of the Jewish king *Solomon*, – Heb. *šᵉlōmōh*.] One who resembles, or is comparable to, Solomon, esp. in respect of wisdom or justice; a sage; also ironically, a wiseacre.

British, English, or *Scotch S.*, King James VI of Scotland and I of England. Hence **Solomo·nic** *a.* ascribed to, originating with, S.; characteristic of S.

Solomon's seal. 1543. [tr. med.L. *sigillum Solomonis*.] **1.** A plant, *Polygonatum multiflorum*, the stems of which bear on the upper part broad sessile leaves and drooping green and white flowers. **2.** Applied to various other plants, as *Smilacina*, False Solomon's Seal, *Convallaria trifoliata*, Three-leaved Solomon's Seal 1760.

Solon (sōᵘ·lǫn). 1625. [– L. *Solon*, Gr. Σόλων, the early Athenian legislator and one of the seven wise men of Greece.] A sage; a wiseacre. Hence **Solo·nian, Solo·nic** *adjs.*

So long: see LONG *adv.* 1.

‖**Solpuga** (sǫlpiū·gă). 1601. [L., also *solipuga, solifuga*.] **1.** A venomous ant or spider mentioned by classical authors. **2.** *Ent.* A genus of tropical or semi-tropical spiders belonging to the group *Solpugidæ* or *Solifugæ*; a weasel-spider 1815. Hence **Solpugid** (sǫlpiū·dʒid), one of the *Solpugidæ*.

Solstice (sǫ·lstis). ME. [– (O)Fr. *solstice* – L. SOLSTITIUM.] **1.** One or other of the two times in the year, midway between the two equinoxes, when the sun, having reached the tropical points, is farthest from the equator and appears to stand still, i.e. about 21st June (the summer s. of the northern hemisphere and winter s. of the southern) and 22nd December (the winter s. of the northern hemisphere and summer s. of the southern). **b.** *spec.* The summer solstice, or the heat of this 1643. **2.** A solstitial point 1601. **3.** *fig.* A turning, culminating, or stopping point; a farthest limit; a crisis 1631. **4.** *transf.* A standing still (*of* the sun). SIR T. BROWNE.

Solstitial (sǫlsti·făl), *a.* and *sb.* 1559. [– (O)Fr. *solsticial*, †*-tial*, or L. *solstitialis*, f. *solstitium*; see prec., -AL¹.] **A.** *adj.* **1.** Of or belonging to, connected with, a solstice or solstices. **2.** Occurring, taking place, etc., at the time of a solstice 1610. **3.** Of heat, etc.: Characteristic of the summer solstice. Also as an epithet of the sun, etc., in this connection. 1642. **4.** †**a.** Of plants (after L. *solstitialis herba*): Coming up at the summer solstice; growing or fading rapidly –1783. **b.** Of insects, etc.: Appearing about the time of the summer solstice 1812. **5.** Connected with the observation of the solstices 1834.

3. From the South to bring S. summers heat MILT.

†**B.** *sb.* A solstice (*rare*) –1612.

‖**Solstitium** (sǫlsti·ʃⁱŏm). *Pl.* **-ia.** 1515. [L., f. *sol* SOL¹ + *stit-*, pa. ppl. stem of *sistere* stand still.] = SOLSTICE.

Solubility (sǫliŭbi·liti). 1628. [f. next + -ITY; see -ILITY.] **1.** The quality or property of being soluble. **2.** *Bot.* Capability of easy separation into parts 1832. **3.** Capability of being solved or explained 1882.

1. The s. of salt in water 1794.

Soluble (sǫ·liŭb'l), *a.* late ME. [– (O)Fr. *soluble* – late L. *solubilis*, f. *solvere* loosen, SOLVE; see -BLE.] **1.** *Med.* **a.** Of the bowels, etc.: Free from constipation or costiveness; relaxed. Now *rare* or *Obs.* †**b.** Laxative –1704. **2.** Capable of being dissolved. late ME. **b.** Dissolving, solvent (*rare*) 1846. **3.** Capable of being untied or loosed (*rare*) 1613. **4.** Capable of being solved or explained 1705. **5.** Reducible *into* 1826.

1. a. Dry figges and old make the bodye s. 1539. **2.** There results a soap which is s. in water 1794. **3.** More s. is this knot, By gentleness than war TENNYSON. **4.** Questions not very s. at present CARLYLE. Hence †**So·lubleness.**

‖**Solus** (sōᵘ·lŏs), *a.* 1590. [L.; see SOLE *a.*] Of male persons: Alone; by oneself. Also of females.

The Famous Blunder in an old Play of *Enter a King and two Fidlers S.* ADDISON.

Solute (sŏlⁱū·t), *ppl. a.* 1440. [– L. *solutus*, pa. pple. of *solvere* loosen, SOLVE *v.*] †**1.** Of loose open texture or composition –1653. †**2.** Of discourse: Free, loose, discursive –1680. †**3.** Relaxed, free from care. YOUNG. **4.** *Bot.* Not adhering; separate 1760. **5.** Dissolved; in a state of solution 1890. **B.** *sb.* A dissolved substance 1904.

2. A s. and lax discourse 1680. **3.** A brow s., and ever-laughing eye 1742. Hence †**Solu·teness,** want of solidity.

†**Solu·te**, *v.* 1533. [– *solut-*, pa. ppl. stem of L. *solvere* SOLVE.] **1.** *trans.* To solve, explain clear up –1654. **2.** To dissolve, nullify (*rare*) –1550.

1. Of the loosing or soluting of Fallacies 1654.

Solution (sŏlⁱū·ʃən), *sb.* late ME. [– (O)Fr. *solution* – L. *solutio, -on-*, f. as prec.; see -ION.] **I. 1.** The action or process of solving; the state, condition, or fact of being solved. **b.** A particular instance or method of solving or settling; an explanation, answer, or decision. late ME. **c.** *Med.* The termination or crisis of a disease 1851. †**2.** The action of releasing or setting free; deliverance –1659. †**3.** The action of paying; a payment –1722.

1. A difficult problem of mixed law and fact for s. by the judges 1879. **b.** It provides a s. for every difficulty 1854.

II. 1. The action of dissolving, or changing from a solid or gaseous to a liquid state, by means of a fluid or solvent; the state or fact of being so dissolved. late ME. **b.** *transf.* Fusion, combination (*poet.*) *rare.* 1820. **2.** A more or less fluid substance produced by the process of solution; a liquid or semi-liquid preparation obtained by the combination of a solid with a solvent 1594. **3.** A dissolved state or condition. Freq. *state of s.* 1802.

1. Mechanical agitation facilitates s. 1800. **b.** The rose Blendeth its odour with the violet,—S. sweet KEATS. **2.** A good solucion of salt in oile 1594. **b.** In full *rubber solution*: a liquid preparation of caoutchouc, used chiefly in repairing rubber tyres 1894.

III. 1. *S. of continuity*: **a.** *Med.* (Also *of connection, of unity.*) The separation from each other of normally continuous parts of the body by external or internal causes 1541. **b.** *transf.* and *fig.* A breach, break, or interruption 1654. **2.** The action of breaking up or separating; dissolution; bringing to an end 1655.

1. a. A wound or S. of Continuity is worse then a Corrupt Humor BACON. **b.** Magnificent gradations of color, one fading into another without s. of continuity 1863. **2.** Easie and frequent Solutions of Conjugal Society LOCKE. Hence **Solu·tion** *v. trans.* to treat with, fasten or secure by, a s.

†**Solu·tive**, *a.* and *sb.* 1564. [– med.L. *solutivus* adj. laxative, also *-um* sb., f. as prec.; see -IVE.] **A.** *adj.* **1.** Laxative, relaxing –1750. **2.** Capable of releasing or setting free. EVELYN. **3.** Capable of dissolving –1732. **B.** *sb.* **1.** A laxative or purgative medicine –1674. **2.** A solvent –1712.

Solvable (sǫ·lvăb'l), *a.* Also †**solvible.** 1647. [f. SOLVE *v.* + -ABLE; in sense 1 after Fr. *solvable*.] †**1.** Able to pay; solvent –1773. **2.** Capable of being solved 1676. **3.** Capable of being dissolved. Also *absol.* 1669. **4.** Capable of being resolved *into* something 1804.

1. Imprisonment was imposed by law on persons not s. 1655. Hence **Solvabi·lity. So·lvableness.**

Solvate (sǫ·lveⁱt), *sb.* 1910. [irreg. f. SOLVE *v.* + -ATE⁴.] *Phys. Chem.* A compound of a dissolved substance with the solvent. So **So·lvate** *v. intr.* of a solute: to enter into combination with the solvent. **Solva·tion.**

Solve (sǫlv), *v.* 1440. [– L. *solvere* unfasten, free, pay.] †**1.** *trans.* To loosen; to break –1450. **2.** To explain, clear up, resolve, answer 1533. **b.** *Math.* To find the answer or solution to (a problem, etc.); to work out 1737. **3.** To clear off; to pay or discharge

1558. **4.** To dissolve, put an end to, settle 1667. **5.** To dissolve; to melt. Now *rare*. 1662.

2. That Theban Monster that proposed Her riddle, and him, who solv'd it not, devour'd MILT. **3.** Minos returned..And solved his vows 1866. **4.** *P. L.* viii. 55. Hence **So·lver,** one who solves.

†So·lvend. 1738. [– L. *solvendum*, n. gerundive of *solvere* SOLVE.] Something to be dissolved –1867.

Solvent (sǫ·lvĕnt), *a.* and *sb.* 1653. [– L. *solvens, -ent-*, pr. pple. of *solvere*; see SOLVE, -ENT.] **A.** *adj.* **1.** Able to pay all one's debts or liabilities. **2.** Dissolving; causing solution 1686. **3.** Helping to solve or explain 1872.

1. *Comb.*: A s. looking gentleman, solus in a buggy, is the very thing for a highwayman 1852.

B. *sb.* **1.** A substance (usually a liquid) having the power of dissolving other substances 1671. **b.** *fig.* A dissolving or disintegrating influence 1841. **2.** Something which solves, explains, or settles 1865. **3.** A laxative; a loosener 1815. **4.** A person able to pay all his debts 1825.

1. Water..is found the most universal s. of the food of man and other animals 1756. **2.** That only universal s., a cash payment 1890. **3.** He took it [tobacco], he would say, as a s. of speech LAMB. Hence **So·lvency,** the state of being s. **So·lvently** *adv.*

‖**Soma**[1] (sōᵘ·mă). 1827. [Skr. *sōma*. See HOM.] **1.** An intoxicating drink holding a prominent place in Vedic ritual and religion. **2.** *S. plant*, the plant (perh. *Asclepias acida* or *Sarcostemma viminale*) yielding the soma-juice. Also *ellipt.* 1827.

‖**Soma**[2] (sōᵘ·mă). 1889. [– Gr. σῶμα body.] *Biol.* The body of an organism in contrast to the germ-cells. Also *attrib.* in *somaplasm*. Hence **So·mal** *a.*

Somatic (somæ·tik), *a.* and *sb.* 1775. [– Gr. σωματικός, f. σῶμα, σωματ- body; see -IC.] **A.** *adj.* **1.** Of or pertaining to the (or a) body; bodily, corporeal, physical. **b.** *Anat.* and *Phys.* of parts of the body 1859. **c.** *spec.* Pertaining to the soma 1888. **2.** Affecting the body 1835.

1. Motions and emotions, both s. and psychical 1884. **b.** The termination of the s. nerves 1899. **2.** Hypnotism could do nothing in s. affections 1899.

B. *sb. pl.* Somatology 1816. Hence **Soma·tical** *a.* corporeal, bodily, substantial; **-ly** *adv.*

Somatist (sōᵘ·mătist). 1676. [f. as prec. + -IST.] **†1.** A materialist –1694. **2.** *attrib.* Pertaining to, connected with, the soma 1908.

Somato- (sōᵘ·măto), – Gr. σωματο-, comb. form of σῶμα, σωματ- body (see SOMA[2]), as in **so·matocyst,** a sac forming the proximal end of the hydrosoma in oceanic hydrozoa; **so·matoplasm,** somaplasm; **so·matopleure,** the upper (or outer) leaf of the blastoderm, as giving rise to the body-walls; **somatopleu·ric** *a.*, of or belonging to the somatopleure; **somato·tomy,** anatomy.

Somatology (sōᵘmătǫ·lŏdʒi). 1736. [f. SOMATO- + -LOGY.] **1.** A treatise or science dealing with the properties of bodies. **2.** A treatise or science dealing with the human body in some respect 1851. Hence **So:matolo·gical** *a.*, **-ly** *adv.* **Somato·logist.**

Sombre (sǫ·mbəɹ), *a.* and *sb.* 1760. [– (O)Fr. *sombre*, adj. use of OFr. sb. (= Cat., Sp., Pg. *sombra* shade), first in *sombre coup* 'dark blow', bruise, based on Rom. *subombrare*, f. L. *sub* SUB- + *umbra* shade, shadow.] **A.** *adj.* **1.** Of inanimate natural objects and their attributes: Characterized by the presence of gloom or shadow; depressingly dark, dusky, or obscure. **2.** Of persons, etc.: Gloomy, lowering, dark and sullen or dejected 1767. **b.** Of thoughts, feelings, etc.: Melancholy, dismal, darksome 1821. **3.** Conveying gloomy ideas or suggestions 1768. **4.** Of colours or colouring: Of a dark shade or tinge; dark, dull 1805. **b.** Of things in respect of colour 1829.

1. This coast..dark, gloomy, and silent;—a savage s. air spread over the whole YOUNG. **2.** The man..was a s. ill-looking fellow 1865. **b.** In s. mood 1821. **4. b.** A s. garb was worn by the nuns 1872.

B. *sb.* Sombre character; sombreness (*rare*) 1795. Hence **So·mbre-ly** *adv.*, **-ness.**

Sombre (sǫ·mbəɹ), *v.* 1787. [f. SOMBRE *a.*] To make, or become, sombre.

Day again had sombred into night 1893.

‖**Sombrero** (sǫmbrēᵊ·ro). 1598. [Sp., f. *sombra* shade.] **†1.** An Oriental umbrella or parasol –1727. **2.** A broad-brimmed hat, usually of felt or some soft material, of a type common in Spain and Spanish America 1770.

Sombrous (sǫ·mbrəs), *a.* 1730. [f. SOMBRE + -OUS. Cf. Fr. †*sombreux* mournful, lugubrious.] Sombre.

Where..the s. pine And yew-tree o'er the..rocks recline WORDSW. Hence **So·mbrous-ly** *adv.*, **-ness.**

Some (sɒm), *indef. pron.*, *a.*, *adv.*, and *sb.* [OE. *sum* = OFris., OS., OHG. *sum*, ON. *sumr*, Goth. *sums* :– Gmc. **sumaz* :– IE. **smmos*, the base of which is also repr. by Gr. ἁμῶς somehow, ἁμόθεν from some place, Skr. *samáṣ* any, every.] **A.** *indef. pron.* **I.** In sing. uses. **†1.** One or other of a number of persons; some one, somebody. In later use also in phr. *s. or other*. –1729. **2.** A certain indeterminate part of something; a portion. Also *s. . . , s.* OE.

1. When somme good cometh to somme, it ought not to be reffused CAXTON. S. or other hath abused him in this Letter 1664. Phr. *S. of these* (. .) *days*, some day soon; before very long. **2.** Bate me s., and I will pay you s. SHAKS. S. of it, much of it, has ceased to be alive for us now 1872.

II. In pl. senses. **1.** An indefinite or unspecified (but not large) number of persons, animals or things; certain persons not named or enumerated OE. **2.** *S. . . , s.*, = Some . . , others OE. **b.** So *S. . . , others* (†*other*) OE. **†3.** *S. and s.*, a few at a time, gradually –1769.

1. And the while he soweth, sum felden byside the weye WYCLIF *Matt.* 13:4. Neuer was Woolfe seene, many nor s. SPENSER. **2.** S. are gold, s. silver 1750. **b.** S. have a smacke of Christ, others of Mahomet 1634. **3.** The swallow kind disappear s. and s., gradually, as they come 1769.

B. *adj.* **I.** With sing. nouns. **†1.** A certain (person or place) –1578. **2.** One or other; an undetermined or unspecified OE. **†3.** Used with an indefinite or generalizing force similar to that of the plural –1638. **4.** A certain (unspecified) amount, part, degree, or extent of (something), freq. implying 'not little, considerable' OE. **b.** With adjs., as *little, small, considerable*, etc. late ME. **c.** *U.S.* Of some account; deserving of consideration (cf. PUMPKIN 2 b) 1848. **5.** *S. other* (see OTHER *a.* 5b) OE. **6.** Followed by *certain* or *one* with limiting force 1561.

2. He hopis sum day to see his sone 1550. Som neighbour Wood-man, or..Som roaving Robber MILT. He must write s. day or other 1881. **4.** 'Twixt which Regions There is s. space SHAKS. Where he feathered his nest to s. purpose MARVELL. **b.** S. brief time hence SCOTT. **c.** She's 's.' now, that is a fact 1848. **d.** In attrib. use: Such in the fullest sense, 'something like a', worthy of the name (*U.S.* and *slang*) 1914. **5.** Sette scolers to scole or to sum oþer craft LANGL. **6.** In s. one Excellence their Merit lies 1746.

II. With pl. nouns. **1.** Certain (taken individually) OE. **2.** A certain number of; a few at least ME. **3.** Used with numbers to indicate an approximate amount or estimate, and passing into an adv. with the sense 'about, nearly, approximately' OE. **b.** With numerals denoting the time of day 1596. **c.** Hence with singular nouns expressing time, distance, etc. 1592.

1. S. certaine dregges of conscience are yet within mee SHAKS. **2.** S. flaggons of rich wine, s. very white bisket, s. pruines and raisins 1617. For s. few gasping moments KEATS. **3.** I have s. three hundred pistoles by me DRYDEN. **b.** 'Tis now s. seuen a clocke SHAKS. **c.** S. halfe musket shot distance 1617.

III. With *other, one, few*, etc., used absol. in sing. or pl. OE.

S. certaine of the Noblest minded Romans SHAKS.

C. *adv.* **1.** With comparatives: A little; slightly; somewhat. Chiefly *Sc.* and *north.* 1560. **2.** With vbs.: **a.** A certain amount; a little 1699. **b.** *U.S.* To some extent; in some degree; somewhat 1825. **c.** *U.S.* In emphatic use: Very much, very well 1866. **3.** *dial.* and *U.S.* With adjs.: Somewhat 1817.

2. a. I hunt s., and snake a little 1834. **c.** Thet night, I tell ye, she looked *some*! 1866. **3.** His clothes were s. bloody 1817.

D. *sb.* An unspecified amount, person, thing, etc. (*rare*) 1830.

-some, *suffix*[1], repr. OE. *-sum* = OFris. *-sum*, rel. by gradation to OS., OHG. *-sam* (Du. *-zaam*, G. *-sam*), ON. *-samr*, Goth. **-sams*, used to form adjs. from nouns and adjs., as *fulsome, gladsome, loathsome, winsome*, rarely from verbs, as *tiresome, wearisome*, etc. (cf. BUXOM).

-some, *suffix*[2], repr. OE. *sum* after numerals in the genitive pl. In ME. the inflexion disappeared, and the pronoun was finally treated as a suffix to the numeral, chiefly with the simple numbers from two to ten. See TWOSOME, THREESOME, etc.

-some, *suffix*[3], later variant of *-sum*, repr. Scand. *sum, som*, as in †*whosome* (= whoever) cf. SOMEVER.

Somebody (sɒ·mbǫdi), *pron.* and *sb.* Also **†some body.** ME. [f. SOME *a.* + BODY *sb.*] **1.** A person unknown, indeterminate, or unnamed; some one, some person. **b.** Used as a substitute for a personal name 1825. **2.** A person of some note, consequence, or importance. Freq. *depreciatory* or *sarcastic.* 1566. **b.** With *a* and *pl.* 1601. **3.** A person whose name is intentionally suppressed; occas., the Devil 1606.

1. I heard some body at a Distance hemming after me ADDISON. *S. else*, some other person. **b.** General S. ordered him to bring up his guns 1842. **2.** A desire to be s...seems to be the rule of his life 1704. **b.** People who are somebodies MARRYAT. **3.** There is a deeper impression of Somebody's Hoof here DICKENS.

Somedeal (sɒ·mˌdīl), *sb.* and *adv.* Now *arch.* or *dial.* [OE., f. *sum* SOME *a.* + *dǣl* DEAL *sb.*[1]] **A.** *sb.* Some part or portion *of* some thing or things; some, somewhat.

Somdeale of our birth our countrey, somedeale our parentes..do claime 1553.

B. *adv.* In some degree or measure; to some extent; somewhat; partly OE.

I doubte not..but that it doth some deal vexe you 1533.

Somehow (sɒ·mhau), *adv.* 1664. [f. SOME *a.* + HOW *adv.*] **1.** In some manner or by some means not understood or defined; one way or another; someway 1740. **2.** In phr. *S. or other, or another* 1664.

1. Somewhere, s., there was a fault BYRON. **2.** We contrived at last, s. or other, to agree 1875.

Some one, someone (sɒ·mwɒn), *pron.* and *sb.* ME. [f. SOME *a.* + ONE.] Some person, somebody.

Some one intent on mischief MILT.

Somersault (sɒ·məɹsǫlt), *sb.* Also **†-saut.** 1530. [Also occas. †*sombersault* – OFr. *sombresau(l)t*, alt. of *sobresault* (whence Eng. †*sobersault* XVI–XVII), mod. *soubresaut* – Pr. **sobresaut*, f. *sobre* (:– L. *supra*) above + *saut* (:– L. *saltus*) leap; see next. In XVI–XVII spelt also *-saut.* The sp. with *l*, after Fr. *-sault*, influenced the pronunc. Cf. FAULT.] A leap or spring in which a person turns heels over head in the air and alights on his feet; esp. such a feat as performed by acrobats or tumblers; a pitchpoll. Hence, a turning over in this fashion; a complete overturn, upset, etc.

fig. The summersaults, spells, and resurrections wrought by the imagination EMERSON. Hence **So·mersault** *v. intr.* to make or turn a s.

Somerset (sɒ·məɹset), *sb.* 1591. [var. of *somersaut*; see prec.] = prec. Hence **So·merset** *v. intr.* to somersault; *trans.* to cause (a person) to turn a somersault.

Something (sɒ·mþiŋ), *sb.*, (*adj.*,) and *adv.* OE. [f. SOME *a.* + THING *sb.*[1] Orig. written as two words.] **A.** *sb.* **1.** Some unspecified or indeterminate thing (material or immaterial). **b.** Used as a substitute for a name or part of one, or other particular, which is not remembered or is immaterial, etc. 1764. **c.** Some liquor, drink, or food; esp. in phr. *to take s.* 1778. **d.** Used (with *between*) to denote an intermediate stage or grade 1821. **e.** Used to denote an undefined or unknown occupation, or a person in respect of this 1874. **2.** A certain part, portion, amount, or share (*of* some thing, quality, etc.); freq. a small part or amount, a slight trace ME. **3.** Followed by an adj. (see below). late ME. **4.** In more emphatic use: A thing, fact, person, etc., of some value, consideration or regard

1582. **5.** As *adj.* Used euphemistically for 'damned' or other expletive 1859.

1. Yet s. must be done for examples sake 1638. *S. like*, see LIKE A. 2. *S. or other*, one thing or another; anything whatever; a thing which it is unnecessary to specify. *Or s.*, vague addition to a word or phrase = 'or the like'. **b.** Lady S. Grey is here 1764. **c.** The restless gentlemen who are 's. in the city', but no one knows what 1886. **2.** S. of the tone, and manners, and feeling of a gentleman SCOTT. *S. of a(n*, to a certain extent or degree a (person or thing of the kind specified). **3.** Slang or colloq. phr *S. damp* or *short*, a drink; spirits. *S. good*, a good racing tip. **4.** *S. in the wind*: see WIND *sb.* *There's s. in it*, etc. *To make s. of*, to make important or useful; to improve in some way; to succeed in utilizing to some extent. **5.** It's the somethingest robbery I ever saw in my life 1859.

B. *adv.* In some degree; to some extent; somewhat; rather, a little ME.

Conies..s. resemble a wilde Cat 1634. Our Guide being s. before us DE FOE. Sir George is s. nervous 1791. 'O!' said I, s. snappishly DICKENS. Now this song..is s. less than just to me STEVENSON. Hence **So·mething** *v. trans.* used *colloq.* in pa. pple. as a euphemism for 'damned' or the like. **So·methingness,** the fact or state of being s.; entity. **Somethingth** (sɒ·mþiŋþ) *a.* used to supply the place of an ordinal number which is not remembered or is immaterial.

Sometime (sɒ·mtəim), *adv.* (and *a.*). ME. [f. SOME *a.* + TIME *sb.*] **1.** At one time or another, with the possibility of recurrence; now and then; occasionally. Now *rare* or *Obs.* **2.** †**a.** At a certain time in the past; once –1661. **b.** At one time; in former times, formerly ME. **3.** At some future time; on a future occasion. Also in phr. *s. or other*. late ME. **4.** At some indefinite or indeterminate point of time; at some time or other 1590. **5.** With *since*, = some time ago (*rare*) 1700.

1. My heart is s. heavy, when I smile 1622. **2. a.** Let the power speak, which s. said, 'Lazarus arise!' 1653. **b.** Of Inde Somtyme ther was a nobyll kyng 1440. Our s. constable, the tipsiest.. of men 1824. **3.** You may s. or other come to Bath BERKELEY. *attrib.* The s. resurrection of the body 1805. **4.** It was s. in the 11th century SOUTHEY.

Sometimes (sɒ·mtəimz), *adv.* 1526. [f. SOME *a.* + *times* pl. of TIME *sb.*] **1.** On some occasions; at times; now and then. **2.** = SOMETIME 2 a, b –1665. †**3.** *At s.*, = sense 1. –1719.

1. Hither s. the King repaires 1634. Somtimes sighingly, and sometimes comfortably BUNYAN. S. The Devil is a gentleman; At others a bard SHELLEY. **2.** Farewell old Gaunt, thy s. brothers wife..must end her life SHAKS.

†**Some·ver,** *adv.* 1440. [f. ME. *sum* (Scand. *sum, som* rel. adv.) + EVER *adv.*] = SOEVER 2; cf. dial. *whatsomever*, etc.

Someway (sɒ·mweⁱ), *adv.* Now *rare* exc. *dial.* Also **some way.** 1450. [f. SOME *a.* + WAY *sb.*] **1.** In some way or manner; by some means; somehow. **2.** At some distance. Also *transf.* of time. (Usu. as two words.) 1859.

1. We s. think that contentment is to feel no want 1890. So **Someways** (sɒ·mweⁱz) *adv.* (in sense 1); now chiefly *dial.* 1440.

Somewhat (sɒ·mhwǫt), *sb.* and *adv.* ME. [f. SOME *a.* + WHAT *pron.* Freq. written as two words down to the end of XVI.] = SOMETHING *sb.* and *adv.* **A.** *sb.* **1.** A certain amount, esp. in the way of statement, information, etc. Freq. with *of* (= concerning). Now *arch.* **b.** Some (material or immaterial) thing of unspecified nature, amount, etc. Now *arch.* or *dial.* ME. **2.** With dependent genitive: Some part, portion, amount, etc. *of* something ME. **b.** *S. of a(n*, = *something of a(n* (see SOMETHING A. 2.) 1841. **3.** A thing, quality, etc., worth considering; a person of importance. late ME. **4.** With *a, the*, etc., and *pl.* A certain undefined or unknown thing, quality, amount, etc. 1598.

1. It is strange, how long some Men will lie in wait, to speake s., they desire to say BACON. **b.** He's..turned miser, or s. 1855. **2.** By quitting s. of his royal prerogative HUME. **3.** The fool is a handsome fool, that's s. DRYDEN. **4.** Thus achievement lacks a gracious s. BROWNING.

B. *adv.* In a certain degree or measure; to some (slight or small) extent; slightly, a little; rather ME.

Ye be diligent To forthren me somwhat in my labour CHAUCER. His vtterance was somewhat vnready 1595. Tell me.., in s. plainer terms, what you mean! 1875.

Somewhen (sɒmhwen), *adv.* ME. In mod. use casual and freq. jocular. [f. SOME *a.* + WHEN *adv.*] At some (indefinite or unknown) time; sometime or other.

Somewhere (sɒ·mhwēᵊɹ), *adv.* and *sb.* ME. [f. SOME *a.* + WHERE *adv.*] **A.** *adv.* **1.** In or at some place unspecified, indeterminate, or unknown. **2.** To some (unspecified or unknown) place. Usu. with *go*. late ME. **3.** In some part or passage of a book, etc.; in some work or other 1634. **4. a.** At some time *about* or *in* (a certain specified year, date, etc.) 1839. **b.** *S. about*, approximately 1846.

1. What malicious Foe..somwhere nigh at hand Watches MILT. **3.** As some one s. sings about the sky BYRON. **4. b.** S. about two months 1846.

B. *sb.* Some unspecified or indefinite place 1647. So **So·mewheres** *adv.* (*dial.* or *vulgar*).

Somewhile (sɒ·mhwəil), *adv.* Now *rare.* ME. [f. SOME *a.* + WHILE *sb.*] **1.** †**a.** At or in some former time; formerly –1654. **b.** *attrib.* or *adj.* Former, sometime 1860. †**2.** Once; at one time –1631. **3.** At some (unspecified) time; at one time or other; at times, sometimes ME.

1. b. Richard Doyle, s. illustrator of *Punch* 1888. **3.** Tho vnder colour of shepeheards, s. There crept in Wolues, ful of fraude and guile SPENSER. So **So·mewhiles** (*dial.* or *arch.*) ME.

Somewhither (sɒ·mhwi:ðəɹ), *adv.* late ME. [f. SOME *a.* + WHITHER *adv.*] **1.** In some direction. **2.** To some place 1530.

2. Like ghosts waiting for Charon to take them s. 1877.

Somewise (sɒ·mwəiz), *adv.* Now *arch.* 1440. [f. SOME *a.*; see -WISE.] In some way or manner; to some extent. In recent use with *in*.

I..knew In s. he was well awake SWINBURNE.

Somite (sōᵘ·məit). 1869. [f. Gr. σῶμα body, SOMA[2] + -ITE[1] 3.] *Zool.* One or other of the more or less distinct segments into which the bodies of many animals are divided. Hence **So·mital, Somi·tic** *adjs.* of or pertaining to, having the form or character of, a s.

Somn-, comb. form of L. *somnus*, used in words based on L. *ambulare* to walk. **Somna·mbulance,** sleep-walking. **Somna·mbulant** *a.*, walking in sleep; *sb.*, a somnambulist. **Somna·mbular** *a.*, of or pertaining to sleepwalking; also *erron.*, connected with, of the nature of, sleep. **Somna·mbulate** *v. intr.*, to walk during sleep; *trans.*, to walk along (a place) while asleep. **Somna:mbula·tion,** the action or fact of walking in sleep. **Somna·mbulator,** = next. **Somna·mbule** [– Fr.], a somnambulist. **Somna·mbulic** *a.*, of the nature of or pertaining to somnambulism; walking during sleep. **Somna·mbulism,** the fact or habit of walking about and performing other actions while asleep; sleep-walking. **Somna·mbulist,** one who walks, etc., while asleep; **Somna:mbuli·stic** *a.*, somnambulic.

†**Somne,** *v.* ME. [Syncopated var. of *somony*, etc.; see SUMMON *v.*] *trans.* To summon –1530.

†**So·mner.** ME. [f. prec. + -ER[1], or contr. f. SUMMONER.] An official summoner –1608.

Somni-, comb. form of L. *somnus* sleep, occurring in a number of L. compounds, as *somnifer, somnificus*, and in English adaptations or imitations of these.

Somni·loquence, = *somniloquy*. **Somni·loquent** *a.*, talking in sleep. **Somni·loquism,** = *somniloquy*. **Somni·loquist,** one who speaks or talks while asleep. **Somni·loquous** *a.* apt to talk in sleep. **Somni·loquy,** the act or habit of speaking during sleep. **Somni·pathy,** sleep induced by mesmerism. **Somni·pathist,** a person in a state of somnipathy.

Somnial (sǫ·mnial), *a. rare.* 1693. [– Fr. †*somnial* or late L. *somnialis*, f. L. *somnium* dream; see -AL[1].] Of or relating to dreams.

The S. magic superinduced on..the active powers of the mind COLERIDGE.

†**So·mniate,** *v.* 1657. [– *somniat-*, pa. ppl. stem of L. *somniare*, f. *somnium* dream; see -ATE[3].] **1.** *trans.* To dream (something). †**2.** To stupefy, make drowsy. DE FOE. Hence †**So·mniative** *a.* relating to, or producing, dreams. †**So·mniatory** *a.* of or pertaining to dreams or dreaming (*rare*).

Somni·culous, *a. rare.* 1656. [f. L. *somniculosus* (f. *somnium* dream) + -OUS; see -ULOUS.] **a.** Drowsy, sleepy. **b.** Inducing sleep.

Somniferous (sǫmni·fĕrəs), *a.* 1602. [f. L. *somnifer*, f. *somnium* dream; see -FEROUS.] **1.** Inducing sleep; soporific. **2.** Somnolent 1798.

1. The wine had exerted its s. influence DICKENS.

Somnific (sǫmni·fik), *a.* 1721. [– L. *somnificus*; see SOMNI-, -FIC.] Causing sleep; somniferous.

Somnolence (sǫ·mnŏlĕns). late ME. [– OFr. *sompnolence* (mod. *somn-*) or late L. *somnolentia* (med.L. *somp-*), f. L. *somnolentus*; see next, -ENCE.] Inclination to sleep; sleepiness, drowsiness. So **So·mnolency.**

Somnolent (sǫ·mnŏlĕnt), *a.* 1475. [– OFr. *sompnolent* (mod. *somn-*) or L. *somnolentus* (med. L. *somp-*), f. *somnus* sleep; see -ENT.] **1.** Tending to cause sleepiness or drowsiness; inclining to sleep. **b.** Marked by sleepiness or slowness 1812. **2.** Of persons: Inclined to sleep; drowsy. Also *transf.* 1547.

1. b. He served me well in his own s. fashion 1877. Hence **So·mnolently** *adv.* sleepily.

‖**Somnus** (sǫ·mnɒs). 1599. [L., sleep, also personified as a divinity.] The god of sleep.

†**Sompnour.** late ME. Variant of SOMNER. See -OUR. –1555.

Son (sɒn). [OE. *sunu* = OFris., OS., OHG. *sunu* (Du. *zoon*, G. *sohn*), ON. *sunr, sonr*, Goth. *sunus* :– Gmc. **sunuz*, rel. to Gr. υἱός.] **1.** A male child or person in relation to either or both of his parents. Sometimes said of animals. **b.** = SON-IN-LAW 1533. **2.** *Theol.* The second person of the Trinity OE. **3.** One who is regarded as, or takes the place of, a son OE. **b.** Used as term of affectionate address to a man or boy by an older person or by one in a superior (esp. ecclesiastical) relation OE. **4.** *S. of God* **a.** Jesus Christ OE. **b.** A divine being; an angel. late ME. **c.** One spiritually attached to God OE. **5.** *S. of man*: **a.** One of the human race; a mortal OE. **b.** *spec.* Jesus Christ OE. **6.** A male descendant *of* some person or representative *of* some race OE. **b.** One who inherits the spirit, or displays the character, *of* some person, etc. late ME. **c.** A member or adherent of a religious body or order, or a follower of the founder of one. late ME. **7. a.** One who is characterized by the presence, possession, influence, use, etc., *of* some quality or thing OE. **b.** A person regarded as the product or offspring *of* a certain country or place 1595. **c.** In terms of abuse or contempt. (See GUN *sb.*, WHORE *sb.*)

1. Lord Colchester, s. to the earl of Rivers 1764. Phr. *S. and heir*. **2.** We seeme more inwardly to knowe the Sonne 1628. **3.** For thy children dead I'll be a s. to thee! WORDSW. **b.** 'Prove thy strength, my s., in the name of God!' said the preacher SCOTT. **4. a.** Beyond compare the S. of God was seen Most glorious MILT. **b.** The Angels ..are the Sons of God by temporal Creation 1643. **5. a.** Deciduous Forests that die and are born again..like the sons of men CARLYLE. **b.** Shall the stones cry out..that they are the only pillows where the S. of Man can lay His head? RUSKIN. **6.** Adams sonnes are my brethren SHAKS. **b.** Thay were the sons of Belial, that is, the devel CHAUCER. **7. a.** Certain Sons of Parchment, call'd Solicitors and Barristers 1700. **b.** We, the sonnes and children of this Isle SHAKS. *fig.* Easie..thou s. of night, Pass by his troubled senses FLETCHER. *S. of the soil*: see SOIL *sb.*[1] Hence **So·nhood** = SONSHIP.

Sonance (sōᵘ·năns). 1599. [f. L. *sonare* to sound + -ANCE.] Sound; quality of sounding.

Let the Trumpets sound The Tucket Sonuance SHAKS.

Sonant (sōᵘ·nănt), *a.* and *sb.* 1846. [– L. *sonans, -ant-*, pr. pple. of *sonare* to sound; see -ANT.] *Phonetics.* **A.** *adj.* Uttered with voice or vocal sound; voiced.

Final *a* is changed to *o* before all s. consonants 1846.

B. *sb.* A sonant articulation or letter 1875. Hence **Sonantal** (sōᵘnæ·ntăl) *a.*

Sonata (sŏnā·tă). 1694. [It., fem. pa. pple. of *sonare* to sound.] †**1.** A musical composition for instruments (opp. to a *cantata*). **2.** An instrumental piece of music, usually for the pianoforte, in several (commonly three or four) movements 1801. **b.** Without article: The class of music represented by sonatas 1883.

2. *Double s.*, a s. for two solo instruments, as pianoforte and violin, or two pianofortes 1880.

Sonatina (sǫnătī·nă). 1801. [It., dim. of prec.] A short, simple form of sonata.

Song (sǫŋ). [OE. *sang* (*song*) = OFris. *sang, song*, OS. *sang* (Du. *zang*), OHG. *sanc* (G. *sang*), ON. *songr*, Goth. *saggws* :– Gmc. **saŋgwaz*, f. **saŋgw-* **seŋgw-* SING *v*.] **1.** The act (†or art) of singing; the result or effect of this, vocal music; that which is sung (in general or collective sense). **b.** The musical utterance of birds OE. **c.** *transf.* A sound as of singing 1822. **2.** A poem, lay; also *gen.* poetry, poetical composition. Now *arch.* OE. **3.** A metrical composition adapted for singing, esp. one having a regular verse-form; such a composition as actually sung OE. **b.** A musical setting or composition of the character of or suggestive of a song, e.g. Mendelssohn's 'Songs without Words' 1871. **4.** *transf.* and *fig.* OE. **b.** A fuss or outcry *about* something 1843. **5.** Used to denote a very small sum, amount, or value, or a thing of little worth or importance 1601.

1. The world is full of s.! 1878. **b.** The night-warbling Bird, that now awake Tunes sweetest his love-labor'd s. MILT. **2.** Our sweetest songs are those that tell of saddest thought SHELLEY. *The S. of Solomon, S. of Songs*, one of the books of the O.T. **3.** We'll hear that s. again SHAKS. My Book of Songs SHAKS. **4.** Out on ye, Owles, nothing but Songs of Death SHAKS. Phr. *To change one's s., sing another* (or *a different*) *s.*, to 'change one's tune'. **b.** She had foreborne likewise and no one made a s. about it 1863. **5.** They were acquired 'for an old s.' 1889.

Comb.: **s.-box**, the syrinx of a bird; **-form** *Mus.*, the simplest form of instrumental composition, consisting of one or more melodic themes as in a vocal song; **-grosbeak**, one or other species of the American genus *Zamelodia*; **-sparrow**, a common North American bird of the genus *Melospiza*, esp. *M. fasciata* (or *melodia*) and *cinerea*; **-thrush**, the common thrush (*Turdus musicus*). Hence **So·ngful** *a.* abounding in s.; musical, melodious. **So·ngless** *a.* devoid of s.; not singing; (of birds) lacking the power of s.

So·ng-bird. 1774. A bird having the power of song; a singing-bird.

So·ng-book. OE. **1.** A book of hours with music. *Hist.* **2.** A book of songs 1489.

So·ng-school. 1537. A school devoted to the teaching of singing or the practising of vocal music.

So·ng-smith. 1795. A composer or maker of songs. Also as a book-title.

Songster (sǫ·ŋstəɹ). [OE. *sangestre*; see SONG, -STER.] **1.** One who sings, a singer; orig. a female singer, a songstress. **2.** A poet; a writer of songs or verse 1585. **3.** A bird that sings; a song-bird 1700. Hence **So·ngstress.** (*a*) a female singer; a poetess; (*b*) a female singing-bird.

Soniferous (soni·fĕrəs), *a.* 1713. [f. L. *soni-*, comb. form of *sonus* sound + -FEROUS.] Sound-bearing; conveying or producing sound.

Son-in-law (sʊ·n,in,lǭ). ME. [See -IN-LAW] A daughter's husband.

How should you like him for a s.? 1811.

Sonless (sʊ·nlĕs), *a.* late ME. [f. SON + -LESS.] Having no son; destitute of a son or sons.

Sonlike (sʊ·nləik), *a.* 1583. [f. SON + -LIKE.] Resembling that of a son; filial.

Sonnet (sǫ·nĕt), *sb.* 1557. [– Fr. *sonnet* or its It. source *sonetto*, dim. of *suono* SOUND *sb.*[2]] **1.** A piece of verse (properly expressive of one main idea) consisting of fourteen decasyllabic lines, with rhymes arranged according to one or other of certain definite schemes. **2.** A short poem or piece of verse; in early use esp. one of a lyrical or amatory character. Now *rare* or *Obs.* 1563.

1. He is a fool which cannot make one S., and he is mad which makes two DONNE. **2.** Some thinke that all Poemes (being short) may be called Sonets GASCOIGNE.

Sonnet (sǫ·nĕt), *v.* 1589. [f. prec.] **1.** *intr.* To compose sonnets; to sonnetize. **2.** *trans.* To celebrate in a sonnet or sonnets 1598.

1. Come, now, you're sonnetting again TENNYSON.

Sonneteer (sǫnĕtī°·ɹ), *sb.* Also **sonnetteer.** 1665. [– It. *sonettiere* (f. *sonetto*), or f. SONNET *sb.* + -EER.] A composer of sonnets; freq. in disparaging sense, a minor or indifferent poet.

Our little Sonnettiers..have too narrow Souls to judge of Poetry DRYDEN. Hence **Sonnetee·r**, **Sonnettee·r** *v. trans.* to celebrate in sonnets; *intr.* to compose sonnets.

Sonnetize (sǫ·nĕtəiz), *v.* 1798. [f. SONNET *sb.* + -IZE.] **1.** *intr.* To compose a sonnet or sonnets. **2.** *trans.* To celebrate in a sonnet or sonnets 1799.

Sonny (sʊ·ni). *colloq.* Also **sonnie.** 1870. [f. SON *sb.* + -Y[6].] A familiar term of address to a boy or to a man younger than the speaker.

Sonometer (sonǫ·mĭtəɹ). 1808. [f. *sono-*, used as comb. form of L. *sonus* sound + -METER. Cf. Fr. *sonomètre*.] **1.** An instrument for determining the number of vibrations made by a sonorous cord. **2.** An instrument for testing the sense of hearing 1849. **3.** *Electr.* A telephone attached to an apparatus for testing metals by means of an induction-coil 1879.

Sonority (sŏnōᵊ·rĭti, sŏnǫ·rĭti). 1623. [– Fr. *sonorité* or late L. *sonoritas*, f. *sonorus*; see next, -ITY.] The quality of being sonorous.

The richness and s. of his [Milton's] language 1876.

Sonorous (sŏnōᵊ·rəs, sǫ·nŏrəs), *a.* 1611. [f. L. *sonorus*, f. *sonor, sonor-* sound; see -OUS.] **1.** Of things: Giving out, or capable of giving out, a sound, esp. of a deep or ringing character. **b.** Of places, etc.: Resounding, roaring, noisy 1729. **2.** Of sounds: Having a loud, deep, or resonant character 1668. **3.** Of language, diction, etc.: Having a full, rich sound; strong and harmonious 1693. **b.** Of persons: Having a full and rich style or voice 1728.

1. S. mettal blowing Martial sounds MILT. **b.** The s. Shore 1729. **2.** Nestor, brave Gerenian, with a voice S. COWPER. S. vibrations convey the sensation of sound to the ear 1839. **3.** The Italian Opera..has something beautiful and s. in the Expression ADDISON. **b.** Santerre, the s. Brewer of the Suburb Saint-Antoine CARLYLE. Hence **Sonorous-ly** *adv.*, **-ness.**

Sonship (sʊ·nʃip). 1587. [f. SON + -SHIP.] The position, state, or relation of a son.

Sonsy (sǫ·nsi), *a.* orig. *Sc.*, *Ir.*, and *n. dial.* 1533. [f. (dial.) *sonse* (XIV) abundance, prosperity – Ir., Gael. *sonas* good fortune, f. *sona* fortunate, happy; see -Y[1].] **1.** Bringing luck; lucky, fortunate. **2.** Plump, buxom, comely and pleasant; comfortable-looking, etc. 1725. **3.** Of animals: Tractable, manageable 1786.

2. Twa s. lasses, young and fair 1725. Trousers of s. grey homespun 1870.

‖**Soojee** (sū·dʒī). Also **-y, -ie.** 1810. [Hindi *sūjī*.] A flour obtained by grinding Indian wheat; a nutritious food prepared from this.

Soon (sūn), *adv.* [OE. *sōna* = OFris. *sōn*, OS. *sāno, sān(a*, OHG. *sān* :– WGmc. **sǣnō* (obs. in nearly all Continental langs.), perh. rel. to Goth. *suns* immediately.] **1.** Within a short time (after a particular point of time specified or implied), before long, quickly; without delay, forthwith, straightway. **2.** Early, betimes; before the time specified or referred to is much advanced ME. **b.** At an early stage, date, period 1615. **3.** *So s.*, so quickly, so early ME. **4.** *As* or *so s. as*: **a.** At the very time or moment when, whenever ME. **b.** As quickly, as early (as) 1548. **c.** As readily, as willingly, (as) 1590. **d.** With as much reason or probability 1591.

1. Small lights are s. blown out, huge fires abide SHAKS. S. I must drink the poison 1875. S. afterwards a direct charge of plagiarism was made 1875. **2.** I went s. To bedde CHAUCER. Late and s., Getting and spending, we lay waste our powers WORDSW. **3.** What, all so soone asleepe? SHAKS. **4. a.** This Law..fell into disuse as soon as made 1710. **c.** For he'll abuse a stranger just as s. as his best friend SHERIDAN. **d.** *Two Gent.* II. vii. 19. Hence **Soo·nness.**

Soon (sūn), *a.* late ME. [attrib. use of prec.] Taking place, coming about, happening, etc., soon or quickly; early, speedy.

Soone sowing sometime deceaveth 1546.

Sooner (sū·nəɹ), *adv.* ME. [comp. of SOON *adv.*; see -ER[3].] Earlier, more readily; preferably, rather (1457). So **Soo·nest** superl. ME.

Phr. *Sooner or later*, at some time or other (usu. with ref. to the future). *With the soonest*: †**a.** Rather, or very early. †**b.** As soon as possible. **c.** *dial.* Too soon. *At (the) soonest*, at the earliest.

Soot (sut), *sb.*[1] [OE. *sōt* = MLG. *sōt* (G. dial. *sott*), MDu. *soet*, (also mod. dial.) *zoet*, ON. *sót* :– Gmc. **sōtam* 'that which settles', f. IE. **sōd-* **sĕd-* SIT. For the standard pronunc., cf. *book, shook*; for the dial. (sʊt) cf. *blood, flood*.] **1.** A black carbonaceous substance or deposit consisting of fine particles formed by the combustion of coal, wood, oil, or other fuel. **2.** With *a* and *pl.* **a.** A particular kind of soot 1601. **b.** A flake of soot; a smut 1906.

1. *fig.* Al sugre and hony, al minstralsy..ben but s. and galle in comparison T. USK.

†**Soot,** *a.*, *adv.*, and *sb.*[2] [OE. *swōt* var. of *swēte* SWEET *a.*, infl. by *swōte* adv.] **A.** *adj.* Sweet –1614.

As þe fayre and swoote rose spryngeth amonge þe thornes 1430.

B. *sb.* That which is sweet; a person of sweet disposition –1682. **C.** *adv.* Sweetly –1579.

Soot (sut), *v.* 1602. [f. SOOT *sb.*[1]] **1.** *trans.* To smear, smudge, or foul with soot; to cover with or as with soot. **2.** To sprinkle or manure with soot 1707.

2. Part was dunged; part, sooted 1778.

Sooterkin (sū·təɹkin). Now *rare.* 1530. [In sense 1 app. – early Du. or Flem. **soetekijn*, f. *soet* sweet. In sense 2 perh. f. SOOT *sb.*[1]] †**1.** Sweetheart, mistress. **2.** An imaginary kind of afterbirth formerly attributed to Dutch women 1658. **b.** *transf.* Applied to persons; sometimes = Dutchman 1680. **c.** Applied to literary compositions, etc., of a supplementary or imperfect character 1668.

2. There goes a Report of the Holland Women, that together with their Children, they are delivered of a S., not unlike to a Rat, which some imagine to be the Off-spring of the Stoves 1658. **c.** Fruits of dull Heat, and Sooterkins of Wit POPE.

Sooth (sūþ), *sb. arch.* [OE. *sōþ* = OS. *sōð*, f. the adj.; see next.] **I.** Without article. Truth, verity. Also *personif.*

Phrases *S. to say. To speaks s. In s. In good* or *very s.* (also with ellipsis of *in*). *By my, your*, etc. *s.* (also with ellipsis of *by*).

II. With article (or pronoun). **1.** *The s.*, the truth; the real or actual facts, circumstances, etc. Freq. with the verbs *say, speak, tell*, etc. OE. †**2.** A true thing or saying; a truth –1641. †**3.** Soothsaying; prognostication –1582.

1. He goth ful neigh the soth CHAUCER. To say the s.,..My people are with sickness much enfeebled SHAKS. **3.** Time..taught me..: The soothe of byrds by beating of their wings SPENSER.

†**III.** assoc. w. senses of SOOTHE *v.*: Blandishment, flattery; a smooth or plausible word or speech. Also *personif.* –1609.

When *signior* s. here does proclaime peace, He flatters you, makes warre vpon your life SHAKS.

Sooth (sūþ), *a. arch.* [OE. *sōþ* = OS. *sōð*, ON. *sannr, saðr* :– Gmc. **sanþaz* :– IE. **sontos*, rel. to Goth. **sunjis* true :– IE. **sn̥tyós* (cf. Skr. *satyás*).] †**1.** True, veritable, real, genuine –ME. **2.** True; in accordance with truth; not false or fictitious OE. **3.** Of persons, etc.: Telling or speaking the truth; truthful. Also const. *in* (speech, etc.), *of* (one's word). ME. **4.** *poet.* Soothing, soft; smooth. KEATS.

2. If thy speech be s. SHAKS. **3.** Melibœus.., The soothest Shepherd that ere pip't on plains MILT. **4.** Jellies soother than the creamy curd KEATS. Hence **Soo·th-ly** *adv.* (now *arch.*); †**-ness** –1587.

Sooth (sūþ), *adv.* Now *arch.* and *rare.* [OE. *sōþe*, f. the adj.; see prec.] Truly; truthfully; in truth.

And s., men say that he was not the sonne Of mortall Syre SPENSER.

Soothe (sūð), *v.* [OE. (*ġe*)*sōþian*, f. *sōþ* SOOTH *a.*] †**1.** *trans.* To prove or show (a fact, statement, etc.) to be true; to verify, demonstrate –1588. †**2.** To declare (a statement) to be true; to uphold as the truth; to corroborate, support –1616. †**b.** To maintain or put forward (a lie or untruth) as being true –1616. †**3.** To support, or back *up*, (a person) in a statement or assertion –1623. †**4.** To confirm, encourage, or humour (a person) *in* something by expressing assent or approval. Also with *up*. –1705. †**5.** To blandish, cajole, or please (a person) by agreement or assent; to flatter in this way; to humour. Also with *up*. –1814. †**6.** To smooth or gloss over (an offence, etc.). Also with *up*. –1645. **7.** To render (an animal, a person, the feelings) calm or quiet; to mollify or appease 1697. **8.** To bring to a calm or composed condition; to affect in a tranquillizing and agreeable manner 1742. **9.** To reduce the force or intensity of (a passion, pain, etc.); to allay, assuage, mitigate, etc. 1711. **10.** *absol.* To have or exercise a soothing or tranquillizing influence 1728.

5. Like shrill-tongued tapsters answering every call, Soothing the humour of fantastic wits SHAKS. **6.** 3 *Hen. VI.* III. iii. 175. **7.** *transf.* The loveliness of heaven Soothes the unquiet sea SHELLEY. **8.** Poetry of a certain kind soothed him 1891. **9.** An intimate Friend..will..s. and asswage their secret Resentments ADDISON. **10.** 'Twill s. to be where thou hast been BYRON. Hence **Soo·ther,** one who or that which soothes. **Soo·thingly** *adv.*

Soothfast (sū·þfɑst), *a.* and *adv. arch.* [OE. *sōþfæst*; see SOOTH *sb.* and FAST *a.*] **A.** *adj.* **1.** Of persons: Veracious, truthful; true, faithful, loyal. **2.** In accordance with the truth; true, veracious; †just, equitable OE. †**3.** Truly or actually that which the name implies; true, real, veritable, very. Said esp. of God or of the persons of the Trinity. –1470.

1. Edie was ken'd to me..for a true, loyal, and s. man SCOTT. **2.** It was a southfast sentence..That hastye men shal never lacke much woe 1559.

B. *adv.* Soothfastly OE. Hence **Soo·th-fastly** *adv.*, **-ness.** Now *arch.*

Soothsay (sū·þsēⁱ), *sb.* 1549. [Back-formation from SOOTHSAYER or SOOTHSAYING.] †**1.** A true or wise saying; a proverb, saw. LATIMER. **2.** A prediction, prognostication, or prophecy; an omen or portent 1582. **b.** Without article. (Good) omen; soothsaying, prognostication (*rare*) 1590.

2. Shewes, visions, sooth-sayes, and prophesies SPENSER. **b.** God turne the same to good s. SPENSER. So **Soo·thsay** *v. intr.* to make predictions; to prophesy (*rare*).

Soothsayer (sū·þsēⁱ:əɹ). ME. [f. SOOTH *sb.* or *a.* + SAYER *sb.*[1]] †**1.** One who speaks the truth –1642. **2.** One who claims or pretends to the power of foretelling future events; a predicter, prognosticator. late ME. **3.** An insect of the family *Mantidæ*; a mantis 1855.

Soothsaying (sū·þsē:iŋ), (*vbl.*) *sb.* 1535. [f. SOOTH *sb.* or *a.* + SAYING *vbl. sb.* Cf. OE. *sōþsecġan* tell the truth.] **1.** The practice of foretelling the future or the course of future events; prediction, prognostication. **2.** A prediction or prophecy 1535.

1. Soythsayenge, witchcraft, sorcery, and dreaminge is but vanyte COVERDALE *Ecclus.* 34:5. **2.** Hearkning to impious South-sayings 1653.

Sooty (su·ti), *a.* ME. [f. SOOT *sb.*[1] + -Y[1].] **1.** Foul or dirty with soot; covered or smeared with soot; full of soot. †**b.** Of the soul: Foul with sin –1680. †**c.** Of grain: Affected by smut; blackened DRYDEN. **2.** Resembling soot in colour; dusky or brownish black 1593. †**b.** *fig.* Black, dismal. –1673. **3.** Of colours: Having a dark, dusky, blackish, or dirty tinge 1597. **4.** Consisting of soot; of the nature of soot 1651.

1. In thunder Jove his s. bolt down threw HOBBES. **2.** Not like that s. devil of Othello's BYRON. The S. Tern (*Sterna fuliginosa*) inhabits the bays and gulfs of the Mediterranean 1870. **3.** By the heat of the sun the skin is scorched, and so acquires a s. hue JOHNSON. Hence **Soo·tied** *pa. pple.* made s., blackened. **Soo·tily** *adv.* **Soo·tiness.**

Sop (sǫp), *sb.* [Late OE. *sopp*, corresp. to MLG. *soppe*, OHG. *sopfa* bread and milk, ON. *soppa* (a foreign word), prob. f. wk. grade of the base of OE. *sūpan* SUP *v.*[1]] **1.** A piece of bread or the like dipped or steeped in water, wine, etc., before being eaten or cooked. **b.** Const. *in* (or †*of*) the liquid in which the bread, etc., is dipped or steeped. late ME. **c.** A dish composed of soaked bread 1845. **2.** *transf.* and *fig.* †**a.** A thing of small value –1526. †**b.** Used of persons in respect of some pervading quality or property –1605. **c.** = MILKSOP 1625. **d.** A person or thing thoroughly soaked or steeped in some way 1594. **e.** Something given to appease or pacify the recipient; a bribe (see CERBERUS) 1665. **3.** A copious collection or accumulation of some liquid; soppy or soaked condition 1700.

1. A s., in honey steep'd DRYDEN. **b.** Thanne he taketh a sope in fyne clarree CHAUCER. **2. b.** *Lear* II. ii. 35. **d.** The bounded Waters Should..make a soppe of all this solid Globe SHAKS. **e.** This bill.. is a s. given to the priests 1845. **4.** A great pool and s. of blood HAWTHORNE.

Sop (sǫp), *v.* [OE. *soppian* (thereafter not till XVI), f. the sb.] **1.** *trans.* To dip, soak, or steep (bread, etc.) in some liquid. Also *absol.* **b.** To drench with moisture; to soak; also *fig.*, to intoxicate 1682. **2.** *intr.* **a.** To be, or become, soaking wet 1831. **b.** Of moisture: To soak *in* or *through* 1844. **3.** *trans.* To propitiate; to bribe CARLYLE.

2. b. The water just sops through the turf 1894. **3.** Danton and needy corruptible Patriots are sopped with presents of cash CARLYLE. Hence **So·pper,** one who sops (*rare*).

Soph (sǫf). *colloq.* 1661. [abbrev. of SOPHISTER and SOPHOMORE.] **1.** = SOPHISTER 3. (In early use also at Oxford.) **2.** *U.S.* = SOPHOMORE 1 b. 1778.

‖**Sophia** (sǫ·fiă). 1649. [L. – Gr. σοφία, f. σοφός wise.] Wisdom, knowledge; *spec.* the Divine Wisdom (freq. personified).

Sophic (sǫ·fik), *a.* 1709. [– Gr. σοφικός, f. σοφία wisdom.] †**1.** Obtained by some secret process. †**2.** Conveying, or full of, wisdom; learned –1773. **3.** Pertaining to knowledge or speculation 1898. So **So·phical** *a.* 1601. **So·phically** *adv.*

Sophism (sǫ·fiz'm). Also †**sophim(e.** [ME. *sophime, -eme* – OFr. *sophime* (mod. *sophisme*) – L. *sophisma* – Gr. σόφισμα clever device, trick, argument, f. σοφίζεσθαι devise, f. σοφός wise, clever; see -ISM.] A specious but fallacious argument, either used deliberately in order to deceive or mislead, or employed as a means of displaying ingenuity in reasoning. **b.** Without article: Sophistry 1768.

But no s. is too gross to delude minds distempered by party spirit MACAULAY. **b.** All that s. and equivocation wherewith it has been..overclouded 1768.

Sophist (sǫ·fist). 1542. [– L. *sophista, sophistes* – Gr. σοφιστής, f. σοφίζεσθαι become wise or learned; see prec., -IST.] **1.** In ancient Greece, one specially engaged in the pursuit or communication of knowledge; *esp.* one who gave instruction in intellectual and ethical matters in return for payment. **2.** A wise or learned man 1614. **3.** One who makes use of fallacious arguments; a specious reasoner 1581.

1. The very Sophists themselves..have declar'd him no S., but a Philosopher BENTLEY. **3.** Thou art and thou remain'st a s., liar 1871. *attrib.* I laugh..At the s. schools EMERSON.

Sophister (sǫ·fistəɹ). late ME. [– OFr. *sophistre* – L. *sophista*; see -ISTER.] †**1.** = SOPHIST 1. –1710. **2.** = SOPHIST 3. late ME. **3.** At Cambridge, a student in his second or third year. Now *Hist.* 1574. **4.** At Trinity College, Dublin, a student in his third or fourth year 1841.

Sophistic (sŏfi·stik), *a.* and *sb.* 1549. [– (O)Fr. *sophistique* or L. *sophisticus*, f. *sophista*; see SOPHIST, -IC.] **A.** *adj.* **1.** Of persons: Given to the use or exercise of sophistry. **2.** Of or pertaining to sophistry or sophists; of the nature of sophistry 1591. **b.** Pertaining to, characteristic of, the ancient sophists 1835.

2. A mystery indeed in their S. Subtilties, but in Scripture a plain Doctrin MILT.

B. *sb.* **1.** Sophistic argument or speculation as a subject of instruction. Also **Sophi·stics.** 1862. **2.** Sophistry, deceptiveness 1868.

Sophistical (sŏfi·stikăl), *a.* 1483. [f. as prec.; see -ICAL. Cf. med. L. *sophisticalis*, perh. partly the source.] **1.** = prec. A. †**2.** Employed for the purpose of adulteration or deception –1680.

1. He is fluent and s.,—a sure token of feeble wisdom 1863. So **Sophi·stically** *adv.* late ME.

Sophisticate (sŏfi·stikĕt), *ppl. a.* late ME. [– med.L. *sophisticatus*, pa. pple. of *sophisticare*; see next, -ATE[2].] = SOPHISTICATED *ppl. a.*

Sophisticate (sŏfi·stikeⁱt), *v.* late ME. [– *sophisticat-*, pa. ppl. stem of med.L. *sophisticare* tamper with, adulterate, quibble, f. L. *sophisticus*; see SOPHISTIC *a.*, -ATE[3].] **1.** *trans.* To mix (commodities) with some foreign or inferior substance; to adulterate. Now somewhat *rare*. **b.** To deal with in some artificial way (*rare*) 1611. **c.** To render artificial; to convert *into* something artificial 1796. **2.** To corrupt or spoil by admixture of some baser principle or quality; to render less genuine or honest 1604. **3.** To corrupt, pervert, mislead (a person, the understanding, etc.) 1597. **4.** To falsify by misstatement or by unauthorized alteration 1598. **5.** *intr.* To practise sophistication 1664.

1. b. His hair, never sophisticated by a comb,.. resembled dark sea-weed 1831. **2.** It is the manner of the world..to s. ever the best things with hypocrisy 1626. **3.** It alwaies behoueth men to take good heede, lest affection..s. the true and sincere iudgement 1597. **4.** Thou..shalt testifie.. What now thy shame-lesse lips s. 1598. Hence **Sophi·sticator,** one who sophisticates or adulterates.

Sophisticated (sŏfi·stikeⁱtĕd), *ppl. a.* 1603. [f. prec. + -ED[1].] **1.** Mixed with some foreign substance; adulterated; not pure or genuine 1607. **2.** Altered from, deprived of, primitive simplicity or naturalness; rendered artificial or wordly-wise 1603. **3.** Falsified in a greater or less degree 1672.

3. I love not a s. truth, With an allay of lye in 't DRYDEN.

Sophistication (sŏfistikēⁱ·ʃən). late ME. [– OFr. *sophistication* or med.L. *sophisticatio, -on-*, f. *sophisticat-*; see SOPHISTICATE *v.*, -ION.] **1.** The employment of sophistry; the process of investing with specious fallacies or of misleading by means of these; falsification. **b.** A sophism, a quibble, a fallacious argument 1491. **2.** Disingenuous alteration or perversion *of* something 1564. **3. a.** An adulterated article. **b.** A substance used in adulteration. late ME. **4.** Adulteration (of commodities, etc.) 1540. **5.** The state or quality of being sophisticated.

1. If you asked her opinion upon any subject you got it, without s. 1882. **2.** The s. of the human intellect formed..language HAWTHORNE. **4.** Food free from s. 1871.

Sophistry (sǫ·fistri). ME. [– OFr. *sophistrie* (mod. *-erie*) or med.L. *sophistria*; see SOPHIST, -RY.] **1.** Specious but fallacious reasoning; employment of arguments which are intentionally deceptive. **b.** A sophism 1673. **2.** The use or practice of specious reasoning as an art or dialectic exercise. late ME. †**3.** Cunning, trickery, craft –1657. **4.** The type of learning characteristic of the ancient sophists; the profession of a Sophist 1837.

1. The parson's cant, the lawyer's s. POPE. **4.** Euripides was nursed in the lap of s. 1837.

Sophoclean (sǫfŏklī·ăn), *a.* 1649. [f. L. *Sophocleus* – Gr. Σοφόκλειος, f. Σοφοκλῆς, -κλέης; see -AN.] Of or pertaining to, characteristic of, Sophocles, the Athenian tragic poet, or his works, style, etc.

Sophomore (sǫ·fŏmōᵊɹ). Now *U.S.* Also **sophimore.** 1688. [Earlier (1653) *sophumer*, f. *sophum, sophom*, obs. vars. of SOPHISM, + -ER[1].] **1.** A student of the second year: †**a.** At Cambridge –1795. **b.** In American universities and colleges 1726. **2.** *attrib.*, passing into adj., as *s. class, year*, etc. 1778.

1. a. The Freshman's year being expired, the next distinctive appellation conferred is A Soph Mor 1795. Hence **Sophomo·ric, -al** *adjs.*, *U.S.*, of or pertaining to, befitting or resembling, characteristic of, a s.; hence, pretentious, bombastic; immature, crude, superficial.

‖**Sophora** (sofōᵊ·ră). 1753. [mod.L. (Linn.).] *Bot.* A genus of leguminous trees, shrubs, or plants, characterized by having odd-pinnate leaves and racemose or paniculate flowers, many species of which are cultivated for their ornamental properties; a tree of this genus.

Sophy (sōᵘ·fi). Now *Hist.* or *arch.* 1539. [– Pers. *ṣafī*, surname of the ruling dynasty of Persia from *c* 1500 to 1736, derived from the Arabic epithet *ṣafī-ud-dīn* 'pure of religion', given to an ancestor of the founder of the dynasty.] **1.** A former title or designation of the supreme ruler of Persia; the Shah. Also *Grand S.* **2.** With *a* and *pl.* A Persian monarch or king 1606. **b.** *transf.* A ruler; a great person 1599.

Sopite (soᵘpəi·t), *v.* Now *rare.* 1542. [– *sopit-*, pa. ppl. stem of L. *sopire* deprive of sense or consciousness, f. *sopor* (see next).] **1.** *trans.* To put or lull to sleep; to render drowsy, dull, or inactive. Also *transf.* (with ref. to the mental or moral faculties). **2.** To put an end to, to settle (a dispute, question, etc.) in some way. Also, to pass over or suppress (something discreditable). 1628.

2. A meeting of the bishops..about sopiting.. the controversies of this present time 1628. So **Sopi·te** *pa. pple.* (*rare*) put to sleep; settled. †**Sopi·tion,** the action of sopiting.

Sopor (sōu·pǫɹ). 1658. [– L. *sopor*, rel. to *somnus* sleep.] **1.** A deep, lethargic, or unnatural sleep or state of sleep. In later use *Path.* 1675. †**2.** *fig.* A state of mental or moral lethargy or deadness –1693.

Soporiferous (sōupŏri·fĕrəs, sǫp-), *a.* Now *rare.* 1590. [f. L. *soporifer* + -OUS; see prec., -FEROUS.] †**1.** Of a disease, morbid state, etc.: Characterized by unnatural or excessive sleep; soporose; lethargic –1681. **2.** = next A 1. 1601. †**3.** = next A 3. –1624.

2. S. Medecines applyed unto them, provoke sleep BACON. Hence **Sopori·ferous-ly** *adv.*, **-ness.**

Soporific (sōupŏri·fik, sǫp-), *a.* and *sb.* 1690. [f.L. *sopor*; see SOPOR, -FIC. Cf. Fr. *soporifique.*] **A.** *adj.* **1.** Inducing or tending to induce sleep; causing a person to sleep or slumber. **2.** Of the nature of, characterized by, belonging to, sleep or sleepiness 1754. **3.** Drowsy, sleepy, somnolent 1841.

1. Its [opium's] s. or anodyne virtues LOCKE. I thought of all sleepy sounds and all s. things SOUTHEY. **2.** The s. tendencies of..a portion of the congregation 1896.

B. *sb.* A substance, esp. a medicament, which induces sleep 1746.

Soporose (sōu·pŏrōus, sǫ·p-). *rare.* 1710. [f. L. *sopor* + -OSE[1].] *Med.* Of diseases, states, etc.: Marked or characterized by morbid sleep or stupor. So **So·porous** *a.* 1684.

Sopping (sǫ·piŋ), *ppl. a.* 1866. [f. SOP *v.* + -ING[2].] Soaking wet; also *advb.*

Soppy (sǫ·pi), *a.* 1611. [f. SOP *sb.* or *v.* + -Y[1].] †**1.** Full of or containing sops. **2.** Soaked or saturated with water or rain; soft with moisture; drenched, sodden 1823. **3.** Of the season or weather: Very wet or rainy 1872. **4.** Sloppy, slovenly 1899. **5.** *slang.* 'Soft', foolishly sentimental.

2. It [Yarmouth] looked rather spongey and s. DICKENS. Hence **So·ppiness.**

Soprano (sŏprā·no), *sb.* (and *a.*). *Pl.* **sopranos,** also **soprani.** 1730. [– It. *soprano*, f. *sopra* above.] *Mus.* **1.** The highest singing voice in women and boys, having a compass from about middle C to two octaves above it; the quality or range of this voice. **b.** A part for or sung by such a voice 1801. **2.** A singer having a soprano voice; one who sings the soprano part 1738. **3.** *attrib.* or as *adj.* **a.** Of persons: Having a soprano voice; singing a soprano part 1730. **b.** *transf.*, as *s. cornet*, *trombone* 1856. **4.** Of or belonging to the soprano 1801.

4. **S. clef,** the C-clef upon the first line of the treble stave. Hence **Sopra·nist,** a s. singer.

Sops-in-wine. 1573. [See SOP *sb.* Cf. Fr. *soupe-en-vin.*] †**1.** The clove-pink or gillyflower –1625. **2.** A variety of apple 1764.

Sora (sōə·ră). 1705. [prob. native name.] The Carolina rail (*Porzana carolina*). Also *attrib.* with *gallinule, rail.*

Sorabian (sŏrēi·biăn), *a.* and *sb.* 1788. [f. med.L. *Sorabi*; see SORB[2].] **A.** *adj.* Of or belonging to the Slavonic race formerly dominant in Saxony; Sorbian. **B.** *sb.* A Sorb; the Sorbian language.

†**So·rance.** 1440. [f. SORE *a.*[1] + -ANCE, prob. after GRIEVANCE 4.] A sore, or a morbid state producing a sore, in an animal, esp. in a horse –1749.

Sorb[1] (sǫɹb). 1530. [– Fr. *sorbe* or L. *sorbum* service-berry, *sorbus* service-tree.] **1.** The fruit of the service-tree (*Pyrus domestica*); a service-berry. **2. a.** The service-tree 1555. **b.** = SERVICE-TREE 2. 1777. **c.** The rowan-tree 1796. Hence **So·rbin** *Chem.*, = SORBITOL.

Sorb[2] (sǫɹb). Also **Sorbe.** 1843. [– G. *Sorbe*, var. of *Serbe* SERB.] **1.** A member of the Slavonic race inhabiting Lusatia in the east of Saxony; a Wend. **2.** The language spoken by this race 1862. Also **So·rbian** 1836.

So·rb-a:pple. 1548. [– G. *sorbapfel*, older LG., Flem. *sorbappel*; see SORB[1].] The fruit of the service-tree, or the tree itself.

Sorbate (sǫ·ɹbĕt). 1823. [f. SORBIC *a.* + -ATE[1] 1 c.] *Chem.* A salt of sorbic acid.

Sorbefacient (sǫɹbĭfēi·ʃ'ĕnt), *a.* and *sb.* 1847. [f. L. *sorbēre* absorb + -FACIENT.] **A.** *adj.* Causing or promoting absorption. **B.** *sb.* A substance or preparation causing absorption.

Sorbet (sǫ·ɹbĕt). 1585. [– Fr. *sorbet* – It. *sorbetto* – Turk. *şerbet* – Arab. *šarbāt*, pl. drinks; cf. SHERBET.] **1.** = SHERBET. **2.** A variety of sweetmeat or ice 1864.

Sorbic (sǫ·ɹbik), *a.* 1815. [f. SORB[1] + -IC.] *Chem.* Contained in or derived from the berries of the mountain-ash, *Sorbus* (now *Pyrus*) *aucuparia.* Chiefly in *s. acid.*

Sorbile (sǫ·ɹbəil), *a.* Now *rare.* 1620. [– L. *sorbilis*, f. *sorbēre* to drink; see -ILE. Cf. Fr. †*sorbile.*] That may be drunk or supped; liquid.

Sorbite (sǫ·ɹbəit). 1867. [f. SORB[1] + -ITE[1] 4 a.] *Chem.* = SORBITOL. Hence **Sorbi·tic** *a.*

Sorbitol (sǫ·ɹbitǫl). 1895. [f. SORBITE + -OL.] *Chem.* An unfermentable saccharine principle found in the berries of the mountain-ash.

Sorbonist (sǫ·ɹbŏnist). Also †**-onnist.** 1560. [– Fr. *Sorboniste*; see next, -IST.] A doctor or student at the Sorbonne.

Sorbonne (sǫɹbǫ·n, Fr. sorbon). 1560. [– Fr. *Sorbonne*, f. the place-name *Sorbon* in the Ardennes.] A theological college at Paris founded by Robert de Sorbon early in the 13th c.; the faculty of theology in the old University of Paris, of great importance down to the 17th c.; later, (the seat of) the university of Paris.

‖**Sorbus** (sǫ·ɹbŏs). 1706. [L. Cf. SORB[1].] A Linnæan genus (now placed under *Pyrus*) including the service-tree, mountain-ash, etc.; a tree of this genus.

Sorcerer (sǫ·ɹsərəɹ). 1526. [Extension, with -ER[1] 3, of late ME. *sorser* – (O)Fr. *sorcier* :- Rom. *sortiarius, f. *sors, sort-* lot, SORT *sb.*[1]; see -ER[2].] One who practises sorcery; a wizard, magician.

The sorserar Elemas..withstode them TINDALE *Acts* 13:8.

Sorceress (sǫ·ɹsərĕs). late ME. [– AFr. *sorceresse*, fem. of *sorc(i)er*; see prec., -ESS[1].] A female sorcerer; a witch. **b.** In playful use 1800.

Sorcerous (sǫ·ɹsərəs), *a.* 1546. [f. SORCERER + -OUS.] **1.** Of the nature of, pertaining to or connected with, sorcery. **2.** Dealing in or exercising sorcery 1550. Hence **So·rcerously** *adv.*

Sorcery (sǫ·ɹsəri). ME. [– OFr. *sorcerie*, f. *sorcier*; see SORCERER, -ERY.] **1.** The use of magic or enchantment; the practice of magic arts; witchcraft. **b.** *pl.* Particular forms or instances of this ME. **2.** *transf.* and *fig.* 1576.

1. By enchauntement and sorssery she hath ben the destroyer of many good knyghtes MALORY. **2.** What drugs, what sorceries..doe our curious Dames vse to inlarge our withered beauties? 1592.

‖**Sordes** (sǫ·ɹdīz). 1640. [L. (pl., rare in sing.) filth, etc., rel. to *sordēre* be dirty or foul. Construed either as sing. or pl.] **1.** Dirt, filth; foul or feculent matter; refuse or rubbish removed or separated by or during the treatment, manufacture, or working of something. **2.** Filthy or feculent matter attaching to, or collecting on or in, the bodies of persons or animals 1670. **b.** Impure matter collecting about the teeth, gums, etc.; *spec.* in *Path.*, the foul crusts formed upon the teeth and lips in typhoid or other fevers 1746.

Sordid (sǫ·ɹdid), *a.* 1597. [– Fr. *sordide* or L. *sordidus*, f. *sordēre* be dirty; see -ID[1].] **1.** *Path.* **a.** Of suppurations, etc.: Corrupt, foul, repulsive; of the nature of sordes. **b.** Of an ulcer, wound, etc.: Yielding or discharging matter of this kind 1597. **2.** Dirty, foul, filthy; in later use, mean and squalid 1611. †**3.** Of persons (or animals): Dirty or sluttish in habits or appearance –1712.

2. Their houses..within are poore and s. 1634. Tattered raiment, and all the outward signs of s. misery 1850. **3.** The Person he chanced to see was ..an old s. blind Man ADDISON.

II. †**1.** Of a coarse, gross, or inferior character or nature; menial –1751. **2.** Of actions, habits, etc.: Of a low, mean, or despicable character; marked by or proceeding from ignoble motives, esp. of self-interest or monetary gain 1611. **b.** Low, coarse, rough 1668. **3.** Of persons, their character, etc.: Inclined to what is low, mean, or ignoble; *esp.* moved by mercenary motives; influenced only by material considerations 1636.

2. His courage, his abilities,..had made him, in spite of his s. vices, a favourite with his brethren in arms MACAULAY. **3.** He s. is, who..dies wrangling in a worthlesse cause 1636. Hence **Sordi·dity** (*rare*) sordidness 1584. **So·rdid-ly** *adv.*, **-ness.**

Sordine (sǫ·ɹdīn). 1591. [– It. *sordina*, *-ino*, f. *sordo* :- L. *surdus* deaf, mute; see SURD *a.*, -INE[1].] †**1.** A small pipe or mouthpiece placed in a trumpet or bugle in order to muffle or reduce the sound; a trumpet fitted with this –1611. **2.** *Mus.* = MUTE *sb.*[1] 4 a. 1776.

Sordor (sǫ·ɹdǫɹ). 1823. [f. SORDID, after *squalor, squalid.*] Physical or moral sordidness.

Sore (sōəɹ), *sb.*[1] [OE. *sār* = OFris., OS., OHG. *sēr* (Du. *zeer*, G. †*sehr*), ON. *sár*, Goth. *sair* :- Gmc. *sairam (-az).] †**1.** Bodily pain or suffering –1583. †**2.** Sickness, disease; a disease, ailment, or bodily affliction –1648. **3.** A bodily injury; a wound. *Obs.* exc. *dial.* OE. **4.** A place in an animal body where the skin or flesh is diseased or injured so as to be painfully tender or raw; a sore place, such as that caused by an ulcer OE. **5.** In fig. uses, esp. coupled with *salve* ME. †**6.** Mental suffering, pain, or trouble; grief, sorrow, anxiety, or the cause of this –1575.

4. Another [hound] licking of his wound, 'Gainst venom'd sores the only sovereign plaster SHAKS. **5.** That infectious soare of iealowsie GREENE.

Sore (sōəɹ), *sb.*[2] late ME. [subst. use of SORE *a.*[2] Cf. AL. *sourus* (XIII).] †**1.** *Venery.* A buck in its fourth year –1865. **2.** *Falconry.* A hawk in its second year. Also *transf.* 1600.

Sore (sōəɹ), *a.*[1] [OE. *sār* = OFris. *sēr, OS., OHG. *sēr* (Du. *zeer*, G. *sehr*), ON. *sárr* :- Gmc *sairaz (whence Finnish *sairas* sick, ill).] **I.** Now mainly *arch.* or *dial.* **1.** Causing or involving bodily pain; painful, grievous; distressing or severe in this respect. **2.** Causing, involving, or accompanied by mental pain, trouble, or distress OE. **b.** Of manifestations of grief: Bitter, painful ME. **3.** Involving great hardships, painful exertion, unusual difficulty, etc. OE. **b.** Of battle, etc.: Severe, fierce, hot. late ME. **4.** Pressing hardly upon one; difficult to bear or support 1500. **b.** In intensive use: Very great or serious 1555. **5.** Severe, stern, hard, or harsh 1526. **6.** Of a strong, severe, or violent character in respect of operation or effect 1449. †**7.** Strong, weighty, valid –1551. **8.** *dial.* = SORRY *a.* 4. 1825.

1. The Lord with his s. and great and strong sworde *Isa.* 27:1. **2. b.** They mourned with a great and very s. lamentation *Gen.* 50:10. **3.** Sleepe,..The death of each dayes Life, s. Labors Bath SHAKS. **b.** In that s. battel when so many dy'd MILT. **4.** Man is to man the sorest, surest ill YOUNG. **b.** Henry was now in s. want of money 1875. **6.** Soch a s. snowe & a frost 1556.

II. 1. Of parts of the body: In pain; painful, aching. Now *spec.*, having the skin broken or raw. OE. **b.** Of the eyes, throat, etc.: Painful through inflammation or other morbid condition. late ME. **2.** Of persons: Suffering pain (from wounds, disease, etc.). Also *absol.* ME. **3.** Afflicted with sorrow or grief; pained, distressed ME. **4.** Of persons or their feelings: Inclined to be irritated or grieved; irritable, sensitive 1694.

1. I'm tyr'd, my Bones are s. 1704. *A bear with a s. head*, used allusively for a type of sullen irritability, peevishness, or sensitiveness. **b.** May not honey's self be turn'd to gall..by marriage, and s. eyes? GRAY. *Clergyman's sore-throat*, chronic follicular pharyngitis 1898. **4.** Malice and hatred are..apt to make our minds s. and uneasy 1694. *S. point, spot*, a matter in respect of which one is easily annoyed or grieved. Hence **So·reness.**

Sore, *a.*[2] *Obs.* exc. *Hist.* late ME. [– AFr., OFr. *sor* (mod. *saur*), in med.L. *sorus*; see SORREL *a.*] **1.** *Falconry.* Applied to a hawk of the first year that has not moulted and still has its red plumage (now called a *red hawk*); hence applied to the plumage itself; occas. extended to other birds of prey, as the kite and eagle 1450. †2. Of a horse: Of a reddish-brown colour –1679.

Sore (sōᵊɹ), *v.* In mod. use *U.S.* ME. [f. SORE *a.*[1]] *trans.* To make sore; to give (physical or mental) pain to; †to wound.

Sore (sōᵊɹ), *adv.* Now chiefly *arch.* and *dial.* [OE. *sāre* = OFris. *sēre*, OS., OHG. *sēro* (Du. *zeer*, G. *sehr* greatly, very).] **1.** Severely, dangerously, seriously. **2.** With verbs of grieving, annoying, etc.: So as to cause mental pain or irritation; deeply, intensely OE. **3.** With great grief, distress, or perturbation of mind; in such a manner or to such an extent as to involve or manifest this. (Passing into a mere intensive.) OE. **4.** To a painful or distressing degree OE. **5.** With great exertion or effort; laboriously, toilsomely, hard ME. **b.** Severely 1483. **6.** Eagerly, earnestly ME. **7.** To a great extent; greatly, very much 1440.

1. Fast his blood was flowing; And he was s. in pain MACAULAY. **2.** It griev'd him s. COWPER. **3.** And the people..lift vp their voices, and wept s. *Judges* 21:2. **4.** The torrid Clime Smote on him s. besides MILT. **6.** Because thou s. longedst after thy fathers house *Gen.* 31:30. **7.** A shameless wight, S. given to revel and ungodly glee BYRON.

Soredi- (sŏrī·di), comb. form of SOREDIUM, as in **Sore·dial** *a.*, of the nature of, pertaining to, a soredium; **Sore·diate** *a.*, bearing or characterized by the presence of soredia; **Soredi(i)·ferous** *a.*, bearing soredia; caused by producing soredia; etc.

‖**Soredium** (sŏrī·diŏm). *Pl.* **-ia.** 1829. [mod.L., f. Gr. σωρός a heap.] *Bot.* A thallus-bud or cell in lichens. Usu. in *pl.*

So·re-head, *a.* and *sb.* 1862. [See SORE *a.*[1] II. 1.] **A.** *adj.* Irritable or out of temper 'like a bear with a sore head'; discontented, dissatisfied. **B.** *sb. U.S. political slang.* A dissatisfied or disappointed politician 1862.

Sorely (sōᵊ·ɹli), *adv.* [OE. *sārlīće*; see SORE *a.* and -LY[2].] In a manner involving pain, grief, distress, or oppression; hardly, severely (chiefly with words expressing injury, evil, or want) greatly, highly.

Sorghum (sǭ·ɹgŏm). Also †**sorgum.** 1597. [– mod.L. *sorghum* – It. *sorgo*, perh. :– Rom. **syricum* (cf. med.L. *sur(i)cum*) Syrian (sc. *gramen* grass).] **1. a.** The cereal plant known as Indian millet, Guinea-corn, durra, etc. (*Andropogon sorghum*, also called *Holcus sorghum* and *Sorghum vulgare*). **b.** The Chinese sugar-cane (*Andropogon saccharatus*). Usually *Sweet s.* 1859. **2.** A genus of grasses belonging to the tribe *Andropogoneæ* and including the species mentioned above; also, with *a* and *pl.*, a variety belonging to this genus 1842. **3.** *U.S.* A kind of molasses made from sorghum-juice 1883. So **So·rgho.**

‖**Sorites** (sŏrəi·tīz). 1551. [L. – Gr. σωρείτης, f. σωρός heap.] **1.** *Logic.* A series of propositions in which the predicate of each is the subject of the next, the conclusion being formed of the first subject and the last predicate. **b.** An instance of this type of syllogism. 1581.

In the GOCLENIAN form, the subject of each proposition is the predicate of the next, the conclusion being formed of the last subject and the first predicate.

2. *transf.* A series, chain, or accumulation *of* some thing or things 1664. **3.** A sophistical argument turning on the definition of a 'heap' 1768.

1. The S. can be resolved into as many simple syllogisms as there are middle terms between the subject and predicate of the conclusion 1838. Hence **Sori·tic, -al** *adjs.*

Sorn (sǭɹn), *v. Sc.* 1563. [f. SORREN.] †**1.** *trans.* To exact 'sorren' from –1589. **2.** *intr.* To take up free quarters or exact maintenance unjustifiably; to sponge *upon* 1575. So **So·rner,** a sponger 1449.

Sororal (sŏrōᵊ·răl), *a.* 1654. [f. L. *soror* sister + -AL[1].] **1.** By one's sister; on a sister's side (*rare*). **2.** That is a sister. LAMB. **3.** Of, pertaining to, or characteristic of a sister or sisters; sisterly 1854.

Sororicide[1] (sŏrǫ·risəid). 1656. [– L. *sororicida*, f. L. *soror* sister; see -CIDE 1.] One who kills his or her sister.

Sororicide[2] (sŏrǫ·risəid). 1727. [– late L. *sororicidium*, f. L. *soror*; see -CIDE 2.] The action of killing one's sister. Hence **Soro·ricidal** *a.*

Sorority (sŏrǫ·rĭti). 1532. [– med.L. *sororitas*, or f. L. *soror* + -ITY, after *fraternity*. Cf. Fr. †*sororité*.] **1.** A body or company of women united for some common object, esp. for devotional purposes. **2.** *U.S.* A women's society in a college or university 1900.

Sororize (sǫ·rŏrəiz), *v. rare.* 1875. [f. L. *soror* + -IZE, after *fraternize*.] *intr.* To associate *with* a person or persons as a sister or sisters; to form a sisterly friendship.

‖**Sorosis** (sŏrōᵘ·sis). 1831. [mod.L., f. Gr. σωρός a heap; see -OSIS.] **1.** *Bot.* A spike or raceme converted into a fleshy fruit by the cohesion in a single mass of the ovaria and floral envelopes. **2.** *U.S.* A woman's society or club.

Sorrel (sǫ·rĕl), *sb.*[1] late ME. [– OFr. *sorele, surele* (mod. dial. *surelle*), f. *sur* – Gmc. **sūraz* SOUR; see -EL.] **1.** One or other of certain small perennial plants belonging to the genus *Rumex*, characterized by a sour taste, and to some extent cultivated for culinary purposes; esp. the common wild species, *R. acetosa* 1440. **2.** The leaves of species of *Rumex* used in cookery or medicine, or as a salad; a decoction or drink made from one or other of these plants. late ME. †**3.** *S. de boys*, = WOODSORREL –1647. **4.** With distinguishing epithet: One or other of various plants of other genera in some way resembling sorrel 1753. **5.** *pl.* Species of sorrel; sorrel plants 1596. **6.** *Salt of s.*, binoxalate of potash 1800.

4. S., Indian or red, *Hibiscus sabdarifa* 1864. *Oxyria reniformis*..Mountain S. 1843.

Comb.: **s.-tree,** the sour-wood or elk-tree of N. America, *Oxydendron arboreum*.

Sorrel (sǫ·rĕl), *a.* and *sb.*[2] late ME. [– OFr. *sorel* adj., f. *sor* yellowish – Frankish **saur* dry; see -EL. So med.L. *sorellus* (XIII).] **A.** *adj.* Of a bright chestnut colour; reddish brown 1469.

Behind him there were horses, red, s., and white BIBLE (1884) *Zech.* 1:8.

B. *sb.* **1.** A horse of a bright chestnut colour; also as the name of a horse. late ME. **2.** A buck in its third year. Now *Obs.* or *Arch.* 1486. **3.** A sorrel or reddish-brown colour 1530.

Sorren (sǫ·rən). *Sc.* and *Ir.* Now *Hist.* ME. [– obs. Ir. *sorthan*, 'free quarters, living at free expense'. Cf. SORN *v.*] A service formerly required of vassals in Scotland and Ireland, consisting in giving hospitality to the superior or his men; a sum of money or other contribution given in lieu of this.

Sorrow (sǫ·roᵘ), *sb.* [OE. *sorh, sorg* = OFris. **sorge*, OS. *sorga* (Du. *zorg*), OHG. *sor(a)ga* (G. *sorge*), ON. *sorg*, Goth. *saurga*; Gmc., of unkn. origin.] **1.** Distress of mind caused by loss, suffering, disappointment, etc.; grief, deep sadness or regret; also, that which causes grief or melancholy; affliction, trouble. Occas. *personified.* **2.** With *a* and *pl.* An instance or cause of grief or sadness; an affliction or trouble OE. **b.** Applied to persons 1637. **3.** In phrases of imprecation or emphasis ME. **4.** The outward expression of grief; lamentation, mourning; *poet.*, tears ME.

1. A countenance more in s. then in anger SHAKS. S.,..the mother and daughter of melancholy BURTON. **2.** When sorrowes come, they come not single spies, But in Battaliaes SHAKS. *The Man of Sorrows*, Jesus Christ (after *Isa.* 53:3). **3.** S. on thee, and all the packe of you SHAKS. **4.** She nothing said but,..wept a rain Of sorrows at his words KEATS.

Comb., as *s.-blinded, -bound, -laden*, etc. Hence **So·rrowless** *a.* free from s.

Sorrow (sǫ·roᵘ), *v.* [OE. *sorgian*; cf. OS. *sorgon*, OHG. *sorgēn* (Du. *zorgen*, G. *sorgen*), beside ON. *syrgja* and Goth. *saurgan*; Gmc., f. the sb.] **1.** *intr.* To feel sorrow or sadness; to regret or grieve; also, to exhibit signs of grief, to mourn. **2.** *trans.* To think of with sorrow; to feel sorrow on account of; to lament ME. **3.** To give pain to; to grieve, make sorrowful ME.

1. The miserable change..Lament nor s. at SHAKS. I shall..So send them forth, though sorrowing, yet in peace MILT. **2.** The redde rose waxed..pale when the vyrgyn sorowed the dethe of her sonne 1450. **3.** The bitterness of her tone sorrowed him 1890. Hence **So·rrower,** one who sorrows; a mourner.

Sorrowful (sǫ·rŏfŭl), *a.* [OE. *sorhful*, of Gmc. range; see SORROW *sb.*, -FUL.] **1.** Full of or oppressed by sorrow or grief; sorrow-laden, grieved. Also *absol.* (chiefly *pl.*). **2.** Indicative or expressive of sorrow or grief ME. **3.** Distressing, lamentable, doleful OE. **4.** quasi- *adv.* Sorrowfully. late ME.

1. I rent my holy garmentes, and..sat me downe sorowfull & heuy COVERDALE 1 *Esdras* 8:71. **2.** Sorowfull blacke apparell 1565. **3.** Sounds and odours, s. Because they once were sweet SHELLEY. Hence **So·rrowful-ly** *adv.*, **-ness.**

Sorry (sǫ·ri), *a.* [OE. *sāriġ* = OS., OHG. *sērag* (G. dial. *sērich*) :– W.Gmc. **sairaȝ*, *-iȝ-*; f. **sairaz* SORE *sb.*[1]; see -Y[1]. The change of *ā* to *ō* and subsequent shortening have given the word an apparent connection with unrelated SORROW *sb.*] **1.** Pained at heart; distressed or sad; full of grief or sorrow. (In later use freq. expressing mere sympathy or apology, as in the phrase 'I'm sorry'.) †**2.** Expressive or suggestive of distress or sorrow –1567. †**3.** Causing distress or sorrow; painful, grievous, dismal –1605. **4.** Vile, wretched, mean, poor; of little account or value ME.

1. No soryer man in erth may dwel Than I 1430. I do not wonder that they are s. BURKE. **2.** A sory song we myght all synge CHAUCER. **3.** This is a s. sight SHAKS. **4.** One s. room in a miserable tavern 1716. One man, with a couple of s. horses HUME. The baron..grew fat and wanton, and a s. brute EMERSON. Hence **So·rrily** *adv.* **So·rriness** (now *rare*). **So·rryish** *a.* somewhat s.

†**Sort,** *sb.*[1] ME. [– (O)Fr. *sort* or L. *sors, sort-*, lot, share, fortune, etc.] Lot, fate, destiny; share, portion –1606.

Part is not to thee, nethir s., in this word WYCLIF *Acts* 8:21. Make a Lott'ry, And by deuice let blockish Aiax draw The s. to fight with Hector SHAKS.

Sort (sǭɹt), *sb.*[2] late ME. [– (O)Fr. *sorte* = It. *sorta* :– Rom. **sorta*, alt. of L. *sors, sort-* wooden voting tablet, lot, share, condition, (late) rank (AL. *sorta* sort, kind).] **I.** A (definite or specified) kind, species, variety, or description of persons or things. **1.** Preceded by *of*. **2.** Followed by *of*: A particular kind, etc., *of* thing(s or person(s 1526. **b.** Used collectively, after *kind of* (see KIND *sb.* II) esp. with *these* or *those* 1551. **3.** *ellipt.* or *absol.* **a.** A particular class, order, or rank of persons 1529; a kind, variety, etc., of thing(s 1523. **b.** *Typog.* One or other of the characters or letters in a fount of type. Usu. in *pl.* 1668. †**4.** Without article: Rank, class. MILT.

1. *Of a* (certain) *s.*, of a certain kind, etc.; The moment a topic of that solemn s. is started 1787. *Of* (various) *sorts*; Plays of all sorts ADDISON. †*Of s.*, of (high) quality or rank; Persons of good S. and Credit DE FOE. *Of a s.*, of the same kind or description (now *dial.*). *Of sorts*: (*a*) of different or various kinds (now *rare*); They [*sc.* bees] haue a King, and Officers of sorts SHAKS; (*b*) *colloq.* of a kind which is not very satisfactory; rather poor. *Something of the s.*, something similar to that previously indicated, mentioned or specified. *Nothing of the s.*, no such thing. **2.** A fair specimen of the s. of letter they ought not to write TROLLOPE. *All sorts of* (things or persons) = things or persons of all kinds or descriptions. All sorts of Ven'son DRYDEN. *A s. of* = something in the nature of. So *a* (or *some*) *s. of a...* *In a s. of way*, imperfectly. *No s. of..*, used as an emphatic neg. phrase to denote the complete absence of anything of the kind specified. *That* or *this s. of thing*, used to denote in a general way a thing, quality, etc., of a like or similar nature to that specified. **b.** These s. of details gave my poor father great delight 1798. Such s. of questions..are not merely innocent subtleties SYD. SMITH. **3. a.** All sorts and conditions that stood by..bore witness to the prophecy BROWNING. There's a shop of all sorts, that sells every thing HOOD. Phr. *A* (*bad, good*, etc.) *s.*, applied to a single person. (*colloq.*). *Out of sorts*: (*a*) not in the normal condition of good health or spirits; slightly unwell; (*b*) †out of or without certain kinds of articles or goods (*rare*).

II. †**1.** A number of persons associated together in some way; a band, company, group, or set of persons (or animals) –1612. **2.** A (great, good, etc.) number or lot of persons or things; a considerable body or quantity; a multitude. Now *dial.* 1475. †**3.** A (great, etc.) part or portion *of* a number of persons or things –1669.

1. †*In s.*, in a body or company. **2.** See what a s. of rebels are in arms MIDDLETON.

III. Manner, method, or way. *arch.* **1.** In phrases with *in* 1533. **2.** *After this, what*, etc., *s., after a* (..) *s.* 1551.

1. Phr. *In this, that, such, (the) like, what*, etc., *s.* (now *arch.*) *In good, honest*, etc. *s.* (now *rare*). *In* *some* or *a s.*, in a certain undefined or unknown way; to some extent or degree. †*In no s.*, in no way, to no extent, not at all. **2.** Captain Dampmartin.. who loves the Reign of Liberty, after a s. CARLYLE.

Sort (sǭɹt), *v.* ME. [– OFr. *sortir* or L. *sortiri* divide or obtain by lot, f. *sors, sort-* (see prec.); later f. the sb., or aphetic f. ASSORT.] **I. †1.** *trans.* To allot, apportion, or assign –1599. **†b.** To dispose, ordain, order (events). Also *absol.* (*rare*). –1596. **†2.** To arrive at, attain to, result in, or reach (an effect, end, etc.) –1656. **†3.** *intr.* Of events, etc.: To come about, to fall or turn out, in a certain way or with a certain result –1653. **†b.** To come to effect; to be successful (*rare*) –1626. **†4. a.** To come or attain *to* an end, conclusion, effect, etc. –1659. **b.** To end in coming or leading *to* a specified result –1624. **c.** To fall *to* a person as a right or duty (*rare*) –1677. **5.** *trans.* To answer or correspond to, to befit or suit. Now *rare.* 1587.

3. The Experiment sorted in this Manner BACON. **b.** It was tried in a Blowne Bladder..and it sorted not BACON. **5.** Well sorting your high place 1587.

II. 1. *trans.* To arrange (things, etc.) according to kind or quality, or after some settled order or system; to classify; to assort. Also *absol.* ME. **†b.** To separate or distinguish (*from* something else). *rare.* –1599. **2.** To place in a class or sort; to give a place to; to classify 1486. **3.** With *out*: To take *out*, remove, or separate (certain sorts from others) 1534. **b.** To choose or select in this way. Now *rare* or *Obs.* 1553. **c.** To arrange according to sort 1713. **4.** *refl.* **a.** To form sets or groups by some process of combination or separation 1570. **b.** To associate or consort *with* another or others. Now *dial.* 1579. **5.** To adapt, to fit, to make conformable *to* or *with* some thing or person. Now *rare* or *Obs.* 1561. **†6.** To choose or select (time, opportunity, etc.) as fitting or suitable –1634. **†b.** To choose (a thing or person) from others –1638. **7.** *Sc.* and *north.* **a.** (Also with *up.*) To arrange or put in order; to put to rights in some respect 1816. **b.** To deal effectively with (a person) by way of punishment, repression, etc. 1815.

1. Wee have sorted what papers I could at present find 1684. **2.** A bony, yellow, crab-like hand ..easy to s. with the square gaunt face GEO. ELIOT. **3.** They will s. out the good from the evil BURKE. **5.** My will is something sorted with his wish SHAKS. **6.** 1 *Hen. VI*, II. iii. 27. **b.** *Rom. & Jul.* IV. ii. 34. **7. b.** Bid them bring up the prisoner—I trow I'll s. him SCOTT.

III. 1. *intr.* To fit, suit, or agree; to be in harmony or conformity. Now *arch.* 1590. **†b.** Without const.: To be fitting; to accord; to be in place, to exist –1667. **2.** To associate, consort, go in company *with* others or *together*. Also with *among* and without const. Now *rare* or *dial.* 1592.

1. For diff'rent styles with diff'rent subjects s. POPE. **b.** Among unequals what societie Can s., what harmonie or true delight? MILT. **2.** A company, with whom I may not s., Approaches CARY. Hence **†So·rtable** *a.* suitable or appropriate; of a cargo, properly assorted. **†So·rtance,** agreement, correspondence. **So·rtment,** the action or process of sorting; an assortment.

Sorter (sǭ·ɹtəɹ). 1554. [f. prec. + -ER¹.] One who sorts, arranges, selects, or classifies; *esp.* a wool-sorter. **b.** *spec.* A letter-sorter 1700.

Sortie (sǭ·ɹti). 1795. [– Fr. *sortie*, fem. pa. pple. of *sortir* go out.] **1.** A dash or sally by a besieged garrison. Freq. in phr. *to make a s.* **2. a.** A sally-port. **b.** An outlet (of a river). 1848.

Sortilege (sǭ·ɹtilėdʒ). late ME. [– (O)Fr. *sortilège* – med.L. *sortilegium* sorcery, divination, f. L. *sortilegus* sorcerer, diviner, f. L. *sors, sort-* (SORT *sb.*²) + *legere* choose.] **1.** Divination by lots; †sorcery, magic, witchcraft. **2.** An act of this 1600.

2. A woman infamous for sortileges and for witcheries SCOTT. Hence **†Sortile·gious** *a.* of the nature of, relating to, or connected with s. **So·rtileger,** a diviner, fortune-teller. **So·rtilegy,** sortilege.

Sortition (sǫɹti·ʃən). 1597. [– L. *sortitio, -on-*, f. pa. ppl. stem of *sortiri*; see SORT *v.*, -ION.] **1.** The casting or drawing of lots; selection, choice, or determination by lot. **2.** With *a* and *pl.* An act or instance of determining by lot 1634.

‖**Sorus** (sōᵊ·rŏs). *Pl.* **sori** (sōᵊ·rəi). 1832. [mod.L. – Gr. σωρός a heap.] **1.** *Bot.* A cluster of capsules or spore-cases on the under surface of fern-leaves. **2.** A similar formation in algæ, lichens, or fungi 1842.

SOS (e:s,ōᵘ:e·s). 1910. [Arbitrary]. A wireless code-signal of extreme distress, used esp. by ships at sea. Also *transf.*

So so, so-so (sōᵘ·sōᵘ), *adv.* and *a.* 1530. [So *adv.*] **A.** *adv.* In an indifferent, mediocre, or passable manner or degree; indifferently, not quite satisfactorily.

Clo. Art rich? *Will.* Faith sir, so, so SHAKS. He said he had been but so so 1820.

B. *adj.* **1.** Indifferent, mediocre, of middling ity; neither very good nor very bad, but usu. inclining towards bad 1542. **2.** Of persons 1592.

1. Your white or Clarret Is but so so; he cares not greatly for it 1616. As in some Irish houses, where things are so so, One gammon of bacon hangs up for a show GOLDSM. *attrib.* You will..make but a so so Figure, as..a Husband 1767. **2.** Mrs. Harris—a so-so sort of woman 1775. Hence **So-so·-ish** *a.*

Soss, *sb.*¹ Now *dial.* 1691. [perh. imitative of the sound of lapping.] **1.** A sloppy mess or mixture; a dish of food having this character. **2.** A sloven 1611.

Soss (sǫs), *sb.*² Chiefly *dial.* 1718. [imit.] **1.** The sound made by a heavy, soft body falling upon or otherwise coming into contact with a surface; a heavy, awkward fall. Chiefly in the phr. *with a s.* **2.** The sound made by impact upon water 1885.

Soss, *v.* Now *dial.* and *Sc.* 1711. [Cf. prec.] **†1.** *trans.* To put *up* so as to rest softly. SWIFT. **†2.** *intr.* To move gently; to lounge –1723. **3.** To fall with a thud or heavy impact 1789. **4.** *trans.* To throw heavily 1855. So **Soss** *adv.* with a heavy fall or dull thud.

‖**Sostenuto** (sǫstĕnū·to), *a.* Abbrev. **sost.** 1724. [It., pa. pple. of *sostenere* SUSTAIN *v.*] **1.** Of music: To be sung or played in a sustained manner. **2.** Marked or characterized by being sustained or held on 1835.

Sot (sǫt), *sb.* and *a.* [Late OE. *sott* – med.L. *sottus* (c800), of unkn. origin; reinforced from (O)Fr. *sot.*] **A.** *sb.* **†1.** A foolish or stupid person; a blockhead, dolt –1745. **2.** One who dulls or stupefies himself with drinking; a soaker 1592.

1. The one is ever..a s., an ideot for any use that mankind can make of him MILT. **2.** A s., a beast, benumbed and stupefied by excess BERKELEY. Hence **†So·ttery,** a piece of foolishness or folly.

†B. *adj.* Foolish, stupid –1648.

Sot (sǫt), *v.* late ME. [f. prec., or aphetic f. ASSOT.] **1.** *trans.* **†a.** To render foolish or doltish; to besot –1700. **b.** With *away.* To waste or squander by sottish conduct 1746. **2.** *intr.* To play the sot; to drink to excess; to soak 1633.

1. b. I must..have destroyed my health and faculties by sotting away the evenings CHESTERF. **2.** Writers that s. over beer 1815. So **So·tted** *ppl. a.* rendered sottish or stupid; besotted.

Sotadean (sōᵘtădī·ăn), *a.* and *sb.* 1774. [f. L. *Sotadeus*, f. *Sotades*; see next.] = SOTADIC *a.*

Sotadic (sotæ·dik), *sb.* and *a.* 1645. [– L. *Sotadicus*, f. *Sotades*, Gr. Σωτάδης] **A.** *sb.* **1.** A satire after the manner of Sotades, an ancient Greek poet noted for the coarseness and scurrility of his writings. **2.** *Pros.* A catalectic tetrameter composed of ionics *a majore* 1830. **B.** *adj.* **1.** Characterized by a coarseness or scurrility like that of Sotades 1716. **2.** Palindromic 1814. **3.** *Pros.* (see A. 2.) 1830.

Soteriology (sotīᵊriǫ·lŏdʒi). 1864. [f. Gr. σωτηρία salvation + -LOGY.] *Theol.* The doctrine of salvation. Hence **Sote:riolo·gical** *a.* of or pertaining to s. or salvation.

Sothiac (sōᵘ·þiăk), *a.* 1834. [– Fr. *sothiaque*, f. as next + *-aque* -AC.] = next. So **Sothi·acal** *a.*

Sothic (sǫ·þik, sōᵘ·þik), *a.* 1828. [f. Gr. Σῶθις, an Egyptian name of Sirius, the dog-star; see -IC.] **1.** *S. cycle* or *period*, a period of 1460 full years, containing 1461 of the ancient Egyptian ordinary years. **2.** *S. year*, a year of 365¼ days, in contrast to the ordinary Egyptian year of 365 days 1828.

‖**Sotnia** (sǫ·tniă). 1863. [Russ. *sotnya* hundred, f. *sto* (gen. pl. *sot*), related to Skr. *çatam*, L. *centum*, OE. *hund.*] A squadron of Cossack cavalry. So ‖**So·tnik,** a commander of a s.; a local Cossack official 1799.

‖**Sottise** (sotīz). 1673. [Fr., f. *sot* SOT *a.*] A silly remark or saying; a foolish action.

Sottish (sǫ·tiʃ), *a.* 1566. [f. SOT *sb.* + -ISH¹.] **†1.** Foolish, doltish, stupid –1796. **2.** Given to, characterized or affected by, excessive drinking or coarse self-indulgence 1632.

1. How ignorant those s. pretenders to astrology are in their own concerns SWIFT. **2.** His face was sallow and s. 1871. Hence **So·ttish-ly** *adv.*, **-ness.**

‖**Sotto voce** (sǫ·to vō·tʃe), *adv.*, *a.*, and *sb.* 1737. [It. *sotto* under + *voce* voice.] **1.** In a subdued or low voice. **2.** *fig.* Quietly, privately. SCOTT. **3.** as *adj.* Uttered, etc., in an undertone 1809. **4.** as *sb.* A remark made in an undertone 1868.

‖**Sou** (sū). 1556. [Fr., sing. form deduced from *sous*, †*soux*, pl. of OFr. *sout* :– *solidus* (sc. *nummus* coin), subst. use of L. *solidus* SOLID *a.*; see SOLIDUS.] A French coin, formerly the twentieth part of a livre, now used to designate the five-centime piece.

‖**Soubise** (subīz). 1776. [From Charles de Rohan *Soubise* (1715–1787), French general and courtier.] **†1.** A kind of cravat. **2.** A kind of onion-sauce. (Often in Fr. form *Sauce S.*) 1822.

‖**Soubrette** (subrę·t). 1753. [Fr. – mod.Pr. *soubreto*, fem. of *soubret* coy, f. *soubra* (Pr. *sobrar* :– L. *superare* be above).] **1.** *Theatr.* A maidservant or lady's maid as a character in a play or opera, usually one of a pert, coquettish, or intriguing character; an actress or singer taking such a part. **2.** A lady's maid; a maidservant 1824.

‖**Soubriquet** (sū·brikēⁱ, ‖subrikę), *sb.* 1818. [Fr., older var. of *sobriquet.*] = SOBRIQUET.

‖**Soucar** (sau·kāɹ). 1785. [– Urdu (Hindi) *sāhūkār* great merchant.] A Hindu banker or moneylender.

The Indian Sowcar has..a notoriety hardly surpassed by that of the European Jew 1883. Hence **Sou·caring,** moneylending.

Souchong (sūʃǫ·ŋ). 1760. [– Chinese *siao chung* (Cantonese *siu chung*) small sort.] One of the finer varieties of black tea.

Soudan, Sudan (sudā·n). 1875. [Arab. *sūdān*, pl. of *aswad* black.] The part of Africa lying between the Sahara and the Equator. Hence **Soudane·se** *sb.* an inhabitant of the S. (also as *pl.*); *adj.* of or pertaining to the S.

‖**Souffle** (sufl'). 1879. [Fr.] *Path.* A murmuring or breathing sound.

‖**Soufflé** (sū·flēⁱ, sufle), *sb.* and *a.* 1813. [Fr., pa. pple. of *souffler* :– L. *sufflare*, f. *sub* under + *flare* blow.] **A.** *sb.* A light dish, either sweet or savoury, made by mixing materials with white of egg beaten up to a froth, and heating the mixture in an oven until it puffs up. **B.** *adj.* Of ceramic ware: Having liquid colour applied by means of blowing 1878.

‖**Souffleur** (suflō̈r). [Fr., f *souffler* blow.] A prompter.

Sough (sau, sɒf, Sc. sux), *sb.*¹ [Late ME. *swo(u)gh, swow*, f. *swoghe*, OE. *swōgan*; see SOUGH *v.*¹] **1.** A rushing or murmuring sound as of wind, water, or the like, esp. one of a gentle or soothing nature. **2.** A deep sigh or breath. late ME. **3.** A rumour; a report 1716.

1. Pine-wood's steady sugh WORDSW. **2.** From the loch would come the s. of a porpoise 1885. **3.** There was a s. in the country about it SCOTT.

Phr. *To keep a calm* (or *quiet*) *s.*, to say little or nothing, to keep quiet (Sc.).

Sough (sɒf), *sb.*² ME. [Of unkn. origin.] **1.** A boggy or swampy place; a small pool. **2.** A drain, sewer, trench 1440. **3.** An adit of a mine 1619.

Sough (sau, sɒf, *Sc.* sux), *v.*¹ [OE. *swōgan* = OS. *swōgan* resound, rel. to OE. *swēgan* sound, Goth. *ga-, uf|swōgjan, swōgatjan, swēgnjan* sigh (see SWOON *v.*).] **1.** *intr.* To make a rushing, rustling, or murmuring sound. **2.** To draw the breath heavily or noisily; to sigh deeply 1475. **b.** With *away*: To breathe one's last. *dial.* 1816. **3.** *trans.* **a.** To hum (a tune) 1711. **b.** To utter in a sighing or whining tone 1816.

1. The wind soughed through the..branches..in long monotonous swell 1884.

Sough (sɒf), *v.*² 1688. [f. SOUGH *sb.*²] **1.** *trans.* **a.** To face or build up (a ditch) *with* stone, etc. **b.** To make drains in (land); to drain by constructing proper channels. Also *absol.* **2.** *intr.* To reach, or get into, a sough 1898.

Sought (sǫt), *ppl. a.* ME. [pa. pple. of SEEK *v.*] That is, or has been, searched for, desired, etc.

Soul (sōᵘl), *sb.* [OE. *sāwol, sāw(e)l* = Goth. *saiwala*, corresp. to OFris. *sēle*, OS. *sēola* (Du. *ziel*), OHG. *sē(u)la* (G. *seele*) :– Gmc. **saiwalō*, corresp. formally to Gr. αἰόλος quick-moving, easily moved (:– **saiwolos*).] **I.** †**1.** The principle of life in man or animals; animate existence –1697. **2.** The principle of thought and action in man, commonly regarded as an entity distinct from the body; the spiritual part of man in contrast to the purely physical. Also occas., an analogous principle in animals. Freq. in connection with or in contrast to *body*. OE. **3. a.** The seat of the emotions, feelings, or sentiments; the emotional part of man's nature OE. **b.** Intellectual or spiritual power; high development of the mental faculties 1604. **4.** *Metaph.* The vital, sensitive, or rational principle in plants, animals, or human beings. Freq. distinguished as *vegetative, sensitive,* and *rational* or *reasonable*. ME. **5.** *fig.* Applied to persons: **a.** As a term of endearment or adoration 1581. **b.** The personification *of* some quality 1605. **c.** The inspirer or leader of some business, cause, movement, etc. 1662. **6.** *fig.* Of things: **a.** The essential or animating part, element, or feature *of* something 1596. **b.** An element, principle, or trace *of* something 1599. **c.** The *s. of the world* [after L. *anima mundi*, Gr. ψυχὴ τοῦ κόσμου], the animating principle of the world, according to early philosophers 1600. **d.** The essential part or quality *of* a material thing 1658.

1. Þei hated her soules, þat is to say, her bodely lyues, þat þei miȝt kepe hem in to lif euerlasting 1450. **2.** Who can tell yf that the sowle of man ascende, Or with the body of it dye? 1547. So much..as will hold s. and body together SCOTT. God is s., souls I and thou BROWNING. **3. a.** Is it not strange that sheepes guts should hale soules out of men's bodies? SHAKS. Phr. *Heart and s.*, with all one's energy and devotion; entirely. **b.** The mouse that..trusts to one poor hole, Can never be a mouse of any s. POPE. From that moment he could not call his s. his own 1889. **4.** Shall wee rowze the night-Owle in a Catch, that will drawe three soules out of one Weauer? SHAKS. **5. a.** Hang there like fruite, my soule, Till the Tree dye SHAKS. **b.** My brother..was the s. of honour GOLDSM. **c.** He was the author and the s. of the European coalition MACAULAY. **6. a.** Breuitie is the Soule of Wit SHAKS. **b.** There is some soule of goodnesse in things euill SHAKS. **c.** The prophetick soule Of the wide world, dreaming on things to come SHAKS. **d.** The s. of a ship is her engines 1890.

II. 1. The spiritual part of man considered in its moral aspect or in relation to God and His precepts OE. **2.** The spiritual part of man regarded as surviving after death and as susceptible of happiness or misery in a future state OE. **3.** Used in various asseverative phrases or as an exclam. late ME.

1. I begin to think of setting things in order, which I pray God enable me to put both as to s. and body PEPYS. **2.** Beseechinge him to have mercye on my sowle 1536. **3.** *By, for, on* or *upon* (one's) *s.*, etc.; Vpon my Soule, a Lye; a wicked Lye SHAKS.

III. 1. The disembodied spirit of a (deceased) person, regarded as a separate entity, and as invested with some amount of form and personality OE. **2.** A person, an individual; †a living thing. Chiefly in enumeration, or with *every*. ME. **3.** Used with defining adj. to denote a person of a particular character or in respect of some quality; freq. with a touch of contempt, compassion, or familiarity 1519. **4.** One in whom the spiritual or intellectual qualities predominate (*rare*) 1814.

1. It was beleved certenly that dead mens soules dyd walke after they were buried 1560. Devils and damned Souls in hell Fry in the fire with which they dwell 1683. **2.** There were about three hundred souls on board 1894. All alone, without a s. to say a word to 1897. **3.** For his errors, poor s.! were venial 1811.

IV. In spec. or techn. uses. **1.** The lungs of a goose. Now *dial.* 1530. †**2.** The bore of a cannon. (So Fr. *l'âme d'un canon*) –1669. **3.** The sound-post of a violin 1838.

attrib. and *Comb.*, as *s.-concern(ment; s.-curer; s.-adorning, -afflicting, -amazing, -conquering, -saving, -searching* adjs.; *s.-benumbed, -blinded, -felt* adjs.; also, †**s.-ale,** a dirge ale; †**s. chaplain,** = *s.-priest*; **s. pence,** money subscribed by members of a guild to pay for s.-masses; †**s.-priest,** a priest having the special function of praying for the souls of the dead.

Soul (sōᵘl), *v.* late ME. [f. the sb.] †**1.** *trans.* To endow or endue with a soul. Also *fig.* –1646. **2.** *intr.* To go about collecting doles, properly on the eve of All Souls' Day. Chiefly in the phr. *to go a-souling*. 1779.

Sou·l(-)bell. 1599. [f. SOUL *sb.* II. 2.] The passing-bell.

The great Soul Bell of St. Swithun's was sobbing in the winter wind 1893.

Souled (sōᵘld), *ppl. a.* 1602. [f. SOUL *sb.* + -ED[2].] As the second element of parasynthetic combs.: Endowed with a soul of a specified kind, as *great-, high-, large-, mean-s.* adjs.

Soulful (sōᵘ·lfŭl), *a.* 1863. [f. SOUL *sb.* + -FUL 1.] **1.** Full of soul or feeling; in recent use freq. affectedly or unduly æsthetic or emotional. **2.** Expresssive or indicative of deep feeling or emotion 1868.

1. Who can be s. and an athlete? 1882.

Soulish (sōᵘ·liʃ), *a.* 1550. [f. SOUL *sb.* + -ISH[1].] **1.** = PSYCHICAL *a.* 2. **2.** Soul-like 1581.

Soulless (sōᵘ·l,lės), *a.* 1553. [f. SOUL *sb.* + -LESS.] **1.** Having no soul; from whom or which the soul has departed. **2.** Of persons; Destitute of the noble qualities of the soul; lacking spirit, courage or elevation of mind or feeling 1587. **b.** Of the eyes: Lacking animation or expression: dull 1835. **3.** Of things, qualities, etc.: Characterized by a lack of animation, ardour, or vivacity; dull, insipid, uninteresting 1632. **b.** Of writings, etc.: Devoid of inspiration or feeling 1856.

1. A brainlesse head and a soule-lesse body 1599. **2.** Trembling, and Soul-less half the Nation stood DE FOE. **3.** I see things as they are, bleak and bare, and s. 1833. Hence **Sou·lless-ly** *adv.*, **-ness.**

Sou·l-mass. Now *Hist.* or *dial.* 1450. [f. SOUL *sb.* II. 2 + MASS *sb.*[1]] **1.** A mass for the soul of a dead person 1488. **2.** *Soul-mass* (*Day*), All Souls' Day, 2 Nov. 1450.

Sou·l-scot. *Hist.* 1670. [f. SOUL *sb.* II. 2 + SCOT *sb.*[2]] A due paid on behalf of a deceased person to the church of the parish to which he belonged; a mortuary.

Sou·l-shot. *Hist.* 1647. [f. SOUL *sb.* + SHOT *sb.*[1]] = prec.

Sou·l-sick, *a.* 1598. [f. SOUL *sb.*] **1.** Of persons: **a.** Suffering from spiritual indisposition or depression. **b.** Sick at heart; deeply dejected 1609. **2.** Characterized by dejection of spirit 1880.

2. A soul-sick longing comes over us for the silent heather hill 1899. So **Sou·l-sickness.**

Soum (sum). *Sc.* (*Hist.*) 1500. [app. identical with SUM *sb.*] The amount of pasturage that will support one cow or a proportional number of sheep; the number of sheep or cattle so maintained.

Sound (saund), *sb.*[1] [OE. *sund* = ON. *sund* swimming, strait (Norw. *sund* swimming, swimming-bladder, strait, ferry, Sw., Da. *sund* strait) :– Gmc. **sundam*, f. **swum-* **swem-* SWIM *v.*] **I.** †**1.** The action or power of swimming –ME. **2.** The swimming bladder of certain fish, esp. of cod or sturgeon ME.

2. This day dined..upon a fin of ling and some sounds PEPYS.

II. A relatively narrow channel or stretch of water, esp. one between the mainland and an island, or connecting two large bodies of water; a strait. Also, an inlet of the sea. ME. **b.** *The S.*, the strait between Denmark and Sweden which connects the Cattegat with the Baltic Sea 1633.

Sound (saund), *sb.*[2] [ME *sun, son, soun*–AFr. *sun, soun,* (O)Fr. *son* :– L. *sonus*. The form with *d* appears XV, and is established XVI.] **1.** The sensation produced in the organs of hearing when the surrounding air is set in vibration in such a way as to affect these; also, that which is or may be heard; the external object of audition, or the property of bodies by which this is produced. **2.** The particular auditory effect produced by a special cause ME. **b.** The distance or range over which the sound of something is heard. In phr. *in* or *within* (*the*) *s. of* (something). 1617. **3.** A particular cause of auditory effect; an instance of the sensation resulting from this ME. **4.** In restricted sense: The auditory effect produced by the operation of the human voice; utterance, speech, or one of the separate articulations of which this is composed ME. **b.** The audible articulation(s) corresponding to a letter, word, name, etc. late ME. **c.** Used with implication of richness, euphony, or harmony 1553. †**d.** Import, significance –1719. **e.** Mere audible effect, without significance or real importance 1605. **5.** Fame or knowledge, report or rumour, news or tidings (*of* some thing or person). *Obs.* exc. *arch.* late ME.

1. He loudly brayd with beastly yelling s. SPENSER. Linnets fill the Woods with tuneful S. DRYDEN. **2.** The sowne Of swarming Bees SPENSER. After s. of trumpets and silence made EVELYN. **b.** Whether he first sees light..in s. of the swallowing sea M. ARNOLD. **3.** Oft in the Winds is heard a plaintive S. Of melancholy Ghosts ADDISON. **4.** Idle words,..Unprofitable sounds SHAKS. **b.** The very s. of the name of a royal maiden SCOTT. **c.** Woordes that fill the mouthe and haue a s. with them 1553. **e.** A Tale Told by an Ideot, full of s. and fury, Signifying nothing SHAKS.

attrib. and *Comb.*, as *s.-carrier, -wave; s.-conducting, -producing* adjs.; also **s.-body** *Mus.*, the hollow part of a stringed instrument which strengthens its s.; **-bow,** the thickest part of a bell, against which the hammer strikes; **-box,** s.-body; in a gramophone, the box which carries the reproducing or recording stylus; **-change** *Philol.*, the passage of one sound into another; so **-law; -house,** a marine alarm station from which audible alarms or signals are given in foggy weather; **-proof** *a.* (see PROOF *a.* 1 b). **b.** Denoting instruments, etc. for the recording of sound or the resulting record, as *s. camera, record*; **s.-film,** a cinema film with audible dialogue, music, etc.

Sound, *sb.*[3] Now *dial.* late ME. [var., with parasitic *d*, of SWOON *sb.* Cf. SOUND *v.*[3], SWOUND.] A swoon or fainting-fit.

Sound (saund), *sb.*[4] 1584. [Partly f. SOUND *v.*[2]; partly – Fr. *sonde* in same senses.] **1.** An act of sounding with the lead; also *fig.*, power of sounding or investigating (*rare*). **2.** *Surg.* An instrument for probing parts of the body, usually long and slender and having a slightly enlarged end 1797.

Sound (saund), *a.* [Early ME. *sund*, aphetic of *isund*, OE. *ġesund* = OS. *gisund* (Du. *gezond*), OHG. *gisunt* (G. *gesund*) :– WGmc. **ȝasunda*.] **I. 1.** Of persons, animals, etc.: Free from disease, infirmity, or injury; having or enjoying bodily health; healthy, robust. Usu. predicative. Also *absol.* **b.** Said of appetite, health, etc. 1591. **2.** Not affected by disease, decay, or injury ME. **3.** Free from damage, decay, or special defect; unimpaired, uninjured; in good condition or repair ME. **b.** Of air, liquor, or food; Not spoiled or vitiated in any way; hence, wholesome, good and strong 1460. **c.** Financially safe 1601. **4. a.** Of things or substances: Solid, massive, compact. late ME. **b.** Of land: Dry in subsoil; not boggy or marshy. Now *dial.* 1523. **5.** Of sleep, etc.: Deep, profound; unbroken or undisturbed. Hence with *sleeper*. 1548. **6.** Of a solid, substantial, ample, or thorough nature or character 1565. **b.** Of blows, a beating, etc.: Dealt or given with force or severity 1607.

1. They were known to be all s. and in good health DE FOE. Phr. *As s. as a bell.* **b.** Things unsavory to s. appetites 1591. **2.** A s. heart is the life of the flesh: but enuie is the rotting of the bones BIBLE (Geneva) *Prov.* 14:30. A prince of.. sound intellectuals EVELYN. **3.** Our men healthy, and our ships s. DE FOE. *fig.* My loue to thee is s., *sans* cracke or flaw SHAKS. **b.** Some s. old ale, and a glass of stiff negus SCOTT. **c.** He lent his money..with s. securities and at usurious interest 1879. **4.** A small Gothic chapel, hewn..out of the s. and solid rock SCOTT. **5.** This sleepe is s. indeede SHAKS. **6.** School-friendships are not always..permanent and s. COWPER. **b.** A s. rap on the pate 1607.

II. 1. In full accordance with fact, reason, or good sense; free from error, fallacy, or logical defect; good, strong, valid 1440. **b.** Theologically correct; orthodox 1575. †**c.** Of a book or writing: Accurate, correct –1700. **2.** Of judgement, sense, etc.: Based on or characterized by well-grounded principles or good practical knowledge 1577. **3.** Of persons, disposition, etc.: Morally good; honest, straightforward 1580. **b.** Sincere, true; trusty, loyal 1581. **c.** Having a healthy national or moral tone 1822. **4.** Of persons: Orthodox, esp. in regard to religious belief 1526. **5.** Of sober or solid judgement; well-grounded in principles or knowledge; thoroughly versed and reliable 1615.

1. Remarks..as s. as they are acute and ingenious BURKE. Their..theory, s. or unsound, was..complete and coherent MACAULAY. **b.** He ordinarily preach'd s. doctrine EVELYN. **2.** It is a Maxim of the soundest Sense 1718. **4.** He came from Scotland s. as a bell on the five points of Calvinism 1874. **5.** As s. in iudgement as ripe in experience 1615. Hence **Sou·nd-ly** *adv.* late ME., **-ness** late ME.

Comb., as *s.-headed, -hearted, -minded*, adjs.

Sound (saund), *adv.* late ME. [f. prec.] Soundly.

So s. he slept, that nought mought him awake SPENSER. *S.* (*asleep*), fast asleep.

Comb., as *s.-judging, -thinking*, adjs.

Sound (saund), *v.*[1] [ME. *sune, sone, soune* – AFr. *suner*, OFr. *soner* (mod. *sonner*) :– L. *sonare*, f. *sonus*; see SOUND *sb.*[1]] **I.** *intr.* **1.** Of things: To make or emit a sound. **b.** To resound; to be filled with sound ME. **c.** Of instruments: To give a call *to* arms, battle, etc. 1705. **2.** Of persons: To make a sound by blowing, or playing upon, some instrument. late ME. **3.** To strike the ears, to be heard, as a sound. late ME. **b.** To be mentioned or spoken of 1635. **4.** To convey a certain impression or idea by the sound; to appear to have a certain signification when heard (or read). late ME. †**5.** To have a suggestion or touch of, a tendency towards, some connection or association with, a specified thing –1661. **6.** *To s. in damages*, in legal use, to be concerned only with damages 1780.

1. The Trumpet alwaies sounding when the meat was carried up 1662. **b.** The street sounds to the soldiers' tread 1896. **c.** The trumpets sounded to horse DE FOE. **3.** I hear the far-off Curfeu s. MILT. As if the words of an oracle sounded in his ears SCOTT. **b.** Wherever I went my name sounded DISRAELI. **4.** I tell you 'twill s. harshly in her eares SHAKS. **5.** I promise you that this matter sowndeth moche to your dishonour 1530.

II. *trans.* **1.** To cause (an instrument, etc.) to make a sound; to blow, strike, or play on ME. **2.** To utter in an audible tone; to pronounce or repeat. Sometimes implying loudness of tone. ME. †**b.** To express in words (*rare*). –1592. **c.** To utter or pronounce in a certain way 1542. **3.** To give intimation of, a signal or order for (something) by the sound of a trumpet, drum, etc.; to announce, order, or direct by such means 1568. **b.** To blow (a blast) 1806. **4.** To declare, announce, proclaim; to make known or famous; to celebrate. late ME. †**5.** Of words: To signify or mean; to import or imply –1671. **6.** To examine (a person) by auscultation 1887.

1. Or say we s. The trump of liberty GRAY. **2.** Hearing these tearmes of hell and eternall, so often souned in our eares 1593. **b.** No words can that woes s. SHAKS. **3.** The besieged sounded a retreat 1734. **4.** To him The Sabbath bell sounds peace 1804.

Sound (saund), *v.*[2] ME. [– (O)Fr. *sonder*, corresp. to Sp., Pg. *sondar* use the sounding-lead :– Rom. *subundare*, f. L. *sub* SUB- + *unda* wave.] †**1.** *intr.* To sink in, penetrate, pierce. –late ME. **2.** *Naut.* To employ the line and lead, or other means, in order to ascertain the depth of the sea, a channel, etc., or the nature of the bottom 1485. **b.** *fig.* To make inquiry or investigation 1793. **3. a.** Of the lead: To go down; to touch bottom 1610. **b.** Of a whale: To go deep under water; to dive 1839. **4.** *trans.* To investigate (water, etc.) by the use of the line and lead or other means, in order to ascertain the depth or the quality of the bottom; to measure or examine in some way resembling this 1460. **b.** To measure (depth) in this way 1628. **5.** In fig. contexts: To measure, or ascertain, as by sounding 1589. **6.** To examine or question (a person) in an indirect manner 1575. **b.** To investigate (a matter, a person's views, etc.), esp. by cautious or indirect questioning; to make trial of in this way 1579. †**7.** To understand; to fathom –1655. **8.** *Surg.* To examine by means of a sound, esp. for the stone; †to probe 1597.

2. There sounding with our plummet, sand of Amber stuck thereto 1617. Men went overboard with poles in their hands, sounding..for deeper water DE FOE. **b.** His thoughts..had sounded into the depths of his own nature CARLYLE. **3. a.** And deeper then did euer Plummet s. Ile drowne my booke SHAKS. **b.** The whale suddenly disappears; he has 'sounded' 1839. **4.** It is so deepe in some places that it cannot be sounded 1604. **5.** He..sounded the depth of my character 1824. **6.** It is better to s. a person..a farre off, then to fal vppon the pointe at first BACON. Hence **Sou·ndable** *a.* (*rare*) of the sea, capable of being sounded. †**Sou·ndage**, a due paid for the taking of soundings. **Sou·nder**[3], an apparatus for sounding the sea.

Sound *v.*[3] Now *dial.* late ME. [Cf. SOUND *sb.*[3]] Variant of SWOON *v.*

Sou·nd-board. 1500. [SOUND *sb.*[2]] **1.** A thin board or plate of wood forming part of a musical instrument and placed in such a position as to strengthen or increase its sound. **2.** = SOUNDING-BOARD 1. 1766.

1. As in an Organ from one blast of wind To many a row of Pipes the s. breaths MILT.

Sounder[1] (sau·ndəɹ). late ME. [– OFr. *sundre*, (also mod. dial.) *sonre*, of Gmc. origin.] A herd of wild swine.

Sounder[2] (sau·ndəɹ). 1591. [f. SOUND *v.*[1] + -ER.[1]] **1.** One who causes or utters a sound or sounds; one who causes something, esp. an instrument, to sound. **2.** A telegraphic device which enables the communications or signals to be read by sound 1860. **b.** A telegraphist who operates or has experience with this 1887. **3.** A device which gives a signal, etc., by sounding; also, the signal so given 1884.

Sou·nd-hole. 1611. [SOUND *sb.*[2]] **1.** *Mus.* Either of the curvilinear openings in the belly of a stringed instrument, one on each side of the bridge. **2.** *Arch.* An opening in a tower or belfry 1848.

Sounding (sau·ndiŋ), *vbl. sb.*[1] late ME. [f. SOUND *v.*[1] + -ING[1].] **1.** The fact of giving out a sound or sounds, or the power of doing this; the sound produced by something. **2.** Vocal utterance or pronunciation; resonant or sonorous quality of this. late ME. **3.** The (or an) act of causing a trumpet, bell, etc., to sound; the blowing *of* a bugle or trumpet, esp. as a signal 1523. **4.** The action of examining by percussion; *spec.* auscultation 1883.

1. A blast so hye, That made an eckow in the ayer and sowning through the sky 1557.

Comb.: **s.-post,** = SOUND-POST.

Sounding (sau·ndiŋ), *vbl. sb.*[2] ME. [f. SOUND *v.*[2] + -ING[1].] **1.** The action of sounding or ascertaining the depth of water by means of the line and lead; an instance of this. **b.** *fig.* Investigation 1592. **2.** A place or position at sea where it is possible to reach the bottom with the ordinary deep-sea lead. Chiefly *pl.* late ME. †**b.** *spec.* with *the.* Such places in the mouth of the English Channel 1666. **3.** *pl.* The depths of water in the sea or (rarely) in a river, ascertained by sounding with the line and lead; also, the entries in a log-book, etc., giving these, together with particulars of the nature of the bottom reached by the lead 1570. **4.** *Surg.* The action of examining with a sound or probe 1597. **5.** *attrib.*, chiefly in sense 1, as *s.-machine, -plumb, -plummet* 1555.

2. We were soon out of soundings, and well into the Bay of Biscay MARRYAT.

Sounding (sau·ndiŋ), *ppl. a.* ME. [f. SOUND *v.*[1] + -ING[2].] **1.** Having a sound; causing, emitting, producing a sound or sounds, esp. of a loud character; resonant, sonorous; reverberant. **2.** Of language, names, titles, etc.: Having a full, rich, or imposing sound; high-sounding, pompous, bombastic 1683.

1. The s. cataract Haunted me WORDSW. **2.** The orator has been apt to..deal in s. commonplaces 1888.

Sou·nding-board. 1766. [SOUNDING *vbl. sb.*[1]] **1.** A board or screen placed over or behind a pulpit, etc., in such a manner as to reflect the speaker's voice towards the audience. **2.** *Mus.* = SOUND-BOARD 1. 1776.

Sou·nding-lead. late ME. [SOUNDING *vbl. sb.*[2]] *Naut.* The lead or plummet attached to the sounding-line.

Sou·nding-line. ME. [f. as prec.] *Naut.* A line used in sounding the depth of water; also, material forming this.

Soundless (sau·ndlės), *a.*[1] 1586. [f. SOUND *v.*[2]] That cannot be sounded; unfathomable. *lit.* and *fig.*

Soundless (sau·ndlės), *a.*[2] 1601. [f. SOUND *sb.*[2]] **1.** Having, making, etc., no sound; quiet, silent. **2.** In which no sound is heard; still 1816.

2. A s. waste, a trackless vacancy! WORDSW. Hence **Sou·ndless-ly** *adv.*, **-ness.**

Sou·nd-post. 1687. [f. SOUND *sb.*[2] + POST *sb.*[1]] A small peg of wood fixed beneath the bridge of a violin or similar instrument, serving as a support for the belly and as a connecting part between this and the back.

Soup (sūp), *sb.* 1653. [– (O)Fr. *soupe* (i) sop, (ii) broth poured on slices of bread :– late L. *suppa* (Oribasius), f. **suppare* soak, of Gmc. origin; cf. SOP *sb.*, SUP *v.*[1]] **1.** A liquid food prepared by boiling, usually consisting of an extract of meat with other ingredients and seasoning. **2.** *colloq.* or *slang.* **a.** Briefs for prosecutions given to members of the Bar at Quarter Sessions or other courts; the fees attaching to such briefs. Also in *pl.* 1856. **b.** *In the s.*, in a difficulty. orig. *U.S.* 1889.

Comb.: **s.-house, -kitchen,** an establishment for preparing s. and distributing it to the poor or unemployed, either free or at a very low charge; **-ticket,** a ticket given to poor people enabling them to receive s. from a s.-kitchen. Hence **Soup** *v. trans.* to provide with s. **Sou·py** *a.* like s.; having the appearance or consistency of s.

‖**Soupçon** (supsoṅ). 1766. [Fr., repr. OFr. *sou(s)peçon* :– late L. *suspectio, -on-*, for L. *suspicio* SUSPICION.] A suspicion, a suggestion, a very small quantity or slight trace, *of* something.

Souper (sū·pəɹ). 1851. [f. SOUP *sb.* or *v.* + -ER[1].] **1.** In Ireland, a Protestant clergyman seeking to make proselytes by dispensing soup in charity. **2.** One converted to Protestantism by the receipt of soup or other charity 1871.

Soup maigre (sūp₁mē[1]·gəɹ). 1754. [– Fr. *soupe maigre*; see SOUP *sb.*, MAIGRE *a.*] Thin soup, made chiefly from vegetables or fish. So †**Soup-mea·gre** 1737.

Sour (sau[ə]ɹ), *a.* and *sb.* [OE. *sūr* = OS., OHG. *sūr* (Du. *zuur*, G. *sauer*), ON. *súrr* :– Gmc. **sūraz.*] **A.** *adj.* **I. 1.** Having a tart or acid taste, such as that of unripe fruits or vinegar. (Opp. to *sweet*, and dist. from *bitter.*) **b.** *transf.* Producing tart or acid fruit OE. **c.** In fig. or allusive uses. late ME. **2.** Rendered acid by fermentation or similar processes; fermented; affected or spoiled in this way by being kept or exposed too long OE. **b.** Of smell, breath, eructations, etc. ME. **3. a.** Of land, etc.: Cold and wet; uncongenial through retaining stagnant moisture 1532. **b.** Of pasture: Having a harsh, unpleasant taste; coarse, rank. Now *dial.* 1654.

1. [The fox] sayd these raysyns ben sowre CAXTON. More sowr then the strongest Vinegar 1666. **b.** The soure crabtree 1560. **c.** *Prov b.* He has given me sweet Meat, but sowr Sauce 1687. *Sour grapes*, in allusion to Æsop's fable of 'The Fox and the Grapes', when a person disparages something which it is suspected he would be glad to possess if he could. **2.** *fig.* Ephraim is ioyned to idoles:.. Their drinke is sowre *Hosea* 4:18.

II. 1. Extremely distasteful or disagreeable; bitter, unpleasant ME. **2.** Having a harsh, morose, or peevish disposition; sullen, austere; gloomy, discontented, embittered ME. **3.** Displaying, expressing, or implying displeasure or discontent; peevish, cross, 1440. **b.** Wry, distorted 1611. **4.** Of weather, etc.: Cold and wet; inclement. Now *Sc.* 1582. **5.** Of animals: Heavy, coarse, gross. *dial.* 1713.

1. Al though it be soure to suffre, þere cometh swete after LANGL. **2.** His temper was s., arrogant, and impatient of opposition MACAULAY. **3.** He..from his sower Looks is commonly called Vinegar Jones 1720. A s. discourse on the wickedness of the others 1851. **b.** Make what s. mouths he would for a pretence LAMB. **4.** The Earth.. weeps and blears itself, in s. rain, and worse CARLYLE.

Comb.: **s. cake,** an oat- or rye-cake made of fermented dough; **s. gourd,** (the fruit of) the Baobab, *Adansonia digitata*, or the related species *A. gregorii*; **s. grass,** (*a*) the grass *Paspalum*; (*b*) sorrel; **s. gum** *U.S.*, *Nyssa villosa* or *multiflora*, also called tupelo; **s. plum,** *Owenia acidula*; **s. wood** *U.S.*, the sorrel-tree. Hence **Sou·r-ly** *adv.*, **-ness** OE.

B. *sb.* **1.** That which is sour OE. **2.** In

bleaching and tanning, a bath or steep of an acid character 1756. **3.** *U.S.* An acid drink, usu. whisky or other spirit with lemon added 1885.

1. The sweets we wish for, turne to lothed sowrs SHAKS.

Sour (sauəɹ), *adv.* [ME. *sūre*, f. *sūr* SOUR *a.*] †**1.** Bitterly, dearly; severely –1450. **2.** Disagreeably, unpleasantly; crossly, gloomily, unfavourably. Chiefly in phr. *to look s.* 1500.

Sour (sauəɹ), *v.* ME. [f. SOUR *a.*] **1.** *intr.* To become sour; to acquire a sour taste. **b.** To become embittered, morose, or peevish 1748. **c.** *To s. on*, to take a dislike to. orig. *U.S.* 1862. **2.** *trans.* Of leaven: To cause fermentation in (dough, etc.) ME. **3.** To make sour or acid; *esp.* to cause to have a tart or sour taste; to spoil in this way 1460. **b.** To make (land) cold and wet 1842. **c.** *Bleaching.* To subject to the action of diluted acids 1756. **4.** To render sour, gloomy, or morose; to embitter (the mind, temper, etc.) 1599. †**b.** To invest with a sour expression. SHAKS.

1. Milk when it sours on the Stomach 1632. *fig.* Hote loue often after wil soure ME. **b.** She sour'd To what she is: a nature never kind! TENNYSON. **2.** *fig.* Sowred with the leauen of their superstition 1611. **3.** *fig.* This sowers all thy sweets, sads all thy Rest 1645. **4.** A man..whose conscience..had soured him 1878. Physical and mental misery,..soured her disposition 1882. **b.** *Ven. & Ad.* 185.

Source (sōəɹs). [ME. *sours* and *sourse* – OFr. *sours, sors* masc. and *sourse*, (also mod.) *source* fem., subst. uses of masc. and fem. pa. pple. of *sourdre* rise, spring :– L. *surgere* rise, SURGE.] †**1.** 'A support or under-prop'. ME. only. †**2.** *Hawking.* The act of rising on the wing, on the part of a hawk or other bird –1612. **3.** The fountain-head or origin of a river or stream; the spring or place from which a flow of water takes its beginning. late ME. **b.** With *a* and *pl.* A spring; a fountain 1477. **4.** *fig.* The chief or prime cause *of* something of a non-material or abstract character; the quarter whence something of this kind originates. late ME. **b.** The origin, or original stock, *of* a person, family, etc. 1669. **c.** The originating cause or substance *of* some material thing or physical agency 1803. **d.** A work, etc., supplying information or evidence (esp. of an original or primary character) as to some fact, event, or series of these 1788. **5.** *Physics.* A point or centre from which a fluid or current flows 1878.

2. Right as an hauk upon a sours Upspringeth into thaer, right so prayeres..Maken her sours to Goddis eeres tuo CHAUCER. **3.** The flouds do gaspe, for dryed is theyr sourse SPENSER. **b.** Like torrents from a mountain s. TENNYSON. **4.** O swerd of knighthod, sours of gentilesse! CHAUCER. This s. of ideas, every man has wholly in himself LOCKE.

Comb. **s.-book** [tr. G. *quellenbuch*], a book or collection of 'sources' or original documents serving as materials for the historical study of a subject.

Sour(-)crout. 1617. [Anglicized form of SAUERKRAUT.] A fermented preparation of cabbage.

†**Sourd,** *v.* late ME. [– (O)Fr. *sourdre* :– L. *surgere* rise; see SOURCE, SURGE.] **1.** *intr.* Of conditions, events, etc.: To arise, take rise, spring or issue –1567. **2.** Of fountains, etc.: To spring up, to issue from the ground –1606.

1. Now myghte men axe, wher-of that pride sourdeth and spryngeth CHAUCER.

Sour(-)dock. Now *dial.* ME. [SOUR *a.* and DOCK *sb.*[1]] Common sorrel.

Sour-dough (sauə·ɹ,dōu). ME. [See SOUR *a.* and DOUGH *sb.*] **1.** Leaven. Now *dial.* and *rare.* **2.** *Amer.* One who has spent one or more winters in Alaska 1902.

Souring (sauə·riŋ), *vbl. sb.* late ME. [f. SOUR *v.* + -ING[1].] **1.** A substance which renders sour or acid; *spec.* leaven, lemon-juice, or vinegar. Now chiefly *dial.* **2.** The process or fact of becoming or making sour 1579. **3.** *spec.* The process of subjecting cloth, wool, skins, etc., to the action of diluted acids 1756. **4.** A sourish variety of apple; *dial.* a crab-apple 1846.

2. *fig.* Hazlitt's cynicism is the s. of a generous nature 1874.

Sourish (sauə·riʃ), *a.* late ME. [f. SOUR *a.* + -ISH[1].] Somewhat sour, in various senses.

Bread brownish and sowrish, and made with aniseeds 1617. Hence **Sou·rish-ly** *adv.*, **-ness.**

Sour-sop. 1667. [f. SOUR *a.* + SOP *sb.*] **1.** The fruit of the West Indian tree *Anona muricata.* **2.** The tree itself 1753.

Sou·r-sweet, *a.* and *sb.* 1591. [f. the adjs.] **A.** *adj.* Sweet with an admixture or after-taste of sourness. **B.** *sb.* Something which is sour-sweet; *spec.* an acid sweetmeat 1603.

‖**Sous-** (sū, sūz), *prefix*, repr. OFr. and mod.Fr. *sous* (:– L. *subtus*) 'under', 'sub-', in words directly adopted from French, as *s.-lieutenant, -ministre, -officier, -prefect.*

Souse (saus), *sb.*[1] Now *dial.* and *U.S.* late ME. [– OFr. *sous, souz* – OS. *sultia*, OHG. *sulza* (G. *sülze*) brine, f. Gmc. **sult-* **salt-* SALT.] **1.** Various parts of a pig or other animal, esp. the feet and ears, prepared or preserved for food by pickling. **b.** *transf.* The ears; also in *sing.*, an ear 1658. **2.** A liquid employed as a pickle 1502.

Souse (saus), *sb.*[2] Now *dial.* 1480. [prob. imit.] A heavy blow; a thump.

†**Souse,** *sb.*[3] 1486. [Alteration of SOURCE *sb.* 2.] *Hawking.* **1.** Phr. *at* (*the*) *s.*: (of a hunted bird) in the act of rising from the ground and giving the hawk an opportunity to strike. –1620. **2.** The act of a hawk, in swooping down upon a hunted bird –1638.

2. As a Faulcon faire That once hath failed of her s. full neare SPENSER.

†**Souse,** *sb.*[4] 1502. [– OFr. *sous*, pl. of *sout, solt*, later *sol* SOL *sb.*[3] and *sou* SOU.] **1.** A sol or sou –1823. **2.** Taken as a type of a small coin or amount, with an expressed or implied negative –1815.

Souse (saus), *sb.*[5] 1741. [f. SOUSE *v.*[1]] **1.** An act of sousing; a plunge into, immersion in, or drenching with, water; *dial.* a wash. **b.** An act of getting drunk (*slang*) 1930. **2.** A sound as of water surging against something 1883.

Souse (saus), *v.*[1] late ME. [f. SOUSE *sb.*[1]] **I.** *trans.* **1.** To prepare or preserve (meat, fish, etc.) by steeping in some kind of pickle, esp. one made with vinegar or the like. **2.** To plunge or immerse (a person, etc.) deeply or thoroughly *in* or *into* water, etc. 1470. **3.** To drench or soak with water, etc. 1542. **4.** To dash or pour (a quantity of water or something containing this). Const. *into, on*, etc. 1859.

1. A sheepes heade sawsed in ale 1500. *fig.* Sowse us..in the Powdering-Tub of thy Mercy, that we may be Tripes fit for the Heavenly Table 1704. **2.** To be soused over head and ears in cold water 1660. **3.** Then the engines arrived and soused the burning houses 1871.

II. *intr.* **1.** To soak; to be or become soaked or drenched; to go plunging or sinking in water, etc. **b.** To get drunk (*slang*) 1923. †**2.** To flow or fall in copious streams –1648.

1. Down I soused into the water THACKERAY. **2.** The surging seas came sousing in againe DRAYTON.

Souse (saus), *v.*[2] Now *dial.* 1550. [Related to SOUSE *sb.*[2]] **1.** *trans.* To strike, smite, or beat severely or heavily. †**2.** *absol.* To deliver heavy blows. SPENSER. **3.** *intr.* To fall heavily or with some weight 1596.

1. Soundly did he s. my pate 1787. **2.** Both..souce so sore, that they the heauens affray SPENSER.

Souse (saus), *v.*[3] Now *arch.* 1583. [f. SOUSE *sb.*[3] 2.] **1.** *intr.* Of a hawk, etc.: To swoop down; to descend with speed and force. **2.** *trans.* To swoop or pounce upon (something) in a hostile manner 1595.

1. The sacred eagle..sousing on the quivering hare POPE. **2.** The gallant Monarch..like an Eagle, o're his ayerie towres, To sowsse annoyance that comes neere his Nest SHAKS.

Souse (saus), *adv.*[1] Now chiefly *dial.* 1680. [f. SOUSE *sb.*[3] or *v.*[3]] **1.** Suddenly; without warning. **2.** With a direct and rapid course 1690. **3.** With strong or violent impact 1694.

3. Gundling comes s. upon the ice with his sitting-part CARLYLE.

Souse (saus), *adv.*[2] 1706. [f. SOUSE *sb.*[1] or *v.*[1]] With a deep or sudden plunge.

S. he went into the sea 1882.

Souslik, var. of SUSLIK.

‖**Soutache** (sutaʃ). 1856. [Fr. – Magyar *sujtás.*] A narrow flat ornamental braid of wool, silk, or the like, usually sown upon fabrics in fanciful designs.

‖**Soutane** (sutan). 1838. [Fr. – It. *sottana*, f. *sotto* :– L. *subtus* under.] **1.** An ecclesiastic's cassock. **2.** *transf.* An ecclesiastic 1890.

2. A confederacy of soutanes and petticoats 1890.

‖**Souteneur** (sutnǒr). 1906. [Fr. 'protector'.] A man who cohabits with and lives on the earnings of a prostitute.

Souter (sū·təɹ). Now *Sc.* and *n. dial.* [OE. *sūtere*, corresp. to OHG. *sūtāri*, ON. *sútari* – L. *sutor* shoemaker, f. *suere* sew, stitch; see -ER[1].] A shoemaker or cobbler.

The s. tauld his queerest stories BURNS. Hence †**Sou·terly** *a.* resembling a s.; common, vulgar, appropriate to a s.

Souterrain (sū·tərēin). 1735. [– Fr. *souterrain*, f. *sous* under + *terre* earth, after L. *subterraneus.*] An underground chamber, store-room, passage, etc.

South (sauþ), *adv., prep., sb.*, and *a.* [OE. *sūþ* = OFris., OS. *suth* (LG. *sud*), OHG. *sunt* (-*d*-), ON. *suðr* (:– *sunþr*).] **A.** *adv.* **1.** Towards, or in the direction of, that part of the earth or heavens which is directly opposite to the north. **2.** From the south 1626. **3.** quasi-*sb.* = B. 1. ME. **4.** *ellipt.* as *prep.* At, in, or to the south of 1607.

1. Steering s. and s. by west 1743. **2.** In a Faire and Dry Day,..And when the Wind bloweth not S. BACON. **3.** To S. the Persian Bay MILT. †*By s.*, in the s.; on the s. side. **4.** The Chimney Is S. the Chamber SHAKS.

B. *sb.* (Usu. with *the.*) **1.** That one of the four cardinal points which is opposite to the north ME. **2.** The southern part of a country or region; *spec.* **a.** Of England (below the Wash), Great Britain, Scotland, or Ireland; the south country ME. **b.** The southern lands of Europe, etc. late ME. **c.** The southern States of America. orig. *U.S.* 1779. **3.** The southern part *of* a particular country, etc. late ME. **4.** *transf.* The inhabitants of a southern region or district ME. **5.** The south wind. Chiefly *poet.* ME. **b.** A south wind 1699.

1. The wyndes of the S. Ben most of alle debonaire GOWER. **2. a.** In the S. we usually call marygolds simply *golds* 1691. **b.** Dark-browed cavaliers from the sunny s. 1890. **4.** Between the North and S. there will be feelings of implacable hatred 1861. **5.** Wake North, and com O South, and on my garden blowe 1587. **b.** My wind is turned to bitter north, That was so soft a s. before CLOUGH.

C. *adj.* **1.** With proper names: Situated or dwelling in the south; southerly OE. **2.** With common nouns: Lying towards the south; situated on the side next the south OE. **3.** Of the wind: Blowing from the south OE. **4.** Of or pertaining to the south; belonging or native to the south 1470. **5.** Facing the south 1527. **6.** Tending towards the south 1839.

1. The second Kingdome of the Heptarchy, was of the S. Saxons 1643. They were lordes of Granada in s. Spaine 1600. **2.** The fort near the s. end of the city 1792. **3.** The Southwind rose,..with black wings Wide hovering MILT. *transf.* The South-Fog rot him SHAKS. **4.** For what says the s. proverb SCOTT. **5.** Carnations and mignonette blooming in the s. window 1867. **6.** In a s. direction 1886. Also in comp. †**Sou·ther** *a.*, whence **Sou·thermost** *a.* (now *rare* or *Obs.*).

South (sauþ), *v.* 1659. [f. SOUTH *adv.* or *sb.*] **1.** *intr.* To cross the meridian of a place. **2.** To veer, move, or turn towards the south; to blow more from the south 1725.

2. About sun-down the wind southed 1898.

South- (sauþ), comb. form repr. SOUTH *sb.* or *adv.*, with the sense 'to or towards, in or on, the south', as in *s.-going*, etc.; *s.-bounded, -turned*, etc.

Southard (sɒ·ðəɹd), *adv.* and *sb.* 1470. Reduced form of SOUTHWARD.

Southco·ttian, *sb.* and *a.* Also **-cotian.** 1842. [See def., -IAN.] **A.** *sb.* A believer in the claims or teaching of Joanna Southcott (1750–1814), who announced herself as the woman spoken of in *Rev.* 12. **B.** *adj.* Of or pertaining to Joanna Southcott or her followers 1843.

South country. late ME. [SOUTH *a.* 2.] The southern part of any country; the district or region towards the south; *spec.* of Great Britain (south of the Tweed), of England (south of the Wash), or of Scotland (south of the Forth). Also *attrib.* (freq. hyphened.)

Southdown (sau·þdaun). Also **South Down, South-down.** 1787. [See def.] **1.** One of a breed of sheep, noted for its short, fine wool and for the good quality of its mutton, orig. reared on the South Downs of Sussex and Hampshire. Chiefly in *pl.* **2.** This breed of sheep. Chiefly with *the.* 1827. **3.** *ellipt.* Mutton from this breed of sheep 1859.

South-east (sauþ,ī·st), *adv., sb.,* and *a.* [OE. *sūþēast*; see SOUTH *adv.* and EAST *adv.*] **A.** *adv.* **1.** In the direction lying midway between south and east. **2.** quasi-*sb.* ME.

1. We..stood off to sea, steering still s. DE FOE. The district east and s. of Charter 1896. **2.** Faced all round with a..Rock, except a Bay at South-East 1707

B. *sb.* **1.** The direction or point of the horizon lying between south and east. late ME. †**2.** The south-east wind –1725. **3.** The south-eastern part of a country 1778.

1. He made the signal..to..steer to the s. 1806. **3.** Sardinia rising to invade the Southeast 1837.

C. *adj.* **1.** Lying or situated in or towards, directed to, the south-east 1548. **2.** Of the wind, currents, etc.: Blowing or running from the south-east. late ME.

2. The strong southeast swell 1898. Hence **South-ea·ster,** a wind or gale blowing from the s.

South-ea·sterly, *a.* and *adv.* 1708. [f. SOUTH + EASTERLY.] **A.** *adj.* **a.** Lying, etc., in the direction of south-east. **b.** Blowing or running from the south-east. **B.** *adv.* Towards the south-east 1884.

South-ea·stern, *a.* 1577. [f. SOUTH + EASTERN.] **1.** Lying on the south-east side; situated in the south-east. **b.** Of or pertaining to the south-east of England 1886. **2.** Of the wind: Blowing from the south-east 1842.

South-ea·stward, *adv., sb.,* and *a.* 1528. [f. SOUTH-EAST + -WARD.] **A.** *adv.* In a south-easterly direction; towards the south-east. **B.** *sb.* The south-east quarter or direction 1555. **C.** *adj.* Situated towards or leading to the south-east 1766. Hence **South-ea·stwardly** *adv.* towards the south-east; on the south-east side.

Souther (sau·þəɹ), *sb.* 1862. [f. SOUTH *a.* + -ER[1].] A south wind or gale.

Souther (sɒ·ðəɹ), *v.* 1628. [f. SOUTH *adv.* + -ER[5].] *intr.* To shift, turn, or fly to the south; of the wind, to south.

Southerly (sɒ·ðəɹli), *a.* 1551. [f. SOUTH; cf. *northerly*, etc.] **1.** Situated in or towards the south; southern. **2.** Of the wind: Blowing from the south 1602. **3.** Tending or facing southwards 1789. Hence **Sou·therliness.**

Southerly (sɒ·ðəɹli), *adv.* 1577. [Cf. prec. and -LY[2].] **1.** To the southward; in or towards the south; on the south side. **2.** From the direction of the south 1642.

2. The Wind chop'd up S. 1642.

Southern (sɒ·ðəɹn), *a.* and *sb.* [OE. *sūþerne* = OFris. *sūthern*, OS. *sūthrōni*, OHG. *sundrōni*, ON. *suðrœnn*. Cf. SOUTHRON.] **A.** *adj.* **1.** Of persons: Living or originating in, coming from, the south, esp. of Great Britain (= English), of England, or of Europe. **b.** *U.S.* Belonging to the Southern States 1839. **2.** Of the wind: Blowing from the south OE. **3.** Situated or lying to the southward or in the south; having a position relatively south OE. **b.** *Astron.* In the names of constellations, as *S. Cross, Fish,* etc. 1594. **4.** Of things: Pertaining or belonging to, produced by, found in, characteristic of, the south OE. **b.** *S. lights,* the Aurora Australis 1775. **5.** Facing or directed towards the south 1706. **6.** As *adv.* Towards the south 1678.

3. b. *S. Cross,* see CROSS *sb.* 11. **6.** All S., from yon Hills, the Roman Camp Hangs o'er us black and threatning DRYDEN.

B. *sb.* **1.** Southern men (*rare*). late ME. **2.** A native of the south (see A. 1) 1721.

1. The S. on this side, for Yorke 'a Warwicke' cry 1622. Hence **Sou·thern** *v. intr.* to become more southerly. **Sou·therner,** a native of the south. **Sou·thernly,** *a.* and *adv.* = SOUTHERLY *a.* and *adv.* **Sou·thernmost** *a.* furthest south.

Southernwood (sɒ·ðəɹnwud). [OE. *sūþerne* SOUTHERN *a.*, and *wudu* WOOD *sb.*] A hardy deciduous shrub, *Artemisia abrotanum,* having a fragrant aromatic smell and a sour taste, orig. native to the south of Europe, and formerly much cultivated for medicinal purposes. Also, the genus of *Compositæ* of which this is the type.

Southing (sau·ðiŋ, sau·þiŋ), *vbl. sb.* 1659. [f. SOUTH *adv.* or *v.* + -ING[1].] **1.** Of heavenly bodies: The action of crossing or approaching the meridian of a place. **2.** Progress or deviation towards the south made in sailing, travelling, etc.; difference in latitude due to moving southward. Chiefly in *Navigation.* 1669.

Sou·thland. Now *arch.* or *poet.* Also **south land, south-land.** [OE. *sūþland*; see SOUTH *adv.* and LAND *sb.*] **1.** A land lying in or towards the south. **2.** The southern part of a country or district; the South OE. **3.** *attrib.* or as *adj.* 1470. Hence **Sou·thlander,** a southerner.

†**Sou·thly,** *a.* and *adv.* 1440. [f. SOUTH + -LY.] **A.** *adj.* Southern. **B.** *adv.* Towards or in the south; facing or from the south –1590.

Southmost (sau·þməst, -moᵘst), *a.* OE. [f. SOUTH *adv.*; see -MOST.] Most southerly; southernmost.

Sou·thness. 1852. [f. SOUTH + -NESS.] The quality of indicating the south; the state of being relatively south.

Southron (sɒ·ðrǫn), *a.* and *sb.* 1470. [Sc. var. of *southren* SOUTHERN *a.*] **A.** *adj.* **1.** Belonging to or dwelling in the south, esp. of Britain; southern; *esp.* English as dist. from Scottish. Chiefly *Sc.* **2.** Of or pertaining to, characteristic of, the south; situated in or on the south 1470.

2. A s. mode of speech 1891.

B. *sb.* **1.** A native of the south of Great Britain; an Englishman 1470. **b.** In pl. sense, = Englishmen. Freq. with *the.* 1470. **2.** A native or inhabitant of the south of England, of Europe, etc. 1848.

South Sea. late ME. †**1. a.** The sea to the south of England; the Mediterranean. TREVISA. †**b.** The English Channel –1478. **2.** *pl.* The seas of the southern hemisphere; *esp.* the South Pacific Ocean 1528. **3.** The South Pacific Ocean; †the Pacific Ocean as a whole 1555. **b.** *ellipt.* for 'South Sea bonds', etc. 1717.

3. *fig.* One inch of delay more, is a South-sea of discouerie SHAKS. **b.** The nation then too late will find..South Sea, at best, a mighty bubble SWIFT.

attrib.: **South Sea bubble** = *South Sea scheme*; **South Sea Company,** a company incorporated in 1711 for the purpose of exclusive trade with the South Seas, and of taking up the unfunded National Debt; **South Sea scheme,** a stock-jobbing scheme which was inaugurated by this company in 1720 for taking up the whole National Debt, but which collapsed in the same year.

South-side. [orig. repr. ME. *sūðsīde*; but in later use felt merely as a collocation of SOUTH *a.* and SIDE *sb.*[1]] The side situated in or lying towards the south.

South-south-east, *adv.* late ME. In or from the direction lying midway between south and south-east. Also as *sb.* and *adj.*

South-sou·therly. 1814. [Imitative of its cry.] *Amer.* The long-tailed duck, *Harelda glacialis.*

South-south-west, *adv.* 1513. In or from the direction situated midway between south and south-west. Also as *sb.* and *adj.*

Southward (sau·þwǫɹd, *Naut.* sɒ·ðəɹd), *adv., sb.,* and *a.* [OE. *sūþweard,* f. SOUTH *adv.* + -WARD.] **A.** *adv.* **1.** Towards the south; in a southern direction. **2.** quasi-*sb.* = B. 1842.

1. S. they set their faces TENNYSON. Half a mile s. of the town lies a..rising ground 1896. **2.** So came he far to s. MACAULAY.

B. *sb.* That direction or part which lies to the south of a place, etc. 1555.

It looked black at the s. and eastward 1840.

C. *adj.* That has a southerly situation or direction; lying, facing, moving, etc., towards the south 1611.

With the s. swallow SWINBURNE. Hence **Sou·thwardly** *adv.* in a s. direction; *adj.* situated in or directed towards the south; of the wind, blowing from the south.

Sou·thwards, *adv.* and *sb.* [OE. *sūþweardes*; see -WARDS.] = prec. A, B.

South-west (sauþwe·st), *adv., sb.,* and *a.* [OE. *sūþwest* (see SOUTH and WEST).] **A.** *adv.* **1.** In the direction situated midway between south and west. **b.** From this direction 1725. **2.** quasi-*sb.* **a.** *At s.* = 1. **b.** = B. 1. 1555.

2. a. The wind at s., and the thermometer at 58½ 1777.

B. *sb.* **1.** The direction, district, or region situated between south and west OE. **2.** The (or a) south-west wind 1610.

2. A Southwest blow on yee, And blister you all ore SHAKS.

C. *adj.* **1.** Of the wind: Blowing from the south-west. late ME. **2.** Lying in or situated to the south-west 1440. **3.** Directed towards the south-west 1756.

South-we·ster. Also **southwester.** 1831. [f. prec. + -ER[1].] **1.** A wind or gale blowing from the south-west 1833. **2.** (usu. *sou'wester.*) A large oilskin or waterproof hat or cap worn orig. by seamen to protect the head and neck during wet or rough weather. Also *attrib.* 1831.

South-we·sterly, *a.* and *adv.* 1708. [f. SOUTH-WEST + -LY, after WESTERLY.] **A.** *adj.* **a.** Of the wind: Blowing from the south-west. **b.** Tending south-westward. **B.** *adv.* South-westwardly 1792.

South-we·stern, *a.* and *sb.* [OE. *sūþwesterne* (see SOUTH *adv.* and WESTERN *a.*).] **A.** *adj.* **1.** Of the wind: Blowing from the south-west. **2.** Situated or extending towards the south-west; of or pertaining to the south-west 1828. **B.** *sb.* A wave from the south-west. TENNYSON.

A. 1. Western and s. gales 1835. **2.** The main marks of s. English 1863.

South-we·stward, *adv.* and *sb.* 1548. [f. SOUTH-WEST + -WARD.] = SOUTH-WEST *adv.* and *sb.* So **South-we·stwards** *adv.*

South-we·stwardly, *adv.* 1796. [f. prec. + -LY[2].] = SOUTH-WEST *adv.*

Souvenir (sū·vənīᵊɹ). 1775. [– Fr. *souvenir* memory, keepsake, subst. use of the inf. *souvenir* :– L. *subvenire* come into the mind.] **1.** A remembrance, a memory. **2.** A token of remembrance; a keepsake 1782.

Sou'-we·st, -we·ster, reduced ff. SOUTH-WEST, -WESTER.

Sov (sǫv). 1850. Colloquial abbrev. of SOVEREIGN *sb.* 3 b.

†**Sovenance.** 1477. [– OFr. *sovenance,* (also mod.) *sou-,* f. *so(u)venir*; see SOUVENIR, -ANCE.] Remembrance; memory –1625.

Sovereign (sǫ·vrėn), *sb.* and *a.* [ME. *soverein* – OFr. *so(u)verain, -ein* (mod. *souverain*) :– Rom. **superanus,* f. L. *super* above. Forms in *-gn-* (after *reign*) are found c1400; cf. FOREIGN.] **A.** *sb.* **1.** One who has supremacy or rank above, or authority over, others; a superior; a ruler, governor, lord, or master (*of* persons, etc.). Freq. applied to the Deity in relation to created things. **b.** A person or thing which excels or surpasses others of the kind. Now *rare.* 1500. **2.** *spec.* The recognized supreme ruler of a people or country under monarchical government; a monarch; a king or queen ME. **3. a.** A gold coin minted in England from the time of Henry VII to Charles I, orig. of the value of 22*s.* 6*d.* but later worth only 10*s.* or 11*s.* 1503. **b.** A current British gold coin of the value of twenty shillings 1817.

1. Thy husband is thy Lord, thy life, thy keeper, Thy head, thy soueraigne SHAKS. **b.** This Soveraigne of her Sexe 1635. **2.** How darst thou thus oppose thy Soveraignes will 1652. *fig.* Weak Verses, go, kneel at your Sovereign's feet SHELLEY.

B. *adj.* †**1.** Of persons: Standing out above others or excelling in some respect –1688. **2.** Of things, qualities, etc.: Supreme, paramount; principal, greatest, or most notable ME. **b.** Qualifying *good.* (Freq. = *summum bonum*). ME. **c.** Of contempt: Supreme, unmitigated 1749. **3.** Of remedies, etc.: Efficacious in a superlative degree. Freq. in fig. use. late ME. **4.** Of persons: Having superior or supreme rank or power; *spec.* holding the position of a ruler or monarch ME. **b.** Of states, communities, etc. 1595. **5.** Of power, authority, etc.: Supreme 1532. **6.** Of or belonging to, characteristic of, supremacy or superiority 1600.

2. This is his s. Charm against Fear in an Engagement 1706. **b.** The knowledge of Truth..is the Soueraigne Good of humane Nature BACON. **3.** A soueraine simple against disquiet and feare GREENE. **4.** Partly because, being members of the s. body, they would have it so BENTHAM. **b.** A State is called a *s. State* when this supreme power resides within itself 1868. 6. Full many a glorious morning haue I seene, Flatter the mountaine tops with soueraine eie SHAKS. Hence **So·vereignly** *adv.* in a s. manner.

†**So·vereignize,** *v.* 1601. [f. SOVEREIGN *sb.* + -IZE.] *intr.* To exercise supreme power; to rule as a sovereign –1680.

Sovereignty (sǫ·vrenti). ME. [– OFr. *so(u)vereineté* (mod. *souveraineté*); see SOVEREIGN, -TY¹.] **1.** Supremacy or pre-eminence in respect of excellence or efficacy. **2.** Supremacy in respect of power, domination, or rank; supreme dominion, authority, or rule. late ME. **3.** *spec.* The position, rank, or power of a supreme ruler or monarch; royal authority or dominion. late ME. **b.** *transf.* The supreme controlling power in communities not under monarchical government; absolute and independent authority 1860. **4.** A territory under the rule of a sovereign, or existing as an independent state 1715.

1. *L. L. L.* IV. iii. 234. **2.** The Romans..had acquired the S. of the Sea 1718. **3.** Hee wanne the soueraignty not meerely by the sword 1625. **4.** The United States, with thirty governors, for thirty independent sovereignties 1849.

Soviet (sōᵘ·viet, soᵘvie·t). 1917. [– Russ. *sovét.*] A Russian soldiers' or workmen's council of delegates; since the Russian revolution of 1917 also a congress consisting of representatives of the local soviets (hence *attrib.* as in 'Soviet Republic'); (with *the*) the system of government by soviets. Also *transf.* of similar organizations elsewhere. Hence **So·vietism,** the system of government by soviets. **So·vietize** *v. trans.* to organize on a soviet basis.

Sovran (sǫ·vrăn), *a.* and *sb.* Chiefly *poet.* 1634. [Milton's spelling of SOVEREIGN, after It. *sovrano.*] = SOVEREIGN *a.* and *sb.* Hence **So·vranly** *adv.* **So·vranty,** sovereignty.

Sow (sau), *sb.* [OE. *sugu* = OS. *suga,* MLG., MDu. *soge* (Du. *zeug*), rel. to OE. *sū,* OHG. *sū* (G. *sau*), ON. *sýr* (acc. *sú*); f. IE. base **sŭ-,* repr. also by L. *sūs* (*suis*) pig, Gr. ὗς.] **1.** The female of swine; a full-grown female pig, esp. a domestic one used for breeding. **2.** Applied to persons (male or female) as a term of abuse, esp. to a fat, clumsy, or slovenly woman 1508. **3.** *Mil.* A movable structure having a strong roof, used to cover men advancing to the walls of a besieged town or fortress, and to protect them while engaged in sapping and mining or other operations. Now *Hist.* ME. **4.** A wood-louse or sow-bug. Now chiefly *dial.* late ME. **5.** *techn.* A large oblong mass of solidified metal as obtained from the blast- or smelting-furnace 1481. **b.** In general use: A bar or mass of metal; an ingot. Now *Obs.* or *rare.* 1570. **c.** One of the larger channels, or the main channel, in the hearth of an iron-smelting furnace, serving as a feeder to the smaller channels or 'pigs' 1843. **d.** A mass of metallic iron which has congealed in the hearth of a lead-furnace; a salamander 1871.

Phrases. *To get, have,* or *take the wrong* (or *right*) *s. by the ear,* to get hold of, hit upon, the wrong (or right) person or thing; to arrive at a wrong (or right) conclusion, solution, etc. *As drunk as David's s.* or *as a s.,* blind-drunk.

Sow (sōᵘ), *v.* Pa. t. **sowed** (sōᵘd). Pa. pple. **sowed, sown** (sōᵘn). [OE. *sāwan,* corresp. to OS. *sāian,* OHG. *sāwen, sājen, sā(h)en* (Du. *zaaien,* G. *säen*), ON. *sá,* Goth. *saian*; Gmc. **sǣjan,* repr. IE. base **sē(j-,* as in L. pa. t. *sēvi,* and in SEED, SEMEN.] **1.** *intr.* or *absol.* To perform the action of scattering or depositing seed on or in the ground so that it may grow. **2.** *trans.* To scatter seed on or upon (land, etc.) in order that it may grow; to supply with seed OE. **b.** To strew or sprinkle (land, etc.) *with* something as in the sowing of seed 1611. **c.** Of seed: To be sufficient for (a certain area) 1440. **3.** To cover or strew (a place, etc.) thickly *with* something. Chiefly in pa. pple. late ME. **4.** To scatter or deposit (seed) on or in the ground, etc., for growth, usually by the action of the hand; to place or put (seed) in the ground; to plant (a crop) in this way OE. **b.** *transf.* with ref. to fish, bacilli, etc. 1854. **5. a.** Used with *seed,* etc., in transf. and fig. senses OE. **b.** Contrasted with *reap* in fig. uses. late ME. **6.** *fig.* To disseminate or spread; to endeavour to propagate or extend OE. **7.** To scatter after the manner of seed; to sprinkle, throw or spread about, in this way. late ME. **b.** To distribute or disperse (*rare*) –1535.

1. [I] Plough water, s. on rocks, and reap the wind 1687. **2.** The whole was sowed with barley 1846. *fig.* The daily strife..Which sows the human heart with tares SHELLEY. **b.** And Abimelech..beat downe the citie and sowed it with salt *Judges* 9:45. **3.** Thick as the Galaxy with Stars is sown DRYDEN. **4.** When to turn The fruitful Soil, and when to sowe the Corn DRYDEN. *To s. one's wild oats*: see OAT 3. **5. a.** In all this the seeds of the Conquest were sowing 1868. **b.** What Darkness sowed, the Light shall reap 1878. *To s. the wind and reap the whirlwind*: see WHIRL-WIND. **6.** Between the best of Peoples and the best of Restorer Kings they would s. grudges CARLYLE. He sow'd a slander in the common ear TENNYSON. **7.** Not sowing hedgerow texts and passing by TENNYSON. Hence **Sown** *ppl. a.*

‖**Sowar** (sɒ₁wā·ɹ). *Anglo-Ind.* 1802. [Urdu (Pers.) *sawār* horseman.] A native horseman or mounted orderly, policeman, etc.; a native trooper, esp. one belonging to the irregular cavalry.

Sowarry (sɒ₁wā·ri). *Anglo-Ind.* 1776. [Urdu (Pers.) *sawārī,* f. prec.] The mounted attendants of a person of high rank, a state official, etc.; a number of these forming a cavalcade.

Sow·-back (sau-). 1874. [f. SOW *sb.*] *Geol.* A ridge of glacial origin suggestive of the back of a sow. So **Sow·-backed** *a.* 1728.

Sow·-bread (sau-). Also **sowbread.** 1550. [f. SOW *sb.* + BREAD *sb.,* after med.L. *panis porcinus.* Cf. Flem. *seugenbrood* (Kilian), G. *saubrot* (XVI).] A plant of the genus *Cyclamen,* esp. *C. europæum,* the fleshy tuberous root-stocks of which are eaten by swine.

Sow·-bug (sau-). 1750. [f. SOW *sb.* 4.] **a.** A wood-louse of the genus *Oniscus,* esp. *O. asellus.* **b.** *U.S.* A small marine crustacean of the genus *Idotea.*

Sowens (sōᵘ·ĕnz, sū·-), *sb. pl. Sc.* (and *Ir.*). 1582. [app. – Gael. *súghan, súbhan,* the liquid used in preparing 'sowens', f. *súgh, súbh* sap.] An article of diet formerly in common use in Scotland (and some parts of Ireland), consisting of farinaceous matter extracted from the bran or husks of oats by steeping in water, allowed to ferment slightly, and prepared by boiling.

Sower (sōᵘ·əɹ). OE. [f. SOW *v.* + -ER¹.] One who, or that which, sows.

Sow·-ge:lder (sau-). 1515. [f. SOW *sb.*] One whose business it is to geld or spay sows.

Sowl (saul, sūl), *v.* Now *dial.* 1607. [Of unkn. origin.] **1.** *trans.* To pull, seize roughly, etc., *by* the ear or ears. In later use esp. of dogs: To seize (a pig) by the ears. **2.** To pull or lug (the ears) 1654.

Sow·-me:tal (sau-). 1674. [f. SOW *sb.* 5.] Cast iron in sows or large ingots as it comes from the blasting- or smelting-furnace.

Sown, pa. pple of SOW *v.*

Sow·-pig (sau-). 1548. [f. SOW *sb.*] A young female pig, esp. one that has been spayed; a sow.

Sow-thistle (sau·pi:s'l). Also **sowthistle.** [Early ME. *suȝeþistel.*] One or other of the species of *Sonchus*; a plant belonging to this genus, esp. *S. oleraceus* and *S. asper,* common European weeds characterized by their sharply-toothed thistle-like leaves and milky juice.

Soy (soi). 1696. [– Jap. *soy,* colloq. f. *sho-yu* or *siyau-yu* – Chinese *shi-yu, shi-yau,* f. *shi* salted beans used as condiment + *yu* oil.] **1.** A sauce prepared chiefly in Japan, China, and India, from the beans of *Soja hispida* (*Dolichos soja*), and eaten with fish, etc. **2.** The soy-bean, *Soja hispida* 1880.

attrib.: **s-bean** = 2.

Soya (soi·ă). 1679. [– Du. *soja, soya* – Malay *soi* – Jap. *soy*; see prec.] = SOY.

Sozzle (sǫ·z'l), *sb. dial.* and *U.S.* 1823. [Cf. SOSS *sb.*¹] **1.** *dial.* A sloppy spoon-meat or medicine. **2.** *U.S.* A slattern; a state of sluttish confusion or disorder 1854. So **So·zzle** *v. trans.* to mix or mingle in a sloppy manner; *U.S.* to splash; to perform sluttishly or lazily (also *intr.*). **So·zzled** *ppl. a.* (*slang*) intoxicated.

Spa (spā, spǭ), *sb.* 1565. [A place-name.] **1.** With capital. The name of a watering place in the province of Liège, Belgium, celebrated for the curative properties of its mineral springs. **b.** In generalized sense 1610. **2.** A medicinal or mineral spring or well 1626. **3.** A town, locality, or resort possessing a mineral spring or springs; a watering-place of this kind 1777. Hence **Spa** (also **spaa**), *v. trans.* to subject to spa-treatment; *intr.* to frequent or visit a s. or spas.

†**Spaad.** 1594. [– obs. G. *spad, spade,* vars. of *spat* SPATH; see FELDSPAR.] *Min.* A variety of talc, gypsum, or spar, or a powder prepared from one or other of these, mainly used to form moulds for casting metal objects –1738.

Space (spēˈs), *sb.* ME. [Aphetic – (O)Fr. *espace* – L. *spatium.*] **I.** Denoting time or duration. **1.** Without article: Lapse or extent of time between two definite points, events, etc. Chiefly with *long, short, small,* etc. ME. †**b.** Delay (*rare*) –1554. †**2.** Time, leisure, or opportunity for doing something. Chiefly in *to have* or *give s.* –1675. **3.** With *the* (*that,* etc.): **a.** The amount or extent of time comprised or contained in a specified period ME. **b.** The amount of time already specified or indicated, or otherwise determined ME. **4.** With *a* and *pl.*: A period or interval of time ME.

1. Short s. ensued; I was not held..Long in expectance CARY. **2.** Come on, thou art granted s. SHAKS. Phr. *Time and s., s. and time.* **3. a.** In the s. of a tide, the salt water has not time to..return 1793. **b.** In less than the s...mentioned, the Count..came back SCOTT. †*In the mean s.,* meantime. **4.** He and his defended themselves..a long s. 1568. Phr. (*for*) *a s.,* for a moderate period of time.

II. Denoting area or extension. *Without article, in generalized sense.* **1.** Linear distance; interval between two or more points or objects. late ME. **2.** Superficial extent or area; also, extent in three dimensions. late ME. **b.** Extent or area sufficient for some purpose; room. Also const. *to* with inf. late ME. **c.** Extent or room in a letter, periodical, book, etc., available for or occupied by written or printed matter 1530. **3.** *Metaph.* Continuous, unbounded, or unlimited extension in every direction, regarded as void of matter, or without reference to this. Freq. coupled with *time.* 1656. **4.** *Astr.,* etc. The immeasurable expanse in which the solar and stellar systems, nebulæ, etc., are situated; the stellar depths 1667. **b.** In more limited sense: Extension in all directions, esp. from a given point 1827.

1. 'Twixt Host and Host but narrow s. was left, A dreadful interval MILT. **2.** Affrica in his kynde hap lasse s. TREVISA. The more it is heated, the more s. it takes up 1815. **b.** Crime that leaves no s. for penitence! 1869. **c.** I write no more to you, for lacke of s. 1530. **3.** All our conceptions are defined by conditions of time and s. 1892.

In particularized or limited senses. **5.** A certain stretch, extent, or area of ground, surface, sky, etc.; an expanse ME. **6.** A more or less limited area or extent; a small portion of space (in senses II. 2, 4 b). late ME. **b.** A division, section. late ME. **c.** A void or empty place or part 1837. **7.** An interval; a length of way; a distance. late ME. **b.** A short distance 1813. **8.** The dimensional extent occupied by a body or lying within certain limits 1530. **9.** *Mus.* One or other of the degrees or intervals between the lines of a staff 1597. **10.** An interval or blank between words, or lines, in printed or written matter 1676. **b.** *Typog.* One or other of certain small pieces of cast-metal, of various thicknesses and shorter than a type, used to separate words (or letters in a word), and also to justify the line 1676.

5. The s. around the building was silent 1794. *fig.* Oh indistinguished s. of Woman's will SHAKS. **6.** A viscid secreting s. called the stigma 1845. **7.** The s. which separates the stars 1842. Phr. †*From s. to s.,* at (regular) intervals. **8.** The things do not fill up that s., which the idea of them seemed to take up in his mind LAMB. **10.** Leaving a s. for his own name 1908.

attrib. and *Comb.*: **s.-nerve,** 'that portion of the auditory nerve which supplies the semicircular canals of the inner ear'; **-telegrapher,** one concerned or connected with s.-telegraphy; **-telegraphy,** wireless telegraphy; **-time,** a fusion of the concepts of s. and time regarded as a continuum in which the existent exists. Hence **Spa·ceful** *a.* (*rare*) spacious, commodious; wide, extensive.

Space (spē^{i}s), *v.* 1548. [Aphetic – (O)Fr. *espacer*, f. *espace* (see prec.) or f. the sb.] **1.** *trans.* To limit or bound in respect of space; to make of a certain extent. **2.** †**a.** To divide into spaces or sections (*rare*) 1578. **b.** *dial.* To measure (ground, etc.) by pacing 1808. **3.** To set, to arrange or put, at determinate intervals or distances. Also with *out.* 1703. **4.** *Typog.* **a.** With *out*: To extend to a required length by inserting additional space between the words (or lines) 1683. **b.** To separate (words, letters, or lines) by means of a space or spaces; occas. = a 1771. †**5.** *intr.* To walk, ramble, or roam –1599.

5. That Wolues, where she was wont to s., Should harbour'd be SPENSER.

Spaceless (spē^i·slės), *a.* 1606. [f. SPACE *sb.* + -LESS.] **1.** That is not subject to or limited by space; infinite, boundless. **2.** Occupying no space 1825.

1. There timeless, s., dwells the Eternal One 1819.

Spacer (spē^i·səɹ). 1884. [f. SPACE *v.* + -ER[1].] A device or piece of mechanism for spacing words; a piece of metal, etc., for making a space, interval, or division.

Spacious (spē^i·ʃəs), *a.* late ME. [– OFr. *spacios* (mod. *-ieux*) or L. *spatiosus*, f. *spatium*; see SPACE *sb.*[1], -OUS.] **1.** Of lands, etc.: Of vast, large, or indefinite superficial extent or area; wide, extensive. **2.** Of dwellings, rooms, roads, etc.: Having or affording ample space or room; large, roomy, commodious. late ME. **b.** quasi-*adv.* Spaciously. MILTON. **3.** Of things: Presenting, having, or covering a comparatively wide surface; large, ample, expansive 1631. **4.** *fig.* Great, extensive, ample 1595. **5.** Characterized by greatness, breadth, or comprehensiveness of character, style, or outlook 1600. †**6.** Prolonged –1647.

1. Ouse, slow winding through a level plain Of s. meads COWPER. **2.** The log burnt on the s. hearth 1832. **4.** You may Conuey your pleasures in a s. plenty, And yet seeme cold SHAKS. **5.** The s. times of great Elizabeth TENNYSON. Hence **Spa·cious-ly** *adv.*, **-ness.**

Spade (spē^{i}d), *sb.*[1] [OE. *spadu, spada, -e* = OFris. *spada*, OS. *spado* (Du. *spade, spa*), a word of the LG. area; rel. to Gr. σπάθη blade, paddle, shoulder-blade, broadsword; see next, SPATHE.] **1.** A tool for digging, paring, or cutting ground, turf, etc., now usually consisting of a flattish rectangular iron blade socketed on a wooden handle which has a grip or cross-piece at the upper end, the whole being adapted for grasping with both hands while the blade is pressed into the ground with the foot. **b.** The depth of a spade-blade; a spit 1674. **2.** An implement resembling a spade in form or use; *esp.* a spade-like knife used in flensing a whale 1820.

1. Phr. *To call a s. a s.*, to call things by their real names, without any euphemism; to use plain or blunt language; to be straightforward to the verge of rudeness or indecency.

Comb.: **s.-bayonet**, a broad-bladed bayonet, which may be used in digging shelter-holes or rifle-pits; **-bone**, the shoulder-blade; **-fish**, a fish resembling a s. in form; now *spec.* the moon-fish, *Chætodipterus faber*; **-foot**, (*a*) the foot used in pressing a s. into the ground; (*b*) a toad having a foot specially adapted for digging; **-guinea**, a guinea coined from 1787 to 1799, on which the shield bearing the arms has the form of a pointed s.; **-(s)man**, a labourer accustomed to work with a spade; **-work**, *lit.* work done with a spade; *fig.* pioneer work.

Spade (spē^{i}d), *sb.*[2] 1598. [– It. *spade*, pl. of *spada* SPADO[2].] **1.** One or other of the black spade-shaped marks by which one of four suits in a pack of playing-cards is distinguished; hence *pl.*, the cards belonging to or forming this suit. **2.** A card belonging to the spade-suit 1745.

Spade (spē^{i}d), *v.*[1] 1594. [f. SPADE *sb.*[1]] †**1.** *trans.* To cut in the form of a spade. NASHE. **2.** To dig up or remove with a spade 1647. **3.** To cut or flense with a whaling-spade 1887. **4.** *intr.* To work with a spade 1869.

†**Spade,** *v.*[2] 1611. [f. *spaid, spayed*, pa. pple. of SPAY *v.*, perh. assoc. w. L. *spado* SPADO[1].] *trans.* To spay –1816.

Spa·de-beard. 1598. [f. SPADE *sb.*[1] + BEARD *sb.*] A spade-shaped beard; a beard cut or trimmed to the shape of a (pointed or broad) spade-blade.

Spadeful (spē^i·dful). Also **-full.** 1643. [f. SPADE *sb.*[1] + -FUL.] A quantity that fills a spade; as much as a spade can hold or take up at one time.

Spader (spē^i·dəɹ). 1647. [f. SPADE *v.*[1] + -ER[1].] One who works with a spade; an implement which digs, etc., by means of spades; also *dial.*, a breast-plough.

Spadiceous (spē^{i}di·ʃəs), *a.* Now *Bot.* 1646. [f. L. *spadix, -ic-* SPADIX; see -EOUS.] **1.** Of a reddish or brownish colour. **2.** Having the nature or form of a spadix 1760. So **Spa·dicose** *a.* (in sense 2).

Spadici- (spē^{i}dəi·si), comb. form of SPADIX, used in a few terms of *Bot.*, as *spadiciflo·ral, -form* adjs.

‖**Spadille** (spădi·l). 1728. [Fr. – Sp. *espadilla*, dim. of *espada* sword; cf. SPADE *sb.*[2]] The ace of spades in ombre and quadrille. Also †‖**Spadi·llo** [– Sp.].

‖**Spadix** (spē^i·diks). *Pl.* **spadices** (spē^{i}dəi·sīz), and **spa·dixes.** 1760. [L. – Gr. σπάδιξ palm-branch, palm-coloured.] **1.** *Bot.* A form of inflorescence consisting of a thick fleshy spike, closely set with flowers, and enclosed in a spathe; a succulent spike, whether enclosed in a spathe or not. **2.** *Zool.* A part in cephalopods and hydrozoans having some analogy to a spadix in plants 1871.

‖**Spado**[1] (spā·do). late ME. [L. – Gr. σπάδων.] A eunuch.

†‖**Spado**[2] (spā·do). 1711. [Altered from It. *spada* or Sp. *espada* :– L. *spatha* – Gr. σπάθη; see SPADE *sb.*[1]] A cut-and-thrust sword –1785.

Spadroon (spădrū·n). *Obs.* exc. *Hist.* 1798. [– Genevan dial. *espadron* = Fr. *espadon* ESPADON.] A sword much lighter than a broadsword, and made both to cut and to thrust.

Spae (spē^i), *v.* orig. *north.* and *Sc.* ME. [– ON. *spá*, of unkn. origin.] To foretell, prophesy. Chiefly *trans.* So **Spae** *sb.*

Spae·man. *Sc.* 1480. [– ON. *spámann* (nom. *-maðr*); cf. next.] A soothsayer, wizard.

Spae·wife. *Sc.* 1774. [f. SPAE *v.* + WIFE *sb.*] A female fortune-teller; a sybil; a witch.

‖**Spaghetti** (spăge·ti). 1888. [It. pl., of dim. of *spago* string.] An Italian variety of alimentary paste made in solid cords intermediate in thickness between macaroni and vermicelli.

Spagyric (spădʒi·rik), *sb.* and *a.* *Obs.* exc. *Hist.* 1593. [– early mod.L. *spagiricus* (used and prob. invented by Paracelsus).] **A.** *sb.* †**1.** The science of alchemy or chemistry –1605. **2.** An alchemist 1593. **B.** *adj.* Pertaining to alchemy 1596. So **Spagy·rical** *a.*, **-ly** *adv.*

Spagyrist (spæ·dʒirist). 1652. [– mod.L. *spagirista*; see prec., -IST.] An alchemist.

‖**Spahi** (spā·hī). 1562. [– Turk. (Pers.) *sipāhī*; see SEPOY.] **1.** A horseman forming one of a body of Turkish cavalry which was to some extent organized on a feudal basis. Now *Hist.* **2.** A native Algerian horseman serving under the French Government 1863.

Spake, obs. poet. or arch. pa. t. of SPEAK *v.*

Spald, *v.* *north.* and *Sc.* late ME. [– MLG. *spalden* = OHG. *spaltan* (MHG. and G. *spalten*) split.] **a.** *trans.* To splinter, split, break up, lay open or flat. **b.** *intr.* To go apart, to splay out. Hence **Spa·lding,** a split and dried fish. **Spalding-knife.**

Spale (spē^{i}l), *sb.*[1] *Sc.* and *north.* 1470. [Of unkn. origin.] A splinter or chip, a thin piece or strip, of wood.

Spale, *sb.*[2] 1867. [Cf. SPALL *sb.*[3]] *Shipbuilding. pl.* Temporary cross beams used as internal strengthening.

Spall (spǭl), *sb.*[1] Also **spawl.** 1440. [Cf. SPALE *sb.*[1]] A chip or splinter, esp. of stone.

Spall, *sb.*[2] *rare.* 1590. [In XVI (Spenser) – It. *spalla*; in XIX (Carlyle) Sc. var. (*spaul*) of SPAULD.] A shoulder.

Spall (spǭl), *sb.*[3] Also **spawl.** 1895. [Cf. SPALE *sb.*[2]] A cross-spall; a cross-piece used in staging.

Spall (spǭl), *v.*[1] 1758. [Related to SPALL *sb.*[1]] **1.** *trans.* **a.** *Mining.* To break (ore) into smaller pieces. **b.** To dress (stones) roughly with a hammer 1793. **2.** To split or chip. Also with *off.* 1841. **3.** *intr.* To break *off* in fragments or chips 1853.

Spall (spǭl), *v.*[2] 1850. [Related to SPALL *sb.*[3]] *trans.* To fix (ship-frames) at the proper breadth by means of cross-spalls.

Spalpeen (spælpī·n). *Irish.* 1780. [– Ir. *spailpín* of unkn. origin; see -EEN[2].] **1.** A common workman or labourer; a farm-worker or harvester. **2.** A low or mean fellow; a scamp, a rascal 1815. **3.** A youngster 1891.

Spalt, *a.* Now *dial.* 1567. [Of unkn. origin.] Of wood: Brittle, short-grained; breaking easily through dryness or decay.

Spalt (spǭlt), *v.* *dial.* 1733. [app. var. of SPALD *v.*] *intr.* and *trans.* To split, tear, splinter.

Span (spæn), *sb.*[1] [OE. *span(n* = MLG. *spen(ne*, (M)Du. *spanne*, OHG. *spanna* (G. *spanne*), ON. *spǫnn* (*spann-*); perh. not continuous with OE., but in ME. prob. – OFr. *espan(n)e, espan* (mod. *empan*), of Gmc. origin.] **1.** The distance from the tip of the thumb to the tip of the little finger, or sometimes to the tip of the forefinger, when the hand is fully extended; the space equivalent to this taken as a measure of length, averaging nine inches. **2.** The hand with the thumb and fingers extended, esp. as a means of measuring. *Obs.* exc. *arch.* 1535. **3.** A thing, piece, etc., of the length of a span; a very small extent or space ME. **4.** A short space of time, esp. as the duration of human life; the (short) time during which a person lives 1599. **5.** The distance or space between the abutments of an arch, the supports of a beam, the piers of a bridge, the walls carrying a roof, etc.; the stretch or extent of this 1725. **b.** The maximum lateral dimension of an aeroplane or of a wing 1910. **6.** An arch of a bridge; a section between two piers. Also *transf.*, the vault of the sky. 1806. **b.** A stretch, line, or extent *of* something 1894.

1. Ehud made him a two edged dagger of a spanne longe COVERDALE *Judges* 3:16. **2.** Who hath measured heauen with his spanne? COVERDALE *Isa.* 40:12. **4.** Tymon is dead, who hath outstretcht his s. SHAKS.

Span (spæn), *sb.*[2] 1769. [– LG., Du. *span*, f. *spannen* unite, fasten, etc.; see SPAN *v.*[2]] **1.** *Naut.* One or other of various ropes or chains used as fastenings or means of connection. **2.** *U.S.* and *Canada.* A pair of horses harnessed and driven together, *esp.* a pair as nearly alike in colour and size as possible 1769. **3.** *S. Africa.* A team of oxen or other draught animals consisting of two or more yokes 1812.

1. *S.*, a rope with both ends made fast, for a purchase to be hooked to its bight DANA. *S.*,..a double rope with thimbles seized betwixt the two parts, stretched across the rigging as a fair-leader for ropes 1846.

Span (spæn), *v.*[1] late ME. [f. SPAN *sb.*[1]] **I.** *trans.* †**1.** To grasp, lay hold of, seize –1513. **2.** To measure by means of the outstretched hand; to cover with the hand in this way 1560. †**b.** To measure in any way –1717. †**c.** To measure out; to set a limit or bound to (life, etc.) –1657. **d.** To encircle or encompass (the wrist, waist, etc.) with the hand or hands 1781. **3.** Of the rainbow, a bridge, etc.: To form an arch across or over (the sky, a river, etc.); to cross from side to side 1633. **4.** To throw a bridge across (a river, etc.); to bridge over 1861.

2. My right hand hathe spanned the heauens BIBLE (Geneva) *Isa.* 48:13. **b.** How to s. Words with just note and accent MILT. **c.** My life is spand already SHAKS. **d.** And oft..her wrist she spanned COLERIDGE. **3.** A rainbow spanned the lake SHELLEY. Its waters are spanned by a fine stone bridge 1869. *transf.* Chaucer's life.. spans rather more than the latter half of the fourteenth century 1879.

II. *absol.* To make a span *over* something; to reach with or as with a span; to stretch or range *from* one place or point *to* another. Chiefly *fig.* 1535.

Span (spæn), *v.*[2] 1550. [– (M)Du. or

(M)LG. *spannen* = OE. *spannan*, OHG. *spannan* (G. *spannen*).] **1.** *trans.* To harness or yoke (horses, oxen, etc.); to attach to a vehicle. See also INSPAN *v.* and OUTSPAN *v.* **b.** *dial.* To fetter or shackle (a horse); *trans.* to enclose or confine 1844. **2.** To stretch, extend, make taut or tight; to draw (a bow). Now *arch.* 1597. **3.** †**a.** To wind up the wheel-lock of (a pistol or musket) by means of a spanner –1672. **b.** To screw tight with a spanner 1859. **4.** *Naut.* To fix, fasten, attach, or draw tight in some way. Also with *in.* 1781. **5.** *U.S. intr.* Of horses: To form a span or pair; to match in colour and size 1828.

1. We left Berea, and spanned out on the flat 1836. **2.** New bows I s., new arrows fill my quiver 1878. **5.** The horses s. well 1828.

Span, *a.*: see SPICK AND SPAN.

Span-, stem of SPAN *v.*[1] and SPAN *v.*[2], used in various technical combs., as **s.-dog,** either of a pair of dogs linked together, used to lift timber; **-piece** *dial.*, the collar-beam of a roof; **-shackle,** a large bolt with a triangular ring attached to which anchors or spars are lashed; **-worm** *U.S.*, a caterpillar of the *Geometræ* of Linnæus; a geometer.

Spanæmia (spænī·miă). Also (*U.S.*) **-emia.** 1845. [mod.L., f. Gr. σπανο-, comb. form of σπανός (usu. σπάνιος) scarce, scanty + -αιμία (as in ἀναιμία ANÆMIA), f. αἷμα blood.] *Path.* A morbid condition of the blood characterized by a deficiency of red corpuscles; poorness of the blood. Hence **Spanæ·mic** *a.* of or relating to, inducing, s.; also *sb.* a medicine inducing s.

Spancel (spæ·nsĕl), *sb.* 1610. [– Flem., Du., or LG. *spansel*, f. *spannen* SPAN *v.*[2] Cf. ON. *spennsl* clasp, tie.] A rope or fetter for hobbling cattle, horses, etc.; *esp.* a short, noosed rope for fettering the hind legs of a cow during milking. Hence **Spa·ncel** *v. trans.* to fetter or hobble with a s. or spancels.

†**Span-counter.** 1566. [f. SPAN *sb.*[1] or *v.*[1] + COUNTER *sb.*[3] 1.] A game in which the object of one player was to throw his counters so close to those of his opponent that the distance between them could be spanned with the hand –1815.

Spandrel (spæ·ndrĕl). 1477. [perh. f. AFr. *spaund(e)re*, poss. f. *espaundre* EXPAND *v.*] **1.** The triangular space between the outer curve of an arch and the rectangle formed by the mouldings enclosing it; any similar space between an arch and a straight-sided figure bounding it; also, the space included between the shoulders of two contiguous arches and the moulding or string-course above them. **b.** *transf.* The support of a set of steps; the material with which the space between a stair and the floor is filled in 1833. **2.** An inner border or frame for a picture 1862.

Spane (spēⁱn), *v. north.* and *Sc.* ME. [– MLG., MDu. *spanen*, corresp. to OHG. *spanan* entice, etc., (cf. MHG. *ein kint spanen* wean a child), app. rel. to OE. *spana, spona*, G. dial. *span* teat.] **1.** *trans.* To wean (an infant, lamb, etc.). **2.** *intr.* Of corn: To begin to take root and cast off the seed 1843.

†**Span-farthing.** 1688. [f. SPAN *sb.*[1] or *v.*[1] + FARTHING *sb.*] A game played with farthings after the same manner as span-counter –1777.

Spang, *sb.*[1] late ME. [– MDu. *spange* (Du. *spang*) = OHG. *spanga* (G. *spange*), ON. *spǫng, spang-* clasp, brooch :– Gmc. **spangō.*] †**1.** A small, glittering ornament; a spangle –1625. **2.** *techn.* A stain due to defective bleaching 1839.

1. The same horse Harneis were sette full of tremblyng spanges 1548.

Spang (spæŋ), *sb.*[2] Chiefly *Sc.* and *north.* 1513. [Goes with SPANG *v.*[2]] **1.** A jerk. **2. a.** A spring, bound, leap 1818. **b.** A strong kick 1863.

†**Spang,** *v.*[1] 1552. [f. SPANG *sb.*[1]] *trans.* To spangle; to ornament as with spangles –1621.

Spang (spæŋ), *v.*[2] *Sc.* and *north.* 1513. [Goes with SPANG *sb.*[2]; of unkn. origin.] **1.** *intr.* To spring, leap, bound; to move rapidly. **2.** *trans.* To cast, throw, jerk, bang 1513.

1. The trout slipped off, spanged down the bank, and..was lost 1833.

Spangle (spæ·ŋg'l), *sb.* late ME. [f. SPANG *sb.*[1] + -LE.] **1.** A small round thin piece of glittering metal (usu. brass or steel) with a hole in the centre to admit a thread, used for the decoration of textile fabrics and other materials. **b.** *transf.* A star (*poet.*) 1591. **c.** A glitter as of spangles (*rare.*) 1830. **2.** A condensed particle reflecting light, as of hoarfrost, snow, or dew 1590. **b.** A glittering point or speck of light 1821. **3.** A small or minute glittering particle, esp. of a mineral substance 1611. **4.** A scale, spot, or marking suggestive of a spangle 1796. **b.** An oak-spangle 1842.

1. A tawdry scarf of yellow silk, trimmed with tinsel and spangles SCOTT. **c.** Overhead was the s. of the stars 1893. **2.** The wintry clouds..drop spangles on the mountains 1862. Hence **Spa·ngly** *a.* resembling spangles, covered with spangles.

Spangle (spæ·ŋg'l), *v.* 1548. [f. prec.] **1.** *trans.* To decorate (a garment or the like) with spangles. **b.** To adorn as with spangles; to cause to glitter as if so decorated. Const. *with.* 1591. **2.** Of things: To dot or cover (something) as if with spangles 1596. **3.** In passive: To present an appearance as if decorated with spangles; to be dotted or spotted *with* something suggestive of spangles 1667. **4.** *intr.* To glitter or sparkle with, or in the manner of, spangles 1639.

1. b. A hundred torches play'd, Spangling the wave with lights SCOTT. **2.** What stars do s. heauen with such beautie? SHAKS. **3.** The meadows, spangled with yellow flowers 1874. **4.** Sparks flashing and spangling 1857. Hence **Spa·ngler,** one who or that which spangles.

Spangled (spæ·ŋg'ld), *ppl. a.* 1584. [f. SPANGLE *sb.* or *v.* + -ED.] **1.** Adorned with or as with spangles. **2.** Speckled 1586.

Spanglet (spæ·ŋglĕt). 1610. [f. SPANG *sb.*[1] + -LET, or SPANGLE *sb.* + -ET.] A little spangle.

Sweet star..S. of light on evening's shadowy veil SHELLEY.

Spaniard (spæ·nyăɹd), *sb.* (and *a.*). [Late ME. *Spaynard*, aphet. – OFr. *Espaignart, Espaniard*, f. *Espaigne* (mod. *Espagne*); see -ARD.] **1.** A native of Spain; one of Spanish descent. Occas. (with *the*) in collect. sing. = the Spanish nation or people. **2.** A Spanish ship or vessel 1537. **3. a.** New Zealand bayonet- or spear-grass 1851. **b.** A species of willow 1871. **4.** *attrib.* (or as *adj.*) 1485.

Spaniel (spæ·nyĕl), *sb.* (and *a.*) [Late ME. *spaynel* – OFr. *espaigneul* (mod. *épagneul*) :– Rom. **spaniolus*, for *Hispaniolus* Spanish, f. *Hispania* Spain.] **1.** A small or medium-sized variety of dog characterized by large drooping ears, long silky hair, keen scent, and affectionate nature, some breeds of which are used for sporting purposes, esp. for starting and retrieving game, while others are favourite pet- or toy-dogs. **2.** *fig.* **a.** One who pries into, or searches out, something 1562. **b.** A submissive, cringing, or fawning person 1592. **3.** *attrib.*, passing into *adj.* in the sense 'meanly submissive, cringing, fawning', etc. 1601.

1. For, as a spaynel, she wol on hym lepe CHAUCER. *Alpine, Blenheim, cocker, English, King Charles, Norfolk* (etc.) *s.* **2. b.** You are the Spaniels of the court HEYWOOD. Hence **Spa·niel** *v. rare, intr.* to act like a s., to be meanly submissive or subservient; *trans.* to follow, or fawn upon, like a s.

Spaniolize (spæ·niŏləiz), *v.* Now *rare.* 1598. [Aphetic f. HISPANIOLIZE, perh. after Fr. †*espagnoliser*. Cf. contemp. *Spaniolate* vb.] *trans.* To make Spanish; to imbue with Spanish notions or tendencies; to cause to follow Spanish fashions. (Chiefly in pa. pple.) So **Spa·niolate** *v. trans.* (*rare*) 1577.

Spanish (spæ·niʃ), *a.* (*adv.*) and *sb.* ME. [f. SPAIN + -ISH[1], with later shortening of the first element.] **A.** *adj.* **1.** Of or pertaining to Spain or its people; inhabiting, native to, characteristic of, Spain. **2.** Of things: Of actual or attributed Spanish origin; made, manufactured, or produced in Spain (or Spanish America); associated or connected with Spain on this account 1483. **b.** Of articles of dress, etc.: Made in Spain, of Spanish materials, or after the Spanish fashion 1530. **3.** Of a type or kind characteristic of, or exemplified by, the Spaniards 1530. **4.** Of or pertaining to, dealing or connected with, the language or literature of Spain 1599.

1. *S. Main*, the mainland of America adjacent to the Caribbean Sea, esp. that portion of the coast stretching from the Isthmus of Panama to the mouth of the Orinoco; in later use also, the sea contiguous to this, or the route traversed by the Spanish register ships. Now *Hist.*

Special collocations. **S. black,** a pigment obtained by burning cork in closed vessels. **S. brown,** a kind of earth having a reddish brown colour, used as a pigment; also, the colour which this imparts. **S. burton** *Naut.*, a purchase composed of three single blocks, or two single blocks and a hook. A double S. burton has one double and two single blocks. †**S. chalk,** a variety of steatite found in Spain. **S. fox** *Naut.*, a rope-yarn twisted contrary to the lay. **S. juice, liquorice** (see LIQUORICE 1). **S. red,** an ochre resembling Venetian red, but slightly yellower. **S. reef** *Naut.*, a form of reefing in which the yards are lowered on the cap of the mast to reduce the spread of square sails; also, a knot tied in the head of the jib to reduce its area. **S. white,** (*a*) finely powdered chalk used as a pigment or for its cleansing properties; (*b*) a fine quality of flour. **S. windlass** *Naut.*, a windlass with an iron bolt inserted through the bight of the rope to serve as a lever.

b. In the specific names or designations of animals; esp. **S. fly,** = CANTHARIDES. **S. mackerel** (see MACKEREL[1] 1.).

c. In the names of plants, trees, etc. denoting either varieties or distinct species found in Spain or Spanish America (esp. the West Indies). **S. bayonet** (see BAYONET *sb.*). **S. bean,** (*a*) a variety of broad bean; (*b*) *U.S.*, the scarlet runner. **S. chestnut,** *Castanea vesca*, a native of Asia Minor and the region eastward of the Himalayas. **S. dagger,** a West Indian name for *Yucca aloifolia*. **S. elm,** an evergreen timber-tree (*Cordia geraschanthus*) of the West Indies. **S. grass,** esparto grass. **S. iris,** a bulbous iris of the genus *Xiphium*, esp. *X. vulgare*. **S. moss,** *U.S.*, the epiphytic plant, *Tillandsia usneoides*, of the Southern States; long-beard. **S. needles,** the American plant *Bidens bipinnata* or its prickly fruit. **S. nut,** (*a*) an iridaceous plant, *Moræa sisyrinchium*, the bulbs of which are eaten in Spain; (*b*) a variety of hazel-nut, *Corylus colurna*. **S. potato** (see POTATO *sb.* 1.).

B. *sb.* or *ellipt.* The Spanish language 1485. **C.** *adv. U.S. To walk S.*, to (cause to) walk under compulsion, prop. with some one holding the collar and the seat of the trousers 1848.

Spanish broom. 1562. [SPANISH *a.*] The plant *Spartium junceum* (or *Cytisus junceus*) common to the Mediterranean region, the rush-like branches or twigs of which are used in basket-work and yield a fibre employed in the manufacture of cords, coarse cloth, etc.

Spanishly (spæ·niʃli), *adv.* 1641. [f. SPANISH *a.* + -LY[2].] Towards Spain or Spanish policy; like Spanish; in a characteristically Spanish manner.

Spank (spæŋk), *sb. dial.* or *colloq.* 1785. [f. SPANK *v.*[1]] A smart or sounding blow, esp. one given with the open hand; a slap or smack. **b.** The sharp sound produced by this 1833.

Spank (spæŋk), *v.*[1] *dial.* and *colloq.* 1727. [perh. imit. of the sound.] **1.** *trans.* To slap or smack (a person, esp. a child) with the open hand. Also *absol.* **2.** *intr.* **a.** To drop or fall with a spank or smack 1800. **b.** Of a boat: To pound, beat, or slap the water in sailing (*rare*) 1891.

Spank (spæŋk), *v.*[2] *dial.* and *colloq.* 1807. [prob. a back-formation from SPANKING *ppl. a.* 2.] **1.** *intr.* To move or travel with speed and elasticity; to go quickly and vigorously; to ride or drive at a sharp trot and in a smart or stylish manner. **b.** *spec.* Of horses, or of persons driving or riding them 1811. **c.** Of ships: To sail quickly and smartly; to bowl *along* 1834. **2.** *trans.* To drive (horses) quickly and smartly 1825.

2. How knowingly did he s. the horses along THACKERAY.

Spanker (spæ·ŋkəɹ). 1663. [Related to SPANKING *ppl. a.* or (in later use) f. SPANK *v.*[2]] †**1.** *slang.* A gold coin, usu. in *pl.*, coin, money –1785. **2.** *dial.* and *colloq.* Anything exceptionally large or fine 1751. **b.** A heavy blow or smack 1772. **3.** *Naut.* A fore-and-aft sail, set with a gaff and boom at the aftermost part of the ship 1794. **4.** *dial.* A person who takes long rapid strides 1808. **5.** *dial.* and *colloq.* A fast-going horse 1814.

Comb.: **s.-boom** *Naut.*, the boom on which the s. is set.

Spanking (spæ·ŋkiŋ), *vbl. sb.* 1854. [f. SPANK *v.*[1] + -ING[1].] The action of beating or slapping with the open hand by way of punishment.

Spanking (spæ·ŋkiŋ), *ppl. a.* Chiefly *dial.* and *colloq.* 1666. [perh. of symbolic origin; cf. *whacking, thumping.*] **1.** Very big, large, or fine; exceptionally good in some respect. **2.** Of horses; *esp.* in later use: Moving or travelling at a rapid pace and in a smart and vigorous manner 1738. **3.** Of a breeze: Blowing strongly or briskly; rattling 1849. **4.** Of a pace, etc.: Rapid, smart, vigorous 1857.

4. The wheelers in a s. trot, and leaders cantering 1857.

Spanless (spæ·nlės), *a.* 1847. [f. SPAN *v.*[1] + -LESS.] That cannot be spanned.

Spa·n-long, *a.* 1593. [f. SPAN *sb.*[1] + LONG *a.*] Having the length of a span; hence, brief, short.

White faies..And span-long elves that dance about a pool B. JONS.

Spanner (spæ·nəɹ). 1639. [– G. *spanner*, f. *spannen* SPAN *v.*[2]] †**1.** An instrument by which the spring in a wheel-lock firearm was spanned or wound up –1863. **2.** A hand-tool, usually consisting of a small bar of steel, having an opening, grip, or jaw at the end which fits over or clasps the nut of a screw, a bolt, coupling, etc., and turns it or holds it in position; a wrench 1790. **3.** *Mech.* A bar or lever for opening the valves of a steam-engine 1773.

Span-new (spæ·n,niū), *a.* Now chiefly *dial.* Also **span new.** ME. [– ON. *spán-nýr*, f. *spánn* chip + *nýr* new.] Quite or perfectly new.

A maker of s. governments and religions COBBETT.

Span-roof (spæ·n,rūf). 1823. [SPAN *sb.*[1]] A roof consisting of two inclined sides.

Spar (spāɹ), *sb.*[1] [ME. *sperre, sparre* – ON. *sperra* or aphetic – OFr. *esparre* (mod. *épare, épar*) or its Gmc. source, repr. by MLG., MDu. *sparre* (Du. *spar*), OHG. *sparro* (G. *sparren*), ON. *sparri*; f. Gmc. base of unkn. origin.] **1.** One of the common rafters of a roof. Now chiefly *dial.* **2.** A pole or piece of timber of some length and moderate thickness; *spec.* an undressed stem of fir, etc., under six inches in diameter. late ME. **3.** †**a.** A bar of wood used to fasten a gate or door –1668. **b.** A spoke, bar, or cross-bar 1687. **4.** *Naut.* A general term for masts, yards, booms, gaffs, etc. 1640.

4. b. Each of the main lateral members of the wing of an aeroplane 1913.

Comb.: **s.-buoy,** a buoy designed with a s. or mast which stands almost perpendicularly out of the water; **-deck,** a light upper deck in a vessel; **-torpedo,** a torpedo fastened on the end of a s. projecting from the bows of the boat.

Spar (spāɹ), *sb.*[2] 1581. [– MLG. *spar*, rel. to OE. *spæren* of plaster or mortar, *spærstān* gypsum. See also FELDSPAR.] *Min.* **1.** A general term for a number of crystalline minerals more or less lustrous in appearance and admitting of easy cleavage. **b.** *pl.* Different varieties of this 1668. **2. a.** A fragment or particle of spar. Also *transf.* 1855. **b.** An ornament made of spar 1851.

1. *Calcareous, Derbyshire, Iceland s.*: see these words and CALC-, FELD-, FLUOR-SPAR.

Spar (spāɹ), *sb.*[3] late ME. [f. SPAR *v.*[2]] †**1.** A thrust. late ME only. **2.** A boxing-match; a display of boxing; a motion of sparring 1814. **3.** A cock-fight 1849. **4.** *transf.* A wordy contest or dispute. *colloq.* 1836.

Spar (spāɹ), *v.*[1] [ME. *sperre, sparre* – MDu. *sperren* = (O)HG. *sperren*, f. the stem *sparr-* of SPAR *sb.*[1]] **1.** *trans.* To fasten (a door or gate) with a bar or bolt; to shut securely. Also occas. with *up*. Now *arch.* †**2.** *gen.* To close; fasten, secure, lock (*up*), etc. –1615. †**3.** To confine, enclose, or imprison; to shut *up*, in a place –1600. †**4.** To shut (a person or thing) *in* or *out* –1535.

1. Sperre the yate fast for feare of fraude SPENSER.

Spar (spāɹ), *v.*[2] [OE. *sperran, spyrran*, **spierran*, corresp. to ON. *sperrask* kick out, of unkn. origin.] †**1.** *intr.* To dart or spring; to strike or thrust rapidly –1450. **2.** Of cocks: To strike with the feet or spurs; to fight 1570. **b.** *trans.* To cause (a cock) to spar; to exercise in sparring 1686. **3.** To engage in or practise boxing; to make the motions of attack and defence with the arms and fists; to box. Also const. *at.* 1755. **4.** To dispute; to bandy words 1698.

2. A young cock will s. at his adversary before his spurs are grown 1776. **Spa·rring** *vbl. sb.* attrib. *s. partner*, a boxer employed to practise with another.

Spar (spāɹ), *v.*[3] 1657. [f. SPAR *sb.*[1]] **1.** *trans.* To furnish, make, or close *in*, with spars. **2.** *Naut.* **a.** In pa. pple: Provided with spars 1840. **b.** To fix spars across (the rigging) preparatory to rattling down 1860.

Sparable (spæ·răb'l). 1627. [Reduced form of SPARROW-BILL.] A small headless wedge-shaped iron nail (stouter than a *sprig*), used in the soles and heels of boots and shoes.

†**Sparadrap.** 1543. [– (O)Fr. *sparadrap* – It. *sparadrappo*, of unkn. origin.] *Med.* A piece of linen or other cloth dipped in, or spread with, some ointment or medicament for use as a bandage or plaster –1728.

†**Spa·rage.** 1565. [ult. – med.L. *sparagus*, whence Fr. †*esparge*, It. *sparagio*. See ASPARAGUS.] Asparagus –1612. So †**Spa·ragus** 1543.

Spare (spēəɹ), *sb.* ME. [f. SPARE *v.* and *a.*] †**1.** The fact of leaving unhurt or unharmed; sparing; leniency, mercy –1633. **2.** The exercise of economy, frugality, or moderation. Chiefly in the phr. *to make* (*no*, etc.) *s.* 1577. **3.** *ellipt.* A spare or reserve sum of money; a spare room; a spare part, tool, tyre, etc., carried esp. by motorists to replace a breakage, etc. 1642. **4.** In skittles and ten-pins (*U.S.*): The knocking down of all the pins with two bowls (thus leaving one 'to spare'), or with the first bowl (= *double s.*); the score for doing this 1879.

1. Cut them off..and make no s. of any of them 1633. **2.** At our meal there was no spare of liquor 1655.

Spare (spēəɹ), *a.* and *adv.* [OE. *spær* sparing, frugal = OHG. *spar*, ON. *sparr*; see next.] **I. 1.** Not in actual or regular use at the time spoken of, but carried, held, or kept in reserve for future use or to supply an emergency; orig. *Naut.*; additional, extra. †**b.** Of land, ground, etc.: Uncultivated, unoccupied, vacant –1669. **2.** That can be spared, dispensed with, or given away, as being in excess of actual requirements; superfluous 1553. **b.** Of time: Leisure 1610.

1. A small s. Mast, Such as sea-faring men prouide for stormes SHAKS. One or more s. beds for lodging of strangers 1702. A spare part (1897), room (1837). **2.** When I..have enough s. gold To boil away, you shall be welcome to me 1613. **b.** The female world..have more s. time upon their hands ADDISON.

II. †**1.** Of speech: Sparing; marked by reticence or reserve (*rare*) –1460. **2.** Of persons, their limbs, etc.: Having little flesh; not fat or plump; lean, thin 1548. **b.** Const. *in* or *of* (flesh) 1632. **c.** *poet.* Growing thinly or sparsely 1815. †**3.** Of persons: Sparing *of* or *in* something, esp. diet or speech –1697. †**b.** Not lavish, liberal, or profuse; frugal, niggardly; abstemious –1633. **4.** Characterized by meanness, bareness, economy, or frugality, esp. in regard to food 1560. **b.** Of diet, fare, meals, etc.: Consisting of a comparatively small amount of food, esp. of a plain kind; not plentiful 1570. **c.** *poet.* Scanty, meagre, rare 1813. **5.** As *adv.* Sparely; with spare diet. SCOTT.

2. O, giue me the s. men, and spare me the great ones SHAKS. **c.** Grey rocks did peep from the s. moss SHELLEY. **3.** Are they s. in diet SHAKS. **4.** As it is a s. life..it fits my humor well: but as there is no more plentie in it, it goes much against my stomacke SHAKS. **b.** S. feast!—a radish and an egg! COWPER. **5.** The warrior.. Feeds hard and s., and seldom sleeps SCOTT. Hence **Spa·re-ly** *adv.*, **-ness.**

Spare (spēəɹ), *v.* [OE. *sparian* = OFris. *sparia*, OS., OHG. *sparōn* (Du., G. *sparen*), ON. *spara* :– Gmc. **sparōjan.*] **I. 1.** *trans.* To leave (a person) unhurt, unharmed, or uninjured; to refrain from inflicting injury or punishment upon; to allow to escape, go free, or live. **b.** To allow to be free or exempt *from* some task –1794. **c.** To deal leniently or gently with 1535. **d.** To refrain from afflicting or distressing 1794. **2.** *absol.* To exercise or show mercy, forbearance, or leniency ME. **3.** *trans.* **a.** To abstain from visiting (a sin, etc.) with due punishment; to forgive or pardon. late ME. **b.** To preserve or save (life) in place of destroying; to allow to continue or last 1594. **4.** To abstain from destroying, removing, damaging, or injuring (a thing) OE.

1. Spare my gray-beard, you wagtaile? SHAKS. Whom ev'n the savage Beasts had spar'd, they kill'd DRYDEN. **c.** My lady used not to s. Colonel Esmond in talking of him THACKERAY. **2.** He will not s. in the day of vengeance *Prov.* 6:34. **3. b.** He hoped that the squire's life would be long spared TROLLOPE. **4.** Shee..was now about to put out his eyes, which all this while were spared SIDNEY.

II. 1. To refrain from using or consuming; to use in a frugal or economical manner. Now *rare.* OE. †**b.** To save, hoard, or store up –1683. **c.** *absol.* To use or practise economy or frugality; to be parsimonious or niggardly; to live or act sparingly. late ME. **d.** In passive: To be left over or unused 1577. **2.** To abstain from using, employing, exercising, etc.; to forbear, omit, or avoid the use or occasion of; also, to use or deal in, with moderation, economy, or restraint OE. **b.** *ellipt.* To refrain from doing something. Now *rare* or *Obs.* late ME. **3.** To avoid incurring or being involved in, to save (expense or labour) ME. **b.** To avoid, shun, keep clear of. Now *rare.* late ME. **4.** To dispense with; to part with to another or others, esp. without inconvenience or loss to oneself; to do without ME. **b.** To set aside *for* some particular use or purpose; to keep in reserve ME. **c.** To set apart, save, or give (time) from one's usual duties or avocations; to have (time) free 1548. **5.** With direct and indirect object: **a.** To give or grant; to supply (a person) with (something) out of a stock, quantity, etc. 1593. **b.** To save or relieve (a person, one's feelings, etc.) from (something) 1681.

1. Free Nature's bounty thriftily they spent, And spared the Stock COWLEY. **c.** I, who at some times spend, at others s. POPE. **2.** Had he but spared his tongue and pen, He might have rose like other men SWIFT. S. the rod and spoil the child 1841. **3.** No time, trouble, or expense has been spared in the matter 1892. **b.** Shun me and I will s. your haunts SHAKS. **4.** Kirke could s. no soldiers; but he had sent..some experienced officers MACAULAY. **c.** Let all the citizens who can s. time hear..such causes 1875. **5.** And now A word, but one,..Not one to s. her TENNYSON. **b.** I was, however, spared this infliction 1893.

III. *intr. To s. for*: **a.** To desist or refrain from some action because or on account of (difficulty, opposition, loss, etc.). Now *arch.* ME. **b.** With neg.: To refrain from action in order to save (expense, trouble, etc.); to be sparing of or in (something). late ME.

a. S. not for spoiling of thy steed SCOTT. **b.** S. for no cost MARLOWE. Hence **Spa·reable** *a.* 1688.

†**Spa·reful,** *a.* 1565. [f. SPARE *sb.* or *v.* + -FUL.] Sparing, frugal –1600. Hence †**Spa·reful-ly** *adv.*, †**-ness.**

Spareless (spēə·ɹlės), *a.* and *adv.* late ME. [f. as prec. + -LESS.] †**1.** Unstinted, unlimited –1450. **2.** Unsparing, merciless 1589. **3.** As *adv.* Without stint 1567.

Spare-rib (spēə·rib, spæ·rib). 1596. [prob. – MLG. *ribbesper* (whence dial. *ribspare* XVII), with transposition of the two elements and assoc. with SPARE *a.*] A cut of meat, esp. of pork, consisting of part of the ribs somewhat closely trimmed.

Sparge (spāɹdʒ), *v.* 1560. [In 1 Sc. and north. dial. var. of PARGET *v.*, beside †*sparget* (XV), †*spargen* (XVI–XVII); in 2, 3, app. – L. *spargere* sprinkle.] **1.** *trans.* To plaster; to rough-cast. **2.** To dash, splash, or sprinkle (water) about 1785. **3.** *Brewing.* To sprinkle (malt) with hot water. Also *absol.* 1839. Hence **Sparge** *sb.*, sprinkling; *Brewing*, the spray of water with which the malt is sprinkled. **Spa·rger,** an appliance for sprinkling water, esp. in brewing.

Spargefication (spāɹdʒĕfikē¹·ʃən). Also **-ification.** 1835. [f. L. *spargere*; see -FICATION.] The action of sprinkling or scattering. So **Spargefa·ction.** SWIFT.

Sparhawk (spā·ɹhǫk). Now *arch.* or *dial.*

[OE. *spearhafoc*, = ON. *sparrhaukr*, f. stem of *spearwa* SPARROW + *hafoc* HAWK.] A sparrowhawk.

Spaˑring (spēᵊ·riŋ), *ppl. a.* and *adv.* ME. [f. SPARE *v.* + -ING.²] **1.** Inclined to save, niggard; restrained in discourse or statement; scanty, limited; forbearing, merciful. †**2.** As *adv.* Sparingly –1742. Hence **Spa·ring-ly** *adv.*, **-ness.**

Spark (spāɹk), *sb.*¹ [OE. *spærca*, *spearca*, = (M)LG., MDu. *sparke*, of unkn. origin.] **1.** A small particle of fire or an ignited fragment, thrown off from a burning body or remaining in one almost extinguished, or produced by the impact of one hard body on another. **b.** *fig.* and in fig. context; freq. with allusion to the beginning or immediate cause of a fire or conflagration OE. **2.** A small trace, indication, or portion *of* some quality, feeling, sentiment, etc., in some way comparable to a spark, esp. in respect of its latent possibilities OE. **b.** A small remnant, fragment, piece, atom, or amount *of* something 1548. **3.** The vital or animating principle in man; a trace *of* life or vitality. Freq. in *vital s.*, *s. of life.* late ME. **4. a.** A small ruby or diamond: orig. *diamond* or *ruby s.* and *s. of diamond*, etc. 1629. **b.** A (glittering) fragment or particle *of* some metal, ore, or mineral 1560. **5.** A bright or glittering flash or gleam of light. Also *transf.*, a bright glance. 1542. **6.** *Electr.* In full *electric(al) s.*: A brilliant streak or flash of light produced by a discontinuous discharge of electricity between two conductors at a short or moderate distance apart 1748. **b.** *spec.* An electric spark serving to fire the explosive mixture in the oil-engine of a motor.

1. Yet man is borne vnto trouble, as the sparkes flie vpward *Job* 5:7. **b.** Left alone they might have remained quiet; but they only wanted the s. DISRAELI. Phr. *A s. in one's throat* (slang), a constant thirst. **2.** They still kept alive the sparks of future friendship 1820. **4. a.** All the haft twinkled with diamond sparks TENNYSON. **b.** This bluish stone was filled with sparks of virgin copper 1796. **6.** *fig.* Animated by the electric s. of genius 1846. *Sparks* (slang), a wireless operator.

attrib. and *Comb.*: **s.-arrester,** a device for arresting sparks in locomotive funnels or chimneys; **-gap,** a space between two terminals through which an electric spark passes; **-plug** *U.S.* = sparking-plug. Hence **Spa·rker,** a s.-arrester.

Spark (spāɹk), *sb.*² 1513. [prob. a fig. use of prec.] †**1.** A woman of great beauty, elegance, or wit –1676. **2.** A young man of an elegant or foppish character; one who affects smartness 1513. **3.** A beau, lover, suitor (*arch.*) 1706.

1. The louely sparke, the bright Laodice CHAPMAN. **2.** Hark'ee, my s., none of your grinning! MISS BURNEY. **3.** A very woman..daring death..for the sake of thee, her handsome s.! BROWNING.

Spark (spāɹk), *v.*¹ ME. [f. SPARK *sb.*¹] **1.** *intr.* To emit or give forth a spark or sparks; to sparkle. **2.** To issue, come forth, fall, etc., as or in the manner of sparks 1513. **3.** *trans.* **a.** To send *out*, or emit, in or as sparks 1596. **b.** *Electr.* To affect, act or operate upon, by the emission or transmission of electric sparks. Also *absol.*, to send a spark *across*, etc. 1889.

1. *transf.* Her eyes did sparke, At every glance, like Diamonds in the darke QUARLES. Hence **Spa·rking** *vbl. sb.*, esp. in *sparking-plug*, a device for firing the explosive mixture in a motor engine.

Spark (spāɹk), *v.*² 1676. [f. SPARK *sb.*²] †**1.** *intr.* With *it.* To play the spark or gallant; to show off –1709. **2.** *U.S.* To engage in courtship; to play the suitor, wooer, or beau. Also with *it.* 1807. **b.** *trans.* To court 1888.

2. He used to go sparkin' round among the girls 1884.

Sparkish (spā·ɹkiʃ), *a.* 1641. [f. SPARK *sb.*² + -ISH¹.] **1.** Of persons: Having the character, airs, or manner of a spark or gallant. **2.** Of things: Characteristic of, or appropriate to, a spark; of a smart or elegant make 1657. Hence **Spa·rkish-ly** *adv.*, **-ness.**

Sparkle (spā·ɹk'l), *sb.* ME. [f. SPARK *sb.*¹ + -LE 1.] **1.** A small spark; an ignited or luminous particle. **b.** *fig.* and in fig. context; freq. with allusion to the kindling of a fire or conflagration. late ME. **2.** A slight beginning, trace, indication, or manifestation *of* something. late ME. †**3.** A vital or animating principle (*rare*). late ME. †**4.** A small ruby or diamond (*rare*) –1704. **5.** A glittering or flashing point of light. Also *fig.* 1490. **b.** A flashing or fiery glance 1590. **6.** Glittering or flashing appearance or quality; lively brightness 1589. **b.** Liveliness of spirit; smartness; wittiness 1611. **c.** *spec.* The appearance characteristic of certain wines, due to the presence of carbonic-acid gas 1833. **7.** A small piece, part, spot, etc. *of* something; now only, a (glittering) particle 1570.

1. Smoak and bickering flame, and sparkles dire MILT. **b.** Some unlucky s. from a Tory paper set Steele's politicks on fire JOHNSON. **2.** Sparclis of grace þat we felen WYCLIF. **5.** Swift as the S. of a glancing Star MILT. **6.** The occasional s. of the long line of spears SCOTT. **7.** Sparkles of blood on the white foam are cast SHELLEY.

Sparkle (spā·ɹk'l), *v.*¹ ME. [f. SPARK *sb.*¹ + -LE 3; cf. (M)Du. *sparkelen.*] **I.** *intr.* **1.** To issue, fly, spring *out* or *forth* in sparkles or small particles. **2.** To emit sparks or sparkles of fire 1480. **b.** Of the eyes: To flash with anger or rage 1593. **3.** To reflect or emit numerous separate rays or points of light; to glitter or flash. late ME. **b.** To move, proceed, flow, etc., in a glittering or sparkling manner 1823. **4.** Of wines, etc.: To effervesce with small glittering bubbles. late ME. **5. a.** Of feelings, etc.: To appear or be evident *in* (or *through*) the eyes by the brightness or animation of these 1592. **b.** Of the eyes: To be bright or animated; to shine; to glisten 1700.

1. When some heat of difference sparkled out TENNYSON. **2. b.** Mine eyes should s. like the beaten Flint SHAKS. **3.** Sparkles this Stone as it was wont? SHAKS. *fig.* His Wit sparkles as well as his Eyes 1699. **b.** To trace your..waters sparkling through green Hertfordshire LAMB. **5. a.** Disdaine and Scorne ride sparkling in her eyes SHAKS. **b.** A burly man..whose little eyes seemed always sparkling with unclerical humour 1883.

II. *trans.* **1.** To cause to sparkle or glitter 1553. **2.** To emit or eject (fire, etc.) as or like sparks 1588. **b.** Of the eyes: To indicate (a feeling) by brightness or animation 1601.

1. Aurora now..Sparkled with rosy light the dewy lawn POPE. **2.** Womens eyes..sparcle still the right promethean fire SHAKS. Hence **Spa·rkling-ly** *adv.*, **-ness.**

Spa·rkle, *v.*² *Obs.* or *dial.* late ME. [Alteration of SPARPLE *v.* Cf. DISPARKLE.] **1.** *intr.* Of persons: To scatter, disperse 1440. **2.** *trans.* To cause to scatter or disperse; to drive in different directions 1470. **3.** To cast abroad; to scatter, sprinkle, or strew 1440. **4.** To sprinkle, bestrew or bespatter *with* something; to dot thickly. late ME. **5.** To disseminate or diffuse; to spread or circulate 1532.

2. Then went the kyng..and sparcled them then so That North they went 1470. **4.** The pauement of the temple is all sparcled with bludde 1555.

Sparkler (spā·ɹkləɹ). 1713. [f. SPARKLE *v.*¹ + -ER¹.] **1.** One who sparkles; *esp.* a vivacious, witty, or pretty young woman. **2.** A bright or sparkling eye. Chiefly *pl.* Latterly *colloq.* or *slang.* 1746. **3.** A sparkling gem; a diamond; esp. *pl.* 1822. **4.** Something which shines or sparkles: a sparkling firework which is noiseless 1879. **5.** A tiger-beetle 1860.

Sparkless (spā·ɹklės), *a.* 1821. [f. SPARK *sb.*¹ + -LESS.] Free from or devoid of sparks; emitting no sparks; *spec.* in *Electr.*

Sparklet (spā·ɹklėt). 1689. [f. as prec. + -LET.] **1.** A small spark or sparkle. **2.** A small sparkling ornament for a dress 1902. **3.** (*pl.*) Trade name for a capsule containing carbonic acid gas under pressure used with a siphon for making aerated water 1904.

Sparkling (spā·ɹkliŋ), *ppl. a.* ME. [f. SPARKLE *v.*¹ + -ING².] **1.** That emits sparks or sparkles. **2.** Of the eyes: Flashing, bright, animated. late ME. **3.** Reflecting or emitting rays of light; flashing, glittering, brilliant, resplendent. late ME. **4.** Characterized by brilliancy and liveliness; brilliant, animated, sprightly 1647. **5.** Of pleasure: Characterized by a high degree of delight or enjoyment 1789.

1. A large s. fire of turf and bog-wood SCOTT. **2.** His s. Eyes, repleat with wrathfull fire SHAKS. **3.** Drynke grene wyne, clere, sharpe and sparklynge in tempure 1422. **4.** A piece of s...rhetoric CARLYLE. Hence **Spa·rkling-ly** *adv.*, **-ness** (*rare*).

Sparling (spā·ɹliŋ). Now chiefly *north.* and *Sc.* ME. [Aphetic – OFr. *esperlinge* (mod. *éperlan*), of Gmc. origin (cf. MLG., MDu. *spirlinc*, G. *spierling*).] **1.** The common European smelt, *Osmerus eperlanus.* **2.** Applied to other small fish; †**a.** The sprat, *Clupea sprattus* (*rare*) –1740. **b.** *U.S.* A young or immature herring 1884.

Sparoid (spæ·roid, spēᵊ·roid), *a.* and *sb.* 1836. [– mod.L. *Sparoides*, f. SPARUS; see -OID.] Of or belonging to, characteristic of, the *Sparidæ* or sea-bream family; a fish of this family.

†**Sparple,** *v.* Also **sparpoil,** etc. ME. [– OFr. *esparpeillier* (mod. *éparpiller*); cf. DISPARPLE.] = SPARKLE *v.*² –1819.

Sparred (spāɹd), (*ppl.*) *a.* 1805. [f. SPAR *sb.*¹ or *v.*³ + -ED.] **1.** Made or constructed of, having or fitted with, spars, narrow boards, or planks, set with intervals or spaces between them. **2.** Of a ship: Furnished with spar 1905.

Sparrow (spæ·roᵘ). [OE. *spearwa* = OHG. *sparo*, ON. *spǫrr*, Goth. *sparwa* :– Gmc. **sparwon*, **sparwaz.*] **1.** A small brownish-grey bird of the family *Fringillidæ*, indigenous to Europe, where it is very common, and naturalized in various other countries; esp. the house-sparrow, *Passer domesticus.* **2.** With distinguishing terms, denoting varieties of the true sparrow, or other small birds in some way resembling these 1668.

2. *Field-, house-, Java, Savannah, song-, swamp-s.*, HEDGE-, REED-, TREE-SPARROW: see these words.

Comb.: **s.-bunting,** *Zonotrichia albicollis*, differing from the true bunting in having exposed nostrils; **-owl,** one or other of various small owls, esp. of the genus *Glaucidium*; **-pie, -pudding,** a dish proverbially supposed to make the eater sharp-witted; **-wort,** *Erica passerina*, native to South Africa.

Spa·rrow-bill. 1629. [f. prec. + BILL *sb.*²] = SPARABLE.

†**Spa·rrow-bla:sting.** 1589. [f. SPARROW, with joc. or contemptuous force.] The fact of being blasted or blighted by some mysterious power, sceptically regarded as unimportant or non-existent –1633. So †**Spa·rrow-blasted** *a.* balefully stricken or blighted; dumbfounded.

Spa·rrow(-)grass. Now *dial.* or *vulgar.* 1649. [Illiterate alt. of †*sparagus* (XVI) – med.L. aphetic form of ASPARAGUS, by assim. to *sparrow* and *grass.*] Asparagus.

Spa·rrow-hawk. late ME. [f. SPARROW; repl. SPARHAWK.] **1.** A species of hawk (*Accipiter nisus*) which preys on small birds, common in the British Islands and widely distributed in northern Europe and Asia. Occas., one or other species of hawk resembling this. **2.** A small anvil used in silver-working 1869.

Sparry (spā·ri), *a.* 1695. [f. SPAR *sb.*² + -Y¹.] **1.** Consisting of or abounding in spar; of the nature of spar. **b.** Of places: Rich in spar 1789. **2.** In specific terms denoting mineral substances of the nature of or containing spar, as *s. iron* (*ore*) 1796. **3.** Of lustre, etc.: Resembling that of spar 1792.

Sparse (spāɹs), *a.* 1727. [– L. *sparsus*, pa. pple. of *spargere* scatter.] **1.** *Sc.* Of writing: Having wide spaces between the words. **2.** Separated by fairly wide intervals or spaces; thinly scattered; placed or set here and there over a relatively extensive area; not crowded, close, or dense 1753. **3.** Characterized by wide distribution or intervals 1801. **b.** Characterized by sparseness or scantiness 1871.

2. A wide-spread though s. population 1870. A man with s. grey hair 1875. **3. b.** The gleaning has been somewhat s. 1889. Hence **Spa·rse-ly** *adv.*, **-ness. Spa·rsity,** s. state or condition; comparative scarcity or fewness.

†**Sparse,** *v.* 1535. [– *spars-*, pa. ppl. stem of L. *spargere* scatter.] **1.** *absol.* To scatter *abroad* in giving –1614. **2.** *trans.* To spread or disseminate (a rumour, doctrine, etc.). Freq. with *abroad.* –1651. **3.** To break up, scatter; to dispose, sprinkle, etc., in a scattered manner –1614. Hence **Spa·rsedly** *adv.* (now *rare*), sparsely.

‖**Sparsim** (spā·ɹsim), *adv.* 1586. [L.; cf. prec.] In various places; here and there; sparsely.

Spart (spāɹt). 1600. [– L. *spartum* or Sp. *esparto.*] Esparto. Also *s.-grass.*

Spartacist (spā·ɹtăsist). 1916. [– G. *Spartakist*, f. *Spartacus*, name of the leader in the servile war against Rome (73–71 B.C.); see -IST.] A member of the Spartacus group of communistic revolutionists in Germany.

Spartan (spā·ɹtăn), *sb.* and *a.* late ME. [– L. *Spartanus*, f. *Sparta* (Gr. Σπάρτα, Σπάρτη) capital of the ancient Doric state of Laconia; see -AN.] **A.** *sb.* **1.** A native or inhabitant of Sparta; a Laconian or Lacedæmonian. **2.** One who resembles the ancient Spartans in character 1810. **B.** *adj.* **1.** Of or pertaining to Sparta or its inhabitants; Laconian, Lacedæmonian 1582. †**b.** *S. dog*, etc.: A kind of bloodhound –1697. **2.** Characteristic or typical of Sparta, its inhabitants, or their customs; *esp.* distinguished by simplicity, frugality, courage, or brevity of speech 1644.

1. b. *fig.* Oh Sparton Dogge: More fell then Anguish, Hunger, or the Sea SHAKS. **2.** The fare is S. in its extreme frugality 1885.

Sparteine (spā·ɹtī|in). 1850. [irreg. f. L. *spartum* broom (Stenhouse 1851), perh. after *coneine* CONIINE; see -INE⁵.] *Chem.* An alkaloid obtained from common broom, used to some extent in medicine.

Sparth. *Obs.* exc. *Hist.* ME. [– ON. *sparða.*] A long-handled broad-bladed battle-axe, used esp. by the Irish down to the 16th c.

He hath a s. of twenti pound of wighte CHAUCER.

Spartiate (spā·ɹʃiĕt). *rare.* late ME. [– L. *Spartiates* – Gr. Σπαρτιάτης, f. Σπάρτη Sparta.] A Spartan.

‖**Sparus** (spēᵊ·rɒs). *Pl.* **spari** (spēᵊ·rəi). 1668. [L. – Gr. σπάρος.] A sea-bream or gilt-head.

Spasm (spæ·z'm). late ME. [– (O)Fr. *spasme* or L. *spasmus, spasma* – Gr. σπασμός, σπάσμα, f. σπᾶν draw, pull.] **1.** Sudden and violent muscular contraction of a convulsive or painful character. **2.** With *a* and *pl.* A convulsive twitch or throe 1477. **3.** *fig.* Any sudden or convulsive movement of a violent character; a convulsion 1817.

3. As with an earthquake's s. SHELLEY. A mere s. of suspicious jealousy 1874. So †‖**Spa·sma** (in senses 1 and 2). †‖**Spa·smus. Spasma·tic, Spa·smic** *adjs.* spasmodic, convulsive.

Spasmodic (spæzmǫ·dik), *a.* 1681. [– mod.L. *spasmodicus*, f. Gr. σπασμώδης, f. σπάσμα SPASM; see -ODE, -IC.] **1.** Of the nature of a spasm; characterized by spasms or convulsive twitches; marked by jerkiness or suddenness of muscular movement; *spec.* in *Path.* **2.** Occurring or proceeding by fits and starts; irregular, intermittent; not sustained 1837. **3.** Agitated, excited; emotional, highly-strung; characterized by a disjointed or unequal style of expression 1848.

1. The use of ipecacuan in s. asthma 1811. **2.** Acquiescence in disorder would be followed by a s. severity 1856. So **Spasmo·dical** *a.*, **-ly** *adv.*

Spastic (spæ·stik), *a.* 1753. [– L. *spasticus* (Pliny) – Gr. σπαστικός, f. σπᾶν draw, pull; see -IC.] **1.** *Path.* Of the nature of a spasm or sudden contraction; characterized or affected by spasmodic symptoms or movements. **2.** *Physiology.* Performing involuntary contractile movements 1822. Hence **Spasti·city,** s. condition or quality.

Spat (spæt), *sb.*¹ 1634. [– AFr. *spat* (XIV), of unkn. origin.] **1.** The spawn of oysters or other shell-fish. Freq. used in *pl.* 1667. †**2.** The eggs of bees –1657.

Spat (spæt), *sb.*² Chiefly *dial.* or *colloq.* 1804. [prob. imit.; cf. SPAT *v.*²] **1.** A tiff or dispute; a quarrel. Orig. *U.S.* **2.** A smart blow, smack, or slap 1823. **3.** A sharp smacking sound 1881.

Spat (spæt), *sb.*³ 1802. [abbrev. of SPATTERDASH.] A short gaiter worn over the instep and reaching only a little way above the ankle, usually fastened under the foot by means of a strap. Chiefly in *pl.*

Spat (spæt), *sb.*⁴ 1876. [app. – Du. *spat* in the same sense.] A small splash *of* something.

Spat (spæt), *v.*¹ 1667. [f. SPAT *sb.*¹] *intr.* and *trans.* Of oysters: To spawn.

Spat (spæt), *v.*² 1809. [prob. imitative. Cf. SPAT *sb.*²] **1.** *intr.* To start *up* sharply or actively; to engage in a dispute. *U.S.* **2.** *trans.* To clap, slap, or smack 1832. **3.** *intr.* To administer slaps or pats; to strike sharply; to spatter. Also used advb. 1868.

2. The little Isabel leaped up and down spatting her hands 1845. **3.** Bill fired again..and I heard the ball go 's.!' 1890.

Spatangoid (spætæ·ŋgoid), *sb.* and *a.* 1857. [– mod.L. *Spatangoides*, f. *Spatangus* (late L. *spatangius*, Gr. σπατάγγης); see -OID.] *Zool.* **A.** *sb.* A sea-urchin belonging or related to the genus *Spatangus* (heart-urchins). **B.** *adj.* Having the characteristics of this.

Spatch-cock, spatchcock (spæ·tʃkǫk), *sb.* 1785. [Connected by Grose (1785) with DISPATCH, but cannot be dissociated from SPITCHCOCK.] A fowl split open and grilled after being killed, plucked, and dressed in a summary fashion.

Spatchcock (spæ·tʃkǫk), *v.* 1865. [f. prec.] **1.** *trans.* To cook as, or in the manner of, a spatchcock. **2.** To insert, interpolate, or sandwich (a phrase, sentence, etc.) 1901. **b.** To add to, or modify, by interpolation 1901.

2. We read phrases of apparent sincere religious fervour spatchcocked in between these bloodthirsty expressions 1903. ¶Also used for SPITCHCOCK *v.*

Spate (spēˡt), *sb.* Orig. *Sc.* and *north.* late ME. [Of unkn. origin.] **1.** A flood or inundation; *esp.* a sudden flood or rising in a river or stream caused by heavy rains or melting snow. Also *transf.* and *fig.*, esp. a sudden outburst, rush, or 'flood'. **2.** Without article: Flooding or inundation, swollen condition *of* water, etc.; copious downpouring *of* rain. Now usu. without const. 1513. Hence **Spate** *v. trans.* and *intr.* to flood.

1. Heaps of drifted rubbish..to mark the tide-line of the winter spates 1889. **2.** *In s.*, in flood.

Spath (spæþ). Now *rare.* 1763. [– G. *spath*, var. sp. of *spat*; see FELDSPAR.] = SPAR *sb.*² Hence **Spa·thic** *a.* = SPATHOSE.

‖**Spatha** (spēˡ·pă). *Pl.* **-æ** (-ī). 1753. [L.; see SPATHE.] **1.** *Bot.* A spathe. **2.** A flat blade-shaped implement 1881.

Spathaceous (spăþēˡ·ʃəs), *a.* 1760. [f. prec. + -ACEOUS.] *Bot.* Furnished with or enclosed by a spathe; of the nature of or resembling a spathe.

Spathe (spēˡð). 1785. [– L. *spatha* – Gr. σπάθη; see SPADE *sb.*¹] **1.** *Bot.* A large bract or sheathing-leaf enveloping the inflorescence (usu. a spadix) of certain plants, as arums, palms, etc., in such a way as completely to enclose it before expansion. **2.** *Zool.* A spatulate or spoon-shaped part, process, etc. 1891. Hence **Spa·thal** *a.* furnished with a s. **Spathed** (spēˡðd) *a.* having a s. **Spa·thiform** *a.*² having the form of a s.

Spathiform (spæ·þifǭɹm), *a.*¹ 1793. [f. SPATH + -FORM.] *Min.* Resembling spath or spar in form or appearance; lamellar.

The s., or uranite spar 1793.

Spathose (spæþōᵘ·s), *a.* 1776. [f. SPATH + -OSE¹.] *Min.* **1.** Of the nature of or resembling spath or spar; abounding in, consisting of, spar; foliated or lamellar in structure or texture; sparry. †**2.** Derived from fluor-spar –1811.

1. *S.-iron, iron-ore, ore* = SIDERITE 6. **2.** *S. acid*, hydrofluoric acid.

Spathulate (spæ·þiŭlĕt), *a.* 1821. [f. L. *spathula* (see SPATULA) + -ATE².] Chiefly *Bot.* Spatulate, spatular. So **Spa·thulated** *ppl. a.* (*rare*).

Spatial (spēˡ·ʃăl), *a.* 1847. [f. L. *spatium* SPACE *sb.* + -AL¹.] **1.** Having extension in space; occupying or taking up space; consisting of or characterized by space. **2.** Of, pertaining, or relating to space; subject to, or governed by, the conditions of space. Chiefly *Metaph.* and opp. to *temporal.* 1857. **3.** Happening or taking place in space; caused or involved by space 1866. **4.** Of faculty or sense: Apprehending or perceiving space or extension 1886.

1. An independent s. world 1886. **2.** Ideas.. which have been formed from a vast quantity of temporal and s. experience 1886. **4.** The origin of the s. faculty 1886. Hence **Spa·tially** *adv.* as regards, in or with reference to, or by means of space.

Spatiate (spēˡ·ʃieˡt), *v.* 1626. [– *spatiat-*, pa. ppl. stem of L. *spatiari*, f. *spatium* SPACE *sb.*; see -ATE³.] *intr.* To walk about; to stroll, wander, range, or roam.

Spattee (spæti·). 1926. [f. SPAT *sb.*³ + -EE².] A kind of gaiter for women and girls made in imitation of Highland stockings. Chiefly *pl.*

Spatter (spæ·təɹ), *sb.* 1797. [f. next.] A slight splash or sprinkle; a spattering.

Spatter (spæ·təɹ), *v.* 1582. [frequent. of imit. base repr. also in LG., Du. *spatten* burst, spout, WFlem. *spatteren*, WFris. *spatterje*; see -ER⁵.] **I.** *trans.* **1.** To scatter or disperse in fragments. **b.** With *out*: To sputter, or cause to sputter 1586. **c.** To dash, cast, send flying, in drops or small particles 1721. **2.** To splash or stain with drops of fluid, mud, etc.; to bespatter; *fig.* to assail with obloquy or detraction 1645. **b.** To cover in a dispersed manner 1647. **3.** Of fluids, etc.: To fall or strike upon (something) in scattered drops 1837.

1. With..my battle-axe..To s. his brains TENNYSON. **c.** The..puffs of wind spattered the snow against the windows 1852. **2.** Bend all your force to s. merit GAY. **b.** Natures carelesse pencill dipt in light With sprinkled starres hath spattered the Night 1647.

II. *intr.* **1.** To spring, fly, or spirt in drops or particles; to throw off drops or small fragments 1600. **b.** To fall, descend, strike, in heavy drops or with a sound suggestive of these 1675. **2.** To eject small drops of saliva or particles of food, etc., from the mouth; to splutter while speaking; to cause spattering in any way 1618. **b.** To scatter drops of ink 1640. **3.** To walk or tread in some splashy substance 1806.

1. b. The musket-balls spattering in the water 1887. **2.** That mind must needs be irrecoverably deprav'd, which..tasting but once of one just deed, spatters at it, and abhorrs the relish ever after MILT.

Comb.: **s.-dock,** the yellow pond-lily, *Nuphar.*

Spatterdash (spæ·təɹdæʃ). 1687. [f. SPATTER *v.* + DASH *v.*] A kind of long gaiter or legging of leather, cloth, etc., to keep the trousers or stockings from being spattered, esp. in riding. Chiefly in *pl.* Hence **Spa·tterdashed** (dæʃt) *ppl. a.* clad in, provided with, spatterdashes.

Spattle (spæ·t'l), *sb.*¹ *Obs.* exc. *dial.* [OE. *spātl*, f. *spāt-*, stem of *spǣtan* to spit.] Spittle.

Spattle (spæ·t'l), *sb.*² 1440. [contr. f. SPATULE. Cf. Du. (etc.) *spatel.*] **1.** A spatula. Now *rare* or *Obs.* **2.** *techn.* A tool for mottling a moulded article with pigment 1875.

†**Spa·ttle,** *v.*¹ [OE. *spātlian*, f. *spātl* SPATTLE *sb.*¹] *intr.* and *trans.* To spit –1611.

Spattle (spæ·t'l), *v.*² Now *techn.* and *dial.* 1611. [Related to SPATTER *v.*] *trans.* To spatter or sprinkle; to mottle.

‖**Spatula** (spæ·tiŭlă). 1525. [L., var. of *spathula*, dim. of *spatha* SPATHA.] A simple instrument of wood, ivory, or metal, having a flat elongated form with various modifications of shape and size, used for a variety of purposes: *esp.* **a.** For stirring mixtures, spreading ointments or plasters, etc. **b.** For minor surgical operations or for the medical examination of certain organs 1684. So **Spa·tule.** late ME.

Spatulate (spæ·tiŭlĕt) *a.* 1760. [f. SPATULA + -ATE².] Having a broadened and rounded end like that of a common form of spatula. So **Spa·tulated** *a.*

Spatulous (spæ·tiŭləs), *a.* 1828. [f. SPATULA + -OUS.] Resembling a spatula in form; spatulate. So **Spa·tulose** *a.*

Spauld (spǫld). Now *Sc.* and *north.* ME. [– OFr. *espalde*, etc. (mod. *épaule*) :– L. *spatula* shoulder-blade.] **1.** The shoulder in man or animals; a shoulder of an animal used for food. **2.** *transf.* A limb, leg, etc.; any joint of the carcass of a beast or bird 1500.

Spavin (spæ·vin). [Late ME. *spaveyne*, aphetic – OFr. *espavin*, var. of *esparvain* (mod. *éparvin*) – Gmc. *spadwāni*, f. base repr. by EFris. *spadde, sparre* + *wan-* (see WANE *v.*).] *Farriery.* **1.** A hard bony tumour or excrescence formed at the union of the splint-bone and the shank in a horse's leg, and produced by inflammation of the cartilage uniting those bones; a similar tumour caused by inflammation of the small hock bones. **b.** A malady of horses due to the above cause 1500. **2.** With distinguishing terms, as *blood s.*, a soft swelling of the hock vein caused by the accumulation of blood; freq. taken as synonymous with *bog s.* (see BOG *sb.*^{1}); *dry* or *bone s.* (see BONE *sb.*) 1523.

Spavined (spæ·vind), *a.* late ME. [f. prec. + -ED^2.] Of horses, etc.: Affected with spavin; having a spavin. **b.** *fig.* Lame, halting 1647.

Spa·-wa:ter. 1589. Water from a mineral spring (orig. from the springs at Spa).

Spawl (spǭl), *v. arch.* 1598. [Of unkn. origin.] **1.** *intr.* To spit copiously or coarsely; to expectorate. **2.** *trans.* To utter in a coarse manner 1616.

1. Why must he sputter, s., and slaver it In vain..against the people's fav'rite? SWIFT.

Spaw·ling, *vbl. sb. arch.* 1609. [f. SPAWL *v.* + -ING^1.] **1.** The action of the vb.; expectoration. **2.** *pl.* Spittle, spittings, saliva 1614.

Spawn (spǭn), *sb.* late ME. [f. next.] †**1.** The milt of a fish –1450. **2.** The minute eggs of fishes and various other oviparous animals, usu. extruded in large numbers and forming a more or less coherent or gelatinous mass; also, the young brood hatched from such eggs, while still in an early stage of development 1491. **b.** With *a* and *pl.* A fish-egg; an undeveloped fish 1563. **3.** A brood; a numerous offspring. Chiefly *fig.* 1590. **4.** *fig.* A person contemptuously regarded as the offspring of some parent or stock 1589. **b.** So in collective use 1601. **5.** *fig.* A product, result, or effect *of* something 1624. **6.** *fig.* The source or origin *of* something 1591. **7.** The mycelium of mushrooms or other fungi 1731.

4. Thou s. of the old serpent, fruitful in nothing but in lies DRYDEN. **5.** Libels are her spawns 1646.

attrib. and *Comb.*: **s.-brick,** a brick-shaped mass of compost containing mushroom-spawn; **-eater** *U.S.*, the smelt (*Leuciscus hudsonicus*).

Spawn (spǭn), *v.* late ME. [Aphetic – AFr. *espaundre* shed roe, var. of OFr. *espandre* (mod. *épandre*) shed, spill, pour out :– L. *expandere* EXPAND.] **I.** *intr.* **1.** Of fish, etc.: To cast spawn. **2.** To increase or develop after the manner of spawn; to become reproductive 1607. **3.** To issue or come forth like or after the manner of spawn 1657. **4.** To swarm or teem *with* something 1818.

1. The sun comes forth, and many reptiles s. SHELLEY. **4.** The rivers and the surrounding sea s. with fish EMERSON.

II. *trans.* **1.** To produce or generate as spawn or in large numbers; also, in contemptuous use, to give birth to (a person) 1603. **2.** To engender, produce, bring forth, give rise to 1594. **b.** *spec.* in contemptuous use with reference to literary work, utterances, etc. 1631. **3.** To supply with spawn or mycelium 1786. **4.** To extract spawn from (fishes) 1884.

2. b. The Press..hath Spawn'd so many Blasphemous..Pamphlets 1713. Hence **Spawned** *ppl. a.* cast or deposited as spawn; that has emitted spawn, spent.

Spawner (spǭ·nəɹ). 1601. [f. SPAWN *sb.* or *v.* + -ER^1.] **1.** A female fish, esp. at spawning time. †**b.** Applied to a woman –1675. **2.** One who, or that which, spawns, produces, etc., in various senses 1650.

Spay (spē^i), *v.* late ME. [Aphetic – AFr. *espeier*, OFr. *espeer*, f. *espee* (mod. *épée*) sword :– L. *spatha*; see SPATHE.] †**1.** *trans.* To pierce or cut (a deer) so as to kill. late ME. only. **2.** To operate upon (a female, esp. the female of certain animals) so as to remove the ovaries and destroy the reproductive power. late ME.

Spaya(r)d, spayd. Now *arch.* late ME. [Of unkn. origin.] A male deer in its third year.

Speak (spīk), *v.* Pa. t. **spoke** (spō^{u}k), (*arch* or *poet.* **spake.** Pa. pple. **spoken** spō^u·k'n). [Late OE. *specan*, superseding parallel OE. *sprecan*, which did not survive beyond XII, = OFris. *spreka*, OS. *sprekan*, OHG. *sprehhan* (Du. *spreken*, G. *sprechen*); W. Gmc. str. vb., with which cf. ON. *spraki* rumour, *forsprakki* spokesman.] **I.** *intr.* **1.** To utter or pronounce words or articulate sounds; to exercise the faculty of speech; to express one's thoughts in words. Also said of the mouth. **b.** To hold talk with others or with each other. Also, in mod. use, to be on speaking terms. OE. **c.** To deliver a speech or formal address; to express one's opinions or views in an assembly of any kind 1577. **2. a.** Followed by direct quotation of the words uttered OE. **b.** In pa. t. used in narrative poetry (after L. *dixit*) at the end of a speech 1667. **3.** Of a writer, literary composition, etc.: To make a statement or declaration in words; to state or say ME. **4.** *fig.* Of things: To be expressive or significant to make some revelation or disclosure 1535. **b.** To take effect legally; to be valid 1837. **5.** *transf.* **a.** Of musical instruments, etc.: To emit a sound; *spec.* to utter a full and proper note. Chiefly *rhet.* or *techn.* 1602. **b.** Of natural forces, etc.: To emit noise, make a sound; to reverberate 1604. **c.** Of firearms: To emit a report on being fired 1706. **d.** Of a hound: To give tongue; to bay 1826.

1. I speake but as I finde SHAKS. Christ bids the dumb tongue s.; it speakes CRASHAW. I had taught my Poll, as I noted before, to s. DE FOE. I am speaking like a book 1875. **b.** Going a side, they spake among them selues N.T. (Rhem.) *Acts* 26:31. There is Courtown, but we do not s. DISRAELI. **c.** Heere..Come I to speake in Cæsars Funerall SHAKS. **2. a.** Again th' Almightie spake Let there be Lights MILT. **b.** He spoke, and headlong..plunged to endless night GRAY. **3.** A law of the Twelue Tables at Rome speaks to the same effect 1869. Phr. with advbs., e.g. *to s. generally, generally speaking*, to make a general statement. *So to s.* **4.** His words were ended, but his meek aspect Silent yet spake MILT. **b.** A will now speaks from the death of testator 1845. **5. a.** Let the Kettle to the Trumpets speake SHAKS.

Comb. with preps. **Speak for —. a.** To make a speech in place of or on behalf of (a person); *esp.* to plead for. **b.** To beg or request; to ask for. **c.** To order; to bespeak; to engage. **d.** To indicate. **e.** *To s. for itself*, to be significant or self-evident. **S. of —. a.** To mention, or discourse upon, in speech or writing. **b.** In the phr. *to s. of* (in later use = 'worth mentioning'). Chiefly in neg. constructions. **c.** With vbl. sbs.: To suggest, propose, hint at (doing something). **S. to —. a.** To address words or discourse to (a person); to talk to, converse with. *To s. to*: so as to have personal conversation with. **b.** To apply to (a person) for a special purpose, esp. for help or service; to influence or bribe. **c.** To treat of or deal with (a subject) in speech or writing. **d.** To give (†or constitute) evidence regarding (a thing); to attest, bear testimony to. **e.** To address with reproof; to admonish. **S. with —. a.** To converse with, talk to; to consult or confer with. **b.** *Naut.* To hold communication with (another vessel).

With advs. **S. out. a.** To talk in a loud voice. **b.** To talk freely or unreservedly. **S. up. a.** To speak strongly *for* (= on behalf of, in defence of) a person. **b.** To raise the voice in speaking; to talk boldly; to break into speech.

II. *trans.* **1.** With cognate object: To articulate or utter (a word or words); to utter, make, or deliver (a speech, statement, etc.) OE. **2.** To utter or say (something) by way of a remark or statement OE. **3.** To utter or express (truth, falsehood, etc.) in words or speech OE. **4.** To declare in words; to make known by speech; to tell (of) OE. **b.** To state or declare in writing, etc. ME. **c.** *transf.* Of musical instruments: To announce, indicate, or proclaim by sound 1702. **5.** To use as a language; to talk ME. †**6.** To make mention of (a person); to speak of or mention in a certain way; to commend (a person) *to* another –1657. **7.** To indicate, denote, or betoken; to reveal, make known 1588. **b.** Of the countenance, eyes, etc.: To indicate or manifest by expression 1601. **8.** To manifest or show (a person, thing, etc.) to be or do a certain thing, or to possess a certain quality or character. Now *arch.* 1605. **b.** To term; to describe as (*rare*) 1617. **c.** To describe (a person). Now *arch.* 1623. **9.** To express or signify. Now *rare.* 1645. **10.** To send *to*, to cause to pass or enter *into* (another state, condition, or position) by speaking 1684.

1. Phr. *To s. not a word of*, to make no mention or suggestion of. *To s. a good (word) for*: see WORD *sb.* I. 2 d. Speeches are spoken..audible within doors and without CARLYLE. *fig.* He speakes all creame, skimd B. JONS. **2.** To s. the matter in a word 1662. **3.** Beleeue it (Page) he speakes sence SHAKS. That Vision spake Fear to my Soul WORDSW. **4.** Phr. *To s. one's mind*: see MIND *sb.* I. 2. **c.** These Trumpets s. his Presence 1702. **5.** Can they s. Dutch? DE FOE. **6.** *Hen. VIII*, IV. ii. 32. **7.** The loud laugh that spoke the vacant mind GOLDSM. **b.** Her look spoke affection 1859. **8.** His whole Person is finely turned, and speaks him a Man of Quality STEELE. **9.** Phr. *To s. volumes*: see VOLUME *sb.* I. 3. **10.** Too just to wink, or s. the guilty clear COWPER.

III. 1. To talk or converse with; to address OE. **b.** To communicate with (a passing vessel) at sea, by signal, speaking trumpet, etc. 1792. **2.** *To s.* (a person) *fair*, to address (a person) courteously or kindly. late ME.

1. b. We saw several vessels, but spoke none 1816. **2.** *fig.* Heaven speaks me fair DRYDEN.

IV. Speak out. *trans.* To utter, declare openly or plainly. late ME.

Comb.: **s.-easy** *U.S. slang*, an illicit liquor-shop.

Speakable (spī·kăb'l), *a.* 1483. [f. prec. + -ABLE.] **1.** That may or can be spoken; fit to be expressed in speech. †**2.** Having the power of speech, able to speak (*rare*) –1676.

2. Redouble then this miracle, and say, How cam'st thou s. of mute? MILT.

Speaker (spī·kəɹ). ME. [f. SPEAK *v.* + -ER^1.] **1.** One who speaks or talks. **b.** *spec.* One who addresses an audience; an orator. late ME. **2.** The member of the House of Commons who is chosen by the House itself to act as its representative and to preside over its debates. Also called *Mr. S.* late ME. **b.** More fully in *S. of (the) Parliament* 1460. **c.** The presiding officer or chairman of the House of Lords, now the Lord Chancellor, or one acting as his deputy or substitute 1660. **d.** A similar president in other assemblies 1656. †**3.** One who proclaims or celebrates. SHAKS. **4.** As a title of books containing pieces adapted for recitation or reading aloud 1774.

1. Let not an euill s. be established in the earth *Ps.* 140:11. We of the Lower House..have likewise the most able speakers MISS BURNEY. **Loud s.,** a device for converting electrical energy into sound energy with the object of producing a large volume of sound. Hence **Spea·kership,** the office of Speaker in a legislative or other assembly.

Speakie (spī·ki). *U.S.* 1928. [See -Y^6, -IE.] = TALKIE.

Speaking (spī·kiŋ), *vbl. sb.* ME. [f. SPEAK *v.* + -ING^1.] **1.** The action of the vb.; talking, discoursing. **b.** Speech-making 1763. **2.** With possessive prons., etc.: Speech, talk; conversation, discourse ME. **b.** An instance or occasion of speech or talk; a discourse, discussion, etc. ME. **3.** *attrib.*, as *s. acquaintance, voice*, etc. 1687.

2. b. A s. to instruction and edification CROMWELL.

Phr. *On (upon) s. terms*: see TERM *sb.* III. 2.

Comb.: **s.-front,** an organ-front composed of pipes which actually sound, as contrasted with dummy pipes.

Speaking (spī·kiŋ), *ppl. a.* ME. [f. as prec. + -ING^2.] **1.** That speaks; capable of articulate speech. **2.** *fig.* and *transf.* esp. **a.** Expressive, significant, eloquent 1586. **b.** Of the eyes, countenance, etc.: Highly expressive 1592. **3.** Of a likeness: Faithful or true (so that it gives the impression of one speaking) 1582.

1. The s. head which uttered its oracular responses at Lesbos 1832. **2. a.** Still borne Silence.. Admirations speakingst Tongue 1653. **b.** I vow she has s. eyes! RICHARDSON. **3.** Anybody.. could still draw a s., nay scolding, likeness of Keate 1844. Hence **Spea·kingly** *adv.* in a s. manner; strikingly.

Spea·king-tru:mpet. (Also unhyphened.) 1671. [SPEAKING *vbl. sb.*] A kind of trumpet (chiefly used at sea), so contrived as to carry the voice to a great distance, or to cause it to be heard above loud noises.

Spea·king-tu:be. (Also unhyphened.) 1833. [SPEAKING *vbl. sb.*] **1.** A tube or pipe for speaking, or communicating orders, from one room, building, etc., to another. **2.** A speaking-trumpet 1889.

Spear (spī^{ə}ɹ), *sb.*^{1} [OE. *spere* = OFris. *spiri, spere*, OS., OHG. *sper* (Du., G. *speer*), ON. (pl.) *spjǫr*, doubtfully rel. to L. *sparus* hunting-spear.] **1.** A thrusting weapon consisting of a stout wooden staff of some length, on which a sharp-pointed head, usually of iron or steel, is socketed or otherwise fixed; also, a shorter weapon of this kind used for throwing. **b.** Without article, freq. in a collective sense ME. **c.** One of the transverse spikes or poles of a cheval-de-frise 1823. **2.** A spearman. Now *arch.* ME. **3.** A sharp-pointed weapon used for various purposes; esp. one for catching fish, a leister 1551. **4. a.** *pl.* The thorns or prickles of a plant, the spines or spikes of a hedgehog, sharp fins of a fish, etc. Chiefly *poet.*; now *rare.* 1607. **b.** The sting of a reptile or insect, esp. of a bee. Now *Sussex dial.* 1608.

1. His S., to equal which the tallest Pine Hewn on Norwegian hills..were but a wand MILT. *fig.* Slanders venom'd speare SHAKS. The s. of Butler's reasoning M. ARNOLD. Phr. †*To sell at the s., to put*, etc., *under the s.*, to sell by auction. †*To pass under the s.*, to 'come under the hammer'. †*Stroke of the s.*, the feather of a horse (see FEATHER *sb.* III. 1.). **b.** They shall lay hold on bowe and speare *Jer.* 6:23. **3.** Abounding in trouts catch'd by speare in the night EVELYN. *Eel-, fish-, salmon-, trout-s.*

attrib. and *Comb.*: as *s.-point, -shaft* (OE. *sperescreaft*), *-staff*; **s.-axe**, a s. with an axe-shaped head; †**-foot**, the off hind foot of a horse; **-hand**, the hand with which a s. is usually held, thrown, etc.; the right hand or side; **-side** (after OE. *on sperehealfe*), the male line of descent. **b.** In names of plants, etc.: **s.-thistle**, *Cnicus lanceolatus*; **-wood**, *Acacia doratoxylon*, also *Eucalyptus doratoxylon*. **c.** In names of fishes; **s.-dog**, *Spinax acanthias*; **-fish**, *Tetrapturus albidus*, also called Bill-fish.

Spear (spīᵊɹ), *sb.*[2] 1490. [irreg. var. of SPIRE *sb.*[1], perh. infl. by prec.] †**1.** A spire of a church or other building; a pyramid –1755. **2.** The plumule or rudimentary shoot of a seed; *spec.* the acrospire of grain 1647. **b.** A blade, shoot, or sprout (*of* grass, etc.) 1841.

2. Tell me the motes, dust, sands, and speares Of corn, when Summer shakes his eares HERRICK.

Spear (spīᵊɹ), *sb.*[3] 1543. [var. of SPIRE *sb.*[2]] **1.** A young tree, esp. a young oak; a sapling. Also *attrib.* in *s. oak, tree.* **2.** *techn.* A pump-rod. Also *attrib.* 1729.

Spear (spīᵊɹ), *sb.*[4] *rare.* 1903. [f. SPEAR *v.*[2]] The act of spearing or striking with a spear, *spec.* in pig-sticking.

Spear (spīᵊɹ), *v.*[1] 1573. [irreg. var. of SPIRE *v.*[1] Cf. SPEAR *sb.*[2]] *intr.* Of corn, etc.: To sprout, germinate. Also with *out.*

Spear (spīᵊɹ), *v.*[2] 1755. [f. SPEAR *sb.*[1]] **1.** *trans.* To pierce or transfix with a spear. **2.** *intr.* To rise *up* like a spear 1822.

1. The King saw his men speared and shot down 1869. *transf.* The sparrow [is] spear'd by the shrike TENNYSON.

Spearer (spīᵊ·rəɹ). 1573. [f. SPEAR *sb.*[1] or *v.*[2] + -ER[1].] One who is armed with, or strikes with, a spear.

Spea·r-grass. Also as one or as two words. 1548. [f. SPEAR *sb.*[1]] A name for many grasses or grass-like plants having spear-like parts.

†**1.** = SPEARWORT 2. –1596. **2.** One or other of various British grasses, *esp.* couch-grass (*Triticum repens, Agrostis*, etc.) 1784. **3.** *Amer.* One or other of several species of meadow-grass, esp. *Poa pratensis* 1747. **4.** One or other of many Australasian and Asiatic grasses 1847.

Spea·r-head. Also as one word. late ME. [f. SPEAR *sb.*[1]] **1.** The sharp-pointed head or blade forming the striking or piercing end of a spear. **b.** *fig.* A person or body of persons chosen to lead a thrust or attack 1929. **2.** *transf.* A thing having the pointed form characteristic of the head of a spear 1894. So **Spearhead** *v.* act as s. of (movement, attack, etc.).

Spea·rman. ME. [f. SPEAR *sb.*[1]] **1.** A soldier armed with a spear; one who carries a spear as a weapon. **2.** A spearer of fish. SCOTT.

Spearmint (spīᵊ·ɹmint). 1539. [f. SPEAR *sb.*[1]] The common garden mint, *Mentha viridis*, much used in cookery; (with pl.) †a plant of this. Also *attrib.*

Spea·r-shaped, *a.* 1763. Resembling a spear in shape; pointed like a spear.

Spearwort (spīᵊ·ɹwɒɹt). OE. [f. SPEAR *sb.*[1] + WORT[1].] †**1.** Elecampane –ME. **2.** One or other of several species of ranunculus, esp. *R. flammula* (lesser or small s.) and *R. lingua* (great s.). late ME. **b.** Mentioned as used by beggars to produce artificial sores –1673.

Speary (spīᵊ·ri), *a.* 1577. [f. SPEAR *sb.*[1] + -Y[1].] †**1.** Of grass: Hard and stiff –1653. **2.** Resembling a spear or spears; slender and sharp-pointed; keen 1820. **3.** Consisting of spears; waged with spears 1810.

2. S. sleet and driving snow 1855.

Spec (spek), *sb. colloq.* or *slang*; orig. *Amer.* 1794. [Short for SPECULATION.] A commercial speculation.

Phr. *A good* (*bad*, etc.) *s. On s.*, on the chance of obtaining something, gaining some profit, etc.

†**Spece.** ME. [– (O)Fr. *espèce* sort, kind, appearance, etc. – L. SPECIES.] **1.** Appearance, form –1490. **2. a.** A spice. **b.** A medical substance, drug. –1605. **3.** A species, kind –1647.

Special (spe·ʃăl), *a.*, *adv.*, and *sb.* ME. [Aphetic – OFr. *especial* ESPECIAL or – L. *specialis*, f. *species*; see -AL[1].] **A.** *adj.* **1.** Of such a kind as to exceed or excel in some way that which is usual or common; exceptional in character, quality, or degree. **2.** Of friends: Admitted to particular intimacy; held in particular esteem ME. **3.** Marked off from others of the kind by some distinguishing qualities or features; having a distinct or individual character; also, in weakened sense, particular, certain ME. **b.** Additional to the usual or ordinary 1840. **4.** Of persons: **a.** Appointed or employed for a particular purpose or occasion ME. **b.** Devoted to a particular or limited field of study or research 1899. **5.** Having an individual, particular, or limited application, object, or intention; concerning a single person, thing, or circumstance, or a particular class of these ME. **6.** Having close, intimate, or exclusive connection or relationship with one person or thing (or set of these); peculiar. late ME. **7.** *Law.* Used to denote particular or distinctive instances or cases of the thing, action, or person in question, as *s. bail, bailiff, bastard(y, occupant, tail, verdict* 1495.

1. She's a s. favourite 1854. Men of no s. celebrity 1867. **3.** Aristotle saith, a man is the most speciall 1620. A s. Idea is call'd by the Schools, a Species 1725. **b.** S. Trains may be engaged for large Parties 1847. **4. a.** The s. correspondent of the 'Times' in the Crimea 1856. **b.** Some well-known (and not too s.) specialist 1899. **5.** It is a s. purpose, specially consulted throughout 1802. *S. intention*: see INTENTION II. 4. **6.** The Lord thy God hath chosen thee to be a s. people vnto himselfe *Deut.* 7:6. Each region has its s. treasures 1870.

B. *adv.* In a special manner; especially, particularly. Now only *colloq.* or *dial.* ME.

Great plenty of dates, which..are speciall good 1600.

C. *sb.* †**1.** A particularly intimate or favourite friend, associate, or follower –1660. †**2.** A particular point, part, detail, concept, statement, thing, or article –1628. †**b. In s.:** (*a*) Specially, particularly –1680. (*b*) In detail –1573. †**3.** Species, kind –1654. **4.** *ellipt.* A special constable, correspondent, etc.; an advocate at a special fee 1837. **b.** A special train, examination, prize, etc. 1866. Hence **Spe·cialness,** the quality of being s.

Specialism (spe·ʃăliz'm). 1856. [f. prec. + -ISM.] **1.** Restriction or devotion to a special branch of study or research; limitation to one department or aspect of a subject. **2.** With *a* and *pl.* A special study or investigation; an instance of specializing 1868.

1. The evils of s. [in medicine] 1891.

Specialist (spe·ʃălist). 1856. [f. as prec. + -IST.] **1.** A medical practitioner or authority who specially devotes his attention to the study or treatment of a particular disease or class of diseases. **2.** *gen.* One who specially or exclusively studies one subject or one particular branch of a subject 1862.

1. He was a famous nerve s. 1889. Hence **Speciali·stic** *a.* of or pertaining to specialism or specialists.

Speciality (speʃiæ·lĭti). late ME. [– OFr. *especialité*, or late and med.L. *specialitas*, f. L. *specialis*, see SPECIAL, -ITY.] **1.** A special, particular, or individual point, matter, or item; freq. *pl.*, particulars, details. **2.** The quality of being special, limited, or restricted in some respect (occas. implying particularity of application or treatment) 1456. **3.** A special or distinctive quality, property, characteristic, or feature; a peculiarity 1625. **b.** With *the*: The distinctive quality, etc., *of* a particular thing or class 1829. **4.** *Law.* = SPECIALITY II. 3. 1681. **5.** A special aptitude, skill, occupation, or line of business 1867. **b.** A special subject of study or research; that branch of work in which one is a specialist 1858. **c.** A thing or article specially characteristic of, produced or manufactured by, a particular place, business firm, etc. 1863. **6.** A thing or article of a special kind, as dist. from what is usual or common 1867.

1. A practical position..chains the mind to specialities and details 1865. **2.** Phr. *In s.*, especially, particularly. **3.** Think of this, Sir,.. apart from the specialities..of prejudice DICKENS. **b.** It is the s. of all vice to be selfishly indifferent to..injurious consequences 1882. **5. b.** His s. was Entomology 1880.

Specialization (spe:ʃăləizē[i]·ʃən). 1843. [f. next + -ATION.] The action or process of specializing or of becoming specialized. **a.** Of language, legislation, etc. **b.** *Biol.* Of animals or plants, or of the parts or organs of these 1862. **c.** Of employment, studies, etc. 1865.

c. The increasing specialisation of all employments..is not without inconveniences 1865.

Specialize (spe·ʃăləiz), *v.* 1613. [– Fr. *spécialiser*; see SPECIAL *a.* and -IZE.] **1.** *trans.* To mention or indicate specially; to specify, particularize 1616. **b.** *absol.* To enter into particulars or details 1613. **2.** To render special or specific; to invest with a special character or function 1628. **b.** *spec.* in *Biol.* In pa. pple.: Adapted to a special function or environment; modified by development tending to this end 1851. **3.** To make narrower and more intensive 1855. **4.** *intr.* **a.** To engage in special study or some special line of business, etc. 1881. **b.** To develop in a special direction 1889.

1. b. First lash the Great-ones; but if thou be wise, In generall and doe not speciallize 1613. **4. a.** They will not allow their scholars to s. 1881.

Specially (spe·ʃăli), *adv.* ME. [f. SPECIAL *a.* + -LY[2], after OFr. (*e*)*speciaument*, L. *specialiter.*] **1.** In a special manner; particularly. **2.** Of special purpose; expressly ME. **3.** In a supreme degree; pre-eminently ME. †**4.** With particularity or detail –1620.

1. The military results..were not s. glorious 1871. **2.** It is better to make them s. for each patient 1879. **3.** Phr. *And s.*, used to introduce a clause following upon a previous statement; In the Writings of Divines, and s. in Sermons HOBBES.

Special pleader. 1804. [See PLEADER.] **1.** *Law.* A member of an Inn of Court who devotes himself mainly to the drawing of pleadings and to attending at Judges' chambers. **2.** One who uses special pleading; a disingenuous or sophistical disputant 1809.

Special pleading. 1684. [See PLEADING *vbl. sb.*] **1.** A pleading drawn with particular reference to the circumstances of a case, as opposed to general pleading. **2.** The putting forward of special pleadings; the art or science of drawing pleadings 1768. **b.** *fig.* Exparte or one-sided argumentation; disingenuous pleading; sophistry 1872.

Specialty (spe·ʃălti). ME. [– OFr. (*e*)*specialté*, f. (*e*)*special* SPECIAL *a.*; see -TY[1].] **I.** †**1.** Particularity or detail in description or discussion –1577. **2.** *In s.*, in a special or particular manner or degree 1451. **3.** Special or particular character or quality; a special feature or characteristic 1575. **b.** The quality of being limited or determined by special cases or circumstances 1619. **c.** Special knowledge; tendency to specialism 1868.

3. The s. of Rule hath beene neglected SHAKS. **c.** The favorite charge against the academies is their 'one-sidedness' or s. 1868.

II. †**1.** A thing specially belonging or attached to one person; a special possession, distinction, favour, or charge –1628. **2.** A special or particular matter, point, or thing. late ME. **3.** *Law.* A special contract, obligation, or bond, expressed in an instrument under seal 1482. **4.** A special line of work or business; a special manufacture or product; an article specially dealt in or stocked 1860. **b.** A special subject of study or research 1861.

3. Marriage-settlements, mortgage-deeds, and specialties of various kinds 1781. **4.** The brass work of Birmingham has long been one of its specialties 1883. **b.** He had selected as his s. currency and finance 1883.

Specie (spī·ʃi, spī·ʃī, spī·ʃiī). 1551. [– L.

specie, abl. sing. of *species* SPECIES, orig. adopted in the phr. *in specie*.] **I.** In the phr. **in specie** **1.** In kind; in respect of kind; specifically 1562. **2.** In the real, proper, precise, or actual form; without any kind of substitution. In later use only in *Law*. 1551. **3.** †**a.** In the actual coin specified –1630. †**b.** Of coin or money: In the actual form of minted pieces of metal –1714. **c.** Of sums or amounts: In actual coin; in money 1636. †**4.** Of goods, etc.: In kind –1738. †**b.** *transf.* Of requital or repayment: In a similar fashion; with like treatment –1772.

2. The covenant will be decreed to be performed in s. 1818. **3. b.** Our Coin..whether we send it in S., or whether we melt it down here to send it in Bullion LOCKE. **c.** He has wealth in s. DRYDEN. **4. b.** Kindnesses are to be paid in S. as well as Money 1702.

II. 1. Coin; coined money 1671. **2.** Species; kind. Now *rare* or *Obs.* 1711.

1. Money may mean either s., or bank-notes 1864. **2.** A very large s. of gull 1800.

Species (spī·ʃīz, -iz, spī·ʃiīz). *Pl.* **species.** 1551. [– L. (sing. and pl.) *species* appearance, form, kind, etc., f. *spec-* of *specere* look, behold. Cf. SPICE *sb.*] **I.** †**1.** Appearance; outward form –1651. **b.** *Geom.* Form, irrespective of size 1660. **2.** *Eccl.* The sensible form of the consecrated bread and wine in the sacrament of the Eucharist; one or other of these (cf. KIND *sb.* II. 4) 1579. †**3.** The outward appearance or aspect, the visible form or image, *of* something, as constituting the immediate object of vision –1700. †**b.** The image of something as cast upon, or reflected from, a surface; a reflection –1790. †**4.** A thing seen; a spectacle; *esp.* a phantom or illusion –1661. †**5.** *Metaph.* A supposed emission or emanation from outward things, forming the direct object of cognition for the various senses or for the understanding –1756. †**b.** A mental impression; an idea –1711. †**6.** In Platonic philosophy, = IDEA *sb.* 1. –1792.

1. b. A triangle is said to be given in s. when its angles are given 1881. **2.** The Ceremony of mixing a Particle of the Host with the S. of Wine in the Chalice 1737. **3.** As the two Eyes, two S. entertain 1700. **5. b.** There are certain moral Species or Appearances so striking..that..they bear down all contrary Opinion 1711.

II. 1. *Logic.* The second of the five predicables (q.v.), connoting the common attributes or essential qualities of a class of persons or things as dist. from the genus on the one hand and the individual on the other 1551. †**b.** The essential quality or specific properties *of* a thing –1651. **2.** A class composed of individuals having some common qualities or characteristics, freq. as a subdivision of a larger class or genus 1630. **3.** A distinct class, sort, or kind, of something specifically mentioned or indicated. Freq. const. *of*. 1561. **b.** *A s. of*, a kind of (cf. KIND *sb.* I. 7); also with *the* 1620. **c.** Applied to individuals as unique or as typical of a class 1644. **d.** *The s.*, the human race 1711. **4.** *Zool.* and *Bot.* A group or class of animals or plants (usu. constituting a subdivision of a genus) having certain common and permanent characteristics which clearly distinguish it from other groups 1608. †**5. a.** *pl.* The separate materials or ingredients used in compounding a perfume, drug, or the like –1693. †**b.** *pl.* Spices. CRASHAW. †**6. a.** A particular kind or sort of coin or money –1756. **b.** Coinage, coin, money, bullion –1804. **c.** Metal (gold or silver) used for coinage. BURKE. †**7.** *pl. Naut.* Sorts of provisions –1806.

1. That common nature which is communicable to several Individuals, is called S., Sort or special kind 1668. **2.** A s. is any class regarded as forming part of the next larger class 1870. **3.** Aristotle..divides mankind into two distinct species: that of freemen and that of slaves BENTHAM. Such history is a distinct s. of composition 1845. **b.** Their gratitude is a s. of revenge JOHNSON. **c.** The Phœnix Pindar is a vast S. alone COWLEY. **d.** If individuals were happy, the s. would be happy GODWIN.

Specifiable (spe·sifəiăb'l), *a.* 1661. [f. SPECIFY *v.* + -ABLE.] Capable of being specified.

Specific (spėsi·fik), *a.* and *sb.* 1631. [– late L. *specificus* (Boethius), f. L. *species*; see SPECIES, -FIC.] **A.** *adj.* **1.** Having a special determining quality. **2.** Of qualities, properties, effects, etc.: Specially or peculiarly pertaining to a certain thing or class of things and constituting one of the characteristic features of this 1650. **b.** Peculiar *to*, characteristic *of*, something 1667. **3. a.** *Med.* Of remedies, etc.: Specially or exclusively efficacious for, or acting upon, a particular ailment or part of the body 1677. **b.** *Path.* Of a distinct or characteristic kind 1804. **4. a.** Precise or exact in respect of fulfilment, conditions, or terms; definite, explicit 1740. **b.** Exactly named or indicated, or capable of being so; precise, particular 1766. **5.** *Zool.* and *Bot.* Of or pertaining to, connected with, etc., a distinct species of animals or plants; esp. in *s. character, name* 1753.

2. The s. taint or peculiar cause of the malady BERKELEY. This feature in the case..constitutes the s. difference between justice, and generosity MILL. Phr. *S. gravity, heat*: see GRAVITY II. 1 c, HEAT *sb.* 2. *S. difference* = DIFFERENTIA. **3. a.** Garlick..I believe is..a Specifick Remedy of the Gout 1680. **b.** The s. irritation of the skin termed scabies 1843. **4. a.** A command must by its very nature be s. 1871. **b.** The s. cause of the quarrel 1880. **c.** Of a duty or tax: Assessed by quantity or amount without reference to value 1845.

B. *sb.* **1.** A specific remedy. (See A. 3 a.) 1661. **2.** A specific difference, quality, statement, subject, disease, etc. 1697.

1. How did you light on your specifick for the tooth-ach? JOHNSON. *transf.* and *fig.* A more infallible s. against tedium and fatigue 1779. Hence **Speci·fical** *a.* (now *rare*) = A.; *sb.* = B. 1. **Speci·fically** *adv.* **Speci·ficness**, s. character or quality (*rare*).

Specificate (spėsi·fikeʹt), *v.* Now *rare* or *Obs.* 1620. [– *specificat-*, pa. ppl. stem of late and med.L. *specificare*; see SPECIFY *v.*, -ATE[3].] **1.** *trans.* To distinguish as belonging to a particular species, group, or kind; to determine specifically. **2.** To apply specifically or especially *to*; to confine or limit *to* 1631. **3.** To give specific or explicit details of or concerning; to mention specifically or in detail; to particularize or specify 1649. **4.** To render specific in character or qualities 1650. **5.** *intr.* To become specific COLERIDGE. Hence **Speci·ficate** *sb.* something specified.

Specification (spe:sifikēʹ·ʃən). 1615. [– med.L. *specificatio*, *-on-*, f. as prec.; see -ION.] †**1.** The action of investing with some specific or determinate quality; conversion to something specific –1701. **b.** *Roman* and *Scots Law.* The formation of a new species of property out of material belonging to another by converting it into a different form 1651. †**2.** A specific character, quality, or nature –1710. **3.** Specific definition or description 1633. **4.** Specific, explicit, or detailed mention, enumeration, or statement *of* something 1642. **b.** *spec.* A document, drawn up by the applicant for a patent and submitted to the proper authority, giving an explicit description of the nature, details, construction, and use of an invention 1791. **c.** *techn.* A detailed description of the particulars of some projected work in building, engineering, or the like, giving the dimensions, materials, quantities, etc., of the work, together with directions to be followed by the builder or constructor; the document containing this 1833. **d.** A specified article, item, or particular 1828.

3. The second element in the s. of a force is its direction..The third element in the s. of a force is its magnitude 1879. **4.** By demanding a S. of the powers claimed 1719.

Specificity (spesifi·sĭti). 1876. [f. SPECIFIC + -ITY, perh. after Fr. *spécificité*.] Chiefly *Med.* The quality or fact of being specific.

Specify (spe·sifəi), *v.* ME. [– (O)Fr. *spécifier* or late or med.L. *specificare*, f. *specificat-*; see SPECIFICATION, -FY.] †**1.** *intr.* To speak or make relation *of* some matter fully or in detail –1489. **2.** *trans.* To mention, speak of, or name (something) definitely or explicitly; to set down or state categorically or particularly; to relate in detail ME. **3.** To invest with a specific character 1645.

2. There must many requisites be observed, which the statute specifies BLACKSTONE. Take..double the quantity above specified 1799. Hence **Spe·cified** *ppl. a.*

Specimen (spe·simĕn). 1610. [– L. *specimen*, f. *specere* look, look at.] †**1.** A means of finding out; an experiment. †**2.** A pattern or model –1697. **3.** An example, instance, or illustration *of* something, from which the character of the whole may be inferred 1659. **4.** A single thing selected or regarded as typical of its class; a part or piece *of* something taken as representative of the whole 1654. **b.** *spec.* An animal, plant, or mineral, a part or portion of some substance or organism, etc., serving as an example of the thing in question for purposes of investigation or scientific study. Also *transf.* 1765. **5.** Of persons as typical of certain qualities or of the human species. Also *colloq.* or *slang*, with derogatory force. 1817. **6.** *attrib.*, passing into *adj.* (freq. hyphened): Serving as or intended for a specimen; typical. (Often implying 'exceptionally large or fine'.) 1860.

3. Our English Bible is a wonderful s. of the strength and music of the English language EMERSON. **4.** Things..of which they had brought specimens DE FOE. **b.** I have found..a s. of another yellow trefoil 1765. **5.** There were some curious specimens among my visitors 1854. *A bright, fine, poor, sad s.* **6.** A number of 's.' fish have lately been caught in the Thames 1896.

Specio-, comb. form of L. *species*, as in *speciology*, the doctrine of species, etc.

Speciosity (spīʃiǫ·sĭti). Now *rare.* 1470. [– late L. *speciositas* beauty, etc., f. L. *speciosus*; see next, -ITY. Later f. next.] †**1.** The quality of being beautiful; beauty. Also, a beautiful thing. –1731. **2.** The quality of being specious; speciousness 1608. **b.** *pl.* Specious actions, promises, etc. CARLYLE.

2. S. in all departments usurps the place of reality..; instead of performance, there is appearance of performance CARLYLE.

Specious (spī·ʃəs), *a.* late ME. [– L. *speciosus* fair, fair-seeming, etc., f. *species*; see SPECIES, -OUS.] †**1.** Fair or pleasing to the eye or sight; beautiful, handsome, lovely; resplendent with beauty –1818. **2.** Having a fair or attractive appearance or character, but in reality devoid of the qualities apparently possessed; *occas.*, merely apparent 1612. **3.** Of language, statements, etc.: Fair, attractive, or plausible, but wanting in genuineness or sincerity 1651. **b.** Of reasoning, etc.: Plausible, apparently sound or convincing, but in reality sophistical or fallacious 1651. **4.** Of material things: showy, but of little intrinsic worth (*rare*) 1816. **5.** Of persons: Characterized by conduct, actions, or reasoning of a specious nature; †outwardly respectable 1740. †**6.** Of algebra: Performed by means of, expressed in, letters –1728. **7.** *Psychol.* Appearing to be actually known or experienced 1890.

1. Successive acquists of fair and s. Plants SIR T. BROWNE. There is thy Saviour..looking like a s. Bridegroom 1670. **2.** Traiterous requests..he was now willing to maske with the s. pretext of iustice and deuotion 1611. It appeared that this plan, though s., was impracticable MACAULAY. A policy which had a s. show of liberality MACAULAY. **3.** The meaning latent under this s. phrase MACAULAY. **b.** This s. reasoning is neverthelesse false HOBBES. **5.** You are a s. fellow,..and carry two fans under your hood DICKENS. Hence **Spe·cious-ly** *adv.*, **-ness.**

Speck (spek), *sb.*[1] [OE. *specca*, repr. otherwise only in SPECKLE *sb.*] **1.** A small spot of a different colour or substance from that of the material or surface upon which it appears; a minute mark or discoloration. **b.** Applied to things rendered extremely small by distance or by comparison with their surroundings 1656. **c.** Applied to a very small or distant cloud. Freq. in fig. context. 1726. **2.** A small or minute particle *of* something. late ME. **b.** A small piece, portion, etc., of ground or land 1538. **3.** A small spot as indicative of a defective, diseased, or faulty condition; a blot, blemish, or defect 1825.

1. The smallest s. is seen on snow GAY. **b.** We find..that the whole solar system is but a mere s. in the universe 1868. **2.** These bunches frequently containing strings and specks of ore 1839. He..deemed it a duty..to magnify faults and dwindle virtues to specks 1883. **3.** The..little pitted s. in garner'd fruit TENNYSON. *fig.* Can all the pearls of the East atone for a s. upon England's honour? SCOTT.

Speck (spek), *sb.*[2] Now *U.S.* and *S. African.* 1633. [– Du. *spek* (MDu. *spec*, MLG. *speck*) or G. *speck* (OHG. *spec*) = OE. *spec*, var. of *spic* = ON. *spik*.] **1. a.** Fat meat, esp. bacon or pork. **b.** The fat or blubber of a whale 1743. **c.** The fat of a hippopotamus 1863. **2.** *attrib.* in the names of tackle or apparatus used in dealing with whale-s., as *s.-block, -purchase* 1820.

Speck (spek), *v.* 1580. [f. SPECK *sb.*[1], or back-formation from *specked* ppl. a. (XIV).] **1.** *trans.* To mark with specks; to dot after the manner of specks. **b.** In passive: To be covered, marked, or diversified *with* (or *by*) specks or spots 1667. **2.** To go over (a woven fabric) and remove specks or other blemishes 1895. **3.** To convert into a mere speck. MEREDITH.

1. b. Each Flour of slender stalk, whose head though gay Carnation, Purple, Azure, or spect with Gold, Hung drooping unsustained MILT. **3.** Specked overhead, the imminent vulture wings At poise MEREDITH.

Speckle (spe·k'l), *sb.* 1440. [– MDu. *spekkel* (Du. *spikkel*); cf. SPECKLED.] **1.** A speck, small spot, or mark, esp. one occurring on the skin or body; a natural marking of this nature; a small patch or dot of colour. **2.** Speckled colouring, speckling. HAWTHORNE.

1. An huge great Serpent all with speckles pide SPENSER.

Comb.: **s.-belly,** (*slang*) a Nonconformist or Dissenter; (*U.S.*) one or other of various birds or fishes having speckled markings on the abdomen. Hence **Spe·ckly** *a.*, full of or covered with speckles; speckled or spotted; freckly.

Speckle (spe·k'l), *v.* 1570. [f. SPECKLE *sb.* or back-formation from SPECKLED; cf. MDu. *speckelen, spekelen* (WFlem. *spekelen*, Du. *spikkelen*), which may be partly the source.] **1.** *trans.* To mark with, or as with, speckles; to cover or dot (a surface, etc.) as if with speckles. **2.** *intr.* To form speckles; to be dotted about like speckles. (*rare.*) 1820.

Speckled (spe·k'ld), (*ppl.*) *a.* and *pa. pple.* late ME. [perh. after MDu. *spekelde, gespekeld* (Du. *gespikkeld*); cf. SPECKLE *sb.*] Covered, dotted, or marked with (numerous) speckles or specks; variegated or flecked with spots of a different colour from that of the main body; spotted. **1.** In predicative use. **2.** In attrib. use 1482. **b.** *fig.* Of sin, vice, etc.: Characterized by, full of, moral blemishes or defects 1603. **c.** *colloq.* Of a mixed character or nature; motley 1845.

1. She usually lays but one [egg], which is s. GOLDSM. Trophies..s. with blood SCOTT. **2.** A clean old woman..talking to some s. fowls GEO. ELIOT. **b.** And speckl'd vanity Will sicken soon and die MILT. **c.** They are usually a s. lot 1909. Hence **Spe·ckledness,** the state of being s.; spottiness.

Spe·ckless, *a.* 1788. [f. SPECK *sb.*[1] + -LESS.] Having no speck or speckle; free from specks, blemishes, flaws, etc. **b.** Free from specks of dirt, dust, etc.; spotlessly clean 1827. Hence **Spe·ckless-ly** *adv.*, **-ness.**

Specksioneer (spekʃənī^ə·ɹ). 1820. [– Du. *speksnijer*, colloq. form of *speknijder*, f. *spek* SPECK *sb.*[2] + *snijden* cut.] *Whale-fishing.* A harpooner, usu. the chief harpooner, of a whaler, who directs the operation of flensing the whale or cutting up the blubber.

Specky (spe·ki), *a.* late ME. [f. SPECK *sb.*[1] + -Y[1].] Covered or marked with specks; having specks or spots of disease, discoloration, etc.

Spec(k)s. 1807. [colloq. abbrev. of pl. of next II. 2.] Spectacles for the eyes.

Spectacle[1] (spe·ktăk'l). ME. [– (O)Fr. *spectacle* – L. *spectaculum* public show, f. *spectare*, frequent. of *specere* look at.] **I. 1.** A specially prepared display of a more or less public nature (esp. one on a large scale), forming an impressive or interesting show for those viewing it. Also without article. **2.** A person or thing exhibited to the public gaze as an object either of curiosity or contempt, or of marvel or admiration. late ME. **3.** A thing seen or capable of being seen; a sight. late ME. **b.** The sight or view *of* something 1625. **4.** A sight, show, or exhibition *of* a specified character or description 1484.

1. They abhorred Theaters, and publique spectacles, especially of blood 1641. **2.** We are made a s. to the world, and to Angels and men N.T. (Rhem.) 1 *Cor.* 4:9. **3.** *A.Y.L.* II. i. 44. **b.** The s. of their hurried and harassed retreat SCOTT. **4.** A s. of suffering royalty BURKE.

II. †**1.** A means of seeing; something made of glass; a window or mirror –1630. †**b.** *fig.* A mirror, model, pattern, or standard –1575. †**c.** An illustrative instance –1656. **2.** A device for assisting defective eyesight, or for protecting the eyes from dust, light, etc., consisting of two glass lenses set in a frame which is supported on the nose, and freq. kept in place by 'legs' passing over the ears. Usu. in *pl.* late ME. **b.** *fig.* A means or medium through which anything is viewed or regarded; a point of view, prepossession, prejudice, etc. late ME. **3.** *pl.* A batsman's score of two zeros or 'ducks eggs' in a cricket match of two innings. Freq. in *a pair of spectacles.* 1892.

2. Reading much, yet never used s. or other help 1640. I this evening did buy me a pair of green spectacles PEPYS. **b.** False informations, which are rightly called the spectacles of error 1606.

attrib. and *Comb.*: **s.-case,** a case of leather, etc., in which spectacles are kept when not in use; **s. owl,** *Strix perspicillata*; **s. warbler,** a bird of the family *Sylviidæ*, having naked yellowish wrinkled skin round the eye suggesting spectacles.

‖**Spectacle**[2] (spe·ktak'l). 1749. [Fr.; see prec.] **1.** = prec. I. 1. **2.** *spec.* A piece of stage-display or pageantry, as contrasted with real drama 1752.

Spectacled (spe·ktăk'ld), *a.* 1607. [f. SPECTACLE[1] + -ED[2].] **1.** Provided with or wearing spectacles. **2.** In names of birds, animals, etc., having spectacle-shaped markings or the appearance of wearing spectacles 1829.

1. The bleared sights Are spectacled to see him SHAKS. **2.** Named S. Serpent, from a black line drawn on the widened part of its disk in the form of spectacles 1831. The S. Bear, *Ursus ornatus*.. inhabits the Cordilleras of the Andes in Chili 1835.

Spectacular (spektæ·kiŭlăɹ), *a.* 1682. [f. SPECTACLE[1], after pairs like *oracle/oracular*; see -ULAR.] **1.** Of the nature of a spectacle or show; striking or imposing as a display. **b.** *absol.* That which appeals to the eye 1876. **2.** Pertaining to, characteristic of, spectacles or shows 1864. **3.** Addicted to spectacles 1894.

1. The Lord Mayor's Show was a more..s. pageant than ever 1884. **3.** The most s. nation in the world 1894. Hence **Specta·cularly** *adv.*

Spe·ctant, *a.* 1683. [– L. *spectans, -ant-*, pr. pple. of *spectare*; see SPECTACLE[1], -ANT.] *Her.* At gaze, looking forward.

Spectator (spektēⁱ·təɹ). 1586. [– Fr. *spectateur* or L. *spectator*, f. pa. ppl. stem of *spectare*; cf. prec. and see -OR 2.] **1.** One who sees, or looks on at, some scene or occurrence; a beholder, onlooker, observer. **2.** *spec.* One who is present at, and has a view or sight of, anything in the nature of a show or spectacle 1590. **3.** Used as the title of various periodical publications 1711.

1. There is a true saying, 'That the s. oft times sees more than the gamester' 1645. **2.** Gods..sit Amus'd spectators of this bustling stage COWPER. Hence **Spectato·rial** *a.* pertaining to, characteristic of, a s.; having the characteristics of one or other of the periodicals bearing the title of *Spectator.* **Specta·tress, Specta·trix,** a female s.

Spectatorship (spektēⁱ·təɹʃip). 1607. [f. prec. + -SHIP.] †**1.** Presentation to the eyes of spectators. SHAKS. **2.** The state of being a spectator; the fact of (merely) looking on 1712.

Spectral (spe·ktrăl), *a.* 1718. [f. SPECTRE + -AL[1].] †**1.** Capable of seeing spectres. **2.** Having the character of a spectre; ghostly, unsubstantial, unreal 1815. **b.** Resembling or suggestive of a spectre or spectres. Also *spec.* in *Zool.* 1828. **3.** Characteristic of or appropriate to a spectre 1820. **4.** Produced merely by the action of light on the eye or on a sensitive medium 1839. **5. a.** Of or pertaining to, appearing or observed in, the spectrum 1832. **b.** Carried out by means of the spectrum. Freq. in *s. analysis.* 1862.

2. A wild vision of a pair of s. horses apparently in mid-air 1877. **b.** The old s. Lombard friezes RUSKIN. *Strix cinerea*,..S. Owl 1884. **3.** A s. voice, Which shook me in a supernatural dream BYRON. **5. a.** S. colours, when re-united, produce white 1832. **b.** S. observations on stars 1881. Hence **Spe·ctrally** *adv.*

Spectre (spe·ktəɹ). Also (now *U.S.*) **specter.** 1605. [– Fr. *spectre* or L. *spectrum*, f. *specere* look, see.] **1.** An apparition, phantom, or ghost, esp. one of a terrifying nature or aspect. **b.** *fig.* A phantasm of the brain (*rare*) 1711. **c.** *fig.* An object or source of dread or terror, imagined as an apparition 1774. **d.** *transf.* One whose appearance is suggestive of an apparition or ghost 1807. **2.** One of the images or semblances supposed by the Epicurean school to emanate from corporeal things 1785. **3.** An image or phantom produced by reflection or other natural cause 1801. **4.** *Zool.* Any insect or animal distinguished by the epithet *spectre-* (see combs.), esp. an insect of the family *Phasmidæ* 1797.

1. A terror..As when a sudden s. at mid-day Meets us 1871. **c.** That same cloud-capt, fire-breathing S. of Democracy CARLYLE. **3.** Before each of us..stood a spectral image of a man... We stretched forth our arms; the spectres did the same TYNDALL.

Comb.: **s.-bat,** a tropical species of bat (*Vespertilio* or *Phyllostoma spectrum*); **-candle,** a belemnite; **-crab,** a glass-crab; **s. insect,** an insect of the genus *Phasma*; **-lemur,** = *spectre tarsier*; **-shrimp,** a slender-bodied amphipod of the genus *Caprella*; **s. tarsier,** a small lemuroid animal (*Tarsius spectrum*).

Spectro- (spe·ktro), comb. form (on Gr. analogies) of SPECTRUM, chiefly employed in a number of recent terms, as **Spe·ctrogram,** a photograph of a spectrum; **-graph,** (*a*) an instrument for photographing a spectrum; (*b*) = *spectrogram*; **-he·liograph,** an instrument for photographing the sun; **-heliogra·phic** *a.*, **-phone, -photo·meter, -te·lescope,** etc.

Spectrology (spektrǫ·lŏdʒi). *rare.* 1820. [f. SPECTRO- + -LOGY.] **1.** The science or study of spectres. **2.** The scientific study of spectra 1862. Hence **Spectrolo·gical** *a.* of or pertaining to s.

Spectrometer (spektrǫ·mĭtəɹ). 1874. [– G. *spektrometer* or Fr. *spectromètre*; see SPECTRO-, -METER.] An instrument used for measuring the index of refraction. Hence **Spectrome·tric** *a.* **Spectro·metry.**

Spectroscope (spe·ktrŏskōᵘp), *sb.* 1861. [– G. *spektroskop* or Fr. *spectroscope*; see SPECTRO-, -SCOPE.] An instrument specially designed for the production and examination of spectra. Hence **Spe·ctroscope** *v. trans.* to examine by means of a s. **Spectroscopist** (spektrǫ·skŏpist), one who pursues researches with the s. **Spectroscopy** (spektrǫ·skŏpi), the art of using the s.; that branch of science which involves the use of the s.

Spectroscopic (spektrŏskǫ·pik), *a.* 1864. [f. prec. + -IC; cf. Fr. *spectroscopique.*] **1.** Performed by means of the spectroscope. **2.** Presented or afforded by, pertaining or belonging to, the spectroscope 1869. **3.** Occupied or dealing with spectroscopy 1871. So **Spectrosco·pical** *a.*, **-ly** *adv.*

Spectrous (spe·ktrəs), *a.* 1652. [f. SPECTRE 1 + -OUS.] Spectral.

Spectrum (spe·ktrŏm). *Pl.* **spectra** (also **-ums**). 1611. [– L. *spectrum* image of a thing, apparition; see SPECTRE.] **1.** An apparition or phantom. **2.** An image or semblance (*rare*) 1693. **3.** The coloured band into which a beam of light is decomposed by means of a prism or diffraction grating 1671. **4.** The image retained for a time on the retina of the eye when turned away after gazing fixedly for some time at a bright coloured object 1786. **5.** *attrib.*, as *s. analysis* (cf. SPECTRAL *a.* 5 b); *s. band, -line, microscope* 1866.

4. This appearance in the eye we shall call the ocular s. of that object 1786.

Specular (spe·kiŭlăɹ), *a.* 1577. [– L. *specularis*, f. *speculum* SPECULUM; or, in branch II, f. L. *speculari* spy, observe, *specula* watch tower.] **I. 1.** *S. stone* (after L. *specularis lapis*): a transparent or semi-transparent substance formerly used as glass or for ornamental purposes; a species of mica, selenite, or talc; a piece or flake of this. *Obs.* exc. *arch.* †**2.** Of vision: Obtained by reflection only; not direct or immediate. (Based upon 1 *Cor.* 13:12.) –1704. **3.** Having the reflecting property of a mirror; presenting a smooth, polished, and reflecting surface; of a brilliant metallic lustre. Now *Min.* 1661. **4.** Of a telescope: Fitted with a speculum; reflecting 1676. **5.** Performed by means of a surgical speculum 1898.

3. *S. iron* or *iron ore*, hæmatite, esp. the brilliant crystalline form of this. 5. In every case in which there is probability of rectal disease digital or s. examination must be made 1898.

II. 1. Of or pertaining to sight or vision; esp. *s. orb* (poet.), the eye 1656. **2.** *poet.* Of heights, etc.: Affording a wide view 1671.

2. Look once more e're we leave this s. Mount Westward MILT.

Speculate (spe·kiŭleit), *v.* 1599. [– *speculat-*, pa. ppl. stem of L. *speculari* spy out, watch, f. *specula* lookout, watch tower, f. *specere* see, look; see -ATE[3].] **1.** *trans.* To observe or view mentally; to consider or reflect upon with close attention; to contemplate; to theorize upon. *Obs.* or *arch.* †**2.** To look at (something); to examine or observe closely or narrowly –1805. **b.** *spec.* To observe (the stars, heavens, etc.), esp. as an object of study 1630. **3.** *intr.* To engage in thought or reflection, esp. of a conjectural or theoretical nature, *on* or *upon, about, as to*, etc., a subject 1677. **4.** To engage in the buying and selling of commodities or effects in order to profit by a rise or fall in their market value; to undertake, or take part or invest in, a business enterprise or transaction of a risky nature in the expectation of considerable gain 1785. **b.** To count or reckon *on* something as probable or certain 1797.

1. If we do but s. the folly and indisputable dotage of avarice SIR T. BROWNE. 2. b. The sun and moon, which, he said, he was born to s. 1890. 3. Nearly every body whose death was worth speculating about 1847. 4. Would he be what he is if he hadn't speculated? DICKENS.

Speculation (spekiŭlē·ʃən). late ME. [– (O)Fr. *spéculation* or late L. *speculatio, -on-*, f. as prec.; see -ION.] **I. 1.** The faculty or power of seeing; sight, vision, *esp.* intelligent or comprehending vision. Now *arch.* 1471. †**2.** The exercise of the faculty of sight; the action, or an act, of seeing, viewing, or looking on or at; examination or observation –1774. †**b.** Observation of the heavens, stars, etc. –1652. †**3.** An observer or watcher; a spy. SHAKS.

2. †*Top* or *turret of s.* (after L. *turris speculationis*), one from which a wide view is obtained.

II. 1. The contemplation, consideration, or profound study *of* some subject. Now *rare* or *Obs.* late ME. **2.** An act of speculating, or the result of this; a conclusion, opinion, view, or series of these, reached by abstract or hypothetical reasoning. late ME. **b.** A conjectural consideration or meditation; an attempt to ascertain something by probable reasoning 1796. **3.** Without article: Contemplation of a profound, far-reaching, or subtle character; abstract or hypothetical reasoning on subjects of an abstruse or conjectural nature; freq. in disparaging use, usu. with adjs.; also simply = conjecture, surmise 1450. **b.** *In s.*, in conjecture or theory; not actually or practically; also, under consideration, in view 1638. **4.** The action or practice of buying and selling goods, stocks and shares, etc., in order to profit by the rise or fall in the market value, as distinct from regular trading or investment; engagement in any business enterprise or transaction of a venturesome or risky nature, but offering the chance of great or unusual gain 1774. **5.** An act or instance of speculating 1776. **6.** *Cards.* A round game of cards, the chief feature of which is the buying and selling of trump cards, the holder of the highest trump card in a round winning the pool 1804.

2. In consequence of these speculations, I ordered a well to be sunk near the middle of the peninsula 1793. 3. Your courtier theorique..doth ..know the court, rather by s., than practice B. JONSON. Because slavery is of all things the greatest clog and obstacle to s. SWIFT. The mere romantic s. of political dreamers 1861. 4. That species of gambling named s. 1834. Phr. *On s.*, on chance; on the chance of gain or profit.

Speculatist (spe·kiŭleitist). 1613. [f. SPECULATE *v.* + -IST.] **1.** One who speculates, or indulges in abstract reasoning; a theorist. **2.** One who speculates in commerce or finance 1812.

1. The s. is only in danger of erroneous reasoning JOHNSON.

Speculative (spe·kiŭlătiv), *a.* and *sb.* late ME. [– (O)Fr. *spéculatif, -ive* or late L. *speculativus*, f. *speculat-*; see SPECULATE, -IVE.] **A.** *adj.* **1.** Of the nature of, based upon, or characterized by speculation or theory in contrast to practice or positive knowledge. **2.** Given to speculation or conjectural reasoning 1546. †**b.** Given to pry or search *into* something. BACON. **3.** Of life, etc.: Spent in, devoted to, speculation –1849. **4.** Of faculties, etc.: Adapted for or exercised in speculation 1604. **5.** Suitable for observation or watching. Chiefly *poet.* 1709. **6. a.** Of persons: Given to or engaging in commercial or financial speculation 1763. **b.** Of the nature of, characterized by, or involving speculation 1799.

1. She has a world of knowledge: knowledge s., as I may say, but no experience 1748. He..had a languid s. liking for republican institutions MACAULAY. 2. Too s. a writer 1813. 4. Thoughts speculatiue, their vnsure hopes relate SHAKS. 5. High on her s. tower Stood Science WORDSW. 6. a. A s. bookseller SCOTT. b. Heavy s. transactions 1907. Hence **Spe·culative-ly** *adv.*, **-ness.**

B. *sb.* †**a.** Speculation; hypothetical reasoning; theory. (After late L. *speculativa* sb.) –1509. †**b.** *pl.* Speculative matters; the speculative sciences –1678. **c.** With *the*: That which rests only on speculation 1877.

Speculator (spe·kiŭleitəɹ). 1555. [– L. *speculator*, f. as prec.; see -OR 2. In sense 4 f. SPECULATE + -OR 2.] **1.** One who speculates on abstruse or uncertain matters; one who devotes himself to theoretical reasoning. **2.** A watchman, sentry, or look-out 1607. †**3.** One who engages in occult observations or studies –1691. **4.** One who engages in commercial or financial speculation 1778.

1. The most enthusiastic s. cannot suppose a greater increase MALTHUS.

Speculatory (spe·kiŭlătəri), *sb.* and *a.* Now *rare.* 1569. [– L. *speculatorius* pertaining to spies or scouts, in various applications; see SPECULATE, -ORY[1,2].] **A.** *sb.* †**1.** The observation or study of occult phenomena –1676. †**2.** = SPECULATOR 2. –1775. **B.** *adj.* †**1.** Of the nature of or pertaining to, occult speculation –1676. **2.** Serving for observation; affording an outlook or view 1781.

Speculatrix (spe·kiŭlēitriks). 1611. [f. SPECULATOR; see -TRIX.] A female speculator.

Speculist (spe·kiŭlist). 1707. [f. SPECULATE *v.* + -IST.] = SPECULATIST.

‖**Speculum** (spe·kiŭlŏm). *Pl.* **specula** and **-ums.** 1597. [L., f. base of *specere* look, see; cf. -ULE.] **1.** A surgical instrument for dilating orifices of the body so as to facilitate examination or operations. **2.** A mirror or reflector (of glass or metal) used for some scientific purpose; †a lens 1646. **b.** *spec.* A metallic mirror forming part of a reflecting telescope 1704. **3.** *Ornith.* A lustrous mark on the wings of certain birds; = MIRROR *sb.* III. b. 1804.

attrib.: **s.-forceps,** long, slender forceps, used for dressing wounds or operating on parts not accessible except through a speculum. **s. metal,** an alloy of copper and tin used for making specula.

Speech (spītʃ), *sb.* [OE. *spēć*, WS. *spǣć*, rel. to *specan* SPEAK, repl. earlier *sprǣć* = OFris. *sprēke, sprētze*, OS. *sprāka* (Du. *spraak*), OHG. *sprāhha* (G. *sprache*), WGmc. sb. f. ***sprǣk-, *sprek-** SPEAK.] **I. 1.** The act of speaking; the natural exercise of the vocal organs; the utterance of words or sentences. **b.** *transf.* The speaking or sounding of a musical instrument, organ-pipe, etc. 1862. **2.** Talk, speaking, or discourse; colloquy, conversation, conference. Commonly const. *with* or *of* (a person). OE. **b.** With possess. pron., or *the* and genitive: The opportunity of speaking or conversing with a person; an audience or interview with a person. Now *arch.* or *Obs.* OE. **c.** Mention *of* a thing. Also with *no.* Now *rare.* ME. **3.** Common or general talk; report, rumour, or current mention *of* something. Now *rare* or *Obs.* ME.

1. Men..express their thoughts by s. BERKELEY. 2. Deserue well at my hands, by helping mee to the s. of Beatrice SHAKS. He desires Some priuate s. with you SHAKS. 3. Dr. Clement, what's he? I haue heard much s. of him B. JONS. †*In s.*, spoken about, mentioned.

II. 1. The form of utterance peculiar to a particular nation, people, or group of persons; a language, tongue, or dialect OE. **2.** The faculty or power of speaking, or of expressing thoughts by articulate sounds OE. **3.** Manner or mode of speaking; *esp.* the method of utterance habitual to a particular person OE.

1. The Iewes speche COVERDALE 2 *Kings* 18:26. The several families who understood one another's s. kept together DE FOE. 2. The s. of the dying man failed MACAULAY. 3. Thou art a Galilean, and thy speach soundeth euen alike COVERDALE *Mark* 14:70.

III. 1. The result of speaking; that which is spoken or uttered OE. **2.** A certain number of words uttered by a person at one time; *esp.* a more or less formal utterance or statement with respect to something OE. †**b.** A talk or discourse between persons or *with* another –1633. **c.** A more or less formal discourse delivered to an audience; an oration; also, the manuscript or printed copy or report of this 1583. **d.** A school composition declaimed on speech-day 1886. †**3. a.** A report or rumour –1660. †**b.** A current saying or assertion –1642. †**c.** A phrase, term, or idiom –1675. †**4.** A law-plea –1450.

1. Blessed be thy speach, and blessed be thou COVERDALE 1 *Sam.* 25:33. Ten Kabs of s. descended into the world, and the women took away nine of them 1647. 2. Many have been the wise speeches of fools, though not so many as the foolish speeches of wise men FULLER. c. *King's S.*, the sovereign's address to parliament at its opening and closing; His Majesty's s. of 13th November 1770 *'Junius' Lett.* 3. b. The common s. is, spend and God will send GASCOIGNE.

Comb.: **s.-centre,** the nervous brain-centre controlling the power of speech; **-craft,** the knowledge or science of s.; **-day,** the day at the end of the school year on which exercises are declaimed and the annual prizes distributed in certain public schools; also, a similar day in other schools marked by prize-giving and s.-making; **-reading,** the action on the part of deaf and dumb persons of comprehending s. by watching the movements of a speaker's mouth.

Speech (spītʃ), *v.* 1682. [f. prec.] **1.** *trans.* To say or state in a speech or speeches (*rare*). **2.** To make a speech to; to address in a speech 1818. **3.** *intr.* To make a speech or speeches. Now *rare.* 1684.

Speechful (spī·tʃfŭl), *a.* 1842. [f. SPEECH *sb.* + -FUL.] Full of speech; possessing the power of speech; loquacious, talkative. **b.** Of the eyes, etc.: Full of expression; speaking 1849. Hence **Spee·chfulness.**

Speechification (spī:tʃifikē·ʃən). 1809. [f. SPEECHIFY *v.*; see -FICATION.] **1.** An instance or occasion of speech-making; a speech, oration, harangue. **2.** The action of making speeches; oratory 1825.

Speechifier (spī·tʃifəi,əɹ). 1778. [f. next + -ER[1].] One who speechifies or delivers speeches; one given to, or having some aptitude for, public speaking.

Speechify (spī·tʃifəi), *v.* Chiefly *joc.* or *depreciatory.* 1723. [f. SPEECH *sb.* + -IFY.] **1.** *intr.* To make a speech or speeches; to 'hold forth'; to speak or talk at some length or with some degree of formality. **2.** *trans.* To address in a speech or speeches 1862.

Speechifying (spī·tʃifəi,iŋ), *vbl. sb.* 1723. [f. prec. + -ING[1].] **1.** The action of making speeches; the practice of oratory. **b.** The action of speaking or talking, esp. in a formal manner or at excessive length 1777. **2.** An instance or occasion of public speaking 1843.

1. Then came the feast, and afterwards the meeting, with music and s. in the church C. BRONTË.

Speeching (spī·tʃiŋ), *vbl. sb.* 1664. [f. SPEECH *sb.* or *v.* + -ING[1].] The action or practice of making speeches; the art of speaking; a speech.

Speechless (spī·tʃlės), *a.* [Late OE. *spǣclēas*; see SPEECH *sb.*, -LESS.] **1.** Destitute of the faculty of speech; naturally or permanently dumb. **b.** Of a state or condition: Characterized by the lack of speech 1593. **2. a.** Unable to speak on account of illness, injury, or extreme exhaustion ME. **b.** Deprived for the time being of speech through astonishment, fear, etc., or through excessive drinking; temporarily dumb. late ME. **3.** Refraining from speech; silent. Also, reticent, taciturn. late ME. †**4.** Not uttered or expressed in speech. SHAKS. **5.** Of an emotion, etc.: Characterized by loss of speech 1593. **6.** Free from, unaccompanied or undisturbed by, speech 1726. **7.** *poet.* Incapable of expression in or by speech 1813.

1. They mouthes, but speechlesse, have: Eyes sightlesse 1586. **b.** As pure as s. infancy! SHELLEY. **2. a.** Some powere strike me s. for a time! 1591. **b.** S. with surprise 1891. **3.** *transf.* A silence in the Heauens,..The bold windes speechlesse SHAKS. **4.** For in her youth There is a prone and speechlesse dialect, Such as moue men SHAKS. **5.** She gave herself up to s. joy 1794. **6.** The great..darkness Of the speechless days that shall be! LONGFELLOW. Hence **Spee·chless-ly** *adv.*, **-ness.**

Spee·ch-ma:ker. 1710. [f. SPEECH *sb.*] One who makes a speech or speeches, esp. in public; an orator. So **-ma:king** 1718.

Speed (spīd), *sb.* [OE. *spēd*, earlier *spǣd* = OS. *spōd*, OHG. *spuot*; f. Gmc. **spōan* (OE. *spōwan*, OHG. *spuo(e)n* prosper, succeed).] **I. 1.** Success, prosperity, good fortune; profit, advancement, furtherance. *Obs.* exc. *Sc.* or *arch.* †**2. a.** Assistance, aid, help –1500. †**b.** One who, or that which, promotes successs or prosperity –1681.

1. The king wished us good s. DE FOE. **2. b.** Good-manners be your speede SHAKS. Christ be our s. 1681.

II. 1. Quickness in moving or making progress from one place to another, usually as the result of special exertion; celerity, swiftness; also, power or rate of progress OE. **b.** Of things: Swiftness, rapidity, velocity, of direct or circular movement; rate of motion or revolution ME. **2.** Quickness, promptness, or dispatch in the performance of some action or operation OE. **b.** *Photogr.* The relative rapidity with which a plate, film, etc., is acted upon by light or by a developer 1892. **3.** A section of a cone-pulley giving a particular rate of speed 1881.

1. Madam, I goe with all conuenient s. SHAKS. **b.** The slowness of the s. 1857. Phr. †*At s.*, at a rapid rate of movement. *At* (or †*on*) *full s.*, or, simply, *full s.*, with the utmost s. possible. *To make s.*, to hurry, make haste. †*To have*, or *get*, *the s. of*, to outdistance, to get ahead of (a person). **2.** Get them transcribed by good hands with all s. 1701.

attrib. and *Comb.*: **a.** In the names of devices or apparatus for regulating or indicating s., as *s.-check*, *-clock*, *-cone*, *-gauge*. **b.** Denoting the attainment of, or capacity for, high s., as *s.-boat*, *-car*, *lathe*. **c.** Miscellaneous, as *s.-capacity*, *-limit*, *-trial*. **s.-cop** *U.S. slang*, a policeman who is detailed to observe the s. of motorists; **-gear,** a device for regulating the s. of a bicycle, etc.; **-man,** a cyclist who rides at a high rate of s.; **-merchant,** orig. *U.S. slang*, one who indulges in motoring, etc. at high s.; **speedway** *U.S.*, a special track for rapid cycling or motoring.

Speed (spīd), *v.* Pa. t. and pa. pple. **sped, speeded.** [OE. *spēdan*, usu. *ġespēdan* = OS. *spodian* (Du. *spoeden*), OHG. *spuoten* (G. *spuden*, *sputen* from LG.), f. **spōd-* (see prec.).] **I. 1.** *intr.* Of persons: To succeed or prosper; to attain one's purpose or desire. Now *arch.* †**b.** Const. *of*: To succeed in getting, obtaining, or accomplishing –1643. **2.** *impers.* To go or fare (well or ill) *with* a person, etc. ME. **3.** Of things: To prove successful; to thrive ME. **4.** *trans.* To further or assist (a person); to cause to succeed or prosper. Now *arch.* ME. †**b.** Const. *of* or *with*: To provide or furnish (a person) with something. Chiefly in *pa. pple.* –1665. **5.** In *pa. pple.*: **a.** Furthered or brought to the end or condition desired; so dealt with as to be satisfied or well situated ME. **b.** In contexts implying an evil plight or awkward situation 1530. **c.** Appointed or elected *to* (or *as*) something (*rare*) ME. **6.** To promote or further (a matter); to accomplish or carry out ME. **b.** *spec.* To promote, expedite, prosecute (a bill, plea) as a matter of official or legal business. late ME. **7.** *arch.* **a.** †To deal with, finish, or dispatch (a matter) ME. **b.** To dispatch, destroy, kill (a person, etc.) 1594.

1. Soonest he spedes, that most can lye and fayn WYATT. **2.** It has constantly sped worse with philosophy, instead of speeding better 1854. **3.** Philip's suit no longer sped so favorably as before 1855. **4.** For let the Gods so s. mee, as I loue The name of Honor, more then I feare death SHAKS. Phr. *God s. the plough*, etc. **5. b.** We three are married, but you two are sped SHAKS. **c.** His father got him to be sped a Kings-scholar at Westminster 1691. **6.** S. his hunting with thy Pow'r divine DRYDEN. **b.** To s. the action, that is to prosecute the action with due diligence 1884. **7. a.** Go, s. thine office quickly, sirrah SCOTT. **b.** 'Yes. I am sped,' he said in a faint voice 1845.

II. 1. *trans.* To send with speed or haste; also, to force to go ME. **b.** To send out, cast, discharge, or direct, with some degree of quickness and force 1569. **c.** To enable (a person) to make speed in departing or travelling; to further the going or progress of; sometimes simply, to bid farewell to 1725. **2.** To give speed to (a course, etc.); to hasten; to cause to be rapid in movement ME. **b.** To press or urge on, *esp.* in order to bring to an early result or termination; to expedite. late ME. **c.** To cause (time) to pass (*away*) quickly 1818. **d.** To increase the working rate of. In recent use chiefly with *up*. 1856. **e.** To give a specified speed to (a machine) 1881. **3.** *refl.* **a.** To go with speed. Now *literary*. ME. **b.** To act with speed; to make haste in doing, or to do, something. Now *arch.* ME. **4.** *intr.* **a.** To go or move with speed. late ME. **b.** Of time: To pass quickly ME. **c.** To make haste *to* do something; to be speedy in action. late ME. **d.** To drive a motor vehicle at a high rate of speed. Chiefly in *vbl. sb.* Also *trans.* 1904.

1. The cry in all thy ships is still the same—S. us away to battle and to fame COWPER. **b.** His last arrow is sped TENNYSON. **c.** I..Welcome the coming, s. the going guest POPE. **2.** The king.. Repels their hordes, and speeds their flight afar 1807. **b.** Command thy maids to s. the work 1870. **e.** Similar automatic machines, speeded alike 1897. **4. a.** Streams sped downwards, falling over the rocks 1860. *fig.* Your wit's too hot, it speeds too fast, 'twill tire SHAKS. **c.** First to Watch, and then to S. BACON.

Speeder (spī·dəɹ). late ME. [f. prec. + -ER[1].] **1.** One who speeds, aids, or furthers; a helper or forwarder. Now *arch.* †**2.** One who prospers, *esp.* in a suit –1671. **3.** A device for quickening or regulating the speed of machinery; also, a kind of roving-machine used in cotton-manufacture 1875.

Spee·dful, *a.* ME. [f. SPEED *sb.* + -FUL.] †**1.** Profitable, advantageous, expedient, helpful, efficacious –1573. **2.** Speedy, quick, swift, rapid. Now *rare*. late ME. **Spee·dfully** *adv.*

Speedless (spī·dlės), *a.* ME. [f. SPEED *sb.* + -LESS.] Profitless, ineffectual, unsuccessful.

Speedometer (spīdǫ·mǐtəɹ). 1904. [f. SPEED *sb.* + -METER.] A speed-indicator, esp. one affixed to an automobile.

Speedster (spī·dstəɹ). 1918. [f. as prec. + -STER, after *roadster*.] **a.** A person who drives, etc. at high speed. **b.** A fast motor car, etc.

Speedwell (spī·d,wėl). 1578. [app. f. SPEED *v.* I. 1 + WELL *adv.*, in ref. to the fugacious petals.] Any herb of the genus VERONICA.

Speedy (spī·di), *a.* late ME. [f. SPEED *sb.* + -Y[1].] †**1.** Advantageous, expedient, helpful –1449. **2.** Moving, or able to move, with speed; swift. Now *rare*. late ME. **3.** Acting with speed; active, prompt, quick 1504. **4.** Characterized by speed of motion or action. late ME. **b.** Rapidly brought to pass or to an end; quickly accomplished, arrived at, or obtained 1607. **5.** quasi-*adv.* Speedily 1601.

2. The Barbary Horse is more s. than the rest 1630. **3.** Speak out, and be s. SCOTT. **4.** Some s. remedy should be applied 1764. Favourable winds seemed..to promise them a s. navigation 1797. **b.** I will wish her s. strength SHAKS.

Comb.: **s. cut,** an injury on the inner side of a horse's fore leg, near the knee, caused by the foot of the opposite leg when in motion; also as *vb.* and *attrib.* So **Spee·di-ly** *adv.* ME., **-ness.**

†**Speer,** *sb.* Also **spear.** 1607. [var. of SPIRE *sb.*[1] Cf. SPEAR *sb.*[2]] A branch or prong of a deer's horn –1774.

Speer (spīᵊɹ), *v.*[1] Also **speir.** Chiefly *Sc.* and *north.* [OE. *spyrian* = OFris. *spera*, OS. **spurian*, OHG. *spur(r)en* (G. *spüren*), ON. *spyrja* :– **spurjan*, f. Gmc. **spur-* (see SPOOR).] **I.** *intr.* **1.** To put a question or questions; to ask. †**2.** To inquire one's way –1615.

1. S. as little about him as he does about you SCOTT.

II. *trans.* **1.** With objective clause: To inquire or ask *how*, *what*, *who*, etc. OE. **2.** To make inquiries concerning, to ask questions regarding (a thing or fact) ME. **3.** To trace or find out by inquiry. Usu. with *out*. late ME. **4.** To ask (a question) 1460. **5.** To question or interrogate (a person) ME.

Speer (spīᵊɹ), *v.*[2] *dial.* and *U.S.* 1866. [perh. identical w. prec., infl. by PEER *v.*] *intr.* To peer.

†**Speight.** 1450. [Either repr. OE. **speht*, or – MLG., MDu. *specht*, OHG. *speht* (Du., G. *specht*).] The green woodpecker –1656.

Speiss (spəis). 1796. [– G. *speise* in the same sense, spec. use of *speise* food, nourishment.] **1.** An impure metallic compound, containing nickel, cobalt, iron, etc., produced in the smelting of certain ores; *esp.* an arsenide obtained in the manufacture of smalt and used as a source of nickel. **2.** **Speiss-cobalt,** tin-white cobalt; smaltine 1872.

‖**Spek-boom** (spe·kbōm). Also **speck-.** 1823. [S. Afr. Du., f. *spek* SPECK *sb.*[2] + *boom* tree.] The purslane-tree (*Portulacaria afra*) of South Africa; the wood of this.

Spelæan (spĭlī·ăn), *a.* Also **spelean.** 1839. [f. L. *spelæum* (– Gr. σπήλαιον cave) + -AN.] **1.** Inhabiting a cave or caves; frequenting caverns; cave-dwelling. **2.** Of the nature of a cave 1882.

Spelæology (spīli,ǫ·lŏdʒi). Also **speleo-.** 1895. [– Fr. *spéléologie*: see prec. and -LOGY.] The scientific study of caves. Hence **Speleolo·gical** *a.*, **-lo·gically** *adv.* **Speleo·logist.**

Spelding (spe·ldiŋ). *Sc.* 1537. [f. Sc. *speld* slit open + -ING[1]. See SPALD *v.*] A small split fish, preserved by being dried in the sun.

Spelk. Chiefly *north.* and *Sc.* [OE. *spelc* (also *spilc*), = LG. *spalke*, Icel. *spelka*.] **1.** A surgical splint. **2.** A splinter or chip; a small strip of wood 1440. **3.** A thatching-rod 1563.

Spell (spel), *sb.*[1] [OE. *spel(l* = OS., OHG. *spel*, ON. *spjall*, Goth. *spill* recital, tale :– Gmc. **spellam*. Cf. GOSPEL.] †**1.** Without article: Discourse, narration, speech; occas. idle talk, fable. –late ME. †**2.** A discourse or sermon; a narrative or tale –1653. **3.** A set of words, a formula or verse, supposed to possess occult or magical powers; a charm or incantation 1579. **b.** *transf.* and *fig.* An occult or mysterious power or influence; a fascinating or enthralling charm 1592.

3. She workes by Charmes, by Spels, by th' Figure, & such dawbry as this is SHAKS. **b.** The s. is removed; I see you as you are JANE AUSTEN. Hence **Spe·llful** *a.* full of, abounding in, spells or magical power.

Spell (spel), *sb.*[2] Now *dial.* 1545. [perh. a later form of †*speld* sb. (as in SPELDING) in the same sense. See also SPALD *v.*] **1.** A splinter, chip, fragment. **2.** A bar, rail, or rung 1559. **3.** The trap used in the game of *knur and s.* 1781.

Spell (spel), *sb.*[3] 1593. [f. SPELL *v.*[3]] **1.** A set of persons taking a turn of work in order to relieve others; a relay, relief-gang, or shift. Now *rare*. **2.** A turn of work taken by a person or set of persons in relief of another 1625. **3.** A continuous course or period *of* some work, occupation, or employment; a turn or bout *at* something. Also without const. 1706. **4.** A period or space of time of indefinite length 1728. **b.** A period having a certain character or spent in a particular way 1830. **5.** A continuous period or stretch *of* a specified kind of weather 1728. **6.** *U.S.* A period of being indisposed, out of sorts, or irritable 1856.

1. Yet I sent them an other fresh s. of men 1628. **2.** The men gave way..with a good will, the passengers taking spells to help them STEVENSON. **3.** The Termagant Sloop..has had a long s. of service NELSON. *S. oh!* (or *ho!*), a call or signal usu. to rest or cease working. **4.** I hope to take a pretty long s. in town GIBBON. **b.** A grievous s. of eighteen months on board the French galleys 1885. **5.** A severe s. of cold weather 1775. No man ever knew so winter-like a s. so early in the year 1740.

Spell, *v.*[1] *Obs.* or *dial.* [OE. *spellian*, f. *spel(l* SPELL *sb.*[1]; = MLG., MDu. *spellen*, OHG. *-spellōn*, ON. *spjalla*, Goth. *spillōn*.] **1.** *intr.* To discourse or preach; to talk, converse, or speak. **2.** *trans.* To utter, declare, relate, tell OE.

Spell (spel), *v.*[2] Pa. t. and pa. pple. **spelled, spelt.** ME. [Aphetic – OFr. *espel(l)er* (mod. *épeler*), for older **espeldre*, *espeaudre* – Frankish **spellōn*; see prec.] **I.**

trans. **1.** To read (a book, etc.) letter by letter; to peruse, or make out, slowly or with difficulty. **2.** *fig.* **a.** To find out, to guess or suspect, by close study or observation 1587. **b.** To make out, understand, decipher, or comprehend, by study 1635. **c.** To consider, contemplate, scan intently 1633. **3.** To name or set down in order the letters of (a word or syllable); to denote by certain letters in a particular order 1588. **b.** Of letters: To form (a word) 1738. **4.** To amount to; to signify, imply, or involve 1661.

1. He was spelling the paper, with the help of his lips THACKERAY. **2. a.** That there should be a God, heathens might s. out 1879. **b.** He..spells a horse's teeth divinely 1820. **c.** Will great God measure with a wretch? Shall he thy stature s.? G. HERBERT. **3.** What is Ab speld backward with the horn on his head? SHAKS. **c.** *U.S.* To put to the test in spelling; to put (a person) *down* in spelling 1853.

II. *intr.* **1.** To form words by means of letters; to repeat or set down the letters of words; to read off the separate letters forming a word or words. late ME. **b.** *fig.* To engage in study or contemplation *of* something. *poet.* 1632. **2.** To intimate or suggest a desire *for* something; to ask *for*, either by hints or direct request 1790.

1. A foolish opinion..that we ought to s. exactly as we speak SWIFT. **b.** The..Mossy Cell, Where I may sit and rightly s. Of every Star that Heav'n doth shew MILT. **2.** It will be observed.. that he 'spelled' for the curacy 1860.

Phrases: *To s. able* (U.S. slang), to be able; to have all the ability and strength needed (for some particular purpose). †*To s.* (a person) *backward*, to misrepresent, to pervert. *To s. short*, to express by a blunter term. Hence **Spe·llable** *a.* capable of being spelled or denoted by letters.

Spell (spel), *v.*[3] 1595. [Later form of †*spele* take the place of, OE. *spelian*, rel. to *ġespelia*, *spala* substitute, of unkn. origin.] **1.** *trans.* To take the place of (a person) at some work or labour; to relieve (another) by taking a turn at work. Now *U.S.* **b.** To relieve by an interval of rest; to rest (*esp.* a horse). Chiefly *Austral.* 1846. **2.** *Naut.* To take a turn or turns of work at (the pump, etc.) 1769. **3.** *intr.* **a.** To replace one set of workers by another; to take turns 1861. **b.** *Austral.* To take an interval of rest 1880.

1. Sometimes there are two ostensible boilers to s. and relieve one another 1823.

Spell (spel), *v.*[4] 1591. [f. SPELL *sb.*[1] 3.] **1.** *trans.* To charm, fascinate, bewitch, bind by (or as by) a spell; to act as a spell upon. **b.** To protect (a person) *from*, to drive *away*, by means of a spell or charm 1691. **2.** To invest with magical properties 1697.

1. When..thy roses came to me My sense with their deliciousness was spell'd KEATS. **b.** Thy soft voice spelled away All my dearth 1876. **2.** This,..spell'd with Words of Pow'r, Dire Stepdames in the Magick Bowl infuse DRYDEN.

Spell-bind (spe·lbaind), *v.* 1808. [f. SPELL *sb.*[1] 3, after next.] *trans.* To bind by, or as by, a spell; to fascinate, enchant. So **Spe·llbinder** *U.S.* a speaker capable of holding an audience spell-bound.

Spell-bound (spe·lbaund), *ppl. a.* 1799. [f. SPELL *sb.*[1] 3.] Bound by, or as by, a spell; fascinated, enchanted, entranced.

Speller (spe·ləɹ). 1440. [f. SPELL *v.*[2] + -ER[1].] **1.** One who spells; an authority on spelling. **2.** *U.S.* A spelling-book 1864.

Spelling (spe·liŋ), *vbl. sb.* 1440. [f. SPELL *v.*[2] + -ING[1].] **1.** The action, practice, or art of naming the letters of words, of reading letter by letter, or of expressing words by letters. **2.** Orthography; a particular instance of this 1661.

Comb.: **s.-book**, a book designed to teach s.

Spelt, *sb.* [In late OE., ME., and mod. Eng. due to independent adoptions from the Continent of OS. *spelta*, MLG., MDu. *spelte* (Du. *spelt*) = OHG. *spelza*, *spelta* (G. *spelz*).] A species of grain (*Triticum spelta*) related to wheat, formerly much cultivated in southern Europe and still grown in some districts.

Spelt (spelt), *v.* Now *dial.* 1570. [Related to †*speld* vb. (as in SPELDING) in the same way as SPALT *v.* to SPALD *v.*] *trans.* To husk or pound (grain); to bruise or split (*esp.* beans).

Spelter (spe·ltəɹ). 1661. [corresp. to OFr. *espeautre*, MDu. *speauter* (Du., G. *spiauter*), G. *spialter*, and rel. indeterminately to PEWTER.] **1.** Zinc. (Now only *Comm.*) **2.** An alloy or solder of which zinc is the principal constituent 1815.

Speluncar (spelɒ·ŋkăɹ), *a.* 1855. [f. L. *spelunca* cave + -AR[1].] Having relation or reference to a cave.

Spence (spens). late ME. [Aphetic – OFr. *despense* (mod. *dépense*) :– subst. use of fem. pa. pple. of L. *dispendere* DISPENSE *v.*] **1.** A room or separate place in which victuals and liquor are kept; a buttery or pantry; a cupboard. Now *dial.* or *arch.* **2.** *Sc.* An inner apartment of a house; a parlour 1783.

1. In one large aperture, which the robber facetiously called his *s.* (or pantry) SCOTT.

†**Spencer**[1]. ME. [Aphetic – AFr. *espenser*, var. of *despenser*, OFr. *despensier* DISPENSER.] A steward or butler –1580.

Spencer[2] (spe·nsəɹ). 1700. [From the family name *Spencer*. In sense 1 prob. from that of Charles *Spencer*, third Earl of Sunderland (1674–1722); in sense 2 from that of George John *Spencer*, second Earl Spencer (1758–1834).] †**1.** A kind of wig –1753. **2.** A short double-breasted overcoat without tails worn by men in the end of the 18th c. and the beginning of the 19th 1796. **b.** A kind of close-fitting jacket or bodice commonly worn by women and children early in the 19th c., and since revived 1803. **c.** A short coat or jacket 1851.

Spencer (spe·nsəɹ), *sb.*[3] 1840. [perh. f. the name of Mr. Knight *Spencer*.] *Naut.* A fore-and-aft sail, set with a gaff, serving as a try-sail to the fore or main mast of a vessel.

Spencerian (spensɪ͡ə·riăn), *a.* and *sb.* 1881. [f. name of the philosopher Herbert *Spencer* (1820–1903); see -IAN.] **A.** *adj.* Of or pertaining to Herbert Spencer or his philosophical views. **B.** *sb.* A follower of Spencer 1888.

Spend (spend), *sb.* 1688. [f. SPEND *v.*] The action of spending money. Only in phr. *on* or *upon the s.*

Spend (spend), *v.* Pa. t. and pa. pple. **spent.** [Partly (i) OE. *spendan*, corresp. to MLG., MDu. *spenden*, OHG. *spentōn* (G. *spenden*), ON. *spenna* – L. *expendere* EXPEND; partly (ii) aphetic f. DISPEND.] **I.** *trans.* **1.** Of persons: To pay out or away; to disburse or expend; to dispose of, or deprive oneself of, in this way. †**b.** To levy charges on (a person). Only in phr. *s. me and defend me.* –1596. **2.** *absol.* To exercise, make, or incur expenditure of money, goods, means, etc. ME. **3.** To expend or employ (labour, material, thought, etc.) in some specified way ME. **4.** To employ, occupy, use, or pass (time, one's life, etc.) *in* or *on* some action, occupation, or state ME. **b.** *ellipt.* To pass (the day, evening, etc.) in social intercourse or entertainment, or as a guest 1697. **5.** To use up; to exhaust or consume by use; to wear out. In later use freq. with *force*, *fury*, etc., as object. ME. **b.** To bring to a violent end; to destroy; to consume by destruction or wasting; to reduce or convert *into* something. late ME. **c.** *refl.* Of persons or things: To exhaust or wear out (oneself or itself); to become incapable of further activity; to cease to operate 1593. **6.** To suffer the loss of (blood, life, etc.); to allow to be shed or spilt ME. †**b.** *Naut.* To lose or incur the loss of (a mast, yard, sail, etc.) through bad weather or by some accident –1694. **7.** To use for food or drink; to consume in this way; to eat or drink. late ME. **b.** *Agric.* To use (a crop, hay, etc.) as food or fodder for cattle; to eat off 1733. **8.** To make use of; to use or employ. Now *rare.* late ME. **9.** To expend or employ (speech or language); to utter or emit (a word, sound, etc.). late ME. †**b.** *To s. the mouth, tongue*, etc. Of hunting dogs: To bark or give tongue on finding or seeing the game –1682. **c.** To shed (tears, blood, or the like). *arch.* 1602. **10.** To consume, employ, use superfluously, wastefully, or with undue lavishness; to waste or squander; to throw away. late ME. †**b.** To waste (time) –1720. **11.** To allow (time, one's life, etc.) to pass or go by; to live or stay through (a certain period) to the end. late ME. †**12.** To cause or involve expenditure of (something) –1703. †**b.** To involve the expenditure of (time) –1649.

1. I have..spent very many hundred powndes 1574. Wherefore doe yee s. money for that which is not bread? *Isa.* 55:2. **2.** He spendeth a pace and getteth nothyng 1530. **3.** I s. my Breath in Groans 1696. Why do you s. many words..on this subject? 1875. **4.** He spent his time in training horses 1802. **5.** The Thunder..Perhaps hath spent his shafts MILT. **c.** Man after man spends himself in this cause CARLYLE. **7. b.** To spend all the stover, straw, and turnips on the land 1823. **9. b.** *absol.* For then reason like a bad hound spends upon a false sent SIR T. BROWNE. **10.** I am a fool..to s. my words upon an idle.. unintelligent boy SCOTT. **11.** I have been spending six weeks in Ireland 1854.

II. *intr.* †**1.** Of time, the season, etc.: To pass, elapse –1681. †**2.** To be consumed, dispersed, exhausted, or used up; to pass off or *away* –1704. **3.** Of foodstuffs, wheat, hay, etc.: To turn out or prove in use to be of a certain quality; to last or hold out *well*. Now *dial.* 1673. †**4.** Of a liquid; To flow or run –1811.

2. The Sound spendeth, and is dissipated in the Open Aire BACON. **3.** Meat that spends well 1687. Hence **Spe·ndable** *a.* that can be spent.

Spe·nd-all. Now *rare.* 1553. [f. SPEND *v.* + ALL *sb.*] One who spends all his goods, money, etc.; a spendthrift.

Spender (spe·ndəɹ). late ME. [f. SPEND *v.* + -ER[1].] **1.** One who spends; *spec.* a spendthrift. **2.** One who, or that which, consumes, employs, or uses up; a consumer or waster *of* something 1565. **3.** *Tanning.* A pit in which the bark is leached. Also *attrib.* in *s. pit.* 1882.

Spending (spe·ndiŋ), *vbl. sb.* OE. [f. SPEND *v.* + -ING[1].] **1.** The action of SPEND *v.*, in various senses. †**2.** That which may be expended or spent; means of support; goods, money, cash –1650.

Spe·nding-mo:ney. 1598. [f. SPENDING *vbl. sb.*] Money used or available for spending; a sum allowed for this purpose; pocket-money.

Spendthrift (spe·ndþrift), *sb.* (and *a.*). 1601. [f. SPEND *v.* + THRIFT *sb.*] **1.** One who spends money profusely or wastefully; one who wastes his patrimony by foolish or lavish expenditure; an improvident or extravagantly wasteful person (freq. connoting moral worthlessness). **2.** *transf.* A prodigal consumer, user up, or waster, *of* something 1610. **3.** *attrib.* passing into *adj.* **a.** Acting as or like, having the qualities of, a spendthrift 1607. **b.** Wasteful 1790.

2. Fie, what a spend-thrift is he of his tongue SHAKS. **3. a.** These rich plebeians are a harvest for us spend-thrift nobles 1834. **b.** The improvident resource of a s. sale BURKE. Hence **Spe·ndthri:fty** *a.* prodigal or wasteful in expenditure.

Spenserian (spensɪ͡ə·riăn), *a.* and *sb.* 1818. [f. name of the poet Edmund *Spenser* (?1552–1599) + -IAN.] **A.** *adj.* Of or belonging to, characteristic of, Spenser or his work.

S. stanza, the stanza employed by Spenser in the *Faerie Queen*, consisting of eight decasyllabic lines and a final Alexandrine, with the rhyming scheme *ab ab bc bcc*.

B. *sb.* **1.** A Spenserian stanza, or a poem in this metre 1818. **2.** A follower or imitator of Spenser; a poet of Spenser's school 1894.

Spent (spent), *pa. pple.* and *ppl. a.* 1440. [f. SPEND *v.*] **I.** In predicative uses. **1.** Of material things: Expended, consumed, used up completely. **2.** Passed, gone; come to an end; over 1528. **3.** Of persons or animals: Deprived of force or strength; tired or worn out; completely exhausted 1591. **4.** Of things: Exhausted of the active or effective power or principle 1596.

1. Their powder and ball were s. MACAULAY. **2.** The time is farre spente 1560. The raine is s. 1634. **3.** Now thou seest me S., overpower'd, despairing of success ADDISON. **4.** Though their lustre now was s. and faded SHELLEY.

II. In attrib. uses. **1.** Of persons or animals: = sense I. 3. 1568. **b.** Of fish: Exhausted by spawning; having recently spawned 1864. **2.** Of things: Exhausted, worn out, used up; no longer active, effective, or serviceable 1697.

1. The talke of a s. old man ASCHAM. **2.** Heaps of s. Arrows fall and strew the Ground DRYDEN. The s. liquor..is discharged into the stream 1877.

‖**Speos** (spī·ɒs). 1843. [Gr. σπέος cave, grotto.] *Egyptol.* A cave temple or tomb, esp. one of some architectural importance. Hence **Speo·logy**, the study of caves.

†**Spe·rage.** 1440. [var. of SPARAGE.] Asparagus –1760.

Spe·rate, *a. Obs.* or *arch.* 1551. [– L. *speratus*, pa. pple. of *sperare* hope; see -ATE².] **1.** Of debts: Having some likelihood of being recovered; not desperate. **2.** *gen.* Giving or leaving room for hope; of a promising nature 1808.

Spere, obs. f. SPHERE.

Sperling, variant of SPARLING.

Sperm (spə̄ɹm). late ME. [– late L. *sperma* – Gr. σπέρμα, f. base of σπείρειν sow.] **I. 1.** The generative substance or seed of male animals (esp. of vertebrates). **b.** A spermatozoon 1904. †**2.** Offspring, brood (of persons). MILT. **3.** *transf.* The generative matter or source from which anything is formed or takes its origin 1610. **II.** (Short for SPERM WHALE or SPERMACETI.) **1. a.** *S. oil*, an oil found together with spermaceti in the head of various species of whales 1839. **b.** *S. candle*, a spermaceti candle 1856. **2.** A sperm whale. Also *collect.* and *attrib.* 1840. **3.** Sperm candles or oil 1856.

‖**Sperma** (spə̄·ɹmă). Now *rare*. *Pl.* **spermata.** late ME. [Late L. or Gr.; see prec.] Sperm; seed. Hence **Sperma-**, comb. form.

Spermaceti (spə̄ɹmăse·ti, -sī·ti). 1471. [– med.L. *spermaceti* (so named from an erron. notion of the nature of the substance), f. *sperma* (see prec.) + *ceti*, gen. of *cetus* – Gr. κῆτος whale.] A fatty substance, which in a purified state has the form of a soft white scaly mass, found in the head (and to some extent in other parts) of the sperm-whale (*Physter macrocephalus*) and some other whales and dolphins; it is used largely in medicinal preparations, and in the manufacture of candles. Also *attrib.*, as *s.-candle*, etc.; **s. whale**, the sperm whale.

Spermaduct (spə̄·ɹmădɒkt). 1847. [f. SPERMA- + DUCT.] *Zool.* A spermatic or seminal duct or passage in a male animal. Also **Spe·rmaphore** *Bot.*, = SPERMOPHORE.

Spermary (spə̄·ɹmări). 1864. [Anglicized f. mod.L. *spermarium* (f. late L. *sperma* sperm), also used; see -ARY¹.] The organ or gland in which spermatozoa are generated in male animals.

‖**Spermatheca** (spə̄ɹmăþī·kă). *Pl.* **-thecæ** (þī·si). 1826. [f. SPERMA + THECA.] A receptacle in the oviduct of female insects and invertebrates, in which fecundation of the ova takes place. Hence **Spermathe·cal** *a.*

Spermatic (spəɹmæ·tik), *a.* (and *sb.*). 1539. [– late L. *spermaticus* – Gr. σπερματικός, f. σπέρμα, -ματ- SPERM.] **1.** Containing, conveying, or producing sperm or seed; seminiferous. **b.** Full of sperm; generative, productive 1619. **2.** Of the nature of sperm; resembling sperm 1541. †**3.** Directly derived from sperm (according to old physiological views) –1728. **4.** Of qualities: Characteristic of, peculiar to, or derived from, sperm 1642. **5.** Existing in sperm 1837. **6.** As *sb.* in *pl.* The spermatic vessels 1690.

1. A disease of the s. chord 1797. **b.** Spermatick Nile, which brings Choise Monsters forth 1648. **4.** Spermatick Vigour spreads the poison'd Race DE FOE. **5.** S. animalcules 1837. So †**Sperma·tical** *a.* (in senses 1–4); **-ly** *adv.*

Spermatin (spə̄·ɹmătin). 1836. [– Fr. *spermatine*, f. late L. *sperma*, *-mat-*; see SPERM, -IN¹, -INE⁵.] *Chem.* An albuminic constituent of the spermatic fluid.

Spermatium (spəɹmē¹·ʃⁱɒm). *Pl.* **-atia.** 1856. [mod.L. – Gr. σπερμάτιον, dim. of σπέρμα seed; see -IUM.] *Bot.* A minute linear sporule forming part of the reproductive system of lichens and fungi. (Chiefly in *pl.*)

Spermato- (spə̄·ɹmăto, spə̄ɹmătǫ·), repr. Gr. σπερματο-, comb. form of the stem of σπέρμα SPERM, employed in terms (chiefly of recent origin) relating to the reproductive organs or activities of animals and plants. Some of these have alternative forms in *sperma-* or *spermo-*. **a.** In terms denoting special reproductive organs, or parts of these, as **Spe·rmatoblast, -cyst, -cyte, -ge·mma, -gone, -go·nium, -mere, -spore. b.** In some other sbs. and adjs. with second elements of obvious meaning, as **Spermatoge·nesis, -gene·tic** *a.*, **-ge·nic** *a.*, **-o·logy, -o·phoral** *a.*, **-o·phorous** *a.*, **-rrhœ·a, -spore.**

‖**Spe·rmatocele** (-sīl). 1693. [f. SPERMATO- + CELE.] *Path.* A swelling of the testes or epididymis, from an accumulation of semen.

Spe·rmatophore (-fō³ɹ). 1847. [f. SPERMATO- + -PHORE.] **1.** *Biol.* In certain of the lower forms of animal life, a structure containing a compact mass of spermatozoa. **2.** *Bot.* A part of the spermogonium of lichens or fungi, on which the spermatia are borne 1861.

Spe:rmatozoid (-zōᵘ·id). 1857. [f. next + -ID², ³.] **1.** *Bot.* A minute fertilizing body or cell in Cryptogamia and Algæ. **2.** *Phys.* = next 1861.

‖**Spe:rmatozoon** (-zōᵘ·ǫn). *Pl.* **-zoa.** 1836. [f. SPERMATO- + Gr. ζῷον living thing, animal.] One of the numerous minute and active filaments present in the seminal fluid, by which the fecundation of the ovum is effected. Hence **Spe:rmatozo·al** *a.*

Spermi-, irreg. comb. form of L. *sperma* SPERM, as in **Spe·rmiduct** (= SPERMADUCT).

Spermism (spə̄·ɹmiz'm). 1889. [f. SPERMA + -ISM.] *Biol.* The theory that the male sperm contains the whole germ of the future animal.

Spermo-, irreg. comb. form (for SPERMATO-) of late L. *sperma* or Gr. σπέρμα SPERM, used in various terms of *Phys.*, *Zool.*, and *Bot.*

Spe·rmoderm [mod.L. *spermoderma*, *-dermis* (De Candolle)] *Bot.*, the combined outer and inner integuments of a seed, or the outer of these by itself. ‖**Spermogo·nium** [mod.L.], (*a*) *Bot.* one of the receptacles in lichens and fungi in which the spermatia are produced; (*b*) *Phys.* a sperm-cell. **Spe·rmophile** [mod.L. *Spermophilus* (Cuvier)] *Zool.*, a rodent belonging to the squirrel-like genus *Spermophilus*; a pouched marmot. **Spe·rmophore** [mod.L. *spermophorum*] *Bot.*, the placenta in plants. **Spe·rmophyte** *Bot.*, a seed-bearing plant. **Spermophy·tic** *a.* 'capable of producing true seeds'. **Spe·rmospore** *Phys.*, a compound cellular mass from which sperm filaments are developed. **Spermoto·xin** *Chem.*, a serum destructive to spermatozoa.

Sperm whale. Also **sperm-whale.** 1830. [Short for *spermaceti whale*; cf. SPERM II.] The spermaceti whale; = CACHALOT. **b.** Applied, with distinguishing epithets, to species of whales resembling, or related to, this 1882. Hence **Sperm-whaler,** a person or vessel engaged in the capture of sperm-whales.

‖**Speronara** (speronā·ră). 1783. [It.] A large rowing and sailing boat used in southern Italy and Malta.

Sperse (spə̄ɹs), *v.* Now *arch.* 1580. [Aphetic f. DISPERSE *v.*, prob. in part after It. *sperso*.] **1.** *trans.* To cause to scatter or disperse; to drive in different directions. **2.** *intr.* To take different directions 1819.

Spessartine (spe·săɹtin). 1850. [– Fr. *spessartine* (Beudant, 1832), f. *Spessart*, a hilly district in north-western Bavaria, where it is found; see -INE⁵.] *Min.* A species of manganese garnet. So **Spe·ssartite.**

Spet, *v.* Now *dial.* late ME. [Alteration of SPETE *v.*, after pa. t. and pa. pple. *spet(te)*.] *intr.* and *trans.* To spit. Hence **Spet** *sb.* spit.

Spetch (spetʃ). 1611. [Later f. north. dial. *speck* (XV), of unkn. origin.] A piece or strip of undressed leather, a trimming of hide, used in making glue or size.

†**Spete**, *v.* [OE. *spǣtan*, f. ***spāt-**; cf. SPATTLE *sb.*¹ and *v.*¹ See SPIT *v.*²] To spit. –late ME.

†**Spettle.** late ME. [repr. OE. *spǣtl*, var. of *spātl* SPATTLE *sb.*¹, or modification of *spattle* after SPETE *v.* and SPET *v.* Cf. SPITTLE *sb.*²] Spittle –1693.

Spew (spiū), *sb.* Also †**spue.** 1609. [f. the vb.] That which is spewed or cast up from the stomach; vomit.

Spew (spiū), *v.* Also †**spue.** [(i) OE. *spīwan* = OFris. *spīa*, OS., OHG. *spīwan* (G. *speien*), ON. *spýja*, Goth. *speiwan*; Gmc. str. vb.; (ii) OE. *spēowan*, *spīowan*, wk. vb.; corresp. to L. *spuere*, Gr. πτύειν (:– *spjūj-), and Balto-Sl. formations on an IE. base of imit. origin.] **1.** *intr.* To bring up and discharge the contents of the stomach through the mouth; to vomit. Not now in polite use. **2.** *trans.* To bring up (food or drink) from the stomach and eject through the mouth; to cast up or vomit; to cast out or discharge (blood, poison, etc.) from the mouth OE. **3.** To cast *out* (†or *up*), to eject or reject, with abhorrence, contempt, or loathing. late ME. **4.** To eject, cast or throw up or out, as if by vomiting; *spec.* to eject by volcanic action 1594. **5.** *intr.* Of water, liquids, etc.: To flow, pour, or run in a more or less copious stream; to ooze or be forced *out* or *up*. Now chiefly *dial.* 1670. **b.** Of ground: To swell through excess of moisture; to slip or run when left unsupported 1839.

2. *fig.* My sonne, beholde you deserue to be burnt quicke.., Spewing forth..this Fæminine Latine 1632. **3.** Because thou arte..nether colde ner hott, I will s. the oute of my mought TINDALE *Rev.* 3:16. **4.** A crater-crust which may crack and spue fire any day C. BRONTË. Phr. *To s. the oakum*, said of a vessel when the oakum starts out from the seams of her planks. **5. b.** In constructing a 'sike' for the drainage of land, gravelly earth will often break edge, and spew 1876. Hence **Spew·er** OE.

Spewy (spiū·i), *a.* 1669. [f. prec. + -Y¹.] Of ground: Tending to excessive wetness; from which water oozes out. Chiefly *Agric.* Hence **Spew·iness** s., boggy, or undrained condition (of land) 1653.

Sphacelate (sfæ·silē¹t), *v.* 1653. [f. SPHACELUS + -ATE³, perh. after Fr. *sphacéler*, *sphacélé* (XVI).] *Path.* **1.** *trans.* To affect with sphacelus; to cause to gangrene or mortify. **2.** *intr.* To become gangrenous or mortified 1684. So **Spha·celated** *ppl. a.* (*a*) *Path.* mortified, gangrened 1612; (*b*) *Bot.* withered, dead.

Sphacelation (sfæsilē¹·ʃən). 1657. [f. prec.; see -ATION.] *Path.* The fact or process of becoming mortified; the formation of a sphacelus.

‖**Sphacelia** (sfæsī·liă). 1879. [mod.L., f. *sphacelus*, with reference to its effects when eaten; see -IA¹.] *Bot.* The first stage of the fungus which produces ergot in rye.

‖**Sphacelus** (sfæ·silɒs), *a.* 1575. [mod.L. – Gr. σφάκελος convulsive movement, painful spasm, gangrene (Hippocrates). Cf. Fr. *sphacèle* (XV).] *Path.* **1.** Necrosis, mortification; an instance of this. **2.** A mass of mortified tissue; a slough 1880. Hence **Spha·celous** *a.* necrotic.

‖**Sphæridium** (sfiᵊri·diɒm). *Pl.* **-idia.** 1877. [mod.L. (Lovén), f. *sphæra* SPHERE *sb.* + Gr. dim. suffix -ιδιον; see -IUM.] *Zool.* One of the numerous minute rounded bodies attached to certain parts of sea-urchins.

Sphæro- (sfiᵊ·ro), – Gr. σφαιρο-, comb. form of σφαῖρα ball, SPHERE, as in **Sphæ·rospore** *Bot.*, the quadruple spore of some algals.

Sphærosiderite (sfiᵊrosi·dərəit). 1837. [f. SPHÆRO- + SIDERITE 1.] *Min.* A variety of siderite which occurs in spherical concretions.

Sphagnous (sfæ·gnəs), *a.* 1828. [f. next + -OUS.] **1.** Of the nature of, consisting of, sphagnum. **2.** Producing, or abounding in, sphagnum 1845.

‖**Sphagnum** (sfæ·gnɒm). *Pl.* **-a, -ums.** 1753. [mod.L., f. Gr. σφάγνος kind of moss.] *Bot.* **1.** A genus of mosses growing in boggy or swampy places; bog-moss, peat-moss; also, one or other of the species or plants composing this genus. **2.** The mossy substance of which plants of this genus are composed 1840.

Sphalerite (sfæ·lĕrəit). 1868. [f. Gr. σφαλερός deceptive + -ITE¹ 2 b; named by E. F. Glocker (1847).] *Min.* Zinc-blende.

‖**Sphendone** (sfe·ndŏnī). 1850. [– Gr. σφενδόνη.] *Archæol.* A head-band or fillet, shaped like a common form of sling, worn by women in ancient Greece.

Sphene (sfīn). 1815. [– Fr. *sphène* (Haüy, 1801), f. Gr. σφήν wedge, from the shape of its crystals.] *Min.* = TITANITE.

Sphenethmoid (sfīne·þmoid), *sb.* and *a.* 1875. [f. Gr. σφήν wedge + ETHMOID.] *Zool.* One of the cranial bones in batrachians, situated at the base of the skull; the girdle bone. Also *s. bone.*

Spheniscan (sfī·ni·skăn). 1840. [f. mod.L. *Spheniscus* (Brisson) + -AN.] A penguin of the genus *Spheniscus*; a jackass penguin.

Spheno- (sfī·no), – Gr. σφηνο-, comb. form of σφήν wedge.

1. *Anat.* In adjs. which designate something belonging to the sphenoid bone together with the part specified by the second element of the compound, as **S.-ba·silar, -maxi·llary, -te·mporal. 2.** In names of genera of animals or plants, as **Sphe·nodon,** a New Zealand lizard, called also *Tuatera* or *Hatteria*; **Sphenophy·llum,** a genus of fossil plants peculiar to the coal measures and the transition formations.

Sphenoid (sfī·noid), *a.* and *sb.* 1732. [– mod.L. *spheno(e)ides* – Gr. σφηνοειδής, f. σφήν wedge; see -OID.] **A.** *adj. S. bone*, a bone of irregular form situated at the base of the skull, where it is wedged in between the other bones of the cranium. **B.** *sb.* **1.** *Anat.* The s. bone; one or other of the separate parts of this 1828. **2.** *Cryst.* A wedge-shaped crystal bounded by four equal and similar triangular faces 1855.

Sphenoidal (sfīnoi·dăl), *a.* 1726. [f. prec. + -AL¹.] **1.** *S. bone*, the sphenoid bone. **2.** Of or pertaining to, connected with, this bone 1726.

Sphenotic (sfīnǫ·tik), *a.* and *sb.* 1872. [f. SPHEN(O- + OTIC *a.*] *Zool.* **A.** *adj.* Of or pertaining to, formed by combination of, the sphenoid bone and otic structures in certain fishes and in birds 1884. **B.** *sb.* The sphenotic bone or ossification 1872.

Spheral (sfīᵊ·răl), *a.* 1571. [– late L. *spher-*, *sphæralis*, f. *sphæra* SPHERE *sb.*; see -AL¹ 1.] **1.** Of or pertaining to a sphere or round body; having the rounded form of a sphere; spherical. **b.** *fig.* Symmetrically rounded or perfect 1841. **2.** Of or pertaining to the cosmic spheres or the heavenly bodies 1829.

1. b. There is somewhat s. and infinite..in every genius EMERSON. **2.** As the Ancients fabled of the S. Music CARLYLE.

Sphere (sfīᵊɹ), *sb.* [ME. *sper(e* – OFr. *espere*, later (with assim. to Gr. or L.) *sphère* – late L. *sphēra*, earlier *sphæra* – Gr. σφαῖρα ball, globe.] **I. 1.** The apparent outward limit of space, conceived as a hollow globe enclosing (and at all points equidistant from) the earth; the visible vault of heaven, in which the celestial bodies appear to have their place. **b.** A globe or other construction illustrating the place and motions of the celestial bodies. late ME. **2.** One or other of the concentric, transparent, hollow globes imagined by the older astronomers as revolving round the earth and respectively carrying with them the several heavenly bodies (moon, sun, planets, and fixed stars). late ME. **b.** In ref. to the harmonious sound supposed to be produced by the motion of these spheres. late ME. **c.** A place of abode different from the present earth or world; a heaven 1592. **3.** One or other of the concentric globes formerly supposed to be formed by the four elements, earth, water, air, and fire. Now *Hist.* late ME. **4.** With possess. pron. or genitive: The particular sphere (in sense 2) appropriate to, or occupied by, each of the planets (or the fixed stars). late ME. **5.** A place, position, or station in society; an aggregate of persons of a certain rank or standing 1601. **b.** The group of persons with whom one is directly in contact in society 1839. **6.** A province or domain in which one's activities or faculties find scope or exercise, or within which they are naturally confined; range or compass of action or study 1606. **7.** The whole province, domain, or range *of* some quality or activity 1602.

1. Sweet Echo,..Sweet Queen of Parly, Daughter of the Sphear MILT. *fig.* God is our circumambient S. KEN. *Oblique, parallel, right s.*: see OBLIQUE *a.* 2 b, PARALLEL *a.* 1 b, RIGHT *a.* I. 3. **b.** *Armillary s.*: see ARMILLARY. **2. b.** His voyce was propertied As all the tuned Spheres SHAKS. **3.** The principle that each element seeks its own place, led to the doctrine, that, the place of fire being the highest, there is, above the air, a s. of fire 1837. **4.** Certaine starres shot madly from their Spheares SHAKS. **5.** The young lady,.. seemed to have dropped amongst them from another s. of life SCOTT. **6.** A village is..too narrow a s. for him 1776. **7.** In this course, he came within the s. of the trade wind 1777. The s. of architecture proper RUSKIN. Phr. *S. of action*, *influence*, or *interest*, a region or territory within which a particular nation is admitted to have a special interest for political and economic purposes; also *ellipt.*

II. 1. *Geom.* A figure formed by the complete revolution of a semicircle about its diameter; a round body of which the surface is at all points equidistant from the centre. late ME. **2.** A body of a globular or orbicular form; a globe or ball. late ME. **b.** The rounded mass *of* such a body 1555. **3.** †**a.** = GLOBE *sb.* 4. –1548. **b.** An orb of the mundane system; a planet or star 1598.

2. Of Celestial Bodies first the Sun A mightie Spheare he fram'd MILT. **b.** Until the flat surface is nearly equal to the diameter of the s. of the ball 1858.

Sphere (sfīᵊɹ), *v.* Chiefly *poet.* 1605. [f. prec.] **1.** *trans.* To enclose in or as in a sphere; to encircle, engirdle 1607. **2.** To make into a sphere; to fill up or 'crown' *with* liquor 1605. **b.** *fig.* To form into a rounded or perfect whole 1615. **3.** To place in a sphere or among the spheres; to set in the heavens 1606. **b.** *fig.* To set aloft or aloof 1615. **4.** To send *about* in a circle; to turn *round* in all directions 1648.

1. Spreading all our reaches As if each private arm would s. the earth CHAPMAN. **2.** An urn sphered with wine B. JONS. **3.** Therefore is the glorious Planet Sol In noble eminence, enthron'd and sphear'd Amid'st the other SHAKS. **b.** Maiestie should be sphear'd Beyond the common Eye 1649.

Sphereless (sfīᵊ·ɹlės), *a.* 1819. [f. SPHERE *sb.* + -LESS.] **a.** Having no proper sphere; wandering. **b.** Starless.

Spheric (sfe·rik), *a.* and *sb.* 1559. [– late L. *spher-*, *sphæricus* – Gr. σφαιρικός, f. σφαῖρα SPHERE *sb.*; see -IC.] **A.** *adj.* **1.** Of or relating to the sphere as a geometrical figure. **2.** = next 1. 1610. **3.** Of, pertaining to, or connected with, the spheres or heavenly bodies 1648.

1. Cutting the Equinoctiall at right Spherick Angles 1594. **3.** We shall leap up..To join the s. company E. B. BROWNING.

B. *sb.* (Chiefly *pl.*) The mathematical study or science of the sphere; spherical geometry and trigonometry 1660.

Spherical (sfe·rikăl), *a.* 1523. [f. as prec.; see -ICAL.] **1.** Having the form of a sphere (or a segment of a sphere); globular. **b.** Of form or figure: Characteristic of a sphere 1527. **2.** *Math.* **a.** Of lines or figures: Drawn in, or on the surface of, a sphere; esp. *s. triangle* 1571. **b.** Dealing with the properties of the sphere or spherical figures 1728. **c.** Of or pertaining to, characteristic of, or arising from the sphere or its properties 1840. **3.** Of or pertaining to the celestial spheres 1605.

1. †*S. number*, a number whose powers always terminate in the same digit as the number itself, viz 5, 6, and 10. **2. c.** *S. aberration, excess, harmonic, inversion*, etc.: see the sbs. **3.** As if we were ..Knaues, Theeues, and Treachers by Sphericall predominance SHAKS. Hence **Spherica·lity**, the quality of being s. **Sphe·rical-ly** *adv.*, **-ness** (*rare*).

Sphericity (sferi·sĭti). 1625. [f. SPHERIC + -ITY. Cf. Fr. *sphéricité* (XVII).] The quality of being spherical or having the form of a sphere.

The S. of the drops of Rain 1719.

Spherico- (sfe·riko), used as comb. form of SPHERIC *a.*, as in *s.-cylindrical, -tetrahedral, -triangular* adjs.

Spheriform (sfīᵊ·rifǫɹm), *a.* 1678. [f. SPHERE *sb.* + -FORM.] = SPHERICAL *a.* 1.

Sphero- (sfīᵊ·ro), var. of SPHÆRO-, used as comb. form of SPHERE *sb.*, as in **Spheroco·nic** *Math.*, the section of a sphere by a quadric cone having its vertex at the centre of the sphere. **Sphe·rograph** *Naut.*, a device serving to facilitate the calculation of spherical problems. **Spheroma·niac**, one who is passionately fond of playing at ballgames, esp. bowls.

Spheroid (sfīᵊ·roid), *sb.* and *a.* 1664. [– L. *sphæroides* – Gr. σφαιροειδής, f. σφαῖρα ball; see -OID. Cf. Fr. *sphéroïde* (XVI).] **A.** *sb.* A body approaching in shape to a sphere, *esp.* one formed by the revolution of an ellipse about one of its axes. **B.** *adj.* = next 1767.

Spheroidal (sfīroi·dăl, sfe-), *a.* 1781. [f. SPHEROID *sb.* + -AL¹ 1.] **1.** Of form, figure, etc.: Approximately spherical. **2.** Having the form of a spheroid 1798. **3.** Dealing with the properties of spheroids 1876.

1. *S. condition* or *state*, the condition in which a liquid, as water, assumes drops of a s. form on being placed on a highly-heated surface, the drops being supported by a thin badly-conducting layer of vapour. **3.** S. Trigonometry 1876. Hence **Spheroi·dally** *adv.* after a s. manner, so as to form spheroids.

Spheroidical (sfīroi·dikăl, sfe-), *a.* 1698. [f. SPHEROID *sb.* + -ICAL.] = prec. 1, 2. Hence **Spheroi·dically** *adv.* **Sphe:roidi·city**, the state or character of being spheroidal.

Spherometer (sfīrǫ·mĭtəɹ, sfe-). 1827. [– Fr. *sphéromètre*; see SPHERO-, -METER.] An instrument for measuring the sphericality or curvature of bodies or surfaces.

Spherule (sfe·riul). 1665. [– late L. *spher-*, *sphærula*, dim. of L. *sphæra* SPHERE *sb.*; see -ULE.] A little sphere; a small or minute spherical body. Hence **Sphe·rular** *a.* having the form of a s.

Spherulite (sfe·riŭləit). 1823. [f. late L. *sphærula* SPHERULE + -ITE¹ 2 a and 2 b.] **1.** *Min.* A concretionary substance found in small spherular masses in certain rocks. **b.** A spherular concretion of this nature 1863. **2.** *Palæont.* A genus of fossil molluscs 1834.

Spherulitic (sferiŭli·tik), *a.* 1833. [f. prec. + -IC.] *Geol.* and *Min.* **1.** Of rocks, etc.: Containing, or composed of, spherulites. **2.** Pertaining to or characteristic of spherulites 1878.

Sphery (sfīᵊ·ri), *a.* 1590. [f. SPHERE *sb.* + -Y¹.] **1.** Of or pertaining to, connected with, the spheres or heavenly bodies; sphere-like. **2.** Having the form of a sphere 1600.

1. Hermias s. eyne SHAKS. Love vertue,..She can teach ye how to clime Higher then the Spheary chime MILT.

‖**Sphex** (sfeks). *Pl.* **spheges** (sfī·dʒīz). 1797. [– Gr. σφήξ (pl. σφῆκες) wasp.] *Entom.* A genus of digger-wasps; a wasp of this genus.

Sphincter (sfi·ŋktəɹ). 1578. [– L. *sphincter* – Gr. σφιγκτήρ band, contractile muscle, f. σφίγγειν bind tight.] *Anat.* A contractile muscular ring by which an orifice of the body (in man or animals) is normally kept closed. **b.** *attrib.*, as *s.-fibre, -muscle, -power* 1615.

The Fibres that compose the S. of the Bladder 1691. Hence **Sphincte·ric** *a.* of or pertaining to, of the nature of, a s.

Sphinx (sfiŋks). *Pl.* **sphinges** (sfi·ndʒīz), **sphinxes.** late ME. [– L. *Sphinx* – Gr. Σφίγξ (stem Σφιγγ-), app. f. σφίγγειν draw tight. In generalized senses usu. with small initial; otherwise with capital S.] **1.** *Gr. Myth.* A hybrid monster, usually described as having the head of a woman and the (winged) body of a lion, which infested Thebes until the riddle it propounded was solved by Œdipus; also, any monster of a similar form and character. **b.** *transf.* One who propounds or presents a difficult question or problem 1603. **c.** *fig.* A thing or subject of an inscrutable or mysterious nature 1610. **2.** A sculptured, carved, or moulded figure of an imaginary creature having a human head and breast combined with the body of a lion 1579. **b.** *spec.* The colossal stone image of this kind near the pyramids of El-Gizeh in Egypt 1613. **3.** A kind of ape; in mod. use, a sphinx-baboon 1607. **4.** An insect belonging to the lepidopterous genus *Sphinx* or to the family represented by this, so called from the attitude frequently assumed by the caterpillar 1753.

1. Subtill as S., as sweet and musicall, As bright Apollos Lute SHAKS. **b.** Mr. Dodson has for many years been a political s. 1884. **2.** He had a S. of Yvory geven him by Verres NORTH.

attrib. and *Comb.*, as *s.-enigma, -form, -question*, etc.; *s.-like* adj.; **s.-baboon**, the Guinea baboon (*Cynocephalus* or *Papio sphinx*); **-moth** = sense 4.

Sphragistic (sfrădʒi·stik), *sb.* and *a.* 1836. [– Fr. *sphragistique* – Gr. σφραγιστικός, f. σφραγίς seal.] **A.** *sb. pl.* The scientific study or knowledge of seals or signet rings. **B.** *adj.* Of or pertaining to, relating to or dealing with, seals or signet rings 1884.

Sphygmic (sfi·gmik), *a.* 1707. [– Gr. σφυγμικός, f. σφυγμός pulse; see -IC.] Of or pertaining to the pulse. Also *sb. pl.*

Sphygmo- (sfi·gmo), – Gr. σφυγμο-, comb. form of σφυγμός pulse.

Sphy·gmogram, a diagram of pulse-beats as traced by the sphygmograph. **Sphy·gmograph,** an instrument which records the movements of the pulse by means of tracings; hence **Sphy·gmograph** *vb.* **Sphygmogra·phic** *a.*, of or pertaining to, effected or produced by, the sphygmograph. **Sphygmo·graphy,** the scientific description of the pulse or registration of pulse-beats. **Sphy:gmomano·meter, Sphygmo·meter,** an instrument for measuring the force or rate of the pulse. **Sphygmome·tric** *a.*, relating to the measurement of the pulse. **Sphy·gmophone,** an instrument by which pulsations are rendered audible. **Sphy·gmoscope,** an instrument for examining the pulse.

‖**Sphyræna** (sfəirī·nă). 1849. [mod. use of L. *sphyræna* – Gr. σφύραινα, f. σφῦρα hammer.] *Zool.* A pike-like fish belonging to the genus *Sphyræna* or the family represented by this; one of the common species is the barracuda. Hence **Sphyræ·noid** *a.* related to or resembling the genus *S.*; *sb.* a fish of this kind.

†**Spi·al.** late ME. [Aphetic f. ESPIAL.] **1.** Spying; observation, watch –1611. **2.** A spy, scout –1837.

‖**Spica** (spəi·kă). late ME. [L., = ear of grain, etc. In senses 3 and 4 after Gr. στάχυς.] †**1.** *Oil of s.*, oil of spike. –late ME. **2.** *Bot.* A flower-spike 1693. **3.** *Astr.* A bright star in the constellation Virgo 1728. **4.** *Surg.* A form of bandage, the arrangement of which is suggestive of an ear of wheat or barley 1731.

Spicate (spəi·kět), *a.* 1668. [– L. *spicatus*, pa. pple. of *spicare* furnish with spikes, f. *spica* SPIKE *sb.*[1]; see -ATE[2].] *Bot.* and *Zool.* Having the form of a spike; arranged in a spike. So **Spi·cated** *a.* having the form of a spike; furnished with spikelets 1661.

Spice (spəis), *sb.* ME. [Aphetic – OFr. *espice* (mod. *épice*) :– L. *species* appearance, specific kind, SPECIES, (late) pl. wares, merchandise, after late Gr. use of pl. of εἶδος 'form' in the senses 'goods', 'groceries', 'spices'.] **1.** One or other of various strongly flavoured or aromatic substances of vegetable origin, obtained from tropical plants, commonly used as condiments, etc. **b.** An odour or perfume arising from, or resembling that of, spices 1560. **2.** Without article, as a substance or in collective sense ME. †**3.** A sort, kind, or species –1601. **4.** A slight touch or trace, a dash, *of* something 1479.

1. Let our Merchants answer, which owe their Spices to Arabia 1625. *fig.* Variety's the very s. of life, That gives it all its flavour COWPER. **b.** The woodbine spices are wafted abroad TENNYSON. **2.** A man all vertue, like a pye all s., will not please 1694. **3.** The spices of penitence ben thre CHAUCER. **4.** The horse..had a considerable s. of devil in his composition 1835.

attrib. and *Comb.*, as *s.-bag, -bread, -merchant*, etc.; **s.-bush** *U.S.*, wild allspice, fever-bush (*Benzoin odoriferum*); **-islands,** the islands in the East from which spices were imported; **-nut,** a gingerbread nut; **-tree,** a s.-bearing tree; **-wood,** (*a*) *U.S.*, the s.-bush; (*b*) wood of s.-bearing shrubs

Spice (spəis), *v.* late ME. [Aphetic – OFr. *espicer* (mod. *épicer*), f. *espice* SPICE *sb.*; or from the sb.] **1.** *trans.* To prepare or season (food, etc.) with a spice or spices. **b.** *fig.* To season, to affect the character or quality of, by means of some addition or modification. Usu. const. *with.* 1529. **2.** †**a.** To embalm, to preserve with spices –1598. †**b.** To perfume with or as with spices –1648. **c.** To dose (a horse) with spice in order to mislead the buyer 1841.

1. Consume the flesh, and s. it well, and let the bones be burnt *Ezek.* 24:10. **b.** O, why should Love..S. his fair banquet with the dust of death? TENNYSON. Hence **Spi·cer**[2], one who seasons with s.

Spi·ce-box. 1527. [SPICE *sb.*] **1.** A box having several compartments, to keep spices in. **2.** A small decorated box, usually of Oriental workmanship 1880.

Spi·ce-cake. 1530. [SPICE *sb.*] A cake seasoned with spice; *dial.* a rich fruit cake.

Spiced (spəist), *ppl. a.* ME. [f. SPICE *sb.* or *v.* + -ED.] **1.** Seasoned or flavoured with spice or spices; cured with spices. †**2.** Of conscience, etc.: Nice, dainty, delicate; over scrupulous –1631. **3.** Fragrant, aromatic; spice-laden 1590.

1. Carmela seeing her brother refuse his spicte drinke, thought all was not well 1589. **3.** In the s. Indian aire SHAKS.

†**Spi·cer**[1]. ME. [Aphetic – OFr. *espicier* (mod. *épicier* grocer), f. *espice* SPICE *sb.*; see -ER[2] 2.] A dealer in spices; an apothecary or druggist –1609.

Spicery (spəi·səri). ME. [Aphetic – OFr. *espicerie* (mod. *épicerie*), f. *espice* SPICE *sb.*; see -ERY.] **1.** *collect. sing.* or *pl.* Spices. **2. a.** The department of the royal household connected with the keeping of spices; esp. in *Clerk of the S.* Now *Hist.* late ME. **b.** A room or part of a house set apart for the keeping of spices. Now *Hist.* 1536.

1. While on the veined pavement lie The honied things and s. MORRIS.

Spici- (spəisi), comb. form of L. *spica* ear of corn, SPIKE *sb.*[1], as in **Spici·ferous** *a.* [L. *spicifer*], bearing ears of corn. **Spi·ciform** *a.*, having the form of a (flower-) spike. **Spi·cilege,** ‖**Spicile·gium** [L. *spicilegium*], a gleaning; a collection or anthology.

Spick(-)and(-)span, *a.*, *sb.*, and *adv.* 1665. [Shortening of next.] **A.** *adj.* Particularly neat, trim, or smart; suggestive of something quite new or unaffected by wear.

1. New spicke and span white shoes PEPYS. A dog-cart,..driven by a spick-and-span groom 1886.

B. *sb.* That which is quite new or particularly trim and smart 1758. **C.** *adv.* In a spick and span manner 1815. Hence **Spick-span** *a.*

Spick(-)and(-)span new. Also †**speck-.** 1579. [Extension of SPAN-NEW; the element *spick* is prob. due to synon. Du. *spikspelldernieuw, -splinternieuw* 'spike-, splinter-new' (cf. G. *nagelneu* 'nail-new').] Absolutely or perfectly new; brand-new; perfectly fresh or unworn.

Spicket (spi·kėt). late ME. [alt. of SPIGOT *sb.*] Now *dial.* and *U.S.* = SPIGOT *sb.*

†**Spi·cous,** *a.* 1658. [f. L. *spica* spike + -OUS.] *Bot.* Spicate; spiky, pointed –1775.

‖**Spicula** (spi·kiŭlă). *Pl.* **-læ** (-lī). 1747. [mod.L., dim. of L. *spica* SPIKE *sb.*[1]; see -ULE.] **1.** A sharp-pointed or acicular crystal or similar formation. **2.** A small sharp-pointed process on some part of a plant or animal; a prickle 1753. **3.** *Bot.* A floral spikelet (*rare*) 1760. **4.** A slender pointed fragment *of* bone, etc. 1835. **5.** = SPICULUM 3. 1845. Hence **Spi·cular** *a.* of the nature of a spicule or s.; slender and sharp-pointed; also, characterized by the presence of spicules.

Spiculate (spi·kiŭlět), *a.* 1832. [f. SPICULE or SPICULA + -ATE[2].] *Bot.* Covered with spicules; composed of several spicules crowded together.

Spiculated (spi·kiŭlēˡted), *a.* 1738. [f. as prec.; see -ED[1] 2.] **1.** Containing spiculæ –1794. **2.** Having the form of a spicula; slender and sharp-pointed 1744. **3.** Furnished with sharp points or spikelets 1762.

Spicule (spi·kiul). 1785. [Anglicized f. SPICULA, SPICULUM.] **1.** *Bot.* A floral spikelet. **2.** One or other of the points of the basidia or sporophores in fungals 1843. **3.** = SPICULUM 3. 1846. **4.** *Zool.* A needle-like or sharp-pointed process or part 1861. **5.** A fine-pointed piece, splinter, or fragment of some hard substance; a spicula or spiculum 1878.

Spiculi- (spi·kiŭli), comb. form, after L. models, of SPICULA, SPICULE, and SPICULUM, occurring in a few *Zool.* terms, as **Spiculi·ferous** *a.*, bearing spicules. **Spi·culiform** *a.*, formed like a spicule; sharp-pointed. **Spiculi·genous** *a.*, containing spicules.

‖**Spiculum** (spi·kiŭlŏm). *Pl.* **-la.** 1746. [mod.L., irreg. dim. f. L. *spica* SPIKE *sb.*[1]] **1.** = SPICULA 1. **2.** *Zool.* A sharp-pointed process or formation 1762. **b.** The excitatory dart in snails 1838. **3.** One of the calcareous or siliceous needles found in sponges. Usu. in *pl.* 1842. **4.** = SPICULA 4. 1872.

Spicy (spəi·si), *a.* 1562. [f. SPICE *sb.* + -Y[1].] **1.** Having the characteristic qualities of spice; of the nature of spice. **b.** Flavoured or mixed with spice 1632. **2.** Having the fragrance of spice; sweet-scented, aromatic 1650. **3.** Containing or producing, abounding in, spices 1648. **b.** Consisting of spice; conveying spice 1712. **4.** Of qualities: Appropriate to, or characteristic of, spices 1652. **5.** *slang.* **a.** Full of spirit, smartness, or 'go' 1828. **b.** Smart-looking; neat 1846. **6.** Of writing or discourse: Smart and pointed; having a flavour of the sensational or scandalous; somewhat improper 1844.

1. Whence Merchants bring Thir spicie Drugs MILT. **b.** The S. Nut-brown Ale MILT. **2.** Led by new stars, and borne by s. gales! POPE. The s. myrtle sent forth all its fragrance 1797. **3.** The spicie shoare Of Arabie the blest MILT. **b.** The s. traffick of the East 1712. **5. a.** A remarkably s. team 1828. **b.** *advb.* That young Tom! He've come to town dressed that s. MEREDITH. **6.** The articles were so clever, and so very 's.' 1844. Hence **Spi·cily** *adv.* **Spi·ciness.**

Spider (spəi·dəɹ). [OE. *spīþra*, ME. *spiþre, spiþer* :– **spinþron*, f. *spinnan* SPIN; cf. OHG. *spinna*, G. *spinne* (lit. female spinner), Eng. dial. *spinner* (XIII).] **1.** One or other of the arachnids belonging to the insectivorous order *Araneidæ*, many species of which possess the power of spinning webs in which their prey is caught.

The cunning, skill, and industry of the spider, as well as its power of secreting or emitting poison, are frequently alluded to in literature.

b. Applied to persons as an opprobrious or vituperative term 1568. **2.** Applied to other allied species of *Arachnida* resembling spiders in appearance; esp. the harvest-spider; the spider-mite. See also RED *spider*, SEA SPIDER. 1665. **3.** A kind of frying-pan having legs and a long handle; also loosely, a frying-pan. Orig. *U.S.* 1830. **b.** *U.S.* A trivet or tripod; a griddle 1875. **4.** *Naut.* An iron outrigger to keep blocks clear of the ship's side. Cf. *s.-hoop.* 1860. **5.** *techn.* One or other of various parts or pieces of machinery, *esp.* one consisting of a framework or metal casting with radiating arms or spokes suggestive of the legs of a spider 1875. **6.** A lightly-built cart, trap, or phaeton with a high body and disproportionately large and slender wheels. Orig. *S. Afr.* 1879. **7.** Short for *s.-cell, -rest, -table* 1893.

Comb.: **s.-cell,** (*a*) *Biol.* a bacillus having the appearance of a s.; (*b*) *Anat.* one of the characteristic cells of the neuroglia, having numerous delicate processes resembling the legs of a s.; **-hoop** *Naut.*, a hoop passing round a mast in order to secure the shackles to which the futtock-shrouds are attached; **-rest,** a billiard-rest with legs of sufficient length to allow of its being placed over a ball without touching it; **-shanks,** a person having long thin legs; **-table,** a slightly-constructed occasional table with s.-like legs; **-work,** work having the characteristics or appearance of a spider's web.

b. In the names of beasts, insects, birds, etc. which bear some resemblance to or are associated with spiders: **s.-ant,** an insect of the genus *Mutillæ*; **-fly,** a pupiparous dipterous insect, as a bee-louse, bat-louse, sheep-tick, etc.; **-hunter,** = next 2 (*b*); **-mite,** (*a*) a parasitic mite of the family *Ganasidæ*; (*b*) a small mite injurious to plants; **-shell,** any shell of the genus *Pteroceras*; a scorpion-shell. Hence **Spi·dered** *a.* infested by spiders, cobwebbed.

Spi·der-ca:tcher. 1579. [SPIDER *sb.*] **1.** One who catches spiders. Chiefly *fig.*, and freq. as a vague term of abuse (*obs.*). **2.** One or other of certain birds which catch or eat spiders, as (*a*) the wall-creeper; (*b*) any East Indian sunbird of the genus *Arachnothera* 1668.

Spi·der-crab. 1710. [SPIDER *sb.*] One or other of several crabs belonging to the group *Oxyrhyncha*, esp. to the family *Maioidea*, and characterized by their long slender legs and spider-like appearance; a maia or maioid crab.

Spi·der-leg. 1760. [SPIDER *sb.*] **1.** A thin long leg like that of a spider. **2.** *transf.* A long irregular marking, crack, etc., resembling in shape the leg of a spider. Also *attrib.* in *s. gold.* 1873.

Spi·der-like, *adv.* and *a.* 1604. [f. SPIDER *sb.* + -LIKE.] **A.** *adv.* In or after the manner of a spider; with the power or faculty (real or supposed) of a spider. **B.** *adj.* Like or resembling a spider or that of a spider; spidery 1653.

Spi·der line. Also **spider's line.** 1829. [SPIDER *sb.*] One of the threads or filaments of spider-web used to form the reticle of various optical instruments, esp. of micrometers, and serving to obtain minute measurements; also loosely, any slender thread or wire used for this purpose.

Spi·der(-)mo:nkey. 1764. [SPIDER *sb.*] One or other of the monkeys belonging to the South and Central American genus *Ateles*, characterized by their long spider-like limbs and prehensile tail.

Spi·der-web. Also **spider's web.** 1535. **1.** A cobweb. **2.** *transf.* and *fig.* Something resembling a cobweb in nature or appearance 1700.

1. His confidence shalbe destroyed, for he trusteth in a spyders webbe COVERDALE *Job* 8:14.

Spi·derwort. 1597. †**1.** One or other plant of the lilaceous genus *Anthericum* (earlier *Phalangium*) –1763. **2.** Any plant belonging to the genus *Tradescantia*, or (later) to the family *Commelynaceæ*, which includes this genus 1629.

Spidery (spəi·dəri), *a.* 1837. [f. SPIDER *sb.* + -Y[1].] **1.** Like a spider in appearance or form. **2.** Of legs or arms: Resembling those of a spider; long and thin 1845. **b.** Suggestive of the appearance of a spider with long and thin legs 1862. **c.** Like a spider-web in formation 1860. **3.** Suggestive of that of a spider, in respect of entanglement, cunning, etc. 1843. **4.** Infested by spiders 1889.

1. That hideous s. crustacean, the crab 1881. **2. b.** The marchesa wrote..in her long s. characters 1862.

‖**Spiegeleisen** (ʃpī·gəlˌəiːzən). 1868. [G., f. *spiegel* mirror + *eisen* iron.] A crystalline and lustrous variety of white manganiferous cast-iron much used in the Bessemer process for the manufacture of steel. So (semi-translated) **Spiegel iron.**

Spiffing (spi·fiŋ), *a. colloq.* and *dial.* 1872. [Of unkn. origin; of pr. ppl. form, like *clinking, ripping, topping*, and rel. to next.] Excellent, first-rate, very good. Also as *adv.*

Spiffy (spi·fi), *a. colloq.* and *dial.* 1860. [Of unkn. origin; see prec.] Smart, spruce.

Spif(f)licate (spi·flikeˈt), *v. joc.* or *colloq.* 1785. [Of fanciful formation.] *trans.* To treat or handle roughly or severely; to crush, destroy. Hence **Spiflica·tion**, complete destruction.

Spignel (spi·gněl). 1502. [perh. contr. of obsc. ME. †*spigurnel* (XIV–XV) – med.L. *spigurnellus* (XII).] †**1.** The aromatic root of the umbelliferous plant *Meum athamanticum*, used, when dried and ground, in medicine as a carminative or stimulant, or as a spice in cookery –1718. **2.** The plant itself; meum; baldmoney 1548.

Spigot (spi·gǒt), *sb.* late ME. [perh. with change of suffix – Pr. *espigoun*, *-gou* = Sp. *espigón*, It. *spigone* rung of a ladder, bar of a chair, bung; cf. Pg. *espicho* spigot :– L. *spiculum*, dim. of *spicum*, var. of *spica* SPIKE *sb.*¹] **1.** A small wooden peg or pin used to stop the vent-hole of a barrel or cask; a vent-peg; a similar peg inserted into the opening or tube of a faucet and used to regulate the flow of liquor. **b.** *fig.* That which controls, lets out, or restrains 1780. †**2.** A faucet –1725. **3.** A plain end of a pipe entering an enlargement of another as a means of forming a joint. Chiefly in attrib. phrases, as *s. and faucet joint*, etc. 1797. **4.** *attrib.*, as **s. joint**, a spigot and faucet joint 1611.

1. b. Something which he called the rudder of Government, but which was rather the s. of Taxation CARLYLE. Hence **Spi·got** *v. trans.* to thrust a s. into.

Spike (spəik), *sb.*¹ late ME. [– L. *spica* (*-us*, *-um*) ear of corn, plant-spike, rel. to *spina* SPINE.] **1.** An ear of grain. Chiefly *poet.* **b.** Astr. *The Virgin's s.* [tr. L. *spica Virginis*], = SPICA 3. 1559. **2.** *Bot.* A form of inflorescence consisting of sessile flowers borne on an elongated simple axis 1578. †**3.** French lavender (*Lavandula spica*) –1712.

3. *Oil of s.*, an essential oil obtained by distillation from *Lavandula spica* (and *L. stœchas*), employed in painting and in veterinary medicine 1577.

attrib. and *Comb.*, as *s. corn, -lavender, -stalk*; **s.-grass,** *Uniola paniculata*; **-oil,** = *oil of s.*; **-rush,** any sedge of the genus *Eliocharis*.

Spike (spəik), *sb.*² [ME. *spyk*, (also *spik-nail*), of unc. origin, but corresp. to OSw. *spīk*, *spijk* (Sw., Norw. *spik* nail), and perh. a shortening of (M)LG., MDu. *spīker* (Du. *spijker*), or of MDu. *spiking*; rel. to SPOKE *sb.*] **1.** A sharp-pointed piece of metal (esp. iron) or wood used for fastening things together; a large and strong kind of nail. **b.** A pointed piece of steel used for driving into the touch-hole of a cannon in order to render it unserviceable 1617. **2.** A sharp-pointed piece of metal (or other hard material) which is, or may be, so fixed in something that the point is turned outwards; a stout sharp-pointed projecting part of a metal object 1470. **b.** *transf.* A stiff sharp-pointed object or part 1718. **c.** [back-formation f. SPIKY *a.*² 2 b.] A 'spiky' churchman or churchwoman 1902.

2. b. Then shot up on high A steady s. of light MORRIS.

attrib. and *Comb.*, as *s. bit, gimlet, rod*; **s.-buck** *U.S.*, a buck in its first year; **-fish** *U.S.*, the sail-fish (*Histiophorus americanus*); **-tail** *U.S.*, a dress-coat; **-team** *U.S.*, a waggon drawn by three animals, arranged as one leader and two wheelers. Hence **Spi·kelet**² a small s. or spike-shaped object; a prickle or thorn.

Spike (spəik), *v.*¹ 1624. [f. prec.] **1.** *trans.* With *up*. **a.** To fasten or close firmly with spikes or strong nails. †**b.** *spec.* = sense 2. –1799. **2.** To render (a gun) unserviceable by driving a spike into the touch-hole; also, to block or fill up (the touch-hole) with a spike 1687. **3.** To fix or secure by long nails or spikes 1703. **4.** To provide, fit, or stud with spikes 1716. **5.** To pierce with, or as with, a spike 1687.

2. *fig.* All the batteries of noise are spiked 1871.

Spike (spəik), *v.*² 1711. [f. SPIKE *sb.*¹ 2.] *intr.* Of plants: To form a spike or spikes of flowers. Also with *up*.

Spiked (spəikt), *a.*¹ 1597. [f. SPIKE *sb.*¹ + -ED².] Of plants: Having an inflorescence in the form of a spike; bearing ears, as grain.

Spiked (spəikt), *a.*² 1681. [f. SPIKE *sb.*² + -ED².] Provided with spikes or sharp points.

Spikelet¹ (spəi·klėt). 1793. [f. SPIKE *sb.*¹ + -LET.] *Bot.* **1.** A small group of florets in grasses, forming part of the spike. **2.** A subdivision of an ear of grain 1860.

Spi·ke-nail. ME. [See SPIKE *sb.*²] A large and strong nail, now *spec.* one upwards of three (or four) inches in length, with a small head.

Spikenard (spəi·knaɹd). ME. [– med.L. *spica nardi* (see SPIKE *sb.*¹, NARD), rendering Gr. νάρδου στάχυς, ναρδόσταχυς; or more immed. – OFr. *spicanard(e* or MLG. *spīkenard*, MDu. *spīkenaerde* (Du. *spijknardus*).] **1.** An aromatic substance (employed in ancient times in the preparation of a costly ointment or oil) obtained from an Eastern plant, now identified as the *Nardostachys jatamansi* of Northern India. **2.** The plant yielding this substance 1548. **3.** With defining term, applied to other fragrant plants, as American S., *Aralia racemosa*, Ploughman's S., *Inula conyza* 1597. **4.** *Oil of s.*, a name given to various fragrant oils 1565.

Spiky (spəi·ki), *a.*¹ 1578. [f. SPIKE *sb.*¹ + -Y¹.] Having the form of a flower-spike; characterized by the production of spikes or ears.

Spiky (spəi·ki), *a.*² 1720. [f. SPIKE *sb.*² + -Y¹.] **1.** Fitted with a spike or spikes; having sharp projecting points. **2.** Having the form of a spike or spikes; stiff and sharp-pointed 1742. **b.** *fig.* Extremely sharp or aggressive; (*slang*) extreme and uncompromising in Anglo-Catholic belief or practice 1881.

1. The s. Wheels thro' Heaps of Carnage tore; And thick the groaning Axles dropp'd with Gore POPE. **2.** A dozen s. thorns sticking into him 1894.

Spile (spəil), *sb.*¹ 1513. [– MLG., MDu. *spīle* (NFris. *spīl*, G. dial. *speil*), splinter, wooden pin or peg, skewer, etc.; rel. to SPILL *sb.*¹] **1.** *north.* and †*Sc.* A splinter, chip, or narrow strip, of wood; a spill. **2.** A small plug of wood for stopping the vent of a cask; a vent-peg; a spigot. Chiefly *dial.* 1707. **b.** *U.S.* A small wooden or metal spout for conducting sap from the sugar-maple 1875.

Spile (spəil), *sb.*² 1513. [app. an alteration of PILE *sb.*¹ after prec. or by wrong analysis of combs.] = PILE *sb.*¹ 3. **b.** *Mining.* A sharp-pointed post used in sinking by means of cribs 1841. Hence **Spile** *v.*² *trans.* = PILE *v.*¹ 1.

Spile (spəil), *v.*¹ 1691. [f. SPILE *sb.*¹] **1.** *trans.* To stop up (a hole) by means of a spile. Also with *up*. **2.** To draw (liquid) from a cask by spiling or broaching. Now *dial.* 1772. **3.** To provide (a cask, tree, etc.) with a spile ,in order to draw off liquid. Now *dial.* or *U.S.* 1832.

Spiling (spəi·liŋ), *vbl. sb.* 1841. [Of unkn. origin.] *Naut. pl.* The dimensions of the curve or sny of a plank's edge 1846.

Spill (spil), *sb.*¹ ME. [Obscurely rel. to SPILE *sb.*¹] **1.** A splinter; a sharp-pointed fragment of wood, bone, etc.; a slip or sliver. **2.** A thin slip of wood, a folded or twisted piece of paper, used for lighting a candle, pipe, etc. 1839. **3.** A small peg or pin for stopping a hole 1875.

Spill (spil), *sb.*² 1594. [prob. – (M)LG., (M)Du. *spil(l)e* = OHG. *spilla* (G. *spille* spindle, axis, stalk) :– WGmc. **spinla*, f. **spin-* SPIN *v.*] †**1.** A spool –1615. **2.** A rod or stalk of wood, metal etc. 1594. **3.** A pin or slender rod on which anything turns; a spindle 1730.

Spill (spil), *sb.*³ 1845. [f. SPILL *v.*] **1.** A throw from a horse or vehicle; a fall or tumble; an upset. **2.** A downpouring or dropping of liquid; a quantity spilled 1848.

Spill (spil), *v.* Pa. t. and pple. **spilled** (spild); **spilt.** [OE. *spillan* = (M)LG., (M)Du. *spillen*, rel. to OE. *spildan* destroy = OS. *spildian*, OHG. *spilden*, ON. *spilla* (:– **spilþjan*), of unkn. origin.] **I. 1.** *trans.* To destroy by depriving of life; to put (or bring) to death; to slay or kill. Now *arch.* †**b.** *absol.* To cause death; freq. contrasted with *save, spare*, etc. –1627. **2.** To destroy or put an end to (life). Now *arch.* OE. †**3.** To destroy, ruin, or overthrow (a person); to bring to ruin or misery –1642. †**4.** To wreck, destroy, or devastate; to spoil or ruin by demolition, etc. –1623. **5.** To spoil by injuring or damaging in some way; to render imperfect or useless; to destroy the goodness or value of (a thing). Now *dial.* ME. †**6.** To waste by scattering, squandering, or misusing; to employ or expend wastefully –1786. †**7.** *intr.* To perish; to be destroyed or lost –1592. **8.** To fall off or decline in respect of good qualities; to degenerate or deteriorate; to spoil. *Obs.* exc. *dial.* ME.

1. Caring no more in their fury to s. a man, then to kill a dogge 1612. **2.** You must carry your body steadily, or else s. your life 1668. **3.** *Haml.* IV. v. 20.

II. 1. *trans.* To shed (blood) ME. **2.** To allow or cause (a liquid) to fall, pour, or run out (esp. over the edge of the containing vessel), usually in an accidental or wasteful manner; to lose or waste in this way ME. **3.** To scatter, esp. by emptying from some receptacle or the like; to disperse ME. **b.** *To s. the beans, s. it*: to reveal or divulge something. *U.S. slang.* 1919. **4.** *Naut.* To empty (the belly of a sail) of wind in order that it may be reefed or furled more easily 1625. **b.** To discharge (wind) from a sail 1875. **5.** *colloq.* To cause to fall from a horse or vehicle; to throw or throw out. So in other contexts. 1731. **6.** *intr.* To flow or run over the brim or side; to escape or be wasted in this manner 1655. **b.** *Naut.* To become void of wind 1762. **7.** *trans.* To divulge (*U.S. slang*) 1920.

1. The red life spilt for a private blow TENNYSON. **2.** Their arguments are as fluxive as liquor spilt upon a table B. JONS. **3.** As ruthless Winds the tender Blossoms s. 1710. **4. b.** *Spilling-line*, a line to s. the wind out of a sail, by keeping it from bellying out when clewed up 1875. **5.** I..call'd to the Coachman, Pray, Friend, don't s. us SWIFT. **6.** The Mettal may s. or slabber over the Mouth of..the Mold 1683.

Spill- (spil), the stem of SPILL *v.* in comb., *esp.* in the sense 'constructed for (or by) the passage of surplus water, for receiving overflow liquid, etc.', as *s.-box, channel, -trough, -way*.

Spiller¹ (spi·ləɹ). 1530. [f. SPILL *v.* + -ER¹.] One who sheds or spills; *esp.* a shedder of blood.

Spiller². *arch.* 1576. [alt. of *speller* (XVI), aphet. f. *espeler* (1486).] A branchlet of a deer's horn.

Spiller³ (spi·ləɹ). Chiefly *Cornish dial.*, *Ir.*, and *Amer.* Also **-(i)ard.** 1602. [Of unkn. origin.] A long fishing-line provided with a number of hooks; a trawl-line. So **Spi·llet.**

Spillikin (spi·likin), **spellican** (spe·likăn). 1734. [f. SPILL *sb.*¹ + -KIN.] **1.** *pl.* A game played with a heap of slips or small rods of wood, bone, or the like, the object being to pull off each by means of a hook without disturbing the rest. **b.** One of the slips with which this is played 1883. **2.** *fig.* In *pl.*, Splinters, fragments 1857.

Spilt (spilt), *ppl. a.* of SPILL *v.* late ME.

Phr. *To cry over s. milk* (or variants of this), to fret about some loss, mistake, etc., that cannot be remedied.

Spilth (spilþ). 1607. [f. SPILL *v.* + -TH¹.] That which is spilled; the action or fact of spilling.

To avenge..The s. of brother's blood 1830.

Spin (spin), *sb.* 1831. [f. the vb.] **1.** An act or spell of spinning; also *techn.*, capacity for being twisted or spun; the product resulting from spinning 1853. **2.** An act or spell of revolving or whirling round; a circular or rotatory movement 1831. **b.** *Cricket*, etc. A twisting motion given to the ball when bowled, thrown, or hit 1862. **3.** The act of causing something to spin 1840. **b.** The act of spinning a coin 1882. **4.** A spell of continuous movement by way of exercise or pastime; a fairly rapid ride or run of some duration 1856. **b.** A spell of quick rowing or sailing 1875. **5.** *Aviation.* An act of spinning (see SPIN *v.* II. 4 c, quots.) 1915.

4. A ten-mile s. with a greatcoat on 1890.

Spin (spin), *v.* Pa. t. **spun** (spɒn), **span** (spæn). Pa. pple. **spun.** [OE. *spinnan* = (M)Du. *spinnen*, OHG., Goth. *spinnan* (G. *spinnen*), ON. *spinna*; Gmc. str. vb.] **I. 1.** *intr.* To draw out and twist the fibres of wool, flax, etc., so as to form a continuous thread; to be engaged in or to follow this occupation. **b.** Of insects: To produce glutinous threads from the body by means of special organs 1511. **2.** *trans.* To draw out (wool, flax, etc.) and convert into threads either by the hand or by machinery OE. **b.** To convert (or *intr.*, to admit of being converted) *into* thread, etc., by spinning 1669. **3.** To form or fabricate (a thread, etc.) by the process of drawing out (and twisting) some suitable material; to prepare the material for (a fabric or garment) by this process ME. **4.** *fig.* **a.** Of the Fates or other powers: To devise or appoint (one's destiny or fortune). late ME. **b.** To evolve, produce, contrive, or devise, in a manner suggestive of spinning 1555. **c.** To draw out, prolong 1629.

1. When Adam dalve, and Eve span, Who was than a gentleman? 1560. **2.** The farmers' wives began..to s. their wool from their own sheeps' backs 1874. **b.** It will not s. into good yarn 1842. **c.** To convert (a viscous solution or pulp) into artificial silk; to form (artificial silk filaments) 1894. **3.** All the yearne she spun in Vlisses absence SHAKS. *transf.* and *fig.* Insects s. silk for his service 1660. [A grave] so fresh made that the spring had scarce had time to s. a coverlet for it THACKERAY. *To s. a yarn* (to tell a story): see YARN *sb.* **4. a.** On David's head, God doth not s. good hap 1606. **b.** Many secret agents..were spinning their dark intrigues D'ISRAELI.

S. off: *trans.* To finish or clear *off* (a distaff, etc.) by spinning. **S. out:** *trans.* **a.** To protract, prolong. **b.** To spend or occupy (time) in inactivity or without effect. **c.** To evolve or devise by mental effort; to express at length. **b.** To draw out, prolong, in length or duration. **e.** To cause to last out; to use sparingly. **f.** *intr.* To run out; to extend; to last out.

II. 1. *intr.* To shoot or spring *up*; to grow or rise rapidly (*rare*). late ME. **2.** Of blood, etc.: To issue in a rapid stream; to gush or spurt. late ME. **3.** To move rapidly; to run quickly; now *esp.* to ride or drive at a rapid and even rate. late ME. **b.** To pass or be spent quickly 1850. **c.** *trans.* To cause to pass *away*; to carry *away* or convey rapidly 1696. **4.** *intr.* To revolve or gyrate; to whirl *round* 1667. **b.** Of the brain or head: To whirl; to be giddy or dazed 1819. **5.** *trans.* To cause to turn or revolve rapidly; to twirl or whirl 1612. **b.** To shape (articles of sheet-metal) by pressure applied during rotation on a lathe 1853. **6.** *Angling.* **a.** *trans.* To cause (a minnow or other bait) to revolve in the water by fastening it on the hook in a particular manner 1814. **b.** *intr.* To fish with a spinning bait 1863. **c.** *trans.* To fish (a pool, etc.) by means of a spinning bait 1886. **7.** *slang.* To reject (a candidate) at an examination; to plough. Usu. in *pass.* 1860.

2. One raz'd Achilles' hand; the spouting blood Spun forth POPE. **3. b.** The young one is making the money s. THACKERAY. **4.** The Earth..With inoffensive pace that spinning sleeps On her soft Axle MILT. **c.** *Aviation.* (*a*) *intr.* To make a diving descent combined with a continued rotation of the aeroplane 1915; (*b*) *trans.* to make (an aeroplane) perform this evolution 1918. **d.** Of a motor clutch: To continue to revolve after being disengaged 1918. **5.** When you spun tops and snapped marbles EMERSON. *To s. a coin* (also absol.): to toss a coin with a spinning motion (see TOSS *v.* III. 3).

‖**Spina** (spəi·nă). late ME. [L. *spina* SPINE.] **1.** The backbone. Now only *Path.* in *spina bifida*, dropsy of the spine. **2.** *Rom. Antiq.* The barrier running up the middle of a Roman circus 1766.

Spinaceous (spinēⁱ·ʃəs), *a.* 1822. [f. mod.L. *Spinacia* spinach; see -IA¹, -EOUS.] Belonging to the spinach family.

Spinach (spi·nėdʒ). Also †**spinage.** 1530. [prob. – MDu. *spinaetse, spinag(i)e* (Du. *spinazie*) – OFr. *espinache, -age* (mod. *épinard*) – med.L. *spinachia, -ium, -acia, -acium* – Arab. *'isfānāḵ* (– Pers. *ispānāḵ*), perh. by assim. to L. *spina* SPINE, with ref. to the prickly seeds of some species.] **1.** A plant (*Spinacia oleracea*) belonging to the family *Chenopodiaceæ*, extensively cultivated for culinary purposes; the succulent leaves of this plant used as a vegetable. **b.** Applied (with distinguishing terms) to other species of *Spinacia*, or to plants in some way resembling or taking the place of this, as *Australian, mountain, New Zealand, wild s.* 1710. **2.** *ellipt.* As a moth-name 1832.

1. b. The Orach, or Mountain S., *Atriplex hortensis* 1822. New Zealand S., *Tetragonia expansa* 1824. Australian S. (*Chenopodium erosum*) 1866.

Spinal (spəi·năl), *a.* 1578. [– late L. *spinalis*, f. *spina* SPINE; see -AL¹.] **1.** Of or pertaining to, forming part of, or located in, the spine or backbone. **2.** Of diseased conditions: Affecting the spine 1838. **3.** Resembling a spine or backbone in form or function 1841. **4.** Of qualities: Arising from or seated in the spine 1855. **5.** Of appliances: Adapted to or intended for application to the spine 1864.

1. The spinall marrow, which is but the braine prolonged SIR T. BROWNE. *S. artery, bone, canal*, etc. **2.** S. hemorrhage 1878. **3.** Everywhere else the s. ridge seemed unbroken 1856. **5.** *S. brace*, a brace for remedying posterior curvature of the spine 1875.

Spindle (spi·nd'l), *sb.* [OE. *spinel*, corresp. to OFris. *spindel*, OS. *spinnila*, (M)Du. *spindel*, OHG. *spin(n)ila* (G. *spindel*), f. **spin-* SPIN *v.*; see -LE. For intrusive *d* cf. Du. and G. forms.] **I. 1.** A simple instrument employed in spinning by hand, consisting of a slender rounded rod (usually of wood), tapering towards each end, which is made to revolve and twist into thread the fibres drawn out from a bunch of wool, flax, etc. **b.** In a spinning frame, one of many steel rods, by each of which a thread is twisted and wound on a bobbin 1790. **c.** A spool or bobbin 1837. **2.** *fig.* In allusion to the Fates imagined as spinning the thread of life or destiny 1577. **3.** Such an amount of thread or yarn as can be prepared on a spindle at one time; hence, a certain measure or quantity of yarn, varying according to the material 1452. **4. a.** *Her.* = FUSIL¹ 1486. **b.** *Anat.* A dilatation of the fœtal aorta resembling a spindle in shape; the spindle-shaped part of a muscle 1898.

II. 1. A rod, usually of iron or other metal, serving as an axis upon which, or by means of which, something revolves or is turned round ME. **2. a.** A cylindrical rod or bar provided with grooves so as to act as a screw; *spec.* that by which the platen of a hand printing-press is lowered and raised. late ME. **b.** A revolving frame used for stirring a mixture 1793. **c.** A rod upon which the core of a gun-shell is moulded 1842. **3.** A machine for recessing an aeroplane spar (cf. SPINDLE *v.* 4) 1920. †**4.** A stalk, stem, or shoot of a plant; esp. of cereals –1750. **5.** *Naut.* The upper part or section of a made wooden mast 1597.

Comb.: **s. cross** *Her.*, a cross having arms shaped somewhat like a s.; **-shell**, (*a*) = *s.-stromb*; (*b*) a gasteropod of the genus *Fusus*; **-stromb**, any marine gasteropod of the genus *Rostellaria*; **-wood**, the s.-tree, or the wood of this; **-worm** *U.S.*, the maize-eating larva of a noctuid moth, *Achatodes zeæ*.

Spindle (spi·nd'l), *v.* 1577. [f. the sb.] **1.** *intr.* Of cereals: To shoot up into the slender stalks on which the ear is formed. **b.** Of flowering plants: To form the stalk or stem on which the flowers are produced 1601. **c.** With *up* or *upward(s)*. In later use sometimes implying too slender a growth. 1601. **2.** To shoot out or up, to develop by rapid growth or attenuation, *into* something thin or unsubstantial 1784. **3.** *trans.* To fit with or fix upon a spindle or axis 1833. **4.** To recess and taper (an aeroplane spar) 1919.

2. That fairest variety of mortal grass which with us is apt to s. soon into a somewhat sapless womanhood 1854.

Spindleage (spi·nd'lėdʒ). 1921. [f. SPINDLE *sb.* + -AGE.] The total number of cotton spindles in use at a given time and in a specified area.

Spi·ndle-legged, *a.* 1710. [SPINDLE *sb.*] Having long and slender legs.

Spindle(-)shank. 1570. **1.** A long and slender leg. (Chiefly *contempt.* and in *pl.*) **2.** *transf.* A spindle-legged person 1602. So **Spi·ndle-shanked** *a.*

Spi·ndle-shaped, *a.* 1776. [SPINDLE *sb.*] Fusiform.

Spi·ndle-side. 1851. [Used as a rendering of OE. *spinlhealf.*] The female line of descent.

Spi·ndle-tree. 1548. [f. SPINDLE *sb.*, after G. *spindelbaum*, MDu. *spindelboom.*] **1.** An ornamental European shrub (*Euonymus europæus*), furnishing a hard fine-grained yellowish wood formerly much used for spindles. **2.** *pl.* The family *Celastraceæ*, to which the genus *Euonymus* belongs 1846.

Spi·ndling, (*vbl.*) *sb.* 1626. [f. SPINDLE *sb.* or *v.* + -ING¹.] **1.** The formation of a stem, stalk, or shoot, in plants. **2.** A spindly plant, animal, etc. 1842.

2. Half-conscious of the garden-squirt, The spindlings look unhappy TENNYSON.

Spi·ndling, *ppl. a.* 1750. [f. SPINDLE *v.* + -ING².] **1.** Of plants: Growing or shooting out into (long) stalks or stems, esp. of a slender or weakly kind. **2.** Of things: Slender, spindly 1858.

1. Five s. pines stand in the midst of a sandy waste 1885.

Spindly (spi·ndli), *a.* 1651. [f. SPINDLE *sb.* + -Y¹.] **1.** Of plants: Of a slender and weakly growth. **b.** Of growth: Characterized by slimness or attenuation and weakness 1856. **2.** *gen.* Having a slender elongated form implying, or suggestive of, weakness 1827.

Spi·ndrift. orig. *Sc.* 1600. [var. of SPOONDRIFT, app. due to local Sc. pronunciations of *spoon.*] Continuous driving of spray.

Spine (spəin). late ME. [Aphetic – OFr. *espine* (mod. *épine*), or its source L. *spina* thorn, prickle, backbone, rel. to *spica* SPIKE *sb.*¹] **I. 1.** *Bot.* A stiff sharp-pointed process produced or growing from the wood of a plant, consisting of a hardened or irregularly developed branch, petiole, stipule, or other part; a thorn; a similar process developed on fruit or leaves. Cf. PRICKLE *sb.* 2. **2.** *Anat.* One or other of several sharp-pointed slender processes of various bones 1706. **3.** *Zool.* A stiff, pointed, thorn-like process or appendage developed on the integument of certain fishes, insects, or lower forms of animal life 1721. **b.** One of the prickles of a hedgehog, the quills of a porcupine, or similar growth on other animals 1753. **c.** *Ichth.* A spinous or spiny fin-ray; a fin-spine 1774. **4.** Any natural formation having a slender sharp-pointed form 1750. **II. 1.** The spinal or vertebral column in man and vertebrates; the backbone. late ME. **b.** *transf.* A part or formation having the function of a backbone 1665. **2.** The heart-wood or duramen of a tree 1630. **3.** A ridge or elevated stretch of ground, rock, etc., having a position analogous to that of the backbone, or resembling it 1796. **4.** The 'back' of a book 1922.

Comb.: **s.-bill**, one or other of two species of Australian honey-eaters, characterized by their long spine-like bills; **-bone**, the spine; **-eel**, a spiny eel; **-oak**, the heart-wood of an oak. Hence **Spined** (spəind), *a.* (*a*) having, provided with, or covered with, spines; spinous, spiny; (*b*) having a spine or spinal column.

Spinel (spi·nĕl). 1528. [– Fr. *spinelle* – It. *spinella*, dim. of *spina* SPINE; see -EL.] **1.** A gem or precious stone of a red or scarlet colour closely resembling the true ruby, now classed as belonging to the typical species of the spinel group of minerals. More fully *s. ruby.* **2.** *Min.* The typical species of a group of minerals (the *s. group*) which are compounds of sesquioxides with protoxides, and crystallize in the isometric system 1807. **b.** Any mineral belonging to this group 1837.

Spineless (spəi·nlės), *a.* 1827. [f. SPINE + -LESS.] **1.** Having no spines or sharp-pointed processes; not spinous. **2.** Having a weak or diseased spine; deprived of the natural support of the spine; exhausted, limp 1860. **b.** Lacking moral force or vigour; irresolute, flabby 1885.

2. b. We are sick of this s. way of treating violators of law 1885.

Spinelle (spine·l). 1555. – SPINEL.

Spinescent (spəine·sěnt), *a.* 1793. [– *spinescens, -ent-*, pr. pple. of late L. *spinescere* grow thorny, f. L. *spina* thorn; see -ESCENT.] **1.** *Bot.* Developing into or terminating in a spine or thorn; also, bearing or covered with spines; spiniferous. **2.** *Zool.* Tending to become a spine or spinous process; spinous, spinulous 1856. Hence **Spine·scence.**

Spinet[1] (spi·nét, spine·t). Also **spinette.** 1664. [Aphetic – Fr. †*espinette* (mod. *épinette*) – It. *spinetta* virginal, spinet, dim. of *spina* thorn, etc., the strings of both instruments being plucked by quills, etc.] A keyed musical instrument, common in England in the 18th c., closely resembling the harpsichord, but smaller and having only one string to each note.

†**Spi·net**[2]. 1603. [– L. *spinetum* (f. *spina* thorn). See SPINNEY.] A thicket; a spinney –1848.

Spi·ne-tail. 1839. [SPINE.] One or other of several birds of unrelated genera characterized by their stiff, spine-like, or mucronate tail-feathers. So **Spi·ne-tailed** *a.* 1802.

Spi·n-house. Now *Hist.* 1700. [– Du. *spinhuis*. Cf. SPINNING-HOUSE.] A house or building in which persons are employed in spinning; (in ref. to Continental usage) a house of correction for women.

Spini- (spəi·ni), comb. form of L. *spina* spine, as in *s.-acute, -dentate, -spirulate* adjs.

Spiniferous (spəini·fěrəs), *a.* 1656. [f. L. *spinifer* (f. *spina* SPINE) + -OUS.] Bearing, covered with, or having spines; spinose. Chiefly *Zool.* or *Bot.*

‖**Spinifex** (spei·nifeks). 1846. [mod.L., f. L. *spina* SPINE + *-fex* maker, f. *facere* make.] *Bot.* One or other of a number of coarse grasses (now classed in the genus *Tricuspis*) which grow in dense masses on the sand-hills of the Australian deserts, and are characterized by their sharp-pointed spiny leaves; esp. the porcupine-grass, *Triodia irritans*.

Spiniform (spəi·nifǭɹm), *a.* 1833. [f. SPINI- + -FORM.] *Bot.* and *Zool.* Having the form of a spine or spinous process.

Spinigerous (spəini·dʒěrəs), *a.* 1852. [f. SPINI- + -GEROUS.] *Bot.* and *Zool.* = SPINIFEROUS *a.*

Spink (spink), *sb.* Now *dial.* late ME. [prob. imitative of the note of the bird.] **1.** One or other of the finches; esp. the chaffinch. **2.** Used to imitate or represent the characteristic note or cry of certain birds 1898. Hence **Spink** *v. intr.*

Spinnaker (spi·năkəɹ). 1866. [Said to be a fanciful formation on *spinx*, mispronunciation of *Sphinx*, name of the first yacht that carried the sail; perh. with reminiscence of SPANKER 3.] A large three-cornered sail carried by racing-yachts, boomed out at right angles to the vessel's side opposite to the mainsail, and used in running before the wind.

Spinner (spi·nəɹ). ME. [f. SPIN *v.* + -ER[1].] **I. 1.** A spider, esp. one which spins a web. **2.** One who spins cotton, wool, yarn, etc.; *esp.* one whose occupation it is to do this; one who attends to or works a spinning machine. late ME. **b.** A manufacturer engaged in spinning, esp. cotton-spinning; a master-spinner 1834. **3.** *fig.* One who spins, tells, or relates (a story, yarn, etc.) 1770. **4. a.** = next 1815. **b.** *techn.* A spinning-machine 1875.

3. I am a s. of long yarns HAWTHORNE.

II. 1. *Angling.* **a.** One or other of several flies, or imitations of these, used esp. in trout-fishing 1787. **b.** An angler who uses spinning-tackle 1836. **2. a.** A teetotum; a top 1794. **b.** A cricket-ball bowled with a spin 1895. **3.** *Aircraft.* A metal fairing attached to the propeller boss and revolving with it 1924.

Spinneret (spi·nəret). 1826. [dim. of SPINNER; see -ET.] An organ or process by which the silk, gossamer, or thread of certain insects, esp. silkworms and spiders, is produced; a spinning-organ; *spec.* (*a*) one of the pores or tubules on the lower lip of a silkworm or caterpillar; (*b*) one of the nipple-like mamillæ on the abdomen of a spider. **b.** *Artificial Silk Manuf.* A tube, or a small plate with fine holes, through which the viscous solution passes into the solidifying medium to form filaments 1894.

Spinney (spi·ni). ME. [Aphetic – OFr. *espinei* (mod. *épinaie*) :– Rom. **spineta*, colloq. form of L. *spinetum* SPINET[2].] †**1.** A thorn-hedge (*rare*). **2.** A small wood or copse, esp. one planted or preserved for sheltering game-birds; a small clump or plantation of trees 1597.

Spinning (spi·niŋ), *vbl. sb.* ME. [f. SPIN *v.* + -ING[1].] **1.** The action of SPIN *v.*; an instance of this. **2.** The thread or yarn spun 1511. *attrib.*, as *s.-engine, -factory, -mill, -organ*; **s.-gland,** one of the glands which form the material for spinning the thread of silkworms, etc.; **-top,** = TOP *sb.*[2] 1.

Spi·nning, *ppl. a.* 1634. [f. SPIN *v.* + -ING[2].] **1.** That spins or produces thread. **2.** That revolves, gyrates, or turns round 1854.

Spi·nning-house. 1463. [SPINNING *vbl. sb.* Cf. SPIN-HOUSE.] **1.** A room or building set apart for the purpose of spinning. **2.** A house of correction for women, esp. at Cambridge 1803.

Spi·nning-je·nny. 1783. [f. SPINNING *vbl. sb.* or *ppl. a.*; cf. JENNY II. 1.] An early form of spinning-machine in which several spindles were set in motion by a band from one wheel.

Spi·nning-wheel. late ME. [f. SPINNING *vbl. sb.*] A simple apparatus for spinning, formerly in common use, in which the formation of the thread is carried out by the help of a wheel worked either by the hand or foot.

Spino- (spəi·no), used as comb. form of L. *spina* spine, in a few terms of *Anat., Bot.*, etc.

Spinode (spəi·nōᵘd). 1852. [irreg. f. L. *spina* SPINE *sb.* + NODE *sb.*] *Geom.* A stationary point on a curve; a cusp.

Spinose (spəinōᵘ·s), *a.* 1660. [– L. *spinosus*, f. *spina* thorn; see SPINE, -OSE[1].] = SPINOUS 2, 3.

Spinosity (spəinǫ·sĭti). 1605. [– late L. *spinositas*, f. as prec.; see -ITY.] †**1.** *fig.* The quality of being spinose or thorny –1660. **2.** A disagreeable remark; an argument or theory of a difficult and unprofitable character 1653.

2. Amid the dry spinosities and tortuous labyrinths of theology 1836.

Spinous (spəi·nəs), *a.* 1638. [– L. *spinosus*, f. *spina* thorn; see SPINE, -OUS.] **1.** *fig.* Resembling or suggestive of a thorn or thorns in respect of sharpness and aridity; unpleasant and difficult or unprofitable to handle or deal with. **2.** *Bot.* Furnished with spines or thorns; thorn-bearing, thorny 1668. **3.** Spinigerous. Chiefly *Zool.* 1774. **4.** Having the form of a spine or thorn; slender and sharp-pointed 1732.

4. *S. process*, a process or apophysis of a spine-like form, esp. one of those on the vertebræ.

Spinozism (spinōᵘ·ziz'm). 1728. [f. the name of the philosopher Baruch or Benedict de *Spinoza* (1632–77). So Fr. *spinosisme*.] The philosophical doctrines of Spinoza, or the general principles underlying these; pantheism as represented by Spinoza.

Spinozist (spinōᵘ·zist). 1728. [f. as prec. + -IST. So Fr. *spinosiste*.] One who accepts or advocates the philosophical doctrines of Spinoza. Hence **Spinozi·stic, -osistic** *a.* of, pertaining to, or characteristic of Spinoza or his philosophical views.

Spinster (spi·nstəɹ). late ME. [f. SPIN *v.* + -STER; perh. after (M)Du. *spinster* (cf. MLG. *spinsterinne*).] **1.** A woman (or, rarely, a man) who spins, *esp.* as a regular occupation. **b.** A spider, or other insect that spins (*rare*) 1636. **2.** Appended to the names of women, orig. to denote their occupation, but subsequently as the proper legal designation of one unmarried. late ME. **b.** An unmarried woman; *esp.* an 'old maid' 1719.

1. Ther were..ther dwelling..dyuers good spynsters & carders 1543. **2.** Joan Lambe, widow of London, spynster 1564. I write myself s., because the laws of my country call me so 1719. **b.** Plain little spinsters with a knack of making themselves useful 1882. Hence **Spi·nsterdom** = next. **Spi·nstry,** the art or occupation of spinning, the product of spinning.

Spi·nsterhood. 1823. [f. prec. 2b + -HOOD.] **1.** The condition of being an unmarried woman, esp. one advancing in years. **2.** The collective body of spinsters 1844.

Spinstress (spi·nstrés). 1643. [f. SPINSTER + -ESS[1].] **1.** A female spinner. **2.** A maiden lady; a spinster 1716.

Spi·n-text. 1693. [f. SPIN *v.* + TEXT *sb.*, orig. as a suggestive surname.] A parson, *esp.* one who preaches long or weak sermons.

Spintha·riscope. 1903. [irreg. f. Gr. σπινθαρίς spark; see -SCOPE.] An instrument in which the rays emitted from the metal radium are evidenced by the production of tiny sparks.

Spinule (spəi·niul). 1752. [– L. *spinula*, dim. of *spina*; see SPINE, -ULE.] **1.** A small or minute spine or thorn-like formation, esp. in lower forms of animal life. **2.** A particular kind of larva 1857. Hence **Spinule·scent** *a.* having a tendency to produce small spines. **Spi·nulous** *a.* = SPINULOSE *a.*

Spi·nuli-, comb. form of L. *spinula* spinule, as in *spinuli·ferous, spinu·liform* adjs.

Spinulose (spəi·niulōᵘs), *a.* 1819. [f. SPINULE or L. *spinula* + -OSE[1].] *Zool.* and *Bot.* **1.** Furnished or covered with spinules. **2.** Having the form of spinules 1848. So **Spinulo·so-,** comb. form.

Spiny (spəi·ni), *a.* 1586. [f. SPINE *sb.* + -Y[1].] **1.** Having the characteristics of a thorn or thorns. **b.** Thin and hard or dry; spare, lean 1598. **2.** Abounding in, furnished or thickly set with, thorns 1604. **3.** Furnished or set with spines 1615. **4.** Having the form of a spine; stiff and sharp-pointed 1828.

1. And so much for this little s. objection COWLEY. **2.** The spiney Desarts of Scholastic Philosophy 1727. **3.** Two..lizards with remarkable spiney skins 1883. **4.** S. developments of the epidermis HUXLEY. Hence **Spi·niness.**

Spiracle (spəiᵊ·răk'l). late ME. [– L. *spiraculum* breathing-hole; see next.] †**1.** Breath, spirit. (orig. after L. *spiraculum vitæ* in Gen. 2:7, 7:22) –1654. **2.** A small opening by which a confined space has communication with the outer air; *esp.* an air-hole or air-shaft 1620. **b.** *spec.* A volcanic vent-hole 1671. **3. a.** A breathing-pore in the epidermis of plants; a stoma (*rare*) 1774. **b.** *Zool.* A special aperture, orifice, or pore, chiefly in lower forms of animal life, by which respiration is effected 1775. **c.** The blow-hole of a cetacean (and of certain sharks) 1796. Hence **Spira·cular** *a.* of, pertaining to, or serving as a s. or spiracles.

‖**Spiraculum** (spəiræ·kiŭlŏm). *Pl.* **-acula.** 1668. [L., f. *spirare* breathe.] = prec. 2, 2 b, 3 b.

Spiræa (spəirī·ă). Also **spirea.** 1669. [– L. *spiræa* – Gr. σπειραία, f. σπεῖρα SPIRE *sb.*[3]] *Bot.* **1.** One or other species of an extensive genus of rosaceous plants or shrubs, many of which are largely cultivated for their handsome foliage and flowers. **b.** With *a* and *pl.* A single plant or shrub, or one particular species, of this genus 1731. **2.** The genus composed of these plants 1753.

Spiral (spəiᵊ·răl), *sb.* 1656. [subst. use of next.] **1.** *Geom.* A continuous curve traced by a point moving round a fixed point in the same plane steadily increasing (or diminishing) its distance from this. **2.** A curve traced by a point moving round, and simultaneously advancing along, a cylinder or cone; a helix or screw-line 1670. **b.** The degree in which the successive circles of such a curve approach each other 1846. **3. a.** A piece of wire coiled into a spiral form 1825. **b.** *Bot.* A spiral vessel in plants 1837. **c.** *Astr.* A spiral nebula 1866. **d.** *gen.* Any object having a spiral form 1853. **e.** *Aviation.* A spiral mode of ascent or descent 1918. **4.** One of the separate circles or coils of a spiral or helical object 1728.

1. *S. of Archimedes*, a curve traced by a point moving uniformly along a line which at the same time revolves uniformly round a fixed point in itself. *Equiangular, Logarithmic s.*: see these words. **3. d.** The staircase was of those narrow, twisting spirals 1853. **e.** When I came out of my s. 1918.

Spiral (spəiᵊ·răl), *a.*[1] 1551. [– Fr. *spiral* or med.L. *spiralis* (XIII), f. L. *spira* SPIRE *sb.*[3]; see -AL[1].] **1.** Forming a succession of curves arranged like the thread of a screw; coiled in a cylindrical or conical manner; helical. **2.** Curving continuously round a fixed point in the same plane, at a steadily increasing (or diminishing) distance from it 1639.

1. As woodbine..In s. rings ascends the trunk COWPER. Where upward..The noisy bittern wheeled his s. way LONGF.

Special collocations: *s. gearing, spring, staircase*; Bot., *s. cell, tube, vessel*. Hence **Spira·lity**, *s.* character, the degree of a s. curve. **Spi·rally** *adv.*

Spiral (spəiᵊ·răl), *a.*[2] 1658. [SPIRE *sb.*[1] + -AL[1].] Rising like a spire; tall and tapering or pointed.

Spiral (spəiᵊ·răl), *v.* 1834. [f. SPIRAL *sb.*] **1.** *intr.* To wind or move in a spiral manner; to form spiral curves; *Aviation*, to fly in a spiral. **2.** *trans.* To twist spirally 1867.

Spirant (spəiᵊ·rănt), *sb.* and *a.* 1866. [– L. *spirans, spirant-*, pr. pple. of *spirare* breathe; see -ANT.] *Phonetics.* A consonant uttered with a continued emission of breath, so that the sound is capable of being prolonged. Also *attrib.* or as *adj.* = **Spira·ntal** *a.*

Spi·rated, *ppl. a.* 1871. [f. SPIRE *sb.*[3] (sense 2) + -ATE[2] + -ED[1].] Spirally twisted.

The males..have long straight s. horns DARWIN.

Spiration (spəirēⁱ·ʃən). 1526. [– L. *spiratio, -on-*, f. pa. ppl. stem of *spirare* breathe; see -ION.] **1.** *Theol.* †**a.** The creative function of the Deity conceived as the action of breathing –1765. **b.** The procession of the Holy Ghost regarded as an emanation of spirit 1602. †**2.** The action of breathing or drawing breath in man and animals –1674.

Spire (spəiᵊɹ), *sb.*[1] [OE. *spīr* = MLG., MDu. *spier, spīr*, MHG. *spīr* (G. *spier* tip of blade of grass).] **1.** A stalk or stem of a plant, esp. one of a tall and slender growth. Now *rare.* **b.** The tapering top of a tree 1657. **c.** A flower-spike 1850. **d.** Reeds; a reed. Now *south.* or *s. w. dial.* ME. **2.** *Mining.* The tube carrying the train to the charge in the blast-hole 1875. **3.** A young or tender shoot or sprout; *esp.* the rudimentary shoot of a seed; the acrospire of grain ME. **b.** A blade or shoot *of* grass, etc. Now *rare.* 1646. **4.** A long slender and tapering growth in a plant; *esp.* the awn or beard of grain. Now *Obs.* or *dial.* 1530. **5.** An elongated or pointed shoot or tongue of fire or flame 1450. **6.** A conical, tapering, pointed body or part of something; a sharp point 1551. **b.** A prong of a deer's horn 1607. **7.** A tall, slender, sharp-pointed summit, peak, rock, or column 1586. **8.** A tall structure rising from a tower, roof, etc., and terminating in a slender point; *esp.* the tapering portion of the steeple of a cathedral or church 1596. †**9.** *fig.* The highest point, summit, or top *of* something –1611.

1. Tall spires of windlestrae SHELLEY. **c.** Where ..asphodel is pale with spires of faintest rose 1874. **3.** As an oke comyth of a littil s. CHAUCER. **5.** The flames Drivn backward slope their pointing spires MILT. **6.** The narrow'r end I sharpen'd to a s. POPE. **7.** These two Pyramides, the mighty spires and steeples whereof..do arise out of the very water HOLLAND. **8.** And that sweet city with her dreaming spires..Lovely..she lies M. ARNOLD. **9.** The s., and top of prayses SHAKS. Hence **Spi·relet,** a small s.

Spire, *sb.*[2] Chiefly *Sc.* and *n. dial.* late ME. [app. of Continental origin; corresp. in sense 1 to ON. *spíra*, LG. *spiere, spier*.] †**1.** A spar or pole of timber; a bar or moderately long piece of wood –1609. **2.** A young tree suitable for making into a spar; a sapling. late ME.

Spire (spəiᵊɹ), *sb.*[3] 1572. [– Fr. *spire* – L. *spira* – Gr. σπεῖρα coil, winding.] **1.** One of the series of complete convolutions forming a coil or spiral. **2.** A spiral; a series of spiral curves or coils 1611. **3.** *Conch.* The upper convoluted portion of a spiral shell, consisting of all the whorls except the body-whorl 1822.

Spire (spəiᵊɹ), *v.*[1] ME. [f. SPIRE *sb.*[1]] **1.** *intr.* Of seeds, grain, etc.: To send forth or develop shoots, esp. the first shoot or acrospire; to germinate, sprout. Now *rare* or *Obs.* **2.** Of plants, corn, etc.: To run up into a tall stem, stalk, or spike; to grow upwards instead of developing laterally. Now *dial.* late ME. **3.** To rise or shoot up into a spire or spire-shaped form; to mount or soar aloft 1591.

3. The crowded firs S. from thy shores, and stretch across thy bed COLERIDGE.

†**Spire,** *v.*[2] late ME. [– OFr. *spirer, espirer* or its source L. *spirare* breathe.] **1.** *intr.* or *absol.* To breathe; to blow gently; to come *forth* or *out* as breath –1535. **2.** *trans.* To breathe (air, etc.). Const. *into.* –late ME. **3.** To breathe forth or out, to create or produce by the agency of the breath –1645.

Spire (spəiᵊɹ), *v.*[3] 1607. [f. SPIRE *sb.*[3]] *intr.* To curl, twist, or wind spirally; to make a spiral curve; *esp.* to mount or soar with spiral movement.

Spired (spəiᵊɹd), (*ppl.*) *a.* 1610. [f. SPIRE *sb.*[1] + -ED[2].] **1.** Having a tapering, sharp-pointed top; peaked 1611. **b.** Of a steeple, tower, etc.: Provided with or carrying a spire 1610. **2.** Of plants: Stemmed, spiked 1780.

†**Spire-steeple.** 1559. [SPIRE *sb.*[1]] A steeple surmounted by a spire; a church spire –1809.

Spiricle (spəiᵊ·rik'l). 1891. [dim. of SPIRE *sb.*[3]] *Bot.* A minute coiled thread in the coating of certain seeds and achenes, which uncoils when moistened.

Spirifer (spəiᵊ·rifəɹ). 1835. [mod.L. *spirifer* (Sowerby, 1816), f. L. *spira* SPIRE *sb.*[3] + *-fer*; see -FEROUS.] *Palæont.* A genus of fossil brachiopods, characterized by long highly developed spiral appendages; a member or species of this genus, or of the family *Spiriferidæ* of which it is the type.

Spiriform (spəiᵊ·rifǫɹm), *a.* 1841. [f. *spiri-*, taken as comb. form of L. *spira* (SPIRE *sb.*[3]) + -FORM.] Having the form of a spire or spiral.

Spirillum (spəiᵊri·lŏm). *Pl.* **-a.** 1875. [mod.L., irreg. dim. of L. *spira* SPIRE *sb.*[3]] *Bacteriology.* A genus of bacteria characterized by a spiral structure; any member of this genus, esp. the species found in the blood in relapsing fever. Hence **Spiri·llar** *a.*

Spiring (spəiᵊ·riŋ), *ppl. a.* 1538. [f. SPIRE *v.*[1] + -ING[2].] **1.** That spires or rises up taperingly to a point; soaring aloft or reaching to a great height. freq. *poet.* or *rhet.* **2.** Of grass or plants: Shooting, sprouting; running up into a spire or stem 1612.

1. The lofty, s. tops of the spruce and fir 1857. **2.** The s. grass DRAYTON.

Spirit (spi·rit), *sb.* [ME. *spirit* (later (XV) also *sperit*) – AFr. *spirit*, aphetic of *espirit*, OFr. *esperit*, (also mod.) *esprit* – L. *spiritus* breathing, etc. (in Christian use incorporeal being), f. *spirare* breathe.] **I. 1.** The animating or vital principle in man (and animals); that which gives life to the physical organism, in contrast to its purely material elements; the breath of life. **b.** In contexts relating to temporary separation of the immaterial from the material part of man's being, or to perception of a purely intellectual character. Chiefly in phr. *in s.* late ME. **c.** Incorporeal or immaterial being, as opp. to *body* or *matter*; being or intelligence conceived as distinct from, or independent of, anything physical or material. late ME. **2.** The soul of a person, as commended to God, or passing out of the body, in the moment of death. late ME. **b.** = SOUL III. 1. late ME. **3.** A supernatural, incorporeal, rational being or personality, usually regarded as imperceptible at ordinary times to the human senses, but capable of becoming visible at pleasure, and freq. conceived as troublesome, terrifying, or hostile to mankind ME. **b.** A being of this nature imagined as possessing and actuating a person. late ME. **c.** With *the* and qualifying term, denoting some particular being of the above nature. late ME. **4.** A being essentially incorporeal or immaterial ME.

1. The s. when it is gone foorth returneth not; neither the soule receiued vp, commeth againe *Wisd.* 16:14. **b.** In S. perhaps he also saw Rich Mexico..And Cusco in Peru MILT. **c.** The Egyptians are men and not God, and their horses flesh and not s. *Isaiah* 31:3. **2.** Father, into thy hands I commend my s. *Luke* 23:46. **b.** Where I may..unsphear The s. of Plato MILT. **3.** For Spirits when they please Can either Sex assume, or both MILT. As if God bade some s. plague a world BROWNING. Phr. *Evil, familiar, guardian, wicked s.*, etc. **b.** Sum wenche hauynge a s. of dyuynacioun WYCLIF *Acts* 16:16. **c.** The Evil S. is pulling you towards him 1842. **4.** Man *has* a body, but he *is* a s. 1876.

II. 1. *The S. of God* (or *the Lord*), the active essence or essential power of the Deity, conceived as a creative, animating, or inspiring influence ME. **b.** *The Holy S., the S., the S. of truth*, etc. = HOLY GHOST 1. ME. **2.** The active or essential principle or power *of* some emotion, frame of mind, etc., as operating on or in persons. late ME. **b.** With *a*: A tendency, inclination, or impulse. *of* a specified kind. late ME. **3.** A particular character, disposition, or temper existing in, pervading, or animating, a person or set of persons; a special attitude of mind characterizing men individually or collectively 1561. **b.** The disposition, feeling, or frame of mind with which something is done, considered, or viewed 1601. **4.** A person considered in relation to his character or disposition; one who has a spirit of a specified nature 1591. **5.** The essential character, nature, or qualities *of* something; that which constitutes the pervading or tempering principle of anything 1690. **b.** The prevailing tone or tendency *of* a particular period of time 1820. **c.** The broad intent or meaning *of* a statement, enactment, etc.; opp. to *letter* 1802.

1. The Spirit of the Lord is God the Holy Ghost 1875. **2.** O s. of Loue, how quicke and fresh art thou SHAKS. **b.** A slight s. of mockery played over his speech DISRAELI. **3.** The money-making s. was..driven back 1856. **b.** It is not thy works..but only the S. thou workest in, that can have worth or continuance CARLYLE. **4.** Let thirsty Spirits make the Bar their Choice 1746. **5.** The s. of the hills is action, that of the lowlands repose RUSKIN. **b.** It is the s. of the age, and we are all infected with it SHELLEY.

III. 1. The immaterial, intelligent, or sentient part of a person, freq. in implied or expressed contrast to the body. late ME. **2.** The emotional part of man as the seat of hostile or angry feeling. late ME. **3.** Mettle; vigour of mind; courage; disposition to assert oneself or hold one's own 1596. **4.** A brisk or lively quality, vivacity or animation, in persons or things 1588.

1. My spirite reioyseth in god my sauiour BIBLE (1551) *Luke* 1:47. Saddened and humbled in s. THACKERAY. **2.** She was prepared for war and her s. was hot within her 1862. **3.** A man of more s. than discretion 1715. Phr. *With s. A man of s.* **4.** Wine hath Briskness and S. in it 1686. The absence of Dr. Johnson..took off the s. of the evening MME. D'ARBLAY.

IV. 1. A movement of the air; a wind; a breath (of wind or air). Now chiefly *poet.* late ME. **b.** *Gram.* An aspirate or breathing; a conventional mark indicating this; *spec.* in the writing or printing of Greek 1555. †**2.** One of certain subtle highly-refined substances or fluids (dist. as *natural, animal*, and *vital*) formerly supposed to permeate the blood and chief organs of the body. Chiefly used in *pl.* late ME. **b.** *pl.* Vital power or energy; the normal operation of the vital functions. late ME. **3.** *pl.* The mind or faculties as the seat of action and feeling, esp. as liable to be depressed or exalted by events or circumstances. late ME. **b.** Vigour or animation of mind; cheerfulness, vivacity, liveliness 1716. †**4.** *pl.* The faculties of perception or reflection –1697. †**b.** Disposition. SHAKS. †**5.** A subtle or intangible element or principle in material things –1725.

1. The balmy s. of the western gale POPE. **b.** The book has neither spirits..nor accents 1861. **2. b.** Thy spirits have a fainter flow, I see thee daily weaker grow COWPER. **3.** Depressed in spirits 1893. Phr. *In good, high*, etc. *spirits.* **b.** I..have had spirits enough to go and see all that is curious in the town 1716. *In spirits*, in a cheerful mood. *Out of spirits*, low-spirited. **4. a.** His Spirits should hunt After new Fancies SHAKS.

V. †**1.** One or other of four substances so named by the mediæval alchemists; *spec.* mercury –1728. **2.** A liquid of the nature of an essence or extract from some substance, esp. one obtained by distillation; a solution in alcohol of some essential or volatile principle 1610. **b.** Without article: Liquid such as is obtained by distillation, *spec.* that which is of an alcoholic nature. Also *pl.* 1610. **c.** orig. *pl.* Strong alcoholic liquor for drinking, obtained by distillation from various substances; *sing.* any particular kind of this 1684. **3.** An essence, distilled extract, or alcoholic solution *of* a specified substance. Freq. *pl.*, esp. in later use. 1700. **b.** *Dyeing.*

Any of various solutions used as mordants 1875.

2. b. M. Palm..shot one, and forwarded it to Batavia in s. 1863. c. He gave me also..a little Bottle of Spirits BUNYAN. Quilp..drank three.. glassfulls of the raw s. DICKENS. 3. Aromatic S. of Ammonia 1871. Sweet Spirits of Nitre 1871. See also TURPENTINE 3, VITRIOL 1, WINE *sb.* 5.

attrib. and *Comb.*: *s. flask, grocer*; **s. fresco,** a method of fresco-painting, in which the colours are ground in a medium of wax, elemi, rosin, artist's copal, oil of spike or spirits of turpentine; **-gum,** a quick-drying gum used in theatrical make-up; **-licence,** a legal permit to sell spirits; **-merchant,** a vendor of spirits; **-stove,** a stove fed by methylated or other s.; **s. varnish,** a varnish prepared by dissolving a resin in s.; also as vb.

Spirit (spi·rit), *v.* 1599. [f. SPIRIT *sb.*] **I. 1.** *trans.* To make (the blood, a liquor) of a more active or lively character. **2.** To infuse spirit, life, ardour, or energy into (a person); to inspirit, animate, encourage 1608. **b.** To excite, instigate, or stir up (*rare*) 1680. **†3.** To invest with a spirit or animating principle –1741. **4.** With *up*: To stimulate, animate, encourage, stir up, or excite (a person) 1712.

1. And shall our quick blood, spirited with Wine, Seeme frostie? SHAKS. 2. Spirited with this advantage, he pushed onwards 1758. Phr. *To spirit* (a person) *on*, to urge him on by encouragement. 3. Thy high commands must s. all our wars POPE. 4. Spiriting them up to heroic deeds W. IRVING.

II. 1. To carry off or away; to make away with or remove in a mysterious or dexterous manner 1666. **2.** With *away*: To kidnap, carry off, or abduct (a person) 1670. **b.** To take away or carry off by some mysterious means or power; to transport with speed 1696. **c.** Said of the action of spirits 1825.

1. [He] seemed to s. the things off the table without sound or effort 1858. 2. The archbishop spirited away the preacher into Kent 1858. b. She was spirited away in a moment 1861.

†Spi·rital, *a.* 1598. [Aphetic – OFr. *esperital, espirital*, or – late L. *spiritalis*, f. L. *spiritus*; see SPIRIT *sb.*, -AL[1].] Of the nature of spirit; of or pertaining to the spirit –1707.

Spirited (spi·ritėd), *a.* 1599. [f. SPIRIT *sb.* + -ED[2].] **†1.** Impregnated with spirit or active properties –1677. **2.** Of persons: Full of spirit or animation; lively, energetic; prompt to act in a worthy manner 1599. **b.** Of horses, etc.: Mettlesome 1774. **3.** Of things: Characterized by, displaying, or suggestive of spirit, animation, vigour, or energy 1715. **†4.** Of persons: Occupied or possessed by a (good or evil) spirit (*rare*) 1667.

2. The s. little garrison 1852. b. A remarkably fine and s. horse 1828. 3. A very s. critique upon the party JANE AUSTEN. What clearly cut, s. features! C. BRONTË. 4. So talk'd the s. sly Snake MILT.

Freq. as second element of parasynthetic combs.; as *high-, low-, mean-, public-s.* Hence **Spi·rited-ly** *adv.*, **-ness.**

Spi·ritful, *a. Obs.* or *dial.* 1546. [f. SPIRIT *sb.* + -FUL.] **1.** Having a spiritual or refined character. **2.** Of persons: Spirited, vigorous, energetic 1598. **3.** Of actions, etc.: Performed with, characterized by, spirit or vigour 1614. **4.** Of liquor: Spirituous 1608.

1. The spiritfull and orderly life of our grown men MILT. 2. Miss Howe is..confoundedly smart and s. RICHARDSON. Hence **†Spi·ritful-ly** *adv.* **†-ness.**

Spi·riting, *vbl. sb.* 1768. [f. SPIRIT *v.* + -ING[1].] The action or work of a spirit; the ministering of spirits.

Spiritism (spi·ritiz'm). 1864. [f. SPIRIT *sb.* + -ISM.] = SPIRITUALISM 2.

Spi·ritist. 1858. [f. SPIRIT *sb.* + -IST.] **1.** One who believes in spiritism; a spiritualist. Also *attrib.* **2.** = SPIRITUALIST 3. 1878. Hence **Spiriti·stic** *a.*

Spi·rit(-)lamp. 1802. [SPIRIT *sb.* V. 2.] A lamp fed by methylated or other spirits, and used esp. for heating or boiling.

Spi·ritless, *a.* 1570. [f. SPIRIT *sb.* + -LESS.] **1.** Deprived of the spirit or animating principle; not having or possessing a spirit; lifeless. **2.** Devoid of lively or cheerful spirits; dejected, dull or melancholy 1597. **3.** Destitute of spirit, animation, or courage; lacking ardour or boldness 1628. **b.** Destitute of energy or enterprise (*rare*) 1799. **4.** Marked or characterized by lack of animation, vivacity, or energy 1651.

1. The s. Body should be restored to the Earth 1705. 2. Euen such a man, so faint, so spiritlesse, So dull SHAKS. 3. As a swordless and s. nation SWINBURNE. 4. The evening was passed in s. conversation MME. D'ARBLAY. Hence **Spi·ritless-ly** *adv.*, **-ness.**

Spi·rit(-)le:vel. 1768. [f. SPIRIT *sb.* + LEVEL *sb.* 1.] A levelling instrument used for determining a horizontal line or surface, usu. consisting of a hermetically-sealed glass tube filled with spirit and containing an air-bubble, which when the tube lies exactly horizontal, occupies a position midway in its length.

†Spi·ritous, *a.* 1605. [f. SPIRIT *sb.* + -OUS.] **1.** Of the nature of spirit; having the qualities of an essence; highly refined or dematerialized –1766. **b.** Of liquors: Alcoholic –1836. **2.** Of persons: Lively, vivacious, high-spirited –1763.

Spi·rit-ra:pper. 1854. [f. next.] One who professes that he can induce spirits to communicate with him by means of rapping.

Spi·rit-ra:pping. 1853. [f. SPIRIT *sb.* + *rapping* vbl. sb.] **1.** *pl.* Rappings alleged to be made by spirits in answer to questions addressed to them. **2.** Professed communication from or with spirits by means of raps made by them 1854.

Spi·rit-sti:rring, *a.* 1604. That stirs or animates the spirits.

Spiritual (spi·ritiuăl), *a.* and *sb.* ME. [– (O)Fr. *spirituel* – L. *spiritualis*, f. *spiritus*; see SPIRIT *sb.*, -AL[1].] **A.** *adj.* **1.** Of, pertaining to, affecting or concerning, the spirit or higher moral qualities, esp. as regarded in a religious aspect. (Freq. dist. from *bodily, corporal*, or *temporal*.) late ME. **b.** Applied to material things, substances, etc., in a fig. or symbolical sense. late ME. **†c.** Of songs, etc.: Devotional, sacred –1660. **2.** Of, belonging or relating to, or concerned with sacred or ecclesiastical persons or things, as dist. from secular; pertaining to the church or the clergy; ecclesiastical ME. **3.** Of persons: **a.** Standing to another in a relationship based on a sacred or religious obligation. late ME. **b.** Ecclesiastical, religious. Freq. in *s. lords* and *s. man* (or *person*). late ME. **c.** Devout, holy, pious; morally good; having religious tendencies or instincts. late ME. **4.** Of, pertaining to, or consisting of spirit, regarded in either a religious or intellectual aspect; of the nature of a spirit or incorporeal supernatural essence; immaterial ME. **5.** Consisting of pure essence or spirit; volatile; alcoholic. Now *rare* or *Obs.* 1477. **6.** Of or pertaining to, emanating from, the intellect or higher faculties of the mind; intellectual 1725. **7.** Characterized by a high degree of refinement of thought or feeling. (Cf. SPIRITUEL *a.*) 1784. **8.** Clever, smart, witty. (Cf. SPIRITUEL *a.*) 1791. **9.** Concerned with spirits or supernatural beings 1841.

1. For they doo spirytuell and also corporall werkis CAXTON. b. The Spirituall and sincere milke of the word 1611. 2. The duties of life, which are either s. or secular DE FOE. *S. court*, a court having jurisdiction in matters of religion or ecclesiastical affairs. 3. a. He preferrs his own parish priest..as being his s. father 1697. b. The Lords S. and Temporal form one legislative assembly 1863. 4. Millions of s. Creatures walk the Earth Unseen MILT. 6. Blunting the keenness of his s. sense With narrow schemings and unworthy cares SHELLEY. 7. Those sad eyes were s. and clear KEATS. 8. We French are extremely s., and..are never at a loss for an answer 1872. Hence **Spi·ritual-ly** *adv.*, **-ness.**

B. *sb.* **1. a.** A spiritual or spiritually-minded person 1532. **b.** *Eccl. Hist.* (With initial capital.) A member of the Congregation of Narbonne, a branch of Franciscans, pronounced schismatic in 1318, which advocated a stricter observance of the rule of poverty and simplicity of dress 1791. **2.** *pl.* **a.** Spiritual matters, affairs, or ideas 1582. **b.** Matters which specially or primarily concern the church or religion 1647. **c.** Spiritual or ecclesiastical goods or possessions; spiritualities 1827. **3.** A 'spiritual' song of American Negro origin 1870.

2. a. Such was the prevailing tone of English belief in temporals; what was it in spirituals? MILL. b. It did not belong to the secular power to meddle in spirituals 1794.

Spiritualism (spi·ritiuăliz'm). 1831. [f. SPIRITUAL *a.* + -ISM.] **1.** Tendency towards, or advocacy of, a spiritual view of things, esp. as a leading principle in philosophy or religion 1836. **2.** The belief that the spirits of the dead can hold communication with the living, or make their presence known to them in some way, esp. through a 'medium'; the system of doctrines or practices founded on this belief 1855. **3.** Belief in the existence and influence of spiritual beings 1871.

2. Witchcraft, demonology, possession, and the like, revived in the modest phrase of S. 1860.

Spiritualist (spi·ritiuălist). 1649. [f. as prec. + -IST.] **1.** One who regards things from a spiritual point of view; one whose ideas and doctrines have a purely spiritual basis or tendency. **2.** An adherent of spiritualism as a philosophical doctrine 1836. **3.** A believer in spiritualism (sense 2); a spiritist 1859.

Spiritualistic (spi:ritiuăli·stik), *a.* 1852. [f. prec. + -IC.] **1.** Of or pertaining to, characterized by, philosophical or theological spiritualism; of the nature of spiritualism. **2.** Of or pertaining to, associated or connected with, spiritualism (sense 2); spiritistic 1865.

Spirituality (spi:ritiuæ·lĭti). late ME. [– (O)Fr. *spiritualité* or late L. *spiritualitas*, f. *spiritualis* SPIRITUAL; see -ITY.] **1.** The body of spiritual or ecclesiastical persons; the clergy. Now *Hist.* 1441. **2.** That which has a spiritual character; ecclesiastical property or revenue held or received in return for spiritual services. Now *arch.* 1456. **b.** *pl.* Spiritual or ecclesiastical things; ecclesiastical possessions, rights, etc., of a purely spiritual character. Now *Hist.* late ME. **3.** The quality or condition of being spiritual 1500. **b.** With *a* and *pl.* A spiritual thing or quality as distinct from a material or worldly one 1676. **4.** The fact or condition of being spirit or of consisting of an incorporeal essence 1681.

1. He blamed both S. and laity 1709. 2. b. They [the Dean and Chapter] are Guardians of the Spiritualities during the Vacancy of the Bishoprick 1726. 3. His Life..is full of excellent Lessons of S. 1753. 4. That He is invisible is accounted for by His s. 1884.

Spiritualization (spi:ritiuăləizē¹·ʃən). 1665. [f. next + -ATION.] **1.** The action of changing into spirit; conversion or transformation of a corporeal or material substance into a spiritual condition. **2.** The action of spiritualizing; the state of being spiritualized 1809.

Spiritualize (spi·ritiuăləiz), *v.* 1631. [f. SPIRITUAL *a.* + -IZE, partly after Fr. *spiritualiser* (XVI) in same sense.] **1.** *trans.* To render spiritual; to raise or change to a spiritual (a more spiritual) condition. **b.** To convert into, invest with, a spiritual sense or meaning; to expound in a spiritual sense; to explain *away* in this manner. Also *absol.* 1645. **c.** To render spiritual in appearance; to refine in a high degree 1889. **2. †a.** To render volatile or spirituous –1741. **b.** To invest with the nature of a spirit 1659.

1. Christ more spirituallized their Joy, rather to rejoyce that their Names were written in Heaven FULLER. b. To spiritualise away the pains of what is technically called Hell 1833. c. The softened light spiritualises the landscape 1889. Hence **Spi·ritualizer,** one who spiritualizes.

Spi:ritual-mi·ndedness. 1647. [After *spiritually-minded* (Tindale), tr. *geistlich gesinnet* (Luther).] The quality or state of being spiritually-minded or of having the mind set on spiritual things.

Spiritualty (spi·ritiuălti). late ME. [– OFr. *spiritualté* – late L. *spiritualitas*; see SPIRITUALITY.] = SPIRITUALITY 1, 2, 2b, 3.

‖Spiritue·l, -e·lle, *a.* 1673. [Fr. *spirituel* masc., *-elle* fem.; see SPIRITUAL *a.*] Of a highly refined character or nature, esp. in conjunction with liveliness or quickness of mind.

Spirituosity (spiritiuǫ·sĭti). 1669. [f. next + -ITY.] The state or quality of being spirituous, esp. through distillation.

Spirituous (spi·ritiuəs), *a.* 1599. [– Fr. *spiritueux* or f. L. *spiritus* SPIRIT + -OUS.] **1.** Spirited, animated, lively, vivacious. Now *rare.* **2.** Of the nature of, having the properties of, spirit; containing spirit or volatile principle in a natural state 1605. **3.** Containing or impregnated with spirit or alcohol obtained by distillation; containing an infusion of alcohol; alcoholic, ardent 1681. **4.** Of or belonging to spirit or alcohol; like or resembling that of spirit 1667. †**5.** = SPIRITUAL, in various senses –1745.

1. The Emir in his s. humour, and haughty familiar manners 1888. **3.** Strong Waters or S. liquors 1732. Hence **Spi·rituousness** = SPIRITUOSITY.

Spirketting (spə̄·ɹkėtiŋ). Also †**spirkiting, spar-.** 1748. [f. †*spirket*, †*spurket* pl. spaces between the rungs along a ship's side.] *Naut.* Inside planking between the waterways and the ports of a vessel.

Spirling (spə̄·ɹliŋ). Now only *Sc.* late ME. [– MLG. *spirling*, MDu. *spierling* (AL. *sper-*, *spirlingus*, XIV). Cf. SPARLING, SPURLING.] The smelt, *Osmerus eperlanus*.

Spiro- (spəi·ro), comb. form of L. *spira*, Gr. σπεῖρα SPIRE *sb.*[3], as in: **Spirobacte·ria,** bacteria with spirally twisted cells; **Spirochæte** (-kī·tī), a genus of bacteria having a highly twisted spiral form.

Spirometer (spəirǫ·mĭtəɹ). 1846. [f. L. *spirare* breathe; see -METER.] An instrument for measuring the breathing power of the lungs. Hence **Spirome·tric, -al** *adjs.*

Spirometry (spəirǫ·mĭtri). 1859. [See prec., -METRY.] Measurement of breathing-power; the use of the spirometer.

Spirt (spə̄ɹt), *sb.*[1] 1550. [var. of contemp. SPURT *sb.*[1]; of unkn. origin.] †**1.** A brief period of time; a short space –1612. **2.** *Naut.* A short or slight spell *of* wind 1726. **3.** A sudden outbreak or brief spell of activity or exertion; a spurt 1829.

Spirt (spə̄ɹt), *sb.*[2] 1716. [f. SPIRT *v.*[1]; cf. SPURT *sb.*[2]] **1.** A jet or slender spout of water or other liquid. **2.** A sudden jet of fire or puff of smoke 1851.

1. A great s. of blood DICKENS. **2.** Little spirts of fire 1851.

Spirt (spə̄ɹt), *v.*[1] 1582. [var. of contemp. SPURT *v.*[1]; of unkn. origin.] **1.** *intr.* Of liquids (or small objects): To issue in a jet. **2.** *trans.* To send out in a jet or slender rapid stream; to squirt 1582.

Spirt (spə̄ɹt), *v.*[2] 1599. [f. SPIRT *sb.*[1] Cf. SPURT *v.*[2]] *intr.* To make a spurt; to exert oneself for a short time.

Spirtle (spə̄·ɹt'l), *sb. dial.* 1881. [Cf. next.] A small spirt or jet; a sprinkle.

Spirtle (spə̄·ɹt'l), *v.* Now *dial.* 1603. [f. SPIRT *v.*[1] + -LE.] **1.** *trans.* To sprinkle, spatter, or splash *with* something. **2.** To cause to spatter or splash; to disperse in small particles 1612. **3.** *intr.* To become dispersed or scattered 1725.

‖**Spirula** (spəiᵊ·riŭlă). 1835. [mod.L., dim. of L. *spira* SPIRE *sb.*[3]] *Zool.* A genus of cephalopods having a flat spiral shell in the hinder part of the body; an animal of this genus, or one of the shells. So **Spi·rule.**

Spiry (spəiᵊ·ri), *a.*[1] 1602. [f. SPIRE *sb.*[1] + -Y[1].] **1.** Of grass or other plants, stems, etc.: Forming slender pointed shoots. **b.** Of trees: Rising in a tapering form without much branching 1664. **2.** Having the characteristic form of a spire; tapering up to a point 1664. **3.** Of form: Resembling that of a spire 1777. **4.** Of places: Full of spires; spire-crowned 1728. **5.** Characterized by slenderness or slimness of growth or form 1853.

1. Heath and Spirie Grasse 1602. **b.** A range of meadows, set with s. poplars STEVENSON. **2.** London's s. turrets THOMSON. Two s. cliffs.. bound the lake 1840. **4.** The s. habitable city STEVENSON.

Spiry (spəi·ri), *a.*[2] 1676. [f. SPIRE *sb.*[3] + -Y[1].] Curving or coiling in spirals.

Hid in the s. volumes of the snake, I lurked within the covert of a brake DRYDEN.

†**Spiss,** *a.* 1530. [– L. *spissus.*] Thick, dense, compact, close –1784.

Boil these to a spisse Cataplasme 1658.

Spissitude (spi·sitiud). Now *rare.* 1440. [– L. *spissitudo*, f. *spissus* SPISS *a.*; see -TUDE.] Density, thickness, compactness.

Spit (spit), *sb.*[1] [OE. *spitu* = MLG., MDu. *spit*, *spet* (Du. *spit*), OHG. *spiz* (G. *spiess*) :– WGmc. **spitu.*] **1.** A slender sharp-pointed rod of metal or wood, used for thrusting into or through meat which is to be roasted at a fire; a broach. †**2.** = OBELISK *sb.* 2. –1627. **3.** *Printing.* An iron rod carrying the wheel by which the carriage of a hand-press is run out or in 1728. **b.** A rod or skewer on which fish are strung and hung up to dry 1833. **4.** A sword. (Chiefly contemptuous.) 1642. **5.** A small, low point or tongue of land, projecting into the water; a long narrow reef, shoal, or sandbank extending from the shore 1673.

4. Out with your s. without delay! You've but to lunge and I will parry 1871. **5.** Above the third buoy..lies a dangerous s. 1802.

Spit (spit), *sb.*[2] ME. [f. SPIT *v.*[2]] **1.** The fluid secreted by the glands of the mouth, esp. when ejected; saliva, spittle; a clot of this. See also CUCKOO-SPIT. **2.** The act of spitting; an instance of this 1658. **3.** *The very s. of*, the exact image, likeness, or counterpart of (a person, etc.). *colloq.* 1825. **4.** A slight sprinkle or shower of rain or snow 1849.

2. *A s. and a stride* (dial.), a very short distance. **3.** A daughter,..the very s. of the old Captain 1825.

Spit, *sb.*[3] 1507. [– (M)LG., (M)Du. *spit*, rel. to OE. *spittan* SPIT *v.*[3]] **1.** Such a depth of earth as is pierced by the full length of a spade-blade; a spade-graft. **b.** A thrust *of* the spade in digging 1844. **2.** A layer of earth of a spade's depth 1663. **3.** The quantity of earth taken up by a spade at a time; a spadeful 1675. **b.** A series of spadefuls taken in a line 1722.

1. The ground is delved two s. deep 1670.

Spit, *v.*[1] ME. [f. SPIT *sb.*[1]] **1.** *trans.* To put on a spit; to thrust through with a spit. **b.** *transf.* To pierce, transfix, or stab with a sharp weapon, etc.; to impale *on* or *upon* something sharp. late ME. **2.** To fix (herrings, etc.) on a spit or rod for drying or smoking 1617.

1. He lighted a fire, spitted a leg of mutton SMOLLETT. **b.** Your naked Infants spitted vpon Pykes SHAKS.

Spit, *v.*[2] Pa. t. **spit, spat.** Pa. pple. **spit, spat.** [OE. (late Northumb.) (*ġe*)*spittan* = G. dial. *spützen*, f. imit. base **spit-*. Cf. SPEW *v.*, SPITTLE *sb.*[2]] **I.** *trans.* †**1.** To eject saliva on (a person) as a sign of contempt –ME. **2.** To eject from the mouth by the special effort involved in expelling saliva OE. **3. a.** To emit, cast, throw, in a manner similar to the ejection of saliva. late ME. **b.** To extrude or lay (eggs or spawn) 1847. **4.** With *out* (or †*forth*): To utter in a proud, spiteful, plain, or unreserved manner. Also without adv.: To speak (a language). 1595.

2. The wulf..spytte blood CAXTON. fig. *To s. venom, poison, fire*, etc. *To s. in one's face, teeth*, etc. (chiefly *fig.*); He bit off his tongue and s. it in her face 1636. **3. a.** The Canons..ready mounted ..to s. forth Their Iron indignation gainst your walles SHAKS. **4.** Thus Michael spits out bitter reproaches against David 1657. He spits French like a Magpy 1701.

II. *intr.* **1.** To eject saliva (at or on a person or thing) as a means of expressing hatred or contempt OE. **2.** To eject saliva from the mouth; to expectorate ME. **b.** Of certain animals when angry 1668. **3.** To sputter 1611. **4.** Of rain or snow: To fall in scattered drops or flakes. (Usu. impers.) 1567. **5.** *S. and polish*, the occupation of cleaning up or furbishing, as part of the work of a sailor or soldier 1895.

Spit, *v.*[3] Now *dial.* [OE. *spittan* dig with a spade, prob. ult. rel. to SPIT *sb.*[1] Cf. SPIT *sb.*[3]] **1.** *intr.* To dig with a spade; to delve. late ME. **2.** *trans.* To plant with a spade 1610. **3.** To dig (*up*) with a spade; also, to turn up with a plough OE.

Spital (spi·tăl). 1634. [Late respelling of SPITTLE *sb.*[1] after HOSPITAL.] **1.** = SPITTLE *sb.*[1] 1, 2. **b.** *S. sermon*: see SPITTLE *sb.*[1] 1755. **2.** *fig.* A foul or loathsome place. SMOLLETT. **3.** A shelter for travellers. WORDSW.

1. Defrauding the Poor..or, to see it under the most opprobrious Colours, robbing the Spittal FIELDING.

Spi·t-ball. *U.S.* **1.** Paper chewed and rolled into a ball, to be thrown as a missile. Also *fig.* 1846. **2.** *Baseball.* A pitched ball moistened on one side with saliva 1912.

Spitchcock (spi·tʃkǫk), *sb.* 1597. [Of unkn. origin. See SPATCHCOCK.] †**1.** A method of preparing an eel for the table (see sense 2) –1771. **2.** An eel cut into short pieces, dressed with bread-crumbs and chopped herbs, and broiled or fried 1601.

Spitchcock (spi·tʃkǫk), *v.* 1675. [f. prec.] **1.** *trans.* To prepare (*esp.* an eel) for the table as, or after the manner of, a spitchcock. **2.** To deal with (a person) in a similar manner; *fig.* to handle severely 1674. So **Spitchcocked** (spi·tʃkǫkt) *ppl. a.* 1643.

Spite (spəit), *sb.* †Also **spight.** ME. [Aphetic – OFr. *despit* DESPITE *sb.*] †**1.** Action arising from, or displaying, hostile or malignant feeling; outrage, injury, harm; insult, reproach –1658. **2.** A strong feeling of (†contempt,) hatred, or ill-will; intense grudge or desire to injure; rancorous or envious malice ME. **b.** *fig.* Of fortune, nature, the elements, etc. 1562. **3.** With *a* and *pl.* A particular instance of malignant or rancorous feeling directed towards a special object. late ME. †**4.** An annoying matter, affair, or thing; a feeling of irritation –1670.

2. Much have I borne from canker'd critic's s. GRAY. Phr. *For* or *in spite.* **b.** He defied the spight of Fortune 1562. **3.** Phr. *To have a s. at*; This Preacher..hath some s. at me 1612. *Phr.* **In s. of** (also, now *arch.*, **s. of**), in defiance (†scorn or contempt) of; in the face of; notwithstanding. **5.** *attrib.* **s. fence** *U.S.* an unsightly fence erected for the purpose of injuring a neighbour.

Spite (spəit), *v.* ME. [Aphetic – OFr. *despiter* DESPITE *v.*] †**1.** *trans.* To regard with contempt or spite –1690. **2.** To treat spitefully or maliciously; to annoy or thwart in a spiteful manner 1592. **3.** To fill with spite or vexation; to annoy, offend, irritate 1563. †**4.** *intr.* To be angry or annoyed; to cherish spite –1580.

2. Not caring what they suffer themselves, so they may s. their enemy 1658. Phr. *To s.* (*one*), in order to vent spite or spleen upon (another); with the object of vexing or annoying. **3.** There is nothing spites us more, than to heare a man commend himselfe 1581.

Spiteful (spəi·tfŭl), *a.* 1440. [f. SPITE *sb.* + -FUL.] †**1.** Expressive of, characterized by, contempt or disdain –1700. †**b.** Bringing contempt or opprobrium; disgraceful, shameful –1586. **2.** Full of, possessed or animated by, spite; malicious, malevolent. Also *fig.* of things 1490. †**3.** Distressing, annoying, vexing –1633.

2. A s. Saying gratifies so many little Passions ADDISON. Hence **Spi·teful-ly** *adv.*, **-ness.**

Spitfire (spi·tfəiᵊɹ), *a.* and *sb.* 1600. [f. SPIT *v.*[2]] **A.** *adj.* **1.** That spits fire; fire-spitting; *fig.* irascible; displaying anger or hot temper. **2.** Naut. *S.-jib*: in cutters, a small storm-jib of very heavy canvas 1867.

1. Where..spit-fire cats their midnight revels keep 1791.

B. *sb.* **1.** A thing which emits or vomits fire; *esp.* a cannon 1611. **2.** One whose temper is fiery; a passionate quick-tempered person 1680. **3.** A cat in an angry state 1825.

1. That s., the Rock of Gibraltar 1785. **2.** What a little s. was this Nancy of mine! 1881.

Spi·tful. 1842. [f. SPIT *sb.*[3]] A spadeful.

†**Spi·tous,** *a.* and *adv.* ME. [Aphetic – AFr. *despitous*, f. *despit*; see SPITE *sb.*] **1.** = DESPITOUS *a.* –1481. **2.** As *adv.* = DESPITOUSLY *adv.* –1400. So †**Spi·tously** *adv.*

†**Spi·tter**[1]. 1565. [Also *spittard* (XVI–XVII); app. f. SPIT *sb.*[1] Cf. Du. *spithert*, G. *spiessert*, *spiesser.*] A young deer with simple unbranched horns; a brocket or pricket –1661.

Spitter[2] (spi·təɹ). late ME. [f. SPIT *v.*[2] + -ER[1].] One who spits or ejects saliva. Also *fig.*

Spi·tter[3]. Now *dial.* 1600. [f. SPIT *v.*[3] + -ER[1].] **1.** A spade or spud. **2.** A spademan; a delver or digger 1648.

†**Spittle,** *sb.*[1] [ME. *spit*(*t*)*el*, repr. (ult.) an aphetic form of HOSPITAL, modified after native words in *-el*, *-le.*] **1.** A house or place for the reception of the indigent or diseased; a charitable foundation for this purpose, *esp.* one chiefly occupied by persons of a low class or afflicted with foul diseases; a lazar-house. (Now written SPITAL.) –1839. **2.** Phr. *To rob the s.*, to make gain in a particularly mean or dastardly manner –1708. **3.** *fig.* A foul receptacle or collection. Const. *of.* –1652.

2. Of all men, Vs'rers are not least accurst; They robb the S.; pinch th' Afflicted worst QUARLES.

Comb.: **s.-house** = sense 1; **S. sermon,** one of

the sermons preached on Easter Monday and Tuesday from a special pulpit at St. Mary Spital (afterwards at St. Bride's and finally at Christ Church in the City).

Spittle (spi·t'l), *sb.*^{2} 1480. [alt., by assoc. with SPIT *sb.*^{2}, of SPATTLE *sb.*^{1}] **1.** Saliva, spit. **2.** The frothy secretion of an insect. Cf. CUCKOO-SPIT. 1821.

Phr. †*S. of the stars*, honey-dew, nostoc. †*S. of the sun*, gossamer.

Comb.: **s.-fly, -insect,** *U.S.*, an insect forming, or bred in, a frothy secretion.

Spi·ttle, *sb.*^{3} Now *dial.* [OE. *spitel*, related to SPIT *sb.*^{3} and *v.*^{3}] **1.** A spade or small spade; a spud. **2.** A hoe or scraper 1832.

Spittle (spi·t'l), *v.*^{1} *rare.* ME. [alt., by assoc. with SPIT *v.*^{2}, of SPATTLE *v.*^{1}; later f. SPITTLE *sb.*^{2}] *intr.* To eject spittle; to spit.

Spittle, *v.*^{2} *rare.* 1727. [f. SPITTLE *sb.*^{3}] *trans.* To dig (*in*), to pare, etc., with a spittle.

Spittoon (spitū·n). 1840. [f. SPIT *v.*^{2} + -OON.] A receptacle for spittle; usually a round flat vessel of earthenware or metal, sometimes having a cover in the form of a shallow funnel with an opening in the middle, and frequently containing sawdust.

‖**Spitz** (spits). 1845. [G. (also *spitzhund*), special use of *spitz* pointed, peaked.] A species of dog having a very pointed muzzle; a Pomeranian dog.

Spla·cknuck. 1726. [Invented by Swift.] An imaginary animal of Brobdingnag; a strange animal or person.

Your modern ladies shriek at a pipe as if they saw a 's.' TENNYSON.

Splanchnic (splæ·ŋknik), *a.* and *sb.* 1681. [— mod.L. *splanchnicus* — Gr. σπλαγχνικός, f. σπλάγχνον, usu. pl. σπλάγχνα inward parts; see -IC.] **A.** *adj.* **1. a.** Situated in, connected with, the viscera or intestines. Freq. in *s. nerve(s.* 1694. **b.** Occupied by the viscera (esp. in *s. cavity*); of a visceral character 1830. **2.** Affecting, pertaining or relating to, the viscera 1681. **B.** *sb.* A splanchnic nerve. Chiefly in *pl.* 1840.

Splanchno- (splæ·ŋkno), comb. form of Gr. σπλάγχνον (see prec.), as in:

Splanchno·graphy, an anatomical description of the viscera. **Splanchnopleu·ral** *a.*, pertaining to the splanchnopleure. **Spla·nchnopleure,** one of the two layers or divisions of the mesoblast. **Splanchnopleu·ric** *a.*, = *splanchnopleural*. **Splanchnoske·letal** *a.*, relating or belonging to the visceral skeleton. **Splanchnoske·leton,** the visceral skeleton, consisting of hard or bony parts developed in the viscera or sense-organs. **Splanchno·tomy,** dissection or anatomy of the viscera.

Splanchnology (splæŋknǫ·lŏdʒi). 1706. [f. prec. + -LOGY.] **1.** The scientific study of the viscera. **2.** The visceral system 1842.

Splash (splæʃ), *sb.* 1736. [f. SPLASH *v.*] **1.** A quantity of some fluid or semi-fluid substance dashed or dropped upon a surface. **b.** The fragmentary metal resulting from the shattering of bullets upon impact 1865. **2.** *colloq.* A striking or ostentatious display, appearance, or effect; a dash 1806. **3.** The act or result of suddenly and forcibly striking or dashing water or other fluid; the sound produced by this 1819. **4.** The act, result, or sound of water falling or dashing forcibly upon something 1832. **5.** A large or irregular patch of colour or light 1832.

2. Phr. *To make* or *cut a s.* **3.** That pebble which falls into the water with a s. 1898. **5.** [The light] fell in a great s. upon the thicket STEVENSON.

Splash (splæʃ), *v.* 1715. [Expressive alt. of PLASH *v.*^{2}] **I.** *trans.* **1.** To bespatter, to wet or soil, by dashing water, mud, etc. 1722. **b.** To stain, mark, or mottle with irregular patches of colour or light. Chiefly in *pa. pple.* 1833. **2.** To cause (a liquid or semi-liquid substance) to fly about 1762. **3.** To cause (something) to dash or agitate a liquid, esp. so as to produce a sound 1879. **4.** To make (one's way) with splashing 1830.

3. Splashing their oars, and making as much noise as possible FROUDE.

II. *intr.* To cause dashing or noisy agitation of a liquid; to move or fall with a splash or splashes 1715. **2.** Of liquids: To dash or fly in some quantity and with some degree of force 1755. **3.** Of bullets: To throw off fragments on striking an object 1894. Hence **Splash** *adv.* in a splashing manner; with a splash or splashing sound.

Splash-, the stem of SPLASH *v.*, as in **s. lubrication, method, system,** a method of keeping machinery oiled by regular splashing of oil from a receptacle; **s.-net,** a small fishing-net; hence *splash-netting* vbl. sb.; **-paper,** paper coloured in irregular patches; **-work,** spatter-work.

Spla·sh(-)board. 1842. [f. prec.] **1.** A guard or screen in front of the driver's seat on a vehicle, to protect him from being splashed with mud from the horse's hoofs. **2.** A board fixed over or beside a wheel to intercept splashings 1850. **3.** *Naut.* A screen above the deck-line 1907.

Splasher (splæ·ʃəɹ). 1848. [f. SPLASH *v.* + -ER^1.] **1. a.** A guard placed over or beside a wheel to prevent splashing or accidental contact. **b.** A splash-board 1887. **2.** A flat board strapped to the foot for walking on soft ground or mud 1859.

Spla·shy, *a.*^{1} 1727. [Alteration of PLASHY *a.*^{1}] Full of shallow pools or puddles; wet and soft.

Splashy (splæ·ʃi), *a.*^{2} 1834. [f. SPLASH *sb.* or *v.* + -Y^1.] **1.** Of a splashing character; falling, etc., with a splash or in splashes 1856. **2.** Of sounds: Such as are made by a splash 1834. **3.** Making a show or stir; sensational 1836. **4.** Done in splashes; not even or regular 1880.

1. Brown leaves, s. rains, and winds moaning CARLYLE. **4.** Fine, but s., sketches 1880.

Spla·tter, *v.* Chiefly *dial.* and *U.S.* 1784. [Imitative.] **1.** *intr.* To splash continuously or noisily. **2.** *trans.* To spatter or sputter (something); to cause to spatter 1785.

Splay (splēⁱ), *sb.* 1507. [f. SPLAY *v.*^{1}] *Arch.* A slope or bevel; applied esp. to the sides of a door or window by which the opening widens from the door or window toward the face or faces of the wall. **b.** The degree of bevel or slant given to the sides of an opening, etc. 1860. **c.** The outward spread of a bowl or cup 1874.

Splay, *adv.* and *a.* 1734. [Back-formation from SPLAY-FOOTED.] **A.** *adv.* **a.** = SPLAY-FOOT 3. **b.** In an oblique manner; slantingly. **B.** *adj.* Oblique; awry; off the straight 1876.

In the German mind, as in the German language, there does seem to be something s. M. ARNOLD.

Splay (splēⁱ), *v.*^{1} ME. [Aphetic f. DISPLAY *v.*] †**1.** *trans.* = DISPLAY *v.* 1. –1594. **2.** To spread out, expand, extend; to open out in a spreading manner. late ME. †**b.** = DISPLAY *v.* 3. –1575. **3.** *trans.* To bevel or make slanting; to construct with a splay 1598. **4.** *intr.* **a.** To have, take, or lie in, an oblique or slanting direction 1725. **b.** To spread out in an awkward manner 1848.

1. Swerd or septer..There was none nor baners splayde wyde LYDG. **3.** The simplest method..is to s. the jambs and arch of the window 1878.

Splay, *v.*^{2} Now *dial.* 1601. [Alteration of SPAY *v.*] *trans.* To spay (female animals).

Splay(-)foot. 1548. [f. SPLAY *v.*^{1}] **1.** A flat, spread out, clumsy foot, esp. one which turns outwards. †**2.** *attrib.* = next –1766. **3.** As *adv.* In a splay-footed manner 1626.

Splay-footed, *a.* 1545. [f. as prec. + -ED^2.] Having splay feet. **b.** *fig.* Clumsy, awkward; sprawling 1716.

†**Splay-mouthed,** *a.* 1651. [f. SPLAY *v.*^{1}] Having a wide or wry mouth –1812. So †**Splay-mouth** a distorted mouth. DRYDEN.

Spleen (splīn), *sb.* ME. [Aphetic — OFr. *esplen* — L. *splen* — Gr. σπλήν, prob. rel. to Gr. σπλάγχνον (see SPLANCHNIC), L. *lien*, Skr. *plīhán*.] **1.** *Anat.* An abdominal organ consisting of a ductless gland of irregular form, which in mammals is situated at the cardiac end of the stomach and serves to produce certain changes in the blood; the milt or melt. †**b.** Regarded as the seat of melancholy or morose feelings - 1665. †**c.** Regarded as the seat of laughter or mirth –1681. †**2.** Merriment, gaiety, sport. SHAKS. †**3. a.** A sudden impulse; a whim or caprice –1625. **b.** Caprice; changeable temper. SHAKS. †**4.** Hot or proud temper; high spirit, courage, resolute mind –1605. †**b.** Impetuosity, eagerness. SHAKS. **5.** Violent ill-nature or ill-humour; irritable or peevish temper 1594. **6.** With *a*: **a.** A fit of temper; a passion. *Obs.* exc. *arch.* 1589. †**b.** A grudge –1722. **7.** Excessive dejection or depression of spirits, gloominess and irritability; moroseness; melancholia. Now *arch.* 1664.

1. c. Come burst your spleens with laughter to behold A new found vanity QUARLES. **2.** *Tam. Shr.* Induct. i. 137. **3. a.** A thousand spleens bear her a thousand ways SHAKS. **b.** 1 *Hen. IV*, II. iii. 81. **4.** *Rom. & Jul.* III. i. 163. **5.** Whereat Geraint flash'd into sudden s. TENNYSON. **6. a.** *Mids. N.* I. i. 146. **7.** This quiet room gives me the s. LYTTON. He is the victim of English s. 1860. Hence **Splee·nish** *a.* somewhat spleenful or splenetic; **-ly** *adv.*, **-ness.**

†**Spleen,** *v.* 1629. [f. the sb.] **1. a.** *trans.* To regard with spleen; to have a grudge at –1675. **b.** To fill with spleen; to make angry or ill-tempered –1801. **2.** *trans.* To deprive of the spleen 1735.

Spleenful (splī·nfŭl), *a.* 1588. [f. SPLEEN *sb.* + -FUL.] Full of spleen; passionate, irritable, peevishly angry.

My selfe haue calm'd their spleenfull mutinie SHAKS. Then rode Geraint, a little s. yet, Across the bridge TENNYSON.

Spleenless (splī·nlės), *a.* *rare.* late ME. [f. SPLEEN *sb.* + -LESS.] **1.** Destitute of a spleen. †**2.** *fig.* Mild, gentle 1615.

Spleenwort (splī·nwɒɹt). 1578. [f. SPLEEN *sb.*, after L. *splenion* or *asplenon* — Gr. σπλήνιον, ἄσπληνον, f. σπλήν spleen.] **1. a.** One or other of various ferns belonging to the genus *Asplenium*; also, the genus itself. †**b.** Hart's-tongue; scolopendrium –1796. **2.** *U.S.* A species of cactus 1846.

Spleeny (splī·ni), *a.* 1604. [f. SPLEEN *sb.* + -Y^1.] Spleenful, splenetic.

Splen-, var. of SPLENO- bef. vowels, as in **Splena·lgia,** pain in the spleen, etc.

†**Splenative,** *a.* 1592. Also †**spleen-.** [var. of contemp. †*splenatic* (— med.L *splenaticus* = late L. *spleneticus* SPLENETIC), by substitution of suffix.] **1.** Acting on the spleen. NASHE. **2.** Of a hot or hasty temper –1660.

Splendacious (splendēⁱ·ʃəs), *a.* 1843. [Fancifully f. SPLEND(ID + -ACIOUS.] Very splendid.

Splendent (sple·ndĕnt), *a.* 1474. [— L. *splendens, -ent-*, pr. pple. of *splendēre* be bright or shining; see -ENT.] **1.** Shining brightly by virtue of inherent light. Also *fig.* **2.** Reflecting light with great brilliancy; bright, gleaming, resplendent 1578. **b.** Extremely brilliant, gorgeous, or magnificent 1567. **3.** *fig.* Having qualities comparable to material brightness or brilliancy; pre-eminently beautiful, grand, or great 1509.

1. Whan the golden sterres clere were s. 1503. **2.** The best Grey-hound hath..a neate sharpe head, and s. eyes 1607. **b.** Giants, s. in gold-lace and grenadier-caps CARLYLE. **3.** The s. brightnes of the Trueth, which burnes..so gloriously 1599. Hence †**Sple·ndently** *adv.*

Splendid (sple·ndid), *a.* 1624. [— Fr. *splendide* or L. *splendidus*, f. *splendēre*; see prec., -ID^1.] **1.** Marked by much grandeur or display; sumptuous, grand, gorgeous. **b.** Of persons: Maintaining, or living in, great style or grandeur 1658. **2. a.** Resplendent, extremely bright, in respect of light or colour (*rare*) 1634. **b.** Magnificent in material respects 1685. **c.** Having or embodying some element of material grandeur or beauty 1815. **3.** Impressive by greatness, grandeur, or some similar excellence 1653. **b.** Dignified, haughty, lordly 1833. **4.** Excellent; very good or fine 1644. **5.** Used, by way of contrast, to qualify nouns having a different connotation 1667.

1. Accommodation so s. I know not that I should desire were I a prince 1797. **b.** Ambitious of s. acquaintance 1779. **2. a.** The topaz is a most s. and famous stone 1750. **b.** A s. Hindoo temple 1863. **c.** The splendider scenery of the Alps 1851. **3.** Persons of..splendider fortunes 1653. **b.** A s. contempt for female intellect 1833. **4.** A s. shot 1882. **5.** Our state Of s. vassalage MILT. Hence **Sple·ndid-ly** *adv.*, **-ness.**

†**Splendi·dious,** *a.* late ME. [f. L. *splendidus* + -IOUS.] Splendid, magnificent, brilliant –1653. So †**Sple·ndidous** *a.*

Splendiferous (splendi·fĕrəs), *a.* 1460. [f. med.L. *splendifer* (XII), for late L. *splendorifer*. In mod. use joc. and orig. U.S.] †**1.** Full of or abounding in splendour –1546. **2.** *colloq.* Remarkably fine 1843.

Splendorous (sple·ndŏrəs), *a.* Also †**splendrous.** 1591. [f. next + -OUS.] Full of splendour; resplendent, bright.

In splendrous Armes he road DRAYTON.

Splendour (sple·ndəɹ). Also (now *U.S.*) **splendor.** 1450. [– (O)Fr. *splendeur* or L. *splendor*, f. *splendēre* shine; see -OUR.] **1.** Great brightness; brilliant light or lustre. **2.** Magnificence; great show of riches or costly things; pomp, parade 1616. **3.** Brilliant distinction, eminence, or glory; impressive character 1604. **4.** Brilliant or ornate appearance or colouring 1774.

1. And swift and swift beyond conceiving The splendor of the world goes round 1871. **2.** The antique s. of the ducal house 1837. **3.** The s. of the present progress had not..been equalled D'ISRAELI. **4.** *Comb.* Like s.-winged moths SHELLEY.

Splenetic (splĭne·tik), *a.* and *sb.* 1544. [– late L. *spleneticus*, f. *splen* SPLEEN. Until the beginning of XIX the stress was on the first syllable.] **A.** *adj.* **1.** Of or pertaining to, connected with, the spleen; splenic. Also *fig.* **†2.** Affected with disease or disorder of the spleen; in later use, affected with melancholia or hypochondria –1766. **†b.** Characterized by, tending to produce, melancholy or depression of spirits –1781. **3.** Having an irritably morose or peevish disposition or temperament; ill-humoured, testy, irascible 1592. **4.** Characterized by, arising from, displaying or exhibiting, spleen or ill-humour 1693. **†5.** Of medicines: Acting on the spleen –1728.

1. The Splenetick Vein, or Artery 1722. **2.** If he be s., he may..meet companions..with whose groans he may mix his own GOLDSM. **b.** Our cloudy and s. country EVELYN. **3.** A s. woman, who must have somebody to find fault with RICHARDSON. **4.** The overflowing of a s. moment 1775.

B. *sb.* **1.** One who has a splenetic disposition; a splenetic, peevish, or ill-humoured person 1703. **†2.** A splenetic medicine or remedy –1718. Hence **†Splene·tical** *a.* and *sb.*, **-ly** *adv.*

Splenial (splī·niăl), *a.* and *sb.* 1848. [f. L. *splenium* (Pliny) – Gr. σπλήνιον bandage or compress; see -AL¹.] *Zool.* and *Anat.* **A.** *adj.* **1.** *S. bone* or *piece*, a splint-like bone or process applied to the inner side of the lower mandible in certain classes of vertebrates below Mammalia. **2.** *S. border*, the posterior border of the corpus callosum 1891. **B.** *sb.* The splenial bone or process 1854.

Splenic (sple·nik), *a.* 1619. [– Fr. *splénique* (Paré) or L. *splenicus* – Gr. σπληνικός, f. σπλήν SPLEEN *sb.*; see -IC.] **1.** *Anat.* Of, pertaining to, connected with, or situated in the spleen. **b.** *S. flexure*, the bend of the colon near the spleen 1808. **2.** *Path.* Of diseases, etc.: Of or affecting the spleen; esp. *s. fever*, malignant anthrax 1867. Hence **†Sple·nical** *a.*

‖**Splenitis** (splĭnəi·tis). 1753. [– Gr. σπληνῖτις, f. σπλήν SPLEEN *sb.*; see -ITIS.] *Path.* Inflammation of the spleen, or a particular form of this.

‖**Splenius** (splī·niŏs). 1732. [mod.L., f. Gr. σπλήνιον; cf. SPLENIAL *a.*] *Anat.* A broad muscle, or either of the two portions (the *splenius capitis* and *colli*) composing it, which occupies the upper part of the back of the neck and is attached to the occipital bone.

Splenization (splenizē¹·ʃən). 1849. [– Fr. *splénisation*, f. L. *splen* SPLEEN *sb.*] *Path.* The conversion of substance into tissue resembling that of the spleen; *esp.* the diseased condition of the lungs when this has taken place.

Spleno- (splĭ·no) – Gr. σπληνο-, comb. form of σπλήν SPLEEN *sb.*, as in: **Sple·nocele**, a rupture of the spleen. **Spleno·graphy**, a description of the spleen. **Spleno·logy**, the science of the spleen. **Spleno·tomy**, dissection or anatomy of the spleen.

Spleuchan (splū·χăn). *Sc.* (and *Ir.*). 1785. [– Gael. *spliùchan*, Ir. *spliuchán*.] A tobacco pouch, freq. used as a purse.

Splice (spləis), *sb.* 1627. [f. the vb.] **1.** A joining or union of two portions of rope, cable, cord, etc., effected by untwisting and interweaving the strands at the point of junction. Chiefly *Naut.* **b.** *techn.* A joining of two pieces of wood, etc., formed by overlapping and securing the ends; a scarf-joint 1875. **2.** *slang.* Union by marriage; a marriage, wedding 1830.

attrib. and *Comb.*: **s.-grafting**, a method of grafting in which the scion and stock are cut obliquely and bound firmly together; whip- or tongue-grafting; hence **Splice-graft** *vb.*; **-joint**, the connecting joints between rails on railways; **-piece**, a fish-plate or break-joint piece at the junction of two rails.

Splice (spləis), *v.* 1524. [prob. – MDu. *splissen* (whence also Du. dial., G. *splissen*, *spleissen*), but agreeing in vocalism with G. *spleissen* in the same sense.] **1.** *trans.* To join (ropes, cables, lines, etc.) by untwisting and interweaving the strands of the ends so as to form one continuous length; to unite (two parts of the same rope) by interweaving the strands of one end into those of another part so as to form an eye or loop; to repair (rigging) in this way. Also *absol.* Chiefly *Naut.* **b.** To form (an eye or knot) in a rope by splicing 1773. **2.** To join (two pieces of timber, etc.) by overlapping or scarfing the two ends together in such a way as to form a continuous length; to fasten *together* in this way; to graft by a similar process 1626. **b.** *transf.* To unite in this manner by means of surgery or natural healing 1755. **c.** To unite, combine, join, mend 1803. **3.** *slang.* To join in matrimony; to marry. Chiefly *pass.* 1751.

1. Phr. *To s. the main-brace*: see MAIN-BRACE¹.

Spline (spləin), *sb.* 1756. [orig. E. Anglian dial.; perh. related to SPLINTER *sb.*] **1.** A long, narrow, and relatively thin piece or strip of wood, metal, etc.; a slat. **b.** *spec.* A flexible strip of wood or hard rubber used by draftsmen in laying out broad sweeping curves, especially in railroad work 1891. **2.** *techn.* A rectangular key fitting into grooves in a shaft and wheel or other attachment so as to allow longitudinal movement of the latter 1864. Hence **Spline** *v. trans.* to fit with a s. **Spli·ning** *vbl. sb.*, used attrib. in *splining-machine*, one for cutting key-seats and grooves.

Splint (splint), *sb.* ME. [– MLG. *splente*, *splinte*, MDu. *splinte* (Du. *splint*); rel. to SPLINTER *sb.*, but no cognates are known. In AL. *splinta* (XIII).] **1.** One of the plates or strips of overlapping metal of which certain portions of mediæval armour were sometimes composed; *esp.* one of a pair of pieces of this nature used for protecting the arms at the elbows. **2.** A slender, moderately long and freq. flexible, rod or slip of wood cut or cleft off and serving for some particular purpose, esp. as a lath or wattle, or prepared for use in some manufacture ME. **3.** A splinter of wood or stone; a chip or fragment. Now chiefly *n. dial.* late ME. **4.** *Surg.* A thin piece of wood, etc., used to hold a fractured or dislocated bone in position during the process of reunion; hence, any appliance serving this purpose. late ME. **5.** *Farriery.* A callous tumour developing into a bony excrescence on the metacarpal bones of a horse's or mule's leg, occurring usually on the inside of the leg along the line of union of the splint-bones with the cannon-bone 1523. **b.** The growth of this, as a specific malady in horses 1594. **6.** A laminated, coarse, hard coal. (See also SPLINT COAL.) 1789.

1. The knees and feet were defended by splints, or thin plates of steel, ingeniously jointed upon each other SCOTT.

Splint (splint), *v.* late ME. [f. the sb. Cf. AL. *splintare* (XIII) fit with laths.] **†1.** *trans.* To cover, furnish, or construct with splints or thin strips of wood, etc. –1639. **2.** To adjust, bind, or fit a surgical splint to (a fractured bone, etc.); to put into splints; to secure by means of a splint or splints 1543. **b.** *transf.* and *fig.* To strengthen or support as if with splints 1634. **†3.** To cut or split (wood, etc.) into splints or splinters; to cleave apart –1600.

Splint(-)bone. Also **†splent bone.** 1704. [SPLINT *sb.*] **1.** *Farriery.* **†a.** = SPLINT *sb.* 5. **b.** Either of the two metacarpal bones of the foreleg of a horse, lying behind and in close contact with the cannon-bone or shank. **2.** = FIBULA 2. 1859.

Splint coal. 1789. [Cf. SPLINT *sb.* 6.] Coal with a more or less splintery fracture; orig. a less bituminous variety of Scotch cannel coal; now chiefly, a hard and highly bituminous coal burning with great heat.

Splinter (spli·ntəɹ), *sb.* late ME. [– (M)Du. *splinter*, MDu. *splenter* = LG. *splinter*, *splenter*, rel. to SPLINT *sb.*] **1.** A rough (usu. comparatively long, thin, and sharp-edged) piece of wood, bone, etc., split or broken off, esp. as the result of violent impact; a chip, fragment, or shiver. **b.** Used (chiefly with negs.) to denote a very small piece or amount, or something of little or no value 1606. **2.** A surgical splint. *Obs.* or *dial.* 1597. **3.** A comparatively thin piece or slender strip of wood prepared or used for some particular purpose 1648. **b.** Used as a torch, or dipped in tallow and used as a candle 1751. **4.** *ellipt.* = SPLINTER-BAR 2. (*rare*) 1794.

1. The bomb,..a s. of which struck the lady 1711. Phr. *In* or *into splinters.* **b.** The Grecian Dames are sun-burnt, and not worth The s. of a Lance SHAKS. **3. b.** Perusing a hymn-book by the light of a pine s. 1862.

attrib. and *Comb.*: **s. net, -netting** *Naut.*, a net or netting of small rope spread on board a warship during action to protect the men from falling splinters; **-new** *a.* (*dial.*) quite new.

Splinter (spli·ntəɹ), *v.* 1582. [f. the sb.] **1.** *trans.* To break or split into splinters or long narrow pieces, or in such a way as to leave a rough jagged end or projections. **†2.** = SPLINT *v.* 2. Also with *up.* –1720. **3.** *intr.* To split 1625. **b.** *poet.* To pierce *through* in the form of, or after the manner of, splinters 1821.

1. A strong bull..splintered with his horns the upper post 1806. *fig.* The Courtier, Scholler, Souldier, all in him, All dasht and splinterd thence SHAKS. **3. b.** The moon..Splinters through the broken glass CLARE. Hence **Spli·nterless** *a.* that will not s.

Splinter-bar. Also **splinter bar.** 1765. [SPLINTER *sb.*] **1.** A swingle-tree or whipple-tree. **2.** A cross-bar in a carriage, coach, etc., which is fixed across the head of the shafts, and to which the traces are attached 1794.

Splinter-proof, *sb.* and *a.* 1805. [See PROOF *a.*] *Mil.* **A.** *sb.* A structure serving for protection from the splinters of bursting shells. **B.** *adj.* Of sufficient strength to ward off the splinters of bursting shells 1834.

Splintery (spli·ntəri), *a.* 1796. [f. SPLINTER *sb.* and *v.* + -Y¹.] **1.** *Min.* Of fracture: Characterized by the production of small splinters. **2.** Of stone, minerals, etc.: Liable to split into splinters; breaking or separating easily into splinters; *spec.* having a splintery fracture 1807. **b.** Of rocks, etc.: Marked by splintering; rough or jagged 1829. **3.** Of the nature of a splinter; resembling a splinter in shape or form 1839. **4.** Full of splinters 1857.

Split (split), *sb.* 1597. [f. SPLIT *v.* and *ppl. a.*] **1.** A narrow break or opening made by splitting; a cleft, crack, rent, or chink; a fissure. **b.** *techn.* An angular groove cut on glass vessels 1850. **2.** A piece of wood separated or formed by splitting. Now *U.S.* 1617. **b.** *techn.* In the leather trade, a section of a skin obtained by splitting it into several thicknesses 1858. **3.** A rupture, division, or dissension in a party or sect, or between friends 1729. **4.** *Mining.* A division of a ventilating air-current 1883. **5.** *slang.* An informer; a detective 1812. **6.** *colloq.* **a.** A split soda; a bottle of mineral water half the usual size 1884. **b.** A split roll or bun 1905. **c.** A split vote 1894.

The splits: the acrobatic feat of lowering oneself to the floor with the legs in a straight line 1861.

Split (split), *v.* Pa. t. and pa. pple. **split** (also **†splitted, †splitten**). 1590. [In earliest use naut., – (M)Du. *splitten*, obscurely rel. to *spletten*, whence earlier Eng. (dial.) *splet*, *spleet*, and to OFris. *splita*, MLG., MDu. *spliten*, MHG. *splīzen* (G. *spleissen* split, cleave); of obscure ult. origin.] **I.** *trans.* **1.** Of storms, rocks, etc.: To break up (a ship); to cause to part asunder. Chiefly in *pass.* **b.** Of persons: In *pass.*, to suffer shipwreck. Also *fig.* 1602. **2.** To divide longitudinally by a sharp stroke or blow; to cause to burst or give way along the grain or length; to cleave or rend 1593. **b.** *Naut.* Of wind: To rend or tear (a sail). Also of persons or a vessel: To have (a sail) rent or torn by the wind. 1625. **3.** *fig.* **a.** Of violent grief or pain 1594. **b.** Of loud noise 1602. **c.** Of excessive laughter 1687. **4. a.** To divide or apportion to, or between, two or more persons 1670. **b.** To divide or break up into separate parts or portions 1706. **c.** To divide or separate (persons) into parties, factions, groups, etc. 1712. **d.** To divide or separate by the interposition of something 1824. **5.** *slang.* To disclose, reveal, let out 1850.

1. Our helpefull ship was splitted in the midst SHAKS. **2.** At Cajeta, in Italy, a mountain was split in this manner by an earthquake GOLDSM. *fig.* Blow, and s. thyself SHAKS. **b.** We split our maintop-sail 1748. **3. a.** Let sorrow s. my heart, if euer I Did hate thee SHAKS. **b.** The air was split with shrill outcries 1865. **c.** He laughed ready to s. his sides 1809. **4. a.** Not worth splitting a guinea;..toss who shall pay for both DICKENS. **b.** He..falls to splitting his Text most methodically 1706. **c.** They are easily split into parties by intrigue 1861. **d.** Mrs. Williamson splits her infinitives 1895.

Phrases. *S. me* (or *my windpipe*), used as an imprecation. *To s. a hair* or *hairs, straws, words,* to make fine or subtle distinctions, to be over-subtle or captious. *To s. the difference,* to halve an amount in dispute between two parties; to take the mean between two sums or quantities; to compromise on this basis.

II. *intr.* †**1.** As predicate to *all*: To go to pieces –1611. **2.** Of a ship: To part or break by striking on a rock or shoal, or by the violence of a storm 1593. **b.** Of persons: To suffer shipwreck in this manner. Freq. *fig.* 1610. **3.** To part asunder, to burst, to form a fissure or fissures, esp. in a longitudinal direction 1625. **b.** Used hyperbolically to denote the effect of excessive laughter, pain, or repletion 1677. **c.** To admit of being cleft 1846. **4.** To part, divide, or separate in some way 1712. **b.** To break up into separate groups or parties 1824. **5.** To break up *into* factions, sects, etc.; to separate through disagreement or difference of opinion; to fall out or disagree 1730. **b.** *slang.* To break or quarrel *with* a person 1835. **6.** *slang.* To turn evidence or informer; to peach; to betray confidence 1795.

1. *Mids. N.* I. ii. 32. **2.** This is the most dangerous Rock to s. upon, in all the Archipelago 1718. **b.** Mercy on vs. We s., we s. SHAKS. **3. b.** I laugh'd till I thought I should s. SWIFT. My head was like to s. 1756. **c.** The wood splits clean and easy 1846. **4.** At the point where Hermon splits into its two parallel ranges 1856. **5.** 'Don't let us s. on a small point of detail,' he began 1890. **6.** If anybody is to s., I had better be the person DICKENS.

Split-, the verbal stem in combs., as **s.-farthing** *a.*, mean, miserly.

Split (split), *ppl. a.* 1648. [f. SPLIT *v.*] **1.** That has undergone the process of splitting; divided in this manner; riven, cleft. **b.** Of a surface: Exposed by splitting 1715. **c.** *Bot.* Cleft or divided very deeply 1832. **2.** Separated, divided, parted, or apportioned in some way 1839.

Special collocations: **s. brilliant,** a brilliant the foundation squares of which are divided horizontally into two triangular facets; **s. infinitive** (see INFINITIVE); **s. peas,** peas shelled, dried, and split for making pease-puddings, soup, etc.; **-pin,** a pin or cotter split at one end; **-ring,** a metal ring split spirally, on which keys, etc. may be hung; **s. second(s,** applied to chronographs having two independent centre second hands, one under the other; **-shot, -stroke,** in various games, a shot or stroke which sends in divergent directions two or more balls placed in contact; **-tail,** (*a*) a Californian fish of the carp family; (*b*) the pintail duck.

Splitter (spli·təɹ). 1623. [f. SPLIT *v.* + -ER[1].] One who, or that which, splits or cleaves, in various senses 1648. **b.** *spec.* One employed in splitting fish 1623.

Splodge (splǫdʒ). 1854. [Expressive alt. of SPLOTCH; cf. WODGE.] A thick, heavy, or clumsy splotch. Hence **Splo·dgy** *a.*

Splosh (splǫʃ), *adv.* 1901. [Blending of SPLASH and PLOP.] With a sudden noisy splash.

Splotch (splǫtʃ), *sb.* 1601. [perh. blend of SPOT and †*plotch* (XVI), BLOTCH.] A large irregular spot or patch of light, colour, or the like. Hence **Splotch** *v. trans.* to cover with splotches; to splash or stain in patches. **Splo·tchy** *a.* covered with or having the appearance of splotches.

Splurge (splǒɹdʒ), *sb. U.S.* 1834. [Of symbolic origin.] **1.** An ostentatious display or effort. **2.** A heavy splash or downpour 1879. So **Splurge** *v. U.S. intr.* (*a*) to make an ostentatious display, to show off; (*b*) to splash heavily.

Splutter (splɒ·təɹ), *sb.* 1677. [alt. of SPUTTER *sb.*, by assoc. with *splash.*] **1.** A noise or fuss. **b.** Violent and confused declamation, discourse, or talk; an instance of this 1688. **2.** A loud, or violent sputter or splash 1815.

1. b. Dinner..with a confused s. of German to the neighbours on my right HUXLEY. **2.** A couple of ducks..made away with a great s. 1873.

Splutter (splɒ·təɹ), *v.* 1728. [f. prec.] **1.** *trans.* To utter hastily and indistinctly 1729. **2. a.** To scatter in small splashes 1835. **b.** To bespatter (a person) 1869. **3.** *intr.* To talk or speak hastily and confusedly 1728. **4.** To make a sputtering sound or sounds 1818. **5.** Of a pen: To scatter ink in writing 1837. **6.** To fly in small splashes or pieces 1849.

1. King James spluttered out his alarm at Jesuit plots in clumsy Latin 1870. **4.** Waning candles s. in the sockets 1860.

Spode (spōᵘd). 1893. The surname of a maker of china, Josiah *Spode* (1754–1827), used *attrib.* to designate ware made by him. Also *ellipt.*, = Spode-ware.

‖**Spodium** (spōᵘ·diǒm). Now *rare.* late ME. [L. – Gr. σπόδιον, = σποδός ashes.] A fine powder obtained from various substances by calcination.

Spodo- (spǫ·do, spǫdǫ·), – Gr. σποδο-, comb. stem of σποδός ashes, dross, as in **Spodoge·nic** *a.*, **Spodo·genous** *a.*, *Path.* characterized by the production of waste organic matter. **Spo·domancy,** divination by means of ashes. **Spodoma·ntic** *a.*

Spodumene (spǫ·diumīn). Also **spodumen.** 1805. [– Fr. *spodumène*, G. *spodumen* (B. J. d'Andrada, 1800) – Gr. σποδούμενος, pr. pple. of σποδοῦσθαι be burnt to ashes, f. σποδός ashes.] *Min.* A silicate of aluminium and lithium, of varying colour, found both in crystals and massive.

Spoil (spoil), *sb.* ME. [Aphetic – OFr. *espoille*, f. *espoillier*; see next.] **I. 1.** Goods taken from an enemy or captured city in time of war; the possessions of which a defeated enemy is deprived by the victor; any goods, property, territory, etc., seized by force, acquired by confiscation, or obtained by similar means; booty, loot, plunder. **b.** *transf.* That which is or has been acquired by special effort or endeavour; esp. objects of art, books, etc. so acquired 1750. **c.** The public offices or positions of emolument distributed among the supporters of a successful political party on its accession to power. Chiefly *U.S.* and in *pl.* 1770. **2.** The action or practice of pillaging or plundering; rapine, spoliation. *Obs.* or *arch.* 1532. †**3.** A marauding expedition or raid –1646. **4.** An object or article of pillage, plunder, or spoliation; a prey 1594.

1. Why did they not..preserve the spoiles of the cloisters for publick and charitable uses? 1654. He led his army back..laden with the s. of Locris 1838. *fig.* New islands..are sometimes formed from the spoils of the continent GOLDSM. Phr. *The spoils of war.* **b.** But Knowledge to their eyes her ample page Rich with the spoils of time did ne'er unroll GRAY. **c.** My vote was counted in the day of battle, but I was overlooked in the division of the s. GIBBON. **2.** So was the citie of Constantinople..for that time saued from saccage and spoile 1603. Phr. *To make s. of,* to pillage or plunder. **4.** Oh, Greece! thy flourishing cities were a s. Unto each other 1821.

II. 1. The arms and armour of a slain or defeated enemy as stripped off and taken by the victor; a set or suit of these. Usu. *pl.* 1547. **b.** A single article acquired in this way 1697. **2.** The skin of a snake (or of any animal) stripped or cast off; the slough. Also *pl.* Now *Obs.* or *arch.* 1601. **b.** *pl.* The remains of an animal body; the parts left intact or uneaten 1695.

1. That Hector..Which erst returnd clad with Achilles spoiles 1547. **2.** Lige the old Skin, or Spoile of Serpents 1638. Skins of Beasts, the rude Barbarians wear; The Spoils of Foxes, and the furry Bear DRYDEN. **b.** Numbers of flies, whose spoils lay scattered before..his [the spider's] palace SWIFT.

III. 1. The action or fact of spoiling or damaging; damage, harm, impairment, or injury, esp. of a serious or complete kind. Now *rare.* 1572. †**2.** An act or instance of this –1722. **3.** *techn.* Earth or refuse material thrown or brought up in excavating, mining, dredging, etc. 1838.

1. Sir John Wallop..did much s. upon the French 1648.

Comb.: **spoils system,** the system or practice of a successful political party giving government or public offices, etc., to its supporters. Hence **Spoi·lsman** *U.S.*, one who obtains, or seeks to obtain, a share of political spoils.

Spoil (spoil), *v.* Pa. t. and pple. **spoiled, spoilt.** ME. [Aphetic – OFr. *espoillier* :– L. *spoliare*, f. *spolium*, pl. *-ia* skin stripped from an animal, booty; or aphetic f. DESPOIL *v.*] **I. 1.** *trans.* To strip or despoil (a dead or helpless person); *esp.* to strip (a defeated or slain enemy) of arms and armour. Now *arch.* **2.** To strip (persons) of goods or possessions by violence or force; to plunder, rob. Now *rare* or *arch.* ME. **3.** To pillage or plunder (a country, city, house, ship, etc.); to clear of goods or valuables by the exercise of superior force; to ravage or sack. Now *arch.* late ME. **4.** To seize (goods) by force or violence; to carry off as spoil; to rob or steal; to take away improperly. *arch.* late ME. **5.** *absol.* To commit or practise spoil or pillage; to plunder, ravage. *arch.* late ME.

1. The Greeks with shouts press on, and s. the dead POPE. **2.** Thy hands..have spoyl'd The hopelesse Widdow 1624. **3.** To slay the folk, and s. the land TENNYSON. **4.** No man can..spoile his goods, except he will first bind the strong man *Mark* 3:27. **5.** On this manner he went spoyling through Fraunce 1597.

II. 1. To strip (a person, body, etc.) *of* arms, clothes, or the like. Now *arch.* ME. **2.** To deprive, despoil, or rob *of* something, *of* some quality, distinction, etc. late ME.

2. When you do this, you s. it of every thing sublime BURKE.

III. †**1.** To destroy, bring to an end –1726. †**b.** To inflict serious bodily injury upon (an animal or person). Now merged in next. –1665. **2.** To damage, impair, or injure, esp. to such an extent as to render unfit or useless; to mar or vitiate completely or seriously 1563. **3.** With immaterial obj.: To affect injuriously or detrimentally, esp. to an irretrievable extent 1578. **4.** To injure in respect of character, esp. by over-indulgence or undue lenience. Also, to treat with excessive consideration or kindness. 1694. **5.** *intr.* To become unfit for use; to deteriorate; to go bad, decay 1692.

1. For Gods sake take a house, This is some Priorie, in, or we are spoyl'd SHAKS. **2.** A great flood, all grass spoyl'd 1692. **3.** If the sudden coming of the King of Barma, had not spoiled his markets 1652. Phr. *To s. all* or *everything.* **4.** I swear, my dear, you'll s. that child CONGREVE. **5.** Cargoes that are liable to s., such as all kinds of grain SOUTHEY. Phr. *To be spoiling for* (a fight, etc.), to long for, desire ardently (orig. *U.S.*). Hence **Spoi·lable** *a.* that may be spoiled; capable of being spoilt.

Spoil-, the stem of SPOIL *v.* in comb. with sbs., as **s.-five,** a round game of cards which is said to be 'spoiled' if no player wins three out of a possible five tricks; †**-paper,** a petty author; **-sport,** one who acts so as to spoil the sport or plans of others.

Spoilage (spoi·lėdʒ). 1816. [f. SPOIL *v.* + -AGE.] **1.** The action of spoiling; the fact of being spoilt. **2.** That which is or has been spoilt, *spec.* applied to sheets of paper which have been spoiled in printing 1888.

Spoil(-)bank. *local.* 1830. [f. SPOIL *sb.*] A bank or large mound consisting of refuse earth or similar waste material.

†**Spoi·lful,** *a.* 1590. [f. SPOIL *sb.* + -FUL.] Causing or characterized by destruction or pillage; plundering, spoliatory –1670.

Spoke (spōᵘk), *sb.* [OE. *spāca* = OFris. *spēke*, *spāke*, OS. *spěca*, OHG. *speihha* (Du. *speek*, G. *speiche*) :– WGmc. **spaika*, f. Gmc. **spaik-* **speik-* SPIKE *sb.*[2]] **1.** One of the set of staves, bars, or rods radiating from the hub or nave of a wheel and supporting the felloes or rim. Also *fig.*, esp. in ref. to the wheel of Fortune. **b.** One of a set of radial handles projecting from a cylinder or wheel (esp. a steering-wheel) 1648. **2.** A bar or rod of wood, esp. one used or shaped for a particular purpose; a stake or pole; a handspike; a weaver's beam 1467. **b.** A round or rung of a ladder, etc. 1658. **c.** A contrivance for locking a wheel in descending a hill 1858.

1. The wheel of fortune keeps turning for the comfort of those who are at the lowest s. 1834.

Phrases. *To put in one's s.*, etc., (*a*) to attempt to

give advice or have some say in a matter; (*b*) to attempt to advance a person's interests (*rare*). *To put a s. in* a person's *wheel*, to act in a manner calculated to thwart, obstruct, or impede his actions or purposes; so *a s. in* a person's *wheel*, an impediment or obstacle.

Comb.: **s.-bone** *Anat.*, = RADIUS 1 b.

Spoke (spōᵘk), *v.* 1720. [f. the sb.] **1.** *trans.* To furnish or provide with spokes or bars; to mark *with* spoke-like lines or rays. **2.** To thrust a spoke into (a wheel, etc.) in order to check movement; *fig.* to block, impede, or obstruct 1854. **3.** To force (a wheel or vehicle) *forward* by pushing the spokes 1860.

Spoken (spōᵘ·k'n), *ppl. a.* 1460. [pa. pple. of SPEAK *v.*] **1.** As the second element in combs.: Speaking or given to speaking in a specified way, as *broad-*, *civil-*, *out-*, *plain-spoken.* **2.** Of language, words, etc.: Uttered in speech, oral. Also, colloquial as dist. from *literary*. 1837. **b.** Expressed, declared, made known by speech or utterance 1851. **c.** Of a phrase in or in connection with a song: Uttered with the ordinary speaking voice; also *ellipt.* a phrase or part of this nature 1865.

2. b. There is a vast difference between the silent and the s. protest 1879. **c.** A comic song.. with 'S.' in it DICKENS.

Spokeshave (spōᵘ·kʃēⁱv), *sb.* 1510. [f. SPOKE *sb.* + SHAVE *sb.*¹] A form of drawing-knife or shave used for shaping and finishing spokes; a transverse plane. Hence **Spo·keshave** *v. intr.* to use a s.

Spokesman (spōᵘ·ksmǣn). 1540. [irreg. f. *spoke*, pa. pple. of SPEAK *v.*, after *craftsman*, etc.] **1.** One who speaks for or on behalf of another or others, *esp.* one deputed to voice the opinions of a body, etc.; a mouthpiece. **b.** *transf.* The chief representative or exponent *of* a movement, period, etc. 1828. **2.** A public speaker 1663.

1. He hath been an earnest s. in your cause 1585. **b.** Dante is the s. of the Middle Ages CARLYLE. **2.** There is many an excellent S. that makes a bad Writer 1693.

Spokeswoman (spōᵘ·kswu:măn). 1654. [Cf. prec.] A woman who speaks for another or others; a female advocate or representative.

Spoliate (spōᵘ·lieⁱt), *v.* 1722. [– *spoliat-*, pa. ppl. stem of L. *spoliare* SPOIL *v.*; see -ATE³.] *trans.* To spoil or despoil; to rob or deprive *of* something.

Spoliation (spōᵘliēⁱ·ʃən). late ME. [– L. *spoliatio*, *-ōn-*, f. as prec.; see -ION.] **1.** The action of spoliating; seizure of goods or property by violent means; depredation, robbery. Also, the condition of being despoiled or pillaged. **b.** An act or instance of despoiling or plundering; a robbery; an exaction of a spoliatory nature 1800. **2.** *Eccl.* A writ or suit brought by one incumbent against another holding the same benefice by an illegal or questionable title 1498. **b.** The action on the part of one incumbent of depriving another of the emoluments of a benefice 1726. **3.** *Law.* The action of destroying a document, or of injuring or tampering with it in such a way as to destroy its value as evidence 1752. **4.** The action of spoiling or injuring 1867.

1. He brought Rome into a state of poverty and s. hitherto unexampled 1832.

Spoliative (spōᵘ·liĕtiv), *a.* 1876. [f. SPOLIATE + -IVE. Cf. Fr. *spoliatif*, *-ive* in same sense.] *Med.* Having the effect of seriously diminishing the amount of the blood.

Spoliator (spōᵘ·lieⁱtəɹ). 1831. [f. SPOLIATE + -OR 2.] One who commits spoliation; a pillager; a spoiler.

Spoliatory (spōᵘ·liătəri), *a.* 1790. [f. as prec. + -ORY².] Of the nature of or characterized by, spoliation or robbery; pillaging, plundering.

Spondaic (spǫndē·ik), *a.* and *sb.* 1722. [– Fr. *spondaïque* or late L. *spondaicus*, alt. of *spondiacus* – Gr. σπονδειακός, f. σπονδεῖος SPONDEE.] **A.** *adj.* **1.** Of verses (or parts of these): **a.** Composed of spondees. **b.** Having a spondee in positions where a different foot is normal; *esp.* of hexameters, having a spondee in the fifth foot. **2.** Characterized by a spondee or spondees 1751. **3.** Of words: Consisting of two long syllables 1849. **B.** *sb.* A spondaic foot or line 1839.

Spondee (spǫ·ndī). late ME. †Also in L. form. [– (O)Fr. *spondée* or L. *spondeus* – Gr. σπονδεῖος subst. use (sc. πούς foot) of adj. f. σπονδή libation, the spondee being a foot characteristic of melodies accompanying libations.] *Pros.* A metrical foot consisting of two long syllables. Hence **Sponde·an** *a.* (*rare*).

Spondulicks (spǫndiū·liks). *slang.* orig. *U.S.* Also **-ics, -ix.** 1857. [Of unkn. origin.] Money, cash.

Spondyl(e (spǫ·ndil). Now *rare*. late ME. [– (O)Fr. *spondyle* or L. *spondylus* – Gr. σπ-, σφόνδυλος.] †**1.** One or other of the joints of the spine; a vertebra –1667. †**2.** A joint *of* a wheel, vessel, etc. –1662. **3.** *Zool.* = next 1668.

‖**Spondylus** (spǫ·ndilŏs). *Pl.* **-li.** 1601. [L.; see prec.] *Zool.* One or other of the species of bivalves belonging to the genus *Spondylus*, characterized by foliaceous spines.

Sponge (spɒnᵈʒ), *sb.*¹ Also †**spunge.** [OE. *sponge*, corresp. to OS. *spunsia* (Du. *spons*) – L. *spongia* – Gr. σπογγιά, f. σπόγγος, σφόγγος; reinforced in ME. by OFr. *esponge* (mod. *éponge*) – L.] **I. 1.** The soft, light, porous, and easily compressible framework which remains after the living matter has been removed from various species of porifers, characterized by readily absorbing fluids and yielding them on pressure, and much used in bathing, cleansing surfaces, etc. **2.** Without article: The material of which this is composed. late ME. **3.** *Zool.* One or other of various aquatic (chiefly marine) animals (or colonies of animals) of a low order, belonging to the group *Porifera*, characterized by a tough elastic skeleton of interlaced fibres 1538. **4.** A moistened piece of the above substance (sense 1) as used for wiping a surface in order to obliterate writing, etc. Also *fig.* 1555. **b.** A method of cancelling or wiping off debts without payment 1717. **5.** A kind of mop or swab for cleansing a cannon-bore after firing 1625.

1. Phr. *To throw up the s.* (of a boxer or his attendant) to throw the s. used between rounds into the air in token of defeat; *fig.* to submit or yield; to abandon a contest or struggle. **3.** The finest type of all, the Levant toilet or Turkish cup-sponge (*Spongia officinalis*) 1883. *Glass-sponge*, the genus *Hyalonema.* **4. b.** A spunge..is the only needful and only availing remedy BENTHAM. Phr. *To pass the s. over*, to agree to forget (an offence, etc.).

II. 1. a. = BEDEGUAR 2. 1608. **b.** The soft fermenting dough of which bread is made. Freq. in the phr. *to set* (or *lay*) *the s.* 1822. **c.** A stretch of ground of a swampy nature 1856. **d.** *techn.* Metal in a porous or sponge-like form, usu. obtained by reduction without fusion 1861.

III. *fig.* **1.** An immoderate drinker; a soaker 1596. **2.** One who or that which absorbs, drains, or sucks up, in a sponge-like manner 1603. **b.** *spec.* One who or that which appropriates or absorbs material or other advantages, wealth, etc.; a person of this kind as a source from which something may be recovered or extracted 1601. **c.** An object of extortion; a source of profit or pecuniary advantage 1625. **3.** A sponger 1838.

1. I will doe any thing Nerrissa ere I will be married to a spunge SHAKS. **2.** *Haml.* IV. ii. 12. He is a s. full of knowledge, which you may squeeze at your leisure 1779. **c.** Thy monarchs.. in distress Found thee a goodly s. for Power to press COWPER.

attrib. and *Comb.*, as *s.-bag*, *-bath*, *-bed*, *-fishery*; **s.-biscuit,** a biscuit of a similar composition to sponge-cake; **-cloth,** (*a*) a peculiar kind of cloth, moist with oil, for cleaning machinery and fire-arms; (*b*) a soft, loosely-woven fabric with a roughish surface; **-finger,** a long, narrow sponge-biscuit; **-gold,** gold as it remains after the silver has been removed in the process of 'parting'; **-iron,** iron ore rendered light and porous by the removal of foreign matter.

Sponge, *sb.*² 1693. [f. the vb.] **1.** The act of living parasitically on others. **2.** An act of wetting or wiping (off) with or as by means of a sponge 1720.

Sponge (spɒnᵈʒ), *v.* late ME. [f. SPONGE *sb.*¹, perh. partly after OFr. *esponger* (mod. *éponger*).] **I. 1.** *trans.* To wipe or rub with a wet sponge for the purpose of cleaning. **b.** To swab the bore of (a cannon), esp. after a discharge. Also *absol.* 1625. **c.** To wipe, wet, or moisten, *with* some liquid applied by means of a sponge 1800. †**2.** With *up*: To make spruce, smart, or trim –1626. **3.** To remove with a sponge 1624. **4.** To convert (flour or dough) into 'sponge' 1772. **5.** *intr.* To issue or rise in a spongy form; to foam 1790.

1. Planning how her..gown..might be sponged, and turned MRS. GASKELL. **c.** The patient should be..sponged with tepid water 1876. **5.** She did not even s. at her mouth 1867.

II. *fig.* **1.** To rub or wipe out; to efface or obliterate 1548. **2. a.** To drain or empty; to clear out (*rare*) 1610. †**b.** To deprive (a person) *of* something by sponging; to press (a person) *for* money; to squeeze –1724. **3.** To get from another in a mean or parasitic manner 1676. **4.** *intr.* To live *on* others in a parasitic manner; to obtain assistance or maintenance by mean arts 1673. **5.** To go about in a sneaking or loafing fashion, esp. in order to obtain something 1825.

1. Its gloom saturated the forest rim, and then sponged it out of sight 1887. **2. b.** Those Hogs hee must feed, till they spunge him of all his substance 1631. **3.** They spunged up my money while it lasted GOLDSM. **4.** Humbugs, ready to..s. upon his benevolence 1902.

Spo·nge-cake. 1808. [SPONGE *sb.*¹] A very light sweet cake made with flour, milk, eggs, and sugar.

Spongelet (spɒ·nᵈʒlét). 1835. [f. SPONGE *sb.*¹ + -LET.] **1.** *Bot.* = SPONGIOLE. **2.** A small sponge 1887.

Spongeous (spɒ·ndʒəs), *a.* late ME. [– L. *spongeosus*, f. *spongea* SPONGE *sb.*¹; see -EOUS.] **1.** Of the nature or character of a sponge; porous, spongy. **2.** Characterized by porousness or sponginess 1600.

Sponger (spɒ·ndʒəɹ). 1677. [f. SPONGE *v.* or *sb.*¹ + -ER¹.] **1.** One who lives meanly at another's expense; a parasite. **2.** One who uses a sponge, esp. in order to cleanse the bore of a cannon 1828. **3.** A gatherer of, a diver or fisher for, sponges 1880.

Spongi- (spɒ·ndʒi), comb. form, after L. types, of SPONGE *sb.*¹, as in **Spo·ngiculture, Spongi·ferous** *a.*, **Spo·ngiform** *a.*

Spongin (spɒ·ndʒin). 1868. [irreg. f. SPONGE *sb.*¹ + -IN¹.] = KERATOSE *sb.*

Sponginess (spɒ·ndʒinės). 1610. [f. SPONGY *a.* + -NESS.] **1.** Spongy or porous character, nature, or quality. **2.** *Path.* The characteristic soft fungous condition of the gums in scurvy 1873.

Sponging (spɒ·ndʒiŋ), *vbl. sb.* 1575. [f. SPONGE *v.* or *sb.*¹ + -ING¹.] **1.** The action of SPONGE *v.* **2.** The practice or occupation of gathering sponges 1868.

Spo·nging-house. 1700. [f. prec.] A house kept by a bailiff or sheriff's officer, formerly in regular use as a place of preliminary confinement for debtors.

His creditors..become more pressing, and at last he gets into a s. 1874.

Spongio- (spǫ·ndʒio), comb. form, on Gr. analogies, of Gr. σπογγιά, L. *spongia* SPONGE *sb.*¹, as in **Spongio·logist** (ǫ·lŏdʒist), **-logy,** = SPONGOLOGIST, -LOGY.

Spongiole (spɒ·ndʒ-, spǫ·ndʒioᵘl). 1832. [– Fr. *spongiole* (De Candolle) – L. *spongiola* asparagus-root, rose-gall, dim. of *spongia* SPONGE *sb.*¹] *Bot.* The tender extremity of the radicle of a plant, characterized by loose sponge-like cellular tissue.

Spongiopiline (spɒ:ndʒiopəi·ləin, -in). Also **-ene, -in.** 1851. [f. SPONGIO- + Gr. πῖλος felt + -INE⁵.] *Med.* Wool or cloth felted together with small pieces of sponge and having an impermeable back, used as a substitute for a poultice when moistened with hot water.

Spongiose (spɒ·ndʒioᵘs), *a.* 1755. [– L. *spongiosus*, f. *spongia* SPONGE *sb.*¹; see -OSE¹.] Of a spongy texture; porous.

Spongious (spɒ·ndʒiəs), *a.* Now *rare*. late ME. [– L. *spongiosus*; see prec., -OUS.] **1.** Of the nature of a sponge; spongy. **2.** Of or pertaining to a sponge 1846.

1. The s. bones of the upper jaw 1778.

Spongo- (spǫ·ŋgo, spǫŋgǫ·), – Gr. σπογγο-, comb. form of σπόγγος sponge, as in **Spo·ngoblast,** one of the pear-shaped cells which secrete the hyaline lamellæ in sponges.

Spongo·logist, an authority on sponges. **Spongo·logy,** the science or knowledge of sponges.

Spongoid (spǫ·ŋgoid), *a.* Also **spungoid.** 1808. [f. Gr. σπόγγος SPONGE *sb.*[1] + -OID.] **1.** *S. inflammation*, a kind of soft cancer or morbid growth. **2.** Having the form or structure of a sponge 1833. **3.** Like that of a sponge 1847.

Spongy (spɒ·ndʒi), *a.* 1539. [f. SPONGE *sb.*[1] + -Y[1].] **1.** Having a soft elastic or porous texture resembling that of a sponge; deficient in solidity or firmness, so as to be readily compressible. **2.** Of hard substances: Having an open porous structure resembling that of a sponge 1591. **3.** Resembling a sponge in respect of moisture or capacity for containing moisture; absorbent 1598. **4.** *fig.* Of diction or style: Deficient in substance or solidity 1603. **5.** Of texture or other qualities: Resembling that of a sponge 1611. **6.** Resembling that pressed from a sponge 1605.

1. The ground..being very spungy in wet weather 1677. The muscular, s. flesh of the tongue GOLDSM. Spungy rushes hide the plashy green CRABBE. **2.** A Splent is a spungy harde grissell or bone, growing fast on the inside of the shin-bone of a Horse 1607. This Ice becometh..spungy by the dashing of the Sea 1694. **3.** The spungy South SHAKS. There is no Lady..More spungie, to sucke in the sense of Feare SHAKS. **4.** To set a petty Gloss upon a spungy Conjecture 1665. **5.** The soil may be of a spungy nature 1765. **6.** With a s. moisture diffused through the atmosphere HAWTHORNE.

Sponsal (spǫ·nsăl), *a.* 1656. [– L. *sponsalis*, f. *sponsus, -a* spouse; see -AL[1].] Of or pertaining to marriage; spousal; wedded.

Sponsible (spǫ·nsĭb'l), *a.* Now *dial.* 1721. [Aphetic f. RESPONSIBLE *a.*] Responsible, reliable. Hence †**Sponsibi·lity** (*rare*).

Sponsion (spǫ·nʃən). 1632. [– L. *sponsio, -ōn-*, f. *spons-*, pa. ppl. stem of *spondēre* promise solemnly; see -ION.] **1.** A solemn or formal engagement, promise, or pledge, freq. one entered into or made on behalf of another person 1677. **b.** *International Law.* An engagement made on behalf of the supreme authority by a person not having a commission to make such engagement 1776. **2.** *Rom. Law.* An engagement to pay a certain sum to the other party in a suit, in the event of not proving one's case 1632. Hence †**Spo·nsional** *a.* entering into an engagement or pledge.

Sponson (spǫ·nsən), *sb.* 1835. [Formerly also *sponsing*; of unkn. origin.] **1.** *Naut.* One or other of the triangular platforms before and abaft the paddle-boxes of a steamer. **2.** A gun platform standing out from the side of a vessel 1862. Hence **Spo·nson** *v. trans.* to support, or set *out*, on a s.

Sponsor (spǫ·nsǫɹ), *sb.* 1651. [– L. *sponsor*, f. *spons-* (see SPONSION) + *-or* -OR 2.] **1.** *Eccl.* One who answers for an infant at baptism; a godfather or godmother. **2.** One who enters into an engagement on behalf of another; a surety 1677. **3.** A business firm or person who pays for a broadcast programme which introduces advertisements of a commercial product 1931.

Hence **Spo·nsor** *v. trans.* to be surety for, to support strongly; also in ref. to sense 3 above. **Spo·nsorship,** the state of being a s.; the office of a s.

Sponso·rial, *sb.* and *a.* 1797. [f. prec.; see -ORIAL.] **A.** *sb.* A baptismal sponsor 1836. **B.** *adj.* Of or pertaining to a sponsor 1797.

Spontaneity (spǫntănī·ĭti). 1651. [f. next + -ITY.] **1.** Spontaneous, or voluntary and unconstrained, action on the part of persons; the fact of possessing this character or quality. **2.** Spontaneous or voluntary action or movement on the part of animals (or plants); activity of physical organs in the absence of any obvious external stimulus 1721. **3.** The fact or quality in things of being spontaneous in respect of production, occurrence, etc. 1751. **b.** The fact or quality of coming without deep thought or premeditation 1826.

1. Actions performed without the s. of the agent, are automatic 1804. **3. b.** Poets who, delighted with the s. of their ideas, never reject any that arise 1839.

Spontaneous (spǫntē[i]·nĭəs), *a.* 1656. [f. late L. *spontaneus*, f. L. (*sua*) *sponte* of (one's) own accord, abl. of **spons*; see -OUS.] **1.** Arising, proceeding, or acting entirely from natural impulse, without any external stimulus or constraint; voluntary. **2.** Of motion: Arising purely from or entirely determined by the internal operative or directive forces of the organism 1659. **3.** Of natural processes: Having a self-contained cause or origin 1664. **4. a.** *S. generation*, the development of living organisms without the agency of pre-existing living matter, usually considered as resulting from changes taking place in some inorganic substance 1656. **b.** *S. combustion*, the fact of taking fire or burning away, through conditions produced within the substance itself; *spec.* the alleged occurrence of this fact in persons addicted to the excessive use of alcohol 1795. **5.** Growing or produced naturally without cultivation or labour 1665. **b.** Produced, developed, or coming into existence by natural processes or changes 1732. **6.** Quasi-*adv.* Spontaneously 1667.

1. That all voluntary actions,..are called also s., and said to be done by a man's own accord HOBBES. **2.** Vegetables..have in some instances s., though we know not that they have voluntary, motion 1807. **3.** Regions of s. fertility JOHNSON. **4. a.** The idea of a s. generation of organic bodies is now exploded 1857. The first and simplest plants had no ancestors; they arose by s. generation 1882. **b.** The s. combustion..of masses of tow, cotton, or rags saturated with oil 1863. **5.** When men lived on the s. fruits of the earth 1839. **6.** Chariots wing'd..now came forth S. MILT. Hence **Sponta·neous-ly** *adv.*, **-ness.**

Spontoon (spǫntū·n). Now *Hist.* 1708. [– Fr. †*sponton* (mod. *esponton*) – It. *spuntone*, f. *spuntare* blunt, f. *s-* EX-[1] + *punto* POINT *sb.*; see -OON.] A species of half-pike or halberd carried by infantry officers in the 18th c.

Spoof (spūf), *sb. slang.* 1889. [Invented by Arthur Roberts (1852–1933), comedian.] **1.** A game of a hoaxing and nonsensical character. Also, a round game of cards in which certain cards when occurring together are termed 'spoof'. **2.** Hoax, humbug; an instance of this 1897. **3.** *attrib.* Hoaxing, humbugging 1895. Hence **Spoof** *v. trans.* to hoax or humbug. **Spoo·fer. Spoo·fery.**

Spook (spūk). 1801. [– Du. *spook* = (M)LG. *spōk* (whence G. *spuk*), of unkn. origin.] A spectre, ghost. Hence **Spoo·kish** *a.*

Spool (spūl), *sb.* ME. [Aphetic – OFr. *espole* (mod. *époule*), or – its source, MLG. *spōle* = MDu. *spoele* (Du. *spoel*), OHG. *spuolo, -a* (G. *spule*); WGmc., of unkn. origin.] **1.** A small cylindrical piece of wood or other material on which thread is wound as it is spun, esp. for use in weaving; a bobbin. **b.** A reel 1852. **c.** Any cylinder on which cord, wire, tape, etc., is wound for convenience or for a special purpose 1864. **2.** A mesh-pin used in net-making 1838. **3.** *attrib.*, as *s.-stand, -ticket, -wheel* 1538.

Spool (spūl), *v. rare.* 1603. [f. prec.] **a.** *intr.* To wind spools. **b.** *trans.* To wind (thread) on spools. So **Spoo·ler,** one engaged in winding thread on spools 1554.

†**Spoom,** *v.* 1620. [Expressive alt. of SPOON *v.*[1]] *intr.* To run *before* the sea, wind, etc.; to scud –1830.

fig. When vertue spooms before a prosperous gale, My heaving wishes help to fill the sail DRYDEN. Hence **Spoo·ming** *ppl. a.* foaming.

Spoon (spūn), *sb.* [OE. *spōn* = MLG. *spān*, MDu. *spaen*, OHG. *spān* (G. *span* shaving), ON. *spónn, spánn*. Sense 2 is specifically Scand. (Norw. and Icel.).] †**1.** A thin piece of wood; a chip, splinter, or shiver –1513. **2.** A utensil consisting essentially of a straight handle with an enlarged and hollowed end-piece (the bowl), used for conveying soft or liquid food to the mouth, or employed in the culinary preparation or other handling of this (often distinguished as *dessert-, sugar-, tea-s.*) ME. **3.** An implement of the form described above, or something similar to this, used: **a.** As a surgical instrument. late ME. **b.** In melting, heating, or assaying substances 1496. **c.** A wooden golf-club having a slightly concave head 1808. **d.** A kind of artificial bait having the form of the bowl of a spoon, used in spinning or trolling 1851. **4.** The student last in each class in the list of mathematical honours at Cambridge; *spec.* the 'wooden spoon' (see WOODEN *a.*) 1824. **5.** *slang* or *colloq.* A shallow, simple, or foolish person; a simpleton, ninny, goose 1799.

2. A spone of golde, full of hony swete SKELTON. Phrases. *He should have a long s. that sups with the Devil. To be born with a silver s. in one's mouth*, to be born in affluence or under lucky auspices. *To make a s. or spoil a horn*, to make a determined effort to achieve something, whether ending in success or failure (orig. *Sc.*). †*S. of the brisket*, the hollow at the lower end of the breast-bone. **5.** Phr. *To be spoons with* or *on* (slang), to be sentimentally in love with (a girl).

Comb.: **s.-bait, -hook,** = sense 3 d; **-wood,** *Kalmia latifolia*, the Mountain Laurel of America.

Spoon, *v.*[1] *Obs.* exc. *arch.* 1576. [Of unkn. origin.] *Naut.* **1.** *intr.* In sailing, to run *before* the wind or sea; to scud. **2.** To move rapidly *on* or *upon* another vessel 1608.

1. He went spooning away large with the wind for one of the islands DE FOE.

Spoon (spūn), *v.*[2] 1715. [f. SPOON *sb.*] **I. 1.** *trans.* To lift or transfer by means of a spoon. **2.** In games: **a.** *Croquet.* To push (a ball) without an audible knock 1865. **b.** *Cricket.* To hit or lift (the ball) up in the air with a soft or weak stroke 1879. **c.** *Golf.* To hit (a ball) in putting so as to lift it 1896. **3.** *intr.* To lie close together, fit into each other like spoons 1887. **4.** *trans.* To hollow out, make concave, after the fashion of a spoon 1897.

1. *fig.* A pewter age,..An age of scum, spooned off the richer past E. B. BROWNING.

II. 1. *intr.* To make love, esp. in a sentimental or silly fashion. *colloq.* 1831. **2.** *trans.* To court or pay addresses to (a person), esp. in a sentimental manner 1877.

Spoonbill (spū·nbil). 1678. [f. SPOON *sb.* + BILL *sb.*[2], after Du. *lepelaar*, f. *lepel* spoon.] **1.** One or other of various species of birds belonging to the widely distributed genus *Platalea*, characterized by having a long spatulate or spoon-shaped bill; esp. the common white species, *P. leucorodia*. **b.** *pl.* The genus *Platalea* 1819. **2.** A spatulate or spoon-shaped bill 1802. **3.** The paddle-fish 1892.

Comb.: **S. duck,** the Scaup-duck; also, the Shoveller, *Spatula clypeata*. So **Spoo·n-billed** *a.*, having a spoon-shaped bill 1668.

Spoondrift (spū·ndrift). 1769. [f. SPOON *v.*[1] + DRIFT *sb.*] Spray swept from the tops of waves by a violent wind and driven continuously along the surface of the sea. Now commonly SPINDRIFT.

Spoonerism (spū·nəriz'm). 1900. [f. the name of the Rev. W. A. *Spooner* (1844–1930); see -ISM.] An accidental transposition of the initial sounds, or other parts, of two or more words.

Spoon-feed (spū·nfīd), *v.* 1615. [f. SPOON *sb.* + FEED *v.*] *trans.* To feed with a spoon. Chiefly *fig.*, esp. in *pa. pple.* **Spoo·n-fed,** fed with a spoon like a child or an invalid; artificially nourished or supported; encouraged by doles or the like.

Spoonful (spū·nful). ME. [f. SPOON *sb.* + -FUL.] As much as fills a spoon; such a quantity as can be lifted in a spoon. **b.** *transf.* A very small quantity or number 1531.

Throw this mixture by spoonfuls into a crucible 1800.

Spoo·n-meat. 1555. [f. SPOON *sb.* + MEAT *sb.*] Soft or liquid food to be taken with a spoon, esp. by infants or invalids. Also with *a* and *pl.*

A fortnight's s. reduced me to inanity 1884.

†**Spoo·nwort.** 1578. [f. SPOON *sb.*, after the L. name or Du. *lepelblad*.] The common scurvy-grass, *Cochlearia officinalis* –1760.

Spoony (spū·ni), *sb.* Also **spooney.** 1795. [f. SPOON *sb.* 5 + -Y[1].] **1.** A simple, silly, or foolish person; a noodle. **2.** One who spoons or is foolishly amorous 1857.

1. What the deuce can she find in that spooney? THACKERAY.

Spoony (spū·ni), *a.* Also **spooney.** 1812. [f. as prec. + -Y[1].] **1. a.** Of persons, etc.: Foolish, soft, silly. **b.** Of things: Characterized by foolishness or silliness 1843. **2.** Sentimentally or foolishly amorous 1836. **b.** Expressive of sentimental fondness 1882.

1. a. Then you think that Priests are bound to be mild and s.? 1876. They are not a bit a spooney couple 1882. Hence **Spoo·ni-ly** *adv.*, **-ness.**

Spoor (spūᵊɹ), *sb.* 1823. [– Du. *spoor* (in S. African use), repr. MDu. *spo(o)r* = OE.,

OHG., ON. *spor* (G. *spur*); rel. to SPEER *v.*[1]] **1.** The trace, track, or trail of a person or animal, esp. of a wild animal pursued as game. **b.** *collect.* (without article) 1850. **2.** The track of a vehicle 1850.

Spoor (spūᵊɹ), *v.* 1850. [f. prec. or – Du. *sporen.*] **1.** *trans.* To trace (an animal) by the spoor. **2.** *intr.* To follow a spoor or trail 1865. Hence **Spoo·rer**, a tracker.

Sporadic (spŏræ·dik), *a.* 1689. [– med.L. *sporadicus* – Gr. σποραδικός, f. σποράς, σποραδ- scattered, dispersed, f. base of σπορά sowing, seed. Cf. Fr. *sporadique.*] **1.** *Path.* Of diseases: Occurring only here and there; not epidemic. **2.** Scattered or dispersed in respect of locality or local distribution 1830. **b.** Occasional 1847. **c.** Of single persons or things: Accidental; isolated 1821. **3.** Characterized by occasional or isolated occurrence, appearance, or manifestation 1842.

1. A man who died of s. cholera 1845. 2. b. The continuance of s. troubles in Basutoland 1882. So **Spora·dical** *a.* 1654. **Spora·dically** *adv.*

Sporange (sporæ·ndʒ). 1857. [Anglicized f. *sporangium*, or – Fr. *sporange.*] *Bot.* = SPORANGIUM.

Sporangiophore (sporæ·ndʒiofōᵊɹ). 1875. [See next and -PHORE.] *Bot.* A structure bearing sporangia.

‖**Sporangium** (sporæ·ndʒiŏm). 1821. [mod.L., f. Gr. σπορά SPORE + ἀγγεῖον vessel; see -IUM.] *Bot.* A receptacle containing spores; a spore-case or capsule. Hence **Spora·ngial** *a.*

Spore (spōᵊɹ). 1836. [– mod.L. *spora* – Gr. σπορά sowing, seed; see SPORADIC.] **1.** *Bot.* One of the minute reproductive bodies characteristic of flowerless plants. **2.** *Zool.* and *Biol.* A very minute germ or organism 1876.

attrib., as *s.-capsule*, *-cell*, etc.; **-case** (*Bot.*), a receptacle containing spores; a sporangium.

Sporidiiferous (sporidii·fĕrəs), *a.* Also **sporidiferous.** 1836. [f. comb. form of next + -FEROUS.] *Bot.* Bearing sporidia.

‖**Sporidium** (spori·diŏm). 1821. [mod.L., dim. (after Gr. types) of σπορά SPORE.] *Bot.* **a.** A case or cell containing sporules. **b.** A sporule.

Sporiferous (spori·fĕrəs), *a.* 1836. [f. mod.L. *spora* SPORE + -FEROUS.] *Bot.* Bearing spores. So **Sporifica·tion,** the process of forming spores. **Spori·genous** *a.* producing spores.

Sporo- (spǫ·ro, sporǫ·), comb. form of Gr. σπορά SPORE, employed in many scientific terms relating to the spores of plants or elementary forms of animal life, as **Spo·ro-blast, -o·genous,** *a.* **-o·phorous,** *a.*

Spo·rocarp [Gr. καρπός fruit] *Bot.*, a fructification containing sporangia; a spore-case. **Spo·rocyst,** (*a*) *Zool.* a cyst or capsule containing spores, forming a stage in the development of Trematodes, etc.; (*b*) *Bot.* the spore-case of algals. **Spo·rophore,** (*a*) a spore-bearing process or stalk; (*b*) the asexual generation of plants. **Spo·rosac** *Zool.*, a simple form of gonophore.

Sporran (spǫ·răn). Also **sporan.** 1818. [– Gael. *sporan* = Ir. *sparán* purse, MIr. *sboran*, W. *ysbur* – L. *bursa* PURSE.] A pouch or large purse made of skin, usu. with the hair left on and with ornamental tassels, etc., worn by Scottish Highlanders in front of the kilt.

Sport (spōᵊɹt), *sb.* 1440. [Aphetic f. DISPORT *sb.*] **I. 1.** Pleasant pastime; amusement; diversion. †**b.** Amorous dalliance or intercourse –1796. **c.** *spec.* Pastime afforded by the endeavour to take or kill wild animals, game, or fish 1653. **d.** Participation in games or exercises, esp. those pursued in the open air; such games collectively 1863. **2.** Jest, jesting; mirth or merriment 1671.

1. Great s. to them was jumping in a sack 1821. c. The higher an angler goes up the Thames,..the more s...he will meet with 1787. 2. Thrice I deluded her, and turn'd to s. Her importunity MILT.

Phr. *In s.*, in jest or joke; not seriously. *To make s.*: (*a*) to provide entertainment or diversion; (*b*) to furnish oneself with, or find, recreation or diversion.

II. 1. A matter affording entertainment; a jest or joke 1450. **2.** An occupation or proceeding of the nature of a pastime or diversion 1526. **b.** *spec.* A game, or particular form of pastime, esp. one carried on in the open air 1523. **c.** *pl.* A series of athletic contests engaged in or held at one time and forming a spectacle or social event 1594. †**d.** A theatrical performance –1593. †**3.** *S. of nature*, = LUSUS NATURÆ –1827. **b.** A plant (or part of a plant), animal, etc., which exhibits abnormal variation from the parent stock or type in some respect, esp. in form or colour; a new variety produced in this way 1842. **4.** That with which one plays or sports; that which forms the sport *of* some thing or person 1667. **5.** One concerned with or interested in sport. **a.** *U.S. slang.* A gambler 1861. **b.** = SPORTSMAN 1, 3. 1873.

1. Especially, it is a S. to see, when a Bold Fellow is out of Countenance BACON. Phr. †*To make a s. of*, to make a jest of. 2. Your present kindness Makes my past miseries sports SHAKS. Phr. †*A s. of terms, wit, words*, a playing upon or trifling with terms, etc.; a passage or piece of writing characterized by this. b. In such a state of things hunting might be a s. FREEMAN. c. The Oxford and Cambridge Sports 1892. d. *Mids. N.* III. ii. 14. 4. The s. and prey Of racking whirlwinds MILT.

Comb. with *pl.*: **sports-car**, an open low-built fast motor car; **-coat, -jacket**, a loose-fitting coat or jacket such as is worn for some games.

Sport (spōᵊɹt), *v.* late ME. [Aphetic f. DISPORT *v.*] **I.** †**1.** *refl.* To amuse, recreate (oneself); to take one's pleasure. Also *transf.* of things. –1779. **2.** *intr.* To amuse or recreate oneself, *esp.* by active exercise in the open air; to take part in some game or play; to frolic or gambol. Also *transf.* and *fig.* 1483. **b.** To engage in or practise field-sports, etc.; to hunt or shoot for sport or amusement 1812. **3.** To indulge in sport, fun, or ridicule *at*, *over*, or *upon* a person or thing 1533. **b.** To deal *with* in a light or trifling way; to trifle, dally, or play *with* something 1630. **4.** †**a.** Of Nature: To produce or develop abnormal or irregular forms or growths as if in sport –1769. **b.** Of plants, animals, etc.: To vary abnormally from the parent stock or specific type; to exhibit or undergo spontaneous mutation 1768. †**5.** *trans.* To amuse or divert (a person); to provide with sport; to cheer, enliven –1763. **6.** To pass (time) in sport or amusement 1760. **7.** To take or cast *away* in or as in sport; to scatter or squander. Now *rare.* 1713.

2. See the Children s. upon the shore WORDSW. The wind sported with her gown HAWTHORNE. b. Any fellow who has sported on the estate at Bradford Wood 1812. 3. I find there simple folke, at whom I maie s. 1533. b. My misery is too great to be sported with 1861. 4. b. All flowers, as we know, easily s. a little in colour 1882. 6. Laughing and sporting Life away 1760. 7. He had sported away thirty thousand lives 1778.

II. In slang or colloq. uses. †**1.** To invest or stake (money) in some sport or in a highly speculative undertaking; to bet or wager. Also, to lay or make (a bet). –1850. **b.** To spend (money) freely or extravagantly and with ostentation 1859. **2.** To display or exhibit, esp. in public or company. Freq. with implication of some degree of parade. 1712. **b.** To display on the person; to wear 1778. **c.** To set up, go in for, keep, support, or use (a carriage, etc.) 1806. **3.** To keep (one's door) shut as a sign that one is absent or does not wish to be disturbed; now only in Univ. slang. *to s. one's oak.* Also formerly *refl.* and *pass.* of a person. 1785. **4.** To entertain or treat (a person) with food or drink by way of compliment or hospitality (*rare*) 1828.

1. The chaps will win your money as sure as you s. it THACKERAY. 2. If a man..sports loose views on morals at a decent dinner party,..he is not invited again FROUDE. b. Sported my Peninsular medal this day at the Queen's Levée 1849. c. We hope some day to s. buttons 1858. 3. His door was always sported; he had but little intercourse with the other Fellows 1889.

Sporter (spōᵊ·ɹtəɹ). 1611. [f. SPORT *v.* + -ER[1].] One who is given to or takes part in sport of any kind; a gamester; a sportsman or sporting man.

The beast [a horse] was too keen a s. to choose any other way than that which the stag followed 1751.

Sportful (spōᵊ·ɹtfŭl), *a.* late ME. [f. SPORT *sb.* + -FUL.] **1.** Yielding sport; having an element of recreation, play, or frolic. **b.** Devised or carried on merely in sport; not serious 1601. **c.** Of movements: Lively, frolicsome 1691. **2.** Of persons, their minds, etc.: Having an inclination or tendency to engage in sport or play; sportive, playful. Also of animals, etc. 1593.

1. A young fool, bent on s. pursuits instead of serious CARLYLE. b. Though 't be a sportfull Combate, Yet in this triall much opinion dwels SHAKS. c. The s. leap of a trout 1848. 2. The s. fawn 1768. They who were then s. on the green are now serious in the church CARLYLE. Hence **Spo·rtful-ly** *adv.*, **-ness.**

Sporting (spōᵊ·ɹtiŋ), *vbl. sb.* 1480. [f. SPORT *v.* + -ING[1].] The action of the verb; an instance or occasion of this.

attrib. and *Comb.*, as *s. celebrity*; *s. magazine*; *s. dog, gun*; also, **s. box**, a small residence for use during the sporting season; **-house**, a house, hotel, or inn frequented by sportsmen; *U.S.* a betting or gambling house; a brothel or disorderly house.

Sporting (spōᵊ·ɹtiŋ), *ppl. a.* 1600. [f. SPORT *v.* + -ING[2].] In the senses of the verb.

Special collocations: **s. chance** *colloq.*, a chance such as is met with or taken in sport; one of an uncertain or doubtful nature; so *s. offer*; **s. man**, now used to denote a sportsman of an inferior type or one who is interested in sport from purely mercenary motives. Hence **Spo·rtingly** *adv.*

Sportive (spōᵊ·ɹtiv), *a.* 1590. [f. SPORT *sb.* or *v.* + -IVE.] **1.** Inclined to jesting or levity. **b.** Characterized by lightness or levity; not serious 1593. **2.** Of the nature of or inclined to amorous sport or wantonness. *arch.* 1594. **3.** Disposed to be playful or frolicsome 1637. **4.** Of or pertaining to, marked or characterized by sport; of the nature of sport or amusement; affording or providing diversion 1705. **b.** Undertaken, given, etc., in (mere) sport 1743. **5.** Produced in or as in sport; *spec.* of the nature of a sport or abnormal variation; anomalous. Now *rare* or *Obs.* 1796. **b.** Of plants, etc.: Liable to vary from the true type 1850.

1. I am not in a sportiue humor now: Tell me, and dally not, where is the monie? SHAKS. b. Severall select Pieces of s. Wit 1655. 2. *Rich. III*, I. i. 14. 3. A shoal of s. dolphins 1762. 4. b. It was now not a s. combat, but a war to the death MACAULAY. Hence **Spo·rtive-ly** *adv.*, **-ness.**

Spo·rtless, *a.* 1621. [f. SPORT *sb.* + -LESS.] Destitute or devoid of sport; marked by the absence of sport.

Sportsman (spōᵊ·ɹtsmæ̆n). 1706. [f. SPORT *sb.*] **1.** A man who follows, engages in, or practises sport; esp. one who hunts or shoots wild animals or game for pleasure. **2.** *U.S.* A gambler, betting man 1848. **3.** *transf.* One who displays the typical good qualities of a sportsman 1894. Hence **Spo·rtsmanlike** *a.* resembling a s.; like that of a s.; consonant with the character or conduct of a s. **Spo·rtsmanship,** skill in, or knowledge of, sport; conduct characteristic or worthy of a s. So **Spo·rtswo:man.**

Sporulate (spǫ·riŭleⁱt), *v.* 1885. [f. SPORULE + -ATE[3].] **1.** *trans.* To convert into spores. **2.** *intr.* To form spores or sporules 1891. So **Sporula·tion,** conversion into spores; spore-formation 1876.

Sporule (spǫ·riul). 1819. [– Fr. *sporule* or mod.L. *sporula* (Hedwig); see SPORE, -ULE.] **1.** *Bot.* and *Zool.* A spore or spore-granule. **2.** *fig.* A germ 1861. Hence **Sporuli·ferous** *a.*

Spot (spǫt), *sb.* ME. [perh. – MDu. *spotte*, LG. *spot*, corresp. to ON. *spotti* small piece, bit (Norw. *spott* speck, spot, plot of ground), obscurely rel. to OE. *splott* spot, plot of land.] **I. 1.** *fig.* A moral stain, blot, or blemish; a stigma or disgrace. Also applied to persons. **2.** A small discolouring or disfiguring mark; a speck or stain ME. **3.** In special senses: †**a.** A mark or speck on the eye; also, a disease characterized by this –1639. **b.** An eruptive or other disfiguring mark on the skin. late ME. **c.** A dark mark on the face of the sun, moon, or a planet. (Cf. *sun-spot.*) 1605. **d.** A discoloration produced by various fungi upon the leaves or fruit of a plant 1852.

1. Spottes they are and filthynes TINDALE 2 *Pet.* 2:13. This s. of synne god dothe away 1526. Sublimely mild, a Spirit without s. SHELLEY. 2. The Moone was like a glasse all voyd of s. 1591. An innocent hand, Not painted with the Crimson spots of blood SHAKS. 3. c. The spots, which have served for determining the period of the rotation of Mars 1854.

II. 1. A small, usu. roundish, mark of a

different colour from the main surface ME. †**b.** A patch worn on the face; a beauty-spot –1735. **2.** A variety of domestic pigeon, having white plumage with a spot of another colour above the beak 1672. **b.** A spotted textile material 1798. **c.** *U.S.* The red fish or red drum 1882. **3.** *Billiards.* **a.** One or other of the marked places on a billard-table, esp. the one at the upper end on which the red ball is placed. **b.** *ellipt.* The spot-ball, or the person who plays it; a spot-stroke, or the score obtained by this 1844.

1. Like as the man of Inde maye chaunge his skynne, & the cat of the mountayne hir spottes COVERDALE *Jer.* 13:23. Phr. *To knock* (*the*) *spots off* or *out of*, to beat thoroughly (orig. *U.S.*).

III. 1. A small piece, amount, or quantity; a particle, a drop. Usu. with *of*. late ME. †**b.** A piece *of* work –1821. **c.** A drop *of* liquor; hence, a small amount *of*. *slang* or *colloq.* 1885. **2.** A particular place or locality of limited extent. late ME. **b.** A small space or extent *of* ground, etc. 1440. **3.** A particular small area, part, or definite point in any surface or body 1827. **4.** *Comm.* **a.** *ellipt.* as *adv.* At immediate cash rates; for cash payment 1884. **b.** *pl.* and *collect. sing.* Goods at immediate cash rates 1890.

1. A few spots of rain 1881. **2.** The most pleasant s. in Italy EVELYN. Phr. **On** (or **upon**) **the s.: a.** Without having time to move from the place; straightway, at once. **b.** At the very place in question. **c.** Doing exactly what is necessary. **d.** In a position prearranged for one's assassination. *U.S. slang. Off the s.*, inexact, irrelevant. **b.** Lab'ring well his little S. of Ground DRYDEN. **3.** *Soft, sore, tender s.*, a point on which one is touchy or easily affected; Mr. Ambrose touched a very tender s. in Camilla's heart 1887. **4. a.** Linseed oil..s...18s. 7½d. 1884.

attrib. and *Comb.*, as *s.-break, -stroke; s. cash, price, sale*; **s.-barred** *a. Billiards*, (a game) in which only one winning hazard is allowed to be made in the top pockets; **-lens,** a lens having the central portion obstructed by a s.; **s. light,** a light that is or can be played upon a particular s.; also as vb., to direct a spot light upon; **s. pigeon** = sense II. 2.

Spot (spǫt), *v.* late ME. [f. prec.] **I. 1.** *trans.* To stain, sully, or tarnish, in respect of moral character or qualities. †**b.** To asperse or vilify –1718. **2.** To mark with spots; to stain in spots 1440. **3.** *intr.* To be liable to spots; to become spotted 1879.

1. Who might be spotted merely with the errors introduced by Luther 1855. **2.** It spotteth and staineth the linnen so mightily, as that such staines will neuer be got out 1600.

II. 1. *trans.* To mark, cover, or decorate with spots 1591. †**b.** To ornament (the face) with a patch or patches –1711. **c.** *U.S.* To mark (a tree) by cutting out a piece of the bark 1792. **2.** To form or appear as spots upon (a surface); to stud 1801. **3.** *Billiards.* To place (a ball) on some particular spot 1844. **4.** *impers.* of rain falling in scattered drops 1849.

2. Many ships spotting the dark blue deep SHELLEY.

III. 1. *Cant.* To mark or note as a criminal or suspected person 1718. **2.** *colloq.* **a.** To single out beforehand (the winner in a race) 1857. **b.** To catch sight of; to recognize or detect; to mark or note the position of 1860.

1. At length he became 'spotted'. The police got to know him. 1851. **2. a.** I spotted a few winners 1888. **b.** *spec.* (*Mil.*) To locate (the fall of a shot or an enemy position) 1914.

Spotless (spǫ·tlės), *a.* late ME. [f. SPOT *sb.* + -LESS.] **1.** Free from spot or stain; of a pure or uniform colour. **2.** *fig.* Immaculate, pure 1577.

1. Vntrodden snow is not so s. 1606. **2.** How have ye..banisht from mans life..Simplicitie and s. innocence MILT. Hence **Spo·tless-ly** *adv.*, **-ness.**

Spotted (spǫ·tėd), *a.* and *ppl. a.* ME. [f. SPOT *sb.* and *v.* + -ED.] **1.** Marked or decorated with spots. **b.** *Mining.* Having the ore irregularly distributed through the workings 1874. **2.** Disfigured or stained with spots 1532. **b.** *fig.* Morally stained or blemished 1522. **c.** Marked, suspected 1864.

1. *S. Dick* (colloq.), a boiled pudding with currants in it; plum-duff. *S. dog*, (*a*) a white dog with black spots; (*b*) = s. Dick. *S. fever*, a fever characterized by the appearance of spots on the skin; now *spec.* epidemic cerebro-spinal meningitis, and typhus or petechial fever. So *s. death, pestilence, sickness*. Often in specific names of animals and plants. **b.** The ground is s. and very rich in places 1874. Hence **Spo·ttedness,** s. quality or state.

Spotter (spǫ·təɹ). 1611. [f. SPOT *v.* or *sb.* + -ER¹.] **1.** One who makes spots. **2.** *U.S.* A spy or detective, esp. one employed by a company to keep watch on employees, or one who watches for infringements of the prohibition-laws 1878. **3.** In target practice, one who notes the point where a shot strikes; one who 'spots' the position of a naval or military unit, etc. 1893. **4.** An aviator detailed to locate enemy positions 1914.

Spotty (spǫ·ti), *a.* ME. [f. SPOT *sb.* + -Y¹.] **1.** Full of, marked with, spots; spotted. **2.** Patchy; lacking in uniformity or harmony 1812. **3.** Occurring in spots; characterized by such occurrence 1821. **Spo·tti-ly** *adv.*, **-ness.**

Spou·sage. *Obs.* exc. *arch.* ME. [Aphetic f. AFr. *esposage*, OFr. *espousage* (cf. ESPOUSAGE), f. *espo(u)ser* SPOUSE *v.*] **1.** Wedlock. **2.** = next 2. ME.

Spousal (spau·zăl), *sb.* ME. [Aphetic f. OFr. *espo(u)saille* (freq. in pl.); see ESPOUSAL.] †**1.** The condition of being espoused or married; the married state; wedlock –1621. **2.** The action of espousing or marrying; the celebration of a marriage or betrothal; an instance or occasion of this. Freq. in pl. Now *arch.* ME.

2. My hoped day of spousall shone SPENSER. With the morrow the Church blessed the spousals 1874.

Spousal (spau·zăl), *a.* 1513. [attrib. use of prec.] **1.** Of, pertaining or relating to, espousal or marriage; nuptial, matrimonial. **2.** Of a hymn, poem, etc.: Celebrating or commemorating an espousal or marriage 1596.

1. There shall we Consummate our Spousall rites SHAKS. So **Spou·sally** *adv.* 1501.

Spouse (spauz), *sb.* [Early ME. *spūs(e* – OFr. *spus, spous* masc., *spuse, spouse* fem., aphetic vars. of *espous, espouse* (mod. *époux, épouse*) :- L. *sponsus* bridegroom, *sponsa* bride, subst. uses of masc. and fem. pa. pple. of *spondēre* betroth.] **1.** A married woman in relation to her husband; a wife; †a bride. **2.** A married man in relation to his wife; a husband; †a bridegroom ME. **3.** *fig.* In religious use: **a.** Applied to the Church, or to a woman who has taken religious vows, in relation to God or Christ ME. **b.** Applied to God or Christ in relation to the Church (or its members), or to women of religion ME.

1. So qualified, as may beseeme The S. of any noble Gentleman SHAKS. **2.** The lady thus address'd her s. COWPER. **3. a.** Their..religious sister..a moste chaste s. of Christ 1610. The Church, the holy s. of God 1827. Hence †**Spousess.**

Spouse (spauz), *v. Obs.* exc. *arch.* ME. [Aphetic – OFr. *espus-*, *espo(u)ser*; see ESPOUSE *v.*] †**1.** *trans.* To join in marriage or wedlock. Chiefly in *pass.* –1667. **2.** To give in marriage; to promote or procure the marriage of; to marry (*esp.* a woman *to* a man) ME. **3.** To take (a woman) as a wife; to marry, wed ME.

1. It was not lawfull for a Christian woman and virgin to be maried, or spoused to a paynime 1565. **2.** I haue spoused you to one husband 1565. **3.** To Faerie land; Where he her spous'd, and made his ioyous bride SPENSER.

†**Spou·se-breach.** ME. [f. SPOUSE *sb.* + BREACH *sb.*] Adultery –1637.

Spousehood (spau·zhud). Now *arch.* ME. [f. SPOUSE *sb.* + -HOOD.] The married state; matrimony; wedlock.

Spouseless (spau·zlės), *a.* 1460. [f. SPOUSE *sb.* + -LESS.] **1.** Of a person: Having no spouse; bereaved or deprived of a spouse. **2.** Characterized by the absence of a spouse 1812.

Spout (spaut), *sb.* late ME. [corresp. to Flem. *spuyte*, Du. *spuit*, but prob. immed. f. SPOUT *v.*] **I. 1.** A pipe by which rain-water is carried off or discharged from a roof. **b.** A pipe or similar conduit through which water or other liquid flows and is discharged. late ME. †**c.** = SPOUT-HOLE 1. –1774. **d.** *Mining.* A short passage connecting an air-head with a gate-road 1839. **2.** A tubular or lip-like addition to, or projection from, a vessel to facilitate the pouring out of liquid from it 1444. **3.** A contrivance having the form of a trough or box with open ends by which flour, grain, coals, etc., are discharged from or conveyed to a receptacle; a shoot 1557. **4.** A lift formerly in use in pawnbrokers' shops, up which the articles pawned were taken for storage. Also *transf.*, a pawnshop. 1837.

1. A S...from the Roof down to the Ground, to carry off..the Water 1823. **b.** She dreampt..she saw my Statue, Which like a Fountaine with an hundred spouts Did run pure blood SHAKS. **4.** Phr. *To put* (or *shove*) *up the s.*, to pawn. *Up the s.* Pawned, pledged; also *fig.*, in a hopeless condition.

II. 1. A waterspout 1555. **b.** A heavy downpour (*of* rain). Now *rare.* 1648. **2.** A discharge of water or other liquid, in some quantity and with some degree of force, from the mouth of a pipe or similar orifice 1500. **b.** *Agric.* A spring of water forcing its way up through the soil 1791. **c.** The column of spray thrown into the air by a whale in the act of respiration 1650. **3.** An outpour or rush of water falling from a higher to a lower level, esp. in a detached stream; a waterfall or cascade of this kind 1700. **b.** A similar fall of earth or rock 1883.

1. The dreadfull s., Which Shipmen doe the Hurricano call SHAKS. **2. c.** Its s...flashes up from the ocean just like smoke 1850.

Comb.: **s.-fish,** a mollusc which spouts or squirts out water, *esp.* a razor-fish; **-shell** *Zool.* any shell of the genus *Aporrhais* or family *Aporrhaidæ*; **-whale,** a spouting whale. Hence **Spou·tless** *a.* deprived of a s., having no s. **Spou·ty** *a.* given to spouting or discharging water.

Spout (spaut), *v.* ME. [– MDu. *spouten* (Du. *spuiten*), f. imit. base **spūt-*, repr. also in ON. *spýta* spit.] **I.** *intr.* **1.** To discharge a liquid or other substance in a copious jet or stream; to gush with water, blood, etc. **b.** *spec.* Of a whale: To throw up spray in the act of respiration; to blow 1796. **2.** Of liquids: To issue with some force and in some quantity from a narrow orifice; to spurt copiously. Also with *out* or *up*. 1500. **3.** *fig.* To engage in declamation or recitation; to make a speech or speeches, esp. at great length or without much matter 1756.

2. A ribbon of white surf, which spouts up in pillars of foam 1885. **3.** The far-sounding Street-orators cease, or s. milder CARLYLE.

II. *trans.* **1.** To discharge, cast out, or pour forth (water, etc.) in a stream of some force or volume. Also with *out* or *up*. ME. **2.** To wet or drench by a stream of liquid 1575. **3.** To utter readily or volubly; to talk (a language); to declaim or recite 1594. **4.** [f. SPOUT *sb.*] To pawn. *slang.* 1811. **5.** To fit or furnish with spouts 1853.

1. Who kepte Ionas in the fisshes mawe Til he was spouted vp at Nynyuee? CHAUCER. The Parish Engine spouts excessive Streams To quench the Blaze 1739. **3.** Pray s. some French BEAUM. & FL. I heard Macaulay s. the first chapter of Isaiah RUSKIN. **4.** The dons are going to s. the college plate HUGHES.

Spouter (spau·təɹ). 1760. [f. SPOUT *v.* + -ER¹.] **1.** A spouting whale 1830. **b.** A whaling-vessel 1840. **2.** †**a.** A reciter or amateur actor –1809. **b.** A fluent or voluble declaimer or speaker 1782. **3.** A spouting oil-well 1886.

Spou·t-hole. 1694. [f. SPOUT *v.*] **1.** The blow-hole or spiracle of a whale or other cetacean. **2.** A natural opening in rocks through which the sea spouts 1849.

Sprack (spræk), *a.* Chiefly *dial.* 1747. [var. of SPRAG *a.*] Brisk, active; alert, smart; in good health and spirits.

Sprag (spræg), *sb.*¹ 1706. [Of unkn. origin.] †**1.** A lively young fellow. **2. a.** A young salmon 1790. **b.** A young cod 1875.

Sprag, *sb.*² 1841. [Of unkn. origin.] **1.** *Mining.* A prop used to support the coal or roof during the working of a seam. **2.** A stout piece of wood used to check the revolution of a wheel (or roller), usually by inserting it between two of the spokes 1878; also, in an early motor vehicle, a device for preventing it from running downhill on a steep incline 1902.

Sprag, *a. rare.* 1598. [Of unkn. origin.] Smart, clever. (Only in Shaks. and imitators.)

M. Pag. He is a better scholler then I thought he

was. *Eu.* He is a good sprag-memory. *Merry W.* IV. i. 84.

Sprag, *v.* 1841. [f. SPRAG *sb.*^{2}] **1.** *trans.* To prop up or sustain (esp. coal in a mine) with a sprag or sprags. **2.** To check or stop (a wheel) by inserting a sprag 1878.

Sprain (sprē^{i}n), *sb.* 1601. [prob. f. SPRAIN *v.*] **1.** A severe wrench or twist of the ligaments or muscles of a joint, causing pain and swelling of the part. **2.** Without article: The condition of being sprained 1805.

2. The analogy of common s. to gout 1805.

Sprain (sprē^{i}n), *v.* 1622. [Of unkn. origin.] *trans.* To wrench or twist (a part of the body) so as to cause pain or difficulty in moving.

He would see my leg. It was sprained sore, and swelled at the ankle. READE.

Spraints, *sb. pl.* late ME. [– OFr. *espreintes* (mod. *épreintes*), subst. use of fem. pa. pple. of *espraindre* squeeze out, for earlier **espriembre* :– Rom. **expremere*, for L. *exprimere* EXPRESS.] The excrement of the otter.

Sprat (spræt), *sb.* 1597. [Later var. of †*sprot*, OE. *sprot* = MLG., (M)Du. *sprot* (whence G. *sprotte*), of unkn. origin. For the vocalism cf. STRAP *sb.*] **1.** A small sea-fish, *Clupea sprattus*, common on the Atlantic coasts of Europe. **b.** *collect.* Fish of this species 1611. **2.** One or other of various small fishes, usually one resembling a sprat 1603. **3.** *fig.* **a.** Applied to persons, usually as a term of contempt 1601. **b.** In phrases denoting the venturing of a small expenditure in the hope of a large gain 1810. **4.** *slang.* A sixpence 1839.

3. a. When his disguise and he is parted, tell me what a s. you shall finde him SHAKS. **b.** Give a S. to catch a Mackarel 1864.

Comb.: **s.-borer,** the young of the Red-throated Diver, *Colymbus septentrionalis*; **-diver** (see DIVER); **-loon,** the Speckled Diver; **-mowe,** the herring-gull. Hence **Sprat** *v. intr.* to fish for sprats.

Spra·t-ba:rley. 1523. [perh. f. SPRAT *sb.*] A species of barley, *Hordeum zeocriton*, with short broad ears and long awns.

Sprawl (sprǭl), *sb.* 1719. [f. SPRAWL *v.*] **1.** The, or an, act of sprawling; an awkward or clumsy spreading out of the limbs. **b.** A straggling array or display *of* something 1827. **2.** *dial.* and *U.S.* Activity, energy, go 1888.

1. To the iron porch they glide, Where lay the Porter, in uneasy s. KEATS.

Sprawl (sprǭl), *v.* [OE. *spreawlian*, formed with expressive initial group *spr-* (cf. the foll. words); for the element *-awl* cf. *crawl*. Obscurely rel. to similar NFris. *spraweli*, Da. *sprelle, sprælle* kick or splash about, Sw. dial. *sprall(l)a*, Norw. dial. *sprala* struggle.] **1.** *intr.* To move the limbs in a convulsive effort or struggle; to toss about or spread oneself out; later, to be stretched out on the ground, etc., in an ungainly or awkward manner. **b.** To crawl from one place to another in a struggling or ungraceful manner. Also *fig.*, to proceed, issue. 1582. **2.** Of things: To spread out, extend, climb, etc., in a straggling fashion 1745. **3.** *trans.* To spread or stretch out (something) in a wide or straggling manner. Usu. with *out*. 1541.

1. Before the child can crawl, He learns to kick.. and s. PRIOR. **2.** His long mis-shapen legs sprawling abroad SCOTT. Is it not a sweet name? It sprawls over half the paper. THACKERAY. Hence **Spraw·ler,** one who or that which sprawls. **Spraw·ling** *ppl. a.* **Spraw·ly** *a.* of a sprawling character; straggly.

Spray (sprē^{i}), *sb.*^{1} ME. [Earlier in Devon place-name *Spreyton*, in Domesday Book *Espreitone, Spreitone* 'farm in brushwood country'. The ult. origin of OE. **spræġ* and synon. *spræc* is unknown.] **1.** *collect.* Small or slender twigs of trees or shrubs, either as still growing or as cut off and used for fuel, etc.; fine brushwood. Also with *the* (or †*that*). **2.** A slender shoot or twig. late ME. **b.** *pl.* Hazel, birch, or other twigs used in thatching 1520. **c.** A graceful shoot or twig of some flowering or fine-foliaged plant or tree, used for decoration or ornament; an artificial imitation of this 1862. **3.** A metal casting resembling a set of twigs 1831.

1. Majestic trees..with spreading tortuous branches and s. 1852. **2.** No more the birds shall..hearken from the sprays POPE. **c.** He would never meet me without some s. of roses, or some boughs of lemon 1873.

attrib.: **s. drain,** a drain formed by burying the branches of trees under the earth.

Spray (sprē^{i}), *sb.*^{2} †Also **spry(e.** 1621. [orig. *spry*, and so commonly XVII–XVIII; immed. source unkn.; formally corresp. to MDu. vb. *spra(e)yen* (whence occas. Eng. †*spray* sprinkle XVI) = MHG. *spræjen, spræwen.*] **1.** Water blown from or thrown up by the waves of the sea in the form of a fine shower or mist. **b.** Water or other liquid dispersed by impact, etc., in fine mist-like particles 1750. **2.** A jet of medicated vapour or the like, used esp. as a disinfectant or a deodorizer 1875. **3.** An instrument used for applying such a jet 1881.

1. In great storms the s. of the sea has been carried more than 50 miles from the shore 1813.

Spray (sprē^{i}), *v.* 1829. [f. SPRAY *sb.*^{2}] **1.** *trans.* To diffuse or send in the form of spray; to scatter in minute drops. **2.** To sprinkle with or as with spray; to wet with fine particles of water or other liquid, esp. by means of a special apparatus 1861. **3.** *absol.* To scatter or throw up spray 1891.

1. Where the nich'd snow-bed sprays down Its powdery fall M. ARNOLD.

Sprayer (sprē^{i}·əɹ). 1891. [f. prec. + -ER^{1}.] One who or that which sprays; *esp.* a machine for diffusing insecticides over plants and trees.

Spread (spred), *sb.* 1626. [f. the verb.] **I. 1.** The act of spreading in space; degree or extent of this. **b.** With *the*: The extent, expanse, or superficial area *of* something 1691. **c.** Capacity for spreading 1772. **d.** Increased girth of the body 1930. **e.** The difference between two rates or prices 1919. **2.** With *a*: An expanse or stretch *of* something 1712. **b.** *Naut.* A display *of* sails 1849. **3.** The fact of being spread abroad, diffused, or made known; diffusion, dispersion 1675. **4.** *U.S. Stock Exchange.* = STRADDLE *sb.* 2. 1911.

1. No Flower hath that kinde of S. that the Woodbine hath BACON. **b.** Under the immense s. of the starry heavens STEVENSON. **2.** I have got a fine S. of improveable Lands ADDISON. **b.** A.. ship..carrying a large s. of canvas 1889. **3.** The translation..had a wonderful s. among the people 1732.

II. 1. *colloq.* A banquet, feast, meal 1822. **2.** A bed-cover, coverlet. orig. *U.S.* 1852.

Spread (spred), *v.* Pa. t. and pple. **spread** (spred). [OE. *-sprǣdan* = OS. *tō|spreidan*, MLG., MDu. *sprēden* (Du. *spreiden, spreien*), OHG. *spreitan* (G. *spreiten*) :– WGmc. **spraidjan*, causative of **sprīdan*, repr. by OHG. *sprītan* be extended, with no certain cognates.] **I.** *trans.* **1.** To stretch or draw out (a cloth, etc.) so as to display more or less fully; to open out or lay out so as to cover or occupy some space ME. **b.** *spec.* To expand, unfurl, or set (sails) ME. **c.** To display in wide extension 1600. **d.** To flatten out; to make of a thin flat form 1704. †**2.** To draw or stretch out (the limbs or a person) in some form of punishment or torture –1526. **3. a.** To send out in various directions so as to cover or extend over a larger space ME. **b.** To hold out, stretch out, extend (the hands or arms) ME. **c.** To extend, open out (the wings, etc.). late ME. **d.** To extend, make larger or wider (*rare*). late ME. **4.** To distribute or disperse (a substance or a number of things) over a certain superficies or area; to scatter ME. **b.** To distribute in a thin layer; *esp.* to smear 1558. **c.** To place in an open or expanded manner; to distribute *over* a certain space, time, etc. 1592. **d.** To lay out (a meal, banquet, etc.) 1784. **5.** In *pass.* of persons, animals, etc.: To be distributed over or throughout some area ME. **6.** To disseminate or diffuse; to cause to become prevalent or (more) widely existent, present, known, felt, etc. ME. **7.** *refl.* **a.** To extend, expand, etc., in various senses ME. **b.** *U.S.* To exert oneself; also, to show off 1857. **8.** To cover, overlay, deck, or strew, *with* something. Also without const. ME. **b.** To lay (a table) for a meal or other purpose 1460. **c.** To cover with a thin layer of some soft substance, esp. butter; to prepare in this way 1579. **9.** †**a.** To overrun or overspread (an area) –1722. **b.** To cover, extend over. *poet.* 1700.

1. He spread the newspaper on the table before him 1902. **b.** He spreads his canvas; with his pole he steers DRYDEN. **c.** The Euxine spread its waters before their eyes THIRLWALL. **d.** The Diamond weighing near 11 Grains, well spread, and of a perfect Water 1706. **3. a.** Pleasant the Sun When first on this delightful Land he spreads His orient Beams MILT. **b.** Trent, who like some earth-born Giant spreads His thirsty Armes MILT. **4.** The flourie lap Of som irriguous Valley spread her store MILT. **b.** 1 *Kings* 6:32. **c.** The repayment of the money to be borrowed shall be spread over a series of years 1885. **e.** *U.S.* To record, enter in a documentary record 1858. **5.** This sect was now wonderfully spread EVELYN. **6.** Missionaries for spreading the gospel among their countrymen BERKELEY. His arrival spread dismay through the whole English population MACAULAY. **8.** Silence spreads the couch of ever welcome rest BYRON. **b.** A Table richly spred, in regal mode, With dishes pil'd MILT. **c.** Every old woman..can..s. a plaster SCOTT. **9. a.** The Gangren..had spread her whole Body DE FOE. **b.** A purple carpet spread the pavement wide POPE.

II. *intr.* **1.** To receive extension or expansion; to cover or occupy a wider space by this means ME. **b.** Of conditions, qualities, etc. 1565. **c.** To become larger; to increase in size 1630. **d.** To go apart; to separate 1839. **2.** Of immaterial things: To become diffused or disseminated ME. **3.** Of flowers, leaves, etc.: To unfold, expand ME. **4.** To extend by growth; *spec.* of trees, to grow outwards ME. **5.** To extend over a larger area by increase or by separation; to disperse ME. **6.** To stretch out, extend ME.

1. A fire broke out and spread with great rapidity 1885. **b.** The mortification seemed to s. DE FOE. **d.** The toes s. widely upon soft ground 1890. **2.** I am informed that this Fashion spreads daily ADDISON. His fame may s., but in the past Her spirit finds its centre WORDSW. **3.** To sen these flouris agen the sunne to sprede CHAUCER. **4.** The she oaks were more inclined to s. than grow tall 1802. **5.** So the men of armes sprad abrode 1523. **6.** Below their breezy crowns.. Spreadeth the infinite smile of the sunlit sea R. BRIDGES. Hence **Sprea·dingly** *adv.*

Spread eagle, *sb.* Also **spread-eagle.** 1570. [*Spread* ppl. adj.] **1.** A representation of an eagle, with body, legs, and both wings displayed, esp. as the emblem of various states or rulers, or as an inn-sign. **2.** A person secured with the arms and legs stretched out, esp. in order to be flogged 1785. **3.** A fowl flattened out for broiling 1854. **4.** *attrib.* Bombastic, ridiculously boastful, esp. in laudation of the United States. *U.S.* 1858.

1. At the Spread Eagle (commonly called the Spread Crow) 1685. **b.** *U.S. Stock Exchange.* = STRADDLE *sb.* 2. 1857. **4.** 'The spread-eagle style'—a compound of exaggeration, effrontery, bombast, and extravagance 1858. Hence **Spread-ea·gleism,** extravagant laudation of the United States; tendency to bombast or grandiloquence in this or similar connections.

Spread-eagle, *v.* 1829. [f. prec.] **1.** *trans.* To tie up (a person) for punishment. **b.** To fasten, pin firmly, stretch out, etc., in the form of a spread eagle 1894. **2.** To beat completely, esp. in racing 1864. **3.** *intr.* To speak or act in a spread-eagle fashion 1866.

Spreader (spre·dəɹ). 1843. [f. SPREAD *v.* + -ER^{1}.] **I. 1.** One who spreads, strews, or scatters. **2.** A diffuser, disseminator, or promulgator *of* something 1551. **3.** A piece of wood, metal, etc., by which things or parts are stretched out or kept asunder 1839. **b.** *Naut.* A bar attached to the mast of a yacht in order to tighten the shrouds 1895. **4.** An apparatus or device by which something is spread or scattered 1853. **II. 1.** Something which spreads or grows outwards 1639. **2.** A catch which operates by spreading 1884.

1. The oak is naturally a wide s. 1845.

Sprea·d-o:ver. 1923. [f. verbal phr. *spread over.*] The accommodation of a limited number of working hours to the requirements of special needs.

Spreagh (sprex). 1809. [alt. of *spreath* (– Gael. *sprèidh* cattle), prob. by assoc. with CREAGH.] A cattle-raid; a foray. Hence **Sprea·ghery,** cattle-raiding; plunder. SCOTT.

Spree (sprī). Chiefly *colloq.* 1804. [Of unkn. origin; former vars. *spray, sprey.*] **1.** A lively or boisterous frolic; an occasion or spell of noisy enjoyment (freq. accompanied by drinking). **b.** *spec.* A drunken carousal

1811. **2.** Rough amusement, merrymaking, or sport; prolonged drinking or carousing; indulgence or participation in this 1808.

1. Phr. *On a s., on* or *upon the s.*

Sprenge (sprendʒ), *v. Obs.* exc. *arch.* in pa. t. and pa. pple. **sprent.** [OE. *sprenġan* :- **sprangjan*, causative of **springan* SPRING *v.*¹; corresp. to OFris. *sprendza*, MLG., (O)HG. *sprengen*, ON. *sprengja.*] **1.** *trans.* To sprinkle (a liquid, etc.). Also *absol.* **b.** To scatter, disperse, distribute, spread abroad or about. Also *absol.* OE. **2.** To sprinkle (a person or thing) with some liquid OE. **3.** In *pa. pple.* and const. *with*: Besprinkled, besprent. late ME.

3. All the ground with purple bloud was sprent SPENSER. The cheek grown thin, the brown hair sprent with grey M. ARNOLD.

Sprew (sprū). *S. Afr.* 1897. [- Du. *spreeuw* starling.] A bird belonging to the genus *Spreo* (of the family *Sturnidæ*), esp. *S. bicolor*, a glossy starling.

Sprig (sprig), *sb.*¹ ME. [Of unkn. origin.] **1.** A small slender nail, either wedge-shaped and headless, or square-bodied with a slight head on one side. **b.** *Naut.* A small eye-bolt, ragged at the point 1794. **c.** A wedge-shaped piece of tin used to hold glass in a sash until the putty dries 1823. **2.** A small projecting part or point 1679.

attrib., as *s.-nail*; **s.-awl, -bit,** a bradawl.

Sprig (sprig), *sb.*² late ME. [- or rel. to synon. LG. *sprick*; for the final *-g*, see SMUG *a.*] **1.** A shoot, twig, or spray of a plant, shrub, or tree; †a rod. **b.** A small spray *of* a particular plant 1563. **2.** *fig.* **a.** An offshoot, a minor development, part, or specimen, of something 1576. **b.** Applied to persons (usu. in disparagement): A scion *of* some person, class, institution, etc. 1601. **c.** Without const.: A stripling; a young fellow 1661. **3.** †**a.** A branch of a nerve, vein, etc. -1730. **b.** A piece of some substance or material resembling a sprig of a plant 1660. **4.** An ornament in the form of a sprig or spray; in later use esp. one made of diamonds 1591. **b.** A design, imitative of a sprig, embroidered, woven, or stamped on a textile fabric, or applied to ceramic ware, etc. 1771. **c.** A small detached piece of pillow-lace, made separately for subsequent use in composite work 1851.

1. Where there are several Sprigs upon one Stem, as in Fenil, Hemlock, and the like 1676. **b.** Sprigs of Rosemarie SHAKS. **2. a.** The following s. of sepulchral poetry SCOTT. **b.** The illustrious sprigs of our Nobility 1768. **c.** A s. whom I remember with a whey face and a satchel not so very many years ago SCOTT. **3. b.** Half-a-score Sprigs of Coral BOYLE.

Sprig, *v.*¹ 1713. [f. SPRIG *sb.*¹] **1.** *trans.* To fasten with sprigs or brads. **2.** *intr.* To drive in sprigs 1898.

Sprig, *v.*² 1731. [f. SPRIG *sb.*²] *trans.* To decorate or cover with designs representing sprigs.

A blue satin tie sprigged with gold 1850.

Sprigged (sprigd), *ppl. a.* 1613. [f. SPRIG *sb.*² or *v.*² + -ED.] **1.** Adorned or ornamented with sprigs. **2.** Having the form of a sprig or sprigs; minutely branched 1714.

Spriggy (spri·gi), *a.* 1597. [f. SPRIG *sb.*² + -Y¹.] Abounding in sprigs or small branches; suggestive of a sprig or sprigs.

Spright (sprəit), *sb.* 1533. [var. of SPRITE *sb.*, after words in *-ight.*] †**1.** = SPIRIT *sb.* in various senses -1700. **2.** A disembodied spirit, a ghost; a supernatural being, goblin, fairy, etc. 1533.

My weryed spryght 1563. Come Sisters, cheere we vp his sprights, And shew the best of our delights SHAKS. **2.** Glad was Huon when he had loste the syghte of the spryghte 1533. And sweete Sprights beare the burthen SHAKS. Hence †**Spright** *v. trans.* to haunt, as by a s. SHAKS. †**Spri·ghtless** *a.* devoid of spirit or animation -1710.

Sprightful (sprəi·tfŭl), *a.* Now *rare.* 1591. [f. SPRIGHT *sb.* + -FUL.] **1.** Of persons: Full of spirit; animated, lively. †**b.** Of horses: Spirited -1674. **2.** Of actions, sounds, etc.: Marked by spirit, animation, or liveliness 1628. †**3.** Of liquids, etc.: Impregnated with spirit; spirituous -1669.

1. Spoke like a sprightfull Noble Gentleman SHAKS. **b.** The Horses were..The noblest, sprightfulst breed COWLEY. **2.** The right jolly and sprightfull tune of *Ca Ira* W. IRVING. Hence **Spri·ghtful-ly** *adv.*, **-ness.**

Sprightly (sprəi·tli), *a.* and *adv.* 1596. [f. SPRIGHT *sb.* + -LY.] **A.** *adj.* **1.** Of persons: Full of vivacity or animation; cheerful, gay, brisk. **b.** Of animals: Lively, sportive 1735. **2.** Characterized by animation or cheerful vivacity 1606. **3.** Of things: Having lively qualities or properties; naturally brisk; suggestive of animation or gaiety 1605. †**4.** Ghostly, spectral. SHAKS.

1. Seest thou that s. youth? MARSTON. **b.** The crowing of the s. cock 1830. **2.** My bones are full of unctious marrow, and my blood, of s. Youth 1646. Gay s. land of mirth and social ease GOLDSM. **3.** Let..Bacchus fill the s. Bowl PRIOR. It is a noble, s. Sound. The Trumpet's Clangor, and the Clash of Arms! DRYDEN.

B. *adv.* In a sprightly manner; with vigour and animation 1604. Hence **Spri·ghtlily** *adv.* (*rare*). **Spri·ghtliness.**

Spri·g tail, spri·gtail. 1676. [f. SPRIG *sb.*¹] **1.** A short pointed tail. **2.** *U.S.* = PINTAIL 1. 1782. So **Sprig-tailed** *a.* 1676.

Spring (spriŋ), *sb.*¹ [OE. *spring* and *spryng*, f. **spreŋg-* and **spruŋg-* respectively of the base of SPRING *v.*¹ With branch I, cf. (M)Du., (M)LG., OHG. *spring.*] **I. 1.** The place of rising or issuing from the ground; the source or head, *of* a well, stream, or river; the supply of water forming such a source. Now *rare.* **2.** A flow of water rising or issuing naturally out of the earth; a similar flow obtained by boring, etc. ME. **b.** A flow of water possessing special properties, esp. of a medicinal or curative nature 1787. **c.** *pl.* A place or locality having such springs to which invalids or pleasure-seekers resort 1849. **3.** *fig.* A source or origin *of* something. Also occas. without const. ME.

1. Great riuers, whose mouthes are knowne, but not their springs 1600. **2.** It has also some Springs of good Water 1665. *fig.* When old age approaches, ..the springs of life dry up 1771. **b.** *Chalybeate, hot, mineral, thermal, warm,* etc. *springs.* **3.** The S., the Head, the Fountaine of your Blood Is stopt SHAKS. Language reveals the deepest springs of thought 1892.

II. 1. The action or time of rising or springing into being or existence: **a.** The first sign *of* day, morning, etc.; the dawn. Also, the beginning of a season. Now *Obs.* exc. *poet.* ME. †**b.** *S. of the leaf*, the time when trees begin to burst into leaf again -1670. **2.** orig. †*Spring of the year* (1530): The first season of the year, or that between winter and summer, reckoned astronomically from the vernal equinox to the summer solstice; in pop. use in Great Britain comprising the months of February, March, and April, or (according to some) March, April, and May. Also *transf.*, a season resembling this in some respect. 1547. **b.** The first or early stage or period *of* life, youth, etc. 1590. **c.** Contrasted with *fall* (cf. FALL *sb.*¹ I. 2). Now *arch.* 1643. **d.** This season in a particular year 1621.

1. It came to passe about the s. of the day 1 *Sam.* 9:26. **2.** O, Wind, If Winter comes, can S. be far behind? SHELLEY. **b.** Oh, how this s. of loue resembleth The vncertaine glory of an Aprill day SHAKS. **d.** I am going to the same place I went last s. 1711.

attrib. in senses 'of or pertaining to the s.', 'appearing, happening, etc., in the s.', as *s.-ague*; **s. pottage, soup,** pottage or soup made of or from fresh green vegetables; 'sown or suitable for sowing in the s.', as *s. barley, onion, wheat.*

Comb.: **s.-beauty,** any plant of the genus *Claytonia*; **-grass,** *Anthoxanthum odoratum*, a native of Britain; **-herring,** the alewife.

III. †**1. a.** A young growth on a tree, plant, or root; a shoot, sprout, sucker; a small branch, sprig, or twig; the rudimentary shoot of a seed -1660. **b.** A growth of this nature cut or slipped off, esp. for planting -1657. **2.** A copse, grove, or wood consisting of young trees springing up naturally from the stools of old ones; a plantation, esp. one inclosed and used for rearing or harbouring game. Now *dial.* late ME. **b.** *collect.* Young growth, shoots, or sprouts, esp. the under growth of trees or shrubs. Now *dial.* 1482. **3.** A springing up, growing, or bursting forth of plants, vegetation, etc.; also, a race or stock of persons. Now *rare.* 1624.

2. Yonder S. of Roses intermixt With Myrtle MILT.

IV. †**1.** Rise, beginning, first appearance, or birth (*of* something) -1682. **2.** †**a.** The rising *of* the sea (to an exceptional height) at particular times -1585. **b.** = SPRING-TIDE 2. Chiefly *pl.* 1584. **3.** An act of springing or leaping; a bound, jump, or leap 1450. **b.** A recoil or rebound 1680. **c.** A quick, convulsive, or elastic movement made by certain plants or animals in dispersing or depositing seed, eggs, etc. 1801. **d.** A distance capable of being covered by a spring or leap 1817. **4.** A flock *of* teal. Now *arch.* 1450. **5.** A cut or joint of pork consisting of the belly or lower part of the fore-quarter. *Obs.* exc. *dial.* 1598. **6.** *Naut.* A split or opening in a †vessel, mast, or spar, esp. one of such a size as to render it unsafe to carry the usual amount of sail 1611. **7.** The quality or capacity of springing; elastic energy or force; elasticity 1660. **b.** Elasticity or springiness as possessed by persons or the limbs; buoyancy and vigour in movement 1700. **8.** *transf.* Buoyancy, activity, vigour *of* mind, temper, etc.; active power or faculty 1682. **9.** *Arch.* The point at which an arch or vault springs or rises from its abutment or impost; the commencement of curvature in an arch 1726. **10.** *Naut.* The sheer, the upward curvature or rise, of the deck planking of a vessel or boat 1838.

1. Phr. *To take* (..) *s. from* or *out of*, to have source or origin in, to rise or originate in. **2. b.** The tide rises six feet on the springs 1779. **3.** *fig.* When Science was pausing for the s. she has since made 1878. **b.** The s. of a well-drawn bow 1853. **6.** We..discover'd a great S. in the Foremast 1744. **7.** The air's s. or elasticity GOLDSM. Yielding few..woods that have sufficient s. for the construction of the bow 1874. **b.** Th' elastic s. of an unwearied foot COWPER. **8.** A selfish villain may possess a s. and alacrity of temper HUME.

V. 1. An elastic contrivance or mechanical device, usu. consisting of a plate or strip of steel (or a number of these) suitably shaped or adjusted, which, when compressed, bent, coiled, or otherwise forced out of its normal shape, possesses the property of returning to it; used chiefly for imparting motion, regulating movement, or for lessening or preventing concussion. late ME. **2.** *fig.* That by which action is produced, inspired, or instigated; a moving, actuating, or impelling agency, cause, or force; a motive. Freq. const. *of* action (or conduct). 1616. **3.** *Naut.* A rope put out from the end or side of a vessel lying at anchor, and made fast to the cable 1744. **b.** A hawser laid out to some fixed object to slew a vessel in any required direction 1769.

1. A helical s. has coils of decreasing diameter as they approach the center KNIGHT. **2.** These men are..able..to put all the springs of a perfect culture in motion 1767. It is difficult..to come at the true springs of action 1779.

attrib.: in senses 'fitted with a spring or springs', 'acting like a spring', 'of or pertaining to a spring', as *s.-arbor, -balance, -bar, -barrel, -bed*; 'having springs, hung or suspended on springs', as *s.-ambulance, -carriage, -cart*; in similar combs. used attrib., as *s.-blade knife*; in parasynthetic combs. as *s.-framed, -jointed* adjs.; *spring-heeled Jack*, a person who from his great activity or agility is imagined to have springs in the heels of his boots.

Spring (spriŋ), *sb.*² late ME. [prob. rel. to OFr. *espring(u)er, -ier* to dance; see SPRING *v.*¹] †**1.** Some kind of dance -1460. **2.** A tune upon the bagpipes or other musical instrument, esp. a quick or lively tune; a dance-tune. Chiefly, and now only, *Sc.* 1475.

2. *fig.* I've play'd mysel a bonie s., An' danc'd my fill! BURNS.

Spring, *sb.*³ *Obs.* exc. *dial.* 1604. [Alteration of SPRINGE *sb.*] A snare or noose.

I set no springs for Woodcocks 1604.

Spring (spriŋ), *v.*¹ Pa. t. **sprang** (spræŋ), **sprung** (sprɒŋ). Pa. pple. **sprung.** [OE. *springan* = OFris. *springa*, OS., OHG. *springan* (Du., G. *springen*), ON. *springa* :- Gmc. **spreŋgan.*] **I.** **Intr. senses.* **1.** Of things: To change place or position by sudden and rapid movement without contact; to move with a sudden jerk or bound (in later use esp. by resilient force); to dart or fly. **b.** To be resilient or elastic; to shift or move on account of this 1667. **c.** To rise or come suddenly *to, into* the eyes, lips, etc. 1848. †**2.** Of fame, rumour, etc.: To spread, extend –1578. **3. a.** Of persons or animals: To bound or leap. Const. with advs. or preps. Also *spec.*, of partridges, to rise from cover. ME. **b.** To rise quickly, or with a bound, from a sitting or recumbent posture 1474. **4.** To fly asunder or in pieces; to burst, break, crack, or split; to give way. Also *fig.* of the heart. ME. **b.** In pa. pple. †(*a*) Of horses: Foundered –1696. (*b*) Of planks, masts, etc.: Split, cracked 1704. (*c*) *slang.* Of persons: Intoxicated 1826. **c.** Of mines: To go off, explode 1658. **5.** To swell *with* milk; to give signs of foaling or calving. Now *dial.* 1607.

1. As fire ys wont to quyk and goo From a sparke spronge amys CHAUCER. **c.** An indignant refusal sprang to his lips 1891. **3. a.** Like Pallas springing arm'd from Jove COWPER. **b.** Good news caused me to s. from my bed 1860. **4.** Splicing a favourite old fives'-bat which had sprung 1857. **b.** (*b*) It will not be possible to race this cutter..owing to her mast being sprung 1894.

II. 1. To issue or come forth suddenly, to break out, esp. in a jet or stream. Freq. with *forth* or *out.* OE. **b.** *esp.* Of water: To rise or flow in a stream out of the ground. Freq. with *out* or *up.* ME. **2.** Of morning, etc.: To come above the horizon; to begin to appear ME.

1. The perspiration which sprung from his brow SCOTT. **b.** I have sene the place where Temmes springeth 1530. **2.** When the day began to s. *Judges* 19:25. *fig.* The Gentiles shal come to thy light, & kynges to the brightness y^t springeth forth vpon ye COVERDALE *Isa.* 60:3.

III. 1. Of vegetation: To grow; to arise or develop by growth OE. **2.** Of conditions, qualities, etc.: To take rise, to originate or proceed ME. **3.** Of persons (or animals): To originate by birth or generation; to issue or descend. Usu. const. *from, of,* or *out of.* ME. **b.** To come into being 1667. **c.** To arise as an offshoot *from* a society 1782. **4.** To grow (*up*); to increase or extend in height or length; to grow out *from* some thing or part. late ME. **b.** To attain to a certain height or point by growth. late ME. **c.** Of arches, etc.: To take a curving or slanting upward course *from* some point of support. Also without const. 1739. **5.** With *up.* Of a breeze: To begin to blow 1719.

1. From the cedar tre..euen vnto the hyssope that springeth out of the wall BIBLE (Geneva) 1 *Kings* 4:33. For her the green grass shall not s. TENNYSON. **2.** The scholastic philosophy sprung up in the schools of Paris 1874. Out of the union of wisdom and temperance with courage, springs justice 1875. **3.** Thou, sprung of the seed of the seas As an ear from a seed of corn SWINBURNE. **b.** The isles of Greece!..Where Delos rose, and Phœbus sprung! BYRON. **4. b.** Corne as yet not sprong To the full height 1627. **c.** Doubtless an arched roof sprung from the side walls SCOTT. **5.** As the breeze is now springing up from the NW. NELSON.

** *Trans. senses.* **IV. 1.** †**a.** = SPRENGE *v.* 1. –1581. **b.** = SPRENGE *v.* 2. Usu. const. *with.* *Obs.* exc. *dial.* late ME. †**2.** To produce, bring forth. Also *fig.* –1697. **3.** To cause (a bird, *esp.* a partridge) to rise from cover. Also *fig.* 1531. **4.** *Naut.* Of a vessel, or those on board: To have (a mast, yard, etc.) split, cracked, or started 1595. **b.** To have or make (a leak) open or start 1611. **5. a.** *Mil.* To explode (a mine) 1637. **b.** To sound (a rattle) 1812. **6.** †**a.** To start (something); to set going –1700. **b.** *colloq.* To give, pay, or disburse (a sum of money); to buy (a certain amount); also (*slang*), to afford to buy 1851. **c.** To bring (an announcement, etc.) suddenly *upon* a person or persons 1884. **7.** To cause (a thing) to spring, move suddenly, fly with a jerk, etc. 1665. **b.** *Mil.* To shift (a weapon, etc.) smartly from one position to another 1780. **c.** To cause (some mechanism, etc.) to work with a sudden movement; to force open by pressure 1828. **d.** To apply or adjust by force applied to some elastic or resilient body 1842. **e.** To bend or deflect from a straight line 1873. **8.** *Arch.* To commence the curve of (an arch) 1703.

2. If, as we dream, Egyptian earth, impregnated with flame, Sprung the first man DRYDEN. **3.** We sprang Ducks and Snipes 1682. **4. b.** The vessel sprang a leak 1851. **5. a.** *fig.* He springs the hushed Volcano's mines WORDSW. **6. c.** The.. arrangement by which Sir Henry Peek's resignation was sprung upon the constituency 1884. **7. c.** He would s. all their traps 1897.

V. To leap over; cover with a spring 1825.

Spring, *v.*[2] 1843. [f. SPRING *sb.*[1]] **1.** *trans.* To give spring or elasticity to. **2.** To provide or fit with a spring or springs 1884.

Spring-, the stem of SPRING *v.* used in a few specific names, as **s.-beetle,** a skipjack; **-hare,** the jumping hare of S. Africa; **-jack,** = *s.-beetle.*

Spri·ngal(d[1]**.** *Obs.* exc. *Hist.* ME. [– OFr. *espringale, -alle* (cf. ESPRINGAL) or AFr. *springalde* (AL. *springaldus, -a, -um* XIII), f. OFr. *espringuer, -gier,* f. Frankish *springan* SPRING *v.*[1]] An engine of the nature of a bow or catapult, used in mediæval warfare for throwing heavy missiles; also, a missile thrown by an engine of this kind.

Spri·ngal(d[2]**.** Now *arch.* 1440. [Presumably f. SPRING *v.*[1], but the ending is obscure. Revived by Scott.] **1.** A young man, a youth, a stripling. **2.** *attrib.* or as *adj.* Youthful, adolescent 1614.

1. Sure the Devil..is in this Springald BEAUM. & FL.

Spri·ng-beam. 1797. [f. SPRING *sb.*[1] or *v.*[1]] The distinctive name of certain strong timbers forming part of the fittings of an engine or paddle-box.

Spri·ng-board. 1866. [f. SPRING *sb.*[1] or *v.*[1]] **1.** A projecting board or plank, from the end of which a person may jump or dive. **2.** An elastic board used to assist in vaulting 1875.

‖**Springbok** (spri·ŋbǫk). Also †**-bock, -boc.** 1775. [S. Afr. Du., f. Du. *springen* to spring + *bok* goat, antelope.] A species of antelope, *Antilope euchore,* abounding in S. Africa, characterized by a habit of springing almost directly upwards when excited or disturbed. **b.** *pl.* A nickname for South Africans. So **Spri·ng-buck** 1775.

Spring-cleaning. 1887. [f. SPRING *sb.*[1]] The general cleaning of a house, etc., usually performed in the spring. Hence **Spring-clean** *v.* and *sb.*

Springe (sprin^dʒ), *sb.* ME. [repr. OE. **sprenċ́* :– **sprangjan*; see SPRENGE *v.*] A snare for catching small game, esp. birds. Freq. *fig.*

fig. Springes to catch Woodcocks SHAKS. He wanted to catch me in his springes of words 1875.

Springe (sprin^dʒ), *v.* 1616. [f. prec.] **1.** *trans.* To catch in a springe or snare. **2.** *intr.* To set snares 1895.

Springer (spri·ŋəɹ). late ME. [f. SPRING *v.*[1] + -ER[1].] **I.** †**1.** A source or origin. CHAUCER. **2. a.** A fish which springs or leaps; now *spec.* a newly-run salmon 1753. **b.** *Zool.* The springbok. Also *s. antelope.* 1781. **3.** One who springs or leaps 1775. **4.** *Arch.* The support from which an arch springs; the impost at each end of an arch 1611. **5.** A cow or heifer near to calving 1844. **II. 1.** One of the larger varieties of spaniel 1808. **2.** One who fires or sets off a mine 1861.

Spri·ng-flood. late ME. [f. SPRING *sb.*[1] + FLOOD *sb.*] †**1.** = SPRING-TIDE 2. –1648. **2.** A river-flood occurring in spring-time 1823.

Spring(-)gun. 1775. [SPRING *sb.*[1]] A gun capable of being discharged by one coming in contact with it, or with a wire or the like attached to the trigger; formerly used as a guard against trespassers or poachers, and placed in concealment for this purpose.

Steel traps and spring guns seemed writ in every wrinkle SHERIDAN.

Springhalt. 1613. [Unexplained alt. of STRINGHALT.] = STRINGHALT.

Spri·ng-head. 1555. [f. SPRING *sb.*[1]] The source or fountain of a river. Also *fig.*

Springing (spri·ŋiŋ), *vbl. sb.* ME. [f. SPRING *v.*[1] + -ING[1].] **1.** The action or process of one who or that which springs, in various senses. **2. a.** *Arch.* = SPRING *sb.*[1] IV. 9. 1703. **b.** The point of growth from the trunk of a tree 1825. **3.** The action of exploding a mine 1665.

1. Thou makest it soft with showres, thou blessest the s. thereof *Ps.* 65:10.

Springle (spri·ŋg'l), *sb.* 1602. [perh. f. SPRING *sb.*[3]] A springe or snare.

Springle (spri·ŋg'l), *v.* Now *rare* or *arch.* 1502. [var. of SPRINKLE *v.*; cf. TINGLE *v.*, TINKLE *v.*[1]] *trans.* To sprinkle. Also *absol.*

Springlet (spri·ŋlėt). 1808. [f. SPRING *sb.*[1] + -LET.] A small spring or fountain.

From out the..hill Oozes the slender s. still SCOTT.

Spri·ng-lock. 1485. [f. SPRING *sb.*[1]] A common form of lock in which a spring presses the bolt outwards, thus rendering it self-locking except when secured by a catch.

Spri·ng-tail. 1797. [SPRING *sb.*[1] or *v.*[1]] *Zool.* One or other of various species of insects which leap or spring by means of their tail.

Spring-tide. 1530. [SPRING *sb.*[1] IV. 2.] **1.** The season of spring; spring-time. **2.** A tide occurring on the day shortly after the new and full moon, in which the high-water level reaches its maximum 1548. **3.** *transf.* A copious flow or large quantity *of* something 1593.

1. *fig.* Happy youth, that shalt possesse Such a spring-tyde of delight 1640. **2.** A sudden land-flood, met by a spring-tide, surrounded and overwhelmed the town 1776. **3.** Woe, wonder, and sensation high, In one spring-tide of ecstasy! SCOTT.

Spri·ng(-)time. 1495. [SPRING *sb.*[1]] **1.** = prec. 1. **2. a.** The earlier period of a person's life; youth 1593. **b.** A time or period comparable in some way to spring. Usu. const. *of.* 1764.

1. As Bees In spring time..Poure forth thir populous youth about the Hive In clusters MILT.

Spri·ng(-)wa:ter. 1440. [SPRING *sb.*[1] I. 2.] Water issuing or obtained from a spring or fountain.

Spri·ng-well. ME. [f. as prec. + WELL *sb.*] A spring or well of water; a spring-head or fountain.

Spri·ng-wood. 1523. [f. SPRING *sb.*[1] III. 2.] **1. a.** Wood growing in a spring or copse of young saplings. **b.** A copse or wood of springs or young trees 1623. **2.** A ring or layer of wood formed round a tree each spring 1884.

Springy (spri·ŋi), *a.* 1641. [f. SPRING *sb.*[1] and *v.*[1] + -Y[1].] **1.** Characterized by the presence of springs of water. **2.** Endowed with spring or elasticity 1660. **b.** Elastic to the tread 1797. **3.** Marked or characterized by spring, elasticity, or resilience 1669. **b.** *esp.* Of the bearing or movements of persons or animals 1818.

1. Lowe, moist, and s. groundes are the best to increase milke in an ewe 1641. **2.** A laughing schoolboy..Riding the s. branches of an elm KEATS. **3. b.** The s. step..reminded Henry Warden of Halbert SCOTT. Hence **Spri·ngily** *adv.* **Spri·nginess.**

Sprinkle (spri·ŋk'l), *sb.* late ME. [rel. to SPRINKLE *v.*; cf. MLG., MDu. *sprinkel,* (M)Du. *sprenkel* speckle, spot, freckle.] †**1.** A sprinkler, *esp.* one for sprinkling holy water –1647. **2.** An (or the) act of sprinkling; a quantity which is sprinkled 1596. **b.** A small number or quantity; a sprinkling 1768. **3.** *techn.* A colour effect produced by sprinkling; a mixture for producing this 1835.

2. Baptizing the Christian infant with a solemne s. MILT.

Sprinkle (spri·ŋk'l), *v.* late ME. [perh. – (M)Du. *sprenkelen* (cf. MLG. *sprinkelt* pa. pple. spotted; so late ME. *sprynkled*); see -LE.] **1.** *trans.* To scatter in drops; to let fall in small particles here and there; to strew thinly or lightly. **b.** *fig.* To disperse, distribute, or scatter here and there 1514. **2.** To bedew, bespatter lightly, or powder (a thing or surface); to besprinkle. Usu. const. *with.* late ME. **b.** To dot, intersperse, diversify *with* something. Usu. in *pass.* 1591. **c.** To colour with small specks or spots. (Chiefly in *pass.*, or *techn.* in bookbinding.) 1750. **3.** *intr.* **a.** To spring or fly *up* in fine drops 1594. **b.** To rain or fall in fine or infrequent drops 1778.

1. S. sordid Ashes all around DRYDEN. **b.** Besides cities, many private dwellings were sprinkled on mount Ephraim FULLER. **2.** The floor was merely sprinkled with rain, and not saturated 1878. **3. a.** It will make the Water friske and sprinckle vp, in a fine Dew BACON. **b.** The rain.. continued to s. 1858.

Sprinkler (spri·ŋkləɹ). 1535. [f. SPRINKLE *v.* + -ER[1].] **1.** A vessel or other device used for sprinkling water, etc. **b.** A machine or vehicle used for this purpose, esp. one for watering the roadway or extinguishing fire 1879. **2.** A brush for sprinkling holy water 1577. **3.** A person who sprinkles 1613.

Spri·nkling, *vbl. sb.* 1440. [f. SPRINKLE *v.* + -ING[1].] **1.** The action of the verb in various senses. **2.** A small quantity sprinkled or to be sprinkled 1657. **3.** *fig.* A small or slight quantity or amount 1594. **b.** A small number scattered or distributed here and there 1621. **4.** *attrib.* as *s.-brush, -can, -cart, -machine* 1596.

1. Baptism..may be perform'd even by Effusion or S. 1726. **2.** A s. of Rain 1700. **3.** Some little S. of Grammer learning NASHE. **b.** A s. of gray hairs 1706.

Sprint (sprint), *sb.* 1865. [f. SPRINT *v.*] A short spell of running, rowing, etc., at full speed. Also *attrib.*, as *s. course, race.*

Sprint (sprint), *v.* 1566. [– ON. **sprinta* (Sw. *spritta*); superseding (dial.) *sprent* (XIV) spring forward, spurt, sprinkle – ON. **sprenta* (Sw. *sprätta*, Da. *sprætte*), prop. the corresp. causative wk. vb., but in Eng. chiefly intr.; ult. origin unkn.] †**1.** *intr.* To dart or spring. **2.** To run, row, etc., at full speed, esp. for a short distance; to race in this manner 1871.

2. By running and walking, or rather sprinting, the whole time 1889. Hence **Spri·nter,** one who sprints or engages in sprint-racing. **Spri·nting** *vbl. sb.*

Sprit (sprit), *sb.*[1] [OE. *sprēot* = (M)LG., (M)Du. *spriet, spret* (whence G. *spriet*), f. Gmc. **spreut-* **sprŭt-*; see SPROUT *v.*] **1.** A pole, *esp.* one used for propelling a boat; a punting-pole; †a spear. **2.** *Naut.* A small boom or pole which crosses the fore and aft sail diagonally from the mast to the upper hindmost corner of the sail, which it extends and elevates. Also *attrib.* late ME.

Sprit (sprit), *sb.*[2] 1622. Now *dial.* [f. the vb.] A shoot, sprout. **Sprit** *v.* [OE. *spryttan.*] *intr.* to sprout.

Sprite (sprəit), †**sprit,** *sb.* ME. [alt. with lengthened vowel of *sprit*, contr. of SPIRIT. Cf. SPRIGHT.] †**a.** = SPIRIT *sb.* in various senses –1847. **b.** A disembodied spirit, a ghost ME. †**c.** The spirit of God; the Holy Spirit –1600.

His sprete was moved in hym TINDALE *Acts* 17:16. Forth with jocund s., I run SHENSTONE. **b.** Where must I lye anight.s? For I am monstrous fraid of Sprites COTTON. **c.** Governe me with thy holy s. 1600.

Spritsail (spri·tsēˈl, spri·ts'l). 1466. [f. SPRIT *sb.*[1] Cf. Du. *sprietzeil*, WFris. *-seil*, etc.] A sail extended by a sprit; formerly also a sail attached to a yard slung under the bowsprit of large vessels.

attrib., as *s. brace, clewline*; *s. barge, vessel*; **s. yard,** a yard slung under the bowsprit to support a s.

Sprocket (sprǫ·kėt). 1536. [Of unkn. origin.] **1.** *Carp.* and *Build.* A triangular piece of timber used in framing, esp. one fastened on the foot of a rafter in order to raise the level of the eaves. **2.** A projection (either forked or simple) from the rim of a wheel, engaging with the links of a chain. Also *attrib.* in *s. wheel.* 1750. **b.** *ellipt.* A sprocket-wheel, esp. that of a cycle 1886. **3.** *Naut.* One of the teeth of a pawl-rim 1903.

Sprod. *n. dial.* 1617. [Of unkn. origin.] A salmon in its second year.

Sprout (spraut), *sb.* ME. [f. SPROUT *v.* or – MLG., MDu. *sprūte* (f. the vb.).] **1.** A shoot from a branch, root, or stump of a tree, shrub, or plant; a new growth developing from a bud into a branch, stalk, sucker, etc. **b.** A rudimentary shoot of a seed; the acrospire of grain 1610. **c.** *pl.* Young or tender shoots or side-growths of various vegetables, esp. of the cabbage kind 1639. **d.** *ellipt.* for *Brussels sprouts* 1858. **2.** *fig.* Applied to persons: A scion 1725. **3.** The action of sprouting or of putting forth new growths (*rare*) 1586.

2. That resuscitated s. of Saxon royalty SCOTT.

Sprout (spraut), *v.* [ME. *sprūten*, OE. **sprūtan* = OS. *sprūtan*, MLG. *sprūten*, (M)Du. *spruiten* :– WGmc. orig. str. vb. **sprūtan*, f. **sprŭt-*, as also in OE. *sprȳtan, spryttan*, OHG. *spriozan* (G. *spriessen*).] **1.** *intr.* To grow, issue, or proceed as a sprout or sprouts; to shoot forth or spring up by natural growth. **b.** Of persons: To originate or spring 1582. **2.** Of a tree, plant, seed, etc.: To put forth, throw up or out, a sprout or sprouts; to develop new growths or shoots; to bud. ME. **b.** *spec.* To germinate, begin to grow, prematurely 1685. **3.** *transf.* Of earth, a surface, etc.: To bear, bring forth, or produce sprouts or sprout-like growths. Freq. const. *with* (a growth). 1591. **4.** *trans.* To cause (branches, leaves, etc.) to grow or shoot; to bear or develop, to put or throw *forth* or *out*, as sprouts 1601. **5.** To cause or induce (plants, seeds, etc.) to develop sprouts or shoots, esp. before planting or sowing them 1770. **b.** *dial.* and *U.S.* To rub or break off the sprouts of (potatoes) 1828.

1. Verse sprouting from verse as simply as leaf from leaf 1879. **2.** *fig.* Should his money s. and yield a thousand fold 1856. **4.** *fig.* When you think he has exhausted his battery of looks,.. suddenly he sprouts out an entirely new set of features LAMB.

Spruce (sprūs), *sb.* late ME. [Alteration of PRUCE Prussia.] †**1.** The country of Prussia. Also *Spruce-land.* –1656. †**b.** *attrib.* in the sense 'brought or obtained from Prussia', as *S. board, canvas* –1875. **2.** *ellipt.* †**a.** Spruce leather –1611. **b.** Spruce beer 1741. **3.** *ellipt.* = SPRUCE FIR 1670. **b.** A species, or a single tree, of spruce fir 1832. **c.** The wood of the spruce fir 1853.

1. b. A Broker, in a s. leather ierkin NASHE. *Spruce-leather*, a sort of Leather corruptly so call'd for Prussia leather 1706. **3.** The black s. is used only for beer... Of this s., is made the essence which is as well known in Europe as in America. 1792.

attrib., as *s. bark, -bough, -cone*; **s.-borer, bud, worm,** U.S. names of insects which attack s. trees; **s. grouse, partridge,** the spotted Canada grouse.

Spruce (sprūs), *a.* and *adv.* 1589. [perh. f. SPRUCE *sb.* 1 b in the collocation *spruce* (*leather*) *jerkin.*] **A.** *adj.* †**1.** Brisk, smart, lively –1749. **2.** Trim, neat, dapper; smart in appearance 1599.

1. A s., lively air, fashionable dress; and all the glitter that a young fellow should have CHESTERF. **2.** A Neat, s., affecting Courtier, one that weares clothes well, and in fashion B. JONS. The s. Night-cap of his Valet STEELE. The Cathedral [of Salisbury], which was finished 600 years ago, has even a s. and modern air EMERSON.

B. *adv.* Sprucely (*rare*) 1618. Hence **Spru·cely** *adv.*, **-ness.**

Spruce (sprūs), *v.* 1594. [f. prec.] **1.** *trans.* To make spruce, trim, or neat. Also with *up.* **2.** With *up* (or †*out*): To make oneself spruce 1709.

2. His Father and grandfather are..profess'd Sparks, and s. up in Cherry and other gaudy colour'd silk Stockings 1709.

Spruce beer. 1500. [SPRUCE *sb.*] †**a.** Beer from Prussia. **b.** A fermented beverage made with an extract from the leaves and branches of the spruce fir.

Spruce fir. 1731. [SPRUCE *sb.*] **1.** A distinct species of fir (*Pinus* or *Abies*) comprising several clearly marked varieties, as *black, red, white, Canadian, Norway spruce*; one or other of these varieties. **2.** A tree belonging to this species 1768.

Sprue[1] (sprū). 1825. [– Du. *spruw*, perh. rel. to Flem. *spruwen* sprinkle.] †**1.** = THRUSH[2] 1. (In Dicts.) **2.** A disease characterized by sore throat, raw tongue, and digestive disturbances, occurring esp. in tropical countries; psilosis 1888.

Sprue[2] (sprū). 1875. [Of unkn. origin.] *Founding.* One of the holes through which metal is poured into the mould.

Sprue[3] (sprū). 1846. [Of unkn. origin.] A poor or inferior quality of asparagus. Also *s. grass.*

‖**Spruit** (sprēˈt). *S. Afr.* 1863. [Du., = SPROUT *sb.*] A small stream or watercourse, usu. almost dry except in the wet season.

Sprung (sprɒŋ), *ppl. a.*[1] 1575. [pa. pple. of SPRING *v.*[1]] **1.** That has sprung up or arisen. **2.** Cracked, split 1597. **3.** Made to fly up, as a *s. partridge* 1598.

Sprung[2], irreg. ppl. adj. of SPRING *v.*[2] *S. rhythm*, a modern form of poetical rhythm based on that of medieval alliterative verse.

Sprunt (sprɒnt), *v.* Now *dial.* 1601. [app. related to SPRENT *v.* and SPRINT *v.*] *intr.* To spring or start; to move in a quick or convulsive manner; to dart or run. Hence **Sprunt** *sb.* a convulsive movement; a start, spring.

Spry (sprəi), *a.* 1746. [Of unkn. origin; cf. SPRACK *a.*, SPRAG *a.*] **1.** Active, nimble, brisk; full of health and spirits. **2.** *dial.* Spruce, neat, smartly dressed 1806. Hence **Spry·-ly** *adv.*, **-ness.**

Spud (spɒd), *sb.* 1440. [Of unkn. origin.] †**1.** A short and poor knife or dagger –1824. **2. a.** A digging or weeding implement of the spade-type, having a narrow chisel-shaped blade 1667. **b.** A digging fork with three broad prongs 1805. **c.** A small instrument with an enlarged end used in ocular and other surgery 1869. **3.** A short or stumpy person or thing 1687. **4.** *slang* and *dial.* A potato 1860.

2. a. We..begun with a spudd to lift up the ground PEPYS. **3.** That baby..everlastingly holds out its spuds of arms 1900.

Spud (spɒd), *v.* 1652. [f. prec. 2.] **1.** *trans.* To dig *up* or *out*, to remove, by means of a spud. **2.** To dig with a spud. Also *intr.* 1828. **3.** To drill (a hole) by a special process in the early stages of sinking an oil-well 1886.

Spulyie (spö·lyi, spö·li), *v.* Chiefly *Sc.* Now *arch.* late ME. [– OFr. *espoillier* SPOIL *v.*] **1.** *trans.* To despoil or plunder (persons, etc.). **2.** To take as spoil or plunder 1470. **3.** *intr.* To commit spoliation 1834. So **Spu·lyie** *sb.* [– OFr. *espoille*] spoiling, spoil 1464.

Spume (spiūm), *sb.* late ME. [– OFr. (*e*)*spume* or L. *spuma.*] **1.** Foam, froth, frothy matter. **b.** *spec.* Foam of the sea 1440. †**2.** = LITHARGE 1. –1661.

1. *fig.* These foul snails..leaving their s. and filth on the fairest flowers of literature RUSKIN. **b.** My forehead was wet with the s. of the spray 1805.

Spume (spiūm), *v.* late ME. [– L. *spumare*, f. *spuma* SPUME *sb.*] **1.** *intr.* To foam or froth. Also with *out.* **2.** *trans.* To send or cast *forth* like foam 1859.

Spumescence (spiūme·sĕns). 1796. [f. SPUME *sb.*; see -ESCE, -ENCE.] Frothiness; the state of being foamy. So **Spume·scent** *a.* having the appearance of froth or foam (*rare*).

Spumous (spiū·məs), *a.* late ME. [– L. *spumosus*, f. *spuma* SPUME *sb.*; see -OUS.] **1.** Of the nature of or resembling froth or foam. **2.** Marked by foam; foaming 1854. So **Spu·mose** *a.* 1576.

Spumy (spiū·mi), *a.* 1582. [f. SPUME *sb.* + -Y[1].] **1.** Covered with, throwing up, or of the nature of sea-foam. **2.** Of a frothy consistency or character; characterized by the presence of froth 1618.

1. The s. Waves proclaim the wat'ry War DRYDEN.

Spun (spɒn), *ppl. a.* 1486. [pa. pple. of SPIN *v.*] **1.** That has undergone the process of spinning; formed, fabricated, or prepared by spinning. **b.** Of butter or sugar: Drawn out or worked up into a thread-like form, esp. for ornamenting confectionery, etc. 1834. **c.** *ellipt.* Spun silk or yarn 1868. **2.** With *out.* Unduly protracted or prolonged 1879. **3.** Tired out, exhausted. *slang.* 1924.

1. *Spun-silk*, a..material produced from short-fibered and waste silk, in contradistinction to the long fibers wound from the cocoon 1875. *S. gold, silver*, a silk thread wound with gold, silver-gilt, or silver wire.

Spunge, var. of SPONGE.

Spunk (spɒŋk). 1536. [Of unkn. origin. Cf. PUNK[2].] **1.** A spark, in various senses. *Sc.* and *dial.* **2.** Touchwood; tinder, match, or amadou prepared from this 1582. **3.** One or other of various fungi or fungoid growths on trees, esp. those of the species *Polyporus*, freq. used in the preparation of tinder 1665. **4.** A match, a lucifer. *Sc.* and *north.* 1755. **5.** Spirit, mettle; courage, pluck 1773.

2. A spark of fire is seen and caught in a piece of s. 1841. **5.** The squire has got s. in him GOLDSM. Phr. *Fellow, man*, etc. *of* (..) *s.* Hence **Spu·nky** *a.* full of s. or spirit; courageous, mettlesome.

Spun(-)yarn. late ME. [f. SPUN *ppl. a.*] **1.** Yarn fabricated by the process of spinning. **2.** *Naut.* Line composed of two or more rope-yarns not laid but simply twisted together by a winch or by hand 1627. **b.** A line or cord of this kind 1685.

Spur (spɒ̄ɹ), *sb.* [OE. *spora, spura* = OS., OHG. *sporo* (Du. *spoor*, G. *sporn*, earlier *sporen*), ON. *spori* :– Gmc. **spuron*, based on IE. **sper-* strike with the foot (cf. SPURN *v.*).] **I. 1.** A device for pricking the side of a horse in order to urge it forward, consisting of a small spike or spiked wheel attached to the rider's heel. **b.** *Her.* The representation of a spur 1688. **2.** A stimulus, incentive, or incitement. Also const. *of* (the particular influence) and *to* (a person or persons). 1548.

1. A pair of Spurs taken from Buonaparte WELLINGTON. They..Set lance in rest, strike s., suddenly move TENNYSON. *Gilt* (or †*gilded*) *spurs*, as the distinctive mark of a knight (now *Hist.*). **2.** With the spurre of Courage, and the bitte of Respect SIDNEY. Avarice, the s. of industry HUME.

Phrases. *On* or *upon the s.* (arch.), at full speed, in or with the utmost haste. *On* (or *upon*) *the s. of the moment* (or *occasion*, etc.), without premeditation; on a momentary impulse; impromptu, suddenly, instantly. *To win one's spurs*, to gain knighthood by some act of valour; hence, to achieve one's first honours. *To put* or *set spurs to*, to impel or urge on by spurring.

II. 1. *Zool.* A sharp, hard process or projection on the tarsus of the domestic cock and certain other fowls and birds; a back-claw 1548. **b.** *Zool.*, *Anat.*, and *Path.* A sharp-pointed or spur-like process, formation, or growth on some part of the body 1681. **2. a.** A sharp-pointed projection from the prow of a war-vessel 1604. **b.** A metal needle or gaff for fastening to the leg of a gamecock for fighting purposes 1688. **c.** *Whaling.* One of a number of metal spikes in a boot-sole to prevent slipping 1820. **d.** Any sharp or short projection, point, or spike suggestive of a spur 1872. **3. a.** A short or stunted branch or shoot, esp. one likely to produce fruit 1700. **b.** *Bot.* A tubular expansion, resembling a cock's spur in form, of some more or less foliaceous part of a flower; a calcar 1731. **c.** = ERGOT 1. 1763.

1. *fig.* Though we are cockerels now, we shall have spurs one day 1571.

III. 1. A short strut or stay set diagonally to support an upright timber; a shore, prop, or sustaining pillar; a sloping buttress 1529. **b.** *Naut.* (*a*) A curved piece of timber serving as a half-beam to support the decks, where a whole beam cannot be placed; (*b*) A piece of timber fixed on the bilge-ways, its upper end being bolted to the vessel's sides above the water; (*c*) A prong or projection on the arm of an anchor to assist in catching hold of the bottom. 1769. **2.** One of the principal roots of a tree 1610. **3.** †**a.** *Fortif.* An angular outwork or projection from the general face of a curtain or wall, to assist in its defence –1702. †**b.** An angular end of the pier of a bridge –1742. **c.** An artificial projection from a river-bank serving to deflect the current 1818. **4.** A range, ridge, mountain, hill, or part of this, projecting for some distance from the main system or mass; an offshoot or offset 1652. **b.** A branch of a lode, railway, etc. 1833.

2. *Temp.* v. i. 47. **4.** A s. or rising ground at the base of the hills 1863.

Comb.: **s. box,** a special form of horseman's boot-heel, to which the rims of the spurs are affixed; **-fowl,** pop. name of *Galloperdix lunulosa*; **s. gear, gearing** *Mech.*, gearing consisting of spur-wheels; **s. line** (cf. 4 b); **s.-nut** *Mech.*, a small spur-wheel; **s. pepper,** *Capsicum frutescens*, a native of the East Indies; **-way,** a bridle-path (*dial.*); **-wheel,** a gear wheel which has cogs or teeth on the periphery projecting radially from the centre; a cog-wheel.

Spur (spɒ̄ɹ), *v.* [ME. *spure, spore*, f. SPUR *sb.*] **I.** *trans.* **1.** To prick (a horse, etc.) with the spur in order to urge to a faster pace; to urge on by the use of spurs. Also *absol.* **2.** *fig.* To drive on or hasten; to incite, impel, or stimulate; to urge or prompt. Freq. const. *to* (do something, or some course of action). ME. **3.** To provide with a spur or spurs; to furnish with gaffs ME. **4.** Of a bird: To strike or wound with the spur. Also *transf.* 1631.

1. He could scarcely make his horse go, though he spurred him continually 1770. He spurred his horse into the waves GIBBON. **2.** Ire, that spurr'd him on to deeds unjust CARY. **3.** They..began to boot and s. one another 1694.

II. *intr.* **1.** To ride quickly by urging on one's horses with the spur 1590. **b.** *transf.* To hasten; to proceed hurriedly 1513. **2. a.** To strike out with the foot; to kick 1590. **b.** Of cocks, etc.: To fight with the spur; to strike *at* 1722.

1. Parthians..spurring from the Fight, confess their Fear DRYDEN. *fig.* Obstinacy spurs on in spight of all perswasions 1659. **2. a.** All day, between his..sleeps, he [an infant] sputters and spurs EMERSON.

III. *trans.* **1.** To support or prop up (a post, etc.) by means of a strut or spur; to strengthen with spurs 1733. **2.** To prune in (a side-shoot, etc.) so as to form a spur close to the stem. Chiefly with *in* or *back*. 1840. **3.** To affect with ergot 1896.

Spu·r-gall, *v. Obs.* exc. *arch.* 1555. [f. SPUR *sb.* + GALL *v.*[1]] **1.** *trans.* To gall (a horse, etc.) with the spur in riding; to injure or disable in this way 1565. **2.** *fig.* To gall severely, in various senses 1555.

Spurge (spɒ̄ɹdʒ), *sb.* late ME. [Aphetic – OFr. *espurge* (mod. *épurge*), f. *espurgier* :– L. *expurgare* (see EX-[1], PURGE *v.*).] **1.** One or other of several species of plants belonging to the genus *Euphorbia*, many of which are characterized by an acrid milky juice possessing medicinal properties. **2.** A particular species or plant of this. Chiefly in *pl.* 1715.

attrib.: **s. flax,** *Daphne gnidium*; **-nettle,** *Cnidoscolus stimulosus*; **-olive,** the shrub *Daphne mezereum*.

Spurge, *v. Obs.* exc. *dial.* ME. [– OFr. *espurgier*; see prec.] †**1.** *trans.* To cleanse, purify (a person, the body, etc.); to rid *of* impurity. Also *fig.* to clear of guilt. –1546. **2.** *intr.* Of ale, wine, or other fermenting liquor: To emit or throw off impure matter by fermentation; to cleanse or purify itself in this way; to ferment or 'work' 1440.

Spurge laurel. Also hyphened. 1597. [SPURGE *sb.*] One or other of the shrubs belonging to the genus *Daphne*, esp. *D. laureola*, the dried bark of which is used in medicine.

Spu·rge-wort. 1562. [f. SPURGE *sb.* or *v.* + WORT[1].] †**1.** The plant *Iris fœtidissima* –1588. **2.** *Bot.* Any plant belonging to the order *Euphorbiaceæ* 1647.

Spurious (spiū°·riəs), *a.* 1598. [f. L. *spurius* illegitimate, false + -OUS.] **1.** Of persons: Begot or born out of wedlock; illegitimate, bastard, adulterous. **b.** Characterized by bastardy or illegitimacy 1770. **2.** Having an illegitimate or irregular origin; not properly qualified or constituted 1601. **3.** Superficially resembling or simulating something; not true or genuine; false, sham, counterfeit 1615. **4.** Of a writing, passage, etc.: Not really proceeding from its reputed origin, source, or author; not genuine or authentic; forged 1624. **5.** Characterized by spuriousness or falseness 1840.

1. Henry came of the s. stock of John of Gaunt 1768. **3.** S. gems our hopes entice COWPER. Statesmen..exist by every thing which is s., fictitious, and false BURKE. Morbid conditions..known as s. dropsies 1877. **4.** The vexed question concerning his reputed works—what are genuine, what s. EMERSON. Hence **Spu·rious-ly** *adv.*, **-ness.**

Spu·r-leather. 1598. [f. SPUR *sb.* + LEATHER *sb.*] **1.** A leather strap for securing a spur to the foot. **2.** *Under spur-leather*, a subordinate, an attendant, a menial. Now *arch.* 1685.

Spurless (spɒ̄·ɹles), *a.* ME. [f. SPUR *sb.* + -LESS.] **1.** Lacking a spur; having no spurs. **2.** Of birds or their legs; Devoid of spurs 1819. **3.** *Bot.* Having no spur or calcar 1839.

Spurling. 1471. var. of SPARLING, SPIRLING.

Spurn (spɒ̄ɹn), *sb.*[1] ME. [f. SPURN *v.*] †**1.** A trip or stumble –1535. **2.** A stroke with the foot; a kick ME. **b.** The act of kicking or spurning 1641. **3.** The act of treating with disdain or contemptuous rejection; an instance of this 1602.

2. *fig.* Death with an equall s. The lofty Turret and low Cottage beats 1612. **3.** The insolence of Office, and the Spurnes That patient merit of the vnworthy takes SHAKS.

Spurn (spɒ̄ɹn), *sb.*[2] 1601. [var. of SPUR *sb.*, prob. after prec. or next.]. **1.** An outward-growing root or rootlet; one of the main roots *of* a tree. *Obs.* exc. *dial.* **2.** A slanting prop or stay; a spur or spur-stone 1620. **b.** *Mining.* A small pillar of coal left within the seam as a temporary support during holing 1837.

Spurn (spɒ̄ɹn), *v.* [OE. *spurnan, spornan*, corresp. to OS. *spurnan*, OHG. *spornōn*, *spurnan*, ON. **spurna*; Gmc. str. vb. cogn. with L. *spernere* scorn. Cf. SPUR *sb.*] **I.** *intr.* †**1.** To strike against something with the foot; to trip or stumble –1734. †**2.** To strike or thrust with the foot; to kick (*at* something) –1740. **3.** *fig.* To kick *against* or *at* something disliked or despised; to manifest opposition or antipathy, esp. in a scornful or disdainful manner 1526.

2. Folly it is to spurne against a pricke CAMDEN. **3.** They spurned at danger, and made several vigorous sallies on the enemy 1781.

II. *trans.* **1.** To strike or tread (something) with the foot; to trample or kick. late ME. **2.** To reject with contempt or disdain; to treat contemptuously; to scorn or despise OE.

1. He with his feet wol spurne adoun his cuppe CHAUCER. You spurne me hence, and he will spurne me hither SHAKS. **2.** Every offer tending to conciliation had been spurned FREEMAN.

Comb.: **s.-water** *Naut.*, a low barrier on the ends of a deck to prevent water from coming aboard.

Spurner (spɒ̄·ɹnəɹ). 1562. [f. SPURN *v.* + -ER[1].] †**1.** One who strikes with the foot –1611. **2.** One who rejects or despises; a scorner 1863.

2. Traitor and trickster, And s. of treaties TENNYSON.

Spurred (spɒ̄ɹd), *a.* late ME. [f. SPUR *sb.* + -ED[2].] **1.** Wearing or provided with a spur or spurs. **2.** Furnished with sharp and hard spikes, claws, or the like 1611. **3.** Of rye, etc.: Affected with ergot or spur 1763. **4.** *Bot.* Of the nature of, provided with, a spur or calcar; calcarate 1824.

1. Others came forth on foot, booted and s. FREEMAN.

Spurrer (spɒ̄·reɹ). 1632. [f. SPUR *v.* + -ER[1].] One who spurs or urges.

Spurr(e)y (spɒ·ri). 1577. [– Du. *spurrie*, earlier *sporie, speurie*, obscurely based on med.L. *spergula* (XIII), whence G. *spergel*, *spörgel*.] **1.** One or other of various species of herbaceous plants or weeds of the genus *Spergula*; esp. the common species corn spurrey (*S. arvensis*), occas. used as fodder for sheep and cattle; also, the genus to which these species belong. **2.** Applied to various species of plants allied to or resembling the genus *Spergula* 1753.

Spurrier (spɒ·riəɹ). ME. [f. SPUR *sb.* + -IER.] A spur-maker.

Spur-rowel. 1611. [f. SPUR *sb.*] The rowel of a spur.

Spur-royal. Now *Hist.* or *arch.* Also **-rial.** 1588. [f. SPUR *sb.* + ROYAL *sb.*] A gold coin of the value of fifteen shillings, chiefly coined in the reign of James I; so called from having on its reverse the form of the sun with rays, resembling a spur-rowel.

Spurry (spɒ̄·ri), *a. rare.* 1611. [f. SPUR *sb.* + -Y[1].] †**a.** Radiating like the points of a spur-rowel. **b.** Of the nature of a spur or prop 1863. **c.** Having spur-like projections 1875.

Spurt (spɒ̄ɹt), *sb.*[1] 1566. [var. of SPIRT *sb.*[1]; of unkn. origin.] **1.** †**a.** A short spell *of* (something) –1699. **b.** A short space of time; a brief period. Now *dial.* 1591. **2.** A brief and unsustained effort; a sudden and short spell of activity or exertion 1591. **b.** A short spell of rapid movement; a marked or sudden increase of speed attained by special exertion 1787. **c.** *transf.* A marked increase or improvement in business; a sudden advance or rise of prices, etc.: also, the period during which this lasts 1814. **3.** *Naut.* A short spell *of* wind 1699.

1. b. Herschel has been in town for short spurts, and back again, two or three times MME. D'ARBLAY. **2.** Quinine..has given me a s. for the last two days 1885. **b.** Their boat..dipped a little when they put on anything like a severe s. HUGHES. Phr. *By* or *in spurts*, in or with brief, unsustained or spasmodic efforts; in intermittent jets.

Spurt (spɒ̄ɹt), *sb.*[2] 1775. [var. of SPIRT *sb.*[2], of unkn. origin.] **1.** A stream or shower of water, etc., ejected or thrown up with some force and suddenness. **b.** A spatter or splash made by a pen 1871. **2.** A sudden manifestation *of* feeling or energy 1859.

2. A sudden s. of woman's jealousy TENNYSON.

Spurt (spɒ̄ɹt), *v.*[1] 1570. [var. of contemp. SPIRT *v.*[1]] = SPIRT *v.*[1] 1, 2.

The milk went on spurting and fizzing into the pail 1833. **2.** *fig.* His stream of meaning..is ever and anon spurting itself up into epigrams CARLYLE.

Spurt (spɒ̄ɹt), *v.*[2] 1664. [f. SPURT *sb.*[1] 2. Cf. SPIRT *v.*[2]] *intr.* To make a spurt, put on increased speed or make greater exertions, for a short time.

Spurtle (spǒ·ɹt'l), *v.* 1633. [f. SPURT *v.*[1] + -LE. Cf. SPIRTLE *v.*] **1.** *trans.* To besprinkle or bespatter (*rare*). **2.** *intr.* To burst or fly out in a small quantity or stream with some force or suddenness; to spirt 1651.

Spu·r-wing. 1842. [Cf. next.] A spur-winged water-hen, goose, etc.

Spu·r-winged, *a.* 1668. [f. SPUR *sb.*[1]] *Ornith.* Having one or more stiff claws or spurs projecting from the pinion-bone of the wing. In specific names, as *s. goose, plover, lapwing*.

Spute, *v. Obs.* or *dial.* ME. [Aphetic f. DISPUTE *v.*] *intr.* To dispute; to contend in disputation. Usu. const. *with*.

Sputter (spɒ·təɹ), *sb.* 1673. [f. SPUTTER *v.*] **1.** = SPLUTTER *sb.* 1 b. **b.** A state of bustling confusion or excitement 1823. **2.** The action or an act of sputtering; the emission of small particles with some amount of explosive sound; the noise characteristic of this. Freq. *fig.* 1837.

1. But he must take some s. rather than be held to the terms of the Question MARVELL. **2.** Nothing breaking the silence but the occasional s. of the rushlight 1845.

Sputter (spɒ·təɹ), *v.* 1598. [– Du. *sputteren*, of imit. origin; cf. SPLUTTER.] **1.** *trans.* To spit out in small particles and with a characteristic explosive sound or a series of such sounds. **2.** To utter hastily and with the emission of small particles of saliva; to ejaculate in a confused, indistinct, or uncontrolled manner, esp. from anger or excitement 1677. **3.** *intr.* Of persons: To eject from the mouth, to spit out, food or saliva in small particles with some force and in a noisy explosive manner 1681. **4.** To speak or talk hastily and confusedly or disjointedly 1681. **5.** To make or give out a sputtering sound or sounds, esp. under the influence of heat 1692.

2. Without the least pretended incitement [to] s. out the basest and falsest accusations SWIFT. **3.** His tongue was too large for his mouth; he stuttered and sputtered 1878. **4.** The Servants.. sputter'd in Dutch, which they understood not 1696. **5.** Like the Green Wood That sputtring in the Flame works outward into Tears DRYDEN. The candle..was sputtering with the rain-drops 1845.

‖**Sputum** (spiū·tǒm). *Pl.* **sputa** (spiū·tă). 1693. [L. subst. use of n. pa. pple of *spuere* spit.] *Med.* Saliva or spittle mixed with mucus or purulent matter, and expectorated in certain diseased states of the lungs, chest, or throat; a mass or quantity of this.

Spy (spəi), *sb.* ME. [Aphetic – OFr. *espie*, f. *espier*; see next. Cf. med.L. *spia* (XIII).] **1.** One who spies upon or watches a person or persons secretly; a secret agent whose business it is to keep a person, place, etc., under close observation; esp. one employed by a government in order to obtain information relating to the naval, military or aeronautical conditions of other countries, or to collect intelligence of any kind. **2.** *Mil.* A person employed in time of war to obtain secret information regarding the enemy; in early use esp. one venturing in disguise into the enemy's camp or territory ME. **3.** The action of spying; an instance or occasion of this. Chiefly in phrases. 1450.

1. Theeves have their spies..in all Innes 1617. I come no Spie With purpose to explore..The secrets of your Realm MILT. **2.** In the early romances, no disguise is so frequently used by a s. as that of a minstrel 1846.

attrib. and *Comb.*, as *s.-system*, etc.; **-money,** payment for the services of a s.; **S. Wednesday,** in Irish use, the Wednesday before Easter Sunday (in allusion to Judas). Hence **Spy·ism,** espionage.

Spy (spəi), *v.* ME. [Aphetic – OFr. *espier* ESPY *v.* – Gmc. *speχ-, as in MLG. *spēen*, MDu, *spien* (Du. *spieden*), OHG. *spehōn* (G. *spähen*), ON. *speja*, *spæja*, repr. IE. **spek*- as in L. *specere* look, behold.] **I.** *trans.* **1.** To watch (a person, etc.) in a secret or stealthy manner; to keep under observation with hostile intent; to act as a spy upon (a person). **b.** To make stealthy observations in (a country or place) from hostile motives. Also with *out*. ME. **c.** To (seek to) discover or ascertain by stealthy observation ME. **2.** To look at, examine, or observe closely or carefully; to see or behold; in mod. use *spec.* to investigate with a spy-glass or telescope ME. **3.** To catch sight of; to descry or discover; to notice or observe ME. **4.** To find *out*, to search or seek *out*, by observation or scrutiny 1530.

1. b. The men, whom Moses sent forth to spye out the lande COVERDALE *Numb.* 13:16. **c.** Goe and spie where he is, that I may send and fetch him 2 *Kings* 6:13. **2.** I spied the whole ground, and never saw a beast 1893. **3.** Feare seeing all, feares it of all is spy'd DRAYTON. By dilating the pupil, the animal..is enabled to s. its prey..in the dark GOLDSM. **4.** I felt ashamed of myself for spying out their follies THACKERAY.

II. *intr.* **1.** To make observations (now *spec.* with a telescope); to keep watch; to be on the look out ME. **2.** To make stealthy or covert observations; to play the spy; to pry 1456.

2. I confesse it is my Natures plague To s. into Abuses SHAKS. I am come to s. upon your vanity and ambition GOLDSM.

Spy-, the stem of SPY *v.* used in combs. in the sense 'that spies', as *s.-all*, or 'from or through which one may spy', as *s.-hole*, *-tower*, *-window*, etc.

Spy-glass. 1706. [f. SPY *v.* + GLASS *sb.*] A telescope; a field-glass.

Squab (skwǫb), *sb.* 1640. [Of unc. origin; cf. Sw. dial. *sqvabb* loose fat flesh, *sqvabba* fat woman, *sqvabbig*, flabby, and Eng. †*quab* (XVII) squat object.] **1.** A newly-hatched, unfledged, or very young bird. Also *fig.* of a person. **b.** *spec.* A young pigeon 1694. **2.** A short fat person 1700. **3.** A sofa, ottoman, or couch 1664. **4.** A thick or soft cushion, *esp.* one serving to cover the seat of a chair or sofa 1687. **b.** A cushion forming part of the inside fittings of a carriage 1794.

2. He is a fat, sallow s. of a man 1823. **3.** On her large s. you will find her spread, Like a fat corpse upon a bed POPE. **4.** She was poking the little fists into the s. of the sofa 1881.

Squab (skwǫb), *a.* 1675. [See prec.] **1.** Of persons: Short and stout; squat and plump. **b.** Having a thick clumsy form 1723. **2.** Young and undeveloped; *esp.* of young birds, unfledged or not fully fledged, newly or lately hatched 1706. †**3.** Abrupt, blunt, curt –1759.

1. A Dutch woman is s. 1703. **b.** Turning his s. nose up in the air SCOTT. **2.** A nest-full of little s. Cupids W. IRVING. **3.** We have returned a *squab* answer, retorting the infraction of treaties H. WALPOLE. So **Squa·bbish** *a.* somewhat s. or squat. **Squa·bby** *a.* squat, thick-set.

Squab (skwǫb), *v.* 1668. [Cf. SQUAB *sb.* and *a.*] **1.** *trans.* To squash. **2.** To stuff or stuff up 1819. **2.** *intr.* To fall or hang in a full or heavy manner 1755.

Squab, *adv.* 1692. [Imitative.] With a heavy fall or squash.

The Eagle took him up a matter of Steeple-high into the Air, and..dropt him down, S. upon a Rock 1692.

Squabash (skwǫbæ·ʃ), *sb.* 1818. [A combination of *squash* and *bash*.] A crushing blow; a squashing. Hence **Squaba·sh** *v. trans.* to crush, squash, demolish.

Squabble (skwǫ·b'l), *sb.* 1602. [prob. imitative; cf. next and Sw. dial. *sqvabbel*.] A wrangle, brawl; a petty quarrel.

Squabble (skwǫ·b'l), *v.* 1604. [See prec.] **1.** *intr.* To wrangle or brawl; to engage in a petty quarrel or dispute; to argue disagreeably or with heat. **2.** *trans.* In *Typog.* to throw (type) out of line; to disarrange or disorder; to twist or skew so as to mix the lines 1674. **b.** *intr.* Of type: To get into disorder 1683.

1. Drunke? And speake Parrat? And s.? Swagger? SHAKS. It agreeth to children..to s. 1677. The Devil comes..and squabbles with him 1677. Hence **Squa·bbler.**

Squab-pie. *local* (*w.* and *s.w.*). 1708. [Cf. SQUAB *sb.*] A pie with a thick crust composed of mutton, pork, apples, and onions.

Squacco (skwa·kko). 1752. [Local It. *sguacco*.] A small crested species of heron, *Ardea ralloides* or *comata*.

Squad (skwǫd), *sb.* 1649. [Aphetic (after *squadron*) – Fr. *escouade*, †*esquade* (XVI), var. of *escadre* – Sp. *esquadra*, It. *squadra*, corresp. to Fr. *écarre* SQUARE *sb.*] **1.** *Mil.* A small number of men, a subdivision or section of a company, formed for drill, or told off for some special purpose. Also in phr. *awkward s.* **2.** A small number, group, or party of persons 1809. **3.** A particular set or circle of people 1786.

1. The awkward s. consists not only of recruits at drill, but of formed soldiers that are ordered to exercise with them, in consequence of some irregularity under arms 1802. **2.** Phr. *Flying s.*, a police detachment equipped for rapid pursuit with motor-cars, cycles, etc. **3.** A rowing s., football s. (*U.S.*).

Squad (skwǫd), *v.* 1802. [f. prec.] **1.** *trans.* To divide or form into squads; to draw up in a squad. **2.** To assign or allocate to a squad 1802.

1. I say, lads, s. your men and form on the road 1841.

Squadron (skwǫ·drən), *sb.* 1562. [– It. *squadrone*, f. *squadra* SQUARE *sb.*; cf. Fr. †(*e*)*squadron* (mod. *escadron*), Sp. *escuadron*; see -OON.] †**1.** *Mil.* A body of soldiers drawn up or arranged in square formation –1656. **2.** *Mil.* A relatively small body or detachment of men 1579. **b.** *spec.* A body of cavalry, usu. composed of between one and two hundred men 1702. **3.** A division of a fleet forming one body under the command of a flag-officer; a detachment of warships told off for some particular duty. Also, a unit of a definite number of aeroplanes with its officers and men. 1588. **4.** A comparatively large group or number of people or animals; an organized body of persons 1617. †**b.** *transf.* A multitude *of* things (*rare*) –1680. **5.** A body of cardinals hovering between the main factions in a conclave 1670.

2. Trump nor pibroch summon here Mustering clans, or squadrons tramping SCOTT. **3.** *Flying s.*: see FLYING *ppl. a.* 4. phr. **5.** Cardinal de Retz and Cardinal Azzolino were of the s. 1906. **S.-commander, -leader,** officers of the Royal Air Force. Hence **Squa·droned** *ppl. a.*, formed into squadrons; drawn up in a s.

Squail (skwē̆ⁱl), *sb.* 1847. [Of unkn. origin. Cf. KAYLES, SKAYLES.] **1.** *pl.* Ninepins, skittles, *s.w. dial.* **2.** *pl.* A table-game in which counters or discs are propelled towards some mark by snapping 1862. **b.** A disc or counter used in this game 1862.

Squail, *v.* Chiefly *dial.* 1626. [Of unkn. origin.] **1.** *intr.* To throw a (loaded) stick or similar missile (*at* some object). **2.** *trans.* To strike or hit by throwing a stick or squailer 1844. **3.** To cast or throw 1876. Hence **Squai·ler,** a loaded stick, esp. used for throwing at small game or apples.

Squalid (skwǫ·lid), *a.* 1591. [– L. *squalidus*, f. *squalēre* be dry, rough, dirty; see -ID[1].] **I. 1.** Naturally foul and repulsive because of the presence of slime, mud, etc., and the absence of all cultivation or care. **b.** *gen.* Repulsive or loathsome to look at 1620. **2.** Foul through neglect or want of cleanliness; repulsively mean and filthy 1596. **3.** Of qualities, conditions, etc.: Marked or characterized by filth, dirt, or squalor 1621. **4.** *fig.* Wretched, miserable, morally repulsive or degraded 1660.

1. S. fields of mud and thistles 1887. **2.** 'Tis a s. den made in the rock EVELYN. The poorest and most s. savage 1875. **3.** Winter is..vgly, foule, s. BURTON.

II. †**1.** Dry, parched; marked by drought –1661. †**2.** Rough, shaggy, unkempt –1722. **3.** Having a pinched and miserable appearance, or a dull unhealthy look. 1661.

3. His complexion sallow and s. LYTTON. Hence **Squa·lid-ly** *adv.*, **-ness.**

Squalidity (skwǫli·dĭti). 1668. [– late L. *squaliditas* or f. prec. + -ITY.] The quality or character of being foul or squalid; filthiness, squalidness.

Squall (skwǭl), *sb.*[1] 1709. [f. SQUALL *v.*] A discordant or violent scream; a loud harsh cry. **b.** The action or habit of squalling or talking in a shrill voice 1755.

The crowing pheasant..Betrays his lair with awkward squalls 1821.

Squall (skwǭl), *sb.*[2] 1719. [perh. f. next.] **1.** A sudden and violent gust, a blast or short sharp storm, of wind. orig. *Naut.* **2.** *fig.* a disturbance or commotion; a quarrel 1813.

1. A very violent and sudden S. took us quite a-head 1745. A *black s.* is attended with a dark cloud, in distinction from a *white s.*, where there are no clouds, and a *thick s.*, accompanied with hail, sleet, &c. CRABB. **2.** Phr. *To look out for squalls*, fig. to anticipate and be on one's guard against sudden danger, disturbance, or trouble.

Squall (skwǭl), *v.* 1631. [prob. alt. of SQUEAL *v.* by assoc. with BAWL *v.*] **1.** *intr.* Of birds or animals: To scream loudly or discordantly. Also in common usage, of persons esp. children. (Freq. with a suggestion of contempt.) 1687. **2.** *trans.* To utter or sing in a loud discordant tone 1703.

1. The parrot scream'd, the peacock squall'd TENNYSON. **2.** She sung, or rather squalled, a song of Sacchini's 1779. Hence **Squa·ller.**

Squally (skwǭ·li), *a.* 1719. [f. SQUALL *sb.*[2] + -Y[1].] **1.** Characterized by the prevalence of squalls. **2.** Of the wind: Blowing in sudden and violent gusts or blasts 1748. **3.** *fig.* Stormy, troublous, threatening. Chiefly *U.S.*, esp. in the phr. *to look s.* 1814.

1. S. Weather, with Hail and Snow 1745. **3.** But for some hours things looked s. enough 1853.

Squalodon (skwē̆ⁱ·lŏdǫn). 1872. [– mod.L. *Squalodon*, f. L. *squalus* SQUALUS + Gr. ὀδούς, ὀδοντ- tooth.] *Palæont.* A genus of fossil cetaceans found in Miocene and early Pliocene formations; a cetacean of this genus. So **Squa·lodont.**

Squaloid (skwē̆ⁱ·loid), *a.* and *sb.* 1836. [f. SQUALUS + -OID.] **A.** *adj.* Shark-like; comprising the sharks. **B.** *sb.* A fish of the shark family 1836.

Squalor (skwǫ·lǝɹ). 1621. [– L. *squalor*, f. *squalēre*; see SQUALID, -OR 2.] The state or condition of being physically squalid; a combination of misery and dirt. **b.** *fig.* The quality of being morally squalid 1860.

Hovel piled upon hovel, —s. immortalized in undecaying stone HAWTHORNE. **b.** The s. of Mesmerism, the deliration of rappings EMERSON.

‖**Squalus** (skwē̆ⁱ·lŭs). *Pl.* **-li** (lǝi). 1753. [L. (Varro, Pliny), some sea-fish] A shark.

‖**Squama** (skwē̆ⁱ·mă). *Pl.* **-mæ** (mī). 1706. [L., scale.] **1.** *Zool.* A scale as part of the integument of a fish, reptile, or insect. **b.** *Path.* A small portion of epidermis morbidly developed in the form of a scale 1876. **2.** *Anat.* A thin scaly portion of a bone, esp. of the temporal bone 1728. **3.** *Bot.* = SCALE *sb.*[2] 3 c. 1738.

Squamate (skwē̆ⁱ·mĕt), *a.* 1826. [f. prec. + -ATE[2].] *Zool.* etc. Provided or covered with squamæ or scales.

Squamation (skwămē̆ⁱ·ʃǝn). 1881. [f. SQUAMA; see -ATION.] *Zool.* The condition or character of being covered with scales; a special mode or form of this.

Squame (skwē̆ⁱ·m). late ME. [– OFr. *esquame* or L. *squama* SQUAMA.] †**1.** A scale (of iron, or on the skin or eyes) –1661. **2.** *Zool.* = SQUAMA 1. 1877.

Squami·ferous (skwă-), *a.* 1748. [f. *squami-*, comb. form of SQUAMA; see -FEROUS.] *Zool.* and *Bot.* Bearing or provided with scales; squamigerous. So **Squami·gerous** *a.* 1656.

Squamiform (skwē̆ⁱ·-), *a.* 1828. [f. as prec.; see -FORM.] *Zool.* and *Bot.* Having the shape of a scale or scales.

Squamo- (skwē̆ⁱ·mo), used as comb. form of SQUAMA, chiefly in terms of *Anat.* relating to the squamous bones, as *s.-occipital*, *-temporal*.

Squamosal (skwămōᵘ·săl), *a.* and *sb.* 1848. [f. next + -AL[1].] *Anat.* **A.** *adj.* **1.** *S. bone*, the squamous bone 1849. **2.** Of or pertaining to the squamous bone 1863. **B.** *sb.* The squamosal bone or squamous portion of the temporal bone 1848.

Squamose (skwē̆ⁱ·moᵘs), *a.* 1661. [– L. *squamosus*, f. *squama* scale; see -OSE[1].] **1.** Covered or furnished with scales; scaly. **2.** *Anat., Bot., Path.* = SQUAMOUS *a.* 1a, b, 2, 5. 1708.

Squamoso- (skwămōᵘ·so), used as comb. form of prec., in the sense 'squamous and —', as *s.-dentated*; or in terms of *Anat.* relating to the squamous bones, as *s.-maxillary*, *-zygomatic*.

Squamous (skwē̆ⁱ·mǝs), *a.* 1541. [– L. *squamosus*, f. *squama* scale; see -OUS. In XVI *scamous* – OFr. *scamoux*.] **1.** *Anat.* **a.** *S. bone, part, portion*, the thin and scaly part of the temporal bone, situated in the temple 1541. **b.** Of a suture: Formed by thin overlapping parts resembling scales 1709. **2.** *Bot.* Furnished or covered with, composed of, squamæ or scales 1658. **3.** = SQUAMOSE *a.* 1. 1668. **4.** Of substances: Composed of scales 1728. **5.** *Path.* Of skin-diseases: Characterized by the development of scales or laminæ of skin 1843. **6.** Of armour: Scaly; laminated 1845.

2. The bracts are described as *s.* or *scaly* 1870. **3.** Blue bellied, s. lizards 1796. **4.** S. epithelium generally consists of many layers of cells, one over the other 1872. Hence **Squa·mous-ly** *adv.*, **-ness.**

‖**Squamula** (skwē̆ⁱ·miŭlă). 1754. [L., dim. of *squama* scale.] *Zool. Ent., Bot.* A small scale. So **Squa·mule.**

Squamulose (skwē̆ⁱ·miŭlōᵘs), *a.* 1846. [f. SQUAMULA + -OSE[1].] *Bot.* Furnished or covered with small scales.

Squander (skwǫ·ndǝɹ), *sb.* 1709. [f. next.] The act of squandering; extravagant expenditure; an instance of this.

Squander (skwǫ·ndǝɹ), *v.* 1593. [Of unkn. origin.] **1.** *trans.* In pa. pple. **a.** Of things: To be scattered over a comparatively wide surface or area 1596. **b.** Brought to disintegration or dissolution 1610. **2.** To cause to scatter or disperse 1657. **3.** To use (money, goods, etc.) recklessly, prodigally, or lavishly; to expend extravagantly, profusely, or wastefully. (The most common usage.) 1593. **4.** To spend or employ (time) wastefully; to waste 1693. **5.** To spend profusely, without securing an adequate return; to use in a wasteful manner 1716. **6.** *intr.* To roam about; to wander 1630. **7.** To scatter 1823.

1. a. In many thousand Islands that lye squandred in the vast Ocean 1645. **2.** All along the sea They drive and s. the huge Belgian fleet DRYDEN. **3.** The public money is squandered away in pensions 1763. **4.** They considered the time occupied in learning as so much squandered away BORROW. **5.** If he s. his Talents in Luxury 1716. Hence **Squa·nderer. Squa·ndering** *vbl. sb.* and *ppl. a.*, **-ly** *adv.*

Squandermania (skwǫndǝɹmē̆ⁱ·niă). 1920. [f. SQUANDER *v.* + -MANIA.] A craze for extravagant expenditure.

Squarable (skwēᵊ·răb'l), *a.* and *sb.* 1706. [f. SQUARE *v.* + -ABLE.] **A.** *adj.* Capable of being squared. **B.** *sb.* A person who can be 'squared'.

Square (skwēᵊɹ), *sb.* Also †**squire.** ME. [Aphetic – OFr. *esquire* (ME. *squire*), *esquar(r)e* (mod. *équerre*) :– Rom. **exquadra*, f. **exquadrare*, f. *ex* EX-[1] + *quadra* square.] **I. 1.** An implement or tool for determining, measuring, or setting out right angles, etc., usually consisting of two pieces or arms set at right angles to each other, but sometimes with the arms or sides hinged or pivoted so as to measure any angle; esp. one used by carpenters and joiners. Freq. without article in phr. *by s.* †**b.** *fig.* In phr. *by the s.*, with extreme accuracy; precisely, exactly –1633. †**2.** *fig.* A canon, criterion, or standard; a rule or guiding principle; a pattern or example –1809.

1. A poet does not work by s. or line, As smiths and joiners perfect a design COWPER. *Bevel-s.* = BEVEL *sb.*; *mitre-s., set-s., T-* or *tee-s., trial-* or *try-s.*: see these words. **b.** *L.L.L.* v. ii. 475. **2.** To governe the body..by the s. of prudence, and rule of season 1604. Is merit everywhere else made the exact s. of preferment? FULLER.

II. †**1.** Rectangular or square shape or form –1663. †**2.** A side of a square, rectangle, or polygon; a face of a cube –1753. **3.** A square or quadrilateral space, esp. one of several marked out on a board, paper, etc., for playing certain games or for purposes of measurement, etc.; a square surface or face 1440. †**b.** *fig.* Affairs, events, matters, proceedings. Only in the phr. *how* (*the*) *squares go.* –1828. **4.** *Geom.* A plane rectilinear and rectangular figure with four equal sides 1551. †**b.** A rectangle with only the opposite sides equal, spec. called *long* or *oblong s.* –1842. †**c.** *Geometrical s.*: two graduated sides of a square marked in the rectangular corner of a quadrant to facilitate its use –1728. **d.** *Logic.* A square diagram used to illustrate the four kinds of logical opposition 1864. **5.** *Math.* The product of a number multiplied by itself; the second power (*of*) 1557. **6.** *Mil.* A body of troops drawn up in a square formation, either with solid ranks or leaving an open space in the centre 1591. **7.** †**a.** A square piece of material covering the bosom; the breast-piece of a dress –1710. **b.** A square or rectangular piece, block, etc. 1601. **c.** A rectangular pane of glass. Now *dial.* 1687. **8.** A square or rectangular area or piece of ground; *spec.* a garden plot of this shape 1615. **9.** An open space or area (approximately quadrilateral and rectangular) in a town or city, enclosed by buildings or dwelling-houses, esp. of a superior or residential kind, freq. containing a garden or laid out with trees, etc.; more generally, any open space resembling this, esp. one formed at the meeting or intersection of streets; also, the group of houses surrounding an area of this kind 1687. **b.** A rectangular building or block of buildings; *U.S.* a block of buildings bounded by streets 1700. **10.** An area of a hundred square feet, forming the measure or standard by which the price of flooring, roofing, tiling, or the like is reckoned 1663. †**11.** *Astrol.* and *Astron.* Quartile aspect; quadrature (*rare*) –1690. **12.** In various techn. uses denoting square parts or structures; also *ellipt.* for *s. cap, dance, drink*, etc. 1688.

1. fig. *Ant. & Cl.* II. iii. 7. **3.** The queen gives a check in the black queen's second s. 1735. *Magic s.*: see MAGIC *a.* **b.** He..then ask'd him how Squares went at Rome 1692. **5.** The law of the inverse s. in electric action 1885. **6.** He..no practise had In the braue squares of Warre SHAKS. *Hollow S.*, a Body of Foot drawn up with an empty space in the middle for the Colours, Drums, and Baggage 1702. *Solid S.*, is a body of foot, where both ranks and files are equal 1802. Men are formed into s. to resist attacks of cavalry 1859. **7. a.** *Wint. T.* IV. iv. 212. **b.** He..bolted his food down his capacious throat in squares of three inches SCOTT. **8.** Within a s. of tall trees, is a basilisc of copper EVELYN. **9.** Going early from his house in the s. of St. James EVELYN.

†**III.** A quarrel, dispute, wrangle; discord, dissension, quarrelling –1627.

They did agree without any S. at all 1627.

Phrases. *To break s.*: see BREAK *v.* *To break no s.*, to make no difference. †*At s.*, at variance; esp. *to be* or *to fall at* (*a*) *s.*, to quarrel or wrangle. *Out of s.*, out of the true, proper, or normal state or condition; out of (right) order or rule.

Square (skwēᵊɹ), *a.* ME. [– OFr. *esquarré*, pa. pple. of *esquarrer* :– Rom. **exquadrare*; see prec.] **I. 1.** Having a rectilinear and rectangular form of equal length and breadth; contained by four equal sides at right angles to each other; quadrate. late ME. **2.** Having an equilateral rectangular section ME. **b.** Having a form more or less approximating to a cube; rectangular and of three dimensions. late ME. **3.** Of limbs, the body, etc.: Approximating to a square section or outline; stoutly and strongly built; solid, sturdy. late ME. **4.** Of a (stated) length on each of the four sides forming a square. late ME. **5.** †**a.** Of an angle: Right. RECORDE. **b.** At right angles; rectangular in position or direction; perpendicular (*to* something) 1571. **6.** Even, straight, level 1814. **b.** *fig.* On equal terms; with all accounts settled 1859. **c.** *Golf.* Having equal scores 1887.

1. EIGHT-, *six-*, THREE-SQUARE: see these words. *S. inch, foot, yard*, etc., a rectangular space measuring an inch, etc., either way, or any equivalent area. *S. measure*, a unit of measurement consisting of a square space; a system of measures based on such units. *S. number*, the product of a number multiplied by itself. *S. root*, the number or quantity constituting such a base of a given number or quantity as to produce this when multiplied by itself. **2.** *fig.* I should but be.. the s. man in the round hole TENNYSON. **3.** He is a S. well-set Man 1709. **4.** The whole were reared in a backyard not ten feet s. 1854. **5. b.** A long low vessel..with immensely square yards 1833. **6. b.** 'To be s. with a man', to be revenged 1859. **c.** They were all s. at the 18th 1898.

II. 1. Of actions: Just or equitable; fair, honest, honourable, straightforward. Also *gen.* 1591. **2.** Of persons: †**a.** Not readily moved or shaken in purpose; steady, reliable –1710. **b.** Honourable, upright 1646. **3.** Precise, exact 1590. **b.** Straight, direct 1804. **c.** Right; in good order; on a proper footing 1836. **d.** Of meals; Full, solid, substantial. Of a drink: Copious; of full measure. orig. *U.S.* 1868.

1. She's a most triumphant Lady, if report be s. to her SHAKS. Phr. *S.* †*play* or *dealing, a s. deal, the s. thing.* **3.** Oh what formalitie, what s. obseruance: liues in a little roome 1590. His ideas being s., solid and tangible HAWTHORNE. **b.** Opportunity for a s. talk 1896. **c.** Phr. *To call* (*it*) *s.*, to regard as balanced or settled. **d.** The one 's. meal' of the day 1876.

Phr. *On* or *upon the s.* **a.** With a square front; face to face; directly, openly (now *rare*). **b.** Without artifice, deceit, fraud, or trickery. †**c.** Upon terms of equality or friendship *with* another or others; also, even or 'quits' *with* another. **d.** In predic. use without const.: Free from duplicity or unfairness; honest, straightforward, upright (now *slang*). **e.** *To set on* or *upon the s.*, at right angles; in a square or solid form; *fig.* to put in proper order (*rare*).

Comb., as *s.-bodied, -built, -faced, -set, -shouldered, -sterned, -tailed* adjs.; **s. bracket** (see BRACKET *sb.* 5); **-headed** *a.* having the head or top of a s. form; **s. hit,** a hit at right angles to the wicket esp. to square leg; **-knot,** = *reef-knot*; **-leg,** the position in the cricket-field to the left of the batsman and nearly in line with the wicket; the fielder stationed at this point; hence as *vb.*; **-rig** *Naut.*, rig in which the lower sails are suspended from horizontal yards, as dist. from *fore-and-aft* rig; so **-rigged** *a.*; **-roof,** one in which the principal rafters meet at a right angle. Hence **Squa·re-ly** *adv.*, **-ness.**

Square (skwēᵊɹ), *adv.* 1570. [f. prec.] †**1.** Steadily, copiously –1608. **2.** Fairly, honestly; in a direct manner. Now *slang* or *colloq.* 1577. **b.** *colloq.* Solidly, without reserve 1867. **3.** So as to be square; in a rectangular form or position; directly in line or in front 1631. **4.** At right angles 1680.

2. 'I reckon the boy means s.', muttered the old man 1891. **b.** N. C. comes out 's.' for the Republican party 1867. **3.** He walked burly and s. LAMB. **4.** Pivot men. .face s. into the new direction 1847.

Square (skwēᵊɹ), *v.* late ME. [– OFr. *esquarrer*; see SQUARE *a.* and *sb.*] **I.** *trans.* **1.** To make (a thing) square; to shape by reduction to straight lines and right angles. **b.** To make (timber, etc.) square or rectangular in cross-section. late ME. **c.** To mark out as a square or in rectangular form; to convert into or draw up in a square; to mark *off* or *out* in squares 1440. **d.** To form by making square; to cut in square or rectangular form 1584. **2. a.** To multiply (a number) by itself 1571. **b.** To convert (a circle) into an equivalent square; to measure exactly in terms of a square 1624. **c.** To calculate in square measure 1811. **3. a.** *Naut.* To lay (the yards) at right angles to the line of the keel by trimming with the braces; to set at right angles to or parallel with some other part 1625. **b.** To adjust so as to make rectilinear or rectangular or to set at right angles to something else 1690. **c.** *Astrol.* To stand in quartile aspect in relation to (another sign) 1697. **d.** To set or place (some part of the body) squarely 1810.

1. Those who. .squared the Portland stone for Saint Paul's MACAULAY. **2. a.** Then do I s. 6, and it is 36. 1674. **b.** Circles to s., and Cubes to double, Would give a Man excessive Trouble PRIOR. **3. b.** *fig.* I feel me. .Well squar'd to fortune's blows CARY. **c.** The Icy Goat, the Crab which s. the Scales 1697. **d.** The Saxon domestics squared their shoulders SCOTT.

II. 1. *fig.* To regulate, frame, arrange, or direct, *by, according to*, or *on* some standard or principle of action 1531. **b.** To adjust or adapt, to cause to correspond *to* or harmonize *with* something 1583. **c.** To arrange, adjust, render appropriate or exact 1596. **2.** To bring to an equality on both sides; to balance 1815. **b.** To put (a matter) straight; to settle satisfactorily, to compound. *colloq.* 1853. **c.** With *up*: To settle (a debt, etc.) by payment 1862. **d.** *intr.* (*Golf*) To make the scores equal 1923. **3.** *slang* or *colloq.* To conciliate, satisfy, or gain over (a person), *esp.* by some form of bribery or compensation; to get rid of in this way 1859.

1. He who squares his actions by this rule can never do amiss BERKELEY. **b.** Eie me, blest Providence, and s. my triall To my proportion'd strength MILT. **2.** She would accept benefits. .but then she insulted her benefactors, and so squared accounts THACKERAY. **b.** We always s. it with the usher 1872. **3.** Rich offenders. .'s. the reporters' 1885.

III. *intr.* †**1.** To deviate or diverge, to vary (*from* something) –1609. †**2.** To fall out, to be at variance or discord, *with* a person, etc. –1561. **3.** To accord, concur or correspond, to agree or fit, *with*, †*to*, †*unto*, something 1592. **b.** *Golf.* To equalize the scores 1923. **4.** To strut or swagger. *Obs.* exc. *dial.* 1590. **5.** To put oneself into a posture of defence; to assume a boxing attitude 1820. **6. a.** To measure (so much) on each of four sides forming a square; to yield a square of (the dimensions specified) 1789. **b.** To become square in form 1902. **c.** *Naut.* To sail *away* with the yards squared 1887.

1. The prophetes somtyme. .dyd s. from the trouthe 1521. **3.** There is no Church, whose every part so squares unto my Conscience SIR T. BROWNE. **4.** At another time, malapert boldnesse will s. it out CAMDEN. **5.** He squared up to his adversary and. .struck him a heavy blow 1893. **6. c.** We squared away to a spanking breeze 1899. Hence **Squa·ring** *vbl. sb.*

Square cap. 1584. [SQUARE *a.*] An academic cap with a square top; a mortar-board, trencher.

Square-cut, *a.* 1622. [SQUARE *a.* or *adv.*] **1.** Cut to or into a square form. **2.** *absol.* A coat with square skirts 1893.

1. The grave man. .with s. antique waistcoat 1848. There's the s. chancellor KEATS.

Squarer (skwēᵊ·rəɹ). late ME. [f. SQUARE *v.* + -ER¹.] **1. a.** One who reduces wood, stone, etc., to a square form. **b.** One who aims at squaring the circle 1852. †**2.** A contentious or quarrelsome person. SHAKS.

Square sail. 1600. [SQUARE *a.*] **a.** A four-sided sail supported by a yard slung across the vessel. **b.** A flying sail set on the foremast of a schooner or the mast of a sloop or cutter.

Square-toed, *a.* 1785. [SQUARE *a.*] **1.** Of shoes: Having broad square toes. **2.** *fig.* Old-fashioned, formal, precise 1795.

2. We old people must retain some s. predilection for the fashions of our youth BURKE.

Squa·re-toes. 1771. [SQUARE *a.*] A precise, formal, old-fashioned person; one having strict or narrow ideas of conduct. Freq. qualified by *old* and usu. with initial capital.

Old Square-toes was obliged to go out of town immediately 1785.

Squa·rewise, *adv.* 1546. [f. SQUARE *a.* + -WISE.] †**1.** Rectangularly –1725. **2.** In the form of a square 1611.

Squarish (skwēᵊ·riʃ), *a.* 1742. [f. SQUARE *a.* + -ISH¹.] Somewhat, more or less, or approximately, square.

Squarrose (skwæ·rōᵘs, skwǫ·rōᵘs), *a.* 1760. [– L. *squarrosus* scurfy, scabby; see -OSE¹.] **1.** *Bot.* **a.** Composed of or covered with, scales or other processes standing out at right angles or more widely. **b.** Of scales: Standing out at right angles or to a greater degree 1829. **2.** *Ent.* Cut into laciniæ which are elevated above the plane of the surface 1826.

Squarro·so-, comb. form of prec., as in *s.-dentate, -laciniate* adjs.

Squarson (skwā·ɹsən). 1857. [joc. combination of SQUIRE *sb.* and PARSON.] A parson who is also the squire in his parish. Hence **Squa·rsonry.**

Squash (skwǫʃ), *sb.*¹ 1590. [rel. to or – SQUASH *v.*] **I. 1.** The unripe pod of a pea. Also applied contemptuously to persons. *Obs.* exc. *arch.* †**2.** *S. pear*, a variety of pear. *S. perry*, a beverage made from this. –1826. **3.** A soft india-rubber ball used in a form of the game of rackets (orig. at Harrow). **b.** Also short for **s. rackets,** a game resembling rackets, played with rackets and soft india-rubber balls in a walled court 1886.

1. As a s. before 'tis a pescod SHAKS. This Kernell, This s., this Gentleman SHAKS.

II. 1. †**a.** The act of squashing; the fact or sound of some soft substance being crushed or dispersed –1739. **b.** The shock or impact occasioned by a soft heavy body falling upon a surface; the sound produced by this. Now *rare.* 1654. **2.** A crush or crowd of persons, etc.; a large number 1884. **3.** Short for *lemon-squash* (LEMON *sb.*¹) 1894.

1. a. Phr. *To go to s.*, to become squashed or ruined. **b.** Hearing a s., he cried, Damn it, what's that? 1812.

Squash (skwǫʃ), *sb.*² 1643. [Short for †(*i*)*squoutersquash* – Narragansett *asquutasquash*, f. *asq* raw, uncooked, the -*ash* being pl. ending, as in SUCCOTASH.] **1.** A gourd produced by plants of the genus *Cucurbita*, esp. a fruit of the bush gourd, *C. melopepo.* **2.** Any species of the genus *Cucurbita* producing the above fruit 1661.

attrib., as *s. pie, vine*; **s.-bug,** one or other of various insects infesting or injurious to squashes; **s. gourd, (-melon) pumpkin,** the common bush gourd or squash, *Cucurbita melopepo.*

†**Squash,** *sb.*³ 1678. [Aphetic f. MUSQUASH.] The musk-rat or musquash, *Fiber zibethicus* –1824.

Squash (skwǫʃ), *v.* 1565. [Expressive var. of QUASH *v.*] **1.** *trans.* To squeeze, press, or crush into a flat mass or pulp; to beat to, or dash in, pieces. **b.** To quash; to suppress or put down; to undo or destroy in a complete or summary manner. Often *colloq.* To silence or discomfit (a person) in a crushing fashion. 1762. **2.** *intr.* To emit or make a splashing sound; to move, walk, etc., in this way; to splash 1671. **3.** To be pressed into a flat mass on impact; to flatten *out* under pressure 1858.

2. Our feet 'squashing' as we step, for our boots are full of rain-water 1893. Hence **Squa·sher.**

Squash, *adv.* 1766. [f. prec.] With or as with a squash. Freq. in *to go s.* (also *transf.*).

Squash-, the vbl. stem used in combs., in the sense 'having the appearance of being squashed', as **squash hat.**

Squashy (skwǫ·ʃi), *a.* 1698. [f. SQUASH *v.* or *sb.*¹ + -Y¹.] **1.** Of fruit, etc.: Having a soft or pulpy consistency; lacking in firmness. **2.** Of ground, etc.: Soft with, full of, water; soaking, marshy 1751. **3.** Of the nature of a squash or squashing 1865. Hence **Squa·shiness,** s. condition or character.

Squat (skwǫt), *sb.*¹ ME. [f. SQUAT *v.*] **1.** A heavy fall or bump; a severe or violent jar or jolt. Now *n. dial.* **b.** A bruise, contusion, or wound, esp. one caused by a fall; a dent or indentation. Now *dial.* 1578. †**2.** *At* (*the* or *a*) *s.*, in a squatting or crouching attitude, esp. that assumed by a hare when sitting –1732. **3.** The act of squatting, *spec.* on the part of a hare 1584. †**4.** The place where an animal squats; *spec.* the form or lair of a hare –1673. **5.** A squatting attitude or posture 1886.

1. Bruises and squats and falls which often kill others can bring little grief or hurt to those that are temperate G. HERBERT.

Squat, *sb.*² *Cornwall.* 1671. [perh. same word as prec.] A small bunch of ore in a vein.

Squat (skwǫt), *pa. pple.* and (*ppl.*) *a.* late ME. [pa. pple. of SQUAT *v.*] **I. 1.** In predic. use: Seated in a squatting or crouching posture; sitting close to the ground. **2.** Hidden from observation; quiet, still. *dial.* 1841.

1. Him there they found S. like a Toad, close at the eare of Eve MILT. The shrub lies s. to the ground 1853.

II. 1. Short and thick; disproportionately broad or wide; podgy 1630. **2.** Characterized by squatness of form or structure 1774.

1. She is a broad, s., pursy, fat thing, quite ugly RICHARDSON. The arches are circular, and the columns s. 1828. Hence **Squa·t-ly** *adv.*, **-ness.**

Squat (skwǫt), *v.* ME. [– OFr. *esquatir, -ter*, f. *es-* EX-¹ + *quatir* press down, crouch, hide :– Rom. **coactire*, f. L. *coactus*, pa. pple. of *cogere* drive or force together.] **I.** *trans.* To crush, flatten, or beat out of shape; to smash or squash; to bruise severely. Now *dial.* **b.** To dash down heavily or with some force. Now *dial.* late ME. **II. 1.** *refl.* To seat (oneself) upon the hams or haunches; to take one's seat in a crouching attitude or posture. late ME. **2.** *intr.* Of hares: To sit close to the ground in a crouching attitude; to crouch or cower down, esp. in order to escape observation or capture. late ME. **3.** Of persons: To sit down with the legs closely drawn up beneath the hams or in front of the body; *esp.* to sit on the ground in this way or in a crouching attitude. Also *joc.*, to sit down. 1573. **4.** *trans.* To cause to squat; to put into, place in, a squatting attitude or posture (*rare*) 1600. **5.** *intr.* †**a.** To sink *into* (something lower or less important). MILT. **b.** To sink in or down 1687. **6.** To settle upon new, uncultivated, or unoccupied land without any legal title and without the payment of rent. orig. *U.S.* 1800. **b.** *Austral.* To rent or take up government or crown land for pasturage as a squatter 1828.

1. The Prince at last squatted himself on the corner of a form MME. D'ARBLAY. **2.** The coy hare squats nestling in the corn 1821. **3.** Down on the grass the Doctor squatted 1812. **6.** He was a Kentucky man, of the Ohio, where he had 'squatted' MARRYAT. Hence **Squa·tty** *a.* somewhat squat.

Squatarole (skwæ·tărōᵘl). Also **-olle.** 1819. [– mod.L. *Squatarola* – local It. *squatarola.*]

The grey or Swiss plover, *Squatarola helvetica*.

Squatter (skwǫ·təɹ), *sb.* 1788. [f. SQUAT *v.* + -ER¹.] **1.** *U.S.* A settler having no normal or legal title to the land occupied by him, *esp.* one thus occupying land in a district not yet surveyed or apportioned by the government. **b.** An unauthorized occupant of land or premises 1821. **2.** *Austral.* One occupying a tract of pastoral land as a tenant of the crown; a grazier or sheep-farmer, esp. on a large scale 1840. **3.** A squatting person or animal 1824.

1. b. Hundreds of squatters from the neighbouring parts of Sutherland and Ross 1860.
attrib.: **s. sovereignty** *U.S.*, the right claimed by the inhabitants of newly-formed territories to settle for themselves the question of slavery, etc.

Squatter (skwǫ·təɹ), *v.* 1611. [prob. imitative.] †**1.** *trans.* To scatter, disperse, spill –1653. **2.** *intr.* To fly or run, to struggle along or make one's way, among water or wet with much splashing or flapping 1785. **b.** To flutter, flap, or struggle among water or soft mud 1808.

2. A little callow gosling squattering out of bounds without leave C. BRONTË.

Squaw (skwǭ). 1634. [– Narragansett Indian *squaws*, Massachusetts *squa* woman.] **1.** A North American Indian woman or wife. **b.** Applied by Indians to white women 1642. **2.** *transf.* An effeminate or weak person 1807. **3.** *Old s.*, the long-tailed duck 1884.

attrib. as **s.-root**, *Conopholis*, cancer-root; †**-sachem**, a squaw chief in certain American Indian tribes; **-weed**, *Senecio aureus*.

Squawk (skwǭk), *sb.* 1850. [f. next.] **1.** A loud grating call or cry; a hoarse squall. **2.** *U.S.* The *Nyctiardea*, or Night Heron 1872.

Squawk (skwǭk), *v.* 1821. [imit.] **1.** *intr.* To call or cry with a loud harsh note; to squall or screech hoarsely. **b.** Of things: To creak or squeak harshly 1859. **2.** *trans.* With *out*: To utter with or as with a squawk 1856.

Squeak (skwīk), *sb.* 1664. [f. the vb.] **1.** The act of squeaking. **2.** A short or slight sound, of a thin high-pitched character, made by animals or persons 1700. **b.** A thin, sharp sound produced by a musical instrument 1805. **3. a.** A slight, narrow, or bare chance *for* something 1716. **b.** A narrow escape, a close shave; usu. with qualifying adjs. *narrow*, *near*, etc. 1822.

3. a. See all ready with the boat,..it may give us a s. for our lives, if a little one 1868. **b.** We had a near s., the wind suddenly coming calm 1889.

Squeak (skwīk), *v.* late ME. [imit., combining the initials of *squeal* and final of *shriek*; but cf. Sw. *skväka* croak.] **1.** *intr.* To emit a short or slight sound of a thin high-pitched character. **2.** *slang.* To confess; to turn informer; to 'split' or 'peach' 1690. **3.** *trans.* To utter, sing or play in a squeaking manner or with a squeaky voice. Usu. derisively 1577.

1. The sheeted dead Did squeake and gibber in the Roman streets SHAKS. Shrill Fiddles s., Hoarse Bagpipes roar 1740. Rats began to s. and scuffle in the night time DICKENS. **2.** If he be obstinate, put a civil Question to him upon the Rack, and he squeaks I warrant him DRYDEN. **3.** Ye s. out your Coziers Catches without any mitigation or remorse of voice SHAKS. Hence **Squea·kingly** *adv.*

Squeaker (skwī·kəɹ). 1641. [f. the vb.] **1.** One who, or that which, squeaks. **2.** One or other of various birds characterized by their squeaking call 1817. **3.** *colloq.* A (young) pig 1861.

2. *Strepera anaphonensis*, Grey Cow-Shrike;..S. of the Colonists 1848.

Squeaky (skwī·ki), *a.* 1862. [f. SQUEAK *sb.* or *v.* + -Y¹.] Characterized by squeaking sounds; tending to squeak.

Squeal (skwīl), *sb.* 1747. [f. the vb.] A more or less prolonged sharp cry; a shrill scream. **b.** A sharp shrill sound 1867.

Squeal (skwīl), *v.* ME. [imit.; in earliest use north.] **1.** *intr.* To utter (or give *out*) a more or less prolonged sharp cry, esp. by reason of pain or sudden alarm; to scream shrilly. **2.** Of things: To emit or produce a shrill or strident sound 1596. **3.** *slang.* To turn informer; to inform or 'peach' *on* a person 1865. **4.** *trans.* To utter or produce with a shrill, grating, or squeaking sound 1675.

1. Ghosts did shrieke and squeale about the streets SHAKS. **2.** Here tortur'd cats-gut squeals amain 1727. Phr. *to make* (a person) *s.*, to blackmail him. **4.** 'Here, sir,' squealed Timothy 1833.

Squealer (skwī·ləɹ). 1854. [f. prec. + -ER¹.] **1.** One who or that which squeals. Also *transf.* 1865. **b.** *slang.* An informer 1865. **c.** *U.S.* A complainer 1889. **2.** Freq. in bird-names 1854.

2. The Swift..This bird's loud piercing cry has obtained for it the name of *s.* 1879. Harlequin Duck,..known also as S. 1888.

Squeamish (skwī·miʃ), *a.* 1450. [alt., by substitution of -ISH¹ for -OUS, of next.] **I. 1.** Readily affected with nausea; easily turned sick or faint; physically unable to support or swallow anything disagreeable. **2.** Slightly affected with or inclined to nausea 1660. †**3.** Characterized by a feeling of nausea (*rare*) –1748.

1. Art thou so squemish that thou canst not see wine but thou must surfet? GREENE. *fig.* The stomach of his Holinesse not being so s., but that he would take a good almes from dirty hands FULLER. **2.** This day..the wind grew high, and..I began to be dizzy and s. PEPYS.

II. †**1.** Averse, unwilling, or reluctant *to* do something –1589. **2.** Averse to freedom or familiarity of intercourse; distant, reserved: coy, cold. Now *dial.* 1561. †**b.** Of actions, etc.; Characterized by coldness or coyness –1603. **3.** Easily shocked; prudish 1567. †**b.** Sensitive; shrinking from contact with anything rude or rough –1785. **4.** Sensitively or excessively fastidious, scrupulous, punctilious, or particular, with regard to standards of action or belief 1581. **b.** Marked or characterized by fastidiousness or scrupulousness 1593. **5.** Fastidious or dainty with respect to what one handles, uses, or comes in contact with 1608.

3. Riddles more or less good, some coarse, and some profane; but the age was not s. 1892. **4.** Trifles magnified into importance by a s. conscience MACAULAY. They are not so s. as to what they say about us 1865. **5.** If delicacies could invite My s. courtier's appetite 1746. **Squea·mish-ly** *adv.*, **-ness.** So **Squea·my** *a.*

Squea·mous, *a.* Now *n. dial.* [ME. *squaymes*, *squeymous*, earlier *scoymus*, *squoymous* (mod. north. dial. *skymous*), aphetic f. AFr. *escoymos*, of unkn. origin.] = SQUEAMISH *a.*

†**Squea·sy,** *a.* 1583. [Alteration of QUEASY *a.*] **1.** Of times: Troublous, disturbed –1662. **2.** Of the stomach: Readily nauseated; easily upset –1656. Hence †**Squea·siness** –1687.

Squeegee (skwī·dʒī, skwīdʒī·), *sb.* 1844. [Arbitrary f. *squeege* (XVIII), expressive alt. of SQUEEZE *v.*; see -EE².] **1.** A scraping implement, usu. a straight-edged blade of india-rubber, gutta-percha, or the like, attached to the end of a long handle, for removing water, mud, etc. **2.** *Photogr.* A strip of rubber mounted on a wooden frame which serves as a handle, for squeezing moisture from a print or pressing a film closer to its mount; a rubber roller serving this purpose; a squeezer 1878.

Squeegee, *v.* 1883. [f. the sb.] **1.** *trans.* To press, squeeze, or force, with a squeegee. **2.** = SQUILGEE *v.* 1886.

Squeezable (skwī·zăb'l), *a.* 1813. [f. SQUEEZE *v.* + -ABLE.] **1.** Capable of being compressed or squeezed. **2.** Capable of being constrained or coerced to yield or grant something 1837. **b.** *esp.* From which money may be extracted 1840.

2. b. The result of their industry is only that they become more s. for taxes 1880.

Squeeze (skwīz), *sb.* 1611. [f. SQUEEZE *v.*] **1.** An act of squeezing; an application of strong or heavy pressure, or of force sufficient to compress. **b.** The pressure *of* a crowd of persons; a crush 1802. **c.** *colloq.* A strong financial or commercial demand or pressure 1830. **2.** A strong or firm pressure of the hand as a token of friendship or affection 1736. **b.** A close embrace; a hug 1790. **3. a.** A (small) quantity or amount squeezed out; a few drops pressed out by squeezing 1761. **b.** A forced exaction or impost made by Asiatic officials or servants; a percentage taken upon goods bought or sold; an illegal charge or levy 1858. **4.** *colloq.* A crowded assembly or social gathering 1779. **5.** *Coal-mining.* A gradual coming together of the floor and roof of a gallery or working; a place where this has occurred; a creep 1789. **6.** A moulding or cast of an object obtained by pressing some plastic substance round or over it; *spec.* in *Archæol.*, an impression or copy of an inscription, design, etc., taken by applying wet paper or other soft material in this way 1857. **7.** Without article: Pressure; constraint used to obtain a concession or gift 1862.

1. d. In full *s. play* (Bridge), leading winning cards until opponent is forced to discard an important card 1928. **3. a.** A s. of lemon-juice 1864. **4.** The weather is getting terribly hot for squeezes 1808. **6.** I saw squeezes of this stone for the first time 1870.

Squeeze (skwīz), *v.* 1599. [var. of earlier †*squise*, *squize* (XVI), intensive of †*queise* (XV), as SQUENCH of QUENCH *v.*; ult. origin unknown.] **1.** *trans.* To press or compress hard, esp. so as to flatten, crush, or force together 1601. **b.** With complement: To reduce to, or bring into, a specified condition by pressure 1660. **c.** To press (the hand) in token of friendship or affection; also, to hug 1687. **2.** To force by pressure. Const. with advs. and preps. 1683. **3. a.** To press upon (a person, etc.) so as to exact or extort money; to fleece. Also const. *of*. 1639. **b.** To subject to strong constraint or pressure 1888. **4.** With *out*: To press or force out 1599. **5. a.** To extort or exact, to obtain by force or pressure, *from* or *out of* a person, etc. Also without const. 1602. **b.** To extract (juice or the like) by pressure 1611. **c.** To put or drop *in* (a fluid extracted by pressure) 1725. **6.** *absol.* **a.** To press hard, esp. with the hand 1692. **b.** To take a squeeze or facsimile impression 1890. **7.** *intr.* To yield to pressure; to admit of being squeezed 1683. **8.** To force a way; to press or push; to succeed in passing by means of compression. Const. with advs. and preps. 1704.

1. *fig.* The six hundred millions of Debt..are now squeezing the borough-mongers 1823. Phr. †*To s. wax*, to set one's seal to a document. *A squeezed orange*, fig. a person or thing from whom or which nothing more can be obtained. **b.** To be squeezed flat against a wall 1871. **2.** Crowl was squeezed into a corner behind a pillar 1892. **3. a.** The Church had been so often squeezed by him 1700. **4.** Lady Kew could..s. out a tear over a good novel too THACKERAY. **5. a.** The above..was the sum squeezed by the judge out of the clerk BENTHAM. **6. a.** He [the fox] squeez'd hard to get out again; but the Hole was too Little for him 1692. **7.** Bran squeezes much more—But plaister of Paris not at all 1771. **8.** The old duke..squeezing into the circle SMOLLETT. Hence **Squee·zy** *a.*

Squeezer (skwī·zəɹ). 1611. [f. SQUEEZE *v.* + -ER¹.] **1.** One who squeezes in various senses. **2.** A mechanical device or apparatus, an implement, by which pressure can be applied 1839. **b.** *spec.* An apparatus by which a ball of puddled iron is reduced to a compact mass 1843.

Squee·zing, *vbl. sb.* 1611. [f. SQUEEZE *v.* + -ING¹.] **1.** The action of pressing or compressing; the fact of being compressed. †**b.** That which is squeezed out –1719. **2.** The action of oppressing by exactions or extortion; the practice of extorting excessive or illicit gain 1681.

Squelch (skwelʹʃ), *sb.* 1620. [imit.; cf. next.] **1.** A heavy crushing fall or blow acting on a soft body; the sound produced by this. **2.** A thing or mass that has the appearance of having been squelched or crushed 1837. **3.** The sound made by a liquid when subjected to sudden or intermittent pressure 1895.

1. I heard a heavy s. and a howl 1829.

Squelch (skwelʹʃ), *v.* 1624. [imit.; cf. QUELCH.] **1.** *trans.* To fall, drop, or stamp upon (something soft) with crushing or squashing force; to crush in this way. **b.** *fig.* To squash or crush; to put down or suppress thoroughly or completely 1864. **2.** *intr.* **a.** To fall with a squelch. Now *dial.* 1755. **b.** To emit a squelch or squelches; to spout in squelches 1834. **c.** To walk or tread heavily in water or on wet ground, or with water in the shoes, so as to make a splashing sound 1849.

1. Oh 'twas your luck and mine to be squelch'd FLETCHER. **b.** It would be so nice to s. that pompous impostor HUXLEY. **2. c.** You'd..pass all your time in squelching about soppy fields 1849. Hence **Sque·lcher** (*colloq.*), a crushing blow, newspaper article, etc.

Squelch, *adv.* 1772. [f. as prec.] With or as with a squelch or heavy splash.

Squench, *v.* Now *dial.* and *colloq.* 1535. [Intensive of QUENCH *v.*; cf. SQUEEZE *v.*] **1.** *trans.* To extinguish (a fire, etc.). **2.** To suppress, put an end to; to quell or stifle 1577. **3.** To satisfy (the appetite); to slake (thirst) 1598. **4.** *intr.* To become extinguished 1643.

Squeteague (skwetī·g). *U.S.* Also **squetee.** 1838. [Narragansett Indian.] The weakfish or sea-salmon, *Cynoscion regalis*, of the eastern United States.

Squib (skwib), *sb.* 1525. [prob. imit. of a slight explosion.] **1.** A species of firework, in which the burning of the composition is usu. terminated by a slight explosion 1530. **2.** †**a.** An explosive device used as a missile or means of attack –1686. **b.** *Mining.* A tubular case filled with a priming of gunpowder used to fire a charge 1881. **3.** A smart gird or hit; a sharp scoff or sarcasm; a lampoon 1525. †**4.** Applied to persons: A mean, insignificant, or paltry fellow –1653. **5.** A squirt. Now *dial.* 1583. **6.** A small measure or quantity (of strong drink). Now *dial.* 1766.

1. The literary gentleman having finished, like a damp s. with a good bang, resumed his seat 1847. *fig.* In 1841 he had thrown a few squibs in the Examiner at Sir Robert Peel and the Tories 1882. **3.** No one was more faithful to his early friends.. particularly if they could write a s. DISRAELI. **4.** Out steps me an infant s. of the Innes of Court NASHE.

Squib (skwib), *v.* 1579. [f. the sb.] **I.** *intr.* **1.** To use smart or sarcastic language; to utter, write, or publish a squib or squibs. **2.** To let off squibs; to shoot 1691. **3.** To move *about* like a squib 1760.

1. To s. in the journals, and write for the stage 1825. **3.** A battered unmarried beau, who squibs about from place to place GOLDSM.

II. *trans.* **1. a.** To cast or throw *forth, off, out* (a remark, quip, etc.) after the manner of a squib 1596. **b.** To let off (a squib); to fire (a gun, etc.), esp. with the priming or powder only; †to shoot (an arrow) 1603. **2.** To assail or attack (a person) with squibs or witty sarcasm; to lampoon or satirize smartly 1631. **3.** To spatter with a squib or squirt 1840.

1. a. Hook squibbed off a few pleasantries 1853. **2.** The mendicant parson, whom I am so fond of squibbing J. R. GREEN.

Squid (skwid), *sb.* 1613. [Of unkn. origin.] **1.** One or other of various species of cephalopods belonging to the family *Loliginidæ*, *Teuthididæ*, or *Sepiidæ*, more esp. to the genus *Loligo*; a calamary, cuttle or pen-fish. **b.** Without article, esp. as a bait or food-stuff 1865. **2.** *Bone-s*, an artificial bait made to imitate a squid 1883.

attrib. and *Comb.*: **s. fish,** = sense 1; **s.-hound,** a name in New England for large sea-going specimens of the Striped Bass. Hence **Squid** *v. intr.* to fish with squid-bait *U.S.*

Squiffer (skwi·fəɹ). *slang.* 1911. [Of unkn. origin.] A concertina.

Squiffy (skwi·fi), *a. slang.* 1874. [Of unkn. origin.] Intoxicated, drunk.

Squiggle (skwi·g'l), *v.* Chiefly *dial.* and *U.S.* 1804. [perh. blend of SQUIRM and WIGGLE, WRIGGLE.] **1.** *intr.* To work wavy or intricate embroidery. **2.** To writhe about; to squirm or wriggle 1816. **Squi·ggle** *sb.* a wriggly twist or curve. **Squi·ggly** *a.* wavy, wriggly.

Squilgee (skwi·ldʒī, skwildʒī·), *sb.* Also **squillage, squiligee.** 1850. [alt. of SQUEEGEE.] *Naut.* = SQUEEGEE 1. **Squilgee** *v.* to use a s.; to swab, clean, or press with a s.

Squill (skwil). late ME. [– L. *squilla*, var. of *scilla* – Gr. σκίλλα.] **1.** A bulb or root of the sea-onion or other related plant (see 2). Chiefly in *pl.* **b.** In names of preparations made from these bulbs 1652. **c.** *Pharm.* Without article, as a substance 1725. **2.** *Bot.* The bulbous-rooted sea-shore plant *Scilla* (or *Urginea*) *maritima*; the sea-onion; also, any other species of the genus *Scilla* 1440. **b.** A plant of the sea-onion or related species. Chiefly *pl.* as a collective term. 1601. **3.** *Zool.* The mantis-shrimp, *Squilla mantis* 1710.

1. b. Galen..gave it to a Dram in Oxymel or Honey of Squills 1712.

‖**Squilla** (skwi·lă). *Pl.* **-æ** (*i*). 1516. [L. (see prec.).] †**1.** = prec. 2. –1611. **2.** = prec. 3. 1658.

†**Squilli·tic,** *a.* 1544. [– med.L. *squilliticus*, var. of L. *scilliticus*, f. *scilla* SQUILL.] Made of squills; containing squill –1725.

Squinacy (skwi·năsi). Now *dial.* ME. [var. (from XIII) of SQUINANCY.] = SQUINSY.

Squi·nancy. Now *rare.* late ME. [– med.L. *squinantia*, app. formed by confusion of Gr. συνάγχη and κυνάγχη CYNANCHE, both denoting diseases of the throat.] **1.** Quinsy. **2.** = SQUINSY 2. 1596.

Comb.: **s. berry,** the black currant, *Ribes nigrum*; **s.-wort,** the quinsy-wort or small woodruff, *Asperula cynanchica*. So †**Squi·nance** –1730.

Squinch (skwinʃ). 1500. [var. of *scunch*, shortened f. SCUNCHEON.] *Arch.* †**1.** A stone cut to serve as a scuncheon –1518. **2.** A straight or arched support constructed across an angle to carry some superstructure 1840. **3.** A small structure, with two triangular faces, sloping back from an angle of a tower against the superimposed side of a spire 1848.

Squinny (skwi·ni), *v.* Now *dial.* Also **squiny.** 1605. [Obscurely rel. to SQUINT *v.* Cf. *squin* adj. (XV).] **1.** *intr.* To squint, look askance; to peer with partly closed eyes. **2.** *trans.* To direct (the eyes) obliquely; to close *up* partly in a short-sighted manner 1825.

Squi·nsy. Now *dial.* 1499. [Reduced f. SQUINACY.] **1.** *Path.* Quinsy; suppurative tonsillitis. **2.** A form or attack of this 1591.

Squint (skwint), *sb.* 1652. [f. SQUINT *a.* or *v.*] **1.** A permanent tendency in the eye to look obliquely or askant; defective coincidence of the optic axes; strabismus. **2.** A directing of the eyes obliquely; a sidelong look or glance; a hasty or casual look; a peep 1673. **3.** An inclination or tendency towards some particular object; a drift or leaning; a covert aim 1736. **4.** An oblique or perverse bent or tendency 1774. **5.** *Arch.* = HAGIOSCOPE 1839.

2. To give damages for all opprobrious language, and especially for all hints, squints, innuendoes, leers, and shrugs SWIFT. **3.** A s. towards radicalism 1895.

Squint (skwint), *a.* 1579. [perh. inferred from SQUINT-EYED *a.*] **1.** Of eyes: Looking obliquely; having a cast or squint; affected with strabismus. Now *rare.* **b.** *fig.* (with *eye* = 'look, regard', and usu. hyphened) 1623. **2.** Characterized by oblique vision 1611. †**3.** Indirect –1681. **4.** Oblique; slanting 1703.

1. He was syrnamed..Strabo, for his s. eyes HOLLAND. **2.** I..gladly banish s. suspicion MILT.

Squint (skwint), *v.* 1599. [Aphetic f. ASQUINT *adv.*] **1.** *intr.* To have the axes of the eyes not coincident; to be affected with strabismus 1611. **b.** Of the eyes 1836. **2.** To look with the eyes differently directed; to glance obliquely; also, to glance hastily or casually, to peep 1610. **b.** *fig.* To have a private eye to something 1642. **c.** To glance *at, on,* or *upon* (a person or thing) with dislike or disapproval, or by means of some covert allusion, hint, or suggestion 1652. **3.** *fig.* To refer or bear indirectly; to incline or tend 1599. **4.** To move or branch off in an oblique direction 1721. **5.** *trans.* To give a permanent or temporary cast to (the eye); to cause to look asquint or obliquely 1605. **b.** To cast or direct (a look, etc.) in a sidelong manner 1631.

1. Can any one be call'd beautiful that squints? WYCHERLEY. **2. b.** Pity but his eyes were out that squints at his own ends in doing God's work FULLER. **3.** The document squints towards treason 1895. **5.** The foule Flibbertigibbet..squints the eye, and makes the Hare-lippe SHAKS. Hence **Squi·nter.**

Squint-eye(s. 1653. [See SQUINT *a.* 1.] A person who has squinting eyes.

Squint-eyed (skwi·nt,əid), *a.* 1589. [f. †*squint*, aphet. f. ASQUINT *adv.*] **1.** Of persons: Having squint eyes; affected with squint or strabismus. **2.** Characterized by squint or oblique vision 1598.

1. *fig.* Heart-gnawing Hatred, and Squint-ey'd Suspition QUARLES.

Squi·nting, *vbl. sb.* 1611. [f. SQUINT *v.* + -ING[1].] **1.** The action of looking with a squint or sidelong glance. **2.** *spec.* = SQUINT *sb.* 1. 1626. So **Squi·nting** *ppl. a.*, **-ly** *adv.* 1593.

Squirage (skwəiᵊ·rédʒ). Also **squireage.** 1837. [f. SQUIRE *sb.* + -AGE.] The body of country squires; a book containing a list or account of these.

Squiralty (skwəiᵊ·rălti). Also **squirealty.** 1856. [f. SQUIRE *sb.*, after *mayoralty, commonalty.*] **a.** The existence of squires as an institution. **b.** The body or class of squires. **c.** The position or status of a squire.

Squire (skwəiᵊɹ), *sb.* ME. [Aphetic – OFr. *esquier* ESQUIRE *sb.*[1]] **1.** In the military organization of the later middle ages, a young man of good birth attendant upon a knight (= ESQUIRE 1 a); one ranking next to a knight under the feudal system of military service and tenure. **b.** A personal attendant or servant; a follower. Also *transf.* late ME. †**c.** In contemptuous use –1618. **2.** Applied to personages of ancient history or mythology holding a position or rank similar to that of the mediæval squire ME. **3.** A gallant or lover 1590. **4.** Employed as a title and prefixed to the surname of a country gentleman. Now chiefly *colloq.* 1645. **b.** A country gentleman or landed proprietor, *esp.* one who is the principal landowner in a village or district 1676. **5.** *U.S.* A Justice of the Peace; also, a lawyer or judge 1817.

1. Each knight was attended to the field by four squires or archers on horseback GIBBON. **b.** †*S. of* (or *for*) *the body* (or *household*), an officer charged with personal attendance upon a sovereign, nobleman, etc. **c.** *Trencher-s.*: see TRENCHER[1]. **2.** And Saul seyde to his squyer, Drawȝe out thi swerd WYCLIF 1 *Chron.* 10:4. **3.** *S. of dames* (Spenser) or *ladies*, one who devotes himself to the service of ladies or pays marked attentions to them. Hence **Squi·ress,** a female s.; the wife of a s.

Squire (skwəiᵊɹ), *v.* late ME. [f. SQUIRE *sb.*] **1.** *trans.* Of a man: To attend (a lady) as, or after the manner of, a squire; to escort. †**b.** *transf.* To act or serve as an escort or guard to; to convoy –1632. **2.** *intr.* With *it*: To act as a squire; to play the squire; to rule or domineer *over* as a country squire 1672.

1. To 'squire a royal girl of two years old SWIFT.

Squirearch (skwəiᵊ·raɹk). 1831. [Back-formation from next, after *monarch*, etc.] A member of the squirearchy; a squire as a local magnate. Hence **Squirea·rchal** *a.* of or belonging to, characteristic of, the squirearchy or a s.

Squirearchy (skwəiᵊ·raɹki). Also **squirarchy.** 1804. [f. SQUIRE *sb.*, after *hierarchy, monarchy*, etc.] **1.** The collective body of squires, landed proprietors, or country gentry; the class to which squires belong, regarded especially in respect of political or social influence. **b.** A class, body, or number of squires 1830. **2.** Rule or government by a squire or squires 1861.

Squiredom (skwəiᵊ·ɹdəm). 1650. [f. SQUIRE *sb.* + -DOM.] **1.** The dignity, position, or status of a squire. **2.** The body of squires; squires collectively 1842.

1. I always direct to you as 'Mr. Barton' because I know not if Quakers ought to endure S. FITZGERALD.

Squireen (skwəiᵊrī·n). orig. *Irish.* 1809. [f. SQUIRE *sb.* + -EEN[2].] A petty squire; a small landowner or country gentleman.

Squirehood (skwəiᵊ·ɹhud). 1680. [f. SQUIRE *sb.* + -HOOD.] **1.** The position or status of a squire or esquire; squireship. **2.** The body of squires; the squirearchy 1792.

Squireling (skwəiᵊ·ɹliŋ). 1682. [f. SQUIRE *sb.* + -LING[1].] **1.** A petty squire. **2.** A young squire 1834.

Squirely (skwəiᵊ·ɹli), *a.* 1612. [f. as prec. + -LY[1].] Of, belonging or relating to, a squire or the squirearchy; befitting a squire.

Squireship (skwəiᵊ·ɹʃip). 1613. [f. SQUIRE *sb.* + -SHIP.] **1.** The state, position, or dignity of a squire or esquire; squirehood. **2.** The personality of a squire 1786.

Squirm (skwə̄ɹm), *sb.* 1839. [f. the vb.] **a.** A squirming or writhing movement; a wriggle. **b.** *Naut.* A twist in a rope.

Squirm (skwə̄ɹm), *v.* 1691. [Of symbolic origin; prob. assoc. with *worm*.] **1.** *intr.* To wriggle or writhe. **2.** To move, proceed, or go with a wriggling or writhing motion 1759. **3.** *fig.* To be painfully affected or sharply touched by something; to writhe under reproof, sarcasm, etc. 1804. **4.** *trans.* With *out*: To utter with a squirm 1889.

1. This harmless snake frequents the branches of Trees and very nimbly squirms among the leaves 1743. These poor little mortals..s. and squall 1890. **3.** I'll write my Lord..such a letter as shall make him s. 1894.

Squirr, *v.* Also **squir.** 1710. [var. of

earlier SKIRR *v.*] *trans.* To throw or cast with a rapid whirling or skimming motion.

Squirrel (skwi·rĕl). late ME. [Aphetic – AFr. *esquirel*, OFr. *esquireul*, *escureul* (mod. *écureuil*) :– Rom. **scuriolus*, dim. of **scurius*, for L. *sciūrus* – Gr. σκίουρος, prob. f. σκιά shade + οὐρά tail.] **1.** One or other of various species of rodents (characterized by a long bushy tail, furry coat, and bright eyes), belonging to the genus *Sciurus*, or to the widely-distributed sub-family *Sciurina* including this; *esp.* the common species *Sciurus vulgaris*, native to Britain, Europe, and parts of Asia. **b.** Applied to other animals or to persons, usu. with contemptuous force 1566. **2.** With *the*, in generalized sense; also, the genus *Sciurus* or the sub-family *Sciurina* to which this belongs. Also *pl.* 1591. **b.** = squirrel-skin, squirrel-fur. late ME. **3.** One or other of various species of fish belonging to the family *Holocentridæ*, esp. *Holocentrus erythræus* 1734.

1. b. A little, cheery, agile, red s. of a Man 1865. *attrib.* and *Comb.*: **s.-cage**, a cylindrical cage in which squirrels are confined, and which revolves as they move; also *transf.* a structure resembling this, *spec.* in *Electr.*; **-corn**, *Dicentra canadensis*; **-fish** = sense 3; **-hake**, *Physis tenuis*, also called White Hake (*U.S.*); **-hawk**, the Californian species, *Archibuteo ferrugineus*; **-headed**, **-minded** *adjs.*, shallow-brained; **-monkey**, one or other of various species of monkeys belonging to the genus *Chrysothrix*.

†**Squi·rrel-tail.** Also **squirrel's tail.** late ME. **1.** The tail of a squirrel. †**2.** A species of lob-worm –1839. **3.** *Squirrel-tail grass*, one or other of various species of grasses belonging to the genus *Hordeum*. Also *ellipt.* 1777. So **Squi·rrel-tailed** *a.* having a tail like that of a squirrel in form or character.

Squirt (skwɔ̄ɹt), *sb.* 1460. [f. SQUIRT *v.*] **1. a.** Diarrhœa; looseness of the bowels; an attack of diarrhœa. Now *dial.* in *pl.* **2.** A small tubular instrument by which water may be squirted; a form of syringe 1530. **b.** A larger instrument of the same type, used esp. as a fire-extinguisher 1590. **3.** A small quantity of liquid that is squirted; a small jet or spray; an act of squirting 1626. **4.** A paltry or contemptible person; a whipper-snapper; a fop. (Chiefly *U.S.* and *dial.*) 1848.

Squirt (skwɔ̄ɹt), *v.* 1460. [Of imit. origin.] **I.** *intr.* **1.** To eject or spirt out water in a jet or slight stream. **b.** To void thin excrement; to have diarrhœa 1530. **2.** To move swiftly or quickly; to dart or frisk 1570. **3.** To issue or be ejected in a jet-like stream; to spirt or spurt 1858.

2. Comes master doctor Glister, as his manner is, squirting in suddenly MIDDLETON.

II. *trans.* **1.** To cause (liquid) to issue or stream (*out*) in a jet from a squirt or syringe 1583. **b.** To eject or propel in a stream from a small orifice, etc. 1601. **2.** To inject (a liquid) by means of a squirt or in a similar manner 1550. **3.** To moisten or cover (a surface) with liquid by means of spirting or squirting; to bring into a certain state in this way 1601. **4.** *techn.* To force or press (a viscous or ductile material) through a small orifice; to form or fashion in this way 1881.

1. *fig.* Versifiers squirting out careless rhapsodies of harmonious billingsgate 1768. **b.** The emphatic way in which. .they squirted their tobacco-juice on the deck 1849. Hence **Squi·rter**, one who or that which squirts.

Squish (skwiʃ), *sb.* 1874. [f. next]. **1.** *Univ. slang.* Marmalade. **2.** A squishing sound 1902. **3.** *slang.* Nonsense, 'rubbish', 'rot', 'bilge' 1912.

Squish (skwiʃ), *v.* 1647. [imit.] **1.** *trans.* To squeeze, to squash. Now *dial.* **2.** *intr.* Of water, soft mud, etc.: To give out a peculiar gushing or splashing sound when walked in or on; to gush up, squirt out, with such a sound 1825.

Squitch (skwitʃ). 1785. [Altered f. QUITCH *sb.*] **1.** Couch-grass, *Triticum repens*. **2.** Applied to certain speices of *Agrostis* and other similar plants 1792.

Squi·tter, *sb.* Now *dial.* 1664. [f. the vb.] Usu. *pl.* Diarrhœa.

Squi·tter, *v.* Now *dial.* 1596. [imit.] **1.** *trans.* and *intr.* To squirt; to spatter, splutter. **2.** *intr.* To void thin excrement 1611.

St (st), *int.* 1552. [repr. a checked sibilation.] **1.** = HIST, HUSH, WHIST. **2.** An exclam. used to drive away an animal, or to urge it to attack 1552.

St. *Abbreviations.* **a.** (with cap.) = SAINT prefixed to a name; **b.** (with cap. or small initial) = STREET preceded by a defining word; **c.** (chiefly with small initial) in references (*a*) = STANZA; (*b*) = STATUTE; **d.** (with small initial) = STONE (weight).

Stab (stæb), *sb.*[1] 1440. [f. STAB *v.*] **1.** A wound produced by stabbing. **2.** An act of stabbing; a thrust with some sharp-pointed instrument 1530. **3.** *Billiards.* A short, stiff stroke which causes the striker's ball to remain dead or to travel but slowly after striking the object ball; more fully *s. stroke*; hence *s. cannon, screw*, a cannon or screw made with this stroke 1873.

1. An important punctured wound, such as the s. of a bayonet 1826. *A s. in the back*, an act of treachery. **2.** A s. that touched the vitals DE FOE. *fig.* A s. was attempted on my reputation BURKE. Phr. *The s.*, death by stabbing. *To have* or *make a s. at*: to try, attempt, make a shot at (*colloq.*, orig. *U.S.*).

Comb.: **s.-awl**, a shoemaker's tool used for piercing leather; **-culture**, a CULTURE (3) in which the medium is inoculated by means of a needle thrust deeply into its substance.

Stab, *sb.*[2] 1865. *Printer's slang.* = ESTABLISHMENT II. 4.

Stab (stæb), *v.* ME. [The relation to synon. dial. *stob* (XVI) is not clear; cf. *sprat/sprot, strap/strop*.] **1.** *trans.* To wound (often to kill) with a thrust of a pointed weapon (chiefly, with a short weapon, as a dagger) 1530. **2.** *absol.* and *intr.* To use a pointed weapon to wound or kill. late ME. **3.** *trans.* To thrust (a weapon) into a person 1610. **4.** *Bookbinding.* To pierce (a collection of sheets) in order to make a hole for a binding thread or wire; to fasten the sheets of (a pamphlet, etc.) together in this way instead of by sewing 1863.

1. Stabbed to the heart by the hand of an obscure villain CLARENDON. *fig.* He fabricates The sword which stabs his peace SHELLEY. Phr. *To s. in the back*, to slander; to behave treacherously towards. **2.** *fig.* Shee speakes poynyards, and euery word stabbes SHAKS. Hence **Sta·bber**, one who or that which stabs. **Sta·bbingly** *adv.*

‖**Stabat Mater** (stēi·bæt mēi·təɹ, stā·bæt mā·təɹ). 1867. [From the opening words, L. *stabat mater dolorosa* 'Stood the mother, full of grief'.] A sequence, composed by Jacobus de Benedictis in the 13th c., in commemoration of the sorrows of the Blessed Virgin Mary. Also, a musical setting of this sequence.

Stabile (stēi·bil, -əil), *a.* 1797. [– L. *stabilis*; see STABLE *a.*] **1.** Firmly established, enduring, lasting. (Used to express more unequivocally the etymological sense of STABLE *a.*) *rare.* **2.** Fixed in position 1896.

†**Sta·biliment.** late ME. [– L. *stabilimentum*, f. *stabilire* render stable, f. *stabilis*; see STABLE *a.*, -MENT.] Something which gives stability or firmness; stay, support –1684.

In the Trailing of the Trunk, they [the Claspers] serve for s., propagation and shade 1673.

Stabilimeter (stæbili·mĭtəɹ). 1907. [f. STABILITY + -METER.] *Aeronautics.* A contrivance for ascertaining the stability of a model airship or aeroplane.

Stabilitate (stăbi·lĭteit), *v. rare.* 1642. [– *stabilitat-*, pa. ppl. stem of med.L. *stabilitare*, f. L. *stabilitas* STABILITY; see -ATE[3].] *trans.* To give stability to.

Stability (stăbi·lĭti). late ME. [In earliest use also *stablete* – OFr. (*e*)*stableté* – L. *stabilitas*, on which (O)Fr. *stabilité* and Eng. *stabilitie* were directly modelled; see STABLE *a.*, -ITY.] The quality or condition of being stable. **1.** Of a person, his character or disposition: The condition of 'standing fast'; fixity of resolution or purpose; firmness, steadfastness. **2.** In physical senses. **a.** Power of remaining erect; freedom from liability to fall or be overthrown. late ME. **b.** Fixity of position in space; freedom from liability to changes of place 1625. **c.** Capacity for resistance to displacement; the condition of being in stable equilibrium, tendency to recover the original position after displacement. Also, of a body in motion: Freedom from oscillation, steadiness. 1542. **d.** Of a system of bodies: Permanence of arrangement; power of resisting change of structure 1855. **e.** Of a chemical compound or combination: Capacity to resist decomposition or disruption 1862. **f.** Of a colour: Permanence 1791. **3.** Of an immaterial thing: Immunity from destruction or essential change; enduring quality 1470.

1. The s. of England is the security of the modern world EMERSON. **2. a.** The S. of a Pyramid 1746. **b.** The doctrine of the motion of the earth and the s. of the sun 1831. **c.** *spec.* with ref. to aircraft.

Stabilizator (stēi·biləizēi:təɹ, stæ·b-). 1902. [– Fr. *stabilisateur*, f. *stabiliser*; see next and -ATOR.] *Aeronautics.* = STABILIZER.

Stabilize (stēi·biləiz, stæ·b-), *v.* 1861. [f. the stem of STABILITY; cf. Fr. *stabiliser*.] **1.** *trans.* To give stability to (a ship or aircraft). **2.** To give a stable character or value to 1875. **b.** To establish a scale of (payments, prices, or the like) 1918. So **Stabiliza·tion.**

Sta·bilizer. 1909. [f. prec. + -ER[1].] **1.** *Aeronautics.* A stabilizing apparatus or device. **2.** A substance added to an explosive to render it less liable to spontaneous decomposition 1911.

Sta·bilizing, *ppl. a.* 1911. [f. STABILIZE *v.* + -ING[2].] That stabilizes or gives stability; *spec.* in *Aeronautics*, that gives stability (to an aeroplane, etc.); that acts or may be used as a stabilizer.

Stable (stēi·b'l), *sb.* ME. [Aphetic – OFr. *estable* masc. and fem. stable, pigsty, etc. (mod. *étable* cow-house) :– L. *stabulum*, Rom. **stabula* (pl. used as fem. sing.), f. base of L. *stare* stand.] **1.** A building fitted with stalls, loose boxes, rack and manger and harness appliances, in which horses are kept. Formerly, a building in which domestic animals, as cattle, goats, etc., are kept. **b.** See AUGEAN *stable* 1903. **2.** A collection (of horses) belonging to one stable 1576. **3.** An establishment where race-horses are trained; a racing-stable. Also, the horses belonging to a particular racing-stable; the proprietors and staff of such an establishment 1810. **4.** *Mil.* Used in *pl.* for: Duty or work in the stables; also the bugle-call for this duty, stable-call 1885.

1. Ful many a deyntee hors hadde he in s. CHAUCER. **b.** Suggestions as to how this particular 's.' must be swept out 1909.

Comb.: **s.-boy**, a boy or man employed in or about a s.; **-call** *Mil.*, a bugle-call to stables (see 4); **s. companion**, a horse from the same s.; *transf.* (colloq.) a member of the same school, club, etc.; **-fly**, any species of the genus *Stomoxys*, esp. *S. calcitrans*; **-lad** = *s.-boy*; **stableman**, one who is employed in a s. to groom, feed, and otherwise look after the horses; **s. room**, stabling; **-yard**, the yard attached to a s.

Stable (stēi·b'l), *a.* ME. [– AFr. *stable*, OFr. *estable* (mod. *stable*) :– L. *stabilis*, f. *sta-*, base of *stare* stand; see -BLE.] **1.** Able to remain erect; secure against falling or being overthrown. **b.** Of a support or foundation: Firm, not likely to give way ME. **c.** Firm in consistency, solid. Now *rare.* 1666. **2.** Stationary, keeping to one place ME. **3.** Of a material thing or its condition: Able to maintain its place or position; presenting resistance to displacement; not easily shaken or dislodged 1560. **b.** Of a system of bodies: Having a permanent structure or constitution; not liable to disintegration 1839. **c.** Of a chemical compound or combination: Not readily decomposing 1850. **4.** Not liable to fail or vary; securely established; firm ME. **5.** Of persons and their dispositions. **a.** Steadfast in purpose or resolution; settled in character, not fickle, changeable, or frivolous ME. †**b.** Of God or a deity: Unchangeable –1700.

1. He which is tottering himselfe, had neede leane unto a s. thing 1591. **b.** If often affords a s. mooring to a ship 1820. **2.** Some seventy miles from the nearest s. ice 1853. **3.** Phr. *S. equilibrium*: see EQUILIBRIUM 1. **4.** Men. .deemed present institutions s., because they had never seen them shaken 1849. An accurate and s. definition of wealth RUSKIN. The s. forces of nature 1878. **5. a.** Things to make me s. In what I have began to take in hand BUNYAN. **b.** He perfect, s.; but imperfect We, Subject to Change, and diff'rent in Degree DRYDEN. Hence **Sta·bleness** (now *rare*), = STABILITY.

†**Stable**, *v.*[1] ME. [var. of ESTABLE *v.*] *trans.* To make stable –1545.

Stable (stēi·b'l), *v.*[2] ME. [f. STABLE *sb.*, or

aphetic – OFr. *establer*.] **1.** *trans.* To put (a horse) into a stable, or into a place which is used as a stable. **b.** Of a building: To afford stabling for 1903. **2.** *intr.* Of an animal: To live in a stable 1508.

2. *transf.* In thir Palaces..Sea-monsters whelp'd and stabl'd MILT.

Stable door. ME. The door of a stable.

Prov. *To shut* (*lock*, etc.) *the s. when the horse is stolen*, to take preventive measures too late.

Stabler (stēⁱ·bləɹ). Now *Sc.* late ME. [– OFr. *establier*, f. *estable*; see STABLE *sb.*, -ER² 2.] A stable-keeper.

†**Stable-stand.** 1598. [f. *stable* var. STABLY *sb.* + STAND *v.*] The position of a man found in a forest standing, with bow bent, ready to shoot at a deer, or standing by a tree with greyhounds in leash, ready to let slip.

Stabling (stēⁱ·bliŋ), *vbl. sb.* 1481. [f. STABLE *v.*² + -ING¹.] The action of placing or accommodating (horses) in a stable; stable accommodation; stable-buildings collectively.

Stablish (stæ·bliʃ), *v.* Now *arch.* ME. [Earlier var. of ESTABLISH *v.*] = ESTABLISH *v.*

And s. quietnesse on euery side SHAKS. As hee went to s. his dominion 1 *Chron.* 18:3. He stablishes the strong, restores the weak COWPER.

Stablishment (stæ·bliʃmĕnt). *arch.* late ME. var. of ESTABLISHMENT.

†**Sta·bly,** *sb.* ME. [– AFr. *establie* (AL. *stabilia* XII), f. *establir* ESTABLISH. Cf. *stabilitiones venationum* (Domesday Book).] **1.** *Hunting.* A besetting of a wood with men, hounds in leash, nets, etc., for the purpose of taking deer, etc. –late ME. **2.** A stand, halt (of armed men) –1450.

Stably (stēⁱ·bli), *adv.* ME. [f. STABLE *a.* + -LY².] In a stable manner, firmly, †steadfastly, †constantly.

†**Stacca·do.** 1612. [Aphetic – Sp. *estacada* (whence Fr. *estacade* ESTACADE), f. *estaca*, rel. to STAKE *sb.*¹; see -ADO.] = STOCKADE –1777.

‖**Staccato** (stăkā·to), *a.* (*adv.*, *sb.*). 1724. [It., pa. pple. of *staccare*, aphetic f. *distaccare* DETACH.] *Mus.* Detached, disconnected, *i.e.* with breaks between successive notes. Used *adj.* or *advb.* as a direction; also as *sb.*, a succession of disconnected notes.

The monotonous s. of the guitar BECKFORD. Hence **Stacca·to** *v. trans.* to play (a piece of music) in a s. manner.

Stack (stæk), *sb.* ME. [– ON. *stakkr* haystack :– Gmc. **stakkaz*, prob. in IE. **stognos* (cf. Russ. *stog* haystack).] **1.** A pile, heap, or group of things, esp. such a pile or heap with its constituents arranged in an orderly fashion. **2.** A pile of grain in the sheaf, of hay, straw, fodder, etc., gathered into a circular or rectangular form, and usu. with a sloping thatched top to protect it from the weather ME. **3.** A pile of sticks, faggots, firewood, poles, etc. late ME. **b.** A measure of volume for wood and coal, usu. 4 cubic yds. (108 cubic feet) 1651. **4.** A number of chimneys, flues, or pipes, standing together in one group 1667. **b.** A chimney of a house, factory, etc.; the chimney or funnel of a locomotive or steamship; also = *stack-furnace* 1825. **5.** *dial.* A columnar mass of rock, detached by the agency of water and weather from the main part of a cliff, and rising precipitously out of the sea 1769. **6.** Often in *pl.* = 'heaps' (*slang*) 1903.

1. b. A structure of bookshelves for compact storage of books; also, a building containing such a structure. **2.** While the Cock..to the s., or the Barn Dore, Stoutly struts his Dames before MILT.

Comb.: **s.-furnace,** a tall circular blast-furnace; **-guard,** a temporary covering to protect a s. of hay or grain in process of formation; **-stand,** a raised staging for a s. of hay grain, to keep it dry and free from the ravages of vermin; **-yard,** a rick-yard.

Stack (stæk), *v.* ME. [f. prec. sb.] **1.** *trans.* To pile (corn, fodder, etc.) into a stack; to make a stack of, to pile (something) up in the form of a stack. **2.** *absol.* and *intr.* To put corn or hay into stacks; to make a stack or stacks 1722. **3.** *trans.* To make a pile of (weapons, etc.) by leaning one against another 1841. **4.** To fill *with* stacks of 1652.

1. At the far end, fleeces of wool stacked up GEO. ELIOT. *To s. the cards* (orig. U.S.), to cheat by shuffling the cards in a particular way; *fig.* to take an unfair advantage. **3.** The men [military cyclists], having dismounted and stacked their machines 1887. Hence **Sta·cker.**

Sta·ck-garth. *north.* ME. [– ON. *stakkgarðr*; see STACK *sb.*, GARTH¹.] A stackyard, rick-yard.

Stacking (stæ·kiŋ), *vbl. sb.* 1531. [f. STACK *v.* + -ING¹.] The action or an act of STACK *v.*

attrib.: **s. stage,** a scaffold used in the building of stacks.

‖**Stacte** (stæ·ktī). ME. [L. – Gr. στακτή, subst. use of fem. of στακτός distilling in drops, f. σταγ-, στάζειν flow, drip.] **a.** A fragrant spice referred to by ancient writers; prop., the finest kind of myrrh, the exudation of the living tree, but the name was also applied to a mixture of storax with fat. In the Bible used as tr. Heb. *nāṭāp*, one of the ingredients of the incense prescribed for the Tabernacle worship, variously conjectured to be opobalsamum, myrrh, storax, or tragacanth. †**b.** *Pharmacy.* Applied to LIQUIDAMBAR and perh. other preparations.

Stactometer (stækto̜·mĭtəɹ). Also **stakto-** 1842. [f. Gr. στακτός (see prec.) + -METER.] *Hydrodynamics.* An appliance consisting of a glass tube having a hollow bulb in the middle, used for measuring liquids in drops.

‖**Stad** (stat). *S. Africa.* Also **stadt.** 1896. [Du.] A town or village.

Staddle (stæ·d'l), *sb.* Also †**stadle.** [OE. *staþol* base, support, tree trunk, fixed position = OFris. *stathul*, OS. *staðal* standing, OHG. *stadal* barn (G.dial. *stadel*), ON. *stǫðull* milking-place :– Gmc. **staþlaz*, f. **sta-* STAND *v.*] †**1.** A foundation –ME. **2.** A young tree left standing when others are cut down. Also *dial.* the root or stump of a tree that has been felled. 1559. **3. a.** The lower part of a stack of corn, hay, etc. 1581. **b.** A platform of timber, stone, etc., on which a stack or rick is placed. Also, in some districts = *s.-stones* 1729.

Comb.: **s.-stones,** the stones on which a s. or stack-frame is supported.

Stade (stēⁱd). *arch.* 1537. Anglicized f. STADIUM.

Stadholder, stadtholder (stæ·thōᵘldəɹ). 1668. [– Du. *stadhouder* (= G. *statthalter*), tr. LOCUM TENENS, f. *stad* place (STEAD) + *houder*, agent noun of *houden* HOLD *v.*] **1.** *Netherlands Hist.* **a.** orig., A viceroy or lieutenant-governor of a province or provinces. **b.** The title borne by the chief magistrate of the Dutch republic. **2.** Used as tr. G. *statthalter*, Da. *statholder*, lieutenant-governor, viceroy 1704. Hence **Sta·dholderate,** the office or dignity of s., a state ruled by a s. **Sta·dholdership.**

Stadia (stēⁱ·diă). 1865. [History obsc.; prob. f. STADIUM, or the pl. *stadia.*] An apparatus for measuring distance by optical means. **a.** *Mil.* A glass plate, or a brass plate with an opening in the form of an isosceles triangle, marked with figures showing the distance at which a foot- or horse-soldier will be when his image covers a certain height on the instrument held at arm's length. **b.** *Surveying.* An apparatus consisting of a rod or staff placed at one end of the distance to be measured and a pair of horizontal lines, hairs or wires on the diaphragm of a telescope placed at the other end.

Stadiometer (stēⁱdio̜·mĭtəɹ). 1862. [f. Gr. στάδιον STADIUM + -METER.] **a.** *Mil.* = STADIA a. **b.** A surveying instrument. In *U.S.* A self-recording theodolite in which the directions are marked upon a small sheet.

‖**Stadium** (stēⁱ·diŏm). *Pl.* **stadia** (stēⁱ·diă); †also **stadias, stadiums,** etc. late ME. [L. – Gr. στάδιον.] **1.** An ancient Greek and Roman measure of length, most commonly = one-eighth of a Roman mile. (In the English Bible rendered by *furlong.*) **2.** A race-course for foot-racing, orig. a stadium in length; hence *occas.* foot-racing as an exercise. In mod. use freq., a place for athletic exercises. 1603. **3.** A stage of a process, disease, etc. 1669. **4.** *Surveying.* = STADIA b. 1861.

‖**Stadthaus** (ʃtat‚haus). 1839. [G., f. *stadt* town + *haus* HOUSE *sb.*] A German town-hall.

Stadthouse (sta·t‚haus). 1646. [Anglicization of G. *stadthaus* or Du. *stadhuis.*] A town-hall.

Staff (stɑf), *sb.*¹ *Pl.* **staves** (stēⁱvz), **staffs** (stɑfs). [OE. *stæf* = OFris. *stef*, OS. *staf* (Du. *staf*), OHG. *stap* (G. *stab*), ON. *stafr* :– Gmc. **stabaz* (cf. Goth. var. **stafs*, dat. pl. *stabim*). Branch III is of continental origin (cf. Du. *staf*, G. *stab*).] **I. 1.** A stick carried in the hand as an aid in walking or climbing. Now chiefly *literary.* **b.** *joc.* as a type of thinness or leanness. late ME. †**c.** A shepherd's crook –1577. **d.** A rod or wand used as an instrument of magic or divination 1610. **2.** A stick, pole, or club used as a weapon. (Cf. QUARTERSTAFF.) OE. **3. a.** The shaft of a spear or lance. *arch.* ME. †**b.** A spear, lance, or similar armed weapon –1868. **4.** *fig.* Something which serves as a support or stay. late ME. **b.** In the Biblical phr. *to break the s. of bread* (literally from Heb.), to diminish or cut off the supply of food. late ME. **c.** Hence *the s. of life* = bread (or similar staple food) 1638. **5.** Part of the insignia of the episcopal office, consisting of a rod or pole of wood, metal or ivory supporting a crook, or, in the case of metropolitans, a cross OE. **6.** A rod or wand, of wood or ivory, borne as an ensign of office or authority; *spec.* as the badge of certain chief officers of the Crown 1535. **7.** A pole from which a flag is flown 1613. †**8.** A strong stick, pole, bar, rod or stake used for various purposes; e.g. for carrying burdens, to support a canopy, the stems of plants, etc. –1708. **9.** *Surveying.* A rod for measuring distances and heights 1556. **b.** The gnomon of a sun-dial 1669. **10.** *Her.* A representation of a stick, stake, bar, etc.; *spec.* = BATON 3, FISSURE *sb.* 2c. See also RAGGED STAFF. 1486. **11.** *Surg.* A grooved steel instrument used to guide the knife in lithotomy 1698. **12. a.** A rung of a ladder ME. **b.** A round cross-bar connecting the handles or stilts of a plough, or the legs of a chair. Also, each of the handles of a plough. *Obs.* or *dial.* 1523. †**c.** A bar or rail used in the construction of a gridiron, gate, cart, cage, etc. –1601. **d.** *Watchmaking.* An arbor or axle 1860.

1. I..dug my s. deeply into the snow TYNDALL. **b.** 2 *Hen. IV*, V. i. 71. **d.** I'le breake my staffe *Temp.* V. 54. **2.** I..with an Oak'n s. will meet thee MILT. **3. b.** Come, put mine Armour on: giue me my Staffe SHAKS. *To break a s.*, to tilt or contend *with* (an antagonist). With defining word, as *Jedburgh* (*Jedworth, Jedwood*, etc.) *s.* **4.** The boy was the verie staffe of my age, my verie prop SHAKS. **12. a.** How many mount Fortunes ladder, and break the staves as they go up 1657.

Phrases. *S. and staple*, the chief elements or ingredients. *To set up* (or †*in*) *one's s.* (*of rest*), to settle down in a place, take up one's abode. *To have the s. in* (*one's*) *own hand*, to keep possession of one's property, to retain authority and obedience.

II. Letter, verse, musical staff. †**1.** A written character, a letter. Cf. RUNE-STAVE. –ME. **2.** †**a.** A line of verse –1540. †**b.** A stanza or set of lines –1697. **c.** A 'verse' or stanza of a song. Now STAVE. 1598. **3.** *Mus.* A set of horizontal lines (now five in number) on, and in the spaces between which, notes are placed so as to indicate pitch. Also STAVE. 1662.

2. b. Mr. Cowley had found out that no kind of S. is proper for a Heroick Poem DRYDEN.

III. (Pl. always *staffs.*) **1.** *Mil.* A body of officers appointed to assist a general, or other commanding officer, in the control of an army, brigade, regiment, etc., or in performing special duties (as the *medical s.*). *General s.*, a body of officers controlling an army from headquarters under the commander-in-chief. [app. of continental Gmc. origin, and prob. developed from the sense 'baton' (= 6 above)] 1781. **2.** *gen.* A body of persons employed, under the direction of a manager or chief, in the work of an establishment or the execution of some undertaking (e.g. a newspaper, hospital, government survey); *esp.* the body of servants (*domestic s.*) employed in any establishment 1837.

attrib. and *Comb.* **a.** In sense 'of or belonging to a military staff', as *s. appointment, pay, surgeon, uniform*; **s. cap,** a flat-topped cap with a peak, such as forms part of various uniforms; **s. college,** a college in which officers are trained for s. appointments; **s. corps,** a body of officers and men organized to assist the commanding officer and his s. in various special departments; in India, a corps formed in each of the three presidencies to supply officers for service; **s.-ride,** a name for exercises on the ground without troops, as a means of teaching strategy. **b.** In the Navy used to designate a senior class of officers, as *s. captain*, etc. **c.** Special: **s.-angle** *Plastering*, a piece of wood fixed to the external angle of the two upright sides of a wall for floating the plaster to, and for defending the angle against accidents; **-head,** the upper end of a s., carved, tipped with metal, etc.; the top of the tripod which supports a theodolite, etc.; **-man,** a workman employed in silk-throwing; **-sling,** a sling the strings of which are attached to the end of a staff (*Obs.* exc. *Hist.*); **-tree,** the genus *Celastrus*; **-vine,** *Celastrus scandens* of U.S.

Staff (stɑf), *sb.*[2] 1892. [Of unkn. origin.] A building material consisting of plaster mixed with fibre, used for temporary ornamental work.

Staff (stɑf), *v.* 1859. [f. STAFF *sb.*[1]] *trans.* To provide with a staff of officers, teachers, servants, etc.

Staffette (stæfe·t). *Obs.* exc. *Hist.* 1545. [– It. *staffetta*, dim. of *staffa* stirrup.] A mounted courier. Cf. ESTAFETTE.

†**Staffier.** 1532. [– It. *staffiero*, *-ere*; see prec.] An attendant; a footman –1734.

†**Sta·ffish,** *a.* 1500. [f. STAFF *sb.*[1] + -ISH[1].] **a.** Rigid, stiff, hard. **b.** *fig.* Stubborn, unmanageable. –1802.

Staff officer. 1702. †**1.** A high officer of the royal household, or minister of state, bearing a white staff. See STAFF *sb.*[1] I. 6. –1728. **2.** *Mil.* †**a.** A non-commissioned officer –1727. **b.** An officer doing duty with the general or departmental staff of an army, division, or brigade 1777. **c.** In the U.S. navy, an officer not exercising military command 1891.

Stafford (stæ·fəɹd). .1460. Name of the county town of Staffordshire, England; used *attrib.* in †*S. blue* (a cloth), †*S. law* ('club law'). So **Sta·ffordshire,** the distinctive name of a kind of earthenware and porcelain 1784.

Stag (stæg), *sb.* ME. [OE. **stacga*, **stagga*, of similar formation to the OE. animal names *docga* DOG, *frocga* FROG, **picga*, **pigga* PIG, etc.] **1.** The male of a deer, esp. the red deer; spec. a hart or male deer of the fifth year. **b.** In the names of various species of the genus *Cervus*, as *Axis S.*, an Indian deer (*C. axis*), *Carolina S.*, the N. Amer. Wapiti (*C. canadensis*) 1859. **2.** *north.* and *Sc.* A young horse, esp. one unbroken ME. **3.** An animal castrated when full-grown. **a.** A bull; more fully *bull s.* Now *dial.*, *Sc.*, and *Austr.* 1680. **b.** A boar, hog, or ram. *dial.* 1784. **4.** Applied to the male of various birds; *esp.* a cock. Also *spec.* in *Cockfighting*, a cock less than one year old. 1730. **5.** *slang.* An informer; esp. in phr. *to turn s.* 1725. **b.** A shilling 1857. **c.** *U.S. slang.* A man who goes to a social gathering unaccompanied by a female partner; phr. *to go stag*; also = *stag-party*; attrib., as *s.-dance*, *-party*, etc. 1848. **6.** *Comm. slang.* A person who applies for an allocation of shares in a joint-stock concern solely with a view to selling immediately at a profit 1845. **7.** *attrib.* and *Comb.* **a.** quasi-*adj.* = male, as *s.-bird*, *-hog*, *-moose*, etc. 1606. **b.** (See 5 c.).

Comb.: **s.-evil,** of a horse, lockjaw; **s. fern,** = staghorn fern (see STAG-HORN 2 c); **-hafted, -handled** *adjs.*, furnished with a haft or handle of stag-horn; **-hog** = BABIROUSSA; †**-match** (*Cockfighting*), a match for young cocks.

Stag (stæg), *v.* 1796. [f. STAG *sb.*] **1.** *slang.* **a.** *trans.* To observe; to take particular notice of; to watch; also, to find out or discover by observation, to detect. Also *absol.* or *intr.* **b.** *intr.* To turn informer; to inform *against* 1839. **2.** *Comm. slang.* To deal in shares as a stag (see STAG *sb.* 6.) 1845.

Sta·g-bee:tle. 1681. A beetle of the genus *Lucanus*, the males of which have large denticulated mandibles resembling the horns of a stag; esp. *L. cervus*, and, in U.S., *L. elaphus.*

Stage (stēⁱdʒ), *sb.* ME. [Aphetic – OFr. *estage* dwelling, stay, situation (mod. *étage* storey) :- Rom. **staticum* standing-place, position, f. L. *stare* stand; see -AGE.] **I.** Standing-place; something to stand upon. **1.** Each of the portions into which the height of a structure is divided; a horizontal partition; *esp.* a storey or floor of a building. **b.** A shelf; *spec.* a tier of shelves for plants; *Geol.* two or more sets of beds; *U.S.* a level (of water) 1465. †**2.** Station, position, seat, esp. with reference to relative height; each of a number of positions or stations one above the other –1625. †**3.** A degree or step in the 'ladder' of virtue, honour, etc.; a 'step' on Fortune's wheel –1634. **4.** A raised floor, platform, scaffold. **a.** A floor raised above the level of the ground for the exhibition of something to be viewed by spectators. Now *rare* or *Obs.* ME. †**b.** A scaffold for execution or exposure in the pillory –1781. **c.** A scaffold for workmen and their tools, materials, etc.; also, each of the levels of scaffolding 1440. **d.** A platform, etc., for drying fish 1535. **e.** A platform used as a gangway, landing place, support or stand for materials, etc. 1773. **f.** A raised plate, ledge, or shelf to support an object, slide, etc., in a microscope or other instrument 1797. **5.** The platform in a theatre upon which spectacles, plays, etc., are exhibited; esp. a raised platform with its scenery upon which a theatrical performance takes place 1551.

3. From the highest S. of Honour, to the lowest staire of disgrace 1622. **4. a.** *Haml.* V. ii. 389. **5.** Then to the well-trod s. anon, If Jonsons learned Sock be on MILT. *fig.* All the world's a s., And all the men and women, meerely Players SHAKS. Phr. *To go on the s.*, to take up the profession of an actor. *To bring* (a person) *on* or *to the s.*, to present (him) as a character in a play. *To bring, put* (an opera, a tragedy, etc.) *on the s.*, to produce (it) in public. *To take the s.*, of an actor, to walk with dignity across the stage after concluding an impressive speech; hence, to assume the chief part, as in a play.

II. Division of a journey or process. **1.** A place in which rest is taken on a journey; *esp.* a regular stopping place on a stage-coach route where horses are changed and travellers taken up and set down 1603. **2.** As much of a journey as is performed without stopping for rest, a change of horses, etc.; each of the several portions into which a road is divided for coaching or posting purposes; the distance travelled between two places of rest on a road 1603. **b.** Short for STAGE-COACH 1671. **3.** A period of a journey through a subject, life, course of action, etc. 1608. **4.** A period of development, a degree of progress, a step in a process 1818. **b.** *Med.* A definite period in the development of a disease, marked by a specific group of symptoms 1747.

2. We proceeded leisurely and by easy stages 1898. **b.** 'Tis like a parcel sent you by the s. COWPER. **3.** The love that cheers life's latest s. COWPER. **4.** It is necessary that at some s. of the Bill the consent of the Crown should be signified 1863. **b.** I found him in the last s. of a dropsy 1780.

attrib. and *Comb.*: **s.-box,** each of the boxes over the proscenium of a theatre; **-craft,** that part of the art of dramatic composition which is concerned with the conditions of representation on the stage; **s. direction,** a direction inserted in a written or printed play where it is thought necessary to indicate the appropriate action, etc.; **-door,** the entrance to that part of a theatre used by the actors; **-fright,** extreme nervousness experienced by an actor on the stage, esp. on his first appearance; hence *transf.*; **-name,** a professional name assumed by an actor; **-property** = PROPERTY *sb.* 3; **-setting,** the disposition of the persons of a play and the accessories on the stage; **-struck** *a.*, smitten with love for the stage or drama or with the desire to become an actor; †**-wagon,** one of the wagons belonging to an organized system of conveyance for heavy goods and passengers by road; **-wait,** a delay or hitch in the course of a theatrical performance; also *transf.*; **-whisper,** a conventional whisper used on the stage, purposely made audible to the spectators; hence any very audible whisper. Hence **Sta·gery,** exhibition on the s.; s. arrangements or contrivances.

Stage (stēⁱdʒ), *v.* ME. [f. STAGE *sb.*] †**1.** To build, erect. ME. only. **2.** To furnish with a stage or staging; freq. with *about.* Now *rare* or *Obs.* 1506. **3.** To put (a person) into a play; to satirize in drama; to represent (a character, incident) on the stage. Sometimes in phr. *to s. to the crowd* or *show.* 1601. **b.** To put (a play, etc.) upon the stage 1879. **4.** To put (plants) on a stage; to exhibit (plants, etc.) at a show. Also *absol.* 1850. **5.** *intr.* To travel by stage or stage-coach; to journey *over* by stages 1695. **6.** Of a play: To lend itself to presentation; esp. *to s. well, badly*, etc. 1924.

3. *Ant. & Cl.* III. xiii. 30. **c.** *U.S.* To arrange to take place dramatically; to make a setting for 1924. **5.** Riding, driving, or staging to London COLERIDGE.

Stage-coach. 1658. [STAGE *sb.* II. 2.] A coach that runs daily or on specified days between two places for the conveyance of parcels, passengers, etc. Hence **Stage-coachman,** the driver of a stage-coach.

Stage-manager. 1817. One whose office it is to superintend the production and performance of a play, and to regulate the arrangements of the stage. So **Stage-manage** *v.* **Stage-management.**

Stage play. 1513. A dramatic performance; also, a dramatic composition adapted for representation on the stage. **b.** Play-acting 1872. So **Stage-player** (1556), = PLAYER 2, **-playing** (1597).

Stager (stēⁱ·dʒəɹ). 1570. [f. STAGE *sb.* + -ER[1]; OFr. *estagier* (f. *estage* STAGE) inhabitant, resident, is a poss. source.] **1.** *Old s.*: one who has become graduated or qualified by long experience; a veteran, an old hand. Also occas. of animals. **b.** Hence *stager* simply, and with other adjs., as *cunning, sly.* Also (rarely) *young s.*, one of small experience, a beginner. 1664. **2.** A stage-player. *Obs.* exc. *arch.* 1580. **3.** A stage-coach or stage-coach horse 1852.

Staggard (stæ·gă̆ɹd). *arch.* late ME. [f. STAG *sb.* + -ARD. Cf. AL. *staggardus.*] A stag in its fourth year.

Stagger (stæ·gəɹ), *sb.* 1577. [f. STAGGER *v.* With sense 2 cf. AL. *stagherum* (XIV).] **1.** An act of staggering; a tottering or reeling motion of the body as if about to fall, as through feebleness, tripping, giddiness, or intoxication. **b.** In a biplane, etc., the amount of advance of the entering edge of an upper wing over that of a lower 1915. **2.** *pl.* (const. as *sing.*) A name for various diseases affecting domestic animals, of which a staggering gait is a symptom 1577.

1. *fig.* I will throw thee from my care for euer Into the staggers, and the carelesse lapse Of youth and ignorance SHAKS. **2.** Phr. (*To have*) *the staggers*, inability to walk steadily.

attrib.: **s. bush** *U.S.*, the shrub *Andromeda mariana*; **-grass,** the atamasco-lily, *Zephyranthes atamasco*; **staggerwort,** the ragwort, *Senecio jacobæa.*

Stagger (stæ·gəɹ), *v.* 1530. [alt. of (now dial.) *stacker* –ON. *stakra*, frequent. of *staka* push, stagger. Cf. for change of cons. *straggle, trigger.*] **I.** *intr.* **1.** Of a person or animal: To sway involuntarily from side to side when trying to stand or walk erect; to totter or reel as if about to fall; to walk with a swaying movement. **b.** Said of the legs or feet 1665. **c.** As the result of a blow or encounter, or of carrying a heavy load. Const. *under.* 1547. **d.** *transf.* Of a ship: To move unsteadily and with difficulty; esp. *under* a press of sail 1840. **2.** *fig.* To begin to doubt or waver in an argument, opinion, or purpose; to become less confident or determined; to hesitate or waver *at.* Now *rare.* 1533. **b.** Of purpose, opinion, faith, etc. 1617. **3.** Of an army, line of battle, etc.: To waver, become unsteady, give way 1544. **4.** Of a material thing: To sway or rock from side to side; to shake, rock, or swing violently; to totter 1530.

1. Hee maketh them to s. like a drunken man *Job* 12:25. **c.** The bearers s. under the heavy coffin 1874. **d.** We are staggering along under all sail 1853. **2.** If you shal haue faith, and s. not N.T. (Rheims) *Matt.* 21:21. **b.** At whose immensity Even soaring fancy staggers SHELLEY.

II. *trans.* **1.** To cause (a person or animal) to reel or totter, esp. from a blow 1593. **2.** *fig.* **a.** To bewilder, perplex, nonplus; to render helpless by a shock of amazement (or *occas.* horror). In *pass.* to be perplexed or astonished *at.* 1556. **b.** To shake the stability of (a country, condition of things) 1613. **c.** To shake, unsettle, cause to waver or falter (a person's faith, opinion, purpose, etc.) 1617. **d.** To cause (a person) to falter or waver (*in* his faith or purpose) 1627. †**e.** To throw doubt upon (a doctrine) –1833. **3.** To cause to waver, throw into confusion (troops) 1721. **4.** *Mech.* To arrange in zig-zag order, or in positions alternately on either side of a median line 1856. **b.** To arrange in such a way that one part is farther forward than another; *spec.* cf. STAGGER *sb.* 1 b. 1909.

1. *Rich. II.* v. v. 110. **c.** Phr. *To s. belief*: to be incredible. **e.** He..staggereth the immortality of the soul SIR T. BROWNE. **4. c.** To arrange (working hours) so that some businesses open and close at different times from others, or so that employees enter and leave in batches at intervals instead of all at the same time (orig. *U.S.*) 1918. Hence **Sta·ggerer** (*lit.* and *fig.*).

Stag-headed, *a.* 1683. **1.** Of an animal: Having a head like that of a stag. **2.** Of a tree or forest of trees: Having the topmost branches bare and withered 1769.

2. Some oaks are old and s. at 100 years 1882.

Stag-horn. Also **stag's horn.** 1663. [STAG *sb.*] **1. a.** *pl.* The horns of a stag. **b.** *sing.* The horn of a stag as a material. **2.** In the names of plants. **a.** The American or Virginian sumach, *Rhus typhina.* More fully *stag('s horn tree, sumach.* 1753. **b.** A kind of moss, esp. *Lycopodium clavatum.* More fully *stag's horn* (also *staghorn*) *moss.* 1741. **c.** A fern of the genus *Platycerium.* In full *staghorn fern.* 1882. **3.** In the names of insects, etc. 1816.

3. The s. capricorn beetle (*Prionus cervicornis*, F.) in America 1816. Among the true stony corals are the S. corals (*Madrepora cervicornis, prolifera,* and *palmata*) 1884. Hence **Stag-horned** *a.* (*a*) epithet of a beetle; (*b*) = STAG-HEADED *a.* 2.

Staghound (stæ·ghaund). 1707. [f. STAG *sb.* + HOUND *sb.*] = DEER-HOUND.

Stagiary (stēi·dʒiări), *sb.*[1] 1868. [– med.L. *stagiarius*, f. *stagium* (XIII) term of residence of a canon – OFr. *estage* STAGE *sb.*; see -ARY[1].] *Eccl. Hist.* A canon residentiary.

Stagiary (stēi·dʒiări), *sb.*[2] and *a.* 1836. [– Fr. *stagiaire*, f. after med.L. *stagiarius*; see prec.] **A.** *sb.* A French law student. **B.** *adj.* In *s. school.* a school in which, according to the French law of 1850, assistants could be employed who had no certificate of capacity, but only a certificate of three years' service (Fr. *stage*).

Staging (stēi·dʒiŋ), *vbl. sb.* Also †**stageing.** ME. [f. STAGE *sb.* and *v.* + -ING[1].] **1.** *concr.* **a.** A temporary platform or structure of posts and boards for support; scaffolding. **b.** *Arch.* The stages of a buttress collectively 1865. **2.** The action, process, or art of putting a play on the stage; stage-setting 1884. **3.** The business of running or managing stage-coaches; the action of travelling by stage-coach or by stages (chiefly *Anglo-Ind.*) 1850.

2. The s. of a play is in itself a work of true art 1884.

Stagirite (stæ·dʒĭrəit). 1595. [– L. *Stagirites* (also *Stagerites*) – Gr. Σταγειρίτης, f. Στάγειρος, also Στάγειρα n. pl.; see -ITE[1] 1.] A native or inhabitant of Stagira, a city of Macedonia; *spec.* the philosopher Aristotle, who was born there.

Welcome, great S., and teach me now All I was born to know COWLEY.

Stagnancy (stæ·gnănsi). 1659. [f. STAGNANT *a.*; see -ANCY.] **1.** The condition of being stagnant or without motion, flow, or circulation. **2.** Anything stagnant 1681.

Stagnant (stæ·gnănt), *a.* 1666. [– L. *stagnans, -ant-*, pr. pple. of *stagnare*; see STAGNATE *v.*, -ANT.] †**1.** Of a fluid: That is at rest in a vessel –1721. **2.** Not flowing or running, of water, air, etc.; without motion or current, as a pool. Often involving unwholesomeness. 1699. **3.** *fig.* Void of activity, excitement, or interest 1749.

3. Immur'd, and buried in perpetual Sloth, That gloomy Slumber of the s. Soul JOHNSON. Trade is s. CARLYLE. Hence **Sta·gnantly** *adv.*

†**Sta·gnate,** *a.* 1706. [– L. *stagnatus*, pa. pple. of *stagnare*; see next, -ATE[2].] = prec. –1845.

The s. sea Under the torrid zone HOOD.

Stagnate (stæ·gnēit), *v.* 1669. [– *stagnat-*, pa. ppl. stem of L. *stagnare*, f. *stagnum* pool; see -ATE[3].] **1.** *intr.* To be or become stagnant; to case to flow, to stand without motion or current; *transf.* of a person or people: to subside into a stagnant mode of existence. **2.** *trans.* To cause to be or become stagnant 1693. **3.** To astonish. *dial.* and *U.S.* 1784.

1. The Air that stagnated in the Shaft 1691. The blood tends to accumulate and to s. in the capillaries and veins 1878. *fig.* Nothing tends more to the corruption of science than to suffer it to s. BURKE. **2.** We have neither bogs nor marshes to s. our waters 1750. *fig.* His credit, the life and blood of his trade, is stagnated DE FOE.

Stagnation (stægnē·ʃən). 1665. [f. prec. + -ATION.] **1.** The condition of being stagnant; an instance of this. **2.** *fig.* Unhealthy absence of activity, energy, etc. 1711.

1. If the water runneth, it holdeth clear..; but s. turneth it into a noisome puddle 1677. They are subject to a S. of blood 1707. **2.** The dulness and s. of a French country town 1907.

Stagy, stagey (stēi·dʒi), *a.* 1860. [f. STAGE *sb.* + -Y[1].] **1.** Of or pertaining to the stage; theatrical in appearance, manner, style, etc. (Chiefly in a depreciatory sense.) **2.** Of a seal or its skin: Out of condition from undergoing the change of coat 1885.

1. A stage hero in stagey heroics MEREDITH. Fechter, the tragedian,—an agreeable man, and not at all stagey LONGF. Hence **Sta·gily** *adv.* **Sta·giness.**

Stagyrite, erron. f. STAGIRITE.

Stahlian (stā·liăn), *a.* and *sb.* 1790. [f. name of G. E. *Stahl*, a German chemist (1660–1734) + -IAN.] **A.** Pertaining to Stahl or his doctrines, esp. his theory of vital action and of disease. **B.** A follower of Stahl; an animist.

‖**Stahlhelm:** see *Steel Helmet* s.v. STEEL *sb.*

Staid (stēid), *a.* 1541. [adj. use of *stayed*, pa. pple. of STAY *v.*] **1.** Of beliefs, institutions, etc.: Fixed, permanent; settled, unchanging. Of a person's gaze: Fixed, set. Now *rare.* †**b.** Of persons: Settled in faith, purpose, etc. –1812. **2.** Settled in character; of grave or sedate deportment; dignified and serious in demeanour or conduct; free from flightiness or caprice 1557. **b.** Characterized by or indicating sedateness 1567. **3.** Of the intellect, etc.: Sober, steady, well-regulated; free from extravagance or caprice 1555.

1. His s. opinion 1863. **2.** By his stayed life God hath bene glorified NORTH. Ore laid with black s. Wisdoms hue MILT. A s. and quiet palfrey SCOTT. **3.** A s. and considerate understanding 1870. Hence **Stai·d-ly** *adv.*, **-ness.**

Stail(e, var. ff. STALE *sb. dial.* handle.

Stain (stēin), *sb.* 1563. [f. STAIN *v.*] †**1.** The action of staining; pollution, disgrace –1607. **2.** A discoloration produced by absorption of or contact with foreign matter; usually, one that penetrates below the surface and is not easily removable 1583. **b.** A mark or discoloration on the skin; a blotch or sore 1595. **c.** *transf.* A spot or patch of colour different from the ground. Common in *Nat. Hist.* 1704. †**d.** A slight tinge *of.* SHAKS. **3.** *fig.* (Often in phrases like *to wash, purge a s.*) **a.** A grave blemish on a person's reputation; a mark of infamy or disgrace; a stigma 1591. **b.** A person or thing that causes disgrace. Now *rare* or *Obs.* 1589. †**c.** One who eclipses or casts into the shade –1605. **4.** A dye or colouring matter used in staining. **a.** A thin liquid preparation used to colour wood, etc. 1758. **b.** A dye or pigment used to render minute and transparent structures visible, or to differentiate tissue elements by colouring, for microscopic purposes; or to produce specific microchemical reactions 1880.

1. *Timon* v. i. 176. **2.** Staynes in thinne silkes and woollen clothe 1583. **b.** You do remember This staine [a mole] vpon her? SHAKS. **c.** Swift trouts diversified with crimson stains POPE. **d.** You haue some staine of souldier in you SHAKS. **3. a.** The probable s. on their birth FREEMAN. **b.** Staine to thy countrymen, thou hear'st thy doom SHAKS. **c.** Staine to all Nimphs, more louely then a man SHAKS.

Stain (stēin), *v.* late ME. [Aphetic f. DISTAIN *v.* Some of the Eng. senses are difficult to account for.] †**1.** *trans.* To deprive of colour –1589. †**b.** Of the sun, etc.: To deprive (feebler luminaries) of their lustre. Also *fig.* of a person or thing: To eclipse. –1649. †**c.** To obscure the lustre of –1657. †**2.** *intr.* To lose colour or lustre –1614. **3.** Of something dyed or coloured: To impart its colour to (something in contact). Also in wider use (e.g. said of a chemical reagent), to alter the colour of (something to which it is applied) 1440. **b.** *transf.* Of the blood: To suffuse with colour. Also *pass.*, to be (naturally) spotted or streaked with colour. 1557. **c.** To absorb colouring matter, take a stain 1877. **4.** *trans.* To damage or blemish the appearance of (something) by colouring a part of its surface; to discolour by spots or streaks of blood, dirt, or other foreign matter not easily removed. In poetic use occas.: To colour, defile (a river) with blood. late ME. **b.** *Hunting.* = FOIL *v.*[1] 2. 1798. **5.** *fig.* **a.** To defile or corrupt morally; to taint with guilt or vice 1446. **b.** To be a permanent reproach to, inflict a stigma upon; to blemish, soil (a person's reputation, honour, conscience, etc.). Also *intr.* of the conscience: †To suffer stain. 1513. †**c.** *To s.* (a person's) *blood*: (*a*) to prove (him) of base descent; (*b*) to cause 'corruption of blood' (see CORRUPTION 2). –1776. †**6.** To ornament with coloured designs or patterns –1615. **7.** To colour (esp. textile fabrics, paper, wood, stone) by the application of pigment that more or less penetrates the substance instead of forming a coating on the surface, or by means of chemical reagents. In microscopical and histological research: To colour (tissues, etc.) with some pigment so as to render the structure clearly visible. 1655. **b.** To colour (glass) with transparent colours. Also to depict in stained glass (*rare*). 1797.

1. b. O voice that doth the Thrush in shrilnesse staine SIDNEY. **2.** Suns of the world may staine when heauens sun staineth SHAKS. **3.** The rouge on her neck had stained her collar 1901. [Flint] stained ferruginous from adjacent red clay 1912. **4.** The walls were stained and discoloured DICKENS. **5. a.** The British kings were stained with every vice 1847. **b.** I have..stain'd the glory of my Royal House DRYDEN. A reputation which his later cruelties might s., but could not efface 1879. **7.** There were rolls of vellum or papyrus, stained saffron-colour at the back 1891.

Stained (stēind), *ppl. a.* late ME. [f. STAIN *v.* + -ED[1].] In the senses of the vb.; freq. in comb. with a prefixed sb., as BLOOD-STAINED.

S. glass, transparent coloured glass, formed into decorative mosaics, used in windows (esp. of churches); also, less correctly, glass which has been decorated with vitrified pigments; so *s. glass window.*

Stainer (stēi·nəɹ). late ME. [f. STAIN *v.*; see -ER[1].] One whose employment is staining; one who colours wood, etc., with pigments which penetrate below the surface. See also PAINTER-STAINER, PAPER-STAINER.

Stainless (stēi·nlės), *a.* 1586. [f. STAIN *sb.* + -LESS.] Without stain, spot, or blemish; in trade use, that does not become stained.

The s. mirror of the lake SHELLEY. The very care he took to keep his name S. CRABBE. Hence **Stai·nless-ly** *adv.*, **-ness.**

Stair (stēəɹ). [OE. *stǣger* = (M)LG., (M)Du. *steiger* scaffolding, quay :– **staiȝri*, f. Gmc. **staiȝ-* **stiȝ-* climb.] **1.** An ascending series or 'flight' of steps leading from one level to another, esp. from one floor to another in a house; a staircase. **b.** *fig.* A means of ascending in rank, power, moral excellence, etc. 1570. †**c.** An ascending series, scale. SIR T. BROWNE. **2.** One of a succession of steps leading from one floor of a building to another 1530. †**b.** *fig.* A step or degree in a (metaphorical) ascent or in a scale of dignity –1640. **3.** *collect. pl.* (of sense 2) = sense 1. Also, in generalized sense, the steps of staircases. late ME. †**b.** construed as *sing.* A flight of steps, a staircase –1830. **c.** *fig.*; *esp.* applied to the means by which a person rises in rank or power. Now *rare* or *Obs.* 1576. **4.** *pl.* (rarely †*sing.*). A landing-stage, esp. on the Thames in and near London 1517.

1. A S. of 20 Steps 1730. **2.** I ascended the same by two hundred and forty staires of marble 1617. **b.** The elder he growes, hee is a stayer lower from God EARLE. **3.** *Pair, flight of stairs*: see PAIR *sb.* II. 1 b, FLIGHT *sb.*[1] 6. *Back-stairs*: see BACK-STAIRS. *Above stairs*: on or to the ground floor or upper floors of a house. *Below stairs*: on or to a lower floor, esp. below the ground floor; hence, in the servants' quarters. *Down, up stairs*: see DOWNSTAIRS, UPSTAIRS. **b.** It is a good way to any bed-chamber, and the stairs is steep 1776. **4.** Just opposite, on the riverside, were the Millbank stairs 1904.

Comb., as *s.-carpet*; **s.-pit** *Mining*, a shallow shaft or staple in a mine fitted with a ladder or steps; **-rod,** a metal or wooden rod fixed in eyes, to secure a stair-carpet in the bend of each step; **-step,** one of the steps in a flight of stairs.

Staircase (stēə·ɹkēis). 1624. [f. STAIR + CASE *sb.*[2]] **1.** Orig., the inclosure of a flight of stairs; now usu. a flight (or series of flights) of stairs, with their supporting framework, balusters, etc. **2.** *Phys.* A continuous series of responses to nerve stimuli 1882.

1. Who lived in the same s. with me at Christchurch WESLEY.

Comb.: **s.-shell,** a shell of the genus *Solarium*, any member of the family *Solariidæ*.

Stai·r-foot. Also rarely **stairs-, stair's-.** 1470. The foot of a staircase; the level space in front of the lowest step of a flight of stairs.

Stai·r-head, stai·rhead. 1534. The level space at the top of a staircase or flight of stairs.

Stairway (stēᵊ·ɹweᶦ). 1767. [f. STAIR *sb.* + WAY *sb.*] A way up a flight of stairs, a staircase.

He walked up the grim s. of the hotel 1872.

Staithe (stēᶦð). Now *local.* Also **staith.** [In sense 2 – ON. **stapwō, stǫð*, rel. to OE. *stæþ* = OS. *stað*, OHG. *stad*, Goth. *staþa* (dat. sing.) bank, shore :– Gmc. **staþaz, -am*, f. **sta-* STAND.] †**1.** The land bordering on water, a bank, shore –ME. **2.** A landing-stage, wharf; esp. a waterside depôt for coals brought from the collieries for shipment, furnished with staging and shoots for loading vessels ME. **3.** An embankment 1698. Hence **Stai·th(s)man,** one who superintends the shipping of coal.

Stake (stēᶦk), *sb.*¹ [OE. *staca*, corresp. to OFris., (M)LG., MDu. *stake* (Du. *staak*); a word of the LDu. area, (G. *stake*, etc., being – MLG.), f. **stak- *stek-* (see STICK *sb.*¹).] **1.** A stout stick or post, usually of wood, with a pointed end for driving into the ground; used e.g. to mark a boundary or site, to support a plant, etc. **b.** A post upon which persons were bound for execution, esp. by burning. Hence *the s.* = the punishment of death by burning. ME. **c.** The post to which a bull or bear was fastened to be baited 1546. **d.** A post pointed at both ends for use in military defensive work ME. **2.** *collect. sing.* Stakes used as a framework or support in fencing and hedging; esp. as a basis for the intertwining, wattling, or plashing of brushwood or other materials 1457. **3.** *techn.* **a.** A small anvil used by metal workers, esp. one with a tang for fitting into a socket on a bench 1660. **b.** *Leather-manuf.* A wooden stake in the top of which is set a broad steel blade over which the skins are drawn to soften and stretch them 1853. **c.** Each of the stanchions or posts which fit into sockets or staples on a trolley, wagon or boat to prevent the load from slipping off 1875. **d.** *Basket-making.* Each of the longest foundation-rods of a basket or the like 1911. **4.** In the Mormon Church: A territorial division; the see or jurisdiction of a Mormon bishop. [perh. suggested by Isa. 54 : 2, 3.] 1882.

1. b. Curse Miscreant, when thou comst to the s. SHAKS. **c.** Let vs do so: for we are at the s., And bayed about with many Enemies SHAKS.

attrib. and *Comb.*: **s.-boat,** a boat moored or otherwise fixed to serve as a starting-point or mark for racing boats; **-driver** *U.S.*, the bittern, *Botaurus mugitans*; **-head,** in *Rope-making*, a s. with wooden pins in the upper side to keep the strands apart; **-presidency,** the presidency of a Mormon s. (see sense 4).

Stake (stēᶦk), *sb.*² 1540. [Of unkn. origin.] **1.** That which is placed at hazard; esp. a sum of money, etc. deposited or guaranteed, to be taken by the winner of a game, race, contest, etc. **2.** In certain phrases: The condition of being staked 1592. **3.** *pl.* in *Horse-racing, Coursing*, etc., the sums of money staked or subscribed by the owners who enter horses or dogs for a contest, the whole to be received as the prize by the owner of the winner or divided among the owners of the animals 'placed'. Hence in *sing.* (cf. SWEEPSTAKE) a race for money thus staked or subscribed. Also in *pl.* with defining words as the designation of particular races or classes of races in which the sum of money staked is the prize as dist. from a Plate, Cup, or the like 1696.

1. Our landlord here shall hold stakes SCOTT. *fig.* The Sword, Which for no less a S. than Life you Draw DRYDEN.

Phrases. *To have a s. in* (an event, concern, etc.): to have something to gain or lose by the turn of events; esp. in *to have a s. in the country* (said of those who hold landed property). *To draw stakes*, to withdraw what is staked as a wager, etc. **2.** †*To be, lay down* or *set* (a thing) *at s.* or *at the s. To be at s., to have at s.*; I see my reputation is at s. My fame is shrowdly gored SHAKS. **3.** *Produce stakes*: (*a*) in *Horse-racing*, a race in which the runners must be the offspring of horses named and described at the time of entry; a produce race; (*b*) in *Coursing*, a race for puppies, i.e. for dogs of from one to two years of age; also called *Puppy stakes. Subscription stakes*: in *Horse-racing*, a race for which subscribers of a fixed amount annually have the right to enter one or more horses.

Comb.: **s.-holder,** one who holds the s. or stakes of a wager, etc.

Stake (stēᶦk), *v.*¹ ME. [f. STAKE *sb.*¹] **1.** *trans.* To mark (land) with stakes. Also with *off, out.* **2.** To protect, support, or obstruct with stakes. Also, to shut *in, off, out, up* with stakes. 1500. **b.** To put a stake or stakes to (a plant) 1664. **3.** To secure with or as with a stake 1544. **4.** To impale (a person) on a stake. Also with *up.* Also, to transfix and fasten down (a person) with a stake. 1577. **b.** *pass.* Of a horse, etc.: To be injured by impalement on a hedge or fence stake. Also *refl.*; hence *trans.*, to cause a horse to stake himself. 1687.

2. Order was giuen that the camp should be entrenched and staked SAVILE. On the bank of loose stones above the mud and stakes that staked the tide out DICKENS. **3.** Our horses were unsaddled and staked on the open plain MAYNE REID. *fig.* I haue a soale of Lead So stakes me to the ground, I cannot moue SHAKS. **4.** Stak'd through the body like a paltry Thief 1786.

Stake (stēᶦk), *v.*² 1530. [Of unkn. origin.] **1.** *intr.* To wager, hazard money, on the event of a game or contest. Now felt as absol. use of sense 3. **2.** trans. *To s. down*: to deposit (a sum of money) as a wager or stake on the result of a game or contest. Also *absol.* 1565. **3.** To put at hazard (a sum of money, an article of value, etc.) upon the cast of dice, the result of a competition or game, the event of a contingency, etc.; to wager 1591. **4.** *fig.* To risk the loss of, to hazard 1670.

2. *Gra.* Weele play. .for a thousand ducats. *Ner.* What and s. downe? SHAKS. **3.** He. .No lesser of her Honour confident. .stakes this Ring SHAKS. **4.** Mary had staked all on her union with Darnley 1874.

Stalactic (stălæ·ktik), *a.* 1756. [– Gr. σταλακτικός, f. σταλακ-; see STALACTITES, -IC.] Deposited by dripping water; pertaining to or consisting of stalactites. So **Stala·ctical** *a.* (now *rare*) 1714.

Stalactite (stæ·læ̆ktəit, (*U.S.*) stălæ·kteit). 1677. [Anglicized f. next.] **1.** An icicle-like formation of calcium carbonate, depending from the roof or sides of a cavern and produced by the dropping of waters which have percolated through, and partially dissolved, the overlying limestone. **b.** A similar formation of other material 1801. **2.** A general term for limestone found in this formation 1796.

1. b. Delicate stalactites and stalagmites of lava 1890. **2.** White crusts of s. 1908. Hence **Stala·ctiform, Stalacti·tiform** *adjs.* having the form of a s.

‖**Stalactites** (stælæ̆ktəi·tiz). Now *rare. Pl.* **stalactitæ** (-tī). 1681. [mod.L. (Olaus Wormius), f. Gr. σταλακτός dropping, dripping, f. σταλακ-, base of σταλάσσειν drip, let drip; see -ITE¹.] = prec.

Stalactitic (stælæ̆kti·tik), *a.* 1770. [f. STALACTITE + -IC.] **1.** Having the form or structure of a stalactite; resembling or pertaining to stalactites. **2.** Covered with, containing or consisting of, stalactites 1845. So **Stalacti·tical** *a.*

‖**Stalagma** (stălæ·gmă). 1693. [mod.L. – Gr. στάλαγμα drop, drip, f. σταλακ-; see STALACTITES.] **1.** A distilled liquor (*rare*). **2.** = next 2. 1903.

Stalagmite (stæ·læ̆gməit, *U.S.* stălæ·gməit). 1681. [– mod.L. *stalagmites*, f. Gr. στάλαγμα; see prec., -ITE¹.] **1.** An incrustation or deposit, more or less like an inverted stalactite, on the floor of a cavern, formed by the dropping from the roof of some material in solution. **2.** Limestone deposited in this manner 1815.

attrib.: **s. marble,** onyx marble. Hence **Stalagmi·tic, -al** *adjs.* formed in the same way as a s., composed of stalagmites or having their form or character. **Stalagmi·tically** *adv.*

Stale (stēᶦl), *sb.*¹ Now *dial.* [OE. *stalu* (corresp. to Flem., Fris. *staal* handle), rel. to *stela*; see STEAL *sb.*¹] **1.** †Each of the two upright sides of a ladder. Also (now *dial.*) a rung or step of a ladder; the stave of a rack in a stable. **2.** A handle, esp. a long, slender handle, as the handle of a rake. Also, the stem of a pipe, etc. ME. **3.** The stem of an arrow or spear 1553.

Stale (stēᶦl), *sb.*² 1440. [prob. – AFr. *estale, estal*, applied to a pigeon used to entice a hawk into the net. Of Gmc. origin; prob. from the root of OE. *steall* place (STALL *sb.*¹), *stellan* to place.] **1.** A decoy-bird; a living bird used to entice other birds of its own species, or birds of prey, into a snare or net. Also, a stuffed bird or figure of a bird used for the same purpose. (Now *dial.*) †**2.** *transf.* and *fig.* A deceptive means of allurement; a person or thing held out as a lure or bait to entrap a person –1692. †**3.** A person who acts as a decoy; esp. the accomplice of a thief or sharper –1633. †**4.** More fully *common s.*: a prostitute of the lowest class, employed as a decoy by thieves –1641. †**5.** = STALKING-HORSE 2, 2 b. –1774. †**6.** A lover or mistress whose devotion is turned into ridicule for the amusement of a rival or rivals –1635.

1. Like vnto the fowlers, that by their stales draw other birdes into their nets NORTH. **2.** *Temp.* IV. i. 187. **4.** *Much Ado* II. ii. 26. **5.** Had he none else to make a s. but me? SHAKS. **6.** *Com. Err.* II. i. 101.

†**Stale,** *sb.*³ ME. [– OFr. *estal* place, position, etc. (mod. *étal* butcher's stall) – Frankish **stal* (= OHG. *stal*); see STALL *sb.*¹] **1.** A fixed position or station –1485. **2.** An ambush –1627. **3.** A body of armed men posted in a particular place for ambush, etc., or detached for reconnoitring, etc. Also, the main body of an army. –1579.

Stale (stēᶦl), *sb.*⁴ late ME. [perh. f. STALE *v.*¹] Urine; now only of horses and cattle.

†**Stale,** *sb.*⁵ late ME. [– AFr. *estale* position, f. *estaler* be placed, f. Gmc., see STALE *sb.*³, *v.*³, STALL *sb.*¹] = STALEMATE –1656.

Stale (stēᶦl), *a.* ME. [prob. – AFr., OFr. **estale* (mod. *étale*, naut., of stationary water), f. *estaler* come to a stand; cf. STALL *v.*¹, STALE *sb.*³] †**1.** Of malt liquor, mead, wine: That has stood long enough to clear; freed from dregs or lees; hence, old and strong –1743. **2.** That has lost its freshness; altered by keeping. (Of bread: opp. to *new*.) 1530. **3.** *fig.* Of an immaterial thing: That has lost its freshness, novelty, or interest; hackneyed, worn out; effete 1562. **b.** *Law.* Of a claim or demand: That has been allowed to lie dormant for an unreasonable time 1769. †**4.** Of persons: Past the prime of life; having lost the vigour or attractiveness of youth. Of a bachelor or spinster: Past the fitting season for marriage –1858. **5.** *Sport.* Of an athlete, a racing animal. etc.: Out of condition through over-severe training or exertion too long continued 1856.

1. Good reed wine þat be s. 1400. **2.** The egg becomes s. or addled 1829. The bread should be s. 1878. **3.** How weary, s., flat, and vnprofitable Seemes to me all the vses of this world? SHAKS. Hence **Sta·le·ly** *adv.* (rare), **-ness.**

Stale (stēᶦl), *v.*¹ *Obs.* exc. *arch.* and *dial.* late ME. [perh. – OFr. *estaler* take up a position, in spec. sense; see STALE *sb.*⁵] **1.** *intr.* To urinate, said esp. of horses or cattle. †**2.** *trans.* To pass (blood) in the urine –1647.

Stale (stēᶦl), *v.*² 1440. [f. STALE *a.*] **1.** *trans.* To render (beer or ale) 'stale'. **b.** *intr.* Of beer: to become 'stale' or old 1742. **2.** *trans.* To render stale, out of date or uninteresting; to diminish interest in 1599. †**b.** To lower (oneself, one's dignity) in estimation by excessive familiarity –1843. **c.** *intr.* To grow stale, get out of fashion, become uninteresting 1897.

2. Age cannot wither her, nor custome s. Her infinite variety SHAKS. **b.** Not content To s. himselfe in all societies, He makes my house here common as a mart B. JONS.

Stale, *v.*³ 1470. [prob. – AFr. *estaler*; see STALE *sb.*⁵] *Chess.* **a.** *trans.* = STALEMATE *v.* **b.** *intr.* To undergo stalemate 1585.

Stalemate (stēᶦ·lmēᶦt), *sb.* 1765. [f. STALE *sb.*⁵ + MATE *sb.*¹] *Chess.* A position in which the player whose turn it is to move has no allowable move open to him, but has not his king in check. Also *fig.*, standstill.

According to the modern rules, the game which ends in s. is drawn. See O.E.D.

Stalemate (stē^{i}·lmē^{i}t), *v.* 1765. [f. prec.] *Chess. trans.* To subject to a stalemate. Also *fig.*

Stalk (stǭk), *sb.*[1] [prob. dim. (with *k* suffix) of ME. *stale*; see STALE *sb.*[1]] **1.** The main stem of a herbaceous plant, bearing the flowers and leaves; also, a scape or flower-stem rising directly from the root. **2.** The comparatively slender connecting part by which a vegetable organ is attached to the plant; the petiole of a leaf, the peduncle or pedicel of a flower, fruit, or inflorescence, the stipe of an ovary, etc. ME. **b.** A similar slender connecting part by which an animal organ or structure is attached or supported 1826. **3.** The shaft of a chimney. (Cf. STACK *sb.* 4.) 1821. **4.** The main part of anything long and slender, as dist. from the extremities; e.g. †the shaft of a quill; the tube or stem of a thermometer 1530. **5.** A slender upright support; the stem of a wineglass 1864. **6.** *Arch.* An ornament in the Corinthian which resembles the stalk of a plant 1842.

1. A long green reed, like the s. of the maize 1839. The rough tangle of stalks and stems 1910. **2. b.** The 's.' of the tumour 1899. **5.** Old drinking-glasses, with tall stalks HAWTHORNE.

Comb.: **s.-borer** *U.S.*, the larva of a moth *Gortyna nitela*, destructive to plants; **-eyed** *a.*, having the eye at the end of a s., podophthalmate.

Stalk (stǭk), *sb.*[2] 1450. [f. STALK *v.*] **I.** An act of stalking game. **2.** A striding gait; a stately or pompous mode of walking 1590.

2. An vgly feend,..The which with monstrous stalke behind him stept SPENSER.

Stalk (stǭk), *v.* [Late OE. **stealcian* (repr. in *bistealcian* and vbl. sb. *stealcung*) :– **stalkōjan*, frequent. f. **stal-* **stel-* STEAL *v.*] †**1.** *intr.* To walk softly, cautiously, or stealthily –1587. **2.** †To go stealthily *to*, *towards* (an animal) for the purpose of killing or capturing it. Hence, to pursue game by the method of stealthy approach, esp. by the use of a stalking-horse or of some similar device. late ME. **3.** *trans.* **a.** To pursue (game) by stealthy approach 1823. **b.** To go through (a tract of country) stalking game 1800. **4.** *intr.* To walk with stiff, high, measured steps, like a long-legged bird. Usu. with disparaging notion, implying haughtiness, sullenness, or the like. Freq. said of ghosts, animals, etc. 1530. **b.** *trans.* To march proudly through (a country, etc.) 1610.

1. There stalkte he on, as softe as foote could tread 1587. **2.** One vnderneath his Horse, to get a shoot doth stalke DRAYTON. *fig.* O I, stalke on, stalke on, the foule sits. I did neuer thinke that Lady would have loued any man. SHAKS. **3.** And for shooting him from behind a wall, it is cruelly like to stalking a deer SCOTT. **b.** To s. the bush on foot 1890. **4.** About them round A Lion now he [Satan] stalkes with fierie glare MILT. The Fen-men, stalking through the marshes on their stilts 1787. No heron was seen stalking on the usual haunts of the bird SCOTT. The plague was stalking grimly up and down the land 1889. **b.** Like a hideous phantom stalking the streets at noon-day 1841.

Stalked (stǭkt), *a.* 1731. [f. STALK *sb.*[1] + -ED[2].] Having a stalk or stalks; in *Nat. Hist.*, *Path.*, etc. opposed to *sessile*. Also in parasynthetic combs., *long-s.*, *red-s.*, etc.

One species of S. Barnacle 1863. The s. Crinoids 1874.

Stalker (stǭ·kəɹ). late ME. [f. STALK *v.* + -ER[1].] †**1.** A kind of net used by poachers. Also *s. net.* –1667. **2.** One who stalks game. late ME. **3.** One who walks with long measured steps 1585.

Sta·lking-horse. 1519. [f. *stalking* vbl. sb.] **1.** A horse trained to allow a fowler to conceal himself behind it or under its coverings in order to get within easy range of the game without alarming it. Hence, a portable screen made in the figure of a horse, similarly used. **2.** *fig.* A person whose participation in a proceeding is made use of to prevent its real design from being suspected 1612. **b.** An underhand means for making an attack or attaining some sinister object; usu., a pretext put forward for this purpose 1579.

1. Giovanni d'Udine..is thought to have been the inventor of the s., which poachers now use 1706. **2. b.** He uses his folly like a s. SHAKS.

Stalkless (stǭ·klės), *a.* 1698. [f. STALK *sb.*[1] + -LESS.] Having no stalk; chiefly of vegetable organs, sessile.

Stalklet (stǭ·klėt). 1835. [f. as prec. + -LET.] A small stalk; in *Bot.* = PEDICEL.

Stalky (stǭ·ki), *a.* 1552. [f. as prec. + -Y[1].] Consisting of or abounding in stalks; of the nature of a stalk or stalks; long and slender like a stalk.

Stall (stǭl), *sb.*[1] [OE. *steall* = OFris., (M)Du., OHG. *stal* (G. *stall*), ON. *stallr* pedestal, stall for a horse :– Gmc. **stallaz*, prob. :– **staðlaz*, f. **sta-* STAND. In some ME. senses partly – OFr. *estal* (mod. *étal*); cf. STALE *sb.*[3]] †**1.** *gen.* Standing-place, place, position; place in a series, degree of rank; in OE. occas., state, condition –1618. **2.** [Cf. mod.Fr. *stalle.*] A standing-place for horses or cattle; a stable or cattle-shed; also each division for one animal in a stable, cattle-shed, or cow-house; also, a manger OE. †**3.** A seat of office or dignity –1638. **4.** [Cf. med. L. *stallus*, OFr. *estal(e*, mod.Fr. *stalle.*] A fixed seat enclosed, either wholly or partially, at the back and sides, esp. each of a row of seats in the choir of a church for the use of the clergy or religious, and, in a chapter-house, for the canons; also, each of the seats appropriated to knights of the higher orders of chivalry (e.g. the Knights of the Garter in St. George's Chapel, Windsor, etc.). Hence *occas.* the office, status, dignity or emolument connected with the occupancy of a (cathedral) stall; a canonry or the like. late ME. **b.** A long seat or doorless pew in a church; also, a 'sitting' 1580. **c.** Each of the chair-like seats arranged in rows in front of the pit in a theatre; also each of the corresponding seats in other places of entertainment 1828. **5.** [Cf. OFr. *estal*, Flem. *stal.*] A bench, table, board, or the like, esp. one in front of a shop, upon which goods are exposed for sale; a booth or covered stand for the sale of wares at a market, fair, or in the open street; a stand at a Fancy Fair. late ME. †**b.** The booth or shed to shelter a cobbler at his work –1762. **6.** Applied to a sheath or receptacle of various kinds 1483. †**7.** Each of a series of 'screen' book-cases set at right angles to the walls of a library, each pair forming a bay or alcove –1886. **8.** *Metall.* A 'walled area' or compartment between low walls in which ores are roasted 1887. **9.** [perh. a distinct word.] *Coal-mining.* A working place in a mine, left between pillars in the pillar-and-stall system of mining 1665.

1. Phr. *In stead and s.*, everywhere, continually. **2.** I haue..Sixe-score fat Oxen standing in my stalls SHAKS. At the west end is a s. for one horse 1782. **4.** The eleven vacant stalls of the Most Honorable Order of the Bath 1788. But Wolsey was not satisfied..with six prebendary stalls 1873. **c.** From our places in the stalls we could see our four friends..in the loge THACKERAY. **9.** *Pillar* (or *post*) *and s.*, a method of working coal, etc., in which pillars of coal are left during the first stage of excavation.

Comb.: **s.-edition**, a cheap edition of a work offered for sale on the bookstalls; **s. gate**, the road from a s. to the main road in a coal-mine; **-holder**, (*a*) the holder of an ecclesiastical s.; (*b*) one who is in charge of a s. at a bazaar, etc.; **-literature**, the cheap literature of the bookstalls; **-man**, (*a*) a keeper of a bookstall; (*b*) a man who contracts for and works a s. in a coal-mine; also each of a company of men associated for that purpose; **-plate**, a plate of gilt copper on which the arms of a Knight of the Garter are engraved; **-reader**, one who peruses the books on a bookstall.

Stall (stǭl), *sb.*[2] 1500. [– AFr. *estal*, var. of *estale*; see STALE *sb.*[2]] †**1.** A decoy-bird. Chiefly *fig.* –1592. **2.** A pickpocket's helper who distracts the attention of the victim whose pocket is being rifled; also the action or an act of stalling 1591.

Stall (stǭl), *sb.*[3] 1918. [f. STALL *v.*[1]] *Aviation*, etc. An act of stalling.

Stall (stǭl), *v.*[1] ME. [Partly (i) – OFr. *estaler* stop, sit in choir, f. *estal* (see STALL *sb.*[1]), (ii) f. STALL *sb.*[1], and (iii) aphetic f. INSTALL. Cf. FORESTALL. With sense 3 cf. ESTALL.] **I.** To place. **1.** *intr.* To have one's abode, dwell. *Obs.* exc. *dial.* in *To s. with*, to get on with (another). **2.** *trans.* To assign a particular place to (a person or thing); to place. late ME. †**3.** To agree to the payment of (a debt) by instalments; to fix (days) for payment by instalments –1670.

1. *Ant. & Cl.* v. i. 39. **3.** *fig.* Thou canst never promise thyself to sin..thriftly..and s. the fine DONNE.

II. To place in a 'stall'. †**1.** = INSTALL *v.* 1. –1661. **2.** To put (an animal) in a stall; to keep in a stall, esp. for fattening. late ME. **b.** *intr.* Of cattle: To be lodged in stalls 1805.

1. Where Kings were stall'd, disthron'd..and crown'd 1632. **2.** I much prefer penning to stalling the sheep 1850. *fig.* Praie you leaue mee, s. this in your bosome, and I thanke you for your honest care SHAKS.

III. To come or bring to a stand. **1.** *trans.* To bring to a stand or standstill 1591. **b.** esp. in *pass.* To become stuck (in mud, mire, a snowdrift, etc.) Now *U.S.* or *dial.* 1460. **c.** To cause (an engine) to stop from overloading or insufficient fuel; to stop (a vehicle) undesignedly. Also *absol.* Also *intr.* of an engine or vehicle. 1914. **d.** *intr.* Of a flying machine: To lose flying speed 1914. Also *trans.* To cause (a flying machine) to stall 1913. **2.** *trans.* To take away (a person's) appetite; to satiate, surfeit *with*, *of*. Now *dial.* and *Sc.* 1583. **b.** To cause aversion in, cause to turn away. Also with *off*. Now *rare*. 1642.

1. When as thine eye hath chose the dame, And stall'd the deer that thou shouldst strike 1599. **b.** A teamster whose waggon was stalled in a place where it was somewhat swampy 1897. **2.** Ain't you fairly stalled of waiting? 1875.

IV. To furnish (a choir, etc.) with stalls 1516.

Stall (stǭl), *v.*[2] *slang.* 1592. [f. STALL *sb.*[2]] **1.** *trans.* To screen (a pickpocket or his operations) from observation; also with *off*. Also, to close *up* or surround and hustle (a person who is to be robbed). **2.** *To s. off.* **a.** To get rid of by evasive tactics, a trick, plausible tale, or the like; also, in sporting parlance, to keep the upper hand of (a competitor) 1812. **b.** To get off or extricate (a person) by artifice 1812.

2. a. His very preface should have stalled off denunciations of this kind 1905.

Stallage (stǭ·lėdʒ). late ME. [Aphetic – OFr. *estalage* (mod. *étalage*), f. *estal*; see STALL *sb.*[1], -AGE. So med. L. *(e)stallagium.*] A tax or toll levied for the liberty of erecting a stall in a fair or market; also *attrib.*, as *s. rent*.

Stalled (stǭld), *ppl. a.* 1560. [f. STALL *sb.*[1] and *v.*[1] + -ED.] †**1.** Of a person: Endowed with or occupying a (church) stall –1829. **2.** Of an animal: Confined to a stall; fattened in a stall for killing 1560. **3.** Divided into stalls for animals 1825. **4.** Of a vehicle, etc.: That has stuck fast 1839. **5.** Glutted, satiated 1740.

2. Better is a dinner of grene herbes where loue is, then a s. oxe and hatred therewith BIBLE (Geneva) *Prov.* 15:17.

Staller (stǭ·ləɹ). *Hist.* [– late OE. *stallere*, *steallere*, (AL. *stallarius* 1068), f. *steall* STALL *sb.*[1], after med.L. *stabularius* constable (L. = stable-boy, hostler), and thus a var. of late L. *comes stabuli* (v) CONSTABLE. So ON. *stallari*, title of a Norwegian court officer from X.] The title of a high officer in the reign of Edward the Confessor, equivalent to CONSTABLE 1.

Sta·ll-fed, *ppl. a.* 1554. [f. STALL *sb.*[1] + FED *ppl. a.*] Fed in a stall; hence, luxuriously nurtured.

Sta·ll-feed, *v.* 1763. [Back-formation from prec.] **1.** *trans.* To feed (an animal) in a stall. **2.** *intr.* Of an animal: To undergo feeding or fattening in a stall 1766.

Stalling (stǭ·liŋ), *vbl. sb.* late ME. [f. STALL *v.*[1] + -ING[1].] †**1.** Installation –1535. †**2.** The action of agreeing for the payment of a debt by instalments, or of fixing dates for payment; also, an instance of this –1640. **3.** Stall-accommodation (of or for an animal) 1535. **4.** *Aeronautics.* (Cf. STALL *v.*[1] III. 1 c.) 1916.

3. *A.Y.L.* I. i. 11.

Stallion (stæ·lyən). [Late ME. *staloun* – AFr. var. (cf. AL. *stalonus* XII) of OFr. *estalon* (mod. *étalon*) – Rom. deriv. (cf. -OON) of Gmc. **stall-* STALL *sb.*[1] (stallions for breeding being kept in the stable); the origin of the form *-ion* (XV) is unkn., but cf. It. *stallio.*] **1.** A male horse not castrated, an entire horse, esp. one kept for the purpose of serving mares. †**2.** Applied to a person: A man of lascivious life; in later use, a woman's hired paramour –1796. †**3.** A courtesan –1670.

2. What are you, her S., and her Bravo too? SHADWELL. **3.** *Haml.* II. ii. 616.

†**Stall net.** ME. [prob. f. STALL *sb.*[1]] A net laid across a river, esp. for sprat-fishing.

Stalwart (stǭ·l-, stæ·lwəɹt), *a.* Now *literary.* late ME. [XVI Sc. form of STALWORTH *a.*, brought into Eng. use by Scott.] **A.** *adj.* **1.** Strongly and stoutly built, sturdy, robust 1450. **2.** Of inanimate things: Firmly made or established, strong. Now *rare.* late ME. **3.** Of persons, their attributes, etc.; Resolute, unbending, determined. Chiefly *mod.* late ME. **4.** Valiant in fight, brave, courageous. late ME.

1. A tall and s. bagpiper LOCKHART. **3.** S. opponents of superstition 1905. **4.** A s. knight TENNYSON.

B. *sb.* **1.** A strong and valiant man. (Now only as nonce-use, after 2.) 1470. **2.** A sturdy, uncompromising partisan; esp. as a political designation 1881.

2. *attrib.* The 's.' section of militant Dissent 1907. Hence **Sta·lwart-ly** *adv.*, **-ness** (*rare*).

Sta·lworth, *a.* and *sb. Obs.* exc. *arch,* [OE. *stǣlwierþe* (ME. *stalworþe*, etc.), f. *stǣl* place + *weorþ, worþ* WORTH *a.*] **A.** *adj.* †**1.** Of things: Serviceable. OE. only. **2.** Of persons and animals: = prec. *a.* 1. OE. **3.** Of persons, their actions, etc.: Brave, courageous, valiant, mighty ME. †**B.** *sb.* A strong and valiant man –1500. Hence †**Sta·lworthness,** s. quality. –late ME.

Stamen (stē̆ⁱ·mĕn). *Pl.* **stamens;** also (now *rarely*) **stamina** (stēⁱ·mină). 1650. [– L. *stamen* warp, thread of warp (pl. *stamina*; see STAMINA), applied by Pliny to the stamens of a lily, corresp. to Gr. στήμων warp, στῆμα some part of a plant.] †**1.** The warp of a textile fabric (*rare*) –1681. †**2. a.** The thread spun by the Fates at a person's birth –1753. **b.** The supposed germinal principle or impulse in which the future characteristics of any nascent existence are implicit –1725. **c.** The fundamental or essential element of a thing –1794. **3.** *Bot.* The male or fertilizing organ of a flowering plant, consisting of two parts, the *anther*, which is a double-celled sac containing the pollen, and the *filament*, a slender footstalk supporting the anther 1668. Hence **Sta·mened** *a.* having stamens.

†**Sta·min.** ME. [– OFr. *estamine* (mod. *étamine*) – fem. of L. adj. *stamineus* lit. 'consisting of threads', f. *stamen, stamin-*; see prec.] A coarse worsted cloth; in earliest use usu. an under garment made of this worn by ascetics; later a kind of woollen or worsted cloth, for which Norfolk was formerly noted –1664.

Stamina (stæ·mină). 1676. [– L. *stamina*, pl. of *stamen*; see STAMEN. The senses arise partly from the orig. L. 'warp of cloth', partly from the application of L. *stamina* to the threads spun by the Fates (see STAMEN 2 a).] †**1.** As *pl.* The native or original elements and constitution of anything; the nature, structure, and qualities of an organism, as existing potentially in its nascent state; the rudiments or germs from which living beings or their organs are developed –1824. †**2.** As *pl.*; rarely as *sing.* The congenital vital capacities of a person or animal, on which (other things being equal) the duration of life was supposed to depend; natural constitution as affecting the duration of life or the power of resisting debilitating influences –1863. **3.** orig. as *pl.*; now chiefly as *sing.* Vigour of bodily constitution; power of sustaining fatigue or privation, of recovery from illness, and of resistance to debilitating influences; staying power 1726. †**4.** As *pl.* and *sing.* Source of strength, main support, 'backbone' –1799.

1. *fig.* Enmity to us. .is wrought into the very s. of its constitution BURKE. **3.** Had he been possessed of less s. and less vitality he must have succumbed 1880. *fig.* The British Constitution has considerable s. 1865.

Staminal (stæ·minăl), *a.* 1798. [f. L. *stamin-* STAMEN, STAMINA + -AL[1].] **1.** Belonging to the stamina or natural constitution of a person or thing. **2.** *Bot.* Pertaining to or consisting of stamens 1845.

Staminate (stæ·minĕt), *a.* 1845. [f. L. *stamin-*, stem of STAMEN + -ATE[2].] *Bot.* Furnished with or producing stamens. Of certain flowers: Having stamens but no pistils.

Stamineous (stămi·nĭəs), *a.* 1668. [f. as prec. + -EOUS.] *Bot.* Consisting of, bearing, or pertaining to a stamen or stamens.

Staminiferous (stæmini·fĕrəs), *a.* Also **stameniferous.** 1761. [f. as prec. + -FEROUS.] *Bot.* Having or bearing stamens, applied to a flower having stamens but no pistils.

Staminodium (stæminōᵘ·diŏm). 1821. [mod.L., f. L. *stamin-* STAMEN + mod.L. *-odium* (see -ODE).] *Bot.* **a.** A sterile or abortive stamen, or an organ resembling an abortive stamen, without its anther. **b.** The antheridium of a cryptogam 1848. So **Sta·minode.**

Stammel (stæ·mĕl). Now *arch.* or *Hist.* 1530. [prob. alt. (with variation of suffix) of STAMIN.] **1.** A coarse woollen cloth or linsey-woolsey, usually dyed red; an undergarment of this, worn by ascetics. **2.** More fully *s. colour*: the shade of red in which the cloth was commonly dyed. [Sometimes vaguely = 'red'.) 1567.

Stammer (stæ·məɹ), *sb.* 1773. [f. the vb.] A stammering mode of utterance.

Stammer (stæ·məɹ), *v.* [Late OE. *stamerian* = OS. *stamaron*, (M)LG., (M)Du. *stameren* :– WGmc. **stamrōjan*, f. **stamra-*, **stam-*, repr. by OE. *stam(m*, OHG. *stamm*, ON. *stamr*, Goth. *stamms* stammering, and other formations.] **1.** *intr.* To falter or stumble in one's speech; *esp.* to make one or more involuntary repetitions of a consonant or vowel before being able to pass from it to the following sound. (Cf. STUTTER *v.*) **2.** *trans.* To utter or say with a stammer 1587. **3.** *intr.* To stagger in walking; said esp. of horses. Now *dial.* late ME.

1. The eloquent tongue forgot its office. Cicero stammered, blundered, and sat down. FROUDE. *fig.* That I may dare, in wayfaring, To s. where old Chaucer used to sing KEATS. **2.** I stammer'd that I knew him TENNYSON. *transf.* I stammered out a bow, and. .went home LAMB. Hence **Sta·mmerer,** one who stammers. **Sta·mmeringly** *adv.*

Stammering (stæ·məriŋ), *vbl. sb.* ME. [-ING[1].] **1.** The action of STAMMER *v.*; hesitation and involuntary repetition in speech; also (now *dial.*) staggering and stumbling in gait. **2.** *transf.* in certain *Path.* uses 1855.

2. S. of the Fingers 1855. The s. with the bladder occurs in just the same conditions as the stammering speech 1868. S. with the organs of deglutition 1868.

Stamp (stæmp), *sb.* 1465. [Partly f. STAMP *v.*, partly – (O)Fr. *estampe*, f. *estamper*; see STAMP *v.*] **I.** An act of stamping; a forcible downward blow with the foot 1590.

The repeated stamps of the heel of his heavy boot SCOTT.

II. An instrument for stamping. **1.** An instrument for making impressions, marks, or imprints, on other bodies; a stamping tool, an engraved block or die 1465. **b.** *esp.* A die or the apparatus used in stamping a device upon a coin, token, medal, or the like 1572. **2.** A printing type or types (collectively); hence, a printing press. *To put to s.*, to print 1548 (later, printer's slang). **3.** A bookbinder's tool for embossing bindings. Also *transf.* an ornament produced by this. 1811. **4.** A machine for shaping articles made of sheet-metal; a drop-hammer 1839. **5.** An iron-shod pestle of a mill for stamping ores, esp. each of the several pestles forming a battery; chiefly in *pl.*, a battery of stamps, a stamp-mill 1674.

1. My old silver s., with the double G upon it SCOTT. *fig.* His Sword, Deaths stampe, Where it did marke, it tooke from face to foot SHAKS.

III. The result of stamping. **1.** The mark, impression, or imprint made with an engraved block or die 1542. **2.** *fig.* **a.** A certifying mark or imprint 1611. **b.** The imprint or sign (*of* what is specified) 1596. **c.** Character, fashion, type 1573. **3.** An embossed or impressed mark placed by a government office on paper or parchment to certify that the duty chargeable in respect of what is thereon written or printed has been paid. Hence also, in recent times, an adhesive label (printed with a distinctive device) which is issued by the government for a fixed amount, and which serves the same purpose as an impressed stamp. 1694. **b.** *spec.* = POSTAGE STAMP 1837. **c.** *pl.* (*U.S. slang.*) Money, (properly, paper money) 1872. †**4.** Something marked with a device; a coin, medal –1633. †**5.** A picture produced by printing from an engraved plate, an engraving, print. *In s.*, by means of engraving. [After It. *stampa*, Fr. *estampe.*] –1780. **6.** *Metall.* 'The pieces into which the rough bars shingled from the finery ball are broken, to be piled for subsequent rolling into sheet-iron' (Raymond) 1880.

1. He sold goods, that were not marketable without the s. ARBUTHNOT. The dollar, under its new s., has preserved its name and circulation 1871. The s. acts as a kind of hall-mark 1883. *fig.* The rank is but the guinea's s.—The man's the gowd for a' that BURNS. **2. a.** Truth its radiant s. Has fixed. .Upon her children's brow SHELLEY. **b.** The s. of merit SHAKS. **c.** A yong maid, truly of the finest s. of beautie SIDNEY. Men of the s. of a Washington or a Hampden 1869. **4.** *Merry W.* III. iv. 16. *fig. Rich. III*, I. iii. 256. **5.** The stamps are extremely beautiful, and are representations of the gods and heroes of antiquity 1780.

Comb., as *s.-album*; **S. Act,** each of the various Acts of Parliament for regulating the s. duties; esp. that of 1765 for levying s. duties in the American colonies; also, that of 1712 imposing a s. duty on newspapers; **-battery,** a series of stamps in a stamp-mill; **-collecting,** (*a*) *sb.* = PHILATELY; (*b*) *adj.* that practises philately; **-collector,** (*a*) a collector or receiver of s. duties; (*b*) a PHILATELIST; **-cutter,** an engraver of dies; **-distributor,** an official who issues or sells government stamps; **s. duty,** any of the duties collected by means of stamps impressed on or affixed to the articles taxed; **s. edging,** the gummed marginal paper of a sheet of postage stamps; **s. gold,** gold ore for stamping; **-hammer,** the hammer of a stamping machine; **-head,** the head of a pestle of a s.-mill; **-mill,** (*a*) the apparatus used to crush ores by means of a pestle or series of pestles operated by machinery; (*b*) an oil-crushing mill of similar construction; **s. note,** a permit from a Custom House official granting permission for the loading of goods on board ship; **s. office,** an office where government stamps are issued and where s. duties are received; **s. paper,** (*a*) paper having a government revenue s. impressed on or affixed to it; (*b*) = *s.-edging*; **s. rock,** ore suitable for treatment by stamping; **-tax,** a tax imposed by a s. act. Hence **Sta·mpless** *a.*

Stamp (stæmp), *v.* [prob. OE. **stampian* = (M)LG., (M)Du. *stampen*, OHG. *stampfōn* pound (G. *stampfen* stamp with the foot, pound, crush), ON. *stappa* :– Gmc. **stampōjan*, f. **stampaz, -ōn*, prob. f. nasalized var. of **stap-* tread, STEP; reinforced or infl. in sense in ME. by (O)Fr. *estamper* stamp, f. Gmc. **stamp-*.] **I.** †**a.** *trans.* To bray in a mortar; to beat to a pulp or powder; to pound. Also *absol.* –1764. †**b.** To crush or press (fruit, esp. crabs) to extract the juice; to press (wine) out of grapes –1618. **c.** To crush (ore); in mod. use, by means of the machine called a 'stamp' 1568. **d.** To drive in (a blasting charge) 1899.

a. S. good store of ripe Sloes 1579.

II. To bring down the foot heavily. **1.** *intr.* **a.** To bring the sole of one's foot suddenly and forcibly down (*upon* the ground or floor, etc.), with the object of crushing or beating down something ME. **b.** To strike the ground or floor forcibly with the sole of the foot; *esp.* as an instinctive expression of fury. late ME. **c.** To walk with a heavy, 'pounding' tread; to tramp 1489. **2.** *trans.* **a.** With compl.: To affect in the specified way by stamping; *esp.* to trample violently *down, to the ground* 1470. **b.** To bring down the sole or heel forcibly upon. Now somewhat *rare.* 1602.

1. Shouting clans or squadrons stamping SCOTT. **b.** I have only to s. with my foot, he said, . .to raise legions from the soil of Italy 1850. The Queen. .went stamping about and shouting 'Off with his head!' 'L. CARROLL'. **c.** And Bahrám that great Hunter—the Wild Ass Stamps o'er his Head, and he lies fast asleep FITZGERALD. **2.** Phr. *To s. one's foot* = sense II. 1. *To s. out*, to extinguish (a fire) by trampling on it; hence, *transf.* to extirpate (a disease, a heresy, etc.), suppress (a rebellion); *occas.* to exterminate (a people). **b.** He frets, he fumes, he stares, he stamps the Ground DRYDEN.

III. To strike an impression on something. **1.** To impress with an embossed or intaglio device or lettering by means of a die and the impact of a hammer or machinery; to make (a coin, a medal) by this process 1560. **b.** To impress (a device, lettering, etc.) by means of a die 1589. **c.** To make by cutting out with a die 1798. **2.** To mark (paper or textile material) with a device either impressed in relief or intaglio, imparted to the surface by ink or pigment, or produced by both processes combined. Also, to impress (a device) on paper, etc. by means of a die or engraved plate. 1604. **†b.** [Cf. It. *stampare*.] To print (a book, etc.). –1624. **3.** To impress with a device or lettering indicating genuineness, quality, or official inspection and approval; to impress (a device etc.) on merchandise, weights or measures, or the like, for this purpose 1564. **4.** To impress with an official stamp or mark indicating that a duty or tax has been paid. In later use also, to attach an adhesive 'stamp' to. 1765. **5.** *fig.* **a.** To show to be of a certain quality or nature 1599. **b.** To impress with some conspicuous characteristic 1780. **c.** To impress or fix permanently (an idea, etc.) on the mind or memory 1662.

1. Also they [the Irish] had silver groats,..stamped with the Popes tripple Crowne 1617. **b.** *fig.* What stamps the wrinkle deeper on the brow? BYRON. **2.** This jacket..was stamped in various places with the government broad arrow 1885. The address..was also stamped on the envelope 1908. **4.** We..made another attempt to get the deed stamped 1907. **5. a.** *Leo[nato]* Are they [*sc.* the newes] good? *Old [Man]*. As the euents stamps them. SHAKS. **b.** Its beauty was..stamped with..sadness 1838. The picture of the streets..remained forever stamped upon his memory 1885.

Stamp and go. 1830. [The vbs. in imperative.] *Naut. phr.*

Stamp and go! the order to step out at the capstan, or with hawsers, topsail-halyards, etc., generally to the fife or fiddle (ADM. SMYTH).

Stampede (stæmpī·d), *sb.* 1834. [spec. Mex. use of Sp. *estampida* crash, uproar, subst. use of fem. pa. pple. of Rom. **stampire* – Gmc. **stampjan* STAMP *v.*] A sudden rush and flight of a body of panic-stricken cattle. **b.** *transf.* A sudden or unreasoning rush or flight of persons in a body or mass; in U.S. politics, a sudden unconcerted rush of a political convention for a candidate who seems likely to win 1846.

The shells..only causing a s. among the mules and horses 1884.

Stampede (stæmpī·d), *v.* 1847. [f. the sb.] **1.** *trans.* To cause a stampede amongst (cattle); to cause a stampede of (a person's) cattle. **b.** *transf.* and *fig.* To cause (a body of persons) to fly or rush away through fear or common impulse; in U.S. politics, to induce (a political convention) to vote suddenly in a body (for a particular candidate) 1868. **2.** *intr.* Of a herd of cattle: To become panic-stricken and take to flight 1859. **b.** Of a company of persons: To rush with a common impulse 1849.

1. b. Efforts of the Bears to S. the New York Market 1889. **2. b.** The new regiment broke, stampeded into the other, and threw it into confusion 1884.

Stamper (stæ·mpəɹ). late ME. [f. STAMP *v.* + -ER[1].] **1.** One who stamps. **2.** An instrument used in stamping; *esp.* (chiefly *pl.*) each of the pestles in a crushing or pounding machine, esp. in a stamping-mill 1483.

Stamping (stæ·mpiŋ), *vbl. sb.* ME. [-ING[1].] **1.** The action of STAMP *v.* **2.** *concr.* **a.** *pl.* The materials pounded or crushed 1594. **b.** An article fashioned by stamping 1862.

attrib. and *Comb.*, as *s.-die*, *-machine*, *-mill*, etc.; **s. ground** *U.S.*, an animal's habitual place of resort.

Stance (stæns). Now chiefly *Sc.* and *north.* 1532. [– Fr. *stance* – It. *stanza* station, stopping-place (see STANZA).] **1.** A standing-place, station, position. **b.** *Golf*, etc.: The position of the player in playing a stroke 1897. **2.** A site; esp. an area for building upon. Also *building-s.* 1631.

Stanch, staunch (stanʃ, stǭnʃ), *sb.*[1] late ME. [f. STANCH *v.*] **†1.** That which stops or allays, also a stopping –1790. **2.** Something used for stanching blood, a styptic. late ME. **3.** A kind of after-damp in mines, etc. 1693.

Stanch, staunch (stanʃ, stǭnʃ), *sb.*[2] 1767. [– OFr. *estanche*, related to *estanc* STANK *sb.*] A lock or dam in a river.

Stanch, staunch (stanʃ, stǭnʃ), *v.* ME. [– OFr. *estanchier* (mod. *étancher*) – Rom. **stancare*, f. **stancus* (whence OFr. *estanc*) dried up, weary, of unkn. origin.] **1.** *trans.* To stop the flow of (water, etc.). Now only *poet.* (*rare*). 1481. **2.** To stop the flow of (blood or other issue from the body); to stop the flow of blood from (a wound). Also *intr.* for *refl.* ME. **†3.** To quench, allay, satisfy (thirst, hunger, desire, etc.); also, to repress, extinguish (appetite, rebellion, anger, etc.) –1828. **4.** To arrest the progress of (a disease); to allay (pain); to relieve (a person) *of* pain. late ME. **5.** To stop up, to render water-tight or weather-proof. [After Fr. *étancher*.] 1776.

1. I will staunch his floudes COVERDALE *Ezek.* 31:15. **2.** The bleeding was stanched, the wound was closed. SCOTT. **4.** Aloe..stancheth the heade ake 1551. **5.** The gathered sticks to staunch the wall Of the snow-tower, when snow should fall EMERSON. Hence **Sta·ncher**, one who or that which stanches. **Sta·nchless** *a.* that may not be stanched.

Stanchel (sta·nʃĕl). Now *Sc.* 1586. [perh. – OFr. *estanchele*, *estancele* (dim. of *estance* prop), recorded as the name of an object used in some game.] = next.

Stanchion (sta·nʃən), *sb.* late ME. [– AFr. *stanchon* – OFr. *estanchon*, *estanson*, f. *estance* prop, support :– Rom. **stantia* (cf. STANCE).] An upright bar, stay, or support, as for a ship's deck, awning, etc.; *spec.* of a window.

S., a sort of small pillar of wood or iron used for various purposes in a ship; as to support the decks, the quarter-rails, the nettings, the awnings, &c. 1769.

attrib.: **s.-gun**, a gun mounted in a boat for wild-fowl shooting.

Stanchion (sta·nʃən), *v.* 1528. [f. prec.] *trans.* To provide with stanchions, strengthen or support with stanchions.

Stand (stænd), *sb.*[1] OE. [f. STAND *v.*] **I.** Action or condition of standing. **†1.** A pause, delay (*rare*). OE. only. **2.** The action or an act of standing or coming to a position of rest; a pause, halt, esp. in the phr. *to make a s.* Now *rare* or *Obs.* 1592. **b.** *Theatr.* Each halt made on a tour to give performances 1896. **†3.** A standing in ambush or in cover –1621. **4.** A holding one's ground against an opponent or enemy; a halt (of moving troops) to give battle or repel an attack; esp. in the phr. *to make a* (or *one's*) *s.* 1590. **5.** A state of checked or arrested movement: a standstill; *spec.* the rigid attitude assumed by a dog on finding game 1618. **6.** A state of being unable to proceed in thought, speech, or action; a state of perplexity or nonplus 1599. **7.** A state of arrested progress (of affairs, institutions, natural processes, or the like). Chiefly in the phrases *to be at a s.*, *to come to a s.* 1614. **8.** Manner of standing (of a thing). Now *techn.* 1700.

2. Why he stalkes vp and downe like a Peacock, a stride and a s. SHAKS. **3.** 3 *Hen. VI*, III. i. 3. **4.** Instead of making any S. they retreated continually 1736. *fig.* To make a s. against oppression 1833. **5.** Phr. *To be at a s.*, *to come to a s.*, *to bring* or *put to a s.* **6.** There is one point however that puts me to a s. 1734. **7.** Public business was at a s. 1789.

II. Place of standing. **1.** A place of standing, position, station; also in phr. *to take one's s.* ME. **2.** The post or station of a soldier, sentinel, or watchman 1513. **3.** The standing-place from which a hunter or sportsman may shoot game. late ME. **†4.** *Hawking.* An elevated resting place of a hawk; *spec.* as a 'fault', a position of rest from flight –1678. **5.** A stall or booth 1508. **6.** A plot of land (*S. Afr.*), the position, site, or building for a business (*U.S.*) 1787. **7.** A station for a row of vehicles plying for hire; also, the row of vehicles occupying a station 1692. **8.** A raised platform for spectators at open-air sports as race-meetings, football matches, or for a company of musicians or performers 1615. **9.** An elevated standing place for a speaker; a rostrum, pulpit; *U.S.* the place where a witness stands to testify in court, more fully *witness-s.* 1840.

1. Come, I haue found you out a s. most fit, Where you may haue such vantage on the Duke He shall not passe you SHAKS. *fig.* Their opponents take their s. on a quibble 1850. **3.** Like an old decayed oak.., where the keepers in England take *a s.*,..to shoot a deer DE FOE. **7.** A shabby s. Of Hackney coaches SHELLEY. **8.** *Band s.*: see BAND *sb.*[3] *Grand s.*: see GRAND *a.*

III. An appliance to stand something on. **1.** A base, bracket, stool or the like upon which a utensil, ornament, or exhibit may be set; the base upon which an instrument is set up for use 1664. **2.** A frame or piece of furniture upon which to stand or hang articles 1692.

IV. Something which stands. **1.** *Sc.* and *Anglo-Ir.* A complete set (of things); *Mil.* a set (of arms, colours) 1450. **2.** *S. of pikes*: a compact group of pikemen. *Obs.* exc. *Hist.* 1598. **3.** *Sporting.* An assemblage or group (of certain game birds) 1881. **4.** *U.S.* A standing growth or crop (of wheat, cotton, etc.) 1868.

attrib. and *Comb.*: **s. camera**, a camera for use on a tripod or other stand, as dist. from a hand camera; **s. cock** = STAND-PIPE; **-house**, the grand stand of a race-course with the buildings attached to it.

Stand (stænd), *sb.*[2] *Obs.* exc. *dial.* ME. [– or cogn. with (M)LG., Flem. *stande*, = OHG. *standa* (MHG., G. dial. *stande* fem.); f. base of STAND *v.*] **1.** An open tub; a barrel set on end. **2.** A certain weight (of pitch, coal) 1706.

Stand (stænd), *v.* Pa. t. and pa. pple. **stood** (stud). [OE. *standan* = OFris. *standa*, *stonda*, OS. *standan*, OHG. *stantan*, ON. *standa*, Goth. *standan* :– Gmc. str. vb. **standan*, f. the base **sta-* **stō-* :– IE. **sthə-* **sthā-* stand, cause to stand, repr. by L. *stāre*, Gr. *ἱστάναι*.] **I.** Of persons and animals. **1.** *intr.* To assume or maintain an erect attitude on one's feet (opp. to *sit*, *lie*, *kneel*, etc.). Also said of the feet. Freq. *fig.* **b.** With predicate: To be of a (specified) height when holding oneself upright. Said also of quadrupeds, etc. 1831. **2.** Of a horse: To be kept in a stable or stall. Phr. *To s. at livery.* 1465. **3.** To remain motionless on one's feet; to cease walking or moving on OE. **b.** In imper., a command to come to a halt 1513. **c.** *Hunting.* Of a dog: To point. Const. *upon* (game). 1823. **4.** With predicative extension: To remain erect on one's feet in a specified place, occupation, position, condition, etc. OE. **5.** *Cricket*, etc.: To act as umpire in the field. Also *To s. umpire.* 1846. **6.** To remain firm or steady in an upright position, to support oneself erect on one's feet. Often in neg. contexts. OE. **b.** *fig.* To remain steadfast, firm, or secure ME. **7.** To take up an offensive or defensive position against an enemy; to present a firm front; to await an onset and keep one's ground without budging. Of soldiers: To be drawn up in battle array. OE. **8.** To appear as a candidate, to offer oneself as a candidate 1551. **9.** *Card-playing.* To be willing to play with one's hand as dealt 1824. **10.** *U.S.* **To stand pat.** (*a*) In *Poker*, to play, or declare one's intention of playing, a hand just as it has been dealt, without drawing other cards. (*b*) *transf.* To adhere to an existing state of things or to an avowed policy (esp. a high tariff), refusing to consider proposals for change or reform. Hence **Stand-patter.** 1882. **11.** Uses in which the force of the verb is weakened and approaches that of a copula, the stress being on the complement or predicative extension. late ME. **12.** *fig.* In betting, commercial speculation, etc.: To be in the position of being reasonably certain *to* (win or lose something or a specified amount); to have *to* (win or lose a certain amount in a specified contingency) 1861.

1. Oure fete shal stonde in thy gates, O Jerusalem COVERDALE *Ps.* 121:2. Kneele, and repeate it, I will s., and so shall Trinculo SHAKS. *fig.* phrases. *To s. on one's own feet* or *legs*, *upon a* (specified) *footing*, *not to have a leg to s. on*, *to s. in a person's* or *one's own light* (see LIGHT *sb.* 1 e), *in* (another person's) *shoes* (see SHOE sb.), *in the way* (*of* a person or thing: see WAY *sb.*). **b.** Six foot two, as I think, he stands TENNYSON. **3.** All but Nausicaa fled; but she fast stood CHAPMAN. **b.** He order'd him to S. and Deliver 1714. 'S., Bayard, s.!'— the steed obeyed SCOTT. **4.** The salvage Linxes listning stood DRYDEN. *To s. at attention*, *at ease*, *at gaze*, *on one's own bottom*, (*on*) *tiptoe*, *upright*, see these words. *To s. on one's head*, to take up a position with the crown of the head on the ground and heels in the air; *fig.* (to be ready) to do this as a sign of extreme delight. *To s. sentinel*, *sentry*, see the sbs. **6. b.** They had stood true to the honour of Ireland 1888. Phr. *To s. or fall*, often used *fig.* of a person or thing, to indicate that his or its fate is contingent on the fate of some other person or thing, or must be governed by some event or rule; const. *with* (a person or thing), *together*, also *by* (a rule, an uncertain event). **7.** *To s. fast, firm*; *to s. at bay, in the breach, on* or *upon one's guard, on* or *upon the defensive* or *offensive*. *To s. upon one's trial*, to submit to judicial trial. **8.** How many s. for Consulships? SHAKS. He did not s. for a fellowship 1890. *To s. for a constituency* or *for Parliament*: to offer oneself for election as the representative of a constituency in the House of Commons. **11.** *To s. security, surety*. *To s. godfather, sponsor*. †*To s.* (a person's) *good lord*. *To s. committed, indebted, pledged*. *I s. corrected*, I accept or acknowledge the correction. So *I s. reproved*. *To s. well* or *high* (= to be in high favour or esteem) *with* a person. *To s. fair* (= to be favourably situated) *for* something or *to do* something. *How do you s.* (financially)? **12.** She stood to lose all round 1880.

II. Of things. **1.** To be in an upright position with the lower part resting on or fixed in the ground or other support; opp. to *lie* OE. **b.** Of plants: To grow erect. Said esp. of grass, corn, etc., when left uncut to ripen. OE. **c.** Of the hair: To grow stiff and erect like bristles. *To s. on end*, †*up, upright*: to rise up on the head as a result of fright or astonishment. late ME. **2.** More loosely: To be set, placed, or fixed; to rest, lie (with more or less notion of firmness and steadiness). Of a dish or its contents: To rest flat or on a flat base. ME. **3.** Of a place, country, piece of ground, dwelling, etc.: To be situated in a specified position or aspect. Now chiefly of a town or village. OE. **4.** With predic. extension or complement, indicating the manner or condition OE. **5.** To be inscribed, drawn, †painted, etc. (on a list, sheet, or the like). Hence of words or literary matter: To be set down, recorded, composed in a (specified) context or form. OE. **b.** esp. of numerical figures. To be set down or entered in a list, account, ledger, or the like. Hence of a sum, price, score; also of the game or player whose score is recorded. Const. *at* (a certain figure). 1537. **c.** Of an account: To show a (specified) position of the parties with regard to debit and credit. Also, to continue on the books unsettled. 1710. **d.** Of a word, clause, etc.: To occupy a specified place in a verse or context; to be used in a specified inflexion or construction 1693. **6.** Of water, etc.: To have the surface at a specified level. Of the mercury (or other liquid) in a thermometer, barometer, etc.: To reach to a certain height; hence said of the instrument itself. ME. **7.** Of an edifice, or the like: To remain erect and entire; to resist destruction or decay OE. †**b.** Of the world: To exist: to remain stable, last –1598. **8.** *Naut.* (See quots.) 1669. **9.** Of a pigment or dye: To keep its colour; also, not to blot or run 1811. **10.** Of liquids: To cease flowing; *esp.* of water, to collect and remain motionless, be stagnant OE. **b.** Of land, a ditch, etc.: *To s. with*, to be full of (stagnant water) 1601. **11.** Of tears: To remain collected (in the eyes) without falling. Of a humour, esp. perspiration: To remain in drops (*on* the skin, etc.). 1530. **12.** Of a liquid etc.: To be kept in a vessel without shaking 1467. **13.** Of a star: To appear fixed in the heavens. Of the sun or a planet: To be seen apparently motionless at any point of its course. late ME. **14.** Of a piece of machinery, a timepiece, an implement, a vehicle, etc.: To remain still or motionless; to cease moving, working, or turning. late ME. **b.** Of a mine, factory, etc., also of the men employed: To stop working; to be at a standstill 1733. **c.** Printing. *To be standing*: (of type) to remain undistributed 1888. **15.** Of the wind: To blow from a quarter indicated; also simply, to blow favourably, to continue to blow. Similarly of the weather. *arch.* ME. **16.** *Naut.* Of a vessel (hence of the commander, sailors, etc.): To sail, steer, direct one's course (in a specified direction, to sea, into harbour, etc.) 1627. **17.** With adv., advb. phr., or adj. predicate: To be or remain in a specified condition, relation, situation, etc. OE. **b.** With a relative or demonstrative adv. as predicate; e.g. *the case stands thus, as things s.* (= under present circumstances) OE. **18.** Of a condition, process, or the like: To remain stationary or unchanged, neither progressing nor receding; to be at a standstill. late ME. **19.** To endure, last; to continue unimpaired; to flourish OE. **20.** To be or remain valid or of force, hold good. Freq. with complement or predic. extension, as *to s. good, in force*. OE.

1. Behind the town-hall..stood the parish church 1886. **b.** White wheats should s. somewhat longer 1847. **2.** Some food stood on the table SCOTT. **3.** The village stands pleasantly 1792. **4.** *To s. high, firm, ajar*, etc.; The Gate stood open STEELE. Phr. Of a thing: *As it stands* (= with all its accessories). **5.** Let this pernitious houre S. aye accursed in the Kalender SHAKS. **b.** The score standing at 123 for five wickets 1890. The balance at the Bank stands..at £50. 1913. **c.** Let me know how accounts s. SWIFT. **6.** The thermometer now stood at 20 Fah. 1891. **7.** She had only a foremast standing at day-light 1798. **b.** Whill the worlde stondeth TINDALE 1 *Cor.* 8:13. **8.** *To let all s.*, to leave a ship fully rigged. *All standing*, without dismantling or unrigging; *transf.* with one's clothes on, dressed. *To be brought up all standing*, to be suddenly checked or stopped, without any preparation. *Paid off all standing*, dismissed without unrigging or waiting to return stores. **11.** Cold drops stood on my brow 1849. **13.** Full-faced above the valley stood the moon TENNYSON. **14.** The ploughe standeth, there is no worke done 1549. **15.** The wind stood most easterly 1635. **16.** We discovered a fleet.. standing *athwart* us, i.e. steering across our way FALCONER. We took sail, and stood into the river 1823. **17.** My life stoode in ieopardie HALL. *To s. in awe, in need; s. condemned*, etc. **18.** And while his Fate is in thy Hands, The Bus'ness of the Nation stands SWIFT. **20.** A written Contract.. would s. DE FOE. That charge of murder will not s. law 1890.

III. To cost. late ME.

Phr. *To s.* (a person) *in* (a price, etc.) (the ordinary construction; now restricted in currency, being partly fashionable slang, partly dial.); It stands me in eight shillings a bottle THACKERAY. Now *rare*.

IV. Trans. senses. **1.** To confront, face, oppose, encounter; to resist, withstand, bear the brunt of ME. **2.** To endure, undergo, be submitted to (a trial, test, ordeal, or the like). Usu., to come through or sustain successfully, (be able) to bear (a test, etc.). 1606. **b.** To submit to, offer to abide by (a judgement, decision, vote); to expose oneself to the chances of (a contested election) 1700. **3.** To face, encounter without flinching or retreating (an issue, hazard, etc.). Also, in weaker sense, to be exposed or liable to (hazard, fortunes). 1594. †**4.** To withstand, disobey, hold out against (a command). *rare*. –1800. **5.** To endure (a physical trial, hardship, etc.) without hurt or damage, without succumbing or giving way 1756. **6.** To put up with, tolerate; (to be able or willing) to endure 1626. **7.** To bear the expense of, make a present of, pay for (a treat). Const. *to* or dat. of the recipient. *colloq.* 1835. **8.** *Racing*, etc. To bet on the success of, back (a horse) 1890. **9.** *Hunting*. Of a dog: To set (game) 1863. **10.** *causative*. To cause to stand; to place or leave standing; to set (a thing) upright; to place firmly or steadily in a specified position. Only *colloq.* or in familiar writing. 1837.

1. She was ready to s. fire rather than retreat 1891. **2.** He has stood the ordeal of a London audience 1825. Phr. *To s. one's trial*, to be tried by a court for an offence; also *slang*, in the same sense *to s. the patter*. **b.** All through his career he never stood a contested election 1891. *To s. one's chance*, to take one's chance, submit to what may befall one. **3.** A gallant fellow, who had..stood the hazards of many a bloody day 1792. **4.** *Lear* IV. i. 71 (Qo.). **5.** These dyes will not s. water 1890. Drivers have to s. all weathers 1891. **6.** She..was not going to s. that kind of thing TROLLOPE. **7.** I'll s. you a dinner 1890. Phr. *To s. shot* (*to*), rarely *to s. the shot*, to meet the expenses, pay the bill (for all); see SHOT *sb.* So *to s. Sam, treat*. **10.** I stood my rifle against a tree 1878.

Phrases. *To s. one's ground*, to maintain one's position against attack or opposition. *To s. a chance* (also *a good, poor, little, some, no chance*), to be likely to meet with some piece of fortune, danger, good or ill luck. *To s. watch, to s. a* or *one's watch*: to keep watch, perform the duty of a watch; now chiefly *Naut.*, to take part in the duty of a watch during the prescribed time.

With preps. **S. against —.** To s. and face (an antagonist, etc.); to withstand, oppose, resist. Freq. to resist successfully. **S. at —.** To stick, hesitate, or scruple at; to allow oneself to be deterred, impeded, or checked by. **S. before —. a.** To come or be brought into the presence of, to confront (a person or assembly, a king, judge, tribunal, etc.). **b.** To confront (an adversary). Usu. with *can*, etc. negatively or interrogatively: To maintain one's ground against. **S. by —. a.** *lit.* To station oneself or remain stationed beside (a person); usu. as a helper, advocate, sympathizer, etc. **b.** *Naut.* To prepare to work (a gun, rope, etc.). **c.** *fig.* To support, assist, protect, defend (a person, a cause, etc.); to uphold the interests of, take the side of, be faithful or loyal to. **d.** To adhere to, maintain, abide by (a statement, agreement, or the like). **S. for —. a.** To uphold, defend (a cause, etc.); to support, take the part of (a person). **b.** To be reckoned or alleged for; to be counted or considered as; to serve in lieu of. *To s. for nothing*, to be worthless, of no avail; *to s. for something*, to have some value or importance. **c.** To put up with, 'stand'. *U.S.* **d.** To represent, do duty for. **e.** *Naut.* To sail or steer towards. **f.** To represent by way of symbol or sign; to be an emblem of. **g.** To represent by way of specimen. **S. in —. a.** To be dressed in, to be actually wearing. †**b.** To remain steadfast or obstinate in (a state, course of action, purpose, opinion, assertion). **c.** Of things: To rest or depend upon (something) as its ground of existence (*arch.*). **S. on —. a.** To base one's arguments or argumentative position on, 'take one's stand on'. **b.** Of an immaterial thing: To be grounded or based on. †**c.** To give oneself to, practise (some kind of action or behaviour). **d.** To be meticulously careful or scrupulous about, raise difficulties about (nice points, ceremony, etc.). **e.** To assert, claim respect or credit for (one's rights, qualities, dignity, etc.). †**f.** To value, set store by (something external to oneself). †**g.** To insist on, as essential or necessary, urge, press for, demand. †**h.** *impers.* (It) behoves. **S. over —.** To stand close by and watch or control (one who is seated, lying down, or on a lower level). **S. to —.** †**a.** To submit oneself to, abide by (a trial, award); to obey, accede to, be bound by (another's judgement, decision, opinion, etc.). †**b.** To leave oneself dependent upon (another's mercy, courtesy, etc.). **c.** To apply oneself manfully to (a fight, contest, etc.). *Obs.* exc. in *to s. to it*, to fight stoutly; also, to toil without flagging at painful or severe labour. **d.** Mil. *To s. to one's arms*, also *to s. to*: to stand with one's weapon in readiness for action. *To s. to one's guns, colours*: to maintain one's position, not to retire before an attack. **e.** To confront, present a bold front to (an enemy). †**f.** To abide by (the issue or consequences of an event). †**g.** To endure, bear, put up with (harm, pain); to make good, bear the expense of (damage, loss); to defray, be answerable for (expenses); to accept liability for (a tribute or tax). **h.** To side with, back, help, support (a person); to maintain, uphold (a cause, interest, etc.); to remain faithful or loyal to. **i.** To adhere to, abide by, carry out (a promise, vow, bargain, etc.). **j.** (*a*) To adhere to (a statement, etc.); to persist in affirming or asserting. (*b*) *To s. to it*: to insist upon or maintain a statement or assertion. **k.** *It stands to reason* (dial. *to sense*): it is reasonable, it is natural, evident, or certain (*that*). **l.** To be related to. **S. under —. a.** To be exposed or subject or obnoxious to; to undergo, bear the burden or weight or incidence of; (to be able) to sustain (a charge, etc.). **b.** *Naut.* To make sail with (a specified display of canvas). **c.** Mil. *To s. under arms*, to be ready for action. **S. upon —. a.** In fig. phrases of which the wording is literal. *To s. upon thorns*: see THORN *sb.* *To s. upon the defensive, upon one's guard*, etc.: see sense I. 7. **b.** To rely upon, depend on, trust to. *Obs.* exc. in the sense: To take one's stand upon an argument, argumentative position, etc. **c.** Of an immaterial thing (also *impers.*): To be grounded or based upon. **d.** *To s. upon terms*: (*a*) to be on a specified footing or in a specified situation or condition; (*b*) to insist upon conditions; also, *to s. upon conditions*; (*c*) to take a high line, to hold one's own, refuse to knuckle under. **e.** To be careful or scrupulous in regard to (forms, ceremonies, etc.); to be attentive to or observant of; to allow oneself to be unduly influenced or impeded by. **f.** To pride or value oneself upon; to urge, assert, make the most of, claim respect or consideration for, insist on the recognition of (one's qualities, rank, rights, possessions, dignity, etc.). †**g.** To attach importance to, give prominence or weight to; to value, set store by. †**h.** To dwell with emphasis or at length upon (a topic, argument, etc.). †**i.** *impers.* (It) concerns, behoves, is incumbent upon, is the duty of, is urgent or necessary for (a person). Const. *to* (do something). Usu. in the form *it stands* (a person) *upon* = he ought, he must needs. *Obs.* or *dial.* **S. with —.** To be consistent or consonant with, agree or accord with. *Obs.* exc. *arch.*

With advs. **S. about.** Of a number of persons: To stand here and there, in casual positions or groups. Of an individual: To remain about a locality without a fixed position or definite object. **S. aloof.** To s. at, or withdraw to, some distance (*from*), keep away (*from*). Also *fig.* **S. apart.** To stand separate or at a distance (*from* another or others). **S. away. a.** To withdraw to some distance. **b.** *Naut.* To sail or steer away (from some coast, quarter, enemy, etc.). **S. by. a.** To s. near at hand; to be present. Now chiefly, to be present as an unconcerned spectator. **b.** To draw back and s. apart from the general company or from what is going on. **c.** *Naut.* To hold oneself in readiness, be prepared (*for* something, *to do* something). Often in imper. = be ready! Also *gen.* **S. down. a.** Of a witness: To step down and leave the box after giving evidence. **b.** *Sport.* To withdraw from a game, match, or race; to give up one's place in a team, crew, or 'side'. **c.** *Naut.* To sail with the wind or tide. **S. in. a.** To go shares *with*, join, be a partner (*with*); in wider sense, to have a friendly or profitable understanding with, be in league with, be on good terms with. Also, to share chances with others *for* (a speculative event). **b.** *Naut.* To direct one's course towards the shore. **S. off. a.** To remain at or retire to a distance; to draw back, go farther away. Chiefly in commands. †**b.** *fig.* To be separated in quality, differ. **c.** *fig.* To hold aloof; to be 'distant', uncomplying or unaccommodating. **d.** Of a thing: To protect, protrude, jut out (*from* a surface, etc.). Of a picture: To appear as if in relief. Also *fig.*, to be conspicuous. **e.** *Naut.* To sail away from the shore. **f.** *trans.* To keep off; keep at a distance; to repel, hold at bay. *U.S. colloq.* **g.** To dispense with the services of (an employee) temporarily. **S. off and on.** *Naut.* Alternately to recede from and approach the land while sailing by the wind. **S. on.** *Naut.* To keep one's course, continue on the same tack. **S. out. a.** To move away (from a company, shelter, etc.) and stand apart or in open view. **b.** Not to take part in (an undertaking, joint action, etc.); to refuse to come in or join others; now *esp.* not to take part in a match, game, or dance. **c.** To resist, refuse to yield or comply, hold out. Const. *against* (an opponent, proposal, etc.), *with* (an opponent). **d.** *To s. out for*: to declare oneself for, contend on behalf of. **e.** To haggle; to make an obstinate demand *for* (certain terms). **f.** *Naut.* To sail in a direction away from the shore. Usu. *to s. out to sea.* Hence *gen.*, to start on a journey. **g.** To jut out, project, protrude (*from* a surface); to be prominent. **h.** To be conspicuous; to be seen in contrast or relief *against* a dark object or background. Of figures in painting: To appear as in relief. **i.** *fig.* To be prominent or conspicuous to the mental gaze. **j.** *trans.* To remain standing throughout (a performance). Also *Naut.* To 'stand watch' during (a specified time). **k.** To endure to the end, hold out under or against (a trial, ordeal, severe weather, etc.); to last out (a period of time). **l.** With object-cl.: To maintain, insist, persist in asserting (*that*). **S. over. a.** *Naut.* To leave one shore and sail towards another. **b.** To be left or reserved for treatment, consideration or settlement at a later date. †**S. together.** To agree, be consistent, harmonize. **S. up. a.** To assume an erect position; to rise, get up on one's feet. **b.** To take part in a dance; to dance *with* (a partner). **c.** Of things: To be set upright: to be or become erect. Of hair, spines, etc.: To grow stiff and erect. **d.** To hold oneself boldly erect to confront an opponent; to make a stand *against*. **e.** *To s. up for*: to defend, support, champion (a person, a cause, etc.). **f.** *To s. up to*: to confront or encounter boldly. Also *U.S.*, to meet (an obligation or promise). **g.** *To s. up in* (only in rel. clause), to be actually wearing. **h.** Of an animal: To hold out, endure (in a race, etc.).

Comb.: **s.-easy**, an assumption of the attitude directed by the command 'stand easy'; *fig.* a period of relaxation.

Standage (stæ·ndĕdʒ). 1777. [f. STAND *v.* + -AGE.] **1.** Arrangements or accommodation for standing. **2.** *Mining.* An underground reservoir for water 1842.

Standard (stæ·ndăɹd), *sb.* ME. [Aphetic (in AL. *standard(i)um* XII) f. AFr. *estaundart*, OFr. *estendart* (mod. *étendard*), f. *estendre* EXTEND; see -ARD. The senses of group III are affected by association with STAND *v.*] **A.** *sb.* **I.** A military or naval ensign. **1.** A flag, sculptured figure, or other conspicuous object, raised on a pole to indicate the rallying point of an army (or fleet), or of one of its component portions; the distinctive ensign of a king, great noble, or commander, or of a nation or city. **2.** In a more restricted sense, a military or naval flag of some particular kind usu. rectangular. late ME. **3.** = STANDARD-BEARER. ME. **4.** *Bot.* = VEXILLUM. 1776. **5.** *Ornith.* Each of the two lengthened wing-feathers characteristic of certain birds 1859.

1. Then in the name of God and all these rights, Aduance your Standards, draw your willing Swords SHAKS. Phr. *To raise one's s.*, to take up arms. *Under the s. of*, serving in the army of; so *to join the s. of.* **2.** Barges garnished with standardes, stremers and penons HALL. **3.** *Temp.* III. ii. 19.

II. Exemplar of measure or weight. **1.** The authorized exemplar of a unit of measure or weight; e.g. a measuring rod of unit length; a vessel of unit capacity, or a mass of metal of unit weight, preserved in the custody of public officers as a permanent evidence of the legally prescribed magnitude of the unit. late ME. **b.** The substance or thing which is chosen to afford the unit measure of any physical quantity, such as specific gravity 1805. **2.** (orig. *fig.* from prec.) An authoritative or recognized exemplar of correctness, perfection, or some definite degree of any quality 1477. **b.** A criterion, measure 1563. **3.** Legal rate of intrinsic value for coins; also, the prescribed degree of fineness for gold or silver 1463. **b.** (orig. †*s. of commerce.*) A commodity, the value of which is treated as invariable, in order that it may serve as a measure of value for all other commodities 1683. **4.** A definite level of excellence, attainment, wealth, or the like, or a definite degree of any quality, viewed as a prescribed object of endeavour or as the measure of what is adequate for some purpose 1711. **b.** In British elementary schools: Each of the recognized degrees of proficiency according to which school children are or have been classified 1876. **5.** A definite quantity of timber, differing in different countries 1858. **6.** The market price per ton of copper in the ore 1855. **7.** *Dyeing.* Short for *s. solution* (see B. I. 1 b) 1882.

1. These standards were kept in the royal exchequer 1871. **b.** Water is the s. with which all other bodies are compared 1805. **2.** We always return to the writings of the ancients, as the s. of true taste 1777. **b.** Personal interest is often the s. of our belief as well as of our practice GIBBON. **3.** The standards for gold are 22 and 18 carats of pure metal in every ounce...The coinage is of the higher s...The lower s. is used for all manufacturing purposes 1638. **4.** *S. of living, of comfort*, the view prevailing in a community or class with regard to the minimum of material comfort with which it is reasonable to be content.

III. Senses assoc. w. the verb *stand.* †**1.** A lofty erection of timber or stone, containing a vertical conduit pipe with spouts and taps, for the supply of water to the public –1854. **2.** A tall candlestick. Now *spec.* a tall candlestick (also, latterly, an upright gas or electric candelabrum) rising directly from the floor of a church. late ME. **3.** An upright timber, bar, or rod; e.g. an upright scaffold pole; an upright support or pedestal in various machines. In recent use often, a slender and lofty iron pillar carrying an electric or gas lamp, overhead electric wires, or the like. 1450. **b.** *Naut.* An inverted knee-timber, having the vertical portion turned upwards 1748. **4. a.** *Forestry.* A tree or shoot from a stump left standing when a coppice is cut down 1473. **b.** *Gardening.* A tree or shrub growing on an erect stem of full height, not dwarfed or trained on a wall or espalier 1625. †**5.** A large packing-case or chest –1663. **6.** †**a.** Something permanent; something that has lasted a long time –1655. **b.** One who has been long in a position; an old resident, official, servant, etc. Now only *old s.* (rare exc. dial.). 1661.

1. This paradise, five miles from the s. at Cornhill THACKERAY. **4. b.** [Gardens] part laid out for flowers, others for fruits; some standards, some against walls or palisadoes 1685.

Comb.: **s.-bred** *a.*, of horses, etc. bred up to the s. of excellence prescribed by some authority; **-high** *a.*, of the height of a standard shrub; **s. lamp**, a lamp with a tall s. resting on the floor.

B. *adj.* [attrib. use of sb.] **I. 1.** Serving as a standard of measurement, weight, or value; conformed to the official standard of a unit of measure or weight 1622. **b.** Having the prescribed or normal size, amount, power, degree of quality, etc. 1807. **2.** Of precious metals, coins: Conforming to the legal standard of fineness or intrinsic value. Also said of value or fineness. 1677. **3.** Serving or fitted to serve as a standard of comparison or judgement 1724. **b.** Of a book, an author: That has a permanent rank as an authority, or as an exemplar of excellence 1645. **c.** Of a maxim, etc.: Constantly repeated 1805.

1. b. *S. gauge* (Railways): '4′ 8½″ between centers of rails'. **3.** Applied to a language 1858. *S. English*: that form of the English language which is spoken (with modifications) by the generality of cultured people in Gt. Britain. So *S. American*, etc.

II. 1. Upright, set up on end or vertically 1538. **2.** Of a tree: Grown as a 'standard', not dwarfed or trained on a wall 1685.

2. A tall s. Rose 1908.

Sta·ndard-bea:rer. 1450. **1.** An officer or soldier who bears the standard. **b.** One who carries a banner in a procession 1495. **2.** *fig.* Chiefly, a conspicuous advocate of a cause; one who is in the forefront of a political or religious party 1561.

Standardize (stæ·ndăɹdəiz), *v.* 1873. [f. STANDARD *sb.* and *a.* + -IZE.] **1.** *trans.* To bring to a standard or uniform size, strength, form of construction, proportion of ingredients, or the like. **2.** To test by a standard 1881.

Hence **Sta:ndardiza·tion,** the action of standardizing. **Sta·ndardizer,** one who or that which standardizes.

Sta·ndard-wing. 1869. [STANDARD *sb.* I. 5.] **1.** A species of Bird of Paradise (*Semioptera wallacei*) discovered by Wallace in the island of Batchian. **2.** *attrib.* or *adj.* Of certain birds: Characterized by the possession of 'standards' 1872. So **Standard-winged,** *a.*

Sta·nd-by. 1796. [f. vbl. phr. *stand by*; see STAND *v.*] **1.** *Naut.* **a.** A vessel kept in attendance for emergencies. **b.** An order or signal for a boat to stand by; *attrib.* in *s. bell*, the ringing of a bell in the engine-room of a vessel as a signal to stop the engines 1896. **2.** One who stands by another to render assistance; esp. *fig.* one who upholds or seconds another; a staunch adherent or partisan 1801. **3.** Something upon which one can rely; a main support; a chief resource 1861. **4.** *attrib.* or *adj.*

3. Art and marriage are two very good stand-by's STEVENSON.

Standel (stæ·ndĕl). 1543. [perh. an alteration of STADDLE influenced by STAND *v.*] A young tree left standing for timber.

Stander (stæ·ndəɹ). late ME. [f. STAND *v.* + -ER[1].] **1.** One who stands. †**2.** A person of long standing (in a profession or place); an old hand, an old resident –1832. †**3.** An upright support; a supporting pillar, stem, etc.; also a candlestick –1860. †**4.** = prec. –1712.

S.-by, one who stands by; one who looks on and abstains from interfering; occas. a bystander (now *rare*).

Standergrass (stæ·ndəɹgras). 1578. [f. *stander-* (alt. of *standel-* in †*standelwort* – MLG. *standel-*, *stendelwort*) + GRASS *sb.*] The male orchis (*Orchis mascula*) and allied plants.

Standing (stæ·ndiŋ), *vbl. sb.* late ME. [f. STAND *v.* + -ING[1].] **1.** The action of STAND *v.*; an instance of this. **b.** The condition of being at a standstill. Also *s. still.* 1440. **c.** Erect position; condition of not falling or being overthrown. Now *rare* or *Obs.* 1709. †**2.** Manner of standing. **a.** Relative position –1733. **b.** Situation, site, aspect –1682. **c.** Posture, attitude; position of a thing –1801. **3.** An act of standing erect on one's feet; a period during which a person keeps a standing position 1653. **4.** A standing-place, station; standing-room. late ME. **5.** A position for or occupied by a booth, stall, or the like; a booth or stall occupying such position. Now *dial.* 1547. **6.** Degree of antiquity. (Now only of immaterial things.) Chiefly in phrases, *of old, ancient s.* 1656. **7.** Length of service, experience, or residence; position as determined by seniority 1580. **8.** Status in society, a profession, or the like 1607.

1. He cursed him in sitting, in s., in lying 1840. **4.** Keep all your standings and not stir a foot MARLOWE. *fig.* Some of them believed this; and so kept their s. in the Church 1676. **6.** Tuberculosis of long s. 1891. **7.** One of the fellows, and of Johnson's s. 1790. **8.** Men of some s. in the neighbourhood 1889.

Comb.: **s. room,** space in which to stand; accommodation for persons or a person standing.

Standing (stæ·ndiŋ), *ppl. a.* late ME. [f. STAND *v.* + -ING[2].] **I.** That stands upright or on end. **1.** Of a person, an animal, a statue: That keeps an upright stationary position on the feet 1576. **b.** *transf.* Of an action: Performed in a standing posture 1637. **2.** Of vegetation: That stands erect (in growth); growing. late ME. **3.** Of an inanimate thing: That stands up, upright, or on end; that is set in a vertical position 1539. **b.** Remaining erect; not fallen or overthrown 1700. **4.** Having a foot or feet, a base, or a stem and base upon which to stand, esp. in *s. bowl, cup, piece* (of plate). late ME. **5.** Of a piece of furniture: That rests upon its base when set up for use. 1485. **6.** *Naval Arch.* Of a bevel or bevelling: Forming an angle greater than a right angle; obtuse 1754.

1. Ye shall make you no Idoles..neither reare you vp a s. image *Lev.* 26:1. **b.** That Warr.. sometimes on firm ground A s. fight MILT. **2.** Sheets of Lightning blast the s. Field DRYDEN. **3.** Let vs haue s. Collers, in the fashion 1611. **5.** A s. screen which perpetually belies its name 1806. *S. ladder* = step-ladder.

II. That remains at rest or in a fixed position. **1.** Of air, water, a piece of water: Still, stagnant. late ME. **2.** Of a thing: At a standstill. Of a machine, tool, etc.: Not in operation. 1585. **3.** That is used in a fixed position 1634. **4.** That remains in one spot; stationary. *Obs.* exc. *Mil.* in *s. camp.* 1469. **5.** That remains stationary while another part, or other parts, move; esp. *Naut.* 1680.

1. A sort of men, whose visages Do creame and mantle like a s. pond SHAKS. **2.** Ixion..leans attentive on his s. Wheel DRYDEN. **4.** We got back to our s. camp..about mid-day 1896. **5. S. rigging,** the fixed part of a vessel's rigging which serves as a support for the masts and is not hauled upon, as dist. from the running rigging; **s. ropes** *pl.*, the ropes composing the s. rigging; **s. part** (of a rope, sheet, etc.), that end of a thing which is made fast as dist. from the end hauled upon.

III. That stands or continues. **1.** Continuing without diminution or change; constant, permanent. Of colours: unfading. late ME. **2.** Of employment, wages, prices, attributes, etc.: Fixed, settled; not casual, fluctuating, or occasional 1473. **3.** That continues in existence or operation; that continues to be (what the noun specifies); that does not pass away 1662. **4.** Habitually used; stock 1492. **5.** Permanently and authoritatively fixed or set up; stated, established, organized, regular 1549. **b.** Of a legislative, administrative, or other body: Permanently constituted 1625. **c.** Of troops: Maintained on a permanent footing; esp. in *s. army* 1603. **d.** Of an official: Holding permanent office 1656.

2. My s. allowance from Michaelmas last till Christmas 1670. Two s. characteristics of the Professor's style 1835. **3.** This is the s. joke nightly repeated 1864. *S. order* (Parliament), a continuing regulation for the guidance and order of parliamentary proceedings. *S. order, rule,* (*Mil.*), any one of certain general rules and instructions which are to be invariably followed, and are not subject to the temporary intervention of rank. **4.** The s. excuse of a bad headache 1861. Phr. *s. dish* (at a meal). **5.** A s. caravan commerce with Phenicia 1846. **b.** I commend also s. Commissions; as for Trade; for Treasure BACON. **d.** There should be a s. treasurer 1656.

Sta·nding-place. 1440. [f. STANDING *vbl. sb.*] **1.** A place prepared or assigned for a person or thing to stand in; a place to accommodate persons standing. **2.** A place where a person takes his stand 1736.

Sta·nding stone. ME. [STANDING *ppl. a.*] A large block of stone set upright; a menhir, monolith.

Standish (stæ·ndiʃ). *Obs.* exc. *Hist.* or *arch.* 1474. [Of unkn. origin; presumably based on STAND *v.*, but the ending is obscure.] A stand containing ink, pens and other writing materials and accessories; an inkstand; inkpot.

He wanted pen, ink, and paper. There was an old s. on the high mantel shelf containing a dusty apology for all three. DICKENS.

Sta·nd-off, *attrib. phr.* and *a.* 1837. [f. vbl. phr. *stand off*; see STAND *v.*] That holds aloof from familiar intercourse; contemptuously distant in manner; reserved, unsocial. **b.** *S. half,* in Rugby football, the half-back who stands away from the scrum 1909. Hence **Stand-o·ffish** *a.*, **-ness.**

Stand-patter: see STAND *v.* I. 10.

Sta·nd-pipe, *sb.* 1790. [f. STAND *v.*] **1.** A vertical pipe for the conveyance of water, gas, steam, etc. to a higher level. **2.** A pipe for attachment to a water-main furnished with a spout or nozzle to which a hose may be fixed or with a tap 1850.

Standpoint (stæ·ndpoint). 1829. [f. STAND *v.* + POINT *sb.*[1], after G. *standpunkt.*] A fixed point of standing; the position at which a person stands to view an object; a point of view. Hence, a mental point of view.

Sta·nd(-)still, *sb.* and *a.* 1702. [f. vbl. phr. *stand still*; see STILL *a.*] **A.** *sb.* **1.** A state of cessation of movement; a halt, pause. **2.** The state of being unable to proceed, owing to exhaustion 1811.

1. Phr. *To come, bring to a s., to be at a s.* **2.** To *ride* (a horse) *to a s., to row* (a competitor) *to a s.*

B. *adj.* That stands still; that is deficient in advancement or progress 1856.

Sta·nd-up, *a.* 1811. [f. vbl. phr. *stand up*; see STAND *v.*] **1.** That stands erect; esp. of a collar, upright, not 'turn-down' 1812. **2.** Performed in a standing posture. Of a meal, etc.: Taken standing. 1862. **3.** *Pugilism.* Of a contest: In which the combatants stand up fairly to one another, without wrestling, flinching, or evasion; esp. in (a *fair, square,* etc.) *s. fight* 1811.

Stang (stæŋ), *sb.*[1] *dial.* ME. [– ON. *stǫng* (corresp. to OE. *stenġ*) = OS., OHG. *stanga* (Du. *stang*, G. *stange*) :– Gmc. **staŋʒō*, f. base cogn. with **steŋʒ-* (see STING *v.*).] **1.** A pole or stake, a wooden bar or beam. †**2.** A measure of land –1777.

1. *To make* (a person) *ride the s.*, a method of expressing popular disapproval by having an offender carried on a s. for public derision.

Comb.: **s.-ball,** a variety of bar-shot.

Stang, *sb.*[2] *Sc.* and *north.* ME. [f. next.] A sting; a sharp pain.

Stang (stæŋ), *v.*[1] ME. [– ON. *stanga* prick, goad, spear (fish), etc., f. *stǫng* (*stang-*) STANG *sb.*[1]] *trans.* To sting. Also *absol.*

Stang (stæŋ), *v.*[2] 1674. [f. STANG *sb.*[1]] †**1.** To cause to ride the stang –1777. **2.** To carry (produce) on stangs 1829.

Stanhope (stæ·nəp). 1825. [Proper name.] A light open one-seated vehicle, formerly made with two wheels, but now commonly with four. First made for The Hon. the Rev. Fitzroy *Stanhope* (1787–1864). Often written with small initial.

Comb.: **s. horse,** one suitable for a s.

S. lens, a lens of small diameter with two convex faces of different radii, inclosed in a metallic tube (invented by Charles 3rd Earl *Stanhope* 1753–1816); **S. press,** a hand printing-press invented by the 3rd Earl *Stanhope.*

Staniel, stannel (stæ·nyĕl, stæ·nĕl). [OE. *stān(e)ġella* 'stone-yeller', f. *stān* STONE + **ġella*, f. *ġellan* YELL.] The kestrel, *Tinnunculus alandarius.* Also applied contemptuously to a person, in allusion to the uselessness of the kestrel for the purposes of falconry.

‖**Stanitza** (stăni·tsă). 1662. [Russ. *stanitsa*, dim. of *stan* station, district.] A Cossack community or township.

Stank (stæŋk), *sb.* ME. [– OFr. *estanc* (mod. *étang*) :– Rom. **stancus*, prob. f. **stancare* dam up. See STANCH *v.*] **1.** A pond or pool. Also a ditch or dyke of slowly-moving water, a moat. Now *Sc.* and *dial.* **2.** A dam to hold back water, a weir or flood-gate. Now *dial.* and *techn.* 1604.

Comb.: **s.-hen,** the moor-hen, *Gallinula chloropus*; **-meadow,** a meadow containing a pool. Hence **Stank** *v. trans.* to dam or strengthen the banks of a stream (*dial.* and *techn.*).

Stannary (stæ·nări). 1455. [– med.L. *stannaria* n. pl., f. late L. *stannum*; see STANNUM, -ARY.] **1.** *The Stannaries*: The districts comprising the tin mines and smelting works of Cornwall and Devon formerly under the jurisdiction of the Stannary courts; also, the customs and privileges attached to the mines. **2.** Tin; tin-ware; a locality in a mart or fair appropriated to the sale of tin-ware. *Obs.* exc. *Hist.* 1668.

attrib.: **S. courts,** the courts of law for the administration of justice in the Stannaries. So **Stanna·tor,** a member of the S. convocation or parliament.

Stannic (stæ·nik), *a.* 1790. [f. STANNUM + -IC.] *Chem.* Of a compound: Containing tin as a quadrivalent element.

Stannite (stæ·nəit). 1851. [f. STANNUM + -ITE[1] 2 b, 4 b.] **1.** *Chem.* A salt of stannous acid. **2.** *Min.* Sulphide of tin, copper, iron and zinc, found in steel-grey masses 1896.

Stanno- (stæno), bef. a vowel also **stann-,** used in *Chem.*, as comb. form of late L. *stannum* tin, as **stannamyl, stanno-fluoride,** etc.

Stannoso- (stænōᵘ·so), *Chem.*, used as comb. form of mod.L. *stannosus* STANNOUS.

Stannotype (stæ·notəip). 1883. [See STANNO-, -TYPE.] A form of photo-mechanical engraving in which a mould obtained from a positive instead of a negative is coated with tinfoil.

Stannous (stæ·nəs), *a.* 1849. [f. STANNUM + -OUS.] *Chem.* Of a compound: Containing tin as a bivalent element.

‖**Stannum** (stæ·nŏm). *rare* in Eng. context. 1783. [mod. use of late L. *stannum* tin, properly *stagnum* alloy of silver and tin (Pliny), perh. of Celtic origin.] *Chem.* The chemical Latin name for tin. (Hence the symbol Sn.) Hence **Sta·nnate** *Chem.* a salt of stannic acid. **Stanni·ferous** *a.* producing or containing tin.

Stanza (stæ·nză). 1588. [– It. *stanza* standing, stopping-place, room, strophe :– Rom. **stantia*, f. L. *stans, stant-*, pr. pple. of *stare* STAND *v.*] **1.** *Prosody.* A group of lines of verse (usu. not less than four), arranged according to a definite scheme which regulates the number of lines, the metre, and (in rhymed poetry) the sequence of rhymes; normally forming a division of a song or poem consisting of a series of such groups constructed according to the same scheme. Also, any of the particular types of structure according to which stanzas are framed. **2.** In Italy, an apartment, chamber, room; *spec.* in pl. ‖*stanze* (sta·ntse), applied to certain rooms in the Vatican 1648.

1. I have adopted the s. of Spenser SHELLEY. Hence **Stanzaic** (stænzēⁱ·ik), **-al** *adjs.* of, belonging to, or of the nature of poetry composed in the form of stanzas.

Stap. 1696. Affected pronunciation of STOP *v.*, in the phr. *S. my vitals*, used as an exclam. of surprise, anger, etc., or as an asseveration.

Well, 'tis Ten Thousand Pawnd well given—s. my Vitals VANBRUGH.

Stapedial (stăpī·diăl), *a.* 1875. [f. mod.L. *stapedius* (see next) + -AL[1].] *Anat.* Pertaining to the stapes.

‖**Stapedius** (stăpī·diŏs). 1788. [mod.L., ellipt. use of *stapedius* adj. (sc. *musculus*), f. *staped-* STAPES.] *Anat.* (More fully *s. muscle.*) The small muscle attached to the neck of the stapes.

‖**Stapelia** (stăpī·liă). 1785. [mod.L. (Linn.), f. name of Jan Bode van *Stapel*, a Dutch botanist (died 1636); see -IA[1].] *Bot.* A S. Afr. genus of asclepiadaceous plants, remarkable for the fetid smell of the flowers, whence one species (*S. hirsuta*) is called Carrion-flower. Also, a plant of this genus.

‖**Stapes** (stēⁱ·pīz). 1670. [mod.L. use of med.L. *stapes* (*staped-*) stirrup.] The innermost of the three ossicles in the tympanum of the ear in mammals; named from its stirrup-like shape.

Staphyline (stæ·filəin), *a.* 1820. [– late Gr. σταφύλινος, f. σταφυλή bunch of grapes.] *Min.* = BOTRYOIDAL *a.*

Staphylinid (stæfili·nid), *sb.* and *a.* 1848. [– mod.L. *Staphylinidæ*, f. *Staphylinus* – Gr. σταφυλῖνος a kind of insect, prob. f. σταφυλή bunch of grapes; see -ID[3].] *Entom.* **A.** *sb.* An insect belonging to the *Staphylinidæ* or rove-beetles, a coleopterous order of which the typical genus is *Staphylinus.* **B.** *adj.* Belonging to the *Staphylinidæ.*

‖**Staphylococcus** (stæfilokǫ·kŏs). *Pl.* **-cocci** (-kǫ·ksəi). 1887. [mod.L., f. Gr. σταφυλή bunch of grapes + κόκκος berry.] *Bacteriol.* A form of pus-producing bacteria composed of cocci grouped in irregular masses.

‖**Staphyloma** (stæfilōᵘ·mă). 1597. [mod.L. – Gr. σταφύλωμα a disease of the eye, f. σταφυλή bunch of grapes; see -OMA.] *Path.* Protrusion of the cornea or sclera, resulting from inflammation. Hence **Staphylo·matous** *a.*

Staphyloplasty (stæ:filoplæ·sti). 1846. [f. Gr. σταφυλή bunch of grapes + -PLASTY.] A plastic operation for the closure of cleft palate.

Staphylorrhaphy (stæfilǫ·rāfi). 1846. [f. as prec. + ῥαφή sewing, suture.] *Surg.* The surgical closure of a cleft palate.

Staple (stē̆i·p'l), *sb.*[1] [OE. *stapol*, corresp. to OFris. *stapul*, *-el* rung, anvil, etc., MLG., (M)Du. *stapel* pillar, emporium, etc., OHG. *staffal* foundation, ON. *stǫpull* pillar, steeple :– Gmc. **stapulaz*; see -LE.] †**1.** A post, pillar, column (of wood, stone, metal). –late ME. **b.** *Mining.* A pillar of coal left as a temporary support for a superincumbent mass 1839. **2.** A short rod or bar of iron, etc. bent into the form of a U or of three sides of a rectangle, and pointed at the ends, to be driven into a surface, in order to serve as a hold for a hasp, hook, or bolt to secure a door or box, or as an attachment for a rope or the like. Also any similar contrivance, as the box or case into which the bolt of a lock is shot. ME. **b.** A snout-ring 1688. **c.** A piece of thin wire, driven through papers, etc., and clinched to bind them 1911.

Comb.: **s.-ring** = sense 2 b.

Staple (stē̆i·p'l), *sb.*[2] late ME. [– OFr. *estaple* emporium, mart (mod. *étape* halting-place) – (M)LG., (M)Du. *stapel* (see prec.).] **1.** A town or place appointed by royal authority, in which was a body of merchants having the exclusive right of purchase of certain classes of goods destined for export; also, the body of merchants so privileged. Now *Hist.*

From about 1390 to 1558 the chief s. was at Calais, which is often called 'The S.' There were also staples in many important towns of England, Wales, and Ireland.

b. †(*a*) A town or country which is the principal market or entrepôt for some particular class of merchandise. (*b*) A commercial centre (Now *arch.*). late ME. †**c.** An authorized place of trade for merchants of a foreign country –1892. **2.** [Short for *staple-ware*, etc. (see 3), and ellipt. use of STAPLE *a.*] A staple commodity. **a.** A principal industrial product of a country, town, or district; *occas.* the commodity principally dealt in by a person or class of persons 1616. **b.** *transf.* and *fig.* The thing chiefly 'dealt in'; the principal object of employment, thought, or discourse. Sometimes: The chief component element, the 'substance', 'bulk'. 1826.

1. *Mayor of the S.*: orig., an official specially appointed by the king; latterly, the mayor of some boroughs was *ex officio* mayor of the staple. **2. a.** The manufacture of cotton..has long been the s. of this county 1806.

attrib.: **s.-house**, a warehouse where commodities chargeable with export duties were stored; †**-ware(s**, such goods as were the monopoly of the S.

Staple (stē̆i·p'l), *sb.*[3] 1481. [perh. f. STAPLE *v.*[2]] **1.** The fibre of wool (in later use also of cotton, flax, etc.) considered with regard to its length and fineness; a particular length and degree of fineness in the fibre of wool, cotton, etc. **b.** A lock of wool 1805. **c.** Unmanufactured wool 1885. **2.** The fibre of which a thread or a textile fabric is composed. Hence *gen.* the material of which anything is made. 1588. **3.** The stratum of vegetable mould overlying the rock; a particular depth or quality of this 1722.

1. The s. of mohair is from five to six inches long 1879. **2.** He draweth out the thred of his verbositie finer then the s. of his argument SHAKS.

Comb.: **s.-threaded** *a.*, composed of thread of selected s.

Staple (stæ·p'l), *sb.*[4] *north.* Also **stapple.** 1818. [Of unkn. origin.] **a.** A small shaft joining two different levels in a mine. **b.** A small pit.

Staple (stē̆i·p'l), *a.* 1586. [Extension of attrib. use of STAPLE *sb.*[2], as in *staple-ware.*] orig., qualifying *commodity* or the like: Having a foremost place among the products exported by a country or place. Hence: Having the chief place among the articles of production or consumption, the industries, employments, etc., of a place, a people, or an individual, or among the constituent elements of anything. 1615. †**b.** Of a book, an author: Standard –1745.

The s. commodities are cotton woolles.. chamolets, salt and sope-ashes 1615. The s. trade of Keswick 1872. Phr. In STATUTE STAPLE (the adj. replaces the phr. *of the staple*, on the analogy of *statute merchant*); so *Recognizance s.*, a recognizance taken before the mayor of the s.

Staple (stē̆i·p'l), *v.*[1] 1470. [f. STAPLE *sb.*[1]] To secure with or as with a staple. Hence **Sta·pler**[1], **Sta·pling-machine,** a machine for binding papers together with staples.

Staple (stē̆i·p'l), *v.*[2] Now *Hist.* 1472. [f. STAPLE *sb.*[2]] *trans.* To receive (export goods) at a staple; to cause to be weighed, etc., in accordance with the regulations of the staple.

Stapled (stē̆i·p'ld), *a.* 1594. [f. STAPLE *sb.*[3] + -ED[2].] Having a staple (of a certain kind).

Stapler[2] (stē̆i·plə.ɪ). 1513. [f. STAPLE *sb.*[2] + -ER[1].] **1.** (More fully *merchant s.*) A merchant of the Staple. **2.** = WOOL-STAPLER 1552.

Star (stā.ɪ), *sb.*[1] [OE. *steorra* = OFris. *stēra*, OS. *sterro* (Du. *ster, star*), OHG. *sterro* :– WGmc. *sterro*, with parallel formation in OHG. *sterno* (G. *stern*), ON. *stjarna*, Goth. *stairnō* :– Gmc. **sternōn*; f. IE. **ster-* **stēr-*, repr. by L. *stella* (:– **sterla*), Gr. ἀστήρ.] **1.** Any one of the many celestial bodies appearing as luminous points in the night sky. Now usu. restricted to the *fixed stars* as dist. from planets (exc. in EVENING-STAR, MORNING-STAR), comets, and meteors (exc. in FALLING STAR, SHOOTING STAR). See also SEVEN STARS. Freq. *fig.* **b.** With ref. to the pagan belief that the souls of illustrious persons after death appear as new stars in the heavens. late ME. **c.** *poet.* = LODE-STAR, POLE-STAR. 1599. **2.** In extended use, any one of the heavenly bodies, including the sun and moon; sometimes in *pl.* as a vague designation for the abode of departed spirits. Chiefly *poet.*; cf. L. *sidus*. ME. **3.** In *Astrol.*, used of the planets and zodiacal constellations, as supposed to influence human affairs ME. **b.** *transf.* A person's fortune, rank, or destiny, disposition or temperament, viewed as determined by the stars 1601. **4.** *fig.* A person of brilliant reputation or talents. **a.** *Theatr.*, etc. An actor, singer, etc. of exceptional celebrity, or one whose name is prominently advertised as a special attraction to the public 1824. **b.** *gen.* (Chiefly *colloq.*) One who 'shines' in society, or is distinguished in some branch of art or science 1850. **5.** An image or figure of a star ME.

It is conventionally represented by a number of rays diverging from a central point or circle, or by a geometrical figure of five or more radiating points, such as is formed by producing the sides of a pentagon, hexagon, etc.

6. *Pyrotechny.* A small piece of combustible composition, used in rockets, mines, etc., which as seen burning high in the air resembles a star 1634. **7.** An ornament, usu. of precious metal, representing a star, worn as part of the insignia of an order of knighthood, or as a military decoration. Also occas. applied to the holder or wearer of this decoration. 1712. **8.** A natural object resembling or likened to a star; e.g. the open corolla (or corolla and disc) of a flower 1635. **b.** A spot or patch of white hair on the forehead of a horse or ox. late ME. **c.** A star-like crystalline pattern which appears on the surface of antimony in the process of refining 1660. **d.** *Zool.* A star-shaped zoophyte or its cell. Also, a stellate sponge-spicule. 1755. **9.** = ASTERISK 3. (Cf. Fr. *étoile.*) late ME. **b.** In lists of stockholders, an asterisk prefixed or appended to a person's name when his holding exceeds a certain amount 1845. **10.** Applied to various objects having the conventional form of a star 1672. **11.** A person having a star as a badge 1859. **12.** *Billiards.* The act of 'starring' (see STAR *v.* 7.) 1850.

1. And tell us whence the stars; why some are fix'd, And planetary some COWPER. Thy soul was like a S., and dwelt apart WORDSW. *fig.* Quixote —the errant S. of Knighthood LAMB. Phr. *S. of the sea* = *Stella maris*, a title given to the Virgin Mary. *To see stars* (colloq.), to have a sensation as of flashes of light, produced by a sudden jarring of the head, as by a direct blow. **b.** Heauens make a Starre of him! SHAKS. **c.** Loue..is the s. to euery wandring barke SHAKS. **2.** *Diurnal s.*, *s. of day, of noon*: the sun; Ere this diurnal Starr Leave cold the Night MILT. **3.** You were borne vnder a charitable starre SHAKS. *One's s.* or *stars* the planet or constellation which, by its position at the moment of a man's birth, sways his destinies, moulds his temperament, etc. *My stars!* usu. a trivial expression of astonishment. **b.** Lord Hamlet is a Prince out of thy Starre SHAKS. **5.** *Stars and stripes*, the popular name for the United States flag, which originally contained 13 stripes and 13 stars, representing the 13 States of the Union; it now contains 13 stripes and 50 stars. **8. b.** She Kiss'd the white s. upon his noble front TENNYSON.

attrib. and *Comb.*, as *s.-galaxy*; *s.-watcher*; *s.-embroidered*, *-led*, adjs., etc.; *-eyed*, adj., etc.; *s.-craft*, *-love*, etc. With the sense 'marked or distinguished by a star or asterisk', as *s. days*, *routes*, *prisoners*, etc. In sense 4, as *s. part*, *soprano*, etc.

Comb.: **s.-beam** *poet.*, a ray of starlight; **s.-chart,** a chart which shows the stars in a certain portion of the sky; **-cluster,** a number of stars closely grouped together; **s. connection** *Electr.*, in a polyphase system, an arrangement by which the coils or circuits have a common junction; **-crossed** *a.*, thwarted by a malign s.; **-cut** *a.*, cut with s.-facets; *sb.*, this style of cutting; **-facet,** one of the small triangular facets which surround the table of a brilliant; **-fort,** a small fort having alternate salient and re-entrant angles; **s. fracture** *Med.*, a fracture with radiating fissures **-gauge,** (*a*) a determination by the average of a number of observations of the number of stars visible in a given portion of the heavens; (*b*) a gauge with radiating steel points for measuring the bore of a cannon at any part of its length; **-headed** *a.*, headed with a s.; *spec.* as an epithet of certain stellate flowers; **-lit** *ppl. a.*, lit up or lighted by the stars; **s. lot,** an item in a sale catalogue added after the numbering is completed, and therefore designated by a starred number; **-pagoda,** an Indian gold coin (cf. PAGODA 3); **-proof** *a.*, impervious to starlight; **-pulley** = *s.-wheel*; **-shake,** a shake in timber consisting of radial fissures; **-shell** *Mil.*, a shell which on bursting releases a shower of stars, to illuminate the enemy's position at night; **-shine** = STAR-LIGHT; **-shower,** a shower of falling meteors; **s. system** *Theatr.*, the method of relying on one or two stars to make up for a weak company; **s. turn,** the chief attraction of a performance, company, display, etc.; **-wheel,** a wheel with radial projections or teeth, used in winding-machines, clock-work, etc.; **-worship** = SABAISM. **b.** In names of animals and plants: **s. anemone,** *Anemone stellata* (or *hortensis*); **-anise,** *Illicium anisatum* or its fruit (from the stellate arrangement of the carpels); **-buzzard,** an American hawk of the genus *Asturina*; **-coral,** a coral of the family *Astræidæ*; **-cucumber,** *Sicyos angulatus* of N. America; **-hyacinth,** *Scilla amœna*; **-jelly, -slough,** nostoc. **c. Star of Bethlehem,** the genus *Ornithogalum*, esp. *O. umbellatum*, abundant in Palestine, with white stellate flowers; applied also to other plants; **s. of the earth,** *Plantago coronopus*; **s. of Jerusalem,** *Tragopogon pratensis* or *T. porrifolius*. **d.** In names of precious stones which exhibit asterism, as *s. diamond, quartz, ruby, sapphire*; STAR-STONE.

Star, *sb.*[2] Now *dial.* ME. [– ON. *stǫrr*. In AL. *starrum* (1308).] A name given locally to various coarse seaside grasses and sedges, as *Psamma arenaria* and *Carex arenaria*. Also *s.-grass*.

Star (stā.ɪ), *v.* 1592. [f. STAR *sb.*[1]] †**1.** *trans.* To mark (a horse) with a star. GREENE. **2.** To adorn with an ornament likened to a star or a number of stars; to bespangle as with stars 1718. **3.** To make a radiating crack or fracture in (a surface of glass, ice, etc.) 1788. **b.** *intr.* To become fractured in this way 1842. **c.** *trans.* (*Geol.*) To diversify (strata) by cracks or veins radiating from a centre 1839. **4. a.** To produce the 'stars' on (antimony) in the process of refining. **b.** *intr.* Of antimony: To form 'stars' when solidifying. 1889. **5.** To distinguish (a word, name, etc.) by an affixed star or asterisk. Hence, to single out for notice or recommendation. 1897. **6.** *intr.* Of an actor, singer, distinguished personage, etc.: To appear as a 'star', perform the leading part; to make a tour in the provinces as the 'star' of a dramatic company. Also quasi-trans. *to s. the provinces*. 1824. **7.** *Billiards.* In the game of Pool, to buy an additional life or lives. Similarly in *Dominoes*. Also quasi-*trans.* 1850.

2. Like a sable curtain starr'd with gold YOUNG. The primroses starred the banks 1884. **5.** He maintained that..if the Government meant to proceed with these Bills they ought to have 'starred' them 1897.

Star-apple (stā·ræ:p'l). 1697. The fruit of any tree of the genus *Chrysophyllum*; the tree itself (also *s. tree*).

The fruit is the size of a large apple, and when cut across shows ten cells forming a star-like figure.

Starboard (stā·.ɪbə.ɪd, -bō³.ɪd), *sb.* (and *a.*).

[OE. *stēorbord*, f. *stēor* steering paddle, rudder, STEER *sb.*[2] + *bord* BOARD *sb.*
The etym. sense of the word refers to the mode of steering the early Teut. ships, by means of a paddle worked over the right side of the vessel.]

A. *sb.* The right-hand side of a ship, as dist. from the LARBOARD or PORT side; the side upon which in early types of ships the steering apparatus was worked. **b.** as *adv.* To or on the starboard side 1634. **B.** *attrib.* or *adj.* Of, belonging to or situated on the right side of a boat or vessel 1495.

Starboard (stā·ɹbəɹd, -bōᵊɹd), *v.* 1598. [f. the sb.] *trans.* To put over or turn (the helm) to the starboard side of the ship. Chiefly in the command *S.* (*the helm*)!

Starbolins, starbowlines (stā·ɹbǒlinz), *pl.* 1769. [perh. for **starboardlings*, f. STARBOARD *sb.* + -LING[1].] *Naut.* The men of the starboard watch.

Sta·r-bright, *a.* Chiefly *poet.* 1560. Bright as a star; bright with stars.
Florence!..Thou brightest star of star-bright Italy! COLERIDGE.

Starch (stāɹtʃ), *sb.* 1440. [f. STARCH *v.*; cf. MDu. *stercke*, MHG. *sterke* (G. *stärke*), G. *stärkmehl.*] **1.** A substance obtained from flour by removing some of its constituents (now also from other vegetable sources containing 'starch' in sense 2) used, in the form of a gummy liquid or paste made with water, to stiffen linen or cotton fabrics, to give a finish to the surface of textile materials, to size paper, etc. Also, the paste made from this substance to prepare it for use. **2.** *Chem.* An organic compound found in plant-cells (a member of the amylose group of carbohydrates) being the chief constituent of starch as described in sense 1. 1812. **3.** *fig.* Stiffness, esp. of manner or conduct 1705.
attrib. and *Comb.*, as **s. bandage,** a bandage rubbed with s. paste, to serve as a splint; **s. bath,** a medicinal bath or lotion made with s.; **-gum** = DEXTRIN; **s. sugar** = DEXTROSE; **-water,** a solution of starch and water; **starchwort,** *Arum maculatum.*

Starch (stāɹtʃ), *a.* Somewhat *arch.* 1717. [f. prec.] Of a person, his bearing, etc.: Stiff, unbending; formal.
The s. and unpliant habits of the times H. WALPOLE. Hence **Sta·rch-ly** *adv.* in a stiff or formal manner, **-ness.**

Starch (stāɹtʃ), *v.* [In XV *sterche, starche*, repr. OE. **sterćan* make rigid = OFris. *sterka, -ia*, OS. *sterkian*, OHG. *sterken* (Du. *sterken*, G. *stärken*) strengthen :- WGmc. **starkjan*, f. Gmc. **starkaz* STARK *a.*] **1.** To stiffen (a thing, linen, etc.) with starch. †**b.** *fig.* To make rigid, formal, or precise; to frame (a discourse) in formal or pretentious terms. Also *absol.* –1814. †**2.** To fasten or stick with starch paste –1721.

Sta·r-cha:mber, †starred chamber. late ME. [orig. †*sterred* (starred) *chamber* (XIV), tr. AL. *camera stellata* (1376), AFr. *chambre esteillee* or *des esteilles* (XIV); so called from its decoration; cf. *camera cum stellis depicta* (1375).] **1.** An apartment in the royal palace at Westminster, in which during the 14th and the 15th c. the chancellor, treasurer, justices, and other members of the king's council sat to exercise jurisdiction. **2.** (More fully *Court of S.*) A court, chiefly of criminal jurisdiction, developed in the 15th c. from the judicial sittings of the King's Council in the Star Chamber at Westminster and abolished by the Long Parliament in 1641. From its abuse under James I and Charles I it has become proverbial as a type of an arbitrary and oppressive tribunal. 1487.
2. *attrib.* I will make a Star-Chamber matter of it SHAKS.

Starched (stāɹtʃt), *ppl. a.* 1599. [f. STARCH *v.* + -ED[1].] **1.** Stiffened with or as with starch 1617. **2.** *fig.* Stiff, formal, precise 1599. Hence **Sta·rched-ly** *adv.*, **-ness.**

Starcher (stā·ɹtʃəɹ). 1515. [f. STARCH *v.* and *sb.* + -ER[1].] **1.** One whose employment or trade is to starch linen. **2.** A starched neck-cloth 1818. **3.** A starching machine 1893.

Starchy (stā·ɹtʃi), *a.* 1802. [f. STARCH *sb.* + -Y[1].] **1.** Of or belonging to starch; resembling starch or containing starch grains. **2.** *fig.* Of a person: Stiff, formal, precise 1828. Hence **Sta·rchily** *adv.* **Sta·rchiness.**

Sta·r-dust. 1844. **1.** *Astr.* Innumerable minute stars, likened, as seen in the telescope, to particles of dust. **2.** Meteoric matter in fine particles supposed to fall upon the earth from space; 'cosmic dust'. GEIKIE.

Stare (stēᵊɹ), *sb.*[1] *arch.* and *dial.* [OE. *stær* = MLG. *star(e*, OHG. *star, stara* (G. *star*), ON. *stari* :- Gmc. **staraz, starǒn*, rel. to L. *sturnus.*] = STARLING[1].

Stare (stēᵊɹ), *sb.*[2] late ME. [f. STARE *v.*] †**1.** Power of seeing. late ME. only. †**2.** A condition of amazement, horror, admiration, etc., indicated by staring –1610. **3.** An act or a habit of staring; a fixed gaze with the eyes wide open 1700.
2. Why stand you In this strange s.? SHAKS. **3.** A stony British s. TENNYSON.

Stare (stēᵊɹ), *v.* [OE. *starian* = MLG. *staren*, OHG. *starēn*, ON. *stara*, f. Gmc. **star- *ster-* be rigid.] **1.** *intr.* To gaze fixedly and with the eyes wide open. Said also of the eyes. Also quasi-*trans.* with complement. (In mod. use the verb ordinarily implies rudeness.) **b.** *transf.* and *fig.* Of things: To be obtrusively conspicuous 1657. **2.** Used with implication of a mental state. †**a.** To open the eyes wide in madness or fury; to glare –1837. **b.** To open the eyes wide in astonishment; to be amazed. late ME. **3.** Of hair, a horse's coat, feathers, fibres of any kind: To stand on end. Now chiefly *techn.* 1523.
1. Her bright eyes gan ope, And starde upon him MARSTON. Panurge star'd at him like a dead Pig 1694. I sat for hours together staring on the fire 1806. Phr. *To s.* (a person) *out of countenance*, to disconcert by staring at. *To s.* (a person) *in the face*, to stare at (his) face; *fig.* of a thing, to be glaringly obvious. *To s.* (a person) *up and down*, to survey with a stare from head to foot. **2. a.** Some laught, some swore, some star'd and stamp'd and curst 1615. **b.** Mac-Morlan will s. when he sees the bill SCOTT. **3.** The affected cows were restless and irritable; their coats 'stared' 1888. Hence **Sta·rer,** a person who stares. **Sta·ring** *ppl. a.*, **-ly** *adv.*

Star(-)fish (stā·ɹfiʃ). *Pl.* **-fish, -fishes.** 1538. [cf. SEA-STAR 2.] **1.** Any echinoderm of the genus *Asterias* or of the class *Asteroidea*, having a flattened body, normally consisting of lobes or rays (usually five) radiating from a central disc. These rays are occas. very short or altogether absent, the body having the form of a pentagonal disc. The common star-fish is *Asterias rubens*. **2.** *transf.* A name for certain species of Stapelia 1840.

Sta·r-flo:wer. 1629. A name given to a number of plants with bright stellate flowers, as *Ornithogalum umbellatum* and other species, (in U.S.) *Trientalis americana*, etc. Also, a book-name for *Stellaria* and *Aster*.

Sta·r-gaze, *v.* 1626. [Back-formation from next.] *intr.* To gaze at or study the stars or something compared to a star.

Sta·r-ga:zer. 1560. **1.** One who gazes at the stars. Often used as a familiar or contemptuous substitute for *astrologer* or *astronomer*. **2.** Applied to various fishes; esp. *Uranoscopus scaber*, which has eyes set on the top of the head and directed vertically; also, any fish of this genus or of the family *Uranoscopidæ* 1661. So **Sta·r-ga:zing** *vbl. sb.* the action of gazing at or studying the stars 1576; *ppl. a.* that gazes at the stars 1593.

Sta·r-grass. 1687. [STAR *sb.*[1] Cf. *star-grass* (STAR *sb.*[2]).] A name for various grass-like plants with stellate flowers or stellate arrangements of leaves; as *Aletris farinosa, Callitriche verna* and *C. aquatica, Hypoxis erecta*.

Stark (stāɹk), *a.* and *adv.* [OE. *stearc* = OFris. *stark*, OS., (O)HG. *stark*, (M)Du. *sterk*, ON. *sterkr*, Goth. **starks* :- Gmc. **starkaz.*] **A.** *adj.* **1.** Hard, unyielding. *Obs.* exc. *arch.* **2.** Violent, harsh, severe. *Obs.* exc. *arch.* or *dial.* OE. **3.** Strong, stout, powerful ME. **4.** Rigid, stiff, incapable of movement ME. **b.** Rigid, stiff (in death) 1592. **c.** Of landscape or an object in a landscape: Stiff in outline or formation; hence, bare, barren, desolate 1833. **5.** Sheer, absolute, unqualified. late ME. **b.** Qualifying an unfavourable appellation of a person: Arrant, thorough, unmitigated. late ME. **6.** = STARK-NAKED 1762.
1. Against Tallow-plots, however, the Whig government was s. 1836. **2.** He is..s. as death To those that cross him TENNYSON. The season is early, the weather s. and unpromising 1913. **3.** S. beer boy, stout and strong beer FLETCHER. The dragoons were s. fellows 1895. **4.** That little pug-dog stands s. and stiff 1838. **b.** Each part depriu'd of supple gouernment, Shall stiffe and starke, and cold appeare like death SHAKS. **c.** Among rigid crater rims and s. fields of volcanic sand 1872. **5.** It was s. midnight before they landed W. IRVING. **b.** Beauty is often incident to s. fools 1711. **6.** They bore me to a cavern..And one did strip me s. SHELLEY.

B. *adv.* **1.** In a stark manner; strenuously, vigorously; boldly ME. **2.** To the fullest extent or degree; absolutely, utterly, quite 1489.
2. His conscience accuseth him, hee is stroke starke dumbe NASHE. I am distracted! I am s. raving mad! FIELDING. Hence **Stark** *v.* (*arch.*) to make or †become stiff or rigid. **Sta·rk-ly** *adv.*, **-ness.**

Stark blind, *a.* late ME. [f. STARK *adv.* 2; alt. f. †*stareblind*, after next.] Quite blind.

Stark dead, *a.* late ME. [prob. orig. STARK *a.* (sense 4); afterwards taken as STARK *adv.* 2.] Quite dead.

Starken (stā·ɹk'n), *v.* Now *dial.* late ME. [f. STARK *a.* + -EN[5].] = STARK *v.*

Stark-naked, *a.* and *sb.* 1530. [f. STARK *adv.* 2; altered f. earlier START-NAKED.] **A.** *adj.* Of a person: Absolutely without clothing.
Rather on Nylus mudde Lay me stark-nak'd SHAKS.
B. *sb.* Unadulterated spirit; esp. raw gin. *slang.* 1820.

Stark naught, *a.* Now *rare* and *arch.* 1543. [STARK *adv.* 2.] Utterly worthless or valueless; †utterly bad, vicious, hurtful, etc.

Starless (stā·ɹlės), *a.* late ME. [-LESS.] Destitute of stars or starlight; having no stars visible.
Blacker then a starlesse night COWLEY. The Czar..wore but a s. blue coat BYRON.

Starlet (stā·ɹlėt). 1830. [-LET.] **1.** A small star. Also *transf.* of a flower. **2.** A star-fish of the genus *Asterina* 1854.

Sta·rlight, *sb.* and *a.* late ME. **A.** *sb.* The light of the stars.
By fountaine cleere, or spangled star-light sheene SHAKS.
B. *attrib.* and *adj.* Of or pertaining to starlight; bright as the stars; appearing or accompanied by starlight; lighted by the stars 1585.
A Star-light Evening, and a Morning fair DRYDEN.

Sta·r-like, *a.* 1591. **1.** Resembling a star; shining like a star. **2.** Shaped like a conventional star; stellate, radiate 1611.
1. Those two starrlike eyn 1591. *fig.* You, Whose Starre-like Noblenesse gaue life and influence To their whole being? SHAKS. **2.** A star-like yellow blossom C. BRONTË.

Starling[1] (stā·ɹliŋ). [Late OE. *stærlinc*, f. *stær*; see STARE *sb.*[1], -LING[1].] **1.** Any bird of the passerine genus *Sturnus*, esp. *S. vulgaris*. Now, more widely, any bird of the family *Sturnidæ*. **b.** Applied to birds of the American family *Icteridæ* 1731. **2.** A kind of pigeon. Also *s.-pigeon*. 1867.
1. The Rose S. or Shepherd-bird (*Pastor roseus*) 1869.

Starling[2] (stā·ɹliŋ). Also **†sterling.** 1684. [perh. alt. of synon. *staddling*, f. STADDLE *sb.* + -ING[1].] An outwork of piles, projecting in front of the lower part of the pier of a bridge, so as to form a protection for the pier against the force of the stream or to secure it from damage by the impact of vessels or floating objects.

‖**Starosta** (sta·rǫstā). *Pl.* **-ti** (ti). 1591. [Russ. and Polish, lit. 'elder'.] **1.** In Russia, the head man of a village community. **2.** In the former kingdom of Poland, a noble holding a castle and domain bestowed by the Crown 1670.

‖**Starosty** (sta·rǫsti). 1710. [– G. *starostei* or Fr. *starostie*, f. *starost* STAROSTA.] In the former kingdom of Poland, the domain of a starosta.

Starr. *Hist.* 1614. [– AL. *starrum* (1208) – late Heb. *š'ṭār* a writing.] A Jewish deed or bond, esp. one of release or acquittance of debt.

Starred (stāɹd), *ppl. a.* ME. [f. STAR *sb.*[1] and *v.* + -ED.] **1.** Of the heavens, the sky, etc.: Studded with stars, starry. **2.** Marked with the representation or figure of a star;

studded with star-like figures. Of a horse or cow: Having a star on the forehead. late ME. **b.** Decorated with the star of an order 1826. **c.** Marked with an asterisk 1893. **d.** Of glass or ice; see STAR *v.* 3. 1849. **3.** Star-shaped; stellate. Chiefly *Bot.* 1725. **4.** Influenced by the stars; born under a (lucky or unlucky) star; only with defining adv. or in parasynthetic comb. (as ILL-STARRED) 1611. **5.** Of a person: Made into a star or constellation; elevated to the region of the stars 1632.

1. On a s. night, Prince Lucifer uprose MEREDITH. **2. b.** Gartered peers, and s. ambassadors DISRAELI. **4.** My third comfort (Star'd most vnluckily) SHAKS. **5.** That Starr'd Ethiope Queen MILT.

Starry (stā·ri), *a.* late ME. [f. STAR *sb.*[1] + -Y[1].] **1.** Of the sky, night, etc.: Full of stars, spangled or lit up with stars. **2.** Of or relating to the stars; consisting of stars 1594. **3.** Shining like a star or stars, bright as a star, star-like 1608. **4.** Shaped like the conventional figure of a star; arranged in the form of a star; in *Bot.* = STELLATE 1606. **5.** Sprinkled or studded with star-like forms. Chiefly *Nat. Hist.* 1611.

1. The s. heaven which we behold JOWETT. **2.** The s. system 1878. **3.** Sublime their s. fronts they rear GRAY. Hence **Sta·rrily** *adv.* **Sta·rriness** (*rare*).

Sta·r-shot. Also †**-shoot, -shut.** 1653. [SHOT *sb.*[1]] A pop. name for nostoc, which is supposed to fall from the stars, or to be the remains of a shooting star. *Obs.* or *dial.*

Star-spangled, *ppl. a.* 1591. Spangled with stars; *s. banner*, the U.S. flag.

Sta·r-stone. 1658. [STAR *sb.*[1]] **1.** A name for the pentagonal or star-shaped vertebral joints of pentacrinites. **2.** A precious stone which exhibits asterism 1798.

Start (stāɹt), *sb.*[1] [OE. *steort* = OFris., (M)LG. *stert*, MDu. *staert* (Du. *staart*), (O)HG. *sterz*, ON. *stertr* :– Gmc. **stertaz*.] †**1.** The tail of an animal –ME. **2.** A handle (of a vessel, handbell, broom, etc.). Now *dial.* ME. †**3.** The footstalk of a fruit –1672. †**4.** An outgrowth, a projecting point or spur; *esp.* the point of a stag's horn –1721. **5.** *Mech.* **a.** The innermost segment of the bucket of a water-wheel 1547. **b.** The shaft or lever of a horse-mill 1771.

Start (stāɹt), *sb.*[2] ME. [f. the vb.] †**1.** A short space of time, a moment –1620. **2.** A sudden and transient effort of movement; in early use, †a leap, a rush. late ME. †**b.** A sudden journey; a sudden flight, invasion, etc. *To take the s.*: to decamp. –1894. **c.** A sudden acceleration of progress or growth 1817. **3.** A sudden involuntary movement of the body, occasioned by surprise, terror, joy or grief, or the recollection of something forgotten. late ME. **4.** A starting into activity; a sudden and transient effort or display of energy 1605. **b.** A sudden fit of passion, grief, joy, madness, etc.; an outburst of wit, humour, or fancy. Now *rare* or *Obs.* 1596. **c.** A sudden broken utterance or burst of sound 1601. **5.** A beginning to move; a setting out on a journey or race; the beginning of a career, of a course of action, a series of events, etc. 1566. **b.** An act of setting in motion; an impulse to movement; a signal for starting in a race, etc. 1602. **c.** An opportunity or an assistance given for starting on a career or course of action. Often *a s. in life.* 1849. **6.** Advantage gained by starting first in a race or on a journey; in wider sense, position in advance of competitors whether obtained at the beginning or in the course of a race, etc. Hence *gen.* 1580. **7.** *Mining.* = LEAP *sb.*[1] 5. 1778. **8.** *slang.* = GO *sb.* 3. 1837.

2. Phr. †*At a s.*, with a bound, in an instant; This duc his courser with his spores smoot And at a stert he was bitwix hem two CHAUCER. **3.** Phr. *To give a s.*; He gave a s. of astonishment, and stood still 1863. *To give* (a person) *a s.*, to startle. **4.** Such vnconstant starts are we like to have from him SHAKS. *By starts, by fits and starts* (see FIT *sb.*[2] 4 a). **b.** 1 *Hen. IV*, III. ii. 125. **c.** She did speake in starts distractedly SHAKS. **5.** *False s.*, in *Racing*, a wrong start, necessitating return to the starting-point; hence *gen.* an unsuccessful attempt to begin something. *Flying s.*, a start in a race in which the actual starting-point is passed when one is travelling at full speed; also *fig. From s. to finish.* **b.** The s. shall be by word of mouth 1897. **6.** Phr. *To get, have,* †*take the s.* (*of* a competitor), freq. with words indicating the amount of the advantage as in *ten minutes s.*, *ten yards s.* **8.** That's the rummest s. I ever knew 1880.

Start (stāɹt), *v.* Pa. t. and pa. pple. **started.** [ME. *sterte, starte, stürte*, repr. OE. **stiertan* or **steortian*, **steartian*, **styrtan*, f. Gmc. **stert-* **start-* **sturt-*, repr. on the Continent by (M)LG. *störten*, (M)Du. *storten*, OHG. *sturzen* (G. *stürzen*) overthrow, pour out, rush, fall headlong, gush out.] **I.** *intr.* †**1.** To leap, jump, caper –1567. **2.** To move with a bound or sudden violent impulse from a position of rest. Also with *out.* Freq. *fig.* ME. **b.** To move suddenly from one's place, as to avoid a danger; hence *fig.* to flinch or recoil *from* something in alarm or repugnance. Chiefly with adv. ME. **c.** To awake suddenly *from, out of*; to emerge suddenly *into*, etc. late ME. **3.** Of an inanimate thing: To issue suddenly and violently; to fly, flow, or be projected by a sudden impulse. Of tears: To burst *out* suddenly; to rise suddenly *to* the eyes. late ME. **b.** Of the eyes: To burst out, escape *from* their sockets. Chiefly hyperbolical, expressing the effect of horror or fury. 1526. **c.** *S. out*: to project; to become visible or conspicuous, burst into view 1825. †**4.** To go or come swiftly or hastily; to rush, hasten –1637. **5.** To undergo a sudden involuntary movement of the body, resulting from surprise, fright, sudden pain, etc. Hence *occas.*, to feel startled. 1529. †**6.** To desert or revolt *from* (a leader, a party); to swerve *from* (a cause, purpose, principle); to withdraw *from* (a promise, treaty). Also with *aside, back.* –1781. **7.** Of a material thing: To break away from its place; to be displaced by pressure or shrinkage; to get loose. Chiefly in techn. uses. 1526. **8.** To set out from the starting-point in a race 1645. **9.** To set out, to begin a journey; to begin to move, to leave the point of departure in any kind of progression. Said of a person or animal; also of a vehicle, ship, etc. 1821. **10.** To begin a career, course of action, process, etc. Also of a process: To begin. 1798.

2. Vpon my feet incontinent I s. 1605. Out of the wood he starts in wonted shape MILT. I started out of my Reveries as if I had awak'd from a.. Dream 1737. **b.** The horse, too, upon which the lady rode, started back SCOTT. **c.** When all creation started into birth COWPER. The characters s. into light, life, and identity 1863. **3.** 'Tis said, at times the sullen tear would s. BYRON. *fig.* Fear, pity, justice, indignation s. GOLDSM. **b.** His eyes were starting..and his hair rose up on end 1863. **5.** He starts at every Noise 1695. His fiery steeds Started aside with fright 1870. **7.** Just as the ship floated several rivets started again 1869. Phr. *To s. fair*, to start on equal terms. **9.** Next morning I started with this man up the valley TYNDALL. **10.** Each bowler started with a maiden 1868. Phr. *To s. from* or *with*, (in reasoning) to assume as the point of departure. *To s. in business*, to begin one's career. *To s. in* (U.S. colloq.), to begin. *To s. out*, to set oneself, begin *to do* something.

S. up. a. To rise suddenly; to spring to an erect position; *fig.* to bestir oneself. †**b.** To become suddenly conspicuous. **c.** Of things: To come suddenly into being or notice, to spring up.

II. *trans.* †**1.** To cause to start or flinch; to startle –1871. **2.** *Hunting.* To force (an animal, esp. a hare) to leave its lair, form, or resting-place. late ME. **3.** To propound (a question, an objection); to introduce (a subject of discussion) 1643. **4.** To discharge the contents of, empty (a vessel); to pour or shoot (liquids, coal, etc.) from one vessel into another 1700. **5.** To cause (a material thing) to 'start' or break away from its place; to displace by pressure or strain. Of a ship: To suffer the starting or giving way of (a plank, etc.). 1676. **6.** To cause (a person, an animal, a vehicle) to start or set out in a race, on a journey; to cause to begin moving in any kind of progression. Also with *off.* 1725. **7.** To cause to begin to act or operate; to initiate; *esp.* (freq. **s. up**) to set (machinery) in motion 1666. **b.** To begin to keep as part of one's establishment; to set up (e.g. a horse, carriage) 1851. **8.** To begin (some action or operation). Also said of a thing. 1833.

1. And now..dost thou come To s. my quiet SHAKS. **2.** Little dogs s. the hare, the great one gets her 1659. *transf.* Do but s. An eccho with the clamor of thy drumme SHAKS. **3.** Will you give me liberty to s. one difficulty here? DE FOE. **4.** A small place..wherein the powder is started 1850. **5.** The damage..was trifling,..not a rivet was started 1840. **7.** He started a discourse of a talk he hears about the town PEPYS. The plan for starting the cottager in business 1854. **b.** He is sure to s. a yacht 1873. **8.** The young fellow.. started another ballad 1873. Hence **Sta·rtful** *a.* timorous, fitful. **Sta·rting** *ppl. a.* that starts; **-ly** *adv.* by starts. **Sta·rtish** *a.* apt to jib.

Starter (stā·ɹtəɹ). 1536. [f. START *v.* + -ER[1].] **1.** One who or something which starts. **2.** One who sets out in a race or journey 1818. **3.** A dog trained for starting game 1748. **4.** One who gives the signal to start 1622.

Sta·r-thi:stle. 1578. [STAR *sb.*[1]] A name for the weed *Centaurea calcitrapa*, the flowers of which are surrounded by radiating spines; also for *C. solstitialis*, and as a book-name for the whole genus.

Sta·rting, *vbl. sb.* late ME. [f. START *v.* + -ING[1].] The action of the vb.

Phr. *At s.*: at the beginning or outset.

Comb.: **s.-bolt** *Naut.*, a bolt used to drive out another; it is usually a trifle smaller; **-gate,** a removable barrier for securing a fair start in horse races; **-place,** the place occupied at starting by a competitor in a race; the place from which a person or thing starts; **-point,** the point from which a person or thing starts; a point of departure in a journey, argument, development, etc.; **-post,** a post marking the place from which competitors in a race should start; **-price,** (*a*) the price at which the bidding at an auction starts; (*b*) *Racing*, the final odds on a horse at the time of starting.

†**Sta·rting-hole.** 1530. [f. STARTING *vbl. sb.*] **1.** A place in which a hunted animal or person takes refuge –1618. **2.** *fig.* A means of evasion; a loophole –1801.

Startle (stā·ɹt'l), *sb.* 1714. [f. STARTLE *v.*] An experience of being startled; a start or shock of surprise or alarm. Also (predic.), something that startles.

Burton's death..was quite a s. to me 1836.

Startle (stā·ɹt'l), *v.* [OE. *steartlian*, f. **steart-*; see START *v.*, -LE.] †**1.** *intr.* To kick, struggle. OE. only. **2.** To rush, move swiftly; to caper. Now *dial.* ME. **3.** †**a.** To start. Of a horse: To shy. **b.** To feel sudden astonishment or alarm. Now *rare* or *Obs.* (repl. by passive of sense 4). 1530. †**c.** To awake with a start; to move or change as if surprised or frightened –1847. **4.** *trans.* To cause to start; to frighten; to surprise greatly; †to shock 1595.

2. We see oxen goe to the shambles leaping and startling 1637. **3. b.** The cloister startles at the gleam of arms WORDSW. **c.** The grass that sprung Startled and glanced and trembled even to feel An unaccustomed presence SHELLEY. 4. The garrison, startled from sleep, found the enemy already masters of the towers W. IRVING. *fig.* To hear the Lark..singing s. the dull night MILT. Hence **Sta·rtler,** one who or something which startles. **Sta·rtlingly** *adv.* **Sta·rtlish** *a.* easily startled; apt to take fright; esp. said of a horse.

Start-naked, *a. Obs.* exc. *dial.* ME. [f. START *sb.*[1] + NAKED *a.*; lit. naked to the tail.] = STARK NAKED *a.*

Startup (stā·ɹtɒ̆p), *sb.*[1] *Obs.* exc. *dial.* and *Hist.* 1517. [f. vbl. phr. *start up* (see START *v.*).] Orig., a kind of 'high-low' or boot, worn by rustics; in later use, a kind of gaiter or legging. Chiefly in *pl.*

†**Start-up,** *ppl. a.* and *sb.*[2] 1557. [f. *start*, pa. pple. of START *v.* + UP *adv.*] = UP-START *a.* and *sb.* –1801.

A new S. Sect 1762. A s. baron of yesterday 1801.

Starvation (stāɹvē[i]·ʃən). 1778. [f. STARVE *v.* + -ATION.] **1.** The action of starving or subjecting to famine. **2.** The condition of being starved or having too little food to sustain life or health 1802. **b.** *transf.* Insufficient supply of something necessary to life 1866.

2. b. Oxygen s. and carbonic acid poisoning.. are at work together 1866.

attrib. **s. wages,** wages which are barely sufficient to keep the recipient from s.

Starve (stāɹv), *v.* [OE. *steorfan* = OFris. *sterva*, OS. *sterban* (Du. *sterven*), OHG. *sterban* (G. *sterben*) :– Gmc., str. vb., perh. orig. 'be rigid', extension with *-*bh-* of the base **ster-* be rigid (cf. STARE *v.*).] **I.** *intr.* †**1.** To die. In late use app. to die a lingering death, as from hunger, cold, grief, or slow disease. Also, in spiritual sense, of the soul –1657. **2.** With various constructions, specifying the cause of death. In later use: To be brought gradually nearer to death, to be in process of being killed; to suffer extremely. Now *dial.* ME. †**3.** Of plants or their parts: To die, wither. Of a material substance: To lose its characteristic quality, spoil, deteriorate. –1722. **4.** [orig. *ellipt.*] To die of hunger; to perish or be in process of perishing from lack or insufficiency of food; to suffer extreme poverty and want; more emphatically *to s. to death.* Also hyperbolically in colloq. use: To be extremely hungry. 1578. **5.** [orig. *ellipt.*] To die of exposure to cold; chiefly hyperbolical, to be benumbed or 'dead' with cold. Now *north.* 1602.

2. In paril for to sterue For hungyr CHAUCER. To s. for Food, to perish In Penury SYLVESTER. His Office keeps your Parchment fates entire, He starves with cold to save them from the fire POPE. **4.** No: on the barren Mountaine let him sterue SHAKS. *fig.* I at home starue for a merrie looke SHAKS. **5.** Whether they s. in the snows of Lapland, or burn in the sands of Guinea? 1772.

II. *trans.* †**1.** To cause to die, to kill, destroy –1707. **2.** To cause to perish of hunger; to deprive of or keep scantily supplied with food. Also *transf.* and *fig.* 1530. **b.** To subdue by famine or low diet; also to force *into* (a course of action) by starvation 1625. **c.** To cure (a disease) by abstemious diet 1617. **3.** To produce atrophy in (a plant, an animal or vegetable organ, a morbid growth) by withholding nutriment 1633. **4.** To cause to die of cold, to kill with cold; also hyperbolically, to benumb with cold. Chiefly *pass. Obs.* exc. *dial.* 1600.

1. Aches contract, and sterue your supple ioynts SHAKS. **2.** To s. a man, in law is murther PRIOR. *transf.* We must starue our sight, From louers foode, till morrow deepe midnight SHAKS. **b.** They..were to be starved into compliance 1775. **c.** He had been..starving a cold 1839. **4.** There is not a window or door that shuts; I am starved to death at my fire side 1770. Hence **Sta·rvedly** *adv.* **Sta·rver,** one who or that which starves.

Starveling (stā·ɹvliŋ), *sb.* and *a.* 1546. [f. STARVE *v.* + -LING[1].] **A.** *sb.* A starved person, animal, etc.; one who habitually starves or is stinted of food; one who is emaciated for lack of nutriment.

If I hang, old Sir Iohn hangs with mee, and thou know'st hee's no Starueling SHAKS.

B. *adj.* **1.** That lacks a sufficiency of food; hence, lean and weak for want of nutriment; ill-fed, hungry 1597. **2.** Poverty-stricken. Of circumstances, etc.: Characterized by or exhibiting poverty. 1638. **3.** *fig.* Poor in quality or quantity, lean, thin, meagre, scanty 1641.

1. Staruling Famine comes of large expence 1597. **3.** A s. and comfortless religion COLERIDGE.

Starwort (stā·ɹwɒɹt). late ME. [f. STAR *sb.*[1] + WORT[1].] **1.** The genus *Stellaria*, with white starry flowers; esp. *S. holostea.* **2.** A book-name for the genus *Aster*; esp. *A. tripolium*, Sea Starwort; *A. amellus*, Italian Starwort 1578. **3.** *Water Starwort*, the genus *Callitriche* 1597. **4.** A moth, *Cucullia asteris* 1819.

‖**Stasimon** (stæ·simǫn). *Pl.* **stasima, stasimons.** 1861. [Gr. στάσιμον n. (agreeing with μέλος song) of στάσιμος stationary, f. στα- stand.] In ancient Greek tragedy, a song of the Chorus, occurring after the PARODE, continued without the interruption of dialogue or anapæstics.

‖**Stasis** (stē[i]·sis). 1745. [mod.L. – Gr. στάσις, f. στα- STAND.] *Path.* A stagnation or stoppage of the circulation of any of the fluids of the body, esp. of the blood in some part of the blood-vessels.

-stat, the terminal element in certain names of scientific instruments, *aerostat, heliostat, hydrostat, thermostat,* etc. The earliest example of this formation is *heliostat,* – mod.L. *heliostata*, app. repr. an assumed Gr. type *ἡλιοστάτης, intended to mean an instrument for causing the sun to appear stationary, f. ἥλιος sun + -στατης, agent-n. f. στα- root of ἱστάναι cause to stand. The later words have been formed on the analogy of *heliostat*, app. with some ref. to the Gr. στατός standing, stationary.

Statable (stē[i]·tăb'l), *a.* Also **stateable.** 1802. [f. STATE *v.* + -ABLE.] Capable of being stated.

Statant (stē[i]·tănt), *a.* 1500. [irreg. f. *stat-*, pa. ppl. stem of L. *stare* stand; see -ANT.] *Her.* Of an animal, esp. a lion: Standing in profile with all four feet on the ground.

State (stē[i]t), *sb.* ME. [Partly aphetic f. ESTATE, partly direct – L. *status* manner of standing, condition, f. base of *stare* STAND.] **I.** Condition, manner of existing. **1.** A combination of circumstances or attributes belonging for the time being to a person or thing; a particular manner or way of existing, as defined by the presence of certain circumstances or attributes; a condition. **b.** *colloq.* Implying a state of dirt, untidiness, etc. 1879. **2.** A condition (of mind or feeling) 1538. **b.** *colloq.* An agitated or excited state of mind or feeling 1837. **3.** The mode of existence of a spiritual being; a particular mode or phase of (spiritual) existence ME. **4.** Physical condition with regards internal make or constitution, molecular form or structure, and the like. Also, one of several forms or conditions in which an object—animal, vegetable, or mineral—is found to exist; a phase or stage of existence. ME. †**5.** The height or chief stage of a process; the condition of full vigour. Chiefly *Path.*, the crisis or 'acme' of disease –1717. †**6.** *Rhet.* (after L. *status*). The point in question or debate between contending parties, as it emerges from their pleadings; the issue or main question. In full *s. of the cause, of the plea.* –1776. **7.** *Semitic Gram.* Applied to certain formal and syntactical conditions (see O.E.D.) 1752. **8.** *Engraving.* An impression taken from a plate at a particular stage of its progress and recognizable by special marks 1874. **b.** *Bibliography.* One of two or more differing portions of a single edition of a book 1931.

1. I all alone beweepe my out-cast s. SHAKS. Y[e] violent & desperate s. of their affairs H. WALPOLE. The crowded s. of the port 1890. He attempted to deceive his patient as to her s. 1908. *S. of nature*: see NATURE *sb.* IV. 2. *S. of siege*, the condition of undergoing investment by a hostile army. **b.** Just look what a s. I am in! 1879. **2.** A foolish and unreasonable s. of mind 1728. The term *S.* has.. been applied to all modifications of mind indifferently 1837. **3.** From s. to s. the spirit walks TENNYSON. *Future s.*: see FUTURE *a.* **4.** Water, in the s. of vapour 1815. The most perfect and useful s. of it [iron] is that of ochreous stain RUSKIN. **8.** The best states of the old plates now procurable RUSKIN.

Phrases. *The* (or *a*) *s. of things* or *affairs*, the way in which events or circumstances stand disposed (at a particular time or in a particular sphere). *The s. of the case*, the facts and circumstances of a particular affair, question, etc. †*In s.*, later *in a s.* (now *in a fit s.*) followed by infinitive: fit, likely, ready *to do* or *be* something. *In a great state*, very excited or agitated.

II. Status; high rank; pomp. †**1.** A person's condition or position in life; a person's natural, social, or legal status, profession or calling, rank or degree –1741. †**b.** *Man's s.* = manhood; cf. ESTATE *sb.* 1 b. 1580. **c.** Condition or status as married or single. late ME. †**2.** *contextually* and *pregnantly.* A high rank or exalted position; an office of power or importance –1642. †**b.** High rank, greatness, power –1640. **3.** Costly and imposing display, such as befits persons of rank and wealth; splendour, magnificence ME. **4.** Dignity of demeanour or presence. Now *rare.* 1586. †**5.** A raised chair with a canopy, etc.; a throne –1712. †**b.** A canopy –1828.

1. Having died in the s. of apparency 1741. **2. b.** The glories of our blood and s. 1640. †*To bear* (*great*) *s.*, to hold (high) office; *fig.* (of a thing), to be of importance, involve great consequences. **3.** The gilded coach, indeed, which is now annually admired by the crowd, was not yet a part of his s. MACAULAY. Phr. *of s.*; as in *bed* or *chair of s.* *In s.*, with great pomp and solemnity; with a great train. *To lie in s.*, of a dead body, to be ceremoniously exposed to view before interment. **4.** There is a s. sometimes in decent plainnesse 1642. Phr. *To keep s., one's s.*, to keep one's dignity, behave in a dignified manner (now *rare*). *To hold one's s.*, to appear in pomp and splendour (*arch.*). **5.** This Chayre shall bee my S. SHAKS.

III. A class, rank; a person of rank. †**1.** A class, rank, order, sort or body *of* persons; a 'condition', profession, or occupation; the members of a class or profession collectively. (Cf. ESTATE *sb.* 5 and Fr. *état.*) –1625. †**2.** An ESTATE of the realm –1700. **3.** *pl.* The 'estates of the realm' met to form a constitutional assembly; the princes, dukes, nobles, etc., together with the delegates or representatives of the several ranks, orders, chief cities, etc. of a country, assembled in a parliament or diet. Now *Hist.*, exc. as the title of the legislatures of Jersey and Guernsey. See also STATES GENERAL. late ME. †**b.** Delegates or members of the Dutch government as individuals –1767. †**4.** A person of standing, importance or high rank –1667. †**5.** *pl.* The dignitaries or authorities of a town or district –1609. †**6.** *collect. sing.* The rulers, nobles, or great men of a realm; the government, ruling body, grand council, or court –1617.

2. In full assembly of the three States 1641. **3.** The French States at no time attained the regularity of the English Parliament 1844. In Jersey, besides the Royal Court, there is only one Assembly. It is called the States. 1862. **4.** The bold design Pleas'd highly those infernal States MILT. **6.** *Oth.* I. ii. 96.

IV. Commonwealth, polity. †**1.** The condition of the Church, a country, realm, etc. in regard to its welfare and polity. Occas., a condition of prosperity, of order and settled government. –1651. †**2.** A particular form of polity or government –1701. **3.** *The state*: the body politic as organized for supreme civil rule and government; the political organization which is the basis of civil government; hence, the supreme civil power and government vested in a country or nation 1538. **b.** dist. from 'the church' or eccl. organization and authority. In the phr. *church and s.* the article is dropped. 1589. **4.** A body of people occupying a defined territory and organized under a sovereign government. Hence *occas.* the territory occupied by such a body. 1568. **5. a.** The territory, or one of the territories, ruled by a particular sovereign. *Hereditary states*: spec. (= G. *Erbstaaten*) the kingdoms or principalities held hereditarily by any head of the Holy Roman Empire 1602. **b.** *pl.* (*Hist.*) Applied (perh. after It. *stati*) to the cities and territories included in an Italian principality or republic, esp. the grand duchy of Tuscany and the republic of Venice. Also in *States of the Church, Papal States* (also *sing.*), titles of the former temporal dominions of the Holy See. 1797. **c.** One of a number of polities, each more or less sovereign and independent in regard to internal affairs, which together make up a supreme federal government; as in the U.S. of America, the Commonwealth of Australia 1774. **d.** *The States*: the United States of America 1777. **6.** (Without article.) All that concerns the government or ruling power of a country; the sphere of supreme political power and administration 1582.

1. *Rich. II*, IV. i. 225. **2.** Phr. †*The popular s.*, democracy. †*S. royal*, a monarchy. **3.** The S. is properly..the nation in its collective and corporate capacity M. ARNOLD. **4.** Never any S. was..so open to receive Strangers, into their Body, as were the Romans BACON. States are sovereign within their own territories, independent of other states, and equal as between themselves 1880. **6.** *Reason of S.*: see REASON *sb.* II. 1. *Secretary of S.* (Gt. Britain), a minister in charge of a Government office (defined as *for Foreign Affairs, for War*, etc.); (U.S.) the Foreign Minister. *Department of S., S. Department* (U.S.): see DEPARTMENT 2.

V. Interest in property; possessions. †**1.** *Law.* = ESTATE *sb.* 9 (in a property); right or title to property –1660. †**2.** *Law.* Possession (of property). Chiefly *Sc.* –1768. †**3.** Property, possessions; one's private means –1899.

3. A great s. left to an heire, is as a lure to al the birds of prey round about, to seise on him BACON.

VI. (perh. partly from STATE *v.*) †**a.** A statement; a detailed report of particulars –1818. **b.** *Mil.* A report of the numbers of a corps, regiment, etc. in the field, with details of casualties 1802.

attrib. and *Comb.*, as *s.-bed, s. occasion, entry*, etc.; *s. religion, education, S. Railways, etc.*; *s.-crime, -criminal, -trial.* **s.-cabin** = STATE-ROOM 2, 3; **-church,** a church established by the s.; hence **-churchman; -hospital** *U.S.*, a public asylum for the insane under the direction of a S.; **-paper,** an official document in which some matter concerning the government or the nation is published or expounded; also *attrib.* in *S. Paper Office*; **-prison,** (*a*) a prison for political offenders; (*b*) *U.S.* and *Austral.*, a prison maintained by a S. for the penal confinement of criminals; in *U.S.* also *state's prison*; so **s. prisoner,** a person under arrest for felony, also a political prisoner; **S. rights,** the rights and powers vested in the separate States under the Federal constitution of the U.S.A.; also **States rights; s. secret,** a matter kept secret by the government; *joc.* an important secret; **s. socialism,** a form of socialism which advocates utilizing the power of the state to improve the condition of the working-classes by pensions, etc., and by state administration of industries, railways, etc.; hence **s.-socialist, -socialistic** *a.* Combinations of the genitive or pl.: **State's Attorney** *U.S.* a lawyer commissioned to represent the S. in the Courts, esp. in criminal actions; **states-system** [tr. G. *staaten-system*], the federation of a number of states with the object of preserving the actual balance of power. Hence **Sta·tehood** (chiefly *U.S.*), the condition or status of a political s.

State (stēᶦt), *v.* 1590. [f. prec.] **1.** *trans.* To place, station (*rare*). †**2.** To give a certain rank or position to, to rank; also in *pass.* –1715. †**3.** To place in a specified condition; in early use chiefly to settle, place in safety or quiet –1786. **4.** To set out (a question, problem, etc.) in proper form; spec. in *Logic* 1641. **5.** To declare in words; to represent (a matter) in all the circumstances of modification; to set out fully or in a definite form 1647. **b.** To specify (a number, price, etc.) 1789.

4. An argument thus stated regularly and at full length, is called a Syllogism 1826. Phr. *To s. a case*, to set out the facts of a matter or pleading for consideration by a court. *To s. an account* or *accounts*, to set down formally the debits and credits arising in a course of business transactions. **5.** The contents of the deed were falsely stated 1891.

Statecraft (stēᶦ·tkraft). 1642. [f. STATE *sb.* + CRAFT.] The art of conducting state affairs; statesmanship.

Stated (stēᶦ·tėd), *ppl. a.* 1641. [f. STATE *v.* + -ED¹. In early use perh. rather f. L. *status* appointed, fixed, regular + -ED¹.] **1.** Fixed, regular; settled by authority, agreement or pre-arrangement. **b.** Of a functionary, an employment: Recognized, regular, official 1752. **2.** Of a law, rule, penalty: Formulated, explicitly set forth 1681. **b.** Narrated, alleged as fact 1787. **c.** *S. account*: a statement of account that has been agreed to by the parties to a suit 1765. **d.** Law. *S. case, case s.*: A summary of the points in dispute, drawn up by agreement of the parties to an action, to be presented to a court or an arbitrator in order to facilitate a speedy decision 1899.

2. A penalty in the nature of s. damages; as a rent of 5 *l.* an acre for ploughing up antient meadow BLACKSTONE. Hence **Sta·tedly** *adv.* with regularity, constantly.

Stateful (stēᶦ·tfŭl), *a.* Now *rare* or *Obs.* 1591. [f. STATE *sb.* + -FUL.] Full of state or dignity, stately.

Thou lookest down from heaven, thy s. throne 1624.

Sta·te-house. 1593. [f. STATE *sb.* + HOUSE *sb.* Prob. suggested by Du. *stathuis* (now *stadhuis*) STADTHOUSE.] †**1. a.** A house of state; a building appropriated to state-ceremonies. **b.** = SENATE-HOUSE 1. –1614. †**2.** A town hall –1756. **3.** *U.S.* The building in which the legislature of a State of the Union has its sessions, or in which, formerly the public affairs of a colony or province were transacted 1639.

Stateless (stēᶦ·tlės), *a.* 1609. [f. STATE *sb.* + -LESS.] **a.** Without a state or political community. **b.** Destitute of state or ceremonial dignity.

Stately (stēᶦ·tli), *a.* and *adv.* late ME. [f. STATE *sb.* + -LY.] **A.** *adj.* **1.** Of persons or personal appearance or demeanour. In early use, Befitting or indicating high estate, princely, noble, majestic. In later use, Imposingly dignified. **b.** Of movement, a person or animal in movement: Dignified, deliberate 1593. **2.** Of persons, etc.: †**a.** Haughty, domineering, arrogant –1607. **b.** Showing a sense of superiority; repellently dignified; not affable or approachable 1625. **3.** Of things: Appertaining to or befitting a person of high estate; magnificent, splendid. late ME. **4.** Imposing or majestic in size and proportions 1450. **5.** Of speech or writing or its style; hence of a speaker or writer: Elevated in thought or expression, dignified, majestic 1579.

1. She was..the stateliest of dames 1877. **2. b.** Their ladyships made three s. curtsies THACKERAY. **3.** A s. dinner both of Fish and Flesh 1648. Armorial bearings s. TENNYSON. **4.** Woods high and decked with Stately trees 1586. Garrick and statelier Kemble, and the rest TENNYSON. The s. calmness of the wood-dove's note KINGSLEY. **5.** Choice word and measured phrase..; a s. speech WORDSW.

B. *adv.* In a stately manner. late ME.

A figure..Appeares before them, and with sollemne march Goes slow and s. SHAKS. Hence **Sta·telily** *adv.* (now *rare*). **Sta·teliness.**

Statement (stēᶦ·tmĕnt). 1775. [f. STATE *v.* + -MENT.] **1.** The action or an act of stating; the manner in which something is stated 1789. **b.** *Mus.* A presentation of a subject or theme in a composition 1883. **2.** Something that is stated; an allegation, declaration 1775. **3.** A written or oral communication setting forth facts, arguments, demands, or the like 1787. **b.** *Comm.* (More fully *s. of account*): a document setting out the items of debit and credit between two parties 1897. **4.** *Comm.* In certain branches of industry, a document periodically issued, setting forth the prices to be paid to workmen for various kinds of piece-work. Also *attrib.* as *s. price, wages*. 1889.

1. In s., the late Lord Holland was not successful MACAULAY. A model of cautious and accurate s. 1915. **2.** The s., that truth is appearance only JOWETT.

Sta·te(s)-mo:nger. *Obs.* exc. *arch.* 1616. [See MONGER.] A projector of political constitutions; a pretender to political science.

‖**Stater**¹ (stēᶦ·təɹ). late ME. [Late L. – Gr. στατήρ, f. στα-, base of ἱστάναι STAND used in the sense 'weigh'.] *Antiq.* **1.** An ancient weight equal to half an ounce. **2.** A name of various ancient coins, esp. the Persian stater or DARIC, a gold coin worth about £1 1*s.* 3*d.* late ME.

Stater² (stēᶦ·təɹ). 1702. [f. STATE *v.* + -ER¹.] One who states. *Average s.* = average-adjuster; see AVERAGE *sb.*²

State-room. 1660. **1.** A state apartment; a room in a palace, great house, hotel, etc., splendidly decorated and furnished, and used only on ceremonial occasions. **2.** A captain's or superior officer's room on board ship 1660. **3.** *U.S.* A sleeping apartment with one or two berths on a passenger steamer 1837. **b.** *U.S.* A private compartment in a railway train 1867.

States General. 1585. [= Fr. *états généraux*, Du. *staaten generaal.*] *Hist.* A legislative assembly representing the three estates, viz. clergy, nobles, and commons or burghers of a whole realm, principality, or commonwealth: **a.** in France before the Revolution; **b.** in the Netherlands from the 15th c. to 1796.

Sta·teship. *Irish Hist.* 1917. = TUATH.

Statesman (stēᶦ·tsmăn). 1592. [f. *state's*, gen. of STATE *sb.* + MAN *sb.*, after Fr. *homme d'état*. In sense 2 f. STATE *sb.* V. 1.] **1.** One who takes a leading part in the affairs of a state or body politic; esp. one who is skilled in the management of public affairs. **2.** *dial.* A small landowner 1787.

1. He..in the course of one revolving Moon, Was Chymist, Fidler, States-man, and Buffoon DRYDEN. *Elder statesman*, in Japan: see ELDER *a.* [Lord Dufferin's] wide and varied training had made him not a politician but a s. able to take Imperial views 1891. **2.** A s., which means in Cumberland phrase one who owns the fee-simple of his land, but works on it himself 1813. Hence **Sta·tesmanlike** *a.* having the qualities characteristic of a s.; befitting or worthy of a s. **Sta·tesmanly** *a.* pertaining to or characteristic of a s.; befitting a s.

Sta·tesmanship. 1764. [f. prec. + -SHIP.] The activity or skill of a statesman; skilful management of public affairs.

Stateswoman (stēᶦ·tswu:măn). *Pl.* **-women** (-wimėn). 1609. [f. *state's* gen. of STATE *sb.* + WOMAN, after STATESMAN.] A woman who takes part in the conduct of public affairs; a woman with statesmanlike ability.

The Queen is a theologian as well as a s. 1885.

Static (stæ·tik), *a.* and *sb.* 1570. [– mod.L. *staticus* – Gr. στατικός causing to stand, pertaining to weighing, f. ἱστάναι cause to stand, weigh. Cf. Fr. *statique* (XVII). As sb. – mod.L. *statica* – Gr. στατική (sc. τέχνη art) science of weighing, subst. use of fem. of the adj.] **A.** *adj.* †**1.** Of or pertaining to weighing or the use of the balance –1734. †**2.** Pertaining to the effect of weight or the conditions of the equilibrium of weight. Of a power or principle: Operative in the production of equilibrium. –1775. **3.** Pertaining to forces in equilibrium, or to bodies at rest; opp. to *dynamic* 1850. **b.** Applied *spec.* to designate frictional as opp. to voltaic electricity 1839. **4.** *transf.* and *fig.* = next 5. 1856. **5.** *Path.* and *Phys.* Structural or organic, as opp. to *functional* 1855. **6.** *Machinery.* Of an electric transformer or generator: Having all its parts stationary, non-rotary 1903. **7.** Applied to minor disturbances of an electric current 1911.

1. *S. chair*, the Sanctorian weighing chair (see SANCTORIAN *a.*) for determining the amount of insensible perspiration by weighing the body. **3.** I have used..the terms dynamic and s. to represent the different states of magnetism 1850. **4.** Revelation, like inspiration, is a process, not a s. condition 1909.

B. *sb.* **1.** = STATICS. Now *rare.* 1570. **2.** = STATICS b (*U.S.*) 1913.

Statical (stæ·tikăl), *a.* 1570. [f. as prec.; see -ICAL.] †**1.** = prec. A. 1. –1780. **2.** Of or pertaining to STATICS 1660. †**3.** Of analysis, etc.: Gravimetrical –1813. **b.** Pertaining to the metrology of weight 1846. **4.** = prec. A. 3, 3b. 1802. **5.** *transf.* and *fig.* Of or pertaining to a fixed or stable condition, as dist. from a state of progress or change 1855. **6.** *Math.* Concerned with magnitude alone, without regard to direction (*rare*) 1859. **7.** *Med.* Structural, organic 1896.

4. The s. attributes, shape, size and position 1868. **5.** The fund by which the life of the human race..is sustained is never in a s. condition 1886. Hence **Sta·tically** *adv.*

‖**Statice** (stæ·tisi). 1731. [L. – Gr. στατική, orig. fem. of στατικός causing to stand still (see STATIC *a.*), in the sense 'stopping flow of blood'.] A genus of plumbaginaceous perennial herbs, typical of the *Staticeæ*; a plant of this genus, esp. Sea Lavender.

Statics (stæ·tiks). 1656. [Alteration of STATIC *sb.*, after names of sciences in -ICS.] Orig., the science relating to weight and its mechanical effects, and to the conditions of equilibrium as resulting from the distribution of weight. In mod. use, the branch of physical science concerned with the action of forces in producing equilibrium or relative rest, in contradistinction to *Dynamics* as the science of the action of forces in producing motion. **b.** *Wireless Telegr.* = ATMOSPHERICS 1918.

Phr. *Social s.*; Social philosophy may be aptly divided..into s. and dynamics; the first treating of the equilibrium of a perfect society, the second of the forces by which society is advanced towards perfection SPENCER.

Stating (stēᶦ·tiŋ), *vbl. sb.* 1652. [f. STATE *v.* + -ING¹.] The action of STATE *v.*

Many of our..peevish wranglings are kept up by the ill s. of the Question JER. TAYLOR.

Station (stēᶦ·ʃən), *sb.* late ME. [– (O)Fr. *station* – L. *statio, -ōn-*, f. *sta-*, base of *stare* STAND; see -ION.] **I.** Action or condition of standing. **1.** The action or posture of standing on the feet; manner of standing. Now mainly *techn.* 1526. **2.** The condition or fact of standing still; assumption of a continuance in a stationary condition: opp. to *motion.* Now *rare.* 1606. **3.** A halt; a stand. Now *rare* or *Obs.* 1604. **4.** *Astr.* The apparent standing still of a planet at its apogee and perigee. late ME.

1. A S., like the Herald Mercurie New lighted on a heauen kissing hill SHAKS. *S.*,..the manner of standing or the attitude of live stock, particularly of exhibition game fowls 1891. **2.** His life is a progress, and not a s. EMERSON.

II. Standing-place, position. In lit. applications. **1.** A place to stand in; *esp.* a position assigned to a man on duty, or in games 1556. **b.** A point at which one may stand to obtain a view 1822. **c.** *Boat-racing.* The position (at one side or the other of the river) occupied by a competing crew at starting 1864. **d.** The correct position of a vessel in a squadron 1911. **2.** *Surveying.* Each of the selected points at which observations are taken 1571. **3.** The place in which a thing stands or is appointed to stand. Now *rare* or *Obs.* 1440. **b.** *Biol.* The kind of place in which an animal or a plant is fitted to live, the nature of its habitat 1721. **4.** *Naut.* **a.** More fully *naval s.* In early use, a port, harbour, or roadstead for ships. In mod. use, a place at which ships of the Navy are regularly stationed. late ME. **b.** A place or region to which a government ship or fleet is assigned for duty 1666. **5.** *Mil.* A place where soldiers are garrisoned, a military post 1609. **b.** In India, a place where the English officials of a district, or the officers of a garrison (not in a fortress) reside. Also, the aggregate society of such a place. 1860. **6.** The locality to which an official is appointed for the exercise of his functions 1632. **7.** A place where men are stationed and apparatus set up for some particular kind of industrial work, scientific research, or the like 1823. **b.** = POLICE-STATION 1889. **8.** *Austral.* A stock-farm 1833.

1. I got a s...at the doore of the lobby to the House, and heard much of the debate EVELYN. Phr. *To take (up), keep one's s.* **4. a.** A large Recess,..A S. safe for Ships, when Tempests roar DRYDEN. **b.** She was fit for service on the Australasian S. 1912. **5. b.** Who asked the S. to dinner? 1866. **6.** I am glad my s. is to be here, near my own home PEPYS. **7.** *Fishing. seismological, telegraph, zoological s.*; A wireless telegraph s. at Barfleur 1912.

In fig. applications. **9.** *gen.* A metaphorical standing-place or position, e.g. in a class, in a scale of dignity; and the like 1605. **10.** A person's position in the world; a state of life as determined by outward circumstances or conditions; *spec.* a calling, office, employment. Now *rare* or *Obs.* exc. in *private s.*, an unofficial position. 1675. **11.** Position in the social scale, as higher or lower 1682. **b.** *spec.* Elevated position, high social rank 1731.

9. If you haue a s. in the file, Not i' th' worst ranke of Manhood SHAKS. **11.** Content may dwell in all Stations SIR T. BROWNE. **b.** Many other gentlemen of s. and fortune 1832.

III. A stopping-place. **1.** A stopping-place on a journey; a place of temporary abode in a course of migration. Also (chiefly *U.S.*), a place on a coach route where a stop is made for change of horses and for meals. 1585. **2.** (More explicitly *railway s.*) A place where railway trains regularly stop for taking up and setting down passengers or for receiving goods for transport. Also, and more frequently, a building or group of buildings erected at such a place for purposes connected with the transport of passengers and goods. 1830. **b.** Also with reference to a service of omnibuses, etc. **IV.** Ecclesiastical uses. **1.** *Hist.* A service at which the clergy of the city of Rome assembled at one of a certain number of churches within the city, each of which had its fixed day in the year for this celebration. late ME. **2.** Each of a number of holy places visited by pilgrims in fixed succession; esp. each of those churches in the city of Rome at which 'stations' (see prec. sense) were held, and to the visiting of which on certain days indulgences were attached. Also, a visit to such a holy place, or an assembly held there for purposes of devotion on the appointed day. late ME. **3.** *Stations (of the Cross)*: the series of images or pictures (usually fourteen in number) representing successive incidents of the Passion, placed in a church (or sometimes in the open air) to be visited in order for meditation and prayer; the series of devotional exercises appointed to be used on this occasion 1553. **4.** A special service held at a holy place 1447. **5.** *Hist.* The bi-weekly fast (on Wednesday and Friday) anciently observed 1637. **6.** *Ireland.* A visit of a Roman Catholic parish priest and his curate to the house of a parishioner on a weekday, to give to those in the neighbourhood the opportunity of confession 1830.

Phr. *To go, make, perform one's* (or *the*) *stations, to go on* or *for stations*, to perform the prescribed acts of devotion in succession at certain holy places, or at the Stations of the Cross.

Comb.: **s.-bill** *Naut.*, a list containing the appointed posts of the ship's-company, when navigating the ship; **-hand** *Austral.*, a man employed on a s.; **-line** *Perspective*, the vertical line drawn through the point of sight; **-pointer** *Surveying*, an instrument for placing the observer's position on the chart from angles taken between three objects, the relative positions of which are known; **-staff** *Surveying*, a levelling staff; †**s. time** *Eccl.*, the time when a s. is celebrated.

Station (stēⁱ·ʃən), *v.* 1748. [f. prec. or Fr. *stationner.*] **1.** *trans.* To assign a post, position or station to (a person, troops, ships, etc.); to place or post (a sentinel, etc.) in a station. **b.** To place in a certain position in a list 1865. **c.** *refl.* To take up one's station, post oneself. Also *pass.* Said occas. of a thing. 1780. **2.** *Shipbuilding.* To determine the proper position for (timbers) 1797.

1. The troops stationed near London 1849.

Stational (stēⁱ·ʃənăl), *a.* 1610. [f. STATION *sb.* + -AL¹. Cf. Fr. *stationnal* in the eccl. sense.] Of or pertaining to a station or stations.

Stationary (stēⁱ·ʃənări), *a.* and *sb.* late ME. [– L. *stationarius* (orig. 'belonging to a military station'), f. *statio, -ōn-*; see STATION *sb.*, -ARY¹. Cf. (O)Fr. *stationnaire.*] **A.** *adj.* **1.** Having a fixed station or place. **a.** Not itinerant or migratory 1670. **b.** Not moving 1784. **c.** *Astr.* Said of planets at the portions of their orbits in which they have no apparent motion. late ME. **d.** Having a fixed position. Of a machine, etc.: That remains in one spot when in operation. 1648. **2.** *transf.* Remaining unchanged in condition, quality or quantity; neither advancing nor retrograding 1628. **3.** Of or belonging to a station or stations 1571.

1. A passion for field sports had..kept his brother s. MME. D'ARBLAY. **b.** The sun, being s., could not be said to stand still or to move 1862. *S. air*, the amount of air which remains constantly in the lungs in ordinary respiration. **d.** *S. engines* are used for effecting the ascent and descent of carriages along inclined planes 1840. **2.** It would never do if the world remained s. 1898.

B. *sb.* †**a.** A planet when stationary. HOLLAND. **b.** One of a force of permanent or stationary troops. *Obs.* exc. *Rom. Hist.* 1698. **c.** A politician hostile to progress 1831. Hence **Sta·tionari-ly** *adv.*, **-ness.**

Stationer (stēⁱ·ʃənəɹ). late ME. [– med.L. *stationarius* tradesman having a regular 'station' or shop (i.e. not itinerant), chiefly a bookseller (and 'stationer'); see prec.] **1. a.** A bookseller *Hist.* †**b.** A publishing bookseller, publisher –1673. **2.** A tradesman who sells writing materials, etc. 1656.

The Company of Stationers (or *the Stationers' Company*): one of the Livery Companies of the City of London, founded in 1556, comprising booksellers, bookbinders, and dealers in writing materials, etc. *Stationers' Hall*: the hall of the Stationers' Company, at which a register of copyrights is kept.

Stationery (stēⁱ·ʃənəri). Also †**-ary.** 1727. [f. STATIONER + -Y³.] **1.** The articles sold by a stationer; writing materials, writing-table appurtenances, etc. **2.** *attrib.* as in *s. business, trade, ware* 1679.

2. S. Office, an office in London through which government offices are supplied with s., and which issues the reports, etc. published by the government.

Sta·tion-house. 1836. **1.** The lock-up attached to a police-station 1836. **2.** A railway station; now only, a small country station 1838. **3.** *Austral.* The house belonging to a station 1894.

Stationmaster (stēⁱ·ʃənmāːstəɹ). 1857. [f. STATION *sb.* + MASTER *sb.*] The official who has the control of a railway station. So **Sta·tionmiːstress.**

Statist (stēⁱ·tist). 1584. [– It. *statista*, f. *stato* STATE *sb.*; see -IST. In XVII reinforced by Fr. †*statiste* (XVII).] **1.** A person skilled in state affairs, one having political knowledge, power, or influence; a politician, statesman. Now *arch.* **2.** One who deals with statistics, a statistician 1803.

1. Art thou a S., in the van Of public conflicts trained and bred? WORDSW.

Statistic (stăti·stik), *a.* and *sb.* 1789. [– G. *statistisch* adj., *statistik* sb. (G. Achenwall, 1719–72), whence also Fr. *statistique* – mod.L. *statisticus* (1672), after G. *statist* STATIST.] **A.** *adj.* **1.** = next. Now *rare*. **2.** Of or pertaining to status 1871. **B.** *sb.* **1.** = STATISTICS 1 (*rare*) 1796. **2.** = STATISTICIAN 1804.

Statistical (stăti·stikăl), *a.* 1787. [f. prec. + -AL¹; see -ICAL.] Of or pertaining to statistics, esp. with reference to economic, sanitary, and vital conditions. **b.** Of a writer, etc.: Dealing with statistics 1787.

The..moral and s. features of the period 1841. **b.** Some respectable s. writers 1787. Hence **Stati·stically** *adv.*

Statistician (stætisti·ʃăn). 1825. [f. STATISTIC + -IAN.] One versed in or engaged in collecting and tabulating statistics.

Statistics (stăti·stiks). 1787. [pl. of STATISTIC; see -ICS.] **1.** Construed as *sing.* In early use, that branch of political science dealing with the collection, classification, and discussion of facts bearing on the condition of a state or community. In recent use, the department of study that has for its object the collection and arrangement of numerical facts or data, whether relating to human affairs or to natural phenomena. **2.** Construed as *pl.* Numerical facts or data collected and classified 1837.

Stative (stēⁱ·tiv), *a.* and *sb.* 1631. [– L. *stativus*, f. *stat-*, pa. ppl. stem of *stare* stand; see -IVE.] **A.** *adj.* **1.** Stationary, fixed, having a permanent situation, a fixed recurring date, or the like. Now *Rom. Antiq.* in *s. camp*, etc. **2.** *Heb. Gram.* Epithet of verbs which express a state or condition [= mod.L. *verba stativa*] 1874. **B.** *sb. Heb. Gram.* A stative verb 1874.

Stato- (stæto), repr. Gr. *στατό-ς* standing, used (mainly as virtual comb. form of STATIC, STATICS) in scientific words, chiefly *Biol.*, as **Sta·toblast,** a reproductive gemmule developed in some Polyzoa and Sponges and liberated after the death of the parent organism; hence **Statobla·stic** *a.* **Sta·toscope,** a form of aneroid barometer adapted for recording minute variations of atmospheric pressure.

Stator (stēⁱ·tǫɹ). 1902. [f. *stat-* (as in *stationary*) + -OR 2, after contemp. *rotor.*] **1.** *Electr.* The stationary portion of an electric generator or motor, esp. of an induction motor. **2.** The casing enclosing the revolving blades of a steam turbine 1911.

†**Sta·tua.** late ME. [– L. *statua* STATUE.] = STATUE *sb.* –1691.

I stood A verie S., dull as my owne Mudde 1646.

Statuary (stæ·tiu,ări), *sb.* and *a.* 1563. [– subst. uses of L. *statuarius, -aria* (sc. *ars* art), f. *statua*; see STATUE *sb.*, -ARY¹.] **A.** *sb.* **1.** One who practises the art of making statues 1581. **2.** Sculpture composed of statues, statues collectively. †Also pl., works of sculpture. 1673. **3.** [L. *statuaria*, sc. *ars.*] The art of making statues, sculpture 1563.

1. If Statuaries could By the foote of Hercules set downe punctually His whole dimensions MASSINGER.

B. *adj.* **1.** Of or pertaining to the making of statues 1627. **2.** Consisting of statues or a statue; sculptured 1629. **3.** Of materials: Suitable for statues or statuary work; esp. *s. marble*; *s. vein*, a variety of statuary marble 1815.

Statue (stæ·tiu), *sb.* late ME. [– (O)Fr. *statue* – L. *statua*, f. *stat-*, pa. ppl. stem of *stare* stand.] A representation in the round of a living being, sculptured, moulded or cast in marble, metal, plaster, etc.; esp. a figure of a deity, allegorical personage, or eminent person, usu. of life-size proportions. Also *transf.* and *similative*, as a type of silence or absence of movement or feeling.

And to remember what he does, Build his S. to make him glorious SHAKS. Still as a s...He stood BYRON. Hence **Sta·tueless** *a.*

Statue (stæ·tiu), *v.* 1607. [f. prec.] *trans.* To represent in a statue or in statuary; to honour (a person) by erecting a statue of him. Now only in *nonce-use.*

Statued (stæ·tiūd), *ppl. a.* 1806. [f. STATUE *v.* and *sb.* + -ED.] **1.** Furnished or ornamented with statues or statuary. **2.** Represented in a statue or in statuary 1839.

1. Vased and s. terraces 1806. **2.** The s. satyrs seemed to grin and jibber 1839.

Statuesque (stætiu,e·sk), *a.* 1834. [f. STATUE *sb.* + -ESQUE, after *picturesque.*] Having the qualities of a statue or of sculpture.

The s. native soldiers who stand as sentries 1905. Hence **Statue·sque-ly** *adv.*, **-ness.**

Statuette (stætiue·t). 1843. [– Fr. *statuette*, dim. of *statue*; see STATUE, -ETTE.] A small statue; a statue less than life-size.

Stature (stæ·tiŭɹ, -tʃəɹ), *sb.* ME. [– (O)Fr.

stature – L. *statura*, f. *stat-* (see STATUE) + -*ura* -URE.] **1.** The height of an animal (esp. the human) body in its normal standing position; *transf.* esp. of a tree. †**2.** An effigy, statue –1653.

1. *Two Gent.* IV. iv. 163. *fig.* The men are of meaner moral s. 1875. Hence **Sta·ture** *v.* (*rare* exc. in pa. pple.) *trans.* to give s. to. **Sta·tured** *a.* having (a certain kind of) s.

Status (stēi·tŏs). *Pl.* (*rare*) **status** (stēi·tiūs). 1693. [– L. *status*, f. *stat-* (see prec.).] ‖**1.** *Path.* **a.** The height or acme of a disease. Now *rare* or *Obs.* **b.** Used (with the sense 'state, condition') in many mod.L. combinations with adj., as *s. arthriticus*, *epilepticus*, *lymphaticus*, etc. 1883. **2.** *Law.* The legal standing or position of a person as determined by his membership of some class of persons legally enjoying certain rights or subject to certain limitations; condition in respect, e.g. of infancy or majority. Also applied to things. 1791. **3.** Position or standing in society, a profession, and the like 1820. **4.** Condition of things 1860. **b.** *Finance.* A particular grouping of the conditions bearing on the continuance of an annuity 1838.

2. The legal s. of the Gipsies 1910. The s. of enemy merchant vessels 1914. **4.** The present s. of photography 1889.

‖**Status quo** (stēi·tŏs kwōu·). 1833. [Based on L. phr. *in statu quo ante*, *prius*, or *nunc*.. in the STATE in which (things were) before, (or are) now; see ‖IN 16.] The existing state of things.

Statutable (stæ·tiutăb'l), *a.* 1636. [f. STATUTE *sb.* + -ABLE.] **1.** Prescribed, authorized, or permitted by statute. **2.** Satisfying the requirements of the statutes; †*transf.* of standard quality; that will pass muster 1661. **3.** Recognized by statute; legally punishable 1792.

1. They do not carry with them..any statuteable authority EVELYN. **2.** One s. acre of ground 1758. Hence **Sta·tutably** *adv.*

Statute (stæ·tiūt). ME. [– (O)Fr. *statut* – late L. *statutum* decree, decision, law, subst. use of n. pa. pple. of L. *statuere* set up, establish, decree, f. *status* STATUS.] **I. 1.** A law or decree made by a sovereign or a legislative authority. Now *rare* or *Obs.* in gen. sense. **b.** Applied to an ordinance or decree of God, a deity, fate, etc. late ME. **c.** An enactment made by a corporation for its government. late ME. **2.** An enactment, containing one or more legislative provisions, made by the legislature of a country at one time, and expressed in a formal document; the document in which such an enactment is expressed. late ME. †**b.** *By* (*the*) *s.*: according to the measure, price, or rate appointed by statute –1781. **3.** In international law, [= Fr. *statut personnel*, *réel*] *Personal s.*: the system of law to which an alien party to a process is personally subject, as dist. from *real s.*, the system of law to which the particular transaction is otherwise subject 1907.

1. b. Praysed be thou O Lorde, O teach me thy statutes COVERDALE *Ps.* 118:12. **c.** Oxford..is still governed by the statutes of Archbishop Laud EMERSON. **2.** The famous s., called the Declaration of Right BURKE.

II. Uses originating in ellipsis. †**1.** Applied to certain legal instruments or procedures based on the authority of a statute. **a.** A STATUTE MERCHANT or STATUTE STAPLE –1701. **b.** *S. of bankrupt*, *s. of lunacy*: the process by which a person was declared a bankrupt or a lunatic –1742. **2.** (*sing.* and *pl.*) [Short for †*statute-sessions*.] A fair or gathering held annually in certain towns or villages for the hiring of servants. Also called *statute-fair*, *-hiring*. 1600.

1. a. He that marries her shall give the other a s. upon his estate for two thousand pounds 1701.

III. Misused for STATUE *sb.* late ME.

attrib. and *Comb.*: quasi-*adj.*, with the senses 'fixed by statute', 'recognized by statute', 'statutory'; also *transf.*; as *s.-interest*, *s.-hospitality*, etc.; designating a unit of measure or weight as fixed by statute, as in *s. acre*, *mile*, *ton*, etc. Special comb.: **s.-barred** *a.*, (of debts, claims) barred by the statute of limitations; †**-cap**, the woollen cap ordered by 13 Eliz. c.19 to be worn on Sundays and holy days by all persons not of a certain social or official rank; **s. fair**, **s. hiring** = sense II. 2; **s. labour**, a definite amount of labour on works of public utility, formerly required by statute to be performed by the residents in the district interested; so *s. labourer*; **s. law**, a law contained in a statute; also, the system of law contained in statutes, as dist. from common law; **s. money**, money paid as commutation for statute labour; **-roll**, the roll on which the statutes are engrossed; often = next; **-work** = *s. labour*.

Sta·tute-book. 1648. The book containing the statutes of a nation or state; usu. (*sing.*, occas. *pl.*) the whole series of volumes forming the official record of the statutes. Phr., *on the s.*

Statute merchant. 1442. Now *Hist.* [ellipt. use of **statute of merchants** = med.L. *statutum de mercatoribus* (1285), AFr. *estatut marchand* (XIV), mod.L. *statutum mercatorium*, whence the powers of summary execution of this kind of instrument were derived.] *Law.* A bond of record, acknowledged before the chief magistrate of a trading town, giving to the obligee power of seizure of the land of the obligor if he failed to pay his debt at the appointed time.

Statute staple. 1444. Now *Hist.* [ellipt. use of **statute of the staple**; see STAPLE *sb.*², and cf. prec. In AL. *statutum stapule* (XV).] *Law.* A bond of record, acknowledged before the mayor of the staple, conveying powers similar to those given by the statute merchant.

Statutory (stæ·tiŭtəri), *a.* 1766. [f. STATUTE *sb.* + -ORY².] Pertaining to or consisting in statutes; enacted, created, or appointed by statute; conformable to the provisions of a statute.

S. treason, an offence made treasonable by tatute. *S. declaration*, a declaration in accordance with the Statutory Declaration Act (1835), which substituted simple affirmations for the oaths or solemn affirmations formerly required on certain occasions.

Staunch, stanch (stǭnʃ, stānʃ), *a.* late ME. [– OFr. *estanche*, fem. of *estanc*, used as masc. (mod. *étanche*) – Rom. **stancus*; see STANCH *v.* In British use the spelling *staunch* is the more common for the adj., *stanch* for the vb.] **1.** Impervious to water, not leaking; water-tight. Also occas. air-tight. **2.** Of strong or firm construction, in good or firm condition, substantial 1455. **3.** Of a sporting dog: That may be trusted to find or follow the scent, or to mark the game; dependable 1576. **4.** Of a person: Standing firm to one's principles or purpose, not to be turned aside, determined 1623. **b.** Of personal qualities, actions, etc.: Showing determination or resolution, unwavering 1690.

1. Our ship was staunch, and our Crew all in good Health SWIFT. **2.** The wall of the tower is still stanch and strong HAWTHORNE. **3.** A dog that..is stanch on a covey 1883. **4.** In Politicks, I hear, you'r stanch PRIOR. Hence **Sta(u)·nchly** *adv.* **Sta(u)·nchness.**

Stauro- (stǭ·ro, stǭrǫ·), bef. a vowel **staur-**, comb. form of Gr. σταυρός cross.

Staurolite (stǭ·rŏləit). 1815. [– Fr. *staurolite* (Delamétherie 1792); see prec., -LITE.] Silicate of aluminium and iron, found frequently in cruciform twins. Hence **Stauroli·tic** *a.*

Stauroscope (stǭ·roskōup). 1875. [f. Gr. σταυρός cross (see STAURO-) + -SCOPE.] An instrument used for the microscopic examination of rocks. Hence **Staurosco·pic** *a.*

Staurotide (stǭ·rotəid). 1802. [– Fr. *staurotide* (Haüy, 1801), app. f. Gr. σταυρωτός cruciform, f. σταυρός cross; the suffix is erron. for -ITE¹ 2b.] *Min.* = STAUROLITE.

Stave (stēiv), *sb.* ME. [A back-formation from *staves*, pl. of STAFF *sb.*] **I. 1.** Each of the thin, narrow, shaped pieces of wood which, when placed together side by side and hooped, collectively form the side of a cask, tub or the like. **2.** A rod, bar, pole or the like; e.g. a rung (of a ladder); a cross bar to the legs of a chair. *local.* ME. **II. 1.** A 'verse' or stanza of a poem, song, etc. 1659. **2.** *Mus.* A set of lines for musical notation 1800.

II. 1. Phr. *To tip* (a person) *a s.*, to sing a song to; *joc.*, to send a line to.

Stave (stēiv), *v.* Pa. t. and pa. pple. **staved**; also (chiefly *Naut.*) †**stove.** 1595. [f. prec.] **1.** *trans.* To break up (a cask) into staves; to break into and let out the contents. **b.** To destroy (wine, etc.) by breaking up the cask 1615. **2.** *trans.* To break a hole in (a boat); to break *to pieces*; also, to break (a hole in a boat). *To s. in*, to crush inwards, make a hole in. 1628. **b.** *intr.* for *refl.* of a boat: To break up; hence *trans.* to break a hole in 1743. **3.** *transf.* (*trans.*) To burst in, crush inwards. Chiefly with *in*. 1716. **4.** To renew the staves of (a bucket); to put together the staves of (a cask, etc.) 1627. **5.** To drive off or beat with a staff or stave; esp. in *to s. off*, to beat off (a dog in bear- or bull-baiting; also *transf.* a human combatant); to keep back (a crowd). Now *arch.* 1609. **6.** *fig.* Chiefly *to s. off*. †**a.** To keep (a person) *from* (doing something); to divert *from* (an object, practice, etc.) –1684. **b.** To put off as importune or inopportune; to treat with evasion 1646. **c.** To ward off (something undesirable or hurtful); to prevent the occurrence or event of; to keep back, delay 1662. **7.** *intr.* To go with a rush or dash; to 'drive'. *Sc.* and *U.S.* 1819. **8.** *Forging.* To thicken (bar-iron) by heating and hammering, to UPSET. Also *absol.* **b.** *intr.* Of the iron: To undergo staving 1906.

1. Hogsheads of French wine..were publickly staved 1679. **b.** He..staves all prohibited goods 1694. **2.** A sea..stove in the quarter gallery 1748. **b.** Like a vessel of glass, she stove and sank LONGF. **3.** To break open and s. trunks and chests 1753. **5.** S. off the crowd upon the Spaniard there TENNYSON. **6. b.** This staved the fellows off for a while 1887. **c.** A little fish sufficed to s. off hunger 1879.

Staved (stēivd), *ppl. a.* 1481. [f. STAVE *v.* or *sb.* + -ED.] **1.** Furnished with a stave or staves. **b.** Of a ladder: Furnished with rungs 1603. **c.** *Arch.* Of a column: Having a round convex moulding or bead in the lower part of the fluting 1664. **2.** Broken; also *s. in* 1699. **4.** *Forging.* Thickened by hammering 1906.

Stavesacre (stēi·vzēi:kəɪ). late ME. [– L. *staphisagria* – Gr. σταφὶς ἀγρία wild raisin.] A ranunculaceous plant of the species *Delphinium staphisagria*, native in Southern Europe and Asia Minor; the seeds of this plant, used to destroy vermin, and formerly as an emetic.

Staving (stēi·viŋ), *vbl. sb.* 1491. [f. STAVE *v.* and *sb.* + -ING¹.] **1.** The action of STAVE *v.* 1633. **2.** Staves collectively 1491.

Stay (stēi), *sb.*¹ [Late OE. *stæġ*, corresp. to MLG. *stach*, Du. *stag* (whence G. *stag*), ON. *stag* :– Gmc. **staʒa-*, f. **staʒ-* **stax-* be firm (see STEEL).] *Naut.* A large rope used to support a mast, and leading from its head down to some other mast or spar, or to some part of the ship. **b.** *transf.* A guy or rope supporting a flagstaff, or a pole of any kind 1533.

Phrases. *In stays*, said of a ship when her head is being turned to windward for the purpose of tacking. *To miss*, *lose stays*, of a ship, to fail in the attempt to go about. See *also* BACKSTAY, FORESTAY.

Comb.: **s.-block**, a block buried in the ground as an attachment for the s. of a telegraph pole; **-tackle**, a large tackle attached to the mainstay, and used to hoist heavy bodies in and out of the ship; **-wire**, a wire forming part of a s. for a telegraph pole.

Stay (stēi), *sb.*² 1515. [Partly – OFr. *estaye* (mod. *étai*), partly f. STAY *v.*²] **1.** Something that supports or steadies something else; esp. an appliance for holding up or securing in position some part of a structure; a prop, pedestal, bracket, buttress, or the like. **b.** *fig.* A thing or a person that affords support; an object of reliance. Also, in abstract sense: Support. 1530. **2.** *spec.* Applied to various kinds of supports in technical and mechanical use 1577. **3.** *pl.* (Also *pair of stays.*) = CORSET 2. Rarely in *sing.* 1608.

1. b. From that hour Gerard was looked upon as the s. of the family READE. **3.** The s. he has an invincible aversion to 1731. The deceased died of apoplexy, produced by her stays being too tightly laced 1831.

Comb.: **s.-bar**, a bar for keeping a casement window open at a certain angle; **-bolt**, a bolt connecting plates of a boiler, to secure them against internal pressure; **-rod**, a rod serving to give support, or to connect two parts of a machine or structure to prevent displacement. Hence **Stayed** *a.* provided with stays.

Stay (stēi), *sb.*³ 1525. [f. STAY *v.*¹] **1.** The action of stopping or bringing to a stand or pause; the fact of being brought to a stand or delayed; a stoppage, or suspension of action;

a check, set-back 1537. **b.** *Law.* Suspension of a judicial proceeding 1542. †**2.** Control; restraint; self-control –1622. **3.** A coming to a stand; a cessation of progress or action; a pause, halt 1530. †**4.** Delay, postponement, waiting –1707. †**5.** A cause of stoppage; an obstacle, hindrance –1665. †**b.** A demur, hesitation, scruple –1567. **6.** The action or fact of staying in a place, continued presence; an instance of this, a sojourn 1538. †**b.** Continuance in a state, duration –1700. **c.** Staying power. Now *rare.* 1586. **7.** A stationary condition, a standstill. Now *arch.* 1525.

1. A conqueror who no s. will brook 1862. **b.** The prisoner's counsel then moved for a s. of execution 1856. **3.** Trauailing both day and night without any rest or s. 1585. **5.** Not grudging, that thy lust hath bounds and staies G. HERBERT. **6.** Her s. in London was longer than mine in Paris 1789. **b.** Alas, what s. is there in human state DRYDEN. **7.** Man that is borne of a woman..neuer continueth in one staye *Bk. Com. Prayer, Burial of Dead.* Phr. †*To set in* or *at s.*, to settle. Also *to set a s.*, *to set stays*, to settle matters.

Stay (stē^{i}), *v.*[1] Pa. t. and pa. pple. **stayed** (stē^{i}d), †**staid.** 1440. [prob. – AFr. pres. stem *estai-*, *estei-* of OFr. *ester* :– L. *stare* STAND.] **I.** *intr.* *To cease moving, halt. †**1.** To cease going forward; to stop, halt; to arrest one's course and stand still –1777. **b.** To stop, halt, pause *and* (do something), or in order *to* (do something). Now *rare.* 1577. **2.** To cease or desist from some specified activity. *Obs.* or *arch.* 1576. **b.** In *imper.* used as an injunction to pause, arrest one's course, not to go on doing something. Hence often = give me time to consider, decide, etc.; wait for me to make some remark or give some order 1590. **3.** Of an action, activity, process, etc.: To be arrested, to stop at a certain point, not to go forward. *Obs.* or *arch.* 1563.

1. And the Sunne stood still, and the Moone stayed, vntill the people had auenged themselues vpon their enemies *Josh.* 10:13. **2.** He hearkned, and did s. from further harmes SPENSER. **b.** S., stand apart, I know not which is which SHAKS. S., there is one way FIELDING. **3.** Neither did the matter s. here 1570.

To remain stationary. **4. To remain in a place or in others' company (as opp. to going on or going away) 1575. **b.** With inf.: To remain in order *to* (do something). Also *to s. to* (dinner, etc.). 1591. **c.** Const. *for*: To await in a place, remain to take part in or witness 1554. **5.** Of a thing: To remain (in a place or position); to remain (as opp. to being lost, changing its nature, etc.). Now *rare.* 1593. **b.** Of food, etc.: To be retained by the stomach after swallowing 1643. **6.** With predicative extension: To remain in the specified condition 1573. **7.** With emphasis or contextual colouring: **a.** To delay (as opp. to going on). Chiefly with neg. 1500. **b.** To stand one's ground. Now *rare.* 1593. **8.** To reside or sojourn in a place for a longer or shorter period; to put up *with* a person as his guest 1554. †**9.** To remain inactive or quiet; to wait; to put off action (*until*) –1751. **10.** *Sport.* To last or hold out in a race or run. Also, to hold out for (a specified distance). 1834. **11.** *Poker.* To remain *in* the game when the ante has been raised; so *to s.* out 1882.

4. He comes for half an hour, and stays an hour RICHARDSON. I wish you would s. and talk 1885. **5.** A lesson learned with stroakes, staies with the scholler 1593. **6.** I can bend them up and down and they s. bent RUSKIN. *To s. put* (orig. U.S.): see PUT *v.*[1] II. a. **7.** And Ionathan cryed after the ladde, Make speed, haste, stay not 1 *Sam.* 20:38. **b.** And giue them leaue to flye, that will not s. SHAKS. **8.** He stayed at Rippon one night 1617. While she staid with her uncle 1823. Phr. *To come to s.*, to become permanent or established, to come into regular use or recognition; to assume a secure position in public favour (*colloq.*) **9.** Madam: dinner is ready, and your father staies SHAKS. **10.** [Alcohol] may enable a man 'to spurt' but not 'to s.' 1897.

II. quasi-*trans.* and *trans.* uses derived from I. **1.** quasi-*trans.* To remain for, to remain and participate in or assist at (a meal, ceremony, prayers, etc.); to remain throughout or during (a period of time) 1570. **2.** quasi-*trans.* with *out.* To remain to the end of; to remain and witness the end of. Also, to outstay. 1639. **3.** *trans.* To wait for, await (a person, his coming, an event, etc.); to wait upon, serve (a person's leisure); to abide, sustain (a question, onset). Now *arch.* 1586.

1. I stay'd ye sermon 1661. I'm obliged to ask them to s. tea 1888. **2.** It seemed as if we had stayed our English welcome out HAWTHORNE. **3.** They basely flie and dare not s. the field SHAKS.

III. *trans.* To stop, arrest, check. **1.** To detain, hold back, stop (a person or thing); to hinder from going on or going away; to keep in a fixed place or position. Now *literary.* 1440. **2.** To render motionless or keep immovable; to fix, hold fast 1627. **3.** To prevent, hinder, stop (a person or thing) from doing something; to check, restrain; esp. *to s.* (one's own or another's) *hand* (chiefly *fig.*), to cease or cause to cease from attack or working). Now *arch.* 1560. **4.** To stop, arrest, delay, prevent (an action or process, something which is begun or intended). Freq. in legal parlance. 1525. **b.** To arrest the course or growth of (a disease, something noxious or destructive) 1563. **5.** To leave off, discontinue (doing something, an activity of one's own). Also, to delay, withhold (one's good opinion, thanks). Now *rare* or *Obs.* 1538. **6.** To appease, allay (strife, tumult); to bring under control (rebellious elements). Now *rare.* 1537. **7.** *To s. the stomach*: to stave off hunger. Similarly *to s. one's longing, hunger, appetite,* etc. 1608.

1. And here shal it staye thy proud waues BIBLE (Geneva) *Job.* 38:11. The wet and uncomfortable weather staying us from church EVELYN. **2.** Each Galley doe foure anchors s. 1627. **3.** Rivers are dried, winds stay'd M. ARNOLD. My tongue is tied and my hand is stayed 1880. **4.** I do order.. that until such indemnity be given all further proceedings be stayed 1856. **b.** That the plague may be stayed from the people 2 *Sam.* 24:21. **5.** S. your Thanks a while, And pay them when you part SHAKS. **6.** Old men..Bless'd him who staid the civil strife SCOTT.

Stay (stē^{i}), *v.*[2] Pa. t. and pa. pple. **stayed** (stē^{i}d). 1526. [– OFr. *estayer* (mod. *étayer*), of Gmc. origin; cf. STAY *sb.*[1]] **1.** *trans.* To support, sustain, hold up (a person or thing). Const. *on, upon,* †*unto.* Now chiefly in sense 3. Also *transf.* and *fig.*, to strengthen, comfort. **2.** *fig.* To cause to rest *on, upon* or *in* (a firm support, base or ground); to base or ground *upon*, set firmly *in* 1565. †**b.** *refl.* with *upon*: To rely or build upon, rest or act upon; to abide by; to content oneself with –1709. **3.** (*spec.* and *techn.*) To support, strengthen or secure with stays. Also with *up.* 1556.

1. Because on the bones of the English the English Flag is stayed KIPLING. **2.** Thou wilt keepe him in perfect peace, whose minde is stayed on thee *Isa.* 26:3. **b.** They..staie them selues vpon the God of Israel BIBLE (Geneva) *Isa.* 48:2. **3.** Watch an old building with anxious care..s. it with timber where it declines RUSKIN.

†**To s. on, upon. a.** *intr.* To lean upon, support oneself by (a staff, etc.); of a thing, to be supported by. **b.** To trust to, have confidence in; to depend on. Hence **Stayed** *ppl. a.*, **-ness.**

Stay, *v.*[3] Pa. t. and pple. **stayed** (stē^{i}d). 1613. [f. STAY *sb.*[1]] *Naut.* **1.** *trans.* To secure or steady by means of stays; to incline (forward, aft, or to one side) by means of stays 1627. **2.** To put (a ship) 'in stays'; to put on the other tack 1625. **3.** *intr.* To go about in stays; to turn to windward in order to tack 1613.

Stay-at-home, *a.* and *sb.* 1806. [f. STAY *v.*[1]] **A.** *adj.* That stays at home, not given to travelling or to gadding abroad; hence untravelled. **B.** *sb.* One who stays at home 1841.

Stayer[1] (stē^{i}·əɹ), 1591. [f. STAY *v.*[1] + -ER[1].] **1.** One who stays or remains. **b.** *Sport.* A person or animal having great staying power 1862. **2.** One who or something which stops or restrains 1597.

Stayer[2] (stē^{i}·əɹ). 1579. [f. STAY *v.*[2] + -ER[1].] One who stays or supports. **b.** With reference to the title of Jupiter Stator 1611.

b. Thou Iupiter, whom we do call the S. Both of this Citie, and this Empire B. JONS.

Staying (stē^{i}·iŋ), *vbl. sb.* 1546. [f. STAY *v.*[1] + -ING[1].] The action of STAY *v.*[1] in various senses.

Comb.: **s. power**, in a race or other contest, power to 'stay' or continue in action for a long time; power of persistent effort; hence *gen.*

Staylace (stē^{i}·le^{i}s), *sb.* 1720. [f. STAY *sb.*[2] + LACE *sb.*] A lace or cord used to draw together a woman's stays or bodice. Hence **Stay·lace** *v. trans.* to lace up with staylaces.

Stayless (stē^{i}·lės), *a.*[1] 1572. [f. STAY *sb.*[3] + -LESS.] **1.** Not to be stayed or stopped, ceaseless 1578. **2.** Without stay or permanence, ever-changing 1572.

Stay·less, *a.*[2] 1587. [f. STAY *sb.*[2] + -LESS.] **1.** Without stay or support. **2.** Unsupported by stays or corsets 1880.

Staysail (stē^{i}·se^{i}l, stē^{i}·s'l). 1669. [f. STAY *sb.*[1]] *Naut.* A triangular sail hoisted upon a stay.

Stay-ship (stē^{i}·ʃip). 1567. [f. STAY *v.*[1]] = REMORA.

Stay-tape. 1698. [STAY *sb.*[2]] Tape used by tailors as a support or binding.

‖**Stchi** (ʃtʃī). 1833. [Russ. *shchi.*] Cabbage soup.

Stead (sted), *sb.* [OE. *stede*, corresp. to OFris. *stede*, OS. *stad, stedi* (MLG. *stad, stede* place, town), MDu. *stad, stede*, OHG. *stat* (G. *statt* place, *stätte* place, site, *stadt* town), ON. *staðr*, Goth. *staþs* place :– Gmc. **staðiz* :– IE. **st(h)ətis*, f. **st(h)ə-* **st(h)a-* STAND.] **I.** A point or tract in space. †**1.** A locality; = PLACE *sb.* 2. –1596. †**2.** An inhabited place –1577. †**b. The Steads** [= MLG. *de Steden*]: the Hanse Towns. Also, the corporation of Hanse merchants in London. –1558. **3.** Chiefly with *possessive.* The place assigned to, belonging to, or normally occupied by a thing; appointed or natural place; †a seat. *Obs.* exc. *arch.* OE. †**b.** The place where a body of soldiers is stationed; a military position –1627. **4.** A property or estate in land; a farm ME. **5.** A site for a building; the land on which a building stands. (Cf. *farmstead*, etc.) ME. †**6.** The framework which supports the bedding of a bed. (Cf. BEDSTEAD.) –1858.

1. Great God it planted in that blessed sted With his almightie hand SPENSER. **3.** The mast in its s. we 'stablished and hauled the sails in air MORRIS. **5.** Messuage steads and cottage steads 1773.

II. The place, 'room', 'lieu', or function (of a person or thing) as held by a substitute or a successor. Only in certain phrases. ME.

Phr. *In the s. of* (now *arch.*), (*a*) in the room of, in succession to (one who has died, has retired from or is superseded in an office); (*b*) in lieu of; (*c*) predicatively, *to be in the s. of*, to make up for the want of. *In his*, etc., *s.* (now literary), (*a*) as a successor in his room; (*b*) as his deputy or representative (*arch.*); (*c*) instead of him.

III. Advantage, profit, service, support; esp. in *to stand in s.*; *to do s.* Now *arch.* ME.

Stead (sted), *v.* ME. [f. prec.] **I.** To stand in stead. **1.** *trans.* **a.** *impers.* or with subj. clause, inf., etc.: To avail, profit, be of use to (a person). Also *absol.* Now *arch.* **b.** Of a thing: To be useful or advantageous to. Also *absol.* Now *arch.* (*rare*). 1594. **c.** With subj. a person: To succour, help, render service to. Now *rare.* 1582. †**2.** *To s. up*: to fulfil in the stead of another. SHAKS.

1. a. So it steed you, I will write..a thousand times as much SHAKS. **b.** No adjectives would s. me 1891. **c.** It's like I may pleasure you, and s. your father in his extremity SCOTT. **2.** *Meas. for M.* III. i. 260.

II. To place. †**1.** To establish, fix, place. Chiefly *pass.*, to be situated, stand –1821. †**2.** *pass.* To be placed *in* a certain (evil or difficult) plight or condition; to be burdened *with* (sickness), beset *with* (enemies, etc.) –1818.

1. But it is done..To honour thee..To s. thee as a verse in English tongue KEATS. **2.** Sen we are stad with enemys on ilk syd 1470. We are cruelly sted between God's laws and man's laws SCOTT.

Steadfast (ste·dfăst), *a.* (*adv.*) [OE. *stedefæst*, f. *stede* (see STEAD *sb.*) + *fæst* FAST *a.*] **A.** *adj.* **1.** Fixed or secure in position. Of a person, esp. a soldier in battle: Maintaining his ground. **c.** Of a foundation, etc.: Firmly fixed OE. **2.** Of persons: Unshaken, immovable in faith, resolution, friendship, etc. Also said of belief, purpose, or affection. ME. †**b.** Applied to God: Unchanging –1611. **3.** Of a law, a treaty, an institution, a condition of things: Firmly settled, established, unchangeable ME. **4.** Of sight, the eye (occas. of the mind): Steadily directed ME.

1. These Elements In mutinie had from her Axle torn The stedfast Earth MILT. **2.** COVERDALE *Prov.* 12:4. **b.** *Dan.* 6:26. **4.** MILT. *Hymn Nativ.* 70.

†**B.** *adv.* Steadfastly –1887. Hence **Stea·dfast-ly** *adv.*, **-ness.**

Steading (ste·diŋ). *Sc.* and *north.* 1472. [f. STEAD *sb.* + -ING¹.] **1.** A farm-house and outbuildings; the outbuildings in contrast to the farm-house. **2.** A site for a building 1822.

Stea·dy, *sb.* 1792. [f. STEADY *a.* and *v.*] **1.** Something which is steady or which steadies. **2.** *U.S. slang.* A regular sweetheart 1900.

Steady (ste·di), *a.* (and *adv.*) 1530. [f. STEAD *sb.* + -Y¹, after MLG., MDu. *stēdig*, *stādig* stable, constant.] **A.** *adj.* †**1.** Fixed or immovable in position; not liable to give way or become displaced –1683. **b.** Of affairs: Stable. Of a rule, etc.: Settled, established. 1571. **2.** Firm in standing or movement; not tottering, rocking, or shaking; that is in stable equilibrium 1574. **3.** Of a person or his mind: Not easily perturbed or discomposed; balanced. Of the head: Free from giddiness. Of the eye: Not diverted from its object; unwavering. 1602. **b.** Of troops, their attributes or actions: Firm, disciplined; not liable to panic or loss of self-control. Also *ellipt.* = 'be steady'. 1670. **c.** Of a hound: Not easily diverted from the scent. Of a horse: Not nervous, skittish, or excitable; also, that travels at a moderate and even pace. 1735. **4.** Regular in operation or intensity; uniform, equable 1548. **b.** Of weather, temperature: Free from sudden changes, settled. Of climate: Having little variation of temperature. Hence said of an instrument for recording variations of weather. 1700. **c.** *Comm.* Of prices: Free from sudden rise or fall; hence of the market, goods, shares, etc. 1889. **5.** Persistent, unwavering in resolution, attachment, or in a course of action; persistently devoted *to* a cause, etc. 1602. **6.** Not given to frivolity; staid 1759. **7.** Regular in habits; not given to dissipation or looseness in conduct 1832.

1. b. Their union should be deferred no longer than until Butler should obtain some s. means of support SCOTT. **2.** The hand that held the candle was as s. as a rock 1865. **3.** With folded arms and s. eyes SHELLEY. **b.** They're coming up: s., boys; s. now LEVER. **c.** As a rule, there were four s. horses and a good driver, rarely drunk RUSKIN. **4.** There was a s. trade in all descriptions of barley 1855. The s. rise in the price of wool 1874. **c.** Glorious s. weather EVELYN. **d.** Corn opened s. 1896. **5.** A trusty counsellor and s. friend SMOLLETT. Their own serious and s. attachment to the laws 1818. **6.** A very grave, s. person 1818. Hence **Stea·di-ly** *adv.*, **-ness.**

B. *adv.* In a steady manner, steadily. Chiefly *Naut.* 1605. **b.** *ellipt.* Chiefly *Naut.* = 'steer steady' 1620. **c.** *Comb.*, as *steady-going* adj.

Steady (ste·di), *v.* 1530. [f. STEADY *a.*] **1.** *trans.* To keep from rocking, shaking, tottering, or similar movement. **b.** To keep from falling 1848. **c.** *intr.* for *refl.* 1849. **2.** *trans.* To make (one's mind, troops, etc.) steady 1530. **3.** *Naut.* To keep (a vessel) to the direct line of her course. Also *absol.* and *intr.* for *refl.* 1627. **4.** To bring to a more regular rate of progress. Also *intr.* for *refl.* 1812. **5.** To keep (a person) from irregularity of conduct. Also *intr.* for *refl.*; also with *down.* 1848. **6.** *Comm. intr.* To become more free from fluctuation; also with *up* 1913.

1. The chronic drunkard, who takes a glass of spirits to 's. the hand' 1899. **3.** She doth not tack from side to side..Withouten wind, withouten tide She steddies with upright keel COLERIDGE. **5.** He breaks off..from folly;..he steadies down 1848. Hence **Stea·dy** *sb.* something which is steady; something which steadies, *spec.* a device for holding steady an object in process of being fashioned. **Stea·diment,** a means of studying steady conditions.

Steak (stēⁱk). late ME. [– ON. *steik*, rel. to *steikja* roast on a spit, *stikna* be roasted.] A thick slice or strip of meat cut for grilling, frying, or stewing, sometimes used in a pie or pudding; esp. a piece cut from the hind quarters of the animal; without qualification = BEEF-STEAK. **b.** A thick slice (of cod, salmon, halibut, or hake) 1883. **c.** *transf.* and *fig.* Now *rare* or *Obs.* 1607.

Steal (stīl), *sb.*¹ *Obs.* exc. *dial.* [OE. *stela*, f. OTeut. **stel-*, ablaut-var. of **stal-*, whence STALE *sb.*¹] **1.** The stalk or stem of a plant, leaf, flower, or fruit. **2.** The handle of a tool or utensil (e.g. a hammer, pot, spoon). late ME.

Steal (stīl), *sb.*² 1825. [f. STEAL *v.*] **1.** The, or an, act of stealing; a theft; the thing stolen. Chiefly *U.S. colloq.* **b.** *U.S.* and *Colonial.* A piece of dishonesty or fraud on a large scale; a corrupt or fraudulent transaction in politics 1884. **3. a.** *Golf.* 'A long putt holed unexpectedly.' **b.** *Base-ball.* A stolen run from one base to another. 1842.

Steal (stīl), *v.* Pa. t. **stole** (stōᵘl), †**stale.** Pa. pple. **stolen** (stōᵘ·lən). [OE. *stelan* = OFris. *stela*, OS., OHG. *stelan* (Du. *stelen*, G. *stehlen*), ON. *stela*, Goth. *stilan*, f. Gmc. **stel-* **stæl-* **stul-*, of unkn. origin. *Stole* has been the accepted form of the pa. t. since XVII.] **I.** To take dishonestly or secretly. **1.** *trans.* To take away dishonestly (portable property, cattle, etc., belonging to another); *esp.* to do this secretly or unobserved by the owner or the person in charge. **b.** In wider sense: To take or appropriate dishonestly (anything belonging to another, whether material or immaterial) ME. **c.** *esp.* To plagiarize; to 'borrow' improperly (words, expressions). Also *absol.* 1544. **2.** *absol.* or *intr.* To commit or practise theft OE. **3.** *trans.* To take (*away*) by stratagem or by eluding observation (something that is in the possession or keeping of another) OE. **b.** To carry off, abduct, kidnap (a person) secretly. Now *rare.* late ME. **4.** With immaterial obj. **a.** To cause the loss of, take away (e.g. happiness, a person's life, etc.). late ME. **b.** To take without permission (esp. a kiss). late ME. **c.** To take (time) by contrivance *from* its ordinary employment, sleep, etc. to devote to some other purpose 1526. **d.** To gain possession of, or to entice away (a person's heart, affections, etc.) 1526. **5.** To effect or accomplish clandestinely or unperceived 1625. **b.** To direct (a look), breathe (a sigh) furtively 1586. **6.** To place, move, or convey stealthily. Now somewhat *rare.* ME. **b.** Of a hen: To make (her nest) in a concealed place 1854.

1. Yes; I stole money from Philemon, my beloved master 1891. **b.** No man like you for stealing other men's inventions SCOTT. **c.** It was stolen as Phidias stole from Homer 1841. **2.** To give short weight or measure, is to s. 1871. **3.** Thou who stealest fire From the fountains of the past TENNYSON. **4. a.** How soon hath Time the suttle theef of youth Stoln on his wing my three and twentith yeer! MILT. **c.** They must frequently s. an hour to converse with him whom they love 1758. **d.** So did she steale his heedelesse hart away SPENSER. **5.** He did not s. an interview 1857. *S. runs*, to get a run for a hit, when no run seems reasonably possible 1897. †*To s. a marriage*, to get married secretly. *To s. a march*, Mil. to succeed in moving troops without the knowledge of the enemy; hence *gen.* to get a secret advantage over a rival or opponent. **b.** And, now and then, a Sigh he stole DRYDEN. **6.** Slily s. thy bonnet on,..And wander out with me CLARE.

II. To go secretly or quietly. †**1.** *refl.* To withdraw oneself secretly or quietly. Chiefly with *away.* –1725. **2.** *intr.* To depart or withdraw secretly or surreptitiously from a place ME. **b.** With advb. accus., *to s. one's way.* Now *rare.* late ME. **c.** Hunting. *To s. away.* Of a hunted animal: To leave its lair unperceived and gain a start of the pursuers. late ME. **3.** To go or come secretly or stealthily; to walk or creep softly so as to avoid observation ME. **b.** To come stealthily *on* or *upon* a person for the purpose of attack or injury ME. **4.** Of things. **a.** Of time (with *on, away*): To come or go unobserved. late ME. **b.** Of a condition, esp. sleep, infirmities, etc.: To come insensibly *over* or *on* a person. late ME. **c.** Of a stream, tears, a body of vapour, a ship, etc.: To glide, or move gently or almost imperceptibly 1626. **d.** Of sound, fragrance, light: To become gradually perceptible. Const. *on, upon* (the sense). 1634. †**e.** To develop by insensible degrees *from*; to change insensibly *into, to* something else –1826.

2. Other Captains secretly stole home FULLER. **c.** There was a rustle amongst the long grass, and a fine dog fox..stole away 1872. **3.** Her feet beneath her petticoat, Like little mice stole in and out SUCKLING. *fig.* Calm, independent, let me s. thro' life 1763. **b.** The cat that steals on her prey SCOTT. **4. a.** The houre steales on, I pray you sir dispatch SHAKS. **b.** A kind of pleasant stupor was stealing over me C. BRONTË. **c.** The white ships swim, And s. to havens far R. BRIDGES. **e.** A bright sun-shiny afternoon was stealing into twilight DISRAELI. Hence **Stea·ling** *vbl. sb.* the action of the vb.; concr. in *pl.* gains made by stealing. **Stea·lingly** *adv.* stealthily, furtively (now *rare*).

Stealer¹ (stī·ləɹ). 1500. [f. STEAL *v.* + -ER¹.] One who steals; now only, one who steals something specified.

Stealer² (stī·ləɹ). Also **steeler.** 1805. [The same word as prec.] *Shipbuilding.* The foremost or aftmost plank in a strake, which is dropped short of the stem or stern-post.

Stealth (ste·lþ). [ME. *stalþ, stelþ*, repr. OE. **stælþ*, f. Gmc. **stæl-*; see STEAL *v.*, -TH¹.] †**1.** The action or practice of stealing; theft –1781. †**b.** An instance of stealing; a theft –1797. †**c.** Plagiarism –1653. †**d.** Cunning thievishness. SHAKS. †**2.** Something stolen; something to steal; plunder –1655. †**3.** The action of stealing into or out of a place; the action of stealing or gliding along unperceived –1788. †**4.** Furtive or underhand action; an act accomplished by eluding observation or discovery –1797. **5.** *By s.* †**a.** With ref. to taking: By an act of theft; secretly and without right or permission. **b.** In mod. use: Secretly, clandestinely. late ME.

1. Safeguarded from sand and s., by a defensive wall 1638. **2.** Next morning he was apprehended with his stealths about him 1638. **3.** I told him of your s. vnto this wood SHAKS. **4.** *Meas. for M.* I. ii. 158. Hence **Stea·lthful** *a.* (*poet.*) stealthy; **-ly** *adv.*

Stealthy (ste·lþi), *a.* 1605. [f. prec. + -Y¹.] Of movement or action: Taking place by stealth; proceeding by imperceptible degrees; furtive. Of persons or things: Moving or acting by stealth or secretly; stealing on by imperceptible degrees.

Wither'd Murder..With his s. pace..towards his designe Moues like a Ghost SHAKS. Hence **Stea·lthily** *adv.* **Stea·lthiness.**

Steam (stīm), *sb.* [OE. *stēam* = WFris. *steam*, Du. *stoom* :– Gmc. **staumaz*, of unkn. origin.] **1.** A vapour or fume given out by a substance when heated or burned. **b.** *spec.* An odorous exhalation or fume OE. †**2.** A vapour or exhalation produced as an 'excrement' of the body, e.g. hot breath, perspiration, etc. –1731. **b.** Close and hot air arising from persons crowded together. *arch.* 1609. **3.** An exhalation or watery vapour rising from the earth or sea 1612. †**4.** Matter in the state of gas or vapour; any impalpable emanation or effluvium –1704. **5.** The vapour into which water is converted when heated. In pop. language, applied to the visible vapour which floats in the air in the form of a white cloud or mist. (Also occas. applied to the vapour arising from other liquids when heated.) In mod. scientific and techn. language, applied only to water in the form of an invisible gas. 1440. **6.** The vapour of boiling water used, by confinement in specially contrived engines, for the generation of mechanical power. Hence, the mechanical power thus generated. 1699. **b.** *fig.* Energy, 'go', driving power, and the like 1826. **7.** Short for *s.-coal* 1897.

1. b. The savoury steams of roast and stew.. pervaded the mansion 1827. **2. b.** The dust and din and s. of town TENNYSON. **3.** The Steams and Damps of Mines are detrimental to Health 1695. **5.** *Dry s.*, in Steam-engine working, steam containing no suspended vesicles of water; opp. to *wet s.* **6.** Phrases. *By s.*, (to travel) by steamer. *Under s.*, worked by steam (as opp. to *under sail*). (*At*) *full, half*, etc. *s.*; *with full* or *all one's s. on*; *to have* (all, much, etc.) *s. on*; *to get up, put on s.*; *to blow off, shut off, turn off s.* *Under s., with s. up, in s.*, with the engine working or ready to start working. **b.** Phr. *to get up s.*; *to put on, let off, work off s.*

attrib. and *Comb.*: with reference to operations performed by s., contrivances for managing s. in a steam-engine, or locomotion by s.-power, as *s. chamber, cock, gauge, laundry, packet, tram*; **s.-boiler,** a vessel in which water is heated to generate s., esp. for working a steam-engine; **-car,** a car driven or drawn by s., e.g. a motor-car worked by s. instead of petrol; *U.S.* a railway-carriage; †**-carriage,** a carriage driven or drawn by s.; **-coal,** coal suitable for heating water in s.-boilers; **-colour,** a colour developed and fixed in the cloth by steaming; **-jacket,** a jacket or casing filled with steam in order to preserve the heat of the vessel round which it is placed; **-kettle,** a kettle used in sick-rooms to create a moist warm atmosphere; **-navvy,** a machine for digging or excavating by s.; **-organ,** = CALLIOPE; **-road,** a road prepared for s.-traction; *U.S.* a railroad; **-room, -space,** the space above the water-level in a s.-boiler; **-tight** *a.*, tight enough to resist the ingress or egress of s.; also quasi-*adv.*; **-tug,** a s.-boat specially constructed for towing vessels; **-vessel,** †(*a*) a vessel for holding s.; (*b*) a steamboat or steamship; **†-wheel,** the rotary steam-engine; **-whistle,** a powerful whistle worked by a jet of s. (usu. from a s.-boiler), used as a signal.

Steam (stīm), *v.* [OE. *stēman, stȳman* :- Gmc. **staumjan*, f. **staum-* STEAM *sb.*] **I.** *intr.* †**1.** To emit a scent or odour. Of a scent: To be emitted or exhaled. –1847. **2.** Of vapour, etc.: To be emitted or exhaled; to rise or issue in the form of steam 1582. **3.** To emit, give off, exhale steam or vapour 1614. **4.** Of a surface: To become covered with condensed vapour 1892. **5.** To generate steam for mechanical purposes: said of an engine or boiler 1860. **6.** To move or travel by the agency of steam 1831.

2. The reek of the labouring horses steamed into it DICKENS. *fig.* A waking Dream, Such as from ill-digested Thoughts doth s. 1692. **3.** Several damp gentlemen, whose clothes..began to s. DICKENS. **5.** Some engines s. best with a low fire 1877. Phr. *To s. up*, to turn on steam or set it working; hence *fig.* **6.** Every mile we steamed, the lake assumed a new character 1844. The train was steaming into the station 1863.

II. *trans.* **1.** To exhale (steam or other vapour); to send out in the form of vapour 1666. **2.** To expose to the action of steam; to treat with steam for the purpose of softening, cooking, heating, disinfecting, etc. 1798. **b.** *Calico-printing.* To fix (colours) by the steam-process 1862.

2. Potatoes that are either broiled or steamed 1798. She might easily s. open the envelope 1911.

Stea·mboat. 1787. A boat propelled by steam; esp. a coasting or river steamer of considerable size, carrying either passengers or goods.

Stea·m-e:ngine. 1751. An engine in which the mechanical force of steam is made available as a motive power for driving machinery, etc. **b.** A locomotive engine 1815. **c.** Often in joc. or hyperbolic comparisons. 1833.

c. Daniel Webster struck me much like a s. in trousers 1840.

Steamer (stī·məɹ), *sb.* 1814. [f. STEAM *v.* and *sb.* + -ER¹.] **1.** One who is employed in some process of steaming 1832. **2.** An apparatus for steaming; a vessel in which articles are subjected to the action of steam, as in washing, cookery, etc. 1814. **3.** A vessel propelled by steam; a steamboat, steamship 1825. **4. a.** A steam-propelled road-locomotive, traction-engine, or the like (*rare*). **b.** A motor-car driven by steam. 1837. **5. a.** A fire-engine the pumps of which are worked by steam 1876. **b.** A steam thrashing-machine 1898. **6.** (*transf.* from sense 3.) The duck *Tachyeres* (*Micropterus*) *cinereus* (*brachypterus*) of the Falkland Islands; the logger-head or race-horse. Also *s.-duck.* 1827.

attrib.: **s.-chair,** a lounge-chair such as is used on the deck of a s. (*U.S.*). Hence **Stea·mer** *v. intr.* to travel by steamboat.

Stea·m-ro:ller. 1866. A heavy locomotive engine with wide wheels used for crushing road-metal and levelling roads. **b.** *fig.* (*colloq.*) A crushing power or force 1902. Also as vb.

b. At last Kitchener..set his s. in motion and rolled the enemy flat 1902.

Stea·mship. 1819. A ship propelled by steam.

Steamy (stī·mi), *a.* 1644. [f. STEAM *sb.* + -Y¹.] **1.** Consisting of, abounding in, or emitting steam; resembling steam. **2.** Covered with condensed vapour. *Path.* Of the cornea: Covered or apparently covered with condensed vapour 1869.

1. The climate is s. and enervating 1899. Hence **Stea·mi·ly** *adv.*, **-ness.**

Stean (stīn). [OE. *stǣne* = OHG. *steinna* :- Gmc. **stainjōn*, f. *stainaz* STONE *sb.*] A vessel for liquids (or, in later use, for bread, meat, fish, etc.), usu. made of clay, with two handles or ears; a jar, pot, pitcher, urn. Now *dial.* and *arch.*

Steapsin (sti,æ·psin). 1896. [f. Gr. στέαρ fat, after PEPSIN.] *Phys. Chem.* A ferment of the pancreatic juice which saponifies fat.

Stearate (stī·ăreˈt). 1841. [f. next + -ATE⁴.] *Chem.* A salt of stearic acid.

Stearic (sti,æ·rik), *a.* 1831. [– Fr. *stéarique* (Chevreul *c*1819), f. Gr. στέαρ fat, tallow; see -IC.] *Chem.* Derived from or containing stearin. *S. acid*, an organic acid, $C_{18}H_{36}O_2$, prepared from stearin.

Stearin (stī·ărin). Also **-ine.** 1817. [– Fr. *stéarine* (Chevreul), f. as prec.; see -IN¹.] **1.** *Chem.* A general name for the three glycerids (monostearin, distearin, tristearin) formed by the combination of stearic acid and glycerine; chiefly applied to tristearin, which is the chief constituent of tallow or suet. **2.** The solid portion of any fixed oil or fat, in contradistinction to OLEIN 2. 1910. **3.** (Chiefly spelt *stearine.*) The commercial name of a preparation consisting of purified fatty acids, used for making candles, and formerly also as a material for statuettes 1839. Hence **Ste·ariform** *a.* resembling s.

Stearo- (stī·ăro), used as a comb. form of STEARIC or STEARIN, with the sense 'containing or derived from stearin', e.g. *stearoglucose.*

Stearone (stī·ăroᵘn). 1836. [f. STEARIN + -ONE.] *Chem.* A ketone obtained from stearic acid.

Stearoptene (stī,ărǫ·ptīn). 1836. [– mod.L. *stearoptenum* (Herberger 18..), f. Gr. στέαρ solid fat + πτηνός winged (taken to repr. 'volatile'). See ELÆOPTENE.] The solid crystalline component of a volatile oil, in contradistinction to the liquid part or *elæoptene*; a camphor.

Stearyl (stī·ăril). 1868. [f. STEARIN + -YL.] The radical of stearic acid.

Steatite (stī·ătəit). 1758. [– L. *steatitis, -ites* (Pliny) – Gr. στεατῖτις, -ίτης (λίθος) stone resembling tallow, f. στέαρ, στεατ- tallow; see -ITE¹ 2 b.] *Min.* A massive variety of talc, commonly of a grey or greyish-green colour, with an unctuous or soapy feel; soap-stone. Hence **Steatitic** (stīăti·tik) *a.* of or composed of s., of the nature of s.

Steato- (stī,ăto, -ǫ·), used as comb. form of Gr. στέαρ, στεατ- hard fat, tallow, suet, in many scientific terms, chiefly Medical, as **Stea·togene, -o·genous** *adjs.*, tending to produce steatosis; etc.

‖**Steatoma** (stī,ătōᵘ·mă). 1599. [L. – Gr. στεάτωμα; see prec., -OMA.] *Path.* An encysted fatty tumour. Hence **Steatomatous** (-ǫ·mătəs) *a.* of the nature of or resembling a s.

‖**Steatopyga** (stī:ătopəi·gă). 1822. [mod. L., f. STEATO- + Gr. πυγή rump.] *Phys.* A protuberance of the buttocks, due to an abnormal accumulation of fat in and behind the hips and thighs, found (esp. in women) as a racial characteristic of certain peoples, esp. the Hottentot Bushmen of S. Africa. So ‖**Steatopygia** (-pi·dʒiă), the condition of having a s. **Steatopygous** (stīătǫ·pigəs, stīătopəi·gəs) *a.* pertaining to or characterized by a s.

‖**Steatosis** (stī,ătōᵘ·sis). 1860. [mod.L. f. STEATO- + -OSIS.] *Path.* Fatty degeneration.

Steed (stīd). [OE. *stēda*, f. base of Gmc. **stōđō* STUD *sb.*²] †**a.** In OE., a stud-horse, stallion. †**b.** In ME. and early mod. Eng., a high-mettled horse used on state occasions, in war, or in the lists; a great horse, as dist. from a palfrey. **c.** From the 16th c. used only *poet.* or *rhet.* for: A horse, usu. one for riding.

Thenne they broughte hym a rede spere and a rede stede MALORY. Mounted vpon a hot and fierie S. SHAKS.

Steek (stīk), *v.*¹ Chiefly *Sc.* and *north.* [ME. *steke*, prob. spec. use of next.] To shut.

Steek (stīk), *v.*² Now *dial.* [ME. *steke*, prob. repr. OE. **stecan* = OFris. *steka*, OS. *stekan* (LG., Du. *steken*), OHG. *stehhan* (G. *stechen*), f. **stek-*, WGmc. var. of **stik-* STICK *v.*¹] To pierce; to fix.

Steel (stīl), *sb.* [OE. (Anglian) **stēle*, earlier *stēli, stǣli*, (WS.) **stīele, stȳle* = OFris. **stēl*, OS. *stēhli* :- WGmc. **staχlja*, prop. adj. from Gmc. **staχla-*, repr. by MLG. *stāl*, MDu. *stael* (Du. *staal*), OHG. *stahal* (G. *stahl*), prob. f. **staχ-* **staʒ-*; see STAY *sb.*¹] **1.** A general name for certain artificially produced varieties of iron, dist. from those known as 'iron' by certain physical properties, esp. greater hardness and elasticity, which render them suitable as material for cutting instruments, etc. **b.** A particular variety or sort of steel 1839. **2.** Similative and fig. uses, in which steel is taken as the type of hardness ME. **b.** *Sport.* Power of endurance or sustained effort 1850. **3.** Steel in the form of weapons or cutting tools (occas. spurs, a trap, etc.) Hence used for: A †sword, lance, bayonet, or the like. OE. **4.** Steel as the material of defensive armour ME. **5.** As a material for plates engraved with drawings or designs to be reproduced by printing. Hence, as a trade term: A steel engraving. 1843. **6.** Iron as used medicinally; chalybeate medicine 1647. **7.** The steel part of anything 1450. **8.** As the name of instruments made of steel. **a.** A piece of steel shaped for the purpose of striking fire with a flint ME. **b.** A rod of steel, fluted or plain, fitted with a handle, used for sharpening table or butchers' knives 1541. **c.** A needle; a knitting-needle. *dial.* 1784. **9.** *Dress.* A strip of steel used to give stiffness or support, or to expand a dress 1608. **10.** *pl.* (*Finance*). Shares in steel-manufacturing companies 1912.

1. b. Self-hardening and other special steels 1891. **2.** Like a man of Steele SHAKS. Phr. *True as s.* (said of persons, rarely of things, statements, etc.). †*S. to the (very) back*, thoroughly robust; thoroughly trustworthy. **3.** The stern joy which warriors feel In foemen worthy of their s. SCOTT. *Cold s.*, cutting or thrusting weapons, as dist. from bullets. **4.** In compleat steele SHAKS. *fig.* She that has that [chastity], is clad in compleat s. MILT. **6.** *Flowers of s.*, iron chloride prepared by heating s. filings, etc. with sal-ammoniac. *Tincture of s.*, tincture of iron chloride.

attrib. and *Comb.*: = made of s., as *s. spring*; in similative, objective, or instrumental combs., as *steel-blue, -bound, -clad, -lined, -worker*; **s.-concrete,** concrete reinforced with steel; **-engraving,** the art of engraving upon a s. plate; a print or impression from such a plate; similarly **-engraver; s. grain,** a granular texture like that of s.; **-hardened** *a.*, case-hardened; **-head,** the rainbow-trout of N. America, *Salmo iridens*; **-hearted** *a.*, courageous; hard-hearted, obdurate; **S. Helmet** [tr. G. *stahlhelm*], the designation of an organization of German ex-service men drawn mainly from the Nationalist Party and having a strong conservative bias; also, a member of this; **s. trap,** a trap with jaws and spring of s.

Steel (stīl), *v.* OE. [f. prec.] **1.** *trans.* To overlay, point, or edge with steel. †**b.** To back (a mirror) with steel –1630. **c.** To cover (an engraved metal plate) with a film of iron by electrolysis to render it more durable 1880. **2.** To cause to resemble steel. **a.** *fig.* To make hard, unbending, or strong as steel, to render insensible to impression, to make obdurate, to nerve or strengthen; also to fortify *against* 1581. **b.** To make like steel in appearance (*rare*) 1807.

†Steel-bow¹, stee·l bow. 1607. [BOW *sb.*¹] A bow made of steel; a cross-bow –1671.

Steelbow² (stī·lbōᵘ). *Obs.* exc. *Hist.* late ME. [f. STEEL *sb.* (used fig. = rigidly fixed) + *bow* farmstock (ON. *bú*).] *Sc. Law.* **a.** A quantity of farming stock, which a tenant received from his landlord on entering, and which he was bound to render up undiminished at the close of his tenancy. **b.** The species of tenancy or contract by which farming stock is hired on the condition that the tenant renders up on the expiration of his tenancy the same quantity and value that he received; esp. in phr. *in s.*

Steelify (stī·lifəi), *v.* 1662. [f. STEEL *sb.* + -FY.] †**1.** *trans.* To add steel to, imbue with the properties of steel. **2.** To convert into steel 1807. Hence **Stee:lifica·tion.**

Steeling (stī·liŋ), *vbl. sb.* 1819. [f. STEEL *v.* + -ING¹.] **1.** The giving a steel edge or point to iron, etc. **2.** Conversion into steel 1860. **3.** In *Engraving*, the process of covering a metal plate with steel to render it more durable 1871. **4.** The steel part of a machine 1869.

Steel pen. 1636. **1.** A pen made of steel, split at the tip like a quill. **2.** *colloq.* Applied to the 'swallow-tail' or evening-dress tail-coat 1873.

Steel plate. 1680. A plate of steel used for engraving, for the armour of warships, etc.

Steely (stī·li), *a.* 1509. [f. STEEL *sb.* +

-Y¹.] **1.** Of or belonging to, made or consisting of, steel 1586. **2.** Resembling steel in appearance, colour, hardness, or some other quality 1596. **b.** Of corn, esp. barley: Very hard and brittle 1580. **3.** Of a person, his qualities, etc.: **a.** Hard and cold as steel, unimpressionable, inflexible, obdurate 1509. **b.** Strong as steel 1648.

1. Again the foe discharge the s. show'r POPE. **2.** The s. heavens 1874. **3. a.** That she would unarme her hart of that s. resistance against the sweet blowes of Love SIDNEY. Hence **Stee·liness,** s. quality or condition.

Steelyard¹ (stī·lyaɹd). *Hist.* 1474. [f. STEEL *sb.* + YARD *sb.*¹; mistranslation of MLG. *stālhof*, f. *stāl* sample, pattern (erron. identified with STEEL *sb.*) + *hof* courtyard (= G. *hof*).] The place on the north bank of the Thames above London Bridge where the Merchants of the Hanse had their establishment. Also, the merchants collectively. **b.** A similar establishment in a provincial town 1474. **c.** A tavern within the precincts of the Steelyard where 'Rhenish wine' was sold 1592.

Steelyard² (stī·lyaɹd). 1639. [f. STEEL *sb.* + YARD *sb.*²] A balance consisting of a lever with unequal arms, which moves on a fulcrum; the article to be weighed is suspended from the shorter arm, and a counterpoise is caused to slide upon the longer arm until equilibrium is produced, its place on this arm (which is notched or graduated) showing the weight: = *Roman balance*.

†**Steem** *v.* 1590. [Aphetic var. of ESTEEM *v.*] *trans.* To estimate value –1642.

Steen (stīn), *v.* [OE. *stǣnan* = MLG. *stēnen*, OHG. *gisteinen*, Goth. *stainjan*, f. *stān* STONE *sb.*] †**1.** *trans.* To stone (a person); to put to death by stoning –1450. **2.** To line (a well or other excavation) with stone, brick, or other material 1723. Hence **Stee·ning** *vbl. sb.* (*concr.*) the lining of a well or other excavation.

‖**Steenbok** (stē·nbǫk). 1775. [Du., f. *steen* STONE + *bok* BUCK *sb.*¹] A small S. African antelope, *Rhaphiceros campestris*.

Steenkirk, steinkirk (stī·nkəɹk). *Hist.* 1694. [– Fr. (*cravate à la*) *Steinkerke*, *Steinkerque*, from the victory of Steenkerke (Belgium) gained by the French over the English and their allies on 3 Aug. 1692. Cf. MAGENTA, SOLFERINO.] A kind of neckcloth (worn both by men and women), having long lace ends hanging down or twisted together, and passed through a loop or ring.

Steep (stīp), *sb.*¹ ME. [f. STEEP *v.*] **1.** The process of steeping or soaking; the state of being steeped, esp. in phr. (*to lay*) *in s.* **2.** The liquid in which a thing is placed to undergo soaking or maceration; a prepared liquor used as a dyeing bath or cleansing wash; in *Agric.* a wash for seeds 1759. **3.** = RENNET *sb.*¹ 1688.

Steep (stīp), *a.*, *sb.*², and *adv.* [OE. *stēap* = OFris. *stāp* :– WGmc. **staupa*, f. **staup-* **stŭp-*; see STOOP *v.*] **A.** *adj.* †**1.** Elevated, lofty –1738. **2.** †**a.** Of eyes: Projecting, prominent; staring; glaring with passion –1555. †**b.** Of jewels, eyes, stars: Brilliant –1577. **3.** Of a hill, mountain, cliff: Having an almost perpendicular face or slope; precipitous. Of a gradient or slope, a staircase, etc.: High-pitched. ME. **b.** *transf.* of movement. *poet.* 1603. †**c.** Of water: Having a headlong course, flowing precipitously –1659. **d.** *Coal-mining.* Of a seam or measure: Having a high inclination 1883. **4.** *fig.* **a.** Of an aim, an undertaking, etc.: Arduous, ambitious 1598. †**b.** Of a difficulty: Hard to surmount. MILT. †**c.** = HEADLONG *a.* 4. –1667. **d.** Of inequalities, contrasts: Violent, exteme 1856. **5.** *slang.* Excessive, extravagant, 'stiff', 'tall'. Of a price or amount: Exorbitant. Of a story, etc.: Exaggerated, incredible. 1856.

1. To a roome they came, Steepe, and of state CHAPMAN. **3.** The whole herd of swine ranne violently down a steepe place into the Sea *Matt.* 8:32. **b.** [He] Throws his s. flight in many an Aerie wheele MILT. **c.** And the gilded Car of Day, His glowing Axle doth allay In the steep Atlantick stream MILT. **5.** This is rather a s. statement, even for a party that exists on credit 1895.

B. *sb.* The declivity or slope of a mountain, hill, cliff; a steep or precipitous place 1555. **b.** *poet.* of the sky 1697.

Why art thou heere Come from the farthest steepe of India? SHAKS. **b.** Behold the new morning glittering down the eastern steeps CARLYLE.

†**C.** *adv.* With a steep slope, abruptly 1548. Hence **Stee·pish** *a.* somewhat s., rather precipitous. **Stee·p-ly** *adv.*, **-ness.**

Steep (stīp), *v.* late ME. [repr. formally OE. **stēpan*, **stīepan* = Sw. *stöpa*, Da. *støbe*, Norw. *støypa* steep (seeds, barley for malting) :– Gmc. **staupjan*, f. **staup-*; see STOUP.] **1.** *trans.* To soak in water or other liquid; chiefly, to do so for the purpose of softening, altering in properties, cleansing, or the like. **b.** To plunge or bathe (one's face, eyes, limbs, etc.) in water. Somewhat *rare.* 1579. **c.** *transf.* Of mist, vapour, smoke, light: To 'bathe', envelop like a flood 1798. **2.** To soak, saturate, thoroughly moisten 1590. **b.** To soak or imbrue (a weapon, etc.) *in* blood, poison, etc. 1594. **c.** *hyperbolically.* To 'soak' in alcoholic liquor; chiefly *pass.* Also, to deaden, stupefy (one's memory, senses), to drown (grief, etc.) *in* liquor. 1592 **3. a.** To 'bathe' (the heart, head, limbs, etc.) in slumber or rest 1591. **b.** To soak and stupefy or deaden (grief, the senses) *in* (sleep, etc.) 1597. **c.** To involve deeply in a state or condition; to imbue (with some quality); to make profoundly acquainted (with a subject of study); to absorb *in* (a pursuit). Chiefly *pass.* 1603. **4.** *intr.* To undergo the process of soaking in liquor. late ME.

1. S. your ham all night in water 1769. **c.** A river-mist is steeping The trees BRIDGES. **2.** A Napkin, steeped in the harmlesse blood Of sweet young Rutland SHAKS. **b.** With tongue in Venome steep'd SHAKS. **c.** When thirsty griefe in Wine we steepe LOVELACE. **3. a.** Sleep; Which..In quiet rest his molten heart did s. SPENSER. **b.** O Sleepe,..thou no more wilt.. steepe my Sences in Forgetfulnesse SHAKS. **c.** The whole of modern thought is steeped in science HUXLEY. **4.** *fig.* In a loch at Moy the stars were steeping 1914. Hence **Stee·per,** one who steeps; *spec.* one who carries out the operation of steeping flax, wool, etc.; a vessel used in steeping or infusing.

Stee·p-down, *a. Obs.* exc. *poet.* 1530. [f. STEEP *a.* + DOWN *adv.*] Precipitous.

Wash me in steepe-downe gulfes of Liquid fire SHAKS.

Steepen (stī·p'n), *v.* 1847. [f. STEEP *a.* + -EN⁵.] **1.** *intr.* To become steep or steeper. **2.** *trans. fig.* To increase, 'pile on', 'heap up' 1909.

†**Stee·piness.** 1612. [f. STEEPY *a.* + -NESS.] Steepness –1771.

Steeple (stī·p'l). [OE. *stēpel*, WS. **stīepel*, *stȳpel* :– Gmc. **staupilaz*, f. **staup-* STEEP *a.*; see -LE.] †**1.** A tall tower; a building of great altitude in proportion to its length and breadth –1660. **2.** A lofty tower forming part of a church, temple, or other public edifice (often serving to contain the bells); such a tower together with the spire or other superstructure by which it is surmounted ME. **3.** A spire on the top of the tower or roof of a church or similar edifice. Also *spire s.*, *broach s.* 1473.

attrib. and *Comb.*: **s.-clocked** *a.*, having steeple-shaped clocks (CLOCK *sb.*²); **-crown,** a crown of a hat rising to a point in the middle; also a hat with a s.-crown; hence *s.-crowned* adj.; **s. jack,** a man who climbs steeples or tall chimneys to repair them; **-roofed** *a.*, having very high roofs; **-top,** (*a*) the top of a s.; (*b*) the bowhead, or great polar whale (*Balæna mysticetus*), so called from the spout-holes terminating in a sort of cone. **b.** In names of plants: **s. bells, s. bell-flower,** *Campanula pyramidalis*; **-bush** = HARDHACK. Hence **Stee·pled** *ppl. a.* having the form of a s.; having a s. or steeples. **Stee·plewise** *adv.* after the manner of a s.; in a conical or pyramidal form.

Stee·plechase, *sb.* 1793. [f. prec. + CHASE.] **1.** A horse-race across country or on a made course with artificial fences, water-jumps, and other obstacles. Formerly, a race having a church steeple in view as goal, in which all intervening obstacles had to be cleared. **b.** A parlour game simulating this 1895. **2.** *transf.* A foot-race across country or over a course furnished with hurdles, ditches, etc. 1864. Hence **Stee·plechase** *v. intr.* to ride or run in a s.; to practise riding in steeplechases. **Stee·plechaser,** one who runs or rides in a s., a horse trained for steeplechasing.

Stee·ple-house. 1644. A building with a steeple; used by the early Quakers instead of 'church', on the ground that that word ought not to be applied to a building.

Stee·p-to, *a.* 1748. [f. STEEP *a.* + TO *adv.*] *Naut.* Of a shore: Descending very steeply into the water.

Stee·p-up, *a. arch.* 1565. [f. STEEP *a.* + UP *adv.* Cf. STEEP-DOWN.] Precipitous; perpendicular.

And hauing climb'd the steepe-vp heauenly hill SHAKS.

Steepy (stī·pi), *a. Obs.* exc. *arch.* 1561. [f. STEEP *a.* + -Y¹.] Steep; full of steep places; precipitous.

Now take thy s. flight from Heav'n DRYDEN. *fig.* Ages steepie night SHAKS.

Steer (stīᵊɹ), *sb.*¹ [OE. *stēor* = MLG. *stēr*, OHG. *stior* (Du., G. *stier*), ON. *stjórr*, Goth. *stiur* :– Gmc. **steuraz*.] A young ox, esp. one which has been castrated.

In the U.S. and the colonies applied to male beef-cattle of any age.

Steer, *sb.*² *Obs.* exc. in *Comb.* [OE. *stēor* = OFris. *stiure*, OS. *stior*, MLG. *stūre*, MDu. *stūre*, *stiere* (Du. *stuur*), ON. *stýri* rudder, stem :– Gmc. **steurō*; see next.] **1.** The action of directing or governing; guidance, control, rule, government –1596. **2.** A rudder, helm –1625.

Comb.: **s.-oar,** an oar used at the stern for steering a boat.

Steer (stīᵊɹ), *v.* [OE. *stieran* = OFris. *stiūra*, MLG. *stūren*, MDu. *stūren*, *stieren*, OHG. *stiuren* (G. *steuern*), ON. *stýra*, Goth. *stiurjan* settle :– Gmc. **steurjan*, f. **steurō*; see prec.] **1.** *trans.* To guide the course of (a vessel) by means of a rudder, or of an oar or paddle used like a rudder. **b.** *transf.* of animals. late ME. **c.** To guide (a vessel) to a specified point or in a specified direction 1470. **2.** *absol.* and *intr.* To guide a vessel by means of a rudder or the like OE. **b.** *intr.* in passive sense. Of a ship: To admit of being steered; to answer the helm (well or ill) 1627. **c.** Of a ship: To be guided by the helm in a certain direction 1667. **3.** *trans.* In extended sense, to guide something that is in motion OE. **b.** To guide, lead, 'pilot' (a person) through a crowd, along an intricate path, etc. Also *absol.* Also (*U.S. slang*) to manœuvre or decoy (a person) to a place, or into doing something. 1859. **4.** *intr.* To shape one's course (on land, in the air). Also *trans.* with cogn. obj. 1500. **b.** Of an inanimate thing: To travel in a set course 1692. †**5.** To conduct (one's life) –1699. †**b.** Of reasons, indications, influences: To guide –1683. **c.** *intr.* To direct one's course of action (*by* guiding indications). Often, to find a safe course *between* two evils or two extremes. 1658. †**6.** To govern, rule –1678. †**b.** To manage, administer (government); to conduct (business, negotiations, etc.) –1647.

1. Whanne a fool stereth a barge, Hym self and al the folke is shent 1400. *To s. a (one's) course*; You must s. a middle course HAZLITT. **c.** When Cook..Steer'd Britain's oak into a world unknown COWPER. **2.** Two skilful helmsmen on the poop to s. 1762. They steered by the guidance of the stars GIBBON. *fig.* Yet I..still bear vp and s. Right onward MILT. Phr. *To s. clear of*, to avoid completely. **c.** As when a Ship..where the Wind Veres oft, as oft so steers, and shifts her Saile MILT. **3.** Tapp was the jockey..and 'steered him to victory' 1890. He feeds the pigs and steers the plough 1914. **4.** He was bravely steering his way across the continent W. IRVING. **b.** Thou busy sunny river..Through woodlands steering CLOUGH. **5. c.** Rational animals should use their reason, and s. by it 1722. **6. b.** The great persons who steered the public affairs CLARENDON. Hence **Stee·rable** *a.* that may be steered or guided, dirigible.

Steerage (stīᵊ·rédʒ). 1450. [f. prec. + -AGE.] **1.** The action, practice, or method of steering a boat or ship; the guidance of a balloon or airship, *rarely* of a carriage. **b.** Of a ship: The action, method, or ability of answering to the helm 1653. **2. a.** The direction or government of affairs, the State, one's life 1592. **b.** A course held or steered, esp. a course of conduct 1625. **3.** The steering apparatus of a boat, etc. 1697. **4.** That division of the after part of a ship which is immediately in front of the chief cabin; the second cabin. Also called †*s. room*. (orig. the place from which the ship was steered.) 1612.

5. That part of a passenger ship allotted to the passengers who travel at the cheapest rate. Also quasi-advb. in *to go, travel s.* 1804.

1. These Pilots by their ill s. did split their Vessels 1654. **b.** She..made bad S. 1745. **2. a.** But he that hath the stirrage of my course, Direct my sute SHAKS. **5.** He travelled s. with a ship of emigrants 1906.

attrib. and *Comb.*: **s. passenger,** one who occupies a berth in the s. of a passenger-vessel; **-way,** a way or motion sufficient for the helm to have effect.

Steerer (stīᵊ·rəɹ). late ME. [f. STEER *v.* + -ER¹.] †**1.** A rudder –1633. **2.** A steersman 1585. **3.** *U.S. slang.* A swindler whose business it is to lead his victims to the rendezvous 1883. **4.** A thing which directs its course: **a.** of a ship with adj. referring to its power of answering to the helm or rudder 1887. **b.** Of a cycle, with prefix indicating the position of its steering-wheel 1883.

4. a. The ship is a bad s. 1887. **b.** A front-steerer 1883.

Steering (stīᵊ·riŋ), *vbl. sb.* ME. [f. STEER *v.* + -ING¹.] The action of STEER *v.*

Comb.: **s.-lock,** the turning movement of the wheels of a motor-vehicle; **-wheel,** (*a*) *Naut.* a vertical wheel by which motion is communicated to the rudder through the medium of a tiller-rope or other device; (*b*) a hand-wheel for guiding a motor-vehicle; (*c*) the wheel of a cycle by which steerage is effected.

Stee·ring, *ppl. a.* 1903. [f. STEER *v.* + -ING².] *S. committee* (U.S.), a committee of management.

†**Stee·rless,** *a.* [OE. *stēorlēas*; see STEER *sb.*² and -LESS.] **1.** Not amenable to guidance or control –ME. **2.** Without a rudder –1639.

Stee·rling. 1648. [f. STEER *sb.*¹ + -LING¹.] A young steer.

Steersman (stīᵊ·ɹzmĕn). [OE. *stēoresman*, f. *stēores* gen. of *stēor* STEER *sb.*² + MAN *sb.*] One who steers a boat or ship. **b.** *transf.* One who drives and guides a machine 1828. So **Stee·rman** (now *rare*). †**Stee·rsmate** (*rare*).

Steeve (stīv), *sb.*¹ 1794. [f. STEEVE *v.*¹] *Naut.* The upward inclination of a bowsprit, cathead, etc.; the amount of this.

Steeve (stīv), *sb.*² *U.S.* 1840. [perh. f. STEEVE *v.*²] *Naut.* A long derrick or spar, with a block at one end, used in stowing cargo.

Steeve (stīv), *v.*¹ 1644. [Of unkn. origin.] *Naut. intr.* Of a bowsprit, etc.: To incline upwards at an angle instead of lying horizontally. Also *trans.* to set (a bowsprit) at a certain upward inclination.

Steeve (stīv), *v.*² 1482. [– Fr. *estiver* or its source Sp. *estivar* :– L. *stipare* crowd or press together. Cf. STIVE *v.*¹, ESTIVAGE.] Chiefly *Naut. trans.* To compress and stow (wool, cotton, or other cargo) in a ship's hold, etc.; also, to pack tightly.

Steganography (steganǫ·grăfi). *Obs.* exc. *Hist.* 1569. [– mod.L. *steganographia* (Trithemius 1500), f. Gr. στεγανός covered; see -GRAPHY.] The art of secret writing; cryptography. Also, cryptographic script, cipher. Hence **Stegano·grapher, Stegano·graphist,** a cryptographer. **Steganogra·phical** *a.*

Steganopod (ste·gănopǫd), *sb.* and *a.* 1842. [– mod.L. *Steganopodes*, pl. (Illiger 1811), f. Gr. στεγανόπους, -οποδ- web-footed, f. στεγανός covered + πούς, ποδ- foot.] *Ornith.* **A.** *sb.* A bird belonging to the group *Steganopodes*, which comprises the pelicans, cormorants, frigate-birds, gannets, tropic-birds, and snake birds. **B.** *adj.* Of a bird: Belonging to the group *Steganopodes*. Hence **Stegano·podan, Stegano·podous** *adjs.* belonging to the group *Steganopodes.*

Stego- (stego), used as comb. form of Gr. root στεγ- of στέγειν to cover, στέγη covering, στέγος roof, in certain modern scientific terms.

Stegocephalian (-sĭfē¹·liăn) [Gr. κεφαλή head], *a.* = STEGOCEPHALOUS; *sb.*, a member of the order *Stegocephala* of fossil Batrachians, characterized by having the skull protected by bony plates. **Stegoce·phalous** *a.*, pertaining to or having the characteristics of the order *Stegocephala.* **Ste·gosaur,** ‖**Stegosau·rus** [Gr. σαῦρος lizard], a genus of dinosaurs, characterized by the completeness of their armour; hence ‖**Stegosau·ria** *pl.*, the order of which this genus is typical; **Stegosau·rian** *a.* and *sb.*

‖**Stein** (ʃtəin). Chiefly *U.S.* 1901. [G., lit. 'stone'.] An earthenware mug, esp. for beer.

Steinbock (stəi·nbǫk). Also **-boc.** 1683. [– G. *steinbock*, f. *stein* STONE *sb.* + *bock* BUCK *sb.*¹ Cf. STEENBOK.] A wild goat of the genus *Ibex*; the Alpine Ibex (*Capra ibex*).

Steinkirk: see STEENKIRK.

‖**Stela** (stī·lă). *Pl.* **stelæ** (stī·li), *rarely* **stelas.** 1776. [L. – Gr. στήλη.] = next 1.

Stele (stīl, ‖stīli). 1820. [As a disyllable, repr. Gr. στήλη standing block or slab, f. root **stă-* to stand. As a monosyllable, anglicized form of the Gr. word.] *Antiq.* **1.** An upright slab bearing sculptured designs or inscriptions. Occas. loosely, any prepared surface on the face of a building, a rock, etc., covered with an inscription. **2.** *Bot.* The axial cylinder in the stems and roots of vascular plants, developed from the plerome 1895.

Stell (stel), *v.* [OE. *stellan, stiellan, styllan* = OS. *stellian*, (O)HG. *stellen* :– WGmc. **stalljan*, f. Gmc. **stallaz* STALL *sb.*¹] †**1.** *trans.* To set (an example); to establish (a law) –ME. **2.** *Sc.* To fix, post, place 1470. **3.** To portray, delineate. *Obs.* exc. *arch.* 1598.

3. Mine eye hath play'd the painter and hath steeld Thy beauties forme in table of my heart SHAKS.

‖**Stella** (ste·lă). *Pl.* **stellæ** (-*i*). 1828. [L., 'star'.] **a.** *Zool.* A star-shaped projection on the surface of a coralline; also, a star-shaped sponge-spicule. **b.** *Crystall.* A stellate crystal 1844.

Stellar (ste·lăɹ), *a.* 1656. [– late L. *stellaris*, f. L. *stella* star; see -AR¹.] **1.** Pertaining to the stars or a star; of the nature of a star. **2.** Star-shaped, stellate: chiefly of crystals 1670.

1. These soft fires..shed down Thir s. vertue on all kinds that grow On Earth MILT. **2.** A clump of planting of a s. form 1844. So †**Ste·llary** *a.*

Stellate (ste·lĕt), *a.* and *sb.* 1500. [– L. *stellatus*, f. *stella* star; see -ATE².] **1.** Of the sky: Studded with stars. *poet.* **2.** Star-shaped; arranged or grouped in the form of a conventional star or stars; (chiefly in scientific use) radiating from a centre like the rays of a star 1661. **B.** *sb.* A stellate sponge-spicule 1880.

2. The uniform s. form of snow 1755. S. cells 1899. So **Ste·llated** *a.* **Ste·llately** *adv.*

†**Ste·lled,** *a. rare.* 1605. [f. L. *stella* + -ED¹.] Stellar, starred. –1656.

The Sea..Would have buoy'd vp, And quench'd he S. fires SHAKS.

Stellenbosch (ste·lənbǫʃ), *v. Mil. slang.* 1900. [f. *Stellenbosch*, a military base in Cape Colony.] *pass.* 'To be relegated, as the result of incompetence, to a position in which little harm can be done' (Pettman).

Stellerid (ste·lĕrid). 1835. [– Fr. *stelléride* (Lamarck), app. irreg. f. L. *stella* star; see -ID³.] *Zool.* A star-fish. Also **Stelle·ridan** [see -IDAN], †**Stelleri·dean, -ian.**

Stelliferous (steli·fĕrəs), *a.* 1583. [f. L. *stellifer*, f. *stella* star; see -FEROUS.] Bearing stars. **b.** *Biol.* Having star-shaped markings.

Stelliform (ste·lifǫɹm), *a.* 1796. [f. L. *stella* star; see -FORM.] Shaped like a star; existing in the form of star-shaped crystals.

Stellify (ste·lifəi), *v.* late ME. [– OFr. *stellifier* – med.L. *stellificare*, f. L. *stella* star; see -FY.] **1.** *trans.* To transform (a person or thing) into a star or constellation; to place among the stars. †**b.** *fig.* To extol –1721. †**2.** To set with stars, or with something compared to stars –1658. So **Stellifica·tion,** the action of stellifying.

‖**Stellio** (ste·lio). late ME. [L. form of next.] = next. Now only *Zool.* as generic name.

Stellion (ste·liǫn). late ME. [– L. *stellio* -*ōn*-; according to Pliny f. *stella* star; see -ION.] In early use, a kind of lizard with star-like spots, mentioned by ancient writers. In mod. use, a lizard of the genus *Stellio* or family *Stellionidæ*, native in Southern Europe and Asia.

Stellionate (ste·liŏnĕt). 1622. [– L. *stellionatus*, f. *stellio*, -*ōn*- (see prec.) in sense 'fraudulent person'; see -ATE¹.] *Sc. Civil Law.* (See quot.)

The crime of s...includes every fraud which is not distinguished by a special name; but is chiefly applied to conveyances of the same numerical right, granted by the proprietor to different disponees 1754.

Stellular (ste·liŭlăɹ), *a.* 1796. [f. late L. *stellula*, dim. of *stella* star; see -ULAR. Cf. *granular, valvular.*] Having the form of a small star or small stars.

Stem (stem), *sb.*¹ [OE. *stemn, stefn* (see next) :– Gmc. **stamniz*, of which a parallel and synon. formation **stamnaz* is repr. by (M)LG., (M)Du., OHG. *stam* (G. *stamm*), also by OS., ON. *stamn*, recorded only in the naut. sense; f. **sta-* STAND + suffix -*mn*.] **1.** The main body of the portion above ground of a tree, shrub, or other plant; a trunk, stock, stalk. (Ordinarily implying more slenderness than *stock* or *trunk*.) **b.** *Bot.* The ascending axis (whether above or below ground) of a plant, in contradistinction to the descending axis or root 1807. **2.** The stalk supporting a leaf, flower, or fruit; a peduncle, pedicel, or petiole. Also *transf.* in *Anat.* and *Path.* 1590. **3.** The stock of a family; the main line of descent from which the 'branches' of a family are offshoots; the descendants of a particular ancestor. Also *abstr.*, ancestry, pedigree. 1540. **b.** An ethnic stock, a race 1540. †**c.** *fig.* A branch or offshoot of a family –1634. **4.** Applied to various objects resembling the stem of a plant or of a flower, etc. **a.** *Calligraphy* and *Printing.* The upright stroke of a letter 1676. **b.** *Mus.* The vertical line forming part of a minim, crotchet, quaver, etc. 1806. **c.** The long cylindrical body of an instrument, etc., as dist. from the 'head', or from branches or projections; the tube of a thermometer or similar instrument; the tube of a tobacco-pipe 1815. **d.** The upright cylindrical support of a cup, a wineglass, or other vessel 1835. **e.** *Watch-making.* The pendant-shank of a watch 1866. **f.** The SHAFT of a hair, of a feather 1845. **5.** *Philol.* That part of an inflected word that remains unchanged (except for euphonic variations) in the process of inflexion; the theme of a word, to which the flexional suffixes are attached 1851.

1. The sea eryngo..has a s. about a foot high 1850. **2.** Two louely berries molded on one s. SHAKS. **3.** There shall come forth a rod out of the stemme of Iesse *Isa.* 11:1. Where ye may all that are of noble stemm Approach MILT. **b.** The Danishe governement beganne..to bee..hatefull, as a thinge moste..pestilent to the Englishe name and stemme 1540. **c.** This is a S. Of that Victorious Stock SHAKS.

Comb.: **s.-bed** *Geol.*, a stratum containing stems of trees; **-composition** *Philol.*, composition of word-stems, as dist. from syntactical combination of words; **s. stitch** *Needlework*, a stitch usu. employed for stems and single lines in embroidery and lace-making; **-winder** *U.S.* (*a*) a keyless watch; (*b*) a geared logging locomotive; (*c*) *slang*, a person or thing that is first-rate; **-winding,** *a. U.S.* (of a watch) that is wound up by means of a s. **Ste·mless** *a.* having no s. **Ste·mlet,** a small s. **Ste·mmy** *a.* having long bare stems; containing stems.

Stem (stem), *sb.*² [OE. *stemn, stefn*, spec. use of prec.; corresp., with variation, to OFris. *stevene*, LG., Du. *steven* (whence G. *steven*), and OS. *stamn*, ON. *stamn, stafn*. The ON. form was repr. in Eng. by *stam* (XIV–XV) and the LG. in Sc. by *steven* (XVI–XVII); during these periods the native form was rare.] *Naut.* †**1.** The timber at either extremity of a vessel, to which the ends of the side-planks were fastened; the 'stem' (in the mod. sense) or the stern-post. Hence, the prow or the stern. –1497. **2.** The curved upright timber or piece of metal at the bow of a vessel, into which the planks of the bow are scarfed 1538. **3.** The prow, bows, or the whole forepart of a vessel 1555.

2. Phr. *From s. to stern*, along the whole length of a ship. *S. on*, so as to strike with the s. *S. to s.*, (of ships) with their stems facing each other. *To give* (a ship) *the s.*, to ram.

Stem (stem), *v.*¹ 1450. [– ON. *stemma* = (O)HG. *stemmen* :– Gmc. **stamjan*, f. **stam-* check (cf. STAMMER).] **1.** *trans.* To stop, check; to dam up (a stream, or the like). **2.** To set (one's limbs, hand) firmly 1827. **3.** *Mining.* To plug or tamp (a hole for blasting) 1791. Hence **Ste·mmer** (*Mining*), a metal bar used for stemming.

Stem (stem), *v.*² late ME. [f. STEM *sb.*²] **1.** *trans.* Of a vessel, a navigator: To urge the stem against, make headway against (a tide, current, gale, etc.). Hence of a swimmer, a bird, etc.: To make headway against (water or wind), to breast (the waves, the air). 1593. **b.** *transf.* and *fig.* To go counter to, make headway against (something compared to a stream) 1675. **c.** To direct the head of (a vessel) *on* a place; to keep (a vessel) on a fixed course 1594. **d.** *intr.* Of a vessel or a navigator: To head in a certain direction, keep a certain course. late ME. †**2.** *trans.* To dash against with the stem of a vessel; to ram –1810. †**3.** To furnish (a ship) with a stem –1590.

Stem, *v.*³ 1577. [f. STEM *sb.*¹] †**1.** *intr.* To rise erect like a stem –1786. **b.** *fig.* (*U.S.*) To have or trace one's origin *in*; to spring *from* or *out.* **2.** *trans.* To remove the stalk and midrib from tobacco-leaf; to remove the stalk from (a fruit, etc.).

‖**Stemma** (ste·mă). *Pl.* **stemmata** (ste·mătă). 1826. [L. – Gr. στέμμα garland, f. στέφειν to crown.] **1. a.** *Rom. Antiq.* The recorded genealogy of a family. **b.** A genealogical tree; *transf.* the tree of descent of a text. 1879. **2.** *Zool.* A simple eye, or a single facet of the compound eye, in invertebrates 1826.

Stemson (ste·msən). 1769. [f. STEM *sb.*², after *keelson* KELSON. Cf. STERNSON.] *Naut.* In a wooden vessel, the timber fitted into the angle formed by the junction of stem and kelson.

Stench (stenʃ), *sb.* [OE. *stenć*, corresp. to OS., OHG. *stank* (Du. *stank*, G. (*ge*)*stank*); f. **staŋkw- steŋkwa-* STINK *v.*] †**1.** An odour, a smell; also, the sense of smell. OE. only. **2.** A foul, disgusting, or noisome smell, an offensive odour, a stink OE. **3.** Without article. Evil-smelling quality or property, offensive odour, stink ME. **4.** Something that smells offensively 1595.

2. In Köhln..I counted two and seventy stenches, All well defined, and several stinks! COLERIDGE. 3. A narrow winding street, full of offence and s. DICKENS. 4. Thou odoriferous s., sound rottennesse SHAKS.

attrib. and *Comb.*: **s.-pipe,** an extension of a soil-pipe to a point above the roof of a house, to allow foul gases to escape; **-trap,** a device in a drain, etc. to prevent the upward passage of noxious gas. Hence **Ste·nchy** *a.* emitting a s., foul-smelling.

†**Stench** (stenʃ), *v.* [OE. (Northumb.) *stencan* :– **staŋkwjan*, f. **staŋkw-*; see prec.] **1.** *intr.* To have an ill smell, to stink –1570. **2.** *trans.* To cause to emit a stench, to make to stink, render offensive –1838.

Stencil (ste·nsĭl), *sb.* 1707. [f. next.] **1.** A thin sheet of metal, cardboard, etc., in which one or more holes have been cut, of such shape that when a brush charged with pigment is passed over the back of the sheet, a desired pattern, letter, or figure is produced upon the surface upon which the sheet is laid. **2.** A pattern or design produced by stencilling 1899. **3.** The colouring matter used in stencilling. Also (*Ceramics*), a composition used in transfer-printing and enamelling, to protect from the oil those portions of the pattern that are to be left uncoloured. 1853.

Comb.: **s.-brush,** the brush used in stencilling; **-plate** = sense 1.

Stencil (ste·nsĭl), *v.* [In sense 1, late ME. *stansel, stencel* – OFr. *estanceler, estenceler*, f. *estencele* (mod. *étincelle*) :– **stincilla*, f. L. *scintilla* spark. In sense 2 from the sb.] †**1.** *trans.* To ornament with bright colours or pieces of precious metal. late ME. only. **2. a.** To produce (an inscription, design, etc.) by using a stencil 1861. **b.** To mark or paint (a surface) with an inscription or design by means of a stencil 1833. Hence **Ste·nciller.**

‖**Steneosaurus** (stenĭ,ǒsǭ·rǒs). 1836. [mod. L., badly formed (after *Teleosaurus*) on Gr. στενός narrow + σαῦρος lizard.] A fossil genus of saurians characterized by a narrow beak.

Steno- (steno), comb. form of Gr. στενός narrow, as in **Stenocephalic** (-sĭfæ·lik) *a.*, (of a skull) characterized by abnormal or excessive narrowness. **Stenoderm** (ste·nodə̄ɹm), a bat of the genus *Stenoderma* or of the family *Stenodermata*, the members of which are characterized by having a contracted wing-membrane. **Stenode·rmine** *a.*, resembling a stenoderm; *sb.* a stenoderm. **Stenophyllous** (-fi·ləs) *a.*, having narrow leaves. **Stenopæic** (-pī·ik) *a.* [Gr. ὀπή opening], of an eye-piece, having only a narrow translucent aperture.

Stenog (stenǫ·g). *U.S. colloq.* 1906. = STENOGRAPHER. Hence **Ste·nog** *v.*

Stenograph (ste·nŏgrɑf), *v.* 1821. [Back-formation from next.] *trans.* To write in shorthand, to represent by stenography; also *absol.*

Stenographer (stĭnǫ·grăfəɹ). 1809. [f. next + -ER¹.] A shorthand writer.

Stenography (stĭnǫ·grăfi). 1602. [f. Gr. στενός narrow + -GRAPHY.] The art of writing in shorthand. Hence **Stenogra·phic, -al** *adjs.* of, pertaining to, or expressed in s.; **-ly** *adv.* by means of shorthand.

‖**Stenosis** (stĭnōᵘ·sis). *Pl.* **stenoses** (īz). 1866. [mod.L. – Gr. στένωσις narrowing, f. στενοῦν to narrow, f. στενός narrow.] *Path.* The contraction or stricture of a passage, duct, or canal. Hence **Steno·tic** *a.* pertaining to, characterized by or resulting from s.

Stenting (ste·ntiŋ), *sb.* Also **stenton.** 1812. [Of unkn. origin.] *Mining.* A passage between two winning headways.

Stentor (ste·ntǫɹ). 1600. [Gr. Στέντωρ (*Iliad* v. 785).] **1.** The name of a Greek warrior in the Trojan war, 'whose voice was as powerful as fifty voices of other men'; applied allusively to a man of powerful voice. ‖**2.** [mod.L.] A genus of Protozoa; an individual of this genus, a trumpet-shaped protozoan 1863. Hence **Stento·rious** *a.* = next.

Stentorian (stentōᵊ·riăn), *a.* 1605. [f. prec. + -IAN.] **1.** Of the voice: Loud, like that of Stentor; very loud and far-reaching; hence, of uttered sounds. **2.** That utters such sounds 1690.

1. 'Hold' exclaimed the general, in s. tones 1872. 2. S. lungs 1875. *S. trumpet* = STENTOROPHONIC *trumpet.*

Stentorophonic (ste:ntŏrofǫ·nik), *v.* 1678. [– mod.L. *Stentorophonicus* (f. Gr. Στεντορόφωνος having the voice of a Stentor, f. Στεντορ-, STENTOR + φωνή voice).] **1.** *S. horn, trumpet, tube*: a speaking trumpet –1831. **2.** †Loud as a speaking trumpet; in later use (echoed from Hudibras) = prec. 1. 1678.

Stentorphone (ste·ntǫɹfōᵘn). 1921. [f. STENTOR + -PHONE.] A specially powerful loud speaker.

Step (step), *sb.* [OE. *stepe, stæpe* :– WGmc. **stapiz*, f. **stap-*; see next.] **I.** Action of stepping. **1.** An act of bodily motion consisting in raising the foot from the ground and bringing it down again in a fresh position; usu., an act of this kind as constituting by repetition the progressive motion of a human being or animal in walking, running, or climbing. **b.** *contextually.* A footstep or footfall considered in regard to its audibility 1605. **c.** Manner of stepping or treading; one's stride OE. **d.** One of the various paces taught in drill; as *slow* or *quick s.* 1798. **e.** *Dancing.* Any one of the various paces taught by the master; esp. the gliding movement formerly used in the quadrille, etc. Also, a person's individual manner of pacing in the dance. 1678. **2.** *pl.* Progress by stepping or treading; a person's movements, his goings and comings, the course which he follows OE. **3.** *fig.* An action or movement which leads towards a result; one of a series of proceedings or measures 1549. **4.** In phrases which refer to the action of walking evenly with another 1613. **5.** The space traversed by the movement of one foot beyond the other in walking or running; a pace. Hence as a measure of length or distance. OE. **b.** With limitation or negative: A very short distance OE. **6.** A degree in an ascending scale; a remove in an upward process; a grade in rank or promotion OE. **b.** *Mus. By s.*: by progression through a single degree of the scale (i.e. a tone or semitone) 1889. **7.** A footprint ME.

1. If you will walk a few steps this way SCOTT. *False s.*: see FALSE *a.* 6. *Hop, s., and jump*: see HOP *sb.*² 3. **b.** Thou sowre and firme-set Earth Heare not my steps SHAKS. 2. Honour attend thy steps 1598. Phr. *To bend* or *direct* one's *steps* (to a place, etc.); *to retrace* one's *steps* (see RETRACE *v.*); *to guide, dog* a person's *steps.* 3. The next s. was to assert the royal supremacy 1860. 4. Phr. *In, out of, s.* (*with*); *s. for s.* (*with*); *to keep s.* (*with*; also *to* music, etc.). 5. The military s. of 30 inches, of which there are 2112 to a mile 1862. **b.** There is but one s., said Napoleon, from the sublime to the ridiculous 1831. 6. *To get the* or *one's s.* (Mil.), to be promoted to the next higher grade.

S. by s. a. Moving one foot after the other continuously; *fig.* by gradual and regular progress. **b.** Keeping pace with another. **c.** *attrib.* or quasi-*adj.* = that moves or advances s. by s. **To make** or **take a s. a.** To perform the act of moving the foot as in walking or climbing. †**b.** To make a short journey *to.* **c.** *fig. To take a s.* or *steps*: to perform a move or moves in a course of action; to take action towards attaining an end. *To take the necessary steps*: often, to take the action prescribed by law as necessary to attain some implied object.

II. Something on which to place the foot in ascending or descending. **1.** A flat-topped structure, normally made of wood or stone and some six or seven inches high, used, singly or as one of a series, to facilitate a person's movement from one level to another OE. **b.** The height or depth of this 1662. **c.** A foothold cut in a slope of earth or ice 1860. **d.** A flat projecting foot-piece, fixed or made to let down when wanted, for entering or alighting from a vehicle 1837. **e.** *Fortif.* = BANQUETTE 1. 1672. **2.** A rung or stave of a ladder; each of the flat cross-pieces of a step-ladder OE. **b.** *pl.* A step-ladder; also *a pair* or *set of steps. colloq.* 1693.

1. Adèle and I sat down on the top s. of the stairs to listen C. BRONTË. **c.** He cut steps down one side of a *sérac* 1871.

III. Transferred uses of sense II. 1. **1.** *Geol.* A fault or dislocation of strata 1789. **2.** An offset or part resembling a step in outline, singly or in a series; e.g. in the bit of a key 1674. **3.** *Naut.* The block in which is fixed the heel of a mast or capstan OE. **4.** *Mech.* **a.** The lower bearing or block on which a vertical pivot, shaft, or the like rotates 1814. **b.** The lower brass of a journal-box or pillow-block in which a horizontal shaft revolves 1875.

Comb.: **s.-board,** the tread or flat part of a wooden s.; **-collar,** a collar with a V-shaped opening at the junction of the collar and lapel; **-cut** = TRAP-CUT; also as *adj.*; **-dance,** a dance intended for the display of special steps by an individual performer; **-fault** *Geol.*, one of a series of parallel faults with successive falls like steps; **-wheel,** a wheel with an edge formed in twelve steps arranged spirally, used in striking-clocks; **-wise** *adv.* like a series of steps.

Step (step), *v.* Pa. t. and pa. pple. **stepped** (stept). [OE. *steppan, stæppan* = OFris. *stapa, steppa*, OS. **steppian*, (M)LG., (M)Du. *steppen*, OHG. *stapfōn, stepfen* (G. *stapfen*); WGmc. str. vb., f. **stap-*. Weak forms are found from the end of XIII, and became universal by XVI.] **I.** *intr.* To lift the foot and set it down again on the ground in a new position; to lift and set down the feet alternately in walking; to pace, tread. With adv.: To use a (specified) gait or motion of the feet (often of a horse). **b.** To move with measured paces in a dance. Also quasi-*trans.*, to go through the steps of, perform (a dance) 1698. **2.** To move to a new position by extending the foot to a higher or lower level or across an intervening object or space; with adv. or prep., as *across, in, into, off, out of, on* or *upon, over, up* OE. **3.** To go or proceed on foot. Now chiefly to go a 'step' or short distance for a particular purpose: often in polite formulas of request or direction to another person. OE. †**b.** *fig.* To advance, proceed (in an action, argument, etc.) –1644. †**4.** In pa. pple.: **a.** (*Well, far*, etc.) *stepped in age, in* or *into years*: advanced in years, elderly –1629. †**b.** *Far stepped*: far advanced *in* (an action, etc.) –1605. **5.** *colloq.* To go away, make off. late ME. **6.** Of a horse: To go at a good pace. Also joc. of persons. 1856. **7.** *Naut.* and *Mech.* Of a mast or other upright: To be fixed *in* its step. Of other parts: To be fixed or jointed *in* or *into* (a groove, etc.); to rest securely *on* or *against* (a support). 1791.

1. Phr. *As good* (etc.) *a man as ever stepped* (*in shoe-leather*). **b.** He stepped a minuet gravely and gracefully 1893. 2. *To s. short*, to make an insufficiently long stride, so that the foot fails to reach the intended position. 3. *To s. lively* (orig.

U.S. slang), to hurry up. **4. b.** I am in blood Stept in so farre SHAKS. **5.** Well, I must be stepping.. It's getting late 1902.

II. *trans.* (causal, or by omission of prep.) **1.** To move (the foot) forward or through a specified step. Phr. *To s. foot in* (a place). Now only *U.S.* 1540. **2.** To measure (a distance) by stepping over it. Also with *off, out.* 1832. **3.** *Naut.* and *Mech.* To fix (a mast or other upright) *in* or *into* its step; to fit (a piece) *into* (a groove, etc.); to fix securely *on* or *against* (a support) 1711. **4.** *Mech.* To cut steps in (a key); to arrange (the teeth of a toothed wheel or rack) stepwise 1856.

With preps. (*intr.*) **S. between –.** To come between (two persons, a person and thing, etc.) by way of severance, interruption, or interception. **S. into –. a.** See sense I. 3 and INTO *prep.* **b.** To walk into (a vehicle, etc.) by taking one or more steps up or down. **c.** To obtain possession of (an estate, a place, or office) at a single step; to succeed at once to (the place of another person or thing). †**d.** To enter suddenly and incautiously into (a course of action, etc.). **S. over –.** To walk or stride across (an intervening space, cavity, or obstacle); *fig.* to OVERSTEP, transgress; to 'skip', miss, or neglect in passing; also *Mil.* to be promoted to a position above (another who is considered to have a prior claim).

With advs. **S. aside.** *intr.* **a.** To go a little distance away from one's place or from the path one is following; to withdraw or retire for a short distance; to take one or more steps to one's right or left. †**b.** To abscond. **S. back. a.** To go back a little distance. **b.** To go one or more paces backwards without turning the body round. **S. down. a.** To go from a higher level to a lower, esp. by treading on a step or stairway. Also, to go a short distance to a place which is or is regarded as lower. **b.** *trans.* in *Electr.* To lower the voltage of (a current) by means of a transformer. Hence **s.-down,** used attrib. or as adj. designating a transformer that does this. **S. forth.** *intr.* To advance a short distance from one's place or position; to come out to the front or into the midst; to advance with some immediate purpose in view. **S. forward** = *s. forth.* **S. in. a.** To come or go indoors; to enter a house or apartment casually or for a short time. Also, to enter a boat, vehicle, etc. **b.** To come forward and join in what is going on; to enter the fray; to intervene in an affair, a dispute, etc. **c.** In *Wrestling*, to bring one's leg round an opponent's. In *Cricket*, of a batsman: To advance a step to meet a ball. Hence **step-in,** applied to garments made without fastenings, so that one must step into them. **S. off.** *Mil.* To begin to march at a prescribed pace. **S. out. a.** To go or come out from a place, usu. for a short distance or for a short time; esp. to leave the house, go out of doors. Also, to leave a boat or vehicle. Also, to move one or more paces away from one's position. **b.** *Mil.* To lengthen the pace in marching. **c.** To walk with a vigorous step or stride. **S. up. a.** To go up from a lower position to a higher; to mount, ascend (also *fig.*); *spec.* to go up by treading on a step or stairway. Also, in later use, to go a short distance, or pay a short visit, to a place which is regarded as higher. **b.** To mount a pulpit, rostrum, or the like. **c.** To come forward for some purpose; to leave one's place and come close *to* (a person). **d.** *U.S.* To raise the status, rate, quality, etc. (as by 'steps') 1920. **e.** *Electr.* To increase the voltage of (a current) by means of a transformer. Hence **S.-up,** used attrib. or as adj. designating a transformer that does this.

Step-, OE. *stēop-*, corresp. to OFris. *stiāp-*, OS. *stiof-*, (M)Du. *stief-*, MLG. *stēf-*, OHG. *stiof-* (G. *stief-*), ON. *stjúp-*; the prim. sense is indicated by its relation to OE. *āstīeped* bereaved, OHG. *stiufen* bereave, and the meaning 'orphan' of OE. *stēopbearn, -ċild*; a Gmc. combining element, prefixed to terms of relationship to designate the degrees of affinity resulting from the remarriage of a parent.

Stepbrother (ste·pbrɒːðəɹ). 1440. [STEP-.] A son of one's stepfather or stepmother.

Stepchild (ste·pˌtʃəild). [OE. *stēopċild*; see STEP-.] †**1.** An orphan. OE. and ME. only. **2.** A stepson or stepdaughter ME.

Stepdame (ste·pdēⁱm). Now *arch.* late ME. [f. STEP- + DAME *sb.* 8.] A stepmother.

Stepdaughter (ste·pdǭːtəɹ). [OE. *stēopdohtor*; see STEP-.] A daughter, by a former marriage, of one's husband or wife.

Stepfather (ste·pfāːðəɹ). [OE. *stēopfæder*; see STEP-.] The husband of one's mother by a subsequent marriage.

‖**Stephanion** (stĭfēⁱ·niŏn). *Pl.* **-ia, -ions.** 1878. [mod.L. use of Gr. στεφάνιον, dim. of στέφανος crown.] *Craniometry.* The point where the coronal suture crosses the temporal ridge.

Stephanite (ste·fănəit). 1849. [– G. *stephanit* (Haidinger, 1845), named after the Archduke *Stephan* of Austria; see -ITE¹ 2 b.] *Min.* Sulphantimonide of silver, black in colour and very brittle.

Stephanotis (stefănōᵘ·tis). 1870. [mod.L. – Gr. στεφανωτίς fem. adj., fit for a crown or wreath, f. στέφανος crown.] **1.** ‖**a.** *Bot.* A genus of tropical asclepiadaceous twining shrubs having fragrant white flowers. **b.** A plant of this genus; a flower of such a plant. **2.** A perfume said to be prepared from the flowers of *Stephanotis floribunda* 1907.

Ste·p-la:dder. 1751. [STEP *sb.*] A ladder which has flat steps instead of rungs.

Stepmother (ste·pmɒːðəɹ), *sb.* [OE. *stēopmōdor*; see STEP-.] The wife of one's father by a subsequent marriage. **b.** *transf.* Said of a bird that hatches another bird's eggs 1567. Hence **Ste·pmother** *v. trans.* (*a*) to provide with a s.; (*b*) to behave as a s. to, esp. with suggestion of unfairness or cruelty. **Ste·pmotherly** *a.* pertaining to or characteristic of a s.

Stepney (ste·pni). 1907. [Said to be from the name of *Stepney*-street, Llanelly, the place of manufacture.] A spare wheel with ready inflated tyre but no spokes, carried by motorists. Now *Obs.*

Steppe (step). 1671. [– Russ. *step'*.] **1.** One of the vast treeless plains of south-eastern Europe and Siberia. **2.** *transf.* An extensive plain, usu. treeless 1837.

Stepped (stept), (*ppl.*) *a.* 1833. [f. STEP *sb.* and *v.* + -ED.] Having a step or steps; formed in a series of steps.

In this style we have the simple gable of two lines..and the s. gable 1833. A wheel with s. teeth 1869.

Stepper (ste·pəɹ). 1835. [f. STEP *v.* + -ER¹.] A horse with good paces and showy action. Often with *good, sure,* etc. Cf. HIGH-STEPPER.

Ste·pping-stone. ME. [f. *stepping*, vbl. sb. f. STEP *v.*] **1.** A stone for stepping upon. **a.** A stone placed in the bed of a stream or on muddy or swampy ground, to facilitate crossing on foot. Chiefly *pl.* **b.** A raised stone on which the foot can be placed to facilitate a climb or ascent (*rare*) 1837. **c.** *transf.* A place for a break of journey 1849. **2.** *fig.* Something that is used as a means of rising in the world, or of making progress towards some object; often, a position, etc. that affords opportunity for further advancement 1653.

1. Once he fell into the brook crossing at the stepping-stones SCOTT. **2.** I held it Truth..That men may rise on stepping-stones Of their dead selves to higher things TENNYSON. These obstacles his genius had turned into stepping stones MACAULAY.

Stepsister (ste·psiːstəɹ). 1440. [STEP-.] A daughter of one's stepfather or stepmother.

Stepson (ste·psɒn). [OE. *stēopsunu*; see STEP-.] A son, by a former marriage, of one's husband or wife.

-ster, *suffix*, repr. OE. *-istræ, -istre, -estre*, corresp. to MLG. *-(e)ster*, (M)Du. *-ster*, WGmc. **-strja* :– Gmc. **-astrijōn*, **-estrijōn*, added to verbal pres. stems and to sbs., primarily applied to females, but in OE. and LDu. also to males.

In OE. *-estre* was freely used to form fem. agent-nouns, usu. by being appended to the pres.-stems of verbs. The few instances in which it is used as a masc. are renderings of the Latin designations of men exercising functions which among the English were peculiar to women, as *byrdistre* embroiderer (gl. *blaciarius*), *bæcestre* baker (gl. *pistor*), *sēamestre* tailor (gl. *sartor*).

In the south the suffix continued to be predominantly feminine throughout the ME. period, while in the north it came very early to be used, indiscriminately with -ER¹, as an agential ending irrespective of gender; from the 16th c. onwards the older words in *-ster*, so far as they have survived, have been regarded as masculines, in several instances giving rise to feminines in *-ess*, as *seamstress, songstress, huckstress*, etc. In the modern English period the suffix has been freely used, but it is doubtful whether any of the new formations are really derived from verbs; they are usually associated rather with sbs. than with vbs.

Stercobilin (stəɹkoˌbəi·lin). 1880. [irreg. f. L. *stercus* (*stercor-*) dung + *bilis* BILE + -IN¹.] The colouring matter of the fæces.

Stercoraceous (stəɹkŏrēⁱ·ʃəs), *a.* 1731. [f. L. *stercus, stercor-* dung + -ACEOUS.] **1.** Consisting of, containing, or pertaining to fæces. **b.** *Path.* Of vomiting: Consisting of fæces, fæcal 1754. **2.** *Ent.* Of certain beetles, flies, etc.: Frequenting or feeding on dung 1891.

Stercoral (stə̄·ɹkŏrăl), *a.* 1758. [f. L., *stercus, stercor-* dung + -AL¹.] *Path.* = prec.

Stercoranism (stə̄·ɹkŏrăniz'm). 1728. [f. as next + -ISM.] *Eccl. Hist.* The beliefs of the Stercoranists.

Stercoranist (stə̄·ɹkŏrănist). 1686. [– med.L. *stercoranista*, irreg. f. L. *stercus, stercor-* dung + -IST.] *Eccl. Hist.* A nickname given to one who holds that the consecrated elements in the Eucharist undergo digestion in, and evacuation from, the body of the recipient.

Stercorarious (stəɹkŏrēᵊ·riəs), *a.* 1656. [f. L. *stercorarius* (see next) + -OUS.] = STERCORACEOUS 1, 2.

Stercorary (stə̄·ɹkŏrări), *a.* and *sb.* 1664. [– L. *stercorarius*, f. *stercus, stercor-* dung; see -ARY¹.] **A.** *adj.* Of or pertaining to dung. Of insects: Living in or feeding on dung. **B.** *sb.* A place where manure is stored, a dung-heap. Now *rare* or *Obs.* 1759.

Stercorate (stə̄·ɹkŏreⁱt), *v.* 1623. [– *stercorat-*, pa. ppl. stem of L. *stercorare*, f. as prec.; see -ATE³.] *trans.* To manure or dung. So **Stercora·tion,** manuring with dung; †dung, manure 1605.

Stercorin (stə̄·ɹkŏrin). 1873. [– Fr. *stercorine*, f. as prec.; see -IN¹.] A fæcal extractive resembling biliary cholesterin.

Stercorous (stə̄·ɹkŏrəs), *a.* 1542. [– L. *stercorosus*, f. as prec.; see -OUS.] Stercoraceous, excrementitious.

‖**Sterculia** (stəɹkiū·liă). 1771. [mod.L., f. *Sterculius* the god of manuring, f. *stercus* dung.] **1.** *Bot.* A genus of polypetalous plants (typical of the family *Sterculiaceæ*); a plant of this genus. (Some of the species have a fetid odour, whence the name.) **2.** *Ent.* A beetle of the family *Xantholinidæ* 1874. Hence **Sterculia·ceous** *a. Bot.* pertaining to the *Sterculiaceæ*; **Stercu·liad,** a sterculiaceous plant.

Stere, ‖**stère** (stīᵊɹ, Fr. stęr). 1798. [Fr. *stère*, f. Gr. στερεός solid.] The unit of the metric system for solid measures; a cubic metre, equal to about 35.3 English cubic feet.

Sterelminthous (sterelmi·nþəs), *a.* 1843. [f. mod.L., *Sterelmintha* (irreg. f. Gr. στερεός solid + ἕλμινς, ἑλμινθ- intestinal worm) + -OUS.] *Zool.* Of or pertaining to the *Sterelmintha*, Owen's name for a division of the Entozoa comprising the endoparasitic worms having a solid body with no visceral cavity. So **Sterelmi·nthic** *a.*

Stereo¹ (stīᵊ·rio, ste·rio). 1823. abbrev. of STEREOTYPE; also *attrib.*, as *s. forme, matter.*

Stereo² (stīᵊ·rio, ste·rio). 1876. abbrev. of STEREOSCOPE, STEREOSCOPIC.

Stereo- (stīᵊ·rio, ste·rio), bef. a vowel prop. **stere-,** comb. form repr. Gr. στερεός solid, in various (chiefly recent) scientific and technical terms. (In some instances serving as comb. form of *stereoscope* or *stereoscopic*.)

Ste·reobate *Arch.*, a solid mass of masonry serving as a base for a wall or a row of columns; hence **Stereoba·tic** *a.* **Ste·reochrome,** stereochromy; also, a picture produced by this. **Ste·reochro·my,** a process of mural painting in which water-glass is used as a preservative against atmospheric influences. †**Ste:reo-ele·ctric** *a.*, applied to a (thermo-electric) current produced by contact of solids (opp. to HYDRO-ELECTRIC 2). **Stereomo·noscope,** an instrument with two lenses by which an image of an object is projected upon a screen of ground glass so as to appear solid, as in a stereoscope. **Ste·reopla:sm,** (*a*) *Biol.* Nägeli's term for the denser or more solid part of protoplasm (dist. from HYGROPLASM); (*b*) *Zool.* an endothecal structure in corals, enveloping or connecting the septa, or forming a mass in the interior. **Stereo·pticon,** a double magic lantern arranged to combine two images of the same object or scene upon a screen, so as to produce the appearance of solidity as in a stereoscope. **Stereosta·tic** *a.*, *Mech.* applied to an arch constructed to sustain the pressure of a mass of solid matter, as a geostatic arch. **Ste:reosta·tics,** the statics of solid bodies.

Stereochemistry (stīᵊ:rio-, ste:rioke·mistri). 1890. [f. STEREO- + CHEMISTRY.] That department of chemistry which deals with theoretical differences in the relative position in space of atoms in a molecule, in relation to differences in the optical and chemical properties of the substances. So **Ste:reoche·mical** *a.*

Stereogram (stīᵊrio-, ste·riogræm). 1866. [f. STEREO- + -GRAM.] **1.** A diagram representing a solid object on a plane; esp. a drawing in which the inequalities or curvature of a surface are indicated by contour lines or shading 1868. **2.** = next 1. 1866.

Stereograph (stīᵊ·rio-, ste·riograf). 1859. [f. STEREO- + -GRAPH.] **1.** A picture (or pair of pictures) representing the object so that it appears solid, a stereoscopic photograph. **2.** An instrument for making projections or geometrical drawings of skulls or similar solid objects 1877.

Stereographic (stīᵊ:rio-, ste:riogræ·fik), *a.* 1704. [– mod.L. *stereographicus*; see STEREO-, -GRAPHIC. Cf. Fr. *stéréographique.*] **1.** Delineating or representing a solid body on a plane; applied *spec.* to a kind of projection used in maps, etc. in which the centre of projection is a point on the surface of the sphere, and the whole sphere is represented once on an infinite plane, circles being represented as circles, and the angles being retained. **2.** Pertaining to stereoscopic photography 1859. So **Stereogra·phical** *a.* 1675; **-ly** *adv.* 1679.

Stereography (stīᵊri-, steri,ǫ·grăfi). 1700. [– mod.L. *stereographia*; see STEREO-, -GRAPHY. Cf. Fr. *stéréographie* (XVIII).] The art of delineating or representing the forms of solid bodies on a plane, as in perspective.

Stereometer (steri,ǫ·mĭtəɹ). 1801. [– Fr. *stéréomètre*; see STEREO-, -METER.] **1.** An instrument for measuring the specific gravity of porous or pulverulent bodies. **2.** An apparatus consisting of a frame of bars and columns with sliding rods and wires, for illustrating problems in solid geometry 1884.

Stereometry (steri,ǫmĕtri). Now *rare.* 1570. [– mod.L. *stereometria* – Gr. στερεομετρία; see STEREO-, -METRY. Cf. Fr. *stéréométrie* (XVI).] **1.** The art or science of measuring solids; that branch of geometry which deals with solid figures, solid geometry; the practical application of this to measurement of solid bodies. **2.** The art of measuring specific gravities with a STEREOMETER (sense 1) 1886. Hence **Stereome·tric, -al** *adjs.* pertaining to s.; relating to or existing in three dimensions of space.

Stereoscope (stīᵊ·rio-, ste·rioskōᵘp). 1838. [f. STEREO- + -SCOPE.] An instrument for obtaining from two pictures of an object, taken from slightly different points of view (corresponding to the positions of the two eyes), a single image giving the impression of solidity or relief, as in ordinary vision of the object itself. Hence **Ste:reoscopic** (-skǫ·pik) *a.* of, pertaining to, or adapted to the s.; having an appearance of solidity or relief like an object viewed in a s.; so **Ste:reosco·pically** *adv.* **Stereoscopist** (-ǫ·skŏpist), one skilled in the use of the s.; a maker of stereoscopes. **Stereo·scopy,** the art or practice of using the s.

Stereotomy (steri,ǫ·tŏmi). 1728. [– Fr. *stéréotomie*; see STEREO-, -TOMY.] The science or art of cutting, or making sections of, solids; that department of geometry which deals with sections of solid figures; the art of cutting stone or other solid bodies into measured forms, as in masonry. Hence **Ste:reoto·mic, -al** *adjs.* pertaining to s.; **Stereo·tomist,** one skilled in s.

Stereotype (stīᵊ·rio-, ste·riotəip), *sb.* and *a.* **1798.** [– Fr. *stéréotype* adj.; see STEREO-, -TYPE.] **A.** *sb.* **1.** The method or process of printing in which a solid plate of type-metal, cast from a papier-mâché or plaster mould taken from the surface of a forme of type, is used for printing from instead of the forme itself. **2.** A stereotype plate 1817. **b.** In generalized sense 1823. **3.** *fig.* Something continued or constantly repeated without change; a stereotyped phrase, formula, etc.; stereotyped diction or usage 1850.

2. b. The mode of casting s. 1823. **3.** The s. of school, newspaper and department prevails 1908.

Comb.: **s.-block,** (*a*) a s. plate; (*b*) a block of iron or wood on which a s. plate is fixed.

B. *adj.* **1.** *lit.* Of an edition: Printed by the process described in A. 1. Also used as an epithet of the process. 1801. **2.** *fig.* = STEREOTYPED b. Now somewhat *rare.* 1824.

2. He..answers now always with a kind of s. formula CARLYLE.

Stereotype (stīᵊ·rio-, ste·riotəip), *v.* 1804. [– Fr. *stéréotyper,* f. *stéréotype*; see prec.] **1.** *trans.* To cast a stereotype plate from (a forme of type); to prepare (literary matter) for printing by means of stereotypes. Also *absol.* **2.** *fig.* To fix or perpetuate in an unchanging form 1819.

2. Shakespeare and the Bible have stereotyped English 1874. **Ste:reoty:per,** one who makes stereotype plates; one who fixes unchangingly.

Ste·reotyped (-təipt), *ppl. a.* 1820. [f. prec. + -ED¹.] **a.** Cast in the form of, or prepared for printing by means of, stereotype (*rare*). **b.** Usu. *fig.* Fixed or perpetuated in an unchanging form.

b. Uttering..s. commonplaces MRS. GASKELL

Stereotypic (stīᵊ:rio-, ste:rioti·pik), *a. rare.* 1801. [f. STEREOTYPE *sb.* + -IC.] Pertaining to or having the character of a stereotype.

Stereotypy (stīᵊ·rio-, ste·riotəi:pi). 1891. [– Fr. *stéréotypie*; see STEREO-, -TYPE, -Y³.] **1.** The process of making stereotype plates; stereotyping. **2.** *Path.* Persistence of a fixed or stereotyped idea, mode of action, etc., in cases of insanity 1909.

Sterhydraulic (stɜ̄ɹhəidrǭ·lik), *a.* 1866. [– Fr. *stérhydraulique,* irreg. f. Gr. στερεός solid + Fr. *hydraulique.*] Applied to a form of hydraulic press in which pressure is generated by displacement of the contained liquid by a solid body, as a rod, screw, or rope, introduced with a continuous movement through a packed opening.

Steric (ste·rik), *a.* 1898. [irreg. f. Gr. στερεός solid + -IC.] *Chem.* Pertaining or relating to the arrangement in space of the atoms in a molecule.

‖**Sterigma** (stĕri·gmă). 1866. [mod.L. – Gr. στήριγμα support.] *Bot.* A stalk or filament: variously applied.

Sterile (ste rəil, ste·ril), *a.* 1552. [– (O)Fr. *stérile* or L. *sterilis,* cogn. with Skr. *staris,* Gr. στεῖρα barren cow, στέριφος barren, Goth. *stairō* fem. barren.] Barren; not producing fruit or offspring. **1.** Of soil, a country, etc.: Unproductive of vegetation 1572. **2.** Producing no offspring; incapable of producing offspring. (Chiefly of females.) 1552. †**b.** Causing sterility. SHAKS. **3.** Of a plant: Not bearing fruit 1626. **4.** Mentally or spiritually barren. Also, fruitless; barren *in* or *of* (something sought or desired). 1642. **5.** *Biol.* **a.** Of an organ or structure that would normally contain reproductive elements: Barren, infertile 1646. **b.** Of cells, etc.: Not capable of reproduction 1856. **6.** Free from micro-organisms. Now often of surgical instruments, etc. = STERILIZED. 1877.

1. Leane, stirrill, and bare Land SHAKS. Very S. Yeares BACON. **2.** Women frequently become s. after a miscarriage 1741. **3.** *Potentilla Fragaria* (S. Strawberry) 1845. **4.** He seems..to be very steril of Invention 1665. **5. a.** Flowers having stamens only, are staminiferous, staminal, or s. 1849. **6.** A s. needle or lancet 1898. Hence **Ste·rile-ly** *adv.*, **-ness.**

Sterility (stĕri·lĭti). late ME. [– (O)Fr. *stérilité* or L. *sterilitas,* f. *sterilis*; see prec., -ITY.] **1.** The quality of being sterile, barrenness. Also *fig.* **2.** The state of being free from micro-organisms 1877.

Sterilize (ste·riləiz), *v.* 1695. [f. STERILE *a.* + -IZE, or – (O)Fr. *stériliser.*] **1.** *trans.* To cause to be unfruitful; to destroy the fertility of. **2.** To deprive of fecundity; to render incapable of producing offspring 1828. **3.** *Biol.* To render (organs) sterile 1891. **4.** *fig.* To make mentally or spiritually barren; to render unproductive, unprofitable or useless 1880. **5.** To render free from micro-organisms 1878.

1. *absol.* The practice of sowing with salt, in order to s., is alluded to in the Old Testament 1910. **5.** The milk should be sterilized 1899. Hence **Ste:riliza·tion,** the action of sterilizing. **Ste·rilized** *ppl. a.* **Ste·rilizer.**

Sterlet (stɜ̄·ɹlĕt). 1591. [– Russ. *sterlyad'.*] A small species of sturgeon, *Acipenser ruthenus,* found in Russia.

Sterling (stɜ̄·ɹliŋ), *sb.* and *a.* ME. [Recorded earlier in OFr. *esterlin* (XI or XII), med.L. *sterlingus, libræ sterlingorum, libræ sterilensium* 'pounds of sterlings' (XII); plausibly referred to late OE. **steorling,* f. *steorra* STAR + -LING¹, some of the early Norman pennies bearing a small star.] **A.** *sb.* **1.** The English silver penny of the Norman and subsequent dynasties. Often in *pound of sterlings,* orig. a pound weight of silver pennies, afterwards a name for the English pound (240 pence) as a money of account. Also in *mark, shilling,* etc. *of sterlings. Obs.* exc. *Hist.* **b.** Applied to the Scottish penny. late ME. †**2.** = PENNYWEIGHT –1776. **3.** Money of the quality of the sterling or standard silver penny; genuine English money 1565. **4.** English money as dist. from foreign money. Formerly often in contrast to *currency,* i.e., the depreciated pounds, shillings, and pence of certain colonies. 1601. **b.** *attrib.* Related to or payable in sterling 1894. †**5.** Standard degree of fineness –1724.

1. Paid in starlings which were pence so called 1598. **3.** *fig.* You haue tane his tenders for true pay, Which are not starling SHAKS. **4.** The Tenants are obliged by their Leases to pay S., which is Lawful Current Money of England SWIFT. **b.** S. exchange 1912. **5.** Gold and Silver of the Right S. and Standard SWIFT.

B. *adj.* (Formerly often abbreviated *ster., sterl.*) **1.** In *pound,* etc. *s.,* altered from the older *pound,* etc. (*of*) *sterlings* (see A. 1), and orig. used in the same sense. Hence, in later use, appended to the statement of a sum of money, to indicate that English money is meant. 1444. **2.** Prefixed as the distinctive epithet of lawful English money or coin. Now *rare.* late ME. †**b.** *fig.* That has course or currency –1593. **3.** Of silver: †Having the same degree of purity as the penny. Hence, in later use: Of standard quality. 1488. **4.** Of character, principles, qualities, occas. of persons: Thoroughly excellent, capable of standing every test 1645.

1. Many millions s. 1838. **2.** A pennie loafe of Breade (of English starling money) was worth a crowne of gold 1590. Phr. *To pass for* (later *as*) *s.* (chiefly *fig.*). **b.** *Rich. II,* IV. 264. **3.** *S. mark, stamp,* the hall-mark guaranteeing s. quality; The s. mark upon plate 1776. **4.** Many sound and s. principles of conduct 1828. A young man of s. worth, and Spanish gravity W. IRVING.

Stern (stɜ̄ɹn), *sb.*¹ [OE. *stearn.* Cf. OFris. *stern,* etc., tern.] A seabird; the tern, esp. the black tern (*Hydrochelidon nigra*).

Stern (stɜ̄ɹn), *sb.*² ME. [prob. – ON. *stjórn* steering, f. base of *stýra* STEER *v.*; but the existence of OFris. *stiārne, stiōrne* stern, rudder, may indicate that there was a corresp. form in OE.] †**1.** The steering gear of a ship, the rudder and helm together; but often applied to the rudder only –1671. †**b.** *fig.* That which guides or controls affairs, actions, etc.; also, (from the metaphor of the ship of state) government, rule –1708. **2.** The hind part of a ship or boat (as dist. from the bow and midships); in restricted sense, the external rear part of a ship's hull; also *spec.* in vessels of ordinary type, the overhanging portion of the hull abaft the stern-post ME. **3.** The buttocks of a person (chiefly *joc.* and *vulgar*) or beast; the hinder part of any creature 1614. **4.** The tail of an animal, esp. of a sporting-dog or a wolf 1575.

1. b. I intend to..sit at chiefest Sterne of publique Weal SHAKS. **2.** Phr. *Down by the s.*: see BY A. 1 d. *S.-foremost,* backwards, with the s. (senses 2, 3) first. *S. on,* with the s. presented. **3.** We don't want to..fancy them cherubs without sterns FURNIVALL.

attrib. and *Comb.*: **s.-frame,** the framework of a ship's s.; **-knee** = STERNSON; **-port,** a port or window in the s. of a vessel; **s. sea,** a following sea.

Stern (stɜ̄ɹn), *a.* (*adv.*) [OE. **stierne* (implied in *stiernlīće* adv.), late WS. *styrne* :– WGmc. **sternja,* prob. f. **ster-* **star-* be rigid (cf STARE *v.*).] **A.** *adj.* **1.** Of persons and things personified, their dispositions, etc.; Severe, inflexible; rigorous in punishment or condemnation. **b.** Rigorous in morals or principles; uncompromising, austere. late ME. **c.** Of personal attributes, actions, feelings, etc.: Severe, strict, hard, grim, harsh ME. **2.** Of battle, debate, etc.: Stubbornly-contested, fierce, hard ME. **†3.** In a bad sense: Merciless, cruel –1600. **4.** Of looks, bearing, gait: Indicating a stern disposition or mood; expressing grave displeasure; resolute, austere, gloomy. late ME. **b.** *transf.* Of a building: Severe in style; gloomy or forbidding in aspect 1822. **5.** Of the voice: Expressive of a stern disposition or mood ME. **†6.** Of things, in transf. uses; *esp.* of blows, weapons: Inflicting severe pain or injury –1805. **7.** Of a country, or its physical features, the soil, etc.: Unkindly, inhospitable; forbidding in aspect, frowning, gloomy 1812. **8.** Of circumstances and conditions: Oppressive, hard, inexorable; esp. *s. necessity, s. reality* 1830.

1. The s., ambitious, military old bishop 1841. **b.** Lord Nithsdale, who was a s. Catholic 1835. **c.** Ambition should be made of sterner stuffe SHAKS. The s. policy that dictated his execution 1820. **3.** How many Lambs might the sterne Wolfe betray SHAKS. **4.** Gods and men Fear'd her s. frown MILT. **7.** Mountains s. and desolate WORDSW.

B. *adv.* or *quasi-adv.* Sternly, resolutely, severely, harshly. (*Obs.* or *arch.*) ME.

He shook his Miter'd locks, and s. bespake MILT. Hence **Ste·rn-ly** *adv.*, **-ness.**

Stern (stɔ̄ɹn), *v.* late ME. [f. STERN *sb.*²] **†1.** *trans.* and *intr.* To steer, govern –1648. **2.** *trans.* To propel (a boat) stern foremost; also *intr.* to go stern foremost 1845. **3.** To place astern, in the phr. *s. the buoy* 1711.

Sternad (stɔ̄·ɹnæd), *adv.* 1803. [f. STERNUM + -AD II (cf. DEXTRAD, etc.).] Towards the sternum or the sternal aspect.

†Ste·rnage. 1599. [f. STERN *sb.*² + -AGE.] The sterns of a fleet collectively. SHAKS.

Sternal (stɔ̄·ɹnăl), *a.* (and *sb.*) 1756. [f. STERNUM + -AL¹, after *dorsal, ventral.*] *Anat.* and *Zool.* **1.** Of, pertaining to, or connected with the sternum or breast-bone. **2.** Situated on the same side as the sternum; anterior (in man) or inferior (in other animals); ventral; hæmal. (Opp. to *dorsal, tergal,* or *neural.*) 1803. **3.** Of or pertaining to a sternum or sternite in Arthropoda; sternitic 1835. **B.** as *sb.* A sternal bone 1901.

Sternbergite (stɔ̄·ɹnbɔ̄ɹgəit). 1826. [f. name of Count Caspar *Sternberg*; see -ITE¹ 2 b.] *Min.* A native sulphide of silver and iron, occurring in brown flexible laminæ with metallic lustre.

Ste·rn-board. 1815. [f. STERN *sb.*² + BOARD *sb.*] **1.** A board forming the flat part of the stern of a small boat, punt, etc. 1849. **2.** *Naut.* In phr. *to make a s.*, to go backwards as the result of tacking; also, to force a ship astern with the sails 1815.

Ste·rn-chase. 1627. [f. STERN *sb.*² + CHASE *sb.*¹] *Naut.* **1.** A chase in which the pursuing ship follows directly in the wake of the pursued. **†2.** The chase-guns arming the stern of a warship –1798.

1. *Prov.* A stern chase is a long chase 1849.

Ste·rn-cha:ser. 1815. *Naut.* A gun belonging to the STERN-CHASE (sense 2).

‖**Sternebra** (stɔ̄·ɹnībră). *Pl.* **-æ** (-ī). 1846. [mod.L. f. STERNUM, with ending of VERTEBRA.] *Anat.* Any one of the segments of the sternum, each corresponding to a pair of ribs. Hence **Ste·rnebral** *a.* pertaining to or constituting a s.

Sterned (stɔ̄ɹnd), *a.* 1611. [f. STERN *sb.*² + -ED².] Having a stern. Only in combs., as *black-s., square-s.*

Ste·rn-fast. 1569. [f. STERN *sb.*² + FAST *sb.*²] *Naut.* A rope by which a vessel's stern is moored.

Sternite (stɔ̄·ɹnəit). 1868. [f. STERNUM + -ITE¹ 3.] *Zool.* The under or ventral part of each somite or segment of the body of an insect or other arthropod.

Sternmost (stɔ̄·ɹnmōᵘst, -məst), *a.* 1622. [f. STERN *sb.*² + -MOST.] **1.** Farthest in the rear, last in a line of ships. **2.** Nearest the stern 1838.

1. He came alongside the s. ship SOUTHEY.

Sterno- (stɔ̄rno), bef. a vowel **stern-**, comb. form repr. Gr. στέρνον or L. STERNUM, occurring in several terms, usu. denoting muscles, etc. connected with the sternum and some other part.

‖**Sternalgia** (-æ·ldʒiă) [Gr. ἄλγος pain], pain in the region of the sternum; spec. *angina pectoris.* **Ste:rnoclavi·cular** *a.*, pertaining to or connecting the sternum and the clavicle. **Sternoco·stal** [L. *costa* rib] *a.*, pertaining to or connecting the sternum and the ribs. **Sterno-hy·oid** *a.*, pertaining to or connecting the sternum and the hyoid bone; the name of each of the two muscles serving to depress the larynx; also as *sb.* **Sternoma·stoid** *a.*, pertaining to or connecting the sternum and the mastoid process of the temporal bone; also as *sb.* (*sc.* muscle). **Ste:rnomaxi·llary** *a.*, pertaining to or connecting the sternum and lower jaw-bone. **Sternothy·roid** *a.*, pertaining to or connecting the sternum and the thyroid cartilage; also as *sb.* (*sc.* muscle). **Sterno-ve·rtebral** *a.*, connected with the sternum and the vertebræ.

Ste·rn-post. late ME. [f. STERN *sb.*² + POST *sb.*¹] *Naut.* A more or less upright beam, rising from the after end of the keel and supporting the rudder. **b.** *attrib.*, as *s.-knee* (= STERNSON) 1845.

Ste·rn-sheet. 1481. [f. STERN *sb.*² + SHEET *sb.*²] *Naut.* **1.** *sing.* and *pl.* The internal stern portion of a boat; *spec.* that part abaft the hindmost thwart. **2.** *pl.* **a.** The flooring boards in the after portion of a boat or small ship 1644. **b.** The seats with which the after portion of a boat is furnished 1912.

Sternson (stɔ̄·ɹnsən). 1846. [f. STERN *sb.*², after KELSON. Cf. STEMSON] *Naut.* In a wooden vessel, the knee-shaped timber fitted into the angle formed by the junction of stern-post and kelson in order to secure the joint. **b. S.-knee** (in the same sense) 1849.

Sternum (stɔ̄·ɹnǒm). *Pl.* **sterna, sternums.** 1667. [mod.L. – Gr. στέρνον chest, breast.] *Anat.* and *Zool.* **1.** The breast-bone; a long bone or series of bones, occurring in most vertebrates except snakes and fishes, extending along the middle line of the front or ventral aspect of the trunk, usu. articulating with some of the ribs, and with them completing the wall of the thorax. **2.** *Zool.* The ventral part of any somite of an arthropod; opp. to *tergum* 1835.

Sternutation (stɔ̄ɹniutēⁱ·ʃən). 1545. [– L. *sternutatio, -ōn-*, f. *sternutare*, frequent. of *sternuere* sneeze; see -ATION.] The action of sneezing; a sneeze. (Chiefly *Med.* and *Path.*; otherwise, in mod. use, *joc.*)

Sternutative (stəɹniū·tătiv), *a.* and *sb.* Now *rare.* 1666. [Variant of next, by substitution of suffix -IVE.] = next.

Sternutatory (stəɹniū·tătŏri), *a.* and *sb.* 1616. [– late L. *sternutatorius* adj. and med.L. *-orium* sneezing-powder (XV); see STERNUTATION, -ORY. Cf. (O)Fr. *sternutatoire* (XIII).] **A.** *adj.* **1.** Causing or tending to cause sneezing. **2.** Of or pertaining to sneezing 1842. **B.** *sb.* A substance that causes sneezing; *esp.* an errhine 1634.

Ste·rn-wheel. 1816. [STERN *sb.*²] A paddle wheel placed at the stern of a small river or lake steamer. Hence **Ste·rn-whee:ler**, a boat propelled by a s.

Sterol (ste·rǫl). 1913. *Biol. Chem.* The ending of CHOLESTEROL, ERGOSTEROL, etc., used as a separate word to denote one of a group of allied complex solid alcohols of importance in the synthesis of vitamins.

Ste·rro-me:tal (ste·ro). 1865. [Gr. στερεός stiff, hard.] An alloy of copper and zinc, with a small amount of iron and tin. Also *sterro.*

Stertor (stɔ̄·ɹtǫɹ). 1612. [mod.L. (after *rigor*, etc.), f. L. *stertere* to snore; see -OR 1.] A heavy snoring sound accompanying inspiration in profound unconsciousness.

Stertorous (stə·ɹtŏrəs), *a.* 1802. [f. prec. + -OUS.] Characterized by or of the nature of stertor or snoring.

Hence **Ste·rtorously** *adv.* **Ste·rtorousness.**

Stet (stet). 1821. [L., 3rd sing. pres. subj. of *stare.*] *Printing.* 'Let it stand'; a direction on a proof or MS. that matter which has been altered or struck out is to remain uncorrected. Hence as *v. trans.* to cancel a correction by writing 'stet' in the margin and underlining the words with a series of dots.

Stetho- (steþo), bef. a vowel **steth-**, comb. form repr. Gr. στῆθος breast, chest, occurring in medical terms. **Stethe·ndoscope** [Gr. ἔνδον within + -SCOPE], an instrument for examining the inside of the chest by means of Röntgen rays.

Stethograph (ste·þŏgraf). 1876. [f. STETHO- + -GRAPH.] An instrument for automatically recording the movements of the chest in breathing; a recording stethometer; also called *pneumograph.*

Stethometer (stīþǫ·mĭtəɹ, steþ-). 1850. [f. STETHO- + -METER.] An instrument for measuring the extent of the movement of the walls of the chest in breathing. So **Stethome·tric** *a.* pertaining to or obtained by means of the s. **Stethometry** (-ǫ·mĕtri), measurement by a s., the use of the s.

Stethoscope (ste·þŏskoᵘp), *sb.* 1820. [– Fr. *stéthoscope* (Laennec, the inventor, c1819); see STETHO-, -SCOPE.] An instrument used for examining the chest or other part by auscultation, the sound of the heart, lungs, or other internal organs being conveyed by means of it to the ear of the observer. Hence **Ste·thoscope** *v. trans.*, to apply a s. to; to examine with a s. **Stethoscopic** (-skǫ·pik), **-al** *adjs.* pertaining to, of the nature of, observed or obtained by a s.; **-ly** *adv.* by means of the s. **Stethoscopist** (-ǫ·skŏpist), one who uses a s. **Stetho·scopy.**

Stetson (ste·tsən). 1924. [Name of maker.] A slouch hat worn by soldiers of the Australian and New Zealand forces.

Stevedore (stī·vĭdōᵊɹ), *sb.* 1788. [– Sp. *estivador*, f. *estivar* stow a cargo; see STEEVE *v.*²] A workman employed either as overseer or labourer in loading and unloading the cargoes of merchant vessels. Hence **Ste·vedore** *v. trans.* to stow (cargo) in a ship's hold; to load or unload the cargo of (a ship).

Steven (stev'n). *Obs.* exc. *dial.* [OE. *stefn, stemn*, corresp. to OFris. *stifne, stemme*, OS. *stemn(i)a, stemma*, OHG. *stimna, stimma* (G. *stimme*), Goth. *stibna* :– Gmc. *stemnō.] **1.** = VOICE in various applications. In mod. dial. use chiefly: A loud voice. **2.** Outcry, noise, tumult, din. late ME.

1. Sche cryeth 'systyr' with ful loude a steuene CHAUCER.

Stew (stiū), *sb.*¹ late ME. [– Fr. *estui* place of confinement, fish-pond (mod. *étui*; cf. TWEEZERS), f. *estoier* put into the sheath or scabbard, shut up, conceal, reserve :– Rom. *studiare care for, f. L. *studium* STUDY *sb.*] **†1.** In phr. *in s.* [= OFr. *en estui*], said of fish kept in confinement, to be ready for the table –1573. **2.** A pond or tank in which fish are kept until needed for the table. late ME. **3.** An artificial oyster-bed 1610.

Stew (stiū), *sb.*² ME. [– OFr. *estuve* (mod. *étuve*), rel. to *estuver*; see next.] **I.** A stove, heated room. **†1.** A vessel for boiling, a caldron –1603. **†2.** A heated room; a room with a fireplace –1572. **3.** A heated room used for hot air or vapour baths: hence, a hot bath. *Obs.* exc. *Hist.* or *arch.* late ME. **4.** *pl.* A brothel. (Developed from sense 3, on account of the frequent use of the public hot-air baths for immoral purposes.) *Hist.* late ME. **†b.** (*sing.* and *pl.*) A bawd or prostitute –1650.

4. He strongly censured the licensed stews at Rome BOSWELL.

II. Senses derived from STEW *v.* **1.** A preparation of meat slowly boiled in a stew-pan, usually containing vegetables, etc. 1576. **2.** A state of excitement, esp. of great alarm or anxiety 1806. **3.** *colloq.* A state of being overheated or bathed in perspiration 1892.

1. *Irish s.*, a dish composed of pieces of mutton, potatoes, and onions stewed together. **2.** Poor Mr. Allen is in a s. about his sermon 1809.

Stew (stiū), *v.* late ME. [– OFr. *estuver* (mod. *étuver*) :– Rom. *extupare, *extufare (cf. med.L. *stūpa, stūfa*), prob. f. EX-¹ + *tūfus – Gr. τῦφος smoke, steam, with poss. infl. from Gmc. *stub- (see STOVE).] **1.** *trans.* To bathe in a hot bath or a vapour bath –1665. **2.** *Cooking.* **a.** *trans.* To boil slowly in a close vessel; to cook (meat, fruit, etc.) in a liquid kept at the simmering-point. late ME. **b.** *intr.* Of meat, fruit, etc.: To undergo stewing 1594. **c.** In fig. phrases, with the sense: To be left to suffer the natural consequences of one's own actions 1656. **3.** *transf.* **†a.** *trans.* To bathe in perspiration –1687.

†**b.** *fig.* To soak, steep, imbue –1822. **c.** To confine in close or ill-ventilated quarters. Chiefly with *up.* 1590. **d.** *intr.* To stay excessively long in bed. Also, to remain in a heated or stifling atmosphere; hence *slang*, to study hard. 1671.

2. a. Pour it on your pippins, and s. them till they are quite tender 1770. **c.** Phr. *to s. in one's own juice* [cf. Fr. *cuire dans son jus*]. He would let them s. in their own..juice 1885. **3. b.** *Haml.* III. iv. 93. **d.** Stewing over his books 1866.

Steward (stiū·ǝɹd), *sb.* [OE. *stiġweard, stīweard*, f. *stiġ* (prob.) house, hall + *weard* WARD *sb.*] **1.** An official who controls the domestic affairs of a household, supervising the service of his master's table, directing the domestics, and regulating household expenditure; a major-domo. *Obs.* exc. *Hist.* **b.** A member of a college who supervises the catering or presides at table 1749. **c.** A servant of a college who is charged with the duty of catering. Also, the head servant of a club or similar institution 1518. **d.** An officer in a ship who, under the direction of the captain or the purser, keeps the stores and arranges for the serving of meals; now applied to any attendant who waits upon the passengers 1450. **2.** As the title of an officer of a royal household. **a.** *gen.* Orig., an officer with similar functions to the 'steward' of an ordinary household (see sense 1). *Obs.* exc. *Hist.* OE. **b.** (**Lord**) **S. of the King's Household.** A peer whose nominal duty it is to control the King's household above stairs, and to preside at the Board of Green Cloth. late ME. **3.** One who manages the affairs of an estate on behalf of his employer. late ME. **b.** The administrator, often with merely nominal duties, of certain estates of the Crown, as †*S. of the Duchy of Lancaster* 1444. **c.** In Scotland: A magistrate orig. appointed to administer the crown lands forming a STEWARTRY. late ME. **4.** *fig.* (from senses 1 and 3.) An administrator and dispenser of wealth, favours, etc.; esp. one regarded as the servant of God or of the people OE. **5.** In various societies and corporations, the title of certain officers (e.g. *city s.*; *s. of the Jockey Club*) OE. **6. High S.** In the Universities of Oxford and Cambridge, the title (in academic Latin *seneschallus*) of a judicial officer, in whom is vested the jurisdiction belonging to the university in causes of treason and felony 1450. **b.** In certain English cities, a municipal title of dignity, usu. borne by a nobleman or royal prince 1563. **7.** A person appointed to supervise the arrangements or maintain order at a race meeting, exhibition, dinner, ball, concert, public gathering, etc. 1703. **8.** An overseer of workmen ME. **9.** Among Methodists, a layman appointed to manage the financial affairs of a congregation or of a circuit 1741.

1. Antonio Bologna, s. of the household to the Duchess 1611. **d.** *Bath-, cabin-, deck-, table-s.*; *captain's s.*, etc. **2.** (**Lord High**) **S. of England.** The title of a high officer of state, the earlier *senescallus Angliæ*; since the accession of Henry IV appointed only on the occasion of a coronation at which he presides, or for the trial of a peer. (**Lord High**) **S. of Scotland.** *Hist.* The first officer of the Scottish King in early times. **3.** *S. of the manor*, one who transacts the financial and legal business of a manor on behalf of the lord; he holds the manor-court in the lord's absence, and keeps a copy of its rolls, whence the name *s. of copyhold.* So *S. of the leet, s. of the hundred*, etc. **b.** *S. of the Chiltern Hundreds*: see CHILTERN. **4.** A man of business and a vigilant s. of the public money MACAULAY. **5.** The Stewards and Members of the Jockey Club 1831. Hence **Stew·ard** *v. trans.* to manage, administer; *intr.* to do the duties of a s. **Stew·ardly** *adv.* (*rare*) like a s., with the care of a s. **Stew·ardship**, the office of a s.; conduct of the office of s., administration.

Stewardess (stiū·ǝɹdės). 1631. [f. prec. + -ESS[1].] A female who performs the duties of a steward. **b.** Now chiefly: A female attendant on a ship whose duty it is to wait on the women passengers 1837.

Stewartry, stewardry (stiū·ǝɹtri, stiū·ǝɹdri). Chiefly *Sc.* 1473. [f. as prec. + -RY.] **1.** A former territorial division of Scotland under the jurisdiction of a steward. **2.** The office of steward in such a territory 1483.

Stewed (stiūd), *ppl. a.* [f. STEW *v.* + -ED[1].] Cooked by slow boiling in a closed vessel. Of tea: made strong and bitter by being kept too long in the pot.

Stewpan (stiū·pæn). 1651. [f. STEW *sb.*[2] or *v.* + PAN *sb.*] A saucepan for stewing.

Stewpot (stiū·pǫt). 1628. [f. as prec. + POT *sb.*] A covered pot for stewing meat, etc.

Sthenic (spe·nik), *a.* 1788. [f. after contemp. ASTHENIC; cf. STHENIA (O.E.D.) and ASTHENIA.] *Path.* Applied to diseases characterized by a normal or excessive accumulation of 'excitability' or vital power in the system. In later use, of diseases, symptoms, etc.: Marked by normal or excessive vital or nervous energy. Opp. to *asthenic.*

Stib-. 1852. Used in *Chem.* as comb. form of STIBIUM: cf. STIBIO-.

Stibic (sti·bik), *a. rare.* 1609. [f. STIBIUM + -IC.] Of or belonging to antimony; antimonic.

Stibiconite (sti·bikŏnǝit). 1843. [f. STIBIUM + Gr. κόνις dust + -ITE[1] 2 b.] *Min.* A hydrous oxide of antimony, sometimes found in a pulverulent form.

Stibine (sti·bǝin). 1843. [– Fr. *stibine* (Beudant, 1832); see STIBIUM, -INE[5], and cf. STIBNITE.] **1.** *Min.* = STIBNITE. **2.** *Chem.* Any of the antimony-compounds on the type of ammonia, SbH_3. 1852.

Stibio- (sti·bio). 1857. Comb. form of STIBIUM, used in *Chem.* and *Min.*

Stibium (sti·biŏm). late ME. [– L. *stibium* – Gr. στίβι, στίμμι – Egyptian *stm.*] 'Black antimony', i.e. trisulphide of antimony calcined and powdered, used as a cosmetic for blackening the eyelids and eyebrows. †Formerly used also for metallic antimony or any of its salts, esp. as a poison or an emetic.

Stibnite (sti·bnǝit). 1854. [Refashioning of STIBINE after names of minerals in -ITE[1] 2 b; see -INE[5].] *Min.* Native trisulphide of antimony, 'gray antimony', the most common ore of the metal.

Sticcado (stikā·do). 1776. [perh. – It. *steccato.*] *Mus.* A kind of xylophone.

Stich (stik). 1723. [– Gr. στίχος row, line, verse.] A portion or division of prose or verse writing, of a measured or average length; a line, verse.

Stichic (sti·kik), *a.* 1864. [– Gr. στιχικός, f. στίχος STICH; see -IC.] **1.** Pertaining to or consisting of verses or lines. **2.** *Pros.* Consisting of successive lines of the same metric form 1886. So **Sti·chical** *a.* (in sense 1) 1787.

Stichidium (stiki·diŏm). *Pl.* **-ia** (-iă). 1855. [mod.L., f. Gr. στίχος STICHOS + dim. suffix *-idium* (= Gr. -ιδιον).] *Bot.* A pod-like receptacle for tetraspores in some rose-spored Algæ.

Stichochrome (sti·kokrōᵘm). 1899. [f. Gr. στίχος row, etc. + χρῶμα colour.] *Phys.* Any nerve-cell having the chromophilic bodies arranged in more or less regular layers.

Stichometrical (stikome·trikăl), *a.* 1845. [f. next + -ICAL.] Of or pertaining to stichometry; characterized by measurement by *stichoi* or lines. So **Stichome·tric** *a.* **Stichome·trically** *adv.*

Stichometry (stikǫ·mėtri). 1754. [– late Gr. στιχομετρία, f. στίχος STICHOS; see -METRY.] *Palæogr.* **a.** The measurement of a manuscript text by *stichoi* or lines of fixed or average length into which the text is divided. Also, a list or appendix stating this length. **b.** Occas. used for: The practice of writing a prose text in lines of nearly equal length corresponding to divisions in the sense. Also, *stichoi* collectively. 1875.

b. S. was really nothing but a cumbrous substitute for punctuation 1881.

‖**Stichomythia** (stikomi·piă). Also **stichomuthia** (miū·piă). 1861. [mod.L. – Gr. στιχομυθία, f. στίχος STICHOS + μῦθος speech, talk.] In classical Greek Drama, dialogue in alternate lines, employed in sharp disputation, and characterized by antithesis and rhetorical repetition or taking up of the opponent's words. Also applied to modern imitations of this.

‖**Stichos** (sti·kǫs). *Pl.* **stichoi** (sti·koi). 1863. [– Gr. στίχος STICH.] **1.** In the Greek Ch., a verse or versicle. **2.** *Palæogr.* A line of a stichometrically written text; a line of average length assumed in measuring the contents of a text or codex 1885.

Stick (stik), *sb.*[1] [OE. *sticca* stick, peg, spoon = OFris. *stekk*, MDu. *stecke* (Du. *stek* slip, cutting), OHG. *stecko* (G. *stecken* stick, staff) :– WGmc. **stikka*, synon. vars. of which with single *-*k*- are repr. by OHG. *stehho*, ON. *stika*; f. **stik*- **stek*- pierce, prick; see STICK *v.*[1]] **I.** A rod or staff of wood. **1.** A short piece of wood, esp. a piece cut and shaped for a special purpose. **2.** A slender branch or twig of a tree or shrub, esp. when cut or broken off. Now *rare.* OE. **b.** *pl.* Pieces of cut or broken branches, also pieces of cut and chopped wood, used as fuel ME. **c.** A twiggy bough or long rod stuck in the ground for a plant to 'run' upon 1577. **3.** A stem or thick branch of a tree cut and trimmed and used as timber for building, fencing, etc.; a stave, stake. late ME. **4.** A long and relatively slender piece of wood, whether in natural form or shaped with tools, cut or broken of a convenient length for handling. late ME. **b.** A staff, club, cudgel used as a weapon. late ME. **c.** (Chiefly *the s.*) A beating with a stick. *colloq.* 1856. **d.** = WALKING-STICK 1620. **e.** A rod of dignity, or office, a baton; also the bearer of such a stick 1688. The rod of a sky-rocket 1651. **5.** *spec.* in various games. **a.** A staff for striking or pushing, as in Hockey; also applied to a billiard cue, a golf club, etc. 1674. **b.** Hence in Hockey, *Sticks*, the word used by the umpire in declaring a breach of rule committed by improperly handling the stick; a breach of rule of this kind 1896. **c.** *Cricket.* pl. The stumps of a wicket, the wicket. *rare* in *sing.* Also *Football* the goalposts 1862. **6.** A timber-tree; also, a tree-trunk when cut for timber; more fully *s. of timber* 1748. **7.** *Naut.* A mast or portion of a mast; also a yard. *The sticks*, the masts and yards. 1802.

2. b. Come, Hostis,..lay a few more sticks on the fire WALTON. **3.** *Every s.* (*and stone*), the whole materials of a building. **4.** *Cleft s.*: see CLEFT *ppl. a.* **c.** Come in,..or I'll give you the s. 1856.

II. Transf. uses. **1.** A piece of material rolled, moulded, or cut for convenience of use into a long and slender form like that of a stick: e.g. of sweetstuff; of glass; of lac or sealing-wax 1460. **2.** The stem of a culinary plant when trimmed for use, e.g. a root of celery with its blanched leaf-stems; a leaf-stem of rhubarb; a young shoot of asparagus 1756. **3. a.** A support for a candle, a candlestick 1540. **b.** = COMPOSING-*stick* 1683. **c.** A violin bow, a fiddlestick 1600. **d.** *pl.* The thin pieces of ivory, bone, or other material upon which the folding material of a fan is mounted 1701. **e.** A joy-stick 1914. **4.** *slang.* **a.** *pl.* Furniture, household goods; more fully *sticks of furniture.* Rarely *sing.* in *every s.*, every article of furniture. 1809. **b.** (Now *U.S.* and *colonial.*) *With a s. in it*: said of tea coffee, etc., with a dash of brandy 1804. **5.** Applied to a person, as *tough s.*, *queer s.* 1682. **b.** A 'wooden' person; one lacking in capacity for his work, or in geniality of manner; *Theatr.* an indifferent actor 1800.

1. Pink sticks of barley sugar THACKERAY. **5.** *Crooked s.*, a perverse, cross-grained person. Phr. (*To have* or *get*) *the right* or *the wrong end of the s.*, to have the advantage or the contrary in a bargain or a contest. Also, *to have got hold of the wrong end of the s.*, to have got a story wrong, not know the facts of the case. *To hold sticks with*, to compete on equal terms with.

Comb.: **s.-bug** *U.S.* (*a*) = *s.-insect*; (*b*) a predaceous reduvioid bug, *Emesa longipes*; **-caterpillar, -looper**, a geometrid larva resembling a bit of stick; **s. chimney** *U.S.*, a log-house chimney composed of sticks piled up crosswise and cemented with mud or clay; **-insect**, any insect of the family *Phasmidæ*, from its resemblance to the branches and twigs of the trees in which it is found.

Stick (stik), *sb.*[2] *Obs.* exc. *Hist.* [First in AL. (Domesday Bk. etc.) *stica, sticha, sticka, estika*; it is not clear whether the word thus latinized was English (= STICK *sb.*[1]); cf. MLG. *sticke* in 'xx sticken anguillarum'.] A measure of quantity in small eels (app. 25 or 26).

Stick (stik), *sb.*[3] 1646. [f. next.] **1.** A temporary stoppage, a hitch; a boggle. *Obs.* exc. *arch.* **2.** Something which causes hindrance or delay, a difficulty, an obstacle. *Obs.*

exc. *arch.* 1657. **3.** The power of adhering or of causing a thing to adhere 1853. **4.** A batsman who is not easily 'got out' 1863.

1. When we came at the Hill Difficulty, he made no s. at that BUNYAN.

Stick (stik), *v.*[1] Pa. t. and pa. pple. **stuck** (stɒk). [OE. *stician* = OHG. *stehhan* prick, stab, with parallel forms in (M)LG., (M)Du. *stikken*, OHG. *sticchen, sticken* (G. *sticken* embroider); Gmc. **stik-* pierce, be sharp (see STICK *sb.*[1], STITCH) :– IE. **stig-* **steig-*, repr. by Gr. στίζειν prick, στίγμα STIGMA, L. *instigare* spur on, INSTIGATE. Cf. STEEK *v.*[2]] **I.** To pierce, thrust. **1.** *trans.* To stab, pierce, or transfix with a thrust of a spear, sword, knife, or other sharp instrument; to kill by this means. Not now in dignified use. **b.** To kill (an animal, esp. a pig) by thrusting a knife into its throat ME. **c.** *Sport.* To spear (a salmon). *To s. a pig*: (in India) to hunt the wild boar with a spear. 1820. **2.** To thrust (a dagger, a spear, a pointed instrument) *in, into, through.* late ME. **3.** To thrust, push forward, protrude (one's head, hand, etc.) *in, into, out (of), over* 1627. **b.** *intr.* To project, protrude. Now only const. *from, out of.* 1580.

1. Like a Storme suddenly, The English Archery Stuck the French Horses DRAYTON. **2.** Thou stick'st a dagger in me SHAKS. **3.** A lean old gentleman. .stuck his head out of the window 1907.

II. To remain fixed. **1.** *intr.* Of a pointed instrument: To remain with its point imbedded; to be fixed by piercing OE. †**2.** Of things: To be fastened in position; to be fixed in or as in a socket; to be attached –1673. **b.** In phr. with *full, close,* expressive of crowding to the utmost. *colloq.* 1776. **3.** Chiefly of persons: To continue or remain persistently in a place. Now only *colloq.* **b.** *fig.* Of feelings, thoughts, etc.: To remain permanently in the mind ME. †**4.** To remain firm, continue steadfast, stand *fast*; to be determined *to do* something; to persist *in* (an opinion, etc.); to be persistently engaged *upon* –1698. **b.** To keep persistently *at* 1886. **c.** *trans.* (*slang.*) To put up with, endure association with, tolerate (a person or thing). Also *to s. it (out)*, to continue what one is doing without flinching. 1899. **5.** *intr.* Of things: To remain attached or fastened by adhesion, to adhere, hold, cleave 1558. **b.** *fig.* Of a fact, a saying: To abide in one's memory. Of an imputation: To be fastened upon a person. Of opinions, feelings, habits: To be fixed, not to be shaken off. 1535. **6.** Of a living creature: To cling *to, on, upon. To s. on, to* (a horse), to keep one's seat on. Also *absol.* 1596. **7.** To be set fast or entangled in sand, clay, mud, mire, or the like; similarly of a boat, to become fixed or grounded on sand, a rock, etc.; more explicitly *to s. fast* OE. **8.** To become fixed or stationary in or on account of some obstruction, to be arrested or intercepted. Of a thing made to run, swing, or slide: To become unworkable, to jam. 1531. **b.** Of food, etc.: To lodge (in the throat) 1553. **c.** Of words, *To s. in one's throat,* †*teeth*: 'to resist emission' (J.) 1605. **9.** Of a matter: To be at a stand, to suffer delay or hindrance 1530. **b.** Of a person or thing: To remain in a stationary condition, to be unable to make progress. Of a commodity, etc.: Not to 'go off'; to remain unsold. 1641. **10.** To be in difficulty or trouble; to stop or stand in a state of perplexity; to be embarrassed, puzzled, or nonplussed 1577. **b.** To be unable to proceed in narration or speech, through lapse of memory or embarrassment 1579. **11.** To hesitate, scruple, be reluctant or unwilling. Const. *to* (do something). Only with neg. Now *rare.* 1532.

1. By the light he spies Lucrecias gloue, wherein her needle sticks SHAKS. **3.** I'll s. where I am, for here I am safe as to food and shelter HARDY. **b.** His speech stickes in my heart SHAKS. **4. c.** Sergeant Chambers shouted back, 'Go to hell!' and to his men he cried 'S. it!' 1905. **5.** *Provb.* If you throw mud enough, some of it will s. 1911. Phr. *To s. to a person's fingers,* said *fig.* of money dishonestly retained. **b.** A bad character sticks to a country as well as to an individual 1845. Phrases . .which s., like barbed arrows, in the memory of every reader KINGSLEY. **7.** They ranne the shippe a ground, and the forepart stucke fast *Acts* 27:41. Phr. *To s. in the mud,* now usu., to remain content in a mean or abject condition. (Cf. STICK-IN-THE-MUD.) **8. c.** Amen stuck in my throat SHAKS. **10. b.** He always stuck in the middle, everybody recollecting the latter part excepting himself W. IRVING. **11.** They will not sticke to say, you enuide him SHAKS.

III. To fix, cause to adhere. **1.** *trans.* To fasten (a thing) in position by thrusting in its point ME. **b.** To secure (a thing) by thrusting the end of it *in, into, behind, through* (a receptacle) 1664. **c.** To fix on a point ME. **2.** *gen.* To fasten in position; also in weaker sense, to place, set, put. Now chiefly, to place obtrusively, inappropriately, or irregularly. late ME. **b.** To fasten as an adornment or garnishing. late ME. **c.** *Joinery.* To work (moulding, a bead) with a plane fashioned for that purpose 1769. **3.** To set (a surface) *with*, to furnish or adorn with on the surface, to cover or strew with ME. **b.** *Cookery.* To set with a garnish 1530. **4.** To cause to adhere; to fasten, fix, secure (a thing) *against, on, upon, to* (a surface) by means of an adhesive, pins, etc. Also said of the adhesive. late ME. **b.** *fig.* To fasten (one's choice, opinion, an imputation, a nickname, dishonour, etc.) *on, upon* 1601. **5.** *colloq.* To bring to a stand, render unable to advance or retire. Chiefly *pass.* 1829. **b.** *colloq.* To pose, nonplus 1884. **6.** *slang* and *colloq.* **a.** To cheat (a person) out of his money, to cheat or take in in dealing; to 'saddle' *with* something counterfeit or worthless in purchase or exchange 1699. **b.** To 'let in' *for* 1895. **c.** *To s. it in* or *on*: to make extortionate charges 1844. **d.** *To be stuck on* (U.S. slang): to be captivated with 1886.

1. Then s. a skewer into it 1756. **b.** Sticking his pen behind his ear SCOTT. **2.** Two pitch bals stucke in her face for eyes SHAKS. **3.** My shrowd of white, stuck all with Ew, O prepare it SHAKS. *fig.* Supposition, all our liues, shall be stucke full of eyes SHAKS. **b.** A good piece of beef, stuck with Rose-mary 1611. **4.** *S. no bills,* the usual form of the notice placed on a building forbidding placards to be posted upon it. **b.** His foul esteeme Sticks no dishonor on our Front MILT. **6.** I'm stuck with a counterfeit note 1848. **b.** I'm awfully sorry I stuck you for such a lot 1915.

With preps. (*intr.*) **S. at —. a.** To scruple at; to hesitate to accept or believe, to take exception to, to be deterred by. (Chiefly neg.) *To s. at nothing,* to be unscrupulous. **b.** To be impeded or brought to a stand at (a difficulty). **S. by —. a.** To remain resolutely faithful to (a person) as a follower, partisan, or supporter. †**b.** Of a thing: To remain with, cling to (a person); to remain in (a person's) memory. **c.** To hold to, be constant to (a principle, one's word). Now *rare.* **S. to —. a.** To remain resolutely faithful to (a person or party), not to desert. Now chiefly *colloq.* **b.** To adhere, keep, or hold to (an argument, demand, resolve, opinion, bargain, covenant, and the like); to refuse to renounce or abandon; to persist in. **c.** To refuse to be enticed, led or turned from; to attend unremittingly to (an occupation, course of action, work, etc.). **d.** To keep exclusively to. **e.** To remain by or in (a place, etc.); to refuse to desert or leave. **f.** To follow closely (an original, etc.). **g.** To keep close to (in a pursuit or race). **h.** To keep possession of, refuse to part with.

With advs. **S. down.** To put down in writing (*colloq*). **S. out. a.** *intr.* To jut out, project. **b.** To be prominent or conspicuous (*colloq.*). **c.** To persist in resistance; to hold out. *To s. it out,* to endure to the end. **c.** To persist in one's demand *for* (*colloq*). **S. together. a.** Of things: To adhere one to another. **b.** Of persons, etc.: To keep together; chiefly *fig.*, to make common cause. **S. up. a.** *intr.* To stand out from a surface; to project. **b.** *To s. up for*; to defend the cause of, to champion (*colloq.*). **c.** To offer resistance *to* (colloq.). **d.** To set up in position, to set up (a stake, etc.) on its own point, or (a head, body) by impalement. Also, to put up (one's hands) in surrender. **e.** To affix or post. **f.** To stop and rob on the highway; also, to rob (a bank, etc.). **g.** To hinder from proceeding (on a journey, in work, etc.); hence to puzzle, nonplus. **h.** *Austral.* To bring (an animal) to bay.

Comb.: **s.-culture,** a bacterial culture made by thrusting a platinum needle into the culture medium; **-jaw** *colloq.*, a pudding or sweetmeat difficult of mastication; **-pin** *U.S.*, a pin that is merely stuck in as an ornament; **-seed,** a plant of the genus *Echinospermum,* the seeds of which are furnished with hooked adhesive prickles; **sticktight,** a composite weed, *Bidens frondosa,* whose flat achenia bear two barbed awns; also one of the seeds.

Stick (stik), *v.*[2] Pa. t. and pa. pple. **sticked** (stikt). 1573. [f. STICK *sb.*[1]] **1.** *trans.* To lay sticks between (pieces of timber) in stacking them. **2.** To furnish (a plant) with a stick as a support 1636. **3.** *intr.* To gather fallen wood for firewood: chiefly in *to go sticking. local.* 1870.

Sticker (sti·kəɹ). 1585. [f. STICK *v.*[1] + -ER[1].] One who or that which sticks. **1.** One who sticks or stabs, esp. one who kills swine by sticking. **2.** A weapon used for piercing or stabbing; as dist. from cutting or slashing; esp. a sticking-knife, a fishing-spear, an angler's gaff. Chiefly *colloq.* 1896. **3.** One who remains constant; one who persists in a task 1674. **4.** Something which causes a person to stick or to be at a nonplus; a poser. *colloq.* 1849. **5.** A rod in the mechanism of an organ or pianoforte 1845. **6.** *U.S.* An adhesive label; *spec.* = PASTER 2. 1872.

Sti·ckful. 1683. [f. STICK *sb.*[1] + -FUL.] As much type as a composing-stick will hold.

Stickiness[1] (sti·kinės). 1727. [f. STICKY *a.*[2] + -NESS.] The quality of being sticky; adhesiveness, glutinousness.

Stickiness[2] (sti·kinės). 1910. [f. STICKY *a.*[1] + -NESS.] Stiffness, woodenness.

Sticking (sti·kiŋ), *vbl. sb.* late ME. [-ING[1].] **1.** The action of STICK *v.*[1] **2.** *concr.* **a.** *Mining.* = SELVAGE 3. 1653. **b.** *pl.* Coarse, bruised, inferior meat; *spec.* the portions damaged by the butcher's knife 1851.

Sticking (sti·kiŋ), *ppl. a.* ME. [f. STICK *v.*[1] + -ING[2].] That sticks.

Comb.: **s.-grass** = CLEAVERS; **-piece,** the lower part of the neck-piece of a carcass of beef; **-place,** the place in which a thing stops and holds fast; **-plaster,** a material for covering and closing superficial wounds, consisting of linen, silk, etc., spread with an adhesive substance; **-point** = *s.-place.*

Sti·ck-in-the-mu:d. 1733. [f. phr. *to stick in the mud*; see STICK *v.* II. 7.] A helpless or unprogressive person; one who lacks resource of initiative. Also, a contemptuous substitute for WHAT'S-HIS-NAME.

Stickit (sti·kit), *a. Sc.* 1787. [Sc. form of *sticked* ppl. a. f. STICK *v.*[1]] **1.** Of a task, a product of labour: Imperfect or bungled, unfinished. **2.** That has relinquished his intended profession from want of ability or means to pursue it 1815.

Sticklac (sti·klæk). 1704. [f. STICK *sb.*[1] + LAC[1].] Lac in its natural state of incrustation on twigs.

Stickle (sti·k'l), *v.* 1530. [alt. of †*stightle* (ME. *stiȝtil,* also *stichle*) arrange, control, bestir oneself, strive, frequent. of †*stight,* OE. *stihtan, stihtian* arrange, corresp. to ON. *stétta* support, help; see -LE.] †**1.** *intr.* **a.** To act as an official regulator of a tournament, wrestling match, or the like, in order to ensure fair play. **b.** Hence, to act as mediator or umpire; to interpose or intervene (*between* or *among* combatants, etc.). –1692. †**2.** *trans.* To compose (a dispute, disputants); to stop, quell (a strife or contest) –1630. †**3.** *intr.* To be busy, stirring, or energetic; to strive or contend pertinaciously; to take an active part (*in* a cause, affair) –1706. †**b.** To strive *to* (do something) –1732. **4. S. for —. a.** To strive or contend for (a desired object, an issue, principle, etc.) 1642. †**b.** To take the part of, stand up for (a person) –1748. **5.** To make difficulties, raise objections, haggle (*about*); to be tardy in giving one's acceptance; to hesitate, scruple, take offence *at* 1819.

1. The same Angel. .when half of the Christians are already kill'd. .stickles between the Remainders of God's Host, and the Race of Fiends DRYDEN. **3.** Oh how we can s. in our own causes! 1630. **b.** The Devil. .will s. to do as much mischief as he can among you 1680. **4. a.** The plot. . will. .please those who s. for happy endings 1905. **b.** When Fortune (as she's wont) turn'd fickle And for the foe began to s. 1663. **5.** Flying for life, one does not s. about his vehicle CARLYLE.

Sti·ckleback. late ME. [f. OE. *sticel* sting, goad, thorn = OHG. *stihhil* goad, ON. *stikill* point of a horn, f. **stik-* **stek-* STICK *sb.*[1] + BACK *sb.*[1]] A small spiny-finned fish of the genus *Gasterosteus* or family *Gasterosteidæ.* The common three-spined s., *G. aculeatus,* is found in both fresh and salt water.

Stickler (sti·kləɹ). 1538. [f. STICKLE *v.* + -ER[1].] **1.** A moderator or umpire at a tournament, a wrestling or fencing match, etc. (*Obs.* exc. *s.w. dial.*) †**2.** An active partisan; a (great, chief, etc.) agent, mover, or instigator –1728. †**b.** In unfavourable sense: A factious, seditious, or pragmatic contender; a wrangler; a busybody –1696. †**3.** One who fights or contends *against* (a person, cause, etc.); an opponent, antagonist; one who makes difficulties or raises objections –1846. **4.** With *for*: One who pertinaciously supports or advocates (a cause, principle, person, etc.); one who insists on or stands out for (a form, ceremony, etc.) 1644. †**5.** A second or backer in a contest –1828.

4. Beaufort was no s. for pedantic rules 1879. **5.** Their fathers were honest men and sticklers to their lawful Prince 1711.

Stick-up, *a.* and *sb.* 1857. [f. phr. *to stick up*; see STICK *v.*[1]] **A.** *adj.* That sticks up; esp. of a collar = STAND-UP *a.* 1. 1873. **B.** *sb.* Something which sticks up; *esp.* a stand-up collar 1857. **b.** A thief armed with a revolver who orders his victims to put their hands up; also, a job performed by this type of criminal, a hold-up; also *attrib.* (*U.S.*) 1905.

Sticky (sti·ki), *a.*[1] 1577. [f. STICK *sb.*[1] + -Y[1].] **1.** Of plant-stems: Like a stick; woody. **2.** *Painting.* Characterized by hardness of outline 1753.

Sticky (sti·ki), *a.*[2] 1727. [f. STICK *v.*[1] + -Y[1].] Having the property of sticking or adhering; adhesive; also, viscid, glutinous. **b.** *Racing* and *Cricket.* Of a course, a wicket: Having a yielding surface owing to wet 1888.

Everything s. except postage-stamps LONGF. Hence **Sti·cky** *v. trans.* to smear with something s. (*colloq.*).

Stiff (stif), *a.*, *sb.*, and *adv.* [OE. *stīf*, corresp. to MLG., MDu. *stīf*, Du. *stijf*, ON. *stīfr* :– Gmc. **stīfaz* :– **stīpos*, rel. to L. *stipare* (see STEEVE *v.*[2], CONSTIPATE *v.*).] **A.** *adj.* **I. 1.** Rigid; not flexible or pliant. **2.** Of the body, limbs, joints, muscles, etc.: Lacking suppleness, unable to move without pain ME. **b.** Rigid in death. Often predic. in fig. phr. *to bore* (one) *s.*, to bore 'to death' (*colloq.*). ME. **c.** Of machinery, etc.: Working with excessive friction; hard to move 1848. **3.** Rigid as the result of tension; taut. Now *rare* or *Obs.* late ME. **4.** Of a semi-liquid substance: Thick or viscous, so as to flow with difficulty or to be capable of retaining a definite shape. late ME. **5.** Of soil: Heavy, dense; not porous or friable; difficult to work 1523. **6.** Tight, closely packed. Now *hyperbolically* in colloq. use: Densely crowded (*with*). 1683. **7.** Of a ship: Offering a high resistance to deflexion from the vertical or normal floating position; stable, not crank 1627. **8.** *fig.* Inflexible of purpose, steadfast, resolute, firm, constant ME. **b.** In a bad sense: Obstinate, stubborn, not amenable to reason. Now *rare.* 1526. **c.** Of a battle, debate, etc.: Stubbornly contested, hard ME. **9.** Formal, constrained, lacking ease or grace 1608. **10.** Of price, charges, rates, etc.: Unyielding, firm; having an upward tendency. Hence of a commodity or the dealers in it. 1883.

1. The Gown with s. Embroid'ry shining PRIOR. With sleet and rain, ropes s., and sails half set, very squally, she works like a Cutter 1801. **2.** You and I, ma'am, I think, are too s. to dance THACKERAY. Phr. *To have a s. neck*, to suffer from a rheumatic affection of the neck in which the head cannot be moved without pain. **b.** *S. one, s. 'un*, a corpse (*slang*). **4.** Then work it up into a s. paste MRS. GLASSE. **8. b.** S. in Opinions, always in the wrong DRYDEN. **9.** Too s. a carriage of his fortune WOTTON. S. rectangular walks 1779. His diction..was..pronounced s. and pedantic MACAULAY. Several letters..directed in a s., careful..hand 1885.

Colloq. phrases. *S. as a poker*; *s. in the back*, firm, resolute; *to keep* (*carry, have*) *a s. upper lip*, to be firm or unyielding, esp. in bearing pain or sorrow.

II. Strong. **1.** Of living creatures: Stout, stalwart, sturdy. *Obs.* exc. *dial.* ME. **2.** Of natural agencies: **a.** Strong, violent (of wind); also applied to a steady wind of moderate force ME. †**b.** Of news: Formidable, grave. SHAKS. **3.** Of liquors: Strong, potent. Now only of spirits and water. 1813.

2. a. The winde being contrary, and a stiffe gale 1565. **3.** A good s. glass of brandy grog 1883.

III. Hard, difficult. **1.** Of an ascent or descent: Steep so as to be difficult. In *Hunting*: Difficult (said of an obstacle or a tract of country presenting many obstacles). 1704. **2.** That requires considerable effort; severe; laborious, toilsome 1862. **3.** Of a price, demand, etc.: Unusually high, excessive 1824.

1. The next day's climb proved a stiff one 1903. **2.** A s. examination in the History School 1886. **3.** He naturally thought 3s. an hour pretty s. boat hire 1903.

Comb.: **s.-leaf** *Arch.*, the foliage of conventional form, with stiff leaf-stems, characteristic as a decoration in the Early English style.

B. *sb.* **1.** *slang.* Paper; a document, esp. a promissory note or bill of exchange; a clandestine letter 1823. **2.** *slang.* A corpse 1859. **3.** *slang.* A penniless man; a wastrel 1899.

1. I wish you'd do me a bit of s. THACKERAY.

C. *adv.* Stiffly, tightly, hard, etc. late ME.

Phr. *To give it to someone* (*pretty*) *s.*, to speak severely to, to rate. Hence **Sti·ff-ly** *adv.*, **-ness.**

Stiffen (sti·f'n), *v.* 1500. [f. STIFF *a.* + -EN[5].] To make or become stiff or stiffer. **1.** *trans.* To make stiff or rigid, e.g. by means of starch, or by the addition of a lining or a support 1622. **b.** *Naut.* To increase the initial stability of a ship; to render less liable to heel 1706. **2.** To render stiff in consistency; to thicken, coagulate 1627. **b.** *intr.* To become stiff in consistency; to harden. Also *fig.*, to assume a more definite or permanent form or character. 1697. **3.** *trans.* To make more steadfast, unyielding, or obstinate; *Mil.* to increase the fighting value of a force by the admixture of soldiers of better quality 1500. **b.** *intr.* To become hard or unyielding in temper 1732. **4.** *trans.* To make rigid; to take away the natural suppleness or mobility of (the limbs, joints, muscles, etc.); also *fig.* to make a corpse of, kill (*slang*) 1599. **b.** *intr.* Of persons: To become stiff or rigid; also, to die 1714. **5.** *trans.* To make (a person) formal, cold, or constrained in manner; to make (an artistic composition) pedantic, laboured, or overloaded 1763. **b.** *intr.* To become formal, cold, or constrained 1864. **6.** Of prices, the market, etc.: To become stiffer. **b.** *trans.* To render (prices, etc.) stiffer. 1855. **7.** *intr.* Of wind: To increase in strength or violence 1844. **8.** Of an ascent: To become more steep or difficult 1877.

2. The polar oceans being almost continually stiffened into ice GOLDSM. **b.** *fig.* But gradually the favour will s. into a right 1883. **3.** The Home Secretary wants stiffening 1898. **4.** S. the sinewes, commune [*sic*] vp the blood SHAKS. **5.** I pity Kings Whom Education stiffens into state COWPER. Hence **Sti·ffener**, a workman who stiffens (cloth, hats, etc.); something serving to s.; a reviving drink.

Stiffening (sti·f'niŋ), *vbl. sb.* 1614. [f. prec. + -ING[1].] **1.** The action of the vb.; the process of making or becoming stiff; *concr.* a stiffened substance. **2.** Something that serves to stiffen 1620. **b.** An admixture of soldiers of better quality 1900.

Stiffish (sti·fiʃ), *a.* 1733. [-ISH[1].] Rather stiff.

Stiff-necked (stress var.), *a.* 1526. [f. *stiff neck* + -ED[2]; after Gr. σκληροτράχηλος 'hard of neck'.] Having a stiff neck. Chiefly *fig.* of persons, with Biblical ref.: Obstinate, stubborn, inflexible, haughty.

Ye stiffenecked and of vncircumcised hertes and eares TINDALE *Acts* 7:51. Hence **Sti:ffne·cked-ly** *adv.*, **-ness.**

Stifle (stəi·f'l), *sb.*[1] ME. [Of unkn. origin.] The joint at the junction of the hind leg and the body (between the femur and the tibia) in a horse or other quadruped: corresponding anatomically to the knee in man.

Comb.: **s.-bone, -cap, -pan,** the patella of a horse, the bone in front of the stifle-joint; **-joint** = *stifle.*

Stifle (stəi·f'l), *sb.*[2] *rare.* 1823. [f. next.] The fact of stifling or condition of being stifled.

Stifle (stəi·f'l), *v.*[1] [In XIV *stuf(f)le*, varying with †*stuffe*, superseded (XV) by *stiffle*, *stifle*; perh. orig. frequent. formation on OFr. *estouffer* (mod. *étouffer*) :– Rom. **extuffare*, perh. a blend of **extufare* STEW *v.* and **stuppare* STOP *v.*; see -LE.] **1.** *trans.* To kill by stopping respiration; to kill or deprive of consciousness (a person or animal) by covering the mouth and nose, by depriving of pure air or by introducing an irrespirable vapour into the throat and lungs; to suffocate. Also *absol.* 1513. **b.** In hyperbolic or exaggerated use. late ME. †**2.** To suffocate by immersion; to drown –1705. **3.** To stop the passage of (the breath); to suppress, prevent the emission of, choke in the utterance (the voice, a cry, sob, cough, etc.) 1495. **b.** To make mute or inaudible through intervening space or obstructing medium 1833. **4.** In various fig. uses; *esp.* to conceal, keep from becoming known, suppress (a fact, report, movement; a document, letter) 1577. **5.** To smother or extinguish (a flame) 1726. **6.** To choke up, impede the flow of (running water); to obstruct the passage of, absorb, quench (rays of light) –1794. **7.** *intr.* To be or become suffocated; to perish by stoppage of breath. In weaker sense: To feel in danger of suffocation, to feel almost unable to breathe 1594.

1. Shall I not then be stifled in the Vault? SHAKS. **b.** He almost stifled her with caresses 1832. **3.** He attempted to raise an alarm, but they stifled his cries 1885. **b.** The fog..stifled the roar of the traffic of London KIPLING. **4.** Their former piety was after a manner stifled HOLLAND. This Insurrection was stifled in its very beginning 1705. The rumour may s. the truth for a short time SCOTT. Hence **Sti·fling** *ppl. a.*

Stifle (stəi·f'l), *v.*[2] 1580. [f. STIFLE *sb.*[1]] *Farriery.* (*trans.*) To affect (a horse, etc.) with dislocation of the stifle-bone. Chiefly *pass.*

Stifled (stəi·f'ld), *ppl. a.* 1643. [f. STIFLE *v.*[1] + -ED[1].] **1.** Suffocated, smothered, suppressed, etc. **2.** Devoid of fresh air, close, stuffy 1824.

2. We were shown into a small, s. parlor HAWTHORNE.

Stifler (stəi·fləɹ). 1642. [f. STIFLE *v.*[1] + -ER[1].] One who or something which stifles, suffocates, etc. **b.** *Thieves' slang.* The gallows 1818.

Stigma (sti·gmă). *Pl.* **stigmata** (sti·gmătă) or **stigmas** (sti·gmăz). 1596. [– L. *stigma* – Gr. στίγμα, -ματ- mark made by a pointed instrument, brand, f. *στιγ- as in στίζειν (:– **stigj-*) prick; see STICK *v.*[1]] **1.** A mark made upon the skin by burning with a hot iron (rarely, by cutting or pricking), as a token of infamy or subjection; a brand. **2.** *fig.* A mark of disgrace or infamy; a sign of severe censure or condemnation, regarded as impressed on a person or thing; a 'brand' 1619. **b.** A distinguishing mark or characteristic (of a bad or objectionable kind); in *Path.* a sign of some specific disorder, as hysteria 1859. **3.** *pl.* Marks resembling the wounds on the crucified body of Christ, said to have been supernaturally impressed on the bodies of certain saints and other devout persons 1632. **4.** *Path.* A morbid spot, dot, or point on the skin, esp. one which bleeds spontaneously 1661. **5.** *Zool.* and *Anat.* **a.** Each of the respiratory openings or breathing-pores in insects and other invertebrates; a spiracle. Also applied to other small openings or pores, as that of the pneumatocyst in *Hydrozoa.* (Pl. usu. *stigmata.*) 1747. **b.** The part of an ovisac or Graafian follicle where it ruptures to discharge the ovum 1890. **c.** A natural spot or mark, as one formed by enlargement of a nervure on the fore-wings of certain insects (*pterostigma*), or the pigment- or eye-spot of an infusorian 1826. **6.** *Bot.* That part of the pistil in flowering plants which receives the pollen in impregnation, of very various form, situated either directly on the ovary, or at the summit of the style. Also applied to an analogous structure in cryptogams. (Pl. usu. *stigmas.*) 1753.

1. His flinty Front my S. shou'd retain 1778. **2.** Branded with the s. of illegitimacy 1882. **3.** St. Frances with his inuisible Stigmata 1632.

‖**Stigmaria** (stigmē·riă). *Pl.* **-æ**(*i*). 1845. [mod.L., f. prec., in ref. to the marks or scars on the fossil.] *Geol.* A former genus of fossil plants, whose remains are found abundantly in the coal-measures; they are now commonly believed to be the roots of *Sigillaria* and possibly other trees.

Stigmat (sti·gmæ̆t). 1901. [app. back-formation from STIGMATIC *a.*] *Photogr.* A stigmatic lens or combination of lenses.

Stigmatic (stigmæ·tik), *a.* and *sb.* 1594. [f. L. *stigmat-*, stem of STIGMA + -IC.] **A.** *adj.* **1.** Constituting or conveying a stigma; branding with infamy; ignominious; severely condemnatory 1607. †**2.** Marked with a 'stigma' or brand, branded –1628. †**3.** Marked with or having a deformity or blemish; deformed, ill-favoured, ugly –1827. **4.** Pertaining to or accompanying the stigmata (see STIGMA 3) 1871. **5.** *Path., Zool., Bot.* Pertaining to, constituting, characterized by, or having the nature of a stigma 1830. **6.** [Back-formation from ASTIGMATIC.] Applied to a photographic lens or combination of lenses constructed so as to correct the astigmatic aberration 1896. **B.** *sb.* [the adj. used ellipt.] **1.** A person branded as a criminal; a profligate, villain. *Obs.* (or *rare arch.*) †**2.** A person marked with some physical deformity or blemish –1633. **3.** A person marked with the 'stigmata' (see STIGMA 3) 1885. So †**Stigma·tical** *a.* 1589.

Stigmatism (sti·gmătiz'm). 1664. [In sense 1 f. STIGMATIZE + -ISM; in sense 2 f. L. *stigmat-*, stem of STIGMA.] †**1.** Branding; *collect.* marks made by branding, or by tattooing or the like. **2.** *Path.* The condition of being affected with stigmata (see STIGMA 4) 1900. **3.** Absence of astigmatism 1890.

Stigmatist (sti·gmătist). 1607. [alt. of STIGMATIC (B. 1 and 3) by substitution of -IST.] †**a.** = STIGMATIC B. 1. **b.** = STIGMATIC B. 3.

Stigmatize (sti·gmătəiz), *v.* 1585. [– Fr. *stigmatiser* or med.L. *stigmatizare* – Gr. στιγματίζειν, f. στίγμα, -ματ-; see STIGMA, -IZE.] **1.** *trans.* To mark with a 'stigma' or brand; to brand; also, to tattoo. Now *rare.* **b.** *transf.* To mark with a stain, scar, or blemish 1632. **c.** *Path.* To mark or affect with stigmata; to produce stigmata upon 1822. **d.** To mark with the stigmata: see STIGMA 3. 1844. **e.** To imprint as a brand (*rare*) 1644. **2.** *fig.* To set a stigma upon; to mark with a sign of disgrace or infamy; to 'brand'; *esp.* to characterize by a term implying severe censure or condemnation 1619.

1. God stigmatized him on the forehead with a letter of his own name 1737. **e.** Letters stigmatized in slaves foreheads 1647. **2.** As to their white wines, he stigmatizes them as mere substitutes for cider W. IRVING. Hence **Sti:gmatiza·tion**, the action of stigmatizing, or condition of being stigmatized.

Stigmatose (sti·gmătoᵘs), *a.* 1840. [f. L. *stigmat-* STIGMA; see -OSE¹.] **1.** *Bot.* Said of a style bearing the stigma on some specified part, as along the side instead of (as usual) at the summit. **2.** *Path.* Covered or affected with stigmata 1894.

Stigmatypy (sti·gmătəipi). 1875. [f. Gr. στίγμα (here taken as = στιγμή point, dot) + *-typy.*] The art or process of printing portraits, etc. with small types bearing dots of different sizes, so as to produce an effect of light and shade.

Stilbene (sti·lbīn). 1868. [f. Gr. στίλβειν to glitter + -ENE.] *Chem.* A hydrocarbon produced by the action of heated lead oxide on toluene, and in other ways: used in dye-stuffs. So **Sti·lbin** [see -IN] in same sense.

Stilbite (sti·lbəit). 1815. [– Fr. *stilbite* (Haüy 1796), f. as prec.; see -ITE¹ 2b.] *Min.* A hydrous silicate of aluminium and calcium, in oblique prismatic crystals with pearly lustre.

Stile¹ (stəil). [OE. *stiȝel*, corresp. to OS., OHG. *stigilla* (G. dial. *stiegel*), f. Gmc. **stīȝ-* climb; see STY *v.*¹] An arrangement of steps or the like, contrived to allow passage over or through a fence to one person at a time, while forming a barrier to sheep or cattle.

There was a s. to pass from this field into the next SWIFT. I can..help a lame dog over a s. 1857. *fig.* A lift over the s. at a crisis 1884.

Stile² (stəil). 1668. [prob. – Du. *stijl* pillar, prop, door-post.] *Carpentry*, etc. An upright in a framing or structure, carrying a cross-piece; e.g. each of the vertical bars of a wainscot, sash, panel door, etc.

Stiletto (stile·to), *sb. Pl.* **-oes.** 1611. [– It. *stiletto*, dim. of *stilo* dagger; see STYLUS, -ET.] **1.** A short dagger with a blade thick in proportion to its breadth. **2.** *Needlework*, etc. A small pointed instrument for making eyelet-holes 1828.

Comb.: †**s. beard**, a pointed beard. Hence **Stile·tto** *v. trans.* to stab, esp. mortally, with a s.

Still (stil), *sb.*¹ 1533. [f. STILL *v.*²] **1.** An apparatus for distillation, consisting essentially of a close vessel (alembic, retort, boiler) in which the substance to be distilled is subjected to the action of heat, and of arrangements for the condensation of the vapour produced. Also applied to the alembic or retort separately. 1562. **2.** †**a.** = STILL-ROOM. **b.** A distillery. 1533. **3.** A chamber or vessel for the preparation of bleaching-liquor by the action of hydrochloric acid on manganese dioxide, or for the preparation of chlorine, of alkalis, etc. 1853.

Comb.: **s. burnt** *a.*, of alcoholic spirits, damaged by burning in the process of distillation; **-house**, a distillery.

Still (stil), *a.* and *sb.*² [OE. *stille* = OFris. *stille*, OS., OHG. *stilli* (Du. *stil*, G. *still*) :- WGmc. **stillja*, **stellja*, f. **stel-* be fixed, stand.] **A.** *adj.* **1.** Motionless; stationary; also, remaining in the same position or attitude, quiescent; *spec.* of a photograph, opp. to *moving, motion, picture.* **b.** Of wine and other beverages: Not sparkling or effervescing 1833. **2.** Silent OE. †**a.** *predic.*, of a person –1604. **b.** Habitually silent, taciturn (*dial.*) 1729. **3.** Of a voice, sounds, utterances: Subdued, soft, not loud. Now *arch.* and chiefly after 1 *Kings* 19:12. OE. †**b.** *esp.* of music; hence of instruments, performers, etc. –1816. **4.** Free from commotion. **a.** Of water: Having an unruffled surface; motionless or flowing imperceptibly OE. **b.** Of the air, weather: Quiet. Of rain: Unattended by wind, gentle. late ME. **5.** In mixed sense of 2 and 4. Of places, times, conditions: Characterized by absence of noise and movement; quiet, calm ME. **b.** *contextually* (*poet.*) = That has become still; no longer active or audible 1485. †**6.** Of a child: Dead before birth –1607. †**7.** Constant; continued until now –1615.

1. Hah, no more moouing? S. as the Graue. SHAKS. The charmed water burnt alway A s. and awful red COLERIDGE. **b.** S. champagne 1858. **2.** Phr. *To be* (*hold oneself*) *s.*, to hold one's peace, refrain from speaking. **b.** Phr. *To keep a s. tongue in one's head.* **3.** And after the fire a s. small voice 1 *Kings* 19:12. The s. voice of law and reason was seldom heard or obeyed GIBBON. **b.** The s. flutes sound softly MARSTON. **4. a.** The deep s. Pool 1735. *Provb.* Hers was a case of 'S. waters run deep' 1895. **b.** But our widows sorrow is no storm but a s. rain FULLER. **5.** Now came s. Eevning on MILT. She comes from another stiller world of the dead TENNYSON. **b.** O for the touch of a vanish'd hand, And the sound of a voice that is s.! TENNYSON. **7.** *Rich. III*, IV. iv. 229.

B. *sb.* †**1.** A calm –1626. **2.** Stillness, quiet. Now only *poet.* or *rhet.* 1608. **3.** A 'still' photograph 1918.

1. There is no better sign of *omnia bene*, than when the court is in a s. BACON. **2.** The s. of the night 1608.

Still (stil), *v.*¹ Pa. t. and pa. pple. **stilled** (stild). [OE. *stillan* = OS. (*gi*)*stillian* trans., *stillon* intr., OHG. *stillen* trans., *stillēn* intr., ON. *stilla*; rel. to prec.] To make or become still. Now chiefly *poet.* and *rhet.* **I.** *trans.* **1.** To quiet, calm (waves, winds, etc.). **b.** To subdue, allay (sedition, tumult) 1570. **2.** To relieve (pain); to assuage, allay (an appetite, desire) OE. **3.** To quiet, calm (a person's mind); to subdue (agitation, emotion) ME. **b.** To appease (anger) ME. †**4.** To lull, soothe (a child); to induce (a person) to cease from weeping –1660. **5.** To silence, cause (a sound) to cease. Also *fig.* To cause the cessation of (murmurs, complaints, etc.) late ME. †**b.** To impose silence on –1665. **6.** In occas. uses: To stop the movement or activity of 1850.

1. To s. the wilde winds when they roar MILT. **2.** He tries..to s., or at least to deaden, the undying pain of his spirit 1856. **3.** A turne or two, Ile walke To s. my beating minde SHAKS. **5.** The monks stilled their chant SCOTT. **6.** She stilled her feet 1866.

II. *intr.* To become still or calm OE.

At length the winds began to s. 1851.

Still (stil), *v.*² ME. [Aphetic f. DISTIL *v.*] †**1.** *intr.* = DISTIL *v.* 1. –1690. †**2.** *trans.* To exude, discharge, or give forth in minute drops –1693. †**b.** To cause to distil or fall in drops –1719. **3.** To subject to the process of distillation. Now *rare* or *Obs.* late ME. †**4.** To extract or produce by distillation –1707.

Still (stil), *adv.* [OE. *stille*, OS., OHG. *stillo* (Du. *stil*, G. *still*) :- WGmc. *stillō.*] †**1.** Without noise or commotion; quietly; in a low voice, softly –1560. **2.** At rest, motionless; without change of place or attitude. With certain verbs. OE. **3.** With ref. to action or condition: Without change, interruption or cessation; continually, constantly; invariably; always. *Obs.* exc. *poet.* ME. **b.** †*S. and anon*, †*s. an end*: constantly from time to time. SHAKS. **c.** With words denoting increase or progress: Ever more and more 1596. **4.** Indicating the continuance of a previous action or condition. **a.** Now (or at the time in question) as formerly 1535. **b.** Now (or at the time in question) in contrast to the future; as yet 1632. **c.** After as before some points of time; further. *Obs.* or *arch.* 1526. **d.** In addition; after the apparent ending of a series 1790. **5.** In a further degree; yet 1593. **6.** With adversative notion. **a.** After or at the same time with some event or condition implied to be adverse; even then 1699. **b.** Quasi-*conj.*: In spite of what has been stated or conceded; notwithstanding, yet. Sometimes preceded by *but*, or followed by *however.* 1722. **7.** *Comb.* and quasi-*Comb.* = 'always, ever'; 'now as before' 1593.

2. *To stand s.*; I paused, and my heart stood s. LYTTON. *To sit, lie s.*; I rose at six, tired of lying s. MRS. CARLYLE. **3.** One generacion passeth awaye, another commeth, but the earth abydeth s. COVERDALE *Eccles.* 1:4. Howbeit these..Devise new things and good, not one thing s. SWINBURNE. **b.** *Two Gent.* IV. iv. 67. **c.** Thus s. his courage, with his toils encreas'd POPE. **4. a.** For as you were when first your eye I eyde, Such seemes your beautie s. SHAKS. I wrote a similar epitaph for my wife, though s. living GOLDSM. **c.** Poore haue I been, and poore I am, and poore s. shall I bee 1577. **5.** Next day, he heard the sound s. louder than before 1832. **6. a.** For e'en though vanquished, he could argue s. GOLDSM. **b.** S., however, there was another extreme, which..was also to be avoided MACAULAY. **7.** That s.-closed booke of secrets 1603. Your many acts of s.-continued friendship COWPER.

Stillage (sti·lėdʒ). 1596. [app. – Du. *stellagie*, *stellaedsie* now written *stellage* scaffold, stand, f. *stellen* to place + Fr. suffix *-age*; see -AGE.] **1.** *Brewing.* A stand for casks. **2.** In various industries, a stand for keeping something from the ground 1875.

Stillatitious (stilăti·ʃəs), *a.* 1656. [f. L. *stillaticius* falling in drops (f. *stillare*) + -OUS.] **1.** Falling in drops. Also, †produced by falling in drops, as stalactites. †**2.** Produced by distillation –1704.

Stillatory (sti·lătəri). late ME. [– med.L. *stillatorium* still, alembic, f. L. *stillare* drip, distil; see -ORY¹.] **1.** A still. *Obs.* exc. *Hist.* and *fig.* **2.** A place where distillery is carried on; a stillroom; a distillery 1602.

Still-birth. 1785. [f. STILL *a.* + BIRTH, after next.] Birth of a still-born child; an instance of this. (Cf. next.)

Still-born (stress var.), *a.* 1597. [f. STILL *a.* + BORN *ppl. a.*] Born lifeless; dead at birth; abortive. Also, born in a state of suspended animation.

[His] works one and all fell s. from the press 1894.

Stiller¹ (sti·ləɹ). 1608. [f. STILL *v.*¹ + -ER¹.] One who or something which makes still, quiet, or tranquil.

Stiller² (sti·ləɹ). 1580. [f. STILL *v.*² + -ER¹.] One who distils; a distiller.

Still hunt, *sb. U.S.* 1860. [f. STILL *a.* + HUNT *sb.*] **1.** A pursuit for game in a stealthy manner or under cover; stalking. **2.** *transf.* The pursuit of any object quietly and cautiously 1890. So **Sti·ll-hunt** *v. trans.* and *intr.* **Sti·ll-hunter** 1831. **Sti·ll-hunting** *vbl. sb.* 1831.

Stillicide (sti·lisəid). 1626. [Anglicized f. next.] **1.** A falling of water, etc. in drops; a succession of drops. Now *rare.* **2.** *Civil* and *Scots Law.* The dropping of rain-water from the eaves of a house upon another's land or roof; the right or the servitude relating to this 1656.

‖**Stillicidium** (stilisi·diŏm). *Pl.* **-cidia.** 1727. [L., f. *stilla* drop + *cid-*, weakened root of *cadere* to fall.] **1.** *Civil Law.* = prec. 2. **2.** *Path.* A morbid dropping or trickling 1791.

Stilling (sti·liŋ). 1604. [perh. – Du. *stelling* stand, scaffold, f. *stellen* place. Cf. STILLAGE.] A stand for a cask, a gantry.

Stillion (sti·liən). 1803. [perh. var. of

prec.] **1.** = prec. **2.** A trough to catch yeast 1826.

Still life. 1695. [f. STILL *a.* + LIFE *sb.*, after Du. *stilleven.*] Inanimate objects, such as fruit, flowers, dead game, vessels, etc., as represented in painting.

Stillness (sti·lnės). [OE. *stilnes, -nys,* f. *stille* adj.] The condition or quality of being still. **1.** Absence of movement or physical disturbance; motionlessness. **2.** Freedom from agitation, tranquillity OE. **3.** Silence; freedom from noise; †taciturnity OE. †**4.** Freedom from turbulence or self-assertion –1745.

1. The s. of the Weather SWIFT. **2.** On my Mind A passive s. is enjoined WORDSW. **3.** Soft stilnes, and the night Become the tutches of sweet harmonie SHAKS. **4.** In Peace, there's nothing so becomes a man, As modest stillnesse, and humilitie SHAKS.

Sti·ll-room. 1710. [STILL *sb.*[1]] **a.** *Hist.* Orig., a room in a house in which a still was kept for the distillation of perfumes and cordials. **b.** Later, a room in which preserves, cakes, liqueurs, etc. are kept, and tea, coffee, etc. are prepared. Also *attrib.* in *s. maid,* etc.

A hundred years ago, every lady in the country had her still-room THACKERAY.

Sti·ll-stand. 1597. [f. STILL *a.* + STAND *sb.*] **1.** A stand-still (*rare*). †**2.** *spec.* [After G. (*waffen*)*stillstand.*] An armistice –1819.

Sti·ll wa:ter. 1626. [f. STILL *a.* + WATER *sb.*] = SLACK-WATER 1.

Stilly (sti·li), *a.* ME. [Sense 1 f. STILL *a.* + -LY[1]; sense 2 + -Y[1], after *vasty,* etc.] †**1.** Secret. ME. only. **2.** Characterized by stillness. Chiefly *poet.* 1776.

2. The s. murmur of the distant Sea COLERIDGE. Oft, in the s. night, Ere Slumber's chain has bound me MOORE.

Stilly (sti·li), *adv.* [OE. *stillīce,* f. *stille* STILL *a.* + *-līce* -LY[2].] In a still manner; silently, quietly; †secretly.

From Camp to Camp,..The Humme of eyther Army s. sounds SHAKS.

Stilpnomelane (stilpnǫ·mīlēⁱn). 1850. [– G. *stilpnomelan,* f. Gr. στιλπνός glittering + μέλας, μελαν- black.] *Min.* A hydrous silicate of iron and aluminium, occurring in thin scales, or as a velvety coating, of a black or bronze colour.

Stilt (stilt), *sb.* [ME. *stilte,* corresp. immed. to LG., Flem. *stilte,* Norw. *stilta* :– Gmc. **steltjōn,* and rel. to MLG., MDu. *stelte* (Du. *stelt*), OHG. *stelza* (G. *stelze*) :– **steltōn,* Sw. *stylta,* Da. *stylte* :– **stultjōn*; see STOUT *a.*] **1.** The handle of a plough. *Obs.* exc. *dial.* **2.** A crutch. *Obs.* exc. *dial.* ME. **3.** Each of a pair of props, usu. slender wooden poles with a foot-rest some distance above the lower end, for enabling a person to walk with the feet raised from the ground, the upper end being held by the hand or under the arm, or strapped to the legs 1440. **b.** *transf.* Applied to long slender legs of an animal, esp. a bird 1597. **4.** *techn.* **a.** Each of a set of posts or piles on which a building (esp. of primitive construction) is raised from the ground, or which are fixed under water to support the pier of a bridge, etc. 1697. **b.** *Arch.* A vertical course of masonry placed beneath and continuous with an arch or vault so as to raise the springing of it above the general level, or for a similar purpose beneath or above a column 1835. **5.** Any bird of the genus *Himantopus,* characterized by very long slender legs and slender sharp bills, and inhabiting marshes; a long-legged plover 1813.

3. Fen-men..who stalking on high upon stilts, apply their mindes, to grasing, fishing and fowling HOLLAND. *fig.* Ambition is but Avarice on stilts and masked LANDOR.

attrib. and *Comb.*: **s.-bird,** (*a*) = sense 5; (*b*) any long-legged wading bird, a grallatorial bird; **-plover** = sense 5; **s. sandpiper,** a long-legged N. Amer. species of sandpiper, *Micropalama himantopus*; **-shank** = sense 5.

Stilt (stilt), *v.* 1649. [f. prec.] **1.** *trans.* To raise as on stilts; to elevate artificially. **b.** *Arch.* To raise (an arch, vault, etc.) above the ordinary level by a 'stilt' or other course of masonry beneath 1835. **c.** *Bookbinding.* To bind (a book) so as to make it range with one of larger size 1824. **2.** *intr.* To walk on stilts 1861.

Stilted (sti·ltėd), *ppl. a.* 1615. [f. STILT *sb.* and *v.* + -ED.] **1.** Furnished with or having stilts; raised artificially as if on stilts. **b.** *Arch.* Raised above the general level by a course of masonry beneath, as an arch, vault, etc. 1835. **c.** Of animals, esp. birds: Having very long slender legs resembling stilts 1869. **2.** *fig.* Of (or in ref. to) language, style, or manner: Artificially or affectedly lofty; unnaturally elevated; formally pompous 1820.

2. You are taken in by that false, s., trashy style BYRON.

Stiltified (sti·ltifəid), *a.* Not in dignified use. 1820. [f. as prec. + -FY + -ED[1].] = prec. 2. So **Sti·ltify** *v. trans.* = STILT *v.* 1.

Stilton (sti·ltən). 1736. [Name of a village in Huntingdonshire.] *S. cheese*: a rich quality of cheese made at various places in Leicestershire; so called from having been originally largely sold to travellers at a coaching inn at Stilton. Also *ellipt.* as *sb.*

Stilty (sti·lti), *a.* 1826. [f. STILT *sb.* + -Y[1].] **1.** Resembling stilts. **2.** *fig.* Characterized by stiltedness 1846.

Stimulancy (sti·miŭlănsi). Now *rare.* 1799. [f. next; see -ANCY.] Stimulating quality.

Stimulant (sti·miŭlănt), *a.* and *sb.* 1728. [– L. *stimulans, -ant-,* pr. pple. of *stimulare*; see next, -ANT.] **A.** *adj.* **1.** Stimulating, rousing 1803. **2.** *Phys.* and *Med.* **a.** Exciting an organ, or the organism, to increased activity; quickening some vital function or process 1772. **b.** Acting as a stimulus; exciting the functional activity of an organ (*rare*) 1785. **B.** *sb.* **1.** Something that stimulates, rouses, or incites to action. Now *rare* exc. with some fig. notion of sense 2. 1794. **2.** *Phys.* and *Med.* Something that temporarily quickens some vital process, or the function of some organ 1728. **b.** *spec.* Applied to alcoholic drinks 1865.

1. The pecuniary remuneration..is the direct and immediate s. to exertion and enterprise 1847. **2. b.** The..craving for stimulants LIVINGSTONE.

Stimulate (sti·miŭleⁱt), *v.* 1548. [– *stimulat-,* pa. ppl. stem of L. *stimulare,* f. *stimulus* STIMULUS; see -ATE[3].] †**1.** *trans.* To prick, sting, afflict. HALL. **2.** To rouse to action or exertion as by pricking or goading; to spur on; to incite (a person) *to do* something; to impart additional energy to (an activity, a process) 1619. **3.** *Phys.* To act as a stimulus to (see STIMULUS 1, 3). Also *absol.* 1662. **4.** *intr.* for *refl.* To indulge in (alcoholic) stimulants. Now only *U.S. colloq.* Also *pass.,* To be affected by alcoholic drinks. 1800.

2. To s. production by useful..labour 1832. To..s. him to fresh exertions DICKENS. **4.** We were all slightly stimulated before a move was made 1882. Hence **Sti·mulating** *ppl. a.*

Stimulation (stimiŭlēⁱ·ʃən). 1526. [– L. *stimulatio, -ōn-,* f. as prec.; see -ION. Cf. Fr. *stimulation.*] **1.** The action of stimulating or condition of being stimulated. **2.** *Phys.* and *Med.* The action of a stimulus. **a.** Excitation to increased activity, quickening of some vital function or process. **b.** Excitation of an organ or tissue to its specific activity. 1733.

Stimulative (sti·miŭlĕtiv), *a.* and *sb.* 1747. [f. STIMULATE + -IVE.] **A.** *adj.* Having the property of stimulating; of a stimulating nature or character 1791. **B.** *sb.* Something having a stimulating quality. Now *rare.* 1747.

Stimulator (sti·miŭleⁱtəɹ). 1614. [– L. *stimulator,* f. *stimulat-*; see STIMULATE, -OR 2. In mod. use f. STIMULATE + -OR 2.] One who or that which stimulates.

Stimulatory (sti·miŭlĕtŏri), *a.* and *sb. rare.* 1758. [f. STIMULATE + -ORY[2].] **A.** *adj.* = STIMULATIVE *a.* **B.** *sb. Phys.* and *Med.* = STIMULANT B. 2.

Stimulose (sti·miŭlōᵘs), *a.* 1866. [f. next (in sense 4) + -OSE[1].] *Nat. Hist.* Covered with stings or stinging hairs.

Stimulus (sti·miŭlŏs). *Pl.* **-li** (-ləi). 1684. [– L. *stimulus* goad, spur, incentive, prob. f. **sti-,* repr. also by *stilus* STYLUS.] **1.** *Phys.* Something that acts as a 'goad' or 'spur' to a languid bodily organ; an agency or influence that stimulates, increases, or quickens organic activity. **b.** Stimulating property, action, or effect; stimulation or quickening of organic activity 1684. **2.** *gen.* An agency or influence that stimulates to action or (const. *to*) that quickens an activity or process 1793. **b.** A quickening impulse; also, stimulation 1794. **3.** *Phys.* Something that excites an organ or tissue to a specific activity or function; a material agency that produces a reaction in an organism 1793. **b.** Influence or effect in calling forth some specific reaction of a tissue; irritation of a nerve or other sensitive structure 1785. **4.** *Nat. Hist.* A sting, a stinging hair (*rare,* and perh. only as L.) 1760.

3. c. *Psychology.* A process of stimulation or excitement which affects the area of a sense-organ (*external s.*), or which originates within a sense-organ (*internal s.*). Also *attrib.* 1894.

Sting (stiŋ), *sb.* [OE. *sting, styng,* f. next.] **1. a.** The act of stinging. **b.** The fact or effect of being stung; the wound inflicted by the *aculeus* of an insect, the telson of a scorpion, the fang of an adder, etc.; the pain or smart of such a wound. **c.** The smart or irritation produced by touching a nettle or similar plant 1878. **2.** A sharp-pointed organ in certain insects and other animals (e.g. bees, wasps, scorpions) capable of inflicting a painful or dangerous wound. Applied also to the fang or venom-tooth (and erron. to the forked tongue) of a poisonous serpent. late ME. **3.** *Bot.* A stiff sharp-pointed tubular hair, which emits an irritating fluid when touched. †Also applied to a thorn. 1567. **4.** *fig.* Something which inflicts acute pain; an acute pain or sharp wound inflicted on the mind or heart; the 'point' of an epigram or sarcasm; something which goads to action or appetite. late ME. **b.** *gen.* Stinging quality, capacity to sting or hurt; a (specified) degree or amount of this 1863.

2. Beware the secret Snake that shoots a S. DRYDEN. **4.** The renewed s. of iealosie SIDNEY. They never worked till they felt the s. of hunger MACAULAY. **b.** When once collared the Yorkshire bowling lacks s. 1896.

Comb.: **s.-bull,** the greater weever, *Trachinus draco*; **-fish,** (*a*) the lesser weever, *Trachinus vipera*; (*b*) the sea-scorpion, *Cottus scorpius*; **-moth,** the Australian moth, *Doratifera vulnerans,* the larva of which is able to sting; **-tail,** (*a*) a tail tapering to a point, as in the pointer; (*b*) *U.S.* = STING-RAY. Hence **Sti·ngless** *a.* having no s.

Sting (stiŋ), *v.* Pa. t. and pa. pple. **stung** (stɒŋ). [OE. *stingan* = ON. *stinga,* f. Gmc. **steŋg- *staŋg-* (whence ON. *stanga* pierce).] †**1.** *trans.* To pierce with a sharp-pointed weapon or instrument –1485. **2.** 'To pierce or wound with a point darted out, as that of wasps or scorpions' (J.). Also *absol.* OE. **b.** *transf.* and *fig.* To inflict a sharp or mortal hurt upon. late ME. **c.** *slang.* To rob or cheat, impose upon 1812. **3.** Of certain plants, etc.: To produce by contact a kind of rash or inflammation, accompanied with a burning sensation and itching, in (a person's skin). Also *absol.* 1548. **4.** *transf.* To affect with a tingling pain, a burning sensation, or the like. Also *absol.* 1615. **5.** *fig.* To affect with a sudden sharp mental pain or an access of painful emotion or irritation; to goad or stimulate *to* or *into* (action, rage, etc.). late ME. **6.** *intr.* To smart 1848.

2. With doubler tongue Then thine (thou serpent), neuer Adder stung SHAKS. **b.** Two fired.. 'stinging' one man in the leg 1878. **3.** A pricking of the intire skin, as if stung with Nettles 1665. **5.** Remember'd folly stings JOHNSON. Stung to madness by defeat 1836.

Stingaree (stiŋgărī·, sti·ŋgărī). *U.S.* and *Austral.* 1811. [alt. of STING RAY.] A stingray, esp. *Trygon centrura* (*Dasyatis centrura*).

Stinger (sti·ŋəɹ). 1552. [f. STING *v.* + -ER[1].] **1.** One who stings; applied *fig.* to Death. **2.** An animal or plant that stings 1593. **3.** Something that stings or smarts, e.g. a smart blow; something that causes sharp distress; a pungent speech or crushing argument. Now *colloq.* 1576.

2. The..Nilgiri nettle, a most virulent s. 1880. **3.** I wrote him back a s. 1900.

Stinging (sti·ŋiŋ), *ppl. a.* ME. [f. STING *v.* + -ING[2].] **1.** That stings, that has power to sting; used (often as a specific designation) of animals or plants. **2.** *transf.* That produces a sharp pain or tingling smart, a burning sensation, or the like. Said also of the pain or sensation. late ME. **3.** *fig.* That causes sharp mental pain or irritation, poignant; that goads or stimulates. Of speech: Biting, pungent. ME.

1. Like s. Bees in hottest Sommers day SHAKS. The common s. nettle (*Urtica dioica*) 1887. 2. Fierce showers of s. hail 1866. 3. A s. rejoinder 1885. Hence **Sti·nging-ly** *adv.*, **-ness.**

Stingo (sti·ŋgo). *slang.* 1635. [f. STING *v.*, in allusion to the sharp taste.] Strong ale or beer. **b.** *fig.* Energy, vim.

Sti·ng ray. 1624. [STING *sb.*] Any fish of the genus *Trygon* or family *Trygonidæ*, esp. *T. pastinaca*. The long tapering tail is armed near the middle with a flattened sharp-pointed bony spine, serrated on both sides, capable of inflicting a severe wound.

Sti·ngy (sti·ŋi), *a.*[1] 1615. [f. STING *sb.* or *v.* + -Y[1].] Having a sting; stinging, sharp, virulent. †Often *fig.* of controversy, etc.

Stingy (sti·ndʒi), *a.*[2] 1659. [perh. based on a (dial.) var. *stinge* (stinᵈʒ) of STING *sb.*; see -Y[1].] **1.** Bad-tempered, irritable, peevish, cross. *dial.* 1787 **2.** Of persons, actions, etc.: Niggardly, penurious, mean, close-fisted 1659. **b.** Betokening meanness; doled out sparingly or grudgingly 1849. **3.** Scanty, poor in quantity or amount 1854.

1. Those virulent and stingie Pamphlets 1657. 2. Liberal in promises, and s. in performances 1770. Hence **Sti·ngi-ly** *adv.*, **-ness.**

Stink (stiŋk), *sb.* ME. [f. the vb.] **1.** A foul, disgusting, or offensive smell. **2.** Evil-smelling quality, offensive odour ME. **3.** *pl.* Univ. and Public School slang for Natural Science (orig., for Chemistry) as a subject of study or university examinations 1869.

Comb.: **s.-ball, -bomb,** a missile contrived for the purpose of emitting a suffocating vapour when thrown among the enemy; **-rat** *U.S.* = STINK-POT 4; **-shad,** the mud-shad *Dorosoma cepedianum*; **-trap** = STENCH-TRAP; **-turtle** = STINK-POT 4.

Stink (stiŋk), *v.* Pa. t. **stank** (stæŋk). Pa. pple. **stunk** (stʌŋk). [OE. *stincan* = (M)LG., (M)Du. *stinken*, OHG. *stinkan* (G. *stinken*) :– WGmc. **stiŋkwan*. Cf. STENCH.] †**1.** *intr.* To emit a smell or vapour of any kind; to smell (sweetly or otherwise) –ME. **2.** To emit a strong offensive smell; to smell foully. (In ordinary polite use avoided as unpleasantly forcible.) OE. **b.** *fig.* To be offensive; to be abhorrent; to savour offensively *of* something. Phr. *to s. in* (a person's) *nostrils*. ME. **3.** *trans.* To fill (an animal's earth) with suffocating fumes. Also, to drive (animals or persons) *out* of a place by stench or suffocating fumes. 1781. **4.** To cause to stink ME.

2. b. The name of the vngodly shal stynke COVERDALE *Prov.* 10:7.

Stinkard (sti·ŋkəɹd). 1600. [f. STINK *v.* + -ARD.] **1.** One who stinks. Formerly often as a term of abuse. Now *rare* or *Obs.* **2.** A name given to various ill-smelling animals 1774. **3.** A shark of the genus *Mustelus* 1883. **4.** = STINK-POT 3. 1850.

Stinker (sti·ŋkəɹ). 1607. [f. STINK *v.* + -ER[1].] One who or something which stinks. **1.** = prec. 1. *vulgar*. **2.** A sailor's name for the giant fulmar (*Ossifraga gigantea*) and other ill-smelling petrels 1837. **3.** Anything that emits an offensive smell. *vulgar*. 1898.

Stink-horn (sti·ŋkˌhǭɹn). 1724. [f. STINK *sb.* + HORN *sb.*] A name for various ill-smelling fungi.

†**Sti·nkibus.** *slang.* 1706. [f. STINK *sb.* + *-ibus*, Latin ending of dat. pl. Cf. MUCKIBUS.] Bad liquor, esp. adulterated spirits.

Stinking (sti·ŋkiŋ), *ppl. a.* OE. [-ING[2].] That stinks; offensively smelling. **b.** Used as a vague epithet connoting intense disgust and contempt. Now *vulgar*. ME.

Phr. *To cry s. fish*: see CRY *v.* 5.

Special collocations: **s. badger** = TELEDU; **s. cedar,** any species of *Torreya*; **s. ill,** a disease of sheep; **s. polecat,** one of the skunks or *Mustelidæ*; **s. yew** = *s. cedar*. Hence **Sti·nkingly** *adv.*

Sti·nk-pot. 1665. [f. STINK *sb.* + POT *sb.*, after Du. *stinkpot*.] †**1.** A pot or jar containing a disinfectant. **2.** A hand-missile charged with combustibles emitting a suffocating smoke, used in boarding a ship for effecting a diversion while the assailants gain the deck 1669. **3.** A sailor's name for a petrel 1865. **4.** The musk turtle, *Cinosternum odoratum* or *Aromochelys odorata* 1844.

Sti·nkstone. 1804. [f. STINK *sb.* + STONE *sb.*, after G. *stinkstein*.] *Min.* A name given to various limestones which give out a fetid odour on being scratched or struck.

Sti·nkweed. 1793. [f. STINK *sb.* + WEED *sb.*[1]] **a.** The cruciferous plant *Diplotaxis muralis*. **b.** *U.S.* The Thorn Apple, *Datura stramonium*.

Sti·nkwood. 1731. [f. STINK *sb.* + WOOD *sb.*] A name given in certain colonies to various trees, the wood of which has an unpleasant odour; the wood of any of these trees.

Stint (stint), *sb.*[1] ME. [f. STINT *v.*] **I.** The action of STINT *v.* †**1.** Cessation of action or motion, pause –1613. **2.** Limitation, restriction, esp. excessive restriction in the supply of the necessaries or comforts of life; the condition of being kept scantily supplied 1593.

1. Phr. *To make a s.*, to stop. 2. Phr. *Without s.* with no fixed limit of amount, unstintedly; His.. children had money lavished on them without s. 1876.

II. Limited or fixed amount. **1.** An allotted amount or measure; an allowance. Now *rare* or *Obs.* 1447. **2.** A measure, rate, gauge of amount, price, size, etc. fixed by authority. Chiefly in the phrases *to set*, etc. *at one s.*, *to appoint*, *set a s. Obs.* or *dial.* 1485. **3.** The limited number of cattle, according to kind, allotted to each definite portion into which pasture or common land is divided, or to each person entitled to the right of common pasturage; also, the right of pasturage according to the fixed rate 1437. **4.** An allotted portion of work; a definite task 1530. †**5.** Prescribed, destined, or customary limit 1509.

1. Phr. *One's s.*, an amount which one has resolved not to exceed; My s. [of wine] in company is a pint at noon, and half as much at night SWIFT. 2. A child's s.. .for braiding nets. .is four-pence a day 1794. 4. Their stent was mair than they cou'd well mak out 1789. 5. Every one of our passions and affections hath its natural s. and bound 1729.

Stint (stint), *sb.*[2] 1466. [Of unkn. origin.] Any one of the smaller Sandpipers (genus *Tringa*), esp. the Dunlin.

Stint (stint), *v.* [OE. *styntan*, corresp. to ON. **stynta* shorten, the source of some Eng. uses :– Gmc. **stuntjan*, f. **stunt-*; see STUNT *v.*[1]] **I.** To cut short, stop. **1.** *intr.* To cease action; to desist, forbear. Now only *arch.* and *dial.* ME. †**2.** Of processes, conditions, impersonal agencies: To cease, abate, come to an end –1681. **3.** To cease moving, pause in a journey, to halt, stop ME. †**4.** *trans.* To cause (a person) to cease action, to cause to desist –1653. **5.** To discontinue (an action); to hold in check, restrain (one's own actions or organs of action). Now *arch.* and *dial.* ME. †**6.** To cause to cease, check, stop (an event or state of affairs, actions of others) –1763. †**b.** To assuage, quench (grief, pain, appetite) –1666. **7.** To cause (a fluid, etc.) to stop flowing or emanating; esp. to staunch (blood). *Obs.* exc. *dial.* late ME. **8.** To check the growth of (an animal, plant); to arrest (growth); to force (a plant) *into* bloom by restricting its supply of nourishment 1735.

1. Pretty foole it stinted, and said I SHAKS. 2. Ther saw I how the tempest stent CHAUCER. 3. But come on, what s. ye for? SCOTT. 5. We must not s. Our necessary actions, in the feare To cope malicious Censurers SHAKS. 8. The laborious Chace Shall s. his [a young hound's] growth 1735.

II. To limit, apportion, or appoint definitely. **1.** *trans.* To set bounds to, to limit in extent or scope, to confine to certain limits. Now *rare*. 1513. **2.** To limit (the pasturage of common land) to a certain number of cattle; also, to assign a limited right of pasturage to (a person). late ME. **3.** To restrict (a person, his share or right) with respect to quantity or number; to limit in amount of allowance or indulgence 1567. **4.** To limit unduly in supply; to keep on short allowance, to scant. Const. *of*. 1722. **b.** To limit (a supply) unduly; to give in scanty measure 1838. **5.** *dial.* To apportion a 'stint' of work to (a person); also, to fix upon a definite portion of work as a stint 1794. **6.** *pass.* Of a mare: To be served (by a horse). Also of a ewe: To conceive. 1823.

1. The law of nations does not s. the right of executing justice 1863. 3. We ought to s. our selves in our most lawful Satisfactions ADDISON. 4. They s. themselves in their meals 1885. Hence **Stinted** *ppl. a.* **Sti·nted-ly** *adv.*, **-ness. Sti·nter,** one who or something which stints.

Stintless (sti·ntlės), *a.* 1597. [f. STINT *sb.*[1] + -LESS.] †**1.** That may not be stinted or caused to cease; that may not be assuaged or satisfied –1657. **2.** Supplied without stint 1844.

1. See heere. .The lasting panges: the stintless greefes: the teares 1587. 2. S. charity RUSKIN.

Stipe (stəip). 1785. [– Fr. *stipe* – L. *stipes* log, post, tree-trunk.] **1.** *Bot.* A foot-stalk; = STIPES 1. **2.** *Anat.* 'A stem: applied to two branches, anterior and posterior, of the zygal or paroccipital fissure of the brain' 1891. **3.** *Zool.* = STIPES 2. 1891.

Stipend (stəi·pend), *sb.* late ME. [– OFr. *stipende*, *stipendie* or L. *stipendium*, f. *stips*, *stip-*, money payment, wages, alms + *pendere* weigh, pay.] **1.** The pay of a soldier. Now *rare*. **2.** A salary or fixed periodical payment, made (annually or at shorter intervals) to a clergyman, teacher, or public official, in requital of his services. late ME. †**3.** *gen.* Payment for services, wages –1863. **4.** A fixed periodical payment of any kind, e.g. a pension or allowance, †a tax 1545.

1. Cicero. .earned under the auspices of Strabo his first and only 's.' 1875. 2. The s. of the teacher was precarious enough 1883. 3. For the s. and wages of sin is death 1629. The boys are generally taken away from school as soon as they are able to earn some small s. 1856. 4. Hiring is always for a price, a s., or additional recompense BLACKSTONE. Hence †**Sti·pend** *v. trans.* to provide with a s., salary, or pension. **Sti·pendless** *a.* that has no s.

†**Stipendary,** *a.* and *sb.* 1530. [– AL. *stipendarius* (XIII), var. of L. *stipendiarius*; see next.] = next –1660.

Stipendiary (stəipe·ndiări, stip-), *a.* and *sb.* 1545. [– L. *stipendiarius*, f. *stipendium*; see STIPEND, -ARY[1].] **A.** *adj.* **1.** That receives a stipend. Of a soldier (now *rare*): Serving for pay, mercenary. **2.** Pertaining to a stipend or stipends; of the nature of a stipend. Also of services: Paid for by a stipend. 1659.

1. To make the king a mere s. officer STUBBS. *S. magistrate*, in England, a salaried official exercising judicial functions similar to those exercised by the unpaid justices of the peace. 2. His application for an augmented s. grant 1844.

B. *sb.* One who receives a stipend; a salaried clergyman or teacher; †a pensioner 1584. **b.** A stipendiary magistrate 1875.

I know but three ways of living in society: you must be either a beggar, a robber, or a s. 1849.

Stipendiate (stəipe·ndieɪt), *v.* Now *rare* or *Obs.* 1656. [– *stipendiat-*, pa. ppl. stem of L. *stipendiari* be in receipt of pay, f. *stipendium*; see STIPEND, -ATE[3].] *trans.* To pay a stipend to.

‖**Stipes** (stəi·pīz). *Pl.* **stipites** (sti·pitīz). 1760. [mod. application of L. *stipes* (see STIPE) in the sense 'stalk'.] **1.** *Bot.* A stalk, esp. of some special kind, other than an ordinary leaf- or flower-stalk; e.g. one supporting a carpel or other part of a flower, or the pappus of the 'seed' or fruit of some composites; that of the frond of a fern or seaweed (also, the stem or caudex of a tree-fern); that supporting the pileus or cap of certain fungi. **2.** *Zool.* A part or organ resembling a stalk; *esp.* the footstalk or second joint of the maxilla of an insect; also applied to certain parts of the mouth-appendages in myriapods 1826.

Stipiform (stəi·pifǭɹm), *a.* 1821. [f. *stip-*, var. stem of L. STIPES + -FORM.] *Bot.* and *Zool.* Having the form or character of a stipe: applied esp. to the stems of certain dicotyledonous trees, of simple structure like those of lower classes.

Stipitate (sti·piteɪt), *a.* 1785. [f. *stipit-*, stem of L. STIPES + -ATE[2].] *Bot.* and *Zool.* Having or furnished with a stipes or stipe; stalked.

Stipitiform (sti·pitifǭɹm), *a.* 1859. [f. as var. prec. + -FORM.] *Bot.* and *Zool.* = STIPIFORM.

Stipple (sti·p'l), *sb.* 1669. [In sense 1 – Du. *stippel*, dim. of *stip* point; in sense 2 f. next.] †**1.** *pl.* Dots or small spots, used in shading a painting, engraving, etc. **2.** The method of painting, engraving, etc. by means of dots or small spots, so as to produce gradations of tone; the effect so produced; dotted work done with the point of a brush, a pencil, or a graver. Also *transf.* applied to natural appearances resembling this. **b.** In full *s. engraving*: An engraving thus produced 1864.

Stipple (sti·p'l), *v.* 1675. [–Du. *stippelen*,

frequent. of *stippen* prick, speckle, f. *stip* point; see -LE.] **1.** *trans.* To paint, engrave, or otherwise design in dots; to produce gradations of shade or colour in a design by means of dots or small spots. Also *intr.* or *absol.* **2.** *transf.* in ref. to natural processes or effects resembling this kind of painting or engraving 1774.

2. The Virginia-creeper stipples the church walls with green in summer and..scarlet in winter 1894.

‖**Stipula** (sti·piŭlă). *Pl.* **-læ** (lī), **-las** (lăz). 1762. [mod.L. use of L. *stipula* straw, STUBBLE.] *Bot.* and *Ornith.* = STIPULE *sb.*

Stipulaceous (stipiulēⁱ·ʃəs), *a.* 1760. [f. STIPULA + -ACEOUS.] Of the nature of or composed of stipules; having large stipules.

Stipulant (sti·piŭlănt). 1880. [– L. *stipulans, -ant-*, pr. pple. of *stipulare*; see STIPULATE *v.*, -ANT.] *Rom. Law.* = STIPULATOR 1.

Stipular (sti·piŭlăɹ), *a.* 1793. [f. STIPULA + -AR¹.] *Bot.* Of, belonging to, or furnished with stipules; situated on, near, or in the place of a stipule. Hence **Sti·pulary** *a. Bot.* occupying the place of stipules; formed of stipules.

Stipulate (sti·piŭlĕt), *a.* 1776. [f. STIPULA + -ATE².] *Bot.* Having stipules; with scales that are degenerate stipules.

Stipulate (sti·piŭleⁱt), *v.* 1624. [– *stipulat-*, pa. ppl. stem of L. *stipulari*, according to Paulus (c200) f. OL. *stipulus* firm, but connected by some with *stipula* (cf. STUBBLE) from the custom of breaking a straw in confirmation of a promise.] **1.** *intr.* **a.** *Rom. Law.* To make an oral contract in the verbal form (of question and answer) necessary to give it legal validity. Said *spec.* of the party who asks the question 1656. †**b.** *gen.* To contract, make a bargain, settle terms, covenant (*with* a person or persons) –1785. **2.** *trans.* Of an agreement, or of both contracting parties: To specify (something) as an essential part of the contract 1645. **3.** Of one of the parties to an agreement, or a person making an offer: To require or insist upon (something) as an essential condition. Now only with clause or inf. as obj. 1685. **4.** *intr.* To make an express demand *for* something as a condition of agreement 1790. **5.** *trans.* To promise, give surety for, guarantee. Now only (somewhat *rare*) with clause of inf. as obj. 1737.

1. a. That mutes can neither s. nor promise is quite plain 1880. **2.** The marriage-contract.. stipulates a dowry of twelve ounces of gold and twenty camels GIBBON. **3.** All I s., is to know the day SCOTT. **4.** I had stipulated for ten minutes' sleep on reaching the summit TYNDALL.

Stipulation¹ (stipiulēⁱ·ʃən). 1552. [– L. *stipulatio, -ōn-*, f. as prec.; see -ION.] The action or an act of stipulating. †**1.** An engagement or undertaking to do something –1719. †**2.** A contract, agreement, treaty –1818. **b.** *Rom. Law.* The action of making a contract or agreement in the verbal forms legally binding; a contract or agreement so made 1623. **3.** A giving security for the performance of an undertaking. (Now only in the language of the Admiralty Courts.) 1648. **4.** The action of specifying as one of the terms of a contract or agreement; a formulated term or condition of a contract or agreement 1750. **5.** The action of stipulating for something as a condition of agreement; an instance of this; a condition stipulated for 1792.

4. Next follow the terms or stipulations..upon which the grant is made BLACKSTONE. **5.** Pensions were thrown about indiscriminately... The only s. was, 'Give us your vote'. 1792.

Stipulation² (stipiulēⁱ·ʃən). 1760. [f. STIPULA + -ATION.] *Bot.* The arrangement of the stipules.

Stipulator (sti·piŭleⁱtəɹ). 1610. [– L. *stipulator*, f. *stipulat-*; see STIPULATE *v.*, -OR 2.] *Roman Law.* The person who asks the question (see STIPULATE *v.* 1 a) 1611.

Stipulatory (sti·piulĕtəri), *a.* Now *rare.* 1658. [f. STIPULATE *v.* + -ORY².] Of the nature of or characterized by stipulation.

Stipule (sti·piul), *sb.* 1793. [– Fr. *stipule*, or anglicized form of STIPULA.] **1.** *Bot.* A lateral appendage (often resembling a small leaf or scale) borne in pairs upon the leaf-base of certain plants. **2.** *Ornith.* A newly sprouted feather; a pin-feather 1891. Hence **Sti·puled** *a.* furnished with stipules, stipulate.

Stir (stɔ̄ɹ), *sb.*¹ late ME. [f. STIR *v.*] The action or an act of stirring. **1.** Movement, regarded as an interruption of rest; slight or momentary movement; movement of disturbance, agitation 1470. **2.** Active or energetic movement of a number of persons (or animals); bustle, activity 1586. **3.** Commotion, disturbance, tumult; general excitement; fuss. Now usu. with *a*; the pl. was formerly common, esp. in the sense 'publick disturbance, tumultuous disorder' (J.), riot, insurrection. late ME. **4.** *fig.* Movement of feeling or thought; emotion; intellectual activity 1563. **5.** An act of stirring something; *fig.* a rousing 1818.

1. No s. in the air, no s. in the sea SOUTHEY. **2.** Above the smoak and stirr of this dim spot, Which men call Earth MILT. **3.** For one slight trespass all this s.? COWPER. **4.** *Cymb.* I. iii. 12.

Stir (stɔ̄ɹ), *sb.*² *slang.* 1851. [Of unkn. origin.] A prison.

Stir (stɔ̄ɹ), *v.* Infl. **stirred** (stɔ̄ɹd), **stirring** (stɔ̄·riŋ). [OE. *styrian*, corresp. to OS. *far|sturian* subvert (MLG. *vorsturen*), MHG. *stürn* stir, poke, MSw. *styr(i)a*, Norw. *styrja* make a disturbance :– Gmc. *sturjan, f. *stur-, of which the var. *staur- is repr. by OFris. *to-, ur|stēra*, OHG. *stōren* (G. *stören*).] **I.** *trans.* **1.** To move, set in motion; *esp.* to give a slight or tremulous movement to; to shake, agitate. **b.** To move (a limb); now almost always, in neg. expressions, to make any or the slightest movement with ME. **c.** To move (something) from its place; to shift, displace. Chiefly (now always) with negative or its equivalent (implying ineffectual effort): (to be unable) to move or shift in the slightest degree. Now *rare* or *Obs.* OE. **d.** To rouse or disturb with a push 1590. **2.** *refl.* To move oneself or one's limbs; to take bodily exercise; to move from one's place. Now *rare* or *Obs.* OE. **3.** To agitate with the hand or an implement so as to alter the relative position of the parts of: **a.** a liquid; *esp.* to agitate with a more or less circular continuous movement, as with a spoon OE. **b.** a collection of solid bodies or particles; *esp.* to poke (burning coals, a fire) so as to promote combustion ME. **c.** soil or earth, as with an agricultural implement. Also *absol.* 1483. **4.** *fig.* To move from a fixed or quiet condition; to disturb, trouble, molest; to put into tumult or confusion; to upset. *Obs.* exc. *dial.* OE. **5.** To rouse from rest or inaction ME. **6.** To move to action, urge, incite, instigate, stimulate. Also formerly: To prompt, induce, persuade. OE. **7.** To excite to feeling, emotion, or passion; to move, affect ME. **b.** To move strongly (a person, his spirit, 'blood', etc.) 1489. **8.** To excite, occasion (passion, anger, †laughter, etc.) OE. **9.** To bring into notice or debate; to move, raise, moot (a subject or question). Now *rare.* OE.

1. The shrill sea-wind, whose breath idly stirred My hair SHELLEY. **b.** Unable to arise, or foote or hand to styre SPENSER. 'I will not s. a foot', said the Countess, obstinately SCOTT. *To s. one's stumps*: see STUMP *sb.*¹ 1 c. **3. a.** Idly stirring her little cup of black coffee 1905. **b.** Seizing the poker and stirring the fire vigorously 1888. **5.** Follow forth your own..objects, without stirring a nest of hornets SCOTT. **6.** An Ate, stirring him to bloud and strife SHAKS. Can ye not s. his mind to any pastimes? SCOTT. **7.** The story of a great man's life still stirs the heart 1889. **8.** A fault which stirs the critic's rage 1760. **9.** That..a doubt once decided may be stirred no more PALEY.

II. *intr.* †**1.** To move; to be in motion; *spec.* to move as a living being –1633. **2.** To pass from rest to motion, to begin to move; to move at all or in the least (chiefly with neg.); *occas.* to show signs of life or consciousness (after sleep or a faint) OE. **b.** To go out (from a house or place of abode); almost always with neg. 1567. **c.** *fig.* To begin to show signs of 'life' or activity (as an intellectual movement or the like) 1873. **3.** To move about in a place, to 'be about'; chiefly in *pres. pple.* (often *spec.* = out of bed, up and about) ME. **b.** *transf.* To be in circulation, be current; chiefly in *pres. pple.* Now somewhat *rare.* late ME. **c.** To go on, happen, take place; chiefly in *pres. pple.* = going on, 'on foot' 1526. **4.** To move briskly or energetically; to be on the move, bestir oneself ME. **b.** *fig.* To be active or occupied *about* something; to begin to act ME. **c.** To rise in revolt or insurrection. Now *rare* and merely contextual. ME. **5.** To be roused or excited, as feeling, passion, etc. OE.

1. While rocks stand, And rivers stirre G. HERBERT. **2.** Not a Mouse stirring SHAKS. **b.** I came home at seven, and have never stirred out SWIFT. **3.** When no one in the house was stirring, and the lights were all extinguished DICKENS. **b.** He asked..if there were any news stirring 1850. **c.** No ill luck stirring but what lights a my shoulders SHAKS. **4.** Her husband stirred and bustled about until the requisite leave was obtained THACKERAY. **5.** My Blood stirs at the very thought on 't CIBBER.

Stir up. a. *trans.* To set in motion, agitate; to push or poke so as to displace, disturb, or mix the parts of. **b.** To rouse to action, activity, or emotion; to incite, instigate, stimulate. **c.** To excite, provoke, induce; to raise, set on foot (strife, disturbance, etc.); to arouse (feeling or emotion).

Stirabout (stɔ̄·răbaut). 1682. [See STIR *v.*, ABOUT *adv.*] **1. a.** Porridge made by stirring oatmeal, etc. in boiling water or milk. (orig. *Anglo-Irish.*) **b.** *fig.* A bustle, a state of confusion 1905. **2.** A bustling person 1870.

Stire (stəiᵊɹ). 1483. [Of unkn. origin. Cf. synon. †*stirom* (XVIII).] A kind of cider apple; also, the cider made from it.

Stirk (stɔ̄ɹk). *dial.* [OE. *stirc, styr(i)c*, Kentish *stiorc*, perh. f. *stēor* STEER *sb.*¹ + *-oc, -uc* -OCK; cf. MLG., MDu. *sterke* young cow, MDu. *stierken* bull calf.] **1.** A young bullock or heifer, usu. between one and two years old. **2.** Used as a term of abuse: a foolish person 1590.

Stirless (stɔ̄·ɹlĕs), *a.* 1816. [f. STIR *sb.* and *v.* + -LESS.] Not stirring, motionless.

Mountains..s. as death CARLYLE.

Stirp (stɔ̄ɹp). 1502. [– L. *stirps, stirp-* stock, stem.] **1.** The stock of a family; a line of descent; the descendants of a common ancestor. Now somewhat *rare.* **2.** *Eugenics.* The total of the germs which are found in the newly fertilized ovum 1875.

Stirpiculture (stɔ̄·ɹpikɒltiŭɹ, -tʃəɹ). 1870. [f. *stirpi-*, comb. form of next + *cultura* CULTURE *sb.*] The production of pure races or stocks by careful breeding. Hence **Stirpicu·ltural** *a.* **Stirpicu·lturist.**

‖**Stirps** (stɔ̄ɹps). *Pl.* **stirpes** (stɔ̄·ɹpīz). 1681. [L.; cf. STIRP.] **1.** *Law.* A branch of a family; the person who with his descendants forms a branch of a family. Chiefly in L. phr. *per stirpes*; also *in stirpes.* **2.** *Zool.* Used variously (often vaguely) as a term of classification; a family, subfamily, group, etc. 1863.

Stirrer (stɔ̄·rəɹ). late ME. [f. STIR *v.* + -ER¹.] One who or something which stirs; an instigator; †an agitator; one who moves about; an active person; an instrument or appliance for stirring a liquid or the like.

Stirring (stɔ̄·riŋ), *ppl. a.* OE. [f. STIR *v.* + -ING².] That stirs; that is in motion, or capable of motion; active; energetic in action; that excites or incites.

S. times for you English LYTTON. Cheerful and s. music 1873. Hence **Sti·rringly** *adv.*

Stirrup (sti·rŏp), *sb.* [OE. *stigrāp* = OS. *stigerēp*, MDu. *steegereep*, OHG. *stegareif* (G. *stegreif*), ON. *stigreip*; f. Gmc. *stiʒ- (STY *v.*¹) + *raipaz ROPE *sb.*] **1.** A contrivance suspended from the side of a saddle to serve as a support for the foot of the rider; now, an arched piece of metal (rarely of wood, leather, etc.) closed by a flat plate to receive the sole of the boot. **2.** Applied to various kinds of foot-rest analogous to the stirrup, e.g. in *Shoemaking.* late ME. **3.** *Anat.* = STAPES 1615. **4.** Something shaped like a stirrup; e.g. a U-shaped clamp or support ME. **5.** *Naut.* One of the ropes supporting the foot-ropes 1495.

1. Instead of stirrups we had ropes tied with a loope to put our feete in EVELYN. Phr. *To hold the s.*, lit. in helping a person to mount esp. as a manifestation of homage or reverence; hence *fig.* to be subservient.

attrib. and *Comb.*: **s.-bone** = sense 3; **-cup,** a cup of wine or other drink taken by one already on horse-back setting out for a journey; a parting drink; **-iron** (now *rare*), the metal portion of a stirrup, as dist. from the strap; **-leather,** the leather strap by which a stirrup hangs from the saddle; **-vase** [misrendering of G. *bügelkanne*, formed after *bügeleisen* flat-iron], *Archæol.* a 'pseudamphora' with a square-cut handle on either side of the false spout.

Stirrup (sti·rŏp), *v.* 1610. [f. prec.] **1.** *trans.* To supply with or as with stirrups. **2.** To flog with a stirrup-leather or with a shoemaker's stirrup. *slang.* 1735. **3.** *Naut.* To attach stirrups to 1748.

Stitch (stitʃ), *sb.*[1] [OE. *stiće* = OFris. *steke*, OS. *stiki* prick, stab, OHG. *stih* (G. *stich*) prick, sting, stitch, Goth. *stiks* point :- Gmc. **stikiz*, f. **stik-* STICK *v.*] **I.** A thrust, stab. **†1.** A prick, puncture, or stab, inflicted by a pointed instrument. OE. only. **2.** A sharp sudden local pain, like that produced by the thrust of a pointed weapon; esp. (now only) an acute spasmodic pain in the intercostal muscles, called more fully *a s. in the side* OE. **†3.** *fig.* A grudge, dislike, spite –1679.

2. If you..will laughe your selues into stitches, follow me SHAKS. The agonising s. of pleurisy 1898.

II. A movement in sewing or the like. **1. a.** Each of the movements of a threaded needle in and out of a fabric which is being sewn. Also, a like movement with the awl in shoemaking. ME. **b.** The portion or loop of thread or yarn left in the material as a result of this movement, and forming the means by which the parts of the sewn materials are held together. late ME. **c.** In machine sewing, a single motion of a needle and shuttle carrying the thread through the fabric; the loop or interlocked thread thus produced 1844. **d.** In emphatic phrases with a negative or the like: A single movement with the needle; *fig.* a 'stroke' or work of any kind 1581. **2.** *Surgery.* The movement of the needle through the edges of a wound when it is being sewn up; each loop of thread or other material fastened in the skin or flesh as a result of this operation 1525. **3.** A single complete movement of the needle or other implement used in knitting, crochet, embroidery, lace-making, etc.; the portion of the work produced by such a movement 1599. **4.** A particular mode of using the needle or other implement, in sewing, knitting, embroidery, etc.; the kind or style of work thus produced 1624. **5.** A loop of thread or yarn as an ultimate constituent of a sewn or woven material; hence, the least piece of fabric or clothing 1500. **6.** *A good s.*: a considerable distance (in walking). *dial.* 1684.

1. *Proverb.* A s. in time saves nine. **b.** A s. or two had broke out in the gathers of my stock STERNE. **d.** He never will do a s. of work before Wednesday morning 1768. **3.** Phr. *To drop, take up a s.* **4.** While she is engaged in teaching them a new s. JOHNSON. BACK-, CHAIN-, CROSS-, FEATHER-, HEM-S.; see these words; also LOCK *sb.*,[2] etc. **5.** I haven't a dry s. on my back! 1883. *Every s.*, all the clothes one is wearing; every available piece (of sail); A boat..with every s. of canvas set DISRAELI. **6.** You have gone a good s., you may well be a weary BUNYAN.

Stitch (stitʃ), *sb.*[2] Now *dial.* 1493. [prob. orig. identical w. prec.] A ridge or balk of land; esp. a strip of ploughed land between two water-furrows.

Men at plow..that draue earth here and there, And turnd vp stitches orderly CHAPMAN.

Stitch (stitʃ), *v.*[1] ME. [f. STITCH *sb.*[1]] **†I.** *trans.* To stab, pierce; *transf.* to afflict with a 'stitch' or sharp sudden pain –1620. **II.** To fasten or adorn with stitches. **1.** *trans.* To fasten together (pieces of textile material, leather, etc.) by stitches; to make or mend (a garment, etc.) by thus joining its parts ME. **2.** *Surgery.* To unite the edges of (a wound) by drawing stitches through the flesh 1580. **3.** *Bookbinding.* To fasten together (a number of sheets or sections) by passing the thread or wire through all the sheets at once 1566. **4.** To fasten or attach (something) by sewing 1530. **b.** To enclose *in* or *into* a cover or receptacle secured by stitching 1848. **5.** To ornament with stitches; to embroider 1529. **6.** *absol.* and *intr.* To make stitches; to work with a needle and thread 1697.

1. Court Ladies will..s. a Gown, to pass the time away 1709. **6.** She..stitched in silence 1865.

Stitch up. *trans.* **a.** To make or put together by sewing. **b.** To close (an orifice, a wound), to mend (a rent), by sewing the edges together. **c.** To enclose *in* a cover or receptacle and secure it by sewing. Hence **Sti·tcher**, one who stitches or sews; †(*contempt.*) a tailor; a tool or machine used for stitching.

Stitch (stitʃ), *v.*[2] *dial.* 1805. [Goes w. STITCH *sb.*[2]] *trans.* To turn up (the ground) in ridges in order to cover or protect the roots of potatoes, etc.; to earth *up*.

Stitchery (sti·tʃəri). 1607. [f. STITCH *v.*[1] or STITCHER; see -ERY 2. (App. coined by Shaks.)] Needlework.

Stitching (sti·tʃiŋ), *vbl. sb.* 1521. [f. STITCH *v.*[1] + -ING[1].] **1.** The action of STITCH *v.*[1] **2.** *concr.* **a.** Stitches collectively; i.e. the portions or loops of thread, etc. fastened in the material sewn as the result of sewing. Also, a series of stitches. **b.** The thread, silk, etc., of which stitches are made. Also *pl.* 1614.

Stitchwort (sti·tʃwɒɹt). ME. [f. STITCH *sb.*[1] + WORT[1].] A name for *Stellaria holostea*. Also, a book-name for the genus.

Stithy (sti·ði), *sb.* [ME. *steþi, stiþi* – ON. *steði* :- **staðjon*, f. Gmc. **sta-* STAND. The form is due to assoc. with SMITHY.] **1.** An anvil. **†2.** *Anat.* = INCUS 1 (*rare*) –1615. **3.** A forge, smithy 1602.

3. My imaginations are as foule As Vulcans s. SHAKS. Hence **†Sti·thy** *v. trans.* to forge.

Stive (stəiv), *sb.* 1793. [– Du. †*stuive*, rel. to *stuiven* rise as dust.] Dust; esp. the floating dust of flour during the operation of grinding.

Stive (stəiv), *v.*[1] Now chiefly *Sc.* ME. [In XVII – Fr. *estiver*, whence also STEEVE *v.*[2]] *trans.* To compress and stow (cargo) in a ship's hold. Also *transf.* to pack tightly; to crowd (with things or people). Also with *up*.

Stive (stəiv), *v.*[2] late ME. [app. a var. of STEW *v.* – OFr. *estuver.*] **†1.** *trans.* = STEW *v.* (*rare*) –1743. **2.** To shut up in a close hot place; to stifle, suffocate 1722. **3.** *intr.* To 'stew', suffocate 1806.

2. I have one half of the house to myself.. while..the two musty nieces are stived up in the other half RICHARDSON.

Stiver (stəi·vəɹ), *sb.* 1502. [– Du. *stuiver*, in MLG. *stüver*, prob. based on **stuf-* (cf. STUB).] **1.** A small (orig. silver) coin of the Low Countries; now applied to the nickel piece of 5 cents of the Netherlands, in value about a penny English. **2.** Used as a type of a coin of small value, or of a small amount of money; occas. a small quantity of anything. *Not a s.* = nothing.

‖**Stoa** (stōᵘ·ă). *Pl.* **stoas** (stōᵘ·ăz), **stoai** (stōᵘ·əi). 1603. [Gr. στοά.] *Gr. Antiq.* A portico, roofed colonnade; *spec.* the great hall at Athens (adorned with frescoes of the battle of Marathon), in which Zeno lectured, and from which his disciples were called Stoics.

Stoat (stōᵘt). 1460. [Of unkn. origin.] The European ermine, *Putorius ermineus* or *Mustela erminea*, esp. when in its brown summer coat.

Stoccado (stǫkā·do), *sb. Obs.* exc. *arch.* 1569. [With suffix-substitution – It. *stoccata*, f. *stocco* point of sword, dagger, of Gmc. origin; see STOCK *sb.*[1], -ADO.] A thrust or stab with a pointed weapon. Also as vb.

Stochastic (stokæ·stik), *a.* Now *rare* or *Obs.* 1662. [– Gr. στοχαστικός, f. στοχάζεσθαι aim at a mark, guess, f. στόχος aim, guess.] Pertaining to conjecture.

Stock (stǫk), *sb.*[1] [OE. *stoc*(*c* = OFris. *stokk*, OS., (M)Du. *stok* (G. *stock* stick), ON. *stokkr* trunk, block, log :- Gmc. **stukkaz*; of unkn. origin.] **I.** Trunk or stem. **1.** A tree-trunk deprived of its branches; the lower part of a tree-trunk left standing, a stump. *Obs.* or *arch.* **†b.** A log, block of wood –1806. **c.** As the type of what is lifeless, motionless, or void of sensation. Hence, a senseless or stupid person. ME. **d.** Applied contempt. to an idol or graven image OE. **2.** The trunk or stem of a (living) tree, as dist. from the root and branches ME. **b.** *Bot.* = RHIZOME 1831. **3.** *fig.* **a.** The source of a line of descent; the progenitor of a family or race. In *Law*, the first purchaser of an estate of inheritance. late ME. **†b.** The original from which something is derived –1756. **c.** A line of descent; the descendants of a common ancestor; a family, kindred. late ME. **d.** A race, ethnical kindred; a race or family (of animals or plants); a related group or 'family' (of languages). Also, an ancestral type from which various races, species, etc. have diverged. 1549. **†e.** Pedigree –1657. **f.** Kind, sort. Now *dial.* 1450. **4.** A stem in which a graft is inserted. late ME. **†5.** The 'trunk' of a human body –1590. **†6.** A post, stake –1688. **7.** *pl.* An instrument of punishment now disused, in which the person to be punished was placed in a sitting posture in a frame of timber, with holes to confine the ankles between two planks (and sometimes others for securing the wrists) ME. **8.** [perh. *transf.* from 7.] A frame in which a horse is confined for shoeing 1875.

1. The magpye, lighting on the s., Stood chat-t'ring SWIFT. **c.** I am not so credulous to thinke every S. a Stoicke 1640. **d.** *Phr. Stocks and stones* = gods of wood and stone. **2.** Strong Stocks of Vines it will in time produce DRYDEN. *fig.* The blessid stoke þat ytt on grew Ytt was Mary, that bare Jhesu. *Carol.* **3. a.** Hee that was the stocke of all mankinde 1594. To constitute a new s. of descent a very real possession was necessary 1886. **c.** The Crabbs were of a very old English s. THACKERAY. **d.** A population, sprung from the English s., and animated by English feelings MACAULAY. **4.** He..grafted apples upon the wild stocks 1903. **7.** The pillory, the stocks, and the ducking-stool 1769. fig. *The shoe-maker's stock* (joc.), tight boots.

II. A supporting structure. **†1.** A gun-carriage –1748. **2.** The outer rail of a bedstead; the side of a bed away from the wall; *pl.* a bedstead. *Obs.* exc. *Sc.* 1525. **3.** *pl.* The framework on which a ship or boat is supported while in process of construction. late ME. **b.** *fig.* esp. in phr. *on the stocks*, said e.g. of a literary work planned and commenced 1659. **4.** *dial.* = HOB *sb.*[2] 1. 1592. **5.** *Brick-making.* **a.** = *s.-board* –1753. **b.** Short for *s.-brick* 1738. **6.** The support of the block in which the anvil is fixed, or of the anvil itself ME.

3. **b.** Until my other Play be finished, which is now on the Stocks 1669.

III. (More fully *fulling-s.*) In a fulling-mill: orig., the wooden trough or box in which the cloth is placed to be beaten by the 'faller' or mallet; hence, this receptacle with the 'faller'. In mod. use, often the 'faller' itself. late ME. **IV.** The more massive portion of an instrument or weapon; usu., the body or handle to which the working part is attached. **1.** The heavy cross-bar (orig. wooden) of an anchor ME. **2.** The block of wood from which a bell is hung 1474. **3.** The 'hub' of a wheel 1585. **4.** The wooden portion of a musket or fowling-piece; the handle of a pistol 1541. **5.** The handle (of a whip, fishing-rod, etc.) 1695. **6.** (More explicitly *bit-stock.*) A carpenter's boring tool, a brace 1688. **7.** An adjustable wrench for holding screw-cutting dies 1862. **8.** The shorter and thicker of the two pieces composing a T-square or an L-square 1815. **9.** In a plane, the block in which the plane-iron is fitted 1815. **10.** The wooden case of a lock 1833. **11.** *Flax-dressing.* One of the beaters in a scutching-mill 1776.

1. *S. and fluke* (Naut.), the whole of anything. **4.** Phr. *S., lock*, or *lock, s., and barrel*, the whole of a thing; also *advb.*, every whit, entirely.

V. Concrete senses of uncertain or mixed origin. **1.** A stocking. Now only *dial.* 1456. **2.** A swarm of bees 1568. **3.** The portion of a tally which was given to the person making a payment to the Exchequer 1601. **4.** [Short for *S.-gillyflower.*] **a.** Any plant of the cruciferous genus *Matthiola*. **b.** *Virginia(n) s.*: the cruciferous plant *Malcolmia maritima*, having flowers somewhat resembling those of the s.-gillyflower 1664. **5.** A kind of stiff close-fitting neckcloth, formerly worn by men generally, now only in the army 1700. **b.** An article of clerical attire, consisting of a piece of black silk or other fabric (worn on the chest and secured by a band round the neck) over which the linen collar is fastened 1883.

4. To smell the sucklins and the stocks and to see the new trees grow 1664. **5.** My neckcloths being all worn out, I intend to wear stocks COWPER. The wearing of Stocks may be dispensed with on the line of March 1868.

VI. A fund, store. **†1.** A sum of money set apart to provide for certain expenses; a fund –1718. **†2.** A capital sum to trade with or to invest; capital or principal –1760. **†b.** An endowment for a son; a dowry for a daughter

–1686. †**c.** *fig.* phrase. *Upon the s. of*: on the ground or basis of –1821. †**3.** An estate or property that produces income; a person's total property –1771. †**b.** The aggregate wealth of a nation –1825. †**4.** The business capital of a trading firm or company –1844. **b.** In bookkeeping by double entry, the heading (more fully *s. account*) of the ledger account which summarizes the assets and liabilities of the trader, firm, or company to whom the books belong 1588. †**5.** Money, or a sum of money, invested by a person in a partnership or commercial company –1710. **6.** The subscribed capital of a trading company, or the public debt of a nation, municipal corporation, or the like, regarded as transferable property held by the subscribers or creditors, and subject to fluctuations in market value. Also, a kind of stock, a particular fund in which money may be invested. 1692. **7.** A collective term for the implements (*dead s.*) and the animals (*live s.*) employed in the working of a farm, an industrial establishment, etc. See also ROLLING STOCK. 1519. **8.** *spec.* = LIVE STOCK; the animals on a farm; also, a collective term for horses, cattle, and sheep bred for use or profit 1523. †**b.** Applied to slaves –1837. **9.** A quantity (of something specified, whether material or immaterial) accumulated for future use; a store or provision to be drawn upon as occasion requires 1638. **10.** The aggregate of goods, or of some specified kind of goods which a trader has on hand as a provision for the possible future requirements of customers 1696. **11.** The liquor made by boiling bones or meat (with or without vegetables, etc.) and used as a foundation for soup 1764. **b.** *gen.* The raw material from which anything is made 1873. **12.** *Card-playing.* **a.** In certain games, the portion of the pack of cards which is not dealt out, but left on the table to be drawn from according to the rules of the game 1584. **b.** The set of cards used in a particular game (whether a pack, or one or more incomplete packs) 1584. †**c.** = HAND *sb.* V. 1. –1657.

6. In modern British use, the subscribed capital of a company is called *shares* when it is divided into portions of uniform amount, and s. when any desired amount may be bought or sold. When there is no specific indication, *s.* is usually taken to refer to those portions of the National Debt, the principal of which is not repayable, the government being pledged only to the payment of interest in perpetuity. O.E.D. Phr. (*fig.*) *To take s. in*, to be interested in, attach importance, give credence to (*colloq.* or *slang*). **9.** You have not yet exhausted the whole s. of human infelicity JOHNSON. Phr. *To lay in a s.* **10. Take s.,** In commercial use, to make an inventory of the merchandise, furniture, etc. in one's own (*rarely* in another's) possession, recording its quantity and present value. Hence *fig.*, to make a careful estimate of one's position with regard to resources, prospects, or the like. *To take s. of*, to reckon up, evaluate; also *colloq.*, to scrutinize (a person) with suspicion or interest. See also 6 above. *In s.*, in the possession of the trader.

Combs. **a.** Similatively (with ref. to sense I. 1 c): **s.-blind, -dead, -deaf** *adjs.*, as blind (etc.) as a stock. **b.** In sense VI. 6: **s. certificate,** a document issued by the Treasury, entitling the holder to a certain amount of a particular government stock. **c.** In sense VI. 8: *s.-breeder, -raiser, -run*; indicating an animal selected for breeding purposes, as *s.-dog, -mare*; **s.-rider** *Austral.*, a man employed to ride after cattle on an unfenced station; **-riding,** the occupation of a s.-rider; **-whip** *Austral.*, a whip for driving cattle. **d.** In names of birds: **s. annet,** the common sheldrake, *Tadorna cornuta*; **s. drake, duck,** the mallard or wild duck, *Anas boscas*; **s. pigeon** = STOCK-DOVE. **e.** Special comb.: **s. account** *Book-keeping* (see VI. 4 b.); **-book,** a book in which an account is kept of goods in s.; **-board,** the wooden board which forms the bottom of a brick-mould; **-brick,** a hard solid brick, pressed in the mould; **-company,** a company the capital of which is represented by s.; **-lock,** a lock enclosed in a wooden case, usu. fitted on an outer door; **-market,** (*a*) a place where stocks or securities are brought and sold; the traffic at such a place; (*b*) a cattle-market; trade in live-s.; **-pot,** a pot in which s. for soups is boiled and kept; **-purse,** a fund for the common purposes of a group of persons; **-room,** (*a*) a room in which reserve s. is stored; (*b*) a room in a hotel in which commercial travellers display their samples; **-tackle** *Naut.*, a tackle used for raising the s. of an anchor perpendicular.

B. *adj.* (in attrib. use only). That is kept in stock. **1.** Kept regularly in stock for sale; **s. size,** a size (of ready-made garments) regularly kept in stock; used *attrib.* or predicatively to designate a person whom such a size fits 1625. **b.** Designating a medicinal or chemical preparation which is kept ready for use, or the vessel in which such a preparation is stored 1861. **2.** *Theatr.* **s. piece, play,** etc., one which forms part of a *répertoire*; **s. company,** a company who regularly act together at a particular theatre 1761. **3.** *fig.* In ref. to conventional, intellectual, or literary topics: Kept in stock for use; commonly used or brought forward in conversation, discussion, or composition; hence, commonplace, trite 1738.

3. The s. arguments against utilitarianism MILL. S. quotations from the fathers 1895.

†**Stock,** *sb.*[2] 1513. [Aphetic – (O)Fr. *estoc*, f. *estoquier* (cf. STOCK *v.*[2]) – LG. *stoken*.] **1.** A thrusting sword –1572. **2.** *Fencing.* A thrust with a pointed weapon –1604.

2. *Merry W.* II. iii. 36.

Stock (stǫk), *v.*[1] ME. [f. STOCK *sb.*[1]] **I.** †**1.** *trans.* To set in the stocks; to punish by confining in the stocks; in early use, to subject to rigorous imprisonment –1694. **2.** To fasten to or fit with a stock: esp. **a.** To fix (a bell) to its stock 1483. **b.** To fit (a gun, †crossbow) with a stock 1539. **c.** To fix the stock upon (an anchor) 1769. **d.** Naut. *To s. to*: to haul (an anchor) into a perpendicular position by means of a stock-tackle 1815. †**3.** To cover (hose) with some stronger material; to strengthen (stockings) with pieces of cloth sewn on –1691. **II.** To root up (trees, stumps, weeds, etc.); to extirpate by digging or grubbing; to fell (a tree) by digging round and cutting its roots 1440. **b.** *transf.* To pull up (stones, a fence); to break up or loosen (the surface of the ground with a pick) 1802. **III.** To check in growth; to stiffen. **1.** To stunt, check in growth (a plant or animal). Chiefly in pa. pple. *stocked*. Also *intr.*, to be stunted in growth. *dial.* 1607. **2.** *local.* To indurate (stone) by exposure to the weather 1712. **IV.** To supply with a 'stock', fund, or store. **1.** *trans.* To supply or provide with stock or with a stock; to furnish (a farm, estate, etc.) with live or dead stock; to fill (a pond, river) with fish; to store or supply with goods, commodities, appliances, etc. 1622. **2.** To lay up in store; to form a stock or supply of (a commodity). Also with *up*. 1700. **b.** *esp.* To keep (goods) in stock for sale 1884. **3.** *absol.* To provide stock; to lay in a stock or supply. Also with *up*. 1850.

1. The Fish wherewith you s. the Waters 1683. The country was plentifully stocked with provisions GIBBON. The cellar was stocked with Rhenish Wine 1899. **2. b.** Wholesale Houses regularly S. it 1888.

V. Techn. and dial. senses. **1.** *pass.* Of a female animal: To be impregnated 1478. **2.** *trans.* To leave (a cow) unmilked in order that she may make a good show at market 1683. **3.** To sow (land) with grass or clover. Also with *down*: To lay down to grass, etc. *U.S.* 1828. **4.** To cause to be cropped or eaten by cattle; to use (land) as pasture 1794. **5. a.** To put (playing cards) together in a pack. **b.** To arrange or shuffle fraudulently. 1735.

Stock (stǫk), *v.*[2] Now *dial.* 1625. [f. STOCK *sb.*[2]] †**1.** *trans.* To strike or hit with a thrust of a pointed weapon. **2.** Of a bird: To peck, peck at; to make (a hole) by pecking. Also, to root *up* with the beak. Also *intr.* To peck *away* (*at*). 1653.

Stockade (stǫkē·d), *sb.* 1614. [Aphetic – Fr. †*estocade*, alt. of †*estacade* – Sp. *estacada*, f. *estaca* – Rom. – Gmc. **stak*- STAKE *sb.*[1]; see -ADE.] **1.** A defensive barrier of stakes or piles placed across a harbour or river, around a building, village, or the like; *spec.* in *Fortification*, a barricade for entrenchments and redoubts, usu. made of timber, furnished with loopholes for gun-fire. **b.** *transf.* An enclosure, or pen, made with posts and stakes 1858. **2.** *Hydraul. Engin.* Piling which serves as a breakwater 1891.

Comb.: **s. fort** *Brit. N. Amer.* and *U.S.*, a fortified trading station. Hence **Stocka·de** *v. trans.* to protect or fortify with a s.

†**Stocka·do,** *sb.* 1609. [Altered f. STACCADO, as if f. STOCK *sb.*[1]] = prec. *sb.* 1. –1809. Hence †**Stocka·do** *v.* = STOCKADE *v.*

Sto·ck-bro:ker, sto·ckbro:ker. 1706. [STOCK *sb.*[1]] A broker who, for a commission, buys and sells stock on behalf of clients.

Sto·ck-dove. ME. [Cf. Flem. †*stockduive*, G. *stocktaube*. Prob. so named as living in hollow trees.] The wild pigeon, *Columba œnas*.

Stocker (stǫ·kəɹ). 1641. [f. STOCK *v.*[1] and *sb.*[1] + -ER[1].] **1.** A workman who makes or fits stocks, esp. gun-stocks. **2.** *U.S.* and *Canada*. An animal sold to be finally butchered, but kept as stock until matured or fattened 1881.

Sto·ck excha:nge. 1773. A market for the buying and selling of public securities; the place or building where this is done; an association of brokers and jobbers who transact business in a particular place or market.

Often with capital initials as the name of a particular building, esp. that in the City of London.

Sto·ck-fish. ME. [– (M)LG., (M)Du. *stokvisch*, variously explained.] A name for cod and other gadoid fish cured without salt by splitting open and drying hard in the air. **b.** In fig., proverbial and joc. expressions (often with ref. to the beating of the fish before cooking) 1515. **c.** In contemptuous address to a person. SHAKS.

b. Mute as a s. DICKENS. London is as dead as a s. MEREDITH.

Sto·ck-gi:llyflower. 1530. [Cf. Flem. *stokviolier*.] The plant *Matthiola incana*; so called as having a woody stem, in distinction from clove-gillyflower.

Sto·ckho:lder. 1753. **1.** One who is a proprietor of stock in the public funds or the funds of a joint-stock company, etc. Also (now *U.S.*) used more widely to include the meaning of 'shareholder'. **2.** *Austral.* An owner of large herds of cattle or flocks of sheep 1819.

Stockinette (stǫkine·t). Also **-et.** 1824. [prob. alt., simulating a dim. in -ET, -ETTE, of earlier *stocking-net*.] **1.** A knitted silk or woollen textile fabric of considerable elasticity. **2.** A garment made of stockinette 1837.

Stocking (stǫ·kiŋ), *sb.* 1583. [Of obscure formation with -ING[1], repl. NETHER STOCK, corresp. to †*upper stock*, as Fr. *bas de chausse* (whence *bas* stocking) is parallel to *haut de chausse*.] **1.** A close-fitting article of clothing covering the foot and the leg, and made of knitted or woven material Freq. *pl.* **2.** A stocking used: **a.** as a receptacle for storing one's money; hence, a store of money 1873; **b.** as a receptacle for the presents supposed by children to be deposited in it by 'Father Christmas' (or, latterly, by Santa Claus) on Christmas Eve 1853. **3. a.** A surgical appliance resembling a stocking. **b.** A bandage for the leg of a horse. 1875. **4.** *transf.* Applied to the surface or coat of the leg (or the lower part of it) of a bird or beast, when of different colour from the body 1821.

2. a. She had a 's.' gathered to to meet the wants of an evil day 1876. **3. a.** *Elastic s.*, a covering of elastic webbing worn as a remedial support for the leg, esp. when affected with varicose veins. **4.** A very handsome..bay, with a white s. on his off hind leg 1856.

Comb.: **s.-needle,** a darning-needle; †**-net** = STOCKINETTE; **-sole,** that part of the s. which comes under the tread of the foot; *in one's s. soles*, without one's shoes (cf. STOCKING-FOOT).

Stocking (stǫ·kiŋ), *v.* 1755. [f. prec.] *trans.* To furnish with stockings.

Stockinged (stǫ·kiŋd), *ppl. a.* 1608. [f. STOCKING *sb.* or *v.* + -ED.] **1.** Furnished with stockings or with a stocking. **2.** Of the foot: Covered with a stocking only 1862. **3.** Of a bird: Feathered on the shank 1855.

Stockinger (stǫ·kiŋəɹ). 1741. [f. STOCKING *sb.* + -ER[1].] One who works at a stocking hand-loom; a framework-knitter, stocking-weaver.

Sto·cking-foot. 1766. That part of a stocking which covers the foot. **b.** As a receptacle for money laid by. Chiefly *fig.* 1894.

In, (on) one's stocking feet, with only one's stockings on one's feet, without one's shoes.

Sto·cking-frame. 1710. A machine for

producing material composed of the looped stitch used in knitting; a knitting machine.

Stock-in-trade. 1762. [Earlier †*stock for* or *of trade*.] The goods kept on sale by a dealer, shopkeeper, or pedlar. Also, a workman's tools, appliances, or apparatus.

Such charges were the standing material, the s. of every orator DE QUINCEY.

Stockish (stǫ·kiʃ), *a.* 1596. [f. STOCK *sb.*[1] + -ISH[1].] Resembling a stock or block of wood; esp. of a person, excessively dull, stupid, or 'wooden'.

1. Naught so s., hard, and full of rage, But musicke for time doth change his nature SHAKS.

Stockist (stǫ·kist). 1923. [f. STOCK *sb.*[1] or *v.*[1] + -IST.] A tradesman who keeps (specified goods) in stock.

†**Stock-job,** *v.* 1697. [Back-formation from next.] **a.** *trans.* To apply the methods of stock-jobbing to, employ in stock-jobbing –1721. **b.** *intr.* To practise stock-jobbing –1721.

Sto·ck-jo:bber. 1626. [JOBBER[2] 4.] A member of the Stock Exchange who deals in stocks on his own account.

Sto·ck-jo:bbing, *vbl. sb.* and *ppl. a.* 1692. **A.** *vbl. sb.* The business of a stock-jobber; buying and selling of stock as practised by a jobber; *loosely*, speculative dealing in stocks and shares. (Often with implication of rash or dishonest speculation.) **B.** *ppl. a.* That deals in stocks and shares; concerned with this business or traffic 1692.

Sto·ckman. 1806. **1.** A man employed to look after cattle or other live stock. Chiefly *Austral.* **2.** One who raises live stock; a stock-farmer 1856.

Stock still, stock-still, *a.* 1470. [f. STOCK *sb.*[1] Cf. Du. *stokstil*, G. *stockstill*.] As still as a stock or log; quite motionless.

Sto·ck-ta:king. 1858. [STOCK *sb.*[1]] A periodical examination, inventorying, and valuation of all the stock or goods in a shop, warehouse, etc. Also *fig.* So **Sto·ck-ta:ker.**

Sto·ck-work. 1839. [repr. G. *stockwerk*.] *Mining.* A deposit (esp. of tin) in which the ore is distributed through a large mass of rock.

Stocky (stǫ·ki), *a.* 1622. [f. STOCK *sb.*[1] + -Y[1].] **1.** Of a plant: Of stout and sturdy growth. **b.** Of a root: Woody, as dist. from fibrous 1915. **2.** Of a person, etc.: Short and thick-set 1676.

2. Sturdy and s. as a Jersey bull 1888.

Stodge (stǫdʒ), *sb.* 1825. [f. next.] **1.** A thick liquid mixture. **a.** Thick, tenacious mud or soil. **b.** Food of a semi-solid consistency, esp. stiff farinaceous food 1841. **2. a.** 'Stodging', gorging with food. **b.** A heavy, solid meal. Chiefly *school slang.* 1894. **3.** 'Stodgy' notions. *slang.* 1902.

Stodge (stǫdʒ), *v.* 1674. [Phonetically symbolic after *stuff* and *podge*.] **1.** *trans.* To fill quite full, to fill to distension. **b.** esp. To gorge with food. *slang.* 1854. **2.** *pass.* To be stuck in the mud, to be bogged 1873. **3.** *intr.* To work steadily *at* (something 'stodgy' or tedious). *colloq.* 1889. **4.** To walk or trudge through mud or slush, or with short heavy steps; also *trans.* to trample (mud). *dial.* or *colloq.* 1854. **Sto·dger,** a stodgy person.

Stodgy (stǫ·dʒi), *a.* 1823. [f. prec. + -Y[1].] **1.** Of a thick, semi-solid consistency. **b.** *dial.* Of food, esp. of farinaceous food: Thick, glutinous 1858. **c.** Of food or a meal: Heavy, solid, hard to 'get through' 1884. **2.** *fig.* Dull, heavy; wanting in interest, gaiety, or brightness 1887. **3.** Of a person: Bulky in figure (usu. connoting stiffness and clumsiness in movement) 1854. **4.** Of things: Bulky, 'fat'; distended 1860.

1. b. This cannibal meal was succeeded by s. pudding 1890. 2. The wedding was a s. affair 1904. S. sonnets to the moon 1907.

Stœch-: see STOICH-.

‖**Stœchas** (stī·kæs). 1548. [L. – Gr. στοιχάς.] The plant French Lavender.

‖**Stoep** (stūp). *S. Afr.* 1822. [Du., related to STEP *sb.* and *v.*] A raised platform or verandah running along the front and sometimes round the sides of a house of Dutch architecture.

Stogy (stōᵘ·gi), *a.* and *sb. U.S.* 1847. [orig. *stoga*, short for *Conestoga*, name of a town in Pennsylvania.] **A.** *adj.* The distinctive epithet **a.** of a rough heavy kind of boots or shoes; **b.** of a long, slender, roughly made kind of cigar or cheroot. **B.** *sb.* **a.** A 'stogy' boot 1853. **b.** A 'stogy' cigar 1892.

Stoic (stōᵘ·ik), *sb.* and *a.* late ME. [– L. *stoicus* – Gr. στωϊκός, f. στοά 'the Porch' in which Zeno lectured; see STOA.] **A.** *sb.* **1.** One of a school of Greek philosophers (founded by Zeno, fl. *c*300 B.C.), characterized by the austerity of its ethics and practices on account of which the name has become proverbial (see 2). **2.** One who practises repression of emotion, indifference to pleasure or pain, and patient endurance 1579.

2. I..smile a hard-set smile, like a s...and let the world have its way TENNYSON.

B. *adj.* **1.** Of or belonging to the school of the Stoics or to its system of philosophy 1607. **2.** = next 2 1596.

Stoical (stōᵘ·ikăl), *a.* late ME. [f. as prec. + -AL[1]; see -ICAL.] **1.** Of or belonging to the Stoics; characteristic of the Stoic philosophy. **2. a.** Of temper or disposition, or its manifestations: Conformable to the precepts of the Stoic philosophy; characterized by indifference to pleasure and pain 1571. **b.** Of a person: Resembling a Stoic in austerity, indifference, fortitude, repression of feeling, or the like 1577.

2. a. He looked around him in agony, and was surprised..to see the s. indifference of his fellow-prisoners SCOTT. Hence **Sto·ically** *adv.*

Stoicheiology (stoikəiǫ·lŏdʒi), **stœchiology** (stīkiǫ·lŏdʒi). *rare.* 1837. [f. Gr. στοιχεῖον element + -LOGY. Orig. – the G. form *stöchiologie*.] The science of elements. **a.** In Oken's use: A treatise on, or the theory of, elementary substances 1847. **b.** *Logic.* The division of Logic which treats of its elementary or constituent processes 1837. **c.** *Phys.* The study of the principles of animal tissues; a system of therapeutics based on this 1875. Hence **Stoicheiolo·gical, stœchiolo·gical** *a.*

Stoicheiometry (stoikəiǫ·mėtri), **stœchiometry** (stīkiǫ·mėtri). 1807. [f. as prec. + -METRY.] *Chem.* The process or art of calculating or determining the equivalent and atomic weights of the elements participating in any chemical reaction; the science of estimating chemical elements; the branch of science concerned with the determination of atomic weights. Hence **Stoicheio-, stœchiome·tric, -al** *adjs.*

Stoicism (stōᵘ·isiz'm). 1626. [f. STOIC + -ISM. Cf. Fr. *stoïcisme* (XVII).] **1.** The philosophy of the Stoics. **2.** Stoic conduct or practice; austerity, repression of feeling, fortitude 1630. So †**Stoi·city,** a stoical attitude. B. JONS.

Stoke (stōᵘk), *v.* 1683. [Back-formation from STOKER.] **1.** *trans.* To feed, stir up, and poke the fire in (a furnace); to tend the furnace of (a boiler). Also with *up.* **2.** *transf.* (*joc.*) To feed oneself or another as if stoking a furnace; to 'shovel' food into one's mouth steadily and continuously. Also *absol.* 1882.

Stokehold (stōᵘ·khoᵘld). 1887. [f. prec. + HOLD *sb.*[2]] *Naut.* The compartment containing a ship's boilers, where the stokers tend the furnaces.

Sto·ke-hole. 1660. [tr. Du. *stookgat*, f. *stoken* stoke + *gat* hole.] The space in front of a furnace where the stokers stand to tend the fires; the aperture through which the fire is fed and tended.

Stoker (stōᵘ·kəɹ). 1660. [– Du. *stoker*, f. *stoken* feed (a furnace), MLG., MDu. *stoken* push, poke, f. **stok-*, rel. to **stek-* thrust, prick, STICK *v.*; see -ER[1].] **1.** One who feeds and tends a furnace. **2.** *pl.* Small particles of black gritty matter which escape through the funnel of a steam-engine 1899.

1. *Mechanical s.*, an apparatus for automatically feeding fuel into a furnace.

‖**Stola** (stōᵘ·lă). 1728. [L. – Gr. στολή; see next.] *Antiq.* A long robe worn by Greek and Roman women; chiefly referred to as the distinctive dress of Roman matrons.

Stole (stōᵘl), *sb.*[1] [OE. *stole* fem., *stol* n. – L. *stola* – Gr. στολή equipment, array, clothing, garment, f. **stol-* **stel-* base of στέλλειν place, array.] **1.** A long robe. Chiefly used in translation from Gr. and L., ref. to classical antiquity; also *poet.* and *rhet.* ¶**b.** Some writers have carelessly or ignorantly supposed the ecclesiastical 'stole' (sense 2) to be a gown or surplice 1805. **2.** *Eccl.* A vestment consisting of a narrow strip of silk or linen, worn over the shoulders (by deacons over the left shoulder only) and hanging down in front or crossed over the breast OE. **3.** A woman's fur or feather garment, or the fabric collar of a dress or coat, made somewhat in the shape of an ecclesiastical stole, and worn over the shoulders 1889.

1. b. Behind, four priests, in sable s., Sung requiem for the warrior's soul SCOTT.

Stole (stōᵘl), *sb.*[2] 1455. [var. of STOOL *sb.* in sense 3.] **1.** *Groom of the s.*: the title of a high officer of the king's household, ranking next below the vice-chamberlain of the household. Also †*yeoman of the s.* **2.** The office of Groom of the Stole 1911.

1. Groom of the S., which hath the..benefit of being first Gentleman of the Bed-Chamber CLARENDON.

Stole (stōᵘl), *sb.*[3] 1806. [irreg. – L. STOLO; see STOLON.] *Bot.* = STOLON.

Stole (stōᵘl), *v.* 1824. [f. prec.] *intr.* Of a plant: To develop stolons.

Stole, pa. t. and pa. pple. of STEAL *v.*

Stoled (stōᵘld), *ppl. a.* 1546. [f. STOLE *sb.*[1] + -ED[2].] Wearing a stole (in various senses of the sb.).

The sable-stoled Sorcerers MILT.

Stolen (stōᵘ·lən), *ppl. a.* ME. [pa. pple. of STEAL *v.*] **1.** Obtained by theft. **2.** Accomplished or enjoyed by stealth; secret. late ME. †**3.** Of time: Obtained by contrivance –1611.

Stolid (stǫ·lid), *a.* 1600. [– Fr. †*stolide* or L. *stolidus*, perh. rel. to *stultus* foolish; see -ID[1].] Dull and impassive; having little or no sensibility; incapable of being excited or moved. Also, of actions, demeanour, etc. Hence **Sto·lidly** *adv.*

Stolidity (stŏli·dĭti). 1563. [– Fr. †*stolidité* or L. *stoliditas, -tat-*, f. *stolidus*; see prec., -ITY.] The attribute of being stolid; dull impassiveness; incapacity for feeling.

The look of complacent and pompous s. DISRAELI.

‖**Stolo** (stōᵘ·lo). *Pl.* **stolones** (stŏlōᵘ·nīz). 1725. [L.; see next.] *Bot.* and *Zool.* = next. *S. profiler*, the germ-stock of certain compound organisms.

Stolon (stōᵘ·lǫn). 1601. [– L. *stolo, stolōn-* shoot, scion.] **1.** *Bot.* (see quot.) **2.** *Zool.* Each of the connecting processes of the cœnosarc of a compound organism 1846.

1. A S. is a prostrate or reclined branch which strikes root at the tip, and then develops an ascending growth, which becomes an independent plant 1880.

Stoloniferous (stoᵘ-, stǫlŏni·fĕrəs), *a.* 1777. [f. prec. + -FEROUS.] *Bot.* and *Zool.* Producing stolons.

‖**Stoma** (stōᵘ·mă). *Pl.* **stomata** (stǫ·mătă). 1684. [mod.L. use of Gr. στόμα mouth.] **1.** *Anat.* and *Zool.* A small opening in an animal body; an aperture, orifice, pore (as of a lymphatic or other vessel, an air-tube, etc.). **2.** *Bot.* One of the minute orifices in the epidermis of plants, esp. of the leaves, occurring as a slit between two (or more) cells of special structure (guard-cells), and opening into intercellular spaces in the interior tissue so as to afford communication with the outer air; a breathing-pore 1837.

Stomach (stʊ·măk), *sb.* [ME. *stomak* – OFr. *stomaque*, (also mod.) *estomac* – L. *stomachus* – Gr. στόμαχος throat, gullet, mouth of an organ, as of the stomach, (later) stomach, f. στόμα mouth.] **1.** In a human or animal body: The internal pouch or cavity in which food is digested. **b.** Viewed as the organ of digestion. Often with epithet, as *weak, strong*, etc. late ME. **c.** as the seat of hunger, nausea, discomfort from repletion, etc. late ME. **d.** as the part of the body that requires food; hence, put for the body as needing to be fed 1530. **2.** The part of the body containing the stomach, the belly, abdomen; occas. (formerly often) applied to the chest. late ME. **3.** Appetite or relish for food. Now somewhat *arch.* (const. *for*). late ME. **b.** *fig.* Relish, inclination, desire (for something immaterial) 1513. †**4.** Used to designate the inward seat of passion, emotion, secret thoughts, affections, or feelings –1721. †**5.** Temper, disposition; state of feeling with regard to a person –1610. **b.** With various adjs. (e.g. *bold, high, proud*) or other qualifying words 1510. **6.** In various senses relating to disposition or state of feeling. †**a.** Spirit, courage, valour, bravery –1663. †**b.** Pride, haughtiness; obstinacy, stubbornness –1765. †**c.** Anger, irritation; malice, ill-will, spite; vexation, pique –1825.

1. Phr. *On an empty s.*, fasting. *On a full s.*, immediately after a copious meal. **c.** Phr. *To lie (heavy) on one's s.*, (of food) to cause indigestion. **d.** An army marches on its s. 1904. **2.** Good crawled upon his s. 1888. **3.** Heaven send us all as good food as I have a good s. 1841. **b.** You cram these words into mine eares, against the stomacke of my sense SHAKS. I had no s. for more mysteries 1902. **5. b.** His s. is too high for that now LYTTON. **6. a.** Lustie and couragious captaines, valiaunt men of stomacke 1571. **c.** Others of the nobility.. took s. against him 1643.

attrib. and *Comb.*: **s.-cough,** a cough supposed to proceed from indigestion; **-pump,** a kind of pump or syringe for emptying the s. (esp. in cases of poisoning) or for introducing liquids into it; **-staggers,** a variety of staggers caused by distension of the s.; **-syringe** = *s.-pump*; **-tube,** (*a*) a siphon used in washing out the s.; (*b*) a feeding-tube; **-worm,** a common intestinal round worm, *Ascaris lumbricoides*, sometimes found in the human s.

Stomach (stɒ·măk), *v.* 1523. [orig. – Fr. *s'estomaquer* (refl.) be offended, L. *stomachari* be resentful, be angry with, f. *stomachus* (see prec.).] †**1.** *trans.* To be offended at, resent –1825. †**b.** To be offended with (a person) –1671. †**c.** *intr.* To take offence, feel resentment –1706. **2.** *trans.* To turn the stomach of, to nauseate (*rare*) 1796. **3.** To endure, put up with, tolerate 1677.

1. An Englishman would have stomached it, and been sulky JOHNSON. **3.** The study of the Latin language..he could not s. 1887.

Stomach-ache (stɒ·măk,ēⁱk). 1763. Pain in the stomach or abdomen. Also *fig.*

Stomachal (stǫ·măkăl), *a.* 1582. [– Fr. *stomacal* (XVI *stomachal*), f. *stomaque*; see STOMACH *sb.*, -AL¹.] **1.** Pertaining to the stomach, gastric; of the nature of or serving the purpose of a stomach. †**2.** Of remedies: Good for the stomach –1707.

Stomacher¹ (stɒ·măkəɹ, stɒ·mătʃəɹ). 1450. [prob. aphetic – OFr. *estomachier* (perh. AFr. but recorded only once, PALSGR. 1530), f. *estomac* STOMACH *sb.* + -IER, -ER² 2.] †**1.** A kind of waistcoat worn by men –1715. **2.** An ornamental covering for the chest (often covered with jewels) formerly worn by women under the lacing of the bodice 1535.

2. Their stomatchers some were all Diamonds 1710.

Stomacher² (stɒ·măkəɹ). 1814. [f. STOMACH *sb.* + -ER¹.] *Pugilism.* A blow on the stomach.

†**Sto·machful,** *a.* 1600. [f. as prec. + -FUL¹.] Full of 'stomach'. **1.** Obstinate, self-willed. (Often said of horses; also of children.) –1828. **2.** Resentful, angry, malignant –1765. **3.** Spirited, courageous –1809. Hence †**Sto·machful-ly** *adv.*, †**-ness.**

Stomachic (stomæ·kik), *a.* and *sb.* 1656. [– Fr. *stomachique* or L. *stomachicus* – Gr. στομαχικός, f. στόμαχος STOMACH *sb.*; see -IC.] **A.** *adj.* **1.** Of or pertaining to the stomach; gastric. **2.** Good for the stomach 1665.

1. The author..treats..of the great s. gland 1799.

B. *sb.* A stomachic medicine 1735. So **Stoma·chical** *a.* (now *rare*) 1601.

Stomaching (stɒ·mākiŋ), *vbl. sb.* 1549. [f. STOMACH *v.* + -ING¹.] The action of STOMACH *v.*; †feeling or cherishing indignation or bitterness.

Tis not a time for priuate stomacking SHAKS.

Stomachless (stɒ·măklės), *a.* 1626. [f. STOMACH *sb.* + -LESS.] †**1. a.** Having no appetite. **b.** Unresentful –1727. **2.** Destitute of a stomach 1865.

†**Sto·machous,** *a.* 1547. [– L. *stomachosus*, f. *stomachus* STOMACH *sb.*; see -OUS.] **a.** Spirited, courageous. **b.** Resentful, bitter, irascible; stubborn, obstinate. –1658.

Who..with sterne lookes, and s. disdaine, Gaue signes of grudge SPENSER.

Stomachy (stɒ·măki), *a. dial.* 1825. [f. STOMACH *sb.* + -Y¹.] **1.** Ready to take offence, irritable. **2.** High-spirited 1896. **3.** Paunchy 1889.

3. A little, bald, solemn, s. man STEVENSON.

Stomapod (stǫ·măpǫd), *a.* and *sb.* 1833. [f. mod.L. *Stomapoda* n. pl., irreg. f. Gr. στόμα mouth + πούς, ποδ- foot.] *Zool.* = STOMATOPOD.

Stomatal (stǫ·mătăl), *a.* 1861. [f. *stomat-*, stem of STOMA + -AL¹.] *Bot.* and *Zool.* Pertaining to or connected with a stoma or stomata; of the nature of a stoma; *loosely*, having stomata, stomatous.

Stomate (stōᵘ·mėt). 1835. [app. an Eng. sing. for the pl. **stomata** (see STOMA).] *Bot.* = STOMA 2.

Stomatic (stomæ·tik), *a.* and *sb.* 1656. [– late and med.L. *stomaticus* adj., *-cum* sb. – Gr. στοματικός, -ον, f. στόμα, στοματ-; see -IC.] †**1. a.** *adj.* Of a medicine: Good for diseases of the mouth. **b.** *sb.* A 'stomatic' medicine. –1857. **2.** *Bot.* and *Zool.* = STOMATAL 1835.

Stomatiferous (stǫmăti·fĕrəs), *a.* 1866. [f. *stomat-*, stem of STOMA + -FEROUS.] *Bot.* Bearing stomata.

‖**Stomatitis** (stǫmătəi·tis). 1859. [mod.L., f. as prec. + -ITIS.] *Path.* Inflammation of the mucous membrane of the mouth. Hence **Stomatitic** (i·tik) *a.*

Stomato- (stǫ·măto), repr. Gr. στοματο-, στόμα mouth (see STOMA): occurring in modern scientific terms, chiefly zoological.

Stomatodæ·um, *Embryol.* = STOMODÆUM. ‖**Sto:matode·ndron** (pl. **-dendra**) [Gr. δένδρον tree], each of the dendritic branches bearing minute polyps in the family *Rhizostomidæ* of hydrozoans. **Sto:matoga·stric** [GASTRIC] *a.*, pertaining to or connected with the mouth and stomach; applied to a system of visceral nerves in invertebrates. **Sto·matopla:sty** [-PLASTY], plastic surgery of the mouth (or of the *os uteri*); hence **Sto:matopla·stic** *a.*, pertaining to stomatoplasty. **Sto·matosco:pe** (-skōᵘp) [-SCOPE], an instrument for examining the interior of the mouth.

Stomatode (stǫ·mătoᵘd), *a.* and *sb.* 1870. [– mod.L. *Stomatoda* n. pl., irreg. f. Gr. στόμα, στοματ- mouth, after *Nematoda*, etc.] *Zool.* **A.** *adj.* Pertaining to the *Stomatoda*, a group of *Protozoa* characterized by having a mouth. **B.** *sb.* A member of the *Stomatoda*.

Stomatopod (stǫ·mătopǫ:d), *a.* and *sb.* 1877. [– mod.L. *Stomatopoda* n. pl.; see STOMATO- and cf. STOMAPOD.] *Zool.* **A.** *adj.* Belonging to the *Stomatopoda*, an order of malacostracous crustaceans, orig. (in form *Stomapoda*) synonymous with *Gastrura*, now restricted to the family *Squillidæ*. **B.** *sb.* A s. crustacean.

Stomatous (stǫ·mătəs), *a.* 1880. [f. *stomat-* stem of STOMA + -OUS.] Having or furnished with stomata.

‖**Stomodæum, -eum** (stǫmodī·ɒm). *Pl.* **-æa, -ea** (-ī·ă). 1876. [mod.L., irreg. f. Gr. στόμα mouth + ὁδαῖος that is on or by the road.] *Embryol.* and *Zool.* The anterior portion of the digestive tract, beginning as an invagination of the epiblast. Hence **Stomodæ·al, -e·al** *a.* belonging to or constituting a s.

Stone (stōᵘn), *sb.* [OE. *stān* = OFris., OS. *stēn* (Du. *steen*), (O)HG. *stein*, ON. *steinn*, Goth. *stains* :– Gmc. *stainaz.] **I. 1.** A piece of rock or hard mineral substance (other than metal) of a small or moderate size. †**b.** A rock, cliff, crag; a mass of rock; rocky ground –1700. **2.** The hard compact material of which stones and rocks consist; hard mineral substance other than metal ME. **b.** as material for lithography 1806. **c.** A particular kind of rock or hard mineral matter. late ME. **d.** *spec.* = PHILOSOPHER'S STONE. late ME. †**e.** A mirror. SHAKS. **3.** As a type or emblem of motionlessness or fixity, hardness, insensibility, stupidity, etc. ME. **4.** *transf.* and *fig.* Something resembling stone or a stone. late ME. **5.** A piece of stone of a definite form and size (usu. artificially shaped), used for some special purpose, e.g. for building, paving, as a memorial, etc. OE. **b.** *spec.* = GRAVESTONE, TOMBSTONE. ME. **c.** A rounded stone or pebble formerly used as a missile in war ME. **d.** A shaped piece of stone for grinding or sharpening something, as a GRINDSTONE 2, MILLSTONE 1. 1578. **e.** A flat slab or tablet for grinding something upon, or for smoothing or flattening something; also a slab of stone for lithography. late ME. **f.** A heavy stone used in athletic sports. Phrases. *To cast, put,* or *throw the s.* ME. **6.** A precious stone OE. **7.** A lump of metallic ore. *Obs.* exc. in *s. of tin*, a lump of tin ore. OE. †**b.** = LOADSTONE 1. –1631. †**8.** = HAILSTONE –1753. **9.** = CALCULUS 1. Also, the disease caused or characterized by the formation of a calculus; lithiasis. OE. **10.** A testicle; chiefly in *pl. Obs.* exc. in vulgar use. ME. **11.** The hard wood-like endocarp of a *s.-fruit* or drupe, enclosed by the pulpy pericarp, and enclosing the seed or kernel. Also, applied to the hard seeds of some pulpy fruits, as the grape. 1523. **12.** A measure of weight, usu. equal to 14 pounds avoirdupois, but varying with different commodities from 8 to 24 pounds. The stone of 14 lb. is the common unit used in stating the weight of a man or large animal. (Collective pl. usu. *stone.*) late ME.

1. Aerolites, called also Meteoric Stones 1833. **2. c.** Semitransparent Stones, as Agat 1731. **d.** Lend me a Looking-glasse, If that her breath will mist or staine the s., Why then she liues SHAKS. **3.** Me thynketh myn hert ys harder than a ston 1400. She was deaf as a s. 1841. **4.** Nor wept, for all Within was S. GRAY. The widow's lamentations..would have pierced a heart of s. DICKENS. **5.** The stones on Salisbury-plain, which can never be settled to any certain number ADDISON. Horses clattered on the uneven stones DICKENS. Built up, s. by s., from the level of the earth 1867. **b.** The s. closes over Harry the Fourth THACKERAY. **c.** Like..a s. from a sling 1867. **6.** Sparkles this S. as it was wont? SHAKS. **12.** Of Sugar and Spice 8 pound make the s. 1674. A drayman weighing about eighteen s. 1887.

Phrases. *To kill two birds with one s.*, to accomplish two different purposes by the same act or proceeding. *To leave no s. unturned*, to try every possible expedient in order to bring about a desired result. *To set a s. rolling*, to start a course of action which may lead to unforeseen, esp. disastrous, consequences. Prov. *A rolling s. gathers no moss*: see MOSS *sb.* II. 1, ROLLING STONE 1. *To throw (cast) a s.* or *stones (at)*, to make an attack (upon) or bring an accusation (against) so *to cast the first s.* (in allusion to John 8:7). *S. of stumbling* (arch.), an occasion of scandal or stumbling, a stumbling-block (Vulg. *petra scandali*).

II. *attrib.* passing into *adj.* **a.** Consisting of stone; made or built of stone OE. **b.** Made of stoneware; also, *transf.* of ginger-beer contained in stoneware bottles OE. **c.** Applied to substances in a solid or massive (as dist. from liquid or powdered) form, as *stone alum, stone ochre*, etc. 1608. **d.** Of, pertaining or relating to stone or stones (in various senses) 1826. **e.** *ellipt.* Belonging to the STONE AGE 1864. **f.** (from 10.) Of male domestic animals: Not castrated, entire; †hence allus. of men: lascivious, lustful 1602. **g.** With preceding numeral, forming an attrib. or adj. phrase, in sense (*a*) set with a (specified) number of (precious) stones; (*b*) weighing (so many) stone; hence *transf.* applied to the prize in a race in which the horses carry the specified weight 1683.

a. The lion on your old s. gates TENNYSON. **b.** Beate them well in a s. morter 1600. While I sipped my stone-ginger 1904. **e.** The earlier S. folk are known to us only by their graves 1880. **g.** A Seven S. Diamond Ring 1683.

Comb.: **s.-bark** *Bot.*, bark consisting chiefly of hardened and thickened cells; **-blue,** a compound of indigo with starch or whiting, used by laundresses; **-boat,** a boat (*U.S.* a sled) for transporting stones; **-boiling,** the primitive process of boiling water by putting hot stones in it; **-breaker,** a person employed in, or a machine used for, breaking stones; so **-breaking; -broke** *a. slang*, = *stony-broke*; **-butter** [after G. *steinbutter*], alum occurring in soft masses greasy to the touch; **-canal** *Zool.*, a canal forming part of the water-vascular system in Echinoderms, usu. with calcareous walls, leading from the madreporic plate to the circumoral water-vessel; **-cast** = STONE'S THROW; **-cell** *Bot.*, one of a number of greatly hardened and thickened cells occurring in certain plants; **-china,** a variety of earthenware in common domestic use; **s. circle** *Archæol.*, = CIRCLE *sb.* II. 2; **-coal,** †(*a*) mineral coal as dist. from charcoal; (*b*) any hard variety of coal, esp. anthracite; **-colour,** the (usual) colour of s., a yellowish or brownish grey, also *attrib.*; **-crusher,** a machine for crushing or grinding s., a s.-breaker; **-dike, -dyke,** a dike constructed of s.; a s. fence or embankment; **-dresser,** one who dresses or shapes s. for building; also, a machine for this purpose; **-engraving,** the art or process of engraving on s., lithography; **s. era** = STONE AGE; **-fall,** a fall of meteoric stones, or of loose stones on a mountain slope; **s. fence,** (*a*) a fence made of stones, a s. wall; (*b*) *U.S. slang*, name for various intoxicating drinks; **-ground** *a.*, ground by means of millstones; **-hammer,** a hammer for breaking or rough-dressing stones; **-heading** *Coal-mining*, a heading driven through s. or rock; **-horse** (now *dial.*), an uncastrated horse, a stallion; **-lily,** a fossil crinoid or encrinite, from its resemblance to a lily on its stalk; **-mill,** (*a*) a mill for grinding; (*b*) a machine for dressing stones; (*c*) a mill in which millstones (not rollers) are used for grinding the flour; so **-milled** *a.* = *s.-ground*; **-oil,** a kind of bitumen; petroleum or rock-oil; **s. period** *Archæol.*, = STONE AGE; also, a portion of the Stone age; **-pit,** a quarry; **†-pitch,** pitch in the solid form, hard or dry pitch; **-pock** *Path.*, a hard suppurating pimple; a disease characterized by such pimples, as acne; **-saw,** a saw, usu. without teeth, for cutting stone into blocks or other shapes for building, etc.; **-shot,** (*a*) stones used as missiles, esp. as shot for cannon; (*b*) = STONE'S-THROW; **-shower,** a shower or fall of meteoric stones; **-slate,** a roofing slate made of thin s.; **-weight,** = sense I. 12; also, a piece of metal of this weight, used in weighing; **-yard,** a yard in which s.-breaking or s.-cutting is done.

b. In names of animals, as **s.-bass,** a fish of the genus *Polyprion* (family *Serranidæ*), characterized by a bony ridge on the operculum and serrated spines on the anal and ventral fins; **-bird,** (*a*) the vinous grosbeak; (*b*) = *s.-snipe* (*a*); **-borer,** a bivalve mollusc that bores into stones or rocks; **-buck** = STEINBOCK; **-cat,** a N. Amer. freshwater cat-fish of the genus *Noturus*; **-coral,** hard or sclerodermatous (as dist. from sclerobasic), or massive (as dist. from branching) coral; **-crab,** (*a*) a name for various species of crab; (*b*) applied locally in *U.S.* to the dobson or hellgrammite, the larva of a neuropterous insect, used as a bait in angling; **-crawfish,** a European species of crawfish or crayfish, *Astacus torrentium*; **s. curlew,** see CURLEW 3; **-eater,** = *s.-borer*; **s. falcon** [G. *steinfalke*], the merlin; **-fly,** an insect of the family *Perlidæ*, whose larvæ are found under stones in streams, esp. *Perla bicaudata*, much used as a bait in angling; also, an artificial fly made to imitate this; **-hawk,** = *s. falcon*; **-marten,** the beech-marten (*Mustela foina*), or its fur; **-plover,** see PLOVER 2; **-roller,** name for two N. Amer. freshwater fishes, *Catostomus nigricans*, and *Campostoma anomalum*; **-runner,** the ringed plover or the dotterel; also applied to some species of sandpiper; **-smatch, -smitch** = STONECHAT; **-snipe,** (*a*) the s.-curlew, *Œdicnemus scolopax*; (*b*) a large N. Amer. bird of the snipe family, *Totanus melanoleucus*; also applied to other species of *Totanus*.

c. In names of plants (either growing in stony places, or having some part hard like stone), or their fruits; as **s. basil,** the wild basil, *Calamintha clinopodium*, or basil-thyme, *C. acinos*; **s. bramble,** a species of bramble, *Rubus saxatilis*, growing in stony places, and having bright red fruit; **-break** = SAXIFRAGE; **-fern,** *Asplenium ceterach*; also applied to other ferns growing in stony places; **-mint,** the Amer. dittany, *Cunila mariana*.

Stone (stō^{u}n), *v.* [Early ME. *stānen*, f. *stān* STONE *sb.*] **1.** *trans.* To throw stones at, pelt with stones; *esp.* to put to death by pelting with stones. **†2.** To turn into stone, or make hard like stone; to petrify. (Chiefly *fig.*) –1853. **3.** To furnish or fit with stones; to pave, or build up, with stone or stones 1600. **4.** To rub or polish with a stone; to sharpen on a whetstone; in *Leather Manuf.* to scour and smooth with a stock-stone 1688. **5.** To take the stones out of (fruit) 1639. **6.** *intr.* Of a fruit (drupe): To form a stone in the process of growth 1842.

1. Cowards were stoned to death GIBBON. 2. O periur'd woman, thou do'st s. my heart SHAKS. 5. S. a pound and a half of cherries 1769. Hence **Sto·ner**[1], one who pelts with stones, esp. so as to kill.

Sto·ne age. 1864. *Archæol.* The period or stage in the development of human culture which is marked by the exclusive or greatly predominant use of stone as material for weapons and implements, in contradistinction to the later 'ages' in which bronze or iron was used.

The *Stone age* is divided into the PALÆOLITHIC and NEOLITHIC periods O.E.D.

Sto·ne-axe. OE. **1.** A two-edged axe used for hewing stone. **2.** An axe made of stone 1864.

Stone-blind (stō^u·n,bləi·nd), *a.* (*sb.*) late ME. [STONE *sb.*] Blind as a stone; completely blind.

Stone-bow (stō^u·nbō^u). OE. [BOW *sb.*[1] 3, 4.] **1.** An arch of stone. *Obs.* exc. as the name of one of the gates of Lincoln. **†2.** A kind of cross-bow or catapult used for shooting stones –1660.

Stonechat (stō^u·n,tʃæt). 1783. [f. STONE *sb.* + CHAT *sb.*[2], from its alarm note which resembles the striking together of two pebbles. Cf. AL. *stonchattera* (XVI).] A small bird, *Pratincola* (or *Saxicola*) *rubicola*, inhabiting heaths, commons, etc. in Britain and various parts of Europe. (Also called *s. warbler.*) Also improperly applied to the whinchat, *P. rubetra*, and the wheatear, *S. œnanthe*, etc.

Stonecrop (stō^u·nkrǫp). [OE. *stāncrop*; see STONE *sb.*; the second element is not identified.] The common name of *Sedum acre*, a herb with bright yellow flowers and small cylindrical fleshy sessile leaves, growing in masses on rocks, old walls, etc.; also applied to other species of *Sedum*, and of allied genera, as the N. Amer. *Penthorum*.

Stone-cutter (stō^u·n,kɒ:tə.ɹ). 1540. **1.** One who cuts or carves stone; one who carves figures or inscriptions on stone. **b.** A machine for cutting or shaping stone 1875. **†2.** A lithotomist –1787.

1. *Stone-cutter's disease*, an affection of the lungs, incident to stone-cutters, caused by inhaling the fine dust of the stones. So **Sto·ne-cu:tting,** the process or art of cutting or shaping stone.

Sto·ne-fruit. 1523. **1.** A fruit having the seed or kernel surrounded by a 'stone' or hard endocarp within the pulp; a drupe. (Also collectively.) **2.** (As two words.) Imitation fruit made of stoneware, used as chimney ornaments 1851.

Stonehatch (stō^u·nhætʃ). 1852. [STONE *sb.*] The ring-plover or stone-plover, *Ægialitis hiaticula*.

Stonehenge (stō^u·nhe·ndʒ). OE. [f. STONE *sb.*; the second element is derived from HANG *v.*; cf. OE. *hengen* hanging, gibbet, the meaning being here 'that which is hung up' (Ekwall).] Name of a celebrated stone circle on Salisbury Plain; hence applied allus. to similar structures elsewhere.

Stone(-)jug. 1596. **1.** A jug made of stoneware. **2.** *slang.* A nickname for Newgate prison, or for a prison in general 1796.

Stonemason (stō^u·n,mē^i:s'n). 1809. [f. STONE *sb.* + MASON *sb.*] = MASON *sb.* 1.

Sto·ne-pa:rsley. 1548. The umbelliferous herb *Sison amomum*; also applied to *Seseli libanotis* and other species.

Sto·ne-pine. 1759. [= Fr. *pin de pierre*. The name has been supposed to refer to the hardness of the seeds.] A species of pine-tree, *Pinus pinea*, a native of Southern Europe and the Levant, having edible seeds. Also applied to *P. cembra* (Swiss S.), etc.

Stoner[2] (stō^u·nəɹ). 1862. [f. STONE *sb.* + -ER[1].] In comb. with prefixed numeral: A person weighing, or a horse carrying, (so many) stone.

Stonesfield (stō^u·nzfīld). 1839. Name of a village in Oxfordshire; used *attrib.* in **S. slate** *Geol.*, a stratum of thin-bedded limestone and calcareous sandstone forming part of the Great Oolite series in Oxfordshire and Gloucestershire.

Stone's throw (stō^u·nz,þrō^u). 1581. [THROW *sb.*[2] II. 1.] The distance that a stone can be thrown by the hand; vaguely used for a short or moderate distance.

Stone-still, *adv.* and *predic. a.* ME. [See STONE *sb.* and STILL *adv.* and *a.* Cf. STOCK STILL.] As still as a stone; perfectly still and motionless.

Stone-wall, *sb.* Now usu. as two wds. OE. **1.** A wall built of stones; now esp. of rough stones without mortar, as a fence between fields, etc. **2.** *Austral. Polit. slang.* Parliamentary obstruction, or a body of obstructives 1876. Hence **Stonewall** *v.* (*a*) *intr.*, *Cricket slang*, to block balls persistently; to play solely on the defensive; (*b*) *Polit. slang*, orig. and chiefly *Austral.*, to obstruct business by lengthy speeches, etc., to practise obstruction; also *trans.* to obstruct (business). **Stonewa·ller.**

Stoneware (stō^u·nwē^{ə}ɹ). (Also, with hyphen, or as two wds.) 1683. A hard dense kind of pottery ware, made from very siliceous clay, or a mixture of clay with much flint or sand.

Stonework (stō^u·nwɒɹk). (Also, with hyphen, or occas. as two wds.) OE. [Cf. OS. *stēnwerk.*] **1.** Work built of stone; masonry. **b.** Artistic work of any kind executed in stone 1910. **2.** The process of working in stone, as in building; the labour or task of a mason 1793. **b.** *Coal Mining.* The work of driving headings through stone or rock 1883. Hence **Stoneworker, -works.**

Stonewort (stō^u·nwɒɹt). 1585. [f. STONE *sb.* + WORT[1].] **†1.** The fern *Asplenium ceterach*, also called *stone fern* –1647. **2.** With defining words, applied to species of *Sison* and other umbelliferous plants 1796. **3.** A book-name for the genus *Chara*, from the calcareous deposits on the stem; also, extended to the family *Characeæ* 1816.

Stonify (stō^u·nifəi), *v. rare.* 1610. [f. STONE *sb.* or STONY *a.* + -FY.] *trans.* To make stony, or turn into stone; to petrify.

†Sto·nish, *v.* 1470. [Aphetic f. ASTONISH *v.*] To stun mentally, shock, surprise –1612.

Stony (stō^u·ni), *a.* [OE. *stānig*; see STONE *sb.*, -Y[1].] **1.** Abounding in, or having the character of, stone or rock; full of rocks; rocky. Now *rare* or *Obs.* **b.** Full of or abounding in stones. late ME. **†c.** Of fruits: Having a stone; also, abounding in stone-like seeds –1784. **2. †a.** Made of stone –1776. **b.** Of the nature of stone 1695. **c.** Consisting of stones. Chiefly *poet.* 1586. **3.** Pertaining or relating to stone or stones (*rare*) 1847. **4.** Resembling stone in consistence; hard like stone; very hard 1523. **b.** Of a quality (as hardness, colour): Like that of stone 1565. **5.** *fig.* **a.** 'Hard', insensible, or unfeeling, as if consisting of stone; hardened, obdurate ME. **b.** Rigid, fixed, motionless; destitute of movement or expression: esp. of the eyes or look 1642. **c.** Of fear, grief, etc.: 'Petrifying', stupefying; having no relief 1590. **d.** *slang.* Short for *s.-broke* 1890.

1. Some [seed] fell on a s. grounde TINDALE *Mark* 4:5. **b.** I chatter over s. ways TENNYSON. **2. b.** Ordinary earthy or s. matter FARADAY. **c.** Batter Cadmus walls with s. showers GRAY. **4.** S. haile 1586. **5. a.** A stonie adversary, an inhumane wretch, Vncapable of pitty SHAKS. **b.** A s. British stare TENNYSON. **c.** A s. speechless sorrow 1882.

Comb.: **s.-broke** *a.*, *slang*, 'hard up', without any money, ruined; **s. coral** = *stone-coral*. Hence **Sto·ni-ly** *adv.*, **-ness.**

†Sto·ny, *v.* ME. Aphetic f. ASTONY *v.* (Prob. sometimes confused with STUN *v.*) –1688.

Stony-hearted (stress var.), *a.* 1569. Having a stony heart; unfeeling, merciless.

So then, Oxford Street, s. stepmother. . at length I was dismissed from thee! DE QUINCEY.

Stook (stuk), *sb.* [Late ME. *stouk*, corresp. to or – MLG. *stūke*, formally = widespread Gmc. word (OHG. *stūhha* sleeve, G. *stauche* muff), not agreeing in sense; the present form shows survival of northern vocalism.] **1.** = SHOCK *sb.*[1] 1. **¶b.** Used for: A pile, mass 1865. **2.** A bundle of straw. *dial.* 1571. **3.** *Coal-mining.* [perh. a different word.] The portion of a pillar of coal left to support the roof 1826.

Stook (stuk), *v.* 1575. [f. prec.] *trans.* To set up (sheaves) in stooks. Also with *up*. Also *absol.*

Stool (stūl), *sb.* [OE. *stōl* = OFris., OS. *stōl*, OHG. *stuol* (Du. *stoel*, G. *stuhl*), ON. *stóll*, Goth. *stōls* throne :– Gmc. **stolaz*, f. **stō-* **stā-* stand; see -LE 1.] **†1.** Any kind of seat for one person; often, a chair of authority, state, or office; esp. a royal or episcopal throne –1818. **†b.** A seat for an offender. See CUCKING-, DUCKING-STOOL, *s. of* REPENTANCE. –1750. **2.** A wooden seat (for one person) without arms or a back; a piece of furniture consisting in its simplest form of a piece of wood for a seat set upon legs, usu. three or four in number, to raise it from the ground. late ME. **b.** A high seat of this kind for convenience of writing at a high desk; more fully *office s.* Hence, a situation as clerk in an office. 1837. **c.** A low short bench or form upon which to rest the foot, step, or kneel. Chiefly = FOOTSTOOL. ME. **3.** A seat enclosing a chamber utensil; a commode; more explicitly *s. of ease*. Also, a privy. late ME. **b.** In phrases originally meaning 'the place of evacuation', now (without *the*) the action of evacuating the bowels 1542. **c.** With dem. or poss.: act of discharging fæces 1533. **d.** A discharge of fæcal matter of a specified colour, consistency, etc.; the matter discharged (chiefly *pl.*) 1597. **†4.** A frame upon which to work embroidery or tapestry –1548. **5.** *Naut.* **a.** A minor channel abaft the main channels, for the dead-eyes of the backstays 1711. **b.** The lowest transom of a vessel's stern frame 1797. **6.** *Brick-making.* A brick-moulder's shed or workshop; also, the gang of workmen employed in one shed; also, a moulder's bench 1693. **7.** *Arch.* The sill of a window. *Obs.* exc. *U.S.* 1663. **8.** A base or stand upon which a thing is set to raise it above the ground or general surface 1481. **9.** [Cf. Du. *stoel.*] **a.** The stump of a tree which has been felled; also, the head of the stump from which new shoots are produced 1577. **b.** *Forestry.* A stock or stump of a tree felled or headed for the production of coppice-wood, underwood, saplings, or young timber. Also, a set or group of stumps. 1722. **c.** *Forestry* and *Horticulture.* The base of a plant cut down to produce shoots or branches for layering 1789. **d.** *Horticulture.* The base containing the latent buds in plants which annually throw up new stems or foliage to replace the old 1790. **e.** A cluster of stems or foliage springing from a stool or from the same root; the complement of stalks produced by one grain of corn 1712. **f.** A shoot or layer from the stump or base of a plant. [Confused with L. *stolo*; see STOLON.] 1818. **10.** *U.S.* A decoy-bird (perh. short for *s.-pigeon*), esp. one used in shooting wild-fowl; also a perch upon which a decoy-bird is set 1859.

Phrase. *To fall, come to the ground,* or *sit between two stools,* to incur failure through vacillation between two different courses of action.

Comb.: **s. pigeon** *U.S.*, a pigeon fastened to a s. as a decoy; chiefly *fig.* of a person employed, especially by gamblers, as a decoy

Stool (stūl), *v.* 1545. [f. prec.] **1.** *intr.* To evacuate the bowels; also *trans.*, to evacuate as excrement. **2.** Of a plant: To throw up young shoots or stems; of corn, grass, herbage, to throw out lateral shoots producing a thick head of stems or foliage. Also with *out, forth.* 1789. **3.** *U.S.* (*trans.*) To entice (wild-fowl) by means of a decoy-bird; also *intr.* (of a bird) to come (well) to a decoy 1859.

Stoo·l-ball. 1745. [f. STOOL *sb.* + BALL *sb.* 1.] **1.** An old country game somewhat resembling cricket, played chiefly by young women, or, as an Easter game, between men and women for a 'tansy' as the stake. The 'stool' was the wicket. **2.** A ball used in this game 1690.

Stoop (stūp), *sb.*[1] Now only *dial.* [Late ME. *stulpe, stolpe* – ON. *stólpi.*] **1.** A post, pillar. **2.** *fig.* A person or thing that supports or sustains; a 'prop', 'pillar'. *Sc.* 1572.

Stoop (stūp), *sb.*[2] 1571. [f. STOOP *v.*] **1.** An act of stooping; a bending of the body forwards; a bow. **b.** *fig.* A condescension, a voluntary descent from superiority or dignity 1636. **2.** A stooping attitude; a temporary or permanent bent position of the back or shoulders 1716. **3.** The action of descending from a height; *spec.* the swoop of a bird of prey on its quarry or the descent of the falcon to the lure 1586.

1. b. Can I, can any Loyal Subject see With Patience, such a S. from Sovereignty? DRYDEN. **2.** A tall thin man, with a slight s. 1904.

Stoop (stūp), *sb.*[3] *U.S.* and *Canada.* 1789. [– Du. *stoep* STOEP.] A raised, uncovered platform before the entrance of a house, approached by means of steps. Sometimes incorrectly used for *porch* or *veranda.*

Stoop (stūp), *v.* Pa. t. and pa. pple. **stooped** (stūpt). [OE. *stūpian* = MDu. *stūpen*, ON. *stūpa*, f. Gmc. **stūp-*, rel. to **steup-* STEEP *a.*] **I.** To bow down, to descend. **1.** *intr.* Of a person: To lower the body by inclining the trunk or the head and shoulders forward, sometimes bending the knee at the same time. Often with *down.* **b.** Said of the head or shoulders. late ME. **†c.** Of a quadruped: To crouch –1625. **d.** Of a dog: To put its nose to the ground to find a scent 1523. **2.** *fig.* **a.** To 'bow' to superior power or authority; to yield obedience. Const. *to, under.* Now somewhat *rare.* 1530. **†b.** To submit *to* something burdensome –1647. **c.** To condescend *to* one's inferiors or *to* some position or action below one's rightful dignity 1579. **d.** To lower or degrade oneself morally 1743. **3.** Of a thing: To incline from the perpendicular; to bend down; to slope; to hang over OE. **4.** To stand or walk with the shoulders bent or the upper part of the body inclined forwards; esp. to have habitually or permanently this kind of attitude ME. **†5.** To descend from a height –1847. **6.** Of a hawk or other bird of prey: To descend swiftly on its prey, to swoop (const. *at, on*); also, to descend to the lure 1575. **†b.** *trans.* = To stoop at or on –1618.

1. Angels..stoope down with their faces towards the mercy Seat 1649. **2. a.** Early or late, They s. to fate, And must give up their murmuring breath SHIRLEY. **c.** She stoops to conquer GOLDSM. (*title*). **d.** Incapable of stooping to an act of baseness MACAULAY. **3.** The grasse stoops not, she treads on it so light SHAKS. **4.** Cissy, my Love, don't s. so LYTTON. **6.** *fig.* Whether the priest had stooped at the lure of a cardinal's hat.. I know not 1717.

II. Causative uses. **1.** *trans.* To cause to bow down, bring to the ground; *fig.* to humiliate, subdue. Now *rare.* ME. **2.** To bow (the head, †face, neck, knee); to incline (one's ear) 1634. **b.** *fig.* To condescend to apply (one's thoughts, etc.) to something unworthy 1598. **†3.** To let down, lower, 'vail'. Often *Naut.* and *Mil.* to lower (a sail, an ensign). –1697. **4.** To tilt (a cask). Now *dial.* 1670. **5.** To train (a dog) to 'stoop' for a scent 1781.

1. Shoote, shoote, and stoope his pride CHAPMAN. **2.** MILT. *Comus* 333. **b.** None stoop'd a Thought to base inglorious Flight POPE. Hence **Stooped** (stūpt) *ppl. a.*, that has swooped down; of the head or shoulders: bent downwards; also of a person: stooping. **Stoo·per,** a wedge for tilting a barrel (*dial.*); one who stoops; one who has a stoop. **Stoo·ping** *ppl. a.*, **-ly** *adv.*

†Stoop-gallant. 1551. [f. STOOP *v.* + GALLANT *sb.* = Fr. *trousse-galant.*] Something that humbles 'gallants'; orig., a name for the 'sweating sickness'; also *fig.* –1862.

†‖Stoo·ter. 1598. [Du.] A Dutch coin worth two stuivers and a half –1811.

Stop (stǫp), *sb.* 1450. [f. next.] **I.** Action of stopping. **1.** The action or an act of impeding, obstructing, or arresting; the fact of being impeded or arrested; a check, arrest, or obstruction (of motion or activity) 1544. **2.** *spec.* A veto or prohibition (*against*); an embargo (*upon* goods, trade); a refusal to pass tokens; an order stopping payment of a bank note, cheque, or bill 1634. **3.** The act of filling or closing up an aperture 1593. **4.** The act of coming to a stand; a halt; a cessation of progress or onward movement. Phr. *to make a s.* 1575. **b.** A stay or sojourn made at a place, esp. in the course of a journey 1650. **c.** A place at which a halt is made; a stopping-place 1889. **5.** A block or obstruction of traffic caused by the overcrowding of vehicles 1626. **6.** A cessation, coming to a pause or end (of any activity, process, etc.) 1483. **b.** A pause or breaking-off made by one speaking 1561.

1. If people only made prudent marriages, what a s. to population there would be! THACKERAY. Phr. *To put a s. to,* to check, restrain; to arrest the progress of; to bring to an end, abolish. **4.** Many a s. and stay he makes WORDSW. **b.** From thence [they] rode Post to Paris, where they made some s. 1659. **6.** The band came to a s. 1889. **b.** The smiling and unconscious look of Florence brings him to a dead s. DICKENS.

II. Something that stops, arrests, or blocks. **†1.** Something that hinders motion or activity; an impediment, obstacle –1725. **2.** **†a.** A weir or dam across a river; a sluice or floodgate –1800. **b.** A blind alley in a maze 1666. **3.** A piece of mechanism (e.g. a pin, bolt, shoulder, a strip or block of wood) which checks the motion or thrust of anything, keeps a part fixed in its place, determines the position to which a part shall be brought, etc. 1523. **b.** *Joinery.* Each of the pieces of wood nailed on the frame of a door to form a rebate against which the door shuts 1833. **c.** *Clockwork.* A contrivance to prevent over-winding 1675. **4.** *Naut.* **a.** A piece of small line used to fasten or secure anything 1846. **b.** A projection at the upper part of a mast 1846. **5.** *Arch.* An ornamental termination to a chamfer 1825. **6.** *Optics.* A perforated plate or diaphragm used to cut off marginal rays of light round a lens 1831. **7.** Something that stops an aperture; a plug 1770. **III.** *Music.* **1.** In an organ, a graduated set of pipes producing tones of the same quality 1500. **b.** The handle or knob by which a set of organ pipes is turned on or off; a stop-knob, draw-stop 1585. **c.** In the harpsichord, a handle controlling a lever by which the position of a jack can be varied so as to modify the tone produced 1730. **2. a.** The closing of a finger-hole or ventage in the tube of a wind-instrument so as to alter the pitch. Also, a metal key used for this purpose. Also, the hole or aperture thus closed. 1500. **b.** The act of pressing with the finger on a string of the violin, lute, etc., so as to raise the pitch of its tone. Also, the part of the string where pressure is made in order to produce a required note, sometimes mechanically marked, as by frets. *Full s.*, a chord in producing which all the strings are stopped. 1530. **3.** *fig.* or *transf.* Now chiefly with ref. to the organ. 1576.

1. All Organs of sweet s. MILT. Flourishes..on the trumpet s. RUSKIN. **2. a.** He touch'd the tender stops of various Quills MILT. **b.** *Much Ado* III. ii. 62. **3.** Sweet as stops Of planetary music heard in trance SHELLEY.

IV. *Grammar.* **1.** A mark or point of punctuation 1590. **2. Full stop. a.** The end of a sentence; the single point or dot used to mark this; a period, full point 1596. **b.** *transf.* and *fig.*, as, a complete halt, stoppage, check, or termination 1628. **3.** *Phonetics.* **†a.** The complete closure of the orinasal passages in articulating a mute consonant 1669. **b.** A consonantal sound in the formation of which the passage of the breath is completely obstructed; a stopped consonant, a mute 1873.

2. b. The story..comes unexpectedly to a full s. 1798.

V. 1. a. *Pugilism.* A guard or attack that prevents a blow from getting home 1812. **b.** *Wrestling.* A counter to any particular fall or hold 1840. **2.** A hole in the ground in which the doe-rabbit secures her litter 1669. **3.** *Shooting.* A person posted in order to keep the game within range 1897. **4. a.** The indentation in the face of a dog between the forehead and the nose 1867. **b.** In a cavy: A white marking on the hind feet 1902. **5.** *Card-playing.* In Pope Joan and similar games, a card which stops a sequence. Hence *pl.*, the game of Newmarket. 1808. **b.** *Bridge.* A card that can reasonably be counted on, in conjunction with other cards in the same suit, to take a trick in that suit 1920.

Comb.: **s.-block, -buffer,** a buffer at the termination of a railway-line; **-drill,** a drill with a shoulder or collar to limit the depth of penetration; **-gate,** (*a*) a gate placed across a railway; (*b*) a gate by which the water in one section of a canal can be shut off from the next in case of damage to the bank; **-knob,** the handle which is pulled out to open a particular s. in an organ; **-net,** (*a*) a net thrown across a river or tidal channel to intercept fish; (*b*) a net to stop the ball, in various games; **-order,** (*a*) an order issued by the Court of Chancery to stay payment of funds in the custody of the Court; (*b*) an order directing a broker to buy or sell stock at a specified price, in order to limit loss; **-piece, -pin,** a piece or pin serving to arrest some moving part; **-quoin, -coin,** a quoin used for keeping a gun steady; **-stroke** *Croquet*, a stroke which drives a croqueted ball to a distance, while leaving the striker's ball more or less stationary; **-tap** = STOPCOCK; **-thrust** *Fencing*, a thrust delivered at the opponent at the moment when he advances for attack; **-valve,** a valve which closes a pipe against the passage of fluid; **-work,** a mechanism to prevent the overwinding of the spring of a watch, etc. Hence **Sto·pless** *a.* without a s. or stops.

Stop (stǫp), *v.* Pa. t. and pa. pple. **stopped** (stǫpt), **stopt.** ME. [OE. **stoppian* in *forstoppian* plug (the ear), corresp. to OFris. *stoppia*, G. *verstopfen*, MLG. *stoppen*, OHG. *stopfōn* (G. *stopfen*); WGmc. – late L. *stuppare* STUFF *v.* The sense 'bring or come to a stand' is a specially Eng. development.] **I.** To fill up, plug, close up. **1.** *trans.* To close up (an aperture) by stuffing something into it, by building it up, or by placing something before it. late ME. **b.** Said of the obstruction: To block, choke up. Also *pass.*, to be choked up *with* (dirt, etc.). Now chiefly with *up*. 1508. **2.** To make (a way) impassable by blocking up its passage or outlet ME. **3.** To fill up, repair, make good (a breach, hole, crevice or defective place of any kind). Also with *up*. So *to s. a leak*. late ME. **b.** To plug (the seams of a boat) with oakum, tow, or other caulking material; †to caulk (a ship). Also *to s. up*. 1535. **c.** *Plastering, House-painting*, etc. To fill up or make good the holes in (a surface to be covered with a wash, paint, etc.); †to close (the joints of brick-work), to 'point' 1557. **d.** *Dentistry*. To fill the cavity of (a decayed tooth) with a stopping: now generally superseded by *fill* 1592. †**4.** To staunch the bleeding of, bind up (a wound) –1602. **5.** To close (a vessel or receptacle) by blocking its mouth with a cover, plug, or other stopper; similarly, to close (the mouth of a vessel); also, to shut up (something) *in* a stoppered vessel. Also with *down, up*. late ME. **6.** To obstruct the external orifice of (a bodily organ) by putting something in or on it or by pressing the parts together OE. **7.** To close up, choke, obstruct (a canal, duct, passage or pipe in the animal body); to block the passage or passages of (a bodily organ). Also with *up*. late ME. †**8.** To shut up, block up (a person or thing *in* a place) –1693. **9.** To press down (the tobacco in a pipe) with or as with a tobacco-stopper 1848.

1. S. the holes of the doore with double Matts 1632. S. all the holes, lest the fox should bolt out unseen 1781. **b.** One of the stack pipes was stopped up with leaves and dirt 1885. **2.** The Countess of Avon's carriage stopping the way 1831. Phr. *To s. one's way*, to stand in one's way, bar one's passage, oppose one. **3.** *To s. a gap*, see GAP *sb.* **c.** The walls..of a light buff colour, rubbed down and stopped 1842. **4.** *fig.* Now ciuill wounds are stopp'd, Peace liues agen SHAKS. **5.** Keep it close stopped in a Bottle for Use 1737. **6.** Phr. *To s.* (one's own or another's) *ear* or *ears*; also *fig.*, to render oneself deaf *to* something, close one's mind against arguments, etc. *To s.* (one's own or another's) *mouth*, lit., as with a gag or muzzle; *fig.* to compel or induce to be silent. **7.** The smoulder stops our nose with stench 1573. **8.** *Rich. III*, I. iv. 38.

II. To bring to a stand. **1.** *trans.* To prevent the passage of by blocking a channel or outlet. late ME. **b.** To intercept (light, air, heat, etc.). late ME. **c.** To stanch (bleeding, blood) 1573. **2.** To arrest the onward movement of (a person or thing); to bring to a stand or state of rest; to cause to halt on a journey; also, to prevent the departure or starting of 1440. **b.** To bring down (a bird) with the gun. Also, to arrest the rush of (a charging enemy or wild beast) with rifle-fire. (Said also of the bullet and of the wound produced.) 1862. **c.** *Fencing, Pugilism*, etc. To check (an adversary, his stroke, weapon, etc.) with a counter movement or stroke; to counter (a blow, a manœuvre in wrestling, etc.) 1714. **3.** *Cricket*. (*a*) Of a batsman: To play (a ball) defensively, without attempting to hit it away. Also *absol.* (*b*) *absol.* Of a fieldsman: To field the ball, to act as fieldsman. *To s. behind*, to act as longstop. 1744. **4.** To intercept and detain in transit 1604. **5.** To withhold (a sum of money) in paying wages or other debt, on the ground of some counter-claim. late ME. †**b.** To withhold (goods) as security or in lieu of payment –1865. **6.** To give instructions to a banker not to cash (a bank-note, bill, or the like). Similarly *to s. payment* (of a cheque, etc.). 1713. **7.** To cause (a person) to desist from or pause in a course of action or conduct. Also, *to s. short*, to check abruptly. late ME. **b.** To cause (a person) to break off in narrative or speech. Also *to s. short*. 1545. **c.** To cause (a thing) to cease action. Now *rare*. late ME. **8.** To restrain or prevent (a person) from a contemplated action 1470. †**b.** *Law*. To bar, hinder, preclude –1711. **c.** *Law*. To stay, suspend (proceedings); to prevent (a decree, etc.) from taking effect 1690. †**9.** To hamper the course or progress of (affairs, a project, etc.); to hinder (a person) in action or in some proceeding –1721. **10.** To cause to cease, put an end to (a movement, activity, course of events). late ME. **b.** To prevent the coming-on of 1538. **11.** To cease from, discontinue (an action, allowance, employment) 1525. **12.** To cause (a machine or mechanism) to cease working or going 1538. **13.** *Mus.* To press down (a string of a violin, lute, or the like) with the finger (*rarely* with a key) in order to shorten its vibrating length and thereby produce certain intermediate sounds; hence, to produce (a note, sound) by this means; to use (a finger) for this purpose 1500. **14.** *Naut.* To bring (a ship) to anchor by gradually checking the cable 1627. **b.** To tie up with thin rope. Also *to s. up*. 1770. **15.** *Horticulture*. To pinch out the head of (a plant); to remove (a shoot or portion of it) by pinching. Also *to s. back*. 1699. **16.** *Arch.* To cause (a rib, shaft, chamfer, etc.) to terminate (in a specified form or position) 1835. **17.** *Phonetics*. To check the flow of (breath or voice) in articulation 1867.

1. By the labour of the Persians, the course of the river was stopped below the town, and the waters were confined GIBBON. Phr. *To s. the breath of*, to prevent the respiration of, to suffocate, stifle, choke; hence, to cause to die. **2.** I was at length stopped by the dislocated ice TYNDALL. The responsibility of stopping a train..is given..to the engine-driver 1876. *S. thief!* a cry for help to arrest an escaping thief. *To s. a bullet*, to be shot. **5.** Nor stops, for one bad cork, his butler's pay POPE. **7.** What can be done to s. him from running headlong on ruin? SCOTT. **c.** Hold, s. your murd'ring hands 1672. **8.** If any one likes to go, nobody will s. them RUSKIN. **b.** *K. John* II. i. 562. **10.** For God's sake s. the grunting of those Pigs! SHELLEY. **b.** With thousand doubts How I might s. this tempest ere it came SHAKS. **11.** She has..stopped his..pocket-money DICKENS. The clock stopped striking 1860. Phr. *To s. payment*, to declare oneself unable to meet one's financial obligations. **13.** Phr. *To s. the press*, to suspend the operation of printing (esp. in order to give the opportunity to make some insertion). **14.** Phr. *To s. the cable*, to prevent it running out too fast. *S. her!*, an order to check the running out of the cable; also, on small steamers and motor-boats, the command to s. the engine. *To s. the tide*, to prevent the ship being carried with the tide.

With advs. **Stop down.** *trans.* To reduce the aperture of (a lens) by means of the stops. **S. off.** (*a*) In *Moulding*, to adapt (a mould) to a new design by shortening or obliterating some part of it. (*b*) In *Etching*, etc. = *s. out*. **S. out.** In *Etching*, to obliterate or cover with a varnish (the parts of the plate which are to be kept from the acid in the process of biting in). Also *absol.*

III. To come to a stand, cease to move or act. **1.** *intr.* To cease from onward movement, to come to a stand or position of rest. More emphatically *to s. dead, s. short*. 1530. **2.** To make a halt on a journey, esp. to halt and remain for rest and refreshment. Of a coach, train, boat, etc.: To halt at a specified place to pick up or set down passengers, etc. 1743. **b.** *To s. over*: to make a halt (*at* a place) and proceed by a later conveyance. So *to s. off*. *U.S.* 1884. **3.** To remain, prolong one's stay in a place; to stay (*to* dinner, *at* home, *with* a person). Also quasi-*trans.*, to remain for (a ceremony, a meal, etc.). 1801. **b.** To sojourn as a visitor, resident, or guest 1797. **4.** To leave off doing what one is actually engaged in for the moment 1594. **b.** To pause in speech or narrative; to break off in the middle of a sentence 1579. **c.** *imper.* Also in the phr. *s. a moment!* 1570. **5.** To leave off, stay, desist (in a course of action or a pursuit, or from one's customary action or employment) 1689. **b.** To limit one's activity *at* a certain point; to refrain from exceeding a certain degree or extent 1737. **c.** To stay in action, to hesitate, 'stick'. Const. *at*. 1676. **6.** Of a thing: To cease its motion or action. Of a process: To come to a pause or end. 1529. **b.** Of a machine, etc.: To cease working or going 1789. **7.** Of an immaterial thing: To have its limit of operation at a specified point. Of a series: To come to an end. 1733.

1. I saw a Coach s. at my Door 1709. **2.** The postilions stopped at the convent..to take up Blanche 1794. **3.** But you'll s. and take a bit of dinner with us? 1858. Phr. *To s. on*, to continue in one place or employment. *To s. up*, (*a*) to remain 'up' at one's college or university; (*b*) to sit up instead of going to bed. **4. b.** *To s. short*, to pause abruptly. **5. b.** His charity would willingly have stopped short at Ashby SCOTT. **c.** *To s. at nothing*, to be prevented by no obstacle. **6.** The ulceration stops and heals 1830. **b.** My watch has stopped DICKENS. **7.** But the severities exercised against catholics did not s. there 1741.

IV. 1. [from STOP *sb.*] *trans.* To furnish with stops, to punctuate 1776. **2.** *Versification*. To conclude or divide (a line of verse) with a 'stop' or sense pause. Also *intr.* 1857.

Comb.: **s.-over** *U.S.*, the act of 'stopping over' or breaking one's journey to go on by a later conveyance; also *attrib.*; **-press**, an interruption of the printing in order to insert a late piece of news (see II. 12); also *attrib.* or *adj.* of an issue of a newspaper, etc., containing late news inserted after printing has begun; **-water** *Naut.*, (*a*) something fixed or towed overboard to retard the motion of a ship; (*b*) a plug, etc., for making a joint watertight.

Stopcock (stǫ·pkǫk). 1584. [f. STOP *sb.* or *v.* + COCK *sb.*[1]] A tap or short pipe furnished with a valve operated from the outside by turning a key or handle, for the purpose of stopping or permitting as required the passage of liquid, air, steam, gas or the like. (Sometimes improperly applied to the key or handle by which the valve is turned.)

Stope (stōᵘp), *sb.* 1747. [app. cogn. w. STEP *sb.*, but the phonological relation is obsc.] *Mining*. †**1.** A step or notch in the side of a pit, or in an upright beam, to receive the end of a stemple or cross-piece –1836. **2.** A step-like working in the side of a pit 1747. **b.** *attrib.*, as in **s. drill**, a portable rock-drill, used in stoping 1908. Hence **Stope** *v. trans.* to cut (mineral ground) in stopes; to excavate horizontally, layer after layer; to extract (ore) by this process.

Sto·p-gap. 1684. [f. STOP *v.* + GAP *sb.*[1]] **1.** Something that temporarily supplies a need; a makeshift. Also, of a person: One who temporarily occupies an office, etc. until a permanent appointment can be made. 1691. **2.** An utterance intended to fill up a gap or an awkward pause in conversation or discourse 1684. **3.** *attrib.* passing into *adj.* 1684.

1. Moral prejudices are the stopgaps of virtue 1827. **3.** What will be known in history as the 'S.' Government J. CHAMBERLAIN.

Stoppage (stǫ·pėdʒ). 1465. [f. STOP *v.* + -AGE.] The action of stopping; the condition of being stopped. **1.** Deduction from payments; a sum 'stopped' from the pay of a soldier, workman, or servant. **2.** Obstruction of a road, passage, stream, or current 1540. **b.** A 'block' of the traffic in a street 1727. **3.** *Path.* Obstructed condition of a bodily organ 1575. **4.** Arrest or detention of a traveller, or of goods being conveyed from place to place 1621. **5.** The action of stopping or causing to cease 1657. **b.** Discontinuance of supply 1865. **6.** Cessation of movement or activity; a stop or halt in a journey 1794. **7.** *Comm.* The action of stopping payment 1817. **b.** A strike or lock-out 1902.

Stopped (stǫpt), *ppl. a.* 1440. [f. STOP *v.* + -ED[1].] In the senses of STOP *v.*; *spec.* in *Phonetics*, of a consonant sound: Formed by complete closure of the orinasal passages; explosive.

Bridge. A Suit is Stopped when you can make one trick in it, or can compel the adversary to quit it and lead something else 1901.

Stopper (stǫ·pəɹ), *sb.* 1480. [f. STOP *v.* + -ER[1].] **1.** A person who stops (see the senses of the verb). **2.** Something that stops up a hole or passage 1591. **b.** *spec.* A plug for closing the neck of a bottle, the end of a tube, or the hole for the egress of fluid from any vessel 1667. **3.** The upper pad of the sole of a greyhound's foot 1853. **4.** Something that causes to cease or brings to a stand 1828. **5.** *West Indian*. A tree of the genus *Eugenia* 1884. **6.** *Naut.* A short piece of rope, usu. knotted at one or both ends, used to suspend or secure something 1626. **7.** *Bridge*. = STOP *sb.* V. 5 b. 1901.

4. Phr. *To put a s. on*, to put a stop to (*colloq.*).

Comb.: **s.-bolt** *Naut.*, a ring-bolt in the deck of a ship to which the stoppers are secured; **-knot** *Naut.*, a kind of knot used for the ends of stoppers.

Stopper (stǫ·pəɹ), *v.* 1769. [f. prec.] **1.** *trans. Naut.* To secure with a stopper. **2.** To close or secure (a bottle, etc.) with a stopper. Also with *down*. 1868. **3.** To fit with a stopper 1827. **4.** *slang*. To stop; to 'put the stopper on' 1821. **Sto·ppered** *a.* fitted with a stopper.

Stopping (stǫ·piŋ), *vbl. sb.* late ME. [f. STOP *v.* + -ING[1].] **1.** The action of STOP *v.* in various senses. †**2.** *Path.* Obstructed conditions of an organ –1741. **3.** Something inserted to stop a hole, crevice, or passage 1585. **b.** *Farriery.* A pad charged with grease inserted within the shoe for the purpose of keeping the horse's foot moist 1580. **c.** A composition used to stop holes or crevices; *Dentistry*, the material used for stopping a hollow tooth, latterly called *filling* 1823. **4.** *Mining.* A partition of boards, etc. in an air passage 1708.

attrib. and *Comb.*: **s.-ground** *Etching*, a mixture used to cover the parts of a plate which are bitten-in enough; **s. mixture** *Etching*, a composition to be used as a stopping-ground; **s.-place,** each customary point on their route at which vehicles carrying passengers stop to allow them to mount or alight.

Stopping (stǫ·piŋ), *ppl. a.* late ME. [f. STOP *v.* + -ING[2].] †**1.** *Med.* Tending to cause stoppage; astringent –1666. **2.** That stops 1529.

S. train, a train which stops at some or all intermediate stations on a particular line.

Stopple (stǫ·p'l), *sb.* late ME. [Partly from STOP *v.* + -EL[1], -LE; partly aphetic f. ESTOPPEL.] **1.** An appliance for closing the orifice of a vessel, tube, etc.; a stopper, cork or plug. Now *rare.* †**2.** The action of stopping; a stoppage, prohibition –1651. Hence **Sto·pple** *v. trans.* to put a s. on; to close with a s.

Sto·p-watch. 1737. A watch which indicates fractions of a second by a hand that may be instantly stopped by pressure on a spring or catch, so as to record an exact moment or period of time; chiefly used for timing races.

Storage (stōᵊ·rėdʒ). 1612. [f. STORE *v.* + -AGE.] **1.** Capacity or space for storing. **2.** The action of storing; the condition or fact of being stored 1828. **b.** The conversion of electric energy into chemical energy from which electricity may be generated again 1881. **3.** A place where something is stored 1775. **4.** Rent paid for warehousing 1775.

2. *Cold s.*, the storing of provisions in refrigerating chambers as a means of preserving them from decay.

Comb.: **s. battery,** a secondary battery in which a supply of electricity is accumulated; **s. cell,** an electrical accumulator; **s. heater,** a heating apparatus operating by means of stored heat; **s. tank,** a tank for s.; **s. tuber,** a tuber forming a reservoir of nourishment for the plant.

Storax (stōᵊ·ræ̆ks). late ME. [– L. *storax* – Gr. στύραξ, var. of στύραξ STYRAX.] **1.** A fragrant gum-resin described by ancient writers. In early mod. use applied to the resin of the tree *Styrax officinalis*; in later commercial and pharmaceutical use to the balsam of the tree *Liquidambar orientale* (more explicitly *liquid s.*). **2.** The tree *Styrax officinalis* 1694.

Store (stōᵊɹ), *sb.* [ME. *stor*, aphetic f. †*astore* – OFr. *estor*, f. *estorer* STORE *v.*] **1. a.** *sing.* (without indef. art.) That with which a household, camp, etc., is stored; food, clothing, and other necessaries, collected for future use. Now *rare.* **b.** *collective pl.* Articles (such as food, clothing, arms, etc.) serving for the equipment and maintenance of an army, a ship; occas. of a household, etc. Cf. MARINE STORES. 1636. †**2.** Live stock –1697. **3.** Sufficient or abundant supply (*of* something needful) 1471. †**b.** Plenty; abundance (of food or necessaries) –1712. **c.** Used *advb.*, or as postpositive or predicative adj. = 'in store', in plenty, abundant(ly). Also *good, great s.* Now *arch.* and *dial.* 1569. **4.** A person's collective possessions; accumulated goods or money. Now *arch.* or *poet.* ME. **5.** In phrases with the sense 'to value, esteem, prize; make account of': †*To tell, make, hold, set* (*great, little, no*) *s. of*. *To set* (*great*, etc.) *s. by, upon.* late ME. **6.** A stock (of anything material or immaterial) laid up for future use. Phr. *to lay in a s.* 1487. **b.** *collect. pl.* Stocks, reserves; often in immaterial sense, treasures, accumulated resources 1520. **7.** Storage, reserve. Now *rare* exc. in phr. *in s.* (*for*). 1487. **8.** A sheep, steer, cow, or pig acquired or kept for fattening 1620. **9.** A place where stores are kept, a warehouse; a storehouse 1667. **10.** A place where merchandise is kept for sale. **a.** Chiefly *U.S.* and *Colonial.* orig., A shop on a large scale, and dealing in a great variety of articles. Now, the usual equivalent for SHOP *sb.* 2. 1740. **b.** In Great Britain from about 1850, current in *co-operative store(s*, the shop in which a co-operative trading society exposes goods for sale. Now commonly in *pl.* ('The Stores'), applied esp. to the establishment of any of the larger co-operative societies of London and other cities, which consists of a number of departments, each dealing in a separate class of goods. In imitation of this, often adopted as the designation of a trading establishment resembling these. 1852. **11.** *attrib.* **a.** Denoting a receptacle, repository, depot or transport for stores or supplies, as *s.-cellar*, STOREHOUSE, STORE-ROOM 1507. **b.** Designating animals kept for breeding or as part of the ordinary stock of a farm, also animals bought lean to be fattened; as *s. beast, cattle*; **s. farm,** a farm on which cattle are reared 1602. **c.** *U.S.* and *Colonial.* Of or belonging to a store or shop; purchased or purchasable at a store, as *s. goods* 1741. **d.** Pertaining to 'the Stores', as *s. price(s* 1889.

1. Small s. will serve, where s., All seasons, ripe for use hangs on the stalk MILT. **b.** The docks were full of triremes and naval stores JOWETT. **3.** Thou hast given them s. Of flowers M. ARNOLD. Prov. *S. is no sore*, i.e. abundance does no harm. **b.** Starving in the Midst of S. SWIFT. **c.** Wolves there are great s. 1694. **4.** Increase thy Wealth, and double all thy S. DRYDEN. **5.** The precious metal, on which they set so high a s. 1797. **6.** My desk usually contained a s. of most miscellaneous volumes SCOTT. A s. of energy 1881. **b.** The Stores of Learning 1699. **7.** The vse of things is all, and not the S. B. JONS. Phr. *To keep* (young animals) *for s.* *In s.*, in reserve, laid up for future use; hence (of events or conditions in the future) *in s. for*, awaiting (a person); What such surprise can be in s. for me? DICKENS.

Store (stōᵊɹ), *v.* ME. [Aphetic f. †*astore* – OFr. *estorer* :– L. *instaurare* renew, repair, RESTORE.] **1.** *trans.* To furnish, supply, stock (a person, place, etc.) *with* something. **2.** To keep in store for future use; to collect and keep in reserve; to form a store, stock or supply of; to accumulate, hoard 1600. **b.** *spec.* To deposit (goods, furniture, etc.) in a store or warehouse for temporary safe-keeping 1899. **3.** Of a receptacle: To hold, keep, contain, have storage-accommodation for 1911.

1. I have storyd my parkes and my pondes 1530. These studies..s. a man's mind with valuable facts W. IRVING. **2.** My capital secret, in what part my strength Lay stor'd MILT. But Dora stored what little she could save TENNYSON. **b.** I shall s. my furniture and spend a year in travelling 1917. **3.** A single cell can s. 2000000 foot-pounds of energy 1911. Hence **Stored** (stōᵊɹd) *ppl. a.* laid up in store, accumulated, hoarded; stocked, furnished or supplied with a store. **Sto·rer,** one who or a thing which stores or keeps in store.

Sto·rehouse. ME. [f. STORE *sb.* + HOUSE *sb.*] **1.** A building in which goods are stored. **2.** *transf.* and *fig.* Often, a store or treasury from which something may be obtained in plenty; an abundant source (*of*) 1578.

1. Which neither have stoore housse ner barne TINDALE *Luke* 12:24. **2.** Memory, which is as it were the Store-house of our Ideas LOCKE.

Storekeeper (stōᵊ·ɹ,kīpəɹ). 1618. **1.** One who has charge of a store or stores; *spec.* an officer in charge of naval or military stores. **2.** *U.S.* and *Colonial.* A shopkeeper 1741.

Sto·re-room. 1746. **1.** A room set apart for the storing of goods or supplies, esp. those of a ship or household. **2.** Room or space for storage 1783.

Sto·re-ship, sto·reship. 1693. A government ship employed to carry naval or military stores.

Storey, Storeyed: see STORY *sb.*[2], STORIED *a.*[2]

‖**Storge** (stǫ·ɹgi). 1637. [Gr. στοργή, related to στέργειν to love.] Natural affection; usu., that of parents for their offspring.

Storiation (stōᵊri,ē¹·ʃən). 1884. [f. STORY *v.* + -ATION.] Decoration with artistic designs representing historical, legendary, or emblematic subjects. Hence **Sto·riate** *v.*

Storied (stōᵊ·rid), *a.*[1] and *ppl. a.* 1481. [f. STORY *sb.*[1] and *v.* + -ED, after med.L. *historiatus*, OFr. *(h)istorié.*] **1.** Ornamented with scenes from history or legend by means of sculpture, painting or other art; also, inscribed with a legend or memorial record. **2.** Celebrated or recorded in history or story 1725.

1. S. Windows richly dight, Casting a dimm religious light MILT. **2.** The s. Past TENNYSON.

Storied (stōᵊ·rid), *a.*[2] Also **storeyed.** 1624. [f. STORY *sb.*[2] + -ED[2].] Having storeys, divided into storeys.

†**Sto·rier.** late ME. [Aphetic var. of *historier.*] A chronicler, historian –1640.

Storify (stōᵊ·rifəi), *v. rare.* 1616. [f. STORY *sb.*[1] + -FY.] *trans.* To picture, delineate, or record (a historical event or fact); to celebrate in history or story. Also *absol.*

Storiology (stōᵊriǫ·lŏdʒi). 1860. [f. STORY *sb.*[1] + -LOGY.] The systematic study of popular tales and legends, with regard to their origin and development. Hence **Sto:riolo·gical** *a.* **Storio·logist.**

Stork (stǭɹk). [OE. *storc* = OS. (Du.) *stork*, OHG. *stor(a)h* (G. *storch*), ON. *storkr* :– Gmc. **sturkaz*, prob. f. **sturk-* **sterk-* (see STARK), the name being supposed to refer to the bird's rigid habit.] **1.** A large wading bird of the genus *Ciconia*, allied to the ibis and heron; characterized by having long legs and a long stout bill.

Usually the name denotes the White Stork (*Ciconia alba*), which stands over three feet high, and has brilliant white plumage with black wing-coverts and quills, and red legs.

b. Applied to birds of allied genera 1869. **c.** *fig.* and *allus.* 1555. **2.** The bird or its flesh as an article of food 1460. **3.** A variety of the domestic pigeon. More fully *s. pigeon.* 1855.

1. b. The Giant Storks (*Mycteria*) 1869. The Field Storks (*Arvicolæ*) 1869. **c.** Like Æsops folish Frogges..if hee proue a Storke, they croke and rayle Against him as a tyranne MASSINGER.

Stork's bill. 1562. [Cf. G. *storchschnabel* in sense 1.] **1.** A book-name for a plant of the genus *Erodium* (family *Geraniaceæ*), esp. *E. cicutarium* or *E. moschatum*. **2.** A plant of the genus *Pelargonium* (*Geraniaceæ*) 1825.

Storm (stǭɹm), *sb.* [OE. *storm* = OS. (Du.) *storm*, (O)HG. *sturm*, ON. *stormr* :– Gmc. **sturmaz*, prob. f. **stur-*, repr. also by STIR *v.*] **I. 1.** A violent disturbance of the atmosphere, manifested by high winds, often accompanied by heavy falls of rain, or snow, by thunder and lightning, and (at sea) by turbulence of the waves. Hence sometimes applied to a heavy fall of rain, hail, or snow, or to a violent outbreak of thunder and lightning, unaccompanied by strong wind. **b.** Used *spec.* as the distinctive appelation of a particular degree of violence in wind. In mod. *Meteorology*: An atmospheric disturbance which in the Beaufort scale is classed as intermediate between a whole gale and a hurricane, having a wind-force estimated at 10–11 and a limit of velocity at from 56–57 miles per hour. 1801. **c.** *Magnetic s.*: a magnetic disturbance observed simultaneously over a considerable portion of the globe 1860. **2.** *transf.* A heavy discharge or downfall (of missiles, blows) OE. **3.** *fig.* and in fig. context. **a.** A violent disturbance of (political, social, etc.) affairs; commotion, sedition, tumult OE. **b.** A tumultuous rush (of sound, tears, etc.); a vehement utterance (of words); a violent outburst (of censure, ridicule, etc.); a passionate manifestation of feeling 1602. **c.** Commotion or unrest (of mind, etc.); a tumultuous assemblage (of thoughts, feelings) 1569. **4.** *Path.* A paroxysm, violent access (of pain or disease) 1545.

1. Heres..another Storme brewing, I heare it sing ith' winde SHAKS. The wind setting in at South-west, blew a s. DE FOE. Prov. phr. *A s. in a tea-cup*, a great commotion in a small community or about a trifling matter. **2.** The Sulphurous Hail Shot after us in s. MILT. **3. a.** Here's to the pilot that weather'd the s.! [i.e. Pitt] CANNING. **b.** The s. of music shakes th' astonish'd crowd COWPER. The s. of invective which burst upon him MACAULAY. A s. of weeping 1891. *S. and stress* [G. *Sturm und Drang*], designation of the movement in German literature about 1770–82, due to a school of young writers characterized by extravagance in the representation of passion, and by energetic repudiation of the 'rules' of the French critics. **4.** *Brain s.*, a succession of sudden and severe phenomena, due to some cerebral disturbance 1894.

II. [f. STORM *v.*] *Mil.* A violent assault on a fortified place 1645.

To take by s., to take possession of by a sudden

attack, to carry by assault; also *fig.*; The Franciscans..were taking the world by s. 1889.

attrib. and *Comb.*: **s.-area,** the area of the earth's surface over which a s. spreads itself; **-belt,** a belt or zone in which storms occur periodically; **s. centre,** the central area of a cyclonic storm, characterized by comparative calmness; *fig.* the central point around which a s. of controversy, trouble, etc. rages; the seat of disease, sedition, or the like; **-cloud,** a heavy cloud which threatens or comes with rain; also *fig.*; **-collar,** a collar fitted to a garment and specially adapted for protection against wind and rain; **-cone,** = CONE *sb.* 5; **s. door** *U.S.*, an outer or supplementary door for use in stormy weather; **-glass,** a hermetically sealed tube containing a solution which becomes flocculent on the approach of a s.; **-proof** *a.*, (*a*) impervious to s.; (*b*) proof against storming or assault; **-sail,** 'a sail made of stout No. 1 canvas, of reduced dimensions, for use in a gale'; **-shutter,** an outside window-shutter for use in stormy weather; **-signal,** a signal exhibited at coast-guard stations, etc., to give warning of the approach and direction of dangerous winds; also *fig.*; **-system,** a group of low-pressure areas constituting a cyclonic s.; **s. track,** the path traversed by the centre of a cyclonic s.; **-troops** = *shock troops* (SHOCK *sb.*[3]); **-wind,** the wind which accompanies a s.; **-window,** an outer window to protect the inner from the effects of storms; **-zone,** = *s.-belt.* **b.** In names of certain birds, the movements or cries of which are supposed to presage a s.; **s.-cock,** the missel-thrush; also locally applied to the fieldfare and the green woodpecker; **-finch, -petrel,** *Procellaria pelagica*; **s. thrush,** the missel-thrush. Hence **Sto·rmful** *a.* abounding in or subject to storms; **-ly** *adv.*, **-ness.** **Sto·rmless** *a.* free from storms.

Storm (stǭɹm), *v.* late ME. [f. prec. (not continuous with OE. *styrman*).] **1.** *intr.* Of the elements or weather: To be tempestuous or stormy, to rage. **b.** *impers.* To blow violently; also to rain, snow, etc. heavily. Now only *U.S.* 1530. **c.** *transf.* To rush with the violence of a storm 1842. **2.** *trans.* To make stormy. Also *fig.*, to trouble, vex, disturb. 1597. **3.** *intr.* To complain with rough and violent language; to rage. Const. *at, against* (a grievance or person). 1553. **4.** *Mil.* To make a vigorous assault on (a fortified position); to take or attempt to take by storm or assault 1645. **5.** *intr.* **a.** *Mil.* To rush to an assault or attack 1632. **b.** *transf.* To rush with violence 1837.

1. b. It is now snowing and storming furiously 1858. **3.** Why looke you how you storme, I would be friends with you SHAKS. I do not want to s. at the man 1889. **4.** They stormed Dundie, and caried the towne 1651. He basely resolves to s. her chastity 1652. **5. a.** All the Norman foot Are storming up the hill TENNYSON. Hence **Sto·rmable** *a.* that can be taken by storm. **Sto·rmer.**

Storming (stǭ·ɹmiŋ), *ppl. a.* 1557. [-ING[2].] **1.** That storms or rages. **2.** That attacks in order to take by storm; chiefly in *s. party* 1802.

Stormy (stǭ·ɹmi), *a.* ME. [f. STORM *sb.* + -Y[1].] **1.** Of the weather, season, air, sky, sea, etc.: Characterized by storm or tempest; tempestuous. Of a place or region: Subject to storms. **2.** *fig.* Of persons, their temper or looks; of times, events, circumstances, etc. ME. **3.** Associated or connected with storms; indicative, predictive, or symbolical of storms. *poet.* 1560.

1. Beyond the s. Hebrides MILT. **2.** Nothing shall hide me from thy s. looke 1592. A s. session 1831. The discussion was long and s. 1891. **3.** *S. Petrel*, the bird *Procellaria pelagica*; also *fig.*, a person who delights in strife, or whose appearance on the scene is a harbinger of coming trouble. Hence **Sto·rmi·ly** *adv.*, **-ness.**

‖**Stornello** (stǫɹne·lo). *Pl.* **-li** (-lī). 1873. [It.] A short popular Italian lyric, usu. improvised.

Storthing (stōᵊ·ɹtiːŋ). 1834. [– Norw. *storting*, former *-thing*, f. *stor* great + *thing* assembly; see THING *sb.*[2]] The Norwegian parliament.

Story (stōᵊ·ri), *sb.*[1] *Pl.* **stories** (stōᵊ·riz). ME. [Aphetic f. AFr. *estorie* (OFr. *estoire*, mod. *histoire*) :– L. *historia* HISTORY.] **I.† 1.** A historical narrative or anecdote –1642. **†2.** A historical work, a book of history –1756. **†3.** Historical writing or records; history as a branch of knowledge, or as opp. to fiction. Also, the events recorded or proper to be recorded by historians. –1768. **4.** A recital of events that have or are alleged to have happened; a series of events that are or might be narrated. late ME. **b.** With possessive: A person's account of the events of his life or some portion of it 1604. **c.** With possessive or followed by *of*: The series of events in the life of a person, or in the past existence of a thing, country, institution, etc., considered as narrated or as a subject for narration 1700. **5.** A narrative of real, or, more usu., fictitious events, designed for the entertainment of the hearer or reader; a series of traditional or imaginary events forming the matter of such a narrative; a tale; *spec.* a nursery or folk tale 1500. **b.** Traditional, poetic, or romantic legend or history 1794. **c.** Succession of incidents, 'plot' (of a novel, poem, or drama) 1715. **d.** An incident, real or fictitious, related in order to amuse or interest, or to illustrate some remark made; an anecdote 1679. **¶e.** Used for: A subject of story. Also, a theme for mirth, a dupe. 1603. **6.** An allegation, statement; an account or representation of a matter; a particular person's representation of the facts in a case 1601. **†b.** A mere tale, a baseless report –1796. **c.** *U.S.* A narrative or descriptive article in a newspaper; the subject or material for this 1892. **7.** Euphemism for: A lie. *colloq.* 1697.

2. Examples of this, we have both in Holy Writ, and also in other Stories 1684. **3.** Who is so unread..in s., that hath not heard of many sects refusing books as a hindrance MILT. **4.** A mournful s. of domestic woes POPE. *transf.* Better the rudest work that tells a s...than the richest without meaning RUSKIN. **b.** And then she told him her whole s. 1894. **c.** The S. of Creation 1888. **5.** Now wee haue Arcadia and the Faery Queene, and Orlando Furioso, with such like friuolous stories 1597. **b.** Or die in fight, to live in s. 1839. **d.** Phr. *Good s.*, often, an amusing anecdote. **e.** *Meas. for M.* I. iv. 30. **6.** Phr. *The s. goes that..*, it is reported. *To be all in one s., to be in the same s.*, (of a number of persons) to agree in their account of a matter (usu. implying collusion). *The whole s.*, the full account of the matter, all that there is to be said. (*That is*) *another s.*, an entirely different matter; a matter requiring different treatment. **7.** You were always good Children, and never told stories WESLEY. *You s.!* = you story-teller, liar (*vulgar* and in nursery use).

†II. A painting or sculpture representing a historical subject. Hence, any work of pictorial or sculptural art containing figures. –1700.

Comb.: **s.-book,** a book containing stories, esp. children's stories; also *occas.* a novel or romance; **-writer,** a historian; a writer of tales. Hence **Storye·tte,** a very short story.

Story, *sb.*[2], **storey** (stōᵊ·ri). *Pl.* **stories, storeys.** late ME. [Aphetic – AL. (*h*)*istoria* (XIII), spec. use of L. *historia* HISTORY, STORY *sb.*[1]; perh. orig. a tier of painted windows (cf. AL. (*hi*)*storia* picture XII).] **1.** Each of the stages or portions one above the other of which a building consists; a room or set of rooms on one floor or level. **b.** *transf.* and *fig.* Anything compared to a story of a building 1625. **2.** Each of a number of tiers or rows (of orders, columns, window mullions or lights, etc.) disposed horizontally one above another. late ME.

1. b. *The* or *one's upper s.*, used joc. for the head as the seat of the mind or intellect; I wuz born weak in th' upper s. 1884.

Story (stōᵊ·ri), *v.* late ME. [f. STORY *sb.*[1]] **1.** *trans.* In early use, †to record historically; in later use, to tell as a story, to tell the story of. Now *rare.* 1450. **2.** To decorate with paintings or sculpture; to represent in painting or sculpture. late ME.

1. Daphnis..storied to her what he had seen 1657.

Sto·ry-te:ller. 1709. [f. STORY *sb.*[1] + TELLER.] **1.** One who is accustomed to tell stories or anecdotes in conversation. **2.** Euphemistically: A liar. *colloq.* 1748. **3.** One whose business it is to recite legendary or romantic stories 1777. **4.** Applied to a writer of stories 1814. **5.** The teller of a particular story 1851.

1. He was also a *bon-vivant*, a diner-out, and a s. 1862. So **Sto·ry-te:lling** *sb.* the action of telling stories 1709. **Sto·ry-te:lling** *a.* that tells stories; *colloq.* lying, mendacious.

‖**Stoss** (stǫs, as G. ʃtos). 1891. [G., = thrust, push.] Applied to the side or end (*s. side, s. end*) of an object that meets the impact of a moving body.

Stot (stǫt). [OE. *stot*(*t*, perh. cogn. with ON. *stútr* bull. Cf. AL. *stottus* steer, *stotta* heifer (XII).] **†1.** A horse –1440. **2.** A young castrated ox, a steer. *north.* ME. **3.** A heifer. *north.* 1677.

Stound (staund, stūnd), *sb.*[1] [OE. *stund* = OFris. *stunde*, OS. *stunda* (Du. *stond*), OHG. *stunta* (G. *stunde* hour), ON. *stund* :– Gmc. **stundō*.] **1.** A time, while; a short time, moment. *Obs.* exc. *dial.* **2. †a.** Contextually: A hard time, a time of trial or pain –1590. **b.** Hence, a sharp pain, a pang; a fierce attack, a shock. Chiefly *north.* ME. **c.** Roar, violent noise 1627.

Stound (staund, stūnd), *sb.*[2] Now *dial.* 1567. [app. f. STOUND *v.*[2]] A state of stupefaction or amazement.

Stound, *v.*[1] ME. [f. STOUND *sb.*[1]] **†1.** *intr.* To remain, stay. –late ME. **2. †a.** *trans.* To affect with a 'stound' or pang; to cause great pain to. **b.** *intr.* To be acutely painful; to smart, throb. Only *Sc.* and *north.* 1500.

Stound (staund, stūnd), *v.*[2] Now *dial.* ME. [Aphetic var. of ASTOUND *v.*] *trans.* To stun as with a blow; to stupefy, benumb; to stupefy with astonishment.

Stoup (stūp). late ME. [– ON. *staup* = OE. *stēap*, MLG. *stōp*, (M)Du. *stoop*, OHG. *stouf* (G. dial. *stauf*) :– Gmc. **staupaz, -am*, rel. to OE. *stoppa*, OS. *stoppo* pail :– WGmc. **stoppa*, f. *stup-*; see STEEP *v.*] **1.** A pail or bucket; also *water-s.* Now only *Sc.* **2.** A drinking-vessel; a cup, flagon, tankard. Also as a measure of definite quantity; often with defining word, as *gill, pint, quart s.* Now *Sc.* and *north.* and as a literary archaism. 1452. **3.** A vessel to contain holy-water; often a stone basin set in or against the wall of the church-porch, or within the church close to the entrance-door 1500.

Stour (stūr). ME. [– AFr. *estur*, OFr. *estour, estor* = It. *stormo* – Gmc. **sturmaz* STORM *sb.*] **I. 1.** An armed combat or conflict; esp. a contest in battle; a fight. *Obs.* exc. *arch.* **†2.** *fig.* A conflict waged with immaterial weapons; a struggle with pain or adversity –1810. **†3.** Used by Spenser and his imitators for: Time of turmoil or stress –1811. **†b.** Used by Greene, Lodge, and others for: Occasion, place –1600. **4.** Tumult, uproar; commotion, fuss. Now *Sc.* and *dial.* 1440. **b.** A (driving) storm. *Sc.* and *north.* 1827.

1. When joins yon host in deadly stowre SCOTT. **3.** I haue beene trained vp in warlike stowre SPENSER. **b.** Oft from her lap at sundry stoures, He leapt, and gathered Sommer flowres LODGE.

II. Flying dust raised by the rapid movement of a person or thing, or by the wind; hence, a deposit of dust; also, dust from material undergoing mechanical treatment. *Sc.* and *north.* 1456.

Stout (staut), *sb.*[1] Now *dial.* [OE. *stūt*; of unkn. origin.] A gadfly, horse-fly; also applied to a gnat.

Stout (staut), *sb.*[2] 1677. [prob. ellipt. for *stout ale* or *stout beer.*] **†a.** 'A cant name for strong beer' (J.). **b.** In present use, a strong variety of porter.

Stout (staut), *a.* and *adv.* ME. [– AFr., OFr. (NE. dial.) *stout*, for *estout* :– WGmc. **stult-* (OFris. *stult*, MLG. *stolt*, (M)Du. *stout*, (O)HG. *stolz* proud), perh. rel. to **stelt-* (see STILT *sb.*).] **A.** *adj.* **I. †1.** Proud, haughty, arrogant –1851. **†2.** Fierce, furious –1600. **3.** Valiant, brave; undaunted in conflict. Now *arch.* (chiefly *attrib.* of soldiers). ME. **b.** Of courage, the 'heart', etc.: Undismayed 1508. **c.** Of a conflict, assault, or resistance: Vigorous 1582. **†4.** Of persons: Firm in resolve, unyielding, determined –1815. **b.** Of utterances or demeanour: Resolute, defiant. *arch.* late ME. **c.** Of a partisan, an advocate, an enemy: Uncompromising 1586. **5. a.** Of a fox: Capable of long runs 1714. **b.** Of a horse: Of great staying power: contrasted with *speedy* 1773.

1. As s. and proud as he were Lord of all SHAKS. **2.** Sterne Strife, and Anger s. SPENSER. **3.** A stouter Champion neuer handled Sword SHAKS. **b.** To quell the valour of the stoutest heart COWPER. **c.** He..Smote fiercest, where resistance was most s. CARY. **4.** Askelon was s., and would not surrender FULLER. **b.** Your words haue bin s. against me, saith the Lord *Mal.* 3:13. **c.** Johnson, who was a s. unbeliever in Rowley 1850.

II. Physical senses. **1.** Strong in body; of powerful build. *arch.* **b.** In robust health, 'strong'. *Obs.* exc. *Sc.* 1697. **2.** Of buildings, rocks, trees, etc.: Capable of defying attack; strong. late ME. **b.** Of a ship: Strongly built; capable of bearing rough weather 1622. **3.** Of plants and their parts: Strong in growth; thick, not slender 1573. †**4.** Of liquor: Having 'body' or density. Chiefly of ale or beer: cf. STOUT *sb.*[2] –1826. **5.** Of persons: Thick in the body and limbs; not lean or slender; inclined to corpulence; often *euphem.* = corpulent, fat 1804. **6.** Of a material object or substance: So thick as to be strong or rigid 1765.

1. The Millere was a s. carl for the nones Ful byg he was of brawn, and eek of bones CHAUCER. **2.** The s. dam with its marble bridge 1909. **b.** A s. fighting ship 1868. **5.** Uncle looks very well, but he grows very s., I think 1866. **6.** A s. pair of scissors 1875. Very s. cardboard 1891.

B. *adv.* Stoutly. Now *rare.* ME.

Comb.: **s.-hearted** *a.* courageous, undaunted; †stubborn, intractable. Hence **Stou·ten** *v. trans.* and *intr.* to make or grow stout. **Stou·tish** *a.* somewhat s. **Stou·t-ly** *adv.*, **-ness.**

Stout (staut), *v.* ME. [f. STOUT *a.*] †**1.** *intr.* To be defiant; to act in a defiant or stubborn manner –1616. **2.** quasi-*trans.* **a.** †*To s. it* = sense 1. –1670. **b.** *To s. it out*: to persist in a defiant attitude; to 'brave it out'. Now *rare.* 1587.

Stovaine (stōᵘ·veɪəin). 1904. [– Fr. *stovaïne*, f. STOVE *sb.* (tr. Fr. *fourneau*) after *cocaïne.*] A local anæsthetic, discovered by Fourneau in 1903. (Proprietary term.)

Stove (stōᵘv), *sb.* 1456. [– MLG., MDu. *stove* (Du. *stoof* foot-warmer) = OHG. *stuba* (G. *stube* living-room), rel. to OE. *stofa* bathroom, *stuf|bæþ* vapour bath, f. **stub-*; connection with STEW *sb.*[2] and *v.* is possible.] †**1.** A hot air bath; a sweating-room –1756. †**2.** A sitting-room or bedroom heated with a furnace. Chiefly with ref. to Germany, the Low Countries, Scandinavia, or Russia. –1706. **3.** A hothouse for plants 1695. **4.** A heated chamber or box for some special purpose 1640. **5.** An apparatus for heating (orig. for heating a 'stove' in sense 1 or 2). **a.** A closed box or vessel of earthenware, porcelain, or (now more usu.) of metal, portable or fixed, to contain burning fuel: often with defining word, as *cooking, electric, gas s.* 1618. **b.** Applied to the metal structure of a more or less open fireplace; a 'grate' 1756. **c.** [after Du. *stoof*] A foot-warmer containing burning charcoal 1716.

1. As they were rubbing of him with oile in his stooue or hotte house NORTH. **2.** How tedious is it to them that liue in Stoues & Caues halfe a yeare together; as in Island, Muscovy, or vnder the Pole it selfe BURTON. **5. c.** Under her feet was a wooden s. 1883.

Comb.: **s.-grate** = sense 5 b; **-house** = sense 3; **-polish,** black lead or other substance used for polishing stoves.

Stove (stōᵘv), *v.* 1456. [f. prec.] †**1.** *trans.* To subject (a person) to a hot-air bath; to sweat (a gamecock) –1686. **2.** To put (plants) in a hothouse 1625. †**3.** To keep (persons) in heated rooms –1802. **4.** To dry in a stove or heated chamber; *Naut.* to dry (ropes) in this manner to prepare them for tarring 1625. **5.** To stew (meat or vegetables). Now *Sc.* and *north.* 1738. **6.** To fumigate with sulphur; to disinfect with sulphur or other fumes 1805.

Sto·ve-pipe. 1699. **1.** Each of the pipes by which hot air is conveyed in a 'stove' or hothouse. **2.** A metal pipe attached to a stove to carry off the smoke 1858. **3.** *colloq.* or *slang.* (orig. *U.S.*) A tall hat of cylindrical shape, a 'top hat', 'chimney-pot'. Also *s. hat.* 1851.

Stover (stōᵘ·vəɹ). Now *dial.* ME. [Aphetic var. of ESTOVER.] †**1.** The provision of food (for persons or animals) necessary for a journey or for a sojourn. ME. only. **2.** †**a.** *gen.* Winter food for cattle –1674. **b.** *spec.* In various applications according to locality: Hay made from clover; broken straw, etc. from the threshing-floor; stubble 1669.

2. a. Thy Turphie-Mountaines, where liue nibling Sheepe, And flat Medes thetchd with Stouer, them to keepe SHAKS.

†**Stow,** *sb.*[1] [OE. *stōw* = OFris. *stō*, ON. *-stó* in *eldstó* fireplace :– Gmc. **stōwō*, f. **stō-*, **stā-* STAND *v.*] = PLACE *sb.* in various senses –ME.

Stow (stōᵘ), *sb.*[2] *Obs.* exc. *techn.* 1614. [var. of STOVE *sb.*] †**1.** In various senses of STOVE *sb.*: A hot-air bath; a heated room or chamber; a hothouse for plants; a closed fireplace –1731. **2.** *Tin-plate making.* A raised structure containing the furnace, etc. 1839.

Stow (stōᵘ), *v.* Pa. t. and pa. pple. **stowed** (stōᵘd). late ME. [Aphetic f. BESTOW (f. STOW *sb.*[1]). The naut. sense perh. infl. by Du. *stouwen.*] †**1.** *trans.* To place; to put in a certain place, position, or situation –1594. **b.** To lodge, quarter, find room for (persons). Now only in derogatory sense. 1604. †**2.** To invest (money); to apply (money or goods) to a particular purpose; to spend –1762. **3.** To place in a receptacle to be stored or kept in reserve 1456. **4.** *Naut.* To place (cargo) in proper order in the hold or other receptacles in a ship; also, to store (provisions, etc.) between decks 1555. †**b.** To fasten down (persons) under the hatches for confinement or safety –1644. **c.** To put (guns, oars, furniture, etc.) in the proper receptacles on board 1595. **d.** To furl (a sail) 1644. †**e.** Of a ship: To have stowage-room for; to hold –1645. **5. a.** *Naut.* To fill (the hold of a ship, etc.) with cargo; to load (a ship). Also, to fit up (a ship), supply with necessaries. 1692. **b.** *transf.* To fill (a receptacle), to pack (*full, close*) with things or persons; to crowd with contents 1710. **6.** *slang.* †**a.** *intr.* To cease speaking, 'shut up'. **b.** *trans.* To desist from. 1567.

1. Till sable Night..in her vaultie prison, stowes the daie SHAKS. **b.** Oh thou foule Theefe, Where hast thou stow'd my Daughter? SHAKS. **3.** Raftered lofts to s. the hay 1874. **4.** The human cargoes were stowed close in the holds of small vessels MACAULAY. **b.** The Marriners all vnder hatches stowed SHAKS. **5. b.** The House was stowed as full as possible, but still many were constrained to stand without WESLEY.

Stow away. a. *trans.* To remove and store until required; to put (a thing) in a secret or not easily accessible place or where it will be out of the way; occas. to put or lodge (a person) in out-of-the-way quarters; *joc.* to 'put out of sight', 'dispose of', eat up (quantities of food). **b.** *intr.* for *refl.* to conceal oneself on board a ship, to be a STOWAWAY.

Stowage (stōᵘ·ėdʒ). late ME. [f. prec. + -AGE. First in AL. *stowagium* (1313).] **1.** The action or operation of stowing cargo on board ship, or goods in a warehouse, etc. **b.** Manner in which the contents of a ship are stowed 1769. **2.** The condition or process of being stowed or placed in a receptacle 1611. **3.** Room or accommodation for stowing anything; internal capacity of a warehouse or receptacle of any kind 1547. **b.** *joc.* Capacity for food 1651. **4.** A place in which something is stowed 1641. **5.** That with which a vessel is or is to be stowed 1622.

1. We had finished the s. of the holds 1784. **b.** Losses by bad s. or deficient dunnage 1867. **3.** The small s. necessary for the silver 1748. **4.** A room under the s. or cooling-room 1848.

Stowaway (stōᵘ·ăwēɪ). 1854. [f. vbl. phr. *stow away*; see STOW *v.*] A person who hides in a ship in order to escape payment of passage-money, or to get to sea unobserved. **b.** *gen.* Something stowed away; also the place 1913.

Stow-blade. Also **stoblade.** 1681. [f. *stow* = STOWCE.] *Mining.* Each of two upright pieces of wood, a foot in length, connected at the top with the sole-trees of a stowce.

Stowce (stōᵘs). 1664. [Of unkn. origin.] *Mining. sing.* and *pl.* A kind of windlass for drawing up ore; also, a model of this, intended not for working, but to comply with the old law which provides that the presence of an owner's 'stowce' on a mining tract secures his right of possession. Hence **Stowce** *v. trans.* to mark (a 'meer' of ground) with 'a pair of stowces'.

Strabism (strēɪ·biz'm). 1656. Anglicized f. STRABISMUS.

‖**Strabismus** (străbi·zmŏs). 1684. [mod.L. – Gr. στραβισμός, f. στραβίζειν to squint, f. στραβός squinting.] *Path.* An affection of the eyes in which the axes of vision cannot be coincidently directed to the same object; squinting, a squint. **b.** *fig.* Perversity of intellectual perception 1844.

Convergent or *internal s.*, a turning inward of the eyes, CROSS-EYE; *divergent* or *external s.*, a turning outward of one or both eyes. Hence **Strabi·smal, Strabi·smic** *adjs.* of, pertaining to, or affected by s. **Strabismometer** (strēɪbizmǫ·mĭtəɹ), an instrument for measuring the degree of s.

Strabotomy (străbǫ·tŏmi). 1857. [– Fr. *strabotomie*, f. *strabisme* STRABISM; see -TOMY.] *Path.* The operation of dividing one or more of the muscles of the eye as a remedy for strabismus.

‖**Stracchino** (strakī·no). 1832. [It.] *S. cheese*, a variety of very soft cheese made in the north of Italy.

Strad (stræd). *colloq.* 1884. Short for STRADIVARIUS.

Straddle (stræ·d'l), *sb.* 1611. [f. next.] **1.** The action of walking, standing, or sitting with the legs wide apart. **b.** The distance between the feet or legs of one who straddles 1864. **2.** *U.S. Exchange slang.* A 'privilege' or speculative contract in any one market or class of commodities giving the holder the right at his option (1) of calling, within a specified number of days, for delivery of an ascertained quantity of the commodity at a stated price, or (2) of delivering to the person to whom the consideration had been paid an ascertained quantity of another (or, less usu., of the same) commodity at a stated price. Hence, applied to an analogous contract on the Stock-exchange. Also called *spread-eagle.* 1883. **3.** *U.S. Politics* (*colloq.*). An attempt to take an equivocal or non-committal position in a party platform 1883. **4.** *Poker.* A doubling of the 'blind' or stake by one of the players 1882.

Straddle (stræ·d'l), *v.* 1565. [alt. of contemp. and synon. *striddle*, back-formation from *striddling*(s astride (XV), f. *strid-* wk. var. of STRIDE *v.*; see -LE.] **1.** *intr.* To spread the legs wide apart in walking, standing, or sitting. **b.** Of the legs: To stand wide apart 1634. **c.** *transf.* of a thing, esp. of a thing having legs; also, to sprawl 1596. **d.** *spec.* Of the spokes of a wheel: To stand with the ends staggered 1875. **2.** To walk with the legs wide apart; *dial.* 'to swagger, strut' 1825. **3.** *trans.* To set (the legs) wide apart (in standing or walking) 1565. **4.** To sit, stand, or walk with one leg on either side of; to stride over; to bestride 1823. **b.** *transf.* To stand or lie across or on both sides of (something) 1890. **5.** *U.S. colloq.* To occupy or take up an equivocal position in regard to; to appear to favour both sides of. Also *intr.* 1884. **6.** *Poker.* To double (a stake, bet). Also *absol.* 1882. **7.** *Gunnery.* To find the range of (an object) by placing shots first on one side of it and then on the other 1916.

4. Straddling a chair..may be pardonable in a bachelor's rooms 1859. **5.** He never straddled the negro question 1884. Hence **Stra·ddling** *ppl. a.* that straddles; *Bot.* divaricate.

Stradiot (stræ·diǫt). 1533. [– It. *stradiotto*; see ESTRADIOT.] *Hist.* = ESTRADIOT.

Stradivarius (strædivēᵊ·riŏs). 1833. [– L. *Stradivarius*, latinized f. the name of Antonio *Stradivari* of Cremona (1649–1737).] A violin or other stringed instrument made by Stradivari or his pupils.

Strafe (strāf), *v. slang.* 1915. [From G. phr. *Gott strafe England* 'God punish England', current as a salutation in Germany in 1914 and the following years.] *trans.* Used (orig. by British soldiers in the war of 1914–18) in various senses: To punish; to do damage to; to attack fiercely; to heap imprecations on. Also *absol.* Hence **Strafe** *sb.* a fierce assault; a period of heavy shell-fire. **Stra·fer.**

Straggle (stræ·g'l), *sb.* 1470. [f. next.] †**1.** Phr. *At, to* (*the*) *s.*, in straggling order. *Sc.* –1549. **2.** A body or group of scattered objects; an irregular or fitful emergence (*of* something) 1865.

Straggle (stræ·g'l), *v.* late ME. [perh. alt. of **strackle*, f. (dial.) *strake* move, go, f. **strak-* of STRETCH; see -LE; for *-gg-* from *-ck-*, *-kk-* cf. *stagger, trigger.*] **1.** *intr.* To wander or stray *from* the proper road, one's companions, etc.; to rove without fixed direction; to go up and down dispersedly. Often conjugated with *be.* **b.** *spec.* of a soldier: To wander from the line of march, stray from one's company. Also of a ship: To stray from the line of battle. Of a sailor: To be absent from his ship without leave or to overstay his leave. 1529. **c.** *transf.* and *fig.* (of persons and things) 1588. **d.** Of a plant, branch, etc.: To grow irregularly or loosely; to spread or shoot too far. Similarly of hair. 1693. **e.** Of inanimate objects: To be arranged dispersedly or irregularly. Of a town, building, etc.: To be built irregularly and without compactness. Of a road, river, fence, etc.: To wind in an irregular course. 1611. **2.** *pass.* To be placed stragglingly. *U.S.* 1898.

1. [They] runne stragling and rouing..from towne to towne 1583. **b.** They sickened or straggled or frankly deserted 1913. **c.** Children.. cannot keep their Minds from straggling LOCKE. **e.** A little hamlet which straggled along the side of a creek SCOTT. Hence **Stra·ggling** *ppl. a.*, **-ly** *adv.*

Straggler (stræ·glǝɹ). 1530. [f. prec. + -ER¹.] **1.** One who wanders or roves without fixed direction; one who strays from his companions or from the regular route; †a gadabout; †a camp-follower, a tramp, vagabond. **2.** *Mil.* A soldier who leaves the line of march or falls out of the ranks. †Also, a scout or skirmisher. 1589. **b.** *Naut.* A sailor who is absent from his ship without leave or who overstays his leave 1670. **3.** An animal that strays from its habitat or companions; esp. a migratory bird found at a place outside its usual range 1552. **4.** A plant, branch, etc., that grows irregularly or shoots too far; also, a plant, fruit, etc., found growing singly or apart from others of its kind. Similarly, a stray lock of hair. 1553.

1. Let's whip these straglers o're the Seas againe SHAKS. The vast pleasure-grounds were cleared of the last s. 1883. **4.** Sometimes his pruning-hook corrects the vines, And the loose stragglers to their ranks confines POPE.

Straggly (stræ·gli), *a.* 1866. [f. STRAGGLE *v.* and *sb.* + -Y¹.] Characterized by straggling.

Straight (strēⁱt), *a.*, *sb.*, and *adv.* [ME. *streȝt*, *straȝt*, pa. pple. of *strecche* STRETCH *v.*] **A.** *adj.* †**1.** As ppl. adj.: Extended at full length –1596. **2.** Not crooked; free from curvature, bending, or angularity ME. **b.** Of a human form, a back: Erect, not crooked or stooping 1599. **c.** Of a limb, etc.: Held with the joint not flexed 1765. **d.** Of hair: Not curly or waved 1748. **e.** *Anat.* The distinctive epithet of certain structures (= mod.L. *rectus*) 1585. **3.** Direct, undeviating. late ME. **b.** *colloq.* Of an utterance: Outspoken, unreserved 1894. **4.** *S. angle.* †**a.** A right angle; **b.** in mod. use, an angle of 180° 1601. **5.** Of conduct: Free from crookedness; honest. Hence used of persons and their attributes. Now *colloq.* 1530. **b.** Of a person: Well-conducted, steady. Chiefly in *to keep s.* Of a woman: Virtuous, chaste. 1868. **6.** Not oblique; either vertical or horizontal. Hence, *a s. eye*: ability to see whether an object is placed straight. 1600. **b.** *Cricket.* Of the bat: Held so as not to incline to either side 1843. **7.** *predic.*: In proper order, not ruffled or disarranged 1831. **b.** *colloq.* Of accounts: Settled up, leaving nothing owing 1613. **c.** Of a person: Having settled one's differences (*with* another); also, having balanced one's account, 'even' 1730. **8.** *U.S.* **a.** Unmixed, undiluted; of spirits, 'neat'. Also qualifying a designation of a political party: Strict, rigid, extreme. 1856. **b.** *S. Poker, Whist*, etc.: the game in its unmodified form. *S. five*: a sequence or rotation of fives. *S. flush*: a sequence of five cards, all of the same suit. 1882. **9.** Of or pertaining to the legitimate drama 1928.

2. And bent the wand that might have growen ful streight 1563. Panicle stiff and s. 1796. *S. line*, a line uniform in direction throughout its length; *Geom.* the shortest distance between two points. **b.** A daughter of our meadows..S., but as lissome as a hazel wand TENNYSON. **3.** Prepare the waye of the Lorde, and make his pathes s. COVERDALE *Luke* 3:4. *The s. tip* (colloq.): see TIP *sb.*⁴ **b.** *S. talk*, a piece of plain speaking. **5.** A s. man, true to his cloth and calling 1893. **6.** *S. play*, play with the bat held s. **7.** Phr. *To keep one's face s.* (colloq.), to refrain from laughing. **8. a.** *To vote the s. ticket* (U.S.), to vote for all the official candidates of one's party.

Comb.: *s.-edged, -legged, -limbed, -veined* adjs.; **s. arch**, an arch having radiating joints but a straight intrados and extrados line; **s. fight**, a direct contest between two candidates; **s. play**, a play in which there is plain dialogue without music, etc.; **-side** *a.*, having straight sides, *spec.* of a pneumatic automobile tyre.

B. quasi-*sb.* and *sb.* **1.** The adj. used *absol.* (quasi-*sb.*) in certain phrases. late ME. **2.** A straight form or position; a level 1645. **3.** A straight portion, e.g. of a racecourse (*the s.*), a railway 1846. **4.** *Geom.* A straight line (*rare*) 1892. **5.** In Poker, etc.: A series of five cards in sequence but not of the same suit 1882.

1. *On the s.*, (*a*) along a straight line, not following irregularities of contour; (*b*) parallel with the side, as opp. to 'on the cross' = diagonally; (*c*) *slang*, behaving reputably. *Out of s.*, deviating from the required s. form or position; not duly rectilinear, level, or perpendicular; awry.

C. *adv.* **1.** In a straight course; directly to or from a place; in a straight line, not crookedly ME. **b.** In a straight direction; directly to a mark or object, or following a moving object without deviation 1535. **c.** With additional notion, which sometimes becomes the substantive sense: All the way, continuously to the end; 'right' *across, through*, etc. 1446. **2.** Immediately, without delay. Now *poet.* or *arch.* ME. **3.** In an erect posture, upright 1535. **4.** Honestly, honourably 1845. **5.** Frankly, outspokenly. Also *s. out.* 1877.

1. We took our way streight to Jerusalem 1687. I cannot write straighter in bed, so you must be content SWIFT. **b.** He..looked this time s. into my eyes 1886. **c.** Apertures..cut s. through a wall 1840. **2.** She burst into tears, and s. quitted the room 1760. *S. away, s. off*, immediately, at once, without deliberation or preparation. **3.** *S. set up*, having an erect figure. **4.** As a rule I believe they [*sc.* jockeys] run very s. 1888. **5.** Speak right s. out and do not be afraid 1877.

Straight (strēⁱt), *v.* late ME. [f. STRAIGHT *a.*] †**1.** *trans.* To stretch (e.g. a body on the rack); to extend, stretch forth (a spear) –1800. **2.** To make straight, straighten. In later use chiefly *Sc.*, to straighten (a stream, a boundary); to lay out (a corpse). 1530.

Strai·ghtaway, *a.* and *sb.* 1874. [phr. *straight away* (STRAIGHT C. 2) used *attrib.*] **A.** *adj.* Of a shot: Aimed at a bird flying 'straight away'. Also said of the bird. Of a ride, a course in rowing or sailing: Continuous in direction and time. **B.** *sb.* A racecourse which is without turn or curve 1895.

Strai·ght-edge. 1812. A narrow strip of hard wood, steel, or brass, with one edge cut perfectly straight, used to test the accuracy of a plane surface, or as a guide for a cutting instrument.

Straighten (strēⁱ·t'n). 1542. [f. STRAIGHT *a.* + -EN⁵.] **1.** *trans.* To make straight (what is bent or crooked). Also with *out.* **2.** To unravel, disentangle, clear up (what is confused or intricate). Now chiefly with *out.* 1577. **3.** To put in order, tidy up 1867. **4.** *intr.* To become straight. *To s. up* (orig. U.S.): to rise to an erect posture; also *slang* to adopt an honest course of life. 1891.

1. The crooked Scythes are streightned into Swords DRYDEN. **3.** I'll send Granny up here to s. things a bit 1901. Hence **Strai·ghtener,** one who or something which straightens.

Straight forth, strai·ghtforth, *adv.* Now *rare.* 1530. [STRAIGHT *adv.*] **1.** Directly in front or onwards. **2.** Immediately, at once 1577.

Straight forward, straightfo·rward, *adv.* and *a.* 1806. [STRAIGHT *adv.*] **A.** *adv.* Directly in front or onwards; in direct order 1809. **B.** *adj.* **1.** Of movement, vision, etc.: Proceeding or directed straight forward 1807. **2.** Of language, narrative, or exposition: Direct, without circumlocution or digression 1806. **3.** Of an action or process: Continuous in one direction, undeviating 1817. **4.** Presenting a clear course; free from difficulties 1833. **5.** Of persons, their dispositions or conduct: Consistent, undeviating in purpose, single-minded. Also (now usu.), free from duplicity or concealment; frank, outspoken. 1834. Hence **Straightfo·rward-ly** *adv.*, **-ness.**

Straight-lined (stress var.), *a.* 1571. Composed of or containing straight lines; having the form of a straight line; rectilinear.

Straightly (strēⁱ·tli), *adv.* late ME. [f. STRAIGHT *a.* + -LY².] **1.** In a straight manner; in a straight line; directly. **2.** Straightway, immediately. *poet.* (*rare*) 1830.

Straightness (strēⁱ·tnės). 1530. [-NESS.] The quality of being straight.

Strai·ght-out, *a.* and *sb.* Chiefly *U.S.* 1840. [attrib. use of the phr. *straight out.*] **A.** *adj.* Unrestrained; going all lengths. In party politics = STRAIGHT *a.* 8. 1856. **B.** *sb.* One who votes a 'straight' party ticket, an uncompromising partisan 1840.

Straightway (strēⁱ·twēⁱ), *adv.* 1461. [f. STRAIGHT *a.* + WAY *sb.*] †**1.** By a direct course –1587. **2.** Immediately; at once. Now only *literary.* 1526.

2. She s. sat down and indited a long letter DICKENS. So **Strai·ghtways** *adv.* (in sense 2). Now *rare* or *Obs.*

Strain (strēⁱn), *sb.*¹ [OE. **strēon* (Northumb. *strīon*), aphetic f. *ġestrēon* = OS., OHG. *gistriuni*, rel. to OE. (*ġe*)*strēonan*, (*ġe*)*strienan* gain, get, beget = OHG. (*gi*)*striunen*, f. Gmc. **streu-* pile up, rel. to L. *strues* pile, heap, *struere* build.] †**I.** Gain, acquisition; treasure –ME. **II.** †**1.** Begetting, generation. ME. only. †**2.** The germinal vesicle in the yoke of an egg –1764. **3.** Offspring, progeny. *Obs.* exc. *arch.* ME. **4.** Pedigree, lineage, ancestry, descent ME. **5.** The descendants of a common ancestor; a race, stock, line ME. **b.** Any one of the various lines of ancestry united in an individual or a family; an admixture of some racial or family element in a genealogy 1863. **6.** A race, breed; a variety developed by breeding 1607. **7.** Inherited character or constitution 1603. **b.** An inherited tendency or quality; hence, in wider sense, an admixture in a character of some quality somewhat contrasting with the rest 1598. **8.** A kind, class, or sort (of persons), as determined by community of character, conduct, or degree of ability. Now *rare.* 1598. **b.** A kind, class, or grade (of things) 1612.

4. Hee is of a noble straine, of approued valour, and confirm'd honesty SHAKS. **5.** Charlemain, And the long Heroes of the Gallic S. PRIOR. **b.** Horses which had any s. of hackney..blood 1897. **6.** Two Kids..Both fleck'd with white, the true Arcadian S. DRYDEN. Begonias, gold medal s. 1908. **7. b.** There was..a s. of insanity in the family 1906. **8.** Thou, who lately of the common s., Wert one of us DRYDEN.

Strain (strēⁱn), *sb.*² late ME. [f. STRAIN *v.*¹] †**I.** A strainer –1655. **II.** Action or result of straining. †**1.** Constraint; compulsion –1648. **2.** A result of straining; an injury done to a limb or part of the body through being forcibly stretched beyond its proper length; often = SPRAIN 1. 1558. **3.** A stretch, extreme degree, height, pitch (of a quality, activity, etc.) Now *rare.* 1576. †**4.** A strained construction or interpretation –1731. **5.** A strong muscular effort; †*spec.* an effort to vomit, a retching; a straining at stool 1590. **b.** Extreme or excessive effort; a straining *at* or *after* some object of attainment 1683. **6.** A forcible stretching of a material thing; force tending to pull asunder or to drag from a position. Later, in wider sense: Force or pressure tending to cause fracture, change of position, or alteration of shape; also, the condition of a body or a particle subjected to such force or pressure 1602. **b.** *Physics.* Any definite change of volume or figure exhibited by a solid or liquid mass 1850. **7.** Pressure or exigency that severely taxes the strength, endurance, or resources of a person or thing, or that imperils the permanence of a feeling, relation, or condition 1853.

3. It is, indeed, a high S. of Generosity in you, to think of making me easy all my Life POPE. **5.** Phr. *At (full, utmost) s., on the s.*, straining, using strong effort; Adonis..spear in hand, with leashed dogs at s. R. BRIDGES. **b.** There shall be strenuousness without s.! 1905. **6.** Table of Breaking Strains 1888. **7.** He had been often driven to borrow money of Sir Ralph..but their friendship had stood the s. 1894. The s. of his responsibility had been too much for him 1897.

III. 1. *Mus.* A definite rhythmical section of a piece of music, divided from what follows by a double bar 1575. **2.** In wider sense, a musical sequence of sounds; a melody, tune; often *collect. pl.* 1579. **b.** *transf.* A passage of song or poetry 1563. †**c.** A stream or flow of impassioned or ungoverned language –1742. **3.** Tone, style, or turn of expression; tone or character of feeling expressed; tenor, drift, character, or general tendency (of a composition or discourse) 1622.

2. That s. I heard was of a higher mood MILT. **b.** Till old experience do attain To something like Prophetic s. MILT. **c.** The Strains of ancient

Eloquence HUME. 3. But his letters to England were in a very different s. MACAULAY.

Strain (strē^{i}n), *v.*^{1} [ME. *streyne, strayne* – OFr. *estrei(g)n-*, stem of *estreindre* (mod. *étreindre*) :– L. *stringere* draw tight, bind tightly.] **I.** To bind tightly; to clasp, squeeze. †**1.** *trans.* To bind fast; to confine in bonds –1532. **b.** To fasten, attach firmly. *Obs.* exc. (*rarely*) with the sense: To attach by compulsion. late ME. **2.** To clasp tightly in one's arms. *Obs.* exc. as in b. late ME. **b.** esp. *to s.* (a person) *to one's bosom, heart*, and the like 1789. **3.** To clasp tightly in the hand. *Obs.* or *arch.* 1518. †**b.** Of a bird (esp. a hawk) or beast: To seize (its prey) in its claws. Chiefly *absol.* –1596. **4.** To constrict painfully, as with an encircling cord. late ME. †**5.** To press hard upon, afflict, distress –1730. †**6.** To bridle, control, restrain –1595. †**7.** To force, press, constrain (*to* a condition or action) –1603. †**b.** To urge, insist upon (a thing). Also *absol.* –1604. †**8.** To extract (liquor or juice) by pressure; to squeeze out. Also *intr.* Of a juice: To exude. –1781. †**b.** To extort (money, confessions, etc.) –1699.

2. *Hen. VIII*, IV. i. 46. **3.** The one in hand an yron whip did strayne, The other brandished a bloudy knife SPENSER. **4.** Was it..For this with fillets [you] strain'd your tender head? POPE. **7.** *John* III. iii. 46. **8.** The Bard..strains, from hard-bound brains, eight lines a year POPE. **b.** The quality of mercy is not strain'd SHAKS.

II. To tighten, draw tight, stretch. **1.** To extend with some effort; to subject to tension, to stretch ME. **b.** To tighten up (the strings of a musical instrument) so as to raise the pitch. Also with *up*. late ME. **2.** *fig.* **a.** To force the meaning or sense of (words, an ordinance, decree, etc.) 1449. **b.** To transgress the strict requirements of (one's conscience), to violate the spirit of (one's oath) 1592. **c.** To force (prerogative, power, etc.) beyond its legitimate extent or scope 1605. †**d.** To apply or use (a thing) beyond its province –1647. **e.** *To s. a point*: to exceed one's usual limits of procedure; to do more than one is bound to do or go further than one is entitled to go in a matter 1596. †**f.** To insist upon unduly –1711. †**g.** To raise to an extreme degree –1697. **h.** To raise to a high state of emotional tension 1667. **i.** To make excessive demands upon, tax severely (resources, credit, friendship, etc.) 1609. **3.** To stretch (sinews, nerves, muscles) beyond the normal degree (as the supposed condition of intense exertion); hence, to force to the utmost (one's limbs, organs, powers) 1446. **4.** To injure or alter by excessive tension 1612.

1. There may be danger in straining too strongly the bonds of government BURKE. The barbed wire fence..was strained to posts..6 ft. high 1893. **2. a.** Defective laws should be altered by the legislature, and not strained by the tribunals MACAULAY. **c.** The Crown retains prerogatives at present which would be fatal to it if strained 1883. **d.** *Much Ado* IV. i. 254. **i.** The King had strained his private credit in Holland to procure bread for his army MACAULAY. **3.** Phr. *To s. every nerve* (fig.), to use one's utmost endeavours. **4.** I have strained the thumb of my left hand with pulling him SWIFT. The ship had strained herself a good deal, owing to the heavy cargo of railway-iron she had stowed in her hold 1868.

III. To press through a filtering medium, to filter. **1.** To press (a liquid) through a porous or perforated medium so as to keep back the denser portions or the solid matter held in suspension; to free (solid matter) from the contained or accompanying liquid by this process; to purify or refine by filtration. Also *absol.* late ME. **b.** To remove (liquid) by filtration, drain off 1558. ¶**c.** To take out (something) from a liquid by straining 1526. **2.** *intr.* for *refl.* To filter; to trickle 1588.

1. *fig. Tr. & Cr.* IV. v. 169. **c.** Ye blinde gydes which strayne out a gnat and swalowe a cammyll TINDALE *Matt.* 23:24. **2.** The Sea water passing or Strayning through the Sandes, leaueth the Saltnesse BACON.

IV. 1. *refl.* To exert oneself physically. In later use, to exert oneself so as to be in danger of injury. Now *rare* or *Obs.* late ME. **2.** *intr.* To make violent and continuous physical effort ME. **b.** *transf.* of a thing viewed as endowed with power to make effort 1819. **c.** To pull forcibly (*at* a rope, leash, rein) 1791. **3.** *intr.* To use one's utmost endeavours; to strive vigorously 1593. **4.** †**a.** To retch, make efforts to vomit –1727. **b.** To make efforts to evacuate the bowels; more fully *to s. at stool* 1645. **5.** *To s. at*: to make a difficulty of 'swallowing' or accepting (something); to scruple at 1609. (This use is due to misunderstanding of the phr. 'strain at a gnat' meaning properly 'which strain the liquor if they find a gnat in it', in Matt. 23:24.)

2. The patience with which he had seen a boatman on a canal s. against an adverse eddy MACAULAY. **b.** The wind sung, cordage strain'd, and sailors swore BYRON. **3.** Straining after novelty 1797.

†**V. a.** *trans.* To use (the voice) in song; to play upon (an instrument) –1648. **b.** To utter in song –1648. **c.** *intr.* To sing –1612.

b. It is the Larke that sings so out of tune, Straining harsh Discords, and vnpleasing Sharpes SHAKS. Hence †**Strai·nable** *a.* coercive, compulsive; violent, exerting great force (chiefly of wind and weather).

†**Strain,** *v.*^{2} 1450. [Aphetic f. DISTRAIN *v.*] *Law.* = DISTRAIN *v.* II. 1–3. –1718.

Strained (strē^{i}nd), *ppl. a.* late ME. [f. STRAIN *v.*^{1} + -ED^1.] In the senses of the verb: Subjected to physical tension; done or produced under compulsion or by an abnormal effort; of conduct, demeanour, etc., artificial, forced, not spontaneous or natural; of language, etc., wrested or distorted from the natural meaning or intention; pressed, forced; injured by over-exertion or excessive tension, etc.

S. ropes 1640. A strange, and very..strained interpretation HOBBES. A s. and powerful voice SCOTT. The s., eye-shirking talk at dinner KIPLING. Hence **Strai·ned-ly** *adv.*, **-ness.**

Strainer (strē^i·nəɹ). ME. [f. STRAIN *v.*^{1} + -ER^1.] A utensil or device for straining, filtering, or sifting; a filter, sieve, or the like. **b.** Applied to natural structures or processes which perform the function of filtering 1626. **2.** A device for stretching or tightening 1527.

Straining (strē^i·niŋ), *vbl. sb.* ME. [f. STRAIN *v.*^{1} + -ING^1.] **1.** The action of the verb, in various senses. **2.** *concr.* Something strained or extracted by straining; usu. a strained liquor 1580.

attrib. and *Comb.*: **s.-arch**, an arch designed to resist end-thrust; **-beam, piece,** a piece of timber placed between *queen-posts*, at their upper ends, to withstand the thrust of the principal rafters.

Straint (strē^{i}nt). *rare.* 1534. [Aphetic – OFr. *estrainte, estreinte* (mod. *étreinte*), f. *estreindre* STRAIN *v.*^{1}] Application of force or pressure.

Strait (strē^{i}t), *a.*, *sb.*, and *adv.* [ME. *streit*, aphetic – OFr. *estreit* tight, close, narrow, sb. narrow place, strait of the sea, distress :– L. *strictus* STRICT. The var. forms show confusion with *streȝt* STRAIGHT at an early date.] **A.** *adj.* **I.** Tight, narrow. **1.** Of a garment, etc.: Tight-fitting *Obs. exc. dial.* **2.** Affording little room; narrow. Of bounds, limits: narrow. Now *rare* exc. in *too s.* ME. **b.** Of a place of confinement 1460. **3.** Of a way, passage, or channel: So narrow as to make transit difficult. Now *rare* in lit. sense. ME.

2. Myn hous is streit CHAUCER. **3.** The s. passe was damn'd With dead men SHAKS. *fig.* Entre ȝe bi the streyt ȝate WYCLIF *Matt.* 7:13.

Special collocations: **s. jacket** *sb.* and *v.* = STRAIT WAISTCOAT *sb.* and *v.*; **s. work,** the system of getting coal by headings or narrow work.

II. †**1.** Strict, rigorous (of conditions, sufferings, of modes of living, a religious order, etc.) –1642. †**2.** Of a person, an agent: Severe, strict, exacting in actions or dealings –1612. **b.** Strict or scrupulous in morality or religious observance. *arch.* 1526. **3.** Of a commandment, law, penalty, vow: Stringent, allowing no evasion. *Obs.* exc. *arch.* late ME. **4.** †**a.** Of actions, proceedings: Conducted with strictness –1599. **b.** Of guard, watch, imprisonment: Rigorous, strict. Now *rare.* late ME.

1. The streit administration of Justice 1550. Neither let them keepe any straight Diette 1582. **2.** His Creditors most straite SHAKS. **b.** After the most straytest secte of oure laye lived I a pharisaye TINDALE *Acts* 26:5. **3.** His..s. charge to all posteritie, that one man should cleaue to one wife 1612. **4. a.** S. inquisition and search is made 1599.

III. 1. Of fortune, circumstances, etc.: Limited (so as to cause hardship or inconvenience). *arch.* †**2.** Strictly specified, exact, precise, definite –1638. **3.** Of friendship, alliance, etc.: Close, intimate. Now *rare.* 1530. †**4.** Reluctant and chary in giving; close, stingy; narrow –1760.

1. My wages been ful streite and ful smale CHAUCER. **4.** I begge cold comfort, and you are so straight.., you deny me that SHAKS.

B. *sb.* **1.** A narrow confined place or space or way generally. Now *rare* or *Obs.* ME. **2.** *fig.* A narrow or tight place; a time of sore need or of awkward or straitened circumstances; a difficulty or fix. Now *rare* in *sing.*; still common in *pl.* 1544. **b.** occas. in generalized sense: Privation, hardship 1837. **3.** A comparatively narrow water-way or passage connecting two large bodies of water. (As a geographical proper name, usu. *pl.* with sing. sense.) late ME. **b.** *pl.* Short for *Straits Settlements*, the British possessions in the Malay peninsula collectively, so named because near the Straits of Malacca 1884. †**4.** A narrow pass or gorge between mountains; a defile, ravine –1778. **5.** *poet.* An isthmus. Now *rare.* 1562. **6.** A narrow part (of a river); *pl.* 'narrows'. Now *rare* or *Obs.* late ME. †**7.** A narrow lane, alley, or passage –1622. **8.** The narrow part (of anything tubular); a narrow passage in the body 1558. †**9.** *pl.* Cloth of single width, as opp. to BROADCLOTH –1706.

1. He brought him through a darksome narrow s. To a broad gate SPENSER. **2.** He keept them in great straits for money 1756. Take me: I'll serve you better in a s. TENNYSON. **3.** They returned home by the pillars and streights of Hercules.. called now the straights of Gybralter RALEGH. *transf.* Where the scattered stars are seen In hazy straits the clouds between WORDSW. *The Straits*, in 17–18th c. usu. = the Straits of Gibraltar; now chiefly = the Straits of Malacca. **4.** The streight of Thermopilæ 1753. **5.** A chapel..That stood on a dark s. of barren land TENNYSON.

C. *adv.* **1.** Tightly. *Obs.* exc. *dial.* ME. †**2.** Close; with narrow opening –1641. †**3.** In strait or careful keeping, securely; in strict custody –1611. **4.** Severely, oppressively; so as to cause hardship. Now *rare.* ME. †**5.** With strictness –1590.

†**Strait,** *v.* ME. [f. STRAIT *a.*] **1.** *trans.* As tr. Vulg. *coartare, artare*, to press together, contract. –late ME. **2.** To narrow –1615. **3.** To shut up in or force into a narrow space –1641. **b.** To bring into straits, subject to hardship –1654. **c.** *pass.* To be hard put to it, to be at a loss –1647. **4.** To restrict; to keep ill supplied, stint –1669.

Straiten (strē^i·t'n), *v.* 1523. [f. STRAIT *a.* + -EN^5; superseding prec.] **1.** *trans.* To render strait or narrow; to narrow, contract (an opening, a passage, road, stream, etc.). Now somewhat *rare.* 1552. **2.** *intr.* To become narrow, to narrow 1601. †**3.** *trans.* To tighten (a knot, cord, bonds) –1742. †**b.** To render more strict or rigorous –1753. **4.** To confine in or force into a narrow space; to hem in closely. Now *rare.* 1570. **5.** To narrow or restrict the freedom, power, or privileges of (now *arch.*); to narrow in range, scope, or amount 1586. †**b.** To abridge *of* (a possession or privilege) –1647. **6.** To reduce to straits; to subject to privation, hardship, or distress 1611. **b.** To inconvenience by insufficiency of something specified (as time, space, supplies of any kind). Now only in *pass.* (somewhat *arch.*). 1620. **c.** To render short of money or supplies 1699. †**7.** To hamper, impede in action –1726.

1. An ancient grant..that a way leading to their common should not be streightened COKE. **4.** Waters, when they..are straitned (as in the falls of Bridges;)..giue a Roaring Noise BACON. If this be our condition, thus to dwell In narrow circuit strait'nd by a Foe MILT. **5.** Is the Spirit of the Lord straitned? *Micah* 2:7. They had no design to s. the rights of the Holy See 1855. **6.** The siege and straitnesse, wherewith their enemies..shall s. them *Jer.* 19:9. **c.** If straitened for provisions, they ate the chargers which carried them to battle J. H. NEWMAN. Often in pa. pples., esp. *straitened circumstances.*

Strait-lace, *v.* 1636. [Back-formation from next.] *trans.* and *intr.* (for *refl.*) To lace tightly, confine.

Strait-laced (strē^{i}t,lē^{i}st; stress var.), *a.* 1546. [f. STRAIT *adv.* + LACED *ppl. a.*] †**1.** Wearing stays or bodice tightly laced –1698. **2.** *fig.* †**a.** Of things: Narrow in range or scope –1686. †**b.** Of persons: Shut up within oneself, uncommunicative, morose –1691. †**c.** Obstinate; grudging in gifts or concessions –1601. **d.** Of persons, their habits, opinions, etc.: Excessively rigid or scrupulous in matters of conduct; over-precise; prudish 1554.

1. We should as certainly have no perfect children born, as we have few well-shaped that are strait-laced LOCKE. **2. d.** Had these strait-lac'd Gentlemen once gain'd their Point against Plays 1707.

Straitly (strē̍·tli), *adv.* ME. [f. STRAIT *a.* + -LY[2].] **1.** Tightly. *Obs.* exc. *arch.* **2.** Narrowly; within narrow limits. late ME. **3.** Strictly, rigorously, stringently (now only *arch.* with respect to commands, questions, etc.) ME. **4.** With ref. to alliance or union: Closely, intimately. *arch.* 1480.

Straitness ((strē̍·tnės). ME. [f. STRAIT *a.* + -NESS.] **1.** The quality of being strait; *esp.* straitened condition (of circumstances). late ME. †**2.** Want of room –1775. **3.** Hardship, distress. privation, straitened circumstances. *arch.* ME.

Strait waistcoat, *sb.* 1753. A garment for the upper part of the body with or without sleeves, made of strong material and admitting of being tightly laced, used for the restraint of violent lunatics or prisoners and sometimes as a means of punishment. Hence **Strait-waistcoat** *v. trans.* to confine in a strait waistcoat.

Strake (strēⁱk), *sb.*[1] [ME. *strake* (in AL. *stracus, straca* XIII), prob. f. **strak-*, base of OE. *streććan* STRETCH *v.*; from XVI largely coincident in form and meaning with *streak.*] **1.** A section of the iron rim of a cart-wheel. **2.** A stripe of different colour from the rest of the surface of which it forms part. late ME. **3.** *Naut.* Each of the several continuous lines of planking or plates, of uniform breadth, in the side of a vessel, extending from stem to stern. Hence, the breadth of a plank used as a unit of vertical measurement in a ship's side. late ME. **4.** A stretch of ground travelled over. Also, length of stride; pace. Now *dial.* 1558.

2. Alabaster is a white stone with strakes of diuerse coloure TREVISA. **3.** *Garboard s.*: see GARBOARD.

Strake (strēⁱk), *sb.*[2] 1758. [Same word as prec., prob. orig. applied in pl. to the lining boards.] *Mining.* **a.** A shallow pit for the purpose of washing ore. **b.** A wooden box without ends, used for the same purpose 1860. **c.** *Gold-mining.* An apparatus for concentrating the stamped ore 1887.

†**Strake** (strēⁱk), *v.*[1] 1537. [f. STRAKE *sb.*[1]] *trans.* To mark with lines, to streak –1718.

Strake (strēⁱk), *v.*[2] 1778. [f. STRAKE *sb.*[2]] *Mining. trans.* To wash (ore) in a strake. Also *Gold mining,* to concentrate (ore) by means of strakes.

Stramash (strămæ·ʃ), *sb.* Chiefly *Sc.* 1819. [Belongs to next.] **1.** An uproar, state of noise and confusion; a 'row' 1821. **2.** A state of ruin, a smash 1819.

Stramash (strămæ·ʃ), *v. dial.* 1788. [app. imit.; cf. SMASH.] *trans.* To smash.

Stramineous (strămi·niǝs), *a.* 1621. [f. L. *stramineus* (f. *stramen* straw) + -OUS.] **1.** Consisting of or relating to straw; *fig.* valueless. **2.** *Bot.* Straw-coloured; dull pale yellow 1845.

Stramonium (strămōᵘ·niǝm). 1677. [– mod.L. *stramonium* (Parkinson, 1629), *strammonium* (F. Columna, 1592), perh. alt. of Tartar *turman* medicine for horses (whence Russ. *durmán* stramonium).] **1.** The solanaceous plant *Datura stramonium,* the THORN-APPLE. **2.** A narcotic drug prepared from this plant 1802.

Stramony (stræ·mŏni). 1842. Anglicized form of prec.

Strand (strænd), *sb.*[1] [OE. *strand* = MLG. *strant, -nd-* (whence Du., G. *strand*), ON. *strǫnd*; of unkn. origin.] The land bordering a sea, lake, or †river; in a more restricted sense, that part of a shore which lies between the tide-marks; sometimes vaguely, coast, shore. Now *poet., arch.,* or *dial.* †**b.** A quay, wharf, or landing-place by the side of navigable water –1859. **c.** Used vaguely for country, region, esp. a foreign country. Chiefly *poet.* late ME.

On the bare s. Upon the sea-mark a small boat did wait SHELLEY. *The Strand,* a street in London, orig. so called as occupying the 'strand' or shore of the Thames between the cities of London and Westminster. **c.** Let Freedom and Peace flee far To a sunnier s. SHELLEY.

Comb.: **s. fishery,** a coast fishery pursued from the shore.

Strand (strænd), *sb.*[2] 1497. [Of unkn. origin.] **1.** Each of the strings or yarns which when twisted together or 'laid' form a rope, line, cord, or cable. Also, a ply (of worsted). *dial.* **b.** Each of the lengths of twisted wire used to form a wire-rope, cable, or electric conductor 1860. **2.** Each of the threads or strips of a woven material; hence, a thread or strip drawn from such material 1802. **3.** *transf.* A tress or filament of hair 1870. **b.** A thread or filament in animal or vegetable structure 1877.

1. A Cabell is a three-s. Roape 1644. *fig.* The dusky s. of Death inwoven here With dear Love's tie TENNYSON.

Strand (strænd), *v.*[1] 1621. [f. STRAND *sb.*[1]] **1.** *trans.* To drive or force aground on a shore, esp. on the sea-shore; also *rarely* of a river, to leave aground (by the ebbing of the tide). **2.** *transf.* and *fig.* Chiefly *pass.* 1837. **3.** *intr.* To run aground 1687.

1. The vessel was stranded in a gale 1843. **2.** I am left utterly stranded and alone in life RUSKIN.

Strand (strænd), *v.*[2] 1780. [f. STRAND *sb.*[2]] **1.** *intr.* Of a rope: To break one or more of its strands. Also *trans.,* to break one or more of the strands of (a rope). **2.** *trans.* To form (a rope) by the twisting of strands 1886. **3.** To insert a strand or filament in (a texture); also *absol.* 1895.

3. Time..has..stranded her..hair with grey 1914.

Strange (strēⁱnᵈʒ), *a.* ME. [Aphetic – OFr. *estrange* (mod. *étrange*) :– L. *extraneus* EXTRANEOUS. Cf. ESTRANGE *a.*] †**1.** Of persons, language, customs, etc.: Of or belonging to another country; foreign, alien –1755. †**b.** Of a country, etc.: Situated outside one's own land –1722. **2.** Belonging to some other place or neighborhood; unknown to the particular locality specified or implied. Of a place or locality: Other than one's own. ME. †**3.** Belonging to others; not of one's own kin or family –1533. **4.** *S. woman,* a harlot 1535. †**5.** Added or introduced from outside, adventitious, external –1672. **6.** Unknown, unfamiliar; not known, met with, or experienced before ME. **7.** Exceptionally great (in degree, amount, intensity, etc.), extreme. late ME. **8.** Unfamiliar, abnormal, or exceptional to a degree that excites wonder or astonishment; queer, surprising, unaccountable. late ME. **b.** quasi-*int.* 'An expression of wonder' (J): an elliptical expression for *it is strange* 1670. †**9.** Of persons: **a.** Unfriendly; having the feelings alienated. **b.** Distant or cold in demeanour; reserved; not affable, familiar, or encouraging. –1763. **10.** Of a person: Unfamiliar or unacquainted with something (specified or implied); fresh *to*; unpractised or unskilled *at* 1561.

1. Ancient Bards, and Poets in s. toungs 1621. **b.** And Palmeres for to seken straunge strondes CHAUCER. **2.** A s. Dog happens to pass through a Flesh-Market SWIFT. **5.** Cleanse the Wound first from all s. Bodies 1672. **6.** Among new men, s. faces, other minds TENNYSON. **7.** Taking Devilish long Strides, and shuffling along at a s. Rate DE FOE. **8.** 'Tis s.—but true; for truth is always s.; Stranger than fiction BYRON. Phr. *S. to say,* etc., used parenthetically. **9.** I should haue beene more s., I must confesse SHAKS. Phr. †*To look s.,* to look at a person as if one did not know him. **10.** I am..As s. vnto your towne, as to your talke SHAKS. [I] am s. to the work 1911.

Phrases †*To make (it) s.,* to make difficulties, be unwilling; to be distant or unfriendly; to affect coyness; to pretend not to understand; to affect or feel surprise, dislike. indignation, etc. Const. *of* (=about) a matter, etc.; *to* (do something); also *to make s. at.*

Strange, *v.* late ME. [Aphetic – OFr. *estrangier* ESTRANGE *v.*] †**1.** = ESTRANGE *v.,* in various senses –1715. **2.** To be surprised, wonder. *Obs.* or *dial.*

Strangely (strē̍·nᵈʒli), *adv.* late ME. [f. STRANGE *a.* + -LY[2].] †**1.** In an unfriendly or unfavourable manner; coldly, distantly –1707. †**2.** In an uncommon or exceptional degree; very greatly, extremely –1719. **3.** Surprisingly, unaccountably, oddly 1450.

1. Look not s. upon him because he differs from thee in some opinions 1707. **2.** Hee was straungely importunate with me to give him leave to goe 1618. **3.** They vanish'd s. SHAKS. This fellow runs s. in my head SHERIDAN. So **Stra·ngeness,** the quality of being strange; quasi-*concr.* something strange; a strange circumstance, object, event, or the like.

Stranger (strē̍·ndʒǝɹ), *sb.* (and *a.*) late ME. [Aphetic – OFr. *estrangier* (mod. *étranger*) :– Rom. **extranearius,* f. L. *extraneus*; see STRANGE *a.,* -ER[2] 2.] **1.** One who belongs to another country, a foreigner; chiefly, (now exclusively), one who resides in or comes to a country to which he is a foreigner; an alien. Now somewhat *rare.* †**b.** Something that comes from abroad; *esp.* an exotic plant –1732. **2.** One who is not a native of, or who has not long resided in, a country, town, or place 1447. **3.** A guest or visitor, in contradistinction to the members of the household. Now chiefly with mixture of sense 4. late ME. **b.** Any of the things which are popularly imagined to forebode the coming of an unexpected visitor, e.g. a floating tea-leaf in the cup; a piece of soot flapping on the bar in the grate 1838. **4.** An unknown person; also, a person with whom one is not yet well acquainted. late ME. **b.** Said playfully of a newborn child 1829. **c.** *vocatively.* (formerly, in rustic use in the U.S., the customary mode of address to one whose name is unknown.) 1817. **d.** Predicatively, said of one whose visits have long ceased 1530. **5.** A non-member of a society. Now *rare.* late ME. **b.** *Parliament.* One who is not a member or official of the House, and is present at its debates only on sufferance 1809. **6.** A person not of one's kin; more fully, *s. in blood.* Also, a person unconnected by ties of friendship or the like. 1535. **7.** *Law.* One not privy or party *to* an act. Also, one not standing towards another in some relation implied in the context. 1543. †**8.** Something alien (*to* a class, the nature of a thing, a person's character, etc.) –1838. **9.** Predicatively, *a s. to* — : Unacquainted with, ignorant of 1697. **10.** *attrib.,* passing into *adj.* **a.** That is a stranger (in senses 1–5). Often hyphened. late ME. **b.** Pertaining to a stranger or strangers; also, situated abroad; foreign 1593. **c.** Not one's own (or its own); alien (*rare*) 1577.

1. In a generation or two the s. ceased to be a s. The foreign spoiler..insensibly changed into the son of the soil FREEMAN. **2.** I cannot show you the way, for I am almost a s. here 1794. **3.** Phr. *To make a s. of,* to treat with ceremony, not as one of the family. **4.** The Duke..hath known you but three dayes, and already you are no s. SHAKS. Phr. *A perfect, a total, an utter s.* **d.** I am surprized to see you, you have been so long a S. DE FOE. **5. b.** *I spy strangers,* the formula used by a member in demanding the expulsion of strangers from the House. **6.** To be told..that henceforth they must be for ever strangers 1860. **7.** No man ought to be bound by proceedings to which he was a s. 1842. **8.** *Macb.* IV. iii. 125. **9.** They are strangers to all discipline 1796. **10. a.** What think'st thou of our s. guest? SCOTT. **b.** You cousin Herford..Shall..tread the s. pathes of banishment SHAKS. **c.** The roofs, that heard our earliest cry, Will shelter one of s. race TENNYSON. Hence **Stra·nger** *v. trans.* †To make a stranger of, alienate; to make strange.

Strangle (stræ·ŋg'l), *sb.* late ME. [f. next.] †**1.** The action of strangling: strangulation –1641. **2.** = *strangle-hold* 1890.

Comb.: **s.-hold** *Wrestling,* a hold which stops the adversary's breath; also *fig.*

Strangle (stræ·ŋg'l), *v.* ME. [Aphetic – OFr. *estrangler* (mod. *étrangler*) – L. *strangulare* – Gr. στραγγαλᾶν, rel. to στραγγάλη halter, cogn. with στραγγός twisted.] **1.** *trans.* To kill by external compression of the throat, esp. by means of a rope or the like passed round the neck. **b.** To constrict painfully (the neck or throat) 1450. **2.** In wider sense: To kill by stoppage of breath; to smother, suffocate, choke. Now *rare.* ME. †**b.** To kill by poison or the like; *rarely,* by the sword –1607. †**c.** said of a wild beast, a devil –1751. **3.** *transf.* To choke, hinder the growth of (a plant) by crowding; to impede the action of (an internal bodily organ) by compression; to suppress (a laugh, a yawn). late ME. **b.** *fig.* To prevent the growth or rise of; to hamper or destroy by excessive restrictions; to suppress 1611. **4.** *intr.* To be choked or suffocated ME.

1. He strangles Alexius with the Bowstring 1663. *fig.* They would be eager to s. this insurrection in the birth 1870. **2.** Shall I not then be stifled in the Vault?..And there die strangled ere my Romeo comes SHAKS. **c.** The lyon wold haue strangled hym CAXTON. **3. b.** Her surest way to s. thought MEREDITH. **4.** He came down..strangling in a tight, cross-barred cravat THACKERAY. Hence **Stra·ngler,** one who or something which strangles.

Strangles (stræ·ŋg'lz), *sb. pl.* 1600. [orig. pl. of STRANGLE *sb.*] †**1.** = STRANGULLION 1. –1686. **2.** An infectious febrile disease of equine animals, caused by the bacterium *Streptococcus equi* 1706.

Strangulate (stræ·ŋgiŭlĕt), *a.* 1866. [– L. *strangulatus*, pa. pple. of *strangulare*; see next, -ATE².] *Bot.* = STRANGULATED *ppl. a.* 3.

Strangulate (stræ·ŋgiŭleᶦt), *v.* 1665. [– *strangulat-*, pa. ppl. stem of L. *strangulare*; see STRANGLE *v.*, -ATE³.] †**1.** *trans.* To choke, stifle, suffocate. **2.** *Path.* and *Surg.* To constrict or compress (an organ, duct, etc.) so as to prevent circulation or the passage of fluid; to remove (a growth) by constricting it with a ligature 1771. **b.** To choke (a plant); to prevent the flow of sap in (a tree) 1835. **3.** = STRANGLE *v.* (*rare*) 1829.

Strangulated (stræ·ŋgiŭleᶦtėd), *ppl. a.* 1771. [f. prec. + -ED¹.] **1.** *Path.* and *Surg.* Of a vessel, an intestine: Congested by constriction and the arrest of circulation. **2.** *Ent.* Of the head, abdomen, or thorax of an insect: Constricted or greatly narrowed 1819. **3.** *Bot.* Of a plant-stem: Contracted by or as if by a ligature 1849.

1. *S. hernia*, a hernia so constricted that the circulation in the protruded part is arrested.

Strangulation (stræŋgiŭlēᶦ·ʃən). 1542. [– L. *strangulatio*, *-ōn-*, f. *strangulat-*; see STRANGULATE *v.*, -ION.] The action or process of strangling; the condition of being strangled. **2.** *Path.* and *Surg.* Constriction (of a bodily organ, duct, etc.) so as to stop circulation or the passage of fluids 1749. **3.** *transf.* Excessive constriction of a channel or passage 1882. **4.** *concr.* A strangulated part; a constriction. *spec.* in *Nat. Hist.* 1828. So **Stra·ngulative** *a.*, that strangles.

Strangullion (stræŋgɒ·lyən). 1481. [– OFr. (*e*)*stranguillon* (mod. *étranguillon*) – It. *stranguglione* :– Rom. **strangulio*, *-ōn-*, f. L. *strangulare* STRANGLE *v.*] **1.** A disease of horses, characterized by inflammation and swelling of the glands of the throat. †¶ **2.** Used incorrectly for STRANGURY –1678.

Strangurious (stræŋgiūᵊ·riəs), *a.* 1733. [– late L. *stranguriosus*; see next, -OUS.] Of, pertaining to, or characteristic of strangury; affected with strangury.

Strangury (stræ·ŋgiŭri). late ME. [– L. *stranguria* – Gr. στραγγουρία, f. στράγξ, στραγγ- drop squeezed out + οὖρον urine; see -Y³.] **1.** A disease of the urinary organs characterized by slow and painful emission of urine; also the condition of slow and painful urination. ¶**2.** Erroneously taken to mean a disease due to strangling or choking; chiefly *fig.* 1698.

Strany (stræ·ni). *local.* 1804. [Of unkn. origin.] The Common Guillemot.

Strap (stræp), *sb.* 1573. [dial. form of STROP *sb.*] **1.** A leather band, thong; in recent use, a flat band or strip of leather or other material of uniform breadth used for securing, holding together, etc. 1685. **b.** as used for flogging. Hence, the application of the strap as an instrument of punishment. 1710. **2.** *Naut.* = STROP *sb.* 2. 1625. **3.** A narrow strip of leather, cloth, or other material fitted with a buckle as a fastening and for adjustment 1688. **4. a.** A short band formerly attached to the bottom of each leg of a pair of pantaloons or trousers passing from side to side under the instep of the boot. Now used on leggings, regimental trousers, etc. Chiefly *pl.* 1837. **b.** = SHOULDER-STRAP 2. 1802. **5.** A looped band of leather for a particular use, e.g. to draw a boot on, to steady oneself in a moving vehicle, etc. 1601. **6.** *Mech.* = BAND *sb.*² 6. 1790. **7.** A razor-strop. *Obs.* exc. *dial.* 1758. **8.** A narrow band of iron or other metal used in the form of a plate, loop, or ring for fastening a thing in position, holding together timbers, parts of machinery, etc. 1620. **9.** A projection on a metal article, narrowed and flattened for screwing down to a wooden surface or for slipping under a metal plate; esp. each or one of the leaves of a strap-hinge 1831. **10.** *Bot.* **a.** An appendage to the leaf in some grasses. **b.** = LIGULE. 1796. **11.** *Anglo-Ir.* A term of abuse applied to a woman or girl 1812. **12.** *slang.* Credit, trust. Phr. *on* (*the*) *s.* 1828.

1. b. A lively Cobler, that..had scarce passed a Day in his Life without giving her the Discipline of the S. ADDISON.

Comb.: **s.-bolt** *sb.*, a bolt with a flattened end for screwing down to a surface; *v. trans.*, to fasten *down* with a s.-bolt; **s. brake,** a brake consisting of a friction s. applied to a cylindrical bearing surface; esp. a dynamometer brake on this plan; **straphanger,** *slang* or *colloq.*, a passenger who is compelled to stand and hold on by the s. in a full omnibus, etc.; so **s.-hang** *v. intr.*; **s. hinge,** a hinge with long leaves or flaps for screwing down to a surface; also, a hinge with one leaf lengthened for insertion into an iron plate; **-oil,** *slang*, flogging with a strap; **-rail** *U.S.*, a flat railroad rail laid upon a continuous longitudinal sleeper; hence **s. railroad, railway, road** *U.S.*, a railroad constructed with s.-rails; **-worm,** a cestoid worm of the family *Ligulidæ*.

Strap (stræp), *v.* 1711. [f. prec.] **1.** *trans.* To furnish with a strap; to fasten, bind, or secure with a strap or with straps. **b.** *Surg.* To apply straps of adhesive plaster to (a wound, etc.); to fasten (dressing) *on* with plaster; *to s. up*, to dress and bandage (a wound or a person, *i.e.* his wound) 1843. **c.** To fasten, bind, or secure (a strap) tightly 1818. **2.** To beat with a strap or leather thong 1735. **3.** = STROP *v.* Now *rare* or *Obs.* 1785. **4.** *intr.* To work closely and energetically (*at* a task); to buckle *to* one's work (*slang*) 1823. **5.** *trans.* To groom (a horse) 1854.

‖**Strapontin** (strapoṅtæṅ). 1926. [Fr.] A bracket seat, such as are used in carriages and cars; also, a similar seat used in playhouses.

Strappado (străpēᶦ·do, -ā·do), *sb. Obs.* exc. *Hist.* 1560. [– Fr. *strapade*, *estrapade* – It. *strappata*, f. *strappare* drag, snatch; see -ADO.] **1.** A form of punishment or of torture to extort confession in which the victim's hands were tied across his back and secured to a pulley; he was then hoisted from the ground and let down half way with a jerk; also, an application of this punishment or torture; also, the instrument used. ¶**2.** Erron. taken to mean 'chastisement by blows' (J.) 1668.

2. He gave me the s. on my shoulders, and the bastinado on the soles of my feet BICKERSTAFFE. Hence †**Strappa·do** *v. trans.* to torture or punish with the s.

Strapper (stræ·pəɹ). 1675. [f. STRAP *v.* + -ER¹.] **1.** A 'strapping' person. (Chiefly applied to women.) **2.** One who grooms horses 1828. **3.** *slang.* An unremitting worker 1851.

Stra·pping, *ppl. a.* 1657. [f. STRAP *v.* + -ING².] Orig. of a young woman: †Full of activity, vigorous, lusty. Now of a person of either sex: Strongly and stoutly built, robust, sturdy. **b.** *transf.* Big, 'whopping' (*rare*) 1819.

They..are..all well-built, s. fellows 1902.

†**Stra·pple,** *sb.* [OE. *strapul*, of unkn. origin.] A covering for the lower part of the leg, consisting of a fillet or band laced or bound round the limb –1483.

Stra·pple, *v. Obs.* exc. *dial.* 1607. [f. prec.] †**1.** *trans.* To furnish with 'strapples' or coverings for the legs. CHAPMAN. **2.** To bind or make fast with bands. Now *dial.* 1611.

Strasburg (stræ·zbɒɹg, ‖ʃtrāsburχ). 1642. [Fr. *Strasbourg*, G. *Strassburg*.] The name of the principal town of Alsace, used *attrib.*

S. linen, a kind of linen imported from Strasburg. *S. pie*, a pie made of fatted goose liver.

Strass (stræs). 1820. [– G. *strass*, Fr. *stras*; from the name of the inventor, Josef Strasser.] A vitreous composition used as a basis in the manufacture of artificial stones; = PASTE *sb.*¹ 5.

Strata, pl. of STRATUM.

Stratagem (stræ·tădʒĕm). 1489. [– Fr. *stratagème* – L. *strategema* – Gr. στρατήγημα a piece of generalship, stratagem, f. στρατηγεῖν be a general, f. στρατηγός STRATEGUS.] **1.** An operation or act of generalship; usu., an artifice or trick designed to outwit or surprise the enemy. **b.** *gen.* Military artifice 1599. **2.** Any artifice or trick; a device or scheme for obtaining an advantage 1588. **b.** *gen.* Skill in devising expedients; artifice, cunning 1588. †**3.** Used loosely for: A deed of blood or violence –1606.

1. He was advertised by spies what stratagems the enemy would use against us 1653. **b.** *Hen. V*, IV. viii. 113. **2. b.** 'Tis pollicie and stratageme must doe That you affect SHAKS. **3.** 3 *Hen. VI*, II. v. 89. Hence †**Stratagema·tic,** †**-al** *adjs.*, relating to, versed in, s. or strategy –1650.

†**Stratagemical** (strætăˌdʒe·mikăl), *a.* 1585. [irreg. f. STRATAGEM + -IC + -AL¹.] Concerned with, of the nature of, stratagem –1838.

Strategetic (strætĭˌdʒe·tik), *a.* 1848. [– Gr. στρατηγητικός, f. στρατηγεῖν; see STRATAGEM, -IC.] = STRATEGIC. So **Stratege·tical** *a.* 1828.

Strategic (străte·dʒik, -ī·dʒik), *a.* and *sb.* 1825. [– Fr. *stratégique* – Gr. στρατηγικός, f. στρατηγός STRATEGUS.] **A.** *adj.* Of or belonging to strategy; useful or important in regard to strategy.

S. point [= Fr. *point stratégique*], a position determined as important in a plan of campaign.

B. *sb.* The strategic art, strategy. *sing.* (rare) and *pl.* 1852. So **Strate·gical** *a.*, **-ly** *adv.*

Strategist (stræ·tĭdʒist). 1838. [– Fr. *stratégiste*, f. *stratégie* STRATEGY; see -IST.] One versed in strategy.

Strategus (strătī·gɒ̆s). *Pl.* **-gi** (-dʒəi). Also **strategos** (strătī·gɒs), *pl.* **-oi.** 1656. [– L. *strategus* – Gr. στρατηγός, f. στρατός army + -αγ-, ἄγειν lead.] *Gr. Hist.* A commander-in-chief or chief magistrate at Athens and in the Achæan league.

Strategy (stræ·tĭdʒi). 1688. [– Fr. *stratégie* – Gr. στρατηγία office or command of a general, generalship, f. στρατηγός; see prec.] †**1.** A government or province under a strategus. **2.** The art of a commander-in-chief; the art of projecting and directing the larger military movements and operations of a campaign 1810. **b.** An instance or species of this 1833. **3.** *Gr. Hist.* The office of a STRATEGUS (*rare*) 1869.

2. S. differs materially from *tactic*; the latter belonging only to the mechanical movement of bodies, set in motion by the former 1810.

Strath (stræþ). *Sc.* 1540. [– Gael. *srath* = Ir. *srath*, *sratha*.] A wide valley; a tract of level or low-lying land traversed by a river and bounded by hills or high ground. †**b.** *loosely.* A stretch of flat land by the waterside –1730.

Strathspey (stræþspēᶦ·). 1653. [f. the Sc. place-name *Strathspey* (= the strath of the river Spey).] **a.** A lively Scottish dance or reel for two dancers. **b.** The music or tune (usu. in common time) used to accompany this dance.

Straticulate (străti·kiŭlĕt), *a.* 1880. [f. *stratum*, after *granulate*, *vermiculate* adjs.; see -ULE, -ATE².] *Geol.* and *Min.* Arranged in thin layers. So **Straticula·tion,** arrangement in thin layers.

Stratification (stræ:tifikēᶦ·ʃən). 1617. [– Fr. *stratification*, f. *stratifier*; see STRATIFY, -FICATION.] †**1.** The action of depositing something in layers –1882. **2.** *Geol.* The formation, by natural process, of strata or layers one above the other; the fact or state of existing in the form of strata, stratified condition; also, the manner in which something is stratified 1795. **b.** *Biol.* and *Path.* The thickening of a tissue by the deposition or growth of successive thin layers 1875. **c.** *Electr.* The striated appearance assumed by an electric discharge passing through a highly rarefied gas 1856. **d.** *transf.* and *fig.*, chiefly with ref. to the geological use 1860.

2.d. By exact observation of s., eight more periods have been distinguished by the explorer of Cnossus 1910.

Stratified (stræ·tifəid), *ppl. a.* 1802. [f. STRATIFY *v.* + -ED¹.] Disposed in strata or layers; *spec.* in *Geol.* and *Electr.*

Stratiform (stræ·tifǭɹm), *a.* 1805. [– Fr. *stratiforme*; see STRATUM, -FORM.] **1.** *Geol.* Disposed in the form of strata; showing apparent stratification. **2.** Forming or formed into strata or layers 1834.

Stratify (stræ·tifəi), *v.* 1661. [– Fr. *stratifier*; see STRATUM, -FY.] **1.** *trans.* 'To range in beds or layers' (J.); *spec.* in *Metall.*, to range in alternate layers (metals and reagent substances) in a crucible. **2.** *Geol.* Of natural agencies: To deposit (rocks) in strata or beds;

to produce (a portion of the earth's crust) in the form of strata; to form strata in. Chiefly *pass.* 1794. **3.** *intr.* To assume the form of strata 1856.

2. *fig.* Society stratifies itself everywhere O.W. HOLMES.

Stratigraphy (străti·grăfi). 1865. [f. L. *strati-*, comb. form of *stratum* STRATUM; see -GRAPHY.] **1.** The branch of geology that is concerned with the order and relative position of the strata of the earth's crust. **2.** The stratigraphical features (of a country, etc.); the order and relative position of the strata 1882. Hence **Strati·grapher,** one versed in s. **Stratigra·phic, -al** (1817) *adjs.* pertaining to s.; **-ly** *adv.* **Strati·graphist.**

Stratiote (stræ·tiōᵘt). 1656. [– Gr. στρατιώτης, f. στρατία army.] *Gr. Hist.* A soldier.

Strato- (strēⁱ·to), comb. form of STRATUS, used to form names for mixed types of cloud-structure in which the 'stratus' form is present as an element modifying one of the other forms.

Strato-ci·rrus, a cloud resembling cirro-stratus, but more compact in structure; hence **Strato-ci·rrous** *a.* **Strato-cu·mulus** = *cumulo-stratus*; hence **Strato-cu·mulous** *a.*

Stratocracy (strătǫ·krăsi). 1652. [f. Gr. στρατός army; see -CRACY.] Government by the army; military rule; a polity in which the army is the controlling power. Hence **Stratocra·tic** *a.* pertaining to s.

Stratose (strēⁱ·toᵘs), *a.* 1881. [f. STRATUM + -OSE¹.] *Bot.* Stratified; arranged in layers.

Stratosphere (strēⁱ·tǒsfīᵊɹ). 1908. [f. STRATUM after ATMOSPHERE; cf. TROPOSPHERE.] That stratum of the atmosphere, lying above the troposphere, in which the temperature is nearly uniform at any height.

Stratum (strēⁱ·tǒm). *Pl.* **strata** (strēⁱ·tă); *rarely* **stratums.** 1599. [mod.L. use of L. *stratum*, lit. something spread or laid down, n. pa. pple. of *sternere* lay or throw down.] **1.** *gen.* A quantity of a substance or material spread over a nearly horizontal surface to a more or less uniform thickness; a layer or coat; esp. one of two or more parallel layers or coats successively superposed one upon another. **2.** A bed of sedimentary rock, usu. consisting of a series of 'layers' or 'laminæ' of the same kind, representing continuous periods of deposition 1671. **3.** A region of the atmosphere, of the sea, or of a quantity of fluid, assumed for purposes of calculation as bounded by horizontal planes 1787. **4.** *Biol.*, etc. One of a number of layers composing an animal or vegetable tissue 1741. **5.** *fig.* (in various applications, chiefly after sense 2) 1807.

1. The broken or perforated s. of new snow TYNDALL. **2.** The..Laurentian strata..are seen to underlie..the Silurian beds 1875. **3.** The temperature of the lower strata of the air 1858. **5.** The habit of reading spread to a lower social s. 1902.

Stratus (strēⁱ·tǒs). 1803. [– L. *stratus*, f. *sternere, strat-* spread, lay down. Cf. prec.] *Meteorol.* One of the simple forms of cloud, having the appearance of a broad sheet of nearly uniform thickness.

†**Stra·vagant,** *a.* and *sb.* 1565. [– It. *stravagante*; see EXTRAVAGANT.] **A.** *adj.* Irrelevant, unsuitable, extraordinary –1613. **B.** *sb.* **a.** Something irrelevant. **b.** A vagrant. –1608.

Straw (strǭ), *sb.* [OE. *strēaw* = OFris. *strē*, OS., OHG. *strō* (Du. *stroo*, G. *stroh*), ON. *strá* :– Gmc. **strawam*, rel. to STREW *v.*] **I.** *collect. sing.* **1.** The stems or stalks of certain cereals, chiefly wheat, barley, oats, and rye. Used e.g. as litter and as fodder for cattle, as filling for bedding, as thatch, etc. **b.** *fig.* with ref. to the small value of straw in comparison with the grain, or to its ready inflammability. late ME. **2.** Applied to the stalks of certain other plants, chiefly pease and buckwheat ME. **b.** *U.S.* Pine needles 1856. **3.** As a material (plaited or woven) for hats and bonnets; a kind or variety of this material, or an imitation of it 1730.

1. A lioun and an oxe schulen ete stree WYCLIF *Isa.* 65:25. Their lean and flashy songs Grate on their scrannel Pipes of wretched s. MILT. **b.** Strongest oathes, are s. To th' fire ith' blood SHAKS. **3.** Plain Dunstable straws continue to be worn 1859.

Phrases. *To make bricks without s.*, (to be required) to produce results without the means usu. considered necessary. *In the s.*, in childbed, lying-in; so *out of the s.*, recovered after childbearing. *To die in the s.* (of warriors, esp. vikings), to die in bed, as opp. to the coveted death in battle. *To run to s.*: see RUN *v.* *Man of s.*, a person or thing compared to a straw image; a counterfeit, sham, 'dummy'; (*b*) an imaginary adversary, or an invented adverse argument, adduced in order to be triumphantly refuted; (*c*) a person of no substance; (*d*) a fictitious or irresponsible person fraudulently put forward as a surety or as a party in an action.

II. A single stem of a cereal, etc. **1.** A stem of any cereal plant, esp. when dry and separated from the grain; also, a piece of such a stem ME. **b.** *poet.* A pipe made of an oaten straw (*rare*) 1588. **c.** A straw, or a similar slender tube made of paper, etc. through which drinks are sucked up 1872. **2.** A small particle of straw or chaff, a 'mote' OE. **3.** Used as a type of what is of trifling value or importance ME. **b.** A trifle 1692. **4.** *Cheese s.*: a thin stick of pastry containing cheese 1877.

1. *Jul. C.* I. iii. 108. *To draw, gather, pick straws*: (of the eyes) to be sleepy. Provbs. and allusive phrases: A drowning man will catch at a s. RICHARDSON. The last s. breaks the laden camel's back DICKENS. Sunstroke may act as 'the last s.' 1897. Such straws of speech show how blows the wind READE. **b.** When Shepheards pipe on Oaten strawes SHAKS. **3.** Phr. *Not to care a s.* (*two, three straws*). **b.** My passions will not..be irritated by straws MISS BURNEY.

III. A straw hat 1863.

attrib. and *Comb.*: *s.-roofed, -thatched*, ppl. adjs.; = made of straw, as *s. hat*; **s. bail,** bail given by 'men of s.'; insufficient or worthless bail; **-bid** *U.S.*, a worthless bid; one not intended to be taken up; **-board,** coarse yellow millboard made from straw pulp; **s. cat,** the pampas cat; **s. colour,** the colour of straw, a pale yellow; **-coloured** *a.* pale yellow; **-drain,** a drain filled with s.; **-dynamite,** a mixture of nitro-glycerine and nitro-cellulose made from s.; **s. hat,** a hat made of plaited or woven straw; **-needle,** a long thin needle used for sewing together s. plaits; **s. paper,** paper made from s. bleached and pulped; **s. plait, plat,** a plait or braid made of s., used for making s. hats, etc.; **s. rope,** a rope made of twisted or plaited s.; **-stem,** a wine-glass stem pulled out of the substance of the bowl; hence, a wine-glass having such a stem; **s. vote** *U.S.*, an unofficial vote taken before an election in order to discover the trend of public opinion; **-worm,** the caddis-worm; **s. yard,** a yard littered with s., in which horses and cattle are wintered.

Straw (strǭ), *v.*¹ Pa. t. and pa. pple. **strawed** (*rarely* pa. pple. **strawn**). *Obs.* exc. *arch.* ME. [Differentiated repr. of OE. *strē(o)wian* STREW *v.*] = STREW *v.*

Straw (strǭ), *v.*² 1440. [f. STRAW *sb.*] *trans.* To supply with straw.

Strawberry (strǭ·běri). [OE. *strēa(w)beriġe, strēow-*; the reason for the name is unknown.] **1.** The 'fruit' of any species of the genus *Fragaria*; a soft bag-shaped receptacle, scarlet to yellowish in colour, full of juicy pulp, and dotted over with small yellow seed-like achenes. **2.** The plant which bears this fruit OE.

1. We may say of Angling as Dr. Boteler said of Strawberries; Doubtless God could have made a better berry, but doubtless God never did WALTON. To Godstow bound..For strawberries and cream 1788.

attrib. and *Comb.* *s. bed, ice, jam*; *s. coloured, crushed s.* etc. **s. bass** *U.S.*, the fish *Pomoxys sparoides*; **s. blite,** *Blitum capitatum* and *B. virgatum*, the fruit of which resembles the s.; **s. bush,** (*a*) = *s. shrub*; (*b*) the shrub *Euonymus americanus* with crimson and scarlet pods; **s. finch,** the amadavat; **s. mark,** a birth-mark or nævus resembling a s.; **s. pear,** the fruit of the W. Indian cactus *Cereus triangularis*, or the plant itself; **s. perch** *U.S.* = *s. bass*; **s. shrub** *U.S.* = CALYCANTHUS; **s. tomato,** *Physalis alkekengi*; **-tree,** †(*a*) = sense 2; (*b*) = ARBUTUS; (*c*) *U.S.* = *s-bush* (*b*); **s. vine** = sense 2.

Strawberry leaf. ME. The leaf of the strawberry plant. **b.** In allusion to the row of conventional figures of the leaf on the coronet of a duke, marquis, or earl 1827.

Straw·-breadth, straw's breadth. Now *rare.* 1577. The breadth of a straw. Formerly, a typically small distance.

Strawy (strǭ·i), *a.* 1552. [f. STRAW *sb.* + -Y¹.] **1.** Consisting of, of the nature of, full of, straw. **2.** Made with straw; filled, thatched, or strewed with straw 1568. **3.** Resembling straw in colour, texture, etc. 1668. †**4.** *fig.* Light, empty, or worthless as straw –1662.

4. *Tr. & Cr.* V. v. 24.

Stray (strēⁱ), *sb.* 1440. [– AFr. *strey*, aphetic of *astrey* adj. used as sb.; partly f. STRAY *v.*] **I. 1.** *Law.* = ESTRAY *sb.* 1498. **2.** An animal that has strayed from its flock, home, or owner 1440. **b.** *fig.* One who has gone astray in conduct, opinion, etc. 1605. **c.** A homeless, friendless person; an ownerless cat or dog 1649. **d.** Something that has strayed from its usual or proper place; something separated from the main body; a detached fragment, an isolated specimen 1798. †**e.** *collect.* A number of stray beasts; a body of stragglers from an army –1717.

1. No Fowle can be a s. but a Swan COKE. *Waifs and strays*: see WAIFS. **2. d.** Not found in the Gulf of Mexico, unless as a s. 1888. If a telephone be used as a telegraphic receiver, strays (atmospheric discharges) may sometimes be distinguishable from signals 1908. **e.** 2 *Hen. IV*, IV. ii. 120.

II. †**1.** The action of straying or wandering –1793. **2.** The right of allowing cattle to stray and feed on common land. *north.* 1736. **b.** = COMMON *sb.* 3. 1889. **3.** *Naut.* = STRAY-LINE 1628. Hence **Stray·ling,** a stray thing or person.

Stray (strēⁱ), *a.* 1607. [Partly aphetic var. of ASTRAY; partly attrib. use of prec.] **1.** Of an animal: That has wandered from confinement or control; that has straggled from a flock; that has become homeless or ownerless. **2.** Of a cable: Loose, slack 1791. **3.** Of a person or thing: Separated from the main body; occurring away from the regular course or habitat; isolated 1796. **4.** *Electr.* (see quot.) 1893.

4. *S. Power*, the proportion of the energy wasted in driving a dynamo, which is lost through friction or other hurtful resistances 1893.

Stray (strēⁱ), *v.* ME. [Aphetic – AFr., OFr. *estrayer* ASTRAY *v.*] **1.** *intr.* To escape from confinement or control, to wander away from a place, one's companions, etc. Also of inanimate things. late ME. **2.** To wander up and down free from control; to roam about. late ME. †**b.** Of a stream: To meander –1754. **3.** *intr.* To wander from the direct way; to deviate 1561. **4.** *fig.* **a.** To wander from the path of rectitude, err ME. **b.** To wander or deviate in mind, purpose, etc. Said also of the mind or thoughts. late ME.

1. Here too, 'tis sung, of old Diana stray'd POPE. **b.** Boughs, that stray'd Beyond their Ranks DRYDEN. **2.** Ah fields belov'd in vain, where once my careless childhood stray'd GRAY. *fig.* Their sober wishes never learn'd to s. GRAY. **c.** Where Thames amongst the wanton Vallies strays DENHAM. **4. a.** We have erred and strayed from thy ways like lost sheep *Bk. Com. Prayer.* **b.** But, sir, I ask pardon, I am straying from the question GOLDSM. Hence **Stray·er,** one who strays.

Stray·-line. 1769. [f. STRAY *a.* (or STRAY *sb.* II. 1) + LINE *sb.*] *Naut.* Deviation (of a sounding line) from the perpendicular.

Streak (strīk), *sb.* [OE. *strica* stroke of the pen, mark, etc., corresp. in sense and vowel-grade to OFris. *strike*, MLG., MDu. *strēke* (Du. *streek*), (O)HG. *strich*, Goth. *striks*, f. **strik-* STRIKE *v.*] †**1.** A line. mark, stroke; esp. a character in writing, or a unit or degree in measurement –1735. **2.** A thin irregular line of a different colour or substance from that of the material or surface of which it forms a part 1577. **b.** A line of colour, less firm and regular than a stripe, occurring as a distinctive mark on the coat of an animal, the plumage of a bird, or the body or wings of an insect 1567. **c.** *Min.* The line of coloured powder produced by scratching a mineral or fossil, or the mark made by rubbing it on a harder surface 1794. **d.** *Biol.* A linear mark, stria. Also, a narrow tract in a tissue. 1837. **3.** A faint line of light (esp. of the dawn) diversifying the darkness 1592. **b.** A flash of lightning, etc. 1781. **4.** A long irregular narrow strip of land, water, etc.; a line of colour representing a distant object in a landscape 1727. **5. a.** The horizontal course of a stratum of coal. **b.** A stratum or vein (of metal ore). 1672. **6.** An intermixture (of some contrasting or unexpected quality); an inherited strain 1647. **b.** A temporary run (of luck) 1882.

2. For streaks of red were mingled there, Such as are on a Katherne Pear SUCKLING. **3.** The West yet glimmers with some streakes of Day SHAKS. **4.** That black s. is the belfry BROWNING. *The silver s.*, the English Channel. **6.** A s. of eccentricity in his character 1865.

Streak (strīk), *v.* 1440. [f. prec.] †**1.** *trans.* To cancel by drawing a line or lines across –1595. **2.** To mark with lines or stripes of a different colour, substance, or texture; to form streaks on or in 1595. **3.** *intr.* Of lightning: To flash forth in a streak 1849. **4.** To become streaked or streaky 1870. **5.** To move fast, like a 'streak' of lightning 1927.

2. Some pieces of Rock streaked with gold and silver 1660.

Streaked (strīkt), *ppl. a.* 1596. [f. prec. + -ED^{1}.] **1.** Marked with streaks; striped, striate. **b.** Of bacon, etc.: = STREAKY 2 b. 1687. **2.** *U.S. dial.* Confused, agitated; scared, uneasy 1833.

Streaky (strī·ki), *a.* 1670. [f. STREAK *sb.* + -Y^{1}.] **1.** Of the nature of a streak or streaks; occurring in, consisting of, streaks. **2.** Marked with streaks; streaked 1745. **b.** Of flesh-meat, esp. bacon: Having lean and fat in alternate streaks 1838. **3.** *fig.* Variable, uneven (in character or quality); changeable, uncertain. *colloq.* 1898. **4.** *slang.* **a.** Ill-tempered, irritable. **b.** *U.S.* = prec. 2. 1848.

2. The blushes of the s. west 1745. Hence **Strea·ki-ly** *adv.*, **-ness.**

Stream (strīm), *sb.* [OE. *strēam* = OFris. *strām*, OS. *strōm*, OHG. *stroum* (Du. *stroom*, G. *strom*), ON. *straumr* :– Gmc. **straumaz* :– **sroumos*, f. IE. **srou-* **sreu-* **srŭ-* flow, repr. also by Gr. ῥεῖν flow, ῥεῦμα stream.] **1.** A course of water flowing continuously along a bed on the earth, forming a river, rivulet, or brook. **b.** *pl.* The waters (of a river). *poet.* 1500. **c.** A rivulet or brook, as contrasted with a river 1806. **2.** Flow or current of a river; force, volume, or direction of flow. late ME. **b.** A current in the sea. Cf. GULF STREAM. late ME. **c.** The middle part of a current or tide, as having the greatest force of flow. late ME. **3.** A flow or current of water or other liquid issuing from a source, orifice, or vessel. Often *hyperbolically* in sing. or pl. for a great effusion of blood or tears. OE. **b.** A current or flow of air, gas, electricity 1722. **4.** *transf.* An uninterrupted succession of persons, animals, or things, moving constantly in the same direction 1600. **5.** *fig.* in various applications: e.g. a continuous flow of words; an outflow (of beneficence, etc.); an influx (of wealth) OE. †**b.** The prevailing direction of opinion or fashion –1669. †**6.** A ray or beam of light; the tail of a comet –1700.

1. For there the streme of Isis breaketh into many armelets LELAND. **2.** Soon after, the River had the wonted s. and was Navigable again 1653. Phrases. *Against, with the s.* (often in fig. context). *Down, up* (*the*) *s.* **3.** Traitors..That would..make poore England weepe in Streames of Blood SHAKS. Wine and ale..flowed in streams 1899. **4.** He followed the s. of people JOHNSON. A constant s. of emigration 1849. **5.** This flowing streame of wordes 1585. The quit-rents..will pour large streams of wealth into the royal coffers JOHNSON. To..hear the mighty s. of tendency Uttering, for elevation of our thought, A clear sonorous voice WORDSW. **6.** Holes..to resseyuen the stremes of the sonne by day CHAUCER.

Comb.: **s.-anchor,** an anchor intermediate in size between the bower and the kedge, used to moor a ship in a sheltered position; **-cable,** the cable or hawser of the s.-anchor; **-gold,** gold in alluvial deposits; **-ice,** pieces of drift ice joining each other in a continuous ridge and following the line of current; **-ore,** ore in alluvial deposits; **-tin,** tin ore found in pebble-like lumps in alluvial beds; **-work(s,** the operation of washing detrital deposits for metal, esp. tin; a place where this is done. Hence **Strea·mless** *a.* having no streams; of water, having no current.

Stream (strīm), *v.* ME. [f. prec.] **I.** *intr.* **1.** Of a body of liquid: To flow or issue in a stream; to flow or run in a full and continuous current. **b.** Of a road, or of land which seems to move in the opposite direction to one who passes along it 1833. **2.** *transf.* and *fig.* Of light, air, vapour, immaterial effluences, etc.: To be carried or emitted in a full and continuous current ME. **b.** Of a star or meteor: To form a continuous trail of light as it moves in its course 1838. **3. a.** Of a flag, or the like: To wave or float outwards in the wind 1560. **b.** Of hair, a garment, etc.: To hang loose and waving; to trail *out, behind* 1784. **4.** Of persons (or animals): To move together continuously in considerable numbers; to flock 1735. **5.** To pour off or exude liquid in a continuous stream; to run, drip, overflow with moisture. late ME. **6.** Of a luminous body: To emit a continuous stream of beams or rays of light. Also *spec.* of a comet, with ref. to its 'tail': To issue in a widening stream of light. late ME. **b.** To be suffused *with* (radiant light) 1830.

1. The river Ock streameth by Stow 1630. She suffered the tears to stream down her cheeks unconcealed 1849. **2.** *All's Well* II. iii. 82. The morning sun was streaming in at the window 1852. **3. a.** Th' Imperial Ensign..Shon like a Meteor streaming to the Wind MILT. **b.** Adorn'd with.. ribbands streaming gay COWPER. **4.** People.. streamed to it from all quarters SCOTT. Flocks of little Auk streaming south 1853. **5.** He was streaming with perspiration 1875. **6. b.** The mountain tops began to s. with golden light 1830.

II. *trans.* **1.** To cause to flow; to pour forth, discharge, or emit in a stream (a liquid, rays of light, etc.); also with adv. as *out, forth, down.* late ME. **2.** To suffuse or overspread (a surface) *with* flowing moisture 1526. †**3.** To ornament with flowing lines or rays –1626. **4.** To cause (a flag) to float outwards in the wind; to wave (a handkerchief) 1593. **5.** Naut. *To s. the buoy*: to throw the anchor-buoy overboard before casting anchor 1769. **6.** *Mining.* To flush (a detrital deposit) with a stream of water, in order to carry off the earthy matter, and leave the ore exposed; usu. absol. *to s. for* (tin, copper, etc.) 1778.

1. It may so please, that she at length will streame Some deaw of grace into my withered hart SPENSER. **3.** The Heralds Mantle is streamed with Gold BACON. **4.** *Rich. II*, IV. i. 94.

Streamer (strī·məɹ), *sb.* ME. [f. prec. + -ER^{1}.] **1.** A flag streaming or waving in the air; *spec.* a long and narrow pointed flag or pennon. **2.** *transf.* **a.** Something long and narrow, that hangs loose in the manner of a streamer 1810. **b.** A long narrow strip of vapour, snow, etc. 1871. **3.** †**a.** A luminous heavenly body emitting a continuous stream of light –1647. **b.** A ray proceeding from the sun; esp. *pl.*, the radiation of the sun's corona seen in eclipses 1697. **c.** *pl.* The Aurora Borealis 1735. **4.** *Mining.* One who washes detrital deposits to procure the ore they contain 1619.

1. Like a stately Ship..With all her bravery on, and tackle trim, Sails fill'd, and streamers waving MILT. **2.** Tying up a bouquet..with long streamers of pale yellow ribbon 1889. Hence **Strea·mer** *v. trans.* to furnish or fill with streamers.

Streaming (strī·miŋ), *vbl. sb.* late ME. [f. STREAM *v.* + -ING^{1}.] The action of STREAM *v.* in various senses; an instance of this. **b.** *Biol.* A peculiar flowing motion of protoplasm in a cell 1875.

Streamlet (strī·mlėt). 1552. [-LET.] A small stream; a brook, rill, or rivulet.

Strea·m-line, *sb.* 1873. **1.** *Hydrodynamics.* See quot. **2.** = *S. form* 1909.

1. A 'line of motion' or 's.' is defined to be a line drawn from point to point, so that its direction is everywhere that of the motion of the fluid 1906.

attrib.: **s. form,** that shape of a solid body which is calculated to meet with the smallest amount of resistance in passing through the atmosphere. Hence **Stre·am-line** *v. trans.* to give a s. form to (a motor-car, etc.) also *transf.* and *fig.* **Stre·am-lined** *ppl. a.*

Streamy (strī·mi), *a.* late ME. [f. STREAM *sb.* + -Y^{1}.] **1.** Abounding in or full of running streams. **2.** Of water, etc.: Flowing in a stream, running 1586. **b.** Of hair, etc.: Flowing 1813. **3.** Of the nature of, having the appearance of, or issuing in, a stream 1718.

1. Fair Scotia's s. vales 1806. **3.** His nodding Helm emits a s. Ray POPE. Hence **Strea·miness.**

Streek, streak (strīk), *v.* Now *Sc.* and *dial.* [Northern ME. *strēk-*, corresp. to Southern ME. *strēch-* :– OE. *streććan* STRETCH *v.*] = STRETCH *v.*, in various senses.

Streel (strīl), *v.* Chiefly *Anglo-Ir.* 1839. [Cf. Ir. *straoillim*, trail, drag along on the ground.] *intr.* To trail on the ground; to float at length. Also of persons, to stroll, wander aimlessly. Hence **Stree·ling** *ppl. a.*

Street (strīt), *sb.* [OE. *strǣt* = OFris. *strēte*, OS. *strāta*, OHG. *strāʒ(ʒ)a* (Du. *straat*, G. *strasse*); WGmc. – late L. *strāta*, subst. use (sc. *via* way) of fem. pa. pple. of L. *sternere* throw or lay down; cf. STRATUM.] †**1.** A paved road; a highway. *Obs.* exc. as surviving in the proper names of certain ancient roads, as Watling S., Icknield S. †**b.** Used vaguely for: A road, way, path –1547. **2.** A road in a town or village (comparatively wide, as opp. to a 'lane' or 'alley'), running between two lines of houses or shops. Also, the road together with the adjacent houses. (As part of the proper name of a street, abbrev. *St.*) OE. **b.** Used for: The inhabitants of the street; also, the people in the street. late ME. **c.** *transf.* A passage between continuous lines of persons or things. late ME.

2. Broadway is undoubtedly the handsomest s. in America 1798. I am sure I could not live again in a s. DISRAELI. *S. of houses* or *shops*, a number of houses or shops built in a double line with a road in the middle, forming a s. Phr. *The s.*: some particular s. to which the merchants or financiers of a city resort for business intercourse. In mod. use primarily *U.S.* (with cap.), applied to Wall S., New York. Hence, the money market. Also, in London, *in the s.* is said with ref. to business done or prices quoted after the hour of closing of the Stock Exchange. *In the street(s*, outside the house, out of doors. *To be on the streets*, to be a prostitute; hence, *the street(s*, as designating a life of prostitution. *To walk the street(s*, to go about on foot in a town; also with ref. to prostitution. *The man in the s.*, the ordinary man as dist. from the expert or the man who has special opportunities of knowledge. *Not to be in the same s. with* (colloq. or slang), to be far behind, far inferior to (a person); so *to be streets ahead, better*, to be far ahead of, far superior to. **b.** There was a mystery about him which the whole s. had tried its skill in fathoming 1856.

attrib. and *Comb.*: *s.-corner, -lamp, -singer, -sweeper*; **s.-Arab** (also written with small *a*), a homeless vagrant (usu. a child) living in the streets (see ARAB *sb.*); **-boy,** a homeless or neglected boy who lives chiefly in the streets; **-car,** *U.S.* a tram-car; **-orderly,** a s.-sweeper or scavenger; **-porter,** a porter employed to lift or carry heavy packages in the s.; **-railway,** a tramway; **-refuge** = REFUGE *sb.* 3; **-urchin,** a mischievous little s.-boy; **-way,** a paved road or highway, the roadway of a s. (now only *poet.*). Hence **Street** *v. trans.* to furnish or provide with streets, to lay out in streets.

Street-door. 1563. The chief external door of a house or other building, opening on the street.

Stree·t-wa:lker. 1592. **1.** One who walks in the street 1618. **2.** *spec.* A common prostitute whose field of operations is the street 1592.

Streetward (strī·twǫɹd), *a.* and *adv.* 1596. [f. STREET *sb.* + -WARD.] **A.** *adv.* Towards the street. **B.** *adj.* Facing or opening on the street.

Strelitz (stre·lits). 1603. [– Russ. *strelétś* archer, f. *strelyát'* shoot, f. *strelá* arrow.] A soldier belonging to a body of Russian troops composed of infantry raised by the Tsar Ivan the Terrible (1533–84) and abolished by Peter the Great in 1682.

Strelitzia (strĕli·tsiă). 1789. [f. *Strelitz* (after Charlotte of Mecklenburg-Strelitz, queen to Geo. III) + -IA^{1}.] A genus of herbaceous plants (of the family *Musaceæ*), natives of S. Africa; also, a plant of this genus.

Strengite (stre·ŋəit). 1881. [– G. *strengit* (named after A. *Streng*); see -ITE^{1} 2 b.] *Min.* Hydrous phosphate of iron, found as a drusy incrustation of a red colour.

Strength (streŋþ), *sb.* [OE. *strengþu* = OHG. *strengida* :– Gmc. **strangiþō*; see STRONG, -TH^{1}.] **1.** The quality or condition of being strong. **a.** Power of action in body or limbs; ability to exert muscular force. **b.** Bodily vigour in general; efficiency of the bodily powers OE. **c.** Power in general, whether physical, mental, or due to the possession of resources; ability for effective action OE. **d.** Capacity for moral effort or endurance; firmness (of mind, character, will, purpose) OE. **e.** Power of contending in warfare; now chiefly, military power derived from numbers, equipment, or resources OE. **f.** In a fortification, fortified place, etc.: Power of withstanding assault or capture. late ME. **g.** In things, material or immaterial: Operative power; capacity for producing effects OE. **h.** Power to sustain the application of force without breaking or yielding. late ME. **i.** Intensity and active force (of movement, wind, fire, a stream, current of electricity, or the like); intensity (of a physical condition, colour, sound, etc.) ME. **j.** Vigour, intensity (of feeling, conviction, etc.). Also, emphasis, positiveness (of refusal). 1550. **k.** Intensity of the specific property, or proportionate quantity of the active ingredient in a substance; potency (of drugs, liquors) 1588. **l.** Of soil: Firmness 1573. **m.** Demonstrative force or weight (of arguments, evidence); amount of evidence for (a case) 1593. **n.** Energy or vigour of literary or artistic conception or execution; forcefulness (of delineation, versification, expression) 1687. **o.** *Cards.* Of a hand (or its holder): Effectiveness due to the value of the cards held; also, the condition of being strong *in* (a specified suit). Of a suit: Number and value of the cards held by a player 1862. **p.** *Billiards.* The measure of force used to make a stroke 1788. **q.** *Comm.* Firmness, steadiness in prices 1891. **2.** Used for: A source of strength; that which makes strong OE. **†3.** Legal power; authority –1689. **4.** A stronghold, fastness, fortress. Now *arch.* or *Hist.*, chiefly with ref. to Scotland. ME. **†b.** A defensive work, fortification –1661. **†c.** One's strong position; the place within which one is most secure –1714. **†5. a.** *collect. sing.* Troops, forces –1703. **b.** A body of soldiers; a force –1627. **6.** *Mil.* and *Naval.* The number of men on the muster-roll of an army, a regiment, etc.; the body of men enrolled; the number of ships in a navy or fleet 1601. **7.** A sufficient number (of persons or things) for some purpose. Now *dial.* 1607. **†8.** The aggregate resources (of a nation) –1711. **9.** Strongest part; *spec.* the strongest part of a stream or current 1530.

1. a. Sampson loste hys streyngthe therfore 1400. You have s., I have brains 1888. **b.** My s. was gone, and..I required to rest once more TYNDALL. **c.** His s. lay in accurate verbal scholarship rather than in philosophy 1894. **d.** If..Thou hast the s. of will to slay thy selfe SHAKS. **f.** An old town, formerly of considerable s. BORROW. **g.** Great is the s. Of words SHELLEY. **h.** The brittle s. of bones MILT. Tensile s. 1876. **i.** The s. of the pulse 1866. **j.** If you did know..You would abate the s. of your displeasure SHAKS. **k.** T' allay the S...of the Wine DRYDEN. **m.** The s. of his opponent's case 1895. **n.** The easy vigour of a line, Where Denham's s., and Waller's sweetness join POPE. **2.** The Lord, my S. and Righteousness WESLEY. **4.** To lay down their Arms, and surrender Chester and other Strengths 1661. **6.** His s. at sea now [is] very small 1718. The fighting s. of the regiment 1894. Phr. *Under s.*, having less than the standard or normal number. *On the s.*, entered on the rolls of a regiment; also said of those soldiers' wives whose marriage has been approved by the authorities and who have therefore a recognized position; opp. to *off the s.* **8.** The Woollen Manufacture is the British S., the staple Commodity..of our Country ADDISON.

Phr. *On the s. of*, encouraged by, relying on, or arguing from. Hence †**Strength** *v. trans.* to give s. to, to make strong or stronger; to strengthen, fortify, confirm –1614. **Stre·ngthful** *a.* full of or characterized by s. **Stre·ngthless** *a.* destitute of s.

Strengthen (stre·ŋþ'n), *v.* ME. [f. prec. + -EN[5].] **1.** *trans.* To give moral support, courage or confidence, to. **2.** To give physical strength to (a person); to make stronger or more robust; to give defensive strength to (a town, etc.), make strong against attack; to reinforce (some material thing) by an additional support, added thickness, etc. 1452. **3.** To make stronger in influence, authority, or security of position 1579. **4.** To add strength or intensity to; to increase the strength or force of (reasons, etc.); to make more effective or powerful 1586. **5.** *intr.* To become strong or stronger; to grow in strength or intensity 1610.

2. Wine..taken in moderation..strengthens the stomach 1789. **3.** He loved to s. his family by a good alliance GEO. ELIOT. **4.** Additional Arguments to s. the Opinion which you have..delivered 1712. **5.** The young disease..Grows with his growth, and strengthens with his strength POPE. Hence **Stre·ngthener**, one who or something which strengthens. **Stre·ngthening** *vbl. sb.* and *ppl. a.*

Strengthily (stre·ŋþili), *adv. rare.* 1456. [f. next + -LY[2].] Strongly.

Strengthy (stre·ŋþi), *a.* Chiefly *Sc.* and *north.* ME. [f. STRENGTH *sb.* + -Y[1].] **†1.** Strong, powerful; difficult to overthrow –1596. **2.** Physically or muscularly strong. Now *rare* exc. *dial.* 1456.

Strenuity (strĭniū·ĭti). Now *rare.* late ME. [– L. *strenuitas*, f. *strenuus*; see next, -ITY.] The quality of being strenuous, strenuousness.

Strenuous (stre·niu,əs), *a.* 1599. [f. L. *strenuus* brisk, active, valiant + -OUS.] **1.** Vigorous in action, energetic; 'brave, bold, active, valiant' (J.). Now usu.: Unremittingly and ardently laborious. **b.** Zealous, earnest, 'strong' as a partisan or opponent 1713. **†2.** Of inanimate things: Strong in operation –1633. **b.** Of voice, etc.: Powerful, loud. *arch.* 1680. **3.** Of action or effort: Vigorous, energetic; now, persistently and ardently laborious. Of conditions, periods, etc.: Characterized by strenuous exertion. 1671.

1. A s. and an expert Souldier 1631. The s. metropolis 1899. **b.** A s. supporter of Mary Stuart 1774. **3.** To love Bondage more than Liberty; Bondage with ease than s. liberty MILT. *S. idleness* (= L. *strenua inertia* Hor. *Ep.* I. xi. 28), busy activity to no useful purpose. Hence **Stre·nuous-ly** *adv.* **-ness.**

Strepent (stre·pĕnt), *a. rare.* 1750. [– L. *strepens, -ent*, pr. pple. of *strepere* make a noise; see -ENT.] Noisy.

Strepitant (stre·pitănt), *a.* 1855. [– L. *strepitans, -ant-*, pr. pple. of *strepitare*, freq. of *strepere*; see prec., -ANT.] Making a great noise, noisy.

Strepitous (stre·pitəs), *a.* 1681. [f. L. *strepitus* noise, clatter (f. *strepere* make a noise) + -OUS.] Noisy, accompanied with much noise. (Now used chiefly in musical criticism.)

Strepsipterous (strepsi·ptərəs), *a.* 1817. [f. mod.L. *Strepsiptera* (f. Gr. στρεψι-, comb. form of στρέφειν to twist + πτερόν wing) + -OUS.] *Ent.* Belonging to the order *Strepsiptera* of insects (named from the twisted front wings). So **Strepsi·pteral** *a.*; **Strepsi·pteran** *a.*, also *sb.* an insect of the order *Strepsiptera.*

Strepto- (stre·pto), bef. a vowel **strept-**, comb. form of Gr. στρεπτός twisted (freq. taken to mean 'chain'). f. στρέφειν to turn, twist; used in many scientific terms.

Stre:ptobaci·lli [BACILLUS] *sb. pl.*, bacilli arranged in chains. **Stre:ptobacte·ria** [BACTERIUM] *sb. pl.*, bacteria linked together like a chain. ||**Streptoca·rpus**, a genus of African gesneraceous plants bearing pistils or fruits spirally-twisted towards the point; a plant of this genus, esp. the Cape Primrose. **Stre·ptocyte** [-CYTE], an amœbiform body occurring in bead-like strings from the vesicles of foot-and-mouth disease. **Streptomycin** (-məi·sin) [Gr. μύκης fungus, -IN], an antibiotic similar in action to penicillin. **Streptoneu·ral, -neu·rous** *adjs.*, pertaining to the *Streptoneura*, a branch of gasteropoda in which the loop of visceral nerves is twisted into a figure-of-eight. **Stre·ptothrix,** genus of bacteria comprising organisms having branching filaments growing in interlacing masses; a micro-organism of this type.

||**Streptococcus** (streptokǫ·kǒs). *Pl.* **-cocci** (-kǫ·ksəi). 1877. [f. STREPTO- + COCCUS.] *Bacteriol.* A form of bacterial organism in which the cocci are arranged in chains or chaplets. Hence **Streptococcal** (-kǫ·kăl), **-coccic** (kǫ·ksik), **-coccous** (-kǫ·kǒs), *adjs.* pertaining to or produced by s.

Stress (stres), *sb.* ME. [Aphetic f. DISTRESS *sb.* or, in part, of OFr. *estrece, -esse* narrowness, straitness, oppression :– Rom. **strictia*, f. L. *strictus* STRAIT *a.*, STRICT.] **I. †1.** Hardship, straits, adversity, affliction –1704. **†2.** Force or pressure exercised on a person for the purpose of compulsion or extortion –1655. **3.** The overpowering pressure *of* some adverse force or influence. Chiefly in *s. of weather.* 1513. **b.** A condition of things compelling or characterized by strained effort; occas. coupled with *storm* 1637. **4.** Strained exertion, strong effort. Now *rare.* 1690. **5.** Physical strain or pressure exerted upon a material object; the strain *of* a load or weight. Now *rare* exc. in scientific use. 1440. **b.** Strain upon a bodily organ or a mental power 1843. **†6.** Testing strain or pressure on a support or basis; weight (of inference, confidence, etc.) resting upon an argument or piece of evidence; amount of risk ventured on some assurance; degree of reliance. Chiefly in phr. *to lay s. on* or *upon*, to rely on, rest a burden of proof upon. –1765. **†b.** Weightiest part, essential point (of a business, argument, question) –1791. **†c.** Argumentative force –1784. **7.** Exceptional insistence on something; emphasis. Chiefly in phr. *to lay s. upon.* 1756. **8.** Relative loudness or force of vocal utterance; a greater degree of vocal force characterizing one part of a word as compared with the rest. Also, superior loudness of voice as a means of emphasizing one or more of the words of a sentence. 1749.

1. [He] began to be reduced to the utmost s. 1704. **3. b.** This age of s. and transition 1883. Phr. *Storm and s.*: see STORM *sb.* **4.** Though the faculties of the mind are improved by exercise, yet they must not be put to a s. beyond their strength LOCKE. **6.** I always put a great deal of s. upon his judgment DE FOE. **7.** Do you consider the forms of introduction, and the s. that is laid on them, as nonsense? JANE AUSTEN.

II. *Law.* A distraint; also, the chattel or chattels seized in a distraint. *Obs.* exc. *dial.* 1440. Hence **Stre·ssful** *a.* full of, or subject to, s. or strain. **Stre·ssless** *a.* having no s., unstressed.

Stress (stres), *v.* ME. [In earliest use aphetic – OFr. *estrecier* :– Rom. **strictiare*, f. L. *strictus* (see prec.). Later senses are f. the sb.] **†1.** *trans.* To subject (a person) to force or compulsion; to constrain or restrain –1581. **†b.** To confine, incarcerate –1556. **†2.** To subject to hardship; to afflict, harass, oppress; *pass.*, to be 'hard up' –1824. **3.** To subject (a material thing, a bodily organ, a mental faculty) to stress or strain; to overwork, fatigue. Now chiefly *Sc.* 1545. **4.** To lay the stress or emphasis on, emphasize (a word or phrase in speaking); to place a stress-accent on (a syllable) 1859. **b.** *fig.* To lay stress on, emphasize (a fact, idea, etc.). Chiefly *U.S.* 1896.

3. A metal structure..must not be stressed to more than one-third of its ultimate breaking stress 1892. **4.** Stressing the epithet to increase the defiance MEREDITH.

Stretch (stretʃ), *sb.* 1558. [f. next.] **1.** The action or an act of stretching physically; the fact of being stretched 1600. **b.** An act of 'stretching one's legs'; a walk taken for exercise 1761. **c.** The condition of being stretched; state of tension 1673. **d.** Capacity for being stretched 1875. **2.** In immaterial sense: A stretching or straining something beyond its proper limits; e.g. an unwarranted exercise *of* power; a straining *of* the law 1689; an undue extension of scope or application 1849. **3.** *Furthest, utmost s.*: the utmost degree to which a thing can be extended. Now *rare* or *Obs.* 1558. **4.** Strain or tension of mental or bodily powers; strained exertion 1622. **5.** Extent in time or space. **a.** An unbroken continuance of some one employment, occupation, or condition, during a period of time; an uninterrupted 'spell' of work, rest, prosperity, etc. 1689. **b.** A (more or less long) period of time 1698. **c.** A continuous journey or march. Now *colloq.* 1699. **d.** *Naut.* A continuous sail on one tack 1675. **e.** A continuous length or distance 1661. **f.** An expanse of land or water (usu., of a uniform character) 1829. **g.** *slang.* A term of hard labour; twelve months as a term of imprisonment 1821. **6.** *Mining* and *Geol.* Course or direction of a seam or a stratum with ref. to the points of the compass 1799.

1. Sometimes he thought to swim the stormy Main, By S. of Arms the distant Shore to gain DRYDEN. He gave a yawn and a s. 1856. **c.** Phr. *On, upon the s.*; An instrument, whose cords, upon the s.,..Yield only discord in his Maker's ear COWPER. **2.** These stretches of power naturally led the lords and commons into some degree of opposition GOLDSM. *S. of language*, the use of words or expressions with undue latitude of meaning. **4.** *On the* (*†full*) *s.*, in a state of mental strain, making intense effort. **5. a.** Phr. *At one* or *a s.*, *upon* or *on a s.*, rarely *at the s.*, without intermission, continuously (during the time specified or implied). **b.** Fretted out of..your mind, for a s. of months together DICKENS. **d.** In the evening, we made a s. toward the land 1823. **e.** This range [Lebanon] has an unbroken s. of a hundred miles 1908. **f.** Windsor, with its wide stretches of park and woodland and river 1885.

Stretch (stretʃ), *v.* [OE. *streććan* = OFris. *strekka*, MLG., MDu. *strecken* (Du. *strekken*), (O)HG. *strecken* :– WGmc. **strakkjan*, of doubtful source; cf. STRAIGHT.] **I.** To place at full length. **1.** *trans.* To prostrate (oneself, one's body); to extend (one's limbs) in a reclining posture; *refl.* to recline at full length. **b.** To lay (a person) flat ME. **2.** To extend (the arms) laterally; to expand (the wings), esp. for flight ME. **3.** *refl.* To straighten oneself; to rise to full height; also, to draw up the body, as from a stooping, cramped, or relaxed posture; to straighten the body and extend the arms, as a manifestation of weariness or languor (chiefly coupled with *yawn*). Also *intr.* for *refl.* ME.

1. There..His listless length at noontide would he s. GRAY. **b.** Andremon first..Of life bereft, lay strech'd upon the sand 1757. **3.** Mop [the dog].. rose and stretched himself 1858. Phr. *To s. one's legs*, to straighten them from a sitting position; usu., to relieve by walking the stiffness or fatigue caused by sitting; to take a walk for exercise.

II. To put forward, protrude. **1.** *trans.* To put forth, extend (the hand, an arm or leg, the neck, head). Now almost always with adv., e.g. *forth, out, forward.* OE. **2.** To hold out, hand, reach (something). Now only *Naut.* 1450.

1. He stretcht his hand, and into it, the Herald put the lot CHAPMAN.

III. To direct a course. **1.** *intr.* To make one's way (rapidly or with effort) ME. **2.** *Naut.* To sail (esp. under crowd of canvas) continuously in one direction 1687.

1. I s. over Putney Heath, and my spirit resumes its tranquillity THACKERAY. **2.** I stretched over for California 1726.

IV. To (make to) reach; to give or have a certain extent. **1.** *trans.* To place (something) so as to reach from one point to another, or across an interval in space ME. **2.** *intr.* (rarely *pass.*) and †*refl.* To have a specified extent in space; to be continuous to a certain point, or over a certain distance or area. late ME. **b.** To have its length in a specified direction. late ME. †**3.** *fig.* **a.** To have a specified measure in amount, degree, power, etc.; to be adequate for some purpose –1648. **b.** To have a specified extent or range of action or application –1659. †**4.** To tend, be serviceable (to some object) –1621.

1. A piece of clothes line, stretched across the room 1907. **2.** A steep slope stretches down to the Mer de Glace TYNDALL. *transf. Ant. & Cl.* I. i. 46. **3. a.** 1 *Hen. IV*, I. ii. 62.

V. To tighten by force, to strain. **1.** *trans.* To pull taut; to bring to a rigid state of straightness or evenness by the application of tractive force at the extremities. late ME. **2.** To pull (a person's) limbs lengthwise; esp. to torture by so doing; to rack. In early use, to place with extended limbs on a cross. ME. **3.** †**a.** *To s. a halter, rope*: to be hanged –1708. **b.** *To s.* (a person, his neck): to hang 1595. †**c.** *intr.* To be hanged –1676. **4.** *To s. a point* = to strain a point; see STRAIN *v.* II. 2 e. 1565. †**5.** *fig.* To strain (one's powers) –1660. †**b.** *refl.* and *intr.* To strain, press forward, use effort –1738.

1. Each eager Hound exerts His utmost Speed, and stretches ev'ry Nerve 1735. **2.** He hates him, That would vpon the wracke of this tough world S. him out longer SHAKS. **5. b.** Phr. *To s. to the oar, to the stroke*, to put forth one's strength in rowing.

VI. 1. *trans.* To lengthen or widen (a material thing) by force; to pull out to greater length or width; to enlarge in girth or capacity by internal pressure. late ME. **b.** To open wide (the eyes, mouth, nostrils) 1599. **2.** *fig.* To enlarge or amplify beyond proper or natural limits; to extend unduly the scope, application, or meaning of (a law, rule, word, etc.) 1553. **b.** To exaggerate in narration; chiefly *absol.* (colloq.) 1674. **3.** *intr.* To be or admit of being forcibly lengthened or dilated without breaking 1485.

1. Gentlemen, You'l breake your wits with stretching them 1632. My business..is to s. new boots for millionaires 1889. **b.** Now set the Teeth and s. the Nosthrill wide SHAKS. **3.** To Love a Enemy is to s. Humanity as far as it will go 1670. **b.** They call anything that is 'stretched' a Yankee story 1883. **3.** I tell you their consciences are like chiuerell skins, that will stretch euery way 1597.

Comb.: **s.-bench** *Leather-manuf.*, a bench on which the stretching of hides is performed; **-wood,** a wooden hand upon which a glove is stretched to dry in dyeing. Hence **Stre·tchable** *a.* capable of being stretched.

Stretcher (stre·tʃəɹ). late ME. [f. prec. + -ER[1].] **I.** One who or something which stretches. **1.** One who stretches; *spec.* a worker employed in various industries to stretch fabrics. **2.** An exaggerated story or yarn; *euphem.* or *joc.* a lie 1674. **II.** Techn. senses. †**1.** *Falconry.* A toe of a hawk or falcon –1677. **2.** An instrument or appliance for expanding material, making it taut, removing its wrinkles, and the like 1532. **b.** A frame upon which an artist's canvas is stretched 1847. **c.** An instrument for easing the fit of boots, gloves, hats, etc. 1858. **3.** A bar serving as a stay or brace. **a.** A buttress in masonry; a tie-beam in joinery; in trench timbering, a temporary strut 1774. **b.** A bar or rod used as a tie or brace in the framework of an article; esp. a cross-piece between the handles of a plough or the legs of a chair 1844. **4.** A bar or rod used to expand and to keep expanded something collapsible; e.g. each of the rods pivoted to the ends of the ribs and the sleeve which slides upon the stick of an umbrella 1843. **5.** A foot-rest in a rowing-boat 1609. **6.** A kind of litter composed of two poles separated by cross-bars upon which canvas is stretched, used to transport a sick or wounded person. Also, a shutter, gate, etc. used in the same way. 1845. **7.** A folding bed or bedstead chiefly for camp or hospital use. Also *pl.* the trestles for a bed. 1841. **8.** *Building.* A brick or stone laid with its length in the direction of the wall. Also *Fortif.*, a sod laid in a similar position. 1693. **9.** *Angling.* The artificial fly at the extremity of a casting line to which two or more flies are attached 1837.

attrib. and *Comb.*: **s.-bearer,** a man who helps to carry a s.; esp. a soldier who assists in carrying the wounded from a battle; **-party** *Mil.*, a party of men equipped with stretchers and appliances for assisting and removing the wounded; **-pole,** a pole of an ambulance stretcher.

Stretching (stre·tʃiŋ), *vbl. sb.* ME. [-ING[1].] The action or an act of STRETCH *v.*

Comb.: **s.-bond,** a bond (BOND *sb.*[1] 13) in which stretchers, not headers, are used; **-course,** a course of bricks or stones laid in the direction of the wall.

Stretching (stre·tʃiŋ), *ppl. a.* 1547. [-ING[2].] That stretches, in the senses of the verb.

Comb.: **s.-beam,** a tie-beam or brace used in building.

Stre·tchy, *a. colloq.* 1854. [f. STRETCH *v.* + -Y[1].] **1.** Having the quality of stretching; elastic. **b.** Liable to stretch unduly 1886. **2.** Inclined to stretch oneself or one's limbs 1872.

‖**Stretto** (stre·t,to), *adv.* and *sb. Pl.* **stretti** (stre·t,ti), also **strettos.** 1753. [It., = narrow.] *Mus.* **A.** *adv.* A direction: In quicker time. **B.** *sb.* (See quot.) 1854.

In a fugue the s. is an artifice by which the subject and answer are, as it were, bound closer together, by being made to overlap 1869.

Strew (strū), *sb. rare.* 1578. [f. next.] A number of things strewed over a surface or scattered about.

Strew (strū), *v.* Also (now *arch.* and *dial.*) **strow** (strōu). Pa. t. and pple. **strewed, strowed;** pa. pple. also **strewn, strown.** [OE. *strewian, streowian*, corresp. to OFris. *strēwa*, OS. *strōian*, OHG. *strewen* (Du. *strooien*, G. *streuen*), ON. *strá*, Goth. **straujan*; commonly taken to be based on IE. **ster-* as repr. in L. *sternere*. Cf. STRAW *v.*[1]] **1.** *trans.* To scatter, spread loosely; to sprinkle over a surface. **2.** To cover (the ground, a floor, any surface) with something loosely scattered or sprinkled ME. **3.** To be spread or scattered upon (a surface) 1513. **4. a.** To spread (a cloth or the like) as a covering. **b.** To cover (a bed) *with* a coverlet. **c.** To make or lay (a bed). *rare.* 1615. **5.** To level with the ground, lay low, throw down, prostrate. Chiefly *poet.* 1460. **6.** To level, calm (stormy waves); to allay (a storm). *arch.* and *poet.* (Cf. L. *sternere æquor*) 1594.

1. The newspapers which were strewn upon the table DICKENS. *fig.* The cleare moone strowes siluer in our path 1602. **2.** All the ground With shiverd armour strow'n MILT. Wild tornadoes, Strewing yonder sea with wrecks COWPER. *transf.* The coast is thickly strewn with islands 1879. **3.** The boulders that strewed the mountain-side 1893. **4.** Hands unseen thy Couch are strewing SCOTT. **5.** They..would have strown it, and are fall'n themselves TENNYSON. Hence **Strew·ing** *vbl. sb.*, the action of the vb.; *concr.* something strewed (now *rare* or *Obs.*). **Strew·ment** (*rare*), something strewed or for strewing; *pl.* flowers, etc. strewed on a grave.

'Strewth. *vulgar.* 1892. Short for *God's truth*, used as an oath.

‖**Stria** (strəi·ă). *Pl.* **striæ** (strəi·i). 1563. [L., furrow, grooving.] **1.** *Arch.* A fillet between the flutes of columns, pilasters, and the like. **2.** Chiefly in scientific use. A small groove, channel, or ridge; a narrow streak, stripe, or band of distinctive colour, structure, or texture; *esp.* one of two or of a series 1673. **b.** *pl. Electr.* The alternate bright the dark bands observed in vacuum-tubes (Geissler tubes) upon the passage of an electrical discharge 1881.

Striate (strəi·ēit), *a.* 1678. [– L. *striatus*, pa. pple. of *striare*, f. *stria*; see prec., -ATE[2].] Marked or scored with striæ, showing narrow structural bands, striped, streaked, or furrowed.

Striate (strəi·eit), *v.* 1709. [– *striat-* pa. ppl. stem of L. *striare*; see prec., -ATE[3].] *trans.* To mark or score with striæ; to furrow or streak.

Striated (strəi·eitėd). *ppl. a.* 1646. [f. as prec. + -ED[1].] **1.** = STRIATE *a.* **2.** *Arch.* Chamfered, channelled, grooved 1727. **3.** Constituting striæ 1854.

1. A deep, thin..finely s. Shell 1705. *Picus striolatus.* The S. Woodpecker. 1840.

Striation (strəi,ēi·ʃən). 1849. [f. as prec.; see -ATION.] **1.** Striated condition or appearance 1851. **2.** One of a set or system of striæ, a streak, a marking; esp. *Geol.*, one of the grooves or glacial marks found on rock-surfaces; *Min. pl.* the fine parallel lines on a crystalline face; *Electr. pl.* (cf. STRIA 2 b).

Striato- (strəi,ēi·to), used in *Zool.* and *Bot.* as comb. form of L. *striatus*, prefixed to adjs. in the sense 'striate and —', as *s.-rugose, -tubular.*

Striature (strəi·ătiŭɹ). 1728. [– L. *striatura* (Vitruvius), f. *striat-* (see STRIATE *v.*) + *-ura* -URE.] Disposition of striæ, striation; also, one of a set of striæ.

Strick (strik), *sb.* late ME. [f. **strik-*, wk. grade of base of STRIKE *v.* Cf. OFr. *estrique* (= sense 3), AL. *strica, stricum* (1185, in sense 2).] **1.** A bundle of broken hemp, flax, jute, etc. for heckling. **2.** A measure of capacity for corn, coal, etc.; also the measuring vessel. Now *dial.* late ME. **3.** A piece of wood with which measures of grain are made level. Now *dial.* late ME.

Strick (strik), *v.* late ME. [f. prec.] **1.** *trans.* To strike off (corn, etc.) level with the rim of the measure. **2.** To prepare (lint) for heckling; also, to heckle (flax, etc.) 1808.

Stricken (stri·k'n), *pa. pple.* and *ppl. a.* late ME. [pa. pple. of STRIKE *v.*] **A.** *pa. pple.* in special sense. (For other uses see STRIKE *v.*) **S. in years:** advanced in years. *arch.* **B.** *ppl. a.* **1.** Of a deer, etc.: Wounded in the chase 1513. **2.** Struck with a blow 1538. **b.** Of a sound, musical note: Produced by striking a blow 1820. **3.** Of a person, community: Afflicted with disease or sickness; overwhelmed with trouble, sorrow, or the like: esp. in *fever-, panic-s.* Of the face: Marked with or exhibiting great trouble. 1611. **b.** Of the mind, heart, soul: Afflicted with frenzy, madness, grief, or the like 1795. **4.** Of a measure: Having its contents levelled with the rim of the measuring vessel, as dist. from *heaped* 1495. **5.** *S. field*: a joined engagement between armed forces or combatants; a pitched battle 1700.

1. Let the s. deere goe weepe SHAKS. **2.** Out of s. helmets sprang the fire TENNYSON. **b.** *S. hour*, (arch.), a full hour as indicated by the striking of the clock; General —..sat talking a s. hour or thereabouts HAWTHORNE. **3.** A drawn, s. face 1896. **5.** I never had the good fortune to see a s. field SCOTT.

Strickle (stri·k'l), *sb.* [OE. *stricel* (perh. also **stricels*) with var. *strićel*, repr. by dial. *strichel*; f. **strick-* (cf. STRICK *sb.*).] **1.** A straight piece of wood with which surplus grain is struck off level with the rim of the measure. **b.** Applied to instruments used for similar purposes in casting or moulding 1688. **2.** A tool with which a reaper whets or sharpens his scythe 1641. Hence **Stri·ckle** *v. trans.* (*Founding*) to strike *off* with a s. (the superfluous sand) in moulding; to shape (a core) or form (a mould) by means of a s.; also *absol.*

Strict (strikt), *a.* 1578. [– L. *strictus*, pa. pple. of *stringere* draw tight.] **I.** Physical senses. †**1.** Drawn tightly together; tight, close –1781. **2.** Restricted as to space or extent; narrow, drawn in. Now *rare* or *Obs.* 1597. **3.** Straight and stiff. *Obs.* exc. *Bot.* and *Zool.* 1592.

1. She wildly breaketh from their s. imbrace SHAKS. **2.** S. passage, through which sighs are brought WORDSW. **3.** The s. stem of some corals 1891.

II. Fig. senses. **1.** Of personal relations, alliance, etc.; Close, intimate. Now *rare* or *Obs.* 1600. **2.** Of correspondence, agreement, or connection between facts, ideas, etc.: Close, exactly fitting 1715. †**3.** Restricted in amount, meaning, application, etc. –1737. **4.** Accurately determined or defined; exact, precise, not vague or loose 1631. **b.** Law *S. settlement*: see quot. 1710. **5.** Of confinement or imprisonment: Rigorous; severely restricted in regard to space or liberty of movement 1667. **6.** Of watch and ward, authority, discipline, obedience, etc.: Rigorously maintained, admitting no relaxation or indulgence 1602. **7.** Of a law, ordinance, etc., or its execution: Stringent and rigorous in its demands or provisions, allowing no evasion 1578. **8.** Of an art or science, its procedure, etc.: In rigid conformity to rules or postulates 1638. **9.** Of a quality or condition, an attitude or line of action: Maintained to the full, admitting no deviation or abatement; absolute, entire 1588. **b.** Of truth, accuracy, etc.: Rigidly observed; exactly answerable to fact or reality 1748. **10.** Rigorous and severe in rule and discipline, in administering justice, etc. 1596. **11.** Of persons: Holding a rigorous and austere standard of living; stern to oneself in matters of conscience and morality 1578. **b.** Of virtue, chastity, etc. 1589. **12.** Undeviating in adherence to the principles or practice implied by the designation 1660. **13.** Of inquiry, investigation, inspection, observation, calculation, and the like: Characterized by close and unrelaxing effort, so as to let nothing escape notice 1596.

2. The strictest explanation is the truest PUSEY. **3.** *Cymb.* v. iv. 17. **4.** The s. Import of the Word 1692. **b.** When land is settled..by a limitation to the parent for life, and after his death to his first and other sons in tail, and trustees are interposed to preserve the contingent remainders, this is called a *s. settlement* 1841. **6.** His temper was under s. government MACAULAY. **7.** This purdah system is strictest in the north 1913. **8.** The only concords recognized in s. counterpoint 1869. **9.** I generally go about In s. incognito SHELLEY. A man of the strictest prudence 1860. **10.** S. disciplinarians 1850. **11.** My mother and sisters are dissenters, and very s. THACKERAY. **12.** The feeling on the subject among s. churchmen 1868. **13.** Upon a s. review, I blotted out several passages SWIFT. Hence **Stri·ct-ly** *adv.*, **-ness.**

Striction (stri·kʃən). 1875. [f. *strict-* (see next) + -ION. Cf. Fr. (*ligne de*) *striction.*] **1.** The action of straining (*rare*) 1889. **2.** *Geom.* In a skew surface, *curve* or *line of s.*: the line that cuts each generator in that point of it that is nearest to the succeeding generator 1875.

Stricture (stri·ktiŭɹ, -tʃəɹ), *sb.*[1] late ME. [– L. *strictura*, f. *strict-*, pa. ppl. stem of *stringere* draw tight, touch lightly; see -URE.] **I.** A binding, tightening. **1.** *Path.* A morbid narrowing of a canal, duct, or passage, esp. of the urethra, œsophagus, or intestine. **2.** *gen.* The action of binding or encompassing tightly; tight closure; restriction (*rare*) 1649. †**II.** A spark, flash of light. *lit.* and *fig.* –1674. Rays and strictures of the divine Glory 1651. **III.** A touching slightly or in passing. †**1.** A touch, slight trace –1695. **2.** An incidental remark or comment; now always, an adverse criticism 1655.

2. We may now and then add a few strictures of reproof JOHNSON. Hence **Stri·cture** *v. trans.* to criticize, censure (*rare*). **Stri·ctured** *ppl. a.* affected with s. **Stri·cturing** *vbl. sb. Path.* formation of a s.

†**Stri·cture,** *sb.*[2] [f. STRICT *a.* + -URE.] Strictness. SHAKS.

Strid (strid). 1807. [app. repr. OE. *stride*; see next.] The proper name of the narrowest part of the channel of the Wharfe between level rocks at Bolton Priory; hence, any similar gorge or chasm.

Stride (strəid), *sb.* [Two formations: (1) OE. *stride*, f. *strid-, wk. grade of the root of STRIDE *v.*; (2) the surviving word, f. the present stem of the vb.] **1.** An act of striding; a long step in walking ME. **b.** The distance covered by a stride; the normal length of a stride used as a measure of distance OE. **2.** A striding gait 1671. **3.** An act of progressive movement of a horse, etc., completed when all the feet are returned to the same relative position which they occupied at the beginning; also, the distance covered by such a movement 1614. **b.** The regular or uniform movement (of a horse) in a race. Also *transf.* 1883. **4.** Divergence of the legs when straddled; also, the distance between the feet when the legs are stretched apart laterally to the utmost 1599.

1. Ile..turne two minsing steps Into a manly s. SHAKS. *fig.* Simplicity flies away, and iniquity comes at long strides upon us SIR T. BROWNE. **2.** I know him by his s. MILT. **3. b.** Phr. *To take in his s.*, of a horse or his rider, to clear (an obstacle) without checking his gallop;. *fig.* to deal with (a matter) incidentally, without interrupting one's course of action, argument, etc. *To get into one's s.*, to settle down to one's pace or rate of progress.

Stride (strəid), *v.* Pa. t. **strode** (strōᵘd), occas. **strided,** pa. pple. **stridden** (strid'n). [OE. *strīdan* (cf. *bestrīden* BESTRIDE) = (M)LG. *strīden* set the legs wide apart.] †**1.** *intr.* To stand or walk with the legs widely diverging; to straddle –1638. **b.** *transf.* (Often said of an arch.) 1598. **2.** To walk with long steps; to stalk ME. **3.** To take a long step; to advance the foot beyond the usual length of a step; to pass *over* or *across* an obstacle by a long step or by lifting the feet ME. **4.** *trans.* To step over with a stride 1572. **5.** To walk about (a street, etc.) with long steps; to pace; hence, to measure by striding 1577. **6.** To bestride ME.

1. b. The arches, striding o'er the new-born stream BURNS. **2.** He then rose up, strided to the fire, and stood for some time laughing and exulting BOSWELL. **3.** They that s. so wide at once will go farre with few paces FULLER. **4.** A hedge to clamber or a brook to s. CLARE. **6.** The tempest is his steed, he strides the air SHELLEY.

Strident (strəi·dĕnt), *a.* 1656. [– L. *stridens, -ent-*, pr. pple. of *stridĕre* creak; see -ENT.] **1.** Making a harsh, grating, or creaking noise; loud and harsh, shrill. **2.** *transf.* and *fig.* 1876.

1. Old Steyne's s. voice THACKERAY. **2.** S. colour 1907. Hence **Stri·dency,** the quality of being s. **Stri·dently** *adv.*

Stridor (strəi·dǭɹ). 1632. [– L. *stridor*, f. *stridĕre*; see prec., -OR 2.] **1.** A harsh, high-pitched sound, a shrill grating or creaking noise. **2.** *Path.* A harsh vibrating noise produced by a bronchial, tracheal, or laryngeal obstruction 1876.

Stridulate (stri·diŭleᵗt), *v.* 1838. [– Fr. *striduler* (Goureau 1837); see -ATE³.] *intr.* To make a harsh, grating, shrill noise; said *spec.* of certain insects. So **Stri·dulant** *a.* that stridulates.

Stridulation (stridiŭlēᵗ·ʃən). 1838. [– Fr. *stridulation* (Goureau 1837), f. *striduler*; see prec., -ATION.] The action of prec. vb.; the stridulous noise produced by certain insects.

Stridulator (stri·diŭleᵗtəɹ). 1880. [f. STRIDULATE *v.* + -OR 2.] **a.** An insect that stridulates. **b.** A stridulating apparatus.

Stridulatory (stri·diŭlătəri), *a.* 1838. [Partly f. STRIDULATE *v.* + -ORY², partly f. prec.] Pertaining to, causing, or caused by stridulation; also, capable of stridulating.

Stridulent (stri·diŭlĕnt), *a.* 1874. [f. L. *stridulus* + -ENT; cf. earlier synon. *stridulant.*] = next.

Stridulous (stri·diŭləs), *a.* 1611. [f. L. *stridulus* (f. *stridĕre*) + -OUS.] **1.** Emitting or producing a shrill grating sound. **2.** Of voice, sound: Harsh, shrill, grating 1646. **3.** *Path.* Pertaining to or affected with stridor 1822.

1. S. guitar with wiry twang 1819. **2.** In piercing accents s. COWPER. Hence **Stri·dulous-ly** *adv.*, **-ness.**

Strife (strəif). ME. [Aphetic – OFr. *estrif*, rel. to *estriver* STRIVE *v.*] **1.** The action of striving together; a condition of antagonism, enmity, or discord; contention, dispute. **b.** An act or instance of contention or antagonism; a contest, quarrel, or dispute ME. **c.** A subject of contention (*rare*) 1535. **2.** Competition, emulation; a contest of emulation 1530. **3.** The act of striving; strong effort (*rare*) 1601.

1. A fell woman and full of s. ME. The diuell hath cast a bone..to set stryfe Betweene you 1546. *transf.* Safe amidst the elemental s. BYRON. *At s.*, at variance. *To make s.*, to cause dissension. **b.** A mere s. of words JOWETT. **c.** Thou hast made vs a very s. vnto our neghbours COVERDALE. *Ps.* 79[80]: 6. **2.** Let our s. be, which can best serve our country 1836. **3.** As if these Mystic Authors made it their s. to imitate Nature 1687. Hence **Stri·feful, Stri·feless** *adjs.*

Strift. 1612. [f. STRIVE *v.* after *drift, thrift*, etc.] The action of striving; an instance of this; also, contention, strife. *Obs.* exc. in the traditional phraseology of the Society of Friends.

Strig (strig). 1565. [Of unkn. origin. Cf. AL. *striggum* (1276).] **1.** The stalk of a leaf, fruit, or flower; a petiole, peduncle, or pedicel. Also, the stem of the hop cone. **2.** A long thin appendage in various tools; the tang of a sword-blade; the stem of a marking-gauge; or the like 1703.

‖**Striga** (strəi·gă). *Pl.* **strigæ** (strəi·dʒī). 1760. [L., swath, furrow.] †**1.** *Arch.* = STRIA 1. –1771. **2.** *Bot.* A row of stiff bristles; now, a stiff bristle (chiefly *pl.*) 1760. **3.** *Ent.* A transverse streak 1826.

Strigate (strəi·gĕt), *a.* 1891. [f. prec. + -ATE².] = STRIGOSE *a.* 2. So **Striga·ted** *a.* having a channelled surface 1728.

‖**Striges** (strəi·dʒiz), *sb. pl.* 1563. [L., *striæ, strigæ.*] The channels of a fluted column.

Strigil (stri·dʒil). 1581. [– L. *strigilis*, f. *strig-, base of *stringere* touch lightly.] **1.** *Antiq.* An instrument with a curved blade, for scraping the sweat and dirt from the skin in the hot-air bath or after gynmastic exercise. Also *transf.* a flesh-brush or other instrument used for the same purpose. **2.** *Ent.* (See quot.) 1873.

2. The sixth segment [of the male *Corixa*] bearing on its upper side a small stalked plate (*strigil*) ..furnished with rows of teeth 1910.

Strigillose (stridʒi·lōᵘs), *a.* 1857. [f. as a var. of next, with epenthesis of the L. dim. suffix *-ill-*; cf. STROMBULIFORM.] *Bot.* Finely strigose.

Strigose (strəi·gōᵘs), *a.* 1793. [f. STRIGA 2 + -OSE¹.] **1.** *Bot.* Covered with strigæ or stiff hairs. Also of hairs: Having the character of strigæ. **2.** *Ent.* Having strigæ, streaked 1826.

Strigous (strəi·gəs), *a. rare.* 1776. [f. as prec. + -OUS.] = prec. 1.

Strike (strəik), *sb.* ME. [f. next.] **1.** = STRICK *sb.* 1. late ME. **2. a.** = STRICKLE *sb.* 1. late ME. **b.** An instrument, usu. a rod or narrow board, used in brickmaking, casting, plumbing, etc., for levelling a surface by striking off the superfluous material 1683. **3.** A denomination of dry measure (not now officially recognized); usu. identical with the bushel, but in some districts equal to a half-bushel, and in others to two or four bushels. Also, the cylindrical wooden measuring vessel containing this quantity. ME. †**4.** The unit proportion of malt in ale or beer –1820. **5.** An act of striking 1587. **6.** *Fishing.* **a.** The jerk by which the angler secures a fish that is already hooked 1840. **b.** A large catch (of fish) 1887. **7.** *Mining* and *Geol.* The horizontal course of a stratum; direction with regard to the points of the compass 1829. **8.** A concerted cessation of work on the part of a body of workers, for the purpose of obtaining some concession from the employer or employers. Formerly occas. *s. of work.* 1810. **9.** An act of 'striking oil'; a discovery of a rich vein of ore in mining. Also *fig.* a stroke of success. 1883. **10.** *U.S. Baseball.* An act of striking at the ball, characterized as *fair* or *foul s.*; a 'foul s.' 1874. **11.** *Printing.* A type matrix struck from the punch 1871. **12.** *Coining.* The amount struck at one time 1891. **13.** *Soap-making.* The proper crystalline or mottled appearance of a soap, indicating complete saponification 1884.

8. It appeared there was a s. for higher wages 1815. Phr. *On s.* **14.** *U.S. Political slang.* The introduction of a bill (a *s. bill*) hostile to some moneyed interest in the hope of being paid to withdraw it 1885.

Comb.: **s.-breaker,** a workman who consents to work for an employer whose workmen are on s., thus contributng to the defeat of the s.; **-pay,** the periodical payment made by a trade-union for the support of men on s.

Strike (strəik), *v.* Pa. t. **struck** (strɒk); pa. pple. **struck,** *arch.* (also *U.S.* in sense III. 2) **stricken** (stri·k'n); see also STRIKED. [OE. *strīcan* = OFris. *strīka,* MLG. *strīken,* MDu. *strijken,* OHG. *strīhhan* (G. *streichen*); WGmc. deriv. of **strīk-* **straik-*. Cf. STREAK *sb.*, STRICKLE, STRIGIL, STROKE *v.*[1]] **I. 1.** *intr.* To make one's way, go. In early use chiefly *poet.* Later, chiefly with adv. (*forth, forward, over*) or phr. indicating the direction. *Obs.* exc. *arch.* ME. **2.** To proceed in a new direction; to make an excursion; to turn in one's journey *across, down,* etc. 1615. **b.** of a road, stream, etc. 1584. **c.** Of a boundary, path, mountain-range, etc.: To take a (specified) direction 1456. **d.** trans. *To s. a line* or *path*: to take a direction or course of movement 1867.

1. The Jews were not long of striking forward STEVENSON. 2. It began raining, and I struck into Mrs. Vanhomrigh's, and dined SWIFT. We struck across the island DARWIN. b. A bridle road.. struck into the fields 1883. c. A range of hills strikes southerly 1881.

II. To stroke, rub lightly, smooth, level. **1.** *trans.* To go over lightly with an instrument, the hand, etc.; to stroke, smooth; to make level. Also *absol.* Now *dial.* OE. **†2.** To smear (soap, blood, etc.) on a surface; also, to spread (a surface) with (something); to coat (a surface) *over* with oil, a wash, etc. –1799. **3.** To make (grain, etc.) level with the rim of the measure by passing a strickle over it. Also with the measure as obj. late ME. **b.** To level (sand) in moulding 1779. **4.** *Bricklaying.* To level up (a joint) with mortar; to spread (mortar) along a joint 1668. **b.** To cut off the superfluous mortar from the edges of (tiling) 1693. **5.** *Tanning.* To smooth and expand (skins) 1764. **6.** *Carpentry.* To fashion (moulding) with a plane 1842.

III. To mark with lines; to draw a line. **1.** To draw (a straight line) esp. by mechanical means; to draw (a circle, an arc) with compasses; †to make (a stroke, written mark) 1611. **2.** To cancel or expunge with or as with the stroke of a pen. *Obs.* exc. in *s. off, s. out, s. through,* and in the phr. *to s.* (a name, a person) *off* or (now rarely) *out of* a list. late ME. **3.** To form (a jury) by cancelling a certain number of names from the list of persons nominated to serve; similarly, to form (a committee), to make (a new register of voters) 1715. **4.** To make or cut (a tally) 1626. **5.** *Agric.* To mark off (land, a ridge) by ploughing once up and down the field; to make (furrows) in this manner; also *absol.* 1573. **b.** To make (a row of holes) with a dibble 1797.

1. Accustome your self to s. your strokes firm and bold 1662. 2. He has struck Thomas out of his will THACKERAY. 3. The Committee was struck late in the summer 1896.

IV. To lower (sails, masts), and derived senses. **1.** *Naut.* To lower or take down (a sail, mast, yard, etc.); esp. to lower (the topsail) as a salute and, more rarely, as a sign of surrender in an engagement ME. **b.** To haul down (a flag), esp. as a salute or as a sign of surrender. Chiefly in the phrases *to s.* (*the*) *flag, to s. one's colours.* Also *to s.* one's *flag* (said of an admiral): see FLAG *sb.*[4] 2. 1628. **c.** *absol.* To lower sail, haul down one's flag. late ME. **2.** trans. *Naut.* To lower (a thing) into the hold by means of a rope and tackle. Chiefly *to s. down* (also *absol.*). Also, *to s. out,* to hoist out from the hold and lower to the dock. 1644. **3.** *Building.* **a.** To remove (scaffolding); in trenchwork, to remove (the timbers with which the sides have been secured) 1694. **b.** To remove (the centre or centering of an arch) 1739. **4.** *Shipbuilding.* To cause (a vessel) to slide *down, off* (the slipway); to release (a boat from the cradle) 1647. **5.** To discharge (a load); to empty (a vessel) of its load 1627. **b.** *Sugar-boiling.* To empty (the liquor, the tache) 1793. **6.** To let down (a tent) for removal; to remove the tents of (a camp or encampment) 1707. **7.** To unfix, put out of use 1793. **b.** *Theatr.* To remove (a scene); to remove the scenery, etc. of (a play); to turn down (a light) 1889. **8.** *intr.* Of an employee: To refuse to continue work; esp. of a body of employees, to cease working by agreement among themselves or by order of their society or union 1768. **b.** More explicitly *to s. work, †tools* (cf. sense 7 above) 1803. **c.** *trans.* Of a workmen's society or union: To order a strike of workmen against (a firm); to order (a body of workmen) to strike 1891.

1. Now s. your sailes ye iolly Mariners, For we be come vnto a quiet rode SPENSER. *fig.* He boarding her, she striking sail to him POPE. 3. a. On striking the scaffolding, part of the south transept.. came down 1868. 6. Next morning we struck camp and turned homewards 1891. 7. Arrange.. the hour for..striking wickets 1851. 8. The London omnibus men struck in a body 1892.

V. To deal a blow, to smite with the hand (*occas.* another limb), a weapon or tool. **1.** *trans.* To deal (a person, an animal) a blow; to hit with some force either with the hand or with a weapon. Also with double obj. *to s.* (a person) *a blow.* ME. **b.** *absol.* and *intr.* To deal or aim a blow with the fist, a stick, etc. 1509. **2.** *trans.* To hit, smite (a material, an object) with an implement, esp. with one designed for the purpose. Also with cogn. obj. ME. **b.** *absol.* and *intr.* To make a stroke with a hammer or other implement; spec. in *Smithing* ME. **c.** trans. *To s.* (a prisoner) *in the boots,* to crush the limbs by driving wedges between them and the iron boots as a form of torture. *Obs.* exc. *Hist.* 1715. **3.** With complementary adv. or phr.: To remove or drive with or as with a blow of an implement or the hand. Now somewhat *rare.* 1450. **4.** To stamp with a stroke. **a.** To impress (a coin, medal, etc.) *with* a device by means of a die; to coin (money); also †*absol.* 1449. **b.** To impress (a device) *upon*; also to impress (a die, etc.) with a device 1551. **c.** To impress or print by means of type, an engraving or the like. *Obs.* exc. in *to s. off.* 1759. **†d.** *fig.* To imprint on the mind –1709. **5.** To tap, rap, knock 1470. **b.** To beat or sound (a drum, etc.); to sound (an alarm) on a drum (said also of the drum). Also *to s. up.* Also *absol. Obs.* exc. *Hist.* 1572. **c.** To touch (a string, a key of an instrument) so as to produce a musical note; *poet.* to play upon (a harp, lyre, etc.) 1565. **6. a.** (*a*) To produce (fire, a spark) by percussion, esp. by the percussion of flint and steel. Chiefly in the phr. *to s. fire.* 1450. (*b*) *transf.* (in recent use). To cause (a match) to ignite by friction. Also *intr.* of a match: To admit of being struck. 1880. **b.** To produce (music, a sound, note) by touching a string or playing upon an instrument; hence *gen.* to sound (a particular note). Also said of the instrument. 1597. **7.** To pierce, stab, or cut (a person, etc.) with a sharp weapon. Also with double obj. Now *rare.* ME. **b.** *fig.* Of a feeling, etc.: To pierce (a person *to* the heart, *to* the quick). late ME. **8.** *absol.* and *intr.* (also with cogn. obj.). To deliver a cut or thrust with a sharp weapon. Also said of the weapon. ME. **b.** *fig.* esp. in *to s. at,* to aim at the overthrow, destruction, or defeat of. late ME. **9.** In various spec. uses of sense V. 7; *esp. Angling.* to cause the hook to pierce the mouth of (a fish) by a jerk; to hook; also said of the hook or the rod. late ME. **10.** To hit with a missile, a shot, etc. Also said of the missile. late ME. **11.** *intr.* To use one's weapons; to fight. Also with cogn. obj. 1579. **b.** *trans.* To fight (a battle). late ME. **c.** *Mil. intr.* To attack. Const. *at.* Also *trans.* to attack (in flank, etc.). 1606. **12.** *trans.* **a.** To deliver a blow with (the hand or something held in the hand), to bang, slap (the fist, hand), to stamp (the foot) *on, upon, against.* Also, to strike a horse with (the spur). Const. *to, against.* 1548. **b.** To cause (a tool, etc.) to make the required stroke. In *Bookbinding,* To cause (a hot tool) to make an impression in tooling. 1600. **13.** Of a serpent, etc.: To wound (a person) with its fangs or sting. Also *absol.* late ME. **14.** Of an animal: To wound or attack with the heels, horns, tusks, claws, or any natural weapon. Also *absol.* Now *rare.* 1538. **b.** *intr.* To aim a blow with a natural weapon; to lash *out* (with the feet, etc.) 1565. **15.** *trans.* †**a.** Of a bird of prey: To dart at and seize (its quarry or prey) –1879. **b.** *intr.* Of a fish: To seize the bait 1891. **16.** Of a piece of mechanism: To make a stroke, hit or beat something 1610. **17.** *intr.* and *trans.* with cognate obj. Of a clock: To make one or more strokes on its sounding part. Hence *trans.* to indicate (the hour of day) by a stroke or strokes; also with obj. a numeral designating the hour. late ME. **b.** *intr.* in passive sense. Of the hour: To be indicated by the striking of the clock. late ME. **c.** *trans.* To cause (a clock, etc.) to sound the time; to cause (bells) to sound *together* 1675. **18.** Of lightning, thunder, a thunderbolt: To descend violently upon and blast (a person or thing). late ME. **b.** *absol.* and *intr.* 1750. **19.** *trans.* Of God: To visit with lightning, esp. as a punishment. Also *to s. dead.* 1577. **20.** To bring suffering or death upon (a person, etc.) as with a blow; to afflict suddenly (*with, by* sickness, infirmity, death), esp. as a punishment. (Said chiefly of God or a deity.) late ME. **b.** Of a disease, etc.: To attack or afflict (a person) suddenly; to make infirm, lay low. Chiefly *pass.* 1530. **c.** *pass.* Of a crop, of cattle: To be tainted or infected with a disease 1750. **21.** To deprive (a person) suddenly of life, or of one of the faculties, as if by a physical blow. Often with compl., as *to s. dead, blind,* etc. Also *pass.*: To become suddenly *blind, dumb,* etc. 1534. **b.** *hyperbolically,* expressing the temporary effect of fear, amazement, etc. 1533. **c.** Vulgarly used in joc. forms of imprecation, as *s. me blind* (*if, but* —), etc. 1696. **d.** To turn as by enchantment *into* 1609. **22.** To prostrate mentally; in weaker sense, to shock, depress. *Obs.* exc. in *To s. all of a heap* (colloq.) 1598. **b.** To cause (a person) to be overwhelmed or seized *with* (terror, amazement, grief, etc.). Also of the feeling: To seize. 1533. **c.** To cause (a feeling, etc.) to fall or come suddenly. Const. *into,* †*in,* †*to.* 1583.

1. [He] struck the boy a violent blow 1824. b. His dwarf..Struck at her with his whip TENNYSON. 2. *fig.* Wit now and then, struck smartly, shows a spark COWPER. b. Phr. *To strike while the iron is hot,* to make one's effort while opportunity serves. 3. [They] now prepared to s. the weapon from his hand 1797. 4. A fine Medal was struck.. on Occasion of the Victory 1736. c. Send it to the printer to s. off a certain number of proofs 1892. 5. He struck the table a blow 1889. b. The kettle-drums struck up MACAULAY. c. But hark! he strikes the golden lyre! POPE. 6. a. Phr. *To s. a light,* to produce a flame with flint and steel or by the friction of a match. (*b*) Matches that s. only on the box 1892. b. Such musick sweet..As never was by mortall finger strook MILT. 7. b. The News of the loss of Bologna, struck Pope Julius the 2d to the Heart 1712. 8. The Fellow..struck at the Spaniard with his Hatchet DE FOE. b. The Revolution..began to s. at Church and King 1892. Phr. *To s. at the root* or *foundation,* to attempt or tend to the utter destruction or overthrow (*of* something). 9. He that strikes The Venison first, shall be the Lord o' th' Feast SHAKS. High authorities say that salmon should not be struck at all 1892. 11. To s. one blow for the King 1847. c. The French centre..was marching to s. it in flank 1893. 12. He struck the stock of his gun violently upon the ground 1862. 13. A hideous snake..had uplifted its triangular head to s. 1893. 14. b. They s. with their claws, they bite each other GOLDSM. 17. The clocke hath strucken twelue vpon the bell SHAKS. *fig.* This day my years s. fiftie 1605. b. I will sit up 'till twelve strikes 1787. c. I struck my repeater again 1893. 18. The house had been struck with lightning 1808. Phr. To *s. dead, blind.* 19. Heau'n with Lightning s. the murth'rer dead SHAKS. 20. b. The Duke had been stricken by paralysis 1891. c. They [lambs] have been struck with the fly 1840. 21. Some Planet s. him dead 1628. b. Her beauty will certainly s. me dumb SHERIDAN. 22. b. Rebecca's appearance struck Amelia with terror THACKERAY. c. His appearance will s. terror into his enemies JOWETT.

VI. To make a vigorous movement (as if striking a blow). **1.** *intr.* To make a stroke with the limbs in swimming. Also *to s. out.* 1660. **b.** To make a stroke with one's oar 1725. **2.** Of a horse: To put down his fore feet *short, close,* etc. 1683. **b.** *trans.* Of a horse: To alter his pace into (a faster movement). Also *intr.* To quicken his pace *into.* Also, to put (a horse) *into* a quicker pace. 1816. **3.** To thrust (the hand, etc.) with a sudden movement. Also *intr.* 1607. **4.** *intr.* To move quickly, dart, shoot 1639. **b.** To start suddenly *into* (a song, tune) 1819. **c.** To thrust oneself suddenly or vigorously *into* (a quarrel, debate, etc.) 1828. **d.** *trans.* (= *s. into*) in phr. *to s. an attitude*: see ATTITUDE 2. 1825. **5.** *intr.* **a.** Of light: To pierce *through* (a medium), break *through* (clouds, darkness) 1563. **b.** Of cold: To go *through*, penetrate *to*. Also of the wind, something damp or cold, *to s. chill, damp*, etc.; also *trans.* 1569. **6.** *trans.* To cause to penetrate, impart (life, warmth, dampness) *to, into, through* 1611. **7.** Of a plant, cutting, etc.: To send down or out (its roots); to put forth (its root or roots) 1707. **b.** *intr.* To put forth roots. Of a root: To penetrate the soil. 1682. **c.** *trans.* To cause (a cutting, etc.) to root; to propagate (a plant) by means of a cutting, etc. 1842. **8.** To change the colour of (a substance) by chemical action *into* (a specified colour); to produce or assume (a specified colour) by this means 1664. **9. a.** *trans.* To cause (a colour, dye) to take or sink in 1769. **b.** *intr.* Of a dye: To sink in; also, to spread, run 1790. **10.** *trans.* To cause (herrings) to become impregnated with salt, or (pork) with saltpetre in curing 1780.

1. He..struck out, and swam for a few yards 1888. **2. b.** He struck his horses into a gallop 1823. **4.** A sudden pain..struck across my heart 1719. **b.** The Jester next struck into another carol SCOTT. **5. b.** The..damp of the place struck to his marrow 1889.

VII. To impinge upon. **1.** *intr.* Of a moving body: To impinge upon or come into collision or contact with something else. Const. *on, upon, against*. ME. **2.** *trans.* To come into forcible contact or collision with 1626. **b.** *fig.* (chiefly after Latin *ferire cælum, sidera*) 1605. **3.** *spec.* Of a ship: **a.** *intr.* To hit (*on* or *upon* a rock, etc.), to run aground 1518. **b.** *trans.* To hit or run upon (a rock, the ground, a mine) 1587. **4.** Naut. *To s. ground, soundings*: to reach the bottom with a sounding line. Also *transf.* of a swimmer: To touch (bottom). 1726. **5.** *trans.* Of a beam or ray of light or heat: To fall on, catch, touch 1586. **b.** *intr.* Of light: To fall, impinge *on* 1662. **6.** *trans.* Of a sound, report, etc.: To fall on, reach, or catch (the ear) 1596. **b.** *intr.* with *on, upon* 1848. **7.** *trans.* Of a thought, an idea: To come into the mind of, occur to (a person) 1606. **8.** To impress or arrest (the eye, view, sight) 1700. **9.** Of something seen or heard: To impress strongly (a person); to appear remarkable to 1672. **b.** *intr.* To make an impression (*on* the mind, senses, observation) 1732. **c.** *trans.* To impress in a specified way 1701. **d.** To impress or catch (the senses, fancy, etc.) 1697. **e.** To catch the admiration, fancy, or affection of (one of the opposite sex) 1599. **10.** *intr.* To hit or light *on, upon* 1616. **11.** *trans.* To come upon, reach in travelling; to come to in the course of one's wanderings. Chiefly *U.S.* and *Colonial*. Also of a line: To hit, come upon (a specified point). 1798. **b.** To come across unexpectedly; also, to hit upon (the object of one's search). Chiefly *U.S.* 1851.

1. Birds killed striking [against the glass of a lighthouse] 1901. **2.** His stool-legs were so loosened that when he sat down he struck the floor with a crash 1899. **b.** Bass, and treble voices s. the skies POPE. **2.** The yacht had struck bow on 1890. **6.** [A] scraping sound struck his quick ear 1891. **7.** It struck me immediately that I had made a blunder SWIFT. Hold..a thought has struck me! SHERIDAN. **9.** His attendant was struck by the unusual change in his deportment SCOTT. **b.** On diff'rent senses, diff'rent objects s. POPE. **c.** Phr. *To s. one as —*, to appear to one as —, to give one the impression of being —. **e.** *To be struck on* (vulg.); I'm glad you're struck on her 1893. **10.** You s. on truth in all things, sir 1616. **11.** At length we successfully struck the spoor BADEN-POWELL. **b.** Phr. *To s. a bonanza* (cf. BONANZA 1). *To s. it rich*, to find a rich mineral deposit. *To s. oil*: see OIL *sb.*[1] 3.

VIII. 1. *To s. hands* (said of two parties to a bargain): to take one another by the hand in confirmation of a bargain; hence, to ratify a bargain *with* (another) 1440. **†b.** *To s.* (a person) *luck*: to give him a 'luck-penny' on making a bargain –1677. **2.** To settle, arrange the terms of, make and ratify (an agreement, treaty, truce, †marriage, †peace, etc.); esp. in phr. *to s. a bargain* 1544. **3.** *trans.* To balance (a book or sheet of accounts) 1539. **4.** To determine, estimate (an average, a mean) 1729. **†5.** *To s. a docket*: see DOCKET *sb.* –1852. **6.** *slang.* **†a.** *trans.* To steal (goods), rob (a person); also *absol.* and with cogn. obj. –1622. **†b.** *intr.* To borrow money –1700. **c.** To beg; also in phr. *to s. it* 1898. **d.** *trans.* To make a sudden and pressing demand upon (a person *for* a loan, etc.). Also *absol.* or *intr.* 1751. **7.** *intr.* In the *U.S.* army: To act as an officer's servant 1891.

3. *To s. a balance*: see BALANCE *sb.* 16.

With advs. **S. down. a.** *trans.* To fell to the ground with a blow. **b.** *intr.* Of the sun: To send down its heat oppressively. **S. home.** *intr.* To make an effective stroke or thrust with a weapon or tool. **b.** Of words, etc.: To tell powerfully; to produce a strong impression. **S. in. †a.** *intr.* To join *with* as a co-worker, etc.; to fall in agreement *with*. **†b.** To enter a competition *for*. **c.** Of an eruption, disease: To disappear from the surface or the extremities with internal effects. **d.** To interpose actively in an affair. **e.** To interpose in a discussion, etc., with a remark, an expression of opinion, etc. **S. off. a.** *trans.* To cancel by or as by a stroke of the pen; to remove from a list or record. **b.** To cut off with a stroke of a sword, axe, etc. **c.** To produce (a picture, literary composition, etc.) quickly or impromptu. **S. out. a.** *trans.* = *Strike off* a. **b.** To produce or elicit as by a blow or stroke. **c.** To produce by a stroke of invention (a plan, scheme, fashion, etc.). **d.** To represent in a working drawing or plan. Also, to sketch rapidly. **e.** To open up, make for oneself (a path, course, line). **f.** *intr.* To go energetically. **g.** To lay about one (with the fists, a weapon, etc.). **S. up. a.** (*a*) *trans.* To begin to play or sing (a piece of music, a song); (*b*) *intr.* (or *absol.*) To begin playing or singing; (*c*) *intr.* Of music: To begin to be played. **b.** To make and ratify (an agreement, treaty, bargain, etc.). In recent use slightly *contempt.* **c.** To start (a friendship, a conversation, trade, etc. *with* another). **d.** *intr.* To rise up quickly, dart or spring up. **e.** *U.S.* in *pass.* (*a*) To be bewildered. (*b*) To be fascinated *with* or 'gone' *on* (a person of the opposite sex).

Striked (strəikt), *ppl. a.* 1581. [f. prec. (II. 3) + -ED[1].] Of a measure: Levelled with a strike or strickle: opp. to *heaped*.

Striker (strəi·kəɹ). ME. [f. STRIKE *v.* + -ER[1].] **I. †1.** One who roams as a vagrant. late ME. only. **†b.** A footpad –1611. **2.** A person (or animal) that strikes. **a.** *gen.* ME. **b.** In indecent sense. Hence, a fornicator. –1665. **c.** One who 'strikes' fish with a spear or harpoon 1697. **d.** In metal-working, the assistant operator who wields the heavy sledge-hammer 1831. **e.** In various games: The player who is to 'strike' 1699. **f.** A workman who 'strikes' or is 'on strike' 1850.

2. a. Against which no blow can be struck but it recoils on the s. EMERSON. **c.** The natives are excellent hunters and strikers of fish 1827. **e.** *S.-out* (in *Tennis*, etc.) the one who plays the ball when first served.

II. A thing that strikes or is used for striking. **1.** *gen.* 1644. **2.** = STRICKLE *sb.* 1. a, b. 1693. **3.** A clock or watch that strikes 1778. **4.** A harpoon 1858. **5.** A steam-hammer designed as a substitute for the blacksmith's 'striker' 1869. **6.** The piece of mechanism in a gun, fuse, etc. which explodes the charge 1824. **7.** The part of a bell, clock, etc. which strikes 1872.

Striking (strəi·kiŋ), *vbl. sb.* late ME. [f. STRIKE *v.* + -ING[1].] The action of STRIKE *v.*, in various senses.

attrib. and *Comb.*: **s. distance,** the distance within which it is possible to strike a blow; **-iron,** a kind of harpoon; **-plate,** the metal plate against which the end of a spring-lock bolt strikes, when the door or lid is being closed.

Striking (strəi·kiŋ), *ppl. a.* 1611. [f. STRIKE *v.* + -ING[2].] That strikes, esp. that strikes the attention of an observer; telling, impressive. Hence **Stri·king-ly** *adv.*, **-ness.**

String (striŋ), *sb.* [OE. *streng* = MLG. *strenge*, MDu. *strenc, stranc*, OHG. *stranc* (G. *strang*), ON. *strengr* :– Gmc. **straŋgiz* (see STRONG).] **I.** A line, cord, thread. **1.** A line for binding or attaching anything; normally one composed of twisted threads of spun vegetable fibre. **†a.** In early use occas. a rope or cord of any thickness. In 16–18th c. applied joc. to the hangman's rope. –1840. **b.** Chiefly applied to a line of smaller thickness than that connoted by *rope*. In mod. use: A thin cord or stout thread. ME. **c.** Thin cord or stout thread used for tying parcels and the like 1827. **d.** A cord used as a snare (*rare*) ME. **e.** A cord for leading or dragging along a person or an animal; a leading-string, a leash ME. **f.** A thread on which beads, pearls, etc. are strung 1612. **g.** A cord for actuating a puppet 1860. **2.** *transf.* A natural string or cord. **a.** A ligament, tendon, nerve, etc.; an elongated muscle or muscular fibre; the frænum of the tongue. *rare* exc. in *s. of the tongue*. OE. **b.** In plants: A cord, thread, or fibre; a 'vein' of a leaf; the tough piece connecting the two halves of a pod (in beans, etc.); a root-filament. late ME. **c.** A tendril; a runner. Now *dial.* 1585. **3.** A cord or line (composed of vegetable fibre, gut, or fine wire) adapted to produce a musical sound when stretched and caused to vibrate OE. **b.** *fig.* and in fig. context 1583. **c.** *pl.* Stringed instruments; now only, such as are played with a bow. Also, in mod. use, the players on these (in an orchestra or band). ME. **4.** A bowstring OE. **5.** A piece of cord, tape, ribbon, etc. for tying up or fastening some portion of dress, for binding the hair, for closing a bag or purse, etc. ME. **†b.** *pl.* The short cords, ribbons, or leather straps, formerly often attached (in pairs) to the edges of book-covers, to be tied in order to keep the book closed (now called *ties*) –1663. **†6.** A cord or ribbon worn as a decoration; the ribbon of a knightly order –1814. **†7. a.** The cord or chain wound on the barrel of a watch. **b.** A chain or cord for carrying a watch. –1701.

1. d. We walk in a world of Plots; strings universally spread, of deadly gins and fall-traps CARLYLE. **e.** *fig. To lead in a s., to have in* or *on a s.*: to be able to do what one likes with. Also *U.S.*, a limitation or restriction attached to something 1897. **g.** fig. *To pull the strings*, to control the course of affairs, to be the concealed operator in what is ostensibly done by another. **2. b.** *fig.* The Enquirye concerning the Rootes of Good and euill, and the strings of those Rootes BACON. **3. b.** But why touch I this s. agayne? 1655. *To harp on one* (*the same*, etc.) *s.*: see HARP *v.* 1. **4.** They make ready their arrow vpon the s. *Ps.* 11: 2. fig. *To have two* (*many*, etc.) *strings to one's bow*, to have two (etc.) alternative resources. *Second s.*, a second resource available if the first should fail; 'First,' 'second,' and 'third' strings are the first, second, and third men chosen to represent a club in any event 1897. **6.** Thou..who hast had my purse, As if y[e] strings were thine SHAKS.

II. A number of objects strung on a thread; hence, a series, succession. **1.** A thread or file with a number of objects strung upon it; a number (of beads, herrings, etc.) strung on a thread. Also, a number of things (e.g. sausages) linked together in a line. 1488. **2.** A number of animals driven in single file tied one to the other; a train of animals, vehicles, or persons one behind the other 1686. **b.** A flock (of birds) flying in single file 1801. **3.** A set or stud of horses, beasts of draught or burden, †slaves 1734. **†b.** A set (of persons); a band, a faction –1699. **4.** A number of things in a line; a row, chain, range 1683. **5.** A continuous series or succession (e.g. of stories, questions, incidents) 1710. **b.** A continuous utterance, a 'screed'. *contempt.* 1766. **c.** The 'thread', sequence (of a narrative). *rare.* 1833.

1. I haue sent you..a s. of Corall Beads 1620. **2.** Smugglers and their strings of pack-horses DARWIN. **5.** I had a s. of questions ready to ask 1797. **b.** It sounds like a s. of mere gabble HAWTHORNE.

III. *transf.* **1.** *Mining.* A thin vein of ore or coal; a ramification of a lode 1603. **2.** *U.S.* A line of fencing 1794. **3.** *Carpentry.* = *s.-board* 1711. **4.** *Arch.* = *s.-course* or *-moulding* 1817.

Comb.: **s.-bean** *U.S.*, the French or kidney bean; **-board,** a board which supports the ends of the steps in a wooden staircase; also *collect. sing.*; **-course,** a distinctive horizontal course, carried round a building; **-galvanometer,** one consisting of a fine conducting fibre, for measuring rapidly-fluctuating currents; **-moulding,** a moulding carried horizontally along a wall; **-piece,** a long piece of timber serving to connect and support a framework (e.g. a floor, bridge); a longitudinal railway-sleeper (*U.S.*) a heavy squared timber carried along the edge of a wharf-front.

String (striŋ), *v.* Pa. t. and pa. pple. **strung** (strɒŋ). late ME. [f. prec.; the str. conjugation is after *ring*.] **1.** *trans.* **a.** To fit (a bow) with its string; to 'bend' or prepare for use by slipping the loop of the bowstring into its notch, so that the string is drawn tight. **b.** To fit or furnish with a string or strings. Also *poet.* to tighten the strings of (a musical instrument) to the required pitch;

to tune. 1530. **2.** To furnish (the body) with nerves or sinews; *spec.* to furnish (the tongue) with its frænum 1632. **3.** *fig.* To make tense, brace, give vigour or tone to (the nerves, sinews, the mind, its ideas, etc.) 1599. **b.** with *up* 1845. **c.** To brace *to*, rarely *for* (action) or *to* (do something) 1748. **d.** To bring to a (specified) condition of tension or sensitiveness 1860. **4.** To bind, tie, fasten, or secure with a string or strings 1613. **5.** To thread or file (beads and the like) on or as on a string 1612. **b.** To hang or suspend by a connecting string 1890. **c.** *fig.* To put together in connected speech 1605. **6.** To hang, kill by hanging. Usu. with *up*. 1727. **7.** To deprive (a bean-pod) of its string or strings; to remove the runners from (a strawberry-bed) 1664. **8.** To furnish, equip, or adorn *with* something suspended or slung 1845. **9.** To draw up in a line or row; to extend in a string or series. Also with *out*, *up*. 1670. **10.** To extend or stretch (something flexible or rigid) from one point to another. Also with *out*. 1838. **11.** *intr.* To move or progress in a string or disconnected line; spec. in *Hunting*, of the hounds 1824. **12.** To form into strings, become stringy 1839. **13.** *trans.* To deceive, humbug. *U.S. slang.* 1901.

1. He tipt his arrow, strung his bow, and shot 1788. **b.** Orpheus Lute was strung with Poets sinewes SHAKS. **2.** Art neuer strung her tongue 1632. **3.** Toil strung the Nerves and purifi'd the Blood DRYDEN. **d.** Too highly strung for banter 1863. **5. c.** It is easy..to s. platitudes together 1884. **6.** They strung him up after a fair trial before Judge Lynch 1893. **10.** Stringing booms across the river—obstructing navigation 1908. **11.** However good the scent, they [staghounds] s. out 1905.

Stringed (striŋd), *a.* OE. [f. STRING *sb.* + -ED[2].] **1.** Having a string or strings; *spec.* of musical instruments such as the violin and guitar. **b.** *Her.* Used in specifying the tincture of a string; e.g. *s. argent* 1572. **2.** *transf.* Produced by strings or stringed instruments 1629.

1. A one-stringed banjo 1873. **2.** Divinely-warbled voice Answering the s. noise MILT.

Stringency (stri·ndʒĕnsi). 1844. [f. next; see -ENCY.] The quality of being stringent; strictness, rigour. **b.** Of reasoning: Compulsive force 1864. **c.** *Comm.* 'Tightness' in the money-market 1877.

Stringent (stri·ndʒĕnt), *a.* 1605. [– L. *stringens*, *-ent-*, pr. pple. of *stringere* bind; cf. STRICT and see -ENT.] **1.** Astringent, constrictive, styptic, esp. with ref. to taste. **2.** Tightly enfolding or compressing (*rare*) 1736. **3.** Of reasoning: That compels assent, convincing 1653. **4.** Of regulations, procedure, obligations, etc.: Rigorous, strict, thorough-going; rigorously binding or coercive 1846. **5.** Of the money-market: Tight 1891.

1. Harsh and s. to the palate, as..unripe fruit 1858. **4.** A more s. test was now added MACAULAY. Hence **Stri·ngent-ly** *adv.*, **-ness.**

Stringer (stri·ŋəɹ). late ME. [f. STRING *v.* and *sb.* + -ER[1].] †**1.** One who makes strings for bows –1688. **b.** The workman who fits a musical instrument with strings 1842. **2.** *fig.* One who strings words together 1774. **3.** *Building*, etc. **a.** A horizontal timber connecting uprights in a framework, supporting a floor, or the like; a tie or tie-beam 1838. **b.** *Shipbuilding.* An inside strake of planking or plating, secured to the ribs and supporting the ends of the beams 1830. **c.** *U.S.* A longitudinal railway sleeper 1881. **4.** *Mining* and *Geol.* A narrow vein of mineral traversing a mass of different material 1874. **5.** *pl.* Handcuffs (*slang*) 1893.

Stringhalt (stri·ŋhǭlt). 1523. [Obscurely f. STRING *sb.* and HALT *a.* and *sb.*[2] See also SPRINGHALT.] An affection of the hind legs of a horse which causes certain muscles to contract spasmodically.

Stringing (stri·ŋiŋ), *vbl. sb.* 1620. [-ING[1].] **1.** The action of STRING *v.* **2.** *concr.* **a.** Strings collectively 1722. **b.** Material for the string-board of a staircase, or for string-courses on a building 1833. **c.** Straight or curved inlaid lines in cabinet work 1812.

Stringless (stri·ŋlĕs), *a.* 1591. [-LESS.] Having no string; lacking strings.

His tongue is now a stringlesse instrument SHAKS.

Stringy (stri·ŋi), *a.* 1669. [f. STRING *sb.* + -Y[1].] **1.** Resembling string or fibre; consisting of string-like pieces. Chiefly of vegetable or animal tissue, esp. meat when its fibres have become tough. **2.** Of a person, the body, etc.: Thin; exhibiting sinew rather than flesh 1833. **3.** Of liquid or viscous matter: Containing or forming glutinous thread-like parts; ropy 1694.

1. Bits and gobbets of lean meat..tough and s. morsels HAWTHORNE. Hence **Stri·nginess.**

Stringy-bark. *Austral.* 1802. A name for many species of *Eucalyptus* (e.g. *E. gigantea*), which have a tough fibrous bark. **b.** The bark of any of these trees 1859. **c.** quasi-*adj.* Belonging to the 'bush' or uncultivated country 1833.

Strip (strip), *sb.*[1] Now only *U.S.* 1516. [Aphetic – AFr. *estrepe*, f. *estreper* ESTREPE *v.*] *Law.* = ESTREPEMENT.

Strip (strip), *sb.*[2] 1459. [– or cogn. w. (M)LG. *strippe* strap, thong, prob. rel. to STRIPE *sb.*[2]] **1.** A narrow piece (primarily of textile material, paper, or the like; hence *gen.*) of approximately uniform breadth. **b.** A long narrow tract of land, wood, etc. 1816. †**2.** An ornamental article of attire worn, chiefly by women, about the neck and upper part of the chest –1658. **3.** *Metall.* **a.** An ingot prepared for rolling into plates 1876. **b.** A narrow flat bar of iron or steel; hence, iron or steel in 'strips' (more fully *s. iron*, *steel*) 1887. **4.** *Mining.* An inclined trough for separating ores by washing 1875.

1. No carpet, except little strips by the bed 1856. Strips of wood about $2\frac{1}{2}$ in. wide 1907.

attrib.: **s. ticket,** a ticket for a journey by a public conveyance, printed with a number of similar tickets on a strip of paper.

Strip (strip), *sb.*[3] 1844. [f. STRIP *v.*[1]] *pl.* Tobacco-leaf with the stalk and midrib removed. Also *s.-leaf.*

Strip (strip), *v.*[1] Pa. t. and pa. pple. **stripped** (stript), **stript.** [ME. *stripe*, *strepe*, *strupe*, pointing to an OE **strȳpan*, **striepan* (as in *bestriepan* plunder, strip), corresp. to (M)Du. *stroopen*, OHG. *stroufen* (G. *streifen*) :– WGmc. **straupjan.*] **I.** To unclothe, denude. **1.** *trans.* To divest (a person, body) of clothing; to undress, make bare or naked. Const. *of* (one's clothing). Also *intr.* for *refl.* **b.** To divest (a person, oneself) of outer garments, or of some specified outer garment. Const. *of.* Also *intr.* for *refl.* spec. of an athlete, etc.: To take off one's ordinary wearing apparel in preparation for a contest. late ME. **c.** *trans.* To deprive *of* armour, insignia, ornaments. late ME. **d.** To remove the clothing of (a racehorse); also *intr.* of a horse, to undergo this process 1730. **2.** *fig.* **a.** To divest or dispossess (a person, oneself) *of* attributes, titles, honours, offices, etc. ME. **b.** To denude or divest (a thing) *of* attributes 1597. **c.** To expose the character or nature of (a person or thing) 1619. **3.** To plunder, spoil; to render destitute ME. **b.** To deprive or rid (a substance or thing) *of* 1675. **4.** To denude (a thing) of its covering, esp. (a tree) of its bark, (a seed) of its skin, (a fruit) of its rind ME. †**5.** To skin (an animal) –1770. **6.** To deprive (a plant *of* its foliage or fruit); to remove (seed or grain *from* the straw) 1697. **7.** To empty, make bare, clean out (a place, thing) *of* its contents, ornaments, etc. 1616. **8.** To take away the accessories, equipment, or furniture of; to dismantle 1683.

1. For there they began to s. her of her clothes SIDNEY. *refl.* The Nymph..Stript her self naked to the skin PRIOR. *transf.* (joc.) Therefore on, or strippe your sword starke naked SHAKS. **b.** He had already stripped himself of his wrappings 1865. **c.** The mutineers were stripped of their uniforms 1866. **d.** The mare stripped beautifully, as fine as a star 1857. **2. a.** Of his Godhead, he could not s. himself BUNYAN. **b.** Your friend, sir, must at least s. his proposals of their fine gilding SCOTT. **c.** He hides behind a magisterial air His own offences, and strips others bare COWPER. **3.** His fate was to be strip'd of all he had in Sweden 1737. **5.** An hart or a bucke is flayed, a hare strypped 1575. **7.** I stripped the house for a sale BRIDGES. **8.** To s. a muzzle-loader, first remove the lock 1881.

II. To doff, take off, peel away. **1.** To remove (the clothes, a garment, trappings, hair) from a person, body ME. †**2.** To take as plunder or spoil –1791. **3.** To remove (an adhering covering of skin, bark, lead, paper, etc.); to pull off (leaves, fruit) from a tree, etc. Also *to s. off.* late ME. **b.** *intr.* Of bark, membrane: To lend or adapt itself to the process of peeling or decortication. Of a layer of metal: To become detached. 1877. †**4.** To remove, roll up (a sleeve) –1815. **5.** To slip off (a jewel) from the arm, (a ring) from the finger 1611.

1. As she spoke she stripped off her gloves 1895. **2.** *Hen. V*, I. i. 11. **3.** Gather your currants.., s. them from the stalks 1769. The covers were stripped from the..chair-bottoms 1780. **4.** Then will he s. his sleeue, and shew his skarres SHAKS. **5.** *Cymb.* II. iv. 101.

III. Technical uses. **1.** *Tin-washing.* To remove tin from (the gravel). Also, to wash out, (gold). 1674. **2.** *Tobacco-manuf.* To remove the leaves from the stems of (tobacco) 1688. **b.** To remove the stalk and midrib from (tobacco-leaf) 1844. **3.** *Mech.* To tear off (the thread from a screw or bolt, the teeth from a wheel) 1873. **b.** To rip off the screw thread of (a cannon-ball or bullet); to render incapable of receiving the rotatory direction from the rifling of the barrel. Also *intr.* for *refl.* 1839. **4.** *Mining.* To lay bare (a mineral deposit, etc.) 1839. **5.** To smooth (a metal surface) by filing or the like; to smooth the surface of (a file-blank) preparatory to cutting the teeth 1831. **6.** *Carding.* To remove fluff, etc. from the teeth of (a card) 1891. **7.** *Electrometallurgy.* To remove (the plating from a plated article, the metal from a positive pole, etc.) by electrolysis. Also *intr.* of a plating: To come off. 1877. Hence **Stri·pping** *vbl. sb.* the action of the vb.; *concr.* something stripped off.

†**Strip,** *v.*[2] late ME. [f. Gmc. base **strīp-*; see STRIPE *sb.*[2]] **1.** *intr.* To move or pass swiftly –1616. **2.** *trans.* = OUTSTRIP *v.* –1774.

1. As the Westerne side shee stript along 1616. **2.** Before he reacht it, he was out of breath, And then the other stript him 1613.

Strip (strip), *v.*[3] 1610. [cogn. w. STRIPE *sb.*[1]; cf. WFlem. *strippen.*] **1.** *trans.* To extract (the milk from a cow's udder). Now *spec.* to extract the milk remaining in the udder after the normal milking, esp. by a particular movement of the hand. **2.** To draw between the finger and thumb, through the closed hand, etc.; e.g. to press out with the hand the ripe roe or milt from (a fish) 1884.

Strip (strip), *v.*[4] 1885. [f. STRIP *sb.*[2]] *trans.* To cut into strips.

Stripe (strəip), *sb.*[1] 1440. [Of unkn. origin; Du. *strippen* to whip does not agree in form, and is later.] †**1.** A blow or stroke with a staff, sword, or other weapon, with a missile, with the claws or hoofs of an animal, etc. –1596. †**b.** A touch on the keys of an instrument; hence, measure, strain –1616. **2.** A stroke or lash with a whip or scourge. Now *arch.*, chiefly in *pl.* 1485. †**3.** The mark left by a lash; a weal (*rare*) –1746.

2. Of the Iewes five tymes receaved I every tyme .xl. strypes saue one TINDALE. Labor exacted with stripes—how do you fancy that? 1839.

Stripe (strəip), *sb.*[2] 1626. [perh. back-formation from STRIPED.] **1.** In textile fabrics, hence *gen.*, a portion of the surface long in proportion to its breadth, of uniform width, and differing in colour or texture from the adjacent parts. **2.** A narrow strip of cloth, braid, or gold lace, sewn on a garment of different colour. Pop. applied to the chevrons worn by a non-commissioned officer, to good conduct badges worn by soldiers on the sleeve, etc. 1827. **3.** A striped textile fabric 1751. **4.** *Geol.* A narrow band of rock interposed between strata of differing character 1799. **5.** A long narrow tract of land (*occas.* of ice) 1801. **6.** A strip, shred; a narrow piece cut out 1785. **7.** *U.S.* A particular shade or variety of political or religious doctrine; in wider sense, a sort, class, type 1853.

1. Waistcoat, blue and yellow stripe, each s. an inch in depth 1860.

Stripe (strəip), *v.*[1] 1460. [Belongs to STRIPE *sb.*[1] Sense 2 is prob. a new formation on the sb.] †**1.** *trans.* To beat, whip –1533. **2.** To punish with stripes (*rare*) 1843.

Stripe (strəip), *v.*[2] 1471. [f. STRIPE *sb.*[2]] **1.** *trans.* To ornament (cloth, a garment) with narrow pieces of material or with stripes of colour. **2.** To mark with a narrow band or with bands of colour; to mark with alternate stripes of colour 1597. **b.** *intr.* Of a plant: To become variegated. Also *trans.* To produce variegation in (a plant). 1725. **3.** To finish (a surface) with grooves or ridges 1842.

2. A goodly Tulip, Stript in Gold and Purple 1645.

Striped (strəipt), *ppl. a.* 1617. [perh. of LDu. origin; cf. MLG., MDu. *strīpe* = MHG. *strīfe*, G. *streifen*.] Marked with a stripe or stripes, having a band or bands of colour, streaked. **b.** In specific names of animals, plants, and minerals 1629. **c.** Of muscular fibre: Divided by transverse bands into striations 1854. **d.** Of a person: Entitled to wear a (good-conduct, etc.) stripe 1890.

Stripling (stri·pliŋ). late ME. [prob. f. STRIP *sb.*[2] + -LING[1]; as if 'one who is slender as a strip', one whose figure is not yet filled out.] **1.** A youth, one just passing from boyhood to manhood. **2.** *attrib.* passing into adj. 1553.

1. *transf.* I'm but a s. In the Trade of War DRYDEN. **2.** The s. Thames at Bab-lock-hithe M. ARNOLD.

Stripper (stri·pəɹ). 1581. [f. STRIP *v.*[1] + -ER[1].] **1.** One who strips or strips off. **2.** A machine or appliance for stripping 1835. **3.** *pl. Gaming.* 'High cards cut wedge-shaped, a little wider than the rest, so as to be easily drawn in a crooked game' (Farmer) 1887.

Stripy (strəi·pi), *a.* 1513. [f. STRIPE *sb.*[2] + -Y[1].] Having, marked with, or suggestive of stripes or bands of colour.

Strive (strəiv), *v.* Pa. t. **strove** (strōᵘv), pa. pple. **striven** (stri·v'n). [ME. *strīven*, aphetic – OFr. *estriver*, rel. to *estrif* STRIFE; of unkn. origin. *Strive* was taken over into the native conjugation of DRIVE, etc., the only vb. of Fr. origin to be so treated.] †**1.** *intr.* To be in a state of variance or mutual hostility –1829. **2.** To quarrel, wrangle. Now *rare* (*poet.*). ME. **3.** To contend, carry on a conflict of any kind ME. **b.** To fight against temptation or the like; to wage spiritual warfare. late ME. **c.** To struggle *with* disease or suffering, †hindrances 1594. **d.** Of things: To come into conflict *with*. late ME. †**4.** To contend in arms, fight *with* –1706. †**5.** To contend in words, dispute –1600. †**6.** To contend in rivalry; to seek to surpass another or each other –1725. †**b.** To vie, to be equal or comparable *with* –1700. **7.** To offer obstinate resistance, struggle *against* ME. **8.** To struggle physically. *Obs.* exc. *dial.* of a horse: To be restive. late ME. **b.** To struggle against a natural force, e.g. winds, waves. Const. *with*, *against*. ME. **9.** To endeavour vigorously, use strenuous effort ME. **b.** *transf.* of things 1586. **10.** To make one's way with effort 1586.

1. They say you cannot live in Rome and s. with the Pope SCOTT. **2.** And still they strove and wrangled TENNYSON. **3.** Two Pretenders oft for Empire s. DRYDEN. **b.** In vain I strove Against the Tempter 1816. **4.** How a knyght & a dwarf stroof for a lady MALORY. **6.** *fig.* Patience and sorrow strove Who should express her goodliest SHAKS. **8. b.** To stryve agenst the streame CROMWELL. **9.** Habits are soon assum'd; but when we s. To strip them off, 'tis being flay'd alive COWPER. He for whose applause I strove TENNYSON. She strove to keep her self-control 1885. **10.** He.. Strives through the surge, bestrides the beach BYRON. Hence **Stri·ver**, one who strives with others, a contender; one who makes strenuous effort.

Stroam, strome (strōᵘm), *v. Obs.* exc. *dial.* 1796. [perh. after *stroll* and *roam*.] *intr.* To walk with long strides. Also, to wander about idly.

‖**Strobila** (strobəi·lă). *Pl.* **strobilæ** (-lī). 1842. [mod.L. – Gr. στροβίλη plug of lint twisted into the shape of a fir-cone. Cf. STROBILUS.] *Zool.* **1.** A stage in the development of certain Hydrozoa. **2.** A segmented tape-worm, consisting of a scolex and a chain of proglottides 1864.

Strobilaceous (strǫbilē·ʃəs), *a.* 1802. [f. STROBILUS; see -ACEOUS.] *Bot.* Relating to, or resembling, a strobilus.

Strobilation (strǫbilē·ʃən). 1878. [f. STROBILA + -ATION.] *Zool.* The formation of strobilæ in Hydrozoa, tapeworms, etc.

Strobile (strǫ·bəil, strōᵘ·bəil, -bil). 1777. [– Fr. *strobile* (in sense 1), or anglicized f. STROBILUS and STROBILA.] **1.** *Bot.* = STROBILUS 1. **2.** *Zool.* = STROBILA 2. 1855.

Strobiliform (strobi·lifǭɹm), *a.* 1830. [f. STROBILUS + -FORM.] *Bot.* Shaped like a strobilus.

Strobiline (strǫ·biləin), *a.* 1842. [f. STROBILA and STROBILUS + -INE[1].] *Zool.* and *Bot.* Relating to or of the nature of a strobila or strobilus; strobilaceous.

Strobilization (strǫ:biləizē·ʃən). 1884. [f. STROBILA + -IZE + -ATION.] *Zool.* = STROBILATION.

Strobiloid (strǫ·biloid), *a.* 1865. [f. STROBILA and STROBILUS + -OID.] *Zool.* and *Bot.* Resembling, or of the nature of, a strobila or strobilus.

‖**Strobilus** (strobəi·lŏs). *Pl.* **strobili** (-ləi). 1753. [Late L. *strobilus* – Gr. στρόβιλος anything twisted, pine-cone.] **1.** *Bot.* A fir-cone, or any fruit resembling a fir-cone; an inflorescence made up of imbricated scales, as that of the hop. **b.** In cryptogams: An aggregation of sporophylls resembling a fir-cone 1891. **2.** *Zool.* = STROBILA 2. 1876.

Stroboscope (strǫ·bŏskoᵘp). 1836. [f. Gr. στρόβος a twisting or whirling round + -SCOPE.] **a.** A scientific toy which produces the illusion of motion by a series of pictures viewed through the openings of a revolving disc. **b.** An instrument for observing the successive phases of a periodic motion by means of light periodically interrupted 1896. Hence **Strobosco·pic, -al** *adjs.* relating to, of the nature of, the s.

Stroke (strōᵘk), *sb.*[1] [ME. *strōk*, north. *strāk* :– OE. **strāc* :– **straikaz*, f. gradation var. of base of **strīkan* STRIKE *v.*] **1.** An act of striking; a blow given or received. **a.** A blow with the hand or a weapon (occas. with the paw of an animal, etc.) inflicted on or aimed at a living being. Sometimes (now rarely) applied to the thrust of a pointed weapon. **b.** A blow struck at an inanimate object; e.g. with a hammer, axe, etc. late ME. **c.** In various games: An act of striking the ball; a hit or an attempted hit. Also, manner of striking. 1744. †**d.** Discharge of an engine of war; the impact of a missile –1771. **e.** †Shock or forcible impact of a moving body; impact or incidence of moving particles, light, etc. (now *rare*) 1534. **2.** *fig.* **a.** With conscious metaphor: An act which causes pain, injury, or death; often, an act of divine chastisement or vengeance ME. **b.** A calamitous event 1700. †**c.** An offensive movement in warfare –1777. †**d.** *To have, bear, carry the s.*: to prevail, rule, have authority; to be highest in excellence –1731. **3.** A damaging or destructive discharge (of lighting) 1542. **4.** An attack of disease; an apoplectic or (now more usu.) paralytic seizure 1599. **5.** The striking of a clock; the sound produced by each striking of the clapper or hammer upon the bell, etc. late ME. †**6.** A touch on a stringed instrument; manner of playing a musical instrument; hence, a tune, strain –1773. **7.** A pulsation, beat (of the heart, pulse) 1538. **8.** A movement of beating time; a beat, measure; metrical ictus, rhythm. Now *rare* or *Obs.* 1576. **9. a.** In neg. context: A minimum amount of work 1568. **b.** A large or considerable amount *of* work, business, trade 1712. **10.** A movement like that of striking a blow. **a.** A single movement of the legs in walking or running, of the wings in flying, etc. 1618. **b.** In swimming, the combined movement of the limbs forming a single impulse of progression; also, any particular manner of effecting this, as the breast-s., side-s. 1800. **c.** A single complete movement in either direction of any piece of machinery having a reciprocating motion (e.g. of a piston, piston-rod, etc.); also, the amplitude or length of such a movement 1731. **11.** *Rowing.* **a.** A single pull of the oar 1583. †**b.** *To keep s.*: to keep time in rowing –1652. **c.** Style of rowing, manner of handling the oars, esp. with regard to the length, speed, or frequency of the 'strokes' 1870. **d.** The oarsman who sits nearest to the stern of the boat, and whose 'stroke' sets the time for the other rowers. Also quasi-*adv.* in *to pull, row s.* 1825. **e.** The station occupied in a boat by the stroke-oarsman 1901. **12.** A vigorous attempt to attain some object; a measure, expedient, or device adopted for some purpose 1699. **b.** In a game: An effective move or combination 1735. **13.** A feat, achievement; a signal display *of* art, genius, wit, etc. 1672. **b.** *S. of luck*: an unexpected piece of good fortune 1853. **14.** A movement of the pen, pencil, graver, etc., in writing, printing, drawing, etc.; a single movement of a brush, chisel, knife, file, etc. over the surface operated on 1668. †**b.** Manner of handling the pencil, graver, etc. –1717. **15.** A linear mark; a mark traced by the moving point of a pen, pencil, etc.; a component line of a written character (cf. *up-*, *down-s.*); also, a dash (in writing or print) 1567. **b.** *Bacteriology.* A line formed by drawing the point of an infected wire over the surface to be inoculated 1893. †**16.** Lineament, line of a face or form –1638. †**b.** *fig.* A characteristic; a trait of character –1780. **c.** *fig.* A felicitous or characteristic expression or thought in literary composition; a 'touch' of description, satire, pathos, or the like 1666. **17.** *Agric.* (See quot.) 1765. **18.** = STRIKE *sb.* 3 1532.

1. He slewe and bette downe.. all that came within his s. 1533. He suddenly..aimed a rapid and furious s. at the woodman's head 1849. Phr. *At one s., at a s.*, with a single blow; *fig.* all at once. **b.** With many strokes is an oke ouerthrowen 1539. **c.** A ball may, under a penalty of two strokes, be lifted out of a difficulty of any description 1879. **d.** The Stroak of an Arrow convinc'd Alexander, that he was not the Son of Jupiter 1678. **2.** Till the mortal s. shall lay me low BURNS. The s. of calamity 1858. **3.** The oak, Rent by the lightning's recent s. SCOTT. **4.** He has had a s., like that of an apoplexy JOHNSON. **5.** *On* or *upon the s.* (*of* a specified hour), on the point of striking; It is on the s. of twelve now C. BRONTË. **9. a.** Work!..thank God, I have never done a s. of work since I was born 1867. **b.** A good s. of business 1825. **10.** A gnat's wings make ten or fifteen thousand strokes per second H. SPENCER. **c.** A new pump..for raising water with a perpendicular s. 1741. **11. c.** Rowing a long easy s. 1870. **e.** University..with Huntley at s. 1901. **12.** Phr. *S. of policy, of business. S. of state*: tr. Fr. *coup d'état* (see COUP *sb.*[3]). **b.** Any of the finer strokes of play 1862. **13.** It is filled with strokes of wit and satire in every line GOLDSM. **14.** Phr. *With a s. of the pen*, often used *hyperbolically*; He changed with a s. of the pen the general aspect of affairs 1804. *Finishing s.* (lit. and fig.); see FINISHING *ppl. a.* **b.** Paulo's free s., and Titian's warmth divine POPE. **16. b.** He discovers in almost every body, some Strokes of vanity LAW. **c.** How bold, how masterly, are the strokes of Virgil! DRYDEN. **17.** Each time land is crossed with harrows it is said to have received a s. or line 1891.

attrib.: **a.** *Golf.* in terms relating to the method of scoring by strokes instead of by holes, as *s.-competition, -game, -play*; **b.** *Bacteriology*, as *s.-culture, -inoculation*; **c. s.-haul**, an apparatus used for illegal capture of fish, formed of three hooks joined back to back, and weighted with lead; hence as *vb.*; **-oar**, (*a*) the oar nearest the stern of a rowing-boat; (*b*) the rower who handles this oar; **-oarsman** = sense 11 d; **-side**, the side of a rowing-boat on which the s. oarsman sits.

Stroke, *sb.*[2] 1631. [f. STROKE *v.*[1]] A stroking movement of the hand, †esp. for purposes of healing.

Stroke (strōᵘk), *v.*[1] Pa. t. and pa. pple. **stroked** (strōᵘkt). [OE. *strācian* = MLG., MDu. *strēken* (Du. *streeken*), OHG. *streihhōn* (G. *streichen*), f. Gmc. **straik-*, **strīk-*, STRIKE *v.*] **1.** *trans.* To rub softly with the hand or some implement; *esp.* to pass the hand softly in one direction over, by way of caress or as a method of healing. Also *absol.* **b.** said of an animal using a foot or paw 1621. **c.** With adv., etc.: To bring into a specified position, condition, etc. by such action 1594. **2.** To draw (a cutting instrument) along a surface in order to sharpen or whet it. *Obs.* or *arch.* late ME. **3.** To milk (a cow); esp. to draw the last milk from (a cow) by pressing the teat 1538. **4.** *Masonry.* To work the face of (a stone) in such a manner as to produce a sort of fluted surface 1842. **5.** *Needlework.* To dispose (small gathers) in regular order and close succession by drawing the point of a blunt needle from the top of each gather downwards 1875.

1. His only gesture is that of stroking his beard GIBBON. *absol.* A good groom will rather s. than strike BERKELEY. *fig.* With these faire Promises he stroked the Senators 1629. Phr. *To s. against the hair, the wrong way* (*of the hair*), to rub (an animal) in the direction opposite to the natural lie of its hair; *fig.* to irritate, ruffle, cross (a person). **c.** With his hands so full that he cannot even s. out his splendid whiskers 1859.

Stroke (strōᵘk), *v.*² 1597. [f. STROKE *sb.*¹] **1.** *trans.* To mark with streaks or stripes. **2.** To draw the horizontal line across the upright of (the letter *t*) 1894. **3.** To row stroke in (a boat); to act as stroke to (a crew) 1866.

Stroker (strōᵘ·kəɹ). 1632. [f. STROKE *v.*¹ + -ER¹.] **1.** One who strokes; *spec.* one who cures diseases by stroking. **2.** An implement used for some operation likened to stroking 1884.

Strokesman (strōᵘ·ksmæ̆n). 1712. [f. gen. of STROKE *sb.*¹ + MAN *sb.*] †**1.** A rubber or masseur. STEELE. **2.** One who pulls the stroke-oar in a boat 1769.

Stroking (strōᵘ·kiŋ), *vbl. sb.* 1587. [f. STROKE *v.*¹ + -ING¹.] **1.** The action of STROKE *v.*¹, in various senses. **2.** *pl.* The last milk drawn from a cow; 'afterings' 1602.

Stroll (strōᵘl), *sb.* 1623. [See next.] **1.** = STROLLER. *Obs.* exc. *U.S.* (*rare*). **2.** A walk or ramble taken leisurely, a saunter 1814.

Stroll (strōᵘl), *v.* 1603. [orig. applied (as prec. and next) to itinerant, vagabond, or vagrant persons; later used of aimless or leisurely walking; prob. – G. *strollen*, *strolchen* wander as a vagrant (*strolch* vagabond), of unkn. origin.] †**1.** *intr.* To roam from place to place without any settled habitation –1765. **2.** To walk or ramble in a careless, haphazard or leisurely fashion as inclination directs, often simply to take a walk 1680. †**3.** *trans.* To walk or pace along (a path) or about (a place) –1810.

1. These Mothers..are forced to employ all their time in Stroling, to beg Sustenance for their helpless Infants SWIFT. **2.** They..then strolled along the sands towards the cliff 1827.

Stroller (strōᵘ·ləɹ). 1608. [f. prec. + -ER¹.] One who strolls. **1.** A vagabond, vagrant; an itinerant begger or pedlar. Now chiefly *Sc.* 1679. **2.** An itinerant actor; a strolling player 1608. **2.** A saunterer; a casual traveller or visitor 1738.

Strolling (strōᵘ·liŋ), *ppl. a.* 1621. [f. STROLL *v.* + -ING².] That strolls; roving, itinerant; chiefly in *s. actor, player*, an actor who wanders about the country, giving performances in temporary buildings or hired rooms.

Strom (strǫm), **strum** (strɒm). *Obs.* exc. *dial.* late ME. [Of unkn. origin.] **1.** *Brewing.* An oblong wicker basket, placed over the bung-hole within the mash-tub to prevent the grains and hops passing through when the liquor is drawn off. **2.** *Mining.* A kind of iron sieve placed round the suction-pipe of a pump to prevent obstruction 1849.

‖**Stroma** (strōᵘ·mă). *Pl.* **stromata** (strōᵘ·mătă). 1832. [mod.L. use of late L. *stroma* bed-covering – Gr. στρῶμα anything spread or laid out for lying or sitting upon, f. στρω- root of στρωννύναι spread.] **1.** *Anat.* The fibrous connective sustentacular tissue or substance of a part or organ. Also, the framework containing the alveoli of cancer-cells. 1835. **b.** The spongy colourless framework of a red blood corpuscle or other cell 1872. **2.** *Bot.* A structure containing the substance in which perithecia or other organs of fructification are immersed 1832. Hence **Stro·mal** *a.* of, pertaining to, or of the character of the s. (sense 1). **Stroma·tic** *a.* of the nature of or resembling a s.

Stromb (strǫm, strǫmb). 1835. [Anglicized form of STROMBUS.] A gasteropod of the family *Strombidæ*, esp. a wing-shell of the genus *Strombus*.

Strombite (strǫ·mbəit). 1811. [f. prec. + -ITE¹ 2a.] A fossil stromb or some similar shell.

Stromboid (strǫ·mboid), *a.* and *sb.* 1859. [f. as prec. + -OID.] **A.** *adj.* Resembling or related to a stromb or strombus. **B.** *sb.* A stromb 1891.

Strombuliform (strǫmbiū·lifǭɹm), *a.* 1846. [f. as a var. of *strombiform* (perh. after Fr. *strombuliforme*), with epenthesis of the L. dim. suffix *-ul-* (see -ULE); see STROMBUS, -FORM. Cf. STRIGILLOSE.] **a.** *Geol.* Shaped like a top. **b.** *Bot.* Twisted in a long spire, so as to resemble the convolutions of the shell *Strombus*.

‖**Strombus** (strǫ·mbŏs). 1601. [L. *strombus* spiral shell – Gr. στρόμβος anything spirally twisted.] *Zool.* The typical genus of the family *Strombidæ* of gasteropods; a species or individual of this genus, a wing-shell or fountain-shell.

Stromeyerite (strōᵘ·məi,ĕrəit). 1835. [Named by Haidinger after Friedrich *Stromeyer*, a German chemist; see -ITE¹ 2 b.] *Min.* Sulphide of silver and copper, of steel-grey colour and metallic lustre.

Strong (strǫŋ), *a.* [OE. *strong, strang* = OS., OFris. *strang*, MDu. *stranc*, ON. *strangr* :– Gmc. **straŋgaz*, f. a base of which the mutated form is repr. in OE. (rare) *strenge* severe, MLG., MDu. *strenge* (Du. *streng*), OS., OHG. *strengi* (G. *streng*), and for which see further STRING *sb.*] **1.** Of living beings, their body or limbs: Physically powerful; able to exert great muscular force. **b.** Of an action: Performed with muscular strength. late ME. **c.** of a runner, swimmer, etc.: Having great staying power. Hence, of his 'going' or pace; Maintained with vigour; that does not flag 1854. **2.** Physically vigorous or robust; capable of physical endurance or effort; not readily affected by disease; hale, healthy ME. **b.** of the vital organ and their functions, the nerves, brain, etc. late ME. **c.** of a plant or its parts. late ME. **d.** *A s. head*: capacity for taking much drink without becoming intoxicated 1822. **3.** Having great moral power for endurance or effort; firm in will or purpose; brave, resolute, steadfast OE. **b.** of actions or attributes ME. **c.** Of looks, voice, etc.: Indicative of strength of character 1815. **d.** Of a statesman, judge, commander: That makes his authority felt 1879. **4.** Of the mind or mental faculties: Powerful. Of the memory: Tenacious, retentive. late ME. **5.** Having great controlling power over persons and things, by reason of the possession of authority, resources, or inherent qualities OE. **b.** *absol.* OE. **c.** Of things, sometimes personified ME. **d.** Having great financial resources, rich 1622. **6.** Eminently able or qualified to succeed in something; well skilled or versed *in* some branch of knowledge or practice OE. **b.** *One's s. point*: that in which one excels, one's forte 1875. **c.** In athletic contests, of a side, crew, etc.: Formidable as an opponent or competitor 1860. **7.** Powerful in arms; formidable as a fighting force (or as a commander) ME. **b.** of an individual: Powerful or formidable as a combatant 1450. **c.** Of a warlike operation: Performed or prosecuted with a powerful fighting force 1560. **d.** With prefixed numerical determination: Powerful to the extent of (a specified number of men, ships, etc.). Hence *gen.*, having the specified number. 1589. **e.** Of a body of persons or things, a sect or party: Numerous 1617. **f.** Abundantly supplied with persons or things of a specified kind. Const. *in*. 1621. **8.** Of a fortress, town, country, or military position: Powerful for resistance; difficult to capture or invade OE. **b.** Of a place of confinement, receptacle for valuables and the like: Difficult to escape from or break into ME. **9.** Of material things: Capable of supporting strain or withstanding force; not easily broken, torn, injured, or forced out of shape; solidly made, massive, stout OE. **b.** Of soil: Firm, tenacious, compact OE. **c.** Of food: Solid, hard of digestion 1526. **d.** *Mining.* Of a vein: Thick, massive 1839. **e.** Of wool: Broad-haired or coarse-fibred 1885. **10.** Powerful in operative effect OE. **11.** Severe, burdensome, oppressive OE. †**b.** Of a crime, evil quality: Gross, flagrant. Of a malefactor: Flagrantly guilty. –1818. **c.** Of a course of action or a measure: Extreme, high-handed 1838. **d.** *colloq.* Of a payment, a charge: Heavy, 'stiff' 1669. **12.** Of movements or conditions: Intense; energetic; powerful OE. **b.** Of the voice, a sound: Powerful, loud and firm OE. **c.** Of illumination, light, shadow, colour: Vivid, intense 1658. **d.** Of feeling, conviction, belief: Intense, fervid. Of party views or principles: Uncompromising, thoroughgoing. ME. **e.** Of a person: Firmly convinced, decided in opinion; *colloq.* laying great stress *on* something 1526. **13.** Having its specific property in a high degree OE. **b.** *S. of*: largely or greatly impregnated or flavoured with (*dial.*) 1617. **14.** Affecting the sense of taste or smell in a high degree; strong smelling; strong-tasting, rank; *spec.* having a powerful unpleasant smell OE. **15.** Having a powerful effect on the mind or will; hard to resist or overthrow ME. **b.** Of a case: Well supported by evidence or precedent 1698. **16.** Having legal force; †valid; effectual 1450. **17.** Vividly perceptible; marked, definite 1697. **b.** Of a line: Broad, thick. Also, vivid in colour. 1731. **c.** *Photogr.* Of a negative: Having marked contrasts of light and shade; dense 1892. **18.** Of language, an expression, a word: Emphatic; signifying or implying much; not moderate. *S. language*: see LANGUAGE *sb.* 3. 1697. **b.** Of a protest, recommendation, etc.: Emphatic, strongly-worded, urgent 1733. **19.** Of literary or artistic work: Vigorous or forceful in style or execution 1746. **20.** *Comm.* Of prices: Tending to steadiness or to a rise 1870. **21.** *Gram.* (Opp. to *weak.*) **a.** Of Teut. sbs. and adjs., their inflexions, etc.: Belonging to any of those declensions in which the OTeut. stem ended otherwise than in *n* 1841. **b.** Of Teut. vbs. and their inflexions: Forming the pa. t. and pa. pple. by means of vowel-gradation in the root-syllable, as the Eng. *give, break*. Hence, occas. used with ref. to other Indo-European langs., e.g. in *s. aorist*, applied in Gr. grammar to the 'second aorist' (ἔλιπον) in contradistinction to the 'weak' or sigmatic aorist (ἔλειψα). 1841. **c.** In Skr. grammar, applied to the unreduced form of noun-stems, and to those cases which are formed on the 'strong' stem 1863. **22.** *Phonetics* and *Prosody*. Of a syllable: Bearing stress or metrical ictus. Of a consonant-sound: Characterized by force of utterance. Also in *Music*, Accented. 1792. **23.** *Card-playing.* Of a player: Holding commanding cards (*in* a specified suit). Of a hand or suit: Composed of commanding cards. Of a card: Of high and commanding value. 1862.

1. He is as s. as a horse 1861. *fig.* The s. arm of the law 1873. *The stronger sex*, the male sex. **2.** Old Nanny..was now quite s. again MARRYAT. **b.** Persons even with s. stomachs 1833. Wearying even to the strongest nerves 1863. **3.** Be s. and prosperous In this resolue SHAKS. **b.** To conquer Sin and Death..By Humiliation and s. Sufferance MILT. **c.** The lady with the s. face, and the piercing grey eyes 1891. **d.** He wants to show.. that he too can be a 'S. Man' on a pinch 1879. **4.** He was not a man of s. sense MACAULAY. **5.** What King so s. Can tie the gall vp in the slanderous tong? SHAKS. **b.** It was a reign of minority, when the strongest had the best right SCOTT. **c.** The old Adam was too s. for her 1865. **d.** 'S. people'—that is, people who can wait..for a rise 1885. **6.** I am not very s. in spelling THACKERAY. **7.** Pompey is s. at Sea SHAKS. **d.** The garrison, thirteen hundred s. MACAULAY. **f.** The king was s. in horse DE FOE. **8.** The king was in Wales, which was a Countrey s. by reason of the Mountaines STOW. **b.** Our prison s. MILT. **9.** S. outer walls for defence were discarded 1861. **c.** Soche as haue nede off mylke, and not of stronge meate TINDALE. Hence *s. meat*, doctrine, etc., suitable only for 'digestion' by vigorous or well-prepared minds. **d.** The vein is very s., and carries a very large proportion of quartz 1877. **10.** The spring is always strongest when first wound up 1675. I hate him like s. poison SCOTT. Only traces of it can be seen under a s. lens 1887. **11.** A s. shuddering fit SCOTT. **b.** Oh heinous, s., and bold Conspiracie SHAKS. **12.** By a stronger heat they are decomposed 1857. *S. breeze*, that which reduces a ship to double-reefed topsails, jib, and spanker. *S. gale*, that strength of wind under which close-reefed topsails and storm-staysails are usually carried when close-hauled. The pulse may be s. or weak 1876. **c.** The southern sash admits too s. a light COWPER. **d.** Hate stronger, under shew of Love well feign'd MILT. S. Free-trade views 1881. **e.** A very s. Papist 1679. Mary, who is so s. on the proprieties 1883. **13.** Ale & bere of the strongest TINDALE. S. antiseptic solution 1899. **b.** German sausages, s. of garlick DICKENS. **14.** They say poore Suters haue s. breaths SHAKS. As s. as Mustard 1659. **15.** A man of..s. passions 1779. A s. impulse SHELLEY. The evidence as to this is too s. to be discarded 1892. **b.** Shakespeare has made out a s. case for Shylock 1863. **16.** One heynous Article..cracking the s. Warrant of an Oath SHAKS. The old laws.. received a stronger sanction 1838. **17.** The local traditions..are still very s. 1894. A very s. family likeness amongst them 1870. A s. Breton accent 1890. **18.** He expressed his indignation in the strongest terms 1836. **19.** What the publishers call a 's.' book 1905. **20.** Coal is very s. in price 1890. **23.** A s. hand is difficult to define, further than as one likely to make many tricks 1864.

Comb.: **a.** in parasynthetic adjs., as *s.-armed, -backed, -brained*, etc. **b. s. bark,** a tree or shrub of the genus *Bourreria*, found in the W. Indies and tropical America.

Strong (strǫŋ), *adv.* [OE. *strange, stronge*; see STRONG *a.*] Qualifying a verb or predication = STRONGLY *adv. Obs.* exc. as in b, c. **b.** Used regularly with certain verbs, as *blow, flow, grow, run, smell*, etc. late ME. **c.** In colloq. phrases 1812.

The Bow-string touch'd her Breast, so s. she drew DRYDEN. **b.** The Whig peers..mustered s. MACAULAY. **c.** *To come it s.*, to go to great lengths; to make statements which are hard to credit. *To come out s.*, to make a big display or impression; to 'launch out'; to declare oneself vigorously. *To go it s.*, to act vigorously or recklessly. *To be going s.*, to be vigorous, thriving, or prosperous. *To pitch it s.*, to indulge in 'tall' talk.

Comb., as *s.-built, -knit, -made*, etc.; *s.-beating, -growing, -smelling*, etc.

Stro·ng-box. 1684. A strongly-made chest or safe for money, documents or other valuables.

Strong drink. late ME. Intoxicating liquor, alcoholic liquors generally. Also, drink of more than ordinary alcoholic strength.

Strong hand. Now *rare*. late ME. The exercise of superior power; the use of force.

I carried it with the strongest hand possible SWIFT.

Strong-headed (stress var.), *a.* 1603. **1.** Headstrong. **2.** Endowed with strong intellectual faculties 1849. Hence **Stro:ng-hea·dedness,** obstinacy.

Stronghold (strǫ·ŋ,hōᵘld). late ME. [f. STRONG *a.* + HOLD *sb.*] A strongly fortified place of defence, a secure place of refuge or retreat, a fastness.

fig. The Northern counties..were the s. of the papal party 1856.

Strongish (strǫ·ŋiʃ), *a.* 1799. [f. STRONG *a.* + -ISH¹.] Somewhat strong.

Strongly (strǫ·ŋli), *adv.* [OE. *strang-, stronglīće*; see STRONG *a.*, -LY².] **1.** In a strong manner; powerfully; forcibly; firmly, securely; violently, vehemently; with fortitude; resolutely; emphatically. **2.** In a strong degree; with strength or intensity of the condition or quality predicated. late ME.

2. He s. resembles her CARLYLE. Sea-water is always s. salt to the taste 1880.

Strong-minded (stress var.), *a.* 1791. Having a strong, vigorous, or determined mind. **b.** Applied (usu. in disparagement) to women who have or affect the qualities of mind regarded as distinctively masculine 1854.

Strong room. 1761. A room made specially secure for the custody of persons or things; esp. a fire- and burglar-proof room in which valuables are deposited for safety, e.g. at a bank.

Strong water. 1580. [tr. med.L. *aqua fortis* (sense 1).] †**1.** = AQUAFORTIS –1694. **2.** Any form of alcoholic spirits used as a beverage. Now only in *pl.* (somewhat *arch.*) 1613.

Strongyle¹ (strǫ·ndʒil). 1847. [– mod.L. *strongylus* – Gr. στρογγύλος round.] A thread-worm of the genus *Strongylus* (or the family *Strongylidæ*, of which this is the type), common as a disease-producing parasite in various animals.

Strongyle² (strǫ·ndʒil). 1887. [– Gr. στρογγύλη fem. (sc. ῥάβδος RHABDUS) of στρογγύλος round.] *Zool.* A sponge-spicule of the rhabdus type, rounded at both ends.

Strongyloid (strǫ·ndʒiloid), *a.* and *sb.* 1879. [f. STRONGYLE¹ + -OID.] *Zool.* **A.** *adj.* Resembling a strongyle. **B.** *sb.* A strongyloid worm.

Strontia (strǫ·nʃⁱă). 1802. [f. next; see -IA¹.] *Chem.* One of the alkaline earths, the monoxide of strontium. Also *attrib.* in *s. water*, the aqueous solution of strontium hydroxide.

Strontian (strǫ·nʃⁱăn). 1789. [Name of a parish in Argyllshire, where are the lead mines in which the mineral was discovered.] (orig. *s. earth, lime, mineral, spar.*) Properly, native strontium carbonate, but applied loosely to strontia, occas. to strontium. Not now in scientific use. *S. yellow*: a yellow colour produced by adding potassium chromate to a solution of a strontium salt.

Strontianite (strǫ·nʃⁱănəit). 1794. [f. prec. + -ITE¹ 2 b.] *Min.* Native strontium carbonate.

Strontium (strǫ·nʃⁱŏm). 1808. [f. STRONTIA; see -IUM.] *Chem.* The metallic base of strontia; a dark-yellow metal, fusible at red heat. Symbol Sr.

Strop (strǫp), *sb.* ME. [– (M)LG., (M)Du. *strop* = OE. *strop* (which did not survive), OHG. *strupf* (G. *strüpfe* fem., also (naut.) *strop* = sense 2); WGmc. – L. *struppus, stroppus*, presumably – Gr. στρόφος (cf. STROPHE).] †**1.** A band, thong; a loop or noose of leather, etc. –1723. **2.** A ring or band of hide or of rope with its ends spliced together, used upon a mast, yard, etc., as a fastening or as a purchase for tackle; esp. a band of rope, iron, or chain fastened round a pulley or block. Chiefly *Naut.* ME. **3.** A strip of leather (or of a special textile), or a strip of wood covered with leather or other suitable material, used for sharpening a razor; a razor-strop 1702.

Strop (strǫp), *v.* 1841. [f. prec.] **1.** *trans.* To sharpen or smooth the edge of (a razor) with a strop. **2.** *Naut.* To furnish (a block) with a strop 1860. Hence **Stro·pping** *vbl. sb. concr.* (*Naut.*) rope for making strops.

‖**Strophanthus** (strŏfæ·nþŏs). 1888. [mod.L., f. Gr. στρόφος twisted cord + ἄνθος flower.] **a.** *Bot.* A genus of plants (family *Apocynaceæ*), native to tropical Africa and Asia, having strongly poisonous qualities; a plant of this genus. **b.** A poisonous drug extracted from the seeds of various species of this genus; in recent pharmacy used as a cardiac tonic. Hence **Stropha·nthin,** a glucoside obtained from this.

Strophe (strōᵘ·fi). *Pl.* **strophes** (-fiz), **strophæ** (strōᵘ·fī). 1603. [– Gr. στροφή (whence late L. *stropha*), lit. 'turning', f. στροφ-, grade-var. of the base of στρέφειν turn.] **1.** In Greek choral and lyric poetry: A series of lines forming a system the metrical structure of which is repeated in a following system called the ANTISTROPHE. Also, one of two or more metrically corresponding series of lines forming divisions of a lyric poem. Hence occas. (after Fr.) used as = STANZA. **2.** *Bot.* Applied to a spiral development of leaves 1846. Hence **Strophic** (strǫ·fik) *a.* pertaining to strophes; consisting of strophes; belonging to the s. as dist. from the antistrophe. **Stro·phical** *a.*, **-ly** *adv.*

Strophiolate (strǫ·fiŏlĕt), *a.* 1821. [f. next + -ATE².] *Bot.* Furnished with a strophiole.

Strophiole (strǫ·fioᵘl). 1839. [– mod.L. *strophiolum* (Gærtner 1788), use of L. *strophiolum*, dim. of *strophium* chaplet – Gr. στρόφιον, f. στροφ- (see STROPHE).] *Bot.* An excrescence or tubercle surrounding the hilum of certain seeds.

Strophoid (strǫ·foid). 1880. [– Fr. *strophoïde*, f. Gr. στρόφος twisted cord; see -OID.] *Geom.* The locus of the intersection of two straight lines which rotate uniformly about two fixed points in a plane. Hence **Stropho·i·dal** *a.* and *sb.*

‖**Strophulus** (strǫ·fiŭlŏs). 1808. [mod.L., app. corrupt. of med.L. *scrophulus* (XV), for L. *scrophulæ* (SCROPHULA), misapplied to an eruptive disease.] *Path.* A papular eruption on the skin of infants; known popularly as *red-gum, white-gum, tooth-rash*, etc.

†**Stro·sser.** 1598. [Of unkn. origin.] = TROUSER –1637.

Stroud (straud). Now *rare* or *Obs.* 1683. [perh. f. *Stroud* in Gloucestershire.] **1.** A blanket manufactured for barter or sale in trading with the N. Amer. Indians. **2.** The material of which these blankets were made 1759.

Stroy (stroi), *v. Obs.* or *dial.* ME. [Aphetic f. DESTROY *v.*] *trans.* To destroy.

Struck (strʊk), *pa. pple.* and *ppl. a.* 1594. [pa. pple. of STRIKE *v.*] †**A.** *pa. pple.* in special use = STRICKEN A. –1787. **B.** *ppl. a.* = STRICKEN *ppl. a.* in various uses 1627.

S. jury, a special jury selected by striking from the pannel of jurors, a certain number by each party, so as to leave a number required by law to try the cause 1856. So **Stru·cken** *pa. pple.* and *ppl. a.* (now *Sc.* and *north.*).

Structural (strʊ·ktiŭrăl, -tʃərăl), *a.* 1835. [f. STRUCTURE *sb.* + -AL¹.] Of or pertaining to structure. **1.** Of or pertaining to the art or practice of building; chiefly in *s. iron, steel*, iron or steel intended for building construction 1867. **2.** Of or pertaining to the structure of a building as dist. from its decoration or fittings 1877. **3.** Of or pertaining to the arrangement and mutual relation of the parts of any complex unity 1870. **4. a.** *Phys.* and *Path.* Of or pertaining to the organic structure of an animal or plant, or a portion of an animal or vegetable body 1845. **b.** *Geol.* Pertaining to the structure of the earth's crust, of a rock, formation, mountain, or the like 1855. **c.** Of a branch of science: Concerned with the study of the structures of natural products 1835.

2. *S. load*, the load due to a structure itself, as dist. from the imposed load. **4. a.** *S. disease*, one involving tissue and causing change visible to the naked eye or the microscope; also, organic disease in contradistinction to functional disease 1898. **c.** *S. botany*, botany dealing with the structure and organization of plants. *S. chemistry*, chemistry treating of the arrangement or order of attachment of atoms in the molecules of compounds. Hence **Stru·cturally** *adv.* with regard to structure.

Structure (strʊ·ktiŭɹ, -tʃəɹ), *sb.* 1440. [– (O)Fr. *structure* or L. *structura*, f. *struct-*, pa. ppl. stem of *struere* build; see -URE.] **1.** The action, practice or process of building or construction. Now *rare* or *Obs.* **2.** Manner of building or construction; the way in which an edifice, machine, etc. is made or put together 1650. **3.** The mutual relation of the constituent parts or elements of a whole as determining its peculiar nature or character; make, frame 1615. **4.** *concr.* That which is built or constructed; a building or edifice of any kind, esp. one of considerable size and imposing appearance 1615. **5.** More widely: A fabric or framework of material parts put together 1677. **6.** An organized body or combination of mutually connected and dependent parts or elements. Chiefly in *Biol.*, applied to component parts of an animal or vegetable organism. 1830.

1. The progress and s. of the Edystone Lighthouse SMEATON. **2.** They..show purchased dirks, of an improved s. CARLYLE. **3.** Of the internal S. of the Earth GOLDSM. The s. of society 1803. The story itself is in s. extremely simple 1887. **4.** A church..which is, indeed, a most stately s. GRAY. **5.** This moveable s. of shelves,..charg'd with octavos and twelves COWPER. **6.** The general law of organization..is that distinct duties entail distinct structures SPENCER. Hence **Stru·cture** *v. trans.* (*rare*) to build or form into a s. **Stru·c-tureless** *a.* lacking organic s.

Struggle (strʊ·g'l), *sb.* 1692. [f. next.] **1.** An act of struggling; a resolute contest; a continued effort to resist force or free oneself from constraint; a strong effort under difficulties. **b.** A strong effort to continue to breathe, as in the death-agony 1794. **2.** *gen.* Contention, determined effort or resistance 1706.

1. The Horrors of an hopeless Soul, and the Struggles and Agonies of one sinking under the dismal Apprehensions of the divine Wrath 1716. Phr. *S. for existence, for life*, in *Biol.* used metaphorically to describe the relation between co-existing organic species when the causes tending to the survival of one tend to the extinction of another; also *gen.*, an effort under difficulties to obtain the means of livelihood. **b.** He died.. without a groan or s. 1854. **2.** The subject of love at s. with death 1901.

Struggle (strʊ·g'l), *v.* late ME. [frequent. (see -LE) f. base of obscure origin, prob. symbolic; connection with ON. *strúgr* ill-will, contention, or with Du. *struikelen*, G. *straucheln* stumble, is dubious.] **1.** *intr.* To contend (*with* an adversary) in a close grapple as in wrestling; also, to make violent bodily movements in order to resist force or free oneself from constraint. **b.** To make violent efforts to breathe (usu. *to s. for breath*); to be in the agony of death 1674. **2.** *fig.* To contend resolutely, esp. with an adversary of superior power; to offer obstinate resistance; to make violent efforts to escape from constraint. late ME. **3.** quasi-*trans.* with adv. or phr. expressing the result of struggling 1633.

4. *intr.* To make great efforts in spite of difficulties; to contend resolutely *with* (a task, burden); to strive *to do* something difficult 1597. **5.** To make progress with difficulty *to, into, out of, through.* Also with adv. *along, forward, on.* 1700.

1. In strugling with him for the knife..hee hurt himselfe therwith 1603. The wind was adverse..and they struggled against it without much assistance from the tide SCOTT. **2.** The sunbeams..struggling with the smoky air SCOTT. The Netherlands are struggling vainly for their liberties 1855. **3.** When the light began to appear, the Ass had strugled her self out 1660. **4.** Phr. *To s. for existence*: cf. STRUGGLE *sb.* 1. **5.** He struggled to his feet 1888. Phr. *To s. on*, occas. to maintain existence, or continue one's course of action, with difficulty. Hence **Stru·ggler**, one who struggles. **Stru·gglingly** *adv.*

Struldbrug (strɒ·ldbrɒg). 1726. [Arbitrary.] In Swift's *Gulliver's Travels*, given as the native appellation of 'the immortals' in the kingdom of Luggnagg, who were incapable of dying, but after the age of eighty contined to exist in a state of decrepitude, regarded as legally dead, and receiving a small pittance from the state. Also *allus.* Hence **Struldbru·ggian** *a.* **Stru·ldbrugism.**

Strum (strɒm), *v.* 1775. [imit.; cf. THRUM *v.*[2]] **1.** *trans.* To play on (a stringed instrument) carelessly or unskilfully; to produce (notes, a tune, etc.) by such playing. **2.** *intr.* To play carelessly or unskilfully on a stringed instrument. Said also of an instrument: To sound when strummed upon. 1785. **3.** quasi-*trans.* with advb. extension 1777.

1. Sitting at the piano strumming a music-hall ditty 1894. **3.** To..s. your father to sleep after a Fox Chase SHERIDAN. Hence **Strum** *sb.* the action of strumming.

‖**Struma** (strū·mă). *Pl.* **strumæ** (-ī). 1565. [L., scrofulous tumour.] **1.** *Path.* **a.** = SCROFULA. **b.** A scrofulous swelling or tumour. Also, a goitre, bronchocele (*rare*). 1654. **2.** *Bot.* A cellular dilatation on a leaf-stalk at the point where the petiole joins the lamina or where the midrib joins the leaflets of a compound leaf 1832. Hence **Struma·tic** *a.* (*rare*) suffering from s. **Stru·miform** *a. Bot.* having the appearance of a s.; *Path.* resembling s. **Stru·mose** *a. Bot.* having a s.

Strumous (strū·məs), *a.* 1590. [– L. *stromosus*; see prec., -OUS.] **1.** Affected with struma; characteristic or indicative of a scrofulous disposition. **2.** Of the nature of or caused by struma 1590. **3.** *Nat. Hist.* Having a natural protuberance on some part of the body 1802.

Strumpet (strɒ·mpėt), *sb.* ME. [Of unkn. origin.] A debauched or unchaste woman; a harlot, prostitute. **b.** *fig.* and of things personified 1545. **c.** as *adj.* That is a strumpet 1596.

b. That s. Fortune SHAKS. **c.** *Merch. V.* II. vi. 16.

†**Stru·mpet,** *v.* 1590. [f. prec.] **1.** *trans.* To bring to the condition of a strumpet –1687. **2.** To repute as a strumpet; to debase (a woman's fame, name, virtue) to that of a strumpet –1633.

Strung (strɒŋ), *ppl. a.* 1687. [pa. pple. of STRING *v.*] **1.** Furnished or fitted with strings or a string. Now *rare* or *Obs.* 1695. **2.** Threaded on a string 1687. **3. a.** Of nerves, etc.: In a state of tension. **b.** With prefixed adj., *finely-, highly-s.*: said of persons with ref. to their nervous organization or condition. 1840.

Strut (strɒt), *sb.*[1] 1587. [prob. f. STRUT *v.*[1]] A bar, rod, or built-up member, of wood, iron, etc., designed to resist pressure or thrust in a framework.

Strut (strɒt), *sb.*[2] 1607. [f. STRUT *v.*[1]] A manner of walking with stiff steps and head erect, affecting dignity or superiority; a stiff self-important gait.

Strut (strɒt), *sb.*[3] 1880. [f. STRUT *v.*[2]] The act of strutting; deflexion (of the spoke of a wheel) from the perpendicular.

Strut (strɒt), *v.*[1] Infl. **strutted, strutting.** ME. [unexpl. alt. of ME. *stroute*, repr. formally OE. *strūtian* ?be rigid; but a short vowel is seen in (M)HG. *strotzen* and in the Scand. langs.] †**1.** *intr.* To bulge, swell; to protrude on account of being full or swollen –1854. †**b.** *trans.* To distend, make protuberant; to puff *out* –1740. †**2.** *intr.* To contend, strive, quarrel, bluster. –late ME. †**3.** To protrude stiffly from a surface or body; to stand *out* –1809. †**b.** *trans.* To protrude, stick *out*, stretch *out* –1681. †**4.** *intr.* To behave proudly or vaingloriously; to triumph, swagger –1754. †**5.** To thrust up one's head and stand erect; to perk *up* –1807. **6.** To walk with an affected air of dignity or importance, stepping stiffly with head erect 1518. (The current sense). **b.** quasi-*trans.* with cogn. or advb. obj. 1605. **c.** *trans.* To walk upon or over (a floor, space) with a strut 1749.

5. Johnson did not s. or stand on tiptoe: He only did not stoop BOSWELL. **6.** Do's he not hold vp his head (as it were?) and s. in his gate? SHAKS. While the Cock..Stoutly struts his Dames before MILT. *fig.* Big passions strutting on a petty stage WORDSW. **b.** A poore Player, That struts and frets his houre vpon the Stage SHAKS.

Strut (strɒt), *v.*[2] 1828. [f. STRUT *sb.*[1]] **1.** *trans.* To brace or support by a strut or struts; to hold in place or strengthen by an upright, diagonal or transverse support. **2.** *intr.* To be fixed diagonally or slantwise; to be bent so as to form a sharp turn or angle 1841.

Struthiin (strū·þi,in). 1835. [f. mod.L. (*Gypsophila*) *struthium* the oriental soapwort (– Gr. στρουθίον soapwort); see -IN[1].] *Chem.* = SAPONIN.

Struthioid (strū·þi,oid), *a.* and *sb.* 1879. [f. as next + -OID.] **A.** *adj.* Ostrich-like, struthious. **B.** *sb.* A struthious bird.

Struthious (strū·þiəs), *a.* 1773. [f. L. *struthio* ostrich + -OUS.] *Zool.* Related to or resembling the ostrich.

Struvite (strū·vəit). 1850. [– G. *struvit* (G. L. Ulex 1846), f. *Struve*, name of Russian minister at Hamburg; see -ITE[1] 2 b.] *Min.* Hydrous phosphate of ammonium and magnesium, found in small yellowish-brown or greyish crystals.

Strychnia (stri·kniă). 1826. [f. STRYCHNOS; see -IA[1].] *Chem.* = STRYCHNINE.

Strychnic (stri·knik), *a.* 1840. [f. STRYCHNOS + -IC.] *Chem.* Pertaining to strychnine. *S. acid* = IGASURIC ACID.

Strychnine (stri·knīn, -in). 1819. [– Fr. *strychnine* (Pelletier and Caventou, 1818), f. L. *strychnos*; see next, -INE[5].] *Chem.* A highly poisonous vegetable alkaloid $C_{21}H_{22}N_2O_2$, obtained chiefly from *Strychnos nux-vomica* and other plants of the same genus. Used in medicine as a stimulant and tonic. **b.** *attrib.*, as in *s. poisoning*; **s.-tree,** *Strychnos psilosperma* 1879.

‖**Strychnos** (stri·knǫs). Also **strychnus,** *pl.* **strychni.** 1836. [mod.L. use (Linnæus 1737) of L. *strychnos* (Pliny) – Gr. στρύχνος, -ον kind of nightshade.] *Bot.* A genus of plants of the family *Loganaceæ*, including the nux vomica (*S. nux-vomica*), the St. Ignatius' bean (*S. ignatia*), and other species. Also, a plant or a species of this genus.

Stub (stɒb), *sb.* [OE. *stub*(*b* =. MLG., MDu. *stubbe*, ON. *stubbr, stubbi* :- Gmc. **stubbaz*, **stubbon*. OE. had also *styb* (:- **stubbjaz*), which coalesced with the other form.] **1.** A stump of a tree or, more rarely, of a shrub or smaller plant; the portion left fixed in the ground when a tree has been felled; also, †a trunk deprived of branches. †**b.** The part of a tree-trunk close to the ground –1637. †**2.** *fig.* A blockhead. MILT. **3.** A short piece of a broken branch remaining on the stem. late ME. **4.** = STUBBLE *sb.* Also *pl.* Now *dial.* ME. **5.** A splinter or thorn in the flesh. Now *dial.* 1531. **6.** A short thick nail; a worn horseshoe nail, esp. in *pl.* as material for making stub-iron. late ME. **7.** Something that looks stunted or cut short, e.g. a rudimentary tail or horn 1670. **b.** A short thick piece of wood 1833. **8.** *Mech.* A stud or projection; *spec.* in a lock, a stud which acts as a detent for the tumblers when their slots are engaged with it 1561. **9.** The remaining portion of something that has been broken or worn down; a stump, fag-end 1530. †**b.** = *s.-pen* –1829. **10.** *U.S.* A counterfoil 1876.

1. Old stockes and stubs of trees, Whereon nor fruit nor leafe was euer seene SPENSER. **4.** But ill it suits thee in the stubs to glean CLARE. **9.** A fellow..smoking an old s. of a clay pipe 1898.

attrib. and *Comb.*: **s. book** *U.S.*, a book containing only the counterfoils of cheques or other documents; **-end,** the butt end of a connecting-rod, a weapon, etc.; **-iron,** a tenacious kind of iron, orig. made out of old horse-shoe nails; **-nail** = sense 6; **-pen,** orig. a worn quill pen; hence a broad-pointed pen; **-twist,** a material for fine gun-barrels, composed of a ribbon of stub-iron twisted into a spiral shape.

Stub (stɒb), *v.* Infl. **stubbed** (stɒbd), **stubbing.** 1440. [f. prec.] **1.** *trans.* To dig up by the roots; to grub up (roots). Chiefly with *up.* **2.** To cut down (a tree, etc.) close to the root 1594. **3.** To remove the stubs from (land). Also, to clear (land) of trees, furze, etc. by uprooting. Chiefly with *up.* 1464. **4.** To reduce to a stub or stump 1577. **5.** To cause (a horse) to be wounded with a stub. Also *refl.* of the horse. 1686. **6.** To strike (the toe) violently against anything in walking or running, orig. *U.S.* 1848. Hence *intr.* to go heedlessly (*U.S. colloq.*) **7.** To cover with stubs 1878. **8.** To extinguish (a cigarette) by pressing the lighted end of the stub against a hard object; also with *out* 1927.

Stubbed (stɒbd), *ppl. a.* 1529. [f. STUB *v.* + -ED[1].] **1.** Of trees: Cut down to a stub; cut off near the ground; also, deprived of branches or pollarded 1575. **2.** Short and thick, stumpy. *Obs.* exc. *dial.* 1529. **3.** Reduced to a stub; (of hair) cut close to the skin, stubbly 1621. **4.** Blunted at the point 1610. **5.** Abounding in stubs 1855.

2. The Tartar is a s. squat fellow, hard bred 1630. **5.** Then came a bit of s. ground, once a wood BROWNING.

Stubble (stɒ·b'l), *sb.* ME. [– AFr. *stuble*, OFr. *estuble* (mod. *éteule*), :- L. *stupla, stupula*, f. earlier *stipula* straw; cf. STIPULA.] **1.** Each of the stumps or lower ends of grain-stalks left in the ground after reaping. Now only in *pl.* **2.** *collect. sing.* The stumps or lower parts of the stalks of wheat or other grain left in the ground by the sickle or reaping-machine ME. **b.** *transf.* A rough surface or short growth likened to this; *esp.* the short bristly growth on a man's unshaven face 1596. **3.** The straw of grain-stalks, etc. gathered after the crop has been harvested. late ME. **4.** A field that has been reaped and not yet ploughed again; a stubble-field. Chiefly *pl.* 1792.

1. Every withered stem and s. rimed with frost EMERSON. **2.** I suppose, that you..Know by the s., what the Corne hath bene CHAPMAN. **b.** Bristly with the s. of a coarse hard beard DICKENS. **3.** One night as I lay on my bed of s. 1760.

attrib. and *Comb.*: **s. goose,** (*a*) a goose fed on the s.; (*b*) the grey-lag goose, *Anser cinereus.* Hence **Stu·bble** *v. trans.* to clear (land) of s. **Stu·bbled** *a.* covered with s., stubbly.

Stubbly (stɒ·bli), *a.* 1600. [f. prec. + -Y[1].] **1.** Covered with stubble. **2.** Resembling stubble; *esp.* of hair, bristly 1849.

Stubborn (stɒ·bəɹn), *a.* [Late ME. *stiborne*, later *stoburn*(*e, stuborn*; of unkn. origin.] **1.** Of persons or animals: Pertinacious or dogged in refusing obedience or compliance; unyielding, inflexible, obstinate; chiefly in bad sense, unreasonably obstinate. **b.** Of dispositions, resolves, speech or action: Characterized by obstinacy 1526. **2.** Of things: Intractable, refractory to treatment; difficult to subdue, work, cure, etc. 1514. **3.** Of material things: Hard, stiff, rigid. *Obs.* exc. of wood or stone (with some notion of sense 2) 1577.

1. A disputatious..and s. female will always offend 1767. The people was as s. as their King GREEN. **b.** Stout were their hearts, and s. was their strife SCOTT. **2.** An old S. Pain in the Back WESLEY. The s. glebe GRAY. *Prov.* Facts are s. things. Hence **Stu·bborn** *v.* (only *poet.*) *trans.* to make s.; to harden. **Stu·bborn-ly** *adv.* **-ness.**

Stubby (stɒ·bi), *a.* 1572. [f. STUB *sb.* + -Y[1].] **1.** Of the nature of a stub; short and thick or broad. **2.** Abounding in or full of stubs. Chiefly of the hair or beard: Composed of short, stiff bristles. 1604. Hence **Stu·bbiness.**

Stubwort (stɒ·bwɒɹt). 1541. [f. STUB *sb.* + WORT[1].] The Wood-sorrel, *Oxalis acetosella.*

Stucco (stɒ·kou), *sb.* 1598. [– It. *stucco*, of Gmc. origin.] **1. a.** A fine plaster, esp. one composed of gypsum and pulverized marble, used for covering walls, ceilings, and floors, and for making cornices, mouldings, and other decorations. **b.** A coarse plaster or calcareous cement used chiefly for covering the rough exterior surfaces of walls in imitation of stone; also called *common s.*; *spec.* the third or last coat of plastering 1779. **c.** Plaster of Paris 1839. **2.** The process of ornamenting walls, ceilings, cornices, etc. with stucco; also, work or ornamentation produced by this process 1697. **3.** *attrib.* or *adj.* 1744.

3. S. houses with asphalte terraces in front THACKERAY.

Stucco (stɒ·ko^u), *v.* Infl. **stuccoed, stuccoing.** 1726. [f. prec.] *trans.* To coat or plaster (a cornice, wall, etc.) with stucco; to ornament with stucco-work. **b.** In mod. building: To coat or plaster (a wall, building) esp. in imitation of stone-work 1790. **c.** *transf.* and *fig.* 1774.

c. Ye must s. and whitewash your faces 1776. Hence **Stu·ccoer,** a modeller in stucco.

†**Stuck,** *sb.* 1601. [perh. var. of STOCK *sb.*[2]] *Fencing.* A thrust or lunge –1614.

Stuck (stɒk), *ppl. a.* 1702. [str. pa. pple. of STICK *v.*] **1.** Of an animal: That has been stabbed or had its throat cut. Chiefly in provb. phr. *to stare like a s. pig.* **2.** Unable to go further, 'stickit' 1885.

Stuck-up (stress var.), *a. colloq.* 1829. [pa. pple. of *stick up,* STICK *v.*[1]] Assuming an unjustified air of superiority, or pluming oneself unduly on real superiority; offensively pretentious.

'He's a nasty stuck-up monkey..' said Mrs. Squeers 1839.

Stud (stɒd), *sb.*[1] [OE. *studu, stuþu* = MHG. *stud,* ON. *stoð,* rel. to G. *stützen* prop, support.] **I.** A post, prop. **1.** †A wooden post of any kind; one of the upright timbers in the wall of a building; now chiefly = QUARTER *sb.* IV. 1. **b.** *collect. sing.* Laths to be used as the uprights in partition walls or the walls of lath-and-plaster buildings 1535. †**2.** *fig.* A prop or support –1652. **3.** *U.S.* The height of a room from floor to ceiling 1850. **4.** †**a.** A stem, trunk (of a tree) –1621. **b.** A short branch, spur (*rare*) 1657.

4. a. Seest not thilke same Hawthorne studde? SPENSER.

II. Something fixed in and projecting from a surface. **1.** An ornamental round knob; a boss or large nail-head standing out on a surface, for decoration or protection. late ME. **b.** *Arch.* A sculptured disc such as was used in the ornamentation of mouldings in the Late Norman period of English architecture 1686. **2.** A kind of button which is passed through one or more eyelet-holes, either in order to fasten some article of dress, or merely for ornament 1555. **3.** *Machinery.* **a.** A lug or projecting socket to receive the end of an axle, pin, etc. 1683. **b.** A short rod or pin fixed in or projecting from something, and serving as a support, axis, or stop 1694. **c.** *Gunnery.* One of a number of protuberances on the surface of a projectile to be fired from a rifled gun, placed spirally to make the shot receive rotatory movement from the grooving of the gun 1866. **d.** = *s.-bolt* 1887. **e.** *Naut.* A transverse bar of cast-iron inserted in the middle of each link of a chain-cable 1863.

1. A belt of straw and Iuie buds, With Corall clasps and Amber studs MARLOWE. **2.** The s. in his shirt sleeve 1772.

Comb.: **s.-bolt,** a cylindrical bolt, threaded at both ends, one end to be screwed into a hole tapped in a casting or the like; while the other end passes through a hole in the cover-plate, which is secured by a nut.

Stud (stɒd), *sb.*[2] [OE. *stōd,* corresp. to MLG. *stōt,* OHG. *stuot* (G. *stute* mare), ON. *stóð* :– Gmc. **stōđam,* **stōđō,* f. **stō-* STAND, Cf. STEED.] **1.** An establishment in which stallions and mares are kept for breeding. Also, the stallions and mares kept in such an establishment. †**b.** A collection of mares kept for breeding –1607. †**c.** A breed, race (of horses); also *transf.* –1557. **2.** In early use: The horses bred by and belonging to one person. In later use: A number of horses (esp. race-horses or hunters) belonging to one owner. Also *transf.* 1661. **3.** *U.S.* [Short for STUD-HORSE.] A stallion 1803.

1. A third [order] establishes a Government S. in the district of Tirhút 1898. **2.** He kept a hunting s. to the last 1910. *transf.* A large s. of sows 1813. His..s. of motor-cars 1907.

Comb.: **s.-book,** a book giving the pedigree of thoroughbred horses; also a similar book relating to dogs, etc.; **-groom,** the head groom attached to a s.; **-poker** *U.S.,* a variety of the game of poker.

Stud (stɒd), *v.* 1505. [f. STUD *sb.*[1]] **1.** *trans.* To supply with studs or upright timbers; to build with studs. **2.** To ornament or cover with or as with studs, bosses, or nail-heads 1570. **3.** To set (a surface) with a number of protuberant or conspicuous objects 1790. **b.** *rarely* in immaterial sense 1849. **4.** Of things: **a.** To be fixed in (a surface) in the manner of studs. **b.** To be placed at intervals over (a surface) 1652. **5.** To insert or place (a number of things) at intervals over a surface 1856. **6.** *Mech.* To secure with studs 1911.

2. Their harnesse studded all with Gold and Pearle SHAKS. A strong door of oak, studded with nails SCOTT. **3. b.** Conversation..studded with execrable jokes 1849. **4.** Coaling-stations s. the ocean highways of the world 1906.

Studding (stɒ·diŋ), *vbl. sb.* 1588. [f. STUD *v.* + -ING[1].] **1.** The woodwork of a lath and plaster wall or partition; also *pl.* wood cut into battens for use as studs. **2.** That with which a surface is studded 1844. **3.** *U.S.* = STUD *sb.*[1] I. 3. 1884.

Studding-sail (stɒ·ns'l). 1549. [The earliest recorded form (*stoytene sale* XVI) has suggested deriv. from MLG., MDu. *stōtinge,* noun of action of *stōten* thrust (Du. *stooten*), cogn. with OS. *stōtan,* OHG. *stōzzan* (G. *stossen*) Goth. *stautan.*] A sail set beyond the leeches of any of the principal sails during a fair wind.

Student (stiū·dĕnt). late ME. [– L. *studens, -ent-,* pr. pple. of *studēre* be eager or diligent, study; the earlier †*studiant* (XIV) was aphetic f. †*estudiant* – OFr. *estudiant* (mod. *étudiant*), subst. use of pr. pple. of *estudier*; see STUDY *v.,* -ENT.] **1.** A person who is engaged in or addicted to study. **2.** A person who is undergoing a course of study and instruction at a university or other place of higher education or technical training. late ME. **3. a.** At Christ Church, Oxford: A member of the foundation, corresp. to the 'fellow' or 'scholar' of other colleges (now restricted to the senior members) 1651. **b.** A person who receives emoluments, during a fixed period, to enable him to pursue his studies and as a reward of merit 1800.

1. I am not..leane enough to bee thought a good Student SHAKS.

Comb.: **s. interpreter,** a civil servant who is appointed to undergo a course of instruction in foreign languages in order to qualify for a post in the diplomatic or consular service; **s.-teacher,** a student who teaches in a school as part of his training for a teacher's diploma. Hence **Stu·dentry** (*rare*), students collectively.

Studentship (stiū·dĕnt,ʃip). 1782. [-SHIP.] **1.** A position, usu. stipendiary, the holding of which constitutes a person a 'student'; see prec. 3 a, b. **2.** *gen.* The condition or fact of being a student 1881.

1. A travelling s. for travel and study abroad, of the value of £200. 1883.

Stu·d-horse. [Late OE. *stōdhors* = ON. *stóðhross*; see STUD *sb.*[2], HORSE.] A stallion kept for breeding.

Studied (stɒ·did), *ppl. a.* 1530. [f. STUDY *v.* + -ED[1].] **1.** Produced or acquired by study, carefully contrived or excogitated; premeditated; deliberate, intentional 1606. **2.** Of a person: Learned, deeply read, skilled, practised, versed 1530. †**b.** Prepared by study or cogitation –1658.

1. Expressed..in terms of s. ambiguity 1769. A s. discourtesy 1859. **2.** *Merch. V.* II. ii. 205. **b.** I ..am well s. for a liberall thanks, Which I do owe you SHAKS. Hence **Stu·died-ly** *adv.,* **-ness.**

Studier (stɒ·diəɹ). late ME. [f. STUDY *v.* + -ER[1].] †**1.** A student –1466. **2.** One who studies a specified subject. Now *rare* or *Obs.* 1593. **3.** One who strives after or pursues (an object or end). Now *rare.* 1597.

2. A s. of character JANE AUSTEN. **3.** The merest S. of Pleasure 1710.

Studio (stiū·dio). 1819. [– It. *studio*; cf. STUDY *sb.* 8.] †**1.** *Fine Art.* = STUDY *sb.* 10. SHELLEY. **2.** The work-room of a sculptor or painter; also that of a photographer 1819. **b.** A room or building for the making of a cinematographic film or for wireless broadcasting 1912.

1. The original s. by Michael Angelo of the 'Day of Judgment' SHELLEY.

Studious (stiū·diəs), *a.* late ME. [– L. *studiosus,* f. *studium* STUDY *sb.*; see -OUS.] **1.** Assiduous in study; devoted to the acquisition of learning. **b.** Of the nature of, pertaining to, or concerned with learning or study 1526. **c.** Of a place: Devoted or suited to study 1591. **2.** Giving careful attention; intent on a purpose or object, heedful, solicitous 1450. **b.** Characterized by or exhibiting careful attention 1532. **c.** Planned with care; studied, deliberate 1750.

1. Master Tindall..was..a man of ryght good lyuynge, studyouse & well lerned in scrypture 1528. *absol.* The S. ought to have stated times for Exercise WESLEY. **b.** Persons of s. habits 1832. **c.** But let my due feet never fail, To walk the s. Cloysters pale MILT. **2.** The work she plied; but s. of delay, By night revers'd the labours of the day POPE. **b.** Agrippa paid s. court to the Jews 1879. **c.** For the frigid villany of s. lewdness,.. what apology can be invented? JOHNSON. Hence **Stu·dious-ly** *adv.,* **-ness.**

Stu·d-mare. OE. [Late OE. *stōdmȳre* = ON. *stóðmerr*; see STUD *sb.*[2], MARE[1].] A mare kept for breeding purposes; a brood-mare.

Stu·d-sail. 1850. [app. erron. for *stu'ns'l* = STUDDING-SAIL.] = STUDDING-SAIL.

Study (stɒ·di), *sb.* ME. [Aphetic – OFr. *estudie* (mod. *étude*) – L. *studium* zeal, affection, painstaking application.] †**1.** (Chiefly in translations from Latin): Affection, friendliness, devotion to another's welfare; partisan sympathy; desire, inclination; pleasure or interest felt in something –1697. †**2.** An employment, occupation –1610. †**3.** A state of mental perplexity or anxious thought –1689. **b.** A state of reverie or abstraction. *Obs.* exc. in BROWN STUDY. late ME. **4.** Thought or meditation directed to the accomplishment of a purpose; studied or deliberate effort or contrivance; also, the object or aim of (a person's) solicitous endeavour. late ME. **5.** Application of mind to the acquisition of learning ME. **b.** The cultivation of a particular branch of learning or science. Often *collect. pl.,* a person's work as a student. 1477. **6.** The action of studying (something specified or implied); mental effort in the acquisition *of* (some kind of learning) ME. **b.** *Theatr.* The action of committing to memory one's part in a play. Hence, *to have* or *be a quick, slow,* etc. *s.,* to be quick, slow, etc. in learning by heart. 1590. **7.** That which is studied; the object of one's study. Chiefly with *poss.* 1535. **b.** Something worth studying, or that requires to be studied; an object presenting effects of colour (and the like) attractive to an artist 1766. **8.** A room furnished with books and used for private study, reading, writing, or the like. Often applied to the private room or office of the master of the house, however it may be used. ME. †**9.** A seat of learning. *General s., s. general* (= med.L. *studium generale*), a university. –1673. **10.** An artistic production executed for the sake of acquiring skill or knowledge, or to serve as a preparation for future work; a careful preliminary sketch for a work of art, or (more usu.) for some detail or portion of it. Also, occas., a drawing, painting, or piece of sculpture designed to bring out the characteristics of the object represented, as they are revealed by especially careful observation. 1769. **b.** A discourse or literary composition devoted to the detailed consideration of some question, or the minute description of some object; a literary exercise or experiment 1866. **11.** *Mus.* A composition intended to develop a player's powers of execution 1875.

4. The acquisition of a fortune is the s. of all 1803. **5.** Of studie took he mooste cure and moost heede CHAUCER. Much studie is a wearinesse of the flesh *Eccles.* 12:12. **b.** He gave a considerable time to sacred studies 1756. **6.** The s...of the effect of art on the mind of nations RUSKIN. *To make a s. of,* to study, observe carefully. **7.** The proper s. of mankind is Man POPE. **b.** The harpist, whose nose is a s. in purples 1894. **8.** Doe you obserue this gallerie?..Here are a couple of studies, at each end one. B. JONS. **10.** A clever s. of a calf being fed 1884.

Study (stɒ·di), *v.* Pa. t. and pa. pple.

studied (stʌ·did). ME. [Aphetic – OFr. *estudier* (mod. *étudier*) – med.L. *studiare* (f. L. *studium* STUDY *sb.*), for L. *studēre* be zealous, apply oneself, study.] **I.** *intr.* **1.** To apply the mind to the acquisition of learning, whether by means of books, observation, or experiment. **b.** To follow one's studies at a university, college, or the like; to be a student of some science or art *under* a professor or master 1450. **2.** To think intently; to meditate; to reflect, try to recollect something or to come to a decision. *Obs.* exc. *dial.* and *U.S. colloq.* ME. †**b.** With indirect question: To debate with oneself, deliberate, consider –1788. †**c.** To search, 'cast about' *for* –1748. **3.** To endeavour, make it one's aim, set oneself deliberately *to do* something. *arch.* ME.

1. I wolde fayne be a great clerke, but I love not to studye 1530. **b.** Vandyke studied under Rubens 1758. **2.** You make me s. of that: She was of Carthage, not of Tunis SHAKS. **b.** I haue beene studying how I may compare This prison where I liue, vnto the world SHAKS. **c.** I found a Moral first and studied for a Fable SWIFT. **3.** No body did ever s. to hurt him 1715.

II. *trans.* **1.** To apply one's mind to the acquiring of (a science, art, language, etc.) 1445. **2.** To be occupied with (a specific branch of learning) as the subject of one's educational course or professional training 1569. **3.** To read (a book, a passage, an author) with close attention. late ME. **b.** Of an actor: To commit to memory and exercise oneself in the rendering of (a part) 1601. **4.** To examine in detail, seek to become minutely acquainted with or to understand (a phenomenon, a state of circumstances, a person's character, etc.); to investigate (a problem) 1600. **b.** To scrutinize (a visible object) in order to ascertain its nature or to be familiar with its appearance; *loosely*, to look at as if examining minutely 1662. **5.** To aim at, seek to achieve. Now only, to aim at (some quality in one's own action). 1606. **6.** To devise, excogitate. Now only with *out*. 1559. **7.** To exercise thought and deliberation in (an action, composition, etc.) 1668. **8.** To 'consider' (a person's wishes, feelings, or interests); hence *colloq.* to humour (a person) 1758.

1. If a Gentleman be to s. any Language, it ought to be that of his own Country LOCKE. **3.** The learned Men who s. Aristotle DE FOE. One cannot be always studying one's own works M. ARNOLD. **b.** *Twel. N.* I. v. 190. **4.** The more he studied the situation, the more apparent it became that..he was in a cleft stick 1885. **b.** By seizing and studying the contents of my dearest portmanteaus KINGLAKE. **5.** The three Villains studied nothing but Revenge DE FOE. **6.** The temple itself is nobly and magnificently studied WARTON. **8.** With no husband to s., housekeeping is mere play MRS. CARLYLE.

Stuff (stʌf), *sb.* [Late ME. *stof(fe, stuff(e*, aphetic – OFr. *estoffe* (mod. *étoffe*), perh. f. *estoffer*; see STUFF *v.*] **I.** Equipment, stores, stock. *Obs.* exc. *Sc.* and *north.*, and in HOUSEHOLD-STUFF *arch.* **II.** Material of which something is or may be made. **1.** Material to work with or upon 1440. **b.** *collect.* Materials for a piece of work, esp. building materials. late ME. †**c.** A manufactured material –1626. **2.** *transf.* and *fig.* 1553. **3.** In various operative trades, applied *spec.* to the kind of material used in the trade. **a.** *Carpentry* and *Joinery*. Timber 1544. **b.** *Paper-making*. Pulp or paper-stock ground ready for use 1745. **c.** *Mining*. Material of rock, earth, or clay containing ore, metal, or precious stones 1853. **4.** Material for making garments; woven material of any kind 1462. **b.** In particularized sense: A kind of stuff; a textile fabric 1604. **c.** *spec.* A woollen fabric 1643. **d.** As the material for the gown worn by a junior counsel. Hence *rarely*, A 'stuff gownsman', i.e. a junior counsel, as dist. from a 'silk' (see SILK *sb.* 3 d) 1889.

1. Let Phidias haue rude & obstinate stuffe to carue,..his worke will lacke that bewtie which otherwise..it might haue had HOOKER. **b.** A small cotage, poore for the stuffe, and rude for the workemanship ASCHAM. **2.** We are such stuffe As dreames are made on SHAKS. He was not naturally of the s. that martyrs are made of HAWTHORNE. **3. a.** Panel s. should be treated in a similar manner 1879. **c.** About 10 tons of s. are washed per hour 1887. **4.** *Tam. Shr.* IV. iii. 119. **b.** The walls were covered with the stuffs of the East LYTTON. **c.** He dresses himself according to the Season in Cloth or in S. STEELE.

III. Matter of an unspecified kind. **1.** The general designation for solid, liquid, or (rarely) gaseous matter of any kind: used indefinitely instead of the specific designation, or where no specific designation exists. Often applied to a preparation or composition used for some special purpose. 1580. **b.** Applied to medicine, esp. liquid mixtures. More definitely *doctor's s.* Now only *colloq.* 1611. **c.** Applied to articles of food or drink 1597. **d.** In certain operative trades e.g. *Plastering*, applied *spec.* to some particular preparation used in the work 1812. **e.** Cultivated produce of a garden or farm; natural produce of land 1687. **f.** In commercial and industrial use, applied *spec.* to the particular commodity dealt in 1708. **2.** *transf.* and *fig.* in non-physical senses. **a.** Literary or artistic matter. Now *rare* exc. disparagingly, and *colloq.* among journalists and professional authors = 'copy'. 1542. **b.** Applied to a person 1588. **3.** What is worthless; rubbish 1668. **b.** Worthless ideas, discourse, or writing; nonsense, rubbish. Freq. in interjectional use. 1579. **4.** *slang.* **a.** Money, cash. Chiefly with article, *the s.* 1775. **b.** Stolen goods 1865.

1. For stuffe to kille myce..ij[s] 1617. **b.** Your very kind letter..did me more good, I think, than any of my doctor's s. 1779. **c.** *Good s.*, *the s.* (colloq.), whisky. War slang, *That's the s.* (*to give the troops*); often fig. **2. b.** *Hot s.* (slang), applied to (*a*) a lustful person; (*b*) a person of fiery courage; (*c*) a strong competitor. **3. b.** It is sad s., Sir, miserably written, as books in general then were JOHNSON. Phr. *S. and nonsense.* — *and s.*, and such-like useless or dull matters (*colloq.*). **4. a.** But has she got the s., Mr. Fag; is she rich, hey? SHERIDAN.

Comb.: **s. gown**, a junior counsel (see II. 4 d above); so also **s. gownsman**; **s. heap**, a heap of coals and slack raised from a mine; **s. mark**, a weaver's mark woven into goods to identify them or attest their quality.

Stuff (stʌf), *v.* late ME. [Aphetic – OFr. *estoffer* (mod. *étoffer*) – late Gr. στύφειν draw together, contract, rel. to στυππεῖον oakum, L. *stuppa*.] †**1.** *trans.* To furnish (a fortified town, an army, a commander, etc.) with men, munitions, and stores; to garrison (a town) –1640. †**b.** To furnish (troops) with support; to support, aid (a war) –1560. †**2.** To supply (a person) with arms, provisions, money, etc. –1656. †**3.** To furnish (a place) with accessories, stock, inhabitants; to store with provisions, etc. –1626. †**b.** To store (goods) in a receptacle or place; to keep (flocks) in a place –1606. **4.** To line or fill with some material as a padding; to distend or expand with padding; esp. to fill (a bed-tick, cushion, etc.) with packing in order to furnish a yielding support 1450. **b.** Of material: To serve as padding or stuffing 1530. †**c.** To distend, expand (as if by padding) –1678. **5.** *Cookery*. To fill (the inside of a bird or animal, a piece of meat, etc.) with forcemeat, herbs, etc. as a stuffing. late ME. **6.** To fill out (the skin of a beast, bird, etc.) with material so as to resemble the living creature 1555. **7.** To fill (a receptacle); esp. to fill by packing the materials closely together, to cram full 1440. **b.** Said of the filling material 1664. **c.** To crowd, cram (a vehicle, room *with* persons). Also *intr.* for *pass.* To be crammed. Now *rare*. 1571. **d.** *U.S.* To put fraudulent votes into (a ballot-box) 1872. **8.** *fig.* **a.** To fill, crowd (speech, etc.) *with* something; to fill (a person, his mind, etc.) with ideas, feelings, etc. 1531. **b.** *slang.* To 'cram', hoax, humbug (a person). Also with *up*. 1844. **9.** To fill (oneself, one's stomach) to repletion with food. Also said of the food. late ME. **b.** To cause (a patient) to eat to repletion. Also, to treat (a disease) by feeding up the patient. 1789. **c.** *intr.* for *refl.* To gorge oneself with food 1726. **d.** *trans.* To gorge (food). Also with *down*. 1743. **10.** To fill (an aperture, cavity, etc.) by thrusting something tightly in; hence, to stop up, to plug. Also of a material: To fill *up* so as to block (an aperture). 1593. †**11.** Of bodily humours: To clog, choke *up* (the body, its organs, vessels, etc.) –1750. †**b.** To cause stuffiness in (the head or nose) –1620. **12.** To thrust (something, esp. loose materials) tightly into a receptacle or cavity 1579. **b.** To pack tightly (a person) in a confined space; to crowd (a number of persons *together*) 1728. **13.** *Leather-manuf.* To dress (a skin) with a coating of dubbing or stuffing 1844.

2. A Gentleman..Stuft as they say with Honourable parts SHAKS. **3. b.** In Iuory cofers I haue stuft my crownes SHAKS. **4.** Giue me your Doublet, and stuffe me out with Straw SHAKS. **b.** *Much Ado* III. ii. 47. **c.** Their very sighs might serve to s. the sail 1631. **5.** As shee went to the Garden for Parseley to stuffe a Rabit SHAKS. **7.** In's Hand a Wallet stuff'd with Papers 1705. **c.** The room as full as it could s. 1799. **8.** The lies and fables with which his work is stuffed WALPOLE. Don't s. up your head with things you don't understand 1889. **9.** Stuffed himself till his hide was stretched as tight as a sausage skin 1903. **b.** S. a cold and starve a cold are but two ways 1849. **c.** Let them neither starve nor s. SWIFT. **10.** *Rich. II*, I. i. 44. **11. b.** I am stuft cosin, I cannot smell SHAKS. **12.** With hands stuffed into his front pockets SURTEES. **b.** There I was..stuffed down between Godmamma and the Marquis's mother 1900. Hence **Stuffed** (stʌft) *ppl. a.* **Stu·ffer**, one who stuffs or fills; a machine or implement used for stuffing.

Stuffiness (stʌ·finės). 1611. [f. STUFFY + -NESS.] †**1.** Thickness or closeness of texture. COTGR. **2.** The condition of being close or ill-ventilated 1859. **3.** The state or sensation of stoppage and obstruction in the nose or throat 1862.

Stuffing (stʌ·fiŋ), *vbl. sb.* 1530. [-ING[1].] **1.** The action of STUFF *v.*, or the result of this action 1533. **b.** Obstruction of the throat, nose, or chest by catarrh; the sensation produced by this 1601. **2.** The material with which a receptacle is stuffed 1530. **b.** *Cookery*. Forcemeat or other seasoned mixture used to stuff meat before cooking 1538. †**c.** *fig.* (e.g. literary 'padding') –1804. **3.** *Leather-manuf.* The process of rubbing with a mixture of fish-oil and tallow; the mixture used for this 1851.

1. These cowled gentry, that think of nothing but quaffing and s.! SCOTT. **2.** Phr. *To knock, beat, take the s. out of* (an animal, person, etc.), to reduce to a state of weakness or flabbiness, take the strength or conceit out of (*colloq.*).

Comb.: **s.-box** *Machinery*, a chamber packed with fluid-tight elastic material, through which a piston-rod or shaft is made to pass in order to prevent leakage at the orifice through which it leaves or enters a vessel; similarly *s.-gland*, *s. ring*; **s. wheel**, a revolving hollow drum in which leather is subjected to 'stuffing'.

Stuffy (stʌ·fi), *a.* 1551. [f. STUFF *sb.* + -Y[1].] †**1.** Full of stuff or substance –1667. **2.** Of a room, etc.: Ill-ventilated, close. Of the air: Wanting in freshness; oppressive to the lungs and head. Of persons: Addicted to living in stuffy conditions. 1831. **b.** *transf.* Lacking in freshness, interest, or smartness 1843. **3.** Of persons: Affected with a sensation of stoppage in the nose or throat. Said also of the sensation. 1847. **4.** *U.S. colloq.* Angry, sulky 1825. **5.** *slang.* Easily offended or shocked 1926.

2. b. Listening to a s. debate in the Senate 1909.

Stull (stʌl). 1778. [perh. – G. *stollen* support, prop. Cf. next.] *Mining*. A platform or framework of timber covered with boards to support workmen or to carry ore or rubbish; also, a framework of boards to protect miners from falling stones.

Stulm (stʌlm). 1684. [perh. – G. *stolln*, *stollen*, of the same meaning. Cf. prec.] *Mining*. An adit or level in a mine.

Stultification (stʌ:ltifikē[i]·ʃən). 1832. [f. next; see -FICATION.] The action of STULTIFY *v.*; the state of being stultified; an instance of this.

Stultify (stʌ·ltifəi), *v.* 1766. [– late L. *stultificare*, f. *stultus* foolish, fool; see -FY.] **1.** trans. *Law*. To allege or prove to be of unsound mind; esp. *refl.*, to allege one's own insanity in order to evade some responsibility. **2.** To cause to be or appear foolish, ridiculous, or absurdly inconsistent 1809. **b.** To render nugatory, worthless, or useless 1865. **3.** To regard as a fool or as foolish (*rare*) 1820.

2. This witness, however, stultified himself by admitting that he was too far off to hear what Clement said 1871. **b.** The blind folly of his servants had stultified his efforts 1888. **3.** The modern sciolist stultifies all understanding but his own, and that which he conceives like his own HAZLITT.

Stultiloquence (stɒlti·lŏkwĕns). 1721. [– L. *stultiloquentia*, f. *stultiloquus*, f. *stultus* foolish + *-loquus* that speaks; see -ENCE.] Foolish or senseless talk, babble, twaddle. So **Stulti·loquent** *a.* (*rare*) talking foolishly; **-ly** *adv.*

Stultiloquy (stɒlti·lŏkwi). 1653. [– L. *stultiloquium*, f. *stultiloquus*; see prec.] A speaking foolishly, a foolish babbling.

Stum (stɒm), *sb.* 1662. [– Du. *stom*, subst. use of *stom* dumb. Cf. Fr. *vin muet* in the same sense.] **1.** Unfermented or partly fermented grape juice, must; esp. must in which the fermentation has been prevented or arrested by fumigation with sulphur. **b.** Must as used for renewing vapid wines. Also occas. applied to apple-juice similarly used. 1679. **2.** Vapid wine renewed by the mixture of stum 1664.

1. b. Let our Wines without mixture, or S. be all fine 1692. *fig.* Thy bellowing Renegado Priests, That..with thy Stumm ferment their fainting Cause DRYDEN.

Stum (stɒm), *v.* Infl. **stummed, stumming.** 1645. [– Du. *stommen*, f. *stom* STUM *sb.*] **1.** *trans.* To renew (wine) by mixing with stum or must and raising a new fermentation. **2.** To fumigate (a cask) with burning sulphur, in order to prevent the contained liquor from fermenting; to stop the fermentation of (new wine) by fumigation 1787.

Stumble (stɒ·mb'l), *sb.* 1547. [f. next.] **1.** An act of stumbling; a missing one's footing; a blunder, slip. **b.** A moral lapse 1702. **c.** A stumbling or coming by accident upon something 1865. **2.** *gen.* The action of stumbling 1641.

1. b. One s. is oftentimes enough to deface the character of an honourable life 1702.

Stumble (stɒ·mb'l), *v.* ME. [– ON. **stumla* (repr. by Norw., Sw. dial. *stumla*, Da. dial. *stumle*), parallel to synon. *stumra*, f. Gmc. **stum-*, **stam-* (see STAMMER).] **1.** *intr.* To miss one's footing, or trip over an obstacle, in walking or running, so as to fall or be in danger of falling. **b.** To knock or jostle *against* (a person or thing) involuntarily 1440. **2.** *fig.* **a.** To trip morally ME. **b.** To make a slip in speech or action; to blunder through inadvertence or unpreparedness 1450. **c.** To come *on* or *upon* by chance and unexpectedly; to come *in* or *into* (a place) by chance 1555. **d.** To take offence; to find a stumbling-block or obstacle to belief 1526. **3.** To walk unsteadily and with frequent stumbles. late ME. **b.** *fig.* To proceed, speak, or act in a blundering or hesitating manner. late ME. **4.** *trans.* (causatively). †**a.** To trip up, overthrow –1652. **b.** To puzzle; to give pause or offence to; to embarrass, nonplus 1605. †**c.** To shake (a resolve, an opinion) –1651.

1. How oft to night Haue my old feet stumbled at graues SHAKS. The horse stumblinge threw them both 1659. *To s. at* (*on*) *the threshold*, chiefly *fig.* to fail, take offence, meet with an ominous check at the beginning of an enterprise. Phr. 2. a. They sinned and stumbled..with debt, with drink THACKERAY. b. T'is better s. with thy feet Then s. with thy tongue 1607. c. The founders..appear to have stumbled upon their discovery by a kind of accident 1874. d. In case the Prelacy for England should s. at the Supremacy of Rome 1647. 3. But..blind be blinded more, That they may s. on, and deeper fall MILT. b. My tongue should s. in mine earnest words SHAKS. 4. b. By these..Reproaches, many were stumbled at his Testimony 1724. Hence **Stu·mbler,** one who, or something which stumbles; a cause of stumbling, a 'poser'. **Stu·mblingly** *adv.*

Stu·mbling-block. 1526. [f. *stumbling* vbl. sb.] Something to stumble at or over; a cause of stumbling. Chiefly *fig.*

That no man putt a stomblinge blocke or an occasion to faule [Gr. πρόσκομμα ἢ σκάνδαλον] in his brothers waye TINDALE *Rom.* 14:13.

Stumer (stiū·məɹ). *slang.* 1890. [Of unkn., prob. symbolic, origin.] A worthless cheque; a counterfeit note or coin. **b.** A racehorse fraudulently run; also, a dud.

Stump (stɒmp), *sb.*¹ late ME. [– MLG. *stump*, *stumpe*, (M)Du. *stomp* = OHG., G. *stumpf* subst. uses of corresp. adjs.; perh. rel. to STUB and STAMP *v.*] **1.** The part remaining of an amputated or broken-off limb or portion of the body. **b.** A rudimentary limb or member, or one that has the appearance of being mutilated 1555. **c.** *joc.* A leg. Chiefly in *to stir one's stumps*, to walk or dance briskly. 1460. **d.** A wooden leg 1679. **2.** The portion of the trunk of a felled tree that remains fixed in the ground; also, a standing tree-trunk from which the upper part and the branches have been cut or broken off 1440. **b.** The base of a growing tree 1902. **3.** = STUB *sb.* 9. 1516. **b.** The part of a broken tooth left in the gum. late ME. **c.** A docked tail 1544. **d.** *Naut.* The lower portion of a mast when the upper part has been broken off or shot away 1725. **e.** The remaining portion of a leaf cut out of a volume; the counterfoil of a cheque 1887. **4.** A block-head; a man of short stumpy figure 1601. **5.** The stalk of a plant (esp. cabbage) when the leaves are removed 1819. **b.** *pl.* Hair cut close to the skin. Also, remains of feathers on a plucked fowl. 1584. **6.** A post, a short pillar not supporting anything 1700. **7.** *Cricket.* Each of the three (formerly two) upright sticks which, with the bails laid on the top of them, form a wicket 1735. **8.** A projecting stud in a lock or a hinge 1808. **9.** orig. *U.S.* **a.** In early use, the stump (sense 2) of a felled tree used as a stand or platform for a speaker 1775. **b.** Hence, a place or an occasion of political oratory 1816.

1. The stumps that beggars thrust into coaches to excite charity and miscarriages H. WALPOLE. 2. b. Phr. *To buy* (timber) *on the s.*, before felling. 3. A black s. of a tobacco-pipe was in his mouth 1829. Phr. (*To wear*) *to the stumps* (chiefly *fig.*; *rare* or *Obs.*). 5. b. He said..that the Stumps of my Beard were ten times stronger than the Bristles of a Boar SWIFT. 7. *To draw* (*the*) *stumps*, to pull up the stumps, as a sign of the discontinuance of play or of the termination of a match or game. 9. b. The first of our Presidents who has descended to the s. 1866. Phr. *To go on the s.*, *to take the s.*, to go about the country making political speeches, whether as a candidate or as the advocate of a cause.

Comb.: **s. bed, bedstead,** a bedstead without posts; **s.-end,** (*a*) the end of the s. of a tail; (*b*) the remnant of a cheque-book containing the 'stumps'.

Stump (stɒmp), *sb.*² 1778. [prob. – Fr. *estompe* – Du. *stomp* stub, stump, with support from prec.] A kind of pencil consisting of a roll of paper or soft leather, or of a cylindrical piece of india-rubber or other soft material, usu. cut to a blunt point at each end, used for rubbing down hard lines in pencil or crayon drawing, for blending the lines of shading, and for other similar purposes.

Stump (stɒmp), *sb.*³ 1690. [f. STUMP *v.*¹] **1.** A heavy step or gait, as of a lame or wooden-legged person 1770. **b.** Reiterated, with echoic intention. Also quasi-*adv.*, (to go, come) *s.*, *s.* 1690. **2.** *U.S. colloq.* A challenge to do something difficult or dangerous 1871.

Stump (stɒmp), *a.* 1563. [Partly from attrib. use of STUMP *sb.*¹, perh. partly – Du., LG. *stomp*.] **1.** Worn down to a stump 1624. **2.** Said of mutilated or malformed limbs 1563.

2. *S. foot*, a club-foot. *S. leg*, a leg without a foot or with a club foot.

Comb.: **s.-tail,** a stump-tailed dog; also *Austral.* a stump-tailed lizard (*Trachysaurus*).

Stump (stɒmp), *v.*¹ ME. [f. STUMP *sb.*¹] †**1.** *intr.* To stumble over a tree-stump or other obstacle –1607. **2.** To walk clumsily, heavily, or noisily, as if one had a wooden leg 1600. **b.** *slang.* 'To go on foot'; also *s. it* 1841. **3.** *trans.* To reduce to a stump; to truncate, mutilate 1596. **4.** *Colonial.* To stub; to dig up by the roots 1790. **5.** To remove the stumps from (land). Also *absol.* 1796. **6.** *Cricket.* Of the wicket-keeper: To put (a batsman) out by dislodging a bail (or knocking down a stump) with the ball held in the hand, at a moment when the batsman is off his ground. Also with *out*. 1744. **7.** *slang.* To render penniless. Chiefly in *pass.*, to be 'stony broke'. 1828. **8.** *U.S. colloq.* To strike (the toe) unintentionally against a stone or something fixed 1828. **9.** orig. *U.S.* To cause to be at a loss; to nonplus 1807. **10.** *U.S.* To challenge, 'dare' (a person) to do something 1766. **11.** Chiefly *U.S.* **a.** *intr.* To make stump speeches; to conduct electioneering by public speaking 1838. **b.** *trans.* To travel over (a district) making stump speeches; to canvass or address with stump oratory 1856.

6. He caught three batsmen at the wicket and stumped one 1884. 9. That beastly Euclid altogether stumps me 1854. 11. a. Stumping it through England for seven years made Cobden a consummate debater EMERSON.

S. up. a. *trans.* To dig up by the roots. **b.** *slang.* (*a*) To pay down, 'fork out' (money). *rare.* (*b*) *absol.* or *intr.* (*c*) *trans.* To wear out, exhaust (a horse) by excessive strain.

Stump (stɒmp), *v.*² 1807. [f. STUMP *sb.*², after Fr. *estomper*.] *Drawing. trans.* To tone or treat with a 'stump'

Stumpage (stɒ·mpėdʒ). *local U.S.* 1848. [f. STUMP *sb.*¹ + -AGE.] **1.** The price paid for standing timber; also, a tax charged in some states for the privilege of cutting timber on State lands. **2.** Standing timber considered with reference to its quantity or marketable value 1854.

2. We assume a pine s. of 5000 feet to the acre 1894.

Stumper (stɒ·mpəɹ). 1776. [f. STUMP *v.*¹ + -ER¹.] **1.** One employed or skilled in stumping trees 1828. **2.** *Cricket.* A wicket-keeper 1776. **3.** Something that 'stumps' one; a poser 1807. **4.** *U.S.* A stump speaker 1863.

Stumpy (stɒ·mpi), *sb.* 1828. [f. STUMP *sb.*¹ + -Y⁶.] **1.** A spritsail barge 1881. **2.** *slang.* Money 1828.

Stumpy (stɒ·mpi), *a.* 1600. [f. STUMP *sb.*¹ + -Y¹.] **1.** Like a stump; short and thick. Of grass, etc. Full of stumps or short hard stalks. **2.** Worn down to a stump 1794. **3.** *U.S.* Of ground: Full of stumps 1838.

1. Turner was a s., ill-dressed man, with a red face 1862. Hence **Stu·mpi-ly** *adv.*, **-ness.**

Stun (stɒn), *sb.* 1727. [f. STUN *v.*] **1.** The act of stunning; a stunning effect; stunned condition. **2.** A flaw on the surface of a piece of stone 1850.

Stun (stɒn), *v.* ME. [Aphetic – OFr. *estoner* ASTONE.] **1.** *trans.* To deprive of consciousness or of power of motion by a blow, a fall, or the like. **2.** To daze or astound with some strong emotion or impression ME. **3.** To daze or bewilder with noise or din. Also *absol.* 1621. **4. a.** To bruise or loosen the surface of (stone, a mineral), so that it splinters or exfoliates. Also, to scratch or tear (a surface) in sawing. **b.** *intr.* Of stone, etc.: To exfoliate, peel off in splinters or laminæ. 1676.

1. She was as one stunned into unconsciousness; ..she hardly breathed 1853. 2. The multitude,.. are captivated by whatever stuns and dazzles them MACAULAY. I sat stunned with my good fortune 1886. 3. The ear is stunned by the not unmusical roar of the Falls 1910.

Stundist (ʃtu·ndist, stu·ndist). 1878. [– Russ. *shtundist*, f. G. *stunde* hour, said to be used by the German settlers as the name for their religious meetings; see -IST.] A member of a large Evangelical sect (called *shtúnda*) which arose among the peasantry of South Russia about 1860, as a result of contact with German Protestant settlers. Hence **Stu·ndism,** the teaching and practice of the Stundists.

Stung (stɒŋ), *ppl. a.* ME. [See STING *v.*] Wounded or hurt by a sting.

Stunner (stɒ·nəɹ). 1847. [f. STUN *v.* + -ER¹.] **1.** Something that stuns or dazes, that amazes or astounds. **2.** *colloq.* A person or thing of extraordinary excellence or attractiveness 1848.

2. The cook..was really a s. for tarts THACKERAY.

Stunning (stɒ·niŋ), *ppl. a.* 1667. [-ING².] **1.** That stuns or stupefies; dazing, astounding; deafening. **2.** *colloq.* Excellent, first-rate, 'splendid', delightful; extremely attractive or good-looking 1849.

2. Those regular s. slap-up out-and-outers THACKERAY. The most s. girl I ever set my eyes on 1856. Hence **Stu·nningly** *adv.*

Stunsail (stɒ·ns'l). 1762. *Naut.* Contraction, repr. the ordinary pronunciation, of STUDDING-SAIL.

His ears large and outstanding, like a couple of stunsails 1913.

Stunt (stɒnt), *sb.*¹ 1725. [f. STUNT *v.*¹] **1.** A check in growth; also, a state of arrested growth or development 1795. **2.** A creature which has been hindered from full growth or development 1725. **3.** *dial.* A fit of sulkiness or obstinacy; in phr. *to take* (*the*) *s.* 1837.

Stunt (stɒnt), *sb.*² *colloq.* 1878. [orig. U.S. college slang, of unkn. origin.] **a.** An 'event' in an athletic competition or display; a feat undertaken as a defiance in response to a challenge; an act which is striking for the skill, strength, or the like, required to do it; a feat; something performed as an item in an entertainment. **b.** In recent use, An enterprise set on foot with the object of gaining reputation or signal advantage. In soldiers' use often vaguely: An attack or advance, a 'push', 'move'. **c.** In wider use, an enterprise, performance 1913.

Hence **Stunt** *v.*² *intr.* to perform stunts; *spec.* of a motorist, an airman, etc., to perform spectacular and daring feats. **Stu·nter. Stu·ntist.**

Stunt, *a. Obs* exc. *dial.* [OE. *stunt* foolish = MHG. *stunz*, ON. *stuttr* (:– **stuntr*) short :– Gmc. **stuntaz*, perh. f. base of STUMP *sb.*¹] †**1.** Foolish, stupid –ME. **2.** Obstinate, stubborn; rudely or angrily curt or blunt 1581. **3.** Stunted. **a.** Short and thick 1788. **b.** Dwarfed in growth 1819. **4.** Of a turn, bend: Abrupt 1851.

Comb.: **s.-head** *Engineering*, the vertical timbered end of a trench which has been excavated for the purpose of laying a sewer or a water-main.

Stunt (stɒnt), *v.*¹ 1583. [f. prec.] †**1.** *trans.* **a.** To irritate, provoke to anger. †**b.** To bring to an abrupt stand; to nonplus. –1642. **2.** To check the growth or development of (a person, plant, etc.); to decrease (growth or production); hence, to dwarf 1659. †**3.** *intr.* To become arrested in growth –1796.

2. *transf.* When by a cold penury, I blast the abilities of a nation, and s. the growth of it's active energies, the ill I may do is beyond all calculation BURKE. Hence **Stu·nted** *ppl. a.*, **-ly** *adv.*, **-ness.**

‖**Stupa** (stū·pă). 1876. [Skr. *stūpa.*] A Buddhist monument; = TOPE *sb.*⁴

Stupe (stiūp), *sb.*¹ late ME. [In XV *stup(p)e* – L. *stup(p)a* tow – Gr. στύπ(π)η.] A piece of tow, flannel, or the like, wrung out of hot liquor and medicated, for fomenting a wound or ailing part. Hence **Stupe** *v. trans.* to foment with a s. or stupes.

Stupe (stiūp), *sb.*² *colloq.* Now chiefly *dial.* 1762. [Shortened f. STUPID.] A stupid person, a fool.

Stupefacient (stiūpǐfēⁱ·ʃěnt), *a.* and *sb.* 1669. [– L. *stupefaciens, -ent-*, pr. pple. of *stupefacere*; see STUPEFY, -FACIENT.] *Med.* **A.** *adj.* Stupefying, producing stupor. **B.** *sb.* A medicine producing stupor (*rare*) 1855.

Stupefaction (stiūpǐfæ·kʃən). 1543. [– Fr. *stupéfaction* – med.L. *stupefactio*, f. *stupefact-* pa. ppl. stem of L. *stupefacere*; see STUPEFY, -ION.] **1.** The action of stupefying or state of being stupefied. **2.** Overwhelming consternation or astonishment 1597.

1. Tobacco is the delight of Dutchmen, as it diffuses a torpor and pleasing s. BURKE.

Stupefactive (stiū·pǐfæ̆ktiv), *a.* and *sb.* 1527. [– Fr. *stupéfactif, -ive* or med.L. *stupefactivus*, f. as prec.; see -IVE.] = STUPEFACIENT *a.* and *sb.* Now *rare* or *Obs.*

Stupefy (stiū·pǐfəi), *v.* Also **stupify** (now unusual). 1596. [– Fr. *stupéfier* – L. *stupefacere*, f. *stupēre*; see STUPID, -FY.] **1.** *trans.* To make stupid or torpid; to deprive of apprehension, feeling, or sensibility; to benumb, deaden. Also *absol.* 1600. **2.** To stun with amazement, fear, or the like; to astound 1596. **3.** *intr.* To become stupid or torpid; to grow dull or insensible. Now *rare*. 1631.

1. Those [drugs] she ha's, Will stupifie and dull the Sence a-while SHAKS. **2.** He sat, stupified with shame and remorse 1779.

Stupend (stiupe·nd), *a. Obs.* exc. *joc.* 1621. [– L. *stupendus*; see STUPENDOUS.] Stupendous.

The s. Variety of Human Faces 1702.

†**Stupe·ndious,** *a.* 1547. [irreg. f. L. *stupendus*, after adjs. in -IOUS; cf. *tremendious*, vulgar f. *tremendous.*] Stupendous –1800.

Stupendous (stiupe·ndəs), *a.* 1666. [f. L. *stupendus*, gerundive of *stupēre* be struck senseless, be amazed at; see -OUS.] Such as to cause stupor or astonishment; amazing, astounding; marvellous, prodigious; amazingly large or great.

All are but parts of one s. whole POPE. The man who thinks to outwit three women. .must indeed be a s. ass 1863. Hence **Stupe·ndous-ly** *adv.*, **-ness.**

Stupent (stiū·pěnt), *a. rare.* 1843. [– L. *stupens, -ent-*, pr. pple. of *stupēre*; see STUPID, -ENT.] That is in a state of stupor or amazement.

Stupeous (stiū·pǐ,əs), *a.* Also **stuppeous** (stɒ·pǐ,əs). 1826. [f. L. *stuppeus* made of tow, f. *stuppa* STUPE *sb.*¹; see -OUS.] *Zool.* and *Bot.* Having, or covered with, matted or tufted hairs or filaments.

Stupid (stiū·pid), *a.* and *sb.* 1541. [– Fr. *stupide* or L. *stupidus*, f. *stupēre* be stunned or benumbed, f. base **stup-* strike, thrust; see -ID¹.] **A.** *adj.* **1.** Having one's faculties deadened or dulled; in a state of stupor, stupefied, stunned; esp. *hyperbolically*, stunned with surprise, grief, etc. *Obs.* exc. *arch.* (*poet.*) 1611. †**2.** As the characteristic of inanimate things: Destitute of sensation, consciousness, thought, or feeling –1744. **3.** Wanting in or slow of mental perception; lacking ordinary activity of mind; slow-witted, dull 1541. **b.** Of attributes, actions, ideas, etc.: Characterized by or indicating stupidity or dullness of comprehension 1621. †**c.** Of the lower animals: Irrational; senseless, dull –1867. **4.** Void of interest, tiresome, boring, dull 1778.

1. Is he not s. With Age, and altring Rheumes? Can he speake? heare? Know man, from man? SHAKS. **2.** Matter is incapable of acting, passive only, and s. 1722. **4.** No man who knows aught, can be so s. to deny that all men naturally were borne free MILT. **b.** Let us not. .persist in such a s. error 1707. **4.** We were quartered at a s. seaport town 1862. If my letter is very s., forgive me 1884.

B. *sb.* A stupid person. *colloq.* 1712. Hence **Stu·pid-ly** *adv.* **-ness.**

Stupidity (stiupi·diti). 1541. [– Fr. *stupidité* or L. *stupiditas*, f. *stupidus*; see prec., -ITY.] †**1.** Numbness, incapacity for sensation –1737. †**2.** A state of stupor –1831. †**3.** Incapacity for emotion; apathy, indifference –1748. †**b.** Insensibility to pain or sorrow; blameable absence of resentment under injury or insult –1673. **4.** Dullness or slowness of apprehension; gross want of intelligence 1541. **b.** A stupid idea, action, etc. 1633.

4. With S. and sound Digestion man may front much CARLYLE. **b.** The dull stupidities and senseless flippancies of Roman architecture 1851.

Stupor (stiū·pəɹ; as scientific L. ‖stiū·pǫɹ). late ME. [– L. *stupor*, f. *stupēre*; see STUPID, -OR 2.] **1.** A state of insensibility or lethargy; spec. in *Path.*, a disorder characterized by great diminution or entire suspension of sensibility. **b.** = DEMENTIA 1. 1899. **2.** A state of mental stupefaction; apathy or torpor of mind (now only torpor due to sorrow, painful surprise, or the like) 1672. **b.** Admiring wonder. Also (after med.L. *stupor mundi*), the object of wonder, 'the marvel *of*' (the world, etc.). 1482.

1. James sank into a s. which indicated the near approach of death MACAULAY. **2.** With her mouth wide open, staring vacantly at the collector, in a s. of dismay DICKENS. Hence **Stu·porous** *a.* affected with or characterized by s.

Stupose (stiū·pōᵘs), *a.* 1835. [f. *stupa* (Bot.) tuft of long hairs, etc.; see -OSE¹.] *Bot.* = STUPEOUS.

Sturdy (stɒ̄·ɹdi), *a.* and *sb.* ME. [Aphetic – OFr. *esturdi, estourdi*, stunned, dazed, reckless, violent (mod. *étourdi* thoughtless) :– Rom. **exturdire*, f. L. *ex-* EX-¹ + *turdus* thrush (taken as a type of drunkenness).] **A.** *adj.* **I.** Giddy. Said of sheep affected with the 'sturdy': see B. 1. Now *dial.* 1641. **II.** †**1.** Impetuously brave, fierce in combat –1684. †**2.** Recklessly violent, furious, ruthless, cruel –1603. †**b.** Of waves, a stream, a storm, etc.: Violent, rough –1823. †**3.** Of countenance, speech, demeanour: Stern, Harsh, rough, surly –1611. †**4.** Hard to manage, intractable, refractory; rebellious, disobedient –1781. †**b.** Obstinate –1781. **c.** Epithet of beggars or vagabonds who are able-bodied and apt to be violent. late ME. **5.** Of material things: Refractory, defiant of destructive agencies or force; strong, stout. late ME. **b.** Of a plant: Hardy 1695. **6.** Of persons or animals; Solidly built; stalwart, strong, robust, hardy. late ME. **b.** Of movements, etc.: Displaying physical vigour 1697. **7.** *transf.* Of persons, their actions and attributes: Robust in mind or character; 'downright', uncompromising 1775. **b.** Of expressions: Vigorous, lusty 1822.

4. The most s. and refractory Non-conformists FULLER. **b.** Your blund'rer is as s. as a rock COWPER. **c.** Like s. Beggars, that intreat for Charity at once, and threat 1680. **5.** On the vext Wilderness, whose. .sturdiest Oaks Bow'd thir Stiff necks MILT. **b.** Lichen and moss and s. weed C. ROSSETTI. **6.** A rugged land. .well fitted to produce a s. race JOWETT. **b.** With s. steps he walks PRIOR. **7.** I respect that fine old s. fellow Hobbes HAZLITT. **b.** Here crash'd a s. oath of stout John Bull BYRON.

B. *sb.* **1.** A brain-disease in sheep and cattle, which makes them run round and round; the turnsick 1570. **2.** A name for darnel or some similar stupefying weed 1683. **3.** A sturdy person 1704.

Sturgeon (stɒ̄·ɹdʒən). ME. [– AFr. *sturgeon*, (O)Fr. *esturgeon* :– Rom. **sturione* (med.L. *sturio*) – Gmc. **sturjon*, whence OE. *styrġa*, MLG., MDu. *störe* (Du. *steur*), OHG. *sturjo* (G. *stör*), ON. *styrja.*] A large fish of the family *Acipenseridæ*, having an elongated, almost cylindrical, body protected by longitudinal rows of bony scutes and a long tapering snout, found widely distributed in the rivers and coastal waters of the north temperate zone; esp. a fish belonging to either of the genera *Acipenser* and *Scaphirhynchops*, *A. sturio* being the common s. of the Atlantic. It is a 'royal' fish (see FISH *sb.*¹), esteemed as an article of food, and the source of caviar and isinglass. **b.** With qualifying word, as **black, lake, Ohio, red, rock, stone s.,** *Acipenser rubicundus*, the s. of the great lakes of N. America; **great white, isinglass, Russian s.,** *A. huso*, the BELUGA or HUSO; **small** or **Ruthenian s.,** the STERLET.

Sturionian (stiūᵊriōᵘ·niăn). 1835. [f. mod. L. *Sturiones* (pl. of med.L. *sturio*; see prec.) + -IAN.] A fish belonging to the *Sturiones*, a former order of fishes including the sturgeons (*Acipenseridæ*) and related families.

‖**Sturm und Drang** [G.]: see STORM *sb.* 3.

Sturnoid (stɒ̄·ɹnoid), *a.* 1874. [f. L. *sturnus* starling + -OID.] *Ornith.* Resembling the *Sturnidæ* or Starlings in form or characteristics.

Sturt (stɒ̄ɹt). 1849. [perh. identical with *sturt* (XVII) sudden impulse, perh. var. of START *sb.*²] *Tin-mining.* A great profit made by a 'tributer' in tribute mining.

Stut (stɒt), *v. Obs.* exc. *dial.* [Late ME. *stutte*, the stem of which is repr. also in ME. *stotaye* falter, totter, Gmc. **stut-*, **staut-*, as in MLG. *stöten*, OHG. *stōzan* (G. *stossen*) strike against.] *intr.* To stutter.

Stu·tter, *sb.*¹ *Obs.* exc. *dial.* 1529. [f. prec. + -ER¹.] = STUTTERER.

Stutter (stɒ·təɹ), *sb.*² 1854. [f. next.] An act or a habit of stuttering.

Stutter (stɒ·təɹ), *v.* 1570. [frequent. f. STUT *v.* (+ -ER⁵); cf. (M)LG. *stötern*, Du. *stotteren*, G. *stottern.*] **1.** *intr.* To speak with continued involuntary repetition of sounds or syllables owing to excitement, fear, or constitutional nervous defect; to stammer. **2.** *trans.* To say or speak with a stutter 1645.

1. And though you hear him stut-tut-tut-ter, He barks as fast as he can utter SWIFT. Hence **Stu·tterer. Stu·tteringly** *adv.*

Sty (stəi), *sb.*¹ *Pl.* **sties** (stəiz). [repr. OE. *stī* (as in *stīfearh* 'sty-pig'), perh. identical with *stiġ* hall (cf. *stiġweard* STEWARD, corresp. to ON. **stí* (only in *svínstí* swine-sty) :– Gmc. **stijam*, of which a parallel formation **stijōn* is repr. by MLG. *stege*, MDu. *swijnstije*, ON. *stía* pen, fold.] **1.** An enclosed place where swine are kept, usu. a low shed with an uncovered forecourt, a pigsty. **2.** *transf.* and *fig.* **a.** A human habitation (or sleeping-place) no better than a pigsty 1598. **b.** An abode of bestial lust, or of moral pollution generally. late ME.

2. b. The painted booths and sordid sties of vice and luxury BURKE.

Sty (stəi), *sb.*² 1617. [Deduced from STYANY, apprehended as *sty-on-eye.*] An inflammatory swelling on the eyelid.

†**Sty,** *v.*¹ [OE. *stīġan*, corresp. to OFris. *stīga*, OS., OHG. *stīgan* (Du. *stijgen*, G. *steigen*), ON. *stíga*, Goth. *steigan* :– Gmc. str. vb. **stīʒan*, f. **stīʒ-* **staiʒ-* :– IE. **steigh-* **stoigh-* **stĭgh-* advance, go, rise, repr. by Gr. στείχειν, στίχος STICH, στοῖχος row.]

1. *intr.* To ascend, rise or climb to a higher level –1652. **2.** With *down* adv., etc.: To descend. Also *gen.* To ascend or descend. –ME.

1. From this lower tract he dar'd to stie Up to the clowdes SPENSER.

Sty (stəi), *v.*[2] [OE. *stiġian*, f. *stiġ* STY *sb.*[1] Cf. OHG. *stīgōn*, ON. *stía.*] **1.** *trans.* To place or confine (swine) in a sty. **b.** *transf.* To confine as in a sty; to pen *up* 1610. **2.** *intr.* To share a sty *with*; to dwell as in a sty 1748.

1. b. And here you s. me In this hard Rocke SHAKS.

Styan (stəi·ăn). Now *dial.* [OE. *stīġend*, lit. 'riser', pr. pple. used subst. of *stīġan* STY *v.*[1]] = STY *sb.*[2]

Styany (stəi·əni). Now *dial.* 1440. [f. prec. + EYE *sb.*] = STY *sb.*[2]

Styca (stəi·kă). 1705. [Assumed sing. from ONorth. *stycas*, dial. pl. of OE. *styćće* piece (of money).] *Numism.* A small copper coin current in Northumbria in the seventh, eighth, and ninth centuries.

Stygian (sti·dʒiăn), *a.* 1566. [f. L. *Stygius* – Gr. Στύγιος, f. Στύξ; see STYX, -IAN.] **1.** Pertaining to the river Styx or to the infernal regions of classical mythology. **b.** Of an oath: Supremely binding, like the oath by the Styx, which the gods themselves feared to break 1608. **2.** Infernal, hellish 1601. **3.** Black as the river Styx; dark or gloomy as the region of the Styx 1599.

1. *S. Jove, Jupiter*, Pluto, the god of the lower world; Thus will I pay my Vows, to S. Jove DRYDEN. **3.** Will I not turne a glorious bridall morne Unto a S. night? MARSTON.

Phr. †*S. water, liquor* [tr. mod. L. *aqua Stygia*], in Old Chemistry, a name for nitrohydrochloric acid and other strong mineral acids.

Stylar (stəi·lăɹ). 1614. [f. STYLE *sb.* + -AR[1].] †**1.** Pertaining to the 'style' or gnomon of a dial –1668. **2.** 'Having the character of or pertaining to a style for writing' 1891.

‖**Stylaster** (stəilæ·stəɹ). 1831. [mod.L. (Gray 1831), f. Gr. στῦλος column + ἀστήρ star.] *Zool.* A genus of hydrozoa, closely related to the *Millepora*; a species or an animal of this genus, or of the family *Stylasteridæ*, of which it is the type.

Stylate (stəi·lĕt), *a.* 1866. [f. STYLE *sb.* I. 7, 9 + -ATE[2].] **a.** *Bot.* Having a persistent style. **b.** *Zool.* Having a style or stylet. Also, having the form of a pen or pin, styliform, styloid.

Style (stəil), *sb.* ME. [– (O)Fr. *style*, †*stile* – L. *stilus*. The sp. with *y* is due to assoc. with Gr. στῦλος column.] **I.** Stylus, pin, stalk. **1.** *Antiq.* An instrument made of metal, bone, etc. having one end sharp-pointed for incising letters on a wax tablet, and the other flat and broad for smoothing the tablet and erasing what is written. Also applied to similar instruments in later use. **b.** Used as a weapon of offence, for stabbing etc. 1669. **c.** *fig.* or as a symbol of literary composition 1579. **2.** An engraving-tool; a graver 1662. **3.** *Surg.* A blunt-pointed probe 1631. **4.** A hard point for tracing, in manifold writing; the marking point in a telegraph or phonograph 1871. **5.** *gen.* A fixed pointer, pin, or finger for indicating a point or position 1555. **6.** The pin, rod, or triangular plate which forms the gnomon of a sun-dial 1577. **7.** *Bot.* A narrowed prolongation of the ovary, which, when present, supports the stigma at its apex 1682. **8.** *Ent.* **a.** A slender bristle-like process in the anal region. **b.** The bristle or seta of the antenna of a dipter. 1826. **9.** *Zool.* A small slender pointed process or part; a stylet 1851. **b.** A sponge-spicule pointed at one end 1879.

1. Phr. †*To turn one's s.*, to change *to* another subject; also, to speak on the other side. [So *stilum vertere* in late L.]

II. Writing; manner of writing (hence also of speaking). †**1.** A written work or works; literary composition –1595. †**b.** An entry, clause, or section in a legal document –1649. **2.** The manner of expression characteristic of a particular writer (hence of an orator), or of a literary group or period; a writer's mode of expression considered in regard to clearness, effectiveness, beauty, and the like ME. **3.** *gen.* Those features of literary composition which belong to form and expression rather than to the substance of the thought or matter expressed. Often used for: Good or fine style. 1577. **4.** A manner of discourse, or tone of speaking, adopted in addressing others or in ordinary conversation 1567. †**5.** A form of words, phrase, or formula, by which a particular idea or thought is expressed –1736. **6.** *Scots Law.* The authorized form for drawing up a deed or instrument 1480. **b.** *gen.* Legal technicality of language or construction 1743. **7.** A legal, official, or honorific title; the proper name or recognized appellation of a person, family, trading firm, etc.; the ceremonial designation of a sovereign ME. **b.** *gen.* Any distinguishing or qualifying title, appellation or denomination. Now *rare* or *Obs.* late ME.

2. Proper words in proper places, make the true definition of a s. SWIFT. The incomparable s. of Mr. Ruskin SWINBURNE. **3.** S. is the dress of thoughts CHESTERF. **4.** He talked in his usual s. with a rough contempt of popular liberty BOSWELL. **7.** The Kings Stile, is now no more of England, but of Britaine BACON. I have always been shy of assuming the honourable s. of Professor M. ARNOLD. **b.** The S. of *Maritime Powers*, by which our Allies, in a sort of contemptuous manner, usually couple us with the Dutch SWIFT.

III. Manner, fashion. †**1.** A method or custom of performing actions or functions, esp. one sanctioned by usage or law –1773. **2.** A particular mode or form of skilled construction, execution, or production; the manner in which a work of art is executed; one of the modes recognized in a particular art as suitable for the production of beautiful or skilful work 1706. **b.** *gen.* Often used for: Beauty or loftiness of style 1801. **c.** A definite type of architecture, distinguished by special characteristics of structure or ornamentation 1777. **d.** *Printing.* The rules and methods, in regard to typography, display, etc., observed in a particular printing-office 1871. **3.** A kind, sort, or type, as determined by manner of composition or construction, or by outward appearance 1794. **b.** *transf.* Said predicatively of a person or thing: What suits (a person's) taste; the 'sort' that (a person or set of persons) would choose or approve 1811. **4.** Manner of executing a task or performing an action or operation. Often with ref. to athletics, racing, games: The manner of action of a particular performer, racehorse, etc. 1774. **b.** Used *absol.* for: Good or fine style 1864. **5.** A mode of deportment or behaviour; a mode or fashion of life, esp. in regard to expense, display, etc. 1770. **b.** Used *absol.* for: Fashionable air, appearance, deportment, etc. 1807. **6.** A particular mode or fashion of costume 1814. **7.** A person's characteristic bearing, demeanour, or manner, esp. as conducing to beauty or striking appearance 1826.

1. The S. of Court is properly the Practice observ'd by any Court in its way of Proceeding 1726. I like to give them a hearty reception in the old s. at my gate GOLDSM. **2.** At Lausanne we only stopped for dinner (which we obtained in sufficiently bad s. at the *Lion d'Or*) 1832. **c.** A very handsome church..in the Gothic stile 1777. **3.** There was something in her s. of beauty to please them [*i.e.* men] particularly JANE AUSTEN. **b.** She is not the s. of the day at all, you know 1880. **4.** A barge was coming up in fine s. 1833. The s. in which he [*sc.* a horse] ran, his nose almost sweeping the ground 1833. **5.** The society is noisy and in bad s. 1792. That gentleman..lived in what is called great s. SCOTT. **b.** A plain German city, with little or no pretensions to s. 1835. Phr. *In s.*, splendidly, showily, according to fashionable requirements. **6.** His daughters look very well in their better s. of dress 1833. **7.** Most amusing, delightful girl, great s.! DISRAELI.

IV. A mode of expressing dates. *Chiefly*, Either of the two methods of dating that have been current in the Christian world since the introduction of the Gregorian calendar in 1582: viz., the *New Style* (abbrev. N.S.), which is the result of the Gregorian reform, and the *Old Style* (O.S.) which follows the unreformed calendar. The New Style is occas. called the *Roman Style*, and the Old Style the *English Style*. In historical dates earlier than 1582, however, *Roman Style*, as used by modern writers, means only that the year mentioned is to be understood as beginning on 1 January. 1590.

The Julian calendar assumed that the tropical year consisted of 365¼ days. To give the average calendar year this length, it was provided that the normal year should contain 365 days, but every fourth year 366 days. In England the beginning of the legal year was 25 March.

The Julian estimate of 365¼ days for the length of the year was too great by about 11 minutes, an error which amounts to one day in about 128 years. Hence in 1581 the date of 21 March for the vernal equinox, assumed since the early 4th c. in the rule for computing Easter, was 10 days too late. To remedy this, Pope Gregory XIII ordained that in A.D. 1582 the day after 4 Oct. should be reckoned as 15 Oct., and that in future the years which had a number ending in two cyphers should not be leap years unless the number were divisible by 400. The Julian date for the beginning of the year, viz., 1 Jan., was retained.

In England and Scotland the Gregorian calendar was established by the Act 24 Geo. II. c. 23 (1751), which provided that the year 1752 and all future years should begin on 1 Jan. instead of 25 Mar., that the day after 2 Sept. 1752 should be reckoned the 14 Sep., and that the reformed rule for leap year should in future be followed.

Style (stəil), *v.* 1563. [f. prec.] **1.** *trans.* To give a name or style; to call by a name or style. †**2.** To relate or express in literary form –1605. **3.** To execute (a design) with a stylus on a prepared ground 1864.

Stylet (stəi·lĕt). 1697. [– Fr. *stilet* – It. *stiletto* STILETTO.] **1.** *Surg.* A slender probe. Also, a wire run through a catheter or canula in order to stiffen it or to clear it. **2.** †**a.** *Bot.* = STYLE *sb.* I. 7. –1723. **b.** *Zool.* = STYLE *sb.* I. 8, 9. 1834. **3.** A kind of pencil for the use of the blind 1819. **b.** A pointed marking instrument; a graving tool 1853. **4.** A stiletto, dagger 1820.

3. b. The strong hieroglyphics graven as with iron s. on his brow C. BRONTË.

‖**Stylidium** (stəili·diŏm). 1829. [mod.L. (Swartz 1807), f. Gr. στῦλος column + -ίδιον dim. suffix (here used loosely).] *Bot.* A genus of gamopetalous plants, native in Australia, India, and Ceylon, remarkable for the irritability of the column formed by the union of the stamens and style.

Styliferous (stəili·fĕrŏs), *a.* 1826. [f. STYLE *sb.* I. 7, 9 + -FEROUS.] *Bot.* and *Zool.* Bearing a style or styles.

Styliform (stəi·lifǭɹm), *a.* 1578. [f. as prec. + -FORM.] *Anat., Zool., Min.* Shaped like a stylus.

Stylish (stəi·liʃ), *a.* 1797. [f. STYLE *sb.* + -ISH[1].] **1.** Of persons, their appearance or manners, also of dress, equipage, etc.: Noticeable for 'style' or conformity to the fashionable standard of elegance; showily fashionable. **2.** In occas. uses: Having 'style' (in various senses: see STYLE *sb.*) 1892.

2. A most patient and s. innings of 65. 1895. Hence **Sty·lish-ly** *adv.*, **-ness.**

Stylist (stəi·list). 1795. [f. STYLE *sb.* + -IST, after G. *stilist.*] A writer who is skilled in or cultivates the art of literary style; a writer as characterized by his style.

[Addison] while notably distinguished, as a s., for ease,..combines with it the extreme of inexactness 1873.

Stylistic (stəili·stik), *a.* and *sb.* 1860. [f. STYLE *sb.* + -IST + -IC, after G. *stilistisch* adj., *stilistik* sb.] **A.** *adj.* Pertaining to literary style. **B.** *sb.* The science of literary style; the study of stylistic features. Also (more commonly) **Styli·stics.** 1882.

Stylite (stei·ləit). Also in Gr. form **stylites** (stəiləi·tīz). 1638. [– eccl. Gr. στυλίτης, f. στῦλος pillar; see -ITE[1] 1.] *Eccl. Hist.* An ascetic who lived on the top of a pillar. Also *attrib.* or as *adj.*

Peter à Metra, a famous S., or Pillar-Monk 1638. Hence **Styli·tic** *a.* **Sty·litism,** the mode of life or the ascetic principles of the Stylites.

Stylize (stəi·ləiz), *v.* 1898. [f. STYLE *sb.* + -IZE, after G. *stilisiren.*] *trans.* To conform (an artistic representation) to the rules of a conventional style; to conventionalize. Chiefly in pa. pple.

Stylo (stəi·lo). 1890. Short for STYLOGRAPH or STYLOGRAPHIC (*pen*).

Stylo- (stəi·lo), bef. a vowel **styl-**, used as comb. form of Gr. στῦλος pillar in scientific words.

Styloglo·ssal [Gr. γλῶσσα tongue], *a.* pertaining to the styloid process and the tongue; *sb.* = *styloglossus*. ‖**Styloglo·ssus**, a muscle arising from the styloid process and inserted in the tongue. **Stylohy·al**, *a.* epithet of one of the bones of the hyoid arch, constituting in man the styloid process of the temporal bone; *sb.* this bone. **Stylohy·oid,** *a.* of or pertaining to the stylohyal and the hyoid bone; *sb.* the stylohyoid muscle, a muscle connecting the styloid process and the hyoid bone. ‖**Stylomandi·bular, Stylomaxi·llary,** *adjs.* used to designate a ligament which connects the styloid process and the lower jawbone. **Styloma·stoid,** *a.* common to the styloid and mastoid processes of the temporal bone. **Stylommato·phorous** [Gr. ὄμμα, ὀμματ- eye, -φόρος bearing], *a.* belonging to the suborder *Stylommatophora* of pulmonate gasteropods (land-snails and slugs) which have eyes borne on the tips of a pair of retractile tentacles. ‖**Stylopo·dium,** *Bot.* the double fleshy disc from which the style of the *Umbelliferæ* arises. **Sty·lospore,** *Bot.* one of the naked spores in certain fungals, which are produced at the tips of short thread-like cells. ‖**Styloste·gium** [Gr. στέγη roof], **Stylote·gium** [Gr. τέγος roof], the inner corona enveloping the style in some asclepiads.

Stylobata (stəilǫ·bătă). 1563. [– L. *stylobata* – Gr. στυλοβάτης, f. στῦλος pillar + -βατης, f. base of βαίνειν walk.] *Arch.* = next.

Stylobate (stəi·lŏbēit). 1694. [– L. *stylobata*; see prec.] *Arch.* A continuous basement upon which a row of columns is supported.

Stylograph (stəi·lŏgrɑf). 1866. [f. STYLUS + -GRAPH.] †**1.** Any drawing or writing made with a style. **2.** A stylographic pen. Also *s. pen.* 1882.

Stylographic (stəilogræ·fik), *a.* 1808. [f. as prec. + -GRAPHIC.] †**1.** Relating to stylography or writing with a style –1854. **2.** *S. pen*: a variety of fountain pen, having no nib, but a fine perforated writing-point fed with ink from the reservoir in the stem; in this point is fitted a fine needle, which when pushed back in the act of writing opens a valve so as to permit the flow of ink 1880.

Stylography (stəilǫ·grăfi). Now *rare* or *Obs.* 1840. [f. as prec. + -GRAPHY.] A method of writing, drawing, or engraving with a style.

Styloid (stəi·loid), *a.* 1709. [– mod.L. *styloides* – Gr. στυλοειδής (Galen) like a style, f. στῦλος pillar; see -OID.] *Anat.* and *Zool.* Resembling a style in shape; styliform. Applied chiefly to several slender-pointed processes of bone, e.g. the spine that projects from the base of the temporal bone.

Stylolite (stəi·lŏləit). 1866. [f. Gr. στῦλος pillar + -LITE.] *Geol.* A cylindrical or columnar formation in some limestones, marls, etc. 'varying in length up to more than four inches and in diameter to two or more inches'. Hence **Styloli·tic** *a.*

‖**Stylus** (stəi·lŏs). Also **stilus.** 1728. [erron. sp. of L. *stilus*; see STYLE *sb.*] **1.** = STYLE *sb.* I. 1. 1807. **2.** The tracing-point applied to the record of a phonograph or gramophone 1875. **3.** The gnomon of a sundial 1796. **4.** *Bot.* = STYLE *sb.* I. 7. 1728. **5.** *Zool.* A style or stylet 1856.

Stymie (stəi·mi), *sb.* 1857. [Of unkn. origin.] *Golf.* An opponent's ball which lies on the putting green in a line between the ball of the player and the hole he is playing for, if the distance between the balls is not less than six inches; also, the occurrence of this; often in phr. *to lay a s.* Hence **Sty·mie** *v. trans.* to put (one's opponent or oneself) into the position of having to negotiate a s.; freq. *fig.*; also *intr.* (of a ball) to intervene as a s.

Stymphalian (stimfē·liăn), *a.* 1653. [f. L. *Stymphalius* (f. *Stymphalus* or *-um* – Gr. Στύμφαλος) + -AN.] *Myth.* Of or belonging to Stymphalus, a district in Arcadia, haunted by a species of odious birds of prey, the destruction of which was the sixth of the 'labours' of Hercules. So **Sty·mphalid** *a.* and *sb.* 1560.

Styphnate (sti·fnĕt). 1857. [f. STYPHNIC + -ATE[4].] *Chem.* A salt of styphnic acid.

Styphnic (sti·fnik), *a.* 1850. [f. supposed Gr. *στυφνός (a mistake for στρυφνός) astringent + -IC.] *Chem. S. acid*, a dibasic astringent acid obtained by the action of nitric acid on asafœtida and other gum resins. Also called *oxypicric acid.*

‖**Stypsis** (sti·psis). 1890. [Late L. – Gr. στῦψις, f. στύφειν; cf. next.] *Med.* The application or use of styptics.

Styptic (sti·ptik), *a.* and *sb.* late ME. [– L. *stypticus* – Gr. στυπτικός, f. στύφειν contract; see -IC.] **A.** *adj.* Having the power of contracting organic tissue; having an austere or acid taste; harsh or raw to the palate; having a binding effect on the stomach or bowels. **b.** Of a medicament, etc.: That arrests hæmorrhage. late ME. **B.** *sb.* A substance having the power of contracting organic tissue. late ME. So **Sty·ptical** *a.* 1528.

Stypticin (sti·ptisin). 1910. [f. STYPTIC + -IN[1].] The phthalate of cotarnine used as a hæmostatic and an analgesic. So **Styptol** (sti·ptǫl), the hydrochloride of cotarnine, similarly used 1908.

Stypticity (stipti·sĭti). late ME. [– med.L. *stypticitas*, f. L. *stypticus*; see -ITY. Cf. (O)Fr. *stipticité.*] Styptic quality; astringency.

Styracin (stəiᵊ·răsin). 1838. [– Fr. *styracine*, f. L. *styrax, -ac-*; see next, -IN[1].] *Chem.* A crystalline substance obtained from storax and balsam of Peru.

Styrax (stəiᵊ·ræks). 1558. [– L. *styrax* – Gr. στύραξ; cf. STORAX.] **1.** = STORAX 1. **2.** A styrax-tree 1832.

Comb.: **s.-tree**, a tree of the genus *Styrax*, esp. *S. officinalis.*

Styrian (sti·riăn), *a.* and *sb.* 1621. [f. *Styria* + -AN.] Of or belonging to, an inhabitant of, the province of Styria, formerly a crown-land and duchy of the Austrian empire.

Styrol (stəiᵊ·rǫl). 1845. [f. STYRAX + -OL.] *Chem.* An oil obtained from storax and the resin of balsam of Peru; oil of storax.

Styrolene (stəiᵊ·rŏlīn). 1881. [f. prec. + -ENE.] *Chem.* = prec.

Styrone (stəiᵊ·roᵘn). 1852. [f. STYRAX + -ONE.] *Chem.* An alcohol in crystalline form obtained from the decomposition of styracin; used as an antiseptic and a bleaching agent.

Styryl (stəiᵊ·ril). 1852. [f. STYRAX + -YL.] *Chem.* The radical, C_9H_9, of styrone. Also *attrib.*, as in *s. alcohol* = STYRONE.

Stythe, styth (stəið, stəiþ). *dial.* 1708. [alt. from *ʒtive, cogn. w. STIVE *v.*[2]] **1.** = CHOKE-DAMP. **2.** A suffocating smell 1823.

‖**Styx** (stiks). late ME. [L. – Gr. Στύξ (Στυγ-), rel. to στυγεῖν hate, στυγνός hateful, gloomy.] *Myth.* A river of the lower world or Hades, over which the shades of the departed were ferried by Charon, and by which the gods swore their most solemn oaths.

Suable (siū·ăb'l), *a.* Now chiefly *U.S.* 1623. [f. SUE *v.* + -ABLE.] Capable of being sued, liable to be sued; legally subject to civil process. Hence **Suabi·lity,** liability to be sued.

Suade (swēᵗd), *v.* Now *rare* or *dial.* 1531. [Partly – L. *suadēre*; partly by aphæresis from PERSUADE.] = PERSUADE *v.*

Suant (siū·ănt), *a.* Now *dial.* 1547. [– AFr. *sua(u)nt*, OFr. *suiant, sivant*, pr. pple. of *sivre* (mod. *suivre*) follow :– Rom. **sequere* for L. *sequi*; see -ANT.] Working or proceeding regularly, smoothly, or easily; even, smooth, regular. Also *advb.* Hence **Su·antly** *adv.* (now *dial.*) 1547.

Suasible (swē·sib'l), *a. rare.* 1582. [– late and med.L. *suasibilis*, f. L. *suas-*; see next, -IBLE.] Capable of being persuaded; that is easily persuaded.

Suasion (swē·ʒən). late ME. [– OFr. *suasion* or L. *suasio, -ōn-*, f. *suas-*, pa. ppl. stem of *suadēre* urge, PERSUADE; see -ION.] **1.** The act or fact of exhorting or urging; persuasion. **2.** An instance of this. late ME.

1. *Moral s.*, persuasion exerted or acting through and upon the moral nature or sense.

Suasive (swē·siv), *a.* and *sb.* 1601. [var. of SUASORY by suffix-substitution.] **A.** *adj.* Having or exercising the power of persuading or urging; consisting in or tending to suasion; occas. const. *of*, exhorting or urging to. **B.** *sb.* A suasive speech, motive, or influence 1670.

A. Thanks to the s. influence of British gold 1897. Hence **Sua·sive-ly** *adv.*, **-ness.**

Suasory (swē·səri), *a.* Now *rare.* 1576. [– L. *suasorius*, f. *suas-*; see SUASION, -ORY[2]. Cf. Fr. †*suasoire.*] Tending to persuade; persuasive.

Suave (swēᵗv, swāv), *a.* 1560. [– (O)Fr. *suave* or L. *suavis* sweet, agreeable (see SWEET *a.*).] **1.** Pleasing or agreeable to the senses or the mind; sweet. **2.** Of persons, their manner: Blandly polite or urbane; soothingly agreeable 1847. Hence **Sua·vely** *adv.*

Suaviloquence (sweᵗvi·lŏkwĕns). *rare.* 1649. [– L. *suaviloquentia*, f. *suaviloquens*, f. *suavis* sweet + *-loquens* speaking, f. *loqui* speak; see -ENCE.] Pleasing or agreeable speech or manner of speaking.

Suavity (swæ·vĭti, swē·vĭti). 1450. [– L. *suavitas* (partly through Fr. *suavité*), f. *suavis* SUAVE; see -ITY.] †**1.** Sweetness or agreeableness to the senses –1661. †**b.** Sweetness (of sound, harmony, expression) –1821. **2.** Pleasurableness, agreeableness; *pl.* delights, amenities. Now only as coloured by sense 3. 1594. **3.** The quality or condition of being suave in manner or outward behaviour; bland agreeableness or urbanity 1815.

2. The common suavities of social life 1823. **3.** These words, delivered with a cutting s. DICKENS.

Sub (sɒb), *sb.* 1696. [Short for various subst. compounds of SUB-.] **1.** = SUBORDINATE. **b.** For various titles of subordinate officials, as *sub-editor, sub-lieutenant, sub-warden* 1837. **2.** = SUBALTERN *sb.* 2. 1756. **3.** = SUBSTITUTE; *U.S.* esp. of substitute printers 1830. **4.** = SUBSCRIPTION 1903. **5.** = SUBSIST *(money)*: money in advance on account of wages due at the end of a certain period. *local.* 1866.

Sub (sɒb), *v.* 1879. [Short for various vbl. compounds of SUB-; or f. prec.] **1.** *intr.* To work as a printer's substitute. **2.** To pay or receive 'sub' 1886. **3.** = 'SUB-EDIT 1890.

‖**Sub** (sɒb). 1592. The L. prep. *sub* (with the ablative) 'under', in a few legal and other phrases, now or formerly in common use.

sub dio, under the open sky, in the open air. **sub forma pauperis** = *in forma pauperis* (see ‖IN). **sub hasta,** lit. 'under a spear', i.e. by auction. **sub Jove frigido,** under the chilly sky, in the open air. **sub judice,** lit. 'under a judge'; under the consideration of a judge or court; undecided, still under consideration. **sub lite,** in dispute. **sub modo,** under certain conditions, with a qualification, within limits. **sub rosa,** 'under the rose' (see ROSE *sb.* II), in secret, secretly. **sub sigillo,** under the seal (of confession); in confidence, in secret. **sub silentio,** in silence, without remark being made. **sub voce,** under the word (so-and-so); abbrev. s.v.

Sub- (sɒb, səb) *prefix*, repr. L. *sub-* = the prep. *sub* under, close to, up to, towards, used in composition with various meanings.

The *b* of L. *sub-* remained unchanged when it preceded a radical beginning with *s, t*, or *v*; before *m* and *r* it was frequently assimilated (see e.g. SUMMON, SURROGATE), and before *c, f, g*, and *p* it was almost invariably assimilated (see e.g. SUCCEED, SUFFER, SUGGEST, SUPPOSE). A by-form *subs-* was normally reduced to *sus-* in certain compounds with words having initial *c, p, t* (see SUSCEPTION, SUSPEND, SUSTAIN); and before *sp-* the prefix becomes *su-* (see SUSPECT, SUSPICION).

The original force of the prefix is either entirely lost sight of or to a great extent obscured in many words derived from old L. compounds, such as *subject, suborn, subscription, subserve, subsist, substance.* As a living prefix in English it bears a full meaning of its own and has become capable of being prefixed to words of native English or any other origin.

Under, underneath, below, at the bottom (of). **1.** Forming adjs. in which *sub-* is in prepositional relation to the sb. implied in the second element, as in L. *subaquaneus* = that is *sub aqua* under water, *subterraneus* = that is *sub terra*, SUBTERRANEOUS.

a. Compounds of a general character (mainly nonce-words), and miscellaneous scientific terms. **Subae·rial,** taking place, existing, operating, or formed in the open air or on the earth's surface. **Suba·stral,** situated beneath the stars, mundane, terrestrial. **Su:bcarboni·ferous,** *Geol.* designating the mountain-limestone formation of the carboniferous series or that lying beneath the millstone grit, lower carboniferous. **Subgla·cial,** existing or taking place under the ice. **Submu·ndane,** existing beneath the world. **Subpe·ctoral,** emanating from the depths of the chest. **Subse·nsible,** below or deeper than the range of the senses; so **Subse·nsual, Subse·nsuous. Subso·lar,** *Meteorol.* directly underneath the sun, having the sun in the zenith. **Subtarta·rean,** below or living under Tartarus. **Su·bterrane** (now *rare*), †**Subterra·neal,** = SUBTERRANEAN; also as *sb.*

b. *Anat.* (*Path., Surg.*) and *Zool.* = Situated or

occurring under or beneath (occas. behind) the part or organ denoted by the radical element, or lying on the ventral side of it or ventrally with respect to it; as in (late) L. *subocularis*.

In most of these compounds the meaning is readily inferred from that of the prefix and of the second element; as *subabdo·minal* (= situated or occurring under, below, or beneath the abdomen), *-ara·chnoid* (the arachnoid membrane) *-clavi·cular, conjuncti·val* (the conjunctiva), *-cra·nial, -cuti·cular, -du·ral* (the dura mater), *-epide·rmal, -ic, -epithe·lial, -glo·ttic* (the glottis), *-intesti·nal, -lo·bular* (a lobule of the liver), *-me·ntal* (the chin), *-mu·scular, -notocho·rdal, -o·cular, -pe·ctoral, -peritone·al, -pi·al* (the pia mater), *-pleu·ral, -pu·bic, -spi·nal, -spi·nous, -tenta·cular* (the tentacles or tentacular canal), *-u·ngual, -vagi·nal, -ve·rtebral, -zo·nal* (the zona pellucida of an ovum). (*b*) in derived advs.; e.g. *subdu·rally, su:bperio·steally*.

c. *Bot.* in the same sense as b; e.g. *subpe·tiolar*.

d. *Anat.* In adj. compounds in L. form, designating parts of the body, used absol. by ellipsis of sb. (e.g. *musculus* muscle, *membrana* membrane). ||**Su:bancone·us,** a small muscle arising from the triceps and humerus above the elbow-joint and inserted in the posterior ligament of the elbow. ||**Subcrure·us,** a small band of muscular fibres extending from the anterior surface of the femur to the synovial membrane of the knee-joint.

e. With sbs. forming attrib. compounds. **Subatla·ntic,** under the Atlantic. **Sub-tu·rbary,** found under turf-ground.

f. With sbs. forming sbs. designating a part, organ, or substance lying under the part denoted by the radical element. **Subli·ngua,** in some animals, a process consisting of a fold of mucous membrane under the tongue. **Subme·ntum,** *Ent.* the basal part of the labium. **Subumbre·lla,** *Zool.* the internal ventral or oral disc of a hydrozoan; the concave muscular layer beneath the umbrella of a jelly-fish.

g. Forming vbs., as in L. *subjugare* to SUBJUGATE.

2. With adverbial force (= underneath, below, down, low, lower), prefixed to adjs., vbs., and pples. (and less freq. to sbs.), as in *subadja·cent* adj.; *subaera·ted, -concea·led* pples.; *subi·rrigate* vb. **Su:blinea·tion,** underlining. **Subna·scent** *a.* growing under or up from beneath. **Subnota·tion** = RESCRIPT 2.

b. Hence = in or into subjection, as in *subicere* to SUBJECT.

3. Prefixed to sbs. with adjectival force = lying, existing, occurring below or underneath, under-, (hence, by implication) underground; e.g. *subarmour; sub-current, -deposit; sub-note, -text; sub-crossing, -railway*; in designations of architectural features, indicating a secondary member, feature, chamber, etc. placed under one of the same kind, e.g. *sub-basement, -member, -shaft*; so *subtrench*. Also SUB-ARCH, etc. (Stress even, or on the prefix.)

b. *Anat.* (*a*) Designating the lowest or basal part of the organ denoted by the second element; e.g. *subface, subilium*. (*b*) Denoting a part concealed or encroached upon; e.g. *subfissure, subgyre*.

c. *Agric.* Short for *subsoil-*, as *sub-pulverizer*.

4. *Mus.* With adj. force combining with sbs. to form terms designating: (*a*) an interval of so much below a given note; e.g. *subdiapente*: (*b*) a note or an organ-stop an octave below that denoted by the original sb.; e.g. SUBOCTAVE; *sub-bass, -diapason*; (*c*) a note lying the same distance below the tonic as the note designated by the radical sb. is above it; e.g. SUBDOMINANT, SUBMEDIANT.

5–9. Subordinate, subsidiary, secondary; subordinately, subsidiarily, secondarily. (Stress on the prefix.) **5.** Having a subordinate or inferior position; of inferior or minor importance or size; subsidiary, secondary. **a.** of persons; e.g. *subadvocate, -substitute*. **b.** of material objects; e.g. *sub-affluent, -constellation, -piston*. **c.** of something immaterial, a quality, state, or action; e.g. *subappearance, -cause, -commission, -element, -flavour, -plot, -type*.

6. With names of officials, etc., forming titles designating one immediately subordinate to the chief official; e.g. *sub-abbot, -captain, -collector, -commissioner, -delegate, -governor, -king, -minister, -preceptor, -prefect, -rector, -vicar, -warden*. **Su·b-al:moner,** a subordinate almoner, one of the officials of the Royal Almonry. **Su·b-ma:rshal,** a deputy or under-marshal, an official in the Marshalsea acting as the knight-marshal's deputy (*Obs.* exc. *Hist.*). (*b*) in derived adjs.: e.g. *subsecretarial* pertaining to a sub-secretary. **b.** In the designation of corresponding offices or functions; e.g. *sub-administration, -inspectorship*.

7. Compounded with sbs., to express division into parts, sections, or branches. **a.** Of material objects; e.g. *sub-cavity*, one of the smaller cavities into which a cavity is divided. **Su·b-atom,** *Chem.* a constituent part of an atom; hence **Subato·mic** *a.* **b.** Of a body or assembly of people as in SUBCOMMITTEE, or of a division of animals or plants, as in SUBGENUS; e.g. *subdenomination, -group, -tribe*. (*b*) in derived adjs; e.g. *subsynodical* pertaining to a sub-synod. **c.** Of a region or an interval of time, as in *sub-age* a division of an age, *-zone*, SUB-DISTRICT. **d.** = branch-; e.g. *sub-bureau* a bureau depending on the principal bureau, *sub-office*, a branch office.

8. With advb. force, combined with adjs. and vbs. = in a subordinate or secondary manner or capacity, by subsidiary means.

9. (*a*) On the analogy of SUBDIVIDE and SUBDIVISION, *sub-* is used to denote a further division or distinction; e.g. *sub-classify; sub-articulation*; (*b*) on the analogy of SUBCONTRACT *sb.* and *v.*, SUBLET, to denote a second or further action or process of the same kind as that denoted by the radical; e.g. *subcolonize* to colonize from a colony, *sub-infer* to draw as a further inference, *sub-rent* to rent from one who himself rents, *sub-purchaser* one who purchases from a previous purchaser; *subsecession* a secession from a body that has seceded; *subtenure*, the subfeudation of land.

10. *Math.* Compounded with adjs. expressing ratio, *sub-* denotes a ratio the opposite of that expressed by the radical element, as in late L. *submultiplus* SUBMULTIPLE; e.g. *subdecuple* the ratio 1:10, *subtriple*. Analogously, in SUBDUPLICATE, etc., the prefix is employed to express the ratio of the square (etc.) roots of quantities; e.g. *subtriplicate* (of the cube roots of the quantities).

11–18. Next below, near or close (to); subsequent (to). (As a living prefix *sub-* is restricted in this sense to prepositional uses; the advb. use is seen in SUBSEQUENT.) **11.** Near to (a particular region or point), as in L. *suburbanus* SUBURBAN; e.g. *suba·pical, -basal, -caudal, -dorsal, -lateral, -littoral, -marginal*.

12. *Geog.* and *Geol.* **a.** Lying about the base of or subjacent to mountains designated by the second element, hence, of less height than mountains of similar height to these, characteristic of regions of such altitude; e.g. *sub-Andean, -Etnean, -Himalayan*. **Suba·pennine,** applied to a series of strata of Pliocene age, such as are characteristic of the flanks of the Apennines in Italy; belonging to or characteristic of these strata. **b.** Denoting a region or zone adjacent to or on the borders of that designated by the second element; e.g. *subantarctic, -frigid, -torrid*.

13. *Mus.* Designating a note next to or next below some principal note; e.g. SUBTONIC. (Cf. 4.) **Subse·mitone,** the leading note of a scale.

14. Combined with adjs. with the sense 'of lower condition or degree (or size) than' that denoted by the original adj.; e.g. *sub-angelical, -elementary, -judicial, -regal*.

15. *Zool.* In names of divisions of animals regarded as having only imperfectly developed the characteristics denoted by the word to which *sub-* is prefixed, as *Subungulata*, etc.; also, in derivatives; e.g. *subostracean*, a mollusc of the family *Subostracea*.

16. In craniometry, forming adjs. designating a type of skull having an index next below that of the type denoted by the second element; e.g. *subbrachycephalic* (hence *-cephaly*).

17. In names of certain sectaries, = after, consequent upon: opp. to SUPRA- e.g. SUBLAPSARIAN.

18. In designations of periods immediately 'below' or posterior to a particular period. **Subaposto·lic,** belonging to or characteristic of the period in the history of the Church immediately following that of the Apostles.

19–23. Incomplete(ly, imperfect(ly, partial(ly. * *With adverbial meaning.* **19.** Prefixed to adjs. or pples. of a general character; e.g. *subanalogous* somewhat similar, *subaudible* imperfectly, slightly, or barely audible, *subobscure, subtypical*. (The force of *sub-* may vary contextually from 'only slightly' to 'not quite, all but'.)

20. In techn. use, chiefly *Nat. Hist.* **a.** With adjs. of colour; e.g. *sub-pale, -red, -vivid*. **b.** With adjs. denoting surface texture, contour, or marking, substance, consistency, composition, taste, odour; e.g. *subacrid, -astringent, -cartilaginous, -coriaceous, -fossil, -granular, -spinous, -stony, -villose, -villous*, etc. **c.** With adjs. expressing shape, conformation, or physical habit; e.g. *sub-acuminate, -angular, -arborescent, -arcuate, -equal, -globular, -globose, -hooked, -lunate, -orbicular, -oval, -ovate, -ovoid, -ramose, -rotund, -sessile*. **d.** With adjs. denoting position, as in SUBCENTRAL, SUBLATERAL; e.g. *sub-erect, -internal, -terminal*. **e.** With adjs. designating geometrical forms; e.g. *subcylindric(al, -pentagonal* (= five-sided but not forming a regular pentagon), *-oblong, -spherical, -triangular*, etc. **f.** With adjs. denoting a numerical arrangement or conformation; e.g. *subbifid* imperfectly bifid, *-bipinnate, -dichotomous* somewhat divided or branched. **g.** *Med.* e.g. *subacute, subchronic* not entirely chronic, more chronic than acute; **subconti·nued,** almost continuous, remittent; *subfebrile*. **h.** Forming advs. corresponding to adjs. of any of the above classes, e.g. *subacutely*.

21. With vbs., as in L. *subaccusare* to accuse somewhat; e.g. *sub-blush, -cachinnate, -indicate, understand*. **Subo·dorate** (*rare*) to smell or scent out.

** *With adjectival meaning.* **22.** With sbs. denoting action or condition, in the sense partial, incomplete, 'slight'; e.g. *sub-animation, -saturation*; *Med.* often = 'less than the normal, mild, gentle'; e.g. *sub-delirium, -purgation*; also occas. with sbs. denoting material objects, e.g. *sub-relief*. **Subima·go,** *Entom.* in Ephemeridæ, the stage immediately preceding the imago; the insect at this stage. **Subluxa·tion,** a partial dislocation, a sprain.

23. *Chem.* In names of compounds *sub-* indicates that the ingredient of the compound denoted by the term to which it is prefixed is in a relatively small proportion, or is less than in the normal compounds of that name; e.g. *subacetate*, an acetate in which there are fewer equivalents of the acid radical than in the normal acetate, a basic acetate, *subsalt* a basic salt.

24. Secretly, covertly, as in L. *subornare* to SUBORN. †**Subai·d** *v.* (*rare*), to give secret aid to. †**Subingre·ssion,** subtle or unobserved entrance. **Su:bintrodu·ce** *v.* to introduce in a secret or subtle manner. **Subtru·de,** to thrust itself in stealthily.

25. From below, up, (hence) away; e.g. SUCCOUR, SUGGEST, SUSPICION, etc. **b.** Hence *sub-* implies taking up so as to include, as in SUBSUME.

26. In place of another, as in L. *substituere* to SUBSTITUTE.

27. In addition, by way of or as an addition, after L. *subjungere* to SUBJOIN; e.g. *subinsert* vb.

Subacid (sʌbæ·sid), *a.* and *sb.* 1669. [– L. *subacidus*; see SUB- 20 b and ACID.] **A.** *adj.* **1.** Somewhat or moderately acid. **b.** *Chem.* Containing less than the normal proportion of acid 1808. **2.** Of character, speech, etc.: Somewhat acid or tart; verging on acidity or tartness 1765.

2. An excellent temper, with a slight degree of s. humour SCOTT.

B. *sb.* **1.** Subacid quality or flavour 1838. **2.** A subacid substance 1828.

1. The s. of the strawberry 1884. Hence **Subaci·dity.**

†**Suba·ct,** *v.* 1614. [– *subact-*, pa. ppl. stem of L. *subigere*, f. *sub-* SUB- 2, 25 + *agere* bring.] **1.** *trans.* To work up, as in cultivating the ground, kneading, the process of digestion, etc. –1822. **2.** To bring into subjection; to subdue –1680. So †**Suba·ction,** the action of working up, reducing, or kneading –1822.

Su·b-a:gent. 1683. [SUB- 6.] A subordinate agent; the agent of an agent; *spec.* in *U.S. Law*. Hence **Su·b-a:gency,** the position, condition, or residence of a s.

||**Subah** (sū·ba). *Anglo-Ind.* 1753. [Urdu = Arab *ṣūba*.] **1.** A province of the Mogul empire. **2.** = next 1753. Hence **Su·bahship** = sense 1. 1753.

||**Subahdar** (sūbadā·ɹ). *Anglo-Ind.* 1698. [Urdu *ṣūbahdār*, f. prec. + Pers. *dār* possessor, master.] **1.** A governor of a subah or province. **2.** The chief native officer of a company of sepoys 1747.

attrib.: **s.-major,** the native commandant of a regiment of sepoys. Hence **Subahdary** (sūbadā·ri), subahship.

Suba·lpine, *a.* 1656. [– L. *subalpinus*; see SUB- 12 and ALPINE.] **1.** Belonging to regions lying about the foot of the Alps. **2.** Partly alpine in character or formation; pertaining to or characteristic of elevations next below that called *alpine*; belonging to the higher slopes of mountains (of an altitude of about 4,000 to 5,500 feet) 1833.

Subaltern (sʌ·bǎltəɹn, sʌbǭ·ltəɹn), *a.* and *sb.* 1581. [– late L. *subalternus*; see SUB- 11–18, ALTERN *a.* Cf. Fr. *subalterne* (XV).] **A.** *adj.* †**1.** Succeeding in turn (*rare*) –1762. **b.** Logic. *S. genus* (or *species*): a genus that is at the same time a species of a higher genus 1654. **2.** Of inferior status, quality, or importance 1581. **3.** *S. officer*: an officer of junior rank in the army, i.e. below that of captain. Hence *s. rank*, etc. 1688. **4.** Of a vassal: Holding of one who is himself a vassal. Hence of a feu or right. 1681. **5.** *Logic.* Of a proposition: Particular, in relation to a universal of the same quality 1656.

1. b. Iron-ore is a s. species or genus, being both the genus of magnet, and a species of mineral 1826. **2.** All such s. actors as played between the acts 1734. Fighting his way through every s. degree of his profession 1817. **5.** *S. opposition*, opposition between a universal and a particular of the same quality.

B. *sb.* **1.** A person (or †thing) of inferior rank or status; a subordinate 1605. **2.** A subaltern officer in the army 1690. **3.** *Logic.* A subaltern proposition 1826.

Subalternate (sʌbǫltā·ɹnět), *a.* (*sb.*) late ME. [– late L. *subalternatus*, pa. pple. of *subalternare*; see prec., -ATE².] †1. Subordinate, inferior –1874. †2. [f. SUB- 20 d and ALTERNATE *a.*] *Nat. Hist.* Alternate, but with a tendency to become opposite 1829.

1. The several kinds of s. Species of Plants 1704.

B. *sb. Logic.* A particular proposition 1826.

Subalternation (sɒ:bǫltəɹnē¹·ʃən). 1597. [– med.L. *subalternatio*, *-ōn-*; see prec., -ION.] †1. Subordination. †2. Succession by turn –1627. 3. *Logic.* The relation between a universal and a particular of the same quality; also, an immediate inference from a universal to a particular under it 1650.

Subalternity (sɒbǫltə·ɹnĭti). 1620. [f. SUBALTERN + -ITY; cf. Fr. *subalternité*. In XVII (logic) – med.L. *subalternitas*.] Subordinate position.

Subaqua·tic, *a.* 1789. 1. [SUB- 1 a.] = next 1. Also, pertaining to plants growing under water. 2. [SUB- 20 c.] *Zool.* and *Bot.* Partly aquatic 1844.

Subaqueous (sɒbē¹·kwĭəs), *a.* 1677. [See SUB- 1 a, AQUEOUS.] 1. Existing, formed, or constructed under water. **b.** Performed or taking place under water; adapted for use under water 1774. 2. Reflected as if in depths of water 1798.

1. Vast s. precipices 1774. **b.** *Sub-aqueous Helmet*, a diver's head-dress, supplied with air by pump from above 1875.

Su·b-arch. 1835. [SUB- 3, 5 b.] *Arch.* A subsidiary or secondary arch; one of two or more arches grouped in a larger arch; the lowest member in an arch of two or more 'orders'.

Suba·rctic, *a.* (*sb.*) 1854. [SUB- 12 b.] Nearly Arctic; somewhat south of the Arctic circle or regions; belonging to such a region. Also *sb.*, *pl.*, subarctic regions.

Su:barcua·tion. 1845. [SUB- 2.] *Arch.* The construction of two or more subordinate arches under a main arch; the system of arches so constructed. Hence **Suba·rcuated** *a.* having two or more such arches under a main arch.

Subarrhation (sɒbarē¹·ʃən). 1623. [– med. L. *subarrhatio*, *-ōn-*, f. *subarrhare* pay earnest money, f. *sub-* SUB- 1 g + ARRHA; see -ION.] An ancient form of betrothal in which pledges in the form of money, rings, etc. were bestowed by the man upon the woman.

‖**Subashi** (sūbā·ʃi). 1599. [Turk. *subaşı*, f. *su* water + *baş* head, chief.] A Turkish official in command of a district or village; a 'police magistrate under the timariot system' (Redhouse).

Subaudition (sɒbǫdi·ʃən). 1798. [– late L. *subauditio*, *-ōn-*, f. *subaudire* supply mentally, f. *sub* + *audire* hear, after Gr. ὑπακούειν; see SUB- 24.] Chiefly *Gram.* The act of mentally supplying something that is not expressed; something that is mentally supplied or understood; implied or understood meaning.

'Policeman' has no evil s. 1859.

‖**Subauditur** (sɒbǫdəi·tɒɹ). 1803. [L. 'it is understood', 3rd. pers. sing. ind. pass. of *subaudire*; see prec.] = prec. Phr. *In a s.*: by implication.

Suba·xillary, *a.* (*sb.*) 1769. [SUB- 1 b, c.] 1. *Zool.* Situated beneath the axilla; *Ornith.* = AXILLARY. 2. *Bot.* Beneath the axil or the angle made by a branch with the stem or a leaf with the branch 1802.

Su·b-base. 1826. 1. [SUB- 3.] **a.** *Arch.* The lowest part of a base which is divided horizontally. **b.** A base placed under the bottom of a machine or other apparatus to raise it higher from the ground 1904. 2. [SUB- 5 b.] A secondary base 1903.

Subbra·chial, *a.* 1836. [See SUB- 1 b and BRACHIAL.] 1. *Ichth.* Situated under or near the pectoral fins; (of a fish) having the ventral fins so situated. 2. Under the pectoral muscles 1896. 3. Beneath the brachium (in cerebral anatomy) 1913. So **Subbra·chian** *a.* = sense 1; *sb.* a s. fish; one of the *Subbrachiati*.

Subcele·stial, *a.* and *sb.* 1561. [f. late and med.L. *subcelestis*; see SUB- 1 a, CELESTIAL. Cf. OFr. *sous-céleste*.] **A.** *adj.* Situate or existing beneath or below the heavens; chiefly *transf.* terrestrial, mundane, sublunary. **B.** *sb.* A subcelestial being 1652.

Subce·ntral, *a.* 1822. 1. [SUB- 11, 20 d.] Nearly or not quite central; near or close to the centre. 2. [SUB- 1 a.] Being under the centre 1828. 3. [SUB- 1 b.] *Anat.* Beneath the central sulcus of the brain; beneath the centrum of a vertebra 1882.

Su·bcha:nter. 1515. [f. SUB- 6 + CHANTER, after med.L. *subcantor*, *subcentor*. Cf. (O)Fr. *souschantre*, and see SUCCENTOR.] A precentor's deputy, succentor; now, a vicar-choral or lay-clerk of a cathedral, who assists in chanting the litany.

Subche·late, *a.* 1852. [SUB- 20 c.] Imperfectly chelate.

Subclass (sɒ·bklɑs). 1819. [SUB- 7 b.] A subdivision of a class; *Nat. Hist.* a group of orders ranking next to a class. So **Su·bclass** *v. trans.* to place in a s.

†‖**Subcla·via.** 1733. [mod.L. *subclavia* (sc. *arteria*), fem. of SUBCLAVIUS.] *Anat.* The subclavian artery –1771.

Subclavian (sɒbklē¹·viăn), *a.* and *sb.* 1646. [f. mod.L. SUBCLAVIUS + -AN. Cf. Fr. *sous-clavier* (XVI).] **A.** *adj.* Lying or extending under the clavicle 1681. **b.** Pertaining to the s. artery, vein, or muscle 1646.

S. artery, the principal artery of the root of the neck, being the main trunk of the arterial system of the upper extremity. *S. muscle* = SUBCLAVIUS. *S. vein*, the continuation of the axillary vein from the first rib until it joins the internal jugular vein.

B. *sb.* A s. vessel, nerve, or muscle 1719.

‖**Subclavius** (sɒbklē¹·viɒs). 1704. [mod.L. *subclavius* (sc. *musculus*), f. *sub-* SUB- 1 b + *clavis* key.] *Anat.* In full *s. muscle*: A small muscle extending from the first rib to the clavicle.

Su·bcommi:ttee. 1610. [SUB- 7 b.] A committee formed from and acting under a main committee; a part of a committee appointed for special purposes.

Subconscious (sɒbkǫ·nʃəs), *a.* 1832. [SUB- 19.] 1. *Psych.* **a.** Partially or imperfectly conscious; belonging to a class of phenomena resembling those of consciousness but not clearly perceived or recognized. **b.** Belonging to that portion of the mental field the processes of which are outside the range of attention. 2. Partly or imperfectly aware 1864.

1. *transf.* A sketch of himself..has a s. humour one would not have suspected 1899. Hence **Subco·nscious-ly** *-adv.*, **-ness.**

Sub-co·nstable. Now *Hist.* 1512. [– AL. *subconestabulus* (1273); see SUB- 6.] An under-constable, *esp.* in the Royal Irish Constabulary.

Su·bco:ntinent. 1863. [SUB- 5 b.] A land mass of great extent, but smaller than those usu. called continents; a large section of a continent having a certain geographical or political independence; in recent use, *spec.* South Africa.

Su·bco:ntract, *sb.* 1817. [SUB- 9.] A contract, or one of several contracts, for carrying out a previous contract or a part of it.

Subcontra·ct, *v.* 1605. [SUB- 9.] †1. *pass.* To be betrothed for the second time. SHAKS. 2. *intr.* To make a subcontract 1842. 3. *trans.* To make a subcontract for 1898. Hence **Subcontra·ctor,** one who enters into a subcontract.

Su:bcontrari·ety. 1697. [f. next.] *Logic.* The relation existing between subcontrary propositions.

Subco·ntrary, *a.* and *sb.* 1603. [– late L. *subcontrarius* (Boethius), tr. late Gr. ὑπεναντίος; see SUB- 19 and CONTRARY *a.*] **A.** *adj.* 1. Somewhat or partially contrary. 2. *Logic.* Applied to particular propositions (or the relation of opposition between them) agreeing in quantity but differing in quality 1656. 3. *Geom.* **a.** Applied to the relative position of two similar triangles having a common angle at the vertex and their bases not parallel, so that the basal angles are equal but on contrary sides 1704. **b.** Applied to any circular section of a quadric cone in relation to the base or to another circular section not parallel to it 1706. **B.** *sb.* 1. *Logic.* A s. proposition 1697. 2. *Geom.* A s. section of a cone 1842.

Subco·rtical, *a.* 1815. [SUB- 1 a.] 1. Lying, situated, or formed under the bark of a tree; (of insects) living or feeding under bark. 2. Situated under or pertaining to the region underlying (*a*) the cortex of a sponge, (*b*) the cortex of the brain 1887.

Subco·stal, *a.* and *sb.* 1733. [– mod.L. *subcostalis*; see SUB- 1 b, COSTAL.] **A.** *adj.* 1. *Anat.* Situated below a rib or beneath the ribs; lying on the under side of a rib, as a groove for an artery 1872. 2. *Entom.* Situated behind or near the costal vein or nervure of an insect's wing 1826. **B.** *sb.* A s. muscle (usu. in L. form *subcostalis*); a s. artery or nervure 1733.

Subcutaneous (sɒbkiutē¹·nĭəs), *a.* 1651. [f. late L. *subcutaneus*, f. *sub-* SUB- 1 b + *cutis* skin + *-aneus*; see -EOUS.] 1. Lying or situated under the skin 1656. 2. Living under the skin 1664. 3. Of operations, etc.: Performed or taking place under the skin; characterized by application of a remedy beneath the skin; hence, of instruments by which such operations are performed or remedies administered; hypodermic 1651.

3. The s. administration of anti-toxic serum 1899. Hence **Subcuta·neously** *adv.*

Subdeacon (sɒbdī·kən). ME. [– eccl.L. *subdiaconus*, also *subdiacon* (V) – eccl.Gr. ὑποδιάκονος; in XIV–XV *su-*, *sodekne* – AFr., OFr. *su-*, *soudeacne* – eccl.L.; see SUB- 6.] *Eccl.* 1. The name of the order of ministers in the Christian church next below that of deacon.

The duty of subdeacons is to assist in the celebration of the Eucharist by preparing the sacred vessels and (in the Western Church) by reading the epistle. The subdiaconate does not exist in the Church of England.

2. The cleric (orig. one in subdeacon's orders) or clerk who acts as assistant next below the deacon at a solemn celebration of the Eucharist; the 'epistoler' 1440. Hence **Subdea·conate, †-dea·conry, -dea·conship** = SUBDIACONATE.

Subdean (sɒbdī·n). late ME. [– AFr. *sodean, *subdene = OFr. *sou(z)deien*, f. *sou(s-*, *sub-* (see SUB- 6) + *deien* DEAN¹, after med.L. *subdecanus*.] An official immediately below a dean in rank, and acting as his deputy. Hence **Subdea·nery,** the office, position, or residence of a s.

Subdeca·nal, *a.* *rare.* 1846. [f. med.L. *subdecanus* SUBDEAN + -AL¹ 1.] Of or pertaining to a subdean or subdeanery.

Subdia·conate. 1725. [– late and med.L. *subdiaconatus*, f. *subdiaconus*; see SUBDEACON, -ATE¹.] The office or rank of subdeacon.

Su·bdi:alect. 1642. [SUB- 7.] A subordinate dialect; a division of a dialect.

Subdisju·nctive, *a.* and *sb.* 1656. [– late and med.L. *subdisjunctivus*; see SUB- 19, DISJUNCTIVE.] *Logic* and *Gram.* **A.** *adj.* Partly disjunctive. **B.** *sb.* A subdisjunctive proposition or word 1656.

In English we use the conjunction *or* indifferently as a disjunctive or s.; that is, we say 'Alexander *or* Paris', whether Alexander and Paris be two different persons, or only two different names for the same person 1818.

Subdisti·nction. 1636. [In sense 1 – late L. *subdistinctio* (= Gr. ὑποστιγμή), f. *subdistinguere* (= Gr. ὑποστίζειν) put a comma or one of the lesser stops; cf. SUB- 22. In senses 2 and 3, f. SUB- 5 c and 7 b + DISTINCTION.] †1. A comma or semicolon –1825. 2. A subordinate distinction 1655.

†**Subdisti·nguish,** *v.* 1620. [f. SUB- 9 + DISTINGUISH, after late L. *subdistinguere*; see prec.] *trans.* To distinguish into subordinate kinds, classes, species, etc. –1789.

Su·b-di:strict. 1816. [SUB- 7 c.] A division or subdivision of a district.

Subdivide (sɒbdivəi·d), *v.* late ME. [– late L. *subdividere*; see SUB- 9, DIVIDE *v.*] 1. *trans.* To divide (a part of a divided whole); to divide again after a first division. 2. *intr.* To break up into subdivisions 1597.

1. The army formed into two grand divisions, each of which was subdivided into a battle and two wings 1823. The use of machinery tends still further to s. labour 1868. Hence **Subdivi·der,** one who subdivides; *spec.* one who settles on a portion of an estate. **Subdivi·sible** *a.*

Subdivision (sɒbdivi·ʒən). 1553. [– late L. *subdivisio*, *-ōn-*; see SUB- 9, DIVISION.] 1. The act or process of subdividing, or the fact of being subdivided 1599. **b.** An instance of this 1577. 2. One of the parts into which a whole is subdivided; part of a part; a section resulting from a further division; *Nat. Hist.* a subordinate division of a group 1553. **b.** *Mil.* The half of a division. Also, at various times, the half of a company; in the artillery, a gun with its waggons (now called SUBSECTION). 1625.

1. The increase of wealth had produced its natural effect, the s. of labour MACAULAY. **2.** The Gnosticks and the severall subdivisions of them 1662. Hence **Subdivi·sional** *a.* of the nature of s.; pertaining to s., or a s.; consisting of a s.

Subdivi·sive, *a.* 1838. [f. SUBDIVIDE, SUBDIVISION, after *decide*/*decision*/*decisive*.] Resulting from subdivision.

Subdolous (sʊbdǒləs), *a.* Now *rare.* 1588. [f. L. *subdolus* (f. *sub-* SUB- 19 + *dolus* cunning) + -OUS.] Crafty, cunning, sly. Hence **Su·bdolous-ly** *adv.*, **-ness.**

Subdo·minant, *sb.* 1793. [SUB- 4.] *Mus.* The note next below the dominant of a scale; the fourth note in ascending and the fifth in descending a scale.

Subdo·minant, *a.* 1826. [SUB- 14.] Less than dominant, not quite dominant.

Subduable (sǒbdiū·ăb'l), *a.* *rare.* 1611. [f. SUBDUE *v.* + -ABLE.] That may be subdued.

Subdual (sǒbdiū·ăl). 1675. [f. SUBDUE *v.* + -AL[1].] The act of subduing or state of being subdued; subjection.

†**Subdu·ce,** *v.* 1542. [– L. *subducere*, f. *sub-* SUB- 25 + *ducere* lead, bring.] **1.** *trans.* To take away, withdraw –1761. **b.** *refl.* (occas. *intr.*) To withdraw oneself or itself *from*; to secede –1660. **2.** To subtract, as a mathematical operation –1676.

Subduct (sǒbdʊ·kt), *v.* Now *rare.* 1571. [– *subduct-*, pa. ppl. stem of L. *subducere*; see prec.] **1.** *trans.* To take away from its place or position, withdraw from use, consideration, influence, etc. 1614. **2.** To take away (a quantity) *from*, †*out of* another; to subtract, deduct 1571. †**b.** *intr.* To take something away *from* –1798. **3.** To take away or remove surreptitiously or fraudulently. Also *absol.* 1758. **4.** To draw up 1837.

2. When we..s. the vapour pressure from the barometric height 1881. **b.** Nature..from my side subducting, took perhaps More then enough MILT. **3.** Purchased with money subducted from the shop JOHNSON.

Subduction (sǒbdʊ·kʃən). Now *rare.* 1579. [f. prec. + -ION.] **1.** The action of subducting; subtraction, withdrawal. **2.** The action of subduing or fact of being subdued 1670.

Subdue (sǒbdiū·), *v.* [In XIV *sodewe*, *sudewe*, later *subdewe* – AFr. **soduer*, **su(b)duer* = OFr. *so(u)duire*, *suduire* deceive, seduce – L. *subducere* withdraw, evacuate (see SUBDUCE), with sense derived from †*subdit* subject – L. *subditus*, pa. pple. of *subdere* bring under, subdue, f. *sub* SUB- 2b + *-dere* put.] **1.** *trans.* To conquer (an army, an enemy, a country or its inhabitants) in fight and bring them into subjection. †**b.** To overcome (a person) by physical strength or violence –1604. **2.** To bring (a person) into mental, moral, or spiritual subjection; to render (a person or animal) submissive; to prevail over, get the better of. Const. *to* (that which exercises control, the control exercised). 1509. **b.** With a person's body, soul, mind, actions, etc. as obj. 1520. †**c.** To bring *to* a low state, reduce. SHAKS. **3.** To bring (land) under cultivation 1535. †**4.** In medical use: To reduce, allay –1829. **5.** To reduce the intensity, force, or vividness of (sound, colour, light); to make less prominent or salient 1800.

1. Iohn of Gaunt, Which did s. the greatest part of Spaine SHAKS. **b.** If he do resist S. him, at his perill SHAKS. **2.** Swords Conquer some, but Words s. all men PRIOR. **b.** My heart and hands thou hast at once subdu'd SHAKS. **c.** *Lear* III. iv. 72. **5.** The warm colours of distance, even the most glowing, are subdued by the air RUSKIN. Hence **Subdue·d** *ppl. a.* reduced to subjection, overcome; reduced in intensity, force, or vividness; toned down. **Subdue·ment** (*rare*), subdual. **Subdu·er,** one who or that which subdues.

Subduple (sʊbdiū·p'l, sʊ·bdiup'l), *a.* 1598. [– late L. *subduplus* (Boethius); see SUB- 10, DUPLE *a.*] *Math.* That is half of a quantity or number; denoting a proportion of one to two; (of a ratio) of which the antecedent is half the consequent.

Subdu·plicate, *a.* 1656. [– mod.L. *subduplicatus* (Newton), pa. pple. of med.L. *subduplicare* halve (XIII–XIV); see SUB- 10, DUPLICATE.] *Math.* Of a ratio or proportion: Being that of the square roots of the quantities; thus, 2:3 is the subduplicate ratio of 4:9.

Sub-e·dit, *v.* 1862. [Back-formation from next.] *trans.* To edit (a paper, periodical, etc.) under, to prepare (copy) for, the supervision of a chief editor.

Sub-e·ditor. 1837. [SUB- 6.] A subordinate editor; one who sub-edits. Hence **Su:b-edito·rial** *a.*

‖**Suber** (siū·bəɹ). 1859. [L., = cork, cork-oak.] *Bot.* (*Chem.*) The bark or periderm of the cork-tree; cork. Also, a vegetable principle found in this. So **Suberate,** *Chem.* a salt of suberic acid. **Sube·reous** (siubīᵊ·rĭəs) *a.* suberous, suberose. **Su·berin,** *Chem.* the cellular tissue which remains after cork has been exhausted by various solvents. **Su·berize** *v. Bot. pass.* to be converted into cork-tissue by the formation of suberin. **Su·berone,** *Chem.* an aromatic oil formed by the distillation of suberic acid with lime. **Su·beryl,** *Chem.* the diatomic radical of suberic acid.

Suberic (siube·rik), *a.* 1799. [– Fr. *subérique* (Lagrange 1797); see SUBER; -IC.] *Chem.* Of or pertaining to cork. *S. acid*, a white crystalline dibasic acid prepared by the action of nitric acid on cork, paper, linen rags, fatty acids, and other bodies.

Subero- (siū·běro), comb. form of SUBER in names of chemical compounds containing or obtained from suberic acid.

Suberose (siū·běrōᵘs), *a.* 1845. [f. SUBER + -OSE[1].] *Bot.* Having the appearance of cork; like cork in form or texture. So **Su·berous** *a.* 1679.

Su·bfa:mily. 1833. [SUB- 7 b.] *Nat. Hist.* A primary subdivision of a family.

Subfief (sʊ·bfīf), *sb.* 1845. [f. SUB- 9 + FIEF *sb.*] A fief which is held of an intermediary instead of the original feoffor; *spec.* in Germany, a minor state, holding of a more important state instead of directly of the German crown. Hence **Subfie·f** *v. trans.* to grant as a s.

Subfusc, -fusk (sʊbfʊ·sk), *a.* and *sb.* 1710. [– L. *subfuscus*; see SUB- 20 a, FUSK.] Of dusky, dull, or sombre hue 1763. **b.** (*a*) *absol.* with *the*; (*b*) as *sb.* subfusc colour 1710. So **Subfu·scous** *a.* (*rare*).

Subgeneric (sʊbdʒěne·rik), *a.* 1836. [f. next after *generic*.] Of or pertaining to a subgenus; having the characteristics of, constituting, or typifying a subgenus.

Su·bge:nus. *Pl.* **su·bge:nera.** 1813. [SUB- 7 b.] A subordinate genus; a subdivision of a genus of higher rank than a species.

Subhastation (sʊbhæstē̆ɪ·ʃən). *Obs.* exc. *Hist.* 1600. [– late L. *subhastatio*, *-ōn-*, f. *subhastare*, f. *sub hasta* under the spear, from the Roman practice of setting up a spear where an auction was to be held.] A public sale by auction.

Su·b-hea·d. 1588. [SUB- 5, 6.] **1.** An official next in rank to the head (of a college, etc.). *rare.* **2.** One of the subordinate divisions into which a main division of a subject is broken up 1673. **3.** A subordinate heading or title in a book, chapter, article, etc. 1875. So **Su·bheading** (in senses 2, 3).

Sub-hu·man, *a.* 1793. [SUB- 14, 19.] **1.** Not quite human, less than human; *occas.* almost human. **2.** Belonging to or characteristic of the part of creation that is below the human race 1837.

‖**Subiculum** (siubi·kiŭlǒm). 1836. [mod.L. (Link), dim. (see -ULE) f. *subic-*, stem of L. *subices* (pl.) supports, f. *subicere* (see SUBJECT).] **1.** *Bot.* In certain fungi, the modified tissue of the host bearing the perithecia. **2.** *Anat.* The uncus or uncinate gyrus 1891.

Subindu·ce, *v. rare* or *Obs.* 1623. [Partly – late L. *subinducere*, partly f. SUB- 24 + INDUCE.] **1.** *trans.* To insinuate, suggest indirectly 1640. **2.** To induce by indirect or underhand means 1623. **3.** To bring about (a thing) as a result or in succession to another 1855.

Su:binfeuda·tion. 1730. [– med.L. *subinfeudatio*, *-ōn-*; see SUB- 9 (b), INFEUDATION. Cf. Fr. †*subinfeudation* (COTGR.), *sous-infeudation*.] **1.** The granting of lands by a feudatory to an inferior to be held of himself on the same terms as he held them of his superior; the relation or tenure so established. **2.** An instance of this; also, an estate or fief created by this process 1766. So **Subinfeu·d** *v. trans.* to grant (estates) by s.; to give (a person) possession *of* estates by s.

‖**Subintelligitur** (sʊ:binteli·dʒitǒɹ). 1649. [L., 3rd pers. sing. pres. indic. pass. of *subintelligere*, f. *sub-* SUB- 24 + *intelligere*.] An unexpressed or implied addition to a statement, etc. (Cf. SUBAUDITUR.)

We pray to God as a Person, a larger self; but there must always be a s. that He is not a Person JOWETT.

Subintrant (sʊbi·ntrănt), *a.* (*sb.*) 1684. [– late L. *subintrans*, *-ant-*, pr. pple. of *subintrare* steal into, f. *sub-* SUB- 24 + L. *intrare* ENTER.] *Path.* Of fevers: Having paroxysms so rapidly that before one is over another begins; also said of the paroxysms. **B.** *sb.* A s. fever 1899.

Subitaneous (sʊbitē̆ɪ·nĭəs), *a.* Now *rare.* 1651. [f. L. *subitaneus* sudden (f. *subitus*) + -OUS.] Sudden, unexpected; hastily produced or constructed. So †**Subitany** *a.* 1603.

‖**Subito** (su·bito), *adv.* 1724. [It.] *Mus.* A direction: Quickly; usu. in phr. *volti subito*, turn quickly.

Subjacent (sʊbdʒē̆ɪ·sěnt), *a.* 1597. [– L. *subjacens*, *-ent-*, pr. pple. of *subjacēre*; see SUB- 2, ADJACENT.] **1.** Situated underneath or below; underlying. **b.** *transf.* and *fig.* Forming the basis or substratum 1677. **2.** Lying or situated at a lower level, at or near the base (e.g. of a mountain) 1650. **3.** Taking place underneath or below (*rare*) 1862.

1. The skin and s. cellular membrane 1813. S and intercalated beds GEIKIE. **2.** The rivers that water the s. plains 1760. Hence **Subja·cently** *adv.*

Subject (sʊ·bdʒěkt), *sb.* [ME. *soget*, etc., later *subiect* – OFr. *suget*, *sug(i)et* (mod. *sujet*) – L. *subjectus* masc., *-um* n., pa. pple. of *subicere*, f. *sub-* SUB- 2 b + *jacere* throw, cast.] **I. 1.** One who is under the dominion of a monarch or reigning prince; one who owes allegiance to a government or ruling power, is subject to its laws, and enjoys its protection. †**b.** *collect. sing.* The subjects of a realm. SHAKS. †**2.** One who is bound to a superior by an obligation to pay allegiance, service, or tribute; *spec.* a feudal inferior or tenant; a vassal, retainer; a dependant, subordinate; an inferior –1681. **3.** A person (rarely, a thing) that is in the control or under the dominion of another; one who owes obedience *to* another ME. **4.** *Law.* A thing over which a right is exercised 1765. **b.** *Sc.* A piece of property 1754.

1. I have the honour to be a British s. BENTHAM. The..kings of our own day very much resemble their subjects in education and breeding JOWETT. **b.** transf. *Per.* II. i. 53. **3.** By Nature woman was made mans subiect KYD. **4.** By the s. of a right is meant the thing..over which the right is exercised. My house, horse, or watch is the s. of my right of property. 1875.

II. Senses derived ultimately (through L. *subjectum*) from Aristotle's use of τὸ ὑποκείμενον in the threefold sense of (1) material out of which things are made, (2) subject of attributes, (3) subject of predicates. †**1.** The substance of which a thing consists or from which it is made –1775. **2.** *Philos.* The substance in which accidents or attributes inhere. late ME. †**b.** A thing having real independent existence. SHAKS. **3.** *Logic.* **a.** That which has attributes; the thing about which a judgement is made 1551. **b.** The term or part of a proposition of which the predicate is affirmed or denied 1620. **4.** *Gram.* The member or part of a sentence denoting that concerning which something is predicated (i.e. of which a statement is made, a question asked, or a desire expressed); a word or group of words constituting the 'nominative' to a finite verb 1638. **5.** *Mod. Philos.* More fully *conscious* or *thinking s.*: The mind, as the 'subject' in which ideas inhere; that to which all mental representations or operations are attributed; the thinking or cognizing agent; the self or ego. (Correl. to OBJECT *sb.* 6.) 1796.

2. Two Contraries can never subsist in the same

S. 1728. **5.** Every state of consciousness necessarily implies two elements at least; a conscious s., and an object of which he is conscious 1851.

III. 1. The subject-matter of an art or science 1541. **2.** A thing affording matter for action of a specified kind; a ground, motive, or cause 1586. **b.** That which can be drawn upon or utilized, means of doing something (*rare*) 1752. **3.** That which is or may be acted or operated upon; a person or thing towards which action or influence is directed 1592. **b.** An object with which a person's occupation or business is concerned or on which he exercises his craft; that which is operated upon manually or mechanically 1541. **c.** A body used for anatomical examination or demonstration; a dead body intended for or undergoing dissection 1694. **d.** A person who presents himself for or undergoes medical or surgical treatment; hence, one who is affected with some disease 1822. **e.** A person upon whom a psychic or other experiment is made 1883. **f.** With epithet: A person in respect of his conduct or character(*rare*). (Cf. Fr. *mauvais sujet*.) 1848. **4.** That which forms or is chosen as the matter of thought, consideration, or inquiry; a topic, theme 1586. **b.** An object of study in relation to its use for pedagogic or examining purposes; a particular department of art or science in which one is instructed or examined 1843. **5.** The theme *of* a literary composition; what a book, poem, etc. is about 1586. **b.** The person of whom a biography is written 1741. **6.** An object, a figure or group of figures, a scene, an incident, etc., chosen by an artist for representation 1614. **7.** *Mus.* The theme or principal phrase of a composition or movement; in a fugue, the exposition, dux, or proposition 1753.

1. All sciences have a s., number is the s. of arithmetic JOWETT. **2.** Which had never given..the least s. of complaint SCOTT. **3.** To be Shames scorne, and subiect of Mischance SHAKS. The S. of Conversation at Several Tea-Tables STEELE. **d.** Phr. *A good* (*bad*) *s.*, a patient who has (has not) good prospects of improvement or recovery. **4.** As for politics, it was a s. far beyond the reach of any female capacity 1780. **b.** If an officer only pass in the subjects necessary for a subaltern 1887. **6.** The next thing is to make choice of a S. beautifull and noble DRYDEN. Subjects after Watteau 1867.

attrib. and *Comb.*, as (sense III. 5, chiefly with ref. to cataloguing books according to their subjects) *s. catalogue, index, list, reference*; **s. picture**, a genre painting.

Subject (sɒ·bdʒěkt), *a.* ME. [– OFr. *suget*, *subject* (mod. *sujet*) – L. *subjectus*, pa. pple. of *subicere*; see prec.] **I. 1.** That is under the dominion or rule of a sovereign, or a conquering or ruling power; owing allegiance or obedience *to* a sovereign ruler or state, a temporal or spiritual lord, or other superior. **b.** *to* a law, a jurisdiction. late ME. **2.** *transf.* and *fig.* In a state of subjection or dependence; under the control or influence of something; subordinate ME. **b.** *to* the power, law, command, etc. of another. late ME.

1. All round about are subiect vnto the King of Tunis 1600. The relations between..governing race and s. race MORLEY. **2.** The military power ought always to be s. to the civil BURNET. **b.** He would no longer be s. to the caprice of any woman 1876.

II. (Const. *to*.) **1.** Exposed or open *to*; prone *to* or liable to suffer from something damaging, deleterious, or disadvantageous. late ME. **b.** Exposed *to* violent treatment, damaging weather, or the like 1490. **c.** Liable *to* disease 1577. **2.** Liable *to* the incidence or recurrence of an action, process, or state 1559. **b.** *absol.* Without *to*, in bookselling parlance: Subject to discount 1906. **†3.** Having a tendency, prone or disposed, *to* an action, or *to do* something –1793. **†4.** That may be brought under the operation of a faculty or sense –1668. **5.** Dependent upon a certain correcting or modifying condition; conditional upon. Freq. *advb.*, conditionally upon, with the assumption of. 1832.

1. Lord! what miseries are mortal men s. to EVELYN. **b.** This Region is very moist and subiect to raine 1604. **c.** He became s. to epileptic fits FROUDE. **2.** A man of my Kidney..that am as subiect to heate as butter SHAKS. **3.** A widdow, husbandles, subiect to feares SHAKS. **4.** Be subiect to no sight but thine, and mine SHAKS. **5.** All other business should be transacted by single judges s. to appeal 1883.

III. 1. Lying in the neighbourhood below a certain level, as that of a spectator; subjacent. *Obs.* or *arch.* late ME. **†2.** Forming the substratum or substance. Chiefly in *matter s.*: see SUBJECT-MATTER. –1744.

1. Long he them bore aboue the subiect plaine SPENSER.

Subject (sɒ̆bdʒe·kt), *v.* late ME. [– (O)Fr. *subjecter* or L. *subjectare*, frequent. of *subicere, subject-*; see prec.] **1.** *trans.* To make (persons, a nation or country) subject *to* a conquering or sovereign power; to bring into subjection *to* a superior; to subjugate. *Obs.* or *arch.* **b.** *to* the rule, government, power, or service of a superior 1552. **2.** To render submissive or dependent. late ME. **†3.** *intr.* To submit *to* –1720. **†4.** *trans.* To make subjacent *to*. Chiefly *pass.* –1807. **†b.** To lay before a person's eyes. Const. *to*. –1776. **5.** To lay open or expose to the incidence, occurrence, or infliction of, render liable *to* something. †Also *occas.* to render susceptible *to*, predispose *to*. 1549. **†6.** *pass.* To be attributed *to*, inhere *in* a subject (SUBJECT *sb.* II. 2) –1690. **7.** *Logic.* To make the subject of a proposition 1628. **8.** To bring under the operation of an agent, agency, or process; to submit *to* certain treatment; to cause to undergo or experience something 1794.

1. Men..consequently may s. themselves, if they think good, to a Monarch HOBBES. **b.** Subjecting them to an unheard of tyranny 1839. **2.** He.. was unwilling to s. himself to that which was exacted in polite society SCOTT. **4. b.** In one short view subjected to our eye Gods, Emp'rors, Heroes, Sages, Beauties, lie POPE. **5.** Clauses, subjecting the whole to forfeiture, in case the prohibition was infringed 1758. **8.** When people began to s. the principal historical religions to a critical analysis 1870.

Subjected (sɒ̆bdʒe·ktėd), *ppl. a.* 1586. [f. SUBJECT *v.* + -ED[1].] **1.** Placed or set underneath; underlying, subjacent. *Obs.* or *arch.* 1597. **2.** Reduced to a state of subjection; under the dominion or authority of another. Hence, submissive, obedient. 1586.

1. The hastning Angel..Led them direct, and down the Cliff as fast To the s. Plaine MILT. Hence **Subje·cted-ly** *adv.*, **-ness.**

Subjectify (sɒ̆bdʒe·ktifəi), *v.* 1868. [f. SUBJECT *sb.* + -FY.] *trans.* To identify with or absorb in the subject; to make subjective.

Subjection (sɒ̆bdʒe·kʃən). ME. [– (O)Fr. *subjection* or L. *subjectio*, *-ōn-*, f. *subject-*, pa. ppl. stem of *subicere*; see SUBJECT *sb.*, -ION.] **†1.** The act, state, or fact of exercising lordship or control; dominion, domination, control –1667. **b.** Phr. *In, into, †to, †under s.*: in, into, under the dominion or control of a superior power ME. **2.** The act or fact of being subjected, as under a monarch, etc.; the state of being subject to, or under the dominion of, another; hence *gen.*, subordination. late ME. **†3.** Submission; obedience; homage –1674. **4.** Subjugation (*rare*) 1597. **†5.** The condition of a subject, and the obligations pertaining to it –1635. **6.** Legal or contractual obligation or liability 1450. **†7.** The condition of being under some necessity or obligation; a duty or task; an 'infliction' –1719.

2. Now we read no where of the s. of one Bishop and his charge to an other 1641. The s. of women 1869. **6.** The obligation of civil s., whereby the inferior is constrained by the superior to act contrary to what his own reason and inclination would suggest BLACKSTONE. Hence **Subje·ctional** *a.* (*rare*) involving or based upon s.

Subjective (sɒ̆bdʒe·ktiv), *a.* (*sb.*) 1450. [– L. *subjectivus*, f. as prec.; see -IVE.] **†1.** Pertaining or relating to one who is subject; belonging to or characteristic of a political subject; hence, submissive, obedient –1706. **2.** Pertaining to the subject as that in which attributes inhere; inherent; hence, pertaining to the essence or reality of a thing; real, essential 1642. **3.** Relating to the thinking subject; proceeding from or taking place within the subject; having its source in the mind; (in the widest sense) belonging to the conscious life. (Correl. to OBJECTIVE *a.* 2 b.) 1707. **4.** Pertaining or peculiar to an individual subject or his mental operations; personal, individual 1767. **b.** *Art* and *Literature.* Expressing, bringing into prominence, or deriving its materials mainly from, the individuality of the artist or author 1840. **c.** Excessively introspective or reflective 1842. **d.** Existing in the mind only; illusory, fanciful 1869. **e.** *Physiol.* and *Path.* Due to internal causes and discoverable by oneself alone; said of sensations, symptoms, etc. 1855. **5.** Having the character of the subject of a sentence as expressing the doer of an action 1864. **6.** *absol.* with *the*: That which is subjective; rarely *sb.*, a subjective fact or thing 1817.

3. The motives to consider a proposition as true, are either objective, i.e. taken from an external object,..or..s., i.e. they exist only in the mind of him who judges 1801. *S. idealism*: see IDEALISM 1. *S. method*, the method of investigation which starts from conceptions and *a priori* assumptions, from which deductions are made. **4. b.** The whole s. scheme (damn the word!) of the poems I did not like E. FITZGERALD. **e.** The boomings in the ear and the s. buzz 1876. **5.** The confounding of s. with objective genitives 1864. Hence **Subje·ctive-ly** *adv.*, **-ness.**

Subjectivism (sɒ̆bdʒe·ktiviz'm). 1857. [f. prec. + -ISM.] **1.** The philosophical theory according to which all our knowledge is merely subjective and relative, and which denies the possibility of objective knowledge. **2.** The subjective method (see prec. 3) 1882. **3.** A theory or method based exclusively on subjective facts 1865. **b.** An ethical theory which conceives the aim of morality to be based upon, or to consist in, the attainment of states of feeling 1897. So **Subje·ctivist,** one who believes in or advocates s.

Subjectivity (sɒbdʒěkti·vĭti). 1821. [f. as prec. + -ITY.] **1.** Consciousness of one's perceived states. **b.** A conscious being 1830. **2.** The quality or condition of viewing things exclusively through the medium of one's own mind or individuality; hence, individuality, personality 1827. **b.** That quality of art which depends on the expression of the personality or individuality of the artist; the individuality of an artist as expressed in his work 1830. **3.** = SUBJECTIVISM 1. 1839. **4.** The quality or condition of resting upon subjective facts or mental representation; the character of existing in the mind only 1877.

4. The pure s. of Religion 1884.

Subjectivize (sɒ̆bdʒe·ktivəiz), *v.* 1868. [f. as prec. + -IZE.] *trans.* To make subjective.

Subjectivo- (sɒbdʒěktəi·vo), comb. form of SUBJECTIVE = subjective and.., subjectively.

Su·bjectless, *a.* 1803. [f. SUBJECT *sb.* + -LESS.] Having no subject or subjects.

Su·bject-ma·tter. 1542. [See SUBJECT *a.* III. 2, MATTER *sb.* II. 1. Earlier †*matter subject*, tr. late L. *subjecta materia* (Boethius), tr. Gr. ἡ ὑποκειμένη ὕλη (Aristotle).] **I. 1.** The matter operated upon in an art, a process, etc.; the matter out of which a thing is formed. **†2.** The ground, basis, or source *of* something –1683. **II. 1.** Material for discourse or expression in language; facts or ideas as constituting material *for* speech or written composition, occas. for artistic representation 1702. **2.** The subject or theme of a written or spoken composition 1598. **3.** The substance of a book, speech, etc. as dist. from the *form* or *style* 1633. **4.** That with which thought, deliberation, or discussion, a contract, undertaking, project, or the like is concerned; that which is treated of or dealt with 1657. **b.** That with which a science, law, etc. deals 1660. **c.** *Law.* The matter in dispute 1843.

1. Subject-matter for his satyrical muse, he never wanted 1759. **4.** If subject-matters more than one are included in the deed, mention them accordingly BENTHAM.

Subject-object. 1821. *Philos.* A subjective object; the immediate object of cognition presented to the mind as dist. from the real object; applied by Fichte to the ego.

Subjoin (sɒ̆bdʒoi·n), *v.* 1573. [In early use Sc., – Fr. †*subjoindre* – L. *subjungere*; see SUB- 27, JOIN *v.*] **1.** *trans.* To add at the end of a statement, argument, or discourse; *occas.*, to add (a note) at the bottom of a page. **2.** To place in immediate sequence or juxtaposition; to add as a concomitant or related element 1668.

1. According to your request I s. my Epitaph on Dr. Johnson COWPER.

Subjugate (sɒ·bdʒŭgeɪt), *v.* late ME. [–

subjugat-, pa. ppl. stem of L. *subjugare*, f. *sub-* SUB 1 g + *jugum* YOKE; see -ATE³.] **1.** *trans.* To bring under the yoke or into subjection; to reduce to the condition of a subject country or people. **2.** *transf.* and *fig.* To bring into bondage or under complete control; to make subservient or submissive 1589.

1. The special commissions given to the children of Israel to s. the land of Canaan 1845. **2.** Aristotle..had subjugated the minds of generation after generation D'ISRAELI. Hence **Su·bjugate** *pa. pple.* (*Obs.* or *arch.*) subjugated.

Subjugation (sʊbdʒŭgēⁱ·ʃən). 1658. [– late L. *subjugatio*, *-ōn-*, f. as prec.; see -ION.] **1.** The action of subjugating or condition of being subjugated. **2.** *transf.* and *fig.* Intellectual or moral subjection; reduction to a state of subserviency or submission 1785.

Subjugator (sʊ·bdʒŭgeⁱtəɹ). 1834. [– L. *subjugator*, f. as prec.; see -OR 2.] One who subjugates; a conqueror.

Subjunction (sŏbdʒʊ·ŋkʃən). Now *rare.* 1633. [– late L. *subjunctio*, *-ōn-*, f. *subjungere* SUBJOIN; see next, -ION.] The action of subjoining; the condition of being subjoined.

Subjunctive (sŏbdʒʊ·ŋktiv), *a.* and *sb.* 1530. [– Fr. *subjonctif*, *-ive* or late L. *subjunctivus*, f. *subjunct-*, pa. ppl. stem of L. *subjungere* SUBJOIN; see -IVE.] **A.** *adj. Gram.* That is subjoined or dependent 1583. **b.** Designating a mood (L. *modus subjunctivus*, Gr. ὑποτακτικὴ ἔγκλισις) the forms of which are employed to denote an action or a state as conceived (and not as a fact) and therefore used to express a wish, command, exhortation, or a contingent, hypothetical, or prospective event. Also, belonging to this mood, e.g. *s. present* or *present s.* (So named because it was regarded as specially appropriate to 'subjoined' or subordinate clauses.) 1530. **c.** Characteristic of what is expressed by the subjunctive mood; contingent, hypothetical 1837.

b. No s. mood existed in the common Sanskrit 1853.

B. *sb. Gram.* The subjunctive mood; a form of a verb belonging to the subjunctive mood 1532. Hence **Subju·nctively** *adv.* in the s. mood.

Su·bki:ngdom. 1825. [SUB- 7 b.] One of the primary groups into which the animal and vegetable kingdoms are divided.

Sublapsarian (sʊblæpsēᵊ·riăn), *sb.* and *a.* 1633. [f. mod.L. *sublapsarius*, f. L. *sub-* SUB- 17 + *lapsus* LAPSE; see -ARIAN.] *Theol.* **A.** *sb.* = INFRALAPSARIAN A. 1656. **B.** *adj.* = INFRALAPSARIAN B. 1633. Hence **Sublapsa·rianism,** the s. doctrine.

Sublate (sŏblēⁱ·t), *v.* 1548. [f. L. *sublat-*, f. *sub-* SUB- 25 + *lat-*, pa. ppl. stem of *tollere* take away.] **†1.** *trans.* To remove, take away –1672. **2.** *Logic.* To deny, contradict, disaffirm; opp. to POSIT 2. 1838. **3.** *Hegelian Philos.* (tr. G. *aufheben*, used by Hegel as having the opposite meanings of 'destroy' and 'preserve') 1865.

Sublation (sŏblēⁱ·ʃən). 1626. [– L. *sublatio*, *-ōn-*, f. as prec.; see -ION.] The act of taking away, removal. **b.** *Logic.* (See prec. 2.) 1864. **c.** *Hegelian Philos.* (See prec. 3.) 1865.

Su·b-lease, *sb.* 1826. [f. SUB- 9 (*a*).] A lease granted by one who is a lessee or tenant, an underlease.

Sub-lea·se, *v.* 1828. [f. SUB- 9 (*b*).] *trans.* To sub-let. So **Sub-lessee·**, one who holds or receives a sub-lease; **Sub-le·ssor,** one who grants a sub-lease.

Sub-le·t, *v.* 1766. [f. SUB- 9 (*b*) + LET *v.*¹] *trans.* To let (property, a tenement) to a subtenant; to lease out (work, etc.) under a subcontract; to underlet, sub-lease. Hence **Su·blet** *sb.* a sub-lease.

†Subleva·tion. 1556. [f. †*sublevate* (XVI–XVII) raise, lift up + -ION; see -ATION.] **1.** The action of raising or lifting; elevation; also, a particular point of elevation or height –1708. **2.** A rising, revolt –1699.

Su:b-lieute·nant. 1702. [SUB- 6.] **1.** An army officer ranking next below a lieutenant; formerly, an officer in certain regiments of the British Army, corresponding to the ensign in others. **2.** An officer in the British Navy ranking next below a lieutenant. Formerly called *mate.* 1804. Hence **Sub-lieute·nancy.**

Sublimable (sŏbləi·măb'l), *a.* Now *rare.* 1666. [f. SUBLIME *v.* + -ABLE.] Capable of sublimation or of being sublimated. Hence **Subli·mableness** 1661.

Sublimate (sʊ·blimĕt), *sb.* 1543. [– L. *sublimatum*, n. pa. pple. used subst. of *sublimare* (in med.L. (*Alch.*) sublimate, vaporize); see SUBLIME *v.*, -ATE¹.] **1.** A solid product of sublimation, *esp.* in the form of a compact crystalline cake 1626. **b.** *fig.* A refined or concentrated product 1683. **2.** 'Mercury s.'; mercuric chloride (bichloride or perchloride of mercury), a white crystalline powder, which acts as a violent poison 1543. **b.** Now usu. *corrosive s.* 1685. **c.** *attrib.* = containing or impregnated with corrosive s., as *s. gauze, lotion* 1753.

†Su·blimate, *pa. pple.* and *ppl. a.* late ME. [– L. *sublimatus*, pa. pple. of *sublimare*; see SUBLIME *v.*, -ATE².] **A.** *pa. pple.* Raised, elevated, exalted –1646. **B.** *ppl. a.* **1.** *Mercury s.*: = prec. 2. –1799. **2.** Refined, purified; elevated, sublime –1720.

Sublimate (sʊ·blimeⁱt), *v.* 1566. [– *sublimat-*, pa. ppl. stem of L. *sublimare*; see SUBLIME *v.*, -ATE³.] **†1.** *trans.* = SUBLIME *v.* 7. –1637. **2.** = SUBLIME *v.* 1. Now *rare.* 1591. **b.** *gen.* To act upon (a substance) so as to produce a refined product 1601. **†3.** = SUBLIME *v.* 2. –1644. **b.** *pass.* and *intr.* To be produced as the result of sublimation 1682. **4.** To exalt or elevate *to* a high or higher state 1599. **5.** = SUBLIME *v.* 5. 1624. **6.** To refine away *into* something unreal or non-existent; to reduce to unreality 1836.

2. b. The heat of Milton's mind may be said to s. his learning JOHNSON. **4.** Moral ideas in a thousand forms have been sublimated, enlarged and changed 1869. **5.** Their understandings were too direct to s. absurdities into mysteries FROUDE.

Sublimated (sʊ·blimeⁱtĕd), *ppl. a.* 1599. [f. prec. + -ED¹.] **1.** Produced by sublimation 1605. **2.** *fig.* Exalted, elevated; raised to a high degree of purity or excellence; lofty, sublime 1599. **3.** Of physical things: Purified, refined, rarefied (*rare*) 1676.

2. In words, whose weight best sute a s. straine DRAYTON. **b.** *Psychoanalysis.* (Cf. next, 3 c.) 1920. **3.** The s. air, diffusing itself by its mobility 1860.

Sublimation (sʊblimēⁱ·ʃən). late ME. [– (O)Fr. *sublimation* or med.L. *sublimatio*, *-ōn-* vaporization, 'sublimation', f. L. *sublimat-*; see SUBLIMATE *v.*, -ION.] **1.** The physical action or process of subliming or converting a solid substance by means of heat into vapour, which resolidifies on cooling. **b.** *Geol.* Applied to a (supposed) analogous process by which minerals are thrown up in a state of vapour from the interior of the earth and deposited nearer its surface 1829. **c.** (The condition of) being in the form of vapour as the result of sublimation 1808. **2.** A solid substance deposited as the result of the cooling of vapour arising from sublimation or a similar process 1646. **3.** Elevation to a higher state or plane of existence; transmutation into something higher, purer, or more sublime 1615. **b.** An elated or ecstatic state of mind 1816. **c.** *Psychoanalysis.* The action of directing an obstructed impulse away from its primitive aim to activities of a higher order 1916. **4.** The result of such elevation or transmutation; the highest stage or point (*of*) 1691.

†Sublimatory, *a.* 1605. [f. med.L. *sublimator* (XII) vaporizer, f. as prec.; see -OR 2, -ORY².] **1.** Suitable for subliming. **2.** Used in sublimation –1666.

Sublime (sŏbləi·m), *a.* and *sb.* 1586. [– L. *sublimis*, *-us*, f. *sub* SUB- + an element variously identified with *limen* threshold and *limus* oblique.] **A.** *adj.* **1.** Set or raised aloft, high up. *arch.* 1604. **b.** Of flight; only in fig. context with implication of senses 4–7. 1684. **c.** *Anat.* Of muscles: Lying near the surface, superficial 1855. **2.** Of buildings, etc.: Rising to a great height, lofty, towering. *arch.* 1635. **3.** Of lofty bearing or aspect; in a bad sense, haughty, proud. Chiefly *poet.* 1596. **†b.** Exalted in feeling, elated. MILT. **4.** Of ideas, truths, subjects, etc.: Belonging to the highest regions of thought, reality, or human activity 1634. **5.** Of persons, their attributes, feelings, actions: Standing high above others by reason of nobility or grandeur of nature or character; of high intellectual, moral, or spiritual level. Hence: Supreme, perfect; freq. *mod. colloq.* with ironical force 1643. **6.** Of language, style, or a writer: Expressing lofty ideas in a grand and elevated manner 1586. **7.** Of things in nature and art: Calculated to inspire awe, deep reverence, or lofty emotion, by reason of beauty, vastness, or grandeur 1700. **8.** Of rank, status: Very high, exalted. *arch.* 1702. **b.** As an honorific title of the Sultan or other potentates; also *transf.* of their actions. Cf. *Sublime Porte* (see PORTE). 1820. **c.** Refined; now used in trade names to designate the finest quality 1694.

1. Hee on the wings of Cherub rode s. On the Crystallin Skie MILT. **3.** The proud Souldan with ..countenance s. and insolent SPENSER. His fair large Front and Eye s. declar'd Absolute rule MILT. **4.** England's sublimer battle cry of 'Duty' 1853. **5.** Others more s...Have sunk, extinct in their refulgent prime SHELLEY. A s. piece of impertinence 1917. **6.** The s. Dante COLERIDGE. **7.** A very s. and stately Corinthian columne EVELYN. **8.** Meek Newton's self bends from his state s. GRAY.

B. *sb.* **1.** Now always with *the*: That which is sublime; the sublime part, character, property, or feature *of* 1679. **2.** With *the*: The highest degree or point, summit, or acme *of*. Now *rare.* 1813.

1. The S. of Nature is the Sky, the Sun, Moon, Stars, &c. POPE. The s. of Homer in the hands of Pope becomes bloated and tumid COWPER. **2.** With that s. of rascals your attorney BYRON. Hence **Subli·me-ly** *adv.*, **-ness.**

Sublime (sŏbləi·m), *v.* late ME. [– (O)Fr. *sublimer* or L. *sublimare* lift up, elevate (in med.L. = sense 1), f. *sublimis*; see prec.] **1.** *trans.* To subject (a substance) to the action of heat in a vessel so as to convert it into vapour, which is carried off and on cooling is deposited in a solid form. **2.** To cause to be given off by sublimation or an analogous process (e.g. volcanic heat); to carry over as vapour which resolidifies on cooling; to extract by or as by sublimation 1460. **3.** *intr.* **a.** To undergo this process; to pass from the solid to the gaseous state without liquefaction 1622. **b.** To be deposited in a solid form from vapour produced by sublimation 1682. **4.** *trans.* To raise to an elevated sphere or exalted state; to make (esp. morally or spiritually) sublime 1609. **5.** To transmute *into* something higher, nobler, or more excellent. Also *intr.* 1669. **6.** To raise up or aloft, to cause to ascend 1632. **b.** To cause (vapour, etc.) to ascend, as by the action of the sun's heat 1633. **†c.** To cause (the juices of a plant, etc.) to rise, and thereby rarefy and purify them –1712. **†7.** To exalt (a person), raise to a high office or degree –1638.

4. A judicious use of metaphors wonderfully raises, sublimes, and adorns oratory GOLDSM. The blest sherbet, sublimed with snow BYRON. A soul sublimed by an ideal above the region of vanity and conceit 1866. **5.** His very selfishness therefore is sublimed into public spirit MACAULAY. Hence **Subli·ming** *vbl. sb.*; freq. *attrib.* as *subliming-glass, -tube.*

Sublimed (sŏbləi·md), *ppl. a.* late ME. [f. prec. + -ED¹.] **1.** That has undergone the chemical process of sublimation; produced by sublimation. **†2.** *fig.* Elevated, exalted, sublime; purified, refined –1823.

1. *S. mercury*, mercury sublimate.

Sublimification (sŏbli:mifikēⁱ·ʃən). 1791. [f. as prec. + -FICATION.] The act or fact of making or being made sublime.

Subliminal (sŏbli·minăl), *a.* 1886. [f. SUB- 1 a + L. *limen, limin-* threshold + -AL¹, repr. G. *Unter der Schwelle*, sc. *des Bewusstseins* below the threshold of consciousness (Herbart, 1824).] *Psych.* Below the threshold (see LIMEN) of sensation or consciousness: said of states supposed to exist but not strong enough to be recognized. Also, pertaining to 'the s. self'. **b.** *absol.* That which is s.; the s. self 1901.

Sublimity (sŏbli·mĭti). 1526. [– L. *sublimitas*, *-tat-*, f. *sublimis*; see -ITY. Cf. (O)Fr. *sublimité.*] The state or quality of being sublime. **b.** An instance of this; a sublime thing or being 1642.

S. is produced by aggregation, and littleness by dispersion JOHNSON. Bursts of rapture and of unparalleled s. PALEY. **b.** He loved to talk of great sublimities in religion 1715.

Sublinear (sɒbli·niăɹ), *a.* 1777. **1.** [SUB- 20 c.] *Bot.* and *Zool.* Nearly linear. **2.** [SUB- 1 a.] Placed below a written or printed line 1868.

Sublingual (sɒbli·ŋgwăl), *a.* (*sb.*) 1661. [f. SUB- 1 a, b + L. *lingua* tongue + -AL¹.] **A.** *adj.* †**1.** *Med.* Of a pill, etc.: That is placed under the tongue to be sucked –1666. **2.** *Anat.* Situated under the tongue or on the under-side of the tongue 1694. **B.** *sb.* A s. gland, artery, etc. 1720.

2. *S. gland*, the smallest salivary gland situated at the side of the jaws and underneath the tongue. So *s. artery*, supplying the s. gland, side of the tongue, etc.

Sublunar (sʊ̆blⁱū·năɹ), *a.* and *sb.* 1610. [– late and med.L. *sublunaris*; see SUB- 1 a, LUNAR. Cf. Fr. *sublunaire*.] **A.** *adj.* = next A. Now *rare*. †**B.** *sb.* = next B –1686.

Sublunary (sɒ·blⁱunări, sʊ̆blⁱū·nări), *a.* (*sb.*) 1592. [f. as prec.; see -ARY², and cf. SUPERLUNARY, SUPRALUNARY.] **A.** *adj.* **1.** Existing or situated beneath the moon; lying between the orbit of the moon and the earth; hence, subject to the moon's influence 1613. **2.** Of or belonging to this world; earthly, terrestrial 1592. †**3.** Characteristic of this world and its affairs; mundane; material, gross; temporal, ephemeral –1814.

1. The s. Aereal Heavens 1692. **2.** The uncertainty of all s. things 1650. **3.** Can ye hope to finde rest in any of these s. contentments? 1648.

†**B.** *sb.* A s. thing or creature –1748.

Sub-man (sɒ·bmæn). 1921. [SUB- 5.] A human being of a subnormal type. (Opp. to SUPERMAN.)

Submarine (sɒ·bmărīn, *in the adj. also* sɒbmărī·n), *a.* and *sb.* 1648. [f. SUB- 1 a + MARINE, after med.L. *submarinus* adj. So Fr. *sous-marin*.] **A.** *adj.* **1.** Existing or lying under the surface of the sea 1668. **2.** Operating or operated, constructed or laid, intended for use under the surface of the sea 1648.

1. A sub-marine Plant 1668. S. volcanoes 1877. **2.** S. cables 1855. *S. boat*, a boat so designed that it can be submerged, and navigated when under water. *S. mine*, a charge of explosives moored at or beneath the surface of the sea and exploding on impact.

B. *sb.* **1.** A submarine creature; †a submarine plant, coral, etc. 1703. **2.** A submarine mine 1886. **3.** A submarine boat 1899. Hence **Su·bmarine** *v. trans.* to attack with a s.; **Su·bmarining** *vbl. sb.* **Su·bmariner.**

‖**Submaxilla** (sɒbmæksi·lă). 1891. [mod. L.; see SUB- 3 and MAXILLA.] *Anat.* The lower jaw or jaw-bone.

Submaxi·llary, *a.* (*sb.*) 1787. [f. SUB- 1 b + MAXILLARY.] *Anat.* **1.** Situated beneath the inferior maxilla; pertaining to the s. gland; also as *sb.* **2.** [f. prec.] Pertaining to the submaxilla 1884.

1. *S. gland*, a salivary gland situated on either side below the lower jaw.

Subme·dial, *a.* 1849. **1.** [SUB- 11, 20 d.] Near the middle or median line; almost medial. **2.** *Geol.* [SUB- 1 a.] Lying below the middle group of rocks 1855. So **Subme·dian** *a.* near or behind a median part.

Subme·diant. 1806. [SUB- 4 (*c*).] *Mus.* The sixth note of a scale, lying midway between the subdominant and the upper tonic.

Submerge (sʊ̆bmɜ̄·ɹdʒ), *v.* 1606. [– L. *submergere*; see SUB- 2, MERGE *v.*] **1.** *pass.* To be covered with water; to be sunk under water. **2.** *trans.* To cause to sink or plunge into water; to place under water 1611. **3.** *intr.* To sink or plunge under water; to undergo submersion: now freq. of submarines 1652.

1. Continents submerged, and..ocean bottoms lifted up to become mountains 1880. **2.** The shallow and tideless Baltic has scarcely a sounding that could s. St. Paul's Cathedral 1870. **3.** He submerged, and we lost sight of him 1863.

Submerged (sʊ̆bmɜ̄·ɹdʒd), *ppl. a.* 1799. [f. prec. + -ED¹.] Sunk under water; covered or overflowed with water; *Bot.* growing entirely under water. Now freq. of submarines.

S. tenth (fig.), that part of the population which is permanently in poverty and misery.

Submergence (sʊ̆bmɜ̄·ɹdʒĕns). 1832. [f. SUBMERGE *v.* + -ENCE.] The condition of being submerged or covered with water (also *Geol.*, with glacier ice); the state of being flooded or inundated. **b.** *fig.*, e.g. a being plunged in thought; the 'swamping' of one thing by another; a sinking out of sight or into obscurity 1872.

Submerse (sʊ̆bmɜ̄·ɹs), *v. rare.* 1837. [– *submers-*, pa. ppl. stem of L. *submergere* SUBMERGE.] *trans.* To submerge, drown. So **Submersed** (sʊ̆bmɜ̄·ɹst) *pa. pple.* and *ppl. a.* (now chiefly *Bot.*) submerged 1727.

Submersible (sʊ̆bmɜ̄·ɹsĭb'l), *a.* and *sb.* 1866. [f. SUBMERSE + -IBLE, prob. after Fr. *submersible*.] **A.** *adj.* That may be submerged, covered with, plunged into, or made to remain under water; *esp.* of a boat. **B.** *sb.* A submersible boat 1900.

Submersion (sʊ̆bmɜ̄·ɹʃən). 1572. [– late L. *submersio*, *-ōn-*, f. *submers-*; see SUBMERSE, -ION.] The action of submerging or condition of being submerged; plunging into, sinking under, or flooding with water; *occas.* drowning.

Subminister (sʊ̆bmi·nistəɹ), *v.* Now *rare.* 1601. [– L. *subministrare*; see SUB- 8, MINISTER *v.*] **1.** *trans.* To supply or furnish (sometimes in a secret manner). †**2.** *intr.* To minister *to* (lit. and fig.) –1692.

2. Our Passions..S. to the Best, and Worst of Purposes, at once 1692.

Submiss (sʊ̆bmi·s), *a.* 1570. [– L. *submissus*, pa. pple. of *submittere* SUBMIT *v.*] **1.** = SUBMISSIVE. *Obs.* exc. *arch.* †**2.** Of the voice, speech: Low, uttered in an undertone, subdued –1787.

1. With aw In adoration at his feet I fell S. MILT. A Simple, S., Humble Style 1702. Hence **Submi·ss-ly** *adv.*, **-ness** (*arch.*).

Submission (sʊ̆bmi·ʃən). late ME. [– OFr. *submission* or L. *submissio*, *-ōn-*, f. *submiss-*, pa. ppl. stem of *submittere* SUBMIT *v.*; see -ION.] **1.** *Law.* Agreement to abide by a decision or to obey an authority; reference to the decision or judgement of a (third) party; in recent use *spec.*, the referring of a matter *to* arbitration. **b.** In wider use, the act of submitting a matter *to* a person for decision or consideration 1911. **c.** The theory of a case put forward by an advocate 1922. **2.** The condition of being submissive; submissive conduct or bearing; deference; †*occas.* humiliation, abasement. *arch.* 1449. **b.** *pl.* Acts of deference or homage; demonstrations of submissiveness. *arch.* 1617. **3.** The action of submitting *to* an authority, a conquering or ruling power; the act of yielding to the claims of another, or surrendering to his will or government; the condition of having submitted 1482. †**4.** Used for: Admission, confession. SHAKS.

2. Luther..writeth to the Bishop of Rome letters full of s. 1560. †Phr. *With (great) s.*, subject to correction. **3.** To save his own life..by s. to the enemy HOBBES. *transf.* I learn'd at last s. to my lot COWPER. **4.** *Rom. and Jul.* III. i. 76.

Submissive (sʊ̆bmi·siv), *a.* 1586. [f. SUBMISSION, after *remission*/*remissive*, etc.] Disposed or inclined to submit; yielding to power or authority; marked by submission or humble and ready obedience.

A lowe submissiue reuerence SHAKS. Pious and s. prayers SCOTT. As little s. to lawful authority as his forefather FREEMAN. Hence **Submi·ssive-ly** *adv.*, **-ness.**

Submit (sʊ̆bmi·t), *v.* late ME. [– L. *submittere*, f. *sub-* SUB- 2 + *mittere* send, put.] **I. 1.** *refl.* and *intr.* To place oneself *under* the control of a person in authority or power; to become subject, surrender oneself, or yield *to* a person or his rule, etc. **2.** To surrender oneself *to* judgement, criticism, correction, a condition, treatment, etc.; to consent to undergo or abide by a condition, etc. late ME. †**b.** Const. *to* with inf. or gerund: To yield so far as *to do* so-and-so, consent *to*; *occas.* to condescend *to* –1852. †**3.** *refl.* To expose oneself *to* danger, etc. –1601.

1. When a man maketh his children, to s. themselves..to his government HOBBES. To thy Husband's will Thine shall s. MILT. **2.** Submitting to what seemd remediless MILT. **b.** Where the mortgagee submits to be redeemed 1818. **3.** *Jul. C.* I. iii. 47.

II. 1. *trans.* To bring under a certain control, government, or rule; to make subject, cause to yield *to* a person; to cause (a thing) to be subordinated *to* another. Now *rare.* late ME. **2.** To subject *to* a certain condition or treatment. Now *rare.* 1450. **b.** To subject *to* an operation or process 1815. **3.** To bring under a person's view, notice, or consideration; to refer *to* the decision or judgement of a person; to bring up or present *for* criticism, consideration, or approval 1560. **b.** In *Sc. Law*, to refer to arbitration 1799. **4.** To put forward as a contention or proposition; to urge or represent with deference (*that*..). Now freq. in legal parlance. 1818.

1. We submitte our reason to our fayth 1558. **2. b.** When alcohol is submitted to distillation 1857. **3.** Dare to be true, s. the rest to Heaven PRIOR. Such proceedings may be submitted for the sanction of Parliament 1905. **4.** Counsel,..submitted that the plaintiff was entitled to recover damages 1907.

†**III.** *trans.* To let or lay down, lower, sink, lay low; to place (one's neck) under the yoke or the axe –1807.

Will ye s. your necks, and chuse to bend The supple knee? MILT. Hence **Submi·tter,** one who submits.

Submo·ntane, *a.* 1819. **1.** [SUB- 1 a.] Passing under, or existing below, mountains. **2.** [SUB- 12 a.] Lying about the foot of mountains; belonging to the foot-hills of a range; belonging to the lower slopes of mountains 1830.

Submu·cous, *a.* 1684. [In XVII – mod.L. *submucosus* (Bonet).] **1.** *Path.* [SUB- 20.] Somewhat mucous; partly consisting of or attended by mucus; of an indistinctly mucous character. **2.** [SUB- 1 b.] **a.** *Anat.* Situated beneath the mucous membrane; pertaining to the areolar tissue so situated 1835. **b.** *Path.* and *Surg.* Occurring or introduced under the mucous membrane; affecting the submucous areolar tissue 1875.

Submu·ltiple, *a.* and *sb.* 1696. [f. SUB- 10 + MULTIPLE, after late L. *submultiplex* (Boethius).] **A.** *adj.* Of a ratio: In which the antecedent is an aliquot part of the consequent: the converse of *multiple*. Of a number, etc.: That is an aliquot part *of* another. Now *rare* or *Obs.* **B.** *sb.* A submultiple or aliquot part (*of*) 1758.

†**Subne·ct**, *v.* 1583. [– L. *subnectere*, f. *sub-* SUB- 2, 27 + *nectere* bind.] **1.** *trans.* To subjoin. Also *absol.* –1704. **2.** To fasten underneath. POPE.

Su·bnormal, *sb.* 1710. [– mod.L. *subnormalis* (sc. *linea* line); see SUB- 1, NORMAL.] *Geom.* That part of the axis of abscissas which is intercepted between the ordinate and the normal at any point of the curve.

Subno·rmal, *a.* 1890. [SUB- 14.] Less than normal, below the normal. Chiefly *Med.* Hence **Subnorma·lity** 1890.

Subocci·pital, *a.* 1733. [SUB- 1 b.] *Anat.* **1.** Situated under the occiput or below the occipital bone. **2.** Situated on the under surface of the occipital lobe of the brain 1889.

1. *S. nerve*, the first cervical nerve.

Subo·ctave. 1659. †**1.** [SUB- 10.] An eighth part (*rare*) –1705. **2.** *Mus.* [SUB- 4 (*b*).] The octave below a given note. Also *attrib.* in *s. coupler*. 1659.

Su·b-o:fficer. 1618. [SUB- 6.] A subordinate officer.

Subope·rcular, *a.* (*sb.*) 1854. [f. next + -AR¹.] *Ichth.* Designating a bone in the lower part of the operculum of a fish; pertaining to the suboperculum.

‖**Suboperculum** (sɒbopɜ̄·ɹkiŭlɒ̆m). 1834. [mod.L., f. *sub-* SUB- 2 b (*a*) + OPERCULUM.] **1.** *Ichth.* The bone situated below the operculum in the gill-cover of a fish. **2.** *Anat.* The part of an occipital orbital gyre which overlies the insula of Reil 1889.

Subo·rbital, *a.* and *sb.* 1822. [SUB- 1 b.] **A.** *adj.* Situated below or under the orbit of the eye; infraorbital. **B.** *sb.* A s. structure; a s. bone, cartilage, nerve, etc. 1834. So **Subo·rbitar, -o·rbitary** *adjs.* and *sbs.*

Su·border. 1826. **1.** [SUB- 7 b.] *Zool.* and *Bot.* A subdivision of an order; a group next below an order in a classification of animals or plants. **2.** [SUB- 5 b.] *Arch.* A secondary or subordinate 'order' in a structure of arches 1890.

Subordinacy (sʊ̆bǭ·ɹdinăsi). 1627. [f. SUBORDINATE *a.*; see -ACY.] The state of being subordinate; subordination.

Lifted out of s. into supremacy 1893.

Subo·rdinal, *a.* 1870. [f. SUBORDER, after *order/ordinal.*] Of, pertaining to, or of the rank of, a suborder.

Subo·rdinary. 1791. [f. SUB- 5 + ORDINARY *sb.*] *Her.* A charge of frequent occurrence but considered of less importance than an ordinary; a subordinate ordinary.

Subordinate (sɒbǭ·ɹdinĕt), *a.* and *sb.* 1456. [– med.L. *subordinatus*, pa. pple. of *subordinare*; see next, -ATE[2,1].] **A.** *adj.* **1.** Belonging to an inferior rank, grade, class, or order, and hence dependent upon the authority or power of another. So of power, position, etc. **2.** Of things, material and immaterial: Dependent upon or subservient *to* the chief or principal thing. Chiefly in techn. use. 1588. **3.** Of inferior importance; not principal or predominant; secondary, minor 1661. **4.** *Geol.* Underlying; subjacent 1833.

1. The s. officer must receive the commands of his superior GOLDSM. In his s. official position 1862. **2.** A S. End is that which is referred to some farther End 1697. When a s. clause acts the part of object to a verb 1844. **3.** My expectations from it were of a s. nature only 1786. **4.** Consisting.. partly of clay and sand, with s. beds of lignite 1833.

B. *sb.* **1.** A subordinate person; one in a position of subordination; one who is under the control or orders of a superior 1640. **2.** A subordinate thing, matter, etc. 1839.

1. What the jurisdiction of bishops over their subordinates is to be BURKE. Hence **Subo·rdinate-ly** *adv.*, **-ness** (*rare*).

Subordinate (sŏbǭ·ɹdineit), *v.* 1597. [– *subordinat-*, pa. ppl. stem of med.L. *subordinare* (XIV), f. *sub-* SUB- 2 + *ordinare* ORDAIN; see -ATE[3].] **1.** *trans.* To bring into a subordinate position; to render subordinate, dependent, or subservient. Now *rare* with personal obj. **2.** To place in a lower order, rank, etc.; to make secondary or consider as of less importance or value 1624. **3.** *Arch.* To arrange (arches) in 'orders' 1878.

1. He to whose will our wills are to be subordinated CARLYLE. **2.** The teacher, who subordinates prudence to virtue COLERIDGE.

Subo·rdinating, *ppl. a.* 1751. [-ING[2].] That subordinates; involving subordination. *S. conjunction*, (Gram.) one that serves to join a subordinate to a principal clause.

Subordination (sŏbǭɹdinēi·ʃən). 1616. [– Fr. *subordination* or med.L. *subordinatio*; see SUBORDINATE *v.*, -ION.] **1.** The arrangement *of* persons or things in a series of successively dependent ranks or degrees. Also, †an instance of this. Now *rare* or *Obs.* †**b.** A rank in a graded series –1751. **2.** The condition of being subordinate, inferior, or dependent; subjection, subservience 1651. **b.** *Gram.* The dependence of one clause upon another 1857. **3.** The condition of being subservient *to* some end, object, or need 1673. **4.** The condition of being duly submissive to authority or discipline; submission or subjection to the rule of a superior officer or the government of a higher power 1736. **5.** *Arch.* The act or fact of forming arches into 'orders' 1878.

1. The s. of superior and vassal having soon ceased to be strict 1758. **b.** An insolent leveller.. eager.. to confound the subordinations of society JOHNSON. **2.** Their independent spirit disdained the yoke of s. GIBBON. **3.** A certain s. of individual actions to social requirements 1862. **4.** S. must be preserved in the Army 1760. Hence **Subordina·tionism** *Theol.*, the doctrine that the Second and Third Persons of the Trinity are inferior, in order or in essence, to the First Person.

Subo·rdinative, *a. rare.* 1642. [f. SUBORDINATE *v.* + -IVE.] Tending to subordinate, involving subordination. **b.** *Gram.* Containing a subordinate clause or clauses 1857.

Suborn (sŏbǭ·ɹn), *v.* 1534. [– L. *subornare*, f. *sub* SUB- 24 + *ornare* equip.] **1.** *trans.* To bribe, induce or procure (a person) by underhand or unlawful means *to* commit a misdeed. When used *absol.* often = to draw away from allegiance, corrupt the loyalty of. **2.** *spec.* To bribe or unlawfully procure (a person) *to* make accusations or give evidence; to induce *to* give false testimony or *to* commit perjury. Also, to procure (evidence) by such unlawful means. 1557. **b.** To procure the performance or execution of (a thing) by bribery or other corrupt means 1817. †**3.** To prepare, provide, or procure, *esp.* in a secret, stealthy, or underhand manner –1721. †**4.** To furnish, equip, adorn –1605. †**5.** To introduce or bring to one's aid with a sinister motive –1677.

1. Different persons were suborned to cut off the duke by assassination 1783. **2.** Then they suborned men, which sayd, We haue heard him speake blasphemous wordes *N.T.* (Geneva) *Acts* 6:11. **3.** In a golden boule She then subornd a potion CHAPMAN. Hence **Subo·rner.**

Subornation (sɒbǫɹnēi·ʃən). 1528. [– med. L. *subornatio*, f. *subornat-*, pa. ppl. stem of L. *subornare*; see prec., -ION.] **1.** The act of inducing or procuring a person to commit an evil action, by bribery, corruption, or the like; an instance of this. Also, †underhand action. 1548. **2.** The act of procuring a person to give false evidence. Also, an instance of this. 1528.

1. Without Bribery, or S., he had attain'd to the dignity of the Purple 1670. **2.** A perjury as bloody as that of Oates and Bedlow;—a s. as audacious BURKE. Phr. *S. of perjury*, the act of procuring a witness on oath to commit perjury.

‖**Subpœna** (sŏbpī·nă, sŏpī·nă), *sb.* late ME. [Law-L., = L. *sub pœna* under a penalty, being the first words of the writ.] *Law.* **1.** A writ issued by chancery commanding the presence of a defendant to answer the matter alleged against him. Also *writ of s.* **2.** A writ issued from a court of justice commanding the presence of a witness under a penalty for failure 1467. **b.** *attrib.* in *s. office* 1688. Hence ‖**Subpœ·na** *v. trans.* to serve with a writ of s.; to summon as a witness in a court of justice.

Subpo·lar, *a.* 1826. [Cf. Sp. *subpolar.*] **1.** [SUB- 12 b.] Adjacent to the poles or polar sea. **2.** [SUB- 1 a.] Beneath the pole of the heavens 1876.

Su·b-pre:fect. 1845. [f. SUB- 6 + PREFECT, after Fr. *sous-préfet.*] An assistant or deputy prefect; *spec.* an administrative official of a department of France immediately subordinate to the prefect; the administrator of a province of Peru. Hence **Subprefe·cture,** the office of a s., a division of a prefecture.

Su·bpri:ncipal. 1597. **1.** [SUB- 6.] A vice-principal of a university, etc. **2.** *Arch.* [SUB- 5 b.] An auxiliary rafter or principal brace 1842. **3.** *Mus.* [SUB- 13.] An open diapason sub-bass 1876.

Su·bpri:or. ME. [– OFr. *subprieur*, med. L. *subprior*, var. of *supprior*; see SUB- 6 and PRIOR *sb.*] A prior's assistant and deputy. So **Su·bpri:oress.**

Su·bre:gion. 1864. [SUB- 7 c.] A division or subdivision of a region, *esp.* of a geographical region, with ref. to the distribution of animals.

Subreption (sŏbre·pʃən). 1600. [– L. *subreptio, -ōn-*, f. *subrept-*, pa. ppl. stem of *subripere*, f. *sub-* SUB- 24 + *rapere* snatch. Cf. SURREPTION[1].] **a.** *Eccl. Law.* The suppression of the truth or concealment of facts with a view to obtaining a faculty, dispensation, etc. (Opp. to *obreption.*) **b.** A fallacious or deceptive representation; an inference derived from such a misrepresentation 1865.

Subreptitious (sɒbrepti·ʃəs), *a.* 1610. [f. L. *subrepticius, -tius*, f. as prec.; see -OUS, -ITIOUS[1].] **a.** *Law.* Obtained by subreption. **b.** Clandestine, SURREPTITIOUS. Hence **Subrepti·tiously** *adv.* by subreption.

Subreptive (sŏbre·ptiv), *a.* 1611. [– late L. *subreptivus*, f. as prec.; see -IVE.] Surreptitious; *spec.* in *Kantian Philos.*

Subrogate (sɒ·brŏgeit), *v.* 1538. [– *subrogat-*, pa. ppl. stem of L. *subrogare*, f. *sub-* SUB- 26 + *rogare* ask, offer for election; see -ATE[3].] †**1.** *trans.* To elect or appoint in the place of another; to substitute in an office –1728. **2.** To substitute (a thing) for another. Now *rare.* 1548. **3.** *Law.* To put (a person) *in the place of*, or substitute (him) *for*, another in respect of a right or claim; to cause to succeed *to* the rights of another; see next 2. 1818.

Subrogation (sɒbrŏgēi·ʃən). late ME. [– late and med.L. *subrogatio, -ōn-*, f. as prec.; see -ION. Cf. Fr. *subrogation* (XV).] †**1.** Substitution –1681. **2.** *Law.* The substitution of one party for another as a creditor; the process by which a person who pays a debt for which another is liable succeeds to the rights of the creditor to whom he pays it; the right of such succession 1710.

Sub rosa: see ‖SUB.

Subscapular (sɒbskæ·piŭlăɹ), *a.* 1831. [– mod.L. *subscapularis*; see next.] **a.** *Anat.* Situated below, or on the under surface of, the scapula. **b.** *Path.* Occurring under the scapula 1897.

a. *S. muscle* = next. So **Subsca·pulary** *a.* 1705.

‖**Subscapularis** (sɒ:bskæpiŭlēə·ris). 1704. [mod.L., see SUB 1 d and SCAPULAR.] *Anat.* In full *s. muscle*: A muscle originating in the venter of the scapula and inserted in the lesser tuberosity of the humerus.

Subscribable (sŏbskrəi·băb'l), *a.* 1824. [f. next + -ABLE.] Capable of being subscribed.

Subscribe (sŏbskrəi·b), *v.* late ME. [– L. *subscribere*, f. *sub* SUB- 2 + *scribere* write.] **1.** *trans.* To write (one's name or mark) on, orig. at the bottom of, a document, esp. as a witness or consenting party; to sign (one's name) *to.* Now *rare.* **b.** To write, set down, or inscribe below or at the conclusion of something. Now *rare.* 1579. †**c.** To put (a person) down *for* so much. SHAKS. **2.** With compl.: **a.** *refl.* To put oneself down as so-and-so, at the foot of a letter or other document. Now *rare.* 1678. †**b.** *trans.* To 'write (a person) down' so-and-so. SHAKS. **3.** To sign one's name to; to signify assent or adhesion to, by signing one's name; to attest by signing 1440. †**4.** To give one's assent or adhesion to; to countenance, support, favour, sanction, concur in –1781. †**5.** To sign away, yield up. SHAKS. **6.** *intr.* To write one's signature; *esp.* to put one's signature *to* in token of assent, approval, or testimony; to sign one's name as a witness, etc. 1535. **7.** To give one's assent *to* a statement, opinion, proposal, scheme, or the like; to express one's agreement, concurrence, or acquiescence 1549. **b.** To agree or be a party *to* a course of action or condition of things; to give approval, sanction, or countenance *to*; also *occas.* to consent or engage *to*; to agree *that*... Now *rare* or *Obs.* 1566. **8.** To give one's adhesion or allegiance, make one's submission *to* another; *gen.* to submit, yield, give in. Now *rare* or *Obs.* 1590. †**b.** To submit or subject oneself *to* law or rule; to conform or defer *to* a person's will, etc. –1772. †**c.** To admit one's inferiority or error, confess oneself in the wrong. SHAKS. **9.** Const. *to*: **a.** To admit or concede the force, validity, or truth of. Now *rare* or *Obs.* 1591. †**b.** To make acknowledgement or admission of. SHAKS. †**10.** To vouch or answer *for* a person. SHAKS. **11.** *trans.* To promise over one's signature to pay (a sum of money) *for* shares in an undertaking, or *to* or *towards* a particular object; to undertake to contribute (money) in support of any object. Also, to take up (shares). 1640. **12.** *absol.* or *intr.* To undertake to contribute money *to* a fund, *to* a society, party, etc. 1642. **b.** *To s. for*: to put one's name down as a purchaser of shares, a periodical, newspaper, or book, etc. 1711. **13.** *Book trade.* **a.** Of a bookseller: To agree beforehand to take (a certain number of copies of a book); also *s. for.* Also occas. *intr.* Of a book: To be taken by the trade. 1867. **b.** Of a publisher: To offer (a book) to the trade 1910.

1. They must all s. their names as witnesses BLACKSTONE. **c.** *Rich. II*, I. iv. 50. **2. b.** *Much Ado* V. ii. 59. **3.** He subscribed the will as a witness in the same room 1818. **4.** *Tr. & Cr.* II. iii. 156. **6.** He proceeded in Divinity, having..subscribed to the 34 Articles WOOD. **7.** If ye all doo s. to this opinion 1549. **b.** Shall..I..tamely s. to my own degradation? 1844. **8.** *Tr. & Cr.* IV. v. 105. **b.** Sir, to your pleasure humbly I s. SHAKS. **c.** I will s., and say I wrong'd the Duke SHAKS. **9. a.** I must warmly s. to the learning..of Mr. Hume's history GOLDSM. **11.** The large sum of 10,000*l.* was subscribed at once 1871. **12.** I s. to the club here DICKENS. **b.** The maids of honour..are teazing others to s. for the book SWIFT. **13. a.** Of Mr. Disraeli's 'Lothair' 1500 copies were at first subscribed 1873.

Subscriber (sŏbskrəi·bəɹ). 1599. [f. prec. + -ER[1].] **1.** One who subscribes, or affixes his signature *to*, a letter or document, articles of religion, etc. **2.** One who subscribes *to* a specified object or institution, the funds of a company, etc. *for* shares, a book, etc. 1697.

Subscript (sɒ·bskript), *sb.* and *a.* 1704. [– L. *subscriptus*, pa. pple. of *subscribere* SUBSCRIBE.] **A.** *sb.* **1.** That which is written underneath; a writing at the bottom or end of a document, etc.; a signature. **2.** A subscript letter or symbol 1901. **B.** *adj.* Written underneath; chiefly in *iota s.* (see IOTA 1), the small ι written underneath in ᾳ, ῃ, ῳ 1861.

Subscription (sɒ̆bskri·pʃən). 1450. [– L. *subscriptio, -ōn-*, f. *subscript-*, pa. ppl. stem of *subscribere* SUBSCRIBE; see -ION.] **1.** A piece of writing at the end of a document, *e.g.* the concluding clause or formula of a letter with the writer's signature, the colophon of a book, etc. †**b.** Something written or inscribed underneath, *e.g.* a number written under another, an inscription or title underneath –1814. **2.** A signature, signed name 1483. **3.** A signed declaration or statement; *Rom. Antiq.*, a rescript signed by the emperor. *Obs.* exc. *Hist.* 1599. **4.** The action or an act of affixing a signature; the signing *of* one's name or *of* a document 1492. **5.** A declaration of one's assent *to* articles of religion, or some formal declaration of principles, etc. by signing one's name; *spec.* in the Church of England, assent to the Thirty-nine Articles 1588. †**6.** Assent, approval. Also, an instance of this. –1650. †**b.** Submission, allegiance. SHAKS. **7.** The action or an act of subscribing money to a fund or for stock; the raising of a sum of money for a certain object by collecting contributions from a number of people; †a scheme for raising money in this way. Also, an undertaking or agreement to subscribe so much. 1647. **8.** A contribution of money for a specified object; *spec.* the fixed sum promised or required as a periodical contribution by a member of a society, etc. to its funds, or for the purchase of a periodical publication, or in payment for a book published 'by subscription' 1679. **b.** A sum of money subscribed by several parties; a fund. Now chiefly in phr. *to raise, get up a s.*, U.S. *to make* or *take up a s.*, to make a collection. 1730. †**c.** *spec.* A share in a commercial undertaking or a loan. Also *collect. sing.* –1762. **9.** *Book-trade.* **a.** A method of bringing out a book, by which the publisher or author undertakes to supply copies of the book at a certain rate to those who agree to take copies before publication. Freq. in phr. *by s.* 1706. **b.** (*a*) The taking up of a book by the trade; (*b*) The offering of a book to the trade. 1895. **c.** *U.S.* The house-to-house sale of books by canvassers 1880.

1. The s. of the first epistle to the Corinthians states that it was written from Philippi PALEY. **6. b.** I neuer gaue you Kingdome, call'd you Children; You owe me no s. SHAKS.

attrib. and *Comb.* in the sense 'supported by subscription', as **s.** *concert*; **s. book,** (*a*) a book containing the names of subscribers to any object (with the amounts of their subscriptions); (*b*) *U.S.* a book, sold from house to house by canvassers; **-list,** a list of subscribers' names (often with the amounts of their subscriptions); **s. price,** (*a*) the price at which a book is offered before publication to those who promise to take copies; (*b*) the price at which a periodical publication is supplied to those who promise to take so many numbers; **s. room,** a room (e.g. belonging to a club, an exchange) which is open to subscribers only.

Subscriptive (sɒ̆bskri·ptiv), *a. rare.* 1748. [f. prec., after *description/descriptive*, etc.] **1.** Pertaining to the 'subscription' of a letter. **2.** Pertaining to the subscribing of money 1897.

Subsecive (sɒ·bsĭsiv), *a.* Now *Obs.* or *rare.* 1613. [– L. *subsecivus* cut off and left remaining, f. *sub* SUB- 25 + *secare* cut; see -IVE.] Remaining over, spare: chiefly in *s. hours.*

Su·bsection. 1621. [f. SUB- 7 + SECTION.] A division of a section. **b.** *Nat. Hist.* A subordinate division of a section or group 1826. Hence **Su·bsectioned** *a.* divided into subsections.

‖**Subsellium** (sɒ̆bse·liɒ̆m). *Pl.* **-ia** (-iă). 1701. [L., f *sub* SUB- 3 + *sella* seat.] **1.** *Rom. Antiq.* A seat in an amphitheatre. **2.** *Church Arch.* = MISERICORD 2 c. 1806. So ‖**Subse·lla** (in sense 2).

Subsequence (sɒ·bsĭkwĕns). 1500. [f. next; see -ENCE.] **1.** That which is subsequent; a subsequent event; the sequel. **2.** The condition or fact of being subsequent 1668.

2. With such an order of precedence and s. as their natures will bear 1668.

Subsequent (sɒ·bsĭkwĕnt), *a.* and *sb.* 1460. [– (O)Fr. *subséquent* or L. *subsequens-, -ent-*, pr. pple. of *subsequi*, f. *sub-* SUB- III + *sequi* follow.] **A.** *adj.* **1.** Following in order or succession; coming or placed after, *esp.* immediately after. **2.** Following or succeeding in time; existing or occurring after, *esp.* immediately after, something expressed or implied; coming or happening later 1503.

1. But more of this in a s. chapter SCOTT. **2.** The day from which all his s. years took their colour MACAULAY. It was long s. to the death of both his parents 1871. Phr. *Condition s.*: see CONDITION *sb.*

†**B.** *sb.* A person or thing that follows or comes after another –1824. Hence **Subseque·ntial** *a.*, **-ly** *adv.* **Su·bsequently** *adv.*

Subserous (sɒ̆bsīᵊ·rəs), *a.* 1833. [f. SUB- + SEROUS.] **1.** [SUB- 1 b.] **a.** *Anat.* Situated or occurring beneath a serous membrane, as *s. tissue.* **b.** *Path.* Affecting the subserous tissue. **2.** [SUB- 20 b.] Somewhat serous 1891.

Subserve (sɒ̆bsɔ̄·ɹv), *v.* 1619. [– L. *subservire*, f. *sub-* SUB- 8 + SERVE *v.*] **1.** *intr.* To be subservient *to.* **2.** *trans.* To be instrumental in furthering or assisting (a purpose, object, action, function, or condition); to promote or assist by supplying an instrument or means 1677. **b.** To be instrumental in furthering the purpose, interest, or function of (a person or thing). *rare.* 1661. †**3.** *intr.* To act in a subordinate position. MILT.

1. It subserves..to the Trade of this Place 1759. **2.** It might s. the double purpose of ridding us of a nuisance, and relieving the public pressure 1815. **b.** Portions of bone are also developed to protect and otherwise s. the organs of the senses 1854. **3.** Not made to rule, But to s. where wisdom bears command MILT.

Subservience (sɒ̆bsɔ̄·ɹviĕns). 1676. [f. next; see -ENCE.] **1.** The condition or quality of being serviceable, as a means *to* an end. **2.** A condition of subordination or subjection *to* another. Now *rare* exc. as implied in 3. 1701. **3.** Subservient behaviour, attitude, or conduct; servile subordination, submissiveness, obsequiousness 1819.

1. To order al means and affaires in s. to his end and designe 1677. **3.** A young Persian monarch, corrupted by universal s. around him 1849. So **Subse·rviency** 1651.

Subservient (sɒ̆bsɔ̄·ɹviĕnt), *a.* 1632. [– L. *subserviens, -ent-*, pr. pple. of *subservire*; see SUBSERVE, -ENT.] **1.** Being of use or service as an instrument or means; serviceable. **2.** Acting or serving in a subordinate capacity; subordinate, subject 1641. **3.** Of persons, their actions, etc.: Slavishly submissive; truckling, obsequious 1794.

1. Scarce ever reading any thing which he did not make s. in one kinde or other 1661. Every particular affection..is s. to self-love 1729. **2.** Can we think he will be patient thus to be made s. to his enemy? 1667. **3.** The lawyers had been s. beyond all other classes to the Crown GREEN. Hence **Subse·rviently** *adv.*

Subside (sɒ̆bsəi·d), *v.* 1681. [– L. *subsidere*, f. *sub-* SUB- 2 + *sidere* sit down.] **1.** *intr.* To sink down, fall to the bottom, precipitate. **2.** To sink to a low or lower level, *esp.* of liquids or soil sinking to the normal level; (of valleys) to form a depression; (of a swelling or something inflated) to be reduced so as to become flat 1706. **b.** Of a mass of earth, etc.: To fall or give way as the result of dynamic disturbance, etc. 1773. **c.** Of persons: To sink down *into* or *on to* a chair, etc. 1879. **3.** Of the sea, wind, storm: To sink to rest, abate 1721. **4.** Of strong feeling, excitement, clamour, and the like: To cease from agitation, fall *into* a state of quiet or of less violence or activity 1700. **b.** Of a condition: To die down, pass away, wear off. Of an action: To be discontinued. 1751. **5.** Of persons: To fall *into* an inactive or less active or efficient state 1728. **b.** To cease from activity *esp.* to lapse into silence 1871. **6.** To be merged *in*; to pass *into* (rare) 1781.

2. The waters of the Nile had subsided 1863. **3.** The wind had already subsided 1839. **4.** Our desire of revenge had by this time subsided EVELYN. The hubbub gradually subsides 1892. **5. b.** Being told that he must be kept quiet or be arrested he subsided 1880.

Subsidence (sɒ·bsidĕns, sɒ̆bsəi·dĕns). 1646. [– L. *subsidentia* sediment, f. *subsidere* SUBSIDE; see -ENCE.] †**1.** A sediment, precipitate –1890. **2.** The settling (of solid or heavy things) to the bottom, formation of sediment, precipitation 1656. **3.** The sinking (of liquids) to a normal or lower level; also, a fall in the level of ground 1669. **b.** A fall in rhythm or accent 1824. **4.** A sinking *into* inactivity or quiescence 1731. **5.** (orig. *Geol.*) A gradual lowering or settling down of a portion of the earth due to dynamic causes, mining operations, or the like 1802. **6.** *attrib.*, applied to vessels in which liquids are put in order to precipitate their suspended solid matter 1858.

2. Separate the liquid part by filtration or by s. 1800. **4.** A decided s. of her animosity DICKENS. So **Subsidency** (stress var.).

Subsidiary (sɒ̆bsi·diări), *a.* and *sb.* 1543. [– L. *subsidiarius*, f. SUBSIDIUM; see -ARY[1].] **1.** Serving to help, assist, or supplement; auxiliary, tributary, supplementary. (Chiefly of things). **b.** Of a stream: Tributary. Similarly of a valley. 1834. **2.** Subordinate, secondary 1831. **3.** †**a.** Consisting of a subsidy or subsidies –1640. **b.** Depending on a subsidy or subsidies: in *s. treaty* 1755. **c.** Maintained by subsidies 1802.

2. *S. company*, a company controlled by another holding more than 50 per cent of its issued share capital.

B. *sb.* A subsidiary thing; something which furnishes assistance or additional supplies; an aid, auxiliary. Now *rare.* 1603. **b.** An assistant 1807. **c.** *Stock Exch.* A subsidiary company 1898. **d.** *Polo.* A subsidiary goal 1903.

‖**Subsidium** (sɒ̆bsi·diɒ̆m). *Pl.* **-ia** (iă). 1640. [L.; see SUBSIDY.] A help, aid, subsidy.

Subsidize (sɒ·bsidəiz), *v.* 1795. [f. next + -IZE.] **1.** *trans.* **a.** To make a payment for the purpose of securing the services of (mercenary or alien troops). **b.** To furnish (a country, nation, princes) with a subsidy for the purpose of securing their assistance or their neutrality in war 1797. **2.** *transf.* **a.** To secure the services of by payment or bribery 1815. **b.** To support by grants of money: now *esp.* of the government or some central authority contributing to the upkeep of an institution, etc. 1828.

1. a. He..subsidized a corps of 8000 Swiss 1838. **b.** To s. one power against another 1860. **2. a.** To s. a venal pen 1815. **b.** The schools..have been subsidised by grants from the county magistrates 1885.

Subsidy (sɒ·bsĭdi), *sb.* late ME. [– AFr. *subsidie* = (O)Fr. *subside* – L. *subsidium* reserve of troops, support, assistance, rel. formally to (rare) *subsidēre*, f. *sub* SUB- 5 + *sedēre* SIT.] **1.** Help, aid, assistance. Also with *a* and *pl. Obs.* or *arch.* **2.** *Eng. Hist.* A pecuniary aid granted by parliament to the sovereign to meet special needs. late ME. **b.** *transf.* A pecuniary aid exacted by a prince, lord, etc. 1450. **3.** A grant or contribution of money. **a.** *gen.* late ME. **b.** A sum of money paid by one country to another for the promotion of war or the preservation of neutrality 1668. **c.** Financial aid furnished by a state or a public corporation in furtherance of an undertaking or the upkeep of a thing 1867.

2. The perils of her reign drove her at rare intervals to the demand of a s. 1874. **3. a.** A S. for a Prince in Misfortune STEELE. **c.** Subsidies as a means of restoring American shipping 1882. Hence **Su·bsidy** *v. trans.* and *intr.* to subsidize. CARLYLE.

†**Subsi·gn,** *v.* 1572. [– L. *subsignare*, f. *sub* SUB- 2 + *signare* SIGN *v.*[1]] **1.** *trans.* To sign one's name under, subscribe, attest *with* one's signature or mark. Also, to subscribe (one's name). –1700. **2.** *absol.* or *intr.* To append one's signature; (with clause) to testify *that*... –1653. So †**Subsigna·tion,** signature; affixing a seal –1726.

Subsist (sɒ̆bsi·st), *sb.* 1855. [Short for SUBSISTENCE.] Payment of wages on account. *attrib.*: **s. money,** = SUBSISTENCE MONEY 1; **s. week,** a week for which s. money is paid.

Subsist (sɒ̆bsi·st), *v.* 1549. [– L. *subsistere* stand still, stand firm, cease, etc., f. *sub-* SUB- 25 + *sistere* stand.] **I. 1.** *intr.* To have an existence as a reality; to exist as a substance or entity. **2.** To have its being or existence *in* a certain manner, form, or state, or *by* a certain condition. *Obs.* or *arch.* 1594. **3.** †**a.** *Philos.* To exist *in* a substance or *in* accidents –1821. **b.** *gen.* To consist, lie, or reside *in* some specified thing, circumstance, fact, etc. 1633. **4.** To preserve its existence or continue to exist; to remain in existence, use, or force 1600. †**b.** To continue in a condition or position; to remain (so-and-so) –1650. †**5.** Of physical objects: To be or live in a certain place or state –1813. **6.** Of a condition or quality: To exist 1729.

1. Matter abstractly consider'd cannot have subsisted eternally BENTLEY. **2.** By ceaseless action all that is subsists COWPER. **4.** So long as braine and heart Haue facultie by nature to s. SHAKS. Which charter subsists to this day, and is called Magna Charta CHESTERF. **6.** Granted upon a condition which did not yet s. 1777.

II. †**1.** To make a stand, stand firm, hold out –1726. †**2.** To cease, stop at a certain point –1680.

1. Firm we s., yet possible to swerve MILT.

III. 1. *trans.* To provide sustenance for; to maintain, support, keep: said of provisions, funds, etc., or of the persons dispensing them 1683. **b.** To maintain, provide for, provision (troops) 1687. **2.** *intr.* and *refl.* To maintain or support oneself; to live *upon* food or money, or *by* a particular occupation 1646. †**3.** *intr.* To support life, keep alive, live –1794.

1. Cultivating just as much land as would s. them 1854. **b.** The Charge of Subsisting these Officers and Men must be very great 1704. **2.** From that time he subsisted by literature 1885. **3.** It is difficult to conceive how man can s. without a News-paper JOHNSON.

Subsistence (sŏbsi·stĕns). late ME. [– late L. *subsistentia*, f. *subsistens* SUBSISTENT; see -ENCE.] **I. 1.** Existence as a substance or entity; substantial, real, or independent existence. **2.** A thing that has substantial or real existence 1605. **3.** Continued existence; continuance. Now *rare.* 1616. †**4.** *Theol.* = HYPOSTASIS 5. –1685.

1. He believed the soul had a distinct s. BURNET. **3.** This barbarous outrage committed during the s. of truce 1769.

II. 1. The provision of support for animal life; the furnishing of food or provender. Now *rare* exc. in *means of s.* 1645. **b.** The upkeep *of* an army; the provision of supplies for troops 1746. **2.** Means of supporting life in persons or animals; means of support or livelihood 1639. **b.** A living, livelihood 1690. †**c.** Food-supply, food, provender –1788. **d.** = SUBSISTENCE MONEY 1. 1702.

1. b. I have always taken most especial care of the s. of my troops WELLINGTON. **2.** The country . . but just affording s. 1760. **b.** You offered your labour in return for a s. paid out of our capital 1832. **c.** The seal . . being their principal s. 1788.

Comb.: **s. diet**, the minimum amount of food requisite to keep a person in health.

Subsistence money. 1687. **1.** Money paid in advance to soldiers, workmen, etc. to supply their needs until the regular pay-day. **2.** An allowance for maintenance granted under special circumstances 1720.

†**Subsi·stency.** 1592. [f. as SUBSISTENCE; see -ENCY.] = SUBSISTENCE I. –1768.

Subsistent (sŏbsi·stĕnt), *a.* and *sb.* Now *rare* or *Obs.* 1526. [– L. *subsistens, -ent-*, pr. pple. of *subsistere* SUBSIST *v.*; see -ENT.] **A.** *adj.* **1.** Existing substantially or really; existing of or by itself 1617. †**2.** Inherent or residing *in* –1692. **3.** Subsisting at a specified or implied time 1832.

1. Those which deny there are spirits s. without bodies SIR T. BROWNE. **2.** How . . those iii persones be s. in one deite 1526. **3.** Serious indications of s. evil 1849.

B. *sb.* **1.** A being or thing that subsists 1656. †**2.** *Theol.* = HYPOSTASIS 5. –1802.

Subsistential (sɒbsiste·nʃăl), *a.* 1620. [f. late L. *subsistentia* SUBSISTENCE + -AL[1].] Pertaining to subsistence, *esp.* to the divine subsistence or hypostasis.

Subsizar (sɒ·bsəi:zăɹ). 1590. [SUB- 6.] In the University of Cambridge (now only at Trinity and Emmanuel colleges) an undergraduate (having special need of pecuniary assistance and formerly of performing menial offices) ranking below a sizar.

Subsoil (sɒ·bsoil), *sb.* 1799. [f. SUB- 3 + SOIL *sb.*[1]] **1.** The stratum of soil lying immediately under the surface soil. **2.** *attrib.* as *s. cultivator, draining* 1831. **b.** *fig.* with adj. force = penetrating deep down 1882.

2. b. German is used by s. research men 1882. Hence **Su·bsoil** *v. trans.* to plough so as to cut into the s., use a s. plough upon.

Subsoil plough, *sb.* 1831. A kind of plough with no mould-board, used in ploughed furrows to loosen the soil at some depth below the surface without turning it up. Hence **Subsoil-plough** *v. trans.* to use a subsoil plough upon.

Su·bspe:cies. 1699. [f. SUB- 7 + SPECIES.] A subdivision of species; a more or less permanent variety of a species. Chiefly *Nat. Hist.* Hence **Subspeci·fic** *a.* of, pertaining to, or of the nature of a s.

Substage (sɒ·bstē[i]dʒ). 1859. **1.** [SUB- 7.] *Geol.* A subdivision of a stage. **2.** [SUB- 3.] An apparatus fixed beneath the ordinary stage of a compound microscope for the purpose of supporting mirrors and other accessories 1885.

Substance (sɒ·bstăns). ME. [– (O)Fr. *substance* – post-Augustan (esp. Chr.) L. *substantia* being, essence, material property (formally rendering Gr. ὑπόστασις HYPOSTASIS, but also used for οὐσία ESSENCE), f. *substare*, f. *sub-* SUB- 2 + *stare* stand.] **1.** Essential nature, essence; esp. *Theol.*, with regard to the being of God, the divine nature or essence in respect of which the three Persons of the Trinity are one. **2.** *Philos.* A being that subsists by itself; a separate or distinct thing; hence *gen.*, a thing, being ME. **3.** *Philos.* That which underlies phenomena; the permanent substratum of things; that which receives modifications and is not itself a mode; that in which accidents or attributes inhere. late ME. †**4.** That which underlies or supports; a basis, foundation; a ground, cause –1595. **5.** The matter, subject-matter, subject (of a study, discourse, written work, etc.). late ME. **6.** That of which a physical thing consists; the material of which a body is formed and in virtue of which it possesses certain properties. late ME. **b.** of incorporeal things ME. **7.** The matter or tissue composing an animal body, part, or organ. late ME. **b.** The muscular tissue or fleshy part of an animal body 1695. **8.** Any particular kind of corporeal matter. late ME. **b.** A species of matter of a definite chemical composition 1732. **c.** *Anat.* and *Zool.* With qualifying word or phr. forming specific designations 1815. **9.** A piece or mass of a particular kind of matter; a body of a specified composition or texture. Now *rare.* 1595. **10.** A solid or real thing, as opp. to an appearance or shadow. Also, reality. 1576. **11.** What is embodied in a statement; the meaning or purport of what is expressed in writing or speech; what a writing or speech amounts to. late ME. †**12.** The vital part –1605. **13.** That which gives a thing its character; that which constitutes the essence of a thing; the essential part, essence 1585. **b.** in legal use 1592. †**14.** The amount, quantity, or mass (*of* a thing) –1596. †**15.** The greater number or part, the majority, mass, or bulk *of* –1553. **16.** Possessions, goods, estate; means, wealth. *arch.* ME. †**17.** A supply or provision *of* –1535. **18.** Substantial or solid qualities, character, etc. late ME. **b.** That which makes a material firm, solid, and hard-wearing 1833.

1. That Essence or S. of the Godhead, which all the Three Persons or Hypostases agree in CUDWORTH. **2.** Substances are usually distinguished as Bodies or Minds 1843. *First (primary) s., second (secondary) s.*; The first s. (οὐσία πρώτη) is the individual, which can neither exist in nor be predicated of another. Second s. is the universal, which, as such, does not exist in another, but may be predicated of another. 1903. **3.** *transf.* Thise Cookes, how they stampe, and streyne and grynde And turnen substaunce in-to Accident CHAUCER. **5.** Vnto your Grace doe I in chiefe addresse The s. of my Speech SHAKS. **6.** Surely not in vain My S. from the common Earth was ta'en FITZGERALD. **8.** Thus, from the mixture of two perfectly transparent substances, we obtain an opaque one 1860. **c.** Adipose s. 1815. **10.** He takes false shadowes, for true substances SHAKS. **11.** The s. of what I said to them was this RUSKIN. **12.** *Tit. A.* I. i. 374. **13. b.** The s. of this contract consisteth in the thing solde, and in the price thereof 1592. **14.** *Merch. V.* IV. i. 328. **15.** Phr. *Sum and s.*: see SUM *sb.* **16.** Thy s., valued at the highest rate, cannot amount vnto a hundred Markes SHAKS. **18.** This fact gave great strength and s. to the pretensions of Russia KINGLAKE. **b.** You must learn from the French to give your fabrics more s. 1833.

Phrases. **In s. a.** In reality. **b.** In essentials, substantially. **c.** In effect, virtually. **Of** (. .) **s.** (often *of good* or *great s.*). Substantial, well-to-do, wealthy. Hence **Su·bstanceless** *a.* devoid of s., unsubstantial.

Substanced (sɒ·bstănst), *pa. pple. rare.* 1615. [f. prec. + -ED[2].] †**1.** Furnished with wealth. CHAPMAN. **2.** Made into a substance, made substantial 1873. **3.** Of a specified kind of substance 1624.

Substant (sɒ·bstănt), *a. rare.* 1660. [– L. *substans, -ant-*, pr. pple. of *substare*; see SUBSTANCE, -ANT.] **1.** Subsistent. **2.** Underlying 1883.

Substantial (sŏbstæ·nʃăl), *a.* and *sb.* ME. [– (O)Fr. *substantiel* or Chr. L. *substantialis*, rendering Gr. ὑποστατικός (see HYPOSTATIC), καθ' ὑπόστασιν; see SUBSTANCE, -AL[1].] **A.** *adj.* **1.** That is, or exists as, a substance; having a real existence; subsisting by itself. late ME. **2.** *Philos.* Of, pertaining or relating to, or inherent in substance (esp. as opp. to *accident*); that is substance. late ME. **3.** Relating to or proceeding from the essence of a thing; essential. Now *rare* or *Obs.* late ME. **4.** That is, constitutes, or involves an essential part, point, or feature; essential, material. late ME. **b.** *Law.* Belonging to or involving essential right, or the merits of a matter 1843. **5.** Of food, a meal: Affording ample or abundant nourishment. (In later use the notion of solidity or quantity is predominant.) ME. **6.** Of structures, etc.: Of solid material or workmanship. late ME. **7.** Of ample or considerable amount, quantity, or dimensions 1454. **8.** Based upon a solid substratum; not easily disturbed or damaged; of solid worth or value; weighty, sound. late ME. †**9.** Of acts, measures, etc.: Having weight, force or effect; effective, thorough –1683. **10.** Possessing 'substance', property, or wealth; well-to-do, wealthy; hence, of weight or influence 1450. **11.** Of real worth, reliability, or repute; of good standing or status 1449. **12.** Having a corporeal form: consisting of solid matter. *Obs.* or *rare.* 1589. **13.** Having substance; not imaginary, unreal, or apparent only; true, solid, real 1592. **14.** Pertaining to the substance or tissue of the body or a part or organ 1611. **15.** That is such in the main; real or true for the most part 1771.

1. This hypothesis, that no s. and indivisible thing ever perisheth 1652. **2.** *S. form*, the nature or distinctive character in virtue of possessing which a thing is what it (specifically or individually) is. **4.** Securing them from s. error RUSKIN. **b.** The judge will consider what is the s. fact to be made out 1883. **5.** A s. dinner at three 1902. **6.** Some rich Burgher, whose s. dores, Cross-barrd and bolted fast, fear no assault MILT. **7.** S. reinforcements 1780. **8.** In great matters aske substancial counsell 1547. S. reasons . . why there should be such differences 1687. The s. comforts of a good coal fire 1814. **9.** That s. Order be taken forthwith for the pulling down all Altars 1551. **10.** The Knights, Aldermen, and substantiall Citizens of London 1642. **11.** A sound and s. scholar 1814. **13.** All this is but a dreame, Too flattering sweet to be substantiall SHAKS. **15.** The s. genuineness of the text 1875.

B. *sb.* **1.** *pl.* The things belonging to or constituting the substance; the essential parts or elements; the essentials. late ME. **2.** *pl.* Substantial or solid things 1653. **3.** *pl.* The substantial or solid parts of a meal 1751.

1. His judgement in substantials, like that of Johnson, is always worth having LOWELL. Hence **Substa·ntial-ly** *adv.*, **-ness.**

Substantialism (sŏbstæ·nʃăliz'm). 1881. [f. prec. + -ISM.] *Philos.* The doctrine that there are substantial realities underlying phenomena. So **Substa·ntialist,** one who holds a philosophical doctrine of s.; also, a Flacian.

Substantiality (sŏbstænʃiæ·lĭti). 1545. [– late L. *substantialitas*, f. *substantialis*; see SUBSTANTIAL, -ITY.] **1.** The quality or state of being substantial; existence as a substance or or substratum; substantial or real existence. **2.** Soundness, genuineness; solidity of position or status 1660. **3.** Solidity (of a structure) 1790. **4.** *concr.* (*pl.*) = SUBSTANTIAL B. 3. 1813.

1. The ascription of independent s. to each of the different phases of intellectual life 1877. **3.** A ham and other substantialities composed our meal 1842.

Substantiate (sŏbstæ·nʃie¹t), *v.* 1657. [– *substantiat-*, pa. ppl. stem of med.L. *substantiare* give essence or substance to, f. *substantia*; see SUBSTANCE, -ATE³.] **1.** *trans.* To give substance or substantial existence to, make real or substantial. **2.** To give solidity to, make firm, strengthen 1792. **3.** To give substantial form to, embody, body forth 1784. **4.** To demonstrate or verify by proof or evidence; to make good 1803.

1. Faith substantiateth things not yet seen 1657. **4.** If the Court should wish it, it can be substantiated by evidence WELLINGTON.

Substantiation (sŏbstænʃiē¹·ʃən). 1760. [f. prec.; see -ATION.] **1.** Embodiment (*rare*). **2.** The substitution of substance for shadow 1863. **3.** The making good or proving a statement, etc. 1861.

3. He failed to cite a single case in s. of his words 1886.

Substantival (sɒbstăntəi·văl), *a.* 1832. [f. next + -AL¹ 1.] **1.** *Gram.* Of, belonging to, or consisting of, a substantive or substantives. **2.** Existing substantially 1884. Hence **Substanti·vally** *adv.* as a substantive.

Substantive (sɒ·bstăntiv), *a.* and *sb.* late ME. [– (O)Fr. *substantif, -ive* or late L. *substantivus*, f. *substantia*, see SUBSTANCE, -IVE.] **A.** *adj.* **1. a.** Of persons, nations, etc.: That stands of or by itself; independent, self-existent, self-sufficient 1470. **b.** Of immaterial subjects: Having an independent existence or status; not dependent upon, subsidiary to, or referable to something else 1561. **c.** Of a dye: That attaches itself directly to the stuff, without the necessity of using a mordant 1794. **d.** *Mil.* Definitely appointed to the rank specified; also of an appointment or rank 1883. **2.** *Gram.* Denoting a substance; *noun s.* (late L. *nomen substantivum*): = B. 1. 1509. **b.** Of the nature of, equivalent to, or employed as a substantive; substantival 1668. **3.** *Gram.* Expressing existence; in *s. verb*, formerly *verb s.*: the verb 'to be' (late L. *verbum substantivum*, tr. Gr. ῥῆμα ὑπαρκτικόν) 1559. **4.** Belonging to the substance of a thing; essential 1858. **b.** Of law: Relating to or consisting of the rules of right administered by a court, as opp. to the forms of procedure (*adjective law*) 1786. **5.** Existing as a substance or individual thing; having an actual or real existence; not imaginary or illusory; real 1830. **6.** Having a firm or solid basis; not slight, weak, or transitory 1809. **7.** Having a value or effect because of numbers or quantity; of considerable amount or quantity 1821. **8.** Relating to or affecting the substance or tissue of an organ 1875.

1. That Spain is not a s. power: That she must lean on France, or on England BURKE. **b.** A mere title..rather than a s. office and function 1850. **2. b.** S. clauses, expressing the subject, are placed at the commencement of the sentence 1857. **4.** As a s. part of their message 1858. **6.** Strength and magnitude are qualities which impress the imagination in a powerful and s. manner HAZLITT. **7.** A poem of s. length (above 600 lines) SOUTHEY.

B. *sb.* (for *noun s.*) That part of speech which is used as the name of a person or thing; a noun. late ME. Hence **Substa·ntively** *adv.* as a s. or noun; substantially, inherently. **Su·bstantivize** *v. trans. Gram.* to convert into a s.

Substituent (sɒbsti·tiuĕnt). 1895. [– L. *substituens, -ent-*, pr. pple. of *substituere*; see SUBSTITUTE *v.*, -ENT.] *Chem.* An atom or group of atoms taking the place of another atom or group in a compound.

Substitute (sɒ·bstitiūt), *sb.* late ME. [– L. *substitutus, -um*, masc. and n. of pa. pple. of *substituere* (see next).] **I. 1.** One exercising deputed authority; a deputy, delegate. **†b.** *By s.*: by proxy. SHAKS. **2.** *Law.* A person nominated in remainder 1758. **3.** *Mil.* One who for a remuneration agrees to serve in place of another balloted for the militia 1802. **4.** *gen.* One who acts in place of another 1836.

1. My Substitutes I send ye, and Create Plenipotent on Earth MILT. **4.** In China, where a Criminal can buy a s. to be executed in his stead 1873.

II. A thing put in the place of another. **1.** That which is used or stands in place of something else 1589. **2.** *techn.* **a.** An artificial foodstuff intended to supply the place of a natural food; also, a cheaper article or ingredient substituted for one that is recognized or patented 1879. **b.** *Chem.* A new compound formed by substitution 1852.

Substitute (sɒ·bstitiūt), *v.* 1532. [– *substitut-*, pa. ppl. stem of L. *substituere*, f. *sub* SUB- 2b + *statuere* set up.] **†1.** *trans.* To appoint (a person) *to* an office as a deputy or delegate –1712. **†b.** To set up or appoint as a ruler or official *in the place (stead, room) of* another –1831. **†c.** To depute, delegate –1700. **2.** To put (one) in place of another 1588. **3.** *Law.* To nominate in remainder 1560. **4.** To take the place of, replace. (orig. in *pass.* Now regarded as incorrect.) 1675. **b.** *intr.* To act as a substitute. *U.S.* 1888.

1. b. The Pope substituted John de Columna, a Cardinall, Legate in the place of Pelagius FULLER. **2.** For real wit he is obliged to s. vivacity GOLDSM. The reader by substituting various terms can easily make propositions 1870. **4.** A means of judging how far touch can s. sight 1855. Hence **Su·bstituted** *ppl. a.* put in place of another; created or produced by substitution.

Substitution (sɒbstitiū·ʃən). late ME. [– late L. *substitutio, -ōn-*, f. as prec.; see -ION. Cf. (O)Fr. *substitution.*] **†1.** The appointment of a deputy (or successor); deputation, delegation –1758. **2.** The putting of one person or thing in place of another 1612. **b.** With ref. to the principle in religious sacrifices of replacing one kind of victim by another or a bloody by an unbloody offering; *esp.* in *Christian Theol.* used to designate a doctrine of the Atonement according to which Jesus Christ suffered punishment vicariously for man 1836. **3.** *Law.* The designation of a person or series of persons to succeed as heir or heirs on the failure of a person or persons previously named 1590. **4.** *Alg.* **a.** The method of replacing one algebraic quantity by another of equal value but differently expressed. **b.** The operation of passing from the primitive arrangement of *n* letters to any other arrangement of the same letters. 1710. **5.** *Chem.* The replacement of one or more equivalents of an element or radical by a like number of equivalents of another 1848. **6.** *Biol.* The replacement of one organ or function by another 1870. **7.** *Philol.* A sound-change consisting in the replacement of one vowel or consonant by another 1876. *Trade.* The dishonest replacement of one article of commerce by another, usu. of inferior quality; the passing off of one manufacturer's goods for another's 1902.

1. *Temp.* I. ii. 103. **2.** A mere s. of words for reasons PALEY. The s. of a yellow-stained belt for a plain uncoloured one 1876. Hence **Substitu·tional** *a. Theol.* of or pertaining to, based upon the principle of, sacrificial s.; involving a s.; constituting or forming a substitute; **-ly** *adv.* **Substitu·tionary** *a.* substitutional.

Substitutive (sɒ·bstitiūtiv), *a.* 1600. [In 2 b – L. *substitutivus*, f. as prec.; see -IVE. In other senses f. SUBSTITUTE *v.*] **†1.** Belonging to, characteristic of, or involving the appointment of a substitute or deputy –1640. **2.** Taking, or fitted to take, the place of something else 1668. **b.** *Logic.* Of a proposition or judgement: = CONDITIONAL *a.* 2. 1656. **3.** *Theol.* Involving a theory of substitution 1865. **4.** Dependent upon a designation of heirs in remainder 1853.

Substract (sɒbstræ·kt), *v.* Now *illiterate.* 1550. [– late L. *substract-*, f. *substrahere*, alt. (after *abstrahere* ABSTRACT) of *subtrahere*; see SUBTRACT.] = SUBTRACT *v.* So **Substra·ction.** **†Substra·ctor,** a calumniator. SHAKS.

Substrate (sɒ·bstre¹t). 1810. [Anglicized form of next.] = next.

‖**Substratum** (sŏbstrē¹·tŏm). *Pl.* **substrata** (sŏbstrē¹·tă); also **substratums.** 1631. [– mod.L. subst. use of n. pa. pple. of L. *substernere*; see SUB- 2, STRATUM.] **1.** *Metaph.* That which is regarded as supporting attributes or accidents; the substance in which qualities inhere 1653. **2.** That which underlies, or serves as the basis or foundation of, an immaterial thing, condition, or activity; the basis on which an immaterial 'structure' is raised 1631. **3.** That upon which a material thing is 'built up' or from which it is created; the subject-matter or matter operated upon 1676. **4.** An under-layer of any material substance 1730. **b.** An under-layer of soil or earthy matter 1730. **c.** In immaterial sense 1855.

1. Something..which we take to be the *s.*, or support, of those Idea's we do know LOCKE. **4. c.** Children belonging to the s. of society 1876.

Substruct (sŏbstrɒ·kt), *v. rare.* 1847. [– *substruct-*, pa. ppl. stem of L. *substruere*, f. *sub-* SUB- 2 + *sternere* build, erect.] *trans.* To construct beneath; to lay as a foundation.

Substruction (sŏbstrɒ·kʃən). 1624. [– Fr. *substruction* or L. *substructio, -ōn-*, f. as prec.; see -ION.] **1.** *Arch.* The under-structure of a building or other work. **2.** *fig.* A basis, foundation 1765.

1. The massy substructions of the Capitoline temple 1838. **2.** A scaffolding or s. for the doctrine 1822.

Substructure (sɒ·bstrɒktiŭɹ,-tʃəɹ). 1726. [f. SUB- 3 + STRUCTURE, after prec.] *Arch.* That part of a building which supports the superstructure; an under-structure, substruction. Hence **Substru·ctural** *a.* of the nature of a s.

Substylar (sɒ·bstəilăɹ), *a.* (*sb.*) 1669. [f. next + -AR¹, after Fr. *soustylaire* sb.; see SUB- 1, STYLE *sb.* I. 6.] *S. line* = next. Also *ellipt.* as *sb.*

Substyle (sɒ·bstəil). 1593. [f. SUB- 1 + STYLE *sb.* I. 6.] In dialling, the line on which the style or gnomon stands.

Subsultory (sŏbsɒ·ltəri), *a.* 1638. [f. †*subsult* vb. (– L. *subsultare*) + -ORY²; see SUB- 25, RESULT *v.* Cf. AL. *subsultorius* (Bacon) fitful.] Making or moving by sudden leaps, bounds, or starts. So **Subsu·ltive** *a.* (*rare*).

‖**Subsultus** (sŏbsɒ·ltŏs). 1806. [mod.L., f. *subsult-*, pa. ppl. stem of L. *subsilire* jump up.] *Path.* A convulsive or twitching movement. Often short for *s. tendinum*, a convulsive twitching of the muscles and tendons present in certain fevers.

Subsu·mable, *a. rare.* 1882. [f. next + -ABLE.] Capable of being subsumed.

Subsume (sŏbsiū·m), *v.* 1535. [– med.L. *subsumere* (in logic: *a* 1360), f. L. *sub* SUB- 2, 25 b + *sumere* take.] **†1.** *trans.* To bring (a statement, instance, etc.) under another; to subjoin, add –1660. **2.** intr. *Logic.* To state a minor premiss: freq. with the words of the proposition following 1589. **3.** trans. *Logic.* To state as a minor proposition or concept *under* another 1697. **4.** To bring (one idea, principle, term, etc.) *under* another, (a case, instance) under a rule; to take up *into*, or include *in*, something larger or higher 1812. **†5.** *gen.* To assume; to infer –1694.

3. In the judgment, 'all horses are animals', the conception 'horses' is subsumed under that of 'animals' 1876. **4.** A principle under which one might s. men's most strenuous efforts after righteousness PATER.

Subsumption (sŏbsɒ·mᵖʃən). 1639. [– med. L. *subsumptio* (in logic: *a* 1360), f. pa. ppl. stem of *subsumere*; see prec., -ION.] **1.** *Logic.* A proposition subsumed under another; a minor premiss; *gen.*, an assumption 1651. **b.** Sc. Law. *S. of the libel*, a narrative of the alleged crime 1639. **2.** Chiefly *Logic* and *Philos.* The bringing of a concept, cognition, etc. *under* a general term or a larger or higher concept, etc.; the instancing of a case *under* a rule, etc. 1652.

1. It is the nature of a syllogisme to haue the s. in the second proposition 1672. **2.** A casuistry that is, a s. of the cases most frequently recurring in ordinary life DE QUINCEY.

Subsumptive (sŏbsɒ·mᵖtiv), *a. rare.* 1834. [f. SUBSUMPTION, after *assumption/assumptive*, etc.] Involving subsumption.

Subsurface (sɒ·bsɒ̄ːɹfės). 1778. [SUB- 1–4.] **1.** That which lies immediately below the surface, e.g. the subsoil. **2.** *Math.* In five-dimensional geometry, a three-dimensional continuum 1873. **3.** as *adj.* [see SUB- 1 e.] Existing, lying, or operating under the surface (as of the earth or water) 1875.

3. The construction of sub-surface torpedo boats 1902.

Su·bta:ngent. 1715. [f. SUB- 1 + TANGENT; cf. Fr. *sous-tangente* (XVII).] *Math.* That part of the axis of a curve which is contained between the tangent and the ordinate.

Su·bte:nancy. 1861. [f. next; see -CY.] The status, right, or holding of a subtenant.

Subtenant (sɒ·bte:nănt). 1445. [SUB- 9 (*b*). In med.L. *subtenens* (XIII).] One who holds of a tenant; an under-tenant.

Subtend (sŏbte·nd), *v.* 1570. [– L. *subtendere*, f. *sub-* SUB- 1 + *tendere* stretch; see TEND *v.*²] **1.** trans. *Geom.* To stretch or extend under, or be opposite to: said *esp.* of a line or side of a figure opposite an angle; also, of a chord or angle opposite an arc. Also in *Astron.* and *Optics.* **2.** *Bot.* To extend under, so as to embrace or enfold 1871.

1. Standing upon a semicircular tract of ground, subtended by the great bay or roadstead KINGLAKE.

Subtense (sŏbte·ns). 1614. [– mod.L. *subtensa* (sc. *linea* line), fem. pa. pple. of *subtendere* SUBTEND.] *Geom.* A subtending line; *esp.* the chord of an arc.

attrib. **s. method,** a method of tacheometry in which the angle at the instrument is variable and the distance base is either constant or specially measured.

Subter- (sɒ·btəɹ) *prefix*, repr. L. *subter-* = the adv. and prep. *subter* below, underneath, used in composition = (1) below, beneath; (*a*) advb. as in *subterfluere* to flow beneath, (*b*) prep. as in *subtercutaneus* lying under the skin; (2) secretly, as in *subterfugere* to flee secretly (see SUBTERFUGE); and, in some rare Eng. compounds, = (3) lower or less than (cf. SUB- 14).

Subtera·queous, *a.* living, situated, performed, etc. under water (*rare*). **Su:btercuta·neous** *a.* = SUBCUTANEOUS *a.* **Su:btererога·tion,** the performing of less than is required. **†Subterflu·ent, †Subte·rfluous** *adjs.*, flowing underneath. **Subterna·tural,** *a.* below what is natural, less than natural.

Subterfuge (sɒ·btəɹfiūdʒ). 1573. [– Fr. *subterfuge* or late L. *subterfugium*, f. L. *subterfugere* escape secretly, f. *subter-* SUBTER- (2) + *fugere* flee.] **1.** An article or device to which a person resorts in order to escape the force of an argument, to avoid condemnation or censure, or to justify his conduct; an evasion or shift. Chiefly of discourse, argument, debate, but also of action in general. **b.** contextually: A means of escape (*from* censure, etc.); an excuse 1755. **†2.** A place to which a person escapes, a retreat, refuge –1844. **†3.** That which conceals; a 'cloak' –1733.

1. Do not affect little shifts and subterfuges to avoid the force of an argument WATTS. **b.** The queen of Scots had no other s. from these pressing remonstrances HUME. **2.** They depended on these under ground subterfuges 1737.

Subterranean (sɒbtĕrēⁱ·niăn), *a.* and *sb.* 1603. [f. L. *subterraneus*, f. *sub-* SUB- 1 a + *terra* earth; see -AN, -EAN.] **A.** *adj.* **1. a.** Of inanimate objects: Existing, lying, or situated below the surface of the earth; formed or constructed underground, either by nature or the hand of man; underground 1610. **b.** Of animate beings: Living or working under ground 1621. **c.** Of physical phenomena, forces or movements, actions, etc.: Operating or performed under ground 1603. **d.** *Bot.* Of parts of a plant: Growing under ground 1839. **2.** Existing under the earth; belonging to the lower regions or underworld 1619. **3.** *fig.* Existing or working out of sight, in the dark, or secretly 1651.

1. His taste in cookery, formed in s. ordinaries and *Alamode* beefshops, was far from delicate MACAULAY. **b.** S. colliers, tinners [&c.] RICHARDSON. **c.** A noise like s. thunder SCOTT. **2.** The celestial, terrestrial, and s. deities EVELYN. **3.** The entire town..was honeycombed with s. revolt 1891.

B. *sb.* **1.** One who lives under ground; a cave-dweller 1625. **2.** An inhabitant of the lower regions 1836. **3.** An underground cave, chamber, or dwelling 1797. Hence **Subterra·neanly** *adv.* So **Su·bterrane** *a.* and *sb.* (now *rare*).

Subterraneous (sɒbtĕrēⁱ·niəs), *a.* Now *rare.* 1607. [f. L. *subterraneus* (see prec.) + -OUS: see -EOUS.] = prec. A. Hence **†Subterrane·ity** the condition of being s. (*rare*). **Subterra·neous-ly** *adv.*, **-ness** (*rare*).

Subterra·nity. *Obs.* or *rare.* 1646. Irregular var. of SUBTERRANEITY.

†Su·bterrany, *a.* (*sb.*) *rare.* 1626. [– L. *subterraneus*, after Fr. †*sousterrané*; cf. MOMENTANY (– Fr. *momentané*).] = SUBTERRANEAN –1656.

Subterrene (sɒbtĕrī·n), *a.* and *sb.* 1610. [– L. *subterrenus*; see SUB- 1 a, TERRENE.] **A.** *adj.* = SUBTERRANEAN A. 1, 2. **B.** *sb.* An underground dwelling, etc.; (with *the*) the underworld 1854.

Subterrestrial (sɒbtĕre·striăl), *a.* and *sb.* Now *rare.* 1613. [See SUB- 1 a, TERRESTRIAL.] **A.** *adj.* **1.** = SUBTERRANEAN A. 1. **†2.** = SUBTERRANEAN A. 2. –1702. **B.** *sb.* A creature living under ground 1800.

Subtile (sɒ·til, sɒ·btil), *a.* late ME. [– Fr. *subtil*, latinized refashioning of OFr. *s(o)util* SUBTLE *a.*] **1.** Chiefly of fluids: Not dense, thin, rarefied; penetrating, etc. by reason of tenuity. **2.** Of fine or delicate texture; also, delicately formed or moulded. late ME. **3.** = SUBTLE *a.* 3, 4, 5, 6, 9, 10. late ME. **4.** Of feeling, sense: Acute, keen 1610.

1. The belief in ghosts, or spirits of s. bodies HALLAM. **3.** Many a subtil resoun forth they leyden CHAUCER. Frenchemen are ryght subtyl in gyuyng of good counsell BERNERS. The Goats were so shy, so s., and so swift of Foot DE FOE. Arachne's s. line POPE. Their s. shades of meaning 1888. **4.** A secret S. sense crept in of pain LONGF. Hence **†Su·btileness** –1676.

†Subti·liate, *v.* late ME. [– *subtiliat-*, pa. ppl. stem of med.L. *subtiliare* rarefy, refine, f. L. *subtilis* SUBTLE; see -ATE³.] *trans.* To make thin or tenuous; *esp.* to rarefy (a fluid); to sublime; to refine, purify –1678. Hence **†Subtilia·tion** –1685.

Subtility (sɒbti·lĭti). late ME. [– OFr. *soutilité, subtilité* – L. *subtilitas, -tat-*, f. as prec.; see -ITY.] **1.** = SUBTLETY 1. **†2.** = SUBTLETY 3. –1761. **3.** (Excessive) nicety or refinement in argument, etc. late ME. **4.** An instance of this 1589. **5.** = SUBTLETY 7. late ME.

3. This same vnprofitable subtilitie or curiositie is of two sorts BACON. **4.** The subtilities of philosophers 1845.

Subtilization (sɒ:ᵇtiləizēⁱ·ʃən). 1603. [– Fr. *subtilisation* or med.L. *subtilizatio, -ōn-*, f. *subtilizare*; see next, -ION.] **1.** The action of SUBTILIZE *v.*; the sublimation or rarefaction of a substance. **2.** The drawing of subtle distinctions; over-refinement of argument, etc. 1755.

2. The oriental subtilizations about points of faith 1812.

Subtilize (sɒ·ᵇtiləiz), *v.* 1592. [– Fr. *subtiliser* or med.L. *subtilizare*, f. L. *subtilis* SUBTLE; see -IZE.] **1.** *trans.* To render thin or rare, less gross or coarse, more fluid or volatile; to rarefy, refine. Now *rare* or *Obs.* 1597. **2.** *fig.* To exalt, elevate, sublime, refine 1638. **3.** To render (the mind, the senses, etc.) acute or penetrating 1642. **4.** To render subtle, introduce subleties or nice distinctions into; also, to argue subtly upon 1599. **5.** *intr.* To make subtle distinctions; to argue or reason in a subtle manner; to split hairs 1592.

1. Fire only subtilizes and attenuates the earthy matter 1758. **5.** Men..who s. upon the commonest Duties until they no longer appear binding GOLDSM.

Subtilly, subtilely (sɒ·ᵇtili), *adv.* Now *rare* or *Obs.* late ME. [f. *subtil* SUBTILE *a.* + -LY².] **1.** Thinly; finely; in a rarefied manner or form. **2.** = SUBTLY, in various senses. late ME.

Subtilty (sɒ·ᵇtilti). late ME. [Alteration of ME. *sutilte* SUBTLETY, after SUBTILE. Now used as an occasional var. of SUBTLETY in moral and intellectual senses.] **†1.** = SUBTLETY 1. –1748. **2.** = SUBTLETY 2. late ME. **†3.** = SUBTLETY 3. –1734. **†4.** = SUBTLETY 7. –1815. **5.** Excessive nicety or refinement in argument, etc. 1550. **b.** An instance of this, esp. *pl.* = SUBTLETY 6. 1474. **†6.** Delicacy, fineness (of physical objects, movements) –1794.

1. A better stratagem, than any that can proceed from s. of Wit HOBBES. **5.** These reasons savour of a wonderful s. 1818. **b.** Conversant in subtilties of Logick, Philosophy, and the Schoolmen 1668.

Su·b-ti:tle, *sb.* 1878. [SUB- 5b.] **1.** A subordinate or additional title of a literary work. **2.** A repetition of the chief words of the full title of a book at the top of the first page of text; also, a half-title 1890. **3.** *Cinema.* Any of the series of captions which constitute the running commentary on a moving picture. So **Su·btitle** *v. trans.* to furnish with a specified s.; to furnish (a film) with sub-titles.

Subtle (sɒ·t'l), *a.* [ME. *sutil, so^u^til* – OFr. *sutil, so(u)til* – L. *subtilis.*] **1.** Of thin consistency, tenuous; not dense, rarefied; hence, penetrating, pervasive or elusive by reason of tenuity (now chiefly of odours). late ME. **2.** Of fine or delicate texture or composition. *Obs.* exc. *arch.* late ME. **†3.** Of small thickness or breadth; thin, slender, fine –1680. **†4.** Finely powdered; (of particles) fine, minute –1753. **5.** Of immaterial things: Not easily grasped, understood, or perceived; †intricate, abstruse ME. **6.** Fine or delicate, esp. to such an extent as to elude observation or analysis 1639. **7.** Of craftsmen, etc.: Skilful, clever, expert, dexterous. *arch.* ME. **b.** Of animals (*rare*) 1605. **†8.** Of things: Characterized by cleverness or ingenuity in conception or execution; cleverly designed or executed, artfully contrived –1667. **9.** Of persons, their faculties, actions: Characterized by penetration, acumen, or discrimination. Now with implication of (excessive) refinement or nicety of thought, speculation, or argument. ME. **†10.** Of persons or animals: Crafty, cunning; treacherously or wickedly cunning, insidiously sly, wily –1781. **†b.** Of actions, thoughts, etc. –1671. **†c.** Of ground: Tricky –1630. **11.** Working imperceptibly or secretly, insidious 1601.

1. The material theory supposes heat to be..a s. fluid stored up in the inter-atomic spaces of bodies TYNDALL. **2.** Thinner than the subtlest lawn KEBLE. **3.** *Tr. & Cr.* v. ii. 151. **5.** Things remote From use, obscure and suttle MILT. **6.** The seven are in a most s. alternating proportion RUSKIN. **8.** From the arched roof Pendant by suttle Magic many a row Of Starry Lamps MILT. **9.** The s. dexterity of a scholastic metaphysician 1769. **10.** How soon hath Time the suttle theef of youth, Stoln on his wing my three and twentith yeer! MILT. **b.** Is not thy kindnesse s., couetous? SHAKS. **c.** Like to a Bowle vpon a s. ground I haue tumbled past the throw SHAKS. Hence **Su·btleness**, subtlety.

Subtlety (sɒ·t'lti). ME. [– OFr. *su-, soutillé* :– L. *subtilitas, -tat-*, f. *subtilis*; see prec., -TY¹.] **1.** Of persons, the mind, etc.: Acuteness, sagacity, penetration: in mod. use chiefly with implication of delicate or keen perception of fine distinctions or nice points. **2.** Craftiness, cunning, esp. of a treacherous kind; guile, treachery. late ME. **†3.** An ingenious contrivance; a crafty or cunning device; an artifice; *freq.* in unfavourable sense, a wily stratagem or trick –1671. **4.** *Cookery.* A highly ornamental device, wholly or chiefly made of sugar. *Obs.* exc. *Hist.* late ME. **†5.** Abstruseness, complexity, intricacy; also *pl.*, abstruse or intricate matters –1591. **6.** A refinement or nicety of thought, speculation, or argument; a fine distinction; a nice point 1654. **7.** Thinness, tenuity, exility; penetrativeness arising from lack of density 1691. **8.** Fineness or delicacy of nature, character, manner, operation, or the like; an instance of this 1820.

2. The laws were violated by power, or perverted by s. GIBBON. **6.** Curious in Subtleties, and ignorant in things of solid Knowledge 1680. **8.** Religious controversy sharpens the understanding by the s. and remoteness of the topics it discusses HAZLITT.

Subtly (sɒ·tli), *adv.* ME. [f. SUBTLE *a.* + -LY².] **1.** Cleverly, dexterously, skilfully; ingeniously, artfully, cunningly. *arch.* **2.** With subtle thought or argument; with nice or fine-drawn distinctions ME. **†3.** With craft or guile –1727. **4.** Delicately, finely 1732. **5.** In a manner that defies observation, analysis, or explanation 1854.

1. Thou seest How suttly to detaine thee I devise MILT. **3.** The same dealte suttely with oure kynred COVERDALE *Acts* 7:19. **4.** The Pisan front is far more s. proportioned RUSKIN. **4.** Apology and demonstration are s. blended throughout his appeal 1879.

Subtonic (sɒbtǫ·nik), *a.* and *sb.* 1833. [f. SUB- 19, 13.] **A.** *adj. Phonetics.* Of sounds: Having properties analogous to those of the tonics, but inferior in degree. **B.** *sb.* **1.** *Phonetics.* A subtonic sound 1833. **2.** *Mus.* The note a semitone immediately below the upper tonic of a scale; the leading note 1854.

Subtract (sǒbtræ·kt), *v.* 1540. [– *subtract-*, pa. ppl. stem of L. *subtrahere*, f. *sub* SUB- 25 + *trahere* draw.] **1.** *trans.* To withdraw or withhold (a thing that is or may be used or enjoyed). *Obs.* exc. *arch.* 1548. †**2.** To remove *from* a place or position –1676. **b.** *refl.* 1540. **3.** *Math.* To take away or deduct (one quantity *from*, †*out of* another): see SUBTRACTION 2. Also *absol.* or *intr.* 1557.

3. Podex can..Adde, Multiply, S., Divide 1652. *transf.* That is what I suppose you to say,..you may, if you wish, add or s. anything JOWETT.

Subtraction (sǒbtræ·kʃən). late ME. [– late L. *subtractio*, *-ōn-*, f. as prec.; see -ION.] **1.** The withdrawal or withholding of something due, necessary, or useful. Also, an instance of this. *Obs.* exc. *arch.* 1450. **b.** *Law.* The withdrawal or withholding from a person of any right or privilege to which he is lawfully entitled 1660. **c.** *Logic.* The exception of one class from another in which the excepted class is naturally included 1909. **2.** *Math.* The taking of one quantity *from* (†*out of*) another; the operation of finding the difference between two quantities, the result being termed the *remainder*. Also, an instance of this. late ME. **b.** *transf.* and *fig.* Abstraction, deduction, removal 1534.

1. b. Ecclesiatical laws relate to..s. and right of tythes, oblations, &c. COKE.

Subtractive (sǒbtræ·ktiv), *a.* 1690. [f. SUBTRACT *v.* + -IVE.] Involving or denoting subtraction, deduction, or diminution; (of a mathematical quantity) that is to be subtracted, negative, having the minus sign.

Subtrahend (sʊ·btrăhend). 1674. [– L. *subtrahendus* (sc. *numerus* number), gerundive of *subtrahere* SUBTRACT.] *Math.* The quantity or number to be subtracted. **b.** *transf.* A sum of money to be deducted 1845.

Su·btrea:surer. 1546. [SUB- 6.] An assistant or deputy treasurer. (The specified designation of an official of Hereford and Truro Cathedrals, and of the Inner Temple; in *U.S.* of the official in charge of a subtreasury.)

Su·btrea:sury. 1837. [SUB- 7 d.] A subordinate or branch treasury; *U.S.* the organization by which the separate safe-keeping of the public funds is entrusted to specially appointed officers; any of the branches of the Treasury established in certain cities of the States for the receipt and safe-keeping of public monies.

Su·btro:pic, *a.* and *sb.* 1886. [SUB- 12 b, 19.] **A.** *adj.* = next 1891. **B.** *sb. pl.* **Subtropics:** the regions adjacent to or bordering on the tropics 1886.

Su·btro:pical, *a.* 1842. [SUB- 12 b, 19.] **1.** Bordering on the tropics 1865. **2.** Characteristic of subtropical regions; almost tropical 1842.

Subulate (siū·biŭlět), *a.* 1760. [f. L. *subula* awl + -ATE².] *Bot.* and *Zool.* Awl-shaped; slender and tapering to a point. So **Su·bulated** *a.* 1752.

Subuliform (siubiū·lifǭɹm), *a.* 1859. [f. as prec. + -FORM.] Subulate.

Suburb (sʊ·bʊɹb). late ME. [– (O)Fr. *suburbe*, pl. *-es* or L. *suburbium*, pl. *-ia*, f. *sub* SUB- 11 + *urbs* city.] **1.** *collect. pl.* The country lying immediately outside a town or city; more particularly those residential parts belonging to a town or city which lie immediately outside and adjacent to its walls or boundaries. **2.** Any of such residential parts, having a definite designation, boundary, or organization. late ME. **3.** *transf.* and *fig.* (*pl.*, rarely *sing.*) Outlying parts, outskirts, confines, purlieus. late ME. **4.** *attrib.* and *Comb.* **a.** = SUBURBAN. Now *rare.* 1592. †**b.** = Belonging to or characteristic of the suburbs (of London) as a place of inferior, debased, and *esp.* licentious habits of life –1668.

1. That part of the Suburbs of London commonly called Covent Garden 1665. **2.** I went to the Ghetto, where the Jewes dwell as in a suburbe by themselues EVELYN. **3.** In the Suburbs and expectation of sorrowes JER. TAYLOR. [Bees] Flie to and fro, or on the smoothed Plank, The s. of thir Straw-built Cittadel,..confer Thir State affairs MILT. **4. a.** From the slope side of a s. hill KEATS. **b.** *S. sinner*, a loose woman, a prostitute.

Suburban (sǒbʊ̄·ɹbăn), *a.* and *sb.* 1625. [– L. *suburbanus*, f. as prec.; see -AN.] **A.** *adj.* **1.** Of or belonging to a suburb or the suburbs of a town: living, situated, operating, or carried on in the suburbs. **2.** *transf.* Having characteristics that are regarded as belonging especially to life in the suburbs of a city; having the inferior manners, the narrowness of view, etc., attributed to residents in suburbs 1817.

1. S. villas, highway-side retreats COWPER. **2.** A fifth's look's vulgar, dowdyish, and s. BYRON.

B. *sb.* A s. residence. **b.** A resident in the suburbs. 1856. Hence **Subu·rbanite,** a resident in the suburbs. **Suburba·nity,** the condition of being s., an instance of this. **Subu·rbanize** *v. trans.* to render s.

Suburbia (sǒbʊ̄·ɹbiă). 1896. [f. SUBURB + -IA¹.] A quasi-proper name for: The suburbs (*esp.* of London).

†**Subu·rbian,** *a.* and *sb.* 1606. [f. L. *suburbium* SUBURB + -AN.] **A.** *adj.* Suburban: in 17th c. often with ref. to the licentious life of the (London) suburbs –1810. **B.** *sb.* A resident in the suburbs –1825.

Suburbican (sǒbʊ̄·ɹbikăn), *a.* 1659. [alt. f. next.] = next.

Suburbicarian (sǒbʊ̄ɹbikēᵊ·riăn), *a.* 1654. [– late L. *suburbicarius*, f. L. *suburbium* SUBURB, after *urbicarius* †urbicary (XVII); see -ARIAN.] Applied to the dioceses (now six in number) around Rome, and to their churches, etc., which are subject to the jurisdiction of the Pope as metropolitan and the bishops of which form the body of cardinal bishops. So **Subu·rbicary** *a.* 1654.

Su·bvari:ety. 1802. [SUB- 7 b.] A subordinate or minor variety, *esp.* of a domestic animal or cultivated plant.

Subvention (sǒbve·nʃən), *sb.* late ME. [– (O)Fr. *subvention* – late L. *subventio*, *-ōn-*, f. L. *subvenire* come to the help of, f. *sub* SUB- 25 + *venire* come; see -ION.] **1.** A subsidy levied by the state. *Obs.* exc. *Hist.* †**2.** The provision of help, support, or relief. Also, an instance of this. –1737. **3.** A grant of money for the support of an object or institution; *occas.* a grant in aid of necessitous persons; now *esp.* a grant from government or some other authority in support of an enterprise of public importance 1851. **4.** The granting of pecuniary aid for the support of an undertaking 1868.

3. The Crown-Prince..begged some dole or s. for these poor people CARLYLE. **4.** The s. of rural roads 1894. Hence **Subve·ntion, Subve·ntionize** *vbs. trans.* to support or assist by the payment of a s.

Subverse (sǒbvɔ̄·ɹs), *v. rare.* 1590. [– *subvers-*, pa. ppl. stem of L. *subvertere* SUBVERT *v.*] *trans.* To subvert, upset.

Subversion (sǒbvɔ̄·ɹʃən). late ME. [– (O)Fr. *subversion* or late L. *subversio*, *-ōn-*, f. as prec.; see -ION.] **1.** Overthrow, demolition (of a city, stronghold, etc.). Now *rare* or *Obs.* **2.** The turning (of a thing) upside down or uprooting it from its position; overturning, upsetting (of an object). Now *rare.* 1670. **3.** In immaterial senses: Overthrow, ruin. late ME.

2. The s. of woods and timber..through my whole estate..is almost tragical EVELYN. **3.** The decaye of healthe, and subuersion of reason 1558. The s. of several powers and states upon the continent 1798. Hence **Subve·rsionary** *a.* (*rare*) = next.

Subversive (sǒbvɔ̄·ɹsiv), *a.* 1644. [– med. L. *subversivus*, f. as prec.; see -IVE.] Having a tendency to subvert or overthrow; tending to subversion.

There is a poignant delight in study, often s. of human happiness 1812.

Subvert (sǒbvɔ̄·ɹt), *v.* late ME. [– OFr. *subvertir* or L. *subvertere*, f. *sub-* SUB- 25 + *vertere* turn.] †**1.** *trans.* To overthrow, raze to the ground (a town or city, a structure, edifice) –1792. †**2.** To upset, overturn (an object); *occas.* to break up (ground) –1700. **3.** To undermine the character, loyalty, or faith of, corrupt, pervert (a person). Now *rare.* late ME. **4.** To disturb (the mind, soul); to overturn, overthrow (a condition or order of things, a principle, law, etc.) late ME. **5.** To bring about the overthrow or ruin of (a †person, people, or country, a dynasty, etc.) 1529.

4. This cursed opynion..wyll s. all good lawes 1530. *absol.* They have a power given to them,..to s. and destroy BURKE. **5.** By things deemd weak Subverting worldly strong MILT. Hence **Subve·rter,** one who subverts or overthrows. **Subve·rtible** *a.* capable of being subverted.

Subway (sʊ·bwe¹). 1828. [SUB- 3.] An underground passage for conveying water-pipes, gas-pipes, telegraph wires, etc.; an underground tunnel which enables pedestrians to get from one point to another by passing below a road, railway, etc., and thus avoiding its traffic. **b.** *U.S.* An underground railway 1904.

Succade (sʊkē¹·d). 1463. [– AFr. *sukade*, ONFr. *succade* (also *chuc(c)ade*), of unkn. origin; see -ADE 1 c.] Fruit preserved in sugar, either candied or in syrup; *pl.* sweetmeats of candied fruit or vegetable products. Now *Obs.* or *rare.* **b. S. gourd,** the vegetable marrow 1866. So †**Succate** –1715.

†**Succeda·neous,** *a.* 1646. [f. L. *succedaneus*, f. *succedere* come close after; see SUCCEED, -EOUS.] Taking, or serving in, the place of something else; acting as a succedaneum or substitute.

‖**Succedaneum** (sʊksĭdē¹·nĭǒm). *Pl.* **-ea, -eums.** 1643. [mod.L. use of n. of L. *succedaneus*; see prec.] **1.** A thing which (*rarely*, a person who) replaces or serves in the place of another; a substitute 1662. **2.** *Med.* A drug, frequently of inferior efficacy, substituted for another 1643. †**3.** Misused for: A remedy, cure –1789.

1. In lieu of me, you will have a charming s., Lady Harriet Stanhope H. WALPOLE.

Succedent (sǒksī·děnt), *a.* and *sb.* Now *Obs.* or *rare.* late ME. [– L. *succedens*, *-ent-*, pr. pple. of *succedere* SUCCEED; see -ENT.] **A.** *adj.* **1.** Following, succeeding, subsequent 1450. **2.** Astrol. *S. houses*: the 2nd, 5th, 8th, and 11th houses 1591. **B.** *sb.* †**1.** A thing that follows another –1608. **2.** *Astrol.* A 'succedent house'. late ME.

Succeed (sǒksī·d), *v.* [In XIV *succede* – (O)Fr. *succéder* or L. *succedere* go under or up, come close after, go near, go on well, f. *sub* SUB- 11–18 + *cedere* go.] **1.** *intr.* To come next after and take the place of another, either by descent, election, or appointment, in a position of rule or ownership; to be the immediate successor in an office or in an estate. **b.** *transf.* Const. *to* (†*into*): To follow another in the enjoyment or exercise of; to be the next to share or take part in 1612. **2.** *trans.* To take the place of, as successor in an office or heir to an estate; to be successor or heir to 1503. †**3.** To fall heir to, inherit, come into possession of –1725. **4.** *intr.* To come next in an order of individual persons or things; to follow on; also, †to occupy the space vacated by something. late ME. **5.** To follow or come *after* in the course of events, the sequence of things, the order of development, etc.; to take place or come into being subsequently 1450. †**b.** To follow as a consequence *of* or *upon*; to proceed *from* a source; to ensue, result –1710. †**6.** To follow *in*, or come *into, the place of* someone or something –1701. **b.** Const. *to*: To take the place of 1700. †**7.** Of an estate, etc.: To descend in succession; to devolve *upon*, to come down *from.* Chiefly *Sc.* –1604. **8.** *trans*: To come after in the course of time or the sequence of events 1525. †**9.** *intr.* To happen, come to pass –1653. †**10.** Of an enterprise, etc.: To have a certain issue; to turn out (well or ill, etc.) –1684. **11.** To have the desired or a fortunate issue; to turn out successfully 1450. **b.** Of growing plants: To do well, thrive 1812. **12.** Of persons: To attain a desired end or object; to be successful in an endeavour; to bring one's labours to a happy issue. Also formerly, with adv., to have 'good' or 'ill success'. 1509. †**13.** *trans.* To give success to; to prosper, further –1843. †**14.** To come up or near *to*, approach (*rare*) –1697.

1. When Sir Ralf died, Sir John succeeded 1891. **b.** The christian saints succeeded..to the honours 1782. **2.** Richard Cromwell succeeded his father 1860. **4.** There was another Malefactor to succeede EVELYN. **5.** Enjoy, till I return, Short pleasures, for long woes are to s. MILT. **6. b.** Revenge succeeds to love, and rage to grief

DRYDEN. 7. *All's Well* III. vii. 23. 8. Shame succeeds the short-liv'd pleasure COWLEY. 10. But euery day things now succeeded worse DANIEL. 11. I only used it in two instances, in both of which it succeeded 1808. 12. Alike my scorn, if he succeed or fail POPE. She succeeded in finding an empty carriage 1898. 13. Pallas.. succeeds their enterprise POPE. 14. Will you to the cooler cave s.? DRYDEN. Hence **Succee·der**, a successor (now *rare*); one who is successful.

Succeeding (sǒksī·diŋ), *vbl. sb.* 1450. [-ING[1].] **1.** Successful issue, success. †**2.** Succession –1679. †**3.** Consequence. SHAKS.

Succentor (sǒkse·ntǫɹ). 1642. [– late L. *succentor*, f. L. *succinere* sing to, accompany, 'chime in', agree, f. *sub* SUB- 8 + *canere* sing. In sense 2 assoc. with SUB- 6 as in SUBCHANTER.] †**1.** A chanter who takes up the chant after the precentor, or who presides over the left choir –1817. **2.** A precentor's deputy 1642.

‖**Succès** (sükse̜). 1859. [Fr., = success.] In *s. d'estime*, a cordial reception given to something out of respect rather than from admiration; *s. fou*, a success marked by wild enthusiasm; *s. de scandale*, the success of a thing, e.g. of a work of art, dependent upon its scandalous character.

Success (sǒkse·s). 1537. [– L. *successus*, f. *success-*, pa. ppl. stem of *succedere* SUCCEED.] †**1.** That which happens in the sequel; the termination (favourable or otherwise) of affairs; the result –1733. †**b.** An event –1753. †**c.** The result (of an experiment), the effect (of a medicine) –1756. **2.** The fortune (good or bad) befalling anyone in a particular situation or affair. *Good s.* = sense 3; *ill s.*: failure, misadventure, misfortune. *arch.* 1548. †**b.** In particularized use. –1764. **3.** (= the older *good s.*) The prosperous achievement of something attempted; the attainment of an object according to one's desire: now often with particular ref. to the attainment of wealth or position 1586. **b.** An instance of this; a successful undertaking or achievement 1666. **c.** *transf.* One who or a thing which succeeds or is successful 1882. †**4.** Succession or sequence in time or occurrence –1690. †**5.** Succession as of heirs, etc. –1611.

1. *All's Well* III. vi. 86. †*In the s.*, eventually. 2. Perplex'd and troubl'd at his bad s. MILT. b. After diuers unfortunat successes in warre DRAYTON. 3. Giue but successe to mine attempting spirit KYD. The argument of s. which is always powerful with men of the world GEO. ELIOT. c. Mrs. Hartwell's dance was a great s. 1885. 5. Our Parents Noble Names, In whose successe we are gentle SHAKS.

Successful (sǒkse·sfŭl), *a.* 1588. [f. prec. + -FUL.] **1.** Of persons: That succeeds or achieves success, *esp.* (in recent use), that attains to wealth or position, that 'gets on'. Also *transf.* of things. **2.** Of actions, conditions, etc.: Attended with, characterized by, or resulting in success 1588.

1. A s. play 1848. It failed; we tried again, and were s. TYNDALL. 2. And welcome Nephews from successful wars SHAKS. Hence **Succe·ssful-ly** *adv.*, **-ness.**

Succession (sǒkse·ʃən). ME. [– (O)Fr. *succession* or L. *successio*, *-ōn-*, f. *success-*; see SUCCESS, -ION.] **I. 1.** The action of a person or thing following, or succeeding to the place of, another; the coming of one thing or person after another; also, the passing from one act or state to another; an instance of this. late ME. †**2.** The course, lapse, or process *of time* –1655. **3.** The transmission (or mode of transmission) *of* an estate, royal or official dignity, or the like ME. **4.** The process by which one person succeeds another in the occupation or possession of an estate, a throne, or the like; the act or fact of succeeding according to custom or law *to* the rights and liabilities of a predecessor; the conditions or principles in accordance with which this is done 1513. **b.** *pregnantly* for: The line or order of succession 1533. **5.** (A person's) right or privilege of succeeding to an estate or dignity 1461. **6.** The act of succeeding to the episcopate by the reception of lawfully transmitted authority by ordination 1565.

1. By reflecting on the appearing of various Ideas, one after another in our Understandings, we get the Notion of S. LOCKE. Phr. *In s.*, one after another in regular sequence, successively. 3. So long as the Earl of Warwick lived, he was not certaine of the Kingdoms s. 1641. 4. He swore consent to your S. SHAKS. Phr. *The s.*, the conditions under which successors to a particular estate, throne, etc. are appointed. *War of S.*, a war to settle a dispute as to the s. to a particular throne. *By s.*, according to the customary or legal principle by which one succeeds another in an inheritance, an office, etc. by inherited right. b. He was in the s. to an earldom MACAULAY. 5. The right to make wills or settlements or successions is the creation of positive law 1894. 6. *Apostolic(al) s.* (or *the s.*), the continued transmission of the ministerial commission, through an unbroken line of bishops from the Apostles onwards.

II. †**1.** Successors, heirs, or descendants collectively; progeny, issue –1697. †**2.** A generation (of men); chiefly *pl.* (future or successive) generations –1720. †**b.** Posterity -1704. **3.** A series of persons or things in orderly sequence; a continued line (*of* sovereigns, heirs to an estate, etc.); an unbroken line or stretch (*of* objects coming one after another) 1579. †**b.** The followers collectively, or a sect of followers, of a school of thought (tr. Gr. διαδοχή) –1699. **4.** A set of persons or things succeeding in the place of others 1647. †**5.** That to which a person succeeds as heir (*rare*) –1751.

1. Their young S. all their Cares employ: They breed, they brood, instruct and educate DRYDEN. 3. A s. of victories MACAULAY. Every progress of Elizabeth..was a s. of shows and interludes 1874.

III. *techn.* **a.** *Mus.* The order in which the notes of a melody proceed. Also = SEQUENCE 3 b. 1752. **b.** *Agric.* and *Hort.* (*a*) The rotation (of crops); (*b*) the maturing of crops of the same kind by a system of successive sowings so that as one is declining another is coming on 1778. **c.** *Geol.*, etc. The continued sequence in a definite order of species, types, etc.; *spec.* the descent in uninterrupted series of forms modified by evolution or development 1834.

attrib.: **s.-crop,** a crop of some plant coming in s. to another; **s. duty,** a duty assessed upon s. to estate; **s. house,** one of a series of forcing-houses having regularly graded temperatures into which plants are moved in s.; **s. powder,** a poison supposed to have been made of lead acetate; **S. States,** the states resulting from the dismemberment of Austria-Hungary under the Treaty of Versailles; **s. tax,** a tax similar to s. duty.

Successional (sǒkse·ʃənăl), *a.* 1600. [f. prec. + -AL[1] 1.] **1.** Pertaining to, characterized by, or involving the succession of persons as heirs, rulers, or the like; passing or proceeding by succession or descent; often with special ref. to the apostolic succession. **2.** Of things: Following one upon another; occurring in succession; involved in a succession 1685.

2. A useful s. crop of flowers 1881. Hence **Succe·ssionally** *adv.* by succession.

Successionist (sǒkse·ʃənist). 1846. [f. as prec. + -IST.] One who maintains the validity or necessity of a succession; *esp.* one who upholds the doctrine of the Apostolic Succession.

Successive (sǒkse·siv), *a.* late ME. [– med.L. *successivus*, f. L. *success-* see SUCCESS, -IVE.] **1. a.** With pl. or compound sb.: Coming one after another in an uninterrupted sequence; following one another in order. **b.** With sing. sb.: Following another of the same kind in a regular sequence or series. Somewhat *rare*. 1597. **2.** Characterized by or involving succession; brought about or produced in succeeding stages 1685. †**3.** = HEREDITARY –1726.

1. a. Three s. Bishops..excommunicated him 1606. b. And three..he assailes;..each s. after other quailes DANIEL. 2. Doctrine of s. development not confirmed by the admission that man is of modern origin 1835. 3. Pleade my Successiue Title with your Swords. I was the first borne Sonne. SHAKS. Hence **Succe·ssive-ly** *adv.*, **-ness.**

Successless (sǒkse·slės), *a.* Now *rare.* 1584. [f. SUCCESS + -LESS.] Without, or having no, success; unsuccessful.

How mighty men made foul s. war Against the gods PEELE. Hence **Succe·ssless-ly** *adv.*, **-ness.**

Successor (sǒkse·səɹ). ME. [– OFr. *successour* (mod. *-eur*) – L. *successor*, *-ōr-*, f. *success-*; see SUCCESS, -OR 2.] One who succeeds another in office, function, or position. (Correlative to *predecessor.*) Also *transf.* of a thing.

A gift to such a corporation, either of lands or of chattels, without naming their successors, vests an absolute property in them so long as the corporation subsists BLACKSTONE. So **Succe·ssorship.** †**Succe·ssory** *a.* hereditary –1641.

Succiferous (sɒksi·fĕrəs), *a. rare.* 1655. [f. L. SUCCUS + -FEROUS.] *Bot.* Producing or bearing sap.

Succin- (sɒksin), comb. form (bef. a vowel) of L. *succinum* amber, in the names of various amide and anilide derivatives of SUCCINIC acid, e.g. *succinamic acid, succinanil.*

Succinate (sɒ·ksineit). 1790. [– Fr. *succinate* (Lavoisier); see SUCCINIC and -ATE[4].] *Chem.* A salt of succinic acid.

Succinct (sǒksi·ŋkt), *pa. pple., ppl. a.*, and *a.* late ME. [– L. *succinctus*, pa. pple. of *succingere*, f. *sub* SUB- 2, 25 + *cingere* gird.] **A.** *pa. pple.* and *ppl. a.* **1.** Girt, engirdled. **2.** Of garments, etc.: Girded up; confined by or as by a girdle. Also of persons. 1604. **3.** *Ent.* Of certain pupæ: supported by a silken filament round the middle 1891.

2. The Priest..s. for sacrificial feast 1866.

B. *adj.* **1.** Of a narrative, etc.: Compressed into small compass; brief and concise 1585. **2.** Of persons, their speech, style, etc.: Characterized by verbal brevity and conciseness; terse 1603. **3.** Of garments: Not ample or full, close-fitting, scant. *arch.* or *poet.* 1667. **4.** Of short duration, brief, curt 1796.

1. A full, though s. and sober Narrative 1711. 2. A s. and dry writer 1759. 3. Some novelties of dress, viz., very low stays, and very s. petticoats 1755. 4. With a s. bow..he took a hasty leave MME. D'ARBLAY. Hence **Succi·nct-ly** *adv.*, **-ness.**

‖**Succinea** (sǒksi·niă). *Pl.* **-eæ, -eas.** 1840. [mod.L. (Draparnaud), fem. of *succineus*, f. *succinum* amber.] *Zool.* Any gasteropod of the genus of this name: so called from the transparent texture and amber colour of the shell.

Succinic (sǒksi·nik), *a.* 1790. [– Fr. *succinique* (Lavoisier), f. L. *succinum* amber; see -IC 1 b.] **1.** Chem. *S. acid*: a dibasic acid obtained by the dry distillation of amber. (Formerly called *salt* or *spirit of amber.*) **b.** So *s. anhydride*, etc. 1805. **2.** Found in amber, as an insect 1836.

Succinimide (sɒksi·nimaid). 1857. [f. prec. + IMIDE.] *Chem.* A crystalline substance obtained by the action of dry ammonia gas on succinic anhydride.

Succinite (sɒ·ksinəit). 1816. [f. SUCCINUM + -ITE[1] 2 b.] **1.** *Min.* **a.** A granular garnet of the colour of amber. **b.** Amber 1854. **2.** *Chem.* The insoluble resinous element in amber 1868.

Succino- (sɒ·ksino), used as comb. form (bef. a consonant) of L. *succinum* amber.

Succinol (sɒ·ksinǫl). 1913. [f. L. SUCCINUM + -OL.] Purified amber tar-oil, used in the treatment of skin-diseases.

Succinous (sɒ·ksinəs), *a. rare.* 1658. [f. next + -OUS.] Of or pertaining to amber.

‖**Succinum** (sɒ·ksinǒm). 1608. [L.] Amber.

Succinyl (sɒ·ksinil). 1868. [f. SUCCINIC + -YL.] *Chem.* The radical of succinic acid. Hence **Succiny·lic** *a.* = SUCCINIC.

Succise (sǒksəi·s), *a.* 1880. [– L. *succisus*, pa. pple. of *succidere*, f. *sub* SUB- 25 + *cædere* cut.] *Bot.* Shaped as if abruptly cut or broken off at the lower end.

Succory (sɒ·kəri). 1533. [alt. of *cicoree*, *sichorie*, early forms of CHICORY, after MLG. *suckerie*, MDu. *sūkerie* (Du. *suikerei*, Flem. †*suykerey*, †*succory*).] **1.** The plant *Cichorium intybus* (family *Compositæ*), with bright blue flowers, found wild in England, esp. by roadsides. Also, its leaves and roots used medicinally and as food. **2.** Applied with qualifying words to other composites, chiefly of the tribe *Cichoriaceæ* 1538.

Succose (sɒ·kous), *a. rare.* 1859. [– L. *succosus*, f. *succus* juice; see -OSE[1].] *Bot.* Full of juice or sap. So †**Succo·sity,** juice, moisture 1530–1579.

Succotash (sɒ·kŏtæʃ). 1778. [– Narragansett (Algonquian) *msiquatash* (inanimate pl.); see SQUASH *sb.*[2]] A dish of N. Amer. Indian origin, usu. consisting of green maize and beans boiled together.

Succour (sɒ·kəɹ), *sb.* Also (now *U.S.*) **succor.** [ME. *sucurs*, *soc(o)urs* – OFr. *sucurs*, *socours* (mod. *secours*) :– med.L. *succursus*, f.

succurs-, pa. ppl. stem of L. *succurrere*; see next.] **1.** Aid, help, assistance. **2.** One who or that which helps; a means of assistance; an aid ME. **3.** Military assistance in men or supplies; *esp.* auxiliary forces; reinforcements ME. **4.** Shelter, protection; a place of shelter, sheltered place, refuge. *Obs.* exc. *dial.* ME.

1. I can no mor, but aske of hem socours 1460. The devotion of life or fortune to the s. of the poor JOHNSON. **2.** Thou art my sucoure, haist the to helpe me COVERDALE *Ps.* 21:19. **3.** Our watchful General had discern'd from far This mighty s., which made glad the Foe DRYDEN.

Succour (sɒ·kəɹ), *v.* Also (now *U.S.*) **succor.** ME. [– OFr. *socorre* :– L. *succurrere*, f. *sub* SUB- 25 + *currere* run, and OFr. *suc(c)ourir* (mod. *secourir*), with change of conjugation.] **1.** *trans.* To help, assist, aid (a person, etc.). **2.** To furnish with military assistance; to bring reinforcements to; *spec.* to relieve (a besieged place) ME. †**3.** To relieve or remedy (a state of want, weakness, etc.); to relieve (a diseased condition) –1645. **4.** To shelter, protect. Now *dial.* late ME. **5.** *Naut.* To strengthen, make firm or taut 1688.

1. He is able to sucker them that are tempted TINDALE *Heb.* 2:18. *transf.* Yet not for me, shine sun to s. flowers 1599. **2.** I will socoure hym with all my puyssaunce MALORY. **3.** That so the Parliament May..s. our just Fears MILT. **5.** To S. a Cable 1706. So **Su·ccourable** *a.* affording succour, helpful (*Obs.* exc. *arch.*). †**Su·ccourer**, one who, or that which aids or assists –1686.

Succourless (sɒ·kəɹlės), *a.* Now *rare.* late ME. [f. SUCCOUR *sb.* + -LESS.] Of persons or conditions: Without help, helpless; *freq.* without resources or means of subsistence, destitute.

Succous (sɒ·kəs), *a. rare.* 1694. [– L. *succosus*, f. *succus* juice; see -OUS.] Containing juice or sap; juicy.

‖**Succuba** (sɒ·kiŭbă). *Pl.* **-bæ** (bī). 1587. [Late L. = strumpet, f. *succubare*, f. *sub*, SUB- 2 + *cub-* to lie.] = SUCCUBUS.

Succubous (sɒ·kiŭbəs), *a.* 1857. [f. L. *sub*, SUB- 2 + *cub-* (*-cumbere*) to lie + -OUS. Cf. INCUBOUS.] *Bot.* Having the upper margin of each leaf covered by the lower margin of the one succeeding it; applied to some of the *Jungermanniaceæ*.

‖**Succubus** (sɒ·kiŭbɒs). *Pl.* **-bi** (bəi), †**-busses.** late ME. [med.L. *succubus* (masc. form with fem. meaning), corresp. to SUCCUBA, after INCUBUS.] **1.** A demon in female form supposed to have carnal intercourse with men in their sleep. **2.** *transf.* **a.** A demon, evil spirit; *occas.* a familiar spirit 1601. **b.** A strumpet, whore 1622.

1. For forty years, he had kept up an amatory commerce with a S., called Hermeline 1818. Hence **Su·ccubine** *a.* (*rare*) of or pertaining to a s.

Succulence (sɒ·kiŭlėns). 1787. [f. as next; see -ENCE.] The quality or condition of being succulent; juiciness. Also, succulent part. So **Su·cculency** 1616.

Succulent (sɒ·kiŭlěnt), *a.* and *sb.* 1601. [– L. *succulentus*, f. *succus* juice; see -LENT, -ULENT.] **A.** *adj.* **1.** Full of juice; juicy. **2.** *transf.* and *fig.* 'Juicy', 'sappy', rich 1626.

1. The fruit, which..is s. in the peach 1785. Rich, deep black, s. mud 1877. **2.** His air of rather s. patronage MEREDITH.

B. *sb. Bot.* A succulent plant 1825. Hence **Su·cculently** *adv.*

Succumb (sŏkɒ·m), *v.* 1489. [– (O)Fr. *succomber* or L. *succumbere*, f. *sub*, SUB- 2 + *-cumbere* lie.] †**1.** *trans.* To bring down, bring low, overwhelm –1549. **2.** *intr.* To yield to pressure or give way to superior force, authority, etc.: said properly of persons or communities, and *transf.* of conditions, designs; occas. of material things 1604. **3.** *spec.* To sink under the attacks of a disease, the effects of wounds, an operation, etc.: hence, to die 1849.

2. Pardon me if I do not s. to curiosity 1825. **3.** He succumbed in a few mon hs to fever LIVINGSTONE.

†**Succu·mbent**, *a. rare.* 1645. [– L. *succumbens, -ent-*, pr. pple. of *succumbere*; see prec., -ENT.] Subject, submissive *to* –1660. Hence **Succu·mbency** (*rare*), submission.

Succursal (sŏkō·ɹsăl), *a.* and *sb.* 1844. [– Fr. *succursale*, f. med.L. *succursus* (see SUCCOUR *sb.*) + *-al, -ale* -AL[1].] **A.** *adj.* Subsidiary; applied *esp.* to a religious establishment dependent upon a principal one.

Its Cathedral, surrounded by its s. churches 1855.

B. *sb.* A subsidiary establishment; a branch institution, society, business, etc. Also in Fr. form **succursale.** 1859.

‖**Succus** (sɒ·kɒs). *Pl.* **succi** (sɒ·ksəi). 1719. [L.] A juice; in scientific terminology applied to (*a*) fluid secretions in an animal or vegetable body, (*b*) juices extracted from plants.

†**Succussa·tion.** 1646. [– med.L. *succussatio, -ōn-*, f. *succussat-*, pa. ppl. stem of L. *succussare*, frequent. of *succutere*; see next, -ION.] Shaking up, violent shaking, jolting –1774. **b.** Trotting (of a horse) –1681.

Succussion (sŏkɒ·ʃən). 1622. [– L. *succussio, -ōn-*, f. *sucuss-*, pa. ppl. stem of *succutere*, f. *sub* SUB- 25 + *quatere* shake; see -ION.] The action of shaking or the condition of being shaken, esp. with violence; an instance of this. **b.** *spec.* (*Med.*) An act or method of diagnosis in pneumothorax, etc., which consists in shaking the thorax to detect the presence of fluid 1747. So **Succu·ss** *v. trans.*

Succussive (sŏkɒ·siv), *a. rare.* 1742. [f. prec. + -IVE.] Characterized by shaking.

Such (sɒtʃ), *dem. adj.* and *pron.* [OE. *swilć, swelć, swylć*, ME. *swich, swech, swuch*, mod. dial. *sich*, and *sech*, standard Eng. *such*; for the loss of *w* cf. SO, SWORD, for the loss of *l* cf. WHICH. Cogn. Gmc. forms are OFris. *sāl(i)k*, etc., OS. *sulīk*, OHG. *solīh* (Du. *zulk*, G. *solch*), ON. *slíkr*, Goth. *swaleiks*; f. **swa*, **swe* So + **līk-* body, form (see LIKE *a.*).] **I. 1.** Of the character, degree, or extent described, referred to, or implied in what has been said. (With a concrete sb., or an abstract sb. used in a particularized sense, now always *s. a* exc. *poet.*) **2.** Standing predicatively at the head of a sentence or clause, and referring summarily to a statement or description just made ME. **3.** Of the same kind or class as something mentioned or referred to; of that kind; similar, the like. *Obs.* or *arch.* exc. in collocation with a numeral, indef. adj., etc. ME. **4.** Equivalent to a descriptive adj. or adv. on which it follows closely and the repetition of which is thus avoided. (*So* is now preferred.) OE. **5.** The previously described or specified; the (person or thing) before mentioned. (In this sense usu. *s.* (not *s. a*) with a sing. sb.). late ME.

1. She thinks not fit s. he her face should see CRASHAW. S. Joy my Soul, s. Pleasures fill'd my Sight DRYDEN. Thou didst ill to speak to s. a man of s. matters SCOTT. **2.** Lo sich it is to haue a tunge loos CHAUCER. Phr. *S. is life!*, now often used trivially as an expression of resignation or acquiescence in things as they are. **3.** Of rotchets, whitings or s. common fish 1613. **4.** A heroic poem, truly s. DRYDEN. **5.** For default of *s.* issue, viz. that issue which is before mentioned 1818.

II. Where the meaning is determined by ref. to a correlative or dependent clause. **1. a.** With *s.* in both clauses; now *s. as..s.* = L. *qualis..talis* OE. **b.** With *what* as the correlative in the dependent clause (*rare*) 1834. †**c.** With advb. *as* as the correlative in the dependent clause –1790. **2.** With correlative *as* pron., also *as that* ME. *S. as* = Of the kind or degree that; the kind of (person or thing) that OE. **3.** In uses marked by special word-order. **a.** In predicative use ME. **b.** *S. as one* or *it is*: having the character that he (it) has; chiefly depreciatory or contemptuous, or apologetic ME. **c.** In attrib. use after its sb. OE. **d.** Hence *s. as* is used to introduce examples of a class: = for example, *e.g.* 1695. **4.** The principal clause may be reduced to *s.* and the words qualified by it for the purpose of producing a terse (exclamatory) form. late ME. **b.** The clause introduced by *as* may be reduced to the subj. only; when this is a pron., it may be either nom. or accus., *e.g.* 's. as *me*' or 's. as *I*' (*sc.* am) OE. **c.** *There is s. a thing as*: a phr. used to hint that the thing referred to exists and therefore must be taken into account; often used *colloq.* to convey a veiled threat 1729. **5.** *S..as* (OE. *swá*): the..that, *pl.* those..that; any or all..that; as many (or as much)..as OE. **6.** With relative *who, which* (*whence*, etc.) or *that*: = 'such..as'. Now *rare* and regarded as incorrect. OE. **7.** Followed by a dependent clause introduced by *that, as that* (now *rare*), etc., or by *as to* (†*to*) with infin., expressing a consequence. The meaning of *s.* tends to be intensive = so great, etc. OE. **b.** predicative ME. **c.** In attrib. use after its sb. 1771. **d.** With the clauses in reverse order, that containing *s.* being explanatory of what precedes. late ME. **8.** By suppression of the clause expressing comparison or relativity, *s.* acquires emphatic force = so great, so eminent, and the like OE. **b.** *colloq.* Used as an absolute intensive 1553. **9.** Preceding an adj. used attrib., *s.*, *s. a* becomes advb. = so, so..a 1522.

1. a. S. as is the tree s. is the fruit 1586. *Prov.* S. master, s. man. **c.** As the man is, soch is also his strength COVERDALE *Judges* 8:21. **2.** We'll each of us give you s. a thrashing as you'll remember HUGHES. **3. a.** Her conduct was s. as might have been expected from the weakness of her principles MRS. RADCLIFFE. **b.** But, s. as the rooms were, there were plenty of them HARDY. **c.** Tears s. as Angels weep MILT. **d.** Many large gold coins s. as the..doubloon 1875. **4.** S. a dinner as we had to-day! 1779. **b.** Others s. as he SHAKS. **c.** There are s. things as horsewhips 1889. **5.** S. ale as he hath brued, let him drynke him self 1539. **6.** S. suffering Soules That welcome wrongs SHAKS. **7.** This filled my Mind with s. a huddle of Ideas, that..I fell into the following Dream ADDISON. He..had borne himself with s. gallantry as to attract the attention of his superior officers 1892. **d.** You still shall liue (s. vertue hath my Pen) SHAKS. **8.** *Merry W.* II. i. 45. **b.** It's ever s. a way off 1803. **9.** This mighty army..collected from s. distant parts 1742.

III. 1. Used to indicate or suggest a name, designation, number or quantity, instead of the specific term that would be required in a particular instance 1460. **2.** *Comb.* (parasynthetic) 1591.

1. That the feoffour pay to the feoffee..s. a sume at s. a day 1544. Phr. *S. and s.*; Number so-and-so in s.-and-s. a street 1861. **2.** S. a coulour'd Perrywig SHAKS.

IV. Absolute and pronominal uses. †**1.** The persons or things before mentioned; those, they; also with sing. ref., that person or thing –1655. **2.** Persons or things such as those mentioned, described, or referred to OE. **3.** With dependent rel. pron.: Such people *as*, those (people) *who, whose*, etc.; all or any *that* OE. **b.** People of the same kind *as* 1823. **4.** Such a thing; the thing mentioned or referred to OE. **5.** *S. and s.*: such and such persons or things; also *sing.*, this and this 1450.

1. To s. my errand is MILT. Phr. *And s.*, and suchlike, and the like. **3.** S. whose fathers were right worshipful MASSINGER. **b.** S. as I are free in spirit when our limbs are chained SCOTT. **4.** A forest became s. by a stroke of the pen, not by any physical change 1912. **5.** We have done s., and s., and s. 1893.

Phrases, *Many* (*more*), *some, all, every, s.*, many (etc.)..of the (same) kind, many..like this. *S. another, another s.*, another..of the kind, another similar. **No s.** *adj.*, **none s.** *absol.* or as *pron.* **a.** No (person or thing) of the kind; none of the kind. **b.** No great; advb. qualifying an adj. = not (a) very, not a. **c.** *No s.* †*matter* or *thing*: nothing of the kind; also exclamatorily, = not at all, not a bit of it, quite the contrary. **S. a(n) one. a.** One of that kind. **b.** Followed by rel. pron. *as*: One of the kind that; one who, a thing which. **c.** Followed by rel. adv. *as*: One of the same kind as; one like (so-and-so). **d.** So-and-so. *Obs.* or *arch.* **As s. a.** In that capacity. **b.** Hence: Accordingly, consequently, thereupon. *colloq.* or *vulgar.* **c.** In itself; *quâ* (so-and-so). *S. kind of*, of s. a kind. *S. time as* (or *that*), the time when, the moment at which.

Su·ch-like, su·chlike, *a.* and *pron.* late ME. [f. SUCH + LIKE *a.*] **A.** *adj.* Of such a kind; of the like or a similar kind; of the before-mentioned sort or character. **b.** Having forward ref., usu. with correl. *as* (*rare*) 1591.

Many other suche lyke thinges ye do TINDALE *Mark* 7:8. **b.** Such like petty crimes as these SHAKS.

B. *pron.* Usu. *pl.* Such-like persons or things; also *sing.*, something of that kind. Chiefly in *and s., or s.* late ME.

These Bushes, Brakes, and suchlike 1669. A smooth marble hearth-stone, or such like GOLDSM.

Suchness (sɒ·tʃnės). Chiefly *Philos.* OE. [f. SUCH *a.* + -NESS.] The condition or quality of being such; quality.

Suchwise (sɒ·tʃ,wəiz), *adv. rare.* late ME. [Short for *in such wise.*] In such a manner.

Suck (sɒk), *sb.* ME. [f. next] **1. a.** The action or an act of sucking milk from the breast; the milk or other fluid sucked at one time. **b.** The application of suction by the mouth either to an external object (e.g. a wound, a pipe) or internally 1760. **2.** A small draught of liquid; a drink 1625. **†3.** Milk sucked (or to be sucked) from the breast; mother's milk –1655. **4.** The drawing of air by suction; *occas.* a draught or current of air; *spec.* in *Coal-mining*, the backward suction of air following an explosion of fire-damp 1667. **5.** The sucking action of eddying or swirling water; the sound caused by this; *locally*, the place at which a body of water moves in such a way as to suck objects into its vortex ME. **6.** *slang.* A deception; a disappointing event or result. Also *s.-in.* 1856. **7.** *pl.* Sweetmeats. Also *collect. sing. colloq.* 1858.

1. a. Phr. *At s.*, engaged in sucking. **b.** I saw the cut, gave it [*sc.* my finger] a s., wrapt it up, and thought no more about it STERNE.

To give s.: see SUCK *v.* III. 2.

Suck (sɒk), *v.* Pa. t. and pple. **sucked.** [OE. *sūcan* str. vb. becoming weak from XIV, corresp. to L. *sūgere*, (O)Ir. *súgim*, f. WIE. **sūg-*, of which a parallel imit. base **sūk-* is repr. by OE. *sūgan*, OS. *sūgan*, MLG., MDu. *sūgen* (Du. *zuigen*), OHG. *sūgan* (G. *saugen*), ON. *súga*; cf. SOAK.] **I. 1.** *trans.* To draw (liquid, *esp.* milk from the breast) into the mouth by contracting the muscles of the lips, cheeks, and tongue so as to produce a partial vacuum. **b.** of flies, etc., drawing blood, of bees extracting honey from flowers ME. **2.** To imbibe (qualities, etc.) *with* the mother's milk 1586. **3.** To extract or draw (moisture, goodness, etc.) *from* or *out of* a thing; to absorb into itself. late ME. **4.** To derive or extract (information, comfort, profit, etc.) *from*, †*of*, or *out of* 1535. **†5.** To draw (air, breath) into the mouth; to inhale (air, smoke, etc.) –1717. **6.** To draw (water, air, etc.) in some direction, esp. by producing a vacuum 1661. **7.** To draw in so as to swallow up or engulf. (Now *rare* or *Obs.*) 1523. **b.** *fig.* To draw *into* a course of action, etc. 1771.

1. The milke thou suck'st from her did turne to Marble SHAKS. *fig.* Death that hath suckt the honey of thy breath SHAKS. *To s. the blood of* (fig.), to exhaust the resources of, drain the life out of. **3.** *Rich. II*, III. iv. 38. **4.** There out sucke they no small auauntage COVERDALE *Ps.* 72:10. **5.** Tobacco suckt through water by long canes or pipes 1634. **7.** When a whirle-poole sucks the circkled waters 1590.

II. 1. To apply the lips to (a teat, breast, the mother, nurse or dam) for the purpose of extracting milk; to draw milk from with the mouth OE. **b.** Of flies, bees, etc. late ME. **2.** To apply the lips and tongue (or analogous organs) to (an object) for the purpose of obtaining nourishment; to extract the fluid contents of by such action of the mouth; to absorb (a sweetmeat) in the mouth by the action of the tongue and the muscles of the cheeks ME. **b.** To apply the tongue and inner sides of the lips to (one's teeth) so as to extract particles of food 1595. **3.** *transf.* To draw the moisture, goodness, etc. from 1693. **b.** To work (a pump) dry 1753. **4.** To draw money, information, or the like from (a person); to rob (a person or thing) of its resources or support; to drain, 'bleed' 1558. **5.** With predicative adj.: To render so-and-so by sucking 1530.

2. *To s.* a person's *brains*: see BRAIN *sb.* **3.** Phr. *To teach one's grandmother to s. eggs*: said of those who offer advice to others who are more experienced. *To s. the monkey*: see MONKEY *sb.* Phrases. **4.** The land sucked of its nourishment, by a small class of legitimates EMERSON. **5.** Phr. *To s. dry*, to extract all the moisture out by suction; *fig.* to exhaust.

III. 1. *intr.* Of the young of a mammal: To perform the action described in sense I. 1; to draw milk from the teat; to feed from the breast or udder OE. **b.** of flies drawing blood, etc. 1610. **2. To give suck** (occas. †*to give to s.*); to give milk from the breast or udder, to suckle. Const. simple dat. or *to*. Now *arch.* (*Suck*, properly infin., is now felt as a sb.) ME. **3.** *To s. at.*: (*a*) to take a draught of; to inhale; (*b*) to take a pull at (a pipe, drinking vessel) 1584. **4.** Of inanimate objects: To draw by suction ME. **5.** Of a pump: To draw air instead of water, as a result of the exhaustion of the water or a defective valve. Also *fig.* 1627.

1. To see my Ewes graze, & my Lambes sucke SHAKS. **b.** Where the Bee sucks, there s. I SHAKS. **2.** *Macb.* I. vii. 54. **5.** *fig.* Even Byron's pump *sucks* sometimes, and gives an unpleasant dry wheeze LOWELL.

With advs. **S. in. a.** *trans.* To draw into the mouth by suction; to inhale (air, etc.); *occas.* to draw in (one's breath) etc. **b.** To imbibe (qualities, etc.) *with* one's mother's milk, *with* a draught. **c.** *gen.* To draw or take in (*lit.* and *fig.*); to absorb. **d.** *dial.* and *slang.* To 'take in', cheat, deceive. **S. out.** *trans.* To draw out by or as by suction. **S. up. a.** *trans.* To draw up into the mouth by suction. **b.** To draw up by suction or the creation of a vacuum; to absorb (liquid); to draw up (moisture) by heat; also, to draw up moisture from. **c.** To swallow up. **d.** intr. *To s. up to*, to curry favour with; to toady *to*. *School-boy slang.*

Suck-, the vb.-stem used in comb., as in **s.-bo:ttle,** an infant's feeding-bottle; a tippler; **s.-fish** = SUCKER *sb.* II. 2; **s.-(a)-thumb,** a child that sucks its thumb.

Su·ck-egg. 1609. [f. SUCK- + EGG *sb.*] **a.** An animal that is reputed to suck eggs, e.g. a weasel, cuckoo; *fig.* an avaricious person. **b.** A young fellow; *slang*, 'a silly person'.

Sucken (sɒ·kən). *Sc.* late ME. [var. of SOKEN; orig. 'resort' (*sc.* to a particular mill).] **1.** The duty and liability of tenants within a district astricted to a mill. **2.** The lands astricted to a mill; also, the population of such lands 1754. **b.** *transf.* The area of a bailiff's jurisdiction; the district within which one practises or carries on business 1688.

Hence **Su·ckener,** one who is bound to have his corn ground at a certain mill.

Su·ckeny. *Hist.* late ME. [– OFr. *souscanie*, etc. (mod. *souquenille*), of Slav. origin.] A smock.

Sucker (sɒ·kəɹ), *sb.* late ME. [f. SUCK *v.* + -ER[1].] **I. 1.** A young mammal before it is weaned; now *spec.* a sucking-pig; a young whale-calf. **b.** *fig.* A greenhorn, simpleton. *U.S.* 1857. **2.** One who or that which sucks with the mouth 1440. **3.** One who lives at the expense of another; one who draws profit or extorts subsistence from some source; *U.S. slang*, a sponger, parasite 1500. **4.** A shoot thrown out from the base of a tree or plant, which in most cases may serve for propagation; now *esp.* such a shoot rising from the root under ground, near to, or at some distance from, the trunk; also, (now *rare*) a runner (as of the strawberry); also, a lateral shoot; in the tobacco plant, an axillary shoot 1577. **b.** *fig.* (freq. with ref. to the withdrawal of nourishment from the parent stem) 1591. **5.** An organ adapted for sucking or absorbing nourishment by suction, *e.g.* the proboscis of an insect 1685. **6.** Any fish having a conformation of the lips which suggests that it feeds by suction; *esp.* N. Amer. cyprinoid fishes of the family *Catostomidæ* 1772. **b.** *U.S.* An inhabitant of the state of Illinois 1833. **7.** Used as a book-rendering of *Suctoria*, the name of various groups of animals having a sucking apparatus 1835. **8.** The embolus, piston, or rising-valve of a pump; the piston of a syringe or an air-pump 1611. **9. a.** A pipe or tube through which anything is drawn by suction; *locally*, a hood over a fire-place 1755. **b.** An air-hole fitted with a valve; a valve for the regulation of the flow of air 1797. **c.** *Bot.* = HAUSTORIUM 1849.

2. In names of animals, as BLOOD-SUCKER, GOAT-SUCKER, HONEYSUCKER. **3.** Flatterers to the kyng..suckers of his purse and robbers of his subiectes HALL. **4. b.** If thou payest nothing, they will count thee a s., no branch FULLER.

II. 1. A part or organ adapted for adhering to an object; the adhesive pad of an insect's foot, etc.; a suctorial disc, foot, etc. 1681. **2.** Any fish characterized by a suctorial disc by which it adheres to foreign objects; *e.g.* fishes of the genus *Cyclopterus*, the genus *Liparis* (sea-snails or snail-fishes), and the remora (*Echeneis*) 1753. **3.** A toy, consisting of a round piece of leather with a string attached at the centre, which, laid wet upon a solid surface and drawn up by the string, adheres by reason of the vacuum created 1681.

attrib. and *Comb.*: **s.-cup, -foot,** a cup or foot acting as a s.; **-fish** = senses I. 6, II. 2; **-rod,** a pump rod. Hence **Su·ckered** *ppl. a.* of an organ: provided with suckers.

Sucker (sɒ·kəɹ), *v.* 1660. [f. prec.] **†1.** *trans.* To fit or provide with a sucker or valve. **2.** To remove superfluous young shoots from (tobacco or maize plants); also, †to remove (the shoots) 1661. **3.** *intr.* To throw up suckers. Also occas. *pass.*, to be thrown up as a sucker. 1802.

†Su·cket. 1481. [Altered f. SUCCATE after SUCK *v.* and -ET.] = SUCCADE –1751.

Sucking (sɒ·kiŋ), *vbl. sb.* late ME. [f. SUCK *v.* + -ING[1].] **1.** The action of SUCK *v.*; suction. Also, an instance of this. **2.** *pl.* What is obtained by suction (*rare*). late ME.

attrib. and *Comb.*: **s.-cushion, -pad,** a lobulated mass of fat occupying the space between the masseter and the external surface of the buccinator; **†-tooth** = MILK-TOOTH; **-tube,** a tube through which liquid is sucked into the mouth.

Sucking (sɒ·kiŋ), *ppl. a.* OE. [f. SUCK *v.* + -ING[2].] **1.** That sucks milk from the breast, that is still being suckled, unweaned. **2.** Of an animal that is still sucking its dam. late ME. **b.** Of a bird: That is still with its mother. Now chiefly in *s. dove*, echoed from Shaks. 1590. **3.** *fig.* Not come to maturity; not fully developed 1648. **4.** That sucks down, under water, into a whirlpool, etc. 1513.

2. My enemies are but s. critics, who would fain be nibbling ere their teeth are come DRYDEN. **b.** I will roare you as gently as any s. Doue SHAKS.

Su·cking-fish. 1697. A fish furnished with a sucker or adhesive organ. **a.** The REMORA, *Echeneis remora*. **b.** Applied to other fishes, e.g. the Cornish sucker, the lump-sucker 1776.

Su·cking-pig. 1566. A new-born or very young pig; a young milk-fed pig suitable for roasting whole. (Formerly often called *roasting pig.*)

Su·cking-pump. 1660. **†1.** An air-pump. BOYLE. **2.** A suction pump. Now *rare.* 1660.

Suckle (sɒ·k'l), *v.* late ME. [prob. back-formation from SUCKLING *sb.*] **1.** *trans.* To give suck to; to nurse (a child) at the breast. **b.** *fig.* To nourish *with*, bring up *on* 1654. **2.** To cause to take milk from the breast or udder; to put to suck 1523. **3.** *intr.* To suck *at* the breast (*rare*) 1688.

1. The brests of Hecuba When she did s. Hector, look'd not louelier Then Hectors forhead SHAKS. **b.** A Pagan suckled in a creed outworn WORDSW.

Suckler (sɒ·kləɹ). 1473. [f. SUCKLE *v.* + -ER[1].] **1.** An unweaned mammal (rarely an infant); *esp.* a sucking calf. **2.** An animal that suckles its young, a mammal (*rare*) 1850.

Suckling (sɒ·kliŋ), *sb.*[1] 1440. [f. SUCK *v.* + -LING[1], prob. after MDu. *sūgeling* (Du. *zuigeling*).] **a.** An infant that is at the breast or is unweaned. **b.** = prec. 1. 1530.

Suckling (sɒ·kliŋ), *sb.*[2] 1440. [app. f. *suckle*, short for HONEYSUCKLE.] **1.** Clover. (Also, *lamb-sucklings.*) *dial.* **2.** = HONEYSUCKLE 2 (*Lonicera perichymenum*). *Obs.* exc. *dial.* 1653.

Sucrate (s[i]ū·kre[i]t). 1868. [– Fr. *sucrate*, f. *sucre* SUGAR + -ATE[4].] *Chem.* A compound of a substance with sucrose.

‖**Sucre** (sū·kre). 1886. [f. name of Antonio José de *Sucre*, a S. Amer. patriot.] A silver coin of Ecuador of the value of two shillings.

Sucro- (s[i]ū·kro), used as comb. form of Fr. *sucre* sugar.

Sucrose (s[i]ū·kro[u]s). 1862. [f. Fr. *sucre* SUGAR + -OSE[2].] *Chem.* Any one of the sugars having the composition ($C_{12}H_{22}O_{11}$) and properties of cane-sugar; = SACCHAROSE.

Suction (sɒ·kʃən). 1626. [– late L. *suctio*, *-ōn-*, f. *suct-*, pa. ppl. stem of L. *sugere* SUCK; see -ION.] **1.** The action of sucking with the tongue and lips (or analogous organs). Also, an instance of this. **b.** Imbibing strong drink, drinking. *slang.* 1817. **2.** The production of a more or less complete vacuum with the result that external atmospheric pressure forces fluid into the vacant space or causes the adhesion of surfaces 1658. **3.** Short for *s.-pipe* 1886.

attrib. and *Comb.*: **s. box, chamber,** a chamber in a pump into which the liquid is conveyed by a s.-pipe; **s. pipe,** (*a*) the pipe leading from the bottom of a pump barrel to the reservoir from which fluid is to be drawn; (*b*) a pipe for the extraction of dust from tow; **s. pump,** a pump of the type in which the barrel is placed above the level of the reservoir, and is connected therewith by a s. pipe; **s. stop**, any of the 'clicks' peculiar to certain S. Afr. languages; **s. valve**, (*a*) the valve at the bottom of the cylinder of a s. pump, below the piston; (*b*) the valve in a steam engine through which the water is drawn from the hot-well into the feed-pump. Hence **Su·ctional** *a.* (*rare*) having a power of s.

Suctorial (sɒktōᵊ·riăl), *a.* 1833. [f. mod. L. *suctorius* (n. pl. *Suctoria*, sc. *animalia*, the name of various zoological groups), f. as prec.; see -ORIAL.] *Zool.* Of an organ: Adapted for sucking. Of an animal: Having organs adapted for sucking or having the power of suction; belonging to any of the groups named *Suctoria* in which the mouth is adapted for sucking, or which possess sucking discs or the like. Of a habit, etc.: Involving or characterized by suction. So **Sucto·rian**, a member of the *Suctoria*; *esp.* a cyclostomous fish. **Sucto·rious** *a.* (now *rare*), suctorial 1815.

‖**Sudamina** (sⁱudæ·mină), *sb. pl.* 1671. [mod. L., pl. of *sudamen*, f. *sudare* to sweat.] *Path.* Minute whitish vesicles or pustules caused by the accumulation of sweat in the upper layers of the skin after copious perspiration, esp. in certain fevers. Hence **Suda·minal** *a.*

Sudan, -ese, variety of SOUDAN, -ESE.

‖**Sudarium** (sⁱudēᵊ·riɒ̆m). 1601. [L.; see next.] **1.** A napkin or cloth for wiping the face; a handkerchief; *spec.* the cloth with which, according to legend, St. Veronica wiped the face of Christ on the way to Calvary, and on which his features were impressed; hence, a portrait of Christ on a cloth. **2.** = SUDATORIUM 1852.

Sudary (sⁱū·dări). *Obs.* or *arch.* ME. [– L. *sudarium*, f. *sudor* sweat; see -ARY¹ 2.] **1.** A napkin or handkerchief used to wipe sweat or tears from the face; a sweat-cloth; *esp.* such a napkin venerated as a relic of a saint. **2.** The napkin which was about Christ's head in the tomb; hence, a shroud or winding-sheet ME. **3.** *Eccl.* A ceremonial cloth of linen or silk, often fringed; *esp.* a humeral veil. *arch.* late ME.

‖**Sudatorium** (sⁱūdătōᵊriɒ̆m). 1756. [L., n. sing. of *sudatorius*; see next, -ORIUM.] A room in which hot-air or steam baths are taken to produce sweating; a sweating-room; esp. *Rom. Antiq.*

Sudatory (sⁱū·dătəri), *a.* and *sb.* 1597. [– L. *sudatorius*, f. *sudat-*, pa. ppl. stem of *sudare* sweat; see -ORY¹,².] **A.** *adj.* Producing, accompanied by, or connected with sweating (*rare*). **B.** *sb.* = prec. 1615.

‖**Sudd** (sɒd). Also **sadd.** 1874. [Arab. *sudd* n. of action f. *sudd* obstruct.] An impenetrable mass of floating vegetable matte which obstructs navigation on the White Nile. **b.** *transf.* A temporary dam constructed across a river 1900.

Sudden (sɒ·d'n), *a.*, *adv.*, and *sb.* [ME. *soden, sodein, -ain* – AFr. *sodein, sudein*, (O)Fr. *soudain* :– late L. *subitanus*, for L. *subitaneus*, f. *subitus* sudden.] **A.** *adj.* **1.** Happening or coming without warning or premonition; taking place or appearing all at once. **b.** Of a turning, etc.: Abrupt, sharp. In *Zool.* and *Bot.* applied to parts that are sharply marked off from the neighbouring parts. late ME. **c.** Of physical objects: Appearing or discovered unexpectedly. Now *arch.* or *poet.* 1460. **2. a.** Of actions, feelings: Unpremeditated, done without forethought. *Obs.* or *arch.* ME. **b.** Of persons: Acting without forethought or deliberation; hasty, impetuous, rash. *Obs.* or *arch.* late ME. **3.** Performed or taking place without delay; speedy; prompt, immediate. *Obs.* exc. of death. late ME. †**4.** Of persons: Swift in action, quick to perform, prompt, expeditious. Also, peremptory, sharp. –1753. †**b.** Of mental faculties: Quick, sharp –1742. †**c.** Of the eye: Glancing quickly –1651. **5.** Made, provided, or formed in a short time. *Obs.* or *arch.* 1599. **6.** Prompt in action or effect; producing an immediate result. *poet.* 1586. †**7.** Done, performed, or prepared on the spur of the moment; extempore, impromptu –1741. †**8.** Brief, momentary –1595. †**9.** Happening at an early date; shortly to come or to be –1749.

1. Hayle, rain, and suddaine darknesse EVELYN. A s. start of surprise SCOTT. **c.** See lilies spring, and s. verdure rise POPE. **2. a.** If one kill another upon a suddaine quarrell, this is manslaughter BACON. **b.** Some men..are more s. in their tempers than others NEWMAN. **3.** Expecting your s. answer, I rest, Your servant, Oliver Cromwell 1650. **4.** Caska be sodaine, for we feare preuention SHAKS. **5.** Neuer was such a sodaine Scholler made SHAKS. **6.** *Rom. & Jul.* III. iii. 45. **7.** *Two Gent.* IV. ii. 12. **9.** To morrow, in my iudgement, is too s. SHAKS.

B. *adv.* **1.** Suddenly. Chiefly *poet.* late ME. **2.** When qualifying an adj. in the attrib. position *sudden* is often hyphened to it 1730.

1. The day with cloudes was suddeine overcast SPENSER. **2.** The sudden-starting tear THOMSON.

C. quasi-*sb.* and *sb.* **1.** In advb. phr. formed with preps. = Suddenly 1558. †**2.** A sudden need, danger, or the like; an emergency –1704. †**3.** *For a s.*: for an instant. BUNYAN.

1. *Of a s.* (†*of the s.*); now usu. with preceding *all*; Is it possible That loue should of a sodaine take such hold? SHAKS. *On* or *upon a* (or *the*) *s.* (arch.); On a s. gleam of hope appeared MACAULAY. †*On such a s.*, so suddenly. **2.** At such a S. I knew not what to doe 1704. Hence **Su·dden-ly** *adv.*, **-ness.**

Suddenty (sɒ·d'nti). Chiefly *Sc. Obs.* exc. *dial.* late ME. [– OFr. *sodeineté* (mod. *soudaineté*), f. *sodein* SUDDEN; see -TY¹.] **1.** Unexpectedness; suddenness; *occas.* an nstance of this, an unexpected attack. **2.** (In Sc. legal language.) An unpremeditated outburst of passion 1469.

‖**Sudder** (sɒ·dəɹ), *a.* (*sb.*) *Anglo-Ind.* 1787. [– Urdu = Arab. *ṣadr* foremost or highest part of a thing, chief place or seat, etc., used in comb. with adj. sense.] Chief, supreme: applied esp. to high government departments or officials. **b.** *ellipt.* as *sb.* = S. Court 1834.

Sudoral (sⁱū·dŏrăl), *a. rare.* 1876. [f. L. *sudor* sweat + -AL¹.] *Path.* Characterized by a disturbance of the function of sweating.

‖**Sudoresis** (sⁱūdŏrī·sis). 1834. [mod.L., f. L. *sudor* + *-esis* as in DIAPHORESIS.] Sweating, exudation.

Sudoriferous (sⁱūdŏri·fĕrəs), *a.* 1597. [f. late L. *sudorifer* (f. *sudor* sweat) + -OUS; see -FEROUS.] **1.** = next A. 1. **2.** = SUDORIPAROUS 1713.

2. The s. Glands and Vessels 1713.

Sudorific (sⁱūdŏri·fik), *a.* and *sb.* 1626. [– mod.L. *sudorificus*, f. as prec.; see -FIC. Cf. Fr. *sudorifique* (XVI).] **A.** *adj.* **1.** Promoting or causing perspiration; diaphoretic. **2.** Connected with the secretion and the exudation of sweat; sudoriparous, perspiratory 1720. **3.** Consisting of sweat (*rare*) 1807.

1. S. toil 1850. **2.** The Sudorifick Pores 1720.

B. *sb.* A medicine or remedy which promotes perspiration; a diaphoretic 1667.

Sudoriparous (sⁱūdŏri·părəs), *a.* 1851. [f. L. *sudor* sweat + -PAROUS. Cf. Fr. *sudoripare* (XIX).] *Phys.* Secreting sweat. **b.** Used loosely for: Connected with the production of sweat or with the sweat-glands 1899.

Sudorous (sⁱū·dŏrəs), *a. rare.* 1646. [f. L. *sudorus* + -OUS, or – med.L. *sudorosus*, f. L. *sudor* sweat.] Sweaty.

‖**Sudra** (sū·dra). *Anglo-Ind.* 1630. [– Skr. *çūdra.*] A member of the lowest of the four great Hindu castes.

Suds (sɒdz), *sb. pl.* 1548. [There is no certain evidence for the orig. sense; prob. – MLG., MDu. *sudde*, MDu. *sudse* marsh, bog; early mod. G. has *seifensod* soap-suds; cf. MHG. *sōt* dish-water, etc. The base is prob. Gmc. **suð-*, wk. grade of SEETHE.] †**1.** Dregs, leavings; hence, filth, muck –1645. †**2.** Flood-water; the water of the fens; water mixed with drift-sand and mud; drift-sand left by a flood –1851. **3. a.** Water impregnated with soap for washing, esp. when hot. **b.** The frothy mass which collects on the top of soapy water in which things are washed; in early use *esp.* a barber's lather. (More fully SOAP-SUDS.) 1581. **c.** *sing.* A soap solution 1835. **4.** Foam, froth. Also *sing.* 1592.

Phr. **In the suds:** chiefly in *to lie* or *be in the suds; to lay, leave in the suds.* **a.** In difficulties; in embarrassment or perplexity. *Obs.* or *slang.* †**b.** Done for; in disgrace. **c.** In the sulks, in the blues. *dial.* †**d.** Unfinished. **e.** Being washed, 'in the wash'.

Sue (sⁱū), *v.* ME. [– AFr. *suer, siwer, sure, suir(e*, f. pres. stem *siu-, sieu-, seu-* of OFr. *sivre* (mod. *suivre*) :– Rom. **sequère*, for L. *sequi* follow.] **I.** *trans.* †**1.** To follow (a person or thing in motion) –1590. †**2. a.** To follow (a person's steps, a track, path). **b.** To go in pursuit of (a person); to chase, pursue –1596. †**c.** To follow in time or as a consequence –1559. †**3.** To follow as an attendant, companion, or adherent; *occas.* to follow (a banner or the like); to frequent (a person's company) –1522. †**4.** To take as guide, leader, or pattern; to follow as a disciple or imitator –1509. †**5.** To comply with (a person's will), follow (another's advice or one's own devices) –1767. †**6.** To follow, adopt, put in practice (a form of belief, a manner of life, a virtue or vice, an occupation or profession); to occupy oneself with (a pursuit) –1799. †**7.** To prosecute (an action); to pursue (a subject); also, to follow up (an achievement) –1596. †**8.** To take (legal action); to institute (a legal process); to plead (a cause) –1572. **9.** To institute a suit for, make a legal claim to; hence *gen.* to petition or appeal for; to seek to obtain. Now *rare* (repl. by *s. for*). ME. **b.** Const. inf. (occas. gerund): To petition to be allowed, (hence) to seek *to do* or *to be* something. *arch.* late ME. **10.** *spec.* To make application before a court for the grant of (a writ or other legal process): often with implication of further proceedings being taken upon the writ, etc.; hence, to put in suit, to enforce (a legal process). More freq. to *s. out*, †*forth.* ME. **11.** To institute legal proceedings against (a person); to prosecute in a court of law; to bring a civil action against. In full, *to s. at law.* late ME. **12.** To petition, appeal to (*rare*) 1521. **13.** To woo, court. *arch.* 1596.

2. c. Shame sueth sinne, as rayne drops do the thunder 1559. **3.** Phr. †*To serve and s.*: to give 'suit and service to' (see SUIT *sb.* I. 2). **6.** Since errant armes to sew he first began SPENSER. **9. b.** Many sued to haue had her to maryage 1509. **10.** *Hen. VIII*, III. ii. 341. It putteth him to s. out his pardon of course BACON. Phr. *To s., s. out, s. forth* (*one's*) *livery*: see LIVERY *sb.* 5. **11.** My opinion is that he will not pay a peny till he is sued 1670. **13.** They would s. me, and woo me, and flatter me TENNYSON.

II. *intr.* †**1.** To follow after a person or thing in motion; to follow as an attendant or adherent; to go in chase or pursuit; freq. with *after, on, upon* –1555. †**2.** To do service or homage; chiefly in phr. *serve and s.* –1590. †**3. a.** To follow in time or in a succession of persons. Nearly always in pr. pple. –1642. **b.** To follow in the sequence of events, as a consequence or result –1597. **4.** To make legal claim; to institute legal proceedings; to bring a suit. late ME. **5.** To make one's petition or supplication *to* a person *for* a person or thing; to plead, appeal, supplicate. late ME. **6.** To be a suitor *to* a woman. *arch.* 1588.

2. What bootes thy seruice bace To her, to whom the heauens do serue and sew? SPENSER. **4.** Infant executors may s. by attorney 1817. To s. for a debt 1858. **5.** We were not borne to s., but to command SHAKS. **6.** *Two Gent.* II. i. 143.

‖**Suède** (swēⁱd). 1884. [Fr. = Sweden.] Orig. in *s. gloves* (= Fr. *gants de Suède*), gloves made of tanned kid-skin; hence *suède* is used for the material and the colour of it, also for a fabric woven to imitate suède.

Suet (sⁱū·ėt). late ME. [– AFr. **suet*, **sewet*, f. *su(e, seu*, OFr. *seu, siu, sif* (mod. *suif*) :– L. *sebum* tallow, suet, grease.] The solid fat round the loins and kidneys of certain animals, *esp.* that of the ox and sheep, which, chopped up, is used in cooking, and, when rendered down, forms tallow. (Occas. applied to the corresponding fat in the human body.) †**b.** *Hunting.* The fat of deer –1700.

attrib., as *s.-chopper, dumpling*: **s. face**, a face of a pale podgy appearance; **s. pudding**, a pudding made of flour and chopped or shredded s. and usu. boiled in a cloth or basin.

Suety (sⁱū·ėti), *a.* 1730. [f prec. + -Y¹.] **1.** Of the nature of suet. **b.** *fig.* Pale-faced 1801. **2.** Full of suet, made with suet 1807.

2. I always spell plumb-pudding with a *b*, p-l-u-m-*b*—I think it reads fatter and more suetty LAMB.

Sueve (swīv). 1901. [– L. *Suevus*; see next.] = next B.

Suevian (swī·viăn), *a.* and *sb.* 1617. [f. L. *Suevus*, var. *Suebus* + -IAN. Cf. SWABIAN.] **A.** *adj.* Of or belonging to a confederation of Germanic tribes called by the Romans *Suevi* (*Suebi*), which inhabited large territories in Central Europe to the east of the Rhine. **B.** *sb.* An individual of these tribes.

Suffect (sŏ·fe·kt), *a.* (*sb.*) 1862. [– L. *suffectus*, pa. pple. of *sufficere* substitute; see SUFFICE.] *Rom. Antiq.* Applied to the office of those additional consuls (or to the consuls themselves) who were elected, as under the Empire, during the official year. Also *sb.*, a consul s.

Suffer (sɒ·fəɹ), *v.* [ME. *suffre, soffre, soeffre* – AFr. *suffrir, soeffrir, -er*, OFr. *sof(f)rir* (mod. *souffrir*) :– Rom. **sufferire*, for L. *sufferre*, f. *sub-* SUB- 25 + *ferre* bear.] **I.** To undergo, endure. **1.** *trans.* To have (something painful, distressing, or injurious) inflicted or imposed upon one; to submit to with pain, distress, or grief. **2.** To go or pass through, be subjected to, undergo, experience (now usu. something evil or painful) ME. **3.** *intr.* To undergo or submit to pain, punishment, or death ME. **b.** *from* or (now *rare*) *under* a disease or ailment 1800. **4.** To be the object of an action, be acted upon, be passive. Now *rare.* late ME. †**5.** To endure, hold out, wait patiently –1611. **6.** *trans.* To endure, bear, stand. *Obs.* exc. *dial.* late ME. **7.** To be affected by, subjected to, undergo (an operation or process, *esp.* of change). Now only as *transf.* of 1. late ME. **8.** *intr.* To undergo the extreme penalty; to be put to death, be executed. Now *rare* in literary use exc. of martyrdom. 1570. †**b.** To be killed or destroyed. SHAKS. **9.** To sustain injury, damage, or loss; to be injured or impaired 1600. **10.** *causative.* To inflict pain upon. *Obs.* exc. *dial.* 1500.

1. I suffered thryse shipwracke TINDALE 2 *Cor.* 11:25. For feare that hee should s. thirst 1617. The plaintiff had suffered no loss 1891. **2.** Three more..suffered the same fate 1839. **3.** A brave man suffers in silence 1889. **b.** He had suffered from delirium tremens 1884. **4.** To be weak is miserable Doing or Suffering MILT. **5.** Love suffreth longe, and is corteous TINDALE 1 *Cor.* 13:4. **7.** Nothing of him that doth fade, But doth s. a Sea-change Into something rich, & strange SHAKS. **8.** Edward Transham..suffered at Tyburn 1877. **b.** But let the frame of things dis-ioynt, Both the Worlds s. SHAKS. **9.** How must he in the meantime be suffering in her opinion? SCOTT. **10.** 2 *Hen. VI*, v. i. 153.

II. To tolerate, allow. **1.** *trans.* To bear with, put up with, tolerate. *arch.* or *dial.* ME. †**b.** To admit of –1793. **2.** Const. *acc.* and *inf.* or *clause*: To allow or permit a person, animal, or inanimate thing to be or to do so-and-so ME. **3.** *refl.* or †*intr.* To allow oneself, submit *to be* treated in a certain way; to endure, consent *to be* or *to do* something ME. **4.** *trans.* To permit or allow (a person) to do a certain thing; †to let alone. Also occas. *absol. arch.* late ME. †**5.** *intr.* **a.** Of a person (*transf.* of a thing): To allow a certain thing to be done –1613. †**b.** Of a condition of things: To allow or admit of a certain thing being done –1612.

1. That nolde she suffre by no wey CHAUCER. We s. religion, and endure the laws of God but we love them not JER. TAYLOR. He suffered his grandmother with a good-humoured indifference THACKERAY. **2.** S. mee, that I may feele the pillars whereupon the house standeth *Judges* 16:26. I was not suffered to stir far from the house, for fear I should run away GOLDSM. **3.** Why rather suffre ye not youre selves to be robbed? TINDALE 1 *Cor.* 6:7. *intr.* I must not s. to have the laws broken before my face GOLDSM. **5. b.** And saye the Lordes prayer, yf the tyme will suffre *Bk. Com. Prayer.*

Sufferable (sɒ·fərăb'l), *a. Obs.* exc. *arch.* ME. [– AFr. *suffrable*, OFr. *so(u)ffrable*, f. *suffrir, soffrir*; see- ABLE.] †**1.** Patient, long-suffering. Also const. *of*: Willing to submit to. –1611. **2.** That can be 'suffered' or put up with; bearable, tolerable. Also, tolerably good. ME. †**3.** Permissible –1653.

1. And sith a man is moore resonable Than womman is, ye moste been suffrable CHAUCER. Hence **Su·fferably** *adv.* (*rare*) patiently; tolerably.

Sufferance (sɒ·fərăns). ME. [– AFr., OFr. *suffraunce, soffrance* (mod. *souffrance* suffering) :– late L. *sufferentia*, f. *sufferre*; see SUFFER, -ANCE.] **I. 1.** Patient endurance, forbearance, long-suffering. *arch.* **2.** The suffering *of* pain, trouble, wrong, etc. *arch.* late ME. †**b.** The suffering of a penalty –1640. **c.** Damage, injury (*rare*) –1823. **3.** A painful condition; pain suffered. *arch.* late ME. †**4.** Capacity to endure, endurance –1823.

1. The best apology against false accusers is silence and s. MILT. **2.** Calm in the s. of wrong 1856. **c.** *Oth.* II. i. 23. **3.** The poore Beetle that we treade vpon In corporall s., finds a pang as great, As when a Giant dies SHAKS. **4.** The two chiefest parts of a soldier, Valour and S. 1604.

II. 1. Sanction, consent, or acquiescence, implied by non-intervention; toleration, indulgence. Now *rare* exc. as in b. ME. **b.** *On* or *upon s.*: by virtue of a tacit assent but without express permission; under conditions of passive acquiescence or bare tolerance 1562. †**c.** An instance of this, a licence –1645. **d.** *Customs.* In full, *bill of s.*: a licence to ship or discharge cargoes at specified ports 1670. **2.** *Law.* The condition of the holder of an estate who, having come in by lawful right, continues to hold it after the title has ceased without the express leave of the owner. Phr. *tenant, estate at s.* 1579. †**3.** Suspension, delay; respite. (Chiefly after OFr. or med.L.) –1738.

1. The Company..possessing their privileges through his s. 1817. †*S. of peace*, a grant of peace, truce. **b.** They were a Ministry on s. when they appealed to the country 1879. **2.** *transf.* This is no highway, but a way of S., by favour 1633. **3.** To treat for a peace, and sufferaunce of warr 1523.

attrib.: **s. goods,** goods shipped or landed under a s.; **s. quay, wharf,** a quay or wharf at which cargo should be shipped or landed under a s.

Sufferer (sɒ·fərəɹ). 1450. [f. SUFFER *v.* + -ER[1].] **1.** One who suffers pain, tribulation, injury, wrong, loss, etc.: one who suffers *from* disease or ill health. **b.** One who suffers death; one who is killed (now only in ref. to martyrdom) 1721. **c.** A patient. Now *rare.* 1809. †**2.** One who permits something to be done –1627.

1. Sad suff'rer under nameless ill COWPER. **c.** At the bedside of the unfortunate s. 1809.

Suffering (sɒ·fəriŋ), *vbl. sb.* ME. [f. SUFFER *v.* + -ING[1].] †**1.** Patient endurance; long-suffering. –late ME. **2.** The bearing or undergoing of pain, distress, or tribulation ME. †**b.** Execution; martyrdom –1700. **3.** A painful condition; pain suffered. late ME. **b.** In particularized use, chiefly *pl.* 1609. **c.** In the Society of Friends, the hardships of those who were distrained upon for tithes, etc. 1657.

2. I..to the evil turne My obvious breast, arming to overcom By s. MILT. **3.** Far less shall be Our S., Sir GRAY. **b.** She is callous to his sufferings 1877.

Su·ffering, *ppl. a.* ME. [-ING[2].] †**1.** That endures patiently; inured to suffering; submissive –1694. †**2.** Passive –1792. **3.** That suffers, or is characterized by the suffering of, pain, affliction, or distress 1597. **b.** In Puritan use, with ref. to hardships endured for the sake of religion, esp. in *s. saint* 1661. **c.** [After Fr. *souffrant.*] Ill, indisposed (*rare*) 1885.

3. Gentle maid Haue of my s. youth some feeling pitty SHAKS. Hence **Su·fferingly** *adv. rare.*

Suffete (sɒ·fīt). 1600. [– L. *suffes, suffet-*, prop. *sūfes*, of Phœnician origin (cf. Heb. *šōpēṭ* judge.] *Antiq.* One of the supreme executive magistrates of the ancient republic of Carthage.

Suffice (sŏfəi·s), *v.* ME. [f. OFr. *suffis-*, pres. stem of *suffire* :– L. *sufficere*, f. *sub* SUB- + *facere* make, do.] **1.** *intr.* To be enough, sufficient, or adequate for a purpose or the end in view. †**2.** *impers.* It is enough –1530. **b.** Const. inf. or clause with (or †without) anticipatory subject *it.* Now chiefly in the subj., *S. it*, occas. short for *S. it to say.* late ME. **c.** With dat. pron. *arch.* late ME. †**3.** To have the necessary ability, capacity, or resources for doing something; to be competent or able *to do* something –1823. **4.** *trans.* To be enough for; to meet the desires, needs, or requirements of (a person); to satisfy. *arch.* late ME. **b.** *pass.* To be satisfied or content. *arch.* late ME. †**5.** To provide enough food for, satisfy the appetite of; also, to satisfy (the appetite). Chiefly *pass.* –1791. †**6.** To satisfy, meet the 'calls' of (a desire, need, sense, emotion, etc.) –1737. †**7.** To make or be sufficient provision for; to supply *with* something. Also, to replenish (a supply). –1700. †**8.** To supply, furnish (a product, etc.) –1725.

1. 'Twixt such friends as wee, Few words s. SHAKS. The fog..every trace of which a few minutes sufficed to sweep away TYNDALL. **2. b.** S. it, that perchance they were of fame BYRON. **4.** The good old rule Sufficeth them WORDSW. **b.** Not half suffic'd, and greedy yet to kill DRYDEN. **6.** Scarce all my herds their luxury s. POPE. **8.** The Iuyce, as it seemeth, not being able to s. a Succulent Colour, and a Double Leafe BACON.

Sufficience (sŏfi·ʃĕns). *arch.* late ME. [– OFr. *sufficience* or late L. *sufficientia*, f. L. *sufficiens, -ent-*; see SUFFICIENT, -ENCE.] **1.** The quality or condition of being sufficient or enough; sufficient supply, means, or resources. †**2.** Capacity; ability; competence. Also, a capable or competent person. –1676. †**3.** That which suffices for one's needs; satisfaction of one's needs; sustenance –1620.

1. This full and perfect s. of life was abruptly disturbed MORLEY.

Sufficiency (sŏfi·ʃĕnsi). 1495. [– late L. *sufficientia*; see prec., -ENCY.] †**1.** Sufficient means or wealth; ability to meet pecuniary obligations –1747. **b.** A sufficient supply; a competence 1608. **c.** Adequate provision of food or bodily comfort 1796. **2.** The condition or quality of being sufficient for its purpose or for the end in view; adequacy 1565. **3.** A sufficient number or quantity *of*; enough 1531. **4.** Sufficient capacity *to* perform or undertake something; adequate qualification; ability, competency. *Obs.* or *arch.* 1567. †**b.** An instance of this; also, an accomplishment –1713. **5.** = SELF-SUFFICIENCY 2. *arch.* 1638.

1. In the fulnesse of his sufficiencie, he shalbe in straites *Job* 20:22. **b.** An elegant s., content, Retirement, rural quiet THOMSON. **2.** There is a doubt about the s. of the assets 1884. **3.** S. of wood for fuel 1832. **4.** We haue there a Substitute of most allowed sufficiencie SHAKS.

Sufficient (sŏfi·ʃĕnt), *a.* (*adv.*, *sb.*) late ME. [– OFr. *sufficient* or L. *sufficiens, -ent-*, pr. pple. of *sufficere* SUFFICE; see -ENT.] **A.** *adj.* **1.** Of a quantity, extent, or scope adequate to a certain purpose or object. **b.** *impers.* with dependent clause or inf. 1538. **c.** Achieving its object; effective (*rare*) 1831. **2.** In techn. language, of legal documents, securities, etc. 1461. †**3.** Qualified by talent or ability; competent, capable, able –1817. †**4.** Of persons: Of adequate means or wealth; having a competence; well-to-do; hence, qualified by means or status for an office or duty –1782. †**5.** Of things: Of adequate quality; of a good standard; substantial; in good condition –1800. †**6.** In full, *s. for oneself*: = SELF-SUFFICIENT 1. –1502. †**7.** = SELF-SUFFICIENT 2. –1709.

1. What thanks s...have I to render thee? MILT. The publiq armoury..s. for 30,000 men EVELYN. Even a threatened interference with a plaintiff's rights..is s. to justify him in taking proceedings 1890. **b.** They thought it not sufficiente in their life time to deserue prayse 1553. **2.** This our Lettre shalbe your s. discharge for the same 1551. *S. grace* (Theol.): see GRACE *sb.* 11. (*Principle* or *law of*) *s. reason* (mod. Philos.), the principle that nothing happens without a reason why it should be so rather than otherwise. **3.** Those that..have a s. Gardener 1719. **4.** An honest and s. farmer 1672. **7.** A s. self-conceited Coxcomb STEELE.

†**B.** *adv.* = Sufficiently –1826. **C.** *sb.* †**1.** The quality or condition of being sufficient –1600. **2.** A sufficient quantity or supply; sufficient means; enough 1470.

2. We saw s. to account for the noise TYNDALL. Hence **Suffi·ciently** *adv.* in a s. manner.

Sufficing (sŏfəi·siŋ), *ppl. a.* 1606. [f. SUFFICE + -ING[2].] That suffices *for* a purpose or object; sufficient, adequate, satisfying.

Draw thy sword, and giue mee, Suffising strokes for death SHAKS. Hence **Suffi·cing-ly** *adv.* so as to suffice; **Suffi·cingness**, sufficiency.

†**Su·ffisance.** late ME. [–(O)Fr. *suffisance*, f. *suffisant*; see next, -ANCE.] **1.** Enough to supply one's needs –1632. **2.** = SUFFICIENCY 3. –1544. **3.** Ample means, wealth –1574. **4.** Ability –1627. **5.** Satisfaction, contentment –1590. **b.** A source of satisfaction –1502.

5. S., that seketh no riche metes ne drinkes CHAUCER. **b.** She was, that swete wife, My suffisaunce, my luste, my lyfe CHAUCER.

†**Su·ffisant**, *a.* ME. [– (O)Fr. *suffisant*, pr. pple. of *suffire*; see SUFFICE, -ANT.] **1.** = SUFFICIENT, in various senses –1570. **2.** Of things (chiefly immaterial): Satisfactory in quality or efficacy; effective –1455.

Suffix (sɒ·fiks), *sb.* 1778. [– mod.L. *suffixum*, subst. use of n. pa. pple. of L. *suffigere*, f. *sub-* SUB- 2 + *figere* FIX.] **1.** *Gram.* A verbal element attached to the end of a word to form an entirely new word (e.g. *short, short-age, short-en, short-er, short-ly*) or as an inflexional formative (e.g. *ox, ox-en*). **2.** *Math.* An inferior index written to the right of a symbol 1842. Hence **Suffi·xion** [after PREFIXION], the act of suffixing or state of being suffixed. **Su·ffixment**, use as a s.

Suffix (sɒ̆fi·ks), *v.* Chiefly in *pa. pple.* 1604. [Partly f. L. *suffixus* (see prec.), partly f. prec.] **1.** *trans.* To fix or place under; to subjoin. **2.** To add as a suffix 1778. So **Suffi·xed** *ppl. a.* used as a suffix.

Sufflaminate (sɒ̆flæ·mineᶦt), *v.* Now *rare.* 1656. [– *sufflaminat-*, pa. ppl. stem of L. *sufflaminare*, f. *sufflamen* clog, break, drag-chain.] *trans.* To put an obstacle in the way of, obstruct.

†**Suffla·te**, *v.* 1616. [– *sufflat-*, pa. ppl. stem of L. *sufflare*, f. *sub-* SUB- 25 + *flare* to blow; see -ATE³.] *trans.* To blow up, inflate –1791.

†**Suffla·tion.** 1599. [– L. *sufflatio, -ōn-*, f. as prec.; see -ION.] The action of blowing (up); inflation (*lit.* and *fig.*); distension with wind; inspiration (by the 'breath' of the Holy Ghost); expiration –1817.

Sufflue (sɒflū·). 1562. [Of unkn. origin.] *Her.* A bearing resembling a clarion.

†**Su·ffocate**, *pa. pple.* and *ppl. a.* 1460. [– L. *suffocatus*, pa. pple. of *suffocare*; see next. -ATE².] **1.** Suffocated by deprivation of air –1632. **2.** Smothered, overwhelmed –1606.

1. For Suffolkes Duke, may he be s. SHAKS.

Suffocate (sɒ·fŏkeᶦt), *v.* 1526. [– *suffocat-*, pa. ppl. stem of L. *suffocare*, f. *sub-* SUB- 1 + *fauces* throat; see -ATE³.] **1.** *trans.* To kill (a person or animal) by stopping the supply of air through the lungs, gills, or other respiratory organs 1599. **2.** To interrupt or impede respiration in (a person); to stifle, choke. Also, †to throttle (the windpipe), stifle (the breath). 1599. **3.** To destroy as if by the exclusion of air; to smother, overwhelm, extinguish 1526. **4.** *intr.* To become stifled or choked 1702.

1. Half suffocated with the loss of breath 1791. **2.** Let not Hempe his Windpipe s. SHAKS. **3.** The plants..will s. every kind of weed near them 1793. That..superstition which..had suffocated the higher truths of religion 1868. Hence **Su·ffocating** *ppl. a.*, **-ly** *adv.*

Suffocation (sɒfŏkēᶦ·ʃən). 1549. [– L. *suffocatio, -ōn-*, f. as prec.; see -ION. Cf. (O)Fr. *suffocation.*] The act of suffocating or condition of being suffocated. †**b.** In full *s. of the womb, matrix, mother*: hysteria –1719.

Suffocative (sɒ·fŏkeᶦtiv), *a.* 1605. [f. SUFFOCATE *v.* + -IVE.] Tending to suffocate; causing or inducing suffocation; attended by suffocation. (Chiefly *Med.*, esp. in *s. catarrh* = capillary bronchitis.)

Suffolk (sɒ·fək). The name of a county of East Anglia; used attrib. in designations of things produced in or peculiar to the county, as *S. cow, pig*; **S. coprolite,** a phosphatic nodule occurring in the Red Crag of Suffolk; **S. crag,** a Pliocene formation occurring in Suffolk; **S. punch,** a small but strong and hardy horse bred largely in Suffolk. **b.** *absol.* = Suffolk brick, cow, horse, pig, sheep, etc. 1831.

Suffragan (sɒ·frăgăn), *sb.* and *a.* late ME. [– AFr., OFr. *suffragan*, med.L. *suffraganeus*, f. L. *suffragium*; see SUFFRAGE, -AN.] **A.** *sb.* **1.** A bishop considered in regard to his relation to the archbishop or metropolitan, by whom he may be summoned to attend synods and give his suffrage. **2.** An assistant or subsidiary bishop; in the Church of England. a bishop appointed to assist a diocesan bishop in a particular part of his diocese. late ME. †**3.** A coadjutor, assistant; a deputy, representative –1760. **B.** *adj.* **1.** *Bishop s., s. bishop*: = A. 1, 2. 1475. **2.** Of a see or diocese: Subordinate *to* a metropolitical or archiepiscopal see 1712. Hence **Su·ffraganship,** the office or status of a s.

†**Su·ffragant,** *sb.* and *a.* 1603. [– (O)Fr. *suffragant* – L. *suffragans, -ant-*, pr. pple. of *suffragari*; see next, -ANT.] **A.** *sb.* One who gives his suffrage or vote; a voter; hence, a supporter, witness –1697. **B.** *adj.* **1.** Auxiliary, subordinate. FLORIO. **2.** Giving support or witness –1656.

†**Su·ffragate,** *v.* 1600. [– *suffragat-*, pa. ppl. stem of L. *suffragari*, f. *suffragium*; see next, -ATE³.] **1.** *trans.* To delegate, appoint. **2.** *intr.* To testify, to bear witness *to* –1676. **3.** To vote (*for*) –1691.

Suffrage (sɒ·frĕdʒ), *sb.* late ME. [– L. *suffragium*, partly through (O)Fr. *suffrage.*] **1.** *collect. pl.* and *sing.* Prayers, *esp.* intercessory prayers, intercessions. *arch.* **b.** *spec.* Prayers for the souls of the departed; *esp.* in phr. *to do s.* (*arch.*) 1440. **c.** *pl.* Liturgical intercessory petitions; *esp.* in the Book of Common Prayer, (*a*) the intercessory petitions pronounced by the priest in the Litany; (*b*) a set of versicles and responses 1532. †**2.** Help, support, assistance. Also, one who helps, a support. –1613. **3.** *orig.* A vote given by a member of a body, state, or society, in assent to a proposition or in favour of the election of a person; in extended sense, a vote for or against any controverted question or nomination 1534. **b.** An object, as a pebble, a marked paper, or the like, used to indicate a vote given (*rare*) 1534. **4.** *gen.* A vote in support of or an opinion in favour of some person or thing; hence (now *Obs.* or *arch.*), in neutral sense, an opinion 1594. **5.** Approval, sanction, consent. Const. *to. arch.* 1600. †**b.** An instance of this; an expression or token of approval –1829. **6.** The collective vote of a body of persons 1610. **7.** The collective opinion of a body of persons; hence, contextually, consensus of opinion; (common or general) consent 1576. **8.** The casting of a vote, voting; the exercise of a right to vote; election by voting 1665. **9.** The right or privilege of voting as a member of a body, state, etc. (orig. *U.S.*) 1789. **b.** With prefixed word denoting the extent, as *female, household, manhood s.*, etc. 1706.

1. Of what use to you then the suffrages of the saints? KINGSLEY. **b.** Their prayers and suffrages for the dead 1848. **c.** After the s. for the Church, those for the ecclesiastical orders usually come first 1855. **3.** The manner of choosing Magistrates ..was by plurality of suffrages HOBBES. **b.** The Grand Master had collected the suffrages SCOTT. **4.** He that finds his knowledge narrow,..and by consequence his s. not much regarded JOHNSON. **5.** I'll giue no s. to 't B. JONS. **6.** The election of a new emperor was referred to the s. of the military order GIBBON. **7.** To prefer their own judgment to the general s. of mankind 1794. **8.** The right of s. is not valued when indiscriminately bestowed 1887. **9.** The s., or qualification of electors, is very various COBBETT. **b.** The universal s. of France 1877.

†**Su·ffrage,** *v.* 1613. [f. prec.] **1.** *intr.* To vote *for* or *against*; hence, to agree or side *with*, to give support *to* –1661. **2.** *trans.* To elect by vote; hence, to give support to; to side with –1838.

Suffragette (sɒfrădʒe·t). 1906. [f. SUFFRAGE *sb.* + -ETTE, after SUFFRAGIST.] A female supporter of the cause of women's political enfranchisement, *esp.* one of a violent or 'militant' type.

Suffragism (sɒ·frădʒiz'm). 1888. [f. next + -ISM.] The advocacy of an extension of the suffrage, e.g. to women.

Suffragist (sɒ·frădʒist). 1822. [f. SUFFRAGE + -IST.] An advocate of the extension of the political franchise, *esp.* (since about 1885) to women.

I am a woman and a s. 1914.

‖**Suffrago** (sɒfrēᶦ·go). 1842. [L.] *Anat.* The 'heel' at the junction of the tibia and the tarsus in quadrupeds and birds.

Suffrutescent (sɒfrute·sĕnt), *a.* 1816. [f. SUB- 20 c + FRUTESCENT.] *Bot.* Somewhat woody or shrubby at the base.

‖**Suffrutex** (sɒ·fruteks). *Pl.* **suffrutices** (sɒfrū·tisīz). 1567. [mod.L., f. *sub* SUB- 22 + FRUTEX.] *Bot.* A plant having a woody base, but a herbaceous annual growth above.

Suffruticose (sɒfrū·tikoᵘs), *a.* 1793. [– mod.L. *suffruticosus*, f. stem of SUFFRUTEX + -OSE¹.] *Bot.* Of the character of a suffrutex; woody at the base but herbaceous above.

Suffumigate (sɒfiū·migeᶦt), *v. rare.* 1588. [– *suffumigat-*, pa. ppl. stem of L. *suffumigare*, f. *sub* SUB- 2, 25 + *fumigare* FUMIGATE.] *trans.* To fumigate from below.

Suffumigation (sɒfiūmigēᶦ·ʃən). Now *arch.* or *Hist.* late ME. [– late and med.L. *suffumigatio, -ōn-*, f. as prec.; see -ION. Cf. Fr. *suffumigation* (XVI).] The action of suffumigating; an instance of this; chiefly *concr.* (usu. *pl.*) fumes or vapours generated by burning herbs, incense, etc.; also *occas.*, a substance used for this purpose. †**b.** *gen.* A fume, vapour –1651.

Suffuse (sɒ̆fiū·z), *v.* 1590. [– *suffus-*, pa. ppl. stem of L. *suffundere*, f. *sub-* SUB- 2, 25 + *fundere* pour.] **1.** *trans.* To overspread as with a fluid, a colour, a gleam of light. **2.** To pour (a liquid) over a surface. Chiefly in fig. context. 1734.

1. His eies vnclos'd, with teares suffus'd 1600. You hazy ridges..Climbing suffused with sunny air WORDSW. *fig.* The amused expression suffused the lawyer's face 1876. Hence **Suffu·sedly** *adv.*

Suffusion (sɒ̆fiū·ʒən). late ME. [– L. *suffusio, -ōn-*, f. as prec.; see -ION.] **1.** The defluxion or extravasation of a fluid or 'humour' over a part of the body; †*concr.* the fluid itself; *spec.* in *Old Med.*, cataract. **2.** The action of suffusing a surface with fluid, moisture, or colour; the condition of being suffused or overspread. Also, an instance of this. 1611. **3.** A colouring or tint spread over a surface, *esp.* over the skin by the action of the blood, etc.; *freq.* a flush of colour in the face, a blush 1700.

1. So thick a drop serene hath quencht thir Orbs, Or dim s. veild MILT. **2.** The s. of the eyes with tears DARWIN. **3.** Would she not be much more modest without that ambiguous S.? STEELE.

‖**Sufi** (sū·fi). 1653. [– Arab. *ṣūfī* lit. woollen, f. *ṣūf* wool.] One of a sect of Moslem ascetic mystics who in later times embraced pantheistic views. Hence **Su·fic** *a.* pertaining to the Sufis or their mystical system.

Sufism (sū·fiiz'm). 1817. [f. prec. + -ISM.] The mystical system of the Sufis. Also **Su·fism** 1836.

Sugar (ʃu·gəɹ), *sb.* [ME. *suker* (XIII), *sucre, sugre* (XIV), *suger* (*sugar* from XVI) – OFr. *çukre, sukere* (mod. *sucre*) – It. *zucchero*, prob. – med.L. *succarum* – Arab. *sūkkar*. Cf. SACCHARIN. For the change of -k- to -g- cf. FLAGON.] **1.** A sweet crystalline substance, white when pure, obtained from a great variety of plant juices, but chiefly from those of the sugar-cane and sugar-beet, and forming an important article of human food. **b.** With qualifying adj., sb., or phr., indicating place of origin, colour, stage of boiling, purification, or crystallization at which, or the form in which, the particular kind is produced, its use, or the plant from which it is made. late ME. **c.** *pl.* Kinds of sugar; also, †cargoes or stocks of sugar 1570. †**d.** = SUGAR-CANE –1785. **2. a.** Sweetness; also, sweet or honeyed words. late ME. **b.** Phr. *To be neither s. nor salt, not to be made of s. or salt*, not likely to be injured by a wetting, not afraid of wet weather 1842. **c.** *slang.* Money 1862. **3.** *Chem.* **a.** In old terminology, applied (with qualification) to certain compounds resembling sugar in form or taste. *S. of lead*: lead acetate. *Acid* (or *essence*) *of s.*: oxalic acid. 1652. **b.** In mod. terminology, a chemical compound having the composition of ordinary sugar and forming a constituent of many substances; also, more widely (with distinctive qualifying word), any member of the saccharose and glucose groups of carbohydrates, all of which are soluble in water, more or less sweet to the taste, and either directly or indirectly fermentable 1826.

1. **b.** *Brown, white s.*; *burnt, caramel, clarified, crystal, granulated, lump, moist, raw, refined s.*; *coffee, preserving s.*; BEET *s.*, CANE *s.*; etc. **d.** I have not told you..that S. is a grass of the first division 1785. **2. a.** She was all s. and honey 1895.

attrib. and *Comb.*; **s.-almond,** a sweetmeat consisting of an almond coated with s.; **-cake,** a rich cake made with s., butter, and cream; **-camp**

U.S., a place in a maple forest or plantation where the sap is collected and boiled for s.; **-caster, -castor** (see CASTOR[2]); **-coat** *v.*, to coat with s.; *fig.* to make palatable; *esp.* in **s.-coated** *ppl. a.* (of pills); **-cone,** a conical mould used in making loaf-sugar; **-disease,** diabetes; **-house,** a s.-factory, s.-works; **-house molasses,** a low-grade molasses produced at s.-factories, now chiefly used in the preparation of certain medicines and chemicals; **-lime,** lime formed in the process of preparing s. from beetroot; **-orchard** *U.S.* = SUGAR-BUSH 1; **-stick,** a stick of sweetstuff; **-tongs,** a metal implement for taking hold of pieces of lump s. (to put them into a beverage), consisting of two limbs connected by a flexible back (or a hinge) and furnished at each end with claws or a spoon-shaped plate; **-vinegar,** vinegar made from the waste juice and washings in s.-manufacture: **-water** *U.S.*, the sap of the s.-maple. **b.** In names of birds, insects and other animals that feed upon or infest s. or sweet things; **s.-mite,** (*a*) a springtail or silverfish, *Lepisma sacchari*; (*b*) a mite of the genus *Tyroglyphus* or *Glyciphagus*; **-squirrel,** a species of flying-squirrel found in Australia, which lives partly on honey. **c.** In the names of plants or fruits, so called on account of their sweetness or their yielding s.; **s. beet,** any variety of the beetroot plant from which s. is manufactured; **-berry,** the N. Amer. nettle-tree, *Celtis occidentalis*; **-fungus,** the fungus of yeast, *Saccharomyces cerevisiæ*; **-grass** (*a*) = SORGHUM 1 b; (*b*) the Australian grass *Pollinia fulva* or *Erianthus fulvus*; **-gum,** the Australian *Eucalyptus corynocalyx* and *E. gunnii*; **-tree,** (*a*) = SUGAR-MAPLE; (*b*) = SUGAR-BUSH 2; (*c*) an Australian shrub, *Myoporum platycarpum*; **-wood** = SUGAR-MAPLE.

Sugar (ʃu·gəɹ), *v.* late ME. [f. prec.] **1.** *trans.* To mix, cover, sprinkle, or sweeten with sugar 1530. **b.** *intr.* To spread sugar mixed with beer, gum, etc. upon trees or the like in order to catch moths. Also *trans.* with the tree as obj. 1857. **2.** *fig.* (*trans.*) To make sweet, agreeable, or palatable. late ME. **3.** *intr.*, usu. *s.-off*: in U.S. and Canada, in the manufacture of maple-sugar, to complete the boiling down of the syrup in preparation for granulation 1836. **4.** *Cambridge Univ. Rowing slang.* To shirk while pretending to row hard. 1890. **5.** *pass.* Euphemistic substitute for an imprecation. *slang.* 1891.

1. Rum and water..sugared to the utmost SOUTHEY. *fig.* One dram whereof is able to s. the most wormwood affliction FULLER. **2.** Then I perceiue there's treason in his lookes That seem'd to s. o're his villanie SHAKS. Hence **Su·garless** *a.* without s., unsugared.

Su·gar-ba:ker. 1650. †**1.** A confectioner. **2.** A sugar-refiner. *Obs.* exc. *Hist.* 1688.

Su·gar-bird. 1688. Applied to various small birds which feed (or were supposed to feed) on the nectar of flowers. †**1.** = CANARY-BIRD 1. **2.** A bird of the genus *Certhiola*, belonging to the family *Cærebidæ*, in the W. Indies and S. America; also applied to the genera *Certhia* and *Dacnis* 1787. **3.** Applied to various members of the family *Nectariniidæ* or Sunbirds of Africa 1822.

Su·gar-bush. 1818. **1.** A grove or plantation of sugar-maples 1823. **2.** [S. Afr. Du. *suikerbos*.] The S. African shrub *Protea mellifera* 1818.

Sugar-candy (ʃu:gəɹkæ·ndi). late ME. [– OFr. *sucre candi* – Arab. *sūkkar ḳandī*, the latter adj. f. *ḳand* sugar – Pers. *kand* – Skr. *khaṇḍa* sugar in pieces, orig. piece, fragment, f. *khaṇḍ* break.] **1.** Sugar clarified and crystallized by slow evaporation. **2.** *fig.* Something sweet, pleasant, or delicious 1591. **b.** *attrib.* or as *adj.* Sugared, honeyed, deliciously sweet 1575.

1. *Brown s.*, that obtained at the first crystallization. *White s.*, that obtained by re-boiling the former and allowing it to crystallize. Hence **Sugar-ca·ndied** *a.* coated with or as with (fine white) sugar; also *fig.* (now usu. with pun on *candid*).

Su·gar-cane. 1568. [f. SUGAR *sb.* + CANE *sb.*[1]] A tall stout perennial grass, *Saccharum officinarum*, cultivated in tropical and subtropical countries, and forming the chief source of manufactured sugar.

Sugared (ʃu·gəɹd), *ppl. a.* late ME. [f. SUGAR *sb.* or *v.* + -ED.] **1.** Containing or impregnated with sugar; sweetened with sugar. **b.** Sugar-coated; candied, 'crystallized' 1855. **2.** *fig.* Full of sweetness; honeyed, luscious, delicious. late ME.

1. Wine Sugred inebriateth lesse, than Wine Pure BACON. **2.** This world of sugred lies 1633. Kisses. Tempting,..sugred, lingring. 1658.

Sugaring (ʃu·gəriŋ), *vbl. sb.* 1740. [f. SUGAR *v.* + -ING[1].] **1.** Sugary or sweet matter; sweetening. Also, the adding of sugar. **2.** *U.S.* The manufacture of sugar from the maple. Also *s. off* (see SUGAR *v.* 3). 1836. **3.** (See SUGAR *v.* 1 b.) 1857.

Su·gar-loaf. late ME. [f. SUGAR *sb.* + LOAF *sb.*[1] 3.] **1.** A moulded conical mass of hard refined sugar (now rarely made). **2.** *transf.* A thing having the shape of a sugar-loaf. **a.** Usu. *s.-hat*: A conical hat, pointed, rounded or flat at the top, worn during the Tudor and Stuart periods and after the French Revolution 1607. **b.** A high conical hill. Also *s. mountain.* 1634. **c.** A kind of cabbage 1766. Hence **Su·gar-loafed** *a.* shaped like a s.

Su·gar-ma:ple. 1753. The N. Amer. tree *Acer saccharinum*, which yields maple-sugar.

Su·gar-plum. 1608. [f. SUGAR *sb.* + PLUM *sb.*] **1.** A small round or oval sweetmeat, made of boiled sugar and variously flavoured and coloured; a comfit 1668. **2.** *fig.* Something very pleasing or agreeable, esp. when given as a sop or bribe 1608. Hence **Su·gar-plum** *v. trans.* to reward or pacify with sweetmeats; hence, to pet, cosset.

Sugar-sop (ʃu·gəɹsǫp). 1581. [f. SUGAR *sb.* + SOP *sb.*] †**1.** *pl.* A dish composed of steeped slices of bread, sweetened and sometimes spiced –1776. **2.** The W. Indian Sweetsop, *Anona squamosa* 1847.

Sugary (ʃu·gəri), *sb.* 1696. [for **sugarery*, f. SUGAR *sb.*; see -ERY and cf. Fr. *sucrerie*.] A sugar-manufactory. *Obs.* exc. as in b. **b.** *U.S.* and *Canada.* A place where maple-juice is collected and boiled for the purpose of making sugar; a sugar-camp 1840.

Sugary (ʃu·gəri), *a.* 1591. [f. SUGAR *sb.* + -Y[1].] **1.** Full of, containing, or impregnated with sugar; pertaining to or resembling (that of) sugar; sweet, sweetened 1597. **2.** *fig.* Deliciously or alluringly sweet; honeyed; deceitfully or flatteringly pleasant; also, excessively or offensively sweet 1591.

2. A s. epistle BECKFORD. Hence **Su·gariness.**

Sugescent (s[i]udʒe·sĕnt), *a. rare.* 1802. [f. L. *sugere* suck + -ESCENT.] Misused for: Pertaining to or adapted for sucking.

Suggest (sŏdʒe·st), *v.* 1526. [– *suggest-*, pa. ppl. stem of L. *suggerere*, f. *sub* SUB- 2 + *gerere* bear, carry, bring.] **1.** *trans.* To cause to be present to the mind as an object of thought, an idea to be acted upon, a question or problem to be solved; in early use said *esp.* of insinuating or prompting to evil. In extended application, to propose as an explanation or solution, as a course of action, as a person or thing suitable for a purpose, or the like. **b.** Said of the conscience, feelings, etc.; hence, of external things, to prompt the execution of, provide a motive for 1583. **c.** Const. clause or inf.: To put forward the notion, opinion, or proposition (*that*, etc.) 1526. **d.** To utter as a suggestion 1837. **e.** *refl.* Of an idea, proposition, etc.: To present itself to the mind 1801. †**2.** To prompt (a person) to evil; to tempt *to* or *to do* something; to seduce or tempt away –1643. †**b.** To insinuate into (a person's mind) the (false) idea *that*, etc. –1689. **3.** To give a hint or inkling of, without plain or direct expression or explanation 1697. **4.** To call up the thought of by association or natural connection of ideas 1709. **b.** To give the impression of the existence or presence of 1816. **5.** *Law.* To put forward in a 'suggestion' 1719. **6.** In hypnotism, to influence by suggestion 1895. **7.** *absol.* or *intr.* †To prompt or tempt to evil; to make or offer a suggestion 1599.

1. Why dost thou then s. to me distrust? MILT. It is difficult to s. a remedy 1901. **b.** Prudence suggested the necessity of a temporary retreat GIBBON. **2.** *Two Gent.* III. i. 34. **b.** We must s. the People, in what hatred He still hath held them SHAKS. **3.** It [*sc.* a statue] suggests far more than it shows HAWTHORNE. **4.** A certain kind of sound suggests immediately to the mind, a coach passing in the street 1764. **7.** When diuels will the blackest sinnes put on, They do s. at first with heauenly shewes SHAKS. Hence **Sugge·ster,** †one who imputes crime to, or brings a charge against, another; one who suggests or prompts. **Sugge·stingly** *adv.*

Suggestible (sŏdʒe·stib'l), *a.* 1890. [f. prec. + -IBLE.] **1.** Capable of being influenced by (hypnotic) suggestion. **2.** That can be suggested 1905. Hence **Suggestibi·lity.**

Suggestion (sŏdʒə·styən, -tʃən). ME. [– (O)Fr. *suggestion* – L. *suggestio*, *-ōn-*, f. *suggest-*; see SUGGEST, -ION.] †**1.** Prompting or incitement to evil; an instance of this, a temptation of the evil one –1667. **2.** The action of prompting one to a particular action or course of action; the putting into the mind of an idea, an object of thought, a plan, or the like; an instance of this, an idea or thought suggested, a proposal. late ME. **b.** *Hypnotism.* The insinuation of a belief or impulse into the mind of a subject by words, gestures, or the like; the impulse or idea thus suggested 1887. †**3.** The act of making a false or suborned statement or supplying underhand information; an instance of this, a false representation or charge. Often *false s.* –1592. **4.** *Law.* An information not upon oath 1485. **5.** The process by which an idea brings to the mind another idea by association or natural connection 1605. **6.** An indication of the presence or existence (*of* something); a hint, an inkling 1863.

1. The first sort by thir own s. fell, Self-tempted, self-deprav'd MILT. **2.** Believe not these suggestions which proceed From anguish of the mind MILT. At the s. of friends a subscription was raised 1842. **b.** Several cases of cure by s. 1887. **4.** *S. upon record*, an information drawn in writing showing cause for a prohibition to a suit. **6.** A faint s. of weariness struggling with habitual patience GEO. ELIOT.

Sugge·stionism. 1892. [f. prec. + -ISM.] The doctrine or practice of hypnotic suggestion. Hence **Sugge·stionist,** one who advocates or practises suggestion; one who treats disease by suggestion.

Suggestive (sŏdʒe·stiv), *a.* 1631. [f. SUGGEST *v.* + -IVE.] **1.** Calculated or fitted to suggest thoughts, ideas, a course of action, etc.; conveying a suggestion or hint; implying something that is not directly expressed. **b.** *euphem.* Apt to suggest something indecent 1889. **2.** Of a method, plan, etc.: That suggests itself 1806. **3.** Pertaining to hypnotic suggestion 1903.

1. Some thoughtful and s. chapters by M. de Remusat 1856. A very s. thinker 1857. Much that is s. of inquiry 1880. Hence **Sugge·stive-ly** *adv.*, **-ness. Suggesti·vity** (*rare*).

†**Sugge·stor.** 1591. [f. SUGGEST *v.* + -OR 2. Cf. med.L. *suggestor*.] = SUGGESTER –1818.

‖**Suggestum** (sŏdʒe·stŏm). *Pl.* **-a (-ums).** 1705. [L., n. pa. pple. of *suggerere*; see SUGGEST.] A platform, stage, tribune.

Sugillate, suggillate (s[i]ū·dʒile[i]t, sɒ·dʒ-), *v.* Now *rare* or *Obs.* 1623. [– *sugillat-*, pa. ppl. stem of L. *sugillare*.] *trans.* To beat black and blue, bruise. Chiefly *Med.* in *pa. pple.*, marked with livid spots or patches, bruised. So **Sug(g)illa·tion,** †beating black and blue; *Med.* a livid or black-and-blue mark; a bruise; ecchymosis.

Suicidal (s[i]ūisəi·dăl), *a.* 1777. [f. SUICIDE *sb.*[2] + -AL[1].] **1.** Of, pertaining to, or involving suicide or self-slaughter; (of persons) having a tendency to suicide 1837. **2.** *fig.* Leading to or involving self-destruction; destructive or fatal to those engaged 1777. Hence **Suici·dally** *adv.*

Suicide (s[i]ū·isəid), *sb.*[1] 1728. [– mod.L. *suicida*, f. L. *sui* of oneself; see -CIDE 1. Cf. Fr. *suicide*.] One who dies by his own hand; one who commits self-murder. Also, one who attempts or has a tendency to commit suicide. Also *attrib.* or as *adj.* (= suicidal).

Suicide (s[i]ū·isəid), *sb.*[2] 1651. [– mod.L. *suicidium*, f. as prec.; see -CIDE 2. Cf. Fr. *suicide*.] The or an act of taking one's life, self-murder. Phr. *to commit s.*

fig. The central tragedy of all the world, the s. of Greece RUSKIN. Hence **Su·icide** *v. intr.* and *refl.* to commit s.; *trans.* (*euphem.*) to do to death.

†**Suici·dical,** *a. rare.* 1755. [f. prec. + -ICAL.] = SUICIDAL –1835.

Suicidism (s[i]ū·isəidiz'm). *rare.* 1807. [f. SUICIDE *sb.*[2] + -ISM.] The doctrine or practice of suicide.

‖**Sui generis** (s[i]ū·əi dʒe·nĕris). 1787. [L.] *lit.* Of one or its own kind; peculiar. †Also illiterately as *sb.*, a thing apart, an isolated specimen.

‖**Sui juris** (s[i]ū·əi dʒū[ə]·ris). 1614. [L., = of

one's own right.] **a.** *Anc. Roman Law.* Of the status of one who was not subject to the *patria potestas.* **b.** *Mod. Law.* Of full age and capacity, legally competent to manage one's own affairs 1675. **c.** *transf.* One's own master 1655.

Suilline (sᶦū ilǝin), *a.* and *sb.* 1880. [var. of *suidian*; irreg. f. L. *suillus* pertaining to swine (f. *sus* swine) + -INE¹.] Pertaining to, an animal of, the family *Suidæ* or swine.

Suine (sᶦū·in). 1881. [f. L. *sus, su-* swine + -INE⁵.] A fatty substance made from pig's lard, used as a butter-substitute.

Suing (sᶦū·iŋ), *vbl. sb.* ME. [f. SUE *v.* + -ING¹.] †**1.** The following of a person or thing; the pursuance of a course of action; the carrying out or execution of something –1465. **2.** 'Pursuing' at law; legal prosecution or suit; application for a writ. Also *s. forth.* 1440. **3.** The action of a suitor; paying court; entreaty, supplication 1591.

Suing (sᶦū·iŋ), *ppl. a.* late ME. [f. SUE *v.* + -ING².] **1.** That sues. **2.** In *absol.* or *advb.* const.: (*a*) In succession, one after another; (*b*) afterwards, after. late ME. Hence †**Su·ingly** *adv.* consequently; in due sequence; hence, subsequently, later; in succession.

Suint (swint). 1791. [– Fr. *suint*, earlier †*suing*, f. *suer* sweat.] The natural greasy substance in the wool of sheep, consisting of fatty matter combined with potash salts: called also *yolk*.

Suiogothic (swiǫgǫ·þik), *a.* and *sb.* 1759. [– mod.L. *Suiogothicus*, adj. of *Suiones Gothique*, used to denote the *Sviar* Swedes, and *Götar*, older *Gautar*, inhabitants of Götland (south Sweden); see -IC.] Swedish; the (Old and Middle) Swedish language.

‖**Suisse** (swis, süis). 1837. [Fr., = Swiss.] The porter of a large house; the beadle of a church (in France).

Suit (sᶦūt), *sb.* [ME. *siute, siwte, s(e)ute* – AFr. *siute*, OFr. *sieute, siute* (mod. *suite*) :– Gallo-Rom. **sequita*, subst. use of fem. pa. pple. of **sequere* follow, SUE *v.*] **I.** *Feudal Law.* **1. a.** In full, *s. of court*: Attendance by a tenant at the court of his lord. **b.** In full, *s. real* (*royal, regal*): Attendance of a person at the sheriff's court or tourn, attendance at the court-leet. **c.** An instance of this. late ME. **2.** *S. and service*: attendance at court and personal service due from a tenant to his lord; hence used as a formula in describing certain forms of tenure. Also *homage and s.* late ME. **3.** The resort of tenants to a certain mill to have their corn ground; the obligation of such resort. *Hist.* 1450. †**4.** A due paid in lieu of attendance at the court of a lord –1660.

1. Phr. *To do, give, owe s.* **2.** *fig.* I, being a cadet of my house, owed s. and service to him who was its head DE QUINCEY.

II. Pursuit; prosecution, legal process. †**1.** Pursuit, chase; also, a pursuit –1772. †**2.** The pursuit *of* an object or quest –1596. **3.** The action of suing in a court of law; legal prosecution; hence, †litigation 1477. †**4.** The prosecution *of* a cause; also, the suing for a writ –1607. **5.** A process instituted in a court of justice for the recovery or protection of a right, the enforcement of a claim, or the redress of a wrong; a prosecution before a legal tribunal. late ME. **b.** More fully, *s. in law* = LAWSUIT. Similarly *s. in chancery, equity.* 1530. **6.** The action or an act of suing, supplicating, or petitioning; (a) petition, supplication, or entreaty; *esp.* a petition made to a prince or other high personage. Now *poet.* 1449. †**b.** *To make one's s.*: to supplicate, petition, sue –1738. **7.** Wooing or courting of a woman; solicitation for a woman's hand. Also, an instance of this, a courtship. 1590.

3. Whose suite is he arrested at? SHAKS. **5.** Ordinary private law..upon which nine-tenths of the suits between man and man are founded 1888. **6.** The King sees me, and faine would heare my sute KYD. **7.** Doubtless, that agreeable figure of his must have help'd his s. surprizingly SHERIDAN.

†**III.** Livery, garb; sort, class. **1.** A livery or uniform; also, in wider sense, a dress, garb –1633. **b.** *Out of suits with*: out of favour with. SHAKS. **2.** Kind, sort, class –1642.

IV. Following, train, suite. A company of followers; a train, retinue, SUITE. Also, a company of disciples. Now *arch.* or *dial.* (repl. by *suite*). ME. **b.** The witnesses or followers of a plaintiff in an action at law. Now *Hist.* 1647.

V. Set, series. **1.** A number of objects of the same kind or pattern intended to be used together or forming a definite set or series, e.g. the whole of the sails required for a ship or for a set of spars; a suite of rooms. late ME. **2.** A set of garments or habiliments intended to be worn together at the same time. **a.** of church vestments 1495. **b.** of men's or boys' outer garments; in full, *s. of apparel, of clothes.* late ME. **c.** of women's attire; in earlier use, an entire set of garments for wear at one time; in recent use, a costume (i.e. coat and skirt) 1761. **d.** of armour 1821. **e.** *transf., fig.*, and *allus.* 1593. **3.** Any of the four sets (spades, clubs, hearts, diamonds) of which a pack of playing-cards consists. Also, the whole number of cards belonging to such a set held in a player's hand at one time 1529.

1. A s. of Ribbands ADDISON. A whole s. of drawing-rooms DICKENS. **2. a.** One priestly cope, with the whole suite EVELYN. **b.** His light travelling s. 1892. **e.** The redbreast's sober s. 1804. If honour be your clothing, the s. will last a life-time 1858. *Birthday suit* (joc.), the bare skin. **3.** I purpose agayne to deale vnto you an other card, almost of the same sute LATIMER. Phr. *To follow s.* (†*in s.*), to play a card of the same s. as the leading card; hence often *fig.*, to do the same thing as somebody (or something) else. *One's strong s.*, one's forte.

VI. Sequence; agreement. †**1.** A succession, sequence (*rare*) –1625. **2.** *In s. with*: in agreement or harmony with. *Of a s. with*: of a piece with. 1797.

attrib. and *Comb.*: †**s.-broker**, one who made a business of procuring a favourable hearing for suits; **-case**, a small rigid portmanteau orig. designed to contain a s. of clothes; **-duty**, obligation to give s. at a mill; **-service** *Feudal Law*, service rendered by attendance at a lord's court. **b.** In Bridge, where *suit* is contrasted with 'no trumps' (see No *a.* II. 3), as *s.-bid, -call*, etc.

Suit (sᶦūt), *v.* 1450. [f. prec.] †**1.** *intr.* To 'do suit' to a court; hence, to have recourse *to* –1540. †**2.** To prefer a suit; to sue *to* a person *for* something –1719. †**3.** To pay court *to* a woman –1749. †**4.** To arrange in a set, sequence, or series; to set in due order, sort out –1695. **5.** *trans.* To provide with a suit of clothes; to clothe, attire, dress. Chiefly *pass. arch.* 1577. **6.** To make appropriate or agreeable *to*; to adapt or accommodate in style, manner, or proportion *to*; to render suitable. Freq. in *pass.* 1596. **7.** To provide, furnish. Chiefly *pass.* (or *refl.*), to be provided (or provide oneself) *with* something desired and in such a manner as to please one 1607. **8.** To be agreeable or convenient to (a person, his inclinations etc.); to fall in with the views or wishes of 1578. **9.** To be fitted for, adapted to, be suitable for, answer the requirements of 1603. **b.** To be good for, 'agree with'; *esp.* to be favourable to the health of (a person) 1814. **c.** To be becoming to 1819. **10.** *intr.* To be suitable, fitting, or convenient 1821. **11.** *To s. with*: to agree, harmonize, or fit in with; to be suitable to. *Obs.* or *arch.* 1605.

5. How odly he is suited, I thinke he bought his doublet in Italie SHAKS. **6.** Sute the Action to the Word, the Word to the Action SHAKS. **7.** I hope you are suited, my dear DICKENS. **8.** That sort of promise which a man keeps when the thing suits his inclination 1779. **9.** The Sofa suits The gouty limb COWPER. His own explanation did not s. all phenomena JOWETT. **10.** Say Saturday; if that does not s. there will be time to tell me MRS. CARLYLE.

Suitable (sᶦū·tăb'l), *a.* (*adv.*) 1582. [f. prec. + -ABLE, after *agreeable.*] †**1.** Of furniture, dress, features, etc.: Conforming or agreeing in shape, colour, pattern, or style; matching, to match –1710. †**2.** Of persons, actions, qualities, conditions, institutions: Conforming or agreeing in nature, condition, or action; accordant; corresponding; analogous; *occas.* congenial –1748. †**b.** Of two or more things: That are in agreement or accord –1684. **3.** That is fitted for, adapted or appropriate to a person's character, condition, needs, etc., a purpose, object, occasion, or the like. Const. *to, for.* 1607. †**4.** as *adv.* = Suitably *to* –1796.

3. Senseless fears not sutable to the occasion 1653. There are 750,000 in Ireland who could earn 2s. a week..if they had sutable employment 1672. The most s. season for transplanting the roots 1812. Hence **Suitabi·lity, Sui·tableness. Sui·tably** *adv.*

Suite (swīt). 1673. [– Fr. *suite*; see SUIT *sb.* Senses 2 b, c, are of English development.] **1.** A train of followers, attendants, or servants; a retinue. **2.** A succession or series; now chiefly said of series of specimens 1722. **b.** A number of rooms together forming a set used by a person, a family or company of persons 1716. **c.** A set of furniture of uniform pattern 1851. **d.** *Mus.* †(*a*) A set or series of lessons, etc.; (*b*) A series of dance tunes arranged for one or more instruments and composed in the same key or related keys 1801. **3.** A sequel, result (*rare*) 1800. **4.** ‖**En s.** (aṅ süit). **a.** In agreement or harmony (*with*) 1797. **b.** Of rooms: In a series leading from one to the other 1818.

2. d. (*c*) A collection of pieces or songs by one composer on one main theme to be performed in sequence at one time 1902.

Suited (sᶦū·tĕd), *ppl. a.* 1632. [f. SUIT *sb.* or *v.* + -ED.] With qualifying word: Wearing a suit or attire of a specified kind.

Till civil-suited Morn appeer MILT.

Suiting (sᶦū·tiŋ), *vbl. sb.* 1561. [f. SUIT *v.* + -ING¹.] †**1.** The action of suing for something; suing out a writ; petitioning; paying court to a woman –1690. **2.** The fitting or adaptation of one thing *to* another 1707. **3.** *concr.* Trade name for: Material for making suits of clothes; usu. *pl.* 1883.

Suitor (sᶦū·tǝɹ), *sb.* late ME. [– AFr. *seutor, suitour, sut(i)er, -or* – L. *secutor, -ōr-* follower, f. *secut-*, pa. ppl. stem of *sequi* follow, SUE, after *suite* SUIT *v.*] †**1.** One of a retinue or suite; hence, an adherent, follower, disciple –1830. **2.** One who owed suit (see SUIT *sb.* I. 1) to a court, and in that capacity acted as assessor or elector. Now only *Hist.* late ME. **3.** One who sues or petitions; a petitioner, suppliant. *arch.* late ME. **4.** A petitioner or plaintiff in a suit 1503. **5.** One who seeks a woman in marriage; a wooer 1586.

3. That you would..be a suter for him unto the heavenly powers GASCOIGNE. **5.** She was rich—..of course she had suitors 1870. Hence **Sui·torship.**

Suitor (sᶦū·tǝɹ), *v.* Now chiefly *dial.* 1668. [f. prec.] **1.** *trans.* To court, woo 1672. **2.** *intr.* To be a suitor or wooer (*to*) 1668.

2. Counts a many, and Dukes a few, A suitoring came to my father's Hall BARHAM.

Suitress (sᶦū·trĕs). *rare.* 1714. [f. SUITOR *sb.* + -ESS¹.] A female suitor.

†‖**Suivante** (süivāṅt). 1698. [Fr., pr. pple. fem. of *suivre* follow.] A confidential maid –1812.

‖**Sula** (siū·lă). 1678. [mod.L. (Willughby 1676) – ON. *súla.*] Applied by Hoier and others to a supposed variety of sea-fowl; in mod. *Ornith.* a genus of gannets (family *Sulidæ*).

Sulcal (sɒ·lkăl), *a.* 1889. [f. SULCUS + -AL¹.] *Anat.* Belonging to or connected with a sulcus.

Sulcate (sɒ·lkeᶦt), *a.* 1760. [– L. *sulcatus*, pa. pple. of *sulcare* plough, f. SULCUS; see -ATE².] *Nat. Hist.* Marked with (parallel) furrows or grooves. So **Su·lcated** *ppl. a.* 1694.

†**Sulcate**, *v.* 1577. [– *sulcat-*, pa. ppl. stem of L. *sulcare*; see prec., -ATE³.] *trans.* To plough (*esp.* the seas) –1656.

Sulcation (sɒlkēᶦ·ʃǝn). *rare.* 1658. [f. SULCATE *a.*; see -ATION. In sense 1 from med. L. *sulcatio.*] **1.** Furrowing, grooving. **2.** A sulcus or set of sulci 1852.

Sulca·to-, used as comb. form of L. *sulcatus* SULCATE *a.* in the sense 'sulcate and...', as *s.-costate* adj.

Sulciform (sɒ·lsifǭɹm), *a.* 1822. [f. next + -FORM.] Having the form of a sulcus.

‖**Sulcus** (sɒ·lkɒs). *Pl.* **sulci** (sɒ·lsǝi). 1662. [L. = furrow, trench, ditch, wrinkle.] **1. a.** A groove made with an engraving tool. **b.** A trench. **c.** A hollow or depression in the land. *rare.* **2.** *Anat.* A groove or furrow in a body, organ, or tissue 1744. **b.** *spec.* A fissure between two convolutions of the brain 1833. **3.** *Bot.* The lamella in some fungi 1856.

Suling (su·liŋ). *Hist.* [OE. *swulung*,

sulung, prob. f. **swul(h)ian*, **sul(h)ian*, f. **swulh*, *sulh* plough, SULLOW. In AL. *sullinga, -us* (1204).] In Kent, the fiscal unit.

Sulk (sɒlk), *sb.* 1804. [f. SULK *v.*[2]] **1.** *pl.* A state of ill-humour or resentment marked by obstinate silence or aloofness from society. Often with *the* and in phr. *in the sulks.* **b.** *sing.* A fit of sulking; the action of sulking 1837. **2.** A person who sulks (*rare*) 1883.

1. b. Mrs. Cadurcis remained alone in a savage s. 1837.

†**Sulk,** *v.*[1] *rare.* 1579. [– L. *sulcare* plough, furrow, f. *sulcus* furrow.] *trans.* To plough (the seas). Also *intr.* –1682.

Sulk (sɒlk), *v.*[2] 1781. [perh. back-formation from somewhat earlier SULKY *a.*] *intr.* To keep aloof from others in moody silence; to indulge in sullen ill-humour; to be sulky.

He sulked with his old landlady for thrusting gentle advice and warning on him READE. Hence **Su·lker,** one who sulks.

Sulky (sɒ·lki), *sb.* 1756. [subst. use of next.] **1.** A light two-wheeled carriage or chaise (occas. without a body), seated for one person: now used chiefly in America for trials of speed between trotting-horses. (So called because it admits only one person.) **2.** *attrib.* passing into *adj.*, applied to (*a*) a set of articles for the use of a single person, (*b*) an agricultural implement having a seat for the driver (*U.S.*) 1786.

Sulky (sɒ·lki), *a.* 1744. [perh. an extension with -Y[1] of an adj. †*sulke* (XVII) hard to dispose of, slow in going off, which may repr. ult. the base **sulk-* of OE. *āseolcan* become sluggish.] **1.** Of persons and their actions: Silently and obstinately ill-humoured; showing a tendency to keep aloof from others and repel their advances by refusing to speak or act. Also of animals; *spec.* of a fish that remains in hiding and motionless when hooked. **2.** Of the weather, etc.: Gloomy, dismal. Of things, with respect to their growth, progress, or movement: Sluggish. Also, *dial.* difficult to work. 1817. Here **Su·lkily** *adv.*

Sullage (sɒ·lėdʒ). 1553. [perh. – AFr. **souillage*, **soullage*, *suillage*, f. *souiller* SOIL *v.*[1], SULLY *v.*; see -AGE.] **1.** Filth, refuse, *esp.* such as is carried off by drains from a house, farmyard, or the like; sewage. †**2.** *fig.* Filth, defilement, pollution –1607. **3.** The silt washed down and deposited by a stream or flood 1691. **4.** *Founding.* Metal scoria or slag 1843.

2. The lightest act of dalliance leaves somthing of stain and s. behind it 1673.

Comb.: **s.-pipe,** a drain-pipe.

Sullen (sɒ·lən), *a.*, *adv.*, and *sb.* 1573. [Later form of †*solein*, †*-eyne* unique, sole, solitary, morose (XIV) – AFr. **solein*, **solain*, f. *sol* SOLE *a.*, after OFr. *soltain*, *soutain* :– late L. *solitaneus*, f. L. *solus* SOLE *a.*] **A.** *adj.* **1.** Of persons, their attributes, aspect, actions: Characterized by, or indicative of, gloomy ill-humour or moody silence. **b.** *transf.* Of animals and inanimate things: Obstinate, refractory; stubborn, unyielding 1577. †**c.** *fig.* Baleful, malignant –1703. †**2.** Solemn, serious –1719. **3.** Of immaterial things, actions, conditions: Gloomy, dismal, melancholy; sometimes with the notion of 'passing heavily, moving sluggishly' 1593. **b.** Of a sound or an object producing a sound: Of a deep, dull, or mournful tone. Chiefly *poet.* 1592. **4.** Of sombre hue; of a dull colour; hence, of gloomy or dismal aspect 1586. **5.** Of water, etc.: Flowing sluggishly. *poet.* 1622.

1. The answer of James was a cold and s. reprimand MACAULAY. **b.** As s. as a beast new-caged TENNYSON. **2.** Such s. Planets at my Birth did shine, They threaten every Fortune mixt with mine DRYDEN. **3.** The s. passage of thy weary steppes SHAKS. A bleak, s. day 1864. **b.** I hear the far-off Curfeu sound..Swinging slow with s. roar MILT. **4.** Like bright Mettall on a s. ground SHAKS. The sullen-purple moor TENNYSON. **5.** S. Mole that runneth underneath MILT.

B. *adv.* = Sullenly (*rare*) 1718. **C.** *sb.* (in *pl.*, usu. *the sullens*; rarely *sing.*) A state of gloomy ill-humour; sullenness, sulks. *arch.* 1580.

Phr. *In the sullens, sick of the sullens.* Hence **Su·llen** *v.* (*rare*) *trans.* to make s. or sluggish. **Su·llen-ly** *adv.*, **-ness.**

Sulliage (sɒ·liėdʒ). 1667. variant of SULLAGE, infl. by SULLY *v.*

Su·llow. Chiefly *w.* and *s.w. dial.* [OE. *sulh*, cogn. w. L. *sulcus* furrow. Cf. SULING.] A plough.

†**Su·lly,** *sb.* 1602. [f. next.] An act of sullying or polluting; a stain, blemish –1762.

Little Spots and Sullies in its Reputation ADDISON.

Sully (sɒ·li), *v.* 1591. [perh. – Fr. *souiller*; see SOIL *v.*] **1.** *trans.* To pollute, defile; to soil, stain, tarnish (in material sense now *rare* or *poet.*). Often in pa. pple. †**2.** *intr.* To become soiled or tarnished –1670.

1. The roofe and sides are..sullied..with the smoke of torches 1615. The purity of his virtue was sullied by excessive vanity GIBBON. **2.** Looke you Francis, your white Canuas doublet will sulley SHAKS.

Sulph- (sɒlf). *Chem.*, var. of SULPHO- before a vowel, as in *sulphamide, -anilic (-ate), -antimonic (-ate), -arsenic (-ate), -iodide.*

Su·lphacid. 1859. [See SULPH-.] = SULPHO-ACID.

Sulphate (sɒ·lfeit, -ĕt), *sb.* 1790. [– Fr. *sulfate*, f. L. SULPHUR; see -ATE[4].] *Chem.* **1.** A salt of sulphuric acid: usu. with term indicating the base, as *s. of ammonia.* **2.** *ellipt.* = Sodium sulphate 1900. Hence **Su·lphate** *v.* *intr.* to become sulphated. **Su·lphating** *vbl. sb.* the formation of a sulphate, *esp.* the deposit of lead sulphate on the plates of a battery.

Sulphated (sɒ·lfeitėd), *ppl. a.* 1802. [f. SULPHATE *sb.* and *v.* + -ED. Cf. Fr. *sulfaté.*] Combined or impregnated with sulphur or sulphuric acid; charged with or containing sulphates.

Sulphato- (sɒlfĕi·to). *Chem.*, bef. a vowel sometimes **sulphat-** (sɒ·lfĕt), a prefix in the name of a compound denoting that it contains a sulphate as an ingredient, as *s.-carbonate.*

Sulphide (sɒ·lfəid). 1836. [f. SULPHUR + -IDE.] *Chem.* **1.** A compound of sulphur with another element (usu. denoted by a qualifying term). **b.** *Hydrogen s.*, sulphuretted hydrogen, H_2S. 1849. **2.** *attrib.*, chiefly with ref. to the treatment of metallic sulphides in manufacturing processes 1893.

Sulphinate (sɒ·lfinĕt). 1877. [f. SULPHINIC + -ATE[4].] *Chem.* A salt of sulphinic acid.

Sulphindigotic (sɒlfindigǫ·tik), *a.* 1857. [f. SULPH- + INDIGOTIC.] *Chem.* In *s. acid*: an acid formed by the action of a sulphuric acid on indigo. Hence **Sulphi·ndigotate,** a salt of s. acid.

Sulphine (sɒ·lfəin). 1880. [f. SULPH- + -INE[5].] *Chem.* Any of a group of compounds containing sulphur united to hydrocarbon radicals; also, the hypothetical radical SH_3 from which these are derived.

Sulphinic (sɒlfi·nik), *a.* 1877. [f. prec. + -IC.] *Chem.* Applied to acids containing the group SO . OH united to carbon, obtained by reducing the chlorides of the sulphonic acids.

Sulphion (sɒ·lfiǫn). 1868. [f. SULPH- + ION.] *Chem.* The hypothetical radical consisting of one equivalent of sulphur and four of oxygen (SO_4).

Sulphite (sɒ·lfəit). 1790. [– Fr. *sulfite*, arbitrary alt. of *sulfate*; see -ITE[1] 4 b.] *Chem.* **1.** A salt of sulphurous acid: usu. with a qualifying term indicating the base. **2.** *attrib.*, chiefly with ref. to the use of sulphite of soda or of lime in certain processes 1892.

Sulpho- (sɒ·lfo), bef. a vowel also SULPH-, used as comb. form of SULPHUR, in names of chemical compounds containing sulphur, or (in mod. use) produced by the substitution of sulphur for oxygen (etc.) in a compound; now largely superseded by THIO-.

Su·lpho-a·cid. 1857. [f. prec. + ACID.] *Chem.* **a.** An acid obtained from another acid by substituting sulphur for oxygen; as SULPHOCYANIC acid, CNHS, from cyanic acid, CNHO, now called THIO-ACID. **b.** An acid which contains the group SO_2. OH united to carbon.

Sulphocyanic (sɒ:lfosəi,æ·nik), *a.* 1819. [f. SULPHO- + CYANIC.] *Chem.* Designating the sulpho-acid related to cyanic acid, occurring in cruciferous plants and in human saliva, and obtainable as a colourless liquid; now THIOCYANIC. Hence **Sulphocy·anate, -cy·anide** (in *Photogr.* short for ammonium sulphocyanide).

Sulphocyanogen (sɒ:lfosəi,æ·nŏdʒĕn). 1841. [f. SULPHO- + CYANOGEN.] *Chem.* A compound of sulphur and cyanogen $(CN)_2S$, obtained as a yellow amorphous powder.

Sulphonal (sɒ·lfŏnăl). 1889. [– G. *sulfonal*, f. *sulfon* SULPHONE.] *Chem.* Diethylsulphone-dimethyl-methane, a white crystalline substance, used as a hypnotic.

Sulphone (sɒ·lfoᵘn). 1872. [– G. *sulfon*, f. *sulfur*; see -ONE a.] *Chem.* Any of a group of compounds containing the radical SO_2 united to two hydrocarbon radicals.

Sulphonic (sɒlfǫ·nik), *a.* 1873. [f. prec. + -IC.] *Chem.* Containing the radical SO_2. OH (called the *s. group* or *radical*). Hence **Su·lphonate.**

Sulphopurpuric (sɒ:lfopɒɹpiūᵊ·rik), *a.* 1838. [– Fr. *sulfo-purpurique* (Dumas, 1836); see SULPHO- and PURPURIC.] *Chem.* Applied to an acid obtained by the action of sulphuric acid on indigo. Hence **Sulphopu·rpurate.**

Sulpho-salt (sɒ·lfosǫlt). 1833. [f. SULPHO- + SALT *sb.*[1] 5.] *Chem.* A salt of a sulpho-acid.

Sulphovinic (sɒlfovi·nik), *a.* 1826. [– Fr. *sulfovinique*, f. *sulfo-* SULPHO- + *vin* wine; see -IC.] *Chem.* *S. acid*: an acid produced by the action of sulphuric acid on alcohol or spirit of wine; ethyl hydrogen sulphate or ethyl suphuric acid. Hence **Sulphovinate** (-vəi·nĕt).

Sulphur (sɒ·lfəɹ), *sb.* late ME. [Late ME. *soufre, solfre, sulph(e)re* – AFr.. *sulf(e)re*, (O)Fr. *soufre* :– L. *sulfur, -phur, -pur* (pl. *-phura*), perh. rel. to the Gmc. word repr. by OE. *swefl.*] **I. 1.** A greenish-yellow nonmetallic substance, found abundantly in volcanic regions, and occurring free in nature as a brittle crystalline solid, and widely distributed in combination with metals and other substances. In pop. and commercial language it is otherwise known as BRIMSTONE. In *Chem.*, one of the non-metallic elements: atomic weight 32, symbol S.

Sulphur exists in two distinct crystalline forms and in an amorphous form. It is manufactured largely from native sulphides of copper and iron; when refined and cast into moulds, it is the *roll* or *stick s.* of commerce. It is highly inflammable, and is used in the manufacture of matches, gunpowder, and sulphuric acid, for vulcanizing rubber, in bleaching, and as a disinfectant.

In popular belief sulphur has been associated with the fires of hell, with devils, and with thunder and lightning.

b. In a refined state, e.g. as flowers of sulphur, it is used medicinally as a laxative, a resolvent, and a sudorific, and as an ingredient of various ointments, esp. for skin diseases. ME. †**c.** *pl.* Masses or deposits of native sulphur –1771. **2.** *Alch.* One of the supposed ultimate elements of all material substances. late ME. †**3.** A compound of sulphur; *esp.* a sulphide –1853. **4.** †**a.** Applied to thunder and lightning, a discharge of gunpowder, etc. –1616. **b.** Applied pop. to minerals containing sulphur or supposed to be sulphurous 1799. **c.** *Vegetable s.*: see VEGETABLE *a.* 1855. **5.** *ellipt.* = *sulphur butterfly* 1832. **6.** *colloq.* or *slang.* Pungent talk, 'sulphurous' language 1897.

1. Thunder hath s. in it COWLEY. A fiery Deluge, fed With ever-burning S. unconsum'd MILT. *Virgin s.*, native s. in the form of transparent amber-coloured crystals. *Volcanic s.*, native s. in opaque, lemon-yellow, crystalline masses. *S. of ivy*, corruption of SULPHUR VIVUM. **4. a.** The Gods throw stones of sulpher on me SHAKS.

Comb.: **s. acid,** an old name for sulphides of electronegative metals, as arsenic, antimony; **s. alcohol,** a compound of the nature of an alcohol in which s. replaces oxygen; **s. bath,** †(*a*) a sulphur spring; (*b*) a bath to which flowers of s. have been added, used in the treatment of skin diseases; **-cast** = *s. impression*; **s. ether,** a compound analogous to ether in which s. replaces oxygen; **-impression,** an impression taken of a seal, medallion, etc. in a composition consisting of s. and wax; **-match,** a lucifer match tipped with s.; **-ore,** an ore which yields s., e.g. iron pyrites; **s. salt,** an old name for salt produced by the combination of a 's. acid' with another metallic base; **-spring,** a spring containing compounds of s. or impregnated with sulphurous gases; **-tree,** a hard-wooded tree, *Morinda lucida*, found in West Central Africa and used for building purposes; **-weed** = SULPHURWORT;

-work(s, a s. manufactory; **-yellow**, (of) the pale-yellow colour characteristic of s.

II. *attrib.* passing into *adj.* = Of the colour of sulphur, sulphur-yellow, as in *s. butterfly*, *pearl*; *s.-breasted*, *-crested*; **s.-bottom** (in full *s.-bottom whale*), a rorqual of the Pacific Ocean, *Balænoptera sulphurea*, having yellow underparts; also **s.-whale.**

Sulphur (sɒ·lfəɹ), *v.* 1759. [f. prec.] *trans.* To fumigate with burning sulphur; to sprinkle (plants) with flowers of sulphur to prevent mould or the like; also, to put (wine) into casks that have been fumigated with sulphur to prevent fermentation.

Sulphurate (sɒ·lfiŭreᶦt), *v. rare.* 1757. [f. SULPHUR + -ATE³.] *trans.* To combine with, or convert into, sulphur; to impregnate with, or subject to the action of, sulphur. Hence **Su·lphurator,** an apparatus for sprinkling plants with flowers of sulphur, for fumigating with sulphur, or the like.

Sulphurated (sɒ·lfiŭreᶦtėd), *ppl. a.* 1747. [f. prec. + -ED¹.] Chiefly *Chem.* Combined or impregnated with sulphur: applied chiefly to sulphides. (Survives chiefly in terms of the Materia Medica.)

Sulphuration (sɒlfiŭrēᶦ·ʃən). Now *rare* or *Obs.* 1713. [In senses 1, 2, f. SULPHUR *v.* + -ATION; in senses 3, 4, f. SULPHURATE *v.* + -ION.] **1.** Anointing with sulphur (*rare*). **2.** Fumigation with sulphur 1791. **3.** Combination with sulphur 1796. **4.** Vulcanization 1853.

†**Sulphure·ity.** 1610. [f. L. *sulphureus* SULPHUREOUS *a.* + -ITY, after med.L. *aqueitas* AQUEITY, *terreitas* 'terreity'.] Sulphureous quality or nature –1676.

Sulphureo- (sɒlfiūᵊ·rĭo), used as comb. form of L. *sulphureus* in the sense of 'sulphureous and..'.

Sulphureous (sɒlfiūᵊ·rĭəs), *a.* 1552. [f. L. *sulphureus*, f. *sulphur* SULPHUR; see -EOUS.] **1.** Of or pertaining to sulphur; full of, containing, or consisting of sulphur 1626. †**b.** *Old Path.* Consisting of 'sulphur' as one of the principles of matter; (of disease) arising from 'sulphurous' matter –1702. **2.** Derived or emanating from sulphur; hence, having the qualities associated with (burning) sulphur 1552. **3.** *allus.* and *fig.* †Hellish, satanic; full of the 'sulphur' of hell 1664. **4.** Sulphur-coloured, sulphur-yellow. Also, of the bluish colour of the flame with which sulphur burns. 1656.

1. The patients lie up to their chins in hot s. water 1792. **2.** A s. smell ensues GOLDSM. Hence **Sulphu·reous-ly** *adv.*, **-ness.**

Sulphuret (sɒ·lfiŭret). 1790. [– mod.L. *sulphuretum*; see SULPHUR *sb.* and -URET.] *Chem.* = SULPHIDE. (Now only in the Materia Medica and in Mining.)

Sulphuretted (sɒ·lfiŭretėd), *a.* 1805. [f. prec. + -ED².] *Chem.* Combined chemically with sulphur; impregnated with sulphur.

S. hydrogen, hydrogen sulphide, H_2S, a colourless gas with a very offensive odour, prepared by the action of diluted hydrochloric or sulphuric acid upon iron (ferrous) sulphide.

Sulphuric (sɒlfiūᵊ·rik), *a.* 1790. [– Fr. *sulfurique*; see SULPHUR *sb.* and -IC.] **1.** *Chem. S. acid*, a highly corrosive oily fluid (hydrogen sulphate, H_2SO_4), also called *oil of vitriol*, in its pure state a dense liquid without colour or smell. **b.** Related to or derived from sulphuric acid 1815. †**2.** Consisting of or containing sulphur –1811.

1. *Anhydrous s. acid*, sulphur trioxide. *Fuming s. acid*, a mixture of sulphuric acid and sulphur trioxide. **b.** *S. anhydride*, sulphur trioxide. *S. ether*, ethylic or vinic ether, a compound formed by the action of sulphuric acid upon spirits of wine. *S. oxide*, sulphur trioxide.

Sulphuring (sɒ·lfəriŋ), *vbl. sb.* 1800. [f. SULPHUR *sb.* or *v.* + -ING¹.] **1.** Exposure to the fumes arising from burning sulphur, to produce whiteness in fabrics, to prevent fermentation in casks, to disinfect, etc. **2.** The sprinkling of plants with flowers of sulphur to prevent or destroy mildew 1891.

†**Sulphu·rious,** *a.* 1471. [– OFr. *sulphurieux*, f. L. *sulphur* SULPHUR + *-ieux* -IOUS.] = SULPHUREOUS, SULPHUROUS –1727.

Sulphurize (sɒ·lfiŭrəiz), *v.* 1794. [– Fr. *sulfuriser* (Lavoisier, 1789); see SULPHUR *sb.* and -IZE.] **1.** *trans.* To cause to combine chemically with or to be impregnated by sulphur; to convert into a sulphur compound. **2.** To treat or dress with sulphur; to vulcanize (rubber) 1846. **3.** To fumigate with burning sulphur 1856. Hence **Su:lphuriza·tion.**

Sulphurous (sɒ·lfiŭrəs, *in Chem. use* sɒlfiūᵊ·rəs), *a.* 1530. [– L. *sulphurosus* or f. SULPHUR *sb.* + -OUS.] **1.** = SULPHUREOUS 1. **2.** = SULPHUREOUS 2. 1607. **b.** Applied to thunder and lightning (*poet.*). Also *occas.* volcanic. 1603. **c.** Of or belonging to (the smoke of) gunpowder 1620. **3.** *allus.* and *fig.* **a.** Pertaining to sulphur or brimstone as an adjunct of hell; hellish, satanic. Also, pertaining to or dealing with hell-fire. 1602. **b.** Fiery, heated 1611. **c.** Of language, expression: Characterized by heat; in recent use, blasphemous, profane 1616. **4.** = SULPHUREOUS 4. Also *advb.* 1837. **5.** *Chem.* Designating compounds in which sulphur is present in a larger proportion than in sulphuric compounds 1790.

2. b. Cracks Of s. roaring SHAKS. **3. a.** There's hell, there's darkenes, there is the s. pit SHAKS. **b.** Duc de Rohan rose, in a s. frame of mind CARLYLE. **c.** He used..s. words, and the very biggest D's, I was assured 1897. **4.** Burning sulphurous-blue..it still shines CARLYLE. **5.** *S. acid*: (*a*) more fully, *s. acid gas*, an old name for sulphur dioxide; (*b*) the acid (H_2SO_3) resulting from the combination of sulphur dioxide with water. *S. oxide* or *anhydride*, sulphur dioxide, SO_2, a transparent colourless gas with a pungent and suffocating smell, obtained by burning sulphur in dry air or oxygen. Hence **Su·lphurously** *adv.*

‖**Sulphur vivum** (sɒ·lfəɹ vəi·vɒm). 1651. [L. = living sulphur. So in med.L. (XIII).] Native or virgin sulphur; also in a fused, partly purified form.

Sulphurwort (sɒ·lfəɹwɒ̄ɹt). 1578. [f. SULPHUR *sb.* + WORT¹.] An umbelliferous plant, *Peucedanum officinale*, having pale yellow flowers; hog's fennel.

Sulphury (sɒ·lfəri), *a.* 1580. [f. SULPHUR *sb.* + -Y¹.] **1.** = SULPHUROUS 1, 2, 2 b, c, 3 a, b. **2.** = SULPHUREOUS 4. 1900.

Sulphuryl (sɒ·lfiŭril). 1867. [f. SULPHUR *sb.* + -YL.] *Chem.* The radical SO_2.

Sulphydrate (sɒlf(h)əi·dreᶦt). 1852. [f. SULPH- + HYDRATE *sb.*, after Fr. *sulfhydrate.*] *Chem.* A salt of sulphydric acid or hydrogen sulphide; a compound of a metallic atom or radical with the group SH; a hydrosulphide.

Sulphydric (sɒlf(h)əi·drik), *a.* 1838. [f. SULPH- + HYDRIC, after Fr. *sulfhydrique.*] *Chem.* = SULPHURETTED. *S. acid* (*gas*), sulphuretted hydrogen.

Sulpician (sɒlpi·ʃᶦăn), *sb.* (*a.*) 1786. [– Fr. *sulpicien*, f. (*St.*) *Sulpice.*] *Eccl.* One of a congregation of secular priests founded in Paris in 1642 by the Abbé Olier, priest of the parish of St. Sulpice, mainly for the training of candidates for holy orders; as *adj.*, belonging to this congregation.

Sultan (sɒ·ltăn), *sb.* 1555. [– Fr. *sultan* (XVI) or med.L. *sultanus* – Arab. *sulṭān* power, dominion, ruler, king, f. *saluṭa* rule, overcome. Cf. SOLDAN.] **1.** The sovereign or chief ruler of a Moslem country; in recent times *spec.* the sovereign of Turkey. Also formerly, a prince or king's son, a high officer. **2.** An absolute ruler; *gen.* a despot, tyrant 1648. **3.** (orig. †*sultan('s) flower.*) Either of two species of sweet-scented annuals, brought orig. from the East, usu. dist. as the purple or white sweet sultan, *Centaurea* (*Amberboa*) *moschata*, and the yellow sweet sultan, *C.* (*A.*) *suaveolens* 1629. **4.** A small white-crested species of domestic fowl, orig. brought from Turkey 1855. Hence **Sultan, Su·ltanize,** *vbs. intr.* to rule as a s. or despot. **Su·ltanry** (*rare*) = SULTANATE 2. **Su·ltanship,** (*a*) = SULTANATE 2; (*b*) the personality of a s.

Sultana (sɒ̆ltā·nă). 1585. [– It. *sultana*, fem. of *sultano* SULTAN.] **1.** The wife (or a concubine) of a sultan; also, the queen-mother or some other woman of a sultan's family. **2.** A mistress, concubine 1702. **3.** Any bird belonging to either of the genera *Porphyrio* and *Ionornis*; the purple gallinule or porphyrio 1837. **4.** In full *s. raisin*: A kind of small seedless raisin produced in the neighbourhood of Smyrna 1841.

Sultanate (sɒ·ltăneᶦt). 1879. [f. SULTAN + -ATE¹.] **1.** A state or country subject to a sultan; the territory ruled over by a sultan. **2.** The office or power of a sultan 1884.

†**Sultane.** 1612. [– Fr. *sultane*, fem. of *sultan* SULTAN.] **1.** = SULTANA 1 –1694. **2.** = SULTANIN –1764. **3.** A rich gown trimmed with buttons and loops, fashionable in the late seventeenth and the eighteenth c. –1798.

Sultaness (sɒ·ltănės). Now *rare.* 1611. [f. SULTAN + -ESS¹.] = SULTANA 1.

Sultanic (sɒ̆ltæ·nik), *a.* 1827. [f. SULTAN + -IC.] Of, belonging to, or characteristic of a sultan; hence, despotic, tyrannical.

†**Su·ltanin.** 1612. [– It. *sultanino*, or Fr. *sultanin* – Arab. *sulṭānī* SULTANY.] A former Turkish gold coin valued at 8*s.* –1749.

†**Sultany.** 1612. [– Arab. *sulṭānī* adj. imperial, sb. kingdom, sultanin, f. *sulṭān* SULTAN.] **1.** = SULTANATE. –1855. **2.** = prec. –1674.

Sultry (sɒ·ltri), *a.* 1594. [f. †*sulter* be sweltering hot (XVI), prob. for **swulter*, rel. to SWELTER; see -Y¹.] **1.** Of the weather, the atmosphere, etc.: Oppressively hot and moist; sweltering. **b.** Of places, seasons of the year, etc.: Characterized by such weather 1620. **c.** Of the sun, etc.: Producing oppressive heat. *poet.* 1697. **2.** *fig.* and *allus.* **a.** Chiefly *poet.* (*a*) Associated with oppressive heat; hot with toil 1637. (*b*) Hot with anger or lust 1671. **b.** *colloq.* or *slang.* (*a*) 'Spicy', 'smutty' 1887. (*b*) Of language: Lurid, 'sulphurous' 1891. (*c*) 'Hot', 'warm', lively 1899.

1. The spring, Whom Sommers pride (with sultrie heate) pursues KYD. **b.** When weary reapers quit the s. field POPE. **c.** The s. Sirius burns the thirsty plains POPE. **2. a.** (*a*) What time the Gray-fly winds her s. horn MILT. (*b*) Stalking ..in a sultrie chafe MILT. Hence **Su·ltri-ly** *adv.*, **-ness.**

Sum (sɒm), *sb.* [ME. *summe*, *somme* – OFr. *summe*, (also mod.) *somme* :– L. *summa* main thing, principal part, substance, sum total, subst. use (sc. *res*, *pars*) of fem. of *summus* highest.] **1.** A quantity or amount of money. **a.** *s. of money, gold, silver*, †*pence*, etc. **b.** *absol.* = 'sum of money'. late ME. **c.** A quantity of money *of* a specified amount. late ME. †**d.** *transf.* A quantity *of* goods regarded as worth so much –1872. †**2.** A number, company, or body (*of people*); a host, band –1601. †**3.** *Arith.* A number; *occas.* a whole number as dist. from a fraction –1709. **4.** The total number (*of* individual persons or things capable of numeration). Now only as transf. use of sense 6. late ME. **5.** The total amount or quantity, the totality, aggregate, or whole (*of* something immaterial) ME. **6.** *Math.* The number, quantity, or magnitude resulting from the addition of two or more numbers, quantities, or magnitudes. late ME. **7.** A series of numbers to be added or cast up 1579. **8.** An arithmetical problem in the solution of which some particular rule is applied; also, such a problem worked out. *colloq.* 1803. **9.** That which a statement, discourse, writing, or a system of laws, etc. amounts to, or is in essence; a summary, epitome. *Obs.* or *arch.* late ME. †**b.** = SUMMA 2. –1770. †**10.** The upshot, issue, conclusion –1670. **11.** The ultimate end or goal; the highest attainable point. *Obs.* or *arch.* ME.

1. He supply'd her..with a convenient Summ of Money 1718. **b.** *Principal s.*: see PRINCIPAL *a.* II. 1. **4.** 'Now', cried I, 'the s. of my miseries is made up' GOLDSM. **5.** The stretching of a span, buckles in his summe of age SHAKS. **7.** They might cast the s. without pen, or counters 1579. **8.** A common multiplication or division s. 1862. **9.** Tell us the s., the circumstance defer MILT. **11.** Thus I have..brought My Storie to the s. of earthly bliss Which I enjoy MILT.

Phr. *In s.* [Fr. *en somme*, L. *in summa.*] **a.** (Expressed) in a few words, briefly or summarily. Now *arch.* and *rare.* **b.** Used *absol.* as an illative phr.: To conclude in few words; to sum up; in brief, in short. *S. and substance*, the essence (*of* anything); the gist or pith (*of* a matter). *The s. of things* [tr. L. *summa rerum*], the highest public interest, the public good, the common weal; also, the totality of being, the universe.

Sum (sɒm), *v.* ME. [– (O)Fr. *sommer* or med.L. *summare* add, reckon up, f. L. *summa* SUM *sb.*] **1.** *trans.* To find the sum or total number or amount of; to add *together*;

to reckon or count up; to cast up (a column of figures, an account). Now *rare*. **b.** To bring *up* to a certain total (*rare*) 1597. **c.** *Math.* To find the sum of (a series); in the calculus of finite differences, to find the aggregate of the successive values of a function 1776. **d.** *intr.* To do sums in arithmetic 1825. **e.** *trans.* In transf. and fig. uses: To reckon, count, or total *up* 1597. **2.** To collect into or embrace in a small compass; also with *up*. Chiefly *pass.* 1606. **3.** To give the substance of in a few words or a brief statement; to summarize, epitomize. Said also of the statement made, etc. (Usu. with *up*.) 1621. **4.** *To s. up*: (of the judge in a trial) to recapitulate (the evidence) to the jury before they retire to consider their verdict, giving an exposition of points of law when necessary. Often *absol.* 1700. **b.** To form an estimate of, summarize the qualities or character of 1889. †**5.** To bring to completion or perfection; also with *up* –1667.

1. b. The howre doth rather summe vp the moments then deuide the daye BACON. **e.** 2 *Hen. IV*, I. i. 167. **2.** She..in her looks summs all Delight MILT. **3.** Go to the Ant, thou Sluggard; (says the Wise-man) which in Few Words Summs up the Moral of This Fable 1692. **4.** The judge summed up dead against the claim 1884. **5.** Creatures animate with gradual life Of Growth, Sense, Reason, all summ'd up in Man MILT.

Sumach, sumac (siū·mæk, ʃū·mæk), *sb.* ME. [– (O)Fr. *sumac* or med.L. *sumac(h* – Arab. *summāḳ*.] **1.** A preparation of the dried and chopped leaves and shoots of plants of the genus *Rhus*, esp. *R. coriaria*, much used in tanning, also for dyeing and staining leather black, and medicinally as an astringent. **b.** The leaves of the sumach used as a substitute for tobacco 1823. **2.** Any of the shrubs or small trees of the genus *Rhus*, esp. *R. coriaria*, indigenous in southern Europe, which is the chief source of the material used in tanning, and *R. vernicifera* (lacquer tree), Japan or varnish sumach 1548. Hence **Sumac(h** *v. trans.* to tan with s.

Sumatran (siumā·trăn), *a.* and *sb.* 1688. [f. *Sumatra*, a large island in the Malay Archipelago + -AN.] **A.** *adj.* Of or pertaining to the island of Sumatra or its inhabitants or language 1783. **B.** *sb.* A native or inhabitant of the island of Sumatra; also, the Sumatran language 1688.

Sumbul (sʊ·mbʊl, su·mbul). 1790. [– Fr. *sumbul* – Arab. *sunbul*.] Applied to the roots of certain plants (and to the plants themselves) which are used medicinally; *esp.* (*a*) the spikenard, *Nardostachys jatamansi*, (*b*) the musk-root, *Ferula* (*Euryangium*) *sumbul*, (*c*) valerian.

‖**Sumen** (siū·men). 1662. [L., f. *sugere* SUCK *v.*] A sow's udder, the dugs of a sow; formerly *Anat.*, the hypogastrium. †Also *transf.*, the fat or rich portion of a thing.

Sumerian (siumīə·riăn), *a.* and *sb.* 1875. [– Fr. *sumérien*, f. *Sumer*.] **A.** *adj.* Pertaining to Sumer or Sumir, one of the districts of ancient Babylonia, or to its population. **B.** *sb.* **1.** A non-Semitic inhabitant of Sumer 1878. **2.** The language spoken by the inhabitants of Sumer 1887.

Sumless (sʊ·mlės), *a.* Chiefly *poet.* 1599. [f. SUM *sb.* + -LESS.] Without number; that cannot be 'summed' or counted; incalculable.

As rich with prayse As is the Owse and bottome of the Sea With sunken Wrack, and sum-lesse Treasuries SHAKS.

‖**Summa** (sʊ·mă). 1442. [L.; see SUM *sb.*] †**1.** A sum-total –1784. **2.** A summary treatise; e.g. the *Summa Theologiæ* of St. Thomas Aquinas 1725. **3.** Phr. **S. rerum** (rīə·rŏm) [L. *rerum* of things or affairs]: the highest public interest 1715.

Summarist (sʊ·mărist). 1873. [f. as next + -IST.] One who compiles a summary.

Summarize (sʊ·măreiz), *v.* 1871. [f. next + -IZE.] *trans.* To make (or constitute) a summary of; to sum up; to state briefly or succinctly. Hence **Su:mmariza·tion** 1865.

Summary (sʊ·mări), *sb.* 1509. [– L. *summarium*, subst. use of n. sing. of *summarius*; see next.] **1.** A summary account or statement. †**2.** The highest point or summit; also, the ultimate outcome. CARLYLE.

Summary (sʊ·mări), *a.* late ME. [– med.L. *summarius* (in class. L. only as prec.), f. *summa* SUM *sb.*; see -ARY[1].] **1.** Of a statement or account: Containing or comprising the chief points or the sum and substance of a matter; compendious (now usu. with implication of brevity). **b.** *transf.* Characterized by or involving conciseness and brevity 1582. **2.** *Law.* Applied to the proceedings in a court of law carried out rapidly by the omission of certain formalities required by the common law. Similarly of a court-martial 1765. **3.** Performed or effected by a short method; done without delay 1713. †**4.** Highest, supreme (*rare*) –1733.

1. A s. and general view of the Vices and Follies reigning in his time DRYDEN. **2.** *S. jurisdiction*, the determination of cases expeditiously without reference to the ordinary requirements of the common law. **3.** It put into their heads the idea of s. vengeance 1833. Hence **Su·mmarily** *adv.* **Su·mmariness.**

Summation (sʊmēi·ʃən). 1760. [f. SUM *v.* (1 c) + -ATION. Cf. (O)Fr. *sommation*.] **1.** *Math.* The process of finding the sum of a series. **2.** The adding up of numbers, quantities, etc.; an addition sum 1816. **b.** The accumulation of a number of stimuli applied to a muscle 1877. **3.** The computation of the aggregate value of conditions, qualities, etc.; summing-up 1836. **4.** The aggregate or sum-total; the resultant or product 1840.

3. Such is Mr. Wyndham's s. of Scott 1908. Hence **Summa·tional** *a.* produced by s. or addition.

Summed (sʊmd), *ppl. a.* late ME. [In branch I, f. OFr. *som(m)é*, pa. pple. of *sommer* sum, complete – med.L. *summare*. In branch II, f. SUM *v.* + -ED[1].] †**I. 1.** Of a stag: Having a complement of antlers. Said also of the antlers. Often *full s.* –1637. **2.** Of a hawk: Having the feathers full grown. Said also of the plumage. Often *full s.* Also *fig.* = equipped. –1688.

2. Like a young Eagle summ'd..Disdaines a shoale of Dawes 1649. A full sumd or consumate Orator 1600.

II. Collected into one sum, forming a sum-total. Also with *up*. 1607.

Summer (sʊ·məɹ), *sb.*[1] [OE. *sumor*, corresp. to OFris. *sumur*, OS., OHG. *sumar* (Du. *zomer*, G. *sommer*), ON. *sumar* :– Gmc.; rel. to Skr. *sámā* half-year, year.] **1.** The second and warmest season of the year, coming between spring and autumn; reckoned astronomically from the summer solstice (21 June) to the autumnal equinox (22 or 23 Sept.); in pop. use comprising in the northern hemisphere the period from mid-May to mid-August; also often, *esp.* in contradistinction to *winter*, the warmer half of the year. (Often with initial capital.) **b.** Applied, with qualification, to a period of fine dry weather in late autumn; see ALL-HALLOW(S 1, INDIAN SUMMER, MARTIN[2] 3; *St. Luke's* (*little*) *s.*, such a period occurring about St. Luke's Day, 18 Oct. **c.** *transf.* Summer weather; summery or warm weather ME. **d.** *fig.* and *allus.* 1535. **2.** In *pl.* with numeral, put for 'year'. Now only *poet.* or in speaking of a young person's age. late ME. **3.** *attrib.* passing into *adj.* **a.** = Of or pertaining to summer, characteristic of summer; suitable or appropriate to summer; existing, appearing, performed, etc. in summer ME. **b.** So *summer's* (now chiefly with *morning*, *evening*, *night*; cf. SUMMER'S DAY). late ME. **c.** Applied to crops, etc. that ripen in summer; also *spec.* in pop. names of early-ripening apples and pears. late ME. **d.** *fig.* with ref. to prosperous, pleasant, or genial conditions 1592.

1. When S. brings the lily and the rose MORRIS. You will find me there all s. 1885. Phr. *s. and winter, winter and s.*, all the year round. **c.** There eternal S. dwels MILT. **d.** For now the wine made s. in his veins TENNYSON. **2.** Summers three times eight save one She had told MILT. **3. a.** An odorous Chaplet of sweet Sommer buds SHAKS. S. Quarters 1708. S. holidays LAMB. **b.** Their's is but a summer's song COWPER. **d.** If't be S. Newes, Smile too't before SHAKS.

Comb.: **s. catarrh** = HAY-FEVER; **s. cholera** = CHOLERA 2; **s. complaint** *U.S.*, s. diarrhœa of children; also, infantile cholera and dysentery; **-field,** (*a*) a field with the s. crop; (*b*) *dial.* a s.-fallow; **-heat,** the heat of s.; *spec.* an arbitrary maximum s. temperature commonly marked on thermometers; **s. lightning,** sheet lightning without audible thunder, often seen in hot weather; also *allus.* and *attrib.*; **s. parlour** *Obs.* or *arch.*, an apartment for s. use; **s. rash,** prickly heat, *Lichen tropicus*; **s. school,** a course of instruction and study in a subject or curriculum of subjects held during some part of the summer at a chosen centre; **-weight** *a.*, adapted in weight and texture to summer wear.

b. In names of animals and plants which are active or flourish in summer (often rendering L. *æstivus*, *æstivalis* as a specific name): **s. cypress** = BELVEDERE 2; **s. duck,** a N. Amer. duck, *Æx sponsa*, the wood-duck; **s. snipe,** the common sandpiper, *Tringoides hypoleucus*; **s. tanager,** the rose tanager, *Pyranga æstiva*, which summers in N. America; **s. teal,** the garganey; **s. yellow-bird,** a N. Amer. wood-warbler, *Dendrœca æstiva*.

Summer (sʊ·məɹ), *sb.*[2] ME. [– AFr. *sumer*, *somer*, OFr. *somier* (mod. *sommier*) – Rom. **saumarius*, for late L. *sagmarius*, f. *sagma* – Gr. σάγμα pack-saddle.] †**I.** A pack-horse –1470. **II. a.** *gen.* A main beam in a structure. *Sc.* –1715. **b.** A horizontal bearing beam in a building; *spec.* the main beam supporting the girders or joists of a floor (or *occas.* the rafters of a roof). When on the face of a building it is prop. called BREAST-SUMMER. ME.

attrib.: **s.-beam, -tree** = sense II. b.

Summer (sʊ·məɹ), *sb.*[3] 1611. [f. SUM *v.* + -ER[1].] One who sums or adds; *colloq.* or *dial.* one who does sums, an arithmetician.

Summer (sʊ·məɹ), *v.* 1440. [f. SUMMER *sb.*[1]] **1.** *intr.* To pass or spend the summer, to dwell or reside during the summer (now chiefly *Sc.* and *U.S.*); (of cattle, etc.) to be pastured in summer. **2.** *trans.* To keep or maintain during summer; *esp.* to provide pasture for (cattle, etc.); said of the land or the grazier 1599. **3.** To make summer-like, balmy, or genial 1863.

1. He is summering at Castellamare 1842. **2.** Dartmoor summers an immense number of sheep 1810.

Phr. *To s. and winter*. *intr.* **a.** To spend the whole year; *transf.* to remain or continue permanently. **b.** *trans.* To maintain one's attitude to or relations with at all seasons; to associate with, be faithful to, or adhere to constantly.

Su·mmer-bird. 1560. **1.** A bird that makes its appearance in summer; a summer migrant 1597. †**2.** With allusion to the cuckoo as the 'summer bird': A cuckold 1560.

Summer-cloud. (Also **summer's cloud.**) 1605. A cloud such as is seen on a summer's day, *esp.* one that is fleeting or does not spoil the fine weather. Also *allus.*

Can such things..ouercome vs like a Summers Clowd, Without our speciall wonder? SHAKS.

Su·mmer-fa:llow, *sb.* 1733. [See FALLOW *sb.* 2.] A lying or laying fallow during the summer; also, land that lies fallow during the summer. **b.** as *adj.* Lying fallow during the summer 1801. So **Su·mmer-fa:llow** *v. trans.* to lay (land) fallow during summer 1669.

Su·mmer-house. ME. **1.** A summer residence in the country. Now *rare*. **2.** A structure in a garden or park, usu. of very simple and often rustic character, designed to provide a cool shady place in the heat of summer 1440.

Summering (sʊ·məriŋ), *vbl. sb.* 1703. [app. f. SUMMER *sb.*[2] + -ING[1].] *Arch.* **a.** *collect.* The beds of the stones or bricks of an arch considered with ref. to their direction. **b.** The radial direction of the joints of an arch. **c.** The degree of curvature of an arch.

Summerish (sʊ·məriʃ), *a.* 1726. [f. SUMMER *sb.*[1] + -ISH[1].] Somewhat summer-like.

Summer-like (sʊ·məɹləik), *a.* 1530. [f. SUMMER *sb.*[1] + -LIKE.] Like, or like that of, summer; summery.

Summerly (sʊ·məɹli), *a.* [OE. *sumerlić*; see SUMMER *sb.*[1], -LY[1].] †**1.** Of or pertaining to summer; taking place in summer –1771. **2.** Having the qualities of summer; summer-like, summery ME.

Summer's day. ME. A day in summer; often put typically for a very long day.

A proper man as one shall see in a summers day SHAKS. To lament his fate In amorous dittyes all a Summers day MILT. Phr. *Some summer's day*, 'one of these fine days'.

Summer solstice. 1549. The time at which the sun reaches the summer tropic, *i.e.* in the northern hemisphere, the tropic of Cancer, in the southern, the tropic of Capricorn.

Su·mmer-tide. Now chiefly *poet.* ME. = SUMMER-TIME 1.

Su·mmer-time. late ME. **1.** The season of summer; the time that summer lasts. **2.** (as two words) The standard time (in advance of ordinary time) adopted in some countries during the summer months 1916.

Summery (sʊ·məri), *a.* 1824. [f. SUMMER *sb.*¹ + -Y¹.] Resembling or pertaining to summer; summer-like. Hence **Su·mmeriness.**

Summist (sʊ·mist). 1545. [– med.L. *summista*, f. *summa* SUM *sb.* + *-ista* -IST.] The author of a summa of religious doctrine, etc., e.g. St. Thomas Aquinas, author of *Summa theologiæ*; often used *gen.* of the schoolmen. †**b.** An epitomizer; *transf.* an epitome –1734.

Summit (sʊ·mit). 1470. [– OFr. *som(m)ete*, also *somet, sumet* (mod. *sommet*), *f. som, sum* :– L. *summum*, n. sing. of *summus* (see SUM *sb.*); the sp. with *-it* is due to assim. to next.] **1.** The topmost part, top; the vertex, apex. **b.** *Geom.* A point of a polyhedron where three or more faces meet, forming a solid angle 1805. **2.** The topmost point or ridge of a mountain or hill. Also, the highest elevation of a road, railway, or canal. 1481. **3.** *fig.* The highest point or degree; the acme 1711.

1. Vpon the somette or toppe of the tour, he maad an ymage of copre CAXTON. **2.** Ætna's smoking s. GRAY. **3.** If love be the s. of all virtue, humility is the foundation PUSEY.

attrib.: **s. angle** = *s. quoin*; **s. level,** (*a*) the highest level reached by a canal, watercourse, railway, or the like; (*b*) a level place in a railway or stretch of water in a canal, with descending planes on either side; **s. quoin,** the solid angle at a s. of a polyhedron. Hence **Su·mmitless** *a.* having no s.

†**Su·mmity.** *Obs.* or *arch.* late ME. [– (O)Fr. *sommité* – late L. *summitas, -tat-*, f. *summus*; see SUM *sb.*, -ITY.] = prec. –1862. **b.** A person or thing that is at the head of a body, series, etc. –1685.

†**Su·mmon,** *sb.* ME. [f. next.] = SUMMONS –1800.

Summon (sʊ·mən), *v.* ME. [– AFr., OFr. *sumun-, somun-, somon-*, pres. stem of *somondre*, (also mod.) *semondre* :– pop.L. **summonĕre* for L. *summonēre*, f. *sub* SUB- 24 + *monēre* warn.] **1.** *trans.* To call together by authority for action or deliberation. **b.** To call (a peer) to parliament by writ of summons; hence, to call to a peerage. late ME. **2.** To cite by authority to attend at a place named, *esp.* to appear before a court or judge to answer a charge or to give evidence; to issue a summons against ME. **3.** *gen.* To require the presence or attendance of; to bid (a person) to approach by a call, ringing a bell, knocking, or the like; with adv., to call (to a person) to go in a specified direction. late ME. **4.** *fig.* with immaterial or inanimate subject: To call, bid come or go. Often with adv. 1549. **5.** To call upon (a person) *to do* something. late ME. **b.** To call upon *to surrender* 1471. †**6.** To give warning or notice of, proclaim, call –1611. **7.** Often with *up*: To call (a faculty, etc.) to one's aid; to call up (one's courage, energy) 1582. **8.** To call *into* existence; to call forth 1742.

1. The Grand Master had summoned a chapter SCOTT. **2.** A witness who will not come of himself may be summoned JOWETT. **3.** They were soon summoned to table 1885. **4.** *absol.* Hearke how these Instruments s. to supper SHAKS. **5.** Coleblack clouds..Do s. vs to part SHAKS. **b.** He first summoned the garrison GOLDSM. **6.** *Wint. T.* II. iii. 202. **7.** He summoned all his fortitude 1802. Hence **Su·mmonable** *a.* that can be or is liable to be summoned.

Summoner (sʊ·mənəɹ). ME. [– AFr. *so-, sumenour* = OFr. *somoneor, se-* (mod. *semonneur*) :– AL. *summonitor, -ōr-*, f. L. *summonēre* SUMMON *v.*; see -ER² 3.] **1.** A petty officer who cites and warns persons to appear in court. Now *Hist.* **2.** One who summons another to a place. Often *fig.* of immaterial or inanimate agents. 1580. **3.** One who takes out a summons 1865.

Summons (sʊ·mənz), *sb.* [ME. *somouns* – OFr. *somonce, sumunse* (mod. *semonce*) :– Gallo-Rom. **summonsa*, for L. *summonita*, fem. pa. pple. used subst. of *summonēre* SUMMON *v.*; cf. prec.] **1.** An authoritative call to attend at a specified place for a specified purpose. **b.** The royal act of calling to the national council or parliament the bishops, earls, and barons by special writ, and the knights and freeholders by a general writ addressed to the sheriffs; hence *spec.* the call to a barony ME. **2.** A call or citation by authority to appear before a court or judicial officer; also (in full *writ of s.*), the writ by which the citation is made ME. **3.** *gen.* A peremptory or urgent call or command; a summoning sound, knock, or the like 1567. **4.** *Mil.* The act of summoning a place to surrender. Also, now only, with inf. 1617.

1. He obeyed the summons with the respect of a faithful subject GIBBON. **b.** The Parliament met according to s. upon the 13th of April in the year 1640 CLARENDON. **2.** Every action in the High Court shall be commenced by a writ of summons 1875. **3.** The Duke of Norfolke..Stayes but the s. of the Appealants Trumpet SHAKS. **4.** Vpon our s. of the Towne, after martiall manner 1617.

Summons (sʊ·mənz), *v.* 1658. [f. prec.] **1.** *trans.* = SUMMON *v.* 1–5 b. Now *rare.* **2.** To cite before a court or a judge or magistrate; to take out a summons against 1780.

‖**Summum bonum** (sʊ·mʊ̆m bōᵘ·nʊ̆m). *Pl.* **su·mma bo·na.** 1563. [L. (Cicero) 'the highest good'.] The chief or supreme good: properly a term of *Ethics*; often *transf.* and in trivial or joc. use.

‖**Summum genus** (sʊ·mʊ̆m dʒī·nʊ̆s). *Pl.* **su·mma ge·nera.** 1592. [L.] The highest or most comprehensive division in a classification; in *Logic*, a genus that is not considered as a species of a higher genus.

‖**Summum jus** (sʊ·mʊ̆m dʒʊs). 1588. [L.] The utmost rigour of the law, extreme severity.

Sumner¹ (sʊ·mnəɹ). late ME. [– AFr. *sum(e)nour*, f. *sumen-, sumon-*; see SUMMON *v.*, -ER² 3.] One who is employed to summon persons to appear in court; *esp.* a summoning officer in an ecclesiastical court. Now surviving in the Isle of Man.

Sumner² (sʊ·mnəɹ). 1881. *Naut.* The name of T. H. *Sumner*, American sea-captain, designating a method of determining one's position on the earth's surface, and the line (*S. line*) which is used in the calculations.

I worked a S., or position by double altitude 1925.

Sump (sʊmp), *sb.* late ME. [– (M)LG., MDu. *sump*, or, in mining use, corresp. to G. *sumpf*, rel. to SWAMP *sb.*] **1.** A marsh, swamp, morass; (now *dial.*) a dirty pool or puddle. **2.** A pit or well for collecting water or other fluid; *spec.* a cesspool; a pond or well from which sea-water is collected for salt-manufacture 1680. **b.** *Mining.* A pit or well sunk at the bottom of an engine shaft to collect the water of the mine 1653. **3.** *Metall.* A pit of stone or metal at a furnace to collect the metal at the first fusion 1674.

attrib.: **s.-fuse,** a waterproof fuse used for blasting under water; **-man,** a pitman's assistant, one who attends to the machinery in an engine-shaft. Hence **Sump** *v. intr.* to dig a s. or (small or temporary) shaft.

Sumph (sʊmf). *Sc.* and *n. dial.* 1719. [Of unkn. origin.] A simpleton, blockhead. Also, a surly or sullen man.

Sumpitan (sʊ·mpităn). 1634. [– Malay *sumpītan*, f. *sumpit* blowpipe, prop. narrow.] A blow-gun made by the Malays from a hollowed cane, from which poisoned arrows are shot.

‖**Sumpsimus** (sʊ·mpsimʊ̆s). 1545. [L., 1st pers. pl. perf. ind. of *sumere* take.] A correct expression taking the place of an incorrect but popular one (*mumpsimus*).

Sumpter (sʊ·mᵖtəɹ). *arch.* ME. [– OFr. *som(m)etier* :– Rom. **saumatarius*, f. late L. *sagma, sagmat-*; see SUMMER *sb.*², -ER² 2. Cf. SEAM *sb.*²] †**1.** The driver of a pack-horse –1601. **2.** A pack or baggage horse; a beast of burden 1570. †**3.** A pack, saddle-bag –1681. **4.** *attrib.* (often = *pack-*). late ME.

4. The s.-mule, in harness'd pride SMOLLETT.

Sumption (sʊ·mᵖʃən). 1440. [– L. *sumptio*, f. *sumpt-*, pa. ppl. stem of *sumere* take; see -ION. Sense 1 in med.L. *sumptio, sumpsio*; sense 2 as in Cicero.] †**1.** The reception (of the Sacrament, of Christ in the Sacrament) –1664. **2.** †**a.** The taking of a thing as true without proof; hence, an assumption, premiss. **b.** The major premiss of a syllogism 1572.

Sumptuary (sʊ·mᵖtiu,ări), *a.* 1600. [– L. *sumptuarius*, f. *sumptus* expenditure, expense, f. *sumpt-*; see prec., -ARY¹. Cf. Fr. *somptuaire.*] Pertaining to or regulating expenditure.

S. law, a law regulating expenditure, esp. with a view to restraining excess in food, equipage, etc.

Sumptuosity (sʊmᵖtiu,ǫ·sĭti). 1559. [f. SUMPTUOUS *a.* 3 + -ITY. Cf. late and med. L. *sumptuositas* costliness.] Lavishness or extravagance of expenditure; magnificence or luxuriousness of living, equipment, decoration, or the like. **b.** An instance of this; a sumptuous thing 1601.

b. To speak of his sumptuosities, of his largesses 1601.

Sumptuous (sʊ·mᵖtiu,əs), *a.* 1485. [– (O)Fr. *somptueux* – L. *sumptuosus*, f. *sumptus*; see prec., -UOUS.] **1.** Of buildings, apparel, repasts, and the like: Made or produced at great cost; costly and (hence) magnificent in workmanship, construction, decoration, etc. **b.** of conditions, functions, etc. 1590. **c.** Of natural objects: Splendid or magnificent in appearance 1594. †**2.** Of charges, expenses, etc.: Involving a great outlay of money –1616. †**3.** Of persons, etc.: Spending largely; (hence) magnificent in equipment or way of living –1781.

1. Thir s. gluttonies, and gorgeous feasts MILT. A fine Lady dressed in the most s. Habit STEELE. **b.** Dressed in the most s. mode of the Court 1841. She spoke and turn'd her s. head TENNYSON. **3.** The bishops..were s. in their fare and apparell HOBBES. Hence **Su·mptuous-ly** *adv.*, **-ness.**

Sum-total (sʊ·m,tōᵘ·tăl). *Pl.* **sum-totals, sums-total.** late ME. [tr. med.L. *summa totalis*; see SUM *sb.*, TOTAL *a.*] The aggregate of all the items in an account; the total amount (of things capable of numeration). **b.** *gen.* The aggregate or totality *of* 1660.

Sun (sʊn), *sb.* [OE. *sunne* (fem.) = OFris. *sunne*, OS., OHG. *sunna* (Du. *zon*, G. *sonne*), ON. (poet.) *sunna*, Goth. *sunnō*, beside OE. *sunna* (masc.), OHG., OS. *sunno* :– Gmc. **sunnōn, -on*; f. IE. **su-* with *n*-formative, beside **sāu-* with *l-* formative in Hom. Gr. ἠέλιος, L. *sōl*, OE. *sōl*, ON. *sól*, Goth. *sauil*, W. *haul.*] **1.** The brightest (as seen from the earth) of the heavenly bodies, the luminary or orb of day; the central body of the solar system, around which the earth and other planets revolve, being kept in their orbits by its attraction and supplied with light and heat by its radiation; in the Ptolemaic system reckoned as a planet, in modern astronomy as one of the stars. **b.** OE. *sunne* being fem., the fem. pronoun was used until the 16th c. in referring to the sun; since then the masc. has been commonly used; the neuter is somewhat less frequent. **c.** As an object of worship in various religions, and thus (and hence generally) personified as a male being, sometimes identified with various gods, esp. Apollo; also in classical mythology said to be drawn in a chariot ME. **d.** As a type of brightness or clearness OE. **2.** With qualifying word, or in *pl.*, with ref. to its position in the sky (or occas. the zodiac), or its aspect or visibility at a particular time or times. late ME. **b.** With ref. to the heat produced by the sun; hence (poet.) = climate, clime. late ME. **3.** *fig.* In allusion to the splendour of the sun or to its being a source of light and heat OE. **4.** The direct rays of the sun; sunlight; sunshine OE. **5.** With qualification or in phr. **a.** Sunrise or sunset as determining the period of a day. *Obs.* or *arch.* late ME. **b.** A (particular) day, as being determined by the rising of the sun. *poet.* or *rhet.* 1606. **c.** The time of the sun's apparent revolution in the zodiac, a year. *poet.* 1742. **6.** *gen.* A luminary; *esp.* a star as the centre of a system of worlds. late ME. **7.** An appearance in the sky like a sun; a mock-sun, parhelion. late ME. **8.** A figure or image of, or an ornament or vessel made to resemble, the sun (*e.g.* a monstrance with rays); *Her.* a representation of the sun, surrounded with rays and usu.

charged with the features of a human face; also freq. as the sign of an inn; hence, the name of an inn or a room in an inn 1450. †9. a. *Her.* In blazoning by the names of heavenly bodies, the name of the tincture Or. b. *Alch.* Gold. –1651.

1. Lett nott the sonne goo doune apon youre wrathe TINDALE *Eph.* 4:26. Phrases, etc. *Under* (or *beneath*) *the s.*, on earth, in the world. (*As*..) *as the s. shines on* = as lives or exists; used in commendatory phrases. *On which the s. never sets*, applied formerly to the Spanish dominions, now to the British Empire. *With the s.*, from left to right; similarly *against the s.* (Chiefly *Naut.*) *To take the s.*, to make an observation of the meridian altitude of the sun. Provb. phrases. *To make hay while the s. shines*: see HAY *sb.*[1] b. For yet the S. Was not; shee in a cloudie Tabernacle Sojourn'd the while MILT. c. Who knows not Circe The daughter of the S.? MILT. A Persian, humble servant of the s. COWPER. 2. A glen which sloped towards the southern s. KINGSLEY. b. Underneath another s. TENNYSON. 3. The Sunne of Rome is set SHAKS. The Lord God is a sunne and shield *Ps.* 84:11. *S. of righteousness*, a title of Jesus Christ (after *Malachi* 4:2). 4. Where the reaper..in the s. all morning binds the sheaves M. ARNOLD. Phr. *One's place in the s.*, an individual share in those things to which all have a right; hence, a position giving scope for the development of personal or national life. 5. b. By the fift houre of the Sunne SHAKS. 6. The Moone moues lowest, siluer Sunne of Night 1623.

attrib. and *Comb.*, as *s.-worship*, *-worshipper*; **s.-bath,** an exposure to the direct rays of the s., esp. as a method of medical treatment; basking in the s.; hence **-bathe** *v. intr.*, **-bather; -blink,** a gleam of sunshine; **-bonnet,** a light bonnet with a projection in front and a cape behind to protect the head and neck from the s.; **-bow,** an arch of prismatic colours like a rainbow, formed by refraction of sunlight in spray or vapour; **-burner,** a circular group of gas-burners with reflectors placed near the ceiling of a large room; **-crack** *Geol.*, a crack produced by the heat of the s. during the consolidation of a rock; **-disc, -disk,** the disc of the s., or a figure or image of this, esp. in religious symbolism; **-dog,** a mock sun, parhelion; **-flag,** the Japanese flag, bearing an image of the s.; **-glade,** a beam or track of sunlight, *esp.* the track of reflected sunlight on water; **-glass,** (*a*) a lens for concentrating the rays of the sun, a burning-glass; (*b*) a screen of coloured glass attached to a sextant for moderating the light of the s.; **-glow,** (*a*) a glow or glare of sunlight; (*b*) a hazy diffused light seen around the s., due to fine solid particles in the atmosphere, as after a volcanic eruption; **-hat,** a broad-brimmed hat worn in hot climates to protect the head from the s.; so **-helmet; -myth,** a myth relating to the s., a solar myth; **-picture,** a picture made by means of sunlight, a photograph; **-proof** *a.*, through which the sunlight cannot penetrate; unaffected by the rays of the s.; **-signalling, -telegraphy,** = HELIOGRAPHY 4; **-trap,** a place adapted for catching sunshine; **-wheel,** (*a*) the wheel around which a planet-wheel turns (see *Sun-and-planet wheels*); (*b*) a figure resembling a wheel, with radiating arms or spokes. b. In names of plants and animals; **s.-animalcule,** a microscopic protozoan of the group *Heliozoa*, esp. the common species *Actinophrys sol*, of a spherical form with numerous long, slender, straight, radiating filaments; **-bear,** a small Malayan species of bear (*Helarctos malayanus*), the *bruang*, having close black fur and a white patch on the breast; also, the Tibetan bear (*Ursus thibetanus*); **-beetle,** any one of various scarabæid beetles of the sub-family *Cetoniinæ*, which appear in sunshine; **-bittern,** a S. Amer. bird *Eurypyga ehlias*, with brilliantly coloured plumage, also called *peacock-bittern*; **-drop(s,** any of the species of *Œnothera* (evening primrose) which open in sunlight; **-gem,** a brilliantly coloured Brazilian species of humming-bird, *Heliactin cornutus*; **-grebe** = SUNBIRD 1 c; **-squall, -squawl** *U.S.*, a jelly-fish; **-star, -starfish,** a starfish having numerous rays, as those of the genus *Solaster*; **-trout,** *local U.S.*, the squeteague. c. **Sun-and-planet wheels,** a form of gearing (invented by James Watt) consisting of a central wheel or *s.-wheel* and an outer wheel or *planet-wheel* (of which there may be more than one) geared together so that the axis of the latter moves round that of the former like a planet round the sun; also extended to other forms of gearing on a similar principle.

Sun, *v.* 1519. [f. prec.] 1. *trans.* To place in or expose to the sun; to subject to the action of the sun's rays; to warm, dry, etc. in sunshine. 2. *refl.* To expose oneself to or bask in the sun 1610. 3. *intr.* To shine as or like the sun (*rare*) 1611. 4. *trans.* To shine upon or illumine as or like the sun. Chiefly *poet.* 1637.

1. *fig.* I sunn'd my heart in beauty's eyes BYRON. 2. He suns himself there after his breakfast when the day is suitable THACKERAY. 3. Shine out, little head, sunning over with curls, To the flowers, and be their sun TENNYSON. 4. A glade Far, far within, sunned only at noonday 1820.

Su·n-baked, *a.* 1628. 1. Baked by exposure to the sun, as bricks, pottery, etc. 1700. 2. Excessively heated by the sun; parched or hardened by the heat of the sun 1628.

Sunbeam (sʌ·nbīm). [OE. *sun(n)bēam*, also (late) *sunne-bēam*; see SUN *sb.* and BEAM *sb.*] 1. A beam of sunlight. 2. Used as a literal rendering of a native word applied to a radiant-coloured humming-bird 1613.

1. The gay motes that people the Sun Beams MILT.

Su·nbird, su·n-bird. 1776. 1. a. Any bird of the passerine family *Nectariniidæ*, which comprises small birds with brilliant and variegated plumage, found in tropical and subtropical regions of Africa, Asia, and Australia; also applied to similar birds of other families. b. The sun-bittern, *Eurypyga helias* 1825. c. Any bird of the family *Heliornithidæ*, comprising swimming birds found in tropical America, Africa, and Asia 1872. 2. (With hyphen.) a. A bird sacred to the sun or connnected with sun-worship. b. A mythical 'bird of the sun', or the sun regarded as a bird. 1871.

Su·n-bright, *a.* Chiefly *poet.* 1579. [OE. *sunbeorht* occurs in sense 2.] 1. Bright as the sun; supremely bright. 2. Bright with sunshine; illumined by the sun 1744.

1. Th'Apostat in his S. Chariot sate MILT.

Sunburn (sʌ·nbɔ̄ɹn), *sb.* 1652. [f. next. OE. had *sunbryne.*] The condition of being sunburnt; discoloration or superficial inflammation of the skin caused by exposure to the sun; the brown colour or tan thus produced.

Su·nburn, *v.* 1530. [Back-formation from SUNBURNING, SUNBURNT.] 1. *trans.* To 'burn', scorch, or discolour (usu. the skin) by exposure to the sun; to affect with sunburn; to tan. 2. *intr.* for *pass.* To be discoloured or tanned by exposure to the sun; also of a plant 1832.

1. The scorching rays had sun-burnt his face 1805. So **Su·nbu:rning,** sunburn 1530.

Su·nburnt, su·nburned, *a.* late ME. [f. SUN *sb.* + *burnt, burned*, pa. pple. of BURN *v.*[1]] 1. Discoloured, tanned, or superficially inflamed by exposure to sunshine; chiefly of the skin or complexion. b. *transf.* Of a brown colour, as if sunburnt 1893. 2. Scorched, parched, or dried up by the heat of the sun, as land or vegetation 1586. 3. = SUN-BAKED 1. 1634.

Su·nburst. 1816. [See BURST *sb.* 3.] 1. A burst of sunlight; a sudden shining of the sun from behind a cloud. 2. A firework, a piece of jewellery, etc., constructed so as to imitate the sun with its rays 1902.

Sundae (sʌ·ndeⁱ). orig. *U.S.* 1904. [Said to be altered spelling of SUNDAY, in *Sunday ice cream*, an ice cream left over from Sunday and on sale later.] A portion of ice-cream with syrup, fruit, nuts, etc.

Sunday (sʌ·ndeⁱ, -di). [OE. *sunnandæġ* (Northumb. *sunnadæġ*) = OFris. *sunnandei*, OS. *sunnundag*, OHG. *sunnuntag* (Du. *zondag*, G. *sonntag*), ON. *sunnudagr*; Gmc. tr. L. *dies solis* = late Gr. ἡμέρα ἡλίου 'day of the sun'; surviving as three sylls. till XIV; cf. MONDAY for the formation.] 1. The first day of the week, observed by Christians as a day of rest and worship, in commemoration of Christ's resurrection; the Lord's Day. b. With specific epithet, as *Advent, Midlent, Mothering, Trinity* ME. 2. *Saint S.*, a rendering of *Sanctus Dominicus* = St. Dominic, due to confusion with *dies Dominica* = Sunday. *local.* 1490.

1. Phr. (colloq.). *When two Sundays come together* (*meet*), never. *A month of Sundays*, a very long time. So *A week of Sundays.*

attrib. and *Comb.*, as *S. book, clothes, dinner, paper*; **S. best,** one's best attire, usu. worn on S. **S. letter,** the dominical letter.

Su·nday-school. 1783. A school in which instruction is given on Sunday; *esp.* such a school for children held in connection with a parish or congregation; such schools are now intended only for religious instruction, but orig. instruction in secular subjects was also given.

Sunder (sʌ·ndəɹ), *a.* ME. [In A, compounds formed after OE. compounds in *sundor-* = separate, peculiar, private; in B, derived from ME. *o(n)sunder*, OE. *onsundran* ASUNDER, by substitution of *in* for *on, o, a.*] †A. *adj.* 1. In compounds, as *sunderred*, private advice, etc. ME. only. 2. Separate; various, sundry. –late ME. **B. In sunder** = ASUNDER *adv.* Now *poet.* or *rhet.* ME.

Sunder (sʌ·ndəɹ), *v.* Now *poet.* or *rhet.* [Late OE. *sundrian* (beside *syndrian*), for earlier *āsundrian* (see ASUNDER *v.*), and *ġe-, on-, tōsundrian*, corresp. to OHG. *sunt(a)rōn, sund(e)rōn* (G. *sondern*), ON. *sundra.*] 1. *trans.* To dissolve connection between two or more persons or things; to separate or part one *from* another. 2. To divide into two or more parts; to split, break up, cleave ME. 3. To keep apart, separate by an intervening space or barrier, *from* something. *rare.* (Chiefly *pass.*) 1606. 4. *intr.* To become separated or severed *from* something; *esp.* of a number of persons, to part ME. 5. To be torn, break, or split in pieces. late ME.

1. When both the Chiefs are sund'red from the Fight DRYDEN. 3. No space of Earth shall s. our two hates SHAKS. 5. Euen as a splitted Barke, so s. we SHAKS.

Sundew (sʌ·ndiū). 1578. [tr. Du. *son-, sundauw*, = G. *sonnentau*, tr. L. *ros solis.*] Any plant of the genus *Drosera*, which comprises small herbs growing in bogs, having leaves covered with glandular hairs secreting viscid drops which glitter in the sun like dew; esp. *D. rotundifolia* (round-leaved or common s.).

Su·n-dial. 1599. [f. SUN *sb.* + DIAL *sb.*] A contrivance for showing the time of day by means of a shadow cast by the sun upon a surface marked with a diagram indicating the hours. (Earlier called simply *dial.*)

Sundown, sun-down (sʌ·ndaun). 1620. [perh. shortening of †*sunne gate downe* (XV), †*sun go downe* (XVI).] 1. The going down of the sun; the time when the sun goes down; also, the glow of sunset; the west. Chiefly *U.S.* and *Eng.* and *Colonial dial.*; occas. *poet.* or *rhet.* 2. A hat with a wide brim. *U.S.* 1888.

Su·ndow:ner *Austral. & U.S. colloq.*, a tramp who makes a practice of arriving at a station about sundown under the pretence of seeking work, so as to obtain food and a night's lodging; also (*S. Africa*) a glass of spirit drunk at sunset. **Su·ndowning,** the practice of a sundowner.

Sun-dried (sʌ·nˌdrəid), *a.* 1600. [f. SUN *sb.* + *dried*, pa. pple. of DRY *v.*] 1. Dried by exposure to the sun, as clay, bricks, articles of food, etc. 2. Dried up or parched by the sun, as vegetation, etc. 1638.

2. As Fire the Sun-dri'd Stubble burnes 1638.

Sundries (sʌ·ndriz), *sb. pl.* 1815. [pl. of SUNDRY *a.* used subst.; cf. ODDS.] Small articles of a miscellaneous kind; *esp.* small items lumped together in an account as not needing individual mention.

Sundry (sʌ·ndri), *a.* [OE. *syndriġ* separate, special, private, exceptional, corresp. to MLG. *sunder(i)ch*, OHG. *sunt(a)ric*; see SUNDER *a.*, -Y[1].] 1. Having an existence, position, or status apart; separate, distinct. *Obs.* exc. *dial.* †2. Belonging or assigned distributively to certain individuals; distinct or different for each respectively –1738. †3. Individually separate. Usu. with pl. sb. or sing. sb. in pl. sense: Various, (many) different. –1754. †4. Different, other. (Const. *from.*) –1668. b. Consisting of miscellaneous items 1790. 5. As an indefinite numeral: A number of, several. (The prevailing use.) late ME. b. *ellipt.* and (chiefly *Sc.*) *absol.* 1470.

2. Experience finds That s. Women are of s. Minds DRYDEN. 4. b. Yield, including s. revenue, £4,855. 1913. 5. The scripture moueth vs in sondrye places, to acknowledge and confess our manyfolde synnes and wyckednesse *Bk. Com. Prayer.*

Phr. *All and s.*, every individual, every single; now only *absol.* = everybody of all classes, one and all. (orig. and chiefly Sc. = L. *omnes et singuli.*)

Sun-dry (sʌ·ndrəi), *v.* Chiefly in **sun-dried, sun-drying.** 1695. [Back-formation from SUN-DRIED.] To dry in the sun, *trans.* and *intr.*

Su·n-fish, *sb.* 1629. A name for various fishes, of rounded form or brilliant appearance, or that bask in the sun.

a. Any fish of the genus *Mola* (also called *Orthagoriscus* or *Cephalus*), comprising large fishes of singularly rounded and ungainly form, found in various seas. **b.** Any one of the various species of *Lepomis, Pomotis*, and related genera, small freshwater fishes abundant in N. America. **c.** A name for the basking shark. **d.** The OPAH, *Lampris luna*. **e.** A local name for fishes of the genus *Silene* = MOON-FISH. Hence **Su·nfish** *v.* (*U.S. colloq.*) *intr.* to act like a s., *spec.* of a bucking horse, bringing first one shoulder down almost to the ground and then the other.

Su·nflower. 1562. [tr. mod.L. *flos solis.*] †**1.** The heliotrope (*Heliotropium*). **b.** Used vaguely of any flower that turns so as to follow the sun; cf. HELIOTROPE 1. 1652. **2.** Any species of the composite genus *Helianthus*, chiefly natives of N. America, having conspicuous yellow flower-heads with disc and ray suggesting a figure of the sun; esp. *H. annuus*, a tall-growing plant commonly cultivated for its very large showy flowers 1597. **b.** Applied (usu. with defining word) to various other composite plants with radiant yellow flower-heads 1731. **3.** Applied to various plants whose flowers open only in sunshine or in daylight; as the pimpernel, the star-of-Bethlehem 1670.

Sung (sɒŋ), *ppl. a.* 1526. [pa. pple. of SING *v.*] Uttered in musical tones (*Liturg.* as dist. from being said without note).

||**Sungar, sangar** (sɒ·ŋgəɹ). 1841. [Pushtu *sangar* = Punjabi *saṅghar.*] A breastwork of stone.

Su·n-god. 1592. The sun regarded or personified as a god; a god identified or specially associated with the sun.

Sunk (sɒŋk), *ppl. a.* late ME. [pa. pple. of SINK *v.* (In present usage this form of the pa. pple. in adj. use tends to be restricted to senses implying deliberate human agency; e.g. *s. fence.*)] **1.** = SUNKEN 2. Now *rare.* **2.** Lowered in character, intensity, value, etc. Now *rare* or *Obs.* 1680. **3.** = SUNKEN 1. 1799. **4.** In mod. techn. use, applied to a surface or area lowered, or to an object let in, so as to lie below the general surface, or to work of which depression of level is a principal feature; as *s. carving, cistern, panel*, etc. 1762.

4. *S. fence* = HA-HA *sb.*[2] 1733.

Sunken (sɒ·ŋk'n), *ppl. a.* late ME. [pa. pple. of SINK *v.* See note on prec.] **1.** That has sunk in water; submerged in, or situated beneath the surface of, water or other liquid. **2.** Of the eyes, cheeks, etc.: Abnormally depressed or hollow; fallen in 1600. **3.** That has sunk below the usual or general level; subsided 1832. **4.** In tech. use: prec. 4. 1808.

4. *S. battery* (Mil.), a battery in which the platform is sunk below the level of the ground.

Sunless (sɒ·nlės), *a.* 1589. [f. SUN *sb.* + -LESS.] Destitute of the sun or of the sun's rays; dark or dull through absence of sunlight.

Sunlight (sɒ·nləit). ME. [f. SUN *sb.* + LIGHT *sb.*] **1.** The light of the sun. **2.** (prop. with hyphen.) = SUN-*burner* 1862.

Artificial s. = artificial sun-rays (SUN-RAY 2).

Sunlike (sɒ·nləik), *a.* and *adv.* 1596. [f. SUN *sb.* + -LIKE.] **A.** *adj.* Like or resembling the sun, or that of the sun; *esp.* very bright or resplendent.

Princes couched under the glow Of s. gems SHELLEY.

B. *adv.* Like or in the manner of the sun 1819.

That eternal honour which should live S., above the reek of mortal fame SHELLEY.

Sunlit (sɒ·nlit), *ppl. a.* 1822. [f. as prec. + LIT *ppl. a.*] Lighted or illumined by the sun.

||**Sunn** (sɒn). *Indian.* 1774. [– Urdu, Hindi *san* (Skr. *çaṇá* hempen).] A branching leguminous shrub, *Crotalarea juncea*, widely cultivated in Southern Asia for its fibre; also, the fibre used for rope, cordage, sacking, etc.

||**Sunna** (sɒ·nă). 1728. [– Arab. *sunna* form, way, course, rule.] The body of traditional sayings and customs attributed to Mohammed and supplementing the Koran.

||**Sunni** (sɒ·ni). 1626. [– Arab. *sunnī* lawful, f. SUNNA.] *collect.* The orthodox Moslems, who accept the Sunna as of equal authority with the Koran. Also *sing.* a Sunnite.

||**Sunnite** (sɒ·nəit). 1718. [f. SUNNA or SUNNI + -ITE[1] 1.] A Moslem who accepts the orthodox tradition as well as the Koran.

||**Sunnud** (sɒ·nɒd). *Indian.* Also **sanad.** 1759. [Urdu – Arab. *sanad* signature, deed, diploma.] A deed of grant; a charter, patent, warrant.

Sunny (sɒ·ni), *a.* ME. [f. SUN *sb.* + -Y[1].] **1.** Characterized by or full of sunshine; in or during which the sun shines; esp. of a day, weather, or the like. **2.** Exposed to, illumined or warmed by, the rays of the sun; on which the sun shines 1567. **3.** Pertaining to the sun; solar (*rare*); of or proceeding from the sun 1579. **4.** Resembling the sun in colour or brightness; appearing as if illumined by the sun; (of the hair) bright yellow or golden 1596. **5.** *fig.* Bright, cheerful, joyous; expressing or awakening gladness or happiness 1545.

1. Far more welcome..Then s. daies to naked Sauages 1592. **2.** Cleer Spring, or shadie Grove, or Sunnie Hill MILT. *S. side*, the best, most desirable; side *of* anything, esp. in phr. like *on the s. side of thirty, forty*, etc., = younger than... **3.** A tall stag..lay..panting in the s. ray POPE. **4.** Her s. locks Hang on her temples like a golden fleece SHAKS. **5.** A sunnie looke of his SHAKS. Hence **Su·nnily** *adv.* **Su·nniness.**

||**Sunnyasee** (sɒnyā·si). *Indian.* 1613. [– Urdu, Hindi *sannyāsī* = Skr. *saṃnyāsin* laying aside, abandoning, ascetic, f. *sam* together + *ni* down + *as* know.] A Brahman in the fourth stage of his life; a wandering fakir or religious mendicant.

Su·n-ray. 1829. **1.** A ray from the sun; a sunbeam. Chiefly *poet.* or *rhet.* **2.** *pl.* (Also *artificial sun-rays*) Ultra-violet rays used therapeutically as a substitute for sunlight 1928.

Sunrise (sɒ·nrəiz). 1440. [app. evolved from clauses such as *forto* (= until), *tofore*, or *before the sun rise*, where *rise* is a verb in the subj. Cf. SUNSET, SUNSHINE.] The rising, or apparent ascent above the horizon, of the sun at the beginning of the day; the time when the sun rises, the opening of day. Also, the display of light or colour in the sky at this time.

The gates I enter'd with S. MILT. *fig.* The first dawn of the arts, which preceded their..s. SCOTT.

Su·nri:sing. Now *rare* or *arch.* ME. [f. SUN *sb.* + pr. pple. or gerund of RISE *v.*, partly after Fr. *soleil levant.*] = prec. **b.** *transf.* The east.

Sunset (sɒ·nset). late ME. [app. f. SUN *sb.* + SET *sb.*[1], but perh. arising partly (like SUNRISE) from a clause (e.g. *ere the sunne set*).] **1.** The setting, or apparent descent below the horizon, of the sun at the end of the day; the time when the sun sets, the close of day. Also, the glow of light or display of colour in the sky when the sun sets. **2.** *fig.* Decline or close, *esp.* of a period of prosperity or the like 1613.

1. In the evenyng after soone sette 1542. **2.** The s. of life CAMPBELL.

attrib.: **s. gun**, a gun fired at s.

Sunsetting (sɒ·nse:tiŋ). Now *rare* or *arch.* 1440. [f. SUN *sb.* + pr. pple. or gerund of SET *v.*, partly after Fr. *soleil couchant.*] **1.** = prec. 1. **2.** *transf.* The west 1601.

Sunshade (sɒ·nʃē[i]d). 1851. [See SHADE *sb.*] **1.** An awning over the outside of a window, to keep the sunlight off. **2.** A parasol; now usu. applied to the larger kinds 1852. **3.** A device used with a telescope, etc. to diminish the intensity of sunlight 1894.

Sunshine (sɒ·nʃəin). [ME. *sunnesin(e* had prob. a similar origin to that of SUNRISE. But cf. OFris. *sunnaskin*, (M)LG. *sunnenschīn.*] **1.** The shining of the sun; direct sunlight uninterrupted by cloud. †**b.** with *a* and *pl.* A burst or spell of sunshine –1747. **2.** *fig.* **a.** A source of happiness or prosperity 1595. **b.** A favourable or gracious influence 1596. **c.** A condition or atmosphere of happiness or prosperity 1593. **d.** Sunny disposition 1742. **3.** *transf.* Light or brightness resembling or suggesting that of the sun 1588. **4.** *attrib.* passing into *adj.* 1579. **b.** With reference to a (saloon) motor car with a top which can be opened to admit sunshine 1929.

1. There was a long fight between mist and s. TYNDALL. Phr. *To have been in the s.* (slang), to be drunk. **2. a.** Mamma's little s. 1901. **b.** That man that sits within a Monarches heart, And ripens in the Sunneshine of his fauor SHAKS. **c.** In the meantime all was s. with Vivian Grey DISRAELI. **d.** The s. of Goldsmith's nature would break out W. IRVING. **3.** Vouchsafe to shew the s. of your face SHAKS. **4.** Her sunshine face 1594. On a S. Holy-day MILT. My s.-friends have turned their backs on me 1876.

Sunshiny (sɒ·nʃəi:ni), *a.* 1590. [f. prec. + -Y[1].] = SUNNY *a.* 1, 2, 4, 5.

The..glorious light of her sunshyny face SPENSER. In warm, sun-shiny weather 1713. A s. landscape 1803. His..daughter—a s. young lady of eighteen 1857.

Su·n-spot. 1818. **1.** *Path.* A spot or marking on the skin caused by exposure to the sun. **2.** *Astr.* A spot or patch on the disc of the sun, appearing dark by contrast with the brighter general surface, and constituted by a cavity in the photosphere filled with cooler vapours 1868.

Su·nstone, su·n-stone. 1677. **1.** A name given to amber, because the Heliades or daughters of the sun, according to a Greek myth, were changed into poplars and wept amber 1849. **2.** *Min.* **a.** A name for several varieties of feldspar, showing red or golden-yellow reflexions from minute embedded crystals of mica, oxide of iron, etc. **b.** = CAT'S-EYE 2. 1677.

Su·nstroke. 1851. [For the earlier 'stroke of the sun', tr. Fr. *coup de soleil.*] Collapse or prostration, with or without fever, caused by exposure to excessive heat of the sun. So **Su·nstri:cken** *ppl. a.* 1844.

Su·nstruck, *pa. pple.* 1839. [f. SUN *sb.* + STRUCK, after prec.] Affected with sunstroke.

||**Sunt** (sɒnt). 1820. [Arab. *sanṭ.*] A species of acacia of northern Africa, or its wood.

Sun-up, sunup (sɒ·nɒp). *local*, chiefly *U.S.* 1847. [f. SUN *sb.* + UP *adv.*, after SUNDOWN.] Sunrise.

Sunward (sɒ·nwǭɹd), *adv.* and *a.* 1611. [f. SUN *sb.* + -WARD.] **A.** *adv.* Toward the sun; in the direction of the sun. **B.** *adj.* Directed toward the sun; moving or facing in the direction of the sun 1769. So **Su·nwards** *adv.* 1574.

Sunwise (sɒ·nwəiz), *adv.* (*a.*) 1865. [f. SUN *sb.*; see WISE *sb.*[1]] In the direction of the apparent daily movement of the sun, i.e. (in the northern hemisphere) from left to right; 'with the sun'.

Sup (sɒp), *sb.* Now *dial.* 1570. [f. next.] A small quantity of liquid such as can be taken into the mouth at one time; a mouthful; a sip.

Phr. (*A*) *bit* (later *bite*) *and* (*a*) *s.*, a little food and drink.

Sup (sɒp), *v.*[1] Pa. t. and pa. pple. **supped.** [OE. *sūpan* = MLG. *sūpen*, OHG. *sūfan* (Du. *zuipen*, G. *saufen* drink, booze), ON. *súpa* :– Gmc. str. vb.] **1.** *trans.* To take (liquid) into the mouth in small quantities (as opp. to a draught). Now chiefly *Sc.* and *n. dial.*; often *spec.* to take (liquid food) with a spoon. **b.** To drink *up* or *off*, esp. by mouthfuls or spoonfuls. late ME. **2.** *intr.* To take a sip or sips; to take drink by mouthfuls or spoonfuls. Now chiefly *Sc.* and *n. dial.* OE. **3.** *fig.* To have experience of; to taste; esp. *to s. sorrow* (cf. L. *haurire dolorem.*) OE.

1. He began to s. his porridge 1889. **2.** Might I of Iove's nectar s. B. JONS. **3.** I'll make you one Day s. Sorrow for this SWIFT.

Sup (sɒp), *v.*[2] ME. [– OFr. *super, soper* (mod. *souper*), f. Gmc. *sup- (see SOP *sb.*, SUP *v.*[1], SOUP).] **1.** *intr.* To eat one's supper; to take supper. **2.** *fig.* (or in fig. context) and *allus.* late ME. **3.** *trans.* **a.** *Falconry* and *Venery.* To give the last feed of the day to (a hawk, horse, or hound) 1575. †**b.** Of food: To furnish a supper for (*rare*) –1653. **c.** To give a supper to, entertain at supper 1619.

1. I kept him to sup, sleep..and breakfast here this morning H. WALPOLE. **2.** *Macb.* V. v. 13. People had supped full of horrors 1873. Phr. †*To s. with our Saviour, with Jesus Christ, to s. in heaven* or *hell*, etc., said of persons who have died or are about to die; You shall s. with Jesu Christ to night SHAKS. **3. c.** They will breakfast you, they will s. you 1865.

||**Supari** (supā·ri). *Indian.* 1638. [Hindi *supārī* betel nut.] The areca palm; also, the areca nut which is chewed with the leaves of the betel plant.

Supawn (sɒpǭ·n). *U.S.* 1793. [Natick

saupáun softened, f. *saupáe, sabáe* it is softened.] A kind of porridge made of maize flour boiled in water until it thickens.

Supe (siūp). *slang.* 1824. Short for SUPER *sb.*

Supellectile (siupěle·ktəil, -til), *a.* and *sb.* 1597. [– late L. *supellectilis*, prob. f. *super* SUPER- I. 1 + *lectus* couch; see -ILE.] **A.** *adj.* Pertaining to or of the nature of household furniture; *transf.* ornamental 1615. **B.** *sb.* Furniture; scientific apparatus or equipment 1597.

‖**Supellex** (siupe·leks). *rare.* 1553. [L.] *lit.* Household furniture; *fig.* the equipment or apparatus for an experiment or operation.

Super (siū·pəɹ), *sb.* 1626. †**1.** [Short for INSUPER.] Something 'standing in super'; a balance remaining over –1642. **2.** *Theatr.* Short for SUPERNUMERARY. Also *gen.* 1853. **3.** = *super-hive* (see SUPER- I. 3); a box containing a certain number of sections of honey 1855. **4.** = SUPERINTENDENT 1870.

Super (siū·pəɹ), *a.* *Trade colloq.* 1833. [Short for various adj. compounds of SUPER-.] **1.** = SUPERFICIAL *a.* 2. (Usu. following the *sb.*) **2.** = SUPERFINE 3. 1842.

1. The price..is 3d. per foot s. 1881. **2.** A roll of cloth which he said was extra s. DICKENS.

Super- (siū·pəɹ, -ər), *prefix*, repr. L. *super-* = the adv. and prep. *super* above, on the top (of), beyond, besides, in addition, used in composition with various meanings.

I. Over, above, at the top (of); on, upon. **1.** Forming adjs. in which *super-* is in prepositional relation to the sb. implied in the second element. **a.** Compounds of a general character, and miscellaneous scientific and technical terms. **Su:perae·rial,** situated above the air or atmosphere. **Su:percreta·ceous** *Geol.*, lying above the Cretaceous series. **Superli·neal, -li·near,** written above the line. **Su:permari·ne,** occurring, performed or moving above or upon the surface of the sea; hence *ellipt.* as sb., a supermarine aeroplane. **b.** *Anat.* and *Zool.* = Situated above, or on the dorsal side of, the part or organ denoted by the second element, as in *su:peracro·mial, superce·ntral* (the centre sulcus of the brain), *supero·rbital* (also as *sb.*). **c.** *Bot.* in same sense as b (varying with SUPRA-), as *supera·xillary*; also *supera·rctic*, etc. **d.** Forming sbs. denoting something placed over or upon that which is denoted by the radical element as in SUPERALTAR, SUPERFRONTAL.

2. With advb. force, = Above, over, on, *occas.* from above (in material or non-material sense), prefixed to vbs., pples., adjs., and nouns of action or state, as in SUPERFLUOUS, SUPERSCRIPTION, SUPERSTRUCTURE. **Superna·tant** *a.*, swimming above, floating on the surface. †**Superse·minate** *v. trans.* to sow on the top of something previously sown. **Su·perstratum,** an overlying or superficial stratum. **Su·pervolute** *a. Bot.* applied to convolute leaves one of which envelops another in the bud, or to vernation in which this occurs. (*a*) Forming intr. vbs. and other parts of speech of cognate meaning. **Supercre·scent** *a.*, growing over or on the top of something; so **Supercre·scence,** a parasitic growth. **Superja·cent** *a.*, lying above or over something else; superincumbent. **Supersa·liency,** the leaping of the male for the act of copulation; so **Supersa·lient** *a.* (*b*) Forming trans. vbs. and related words of cognate meaning. **Su:percolumnia·tion,** the erection of one order of columns upon another. **Su:perindue·** *v.*, to put on as a garment, esp. over another. **Su:perinspe·ct** *v.*, to inspect as a superior official, to oversee (now *rare* or *Obs.*). **b.** with intr. vbs. and their derivatives: = Above (in *fig.* sense); in a higher condition, relation, etc.; nonce-words, as *su:per-exi·st* vb., *-exi·stent* adj.

3. Prefixed to descriptive sbs. with adj. force = Placed or situated above, over, or upon something; forming the upper part of (that which is denoted by the second element); higher, upper. **Su·percharge,** *Her.* a charge borne upon another charge (*rare*). **Su·perhive,** a removable upper compartment of a beehive. †**Su·per-plant,** a plant growing upon another plant; a parasite or epiphyte. **Su·pertunic,** *Antiq.* an outer tunic; *spec.* the vestment worn above the dalmatic by a sovereign at his coronation. **b.** *Anat.* (*a*) Designating the upper of two parts or members; superior; e.g. *supermaxilla*, the upper maxilla or jaw. (*b*) Designating a part overlapping another, or formed by such overlapping; e.g. *su·perfissure, supersulcus.* **c.** *Anat.* Forming adjs. (with *super-* in adj. relation to the sb. or subst. phr. implied in the second element): (*a*) derivs. from sbs. in b, as *su:permaxi·llary* (= pertaining to the upper jaw); (*b*) situated in, or forming, the upper part of, e.g. *su:percerebe·llar, -cerebral, temporal*².

II. Above (in various fig. senses); higher in rank, quality, amount, or degree. **1. a.** Prefixed to adjs.: Above or beyond, more or higher than, above the range, scope, capacity, etc. of (what is denoted or expressed by the radical part); e.g. *su:perange·lic* (= beyond that of an angel), *-essential* (= SUPERSUBSTANTIAL 2), *-intellectual, -organic, -physical, -rational, -regal, -secular, -sensible, -sensuous, -superlative, -temporal*¹. (*b*) In corresponding advs., as *supera·dequately.* **b.** Prefixed to sbs., forming adjs. in the same sense as above; e.g. *su·pergraduate, -standard.*

2. Prefixed to sbs., forming sbs. denoting something above, beyond, greater or higher than what is expressed by the radical part. **a.** *gen.*, as *su·per-Erastian,* †*-essence, -septuagenarian.* **b.** *Mus.* Designating a note next above some principal note, as SUPERTONIC. **Superdo·minant,** the SUBMEDIANT, the sixth of the scale. **c.** *Nat. Hist.* In classification, denoting a group or division next higher than, or including a number of, those denoted by the radical part, as *su·per-family, -order, -species, -suborder.* So **Sup·er-mo:lecule** *Chem.* a complex molecule formed by the combination of molecules of different substances. **d.** *Geom.* In geometry of more than three dimensions, designating a locus or figure having one more dimension than that denoted by the simple word; e.g. *su·percube, -curve, -line.* **e.** Prefixed to the name of a person, forming a vb. in the sense to outdo (the person named) in his characteristic quality or action; as *su·percæsar* (rare).

3. Prefixed to sbs. with adj. force: Higher in rank, quality, degree, or amount; of a higher kind or nature; superior. **a.** With names of officials or persons in authority; e.g. *su·per-arbiter, -sovereign*; also in the names of the corresponding offices or functions, as *su·per-sovereignty.* **b.** With nouns of action or condition, etc.; e.g. *su·per-agency, -comprehension, -good, -organism.* **c.** In recent formations after SUPERMAN, used to designate a person, animal, or thing which typifies the highest point of development or evolution of its class; e.g. *su·per-bride, -critic, -film.* **Su·per-Drea:dnought,** an all-big-gun ship with an armament superior to that of the Dreadnought class. **d.** *Mus.* = Next higher in pitch: in *su·peroctave.*

4. Beyond in time, later. †**Superla·st** *v., trans.* to last beyond, outlast. **b.** With prepositional force: see SUPERANNUATE.

5. Before in time, prior to. **Superlapsa·rian** *sb.* and *a.* = SUPRALAPSARIAN. †**Supervive** *v.* = SURVIVE.

III. In or to the highest or a very high degree; hence, in excess of what is usual, or of what ought to be; superabundant(ly; excessive(ly. **1. a.** Prefixed in advb. relation to adjs.: Exceedingly, very highly, extremely, supremely, extraordinarily; over-. **Super-e·xtra,** applied to commodities, esp. to a style of bookbinding, of the very best quality. **Super-fa·tted, -fa·tty,** (of soap), containing an excess of fat, i.e. more than can combine with the alkali. **-rege·nerative** *a.* *Wireless*, pertaining to regenerative reception in which the oscillations generated in the receiver are interrupted at a frequency above the range of inaudibility. **Supervaca·neous** (now *rare* or *Obs.*), superfluous, redundant. (*b*) In corresponding advs., as *super-infinitely.* **b.** Prefixed to vbs. or pples. (with derivs.), in same senses as in a; e.g. *su:peraccu·mulate* (= to accumulate beyond measure), *-exceed, -excel, -extol, -reward* vbs.; *su:peraci·dulated* (= acidulated to excess), *-civilized, -elated, -peopled* pples. and ppl. adjs.

2. Prefixed with adj. force to abstract sbs.: Very great, or too great; surpassing; excessive, extreme; e.g. *su:peracti·vity, -conformity, -infirmity*; hence occas. agent-nouns, as *su:per-confo·rmist, -individualist.* **Su:per-regenera·tion** (cf. *super-regenerative* above). **b.** (Chiefly *Phys.* and *Path.*) Denoting processes or conditions in excess of the normal; e.g. *su:peralkali·nity, -irritation, -secretion.*

3. In prepositional relation with the radical element, as in SUPERNUMERARY.

4. *Chem.* †**a.** Prefixed to vbs., pa. pples., and cognate nouns of action, denoting a high proportion of the ingredient indicated by the radical element; e.g. *su:perca·rbonate* vb., *-carburetted, -oxygenated* pa. pples., *-oxygenation.* **b.** In names of compounds, indicating that the ingredient denoted by the radical is in the highest proportion; e.g. *superoxide* (= PEROXIDE). Now surviving in the names of salts used in manufactures or the arts, e.g. SUPERPHOSPHATE.

IV. Expressing addition. **1.** In advb. or adj. relation to a vb., sb., or adj.: Over and above, in addition, additional(ly, as in SUPERADD, SUPEREROGATE. **Superca·lender** *v. trans.*, to subject (paper) to additional calendering, so as to produce a highly glazed surface; hence **Superca·lender** *sb.*, a roller used for supercalendering. **Super-eleva·tion,** the (amount of) elevation of the outer above the inner rail at a curve on a railway, or of one side of a road above the other. **Su:per-(in)feuda·tion,** creation of a new feudal estate out of one already established. †**Superimpre·gnate** *v. trans.* to impregnate or imbue in addition; hence **Superimpregna·tion.** †**Superinfu·se** *v. trans.* to infuse in addition. **Superi·nstitute** *v. trans.* to institute to a benefice over the head of another (now *rare* or *Obs.*). †**Superlu·crate** *v. trans.*, to gain in addition, make a profit of (so much). **Su·per-tax** *sb.*, an additional duty of income tax levied upon incomes above a certain value; hence as *vb.*

†**2.** *Math.* In adjs. denoting ratios expressible by unity (or some other integer) with some number of aliquot parts over; as in late L. *superdimidius* (sc. *numerus* number) 'that is a half more', i.e. $1\frac{1}{2}$, denoting a ratio of 3:2, *supertertius* 'that is a third more', i.e. $1\frac{1}{3} = 4:3$, etc.

3. Upon something of the same kind, in a secondary relation; secondary, secondarily; e.g. *supercommentary* (= a commentary on a commentary), *-parasite, -reformation,* etc.

Superable (siū·pərăb'l), *a.* 1629. [– L. *superabilis*, f. *superare*; see -ABLE.] Capable of being overcome or vanquished; surmountable; opp. to *insuperable*.

Antipathies are generally s. by a single effort JOHNSON. Hence **Su·perabi·lity, Su·perableness; Su·perably** *adv.*

Superabound (siū:pərăbau·nd), *v.* 1447. [– late (eccl.) L. *superabundare*; see SUPER- III. 1 b and ABOUND *v.*] **1.** *intr.* To abound beyond something else; to be more abundant (with allusion to *Rom.* 5:20.) **2.** To abound excessively; to be very or too abundant 1520.

2. Cony Ile..also superabounds with Seales 1638.

Superabundance (siū:pərăbɒ·ndăns). late ME. [– late l. *superabundantia*, f. *superabundare*; see prec., -ANCE.] **1.** The quality of being superabundant; the fact or condition of superabounding; excessive abundance or plentifulness; redundance. **2.** That which superabounds; a superabundant quantity or amount; a surplus (*of* something). late ME. So **-abu·ndancy.**

Superabundant (siū:pərăbɒ·ndănt), *a.* late ME. [– late L. *superabundans, -ant-*, pr. pple. of *superabundare* SUPERABOUND; see -ANT.] **1.** Abounding above something else, or above measure; enough and to spare; exceedingly abundant or plentiful. Now *rare.* **2.** Abounding above what is fitting or needful; exceeding the normal or required amount; more than sufficient (in a bad sense). late ME.

2. A s. population 1835. Hence **Su:perabu·ndantly** *adv.*

Su·per-acid, *a.* 1808. [SUPER- III. 4 b.] **1.** *Chem. S. salt* = SUPERSALT. **2.** Excessively acid 1901. Hence **Su·peraci·dity,** excessive acidity.

Superadd (siūpəræ·d), *v.* 1458. [– L. *superaddere*; see SUPER- IV. 1, ADD *v.*] **1.** *trans.* To add over and above; to add *to* what has been added; to put as a further addition. Often a mere strengthening of *add*: To add besides; 'to join any thing extrinsick' (J.) **b.** *absol.* To make a further addition *to* 1660. **2.** *spec.* To add as a further statement; to say, state, or mention in addition 1640.

1. A French war is added to the American; and there is all the reason in the world to expect a Spanish war to be superadded to the French BURKE. **2.** I s. a few essentials more COWPER.

Superaddition (siū:pərădi·ʃən). 1609. [f. prec. after *addition*.] **1.** The action (or an act) of superadding, or the condition of being superadded; further addition. Often a mere strengthening of *addition*. **2.** Something superadded; a further addition 1649.

2. A s. to, not a constituent of, man's moral existence 1866. So **Su:peraddi·tional** *a.*

Superaltar (siū·pərǭ:ltəɹ). late ME. [– med.L. *superaltare*; see SUPER- I. 1 d, ALTAR.] *Eccl.* **1.** A portable consecrated stone slab for use upon an unconsecrated altar, a table, etc. **2.** A structure erected above an altar (at the back); **a.** a reredos; **b.** a retable or gradine 1848.

†**Superannated,** *pa. pple.* and *ppl. a.* 1605. [var. of SUPERANNUATED, after med.L. *superannatus* between one and two years old (of animals).] Superannuated –1654.

Supera·nnuate, *a.* and *sb.* Now *rare.* 1647. [– med.L. *superannuatus*; see SUPERANNUATED.] **A.** *adj.* = SUPERANNUATED. **B.** *sb.* A superannuated person 1822.

Superannuate (siūpəræ·niuᵉit), *v.* 1649. [Back-formation from next.] †**1.** *trans.* To render antiquated or obsolete: said of the lapse of time, etc. –1865. **2.** To dismiss or discharge from office on account of age; *esp.* to cause to retire from service on a pension;

to pension off 1692. **3.** *pass.* and *intr.* To become too old for a position; to reach the age at which one leaves a school retires from an office, etc. 1814.

Superannuated (s'ūpəræ·niue'ted), *pa. pple.* and *ppl. a.* 1633. [f. med.L. *superannuatus*, f. *super-* SUPER- II. 4 b + *annus* year, with assim. to L. *annuus* ANNUAL; see -ATE², -ED¹.] **1.** Of persons (or animals): Disqualified or incapacitated by age; old and infirm 1639. **b.** *transf.* Of personal actions or attributes 1707. **2.** Of things: Impaired by age, worn out; antiquated, obsolete, out of date 1633. **b.** *loosely.* That has lasted a very long time; inveterate; very old (*rare*) 1644. **3.** Discharged from service on a pension after attaining a certain age. Also said of the pension. 1740.

1. A s. cock whose muscles were impenetrable to the teeth 1819. **b.** Her s. Charms 1707. **2.** Thy threadbare Cassock and s. Beaver 1689. **3.** A s. lieutenant on half-pay SMOLLETT.

Superannuation (s'ū:pərænįuē'·ʃən). 1658. [f. SUPERANNUATE *v.* or prec.; see -ATION.] **1.** The condition of being superannuated; impairment of the powers or faculties by old age; senile infirmity or decay. *Obs.* or *rare.* 1755. †**b.** The condition of being out of date (*rare*) –1845. **2.** The action of superannuating an official; also, the allowance or pension granted to one who is discharged on account of age 1704. **b.** At certain schools, the attainment of the specified age at which a boy is required to leave 1831. **3.** *attrib.* as *s. allowance, scheme* 1817.

1. The mere doating of s. 1782. **b.** A monk he seemed by. . the s. of his knowledge DE QUINCEY.

Superb (s'upō·ɹb), *a.* 1549. [– (O)Fr. *superbe* or L. *superbus* proud, superior, distinguished.] **1.** Of buildings, monuments, and the like: Of noble and magnificent proportions or aspect. **2.** Grandly and sumptuously equipped, arrayed, or decorated 1700. **b.** in specific appellations of many gorgeously coloured birds, plants, etc. 1760. **3.** Of conditions, language, thought, etc.: Grand, stately, majestic 1784. **4.** Expressing emphatic approval: Very fine; splendid; magnificent 1729.

1. The s. chapell of Ferdinand I. EVELYN. **2.** Saw the s. funerall of the Protector EVELYN. **b.** **S. bird of paradise,** *Lophorina* (*Paradisea*) *superba*, a species of which the male is violet-black with green iridescence, having a gorget of metallic green feathers, and an erectile hood or mantle of velvet-black plumes on the shoulders. *S. lily*, a plant of the genus *Gloriosa* (*Methonica*), esp. *G. superba. S. warbler*, the blue wren of Australia, *Malurus cyaneus.* **4.** The dinner was sumptuous, the wines s. DISRAELI. Hence **Su·pe·rb-ly** *adv.*, **-ness** (*rare*).

†**Supe·rbious,** *a. rare.* 1510. [– OFr. *superbieus* or med.L. *superbiosus*, f. L. *superbia* pride, f. *superbus* SUPERB; see -IOUS.] **1.** Proud, overbearing, insolent –1700. **2.** Stately, grand, superb –1714. So †**Supe·r-bous** *a.* (*rare*) –1709.

Supercargo (s'ūpəɹkā·ɹgo). 1697. [Alteration of SUPRACARGO by prefix-substitution.] An officer on board a merchant ship whose business it is to superintend the cargo and the commercial transactions of the voyage. †Also formerly, an agent who superintended a merchant's business in a foreign country.

Supercelestial (s'ū:pəɹsīle·stiăl), *a.* 1559. [f. late L. *supercælestis* = Gr. ὑπερουράνιος; see SUPER- I. 1 a, II. 1 a, and CELESTIAL.] **1.** That is above the heavens; situated or existing above the firmament. **2.** More than heavenly; of a nature or character higher than celestial 1561.

Su·percharged, *pa. pple.* and *ppl. a.* 1876. [SUPER- III. 1 b.] Charged to excess; overcharged; *spec.* of an internal combustion engine, having air forced into the carburettor by means of a fan or other device. So **Su·percharger,** a device for supercharging an engine; an engine, car, etc., fitted with such a device.

Superchery (s'upō·ɹtʃəri). *Obs.* exc. in Fr. form **supercherie** (süpɛrʃəri). 1598. [– Fr. *supercherie* – It. *soperchieria*, f. *soperchio* superfluous, excessive.] †**1.** An attack made upon one at a disadvantage; (a piece of) foul play –1656. **2.** Trickery. Also with *a* and *pl.* 1650.

Superciliary (s'ūpəɹsi·liări), *a.* and *sb.* 1732. [f. SUPERCILIUM + -ARY¹.] Of or pertaining to the eyebrow, or to the region of the eyebrow; supra-orbital. **b.** Situated over the eye; also *transf.* having a marking over the eye 1872.

S. arch or *ridge*, a prominence of the frontal bone, over the eye, produced by the development of the frontal sinuses.

B. *sb.* A superciliary ridge or marking 1864.

Supercilious (s'ūpəɹsi·liəs), *a.* 1529. [– L. *superciliosus*, f. SUPERCILIUM; see -OUS.] **1.** Haughtily contemptuous in character or demeanour; having or marked by an air of contemptuous superiority or disdain. †**2.** 'Dictatorial, arbitrary, despotic, overbearing' (J.); exacting in judgement, censorious –1791.

Hence **Superci·lious-ly** *adv.*, **-ness.**

‖**Supercilium** (s'ūpəɹsi·liŏm). *Pl.* **-ia** (-iă). 1563. [L., eyebrow; ridge, summit, f. *super-* SUPER- + *cilium* (lower) eyelid.] **1.** The eyebrow. *Obs.* exc. *Anat.* 1672. **b.** *Zool.* A superciliary streak or marking 1817. **2.** *Arch.* †**a.** A narrow fillet above the cymatium of a cornice. **b.** A fillet above and below the scotia of an Attic base. **c.** The lintel of a door-case. 1563. **3.** *Anat.* The lip or margin of a bony cavity, esp. of the acetabulum 1706.

Su·perconscious, *a.* 1884. [SUPER- II. 1 a; after *subconscious.*] That is above or beyond human consciousness. **Superco·nsciousness.**

Su·percool, *v.* 1907. [SUPER- III. 1 b.] *trans.* To cool (a liquid) below the freezing-point without solidification.

Supere·minence. 1616. [– late L. *supereminentia*, f. *supereminent-*; see next and -ENCE.] The quality or fact of being supereminent; supreme or special eminence; *rarely* in physical sense, supreme height or loftiness. So **Supere·minency** (now *rare* or *Obs.*) 1585.

Supereminent (s'ūpəre·minĕnt), *a.* 1555. [– L. *supereminens, -ent-*, pr. pple. of *supereminēre* rise above; see SUPER- III. 1 a, EMINENT.] **1.** Lofty above the rest; supremely or specially high. Now *rare.* **2.** Exalted above others in rank or dignity; supremely exalted 1583. **3.** Distinguished *above* others in character or attainment; conspicuous *for* some quality 1599. **4.** Of qualities, conditions, etc.: Specially or supremely remarkable in degree 1581.

1. A single s. tower 1892. **3.** Som were s. for holines, and high virtues 1651. **4.** Thy s. gifts 1592. Hence **Supere·minently** *adv.*

Supererogant (s'ūpəre·rŏgănt), *a. rare.* 1737. [– late L. *supererogans, -ant-*, pr. pple. of *supererogare*; see next, -ANT.] = SUPEREROGATORY.

†**Supere·rogate,** *v.* 1582. [– *supererogat-*, pa. ppl. stem of late L. *supererogare*, f. *super-* SUPER- IV. 1 + L. *erogare* pay out; see -ATE³.] **1.** *trans.* To pay over and above; to spend in addition. Also *absol. rare.* –1613. **2.** *intr.* To do more than is commanded or required; *spec.* to perform a work of SUPEREROGATION –1727. **b.** To make up by excess of merit *for* the failing of another –1649.

2. We cannot. . haue any perfection in this life, much lesse s. BURTON. **b.** The fervencie of one man in prayer cannot s. for the coldness of another MILT.

Supererogation (s'ū:pərerŏgē'·ʃən). 1526. [– late L. *supererogatio, -ōn-*, f. as prec.; see -ION.] The action (or an act) of 'supererogating'; chiefly in phr. *work(s of s.* **a.** *R.C. Theol.* The performance of good works beyond what God commands or requires, which are held to constitute a store of merit which the Church may dispense to others to make up for their deficiencies. **b.** *transf.* and *gen.* Performance of more than duty or circumstances require; doing more than is needed 1592.

b. An Act of so great S., as singing without a Voice STEELE.

Supererogative (s'ū:pərĭrǫ·gătiv), *a. rare.* 1599. [– med.L. *supererogativus*, f. as prec.; see -IVE.] = next.

Supererogatory (s'ū:pərĭrǫ·gătŏri, s'ū:pəre·rŏgătŏri), *a.* (*sb.*) 1593. [– med.L. *supererogatorius*, f. as prec.; see -ORY².] Characterized by, or having the nature of, supererogation; going beyond what is commanded or required; *loosely*, superfluous. †**B.** *sb.* A work of supererogation. RICHARDSON. Hence **Su:perero·gatorily** *adv.*

Su:perexa·lt, *v.* 1609. [– late (eccl.) L. *superexaltare*; see SUPER- III. 1 b, EXALT *v.*] **1.** *trans.* To exalt or raise to a higher, or to the highest, position or rank; to exalt supremely 1625. **2.** To extol or magnify exceedingly (*rare*) 1609. So **Su:perexalta·tion.**

Supere·xcellence. 1652. [f. next; see -ENCE.] The quality or condition of being superexcellent; superior or supreme excellence. So **Supere·xcellency** (now *rare*) 1587.

Supere·xcellent, *a.* 1561. [– late L. *superexcellens, -ent-*; see SUPER III. 1 a, EXCELLENT.] That superexcels; excellent in a high degree; very or supremely excellent. Hence **Supere·xcellently** *adv.*

Superfetation (s'ū:pəɹfītē'·ʃən). Also **-fœt-** 1603. [– Fr. *superfétation* or mod.L. *superfetatio*, f. L. *superfetare*; see next, -ATION.] **1.** *Phys.* A second conception occurring after (esp. some time after) a prior one and before the delivery; the formation of a second fœtus in a uterus already pregnant; occurring normally in some animals, and believed by some to occur exceptionally in women. **b.** *Bot.* In early use, applied to processes supposed to be analogous to superfetation in animals, e.g. the growth of a parasite, etc.; in mod. use, the fertilization of the same ovule by two different kinds of pollen. 1626. **2.** *fig.* Additional production; the growth or accretion of one *upon* another; also, an instance of this 1641.

1. The hare is often troubled with s. 1661. **2.** Layers of dust have accumulated (a superfœtation of dirt!) upon the old layers LAMB. Mark the s. of omens—omen supervening upon omen, augury engrafted upon augury DE QUINCEY.

†**Superfete,** *v.* 1645. [– L. *superfetare* (Pliny), f. *super-* SUPER- IV. 1 + *fetus* FŒTUS.] *intr.* and *trans.* To conceive by superfetation –1654.

†**Superfice.** late ME. [– OFr. *superfice* or its source, L. SUPERFICIES.] = SUPERFICIES 1, 2 –1823.

Superficial (s'ūpəɹfi·ʃăl), *a.* (*sb.*) late ME. [– late L. *superficialis*, f. L. SUPERFICIES; see -AL¹. Cf. Fr. *superficiel.*] **A.** *adj.* **1.** Of or pertaining to the surface; that is, lies, or is found at or on the surface; constituting the surface, outermost part, or crust. **b.** Of actions or conditions: Taking place or existing at or on the surface 1815. **c.** *Anat.* Situated just beneath the skin; subcutaneous 1804. **2.** Of or pertaining to a superficies; relating to or involving two dimensions; *esp.* relating to extent of surface. (Dist. from *linear* and *solid.*) *S. measure*, square measure. 1571. **3.** Appearing 'on the surface'; external, outward 1561. **4.** That is only on or near the surface; affecting only the surface; not deep 1594. **5.** Concerned only with what is on the surface, and is therefore apparent or obvious; not deep, profound, or thorough; shallow 1533. **b.** *transf.* of persons, in respect of their actions, attainments, or character 1603. **6.** Of conditions, qualities, actions, occupations: Not involving a profound or serious issue; of insignificant import or influence 1530. **7.** That has only the outward appearance of being what is denoted by the sb.; only apparent, not real or genuine 1623.

1. The rise in the temperature of the s. blood HUXLEY. **c.** The s. veins appear remarkably large ABERNETHY. **2.** *S. foot, yard*, etc., a rectangular space measuring a foot, yard, etc. each way, or a space of whatever shape containing the same amount of area; a square foot, etc. **3.** There is a s. appearance of equity in this tax BURKE. **4.** Small and superficiall Wounds 1676. **5.** To vindicate our author's judgment from being s. DRYDEN. Men of s. understanding, and ludicrous fancy BOSWELL. The accounts. . are s., confused and inexplicable 1777. **b.** A very superficiall, ignorant, vnweighing fellow SHAKS. **6.** Empty noise And s. pastimes WORDSW. **7.** The old quarrel has at least a s. reconcilement JOWETT.

B. *absol.* or as *sb.* **1.** With *the*: That which is superficial (in any sense) 1579. **2.** With *the*: Those who are superficial 1701. **3.** *pl.* Superficial characteristics or qualities 1832.

3. Excepting in the merest superficials, there is a far greater variety in women than in men 1897. Hence **Superfi·cial-ly** *adv.*, **-ness.**

Superfi·cialism. 1839. [f. prec. + -ISM.] Superficial character, superficiality. So **Superfi·cialist,** one whose knowledge, observation, or treatment is superficial 1652.

Superficiality (s¹ūpəɹfiʃiæ·lĭti). 1530. [f. as prec. + -ITY.] The quality or state of being superficial; also, an instance of this.

Superfi·cialize, *v.* 1593. [f. as prec. + -IZE.] †**1.** *trans.* To make a surface of (paint or colour); also *transf.* to paint (the cheeks). *rare.* –1633. **2.** *intr.* To treat a subject or do something superficially 1656. **3.** *trans.* To render superficial 1828.

3. It is a necessary consequence of the advance of education that every subject becomes vulgarized and superficialised 1863.

†**Superficie.** 1545. [– L. *superficies* (see next).] = next –1726.

Superficies (s¹ūpəɹfi·ʃiīz, U.S. also s¹ūpəɹfi·ʃīz). *Pl.* **superficies.** 1530. [– L. *superficies*, f. *super-* SUPER- I. 3 + *facies* FACE *sb.*] **1.** *Geom.* A magnitude of two dimensions, having only length and breadth; that which forms the boundary or one of the boundaries of a solid, or separates one part of space from another; a surface. **2.** The outer surface of a body, which is apparent to the eye, or is immediately adjacent to the air or to another body 1577. **3.** That which constitutes the outermost part of a body; the surface layer. Now *rare.* 1603. **b.** *Rom.* and *Civil Law.* A building or other thing in or on the surface of a piece of land, which is by art or nature so closely connected with as to form part of it; the right possessed by a person over any such building or other thing in or on the surface of another's land 1850. **4.** Superficial area or extent 1656. **5.** †**a.** The 'surface' (of something immaterial, *esp.* of the mind or soul) –1700. †**b.** The outward form or aspect –1781. **c.** That which is merely superficial 1589.

3. To render the S. of the Earth loose 1707. 4. The whole s. of the parish contains 21 square miles 1798.

Superfine (s¹ū·pəɹfəin, s¹ūpəɹfəi·n), *a.* (*sb.*) 1575. [– med.L. *superfinus* (implied in *superfinitas*); see SUPER- III. 1 a, FINE *a.*] **A.** *adj.* **1.** Excessively refined, nice, fastidious, or elegant; over-refined, over-nice. †**2.** Consisting of very fine particles or threads. Also, of a file with extremely fine teeth. 1656. **3.** Of manufactured goods: Extremely fine in quality; of the very best kind; (of liquids) the purest or clearest 1682. **4.** Superlatively fine or excellent 1850. **B.** *sb. pl.* Goods of superfine quality 1812.

A. 1. S. distinctions of the Schools LOCKE. 3. The wax was s., its hue vermilion BYRON. 4. My eyes have not been in s. order 1850. Hence **Su·perfine-ly** *adv.*, **-ness** (*rare*).

Superfluent (s¹upō·ɹfluĕnt), *a. rare.* 1440. [– L. *superfluens, -ent-*, pr. pple. of *superfluere*; see SUPERFLUOUS, -ENT.] **1.** = SUPERFLUOUS. **2.** Flowing or floating above. *Obs.* or *arch.* 1440. **3.** Superabundant 1711. So **Superfluence** (s¹upō·ɹfluĕns). *arch. rare.* Superabundance.

Superfluity (s¹ūpəɹflū·ĭti). late ME. [– (O)Fr. *superfluité* – late L. *superfluitas*, f. L. *superfluus*; see next, -ITY.] The quality of being, or something that is, superfluous. **1.** Superabundant supply, superabundance; the condition of there being (or of one's having) more than enough; an instance of this. **2.** The condition or fact of being more abundant or copious than is necessary; excessive quantity or number; *esp.* excess in diet or dress. late ME. **3.** A thing or part that is in excess of what is necessary, or that can be dispensed with. Chiefly *pl.* late ME. †**4.** Immoderate indulgence or expenditure; an instance of this –1801.

1. Her girlhood with its..s. of sisters GEO. ELIOT. 2. Thus the act of fertilization is completed, and there is no s. in the means employed DARWIN. 3. When we are in want of necessaries we must part with all superfluities ADAM SMITH.

Superfluous (s¹upō·ɹfluəs), *a.* late ME. [f. L. *superfluus*, f. *superfluere*, f. *super-* SUPER- I. 2 + *fluere* flow; see -OUS.] **1.** That exceeds what is sufficient; of which there is more than enough; excessively abundant or numerous. **2.** That is not needed or required; needless, uncalled-for 1450. **b.** *transf.* Of a person: Doing more than is necessary (*rare*) 1596. †**3.** Exceeding what is right, desirable, normal, or usual; immoderate, inordinate –1613. †**4.** Having, consuming, or expending more than enough; superabundantly supplied; extravagant in expenditure –1711.

1. Divesting myself of all s. clothes TYNDALL. 2. This warning was not s. 1898. b. 1 *Hen. IV*, I. ii. 12. 3. Purchas'd At a s. rate SHAKS. 4. *Lear* II. iv. 268. Hence **Supe·rfluous-ly** *adv.*, **-ness.**

Su·perflux. 1605. [f. SUPER- III. 2 + FLUX.] **1.** A superfluity or surplus. **2.** An overflowing, or excessive flow, of water or other liquid 1760.

Superfrontal (s¹ū·pəɹfrɒntăl). 1858. [– med.L. *superfrontale*; see FRONTAL *sb.*] **1.** [SUPER- I. 3.] A covering of silk or stuff hanging over the upper edge of an altar frontal. **2.** [SUPER- I. 1 d.] A dossal 1887.

Superfuse (s¹ūpəɹfiū·z), *v.* 1657. [– *superfus-*, pa. ppl. stem of L. *superfundere*; see SUPER- I. 2, FUSE *v.* In sense 3, a new formation on SUPERFUSION.] **1.** *trans.* To pour over or *on* something. **2.** To sprinkle or affuse; to suffuse in baptism 1657. **3.** To cool (a liquid) below its melting-point without causing it to solidify; to supercool, overcool, undercool 1902.

Superfu·sion. 1657. [– late L. *superfusio*, f. as prec.; see -ION.] The action or result of superfusing.

Su·perheat, *v.* 1859. [f. SUPER- III. 1 b.] *trans.* To heat to a very high temperature; *esp.* to raise the normal temperature of (steam). Hence **Su·perheat** *sb.* the state of being superheated; the excess of temperature of a vapour above its temperature of saturation. **Su·perhea:ter,** an apparatus for superheating steam.

Superheterodyne (s¹ūpəɹhe·tĕrŏdəin). 1922. [f. SUPER(SONIC + HETERODYNE.] *Wireless.* In full *superheterodyne receiver*: A receiving-set producing oscillations differing in frequency from those of the transmitting station and utilizing supersonic beat-notes thus produced. Often abbrev. **Superhe·t.**

Superhuman (s¹ūpəɹhiū·măn), *a.* 1633. [– late L. *superhumanus*; see SUPER- II. 1, HUMAN *a.*] **a.** Of a quality, act, etc.: Higher than that of man; beyond the capacity or power of man. **b.** Of a person or being: Higher than man; having a nature above that of man 1824. **c.** In rhet. or hyperbolical use: Higher or greater than that of any ordinary man; beyond the average human capacity, stature, etc. 1822.

a. S. agencies and powers 1896. b. Christ is a s. person 1866. c. The s. yells which he uttered SCOTT. Hence **Su:perhuma·nity,** the character or quality of being s. **Superhu·manize** *v. trans.* to make, or represent as, s. **Superhu·manly** *adv.*

Superhu·meral. 1606. [– late L. *superhumerale*; see SUPER- I. 1 a, HUMERAL.] An ecclesiastical vestment worn over the shoulders, as the Jewish ephod, or an amice or pallium; *fig.* a burden carried on the shoulders.

Su:perimpose, *v.* 1794. [f. SUPER- I. 2 + IMPOSE *v.*, after next.] **1.** *trans.* To impose or place (one object) *on* or *upon* another; to lay above or on the top; *spec.* in *Geol.* in ref. to stratification (always in pa. pple.) **2.** *fig.* To cause to follow *upon* something else and to exist side by side with it 1855.

1. Four buried forests superimposed one upon the other 1863.

Su:perimposi·tion. 1684. [f. SUPER- I. 2 + IMPOSITION, after L. *superimponere*; see IMPONE *v.*] The action of superimposing, or state of being superimposed; superposition.

Su:perincu·mbent, *a.* 1664. [f. SUPER- I. 2 + INCUMBENT.] Lying or resting upon, or situated on the top of, something else; overlying. (Chiefly in scientific use.) **b.** Situated or suspended above; overhanging 1835. **c.** Of pressure: Exerted from above 1854.

fig. A Power Girt round with weakness;—it can scarce uplift The weight of the s. hour SHELLEY. Hence **Su:perincu·mbence, -ency.** *rare.*

Su:perindu·ce, *v.* 1555. [– L. *superinducere* cover over (= sense 4), in late and med.L. bring in, add; bring in from without; see SUPER I. 2, IV. 1, INDUCE.] **1.** *trans.* To bring (a person) into some position in addition to, or so as to displace, one who already occupies it. *Obs.* or *arch.* **2.** To bring in over and above, or 'on the top of' something already present; to introduce in addition (esp. something extraneous) 1605. **3.** To bring or cause to come *upon* a person or thing; to bring on, induce; *esp.* to induce (a disease, etc.) in addition to one already existing 1615. **4.** In physical sense: To bring, draw, deposit, etc. *over* or *upon* a thing as a covering or addition 1660.

1. It was plain adultery to s. any other wife, his former living 1555. 2. Their improvement cannot come from themselves, but must be superinduced from without MILL. 4. To s. a Doctoral hood over a Friers Coul FULLER. Hence **Su:perindu·cement,** the action or an act of superinducing; something superinduced.

Superintend (s¹ū:pərinte·nd), *v.* 1615. [– eccl.L. *superintendere*, rendering Gr. ἐπισκοπεῖν; see SUPER- I. 2, INTEND *v.*] *trans.* To have or exercise the charge or direction of (operations or affairs); to look after, oversee, supervise the working or management of (an institution, etc.). **b.** To exercise supervision over (a person) 1776. **c.** *intr.* with †*over*, or *absol.* 1663.

The King will appoint Commissioners in the nature of a Council, who may s. the works of this nature, and regulate what concerns the colonies BACON.

Su:perinte·ndence. 1603. [f. as next; see -ENCE.] The function or occupation of a superintendent; the action or work of superintending.

Su:perinte·ndency. 1598. [– med.L. *superintendentia*, f. as next; see -ENCY.] **1.** The office or position of a superintendent; superintendence. **2.** A district (*spec.* in the Lutheran Church, a collection of parishes) under the charge of a superintendent; in China, one of the administrative divisions of the country 1762.

1. The S. of Providence STEELE.

Superintendent (s¹ū:pərinte·ndĕnt), *sb.* and *a.* 1554. [– eccl.L. *superintendens, -ent-*, pr. pple. of *superintendere*; see prec., -ENT.] **A.** *sb.* One who superintends. **1.** An officer or official who has the chief charge, oversight, control, or direction of some business, institution, or works; an overseer. Also *transf.* and *gen.* 1575. **2.** *Eccl.* **a.** As tr. Gr. ἐπίσκοπος 'overseer' (see BISHOP) of the N.T.; used controversially instead of 'bishop' by extreme Protestant reformers of the 16th c., and subsequently by Papists with ref. to bishops of the Church of England. *Obs.* exc. *Hist.* 1554. **b.** *spec.* among the Lutherans, a minister who has control of the churches and pastors of a particular district 1560. **c.** In the Church of Scotland, a minister chosen to preside over a district and to ordain. *Hist.* 1561. **d.** The name given by John Wesley to men whom he ordained to act as bishops in the U.S.; now, among the Wesleyan Methodists, the presiding minister of a circuit 1784.

1. The Super-intendent over all the other Civil and Criminal Ministers 1653.

B. *sb.* Superintending; exercising superintendence or oversight; holding the position of a superintendent. Now (in English use) chiefly in designations of officials. 1597.

The s. visiting officer of the London wards 1913. Hence **Su:perinte·ndentship.**

Superior (s¹upī³·riəɹ), *a.* and *sb.* late ME. [– OFr. *superiour* (mod. *supérieur*) – L. *superior, -ōr-*, compar. of *superus* that is above, f. *super-*; see SUPER-, -IOR.] **A.** *adj.* **1.** Higher in local position; situated above or further up than something else; upper; †heavenly, celestial. Now chiefly in techn. use. **b.** *predic.*, quasi-adv.: In or into a higher position; higher; upward. *poet.* 1718. **2.** Higher in rank or dignity; more exalted in social or official status 1485. **3.** Higher in ideal or abstract rank, or in a scale or series; of a higher nature or character. Sometimes, supernatural, superhuman. 1533. **b.** *Logic.* Having greater extension 1843. **4.** Higher in degree, amount, quality, importance, or other respect; of greater value or consideration 1579. **5.** Const. *to* (†occas. *with, than*). **a.** Higher in status or quality than; hence, greater or better than; †formerly also *advb.* = more or better than, above, beyond 1526. **b.** Too great or strong to be overcome or affected by; above the influence or reach of 1647. **c.** Transcending, on a higher plane than 1841. **6.** Characteristic of one who is superior (in senses 2, 3); also, from sense 5 b, 'free from emotion or concern; unconquered; unaffected' (J.). *poet.* or *rhet.* 1667. **b.** Applied ironically to persons of lofty, supercilious, or dictatorial manner or behaviour (or to their actions, etc.) 1864. **c.** *advb.* In a superior style; with a superior air 1716. **7.** In a positive or absolute sense (admitting comparison with *more* and *most*): Supereminent in degree, amount, or (most commonly) quality; surpassing the generality of its class or kind 1777. **8.** *Astr.* **a.** Applied to those planets whose orbits lie outside that of the earth (orig., according to the Ptolemaic astronomy, as having their spheres above that of the sun). **b.** *S. meridian*: that part of the celestial meridian which lies above the pole: so *s. passage* (of the meridian), etc. 1583. **9.** *Bot.* Growing above some other part or organ: said of the ovary when situated above or free from the (*inferior*) calyx, and of the calyx when adherent to the sides of the (*inferior*) ovary so that the calyx-lobes are above the ovary 1785. **10.** *Anat.* and *Zool.* Applied to parts or organs situated above, or in a higher position than, others of the same kind (dist. as *inferior*), or above the usual or normal position 1733. **11.** *Printing.* Applied to small letters or figures, or other characters, made to range above the line, at or near the top of the ordinary letters 1683.

1. The superiour or high India 1553. The s.. portions of the earth's crust 1838. **2.** He says he obeyed s. orders CARLYLE. *Father* or *Mother S.* = B. 2. **3.** Conscience..supposes some s. law informing men to do, or not do a thing 1660. **4.** She escaped by s. sailing 1798. **5. a.** He was..s. in numbers to the enemy 1907. **b.** To that foible even she was not s. SCOTT. **6.** Here passion first I felt,..in all enjoyments else Superiour and unmov'd MILT. **b.** The 's.' person who posed as an authority on matters of culture 1897. **7.** What a woman she was—what a s. creature! THACKERAY.

B. *sb.* **1.** A person of higher rank or dignity; one who is above others in social or official station; *esp.* a superior officer or official 1483. **2.** The head of a community of religious (a monastery, nunnery, convent, abbey, etc.); also, the head of a religious order or congregation, or of a department of it 1497. **3.** *Feudal Law.* One who (or the successor of one who) has granted an estate of heritable property to another (termed the *vassal*) on condition of the annual payment of a certain sum or the performance or certain services 1538. **4.** A person, or (less commonly) a thing, of higher quality or value than another; one that excels another in some respect 1634. **5.** *Printing.* A superior letter or figure 1726.

1. The Rebukes and Censures of Superiours 1659. In respectable conformity to the commands of my ecclesiastical superiors 1817. **2.** The S. of the Passionist Monks 1844. **3.** *Subject s.*, a s. who holds as subject of a sovereign. **4.** No one is the s. of the invincible Socrates in argument JOWETT. Hence **Supe·rioress**, a female s. a mother s. **Supe·riorly** *adv.* in a s. place, degree, or manner.

Superiority (siupīᵊriǫ·rĭti). 1495. [– (O)Fr. *supériorité* or med.L. *superioritas*, f. *superior*; see prec., -ITY.] The quality or condition of being superior; also, an instance of this.

They lost their s. in Greece by the ill-fought battle of Leuctra 1770. All nobility in its beginnings was somebody's natural s. EMERSON.

Superlative (siupɔ̄·ɹlătiv), *a.* and *sb.* late ME. [– (O)Fr. *superlatif, -ive* – late L. *superlativus*, f. L. *superlatus* (used as pa. pple. of *superferre*), f. *super-* SUPER- II + *lat-*, pa. ppl. stem of *tollere* take away; see -IVE.] **A.** *adj.* **1.** *Gram.* Applied to that inflexional form of an adj. or adv. used in comparing a number of things, to express the highest degree of the quality or attribute denoted by the simple word, as *sweet-est, tru-est, often-est* (or to the periphrasis used in the same sense, as *most sweet, most true, most often*); the adj. or adv. is then said to be in the *s. degree.* Freq. used *allus.* **b.** Exaggerative, hyperbolical 1588. **2.** Raised above or surpassing all others; extremely high, great, or excellent; supereminent, supreme. late ME.

2. Gowere and chaucere,..Superlatiue as poetis laureate 1423. Queene Elizabeth,..worthy of s. praise HOLLAND.

B. *sb.* **1.** *Gram.* The superlative degree; an adjective or adverb in the superlative degree. (Also, by extension, any word denoting the highest degree of some quality.) 1530. **b.** *transf.* An exaggerated or hyperbolical expression; usu. *pl.*, exaggerated language or phraseology 1597. **2.** A person or thing surpassing all others of the class or kind; the highest example (*of* a quality). Now *rare*, and with allusion to sense 1. 1600. **3.** The highest or utmost degree of something; the acme 1583.

1. *fig.* Virginity you say is delightful, yet matrimony more pleasant: Virginity you put in the positiue, but matrimonie in the superlatiue GREENE. **b.** He thought and felt in superlatives 1896. Hence **Supe·rlative-ly** *adv.*, **-ness.**

Superlunary (siūpəɹliū·nări), *a.* 1614. [– med.L. *superlunaris*, f. L. *super-* SUPER- I. 1 + *luna* moon; see -ARY², and cf. SUPRALUNARY, SUBLUNARY.] Situated above or beyond the moon; belonging to a higher world, celestial; *fig.* extravagant: the opposite of *sublunary*. So **Superlu·nar** *a.* 1742.

Superman (siū·pəɹmæn). 1903. [f. SUPER- II. 3 + MAN *sb.*, tr. by G. B. Shaw of G. *übermensch* (Nietzsche).] An ideal superior man conceived by F. W. Nietzsche (German philosopher, 1844–1900) as being evolved from the normal human type. Also *transf.* and *allus.*

Like Nietzsche, the modern German believes that the world must be ruled by a super-man, and that he is the super-man 1912.

Supermu·ndane, *a.* 1677. [– med.L. *supermundanus* (Thomas Aquinas), f. *super-* SUPER- I. 1 + *mundus*; cf. MUNDANE.] Elevated in nature or character above what pertains to the earth or world; belonging to a region above the world.

‖**Supernaculum** (siūpəɹnæ·kiŭlŏm), *adv.* and *sb. slang.* 1592. [mod.L. tr. G. *auf den nagel* on to the nail, in phr. *auf den nagel trinken* to drink off liquor to the last drop.] **A.** *adv.* Used in ref. to the practice of turning up the emptied cup or glass on one's left thumbnail, to show that all the liquor has been drunk; hence, to the last drop, to the bottom.

He drank thy health five times, *s.* DRYDEN.

B. *sb.* **1.** A liquor to be drunk to the last drop; a wine of the highest quality; hence, anything excellent of its kind 1704. **2.** A draught that empties the cup to the last drop; also, a full cup, a bumper 1827. Hence **Superna·cular** *a.* (of drink) excellent.

Supernal (siupɔ̄·ɹnăl), *a.* (*sb.*) 1483. [– OFr. *supernal* or med.L. *supernalis*, f. L. *supernus*, f. *super*; see SUPER-, -AL¹. Cf. EXTERNAL.] **A.** *adj.* **1.** That is above or on high; existing or dwelling in the heavens 1485. **2.** Belonging to the realm or state above this world or this present life; pertaining to a higher state of existence; coming from above 1483. **3. a.** Situated in, or belonging to, the sky or upper regions; celestial, heavenly. *Obs.* or *arch.* 1503. **b.** Situated above or at the top, upper; above ground; lofty in position (*rare*) 1599. **4.** High in rank or dignity, exalted 1549. **5.** Supremely great or excellent, 'divine' 1818. **B.** *sb.* A supernal being (*rare*) 1755.

A. 1. That s. Iudge that stirs good thoughts SHAKS. **2.** Errands of s. Grace MILT. **4.** He hath put downe the mightie ones From their supernall seate 1549. Hence **Supe·rnally** *adv.*

Supernatural (siūpəɹnæ·tiŭrăl, -tʃərăl), *a.* (*sb.*) 1526. [– med.L. *supernaturalis* (Thomas Aquinas), f. *super-* SUPER- II. 1 a + *natura*; see -AL¹.] **A.** *adj.* **1.** That is above nature; transcending the powers or the ordinary course of nature. **b.** *transf.* Relating to, dealing with, or characterized by what is above nature 1569. **2.** More than the natural or ordinary; abnormal, extraordinary. *Obs.* or *arch.* 1533.

1. Inspiration..termed s. properly, in Contradistinction to all Knowledge resulting from the common Laws of Nature 1749. The pestilences which desolated nations were deemed s. 1865. **b.** Lady Hester Stanhope's conversation on s. topics KINGLAKE. **2.** Suddenly animated with s. strength 1797.

B. *absol.* or *sb.* **1.** *absol.* with *the.* That which is supernatural 1830. **2.** *sb. pl.* Supernatural things 1587. **3.** A supernatural being 1729.

1. The introduction of the s. and marvellous SCOTT. Hence **Su:pernatura·lity,** the quality of being s.; something that is s., a s. object, occurrence, etc. **Superna·tural-ly** *adv.*, **-ness.**

Superna·turalism. 1799. [f. prec. + -ISM.] **1.** Supernatural character or quality; a system or collection of supernatural agencies, events, etc. Rarely in *pl.* **2.** Belief in the supernatural; a theory or doctrine which admits or asserts the reality of supernatural beings, powers, events, etc. 1809. So **Superna·turalist,** an adherent of s. 1650. **Su:pernaturali·stic** *a.* holding the belief of a supernaturalist; of or belonging to supernaturalists; pertaining to or involving s.

Superna·turalize, *v.* 1643. [f. as prec. + -IZE.] *trans.* To make supernatural; to impart or attribute a supernatural character to.

Supernature (siū·pəɹnē¹tiŭɹ, -tʃəɹ). 1844. [f. SUPER- + NATURE, after *supernatural.*] A supernatural realm or system of things; something supernatural.

Superno·rmal, *a.* 1868. [SUPER- II. 1 a.] **1.** Exceeding that which is normal. **2.** Applied to phenomena of an extraordinary kind, involving a higher law or principle than those ordinarily occurring, but not necessarily supernatural 1885. Hence **Superno·rmally** *adv.*

Supernumerary (siūpəɹniū·mĕrări), *a.* and *sb.* 1605. [– late L. *supernumerarius* applied to soldiers added to a legion after it is complete, f. *super numerum*; see SUPER- III. 3 and -ARY¹.] **A.** *adj.* **1.** That is beyond or in excess of the usual, proper, regular, stated, or prescribed number or †quantity; additional, extra, left over. Now *rare* in gen. sense. **b.** *spec.* Applied to an official, officer, or employee not formally belonging to the regular body or staff, but associated with it to assist in case of need or emergency 1624. **c.** *Bot.* and *Zool.* Applied to structures or organs occurring (either in individuals or in types) in addition to the normal ones 1733. **2.** That is beyond the number needed or desired; superfluous, unnecessary. Now *rare*. 1610.

1. I have had s. Copies wrought off HEARNE. **b.** To be a s. Usher in his Schoole 1683.

B. *sb.* **1.** A supernumerary person or thing; *esp.* a supernumerary official or employee 1639. **b.** On board ship, a sailor, or one of a body of sailors, over and above the ship's complement 1666. **c.** An additional officer attached to a body of men in the army or navy for some special purpose 1796. **d.** A retired Wesleyan minister 1791. **e.** *Theatr.* A person employed in addition to the regular company, who appears on the stage but does not speak. Colloq. abbrev. *super* (see SUPER *sb.* 2). 1836.

b. The whole crew with our black supernumeraries 1833.

Supero- (siū·pĕro), mod. comb. form of L. *superus* that is above, upper (see SUPERIOR), in terms of anatomy and zoology, designating parts situated above or on the upper side. **a.** in adjs., as **Supero-ante·rior** *a.*, situated above and in front; **Supero-exte·rnal** *a.*, situated above and on the outside. **b.** in derived advs., as *supero-externally, -posteriorly.*

Su:perocci·pital, *a.* and *sb.* 1854. [SUPER- I. 1 b.] *Anat.* and *Zool.* **A.** *adj.* Situated at the upper part of the occiput or back of the head. **B.** *sb.* The s. bone, an element of the skull usu. forming part of the occipital bone, but in some lower vertebrates constituting a distinct bone.

Supero·rdinate, *a.* (*sb.*) 1620. [f. SUPER- II, after *subordinate.*] **A.** *adj.* Superior in rank: opp. to SUBORDINATE. Now only in *Logic.* **B.** *sb.* One who is superior in rank 1802.

Su:perordina·tion. 1655. [– late (eccl.) L. *superordinatio, -ōn-* choice of a bishop's successor, f. *superordinare*; see SUPER- IV. 1, ORDINATION.] **1.** Ordination of a person, while another still holds an office, to succeed him in that office when it shall become vacant. **2.** *Logic.* The action of superordinating or condition of being superordinated; superordinate position or relation 1864.

†**Su:perparti·cular,** *a.* (*sb.*) 1557. [– late L. *superparticularis* (Boethius); see SUPER- IV. 2, PARTICULAR.] *Arith.* Applied to a ratio in which the antecedent contains the consequent once with one aliquot part over (e.g. 1½, 1⅓, 1¼ times), i.e. the ratio of any number to the next below it (³⁄₂, ⁴⁄₃, ⁵⁄₄). Also *sb.*, a superparticular ratio. –1842.

†**Superpa·rtient,** *a.* (*sb.*) 1557. [– late L. *superpartiens, -ent-* (Boethius), f. *super* SUPER- IV. 2 + *partiens*, pr. pple. of L. *partiri* divide; see -ENT and cf. prec.] *Arith.* Applied to a ratio in which the antecedent contains the consequent once with any number (greater than one) of aliquot parts over. Also *sb.*, a superpartient ratio. –1788.

Superpho·sphate. 1797. [SUPER- III, 4 b.] **1.** *Chem.* A phosphate containing an excess of phosphoric acid; an acid phosphate. **2.** In full *s. of lime*: an impure superphosphate of lime prepared by treating bones, coprolites, etc. with sulphuric acid, and used as a manure 1843.

†**Su·perplus.** Chiefly *Sc.* 1561. [– med.L. *superplus*; see SUPER- IV. 1, PLUS, and cf. SURPLUS.] = SURPLUS –1825. So †**Superplusage,** surplusage 1450.

Superpose (s¹ūpəɹpōᵘ·z), *v.* 1823. [– Fr. *superposer*, f. *super-* SUPER- I. 2 + *poser* POSE, after L. *superponere* (see next).] **1.** *trans.* To place above or upon something else. Usu. in *pa. pple.*; often loosely of two or more things in a vertical series (= placed one above or upon another). **2.** *Physics*, etc. To bring into the same position so as to coincide; to cause to occupy or coexist in the same space without destroying one another, as two or more sets of physical conditions (e.g. light-rays, etc.), or one such in relation to another 1831. **b.** *Geom.* To transfer (one magnitude) ideally to the space occupied by another, esp. so as to show that they coincide 1870.

1. *fig.* Bursting through the network superpos'd By selfish occupation M. ARNOLD.

Superposition (s¹ū:pəɹpŏzi·ʃən). 1656. [– Fr. *superposition* or late L. *superpositio, -ōn-*; see SUPER- I. 2, IV. 1, POSITION.] **1.** *gen.* The placing of one thing on or above another; an instance of this 1828. **2.** *Geom.* The action of ideally transferring one figure into the position occupied by another, esp. so as to show that they coincide 1656. **b.** *Physics*, etc. The action of causing two or more sets of physical conditions or phenomena (e.g. undulations) to coincide, or coexist in the same place; the fact of such coincidence or coexistence 1830. **3.** *Geol.* The deposition of one stratum upon another, or the condition of being so deposited 1799. **4.** *Bot.* The relative position of leaves, etc., on an axis, when situated directly above one another, not alternating 1880.

Superre·alism. 1935. = SURREALISM.

Su·per-roy:al, *a.* 1612. [SUPER- II. 1.] **1.** That is above royal or kingly rank; higher than royal (*rare*). **2.** Designating a size of paper next above that called *royal* (ROYAL *a.* II. 4), measuring about 19–21 inches by 27–28 inches 1681.

1. The Popes superroiall power 1612.

Supersalt (s¹ū·pəɹsǫlt). 1806. [f. SUPER- III. 4 b + SALT *sb.*¹] *Chem.* A salt containing an excess of the acid over the base.

Supersa·turate, *v.* 1788. [f. SUPER- III. 1 b; after Fr. *sursaturer*.] *trans.* To saturate to excess; to add more of some other substance to (a given substance) than is sufficient to saturate it; chiefly in *Chem.* and *Physics.* Hence **Su:persatura·tion,** the action of supersaturating or condition of being supersaturated.

Superscribe (s¹ūpəɹskrəi·b, s¹ū·pəɹskrəib), *v.* 1598. [– L. *superscribere*, f. *super* SUPER- I. 2 + *scribere* write.] **1.** *trans.* To inscribe or mark *with* writing on the surface or upper part; to write upon; to put an inscription on or over 1605. **2.** *spec.* To write a name, address, or direction on the outside or cover of; to address (a letter, etc.) *to* a person. *arch.* 1598. **b.** To write (a name or address) upon a letter 1728. **3.** To write one's name at the head of a document 1611. **4.** To write (a letter or word) above another, or above the line of writing 1776.

1. He received a Message. .superscribed *With Speed* STEELE. **2.** An envelope, superscribed *To Mr. Skinner, Merchant* MACAULAY.

Superscript (s¹ū·pəɹskript), *sb.* and *a.* 1588. [– L. *superscriptus, -um*, pa. pple. of *superscribere*; see prec., SCRIPT.] †**A.** *sb.* = next 3. SHAKS. **B.** *adj.* Written above a letter, or above the line of writing: opp. to SUBSCRIPT B. 1861.

A. *L.L.L.* IV. ii. 135.

Superscription (s¹ūpəɹskri·pʃən). late ME. [– late L. *superscriptio, -ōn-*, f. *superscript-*, pa. ppl. stem of L. *superscribere*; see prec., -ION.] That which is superscribed. **1.** A piece of writing or an inscription upon or above something. *arch.* (after Matt. 22:20, etc.). **2.** *spec.* A piece of writing at the head or beginning of a document; a heading. late ME. **3.** The address or direction on a letter. *Obs.* or *arch.* 1518. **4.** A name signed; a signature. *Obs.* or *arch. rare.* 1681.

1. *fig.* I learn. .How counterfeit a coin they are who friends Bear in their S. MILT. **2.** *S.*, the sign ℞ before a prescription 1901.

Supersede (s¹ūpəɹsī·d), *v.* 1527. [In early use often *-cede*; – OFr. *supercéder*, later *-séder* – L. *supersedēre* (in med.L. often *-cedere*) set above, be superior to, refrain from, omit, f. *super* SUPER- I, II + *sedēre* sit.] †**1.** *trans.* To desist from, discontinue (a procedure, an attempt, etc.); not to proceed with –1750. †**b.** *intr.* To desist, forbear, refrain –1850. †**2.** To refrain from (discourse, disquisition); to omit to mention, refrain from mentioning –1689. †**3.** To put a stop to (legal proceedings, etc.); to stop, stay –1838. **b.** *Law.* To discharge by a writ of supersedeas 1817. †**4.** To render superfluous or unnecessary –1797. **5.** To make of no effect; to render void, nugatory, or useless; to annul; to override. Now *rare* or *Obs.* 1654. **6.** *pass.* To be set aside as useless or obsolete; to be replaced *by* something regarded as superior 1642. **7.** To take the place of (something set aside or abandoned); to succeed to the place occupied by; to serve, be adopted or accepted instead of 1660. **8.** To supply the place of (a person deprived of or removed from an office or position) *by* another; also, to promote another over the head of; *pass.* to be removed from office to make way for another 1710. **b.** To supply the place of (a thing) 1861. **9.** Of a person: To take the place of (some one removed from an office, or †promoted); to succeed and supplant (a person) in a position of any kind 1777.

5. The Norman invader superseded Anglo-Saxon institutions 1863. **6.** When this work must be superseded by a more perfect history 1838. **7.** Oxen were superseding horses in farm-work 1866. **9.** Captain Maling takes his passage to s. Captain Nisbet in the Bonne Citoyenne NELSON.

‖**Supersedeas** (s¹ūpəɹsī·diæs). late ME. [L., = you shall desist (see prec.).] **1.** *Law.* A writ commanding the stay of legal proceedings which ought otherwise to have proceeded, or suspending the powers of an officer: so called from the occurrence of the word in the writ. More fully *writ of s.* †**2.** *fig.* Something which stops, stays, or checks –1737.

2. A Supersedias for her loue was euery new-come frend 1592.

‖**Supersedere** (s¹ū:pəɹsīdīᵊ·ri). *Sc. Law.* 1547. [L. (see SUPERSEDE).] A judicial order or a private agreement granting protection to a debtor.

Supersedure (-sī·diŭɹ). *U.S.* 1788. [f. SUPERSEDE + -URE.] = SUPERSESSION.

Superse·nsual, *a.* 1683. [SUPER- II. 1 a.] That is above or beyond (the power of) the senses, or higher than what is perceived by the senses; also, relating to such things as transcend sense; often = spiritual. Also *absol.* with *the*.

Superse·rviceable, *a.* 1605. [SUPER- III. 1 a.] More serviceable than is required or fitting; officious. SHAKS.

Supersession (s¹ūpəɹse·ʃən). 1656. [f. SUPERSEDE *v.*, phonetically after pairs like *concede/concession*, with confusion of *-cede, -sede* as in SUPERSEDE.] The action of superseding or condition of being superseded.

Supersonic (s¹ūpəɹsǫ·nik), *a.* 1919. [f. SUPER- II. 1 a + L. *sonus* SOUND *sb.* + -IC.] **1.** Of or pertaining to sound-waves of such a high frequency as to be inaudible. **2.** Exceeding the speed of sound in the medium concerned 1945.

Superstition (s¹ūpəɹsti·ʃən). late ME. [– (O)Fr. *superstition* or L. *superstitio, -ōn-*, f. *superstare* stand on or over, f. *super-* SUPER- I. 2 + *stare* stand; see -TION.] **1.** Unreasoning awe or fear of something unknown, mysterious, or imaginary, esp. in connection with religion; religious belief or practice founded upon fear or ignorance 1538. **b.** An irrational religious belief or practice; a tenet, scruple, habit, etc. founded on fear or ignorance. late ME. **2.** An irrational religious system; a false, pagan, or idolatrous religion. Now *rare* or *Obs.* 1526. **b.** A religious ceremony or observance of a pagan or idolatrous character. Now *rare* or *Obs.* 1529. **3.** *transf.* (from 1). Irrational or unfounded belief in general; an unreasonable or groundless notion 1794.

1. S. is, when things are either abhord or obserued, with a zealous or fearefull, but erroneous relation to God HOOKER. **b.** When they began to say, that. .all wine was an abomination, they pass'd into a direct s. JER. TAYLOR. **2.** The Turks received the Mahometane s. 1603. **3.** Of the political superstitions,. .none is so universally diffused as the notion that majorities are omnipotent SPENCER.

Superstitious (s¹ūpəɹsti·ʃəs), *a.* late ME. [– (O)Fr. *superstitieux* or L. *superstitiosus*, f. *superstitio*; see prec., -OUS.] **1.** Of the nature of, involving, or characterized by superstition. **2.** Subject or addicted to superstition; believing or practising superstitions 1526. †**b.** Idolatrously or extravagantly devoted –1704. †**3.** Over-scrupulous; punctilious; extremely careful or particular –1816. **4.** Used in or regarded with superstition; venerated, observed, or believed in, in the way of superstition. Now *rare* or *Obs.* 1566. †**b.** Magical; credited with supernatural efficacy –1651. †**5.** Extraordinary; excessive; superfluous –1640.

1. Their S. Belief, of Ghosts, Spirits, Dæmons, Devils, Fayries, and Hob-goblins 1678. *S. uses* (Law), 'where lands, tenements, or goods, are given for the maintenance of persons to pray for the souls of dead men in purgatory, or to maintain perpetual obits, lamps, etc.' **2.** It seem'd. . to a S. eye the haunt Of Wood-Gods and Wood-Nymphs MILT. **b.** *Hen. VIII*, III. i. 131. **5.** They . .have such a s. conceit of their owne merit and temper [etc.] 1638. Hence **Supersti·tious-ly** *adv.*, **-ness.**

Superstruct (s¹ū·pəɹstrɒkt), *v.* Now *rare* or *Obs.* 1642. [– *superstruct-*, pa. ppl. stem of L. *superstruere*, f. *super* SUPER- I. 2 + *struere* build.] To build upon something else; to construct upon a foundation; to erect as a superstructure. Usu. *fig.* or in fig. context. Also *absol.*

Those. .on whose approbation his esteem of himself was superstructed JOHNSON.

Superstructive (s¹ūpəɹstrɒ·ktiv), *a.* (*sb.*) Now *rare.* 1625. [f. prec. + -IVE.] **A.** *adj.* Belonging to the superstructure; opp. to *fundamental* 1642. †**B.** *sb.* Something belonging to or constituting the superstructure –1644. So †**Superstru·ctor,** one who builds a superstructure.

Superstructure (s¹ū·pəɹstrɒktiŭɹ, -tʃəɹ). 1641. [f. SUPER- I. 3 + STRUCTURE.] **1.** A building considered in relation to its foundation; an upper part of a building, erected upon a lower supporting part; any material structure resting on something else as a foundation 1645. **2.** *fig.* An immaterial structure, as of thought, action, etc., figured as being built upon something else as a foundation 1641.

1. In som Places, as in Amsterdam, the Foundation costs more than the S. 1645.

Supersubstantial (s¹ū:pəɹsŏbstæ·nʃăl), *a.* 1534. [– eccl.L. (Vulg.) *supersubstantialis*, f. L. *super-* SUPER- II. 1 a + *substantia* SUBSTANCE; see -AL¹.] **1.** In allusion to late L. *supersubstantialis* in the Vulgate version of Matt. 6:11 (tr. Gr. ἐπιούσιος, which is now usu.

held to mean 'pertaining to the coming day'). Above or transcending material substance; spiritual: esp. in ref. to the eucharistic bread. **2.** Above or transcending all substance or being: chiefly of God 1534. So **Su:persubsta·ntiate** *v.* [after *transubstantiate*] *trans.* to make s.

Superterranean (s¹u:pəɹtĕrēⁱ·nĭăn), *a.* (*sb.*) 1691. [f. after SUBTERRANEAN by prefix-substitution; see SUPER- 1 a.] That is or dwells above, or on the surface of, the earth; above-ground: opp. to *subterranean*. Also *sb.*, a dweller above ground or on the earth.
Numerous chambers both s. and subterranean 1816. So **Su:perterra·neous** *a.* 1671.

Superterrene (s¹ū:pəɹterī·n), *a.* 1709. [f. after earlier SUBTERRENE by prefix-substitution; cf. late L. *superterrenus* (Tertullian).] **1.** = prec. **2.** = next 1. 1755.

Superterrestrial (s¹ū:pəɹtĕre·striăl), *a.* 1727. [See SUPER- I. 1 a and TERRESTRIAL.] **1.** Existing, or belonging to a region, above the earth. **2.** = SUPERTERRANEAN 1875.

Su·pertonic. 1806. [SUPER- II. 2 b.] *Mus.* The note next above the tonic; the second of the scale. Also *attrib.* applied to a chord having this note for its root.

Supervene (s¹ūpəɹvī·n), *v.* 1647. [– L. *supervenire*, f. *super* SUPER- IV. 1 + *venire* come.] **1.** *intr.* To come on or occur as something additional or extraneous; to come directly or shortly after something else, either as a consequence of it or in contrast with it; to follow closely upon some other occurrence or condition. †**2.** *trans.* To come directly or soon after, to follow closely; occas. to come after so as to take the place of, to supersede –1810.
1. Upon a sudden supervened the death of the king 1647. Typhus supervening on a gunshot wound 1870.

Supervenience (s¹ūpəɹvī·niĕns). *rare.* 1644. [f. next; see -ENCE.] The fact of being supervenient, or of supervening; supervention.

Supervenient (s¹ūpəɹvī·niĕnt), *a.* 1594. [– L. *superveniens, -ent-*, pr. pple. of *supervenire*; see SUPERVENE, -ENT.] Supervening; coming on something as an extraneous addition; coming on after (and in connection or contrast with) something else; occurring subsequently.
Some s. cause of discord may overpower this original amity JOHNSON.

Supervention (s¹ūpəɹve·nʃən). 1649. [– late L. *superventio, -ōn-*, f. *supervent-*, pa. ppl. stem of L. *supervenire*; see SUPERVENE, -ION; in later use partly f. SUPERVENE.] The action or fact of supervening; coming on in addition; subsequent occurrence.

Supervisal (s¹ū·pəɹvəizăl). Now *rare.* 1652. [f. SUPERVISE + -AL¹ 2.] = SUPERVISION.

Supervise (s¹ū·pəɹvəiz), *v.* 1588. [– *supervis-*, pa. ppl. stem of med.L. *supervidēre*, f. L. *super* SUPER- I. 2 + *vidēre* see.] †**1.** *trans.* To look over, survey, inspect; to read through, peruse –1711. †**b.** *spec.* To read through for correction; to revise –1751. **2.** To oversee, have the oversight of, superintend the execution or performance of (a thing), the movements or work of (a person) 1645. **3.** †**Supervise** *sb.* SHAKS.

Supervision (s¹ūpəɹvi·ʒən). 1640. [– med. L. *supervisio, -ōn-*, f. as prec.; see -ION.] The action or function of supervising; oversight, superintendence.

Supervisor (s¹ū·pəɹvəizəɹ). 1454. [– med. L. *supervisor*, f. as prec.; see -OR 2. In later use f. SUPERVISE.] One who supervises. **1.** A person who exercises general direction or control over a business, a body of workmen, etc.; one who inspects and directs the work of others. †**b.** = OVERSEER *sb.* 1 b. –1767. **c.** An inspector of highways; now only *U.S.* a road-master on a railway 1555. †**2.** An onlooker, spectator, observer –1610. **3.** One who reads over, esp. for the purpose of correction; a reviser. Now *rare* or *Obs.* 1624.
1. d. In some of the United States, an elected official charged with the administration of a township or other county subdivision 1882. **e.** *U.S.* One who supervises the courses and the teachers in a school. Hence **Su·pervisorship,** the office or function of a s.

Supervisory (s¹ūpəɹvəi·zŏri), *a.* 1847. [f. SUPERVISE + -ORY².] Having the function of supervising; of, pertaining to, or exercising supervision.

Supinate (s¹ū·pineⁱt), *v.* 1831. [Back-formation from next; cf. PRONATE *v.*] *Physiol. trans.* To turn (the hand or fore limb) so that the back of it is downward or backward; to turn (the leg) outwards. Opp. to PRONATE *v.*

Supination (s¹ūpinēⁱ·ʃən). 1666. [– L. *supinatio, -ōn-*, f. *supinat-*, pa. ppl. stem of *supinare*, f. *supinus*; see SUPINE *a.*, -ION.] *Physiol.* The action of turning the hand or fore limb so that the back of it is downward or backward; the position of a limb so turned. (Opp. to PRONATION.)

Supinator (s¹ū·pinēⁱtǫɹ). 1615. [– mod.L. *supinator*, f. as prec.; see -OR 2.] *Anat.* A muscle by which supination is effected or assisted; *spec.* one of two muscles of the forearm or fore limb, *s. radii brevis* and *s. radii longus*.

Supine (s¹ū·pəin), *sb.* 1522. [– late L. *supinum*, n. sing. of L. *supinus* (see next) used subst.; cf. Fr. *supin*; this usage has not been satisfactorily explained.] *Gram.* In Latin grammar, applied to forms of a verbal noun, the one an accus. sing. ending in *-tum* or *-sum*, used with vbs. of motion and called the *first* or †*former s.*, the other a locative sing. ending in *-tu* or *-su*, used with adjs. and called the *second* or †*latter s.* (The term is applied by some grammarians to the English infinitive with *to*, as in OE. *tó scéawienne*, mod. Eng. *to show*.)

Supine (s¹ūpəi·n, s¹ū·pəin), *a.* 1500. [– L. *supinus*, f. Italic **sup-*, root of *super* above, *superus* higher; see -INE¹.] **1.** Lying on one's back, lying with the face or front upwards. Also said of the position. **b.** Of the hand or arm: With the palm upward; supinated 1668. **c.** Of a part of the body: Situated so as to be upward; upper, superior 1661. **d.** *transf.* Sloping or inclining backwards. *poet.* 1697. **2.** *fig.* Morally or mentally inactive, inert, or indolent 1603. **b.** Not active; passive 1843.
1. They buried their dead on their backs, or in a s. position SIR T. BROWNE. **d.** If the Vine On rising Ground be plac'd, or Hills s. DRYDEN. **2.** The s. slaves Of blind authority SHELLEY. The listless and s. life which he had been leading THACKERAY. Hence **Supine-ly** *adv.*, **-ness.**

†**Supi·nity.** 1548. [f. SUPINE *a.* + -ITY.] **1.** Supine behaviour or state of mind; inertness –1750. **2.** Posture with the face upward (*rare*) –1755.

‖**Suppedaneum** (sɒpĭdēⁱ·nĭŏm). 1863. [Late and med.L., = footstool, *scabellum*, subst. use of n. adj. *suppedaneus* under the feet, f. *sub-* SUB- + *pes, ped-* foot.] A support for the feet of a crucified person, projecting from the vertical shaft of the cross. So †**Suppeda·neous** *a. rare.* 1646–1711.

†**Suppe·ditate,** *v.* 1535. [– *suppeditat-*, pa. ppl. stem of L. *suppeditare*.] *trans.* To furnish, supply –1754.

Suppeditation (sɒpeditēⁱ·ʃən). Now *rare* or *Obs.* 1605. [– L. *suppeditatio, -ōn-*, f. as prec.; see -ION.] The action of supplying what is needful; supply.

Supper (sɒ·pəɹ), *sb.* [ME. *supe·r(e, sope·r(e*, and *su·per, so·per*, later *soupper, sopper, supper* – OFr. *soper, super* (mod. *souper*), subst. use of *soper* SUP *v.*²; see -ER⁴.] **1.** The last meal of the day; (contextually) the hour at which this is taken, supper-time. (Formerly, the last of the three meals of the day (breakfast, dinner, and supper); now, the last substantial meal of the day when dinner is taken in the middle of the day, or a late meal following an early evening dinner.) Often without article, demonstrative, possessive, or the like, esp. when governed by a prep. (*to have s.; at, to, for, after s.*). **2.** *spec.* **a.** *The Last S.*: the last meal taken by Jesus Christ with the Apostles before his crucifixion, at which he instituted the Eucharist ME. **b.** *The Lord's S., the Dominical S., the S.*: the Eucharist or Holy Communion 1533.
attrib. and *Comb.*, as *s.-dance, -dish, -table, -things*; **s.-party,** a party assembled at s., a social gathering of this kind; **-quadrille,** the quadrille danced just before s.; **-room,** a room in which s. is served; **-time,** the time at which s. is (normally) taken.

Su·pper, *v.* 1622. [f. prec.] **1.** *trans.* **a.** To provide with supper; to entertain at supper. **b.** To give (horses, cattle, etc.) their evening food and bed them down for the night. Chiefly *Sc.* and *n. dial.* 1816. **2.** *intr.* To take one's supper; to sup 1691.
1. We intend to dinner him and s. him round, and by degrees make him our own 1715.

Supperless (sɒ·pəɹlės), *a.* 1515. [-LESS.] Without supper.
They'le..send him supperlesse to bed B. JONS.

Supping (sɒ·piŋ), *vbl. sb.*¹ late ME. [f. SUP *v.*¹ + -ING¹.] **1.** The action of SUP *v.*¹; drinking by spoonfuls or mouthfuls. **2.** Chiefly *pl.* Food (*sing.* a food) that can be supped; *esp.* broth. Now *dial.* late ME.

Supping (sɒ·piŋ), *vbl. sb.*² late ME. [f. SUP *v.*² + -ING¹.] The action of taking supper.

Supplant (sŏplɑ·nt), *v.* ME. [– (O)Fr. *supplanter* or L. *supplantare* trip up, overthrow, f. *sub-* SUB- 25 + *planta* sole of the foot.] †**1.** *trans.* To trip up, cause to stumble or fall by tripping –1667. †**2.** *fig.* To cause to fall from a position of power, superiority, or virtue; to cause the downfall of, bring low –1780. **3.** To dispossess and take the place of (another), esp. by treacherous or dishonourable means ME. †**4.** To take up by the roots; to root out, uproot (a plant, or something likened thereto) –1644. **5.** To remove from its position, get rid of, oust; occas. to replace or supersede *by* something else. Now *rare.* 1576. **6.** Chiefly of things: To take the place of, supersede 1671.
1. His Armes clung to his Ribs, his Leggs entwining Each other, till supplanted down he fell A monstrous Serpent MILT. **3.** He most unworthily supplanted and turned out the worthy Curate..out of his own cure of souls 1731. **5.** S. the Alpes, and lay them smooth and plaine DRAYTON. **6.** These pantomimes will very soon s. all poetry 1789. Hence **Suppla·nter** ME.

Supplantation (sɒplɑntēⁱ·ʃən). late ME. [– (O)Fr. *supplantation* – eccl.L. *supplantatio, -ōn-* hypocritical deceit, f. L. *supplantare*; see prec., -ION. The senses are infl. by SUPPLANT *v.*] **1.** The dispossession or displacement of a person in a position, esp. by dishonourable means. **2.** The supersession or displacement *of* one thing *by* another 1608.

Supple (sɒ·p'l), *a.* [ME. *souple* – (O)Fr. *souple* :– Rom. **supples*, f. L. *supplex, -plic-* submissive, suppliant, lit. bending under, f. *sub* SUB- 2 + **plic-* bend.] †**1.** Not rigid; soft, tender. –late ME. **2.** That is easily bent or folded without breaking or cracking; pliant, flexible. late ME. **b.** *fig.* Adaptable; elastic 1781. **3.** Of the body, limbs, etc.: Capable of bending easily; moving easily or nimbly 1530. **b.** *transf.* of movements, etc.: Characterized by flexibility of body or limb 1592. **4.** *fig.* Yielding readily to persuasion or influence; compliant ME. **5.** Compliant or accommodating from selfish motives; artfully or servilely complaisant or obsequious 1607. **b.** *transf.* Characterized by ingratiating or fawning complaisance 1633.
2. Whipping the stream with his s. fly-rod 1872. Rubbed in..in sufficient quantity to keep the skin s. and unctuous 1899. **b.** His s. address and determination saved Rome from a revolution 1879. **3.** Limbs so s.; will so stubborn! RICHARDSON. *S. knee*, in ref. to insincere or obsequious obeisance; Will ye submit your necks, and chuse to bend The s. knee? MILT. **b.** Keep a..s. position of the body 1809. **4.** Let me be soft and s. to thy will G. HERBERT. **5.** A s. and flattering courtier EVELYN. **b.** We Britons slight Those s. arts which foreigners delight 1690. Hence **Su·pple-ly** *adv.*, **-ness.**

Supple (sɒ·p'l), *v.* late ME. [f. prec., after OFr. *asouplir* (mod. *assouplir*).] **1.** *trans.* To soften, mollify (the heart or mind); to make compliant or complaisant. *Obs.* or *arch.* **b.** *intr.* and *refl.* To be submissive or compliant *to*. *Obs.* or *arch.* 1440. **2.** To make (skin, leather, and the like) supple, pliant, or flexible 1530. †**3.** To reduce the hardness of, to soften. Also *absol.* –1728. †**4.** To soften or mollify (a wound, swelling, etc.) by applying an unguent, a fomentation, etc.; to anoint with oil –1688. **5.** To make (the limbs, the body, the person) supple or capable of bending easily; *spec.* of the training of saddle-horses 1570. **6.** *gen.* To make pliant, flexible, or smooth; also, to tone down, modify 1530.

1. Suppled with Sicknesse, he confessed his Fault FULLER. 2. Hard new boots not yet suppled by use 1915. 5. In order to s. the recruit,.. he will be practised in the..movements 1847. 6. To set free, to s. and to train the faculties LOWELL.

Su·pple-jack. 1725. [f. SUPPLE *a.* + JACK *sb.*[1]] **1.** A name for various climbing and twining shrubs with tough pliable stems found in tropical and subtropical forests; applied in the West Indies to various sapindaceous plants, as species of *Paullinia* and *Serjania*; in Central America, to the rhamnaceous *Berchemia volubilis*, and to a species of *Zizyphus*; and elsewhere to plants of similar habit. **b.** The stems of these plants as a material 1804. **2.** A walking-stick or cane made of the stem of one of these plants; a tough pliant stick 1748. **3.** A toy representing the human figure, the limbs of which are manipulated by a string (*U.S.*) 1829.

Supplement (sɒ·plĭmĕnt), *sb.* late ME. [– L. *supplementum*, f. *supplēre* SUPPLY *v.*; see -MENT. Cf. Fr. *supplément* (XVI).] **1.** Something added to supply a deficiency; an auxiliary means, an aid; occas. of a person. (Now *rare* in general sense.) **b.** A part added to complete a literary work or any written account or document; *spec.* a part of a periodical publication issued as an addition to the regular numbers and containing some special item or items 1568. **c.** *Math.* (*a*) *S. of an arc or angle*, the amount by which an arc is less than a semi-circle, or an angle less than two right angles. (*b*) An additional term introduced in certain cases in an equation or expression (abbrev. *Supp.*). 1570. †**2.** The action of supplying what is wanting; the making good *of* a deficiency or shortcoming –1660. **b.** Sc. Law. *Oath in s.*, a suppletory oath 1672. †**3.** The reinforcement *of* troops; chiefly *concr.* (*sing.* and *pl.*), reinforcement(s –1665. †**4.** The action of supplying or providing; that which is supplied; supply, provision –1658.

Supplement (sɒ·plĭmĕnt, sɒplĭme·nt), *v.* 1829. [f. prec.] *trans.* To furnish a supplement to, supply the deficiency in; also, to supply (a deficiency).

The two sets of dissimilar conditions s. and throw light upon each other 1868.

Supplemental (sɒplĭme·ntăl), *a.* (*sb.*) 1605. [f. as prec. + -AL[1].] **A.** *adj.* = next A. Const. *to*, *of*. **b.** *Math.* 1798. **B.** *sb.* A supplementary fact, etc. (*rare*) 1670.

A. Womens Supplimentall Art, does but the rather bewray Natures Defects 1629. *S. air*, the air that remains in the lungs after an ordinary expiration. **b.** *S. angle*, either (in relation to the other) of two angles which are together equal to two right angles. *S. arc*, either of two arcs which are together equal to a semi-circle. *S. chord*, the chord of a supplemental arc. Hence **Supple·me·ntally** *adv.*

Supplementary (sɒplĭme·ntări), *a.* (*sb.*) 1667. [f. as prec. + -ARY[1].] **A.** *adj.* Of the nature of, forming, or serving as, a supplement. Const. *to*. Often in techn. uses. **B.** *sb.* A supplementary person or thing 1812.

A. To this Claim..was added a s. paper containing a list of grievances MACAULAY. Hence **Suppleme·ntarily** *adv.*

Supplementation (sɒ:plĭmentē[i]·ʃən). 1854. [f. SUPPLEMENT *v.* + -ATION.] The action of supplementing; also, an instance of this, a supplementary addition.

Suppletion (sɒ̆plī·ʃən). *rare.* ME. [– OFr. *suppletion* – med.L. *suppletio*, *-ōn-*, f. *supplet-*, pa. ppl. stem of L. *supplēre* SUPPLY *v.*; see -ION.] The action or an act of supplying; something supplied.

Suppletive (sɒ̆plĭ·tiv), *a. rare.* 1816. [f. †*supplete* vb. (XVII), f. L. *supplet-* (see prec.) + -IVE.] Having the attribute of supplying deficiencies.

Suppletory (sɒ·plĭtŏri), *a.* and *sb.* 1628. [f. as prec. + -ORY[1,2]. With the adj. cf. AL. *suppletorius* (1684); with the sb., late L. *suppletorium*.] **A.** *adj.* Supplementary. Const. *to*, *of*. Now *rare*. **b.** Law. *S. oath*, an oath (given by a party in his own favour) admitted to supply a deficiency in legal evidence 1726. †**B.** *sb.* A supplement –1707.

The rite of confirmation..is an admirable s. of an early Baptisme JER. TAYLOR.

Supplial (sɒ̆pləi·ăl). Now *rare.* 1752. [f. SUPPLY *v.* + -AL[1] 2.] The act of supplying.

The ..s. of all the wants of life 1819.

Suppliance[1] (sɒ̆pləi·ăns). Now *rare.* 1598. [f. as prec. + -ANCE.] = SUPPLY *sb.*

Suppliance[2] (sɒ·pliăns). *rare. poet.* 1611. [f. SUPPLIANT *a.*[1]; see -ANCE.] The action of a suppliant; supplication. So **Su·ppliancy.**

Suppliant (sɒ·pliănt), *sb.* and *a.*[1] Now *poet.* or *rhet.* late ME. [– Fr. *suppliant*, pr. pple. of *supplier* :– L. *supplicare* SUPPLICATE *v.*; see -ANT.] **A.** *sb.* One who supplicates; a humble petitioner.

Thy s. I beg, and clasp thy knees MILT.

B. *adj.* Supplicating, humbly petitioning 1586. **b.** *transf.* Expressing or involving supplication 1667.

The Rich grow s., and the Poor grow proud DRYDEN. **b.** To bow and sue for grace With s. knee MILT. Hence **Su·ppliantly** *adv.*

†**Suppli·ant**, *a.*[2] 1611. [f. SUPPLY *v.* + -ANT.] Supplementary. SHAKS.

Supplicant (sɒ·plikănt), *sb.* and *a.* Now *rare* exc. *arch.* 1597. [– L. *supplicans*, *-ant-*, pr. pple. of *supplicare* SUPPLICATE; see -ANT.] **A.** *sb.* = SUPPLIANT *sb.* **b.** *spec.* One who supplicates for a degree; see SUPPLICATE *v.* 3. 1649.

The..supplicants, who repair to the churches 1834.

B. *adj.* = SUPPLIANT *a.*[1] 1597. Hence **Su·pplicantly** *adv.*

‖**Supplicat** (sɒ·plikæt). 1660. [L., = he supplicates.] A supplication, petition; *spec.* (now only) in English universities, a formal petition for a degree or for incorporation.

Supplicate (sɒ·plike[i]t), *v.* late ME. [– *supplicat-*, pa. ppl. stem of L. *supplicare*, f. *sub-* SUB- 2 + **plic-* bend.] **1.** *intr.* To beg, or entreat humbly; to present a humble petition. **2.** *trans.* To petition humbly 1642. **3.** *spec. intr.* In Oxford University, to present a formal petition for a degree or for incorporation 1691.

1. O holy Mary..s. for the devout Female Sex 1771. **2.** The Church..did s. protection from the temporall powers 1660. Shall I brook to be supplicated? TENNYSON. So **Su·pplicator,** one who supplicates; a suppliant, petitioner. **Su·pplicatingly** *adv.*

Supplication (sɒplikē[i]·ʃən). late ME. [– (O)Fr. *supplication* – L. *supplicatio*, *-ōn-*, f. as prec.; see -ION.] The action, or an act, of supplicating; humble or earnest petition or entreaty. **b.** A written or formal petition. *Obs.* exc. *Hist.* late ME. **c.** (A) humble prayer addressed to God (or a deity); chiefly pl., *spec.* the petitions for special blessings in litanies 1490. **d.** *Rom. Antiq.* A religious solemnity decreed on the occasion of some important public event, esp. in thanksgiving for victory 1606. **e.** *spec.* In Oxford University, a formal petition for a degree or for incorporation 1691.

Supplicatory (sɒ·plikĕtŏri), *a.* 1450. [– med.L. *supplicatorius*, f. as prec.; see -ORY[2]. Cf. *litteræ supplicatoriæ* (*a*1250).] Expressing, consisting of, or containing supplication.

‖**Supplicavit** (sɒplikē[i]·vit). 1507. [L., = he has supplicated.] *Law.* A writ formerly issuing out of the King's Bench or the Court of Chancery for taking surety of the peace against a person: so called from the first word in the writ.

Supplier (sɒ̆pləi·əɹ). 1607. [f. SUPPLY *v.* + -ER[1].] One who (or that which) supplies.

Supply (sɒ̆pləi·), *sb.* late ME. [f. next.] **I.** The action of supplying, or condition of being supplied. †**1.** Assistance, succour, support, relief –1697. **2.** The act of making up a deficiency, or of fulfilling a want or demand 1500. †**3.** The act of supplying something needed –1673. **b.** Now only in ref. to persons: The act, or position, of supplying a vacancy, or officiating temporarily instead of another, esp. as a minister or preacher; *on s.* = acting in such a capacity 1580. **4.** The provision or furnishing *of* a person, etc. with necessaries 1781. **II.** That which is supplied. †**1.** *collect. sing.* or *pl.* An additional body of persons, esp. reinforcements of troops –1750. **2.** One who supplies a vacancy or acts as substitute for another; *esp.* a minister or preacher who temporarily officiates in a vacant charge or pulpit 1584. **3.** A quantity or amount *of* something supplied or provided 1607. **4.** *absol.* (A) provision of funds or food; (a quantity of) money or provisions supplied or to be supplied: now chiefly *spec.* the food and stores necessary for an armed force 1611. **5.** *collect. sing.* or *pl.* A sum of money granted by a national legislature for expenses of government not provided for by the revenue 1626. **6.** *Pol. Econ.* The amount of any commodity produced and available for purchase: correl. to DEMAND *sb.* 4. 1776.

1. The Earle of Salisbury craueth s. SHAKS. **3.** The wine was passed, and a fresh supply ordered DICKENS. **4.** England..sent Money and other Supplies into Ireland 1687. **5.** The Commons declared..that redress of grievances must precede the grant of supplies GREEN. **6.** If the demand exceeds the s. the price will rise 1900.

Supply (sɒ̆pləi·), *v.* [Late ME. (in earliest use mainly Sc.) *sup(p)le*, *sowple*, late *supplie* – OFr. *so(u)pleer*, earlier *soup(p)leier*, *-oier*, later *supplier* (mod. *suppléer*) – L. *supplēre* fill up, make good, complete, f. *sub-* SUB- 25 + *-plēre* fill (*plenus* FULL).] †**1.** *trans.* To help, aid, assist; to succour, relieve; to support, maintain; *occas.* to deliver *from* –1750. †**2.** To furnish with (additional) troops; to reinforce. Also *absol.* –1825. **3.** †**a.** To supplement –1730. **b.** To add (something that is wanting) 1450. **4.** To make up for, make good, compensate for (a defect, loss, or void); to compensate for (the absence of something) by providing a substitute. late ME. **5.** To fulfil, satisfy (a need or want) by furnishing what is wanted 1567. **6.** To furnish, provide, afford (something needed, desired, or used): now usu. with impersonal subj. 1520. **7.** To furnish (a thing) *with* what is necessary or desirable; in early use, without const., to make provision for 1529. **b.** *transf.* To furnish with an occupant, tenant, or contents; to fill. *poet.* 1607. **c.** *Anat.* and *Phys.* Of a nerve or blood-vessel: To furnish with energy or nourishment (the part or organ to which it is distributed) 1843. **8.** To furnish or provide (a person) *with* something; in early use, without const., to satisfy the wants of, provide for; now usu., to furnish with regular supplies of a commodity 1567. **9.** To fill (another's place); *esp.* (now only) to occupy as a substitute. late ME. †**10.** To fulfil, discharge, perform (an office or function), *esp.* as a substitute for another –1748. **11.** To take the place of; to serve as, or furnish, a substitute for; to replace. Now *rare* or *Obs.* 1606. **12.** Of a cleric or minister: To occupy (a church, pulpit, etc.) as a substitute, or temporarily; to act as 'supply' for (another); also *absol.* 1719.

3. a. Nature is supplide in him by Art 1615. **b.** S. words that are wanting 1824. **4.** That which most supplied their want of experience 1600. **5.** Some private purse Supplies his need with an usurious loan COWPER. **6.** The fresco-paintings..of Crete have supplied the clearest proof of it 1910. **7.** She..With flow'r and fruit the wilderness supplies COWPER. **b.** *Timon* III. i. 18. **8.** Can Sir Reginald Glanville's memory..s. him with no probable cause? 1827. **11.** A comfortable heat.. Which might s. the Sun MILT. **12.** To 's. the pulpits' of ministers who left home 1895. Hence †**Supply·ment** (*rare*), the act of supplying, or what is supplied –1611.

Support (sɒ̆pō[ə]·ɹt), *sb.* late ME. [f. next.] **I.** The action of supporting. **1.** The action, or an act, of preventing a person from giving way, backing him up, or taking his part; assistance, countenance, backing. **b.** Spiritual help; mental comfort 1500. **c.** Corroboration or substantiation (*of* a statement, principle, etc.); advocacy (*of* a proposal, motion, etc.) 1771. **d.** *Mil.* The action of supporting other troops. *In s.*: acting as a second line. 1805. **2.** The action of keeping from failing, exhaustion, or perishing; *esp.* the supplying *of* a living thing with what is necessary for subsistence; the maintenance *of* life 1686. **b.** The action of contributing to the success or maintaining the value of something 1912. **3.** The action or fact of holding up, keeping from falling, or bearing the weight of something; the condition of being so supported 1663.

1. Your gallant s. of me at the Battle of Copenhagen NELSON. **c.** The evidence to be called in s. of their statement 1891. **2.** Alone, it is insufficient for the s. of life 1857. A youth..found about the streets without visible means of s. 1915. **3.** Without any s. of columns EVELYN.

II. One who or that which supports. **1.** A supporter, 'prop', 'stay' 1594. **b.** *Mil.* (*pl.*) A supporting body of troops; the second line in a battle 1852. **2.** That which supports life; means of livelihood or subsistence 1599. **b.** One who or that which furnishes means of livelihood, or maintains a person or community 1745. **3.** Anything that holds up, or sustains the weight of, a body, or upon which it rests 1570.

1. High Ioue the heauens among (Their s. that suffer wrong) KYD. **2.** Liuelyhood and s. fit for their estates 1611. **b.** Her slender earnings were the sole s. of the family LAMB. **3.** A crucible,.. with its cover and a s. FARADAY.

Support (sŏ̆pōᵊ·ɹt), *v.* late ME. [– (O)Fr. *supporter* – L. *supportare*, f. *sub-* SUB- 25 + *portare* carry.] **1.** *trans.* To endure without opposition or resistance; to bear with, put up with, tolerate. (In mod. use often a gallicism.) **†b.** To endure, undergo; to bear up against –1805. **2.** To strengthen the position of (a person or community) by one's assistance, countenance, or adherence; to stand by, back up. late ME. **b.** To uphold or maintain the validity or authority of (a thing); also, to give support to (a course of action) 1638. **3. a.** To back up in a statement or an opinion 1686. **b.** To furnish authority for or corroboration of (a statement, etc.); to bear out, substantiate 1761. **c.** To second or speak in favour of (a proposition, or one who makes a proposition); to maintain the truth of (an opinion, etc.) 1736. **4.** To provide for the maintenance of, bear the expense of. Now only with immaterial obj. late ME. **b.** *Law.* Of an estate: To be such as to provide for (a remainder) 1694. **5.** To furnish food or sustenance for; to supply with the necessaries of life. late ME. **b.** To sustain (the vital functions); also, to keep up the strength of (a sick person) 1704. **6.** To bear, hold, or prop up. late ME. **†b.** *refl.* To hold oneself up, keep an erect position –1727. **†c.** To give one's arm to (a lady); to take (a person) on one's arm –1816. **d.** To sustain (a weight of so much) 1726. **e.** *Her.* in *pass.* To be flanked by supporters 1562. **7.** To constitute the substratum of (a structure); to sustain in position above, have on it or at the top 1617. **†b.** *Metaph.* To be the subject or substratum of –1710. **8.** To keep (a person, his mind, etc.) from failing or giving way; to give courage, confidence, or power of endurance to. Also *†refl.* 1602. **9. a.** To maintain unimpaired, preserve from decay or depreciation 1515. **b.** To preserve from failure, contribute to the success of (an undertaking); also, to maintain (a price) 1779. **c.** To maintain in being or in action; to keep up, to provide the necessary matter for 1738. **d.** Of specie: To guarantee the convertibility of (a paper currency) 1868. **10.** To sustain (a character) in a dramatic performance; *gen.* to act or play (a part), bear (a character) 1709. **11.** To give assistance to in a battle, esp. by a second line of troops; to second (a leading actor); to assist as a subordinate in a contest, a musical performance, etc. 1848. **b.** To occupy a position by the side of, with the object of giving assistance or encouragement; hence, to assist by one's presence or attendance 1886.

1. These things his high spirit could not s. EVELYN. **b.** Prethee how does she s. this news? 1671. **2.** He had no party in the country to s. him 1884. **3. b.** The application was supported by an affidavit of the applicant 1885. **c.** Godolphin.. had supported the Exclusion Bill MACAULAY. **4.** This luxury was supported by a thriving trade MACAULAY. **5.** The burden of supporting the poor ought to be sustained by all ranks 1801. **6.** S. him by the arme SHAKS. **7.** 'Andirons' in front to s. the logs of wood 1907. **9. a.** To s. the ancient character of the corps 1802. **b.** Indian gold shares have been supported 1898. **c.** The conversation.. was well supported till midnight 1785. **10.** In order to s. the *rôle* which they unconsciously fall into 1888. **11. b.** Mr. Gladstone was supported right and left by Lord Hartington and Sir William Harcourt 1886. Hence **†Suppo·rtment**, support.

Supportable (sŏ̆pōᵊ·ɹtăb'l), *a.* 1577. [f. prec. + -ABLE.] Capable of being supported; endurable; defensible. Hence **Supportabi·lity, Suppo·rtableness. Suppo·rtably** *adv.*

†Suppo·rtance. 1490. [f. SUPPORT *v.* + -ANCE, after OFr. *suportance.*] = SUPPORT *sb.* in various senses –1830.

†Supporta·tion. late ME. [– OFr. *supportation* – late and med.L. *supportatio*, f. *supportat-*, pa. ppl. stem of L. *supportare* SUPPORT *v.*; see -ION.] = SUPPORT *sb.* in various senses –1768.

Supporter (sŏ̆pōᵊ·ɹtəɹ). late ME. [f. SUPPORT *v.* + -ER[1].] **1.** One who sides with, backs up, assists, or countenances a person, cause, etc. **2.** One who keeps a person or thing from failing, giving way, or perishing; a sustainer, maintainer 1475. **b.** *Chem.* A substance that maintains some process, esp. combustion 1806. **3.** = SUPPORT *sb.* II. 3. 1595. **b.** A leg. (Now only *joc.*) 1601. **†c.** A sepal –1712. **4.** *Her.* A figure of an animal, mythical creature, or human being, represented as holding up or standing beside the shield; each of two such figures, one on each side of the shield 1572. **5.** One who attends another for the purpose of giving physical or moral support; hence, an attendant, as in a procession 1586.

1. Staunch supporters of the Church 1836. **2.** Loyalty..The great S. of his awful Throne DRYDEN. **3.** A Building set upon Supporters 1707. **c.** The Sockets, and Supporters of Flowers, are Figured: As in the Five Brethren of the Rose BACON. **5.** Ingratitude..sitting in its Throne, with Pride at its Right-hand, and Cruelty at its Left; worthy Supporters of..such a reigning Impiety 1675. **Suppo·rtress,** a female s.

Supportive (sŏ̆pōᵊ·ɹtiv), *a. rare.* 1593. [f. SUPPORT *v.* + -IVE.] Having the quality of supporting; sustaining.

Suppo·rtless, *a.* 1643. [f. SUPPORT *sb.* + -LESS.] **†1.** That cannot be 'supported'; intolerable. MILT. **2.** Destitute of support, unsupported 1681.

Supposable (sŏ̆pōᵘ·zăb'l), *a.* 1643. [f. SUPPOSE *v.* + -ABLE.] Capable of being supposed; that may be thought to exist or to be true, or that can be assumed for the sake of argument; presumable, imaginable. Hence **Supppo·sably** *adv.* (chiefly *U.S.*), presumably.

Supposal (sŏ̆pōᵘ·zăl). late ME. [– OFr. *sup(p)osail(l)e*, f. *sup(p)oser* SUPPOSE *v.*; see -AL[1] 2.] **†1.** The action of supposing, supposition –1839. **2.** An act of supposing; something that is supposed; a supposition, hypothesis; an assumption, conjecture. Now *rare.* late ME. **†3.** A notion, opinion –1612. **†4.** A statement, allegation (as in a writ or indictment) –1651.

1. Phr. *Upon s.* (*of* or *that*..). *By, upon s.*, as is (or was) supposed, supposedly. **3.** *Haml.* I. ii. 18.

Suppose (sŏ̆pōᵘ·z), *sb.* 1566. [f. next.] **1.** An act of supposing; a supposition, hypothesis, conjecture. Now always referring to a supposition expressed or expressible by means of the vb. 'suppose'. **†b.** *gen.* Supposition –1719. **†2.** (An) expectation –1606.

1. Fatted with Supposes of fine Hopes B. JONS.

Suppose (sŏ̆pōᵘ·z), *v.* ME. [– (O)Fr. *sup(p)oser*, f. *sub-* SUB- 2 + *poser* POSE *v.*[1]] **†1.** *trans.* To hold as a belief or opinion; to believe as a fact; to think –1658. **†2.** To form an idea of, conceive, imagine; to apprehend, guess –1781. **†3.** To have in mind or as an object of thought or speculation; to think of, conceive, imagine, contextually, to suspect –1763. **†4.** To expect –1760. **5.** To assume (without ref. to truth or falsehood) as a basis of argument, or for the purpose of tracing the consequences; to frame as a hypothesis; to posit ME. **6.** Often in imper. or pres. pple. absol., introducing a hypothetical statement or case ME. **b.** In imper. parenthetically or ellipt.; often = 'as (for example)', 'say'. Now *rare* or *Obs.* 1577. **7.** *trans.* To infer hypothetically; to incline to think; sometimes implying mistaken belief 1601. **8.** To lay down or assume as true, take for granted. late ME. **b.** To presume the existence or presence of 1696. **9.** Of actions, conditions, facts: To involve as a ground or basis; to require as a condition; to imply, presuppose 1660. **†10.** To state, allege; esp. formally in an indictment –1651. **†11.** To substitute by artifice or fraud –1767. **†12.** To put or place under something; to append –1797.

1. Would you not s. Your bondage happy, to be made a Queene? SHAKS. **5.** Which..might..do more harm than good in the case supposed SCOTT. **6.** S. a man to have riches and honours 1678. S. you go to sleep, that you may get up in time enough 1844. Supposing them sculptors, will not the same rule hold? RUSKIN. **b.** A Person.. breaks his Limbs, s. BUTLER. **7.** Those foibles which are chiefly supposed proper to the female sex SCOTT. He fell and it is supposed was instantaneously killed 1885. **8.** *pass.* (Not) to be expected *to do* or *be* so-and-so. He's not supposed to go into the kitchen (*mod.*). **9.** Patience must s. pain JOHNSON. **11.** Persons guilty of supposing children 1767. Hence **Suppo·sedly** (-ėdli) *adv.* in the way of supposition; as is (or was) supposed. **†Suppo·ser** (*rare*).

Supposition (sɒpŏzi·ʃən). 1449. [– (O)Fr. *supposition* or late (Boethius) and med.L. *suppositio*, *-ōn-* (tr. Gr. ὑπόθεσις HYPOTHESIS), f. *supposit-*, pa. ppl. stem of *supponere* place under, substitute; see SUB- 2, POSITION.] The action of supposing, or what is supposed. **†1.** *Scholastic Logic.* Something held to be true and taken as the basis of an argument –1590. **2.** The action of assuming, or, usu. that which is assumed (which may be either true or false), as a basis of argument or a premiss from which a conclusion is drawn 1596. **3.** A hypothetical inference, or the action of making such inferences; an uncertain (sometimes, by implication, a false or mistaken) belief 1596. **†b.** Used vaguely, with various shades of meaning: Idea, notion; imagination, fancy; *occas.* suspicion, expectation –1784. **†4.** Fraudulent substitution of another thing or person in place of the genuine one –1797. **†b.** Insertion of something not genuine in a writing; that which is so inserted (*rare*) –1662.

2. The s. that the defendant had broken the plaintiff's close 1887. **3.** †*In s.*, in uncertainty, uncertain, doubtful; My meaning in saying he is a good man, is..that he is sufficient, yet his meanes are in s. SHAKS. It is only said to be his [handwriting] by s. PEPYS. **b.** *Com. Err.* III. ii. 50. Hence **Supposi·tional** *a.* of the nature of or based on s.; hypothetical.

Suppositious (sɒpŏzi·ʃəs), *a.* Now *rare* or *Obs.* 1624. [Partly shortened or illiterate form of next, partly directly f. prec.] **1.** = next 1, 2. **2.** = SUPPOSITIONAL 1698.

Supposititious (sŏ̆pǫziti·ʃəs), *a.* 1611. [– L. *supposititius*, *-icius*, f. *supposit-*; see SUPPOSITION, -ITIOUS[1].] **1.** Put by artifice in the place of another; fraudulently substituted for the genuine thing or person; hence, pretended (to be what it is not), spurious, counterfeit; false. **b.** *spec.* of a child, *esp.* one set up to displace the real heir or successor; sometimes used for 'illegitimate'; also said of the birth of such a child 1625. **†2.** Pretended or imagined to exist; feigned; fabulous; fancied, imaginary –1774. **3.** = next 1674.

2. I tearm the gold Mine he went to discover, an ayrie and s. Mine 1645. Hence **Suppositi·tiously** *adv.*, **-ness.**

Suppositive (sŏ̆pǫ·zitiv), *a.* (*sb.*) 1605. [– late L. *suppositivus* (Priscian, rendering Gr. ὑποθετικός), f. as prec.; see -IVE.] Of the nature of, implying, or grounded on supposition. **b.** *Gram.* Expressing a supposition; conditional; as *sb.* a conditional conjunction (*rare*) 1751. Hence **Suppo·sitively** *adv.*

†Suppo·sitor. 1545. [Alteration of next after agent-nouns in -ER, -OR.] = next –1689.

Suppository (sŏ̆pǫ·zitŏri), *sb.* late ME. [– med.L. *suppositorium*, subst. use of n. sing. of late L. *suppositorius* placed underneath, f. *supposit-*; see SUPPOSITION, -ORY[1]. Cf. (O)Fr. *suppositoire* (XIII).] A plug of conical or cylindrical shape to be introduced into the rectum in order to stimulate the bowels to action (or to reduce hæmorrhoids), or into the vagina or urethra for various purposes.

Suppo·sitory, *a.* 1599. [In sense 1 attrib. use of prec.; in sense 2 var. of SUPPOSITIVE by suffix-substitution.] **†1.** Used as, or pertaining to, a suppository –1607. **2.** = SUPPOSITIONAL. Now *rare.* 1644.

‖**Suppositum** (sŏ̆pǫ·zitŏ̆m). *Pl.* **supposita.** 1646. [Scholastic L., n. sing., used subst., of *suppositus*, pa. pple. of *supponere*; see SUPPOSITION.] **†1.** *Metaph.* A being that subsists by itself, an individual thing or person; occas., a being in relation to its attributes –1719. **2.** *Logic.* **a.** Something supposed or assumed, an assumption. **b.** *pl.* The things or objects denoted by a given term. 1833.

Suppost (sɒpōᵘ·st). *Obs.* exc. *Hist.* 1490. [– OFr. *suppost* (mod. *suppôt*) – med.L. *suppositus* sb. subordinate – pa. pple. of L. *supponere*; see prec.] A subordinate; a supporter, follower, adherent.

Suppress (sɒpre·s), *v.* late ME. [– *suppress-*, pa. ppl. stem of L. *supprimere*, f. *sub-* SUB- 2 + *premere* PRESS *v.*[1]] **1.** *trans.* To put down by force or authority; to quell; to vanquish, subdue. **b.** To withhold or withdraw from publication (a book or writing); to prevent or prohibit the circulation of 1560. **2.** To subdue (a feeling, thought, desire, habit) 1526. **3.** To keep secret; to refrain from disclosing or divulging; to refrain from mentioning or stating (either something that ought to be revealed, or that was formerly stated or included, or that may be understood from the context) 1533. **4.** To restrain from utterance or manifestation; not to express 1557. **†5.** To press down; to press or weigh upon –1620. **†6.** *fig.* To bring or keep low, into or in subjection; to weigh down –1649. **7.** To hinder from passage or discharge; to stop or arrest the flow of 1621.

1. To Discountenance, and S. all bold enquiries 1647. To blow up the houses to s. the fire 1679. A..Meeting was suppresst at Gallway 1699. Proclamations suppressing the National League 1887. **b.** Those books..cannot be suppresst without the fall of learning MILT. **2.** No cold repulses my desires suppress'd 1721. **3.** What is told in the fullest..annals bears an infinitely small proportion to what is suppressed MACAULAY. **4.** S. thy Sighs PRIOR. **7.** Hæmorrhage, which..it was impossible to s. 1854. Hence **Suppre·ssor.**

Suppressal (sɒpre·săl). *rare.* 1651. [f. prec. + -AL[1] 2.] = SUPPRESSION 1.

Suppressed (sɒpre·st), *ppl. a.* 1620. [f. as prec. + -ED[1].] In various senses of SUPPRESS *v.* **b.** *Bot.* Said of parts normally or typically present, but not found in the particular case in question 1849.

Suppressible (sɒpre·sĭb'l), *a.* 1837. [f. as prec. + -IBLE.] Capable of being suppressed.

Suppression (sɒpre·ʃən). 1528. [– L. *suppressio, -ōn-*, f. *suppress-*; see SUPPRESS *v.*, -ION. Cf. Fr. *suppression* (XV).] **1.** The action of putting down, as by power or authority. **b.** Withholding or withdrawal from publication; prevention or prohibition of the circulation of a book or writing 1700. **2.** The action of keeping secret; refusal to disclose or reveal; also, the leaving of something unexpressed 1728. **3.** Restraint or stifling (of utterance or expression) 1706. **4.** *Med.* and *Path.* Stoppage or arrest (of a discharge or secretion) 1601. **5.** *Bot.* Absence or non-development of some part or organ normally or typically present 1845.

1. The s. of the last rebellion 1574. The S. of Playhouses 1737. The s. of the Society of Jesus 1784. **2.** Unpardonable..suppressions of facts MACAULAY.

Suppressive (sɒpre·siv), *a.* 1778. [f. SUPPRESS *v.* + -IVE.] Having the quality or effect of suppressing.

†Supprise, *v.* Chiefly *Sc.* late ME. [f. AFr., OFr. *supris-e*, var. of *sur-*, *sourpris-e* or *souspris-e*, pa. pple. of *surprendre* SURPRISE *v.*,] To surprise, esp. with violence.

Suppurate (sɒ·piŭreⁱt), *v.* 1563. [– *suppurat-*, pa. ppl. stem of L. *suppurare*, f. *sub-* SUB- 2 + *pus, pur-* PUS; see -ATE[3].] **†1.** *trans.* To cause (a sore, etc.) to form or secrete pus; to bring to a head. Also *absol.* to induce suppuration. –1779. **2.** *intr.* To form or secrete pus, come to a head 1656.

1. To s. and ripen impostumes 1600. **2.** This Disease..is generally fatal if it suppurates 1732.

Suppuration (sɒpiŭrēⁱ·ʃən). 1541. [– Fr. *suppuration* or L. *suppuratio, -ōn-*, f. as prec.; see -ION.] The process or condition of suppurating; the formation or secretion of pus; the coming to a head of a boil or other eruption.

Suppurative (sɒ·piŭrĕtiv), *a.* and *sb.* 1541. [– Fr. *suppuratif, -ive* (XVI), f. as prec.; see -IVE.] **A.** *adj.* **1.** Having the property of causing suppuration; inducing the formation of pus. **2.** Attended or characterized by suppuration 1794. **B.** *sb.* A medicine or preparation which promotes suppuration 1568.

†Supputa·tion. late ME. [– L. *supputatio, -ōn-*, f. *supputat-*, pa. ppl. stem of *supputare* count up, f. *sub-* SUB-[2] + *putare* reckon.] The action, an act, or a method of calculating or computing; calculation, reckoning –1825. **b.** *transf.* Estimation –1677. So **†Su·pputate,** *v.* to calculate. 1559.

‖**Supra** (sⁱū·prā), *adv.*, (*a.*), *prep.* 1440. [L. (see next).] **A.** *adv.* **1.** Above; previously, before (in a book or writing). Also in L. phr. *ut supra* = as above. (abbrev. *sup.*) **†2.** In addition, further; more –1778. **†B.** *adj.* Additional, extra –1773. **C.** *prep.* in phr. *s. protest* [– It. *sopra protesto* 'upon protest']: see quot. and PROTEST *sb.* 2. 1809.

After a bill has been protested, it is sometimes accepted by a third party, for the purpose of saving the reputation of a drawer or of an endorser. Such an acceptance is called an acceptance 'Supra Protest'. 1809.

Supra- (sⁱū·prā), *prefix*, repr. L. *supra-* = *supra* (related to *super* and ult. to *sub*), adv. and prep., above, beyond, in addition (to), before in time. Its meanings in English are for the most part parallel to, but in much less vogue than those of SUPER-, except in certain scientific uses.

I. Over, above, higher than; (less commonly) on, upon: in a physical sense. **1.** In prepositional relation to the sb. implied in, or constituting, the second element = SUPER I. 1. **a.** Miscellaneous adjs., chiefly scientific: = SUPER I. 1 a, c. **Supra-a·xillary,** *Bot.* arising above an axil, as a branch or bud. **Supraco·ralline,** *Geol.* lying immediately above the Coralline Oolite. **Su:pracreta·ceous,** *Geol.* lying above the Cretaceous series, as the Tertiary and more recent formations. **Su:prafolia·ceous, Suprafo·liar,** *Bot.* situated or arising above (or upon) a leaf. **Su-pragla·cial,** occurring upon the surface of ice, esp. of a glacier. **Su:pramari·ne,** situated or occurring above the sea. **Supramedial,** lying above the middle (e.g. of a series of rocks). **Supratro·pical,** next 'above', i.e. higher in latitude than, the tropical. **b.** *Anat.* and *Zool.* Extensively used to form adjs. in the sense 'Situated above, or on the dorsal side of (occas. upon the upper surface of) the part or organ denoted by the second element'; = SUPER- I. 1 b. *Supra-acro·mial, -a·ngular* (the angular bone in some vertebrates), *-auri·cular, -bra·nchial, -ci·liary* (= SUPERCILIARY; as *sb.*, *spec.* any of the small scales attached to the eyelids in reptiles, below the supra-oculars), *-clavi·cular, -co·ndyloid* (= above a condyle or condyles of the humerus, etc.), *-co·stal, -cra·nial* (= on the upper surface of the cranium), *-do·rsal, -du·ral* (= above the dura mater), *-hepa·tic* (on the upper surface of the liver), *-neu·ral* (= above a neural axis), *-occi·pital, -o·cular* (= above the ocular region, *spec.* of the small scales in reptiles above the superciliaries; also *sb.*), *-œsopha·geal* (= on the dorsal side of the œsophagus, applied to a nervous ganglion in invertebrates), *-o·rbital* (= above the orbit of the eye: also as *sb.*), *-pe·dal* (= above the 'foot' of a mollusc), *-pu·bic, -ste·rnal, -te·mporal*[1], *-vagi·nal, -ventri·cular.* **c.** With sb., denoting a part situated above that denoted by the second element. **Supracla·vicle,** *Anat.* and *Zool.* a superior bone of the scapular arch in some fishes, above the clavicle.

2. In advb. relation to the second element: = SUPER- I. 2. **Su:prasori·ferous** *a.*, *Bot.* bearing sori on the upper surface.

3. In adjectival relation to the sb. constituting or implied in the second element: = SUPER- I. 3. **a.** *Anat.* and *Zool.* = Superior, upper; (a structure) situated above some other, or forming or belonging to the upper part of (that denoted by the second element): chiefly in mod.L. terms, as *supramamma.* **Supraco·mmissure,** a commissure of nerve-fibres above and in front of the pineal body. ‖**Suprasca·pula,** a bone (or cartilage) in the upper or anterior part of the scapular arch, in fishes, and in some batrachians and reptiles. **b.** *Anat.* and *Zool.* Prefixed to adjs., or forming derivative adjs. from sbs. in a (sometimes used ellipt. as sbs.): = Pertaining to or situated on the upper..or the upper part of (what is expressed by the second element), as *suprala·bial* (the upper lip), *supramaxi·llary* (the upper jaw).

II. Above (in various fig. senses); higher in quality, amount, or degree. **1. a.** Prefixed to adjs.: = SUPER- II. 1 a, as *supra-Chri·stian, -ra·tional, -temporal*[2]. **b.** Prefixed to a sb., forming an adj., as *su·pra-state.*

2. Prefixed to a sb. = SUPER- II. 2; as *su·pra-entity.*

3. = Higher, superior, as *supra-consciousness, -world.*

4. Above in degree or amount, beyond, more than (what is expressed by the second element): as *su:pra-centena·rian, supra-o·ptimal.*

5. Before in time; = SUPER- II. 5, as in SUPRALAPSARIAN.

III. In the highest or to a very high degree; very highly, extremely = SUPER- III. 1 a, b, as *supra-censo·rious, -se·nsitive.*

IV. Expressing addition; involving addition or repetition. *Su·pra-compound* (= a compound of a compound, a compound of more than two elements). **Su:pradeco·mpound, Su:pradeco·mposite** *adjs.*, *Bot.* additionally decompound; triply or more than triply compound.

†Supraca·rgo. 1667. [– Sp. *sobrecargo* (f. *sobre* over + *cargo* CARGO).] = SUPERCARGO –1844.

Supralapsarian (sⁱū:prălæpsēᵊ·riăn), *sb.* and *a.* 1633. [f. mod.L. *supralapsarius*, f. *supra* SUPRA- II. 5 + L. *lapsus* LAPSE; see -ARIAN.] **A.** *sb.* A name applied to those Calvinists who held the view that, in the divine decrees, the predestination of some to eternal life and of others to eternal death was antecedent to the creation and the fall: opp. to INFRALAPSARIAN. **B.** *adj.* Of or pertaining to the Supralapsarians or their doctrine; that is a S. 1633. Hence **Su:pralapsa·rianism,** the doctrine of the Supralapsarians. So **†Suprala·psary** *sb.* and *a.*

Supraliminal (sⁱūprăli·minăl), *a.* 1892. [f. SUPRA- I. 1 a + L. LIMEN, *limin-* threshold; after *subliminal.*] *Psych.* Above the limen or threshold of sensation or consciousness; belonging to the ordinary or normal consciousness: opp. to SUBLIMINAL.

Supralunar (sⁱūprălⁱū·năɹ), *a.* 1719. [f. SUPRA- I. 1 a + LUNAR; cf. SUBLUNAR.] = next.

Supralunary (sⁱūprălⁱū·nări), *a.* 1635. [f. SUPRA- I. 1 a + LUNARY; cf. SUBLUNARY, SUPERLUNARY.] = SUPERLUNARY.

Supramundane (sⁱūprămɒ·ndeⁱn), *a.* 1662. [var. of SUPERMUNDANE; see SUPRA- I. 1 a, II. 1 a.] = SUPERMUNDANE.

Supranatural (sⁱūprănæ·tiŭrăl, -tʃərăl), *a.* (*sb.*) *rare.* 1857. [See SUPRA- II. 1 a and NATURAL.] = SUPERNATURAL. So **Supra-na·turalism. Suprana·turalist, -i·stic** *a.* **Su·prana:ture.**

Suprarenal (sⁱūprărī·năl), *a.* (*sb.*) 1828. [See SUPRA- I. 1 b, RENAL.] *Anat.* Situated above the kidney; applied to a pair of ductless glands (*s. bodies, capsules, corpuscles, glands*), one immediately above each kidney; also to other structures connected with these. **b.** *transf.* Of, pertaining to, or affecting the suprarenal capsules 1876. **B.** *sb.* A suprarenal capsule 1841.

‖**Suprasca·pular,** *a.* 1828. [– mod.L. *suprascapularis*; see SUPRA- I. 1 b, 3 b, SCAPULAR *a.*] *Anat.* and *Zool.* Situated above or upon the scapula; belonging to or connected with the upper or anterior part of the scapular arch, or the suprascapula.

Suprascript (sⁱū·prăskript), *a.* 1896. [var. of SUPERSCRIPT by prefix-substitution.] = SUPERSCRIPT *a.*

Supraspinal (sⁱūprăspəi·năl), *a.* 1733. [See SUPRA- I. 1 b, SPINAL.] *Anat.* Situated above or upon a (or the) spine. **a.** Situated above the spine of the scapula: opp. to *infraspinal.* **b.** = SUPRASPINOUS b. 1835.

‖**Supraspinatus** (sⁱū:prăspəinēⁱ·tɒs). 1733. [mod.L., f. L. *supra* SUPRA- I. 1 b + *spina* SPINE; see -ATE[2].] *Anat.* A muscle arising from the supraspinal fossa of the scapula, and inserted into the greater tuberosity of the humerus, serving to raise and adduct the arm.

Supraspinous (sⁱūprăspəi·nəs) *a.* 1828. [f. SUPRA- I. 1 b + SPINE + -OUS.] Situated above or upon a spine. **a.** = SUPRASPINAL a. **b.** Situated above or upon the spinous processes of the vertebræ 1828.

†Supravise, *v. rare.* 1606. [var. of SUPERVISE by prefix-substitution (SUPRA- I. 2).] *trans.* = SUPERVISE *v.* 2. Also *absol.* –1640. So **†Supravi·sion** = SUPERVISION 1 1642–67. **†Supravi·sor** 1566–1694.

Supremacy (sⁱupre·măsi). 1547. [f. SUPREME *a.* + -ACY 2, after PRIMACY.] **1.** The condition of being supreme in authority, rank, or power; position of supreme or highest authority or power. **2.** Supreme position in achievement, character, or estimation 1589.

1. Man disobeying..sinns Against the high Supremacie of Heav'n MILT. Possibly Rome had not then resolved to derive her S. from St. Peter 1714. Phr. *Act of S.* (or *S. Act*), any of the acts of Parliament in which is laid down the position of the sovereign (*royal* or *regal s.*) as supreme head on earth of the Church of England, or as supreme governor of England in spiritual and temporal matters. *Oath of (the King's) S.*, the oath in which this is acknowledged. **2.** The naval s. of Athens over the rest of the Greek states 1872.

Supreme (s'uprī·m), *a.* and *sb.* 1523. [– L. *supremus*, superl. of *superus* that is above, f. *super* above. For the formation cf. EXTREME.] **A.** *adj.* **1.** Highest (in literal sense), loftiest, topmost. Now only *poet.* **2.** Highest in authority or rank; holding the highest place in authority, government, or power 1532. **b.** Said of the authority, command, etc. 1539. **c.** *transf.* and *fig.* 1656. **3.** Of the highest quality, degree, or amount 1593. **b.** Of persons: Highest or greatest in character or achievement 1611. **c.** Of a point or period of time: Of highest or critical importance 1878. **4.** *spec.* Applied to God (or his attributes), as the paramount ruler of the world, or the most exalted being or intelligence; also to the most exalted of heathen deities 1594. **5.** Last, final, as belonging to the moment of death. Now only a gallicism. 1606.

1. Day set on Cambria's hills s. MACAULAY. **2.** When we say that the legislature is s., we mean, that it is the highest power known to the constitution *'Junius' Lett.* **c.** The lower still I fall, onely Supream In miserie MILT. **3.** They have..s. endurance in war and in labour EMERSON. **b.** The S. Quack CARLYLE. **c.** The s. moment of the battle 1883. **4.** Human science is..adverse to the belief in a S. Intelligence 1854.

B. *sb.* †**1.** A person having supreme authority, rank, or power; sometimes = superior –1807. **2.** The highest degree or amount *of* something 1760. **3.** As a title of God (or an exalted deity). *The S.*: the Supreme Being, God. 1702.

2. A drainless shower Of light is poesy; 'tis the s. of power KEATS. Hence **Supre·me-ly** *adv.*, **-ness.**

Supremity (s'upre·mĭti). Now *rare.* 1538. [– late L. *supremitas, -tat-*, f. *supremus*; see prec., -ITY.] = SUPREMACY 1, 2.

Sur- (sǒr, sǒɹ), *prefix* – (O)Fr. *sur-*, earlier *sor-*, *sour(e* :– L. *super*, used in various senses of SUPER-, as in SURCHARGE, SURCOAT, SURNAME, SURPASS, SURVIVE. **Sura·ngular** *a.* = SUPRA-*angular*.

‖**Sura**[1] (su·ra). *India.* 1598. [– Skr. *surā* spirituous liquor, wine.] The fermented sap of various species of palm, as the wild date, the coco-nut, and the palmyra.

‖**Sura**[2] (sū·ra). 1661. [– Arab. *sūra.*] A chapter or larger section of the Koran.

†**Suraddi·tion.** 1611. [f. SUR- + ADDITION. Cf. Fr. *suraddition*, and med.L. *superadditio* further addition (XIII).] An additional name or title. SHAKS.

Surah (s'ūə·rā). 1881. [repr. Fr. pronunc. of SURAT.] A soft twilled silk fabric used for women's dresses.

Sural (s'ūə·răl), *a.* 1615. [– mod.L. *suralis*, f. *sura* calf of the leg; see -AL[1].] *Anat.* Of or pertaining to the calf of the leg; esp. in *s. artery, vein.*

†**Su·rance.** ME. [– OFr. *surance*, f. *sur* SURE *a.*, after ASSURANCE.] = ASSURANCE –1603.

Surat (s'uræ·t, s'ūə·ræt, su·ræt). 1643. Name of a town and district in the presidency of Bombay, India, used *attrib.* to designate (*a*) a kind of cotton produced in the neighbourhood, (*b*) coarse cotton goods, usu. uncoloured; also *ellipt.* and as *sb.* (with *pl.*) = *S. cotton*, etc.

Surbase (sǒ·ɹ,bē's). 1678. [f. SUR- + BASE *sb.*[1]] *Arch.* **a.** A border or moulding immediately above the base or lower panelling of a wainscotted room. **b.** A cornice or series of mouldings above the dado of a pedestal, podium, etc. 1815.

Surbased (sǒɹ,bē·st), *a.* 1763. [repr. Fr. *surbaissé*, f. *sur-* exceedingly = SUPER- III. 1 b + *baissé* lowered.] Arch. *S. arch*, an arch whose rise is less than half the span. So *s. dome.*

†**Surbate**, *v.* 1590. [Back-formation from †*surbated*, f. OFr. *surbatu* (pa. pple. of *surbatre*, f. *sur-* exceedingly = SUPER- III. 1 b + *batre* beat).] **1.** *trans.* To bruise or make sore (the hoofs or feet) with excessive walking; to make (an animal or person) foot-sore –1707. **2.** *intr.* for *pass.* To become foot-sore –1725.

†**Surbe·d**, *v.* 1677. [f. SUR- = 'up' + BED *sb.* II. 5 b.] *trans.* To set (a block of stone) edgeways; also, to set (coal) edgeways on a fire –1767.

Surcease (sǒɹ,sī·s), *sb. arch.* 1586. [f. next.] The action, or an act, of bringing or coming to an end; (a) cessation, stop; *esp.* (a) temporary cessation, suspension or intermission.

If th' Assassination Could trammell vp the Consequence, and catch With his s., Successe SHAKS. All the while he talked without s. LONGF.

Surcease (sǒɹ,sī·s), *v. arch.* late ME. [f. OFr. *sursis*, fem. *-sise* (cf. AFr. *sursise* omission), pa. pple. of *surseoir* refrain, delay, suspend :– L. *supersedēre* SUPERSEDE; early assim. in sp. to CEASE.] **1.** *intr.* To leave off, stop, cease from some action (finally or temporarily). **2.** To come to an end, be discontinued; to cease. late ME. **3.** *trans.* To desist from, discontinue; to give up (a course of action, etc.); also, to refrain from 1464. †**4.** To put a stop to, bring to an end; to stay (legal proceedings) –1695.

1. The great Arch-Angel from his warlike toile Surceas'd MILT. **2.** That the cause being taken away, the effect also might s. 1633. **3.** [She] had surceased her tyranny 1897.

Surcharge (sǒ·ɹ,tʃā·ɹdʒ), *sb.* 1569. [f. next.] **1.** = OVERCHARGE *sb.* 2. 1601. **b.** *Equity.* The act of showing an omission in an account, or a statement showing this 1700. **c.** A charge made by an auditor upon a public official in respect of an amount improperly paid by him 1879. **2.** *Law.* (tr. law-L. *superoneratio.*) The overstocking of a common or forest. *Obs.* exc. *Hist.* 1569. **3.** = OVERCHARGE *sb.* 1. 1603. **4.** The action of surcharging or condition of being surcharged; overloading 1625. **5.** An additional mark printed on the face of a postage-stamp, esp. for the purpose of changing its face value 1881.

3. Any s. of punishment on persons adjudged to penance, so as to shorten their lives BLACKSTONE.

Surcharge (sǒɹ,tʃā·ɹdʒ), *v.* late ME. [– OFr. *surcharger*; see SUR-, CHARGE *v.*] **1.** *trans.* To charge (a person) too much as a price or payment; to overburden with expense, exactions, etc.; to subject to an additional or extra charge or payment. **b.** *Equity.* To show an omission in (an account); *absol.* to show that the accounting party ought to have charged himself with more than he has 1754. **c.** To make a charge upon (a public official or body) in respect of an amount improperly paid by him; hence, to disallow (an item of expenditure in an account) 1885. **2.** *Law.* To overstock (a common, etc.) by putting more cattle into it than the person has a right to do or than the pasture will sustain. Also *absol. Obs.* exc. *Hist.* 1480. **3.** To put an additional or excessive (physical) burden or weight upon; to overload, weigh down 1582. **b.** With ref. to surfeit of food or drink 1603. **c.** To charge to excess *with* moisture, a substance in solution, or the like 1611. **4.** In non-physical senses: To weigh down, overburden; to bear heavily upon 1581. **b.** To oppress or overwhelm (*with* emotion, sorrow, or suffering) 1566. **c.** *pass.* To have an excess of inhabitants, inmates, or members 1572. **5.** To print an additional mark on the face of (a postage-stamp), esp. for the purpose of changing its value 1870.

1. c. If any item of expenditure is illegal it is liable to be surcharged by the auditor 1885. **3.** Like a fair flower surcharg'd with dew MILT. **4. b.** Till his spirit sank, Surcharged, within him WORDSW. Hence **Surcha·rger**, one who surcharges.

Surcingle (sǒ·ɹ,sing'l), *sb.* late ME. [– OFr. *s(o)urcengle*, f. *sor-* SUR- + *cengle* (mod. *sangle*) CINGLE.] **1.** A girth for a horse or other animal; *esp.* a large girth passing over a sheet, pack, etc. and keeping it in place on the animal's back. **2.** A girdle or belt which confines the cassock. Now *rare.* 1672.

†**Surcloy**, *v.* 1594. [f. SUR- + CLOY *v.*, after *surfeit.*] *trans.* To cloy excessively, surfeit –1620.

Surcoat (sǒ·ɹ,koᵘt). ME. [– OFr. *sur-*, *sourcot*; see SUR-, COAT *sb.* Cf. AL. *surcotus*, *supercota* (c1200).] An outer coat or garment, commonly of rich material, worn by people of rank of both sexes; often worn by armed men over their armour, and having the heraldic arms depicted on it.

A long surcote of pers vpon he hade CHAUCER.

Surculose (sǒ·ɹkiŭloᵘs), *a. rare.* 1845. [– L. *surculosus*, f. *surculus* twig; see -OSE[1].] *Bot.* Producing shoots or suckers.

Surd (sǒɹd), *a.* and *sb.* 1551. [– L. *surdus* deaf, silent, mute, (of sound, etc.) dull, indistinct. The mathematical sense 'irrational' arises from L. *surdus* being used to render Gr. ἄλογος (Euclid bk. x. Def.) speechless, irrational, absurd, through the medium of Arab. *jadr aṣamm*, lit. 'deaf root'.] **A.** *adj.* **1.** *Math.* Of a number or quantity (esp. a root): That cannot be expressed in finite terms of ordinary numbers or quantities: = IRRATIONAL A. 3. †**2.** Deaf (*rare*) –1819. **3.** *fig.* †**a.** Insensate, unintelligent –1676. **b.** Irrational, stupid 1610. **4.** *Phonetics.* Uttered without vibration of the vocal chords; voiceless, 'breathed': opp. to SONANT. Now *rare.* 1767.

2. Such a s. and Earless Generation of Men SIR T. BROWNE.

B. *sb.* **1.** *Math.* A surd or irrational number or quantity, esp. root: see A. 1. 1557. **2.** *Phonetics.* A speech-sound uttered without 'voice'; a 'breath' consonant: see A. 4. 1789. So **Surd** *v. trans.* to deaden or dull the sound of, as by a mute.

Surdity (sǒ·ɹdĭti). 1597. [– Fr. *surdité* or L. *surditas, -tat-*, f. *surdus*; see prec., -ITY.] Deafness.

Sure (ʃūəɹ), *a.* and *adv.* ME. [– OFr. *sur-e*, earlier *sëur-e* (mod. *sûr*) :– L. *securus* SECURE *a.*] **A.** *adj.* **I.** Safe, secure: = SECURE *a.* II. 1, 2, 3. –1718.

The Forrest is not three leagues off, If we recouer that, we are s. enough SHAKS. Phr. *To make* (a person or thing) *s.*, to get into one's possession or power, to secure, = *make s. of*; to put beyond the power of doing harm; (contextually) to kill.

II. Trustworthy, firm, steadfast. **1.** That can be depended or relied on; trustworthy, reliable. Now *arch.* or *dial.* ME. **b.** Applied to agents or their actions, almost = Steady, steadfast, unfaltering 1450. **2.** Of material objects (in early use esp. of weapons or armour): Not liable to break or give way, sound, 'trusty'; not liable to be displaced, firm, firmly fixed, immovable. *arch.* late ME. **3.** Firmly established or settled; steadfast, stable; not liable to be destroyed or overthrown. *arch.* late ME. †**b.** Of possessions, etc.: That may be counted on to be received or held –1670. †**4. a.** Engaged to be married, betrothed, affianced (*to make s.*, to betroth); also, joined in wedlock, married –1665. †**b.** Engaged or bound by allegiance or devotion (*to* a person or party). –1715.

1. b. My Promise, Lord, is ever s. 1696. **2.** He hath made the rounde worlde so s., that it can not be moued COVERDALE *Ps.* 92[3]:1. **3.** In s. and certayne hope of resurreccion to eternall lyfe *Bk. Com. Prayer.* **b.** If I thought this would be s. money 1669. *To make s.*: to secure *to* or settle upon a person. **4. a.** *Merry W.* v. v. 237. **b.** *To make s.*, to bind by allegiance, or secure the allegiance of.

III. Subjectively certain; certain in mind; having no doubt; assured, confident. Also, convinced, morally certain. ME.

He..gues'd that it was she, But being mask'd, he was not s. of it SHAKS. Phr. *I'm s. I don't know*, etc. (giving asseverative force to a statement). *Well, I'm s.!* used as an exclam. of surprise. *To be s.* = as one may be sure; for a certainty, certainly, undoubtedly, of course; now colloq. and often concessive = it must be admitted, indeed; also absol. *Well, to be s.!* as an exclam. of surprise.

IV. Objectively certain. **1. a.** That one may count on as about to be; certain to come or happen 1565. **b.** That one may rely on as true; indisputable.. Now *rare.* 1470. **c.** *For s.*: as or for a certainty, undoubtedly. Now *colloq.* 1586. **2. a.** Of methods or means: That may be relied on to attain its end or produce the desired or stated result; unfailing, unerring 1530. **b.** Of signs or signals: Producing or leading to certainty; infallible 1559.

1. a. Luck's a chance, but trouble's s. HOUSMAN. Phr. *S. thing* (orig. *U.S.*): a certainty; often as an ejaculation of strong assent = Yes, indeed! **b.** He haid suire knawledg quhair the king was 1578. **c.** *P.R.* II. 35. **2.** Phr. *S. card*; see CARD *sb.*² 1. *S.-fire* adj., certain to come off, unfailing (*U.S.*).

V. Senses combining III and IV. **1.** With *of*: Certain to receive, get, attain, find, have, or keep. Also with gerund, as *s. of getting* = certain to get. ME. **2.** With inf. (act. or pass.): Certain to do or to be something. late ME.

1. We are s. of Sea there DE FOE. **2.** The.. oration..was s. to be full of pungent criticism 1885.

Phrases. *To make s.* (intr. or with clause). **a.** *absol.*, or with *of* followed by a noun of action: To make something certain as an end or result; to preclude risk of failure. (*b*) with *of* followed by a sb.: To act so as to be certain of getting or winning. **b.** With clause or *of*: To make something certain as a fact; to preclude risk of error; to ascertain. (*b*) *loosely*. To feel certain, be convinced. *Be s.* (*to do* something, or *that*.., also mod. colloq. *and*) = take care, don't fail (only in imper. or inf.).

B. *adv.* **1.** Securely, safely. *Obs.* or *arch.* late ME. **2.** Certainly, with certainty; without risk of failure. Now *dial.* = 'for certain, without fail'. late ME. **3.** Qualifying a statement: Assuredly, undoubtedly. Now *poet.*, exc. *dial.* (Irish) and *U.S.* late ME. **b.** With weakened emphasis, (*a*) concessive = One must admit, admittedly, of course, (*b*) used to guard against overstatement = At any rate, to say the least, or (*c*) = SURELY *adv.* II. b. Now *dial.* 1552. **c.** Used to emphasize *yes* or *no*; also alone = Certainly. *dial.* 1813. **4. a.** In similative phr. (*as*) *s. as* (*death*, '*eggs is eggs*', *fate*, *a gun*, etc.). late ME. **b.** In phr. *s. enough*: without doubt 1545.

1. 1 *Hen. VI*, V. i. 16. **2.** I'll pay you the five dollars a week then, s. 1902. **3.** That name speaks pardon, s. KINGSLEY. **b.** S. no clergyman ever offered so much out of his own purse for the sake of any religion POPE. S. it cannot be! GOLDSM. **4. a.** As s. as the year came round 1833. **b.** The number came up s. enough THACKERAY. Hence **Su·reness**, the quality or condition of being s.

Sure-footed (stress variable), *a.* 1633. [SURE *a.* II. 1 b.] **1.** Sure of foot; not liable to slip, stumble, or fall 1707. **2.** *fig.* Not liable to make a 'slip' or error; unerring 1633.

Surely (ʃūə·ɹli), *adv.* ME. [f. SURE *a.* + -LY².] **I. 1.** Without danger, risk of injury, loss, or displacement; securely, safely; firmly. *arch.* †**b.** Steadfastly –1612. **2.** With certainty, assurance, or confidence; for certain. *arch.* late ME. **3.** Without risk of failure; infallibly. Now chiefly in *slowly but s.* late ME.

1. The Indian must be..s. tied to a post by his hands 1648. **b.** *Tam. Shr.* IV. ii. 36. **2.** As if they s. knew their sovran Lord was by MILT.

II. Certainly, assuredly, undoubtedly. Often as a mere intensive: Truly, verily, indeed ME. **b.** Used to express a strong belief in the statement, or as implying a readiness to maintain it against imaginary or possible denial: = as may be confidently supposed; as must be the case; may not one be sure that..? 1588.

Alas! they seem but too s. to be here SCOTT. **b.** This incident is s. an essential part of the story 1870.

†**Su·resby, su·reby.** 1553. [f. SURE *a.* + -BY 2.] An appellation for a person (and hence for a thing) that is 'sure' or may be depended upon –1675.

Surety (ʃūə·ɹti), *sb.* ME. [– OFr. *surté*, *seurté* (mod. *sûreté*) :– L. *securitas*, *-tat-* SECURITY.] **I.** Condition of being (or something that is) sure. †**1.** Safety, security *from* danger, an enemy, etc. –1620. **2.** Accuracy; sureness (*rare*). late ME. **3.** †**a.** = SECURITY I. 3 –1598. **b.** Certain knowledge. *arch.* 1509. **4.** †**a.** Certainty of an end or result aimed at –1607. †**b.** Certainty of a fact or event –1604. **c.** A certainty, fact. *arch.* 1460.

2. He handled French..with neatness of movement and s. of touch 1892. **4. c.** Phr. *For* or *of a s.* = for certain (*arch.*).

II. Means of being sure. **1.** A formal engagement entered into; a pledge, bond, guarantee, or security given for the fulfilment of an undertaking. Now superseded by SECURITY. ME. **2.** *gen.* Ground of certainty or safety, guarantee. Now *rare.* late ME. **3.** A person who undertakes some specific responsibility on behalf of another who remains primarily liable; one who makes himself liable for the default or miscarriage of another, or for the performance of some act on his part (e.g. payment of a debt, appearance in court for trial, etc.); a bail. late ME. **b.** A sponsor at baptism. *arch.* 1548. **c.** *fig.* Applied to Christ (after Heb. 7:22) 1557.

3. When a man becomes s., let him give the security in a distinct form JOWETT. Phr. †*To call to s.*; She call'd the Saints to suretie That [etc.] SHAKS. **c.** Soon after He that was our S. died COWPER. Hence †**Surety** *v. trans.*, to be s. for. **Su·retyship**, the position or function of a s.

Su:rexcita·tion (sɔ̄r-). 1873. [– Fr. *surexcitation*; see SUR-, EXCITATION.] Excessive excitation.

Surf (sɔ̄ɹf). 1685. [In early use sometimes in phr. *surf of the sea*; continuing in sense and chronology †*suff* (*of the sea*) XVI–XVII, and perh. an alt. of the latter by assoc. with SURGE *sb.* Both *suff* and *surf* are first used with ref. to the coast of India.] **1.** The swell of the sea which breaks upon a shore, esp. a shallow shore. (Now usu. with implication of sense 2.) **2.** The mass or line of white foamy water caused by the sea breaking upon a shore or a rock 1757. Hence **Surf** *v.*, to go surf-riding 1917.

Comb.: **s.-bathing**, bathing in the surf, usu. with a board; **-bird**, a small plover-like bird, *Aphriza virgata*, found on the Pacific coast of America; **-board**, a long narrow board on which one rides over a heavy s. to shore; **-boat**, a boat specially constructed for passing through s.; **-clam**, a large clam, esp. *Mactra* (or *Spisula*) *solidissima*, found on the Atlantic coast of the United States; **-coot**, **-duck**, a N. Amer. species of sea-duck of the genus *Œdemia*, esp. *Œ. perspicillata*, found sometimes in Great Britain; **-fish**, any one of the numerous species of the family *Embiotocidæ*, abundant on the coast of California; **-man** *U.S.*, a member of the crew of a surf-boat; **-riding**, riding on a s.-board as a sport; **-scoter** = *s.-duck*; **-smelt**, a species of smelt, *Hypomesus olidus*, found on the Pacific coast of the United States; **-whiting**, the silver whiting, *Menticirrus littoralis*.

Surface (sɔ̄·ɹfės, -ės), *sb.* 1611. [– Fr. *surface* (XVI), f. *sur-* SUR- + *face* FACE *sb.*, after L. *superficies*.] **1.** The outermost boundary (or one of the boundaries) of any material body, immediately adjacent to the air or empty space, or to another body. **b.** *fig.*, usu. denoting that part or aspect of anything which presents itself to a slight or casual mental view; outward appearance; often in such phrases as *on the s.* = superficial(ly) 1725. **2.** *Geom.* A magnitude or continuous extent having only two dimensions (length and breadth, without thickness), such as constitutes the boundary of a material body or that between two adjacent portions of space; a superficies 1658. **3.** The outermost part of a material body, considered with respect to its form, texture, or extent; *esp.* in art or manufacture, an exterior of a particular form or 'finish' 1698. **b.** *spec.* The upper boundary or top of ground or soil, exposed to the air (in *Mining*, as dist. from underground workings and shafts); the outer (according to ancient ideas, the upper) boundary of the earth 1612. **c.** The upper boundary or top of a body of water or other liquid 1625. **d.** The outside of an animal or plant body, or of any part of it; also, the inner boundary of a hollow or tubular part 1748. **4.** An extent or area of material considered as a subject for operations 1662. **5.** Superficial area or extent 1640.

1. An optical prism..is a solid having two plane surfaces 1831. **c.** The wing of a flying machine, whether plane or curved 1903. **3. b.** The aged Earth agast..Shall from the surface to the center shake MILT. **c.** The smiling s. of the deep COWPER. **d.** Diseases affecting internal surfaces 1822. **4.** To calculate the area of the frictional surfaces 1867.

attrib. and *Comb.*: **s.-car** *U.S.*, a tram-car running on a track level with the s. of the ground, as dist. from an elevated or underground track; **s. condensation**, condensation of steam by a *s.-condenser*; **-condenser**, in a steam-engine, a condenser in which exhaust-steam is condensed by contact with cold metallic surfaces; **-contact**, (*a*) contact of surfaces; (*b*) applied *attrib.* to a system of electric traction in which the current is conveyed to the cars through conductors on the s. of the roadway; **-damage**, damage done to the s. of the ground by mining operations; *pl.* compensation payable for this; **-gauge**, an implement for testing the accuracy of plane surfaces; **-grub**, the larva of various moths, which live just beneath the s. of the soil; a CUTWORM; **-integral** *Math.*, an integral taken over the whole area of a s.; **-plate**, (*a*) a plate or flat bar of iron fixed on the upper s. of a rail on a railway; (*b*) an iron plate for testing the accuracy of a flat s.; **-printing**, printing from a raised s. (as dist. from an incised plate); **s. process**, a process of s.-printing; **-road** *U.S.*, a railway on the s. of the ground, as dist. from an elevated or underground railway; **-tension** *Physics*, the tension of the s.-film of a liquid, due to the cohesion of its particles; **-water**, (*a*) water that collects on the s. of the ground; (*b*) the s. layer of a body of water. **b.** quasi-*adj.* Pertaining to, existing or occurring on, a surface; acting upon or against a s.; *fig.* superficial.

Surface (sɔ̄·ɹfės, -ės), *v.* 1778. [f. prec.] **1.** *trans.* To give a (particular kind of, esp. a smooth or even) surface to; to cover the surface of (*with* something). **2.** *intr.* To mine near the surface 1860. Hence **Su·rfacer.**

Surfaceman (sɔ̄·ɹfėsmæ̆n, -ės-). 1878. [SURFACE *sb.* 3 b.] A miner or other labourer who works at the surface, or in the open air; on a railway, a workman who keeps the permanent way in repair.

Surfeit (sɔ̄·ɹfėt), *sb.* ME. [– OFr. *sur-*, *sorfeit*, *-fet* :– Rom. **superfactum* subst. use of pa. pple. n. of **superficere* (cf. late L. *superficiens* excessive, OFr. *sorfaisant* immoderate), f. *super-* SUPER- III. b + *facere* do, act.] **1.** Excess, superfluity; excessive amount or supply *of* something. **2.** (An) excessive indulgence, (an) excess. (Now only as fig. use of 3, 3 b.) late ME. **3.** Excessive taking *of* food or drink; gluttonous indulgence in eating and drinking ME. **b.** An excessive indulgence in food or drink that overloads the stomach and disorders the system. late ME. †**c.** The excessive amount eaten –1700. **4.** Sickness or derangement of the system arising from excessive eating or drinking 1513. **5.** Disgust arising from excess; nausea, satiety 1644. **6.** *Mining* = CHOKE-*damp* 1708.

1. A s. of the precious metals 1847. **3.** Fasting is only to avoid surfet 1684. **b.** It's possible to have a s. of water as well as wine 1649. **4.** He died of a s. caused by intemperance GOLDSM. **5.** Phr. *To* (*a*) *s.*, to satiety, *ad nauseam*; He enjoys to a s. these bounties of nature 1855.

Su·rfeit, *a. arch.* 1699. [app. contr. from *surfeited.*] Satiated, surfeited.

Surfeit (sɔ̄·ɹfėt), *v.* late ME. [f. SURFEIT *sb.*] **1.** *trans.* To feed to excess or satiety; to sicken or disorder by overfeeding. Also *absol.* **2.** *fig.* or *gen.* To fill or supply to excess; to oppress or disgust with over-abundance of something 1592. **3.** *intr.* To eat or drink to excess *of*. (In early use including sensual indulgence in general.) late ME. **b.** *fig.* To indulge in something to excess; to take one's fill, 'feast', 'revel'. Now *rare* or *Obs.* 1586. **4.** To fall sick in consequence of excess. Now *rare* or *Obs.* 1585. **b.** *fig.* or *gen.* To become disgusted or nauseated by excess of something; to grow sick *of*. Now *rare* or *Obs.* 1605.

1. Pork must be well done, or it is apt to s. MRS. GLASSE. **2.** He is weary and surfeited of business PEPYS. **3.** Ev'n the wholesomest Meats may be surfeited on BOYLE. **b.** *Twel. N.* I. i. 2. **4.** They are as sicke that surfet with too much, as they that starue with nothing SHAKS. **b.** So early dost thou s. with the wealth CARY. Hence **Su·rfeiter**, one who surfeits, a glutton.

Surfuse (sɒɹ,fiū·z), *v.* 1883. [f. SUR- + FUSE *v.*] *Physics.* = SUPERFUSE 3. Hence **Surfu·sion** = SUPERFUSION 2.

Surfy (sɔ̄·ɹfi), *a.* 1814. [f. SURF + -Y¹.] Abounding in, consisting of, or resembling surf.

The countless ranks of s. breakers RUSKIN.

Surge (sɔ̄ɹdʒ), *sb.* 1490. [First used as tr. OFr. *sourgeon* (mod. *surgeon*) and prob. – its base *sourge-*, pres. stem of *sourdre*; see next. In senses 3, 4, f. next.] †**1. a.** A fountain, stream –1567. †**b.** The source of a river or other water –1588. **2.** A high rolling swell of water, esp. on the sea; a large, heavy, or violent wave; a billow 1530. **b.** Such waves or billows collectively; the rising or driving swell of the sea 1567. **c.** *fig.* in ref. to feelings, actions, etc.: Impetuous onset or agitated movement 1520. **d.** *transf.* in ref. to fire, wind, sound, etc.; also to 'rolling' hills or the like 1667. **3.** *Naut.*, etc. The slipping back of a rope or chain wound round a capstan, etc.; more gen., a sudden jerk or strain 1748. **4.** *Naut.* The part of a capstan or windlass upon which the rope surges 1664.

2. The mountain-billows..s. above s., Burst into chaos with tremendous roar THOMSON. **b.** Some boats were overset by the S. of the Sea 1702. **d.** The surges of the warm south-west LOWELL. Hence **Su·rgeful** *a. poet.* (*rare*). **Su·rgeless** *a.* (*rare*).

Surge (sɔ̆ɹdʒ), *v.* 1511. [f. OFr. *sourge-* (see prec.) or – OFr. *sorgir* (mod. *surgir*) – Cat. *sorgir* anchor, *surgir* land (OFr. *sourdre*) :– L. *surgere* rise.] **1.** *intr.* To rise and fall or toss on the waves; to ride (at anchor, or along over the waves). †**2.** To rise, spring, issue, as a stream from its source, or from underground –1661. **3.** To rise in great waves or billows, as the sea; to swell or heave with great force, as a large wave; to move tempestuously 1566. **b.** *transf.*, of a crowd of people, etc., and *fig.* (chiefly *s. up*), of feelings, thoughts, etc. **4.** *trans.* To cause to move in, or as in, swelling waves or billows; to drive with waves 1607. **5.** *Naut.* **a.** *intr.* To slip back accidentally, as a rope or chain round a capstan, windlass, etc.; to slip round without moving onwards, as a wheel 1625. **b.** *trans.* To let go or slacken suddenly (a rope wound round a capstan, etc.); also with the capstan, etc. as obj. Also *absol.* 1769. **c.** *intr.* Of a ship: To sweep, pull, or jerk in a certain direction 1839.

1. The..lighter..made faste to the shippe surging at an anker in the Thames 1611. **3.** The waues of the sea..surged tempestuouslye 1586. **b.** From below there surged up the buzz of voices 1891. **5. b.** It's blowing the devil himself, and I am afraid to s. 1853.

Surgent (sɔ̆·ɹdʒĕnt), *a.* 1592. [– L. *surgens, -ent-*, pr. pple. of *surgere* rise; see prec., -ENT.] Rising or swelling in waves, or as a flood or spring; surging.

Surgeon (sɔ̆·ɹdʒən). ME. [– AFr. *surgien*, also *sirogen, cyrogen, sur(r)igien*, contr. of OFr. *serurgien, cir-* (mod. *chirurgien*); see CHIRURGEON.] **1.** One who practises the art of healing by manual operation; a practitioner who treats wounds, fractures, deformities, or disorders by surgical means. Formerly often a medical man, doctor, now *spec.* one who holds a licence or diploma from the Royal College of Surgeons or any other body, legally qualifying him to practise in surgery. **b.** A medical officer in the army or navy (on board ship = 'ship's doctor') 1591. **2.** = *s.-bird, -fish* 1855.

1. b. *S.-general*: see GENERAL *a.*

Comb.: **s.-bird,** the jacana; **-fish,** a fish of the genus *Acanthurus* (cf. DOCTOR *sb.*); **surgeon's knot,** a knot in which the thread is passed twice through the same loop. Hence **Su·rgeoncy,** the office or position of a s. †**Su·rgeonry,** surgery.

Surgery (sɔ̆·ɹdʒəri). ME. [– OFr. *surgerie*, contr. of *sirurgerie*, f. *sirurgien* (prec.). Cf. CHIRURGERY, CHIRURGY.] **1.** The art or practice of treating injuries, deformities, and other disorders by manual operation or instrumental appliances; surgical treatment. **2.** The room or office, often in a general practitioner's house, where patients are seen and medicine dispensed 1846.

Surgical (sɔ̆·ɹdʒikăl), *a.* 1770. [Alteration of CHIRURGICAL after SURGEON, SURGERY.] Pertaining to, dealing with, or employed in surgery or the surgeon's art. **b.** *Path.* Resulting from surgical treatment 1859.

S. scissors are of many forms 1846. **b.** Not unfrequently followed by S. fever 1859. Hence **Su·rgically** *adv.*

Surgy (sɔ̆·ɹdʒi), *a.* 1582. [f. SURGE *sb.* + -Y[1].] Full of or abounding in surge; pertaining to or characteristic of surge; billowy, tempestuous.

The s. murmurs of the lonely sea KEATS.

Suricate (sⁱūᵊ·rikeⁱt). 1781. [– Fr. *suricate, -kate*, of native S. African origin.] An animal of the genus *Suricata*, esp. *S. zenik* or *S. tetradactyla*, a viverrine burrowing carnivore of Cape Colony; the meerkat or zenick.

Surinam (sⁱūᵊrinæ·m), name of the country in S. America also called Dutch Guiana; used *attrib.* in specific names of animals, plants, and products, as *S. bunting, grass, medlar*, etc.; **S. toad** (also *S. water toad*), a large flat toad, the PIPA.

Surly (sɔ̆·ɹli), *a.* 1572. [Altered spelling of †*sirly* (XIV–XVII), f. SIR *sb.* + -LY[1].] †**1.** Masterful, imperious; haughty, arrogant, supercilious –1726. †**b.** as *adv.* –1693. **2.** Churlishly ill-humoured; rude and cross; 'gloomily morose' (J.) 1670. **3.** *fig.* †'Imperious', stern and rough; (of soil, etc.) obstinate, refractory, intractable; (of weather, etc.) rough and gloomy, threatening and dismal 1600.

1. Be opposite with a kinsman, s. with seruants SHAKS. **b.** *Jul. C.* I. iii. 21. **2.** Nor s. porter stands in guilty state GOLDSM. A s., grumbling manner DICKENS. **3.** In a s. Season EVELYN. Before the s. Clod resists the rake DRYDEN. Hence **Su·rlily** *adv.* **Su·rliness.**

‖**Surma, soorma** (sūᵊ·ɹmă). *India.* 1819. [Urdu – Pers. *surma.*] A black powder consisting of sulphide of antimony or of lead, used by Indian women for staining the eyebrows and eyelids.

Surmark, var. SIRMARK.

Surmaster (sɔ̆·ɹmā:stəɹ). 1512. [alt. of orig. *submaster* (= *hypodidascalus* in Erasmus's letters) – med.L. *submagister*, f. *sub-* SUB- 6 + *magister* MASTER.] The title of the second master at St. Paul's School, London.

Surmisable (sɒɹməi·săb'l), *a.* 1817. [f. SURMISE *v.* + -ABLE.] That may be surmised; conjecturable, supposable.

Surmisal (sɒɹməi·zăl). Now *rare.* 1641. [f. as prec. + -AL[1].] = next.

Surmise (sɒɹməi·z, sɔ̆·ɹməiz), *sb.* 1451. [– AFr., OFr. *surmise*, f. *surmettre*; see next.] †**1.** *Law.* A formal allegation or information; *spec.* in *Eccl. Law*, the allegation in the libel –1713. †**2.** An allegation, charge, imputation; *esp.* a false, unfounded, or unproved charge or allegation –1660. **3.** (A) suspicion. *Obs.* or merged in 4. –1837. **4.** An idea formed in the mind (and, often, expressed) that something may be true, but without certainty, and on very slight evidence, or with no evidence 1594. **b.** *gen.* 1590. †**5.** The formation of an idea in the mind; conception, imagination –1637.

4. Surmises and Sleight probabilities will not serue HOOKER. **b.** This is sure, the rest — s. BROWNING. **5.** For so to interpose a little ease, Let our frail thoughts dally with false s. MILT.

Surmise (sɒɹməi·z), *v.* late ME. [f. AFr., OFr. *surmis(e*, pa. pple. of *surmettre* accuse – late L. *supermittere* (in med.L. accuse), f. *super-* SUPER- + *mittere* put.] †**1.** *trans.* To put upon some one as a charge or accusation; to charge *on* or *upon*, allege *against* a person; *spec.* in *Law*, to submit as a charge or information, allege formally –1623. †**2.** To devise, plan, contrive, *esp.* falsely or maliciously –1632. †**3.** To suppose, imagine (*that* a thing is so); to expect –1725. †**b.** To conceive, imagine. Also *absol.* –1602. **4.** To form a notion that the thing in question may be so, on slight grounds or without proof; to infer conjecturally. Also *absol.* or *intr.* 1700.

4. Whatever the Jewish nation might s. or know concerning a future life 1835. Can I know, who but s.? BROWNING. Hence **Surmi·ser.**

Surmount (sɒ̆ɹmau·nt), *v.* late ME. [– (O)Fr. *surmonter*; see SUR-, SUPER- I. 2, MOUNT *v.*] †**1.** *trans.* To rise above, go beyond, surpass –1776. †**b.** = SURPASS *v.* 4. –1738. †**2.** *absol.* or *intr.* To be superior; to excel; to be greater or more numerous –1687. **3.** *trans.* To prevail over, get the better of, overcome. late ME. **4.** To mount, rise, or ascend above (also *fig.*); also, to surpass in height, overtop. Now *rare.* late ME. †**5.** *intr.* To mount, rise, ascend (above something); to extend in height; *fig.* to exalt oneself; to arise, spring up –1563. **6.** *trans.* To mount upon, get on the top of; *usu.*, to mount and cross to the other side of, climb across, get over; *occas.* to round or weather (a cape); also, to extend over and across 1533. **7.** To stand, lie, or be situated above; to rest on the top of; to top, crown; orig. in *Her.*, said of a crest, or of a charge represented as laid upon another so as to extend across and beyond it. Chiefly in pa. pple.: *surmounted by* = having above or on the top. 1610.

3. The attempts of the rival ministers to s. and supplant each other MACAULAY. **4.** She the highest height in worth surmounts P. FLETCHER. **6.** Simond surmounted the next ridge TYNDALL. **7.** The huge square columns that supported the gate were surmounted by the family crest W. IRVING. Hence **Surmou·ntable** *a.* that may be surmounted. **Surmou·nter.**

Surmou·nted, *ppl. a.* 1728. [f. prec. + -ED[1].] *Arch.* Applied to an arch or vault whose rise is greater than half the span: opp. to SURBASED.

Surmullet (sɒɹmɒ·lĕt). 1672. [– Fr. *surmulet*, f. OFr. *sor* (mod. *saur*) red, of unkn. orig., + *mulet* MULLET.] The red mullet; a name comprising species of *Mullus*, esp. *M. surmuletus*, the Striped S., highly prized as a food-fish, and *M. barbatus*, the Plain S., of a plain red.

Surname (sɔ̆·ɹneⁱm), *sb.* ME. [alt. of †*surnoun* (XIV–XV) – AFr. *surnoun* = (O)Fr. *surnom*, f. *sur-* SUR- + *noun* NAME (cf. NOUN), after med.L. *super-*, *supranomen* (cf. late L. *supernominare*).] **1.** A name, title, or epithet added to a person's name or names, esp. one derived from his birthplace or from some quality or achievement; e.g. William *Rufus*. *Obs.* or *arch.* †**b.** A second, or an alternative, name or title given to a person, place, edifice, etc. –1656. **2.** The name which a person bears in common with the other members of his family, as dist. from his *Christian name*; a family name. late ME. **b.** *transf.*, esp. = COGNOMEN 1, e.g. Publius Cornelius *Scipio*. late ME.

Surname (sɔ̆·ɹneⁱm), *v.* 1512. [f. prec.] **1.** *trans.* To give an additional name, title, or epithet to 1539. **2.** To give such-and-such a surname to 1512.

1. Tamberlaine (sirnamed the Scourge of God) 1634. **2.** Rockbeare..had..lords sirnamed thereof 1630.

Surnominal (sɒɹnǫ·minăl), *a.* 1875. [f. SURNAME *sb.*, after *name, nominal.*] Of or pertaining to surnames.

Surpass (sɒ̆ɹpɑ·s), *v.* 1555. [– Fr. *surpasser*, f. *sur-* = SUPER- I. 2 + *passer* PASS *v.*] **1.** *trans.* To pass over, overstep (a limit); also, to go beyond (a certain period of time). *Obs.* or *arch.* †**2.** To surmount (*rare*) –1769. **b.** To extend above or beyond. Now *rare.* 1601. **3.** To go beyond (another) in degree, amount, or quality; to be superior to, to excel 1555. **b.** To exceed (a specified measure, as weight, speed, etc.). *rare.* 1591. **c.** To do something that is more or better than (something done or existing) 1592. **4.** To be beyond the range, reach, or capacity of; to be too much or too great for 1592.

1. Nor let the Sea S. his bounds MILT. **3.** This would s. Common revenge MILT. **c.** When a Painter would surpasse the life SHAKS. **4.** Thy strength they know surpassing human rate MILT. Hence **Surpa·ssable** *a.* capable of being surpassed, exceeded, or excelled.

Surpa·ssing, *ppl. a.* (*adv.*) 1580. [f. prec. + -ING[2].] That surpasses what is ordinary; greatly exceeding or excelling others; of very high degree. **b.** *adv.* Surpassingly 1598. Hence **Surpa·ssingly** *adv.* in a s. degree; exceedingly, pre-eminently; **-ness** (*rare*).

Surplice (sɔ̆·ɹplis). ME. [– AFr. *surplis*, OFr. *sourpelis* (mod. *surplis*) – med.L. *superpellicium, -eum* (sc. *vestimentum* garment), subst. use of n. of adj. f. *super* SUPER- I. 1 a + *pellicia* fur garment (see PELISSE).] A loose vestment of white linen having wide sleeves and, in its amplest form, reaching to the feet, worn (usu. over a cassock) by clerics, choristers, and others taking part in church services. (Formerly put on over the fur garments which used to be worn in church as a protection against the cold; hence the name.) **b.** *transf.* Applied to various ample or enveloping garments. late ME.

Comb.: **s.-fees,** the dues received by an incumbent for the performance of marriages, burials, and other ministerial offices. Hence **Su·rpliced** (-plist) *a.* wearing or vested in a s.

Surplus (sɔ̆·ɹplɒ̆s), *sb.* and *a. Pl.* **-uses.** late ME. [– AFr. *surplus*, OFr. *so(u)rplus* (mod. *surplus*) – med.L. *superplus, surplus*, f. *super-* SUPER- IV + *plus* more.] **A.** *sb.* **1.** What remains over and above what has been taken or used; an amount remaining in excess. †Also, (a) superabundance. †**2.** What remains to make up a whole; the remainder, the rest –1759. **B.** *attrib.* or as *adj.*

That is in excess of what is taken, used, or needed 1641.

They now exchange their s. peltry, for blankets, firearms, and brandy ADAM SMITH. The natural law gets rid of s. population 1879.

Surplusage (sǝ·ɹplɒ̆sėdʒ). late ME. [– med.L. *surplusagium*, also *super-*, (XII), f. *surplus*; see prec., -AGE.] = prec. A. 1, 2. **b.** An excess or superabundance (*of* words); *spec.* in *Law*, a word, clause, or statement in an indictment or a plea which is not necessary to its adequacy.

Any..cause that generates a surplussage of blood 1607. **b.** Nor is it surplussage to reiterate the same thought or fact 1851.

Surprisal (sɒ̆ɹprəi·zăl). Now *rare* or *Obs.* 1591. [f. SURPRISE *v.* + -AL¹ 2.] = next 1–4.

The surprizal of these three Cities, Glocester, Bathe, and Cirencester 1611. A sudden s. of the tide called the Eager, where he very narrowly escaped drowning 1647. I do desire some time to consider of it: for it is a great S. 1660.

Surprise (sɒ̆ɹprəi·z), *sb.* 1457. [– (O)Fr. *surpris(e*, subst. use of pa. pple. of *surprendre*; see next.] **1.** *Mil.* The (or an) act of assailing or attacking unexpectedly or without warning, or of taking by this means; †formerly also in more general sense, seizure (of a person, a place, or spoil). **2.** *gen.* The (or an) act of coming *upon* one unexpectedly, or of taking unawares; a sudden attack. Now *rare* or *Obs.* exc. as in b. 1598. **b.** *To take by s.*: to come upon unexpectedly, take unawares; hence, to astonish by unexpectedness 1691. †**c.** An attack of illness; a sudden access *of* emotion –1719. **3.** Something that takes one by surprise; anything unexpected or astonishing 1592. **b.** *spec.* A fancy dish, or an ingredient of a dish, a present, or the like, designed to take one by surprise 1708. **4.** The feeling or emotion excited by something unexpected, or for which one is unprepared; the feeling or mental state, akin to astonishment and wonder, caused by an unexpected occurrence or circumstance; †alarm, terror, or perplexity, caused by a sudden attack, calamity, or the like 1608.

1. The s. and combustion of Troy 1635. **2.** This is no casual error, no lapse, no sudden s. BURKE. **c.** In the Heat and Surprize of Passion COLLIER. **3.** Egypt..is the land of surprises 1879. **4.** *Per.* III. ii. 17. Circumstances which give a delightful Surprize to the Reader ADDISON.

Comb.: **s. packet**, a sealed packet with contents designed to surprise, sold at a trivial price; also *fig.*; **-party**, (*a*) a body of troops for an unexpected attack; (*b*) *U.S.* and *Colonial*, a party who meet by agreement at a friend's house without invitation, bringing provisions with them.

Surprise (sɒ̆ɹprəi·z), *v.* 1474. [prob. first in pa. pple., f. (O)Fr. *surpris(e*, pa. pple. of *surprendre* :– med.L. *superprehendere*, f. L. *super-* SUR- + *præhendere* seize.] †**1.** *trans.* To 'take hold of' or affect suddenly or unexpectedly –1720. **2.** *Mil.*, etc. To assail or attack suddenly and without warning; †to take or capture in this way 1548. †**b.** *gen.* To capture, seize; to take possession of by force; to take prisoner –1799. **3.** To come upon unexpectedly; to take unawares; to take or catch in the act; hence *fig.*, to find or discover (something) suddenly, to detect 1592. †**4.** To implicate or ensnare (a person) as by a sudden proposal or disclosure –1702. **b.** To lead unawares, betray *into* doing something not intended 1696. **5.** To affect with the characteristic emotion caused by something unexpected; to excite wonder by being unlooked-for. Often *pass.*, const. *at* or inf.: colloq. *to be surprised*, to be scandalized or shocked. 1655.

1. All on a sudden miserable pain Surpris'd thee MILT. So..temperate, that I have heard he had never been surprised by excesse EVELYN. **2.** Kerioth is taken, and the strong holds are surprised *Jer.* 48:41. **b.** Is the Traitor Cade surpris'd? SHAKS. **3.** High instincts before which our mortal Nature Did tremble like a guilty Thing surprised WORDSW. **4. b.** If by chance he has been surprized into a short Nap at Sermon ADDISON. **5.** I was exceedingly surpriz'd with the Print of a Man's naked Foot on the Shore DE FOE.

Surpri·sing, *ppl. a.* 1580. [-ING².] **1.** That surprises or takes unawares 1645. **2.** Causing surprise or wonder by its unexpectedness 1663. †**b.** Admirable –1831.

2. One of the lions leaped to a s. height EVELYN. **b.** The renowned, and surprizing, Archpoet Homer 1580. Hence **Surpri·sing-ly** *adv.*, **-ness.**

†**Su·rquidry, su·rquedry.** ME. [– OFr. *s(o)urcuiderie*, f. *s(o)urcuidier*, f. *sur-* SUR- + *cuidier* think; see OUTRECUIDANCE, -ERY.] **1.** Arrogance, haughty pride, presumption –1825. ¶**2.** Misused for: Excess, surfeit –1656. So †**Su·rquidy, -edy** –1819.

Surrealism (sɒri·ăliz'm). 1927. [– Fr. *surréalisme* (A. Breton, 1924); see SUR-, REALISM.] A form of art in which an attempt is made to represent and interpret the phenomena of dreams and similar experiences. So **Surre·alist.**

Surrebutter (sɒrĭbɒ·təɹ). 1601. [f. SUR- + REBUTTER, after SURREJOINDER.] *Law.* In old common-law pleading, a plaintiff's reply to a defendant's rebutter. Also *transf.*, a further rejoinder. So **Surrebu·t** *v. intr.* to reply to a rebutter; *trans.* to repel as by a s. **Surrebu·ttal.**

Surrejoin (sɒrĭdʒoi·n), *v.* 1594. [Back-formation f. next, after *rejoin.*] *Law. intr.* To reply, as a plaintiff, to the defendant's rejoinder; to make a surrejoinder.

Surrejoinder (sɒ̆rĭdʒoi·ndəɹ). 1542. [f. SUR- + REJOINDER.] *Law.* In old common-law pleading, a plaintiff's reply to the defendant's rejoinder. Also *transf.* an answer to a rejoinder or reply (in general).

Surrender (sɒ̆re·ndəɹ), *sb.* 1485. [– AFr. *surrender*, OFr. inf. *surrendre* used as sb.; see next, -ER⁴.] The action or an act of surrendering. **1.** *Law.* **a.** The giving up of an estate to the person who has it in reversion or remainder, so as to merge it in the larger estate; *spec.* the yielding up of a tenancy in a copyhold estate to the lord of the manor for a specified purpose; *transf.* a deed by which such surrender is made 1487. **b.** The giving up of letters patent granting an estate or office 1557. **c.** The giving up by a bankrupt of his property to his creditors or their assignees; also, his due appearance in the bankruptcy court for examination, as formerly required by the bankruptcy acts 1745. **d.** The abandonment of an insurance policy by the party assured on receiving part of the premiums. 1755. **2.** The giving up of something (or of oneself) into the possession or power of another who has or is held to have a claim to it; *esp.* (*Mil.*, etc.) of combatants, a town, territory, etc. *to* an enemy or a superior. In wider sense: Giving up, resignation, abandonment. 1485.

1. a. I haue wastfully spente..the s. of my fathers landes 1583. **d.** *S. value*, the amount payable to an insured person on his surrendering his policy. **2.** To speake..About s. vp of Aquitaine SHAKS. With eyes Of conjugal attraction unreprov'd, And meek s. MILT.

Surrender (sɒ̆re·ndəɹ), *v.* 1466. [– AFr. *surrender*, OFr. *surrendre*, f. *sur-* SUR- + *rendre* RENDER.] **1.** *Law.* **a.** *trans.* To give up (an estate) to one who has it in reversion or remainder; *spec.* to give up (a copyhold estate) to the lord of the manor. Also *absol.* †**b.** To give up (letters patent, tithes) into the hands of the sovereign –1662. **c.** *refl.* or *intr.* of a bankrupt: To appear in the bankruptcy court for examination 1707. **d.** *trans.* Of a bail: To produce (the principal) in court at the appointed time. Also *intr.* or *refl.* of the principal, usu. in phr. *to s. to one's bail.* 1747. **2.** To give up (something) out of one's own possession or power into that of another who has or asserts a claim to it; to yield on demand or compulsion, *esp.* (*Mil.*) to give up the possession of (a fortress, town, territory, etc.) to an enemy or assailant 1509. **b.** More widely: To give up, resign, abandon, esp. in favour of or for the sake of another 1509. **3.** *refl.* To give oneself up into the power of another, esp. as a prisoner 1585. **b.** *fig.* To give oneself up *to* some influence, course of action, etc.; to abandon oneself *to* 1713. **4.** *intr.* for *refl.* = 3; chiefly *Mil.* 1560.

2. One..More worthy this place then my selfe, to whom..I would s. it SHAKS. Luxembergh was surrendered to the French EVELYN. To s. up some of those great jurisdictions over the Highlands that were in his family BURNET. **3. b.** We must s. ourselves..to our duties 1833. Hence **Surrenderee·** *Law*, the person to whom an estate, etc. is surrendered; correl. to *surrenderor.* **Surre·nderer**, one who surrenders. **Surre·nderor** *Law*, one who surrenders an estate, etc. to another; correl. to *surrenderee.*

Surrendry (sɒ̆re·ndri). Now *rare.* 1547. [f. SURRENDER; see -RY.] = SURRENDER *sb.*

Surreption¹ (sɒ̆re·pʃən). late ME. [– L. *surreptio, -ōn-*, f. *surrept-*, pa. ppl. stem of *surripere* seize secretly, (Vulg.) make false suggestions, f. *sub-* SUB- 24 + *rapere* seize; see -ION. Cf. SUBREPTION.] †**1.** Suppression of truth or fact for the purpose of obtaining something, or the action of obtaining something in this way; more gen., fraudulent misrepresentation, or other underhand or stealthy proceeding –1720. **2.** The action of seizing or taking away by stealth; stealing, theft. Now *rare* or *Obs.* 1603.

1. Fame by s. got May stead us for the time, but lasteth not B. JONS. **2.** Four soldiers..whose express office was to prevent the s. of the body 1860. *By s.*, by stealth, stealthily.

†**Surreption**². 1502. [– med.L. *surreptio* (= late L. *subreptio* a creeping in; cf. also med.L. *surreptare* creep in stealthily), f. *sub-*, SUB- 24 + *repere* creep; see -ION.] An unperceived creeping or stealing upon one or into one's mind (of evil thoughts or suggestions); hence, a sudden or surprise attack (of temptation, sin) –1711.

Surreptitious (sɒrėpti·ʃəs), *a.* 1443. [f. L. *surreptitius, -icius*, f. *surrept-*; see SURREPTION¹, -ITIOUS, and cf. SUBREPTITIOUS.] **1.** Obtained by 'surreption', suppression of the truth, or fraudulent misrepresentation. **2.** Secret and unauthorized; clandestine 1645. **b.** Of a passage or writing: Spurious, forged. Of an edition or copy of a book: Pirated. 1615. **c.** *transf.* Acting by stealth or secretly; stealthy, crafty, sly 1615.

2. O ladies! how many of you have s. milliners' bills? THACKERAY. **c.** The old man's look..betraying his s. curiosity 1856. Hence **Surrepti·tious-ly** *adv.*, **-ness.**

Surrey (sɒ·ri). *U.S.* 1896. [Named after the county of Surrey, England, where orig. built.] An American four-wheeled two-seated pleasure carriage, the seats being of similar design and facing forwards; a motor-carriage of similar structure.

Surrogate (sɒ·rŏgĕt), *sb.* (*a.*) 1603. [– L. *surrogatus*, pa. pple. of *surrogare*; see next, -ATE¹.] **1.** A person appointed by authority to act in place of another; a deputy 1604. **b.** The deputy of an ecclesiastical judge, of a bishop or bishop's chancellor, esp. one who grants licences to marry without banns 1603. **c.** In New York and some other States: A judge having jurisdiction over the probate of wills and settlement of estates of deceased persons 1816. **2.** *fig.* and *gen.* A person or (usu.) a thing that acts for or takes the place of another; a substitute. Const. *for, of.* 1644. **B.** *attrib.* or *adj.* That is a surrogate; representative 1638. Hence **Su·rrogateship,** the office of a s.

Surrogate (sɒ·rŏgēⁱt), *v.* Now *rare* or *Obs.* 1533. [– *surrogat-*, pa. ppl. stem of L. *surrogare*, var. of *subrogare* put in another's place; see SUBROGATE *v.*] *trans.* = SUBROGATE *v.* 1–3.

Surrogation (sɒrŏgēⁱ·ʃən). Now *rare.* 1533. [– late and med.L. *surrogatio, -ōn-*, f. as prec.; see -ION.] **1.** Appointment of a person to some office in place of another. **2.** *gen.* Substitution 1638.

Surround (sɒ̆rau·nd), *sb.* 1837. [f. next.] **1.** An act of surrounding; *spec.* (*U.S.*) the process of hunting certain wild animals by surrounding them and driving them into a place from which they cannot escape. **2.** A border or edging of a particular material, surrounding the central piece, as of linoleum or felt round a carpet 1893.

Surround (sɒ̆rau·nd), *v.* 1444. [– AFr. *sur(o)under*, OFr. *s(o)uronder* :– late L. *superundare*, f. *super-* SUPER- I. 2 + *undare* rise in waves, f. *unda* wave.] †**I.** *trans.* To overflow, inundate, flood, submerge –1634. **b.** *intr.* To overflow –1599. **II. 1.** To enclose, encompass, or beset on all sides; to stand, lie, or be situated around; also, to form the entourage of; often *pass.* 1616. **b.** *Mil.* To enclose (a place, or a body of troops) on all sides so as to cut off communication or retreat; to invest 1649. **2.** To go or extend round (an object or body, a room, or the like); to encircle, as a frame, border, etc. 1688. †**3.** To go or travel around; *esp.* to circumnavigate –1825. **4.** To cause to be enclosed or encircled *with* something 1635.

1. If the planet Neptune..be surrounded by an atmosphere TYNDALL. **b.** Our men surrounded the swamp..and shot at the Indians 1649. **3.** When I was driven out to Sea..in my Attempt to s. the Island DE FOE.

Surrounding (sŏrau·ndiŋ), *vbl. sb.* 1449. [-ING¹.] **1.** The action of SURROUND *v. rare* or *Obs.* **2.** *pl.* Those things which surround a person or thing, or in the midst of which he or it (habitually) is; things around (collectively); environment 1861. **3.** A number of persons standing around; entourage 1877.

Surrou·nding, *ppl. a.* 1634. [-ING².] That is (or are) around; encompassing, circumjacent.

Surroyal (sŏ·roiăl), late ME. [f. SUR- + ROYAL *sb.* 3.] *Venery.* An upper or terminal branch of a stag's antler, above the 'royal'.

†**Sursolid,** *sb.* and *a.* 1557. [app. an etymologizing alteration of †*surdesolid* – mod.L. *surdesolidus*, app. f. *surde* irrationally.] *Math.* **A.** *sb.* The fifth power of a number or quantity; also, an equation of the fifth degree –1817. **B.** *adj.* Of the fifth degree; that is a fifth power or root; involving the fifth power of a quantity –1706.

Surtax (sŏ·ɹtæks), *sb.* 1881. [– Fr. *surtaxe*; see SUR-, TAX *sb.*] An additional or extra tax on something already taxed. So **Surta·x** *v. trans.* to charge with a s.

Surtout (sɒɹtū·t, sɒɹtū·). 1686. [– Fr. *surtout*, f. *sur* above + *tout* everything.] A man's greatcoat or overcoat. (Applied *c* 1870 to a kind of single-breasted frock-coat with pockets cut diagonally in front.) †**b.** A hood (with a mantle), worn by women –1785.

‖**Surturbrand** (sŏ·ɹtəɹbrænd). 1760. [G. – Icel. *surtarbrandr*, f. *Surtar*, gen. of *Surtr* (rel. to *svartr* SWART *a.*) name of a fire-giant + *brandr* BRAND *sb.*] A name for lignite as occurring in Iceland.

Surveillance (sɒɹvēⁱ·lăns, -vēⁱlyăns, ‖sürvęyaṅs). 1802. [– Fr. *surveillance*, f. *surveiller*; see next, -ANCE.] Watch or guard kept over a person, esp. over a suspected person, a prisoner, or the like; often, spying, supervision; less commonly, superintendence.

General Becker—the officer who was charged with the s. of Buonaparte 1815.

Surveillant (sɒɹvēⁱ·lănt, -lyănt, ‖sürvęyaṅ), *sb.* 1819. [– Fr. *surveillant*, pr. pple., used subst., of *surveiller*, f. *sur* SUR- + *veiller* watch; see -ANT.] One who exercises surveillance; a person who keeps watch over another or others; a superintendent, e.g. of a prison.

Survei·llant, *a. rare.* 1841. [– Fr. pr. pple.; see prec.] Exercising surveillance.

Survey (sŏ·ɹveⁱ, sŏɹvēⁱ·), *sb.* 1535. [f. next.] The action, or an act, of surveying; the object or result of this. **1.** The act of viewing, examining, or inspecting in detail, esp. for some specific purpose; usu. *spec.* a formal or official inspection of the particulars of something, e.g. of an estate, of a ship or its stores, etc. 1548. **b.** *transf.* A written statement or description embodying the result of such examination 1613. †**2.** Oversight, supervision, superintendence –1654. **3.** The, or an, act of looking at something as a whole, or from a commanding position; a general or comprehensive view or look 1589. **b.** *concr.* That which is thus viewed; a view, prospect, scene 1700. **4.** *fig.* A comprehensive mental view, or (usu.) literary examination, discussion, or description, *of* something 1568. **5.** The process (†or art) of surveying a tract of ground, coast-line, or any part of the earth's surface; the determination of its form, extent, and other particulars, so as to be able to delineate or describe it accurately and in detail; also, a plan or description thus obtained; a body of persons or a department engaged in such work 1610.

1. b. The Domesday S. 1876. **3.** He..O'relooks the Neighbours with a wide s. DRYDEN. After a moment's s. of her face DICKENS. **4.** A s. of the various possible modes of punishment BENTHAM. **5.** *Ordnance S.*: see ORDNANCE 5.

Survey (sŏɹvēⁱ·), *v.* 1467. [– AFr. *surveier*, *-veir*, OFr. *so(u)rveeir* (pres. stem *so(u)rvey-*) :– med.L. *supervidēre*, f. L. *super-* SUPER- 2 + *vidēre* see.] **1.** *trans.* To examine and ascertain the condition, situation, or value of, formally or officially, e.g. the boundaries, tenure, value, etc. of an estate, a building or structure, accounts, or the like; more widely, to supervise. **2.** To determine the form, extent, and situation of the parts of (a tract of ground, or any portion of the earth's surface) by linear and angular measurements, so as to construct a map, plan, or detailed description of it. Also *absol.* 1550. **3.** To look carefully into or through; to view in detail; to examine, inspect, scrutinize; to explore (a country). Now *rare* or *Obs.* 1592. **4.** To look at from, or as from, a height or commanding position; to take a broad, general, or comprehensive view of; to view or examine in its whole extent; also *fig.* 1586. †**b.** To observe, perceive, see (*rare*) –1615.

1. The Persian Monarch, st., is reported..to be leaking slightly...She will be surveyed 1880. **2.** I was out surveying the whole morning 1846. **3.** To s. all my letters and actions..with a most rigid and censorious eye 1658. **4.** *absol.* Round he surveys, and well might, where he stood So high above the circling Canopie Of Nights extended shade MILT. **b.** *Macb.* I. ii. 31. Hence **Survey·able** *a.* (*rare*). **Survey·al** (*rare*), the act of surveying; survey.

Surveyance (sŏɹvēⁱ·ăns). *rare.* late ME. [– OFr. **surve(i)ance*, f. *surveeir* SURVEY; see -ANCE. In mod. use directly f. prec. + -ANCE.] Survey; superintendence, oversight; inspection.

Surveying (sŏɹvēⁱ·iŋ), *vbl. sb.* 1467. [f. SURVEY *v.* + -ING¹.] The action of SURVEY *v.* **1.** The action of viewing or examining in detail (esp. officially). **2.** The process or art of making surveys of land 1551. **3.** *attrib.* Applied to instruments or appliances used for, and to ships employed in, surveying 1641.

Surveyor (sŏɹvēⁱ·əɹ). 1440. [– AFr., OFr. *sur-*, *sorve(i)our*, f. *surveeir* SURVEY *v.*; see -OR 2.] One who surveys. **1.** One who has the oversight or superintendence of a person or thing; an overseer, supervisor. **2.** One who designs, and superintends the construction of, a building; a practical architect 1460. **3.** One whose business it is to survey land, etc.; one who makes surveys, or practises surveying 1551. **b.** A name for certain caterpillars 1682. **c.** One whose business it is to inspect and examine land, houses, or other property and to calculate and report upon its actual or prospective value or productiveness for certain purposes 1795. **4.** One who views or looks at something; a beholder (*rare*) 1558. **b.** *fig.* One who takes a mental view of something; an examiner, contemplator 1606. **5.** **S.-general:** a principal or head surveyor; one who has the control of a body of surveyors, or the general oversight of some business. In *U.S.*, a government officer who supervises the surveys of public lands. 1515.

1. *S. of highways, of taxes; borough, district, forest, road, timber s.* **3.** *Surveyor's chain* = Gunter's chain: see GUNTER 1. **4. b.** To the s. of the history of humanity this is the interest which Pelagius possesses 1905. Hence **Survey·orship,** the office of s.

Surview (sŏɹviū·), *sb.* late ME. [– AFr., OFr. *surveue*, f. *surveeir* SURVEY *v.*; see SUR-, VIEW *sb.*] †**1.** = SURVEY *sb.* 1, 2. –1475. **2.** = SURVEY *sb.* 3, 4. Now *rare* or *arch.* 1576.

Surview (sŏɹviū·), *v.* 1567. [f. prec.] = SURVEY *v.* 4. Now *Obs.* or *arch.*

Survival (sŏɹvəi·văl). 1598. [f. SURVIVE *v.* + -AL¹ 2.] **1.** The continuing to live after some event (*spec.* of the soul after death); remaining alive, living on. **2.** *transf.* Continuance after the end or cessation of something else; *spec.* continuance of a custom, observance, etc. after the circumstances in which it originated or which gave significance to it have passed away 1820. **3.** (with *a* and *pl.*) Something that continues to exist after the cessation of something else, or of other things of the kind; a surviving remnant; *spec.* applied to a surviving custom, observance, belief, etc. 1716.

1. *S. of the fittest* (Biol.): a phrase used to describe the process of *natural selection* (see SELECTION 3), expressing the fact that those organisms which are best adapted to their environment continue to live and produce offspring, while those of the same or related species which are less adapted perish. Also *transf.* in trivial use. **2.** The use of stone knives in certain ceremonies is evidently a case of s. 1870.

Survivance (sŏɹvəi·văns). 1623. [– early mod.Fr. *survivance*, f. *survivant*; see next and -ANCE.] **1.** = prec. 1, 2. Now *rare.* **2.** The succession to an estate, office, etc. of a survivor nominated before the death of the existing occupier or holder; the right of such succession in case of survival 1674.

2. His son had the s. of the Stadtholdership BURNET. So †**Survi·vancy.**

†**Survi·vant,** *a.* 1555. [– Fr. *survivant*, pr. pple. of *survivre*; see next, -ANT.] Surviving –1677.

Survive (sŏɹvəi·v), *v.* 1473. [– AFr. *survivre*, OFr. *sourvivre* (mod. *sur-*) – L. *supervivere*, f. *super-* SUPER- I. 2 + *vivere* live.] **1.** *intr.* To continue to live after the death of another, or after the end or cessation of some thing or condition or the occurrence of some event (expressed or implied); to remain alive, live on. **b.** *transf.* To continue to exist after some person, thing, or event; to last on 1593. **c.** *Law.* Of an estate, etc.: To pass *to* the survivor or survivors of two or more joint-tenants or persons who had a joint interest 1648. **2.** *trans.* To continue to live after (a person, an event, point of time, etc.), outlive 1572. **b.** *transf.* To continue to exist after the death or cessation of (a person, condition, etc.); to outlast 1633.

1. There are vastly more creatures born than can ever s. 1894. **b.** Yea though I die the scandale will suruiue SHAKS. **2.** And, for that dowrie, Ile assure her of Her widdow-hood, be it that she suruiue me, In all my Lands and Leases whatsoeuer SHAKS. If I s. my journey, you shall hear from me again 1717. **b.** The principal works that have survived him are his magnificent roads EMERSON. Hence **Survi·ver** = SURVIVOR. **Survi·ving** *ppl. a.* that survives.

Survivor (sŏɹvəi·vəɹ). 1503. [f. prec. + -OR 2.] **1.** One who (or that which) survives or outlives another or others 1624. **2.** *spec.* in *Law.* One of two or more designated persons, esp. joint-tenants or other persons having a joint interest, who outlives the other or others; a longer or the longest liver 1503.

1. Of the band of patriots..he was the sole s. 1874.

Survivorship (sŏɹvəi·vəɹʃip). 1625. [f. prec. + -SHIP.] **1.** *Law*, etc. **a.** The condition of a survivor, or the fact of one person surviving another or others, considered in relation to some right or privilege depending on such survival or the period of it 1697. **b.** A right depending on survival; e.g. the right of the survivor or survivors of a number of joint-tenants or other persons having a joint interest, to take the whole on the death of the other or others 1625. **2.** *gen.* The state or condition of being a survivor; survival 1709.

1. a. *Presumption of s.*, the presumption of the momentary or brief survival of one of a number of persons who have perished by the same calamity, as affecting rights of inheritance.

Surwan (sŏ·ɹwan). *India.* 1821. [– Urdu, = Pers. *sārbān*, f. *sār* camel + *-bān* keeper.] A camel-driver.

Susceptibility (sŏseptibi·lĭti). 1644. [f. next + -ITY.] **1.** The quality or condition of being susceptible; capability of receiving, being affected by, or undergoing something. Const. *of* (now rare) or *to*. **2.** Without const. **a.** Capacity for feeling or emotion; disposition or tendency to be emotionally affected; sensibility 1753. Also *pl.* Capacities of emotion, esp. such as may be hurt or offended; sensitive feelings; sensibilities 1846. **b.** Capacity for receiving mental or moral impressions 1782. **c.** Capability of being, or disposition to be, physically affected (as a living body, or an inanimate thing); *spec.* the capacity of a substance (e.g. iron) for being magnetized, measured by the ratio of the magnetization to the magnetizing force 1816.

Susceptible (sŏse·ptĭb'l), *a.* 1605. [– late L. *susceptibilis* (Boethius), f. *suscept-*; see next, -IBLE.] **1.** Capable of taking, receiving, being affected by, or undergoing something. Const. *of* or *to*. **2.** Without const. **a.** Capable of being affected by, or easily moved to, feeling; subject to emotional (or mental) impression; impressionable 1709. **b.** Subject to some physical affection, as infection, etc. 1875.

1. My little boy..is now s. of instruction EVE-

LYN. Infinitely too s. of criticism 1814. Swift.. was exceedingly s. of female influence 1876. S. to smallpox 1887. **2.** The sanguine and s. people of France 1849. Hence **Susce·ptibleness** = SUSCEPTIBILITY. **Susce·ptibly** *adv.* in a s. manner.

Susception (sǒse·pʃən). 1610. [– L. *susceptio, -ōn-*, f. *suscept-*, pa. ppl. stem of *suscipere*, f. *sub-* SUB- 25 + *capere* take; see -ION.] †**1.** The action of taking up, or taking upon oneself (in various senses): taking, assumption, reception, acceptance, undertaking –1738. †**2.** Susceptibility *of*; also *transf.* an attribute of which something is susceptible (*rare*) –1687. **3.** The action or capacity of taking something into the mind, or what is so taken; passive mental reception (dist. from *perception*). *rare.* 1756.

Susceptive (sǒse·ptiv), *a.* 1548. [– late L. *susceptivus*, f. as prec.; see -IVE.] **1.** Having the quality of taking or receiving; in later use *esp.* = SUSCEPTIBLE 2 a. **2.** With *of*: = SUSCEPTIBLE 1. 1637. Hence **Susce·ptiveness** = next.

Susceptivity (sɒsepti·vĭti). 1722. [f. prec. + -ITY.] The quality of being susceptive; susceptibility.

†**Susce·ptor.** 1655. [– late L. *susceptor*, in med. L. godfather, f. *suscept-*; see SUSCEPTION, -OR 2.] A godfather or sponsor at baptism –1743.

Suscipient (sɒsi·piĕnt), *a.* and *sb.* Now *rare* or *Obs.* 1611. [– L. *suscipiens, -ent-*, pr. pple. of *suscipere*; see SUSCEPTION, -ENT.] **A.** *adj.* Receiving, recipient 1649. **B.** *sb.* One who receives, a recipient (esp. of a sacrament) 1611.

Suscitate (sɒ·siteᶦt), *v.* Now *rare.* 1528. [– *suscitat-*, pa. ppl. stem of L. *suscitare*, f. *sub-* SUB- 25 + *citare* excite; see CITE *v.*] *trans.* To stir up, excite (rebellion, a feeling, etc.); to raise (a person) out of inactivity; †to quicken, vivify, animate.

Suscitation (sɒsitēᶦ·ʃən). Now rare. 1646. [– late L. *suscitatio, -ōn-*, f. as prec.; see -ION. Cf. (O)Fr. *suscitation.*] The action of suscitating or condition of being suscitated; stirring up excitement; quickening; incitement.

‖**Suslik** (sɒ·slik). 1774. [Russ. *súslik*; cf. Fr. *souslic, -lik.*] A species of ground squirrel, *Spermophilus citillus* (or other related species), found in Europe and Asia.

Suspect (sǒspe·kt), *sb.*[1] *Obs.* or *arch.* late ME. [– L. *suspectus*, in class. L. looking up, a height, esteem, respect, in med.L. suspicion, f. *suspect-*; see SUSPECT *v.*] **1.** = SUSPICION 1, 1 b. †**2.** = SUSPICION 3. –1620.

1. You..draw within the compasse of s. Th' vnuiolated honor of your wife SHAKS.

Suspect (sɒ·spekt, sǒspe·kt), *a.* and *sb.*[2] ME. [Disused in the adj. after *c*1700, and in the sb. after *c*1600 until revived in XIX after the Fr. use of the word for 'one suspected of hostility or indifference to the Revolution' (cf. *la loi des suspects* 1793); – (O)Fr. *suspect* or L. *suspectus*, pa. pple. of *suspicere*; see next.] **A.** *adj.* Suspected; regarded with suspicion or distrust; that is an object of suspicion; in early use also, exciting or deserving suspicion, suspicious.

I see What I can do or offer is s. MILT. Phr. †*To have* or *hold* (a person or thing) *s.*, to be suspicious of, suspect.

B. *sb.* A suspected person; a suspicious character, esp. one under surveillance as such 1591.

Arrested as a s. under the Coercion Act 1881.

Suspect (sǒspe·kt), *v.* 1483. [– *suspect-*, pa. ppl. stem of L. *suspicere* look up (to), admire, suspect, f. *sub-* SUB- 24, 25 + *specere* look.] **1.** *trans.* To imagine something evil, wrong, or undesirable in (a person or thing) on slight or no evidence; to believe or fancy to be guilty or faulty, with insufficient proof or knowledge; to be suspicious of 1500. **2.** To imagine or fancy something, esp. something wrong, about (a person or thing) with slight or no proof 1483. **3.** To imagine or fancy (something) to be possible or likely; to have a faint notion or inkling of; to surmise 1549. **4.** *absol.* or *intr.* To imagine something, esp. some evil, as possible or likely; to have or feel suspicion 1592. **5.** *trans.* With ref. to a future possibility: To expect; *esp.* to expect with dread or apprehension. *Obs.* or merged in 3. 1509.

1. The people suspected the gentlemen, the gentlemen feared the people FROUDE. **2.** I do s. this Trash To be a party in this Iniury SHAKS. At thirty man suspects himself a fool; Knows it at forty YOUNG. Tell me, that you do not really s. me of any hand in her death 1802. **3.** You do not ..s. half enough the villany of others BURKE. I did not even s. how ill she would be 1866. **4.** Too young and simple to s. or to doubt 1849. Hence **Suspe·ctable** *a.* that may or should be suspected; open to suspicion. **Suspe·cted** *ppl. a.*, **-ly** *adv.*, **-ness. Suspe·cter, Suspe·ctor.**

Suspectful (sǒspe·ktfŭl), *a.* Now *rare* or *Obs.* 1586. [f. SUSPECT *sb.*[1] + -FUL.] = SUSPICIOUS 2.

Alwaies emulous and suspectfull of her 1640. Hence **Suspe·ctfulness,** proneness to suspicion.

†**Suspe·ction.** ME. [– OFr. *suspection* or med.L. *suspectio, -ōn-*, f. L. *suspect-*; see SUSPECT *v.*, -ION.] = SUSPICION –1728.

†**Suspe·ctless,** *a.* 1591. [f. SUSPECT *sb.*[1] + -LESS.] **1.** Having no suspicion; unsuspecting –1756. **2.** Not liable to suspicion; unsuspected –1637.

Suspend (sǒspe·nd), *v.* ME. [– (O)Fr. *suspendre* or L. *suspendere*, f. *sus-* SUB- 25 + *pendere* hang.] **I. 1.** *trans.* To debar, usu. for a time, from the exercise of a function or enjoyment of a privilege; *esp.* to deprive (temporarily) of one's office. **2.** To put a stop to, usu. for a time; *esp.* to bring to a (temporary) stop; to intermit the use or exercise of, put in abeyance ME. **b.** *intr.* for *pass.* To come to a stop for the time, cease temporarily, intermit (*rare*) 1650. **3.** *trans.* To put off to a later time or occasion; to defer, postpone. *Obs.* or merged in other senses. 1577. †**b.** Of an event, etc.: To defer or delay the accomplishment of –1807. **4.** To keep (one's judgement) undetermined; to refrain from forming (an opinion) or giving (assent) decisively 1553. †**b.** *absol.* To suspend one's judgement, to be in doubt; hence *occas.* to doubt; also, to apprehend, suspect –1749. †**5. a.** To keep in a state of mental fixity, attention, or contemplation; to rivet the attention of –1812. **b.** To keep in suspense, uncertainty, or indecision. *Obs.* or *dial.* 1603. **6.** Sc. Law. *trans.* To defer, stay; *intr.* to present a bill of 'suspension' 1650. **7.** *Mus.* To prolong (a note of a chord) into the following chord, thus deferring the progression of the part in which it occurs, usu. so as to produce a temporary discord 1853.

1. The king had been obliged to s. the sheriffs in several counties FROUDE. **2.** All power of thinking is suspended during a swoon PRIESTLEY. In great danger it was the Senate's business to s. the constitution FROUDE. Phr. *To s. payment*, to cease paying debts or claims on account of financial inability; to become insolvent. **3.** Britain will s. her blow till she can strike very hard 1793. **4.** The publick voice suspends its decision JOHNSON. **5. a.** The harmony..Suspended Hell, and took with ravishment The thronging audience MILT.

II. 1. *trans.* To hang, hang up, by attachment to a support above 1440. **b.** To attach so as to allow of movement about the point of attachment 1827. **2.** *fig.* To cause to depend; *pass.* to depend *on.* Now *rare.* 1608. **3. a.** To hold, or cause to be held up, without attachment 1646. **b.** To hold, or cause to be held, in suspension; to contain in the form of particles diffused through its substance, as a fluid medium; to cause to be so diffused (*in* the medium) 1737.

1. The chandeliers suspended from the roof were of silver 1867. **b.** An index suspended from a cross-bar 1871. **3. a.** That in the Temple of Serapis there was an iron chariot suspended by Loadstones in the ayre SIR T. BROWNE. **b.** Gold and silver inks are writing fluids in which gold and silver,..are suspended in a state of fine division 1880. Hence **Suspe·nded** *ppl. a.*, as in *s. animation.*

Suspender (sǒspe·ndəɹ). 1524. [f. prec. + -ER[1].] **1.** One who or that which suspends. **2.** *Sc. Law.* One who presents a bill of suspension 1650. **3.** That by which something is suspended; *esp.* one of a pair of straps passing over the shoulders to hold up the trousers: usu. in *pl.* Chiefly *U.S.* 1810. **b.** A device attached to the top of a stocking or sock to hold it in place 1895. **4.** An apparatus or a natural structure supporting something suspended 1839.

Suspense (sǒspe·ns), *sb.* late ME. [– AFr., OFr. *suspens* or *suspense* abeyance, delay, repr. med. L. subst. uses of n. and fem. of pa. pple. of L. *suspendere* SUSPEND.] †**1.** (Chiefly *Law.*) *In s.*, not being executed, fulfilled, rendered, paid, or the like; esp. *to put in s.*, to defer the execution, payment, etc. of –1818. †**b.** Hence *gen.* (*a*) = SUSPENSION 2. –1818. (*b*) Deferment, delay –1718. **2.** The state of being suspended or kept undetermined (chiefly *to hold, keep in s.*); hence, the action of suspending one's judgement 1560. **3.** A state of mental uncertainty, with expectation of or desire for decision, and usu. some apprehension or anxiety; the condition of waiting, esp. of being kept waiting, for an expected decision, assurance, or issue; less commonly, a state of uncertainty what to do, indecision; esp. in *to keep* (or *hold*) *in s.* 1440. **b.** Objectively, as an attribute of affairs, etc.: Doubtfulness, uncertainty, undecidedness 1513. **c.** *attrib.* in **s. account** (*Book-keeping*), an account in which items are temporarily entered until their proper place is determined 1882. **4.** = SUSPENSION 7 (*rare*) 1752. †**5.** = SUSPENSION 8 (*rare*) –1727.

2. Suspence of iudgement and exercise of charitie HOOKER. **3.** S. in news is torture, speak them out MILT. **b.** In this s. of his affairs at Rome 1741. Hence **Suspe·nseful** *a.* full of s.

Suspe·nse, *a.* Now *rare* or *Obs.* 1440. [– OFr. *suspens, -e* adj., or its source L. *suspensus*, pa. pple. of *suspendere* SUSPEND.] **1.** In a state of mental suspense; doubtful, uncertain. †**2.** Refraining from hasty decision or action; cautious, deliberate –1684. **3.** Hung, hung up, hanging 1440.

1. Expectation held His look suspence, awaiting who appeer'd To second,..The perilous attempt MILT. Hence †**Suspe·nsely** *adv.* (*rare*) cautiously –1625.

Suspensible (sǒspe·nsĭb'l), *a.* *rare.* 1827. [f. SUSPENSION + -IBLE.] Capable of being suspended. So **Suspensibi·lity,** capability of being suspended 1794.

Suspension (sǒspe·nʃən). 1528. [– (O)Fr. *suspension* or L. *suspensio, -ōn-*, f. *suspens-*, pa. ppl. stem of *suspendere* SUSPEND; see -ION.] The action of suspending or condition of being suspended. **1.** The action of debarring or state of being debarred, esp. for a time, *from* a function or privilege; temporary deprivation of one's office or position. **2.** The action of stopping or condition of being stopped, esp. for a time; temporary cessation, intermission; temporary abrogation (of a law, rule) 1603. **b.** Stoppage of payment of debts or claims on account of financial inability or failure 1889. **c.** *Palæography.* A form of abbreviation consisting in representing a word by its first letter or letters accompanied by the contraction-mark; also, a word abbreviated in this way 1896. **3.** The action of putting off to a later time; deferring, postponement 1645. **4.** *Sc. Law.* The staying or postponement of the execution of a sentence pending its discussion in the Supreme Court; a judicial order or warrant for such postponement and discussion (in full, *letters of s.*) 1581. **5.** The action of keeping any mental action in suspense or abeyance; usu. in phr., e.g. *s. of judgement, opinion* 1568. **6.** The action of keeping or state of being kept in suspense (*spec.* in *Rhet.*); doubt, uncertainty (with expectation of decision or issue). Now *rare* or *Obs.* 1635. **7.** *Mus.* The action of deferring the progression of a part in harmony by prolonging a note of a chord into the following chord, usu. producing a temporary discord; an instance of this, a discord so produced 1801. **8.** The action of hanging something up; the condition of being hung, or of hanging from a support; *occas.* hanging as a form of capital punishment; *spec.* in *Med.* the treatment of disease by suspending the patient 1656. **b.** *concr.* A support on which something is hung 1833. **c.** Attachment such as to allow of movement about the point of attachment; 'hanging' as of a vehicle on straps, springs, etc. 1891. **9.** The action of holding up or state of being held up without attachment 1646. **10.** The condition of being suspended, as particles in a medium; *concr.* a collection of suspended particles. 1707.

1. During your S. you are a Sort of Prisoner at

large and do no Duty 1760. **2.** *S. of arms* or *hostilities*, an armistice.

Comb.: **s.-bridge,** a bridge in which the roadway is suspended from spans of ropes, chains, or wire cables attached to and extending between supports; **s.-chain,** each of the chains which support a s.-bridge or similar structure; **-pier,** a pier supported in the manner of a s.-bridge.

Suspensive (sŏspe·nsiv), *a.* 1575. [– (O)Fr. *suspensif* or med. L. *suspensivus*, f. as prec.; see -IVE. In sense 1 app. f. SUSPENSION 1, SUSPEND I. 1.] †**1.** Liable to be suspended (from office) –1606. **2.** Having the power or effect of suspending, deferring, or temporarily stopping the operation of something; involving such suspension 1623. **3.** Inclined to suspend one's judgement; undecided in mind; of, pertaining to, characterized by, or in a state of suspense 1614. **b.** Of a word, phrase, etc.: Expressing or indicating suspense; keeping one in suspense 1711. **4.** Characterized by physical suspension (*rare*) 1827.

2. The king..declared his preference of the s. veto 1822. S. Conditions are such as suspend the sale and stay the transfer till something be done 1826. **3.** The passion for watching chances—the.. s. poise of the mind GEO. ELIOT. Hence **Suspe·nsive-ly** *adv.*, **-ness.**

Suspensor (sŏspe·nsǫɹ). 1746. [– mod. L. *suspensor*, f. as prec.; see -OR 2.] †**1.** *Surg.* **a.** A kind of catheter. **b.** A suspensory bandage. 1803. **2.** *Bot.* The filament by which the embryo is suspended in the seed of phanerogams; also applied to a similar structure in some cryptogams 1832. **3.** *gen.* That by which something is suspended 1874.

Suspensorial (sɒspensō°·riăl), *a.* 1871. [f. next + -AL[1] 1.] *Anat.* Pertaining to or of the nature of a suspensorium; suspensory.

‖**Suspensorium** (sɒspensō°·riŏm). 1758. [Latinization of next; see -ORIUM.] **1.** *Surg.* A suspensory bag, bandage, etc. **2.** *Zool.* The bone, or series of bones, cartilages, etc., by which the lower jaw is suspended from the skull in vertebrates below mammals 1869.

Suspensory (sŏspe·nsŏri), *a.* and *sb.* 1541. [– Fr. *suspensoire* adj. and sb. (XVI); see SUSPENSION, -ORY[1,2].] **A.** *adj.* **I. 1.** *Surg.* and *Anat.* Having the function of suspending, i.e. supporting something suspended. **II.** †**1.** Marked by or indicating mental suspense; doubtful, lacking certainty or assurance –1682. **2.** = SUSPENSIVE 2. 1884.

2. A short s. period during which actions could be brought that [etc.] 1885.

B. *sb. Surg.* and *Anat.* A suspensory bandage, ligament, etc.; a suspensorium 1699.

Sus. per coll. 1560. Abbrev. of L. *suspendatur per collum* 'let him be hanged by the neck', in the entry of a capital sentence in the jailer's books; an entry of this against a person's name; hence as *adj.* = hanged. Hence **Susperco·llate** *v.* (*joc. nonce-wd.*) to hang.

Suspicable (sɒ·spikăb'l), *a.* Now *rare* or *Obs.* 1614. [– late and med. L. *suspicabilis*, f. L. *suspicari* suspect, f. *sub-* SUB- 24 + *spic-* as in *suspicere* SUSPECT *v.*] **1.** That may be suspected or mistrusted; open to suspicion. **2.** That may be suspected to be so; appearing likely 1651.

2. It is a very s. business that he means no more than empty Space by it 1653.

Suspicion (sŏspi·ʃən). ME. [– AFr. *suspeciun*, var. of OFr. *sospeçon* (mod. *soupçon*) :– med. L. *suspectio*, *-ōn-*; see -ION. The earliest forms *suspecio(u)n* began to be superseded before 1400 by assim. to OFr. *suspicion* or L. *suspicio*.] **1.** The action of suspecting; the feeling or state of mind of one who suspects; imagination or conjecture of the existence of something evil or wrong without proof; apprehension of guilt or fault on slight grounds or without clear evidence. **b.** An instance of this. late ME. †**c.** *transf.* A ground of suspicion; a suspicious circumstance –1687. **2.** *gen.* Imagination *of* something (not necessarily evil) as possible or likely; a slight belief or idea of something, or *that* something is the case; a surmise; a faint notion, an inkling. late ME. †**3.** Surmise of something future; expectation; *esp.* expectation or apprehension of evil –1700. **4.** A slight or faint trace, very small amount, 'hint', 'suggestion' (*of* something) 1809.

1. No one may be discovered to whom s. attaches SCOTT. Phr. *Upon* or *on s.*, on the basis of mere supposition (*of* evil or wrongdoing). *Above s.*, too good or worthy to be suspected of evil. **b.** Svspicions amongst Thoughts, are like Bats amongst Birds, they euer fly by Twilight BACON. **c.** *Rom. & Jul.* V. iii. 187. **2.** This may beget a little s., that even animals depend not on the climate HUME. **4.** A wall-eyed horse, with a s. of spavin 1871.

Suspicious (sŏspi·ʃəs), *a.* ME. [– AFr., OFr. *suspecious*, *suspicious* – L. *suspiciosus*, f. *suspicio* SUSPICION; see -OUS.] **1.** Open to, deserving of, or exciting suspicion; that is or should be an object of suspicion; suspected, or to be suspected; of questionable character. †**b.** with dependent clause, inf., or *of* –1788. **2.** Full of, inclined to, or feeling suspicion; disposed to suspect; suspecting; *esp.* disposed to suspect evil, mistrustful. late ME. **b.** *transf.* Expressing, indicating, or characterized by suspicion 1478.

1. Suspecious was the diffame of this man, Suspect his face, suspect his word also CHAUCER. **b.** The wife of Richard Cornish was found s. of incontinency 1765. **2.** The world is suspitious, And men may think what we imagine not KYD. The king was all his life s. of superior people THACKERAY. **b.** S. and black ideas 1797. Hence **Suspi·cious-ly** *adv.*, **-ness.**

Suspiration (sɒspirē[i]·ʃən). Now *rare.* 1485. [– L. *suspiratio*, *-ōn-*, f. *suspirat-*, pa. ppl. stem of *suspirare*; see SUSPIRE *v.*, -ION.] **1.** Sighing; a sigh. **2.** (Deep) breathing; breath; a (deep) breath 1602.

2. Nor Customary suites of solemne Blacke, Nor windy s. of forc'd breath SHAKS.

†**Suspi·re,** *sb.* 1450. [– OFr. *s(o)uspir* (mod. *soupir*) or L. *suspirium*, f. *suspirare*; see next.] A sigh –1637.

Suspire (sŏspəi°·ɹ), *v.* Now chiefly *poet.* 1450. [– L. *suspirare*, f. *sub-* SUB- 25 + *spirare* breathe.] **1.** *intr.* To sigh; *rare* in lit. sense; chiefly *fig.* to sigh *for*, yearn *after*. **2.** *trans.* To utter with a sigh; to sigh forth. Also, to breathe out. 1549. **3.** *intr.* To breathe 1595.

2. A bolt from heaven..suspiring flame BROWNING. **3.** *John* III. iv. 80.

Suspirious (sŏspi·riəs), *a.* 1657. [– L. *suspiriosus*, f. *suspirium*; see SUSPIRE *sb.*, -OUS.] **1.** Breathing with difficulty or painfully; chiefly *Path.* **2.** Full of sighs, sighing 1751.

Sussex (sɒ·sĕks). 1704. The name (OE. *Sūþseaxe* 'South Saxons') of a maritime county in the south-east of England; used attrib. in designations of breeds of cattle, agricultural implements, etc. produced in or peculiar to the county.

†**Sustain,** *sb.* 1653. [f. next.] That which sustains; means of sustenance. MILT.

Sustain (sŏstē[i]·n), *v.* [ME. *sos-*, *susteine* – AFr. *sustein-*, OFr. *so(u)stein-*, tonic stem of *so(u)stenir* (mod. *soutenir*) – L. *sustinēre*, f. *sub-* SUB- 25 + *tenēre* hold, keep.] †**1.** *trans.* To support the efforts, conduct, or cause of; to succour, support, back up –1802. **b.** Const. clause or (rarely) acc. and inf.: To support the contention, maintain (that). Now *rare.* late ME. **2.** To uphold the validity or rightfulness of; to support as valid, sound, correct, true, or just. late ME. **3.** To keep (a person or community, the mind, spirit, etc.) from failing or giving way ME. **4.** To keep in being; to cause to continue in a certain state; to keep or maintain at the proper level or standard; to preserve the status of ME. **5.** To keep going, keep up (an action or process); to keep up without intermission; to carry on (a conflict, contest) ME. †**6.** To support life in; to provide for the life or bodily needs of; to furnish with the necessaries of life; to keep –1700. †**b.** To supply (a person's need). SHAKS. †**7.** To provide for the upkeep of (an institution, estate, etc.) –1592. **8.** To endure without failing or giving way; to bear up against, withstand. Also †*intr.* ME. **9.** To undergo, experience, have to submit to (evil, hardship, or damage; now chiefly with *injury*, *loss* as obj.); to have inflicted upon one, suffer the infliction of. late ME. **b.** To bear (a burden, charge). late ME. **c.** To support (a part or character); to play the part of 1560. †**10.** To reconcile oneself to doing, to bear to do, something; to tolerate that something should be done –1726. **11.** To hold up, bear the weight of; to keep from falling by support from below; often simply, to carry, bear. Now *rare.* ME. **b.** To be the support of, as in a structure or building; to have resting upon it. late ME. **c.** To bear, support, withstand (a weight or pressure). late ME. †**d.** *refl.* and *intr.* To hold oneself upright; also, to be in or maintain a fixed position –1728. **12.** To be adequate as a ground or basis for 1828.

1. All the Grenadiers of their army, well sustain'd by a good body of other foot 1711. **2.** If.. such objection be sustained 1855. **3.** That hope alone sustains me 1662. **4.** Two Chiefs..Each able to s. a Nations fate DRYDEN. **5.** The arts by which he sustains the reader's interest JOWETT. **6.** Whatever was created, needs To be sustaind and fed MILT. **8.** Capable of sustaining a siege MACAULAY. **9.** His Majesty had sustained a signal defeat abroad 1833. **b.** To s. burdens which would have crushed any other people 1833. **11.** In time the sauuage Bull sustaines the yoake KYD. Sustained in the arms of two sisters of her Order 1850. **b.** Two exceeding great Lyons in red marble, that sustaine two goodly pillars CORYAT. **c.** The same pressure must s. the same weight 1800. **12.** We go beyond what the evidence is able to s. 1866. Hence **Sustai·nable** *a.* †supportable; maintainable. **Sustai·ned** *ppl. a.*, **-ly** *adv.* **Sustai·ner,** one who or that which sustains. **Sustai·ningly** *adv.*

Sustainment (sŏstē[i]·nmĕnt). 1450. [f. prec. + -MENT.] **1.** Means of support. **2.** The action of sustaining; *esp.* maintenance in being or activity, in a certain condition or at a certain level; sustentation 1568.

Sustenance (sɒ·stĭnăns). ME. [– AFr. *sustenaunce*, OFr. *so(u)stenance* (mod. *soutenance*), f. *sostenir* SUSTAIN; see -ANCE.] **1.** Means of living or subsistence; livelihood. **2.** Means of sustaining life; food, victuals ME. **b.** *gen.* and *fig.* Nourishment 1489. **3.** The action of sustaining life by food; the action of supporting with the means of subsistence; the fact or state of being so sustained. late ME. **4.** Something that sustains, supports, or upholds; a means or source of support. late ME.

1. She..Gain'd for her own a scanty s. TENNYSON. **2.** Water is one part, and that not the least of our S. 1691. **b.** Lying is thy s., thy food MILT. **3.** The quantity..requisite for human s. 1842. **4.** The s. of his discourse is Newes OVERBURY.

Sustenant (sɒ·stĭnănt), *a. rare.* 1874. [f. prec.; see -ANT.] Sustaining.

‖**Sustentaculum** (sɒstentæ·kiŭlŏm). *Pl.* **-a.** 1838. [L., f. *sustentare* SUSTENTATE; see -CULE.] *Anat.* A sustaining or supporting part or organ. Hence **Sustenta·cular** *a.* of the nature of, pertaining to, a s.; supporting.

Su·stentate, *v. Obs.* or *arch. rare.* 1564. [– *sustentat-*, pa. ppl. stem of L. *sustentare*, frequent. of *sustinēre* SUSTAIN, see -ATE[3].] *trans.* To sustain.

Sustentation (sɒstĕntē[i]·ʃən). late ME. [– (O)Fr. *sustentation* or L. *sustentatio*, *-ōn-*, f. as prec.; see -ION.] †**1.** The action of bearing or enduring; endurance –1653. **2.** The action of sustaining or the state of being sustained; upkeep, maintenance; support; nourishment. late ME. **b.** *Phys.* The action of those vital functions or processes (as digestion, etc.) which sustain the life and normal activity of an organism 1877. **3.** *concr.* That which sustains life; sustenance, food, nourishment. Also applied to spiritual food. Now *rare.* 1537. **4.** The action of holding up or keeping from falling; the condition of being so supported. †Also *concr.*, a support. Now *rare.* late ME.

attrib.: **s. fund,** a fund in the Free Church of Scotland and other bodies for providing adequate support for ministers.

Sustentative (sɒ·stĕntē[i]tiv, sŏste·ntătiv), *a.* 1640. [– med.L. *sustentativus*, f. as prec.; see -IVE. In later use f. prec.] **1.** Having the quality of sustaining. **2.** *Phys.* Pertaining to sustentation 1877.

Sustention (sŏste·nʃən). 1868. [f. after *detain*, *detention*, etc.] **1.** The action of sustaining or keeping up a condition, etc.; the holding-on of a musical note. **2.** The quality of being sustained in argument or style 1871.

2. A paragraph of fine s. MORLEY.

Sustentive (sŏste·ntiv), *a. rare.* 1662. [– med. L. *sustentivus*, f. *sustent-*, pa. ppl. stem of L. *sustinēre* SUSTAIN; see -IVE.] Having the quality or property of sustaining.

‖**Susu** (sū·sū). 1801. [Bengali.] The Gangetic dolphin, *Platanista gangetica*.

Susurrant (s¹usɒ·rănt) *a.* 1791. [– L. *susurrans, -ant-*, pa. pple. of *susurrare*; see next, -ANT.] Whispering, softly murmuring.

Susurration (s¹usɒrē¹·ʃən). late ME. [– late L. *susurratio, -ōn-*, f. *susurrat-*, pa. ppl. stem of L. *susurrare*, f. *susurrus* whisper; see -ION.] Whispering; *occas.* a whisper; in early use, malicious whispering, tattle. **b.** *transf.* A rustling murmur 1640.

b. No sound but the s. of the taller trees 1867.

Susu·rrous, *a. rare.* 1859. [f. L. SUSURRUS + -OUS.] Of the nature of a whisper.

‖**Susurrus** (s¹usɒ·rɒs). 1831. [L., = humming, muttering, whispering (of imit. origin).] A low soft sound as of whispering or muttering; a whisper; a rustling.

The soft s. and sighs of the branches LONGF.

Sutile (siū·til, -əil), *a. rare.* 1682. [– L. *sutilis*, f. *sut-*, pa. ppl. stem of *suere* SEW *v.*¹; see -ILE.] Made or done by stitching or sewing.

Sutler (sɒ·tləɹ). 1590. [– Du. †*soeteler* (mod. *zoetelaar*), MLG. *suteler, sudeler*, f. †*soetelen* (whence SUTTLE *v.*) befoul, perform mean duties, follow a low trade, f. Gmc. **suð-* (see SUDS).] One who follows an army or lives in a garrison town and sells provisions to the soldiers. †**b.** *gen.* One who furnishes provisions –1793. Hence **Su·tlership.**

Sutlery (sɒ·tləri). 1606. [f. prec. + -Y³.] **1.** The occupation of a sutler; victualling. **2.** A sutler's establishment 1636.

‖**Sutra** (sū·tră). 1801. [Skr. *sūtra* thread, string, (hence) rule, f. *siv* SEW *v.*¹] In Skr. literature, a short mnemonic rule in grammar, law, or philosophy, requiring expansion by means of a commentary. Also applied to Buddhistic text-books.

Suttee (sɒtī·). 1786. [– Hindi, Urdu :– Skr. *satī* faithful wife, f. *sat* good, wise, lit. being, pr. pple. of *as* be.] **1.** A Hindu widow who immolates herself on the funeral pile with her husband's body. **2.** The immolation of a Hindu widow in this way. Phr. *to do, perform s.* 1813. Hence **Suttee·ism,** the practice of s.

†**Suttle** (sɒ·t'l), *a.* 1596. [Old var. of SUBTLE *a.* retained in techn. use. Cf. AFr. *pois sutil.*] *Comm.* Of weight, after tare, or tret, has been deducted –1812.

Suttle (sɒ·t'l), *v. Obs.* or *arch.* 1648. [– Du. †*soetelen*; see SUTLER.] *intr.* To carry on the business of a sutler. Hence **Su·ttling** *vbl. sb.* in *suttling-house*, a house where food and drink are supplied, esp. to soldiers.

Sutural (siū·tiŭrăl), *a.* 1819. [f. next + -AL¹ 1.] Of, pertaining or related to, or situated in a suture. Hence **Su·turally** *adv.*

Suture (siū·tiŭɹ, -tʃəɹ), *sb.* 1541. [– Fr. *suture* or L. *sutura*, f. *sut-*, pa. ppl. stem of *suere* SEW *v.*¹; see -URE.] **1.** *Surg.* The joining of the lips of a wound, or of the ends of a severed nerve or tendon, by stitches; also, an instance of this; a stitch used for this purpose. **b.** *gen.* Sewing, stitching; also, a stitch or seam; *fig.* union, now chiefly of the parts or sections of a literary composition, or a point at which it is made 1600. **2.** *Anat.* The junction of two bones forming an immovable articulation; the line of such junction; *esp.* any of the serrated articulations of the skull 1578. **3.** *Zool.* and *Bot.* The junction, or (more freq.) the line of junction, of contiguous parts, e.g. the line of closure of the valves of a shell, the conflux of the inner margins of elytra 1677. Hence **Su·ture** *v. trans.* to secure with a s. **Su·tured** *ppl. a.* sewn together.

Suzerain (s¹ū·zĕrĕn), *sb.* (*a.*) 1807. [– Fr. *suzerain*, prob. f. *sus* above, up (:– L. *susum*), after *souverain* SOVEREIGN.] A feudal overlord. In recent use, a sovereign or a state having supremacy over another state which possesses its own ruler but cannot act as an independent power. **b.** *attrib.* or *adj.* as s. *lord, state.* So ‖**Su·zeraine,** a woman who is in the position of a s.

Suzerainty (s¹ū·zĕrĕnti). 1823. [f. prec. + -TY¹.] The position, rank, or power of a suzerain.

‖**Svarabhakti** (svarabʰa·kti). 1880. [Skr., lit. 'sound separation'.] *Philology.* The development of a glide vowel between two consonants, e.g. in OE. *buruh* for *burh.*

‖**Svelte** (svelt). 1817. [Fr. – It. *svelto.*] Slim, slender, willowy.

Swab (swǫb), *sb.* 1659. [f. SWAB *v.*] **1.** A mop made of rope-yarn, etc. used for cleaning and drying the deck, etc. on board ship. **b.** Anything used for mopping up; any mass or bundle of stuff that takes up moisture, or that, being soaked, is applied to a surface. Also *Med.* a specimen of a morbid secretion, etc., taken with a s. for bacteriological examination. 1787. **c.** A cylindrical brush or cleaner for cleaning out the bore of a firearm; a soft brush for wetting the mould in founding 1874. **d.** A naval officer's epaulette (*slang*) 1798. **e.** A piece of stuff that hangs loose, trails, etc. 1862. **2.** †**a.** = SWABBER¹ 1. **b.** A term of abuse or (now often mild) contempt. 1687.

Swab (swǫb), *v.* 1719. [Back-formation from next.] **1.** *trans.* To apply a swab to; to cleanse or wipe with or as with a swab; to mop *up.* Also with *down.* **2.** To mop *up* (liquid) with or as with a swab 1745. **3.** To souse as with a mop 1762.

1. Swabbing the forward deck 1883.

Swabber¹ (swǫ·bəɹ). 1592. [– early mod. Du. *zwabber*, f. Gmc. base meaning 'sway about', 'splash in water', as in (M)LG. *swabben* splash, sway, slap, Norw. *svabba* splash, wade, LG. *swabber* (G. *schwabber*) mop, swab, Du. *zwabberen* mop.] **1.** One of a ship's crew whose business it was to swab the decks, etc.; a petty officer who had charge of the cleaning of the decks. **2.** One who behaves like a sailor of low rank; a low or unmannerly fellow: a term of contempt 1609. **3.** A mop or swab 1607.

Swabber² (swǫ·bəɹ). *Obs.* exc. *Hist.* or *dial.* 1700. [perh. same wd. as prec. Cf. synon. *swab* (XVII), now s.w. dial.] Chiefly *pl.* Certain cards at the game of whist, which entitled the holder to part of the stakes.

Swabbers, the Ace of Hearts, Knave of Clubs, Ace and Duce of Trumps 1700. *Whisk and swabbers*, a form of whist in which these cards were so used.

Swabian (swē¹·biăn), *a.* and *sb.* Also **Suabian.** 1785. [f. *Suabia*, latinized f. G. *Schwaben* + -AN.] **A.** *adj.* Belonging or pertaining to, or native of Swabia (Schwaben), a former German duchy, now a province including Würtemberg and part of Bavaria. **B.** *sb.* **1.** A native of Swabia 1845. **2.** A variety of pigeon 1855.

Swad (swǫd), *sb.*¹ Now *dial.* 1570. [perh. of Scand. origin; cf. Norw. dial. *svadde* big stout fellow.] **1.** A country bumpkin; a loutish or clownish fellow: a common term of abuse. **2.** A squat fat person 1606.

Swad (swǫd), *sb.*² *dial.* 1600. [perh. related to SWATHE *sb.*², as if = covering, integument.] The pod or husk of peas, beans, etc.

Swad (swǫd), *sb.*³ 1828. *U.S.* [Of unkn. origin.] A thick mass, clump, or bunch; hence, a great quantity (also *pl.*).

Swaddle (swǫ·d'l), *sb.* 1538. [f. next.] **1.** Swaddling-clothes. Now *U.S.* **2.** A bandage. *Obs.* or *arch.* 1569.

Swaddle (swǫ·d'l), *v.* 1491. [Earliest in *swaðelbond* swaddling-clothes XIII, f. SWATHE *sb.*² + -LE. For the phonology cf. FIDDLE *sb.*] **1.** *trans.* To bind (an infant) in swaddling-clothes. **b.** *fig.*, now esp. with ref. to the restriction of action of any kind 1539. **2.** To wrap round *with* bandages; to envelop with wrappings; to swathe, bandage 1522. †**3.** To beat soundly. *colloq.* –1822.

1. Ye shal fynde the babe swadled, and layed in a maunger COVERDALE *Luke* 2:12. **2.** They immediately began to s. me up in my Night-Gown with long Pieces of Linnen ADDISON.

Swaddler (swǫ·dləɹ). 1747. [f. prec. + -ER¹.] *orig.* A nickname for a Methodist, esp. a Methodist preacher, in Ireland; now, for Protestants in general.

Swaddling (swǫ·dliŋ), *vbl. sb.* 1522. [f. as prec. + -ING¹.] **1.** The action of SWADDLE *v.* **2.** *pl.* (rarely *sing.*) Swaddling-clothes; also, a bandage 1623. †**3.** [After prec.] Methodism; hence, conduct supposed to be characteristic of Methodists –1772.

Swa·ddling, *ppl. a.* 1747. [f. SWADDLER; see -ING².] Of a Methodist character or practice; Protestant; †canting.

Swa·ddling-band, usu. pl. **-bands.** ME. [SWADDLING *vbl. sb.*, BAND *sb.*¹] = next.

Swa·ddling-clothes, *sb. pl.* 1535. [SWADDLING *vbl. sb.*] Clothes consisting of narrow lengths of bandage wrapped round a new-born infant's limbs to prevent free movement. Also *transf.* an infant's long-clothes. Now chiefly *fig.* or *allus.* in ref. to the earliest period of the existence of a person or thing, when movement or action is restricted.

Swa·ddling-clouts, *sb. pl.* 1530. [See SWADDLING *vbl. sb.* and CLOUT *sb.*] = prec.

‖**Swadeshi** (swadē¹·ʃi). *India.* 1905. [Bengali, lit. = own-country things, i.e. home industries.] The name of a movement in India, originating in Bengal, advocating the boycott of foreign goods. Hence **Swade·shism.**

Swag (swæg), *sb.* 1660. [f. next.] **1.** A swaying or lurching movement. **2.** A heavy fall or drop (*local*) 1700. **3.** A wreath or festoon of flowers, foliage, or fruit fastened up at both ends and hanging down in the middle, used as an ornament; also of a natural festoon 1794. **4.** A thief's plunder or booty; *gen.* a quantity of money or goods unlawfully acquired, gains dishonestly made (*slang*) 1812. **5.** *Austral.* The bundle of personal belongings carried by a traveller in the bush, a tramp, or a miner 1864.

Swag (swæg), *v.* Now chiefly *dial.* 1530. [immed. source unc., but prob. Scand.; cf. Norw. dial. *svagga* and *svaga* sway.] **1.** *intr.* To move unsteadily or heavily from side to side or up and down; to sway without control. **2.** To sink down; to hang loosely or heavily; to sag. Also with *down.* 1621. **3.** *trans.* To cause to sway uncertainly; to rock about; also, to cause to sink or sag 1530. **4.** [f. prec. 5.] *Austral.* **a.** intr. *To s. it*: to carry one's 'swag' or bundle of effects. **b.** *trans.* To pack up (one's effects) in a 'swag'. 1861.

1. I swagge, as a fatte persons belly swaggeth as he goth PALSGR. *transf.* The front of battle swagged to and fro 1887.

Swa·g be:lly, swag-belly. 1632. [f. prec. + BELLY *sb.*] **1.** (as two words) A pendulous abdomen. **b.** *Path.* A tumour or swelling of the abdomen 1857. **2.** (with hyphen or as one word) A person having a pendulous abdomen 1611. So **Swa·g-be:llied** *a.* having a pendulous paunch 1604.

Swage (swē¹dʒ), *sb.* late ME. [– OFr. *souage, -aige*, (also mod.) *suage*, of unkn. origin.] **1.** An ornamental grooving, moulding, border, or mount on a candlestick, basin, or other vessel. **b.** A circular or semi-circular depression or groove, as on an anvil 1680. **2.** A tool for bending cold metal (or moulding potter's clay) to the required shape; also, a die or stamp for shaping metal on an anvil, in a press, etc. 1812.

2. *attrib.* The holes in the s. block..are used after the manner of heading tools for large objects 1843.

Swage (swē¹dʒ), *v.*¹ *Obs.* exc. *arch.* or *dial.* ME. [– AFr. *suag(i)er, swag(i)er* :– pop. L. **suaviare*, f. L. *suavis* sweet; partly aphetic f. ASSUAGE *v.*] = ASSUAGE *v.*

Swage (swē¹dʒ), *v.*² 1831 [f. SWAGE *sb.*] *trans.* To shape or bend by means of a swage.

Swagger (swæ·gəɹ), *sb.*¹ 1725. [f. SWAGGER *v.*] The action of swaggering; external conduct or personal behaviour marked by an air of superiority or defiant or insolent disregard of others. **b.** *transf.* Applied to a mental or intellectual attitude marked by the same characteristics 1819.

After much s., he asked the constable if he knew who he was? 1811.

Swagger (swæ·gəɹ), *sb.*² *Austral.* 1855. [f. SWAG *v.* or *sb.* + -ER¹.] One who carries a swag.

Swagger (swæ·gəɹ), *a. colloq.* or *slang.* 1879. [f. next.] Showily or ostentatiously equipped, etc.; smart or fashionable in style, manner, appearance, or behaviour; 'swell'.

Swagger (swæ·gəɹ), *v.* 1590. [Presumably f. SWAG *v.* + -ER⁵.] **1.** *intr.* To behave with an air of superiority, in a blustering, insolent, or defiant manner; now *esp.* to walk or carry oneself as if among inferiors, with an obtrusively superior or insolent air. **b.** *spec.* To talk blusteringly; to hector; also, to grumble. Now only, to talk boastfully, or braggingly. 1597. **c.** *trans.* To influence, force, or constrain by blustering or hectoring language 1605. **2.** *intr.* To sway, lurch 1724.

1. [He] swaggered about like an aide-de-camp at a review R. S. SURTEES. **b.** You may think I s., but as I hope to be saved it is true SHERIDAN. **c.** He would s. the boldest men into a dread of his power SWIFT. Hence **Swa·ggerer.**

Swagger-. 1887. The vb. SWAGGER used in comb.; **s.-cane, -stick** (*colloq.*), an officer's cane or stick; the short cane or stick carried by soldiers when walking out.

Swaggy (swæ·gi), *a. rare.* 1646. [f. SWAG *v.* + -Y[1].] Swagging, pendulous.

Swahili (swahī·li). 1814. [lit. = pertaining to the coasts, f. Arab. *sawāḥil*, pl. of *sāḥil* coast.] A Bantu people (or one of them) inhabiting Zanzibar and the adjacent coast; also, their language, Kiswahili. **b.** *attrib.* or as *adj.*

Swain (swēⁱn), *sb.* [Early ME. *swein* – ON. *sveinn* boy, servant, attendant = OE. *swān* swineherd, MLG. *swēn*, OHG. *swein* (G. dial. *schwein*) :- Gmc. *swainaz. See also BOATSWAIN, COXSWAIN.] †**1.** A young man attending on a knight; hence, a man of low degree. (Often coupled with *knight.*) –1572. †**2.** A male servant, serving-man; an attendant, follower –1579. †**3.** A man; a youth; a boy –1633. **4.** A country or farm labourer, *freq.* a shepherd; a countryman, rustic. *arch.* 1579. **5.** A country gallant or lover; hence *gen.* a lover, wooer, sweetheart, esp. in pastoral poetry 1585. ¶**6.** A freeholder within the forest 1615.

2. Hym boes serue hym selne that has na swayn CHAUCER. **4.** Those Swains with their Sheep-hooks in their hands 1663. **5.** Who is Siluia? what is she? That all our Swaines commend her? SHAKS. Hence **Swain** *v. intr.* (with *it*), to play the lover or wooer.

Swainish (swēⁱ·niʃ), *a.* 1642. [f. prec. + -ISH[1].] Resembling or characteristic of a swain or rustic; rustic, boorish.

An ungentle, and s. breast MILT. Hence **Swai·nishness.**

Swale (swēⁱl), *sb.*[1] *local.* ME. [Of unkn. origin.] Timber, planking.

Swale (swēⁱl), *sb.*[2] *local*; chiefly *East Anglian.* 1440. [prob. Scand.; cf. ON. *svalr* cool.] Shade; a shady place; also, the cool, the cold.

Swale (swēⁱl), *sb.*[3] *local.* 1584. [Of unkn. origin.] A hollow, low place; *esp. U.S.*, a moist or marshy depression in a tract of land, esp. in the midst of rolling prairie.

Swale, *v.*[1]: see SWEAL *v.*

Swale (swēⁱl), *v.*[2] 1820. [prob. freq. f. SWAY *v.* + -LE.] *intr.* To move or sway up and down or from side to side.

Swallet (swǫ·lėt). *local.* (*s.w.*) 1668. [Obscure formation on SWALLOW *v.*] An underground stream of water such as breaks in upon miners at work. Also (in full *s. hole*), the opening through which a stream disappears underground.

‖**Swallo** (swǫ·lo). 1779. [– Malay *suwāla.*] = SEA-SLUG 1, TREPANG.

Swallow (swǫ·loᵘ), *sb.*[1] [OE. *swealwe* = OS. *swala*, OHG. *swal(a)wa* (Du. *zwaluw*, G. *schwalbe*), ON. *svala* :- Gmc. *swalwōn.] **1.** A bird of the genus *Hirundo*, esp. *H. rustica*, a well-known migratory bird with long pointed wings and forked tail, having a swift curving flight and a twittering cry, building mud-nests on buildings, etc., and popularly regarded as a harbinger of summer. **b.** In allusion to the swift flight of the bird ME. **2.** In extended sense, any bird of the swallow kind, or of the family *Hirundinidæ*, e.g. a martin; often misapplied to the swifts, now reckoned as a distinct and unrelated family (*Cypselidæ*) 1758. **b.** With qualifying words, applied to various species of *Hirundinidæ* or *Cypselidæ*; also, to birds of other families resembling swallows 1552. **3.** †**a.** = SEA-SWALLOW 1. **b.** A species of moth (*Leiocampa dictæa*). **c.** A variety of domestic pigeon. 1668.

1. Provb. *One s. does not make a summer.* (Cf. Gr. μία χελιδὼν ἔαρ οὐ ποιεῖ). **b.** True Hope is swift, and flyes with Swallowes wings SHAKS. **2. b.** **Cliff S.,** one of several species of the genus *Petrochelidon*, nesting in cliffs. **Window S.,** the house-martin.

attrib. and *Comb.*: **s.-dive,** a form of dive in which the arms are extended to simulate the outline of a gliding s.; so **s.-diving**; **-fish,** †(*a*) the flying fish; (*b*) the sapphirine gurnard; **-shrike,** a bird of the genus *Artamus* or family *Artamidæ*, found in India and Australia; **swallow's nest,** the nest of a swallow; *transf.* applied to a thing lodged at a height; *spec.* a battery of guns or company of shot placed on a height; **s.-warbler,** an Australian warbler (*Sylvia hirundinacea*), with plumage resembling that of a s.

Swallow (swǫ·loᵘ), *sb.*[2] [Late OE. *ġeswelg*, *swelg*, *-h* gulf, abyss, corresp. to MLG. *swelch* (also *swalh*) throat, whirlpool, ON. *svelgr* whirlpool, f. Gmc. *swelʒ-* *swalʒ-; see next.] **1.** A deep hole or opening in the earth; a pit, gulf, abyss. *Obs.* exc. as in b. **b.** *spec.* An opening or cavity, such as are common in limestone formations, through which a stream disappears underground; also called *s.-pit*, SWALLOW-HOLE, and locally SWALLET 1610. **2.** A depth or abyss of water; a yawning gulf; a whirlpool. *Obs.* or *arch.* OE. †**3.** *fig.* A gulf, abyss, sink (of evil) –1624. **4.** The throat, pharynx, or gullet, or these collectively; the gorge, late ME. **b.** *transf.* Capacity of swallowing; appetite for food or drink; voracity; also *fig.* appetite, relish, inclination 1592. **5.** *fig.* 1607. **6.** A single act of swallowing; a gulp 1822. **b.** A quantity (esp. of liquid) swallowed at once; a mouthful swallowed 1861. **7.** The space between the sheave and the shell in a pulley-block, through which the rope runs 1860.

4. b. 'Twill not down, sir! I have no s. for 't MASSINGER. **5.** His Ungodly s. in gorging down the Estates of helpless Widows 1688. Even the largest minds have but narrow swallows LOCKE.

Swallow (swǫ·loᵘ), *v.* [OE. *swelgan* = OS. *far|swelgan*, OHG. *swel(a)han* (Du. *swelgen*, G. *schwelgen*), ON. *svelga* :- Gmc. str. vb. f. *swelʒ- *swalʒ- *swulʒ-. Cf. prec.] **1.** *trans.* To take into the stomach through the throat and gullet, as food or drink. In early use and still *poet.* also more gen. = to eat or drink up, devour. **b.** *absol.* or *intr.* To take food, drink, etc. into the stomach through the gullet; to perform the act of deglutition, as in an effort to suppress emotion 1700. **2.** *transf.* To take into itself (physically); to cause to disappear in its interior or depths; to engulf ME. **3.** *fig.* **a.** To make away with, destroy, consume, cause to vanish (as if by devouring or absorption into itself) ME. **b.** To cause to be 'lost' in something; to 'drown', 'absorb', engross, occupy wholly. (Now only with *up.*) ME. **c.** To take in eagerly, 'devour' (with one's ears or mind). late ME. **d.** To take for oneself, or into itself, as a territory or other possession; to absorb, appropriate 1637. **4.** To accept without opposition or protest; to take (an oath, etc.) without demur or lightly 1591. **b.** *esp.* To accept mentally without question or suspicion; to believe unquestioningly 1594. **5.** To put up with, submit to, take patiently (something injurious or irksome) 1611. **6.** To refrain from expressing or uttering; to keep down, repress. Also with *down.* 1642. **7.** To take back, retract, recant 1593.

1. [Salmons] s. the bait with the hook down into the stomach JOHNSON. **2.** The earthquake that swallowed man and beast 1905. **3.** Sloughs That s. common sense TENNYSON. **b.** The necessary Provision for Life swallows the greatest part of their Time LOCKE. **c.** *John* IV. ii. 195. **4.** The former laid a wager that there was no flattery so gross, but his friend would s. H. WALPOLE. **b.** He that can s. the raining of Frogs 1691. **5.** If I s. this wrong, let her thanke you 1611. **6.** Hannibal swallowed his resentment 1878. **7.** I have swallow'd my Words already; I have eaten them up 1703.

S. up. a. *lit.* To swallow completely or voraciously; to eat up, devour. **b.** *transf.* To engulf completely; to cause to disappear utterly in its depths. **c.** *fig.* To make away with or destroy completely; to cause to disappear utterly. **d.** To occupy entirely; engross. **e.** To take completely into itself, or for oneself; to appropriate, absorb. **f.** To pass over (a distance) rapidly. Hence **Swa·llower,** one who or that which swallows; also *fig.*

Swa·llow-hole. 1661. [f. SWALLOW *v.* or *sb.*[2] + HOLE *sb.*] = SWALLOW *sb.*[2] 1b.

Swallow-tail, swallowtail (swǫ·loᵘ,tēⁱl). 1545. [f. SWALLOW *sb.*[1] + TAIL *sb.*[1]] **1.** A tail like that of a swallow; a forked tail 1703. **2.** Applied to various animals having a forked tail. **a.** A swallow-tailed butterfly 1819. **b.** A humming-bird of the genus *Eupetomena* 1861. **c.** A swallow-tailed kite. **3.** The white willow (*Salix alba*) 1626. **4.** A broad or barbed arrowhead; an arrow with such a head 1545. **5.** *Fortif.* An outwork characterized by two projections with a re-entrant angle between them, suggesting a swallow's tail 1688. **6.** The cleft two-pointed end of a flag or pennon; also, a swallow-tailed flag 1697. **b.** The cleft tail-end of a vane 1843. **7.** A swallow-tailed coat. *colloq.* 1835. **b.** The tail or skirt of such a coat (*rare*) 1894. **8.** *attrib.* = SWALLOW-TAILED 1596.

7. The boys..exchanged their tweed coats for the regulation swallow-tails 1894.

Swallow-tailed (swǫ·loᵘ,tēⁱld), *a.* 1672. [f. prec. + -ED[2].] Having a tail like that of a swallow, or an end or part like a swallow's tail; also, of the form of a swallow's tail. **I.** Of natural objects. **1.** In names of species or varieties of birds characterized by a long deeply forked tail, as **s. duck,** the long-tailed duck, *Harelda glacialis*; **s. gull,** a rare Amer. gull, *Creagrus furcatus*; **s. hawk, kite,** a widely distributed Amer. kite, *Elanoides forficatus*. **2. a.** Having a pair of projecting parts suggesting a swallow's tail, as a seed. **b. S. willow** = prec. 3. 1712. **3.** Having each of the hind wings prolonged into a 'tail', the two together suggesting the forked tail of a swallow, as the **s. butterfly** (*Papilio machaon* and other species of *Papilionidæ*) and the **s. moth** (*Urapteryx sambucaria*) 1743. **II.** Of artificial objects. **1.** Of a flag or pennon: Having a cleft end with two tapering points 1697. **2.** Dovetailed; also, having a cleft end 1726. **3.** Of a coat: Having a pair of pointed or tapering skirts 1835.

Swallowwort (swǫ·loᵘwɒɹt). 1548. [f. SWALLOW *sb.*[1] + WORT[1].] **1.** The herb *Vincetoxicum officinale*; from the form of the pods, suggesting a swallow with outspread wings. **2.** The Greater Celandine, *Chelidonium majus* 1578.

Swam, pa. t. and obs. pa. pple. of SWIM *v.*

‖**Swami** (swā·mi). Also **-y.** 1773. [– Hindi *swāmī* master, prince – Skr. *svāmin.*] **1.** A Hindu idol. **2.** A title for a Hindu religious teacher 1901. **3.** *attrib.* **s.-house,** an idol temple or shrine 1778. **b.** Applied to jewellery ornamented with figures of Hindu deities 1880.

Swamp (swǫmp), *sb.* 1624. [usu. referred to the root which is the base of the several Germanic formations *swamp-, *swamb-, and *swamm-, with the meaning 'sponge' or 'fungus'.] A tract of low-lying ground in which water collects; a piece of wet spongy ground; a marsh or bog. Orig. and in early use only in the N. Amer. colonies, where it denoted a tract of rich soil having a growth of trees and other vegetation, but too moist for cultivation.

The Pontine Marshes, formerly the abode of thirty nations, are now a pestilential s. J. H. NEWMAN. *fig.* In this flat s. of convalescence, left by the ebb of sickness LAMB.

attrib. and *Comb.*: **s.-fever,** malarial fever prevalent in swampy regions; **-hook** (*U.S.*), a large hook used in swamping logs; **-ore** [G. *sumpferz*], bog iron ore. **b.** In names of animals (mostly birds) inhabiting swamps: **s. blackbird** = MARSH *blackbird*; **s. deer,** *Rucervus duvaucelli*, of India; **s. hare,** *Lepus aquaticus*, of the southern U.S., also called *water-rabbit*; **s. hen,** any of various rails, esp. of the genus *Porphyrio*; **s. partridge,** the spruce partridge or Canada grouse; **s. pheasant,** *Centropus phasianus*, of Australia; **s. quail,** any species of the genus *Synœcus*, of Australia; **s. robin,** the cheewink or ground-robin, *Pipilo erythrophthalmus*, of N. America; **s. sparrow,** (*a*) a species of song-sparrow, *Melospiza palustris*, common in U.S. and Canada; (*b*) *Sphenœacus punctatus* of New Zealand, also called *fern-bird*. **c.** Denoting plants or vegetable products (chiefly of N. America) growing in swamps: **s.-cabbage** = SKUNK-CABBAGE; **s. gum,** various Australasian species of *Eucalyptus*; **s. honeysuckle,** *Rhododendron viscosum* (*Azalea viscosa*); **s. laurel,** the s. sassafras, *Magnolia glauca*; also *Kalmia glauca*; **s. maple,** the red maple, *Acer rubrum*; also several other species, as the silver maple, *A. dasycarpum*, the mountain maple, *A. spicatum*, and the allied

Negundo californicum; **s. sassafras** = *s. laurel*; **s. willow,** the pussy willow, *Salix discolor*; **s. wood,** the N. Amer. leather-wood, *Dirca palustris*.

Swamp (swǫmp), *v.* 1688. [f. prec.] **1.** *pass.* To be entangled or lost in a swamp. *N. Amer. Obs.* or *arch.* **2.** orig. *pass.* To be submerged or inundated with water (or other liquid), as a boat, a piece of ground; hence *actively*, to submerge, inundate, or soak with water, etc. 1772. **3.** *intr.* in passive sense: To be swamped or submerged; to fill with water and sink, as a boat 1795. **4.** *fig.* (*trans.*) To plunge or sink as if in a swamp or in water; to overwhelm with difficulties, or esp. by superior numbers, so as to render inefficient 1818. **b.** To ruin financially 1864. **5.** *U.S.* To make (a logging-road) in a forest or 'swamp' by felling trees, clearing away undergrowth, etc. Also, to haul (logs) to the skidways. 1857.

3. The boats swamped in the current—all were lost SCOTT. 4. The Whigs in 1718 sought to govern the country by 'swamping' the House of Commons DISRAELI. b. Mortgages enough to have swamped any man 1864.

Swa·mp-oak. 1683. **1.** In N. America, any of several species of oak growing in swamps. **2.** In Australia: Any of various species of *Casuarina*; cf. SHE-OAK 1837.

Swampy (swǫ·mpi), *a.* 1697. [f. SWAMP *sb.* + -Y[1].] Of the nature of a swamp; abounding in swamps; marshy, boggy. **b.** Of or pertaining to a swamp; found in swamps, as *s. iron ore* = BOG *iron ore*; proceeding from a swamp 1796. Hence **Swa·mpi-ly** *adv.*, **-ness.**

Swan (swǫn), *sb.* [OE. *swan*, OS., OHG. *swan* (G. *schwan*), ON. *svanr* :- Gmc. **swanaz*, beside **swanōn*, repr. by MLG., MDu. *swane* (Du. *zwaan*), OHG. *swana* (G. dial. *schwane*).] **1.** A large web-footed swimming-bird of the genus *Cygnus* or subfamily *Cygninæ* of the family *Anatidæ*, characterized by a long and gracefully curved neck and a majestic motion when swimming; esp. *C. olor, gibbus*, or *mansuetus*, with pure white plumage in the adult, black legs and feet, and a red bill surmounted by a black knob, named specifically the Domestic, Mute, or Tame Swan.

Other important species are **Black S.,** *Chenopsis atratus* of Australia, with plumage almost entirely black; **Black-necked S.,** *Cygnus* (*Sthenelides*) *nigricollis* or *melanocoryphus*, with black head and neck, and the rest of the plumage pure white; **Trumpeter S.** (see TRUMPETER); **Whistling S.,** (*a*) of Europe, *C.* (*O.*) *musicus* or *ferus*, also called Wild Swan, †Elk, or Whooper; (*b*) of N. America, *C.* (*O.*) *americanus* or *columbianus*.

b. In classical mythology, the swan was sacred to Apollo and to Venus (occas., as by Shaks., wrongly ascribed to Juno) 1592. **2.** *fig.* or *allus.* **a.** Applied to persons or things, in ref. to the pure white plumage of the swan taken as a type of faultlessness or excellence; often in contrast to *crow* or *goose* ME. **b.** In allusions to the fabulous belief that the swan sings immediately or shortly before its death. late ME. **c.** Hence used for: A 'singer', bard, poet 1612. **d.** *Black s.*, provb. phr. for something extremely rare (or non-existent) 1579. **3. a.** A figure of a swan, as in heraldry. late ME. **b.** *Astron.* The northern constellation *Cygnus* 1551.

2. a. *Rom. & Jul.* I. ii. 92. Provb. phr. *To think one's geese all swans*, to magnify the qualities of one's own possessions. **b.** *Oth.* V. ii. 247. Like some full-breasted s...fluting a wild carol ere her death TENNYSON. **c.** *The S. of Avon* = Shakespeare. *The Mantuan S.* = Virgil.

Comb.: **s.-dive** *sb. U.S.*, = SWALLOW-*dive*; hence *s.-dive* vb. intr.; **-drop,** (*a*) the knob on a swan's bill; also *transf.*; (*b*) = *s.-shot*; **-quill,** a swan's feather, or a pen made of one; **swan's bath,** (*pseudo-arch.*) the water, the sea; **s.-shot,** a large size of shot, used for shooting swans; **-song,** a song like that fabled to be sung by a dying s.; the last work of a poet or musician, esp. one composed shortly before his death.

Swang, obs. pa. t. of SWING *v.*

Swanherd (swǫ·nhə̄ɹd). 1482. [f. SWAN *sb.* + HERD *sb.*[2]] One who tends swans; an official having charge of swans.

Swanimote (swǫ·nimo[u]t), **swainmote** (swē[i]·nmo[u]t). *Obs.* exc. *Hist.* ME. [repr. OE. **swāngemōt* 'meeting of swineherds', f. *swān* swineherd (see SWAIN) + *ġemōt* MOOT *sb.* 2.] A forest assembly held three times a year in accordance with the Forest Charter of 1217, probably orig. to enable the forest officers to superintend the depasturing of pigs in the king's woods in the autumn and the clearance of the forest of cattle and sheep while the deer were fawning in the summer; later, applied vaguely or generically to courts of attachment, inquisitions, etc.

Swank (swæŋk), *sb. slang.* 1854. [Goes with next.] Ostentatious or pretentious behaviour or talk; swagger; pretentiousness.

Swank (swæŋk), *v. slang.* 1809. [A word of the midland areas, having a wide application as of activity or vigour, taken into gen. sl. use early in XX.] **1.** *intr.* To behave ostentatiously, to swagger; also, to pretend by one's behaviour to be something superior to what one is; *gen.* to make pretence. **2.** To work hard, to 'swot' 1890.

Swa·nky, *a.* 1842. [f. SWANK *sb.* or *v.* + -Y[1].] Swaggering; pretentiously grand.

Swa·n-like, *a.* (*adv.*) 1591. [f. SWAN *sb.* + -LIKE.] **A.** *adj.* Like a swan or that of a swan. **b.** *esp.* in ref. to the fabled singing of the swan just before its death 1592. **B.** *adv.* Like or in the manner of a swan 1635.

A. b. If he loose, he makes a S. end, Fading in musique SHAKS.

Swa·n-mark. 1560. [MARK *sb.*[1] III. 2.] An official mark of ownership cut on the beak of a swan, on the occasion of SWAN-UPPING.

Swa·n-neck. Also **swan's neck.** 1686. **1.** A neck like that of a swan; a long, slender (white) neck 1837. **2.** Name for various structural parts or contrivances having a curved cylindrical form like a swan's neck 1686. **3.** *attrib.* Of a curved form like a swan's neck 1844.

Swanner (swǫ·nəɹ). 1524. Clipped form of SWANHERD.

Swannery (swǫ·nəri). 1754. [f. as prec.; see -ERY.] A place where swans are kept and reared.

Swannish (swǫ·niʃ), *a. rare.* 1586. [f. SWAN *sb.* + -ISH[1].] Swan-like.

Swanny (swǫ·ni), *a.* 1567. [f. SWAN *sb.* + -Y[1].] **1.** Full of or abounding in swans (*rare*). **2.** Of, pertaining to, or resembling that of, a swan 1598.

2. The s. glossiness of a neck late so stately 1748.

‖**Swan-pan** (swæ·n pæ·n). 1736. [Chinese, lit. reckoning-board.] The Chinese abacus.

Swan's down, swansdown (swǫ·nzdaun). 1606. **1.** The down or soft under-plumage of the swan, used for dress-trimmings, powder-puffs, etc. **2. a.** A soft thick close woollen cloth. **b.** A thick cotton cloth with a nap on one side, also called *Canton* or *cotton flannel*. 1801.

Swanskin (swǫ·nskin). Also **swan's-skin.** 1610. **1.** The skin of a swan (with the feathers on); *transf.* a soft or delicate skin. **2.** A fine thick kind of flannel 1694. **3.** *attrib.* Made or consisting of swanskin 1610.

Swa·n-u:pping. 1810. [UPPING *vbl. sb.*] The action or practice of 'upping' or taking up swans and marking them with nicks on the beak in token of being owned by the Crown or some corporation. So **Swa·n-u:pper,** an official who takes up and marks swans 1557.

Swap, swop (swǫp), *sb.* late ME. [f. next.] **1.** An act of 'swapping' or striking; a stroke, blow. *Obs.* exc. *dial.* **2.** An act, or the action, of 'swapping' or exchanging; (an) exchange. *slang* or *colloq.* 1625.

2. Phr. *To get* (or *have*) *the s.*, to be dismissed from employment (*slang*).

Swap, swop (swǫp), *v.* ME. [prob. imit. of a smart resounding blow; cf. G. dial. *schwappe* in same sense, *schwappen* make a clapping or splashing noise.] **I.** †**1.** *trans.* To strike, hit, smite –1582. **b.** To strike or smite *off, in two*, etc. *Obs.* exc. *arch.* ME. **2.** *intr.* To strike, smite, deal a blow or blows. Now *rare* or *Obs.* late ME. **3.** *trans.* To move (something) quickly or briskly, esp. so as to impinge on something else; to fling, cast, throw (*down*, etc.) forcibly; to bang (a door) *to. Obs.* exc. *dial.* ME. **4.** *intr.* To move with haste or violence, esp. so as to strike or impinge upon something; to sink *into* a swoon. Now *rare* or *Obs.* late ME.

1. b. Who so wol nat sacrifise Swape of his heed CHAUCER. **4.** With chilling fear, the Ladies swapped downe, In deadly sownd 1592.

II. †**1.** *trans.* To strike (a bargain) –1692. **2.** To give or dispose of in exchange *for* something else; to exchange (a thing) *with* another person. Chiefly, now only, *slang* or *colloq.* 1594. **b.** *absol.* To exchange, make an exchange 1778. **3.** *transf.* in various slang uses. **a.** To dismiss or be dismissed from employment. **b.** To cheat. **c.** To change one's clothes. 1862.

2. He bought and sold and swopped horses 1882. As they sat in the tavern, swapping stories 1891.

Swap, swop, *adv.* (*int.*) Now *dial.* 1672. [The stem of SWAP *v.* Cf. G. *schwapp(s)*, LG. *swaps.*] At a blow; suddenly and forcibly.

‖**Swaraj** (swarā·dʒ). 1906. [Skr., = self-ruling.] Home rule or self-government as the aim of Indian nationals. Hence **Swara·jist,** an advocate of swaraj.

Sward (swǭɹd), *sb.* [OE. *sweard* (beside *swearþ*: see SWARTH *sb.*[1]), corresp. to OFris., MLG., MDu. *swarde* hairy skin, MHG. *swarte* (G. *schwarte* bacon rind, crust), ON. *svǫrðr* skin (of the head), walrus hide; of unkn. origin.] **1.** The skin of the body; *esp.* (now *dial.*) the rind of pork or bacon. **2.** †**a.** Usu. with defining phr. *of the earth*, etc.: The surface or upper layer of ground usu. covered with herbage –1626. **b.** The surface of soil covered with grass or other herbage; turf, GREENSWARD 1508. (*b*) A growth of grass; a stretch of greensward 1733.

2. b. The grassy s. 1866. It has become the fashion..to break up the s. of the downs 1879.

Comb.: **s.-cutter,** an implement for cutting a tough s. in preparation for ploughing.

Sward (swǭɹd), *v.* 1610. [f. prec.] **1.** *intr.* To form a sward; to become covered with grassy turf. **2.** *trans.* To cover with a sward; chiefly *pass.* to be covered with grass or herbage 1610. So **Swa·rded** *ppl. a.* covered with a sward or grassy turf; turfed 1513.

Swardy (swǭ·ɹdi), *a.* 1639. [f. SWARD *sb.* + -Y[1].] Covered with sward, swarded, turfy.

Sware, arch. pa. t. of SWEAR.

Swarf (swarf), *sb.*[1] *Sc.* 1470. [rel. to ON. *svarfa* upset.] A swoon, a fainting-fit; a state of faintness or insensibility. So **Swarf** *v.* to faint, cause to faint 1513.

Swarf (swǭɹf, swāɹf), *sb.*[2] 1566. [repr. OE. *ġeswearf, ġesweorf, ġeswyrf* filings, or – ON. *svarf* file-dust; see SWERVE *v.*] The wet or greasy grit abraded from a grindstone or axle; the filings or shavings of iron or steel.

Swarm (swǭɹm), *sb.* [OE. *swearm* = OS., MLG. *swarm*, OHG. *swar(a)m* (G. *schwarm*), ON. *svarmr* :- Gmc. **swarmaz*, usu. referred to the base of Skr. *svárati* it sounds, L. SUSURRUS.] **1.** A body of bees which at a particular season leave the hive or main stock, gather in a compact mass or cluster, and fly off together in search of a new dwelling-place, under the guidance of a queen, (or are transferred at once to a new hive). **b.** *allus.* of 1659. **2.** A very large or dense body or collection; a crowd, throng, multitude. (Often *contempt.*) late ME.

1. A s. of bees in May Is worth a load of hay 1864. **b.** A new s. of Danes came over this year [875] HUME. **2.** England in swarms did into Holland throng FULLER. A s. of fire-flies 1842. Swarms of dust 1890.

Comb.: **s.-cell** (*Biol.*) = *s.-spore*; **-movement,** the movement of s.-spores in 'swarming'; **-spore** (*Biol.*), (*a*) a motile spore in certain Algæ, Fungi, and Protozoa, a zoospore; (*b*) the free-swimming embryo or gemmule of freshwater sponges.

Swarm (swǭɹm), *v.*[1] late ME. [f. prec.] **1.** *intr.* Of bees: To gather in a compact cluster and leave the hive in a body to found a new colony. Also with *off*. **b.** *allus.* 1609. **c.** *Biol.* Of certain spores or reproductive bodies: To escape from the parent organism in a swarm, with characteristic movement; to move or swim about in a swarm, as zoospores ('swarm-spores') do in the cell just before escaping, and in the water after escaping 1864. **2.** To come together in a swarm or dense cloud; to crowd, throng; also, to go or move along in a crowd. late ME. **3.** To occur or exist in swarms or multitudes; to be densely crowded; to be very numerous, abound excessively. (Often in reproach or contempt.) late ME. **4.** *To s. with*: to be crowded or thronged with; to contain swarms or great numbers of. Now only in material sense. 1548. **5.** *trans.* To fill or beset as, or with, a swarm; to crowd densely, throng. Chiefly *pass.* 1555.

1. Take heede to thy bees, that are readie to swarme 1573. **2.** The crowd were swarming now . . about the garden rails TENNYSON. The ideas swarming in men's minds JOWETT. **3.** Native doctors s. in Mongolia 1883. **4.** The river swarmed with alligators 1893. **5.** Your house is so swarmed with rats 1810.

Swarm (swǭɹm), *v.*[2] 1550. [Of unkn. origin.] **1.** *intr.* To climb *up* a pole, tree, or the like, by clasping it with the arms and legs alternately. **b.** *transf.* To climb a steep ascent or the like by clinging with the hands and knees, or in some way compared to this 1681. **2.** *trans.* with the pole, etc. as obj. 1668.

1. b. People . . swarming up a difficult ascent 1851.

Swart (swǭɹt), *a.* (*sb.*) Now only *rhet.*, *poet.*, or *dial.* [OE. *sweart* = OFris., OS. *swart*, OHG. *swarz* (Du. *zwart*, G. *schwarz*), ON. *svartr*, Goth. *swarts* :- Gmc. **swartaz*.] **1.** Dark in colour; black or blackish; dusky, swarthy. **b.** *spec.* Of the skin or complexion, or of persons in respect of these. late ME. **c.** quasi-*adv.* qualifying an adj. of colour. late ME. **2.** *transf.* Producing swarthiness of complexion 1637. **b.** Dressed in black 1688. **3.** *fig.* **a.** 'Black', wicked, iniquitous. **b.** Baleful, malignant. OE.

1. Hitt shalle be swarte as any pyche 1430. **b.** Their countenance s. with the sunbeams SCOTT. **c.** Swart-green and gold BROWNING. **2.** Yȩ valleys low . . On whose fresh lap the s. Star sparely looks MILT. Hence †**Swart** *v. trans.* and *intr.* to make or become s. **Swa·rt-ly** *adv.*, **-ness.**

Swa·rtback, swa·rthback. *local.* 1450. [- Icel. *svartbakur*; see prec., SWARTH *a.*, BACK *sb.*[1]] The Great Black-backed Gull, *Larus marinus.*

Swarth (swǭɹþ), *sb.*[1] Now only *dial.* [OE. *swearþ*, var. of *sweard* SWARD *sb.*] **1.** Skin, rind; *fig.* the surface, outside. **2.** Green turf, grass land, greensward. late ME.

2. Lanes, Of grassy s. close cropt by nibbling sheep COWPER.

Swarth (swǭɹþ), *sb.*[2] Now *dial.* 1552. [unexpl. alt. of SWATH *sb.*[1]] = SWATH 3, 4 a, b.

Swarth, *a.* (*sb.*[3]) 1530. [unexpl. var. of SWART *a.*; cf. next.] Dusky, swarthy, black. **B.** *sb.* Swarthiness; dusky complexion or colour (*rare*) 1661. Hence **Swa·rth-ish** *a.*, **-ness.**

Swarthy (swǭ·ɹði, swǭ·ɹþi), *a.* 1577. [unexpl. alt. of †*swarty*, extension of SWART *a.* with -Y[1] to produce an adjectival appearance.] Of a dark hue; black or blackish; dusky.

S. darknesse MARSTON. A s. Ethiope SHAKS. A queen, with s. cheeks and bold black eyes TENNYSON. Hence **Swa·rthily** *adv.* **Swa·rthiness.**

Swa·rtru:tter. *Obs.* exc. *Hist.* 1557. [- early mod.Du. *swartrutter*; see SWART *a.*, RUTTER.] One of a class of irregular troopers, with black dress and armour and blackened faces, who infested the Netherlands in the 16th and 17th centuries.

Swarty (swǭ·ɹti), *a.* Now *rare* or *Obs.* 1572. [f. SWART *a.* + -Y[1]; see SWARTHY.] = SWARTHY *a.*

Swash (swǫʃ), *int.* or *adv.* and *sb.* Also **swosh.** 1528. [imit.] **A.** *int.* or *adv.* Expressive of the fall of a heavy body or blow: With a crash 1538. **B.** *sb.* **I. 1.** Pig-wash; also, wet refuse or filth 1528. **2.** A body of water moving forcibly or dashing against something 1671. **3.** Chiefly *U.S.* = SWATCH *sb.*[2] 1670. **4.** A heavy blow, esp. of, or upon, some yielding substance; the sound of this 1789. **5.** The action of water dashing or washing against the side of a cliff, ship, etc., or of waves against each other; the sound accompanying this 1847. **6.** A watery condition of land; ground under water 1864. **II. 1.** A swaggerer; a swashbuckler; now *Sc.* an ostentatious person 1549. **2.** Swagger; swashbuckling 1593.

attrib.: **s. channel, -way,** 'a channel across a bank, or among shoals'.

Swash, *a.*[1] 1599. [f. prec.] **1.** Slashing with great force. **2.** †**a.** Swashbuckling, swaggering. **b.** 'Swell', 'swagger', showy. *dial.* 1600.

Swash (swǫʃ), *a.*[2] 1680. [Cf. ASWASH (of unkn. origin).] **1.** *Turning*, etc. Inclined obliquely to the axis of the work. **2.** *Printing.* Applied to old-style capital letters having flourished strokes designed to fill up unsightly gaps between adjacent letters 1683.

Swash (swǫʃ), *v.* 1556. [imit.] **1.** *trans.* To dash or cast violently 1577. **2.** *intr.* To dash or move violently *about*; also occas. *refl.* 1583. **3.** To make a noise as of swords clashing or of a sword beating on a shield; to fence with swords; to bluster with or as with weapons; to lash *out*; hence, to swagger 1556. **4.** *trans.* To dash or splash (water) about; to dash water upon, souse with water or liquid; (of water) to beat with a splash against 1589. **5.** *intr.* Of water or of an object in water: To dash with a splashing sound; to splash *about* 1836.

4. Men swishing and swashing and brooming about 1862. **5.** The sea at the cliff foot—swashing ever louder and louder 1892.

Swashbuckler (swǫ·ʃbɒ:kləɹ). 1560. [f. prec. + BUCKLER *sb.*[2]; hence *lit.* one who makes a noise by striking his own or his opponent's shield with his sword.] A swaggering bravo or ruffian; a noisy braggadocio.

attrib. The s. manners of the youth of fashion in the reign of Elizabeth 1816. Hence **Swa·shbu:ckling** *a.*

Swasher (swǫ·ʃəɹ). 1589. [f. SWASH *v.* + -ER[1].] A swashbuckler; a blustering braggart or ruffian.

Swashing (swǫ·ʃiŋ), *ppl. a.* 1556. [f. SWASH *v.* + -ING[2].] **1.** Swaggering; swashbuckling, dashing. **2.** Applied to a particular slashing stroke in fencing; also of a weapon: Slashing with great force. Now only in reminiscences of Shaks. 1611. **3.** Of water, etc.: Dashing and splashing 1620.

2. Gregorie, remember thy s. blowe SHAKS.

Swashy (swǫ·ʃi), *a.* 1796. [f. SWASH *sb.* or *v.* + -Y[1].] Sloppy, watery.

‖**Swastika** (swæ·stikă). 1871. [Skr. *svastika*, f. *svasti* well-being, luck, f. *sú* good + *asti* being (f. *as* be).] A primitive symbol or ornament of the form of a cross with equal arms with a limb of the same length projecting at right angles from the end of each arm, all in the same direction and (usu.) clockwise.

Swat (swǫt), *sb. n. dial.* and *U.S.* 1800. [f. next. Cf. SQUAT *sb.*[1]] A smart or violent blow.

Swat (swǫt), *v.* 1615. [n. dial. and U.S. var. of SQUAT *v.*] **1.** *intr.* To sit down, squat. *north.* **2.** *trans.* To hit with a smart slap or a violent blow. Now chiefly *U.S.* 1796.

Swatch (swǫtʃ), *sb.*[1] *Sc.* and *north.* 1512. [Of unkn. origin.] **1.** †The 'foil' or 'counter-stock' of a tally; in Yorkshire, a tally attached to a piece of cloth before it is put with others into the dye-kettle. **2.** A sample piece of cloth 1647. **3.** *fig.* A sample, specimen 1697.

Swatch (swǫtʃ), *sb.*[2] *local.* 1626. [In local English use chiefly in Eastern counties. Its relation to SWASH *sb.*[1] 3 is not clear.] A channel of water lying between sandbanks or between a sandbank and the shore.

Comb.: **swa·tchway** = SWASH-*way*.

Swath (swǭþ, swǫþ), **swathe,** *sb.*[1] (swē̆ð). [OE. *swæþ* and *swaþu*, corresp. to OFris. *swethe*, MLG. *swat, swade* (Du. *zwad, zwade*), MHG. *swade* (G. *schwade*). The var. *swathe* is now characteristic of the north.] †**1.** Track, trace. *lit.* and *fig.* –ME. **2.** The space covered by a sweep of the mower's scythe; the width of grass or corn so cut 1475. **b.** As a measure of grass land: A longitudinal division of a field. *local.* ME. **c.** A stroke of the scythe in reaping (*rare*) 1643. **3.** A row or line of grass, corn, or other crop, as it falls or lies when mown or reaped; also *collect.*, a crop mown and lying on the ground ME. **4.** *transf.* and *fig.* **a.** A broad track, belt, strip, or longitudinal extent of something 1605. **b.** Something compared to grass or corn falling before the scythe or sickle 1852.

2. The great mower Time, who cuts so broad a swathe THOREAU. **3.** The grass had been cut, and left in swaths 1857. **4. a.** *Swathe*, the entire length of a sea-wave 1867. **b.** We saw the dead lying in swathes as they had fallen 1895.

Comb. **s.-balk,** a ridge of grass left unmown between the swaths, or between the sweeps of the scythe.

Swathe (swē̆ið), *sb.*[2] [Late OE. **swæþ*, only in dat. pl. *swaþum*; rel. to SWATHE *v.* Cf. SWADDLE *v.*] **1.** A band of linen, woollen, or other material in which something is enveloped; a wrapping; sometimes, a single fold or winding of such; also *collect. sing.* †**b.** *sing.* and *pl.* An infant's swaddling-bands –1786. **c.** A surgical bandage 1615. **2. a.** *transf.* A natural formation constituting a wrapping 1615. **b.** *fig.* Something that restricts or confines like a swaddling-band 1864.

1. Long Pieces of Linen folded about me till they had wrapt me in above an hundred Yards of S. ADDISON. **c.** I turn'd a swath a little broader than the Patient's Hand once round him 1722. **2. a.** Grey swathes of cloud still hung about the hills 1871. **b.** Within the swathes and fetters of civilisation 1906.

Swathe (swē̆ið), *v.* [Late OE. *swaþian*; see prec.] **1.** *trans.* To envelop in a swathe or swathes; to wrap up, swaddle, bandage. **b.** Said of the swathe or wrapping 1856. **c.** To wrap round something, as or like a swathe or bandage 1656. **2.** *transf.* and *fig.* To enwrap, enfold; †to encircle so as to confine 1624.

1. From their Infancy their Feet are kept swathed up with bands 1697. **2.** Who hath swathed in the great and proud Ocean, with a Girdle of Sand 1692.

Sway (swēi), *sb.* late ME. [f. next.] †**1.** The motion of a rotating or revolving body –1610. **2.** The sweeping or swinging motion of a heavy body, a storm, etc.; the impetus or momentum of a body, etc. in motion. *Obs.* or *dial.* late ME. †**3.** Force or pressure bearing or inclining its object in one direction or another –1791. †**4.** Inclination or bias in a certain direction –1820. **5.** Prevailing, overpowering, or controlling influence 1510. **6.** Power of rule or command; sovereign power or authority; dominion, rule 1586. **b.** *contextually.* (*a*) Means of government. (*b*) Position of authority or power. 1645. †**7.** Manner of carrying oneself; deportment –1845. **8.** The action of moving backward and forward or from side to side 1846.

3. Expert When to advance, or stand, or turn the s. Of Battel MILT. **5.** The girl had fallen under the s. of nuns and priests 1879. **6.** The soul . . originally govern'd the body with an absolute s. 1714.

Sway (swēi), *v.* 1500. [corresp. formally to Du. *zwaaien* swing, wave, walk totteringly, LG. *swājen* move to and fro as with the wind; but preceded by late ME. *sweigh, sweye*, applied to sweeping or swinging motion, the vocalism of which corresponds to that of ON. *sveigja* bend (intr.), give way; the history is obsc.] **1.** *intr.* To move or swing first to one side and then to the other, as a flexible or pivoted object. **b.** *fig.* To vacillate (*rare*) 1563. **2.** *trans.* To cause to move backward and forward or from side to side 1555. **3.** *intr.* To bend or move to one side, or downwards, as by excess of weight or pressure; to incline, lean, swerve 1577. †**b.** *transf.* To have a certain direction in movement; to move –1650. **4.** *trans.* To cause to incline or hang down on one side, as from excess of weight; *dial.* to weigh or press down; also, to cause to swerve 1570. **5.** To turn aside, divert (thoughts, feelings, etc.); to cause to swerve *from* a course of action 1596. †**b.** To influence in a specified direction –1807. †**6.** *intr.* To incline or be diverted in judgement or opinion –1659. **7.** *trans.* To wield as an emblem of sovereignty or authority; esp. in phr. *to s. the sceptre* 1575. **b.** *transf.* To wield (an instrument or implement). *poet.* (*rare.*) 1600. **8.** To rule, govern, as a sovereign. Chiefly *poet.* 1595. **b.** *transf.* To control, direct 1587. **9.** *intr.* To rule; to hold sway 1565. †**10.** To have a preponderating weight or influence, prevail –1768. **11.** *trans.* To cause (a person, his actions, conduct, or thoughts) to be directed one way or another; to have weight or influence with (a person) in his decisions, etc. 1593. **12.** To swing (a weapon or implement) about; *dial.* to swing (something) to and fro, or from one place to another. Also *intr.* to swing. 1590. **13.** *Naut.* (usu. with *up*). To hoist, raise (esp. a yard or topmast). Also *absol.* 1743.

1. The dreary estuary, where the slow tide sways backwards and forwards 1874. **2.** He swayed himself backwards and forwards in his chair TROLLOPE. *fig.* He..swayes her conscience Which way he list 1650. **3.** In these personal respects, the balance sways on our part BACON. **b.** 2 *Hen. IV*, IV. i. 24. **4.** As Bowls run true, by being made Of purpose false, and to be sway'd 1678. **5.** An huge advantage may s. him a little aside 1679. **6.** *Hen. V*, I. i. 73. **7. b.** This harp, which erst Saint Modan swayed SCOTT. **8.** A gentle Nymph..That with moist curb sways the smooth Severn stream MILT. **b.** The will of man is by his reason sway'd MILT. **9.** Lawless feasters in thy palace s. POPE. **11.** Swayed in their opinions by men who..are incompetent judges GOLDSM.

Sway-, the vb.-stem or sb. used in comb.: **s.-beam,** an early name for the side-lever in a steam-engine; **-bracing,** diagonal bracing of a bridge, designed to prevent swaying; so **-brace** *sb.*; **-brace** *v.* to strengthen with a s.-brace.

Sway·-backed, *a.* 1680. [Of Scand. origin; cf. obs. Da. *sveibaget,* also Da. *sveirygget, sveg-,* Sw. dial. *svegryggad,* in the same sense.] Of an animal, esp. a horse: Having a downward curvature of the spinal column; strained in the back, as by overwork.

†**Swayed,** *ppl. a.* 1577. [pa. pple. of SWAY *v.*] Of a horse: = prec. –1852.

Swaying (swē̆ⁱ·iŋ), *vbl. sb.* 1598. [f. SWAY *v.* + -ING¹.] **1.** The action of SWAY *v.* 1665. **2.** *S. of* or *in the back*: the condition of being SWAY-BACKED 1598.

Sweal, swale¹ (swīl, swēⁱl), *v.* Now *dial.* [OE. *swǣlan* wk. trans. burn, rel. to OE. *swelan* str. intr. burn (which may in part be also the source of this word) = (M)LG. *swelen* singe, wither (of grass), make hay, etc., ON. *svæla* smoke out. See SWELT.] **1.** *trans.* To consume with fire, burn; to set fire to (e.g. gorse, etc., soot in a chimney); to singe, scorch. **2.** *intr.* To burn with fire, or as a fire; to be consumed with fire; to be scorched; to be burning hot ME. **3.** Of a candle: To melt *away*; to gutter. Also said of the tallow or wax. Hence *fig.* to waste away. 1653. **4.** *trans.* To cause to waste away like a guttering candle. Chiefly *fig.* 1655.

Swear (swēᵊɹ), *sb.* Now *colloq.* 1643. [f. SWEAR *v.*] An act of swearing; an oath; a swear-word; a fit of swearing.

Swear (swēᵊɹ), *v.* Pa. t. **swore** (swōᵊɹ); pa. pple. **sworn** (swǭɹn). [OE. *swerian* = OFris. *swaria, swera,* OS. *swerian,* OHG. *swer(i)en* (Du. *zweren,* G. *schwören*), ON. *sverja* :– Gmc. str. vb. **swarjan* (but Goth. *swaran*), f. **swar-*, repr. also by ON. *svar, svara* answer (sb. and vb.), OE. *and|swaru* ANSWER *sb.*; ult. origin disputed.] **I. 1.** *intr.* To make a solemn declaration or statement with an appeal to God or a superhuman being, or to some sacred object, in confirmation of what is said; to take an oath. **2.** To promise or undertake something by an oath; to take an oath by way of a solemn promise or undertaking, **a.** *intr.* OE. **b.** *trans.* with pron. as obj. ME. **3.** With certain sbs.: To promise or undertake on oath to observe or perform (something) ME. **4.** To affirm, assert, or declare something by an oath; to make an oath to the truth of a statement. **a.** *intr.*: *spec.* to give evidence on oath (*against* a person). Now *rare.* OE. **b.** with clause: often also, to affirm emphatically or confidently (without an oath) OE. **c.** *trans.* with pron. as obj. ME. **5.** *trans.* With certain sbs.: **a.** To take an oath as to the fact or truth of; to confirm (a statement) by oath. late ME. **b.** To proclaim or declare with an oath or solemn affirmation. late ME. **c.** To value on oath *at* so much 1854. **6.** To take or utter (an oath), either solemnly or profanely OE. †**7.** To use (a sacred name) in an oath; to invoke or appeal to (a deity, etc.) by an oath –1605. **8.** *intr.* To utter a form of oath lightly or irreverently, as a mere intensive, or as an expression of anger, vexation, or other strong feeling; to utter a profane oath, or use profane language habitually; more widely, to use bad language. late ME. **b.** To utter a harsh guttural sound, as an angry cat or other animal. *colloq.* 1700. **9.** *trans.* **a.** To bring or get into some specified condition or position by swearing 1588. **b.** To put *upon* or ascribe *to* a person in a sworn statement. *arch.* 1754.

1. Wee dare not sware least we sin against our God 1660. **2. a.** God is said to s. when he binds himself absolutely to performance 1662. I have sworn to speak the truth only 1797. Rokeby sware, No rebel's son should wed his heir SCOTT. **b.** As I best koude I swore hir this CHAUCER. **3.** Then sweare Allegeance to his Maiesty SHAKS. Thou ne're swore our covenant 1649. Repentance oft before I swore FITZGERALD. **4.** Against themselves their Witnesses will S. DRYDEN. Phr. *To s. home, through a two-inch board,* denoting hard swearing. **b.** I dorste swere they weyeden ten pound CHAUCER. **5. a.** He swore treason against his friend JOHNSON. **b.** Phr. *To s. the peace against*; see PEACE *sb.* 9. **c.** The gross personal estate is sworn at £37,405.16.10. 1896. **6.** My lord swore one of his large oaths that he did not know..what she meant THACKERAY. **7.** *Lear* I. i. 163. **8.** Oft haue I seene the haughty Cardinall Sweare like a Ruffian SHAKS. **9. a.** The miller swore himself as black as night that he stopt them SCOTT.

II. 1. orig. *pass.* To be bound by oath; hence *actively* to cause to take an oath; to bind by an oath; to put (a person) upon his oath; to administer an oath to OE. **2.** *spec.* To admit to an office or function by administering a formal oath ME.

1. Tender the oath: if he accepts it, s. him BENTHAM. He swore Harry to secrecy THACKERAY. Phr. *I dare be sworn, I'll be sworn,* expressing strong affirmation, properly implying readiness to take an oath upon the fact (*arch.*). **2.** Richard..had been sworn of the Irish Privy Council 1855. The jury were sworn 1880.

S. at —. **a.** To imprecate evil upon by an oath; to address with profane imprecation; *gen.* to curse. **b.** *fig.* Of colours, etc.: To be violently incongruous or inharmonious with. *colloq.* **S. by** —. **a.** To appeal to (a divine being or sacred object, etc.) in swearing; to say 'by..' as a form of oath. **b.** To swear to or be sure of the existence of; in phr. *enough to s. by,* expressing a very slight amount. *colloq.* or *slang.* **c.** To accept as an infallible authority; to have absolute confidence in. *colloq.* **S. off** —. To abjure, forswear, renounce. *colloq.* or *slang.* **S. to** —. **a.** To promise or undertake with a solemn oath (an act or course of action). Now *rare.* **b.** To affirm with an oath; to express assurance of the truth of (a statement), or the identity of (a person or thing) by swearing. **S. away.** To take away by swearing; to give evidence on oath so as to destroy or cause the loss of. **S. in.** To admit or induct into an office by administering a prescribed oath. **S. off.** To abjure something, esp. intoxicating drink.

Swearer (swēᵊ·rəɹ). late ME. [f. prec. + -ER¹.] **1.** One who takes an oath; *spec.* one who takes or has taken an oath of allegiance. **2.** One who uses profane oaths; a person addicted to profane language. late ME. **3.** One who administers an oath to another (const. *of*) 1597.

1. *False s.,* one who swears falsely, or who breaks his oath; a perjurer.

Swearing (swēᵊ·riŋ), *vbl. sb.* ME. [f. SWEAR *v.* + -ING¹.] The action of SWEAR *v.* *False s.,* perjury. *Hard s.*: see HARD *a.* 18.

Swea·r-word. *colloq.* (orig. *U.S.*) 1883. [f. SWEAR *v.* + WORD *sb.*] A word used in profane swearing, a profane word.

Sweat (swet), *sb.* [ME. *swet, swete,* alt., after SWEAT *v.*, of *swot(e* :– OE. *swāt* = OFris., OS. *swēt* (Du. *zweet*), OHG. *sweiz* (G. *schweiss*) :– Gmc. **swaitaz* :– IE. base **swoid-*, whence also L. *sudor.*] †**I.** The life-blood; in phr. *to tine, leave, lose, the s.*: to lose one's life-blood, die –1513. **II. 1.** Moisture excreted in the form of drops through the pores of the skin, usu. as a result of excessive heat or exertion, or of certain emotions; sensible perspiration. late ME. **2.** A condition or fit of sweating as a result of heat, exertion, or emotion; diaphoresis. late ME. †**b.** = SWEATING-SICKNESS. –1661. **3.** A fit of sweating caused for a specific purpose. **a.** as a form of medicinal treatment or to reduce one's weight 1632. **b.** A run given to a horse (often in a coat) as part of his training for a race 1705. **4.** *transf.* Something resembling sweat; drops of moisture exuded from or deposited on the surface of a body. late ME. **5.** A process of sweating or being sweated; exudation, evaporation, or deposit of moisture, fermentation, partial fusion, etc., as practised in various industries 1573.

1. Phr. *The s. of* (one's) *brow, face,* etc., expressing toil: after Gen. 3:19. *Bloody s.,* (*a*) that of Jesus in the Garden of Gethsemane; see Luke 22:44; (*b*) *Path.*: see HÆMATIDROSIS. **2.** *Cold s.,* sweating accompanied by a feeling of cold, esp. as induced by fear or the like. See also NIGHT-*sweat.*

III. 1. *fig.* Hard work; labour, toil; pains, trouble. Now *slang.* ME. **2.** A state of impatience, anxiety, or the like, such as induces sweat; a flurry, hurry, fume. Chiefly *Sc.* and *U.S.* 1715. **b.** *Old s.,* an old soldier (*slang*) 1919.

Comb.: **s.-band,** a band of leather or other substance forming a lining of a hat or cap for protection against s.; **-box,** (*a*) a narrow cell in which a prisoner is confined or interrogated (*slang*); (*b*) a box in which hides are sweated; (*c*) a large box in which figs are placed to undergo a 'sweat'; **-duct** *Anat.,* the duct of a s.-gland, by which the s. is conveyed to the surface of the skin; **-gland** *Anat.,* each of the numerous minute coiled tubular glands just beneath the skin which secrete s.; **-pore** *Anat.,* each of the pores of the skin formed by the opening of the s.-ducts.

Sweat (swet), *v.* Pa. t. †**sweat, sweated**; pa. pple. †**sweat, sweated.** [OE. *swǣtan* = MLG., MDu. *swēten* (Du. *zweeten*), OHG. *sweizzen* roast (G. *schweissen* weld, fuse) :– Gmc. **swaitjan,* f. **swaitaz*; see prec.] **I. 1.** *intr.* To emit or excrete sweat through the pores of the skin; to perspire (sensibly). **2.** *trans.* To emit or exude through the pores of the skin, as or like sweat. Also with *out.* OE. **b.** *fig.* To give forth or get rid of as by sweating; *slang,* to spend, lay out (money) 1592. **3.** To cause to sweat; to put into a sweat 1621. **b.** To give (a horse) a run for exercise (*rare*) 1589.

1. I have toil'd, and till'd, and sweaten in the sun BYRON. **2.** Thou, who..hast..sweat blood YOUNG. **b.** I could not sweate out from my hart that bitternes of sorrow 1610.

II. 1. *intr.* To exert oneself strongly; to work hard, toil, labour, drudge OE. **b.** *spec.* Formerly, in the tailoring trade, to work overtime at home 1851. **2.** *trans.* **a.** To exact hard work from 1821. **b.** *spec.* To employ in hard or excessive work at very low wages, esp. under a system of sub-contract. Chiefly *pass.* 1879. **3.** To work *out*; to work hard at; to get, make, or produce by severe labour (*rare*) 1589. **b.** *Naut.* To set or hoist (a sail, etc.) taut, so as to increase speed (also *intr.*); also with the ship as obj. 1890. **4.** *intr.* To undergo severe affliction or punishment; to suffer severely. Often *to s. for it,* to suffer the penalty, 'get it hot'. Now *rare* or *Obs.* 1612. **5.** To suffer perturbation of mind; to be vexed; to fume, rage. Now *rare* or *Obs.* late ME.

1. Lovers of money must s. or steal READE. **2. b.** They declared that they were being 'sweated'—that the hunger for work induced men to accept starvation rates 1887. A low type of 'sweated' and overworked labour is employed 1889. **3.** Leigh Hunt is sweating articles for his new Journal BYRON. **5.** I s. to think of that Garret DRYDEN.

III. 1. *intr.* To exude, or to gather, moisture so that it appears in drops on the surface OE. **b.** *spec.* of products in store 1440. **c.** To exude nitroglycerine, as dynamite 1900. **2.** *trans.* To emit (moisture, etc.) in drops or small particles like sweat; to exude, distil. Also with *out.* late ME. **3.** *intr.* To ooze *out* like sweat; to exude. late ME. **4.** *trans.* To cause to exude moisture; *spec.* to subject to a process of sweating 1686. **5.** *slang.* To rob, 'fleece', 'bleed' 1847. **6.** To lighten (a gold coin) by wearing away its substance by friction or attrition 1603. **7.** To subject (metal) to partial fusion; to fasten by applying heat so as to produce partial fusion; *Metall.* to heat so as to melt and extract an easily fusible constituent 1884.

1. Stone or Wainscot that has been used to s. 1731. **b.** Salted hides..require..rather longer to s. 1852. **2.** It is no little thing to make Mine eyes to s. compassion SHAKS. **8.** *U.S. slang.* To use 'third-degree' methods on (a prisoner).

Sweater (swe·təɹ). 1529. [f. prec. vb. + -ER¹.] **1.** *lit.* One who sweats or perspires; *spec.* one who takes a 'sweating bath' 1562. **2.** One who works hard, a toiler; †*spec.* a tailor who worked overtime at home for an employer 1529. **3.** A sudorific, diaphoretic 1684. **4.** One who exacts hard work at very low wages 1850. **5.** One who 'sweats' gold coins 1868. **6.** A woollen vest or jersey worn in rowing or other athletic exercise; also worn before or after exercise to prevent taking cold 1882.

Swea·t-house. 1750. **1.** A hut or other structure in which hot-air or vapour baths are taken, among the N. Amer. Indians and other primitive tribes. **2.** *Tanning.* A building in which hides are sweated 1891.

Sweating (swe·tiŋ), *vbl. sb.* ME. [f. SWEAT *v.* + -ING[1].] The action of SWEAT *v.*

attrib. and *Comb.*: **s.-bath,** one used to induce sweating; **-house** = prec. 1; **-iron,** a piece of iron used to scrape off sweat, esp. from horses; **-room,** (*a*) a room in which persons are sweated, as in a Turkish bath; (*b*) a room in which cheeses are 'sweated' or deprived of superfluous moisture.

Swea·ting-si:ckness. 1502. A febrile disease characterized by profuse sweating, of which highly and rapidly fatal epidemics occurred in England in the 15th and 16th centuries. Now chiefly *Hist.* in ref. to these.

Sweaty (swe·ti), *a.* late ME. [f. SWEAT *sb.* + -Y[1].] **1.** Causing sweat. **a.** Heating, excessively hot. **b.** Toilsome, laborious. **2.** Covered with sweat; wet, moist, or stained with sweat 1590. †**b.** Of persons: Laborious, toiling –1667. **3.** Consisting of sweat 1731.

1. The s. Forge PRIOR. A s. city BYRON. **2.** S. hands 1759. **b.** A sweatie Reaper MILT. Hence **Swea·tily** *adv.* **Swea·tiness.**

Swede (swīd). 1614. [– MLG., MDu. *Swēde* (Du. *Zweed*), prob. – ON. *Svíþjóð* 'people of the Swedes', Sweden, f. *Svíar* Swedes + *þjóð* people.] **1.** A native of Sweden. **2.** A Swedish ship (*rare*) 1799. **3.** (= earlier *Swedish turnip.*) A large variety of turnip with yellow flesh, *Brassica campestris,* var. *Rutabaga,* introduced from Sweden in 1781–2. 1812.

Swedenborgian (swīd'nbǭ·ɹdʒiăn), *a.* and *sb.* 1802. [f. name of Emanuel *Swedenborg* or Svedberg (see below) + -IAN.] **A.** *adj.* Of or pertaining to Emanuel Swedenborg, a Swedish scientific and religious writer (1688–1772), or the body of followers of his religious teachings, organized in 1788 and styled by themselves 'The New Church'. **B.** *sb.* A follower of Swedenborg. Hence **Swedenbo·rgianism,** also *rarely* **Swe·denborgism.**

Swedish (swī·diʃ), *a.* and *sb.* 1605. [f. *Sweden* or SWEDE + -ISH[1], after G. *schwedisch,* etc.] **A.** *adj.* Of or belonging to Sweden or the Swedes 1632.

S. drill, gymnastics, movements, a system of muscular exercises as a form of hygienic or curative treatment. *S. turnip* = SWEDE 3.

B. *sb.* The language of Sweden 1605.

Sweeny (swī·ni). *U.S.* 1855. [prob. f. G. dial. *schweine* emaciation, atrophy.] Atrophy of the shoulder-muscles in the horse. Also *fig.* of the 'stiffness' of pride or self-conceit.

Sweep (swīp), *sb.* 1552. [Mainly f. SWEEP *v.*] **I.** The action of sweeping. **1.** An act of sweeping or clearing up or (usu.) away; a clearance. **b.** An act of passing over an area in order to capture or destroy the occupants of it 1837. **2.** The action of a person or animal moving along with a continuous motion, esp. with a magnificent or impressive air 1607. **3.** The rapid or forcible and continuous movement of a body of water, wind, etc. 1708. **b.** Semi-*concr.* of a forcibly moving body of water 1815. **4.** An action, or a process in expression, thought, etc., figured as movement of this kind 1662. **5.** The action of driving or wielding a tool or weapon, swinging an arm, etc., so as to describe a circle or an arc 1725. **6.** The action of moving in a continuous curve or a more or less circular path or track 1679. **7.** *Astr.* A term used by Sir William Herschel to denote a method of surveying the heavens in sections; also, one of such sections of observation 1784. **8.** An act of sweeping with a broom 1818. **9.** The action of a garment, etc. brushing, or of the hand or an instrument passing in continuous movement, along or over a surface 1820. **10.** *Cards.* **a.** In the game of casino, a pairing or combining all the cards on the board, resulting in the removal of all of them. **b.** In whist, the winning of all the tricks in a hand; a slam. 1814. **11.** *Physics.* A process of settling, or tending to settle, into thermal equilibrium 1903.

1. Phr. *A general,* (now always) *a clean s.* **2.** What a sweepe of vanitie comes this way SHAKS. **4.** The first s. of royal fury being past CARLYLE. **5.** The s. of scythe in morning dew TENNYSON. **9.** A s. of lute-strings BROWNING.

II. Range, extent. **1.** Compass, reach, or range of movement, esp. in a circular or curving course 1679. **2.** Extent of ground, water, etc.; an extent, stretch, or expanse, such as can be taken in at one survey or is included in a wide-spreading curve 1767. **3.** Extent or range of thought, observation, experience, influence, power, etc. 1781.

1. In our wake, and just outside the s. of our oars KANE. **2.** Many a s. Of meadow 1842. A s. Of shops 1858. **3.** The extensive s. of these four great principles 1855.

III. A curve or curved object, etc. **1.** A curved line or form; a curve; also, curvature 1715. **b.** The continuously curved part of an arch 1685. **2.** *concr.* **a.** A curved mass of building or masonry 1766. **b.** A semicircular plank fixed up under the beams near the fore-end of the tiller, which it supports; a similar support on which a gun travels 1756. **c.** A curved carriage drive leading to a house 1797. **IV.** That which is swept up. **1.** *collect. sing.* or *pl.* The sweepings of gold and silver dust from the workshops of goldsmiths, silversmiths, etc. 1771. **2.** = SWEEPSTAKE 3 b. 1849. **3.** = ALMOND-FURNACE. 1706. **V.** Apparatus that sweeps or has a sweeping motion. **1.** An apparatus for drawing water from a well, consisting of a long pole attached to an upright which serves as a fulcrum; hence, a pump-handle 1548. **2.** A ballista. *Obs.* exc. *Her.* 1598. **3.** Applied to various kinds of levers, or to a long bar which is swept round so as to turn a shaft 1657. **4.** A sail of a windmill. Also *occas.* a paddle of a water-wheel 1639. **5.** A long oar used to propel a ship, barge, etc. when becalmed, or to assist the work of steering 1800. **6.** A length of cable used for sweeping the bottom of the sea, in mine-laying, etc. 1775. **7.** An instrument used for drawing curves at a large radius; a beam-compass. Also, a profile tool for cutting mouldings in wood or metal in a lathe. 1680. **8.** *Founding.* A movable templet used in loam-moulding, a striking-board 1864. **VI.** One who sweeps (and derived senses). **1.** A chimney-sweeper 1812. **b.** *The Sweeps*: a nickname for the Rifle Brigade 1879. **c.** A disreputable person; a scamp, blackguard. *slang* and *dial.* 1853. **2. a.** A crossing-sweeper. **b.** *U.S.* A servant who looks after university students' rooms, 1858.

1. Our faces.. became almost as black as sweeps 1861.

Sweep (swīp), *v.* Pa. t. and pa. pple. **swept.** [ME. *swepe,* in earliest use mainly northern, repl. ME. *swōpe* (OE. *swāpan*).] **I. 1.** *trans.* To remove, clear *away, off* (etc.) with a broom or brush, or in a similar way by friction upon a surface; to brush away or off. **2.** To cut *down* or *off* with a vigorous swinging stroke. Now *rare* or *Obs.* late ME. **3.** To remove with a forcible continuous action; to brush *off, away, aside* 1577. **4.** *transf.* and *fig.* To clear out, drive away, or carry off *from* a place or region, (as if) forcibly or by violence 1593. **5.** Chiefly with *away*: To remove forcibly or as at one blow; do away with, destroy utterly 1560. **6.** To carry or drive along with force; to carry *away* or *off* by driving before it, as a wind, tide, stream, etc. 1743. **7.** To drive together or into a place by or as by sweeping; to gather or take *up,* esp. so as to allocate or consign to a place, object, or purpose ME. **b.** *fig.* To include in its scope; to extend to 1692. **8.** To gather in or up, collect wholesale or at one stroke; esp. in phr. *to s. the stakes* (cf. SWEEPSTAKE) 1635. **9.** To carry or trail along in a stately manner, as a flowing garment 1591. **10.** To move or draw (something) over and in contact with a surface 1825. **11.** To move (something) *round* with force and rapidity, or over a wide extent; to take *off* (one's hat) with a sweep of the arm 1845. **12.** *intr.* and *trans.* To row, or to propel (a vessel), with sweeps or large oars. Also *intr.* of the vessel. *rare* or *Obs.* 1799.

1. I am sent with broome before, To sweep the dust behinde the doore SHAKS. **3.** S. the chessmen off the board KINGSLEY. **4.** A..storm..In its fury it had just swept away the pier at Ryde 1831. **5.** Why are thy valiant men swept away? *Jer.* 46:15. **6.** The tide was sweeping us past 1840. **7.** He is sure to s. fifty Pounds at least into his Pocket 1706. **8.** Death's a devouring gamester, And sweepes up all SHIRLEY. **10.** Again sweeping his fingers over the strings SCOTT. **11.** He swept off his hat in continental style 1885.

II. 1. *trans.* To pass a broom or brush over the surface of (something) so as to clear it of any small loose or adhering particles; to cleanse with a brush or broom (as a floor of dust and small refuse, a path of dirt, snow, etc., or a chimney of soot). Also (rarely) said of the broom. ME. **b.** *absol.* or *intr.*; also said of the broom, esp. in prov. *New brooms s. clean* ME. **2.** To pass over the surface of (something) in the manner of a broom or brush; to move over and in contact with; to brush 1500. **3.** *transf.* and *fig.* To clear *of* something by vigorous action compared to that of a broom; *spec.* to clear (a place) *of* enemies or a mob by firing amongst them 1627. **4.** To draw something, as a net or the bight of a rope, over the bottom of (a body of water) in search of something submerged; to drag. Also, to catch (something submerged) in this way. Also *intr.* to search *for* in this way. 1637. **5.** To move swiftly and evenly or with continuous force over or along the surface of; in weakened sense, to pass over or across 1590. **6.** To range over (a region of sea or land), esp. to destroy, ravage, or capture; to scour 1788. **b.** Of artillery: To have within range, to command (an extent of territory) 1748. **7.** To pass the fingers over the strings of a musical instrument so as to cause it to sound. (With the strings, or the instrument, as obj.) Chiefly *poet.* 1637. **b.** *transf.* To produce (music) by such action *poet.* 1815. **8.** To direct the eyes, or an optical instrument, to every part of (a region) in succession; to take a wide survey of. Also *absol.* or *intr.*; in *Astron.* to make systematic observations of a region of the heavens. 1727.

1. Be careful to have the used Chimneys sweep'd once a month 1775. **2.** That garment is decently put on, Which does not s. the dust 1638. **3.** *To s. the board,* see BOARD *sb.* II. 1. *To s. the deck* (or usu. *decks*), to clear the deck of a ship (as by artillery, or as a wave breaking over); also *fig.* **4.** Earine was drown'd!..Have you swept the river, say you, and not found her? B. JONS. **5.** *To s. a constituency, the country*: to have an overwhelming majority of votes in it. **6.** Their artillery swept the waters GIBBON. **7.** Begin, and somewhat loudly s. the string MILT. **8.** I swept with my telescope..the line of the horizon SMEATON.

III. Intr. senses denoting movement (esp. in a curve), and derived uses. **1.** *intr.* To move with a strong or swift even motion; to move along over a surface or region, usu. rapidly, or with violence or destructive effect; sometimes, to come with a sudden attack, to swoop. late ME. **2.** To move or walk in a stately manner, as with trailing garments; to move along majestically; 'to pass with pomp' (J.). Also with *it.* 1590. **3.** To move along a surface or in the track of something like a trailing robe; to trail *after*; to brush *along* 1642. **4.** To move continuously in a long stretch or over a wide extent, esp. *round* or in a curve 1725. **5.** To extend continuously through a long stretch, or widely around; to present a surface of wide extent 1789. **b.** *trans.* with cogn. obj. To perform or execute (such a movement) 1848. **6.** To describe, trace, mark out (a line, esp. a wide curve, or an area) 1664. **7.** *Founding.* To form (a mould) with a sweep (SWEEP *sb.* V. 8) 1885.

1. That I, with wings as swift As meditation.. May sweepe to my Reuenge SHAKS. There were light breezes sweeping up 1845. The plague swept over Europe 1889. **2.** Sweepe on you fat and greazie Citizens SHAKS. **4.** The first flight of the hawks, when they sweep so beautifully round the company SCOTT. **5.** A road swept gently round the hill CLARE. **b.** Becky..swept the prettiest little curtsey ever seen THACKERAY. **6.** They.. found it much easier to s. circles than to design beauties RUSKIN.

Comb.: **s.-net,** a large net used in fishing, enclosing a wide space; a kind of seine; **-saw,** a saw adapted for cutting sweeps or curves; a bow-saw, turning-saw; **-seine** = *s.-net.*

Sweepage (swī·pėdʒ). 1628. [f. prec. + -AGE.] 'The Crop of Hay got in a Meadow' (1672); *gen.* what is mown.

Sweeper (swī·pəɹ). 1530. [f. SWEEP *v.* + -ER¹.] **1.** *gen.* One who or that which sweeps. **2.** A person employed in sweeping a room, chimneys, crossings, etc.; *spec.* in India, a person of the lowest caste 1657. **3.** A mechanical apparatus for sweeping a floor, road, etc.; a sweeping-machine 1862.

Sweeping (swī·piŋ), *vbl. sb.* 1480. [-ING¹.] **1.** The action of SWEEP *v.* **a.** Cleansing or removing, with or as with a broom or brush. **b.** Dragging for something under water; esp. in MINE-*s.* 1704. **c.** Movement over a surface or in an extended curve 1830. **d.** Rowing with sweeps 1831. **2.** That which is swept up; matter, esp. dust or refuse, that is swept, together or away 1480. **b.** *fig.* (*pl.*) Of persons or things: Rubbish, riff-raff 1641.

2. b. The sweepings of the gaols 1832.

Swee·ping, *ppl. a.* 1611. [-ING².] **1.** That sweeps, in various senses; see SWEEP *v.* **2.** Extending through a long stretch or wide space, esp. in a curve 1772. **3.** *fig.* Having a wide scope; extensive, comprehensive; wholesale, indiscriminate 1771.

3. A s. measure of sanitary reform KINGSLEY. Hence **Swee·ping-ly** *adv.*, **-ness.**

Sweepstake (swī·pˌsteⁱk), **sweepstakes** (-steⁱks). 1495. [f. SWEEP *v.* + STAKE *sb.*²] †**1.** One who 'sweeps', or takes the whole of, the stakes in a game, etc.; usu. *fig.* one who takes or appropriates everything –1687. (Occurs first as the name of one of the King's ships.) †**2.** The act of sweeping everything away; a clean sweep: usu. in phr. *to make s.*, *to play (at) s.* –1653. **3.** orig. A prize won in a race or contest in which the whole of the stakes contributed by the competitors are taken by the winner or by a certain limited number of them; hence (now usu.) the race or contest itself 1773. **b.** A betting or gambling transaction in which each person contributes a stake, and the whole of the stakes are taken by one or divided among several under certain conditions 1862.

Sweepy (swī·pi), *a.* Chiefly *poet.* 1697. [f. SWEEP *sb.* or *v.* + -Y¹.] Characterized by sweeping movement or form; sweeping.

Hail furious flew and s. light'ning shone 1790.

Sweet (swīt), *sb.* ME. [SWEET *a.* used as sb.] **1.** That which is sweet to the taste; something having a sweet taste. Chiefly *poet.* **b.** A sweet food or drink. late ME. **c.** *pl.* Syrup added to wine or other liquor to sweeten the taste; hence, wine or other liquor thus sweetened; applied *spec.* to British wines and cordials 1679. **d.** *spec.* A sweet dish forming a separate course at a meal. Usu. *pl.* 1834. **e.** A sweetmeat, esp. in lozenge or 'drop' form 1851. **2.** Sweetness of taste; sweet taste (*rare*). late ME. **3.** That which is pleasant to the mind or feelings; (a) pleasure, (a) delight; the pleasant part of something. In later use chiefly in *pl.* late ME. **5.** Sweetness of smell, fragrance; *pl.* sweet odours, scents, or perfumes. *poet.* 1594. **6.** *pl.* Substances having a sweet smell; fragrant flowers or herbs; †scents, perfumes. Now *rare.* 1602.

1. A dram of s. is worth a pound of sowre SPENSER. **3.** Must..Every s. warn "Ware my bitter'? BROWNING. **4.** She is coming, my own, my s. TENNYSON. **5.** He..riots in the sweets of ev'ry breeze COWPER. **6.** Sweets, to the s. SHAKS.

Sweet (swīt), *a.* and *adv.* [OE. *swēte* = OFris. *swēte*, OS. *swōti* OHG. *s(w)uozi* Du. *zoet*, G. *süss*), ON. *sœtr* :– Gmc. **swōtja-*, **swōti-*, f. **swōt-* :– IE. **swād-* (**swad-*), repr. by Skr. *svādús*, Gr. ἡδύς sweet, L. *suavis* SUAVE.] **A.** *adj.* **1.** Pleasing to the sense of taste; *spec.* having the characteristic flavour of sugar, honey, and many ripe fruits. Often opp. to *bitter* or *sour.* **2.** Pleasing to the sense of smell; having a pleasant smell or odour; fragrant. Also said of the smell or odour. OE. †**b.** *spec.* Scented –1656. **3.** Free from offensive taste or smell; not corrupt, putrid, sour, or stale; free from taint or noxious matter; in a sound and wholesome condition ME. †**b.** *spec.* Of water: Fresh, not salt. Also of butter: Fresh, not salted. –1796. **c.** Of milk: Fresh, not sour 1812. **d.** *Old Chem.* and *Metallurgy.* Free from corrosive salt, sulphur, acid, etc. 1666. **4.** Pleasing to the ear; musical, melodious, harmonious: said of a sound, a voice, an instrument, a singer, a performer on an instrument OE. **5.** Pleasing (in general); yielding pleasure or enjoyment; agreeable, delightful, charming. (Only literary in unemotional use.) OE. **b.** Ironically 1656. **c.** In colloq. use, an emotional epithet expressive of the speaker's personal feelings as to the attractiveness of the object 1779. **6.** In extended use: Having an agreeable or benign quality, influence, operation, or effect. Chiefly techn. late ME. **7.** *transf.* Fond of or inclined for sweet things, esp. in *s. tooth* 1591. **8.** Dearly loved or prized, precious; beloved, dear OE. **b.** In forms of address, freq. affectionate, but also (now *arch.*) respectful or complimentary ME. **c.** *absol.* in affectionate address: Beloved, dear one ME. **d.** Dear to the person himself; usu. *sarcastically*: chiefly qualifying *self* or *will* 1621. **9.** Having pleasant disposition and manners; amiable, kindly; gracious, benignant OE. **10.** *To be s. on (upon)*: †**a.** To treat caressingly –1754. **b.** To be enamoured of or smitten with (one of the opposite sex) 1740.

1. A sugred, sweet and most delitious tast 1596. After s. Meat comes sowr Sauce 1721. **2.** S. muske roses SHAKS. S. after showers, ambrosial air TENNYSON. **b.** *Wint. T.* IV. iv.253. **3.** Preserving Fresh Water s., for the use of Seamen during long voyages 1791. **b.** Living in rivers and other s. waters 1661. **4.** Like s. Bels iangled, out of tune, and harsh SHAKS. **5.** S. are the vses of aduersitie SHAKS. Sweetest Shakespear fancies childe MILT. As s. an Autumn day As ever shone on Clyde CAMPBELL. **c.** Some s. thing in hats or handkerchiefs 1887. **6.** Pleasaunt ground, sweete, blacke, rotten, and mellowed 1577. A s. ship in a seaway if one knew her idiosyncracies 1915. **8.** Thy Life to me is s. SHAKS. **b.** O let me not be mad, not mad, s. Heauen SHAKS. **c.** Tell me not, s., I am unkind LOVELACE. **d.** *At one's own s. will*: just as one likes. **9.** Preise ȝee his name, for swete is the Lord WYCLIF. *Ps.* 99 [100]:5. One of a s. nature, comely presence, courteous carriage FULLER. **10. b.** I think he is s. upon your daughter DICKENS.

B. *adv.* Sweetly; so as to be sweet ME.

What early tongue so s. saluteth me? SHAKS. How s. the moonlight sleepes vpon this banke SHAKS. Then low and s. I whistled thrice TENNYSON.

Combs. and special collocations. **1.** of the adj. **a.** with sbs.: **s.-cake,** a kind of cake having sugar as a principal ingredient; **-mart,** the pine-marten, as dist. from the FOUMART or polecat; **s. milk,** fresh milk having its natural s. flavour, as dist. from skimmed milk, or from 'sour milk', i.e. buttermilk; **s. oil,** any oil of pleasant or mild taste, *spec.* olive oil; **-stuff,** sweetmeats, sweets, confectionery; **s. tooth,** a taste or liking for s. things; **s. wine,** wine having a s. taste (as dist. from *dry* wine); wine in the manufacture of which 'sweets' or syrup is added. **b.** *spec.* in distinctive names of s.-scented or s.-flavoured species or varieties of plants, fruits, etc., as *s. almond, marjoram, potato, violet*; **s.-apple,** = SWEET-SOP; **s. bay,** (*a*) the bay laurel, *Laurus nobilis*; (*b*) in N. America applied to *Magnolia glauca*; also in comb. as **s. bay laurel** = (*a*); **s. bow** *U.S.* a variety of apple; **s. chestnut,** the common or Spanish chestnut, *Castanea vesca*, as dist. from the bitter inedible HORSE-CHESTNUT; **s.-corn** *U.S.*, a s.-flavoured variety of maize; **s. fern,** (*a*) locally in England, the s. cicely, *Myrrhis odorata* (family *Umbelliferæ*); in N. America, the shrub *Comptonia asplenifolia* (family *Myricaceæ*); **s. flag,** a rush-like plant, *Acorus calamus* (family *Araceæ* or *Orontiaceæ*), widely distributed in the North Temperate zone, growing in water and wet places, with an aromatic odour, and having a thick creeping root-stock of a pungent aromatic flavour; **-grass,** any kind of grass (or herb called 'grass') of a s. taste serving as fodder; **s. scabious,** *Scabiosa atropurpurea*; **s. sedge** = *s. flag*; **s. willow,** (*a*) *Salix pentandra*; (*b*) = SWEET-GALE.

2. Miscellaneous Combs., as *s.-tempered, -voiced* adjs.: **s. and twenty,** a Shaks. phrase (see TWENTY A. 2) misunderstood later to mean 'a s. girl of twenty years old'; **-lipped, -lipt** *a.*, having s. lips; usu., speaking sweetly; **-mouthed** (-mauðd) *a.*, †(*a*) fond of s.-flavoured things, dainty; (*b*) speaking sweetly (usu. ironically); **-spoken** *a.*, speaking sweetly (cf. *plain-spoken*); **-toothed** (-tūþt) *a.*, having a s. tooth, fond of s. things. Hence **Swee·t-ly** *adv.*, **-ness.**

Sweet, *v.* Now *rare.* [f. prec.; in OE. *swētan.*] **1.** *trans.* To make sweet, sweeten (*lit.* and *fig.*). **2.** To affect in a sweet or pleasant way; to delight, gratify 1555.

Sweetbread (swī·tbred). (Also formerly as two words.) 1565. [perh. f. SWEET *a.* + BREDE *sb.*¹; but the reason for the name is unkn.] The pancreas or the thymus gland of an animal, esp. as used for food (dist. respectively as *heart, stomach,* or *belly s.* and *throat, gullet,* or *neck s.*): esteemed a delicacy.

Swee·t-bri:er, -bri:ar. (Also as two words.) 1538. [f. SWEET *a.* + BRIER *sb.*¹] A species of rose, the Eglantine, *Rosa rubiginosa* (and some other species, as *R. micracantha*), having strong hooked prickles, pink single flowers, and small aromatic leaves; freq. cultivated in gardens.

Sweeten (swī·t'n), *v.* 1552. [f. SWEET *a.* + -EN⁵.] **1.** *trans.* **a.** To make sweet to the taste; *esp.* to add sugar or other sweet substance to (food or drink); also *absol.* **b.** To make sweet to the smell 1586. **2.** To free from offensive taste or smell; to render fresh; to free from taint, purify, bring into a wholesome condition 1599. **3.** To make sweet to the ear; to impart a pleasant sound to 1578. **4.** To make pleasant or agreeable; sometimes, to make more pleasant 1586. **5.** To make less unpleasant or painful; to alleviate, mitigate 1586. **6.** With personal obj.: **a.** To produce a pleasant disposition in; to make gracious, mild, or kind; to refine 1561. **b.** To make things pleasant for, relieve, comfort, soothe, gratify. Now *rare* or *Obs.* 1647. **c.** To mollify, appease. Now *rare* or *Obs.* 1657. **7.** To persuade by flattery or gifts; to cajole; to take in; to bribe. Now only *slang* or *dial.* 1594. **8.** *techn.* **a.** To cause to work smoothly or easily 1607. **b.** *Printing* and *Drawing.* To free from harshness, soften (a tint, line, etc.) 1688. **c.** To render (soil) mellow and fertile 1733. **d.** To neutralize (an acid) by means of an alkali 1681. **9.** *slang.* **a.** *Cards.* To increase the stakes. **b.** To bid at an auction merely in order to raise the price. **c.** *Finance.* To increase the collateral of a loan by adding further securities. 1896. **10.** *intr.* To become sweet (in various senses) 1626.

1. To get something to s. my husband's toddy with 1833. **b.** With fayrest Flowers..I'le s. thy sad graue SHAKS. **2.** All the perfumes of Arabia will not s. this little hand SHAKS. Measures for airing and sweetning their Houses DE FOE. **3.** Mine aduersary (who as the crafty fowler sweeteneth his voice to deceiue) 1578. **4.** The Influence of Hope in general sweetens Life ADDISON. **5.** To s. melancholy 1844. **6.** To correct and s. the Tempers of Men 1706. **7.** The talke..is..that the Holland Embassador here do endeavour to s. us with fair words PEPYS. **8. b.** Correggio has made his Memory immortal..by sweetning his Lights and Shadows, and melting them into each other so happily, that they are even imperceptible DRYDEN. **10.** The soil laid in a heap to s. 1858. Hence **Swee·tener,** one who, or that which, sweetens; †one who softens, palliates, or extenuates; something that restores pleasant feeling; †*slang,* a decoy, cheat. **Swee·tening** *vbl. sb.* the action of SWEETEN *v.*; that which sweetens. **Swee·tening** *ppl. a.* that sweetens.

Swee·t-field, -veld. 1785. [– S. Afr. Du. *zoetveld*, lit. sweet field.] In South Africa, land of good quality for food-plants.

Swee·t-gale. 1640. [See SWEET *a.* and GALE *sb.*¹] The bog myrtle, *Myrica Gale.*

Sweetheart (swī·thāɹt), *sb.* ME. [See SWEET *a.* and HEART *sb.*] **1.** (prop. two words.) = darling: used chiefly in the vocative. †**2.** A paramour –1796. **3.** A person with whom one is in love 1576.

Swee·theart, *v.* 1798. [f. prec.] **1.** *trans.* To make a sweetheart of; to court, make love to 1804. **2.** *intr.* To be a sweetheart; to court a sweetheart, make love 1798. Hence **Swee·t-hea:rting** *vbl. sb.* and *ppl. a.*

Sweetie (swī·ti). orig. and chiefly *Sc.* 1721. [f. SWEET *a.* + -IE.] **1.** A sweetmeat, lollipop. Also, sweet cake or the like. **2.** A sweetheart.

Sweeting (swī·tiŋ). ME. [f. SWEET *a.* + -ING³.] **1.** A 'sweet' or beloved person; dear one, darling, sweetheart. *arch.* **2.** Name for a sweet-flavoured variety of apple 1530.

1. How fares my Kate, what s. all a-mort? SHAKS.

Sweetish (swī·tiʃ), *a.* 1580. [f. SWEET *a.* + -ISH¹.] Somewhat or slightly sweet. Hence **-ness.**

Sweetling (swī·tliŋ). *rare.* 1648. [f.

SWEET *a.* + -LING[1].] **1.** = SWEETING 1. **2.** A small sweet thing 1840.

Sweetmeat (swī·tmīt). ME. [f. SWEET *a.* + MEAT *sb.* Cf. OE. *swētmettas, swōtmettas* delicacies.] **1.** *collect. pl.* (and †*sing.*) Sweet food, as sugared cakes, etc. (*obs.*); preserved or candied fruits, sugared nuts, etc.; also, globules, lozenges, 'drops', or 'sticks' made of sugar with fruit or other flavouring or filling; *sing.* one of these. **2.** A varnish used in the preparation of patent leather 1875.

Sweet pea. 1732. The common name of *Lathyrus odoratus*, a climbing annual leguminous plant, indigenous to Sicily, and cultivated in numerous varieties for its showy variously-coloured sweet-scented flowers; cf. next.

Sweet-scented (stress variable), *a.* 1591. Having a sweet scent; sweet-smelling, fragrant. **b.** *spec.* in names of species or varieties of plants having sweet-smelling flowers, leaves, etc. 1666.

b. *S. pea*, an early name for the SWEET PEA.

Sweet singer. a. *Hist.* The phr. *sweet singer*, more fully *sweet singer of Israel* (app. with reminiscence of 2 Sam. 23:1, where David is called 'the sweet psalmist of Israel'), designating a sect or sects which flourished in the latter years of the 17th c. 1680. **b.** A (religious) poet 1560.

Swee·t-sme·lling, *ppl. a.* ME. Smelling sweet; sweet-scented.

Swee·t-sop. 1696. [SOP *sb.*] The sweet fruit of a tree or shrub, *Anona squamosa*, allied to the SOUR-SOP, extensively cultivated in tropical countries. Also, the tree or shrub itself.

Sweet water, sweet-water. 1544. **1.** (as two words) Fresh water; *attrib.* (usu. with hyphen or as one word), living in or consisting of fresh water 1608. †**2.** (as two words, or with hyphen) A sweet-smelling liquid preparation; a liquid perfume or scent –1859. **3.** (with hyphen, or as one word) A variety of white grape, of specially sweet flavour 1786.

Sweetweed (swī·t,wīd). 1760. Either of two scrophulariaceous plants of the West Indies and tropical America, *Capraria biflora*, and *Scoparia dulcis*.

Sweet-william (swīt wi·lyăm). 1562. **1.** A species of pink, *Dianthus barbatus*, cultivated in numerous varieties, bearing closely-clustered flowers of various shades of white and red, usu. variegated or parti-coloured. Also in wider use. **2.** †**a.** Applied to the tope or dog-fish 1730. **b.** A local name for the goldfinch 1848.

Sweetwood (swī·twud). 1607. Any of various trees and shrubs, chiefly lauraceous, of the West Indies and tropical America, some of which furnish valuable timber; also, the timber itself.

attrib.: **s. bark,** cascarilla bark.

Sweet-wort (swī·twɒɹt). 1567. [WORT[2].] A sweet-flavoured wort; *esp.* the infusion of malt, before the hops are added in the manufacture of beer.

Swell (swel), *sb.* ME. [In sense 1 prob. repr. OE. *ġeswell*; in the other senses f. SWELL *v.*] †**1.** A morbid swelling. ME only. **2.** The condition of being swollen, distended, or increased in bulk; swelling or protuberant form, bulge; *concr.* a protuberant part, protuberance 1683. **3. a.** The rising or heaving of the sea or other body of water in a succession of long rolling waves, as after a storm; *concr.* such a wave, or, more usu., such waves collectively. (See also GROUND-SWELL.) 1606. †**b.** The rising of a river above its ordinary level –1812. **4.** A piece of land rising gradually and evenly above the general level; a hill, eminence, or upland with a smooth rounded outline and broad in proportion to its height; a rising ground 1764. **5.** Of sound, esp. musical sound: Gradual increase in loudness or force; hence, a sound or succession of sounds gradually increasing in volume 1803. **b.** *spec.* in *Mus.* A gradual increase of force (*crescendo*) followed by a gradual decrease (*diminuendo*), in singing or playing; hence, a character composed of the *crescendo* and *diminuendo* marks together, denoting this: < >. 1757. **6.** A contrivance for gradually varying the force of the tone in an organ or harmonium (also in the harpsichord and some early pianos), consisting of a shutter, a lid, or (now usu.) a series of slats like those of a Venetian blind, which can be opened or shut at pleasure by means of a pedal or (in the harmonium) a knee-lever. Also, short for *s.-box, s. keyboard, s. organ*, or *s. pedal* 1773. **7.** The action or condition of swelling, in fig. senses 1702. **8.** *colloq.*, orig. *slang.* A fashionably or stylishly dressed person; hence, a person of good social position, a highly distinguished person 1811. **b.** *transf.* (*colloq.*) One who is very clever or good *at* something 1816.

2. The s. or belly of the shaft 1726. His legs.. had not..much more symmetry or s. than the lean Court sword which dangled by his side THACKERAY. **3.** Their water-casks..rocking on the long swells of subsiding gales 1865. *fig.* Such ebbs of doubt, and swells of jealousy LANDOR. **4.** An uninterrupted s. of moorland SCOTT. The swells and valleys of the veld 1908. **5.** The choir's faint s., Came slowly down the wind SCOTT. **7.** It Moderates the S. of Joy that I am in, to think of your Difficulties STEELE. The s. of insolence, the liveliness of levity JOHNSON. **8.** I never was a gentleman—only a s. MARRYAT. **b.** Russians are tremendous swells at palaver,..gammon you no end 1886.

attrib. (in sense 6) in names of apparatus connected with or actuating the s., as *s.-keyboard, -manual, pedal*; **s.-box,** the box or chamber, containing a set of pipes or reeds, which is opened and closed by the s. in an organ or harmonium; **-organ,** the set of pipes enclosed in the s.-box.

Swell, *a. colloq.* 1810. [attrib. use of prec. in sense 8.] That is, or has the character or style of, a 'swell'; befitting a 'swell'.

Two very s. coachmen 1826. You don't look as if you had such a s. time 1897. **S. mob,** a class of pickpockets who assume the dress and manners of respectable people in order to escape detection; hence **s.-mobsman,** a man belonging to the s. mob. *slang.*

Swell (swel), *v.* Pa. t. **swelled** (sweld); pa. pple. **swollen** (swōᵘ·l'n), **swelled.** [OE. *swellan* = OFris. **swella*, OS. **swellan* (Du. *zwellen*), OHG. *swellan* (G. *schwellen*), ON. *svella* :- Gmc. str. vb. **swellan*.] **1.** *intr.* To become larger in bulk, increase in size (by pressure from within, as by absorption of moisture, or of material in the process of growth, by inflation with air or gas, etc.); to become distended or filled out, *esp.* to undergo abnormal or morbid increase of size, be affected with tumour as the result of infection or injury. Also with *out, up.* **b.** Of a body of water: To rise above the ordinary level, as a river, or the tide; to rise in waves, as the sea in or after a storm; to rise to the brim, well up. late ME. **c.** Expressing form (not movement or action): To be distended or protuberant; to be larger, higher, or thicker at a certain part; to rise gradually and smoothly above the general level, as a hill 1679. **2.** *trans.* To make larger in bulk, increase the size of, cause to expand; to enlarge morbidly, affect with tumour. Also with *out, up.* late ME. **b.** To cause (the sea, a river) to rise in waves, or (more usu.) above the ordinary level 1605. **3.** In pa. pple., without implication of subject: Increased in bulk, dilated, distended; affected with morbid enlargement or tumour OE. **4.** *intr.* To become greater in amount, volume, degree, intensity, or force: now only in immaterial sense 1450. **5.** *trans.* To make greater in amount, degree, or intensity; to increase, add to. Also with *out, up.* 1599. **b.** To fill (a receptacle) to overflowing. *poet.* and *rare.* 1601. **c.** To magnify; to exalt. Now *rare* or *Obs.* 1600. **6.** *intr.* Of sound, esp. music: To increase in volume, become gradually louder or fuller; to come upon the ear with increasing clearness, or with alternate increase and diminution of force. Also of a musical instrument: To give forth a swelling sound or note. 1749. **b.** *trans.* To utter with increase of force, or with increasing volume of sound (*rare*) 1775. **7.** *fig. intr.* **a.** Of a feeling or emotion: To arise and grow in the mind with a sense as of distension or expansion. late ME. **b.** Of a person, the heart, etc.: To be affected with such an emotion; to be puffed up, become elated or arrogant. Const. *with.* late ME. **8.** *trans.* To affect with such an emotion; to puff up, inflate. (Also said of the emotion.) ME. **9.** *intr.* To show proud or angry feeling in one's action or speech; to behave proudly, arrogantly, or overbearingly; to be 'puffed up'; to look or talk big. *Obs.* or *arch.* ME. **10.** To behave pompously or pretentiously, swagger; to play the 'swell' 1795.

1. His knee swelled, and he walked with great difficulty TYNDALL. Every flower-bud swelleth R. BRIDGES. **b.** Do but behold the teares that s. in me SHAKS. **c.** A varied surface—where the ground swells, and falls 1791. **2.** The Major.. swelling every already swollen vein in his head DICKENS. **b.** Bids the winde..s. the curled Waters 'boue the Maine SHAKS. The upland showers had swoln the rills SCOTT. **4.** The ranks of the unemployed are..daily swelling 1895. **5.** The presence of the monarch swelled the importance of the debate GIBBON. **6.** Choral warblings round him s. GRAY. **7. a.** Remembrance.. Swells at my breast, and turns the past to pain GOLDSM. **b.** He swell'd to see Varus a suppliant growne 1627. **8.** What other notions..could s. up Caligula to think himself a God? MILT. **9.** Thy furious foes now s. And storm outrageously MILT.

Swell-, the verb-stem in comb.: **s.-fish,** a fish that inflates itself by swallowing air, also called *puffer* or *puff-fish*; **-front** *U.S.*, a bow-front of a house; *transf.* a house having such a front; **-head** *colloq.* = *swelled head* (see SWELLED b); also, a person affected with 'swelled head'; **-shark,** (*a*) a small shark, *Scyllium ventricosum*, of the Pacific coast of America; (*b*) a Californian shark, *Catulus uter*, which when caught inflates itself by swallowing air.

Swelldom (swe·ldəm). *colloq.* 1855. [f. SWELL *sb.* 8 + -DOM.] The realm or world of 'swells'; people of distinction of any kind.

Swelled (sweld), *ppl. a.* 1611. [Weak pa. pple. of SWELL *v.*; see -ED[1].] In senses of SWELL *v.*, *lit.* and *fig.*; *esp.* in sense 'morbidly enlarged, affected with tumour'. **b. S. head** (*fig.*): inordinate self-conceit, excessive pride or vanity (humorously regarded as a morbid affection). *colloq.* 1891.

Swelling (swe·liŋ), *vbl. sb.* late ME. [f. SWELL *v.* + -ING[1]. In OE. *swelling* (once).] **1.** The process of swelling, or condition of having swollen 1577. **2.** *concr.* A swollen part of something; a protuberance, prominence; *esp.* an abnormal or morbid enlargement in or upon any part or member; a tumour. late ME.

1. What wilt thou do in the s. of Iorden? *Bible* (Geneva) *Jer.* 12:5. The s. of the buds, and the expansion of the leaves 1842. The proud s. of his heart SCOTT. **2.** Swellings or Tumours in Horses, come by Heats, by hard Riding or by sore Labour 1704. *White s.*, a form of swelling without redness, *spec.* a tuberculous arthritis; strumous synovitis of a joint.

Swe·lling, *ppl. a.* OE. [f. as prec. + -ING[2].] That swells. Hence **Swe·llingly** *adv.*

Swellish (swe·liʃ), *a. colloq.* 1820. [f. SWELL *sb.* 8 + -ISH[1].] Stylish, dandified.

S'welp. 1899. Perversion of *so help*, in the oath 'so help me God'.

Swelt (swelt), *v.* Now *dial.* [OE. *sweltan* die, perish = OS. *sweltan*, OHG. *swelzan*, ON. *svelta*, Goth. *swiltan* :- Gmc. str. vb. f. **swelt- *swalt- *swult-*, perh. a secondary f. **swel-*, repr. by SWEAL.] **I.** *intr.* **1.** To die, perish. **2.** To be overcome, faint, swoon ME. **3.** To be faint with heat. late ME.

2. His olde wo þat made his herte to swelte CHAUCER.

II. *trans.* To overheat, broil, scorch; also in fig. phr. *to s. one's heart*, to exert oneself to the utmost. Now *dial.* late ME.

Swelter (swe·ltəɹ), *v.* late ME. [f. base of SWELT *v.* + -ER[5].] **1.** *intr.* To be oppressed with heat; to sweat profusely, languish, or faint with excessive heat. **b.** To move slowly or painfully (as if) oppressed with heat 1834. **2.** *trans.* To oppress with heat; to cause to sweat, languish, or faint with oppressive heat. Chiefly *pass.* 1601. †**3.** *intr.* and *pass.* To be bathed *in* liquid; hence, to welter, wallow (*lit.* and *fig.*) –1865. **4.** *trans.* with allusion to Shakespeare's *sweltered venom* (see next, 1): To exude (venom); also *absol.*, and *intr.* for *pass.* 1834.

1. A fat official sweltering in his uniform under the burning sun 1880. **b.** The labouring ship sweltered about on the boiling sea 1834. **4.** The fat seemed sweltering and full of poison L. HUNT.

Sweltered (swe·ltəɹd), *ppl. a.* 1605. [f. prec. + -ED[1].] **1.** Exuded like sweat (as if) by heat. Only in *s. venom* in and after Shaks. **2.** Bathed in, or oppressed with, great heat 1776.

1. Toad, that vnder cold stone..ha's..Sweltred Venom sleeping got SHAKS. **2.** S. cattle COLERIDGE.

Sweltry (swe·ltri), *a.* Now *arch.* and *dial.* 1576. [f. SWELTER *v.* + -Y[1]. Cf. SULTRY.] **1.** Of heat, weather, etc.: Oppressively hot, sultry. **2.** Oppressed or languishing with heat 1635.

Swept (swept), *ppl. a.* 1552. [pa. pple. of SWEEP *v.*] In senses of the verb; freq. as second element of compounds, as *wind-s.*

Swerve (swə̄ɹv), *sb.* 1741. [f. next.] An act of swerving, turning aside, or deviating from a course.

Swerve (swə̄ɹv), *v.* [ME. *swerve*, repr. OE. *sweorfan* file, scour, = OFris. *swerva* creep, OS. **swerban* wipe, MDu. *swerven* stray, OHG. *swerban* wipe, move quickly backwards and forwards, ON. *sverfa* file, Goth. *af|swairban* wipe (away). The orig. sense of the radical may be that of agitated, irregular, or deflected movement.] **1.** *intr.* To turn aside; to deviate in movement from the straight or direct course ME. **b.** To turn in a specified direction; to be deflected (statically) 1600. **2.** To turn away or be deflected from a (right) course of action, a line of conduct, an opinion, etc.; †to vacillate. late ME. †**3.** To give way; to sway, totter; *fig.* to shrink *from* action –1818. **4.** To rove, stray. Also *fig.* to digress. 1543. †**5.** = SWARM *v.*[2] –1697. **6.** *trans.* To cause to turn aside or deviate. late ME. **b.** *Cricket, Baseball*, etc. To cause a ball to deflect by imparting a spinning motion to it as it leaves the bowler or pitcher 1906.

1. His lab'ring team, that swerv'd not from the track COWPER. **b.** The road swerves to the left 1883. **2.** Yet swarue not I from thy commaundementes COVERDALE *Ps.* 118[9]:110. Honour that knows the path and will not s. WORDSW. The wealth around him never made Walpole s. from a rigid economy GREEN. **3.** The battel swerv'd, with many an inrode gor'd MILT. **4.** Al are swarued and clene gone out of the way 1543. **5.** Nimbly up, from bough to bough I swerv'd DRYDEN. **6.** My decided opinion..from which nothing shall s. me 1801. Hence **Swe·rveless,** unswerving.

Sweven (swe·v'n). *Obs.* exc. *arch.* [OE. *swef(e)n* sleep, dream = OS. *sweban*, ON. *svefn* :- Gmc. **swefnaz, -am* :- IE. **swepno-*, to which are rel. Gr. ὕπνος, L. *sommus*.] A dream, a vision.

Allas and konne ye been agast of sweuenys No thyng god woot, but vanitee in sweuene is CHAUCER.

Swift (swift), *sb.* 1530. [subst. use of next.] **I. 1.** The common newt or eft. Now only *dial.* **b.** A name for several swift-running small lizards, as the N. Amer. fence-lizard, *Sceloporus undulatus* 1530. **2.** A bird of the family *Cypselidæ*, comprising many and widely distributed species, outwardly resembling swallows, and noted for their swiftness of flight; *esp.* the common swift, *Cypselus apus*, a summer visitant to the British Isles and Europe generally 1668. **b.** Name for a breed of domestic pigeons having some resemblance to swifts 1879. **3.** Collector's name for moths of the genus *Hepialus* or family *Hepialidæ*, distinguished by their rapid flight 1819. **II. 1.** A light kind of reel, usu. of adjustable diameter, upon which a skein of silk, yarn, etc. is placed in order to be wound off 1564. **b.** A cylinder in a carding-machine 1853. †**2.** A rapid current; a rapid –1712. **3.** The sail of a windmill. *dial.* 1763. **4.** *Printers' slang.* A quick or expeditious type-setter 1841.

Swift, *a.* (*adv.*) [OE. *swift*, f. base of *swīfan* move in a course, sweep (see SWIVE) = ON. *svifa*. Cf. SWIVEL *sb.*] **1.** 'Moving far in a short time' (J.); moving, or capable of moving, with great speed or velocity; rapid, fleet. **b.** Of movement, or action regarded as movement: Taking place or executed at high speed; rapid, quick OE. **2.** Coming on, happening, or performed without delay; prompt, speedy OE. **b.** Acting, or disposed to act without delay; prompt, ready. Usu. const. *to* with inf. or sb. ME. **3.** Done or finished within a short time; passing quickly, that is soon over, brief. Chiefly *poet.* ME.

1. A Swalwe s. of winge GOWER. The race is not to the s., nor the battel to the strong *Bible* (Geneva) *Eccles.* 9:11. **b.** A s. but not very legible ..penmanship CARLYLE. **2.** Those proud Towrs to s. destruction doom'd MILT. **b.** Crafty of counsel, and s. of execution 1855. **3.** My dayes are swifter then a weauers shuttle *Job* 7:6.

B. *adv.* (Now chiefly *poet.*) Swiftly. late ME. Hence **Swi·ft-ly** *adv.*, **-ness.**

Swift, *v.* 1485. [prob. rel. to ME. †*swift* (XIV), perh. syn. of SWIFTER; presumably of Scand. or LG. origin, and – base repr. by ON. *svipta* reef (sails), *sviftingar* reefing-ropes, Du. *zwichten* take in (sails), *zwichtlings, zwichtlijnen* cat-harpings, and ult. allied to SWIFT *a.*] *Naut. trans.* To tighten or make fast by means of a rope or ropes drawn taut.

Swiften (swi·ft'n), *v. rare.* 1638. [f. SWIFT *a.* + -EN[5].] **1.** *trans.* To make swift or swifter. **2.** *intr.* To become swift or swifter; *loosely*, to move swiftly, hasten, hurry 1839.

Swifter (swi·ftəɹ), *sb.* 1625. [See SWIFT *v.*] *Naut.* A rope used for swifting. **a.** One of a pair of shrouds, fixed above the other shrouds, for swifting or stiffening a mast. **b.** A rope passed through holes or notches in the outer ends of the capstan-bars and drawn taut. **c.** A rope passed around a boat or ship as a protection against strain or collision. Hence **Swi·fter** *v. trans.* to fasten a s. to, or tighten with a s.

Swi·ft-foot, *a.* and *sb.* 1594. **A.** *adj.* = SWIFT-FOOTED *a.* **B.** *sb.* A swift-footed person or animal, a fast runner; *spec.* = COURSER[3] 1825.

Swift-footed (stress variable), *a.* 1600. Having swift feet; capable of running or going swiftly.

Swiftian (swi·ftiăn), *a.* 1762. [f. name of Jonathan *Swift* (1667–1745) + -IAN.] Pertaining to or characteristic of the satirist Swift or his works.

Swiftlet (swi·ftlėt). 1892. [f. SWIFT *sb.* + -LET.] A little or young swift; a small species of swift, as those of the genus *Collocalia*, which construct the edible birds' nests of China.

Swig (swig), *sb.*[1] *slang* or *colloq.* 1548. [Of unkn. origin.] †**1.** Drink, liquor –1635. **b.** Applied locally to special drinks 1827. **2.** An act of 'swigging'; a deep or copious draught; a 'pull' 1621.

Swig, *sb.*[2] 1807. [Cf. SWIG *v.*[2]] *Naut.* **1.** A tackle the falls of which are not parallel. **2.** The act of 'swigging' at a rope 1904.

Swig, *v.*[1] *slang* or *colloq.* 1654. [f. SWIG *sb.*[1]] *trans.* and *intr.* or *absol.* To drink in deep draughts; to drink eagerly or copiously.

I am..drinking as much tea..as I can s. RUSKIN.

Swig, *v.*[2] 1663. [perh. related to SWAG, with general sense 'to cause to sway about, pull'.] **1.** *trans.* To castrate (a ram) by tying the scrotum tightly with a string. **2.** *Naut.* To pull at the bight of a rope which is fast at one end to a fixed object and at the other to a movable one; to pull (a sail, etc.) *up* in this manner 1794. **3.** *intr.* To sway about, waver; to move with a swaying motion 1833.

Swill (swil), *sb.* 1553. [f. next.] **1.** Liquid or partly liquid food, chiefly kitchen refuse, given to swine; hog-wash, pig-wash. **b.** *transf.* A liquid or partly liquid mess, a slop 1665. **2.** Copious or heavy drinking; liquor, esp. when drunk to excess; †a swig (of liquor) 1602.

Swill (swil), *v.* [OE. *swillan, swilian*, of which no certain cognates are known.] **1.** *trans.* To wash or rinse *out* (a vessel or cavity), or, now usu., to cause water to flow freely upon (a surface, floor, etc.) in order to cleanse it; formerly also, to wash, bathe, drench, soak. **b.** To stir (something) about in a vessel of liquid; to shake or stir (liquid) in a vessel by moving the vessel about 1580. **c.** To carry by a current of water, to wash down, against something, etc. Also, to pour or carry (liquid) freely down. 1598. **2.** *intr.* To move or dash about, as liquid shaken in a vessel; to flow freely or forcibly; to flow or spread over a surface 1642. **3.** To drink freely, greedily, or to excess, like hogs devouring 'swill' or 'wash'. *trans.* and *intr.* (*esp.* to tipple, booze). 1530. **4.** *trans.* To cause to drink freely; to fill with drink; *refl.* to drink one's fill. Const. *with*, †*in*. 1548.

1. A galled Rocke..Swill'd with the wild and wastfull Ocean SHAKS. **2.** The river went swishing, swilling past 1895. **3.** Ye eat, and s., and sleep, and gourmandise SHERIDAN. **4.** Till they can show there's something they love better than swilling themselves with ale GEO. ELIOT. Hence **Swi·ller,** one who swills. **Swi·lling** *vbl. sb.* the action of the vb.; *concr.* (usu. *pl.*) = SWILL *sb.* 1.

Swill-bowl (swi·lbōᵘl). *Obs.* or *arch.* 1542. [f. prec. and BOWL *sb.*[1]] One who habitually 'swills the bowl' or drinks to excess; a toper, drunkard.

Swill-tub (swi·ltʊb). 1575. [f. SWILL *sb.* 1 + TUB *sb.*] A tub for swill or hog-wash. Also *fig.* with allusion to heavy drinking.

Swim (swim), *sb.* 1547. [f. SWIM *v.*] †**1.** The clear part of a liquid which floats above the sediment –1676. †**2.** A smooth gliding movement of the body –1772. †**3.** The swimming-bladder or sound of a fish –1833. **4.** A swimming motion; *colloq.* or *dial.* a swimming or dizzy sensation 1817. **5.** An act of swimming 1805. **6.** A part of a river or other piece of water much frequented by fish, or in which an angler fishes 1828. **b.** fig. phr. *In the s. with*: in the same company with, in league with 1885. **7.** *fig.* The current of affairs or events, *esp.* the popular current in business, fashion, or opinion; chiefly in phr. *in* (*out of*) *the s.* 1869.

Swim (swim), *v.* Pa. t. **swam** (swæm); pa. pple. **swum** (swʊm). [OE. *swimman* = OS., OHG. *swimman* (Du. *zwemmen*, G. *schwimmen*), ON. *svim(m)a* :- Gmc. **swemjan*, f. **swem-* **swam-* **swum-*.] **I.** *intr.* **1.** To move along in or on water by movements of the limbs or other natural means of progression. **2.** To float on the surface of any liquid; not to sink; to form the upper part of a mass of liquid. Sometimes, to rise and float on the surface. OE. **b.** To be supported in a fluid medium 1547. **c.** *fig.* 1547. **3.** To move or float along on the surface of the water, as a ship. Now *poet.* OE. **b.** To be conveyed by a body floating on the water. late ME. **4.** To move as water or other liquid, esp. over a surface; to flow. late ME. **5.** To glide with a smooth or waving motion 1553. **b.** Of a plough (in full, *to s. fair*): To go steadily 1797. **6.** To move, or appear to move, as if gliding or floating on water; *esp.* to move, glide, or be suspended in the air or ether, occas. by mechanical means 1661. **b.** Said of the apparent motion of objects before the eyes of a person whose sight is troubled or blurred 1678. **7.** Of the head or brain: To be affected with dizziness; to have a giddy sensation. Also, of the head, *to s. round* = to be in a whirl. 1702. **b.** Of the eyes: To be troubled or blurred: with mixture of sense 9. 1817. **8.** To float, be immersed or steeped, *in* a fluid 1450. **b.** *fig.* To be immersed or sunk *in* pleasure, grief, etc.; †to abound *in*. late ME. **9.** To be covered or filled with fluid; to be drenched, overflowed, or flooded. Const. *with, in.* 1542. **b.** *fig.* To be full to overflowing *with* 1548.

1. Maoris and Kanakas can s., repeated the old man..White men like you and me can only paddle. 1890. Phr. *To s. between two waters* (tr. Fr. prov. *nager entre deux eaux*), to steer between two extremes. *To s. with* or *down the stream* or *tide*, to act in conformity with prevailing opinion or tendency; so, *to s. against the stream.* **2.** A boat, the only one that could s. 1798. Phr. *sink or s.* (occas. *s. or drown*), used *spec.* in ref. to the ordeal of suspected witches, hence *fig.* = 'whatever may happen'. **3. b.** I will scarce thinke you haue swam in a Gundello SHAKS. **5.** She..swam across the floor as though she scorned the drudgery of walking STEVENSON. **6.** High up the vapours fold and s. TENNYSON. **b.** The arena swims around him—he is gone BYRON. **7.** His brain swam with the thought 1851. **8.** A cotton-wick swimming in oil 1775. **b.** At noon we s. in wine; at night, in tears 1644. **9.** The marble floors of the Temple of Jerusalem swam in blood 1891.

II. *trans.* **1.** To traverse or cover (a certain distance) by swimming. Also, to perform (a stroke or evolution) by swimming. OE. **2.** To pass or cross by swimming; to move in, on, or over by swimming; to swim across 1591. **3.** To cause (an animal) to swim, esp. across a river, etc. 1639. **b.** To cause (something) to pass over the surface of water; to float 1743. **4.** To cause to float; to buoy up 1669. **b.** To put (a person suspected of witchcraft) to the ordeal of being immersed in water, the proof of innocence being that the person did not sink 1718. **c.** To furnish sufficient depth of water for (something) to swim or float in 1815.

1. He could not s. a stroke 1893. **2.** You are ouerbootes in loue, And yet you neuer swom the Hellespont SHAKS. **3.** Sometimes swimming their horses, sometimes losing them and struggling for their own lives SCOTT. **4.** Brine that will s. an egg 1842. **c.** Wide rivers..almost deep enough to s. a horse 1887.

Swi·m-bla:dder. 1837. [f. prec.] A fish's swimming-bladder.

Swimmer (swi·məɹ). late ME. [f. SWIM *v.* + -ER[1].] **1.** A person (or animal) that swims in the water. **2.** An animal that (habitually) swims; *spec.* a bird of the order *Natatores*, a swimming bird. late ME. **3.** A swimming-organ of an animal 1816. **4.** A thing which floats upon the surface of a liquid; *spec.* an angler's float 1609.

Swimmeret (swi·məret). 1840. [f. prec. + -ET.] An abdominal limb or appendage of a crustacean, adapted for swimming; a swimming-foot, pleopod.

Swimming (swi·miŋ), *vbl. sb.* late ME. [f. SWIM *v.* + -ING[1].] **1.** The action of SWIM *v.* **2.** A state of dizziness or giddiness 1530.

attrib. and *Comb.*, as *s.-bath*, *-pool*; **s.-bell,** a bell-shaped part or organ, as a nectocalyx, by which an animal propels itself through the water; **-bladder,** (*a*) the air-bladder of a fish, which enables it to keep its balance in swimming; (*b*) an inflated bladder to assist a person in swimming.

Swimming (swi·miŋ), *ppl. a.* OE. [f. SWIM *v.* + -ING[2].] **1.** That swims. **b.** Of the eyes: Suffused with tears; watery 1729. **2.** Affected with, or characterized by, dizziness or giddiness 1607. **b.** Of the eyes or sight (cf. L. *oculi natantes, lumina natantia*) 1697.

1. Poor Tom, that eates the s. Frog SHAKS. **b.** She rose, and fixt her s. eyes upon him TENNYSON. **2. b.** No trembling of the hand, no error of the s. sight 1827. Hence **Swi·mmingly** *adv.* in a s. manner; smoothly and without impediment; with uninterrupted success or prosperity; with a smooth gliding movement. **Swi·mmingness** (*rare*), a misty appearance (of the eyes); smooth gliding movement.

Swimmy (swi·mi), *a.* 1836. [f. SWIM *v.* + -Y[1].] Inclined to dizziness or giddiness. Hence **Swi·mminess.**

Swindle (swi·nd'l), *sb.* 1852. [f. next.] **1.** An act of swindling; a cheat, fraud, imposition. **2.** Something that is not what it appears or is pretended to be; a 'fraud'. *colloq.* 1866.

Swindle, *v.* 1782. [Back-formation from next.] **1.** *intr.* To act the swindler; to practise fraud, imposition, or mean artifice, esp. for the purpose of obtaining money. **2.** *trans.* To cheat, defraud (a person) *out of* money or property 1803. **3.** To get by swindling 1804.

2. Though she swindles Delphine out of her estate 1803. **3.** Lamotte..had..swindled a sum of three-hundred livres from one of them CARLYLE.

Swindler (swi·ndləɹ). orig. *Cant.* 1775. [– G. *schwindler* giddy-minded person, extravagant projector, cheat, f. *schwindeln* be giddy, act thoughtlessly or extravagantly, swindle.] One who practises fraud, imposition, or mean artifice for purposes of gain; a cheat.

Dupes to the designing arts of the wretches distinguished by the name of Swindlers 1775. A s., living as he can SHELLEY.

Swine (swəin). *Pl.* **swine.** [OE. *swīn* = OFris., OS., OHG. *swīn* (Du. *swijn*, G. *schwein*), ON. *svín*, Goth. *swein* :- Gmc. **swīnam*, subst. use of n. of adj. (cf. L. *suinus* pertaining to swine, and see -INE[1]), f. IE. **suw-*, repr. by L. *sus*, Gr. ὗς (see SOW *sb.*).] **1.** An animal of the genus *Sus* or the family *Suidæ*, comprising bristle-bearing non-ruminant hoofed mammals, of which the full-grown male is called a *boar*, the full-grown female a *sow*; esp. the common species *Sus scrofa*, domesticated from early times by Gentile nations for its flesh, and regarded as a type of greediness and uncleanness. (Now only literary, dialectal, or as a generic term in zoology, etc. being superseded in common use by *pig* or *hog*.) **2.** *fig.* Applied opprobriously to a sensual, degraded, or coarse person; also (in mod. use) as a mere term of contempt or abuse. late ME. **3.** = *swine-fish* 1844.

1. Oh monstrous beast, how like a s. he lyes SHAKS. A herd of Swine MILT. **2.** I shall be butchered to amuse these s. 1891.

Comb. (also with *swine's*): **s.-backed** (bækt) *a.*, having a back like that of a s.; *spec.* in *Archery*, having a convexly curved outline (opp. to *saddle-backed*); **-eyes,** eyes like those of a s., which cannot be directed upwards; **s. fever,** a name for two infectious diseases of swine, *hog-cholera*, chiefly affecting the intestines, and *s.-plague*, chiefly affecting the lungs; **-fish,** the wolf-fish, *Anarrichas lupus*, so called from the movement of its snout; **-plague** (see *s. fever*); **swine's back,** a narrow hill-ridge (*local*); **-cress,** †(*a*) = *swine's-grass*; (*b*) the cruciferous plant *Senebiera coronopus*; (*c*) ragwort (*local*); (*d*) nipplewort *Lapsana communis*; **-grass,** knotgrass, *Polygonum aviculare*; **swine's grease,** the fat of a s., lard (now *dial.*); **swine's thistle** = SOW-THISTLE 1 (*dial.*).

Swine-bread (swəi·nbred). 1591. [Cf. G. *schwein(s)brot*, mod.L. *panis porcinus*.] †**1.** The plant cyclamen –1648. †**2.** Truffles –1755. **3.** The earth-nut or pig-nut (*local*) 1888.

Swine-cote. Now only *Hist.* or *dial.* late ME. [f. SWINE + COTE *sb.*[1]] A pigsty.

Swineherd (swəi·nhəɹd). Not in colloq. use. [Late OE. *swȳnhyrde*; see SWINE, HERD *sb.*[2]] A man who tends swine, esp. for hire.

Swine-pipe (swəi·npəip). 1668. [A book-name; origin unkn.] The redwing.

Swi·ne-pox. 1530. †**1.** Chicken-pox –1676. **2.** An eruptive disease in swine 1704.

Swinery (swəi·nəri). 1778. [f. SWINE *sb.* + -ERY.] **1.** A place where swine are kept; a piggery. **2.** A swinish condition; swine collectively 1849.

Swine's feather. *Mil.* (now only *Hist.*) 1635. [– G. *schweinsfeder*.] A pointed stake or pike, used as a weapon of defence against cavalry, being either fixed in the ground as a palisade or carried in a musket-rest like a bayonet.

Swine-stone (swəi·nstōᵘn). 1794. [– G. *schweinstein* (see SWINE, STONE *sb.*).] An early name for ANTHRACONITE.

Swine-sty (swəi·nstəi). Now chiefly *dial.* ME. [f. SWINE + STY *sb.*[1]] A pigsty.

Swing (swiŋ), *sb.*[1] late ME. [In sense 1 app. repr. OE. *ġeswing* in *hand-*, *sweord-ġeswing* stroke with a weapon in fight; in sense 2 app. a substitute or var. of *swinge*; in other senses f. SWING *v.*] **I.** Abstract senses. †**1.** A stroke with a weapon. late ME. only. †**2.** *To bear the s.*: to have full sway or control. Also (*to have*) *s. and sway*. –1633. **3.** The course of a career, practice, period of time, etc., esp. as marked by vigorous action of some kind. Now chiefly in phr. *in full s., in the full s. of*..1570. †**4.** Impulse; inclination, tendency –1716. **5.** Freedom of action, free scope 1584. **6.** Forcible motion of a body swung or flung. *arch.* 1595. **b.** Continuous vigorous movement or progress 1856. **c.** *Full s.*: at full speed; with the utmost vigour or energy 1848. **7.** The act of swinging or waving about a weapon or other body; a movement describing a curve, such as that made in flourishing a weapon, etc. 1635. **8.** The act of swinging or oscillating, as a suspended body, or a body turning upon a fixed centre or axis; oscillation; also, the amount of oscillation, the arc or curve traced or moved through in this way. Also with adv., as *swing-to*. 1589. **b.** The distance which determines the diameter of the work that can be admitted by a lathe 1875. **c.** The leaning outward from the vehicle of the upper part of a wheel 1875. **9.** Movement of the body or limbs in a manner suggesting the action of swinging 1730. **10.** A steady vigorous rhythm or movement characterizing a verse or musical composition 1829.

3. It was still early..but the fishing was in full s. 1894. **5.** The giving free s. to one's temper and instincts M. ARNOLD. **6.** The Ramme that batters downe the wall, For the great s. and rudenesse of his poize [etc.] SHAKS. **b.** The..eight-oar coming with a steady s. up the last reach 1861. **7.** Instantaneous photographs of first-class players taken when at the top of the s. 1899. **8.** Constant as the swings of a pendulum STEELE. The s. Of measured oars MORRIS. Phr. *On the s.*, oscillating. **9.** An easy s. in my walk W. IRVING. **10.** The 's.' and 'go'..of these popular religious ballads 1884.

II. Concrete senses. **1.** A contrivance used for recreation, consisting of a seat which is suspended from above on ropes or rods and on which a person may sit and swing to and fro; also = *swing-boat*. (Allusive phr.: see ROUNDABOUT 4 b.) 1687. **2.** The rope or chain attached to the tongue of a wagon, along which the horses between the leaders and the wheelers are attached, they being said to be *in the s.*; hence, the horses occupying that position (more fully, *s.-pair*, *-team*) 1891. **b.** The outriders who keep a moving herd of cattle in order. *U.S.* 1903.

Swing, *sb.*[2] Now *Hist.* 1830. Used, chiefly *attrib.*, to designate a system of intimidation practised in districts of the South of England in 1830–1, consisting in sending to farmers and landowners threatening letters over the signature of a fictitious Captain Swing, followed by the incendiary destruction of their ricks and other property.

Swing (swiŋ), *v.* Pa. t. **swung** (swʊŋ), *rarely* **swang** (swæŋ); pa. pple. **swung.** [OE. *swingan* = OFris. *swinga*, etc., (M)LG. *swingen*, OHG. *swingan* (G. *schwingen* brandish, etc.), f. Gmc. **sweng-* **swang-*, parallel to **swenk-* SWINK *v.*] †**1.** *trans.* To scourge, whip, flog, beat (a person); also, to strike with a weapon or the hand –1460. †**2.** To throw with force, fling, hurl –1495. †**3.** *intr.* To move or go impetuously; to rush; to fling oneself –1582. **4.** *trans.* To draw *out* (a sword) with a vigorous movement (*obs.*); to flourish, brandish, wave *about*; in later use: to wield (a weapon or implement), or move (a body held or grasped) with an oscillating or rotatory movement. late ME. **5.** *intr.* To move freely backwards and forwards, as a body suspended from a support above; to oscillate below a point of support, as a pendulum or the like 1545. **b.** Of a person: To move backwards and forwards through the air upon a suspended rope or on a swing, as a sport; to ride in a swing 1545. **c.** Of a (suspended) bell: To give forth a sound by swinging; to sound, ring *out* 1632. **d.** *fig.* To waver, vacillate 1833. **e.** *trans.* To mark or indicate by swinging; *to s. seconds*, to oscillate once in every second 1736. **6.** *trans.* To cause to oscillate, as a body suspended from a support above; to move or sway (something) to and fro in this or a similar manner 1560. **b.** To cause (a person) to oscillate as in a swing; to give (one) a ride in a swing 1615. **c.** To lift and transport (something suspended) as with a crane; *transf.* to convey or transport from point to point 1856. **d.** *refl.* To hoist oneself up or transport oneself from point to point by grasping a support above. Also *intr.* 1899. **7.** *intr.* To be suspended from a support above (without necessarily implying oscillation). **a.** *spec.* To be hanged. *slang* or *colloq.* 1542. **b.** *gen.* To be suspended, to hang; *transf.* to appear as if suspended 1641. **8.** *trans.* To hang, suspend; *rarely*, to hang (a person). *slang* or *colloq.* 1528. **9.** *intr.* To oscillate (without suspension); to move to and fro, or from side to side; to sway; to hover; *spec.* to sway the body backward and forward in rowing 1607. **10.** To turn in alternate directions, or in either direction (usu. horizontally), around a fixed axis or point of support; *spec. Naut.* said of a vessel riding at a single anchor or moored by the head, and turning with the wind or tide 1769. **b.** To go along or round in a curve or with a sweeping motion; to wheel, sweep 1810. **11.** *trans.* To cause to turn in alternate directions, or in either direction, on or as on an axis or pivot; to turn or cause to face in another direction 1768. **b.** *Naut.* To turn (a ship) to all points in succession, in order to ascertain the deviation of her magnetic compass 1859. **c.** To drive or cause to move in a curve; also, to make or execute by moving in a curve (in phr. *to s. a cast*, in hunting) 1854. **12.** *intr.* To go along with undulating or swaying movement, or in a vigorous manner; to walk with swinging step 1854. **13.** *trans. fig.* To direct or control the movement or action of; to sway, wield. *U.S.* 1889. **14. a.** To fix (the work) on the centre or centres in a lathe. **b.** Of a lathe: To have a 'swing' or capacity of (so much). 1884. **4.** He..swung his arms like the sails of a wind-mill SCOTT. **5.** The shrill bell rings, the censer swings TENNYSON. **c.** Oft..I hear the far-off Curfeu sound, Over som wide-water'd shoar, Swinging slow with sullen roar MILT. **d.** He should endeavour..not to invest when the pendulum has swung upwards 1877. **6.** Phr. *To s. a cat* (i.e. holding it by the tail); in *no room to s. a cat in* and similar expressions, said of a confined or narrow space. *To s. the lead*: to tell a 'tall' story; to make pretence. **d.** The Douglas swung himself into the saddle 1899. **7. a.** They all lovingly swung together at Execution-Dock DE FOE. **b.** A lantern swung from the roof of the coach 1898. **9.** A single hawk swung in the atmosphere above us TYNDALL. **10.** While safely she at anchor swings 1812. **11.** Swinging the parlour-door upon its hinge COWPER. **c.** He swings his team into the Avenue de l'Impératrice 1889. **12.** The camels, swinging at a steady trot 1894. **13.** He can s. the market so as to break a man 1908.

Swing- in comb. **1.** In general attrib. or adj. use (mostly without hyphen, as a separate word), applied to a piece of mechanism, apparatus, or utensil suspended, hinged, or pivoted so as to be capable of oscillating or turning to and fro; sometimes var. of SWINGING *ppl. a.* **2.** Special combs.: **s.-back,** the back of a photographic camera, carrying the sensitized plate, arranged so as to be 'swung' or turned on a hinge or pivot into any required position; **-beam,** a beam arranged to turn, or to enable something to turn, on a pivot or the like; **-bed,** a movable stool-bed in a gun-carriage; **-boat,** a boat-shaped swing used for amusement at fairs, etc.; **-bridge,** a form of drawbridge which turns horizontally on a pivot (either at one end or in the centre); **-cart** a spring-cart; **-door,** a door constructed to swing to or shut of itself; **-front,** in a photographic camera (cf. *s.-back*); **-handle,** a handle turning on pivots; **-plough,** a plough without wheels; **-span** *U.S.* = *s.-bridge*; **-wheel,** the escape-wheel of a clock, which drives the pendulum; also, the balance-wheel of a watch.

Swinge (swindʒ), *sb. Obs.* exc. *dial.* 1531. [Related to SWINGE *v.*[1]] †**1.** Sway, power, rule, authority, influence –1636. †**2.** = SWING *sb.*[1] I. 5. –1687. †**3.** Impetus, impulse, driving power (of passion, will, etc.); inclination; drift, tendency –1804. †**4.** Impetus (of motion); impetuous or forcible sweeping or whirling movement –1696. **5.** A leash for hounds 1661.

Swinge (swindʒ), *v.*[1] 1553. [Later form of ME. *swenge* smite, dash, OE. *swenġan* shake, shatter :- **swangwjan*, as in Goth. *afswaggwidai* (rendering ἐξαπορηθῆναι be in doubt).] **1.** *trans.* To beat, flog, whip, thrash. *arch.* or *dial.* †**b.** *fig.* To chastise, castigate; to pay out, serve out –1711. †**2.** To brandish, flourish; to lash (the tail, or something with the tail) –1629.

1. Saint George that swindg'd the Dragon SHAKS. I would so s. and leather my lambkin 1764. **b.** One Boyer, a French dog, has abused me..the Secretary promises me to s. him SWIFT. **2.** Th' old Dragon under ground..Swindges the scaly Horrour of his foulded tail MILT.

Comb.: †**s.-buckler** = SWASHBUCKLER.

Swinge (swindʒ), *v.*[2] Now *dial.* and *U.S.* 1590. [perh. alteration of SINGE, perh. infl. by SWEAL.] *trans.* To singe, scorch.

Swing(e)ing (swi·ndʒiŋ), *ppl. a.* (*adv.*) 1590. [f. SWINGE *v.*[1] + -ING[2].] **1.** That swinges; scourging, flogging (*rare*) 1614. **2.** Very forcible, large, or great; huge, immense. Now only *colloq.* or *slang*; mostly *arch.* or *dial.* 1590. **b.** as *adv.* Hugely, immensely 1690.

2. The jury gave swinging damages 1904. **Swi·ng(e)ingly** *adv.* (*colloq.* or *slang*).

Swinger[1] (swi·ndʒəɹ). 1583. [f. SWINGE *v.*[1] + -ER[1].] †**1.** One who acts vigorously or forcibly; a powerful fellow –1684. **2.** Something forcible or effective; *esp.* something very big, a 'whopper'. *colloq.* or *slang*; now *rare* or *local.* 1599. †**b.** *spec.* A great or bold lie –1781. **c.** A forcible blow or stroke 1836.

Swinger[2] (swi·ŋəɹ). 1543. [f. SWING *v.* + -ER[1] 2.] One who or that which swings.

Swi·nging (-ŋ-), *ppl. a.* 1560. [f. SWING *v.* + -ING[2].] That swings.

Comb. **s.-boom** *Naut.*, a boom swung or suspended over the ship's side, used to stretch the foot of a lower studding-sail, and (when at anchor) for a boat to ride by; **-bridge** = *swing-bridge*; **-tree** *dial.* = SWINGLE-TREE. Hence **Swi·ngingly** *adv.*

Swingle (swi·ŋg'l), *sb.* ME. [– MDu. *swinghel*, corresp. formally to OE. *swingel*, *swingle* stroke with a rod; see SWING *v.*, -LE 1.] **1.** A wooden instrument resembling a sword, used for beating and scraping flax or hemp so as to cleanse it of woody or coarse particles; also called *s.-hand*, *-staff*, or *-wand*, *swingling-bat*, *-knife*, or *-staff*. **2.** The striking part or swipple of a flail (*local*). late ME. **b.** A weapon resembling a flail; a kind of cudgel 1818.

Swi·ngle, *v.*[1] ME. [– MDu. *swinghelen*, f. *swinghel* SWINGLE *sb.*] *trans.* To beat and scrape (flax or hemp) with a swingle, in order to cleanse it of the coarser particles; to scutch.

Swi·ngle, *v.*[2] 1450. [frequent. of SWING *v.*; see -LE 3.] †**1.** *trans.* To swing or flourish about. **2.** *intr.* To swing; to hang, be suspended. *dial.* 1755.

Swingle- in comb.: **s.-bar** = SWINGLE-TREE 2; **-hand, -staff** = SWINGLE *sb.* 1; **-tail,** a species of shark = THRASHER[1] 2; **-wand** = SWINGLE *sb.* 1.

Swingletree (swi·ŋg'ltrī). 1462. [f. SWINGLE *sb.* + TREE *sb.*] **1.** A board used in dressing flax or hemp. *Obs.* or *dial.* **2.** In a plough, carriage, etc., a cross-bar, pivoted at the middle, to which the traces are fastened, giving freedom of movement to the shoulders of the horse or other draught animal 1483.

Swingling (swi·ŋgliŋ), *vbl. sb.* 1462. [f. SWINGLE *v.*[1] + -ING[1].] The process of dressing flax or hemp with a swingle; scutching.

attrib.: **s.-bat, -knife, -staff** = SWINGLE *sb.* 1; **-tow,** the coarse part of flax, separated by swingling.

Swing-swang (swi·ŋswæŋ). 1683. [Reduplicated f. SWING *v.* with change of vowel.] A swinging to and fro; a reciprocating movement; *occas.* see-saw.

Swing-tree (swi·ŋtrī). late ME. = SWINGLETREE 2.

Swinish (swəi·niʃ), *a.* ME. [f. SWINE *sb.* + -ISH[1].] **1.** Having the character or disposition of a swine; hoggish, piggish; sensual, gluttonous; coarse, gross, or degraded in nature. **b.** Of actions, etc.: Characteristic of or befitting a swine; coarse, beastly. late ME. **2.** Pertaining to or fit for swine 1592. **3.** Having the nature of a swine; that is a swine; consisting of swine 1612. **b.** Resembling a swine or that of a swine, in aspect or other physical quality 1805.

1. Drunkards, s. Epicures, heretiques 1606. **b.** In S. sleepe SHAKS. **3. b.** The s. outline of the porpoise 1889. Hence **Swi·nish-ly** *adv.*, **-ness.**

Swink (swiŋk), *sb. arch.* [OE. *swinc*, f. *swincan* SWINK *v.*] †**1.** Trouble, affliction (*rare*) –late ME. **2.** Labour, toil ME.

Swink (swiŋk), *v. arch.* and *dial.* [OE. *swincan*,] parallel formation to *swingan* SWING *v.*] **1.** *intr.* To labour, toil; to exert oneself, take trouble. †**2.** *trans.* and *intr.* To drink deeply, tipple –1590.

1. For they doo swinke and sweate to feed the other SPENSER. Hence **Swi·nker,** *arch.* one who swinks.

Swinked, swinkt (swiŋkt, *also* swi·ŋkėd), *ppl. a. arch.* (after Milton). 1634. [f. prec. + -ED[1].] Wearied with toil; overworked.

What time..the swink't hedger at his Supper sate MILT.

Swipe (swəip), *sb.*[1] 1600. [app. local var. of *swape* sb. or SWEEP *sb.*] A contrivance of the form of a lever for raising a weight, *esp.* for raising water.

Swipe (swəip), *sb.*[2] 1807. [f. next.] A heavy blow; *spec.* a driving stroke made with the full swing of the arms, in cricket or golf; *transf.* one who makes such a stroke. *colloq.* **b.** (*a*) = SWATH 3. 1869. (*b*) A streak or stripe produced as if by swiping 1890.

With the cricketers he was accounted a hard *s.*, an active *field*, and a stout bowler 1825.

Swipe (swəip), *v.* 1825. [perh. local var. of SWEEP *v.*] **1.** *trans.* and *intr.* To drink hastily and copiously; to drink at one gulp 1829. **2.** *intr.* To strike *at* with the full swing of the arms; chiefly in cricket 1825. **b.** *trans.* To deal a swinging blow or hit at (esp. in cricket) 1881. **3.** *intr.* and *trans.* = SWEEP *v.* II. 4. 1881. **4.** *trans.* To steal, 'appropriate'; to loot. *U.S.* 1890.

2. Wilson was now as bold as a lion, swiping at every ball 1869. Hence **Swi·per.**

Swipes (swəips). *slang* or *colloq.* 1796. [perh. f. prec. 1.] Poor weak beer; small beer; hence, beer in general.

Swipple (swi·p'l). 1450. [prob. orig. f. *swēp-* SWEEP *v.* or †*swip* vb. strike, smite + -ELS.] The part of a flail that strikes the grain in thrashing.

Swirl (swəɹl), *sb.* late ME. [orig. Sc., perh. of LDu. origin (cf. Du. *zwirrelen* whirl) and frequent. formation (cf. -LE 3) on the imit. base seen in MLG. *swirren*, G. *schwirren*, Da. *svirre* whirl.] **1.** An eddy, a whirlpool; an eddying or whirling body of water, in later use also of cloud, dust, etc. **2.** A whirling or eddying motion; a whirl, gyration 1818. **3.** A twist or convolution; a curl of hair; a knot in the grain of wood 1786. **b.** A tress of hair or strip of material round the head or hat 1909.

1. Seen though clefts in grey swirls of rain-cloud RUSKIN.

Swirl (swəɹl), *v.* 1513. [orig. Sc.; see prec.] **1.** *trans.* To give a whirling or eddying motion to; to bring into some position by a whirling motion; to whirl, brandish. **b.** To give a twisted or convolute form to; also, to wrap round *with* something 1902. **2.** *intr.* **a.** Of water or of objects borne on water: To move in or upon eddies or little whirlpools 1755. **b.** Of other objects: To move rapidly in eddies or in a whirling or circular course 1858. **3.** Of the head, etc.: To swim; to be giddy 1818.

1. Some withered leaves were swirled round and round, as if by the wind 1818. **2. b.** Starlings swirling from the hedge M. ARNOLD.

Swish (swiʃ), *int.* or *adv.* and *sb.*[1] 1820. [imit.] **A.** *int.* or *adv.* Expressive of the sound described in B. 1; with a swish 1837. S. went the whip 1890.

B. 1. A hissing sound like that produced by a switch or similar slender object moved rapidly through the air or an object moving swiftly in contact with water; movement accompanied by such sound 1820. **2.** A dash of water upon a surface 1851. **3.** A cane or birch for flogging; also, a stroke with this 1860.

1. The s. of the angler's rod 1886.

C. *adj.* (*colloq.*) Smart, 'swell' 1879.

Swish (swiʃ), *sb.*[2] 1863. [perh. native name.] A native building mortar of W. Africa.

Swish (swiʃ), *v.* 1756. [imit.] **1.** *intr.* To move with a swish; to make the sound expressed by 'swish'. **2.** *trans.* To cause to move with a swish; *esp.* to whisk (the tail) about 1799. **b.** *intr.* (const. *with*) 1854. **c.** *trans.* To move or remove with (or as with) a swishing movement 1894. **3.** *intr.* To jump a high hedge, brushing through the twigs at the top and making them bend 1825. **4.** *trans.* To flog, esp. at school 1856.

1. The wheels swished through the pools 1877. **2.** And backward and forward he swish'd his long tail As a Gentleman swishes his cane COLERIDGE. **4.** As he wouldn't tell he must be swished 1872.

Swish-, the vb.-stem used attrib. or advb.: **s.-cane,** a light slender cane such as can be swished; **-tail,** †(*a*) *slang*, a pheasant; (*b*) a long flowing tail which can be swished about.

Swiss (swis), *sb.* and *a.* 1515. [– Fr. *Suisse* – MHG. *Swīz* (G. *Schweiz*).] **A.** *sb.* **1.** (Pl. *the Swiss*; †formerly *the Swisses.*) A native or an inhabitant of Switzerland. **2.** The Swiss dialect of German or other language spoken by the Swiss (*rare*) 1846. **B.** *adj.* **1.** Of, belonging to, or characteristic of the Swiss or Switzerland; native to, or coming from, Switzerland 1530. **2.** In names of things, animals, etc. actually or reputedly coming from Switzerland; e.g. *S. cheese, lace, milk*, etc. 1700.

2. S. guards, mercenary soldiers from Switzerland used as a special body-guard by former sovereigns of France, and other monarchs; still employed at the Vatican. **S. roll,** a 'sweet' consisting of sponge cake rolled up with a layer of jam. **S. stone-pine:** see STONE-PINE. **S. sword,** a basket-hilted sword used in the 16th c. by S. foot-soldiers.

†**Swi·sser.** 1530. [– MDu. *Switser* or

MHG. *S(ch)wycer*, *S(ch)witzer* (G. *Schweizer*), f. *Swiz* Switzerland.] A Swiss –1734.

Switch (switʃ), *sb.* 1592. [In early use also *swits*, *switz*; prob. – LG. word repr. by Hanoverian dial. *swutsche*, var. of LG. *swukse* long thin stick (cf. *zwuksen* bend up and down, make a swishing noise). In sense 5 f. SWITCH *v.*] **1.** A slender tapering riding whip. **2.** A thin flexible shoot cut from a tree 1610. **3.** Name for various mechanical devices for altering the direction of something, making a connection or disconnection, or other purposes. **a.** On a railway: A movable rail or pair of rails pivoted at one end, forming part of the track at a junction with a branch line, etc., and used to deflect or shunt a train, car, etc. from one line to another 1797. **b.** *Electr.* A lever, plug, or other device for making or breaking contact, or altering the connections of a circuit. Also *loosely* = SWITCHBOARD. 1866. **4.** A long bunch or coil of hair, esp. of false hair worn by women to supplement the natural growth of hair 1878. **5.** An act of switching; a blow with a switch 1809.

1. To cut off the heads of some nettles..with his s. JANE AUSTEN. Phr. *S. and spurs* = at full speed, in hot haste. **5. b.** *Bridge.* A change of call from one suit to another 1921.

Comb.: **s.-bar,** a bar connected with a s. (on a railway or electrical apparatus); **-grass,** the couch-grass; **-horn,** a stag's horn without branches; also, a stag having such horns; **-man,** a man who works a s. or set of switches on a railway; **-rail** = sense 3a; **-room,** a room containing the switches of an electrical system; **-tail** = SWISH-*tail*.

Switch, *v.* 1611. [f. prec.] **1.** *trans.* To strike, hit, beat, flog, or whip with or as with a switch. **b.** *intr.* or *absol.* To strike, deal a blow or blows, with or as with a switch 1612. **2.** *trans.* To drive with or as with a switch 1616. **3.** To flourish like a switch, to whisk, lash; to move (something) with a sudden jerk 1842. **4.** To cut off the switches or projecting twigs from; to trim (a tree, hedge, etc.) 1811. **5.** To turn (a railway train, car, etc.) on to another line by means of a switch; to shunt; also *intr.* for *pass.* **b.** *intr.* Of a railway line: To branch or turn *off* at a switch. *U.S.* 1875. **6.** *fig.* To turn *off*, divert. Chiefly *U.S.* 1860. **7.** *trans.* In electrical apparatus: To direct (a current) by means of a switch; to put *on* or *off*; to turn (an electric light) *on* or *off* 1881.

3. He..stood switching his riding-whip 1856. **6.** The Colonel..switched the conversation off to the chances of the morrow 1897. **b.** *intr. Bridge.* To change to another suit in bidding 1921.

Switchback (swi·tʃbæk), *a.* and *sb.* 1887. [f. SWITCH *v.* 5 + BACK *adv.*] **A.** *adj.* **a.** Applied to a form of railway used on steep slopes, consisting of a zigzag series of lines connected by switches, at each of which the train or car is 'switched back' or reversed in direction. **b.** Applied to a railway consisting of steep alternate ascents and descents, on which the train or car runs partly or wholly by the force of gravity, the momentum of each descent carrying it up the succeeding ascent; *esp.* to such a railway constructed for amusement at a pleasure-resort, fair, etc. Hence *transf.* of a road having steep alternate ascents and descents. 1888. **B.** *sb.* A switchback railway (in either sense); also *transf.* and *fig.* 1887.

Switchboard (swi·tʃbōᵊɹd). 1884. [f. SWITCH *sb.* 3b + BOARD *sb.*] A board or frame bearing a set of switches for connecting and disconnecting the various circuits of an electrical system, as of a telegraph, telephone, etc.

Switchel (swi·tʃĕl). *U.S.* 1800. [Of unkn. origin; cf. SWIZZLE *sb.*] A drink made of molasses and water, sometimes with vinegar, ginger, or rum added.

Switching (swi·tʃiŋ), *vbl. sb.* 1625. [f. SWITCH *v.* + -ING¹.] The action of SWITCH *v.*

Comb.: **s.-angle** *Gunnery*, the angle between the lines of fire of the directing gun when the latter is brought to bear on the left of the new target; **-engine, -locomotive,** one used in or for shunting on a railway.

Switchy (swi·tʃi), *a. rare.* 1812. [f. SWITCH *sb.* + -Y¹.] Of the nature of or resembling a switch or slender rod; moving or bending like a switch.

Switzer (swi·tsəɹ). *arch.* 1577. [– MHG. *Switzer*, etc.; see SWISSER.] **1.** = SWISS *sb.* 1. **2.** *pl.* = *Swiss guards* (SWISS *a.* 2); rarely *sing.* 1591. **3.** *attrib.* or *adj.* = SWISS *a.* 1598.

Swive (swəiv), *v. Obs.* or *arch.* late ME. [app. repr., with a specialized meaning, OE. *swīfan* move in a course, sweep; see SWIFT *a.*] **1.** *trans.* To have sexual connection with (a female). **2.** *intr.* To copulate 1440.

Swivel (swi·v'l), *sb.* ME. [f. wk. grade of OE. *swīfan* (see prec., SWIFT *a.*) + *-el* (-LE).] **1.** A simple fastening or coupling device made so that the object fastened to it can turn freely upon it, or so that each half of the swivel itself can turn independently; *e.g.* a ring or staple turning on a pin or the like. **b.** *spec.* A pivoted rest for a gun, *esp.* on the gunwale of a boat, enabling it to turn horizontally in any required direction 1697. **2.** Short for *s.-gun* 1748. **3.** A kind of small shuttle used in ribbon-weaving, etc. 1894.

Comb.: **s.-bridge,** a swing-bridge; **-chair,** a chair the seat of which turns horizontally on a pivot; **s. eye** *colloq.* or *slang*, a squinting eye; an eye that rolls in its socket; hence **s.-eyed** *a.*, squint-eyed; **-gun,** a gun or cannon, usu. a small one, mounted on a s., so as to turn horizontally in any required direction; **-hook,** a hook fastened to something, *e.g.* a pulley-block, by means of a s.; **-shuttle** = sense 3.

Swi·vel, *v.* 1794. [f. prec.] **1.** *trans.* To turn (something) on or as on a swivel. **2.** *intr.* To turn or rotate as, or as on, a swivel 1846. **3.** *trans.* To furnish with a swivel; to fasten *to* something by means of a swivel 1870.

Swizzle (swi·z'l), *sb. slang* or *colloq.* 1813. [Of unkn. origin; cf. SWITCHEL.] A name for various compounded intoxicating drinks; occas. vaguely used for intoxicating drink in general.

Comb.: **s.-stick,** a stick used for stirring drink into a froth.

Swi·zzle, *v. slang* or *colloq.* and *dial.* 1847. [f. prec.] **1.** *intr.* To drink to excess, tipple. **2.** *trans.* To stir with a swizzle-stick 1859.

Swollen (swōᵘ·l'n), *ppl. a.* ME. [str. pa. pple. of SWELL *v.*] **1.** Increased in bulk, as by internal pressure; distended; *esp.* morbidly enlarged, affected with tumour; also, of a distended form, bulging, protuberant. **b.** Increased in amount or degree 1631. **2.** *fig.* **a.** Said of a feeling or mental state such as causes a sense of distension or expansion, or of a person affected with such a feeling, etc.; *esp.* inflated with pride, puffed up. late ME. **b.** Of language: Turgid, inflated 1605.

1. Her s. eyes were much disfigured SPENSER. **b.** The s. shelves of our libraries 1911. **2. a.** His s. heart almost bursting DICKENS. **b.** Swoln panegyrics COLERIDGE.

Swoon (swūn), *sb.* ME. [orig. in phr. *i(n) swowne*, alt. of *aswowne* (cf. ASWOON), repr. OE. *āswogen*, pa. pple. of *āswogan*. Otherwise f. SWOON *v.*] **1.** The action of swooning or the condition of one who has swooned; syncope. **b.** A fainting fit. late ME. †**2.** A (deep or sound) sleep. SPENSER.

Swoon (swūn), *v.* [perh. back-formation from ME. gerund *swoȝning*, etc.; see SWOONING *vbl. sb.*] **1.** *intr.* To fall into a fainting fit; to faint. **b.** *fig.* said of natural phenomena 1818. **2.** *pass.* To fall into a swoon; chiefly *pa. pple.* or *ppl. a.*: In a swoon 1450.

1. Many will s. when they do look on bloud SHAKS. **b.** All round the coast the languid air did s. TENNYSON. **2.** She lies swooned on a paillasse CARLYLE.

Swooning (swū·niŋ), *vbl. sb.* [ME. *swoȝning*, *swouning*, *swoning*, f. *iswoȝen*, *iswowen*, OE. *ġeswogen* overcome, dead, pa. pple. of **swogan*, as in *ā-*, *oferswogan* suffocate, choke (with weeds), of unkn. origin.] **1.** Fainting, syncope. **2.** A fainting-fit ME.

Swooning (swū·niŋ), *ppl. a.* 1646. [f. SWOON *v.* + -ING².] That swoons or faints; characterized by swooning. Hence **-ly** *adv.*

Swoop (swūp), *sb.* 1544. [f. next.] †**1.** A blow, stroke –1711. **2.** The act of swooping down; *esp.* the sudden pouncing of a bird of prey from a height upon its quarry 1605. **b.** A sudden descent, as by a body of troops, esp. *upon* something which it is intended to seize 1824.

2. Swift as the s. of the eagle 1847. Phr. *At one (fell, etc.) s.*, at one sudden descent, as of a bird of prey; hence, at a single blow or stroke. **b.** Influenza came down upon me with a s. HUXLEY.

Swoop (swūp), *v.* 1566. [perh. dial. development of ME. *swōpe*, OE. *swāpan* SWEEP *v.*] †**1.** *intr.* To move or walk in a stately manner as with trailing garments; to sweep along –1622. †**2.** *trans.* To sweep *up*, *away*, *off*, etc. –1888. †**3.** To pounce upon, as a bird of prey; to seize, catch up with a sweeping movement –1822. **4.** *intr.* To make a rapid sweeping descent through the air *upon* its prey, as a bird 1837. **5.** To come down *upon* suddenly with a sweeping movement, esp. with the intention of seizing, as a body of troops 1797.

2. A rich patrimonie..he swoopt away HOLLAND. **3.** Till now at last you came to s. it all DRYDEN. **4.** Sea-gulls were swooping down and around the tall masts 1873. **5.** At other times a breeze would s. down upon us TYNDALL.

†**Swoopstake,** *sb.* and *adv.* 1600. [Altered f. SWEEPSTAKE after SWOOP *v.*] **A.** *sb.* = SWEEPSTAKE 2. **B.** *adv.* By sweeping all the stakes at once; hence, indiscriminately.

Sword (sǭɹd, sōᵊɹd), *sb.* [OE. *sweord*, *sword*, *swyrd* = OFris., OS. *swerd*, OHG. *swert* (G. *schwert*), ON. *sverð* :– Gmc. **swerðam*, of doubtful origin. For the loss of *w* cf. TWO.] **1.** A weapon adapted for cutting and thrusting, consisting of a handle or *hilt* with a cross-guard, and a straight or curved blade with either one or two sharp edges (or sometimes with blunt edges) and a sharp point. **b.** As used on ceremonial occasions as a symbol of honour or authority (*s. of honour*, *of state*, etc.) late ME. **2.** *fig.* Something that wounds or kills, a cause of death or destruction, a destroying agency; also, something figured as a weapon of attack in spiritual warfare OE. **3.** *transf.* The use of the sword in warfare, massacre, etc.; hence, slaughter; warfare; military force or power; also, the military profession or class, the army OE. **4.** As the instrument or symbol of penal justice; hence, the authority of a ruler or magistrate to punish offenders; more generally, power of government, executive power, authority, jurisdiction; also, the office of an executive governor or magistrate. late ME. **5.** A material object resembling a sword. **a.** One of various mechanical devices in the form of a flat wooden blade, bar, or rod 1530. **b.** The sharp projecting jaw-bone of the sword-fish 1641. **c.** A sword-like ray or flash of light 1866.

1. Put vp thy swearde into hys sheath *Bible* (Great) *Matt.* 26:52. Phr. *S.-in-hand*, armed with a s.; *fig.* militant. **2.** This Auarice..hath bin The S. of our slaine Kings SHAKS. **3.** It hath bin oft anough told him, that he hath no more autority over the s. then over the law MILT. Phr. *To put to the s.*, to kill or slaughter with the s. *The power of the s.* **4.** This Power Coercive, or (as men use to call it) the S. of Justice HOBBES. **5. a.** Swords are these parts of the loom that the lay is fixed to 1863.

attrib. and *Comb.*, as *s.-exercise*, *-hilt*, *-thrust*; **s.-and-buckler** *a.*, armed with or using a s. and buckler; pertaining to or performed with s. and buckler; †*fig.* bragging, blustering; **s.-arm,** the arm with which the s. is wielded, the right arm; also *rhet.* = military power or action; **-bayonet,** a form of bayonet which may be used as a s.; **-belt,** a belt by which the s. in its scabbard is suspended; **-bill,** a S. Amer. humming-bird, *Docimastes ensiferus*, with a very long bill; **-blade,** the blade of a s.; **-cane,** a hollow cane or walking-stick containing a steel blade, which may be drawn or shot out and used as a s.; **-dance,** a dance in which the performers go through some evolutions with swords, or in which a person dances among naked swords laid on the ground; so **-dancer, -dancing; -hand,** the hand with which the s. is wielded, the right hand; **-knot,** a ribbon or tassel tied to the hilt of a s.; **-law,** government by the power of the s. or by military force, martial law; **-leaved** *a.*, having s.-shaped or ensiform leaves; **-mat** *Naut.*, a piece of matting used to protect parts of the rigging, etc., so called from the wooden 'sword' with which the fabric is beaten close in weaving; so **-matting; -side,** the male line in descent; **-stick** = *s.-cane*; **-swallower,** one who entertains for money by swallowing or pretending to swallow swords; **-tail,** an animal of the group *Xiphosura*, comprising only the genus *Limulus*, a king-crab; **-taker,** one who 'takes the s.' (Matt. 26:52) without authority or right, a lawless killer; **-whale,** the grampus, also called SWORD-

FISH. **b.** In names of plants having sword-shaped leaves or other parts, as **s.-flag,** the yellow water-flag, *Iris pseudacorus*; **-flax,** a name for the New Zealand flax, *Phormium tenax*; **-lily,** the genus *Gladiolus*; **-rush, -sedge,** an Australian sedge, *Lepidosperma gladiatum*. Hence **Sword** *v.* (*rare*) *trans.* to arm or equip with a s.; to strike or kill with a s.; also *absol.* or *intr.*

Swo·rd-bea:rer. late ME. [Cf. ON. *sverð-berari*.] A person who bears a sword. **a.** *spec.* A municipal official who carries a sword of state before a magistrate on ceremonial occasions. **b.** A ruler or magistrate having authority to punish offenders (with allusion to Rom. 13:4) 1660. **c.** *gen.* One who carries or wears a sword 1530. **d.** One of an order of knights in Poland founded in 1204. 1656.

Sworded (sǭ·ɹdėd, sōə·ɹdėd), *a.* OE. [f. SWORD *sb.* + -ED².] Equipped or armed with a sword. **b.** *trans.* Having some part resembling a sword 1681.

Sworder (sǭ·ɹdəɹ, sōə·ɹdəɹ). 1593. [f. SWORD *sb.* + -ER¹, after L. *gladiator*.] **1.** One who kills another with a sword, an assassin, cut-throat; one who habitually fights with a sword; a gladiator. **2.** One skilled in the use of the sword; a swordsman 1814.

Swo·rdfish. late ME. [f. SWORD *sb.* + FISH *sb.*¹] **1.** A large fish of the Atlantic, Mediterranean, and Pacific, *Xiphias gladius*, having the upper jaw prolonged into a sword-like weapon; the flesh is used for food. Also extended to other species of the genus *Xiphias* and related genera. **2.** The southern constellation Dorado or Xiphias 1771.

Swo·rd-grass. 1598. A name for several plants with sword-shaped leaves, as the sword-lily (*Gladiolus*), *Arenaria* (*Spergularia*) *segetalis*, *Melilotus segetalis* or *sulcata*, and various grasses or sedges, as the reed canary-grass (*Phalaris arundinacea*), *Arundo conspicua* of New Zealand, and *Cladium psittacorum* of Australia.

Swo·rding, *ppl. a. Obs.* or *arch.* 1611. [app. f. SWORD *sb.* + -ING²; cf. SWORDER.] Martial, warlike.

Swordless (sǭ·ɹdlės, sōə·ɹd-), *a.* 1440. [f. SWORD *sb.* + -LESS.] Destitute of a sword; not having, carrying, or using a sword.

Swo·rdman. Now *rare* or *Obs. Pl.* **-men.** late ME. [f. SWORD *sb.* + MAN *sb.*] **1.** = SWORDSMAN 1. **b.** A soldier who fights with a sword; one of a body of troops armed with swords; hence, an armed follower. late ME. **2.** A man 'of the sword'; a warrior, military man, fighter, soldier 1601.

2. *All's Well* II. i. 62.

Swo·rd-play. [OE. *sweordpleġa*, f. SWORD *sb.* + PLAY *sb.*] †**a.** Fight, battle. OE. only. **b.** The action of plying or wielding a sword briskly, as in fencing; the art or practice of fencing 1647. **c.** *fig.* Spirited or skilful controversy or debate 1847. So **Swo·rd-play:er,** (*rare* or *Obs.*) one skilled in s.; chiefly, a gladiator; also, a fencer. late ME.

Swordsman (sǭ·ɹdz-, sōə·ɹdzmǣn). *Pl.* **-men.** 1680. [f. gen. of SWORD *sb.* + MAN *sb.*] **1.** A man who uses, or is skilled in the use of, a sword; *spec.* one skilled in fencing. **b.** = SWORDMAN 1 b. 1865. **2.** = SWORDMAN 2. 1701. Hence **Swo·rdsmanship,** the quality or art of a s.

Swore, pa. t. and obs. pa. pple. of SWEAR *v.*

Sworn (swǭɹn), *ppl. a.* ME. [pa. pple. of SWEAR *v.*] **1.** That has taken or is bound by an oath. **b.** Thoroughly devoted or addicted to some course of action; resolute, out-and-out 1607. **2.** Appointed or admitted with a formal or prescribed oath to some office or function. late ME. **3.** Affirmed or promised by an oath; to which one is sworn 1818.

1. *S. brother*, either of two companions in arms who took an oath according to the rules of chivalry to share each other's good and bad fortunes; hence, a close or intimate friend or companion; so *s. friend*. *S. enemy, foe*, one who has vowed perpetual enmity against another; hence, a determined or irreconcilable enemy. **2.** *S. man* (formerly as one word), a man bound by oath to the performance of a duty or office; hence, a man bound to strict service, a 'vassal'.

Swot, swat (swǫt), *sb. slang.* 1850. [dial. var. of SWEAT *sb.*] **1.** Work or study at school or college; in early use *spec.* mathematics. Hence *gen.* labour, toil. **2.** One who studies hard 1850. Hence **Swot, swat** *v.* (*slang*) *intr.* to work hard at one's studies; *trans.* to 'get *up*', 'mug *up*' (a subject). **Swo·tter.**

Swound (swaund), *sb.* Now *arch.* and *dial.* 1440. [Later form of *swoune* SWOON, with excrescent *d*.] A fainting-fit. So **Swound** *v. intr.* to swoon, faint.

†**Swounds,** *int.* 1589. Euphemistic abbrev. of *God's wounds* used in oaths and asseverations –1620.

-sy, hypocoristic dim. ending used in (i) proper names, as *Betsy, Topsy*, also in the form *-cy*, as *Nancy*; (ii) common nouns, as *babsy, ducksy, mopsy, tootsy*; (iii) adjectives, as *flimsy, pudsy, tipsy, tricksy*.

‖**Syagush** (syā·gūʃ). 1727. [Urdu, Pers. *siyāh gūsh* a type of lynx; lit. 'black ear'.] The caracal, a feline animal.

Sybarite (si·bărəit), *sb.* and *a.* 1598. [– L. *Sybarita* – Gr. Συβαρίτης, f. Σύβαρις Sybaris; -ITE¹ 1. Cf. Fr. *sybarite* (XVI).] **A.** *sb.* **1.** A native or citizen of Sybaris, an ancient Greek city of southern Italy, noted for its effeminacy and luxury. **2.** A person devoted to luxury or pleasure, an effeminate voluptuary or sensualist. (Now usu. spelt with small initial.) 1623.

2. The Lords of Lacedæmon were true soldiers, But ours are Sybarites BYRON. The very room for an artist and a s. 1863.

B. *adj.* = SYBARITIC *a.* 1599. Hence **Sy·baritism,** sybaritic habits or practices, effeminate voluptuousness.

Sybaritic (sibări·tik), *a.* 1619. [– L. *Sybariticus* – Gr. Συβαριτικός; see prec., -IC.] **1.** Of or pertaining to Sybaris or its inhabitants 1786. **2.** Effeminately luxurious 1619.

2. S. dinners WARBURTON. An atmosphere of s. enjoyment 1876. So **Sybari·tical** *a.* (now *rare*) 1617, **-ly** *adv.*

Sycamine (si·kămin, -əin). *arch.* 1526. [– L. *sycaminus* – Gr. συκάμινον mulberry, f. Heb. *šiḳmāh* sycamore, with assim. to σῦκον fig.] The common black mulberry, *Morus nigra*.

Sycamore, sycomore (si·kămoəɹ, si·kŏmoəɹ). ME. [– OFr. *sic(h)amor* (mod. *sycomore*) = L. *sycomorus* – Gr. συκόμορος, f. σῦκον fig. + μόρον mulberry.] **1.** A species of fig-tree, *Ficus sycomorus*, common in Egypt, Syria, and other countries, and having leaves somewhat resembling those of the mulberry. **2.** A large species of maple, *Acer pseudoplatanus*, introduced into Britain from the Continent, and grown as a shady ornamental tree and for its wood 1588. **3.** In N. America, a plane or tree of the genus *Platanus*, esp. the buttonwood, *P. occidentalis* 1814. **4.** The wood or timber of the sycamore. late ME. **5.** Short for *s. moth* 1843.

Comb.: **s.-fig,** the fig-tree, *Ficus sycomorus*, or its fruit; **s. maple** = sense 2; **s.-moth,** a noctuid moth, *Acronycta* (*Apatela*) *aceris*, the larva of which feeds on the s. (sense 2); **-tree** = sense 1, 2, 3.

Syce (səis). *India.* 1653. [– Hind. – Arab. *sā'is, sāyis*.] A groom; also, an attendant who follows on foot a mounted horseman or a carriage.

Sycee (səisī·). 1711. [Chinese *si* (pronounced in Canton *sai, sei*) *sz'* fine silk; 'so called because, if pure, it may be drawn out into fine threads.'] Fine uncoined silver in the form of lumps of various sizes, usu. having a banker's or assayer's seal stamped on them, used by the Chinese as a medium of exchange. Also *s. silver*.

Sychnocarpous (siknokā·ɹpəs), *a.* 1832. [f. Gr. συχνός many + καρπός fruit + -OUS.] *Bot.* Bearing fruit many times, as a perennial plant; polycarpous.

Sycoceric (sikose·rik, -sīə·rik), *a.* 1860. [f. Gr. σῦκον fig + κηρός wax + -IC.] *Chem.* Of, pertaining to, or derived from the waxy resin of an Australian species of fig, *Ficus rubiginosa*; as in *s. acid*, a crystalline compound, $C_{18}H_{28}O_2$. So **Sycoce·ryl,** the hypothetical radical of the s. compounds.

‖**Syconium** (səikōu·niŏm). 1856. [mod.L., f. Gr. σῦκον fig; see -IUM.] *Bot.* A multiple fruit developed from numerous flowers imbedded in a fleshy receptacle, as in the fig. So ‖**Syco·nus,** in same sense 1832.

Sycophancy (si·kŏfănsi). 1622. [– L. *sycophantia* – Gr. συκοφαντία, f. συκοφάντης SYCOPHANT.] The practice or quality of a sycophant. **1.** The trade or occupation of an informer; calumnious accusation, tale-bearing. Now only in *Gr. Hist.* **2.** Mean or servile flattery; the character of a mean or servile flatterer 1657.

2. The people, like the despot, is pursued with adulation and s. MILL.

Sycophant (si·kŏfănt), *sb.* (*a.*) 1548. [– Fr. *sycophante* or L. *sycophanta* – Gr. συκοφάντης, f. σῦκον fig + *φαν-, base of φαίνειν show. The origin of the word has not been satisfactorily accounted for.] **1.** *Gr. Hist.* One of a class of informers in ancient Athens 1579. †**2.** *transf.* and *fig.* An informer, tale-bearer; a calumniator, slanderer –1697. **3.** A mean, servile, cringing, or abject flatterer; a parasite, toady 1575. †**4.** Vaguely used for: Impostor, deceiver –1728.

3. The young monarch was accompanied by a swarm of courtly sycophants 1843.

B. *attrib.* or *adj.* Sycophantic 1692. Hence †**Sy·cophant** *v. trans.* to act the s. towards; *intr.* to play the s. **Sy·cophantism,** = SYCOPHANCY 2.

Sycophantic (sikŏfæ·ntik), *a.* 1676. [– Gr. συκοφαντικός, f. συκοφάντης; see prec., -IC.] **a.** Having the character of, or characteristic of, a sycophant; meanly flattering; basely obsequious. **b.** Calumnious, slanderous.

a. Upon sycophantic knees they bowed before the conqueror 1854. So †**Sycopha·ntical** *a.* 1566, **-ly** *adv.* 1643.

Sycophantish (si·kŏfæntiʃ), *a.* 1840. [f. SYCOPHANT *sb.* + -ISH¹.] Basely obsequious. Hence **Sy·cophantishly** *adv.*

Sy·cophantize, *v. rare.* 1605. [f. as prec. + -IZE.] *intr.* To deal in servile flattery.

‖**Sycosis** (səikōu·sis). 1580. [mod.L. – Gr. σύκωσις, f. σῦκον fig; see -OSIS.] *Path.* **1.** Applied to various kinds of ulcer or morbid growth on the skin, resembling a fig. **2.** An eruptive disease characterized by inflammation of the hair-follicles, esp. of the beard 1822.

Syenite (səi·ĕnəit). 1796. [– Fr. *syénite* – L. *Syenites* (*lapis*), (stone) of Syene, f. *Syene*, Gr. Συήνη, a town of upper Egypt, the modern Assouan; see -ITE¹ 2b.] *Min.* A crystalline rock allied to granite, mainly composed of hornblende and feldspar, with or without quartz. Hence **Syeni·tic** *a.* of, pertaining to, composed of, allied to, or having the character of s.

Sy·llab(e. *Obs.* exc. *dial.* 1440. [– OFr. *sillabe*; see SYLLABLE *sb.*] = SYLLABLE *sb.*

‖**Syllabarium** (silăbēə·riŏm). *Pl.* **-ia.** 1850. [mod.L.; see next.] = next.

Syllabary (si·lăbări). 1586. [– mod.L. *syllabarium*, f. L. *syllaba* + *-arium* -ARY¹, after *abecedarium* ABECEDARY *sb.*² Late and med.L. had *syllabarius* boy in a spelling class.] A collection, set, system, list, or table of syllables.

‖**Syllabatim** (silăbēi·tim), *adv. rare.* 1628. [L., f. *syllaba*, after *gradatim*.] By syllables; syllable by syllable.

Syllabation (silăbēi·ʃən). *rare.* 1856. [f. L. *syllaba* + -ATION.] = SYLLABIFICATION.

Syllabic (silæ·bik), *a.* and *sb.* 1728. [– Fr. *syllabique* or late and med.L. *syllabicus* – Gr. συλλαβικός, f. συλλαβή SYLLABLE; see -IC.] **A.** *adj.* **1.** Of, pertaining or relating to, a syllable or syllables 1755. **b.** Forming or constituting a syllable 1728. **c.** Denoting a syllable; consisting of signs denoting syllables 1865. **2. a.** Applied to singing, or a tune, in which each syllable is sung to one note (i.e. with no slurs or runs) 1789. **b.** Pronounced syllable by syllable 1890.

1. In English pronunciation s. quantity is.. imperfectly marked 1852. **b.** *S. augment*: see AUGMENT *sb.* **c.** A s. writing evidently of immense antiquity 1884. **2. b.** His English was careful, select, s. 1890.

B. *sb.* (ellipt. use of the adj.) **1.** A syllabic sign; a character denoting a syllable 1880. **2.** A syllabic sound; a vocal sound capable by itself of forming a syllable, or constituting the essential element of a syllable 1890. So **Sylla·bical** *a.* (now *rare* or *Obs.*) 1530, **-ly** *adv.* **Sylla·bicness,** the quality of being s.

Syllabication (silæbikēi·ʃən). 1631. [– med.L. *syllabicatio, -ōn-*, f. *syllabicat-*, pa.

ppl. stem of *syllabicare*, f. L. *syllaba* SYLLABLE; see -ION.] = next. **b.** The action of making syllabic; pronunciation as a distinct syllable 1857.

Syllabification (silæ:bifikēⁱ·ʃən). 1838. [f. L. *syllaba* SYLLABLE; see -FICATION.] Formation or construction of syllables; the action or method of dividing words into syllables. What he said was unintelligible; but..the s. was distinct POE.

Syllabism (si·lăbiz'm). 1883. [f. L. *syllaba* + -ISM. Cf. next.] **a.** The use of syllabic characters. **b.** Division into syllables.

Syllabize (si·lăbəiz), *v.* 1656. [– med.L. *syllabizare* – Gr. συλλαβίζειν, f. συλλαβή SYLLABLE *sb.*; see -IZE.] *trans.* To form or divide into syllables; to utter or articulate with distinct separation of syllables.

Syllable (si·lăb'l), *sb.* late ME. [– AFr. *sillable*, alt. of OFr. *sillabe* (mod. *syllabe*) – L. *syllaba* (Plautus) – Gr. συλλαβή, f. συλλαμβάνειν take, put, or bring together, f. σύν SYN- + λαμβάνειν take.] **1.** A vocal sound or set of sounds uttered with a single effort of articulation and forming a word or an element of a word; each of the elements of a spoken language comprising a sound of greater sonority (vowel or vowel-equivalent) with or without one or more sounds of less sonority (consonants or consonant-equivalents); also, a character or set of characters forming a corresponding element of written language. **b.** Used pregnantly of a word of one syllable, or in ref. to a part of a word, considered in relation to its significance. late ME. **2.** The least portion or detail of speech or writing (or of something expressed or expressible in speech or writing); the least mention, hint, or trace *of* something: esp. in neg. context. late ME.

1. Our English tong, hauing in vse chiefly, wordes of one s. ASCHAM. **b.** Those awful syllables, hell, death, and sin COWPER. **2.** To the last S. of Recorded time SHAKS. I know every s. of the matter GOLDSM.

Syllable (si·lăb'l), *v.* 1633. [f. prec.] *trans.* To utter or express in (or as in) syllables or articulate speech; to pronounce syllable by syllable; to utter articulately or distinctly; to articulate. **b.** To read (something) syllable by syllable; to read in detail or with close attention; to spell out (*rare*) 1728. **c.** To represent by syllables (*rare*) 1887.

Airy tongues, that s. mens names On Sands, and Shoars, and desert Wildernesses MILT.

Syllabus (si·lăbŏs). *Pl.* **syllabi** (si·lăbəi) or **syllabuses** (si·lăbŏsėz). 1656. [– mod.L. *syllabus*, originating in a misprint in early editions (1470) of *syllabos* for *sittybas*, in Cicero's Letters to Atticus (IV. iv), acc. pl. of *sittyba* = Gr. σιττύβα title-slip or label; *syllabos* was græcized by later editors as συλλάβους, whence a spurious σύλλαβος was deduced and accepted as a deriv. of συλλαμβάνειν put together (cf. SYLLABLE).] **1.** A concise statement or table of the heads of a discourse, the contents of a treatise, the subjects of a series of lectures, etc.; a compendium, abstract, summary, epitome. **2.** *R. C. Ch.* A summary statement of points decided and errors condemned by eccl. authority; *spec.* that annexed to the encyclical *Quanta cura* of Pope Pius IX, 8 Dec. 1864. 1876.

‖**Syllepsis** (sile·psis). *Pl.* **-es** (-īz). 1577. [Late L. – Gr. σύλληψις, f. σύν SYN- + λῆψις taking.] *Gram.* and *Rhet.* A figure by which a word or a particular form or inflexion of a word, is made to refer to two or more other words in the same sentence, while properly applying to or agreeing with only one of them (e.g. a masc. adj. qualifying two sbs., masc. and fem.; a sing. verb serving as predicate to two subjects, sing. and pl.), or applying to them in different senses (e.g. literal and metaphorical). Cf. ZEUGMA.

Sylleptic (sile·ptik), *a.* 1865. [– Gr. συλληπτικός, f. σύλληψις; see prec., -IC.] Pertaining to, of the nature of, or involving syllepsis. So **Sylle·ptical** *a.* 1846, **-ly** *adv.* 1802.

‖**Sylloge** (si·lŏdʒi). *rare.* 1686. [– Gr. συλλογή, f. συλλέγειν collect.] A collection; a summary.

Syllogism (si·lŏdʒiz'm). [Late ME. *silogisme*, occas. *silogime*, – OFr. *sil(l)ogisme*, earlier *sillogime* (mod. *syllogisme*) or L. *syllogismus* – Gr. συλλογισμός, f. συλλογίζεσθαι, intensive of λογίζεσθαι reckon, compute, conclude, f. λόγος discourse, consideration, account; see SYN-, LOGOS, -ISM.] **1.** *Logic.* An argument expressed or claimed to be expressible in the form of two propositions called the premisses, containing a common or middle term, with a third proposition called the conclusion, resulting necessarily from the other two. Example: *Omne animal est substantia, omnis homo est animal,* ergo *omnis homo est substantia.* **b.** *transf.* and *allus.* An argument or something ironically or humorously regarded as such, *esp.* a specious or subtle argument or piece of reasoning; †in early use, a subtle or tricky speech; a poser; more widely, an artifice, trick. late ME. **2.** *gen.* The form of such arguments, or argumentation in that form; the form or instrument of reasoning from generals to particulars. Also, as a mental act: mediate inference or deduction. 1588.

Syllogist (si·lŏdʒist). 1799. [f. prec. or SYLLOGIZE; see -IST.] One who reasons by syllogisms; one versed in syllogism.

Syllogistic (silŏdʒi·stik), *a.* (*sb.*) 1669. [– L. *syllogisticus* (Quintilian) – Gr. συλλογιστικός, f. συλλογίζεσθαι; see SYLLOGISM, -IC.] Of, pertaining to, of the nature of, or consisting of a syllogism or syllogisms. **B.** *sb.* Reasoning by syllogisms; that department of logic which deals with syllogisms. Also pl. (see -ICS). *rare.* 1833. So **Syllogi·stical** *a.* (now *rare*) syllogistic; also, addicted to reasoning by syllogisms 1529; **-ly** *adv.*

Syllogization (si:lŏdʒəizēⁱ·ʃən). *rare.* 1660. [f. next + -ATION.] The action of syllogizing; syllogistic reasoning.

Syllogize (si·lŏdʒəiz), *v.* late ME. [– OFr. *sil(l)ogiser* – late L. *syllogizare* (Boethius) – Gr. συλλογίζεσθαι; see SYLLOGISM, -IZE.] *intr.* To argue by syllogisms; to reason syllogistically: also *gen.* (Also with *it.*) **b.** *trans.* To deduce by syllogism. (Only in transl. and echoes of Dante *Paradiso* x. 138.) 1867.

To S. is to collect, that is, conclude, or from some certain Propositions to draw up the Summ of an Argument or Proof 1697. **b.** Those who, as Dante says, s. hateful truths LOWELL. Hence **Syllogi·zer.**

Sylph (silf). 1657. [– mod.L. pl. *sylphes* and *sylphi*, G. pl. *sylphen*, of unc. origin, but perh. based by Paracelsus on L. *sylvestris* of the woods and *nympha* nymph.] **1.** One of a race of beings or spirits supposed to inhabit the air (orig. in the system of Paracelsus). **b.** Applied to a slender graceful woman or girl 1838. **2.** Gould's name for various humming-birds with long forked tails 1861. Hence **Sy·lphic, Sy·lphish** *adjs.* pertaining to, resembling, of the nature of, or characteristic of a s.

Sylphid (si·lfid), *sb.* (*a.*) 1680. [– Fr. *sylphide*, f. *sylphe*; see prec., -ID².] A little or young sylph. Also *attrib.* or as *adj.*

Ye Sylphs and Sylphids, to your chief give ear! POPE. If to S. Queen 'twere given, To show our earth the charms of Heaven SCOTT.

‖**Sylva, silva** (si·lvă). 1636. [L. *silva* a wood, woodland; commonly misspelt *sylva* in imitation of Gr. ὕλη wood (see HYLE).] **1. a.** A title for a treatise on forest trees, or a descriptive list or catalogue of trees 1664. **b.** The trees of a particular region or period collectively 1846. †**2.** A title for a collection of pieces, esp. of poems; also, a thesaurus of words or phrases –1787.

Sylvan, silvan (si·lvăn), *sb.* and *a.* 1565. [– Fr. *sylvain*, †*silvain*, or L. *silvanus*, *syl-* (only as the name of a god), f. *silva*; see prec., -AN.] **A.** *sb.* One who (or something that) inhabits a wood or forest; a being of the woods. **a.** *Mythol.* A deity or spirit of the woods. **b.** A forester; a rustic 1589. **c.** An animal, esp. a bird, living in or frequenting the woods 1612.

a. Goate-feete Syluans 1616. **b.** Her private orchards, wall'd on ev'ry side, To lawless sylvans all access deny'd POPE.

B. *adj.* **1.** Belonging, pertaining, or relating to, situated or performed in, associated with, or characteristic of, a wood or woods 1580. **2.** Consisting of or formed by woods or trees 1594. **3.** Furnished with, abounding in, or having as its chief feature, woods or trees; wooded, woody 1667.

1. May all the S. Deityes Bee still propitious to you COWLEY. **3.** O s. Wye! thou wanderer thro' the woods! WORDSW.

Sylvanite (si·lvănəit). 1796. [f. (*Tran*)*sylvania*, where found; see -ITE¹ 2 b.] *Min.* **a.** Native tellurium, with slight admixture of gold, iron, etc. **b.** A telluride of gold and silver (sometimes also containing lead), occurring in crystals or masses of a steel-grey, silver-white, or yellow colour with metallic lustre. Hence **Sylvani·tic** *a.* containing s.

Sylvate, silvate (si·lveⁱt). 1836. [f. SYLVIC + -ATE¹ 1c.] *Chem.* A salt of sylvic acid.

Sylvatic, silvatic (silvæ·tik), *a.* *rare.* 1661. [– L. *silvaticus*, f. *silva* SYLVA; see -ATIC.] Belonging to or found in woods; of the nature of a wood or woodland; sylvan; †*transf.* rustic, boorish.

Sylvester (si·lvėstəɹ). 1838. [Proper name.] St. Sylvester's day, Dec. 31.

Sylvestrian, sil- (silve·striăn), *a.*¹ 1657. [f. L. *silvestris* + -AN.] Belonging to or found in woods; sylvan, rustic.

Sylve·strian, *a.*² and *sb.* 1693. [f. *Sylvester* (see below) + -IAN.] *Ch. Hist.* Belonging to, or a member of, an order of Benedictines founded by Sylvester Gozzolini in 1231.

Sylvian (si·lviăn), *a.*¹ 1871. [– Fr. *sylvien*, f. François de la Boë *Sylvius*, a Flemish anatomist (1614–1672).] *Anat.* Described by or named after the anatomist Sylvius: applied to certain structures in the brain.

Sylvian, *a.*² (*sb.*) 1891. [f. mod.L. *Sylvia* (Scopoli, 1769), f. L. *silva* a wood.] *Ornith.* Belonging to the genus *Sylvia* or family *Sylviidæ* of oscine passerine birds (the warblers). **B.** *sb.* A bird of this genus or family.

Sylvic, silvic (si·lvik), *a.* 1836. [– Fr. *sylvique*, f. L. *sylva*, *silva* a wood; see -IC 1 b.] Chem. *S. acid*: a colourless crystalline substance, isomeric with pinic acid, forming a constituent of colophony or turpentine-resin.

Sylvicoline (silvi·kŏləin), *a.* and *sb.* 1872. [– mod.L. *Sylvicolinæ*, f. *Sylvicola*, a former generic name, = L. *silvicola* inhabiting woods; see -INE¹.] *Ornith.* **A.** *adj.* Belonging to the *Sylvicolinæ*, a former division of the family then called *Sylvicolidæ* (now *Mniotiltidæ*), comprising the typical American warblers. **B.** *sb.* A bird of this division.

Sylviculture, silvi- (si·lvikɒltiŭr, -tʃəɹ). 1880. [– Fr. *sylvi-*, *silviculture*, f. L. *sylva*, *silva* a wood + Fr. *culture* cultivation.] The cultivation of woods or forests; the growing and tending of trees as a department of forestry. Hence **Sylvicu·lturist,** a person engaged or skilled in s.

Sylvine (si·lvin). 1850. [– Fr. *sylvine* (Beudant, 1832) from the old name of the salt, *sal digestivus Sylvii*; see -INE⁵.] *Min.* Native potassium chloride, occurring in some salt-mines and on Mount Vesuvius. Also called **Sy·lvite.**

Sym- (sim), *prefix*, repr. Gr. συμ-, assimilated form of συν- SYN-, before labials (β, μ, π, φ, ψ), hence in words of Gr. derivation in Latin and modern languages before *b*, *m*, *p*. **Symble·pharon,** *Path.* [Gr. βλέφαρον eyelid] adhesion of the eyelid to the eyeball. **Sympelmous** (simpe·lməs), *a.* [Gr. πέλμα sole of the foot] *Ornith.* having the tendons of the deep flexors of the toes united before separating to each of the four digits. **Sympetalous** (simpe·tăləs), *a.* *Bot.*, having the petals united; gamopetalous. **Symphyllous** (simfi·ləs), *a.* [Gr. φύλλον leaf] *Bot.* having the perianth-leaves united; gamophyllous. **Sympolar** (simpōᵘ·lăɹ), *a.* *Geom.* reciprocally polar: said of a pair of polyhedra so related that every face of each corresponds to a summit of the other.

‖**Symbiosis** (simbiōᵘ·sis, -bəi-). 1877. [mod.L. – Gr. συμβίωσις a living together, f. συμβιοῦν live together, f. σύμβιος adj. living together, sb. companion, partner, f. σύν SYM- + βίος life; see -OSIS.] *Biol.* Association of two different organisms (usu. two plants, or an animal and a plant) which live attached to each other, or one as a tenant of the other, and contribute to each other's support. Hence **Symbio·tic** *a. Biol.* associated or living in s.; relating to or involving s.; **-ly** *adv.*

Symbol (si·mbəl), *sb.*[1] 1490. [– Chr.L. *symbolum* – Gr. σύμβολον mark, token, ticket, watchword, outward sign, covenant, f. σύν SYM- + *βολ-, as in βολή, βόλος a throw (cf., e.g., PARABLE).] **1.** A formal authoritative statement of the religious belief of the Christian church, or of a particular church or sect; a creed or confession of faith, *spec.* the Apostles' Creed. †**b.** *transf.* A brief or sententious statement; a formula, motto, maxim; *occas.* a summary, synopsis –1751. **2.** Something that stands for, represents, or denotes something else (not by exact resemblance, but by vague suggestion, or by some accidental or conventional relation); *esp.* a material object representing or taken to represent something immaterial or abstract 1590. **b.** An object representing something sacred; *spec.* (*absol.*) either of the elements in the eucharist, as representing the body and blood of Christ 1671. **c.** *Numism.* A small device on a coin, additional to and usu. independent of the main device or 'type' 1883. **d.** Symbols collectively; symbolism (*rare*) 1856. **3.** A written character or mark used to represent something; a letter, figure, or sign conventionally standing for some object, process, etc. 1620.

1. The credo and symbole of the fayth CAXTON. **b.** The celebrated s. of Pythagoras, ἀνεμῶν πνεόντων τὴν ἠχὼ προσκύνει; 'when the wind blows, worship its echo' JOHNSON. **2.** Salt as incorruptible, was the Simbole of friendship SIR T. BROWNE. The offering of incense is a natural s. of adoration 1865. **3.** *Symboles*, are Letters used for Numbers in Algebra 1700. Table of Symbols of the elementary bodies 1844. Hence **Sy·mbol** *v. trans.* = SYMBOLIZE II. 1.

†**Symbol,** *sb.*[2] 1627. [– L. *symbola* – Gr. συμβολή, f. συμβάλλειν put together, f. σύν SYM- + βάλλειν to throw.] A contribution (properly to a feast or picnic); a share, portion.

The persons who are to be judged..shall all appear to receive ther S. JER. TAYLOR. Let me contribute my Symbole on this Subject FULLER.

Symbolic (simbǫ·lik), *a.* 1656. [– Fr. *symbolique* or late L. *symbolicus* – Gr. συμβολικός, f. σύμβολον; see SYMBOL *sb.*[1], -IC.] **1.** Having the character of a symbol or representative sign or mark; constituting or serving as a symbol (*of* something) 1680. **2.** Consisting of, denoted by, or involving the use of written symbols or significant characters; *spec.* in *Math.* 1656. **3.** Expressed, denoted, or conveyed by means of a symbol or set of symbols; concerning, involving, or depending upon representation by symbols; also dealing with or using symbols 1684. **4.** Pertaining to or of the nature of a formal confession of faith 1867. So **Symbo·lical** *a.* 1607. **Symbolical-ly** *adv.* 1603, **-ness** 1633.

Symbolics (simbǫ·liks). 1657. [pl. of prec. used subst. (see -ICS, -IC 2), chiefly after G. *symbolik* or Fr. *symbolique.*] †**1.** The use of written symbols, as in mathematics. HOBBES. **2.** The study of creeds and confessions of faith, as a branch of theology 1847.

Symbolism (si·mbŏliz'm). 1654. [f. SYMBOL *sb.*[1] + -ISM, partly after Fr. *symbolisme.*] **1.** The practice of representing things by symbols, or of giving a symbolic character to objects or acts; the systematic use of symbols; hence, symbols collectively or generally. **b.** A symbolic meaning attributed to natural objects or facts 1835. **c.** The use of symbols in literature or art; *spec.* the principles or practice of the Symbolists 1866. **2.** The use, or a set or system, of written symbols 1864. **3.** = prec. 2. 1846.

1. Heraldry grew out of s. 1870. **2.** I had.. invented a short-hand s. for crystalline forms RUSKIN.

Symbolist (si·mbŏlist). 1585. [f. SYMBOL *sb.*[1] + -IST; in sense 2 b after Fr. *symboliste.*] **1.** *Ch. Hist.* One who holds that the elements in the Eucharist are mere symbols of the body and blood of Christ. *Obs.* exc. *Hist.* **2.** One who uses symbols, or practises symbolism 1812. **b.** One who uses symbolism in art or literature: (*a*) A painter who aims at symbolizing ideas rather than representing the form or aspect of actual objects; *spec.* applied to a recent school of painters who use representations of objects and schemes of colour to suggest ideas or states of mind; (*b*) One of a recent school of French poets who aim at representing ideas and emotions by indirect suggestion rather than by direct expression, and attach a symbolic meaning to particular objects, words, sounds, etc. 1892. **3.** One versed in the study or interpretation of symbols or symbolism 1839. Hence **Symboli·stic, -al** *adjs.* pertaining to or characteristic of a s.; belonging to or characterized by symbolism; **-ly** *adv.*

Symbolization (si:mbŏləizēⁱ·ʃən). 1603. [– Fr. *symbolisation*, †*-ization* (Rabelais), f. *symboliser*; see next, -ATION.] **1.** †**a.** The fact of 'symbolizing' in nature or quality; agreement or participation in qualities –1693. **b.** The action of 'symbolizing' in tenets or practice; conformity (*with*). Now *rare* or *Obs.* 1633. **2.** The action of symbolizing; representation by a symbol or symbols; *transf.* something in which this is exemplified; a symbol or symbolism 1603. **b.** Representation by written symbols; *transf.* a set of written symbols or characters 1842.

Symbolize (si·mbŏləiz), *v.* 1590. [– Fr. *symboliser*, †*-izer*, f. *symbole*; see SYMBOL *sb.*[1], -IZE.] **I.** †**1.** *intr.* To agree or harmonize in qualities or nature (or in some quality); *s. with*, to partake of the qualities or nature of; hence often = to be like, resemble –1816. †**b.** To combine, unite, as elements having qualities in common; to form a harmonious union or combination –1628. †**c.** *trans.* To mix, combine, unite (elements or substances) –1610. **2.** *intr.* To agree in belief or practice (esp. religious); to comply, conform. Now *rare* or *Obs.* 1605. **II. 1.** *trans.* **a.** To represent by a symbol or symbols. Also *absol.* 1606. **b.** To be a symbol of; to typify 1603. **2.** To make into or treat as a symbol; to regard as symbolic or emblematic (*rare*) 1646. **III.** To formulate or express in a creed or confession of faith 1895. Hence **Sy·mbolizer** (*rare*), one who or that which symbolizes.

Symbolography (simbŏlǫ·grăfi). 1865. [f. SYMBOL *sb.*[1] + -GRAPHY.] Symbolic writing.

Symbology (simbǫ·lŏdʒi). 1840. [irreg. f. SYMBOL *sb.*[1] + -LOGY (cf. prec.).] The science or study of symbols; *loosely*, the use of symbols, or symbols collectively; symbolism. So **Symbolo·gical** *a.* **Symbo·logist** (*rare*).

Symbololatry (simbŏlǫ·lătri). 1828. [f. Gr. σύμβολον SYMBOL *sb.*[1] + λατρεία: worship; see -LATRY.] Worship of or excessive veneration for symbols (in any sense).

‖**Symmelia** (simī·liă). 1894. [mod.L., f. Gr. σύν SYM- + μέλος limb; see -IA[1].] *Path.* A form of monstrosity in which a pair of limbs, esp. the hinder limbs, are fused into one.

Symmetral (si·mĕtrăl), *a.* 1660. [f. med.L. *symmetrus* (XIII) commensurable, f. Gr. σύμμετρος (f. σύν SYM- + μέτρον measure) + -AL[1]. Cf. contemp. †ASYMMETRAL (XVII, Theol.).] †**1.** *fig.* Commensurate with the Divine idea or pattern; agreeing with the word of God: applied to the early church or its times, etc. –1685. **2.** *Geom.* Related to or determining symmetry; about which a figure is symmetrical; as in *s. axis, plane* = axis or plane of symmetry 1878.

†**Symme·trian.** *rare.* 1586. [f. L. *symmetria* SYMMETRY + -AN.] An advocate of, or one studious of, symmetry –1623.

Symmetric (sime·trik), *a.* 1796. [f. SYMMETRY + -IC. Cf. Fr. *symétrique*, †*symm-* (XVI).] = next.

Symmetrical (sime·trikăl), *a.* 1751. [f. SYMMETRY + -ICAL, after *geometrical.*] Characterized by or exhibiting symmetry. **1.** Having the parts or elements regularly and harmoniously arranged; regular in form; well-proportioned; balanced. **2.** *Geom.*, etc. Said of a figure or body whose points or parts are equably distributed about a dividing line, plane, or point, i.e. arranged in pairs or sets so that those of each pair or set are at equal distances on opposite sides of such line, plane, or point; consisting of, or capable of being divided into, two or more exactly similar and equal parts. Also said of the form of such a figure or object, of its parts or their arrangement, or of any part in relation to the corresponding part 1794. **b.** *Alg.* and *Higher Math.* Applied to an expression, function, or equation whose value is never altered by interchanging the values of any two of the variables or unknown quantities 1816. **c.** *Photogr.* Applied to a lens of symmetrical form; also *ellipt.* as *sb.* = symmetrical lens 1890. **3. a.** *Bot.* Of a flower = ISOMEROUS 1. 1849. **b.** *Anat.* and *Zool.* Having similar or corresponding parts or organs on opposite sides of a dividing plane, or regularly arranged around an axis or centre; consisting of two or more similar or corresponding divisions. Also said of the parts. (*b*) *Path.* Of a disease: Affecting such corresponding parts or organs simultaneously. 1851.

1. The s. clauses of Pope's logical metre RUSKIN. **2. b.** *S.* or *symmetric determinant*, a determinant in which the constituents in each row are the same respectively, and in the same order, as those in the corresponding column, and which is therefore symmetrical about its principal diagonal. Hence **Symme·trical-ly** *adv.*, **-ness.**

Symmetrize (si·mĕtrəiz), *v.* 1786. [– Fr. *symétriser* (in sense 1), or f. SYMMETRY + -IZE.] †**1.** *intr.* To be symmetrical; to correspond symmetrically. H. WALPOLE. **2.** *trans.* To make symmetrical; to reduce to symmetry 1796.

Symmetrophobia (si:mĕtrophōᵘ·biă). 1809. [irreg. f. next + -O- + -PHOBIA.] Dread or avoidance of symmetry, as shown or supposed to be shown in Egyptian temples, Japanese art, etc.

Symmetry (si·mĕtri). 1541. [– Fr. †*symmétrie* (mod. *symétrie*) or L. *symmetria* – Gr. συμμετρία, f. σύμμετρος, f. σύν SYM- + μέτρον measure; see -METRY.] †**1.** Mutual relation of parts in respect of magnitude and position; relative measurement and arrangement of parts; proportion –1730. **2.** Due or just proportion; harmony of parts with each other and with the whole; fitting, regular, or balanced arrangement and relation of parts or elements; the condition or quality of being well-proportioned or well-balanced. In stricter use: Exact correspondence in size and position of opposite parts; equable distribution of parts about a dividing line or centre. (As an attribute either of the whole or of the parts composing it.) 1599. **3.** Various spec. and techn. uses. †**a.** *Physiol.* Harmonious working of the bodily functions, producing a healthy temperament or condition –1541. **b.** *Geom.*, etc. Exact correspondence in position of the several points or parts of a figure or body with ref. to a dividing line, plane, or point (or a number of lines or planes); arrangement of all the points of a figure or system in pairs (or sets) so that those of each pair (or set) are at equal distances on opposite sides of such line, plane, or point 1823. (*b*) *Alg.* and *Higher Math.* The fact of being symmetrical, as an expression or function: see SYMMETRICAL 2 b. 1888. **c.** *Anat.* and *Zool.* Arrangement of parts or organs in pairs or sets on opposite sides of a dividing plane, or around an axis or centre; repetition of similar corresponding parts in the two halves, or other number of divisions, of the body. (*b*) *Path.* Affection of such corresponding parts simultaneously by the same disease. 1849. **d.** *Bot.* Equality of the number of parts in the several whorls of the flower 1845.

1. True and native beauty consists in the just composure and symetrie of the parts of the body 1650. **3. b.** *Axis of s., centre of s., plane of s.*, the line, point, or plane about which a figure or body is symmetrical, i.e. which bisects every straight line joining a pair of corresponding points of such figure or body.

Symmory (si·mŏri). 1847. [– Gr. συμμορία, f. σύμμορος sharing (*sc.* the burden of taxation), f. σύν + μορ- (= μέρος portion, share).] *Anc. Gr. Hist.* Each of the companies or fellowships, graded according to wealth, into which the citizens of Athens and other cities were divided for purposes of taxation.

Sympathetic (simpăþe·tik), *a.* (*sb.*) 1644. [f. SYMPATHY, after PATHETIC.] **1.** Pertaining to, involving, depending on, acting or effected by 'sympathy', or a (real or supposed) affinity, correspondence, or occult influence. Now chiefly *Hist.* **b.** *Physiol.* and *Path.* Produced by 'sympathy' (see SYMPATHY 1 b): applied to a condition, action, or disorder induced in a person, or in an organ or part of the body, by a similar or corresponding one in another 1728. **c.** *Anat.* Designating one of the two great nerve-systems in vertebrates (the other being the *cerebro-spinal*), consisting of a double chain of ganglia, with connecting fibres, along the vertebral column, giving off branches and plexuses which supply the viscera and blood-vessels and maintain relations between their various activities; belonging to or forming part of this system. Also applied to a similar set of nerves supplying the viscera in some invertebrates. 1769. **d.** *Physics.* Used in ref. to sounds produced by responsive vibrations induced in one body by transmission of vibrations from another 1832. **2.** †Agreeing, harmonious, befitting, consonant, accordant (*obs.*); according with one's feelings or inclinations, congenial 1673. **3. a.** Feeling or susceptible of sympathy; sharing or affected by the feelings of another or others; sympathizing, compassionate 1718. **b.** Pertaining to, of the nature of, characterized by, arising from, or expressive of sympathy or fellow-feeling 1684.

1. *S. powder* = 'powder of sympathy': see SYMPATHY 1. *S. ink*, a name for various colourless liquid compositions used as ink, the writing with which remains invisible until the colour is developed by heat or some chemical reagent. **2.** Now o'er the soothed accordant heart we feel A s. twilight slowly steal WORDSW. **3. a.** An unusually tender and s. audience DICKENS. **b.** The head of the Coal Miners' Union is opposed to s. strikes 1901.

B. *sb.* **1.** *Anat.* Short for *s. nerve* or *system*: see 1 c above 1808. **2. a.** A person affected by 'sympathy' (SYMPATHY 1 b); one who is susceptible or sensitive to hypnotic or similar influence. **b.** A sympathizer (*rare*). 1888. So †**Sympathe·tical** *a.* 1639, **-ly** *adv.* 1621.

Sympathic (simpæ·þik), *a.* Now *rare* or *Obs.* 1659. [– Fr. *sympathique* (XVII), f. *sympathie*; see SYMPATHY, -IC.] †**1.** = prec. A 1, 1 b, 2. –1684. **2.** = prec. 1 c. 1836.

Sympathist (si·mpăþist). *rare.* 1819. [f. SYMPATHY + -IST.] One who sympathizes, a sympathizer.

Sympathize (si·mpăþəiz), *v.* 1588. [– Fr. *sympathiser*, f. *sympathie* SYMPATHY; see -IZE.] **1.** *intr.* To suffer with or like another; to be affected in consequence of the affection of some one or something else; to respond sympathetically to some influence; *spec.* in *Path.* to be or become disordered in consequence of the disorder of some other part. Const. *with.* 1597. †**2. a.** To have an affinity; to agree in nature, disposition, qualities, or fortunes; to be alike; with *with*, to be like, resemble –1668. †**b.** To agree, be in harmony, accord, harmonize *with* –1711. †**3.** *trans.* To agree with, correspond to, match –1606. †**b.** To represent or express by something corresponding or fitting; to apprehend mentally by the analogy of something else –1645. †**c.** To make up or compound of corresponding parts or elements; to form or contrive harmoniously or consistently –1606. **4.** *intr.* To feel sympathy; to have a fellow-feeling; to share the feelings of another or others; *spec.* to be affected with pity for the suffering or sorrow of another, to feel compassion. Const. *with* a person (or, in extended or *fig.* use, a thing), *in*, *with* (rarely †*at*) a feeling, experience, etc. 1605. **b.** *transf.* To express sympathy; to condole (*with* a person) 1748. **c.** In weakened sense: To agree or be disposed to agree in some opinion or way of thinking, to be of (about) the same mind *with* a person or party; also, with *in* or (now usu.) *with*, to approve or incline to approve, to regard with favour (a scheme, cause, etc.) 1828.

1. The mind will s. so much with the anguish and debility of the body, that it will be..too distracted to fix itself in meditation 1812. **2. a.** *Hen. V*, III. vii. 158. **b.** Nature in aw to him Had doff't her gawdy trim, With her great Master so to s. MILT. **3.** *Rich. II*, V. i. 46. **b.** Thou truly faire, wert truly simpathizde, In true plaine words, by thy true telling friend SHAKS. **c.** *L.L.L.* III. i. 52. **4.** Friends and foes pittyed my case, sympathized with me 1685. **c.** Pope..sympathized with his schemes 1880. Hence **Sy·mpathizer,** one who or that which sympathizes.

Sympathy (si·mpăþi). 1579. [– L. *sympathia* (whence Fr. *sympathie*) – Gr. συμπάθεια, f. συμπαθής having a fellow-feeling, f. σύν SYM- + *παθ- base of πάθος feeling, PATHOS; see -Y^{3}.] **1.** A (real or supposed) affinity between certain things, by virtue of which they are similarly or correspondingly affected by the same influence, affect or influence one another (esp. in some occult way), or attract or tend towards each other. *Obs.* exc. *Hist.* 1586. **b.** *Physiol.* and *Path.* A relation between two bodily organs or parts (or between two persons) such that disorder, or any condition, of the one induces a corresponding condition in the other 1603. **2.** Agreement, accord, harmony, consonance, concord; agreement in qualities, likeness, conformity, correspondence. *Obs.* or merged in 3 a. 1579. **3. a.** Conformity of feelings, inclinations, or temperament, which makes persons agreeable to each other; community of feeling, harmony of disposition 1596. **b.** The quality or state of being affected by the condition of another with a feeling similar or corresponding to that of the other; the fact or capacity of entering into or sharing the feelings of another or others; fellow-feeling. Also, a feeling or frame of mind evoked by or responsive to some external influence. Const. *with* (a person, etc., or a feeling). 1662. **c.** *spec.* The quality or state of being thus affected by the suffering or sorrow of another; a feeling of compassion or commiseration 1600. **d.** In weakened sense: A favourable attitude of mind towards a cause, etc.; disposition to agree or approve 1823.

1. *Powder of s.* (*s.-powder*), a powder supposed to heal wounds by 'sympathy' on being applied to a handkerchief or garment stained with blood from the wound, or to the weapon with which the wound was inflicted; also called *sympathetic powder*. Phr. *In s. with* (Comm.), used in market reports in ref. to a rise or fall in the price of a commodity induced by a rise or fall in that of another. **2.** There should be..simpathy in yeares, Manners, and Beauties: all which the Moore is defective in SHAKS. **3. a.** They enjoy the s. of kindred souls 1876. **b.** With answering looks Of sympathie and love MILT. **c.** To awaken something of s. for the unfortunate natives BURKE. **d.** He had no s. with the anti-opium party 1893.

‖**Symphonia** (simfō^{u}·niă). 1579. [L. – Gr. συμφωνία.] = SYMPHONY 2, 3, 5.

Symphonic (simfǫ·nik), *a.* (*sb.*) 1864. [f. SYMPHONY + -IC, after *harmonic*.] **1. a.** = HOMOPHONOUS 2. **b.** Applied to a shorthand sign denoting more than one sound. 1880. **2.** Harmonious (*rare*) 1864. **3.** *Mus.* Of, pertaining to, or having the form or character of a symphony. Also *transf.* in ref. to poetry. 1864.

3. *S. poem* (tr. G. *symphonische dichtung*), a descriptive orchestral composition of the character and dimensions of a symphony, but freer in form, founded on some special poetic theme or idea. So †**Sympho·nical** *a.* (*rare*) = sense 2. 1589–1650.

Symphonious (simfō^{u}·niəs), *a.* Only *literary.* 1652. [f. L. *symphonia* SYMPHONY + -OUS, after *harmonious*.] **1.** Full of or characterized by 'symphony' or harmony of sounds: = HARMONIOUS 2. **b.** *fig.* or *gen.* = HARMONIOUS 1. Const. *to*, *with*. 1742. **2.** Sounding together or in concert 1816.

1. The sound S. of ten thousand Harpes, that tun'd Angelic harmonies MILT. Hence **Sympho·niously** *adv.* harmoniously.

Symphonist (si·mfŏnist). 1789. [f. next or SYMPHONY + -IST. Cf. med.L. *symphonista* (XI), Fr. *symphoniste* (XVIII).] A composer of symphonies.

Symphonize (si·mfŏnəiz), *v.* Now *rare* or *Obs.* 1491. [– med.L. *symphonizare* (f. L. *symphonia*), or directly f. SYMPHONY; see -IZE.] **1.** *intr.* To sing or sound together, in concert, or in harmony. †**2.** To agree, be in accordance, harmonize (*with* something) –1712.

Symphony (si·mfŏni). ME. [– (O)Fr. †*sim-*, *symphonie* – L. *symphonia* instrumental harmony, voices in concert, (Vulg.) musical instrument – Gr. συμφωνία, f. σύμφωνος harmonious, f. σύν SYM- + φωνή sound.] †**1.** Used vaguely, after late L. *symphonia*, as a name for different musical instruments –1602. **2.** Harmony of sound, esp. of musical sounds; concord, consonance. Also occas. of speech-sounds, as in verse. Now *rare* or *Obs.* 1440. **3.** Harmony (in general), agreement, accord, concord, congruity. Now *rare* or *Obs.* 1598. **4.** (transf. from 2.) Music in parts, sung or played by a number of performers with pleasing effect; concerted or harmonious music; a performance or strain of such music. Chiefly *poet.* or *rhet.* 1599. **b.** *fig.* A collection of utterances, or sounds of any kind, likened to concerted music; a 'chorus' (of praise, etc.) 1654. **c.** Applied to a collection or composition of various colours which harmonize, with pleasing or brilliant effect 1874. **5.** *Mus.* **a.** A passage for instruments alone (or, by extension, for a single instrument) occurring in a vocal composition as an introduction, interlude, or close to an accompaniment; also, a short instrumental movement occurring between vocal movements, as the 'Pastoral Symphony' in Handel's 'Messiah'; also formerly applied to a more extended instrumental piece, often in several movements, forming the overture to an opera or other vocal work of large dimensions 1661. **b.** An elaborate orchestral composition in three or more movements, orig. developed from the operatic overture (see prec. sense), similar in form to a sonata, but usu. of grander dimensions and broader style 1789.

1. With harpe and pype and symphonye CHAUCER. The strings of natures s. Are crackt MARSTON. **3.** Their domestic s. was liable to furious flaws CARLYLE. **4.** From afar I heard a suddain S. of War DRYDEN. **c.** Symphonies of colour, like Whistler's 1874. **5. a.** Thir gold'n Harps they took,..and with Præamble sweet Of charming symphonie they introduce Thir sacred Song MILT.

Symphyo- (si·mfio), before a vowel **symphy-**, used as comb. form of Gr. συμφυής growing or grown together.

Symphysial (simfi·ziăl), *a.* 1835. [f. SYMPHYSIS + -AL^{1}.] Of or pertaining to, situated at, or forming a symphysis. So **Symphy·sian** *a.*

Symphysio-, also **-eo-** (after Fr. *-éo-*, from stem συμφυσε- of Gr. σύμφυσις), comb. form of next. **Sy:mphysio·tomy** [Gr. -τομία cutting], the operation of cutting through the symphysis pubis to facilitate delivery.

Symphysis (si·mfisis). 1578. [– mod.L. *symphysis* – Gr. σύμφυσις, esp. of bones, f. σύν SYM- + φύσις growth.] **1.** *Anat.* and *Zool.* The union of two bones or skeletal elements originally separate, either by fusion of the bony substance (*synostosis*) or by intervening cartilage (*synchondrosis*); the part or line of junction where this takes or has taken place: used esp. of such union of two similar bones on opposite sides of the body in the median line, as that of the pubic bones (*symphysis pubis*) or of the two halves of the lower jaw-bone (*s. mandibulæ* or *menti*). **2.** *Bot.* Coalescence or fusion of parts of a plant normally distinct 1866.

Symphytic (simfi·tik), *a.* *rare.* 1871. [– Gr. συμφυτικός, f. συμφύειν make grow together, f. σύν SYM- + φύειν produce, grow, etc.; see -IC.] Formed by or involving coalescence or fusion of two parts or elements. Hence **Symphy·tically** *adv.* in the way of such coalescence or fusion; so **Sy·mphytism** (tendency to) such coalescence or fusion.

Sympiesometer (si:mpiėsǫ·mĭtəɹ). 1817. [irreg. f. Gr. συμπίεσις compression (f. συμπιέζειν compress, f. σύν SYM- + πιέζειν press) + -METER.] A form of barometer in which the column of liquid in the tube has above it a body of confined air or other gas (instead of a vacuum), so that the pressure of the atmosphere acts against the weight of the liquid and the elastic pressure of the gas; a thermometer is attached for correction of the readings according to the expansion or contraction of the gas with changes of temperature.

Symplectic (simple·ktik), *a.* and *sb.* 1839. [– Gr. συμπλεκτικός, f. σύν SYM- + πλέκειν twine, plait, weave; see -IC.] **A.** *adj.* Epithet of a bone of the suspensorium in the skull of fishes, between the hyomandibular and the quadrate bones. **B.** *sb.* The symplectic bone.

‖**Symploce** (si·mplŏsi). 1577. [Late L. – Gr. συμπλοκή an interweaving, f. σύν SYM- + πλέκειν (see prec.).] *Rhet.* A figure consisting in the repetition of one word or phrase at the beginning, and of another at the end, of successive clauses or sentences; a combination of *anaphora* and *epistrophe*.

Sympode (si·mpoᵘd). 1880. *Bot.* Anglicized form of SYMPODIUM.

‖**Sympodia** (simpōᵘ·diă). 1848. [mod.L., f. Gr. σύμπους, συμποδ- with the feet together + -IA¹.] A malformation in which the legs or lower extremities are united.

Sympodial (simpōᵘ·diăl), *a.* 1875. [In sense 1 f. next; in sense 2 f. prec.; see -AL¹.] **1.** *Bot.* Pertaining or relating to, of the nature of, or producing a sympodium. **2.** *Anat.* Affected with sympodia; having the lower extremities united 1902.

‖**Sympodium** (simpōᵘ·diŏm). *Pl.* **-ia.** 1862. [mod.L., f. Gr. σύν SYM- + πούς, ποδ- foot; see -IUM.] *Bot.* An apparent axis or stem in a dichotomously branched plant, made up of the bases of successive branches so arranged as to resemble a simple or monopodial axis; a pseudaxis.

Symposiac (simpōᵘ·ziæ̆k), *sb.* and *a.* 1603. [– L. *symposiacus* adj., in n. pl. *symposiaca*, or Gr. συμποσιακός adj., f. συμπόσιον SYMPOSIUM; see -AC.] **A.** *sb.* A symposiac meeting or conversation, or an account of one; a symposium. Now *rare* or *Obs.* **B.** *adj.* Of, pertaining to, or suitable for a symposium; of the nature of a symposium; convivial 1642.

Symposiarch (simpōᵘ·ziaɹk). 1603. [– Gr. συμποσίαρχος, f. συμπόσιον SYMPOSIUM + ἀρχός ruler, chief; see -ARCH.] The master, director, or president of a symposium; the leader of a convivial gathering.

Symposiast (simpōᵘ·ziæst). 1656. [f. Gr. συμποσιάζειν drink together (f. συμπόσιον: see next), on Gr. analogies; cf. *enthusiast*.] **1.** A member of a drinking party. **2.** One who contributes to a 'symposium' on some topic 1878.

Symposium (simpōᵘ·ziŏm). *Pl.* **-ia** (rarely **-iums**). 1586. [– L. *symposium* – Gr. συμπόσιον, f. συμπότης fellow-drinker, f. σύν SYM- + πότης drinker.] **1.** A drinking-party; a convivial meeting for drinking, conversation, and intellectual entertainment. **b.** An account of such a meeting or the conversation at it; *spec.* the title of one of Plato's dialogues 1586. **2.** *transf.* A meeting or conference for discussion of some subject; hence, a collection of opinions delivered, or a series of articles contributed, by a number of persons on some special topic 1784.

1. Our s. at the King's head broke up 1787.

Symptom (si·mptəm). late ME. [In XIV–XV *synthoma* – med.L. forms, for late L. *symptoma* – Gr. σύμπτωμα chance, accident, mischance, f. συμπίπτειν fall upon, happen to, f. σύν SYM- + πίπτειν fall.] **1.** *Path.* A (bodily or mental) phenomenon, circumstance, or change of condition arising from and accompanying a disease or affection and constituting an indication or evidence of it; a characteristic sign *of* some particular disease. **2.** *gen.* A phenomenon or circumstance accompanying some condition, process, feeling, etc., and serving as evidence of it (orig. and prop. of something evil); a sign or indication *of* something 1611. **b.** With neg. expressed or implied: A slight, or the least, sign *of* something; a trace, vestige 1722.

1. His skin was hot, and his pulse strong. These symptoms could be attributed to..inflammation of the brain. ABERNETHY. *attrib.*: **s.-complex, -group**, a set of symptoms occurring together and characterizing or constituting a particular disease or affection. **2.** Symptoms of discontent began to appear MACAULAY.

Symptomatic (simptŏmæ·tik), *a.* (*sb.*) 1698. [– Fr. *symptomatique* or late L. *symptomaticus*, f. *symptoma*, *-mat-* SYMPTOM; see -IC.] **1.** *Path.* Of the nature of, or constituting, a symptom of disease; *spec.* applied to a secondary disease or morbid state arising from and accompanying a primary one (opp. to *idiopathic*). **2.** Relating to or concerned with symptoms 1767. **3.** *gen.* That is a symptom of something; characteristic and indicative *of* 1751.

1. S. of a weak state of stomach L. HUNT. **2.** The mere s. practitioner 1843. **3.** The s. smoke has puffed up from the social volcano 1847.

B. *sb.* in *pl.* **Symptoma·tics** = SYMPTOMATOLOGY 1748. So **Symptoma·tical** *a.* in senses 1, 3 (now *rare* or *Obs.*) 1586, **-ly** *adv.* 1615.

Symptomatize (si·mptŏmătəiz), *v.* 1794. [f. Gr. σύμπτωμα, -ματ- SYMPTOM + -IZE.] *trans.* To be a symptom of; to characterize or indicate as a symptom.

Symptomatology (si:mptŏmătǫ·lŏdʒi). 1798. [f. as prec. + -LOGY.] **1.** The study of symptoms; that branch of pathology which treats of the symptoms of disease; also, a discourse or treatise on symptoms 1804. **2.** *transf.* The symptoms of a disease collectively (as a subject of study) 1798.

Syn- (sin), *prefix*, latinized form of Gr. συν- (= σύν prep. with), together, similarly, alike, occurring in many modern scientific terms. (It undergoes assimilation before consonants: before *l* to *syl-*, before labials to SYM- (q.v.), before simple *s* to *sys-*; before *s* + consonant and *z* it is reduced to *sy-*.)

Syna·cmic [Gr. ἀκμή point] *a. Bot.* having the stamens and pistils ripening at the same time; so **Syna·cmy,** simultaneous ripening of the stamens and pistils of a flower. **Synanthe·reous,** *a.* (*rare*) *Bot.* belonging to the *Synantheræ* (= *Compositæ*); having the anthers united. **Synanthe·sis,** *Bot.* simultaneous ripening of the stamens and pistils in a flower; hence **Synanthe·tic** (-þe·tik) *a.* **Syna·nthous,** *a. Bot.* (*a*) applied to plants whose leaves expand at the same time as the flowers; (*b*) characterized by synanthy. **Syna·nthy,** abnormal union or fusion of two or more flowers. **Syna·ptase** [Gr. συναπτός joined together] *Chem.* an albuminous ferment found in almonds and other oily seeds; also called *emulsin*. **Synapti·cula,** each of a number of transverse calcareous processes connecting the septa in certain corals. ‖**Synarthro·sis** [Gr. ἄρθρωσις jointing] *Anat.* a form of articulation in which the bones are firmly fixed so as to be incapable of moving upon one another, as in the sutures of the skull; so **Synarthro·dial** *a.* **Sy·ncarp,** *Bot.* a multiple fruit, i.e. one arising from a number of carpels in one flower. **Synca·rpous,** *a.* consisting of united or adherent carpels. **Synchondro·sis** [Gr. χόνδρος cartilage] *Anat.* the junction of two bones by cartilage; the structure or part in which this takes place; hence **Synchondro·sial,** *a.* **Syncotyle·donous,** *a. Bot.* having the cotyledons united. **Syncrante·rian,** *a. Anat.* having the teeth in a continuous row, as certain snakes. ‖**Syncy·tium** (-si·tiŏm, -si·ʃiŏm) [Gr. κύτος receptacle] *Biol.* (*a*) a single cell or protoplasmic mass containing several nuclei, formed by fusion of a number of cells without fusion of the nuclei, or by division of the nucleus without division of the cell-substance; (*b*) a structure composed of such cells forming the outermost fœtal layer of the placenta; hence **Syncy·tial** *a.* **Synda·ctyl,** *a.* having some or all of the fingers or toes wholly or partly united, as certain mammals and birds; *sb.* a syndactyl animal. **Syndya·smian,** *a. Anthrop.* pertaining to or marked by sexual union without exclusive coition, or with temporary cohabitation. **Synechia** (sine·kiă), *Path.* an affection of the eye, consisting in adhesion of the iris to the cornea (*anterior s.*) or to the capsule of the lens (*posterior s.*). **Syne·nergy** (*rare*) = SYNERGY. ‖**Syne·rgia,** (*a*) *Physiol.* = SYNERGY; (*b*) *Anthropol.* agreement in bodily movements or acts, as a hypothetical stage in the development of sympathy. ‖**Syne·rgida,** *Bot.* either of two naked nucleated cells at the apex of the embryo-sac, regarded as co-operating with the oosphere in the production of the embryo. **Sy·ngamy,** (*a*) free interbreeding between organisms; (*b*) the fusion of two cells, or of their nuclei, in reproduction. **Sy·ngnathous,** *a. Zool.* belonging to the genus *Syngnathus* or sub-order *Syngnathi* of fishes, characterized by the jaws being united into a tubular snout. **Synneuro·sis** [Gr. νεῦρον sinew] *Anat.* connection or articulation of bones by a ligament. **Sy·nocil,** *Zool.* a structure in certain sponges, supposed to be a sense-organ, perhaps analogous to the rods and cones of the retina of the eye. **Synse·palous** *a. Bot.* having the sepals united, gamosepalous. **Sy·ntheme,** *Math.* a system of groups of elements, each of the groups being formed of a certain number of elements, so that each occurs exactly a given number of times among all the groups. **Synthe·rmal,** *a.* having the same temperature; *sb.* an isotherm connecting places having the same temperature at the same moment of time. **Sy·ntype,** *Nat. Hist.* any one of the original set of specimens from which a species has been described and named.

Synæresis (sinīᵊ·rĭsis). 1577. [– late L. *synæresis* – Gr. συναίρεσις, f. σύν SYN- + αἱρεῖν take.] *Gram.* Contraction, esp. of two vowels into a diphthong or a simple vowel.

‖**Synæsthesia** (sinĭzþī·ziă, -siă). *Pl.* **-ae** (*-i*). 1891. [mod.L., f. SYN-, after ANÆSTHESIA.] *Psychol.* **a.** A sensation in one part of the body produced by a stimulus applied to another part. **b.** Agreement of the feelings or emotions of different individuals, as a stage in the development of sympathy. **c.** Production, from a sense-impression of one kind, of an associated mental image of a sense-impression of another kind. So **Synæsthe·tic.**

Synagogal (si·năgōᵘgăl), *a.* 1682. [f. next + -AL¹ 1.] Of, pertaining or relating to, or characteristic of a or the synagogue. So **Synago·gical** *a.* 1621.

Synagogue (si·năgǫg). [ME. *sinagoge* – OFr. *sinagoge* (mod. *synagogue*) – late L. *synagoga* – Gr. συναγωγή meeting, assembly, in LXX. synagogue, f. συνάγειν bring together, assemble, f. σύν SYN- + ἄγειν lead, bring.] **1.** The regular assembly or congregation of the Jews for religious instruction and worship apart from the service of the temple, constituting, since the destruction of the temple, their sole form of public worship; hence, the religious organization of the Jews as typified by this, the Jewish communion. **2.** *transf.* in hostile controversial use, often in phr. *s. of Satan* (see Rev. 2:9) 1464. **3.** A building or place of meeting for Jewish worship and religious instruction ME. †**b.** *transf.* A place of worship; a temple. In post-Reformation use applied disparagingly to abbeys, etc. –1655. **4.** *gen.* An assembly; chiefly as a literalism of biblical translation ME.

1. *The Great S.*, a Jewish council of 120 members, said to have been founded and presided over by Ezra after the return from the Babylonian captivity. **2.** By the incitement..of that unchristian S. [*sc.* Scots Presbytery] at Belfast MILT.

Synallactic (sinălæ·ktik), *a. rare.* 1853. [– Gr. συναλλακτικός, f. συναλλάσσειν exchange, bring into intercourse, reconcile, f. σύν SYN- + ἀλλάσσειν exchange.] Reconciliatory.

Synallagmatic (sinælægmæ·tik), *a.* 1792. [– Gr. συναλλαγματικός, f. συνάλλαγμα covenant, contract, f. συναλλάσσειν; see prec.] Pertaining to or of the nature of a contract or mutual engagement; imposing mutual obligations; reciprocally binding; esp. in *Civil Law*, of a treaty or the like.

Synallaxine (sinælæ·ksəin, -in), *a.* 1862. [– mod.L. *Synallaxinæ* pl., f. *Synallaxis* (Vieillot, 1819), name of the typical genus; see -INE¹.] *Ornith.* Belonging to the subfamily *Synallaxinæ* of dendrocolaptine birds, found in tropical America, in habits and appearance resembling tree creepers.

‖**Synalœpha** (sinălī·fă), **-phe** (*-fi*). 1540. [Late L. (Quintilian) – Gr. συναλοιφή, f. συναλείφειν smear or melt together, f. σύν SYN- + ἀλείφειν anoint.] *Gram.* The coalescence or contraction of two syllables into one; *esp.* the coalescence (in verse) of two vowels at the end of one word and the beginning of the next, by obscuration of the former (or, *loosely*, by suppression of it, in which case more properly called *elision*).

‖**Synangium** (sinæ·ndʒiŏm). *Pl.* **-ia.** 1875. [mod.L., f. Gr. σύν SYN- + ἀγγεῖον vessel; see -IUM.] **1.** *Anat.* and *Zool.* A collective or common blood-vessel from which several arteries branch; *spec.* the terminal part of the arterial trunk in the lower vertebrates. **2.** *Bot.* The oblong mass of coherent sporangia in ferns of the order *Marattiaceæ* 1881. Hence **Syna·ng-ial, -ic** *adjs.*

‖**Synaphe** (si·năfi). 1801. [– Gr. συναφή, f. σύν SYN- + ἅπτειν fasten, fix.] *Anc. Gr. Mus.* The 'conjunction' of two tetrachords.

‖**Synaphea** (sinăfī·ă). 1827. [– Gr. συνάφεια connection, f. συναφής connected, united; see prec.] *Anc. Pros.* Continuity of rhythm; maintenance of the same rhythm throughout, esp. in anapæstic verse.

Synapse (sinæ·ps). 1899. [– Gr. σύναψις; see next.] *Anat.* The junction, or structure at the junction, between two neurons or nerve-cells.

‖**Synapsis** (sinæ·psis). *Pl.* **synapses** (-sīz).

1892. [– Gr. σύναψις connection, junction, f. σύν SYN- + ἅψις joining, f. ἅπτειν join.] **1.** *Biol.* The condensation and fusion of the chromatin to one side of the nucleus, as a stage in the development of a fertilized cell. **2.** *Anat.* = prec. 1897. So **Syna·ptic** *a.*

Synarchy (si·naɹki). *rare.* 1732. [– Gr. συναρχία, f. συνάρχειν rule jointly; see SYN-, -ARCH.] Joint rule or sovereignty; participation in government.

Synastry (sinæ·stri). Also in L. form **synastria.** 1657. [– late L. *synastria* – Gr. συναστρία, f. σύν SYN- + ἀστήρ, ἀστρ- star; see -Y[3].] *Astrol.* Coincidence or agreement of the influences of the stars over the destinies of two persons.

‖**Synaxarion, -ium** (sinæksēᵊ·riǫn, -iŏm). *Pl.* **-ia.** 1850. [eccl. L. – eccl. Gr. συναξάριον, f. σύναξις SYNAXIS.] *Gr. Ch.* An account of the life of a saint, read as a lesson in public worship; also, a collection of such accounts. So **Syna·xarist,** the compiler of a s.

‖**Synaxis** (sinæ·ksis). *Pl.* **-es** (-īz). 1624. [Late (eccl.) L. – eccl. Gr. σύναξις, f. συνάγειν gather together.] *Eccl. Hist.* A meeting for worship, esp. for celebration of the Eucharist.

Syncategorem (sinkæ·tĭgŏrem). 1653. [– late and med.L. *syncategorema* – Gr. συγκατηγόρημα, f. συγκατηγορεῖν (in Logic) predicate jointly.] *Logic.* A word which cannot be used by itself as a term, but only in conjunction with another word or words; e.g. a sign of quantity (as *all, some, no*), or an adverb, preposition, or conjunction.

Syncategorematic (sinkæ:tĭgǫrĭmæ·tik), *a.* 1827. [– med.L. *syncategorematicus* (XII) or its source Gr. συνκατηγορηματικός see prec., -IC.] *Logic.* Of the nature of a syncategorem; opp. to CATEGOREMATIC. So †**Syncategorema·tical** *a.* 1646–1701, †**-ly** *adv.* 1600.

‖**Syncellus** (sinse·lŏs). *Pl.* **-i.** Also in anglicized form **syncel.** 1706. [Late L. *syncellus* cell-mate, later domestic chaplain, – Byzantine Gr. σύγκελλος, f. σύν SYN- + L. *cella* CELL *sb.*] In the Eastern Church, orig. an ecclesiastic who lived continually with a prelate; later, a dignitary who was associated with a prelate and succeeded to his office.

Sy·nchro-mesh, abbrev. of *synchronized mesh,* used *attrib.* to designate a form of automatic gear-changing box; also, a synchromesh gear 1932.

Synchronal (si·ŋkrŏnăl), *a.* Now *rare* or *Obs.* 1660. [f. late L. *synchronus* SYNCHRONOUS + -AL[1] 1.] = SYNCHRONOUS 1, 1 b, 2.

Synchronic (siŋkrǫ·nik), *a. rare.* 1833. [f. as prec. + -IC.] = SYNCHRONOUS 1, 1 b, 2.

Synchronical (siŋkrǫ·nikăl), *a.* Now *rare* or *Obs.* 1652. [f. as prec.; see -ICAL.] = SYNCHRONOUS 1, 1 b, 2. Hence **Synchro·nically** *adv.*

Synchronism (si·ŋkrŏniz'm). 1588. [– Gr. συγχρονισμός, f. σύγχρονος SYNCHRONOUS; see -ISM.] **1.** The quality of being synchronous; coincidence or agreement in point of time; contemporary existence or occurrence. **b.** *Geom.* The property of being synchronous, as a curve; *spec.* of a circle, the property that chords starting from the same point of the circumference will be described in equal times by particles descending under the influence of gravity 1867. **2.** Arrangement or treatment of synchronous events, etc. together or in conjunction, as in a history; agreement in relation to the time of the events described 1612. **b.** (with *a* and *pl.*) A statement or argument that two or more events, etc. are synchronous; a parallel drawn between occurrences, etc. in respect of time; a description or account of different events belonging to the same period; a tabular arrangement of historical events or personages according to their dates 1593. **c.** (*a*) Treatment of details according to identity of period, as in architecture. (*b*) Representation of events of different times together, e.g. in the same picture. 1843. **3.** Recurrence at the same successive instants of time; the fact of keeping time, i.e. proceeding at the same rate and exactly together; coincidence of period, as of two sets of movements, vibrations, or alternations of electric current 1854. Hence **Sy·nchronist** (*rare*) a contemporary.

3. *spec.* of the audible and visible components in cinematography, etc.

Synchroni·stic, *a.* 1685. [f. prec.; see -ISTIC.] Belonging to synchronism; relating to or exhibiting the concurrence of events in time.

Synchronize (si·ŋkrŏnəiz), *v.* Also **-ise.** 1624. [f. as prec.; see -IZE.] **1.** *intr.* To occur at the same time; to be contemporary or simultaneous. Const. *with.* **b.** *trans.* To cause to be, or represent as, synchronous; to assign the same date to; to bring together events, etc. belonging to the same time. Also *absol.* 1806. **2.** *intr.* To occur at the same successive instants of time; to keep time *with*; to have coincident periods, as two sets of movements or vibrations 1867. **b.** *trans.* To cause to go at the same rate; *spec.* to cause (a timepiece) to indicate the same time as another 1879.

2. c. *Cinematogr.* To add (sound effects) in time and harmony with the action of a picture; to furnish (a picture) with such effects; also *intr.* of the audible and visible components. Hence **Sy:nchroniza·tion. Sy·nchronized** *ppl. a.*; spec. *s. gear-changing, -shifting,* a form of gear-changing in a motor vehicle by which both gears are brought to the same speed before the change is made. **Sy·nchronizing** *vbl. sb.* and *ppl. a.*, also, of gun-firing apparatus.

Synchrono·logy. 1736. [f. SYN- + CHRONOLOGY.] Combined or comparative chronology; arrangement of events according to dates, those of the same date being placed or treated together. Hence **Sy:nchronolo·gical** *a.*

Synchronous (si·ŋkrŏnəs), *a.* 1669. [f. late L. *synchronus* – Gr. σύγχρονος, f. σύν SYN- + χρόνος time; see -OUS.] **1.** Existing or happening at the same time; coincident in time; contemporary, simultaneous. **b.** *transf.* Relating to or treating of different events or things belonging to the same time or period; involving or indicating contemporaneous or simultaneous occurrence 1823. **c.** *S. curve* (Geom.), a curve which is the locus of the points reached at any instant by a number of particles descending from the same point down a family of curves under the action of gravity 1867. **2.** Recurring at the same successive instants of time; keeping time *with*; having coincident periods, as two sets of vibrations or the like 1677. **b.** *Electr.* applied to alternating currents having coincident periods; also, to a machine or motor working in time with the alternations of current 1901.

Hence **Sy·nchronous-ly** *adv.*, **-ness.**

Sy·nchrony. 1848. [f. Gr. σύγχρονος; see prec. and -Y[3].] = SYNCHRONISM 1, 2, 2 b.

‖**Synchysis** (si·ŋkisis). 1577. [Late L. (Donatus) – Gr. σύγχυσις, f. συγχεῖν mingle, confuse, f. σύν SYN- + χεῖν pour.] **1.** *Gram.* and *Rhet.* A confused arrangement of words in a sentence, obscuring the meaning. **2.** *Path.* Softening or fluidity of the vitreous humour of the eye; called *sparkling s.* (*s. scintillans*) when minute flakes of cholesterol float in the humour, giving it a sparkling appearance 1684.

Synclastic (sinklæ·stik), *a.* 1867. [f. Gr. σύν SYN- (alike) + κλαστός 'bent', f. κλᾶν break.] *Geom.* Of a curved surface: Having the same kind of curvature (concave or convex) in all directions.

Synclinal (siŋkləi·năl, si·ŋklinăl), *a.* and *sb.* 1833. [f. Gr. σύν SYN- + κλίνειν bend + -AL[1]. Cf. ANTICLINAL.] **A.** adj. *Geol.* Applied to a line or axis towards which strata dip or slope down in opposite directions; also said of the fold or bend in such strata, or of a valley, trough, or basin so formed. Opp. to ANTICLINAL. **b.** *transf.* and *gen.* Inclined or sloping towards each other, or characterized by such inclination 1880. **B.** *sb. Geol.* A s. line, fold or depression 1855. Hence **Sy·ncline,** a s. fold or depression. **Syncli·nical** *a.* = SYNCLINAL A.

Syncopal (si·ŋkŏpăl), *a.* 1689. [f. SYNCOPE + -AL[1] 1, perh. after Fr. *syncopal* (XV).] *Path.* Of, pertaining to, or marked by syncope.

Syncopate (si·ŋkŏpeⁱt), *v.* 1605. [– *syncopat-*, pa. ppl. stem of late and med.L. *syncopare* affect with syncope, f. SYNCOPE; see -ATE[3].] **1.** *Gram. trans.* To contract (a word) by omitting one or more syllables or letters in the middle; also *pass.*, to be produced by syncopation. **2.** *Mus.* **a.** *trans.* To begin (a note) on an unaccented part of a bar and sustain it into the accented part; to introduce syncopation into (a passage). Often in pa. pple. **b.** *intr.* To be marked by syncopation. 1667.

1. *Soldo* is syncopated for *solido* 1857.

Syncopation (siŋkŏpēi·ʃən). 1532. [– med. L. *syncopatio, -ōn-*, f. as prec.; see -ION.] **1.** *Gram.* Contraction of a word by omission of one or more syllables or letters in the middle; *transf.* a word so contracted (*rare*). **2.** *Mus.* The action of beginning a note on a normally unaccented part of the bar and sustaining it into the normally accented part, so as to produce the effect of shifting back or anticipating the accent; the shifting of accent so produced 1597.

‖**Syncope** (si·ŋkŏpi). late ME. [Late L. (also *syncopa*) – Gr. συγκοπή, f. σύν SYN- + κοπ- stem of κόπτειν strike, cut off.] **1.** *Path.* Failure of the heart's action, resulting in loss of consciousness, and sometimes in death. **2.** *Gram.* = prec. 1. Now *rare.* 1530. †**3.** *Mus.* = prec. 2. –1795. **4.** A cutting short; abbreviation, contraction; sudden cessation or interruption (*rare*) 1658.

4. Revelry, and dance, and show, Suffer a s. and solemn pause COWPER. Hence **Sy·ncopist** (*nonce-wd.*), one who syncopates a word; *spec.* one who omits letters and supplies their places with dashes, etc. as in satirical writing ADDISON.

Syncretic (siŋkrī·tik, -kre·tik), *a.* (*sb.*) 1840. [f. next.] Characterized by syncretism; aiming at a union or reconciliation of diverse beliefs, practices, or systems. **B.** *sb.* = SYNCRETIST 1883.

Syncretism (si·ŋkrĭtiz'm). 1618. [– mod. L. *syncretismus* (D. Pareus, 1615) – Gr. συγκρητισμός, f. συγκρητίζειν SYNCRETIZE.] Attempted union or reconciliation of diverse or opposite tenets or practices, esp. in philosophy or religion; *spec.* the system or principles of a school founded in the 17th c. by George Calixtus, who aimed at harmonizing the sects of Protestants and ultimately all Christian bodies. (Usu. derogatory.)

Syncretist (si·ŋkrĭtist). 1758. [f. prec.; see -IST.] One who practises or favours syncretism; *spec.* = CALIXTIN 2. Hence **Syncreti·stic** *a.* of or pertaining to syncretism or syncretists; characterized by syncretism.

Syncretize (si·ŋkrĭtəiz), *v.* 1675. [– Gr. συγκρητίζειν combine, as two parties against a third; of unkn. origin.] **1.** *intr.* To practise syncretism; to attempt to combine different or opposing tenets or systems; †*loosely,* to agree, accord. **2.** *trans.* To combine, as different systems, etc. 1907.

Synderesis: see SYNTERESIS.

Syndesmo- (sinde·smo), bef. a vowel **syndesm-,** repr. Gr. σύνδεσμος a ligament. **Syndesmo·graphy,** description of the ligaments. **Syndesmo·logy,** that branch of anatomy which treats of the ligaments. **Syndesmo·sis,** the union of two bones by a ligament; hence **Syndesmo·tic** *a.* **Syndesmo·tomy,** dissection or surgical section of ligaments.

Syndetic (sinde·tik), *a.* 1621. [– Gr. συνδετικός, f. συνδεῖν bind together.] Serving to unite or connect; connective, copulative. So **Synde·tical** *a.*, **-ly** *adv.*

Syndic (si·ndik). 1601. [– (O)Fr. *syndic,* †*-ique* delegate, chief magistrate of Geneva – late L. *syndicus* delegate of a corporation – Gr. σύνδικος defendant's advocate, f. σύν SYN- + *δικ-, base of δίκη judgement, δείκνυσθαι show.] **1.** An officer of government having different powers in different countries; a civil magistrate, or one of several such, entrusted with the affairs of a city or community; *spec.* each of the four chief magistrates of Geneva. **2.** One deputed to represent and transact the affairs of a corporation, e.g. a university; *spec.* in the University of Cambridge, applied to members of special committees of the senate, appointed by grace for specific duties 1607. †**3.** A censor of the actions of another –1658.

4. *Gr. Hist.* The title of various officials at Athens and elsewhere 1682.

Syndical (si·ndikăl), *a.* 1864. [– Fr. *syndical*, f. *syndic* SYNDIC; see -AL[1] 1.] Only in *s. chamber* (occas. *union*) = Fr. *chambre syndicale*, a union of people engaged in a particular trade, for the protection of their interests; a trade-union.

Syndicalism (si·ndikăliz'm). 1907. [– Fr. *syndicalisme*, f. *syndical*; see prec., -ISM.] A movement among industrial workers having as its object the transfer of the means of production and distribution from their present owners to unions of workers for the benefit of the workers, the method generally favoured for the accomplishment of this being the general strike. So **Sy·ndicalist**, an adherent of s.

Syndicate (si·ndikĕt), *sb.* 1624. [– Fr. *syndicat* – med.L. *syndicatus*, f. late L. *syndicus*; see SYNDIC, -ATE[1].] †**1.** The office, status, or jurisdiction of a syndic –1728. **2.** A council or body of syndics; also, a meeting of such a body 1624. **3.** A combination of capitalists or financiers entered into for the purpose of prosecuting a scheme requiring large resources of capital, esp. one having the object of obtaining control of the market in a particular commodity. Hence, more widely, a combination of persons formed for the promotion of an enterprise; *esp.* a combination for the acquisition of articles, etc. and their simultaneous publication in a number of periodicals; also, a combination of newspapers controlled by such a body 1865.

Syndicate (si·ndikeᶦt), *v.* 1610. [In sense 1 – *syndicat-*, pa. ppl. stem of med.L. *syndicare* subject to an inquiry; in other senses f. prec.; see -ATE[3].] †**1.** *trans.* To judge, censure –1822. **2.** To control, manage, or effect by a syndicate; *esp.* to publish simultaneously in a number of newspapers 1882. **3.** To combine into a syndicate 1889.

2. Dr. Talmage syndicates his sermons, and they are published in Monday's newspapers in all quarters of America 1891.

Syndication (sindikēᶦ·ʃən). 1650. [In sense 1 – med.L. *syndicatio, -ōn-* examination, f. as prec.; see -ION. In sense 2 f. prec.] †**1.** The action of judging. HOBBES. **2.** The action or process of forming a syndicate 1887.

‖**Syndrome** (si·ndrŏᵘm, si·ndrŏmi). 1541. [mod.L. – Gr. συνδρομή, f. σύν SYN- + δρομ-: δραμεῖν run.] **1.** *Path.* A concurrence of several symptoms in a disease; a set of such concurrent symptoms. **2.** *transf.* or *gen.* A concurrence; a set of concurrent things 1646.

Syne (səin), *adv. Sc.* and *n. dial.* ME. [Contracted f. SITHEN.] **1.** = SINCE A. 1 (occas. strengthened by *after*). **2.** At a later time, afterwards, subsequently; esp. in *soon or syne*, sooner or later. late ME. **3.** Since then. late ME. **4.** (So long) before now; ago 1573.

Synecdoche (sine·kdŏki). late ME. [– L. *synecdoche* – Gr. συνεκδοχή, f. συνεκδέχεσθαι, lit. take with something else, f. σύν SYN- + ἐκδέχεσθαι take, take up.] *Gram.* and *Rhet.* A figure by which a more comprehensive term is used for a less comprehensive or *vice versa*; as whole for part or part for whole, genus for species or species for genus, etc. Hence **Synecdo·chic, Synecdo·chical** *adjs.* involving s. or synecdochism. **Synecdo·chically** *adv.* by s.

Synecdochism (sine·kdŏkiz'm). 1854. [f. prec. + -ISM.] **a.** *Gram.* and *Rhet.* Synecdochical style; the use of synecdoche. **b.** *Ethnol.* Belief or practice in which a part of an object or person is taken as equivalent to the whole, so that anything done to, or by means of, the part is held to take effect upon, or have the effect of, the whole.

Synectic (sine·ktik), *a.* 1697. [– late L. *synecticus* – Gr. συνεκτικός, f. συνέχειν, f. συν- SYN- + ἔχειν have, hold.] **a.** Of a cause: Producing its effect directly; immediate; *spec.* in *Old Med.* = CONTINENT *a.* 6. **b.** *Math.* Applied to certain continuous functions 1888.

Synedrian (sine·driăn), *sb.* and *a.* 1606. [f. next + -AN]. **A.** *sb.* A member of a synedrion. **B.** *adj.* Of or belonging to a synedrion.

‖**Synedrion** (sine·driŏn), **synedrium** (-ŏm). *Pl.* **synedria.** 1584. [mod.L. – Gr. συνέδριον, f. σύνεδρος sitting with, f. σύν SYN- + ἕδρα seat.] A judicial or representative assembly, a council, consistory; *spec.* the Jewish SANHEDRIM.

‖**Syneidesis** (sinəidī·sis). 1620. [Gr. συνείδησις consciousness, conscience (in Vulg. tr. *conscientia*), f. συνειδέναι be cognizant of or privy to a thing.] *Theol.* That function or department of conscience which is concerned with passing judgement on acts already performed.

Synergetic (sinəɹdʒe·tik), *a. rare.* 1682. [– Gr. συνεργητικός, f. συνεργεῖν work together, co-operate.] = next.

Synergic (sinə̄·ɹdʒik), *a.* 1859. [f. Gr. συνεργός working together, f. συνεργεῖν work together; see -IC.] *Physiol.* Working together, co-operating, as a group of muscles for the production of some movement; pertaining to or involving synergy.

Synergism (si·nəɹdʒiz'm). 1764. [f. as prec.; see -ISM.] *Theol.* The doctrine that the human will co-operates with Divine grace in the work of regeneration.

Synergist (si·nəɹdʒist). 1657. [f. as prec.; see -IST.] **1.** *Theol.* One who holds the doctrine of synergism. **2.** *Med.* and *Physiol.* A medicine, etc., or a bodily organ (*e.g.* a muscle) that co-operates with another or others. Hence **Synergi·stic** *a. Theol.* of or pertaining to synergism or the synergists; (of a medicine, etc.) acting as a s.

Synergy (si·nəɹdʒi). 1847. [– mod.L. *synergia* – Gr. συνεργία, f. as prec.; see -IA[1].] Combined or correlated action of a group of bodily organs (as nerve-centres, muscles, etc.); hence, of mental faculties, of remedies, etc.

‖**Syngenesia** (sindʒĭnī·ziă, -siă). 1753. [mod.L. (Linnæus, 1730), f. Gr. σύν SYN- + γένεσις GENESIS; see -IA[1].] *Bot.* The nineteenth class in the Linnæan Sexual System, comprising plants having stamens coherent by the anthers, and flowers (florets) in close heads or *capitula*; corresponding to the family *Compositæ*. Hence **Syngene·sian** *a.* = next.

Syngenesious (sindʒĭnī·ʃəs, -ī·siəs), *a.* 1753. [f. prec. + -OUS.] *Bot.* **a.** Belonging to the class *Syngenesia*; having the stamens united by their anthers. **b.** Of the stamens: United by the anthers so as to form a tube, as in the *Syngenesia*; also said of the anthers.

Syngenesis (sindʒe·nĭsis). 1836. [f. SYN- + GENESIS.] *Biol.* Formation of the germ in sexual reproduction by fusion of the male and female elements, so that the substance of the embryo is derived from both parents. Hence **Syngene·tic** *a.*

Syngraph (si·ŋgrɑf). Also in L. form. 1633. [– L. *syngrapha* (*-us*) – Gr. συγγραφή (-ος), f. συγγράφειν compose in writing, draw up, f. σύν SYN- + γράφειν write.] A written contract or bond signed by both or all the parties.

‖**Synizesis** (sinizī·sis). *Pl.* **-ses** (-sīz). 1820. [Late L. – Gr. συνίζησις, f. συνιζάνειν sink down, collapse, f. σύν SYN- + ἱζάνειν seat, sit, settle down, f. ἵζειν seat, sit.] **1.** *Gram.* and *Pros.* Fusion of two syllables into one by the coalescence of two adjacent vowels (or of a vowel and a diphthong) without the formation of a recognized diphthong 1846. **2.** *Path.* Closure of the pupil of the eye 1820.

‖**Synocha** (si·nŏkă). 1801. [med.L., fem. of SYNOCHUS.] *Path.* A continued or unintermitting fever (or a particular variety of this; cf. SYNOCHUS). Hence **Sy·nochal** *a.* of the nature of or pertaining to s. (or synochus) 1541.

‖**Synochus** (si·nŏkŏs). late ME. [med.L. – Gr. σύνοχος, f. σύν SYN- + ὀχ-: ἔχειν have, after συνέχειν hold together, be continuous.] *Path.* = SYNOCHA (but often dist. as a different species).

Synod (si·nŏd). late ME. [– late L. *synodus* – Gr. σύνοδος meeting, f. σύν SYN- + ὁδός way, travel.] **1.** *Eccl.* An assembly of the clergy of a particular church, nation, province, or diocese (sometimes with representatives of the laity) duly convened for discussing and deciding ecclesiastical affairs. †In early use freq. applied to general councils. **b.** In Presbyterian Churches: A body or assembly of ministers and other elders, constituting the ecclesiastical court next above the presbytery, and consisting of the members of, or of delegates from, the presbyteries within its bounds 1593. **2.** *gen.* and *transf.* An assembly, convention, or council of any kind 1578. †**3.** *Astrol.* A conjunction of two planets or heavenly bodies –1686.

2. Sir, we could not have had a better dinner, had there been a S. of Cooks JOHNSON.

Synodal (si·nŏdăl), *a.* and *sb.* 1450. [– late L. *synodalis*, f. *synodus* SYNOD; see -AL[1] 1.] **A.** *adj.* **1.** Done or made by, or proceeding from a synod (†or general council). **2.** Of the nature of or constituted as a synod 1530. †**b.** *transf.* Connected with or related to church government by synodal assemblies, presbyterian –1640. **3.** Of, belonging to, or connected with, having or characterized by, a synod or visitation 1579.

1. The S. decrees of the Council of 214 Bishops at Carthage 1865.

B. *sb.* **1.** A synodal decision, constitution, or decree. *Obs.* exc. *Hist.* 1485. **2.** A payment made by the inferior clergy to the bishop, properly on the occasion of a synod, and hence at an episcopal or archidiaconal visitation 1534.

2. At Easter Visitation the Ministers pay their Pascal Rents, or Synodals 1667.

Synodic (sinǫ·dik), *a.* 1640. [– late L. *synodicus* – late Gr. συνοδικός, f. σύνοδος SYNOD; see -IC.] **1.** *Eccl.* = SYNODAL *a.* **2.** *Astron.* = next 2. 1654.

Synodical (sinǫ·dikăl), *a.* 1561. [f. as prec.; see -ICAL.] **1.** *Eccl.* = SYNODAL *a.* **2.** *Astron.* Pertaining to the conjunction of two heavenly bodies (see CONJUNCTION 3); said *esp.* of the revolution, or period of revolution, of a planet between two successive conjunctions with the sun, or of a satellite between two successive conjunctions with (or occultations or eclipses by) its primary planet 1669.

1. A Synodicall Epistle 1561. S. majorities 1866. 2. *S. month*, the synodic period of the moon, i.e. the time from new moon to new moon; a lunar month, lunation. Hence **Syno·dically** *adv.* by the action or authority of a synod; in synod, as a synod.

Synodist (si·nŏdist). 1626. [f. SYNOD + -IST.] †**1.** A member of a synod –1650. **2.** An adherent of a synod; used disparagingly of those who accepted the decrees of the Council of Chalcedon (*rare*) 1846.

Synœcious (sinī·ʃᶦəs), *a.* 1863. [f. SYN-, after DIŒCIOUS, etc.; cf. Gr. συνοικία community living together.] *Bot.* Having male and female flowers in the same flower-head, as some *Compositæ*, or male and female organs in the same receptacle, as some mosses.

Synœcism (sinī·siz'm). 1886. [– Gr. συνοικισμός, f. συνοικίζειν cause to dwell with, unite under one capital city, f. σύν SYN- + οἰκίζειν found as a colony, colonize, f. οἶκος house.] *Gr. Antiq.* The union of several towns or villages into or under one capital city. So **Synœ·cize** *v. trans.* to unite into or under one capital city.

Synomosy (sinŏᵘ·mŏsi). 1808. [– Gr. συνωμοσία, f. συνομνύναι to confederate, f. σύν SYN- + ὀμνύναι swear.] *Gr. Antiq.* A political society of men leagued by oath.

Synonym (si·nŏnim). late ME. [– L. *synonymum* – Gr. συνώνυμον, subst. use of n. sing. of συνώνυμος, f. σύν SYN- + -ωνυμ- NAME (as in ANONYMOUS).] **1.** Strictly, a word having the same sense as another (in the same language); but more usu., either of any two or more words (in the same language) having the same general sense, but possessing each of them meanings which are not shared by the other or others, or having different shades of meaning appropriate to different contexts, e.g. *serpent, snake*; *ship, vessel*; *glad, happy*; *to kill, slay, slaughter*. **b.** spec. in *Nat. Hist.* A systematic name having the same, or nearly the same, application as another, esp. as another which has superseded it 1659. **c.** The equivalent of a word in another language 1594. **2.** By extension: A name or expression which involves or implies a meaning properly or literally expressed by some other, 'another name *for*' 1631. **3.** *transf.* Either of two or more things of like or identical nature but called by different names, e.g. corresponding geological formations in different regions 1839.

1. Change the structure of the sentence; substitute one synonyme for another; and the whole effect is destroyed MACAULAY. **b.** We cannot have too complete a catalogue of all the species.. together with their synonyms 1833. **c.** Had *life* been used instead of its Latin s. *ens* 1804. **2.** 'Hobbism' became..the popular s. for irreligion and immorality J. R. GREEN.

Synonymic (sinǒni·mik), *a.* (*sb.*) 1816. [f. prec. + -IC, after Fr. *synonymique.*] Of, relating to, consisting of, or exhibiting synonyms. **B.** *sb.* The study of synonyms, as a department of grammar. Also **Synony·mics** 1857.

Synony·mical, *a. rare.* 1645. [f. as prec. + -ICAL.] †**1.** = SYNONYMOUS 1. –1690. **2.** = prec. 1806. Hence **Synony·mically** *adv.* as a synonym or synonyms 1599.

Synonymist (sinǫ·nimist). 1753. [f. as prec. + -IST; cf. Fr. *synonymiste.*] One who treats of, or makes a list of, synonyms.

Synonymity (sinǒni·mĭti). 1875. [f. SYNONYMOUS; see -ITY.] The quality or fact of being synonymous, or having the same meaning 1880. **b.** *transf.* Identity of nature of things having different names 1875.

Synonymize (sinǫ·nimaiz), *v. rare.* 1595. [f. late L. *synonymum* + -IZE.] **1.** *trans.* To give the synonyms of. **2.** *intr.* To use synonyms; to express the same meaning by different words 1700.

1. This worde *fortis* wee maye synnonomize after all these fashions, stoute, hardye, valiaunt, doughtye, Couragious, adueuturous, &c. 1595.

Synonymous (sinǫ·nimәs), *a.* 1610. [f. med.L. *synonymus* – Gr. συνώνυμος; see SYNONYM, -OUS.] **1.** Having the character of a synonym; equivalent in meaning: said of words or phrases denoting the same thing or idea. Const. *to*, (now usu. *with*). **b.** *transf.* Said of things of the same nature denoted by different names, i.e. by synonyms; thus = identical 1789. **2.** In extended sense, said of words or phrases which denote things that imply one another 1659. **3.** *loosely* = HOMONYMOUS 2. 1734.

1. Words are seldom exactly synonimous JOHNSON. To say that a person 'is down in the mouth' is s. with saying that he is out of spirits DARWIN. **2.** The name of soldier was s. with that of marauder 1855. Hence **Syno·nymous-ly** *adv.*, **-ness.**

Synonymy (sinǫ·nimi). 1609. [– late L. *synonymia* – Gr. συνωνυμία, f. συνώνυμος SYNONYM; see -Y³.] †**1.** = SYNONYM 1. –1799. **2.** The use of synonyms or of words as synonyms; *spec.* a rhetorical figure by which synonyms are used for the sake of amplification 1657. **3.** The subject or study of synonyms; synonyms collectively; a set of synonyms 1683. **4.** The quality or fact of being synonymous; identity of meaning 1794.

Synopsis (sinǫ·psis). *Pl.* **synopses** (-sīz). 1611. [– late L. *synopsis* – Gr. σύνοψις, f. σύν SYN- + ὄψις view.] **1.** A brief or condensed statement presenting a combined or general view of something; a table, or set of paragraphs or headings, so arranged as to exhibit all the parts or divisions of a subject or work at one view; a conspectus. **2.** *Eastern Ch.* A book of prayers for the use of the laity 1850.

1. He hath written a s. of the history of man 1611.

Synoptic (sinǫ·ptik), *a.* (*sb.*) 1763. [– Gr. συνοπτικός, f. σύνοψις; see prec., -IC.] **1.** Of a table, chart, etc.: Pertaining to or forming a synopsis; furnishing a general view of some subject. **b.** Of a mental act or faculty, conduct, etc.: Pertaining to, involving, or taking a combined or comprehensive view of something 1852. **2.** Applied distinctively to the first three Gospels (viz. of Matthew, Mark, and Luke) as giving an account of the events from the same point of view or under the same general aspect. Also *transf.* pertaining or relating to these Gospels. 1841. **b.** as *sb.* Any one of the Synoptic Gospels (or of their writers). Usu. in *pl.* 1858. So **Syno·ptical** *a.* 1664, **-ly** *adv.* in the way of a synopsis.

Synoptist (sinǫ·ptist). 1860. [f. prec.; see -IST.] Any one of the writers of the Synoptic Gospels. (Usu. in *pl.*)

Synostose (si·nǫstōᵘz), *v.* 1878. [Back-formation from next. Cf. ANCHYLOSE.] *pass.* and *intr.* To be affected with synostosis; to be united by a growth of bone.

Synostosis (sinǫstōᵘ·sis). *Pl.* **-oses** (-ōᵘ·sīz). 1848. [Contracted from *synosteosis.*] *Anat.* and *Physiol.* Union or fusion of adjacent bones by growth of bony substance (either normal or abnormal). Hence **Synosto·tic** *a.*

‖**Synovia** (sinōᵘ·viă, sәi-). 1661. [mod.L. *sinovia, synovia*, also *sinophia*, an invention, prob. arbitrary, of Paracelsus (died 1541), applied by him to the nutritive fluid peculiar to the several parts of the body, and also to the gout.] *Physiol.* The viscid albuminous fluid secreted in the interior of the joints, and in the sheaths of the tendons, and serving to lubricate them; also called *joint-oil* or *joint-water* 1726. †**b.** *Path.* A morbid condition or discharge of this fluid –1766.

Synovial (sinōᵘ·viăl, sәi-) *a.* 1756. [f. prec. + -AL¹ 1.] Pertaining to, consisting of, containing, or secreting synovia. **b.** *transf.* Occurring in or affecting a synovial membrane 1846.

The s. fluid is viscid, transparent, of a yellow or reddish colour, faintly saline 1846. Hence **Syno·vially** *adv.* by means of synovia, or of a joint containing synovia.

Synovitis (sinǒvәi·tis, sәi-). 1835. [f. SYNOVIA + -ITIS.] *Path.* Inflammation of a synovial membrane.

Syntactic (sintæ·ktik), *a.* 1828. [var. of next; see -IC, -ICAL.] = next.

Synta·ctical, *a.* 1577. [f. Gr. συντακτικός, f. συντάσσειν; see SYNTAX, -IC. Cf. contemp. *syntaxical.*] Belonging or relating to syntax. Hence **Synta·ctically** *adv.* in respect of syntax. **Syntacti·cian,** an expert in syntax.

‖**Syntagma** (sintæ·gmă). *Pl.* **-ata** or **-as.** 1644. [– late and med.L. *syntagma* – Gr. σύνταγμα, f. συντάσσειν; see next.] **1.** A regular or orderly collection of statements, propositions, doctrines, etc.; a systematically arranged treatise. **2.** *Antiq.* **a.** A body of persons forming a division of the population of a country. **b.** A body of troops forming a division of a phalanx. 1813. **3.** *Bot.* An aggregate of 'tagmata' 1885.

Syntax (si·ntæks). 1605. [– Fr. *syntaxe* or late L. *syntaxis* – Gr. σύνταξις, f. συντάσσειν, f. σύν SYN- + τάσσειν arrange.] †**1.** Orderly or systematic arrangement of parts or elements; constitution (of body); a connected order or system of things –1696. **2.** *Gram.* **a.** The arrangement of words (in their appropriate forms) by which their connection and relation in a sentence are shown. Also, the constructional uses of a word or form or a class of words or forms, or those characteristic of a particular author. **b.** The department of grammar which deals with the established usages of grammatical construction and the rules deduced therefrom: dist. from *accidence.* 1613. **c.** Name of a class in certain English Roman Catholic schools and colleges, next below that called *Poetry* 1629.

1. Concerning the S. and disposition of studies, that men may know in what order..to reade BACON. **2.** Neither Sense nor S. would allow of that Signification BENTLEY. Hence **Synta·xian,** a member of the Syntax class in a R. C. school.

†**Synta·xis.** 1540. [Late and med.L. *syntaxis*; see prec.] = prec. 2. –1749.

‖**Synteresis** (sintĭrī·sis). *Pl.* **-eses** (-ī·sīz). Also †**synderesis** (cf. Fr. *syndérèse*). 1594. [med.L. (Aquinas), Gr. συντήρησις careful guarding or watching, f. σύν SYN- + τηρεῖν watch over, guard.] **1.** *Theol.* That function or department of conscience which serves as a guide for conduct; conduct as directive of one's actions: dist. from SYNEIDESIS. Now *Hist.* **2.** *Med.* Prophylactic or preventive treatment. (prob. only a book-term) 1848.

Synthesis (si·nþĭsis). *Pl.* **-es** (-īz). 1606. [– L. *synthesis* – Gr. σύνθεσις composition, etc., f. συντιθέναι; see SYN-, THESIS.] **1.** *Logic, Philos.*, etc. The action of proceeding in thought from causes to effects or from laws or principles to their consequences. (Opp. to ANALYSIS 8.) 1611. †**2.** *Gram.* A figure by which a sentence is constructed according to the sense, in violation of strict syntax –1704. **3.** *Chem.* Formation of a compound by combination of its elements or constituents; esp. applied to artificial production in this way of organic compounds formerly obtained by extraction from natural products 1733. **b.** *Physics.* Production of white or other compound light by combination of its constituent colours, or of a complex musical sound by combination of its component simple tones 1869. **4.** In the philosophy of Kant, the action of the understanding in combining and unifying the isolated data of sensation into a cognizable whole 1817. **5.** In wider philosophical use and *gen.* The putting together of parts or elements so as to make up a complex whole; the combination of immaterial or abstract things, or of elements into an ideal or abstract whole. (Opp. to ANALYSIS 1.) Also the state of being so put together. 1833. **b.** A body of things put together; a complex whole made up of a number of parts or elements united 1865. **c.** *Philol.* Synthetic formation or construction 1869. **6.** *Rom. Antiq.* A loose flowing robe, white or bright-coloured, worn at meals and festivities 1606.

3. Alcohol can also be prepared from its elements by s. 1869. **4.** Experience proves the possibility of the s. of the predicate 'heavy', with the subject 'body'; for these two notions, although neither is contained in the other, are nevertheless parts of a whole, or of experience 1839. **5.** The happiest *s.* of the divine, the scholar, and the gentleman COLERIDGE.

Synthesist (si·nþĭsist). 1863. [f. next; see -IST.] One who uses synthesis, or proceeds by a synthetic method. (Opp. to ANALYST.)

Synthesize (si·nþĭsәiz), *v.* 1830. [f. SYNTHES(IS + -IZE.] *trans.* To make a synthesis of; to put together or combine into a complex whole; to make up by combination of parts or elements. Also *absol.* (Opp. to ANALYSE.) **b.** *Chem.* To produce (a compound, esp. an organic compound) by synthesis 1865.

b. The kidney is capable of synthesising complex organic substances 1897.

Synthetic (sinþe·tik), *a.* 1697. [– Fr. *synthétique* (XVII), or mod.L. *syntheticus* – Gr. συνθετικός, f. συνθετός, f. συντιθέναι put together, f. σύν SYN- + τιθέναι place.] (In most senses opp. to ANALYTIC.) **1.** *Logic, Philos.*, etc. Proceeding from causes or general principles to consequences or particular instances; deductive. **2.** *Chem.* Pertaining to or involving synthesis; of organic compounds, produced by artificial synthesis 1753. **3.** In the philosophy of Kant, (*a*) applied to judgements which add to the subject attributes not directly implied in it; (*b*) pertaining to the synthesis of the manifold 1819. **4.** Of, pertaining to, consisting in, or involving synthesis, or combination of parts into a whole; constructive 1702. **b.** Concerned with or using synthesis 1864. **5.** **5.** *Gram.* and *Philol.* Characterized by combination of simple words or elements into compound or complex words; expressing a complex notion by a single compounded or complex word instead of by a number of distinct words 1835. **6.** *Biol.* Combining in one organism different characters which in the later course of evolution are specialized in different organisms; having a generalized or undifferentiated type of structure 1859.

2. b. Applied gen. to preparations simulating a natural product; hence, artificial 1916. **5.** The s. character of ancient languages 1869. So **Synthe·tical** *a.* 1620, **-ly** *adv.*

Synthetism (si·nþĭtiz'm). 1832. [f. SYNTHETIC or SYNTHETIZE; see -ISM.] A synthetic system or doctrine.

Synthetist (si·nþĭtist). 1848. [f. as prec.; see -IST.] = SYNTHESIST.

Synthetize (si·nþĭtәiz), *v.* 1828. [– Gr. συνθετίζεσθαι, f. συνθετός; see SYNTHETIC, -IZE.] *trans.* = SYNTHESIZE.

‖**Synthronus** (si·nþrǒnǒs). *Eccl.* 1861. [– Gr. σύνθρονος, f. σύν SYN- + θρόνος THRONE.] The joint throne of the bishop and his presbyters.

Syntonic (sintǫ·nik), *a.* 1892. [f. SYN- + TONE + -IC.] *Electr.* Denoting a system of wireless telegraphy in which the transmitting and receiving instruments are accurately 'tuned' or adjusted so that the latter responds only to vibrations of the frequency of those emitted by the former; also said of the instruments so 'tuned'. Hence **Syn·to·nically** *adv.*

Syntonin (si·ntŏnin). 1859. [f. Gr. σύντονος (see SYNTONOUS) + -IN¹.] *Chem.* An acid albuminous substance found in muscular tissue, or produced from myosin by the action of acids.

Syntonize (si·ntŏnəiz), *v.* 1892. [f. SYNTONIC + -IZE.] *Electr. trans.* To make syntonic. Hence **Sy·ntonizer**, an apparatus for syntonizing.

Syntonous (si·ntŏnəs), *a.* 1789. [f. Gr. σύντονος strained tight, high-pitched, f. σύν SYN- + τείνειν stretch; see -OUS.] *Mus.* An epithet for the ordinary form of diatonic scale (διάτονον σύντονον) in ancient Greek music, in which the tetrachord was divided into a semitone and two tones, the third note of it being thus tuned to a higher pitch than in the other scales; nearly corresponding to the modern diatonic scale.

Syntony (si·ntŏni). 1892. [f. SYNTONIC + -Y³.] *Electr.* The condition of being syntonic.

Sypher (səi·fəɹ), *v.* 1841. [var. of CIPHER *v.*] *Carpentry.* To make a lap-joint by overlapping two bevelled or chamfered plank-edges, so as to leave a plane surface. So **S.-joint.**

Syphilide (si·filəid). 1879. [orig. in pl. – Fr. *syphilides*, f. SYPHILIS after names of zoological families; see -ID³.] *Path.* A generic term for any skin affection of a syphilitic nature.

Syphilis (si·filis). 1718. [mod.L. *syphilis* (*syphilid-*), orig. the title (in full, *Syphilis, sive Morbus Gallicus*) of a poem, published 1530, by Girolamo Fracastoro (1483–1553), a physician, astronomer and poet of Verona, but used also as the name of the disease in the poem itself; the name *Syphilis* being formed on the analogy of *Æneis, Thebais*, etc., from that of a shepherd *Syphilus*, the first sufferer from the disease.] *Path.* A specific disease caused by *Treponema pallidum* (*Spirochæte pallida*) and communicated by sexual connection or accidental contact (acquired form) or by infection of the child in utero (congenital form).

Three stages of the disease are distinguished, *primary, secondary,* and *tertiary s.*; the first characterized by chancre in the part affected, the second by affections of the skin and mucous membranes, the third involving the bones, muscles, and brain.

Syphilitic (sifili·tik), *a.* (*sb.*) 1786. [– mod.L. *syphiliticus* (Sauvages), f. SYPHILIS.] *Path.* Of, pertaining to, caused by, or affected with syphilis. **B.** *sb.* A person affected with syphilis 1881.

Syphilize (si·filəiz), *v.* 1854. [– Fr. *syphiliser*; see SYPHILIS, -IZE.] *Med.* and *Path. trans.* To inoculate with the virus of syphilis, as a means of cure or prevention; also, to infect with syphilis. Hence **Sy:philiza·tion.**

Syphilo- (si·filo), used as comb. form of SYPHILIS. **Sy·philoderm, ‖-derma** (pl. *-ata*) [Gr. δέρμα skin] = SYPHILIDE; hence **Syphilode·rmatous** *a.* **Syphilo·grapher,** a writer on syphilis; so **Syphilo·graphy,** the description of syphilis. **Syphilo·logist, -o·logy.**

Syphiloid (si·filoid), *a.* (*sb.*) 1813. [f. SYPHILIS + -OID.] *Path.* Resembling syphilis. **B.** *sb.* A s. disease or affection 1890.

Syphiloma (sifilōᵘ·mă). *Pl.* **-ata.** 1864. [f. SYPHILIS + -OMA, as in *sarcoma.*] *Path.* A syphilitic tumour. Hence **Syphilo·matous** *a.*

Syphilosis (sifilōᵘ·sis). 1898. [f. SYPHILIS + -OSIS.] *Path.* Syphilitic condition.

Syphon: see SIPHON.

Syracusan (səiᵊrăkiū̆·zăn), *a.* and *sb.* 1576. [– L. *Syracusanus*, f. *Syracusæ*, Gk. Συράκουσαι Syracuse + -AN.] Of or belonging to (a native or inhabitant of) Syracuse, a city in Sicily. So †**Syracu·sian** *a.* and *sb.* –1796.

Syracuse (səi·ᵊrăkiūz). 1768. [See prec.] A luscious red muscadine wine made in Italy.

Syriac (si·riæk), *a.* and *sb.* 1602. [– L. *Syriacus* – Gr. Συριακός, f. Συρία; see -AC.] **A.** *adj.* Of or pertaining to Syria: only of or in ref. to the language; written in Syriac; writing, or versed, in Syriac.

A very curious old S. copy of the Four Gospels 1867.

B. *sb.* The ancient Semitic language of Syria; formerly, = ARAMAIC; now, the form of Aramaic used by Syrian Christians, in which the Peshito version of the Bible is written 1611. **b.** A or the Syriac version (of the Bible) 1644. Hence **Sy·riacism** (-ăsiz'm) = SYRIASM. **Sy·riacist** (-ăsist), a S. scholar.

Syrian (si·riăn), *sb.* and *a.* late ME. [– OFr. *sirien* (mod. *syrien*), f. L. *Syrius* – Gr. Σύριος; see -AN.] **A.** *sb.* A native or inhabitant of Syria. **B.** *adj.* Of, belonging to, or characteristic of Syria or the Syrians 1537. Hence **Sy·rianism** = SYRIASM.

Syriarch (si·riaɹk). 1840. [– late L. *Syriarcha, -us* – Gr. Συριάρχης, f. Συρία Syria; see -ARCH.] The director of public games in Syria under the Romans, who was at the same time the chief priest.

Syriasm (si·riæz'm). 1684. [irreg. contr. of earlier *Syriacism* (MILT.), f. SYRIAC + -ISM.] A phrase or construction characteristic of the Syriac language; a Syriac idiom or expression.

It hath. .many Hebraisms and Syriasms 1684.

Syringa (sĭri·ŋgă). 1664. [– mod.L. *syringa*, f. Gr. σῦριγξ, συριγγ- SYRINX; first applied (by Lobel, 1576) to the mock orange, from its stems being used for pipe-stems, later (by Linnæus, 1735) to the lilac (formerly called *pipe tree*), of which it remains the botanical generic name.] Any of the shrubs of the genus *Philadelphus*, esp. *P. coronarius*, the mock-orange (see MOCK *a.*), having creamy-white strongly sweet-scented flowers, cultivated as an ornamental shrub.

Syringe (si·rindʒ), *sb.* late ME. [– med.L. *syringa*, f. L. SYRINX; orig. *siryng, syring*, which in XVI became assim. to obl. cases of the L. *syrinx*, pl. *syringes* (siri·ndʒīz).] **1.** A small cylindrical instrument, in its commonest form consisting of a tube fitted with a piston, used to draw in a quantity of water or other liquid, and to eject it forcibly in a stream or jet for making injections, cleansing wounds, etc.; †also used as a catheter. **b.** A similar instrument used for various purposes, as exhausting or compressing air, squirting water over plants, etc. 1659. **2.** Applied to certain structures in insects 1826.

Syringe (si·rinᵈʒ), *v.* 1610. [f. prec.] **1.** *trans.* To treat with a syringe; to inject or sprinkle fluid into or upon by means of a syringe. Also *absol.* **2.** *intr.* To inject (liquid) by means of a syringe 1653.

2. This Balsam. .is to be syringed. .into the Wound 1737.

Syringeal (siri·ndʒĭăl), *a.* 1872. [f. L. *syring-* SYRINX, + -AL¹ 1.] *Ornith.* Of, pertaining to, or connected with the syrinx in birds.

Syringin (siri·ndʒin). 1843. [– Fr. *syringine*, f. *Syringa*, generic name of the lilac; see -IN¹.] *Chem.* A white crystalline substance, $C_{17}H_{24}O_9$, obtained from the lilac, *Syringa vulgaris.*

Syringo- (siri·ŋgo), comb. form of Gr. σῦριγξ, συριγγ- SYRINX. **‖Syri:ngomye·lia, ‖-my·elus** [Gr. μυελός marrow], dilatation of the central canal of the spinal cord, or formation of abnormal tubular cavities in its substance; so **Syri:ngomyeli·tis,** inflammation of the spinal cord producing syringomyelia. **Syri·ngotome** [mod.L. *syringotomus*, Gr. -τομος cutting], an instrument for cutting a fistula; so **Syringo·tomy,** incision of a fistula.

Syrinx (si·riŋks). *Pl.* **syringes** (siri·ndʒīz), also **sy·rinxes.** 1606. [– L. *syrinx*, *syring-* – Gr. σῦριγξ, συριγγ- pipe, tube, channel, fistula.] **1.** = PAN-PIPE. Also *attrib.* **2.** *Archæol. pl.* Narrow rock-cut channels or tunnels, esp. in the burial vaults of ancient Egypt 1678. **3.** *Ornith.* The organ of voice in birds, the lower larynx, at or near the junction of the trachea and bronchi 1872.

‖Syrma (sɜ̄·ɹmă). 1753. [L. – Gr. σύρμα, f. σύρειν drag or trail along.] *Antiq.* A long trailing garment, as that worn by tragic actors.

‖Syrmæa (səɹmī·ă). Also **surmaia, surmia.** 1833. [– Gr. συρμαία radish, purge, f. συρμός vomiting, purging, f. σύρειν drag along, sweep away, purge.] *Antiq.* A cathartic said to have been used in some Egyptian forms of embalming.

Syro- (səiᵊ·ro), – Gr. Συρο-, comb. form of Σύρος a Syrian, used with adjs. or sbs. denoting other peoples, countries, languages, etc., signifying 'Syrian or in a Syrian way', or 'Syrian and. .', as *Syro-Arabian, -Galilæan, -Roman.*

Syrophœnician (səiᵊ:rofĭni·ʃ¹ăn), *sb.* (*a.*) 1560. [f. L. *Syrophœnix, -ic-* – Gr. Συροφοίνιξ, -ικ-; see SYRO, PHŒNICIAN.] A native or inhabitant of Syrophœnicia, a Roman province of Western Asia, including Phœnicia and the territories of Damascus and Palmyra. Also *adj.* belonging to this country or its inhabitants.

‖Syrphus (sɜ̄·ɹfŏs). *Pl.* **syrphi** (sɜ̄·ɹfəi). 1834. [mod.L. (Fabricius, 1775) – Gr. σύρφος gnat.] *Ent.* A fly of the genus *Syrphus*, typical of the *Syrphidæ*, a large and widely distributed family of two-winged flies, mostly bright-coloured, feeding on pollen and in the larval state often on plant-lice, etc. Hence **Sy·rphian, Sy·rphid** *adjs.* belonging to this family; also as *sbs.*

†**Syrt.** 1575. [– L. SYRTIS. Cf. Fr. (pl.) *sirtes, syrtes.*] = SYRTIS. –1718.

Syrtic (sɜ̄·ɹtik), *a.* 1846. [– L. *syrticus*, f. *Syrtis*; see next, -IC.] Of, pertaining to, or of the nature of a quicksand.

‖Syrtis (sɜ̄·ɹtis). *Pl.* **syrtes** (-īz). 1526. [L. – Gr. Σύρτις, σύρτις, f. σύρειν drag along, sweep away.] Proper name of two large quicksands (*S. major* and *minor*) off the northern coast of Africa; hence *gen.* a quicksand.

Quencht in a Boggie S., neither Sea, Nor good dry Land MILT.

Syrup (si·rəp), *sb.* late ME. [– (O)Fr. *sirop* or med.L. *siropus, sirupus*, ult. – Arab. *šarāb* beverage, drink. Cf. SHRUB², SHERBET.] **1.** A thick sweet liquid; esp. one consisting of a concentrated solution of sugar in water (or other medium, e.g. the juices of fruits). **a.** Such a liquid medicated, or used as a vehicle for medicines. **b.** As used in cookery, confectionery, etc., as a sweetener, preservative, or article of food; also *gen.* (often in ref. to its thick or viscid consistence). late ME. **c.** *spec.* (*a*) = MOLASSES. *local* (*U.S.*, etc.). (*b*) In sugar-manufacture, applied to various stages of the liquid. 1553. **d.** *transf.* A liquid of syrupy consistence 1838. **2.** With qualifying words, indicating the source, or the flavouring or medicinal ingredient, as *s. of almonds, of poppies, of squills, of violets*, etc.; **s. of sugar,** molasses. Also **golden s.,** syrup of a bright golden-yellow colour, drained off in the process of obtaining refined crystallized sugar.

1. a. Not Poppy, nor Mandragora, Nor all the drowsie Syrrups of the world SHAKS. **b.** Lucent syrops, tinct with cinnamon KEATS. *fig.* Words steep'd in syrop of Ambrosia 1600.

Sy·rup, *v.* 1619. [f. prec.] **1.** *trans.* To cover with or immerse in syrup. **2.** To make into or bring to the consistence of syrup 1847.

Syrupy (si·rəpi), *a.* 1707. [f. SYRUP *sb.* + -Y¹.] Partaking of the qualities of syrup; *esp.* having the viscid consistence of syrup.

‖Syssarcosis (sisaɹkōᵘ·sis). 1676. [mod. L. – Gr. συσσάρκωσις, f. συσσαρκοῦν to unite by flesh, cover over with flesh, f. σύν SYN- + σάρξ flesh; see -OSIS.] **1.** *Anat.* The union of bones by means of intervening muscle. **2.** *Path.* and *Surg.* The healing of a wound by granulation or the formation of new flesh 1753.

‖Syssitia (sisi·ʃ¹ă, -i·tiă). 1835. [– Gr. συσσίτια, pl. of συσσίτιον common meal, f. σύν SYN- + σῖτος food.] **a.** Meals eaten together in public. **b.** The custom of eating the chief meal of the day at a public mess, as practised in Sparta and Crete. Also **Syssition** (-i·ʃiǫn, -i·tiǫn), a common meal, mess.

Systaltic (sistæ·ltik), *a.* 1676. [– late L. *systalticus* – Gr. συσταλτικός, f. σύν SYN- + σταλτός, vbl. adj. f. σταλ-: στέλλειν place, put.] *Phys.* Contracting; of the nature of contraction; *spec.* applied to movement, as that of the heart, in which there is alternate contraction (*systole*) and dilatation (*diastole*).

†**Sy·stasis.** 1605. [– Gr. σύστασις composi-

tion, collection, union, alliance, f. σύν Syn- + στα-; see next, Stasis.] **1.** The act, or the result, of setting or putting together; combination, synthesis –1710. **2.** A political union or confederation. Burke.

Systatic (sistæ·tik), *a.* (*sb.*) 1640. [– med. or mod.L. *systaticus* – Gr. συστατικός ('astringent' in Galen, 'commendatory' in eccl. Gr.), f. σύν Syn- + στα- place, after συνιστάναι put together, etc.] **1.** Pertaining to or involving 'systasis'; synthetic. *Obs.* or *rare.* **2.** *Path.* Involving several of the sensory powers simultaneously; *sb.* a disease which does this 1820.

System (si·stėm). 1619. [– Fr. *système* (xvi) or its source late L. *systema* musical interval, in med.L. universe, etc. – Gr. σύστημα organized whole, f. σύν Syn- + στα-, base of ἱστάναι set up.] **I.** An organized or connected group of objects. **1.** A set or assemblage of things connected, associated, or interdependent, so as to form a complex unity; a whole composed of parts in orderly arrangement according to some scheme or plan; rarely applied to a simple or small assemblage of things (nearly = 'group' or 'set') 1638. **b.** *spec.* (with *this*, a possessive, or the like): The whole scheme of created things, the universe 1619. **2.** *Physics.* A group of bodies moving about one another in space under some particular dynamical law, as the law of gravitation; *spec.* in *Astron.* a group of heavenly bodies connected by their mutual attractive forces and moving in orbits about a centre or central body, as the *solar s.* (the sun with its attendant planets, etc.), the *s.* of a planet (the planet with its attendant satellites) 1690. **3. a.** *Biol.* A set of organs or parts in an animal body of the same or similar structure, or subserving the same function, as the *nervous, muscular, osseous*, etc. *systems*, the *digestive, reproductive*, etc. *systems*; also, each of the primary groups of tissues in the higher plants 1740. **b.** With *the* or possessive: The animal body as an organized whole; the organism in relation to its vital processes or functions. (Occas. including the mind.) 1764. **4.** In various scientific and technical uses: A group, set, or aggregate of things, natural or artificial, forming a connected or complex whole 1830. **5.** *Mus.* **a.** In ancient Greek music, A compound interval, i.e. one consisting of several degrees (opp. to Diastem); also, a scale or series of notes extending through such an interval, and serving as the basis of musical composition 1656. **b.** Applied to †a stave, or to a set of staves connected by a brace in a score of concerted music 1672. **6.** *Gr. Pros.* A group of connected verses or periods, esp. in anapæstic metres 1850.

1. The body is a s. or constitution: so is a tree: so is every machine 1729. The universe itself is a s. Paley. **2.** First satellite-systems, then planetary systems, then star-systems, then systems of star-systems 1870. **3. b.** Introducing vaccine virus into the s. 1805. **4.** A s. of telegraph wires 1855. The glacier s. of the region Tyndall. Low pressure s. or cyclone 1893.

II. A set of principles, etc.; a scheme, method. **1.** The set of correlated principles, ideas, or statements belonging to some department of knowledge or belief; a department of knowledge or belief considered as an organized whole; a comprehensive body of doctrines, conclusions, speculations, or theses 1656. **b.** *spec.* in *Astron.* A theory or hypothesis of the arrangement and relations of the heavenly bodies, by which their observed movements and phenomena are or have been explained 1678. **†c.** In weakened sense: A theory or hypothesis; also, theory (as opp. to practice). *colloq.* –1768. **d.** *transf.* A systematic treatise. *Obs.* exc. in titles of books. 1658. **2.** An organized scheme or plan of action; an orderly or regular method of procedure. Now usu. with defining word or phrase. 1663. **b.** A formal, definite, or established scheme or method (of classification, notation, or the like) 1753. **c.** *Cryst.* Each of the six different general methods in which different minerals crystallize, constituting the six classes of crystalline forms 1820. **3.** In the abstract (without *a* or *pl.*): Orderly arrangement or method; systematic form or order 1699.

1. The dry Systems of the Old Philosophers 1699. Morality is not a s. of truths, but a s. of rules 1845. **b.** The Copernican s. 1855. **d.** A S. of Magick; or, a History of the Black Art De Foe. **2.** Subsidising the denominational s. 1873. **b.** The s. of chemical notation now in use 1866. **3.** There is more of s. in the Phædo than appears at first sight Jowett.

Systematic (sistėmæ·tik), *a.* and *sb.* 1680. [– Fr. *systématique* – late L. *systematicus* – late Gr. συστηματικός (both relating to systems of metres), f. σύστημα, -ματ- System; see -ic.] **A.** *adj.* **†1.** = next 1 b. **2.** = next 1. 1725. **3.** Arranged or conducted according to a system, plan, or organized method; involving or observing a system; (of a person) acting according to system, regular, methodical 1790. **b.** Qualifying nouns of unfavourable meaning: Regularly organized (for an evil purpose), or carried on as a regular (and reprehensible) practice. Also said of the agent. 1803. **4.** *Nat. Hist.*, etc. Pertaining to, following, or arranged according to a system of classification; classificatory. Also of a writer: Composing or adhering to a system of classification. 1796.

2. Now we deal much in Essays, and most unreasonably despise s. Learning 1725. S. books of morality 1821. **3.** The systematick proceedings of a Roman senate Burke. He is very s. with the luggage Dickens. **b.** The s. intrigues of the Papal Court D'Israeli. Pope..was a s. appropriator.. of other men's thoughts 1874. **4.** Endeavouring to perfect s. botany 1829.

B. *sb.* **1.** *Nat. Hist.*, etc. A systematist 1771. **2.** *pl.* **Systematics**: the subject or study of systems, esp. of classification 1888.

Systema·tical, *a.* Now *rare* or *Obs.* 1661. [See prec., -ical.] **1.** Of a writing or treatise: Containing or setting forth a system or regular exposition of some subject. Of a subject or study: Set forth, or pursued, in the way of a system or regular scheme. Of a writer: Dealing with a subject in this way. **b.** Belonging to, or dealing in, a 'system' or theory; theoretical 1748. **2.** *gen.* = prec. 3. 1692. **b.** = prec. 3 b. 1750. **†3.** Belonging to the system of the universe, or to the solar system; cosmical –1797. **4.** *Nat. Hist.* = prec. 4. 1813. Hence **Systema·tically** *adv.*

Sy·stematism. *rare.* 1846. [f. Systematize *v.* + -ism.] The practice of systematizing.

Sy·stematist. 1700. [f. Gr. σύστημα, -ατ- System + -ist.] One who constructs, or adheres to, a system, esp. a system of classification in natural history; a classifying naturalist.

Systematize (si·stėmătəiz), *v.* 1764. [f. as prec. + -ize.] *trans.* To arrange according to a system; to reduce to system. **b.** *absol.* or *intr.* To construct a system (e.g. of philosophy, classification, etc.) 1891.

His restless ambition..had systematised intrigue D'Israeli. Hence **Sy:stematiza·tion,** the action or process of systematizing; a systematic arrangement, statement, etc. **Sy·stemati:zer.**

Sy·stematy. 1912. [f. as prec.; see -y[3].] Systematic classification.

Systemic (siste·mik), *a.* 1803. [irreg. f. System + -ic.] **1.** *Physiol.* and *Path.* Belonging to, supplying, or affecting the system or body as a whole; orig. and esp. in ref. to the general circulation as dist. from that supplying the respiratory organs. **b.** Belonging to or affecting a particular system of bodily organs, esp. the nervous system or special parts of it 1887. **2.** *gen.* Of or pertaining to a system (*rare*) 1850.

1. The S. Circulation..divisible into Arterial and Venous 1896. **b.** S. sclerosis of a small but defined tract of the spinal cord 1896.

Systemize (si·stėməiz), *v.* 1778. [irreg. f. System + -ize.] *trans* = Systematize. Hence **Sy:stemiza·tion,** systematization. **Sy·stemizer,** a systematizer.

Systemless (si·stėmlės), *a.* 1851. [f. System + -less.] **1.** Devoid of system or orderly arrangement; unsystematic. **2.** *Biol.* Having no differentiated systems of organs; structureless 1862.

‖**Systole** (si·stŏli). 1577. [Late L. – Gr. συστολή, f. σύν Syn- + *στολ- *στελ- place, after συστέλλειν contract.] **1.** *Phys.* The regular contraction of the heart and arteries that drives the blood outward: opp. to Diastole 1578. **b.** Applied to similar rhythmical contraction in other organs, as the lungs, the intestines, the pulsatile vesicles in protozoans, etc. 1578. **2.** *Pros.* The shortening of a vowel or syllable which is long by nature or position 1577.

1. *fig.* A *s.* and *diastole* of the spiritual life 1899. So **Systo·lic** *a.* pertaining to or marked by s.

Systyle (si·stəil), *a.* and *sb.* 1704. [– L. *systylos* – Gr. σύστυλος, f. σύν Syn- + στῦλος column, pillar.] *Arch.* **A.** *adj.* Applied to architecture in which the columns are close together, viz. at a distance from each other of twice their thickness. **B.** *sb.* A building characterized by such intercolumniation.

Systylous (si·stiləs), *a.* 1863. [f. prec. + -ous.] **a.** In mosses, having the lid permanently fixed to the columella. **b.** Having the styles united into a single column.

Syud, var. Sayyid.

Syzygetic (sizidʒe·tik), *a.* 1850. [Loosely f. Syzygy + *-etic* as in *apologetic*.] *Math.* Of, pertaining to, or constituting a syzygy (sense 4).

Syzygial (sizi·dʒiăl), *a.* 1863. [f. Syzygy + -al[1] 1.] *Astron.* and *Zool.* Pertaining to a syzygy or syzygies; having the character of a syzygy (senses 1b, 3).

Syzygy (si·zidʒi). 1656. [– late L. *syzugia* – Gr. συζυγία yoke, pair, copulation, conjunction, f. σύζυγος yoked, paired, f. σύν Syn- + *ζυγ- (base of ζευγνύναι) Yoke.] **1.** *Astron.* **†a.** Orig. = Conjunction 3. –1704. **b.** Now extended to include both conjunction and opposition (Opposition 3) of two heavenly bodies, or either of the points at which these take place, esp. in the case of the moon with the sun (new and full moon). **2.** *Biol.* **a.** A suture or immovable union of two joints of a crinoid; also, the joints thus sutured. **b.** The conjunction of two organisms without loss of identity, as in the genus Diplozoon; a syzygium. 1873. **3.** *Anc. Pros.* A dipody, or combination of two feet in one metre 1836. **4.** *Math.* A group of rational integral functions so related that, on their being severally multiplied by other rational integral functions, the sum of the products vanishes identically; also, the relation between such functions 1850. **5.** A pair of connected or correlative things; in Gnostic theology, a couple or pair of opposites, or of æons 1838.

T

T (tī), the twentieth letter of the English and the nineteenth of the ancient Roman alphabet, corresponding in form to the Greek Τ (*tau*) from the Phœnician (and ancient Semitic) + X X X (*tau*). It represents the point-breath-stop consonant of Bell's 'Visible Speech', or 'surd dental mute'; in English it is gingival or alveolar, not dental.

In mod. English, besides its proper sound as above described, *t* in the combinations *-tion, -tious, -tial, -tia, -tian, -tience, -tient*, after a vowel or any consonant except *s*, has the sound of *sh* (ʃ), in which the following *i* is absorbed, as in *nation* (nēⁱ·ʃən), *factious* (fæ·kʃəs), *partial* (pā·ɹʃăl), etc.; but in *-ia, -ian, i* is sometimes more or less preserved, esp. in proper names, as in *inertia, Portia*, etc. After *s* the original sound of *t* has remained, as in *bestial, Christian*.

A modern change is the development in southern England of the sound (tʃ) from *t* followed by [iu], [yu] in such combinations as *-tual, -tuous*, and esp. *-ture*, as in *nature* (nēⁱ·tiŭɹ, nēⁱ·tʃəɹ). In rapid speech *ti* after *s* usu. passes similarly into tʃ, as (kwe·stʃən) for (kwe·styən).

T between *s* and syllabic *l* or *n* (*en*), as in *bustle, castle, epistle, christen, fasten, hasten*, is now usu. mute; so between *s* and *m* in *Christmas*, and between *f* and syllabic *n* in *often, soften*.

Th is a consonantal digraph representing

two simple sounds (þ, ð), for which the Roman alphabet has no simple symbols, and is thus phonetically a distinct letter (or two letters), inserted between TE- and TI-.

I. 1. The letter and its sound. The pl. is variously written t's, *t*'s, *ts* (tīz). **b.** In phr. *to cross the t's*: to make the horizontal stroke of *t* (often omitted in hasty writing); *fig.* to be minutely exact or particular in one's account; to make the meaning more distinct; to particularize and emphasize the points. **c.** Phr. *To a T* (also *to a tee*): exactly, properly, to a nicety. **2.** The shape of the letter; an object having the shape T. **3.** *attrib.* (sometimes hyphened): Shaped like the letter T; having a cross piece at the top, as *T hinge, joint.* See also TEE *sb.*[1], TEE-*piece*, etc. **b.** *Special Combs.* (sometimes hyphened). **T branch,** in piping, a right-angled joint of a small pipe to a main; a T joint. **T cart,** an open phaeton, so called from its ground plan resembling the letter T. **T cloth,** a plain cotton cloth exported to India, China, Africa, etc., so called from the large letter T stamped on it. **T rail,** a railway metal or rail having a T section. **T square,** a square of the form of a T or rather ⊢ (with a long stem) used for drawing lines parallel, or at right angles, to each other. **TV,** television.

II. 1. Used to denote serial order; applied e.g. to the twentieth (or more usu. the nineteenth) of any series, to the nineteenth sheet of a book, etc. **2.** A mediæval symbol for the numerical 160, and with a stroke over it (T̄) for 160,000. **3.** *Abbreviations* for various proper names, as Thomas, Theresa, etc.; officially stamped on a letter, = *taxed*, i.e. postage to be paid; in *Music*, = tasto, tempo, tenor, tutti; in a ship's log-book, = thunder; in *Math.*, = time, terms; *t.b.(d.)* = torpedo boat (destroyer); *T.O.* = turn over; *T.U.C.* = Trade Union Congress. Also T.B., T.N.T.

T'[1]. ME. Shortened form of TO, before an infinitive beginning with a vowel, formerly in use, often combined with the following word, as *tabandon* to abandon.

T'[2], north. dial. form of *the*, before a vowel or consonant.

't, shortened form of *it*, initially or finally, as in *'tis, 'twas; do't, see't, on't*; formerly often written without apostrophe as one word; see IT.

-t[1], *suffix* of abstr. sbs. derived from vbs., repr. IE. *-t-* in **-tis, *-tus*, which is preserved in OE. *-þ* and G. *-t*, after guttural, labial, and sibilant consonants, as in *draught, drift, flight, thirst, thrift.*

-t[2], phonetic var. of OE. *þ* (as in *health, truth*: see -TH[1]), e.g. in *drought, height, sleight, theft.*

-t[3], var. of -ED[1], formation of the pa. pple. of weak verbs. From XVI to XVIII commonly (and later in individual usage) *-ed* was replaced by *-t* after a voiceless cons. preceded by another cons. or a short vowel, as in *blest, jumpt, stept*; this sp. has become universal where a long vowel in the stem has been shortened in the pa. pple., as in *crept, dealt, knelt, lost, meant, swept.*

In certain other classes of verbs there has been general contr. of *-ed* which had begun in inflected forms in OE.: after *l, n, r*, the ending *-ded* has become *-t*, as in *gilt, girt, sent*, and in some verbs with *l, m, n* at the end of the stem, *-ed* has also become *-t*, as in *smelt, spilt.* Several verbs have parallel forms without contraction, sometimes with difference of use, e.g. *burned* and *burnt, leaned* and *leant, penned* and *pent, roasted* and *roast, spoiled* and *spoilt.*

Ta (tā), *int.* 1772. An infantile word expressing thanks.

Ta, obs. and dial. form of THE, THEE, THOU. **Ta, taa,** obs. ff. TAKE *v.*

Taal (tāl). *S. Afr.* 1896. [– Du. *taal* language, speech, MDu. *tāle* = OE. *talu* TALE.] *The t.*, Cape Dutch or Afrikaans, a variety of Dutch spoken in South Africa.

Tab[1] (tæb). 1607. [prob. of dial. origin; partly synon. with TAG *sb.*[1]] **I. 1.** A short broad strap, flat loop, or the like, attached by one end to an object, or forming a projecting part by which a thing can be taken hold of, hung up, fastened, or pulled. **b.** *spec.* A shoe latchet, for fastening with a buckle, button, or thong. Chiefly *dial.* 1674. **2.** As an ornament of dress: Each of the projecting square pieces formed by cutting out the lower edge of a jacket or other article of dress, or sewn on to its uncut edge, and usu. embellished with buttons, embroidery, etc. 1880. **b.** A similar piece sewn by its upper edge on the surface of dress, so as to hang loose; or **c.** in recent use, sewn on entirely, and variously adorned with buttons, beads, embroidery, etc. 1834. **d.** *Red t.*: a staff officer: so called from the 'red tab' on his uniform. **3.** A tie-label, a luggage label 1904. **II.** *U.S. colloq.* A table, an account; a check; esp. in phr. *to keep (a) tab* or *tabs on* 1889.

Tab[2], colloq. shortening of CANTAB (a Cambridge man).

Tabac (tăbæ·k), *a.* 1894. [– Fr. *tabac* TOBACCO.] Of a deep shade of brown; tobacco-coloured.

Tabacco, obs. f. TOBACCO.

‖**Tabagie** (tabaʒī). 1819. [Fr. (XVII), irreg. deriv. of *tabac* TOBACCO.] A group of smokers who meet in club fashion; a 'tobacco-parliament'.

Tabanid (tæ·bănid), *a.* and *sb.* 1891. [f. L. *tabanus* gad-fly, horse-fly + -ID[3].] **A.** *adj.* Belonging to the family *Tabanidæ* of flies, of which *Tabanus* is the typical genus. **B.** *sb.* A fly of this family, a gad-fly.

Tabard (tæ·băɹd). ME. [– OFr. *tabart*, of unkn. origin.] †**1.** A garment of coarse material; a loose upper garment without sleeves; formerly worn out of doors by the lower classes, also by monks and foot-soldiers –1568. **2.** A short surcoat open at the sides and having short sleeves, worn by a knight over his armour, and emblazoned on the front, back, and sleeves with his armorial bearings. Now *Hist.* 1450. **3.** The official dress of a herald or pursuivant; a coat or jerkin having short sleeves, or none, and emblazoned with the arms of the sovereign 1598.

1. A Plowman..In a t. he rood vpon a Mere CHAUCER. Hence **Ta·barded** *a.* wearing a t.

Tabaret (tæ·bărĕt). 1851. [mod. trade name, prob. f. TABBY; cf. TABINET.] A fabric of alternate satin and watered silk stripes used in upholstery.

Tabasco (tăbɑ·sko). 1898. [A registered trademark; from *Tabasco*, name of a river and state of Mexico.] More fully *T. (pepper) sauce*: A very pungent sauce made from the pulp of the ripe fruit of a variety of *Capsicum annuum.* Also *fig.*, a story 'highly spiced'.

‖**Tabasheer** (tæbăʃīᵊ·ɹ). 1598. [– Pg. or Fr. form of Urdu (Arab., Pers.) *tabāšīr*, also *ṭabāšīr* chalk.] A siliceous substance, white or translucent, occasionally formed in the joints of the bamboo; also called *bamboo salt*; used medicinally in the East.

‖**Tabatière** (tabatyēr). *rare.* 1823. [Fr. (XVII), for *tabaquière*, f. *tabac* TOBACCO.] A snuff box.

Tabby (tæ·bi), *sb.* and *a.* 1638. [– (O)Fr. *tabis*, †*atabis* (cf. med. L. *attābi*) – Arab. *al-'attābiya*, name of a quarter of Bagdad in which the stuff was manufactured, named after *'attab*, great grandson of 'Umayya. The connection of the other senses is not clear.] **A.** *sb.* **1.** A general term for a silk taffeta, app. orig. striped, but afterwards applied also to silks of uniform colour waved or watered. **b.** Short for *t. gown* or *dress* 1727. **2.** Short for *t. cat*: A cat having a striped or brindled coat 1774. **b.** Also a she-cat: correl. to *tom-cat* 1826. **3.** An old or elderly maiden lady: a dyslogistic appellation; sometimes applied to any spiteful or ill-natured female gossip or tattler 1748. **4.** A collector's name for two pyralid moths, the T., *Aglossa pinguinalis*, and the Small T., *A. cuprealis*, both with fore wings greyish brown, clouded with a darker colour 1819. **5.** A concrete formed of a mixture of lime with shells, gravel, or stones in equal proportions, which when dry becomes very hard. orig. *t. work.* 1802. **B.** *adj.* (The sb. used attrib.) **1.** Made or consisting of tabby (see A. 1) 1638. **2.** Of a brownish, tawny, or grey colour, marked with darker parallel stripes or streaks; brindled; primarily and esp. in **t. cat** or **t.-cat**, a cat of this coloration, or of any other colour similarly marked 1665.

A. 1. His lady in crimson t. HAWTHORNE. **B. 2.** Demurest of the t. kind GRAY. Hence **Ta·bbyhood,** the condition of being an old maid.

Tabby (tæ·bi), *v.* 1728. [f. prec.] **1.** *trans.* To give a wavy appearance to (silk, etc.) by calendering. **2.** To stripe or streak in parallel lines with darker markings. Usu. in pa. pple. **Ta·bbied.** 1860.

Tabefa·ction. *rare.* 1658. [f. pa. ppl. stem of late L. *tabefacere*; see next, -ION.] The action or process of tabefying; the wasting away or consumption of the body.

Tabefy (tæ·bĭfəi), *v. rare.* 1656. [– Fr. †*tabéfier* – late L. *tabefacere* cause to waste (f. *tabēre* waste, melt + *facere* make); see -FY.] **1.** *trans.* To waste away, consume; to emaciate; †to melt down. **2.** *intr.* To waste away gradually, become emaciated (*rare*) 1891.

‖**Tabe·lla.** *Pl.* **-æ** (*i*). 1693. [L., dim. of *tabula* TABLE.] *Pharm.* = TABLET 3.

Taberdar (tæ·bəɹdāɹ). 1648. [In L. form *taberd(i)us, tabardarius*, f. TABARD + *-arius*; see -AR[2].] *lit.* One who wears a tabard; a name formerly given to certain scholars of Queen's College, Oxford, from the gown they wore; still surviving in the name of some of the scholarships at that college and in *Taberdars' Room*, the junior common room.

Tabernacle (tæ·bəɹnæk'l), *sb.* ME. [– (O)Fr. *tabernacle* or L. *tabernaculum* tent, booth, shed, dim. of *taberna* TAVERN; see -CULE.] **1.** A temporary dwelling; usu. moveable, constructed of branches, boards, or canvas; a hut, tent, booth. **2.** *spec.* in *Jewish Hist.* The curtained tent, containing the Ark of the Covenant and other sacred appointments, which served as the portable sanctuary of the Israelites during their wandering in the wilderness and afterwards till the building of the Temple. Also called *t. of the congregation* (or *meeting*), *of testimony*, and *of witness.* ME. **b.** Transferred to the Jewish temple. late ME. **3.** *fig.* In phraseology chiefly of biblical origin: A dwelling-place. **a.** *spec.* The dwelling-place of Jehovah, or of God ME. **b.** *gen.* A dwelling-place, a place of abode. late ME. **c.** Applied to the human body regarded as the temporary abode of the soul or of life. late ME. **4.** A canopied niche or recess in a wall or pillar, to contain an image. late ME. **5.** *Eccl.* An ornamented receptacle for the pyx containing the consecrated host reserved 1487. **6.** A place of worship distinguished in some way from a church. **a.** A temporary place of worship; esp. applied to the structures temporarily used during the rebuilding of the churches destroyed by the Fire of London in 1666. 1693. **b.** A meeting-house or place of worship of Protestant Nonconformists, esp. when not of ecclesiastical architecture. (Now chiefly *contempt.*) 1768. **c.** *fig.* Applied to the 'edifice' which for the time enshrines the principles of a party 1902. **7.** *Naut.* An elevated socket or step for the mast of a river-boat, or a post to which the mast is hinged, so that it may be lowered to pass bridges 1877.

1. *Feast of Tabernacles*, a Jewish festival, commemorating the dwelling of the Israelites in tents during their sojourn in the wilderness, held from the 15th to the 23rd of Tisri (October); it was also called the Feast of Ingathering, and was observed as a thanksgiving for the harvest. **2. b.** At Salem is his t., & his dwellinge in Sion COVERDALE *Ps.* 75 [6]: 2. **3. b.** And all The crowned Gods in their high tabernacles Sigh unawares TENNYSON. **c.** True image of the Father,..enshrin'd In fleshly T., and human form MILT. **6. b.** Pewing which would disgrace a t. of the last century 1878.

attrib. and *Comb.*: **t. roof,** a roof which slopes at the ends, as well as the sides, to a central ridge shorter than the side-walls; **-work,** (*a*) the ornamental carved work or tracery usual in canopies over niches, stalls, or pulpits, and in the carved screens of churches; (*b*) architectural work in which tabernacles or canopied niches form the characteristic feature.

Ta·bernacle, *v.* 1653. [– med.L. *tabernaculare* (1342 in Du Cange: rendering Gr. σκηνοῦν in John 1:14), f. *tabernaculum* (see prec.).] **1.** *intr.* To occupy a tabernacle, tent, or temporary dwelling, or one that can be shifted about; to dwell for a time, to sojourn: usu. *fig.*, said of the sojourning of Christ on earth or 'in the flesh', and of the indwelling of the Spirit of Christ; also of men as spiritual beings dwelling in the 'fleshly tabernacle' of the body. **2.** *trans.* To place in a tabernacle; to enshrine 1822.

1. The Evangelist Saint John..saith, He tabernacled amongst us 1653.

Tabernacular (tæbəɹnæ·kiŭlăɹ), *a. rare.* 1678. [f. L. *tabernaculum*; see -AR[1].] Of or pertaining to a tabernacle. **1.** Of the style or character of an architectural tabernacle; constructed or decorated with open-work and tracery. **2.** Savouring of the language of a 'tabernacle' or conventicle. (*contempt.*) 1847.

2. The word 'shortcomings'..being horridly t. DE QUINCEY.

‖**Tabes** (tē[i]·bīz). 1651. [L., 'wasting away'.] **1.** *Path.* Slow progressive emaciation of the body or its parts; consumption. **2.** Decay of plants caused by disease or injury 1832.

Tabescent (tăbe·sĕnt), *a.* 1890. [– L. *tabescens, -ent-*, pr. pple. of *tabescere*, inceptive of *tabēre* waste away; see -ESCENT.] Wasting away. So **Tabe·scence,** emaciation 1890.

Tabetic (tăbe·tik). *a.* and *sb.* 1847. [irreg. f. L. *tabes*, after *diabetic*, etc.] **A.** *adj.* Of, pertaining to, or affected with tabes or emaciation. **B.** *sb.* One who suffers from tabes 1899.

Tabid (tæ·bid), *a.* Now *rare.* 1650. [– L. *tabidus* wasting, f. *tabēre*; see -ID[1]. Cf. Fr. *tabide* (XVI).] **1.** *Path.* Affected with tabes; wasted by disease; consumptive; marcid 1651. †**2.** Corrupted, decomposed –1657. **3.** Causing consumption, wasting, or decline 1671. **4.** Of the nature of tabes; characterized by wasting away 1747.

1. Sinking..into a premature and t. old age 1822. Hence **Ta·bid-ly** *adv.*, **-ness.**

Tabific (tăbi·fik), *a. rare.* 1669. [– L. *tabificus*, f. TABES; see -FIC.] Causing tabes; consumptive, emaciating, wasting. So †**Tabi·fical** *a.* 1608–1657.

Tabinet (tæ·binėt). 1611. [app. arbitrarily f. TABBY. Cf. TABARET.] A watered fabric of silk and wool resembling poplin: chiefly associated with Ireland.

Tablature (tæ·blătiŭɹ, -tʃəɹ). 1574. [– Fr. *tablature* (XVI) – It. *tavolatura* 'any kind of Prick-song' (Florio), f. *tavolare* 'to set in Musike or Prick-song'.] **1.** *Mus.* An old name for musical notation in general, esp. for systems differing from the ordinary staff notation; *spec.* a peculiar form of notation used for the lute and other stringed instruments, in which the lines of the stave denoted the several strings, and letters or figures were placed upon them to indicate the points at which they were to be 'stopped' with the fingers; also, a similar notation for the flute, etc. *Obs.* exc. *Hist.* **2.** A tabular formation or structure bearing an inscription or design; a tablet. *Obs.* or *arch.* 1606. †**3.** A painting; a picture –1767. †**b.** *collect.* Work consisting or of the nature of paintings or pictures –1819. **c.** *fig.* A 'picture' formed by description or in fancy; *pl.* the 'pictures' of memory, or the faculty of retaining these 1779.

1. Organ T. was a system of writing the notes without the stave by means of letters...Figured bass has also been called T. 1898. **3. c.** Yielding a t. of benevolence and public spirit SHERIDAN.

Table (tē[i]·b'l), *sb.* ME. [– (O)Fr. *table* – L. *tabula* plank, tablet, list, repl. *mensa* in sense II in Gallo-Roman and Italian areas. The L. word was adopted in OE. as *tabule* and *tæfl.*] **I.** A flat slab or board. **1.** A flat and comparatively thin piece of wood, stone, metal, or other solid material (usu. shaped by art); a board, plate, slab, or tablet; also applied to natural formations, as the laminæ of a slaty rock. *Obs.* exc. in special applications. **2.** *spec.* **a.** A tablet bearing or intended for an inscription or device: as the stone tablets on which the ten commandments were inscribed, a votive tablet, etc. *arch.* ME. †**b.** A writing-tablet. Often in phr. *a pair (of) tables.* –1656. **c.** *Anc. Hist.* pl. The tablets on which certain collections of ancient Greek and Roman laws were inscribed; hence the laws themselves; esp. *the Twelve Tables*, drawn up by the decemviri B.C. 451 and 450, embodying the most important rules of Roman Law, and forming the chief basis of subsequent legislation 1726. **d.** *First, second t.*: the two divisions of the decalogue, relating to religious and moral duties respectively, held to have occupied the two 'tables of stone' 1560. †**3.** A board or other flat surface on which a picture is painted; hence, the picture itself –1700. †**4.** The 'board' on which chess, draughts, or any similar game is played –1801. **b.** Each of the two folding leaves of a backgammon board (*inner* and *outer t.*); †hence in *pl.* (often *pair of tables*) a backgammon board. Also, the half of each leaf in relation to the player to whom it belongs. 1483.

1. The inner part of the temple is altogether plastered and couered with great tables of Porphyre 1585. **2. a.** As stern as the statue of Moses breaking the tables 1849. **3.** *fig.* Mine eye hath play'd the painter and hath steeld, Thy beauties forme in t. of my heart SHAKS. **4. b.** Phr. *To turn the tables*, to reverse the relation between two persons or parties; to effect a complete reversal of the state of affairs (a metaphor from the notion of players reversing the position of the board so as to reverse their relative positions.)

II. A raised board at which persons may sit. **1.** An article of furniture consisting of a flat top of wood, stone, or other solid material, supported on legs or on a central pillar, and used to place things on for various purposes, as for meals, for some work or occupation, or for ornament ME. **2.** *spec.* An article of furniture as described in II. 1 upon which food is served, and at or around which persons sit at a meal. late ME. **b.** *transf.* Provision of food for meals; supply of food; fare; entertainment of a family or guests at table; eating, feasting. late ME. **3.** Usu. with defining word, as *the Lord's t.*, *the holy t.*: (*a*) In a church, that upon which the elements are placed at the Communion; the communion table: esp. when the rite is not regarded as a sacrifice. (*b*) *transf.* The Communion. ME. **4.** *transf.* A company of persons at a table ME. **b.** The company at dinner or at a meal 1602. **c.** A 'board' of persons who normally transact their business at a table (in various special uses) 1606. **5.** A table on which some game of chance is played; a gaming-table; also, the company of players at such a table 1750.

1. Phr. *Upon the t.*, under consideration or discussion. *To lay on* or *upon the t.*, of a legislative or deliberative body, to leave (a report, a proposed measure, etc.) for the present, subject to its being considered or called up at any subsequent time; hence, sometimes, to defer its consideration indefinitely; so *to lie on the t.* **2.** Phr. *At t.*, at a meal or meals. *For (the) t.*, for eating at a meal, for food; The greening [of potatoes]..renders them unfit for t. 1855. **4. b.** Your flashes of Merriment that were wont to set the T. on a Rore SHAKS. **5.** The plan will be for two to bank against the t. DISRAELI.

III. An arrangement of numbers, words, or items of any kind, in a definite and compact form, so as to exhibit some set of facts, or relations in a distinct and comprehensive way, for convenience of study, reference, or calculation. Now chiefly applied to an arrangement in columns and lines occupying a single page or sheet, as the multiplication t., tables of weights and measures, insurance tables, TIME-TABLES, etc. Formerly sometimes merely: An orderly arrangement of particulars, a list. late ME. †**b.** *absol.* = *t. of contents* (CONTENT *sb.*[1] 1) –1824. **c.** *Tables*: the common arithmetical tables, esp. as learnt at school 1828. **IV.** Special and techn. senses (chiefly arising out of sense I. 1). †**1.** *pl.* **Tables,** formerly the ordinary name of BACKGAMMON; app. orig. the 'men' or pieces used in playing early forms of this game –1808. **2.** *Arch.* **a.** A general term for a horizontal projecting course or moulding, as a cornice; a string-course. late ME. **b.** A member consisting of a flat vertical surface, usu. of rectangular form, plain or ornamented, sunk in or projecting beyond the general surface of a wall, etc.; a panel 1678. **3.** A flat elevated tract of land; a table-land, plateau; a flat mountain-top; also *Geol.* applied to a horizontal stratum 1587. **4.** *Palmistry.* The quadrangular space between certain lines in the palm of the hand 1460. **5. a.** A large flat circular disc, plate, or sheet of crown-glass, being the form in which it is made 1688. **b.** A crystal of flattened or short prismatic form 1796. **6.** *Anat.* Each of the two dense bony layers of the skull, separated by the diploë 1612. **7.** A flat plate, board, or the like, forming part of a mechanism or apparatus 1677. **a.** In various manufactures, A flat metal plate (often movable or adjustable) for supporting something to be operated upon, etc.; the plate with a raised rim on which plate-glass is made 1727. **b.** In an organ: (*a*) The upper part of the sound-board, above the sound-board bars and grooves, perforated with holes for admitting air to the pipes. (*b*) The upper board of the bellows. 1852. **c.** *Shipbuilding.* = COAK *sb.* 1. 1890. **d.** *Plain t.* (surveying instrument): see PLANE-TABLE. **8. a.** The upper horizontal surface of a table diamond or a brilliant. **b.** Short for TABLE DIAMOND; also applied to other precious stones cut in a similar form. 1530.

3. The ascent to the Sugar-loafe and T. [= Table Mountain], two Hils so named 1634.

attrib. and *Comb.*: **t.-allowance,** an allowance of money for provisions; = *t.-money* (*a*); **-bell,** a small hand-bell placed upon the t. for summoning attendants; **-centre,** a piece of embroidery, decorated work, etc., for the centre of a table, sometimes placed over the table-cloth; **-cover,** a cloth of wool or other fabric used for covering a t. permanently or when not in use for meals; **-faced** *a.* = TABLE-CUT; **-glass,** (*a*) glass made in 'tables' (see sense IV. 5 a); (*b*) a glass (drinking-vessel) for use at t.; **-knife,** a knife used at t., esp. one of the shape or size used in cutting meat on the plate; **-lifting,** the lifting of a table by supposed spiritual agency; **-linen,** linen for use at t., as t.-cloths and t.-napkins; **-money,** (*a*) an extra allowance of money made to the higher officers in the British army and navy for t. expenses; (*b*) a charge made in some clubs for the use of the dining-room; also, an extra charge made in some restaurants; **-mountain,** a flat-topped mountain; *spec.* the name of the mountain which rises behind Capetown; **-napkin,** a napkin used at t. for wiping the fingers and lips; **-shore** *Naut.*, a low level shore; **-tennis** = PING-PONG; **-tilting, -tipping,** the tilting or tipping of a table by supposed spiritual agency; **-work** *Printing*, the setting up of tables (sense III), or of matter between column rules; *concr.* printed matter of this kind, as dist. from ordinary letter-press. Hence **Ta·ble-wise** *adv.* in the manner of a t.; *spec.* of the placing of the Holy Table with its length in the direction of the church or chancel (opp. to *altar-wise*).

Table, *v.* 1450. [f. prec.] **1.** *trans.* To enter in a table or list; to tabulate. Now *rare.* **2. a.** To entertain at table as a guest, or for payment; to provide with meals. Now *rare.* 1457. **b.** *intr.* (for *refl.*) To have a meal, to dine; to take one's meals habitually (at a specified place or with a specified person). Now *rare* or *Obs.* 1562. **3.** *trans.* To picture, depict, represent as in a picture. *Obs.* or *rare arch.* 1607. **4.** To place or lay upon a table. **a.** To lay (an appeal, proposal, etc.) on the table of a deliberative or legislative assembly; hence, to bring forward for discussion or consideration. In the *U.S. Congress*, to lay on the table as a way of postponing indefinitely; to shelve. 1718. **b.** To pay down (money); to throw down or play (a card) 1827. **5.** *Carpentry.* To join two pieces of timber firmly together by means of flat oblong projections (see TABLE *sb.* IV. 7 c) in each alternately, fitting into corresponding recesses in the other. Also *intr.* for *pass.* 1794. **6.** *Sail-making.* To make a broad hem or 'tabling' on the edge of (a sail), to strengthen it in that part which is sewed to the bolt-rope 1794.

2. They haue..ten pound a yeere..and t. themselues also of the same 1583. **b.** Comming to Ordinaries about the Exchange where Merchants do t. for the most part 1602. **3.** This last Powder Treason, fit to be tabled and pictured in the chambers of meditation, as another hell above the ground BACON.

‖**Tableau** (tæ·blo[u], Fr. tablo). *Pl.* **tableaux**(-o[u]z, Fr. -o). 1699. [Fr. *tableau*, OFr. *tablel*, dim. of *table* TABLE *sb.*; see -EL.] **1.** A picture; usu. *fig.* a picturesque or graphic description. **2.** A group of persons and accessories, producing a picturesque effect 1813. **b.** = *T. vivant* 1828. **c.** Used *ellip.* to express the sudden creation of a striking or dramatic situation, a 'scene' which it is left to the hearer or reader to imagine 1885. **3.** A table, a schedule; an official list 1798.

2. T. vivant (tablo vivan), pl. **tableaux vivants**

(same pron.), lit. 'living picture': a representation of a personage, character, scene, incident, etc., or of a well-known painting or statue, by one person or a group of persons in suitable costumes and attitudes, silent and motionless.

Ta·ble-board. 1483. †**1.** = TABLE *sb.* I. 4. –1623. **2.** A board forming the top of a table; also a table (*obs.* or *dial.*) 1603. **3.** Board, i.e. meals, without lodging. *U.S.* 1884.

Ta·ble-book. 1596. †**1.** A book composed of tablets for memoranda; a pocket note-book or memorandum-book –1816. **2.** An ornamental book for a drawing-room table 1845.

Table-cloth (tē¹·b'l,klǫþ; for pl. see CLOTH *sb.*). 1467. A cloth for covering a table. **a.** A cloth, usu. of linen, spread upon a table in preparation for a meal, and upon which the dishes, plates, etc. are placed. **b.** A cloth, usu. of woollen material and often of ornamental design, used to cover a table permanently or when not in use for meals 1610. **c.** Name for a cloud covering the flat top and hanging down over the edge of Table Mountain at the Cape of Good Hope 1836.

Ta·ble-cut *a.* 1688. [f. TABLE *sb.*, used advb. + CUT *ppl. a.* or *sb.*²] Of a diamond, etc.: Cut in the form of a 'table'.

‖**Table d'hôte** (tab(lə),dōt). 1617. [Fr., = host's table.] A common table for guests at a hotel or eating-house; a public meal served there at a stated hour and at a fixed price; an ordinary. Also, in full *t. dinner, lunch*, a dinner or lunch (of several courses) served at a fixed price for the whole, whatever may be actually consumed.

Ta·ble di:amond. 1470. [f. TABLE *sb.* IV. 8 + DIAMOND.] A diamond cut with a table or large flat upper surface surrounded by small facets; esp. a thin diamond so cut having a flat under surface.

†**Table·ity.** 1542. [f. TABLE *sb.* + -ITY; tr. Erasmus's L. *menseitas* = Gr. τραπεζότης.] The abstract quality of a table –1702.

Ta·ble-land. 1697. [f. TABLE *sb.* + LAND *sb.*] An elevated region of land with a generally level surface, of large or considerable extent; a lofty plain; a plateau. **b.** Without *a* or *pl.*: Elevated level ground 1836.

The great irregular tableland of Dartmoor, over a thousand feet above the sea 1899.

Tablement (tē¹·b'lmĕnt). ME. [f. TABLE *v.* + -MENT, after L. *tabulamentum.*] *Arch.* = TABLE *sb.* IV. 2 a; also, a foundation or basement.

Tabler (tē¹·bləɹ). Now *rare.* 1598. [f. TABLE *v.* + -ER¹.] One who gets his meals at another's table for payment.

Ta·ble-ra:pping. 1858. The production of raps or knocking sounds on a table without apparent physical means; by spiritualists ascribed to the agency of departed spirits, and used as a supposed means of communication with them.

Table Round, = ROUND TABLE.

Ta·ble ru:by. 1529. A ruby cut with a large flat upper surface surrounded by small facets.

Ta·ble-spoon. 1763. A spoon (larger than a dessert-spoon) used for taking soup, and, in a larger size, for serving vegetables, puddings, etc. at table. Hence **Ta·ble-spoonful,** as much as a t. will hold.

Ta·ble-stone. 1840. *Archæol.* A flat stone supported by two or more upright stones; a cromlech or dolmen; also, the horizontal stone forming the top of this.

Tablet (tæ·blĕt), *sb.* ME. [– OFr. *tablete* (mod. *tablette*) – Rom. dim. of L. *tabula* TABLE *sb.*; see -ET.] **1.** A small, flat, and comparatively thin piece of stone, metal, wood, ivory, or other hard material, artificially shaped for some purpose. **a.** A small slab of stone or metal bearing or intended to bear an inscription or carving, *esp.* one affixed to a wall as a memorial. **b.** A slab or panel, usually of wood, for a picture or inscription. Chiefly *arch.* or *Hist.* 1581. **c.** A small smooth inflexible or stiff sheet or leaf for writing upon; usu., one of a pair or set hinged or otherwise fastened together 1611. †**2.** An ornament of precious metal or jewellery of a flat form, worn about the person –1620. **3.** A small flat or compressed piece of some solid confection, drug, or the like; a lozenge of flattened (orig. rectangular) form; a flat cake of soap 1582. **4.** *Arch.* = TABLE *sb.* IV. 2 a, b. 1823.

1. b. *Votive t.*, an inscribed panel anciently hung in a temple in fulfilment of a vow, e.g. after deliverance from shipwreck or dangerous illness. **c.** I took out my tablets, and wrote down the address 1836.

Tablet (tæ·blĕt), *v.* 1864. [f. prec.] *trans.* To furnish with a tablet (esp. one bearing an inscription); to affix a tablet to. **b.** To inscribe on a tablet 1878.

Table-talk (tē¹·b'l,tǫk). 1569. Talk at table; familiar conversation at meals. (Now usu. applied to the social conversation of famous men or of intellectual circles, esp. as reproduced in literary form.) Hence **Ta·ble-talker,** one who converses at table; esp. a person of high conversational powers.

Ta·ble-tu:rning. 1853. The action of turning or moving a table without the use of any apparently adequate means, as by a number of persons placing their hands or fingers upon it; such movements being ascribed by some to spiritual agency. So **Ta·ble-tu:rner.**

Tableware (tē¹·b'lwēᵊɹ). 1832. Ware for the service of the table; a collective term for the articles which are used at meals, as dishes, plates, knives, forks.

‖**Tablier** (tæ·blie, Fr. tabliye). 1474. [Fr.] †**1.** A chess-board. CAXTON. **2.** A part of a lady's dress resembling an apron; the front of a skirt cut or trimmed in the form of an apron 1835.

Tabling (tē¹·bliŋ), *vbl. sb.* late ME. [f. TABLE *v.* and *sb.* + -ING¹.] **1.** The action of setting down or entering in a table; tabulation. Now *rare.* 1450. †**2.** Playing at 'tables' or backgammon –1608. **3.** The action of providing or fact of being provided with food; boarding, board. Now *rare* or *Obs.* 1553. **4.** Material for table-cloths; table-linen 1640. **5.** *Arch.* The making of a 'table' or horizontal projecting course; *concr.* such a course itself; *spec.* a coping. late ME. **6.** *Carpentry* and *Shipbuilding.* See TABLE *v.* 5. 1794. **7.** *Sailmaking.* A broad hem made at the edge of a sail to strengthen it 1769.

Tabloid (tæ·bloid). 1898. [A term registered in 1884 by Messrs. Burroughs, Wellcome & Co., as a trademark applied to chemical substances used in medicine and pharmacy, and afterwards for other goods; held by the Court of Appeal to be a 'fancy word' as applied to the goods for which it is registered, and legally restricted to the preparations of the firm named.] In fig., transf., and sometimes joc. use, chiefly *attrib.* or as *adj.*, with relation chiefly to the compressed or concentrated form of the drugs sold under the name. **b.** A newspaper of small format which gives its news in a concentrated form 1926.

The proprietor intends to give in t. form all the news printed by other journals 1902.

Taboo, tabu (tăbū·), *a.* and *sb.* 1777. [orig. – Tongan *ta·bu* (so stressed in all native languages).] **A.** *adj.* (chiefly predic.). As orig. used in Polynesia, Melanesia, New Zealand, etc.; Set apart for or consecrated to a special use or purpose; restricted to the use of a god, a king, priests, or chiefs, while forbidden to general use; prohibited to a particular class (esp. to women), or to a particular person or persons; inviolable, sacred; forbidden, unlawful; also said of persons under a permanent or temporary prohibition from certain actions, from food, or from contact with others. Also *transf.* and *fig.*

transf. The mention of her neighbours is evidently t., since..she is in a state of affront with nine-tenths of them MISS MITFORD.

B. *sb.* **1.** The putting of a person or thing under prohibition or interdict, perpetual or temporary; the fact or condition of being so placed; the prohibition or interdict itself. Also, the institution or practice by which such prohibitions are recognized and enforced. 1777. **2.** *transf.* and *fig.* Prohibition or interdiction generally of the use or practice of anything, or of social intercourse; ostracism 1833.

1. Tabus connected with animals and plants are..part of totemism 1905.
attrib. The t. custom, which is a prohibition with a curse 1897.

Taboo, tabu (tăbū·), *v.* 1777. [f. prec.] **1.** *trans.* To put (a thing, place, action, word, or person) under a (literal) taboo; see prec. B. 1. **2.** *transf.* and *fig.* **a.** To give a sacred or privileged character to (a thing), which restricts its use to certain persons, or debars it from ordinary use or treatment: †(*a*) to consecrate, set apart, render inviolable; (*b*) to forbid, prohibit *to* the unprivileged, or to particular persons 1825. **b.** To put (a person, thing, name, or subject) under a social ban; ostracize, boycott 1791.

1. On the day of a chief's decease work is tabooed 1896. **2. a.** That sacred enclosure of respectability was tabooed to us LOWELL. **b.** I found myself as strictly tabooed as if I had been a leper 1860.

Tabor, tabour (tē¹·bəɹ), *sb.* Now *rare.* ME. [– OFr. *tabur, tabour*, beside *tanbor, tamb(o)ur*; app. of Oriental origin; cf. Pers. *tabīra*, and *tabūrāk*, both meaning 'drum', and Arab. *ṭunbūr* a kind of lute or lyre.] The earlier name of the drum; in later use, A small kind of drum, used chiefly as an accompaniment to the pipe or trumpet; a taborin or tabret. Now *Hist., arch.*, or *poet.* **b.** *transf.* The drummer (with his drum). late ME.

Tabor, tabour (tē¹·bəɹ), *v.* Now *rare.* ME. [f. prec., or – OFr. *taborer.*] **1.** *intr.* To perform upon or beat the tabor; to drum. **b.** *transf.* and *fig.* To beat as upon a tabor; to drum 1579. **2.** *trans.* To beat (a tune, etc.). late ME. †**3.** To beat, thump (anything); to thrash –1655. Hence **Ta·borer,** one who tabors; a drummer.

†**Ta·borin.** 1500. [– Fr. *tabourin* (XV), mod. *tambourin* (XVI), f. OFr. *tabour* TABOR *sb.*] A kind of drum, less wide and longer than the tabor, and struck with one drumstick only, to accompany the sound of a flute which is played with the other hand –1765.

Tabouret (tæ·bŏret, *or as Fr.*). 1656. [– Fr. *tabouret*, dim. of *tabour*; see TABOR, -ET.] †**1.** = TABRET –1885. **2.** A low seat or stool, without back or arms, for one person; so called orig. from its shape 1656. **3.** A frame for embroidery, a tambour-frame 1858.

2. In France the priviledge of the T. is of a stool for some particular Ladies to sit in the Queens presence 1656.

Tabret (tæ·brĕt). late ME. [f. TABOR *sb.* + -ET.] **1.** A small tabor; a timbrel. *Hist.* or *arch.* 1464. †**2.** *transf.* A performer on a tabret –1634.

Tabu, var. f. TABOO.

‖**Tabula** (tæ·biŭlă). *Pl.* **-æ** (-i). 1845. [L., TABLE.] **1.** An ancient writing-tablet; also *transf.* a body of laws inscribed on a tablet 1881. **2.** *Eccl.* A wooden or metal frontal for an altar 1845. **3.** *Palæont.* Name for the horizontal dissepiments in certain corals; cf. TABULATE *a.* 2. 1855.

T. rasa [L. = scraped tablet], a tablet from which the writing has been erased, and which is therefore ready to be written upon again, a blank tablet; usu. *fig.*

Tabular (tæ·biŭlăɹ), *a.* 1656. [– L. *tabularis*, f. *tabula* TABLE; see -AR¹.] **1.** Having the form of a 'table', tablet, or slab; flat and (usu.) comparatively thin; consisting of, or tending to split into, pieces of this form, as a rock; of a short prismatic form with flat base and top, as a crystal; flat-topped, as a hill. **2. a.** Entered in, or calculated by means of, a table or tables, as a number or quantity 1710. **b.** Of the nature of, or pertaining to, a table, scheme, or synopsis; arranged in the form of a table; set down in a systematic form, as in rows and columns 1816. **c.** *Printing.* Applied to matter set up in the form of tables 1771.

1. *T. spar*, a name for WOLLASTONITE, as occurring in masses of t. structure, or rarely in t. crystals. **2. a.** Uranus still deviates from his t. place 1837.

Ta·bularize, *v.* 1853. [f. TABULAR + -IZE.] *trans.* To put into a tabular form, to tabulate. Hence **Ta:bulariza·tion.**

Tabulary (tæ·biŭlări), *sb.* 1656. [– L. *tabularium* record-office, archives, f. *tabula* TABLE; see -ARY¹, -ARIUM.] *Rom. Antiq.* A place where the public records were kept in ancient Rome; hence, in other places.

Ta·bulary, *a.* Now *rare.* 1594. [– L. *tabularis*, f. *tabula* TABLE; see -ARY[2].] = TABULAR 2 a, b.

Tabulate (tæ·biŭlĕt), *a.* (*sb.*) 1826. [– late L. *tabulatus*, pa. pple. of *tabulare*; see next, -ATE[2].] **1.** = TABULAR 1. **2.** *Palæont.* Having *tabulæ* or horizontal dissepiments, as the corals of the group *Tabulata* 1862. †**B.** *sb.* = TABLET 3. SOUTHEY.

Tabulate (tæ·biŭleit), *v.* 1734. [– *tabulat-*, pa. ppl. stem of late L. *tabulare*, f. L. *tabula* TABLE; see -ATE[3].] *trans.* To put into the form of a table, scheme, or synopsis; to arrange, summarize, or exhibit in a table; to draw up a table of. Hence **Ta·bulator,** one who tabulates; a machine or apparatus for this purpose; also, an attachment to a typewriter for typing columns of figures.

We may tabulate the Italic family as follows 1869.

Tabulated (tæ·biŭleitĕd), *ppl. a.* 1681. [In sense 1 f. TABULATE *a.* + -ED[1]; in 2 pa. pple. of prec.] **1.** Shaped with or having a flat upper surface; flat-topped. Also, composed of thin parallel layers. **2.** Arranged or exhibited in the form of a table, scheme, or synopsis 1802.

1. The zoned or t. form of the onyx 1794.

Tabulation (tæbiŭlēi·ʃən). 1837. [f. TABULATE *v.*; see -ATION.] **1.** The action or process of tabulating; arrangement in the form of a table or orderly scheme. **2.** *Arch.* Division into successive stages of height by 'tables' or horizontal mouldings, etc. 1886.

Tacamahac (tæ·kămăhæk), **tacamahaca** (tæ:kămăhă·kă). 1577. [– Sp. †*tacamahaca* (now *tacamaca*) – Aztec *tecomahiyac.*] **1.** An aromatic resin, used for incense, and formerly extensively in medicine. **a.** *orig.* That yielded by a Mexican tree, *Bursera* (*Elaphrium*) *tomentosa.* **b.** Extended in the West Indies and S. America to similar resins obtained from other species of *Bursera* and the allied genus *Protium*, and subsequently to resins imported from Madagascar, Bourbon, and the E. Indies, chiefly the product of species of *Calophyllum.* **2.** The resin of the buds of the N. Amer. Balsam Poplar, *Populus balsamifera*; hence, the tree itself 1739.

‖**Tace** (tei·si). 1697. [L., imper. of *tacēre.*] The Latin for 'Be silent'. *T. is Latin for a candle*, a humorously veiled hint to a person to keep silent about something.

‖**Tacet** (tēi·set). 1724. [L., = 'is silent', f. *tacēre.*] *Mus.* A direction that the voice or instrument is to be silent for a time.

Tache[1] (†tætʃ, ‖taʃ). [ME. *teche* – OFr. *teche*, (also mod.) *tache*, (ult.) – Frankish **tēkan* TOKEN.] **1.** A spot, blotch, blot. In mod. scientific use only as Fr. †**2.** *fig.* A moral spot or blemish; a fault or vice; a bad quality or habit; also, a physical blemish –1602. **3.** A trait, a characteristic, good or bad. *Obs.* exc. *dial.* (tetʃ). late ME.

Tache[2], **tach** (tætʃ). Now *rare.* late ME. [– OFr. *tache* fibula, also a large nail. A doublet of TACK *sb.*[1]] **1.** A contrivance for fastening two parts together; a fibula, a clasp, a buckle, a hook and eye, or the like; a hook for hanging anything on. *Obs.* or *arch.* †**b.** A band or strap that may be fastened round anything (*rare*) –1611. **c.** *fig.* A means of attachment, a bond of connection 1701. **2.** *techn.* A rest for the shank of a punch or drill. Now *dial.* 1683.

1. Thou shalt make fiftie taches of gold, and couple the curtaines together with the taches *Exod.* 26:6.

Tache[3] (tætʃ). 1657. [app. – obs. or dial. Fr. *tache, tèche* plate of iron.] **1.** *Sugar-boiling.* Each pan of the series through which the juice of the sugar-cane is passed in evaporating it; *esp.* the smallest and last of these, the *striking-t.* †**2.** Applied to the flat iron pan in which tea-leaves are dried –1802.

Tacheometer (tækiˌǫ·mĭtəɹ). 1876. [– Fr. *tachéomètre*, f. Gr. ταχε-, stem of ταχύς quick, swift, τάχος swiftness + -METER.] = TACHYMETER. Hence **Tacheome·tric** *a.* pertaining to a t. or tacheometry. **Tacheo·metry,** surveying by means of a t.

Tachometer (tækǫ·mĭtəɹ). 1810. [f. Gr. τάχος speed + -METER.] **a.** An instrument by which the velocity of machines is measured. **b.** An instrument for measuring the velocity of a moving body of water, a current-measurer. So **Tacho·metry,** the scientific use of a t.; the measurement of velocity.

Tachy- (tæ·ki), comb. form of Gr. ταχύς swift, in scientific terms.

Tachhy·drite, Tachy·drite [– G. *tachhydrit*, contr. for **tachyhydrit*, f. Gr. ὕδωρ water + -ITE[1]; from its property of deliquescing readily], *Min.* a chloride of calcium and magnesium found at Stassfurt in Prussian Saxony. **Tachycardia** (-kā·ɹdiă) [Gr. καρδία heart], *Path.* abnormal rapidity of the heart's action. **Ta·chygen** [-GEN], *Biol.* the sudden appearance of an organ in evolution; the part so appearing; so **Tachyge·nesis** [GENESIS], acceleration in development by the shortening or suppression of intervening stages; **Tachyge·nic** *a.*, appearing or developing suddenly. **Tachyglo·ssal** *a.* [Gr. γλῶσσα tongue], *Zool.* of a tongue, capable of being quickly thrust forth and retracted, as that of the ant-eater; so **Tachyglo·ssate** *a.*, having a tachyglossal tongue; belonging to the *Tachyglossidæ*, a family of aculeate monotrematous mammals, of which the typical genus *Tachyglossus* contains the Echidna or porcupine ant-eater of Australia; **Tachyglo·ssid,** an animal of this family.

Tachygraph (tæ·kigrɑf). 1810. [– Fr. *tachygraphe* (XVIII) – Gr. ταχυγράφος swift writer; see TACHY-, -GRAPH.] One who practises tachygraphy; a stenographer; *spec.* one of the shorthand writers of the ancient Greeks and Romans.

Tachygraphic (tækigræ·fik), *a.* 1763. [– Fr. *tachygraphique*; see prec., -IC.] Of or pertaining to tachygraphy or rapid writing; *spec.* applied to a cursive or running handwriting, as opp. to one having separate and fully-formed letters, also to writing with many contractions, ligatures, and compendia. So **Tachygra·phical** *a.*

Tachygraphy (tæ̆ki·grăfi). 1641. [f. Gr. ταχύς swift + -GRAPHY.] 'The art or practice of quick writing' (J.); variously applied to shorthand, and (in palæography) to cursive as dist. from angular letters, to the Egyptian hieratic writing, etc.

Tachylite -lyte (tæ·kiləit). 1868. [– G. *tachylit* (Breithaupt, 1826), f. Gr. ταχύς swift + λυτός soluble, in ref. to its easy fusibility.] *Min.* A black basaltic glass, formerly regarded as a homogeneous mineral.

Tachymeter (tæ̆ki·mĭtəɹ). 1860. [f. Gr. ταχύς + -METER.] Name of a surveying instrument, adapted to the rapid location of points on a survey. So **Tachy·metry,** the use of such an instrument.

Tacit (tæ·sit), *a.* 1604. [– L. *tacitus*, prop. pa. pple. of *tacēre* be silent. Cf. (O)Fr. *tacite.*] **1.** Unspoken; silent, emitting no sound; noiseless, wordless 1605. **b.** Saying nothing; still, silent 1604. **2.** Not openly expressed or stated, but implied; understood, inferred 1637.

1. A t. thankfulness in his looks W. IRVING. **b.** A t. spectator of events 1804. **2.** A t. Consent LOCKE. Hence **Ta·cit-ly** *adv.*, **-ness** (*rare*).

Tacitean (tæsitī·ăn), *a.* 1890. [f. the name of the Roman historian *Tacitus* (c54–117); see -EAN.] Pertaining to Tacitus, or resembling his pregnant sententious style.

Taciturn (tæ·sitǭɹn), *a.* 1771. [– Fr. *taciturne* or L. *taciturnus*, f. *tacitus*; for the ending, cf. NOCTURN.] Characterized by silence or disinclination to conversation; reserved in speech; uncommunicative.

Godolphin, cautious and t., did his best to preserve neutrality MACAULAY. Hence **Ta·citurnly** *adv.*

Taciturnity (tæsitǭ·ɹnĭti). 1450. [– (O)Fr. *taciturnité* or L. *taciturnitas*; see prec., -ITY.] Habitual silence or disinclination to conversation; reservedness in speech; a taciturn character or state.

My natural T. hindered me from shewing my self to the best Advantage ADDISON.

Tack (tæk), *sb.*[1] ME. [This, and TACHE[2], presumably repr. OFr. vars. **taque*, (dial.) *tache*; but the relation with TACK *v.* and with *attack, attach, detach* has not been made out.] **I.** That which fastens or attaches, etc. **1.** That which fastens one thing to another, or things together: applied to a fibula or clasp, a buckle, a nail, or the like. *Obs.* exc. as in 2 and 3. **2.** *spec.* (perh. orig. short for *t.-nail.*) A small sharp-pointed nail of iron or brass, usu. with a flat and comparatively large head, used for fastening a light or thin object to something more solid, esp. in a slight or temporary manner, so as to admit of easy undoing 1574. **3.** *techn.* **a.** *Gardening.* A fastening for shoots, etc., consisting of a strip or band secured at each end to a wall or the like. **b.** *Plumbing.* A strip of lead having one end soldered to a pipe, and the other fastened to a wall or support. 1545. **4.** An act of tacking or fastening together, now esp. in a slight or temporary way; a stitch, *esp.* a long slight stitch used in fastening seams, etc., preparatory to the permanent sewing; a very slight fastening or tie, by which a thing is loosely held, as *hanging by a t.* 1705. **b.** Adhesiveness 1908.

2. *To come* (or *get*) *down to brass tacks*, to deal with actual facts; to come to the real business. **4.** If dear mother will give us her blessing, the parson shall give us a t. VANBRUGH.

II. Nautical and derived senses. **1.** A rope, wire, or chain and hook, used to secure to the ship's side the windward clews or corners of the courses (lower square sails) of a sailing ship when sailing close hauled on a wind; also, the rope, wire, or lashing used to secure amidships the windward lower end of a fore-and-aft sail 1481. **b.** The lower windward corner of a sail, to which the tack (rope or chain) is attached 1769. **2.** An act of tacking (TACK *v.* II. 1); hence, the direction given to a ship's course by tacking; the course of a ship in relation to the direction of the wind and the position of her sails; a course or movement obliquely opposed to the direction of the wind; one of a consecutive series of such movements to one side and the other alternately made by a sailing vessel, in order to reach a point to windward 1614. **b.** *fig.* and *transf.* A zigzag course on land 1788. **3.** *fig.* A course or line of conduct or action; implying change or difference from some preceding or other course 1675.

1. *To bring, get, haul,* or *put the tacks aboard*, to haul the tacks into such a position as to trim the sails to the wind, to set sail. *To bring* or *have the starboard* or *port tacks aboard*, to set the sails to, or sail with, the wind on the side mentioned. **2.** A ship is said to be *on the starboard* or *port t.* as the wind comes from starboard or port O.E.D. **3.** The bill..seemed to proceed upon the wrong t. 1901.

III. That which is tacked on or appended. **1.** Something tacked on or attached as an addition or rider; an addendum, supplement, appendix; *spec.* in parliamentary usage, A clause relating to some extraneous matter, appended, in order to secure its passing, to a bill, esp. a bill of supply 1705. **2.** *dial.* **a.** A hanging shelf 1446. **b.** *Coal-mining.* A temporary prop or scaffold 1849.

1. Some tacks had been made to money-bills in king Charles's time BURNET.

IV. As a quality. Hold; holding quality; adherence, endurance, stability, strength, substance, solidity. Now *dial.* late ME. **b.** Stickiness 1850.

There will neuer bee any holde or tacke in it 1583. Phr. †*To hold* (a person, etc.) *t.* (*to t.*), to be a match for; to hold at bay. †*To bear, hold t.*, to be strong or lasting; to hold out, endure, hold one's own.

Tack (tæk), *sb.*[2] Chiefly *Sc.* and *n. dial.* late ME. [prob. – ON. *tak* (beside *taka*) seizure, hold, bail, security, f. *taka* TAKE *v.*] **1.** Tenure or tenancy, of land, benefice, etc., *esp.* leasehold tenure, the period of tenure. **2.** Pasture for cattle let on hire 1804. **3.** A take of fish 1596.

Tack, *sb.*[3] *Obs.* or *dial.* late ME. [In sense 1 app. a doublet of TACHE[1]. Sense 2 is perh. transf. from 1, but may be of different origin.] †**1.** A spot, a stain; a blemish –1603. **2.** A smack, taste, or flavour (*of* something); *esp.* an alien, peculiar, or ill flavour 1602.

Tack, *sb.*[4] 1833. [Of unkn origin.] Food-stuff; chiefly in HARD-TACK ship's biscuit, SOFT-TACK; also *gen.* stuff, often in depreciatory sense.

Tack, *v.* late ME. [See TACK *sb.*[1]] **I.** To attach. †**1.** *trans.* To attach, fasten (one thing to another, or things together). *Obs.* exc. as in 3. –1843. **b.** *transf.* and *fig.* To attach 1533. †**c.** To join in wedlock (*slang*) –1821. †**2.** To connect or join by an intervening part –1771. **3.** To attach in a slight or temporary manner; *esp.* to attach with tacks (short nails or slight stitches), which can be easily taken out 1440. **4.** To join together (events, accounts, etc.) so as to produce or show a connected whole; to bring into connection. (Often implying arbitrary or artificial union.) 1683. **5.** To attach or add as a supplement; to adjoin, append, annex; *spec.* in parliamentary usage: see TACK *sb.*[1] III. 1. 1683. **6.** *Law.* To unite (a third or subsequent incumbrance) to the first, whereby it acquires priority over an intermediate mortgage 1728.

1. He dried and tacked together the Skins of Goats STEELE. **c.** We will employ this honest gentleman here, to t. our son and daughter together FIELDING. **3.** They are lined with a layer of cotton-wool neatly tacked in 1896. **4.** The Gentleman..tacks these two accounts together BENTLEY. **5.** A strong party in the Commons..proposed to t. the bill which the Peers had just rejected to the Land Tax Bill MACAULAY.

II. Nautical senses. **1.** *intr.* To shift the tacks and brace the yards, and turn the ship's head to the wind, so that she shall sail at the same angle to the wind on the other side; to go about in this way; also *t. about.* Hence, to make a run or course obliquely against the wind; to proceed by a series of such courses; to beat to windward: often said of the ship itself. 1557. **b.** Said of the wind: To change its direction 1727. **2. a.** *transf.* To make a turning or zigzag movement on land 1700. **b.** *fig.* To change one's attitude, opinion, or conduct; also, to proceed by indirect methods 1637. **3.** *trans.* To alter the course of (a ship) by turning her with her head to the wind (sometimes said of the ship); opp. to WEAR *v.* Also, to work or navigate (a ship) against the wind by a series of tacks. 1637.

1. His Ketch Tackt to and fro, the scanty wind to snatch 1600. **2. b.** He is not for a moment diverted, although he sometimes consents to t. STUBBS. **3.** All hands were turned up to t. ship 1860. Hence **Ta·cking** *vbl. sb.* the action of the vb.; *concr.* = tacking threads.

Tacker (tæ·kəɹ). 1704. [f. prec. + -ER[1].] One who tacks; in various senses. **a.** *Eng. Hist.* One who favoured the tacking of other bills in parliament to money-bills, in order to secure their passage through the House of Lords. **b.** In various trades: One who tacks or fastens articles or parts of things; also, a machine for putting or driving in tacks 1727.

Tacket (tæ·két). Now *dial.* ME. [f. TACK *sb.*[1] + -ET.] A nail; in later use, a small nail, a tack; now in *Sc.* and *n. dial.*, a hobnail for studding the soles of shoes.

Tackle (tæ·k'l, *Naut.* tēi·k'l), *sb.* ME. [prob. – (M)LG. *takel* (whence also Du., G. *takel*, Sw. *tackel*), f. *taken* = MDu. *tacken* lay hold of; see -LE.] **1.** Apparatus, utensils, instruments, implements, appliances; equipment, furniture, gear. **2.** The rigging of a ship; in later use *spec.* the running rigging or ropes used in working the sails, etc., with their pulleys; passing into sense 3 ME. **b.** Cordage; a rope used for any purpose 1529. **3.** An arrangement consisting of a rope and pulley-block, or more usu. a combination of ropes and blocks, used to obtain a purchase in raising or shifting a heavy body 1539. **b.** A windlass and its appurtenances, used for hoisting ore, etc. 1874. †**4.** Implements of war, weapons; *esp.* arrows; also, a weapon, an arrow –1663. **5.** Apparatus for fishing; fishing-tackle. late ME. **6.** The equipment of a horse; harness 1683. **7.** Victuals; food or drink; 'stuff' (*slang*) 1857. **8.** [from the vb.] *Football*, etc. **a.** The or an act of tackling; see TACKLE *v.* 4. 1901. **b.** In Amer. football: Each of two players (right and left) stationed next to the end rusher or forward in the rush-line 1894.

1. George wanted the shaving t. 1889. **2.** With all her bravery on, and t. trim, Sails fill'd, and streamers waving MILT. **4.** This said, she to her T. fell, And on the Knight let fall a peal Of Blows so fierce 1663.

attrib. and *Comb.*: **t.-block,** = BLOCK *sb.* 4; **-board,** a frame, placed at the end of a rope-walk, containing the whirls to which the yarns are attached to be twisted; **-fall,** the loose end of a t., to which the power is applied in hoisting; †**-house,** a building in which porters employed in loading and unloading ships kept their tackle.

Tackle (tæ·k'l), *v.* late ME. [f. prec.] †**1.** *trans.* To furnish (a ship) with tackle –1686. †**b.** To handle or work the tackle of (a ship) –1642. **2.** To harness (a horse) for riding or draught. Also *absol.* with *up.* 1714. **3.** *colloq.* **a.** To grip, lay hold of, take in hand, deal with; to fasten upon, encounter (a person or animal) physically 1828. **b.** To 'come to grips with', to enter into discussion or argument with; to attack; to approach or question on some subject 1840. **c.** To grapple with, to try to deal with (a task, a difficulty, etc.); to try to solve (a problem) 1847. **d.** To attack, to begin to eat (food) 1889. **4. a.** *Football.* (*a*) In *Rugby*, To seize and stop (an opponent) when in possession of the ball; (*b*) In *Association*, To obstruct (an opponent) with the object of getting the ball away from him. **b.** *Hockey.* To attempt to take the ball from (an opponent) with the stick. Also *absol.* 1884.

2. I'll get a spare saddle and bridle, and will t. him 1890. **3. b.** He too was tackled on the subject, but when he explained it..he found the electors.. reasonable 1901. **d.** We tackled the cold beef for lunch 1889. Hence **Ta·ckler,** one who tackles.

†**Ta·ckled,** *ppl. a.* 1592. [f. TACKLE *sb.* + -ED[2].] Made of tackle or ropes. SHAKS.

Tackling (tæ·kliŋ), *vbl. sb.* ME. [f. TACKLE *v.* + -ING[1].] †**1.** *concr.* The rigging of a ship; the tackle –1769. †**2.** = TACKLE *sb.* 1. –1813. †**b.** A horse's harness –1787. †**3.** Arms, weapons, instruments –1679. †**4.** Fishing tackle –1727. **5.** The action of TACKLE *v.* 1893.

5. The splendid t. of the Oxford men 1900.

Tacksman (tæ·ksmæ̆n). *Sc.* 1533. [f. *tack's*, poss. of TACK *sb.*[2] + MAN.] One who holds a tack or lease of land, coal-mines, fisheries, tithes, customs, etc.; esp. in the Highlands, a middleman who leases directly from the proprietor of the estate a large piece of land which he sublets in small farms.

Next in dignity to the laird is the T. JOHNSON.

Tacky (tæ·ki), *a.* 1788. [f. TACK *sb.*[1] + -Y[1].] Slightly sticky or adhesive: said of gum, glue, or varnish nearly dry.

Tacnode (tæ·knōᵘd). 1852. [f. L. *tactus* touch + NODE.] *Geom.* A point at which two parts of the same curve have ordinary contact.

Tact (tækt). 1609. [– (O)Fr. *tact* or L. *tactus* touch, f. **tag-*, base of *tangere* touch. In sense 2 immed. after Fr. *tact* (Voltaire, 1769).] **1.** The sense of touch 1651. **b.** *fig.* A keen faculty of perception or discrimination likened to the sense of touch 1797. **2.** Ready and delicate sense of what is fitting and proper in dealing with others, so as to avoid giving offence or to win good will; the faculty of saying or doing the right thing at the right time 1804. **3.** *Mus.* A stroke in beating time 1609.

1. Sight is a very refined t. 1881. **b.** You..must needs have a better t. of what will offend that class of readers COLERIDGE. **2.** A most delicate task; requiring t. CARLYLE. That fine instinct in the management of men which is commonly called t. 1892. Hence **Ta·ctful** *a.* full of or endowed with t.; displaying or inspired by t.; **-ly** *adv.* **Ta·ctless** *a.* destitute of t.; awkward; **-ly** *adv.*, **-ness.**

Tactic (tæ·ktik), *sb.* 1638. [– mod. L. *tactica* (XVII) – Gr. τακτική (sc. τέχνη art), fem. of τακτικός TACTIC *a.*[1] In sense 2 – Gr. τακτικός (sc. ἀνήρ man) tactician.] **1.** = TACTICS. †**2.** A tactician –1641.

Tactic (tæ·ktik), *a.*[1] 1604. [– mod.L. *tacticus* (XVII) – Gr. τακτικός of arrangement or tactics, f. τακτός ordered, vbl. adj. of τάσσειν set in order. Cf. Fr. *tactique* (XVII).] †**1.** = TACTICAL *a.* 1. –1831. **2.** Of or pertaining to arrangement or order 1811.

Ta·ctic, *a.*[2] *rare.* 1625. [– *tact-*, pa. ppl. stem of L. *tangere* touch, + -IC.] Of, belonging or relating to touch; tactual.

Tactical (tæ·ktikăl), *a.* 1570. [f. Gr. τακτικός (see TACTIC *a.*[1]) + -AL[1]; see -ICAL.] **1.** Of or pertaining to (military or naval) tactics. **2.** Of or relating to arrangement, esp. the arrangement of procedure with a view to ends 1876. **3.** Of a person, his actions, etc.: Characterized by skilful tactics; skilful in devising means to ends 1883. Hence **Ta·ctically** *adv.*

Tactician (tækti·ʃăn). 1798. [f. TACTIC *sb.* + -IAN (see -ICIAN), after Fr. *tacticien.*] One skilled in the science or art of tactics.

Tactics (tæ·ktiks), *sb. pl.* 1626. [repr. mod.L. *tactica* (1616 in title of Ælian's 'Taktike Theoria') – Gr. τὰ τακτικά, n. pl. of τακτικός, f. τακτός ordered, arranged, f. base of τάσσειν set in order.] The art or science of deploying military or naval forces in order of battle, and of performing war-like evolutions and manœuvres.

fig. We have seen principles strangled by t. so often 1842.

Tactile (tæ·ktəil), *a.* 1615. [– L. *tactilis*, f. *tact-*, pa. ppl. stem of *tangere* touch; see -ILE.] **1.** Perceptible to the touch; tangible. **2.** Of or pertaining to touch; relating to the sense of touch 1657. **b.** Of organs: Endowed with the sense of touch 1768.

1. Certain visible and t. signs 1898. **2.** T. anæsthesia 1899. *T. values*: the quality of painting which represents the tangibility of objects. **b.** The t. papillæ of the fingers 1768. Hence **Tactility** (tækti·liti), t. quality or condition.

Taction (tæ·kʃən). 1623. [– L. *tactio*, *-ōn-*, f. as prec.; see -ION. Cf. Fr. *taction* (XVII).] The action of touching; contact.

Tactor (tæ·ktǫɹ). 1817. [f. L. *tact-* (see TACTILE) + -OR 2.] A feeler; an organ of touch.

Tactual (tæ·ktiuăl), *a.* 1642. [f. L. *tactus* touch (f. as prec.) + -AL[1]; cf. *visual.*] Of or pertaining to touch; of the nature of or due to touch.

In the lowest organisms we have a kind of t. sense diffused over the entire body TYNDALL.

Tadpole[1] (tæ·dpoᵘl). late ME. [In XV f. ME. *tadde* TOAD + *pol* POLL *sb.*[1]; the notion of 'head' appears in dial. syns., e.g., as *bullhead, pole-, pollhead.*] **1.** The larva of a frog, toad, or other batrachian, from the time it leaves the egg until it loses its gills and tail. Chiefly applied in the early stage when the animal appears to consist simply of a round head with a tail. **2.** Sometimes applied to the tailed larva of a tunicate, the swimming tail of which is afterwards dropped or absorbed 1880. **3.** *U.S.* The Hooded Merganser, *Lophodytes cucullatus*, app. from the size of its head (*local*) 1891.

1. *transf. Tit. A.* IV. ii. 85.

Comb.: **t.-fish, -hake,** a ganoid fish of the North Atlantic, *Raniceps raninus.*

Tadpole[2]. 1844. In *T. and Taper*, names of two political schemers in Disraeli's *Coningsby*; hence allus., in the sense 'professional politicians, the hacks of a political party'.

Tael (tēⁱl). 1588. [– Pg. *tael*, pl. *taeis* – Malay *tahil*, *taïl* weight.] **1.** The trade name for the Chinese *liang* or 'ounce', a weight used in China and the East 1598. **2.** Hence, a money of account, orig. a tael (in weight) of standard silver, the value of which fluctuated with the price of the metal 1588.

Ta'en (tēⁱn), contr. f. *taken*, pa. pple. of TAKE *v.*

‖**Tænia, tenia** (tī·niă). *Pl.* **-æ, -as.** 1563. [L. – Gr. ταινία band, fillet, ribbon.] **1.** *Archæol.* A headband, ribbon, or fillet 1800. **2.** *Arch.* In the Doric order, A band separating the architrave from the frieze 1563. **3.** *Surg.* A long narrow ribbon used as a ligature 1882. **4.** *Anat.* A ribbon-like structure; applied *esp.* to the bands of white nervous matter in the brain and the longitudinal muscles of the colon 1882. **5.** *Zool.* A tapeworm [so in L.]; *spec.* a genus of cestoid worms, including the common tapeworm 1706. Hence **Tænian** (tī·niăn) *a.* pertaining to tapeworms. **Tæ·niate** *a.* tænioid, tæniiform.

Tænii- (tīni,i), comb. form of L. *tænia* ribbon, often contracted to **tæni-**. **Tæ·ni(i)cide** [-CIDE[2]], a destroyer of tapeworms, a tænifuge. **Tæ·ni(i)form** *a.* [-FORM], having the form of a tape or ribbon, tænioid. **Tæ·nifuge** [-FUGE], *sb.* a substance used to expel tapeworms from the body; *adj.* expelling tapeworms.

Tænio- (tī·ni,o), comb. form of Gr. ταινία ribbon. **Tæ:nioglo·ssate** *a.* [Gr. γλῶσσα tongue], in Mollusca, having upon the lingual ribbon one median tooth between three admedian teeth on either side. **Tæ·niosome** [Gr. σῶμα body], one of the sub-order

Tæniosomi of teleocephalous fishes, a ribbon-fish.

Tænioid (tī·ni,oid), *a.* 1836. [f. TÆNIA + -OID.] Of a ribbon-like shape; related to the tapeworms.

‖**Tæniola** (tǐ·niolă). 1884. [mod.L., dim. of TÆNIA.] *Zool.* One of the radial partitions in the body of some acalephans.

Tafferel (tæ·fĕrĕl, tæ·frĕl). 1622. [– Du. *taffereel* panel, picture, for **tafeleel*, dim. of *tafel* TABLE.] †**1.** A panel; *esp.* a carved panel –1632. **2.** *Naut.* The upper part of the flat portion of a ship's stern above the transom, usu. ornamented with carvings, etc. In later use including, and now applied to, the aftermost portion of the poop-rail, and spelt TAFFRAIL. 1704.

Taffeta, taffety (tæ·fėtă, -ėti), *sb.* and *a.* late ME. [– OFr. *taffetas* or med.L. *taffata*, ult. – Pers. *tāfta*, subst. use of pa. pple. of *tāftan* shine.] **A.** *sb.* A name applied at different times to different fabrics; in more recent times, a light thin silk or union stuff of decided brightness or lustre. Latterly misapplied to various mixtures of silk and wool, and even cotton and jute, thin fine woollen material, etc. **B.** *attrib.* or as *adj.* **1.** Of taffeta; of the nature of taffeta 1552. **2.** *fig.* Florid, bombastic; over-dressed; dainty, delicate, fastidious 1588.

2. Taffata phrases, silken tearmes precise SHAKS.

Taffrail (tæ·freⁱl). 1814. [alt. of TAFFEREL, the final syll. being assim. to RAIL *sb.*²] *Naut.* The aftermost portion of the poop-rail of a ship.

Taffy¹ (tæ·fi). 1817. [The earlier form of TOFFEE, now Sc., North Eng., and Amer.] **1.** = TOFFEE. **2.** *U.S. slang.* Crude or vulgar compliment or flattery; 'soft soap'; blarney 1879.

Taffy² (tæ·fi). 1682. [An ascribed Welsh pronunc. of *Davy* or *David*, in Welsh *Dafydd*.] A familiar nickname for a Welshman.

‖**Tafia** (tæ·fiă). 1777. [Given in 1722 as native name in West Indies; but *tāfīa* is also given in Malay dicts. as 'a spirit distilled from molasses'.] A rum-like spirituous liquor obtained from the lower grades of molasses, refuse brown sugar, etc.

Tag (tæg), *sb.*¹ late ME. [Of unkn. origin; an early synonym is DAG *sb.*¹, which was perh. infl. by TACK *sb.*¹] **1.** Orig., one of the narrow, often pointed, *laciniæ* or pendent pieces made by slashing the skirt of a garment; hence, any hanging ragged or torn piece; also, any end or rag of ribbon or the like. **2.** A small pendent piece or part hanging from, or attached more or less loosely to the main body of anything 1640. **3.** A point of metal or other hard substance at the end of a lace, string, strap, or the like, to facilitate its insertion through an eyelet-hole, when externally visible often made ornamental; an aglet 1570. **4.** An ornamental pendent; a tassel; a ribbon bearing a jewel, etc. 1570. **b.** *pl.* A footman's shoulder-knots 1837. **5.** The tip of the tail of an animal; the tail piece of an angler's fly 1681. **6.** The strip of parchment bearing the pendent seal of a deed 1688. **7.** A tab or tie-label attached by one end to a package, to luggage, etc.; also, a label pinned on as a badge, etc. Orig. and chiefly *U.S.* 1864. **8.** Something appended or added to a writing or speech, esp. by way of ornament or improvement, e.g. the moral of a fable, etc. 1734. **b.** A brief and usu. familiar quotation added for special effect; a much used or trite quotation 1702. **c.** The refrain or catch of a song or poem; the last words of a speech in a play, etc. 1793. †**9.** The rabble, the lowest class of people; *esp.* in collocation with *rag*. See also TAG-RAG. –1825. **10.** A disease in sheep; = *t.-sore* 1741.

8. b. The Latin t. holds: 'Quem Deus vult perdere, prius dementat' 1897. **9.** *T. and rag*, all the components of the rabble; all and any, every man Jack, everybody; Tom, Dick, and Harry.

attrib. and *Comb.*: **t.-belt**, = *t.-sore*; **t. day** *U.S.* = *flag-day* (FLAG *sb.*⁴); **-end**, = FAG-END; **-lock**, = DAG-LOCK; **-sore**, pustular excoriation of a sheep's tail set up by the irritation of diarrhœal flux; **-tail**, a worm with a yellow t. or tail.

Tag (tæg), *sb.*² 1738. [app. var. of TIG *sb.*; cf. TICK *sb.*³ 1 b.] = TIG *sb.*

Tag, var. of TEG, a young sheep.

Tag (tæg), *v.*¹ late ME. [f. TAG *sb.*¹] **1.** *trans.* To furnish or mark with or as with a tag (in various senses). **2.** To append as an addition or afterthought; to fasten, tack on, or add as a tag *to* something 1704. †**3.** To fasten or tack together; to join –1750. **b.** To join or string together (verses, rhymes) 1720. **4.** *intr.* To trail or drag behind; to follow closely, follow in one's train 1676. **5.** *trans.* To cut off tag-locks from (sheep) 1707.

1. Canning tags his speeches with poetry 1823. All my beard Was tagg'd with icy fringes in the moon TENNYSON. After inspection each animal will be tagged and described 1896. **3.** His clothes were tagg'd with thorns DRYDEN.

Tag, *v.*² 1891. [f. TAG *sb.*²] *trans.* = TIG *v.*

Tagalog (tăgā·lǫg). 1834. One of the Malayo-Polynesian languages.

Tagel (tēⁱ·gəl), *a.* Also **tegal, tagal.** 1905. [Place-name.] In *t. straw*, a soft fine straw for hats, etc. Also ellipt. as *sb.*

Tagger (tæ·gəɹ). 1648. [f. TAG *v.*¹ or *sb.*¹ + -ER¹.] **1.** One who tags. **2.** A device for tagging a sheep 1891. **3.** *pl.* Very thin sheet-iron, usu. coated with tin. (Also **taggar.**) [prob. so called from being used to make tags of laces.] 1834.

Taglet (tæ·glėt). *rare.* 1578. [f. TAG *sb.*¹ + -LET.] A small tag; *spec.* **a.** A tendril; **b.** A catkin.

Taglioni (talyō·ni). *Hist.* 1832. [Named after a family of ballet-dancers of the early 19th c.] **1.** A dress skirt modelled on a ballet-dancer's skirt, fashionable *c*1835. **2.** A kind of overcoat in use in the first half of the 19th c.

‖**Tagnicati** (tanʸikā·ti). 1827. [– Guarani and Sp. *tañicati*.] Native name of the White-lipped Peccary of Paraguay.

Tag-rag (tæ·g,ræg), *sb., a., adv.* 1582. [orig. two words, = both *tag* and *rag*; cf. TAG *sb.*¹ 9.] **A.** *sb.* The rabble, the riff-raff; also (with *pl.*) a member of the rabble. Now *rare* exc. as in D. 1609. **b.** A ragged tag or appendage 1827. **B.** *adj.* †**a.** Of or belonging to the rabble. **b.** Consisting of tags and rags of dress, etc.; dressed in rags, ragged. 1601.

If the tag-ragge people did not clap him, and hisse him, . . I am no true man SHAKS.

†**C.** *adv.* (for *tag and rag*.) All to tags and rags; also, pell-mell; one and all; promiscuously –1737. **D. Tag, rag, and bobtail** [see BOBTAIL *sb.* Now occas. **tagrag and bobtail.**] A contemptuous term for a number of persons of various sorts and conditions; all and sundry, esp. of the lower classes 1645.

‖**Tagua** (tæ·gwă). 1830. [Native name in Colombia.] The ivory-palm, *Phytelephas macrocarpa*, which produces the ivory-nut or corozo-nut.

‖**Taguan** (tæ·gwăn). 1807. [app. native name in the Philippines.] The Malayan Flying Squirrel, *Pteromys petaurista*.

‖**Tagus** (tēⁱ·gŏs). 1839. [Latinized f. Gr. ταγός ruler, leader, etc.] *Gr. Hist.* A commander, leader, ruler, chief; *spec.* the title of the chief of the confederation of Thessaly.

‖**Taha** (tā·hā). 1836. [Native name.] A S. African species of weaver-bird, *Euplectes taha* of Sir A. Smith, now *Pyromelana taha*, the male of which is chiefly yellow and black.

‖**Tahsildar** (tɒχsī·ldār). *India.* 1799. [Urdu, f. Arab., Pers. *taḥṣīl* collection of tax + *dār*, Pers. agent-suffix.] The chief revenue-officer of a subdivision of a district under the Mogul rule; retained by the British; formerly sometimes applied to the cashier in a business house.

Tail (tēⁱl), *sb.*¹ [OE. *tæġ(e)l* = MLG. *tagel* twisted whip, rope's end, OHG. *zagal* animal's tail (G. dial. *zagel, zāl*), ON. *tagl* horse's (or cow's) tail, Goth. *tagl* hair of the head, of the camel :– Gmc. **taʒlaz*.] **1.** The posterior extremity of an animal, in position opposite to the head, either forming a distinct flexible appendage to the trunk, or being the continuation of the trunk itself behind the anus. Also, a representation or figure of this part.

In most vertebrate animals, consisting of a number of gradually attenuated coccygeal vertebræ covered with flesh and integument; in quadrupeds often clothed with hair, in birds with feathers (see also PEACOCK'S TAIL), and in fishes bearing the caudal fin; in invertebrate animals, sometimes a distinct and well-marked member, at other times not distinctly marked off from the rest of the body.

b. The tail of a horse, of which one, two, or three were borne before a pasha as insignia of rank 1717. **2.** A thing, part, or appendage, resembling the tail of an animal in shape or position ME. **3.** The train or tail-like portion of a woman's dress (now *colloq.*); the pendent posterior part of a man's dress-coat or a peasant's long coat; the loose part of any coat below the waist; (often *pl.*) the bottom or lower edge of a skirt, etc., which reaches quite or nearly to the ground. Also *dial.* the skirt of a woman's dress; *tails*, skirts. ME. **4.** The lower or hinder extremity of anything; the part opposite to what is regarded as the head; the terminal or concluding part of anything. late ME. (Cf. CART-TAIL, PLOUGH-TAIL, etc.) **b.** The reverse side of a coin; esp. in *head(s or tail(s* 1684. **c.** *Surg.* Either end of an incision, which does not go through the whole thickness of the skin 1846. **5.** The lower and hinder part of the human body; the fundament, posteriors, buttocks, backside. Now *dial.* or *low colloq.* ME. **6.** A train or band of followers; a following; a retinue ME. **7.** (Also *pl.*) The inferior, less valuable, or refuse part of anything; foots, bottoms, dregs, sediment 1542. **8.** The inferior, least influential, or least skilful members of a body; e.g. of a profession, a political party, a cricket team, etc. 1604.

1. b. It was governed by beys, and pashas of two tails 1820. **2.** The cipher is turned into 9 by adding the t. 1599. The t. is. . by no means an invariable appendage of comets HERSCHEL. Hair . . plaited in long tails behind 1877. **3.** His friends at home. . hadn't put him into tails 1857. **4.** The Tayles of Mills 1613. (Cf. TAIL-RACE.) At the t. of their conversation 1833. His place is at the t. of a procession 1858. At the plough's t. 1887. *T. of the eye*, the outer corner of the eye. *Out of, with the t. of the eye*, with a sidelong or furtive glance.

Phrases. *Head and* (*or, nor*) *t.*: see HEAD *sb.* *To twist the lion's t.*: see LION 1. *To put salt on the t.*: see SALT *sb.*¹ 1. *With the t. between the legs*, lit. of a dog or other beast; *fig.* with a cowed and dejected demeanour. *To turn t.* (orig. a term of falconry) to turn the back; hence, to run away, take to flight. *Tail(s) up*, (fig.) of persons, in good spirits.

Comb.: **t.-bandage**, a bandage divided into strips at the end; **-bay**, (*a*) the space between a girder and the wall; (*b*) in a canal-lock, the narrow water-space just below the lock, opening out into the lower pond; **-beam**, a beam that is tailed in, as to a wall; a t.-piece; **-coat**, a coat with tails, *esp.* a dress or swallow-tailed coat; **-coverts** (**-covers**), *sb. pl. Ornith.* the feathers that cover the rectrices or quill-feathers of the t. in birds; divided into upper and lower, according to their position on the dorsal or ventral surface; **-joist**, a joist tailed into the wall, a t.-piece; **-lamp**, **-light**, the (usu. red) light or lights carried at the rear of a train, motor car, etc.; **-lock**, a lock at the exit or lower end of a dock; **-pin**, the centre in the tail-spindle of a lathe; **-rod**, a continuation of the piston-rod, which passes through the back cover of the cylinder, and serves to steady the piston and rod by giving the former a double bearing; **-rhyme:** see **Tailed;** **-spin** (cf. SPIN *sb.* 5); **-spindle**, the spindle in the t.-stock of a lathe; **-stock** = DEAD-HEAD 2; **-valve**, (*a*) the air-pump valve in some forms of condenser; (*b*) = SNIFTING-*valve*; **-water**, the water in a mill-race below the wheel, or in a canal or navigable channel below a lock.

Tail (tēⁱl), *sb.*² ME. [– (O)Fr. *taille* cut, division, partition or assessment of a subsidy, tax, f. *taillier* cut, fix the precise form of limit; see TAIL *v.*², and cf. TAILOR, TALLY *sb.*¹] **I.** †**a.** The individual assessment of a subsidy or tallage levied by the king or lord; a tax, impost, due, duty, or payment levied –1645. ‖**b.** Now only as Fr., in form **taille.** A tax formerly levied upon the unprivileged classes in France 1533. **II.** *Law.* The limitation or destination of a freehold estate or fee to a person and the heirs of his body, or some particular class of such heirs, on the failure of whom it is to revert to the donor or his heir or assign. Hence phrase *in t.*, as *estate in t.*, *tenant in t.*, *heir in t.*, i.e.

within or under the limitation in question. late ME.

T. general, limitation of an estate to a man and the heirs of his body lawfully begotten. *T. special*, limitation of an estate to a special class of heirs, e.g. to a man and his wife and the heirs of their bodies lawfully begotten. *T. male* (or *female*), limitation of an estate to male (or female) heirs.

†**III.** A tally; a score, an account; = TALLY *sb.*¹ 1, 2. –1677.

Tail (tēˡl), *a.* 1473. [– AFr. *taile*, OFr. *taillié*, pa. pple. of *taillier*; esp. in FEE-TAIL. For the fall of final *-é* cf. ASSIGN *sb.*²] Of a fee or freehold estate: Limited and regulated as to its tenure and inheritance by conditions fixed by the donor: thus dist. from *fee simple* or absolute ownership. See also FEE-TAIL.

Tail (tēˡl), *v.*¹ 1663. [f. TAIL *sb.*¹] **I.** *trans.* **1.** To furnish with a tail or final appendage 1817. **2.** To grasp or drag by the tail 1663. **3.** To dock the tail of (a lamb, etc.); to cut or pull off that which is regarded as the tail, esp. of a plant or fruit 1794. **4.** To form the tail of (a procession, etc.); to terminate 1835. **5.** To join on behind, annex, subjoin *to* 1523. **6.** *Building.* To insert the tail or end of (a beam, stone, or brick) *into* a wall, etc.; to let in, dovetail 1823.

5. What is this but to t. one folly to another? 1685.

II. *intr.* **1.** Of a ship: To run *aground* stern foremost 1725. **2.** Of a moving body of men or animals: **a.** To lengthen out into a straggling line, as in racing, etc.; to drop behind, fall away 1781. **b.** To move or proceed in the form of a line or tail; to fall into a line or tail 1859. **3.** To take a position in which the tail or rear is directed away from the wind, current, etc. 1849. **4.** *Building.* Of a beam, stone, or brick: To have its end let into a wall, etc. 1842. **5.** Of a fish: To show its tail at the surface 1892.

1. The Formidable..tailed on the..mud 1799. **3.** Sea-weed always 'tails to' a steady or a constant wind 1860.

With advs. **T. away.** *intr.* To fall away in a tail or straggling line; to die away. **T. off (out).** **a.** *trans.* To taper off. **b.** *intr.* To fall away in a tail; to diminish and cease; to subside. **c.** To turn tail, go or run off; to withdraw. *colloq.* **d.** *trans.* To pass and leave behind (other competitors in a race, etc.). **T. on.** **a.** *trans.* To add on as an appendage. **b.** *intr.* To join on in the rear.

Tail (tēˡl), *v.*² [ME. *taille* – OFr. *taillier* (mod. *tailler*) :– Rom. **tal(l)iare* (med. L. *talliare*), f. L. *talea* rod, twig, cutting.] †**I.** *trans.* To cut, esp. to a certain size or shape; to shape, fashion –1562. **II.** †**1.** To decide or determine in a specified way; to settle, arrange, or fix (a matter) –1473. **2.** *Law.* To limit (an estate of inheritance) to the donee and his heirs general or special; to grant in tail; to tie up by entail; to ENTAIL. late ME. †**III.** To impose a 'tail' or tax upon; to tax –1577. †**IV.** **1.** To mark or record on a tally; to charge (a person) with a debt; *transf.* to mark –1655. **2.** *intr.* To deal by tally, or on credit –1570.

Tail-board (tēˡ·lbōᵊɹd). 1805. [f. TAIL *sb.*¹ + BOARD *sb.*] The board at the hinder end of a cart, barrow, van, etc.; usu. one attached to the bottom by a hinge, for convenience in loading, etc.

Tailed (tēˡld), *a.* and *ppl. a.* ME. [f. TAIL *sb.*¹ and *v.*¹ + -ED.] **A.** *adj.* Having, or furnished with, a tail or tails; in *Zool.* and *Bot.* = CAUDATE. **B.** *ppl. a.* Deprived of the tail or tails 1550.

A. *T. rhyme* (rarely *tail-rhyme*), tr. Fr. *rime couée*, applied to a couplet, triplet, or stanza with a tail, tag, or additional short line, either unrhymed or rhyming with another tag further on.

Tail-end (tēˡ:lˌe·nd). 1837. [f. TAIL *sb.*¹ + END *sb.*] The hindmost or lowest end of anything; that part which is opposite the head. **b.** *fig.*; *esp.* the concluding part of an action, period of time, etc. 1845.

Tailing (tēˡ·liŋ), *vbl. sb.* 1495. [f. TAIL *v.*¹ + -ING¹.] **1.** The action of TAIL *v.*¹ 1703. **2.** *pl.* A name for the inferior qualities, leavings, or residue of any product; foots, bottoms 1764. **3.** The end or latter part 1646. **b.** *Arch.* The part of a projecting stone or brick inserted in a wall 1842. **4.** *attrib.* as *t.-rope* = TAIL-ROPE 1495.

‖**Taille** (tay). 1663. [Fr., f. *tailler* cut; see TAIL *sb.*², *v.*²] **1.** Cut, shape, form; shape of the bust from the shoulders to the waist; figure, build, make. In *Dress-making*, the waist or bodice of a gown; the style or fit of this. **2.** See TAIL *sb.*² I. b.

‖**Taille-douce** (taydus). 1650. [Fr., = soft cutting.] Engraving on a metal plate with a graver or burin, as dist. from work with the dry point, and from etching.

Tai·lless (tēˡ·lˌlės), *a.* 1550. [f. TAIL *sb.*¹ + -LESS.] Having no tail; deprived of a tail.

Tailor (tēˡ·ləɹ), *sb.* [ME. *taillour, taylo(u)r* (from XVI *tailor*) – AFr. *taillour*, OFr. *tailleur* cutter :– Rom **tal(l)iator, -ōr-*, f. **tal(l)iare* TAIL *v.*²; see -OR 2.] **1.** 'One whose business is to make clothes' (J.); a maker of the outer garments of men, also sometimes those of women, esp. riding-habits, walking costumes, etc. See also MERCHANT-TAILOR. **b.** *provb.* and *allus.*; often implying disparagement and ridicule 1605. **2.** A name given to several kinds of fish, as **a.** The t.-herring and the t.-shad. **b.** The Silversides. **c.** The Bleak. 1676. **3.** Short for TAILOR-BIRD 1848.

1. They all sit down cross-legg'd, as Taylors do 1704. **b.** They say it takes nine tailors to make a man—apparently, one is sufficient to ruin him SCOTT.

Comb.: **t.-herring, -shad,** a clupeoid fish, *Pomolobus mediocris*, of the Atlantic coast of N. America; **-warbler** = TAILOR-BIRD; **t.'s block, dummy,** a lay figure on which to fit or display clothes.

Tailor (tēˡ·ləɹ), *v.* 1662. [f. prec.] **1.** *intr.* To do tailor's work; to make clothes; to follow the calling of a tailor. **2.** *trans.* To make or fashion (a garment, etc.) by tailor's work. Hence **Tailored** *ppl. a.*, tailor-made. 1856. **3.** To fit or furnish (a person) with clothes; to apparel, to dress 1832. **4.** To shoot at (birds) in a bungling manner, so as to miss or merely damage them (*slang*) 1889.

1. I set to work a Tayloring, or rather indeed a Botching DE FOE. **2.** A tailored suit of tabac brown 1908.

Tailor-bird (tēˡ·ləɹbɔ̄ɹd). 1769. [f. TAILOR *sb.* + BIRD.] One of a number of species of Asiatic passerine singing birds, belonging to the genera *Orthotomus*, *Prinia*, *Sutoria*, etc., which stitch together the margins of leaves with cotton, etc., so as to form a cavity for their nest. Orig. applied to a particular species (*Motacilla sutoria* of Pennant, now variously called *Orthotomus sutorius*, *Sutoria longicauda*, or *S. sutoria*) of India and Ceylon.

Tailoress (teˡ·lərės). 1654. [f. TAILOR *sb.* + -ESS¹.] A woman tailor.

Tailoring (tēˡ·ləriŋ), *vbl. sb.* 1662. [f. TAILOR *v.* + -ING¹.] The action or business of a tailor; the making of garments. **b.** The production of the tailor; tailor's work 1850.

Tai·lor-ma·de, *a.* 1832. **1.** Made by a tailor; esp. said of women's garments of a heavier type, close-fitting and plain in style, prop. when made by a tailor (as dist. from a dressmaker); hence ellipt. as *sb.* 1873. **2.** **a.** *fig.* Made such by the tailor, i.e. by one's dress. **b.** *transf.* Dressed in tailor-made garments. 1832.

1. Braid is the favourite trimming for tailor-mades 1892. **2.** **b.** Some severely tailor-made ladies 1896.

Tail-piece (tēˡ·lpīs). 1601. **1.** The piece of anything forming its tail or end, or tailed into it; the piece at the end. **2.** *Printing.* A small decorative engraving placed at the end of a book, chapter, etc. 1707.

Tail-race (tēˡ·lrēˡs). 1776. [Cf. RACE *sb.*¹ III. 2 b.] The part of a mill-race below the wheel.

Tail-rope (tēˡ·lrōᵘp). ME. †**1.** That part of a horse's harness near the tail, as a breeching or crupper. –late ME. **2.** A rope forming or attached to the tail, or the hinder or lower end of anything; in various techn. applications 1495.

Tailye, tailzie, taillie (tēˡ·lyi, tēˡ·li). *Sc.* late ME. [In form *talȝe, tailȝe* – OFr. *taille* cutting, = TAIL *sb.*²; in form *tailȝie* – OFr. *tailliée, taillée, -ie*, fem. pa. pple. of *taillier* TAIL *v.*²] †**1.** A cut or slice –1819. **2.** *Sc. Law.* = TAIL *sb.*² II, ENTAIL *sb.*² 1. So **Tailye** *v. Sc.* = TAIL *v.*² II. 2.

Taint (tēˡnt), *sb.* late ME. [Two words of distinct origin run together. See A and B.] **A.** [Aphetic f. ATTAINT *sb.*] †**1.** = ATTAINT *sb.* 1. –1611. **2.** = ATTAINT *sb.* 2. 1565. †**3.** = ATTAINT *sb.* 3. –1706. †**B.** [– OFr. *teint, taint* :– L. *tinctus* and *teinte* :– med.L. *tincta* subst. uses of pa. pple. of *tingere* TINGE.] Colour, hue, tint; tinge; dye –1593. **C.** [Senses app. combining A and B.] **1.** A stain, a blemish; a sullying spot; a touch of discredit, dishonour, or disgrace; a slur 1601. **2.** A cause or condition of corruption or decay; an infection 1613. **b.** A trace or tinge of disease in a latent state 1615. †**3.** (Also **tant.**) Short for TAINT-WORM; also, a small red spider –1848.

1. Free from the foul T. of High Treason 1643. **2.** A deep and general t. infected the morals of the most influential classes MACAULAY. **b.** Hereditary nervous t. 1899.

Taint (tēˡnt), *v.* Pa. pple. **tainted**; also formerly †**taint.** late ME. [Two words of distinct origin. See A and B.] †**A.** [Aphetic f. ATTAINT *v.*] **1.** *trans.* = ATTAINT *v.* 2. –1603. **2.** = ATTAINT *v.* 1. –1590. **b.** To break (a lance, staff) in tilting, etc. –1624. †**B.** [– AFr. *teinter*, f. *teint*, pa. pple. of (O)Fr. *teindre* :– L. *tinguere* TINGE.] **1.** *trans.* To colour, dye, tinge –1725. **b.** To dip, bathe. MARLOWE. **2.** To apply tincture, balm, or ointment to (a wound, etc.) –1639. **C.** [Senses in which A and B appear to blend.] **1.** *trans.* To affect (esp. in a slight degree); to touch, tinge, imbue slightly (usu. *with* some bad or undesirable quality) 1591. †**2.** To affect injuriously; to hurt, injure, impair –1623. †**b.** To sully, stain (a person's honour) –1722. †**3.** To affect with weakness –1611. †**b.** *intr.* To lose vigour or courage; to become weak or faint; to fade, wither –1639. **4.** *trans.* To infect with pernicious, noxious, corrupting or deleterious qualities; to touch with putrefaction; to corrupt, contaminate, deprave 1573. **b.** *intr.* To become putrefied, corrupted, or rotten; to tarnish 1601.

1. Nowise tainted with enthusiasm HUME. **2.** *Twel. N.* III. iv. 13. **3.** Fear taints me worthily, Though firm I stand, and show it not CHAPMAN. **b.** *Macb.* V. iii. 3. **4.** One..who tainted a great society by a bad example THACKERAY. **b.** Nay pursue him now, least the deuice take ayre, and t. SHAKS.

Tainted (tēˡ·ntėd), *ppl. a.* 1577. [f. TAINT *v.* + -ED¹.] **1.** In the senses of TAINT *v.* **2.** Imbued with the scent of an animal (usu. a hunted animal). *Obs.* or *arch.* 1704.

1. *Tainted goods*, (in trade-unionism) goods that members of a union must not handle because non-union labour has been employed on them. **2.** [The stag] A moment snuffed the t. gale SCOTT.

Taintless (tēˡ·ntlės), *a.* Chiefly *poet.* 1590. [-LESS.] Free from taint or blemish; immaculate; clean, pure, innocent. Hence **Tai·nt-lessly** *adv.* without taint.

Tainture (tēˡ·ntiŭɹ). Now *rare.* 1593. [– OFr. *tainture*, (also mod.) *teinture* – L. *tinctura* dyeing, TINCTURE.] Tainting, staining, stain, defilement, infection.

Tai·nt-worm. *arch.* 1573. [f. TAINT *sb.* + WORM *sb.*] A worm or crawling larva supposed to infect cattle, etc.

As killing as the Canker to the Rose, Or T. to the weaning Herds that graze MILT.

‖**Tai-ping** (taiˌpiŋ). Also **Taë-ping.** 1860. [Chinese *T'ai-p'ing*, i.e. *t'ai* great, *p'ing* peace.] The name given to the adherents of a great rebellion which arose in Southern China in 1850, under the leadership of Hung-siu-tsuen, styled *T'ai-p'ing-wang*, Prince of great peace, who claimed a divine commission to overthrow the Manchu dynasty and establish one of native origin, to be called *T'ai-p'ing Chao* or Great Peace Dynasty.

Tais(c)h (taiʃ). *Gaelic Folklore.* [– Gael. *taibhs* (taivʃ, taiʃ) = OIr. *taidbse.*] A phantom, esp. of a person about to die.

Take (tēˡk), *sb.* 1654. [f. next.] **1.** The act of taking or leasing (land); the land taken; a holding. *dial.* 1805. **2.** That which is taken or received in payment; *pl.* takings, receipts, proceeds 1654. **3.** An act of taking or capturing an animal, or (usu.) a number of animals (esp. fish) at one time; also, the quantity so caught; a catch 1753. **4.** An act of taking (in general) 1816. **5.** *Printing.* A portion of copy taken at one time to be set up in type 1864. **6.** *Cinematography.* A portion of a scene photographed at one time 1928.

Take (tē^{i}k), *v.* Pa. t. **took** (tuk); pa. pple. **taken** (tē^{i}·k'n). [Late OE. *tacan* – ON. *taka* = WFris. *take*, EFris. *tāken*, MDu. *tāken* grasp, seize, catch, rel. by graduation to Goth. *tēkan*; further connections uncertain.]
†**I.** To touch (*intr.* with *on*, also *trans.*) –ME.
II. To seize, grip, catch, etc. **1.** *trans.* To lay hold upon, get into one's hands by force or artifice; to seize, capture, esp. in war; to make prisoner; hence, to get into one's power, to win by conquest (a fort, town, country). Also, to apprehend (a person charged with an offence), to arrest; to seize (property) by legal process, as by distraint, etc. **b.** To catch, capture (a wild beast, bird, fish, etc.); also of an animal, to seize or catch (prey). ME. **c.** In various games, as chess, cards, etc.: To capture (an adversary's piece, card, etc.) so as to put it out of play; also (*Cards*) to gain possession of (a trick). late ME. **d.** *Cricket.* To catch (the ball) off the bat so as to put the batsman 'out' (also with the batsman as obj.); of the bowler, To 'capture' (a wicket) by striking it with the ball or otherwise 1882. **2.** To lay hold of, grasp (with the hand, arms, etc.); to seize and hold ME. **3.** *intr.* Of a hook, a mechanical device, etc.: To catch, engage. late ME. **b.** *trans.* Of a mechanical appliance, etc.: To 'lay hold of'; to act upon by contact, adhesion, or the like 1659. **4.** *trans.* To strike, hit, impinge upon (a person, etc.), usu. *in*, *on* (*across*, *over*, etc.) some part. late ME. **b.** With double obj.; e.g. *to t.* (a person) *a blow* 1448. **5.** *absol.* or *intr.* Of a plant, seed, or graft: To 'get hold' of that on which it grows; to take root, 'strike', germinate, begin to grow 1440. **6.** *trans.* Of a disease, a pain, an injurious or destructive agency, etc.; also of a notion, fancy, feeling, etc.: To affect, seize, lay hold of, attack. Also in imprecations, as 'plague t. him'. ME. **b.** *pass.* with complemental adj., as *to be taken ill*, to be seized or struck with illness, etc. late ME. **c.** *intr.* for *pass.*, with *compl.*, as *to t. ill* = to be taken ill, to fall ill. *colloq.* and *dial.* 1674. **d.** *intr.* To catch, catch hold; *esp.* of fire, to seize upon combustible substances, to begin burning; also of a condition, humour, fancy, etc. Now *rare.* 1523. **7.** *trans.* To 'catch' or come upon (a person) *in* some action or situation; *fig.* to catch or detect *in* a fault or error 1577. **b.** To come upon suddenly, overtake, catch. *Obs.* or *arch.* exc. in certain phrases, as *t. by* SURPRISE, etc. 1533. **8.** To catch the fancy or affection of; to captivate, delight, charm; to 'fetch' 1605. **b.** *absol.* or *intr.* *To t.* = to take the fancy, gain acceptance; *esp.* to become popular 1635. **9.** *intr.* Of a plan, operation, etc.: To succeed, 'come off'. Now *rare.* 1622. **b.** Of a medicine, inoculation, etc.: To take hold, prove effective 1626.

1. I was taken into custody 1803. I took two guns and retook two 1854. Phr. *To t. by storm*: see STORM *sb.* II. **c.** The king takes the queen 1735. **2.** I took her hand 1825. *To t. in one's arms*, to embrace. **4.** T. him on the Costard, with the hiltes of thy Sword SHAKS. **b.** If he tooke you a box o' th' eare SHAKS. **6.** Fire tooke the Temple 1604. I was going to be taken with a fit 1888. What in the name of wonder has taken the girl? 1892. **c.** Mr. William Pitt..took ill and died after Austerlitz 1903. **d.** The tinder was ready, and the spark took 1803. **7.** The doctor was not easily taken off his guard 1885. **8.** Such sweet neglect more taketh me, Than all th' adulteries of art B. JONS. He was much taken with my little Jeannie CARLYLE. **b.** The new melodrame..takes mightily 1817. **9.** The design took and the Fellow got away 1701.

III. Weakened sense of 'seize', with elimination of the notion of force or art: the ordinary current sense. **1.** *trans.* To perform the voluntary physical act by which one gets (something) into one's hand or hold; to transfer to oneself by one's own physical act. (Now the main sense.) ME. **b.** with the instrumentality not expressed or considered ME. **2.** To receive into one's body by one's own act; to eat or drink, to swallow (food, drink, medicine, opium, etc.); to inhale (snuff, †tobacco-smoke, etc.) ME. **b.** To expose oneself to (air) so as to inhale it or get the physical benefit of it; chiefly in phr. *to t. the air*, to walk or ride out in the open air (now *rare* or *arch.*): see AIR *sb.* 4. So *to t. a bath*, to bathe. late ME. **c.** Phr. *Not to be taking any*..: not to be in the mood for, to be disinclined for. *slang.* 1900. **3.** To bring, receive, or adopt (a person) into some relation to oneself (e.g. into one's service, protection, tuition, care) ME. **b.** *spec.* in ref. to marriage or cohabitation; often in phr. *to t. to wife*, *in marriage* ME. **4.** To transfer by one's own direct act (a thing) into one's possession or keeping; to appropriate; to enter into possession or use of ME. **b.** *absol.* To take possession; *spec.* in *Law*, to enter into actual possession. late ME. **c.** To secure beforehand by payment or contract; e.g. *to t. a house*, etc., to engage (a house or other place) for the purpose of occupying it 1604. **d.** To get or procure regularly by payment (something offered to the public, as a periodical, a commodity) 1593. **5. a.** To assume (a form, nature, character, name, or other attribute); sometimes, to assume the part or character of ME. **b.** To assume, adopt (a symbol, a badge, or something connected with a function): in spec. phrases ME. **6.** To assume, charge oneself with, undertake (a function, responsibility, etc.) ME. **b.** To subject oneself to (an oath, vow, pledge, or the like) 1511. †**c.** *To t. it*: to affirm, asseverate. Const. *on* (one's death, honour). –1631. **7.** *To t. on* or *upon oneself*. **a.** To charge oneself with, undertake (an office, etc.); to make oneself responsible for ME. **b.** With *inf.*: To undertake; to presume (*to do* something) ME. †**c.** To affect, feign (*to do* something) –1606. †**d.** *absol.* or *intr.* To assume authority or importance; usu. in bad sense, = to take too much upon one, assume airs –1720. **8. a.** To undertake and perform, conduct, or discharge (a part, function, duty, service, or the like). late ME. **b.** Phr. *To t. pains*, *trouble*: to take upon oneself and exercise these activities and qualities; to exercise care and diligence ME. **9.** To adopt as one's own (a part or side in a contest, controversy, etc.); to range oneself on, ally oneself with (a side or party). late ME. **10.** To assume as if one's own, to appropriate or arrogate to oneself (credit, etc.); to assume as if granted, e.g. *to t. leave*, *liberty*, etc. 1525. **11.** *Gram.* Of a word, clause, or sentence: To have by right or usage, either as part of itself or with it in construction (a particular inflexion, accent, case, mood, etc.) as the proper one 1818.

1. Iesus then commeth, and taketh bread, and giueth them *John* 21:13. He could t. his hat and go 1833. **b.** T. a quart of shrimps 1771. **2.** He died by taking poison 1875. **3.** He took pupils to increase his income 1891. Colloq. phr. *To t. too much* (sc. drink). **5. a.** France cannot t. the offensive, but she can paralyse Germany and Italy 1887. **b.** *To t. the crown, the throne*, to assume sovereignty. *To t. the ball* (at cricket), to assume the position of bowler. *To t. an oar*, to begin to row. See also HABIT *sb.* I. 2, SILK 2 b, VEIL *sb.* **6.** Grenville refused to t. office without Fox 1890. **b.** She has taken the monastic Vow 1803. **7. b.** I took upon me..to go to Leeds DE FOE. **c.** *Tr. & Cr.* I. ii. 153. **d.** Lord! to see how Duncomb do t. upon him is an eyesore PEPYS. **8. a.** She would t. the grammar class at ten 1890. **10.** We would t. leave to recommend..an alteration 1820. He took credit to himself that..her son remained stanch 1870.

IV. Pregnant senses related to III. **1.** To pick out from a number: either by chance, at random, or with intention; to select, choose ME. **2.** To adopt or choose in order to use in some way; to adopt in some capacity (*as*, *for*); hence, to employ for a purpose, to have recourse to (a means or method); to seize (an opportunity, etc.) ME. **b.** To use (one's hands, a tool, weapon, etc.) for doing something. *To t. a stick* (etc.) *to*, to use it to beat (a person, etc.). 1768. **c.** *esp.* To take into use or employment as a means of progression; to enter or mount (a vehicle, ship, horse, one's limbs, etc.) for a journey or voyage. Often without article, as *to t. boat*, *coach*, *ship*, etc. 1450. **3.** To gain the aid or help of (a place) by betaking oneself to it; to gain, reach, repair to, go into, enter (esp. for refuge or safety); to get into or on to ME. **b.** To adopt and enter upon (a road, way, path, course, etc.): sometimes with mixture of sense 'to choose, select' ME. **c.** *To t.* (*a place* or *person*) *in* (*on*) *one's way*, to touch at or visit in one's journey; to include in one's route 1622. **4.** To proceed or begin to deal with or treat in some way or do something to; hence, 'to take in hand', 'tackle', deal with, treat 1523. **b.** To proceed to deal with mentally; to consider; to reckon. So *to t. into* or *under consideration*. ME. **5.** To proceed to occupy, enter on the occupation of (a place or position) ME. **6.** To use, occupy, use up, consume (so much material, space, time, energy, activity, etc.). Sometimes nearly = 'need' or 'require'. Hence (*colloq.*) to require (a person or thing of so much capacity or ability) *to do* something 1578. †**7.** To begin or start afresh after leaving off, or after some one else; to resume. late ME. (superseded by *t. up* m).

1. Good Commanders in the Warres, must be taken, be they neuer so Ambitious BACON. **2.** *To t.* ADVANTAGE, MEASURE, OCCASION: see the sbs. **c.** They..took train to London 1892. **3.** Vipers occasionally t. the water 1831. A harbour which may be easily taken and left in stormy weather 1880. **b.** The court..left the parties to t. their own course 1895. **4.** To t. the Distemper in its first Stage 1737. Phr. *To take it easy*: see EASY B. *To t. in vain*: see VAIN A. **b.** He was a man, take him for all in all: I shall not look vpon his like againe SHAKS. **5.** Phr. *To t. the* CHAIR, FLOOR, *to t.* PRECEDENCE: see the sbs. **6.** Any ignoramus can construct a straight line, but it takes an engineer to make a curve 1890. Her Mamma took nines in gloves 1897. Phr. *To t.* (*one's*) *time*, to allow oneself ample time (to do something); hence (sarcastically), to be 'quite long enough', i.e. too long; to loiter.

V. To obtain from a source, to derive. **1.** To get, obtain, or derive by one's own act from some source (something material or non-material); to adopt, copy, 'borrow'; to take example of, 'get' or 'learn' *from* some one ME. **b.** *spec.* To obtain from its natural source (e.g. stone from a quarry); to get; to pluck, gather (plants, a crop). Now *rare.* 1477. **2.** To derive, draw (origin, name, character, or some attribute or quality) from some source ME. **3.** To get as a result or product by some special process, e.g. by inquiry, by measurement, scientific observation, etc. late ME. **4. a.** To obtain in writing, make (notes, a copy, etc.); to write down (spoken words), report in writing (a speech, etc.) 1591. **b.** To obtain by drawing, delineating, etc.; also *transf.*, to obtain or make a figure or picture of, to portray; now *esp.* to photograph. Also (*colloq.*) *intr.* for *pass.* (with adv.) of a person: To be a (good or bad) subject for photographing. 1538.

1. The proportions of the three Grecian orders were taken from the human body BERKELEY. **2.** The Turks..took their..taste for poetry from the Persians 1772. **3.** He hastened down to the country to take the sense of his constituents 1817. Isn't it about time for taking the sun?..it is four days since we knew our position 1887. **4. a.** Minutes of the meeting must be taken 1883. **b.** A limner, who..took likenesses for fifteen shillings a head GOLDSM. The photographers..say a woman 'takes' better standing 1889.

VI. To take something given or offered; to receive, accept, exact, etc. **1.** To receive, get (something given, bestowed, or administered); to have conferred upon one; to win, or receive as won (a prize, reward); to acquire (experience, etc.). Also *absol.* ME. **b.** To receive (something inflicted); to have (something) done to one; to suffer, undergo, submit to ME. **c.** To receive information of, to hear; in *imper.* often = 'let me tell you'. Somewhat *arch.* 1595. **2.** To enter into the enjoyment of (pleasure, recreation, rest, or the like) ME. **3.** To receive, as wages, etc., or by way of charge or exaction as a fine, tribute; sometimes with connotation 'accept' or 'charge, exact, demand' ME. **4.** To exact (satisfaction or reparation) for an offence; hence, to execute vengeance, revenge, etc.) ME. **5.** To receive, exact, or accept (a promise, oath, etc.); hence, to administer or witness (an oath) 1450. **6.** To receive (something offered); to receive willingly; to accept ME. **b.** Of a female animal: To admit (the male) 1577. **c.** Of fish: To seize (the bait). Also *absol.* 1863. **7.** To accept (a wager, or the person who offers it). So also in ref. to a proposal, etc. 1602. **8.** To accept and act upon (advice, a hint, warning, etc.) ME. **b.** To accept as true or correct. Also, to accept mistakenly as trustworthy ME. **9.** To accept with the mind or will in some specified way (*well, ill, in earnest*, etc.) ME. **b.** To be content with; to put up with, tolerate, 'stand' 1470. **10.** To face and attempt to get over, through, up, etc.; clear (an obstacle, as a fence, ditch, space, etc.); to mount (a slope), get round (a corner), clear (the points on a railway line), etc. 1579. **11. a.** To admit, let in 1674. **b.** To absorb or become impregnated with (something detrimental, as moisture); to be affected injuriously by; to contract (disease, infection, injury, etc.); to fall into (a fit or trance) ME. **c.** To absorb, become impregnated with (a dye, colour, quality, salt, etc.); to receive (an impression, a polish, or the like) 1592. **d.** *absol.* or *intr.* To become affected in the desired or required way 1599.

1. It is more blessyd to gyue than t. 1450. In the house where the Doctors, and other Graduates take their degrees 1617. **b.** He professed himself ready to t. his trial 1879. **c.** Then t. the worst in brief, Samson is dead MILT. **2.** So perforce I took holiday 1897. **3.** A thousand guilders! Come, t. fifty BROWNING. **5.** Commissioners to t. oaths and affidavits 1873. **6.** T. no repulse, what euer she doth say SHAKS. **c.** Fish always t. best after rain 1889. **7.** I'll t. ten to one on it 1850. Phr. *To t. one's death* (upon a thing), to stake one's life upon it. **8.** They'l t. suggestion, as a Cat laps milke SHAKS. **b.** I would not t. this from report SHAKS. **9.** Phr. *To t. to heart* (HEART *sb.* II. 7); *to t. in good* (etc.) *part* (PART *sb.*). **b.** I had the good sense to t. things as I found them 1809. He must t. the consequences 1896. **11. b.** As men t. diseases, one of another SHAKS. **c.** It takes dyes admirably 1865. **d.** Vaccinated just six weeks ago-o! Took very finely! DICKENS.

VII. Senses related to VI, denoting intellectual action. **1.** To receive and hold with the intellect; to grasp mentally, apprehend, comprehend. (Now only in ref. to the meaning of words.) late ME. **b.** *transf.* To understand (a person, i.e. what he says) 1513. **2. a.** With *adv.* or *advb. phr.* To understand or apprehend in a specified way. Also with person as obj. ME. †**b.** With *simple compl.* To consider as, suppose to be –1709. **c.** With *dependent cl.*: To suppose, be of opinion, assume as a fact (*that*..). Usu. *take it.* late ME. **d.** With *inf.* To understand, suppose, imagine, assume (*to be* or *to do* something) 1548. **3.** *To t...for*: To suppose to be, consider as; often, to mistake for. late ME. **4.** To regard, hold, esteem (*as*); to reckon (*at* so much) 1531. **5.** To begin to have or be affected by (a feeling or state of mind); to conceive; hence, to experience (*delight, pleasure, pride*, etc.) ME. **6.** *trans.* To conceive and adopt with the will (a purpose, resolution, etc.), or with the intellect (an estimate, view, etc.); to form and hold in the mind ME. **b.** To conceive and exercise (*courage, heart, compassion, pity*, etc.); to form in the mind and exhibit in action ME. **c.** To exercise with the mind, in thought (*note, notice*, etc.), or with the mind and will, in action (*care*, etc.) ME.

1. An audience..quick to t. his points 1893. **b.** You t. me right, Eupolis BACON. **2. a.** So was the law taken in Anno 4. H. 3. 1642. **b.** I t. myself obliged in Honour to go on STEELE. **c.** I t. it your owne busines calls on you SHAKS. **3.** Do you t. me for a fool? 1889. Phr. *To t. for granted*: see GRANT *v.* 7. **5.** Persons to whom I had taken so much Dislike 1773. Women do t. prejudices 1888. **6. a.** We do not t. the alarmist view of our correspondent 1891. **b.** The Arabs would have taken fresh heart 1888.

VIII. Various senses, nearly = make, do, perform (some action). **1.** To perform, make, do (an act, action, movement, etc.). late ME. **2.** *To t. counsel*: to get advice, to consult, deliberate ME. †**3.** To arrange, agree upon (a truce, peace, league, etc.) –1656. **4.** *To t. adieu, farewell*: to bid farewell, say good-bye. Const. *of.* 1560. **5.** To lay hold of, raise, make (an objection, an exception, a distinction, etc.) 1542.

1. The salmon took a great leap 1889. *To t. one's departure*, to depart. **2.** She took counsel with witches and magicians 1879. **3.** Betwixt mine eye and heart a league is tooke SHAKS. **5.** The distinction which they took was..ingenious 1849.

IX. Senses denoting movement or removal, and related senses. **1. a.** To carry, convey; to conduct, lead, escort (a person or animal). Also said of a vehicle, etc., and of a road, way, etc.; so of a journey, etc. ME. **b.** To carry or bear (a thing) with one; to carry to some place or person. late ME. **c.** *fig.* To induce (a person) to go; to be the cause of his going 1848. **2.** With *from, off* (hence sometimes *simply*): To carry away, to remove; to extract; to deprive or rid a person or thing of ME. **b.** *To t. the life of*: to deprive of life, to kill 1591. **c.** To remove by death 1552. **d.** To subtract, deduct 1611. **e.** *absol.* with *from*: To detract from, lessen 1625. **f.** *intr.* for *pass.* To be capable of being, or adapted to be, taken *off, out, to pieces*, etc.; to be removable, detachable, etc. 1669. **3.** *fig.* **a.** To carry, draw, or lead in thought, etc.; with *from, off*, to distract 1611. †**b.** *To t.* (a person) *with one*: to speak so that (he) can 'follow'; to be explicit –1695. **c.** To bring or convey to a higher or lower degree; to advance or put back 1589. †**4.** *trans.* To deliver, hand over; to give; to commit, entrust –1533. **5.** *refl.* To devote or give oneself up; to apply oneself *to* (some pursuit, action, or object) ME. **6.** *intr.* To apply oneself *to* a habitual action 1677. **7. a.** To make one's way, go, proceed ME. **b.** Of a road, a river, etc.: To proceed, go, run, strike off (in some direction). *Obs.* or *dial.* 1610. **c.** *refl.* In same sense as a; also to betake oneself *to* 1470.

1. I took my man Friday with me DE FOE. **b.** T. thy face hence SHAKS. **c.** What took you out so late? 1883. **2.** The doing so would..t. the case from under the statute SCOTT. **d.** Twopence in the pound was taken off the tea duty 1890. **e.** It takes greatly from the pleasure 1891. **3. a.** Your heart is full of something, that do 's t. Your minde from feasting SHAKS. **b.** *Rom. & Jul.* III. v. 142. **c.** Phr. *To t. down a peg*, see PEG *sb.*[1] 3. **5.** Art thou a craftsman? t. thee to thine arte GASCOIGNE. **6.** Their taking to smoke tobacco 1890. **7. a.** I took across some fields 1801. **c.** I am to..t. myself elsewhere 1865.

Phrases. **I.** With special obj. **Take aim.** To direct a missile at something with intention to strike it; to aim. **T. alarm.** To accept and act upon a warning of danger; hence, to become alarmed. **T. charge. a.** To assume the care or custody *of*, make oneself responsible. **b.** To get out of control and act automatically. **T. fire. a.** *lit.* = *catch fire* (CATCH *v.* IX). **b.** *fig.* To become 'inflamed' or excited, 'fire up'. **T. hold. a.** = *catch* or *lay hold*: see HOLD *sb.*[1] 1. **b.** *fig.* To get a person or thing into its (or one's) 'hold' or power; of a feeling, a disease, etc.: to seize and affect forcibly and more or less permanently; of fire, to 'lay hold' *of* (something), begin to burn. Also, to seize (an opportunity). **T. horse. a.** To mount a horse (esp. for a journey). **b.** Of a mare: see HORSE *sb.* I. 1 b. **T. possession. a.** To enter into possession. With *of*: to take into one's possession, appropriate. **b.** *fig.* To begin to 'possess', dominate, or actuate. **II.** Intr. uses in idiomatic combination with preps. **T. after —.** To follow the example of; hence, to resemble (a parent, ancestor, superior, etc.) in nature, character, habits, appearance, or other quality. **T. to —. a.** To undertake, take in hand; to take charge of. *Obs.* exc. *dial.* **b.** To have recourse to (esp. some means of progression, as in *t. to the boats, one's heels*, etc.); also (now *dial.*) *to* some resource or means of subsistence). **c.** To betake oneself to (a place); to take refuge in; to enter. **d.** To adopt or take up as a practice, business, habit, or something habitual. **e.** To apply oneself (*well, kindly*); to adapt oneself. **f.** To take a liking to. **III.** In comb. with advs., forming the equivalent of compound verbs, chiefly trans. **T. aback**: see ABACK *adv.* 3. **T. away. a.** *trans.* To remove, withdraw, abstract; to remove by death; to subtract. **b.** *absol.* To clear the table after a meal. **c.** *absol.* To detract *from.* **T. back. a.** *trans.* To take possession of again, resume. **b.** To withdraw, retract, unsay (a statement, promise, etc.). **c.** To carry back in thought to a past time. **T. down. a.** *trans.* To remove from a higher to a lower, or from an upright to a prostrate, position; to lower; to carry down; to cut down, fell (a tree); to pull down (a house, etc.); to distribute (type). **b.** (*a*) To swallow; (*b*) in *Falconry*, to cause (a hawk) to fly down; (*c*) in school, to get above (another scholar) in class; so of a boat in a race, to get in front of (another boat); (*d*) to lead (a lady) down to dinner. **c.** *fig.* To humble, humiliate, abate the pride or arrogance of. **d.** To write down so as to use or preserve (what is said); to take a written report or notes of. **T. in. a.** *trans.* To take, draw, or receive into itself, or into something (see simple senses and IN *adv.*). **b.** To receive (money) in payment, etc.; to receive and undertake (work) to be done at home for pay. **c.** To subscribe for and receive regularly (a newspaper or periodical). **d.** To lead or conduct into a house, room, etc. *To t.* (a lady) *in to dinner.* **e.** To receive or admit as inmate or guest. **f.** To bring into smaller compass, draw in, reduce the extent of, contract, make smaller; to shorten, narrow, or tighten; to furl (a sail). *T. in a reef*, to roll or fold up a reef in a sail so as to shorten the sail. **g.** To enclose (a piece of land, etc.); to take into possession (a territory, a common), or into cultivation (a waste); to include; to annex. **h.** To admit into a number or list; to include, comprise, embrace. **i.** To receive into or grasp with the mind; to comprehend, realize; to learn; to conceive. **j.** To comprehend in one view; to perceive at a glance. **k.** To believe or accept unquestioningly. *colloq.* **l.** To deceive, trick, impose upon. *colloq.* **T. off. a.** *trans.* To remove from the position or condition of being *on* (see simple senses and OFF *adv.*). (*b*) *spec.* To divest oneself, or another, of, doff (a garment). (*c*) To remove or convey (a person) from on shore, from a rock, or from on board ship. **b.** *trans.* To drink to the bottom or at one draught; to 'toss off'. **c.** To lead away summarily; *refl.* to take one's departure, 'be off'. **d.** To lead away or draw off (in *fig.* sense); to divert, distract, dissuade. **e.** To dismiss; to withdraw (a coach, train, etc.) from running. **f.** To remove by death, kill, 'carry off', cut off: said of a person (esp. an assassin), of disease, devouring animals, etc. **g.** To remove (something imposed), esp. so as to relieve those subject to it. **h.** To remove or do away with (a quality, condition, etc.). **i.** (*a*) To make or obtain (an impression) from something; to print off. (*b*) To make (a figure of something); *transf.* to draw a likeness of, to portray. (*c*) To measure off; to mark the position of. **j.** To imitate or counterfeit, esp. by way of mockery; to mimic, caricature, burlesque. *colloq.* **k.** To close the stitches in knitting; to knit off. Also *absol.* **l.** *intr.* To abate, grow less; (of rain) to cease. **m.** To go off, start off, run away; to branch off from a main stream. (*b*) To start in jumping or rising from the ground, etc. (*c*) *Croquet.* To make a stroke from contact with another ball (cf. TAKE-OFF A. 4). **n.** *Aeronautics.* To start from rest, attain flying speed, and become air-borne. **T. on. a.** *trans.* See simple senses and ON *adv.* (*b*) To 'put on' (flesh, etc.). **b.** To assume, 'put on' (a form, quality, etc.): to assume, begin to perform (an action or function); to contract, 'catch'. **c.** To take (a person) into one's employment or upon one's staff; †to accept in marriage; to receive into fellowship. **d.** To undertake; to begin to handle or deal with, to 'tackle'. **e.** To undertake the management of (a farm, etc.), esp. in succession or continuance. **f.** *intr.* To 'go on' madly or excitedly; to be greatly agitated; to make a great fuss, outcry, or uproar; now *esp.* to distress oneself greatly. Now *colloq.* and *dial.* **g.** To take service or employment, to engage oneself; to enlist. **h.** To 'catch on', become popular. *colloq.* **T. out. a.** *trans.* See simple senses and OUT *adv.* (*b*) To remove, extract (a stain, etc.). **b.** To leave out, except, omit. **c.** To lead or carry out or forth. (*b*) Cricket. *To take out one's bat*: see CARRY *v.* III. **d.** To make a copy from an original; to copy (a writing, etc.); *esp.* to extract a passage from a writing or book. (*b*) To extract from data. **e.** To apply for and obtain (a licence, etc.) from the proper authority. **f.** To obtain, spend, the value of (something) *in* another form. **g.** *Bridge.* To remove (one's partner) from the suit he has called by a higher bid. **T. out of. a.** *trans.* See simple senses and OUT OF. **b.** To get, derive, or obtain from. **c.** To deprive a person or thing of (some quality, etc.); *spec.* to deprive of (energy or the like); usu. *to t. it out of*, to exhaust, fatigue (*colloq.*). **d.** To remove from the jurisdiction of; to prove not to come under (a statute). **e.** To take (something) from a person in compensation; *to t. it out of*, to exact satisfaction from (*colloq.*). **T. over. a.** To take by transfer from, or in succession to another. **b.** To carry or convey across, to transport. **T. up. a.** *trans.* To raise, lift; to pick up. Somewhat *arch.* (*b*) With special obj., implying a purpose of using in some way; as, *to t. up one's pen*, to proceed or begin to write; *to t. up a book* (i.e. with the purpose of reading); *to t. up the* (or *one's*) *cross*; *to take up* ARMS, *the* GLOVE, etc., see the sbs. (*c*) To take (a person) from the ground into a vehicle, or on horseback, etc. Said of a person, or of the carriage, horse, train, etc. Also *absol.* of a vehicle, a train, etc., to take up its occupants. **b.** To lead, conduct, convey, or carry (a person or thing), to a higher place or position. **c.** To pull up or in, so as to tighten or shorten; to make fast in this way, as a dropped stitch. (*b*) To tie up or constrict (a vein or artery); 'to fasten with a ligature passed under' (J.). **d.** To take into one's possession, possess oneself of; with various shades of meaning, as: to purchase wholesale, buy up; to get, receive, or exact in payment; to levy; to borrow (at interest); to hire. (*b*) To take (land) into occupation. (*c*) To accept or pay (a bill of exchange); to advance money on (a mortgage); to subscribe for (stocks, shares, a loan) at their original issue. **e.** To receive into its own substance or interstices; to absorb (a fluid); to dissolve (a solid). **f.** To accept. **g.** To take (a person) into one's protection, patronage, or other relation; to adopt as a *protégé* or associate; to begin to patronize. †**h.** To levy, raise, enlist (troops). **i.** To seize by legal authority, arrest, apprehend. **j.** *intr.* for *refl.* To check oneself, 'pull up'; to slacken one's pace; to reform. *Obs.* exc. *dial.* (*b*) Of weather: To improve, become fair. **k.** *trans.* To check (a person) in speaking; to interrupt sharply, esp. with an expression of dissent or disapproval; to rebuke, reprove, or reprimand sharply or severely. Also *to take up short*: see SHORT. †**l.** To oppose, encounter, cope with. **m.** To begin afresh (something left off, or begun by another); to resume. **n.** To adopt (a practice, notion, idea, purpose, etc.); to assume (an attitude, tone, etc.); to 'go in for' (a study, profession, business, etc.). (*b*) To take in hand, proceed to deal practically with (a matter, question, etc.); to interest oneself in, embrace (a cause). †**o.** To make up, settle (a dispute, quarrel, etc.). **p.** To proceed to occupy (a place or position, *lit.* or *fig.*); to station or place oneself in. †(*b*) *absol.* or *intr.* To lodge, 'put up'. **q.** *trans.* To occupy entirely; to fill up (space, time, etc.); to occupy exclusively; to obstruct. (*b*) To engage or occupy fully, engross (a person, his attention, mind, etc.). **r.** intr. *T. up with.* (*a*) To associate with (a person); to consort with (esp. with a view to marriage). (*b*) To adopt, espouse (esp. as a settled practice); to assent to, agree with. *arch.* †(*c*) To put up with, tolerate.

Take-, the vb.-stem in combs. and phrases used as sbs. or adjs.: **t.-down** *colloq.* = SET-DOWN 2; **t.-it-or-leave-it** *a.*, allowing acceptance or rejection; showing indifference; **t.-on**, a state of 'taking on' or mental agitation.

Take-in (tēⁱ·kˌin), *sb. colloq.* 1778. [The vbl. phr. *take in.*] The act of taking in; a cheat, swindle, deception; a thing or person that takes one in; a 'fraud'.

Take-off (tēⁱ·kˌǫf), *sb.* and *a.* 1826. [f. the vbl. phr. *take off.*] **A. 1.** A thing that 'takes off' or detracts from something; a drawback. **2.** An act of 'taking off' or mimicking; a mimic; a caricature. *colloq.* 1855. **3.** The act of 'taking off', or springing from the ground, etc.; usu. *transf.* a place or spot from which one takes or may take off 1869. **4.** *Croquet.* A stroke made from contact with another ball so as to send one's own ball nearly or quite in the direction of aim, the other ball being moved only slightly or not at all 1874. **5.** *Aeronautics.* See *take off* n. (TAKE *v.*) 1914. **B.** *attrib.* or *adj.* **1.** From which one 'takes off' or makes the spring in leaping, as *the t. line* 1889. **2.** Applied to a part of mechanism for taking something off 1896.

Taker (tēⁱ·kəɹ). late ME. [f. TAKE *v.* + -ER¹.] One who or that which takes; one who captures or seizes. **b.** One who takes possession, esp. of land; often with *first* or *next* 1766. **c.** One who accepts a bet 1810.

Take-up (tēⁱ·kˌʋp), *sb.* 1825. [f. the vbl. phr. *take up* (TAKE *v.*).] **1.** The act of 'taking up' the stuff so as to form 'gathers' in a dress; *concr.* one of such 'gathers'. Now *rare.* **2.** A contrivance for taking up; *spec.* a device in a sewing-machine for drawing up the thread so as to tighten the stitch 1877. **3.** In a loom or other machine, the process of winding up the stuff already woven or treated; *concr.* the part of the mechanism by which this is done 1877. **4.** The part between the smoke-box and the bottom of the funnel of a marine engine boiler 1838.

‖**Takin** (tā·kin). 1850. [Native name in Mishmi.] A horned ruminant (*Budorcas taxicolor*) of south-eastern Tibet on the northern frontier of Assam.

Taking (tēⁱ·kiŋ), *vbl. sb.* ME. [f. TAKE *v.* + -ING¹.] The action or condition expressed by TAKE *v.* **1.** Touching, touch. ME only. **2.** Capture, seizure (in warfare, etc.); apprehension, arrest; catching (of fish or other animals) ME. †**b.** A seizure or attack of disease, *esp.* a stroke of palsy or the like; also, malignant influence –1639. **3.** The physical act of possessing oneself of anything, of receiving, accepting, etc. ME. †**b.** Mental acceptance or reception; estimation –1639. **4. a.** Condition, plight (in unfavourable sense). *Obs.* exc. *Sc.* 1522. **b.** *spec.* A disturbed or agitated state of mind; excited condition, passion 1577. **5. a.** That which is received or gained; *esp.* in *pl.*, the receipts or earnings of merchants, tradesmen, or workmen 1632. **b.** That which is captured; *esp.* the fish or other animals caught at one time, a capture, a catch 1809. **c.** *Printing.* = TAKE *sb.* 5. 1808.

3. Their t. of notes at sermons 1660. The t. of the census 1896. **b.** Manifested in his sorrowful t. of her death 1639. **4. a.** The poor boy was in a pitiful t. and pickle PEPYS. **b.** By this time your Mother is in a fine t. 1676.

Ta·king, *ppl. a.* 1483. [f. as prec. + -ING².] That takes; see the vb. **1.** Seizing, getting something into one's possession; rapacious (*rare*). **2.** That takes the fancy or affection; captivating, charming, attractive. Now *colloq.* 1605. **3.** †Blasting, pernicious; infectious, catching (*rare*) 1605.

2. Phillis has such a t. way, She charms my very soul PRIOR. **3.** Strike her yong bones, You t. Ayres, with Lamenesse SHAKS. Hence **Ta·kingly** *adv.*, **-ness.**

‖**Talapoin** (tæ·lăpoin). 1586. [– Pg. *talapão* – Talaing (Old Peguan) *tala pôi* 'my lord', the title of a Buddhist monk.] **1.** A Buddhist monk or priest, properly of Pegu; extended by Europeans to those of Siam, Burma, and other Buddhist countries. **2.** *Zool.* (In full *t. monkey.*) A small W. African monkey, *Cercopithecus talapoin* 1774.

Talar (tēⁱ·lăɹ). 1738. [– L. *talaris*, f. *talus* ankle; see -AR¹.] A long garment or robe, reaching down to the ankles.

‖**Talaria** (tălēᵊ·riă), *sb. pl.* 1593. [L., n. pl. of *talaris*; see prec.] *Anc. Rom. Mythol.* Winged sandals or small wings attached to the ankles of some deities, esp. Mercury.

Talbot (tǭ·lbət). 1491. [Supposed to be derived from the ancient Eng. family name *Talbot.*] **1.** Name of a variety of hound, formerly used for tracking and hunting; a large white or light-coloured hound, having long hanging ears, heavy jaws, and great powers of scent 1562. **2.** A representation of a hound or hunting-dog; *esp.* in *Her.* that borne by the Talbot family 1491.

Talbotype (tǭ·lbŏtəip). Also **Talbot-type.** 1846. [f. W. H. F. *Talbot*, the inventor's name + TYPE *sb.*] = CALOTYPE; also, a picture produced by this process.

Talc (tælk), *sb.* 1601. [– Fr. *talc* or med.L. *talcum* – Arab. *ṭalḳ* – Pers. *ṭalḳ*.] A name applied by the Arabs and mediæval writers to various transparent, translucent, or shining minerals, as talc proper, mica, selenite, etc. Now: **1.** In popular and commercial use, (loosely) applied to MICA or MUSCOVY *glass.* **b.** With *a* and *pl.* A plate of mica used as a microscopic slide 1761. **2.** *Min.* A hydrated silicate of magnesium, usu. consisting of broad flat laminæ or plates, white, apple-green, or yellow, having a greasy feel, and shining lustre, translucent, and in thin plates often transparent; it exists in three varieties—foliated, massive (*steatite* or *soapstone*), and indurated (*talc slate* or *schist*) 1610.

Comb.: **t. powder,** talcum powder; **t. schist, slate,** a schistose rock consisting largely of t. Hence **Talcky** (tæ·lki) *a.* pertaining to, of the nature of, or consisting of t. **Ta·lcoid** *a.* resembling t.; *sb.* a snow-white, broadly-foliated variety of t. **Ta·lcose** *a.* abounding in t. **Ta·lcous** *a.* of the nature of t.; talcose.

‖**Talcum** (tæ·lkŏm). 1558. [med.L.; see prec.] = TALC. *T. powder*, powdered talc or French chalk for toilet use, usu. perfumed.

Tale (tēⁱl), *sb.* [OE. *talu* = OFris. *tale*, OS. *tala* (Du. *taal* speech), OHG. *zala* (G. *zahl* number), ON. *tala* talk, tale, number :– Gmc. **talō*, f. **tal-*, as in **taljan* TELL *v.* Branch II was prob. taken from ON.] **I.** †**1.** The action of telling, relating, or saying; discourse, conversation, talk –1592. **2.** That which one tells; the relation of a series of events; a narrative, statement, information OE. **b.** *pl.* Things told so as to violate confidence or secrecy; idle or mischievous gossip ME. **3.** A true or fictitious story or narrative; a literary composition cast in narrative form ME. **4.** A mere story as opp. to a narrative of fact; a fiction, an idle tale; a falsehood ME. **b.** A thing now existing only in story; a thing of the past 1780.

1. *Rom. & Jul.* II. iv. 99. **2.** The t. of hym wente forth. .in to al. .Galilee WYCLIF. One t. is good, untill anothers told 1601. Phr. *Thereby hangs a t.* (and such phrases) = 'about that there is something to tell'. *In the same t.*, *in a* (= one) *t.*, in the same enumeration, statement, or category; hence, in agreement (*arch.*). **b.** Phr. *To tell* (*bring, carry*) *tales.* Dead men tell no tales 1838. *Tales out of school* (see SCHOOL *sb.*¹ 1 b). **3.** Indeed Sir the best Tales in England are your Canterburie tales 1606. Hates the T. of Troy for Helen's sake GRAY. **4.** There was more of t. than of truth in those things DE FOE. Phr. *A Canterbury t.*, *old wives' tales, travellers' tales, a t. of a tub* (see TUB), etc. **b.** No power. .could have prevented a general conflagration; and at this day London would have been a t. BURKE.

II. 1. Numerical statement or reckoning; enumeration; number ME. **2.** The number all told; the complete sum, enumeration, or list ME. †**3.** An account, a reckoning of numbers –1807. †**4.** Reckoning of value; account, estimation –1496.

1. An exact t. of the dead bodies DE FOE. Phr. *By t.*, by number; as dist. from *by weight, by measure*; Where oysters are. .sold by t. 1594. **2.** Yet shal ye delyuer the hole t. of brycke BIBLE (Great) *Exod.* 5:18. **4.** Phr. *To hold* (*make, give, tell*) *no t. of*, to hold of no account. Hence **Ta·leful** *a.* full of tales; talkative. THOMSON.

Tale (tēⁱl), *v.* Now *rare.* [OE. *talian* reckon = OS. *talon* reckon, OHG. *zalōn* number, reckon (G. *zahlen* pay), ON. *tala* talk, tale, number :– Gmc. **talōjan*, f. **tal-*; see prec.] †**1.** *trans.* To account, reckon (something) to be (so and so). –late ME. **2.** To count up; to deal *out* by number. Now *dial.* 1626. †**3.** *intr.* To discourse, talk, gossip; to tell (*of*); to tell tales –1500.

Talebearer (tēⁱ·lˌbēᵊːrəɹ). 1478. [f. TALE *sb.* + BEARER.] One who officiously carries gossip or reports of private matters to gratify malice or idle curiosity. So **Ta·lebearing,** the carrying of malicious or injurious reports.

‖**Talegalla** (tælĭgæ·lă). 1842. [mod.L. (Fr. *talégalle*) formed by R. P. Lesson (1828) from Malagasy *talèva* and L. *gallus* cock.] *Ornith.* A genus of megapod birds inhabiting Australia and New Guinea. As English, chiefly applied to *T. lathami*, the Brush-turkey of Australia.

Talent (tæ·lĕnt), *sb.* OE. [– OFr. *talent* will, desire :– L. *talentum* in Rom. sense of 'inclination of the mind' – Gr. τάλαντον balance, weight, sum of money, f. **tal-*, **tla-* bear, endure (see THOLE *v.*)] **I.** A denomination of weight, used by the Assyrians, Babylonians, Greeks, Romans, and other ancient nations, varying greatly with time, people, and locality. **b.** The value of a talent weight (of gold, silver, etc.): a money of account OE. †**c.** *fig.* Treasure, riches, abundance –1635.

b. The Babylonian silver t. was equal to 3000 shekels; the Greek t. contained 60 minæ or 6000 silver drachmæ, and the value of the late Attic t. of silver, with pure silver at 4*s.* 9*d.* an oz. troy, has been estimated at £200. O.E.D.

II. †**1.** Inclination, propension, or disposition for anything; 'mind', 'will', wish, desire, appetite –1530. †**2.** An evil inclination, disposition, or passion; esp. and usu. anger –1695.

1. Grete t. and desyre. .to knowe hym 1485. **2.** One that had of a long time borne an ill T. towards the King BACON.

III. Mental endowment, natural ability. [From the parable of the talents, Matt. 25:14–30, etc.] **1.** Power or ability of mind or body viewed as something divinely entrusted to a person for use and improvement. late ME. **2.** A special natural ability or aptitude, usu. for something expressed or implied; a natural capacity for success in some department of mental or physical activity 1660. **b.** *pl.* Aptitudes or faculties of various kinds; mental powers of a superior order 1654. **c.** collect. *sing.* (without *a* or *pl.*). Mental power or ability; cleverness 1622. **d.** Talent as embodied in the talented; *occas.*, persons of ability collectively; rarely, as sing., a person of talent. By the sporting press, applied to backers of horses, as dist. from the bookmakers. 1856. †**3.** The characteristic disposition or aptitude of a person or animal –1774.

1. Though Nature weigh our talents, and dispense To every man his modicum of sense COWPER. **2.** He is chiefly to be considered in his

three different talents, as he was a critic, a satirist, and a writer of odes DRYDEN. **b.** The Duke of Buckingham, a man of talents and power GOLDSM. **c.** He was a person of no t. MORLEY. **d.** (*Administration of*) *All the Talents* (Eng. Hist.), an ironical appellation of the Ministry of Lord Grenville, 1806–7, implying that it combined in its members all the talents. **3.** It is the t. of human nature to run from one extreme to another SWIFT. Hence **Ta·lent** *v.* (*rare*) *trans.* to endow with t. or talents; chiefly in *pa. pple.* (cf. next).

Talented (tæ·lĕntĕd), *a.* 1824. [f. prec. + -ED².] Endowed with talent or talents; possessing talent; gifted, clever, accomplished.

‖**Tales** (tēⁱ·līz). 1495. [L., pl. of *talis* such, in the phrase *tales de circumstantibus* 'such (or the like) persons from those standing about', occurring in the order for adding such persons to a jury.] *Law.* orig., in *pl.*, Persons taken from among those present in court or standing by, to serve on a jury in a case where the original panel has become deficient in number by challenge or other cause, these being persons *such* as those originally summoned; loosely applied in Eng. as a singular (*a tales*) to the supply of men (or even of one man) so provided. Also, contextually applied to the order or act of supplying such substitutes, as *to pray, grant, award a t.* Now restricted to such summoning of common jurors to serve on a special jury; orig., and still in U.S., in general use (including criminal jurisdiction).

Comb.: **t.-book**, the entry-book of persons summoned on a t. Hence **Talesman** (tēⁱ·līz-, tēⁱ·lzmæn), a member of the t. impanelled to complete a jury.

Ta·le-te:ller. late ME. [f. TALE *sb.* + TELLER.] **1.** A teller of tales or stories; a narrator. **2.** A tale-bearer; a tell-tale. late ME.

Taliacotian (tæ:liăkōᵘ·ʃiăn), *a.* 1656. [f. *Taliacotius*, latinized f. It. *Tagliacozzi* + -AN.] *Surg.* Of, pertaining to, or named after Tagliacozzi, a surgeon of Bologna (1546–99); esp. in *T. operation*, a plastic operation described by him for restoration of the nose by means of tissue taken from another part.

Talia·tion. *Obs.* exc. *Hist.* 1591. [XVI, but perh. older; app. an extended form of TALION.] A return of like for like; retaliation; = TALION.

‖**Talio** (tēⁱ·lio). 1611. [L., f. *talis* such.] = next.

Talion (tæ·liən). late ME. [– (O)Fr. *talion* – L. *talio, -ōn-*, f. *talis* such, the like.] Retaliation; *esp.* in the Mosaic, Roman, and other systems of Law, the *lex talionis*, the principle of exacting compensation, 'eye for eye, tooth for tooth'; also, the infliction of the same penalty on the accuser who failed to prove his case as would have fallen upon the accused if found guilty.

‖**Talipes** (tæ·lipīz). 1857. [mod.L., f. L. *talus* ankle + *pes* foot.] **1.** *Path.* Club-foot; clubfootedness. **2.** *Zool.* A twisted disposition of the feet, occurring naturally in sloths 1891.

Talipot (tæ·lipǫt, -pət). 1681. [Malayalam *tālipat*, Sinhalese *talapata*, Hindi *tālpāt* :– Skr. *tālapattra* leaf of the *tāla* or fan-palm.] A South Indian fan-palm, *Corypha umbraculifera*, native in Ceylon and Malabar, noted for its great height, and its enormous fan-shaped leaves, which are much used as a material to write on.

†**Talisman**¹. 1599. [= Fr. *talisman*, of uncertain history.] A name formerly applied to a Turk learned in divinity and law, a Mullah; sometimes to a lower priest of Islam, a religious minister, a muezzin –1668.

Talisman² (tæ·lizmăn). 1638. [– Fr., Sp. *talisman*, It. *talismano* – med. Gr. τέλεσμον, alt. of late Gr. τέλεσμα (whence Arab. *ṭilasm*) completion, performance, religious rite, consecrated object, f. τελεῖν complete, perform (a rite), consecrate, f. τέλος end, result.] **1.** A stone, ring, or other object engraven with figures or characters, to which are attributed the occult powers of the planetary influences and celestial configurations under which it was made; usu. worn as an amulet to avert evil from or bring fortune to the wearer; also, used medicinally to impart healing virtue; hence, any object held to be endowed with magic virtue; a charm. **2.** *fig.* Anything that acts as a charm or by which extraordinary results are achieved 1784.

1. He had stolen from Henry..a T., which rendered its wearer invulnerable STUBBS. Hence **Talisma·nic, -al** *adjs.* of, pertaining to, or of the nature of a t., **-ly** *adv.*

Talk (tǫk), *sb.* 1475. [f. next.] The action or practice of talking. **1.** Speech, discourse; *esp.* conversation (of a familiar kind). With *a* and *pl.* A conversation 1548. **b.** A short lecture 1900. **2.** A more or less formal or public oral interchange of views, opinions, or propositions; a conference; an informal lecture. **b.** A palaver or pow-wow with savages; also, a verbal message to or from these. 1550. **3.** Mention (of a subject); the making of statements and remarks; rumour, gossip, or an instance of this 1560. **4.** The subject, theme, or occasion of topical conversation, esp. of current gossip or rumour 1624. **5.** Utterance of words, speaking (to others), speech; also *contempt.*, empty words, verbiage 1539. **b.** Applied to writing of the nature of familiar or loose speech 1552.

1. We had t. enough, but no conversation; there was nothing discussed JOHNSON. **3.** Great t. of a comet 1677. That would make a t. MRS. GASKELL. Phr. *The t. of the town.* **4.** Just when these letters were the t. of all London MACAULAY. **5.** Phr. *Tall t.*, speaking in a boastful or exaggerated fashion; see also SMALL TALK. **b.** Columns of.. dangerous t. are appearing in most of our newspapers 1884.

Talk (tǫk), *v.* [ME. *talkien, talken* (first in w. midl. texts), deriv. with *k*-suffix of the base **tal-* of TALE, TELL *v.*] **I.** *intr.* **1.** To convey or exchange ideas, information, etc. by means of speech, esp. the familiar speech of ordinary intercourse; to converse. **b.** To communicate by wireless signals 1912. **2.** To exercise the faculty of speech; to speak, utter words, say things; often *contempt.*: to speak trivially, utter empty words, prate. late ME. **b.** To say something as a rumour or matter of gossip; hence, to indulge in idle or censorious gossip 1461. **3.** To utter words, or the sound of words, unconsciously, mechanically, or imitatively, as *to t. in one's sleep, like a parrot*, etc. 1591. **4.** *fig.* Of inanimate things: To make sounds or noises resembling or suggesting speech; to produce the effects of speech. 1793.

1. My mother and I talked at large on the subject 1819. Phr. *T. about..*, often used *colloq.* to contrast something already mentioned with something still more striking; T. about English people being fond of eating, that Canadian party beat all I had ever seen 1891. *T. of*, speak of, about, or in reference to (anything). *To t. of* (doing something), to speak somewhat vaguely, so as to suggest a notion, or express one's probable intention, of doing it. *Talking of..*, apropos of... **2.** What canst thou talke..hast thou a tonge? SHAKS. A disposition to be talking for its own sake 1729. Phr. *To t. to*, to address words to; *colloq.* to rebuke, scold, reprimand. *To t. back*, to answer, esp. impertinently. **b.** They t. heere as if the King would goe a northerne progresse this summer 1669. Phr. *To t. big, tall*, etc., to talk boastfully, to indulge in inflated language. *To t. down* (*to* an audience), to adapt one's discourse to the assumed lower level of their intelligence. *To t. at*, to make remarks intended for some one but not directly addressed to him. **c.** *pregnantly.* To say something to the purpose 1840. **4.** The ship was talking, as sailors say, loudly, treading the innumerable ripples with an incessant weltering splash STEVENSON.

II. *trans.* **1.** To utter or speak in familiar language (words, a tale, etc.); to express in talk or speech (matter, opinions, etc.) ME. **b.** To use as a spoken language, to speak conversationally; as *to t. dialect, French, slang, Somerset.* 1859. **2.** To discourse about, speak of, discuss. Now *colloq.* late ME. **3.** To bring or drive (oneself or another) into some specified state by talking 1599.

1. b. *To t. Greek, Hebrew, Double-Dutch, gibberish*, etc., to use language unintelligible to the hearer. **2.** Phr. *To t. shop*: see SHOP *sb.* 5. **3.** They would talke themselves madde SHAKS. Phr. *To t.* (a person) *over* or *round*, to win over or bring into compliance by talking. *To t.* (a thing) *over, to t. over* (a matter), to discuss it in familiar conference or conversation. *To t. down*, to put down by talking; to out-talk. *To t. out*, to t. to the end of; to carry on the discussion of (a bill in Parliament, etc.) till the time for adjournment is reached, and so frustrate its progress by preventing its being put to the vote. *To t.* (a person) *into* or *out of*, to persuade into, or dissuade from (something) by talking. *To t. through one's hat*, to exaggerate or bluff or make wild statements (*slang*).

Talkative (tǫ·kătiv), *a.* late ME. [f. prec. + -ATIVE.] Given to talking; inclined to talk; chatty, loquacious; garrulous, 'full of prate' (J.). **b.** Said of personal qualities, etc. late ME.

b. Nothing is so t. as misfortune STEELE. Hence **Ta·lkative-ly** *adv.*, **-ness.**

Talkee-talkee (tǫ·ki,tǫ·ki). 1808. [A redupl. deriv. of TALK, with dimin. ending.] **1.** The imperfect or broken English of some native races; *esp.* the lingua franca of Negro slaves in the W. Indies. **2.** Small-talk; chatter; continuous prattle; mere talk. *contempt.* 1812.

Talker (tǫ·kəɹ). late ME. [f. TALK *v.* + -ER¹.] One who talks or is given to talking; a speaker, a conversationalist; a talkative person.

Great Talkers should always be mistrusted 1701.

Talkie (tǫ·ki). 1928. [f. TALK(ING *picture* + -IE, -Y⁶, after MOVIE; cf. SPEAKIE.] A talking film or picture.

Talking (tǫ·kiŋ), *vbl. sb.* ME. [f. TALK *v.* + -ING¹.] The action of TALK *v.*

Words learn'd by rote a parrot may rehearse, But t. is not always to converse COWPER. *T. to*, a reprimand, an admonition (*colloq.*).

Talking (tǫ·kiŋ), *ppl. a.* 1562. [f. TALK *v.* + -ING².] That talks; loquacious.

The hawthorn bush, with seats beneath the shade, For t. age and whispering lovers made GOLDSM. *T. film, picture*, a cinematograph film accompanied by talking (and other sounds).

Talky (tǫ·ki), *a.* 1862. [f. TALK *sb.* + -Y¹.] Inclined to or abounding in talk; talkative, loquacious. Hence **Ta·lky-ta·lky** *a.* (cf. TALKEE-TALKEE) abounding in (mere) talk; not rising above the level of talk.

Tall (tǫl), *a.* ME. [repr. OE. *ġe*|*tæl* swift, prompt = OFris. *tel*, OS. *gital*, OHG. *gizal* quick.] **I.** †**1.** Quick, prompt, ready, active (*rare*) –1542. †**2.** Meet, becoming, seemly –1440. †**b.** Comely, goodly, fair, handsome; elegant, fine –1656. †**3.** Good at arms; doughty, grave, bold, valiant –1825. †**4.** Phr. *t. of* (*his*) *hand*(*s*: sometimes, (cf. sense 1) ready, skilful with (his) hands; sometimes, (cf. sense 3) stout of arm, formidable with weapons –1632.

2. b. That such a base slave as he should be saluted by such a tall man as I am, from such a beautiful dame as you MARLOWE. **3.** Now sirs, quite our selues like t. men and hardie UDALL.

II. 1. Of a person: High of stature; of more than average height. Usu. appreciative. Also of animals, as a giraffe, stag, or the like. 1530. **b.** Having a specified or relative height; measuring in stature (so much): without implication of great height 1588. **2.** Of things, as ships, trees, etc.: High, lofty; esp. of things high in proportion to their width, as *a t. chimney, mast*, etc. 1548. **b.** Of more than average length, measured from bottom to top 1608. **3.** *fig.* †**a.** Lofty, grand, eminent –1827. **b.** High-flown, esp. in *t. talk* (TALK *sb.* 5). *colloq.* 1670. **c.** Exaggerated, highly coloured. *U.S. colloq.* 1846. **d.** Large, in amount; big. *slang* (*orig. U.S.*) 1842. †**4.** *fig.* Great, eminent (*at* something) –1662.

1. Fair Galatea,..T. as a Poplar, taper as the Bole DRYDEN. **b.** If a Man could make himself happy by imagining himself six Foot tall, tho' he was but three 1744. **2.** A t. house in the city of Paris 1852. **b.** The faith they haue in Tennis and t. Stockings, Short blistred Breeches, and those types of Trauell SHAKS. *T. folio, t. copy* (of a book). *T. hat*, a man's silk hat with a high cylindrical crown. **3. c.** 'T. stories' are the perquisite of every traveller 1897. **d.** It's a t. order, but it's worth trying 1893. Hence **Ta·llness.**

Tallage (tæ·lėdʒ), *sb.* ME. [– OFr. *taillage*, f. *taillier* TAIL *v.*² III; see -AGE.] orig., in *Eng. Hist.*, An arbitrary tax levied by Norman and early Angevin kings upon the towns and the demesne lands of the Crown; hence, a tax levied upon feudal dependants by their superiors; also, by extension, a municipal rate; a toll or customs duty; a grant, levy, imposition. Hence **Ta·llage** *v. trans.* to impose t. upon; to tax.

Tallboy (tǫ·lboi). 1676. [f. TALL *a.* + BOY.] **1.** A tall-stemmed glass or goblet.

Now *local*. **2.** A tall chest of drawers (often raised on legs), usu. in two parts, one standing on the other; sometimes applied to a chest of drawers or a bureau standing on a dressing-table 1769. **3.** A tall chimney-pot 1884.

Talliable (tæ·liăb'l), *a.* Now *Hist.* 1531. [– (O)Fr. *taillable* or med.L. *talliabilis* (to which the Eng. sp. conforms), f. *taillier*, *talliare*; see TAIL *v.*[2], -ABLE.] Subject to tallage.

Talliate (tæ·li,e^{i}t), *v.* 1754. [– *talliat-*, pa. ppl. stem of med.L. *talliare*; see TAIL *v.*[2], -ATE[3].] *trans.* = TALLAGE *v.*

Ta·llier. Now only in Fr. form **tailleur** (ta^{i}yör). 1709. [f. TALLY *v.*[3] + -ER[1], and from Fr. *tailler* cut (at cards).] *Cards.* In rouge-et-noir and similar card-games, the name of the dealer or banker.

Tallish (tǫ·liʃ), *a.* 1748. [f. TALL *a.* + -ISH[1].] Inclining towards tallness; rather tall.

‖**Tallith** (tæ·liþ, ‖tal,lī·þ). 1613. [Rabbinical Heb. *ṭallīt*, f. bibl. Heb. *ṭillel* to cover.] The garment or mantle (now often a scarf) worn by Jews at prayer.

Tallow (tæ·lo^{u}), *sb.* [In XIV *talȝ*, *taluȝ*, *talow* – MLG. *talg*, *talch*, of unkn. origin.] **1.** The fat or adipose tissue of an animal, esp. that which yields the substance described in 2; suet. **2.** A substance consisting of a somewhat hard animal fat (esp. that obtained from the parts about the kidneys of ruminating animals), separated from the membranes, etc., naturally mixed with it by melting and clarifying; used for making candles and soap, dressing leather, and other purposes. **3.** Applied to various kinds of grease or greasy substances, e.g. those obtained from plants 1745.

attrib. and *Comb.*: **t. candle,** a candle made of t.; **-chandler,** one whose trade is to make or sell t. candles; **-chandlery,** the business of a t.-chandler; also, the place of work of a t.-chandler; **-tree,** any of various trees yielding substances resembling t.; *spec.* (*a*) *Stillingia sebifera*, a euphorbiaceous tree of China, also cultivated elsewhere for the fatty covering of its seeds; (*b*) *Pentadesma butyracea*, a guttiferous tree of Sierra Leone; (*c*) *Vateria indica* of Malabar; (*d*) *Eucalyptus microcorys* of Australia, called also **t.-wood.**

Ta·llow, *v.* ME. [f. prec.] **1.** *trans.* To smear or anoint with tallow; to grease. †**b.** *intr.* (for *refl.*) –1720. **2. a.** *intr.* Of cattle, etc.: To produce, or yield tallow 1722. **b.** *trans.* To cause (cattle, etc.) to form tallow; to fatten 1765.

2. b. The largest pasture..will neither skin nor t., or, in other words, is fit for nothing but young stock 1765.

Ta·llow-face. Now *rare* or *Obs.* 1592. A pale yellowish-white face; hence, a person having such a face.

Out you baggage, You tallow face SHAKS. So **Ta·llow-faced** *a.*

Tallowish (tæ·lo^{u},iʃ), *a.* 1552. [f. TALLOW *sb.* + -ISH[1] 2.] Of the nature of or resembling tallow.

Tallowy (tæ·lo^{u},i), *a.* 1440. [f. as prec. + -Y[1].] **1.** Having the nature or properties of tallow; sebaceous. **2.** Resembling tallow in colour or complexion 1832. **3.** Of a beast: Abounding in tallow, fat 1495.

Tally (tæ·li), *sb.*[1] 1440. [– AFr. *tallie* = AL. *tallia*, *talia*, for L. *talea* cutting, rod, stick; the corresp. OFr. *taille* was adopted earlier in this sense as *tail*; see TAIL *sb.*[2]] **1.** A stick or rod of wood, usu. squared, marked on one side with notches representing the amount of a debt or payment. The rod being cleft lengthwise across the notches, the debtor and creditor each retained one of the halves, the tallying of which constituted legal proof of the debt, etc. **b.** Such a cloven rod, as the official receipt formerly given by the Exchequer for a tax, tallage, etc. paid, or in acknowledgement of a loan to the sovereign 1604. **c.** *transf.* Any tangible means of recording a payment or amount 1863. †**2.** The record of an amount due; a score or shot, an account –1833. **3.** *fig.* (from 1 and 2). Reckoning, score, account. Now *rare*. 1614. **4.** Each of the two corresponding halves or parts of anything; a thing, or part, that exactly fits or agrees with another thing or corresponding part, a counterpart; *fig.* an agreement, correspondence 1651. **5.** A number, group, series, lot, tale; *esp.* a certain number or group (of things or persons) taken as the unit of computation 1674. **b.** The last of a specified number forming a unit of computation, on the completion of which the t.-man calls 'tally' and notes it down 1886. †**6.** A mark (such as the notch of a tally) representing a unit quantity, or a series or set of units –1807. **7.** A distinguishing mark on a bale or case of merchandise, etc., corresponding to one in a list, for the purpose of comparison or identification; hence, a mark, label, ticket, or tab, used for this purpose, or to denote the weight and contents, etc.; a gardener's plant label 1860.

2. †*Upon* or *on t.*, on credit, 'on tick'. †*Petty t.* (Naut.), a petty account kept of a ship's provisions; hence *transf.* provisions. **4.** So suited in their minds and persons That they were fram'd the tallies for each other DRYDEN. *To live (on) t.*, to cohabit without marriage (*slang*). **5.** Used *spec.* in certain trades.

attrib. and *Comb.*, as *t.-book*, *-stick*, *-trade*; **t.-board,** a board on which an account is notched or chalked; **-clerk,** one who checks merchandise with a list in loading or discharging cargo; **-sheet,** a score-sheet, esp. (*U.S.*) in recording votes; **-stick,** a stick used as or like a t.

†**Tally,** *sb.*[2] 1706. [f. TALLY *v.*[3]] *Cards.* At faro, basset, etc., a deal –1760.

Tally (tæ·li), *v.*[1] 1440. [f. TALLY *sb.*[1] Cf. med.L. *talliare* (XIII) TAIL *v.*[2]] **I. 1.** *trans.* †To notch (a stick) so as to make it a tally; hence, to mark, score, set *down* or enter (a number, etc.) on or as on a tally; *transf.* to record, register. **b.** *spec.* To identify, count, and enter each bale, case, article, etc. of a cargo or lot of goods in loading or discharging 1812. **c.** To distinguish, mark, or identify (a bale of goods, etc.) by or as by a tally 1837. **2.** To count or reckon *up*, to number. Now *rare*. 1542. †**3.** To deal on tally or credit; to open or have a credit account *with* any one –1724.

1. c. Leaving his people to mark and t. the bales MARRYAT. **2.** They anchor'd at morning to t. their spoil 1885.

II. †**1.** *trans. fig.* To cause (things) to correspond or agree; to match; *pa. pple.* matched, suited, adapted –1812. **2.** *intr.* To agree, as one half of a cloven tally with its fellow; to correspond or answer exactly; to accord, conform, fit. (The chief current sense.) 1705.

2. A Theory that does not exactly t. with fact 1738.

Ta·lly, *v.*[2] Now *rare*. 1450. [Of unkn. origin.] *Naut.* **1.** *trans.* To haul taut (the fore or main lee-sheets). **2.** *intr.* To catch hold or 'clap' *on* to a rope 1840.

†**Tally,** *v.*[3] 1706. [– Fr. *tailler* TAIL *v.*[2]] *Cards. intr.* At faro, basset, etc., to be banker (i.e. to deal) –1748.

Tally (tǫ·l,li), *adv.* Now *rare* or *Obs.* ME. [f. TALL *a.* + -LY[2].] In a tall manner. †**1.** In a seemly manner; elegantly; well, bravely –1450. **2.** Highly, loftily 1611.

Tally-ho (tæ:li,hō^{u}·), *int.* and *sb.* 1772. [Cf. Fr. *taïaut* (XVII), †*taho*, †*theau* (XVI).] **1.** The view-halloo raised by huntsmen on catching sight of the fox; used as *int.* and as *sb.* 1787. **2.** orig., The proper name given to a fast day-coach between London and Birmingham, started in 1823; subsequently the name was appropriated by other fast coaches, and treated somewhat as a common noun. Also *t. coach.* 1831. **b.** *U.S.* A large four-in-hand coach or drag 1882.

Ta:lly-ho·, *v.* 1812. [f. prec.] **1.** *trans.* To salute or make known the presence of (a fox) by the cry of 'tally-ho'. **2.** *intr.* To cry 'tally-ho' or a similar call 1826.

Tallyman (tæ·limæn). 1654. [f. TALLY *sb.*[1] + MAN *sb.*] **1.** One who carries on a tally-trade, or supplies goods on credit, to be paid for by instalments. **2.** One who tallies, or keeps account of, anything; *spec.* a clerk who checks a cargo in loading or discharging 1888. **3.** One who 'lives tally' with a woman. *slang.* 1890. So **Ta·llywoman** 1727.

Talma (tæ·lmă). *Pl.* **-as.** 1860. [Named after François Joseph *Talma*, French tragedian (1763–1826). Cf. ROQUELAURE.] A cape or cloak worn by men, and also by women in the 19th c.

‖**Talmud** (tæ·lmɒ̆d, talmū·d). 1532. [– late Heb. *talmûḏ* instruction, f. Heb. *lāmaḏ* learn.] In the wide sense, The body of Jewish civil and ceremonial traditionary law, consisting of the MISHNAH or binding precepts of the elders, additional to and developed from the Pentateuch, and the later GEMARA or commentary upon these, forming a complement to the Mishnah. The term was orig. applied to the Gemara, of which two recensions exist, known respectively as the Jerusalem (or Palestinian) and the Babylonian T.; to the latter of which the name is in strictest use confined. Hence **Talmu·dic, -al** *adjs.* of or pertaining to the T.; contained in the T. **Ta·lmudize** *v.*

Talmudist (tæ·lmɒ̆dist, talmū·dist). 1569. [f. prec. + -IST.] **a.** One of the authors of the Talmud. **b.** One who accepts the authority of the Talmud. **c.** A Talmudic scholar. Hence **Talmudi·stic, -al** *adjs.* = TALMUDICAL.

Talon (tæ·lən). late ME. [– (O)Fr. *talon* heel :– Rom. **talo*, *-ōn-*, f. L. *talus* ankle-bone. The extension to the claws of a bird of prey, etc., is peculiar to English.] **I.** †**1.** The 'heel' or hinder part of the foot of certain quadrupeds, as swine and deer, or of the hoof of a horse –1725. †**b.** The hallux of a bird –1577. **2.** *pl.* The claws (or less usu. in *sing.* any claw) of a bird or beast. late ME. **b.** *spec.* The powerful claws of a bird of prey, or of a dragon, griffin, etc. late ME. **c.** Allusively applied to the grasping hands or fingers of human beings 1588. **d.** *fig.* 1586.

2. A kite..would have certainly carried me away in his talons SWIFT. **d.** That they may yet be able to save something from the talons of despotism BURKE.

II. 1. *transf.* A heel-like part or object. **a.** *Naut.* The curved back of a ship's rudder. *Obs.* or *arch.* 1485. **b.** *Arch.* An ogee moulding 1704. **c.** The projection on the bolt of a lock against which the key presses 1877. **2.** *fig.* **a.** *Cards.* The remainder of the pack after the hands have been dealt 1891. **b.** *Comm.* The last portion of a sheet of coupons 1882.

‖**Talpa** (tæ·lpă). 1693. [L., mole.] **1.** *Zool.* The genus typified by the common mole (*Talpa europæa*) 1706. **2.** *Path.* An encysted cranial tumour; a wen 1693.

‖**Taluk, taluq** (tălu·k). *India.* 1799. [– Urdu *ta'alluḳ* estate, f. Arab. *'aliḳa* adhere, be attached.] *orig.* A hereditary estate belonging to a native proprietor; also, more usu., a sub-division of a *zillah* or district, comprising a number of villages placed for purposes of revenue under a native collector; a collectorate.

‖**Talukdar, taluqdar** (tălu·kdāɹ). *India.* 1798. [f. prec. + *dār*, Pers. agent-suffix.] The holder of a taluk or hereditary estate, or the officer in charge of the district so called.

Talus[1] (tē^{i}·lɒ̆s, Fr. talü). 1645. [– (O)Fr. *talus*, of unkn. origin.] **1.** A slope; *spec.* in *Fortification*, the sloping side of a wall or earthwork, which gradually increases in thickness from above downwards. **2.** *Geol.* A sloping mass of detritus lying at the base of a cliff or the like, and consisting of material which has fallen from its face; also, the slope or inclination of the surface of such a mass 1830. **b.** *gen.* A mountain slope 1830.

‖**Talus**[2] (tē^{i}·lɒ̆s). *Pl.* **tali.** 1693. [L.] **1.** The ankle-bone or astragalus; also applied to an analogous part in birds and insects. **2.** *Path.* A variety of club-foot in which the toes are drawn up, the heel resting on the ground 1864. **3.** A modular concretion somewhat resembling an astragalus bone 1728.

Ta·lwood. *Obs.* exc. *Hist.* ME. [Rendering of OFr. *bois de tail*, f. *tail* cutting, cut. Cf. TAIL *sb.*[2]] Wood for fuel, usu. cut up to a prescribed size.

‖**Tamal** (tămā·l). Also *erron.* **tamale.** 1856. [Mexican Sp. *tamal*, pl. *tamales.*] A Mexican delicacy, made of crushed Indian corn, flavoured with pieces of meat or chicken, red pepper, etc., wrapped in corn-husks and baked.

‖**Tamandua** (tămæ·nduă). 1614. [Pg. – Tupi *tamanduà.*] †**a.** orig., a name for the Brazilian Ant-eaters generally –1774. **b.** Now usu. restricted to the smaller *Tamandua tetradactyla* and its congeners 1834.

‖**Tamanoir** (tamanwār). 1849. [Fr., repr. Carib *tamanoà*, = Tupi *tamanduà*; see prec.] The French name of the Great Ant-eater or Ant-bear, *Myrmecophaga jubata*.

Tamarack (tæ·mǎræk). 1841. [app. a native Indian name in Canada.] **a.** prop., The American Larch (*Larix americana*); also, the timber of this tree. **b.** Also, applied to the Black or Ridge-pole Pine (*Pinus murrayana*) of dry inland regions of western N. America, and app. sometimes to the Scrub Pine of the coast.

Tamarin (tæ·mǎrin). 1780. [– Fr. *tamarin* (La Condamine, 1745) – native name in Carib dial. of Cayenne.] Any of several species of the genus *Midas* of S. Amer. marmosets or squirrel-monkeys.

Tamarind (tæ·mǎrind). 1533. [– med.L. *tamarindus* – Arab. *tamr hindī* date of India (cf. OFr. *tamarinde* XIII, mod. *tamarin* XV).] **1.** The fruit of the tree *Tamarindus indica*, a brown pod containing one to twelve seeds embedded in a soft brown or reddish-black acid pulp, used medicinally, and in cookery as a relish, etc. In *Comm.*, *Med.*, etc. *tamarinds* is used for the pulp. **2.** A large tree, *Tamarindus indica*, of the family *Leguminosæ*, supposed to be a native of the E. Indies, but now cultivated in warm climates generally, bearing dark-green pinnate leaves and racemes of fragrant yellow flowers streaked with red, and producing the fruit described in 1, and a hard and heavy timber 1614. **3.** Applied to various trees (or their fruits) resembling the t. in some respect 1833.

3. Black, Black-crown, Brown, or **Velvet t.,** a small leguminous tree, *Codarium acutifolium* or *Dialium guineense*. **Wild t.,** applied to various leguminous trees or shrubs, as, in the W. Indies, *Pithecolobium filicifolium*; in Jamaica, *Acacia arborea*, etc.

attrib. and *Comb.*: **t.-fish,** a relish made from various kinds of Indian fish preserved with the acid pulp of the t. fruit; **-plum,** an E. Indian tree, *Dialium indicum*, or its fruit; **-tea, -water,** an infusion of tamarinds, used as a cooling drink.

Tamarisk (tæ·mǎrisk). late ME. [– late L. *tamariscus*, var. of L. *tamarix*; of unkn. origin.] A plant of the genus *Tamarix*, esp. *T. gallica*, the Common T. (called in L. *myrica*), a graceful evergreen shrub or small tree, with slender feathery branches and minute scale-like leaves, growing in sandy places in S. Europe and W. Asia, and now much planted by the sea-shore in the south of England. †**b.** A decoction of the leaves of this plant, formerly used in medicine –1718.

attrib. and *Comb.*; **t. salt,** salt found adhering to the trunk of *Tamarix orientalis* in edible quantity; **t. ware,** vessels or dishes of t. wood.

‖**Tamasha** (tǎmā·ʃǎ). *India.* 1872. [Urdu – Arab. (Pers.) *tamāša* walking about for amusement, entertainment, Turk. spectacle.] An entertainment, public function. **b.** A fuss, commotion 1882.

Tambour (tæ·mbuᵊɹ, -bəɹ), *sb.* 1484. [– Fr. *tambour*, expressive of *tabour* TABOR.] **1.** A drum; *spec.* the great or bass drum. ‖**b. T. de basque** [Fr.], a tambourine 1688. **2.** An instrument for recording pulsations, as in respiration 1877. **3.** (Also **tambor.**) A fish which makes a drumming noise, or which resembles a drum in form; as a fish of the genus *Pogonias*, a drum-fish; a globe-fish, swell-fish, or puffer 1854. **4.** A circular frame formed of one hoop fitting within another, in which silk, muslin, etc. is stretched for embroidering 1777. **b.** A species of embroidery in which patterns are worked with a needle of peculiar form on material stretched on such a frame; now superseded by pattern-weaving; in recent use = *t.-lace* 1813. **c.** A kind of fine gold or silver thread 1899. **5.** *Arch.* **a.** The core of a Corinthian or Composite capital. **b.** Any one of the courses forming the shaft of a cylindrical column. **c.** The wall of a circular building surrounded with columns. **d.** A round exterior building surrounding the base of a dome or cupola; also, the circular vertical part of a cupola. **e.** A projecting part of the wall of a tennis court. 1706. **6.** *Mil.* A small defensive work formed of palisades or earth, usu. in the form of a redan, to defend an entrance or passage 1834.

2. Each bag communicates by a separate air-tight tube with an air-tight t. on which a lever rests; so that any pressure on either bag is communicated to the cavity of its respective t., the lever of which is raised in proportion 1877.

attrib. and *Comb.*: **t.-frame,** = sense 4; **-lace,** a modern lace resembling t. (4 b), consisting of needlework designs on machine-made net; **-needle,** the needle used in t.-work; **-stitch,** the loop-stitch used in t.-work; also, a stitch used in crochet.

Tambour (tæ·mbuᵊɹ, tæmbūᵊ·ɹ), *v.* 1774. [f. prec.] **1.** *trans.* To work or embroider in a tambour-frame; to ornament with tambour-work. **2.** *intr.* To work at a tambour-frame; to do tambour-work 1845.

‖**Tambourin** (Fr. tãṅburæ̃ṅ, tæ·mburin). 1797. [Fr., dim. of *tambour*; see TAMBOUR *sb.*, -INE[4].] **1.** The long narrow drum or tabor used in Provence: see TABORIN 1833. **2.** A Provençal dance, orig. accompanied by the tambourin. **b.** Music for such a dance, in duple rhythm and quick time. 1797.

Tambourine (tæmbŭrī·n). 1579. [– Fr. *tambourin*; see prec.] **1.** A musical instrument consisting of a wooden hoop having skin or parchment stretched over one side, and pairs of small cymbals, called jingles, placed in slots round the circumference. It is played by shaking, striking with the knuckles, or drawing the fingers across the parchment. **2. T. pigeon** (also ellipt. *tambourine*): an African species of pigeon, so called from the resonance of its note 1891.

‖**Tambreet** (tæmbrī·t). 1840. [Mallangong lang. of New South Wales.] The Duckbilled Platypus.

Tame (tēⁱm), *a.* [OE. *tam* = OFris., (M)LG., (M)Du. *tam*, OHG. *zam* (G. *zahm*), ON. *tamr* :– Gmc. **tamaz*, f. IE. **dom-*, repr. also by L. *domare*, Gr. δαμᾶν tame, subdue.] **1.** Of animals (rarely of men): Reclaimed from the wild state; brought under the control and care of man; domestic; domesticated. (Opp. to *wild.*) **b.** *joc.* Of a person: Domestic; kept for domestic or private use 1711. **2.** Applied to plants, also (in *U.S.*) to land: Cultivated, improved by culture; garden- as opp. to *wild*. late ME. **3.** Having the disposition or character of a domesticated animal; accustomed to man; not showing the natural shyness, fear of, or fierceness to man; also of persons, their disposition, etc.: made tractable, docile, or pliant OE. **4.** Subdued by taming; submissive; meek, poor-spirited, pusillanimous; servile 1563. **5.** Lacking animation, force, or effectiveness; deficient in striking features; weak, spiritless, insipid, dull 1602. **b.** Of scenery: Wanting boldness; having no striking features 1807.

1. They have also t. Lions 1660. **2.** *fig.* His lordship sowed t. oats now after his wild ones THACKERAY. **3.** *T. cat*, one who is on the footing of a domestic cat; a person who is made a convenience by his friends. **4.** A t. surrender of their rights 1769. **5.** The t. correct paintings of the Flemish school GOLDSM. **b.** A broad expanse of t. arable country 1894. Hence **Ta·me-ly** *adv.*, **-ness**.

Tame (tēⁱm), *v.*[1] [f. TAME *a.*, superseding ME. *teme*, OE. *temian*.] **1.** *trans.* To bring (a wild animal) under the control or into the service of man; to reclaim from the wild state; to domesticate. †**b.** To bring (a wild plant) under or into cultivation; to reclaim or improve (land) by cultivation –1746. **2.** To overcome the wildness or fierceness of (a man, animal, or thing); to subdue, subjugate, curb; to render gentle, tractable, or docile. late ME. **b.** *intr.* To become tame; to grow gentle, submissive, or sedate 1646. **3.** *trans.* To reduce the intensity of, tone *down*; to temper, soften, mellow; also, to render dull or uninteresting 1500.

1. To t. the vnicorne, and Lion wild SHAKS. **2.** She hoped she had tamed a high spirit or two in her day DICKENS. **3.** The first editors had tamed down some of the more startling statements 1847. Hence **Ta·meable, ta·mable** *a.* capable of being tamed. **Ta·meableness. Ta·meability (ta·ma-).**

Tame (tēⁱm), *v.*[2] Now *dial.* late ME. [Aphetic f. ATTAME *v.*, ENTAME *v.*[1]] *trans.* To pierce, cut into (in fighting or carving); to cut or break into, so as to use. †**b.** To broach (a cask, bottle, etc.) –1681.

Tameless (tēⁱ·mlės), *a.* 1597. [f. TAME *v.*[1] + -LESS.] That has never been tamed; that cannot be tamed; untamed, untameable. Hence **Ta·melessness.**

Tamer (tēⁱ·məɹ). 1530. [f. TAME *v.*[1] + -ER[1].] One who or that which tames.

Tamil, Tamul (tæ·mĭl, -ŭl). 1734. [– (partly through Du., Pg. *Tamul*) *Tamiḷ Tamiṛ*, native name, in Pali and Prakrit *Damila, Davila, -iḍa*, Skr. *Dramiḷa, -iḍa, Draviḍa* DRAVIDIAN.] One of a race of people of the Dravidian stock, inhabiting the south-east of India and part of Ceylon. **b.** The language spoken by this people, the leading member of the Dravidian family. Also *attrib.* or as *adj.* Hence **Tami·lian (Tamu·-lian)** *a.* Tamulic; *sb.* a member of the Tamil people. **Tamu·lic** *a.* pertaining to the Tamils or their language, Tamil.

Tammany (tæ·mǎni). 1683. [Name of a Delaware Indian chief who flourished about 1683 and with whom W. Penn had transactions for land.] The name of the central organization of the Democratic party in the City (formerly also in the State) of New York, located in *Tammany Hall*, in 14th Street, New York. In Eng. use associated with political and municipal corruption.

Tammy (tæ·mi), *sb.*[1] 1665. [Of unkn. origin.] A fine worsted cloth of good quality, often with a glazed finish.

Ta·mmy, *sb.*[2] 1769. [app. – Fr. *tamis* assim. to prec.] A strainer. Hence **Ta·mmy** *v. trans.* to strain through a t.

Tammy (tæ·mi), *sb.*[3] 1894. Short for *Tammy Shanter*, = next.

Tam o'Shanter (tæməʃæ·ntəɹ). 1840. [f. name of the hero of Burns's poem of that name (1790).] In full *Tam o' Shanter bonnet, cap*: A soft woollen bonnet with flat circular crown, the circumference of which is about twice that of the head, formerly worn by Scottish ploughmen, etc.; introduced, in a modified form, *c*1887, as a head-dress for girls and young women. Abbrev. *Tam*, TAMMY *sb.*[3]

Tamp (tæmp), *v.* 1819. [app. a XIX workmen's word; a back-formation from *tampin* (var. of TAMPION) taken as = *tamping*.] **1.** *trans. Mining.* **a.** To stop up (a bore-hole) with clay, sand, etc., rammed in upon the charge before firing the shot; also, to pack up (a gallery of a military mine) before firing it, in order to concentrate the effect. **b.** To ram home (the charge) in a bore-hole. Also *absol.* **2.** To ram down hard, so as to consolidate (earth, gravel, etc.); to pun; also, to pack (anything) round with earth so rammed down 1879.

2. The track is raised, the gravel tamped well under the ties, and the track is ready for use 1890. Hence **Ta·mper,** one who tamps a boring, etc.; also, a tamping-bar.

‖**Tampan** (tæ·mpæn). 1880. [perh. Sechuana name.] A S. African species of acarus remarkable for the venom of its bite.

Tamper (tæ·mpəɹ), *v.* 1567. [In all senses the earlier form is *temper*, of which *tamper* was perh. a workman's alteration.] †**I. a.** *intr.* To work in clay, etc. so as to mix it thoroughly. **b.** *trans.* To temper (clay). –1766. **II. 1.** *intr.* To work or busy oneself for some end; to machinate, scheme, plot. Const. *in* some practice, *for* something, *to do* something. 1596. **2.** To try to deal or enter into clandestine dealings *with*; often with connotation of improper interference with a person 1567. **3.** To have to do or interfere *with* improperly; to meddle *with* (a thing) 1601. **4.** To meddle or interfere *with* (a thing) so as to misuse, alter, corrupt, or pervert it 1593.

1. Others tamper'd For Fleetwood, Desborough, and Lambert 1678. The queen dowager tampered in this plot H. WALPOLE. **2.** He was trafficking with her enemies and tampering with her friends 1852. **4.** To have her up for tampering with the evidence DE FOE. Accused of..tampering with ballot boxes 1888. Hence **Ta·mperer,** one who tampers; a schemer, a meddler.

Tamping (tæ·mpiŋ), *vbl. sb.* 1828. [f. TAMP *v.* + -ING[1].] The action of TAMP *v.*; the plugging of a blast-hole above the charge; the packing of the part of a military mine nearest the charge with earth or other material. **b.** *concr.* The material used for this purpose 1828.

Comb.: **t.-bar, -iron,** = STEMMER; **-plug,** a plug or stopper used to block up a bore-hole.

Tampion, tompion (tæ·mpiən, tǫ·mp-). 1460. [– Fr. *tampon* (xv) in same senses, nasalized var. of (O)Fr. *tapon* :- Frankish **tappo*; see TAP *sb.*¹] †**1.** A plug for stopping an aperture –1882. †**2.** A disc-shaped or cylindrical piece of wood made to fit the bore of a muzzle-loading gun, and rammed home between the charge and the missile, to act as a wad –1828. **3.** A block of wood fitting into the muzzle of a gun, and serving to exclude rain, sea-water, etc. 1625. **4.** In the organ: A plug used to stop up the upper end of an organ-pipe 1864.

Tampon (tæ·mpǫ̆n), *sb.* 1860. [– Fr. *tampon*; see prec.] **1.** *Surg.* A plug or tent inserted tightly into a wound, orifice, etc., to arrest hæmorrhage, or used as a pessary. **2.** The dabber or inking ball used in lithography and copperplate printing. (So in Fr.) 1877. Hence **Ta·mpon** *v. trans. Surg.* to fill or stop (a wound, cavity, etc.) with a t.; to plug.

Tan (tæn), *sb.* (*a.*) 1604. [f. TAN *v.* Cf. (O)Fr. *tan*, med.L. *tannum*.] **I. 1.** The crushed bark of the oak or of other trees, an infusion of which is used in converting hides into leather. **b.** Spent bark from the tan-pits, used by gardeners, and for riding-courses, etc. 1739. **2.** The astringent principle contained in oak-bark, etc.; tannin; also, the solution of this, tan-liquor, 'ooze' 1800. **II. 1.** The brown colour of tan; tawny 1851. **b.** *esp.* The bronzed tint imparted to the skin by exposure to the sun or the weather 1827. **2.** *pl.* [ellipt. use of the adj.] Articles of dress, etc., of a tan colour; *esp.* tan shoes or boots 1902.

1. b. With the t. of a southern sun upon his face 1885.

attrib. and *Comb.*: **t.-bark,** = sense I. 1; **-bed,** a hot-bed made of spent t.; a bark-bed; **-ooze, -pickle,** the liquor of a t.-vat; **-ride,** a riding-track covered with t.; **-spud,** a curved chisel for peeling the bark from trees; **-stove,** a bark-stove; also, a hot-house with a bark-bed; **-vat,** the receptacle containing the 'ooze' in which the hides are laid in tanning.

B. *adj.* Of the colour of tan or of tanned leather; of a yellowish or reddish brown 1665.

Black and t. (see BLACK *a.*) Beautiful black and tan spaniels DISRAELI. *Black and Tans*: an armed force raised against the Sinn Feiners in 1921, so named from the mixture (black and khaki) o constabulary and military uniforms worn by them.

Tan (tæn), *v.* [Late OE. *tannian*, prob. – med.L. *tannare*, perh. of Celtic origin; reinforced in ME. from OFr. vb. *tan(n)er*.] **1.** *trans.* To convert (skin or hide) into leather by steeping in an infusion of an astringent bark, as that of the oak, or by a similarly effective process. **b.** *transf.* To treat (fishing-nets, sails, etc.) with tanners' ooze or some preserving substance; also, to act upon as an astringent 1601. **c.** In the manufacture of artificial marble to steep (the composition) in a hardening and preservative preparation 1891. **2.** To make brown (the face or skin), esp. by exposure to the sun or weather; to embrown; hence, to make dark or tawny in colour 1530. **b.** *intr.* (for *refl.*) To become sunburnt or darkened by exposure 1530.

1. Phr. *To t.* (a person's) *hide*, also simply *to t.* (a person), to thrash soundly (*slang* or *colloq.*). **2.** You shall tanne your selfe more upon the see than upon lande PALSGR. Often in pa. pple. **Tanned** (tænd).

Tan, *Math.* abbrev. of TANGENT B. 1.

‖**Tana** (tā·nă). *India.* 1803. [Hindi *thāna, thānā*.] A police station in India; formerly, a military station or fortified post. Hence ‖**Tanada·r,** an officer in charge of this 1802.

Tanager (tæ·năd͡ʒəɹ). 1614. [– mod.L. *tanagra* (Linnæus 1758), alt. of Tupi *tangara* (in Fr. and Eng. use XVII–XIX).] *Ornith.* A bird of the genus *Tanagra* or family *Tanagridæ* of passerine birds, of Central and South America. Hence **Ta·nagrine** *a.* of or pertaining to tanagers; belonging to the family *Tanagridæ*, or subfamily *Tanagrinæ*. **Ta·nagroid (tangaroid)** *a.* resembling the tanagers.

Tanagra (tæ·năgră). 1893. Applied to terra-cotta statuettes found in the neighbourhood of Tanagra in Bœotia.

Tandem (tæ·ndĕm), *sb.* and *adv.* 1785. [orig. sl. punning use of L. *tandem* at length (of time).] **A.** *sb.* **1.** A two-wheeled vehicle drawn by two horses (or other beasts of draught) harnessed one before the other. **b.** *transf.* A pair of carriage-horses harnessed one before the other 1795. **2.** Short for *t. bicycle* (*tricycle*), *canoe, engine* 1884. **B.** *adv.* One behind the other, in single file; orig. of a team of two horses 1795.

A. 1. We shall..proceed in a t...to Inverary BYRON. **B.** Three logs chained t. constituted the load 1893.

attrib. and *Comb.*: **t. bicycle, (tricycle), canoe,** a bicycle (tricycle) or canoe for two persons, one seated behind the other; **t. engine,** a steam-engine with two cylinders one in front of the other, the two pistons working on a common piston-rod.

‖**Tandstickor** (tæ·nd,sti:koɹ). 1884. [– Swed. *tändstickor* matches.] In full *t. match*, a cheap kind of lucifer match imported from Sweden.

Tang (tæŋ), *sb.*¹ ME. [– ON. *tange* point, spit of land, tang of a knife, etc. (Norw., Da. *tange*, Sw. *tång(e)*.] **I. 1.** A projecting pointed part or instrument. **a.** The tongue of a serpent; the sting of an insect. Now *dial.* **b.** *dial.* A sharp point or spike; the pin of a buckle; one of the prongs or tines of a fork; a prong or tine of a stag's horn 1688. **2.** An extension of a metal tool or instrument, as a chisel, file, knife, axe, coulter, pike, scythe, sword, etc., by which it is secured to its handle or stock 1440. **3.** One of various fishes having spines, as the common t. (*Teuthis hepatus*), the blue t. (*T. cæruleus*), etc. 1734. **II. 1.** A penetrating taste or flavour; usu. an after-taste, or a disagreeable or alien taste from contact with something else 1440. **b.** A pungent odour, a penetrating scent 1858. **2.** A slight 'smack' *of* some quality, opinion, habit, form of speech, etc.; a 'suspicion', a suggestion; a trace, a touch *of* something 1593. **b.** Distinctive or characteristic flavour or quality 1868.

1. A strong t. of tallow or onion in your bread and butter 1806. **2.** Some little t. of Gentry 1625. The language has a t. of Shakespear GRAY.

Tang (tæŋ), *sb.*² 1669. [imit.] The strong ringing note produced when a large bell or any sonorous body is suddenly struck with force, or a tense string is sharply plucked; often denoting a sound of a particular tone, esp. one of an unpleasant kind; a twang.

Tang (tæŋ), *sb.*³ *dial.* 1547. [Of Scand. origin (Norw., Da. *tang*, Icel. *þang*).] A collective name for large coarse seaweeds; tangle, sea-wrack; also called *sea-tang*.

Tang (tæŋ), *sb.*⁴ Also **tangue.** 1891. [f. native name.] = TANREC.

Tang (tæŋ), *v.*¹ late ME. [f. TANG *sb.*¹] **1.** *trans.* †To pierce, prick; to sting as a serpent or insect; also *absol.* Now *dial.* **2.** To furnish with a tang, spike, flange, etc. 1566. **3.** To affect with a tang or (unpleasant) taste 1686.

Tang (tæŋ), *v.*² 1556. [Mainly imit.] **1.** *trans.* To strike (a bell or the like) so as to cause it to emit a sharp loud ringing note. **2.** To utter with a tang or ringing tone 1601. **3.** *intr.* To emit a sharp and loud ringing or clanging sound; to ring, clang 1686.

2. Let thy tongue t. arguments of state SHAKS. **3.** The smallest urchin whose tongue could t., Shock'd the Dame with a volley of slang HOOD.

‖**Tanga** (tæ·ngă, ‖tɒ·ngă). *India.* 1598. [– Pg. *tanga* – *ṭaṅka* in various Indian vernaculars :- Skr. *ṭaṅka* a weight.] A name (orig. of a weight) given in India, Persia, and Turkestan to various coins (or moneys of account); still applied in certain places to a copper, in others to a silver coin.

‖**Tangalung** (tæ·ŋgălɒŋ). 1820. [Malay *tanggālung*.] The civet cat of Sumatra and Java, *Viverra tangalunga*; the Sumatran civet.

Tangency (tæ·nd͡ʒĕnsi). 1819. [f. TANGENT; see -ENCY.] The quality or condition of being tangent; state of contact.

Tangent (tæ·nd͡ʒĕnt), *a.* and *sb.* 1594. [– L. *tangens, -ent-*, pr. pple. of *tangere* touch; see -ENT. In mod.L. (*linea*) *tangens*, 1583.] **A.** *adj.* **1.** *Geom.* Of a line or surface in relation to another (curved) line or surface: Touching, i.e. meeting at a point and (ordinarily) not intersecting; in contact. **b.** *transf.* Said of the wheel of a bicycle or tricycle having the spokes tangent to the hub 1886. **2.** *fig.* 'Flying off at a tangent'; divergent, erratic 1787. **3.** *gen.* Touching, contiguous 1846.

1. All the vibrations t. to the little circle..are reflected perfectly polarized TYNDALL. **2.** The voluble loquacity and t. style of reasoning of their new companion 1799.

B. *sb.* **1.** *Math.* (ellipt. for *t. line.*) **a.** *Trigonometry.* One of the three fundamental trigonometrical functions (cf. SECANT, SINE), orig. considered as functions of a circular arc, now usu. of an angle (viz. that subtended by such an arc at its centre); *orig.* The length of a straight line perpendicular to the radius touching one end of the arc and terminated by the *secant* drawn from the centre through the other end; in mod. use, the ratio of this line to the radius, or (equivalently, as a function of the angle) the ratio of the side of a right-angled triangle opposite the given angle (if acute) to that of the side opposite the other acute angle (the t. of an obtuse angle being numerically equal to that of its supplement, but of opposite sign). (Abbrev. *tan*) 1594. **b.** *Geom.* A straight line which touches a curve (or curved surface), i.e. meets it at a point and being produced does not (ordinarily) intersect it at that point 1655. **c.** In general use, chiefly *fig.* from b, esp. in phrases (*off*) *at, in, upon a t.*, i.e. off or away with sudden divergence, from the course or direction previously followed; abruptly from one course of action, subject, thought, etc., to another 1771. **2.** Short for *t. scale, galvanometer* 1861. **3.** A straight section of a railway track. *U.S. colloq.* 1895.

1. c. That manner which they have..of flying off in tangents when they are pressed BENTHAM.

Comb.: **t. backsight,** = *t. scale* (*a*); **galvanometer,** a galvanometer in which the t. of the angle of deflexion of the needle is proportional to the strength of the current passing through the coil; **t. scale,** (*a*) in *Gunnery*, a kind of breech-sight in which the heights of the steps or notches correspond to the tangents of the angle of elevation; (*b*) a graduated scale indicating the tangents of angles; **t. screw,** a screw working tangentially upon a toothed circle or arc so as to give it a slow motion for delicate measurements or adjustments; **t. sight,** = *t. scale* (*a*).

Tangential (tænd͡ʒe·nʃăl), *a.* (*sb.*) 1630. [f. TANGENT + -IAL.] **1.** Of, pertaining to, or of the nature of, a tangent; identical with, or drawn at, a tangent to a curve or curved surface; acting along a tangent. **2.** *fig.* Going off suddenly 'at a tangent'; erratic; divergent; digressive 1867. **b.** That merely touches a subject or matter 1825.

2. A collection of mixed and t. information 1903. **b.** Emerson had only t. relations with the experiment 1885.

B. *sb.* Geom. *T. of a point* (in a curve of the third or higher order): the point at which a tangent at the given point meets the curve again 1858. Hence **Tange·ntially** *adv.*

Tangerine (tænd͡ʒĕrī·n), *a.* and *sb.* 1710. [f. *Tanger, Tangier* + -INE¹.] **A.** *adj.* Of or pertaining to, or native of Tangier, a seaport in Morocco, on the Strait of Gibraltar.

T. orange, a small flattened deep-coloured variety of orange from Tangier, *Citrus nobilis* var. *Tangeriana*.

B. *sb.* **1.** A native of Tangier 1860. **2.** A T. orange 1842. **b.** A deep orange colour 1899.

‖**Tanghin** (tæ·ŋgin). 1788. [– Fr. – Malagasy *tangena, tangen'*.] **1.** A poison obtained from the kernels of *Tanghinia venenifera*, of the family *Apocynaceæ*, a shrub of Madagascar, the fruit of which is a large purplish drupe. The kernels were formerly used by the natives to test the guilt of a suspected person. **2.** The shrub itself: more prop. *tange·na* or *tangi·na* 1866.

Tangible (tæ·nd͡ʒĭb'l), *a.* 1589. [– Fr. *tangible* or late L. *tangibilis*, f. *tangere* touch; see -IBLE.] **1.** Capable of being touched; affecting the sense of touch; touchable. Hence, material, externally real, objective. **2.** That may be discerned or discriminated by the sense of touch; as *a t. property* or *form* 1664. **3.** *fig.* That can be laid hold of or grasped by the mind, or dealt with as a fact;

that can be realized or shown to have substance 1709.

1. Not..much chance of winning t. rewards 1874. 3. T. ideas BERKELEY. Without any t. ground of complaint 1852. Hence **Tangibi·lity. Ta·ngibleness. Ta·ngibly** *adv.*

Tangle (tæ·ŋg'l), *sb.*[1] 1536. [prob. – Norw. *taangel, tongul*, repr. ON. *þongull.*] **1.** = TANG *sb.*[3] **2.** *spec.* Either of two species of seaweed, *Laminaria* (*Fucus*) *digitata* and *L. saccharina*, having long leathery fronds which are edible, as is the young stalk 1724.

2. I never saw it cast ashore anything but dulse and t. SCOTT.

Comb.: **t. fish,** the needle-fish or pipe-fish, *Syngnathus acus*; **-picker,** a bird, the Turnstone (*Strepsilas interpres*).

Tangle (tæ·ŋg'l), *sb.*[2] 1615. [f. TANGLE *v.*] **1.** A tangled condition, or *concr.* a tangled mass; a complication of threads, hairs, fibres, branches, boughs, or the like, confusedly intertwined, or of a single long thread, line, or rope, involved in coils, loops, and knots; a snarl, ravel, or complicated loose knot. Also *transf.* of streams, paths, etc. **b.** *spec.* A dredger for sweeping the sea-bed, consisting of a bar to which are attached a number of hempen 'mops', in the fibres of which the more delicate marine specimens are entangled 1883. **2.** *fig.* A complicated and confused assemblage; a muddle, jumble, complication, puzzle; a confused network of opinions, facts, etc.; also, a perplexed state 1757.

1. The tangles of Neæra's hair MILT. This bow became covered with a tangle of creepers DARWIN. 2. The tangles of metaphysics 1858. He reduced into method and compass the..t. of facts and figures 1883.

Tangle, *sb.*[3] 1857. [perh. belonging to TANGLE *sb.*[1] or [2].] Applied to plants having long, winding, and often tangled stalks, as Water Milfoil and Pondweed; and to plants of tangled growth, as Blue Tangle(s, (U.S.) *Gaylussacia frondosa.*

Tangle (tæ·ŋg'l), *v.* [ME. *tangil, -el*, var. of *tagil* in Rolle's works; thereafter *tangle* (XVI); of obsc. origin.] †**1.** *trans.* = ENTANGLE *v.* 2. Chiefly *refl.* and *pass.* –1671. **2.** To involve in material things that surround or wind about, so as to hamper and obstruct; also, to cover or wreathe with intertwined growth or with something that obstructs 1506. **3.** To catch and hold fast in or as in a net or snare; to entrap 1526. **4.** To intertwist (threads, branches or the like) complicatedly or confusedly together; to intertwist the threads or parts of (a thing) in this way; to put or get (a long thread or a number of threads, etc.) into a tangle. Also *intr.* for *refl.* 1530.

1. Not willingly, but tangl'd in the fold Of dire necessity MILT. 2. A country tangled with rivers 1829. The hedges were tangled with wild rose bushes 1885. 3. Looke how a bird lyes tangled in a net SHAKS. 4. He had cut the knot which the Congress had only twisted and tangled MACAULAY. Hence **Ta·nglingly** *adv.*

Tanglefoot (tæ·ŋg'lfut), *a.* and *sb.* 1860. [f. prec. + FOOT *sb.*] **A.** *adj.* That tangles or entangles the foot. **B.** *sb.* That which tangles or entraps the foot; *spec. U.S. slang*, an intoxicating beverage, esp. whisky.

Tangly (tæ·ŋgli), *a.*[1] 1762. [f. TANGLE *sb.*[1] + -Y[1].] Strewn with, consisting of, or full of tangle.

Helpless, on the t. beach he lay 1762.

Ta·ngly, *a.*[2] 1813. [f. TANGLE *sb.*[2] + -Y[1].] Abounding in tangles; tangled.

The jungle's t. growth 1899.

Tango (tæ·ŋgo^u), *sb.* 1913. [Amer. Sp., Negro or native dance, music for this, (in Honduras) musical instrument of the tambourine kind.] A Spanish (or S. Amer.) dance adapted for the ballroom; the music for this. Hence **Ta·ngo** *v.* to dance the t.

Tangram (tæ·ŋgrǣm). 1864. [Of unkn. origin.] A Chinese geometrical puzzle consisting of a square dissected into five triangles, a square, and a rhomboid, which can be combined so as to make two equal squares, and also so as to form several hundred figures, having a rude resemblance to houses, boats, bottles, glasses, urns, birds, beasts, men, etc.

‖**Tania, tan(n)ier** (ta·nyă, tæ·nyəɹ). 1756. [– Tupi *taña, taya*, Carib *taya.*] A species of *Caladium* or *Xanthosoma* (*X. sagittifolium*), of the family *Araceæ*, cultivated in Brazil, the West Indies, and tropical Africa, for its farinaceous tuberous root.

Tanist (tæ·nist). 1538. [– Ir. and Gael. *tánaiste* anything parallel or second to another, the next heir to an estate.] *Anc. Ir.* and *Gaelic Law.* The successor apparent to a Celtic chief, usu. the most vigorous adult of his kin, elected during the lifetime of the chief.

The T. he to great O'Neale SCOTT.

Tanistry (tæ·nistri). 1589. [f. prec. + -RY.] *Anc. Ir.* and *Gaelic Law.* A system of life-tenure among the ancient Irish and Gaels, whereby the succession to an estate or dignity was conferred by election upon the 'eldest and worthiest' among the surviving kinsmen of the deceased lord. †**b.** The office of a tanist. SCOTT.

Tank[1] (tæŋk). 1616. [– Indian vernacular word such as Gujerati *tānkh*, Marathi *ṭānken*, perh. from Skr. *taḍāga* pond, lake.] **1.** In India, a pool or lake, or an artificial reservoir or cistern, used for purposes of irrigation, and as a storage-place for drinking-water. **b.** A natural pool or pond; a 'stank'. *dial.* and *U.S.* 1678. **2.** An artificial receptacle, usu. rectangular or cylindrical and often of plate-iron, used for storing liquids or gases 1690.

attrib. and *Comb.*: **t.-engine,** a railway engine which carries the fuel and water receptacles on its own framing and not in a separate tender; **-iron, -plate,** plate-iron of a thickness suitable for making tanks; **-steamer,** one fitted with a t. for carrying liquids, esp. mineral oils, in bulk; **-worm,** a nematoid worm inhabiting the mud of Indian tanks, and believed to be the young of the guinea worm.

Tank[2] (tæŋk). [Special use of TANK[1] adopted in December 1915 for the purpose of secrecy during manufacture.] A type of armoured car with caterpillar wheels, equipped with a crew and guns, for attacking an enemy in difficult country.

‖**Tanka** (tæ·ŋkă). Also **tankia, tanchia.** 1839. [f. Chinese *tan* lit. egg + Cantonese *ka*, in South Mandarin *kia*, North Mandarin *chia* family, people.] The boat-population of Canton, who live entirely on the boats by which they earn their living; they are descendants of some aboriginal tribe of which *Tan* was app. the name. *T. boat*, a boat of the kind in which these people live.

Ta·nkage (-ėdʒ). 1866. [f. TANK[1] + -AGE.] **1.** Tanks collectively; a provision or system of storage-tanks, sometimes with special ref. to its capacity. **2.** The act or process of storing liquid in tanks; the price charged for this 1891. **3.** The residue from tanks in which fat, etc. has been rendered, used as a coarse food, and as manure 1886.

Tankard (tæ·ŋkăɹd). ME. [Of unkn. origin, but cf. MDu., Du. *tanckaert*, and AL. *tancardus* (*tank-*), *c*1266.] †**1.** A large open tub-like vessel, usu. of wood hooped with iron, etc.; *spec.* such a vessel used for carrying water, etc. –1688. **2.** A drinking-vessel, formerly made of wooden staves and hooped; now *esp.* a tall one-handled mug or jug, usu. of pewter, occas. with a lid, used chiefly for beer 1485. **b.** *transf.* in COOL *tankard* 1700.

2. Tankards foaming from the tap WORDSW.

Comb.: **t.-turnip,** a variety of turnip with a long tuber.

Tanker (tæ·ŋkəɹ). 1900. [f. TANK *sb.*[1] + -ER[1].] A tank-steamer. Also *t.-ship.*

Ta·nling. *rare.* 1611. [f. TAN *a.* + -LING[1].] One tanned by the sun's rays.

To be still hot Summers Tanlings, and The shrinking Slaues of Winter SHAKS.

Tannage (tæ·nėdʒ). 1662. [f. TAN *v.* + -AGE, perh. partly after (O)Fr. *tannage.*] The art or process of tanning; also *concr.* the produce of tanning.

Tannate (tæ·nĕt). 1802. [– Fr. *tannate* (Proust 1798); see TANNIC, -ATE[4].] *Chem.* A salt of tannic acid.

Tanned: see TAN *v.*

Tanner[1] (tæ·nəɹ). [OE. *tannere*, f. *tannian* TAN *v.*; or – OFr. *tanere* :– med.L. *tannator.*] One whose occupation is to tan hides.

Tanner[2] (tæ·nəɹ). *slang.* 1811. [Of unkn. origin.] A sixpence.

Tannery (tæ·nəri). late ME. [f. TANNER[1] + -Y[3]; see -ERY. Cf. (O)Fr. *tannerie.*] **1.** A place where tanning is carried on 1736. **2.** The process or trade of tanning; tannage. late ME.

Tannic (tæ·nik), *a.* 1836. [– Fr. *tannique* (Pelouze, 1834), f. *tannin*; see next, -IC.] *Chem.* In *t. acid*: orig. applied to the tannin principle obtained from oak-galls, a white amorphous strongly astringent substance, $C_{14}H_{10}O_9$, now dist. from other forms of tannin as GALLOTANNIC *acid.* Now chiefly used in a general sense to include a great number of allied substances, which differ in the proportion of their elements.

Tannin (tæ·nin). 1802. [– Fr. *tanin* (Proust, 1798), f. *tan* TAN *sb.* + *-in* -IN[1].] *Chem.* Any member of a group of astringent vegetable substances, the *tannins*, which possess the property of combining with animal hide and converting it into leather. (Cf. GALLOTANNIN.)

Tanno- (tæ·no). Combining base of *tannic, tannin*, as in **Tannocaffe·ic** *acid* = CAFFETANNIC ACID. **Tannoga·llic** *a.* = GALLOTANNIC.

‖**Tanrec, tenrec** (tæ·n-, te·nrek). 1729. [Fr. – Malagasy *tàndraka, tràndraka.*] An insectivorous mammal, *Centetes ecaudatus*, allied to the hedgehog, and covered with spiny bristles intermixed with silky hairs; the Madagascar hedgehog. Also, any species of the genus *Centetes* or of the family *Centetidæ.*

Tansy (tæ·nzi). late ME. [– OFr. *tanesie* (mod. *tanaisie*), perh. aphetic f. med.L. *athanasia* tansy – Gr. ἀθανασία immortality.] **1.** An erect herbaceous plant, *Tanacetum vulgare*, growing about two feet high, with deeply cut and divided leaves, and terminal corymbs of yellow rayless button-like flowers; all parts of the plant have a strong aromatic scent and bitter taste. **2.** Applied to other plants, esp. the Silverweed or Goose-grass, *Potentilla anserina* (Wild, Dog's or Goose T.). late ME. **3.** A pudding, omelet, or the like, flavoured with juice of tansy. (Said to have been eaten at Easter in memory of the 'bitter herbs' of the Passover.) *arch.* or *dial.* 1450.

3. Spent an houre or two..with her, and eat a t. PEPYS. Phr. †*Like a t.* [origin unkn.], properly, perfectly; perfect.

Tantalate (tæ·ntălĕt). 1849. [f. TANTAL(UM + -ATE[4].] *Chem.* A salt of tantalic acid.

Tantalic (tæntæ·lik), *a.* 1842. [f. TANTALUM + -IC.] *Chem.* Of or derived from tantalum; in names of chemical compounds in which tantalum is pentavalent, as *t. chloride*; *t. oxide, anhydride*, Ta_2O_5.

Tantalite (tæ·ntăləit). 1805. [– G. and Sw. *tantalit* (Ekeberg, 1802), f. TANTALUM (of which it is a source); see -ITE[1] 2 b.] *Min.* Native tantalate of iron or ferrous tantalate, found in black lustrous crystals.

Tantalize (tæ·ntăləiz), *v.* 1597. [f. TANTALUS + -IZE.] **1.** *trans.* To subject to torment like that inflicted on Tantalus; to torment by the sight, show, or promise of a desired thing which is kept out of reach, or removed or withheld when on the point of being grasped. Also *absol.* **b.** *fig.* To tease or torture into an artificial form 1807. †**2.** *intr.* To act Tantalus; to suffer like Tantalus –1673.

1. Our Richard II. was starved at Pomfret Castle by being tantalized TRAPP. Hence **Ta:ntaliza·tion, Ta·ntalizer. Ta·ntalizingly** *adv.*

Tantalous (tæ·ntăləs), *a.* 1868. [f. next + -OUS.] *Chem.* Applied to compounds containing a greater proportion of tantalum than those called *tantalic*, as *t. oxide*, tantalum dioxide, TaO_2.

Tantalum (tæ·ntălŏm). 1809. [f. next, with the ending *-um* (more usu. -IUM) appropriate to metallic elements. So called by Ekeberg, 'partly in allusion to its incapacity, when immersed in acid, to absorb any and be saturated'.] *Chem.* A rare metal, occurring in combination in various rare minerals, and in certain metallic ores; discovered in 1802 by Ekeberg in two minerals, which he named *tantalite* and *yttrotantalite.* It has been isolated as a solid of greyish-white colour and metallic lustre, and has been used for the incandescent filament of electric lamps. Atomic weight 182; symbol Ta. Also *attrib.*, as *t. lamp.*

Tantalus (tæ·ntălŏs). late ME. [– L. *Tantalus* – Gr. Τάνταλος.] **1.** Name of a mythical king of Phrygia, son of Zeus and the nymph Pluto, condemned, for revealing the secrets of the gods, to stand in Tartarus up to his chin in water, which constantly receded as he stooped to drink; he had branches of fruit hanging above him which always evaded his grasp. Hence *allus.* **2.** A stand containing (usu. three) decanters which, though apparently free, cannot be withdrawn until the grooved bar which engages the stoppers is raised 1898. **3.** *Ornith.* A genus of storks, including *T. ibis*; the wood stork or wood ibis 1824.

1. It seems like our cup of T.: we are never to reach it KANE.

†**Ta·ntamount,** *sb.* 1637. [f. TANTAMOUNT *v.*] Something equivalent (*to*); an equivalent –1646.

Tantamount (tæ·ntămaunt), *a.* 1641. [f. TANTAMOUNT *sb.* and *v.*] As much; that amounts to as much, that comes to the same thing; of the same amount; equivalent. Usu. const. *to*.

They are t. to a plain acknowledgement 1659. A t. service should be given in exchange for them 1868.

†**Ta·ntamount,** *v.* 1628. [In XVII – It. *tanto montare*, i.e. *tanto* as much, *montare* AMOUNT, MOUNT *vbs.* Not connected with AFr. *tant amunter* (c1300).] **1.** *intr.* To amount to as much, to come to the same thing; to be or become equivalent –1716. **2.** *trans.* To amount or come up to (something); to equal –1683.

1. It ought to be pardoned specially, or by words which tant amount COKE.

Tantara (tæ·ntără, tæntā·ră), *int.* and *sb.* Also extended **tantara·ra,** etc. 1537. [imit.] **A.** *int.* Imitative of the sound of a flourish blown on a trumpet, or sometimes of a drum. **B.** *sb.* A fanfare, or flourish of trumpets; hence, any similar sound 1584.

‖**Tanti** (tæ·ntəi). 1590. [L., 'of so much (value)', gen. of *tantum*, n. of *tantus* so great.] Of so much value, worth so much; worth while. †As an exclam.: So much *for*..!

Is it *t.* to kill yourself, in order to leave a vas deal of money to your heirs? WARBURTON.

Tantivy (tæ·ntivi, tænti·vi), *adv.*, *sb.*, *a.*, *int.* Now *rare* or *arch.* 1641. [perh. intended to repr. the sound of horses galloping.] †**A.** *adv.* At full gallop; headlong –1823.

Up at five a'Clock in the morning..And T. all the country over, where Hunting..or any Sport is to be made 1641.

B. *sb.* **1.** (from the adv.) A rapid gallop; a ride at this pace 1658. **2.** A nickname given to the post-Restoration High-Churchmen and Tories, esp. in the reigns of Charles II and James II. See O.E.D. 1680. **3.** *erron.* applied to a blast or flourish on a horn 1785. **C.** *adj.* perh. orig. in *t. men* and the like, attrib. use of B. 1; afterwards often of B. 2. 1681.

C. Master Wildrake is one of the old school—one of the t. boys SCOTT.

D. *int.* An imitation of the sound of galloping or scudding feet; later (*erron.*) of the sound of a horn 1697. Hence †**Tantivy** *v.* (*rare*) *intr.* to ride full tilt, to hurry away.

‖**Tanto** (ta·nto), *adv.* 1876. [It. :– L. *tantum* so much.] *Mus.* So, so much: as *allegro non tanto*, fast, but not too fast.

Tantony (tæ·ntəni). 1567. Shortened form of *St. Anthony*, chiefly used *attrib.*; *spec.* **a.** (in full *t. bell*) a hand-bell; a small church bell; **b.** (in full *t. pig*) [St. Anthony the hermit, usu. represented as accompanied by a pig, being the patron of swine-herds; cf. TAWDRY], the smallest pig of a litter 1659.

fig. Dangling after me every where, like a t. pig 1765.

‖**Tantra** (tæ·ntră). 1799. [Skr., loom, warp, hence groundwork, system, doctrine, etc., f. *tan* stretch, extend.] One of a class of Hindu religious works in Sanskrit, of comparatively recent date, chiefly of magical and mystical nature; also, one of a class of Buddhist works of similar character. Hence **Ta·ntrism,** the doctrine of the Tantras. **Ta·ntrist.**

Tantrum (tæ·ntrŏm). *colloq.* 1748. [Of unkn. origin.] An outburst or display of petulance or ill-temper; a fit of passion. Mostly in *pl.*

Taoism (tā·o,iz'm). 1839. [f. Chinese *tao* way, path, right way (of life), reason + -ISM.] A system of religion, founded on the doctrine set forth in the work *Tao tê king* 'Book of reason and virtue', attributed to the ancient Chinese philosopher Lao-tsze (or Lao-tzŭ), born 604 B.C. It ranks with Confucianism and Buddhism as one of the three religions of China. So **Ta·oist**; also *attrib.* or as *adj.*; hence **Taoi·stic** *a.*

‖**Taotai** (tā·otai). 1876. [Chinese *tao* circuit, division, *t'ai* eminence.] A provincial officer in a *tao*.

Tap (tæp), *sb.*[1] [OE. *tæppa* = MLG., MDu. *tappe* (Du. *tap*), OHG. *zapho* (G. *zapfen*), ON. *tappi* :– Gmc. **tappon.*] **1.** A cylindrical stick, long peg, or stopper, for closing or opening a hole bored in a vessel; hence, a hollow or tubular plug through which liquid may be drawn, having some device for shutting off or governing the flow; a cock, a 'faucet', esp. for turning on the water over a sink, bath, etc. **2.** A tap-room or tap-house. *colloq.* 1725. **3.** The liquor drawn from a particular tap; a particular species or quality of drink. Also *fig.* a particular strain or kind of anything. *colloq.* 1623. **4.** *Mech.* A tool used for cutting the thread of an internal screw, consisting of a male screw of hardened steel, grooved lengthways to form cutting edges, and having a square head so that it may be turned by a wrench 1677. **5.** An object having the shape of a slender tapering cylinder, as an icicle; *esp.* a t.-root 1658.

1. Phr. *On* (*in*) *t.*, on draught, ready for immediate consumption or use; *on t.* spec. of treasury bills, etc. obtainable when and as required at a fixed rate; so *t. rate*, etc.

attrib. and *Comb.*, as *t.-boy*, *-man*; **t.-bolt,** a threaded bolt which is screwed into a part, as dist. from one that penetrates it and receives a nut; **-cinder,** the slag or refuse produced in a puddling furnace; **-rivet, -screw,** = *t.-bolt*.

Tap (tæp), *sb.*[2] late ME. [f. TAP *v.*[2]; cf. Fr. *tape* slap.] **1.** A single act of tapping; a light but audible blow or rap; the sound made by such a blow. **2.** *pl.* (*U.S. Mil.*) A signal sounded on the drum or trumpet, fifteen minutes after the tattoo, at which all lights in the soldiers' quarters are to be extinguished. Sounded also over the grave of a soldier. 1862. **3.** A piece of leather with which the worn-down heel or sole of a boot is 'tapped' (*U.S.*); a plate or piece of iron with which the heel is shielded 1688.

Tap-tap, a repeated t.; a series of taps; also *adv.* Comb. *t.-dancing*, exhibition dancing characterized by rhythmical tapping of the feet.

Tap (tæp), *v.*[1] [OE. *tæppian*, f. *tæppa* TAP *sb.*[1] = (M)LG., (M)Du. *tappen*, (M)HG. *zapfen*, f. the cogn. sbs.] **I.** To open (a cask, reservoir). **1.** *trans.* To furnish (a cask, etc.) with a tap or spout, in order to draw the liquor from it. **2.** To pierce (a vessel, tree, etc.) so as to draw off its liquid contents; to broach; to draw liquid from (any reservoir); *slang*, to draw blood from the nose 1694. **b.** *spec.* in *Surg.* To pierce the body-wall of (a person) so as to draw off accumulated liquid; to drain (a cavity) of accumulated liquid 1655. **c.** To divert part of the current from (an electric wire or cable), esp. so as to intercept a telegraphic or telephonic communication 1879. **3.** *fig.* To open up (anything) so as to liberate or extract something from it; to open, penetrate, break into, begin to use 1575.

2. The season for tapping the [maple] trees is in March 1792.

II. To draw off (liquid, etc.). **1.** To draw (liquor) from a tap; to draw and sell in small quantities. late ME. †**b.** *absol.* To draw liquor; to act as a tapster –1625. **2.** To draw off (liquid) from any source 1597. †**b.** *intr. fig.* To spend or 'bleed' freely. *slang.* –1713.

1. b. *Merry W.* I. iii. 11. **2.** *To tap one's claret*, to cause one's nose to bleed; He told Verdant, that his claret had been repeatedly tapped 1853.

III. 1. *Mech.* **a.** To furnish (a hole) with an internal screw-thread, or (any part) with a threaded hole 1808. **b.** To furnish with an external screw-thread; to convert (a bolt or rod) into a screw 1815. **c.** To cause to pass through or in by screwing 1869. **2.** To deprive (a plant) of its tap-root 1792.

Tap (tæp), *v.*[2] ME. [Either – (O)Fr. *taper* or independent imit. formation similar to *flap*, *rap*, *slap*.] **1.** *trans.* To strike lightly, but clearly and audibly; rarely applied by meiosis to a sharp knock or rap. **b.** To strike (the foot, hand, etc.) lightly upon something 1500. **2.** *intr.* and *absol.* To strike a light but distinct blow; to make a sound by so striking, e.g. on a drum; *esp.* to knock lightly *on* or *at* a door, etc. in order to attract attention. late ME. **3.** *trans.* To add a thickness of leather to the sole or heel of (a shoe) in repairing. *dial.* and *U.S.* 1818.

1. He sate there tapping his boot with his cane THACKERAY. **2.** She tapped gently at the door 1791.

‖**Tapa** (ta·pă). Also **tappa.** 1823. [Com. Polynesian *tapa*.] A kind of unwoven cloth made by the natives of Polynesia from the bark of the Paper Mulberry (*Broussonetia papyrifera*). Also *attrib.* as *t. cloth, mat.*

‖**Tapayaxin** (tæpăyæ·ksin). 1753. [Native Mexican.] The orbicular horned lizard, *Phrynosoma orbiculare*, incorrectly called the *Horned Frog* or *Toad*.

Tape (tē[i]p), *sb.* late ME. [OE. *tæppa* or *tæppe*, repr. obscurely by ME. *tāpe* (Chaucer); perh. rel. to OFris. *tapia*, MLG. *teppen* pluck, tear.] **1.** A narrow woven strip of stout linen, cotton, silk, etc. used as a string for tying garments, as binding, as measuring lines, etc. **b.** Without article, as name of the material. Also *fig.*: see RED-TAPE. 1537. **c.** A piece of tape suspended across the course at the finishing point in a race, or (formerly) between the goal-posts in Association football 1867. **2.** A long, narrow, thin and flexible strip of metal or the like; *esp.* such a strip of steel used as a measuring line in surveying 1884. **b.** The paper strip or ribbon on which messages are printed in the receiving instrument of a recording telegraph system 1884. **3.** *slang.* Spirituous liquor, esp. gin (*white t.*); brandy (*red t.*) 1725.

1. A black Box..tied about with a white T. 1690. **b.** *fig.* Twenty years gone in t. and circumlocution 1856. **2.** Base measurement with steel tapes 1900. **b.** Now we watch the t., day by day, and hour by hour 1888.

attrib. and *Comb.*: **t.-fish,** a ribbon-fish; **-grass,** an aquatic herb, *Vallisneria spiralis*, with narrow grass-like leaves; **-line,** a line of t.; *spec.* a strip of linen or steel marked with subdivisions of the foot or metre, sometimes coiling in a cylindrical case with a winch or spring; **-machine,** the receiving instrument of a recording telegraph system, in which the message is printed on a paper t.; **-measure,** a measuring line of prepared t., marked with feet and inches, etc., esp. one of five or six feet long used by tailors, dress-makers, etc.; **-needle,** an eyed bodkin for inserting t.

Tape (tē[i]p), *v.* 1609. [f. prec.] **1.** *trans.* To attach a tape or tapes to; to tie *up*, fasten, bind, or wind with tape; *spec.* in *Bookbinding*, to join the sections of (a book) with tape. **2.** *trans.* To measure with a tape-line 1886. **3.** *intr.* To appear (of such a size) on measurement with a tape; to measure (so much) 1895.

2. fig. phr. (colloq.) *To have* (a person) *taped*: to have taken hs measure, to have summed him up.

Taper (tē[i]·pəɹ), *sb.*[1] [OE. *tapor*, *-er*, *-ur* – (with dissimilation of *p* . . . *p* to *t* . . . *p*) L. *papyrus*, on which the OE. word occurs as a gloss; = 'wick of a candle', for which the pith of the papyrus was used.] *orig.* A wax candle, in early times used chiefly for devotional or penitential purposes; now *spec.* a long wick coated with wax for temporary use as a spill, etc. **b.** *fig.* Something that gives light or is figured as burning; in mod. use esp. a thing that gives a feeble light OE.

b. The Apostles, those holy Tapours of the.. Church 1635. To husband out life's t. at the close GOLDSM.

Taper (tē[i]·pəɹ), *sb.*[2] 1793. [f. TAPER *v.* or *a.*] **1.** Gradual diminution in width or thickness in an elongated object; *fig.* gradual decrease of action, power, capacity, etc. **2.** Anything that gradually diminishes in size towards one extremity, as a tapered tube 1882.

Taper, *sb.*[3]: see TADPOLE[2].

Taper (tē[i]·pəɹ), *a.* 1496. [f. TAPER *sb.*[1]] Diminishing gradually in breadth or thickness towards one extremity (orig., upward); tapering.

To the fine t. fingers' ends 1821. Hence **Ta·perness.**

Taper (tē¹·pəɹ), *v.* 1589. [f. TAPER *a.*] †**1.** *intr.* To rise or shoot up like a flame, spire, or pyramid; *fig.* to rise or mount up continuously in honour, dignity, rank, etc. –1887. **2.** To narrow or diminish gradually in breadth or thickness towards one end; to grow smaller by degrees in one direction. Also *fig.* 1610. **3.** *trans.* To reduce gradually in breadth or thickness in one direction; to make tapering 1675. Hence **Ta·pering** *ppl. a.*, **-ly** *adv.*

Tapered (tē¹·pəɹd), *a.* 1745. [f. TAPER *sb.*¹ + -ED².] Lighted by, or accompanied by the use of, tapers.

Tapered (tē¹·pəɹd), *ppl. a.* 1669. [f. TAPER *v.* + -ED¹.] Made to taper; diminished in thickness or breadth by degrees; tapering, taper.

Tapestry (tæ·pėstri), *sb.* late ME. [alt. of †*tapisery*, †*tapecery* TAPISSERY (XV) – (O)Fr. *tapisserie*, f. *tapissier* tapestry-worker, or *tapisser* cover with carpet, f. *tapis* carpet; see TAPIS *sb.* (In Milton and Dryden a disyllable.)] A textile fabric decorated with ornamental designs or pictorial subjects, painted, embroidered, or woven in colours, used for wall hangings, curtains, etc.; esp., such a decorated fabric in which a weft containing ornamental designs in coloured wool or silk, gold or silver thread, etc., is worked with bobbins or broaches, and pressed close with a comb, on a warp of hemp or flax stretched in a frame. Often loosely applied to imitative textile fabrics.

Comb.: **t.-carpet,** a carpet resembling Brussels, but in which the warp-yarn forming the pile is coloured so as to produce the pattern when woven; **-moth,** a species of clothes-moth, as *Tinea tapetzella*; **-stitch,** used loosely for various stitches used in tapestry work; **-weaving,** the weaving of t.; the method of weaving by bobbin and comb, used in making t., as dist. from weaving in a loom with a shuttle; **-work,** tapestry.

Tapestry (tæ·pėstri), *v.* 1630. [f. prec.] **1.** *trans.* To cover, hang, or adorn with, or as with, tapestry. (Chiefly in *pass.*) **2.** To work or depict in tapestry 1814.

1. My walls..were tapestried with..lichen 1798.

Tapet. *Obs.* exc. *Hist.* [OE. *teped*, later *tæpped*, *-et* (ult.) – late L. *tapetium.*] A piece of figured cloth used as a hanging, table-cover, carpet, or the like.

‖**Tapeti** (tæ·pĕti). 1613. [Tupi.] The Brazilian rabbit, *Lepus brasiliensis.*

‖**Tapetum** (tăpī·tŏm). 1713. [Late and med.L., for L. *tapete* carpet.] **1.** *Comp. Anat.* An irregular sector of the choroid membrane in the eyes of certain animals (e.g. the cat), which shines owing to the absence of the black pigment. **2.** *Bot.* The layer of epithelial cells which lines the inner wall of the sporangium in ferns, etc., or of the pollen-sac in flowering-plants 1882.

Tapeworm (tē¹·pwɒ̈ɹm). 1752. [f. TAPE *sb.* + WORM *sb.*; from its flat ribbon-like form.] A cestoid worm (e.g. *Tænia solium*), which when adult infests the alimentary canal of vertebrates. **b.** *fig.* A parasite 1824.

Tap-hole (tæ·phōᵘl). 1594. [f. TAP *sb.*¹ + HOLE *sb.*] **1.** The hole in a cask, vat, or the like, in which the tap is inserted. **2.** A small opening in a furnace, through which the metal, or slag, or both, may be run out 1825.

Ta·p-house. 1500. [f. TAP *sb.*¹ + HOUSE *sb.*¹] A house where beer drawn from the tap is sold in small quantities; an ale-house; sometimes in connection with a brewery. Also, the tap-room of an inn.

‖**Tapia** (tā·piă). 1748. [Sp., mud-wall.] Clay or mud puddled, rammed, dried, and used for walls.

Tapinocephalic, tapeino- (tăpəi:noˌsĭfæ·lik), *a.* 1878. [f. Gr. ταπεινός low + κεφαλή head + -IC; see CEPHALIC.] *Anthrop.* Of the nature of, or having, a low flattened skull.

Tapioca (tæpiˌōᵘ·kă). 1707. [– Tupi-Guarani *tipioca*, f. *tipi* residue, dregs + *ok*, *og* squeeze out; the present form is due to Fr., Sp., Pg.] A starch used for food, the prepared flour of the roots of the CASSAVA plant.

Tapir (tē¹·pəɹ). 1774. [– Tupi *tapira* or *tapyra.*] An ungulate mammal of tropical America of the genus *Tapirus* or family *Tapiridæ*, somewhat resembling the swine (but more nearly related to the rhinoceros), having a short flexible proboscis.

Orig. applied to the species *Tapirus americanus* of Brazil; thence extended to the two Central Amer. species, *T. dowii* and *T. bairdi* (also *Elasmognathus*), and the Malay t., *T.* (or *Rhinochœrus*) *indicus.* Hence **Ta·pirine** *a.* of or pertaining to the tapirs. **Ta·piroid** *a.* allied to or resembling the tapirs.

Tapis (tæ·pis, ‖ta·pi), *sb.* 1494. [– OFr. *tapiz*, (also mod.) *tapis* :– Rom. **tappetium*, for late L. *tapetium* – Gr. ταπήτιον, dim. of τάπης, ταπητ- tapestry.] †**a.** A cloth worked with artistic designs in colours, used as a curtain, table-cloth, carpet, or the like –1800. **b.** Phr. *On* (*upon*) *the t.* [from Fr. *sur le tapis*], 'on the table-cloth', under discussion or consideration 1690.

b. Several marriages are adjusted, and many others are on the t. 1782.

Tapis, tapish (tæ·pis, -iʃ), *v. Obs.* or *arch.* ME. [– *tapiss-*, lengthened stem of OFr. *tapir* (mod. *se tapir*); see -ISH².] To lie close to the ground, lie low so as to be hid; to lurk, skulk, lie hid. **b.** *trans.* (and *refl.*) To hide 1660.

Ta·pisser. *Obs.* exc. *Hist.* late ME. [– AFr. *tapicer*, OFr. *tapicier* (mod. *tapissier*), f. *tapiz* (mod. *tapis*); see TAPIS *sb.*, -ER² 2.] A maker or weaver of figured cloth or tapestry.

†**Ta·pissery.** late ME. [See TAPESTRY, -ERY.] The early form of the word TAPESTRY –1697.

Tap-lash (tæ·pˌlæʃ). Now *dial.* 1623. [f. TAP *sb.*¹ + LASH *v.*¹] The 'lashings' or washings of casks or glasses; dregs or refuse of liquor; very weak or stale beer.

fig. This the T. of what he said MARVELL.

Tapotement (tăpōᵘ·tmĕnt). 1889. [– Fr. *tapotement*, f. *tapoter* to tap; see -MENT.] *Med.* Percussion, esp. as a part of the treatment in massage.

‖**Tappen** (tæ·pĕn). 1865. [Sw. and Norw. *tapp-en* the plug.] The plug by which the rectum of a bear is closed during hibernation.

Tapper (tæ·pəɹ). 1810. [f. TAP *v.*² + -ER¹.] **1.** One who taps or lightly strikes; a dialect name of the spotted woodpecker. **2.** That which taps or lightly strikes, as a hammer for striking a bell; *spec.* a key in an electric telegraph which is depressed to complete the circuit; in wireless telegraphy, a device for restoring the filings to their original condition 1876.

Tappet (tæ·pėt). 1745. [app. f. TAP *v.*² + -ET.] A projecting arm or part in a machine, which by the movement of the latter comes intermittently into contact with another part, so as to give or receive motion.

Tappit (tæ·pit), *ppl. a. Sc.* 1721. = TOPPED *ppl. a.*; *esp.* crested, tufted; chiefly in **t. hen, a.** a hen having a crest or topknot; hence **b.** a drinking-vessel having a lid with a knob; *spec.* one containing a Scotch quart.

Ta·p-room. 1807. [f. TAP *sb.*¹ + ROOM *sb.*] A room in a tavern, etc., in which liquors are kept on tap.

Tap-root (tæ·pˌrūt). 1601. [f. TAP *sb.*¹ + ROOT *sb.*] A straight root, of circular section, thick at the top, and tapering to a point, growing directly downwards from the stem and forming the centre from which subsidiary rootlets spring.

Tapster (tæ·pstəɹ). [OE. *tæppestre*, orig. fem. of *tæppere*, agent-noun of *tæppian* TAP *v.*¹; see -STER.] †**1.** *orig.* A woman who tapped or drew ale or other liquor for sale in an inn; a hostess –1568. **2.** A man who draws the beer, etc. for customers in a public house; the keeper of a tavern. late ME.

Ta·pstress. 1631. [f. prec. + -ESS¹; formed after *tapster* had ceased to be fem.] A female tapster.

Tar (tāɹ), *sb.* [OE. *teru*, *teoru*, corresp. to MLG. *ter(e* (LG. *teer*, whence Du., G. *teer*), MDu. *tar*, *ter(re*, ON. *tjara* :– Gmc. **terw-* (cf. OE. *tyrwe*, **tierwe* :– **terwjōn*), gen. held to be f. **trew-* TREE, the primary application having been to the black oily liquid produced by trees such as pines.] **1.** A thick, viscid, black or dark-coloured, inflammable liquid, obtained by the destructive distillation of wood, coal, or other organic substance; chemically, a mixture of hydrocarbons with resins, alcohols, and other compounds, having a heavy resinous or bituminous odour, and powerful antiseptic properties; much used for coating and preserving timber, cordage etc. See also COAL-TAR. **b.** *fig.* in ref. to extraction from a Negro or dark-coloured ancestry (cf. TAR-BRUSH b) 1897. **2.** Applied, with distinctive epithets, to natural substances resembling tar, as petroleum or bitumen; see MINERAL *a.* 1747. **3.** A familiar appellation for a sailor: perh. abbrev. of TARPAULIN 1676.

Comb.: **t.-board,** a strong quality of millboard made from junk and old tarred rope; **-weed** *U.S.*, any plant of the genera *Madia*, *Hemizonia*, and *Grindelia*, from their viscidity and heavy scent; **-wood,** resinous wood from which t. is obtained.

Tar (tāɹ), *v.*¹ ME. [f. OE. *teoru*, *teorw-* TAR *sb.*] *trans.* To smear or cover with tar. Also *absol.* **b.** To smear (a person's body) over with tar; esp. in phr. *to t. and feather*, to smear with tar and then cover with feathers: a punishment occas. inflicted by a mob (esp. in *U.S.*) on an unpopular or scandalous character 1769. **c.** To dirty or defile as with tar; esp. in phr. *tarred with the same stick* (or *brush*), stained with the same or similar faults or obnoxious qualities 1612.

Tar, †**tarre,** *v.*² *Obs.* or *arch.* [ME. *terre(n*, app. repr. OE. **terw(i)an*, collateral form of *tergan*, = (M)Du. *tergen*, G. *zergen.* Cf. OFr. *tarier* in same sense.] *trans.* To vex, irritate, provoke. Now only in *tar on*, to incite, hound on.

Pride alone Must tarre the Mastiffes on, as 'twere their bone SHAKS.

Taradiddle, tarradiddle (tæ·rădid'l). *colloq.* 1796. [Cf. DIDDLE *v.*²] A colloquial euphemism for a lie; a 'fib', trifling falsehood.

Tarantara: see TARATANTARA.

‖**Tarantas(s** (ta:ră·ntɑ·s). 1850. [Russ. *tarantás.*] A four-wheeled Russian travelling-carriage without springs, on a long flexible wooden chassis.

‖**Tarantella** (tærănte·lă). 1782. [It., dim. formation from *Taranto* the town of *Tarentum* in southern Italy; pop. assoc. w. *tarantola* TARANTULA.] A rapid whirling South Italian dance popular with the peasantry since the 15th c., when it was supposed to be the sovereign remedy for tarantism. **b.** The music for such a dance, or a composition in its rhythm, formerly in quadruple, but now always in 6–8 time, with whirling triplets, and abrupt transitions from the major to the minor 1833.

Tarantism (tæ·răntiz'm). 1638. [– mod.L. *tarantismus* = It. *tarantismo*, from It. *Taranto* (see prec.), but pop. assoc. w. *tarantola* the tarantula spider.] A hysterical malady, characterized by an extreme impulse to dance, which prevailed as an epidemic in Apulia and adjacent parts of Italy from the 15th to the 17th c., popularly attributed to the bite or 'sting' of the tarantula.

Tarantula (tăræ·ntiŭlă). 1561. [– med.L. *tarantula* – It. *tarantola*, f. *Taranto* :– L. *Tarentum* (– Gr. Τάρας, Ταραντ-), where it is commonly found.] **1.** A large wolf-spider of Southern Europe, *Lycosa tarantula* (formerly *Tarantula apuliæ*), named from the town in the region where it is commonly found, whose bite is slightly poisonous, and was fabled to cause TARANTISM. **b.** Pop. applied to other noxious spiders, esp. to the great hairy spiders of the genus *Mygale*, natives of the warmer parts of America 1794. **2.** Contextually, the bite of the tarantula; hence, erroneously, = TARANTISM 1586. **3.** *fig.* from 1 and 2 1608.

3. Saw the sun ever such a swearing people? Have they been bit by a swearing t.? CARLYLE.

Comb.: **t.-hawk, -killer,** names in Texas for a kind of wasp, *Pepsis formosa.* Hence **Tara·ntulate** *v. trans.* to affect with tarantism.

Taratantara (tārătæ·ntără, -tæntā·ra). 1553. Also **tarantara,** etc. [imit., prob. after L. (Ennius) and It. *taratantara.*] A word imitating, and hence denoting, the sound of a trumpet or bugle.

Taraxacin (tăræ·ksăsin). 1858. [f. next + -IN¹.] *Chem.* A bitter crystalline substance obtained from the juice of dandelion-root.

‖**Taraxacum** (tăræ·ksăkŏm). 1706. [med. L. *taraxacum* – Arab. *ṭarakšakūk* – Pers. *talk* bitter, *chakūk* purslane.] **a.** *Bot.* The genus of Composite plants including the dandelion (*T. dens-leonis*, *T. officinale*, or *Leontodon taraxacum*). **b.** *Pharm.* A drug prepared from the root of the dandelion, used as a tonic and in liver complaints.

Tar-barrel (tā·ɹ,bæ:rĕl). 1450. A barrel containing or that has contained tar: esp. as used for making a bonfire; formerly also in the carrying out of capital punishment by burning. †Also applied opprobiously to a person.

‖**Tarboosh** (taɹbū·ʃ). 1702. [– Egyptian Arab. *ṭarbūš* ult. – Pers. *sar-būš* lit. head cover; lid, hat.] A cap of cloth or felt (almost always red) with a tassel (usu. of blue silk) attached at the top, worn by Moslems either by itself or as part of the turban; the *fez* is the Turkish form.

Tar-brush (tā·ɹ,brʊʃ). 1711. A brush used for smearing anything with tar. **b.** *fig.* esp. in such phrases as *a dash* or *touch of the tar-brush*, i.e. of Negro or Indian blood, showing itself in the complexion 1835.

Knight of the t., a sailor.

Tardigrade (tā·ɹdigrēⁱd), *a.* and *sb.* 1623. [– Fr. *tardigrade* or L. *tardigradus*, f. *tardus* slow + *-gradus* stepping, walking.] **A.** *adj.* **1.** Walking or going slowly; 'slow-going'. **2.** *Zool.* **a.** Belonging to the sub-order (*Tardigrada*) or family (*Bradypodidæ*) of edentate mammals, comprising the sloths 1799. **b.** Belonging to the group *Tardigrada* of Arachnida, comprising the minute aquatic animals called water-bears or bear-animalcules 1847. **B.** *sb.* **a.** An edentate mammal of the sub-order *Tardigrada*; a sloth 1827. **b.** An arachnid of the group *Tardigrada*; a water-bear 1860.

Tardigradous (taɹdi·grădəs), *a.* 1658. [f. L. *tardigradus* + -OUS; see prec.] = prec. A.

Tardity (tā·ɹditi). Now *rare.* 1450. [– OFr. *tardité* – L. *tarditas*, *-tat-*, f. *tardus* slow; see -ITY.] **1.** Slowness of movement or action. In later use, a techn. term of *Physics*, opp. to *velocity*. **2.** The fact of being late; lateness 1599.

Tardive (tā·ɹdiv), *a. rare.* 1905. [– Fr. *tardif*, *-ive*; see TARDY.] Characterized by lateness; of late appearance or development.

Tardy (tā·ɹdi), *a.* (*adv.*) 1483. [In XV, XVI *tardife*, *-ive* –, (O)Fr. *tardif*, *-ive* :– Rom. **tardivus*, f. L. *tardus* slow; see -IVE, -Y¹.] **1.** Slow, in various senses. **a.** Slow in motion, action, or occurrence; of a slow nature, sluggish. **b.** Not acting, coming, or happening until after the proper, expected, or desired time; late, behindhand; delaying or delayed; dilatory; sometimes, delaying through unwillingness, reluctant, 'slow' (*to* some action, or *to do* something) 1667. **c.** *U.S.* Late for a meeting, assembly, class, school, or appointment 1638. †**2.** Phr. *To take* (also rarely, *catch*, *find*) a person *t.*: to overtake; to surprise; hence, to detect, 'catch' in a crime, fault, error, etc. –1690. †**b.** *ellipt.* for 'taken tardy': Detected in a fault, caught tripping –1706. **3.** quasi-*adv.* Behind time, late 1586.

1. a. Thus the firmest timber is of t. growth JOHNSON. **2.** *Rich. III*, IV. i. 52. **3.** Too swift arriues as tardie as too slow SHAKS. Hence **Ta·rdily** *adv.* **Ta·rdiness.**

†**Tardy,** *v.* 1611. [f. prec.] *trans.* To make tardy; to delay, keep back –1623.

Tare (tēᵊɹ), *sb.*¹ ME. [Of unkn. origin; MDu. *tarwe*, *terwe* wheat (rel. to Lith. *dirva* wheat-field) has been compared.] **1.** The seed of a vetch; usu. in ref. to its small size. **2.** A name given to some species of vetch. **a.** In early times, esp. to those occurring as weeds in cornfields. late ME. **b.** Now, in general agricultural use, applied to the cultivated vetch, *Vicia sativa*, grown as fodder 1482. **3.** *pl.* Used to render L. *zizania* (Vulg., *Matt.* 13:25) Gr. ζιζάνια, as name of an injurious weed among corn. *Obs.* exc. as a biblical use, and as in b. late ME. **b.** Hence in fig. and allusive uses 1711.

3. Declare vnto vs the parable of the tares of the field *Matt.* 13:36. **b.** The tares of sedition have been industriously sown among you KEN.

Tare (tēᵊɹ), *sb.*² 1486. [– Fr. *tare* waste in goods, deficiency, also as in Eng., – med.L. *tara* – Arab. *ṭarḥa* that which is thrown away, f. *ṭaraḥa* reject.] The weight of the wrapping, receptacle, or conveyance containing goods, which is deducted from the gross in order to ascertain the net weight; hence, a deduction made from the gross weight to allow for this; also, the weight of a motor vehicle without its fuel and other equipment. **b.** *Chem.* The weight of a vessel in which a substance is weighed, or of another vessel equal to it, deducted in ascertaining the weight of the substance 1888. **c.** *T. and tret*: the two ordinary deductions in calculating the net weight of goods to be sold by retail: see TRET; also, the rule in arithmetic by which these are calculated 1670. Hence **Tare** *v. trans.* to ascertain, allow for, or indicate the t. of. **Tared** *ppl. a.* of which the t. or weight when empty has been ascertained.

‖**Tarfa** (tarfā·). 1858. [– Arab. *ṭarfā'*.] The tamarisk, *Tamarix gallica*, which exudes a gum called manna.

Targe (tāɹdʒ). Now *arch.* and *poet.* OE. [– (O)Fr. *targe* – Frankish **targa*, cogn. with OE. *targa*, *targe*, ON. *targa* shield, OHG. *zarga*, (M)HG. *zarge* edging, border.] A shield; *spec.* a slight shield or buckler, borne esp. by footmen and archers.

Target (tā·ɹgėt), *sb.* late ME. [dim. of prec. (see -ET), but of obsc. history.] **1.** A light round shield or buckler; a small targe. Now chiefly *Hist.* **2.** orig., A shield-like structure, marked with concentric circles, set up to be aimed at in shooting practice; hence, any object used for the purpose 1757. **b.** Something aimed at or to be aimed at; *esp.* a person who is the object of general abuse, derision, or the like 1757. **c.** A shooting match; the score made at such a match 1825. **3.** Applied to various objects resembling a target or shield; *esp.* **a.** *Cookery.* The neck and breast of lamb as a joint; the fore-quarter without the shoulder 1750. **b.** The sliding sight on a levelling staff; a vane 1877. **c.** A disc-shaped signal on a railway switch, etc., indicating its position. *U.S.* 1884.

2. b. A t. for the abuse of the prejudiced, the ignorant and the profane 1889. **c.** The Artists' team have made a magnificent t. 1884. Hence **Ta·rget** *v. trans.* †to protect with or as with a t.; to use (a person) as a t.; *U.S.* to signal the position of (a railway switch, etc.) by means of a t. **Ta·rgeted** (tā·ɹgėtėd) *a.* furnished with a t. or shield, or with something resembling one.

Targeteer (tāɹgėtīᵊ·ɹ). *Obs.* exc. *Hist.* 1586. [prob. – It. *targhettiere*, f. *targhetta* target; see -EER.] A foot-soldier armed with a target; a peltast.

Targum (tā·ɹgŏm, ‖targū·m). 1587. [– Chaldee *trgūm* interpretation, f. *trgēm* interpret; see DRAGOMAN.] Each of several Aramaic translations, interpretations, or paraphrases of the various divisions of the Old Testament, committed to writing from about A.D. 100 onwards. **Targumic** (taɹgū·mik), **-al** *adjs.* **Ta·rgumist,** one of the compilers of the Targums, one versed in the Targums. **Targumi·stic** *a.*

Tarheel (tā·ɹ,hīl). *U.S. colloq.* 1888. A native or inhabitant of N. Carolina, in allusion to tar as a principal product of that State.

Tariff (tæ·rif), *sb.* 1591. [– Fr. *tarif* – It. *tariffa* – Turk. *tarife* – Arab. *taʿrīf*(*a*, f. *ʿarrafa* notify, make known.] †**1.** An arithmetical table or statement; a table of multiplication, a ready reckoner, or the like –1770. **2.** An official list or schedule of customs duties to be imposed on imports and exports; a table or book of rates; any item of such a list, the impost (on any article); also the whole body or system of such duties as established in any country 1592. **3.** A classified list or scale of charges made in any private or public business; as, a hotel tariff, a railroad tariff. *U.S.* 1751.

2. A free-trade t. 1868. **3.** The t. of fares 1867. *Comb.* **t.-wall,** a rate of tariff duties which check imports. Hence **Ta·riff** *v. trans.* to subject to a t.-duty; to fix the price of (something) according to a t.

Ta·riff-refo:rm. 1891. *gen.* The reform of a tariff, or of existing tariff conditions; *spec.* in U.S. politics, a reform favouring a general reduction of import duties, and a movement away from Protection; in British politics since *c*1903 (sometimes with caps. *Tariff Reform*), the extension of the tariff on imports, as opp. to 'Free Trade'. Hence **Ta·riff-refo:rmer.**

Taring (tēᵊ·riŋ). 1622. [f. TARE *sb.*² and *v.* + -ING¹.] The calculation and abatement of the tare on goods.

Tarlatan (tā·ɹlătăn). 1727. [– Fr. *tarlatane*, dissimilated f. *tarnatane*; prob. of Indian origin.] A kind of thin open muslin, used esp. for ball-dresses.

Ta·r maca·dam. 1882. [f. TAR *sb.* + MACADAM *sb.*] A material for making roads, consisting of some kind of broken stone or ironstone slag in a matrix of tar alone, or of tar with some mixture of pitch or creosote. Hence **Ta·rmac,** the registered trade-mark of a kind of tar macadam consisting of iron slag impregnated with tar and creosote.

Tarn (tāɹn). [ME. *terne*, *tarne* – ON. **tarnu* (*tjorn*, *tjǫrn*, Sw. dial. *tjärn*, *tärn*, Norw. *tjörn*, Da. *tjern*).] A small mountain lake, having no significant tributaries. (orig. local northern Eng.)

That sable t., In whose black mirror you may spy The stars, while noon-tide lights the sky SCOTT.

Tarnal (tā·ɹnăl), *a.* (*adv.*) *slang*, chiefly *U.S.* 1790. Aphetic dial. pronunc. of *eternal*, vulg. used as an expression of execration, passing into a mere intensive.

Tarnation (taɹnēⁱ·ʃən), *sb.*, *a.*, *adv. slang*, chiefly *U.S.* 1784. Variant of *darnation*, DAMNATION 3; app. assoc. w. prec.

Tarnish (tā·ɹniʃ), *v.* 1598. [– Fr. *terniss-*, extended stem (see -ISH²) of *ternir*, of unkn. origin; the change of *-er-* to *-ar-* is unparalleled at this date.] **1.** *trans.* To dull or dim the lustre of, to discolour (as a metallic surface by oxidation, etc.); to cause to fade; to spoil, wither. **b.** *fig.* To take away from the purity of, cast a stain upon; to sully, taint; to bring disgrace upon 1697. **2.** *intr.* To grow dull, dim, or discoloured; to fade, wither; *esp.* of metals, to lose external brightness or lustre. Also *fig.* 1676.

1. Her Clothes were very rich, but tarnished ADDISON. **b.** Unwilling that his reputation should be tarnished 1786. **2.** Till thy fresh glories, which now shine so bright, Grow stale, and t. with our daily sight DRYDEN. Hence **Ta·rnish** *sb.* the fact of tarnishing or condition of being tarnished; discoloration; also *concr.* the substance of such discoloration. **Ta·rnisher,** one who or that which tarnishes.

Taro (tā·ro, tæ·ro). 1779. [Native Polynesian name.] A food-plant, *Colocasia antiquorum*, family *Araceæ*, cultivated in many varieties in most tropical countries for its starchy root-stocks, or its succulent leaves or stems, which in a raw state are acrid, but lose their acridity by boiling.

‖**Tarot** (taro). Also **taroc.** 1598. [Fr. – It. **tarocco* (pl. *tarocchi*), of unkn. origin.] **a.** One of a set of playing-cards, first used in Italy in the 14th c. Also used in fortune-telling. **b.** *pl.* The game played with these.

‖**Tarpan** (tā·ɹpæn). 1841. [Kirghiz Tartar name.] *Zool.* The wild horse of Tartary.

Tarpaulin (tā·ɹpǫlin, taɹpǭ·lin), *sb.* 1605. [Of unkn. origin; presumed to be f. TAR *sb.* + PALL *sb.*¹ + -ING¹.] **1.** A covering or sheet of canvas so coated or impregnated with tar so as to make it waterproof, used to spread over anything to protect it from wet. Also without *a* or *pl.*, canvas so tarred. **b.** A sailor's hat made of tarpaulin 1841. **2.** *transf.* A nickname for a mariner or sailor, esp. a common sailor. Now *rare* or *arch.* (Cf. TAR *sb.* 3.) 1647. **b.** Formerly applied to a sea-bred superior officer (captain, etc.) as contrasted with the military officers often appointed to command men-of-war 1690.

2. Every tarpawling, if he gets but to be lieutenant of a press smack, is called captain DE FOE. **b.** Drake and his brother tarpaulins 1894. Hence **Tarpau·lin** *v. trans.* to cover with a t.

Tarpeian (taɹpī·ăn), *a.* 1607. [f. L. *Tarpeius* + -AN, or – L. *Tarpeianus*, f. proper name *Tarpeius* or *Tarpeia*.] Denoting a rock-face on the Capitoline Hill at Rome over which persons convicted of treason to the state were thrown headlong.

Tarpon (tā·ɹpǫn). 1685. [– Du. *tarpoen*, of unkn. origin.] The Jew-fish, *Megalops atlanticus*, a giant representative of the herring tribe found in the warmer waters of the western Atlantic: see JEW-FISH and ELOPS.

Tarragon (tæ·răgǫn). 1538. [Given first (1538, 1548) as repr. med.L. *tragonia* and *tarchon*, the latter of which goes back to med. Gr. ταρχών, which may be an Arab. deformation (*ṭarḵūn*) of Gr. δράκων (assoc. with δρακόντιον dragonwort).] **1.** A composite plant, *Artemisia dracunculus*, of the wormwood genus, a native of Southern Russia and Eastern Europe, the aromatic leaves of which are used to flavour salads, soups, etc. **2.** *attrib.*, as **t. vinegar**, vinegar flavoured with the leaves or oil of t. 1855.

Tarragona (tærăgōᵘ·nă). 1885. [Name of a town in Spain.] A Spanish port-like wine.

Tarras (tæ·răs), *sb.* Now *rare* or *Obs.* 1612. [– early mod. Du. *tarasse*, *terras*, *tiras* (whence Du. *tras*, G. *trass*), of Rom. origin; cf. TERRACE.] A kind of rock, allied in composition to pozzolana, consisting largely of comminuted pumice or other volcanic substance; it is found along the Rhine between Cologne and Mainz, and was formerly imported from Holland for making a mortar or hydraulic cement. Hence, the mortar or cement made of this, used for pargeting, lining cisterns, etc.; also applied to other similar cements.

Tarras, *v.* Now *rare* or *Obs.* 1485. [orig. prob. f. Fr. *terracer*, *terrasser*; later app. f. prec.] *trans.* To cover, coat, or lay with plaster; in later use, with tarras.

Tarriance (tæ·riăns). *arch.* 1460. [f. TARRY *v.* + -ANCE.] **1.** The action of tarrying; delay, procrastination. **2.** Temporary residence or continuance in a place; sojourn, abiding 1530. †**3.** Abiding in expectation; awaiting, waiting –1646.

1. I am impatient of my t. SHAKS.

Tarrier[1] (tæ·riəɹ). *arch.* late ME. [f. TARRY *v.* + -ER[1].] **1.** One who tarries or delays; a lingerer; one who stays or remains. †**2.** A hinderer; an obstruction –1622.

Tarrier[2] (tæ·riəɹ). 1460. [In XV *tarrer(e* – OFr. *tarere* (mod. *tarière*) :– late L. *taratrum* (Isidore) of Gaulish origin; cf. Ir. *tarathar*.] A boring instrument, an auger; now, an instrument for extracting a bung from a barrel.

Tarrier[3], obs. or vulgar f. TERRIER[2].

Tarrock (tæ·rǫ̆k). 1674. [Of unkn. origin; for the (app. dim.) ending cf. PUTTOCK[1].] A name applied locally to various sea-birds: in the Shetland Islands, to the Arctic Tern; elsewhere to the Kittiwake, to the young of the Common Gull, and to the Common Guillemot.

Tarry (tæ·ri), *sb.* late ME. [f. TARRY *v.*] †**1.** The act of tarrying; spending or loss of time; delay, procrastination –1745. **2.** Sojourn; a 'stay'. Now chiefly *U.S.* late ME.

Tarry (tā·ri), *a.* 1552. [f. TAR *sb.* + -Y[1].] **1.** Consisting or composed of tar; of the nature of tar. **b.** Resembling tar; having the consistence, colour, or flavour of tar 1880. **2.** Covered, smeared, soiled, or impregnated with tar; black as if smeared with tar 1585.

Comb.: **t.-breeks** (orig. *Sc.*), **-jacket, -John,** joc. nicknames for a sailor. Hence **Ta·rriness.**

Tarry (tæ·ri), *v.* Now chiefly *literary*. ME. [In earliest use identical in form with TAR *v.*[2], and OFr. *tarier*; but the sense is against identity.] †**1.** *trans.* To delay, put off (a thing, an action); to protract, prolong –1583. †**2.** To delay, keep back (a person or agent) for a time; to keep waiting; to hold in check, impede, hinder –1609. **3.** *intr.* To delay or be tardy in beginning or doing anything, esp. in coming or going; to wait before doing something; to linger, loiter ME. **b.** To linger in expectation of a person or occurrence, or until something is done or happens; to wait. late ME. †**4.** To remain, stay, continue –1814. **b.** To abide temporarily; to stay, remain, lodge (in a place). *arch.* exc. in *U.S.* late ME. **5.** *trans.* To wait for, wait in expectation of; to await, expect; †to stay for (a meal). late ME.

2. Sir kyng, he sayd, tary me noo lenger for I may not tary MALORY. **3.** Why tarie the wheeles of his charets? *Judg.* 5:28. **b.** Time and tide t. for no man SCOTT. **4. b.** There they were to t. through Lent FREEMAN. **5.** I pressed him..to t. your coming 1829. Phr. *To t. a person's leisure*: see LEISURE 3 (*arch.*).

Tarsal (tā·ɹsăl), *a.* and *sb.* 1817. [f. TARSUS + -AL[1].] **A.** *adj.* **1.** *Comp. Anat.* Of or pertaining to the tarsus of the ankle or foot. **2.** Of or pertaining to the tarsi of the eyelids 1839. **B.** *sb.* Short for *t. bone, joint*, etc. 1881.

‖**Tarsia** (tā·ɹsiă). 1665. [It.] A kind of mosaic inlaid work in wood of various colours.

Tarsier (tā·ɹsiəɹ). 1774. [– Fr. *tarsier*, f. *tarse* TARSUS; so named by Buffon from the structure of the foot.] *Zool.* A small lemuroid quadruped, *Tarsius spectrum*, of Sumatra, Borneo, Celebes, and the Philippines, called also malmag or spectre, related to the aye-aye of Madagascar.

The T...The bones of..the Tarsus, are..so very long, that from thence the animal has received its name GOLDSM.

Tarso- (tāɹsǒ), bef. a vowel **tars-,** comb. form of Gr. ταρσός TARSUS, as in **Tarso·rrhaphy** [Gr. ῥαφή seam], plastic suture of the eyelid. **Tarso·tomy** [Gr. τομή cutting], the section or removal of the tarsal cartilages.

Tarso-metatarsal (tā:ɹso,metătā·ɹsăl), *a.* and *sb.* 1835. *Comp. Anat.* **A.** *adj.* **a.** Of or pertaining to the tarsus and the metatarsus, as 'the tarso-metatarsal ligaments'. **b.** Of or pertaining to a tarso-metatarsus. **B.** *sb.* Short for *t. bone* or *ligament*.

‖**Tarso-metatarsus** (tā:ɹso,metătā·ɹsʊ̆s). 1854. *Comp. Anat.* The bone formed by ankylosis of the tarsus and the metatarsus in birds and early reptilian types.

‖**Tarsus** (tā·ɹsʊ̆s). *Pl.* **-i** (əi). 1676. [mod.L. – Gr. ταρσός the flat of the foot between the toes and the heel, the rim of the eyelid.] **1.** The first or posterior part of the foot: a collective name for the seven small bones of the human ankle, arranged in two transverse series, the proximal or tibial, consisting of the astragalus and os calcis, and the distal, or metatarsal, consisting of the naviculare, the cuboides, and the three ossa cuneiformia; also, the corresponding part in mammalia generally, and in some reptiles and amphibia. **b.** In birds: The third segment of the leg, the shank: = TARSO-METATARSUS 1828. **c.** In insects and other arthropods, a series of small articulations forming the true foot; in spiders, the last joint, forming, with the preceding joint or metatarsus, the foot 1826. **2.** The thin plate of condensed connective tissue found in each eyelid. Now *rare* or *Obs.* 1691.

Tart (tāɹt), *sb.*[1] late ME. [– OFr. *tarte* (med.L. *tarta* XII), of unkn. origin.] Name for various dishes consisting of a crust of baked pastry enclosing different ingredients: †**a.** Formerly with meat, fish, cheese, fruit, etc. **b.** In current use: (*a*) a flat, usu. small, piece of pastry, with no crust on the top, filled with fruit preserve or other sweet confection; (*b*) a covered fruit pie.

b. Her rejection of a nice little jam t...'she never touched *patisserie*' 1899.

Tart, *sb.*[2] *slang.* 1887. [Shortened f. SWEETHEART.] Applied (orig. endearingly) to a girl or woman (esp. one of immoral character).

Tart (tāɹt), *a.* [OE. *teart* 'acerrimus', 'asperrimus', of unkn. origin.] †**1.** Of pain, punishment, suffering, law, etc.: Sharp, severe, painful, grievous –1605. **2.** Sharp to the sense of taste; now *esp.* sour, acid, or acidulous. late ME. †**b.** Of the sense of taste: keen. B. JONS. †**3.** Sharp, keen (as an edge, point, weapon) –1600. **4.** *fig.* Of words, speech, a speaker: Sharp in tone or tendency, biting, cutting, acrimonious, caustic 1601.

1. *Lear* IV. ii. 87. **2.** Cherries..the juice of which was agreeably t. 1772. **4.** Sometimes a t. Irony goes for Wit 1691. Entertaining the Company with t. ill-natured Observations ADDISON. Hence **Ta·rt-ly** *adv.*, **-ness.**

Tartan (tā·ɹtăn), *sb.*[1] orig. *Sc.* 1500. [perh. – OFr. *tertaine*, var. of *tiretaine* cloth half wool, half linen or cotton, of unkn. origin.] A kind of woollen cloth woven in stripes of various colours crossing at right angles so as to form a regular pattern; worn chiefly by the Scottish Highlanders, each clan having usu. its distinctive pattern. Also, the pattern or design of such cloth. Also applied to silk and other fabrics having a similar pattern. **b.** *transf.* Applied to one who wears tartan; a Highlander; collectively, those who wear tartan; the body of Highlanders; the men of a Highland regiment 1817.

Shepherds' t., shepherds' plaid (see PLAID 1). Hence **Ta·rtan** *v. trans.* to clothe or array in t.

Tartan, tartane (tā·ɹtăn, ‖tartan), *sb.*[2] 1621. [– Fr. *tartane* – It. *tartana*, perh. – Arab. *ṭarīda*.] A small one-masted vessel with a large lateen sail and a foresail, used in the Mediterranean. So **Tarta·na** 1588.

‖**Tartan,** *sb.*[3] 1880. [Assyrian. See 2 Kings 18:17, Isa. 20:1.] The ancient Assyrian commander-in-chief.

Tartar (tā·ɹtăɹ), *sb.*[1] late ME. [In XIV *tartre* (Chaucer), *tartar* (Trevisa) – med.L. *tartarum* – med. Gr. τάρταρον, of unkn. origin. Cf. mod. Fr. *tartre*, Sp., It. *tartaro*.] **1.** *Chem.* Bitartrate of potash (acid potassium tartrate), present in grape juice, deposited in a crude form in the process of fermentation, and adhering to the sides of wine-casks in the form of a hard crust, also called *argal* or ARGOL, which when purified forms white crystals, which are *cream of t.* **b.** Hence, 'A generic name for salts of tartaric acid' (Watts). **2.** *transf.* Any calcareous or other incrustation deposited from a liquid upon bodies in contact with it 1605. **b.** *spec.* A deposit of calcium phosphate from the saliva, which tends to harden and concrete upon the teeth 1806.

Cream of t.: see sense 1 and CREAM *sb.* **T. eme·tic,** common name in pharmacy of potassio-antimonious tartrate, $C_4H_4K(Sb.O)O_6 + \frac{1}{2}H_2O$, a poisonous substance, used in medicine to excite vomiting.

Tartar (tā·ɹtăɹ), *sb.*[2] (*a.*), **Tatar** (tā·tăɹ). late ME. [In XIV *tartre* (Chaucer), in XV *tartar* – (O)Fr. *Tartare* or med.L. *Tartarus*. The form *Tatar* and its derivatives are now often used in ethnological works in sense 1.] **1.** A native inhabitant of the region of Central Asia extending eastward from the Caspian Sea. First known in the West as applied to the mingled host of Mongols, Tartars, Turks, etc., which under the leadership of Jenghiz Khan (1202–1227) overran and devastated much of Asia and Eastern Europe; hence vaguely applied to the descendants of these now dwelling in Asia or Europe; more strictly and ethnologically, to any member of the Tâtar or Turkic branch of the Ural-Altaic or Turanian family, including the Turks, Kazakhs, and Kirghiz Tartars. **2.** *transf.* †**a.** A strolling vagabond, a thief, a beggar –1697. **b.** As an opprobrious appellation 1590. **3.** *fig.* A savage; a person supposed to resemble a T. in disposition; a rough and violent or irritable and intractable person: when applied to a female, a vixen, a shrew, a termagant 1663. **4.** The language of the Tartars 1884.

1. Looke how I goe, Swifter then arrow from the Tartars bowe SHAKS. **2. a.** *Merry W.* IV. v. 21. **b.** *Mids. N.* III. ii. 263. **3.** The old man was a awful T. DICKENS. Phr. *To catch a T.*, to get hold of one who can neither be controlled nor got rid of.

B. *adj.* Of or pertaining to the Tartars, or their country. Also applied to plants, animals, etc., belonging to Tartary. 1731.

†**Ta·rtar,** *sb.*[3]: see TARTARUS.

Tartarated (tā·ɹtărēⁱtėd), *a.* 1863. [f. TARTAR *sb.*[1] + -ATE[4] + -ED[1].] *Chem.* Combined with tartar; as in *t. iron, soda.*

Tartarean (taɹtēᵊ·riăn), *a.* 1623. [f. L. *Tartareus* + -AN; see -EAN.] Of or belonging to the Tartarus of the ancients; hence, pertaining to hell or to purgatory; infernal.

Mixt with T. Sulphur, and strange fire MILT.

Tartareous (taɹtēᵊ·rĭəs), *a.*[1] 1625. [f. TARTAR *sb.*[1] + -EOUS.] †**1.** *Path.* Of the nature of a tartar, or calcareous or earthy deposit; characterized by such deposits –1677. †**2.** Like tartar in consistence or formation; of the nature of a concretion or crust; gritty –1683. †**3.** *Chem.* Having the quality of tartar or argol; containing or derived from tartar –1822. **4.** *Bot.* Of a crust-like structure like tartar: descriptive of certain lichens 1845.

†**Tarta·reous,** *a.*[2] 1619. [f. L. *tartareus* (f. TARTARUS) + -OUS.] Of or pertaining to Tartarus; infernal, hellish, very wicked –1667.

Tartarian (taɹtēᵊ·riăn), *sb.* and *a.*[1] late ME. [– OFr. *Tartarien*; later f. med.L. *Tartaria* TARTARY + -AN.] **A.** *sb.* = TARTAR *sb.*[2] 1, 2 a. **B.** *adj.* = TARTAR *a.* 1590. **b.** In names of things of actual or supposed Tartar origin; as *T. cherry, lamb* 1805.

Tarta·rian, *a.*[2] *rare.* 1864. [f. L. TARTARUS + -IAN.] = TARTAREAN *a.*

Tartaric (taɹtæ·rik), *a.*[1] 1790. [– Fr. †*tartarique*, f. med.L. *tartarum*; see TARTAR *sb.*[1], -IC.] *Chem.* Of the nature of, related to, or derived from tartar or argol.

T. acid, an organic acid, $C_4H_6O_6 = C_4H_2O_2 + (OH)_4$, or $CO_2H.(CHOH)_2.CO_2H$, of which there are five isomeric forms, differing in their optical properties; spec. one of these (*dextrotartaric* acid), a colourless crystalline compound, occurring largely in the vegetable kingdom, esp. in unripe grapes, and as a potassium salt in argol or tartar of wine, from which it is commercially prepared.

Tartaric (taɹtæ·rik), *a.*[2] Also **Tataric.** 1811. [f. TARTAR *sb.*[2] + -IC.] Of, pertaining to, or connected with the Tartars or Tartary.

Tartarin (tā·ɹtărin, ‖tartaræ̃n). 1903. Name of a bombastic character, 'Tartarin of Tarascon', created by A. Daudet; hence, used *allus.* as sb. or adj.

Tartarize (tā·ɹtărəiz), *v.*[1] 1706. [f. TARTAR *sb.*[1] + -IZE.] Chem. *trans.* To treat or impregnate with tartar; to rectify by means of the salt of tartar.

Ta·rtarize, *v.*[2] Also **Tatarize.** 1877. [f. TARTAR *sb.*[2] + -IZE.] *trans.* To convert or transform into a Tartar.

Tartarly (tā·ɹtărli), *a. nonce-wd.* 1821. [f. TARTAR *sb.*[2] + -LY[1].] Rough and fierce.

Who killed John Keats? 'I' says the Quarterly, So savage and T. BYRON.

†**Tartarous** (tā·ɹtărəs), *a.* 1605. [f. TARTAR *sb.*[1] + -OUS; cf. Fr. *tartareux* (f. med.L. *tartarum*).] **1.** Of the nature of, consisting of, or containing tartar or argol –1768. **2.** *Path.* Said of indurations, inspissated fluids, phlegms, etc., attributed to the presence of tartar in the body –1744. **3.** Of the nature of or derived from tartar; *t. acid*, an earlier name of TARTARIC *acid* 1790.

‖**Tartarus** (tā·ɹtărŏs). 1586. [L. – Gr. Τάρταρος.] The infernal regions of ancient Greek and Roman mythology, or the lowest part of them; hence sometimes used for: Hell. **b.** A place likened to Tartarus, in situation or character 1821. Also †**Tartar** 1500–1601.

b. She never emerged from the dismal T. of the kitchens, &c., to the upper air DE QUINCEY.

Tartary (tā·ɹtări). late ME. [–(O)Fr. *Tartarie* – med.L. *Tartaria* land of the Tartars; assoc. w. TARTARUS; see -Y[3].] **1.** The country of the Tartars; see TARTAR *sb.*[2] †**2.** Tartarus, as a region –1620.

‖**Tartine** (tartīn). 1826. [Fr., f. *tarte* TART *sb.*[1]] 'A slice of bread spread with butter or preserve.'

Tartish (tā·ɹtiʃ), *a.* 1712. [f. TART *a.* + -ISH[1].] Somewhat tart, slightly pungent or acid; also *fig.*

Tartlet (tā·ɹtlét). late ME. [– (O)Fr. *tartelette*, dim. of *tarte* TART *sb.*[1]; in XVIII formed anew on TART; see -LET.] A small tart.

Tartralic (taɹtræ·lik), *a.* 1857. [– Fr. *tartralique* (Frémy, 1838), arbitrarily f. *tartrique* (f. *tartre* TARTAR *sb.*[1]), to indicate derivation from tartaric acid; cf. TARTRELIC.] *Chem.* In *t. acid* (also called *ditartaric* or *isotartaric acid*), $C_8H_{10}O_{11}$, an amorphous deliquescent substance obtained by heating tartaric acid. Its salts are **Ta·rtralates.**

Tartramic (taɹtræ·mik), *a.* 1857. [f. TARTRO- + AMMONIUM + -IC.] *Chem.* In *t. acid*, $C_4H_7NO_5$, an amidated derivative of tartaric acid. Its salts are **Ta·rtramates.**

Ta·rtrami:de. 1868. [f. TARTRO- + AMIDE.] *Chem.* The amide of tartaric acid, $C_4H_4(NH_2)_2O_4$, a crystalline body produced by passing dry ammonia gas into an alcoholic solution of tartaric ether.

Tartrate (tā·ɹtrĕt). 1794. [– Fr. *tartrate*, f. *tartre* TARTAR *sb.*[1]; see -ATE[4].] *Chem.* A salt of tartaric acid. Hence **Ta·rtrated** *ppl. a.* made into a t.; tartarated.

Tartrelic (taɹtre·lik), *a.* 1838. [– Fr. *tartrélique* (Frémy, 1838), arbitrarily formed, along with TARTRALIC, to indicate derivation from tartaric acid by further heating; the *a* and *e* indicating the order of production of these modifications.] *Chem.* In *t. acid*, soluble tartaric anhydride, $C_4H_4O_5$, obtained as a yellowish deliquescent mass by quickly heating small quantities of tartaric acid. Its salts are **Ta·rtrelates.**

Tartro-, bef. a vowel **tartr-** [f. Fr. *tartre* TARTAR *sb.*[1]], in names of chemical compounds containing or derived from tartaric acid; as **Ta·rtrazine** [AZO- + -INE[5]], a fast and brilliant dye-stuff of rich orange yellow; **Tartrethy·lic** *acid*, $C_6H_{10}O_6$; **Tartrovi·nic** *acid* = *tartrethylic acid.*

Tartronic (taɹtrǫ·nik), *a.* 1866. [– Fr. *tartronique* (Dessaignes, 1854), arbitrarily f. *tartrique* (perh. with *ni-* of *nitro-*).] *Chem.* In *t. acid*, a dibasic acid, $C_3H_4O_5$, produced by the spontaneous decomposition of nitro-tartaric acid, crystallizing in large prisms. Its salts are **Ta·rtronates.**

‖**Tartuffe, Tartufe** (taɹtu·f, ‖tartüf). 1676. [Fr., name of the principal character (a religious hypocrite) in a comedy by Molière (1664); taken from It. *Tartufo*, a use of *tartuffo* truffle, as a concealed production.] A hypocritical pretender to religion, or, by extension, to excellence of any kind. Hence **Tartu·fferie, -ery,** the character or conduct of a T., hypocrisy. **Tartu·ffian, Tartu·f(f)ish** *adjs.* pertaining to or characteristic of a T.; hypocritical, pretentious.

Ta·r-wa:ter. 1740. [f. TAR *sb.* + WATER *sb.*] **1.** An infusion of tar in cold water, formerly in repute as a medicine. **2.** The ammoniacal water of gas-works 1858.

‖**Tasajo** (tasā·χo). 1783. [Sp.] Buffalo meat cut into strips and dried in the sun.

Tasimeter (tăsi·mĭtəɹ). 1878. [f. Gr. τάσις tension + -METER.] An electrical apparatus for measuring minute variations of temperature, length, moisture, etc. by means of changes in the electrical conductivity of carbon resulting from alterations of pressure caused by these variations.

Task (tɑsk), *sb.* ME. [– ONFr. *tasque*, var. of OFr. *tasche* (mod. *tâche*) – med.L. *tasca*, alt. of *taxa*, f. L. *taxare* TAX *v.*] †**1.** A fixed payment to a king, lord, or feudal superior; an impost, tax; tribute –1766. **2.** A piece of work imposed, exacted, or undertaken as a duty or the like; orig., a fixed or specified quantity of work imposed on or exacted from a person; later, the work appointed to one as a definite duty ME. **b.** *spec.* A portion of study imposed by a teacher; a lesson to be learned or prepared. Now *arch.* 1742. **3.** *gen.* Any piece of work that has to be done; something that one has to do (usu. involving labour or difficulty) 1593.

2. The silk-worm, after having spun her t., lays her eggs and dies ADDISON. She..appoints them a t. of needle-work JOHNSON. **3.** He had taken upon himself a t. beyond the ordinary strength of man FROUDE. Phr. *To take to t.*, to deal with in the way of fault-finding or censure, to call to account about a matter.

Task (tɑsk), *v.* 1483. [f. prec.] **I.** †**1.** *trans.* To impose a tax upon; to tax; to exact tribute from –1642. **2.** To force, put, or set (a person) to a task; to impose a task on; to assign a definite amount of work to 1530. **3.** *transf.* and *fig.* To occupy or engage fully or burdensomely; to put a strain upon; to put in a condition of stress or difficulty; to put to the proof 1598. **b.** *spec.* To test the soundness of (a ship's timbers, a plank, etc.) 1803.

2. But now to taske the tasker SHAKS. Man alone ..tasks creation to assist him in murdering his brother worm! W. IRVING. **3.** Some things of weight, That taske our thoughts SHAKS. You must not t. me too high RICHARDSON.

†**II.** To take to task; to reprove –1632.

Tasker (tɑ·skəɹ). late ME. [f. TASK *v.* (or *sb.*) + -ER[1].] †**1.** One who assesses or regulates a rate or price (e.g. of things brought to market, etc.) –1614. **2.** One who imposes or sets a task; a taskmaster 1588. **3.** One who works or is paid by the task or piece, as dist. from a day-labourer, etc. *dial.* 1621. **b.** *spec.* One who threshes corn with a flail, as TASK-WORK or piece-work. late ME.

Ta·skma:ster. 1530. [f. TASK *sb.* + MASTER *sb.*[1]] One whose office is to allot tasks and see to their performance; an overseer; a middleman; also *fig.* one who allots a duty, or imposes a heavy burden or labour.

All is, if I have grace to use it so, As ever in my great task Masters eye MILT. So **Ta·skmi:stress.**

Ta·sk-work. 1486. [f. TASK *sb.* + WORK *sb.*] **1.** Work performed as a task; forced labour; hence, burdensome or oppressive work 1582. **2.** Piece-work 1486.

Tasmanian (tæzmēⁱ·niăn, tæs-), *a.* Of or pertaining to Tasmania in Australasia. In names of animals, plants, etc., native to Tasmania, as *T. devil* (see DEVIL 7), *T.* WOLF.

Tass[1] (tɑs). Now *dial.* ME. [– (O)Fr. *tas* masc., OFr. *tasse* fem. – Frankish **tas*, whence MDu. *tass*, Du. *tas*, whence prob. the later Eng. use (from XV). Cf. AL. *tassa* haycock (XIII).] A heap, pile, stack.

Tass[2] (tæs). Now chiefly *Sc.* 1483. [– (O)Fr. *tasse* – Arab. *ṭāsa* basin – Pers. *tast.*] A cup or small goblet; the contents of this; a small draught of liquor.

Tasse (tæs). *Obs.* exc. *Hist.* 1548. [In form the same word as OFr. *tasse* purse; in sense = Fr. *tassette*, †*tassete* small pouch, steel plate to guard the thigh, dim. of *tasse.*] *pl.* A series of articulated splints or plates depending from the corslet, placed so that each slightly overlapped the one below it, forming a sort of kilt of armour to protect the thighs and the lower part of the trunk.

Tassel (tæ·s'l), *sb.*[1] ME. [– OFr. *tas(s)el* clasp, of unkn. origin; cf. AL. *tassellus, -um* (XII) tassel, fringe.] †**1.** A clasp or fibula by which the two sides of a cloak or the like are held together. late ME. **2.** A pendent ornament consisting of a bunch or thick fringe of threads or small cords hanging in a somewhat conical shape from a solid rounded knob or mould, or from a knot formed by their junction with a cord. Frequently attached to a curtain, cushion, cap, umbrella, etc., or forming the pull of a blind-cord or bell-cord. late ME. **3.** Anything resembling or suggesting a tassel; as a pendent catkin, blossom, or bud; *spec.* the staminate (terminal) inflorescence of the maize-plant (*U.S.*) 1646.

2. A knotted girdle, ending in tassels encircled the loins 1849. **3.** The yellow tassels on the hazel MISS MITFORD.

Comb.: **t.-flower,** (*a*) a tassel-like flower; *spec.* the orange, scarlet, or yellowish blossom of *Emilia sagittata*, family *Compositæ*, or the plant itself; (*b*) a shrub or tree of the genus *Inga*; **-grass,** an aquatic herb, *Ruppia maritima*, of which the seed-vessels are borne on clusters of pedicels; **-hyacinth,** *Muscari comosum*, the stalk and flower of which resemble a t. Hence **Tassel(l)ed** (tæ·s'ld) *a.* 1611.

Tassel, torsel (tæ·s'l, tǫ·s'l, tǭ·ɹs'l), *sb.*[2] 1632. [– OFr. *tassel* (mod. *tasseau*) – pop.L. **tassellus*, a blending of L. *taxillus* small die and *tessella* small square piece of stone.] *Arch.* A short board or 'templet' placed under the end of a beam or other timber where it rests on brickwork or stonework.

Tassel (tæ·s'l), *v.* late ME. [f. TASSEL *sb.*[1]] **1.** *trans.* To furnish or adorn with or as with a tassel or tassels. **2.** *intr.* Of maize and sugar-cane: To form 'tassels', i.e. to flower, bloom. Chiefly *U.S.* 1785.

Tassets (tæ·séts), *sb. pl.* 1834. [– Fr. *tassette*; see TASSE.] = *tasses*; see TASSE. (Only in recent archæological or romantic use.)

Taste (tēⁱst), *sb.*[1] ME. [– OFr. *tast*, f. *taster* TASTE *v.*] **I.** †**1.** The sense of touch, feeling (with the hands, etc.); the act of touching, touch. late ME. †**2.** A trying; a trial, test –1633. **II.** †**1.** The act of tasting or perceiving the flavour of a thing with the organ of taste; the fact of being tasted –1766. **b.** *transf.* The means of tasting; hence, such a small quantity as admits of being tasted; a very small quantity (esp. of spirits), a sip 1530. **c.** *fig.* A slight experience, received or given; a slight show or sample *of* any condition or quality. late ME. **2.** The faculty or sense by which that particular quality of a thing described in 3 is discerned; one of the five bodily senses. late ME. **3.** That quality or property of a body or substance which is perceived when it is brought into contact with certain organs of the mouth, etc., esp. the tongue; savour, sapidity; the particular sensation excited by anything in this manner. late ME.

1. The Fruit Of that Forbidden Tree, whose mortal tast Brought Death into the World, and all our woe MILT. **2.** Second childishnesse, and meere obliuion, Sans teeth, sans eyes, sans t., sans euery thing SHAKS. **3.** Iron..has a styptic t., very sensible 1800. *fig.* I haue..forgot the t. of Feares SHAKS. The poems leave a nasty t. in the mouth; the t. of a snarl and a sneer 1904.

III. †**1.** Mental perception of quality; judgement, discriminative faculty. *Obs.* exc. as in 3 below –1692. **2.** The fact or condition of liking or preferring something; inclination, liking *for*; †appreciation 1477. **3.** The sense of what is appropriate, harmonious, or beautiful; *esp.* discernment and appreciation of the beautiful in nature or art; *spec.* the faculty of perceiving and enjoying what is excellent in art, literature, and the like 1671. **b.** Style or manner exhibiting æsthetic discernment; good or bad æsthetic quality; the style or manner favoured in any age or country 1739.

2. Whoever hath a t. for true humour SWIFT. The other girl is more amusing, more to my t. LYTTON. **3.** No, no, hang him, he has no Taste CONGREVE. A fine Musical t. is soon dissatified with the Harmonica 1834. **b.** Nothing could be.. 'in better t.' DISRAELI. It was..built something in the Moorish t. 1843.

attrib. and *Comb.*: **t.-beaker, -bud, -bulb, -goblet,** one of the flask-shaped bodies in the epithelium of the tongue, believed to be organs of taste; †**-paper,** in the (old) Greats examination at Oxford, the paper in which passages were set from the classical authors for critical and exegetical treatment.

Taste (tēⁱst), *sb.*² *U.S. local.* 1788. [Of unkn. origin.] A kind of narrow thin silk ribbon used for edge-binding: now commonly called taffeta-binding.

Taste (tēⁱst), *v.* ME. [OFr. *taster* (mod. *tâter*) touch, feel, try, taste :– Rom. **tastare*, supposed to be a blend of L. *tangere* touch and *gustare* taste.] **I.** †**1.** *trans.* To try, examine, or explore by touch; to feel; to handle –1648. †**2.** *trans.* To put to the proof; to try, test –1670. **b.** spec. *Shipbuilding.* To chip (a plank or timber) with an adze for the purpose of finding any defects 1711. **3.** *fig.* To have experience or knowledge of; to experience, feel; to have a slight experience of ME. †**b.** To have carnal knowledge of –1752.

3. You have tasted the Pleasures of the Town 1693. **b.** *Cymb.* II. iv. 57.

II. 1. *trans.* To perceive by the sense of taste; to perceive or experience the taste or flavour of ME. †**b.** *fig.* To perceive as by the sense of taste –1616. **c.** *absol.* or *intr.* To experience or distinguish flavours; to have or exercise the sense of taste. late ME. **2.** *transf.* (*trans.*) To perceive by some other sense, esp. smell. Now only *poet.* or *dial.* 1656. **3.** To try the flavour or quality of by the sense of taste; to put a small quantity of (something) into the mouth in order to ascertain the flavour, etc.; *spec.* to test the quality of by tasting, for trade purposes. Also *absol.* ME. **b.** *spec.* (*trans.*) To test or certify the wholesomeness of (food provided) by tasting it; also *absol.* to act as taster *to* a person 1595. **c.** *fig.* To make trial of as by the sense of taste; to try the quality of. Also *absol.* or *intr.* late ME. **4.** To have or take a taste of (food or drink); to eat or drink a little; but often by meiosis, simply for 'eat' or 'drink'. Negatively, *not to t.* = not to eat or drink at all. ME. **5.** To like the taste of (usu. *fig.*); to like, take pleasure in; formerly sometimes in neutral sense: to appreciate. Now *arch.* or *dial.* 1605. **6.** *intr.* Of a substance: To have a taste of a specified or implied kind; to have a taste or flavour *of* 1552. **b.** *fig.* To partake of the nature, character, or quality *of*; to savour *of* 1599. **7.** *trans.* To impart a taste or flavour to. Now *rare.* 1577.

1. This daye am I foure score yeare olde. How shulde I..taist what I eate or drynke? COVERDALE 2 *Sam.* 19:35. **b.** Nay, then I t. a Trick in't B. JONS. **c.** O, you are sicke of selfe-loue, Maluolio, and t. with a distemper'd appetite SHAKS. **2.** To t. the cold breath of the earliest morn KINGLAKE. **3.** The ale teaster to teast the ale before they sell it 1604. **b.** How did he take it [poison]? Who did t. to him? SHAKS. **c.** O taist and se how frendly the Lorde is COVERDALE *Ps.* 33:9. **4.** I often..t. a cup of Ale there WALTON. **5.** The King seemed to t. the Duke of Grafton, and commended his parts 1768. **6.** Let him drink deeply..nor grumble if it tasteth of the cork 1871. **b.** The place, the air Tastes of the nearer north CLOUGH. **7.** We will have a bunch of radish and salt to t. our wine B. JONS.

T. of: a. = II. 3. **b.** = II. 7. **c.** = I. 3.

Tasteable, tastable (tēⁱ·stăb'l), *a.* 1572. [f. TASTE *v.* + -ABLE.] **1.** Capable of being tasted. †**2.** Pleasant to the taste –1791.

Tasteful (tēⁱ·stfŭl), *a.* 1611. [f. TASTE *sb.*¹ + -FUL.] †**1.** Having the capacity of tasting or trying. CRASHAW. **2.** Having an agreeable taste; palatable, toothsome, tasty. Now *rare.* 1611. **3.** Having or showing good taste, as a person; displaying good taste, as a work of art, etc. 1756.

2. T. food 1747. A t. dish 1887. **3.** The t. pencil of Stothard 1816. The t. publisher of the 'Aldine Poets' 1849. Hence **Ta·steful-ly** *adv.*, **-ness.**

Tasteless (tēⁱ·stlės), *a.* 1591. [f. TASTE *sb.*¹ + -LESS.] **1.** Destitute of the sense of taste; unable to taste. Also *fig.* Now *rare.* **2.** Without taste or flavour; insipid 1611. **3.** Devoid of good taste; of things, showing want of good taste 1676.

1. The t. palate of age 1820. **2.** Very dry and t. food 1748. *fig.* A while on trivial things we held discourse, To me soon t. WORDSW. **3.** The t. fashion of an artificial and decaying civilization KINGSLEY. Hence **Ta·steless-ly** *adv.*, **-ness.**

Taster¹ (tēⁱ·stəɹ). late ME. [orig. – AFr. *tastour* = OFr. *tasteur*, f. *taster* TASTE *v.* Later f. TASTE *v.* + -ER¹.] **1.** One who tastes, or tries the quality of a thing by tasting; *spec.* one whose office, business, or employment is to test by taste the quality of victuals sold to the public, as ales, wines, teas, etc. 1440. **2.** A domestic officer whose duty it is to taste food and drink about to be served to his master, in order to ascertain their quality, or to detect poison. late ME. **3.** An implement by which a small portion of anything is taken for tasting. **a.** A small shallow cup of silver, for tasting wines. late ME. **b.** An instrument by which a small portion is taken from the interior of a cheese; a skewer for testing the condition of hams 1784. **4.** A small portion of food, etc., for a sample 1826.

2. Princes have their tasters before they eat, lest there should be poison in the dish 1662.

‖**Taster**² (tɑ·stəɹ). 1884. [G., feeler, antenna, f. *tasten* to feel, touch.] *Zool.* In certain Hydrozoa, A modified zooid situated on the polyp-stem, and somewhat resembling the polypites, but having no mouth; a hydrocyst or feeler.

Tasting (tēⁱ·stiŋ), *vbl. sb.* ME. [-ING¹.] **1.** The action of the vb. TASTE; now, the action of TASTE *v.* II; †also formerly, the faculty or sense of taste, and the quality of a substance so apprehended. **2.** quasi-*concr.* A small portion taken to try the taste; a taste (esp. of spirituous liquor) 1526.

Comb.: **t.-knife,** a cheese-taster.

Tasty (tēⁱ·sti), *a.* Now *colloq.* and *dial.* 1617. [f. TASTE *sb.*¹ + -Y¹.] **1.** Pleasing to the taste; appetizing, savoury. **2.** Tasteful, elegant. Now *rare.* 1762.

1. A t. bird, that pheasant 1795. **2.** [The silk] is at once rich, t., and quite the thing GOLDSM. Hence **Ta·stily** *adv.* **Ta·stiness.**

Tat (tæt), *sb.*¹ *slang.* 1688. [Of unkn. origin.] *pl.* **Tats:** Dice; *esp.* false or loaded dice.

Tāt (tāt), *sb.*² *India.* Also **taut.** 1820. [Hindi *ṭāṭ*.] Coarse canvas made from various fibres, esp. jute, and used as sacking.

Tat, tatt (tæt), *sb.*³ *India.* 1840. Short for TATTOO *sb.*³, a native pony of India.

Tat, *sb.*⁴, in phr. *tit for tat*: see TIT.

Tat, *v.* Also **tatt.** 1842. [Of unkn. origin; cf. TATTING.] *intr.* To do tatting. *trans.* To make by tatting.

Ta-ta (tætā·), *int.* 1837. A nursery expression for 'Good-bye': also used playfully by adults.

Tatar: see TARTAR².

‖**Tatou, tatu** (ta·*tu*). 1568. [Native name in Tupi.] An armadillo. **b.** In comb. with defining words, applied (in Tupi and Guarani) to various species, as **ta:touay·** (**tatou-áiba**), the wounded armadillo; **ta:touhou·, ta:toupe·ba,** = PEBA.

Tatter (tæ·təɹ), *sb.*¹ late ME. [– ON. **taturr* (Icel. *töturr*, Norw. dial. *totra*), pl. *tǫtrar* rags, rel. to OE. *tættec* rag.] **1.** An irregularly torn piece, strip, or scrap of cloth or similar substance, hanging loose from the main body, esp. of a garment; more rarely applied to the separate pieces into which a thing is torn; a rag. In *pl.* often = tattered or ragged clothing; rags. †**2.** *transf.* A person wearing tattered or ragged clothes; a tatterdemalion –1637.

1. *fig.* To see a robustious Pery-wig-pated Fellow, teare a Passion to tatters, to verie ragges SHAKS.

Tatter, *sb.*² *rare.* 1881. [f. TAT *v.*] One who tats or does tatting.

Tatter (tæ·təɹ), *v.* late ME. [app. a back-formation from TATTERED.] *trans.* To tear or reduce to tatters; to make ragged; to tear in pieces. **b.** *intr.* To be or become tattered 1595.

fig. A Nation so exhausted and tattered by divisions 1652.

Tatterdemalion, -demallion (tæ:təɹdimēⁱ·liən, -mæ·liən). 1608. [f. TATTER *sb.*¹, or more prob. TATTERED *a.*, + a factitious element suggesting a descriptive derivative; cf. RAMPALLION, RAPSCALLION.] A person in tattered clothing; a ragged or beggarly fellow; a ragamuffin. Also *attrib.* or as *adj.*

Tattered (tæ·təɹd), *a.*, *ppl. a.* late ME. [app. orig. f. TATTER *sb.*¹ + -ED².] †**1.** Having 'tatters', jags, or long pointed projections; denticulated; slashed or laciniated, as a garment –1501. **2.** Torn or rent so as to hang in tatters; ragged 1596. **3.** *transf.* Having tattered or ragged garments 1623. †**4.** Of a ship, building, or other solid structure: Dilapidated, battered, shattered –1798. †**b.** Of troops: Routed and broken up –1728.

2. Crowds of People in t. Garments ADDISON. **3.** This is the man all t. and torn *Nursery Rhyme.* **4.** [He] warns his t. fleet to follow home DRYDEN. I do not like ruined, t. cottages JANE AUSTEN.

Tatting (tæ·tiŋ). 1842. [Of unkn. origin.] **A.** *sb.* A kind of knotted lace, netted with a small flat shuttle-shaped instrument from stout sewing-thread; used for edging or trimming, etc. **B.** *vbl. sb.* The action or process of making this. Also *attrib.*, as *t.-cotton, -shuttle.*

Tattle (tæ·t'l), *sb.* 1529. [f. next. Cf. LG. *tätel* in same sense.] The action of tattling; idle or frivolous talk; chatter, gossip. Also with *a* and *pl.* (now *rare*).

Like olde wiues tales, or tattles 1612. They.. told the t. of the day SWIFT.

Tattle (tæ·t'l), *v.* 1481. [– MFlem. *tatelen*, parallel to the more usual MFlem., MDu., MLG. *tateren*; of imit. origin; see -LE.] †**1.** *intr.* To speak hesitatingly, falter, stammer; *esp.* to prattle as a young child. **2.** To utter small talk; to talk idly or lightly; to chatter, babble; to chat, gossip 1547. **3.** To talk without reticence so as to reveal private affairs. (Now usu. with mixture of sense 2.) 1581. **4.** *trans.* To utter, say, or tell over in tattling. Now *rare.* 1588.

2. I must tell you, sir, you have tattled long enough DRYDEN. **3.** She never tattled 1876.

Tattler (tæ·tləɹ). 1550. [f. TATTLE *v.* + -ER¹.] **1.** One who tattles; an idle talker; a gossip; a telltale. †**2.** *slang.* A striking watch, a repeater; a watch in general –1844. **3.** *Ornith.* Any of the sandpipers of the genus *Totanus* or subfamily *Totaninæ*; so called from their vociferous cry 1831.

Ta·ttling, *ppl. a.* 1576. [f. as prec. + -ING².] That tattles; chattering; gossiping; tale-telling. Hence **Ta·ttlingly** *adv.*

Tattoo (tætū·), *sb.*¹ 1644. [In XVII *taptoo* – Du. *taptoe* in same sense; f. *tap* the tap (of a cask) + *toe* = *doe toe* 'shut'. Cf. G.

zapfenstreich, LG. *tappenslag* lit. 'tap-blow'.] **1.** *Mil.* A signal made, by beat of drum or bugle-call, in the evening, for soldiers to repair to their quarters in garrison or tents in camp. **b.** A military entertainment consisting of an elaboration of the tattoo by extra music and military exercises, usu. at night and by torch or other artificial light 1742. **c.** A drum-beat in general, as a means of raising an alarm, attracting attention, etc. 1688. **2.** *transf.* A beating or pulsation as of a drum; the action of beating, thumping, or rapping continuously upon something 1755.

2. Beginning to play a rapid t. with her feet THACKERAY. Phr. *Devil's t.*, the action of idly tapping or drumming with the fingers, etc. upon a table or other object, in an irritating manner, or as a sign of vexation, impatience, or the like.

Tattoo (tætū·), *sb.*[2] 1777. [In XVIII *tattow*; of Polynesian origin; in Tahiti, Samoa, Tonga *ta-tau*; in Marquesa *ta-tu*.] The act or practice of tattooing the skin (see the vb.); the mark or design made by tattooing.

Tattoo (tæ·tu), *sb.*[3] *India.* 1629. [– Hindi *ṭaṭṭū*.] A native-bred Indian pony.

Tattoo·, *v.*[1] 1780. [f. TATTOO *sb.*[1]] **1.** *trans.* To beat (a drum, etc.); to strike (something) with a succession of blows, to thump. **2.** *intr.* To beat as upon a drum 1806.

Tattoo·, *v.*[2] 1769. [f. TATTOO *sb.*[2]] *trans.* To make permanent marks or designs upon the skin by puncturing it and inserting a pigment or pigments: practised by various tribes of low civilization, and by individuals in civilized communities. Hence **Tattoo·er.**

‖**Tatty** (tæ·ti), *sb.* *India.* 1792. [– Hindi *ṭaṭṭi*.] A screen or mat, usu. made of the roots of the fragrant cuscus grass, which is placed in a frame so as to fill up the opening of a door or window, and kept wet, in order to cool and freshen the air of a room.

Tau (tǭ, tau). ME. [– Gr. ταῦ, name of the letter T in the Greek alphabet; see T, the letter.] **1.** The name of the letter T in the Greek, Hebrew, and ancient Semitic alphabets. Often in the sense 'last letter', as *tau* was orig. in Greek, and continued to be in Hebrew, etc. **2.** A mark of the shape of the letter T, a St. Anthony's cross; a figure of this as a sacred symbol ME. **3.** The Amer. toad-fish (*Batrachus tau*): so called from having markings resembling the letter T.

Comb.: **tau-cross** = sense 2.

‖**Taube** (tau·bə). 1913. [G., pigeon; cf. DOVE.] A type of German aeroplane.

Taught (tǭt), *ppl. a.* ME. Pa. t. and pa. pple. of TEACH *v.*

Taunt (tǭnt), *sb.* 1529. [orig. – Fr. phr. *tant pour tant* 'so much for so much', like for like (L. *tantum*, n. of *tantus* so great).] †**1.** In phr. *t. for* (*pour*) *t.*, like for like, tit for tat, in reply or rejoinder –1620. (Also *tint for t.* 1620–1828.) †**2.** A smart or clever rejoinder; banter –1625. **3.** An insulting or provoking gibe or sarcasm; a mocking or scornful reproach or challenge; a casting of something in any one's teeth 1529. †**b.** *transf.* An object of scornful gibes (*biblical*) –1611.

3. Haue I liu'd to stand at the t. of one that makes Fritters of English? SHAKS. With ireful taunts each other they oppose POPE. **b.** *Jer.* 24:9.

Taunt (tǭnt), *a.* 1579. [prob. aphetic f. ATAUNT (naut.) with all sails set – (O)Fr. *autant* as much; but the development is obscure.] *Naut.* Of masts: Excessively tall or lofty.

Taunt (tǭnt), *v.* 1513. [f. TAUNT *sb.*] †**1.** *intr.* To make an effective rejoinder; to exchange banter –1548. †**2.** *trans.* To 'chaff', banter –1596. **3.** To reproach (a person) *with* something in a sarcastic, scornful, or insulting way 1560. **b.** *intr.* To utter taunts or stinging reproaches 1560. **4.** *trans.* To drive or get by taunting; to provoke 1813.

3. They taunted him with cowardice FROUDE. **4.** Proscribed at home, And taunted to a wish to roam BYRON. Hence **Tau·nter.**

Tau·nting, *ppl. a.* 1548. [f. prec. + -ING[2].] That taunts or reproaches provokingly.

They accompanied their notice . with every kind of insolent and t. reflection BURKE. Hence **Tau·ntingly** *adv.*

Tauric (tǭ·rik), *a.* 1816. [f. Gr. ταῦρος or L. *taurus* bull + -IC.] Taurine.

Taurid (tǭ·rid). 1888. [f. TAURUS, after LEONID, PERSEID.] *Astron.* In *pl.* A system of meteors which appear to radiate from a point in the constellation Taurus about the 20th of November.

Tauriform (tǭ·rifǭɹm), *a.* 1721. [– L. *tauriformis*, f. *taurus* bull; see -FORM.] Having the form of a bull.

Taurine (tǭ·rəin), *sb.* 1842. [f. TAURO- in TAUROCHOLIC + -INE[5].] *Chem.* A neutral crystallizable substance, $C_2H_7NSO_3$, amido-ethyl-sulphonic acid, obtained in 1826 by L. Gmelin from ox-bile, and contained in the bile of most other animals, resulting from the transformation of taurocholic acid under the influence of acids and alkalis.

Taurine (tǭ·rəin), *a.* 1613. [– L. *taurinus*, f. *taurus* bull; see -INE[1].] Of, pertaining to, of the nature of, or resembling a bull.

Tauro-, repr. Gr. ταυρο-, comb. form of ταῦρος (= L. *taurus*) bull, occurring in a few words derived from Greek, and modern chemical terms.

Tauro·boly [L. *taurobolium*, f. Gr. ταυροβόλος] the sacrifice of bulls. **Tauro·cho·lic** *a.*, *Chem.* in *t. acid*, an acid ($C_{26}H_{45}NSO_7$) found in the bile of the ox and of most animals, mostly together with glycocholic acid. **Tau·rocol(l** [Gr. ταυρόκολλα], glue made from bulls' hides (*rare*). **Tauro·machy** [Gr. ταυρομαχία], the practice or custom of bull-fighting; with *a* and *pl.*, a bull-fight; so **Tauroma·chian**, *a.* of or pertaining to tauromachy.

‖**Taurus** (tǭ·rŏs). late ME. [L.] *Astron.* **a.** The second of the zodiacal constellations, the Bull, in which are included the groups of the Pleiades and Hyades. **b.** Also, the second of the divisions or signs of the Zodiac, into which the sun enters on or near the 21st of April: orig. identical with the constellation. Symbol ♉.

Taurylic (tǭri·lik), *a.* 1868. [f. L. *taurus* bull + -YL + -IC.] *Chem.* In *t. acid*, a colourless oil (C_7H_8O) obtained together with phenol from human urine and that of cows and horses.

Taut, taught (tǭt), *a.* ME. [*Taut* for earlier *taught*, alt. (cf. *daughter*) of *tought*, ME. *touht*, *toȝt*, prob. identical with the common var. *tought* of TOUGH, with the sense influenced by assoc. with *toȝ-*, pa. ppl. stem of TEE *v.*[1]] †**1.** Tense, as a surface; tight, distended –1612. **2.** Tightly drawn, as by longitudinal tension; stiff, tense, not slack 1604. **b.** Tightly or trimly done up; put into good order. Of a person: Neat in appearance. 1870. **c.** *fig.* Of a person: Strict or severe as to duty 1833.

2. The hawser was as t. as a bowstring STEVENSON. **b.** A fair wind, and the ship t. and trim 1887. Hence **Tau·tly** *adv.* **Tau·tness.**

Tautegorical (tǭtigǫ·rikăl), *a.* *nonce-wd.* 1825. [f. TAUTO-, after ALLEGORICAL.] Expressing the same subject but with a difference; opp. to *metaphorical*, etc. COLERIDGE.

Tauten (tǭ·t'n), *v.* 1814. [f. TAUT *a.* + -EN[5].] *trans.* and *intr.* To make, or become, taut.

Tauto- (tǭto), bef. a vowel properly **taut-**, repr. Gr. ταὐτο-, comb. form of ταὐτό, contr. of τὸ αὐτό the same; occurring in TAUTOLOGY, TAUTOMERISM, and their derivs.; also in various rare technical words.

Tauto,ou·sian, -ious *adjs.* [f. eccl. Gr. ταὐτοούσιος, f. οὐσία essence], *Theol.* having absolutely the same essence. **Tauto·phony** [med. Gr. ταὐτοφωνία, f. φωνή voice], repetition of the same (vocal) sound; so **Tautopho·nic, -al** *adjs.* repeating the same sound. **Tautozo·nal** *a.*, *Cryst.* belonging to or situated in the same zone.

Tautochrone (tǭ·tŏkroᵘn). 1774. [f. TAUTO- + Gr. χρόνος time. Cf. Fr. *tautochrone* (Dict. Trévoux, 1771).] *Math.* That curve upon which a particle moving under the action of gravity (or any given force) will reach the lowest (or some fixed) point in the same time, from whatever point it starts. So **Tauto·chronous** *a.* having the character of a t.; occupying the same time; isochronous.

Tautog (tǭtǫ·g). Also **tautaug.** 1643. [– Narragansett *taut-auog*, pl. of *taut*, name of the fish.] A labroid fish, *Tautoga americana* (*T. onitis*), also called *black-fish* or *oyster-fish*, abundant on the Atlantic coast of N. America, and esteemed for food.

Tautologic (tǭtolǫ·dʒik), *a.* *rare.* 1818. [var. of next; see -IC, -ICAL.] = next 1.

Tautological (tǭtolǫ·dʒikăl), *a.* 1620. [f. TAUTOLOGY, after similar pairs; see -LOGY (ad fin.), -ICAL.] **1.** Pertaining to, characterized by, involving, or using tautology; repeating the same word, or the same notion in different words. **2.** Of an echo: Repeating a sound several times. Now *rare* or *Obs.* 1677. Hence **Tautolo·gically** *adv.*

Tautologize (tǭtǫ·lŏdʒəiz), *v.* 1607. [f. TAUTOLOGY + -IZE, after *apology/apologize*.] *intr.* To repeat the same thing in the same or different words; to use tautology. Hence **Tauto·logism,** the use or practice of tautology; an instance of this. **Tauto·logist,** one who practises tautology.

Tautologous (tǭtǫ·lŏgəs). *a.* 1714. [f. next + -OUS, after *analogy/analogous*.] = TAUTOLOGICAL 1.

Tautology (tǭtǫ·lŏdʒi). 1579. [– late L. *tautologia* – Gr. ταὐτολογία, f. ταὐτολόγος repeating what has been said; see TAUTO-, -LOGY.] **a.** A repetition of the same statement. **b.** The repetition (esp. in the immediate context) of the same word or phrase, or of the same idea or statement in other words: usu. as a fault of style. With *a* and *pl.*, an instance of this. **c.** Applied to the repetition of a statement as its own reason, or to the identification of cause and effect 1659. **d.** *transf.* A mere repetition of acts, incidents, or experiences 1650.

b. That villanous t. of lawyers, which is the scandal of our nation WESLEY. **d.** Our whole Life is but a nauseous T. 1687.

Tautomerism (tǭtǫ·mĕriz'm). 1885. [f. TAUTO- + Gr. μέρος part, after ISOMERISM.] *Chem.* The property exhibited by certain organic compounds of behaving in different reactions as if they possessed two (or more) different constitutions, that is, as if the atoms of the same compound or group were arranged in two (or more) different ways, expressible by different structural formulæ (e.g. the group —CH:C(OH)—, or —CH_2.CO—, in ethyl aceto-acetate). So **Tau·tomer,** any one of the forms of a tautomeric compound in relation to another. **Tautomeric** (tǭtome·rik) *a.* pertaining to or exhibiting t.

Tavern (tæ·vəɹn). ME. [– (O)Fr. *taverne* :– L. *taberna* hut, booth, etc., also a tavern or inn.] **1.** In early use, a public house or tap-room where wine was retailed; a dram-shop; now = PUBLIC HOUSE 2 b. †**2.** A shop or workshop attached to, or (often) under, a dwelling-house. *dial.* –1703.

Taverner (tæ·vəɹnəɹ). ME. [– AFr. *taverner* = OFr. *tavernier*, f. *taverne*; see prec., -ER[2] 2.] **1.** A tavern-keeper. *arch.* †**2.** One who frequents taverns; a tippler –1612.

†**Taw,** *sb.*[1] *rare.* 1562. [f. TAW *v.*] **1.** Tawed leather; white leather. **2.** A thong, whip. [app. the sing. of TAWS, TAWSE.] –1853.

Taw (tǭ), *sb.*[2] 1709. [Of unkn. origin.] A large fancy marble, often streaked or variegated, being that with which the player shoots. **b.** *transf.*, often *pl.* A game played with such marbles 1709. **c.** The line from which the players shoot in playing the game 1740.

Taw (tǭ), *v.* [OE. *tawian*, rel. to OS. *tōgean*, MLG., MDu. *touwen*, OHG. *zouwen*, Goth. *taujan* :– Gmc. **tawōjan*, **tawjan* do, make, prepare.] **1.** *trans.* To prepare or dress (some raw material) for use, or for further manipulation; e.g. to soften (hides) by beating, to heckle (hemp), etc. **2.** *spec.* To make (skins) into leather by steeping them in a solution of alum and salt; the product is white and pliant, and is known as *alum*, *white*, or *Hungarian leather* ME. †**3.** *fig.* To treat (a person) abusively or with contumely –1549. **b.** To flog. *Obs.* exc. *dial.* 1600.

Tawdry (tǭ·dri), *sb.* and *a.* 1612. [As sb., short for TAWDRY LACE; hence referring to the showy but cheap quality of these in XVII.] **A.** *sb.* †**1.** Short for next. DRAYTON. **2.** Cheap and pretentious finery 1680.

1. Of which the Naïdes, and the blew Nereïdes make Them Taudries for their necks DRAYTON. **2.** A poor bedizened creature, clad in t. 1867.

B. *adj.* **1.** Of the nature of cheap finery; showy or gaudy without real value 1676. **2.** *transf.* Of persons or their condition:

Tawdrily dressed or decked out; cheaply adorned 1676. **3.** *fig.* esp. of style, diction, etc.; hence of a speaker or writer: Pretentiously fine 1696.

1. The high altar is wretchedly t. 1859. **2.** Taudry affected Rogues, well drest WYCHERLEY. **3.** 'Tis but Taudry Talk, and next to very Trash PENN.

†**Tawdry lace.** 1548. [f. *t* (final letter of *Saint*) + *Audrey*. For the metathesis of *t* cf. *Tooley* (Street) from *St. Olave's*.] orig. *St. Audrey's lace*, i.e. lace of St. Audrey or Etheldrida (patron saint of Ely): A silk 'lace' or necktie, much worn by women in the 16th and early 17th c.; sometimes taken as a type of female adornments –1750.

Taudrey Lace, so called from St. Audrey..who thought her self punished for wearing rich Necklaces of Jewels; and therefore women after that wore Necklaces of fine silk, called Taudrey laces BLOUNT.

Tawer (tǭ·əɹ). late ME. [f. TAW *v.* + -ER[1].] One who taws or who prepares white leather.

Tawery (tǭ·əri). *rare.* 1830. [f. prec. or TAW *v.*; see -Y[3], -ERY.] An establishment where skins are tawed.

Tawny (tǭ·ni), *a.* and *sb.* [In XIV *tauny, tawne* – AFr. *tauné*, OFr. *tané* dark like tan, f. TAN *sb.* Cf. TENNÉ, TENNY.] Name of a colour consisting of brown with a preponderance of yellow or orange; but formerly applied also to other shades of brown. **A.** as *adj.* Having, or being of, this colour.

A lion's t. skin COWPER. A light and t. wine DICKENS.

B. as *sb.* **1.** Tawny colour. In *Her.* = TENNÉ. late ME. †**2.** Cloth of a tawny colour –1587. **3.** = TAWNY-MOOR. *arch.* 1660. Hence **Taw·niness**, t. quality or condition.

†**Taw·ny-moor.** 1603. [f. prec. + MOOR *sb.*[2] Cf. BLACKAMOOR.] A name given to the tawny or brown-skinned natives of foreign lands; prob. orig. to natives of northern Africa –1849.

Taws, tawse (tǭz), *sb.* Chiefly *Sc.* 1585. [pl. of TAW *sb.*[1] (but evidenced much earlier); occas. treated as a sing.] An instrument of family or school discipline, used in Scotch and some English schools, consisting of a leathern strap or thong, divided at the end into narrow strips.

A pedagogue called Fate; ..his fees are very high, and his tawse are rather heavy CARLYLE. Hence **Tawse** *v. trans.* to chastise with the t.

Tax (tæks), *sb.* ME. [f. next. In ME. *taxe* and *taske* TASK *sb.* were at first almost synonymous. Cf. Fr. *taxe* (XV), med.L. *taxa*.] **1.** A compulsory contribution to the support of government, levied on persons, property, income, commodities, transactions, etc., now at fixed rates, mostly proportional to the amount on which the contribution is levied. (In British practice few of the individual imposts are called by the name, the most notable being the INCOME TAX, LAND TAX, and PROPERTY TAX, also *dog-t.*, *match-t.*, *window-t.* In U.S. 'tax' is more generally applied to every federal, state, or local exaction of this kind). **2.** *fig.* Something compared to a tax in its incidence, obligation, or burdensomeness; an oppressive or burdensome charge, obligation, or duty; a burden, strain, heavy demand 1628. †**3.** = TASK *sb.* I. 2, 2 b. (*rare*) –1564. †**4.** A charge, accusation; censure –1642.

1. A tax on German linen encourages home manufactures HUME. A t...is said to be *direct* when it is immediately taken from income or capital; and *indirect* when it is taken from them by making their owners pay for liberty to use certain articles, or to exercise certain privileges 1840. **2.** The greatness of the question..justifies even a heavier t. on the reader's attention 1862. *Comb.*, as *t.-collector*.

Tax (tæks), *v.* ME. [– (O)Fr. *taxer* – L. *taxare* (perh. f. Gr. τάσσειν order, fix) censure, charge; rate, value, etc.; in med.L. also impose a tax.] **I. 1.** To determine the amount of (a tallage, fine, penalty, damages, etc.); to assess; rarely, to impose, levy (a tax); also, to settle the price or value of. *Obs.* exc. in *Law*, to assess (costs). †**2.** To impose, ordain, prescribe (a thing) *to* a person; also, to order (a person) *to* or *to do* something –1814. **3.** To impose a tax upon; to subject to taxation ME. **4.** *fig.* To burden; to make serious demands upon; to put a strain on 1672.

1. The costs to be taxed to the vttermost charge approved due 1592. **3.** The King cannot t. any by way of Loans SIR E. COKE. The right of the people to be taxed entirely by their representatives 1857. **4.** My ingenuity was often taxed for expedients KANE.

II. 1. To censure; to reprove, blame (a person, his action, etc.); to accuse, charge; to take to task, call to account; freq. const. *with*. 1569. †**2.** To call in question; to challenge, dispute (a statement, etc.) –1777.

1. None shall t. me with base Perjury DRYDEN. **2.** Prone to taxe Gods wisedom, and call him to our barre 1642.

†**III.** Used in translations of the Bible as tr. Gr. ἀπογράφειν, to enter in a list, enrol –1611.

Taxable (tæ·ksăb'l), *a.* (*sb.*) 1474. [– AFr., OFr. *taxable* (AL. *taxabilis*), f. *taxer*; see prec., -ABLE. Later directly f. TAX *v.*] **A.** *adj.* †**1.** Liable to be assessed (*to* a tax, etc.); assessable –1569. **2.** Liable to be taxed; subject to a tax or duty 1583. †**3.** Liable to a charge or accusation; chargeable (*with* some fault); censurable, blamable –1792. **4.** *Law.* Of legal costs or fees: Liable to be taxed or reduced by the taxing-master 1828. **B.** *sb.* One who or that which is subject to a taxation; *esp.* in *pl.* persons or things liable to a tax. orig. *U.S.* 1662.

2. To learn..the t. capacities of their farms COBBETT. Hence **Taxabi·lity, Ta·xableness**, t. quality or condition; liability to taxation. **Ta·xably** *adv.*

Taxaceous (tæksēⁱ·ʃəs), *a.* 1846. [f. mod. L. *Taxaceæ* (f. L. *taxus* yew) + -OUS; see -ACEOUS.] *Bot.* Belonging to the family *Taxaceæ*, including the yew.

Taxaspidean (tæksăspi·diăn), *a.* 1899. [f. mod.L. *Taxaspidea* (f. Gr. τάξις arrangement + ἀσπίς shield) + -AN; see -EAN.] *Ornith.* Belonging to the division *Taxaspidea* of passerine birds, having the metatarsus regularly scutellated behind.

Taxation (tæksēⁱ·ʃən). ME. [– AFr. *taxacioun*, (O)Fr. *taxation* – L. *taxatio* rating, (later) blame, in med.L. assessing for taxation, f. *taxare* TAX *v.*; see -ATION.] **1.** The fixing of the sum of an impost, damages, price, etc.; assessment, valuation. *Obs.* exc. *Hist.* **b.** *T. of costs*, the allowing or disallowing, by certain officials of courts of law, of the charges made by solicitors or other persons (e.g. arbitrators) subject to the jurisdiction of the court 1552. **2.** The imposition or levying of taxes (formerly including local rates); the action of taxing or the fact of being taxed; also *transf.* the revenue raised by taxes. With *a* and *pl.*, an instance of this. 1447. †**3.** Accusation; censure, reproof, blame –1653.

Taxative (tæ·ksătiv), *a.* *rare.* 1862. [f. TAX *v.* + -ATIVE.] Having the function of taxing; of or pertaining to taxation.

Taxator (tæksēⁱ·tǭɹ). *Hist.* late ME. [– med. and mod.L. *taxator*, f. med.L. *taxare* assess; see TAX *v.*, -ATOR.] = TAXER.

†**Ta·x-cart.** orig. **taxed cart.** 1795. [f. TAX *sb.* or *taxed* pa. pple. of TAX *v.* + CART *sb.*] A two-wheeled (orig. springless) open cart drawn by one horse, and used mainly for agricultural or trade purposes, on which was charged only a reduced duty (afterwards taken off entirely) –1884.

Taxeopodous (tæksiˌǫ·pŏdəs), *a.* 1887. [irreg. f. Gr. τάξις arrangement + -ποδος footed (f. πούς foot) + -OUS.] *Zool.* Having each one of the carpal or tarsal bones of one row articulated with one of the other row; opp. to *diplarthrous*. So **Ta·xeopod** *a.* = *taxeopodous*; *sb.* a member of the division *Taxeopoda* of ungulate mammals, having this arrangement of the tarsal bones.

Taxer, taxor (tæ·ksəɹ, -ǭɹ). late ME. [– AFr., f. *taxer* TAX *v.*; see -ER[2] 3.] †**1.** An assessor –1695. **b.** *spec.* In the ancient universities, an officer (one of two) who fixed the rents of students' lodgings. At Cambridge, they also regulated the prices of commodities, kept the standard of weights and measures, and punished those who offended in these matters. Now *Hist.* 1532. **2.** One who levies a tax or taxes 1603.

Ta·x-ga:therer. *arch.* 1693. A collector of taxes.

Taxi (tæ·ksi), *sb.* 1907. Colloq. abbrev. of TAXIMETER; also of TAXI-CAB, -PLANE.

Comb. **t.-dance** *U.S.*, a dance at which a partner may be hired: so **t.-dancer.**

Taxi (tæ·ksi), *v.* 1914. [f. prec.] **1.** To travel by taxi-cab 1915. **2.** Of an aeroplane: To run along the ground before taking off or after alighting 1914.

Taxiarch (tæ·ksiˌaɹk). 1808. [– Gr. ταξίαρχος, f. τάξις TAXIS; see -ARCH.] *Anc. Gr. Hist.* The commander of a taxis.

Taxi-cab, taxicab (tæ·ksiˌkæb). 1907. [Short for TAXIMETER *cab*, and itself shortened to TAXI.] A cab for public-hire, fitted with a taximeter; *esp.* a motor-cab so furnished.

Taxicorn (tæ·ksikǭɹn), *a.* and *sb.* 1842. [– mod.L. *Taxicornes* pl. (Latreille, 1817), f. Gr. τάξις (see TAXIS) + L. *cornu* horn.] *Ent.* **A.** *adj.* Having perfoliate antennæ, as the beetles of the obsolete family *Taxicornes*. **B.** *sb.* A beetle of this family.

Taxidermal (tæksidə̄·ɹmăl), *a.* 1877. [f. TAXIDERMY + -AL[1] 1.] Of or pertaining to taxidermy. So **Taxide·rmic** *a.* 1847.

Taxidermy (tæ·ksidə̄ːɹmi). 1820. [f. Gr. τάξις (see TAXIS) + δέρμα skin; see -Y[3].] The art of preparing and preserving the skins of animals, and stuffing and mounting them so as to present the appearance, attitude, etc., of the living animal. Hence **Taxide·rmist**, one skilled in t.

Taximeter (tæksi·mǐtəɹ). 1898. [– Fr. *taximètre*, f. *taxe* tariff (see TAX) + *-mètre* -METER; slightly earlier *taxameter*, after G. (which earlier still, *c*1875, had *taxanom*), with assim. to Gr. τάξις TAXIS.] An automatic contrivance fitted on a cab, etc., to indicate to the passenger at any point the distance traversed and the fare due.

attrib., as *t.-cab*, *-driver*.

Taxin (tæ·ksin). 1907. [f. L. *taxus* yew + -IN[1].] *Chem.* 'A resinous substance obtained from the leaves of the yew-tree' (Watts). So **Ta·xine** (-əin), a poisonous alkaloid found in these leaves 1899.

Ta·xing, *vbl. sb.* late ME. [f. TAX *v.* + -ING[1].] The action of the vb. TAX.

Comb.: **t.-master**, an officer in a court of law who examines and allows or disallows items in a solicitor's bill of costs when disputed.

Taxinomy (tæksi·nŏmi). 1865. A more etymological form of TAXONOMY.

Ta·xiplane. 1920. [f. TAXI *sb.* + PLANE *sb.*[3]] A light aeroplane for public hire.

‖**Taxis** (tæ·ksis). 1758. [– Gr. τάξις arrangement, f. τάσσειν arrange.] **1.** *Surg.* A manipulative operation employed for replacing displaced parts, reducing hernia, etc. **2.** *Anc. Gr. Hist.* A company of soldiers, esp. foot-soldiers, variously answering in size to a modern company, battalion, regiment, or brigade 1850. **3.** *Biol.* The reaction of a free organism to external stimulus by movement in a particular direction 1904.

Taxless (tæ·ksles), *a.* 1615. [f. TAX *sb.* + -LESS.] Free from taxes or taxation; untaxed.

Taxonomy (tæksǫ·nŏmi). 1828. [– Fr. *taxonomie* (De Candolle, 1813), irreg. f. Gr. τάξις; see TAXIS, -NOMY.] Classification, esp. in relation to its general laws or principles; that department of science, or of a particular science or subject, which consists in or relates to classification. So **Taxo·nomer**, a scientific classifier. **Taxono·mic, -al** *adjs.* classificatory. **Taxo·nomist** = *taxonomer*.

Ta·x(-)pay:er. 1816. One who pays a tax or the taxes generally; one who is liable to taxation; in U.S. including local rate-payers.

‖**Tayassu, tayaçu** (tāˌyăsū·). 1698. [Tupi *tayaçu* = tania-eater, f. *taña, taja* TANIA + *çu* eat.] The Common or Collared Peccary, *Dicotyles torquatus* (*D. tajacu*).

‖**Tayra** (tai·ră). 1854. [Tupi *taira*.] Native name in Brazil of a mammal of the weasel family, *Galera barbara*.

‖**Tazza** (ta·ttsa). *Pl.* **tazze** (ta·ttse). 1828. [It. – Arab.; see TASS[2].] A shallow ornamental bowl or vase; prop., one supported on a foot.

T.B., colloq. abbrev. of TUBERCLE *bacillus*, pop. of TUBERCULOSIS.

Tcheka, cheka (tʃē·kă). 1921. [– Russ. *cheká*, f. names (*che, ka*) of initial letters of *Chrezvy̆chaĭnaya komissiya* Extraordinary Commission.] An organization set up in 1917 under the Soviet régime in Russia for the secret investigation of counter-revolutionary activities, superseded in 1922 by the OGPU.

Tchetvert (tʃe·tvəɹt). 1544. [– Russ. *chétvert'* quarter.] A Russian measure of capacity for grain.

Tchick (tʃik), *sb.* 1823. A representation of the click made by pressing some part of the tongue against the palate and withdrawing it with suction; prop. the unilateral palatal click used to urge on a horse, etc. So **Tchick** *v.*

Tea (tī), *sb.* 1655. [Early forms also *tay*, *tey*, repr. the pronunc. (tē, tēⁱ), still in dial. use, prob. immed. – Du. *tee* – Chinese (Amoy) *t'e*, in Mandarin dial. *ch'a*, whence earlier CHA, *chaa*, *chia* (XVI). Cf. Fr. *thé*, Sp. *te*, It. *tè*, G. †*thee*, *tee*.] **1.** The leaves of the tea-plant (see 3), usu. in a dried and prepared state for making the drink (see 2); first imported into Europe in the 17th c. **b.** With qualifying words, denoting various kinds 1704. **2.** A drink made by infusing these leaves in boiling water, having a somewhat bitter and aromatic flavour, and acting as a moderate stimulant; largely used as a beverage 1658. **3.** The plant from which tea is obtained, a shrub of the genus *Thea* (now often included in *Camellia*), family *Ternstrœmiaceæ*, with white flowers, and oval pointed slightly-toothed evergreen leaves; grown in China, Japan, India, and adjacent countries. (Now chiefly in comb., as *t.-leaf*, *-plant*.). 1663. **4.** A meal or social entertainment at which tea is served; *esp.* an ordinary afternoon or evening meal, at which the usual beverage is tea 1738. **5.** Used as a general name for infusions made in the same way as tea; mostly used medicinally; e.g. *camomile t.*, *senna t.* 1665. **6.** With defining words, applied to various plants whose leaves, flowers, etc. are used in the same way as tea (also to the leaves, etc. themselves, or the drink, infused from them) 1727.

1. A small parcel of most excellent t... to be sold, ..the lowest price is 30s. a pound 1680. **b. Black t.** is exposed to the air for some time, so as to produce fermentation, before roasting. **Green t.** is roasted almost immediately after gathering, and often artificially coloured. **2.** I did send for a cup of tee (a China drink) of which I never had drunk before PEPYS. Here, thou, great Anna! whom three realms obey, Dost sometimes counsel take—and sometimes Tea POPE. **4.** The now universally-honoured institution of 'five o'clock tea' 1882. *High t.*, *meat t.*: see HIGH *a.*, MEAT *sb.* **5.** Valerian, or rosemary, t. 1783. Poppy t. 1893. **6. Arabian t.**, *Catha edulis*, whose leaves furnish a stimulating beverage used in Arabia. **Australian t.**, **Botany Bay t.**, an Australian species of sarsaparilla, *Smilax glycyphylla*, also called *sweet tea*. **Brazil** or **Brazilian t.**, *Stachytarpha jamaicensis*. **Labrador t.**, *Ledum latifolium* and *L. palustre*. **New Jersey t.**, *Ceanothus americanus*. **New Zealand t.**, *Leptospermum scoparium*. **Oswego t.**, a N. Amer. aromatic labiate, *Monarda didyma*, used as a tonic and stomachic. **Paraguay t.**, *Ilex paraguayensis*, used in S. America as a substitute for t. **Sweet t.** = *Botany Bay t.*

attrib. and *Comb.*: *t.-drinker*, *-duty*, *-planter*, *-shop*; **t.-basket**, a basket containing the requisites for afternoon t.; **-berry**, the Amer. wintergreen *Gaultheria procumbens*, also called *Canada t.* or *mountain t.*; also, the fruit of this; **-board** (now *local*), a t.-tray, esp. a wooden one; **-bug**, a destructive insect which infests tea-plants; **-caddy**, a small box, formerly with divisions, for holding t.; **-cake**, a light kind of flat cake to be eaten at t.; **-canister** = *t.-caddy*; **-clam**, *U.S.* a very small clam; **-clipper**, a clipper or fast-sailing vessel formerly employed in the t.-trade; **-cloth**, a cloth used for wiping the utensils used for a meal after washing them; (*b*) *afternoon t.*, a small table-cloth used at afternoon t.; **-cosy**, a covering for a t.-pot to keep it hot; **-fight**, *colloq.* or *slang*, joc. name for a t.-party or t.-meeting; **-gown**, a special fashion of garment worn by girls and women at t.; **-house**, a refreshment-house where t. is served (esp. in China or Japan); **-kettle**, a kettle in which water may be boiled for making t.; **-meeting**, a public social meeting (usu. in connection with a religious organization) at which t. is taken; **-room**, a room in which t. is served in a refreshment-house, etc.; notably, that of the British House of Commons, the scene of numerous informal meetings of members; **-scented** *a.*, having a scent like that of t. (applied to a variety of rose); **-service**, **-set**, a set of articles used in serving t. at table, comprising t.-pot, milk-jug, sugar-basin, cups and saucers, etc.; **-things** *sb. pl.* articles used in serving t.; **-time**, the time at which the meal called t. is usu. taken; **-urn**, an urn with a tap, placed upon a t.-table, to hold hot water for making t.

Tea, *v. colloq.* 1812. [f. prec.] **1.** *trans.* To supply or regale with tea; to give a tea to. **2.** *intr.* To drink tea; *esp.* to have one's tea 1823.

Teach (tītʃ), *v.* Pa. t. and pa. pple. **taught** (tǫt). [OE. *tǣćan* (pa. t. *tǣhte*, Northumb. *tāhte*) :- **taikjan* (see TOKEN), f. Gmc. **teik-* **taik-* **tik-* show :- IE. **deig-* **dig-*, also **deik-*, repr. in Gr. δεικνύναι show, δεῖγμα sample.] **I.** †**1.** *trans.* To show –1567. **2.** *Shipbuilding.* (*absol.*) Of a line: To point in a particular direction 1850. **II.** To show by way of information or instruction. **1.** *To t. a thing*: to impart or convey the knowledge of; to give instruction or lessons in (a subject); †to make known (a message) OE. **2.** *To t. a person a thing, a thing to a person* (or *agent*): to communicate something to a person, by way of instruction; †to inform OE. **b.** To show or make known to a person (how to do something) OE. **c.** Used by way of threat: To let a person know the cost or penalty of something 1575. **3.** *To t. a person* or *agent* (with personal object only): to impart knowledge to, give instruction to; to inform, instruct, educate, train, school. OE. *To t.* (*a*) *school* (now *dial.* and *U.S.*): to teach in a school 1590. **4.** *absol.* or *intr.* To communicate knowledge; to act as a teacher OE.

1. He cam first hom..and þer taute he gramer 1451. **2.** Thynges that I shal teche the LYDG. I am being taught French 1825. **b.** Education.. means teaching children to be clean, active, honest, and useful RUSKIN. **c.** I'll t. you to be too clever, my lad 1889. **3.** All Nations they shall t. MILT. †*To t. to*: to train to. **4.** One that teacheth by publique Authority HOBBES.

Teachable (tī·tʃăb'l), *a.* 1483. [f. TEACH *v.* + -ABLE.] †**1.** Able to teach –1695. **2.** Capable of being taught (as a person); docile 1483. **3.** Capable of being taught (as a subject); that may be communicated or imparted by instruction 1669.

2. These old Greeks were t., and learnt from all the nations round KINGSLEY. **3.** To teach you.. everything that is t. RUSKIN. Hence **Teachabi·lity**, **Tea·chableness**, docility; †instructiveness; the quality of being communicable by instruction. **Tea·chably** *adv.*

Teacher (tī·tʃəɹ). ME. [f. as prec. + -ER¹.] One who or that which teaches or instructs; *spec.* one whose function is to give instruction, esp. in a school.

A t. of anatomy 1799. His daily teachers had been woods and rills,..The sleep that is among the lonely hills WORDSW. Hence **Tea·chership**, the office, function, or position of a t.

Tea·-chest. 1740. [f. TEA *sb.* + CHEST *sb.*¹] †**1.** = *tea-caddy* –1850. **2.** A large box or chest of cubical form, lined with sheet-lead, in which tea is packed for transport 1801.

Tea·ching, *vbl. sb.* ME. [f. TEACH *v.* + -ING¹.] The imparting of instruction; the occupation or function of a teacher. **b.** That which is taught; a thing taught, doctrine, instruction, precept ME.

Tea·-cup. 1700. A cup from which tea is drunk; usu. of small or moderate size, with a handle.

Phr. *A storm in a tea-cup*, a great commotion in a circumscribed circle, or about a small matter. Hence **Tea·cupful**, as much as a tea-cup will hold, a gill.

Tea·-ga:rden. 1802. **1.** An open-air enclosure, connected with a house of entertainment, where tea and other refreshments are served. **2.** A plantation in which tea-plants are grown 1882.

Teague (tēg, tīg). *colloq. Obs.* or *arch.* 1661. [Anglicized spelling of the Irish name *Tadhg*, variously pronounced (tēg, tīg, taig).] A nickname for an Irishman.

Teak (tīk). 1698. [– Pg. *teca* – Malayalam *tēkka*.] **1.** A large E. Indian tree *Tectona grandis* (family *Verbenaceæ*), with opposite egg-shaped leaves and panicles of white flowers; more usu., its timber, a dark, heavy, oily wood of great strength and durability, used largely in the construction of ships and railway carriages, and for other purposes; distinctively called *Indian t.* **2.** Applied, usu. with defining word, to other trees which produce strong or durable timber, or otherwise resemble the Indian t. 1842.

2. African T., *Oldfieldia africana* (family *Euphorbiaceæ*), or its wood, which is too heavy to be exclusively used in shipbuilding; **T. of New Zealand**, *Vitex littoralis*.

Teal (tīl). [rel. to MLG. *telink*, MDu. *tēling*, *teiling* (Du. *teling*); ult. origin unkn.] **1.** A small freshwater fowl, *Querquedula* or *Anas crecca*, or other species of the genus, the smallest of the ducks, widely distributed in Europe, Asia, and America; also locally applied to other genera of the *Anatidæ*. Also as collect. pl. **b.** The flesh of this bird as food 1475. **2.** With distinctive prefixes, applied to various species of *Querquedula* and allied genera 1678.

2. American or **Green-winged T.**, *Q. carolinensis*; **Blue-winged T.** of N. and S. America, *Q. discors* or *cyanoptera*; **Garganey T.**, the GARGANEY, *Q. circia*; **Chinese T.**, the mandarin duck, *Aix galericulata*. Hence **Tea·lery**, a place where teal are kept and fattened.

Tea·-leaf. 1756. The leaf of the tea-plant; *esp.* in *pl.* the leaves after being infused to make the beverage.

Team (tīm), *sb.* [OE. *tēam* = OFris. *tām* bridle, progeny, OS. *tōm*, OHG. *zoum* (G. *zaum*), ON. *taumr* bridle, rein :- Gmc. **taumaz*, prob. for **tauȝmaz*, f. **tauȝ-* draw, rel. to L. *ducere*. Cf. TEE *v.*¹, TEEM *v.*¹] **I.** †**a.** Child-bearing –ME. **b.** A family or brood of young animals; now *dial.* applied to a litter of pigs, a brood of ducks OE.

b. We have a few teams of ducks, bred in the moors G. WHITE.

II. 1. A set of draught animals; two or more oxen, horses, dogs, etc. harnessed to draw together. (Pl., after a numeral, *team*.) OE. **2. a.** *fig.* Applied to persons drawing together 1614. **b.** *transf.* A number of persons associated in some joint action; now *esp.* a definite number of persons forming a side in a match, e.g., in a football match or a 'tug-of-war' 1529. **3.** Two or more beasts, or a single beast, along with the vehicle which they draw; a horse and cart, or waggon with two horses. Now *dial.* and *U.S.* **4.** A flock of wild ducks or other birds flying in a line or string 1688.

3. He was returning..with a loaded t. 1798. **b.** *fig.* (*U.S.*) Usu. *a whole* (or *full*) *t.* 1833. **4.** Like a long t. of snowy swans on high DRYDEN.

III. In Anglo-Saxon Law. **a.** In a suit for the recovery of goods alleged to have been stolen, the action or procedure by which the holder transferred or referred it back to a third person to defend the title to them; vouching to warranty. *Obs.* exc. *Hist.* **b.** The right or prerogative of jurisdiction in a suit of *tēam*, together with the fees and profits thence accruing; from the 11th c. usually included in charters granting land (in which it regularly followed *toll*, esp. in the formula *with sac and soc, toll and team, infangthief*, etc.).

Comb.: **t.-work**, (*a*) work done with a t. of beasts; (*b*) the combined action of a t. of players, etc.; (*c*) work done by a t. of operatives; (*d*) work done by persons working as a team, i.e. with concerted effort.

Team (tīm), *v.* 1552. [f. prec. II.] **1.** *trans.* To harness (beasts) in a team; to yoke. **2.** To transport by means of a team. **b.** *absol.* or *intr.* To drive a team. *U.S.* 1841. **c.** *fig.* (*U.S.*) *To t. up with*: to join forces with. **3.** *trans.* To get (work) done by a team or teams of workmen; to let (work) to a contractor who employs teams of workmen. *U.S.* 1877.

Teamster (tī·mstəɹ). 1779. [f. TEAM *sb.* + -STER.] The driver or owner of a team.

Tea·-pa:rty. 1778. A party assembled to take tea together; a social entertainment at which tea is taken.

Boston t.: the revolutionary proceeding (1773) when tea was thrown overboard in Boston harbour as a protest against British taxation; hence, a lively proceeding.

Tea·-plant. 1727. = TEA *sb.* 3, 6.

Tea·-pot. 1705. A pot with a lid, spout, and handle, to contain an infusion of tea.

‖**Teapoy** (tī·poi). *India.* Also **tepoy.** 1828. [f. Hindi *tīn*, in comb. *tir-* three + Pers. *pāī* foot.] A small three-legged table or stand, or any tripod; (by erron. association with *tea*), such a table with a receptacle for tea.

Tear (tīᵊɹ), *sb.*¹ [OE. *tēar* (contr. of **teaxor*), ONorth. *tehher*, *tæher* (in MSc. *techyr*) = OFris.

tār, OHG. *zah(h)ar* (G. *zähre*, orig. pl.), ON. *tár*, Goth. *tagr* :– IE. **dakru-*, repr. also by OL. *dacruma* (L. *lacruma*, *-ima*), Gr. δάκρυ.] **1.** A drop of the limpid fluid secreted by the lachrymal gland appearing in or flowing from the eye; chiefly as the result of emotion, esp. grief, but also of physical irritation or nervous stimulus: usu. in *pl.* **b.** As the visible feature of weeping: hence, put for this, or as the expression of grief or sorrow ME. **2.** *transf.* and *fig.* A drop of any liquid; *spec.* a drop or bead of liquid spontaneously exuding OE. **3.** *spec.* Applied to various gums that exude from plants in tear-shaped or globular beads, which then become solid or resinous OE. **4.** Anything resembling or suggesting a tear; e.g. (*a*) a defect in glass caused by a small particle of vitrified clay; (*b*) a detonating bulb, or Prince Rupert's drop 1832.

1. There are also tears of joy 1855. **b.** He must not flote upon his watry bear..Without the meed of som melodious t. MILT. He gave to Mis'ry all he had, a t. GRAY. *In tears*, weeping, in sorrow or commiseration. **2.** I would these dewy teares were from the ground SHAKS.

attrib. and *Comb.*, as *t.-drop*; **t.-bag**, (*a*) = *t.-pit*; (*b*) = *t.-gland*; **-bomb, -shell,** a bomb or shell charged with lachrymatory gas; **-gas,** lachrymatory gas; **-gland,** the lachrymal gland; **-mask,** a gas-mask; **-pit,** the lachrymal or sub-orbital sinus found in many species of deer, a fold or cavity beneath the inner corner of the eye, containing a thin waxy secretion.

Tear (tēᵊɹ), *sb.*² 1611. [f. TEAR *v.*] **1.** An act of tearing or rending; the action of tearing; hence, damage caused by tearing (or similar violent action): also used *fig.* in ref. to body or mind 1666. **2.** *concr.* A torn part or place; a rent or fissure 1611. **3. a.** A rushing gallop or pace 1838. **b.** A spree. *U.S. slang.* 1869. **c.** A rage or passion; a violent flurry 1880.

1. Phr. *t. and wear, wear and t.*, including damage due to common use and ordinary wear; *fig.* The t. and wear of the campaign is telling severely on the..Yeomanry 1901.

Tear (tēᵊɹ), *v.* Pa. t. **tore** (tōᵊɹ), *arch.* and *dial.* **tare** (tēᵊɹ). Pa. pple. **torn** (tǭɹn). [OE. *teran* = OS. *terian*, MLG., (M)Du. *teren*, OHG. *zeran* (G. *zehren*) destroy, consume, Goth. *dis|tairan*; the IE. base **der-* is repr. by Gr. δέρειν flay.] **I. 1.** *trans.* To pull asunder by force (a body or substance, now esp. one of thin and flexible consistence, as cloth or paper), usu. so as to leave ragged or irregular edges; to rend. **b.** *transf.* To make a (hole, etc.) by tearing 1593. **c.** To shatter, split, rive (a hard solid body). Now *dial.* 1582. †**d.** Phr. *To t. a (the) cat*: to rant and bluster. SHAKS. **2.** To wound or injure by rending; to lacerate OE. **3.** In various *fig.* applications; *esp.* in later use, to split into parties or factions OE. **b.** Used of the effect of sounds, esp. loud or 'piercing' noises, on the air, etc. 1592. **c.** To harrow, wound (the heart, soul, feelings, etc.) 1666. **4.** *To t. (out) the hair* in a frenzy of grief or anger: now a hyperbolical expression OE. **5.** To pull, wrench, or drag by main force from its attachment or fixed place ME. **b.** *fig.* To take or remove by force or violence; to force; *refl.* to force oneself away 1574. **6.** *intr.* To perform the act of tearing; to make a tear or rent 1526. **7.** *intr.* (for *refl.* and *pass.*) To become torn or rent; *dial.* to burst asunder, split, snap 1526.

1. He hath torne my gowne a foote and more 1530. The unpopular minister of finance was torn in pieces by the mob 1841. Phr. (vulgar slang), *That's torn it*, that has spoilt or ruined everything. **c.** Their Fregates..were torne in pieces and sunke 1582. **2.** Their defenceless Limbs the Brambles t. DRYDEN. **3. b.** What noise or shout was that? it tore the Skie MILT. That man torn by domestic affliction 1859. **5.** By tearing up the Trees by the Roots 1699. Ships from their Anchors torn ADDISON. **b.** At length he tore himself away 1797. **7.** The Boards will T. or Shake, which is in vulgar English, Split or Crack 1703.

II. 1. *intr.* †To rant and bluster as a roisterer; †to vociferate; to 'go on' violently, to rave, to rage (*dial.*) 1601. **2.** To move with violence or impetuosity; to rush or 'burst' impetuously or violently. *colloq.* 1599.

1. He goes through life, tearing, like a man possessed with a devil THACKERAY. **2.** This river tore down the narrow valley with headlong violence 1894.

Tear-, the stem of TEAR *v.* in comb., as in **tear-away** *adj.*, characterized by impetuous speed, tearing; *sb.*, one who or that which 'tears' or rushes away, or acts with great impetuosity; **tear-off** *adj.*, adapted to be torn off; *sb.*, a sheet or slip of paper so attached as to be easily torn off; **tear-thumb,** two species of *Polygonum*, the halberd-leaved tear-thumb, *P. arifolium*, and the arrow-leaved, *P. sagittatum*; so called from the hooded prickles on the petioles and angles of the stems.

Tear-bottle (tīᵊ·ɹ,bǫ:t'l). 1658. A bottle containing tears (cf. Ps. 56:8); *spec.* = LACHRYMATORY B. 1.

Tearer (tēᵊ·rəɹ). 1625. [f. TEAR *v.* + -ER¹.] **1.** One who or that which tears or rends. **2.** A person who tears or rushes along or about; a ranter, roisterer, swaggerer, bully 1625.

Tearful (tīᵊ·ɹfŭl), *a.* 1586. [f. TEAR *sb.*¹ + -FUL.] Full of tears; weeping; lachrymose. Sory and fearefull, yea penitent and tearefull 1597. Hence **Tea·rful-ly** *adv.*, **-ness.**

Tearless (tīᵊ·ɹlės), *a.* 1603. [f. TEAR *sb.*¹ + -LESS.] Void of tears; shedding no tears, not weeping. Hence **Tea·rless-ly** *adv.*, **-ness.**

Tea·-rose. 1850. A variety (or group of varieties) of cultivated rose, derived from the species *Rosa indica*, var. *odorata*, having flowers of a pale yellow colour, with a delicate scent supposed to resemble that of tea. (Orig. *tea-scented rose*.) **b.** The colour of this rose 1884.

Teary (tīᵊ·ri), *a.* late ME. [f. TEAR *sb.*¹ + -Y¹.] **1.** Full of or suffused with tears; tearful. Now *colloq.* **2.** Of the nature of or consisting of tears (*rare*). late ME.

Tease, *sb.* 1693. [f. next.] **1.** The action of teasing. **2.** A person addicted to teasing. *colloq.* 1852.

Tease (tīz), *v.* [OE. *tǣsan* = (M)LG., MDu. *tēzen* (Du. *teezen*), OHG. *zeisan* (G. dial. *zeisen*) :– WGmc. **taisjan* (**taisan*). Cf. TOZE, TOSE.] **1.** *trans.* To separate or pull asunder the fibres of; to comb or card (wool, flax, etc.) in preparation for spinning; to open *out* by pulling asunder; to shred. **b.** To comb the surface of cloth, after weaving, with teasels, which draw all the free hairs or fibres in one direction, so as to form a nap 1755. **2.** To worry or irritate by persistent action which vexes or annoys; now *esp.* in lighter sense, to disturb by persistent petty annoyance, out of mere mischief or sport; to bother or plague in a petty way. Also *absol.* and *intr.* 1627.

1. To ply The sampler, and to teize the huswifes wooll MILT. **2.** Harry ceased to t. and torment them with little tricks and devices of mischief 1881. *fig.* The earth..constantly teized more to furnish..luxuries..than..necessities GOLDSM.

Teasel, teazle (tī·z'l), *sb.* [OE. *tǣs(e)l* = OHG. *zeisala* (MHG. *zeisel*), f. base of **taisan* TEASE; see -EL¹, -LE.] **1.** A plant of the genus *Dipsacus*, comprising herbs with prickly leaves and flower-heads; *esp.* **Fullers' T.,** *D. fullonum*, the heads of which have hooked prickles between the flowers, and are used for teasing cloth (see 2); **Wild T.,** *D. sylvestris*, having straight instead of hooked prickles. **2.** The dried prickly flower-head or bur of the fullers' teasel (see 1), used for teasing or dressing cloth, so as to raise a nap on the surface. late ME. **3.** *transf.* A mechanical substitute for the natural teasel in cloth-working 1835.

Comb.: **t.-frame,** a frame in which t. heads are fixed for dressing cloth (so **t.-board, -cylinder, -rod**). Hence **Tea·sel, tea·zle** *v. trans.* to raise a smooth nap on (cloth) with or as with teasels.

Teaseler (tī·z'ləɹ). late ME. [f. prec. + -ER¹.] **1.** One whose occupation is to teasel cloth. **2.** An implement for teaseling 1607.

Teaser (tī·zəɹ). late ME. [f. TEASE *v.* + -ER¹.] One who or that which teases, in various senses. **b.** Local name of several birds which chase gulls and force them to disgorge their prey, as the skua 1833. **2.** Something that teases, or causes annoyance; something difficult to deal with, a 'poser'. *colloq.* 1759.

Tea·-spoon. 1686. A small spoon, usu. of silver or silvered metal, of a size suitable for stirring tea or other beverage in a cup. Hence **Tea·spoonful,** as much as a tea-spoon will hold; in medical prescriptions = 1 fluid-drachm.

Teat (tīt). [ME. *tete* – OFr. *tete* (later and mod. *tette*), prob. of Gmc. origin (see TIT *sb.*³, which it repl. in the standard language).] **1.** The small protuberance at the tip of each breast or udder in female mammalia (except monotremes), upon which the ducts of the mammary gland open, and from which the milk is sucked by the young; the nipple. Formerly also applied to the whole breast or udder. Now usu. only of quadrupeds. †**b.** *fig.* A source of nourishment or supply –1675. **2.** *transf.* A structure, natural or artificial, resembling a teat; a nipple 1587. Hence **Tea·ted** *a.* furnished with or having teats.

Tea·-ta:ble. 1688. [f. TEA *sb.* 4 + TABLE *sb.*] **1.** A table at which tea is taken, or on which tea-things are placed for a meal. **2.** *transf.* The company assembled at tea 1712. **3.** *attrib.* chiefly in ref. to social gatherings 1700.

3. T. Talk—Such as mending of Fashions, spoiling Reputations, railing at absent Friends CONGREVE.

Tea-taster (tī·tēⁱ:stəɹ). 1858. One whose business is to test the quality of samples of tea by tasting them; a tea-expert. So **Tea·-ta:sting.**

Tea·-tray. 1773. [TRAY *sb.*¹] A tray for holding tea-things.

Tea·-tree. 1760. **1.** *prop.* = TEA *sb.* 3. **2.** *transf.* Applied in Australia, Tasmania, and New Zealand to various shrubs or trees of the myrtle family, of which the leaves have been used as a substitute for tea 1790.

Tec, 'tec (tek), *sb. slang.* 1888. Abbreviation for DETECTIVE.

Technic (te·knik), *a.* and *sb.* 1612. [– L. *technicus* – Gr. τεχνικός of or pertaining to art, f. τέχνη art, craft; see -IC.] **A.** *adj.* Pertaining to art, or to an art: = TECHNICAL. Now *rare.* **B.** *sb.* **1.** A technical term, expression, point, or detail; a technicality. Chiefly *U.S. rare.* 1826. **2.** Technical details or methods collectively; the technical department of a subject; *esp.* the formal and mechanical part of an art (now more commonly TECHNIQUE) 1855. **b.** Collective pl. **Technics** in same sense; also constr. as a sing. 1850. **3.** = TECHNOLOGY 1. Usu. in pl. **Technics.** 1864.

2. Icelandic poetry..shows a powerful and developed t. M. ARNOLD. **b.** Literary technics, especially that of the novel, depends on reproducing experiments from life 1909.

Technical (te·knikăl), *a.* (*sb.*) 1617. [f. as prec. + -AL¹; see -ICAL.] **1.** Of a person: Skilled in or practically conversant with some particular art or subject (*rare*). **2.** Belonging or relating to an art or arts; appropriate or peculiar to, or characteristic of, a particular art, science, profession, or occupation; also, of or pertaining to the mechanical arts and applied sciences generally, as in *t. education, t. school* 1727. **b.** *spec.* said of words, terms, phrases, etc., or of their senses or acceptations; as, the *t. terms* of logic; the *t. sense* of 'subject' in logic 1652. **c.** *transf.* Of an author, a treatise, etc.: Using technical terms; treating a subject technically 1779. **d.** That is such from the technical point of view 1860. **B.** *sb.* In *pl.* Technical terms or points; technicalities 1790.

2. *T. difficulty*, a difficulty arising in connection with the method of procedure (esp. legal). **e.** Legally such, in the eyes of the law, as *t. assault* 1911. Hence **Te·chnicalism,** t. style, method, or treatment; addiction to technicalities. **Te·chnical-ly** *adv.*, **-ness.**

Technicality (teknikæ·lĭti). 1814. [f. prec. + -ITY.] **1.** Technical quality or character; the use of technical terms or methods 1828. **2.** A technical point, detail, term, or expression; something peculiar or specially belonging to the art or subject referred to. Usu. in *pl.* 1814.

2. To translate the technicalities of Kant into plain English 1874.

Technician (tekni·ʃăn). 1833. [f. TECHNIC + -IAN.] **a.** A person conversant with the technicalities of a particular subject. **b.** One skilled in the technique or mechanical part of an art, as music or painting.

Technicist (te·knisist). 1881. [f. as prec. + -IST.] = prec.; one who has technical knowledge.

Technico-, comb. element from Gr. τεχνικός

(see TECHNIC). **Technico·logy**, = TECHNOLOGY 1, 2.

Technique (tekni·k). 1817. [– Fr. *technique*, subst. use of adj. – L. *technicus* TECHNIC.] Manner of artistic execution or performance in relation to formal or practical details (as dist. from general effect, expression, sentiment, etc.); the mechanical or formal part of an art, esp. of any of the fine arts; also, skill or ability in this department of one's art; mechanical skill in artistic work (esp. painting or music).

A player may be perfect in t., and yet have neither soul nor intelligence GROVE.

Technocracy (teknǫ·krăsi). 1932. [f. *techno-* (see next) + -CRACY.] The organization of the social order based on principles established by technical experts. Hence **Te·chnocrat, -cra·tic** *a.*

Technology (teknǫ·lŏdʒi). 1615. [– Gr. τεχνολογία systematic treatment, f. τέχνη art, craft; see -LOGY.] **1.** A discourse or treatise on an art or arts; the scientific study of the practical or industrial arts. **b.** *transf.* Practical arts collectively 1859. **2.** The terminology of a particular art or subject; technical nomenclature 1658.

2. An engine, called, in the t. of that day, *fork* BENTHAM. So **Technolo·gical** *a.* pertaining or relating to. **Techno·logist.**

Tecno- (also **tekno-**), repr. Gr. τεκνο-, comb. form of τέκνον child; used in Eng. in a few rare technical words, as **Tecnology** (teknǫ·lŏdʒi) [-LOGY], the scientific study of children.

Tectibranch (te·ktibræŋk), *a.* and *sb.* 1851. [f. L. *tectus* covered + *branchiæ* (Gr. βράγχια) gills.] *Zool.* **A.** *adj.* Belonging to the order or sub-order *Tectibranchiata* of gasteropod molluscs, comprising marine forms having the gills covered by the mantle, and small shells often concealed by the mantle. **B.** *sb.* A gasteropod belonging to this division. So **Tectibra·nchian** *a.* 1839. **Tectibra·nchiate** *a.* 1836.

Tectiform (te·ktifǭɹm), *a.* 1834. [f. L. *tectum* roof + -FORM.] *Zool.* **a.** Roof-shaped; sloping downwards on each side from a central ridge. **b.** Serving as a covering or lid.

Tectology (tektǫ·lŏdʒi). 1883. [– G. *tektologie* (Haeckel), irreg. f. Gr. τέκτων carpenter, builder; see -LOGY.] *Biol.* A subscience of morphology, which regards the organism as composed of organic individuals of different orders: cf. PROMORPHOLOGY.

Tectonic (tektǫ·nik), *a.* 1656. [– late L. *tectonicus* – Gr. τεκτονικός, f. τέκτων, -ον- carpenter, builder.] **1.** Of or pertaining to building, or construction in general; constructional, constructive: used esp. in ref. to architecture and kindred arts. **2.** *Geol.* Belonging to the actual structure of the earth's crust, or to general changes affecting it 1893. So **Tecto·nics** [= G. *tektonik*], the constructive arts in general.

Tectorial (tektōᵊ·riăl), *a.* 1890. [f. L. *tectorium* covering, a cover + -AL[1] 1.] *Anat.* Covering like a roof: applied to a membrane in the internal ear.

‖**Tectrix** (te·ktriks). Usu. in pl. **tectrices** (tektrəi·sīz). 1874. [mod.L. *tectrix*, f. *tect-*, pa. ppl. stem of L. *tegere* cover; see *-trix*.] *Ornith.* = COVERT *sb.* 4. Hence **Tectri·cial** *a.* pertaining to the tectrices.

Ted (ted), *v.* late ME. [– ON. *teðja*, pa. t. *tadda*, rel. to *tad* dung, *toddi* small piece (see TOD *sb.*[2]), OHG. (G. dial.) *zetten* spread.] **1.** *trans.* To spread out, scatter, or strew abroad (new-mown grass) for drying. Also *absol.* **2.** *transf.* and *fig.* To scatter; to dissipate 1560.

1. The Grasse being cutte, must be well tedded and turned in the Sommer 1577. Hence **Te·dded** *ppl. a.* spread out for drying, as grass. **Te·dder,** one who teds new-mown grass; also, a machine for doing this.

Teddy-bear (te·dibēᵊ:ɹ). 1907. [*Teddy* pet form of *Theodore*.] A stuffed figure of a bear in plush, used as a toy: called after Theodore Roosevelt (President of U.S.A. 1901–9). Also simply **Te·ddy.**

‖**Tedesco** (tede·sko), *a.* (*sb.*) *Pl.* **tedeschi** (-ki). 1814. [It., = German.] The Italian word for German; esp. used to express Teutonic influence as shown in some spheres of Italian art.

Te Deum (tī· dī·ŏm). OE. [From the opening words of the L. original, *Te Deum laudamus* 'Thee, God, we praise'.] An ancient Latin hymn of praise in the form of a psalm, sung as a thanksgiving on special occasions, as after a victory or deliverance; also regularly at Matins in the R. C. Ch., and (in an Eng. translation) at Morning Prayer in the Ch. of England. **b.** With *a* and *pl.* **(Te Deums)**, in ref. to a recital of this, or (*allus.*) to any public utterance of praise to God; also, a service of (public) thanksgiving marked by the singing of this hymn 1679. **c.** A musical setting of this hymn 1864.

Tedious (tī·diəs), *a.* late ME. [– OFr. *tedieus* or late L. *tædiosus*, f. L. *tædium* TEDIUM; see -OUS, -IOUS.] **1.** 'Wearisome by continuance' (J.); long and tiresome; *esp.* of a speech or narrative, hence of a speaker or writer: prolix, so as to cause weariness. †**b.** *joc.* Long (in time or extent) –1630. **2.** Wearisome in general; annoying, irksome, disagreeable, painful. *Obs.* exc. *dial.* 1454. **3.** Late, tardy, dilatory, slow. *Obs.* exc. *dial.* 1485.

1. Come: you are a t. foole: to the purpose SHAKS. **2.** I may be t., but I will not be long TILLOTSON. Hence **Te·dious-ly** *adv.*, **-ness.**

Tedium (tī·diŏm). Also †**tædium.** 1662. [– L. *tædium* weariness, disgust, f. *tædēre* be wearisome.] The state or quality of being tedious; wearisomeness, tediousness, ennui.

The charge and t. of travelling 1662. When he remembered the tædium of his quarters SCOTT.

Tee (tī), *sb.*[1] 1610. **1.** The name of the letter T; also applied to objects having the form of this letter (T or ⊢). See also T (the letter) 2. **2.** *attrib.* Shaped like a T, having a cross-piece at the top or end, as *t.-joint, -piece, -square*; also, *t.-headed, -shaped* adjs. 1819.

Tee (tī), *sb.*[2] orig. *Sc.* 1673. [Clipped form of earlier †*teaz* (XVII), of unkn. origin.] *Golf.* The starting-place, usu. a little heap of sand, from which the ball is driven in beginning to play each hole.

Tee (tī), *sb.*[3] orig. *Sc.* 1789. [Of unkn. origin; perh. identical with TEE *sb.*[1]] *Curling*, etc. The mark, a cross made on the ice and surrounded by circles, at which the stones are aimed; applied also to the 'jack' at bowls, and the 'hob' at quoits.

‖**Tee** (tī), *sb.*[4] Also **htee.** 1800. [Burmese *h'ti* umbrella.] A metallic decoration, in the shape of an umbrella, usu. gilded and hung with bells, surmounting the topes and pagodas of Burma and adjacent countries.

†**Tee,** *v.*[1] [OE. *tēon* = OFris. *tiā*, OS. *tiohan*, OHG. *ziohan* (G. *ziehen*), ON. pa. pple. *toginn*, Goth. *tiuhan* draw, lead, f. Gmc. base rel. to that of TEAM *sb.*] *trans.* To draw, pull, drag, tug –1446. **b.** *intr.* To proceed, go –1450.

Tee (tī), *v.*[2] 1673. [f. TEE *sb.*[2]] *Golf.* **a.** *trans.* To place (a ball) on the tee. **b.** *intr.* With *off*: To play a ball from the tee. Hence **Tee·ing-ground,** a small patch of ground from which the ball is teed off.

Teem (tīm), *v.*[1] [OE. *tēman* (WS. *tīeman*) :- **taumjan*, f. Gmc. **taumaz* TEAM.] **1.** *trans.* To bring forth, produce, give birth to, bear (offspring). *Obs.* or *arch.* †**2.** *intr.* To bring forth young, bear or produce offspring; to be or become pregnant –1636. **3.** To be full, as if ready to give birth; to be prolific or fertile; to abound, swarm 1593.

1. Nothing teemes But hatefull Docks, rough Thistles, Keksyes, Burres SHAKS. **3.** The housetops teemed with people DICKENS. Hence **Tee·mful** *a.* prolific, productive, fruitful, teeming. †**Tee·mless** *a.* barren. DRYDEN.

Teem (tīm), *v.*[2] Now *dial.* and *techn.* [ME. *tēmen* – ON. *tœma* to empty, f. **tômjan*, f. *tómr* TOOM *a.*] **1.** *trans.* **a.** To empty (a vessel, etc.); to discharge or remove the contents of; to empty (a wagon, etc.). **b.** To empty out, pour out 1482. **2.** *intr.* Of water, etc.: To pour, flow in a stream, flow copiously; of rain, to pour 1828.

1. b. You immediately t. out the remainder of the ale into the tankard SWIFT.

Teeming (tī·miŋ), *ppl. a.* 1535. [f. TEEM *v.*[1] + -ING[2].] **1.** That bears or breeds offspring; pregnant, gravid. *arch.* and *dial.* †**b.** Germinating, sprouting –1835. **2.** Fertile, prolific 1593. **b.** *transf.* Abounding; swarming; crowded 1715.

2. The t. Autumne big with ritch increase SHAKS. **b.** The t. streets of Jerusalem 1873. Hence **Tee·ming-ly** *adv.*, **-ness.**

Teen (tīn), *sb. arch.* [OE. *tēona* = OFris. *tiona, tiuna*, OS. *tiono*, and OE. *tēon* = ON. *tjón*, rel. to Gr. δύη misfortune, misery, Skr. *dunōti*.] †**1.** Harm inflicted or suffered; injury, hurt, mischief; damage –1609. **2.** Irritation, annoyance; anger, rage; spite, ill-will, malice. *Obs.* exc. *Sc.* ME. **3.** Affliction, suffering, grief, woe. *arch.* ME.

3. Each howres ioy wrackt with a weeke of teene SHAKS.

Teen, *v. Obs.* or *dial.* [OE. *tēonian*, f. *tēon* TEEN *sb.*] **1.** *trans.* To vex, anger, enrage. **2.** To grieve, distress. *trans.* and *intr.* for *refl.* –1611.

-teen (tīn). [OE. **-tīene, -tēne, -tȳne* = OFris. *-ten(e, -tīne*, OS. *-tein*, OHG. *-zehan*, Goth. *-taihun* (Du. *-tien*, G. *zehn*).] An inflected form of TEN, added to the numerals from *three* to *nine*, to form those from *thirteen* to *nineteen*. The stressing of these forms depends on their position in the sentence, e.g. *she is se·venteen years old*; *she is seventee·n*, *sweet seventee·n*. Hence **-teenth** (tīnþ), forming the ordinals of the cardinals in *-teen*, from *thirteenth* to *nineteenth*.

Teens (tīnz), *sb. pl.* 1673. [-TEEN treated as a separate word with pl. suffix.] The years of a person's life (rarely, of a thing's age) of which the numbers end in *-teen*, namely 13 to 19; chiefly in phr. *in one's t.*, *out of one's t.* Hence **Tee·n-a:ger,** a person in his or her teens.

Teeny (tī·ni), *a.*[1] *Obs.* exc. *dial.* 1594. [f. TEEN *sb.* + -Y[1].] Characterized by 'teen'; malicious; peevish.

Tee·ny, *a.*[2] *dial.* and *colloq.* 1847. An emphasized form of TINY; esp. in childish use. Also in jingling comb. *teeny-weeny*.

Teer (tīᵊɹ), *v. dial.* and *techn.* late ME. [– OFr. *terrer* plaster, etc. (mod. Fr. cover with earth, etc.), f. *terre* earth.] **1.** *trans.* To daub with earth, clay, or plaster. **2.** To spread (colour) 1839.

‖**Teetee**[1] (tī·tī). Also **titi.** 1832. [Native name in Tupi.] Any Brazilian monkey of the genus *Callithrix*; a sagoin.

Teetee[2] (tī·tī). Also **ti-ti.** 1882. [Maori name.] A name in New Zealand for the Diving Petrel (*Pelecanoides* or *Halodroma urinatrix*), and for allied species.

Teeter (tī·təɹ), *sb. dial.* and *U.S.* 1867. [f. next.] A see-saw; a see-sawing or swaying motion; the game of see-saw; also *fig.*, hesitation between two alternatives, vacillation.

Teeter (tī·təɹ), *v. dial.* and *U.S.* 1846. [var. of dial. *titter* totter, move unsteadily.] **1.** *intr.* **a.** To see-saw. **b.** To move like a see-saw; to sway from side to side; to move unsteadily; *esp.* of a person or animal, to balance oneself unsteadily on alternate feet 1850. **2.** *trans.* To move (anything) with a see-saw motion; to tip up and down, to tilt 1874.

1. b. The peetweets..'teter' along its stony shores all summer THOREAU.

Teeth, pl. of TOOTH.

Teethe (tīð), *v.* late ME. [f. *teeth*, pl. of TOOTH.] **1.** *intr.* To develop or 'cut' teeth. (Now only in pr. pple. and vbl. sb.) **2.** *trans.* To furnish with teeth, to set teeth in. Chiefly *dial.* 1775.

Teething (tī·ðiŋ), *vbl. sb.* 1732. [f. TEETHE *v.* + -ING[1].] The action of TEETHE *v.*; the process of developing teeth, dentition; usu. applied to the cutting of the milk-teeth.

attrib. and *Comb.*, as *t.-rash*; **t. powder,** a medicinal powder given to children when teething.

Teetotal (tītōᵘ·tăl), *a.* (*sb.*) 1834. [A reduplication or extension of the word TOTAL, app. first used (in sense 1) by a working-man, Richard Turner of Preston, in a speech advocating total abstinence from intoxicating liquors, in preference to abstinence from ardent spirits only.] **1.** Of or pertaining to total abstinence from alcoholic drinks; pledged to, or devoted to the furtherance of, total abstinence. **2.** *dial.* Absolute, complete, perfect, entire. (More emphatic than *total*.) 1840. **B.** *sb.* (The adj. used *absol.*; now *rare* or *dial.*) **a.** The total abstinence principle or pledge; teetotalism; a society for the promotion of total abstinence. **b.** A teetotaller (*rare*) 1834. Hence **Teeto·talism,** total abstinence from alcoholic liquors. **Teeto·tal(l)er,** a total abstainer.

Tee:to·tally, *adv. dial.* and *U.S.* 1832. [redupl. form of TOTALLY.] Entirely, wholly.

Teetotum (tītōᵘ·tŏm). 1720. [orig. *T totum*, formed by prefixing to L. *totum* 'all, the whole', its initial T, which stood for it on one of the sides of the toy (itself in earlier use called simply a *totum*).] **1.** A small four-sided disc or die having an initial letter inscribed on each of its sides, and a spindle passing down through it by which it could be twirled or spun with the fingers like a small top, the letter which lay uppermost, when it fell, deciding the fortune of the player; now, any light toy spun with the fingers, used as a toy. **2.** A game of chance played with this device 1753.

1. The letters were orig. the initials of Latin words, viz. T *totum*, A *aufer*, D *depone*, N *nihil*. Later they were the initials of English words, T *take-all*, H *half*, N *nothing*, P *put down* (i.e. a stake equal to that you put down at first). *attrib.* His own t. brain is upset 1863.

‖**Teff** (tef). 1790. [Amharic *ṭêf*.] The principal cereal of Abyssinia, *Poa abyssinica*.

Teg (teg), **tag** (tæg). 1530. [ME. **tegge*, **tagge* in place-names, repr. OE. **tegga*, **tagga*, parallel to OSw. *takka*, Sw. *tacka* ewe. In the formation cf. *earwig*, †*haysugge* hedge-sparrow, *pig*, *stag*.] **1.** A sheep in its second year, or from the time it is weaned till its first shearing; a yearling sheep. Formerly restricted to the female. 1537. **b.** *T. wool*, also ellipt. *teg* 1854. †**2.** A doe or female deer in its second year –1774.

1. b. T. wool is the wool of the first shearing when the sheep is little more than a year old 1854.

‖**Tegmen** (te·gmen). *Pl.* **tegmina.** 1817. [L., covering, f. *tegere* to cover.] A cover, covering, coating, integument. (Only in scientific use.) **a.** *Ent.* (*pl.*) The wing-covers, i.e. the fore wings when modified so as to serve as coverings for the hind wings; esp. those of orthopterous insects (corresp. to the *elytra* of beetles). **b.** *Bot.* The thin inner coat of a seed, immediately enveloping the nucleus; the *endopleura* 1857. **c.** *Ornith.* (*pl.*) = *Tectrices*: see TECTRIX 1891.

Tegmental (tegme·ntăl), *a.* 1890. [f. next + -AL[1] 1.] Of or pertaining to the tegmentum.

‖**Tegmentum** (tegme·ntŏm). *Pl.* **-a.** 1832. [L., collateral form of *tegumentum* TEGUMENT.] **1.** *Bot.* Each of the scales forming the covering of a leaf-bud; a bud-scale. **2.** *Anat.* The upper and hinder portion of each of the *crura cerebri* 1879.

‖**Teguexin** (tegwe·ksin). 1879. [– Aztec *tecoixin*, *tecouixin* lizard.] *Zool.* A large S. Amer. lizard of the genus *Teius*, esp. *T. teguexin*.

‖**Tegula** (te·giŭlă). *Pl.* **-æ** (*i*). 1826. [L., tile, f. *tegere* to cover.] *Ent.* **a.** A small scale-like structure covering the base of the fore wing in hymenopterous and other insects. **b.** Each of a pair of membranous scales (*prehalteres*) in front of the halteres in dipterous insects.

Tegular (te·giŭlăɹ), *a.* 1796. [f. as prec. + -AR[1].] **a.** Pertaining to or of the nature of a tile; composed of or arranged like tiles. **b.** *Ent.* Pertaining to or of the nature of a *tegula* 1891. So **Te·gulary** *adv.* in the manner of tiles; so as to overlap like tiles. **Te·gulated** *a.* (of armour) composed of overlapping plates.

Tegument (te·giŭmĕnt). 1440. [– L. *tegumentum* covering, f. *tegere* to cover; see -MENT.] Something that serves to cover; a covering, coating, envelope, investment, integument. **a.** *gen.* **b.** *Nat. Hist.* and *Anat.* The natural covering of the body, or of some part or organ, of an animal or plant; a skin, coat, shell, husk, or the like; *spec.* = TEGMEN a. Now *rare* or *Obs.*; mostly repl. by INTEGUMENT. 1646. Hence **Tegume·ntal** *a.* = next.

Tegumentary (tegiŭme·ntări), *a.* 1828. [f. prec. + -ARY[1].] Constituting, or serving as, a tegument; pertaining to or occurring in the tegument; integumentary.

Tehee (tīhī·), *int.* and *sb.* late ME. **A.** *int.* A representation of the sound of a light laugh, usu. derisive.

And all the Maids of Honour cry Te! He! 1773.

B. *sb.* A laugh of this kind; a titter, a giggle 1593. So **Tehee·** *v.* to utter *t.* in laughing; to titter, giggle ME.

‖**Teichopsia** (təikǫ·psiă). 1872. [mod.L., f. Gr. τεῖχος wall + ὄψις sight + -IA[1].] *Path.* Half-blindness accompanied by an appearance as of the zigzag outline of battlements.

‖**Te igitur** (tī i·dʒitŏɹ). 1819. [L., = 'Thee therefore', the opening words of the prayer.] The first prayer in the Canon of the Mass in the Roman and some other Latin liturgies.

Teil (tīl). Now *rare* or *Obs.* 1589. [– OFr. *teil*, var. of *til* :– Rom. **tilium*, for L. *tilia* linden tree, whence Fr. *teille*, *tille* linden-bast.] The lime or linden-tree, *Tilia europæa*. Usu. *t.-tree*.

Teind (tīnd), (*a.*) *sb. Sc.* and *north.* [Early ME. *tende*, adj. and sb., collateral form of TENTH; cf. also TITHE.] **A.** *adj.* See TENTH A. 1, and 3. **B.** *sb.* †**1.** The tenth part (of anything); a tenth –1475. **2.** *spec.* = TITHE *sb.* 1; now, in Scotland, that portion of the estates of the laity which is liable to be assessed for the stipend of the clergy of the established church. Now chiefly in pl. ME. **b.** *transf.* The payment, institution or system of teinds 1817.

Teinoscope (təi·noskōᵘp). 1822. [f. Gr. τείνειν stretch, extend + -SCOPE.] An optical instrument in which prisms are so arranged and combined as to increase or diminish the apparent linear dimensions of objects, while the chromatic aberration of the light is corrected.

†**Teise,** *v.* Also **tease.** late ME. [Of unkn. origin.] *trans.* app. To drive (esp. a hunted beast); to chase; to urge on –1819.

They..did tease Their horses homeward, with convulsed spur KEATS. Hence †**Tei·ser,** one who rouses the game; *spec.* one of the first brace or leash of deer-hounds let slip.

‖**Telæsthesia** (telĭspī·ziă, -siă). 1882. [mod. L. (Myers, 1882), f. Gr. τῆλε TELE- + αἴσθησις perception + -IA[1].] *Psychics.* Perception at a distance; direct sensation or perception of objects or conditions independently of the recognized channels of sense. So **Telæsthe·tic** *a.* having physical perception of things at a distance; of or belonging to t.

‖**Telamon** (te·lămǫn). *Pl.* **Telamones** (telămōᵘ·niz). 1706. [In pl. – L. *telamones*, = Gr. τελαμῶνες, pl. of Τελαμών name of a hero in mythology.] *Arch.* A figure of a man used as a column to support an entablature or other structure.

‖**Telangiectasis** (tĭlændʒiˌe·ktăsis). *Pl.* **-ses** (-sīz). 1831. [mod.L., f. Gr. τέλος end + ἀγγεῖον vessel + ἔκτασις extension, dilatation.] *Path.* Dilatation of the small blood-vessels, producing small red or purple tumours in the skin; one of such tumours. Also **Telangie·ctasy.** Hence **Telangiectatic** (-tæ·tik) *a.* pertaining to or resulting from t.

Telautograph (telǭ·tǒgrɑf). 1884. [f. TELE- + AUTOGRAPH, after *telegraph*.] Proprietary name for a telegraphic apparatus by which writing or drawing done at the transmitting end is reproduced in facsimile at the receiving end, by means of an electric current conveyed along a wire. Hence **Telautogra·phic** *a.* pertaining to the t. **Telauto·graphy,** the use of the t.

Tele- (te·lĭ) (bef. a vowel properly **tel-**, but more often in the full form), repr. Gr. τηλε-, comb. form of τῆλε far off.

Telacou·stic *a. Psychics*, pertaining to or involving the perception of a sound beyond or apart from the possibility of ordinary hearing. **Tele·gony,** [Gr. -γονια begetting] *Biol.* the (hypothetical) influence of a previous sire seen in the progeny of a subsequent sire from the same mother; hence **Telego·nic** *a.* **Tele·graphone,** a form of telephone in which the spoken message is recorded at the receiving end magnetically on an iron ribbon, so as to be capable of reproduction. ‖**Telekine·sis** [Gr. κίνησις motion] *Psychics*, movement of or in a body occurring at a distance from, and without material connection with, the motive cause or agent. **Telelec·tric** *a.*, producing mechanical motions or effects at a distance by electrical means. **Telemecha·nics,** the art of transmitting power to a distance, esp. by etherial vibrations as in wireless telegraphy. **Te·lemo:tor,** an apparatus for transmitting motive power to a distance; *esp.* a device for steering a ship from some part distant from the tiller, by means of hydraulic or pneumatic pressure, etc. **Telepho·nograph,** an instrument consisting of a combination of telephone and phonograph, by which telephone messages can be recorded and subsequently reproduced; also (*U.S.*) = *telegraphone*. **Te·lergy** [after *energy*] *Psychics*, the supposed force operating in telepathy, regarded as correlated with the various forms of physical energy, or as directly affecting the brain or organism of the percipient. **Te·leseme** [Gr. σῆμα sign], an electric signalling apparatus used in hotels, etc., fitted with an indicator which shows the article or service required. **Te·letype,** a type-printing telegraph. **Telewriter** (te·lĭrəi:təɹ), an instrument which electrically reproduces in facsimile a written message.

‖**Teledu** (te·lĕdu). 1824. [Native name in Javanese.] A carnivorous animal of Java and Sumatra (*Mydaus meliceps*), allied to the skunk and of similar habits; also called *stinking badger* or *stinkard*.

‖**Telega** (telēⁱ·gă). 1558. [Russ. *teléga*.] A four-wheeled Russian cart, of rough construction, without springs.

Telegram (te·lĭgræm). 1852. [f. TELE- + -GRAM, after *telegraph*.] A message sent by telegraph; a telegraphic dispatch or communication.

'A t.'—a new Yankee word for a telegraphic despatch 1857. Hence **Te:legramma·tic, Telegra·mmic** *adjs.* of or pertaining to telegrams; concise or condensed like a t. *rare*.

Telegraph (te·lĭgrɑf), *sb.* 1794. [– Fr. *télégraphe* (Miot de Mélito, 1792); see TELE-, -GRAPH.] **1.** An apparatus for transmitting messages to a distance, usu. by signs of some kind. The name was first applied to that invented by Chappe in France in 1792, consisting of an upright post with movable arms, the signals being made by various positions of the arms according to a pre-arranged code. Hence applied to later devices operating by movable discs, shutters, etc., flashes of light, sounds of bells, horns, etc., or other means. (Now *rare* in this sense, such contrivances being usu. called *semaphores* or *signalling apparatus*.) **2.** In full, *electric* or *magnetic t.*: An apparatus consisting of a *transmitter*, a *receiver*, and a line or wire of any length connecting these, along which an electric current from a battery or other source passes, the circuit being made and broken by working the transmitter, so as to produce movements, as of a needle or pointer, in the receiver, which indicate letters, etc., either according to a code of signs, or by pointing to characters upon a dial; in some forms the receiver works so as to print or trace the message upon a prepared strip of paper. Also, an apparatus for wireless telegraphy. 1797. †**3.** A telegram –1862. **4.** In *Cricket*, A board upon which the number of runs obtained and wickets taken are exhibited during a match in large figures so as to be visible at a distance; a scoring-board. Also, a similar device used in other athletic sports. 1859. **5.** Used as individual name of a newspaper, a variety of plant, etc. 1794.

attrib. and *Comb.*, as *t. boy*, *cable* (CABLE *sb.* 3), *line*, *message*, *office*, *wire*, etc.; **t.-board** = sense 4; **t. form,** a paper printed with spaces in which the words of a telegram are to be written for dispatch; **-key,** a small lever or other device in a telegraphic transmitter, worked by the hand, for making and breaking the circuit; **-plant,** an E. Indian leguminous plant, *Desmodium gyrans*, remarkable for the spontaneous movements of its leaflets, suggesting signalling; also called *moving plant*; **-pole, -post,** one of a series of poles upon which a telegraph wire or wires are carried above the ground; **-register,** a telegraphic receiver, or part of one, which gives a permanent record of the messages received.

Telegraph (te·lĭgrɑf), *v.* 1805. [f. prec.] **1. a.** *intr.* To signal or communicate by telegraph; to send a telegram 1815. **b.** *trans.* To send, transmit, or announce (a message, news, etc.) by telegraph. In *Cricket*, etc., to exhibit (the score, etc.) on the telegraph-board. 1805. **c.** To send a message to (a person) by telegraph, summon by a telegram 1810. **2.** *fig.* **a.** *intr.* To make signs, signal (*to* a person). **b.** *trans.* To make (a signal), convey or announce by signs. **c.** To signal to (a person). Now *rare*. 1825.

Telegrapher (te·lĭgrɑfəɹ). 1795. [f. TELE-

GRAPH *sb.* or *v.* + -ER¹.] **1.** One who works a telegraph. (Now *rare* exc. in U.S.: the techn. term being *telegraphist.*) **2.** The sender of a telegram 1865.

Telegraphese (te:lĭgrɑfī·z). *colloq.* or *joc.* 1885. [f. TELEGRAPH *sb.* + -ESE.] **1.** The concise and elliptical style in which telegrams are worded. **2.** *joc.* An elaborate or inflated style, such as that of leading articles in the (London) *Daily Telegraph* newspaper 1885.

1. Electric T. is as short and spare as Daily T. is longwinded and redundant 1885.

Telegraphic (telĭgræ·fik), *a.* 1794. [f. as prec. + -IC.] **1.** Of, pertaining to, of the nature of, or connected with a telegraph; made, sent, or transmitted by telegraph. **2.** *fig.* †**a.** Making signals (as by glance or gesture); conveyed by a sign or signal. **b.** Resembling an (electric) telegraph; conveying impulses or intelligence as by electricity. **c.** Abbreviated or concise like a telegram. 1820.

1. Lord Nelson made the t. signal, 'England expects that every man will do his duty' 1805. As if on t. wires 1854. **2. c.** His speech as t. as though each word were paid for 1896.

Telegraphist (tĭ-, tele·grăfist, te·lĭgrɑfist). 1854. [f. as prec. + -IST.] A person employed, or skilled, in working a telegraph; a telegraph-operator.

Telegraphy (tĭle·g-, tele·grăfi, te·lĭgrɑfi). 1795. [f. as prec. + -Y³.] The art or science of constructing or using telegraphs; the working of a telegraph or telegraphs. *Wireless t.*: see WIRELESS.

Telemark (te·lėmaɹk). 1910. [Name of a district of Norway.] An expert swing turn in ski-ing, used in changing direction or stopping short.

Telemeter (tĭ-, tele·mĭtəɹ). Also **telometer.** 1860. [f. TELE-, TELO-² + -METER.] **1.** An instrument for ascertaining the distances of objects: applied to instruments of various kinds used in surveying, and in military operations. **2.** An apparatus for recording the readings of any physical instrument at a distance by means of an electric current 1891. Hence **Teleme·tric, -al** *adjs.*

Teleo-¹ (te·li,o), bef. a vowel **tele-**, repr. Gr. τελεο- (τελειο-), comb. form of τέλεος, τέλειος perfect, complete, f. τέλος end.

Teleocephalous (-se·făləs) [Gr. κεφαλή head] *a.*, *Ichth.* belonging to the order *Teleocephali* of teleostean fishes, having the full number of bones in the skull; so **Teleoce·phal,** a teleocephalous fish. **Te·leosaur** (-sǭɹ) [Gr. σαῦρος lizard], *Palæont.* a crocodile of the extinct genus *Teleosaurus* or family *Teleosauridæ*; so **Teleosau·rian** *a.* belonging to this genus or family; *sb.* = *teleosaur.* **Teleozoon** (-zōᵘ·ǫn) [Gr. ζῷον animal], *Biol.* an animal of perfect or complete organization; one of the higher animals; hence **Teleozoic** (-zōᵘ·ik) *a.*, pertaining to the teleozoa.

Teleo-², bef. a vowel **tele-**, comb. form repr. Gr. τέλος end (stem τελε-), as in TELEOLOGY and its derivs; also in **Teleorga·nic** *a.*, serving the purposes of an organism; necessary to organic life.

Teleologic (teli,olǫ·dʒik), *a.* and *sb.* 1842. [f. as next + -IC.] **A.** *adj.* = next. **B.** *sb.* The science of final causes; that branch of knowledge which deals with ends or purposes 1865.

Teleological (teli,olǫ·dʒikăl), *a.* 1809. [f. TELEOLOGY + -ICAL.] Of, pertaining to, or involving teleology; relating to ends or final causes; dealing with design or purpose, esp. in natural phenomena. **Teleolo·gically** *adv.*

Teleologist (teli,ǫ·lŏdʒist). 1864. [f. as prec. + -IST.] A believer in or maintainer of the doctrine of teleology; one versed in this.

Teleology (teli,ǫ·lŏdʒi). 1740. [– mod.L. *teleologia* (Chr. Wolf, 1728), f. Gr. τέλος end (see TELEO-²) + -λογια (see -LOGY).] The doctrine or study of ends or final causes, esp. as related to the evidences of design or purpose in nature; also *transf.* such design as exhibited in natural objects or phenomena.

Teleostean (teli,ǫ·stiăn), *a.* and *sb.* 1859. [f. TELEO-¹ + Gr. ὀστέον bone + -AN.] *Ichth.* **A.** *adj.* Belonging to or characteristic of the order *Teleostei*, having the skeleton (usu.) completely ossified. **B.** *sb.* A fish of this order. So **Te·leost** *sb.* and *a.* **Teleo·steous** *a.* = t.

Teleostome (te·li,ŏstoᵘm). 1896. [– mod. L. *teleostomus*, f. TELEO-¹ + Gr. στόμα mouth.] *Ichth.* A fish of the division *Teleostomi*, including the teleosts and ganoids (i.e. all the higher fishes), characterized by well-developed maxillary, dentary, and membrane bones.

Telepathy (tĭ-, tele·păþi, te·lĭpæþi). 1882. [f. TELE- + -PATHY.] *Psychics.* The communication of impressions from one mind to another, independently of the recognized channels of sense. So **Te·lepath, Tele·pathist,** an adept in, a subject of, or believer in t. **Telepa·thic** *a.* pertaining to, of the nature of, or effected by t.

Telephone (te·lĭfōᵘn), *sb.* 1835. [f. TELE- + -PHONE. Cf. TELEPHONY.] **1.** An instrument, apparatus, or device for conveying sound to a distance. Now chiefly *Obs.* **2.** An apparatus for reproducing sound, esp. that of the voice, at a great distance, by means of electricity; consisting, like the electric telegraph, of transmitting and receiving instruments connected by a line or wire which conveys the electric current 1866.

1. *Lovers'* or *String T.*, a toy consisting of two stretched membranes or metal discs connected by a tense cord which mechanically transmits sound-waves from the one to the other. **2.** The t. proper differs from other instruments of a like class, in that it reproduces instead of merely conveying vibrations 1884. (The first electrical telephone was described by P. Reis in 1861; the first of practical use was A. G. Bell's of 1876.) Phr. *On the t.*, connected with a system of telephonic intercommunication.

attrib. and *Comb.*, as *t. message, operator, receiver*; **t. exchange,** the office or central station of a local t. system, where the various lines are brought to a central switchboard, and communication between subscribers is effected; sometimes applied to the switchboard itself, as in an 'automatic exchange'; **t. girl,** a girl employed at the switchboard to connect the wires so as to put two persons into communication.

Telephone (te·lĭfōᵘn), *v.* 1879. [f. prec.] **1. a.** *intr.* To convey sound to a distance by or as by a telephone; *esp.* to send a message or communicate by speaking through a telephone 1880. **b.** *trans.* To convey or announce by telephone 1879. **c.** To speak to or summon by telephone 1889. **2.** To furnish with telephones; to establish a system of telephones in (a place) 1901.

2. Estimates for telephoning London 1901. **c.** She telephoned you on the impulse of the moment 1894.

Telephonic (telĭfǫ·nik), *a.* 1834. [f. TELEPHONE *sb.* + -IC.] Transmitting, or relating to the transmission of, sound to a distance; of, pertaining to, of the nature of, or conveyed by a telephone. Hence **Telepho·nically** *adv.* in the manner of or by means of a telephone.

Telephonist (tĭ-, tele·fŏnist, te·lĭfōᵘnist). 1882. [f. TELEPHONE *sb.* + -IST.] A person employed in transmitting messages by telephone.

Telephony (tĭ-, tele·fŏni, te·lĭfōᵘni). [See TELEPHONE, -Y³. In sense 1 – Fr. *téléphonie* (Sudré, 1835); in sense 2 earliest in G. *telephonie* (P. Ries, 1861); in Eng., A. Graham Bell, 1876.] †**1.** Name for a system of signalling by means of musical sounds, and for the practice of other early forms of telephone –1835. **2.** The art or science of constructing telephones; the working of a telephone or telephones. *Wireless t.*; see WIRELESS. 1876.

Telephote (te·lĭfōᵘt), *sb.* 1880. [f. Gr. τῆλε TELE- + φῶς, φωτ- light.] A name employed or proposed for various devices or apparatus used or projected. **a.** A means of transmitting signals or messages from a distance by means of light. **b.** A device for the electric transmission of pictures, so that they are reproduced as pictures at a distance. **c.** An apparatus for photographing at a great distance; a telephotographic lens or camera. Hence **Te·lephote** *v. trans.* to transmit (an optical image) to a distance by means of electricity. **Telepho·tic** (-fǫ·tik) *a.* of or pertaining to a t., or to TELEPHOTY.

Telephoto. 1898. Abbrev. of TELEPHOTOGRAPHIC *a.*²

Telephotograph (telĭfōᵘ·tŏgrɑf), *sb.*¹ 1881. [f. as TELEPHOTE *sb.* + -GRAPH.] A picture or image electrically reproduced at a distance; also, an apparatus for doing this. So **Te:lephotogra·phic** *a.*¹ **Te:lephoto·graphy**¹, = TELEPHOTY.

Telepho·tograph, *sb.*² 1900. [f. TELE- + PHOTOGRAPH; a back-formation from next.] A photograph of a distant object taken with a telephotographic lens. So **Telepho·tograph** *v. trans.* to photograph with a telephotographic lens or apparatus. **Te:lephoto·graphy**², the art or practice of taking photographs of distant objects by a camera with a telephotographic lens.

Telephotographic (te:lĭfōᵘto,græ·fik), *a.*² 1892. [f. TELE- + PHOTOGRAPHIC.] Of, pertaining to, or used in the photographing of distant objects, within the field of sight but beyond the limits of distinct vision, esp. in *t. lens,* a lens or combination of lenses for this purpose.

Telephoty (te·lĭfōᵘti). 1908. [f. as TELEPHOTE + -Y³.] The art or practice of reproducing pictures or views at a distance by means of the electric current; the theory and practice of the telephote.

Telescope (te·lĭskoᵘp), *sb.* 1648. [– It. *telescopio* (Galilei) or mod.L. *telescopium* (Porta); see TELE-, -SCOPE.] An optical instrument for making distant objects appear nearer and larger, consisting of one or more tubes with an arrangement of lenses, or of one or more mirrors and lenses, by which the rays of light are collected and brought to a focus and the resulting image magnified. Telescopes are of two kinds: *refracting,* in which the image is produced by a lens (the object-glass), and *reflecting,* in which it is produced by a mirror or *speculum*; being magnified in each case by a lens or combination of lenses (the EYE-PIECE). The smaller hand-telescopes are always refracting, and consist of two or more tubes made to slide one within another for convenience of packing into a narrow compass and for adjusting the lenses as required for focusing the image. **b.** *Astr.* A constellation south of Sagittarius 1891.

1. By what strange Parallax or Optic skill Of vision multiplyed through air, or glass Of Telescope MILT.

Comb.: **t.-carp,** a monstrous variety of goldfish, having protruding eyes; **-driver,** a clockwork apparatus for driving an astronomical t. so as to follow the apparent movements of the heavenly bodies and thus keep the same object continually in the field of view; **-eye,** an eye which can be protruded and retracted like a t.-tube, as in gasteropod molluscs; **-fish** = *t. carp*; **-fly,** a fly of the genus *Diopsis,* having the eyes on long stalks; **-shell,** the long conical shell, with numerous whorls, of an Indian gasteropod (*Telescopium fuscum*); **-sight,** a small t. mounted as a sight upon a firearm or surveying instrument.

Telescope (te·lĭskoᵘp), *v.* 1861. [f. prec.] **1. a.** *trans.* To force or drive one into another (or into something else) after the manner of the sliding-tubes of a hand-telescope: usu. said in ref. to railway carriages in a collision 1872. **b.** *intr.* To slide, run, or be driven one into another (or into something else); to have its parts made to slide in this manner; to collapse so that its parts fall into one another 1877. **2.** *trans.* To make into or use as a telescope 1861.

1. b. They telescoped like cars in railroad smashes O. W. HOLMES. **2.** Looking through his telescoped hand 1861.

Telescopic (telĭskǫ·pik), *a.* 1705. [f. as prec. + -IC.] **1.** Of or pertaining to a telescope; of the nature of or consisting of a telescope, as *t. sight* = telescope-sight; done by means of a telescope, as *t. observations.* **2.** Seen by means of a telescope; *spec.* of a heavenly body, visible only through a telescope 1714. **3.** Having the property of a telescope; having the power of distant vision, far-seeing; contemplating something distant (*lit.* and *fig.*) 1781. **4.** Consisting of parts made to slide one within another like the tubes of a hand-telescope 1846.

1. The limits of t. vision have not been reached 1855. **2.** These asteroids..are..entirely t. 1893. **3.** These Saxons..have..the t. appreciation of distant gain EMERSON. So **Telesco·pical** *a.* (now *rare*), in senses 1 and 2. 1665. **Telesco·pically** *adv.*

Telescopist (tĭ-, tele·skŏpist, te·lĭskōᵘpist). 1870. [f. TELESCOPE + -IST.] One skilled in using a telescope; one who makes telescopic observations.

Telescopy (tĭ-, tele·skŏpi, te·lĭskŏpi). *rare.* 1861. [f. TELESCOPE + -Y³.] The art or practice of using the telescope, or of making telescopes.

†**Te·lesm.** 1646. [– late Gr. τέλεσμα completion, f. τελεῖν complete, fulfil, f. τέλος end.] = TALISMAN² 1. –1693. So **Telesma·tic** (*rare*), †**Telesma·tical** *adjs.* of or pertaining to a t.; talismanic; magical.

Telestich (tĭ-, tele·stik, te·lėstik). 1637. [irreg. f. Gr. τέλος, τελε- end + στίχος row, line of verse, after ACROSTIC.] A short poem (or other composition) in which the final letters of the lines, taken in order, spell a word or words.

Teleutospore (tĭ-, teliū·tŏspoᵊɹ). 1874. [f. Gr. τελευτή completion, end (f. τέλος end) + SPORE.] *Bot.* A special form of spore, usu. produced at the end of the period of fructification, in parasitic fungi of the family *Uredineæ.* **Teleutospo·ric** *a.*

Television (te·lĭvizən). 1909. [f. TELE- + VISION.] Vision of a distant (moving) object or scene electrically transmitted and reproduced; also, the process by which this is effected. Hence **Te·levise** *v. trans.*, to transmit by t. **Te·levisor,** a t. apparatus.

Telic (te·lik), *a.* 1846. [– Gr. τελικός final, f. τέλος end; see -IC.] **1.** *Gram.* Of a conjunction or clause: Expressing end or purpose. **2.** Directed or tending to a definite end; purposive 1889.

Telinga (tĕli·ŋgă), *sb.* and *a.* 1698. [Of unkn. origin.] **1.** The Telugu language. (As *sb.* or *a.*) **2.** One of the Telugu people 1800. †**b.** *spec.* A native Indian soldier disciplined and dressed in quasi-European fashion; a sepoy –1883.

Tell (tel), *sb.*¹ Now *dial.* 1742. [f. TELL *v.*] **1.** What one tells or has to tell; a tale, statement, account. **2.** A talk, conversation, gossip 1864.

1. I am at the end of my t. H. WALPOLE.

‖**Tell** (tel), *sb.*² Also **tel.** 1864. [– Arab. *tall* a hillock.] Arab name for an artificial hillock or mound, usu. one covering the ruins of an ancient city.

Tell (tel), *v.* Pa. t. and pa. pple. **told** (tōᵘld). [OE. *tellan* = OFris. *talia, tella,* OS. *tellian,* (M)LG., (M)Du. *tellen,* OHG. *zellen,* G. *zählen* reckon, count (cf. *erzählen* recount, relate), ON. *telja* :– Gmc. **taljan,* f. **talō* TALE *sb.*] **I.** To mention in order, narrate, make known. †**1.** *trans.* To recount, enumerate; to give a list of –1440. **2.** To give an account or narrative of (facts, actions, or events); to narrate, relate. Also *to t. over.* OE. **b.** *intr.* for *pass.* To sound (well, etc.) when told 1584. **3.** To make known by speech or writing; to communicate (information, facts, ideas, news, etc.); to state, announce, report, intimate ME. **b.** To declare, state formally or publicly; to announce, proclaim, publish ME. **4.** To utter (words); to say over, recite (a passage, composition, etc.); to say. Now *dial.* ME. **b.** To utter, speak, say (things). *rare.* late ME. **c.** To express in words (thoughts, things known). Now *rare.* ME. **5.** To disclose or reveal (something secret or private) late ME. **6.** To discern so as to be able to say with knowledge or certainty; hence, to distinguish, recognize, decide, determine 1687. **b.** Preceded by *can*: To be able to state; to know; to make out, understand. Usu. in neg. or interrog. sentences, as *Nobody can t., Who can t.?* late ME. **7.** trans. *To t. a person*: To inform (a person) of something; to make aware, apprise, acquaint; to instruct ME. **8.** To assert positively to; to assure (a person). Often *parenthetically.* 1440. **9.** To order or direct (a person) *to do* something; to bid 1599. **10.** *intr.* To give an account, description, or report ME. **11.** *fig.* To give evidence, be an indication *of* 1798. **12.** To disclose something wished to be kept secret, to play the informer, tell tales, blab 1539.

2. Others of some note, As story tells, have trod this Wilderness MILT. **3.** I'le t. you one piece of my mind 1673. Tell me not, in mournful numbers, Life is but an empty dream! LONGFELLOW. **b.** Phr. *T. it not in Gath* (from 2 *Sam.* 1:20), publish it not to the enemy, or to the Philistine, or to the world. **4. b.** The lippes of the vnwyse wylbe tellynge foolish thinges COVERDALE *Ecclus.* 21:25. **5.** She neuer told her loue SHAKS. *To t. tales*: see TALE *sb.* 2 b. **6.** They can be told by their complexions, dress, manner, and..speech 1840. **7.** He..tolde me of my fault 1573. Wherefore was I not told of all this? SCOTT. **8.** I t. you, it got on my nerves 1905. **9.** Tell the Sergeant to keep his eye open KIPLING. **10.** He told of bloody fights CRABBE. **11.** Blocks of basalt..telling of a still more ancient Moabite city 1873. **12.** He didn't want to 't.' of Maggie GEO. ELIOT.

Phrases. *To t. a tale, a story,* to relate a story or narrative. *To t. a tale, t. its own tale*: to be significant of itself. *To t. the tale,* to pitch a yarn. *To t. one's tale,* to relate one's story; also, to say what one has to t., to deliver one's message. *To t.* (*the*) *truth,* to make a true statement; to state the fact or circumstance as it really is; also, used parenthetically to emphasize a statement. So *to t. a lie,* to make a wilfully false statement or report. *To hear t.*; usu. const. *of*: see HEAR *v.* 2; now chiefly *dial.* and *colloq. Never t. me, don't t. me,* expressing incredulity or impatience. *I can t. you,* I can assure you. *I'll t. you what* = 'I'll t. you what it is', or 'I'll t. you something'. *To t. any one his own,* to t. him frankly of his faults. *To t.* (a person) *good-bye*: to say goodbye (*U.S.*). *To t. the world*: to announce openly (*U.S.*).

II. To mention numerically, to count, reckon. **1.** *trans.* To mention or name (the single members of a series or group) one by one, specifying them as *one, two, three,* etc.; hence, to enumerate, reckon in; to reckon up, count, number. Also *absol.* Now *arch.* or *dial.* OE. **b.** *spec.* To count (voters or votes). Also *absol. To t. noses*: To count heads; see NOSE *sb.* **2.** To count out (pieces of money) in payment; hence, to pay (money). *arch.* or *dial.* ME. **b.** To reckon up or calculate the total amount or value of (money or other things). *arch.* OE.

1. Phr. *To t. one's beads*: see BEAD *sb.* 2. †*To t. the clock,* to count the hours as shown by a clock; hence, to pass one's time idly. *To t.* (so many) *years,* to have lived (so many) years. *Obs.* or *arch. All told,* when all are counted; in all. **b.** The House was told by Mr. Speaker 1899. **2.** He told the money into my hand DE FOE. **b.** Those who weigh and t. over money MARVELL. As a miser tells his gold 1827.

With advs. **T. off. a.** To count off from the whole number or company; to separate, detach, esp. so many men for a particular duty; hence *gen.* to appoint to a particular task, object, position, or the like. **b.** To scold; to rebuke strongly (*slang*). **c.** *intr.* for *refl. Mil.* Of a rank or troop of men: To number themselves in succession. **T. out,** to separate by counting: to count out (*arch.* or *dial.*).

III. To account, or estimate, qualitatively. †**1.** To account, esteem as being (something) –1430. **2.** *intr.* To count (for something); to have its effect, be effective, act or operate with effect; to make an impression 1797.

1. Wordly selynesse Which clerkes tellyn fals felicite CHAUCER. **2.** Every blow..tells 1797. Everything in the print, to use a vulgar expression, tells LAMB. It tells somewhat against his interpretation 1870. Hence **Te·llable** *a.* capable of being told or narrated; fit to be told; worth telling.

Tellen (te·lĕn). 1711. [– mod.L. *tellina* – Gr. τελλίνη kind of shell-fish.] A bivalve of the genus *Tellina* or family *Tellinidæ.*

Teller (te·ləɹ). ME. [f. TELL *v.* + -ER¹.] One who or that which tells, in various senses; *esp.* **a.** One who counts or keeps tally; now *esp.* one who counts money; *spec.* an officer in a bank who receives or pays money over the counter 1480. **b.** One of four officers of the Exchequer formerly charged with the receipt and payment of moneys 1488. **c.** In a deliberative assembly (esp. the House of Commons), A person (usu. one of two or more) who counts the votes on a division 1669. Hence **Te·ller-ship,** the office or position of a t.

Telling (te·liŋ), *vbl. sb.* ME. [f. TELL *v.* + -ING¹.] The action of TELL *v.*

Phr. That's (or *that would be*) *telling* (trivial colloq.), that would be to divulge something secret.

Te·lling, *ppl. a.* 1852. [-ING².] That tells; effective, forcible, striking.

A *t.* reply 1852. Drawn up with t. force 1870. Hence **Te·llingly** *adv.*

Tell-tale (te·l₁tēᶦl), *sb.* (*a.*) 1548. **1.** One who tells tales; one who idly or maliciously discloses private or secret matters; a tale-bearer, a tattler. Also *transf.* of things. **b.** A name of a species of Sandpiper (*spec.* in *U.S.*), so named from their loud cry 1824. **2.** *Mech.* A device for mechanically indicating or recording some fact or condition not otherwise apparent; an indicator, a gauge 1801. **3.** *attrib.* or as *adj.* **a.** That tells tales, that is a tell-tale. Now *rare* or *Obs.* in *lit.* sense. 1594. **b.** Applied to a thing: That betrays something meant to be kept secret 1577. **c.** That gives notice or warning of something 1867.

3. a. *Rich. III,* IV. iv. 149. **b.** These tell-tale articles must not remain here SCOTT. **c.** *T. clock,* a clock with an attachment of some kind requiring attention at certain intervals, by which the vigilance of a watchman may be checked. *T. compass,* a compass suspended overhead in the captain's cabin, enabling him to detect any deviation from the course.

†**Te·ll-truth.** 1558. **1.** One who or that which tells the truth –1810. **2.** The telling of the truth; candour (*rare*) –1734.

Te·llur-, tellu·ri-, *Chem.,* used as comb. forms of TELLURIUM; as in **Tellurhy·dric** *acid,* hydrogen telluride.

Tellurate (te·liŭreᶦt). 1826. [f. TELLURIC + -ATE⁴.] *Chem.* A salt of telluric acid.

Telluret (te·liŭret). Now *rare.* 1842. [f. TELLURIUM; see -URET.] *Chem.* A compound of tellurium with hydrogen or a metal, as *t. of sodium,* $TeNa_2$: now usu. TELLURIDE.

Telluretted (te·liŭretėd), *a.* Now *rare.* 1819. [f. as prec. + -ED².] *Chem.* Combined with tellurium, as in *telluretted hydrogen,* a gaseous compound of hydrogen and tellurium, TeH_2, formerly also called *hydrotelluric* or *tellurhydric acid,* and now *hydrogen telluride.*

Tellurian (teliūᵊ·riăn), *a.* and *sb.* 1846. [f. L. *tellus, tellur-* earth + -IAN.] **A.** *adj.* Of or pertaining to the earth; earthly, terrestrial. **B.** *sb.* An inhabitant of the earth 1847.

Telluric (teliūᵊ·rik), *a.*¹ 1800. [f. TELLURIUM + -IC.] *Chem.* and *Min.* Derived from or containing tellurium. Applied to compounds in which tellurium is present in a smaller proportion than in tellurous compounds, as *t. acid,* H_2TeO_4. Also in *t. gold, silver, bismuth,* the tellurides of these metals occurring as native alloys.

Telluric (teliūᵊ·rik), *a.*² 1836. [f. L. *tellus, tellur-* earth + -IC.] Of or belonging to the earth, terrestrial; pertaining to the earth as a planet; of or arising from the earth or soil.

A 't. poison' is generated in it [the Campagna] by the energy of the soil 1884.

Telluride (te·liŭrəid). 1849. [f. TELLURIUM + -IDE.] *Chem.* A combination of tellurium with an electro-positive element (e.g. hydrogen or a metal), or with a radical; as *t. of hydrogen.*

T. of bismuth, telluric bismuth, tetradymite, or bornite. *T. of gold and silver* = SYLVANITE.

Tellurion (teliūᵊ·riŏn). Also **tellurium.** 1831. [f. L. *tellus, tellur-* + (in quasi-Gr. form) -IUM.] An apparatus for showing the effect of the earth's motions and obliquity of axis in causing the alternations of day and night and the succession of the seasons; a simple kind of orrery.

Tellurism (te·liŭriz'm). 1843. [f. as prec. + -ISM.] **1.** A magnetic influence or principle supposed by some to pervade all nature and to produce the phenomena of animal magnetism; also, the theory of animal magnetism based on this, propounded in 1822 by Kieser in Germany. **2.** Influence of the soil in producing disease 1890.

Tellurite (te·liŭrəit). 1799. [f. TELLURIUM + -ITE¹ 2 b, 4 b.] **1.** *Min.* Native oxide of tellurium, found in minute whitish or yellow crystals; telluric ochre. **2.** *Chem.* A salt of tellurous acid 1847.

Tellurium (teliūᵊ·riŏm). 1800. [f. L. *tellus, tellur-* earth + -IUM; named by Klaproth, 1798, prob. in contrast to *uranium* (Gr. οὐρανός heaven), a metal which he had discovered in 1789.] *Chem.* One of the rarer elements, a tin-white shining brittle substance, formerly from its outward characteristics classed among the metals, but chemically belonging to the same series as sulphur and selenium. It occurs native in rhombohedral crystals, isomorphous with those of antimony, arsenic, and bismuth. Symbol Te; atomic weight 128. **b.** *Graphic t.* = SYLVANITE.

Comb.: **t. glance** *Min.* nagyagite or black telluride of lead.

Tellurous (te·liŭrəs), *a.* 1842. [f. TELLURIUM + -OUS.] *Chem.* Characterized by or of the nature of tellurium; said of compounds containing a greater proportion of tellurium than those called *telluric*; as *t. acid*, H_2TeO_3.

‖**Tellus** (te·lŏs). late ME. [L.] In Roman mythology, the goddess of the earth; the earth personified; the terrestrial globe.

Telly (te·li), colloq. abbrev. of TELEVISION.

Telo-[1] (telo), comb. form repr. Gr. τέλος, τέλεος end; as in **Te·loblast** [Gr. βλαστός germ], each of a number of proliferating cells at one end of the embryo in segmented animals, as insects and annelids.

Telo-[2], repr. Gr. τηλο-, comb. form of τῆλε or τηλοῦ far off, occurring exceptionally instead of τηλε- (TELE-). See next and TELOTYPE.

Telodynamic (te:lodinæ·mik, -dəi-), *a.* Also **teledynamic.** 1870. [f. TELO-[2] + DYNAMIC.] Term applied to a cable transmitting mechanical power to a distance.

‖**Telos** (te·lǫs). 1904. [– Gr. τέλος end.] End, purpose, ultimate object or aim.

Telotroch (te·lotrǫk). 1877. [f. TELO-[1] + Gr. τροχός wheel. Cf. mod.L. *Telotrocha* n. pl., as name for larvæ having this structure.] *Zool.* A zone of cilia circling either or each end of the preoral (and perianal) segments of a free-swimming polychætus annelid larva. **b.** A larva of this kind. Hence **Telo·trochal, Telo·trochous** *adjs.* possessing a t. or telotrochs; of the nature of a t.

Telotype (te·lotəip). 1858. [f. TELO-[2] + TYPE.] An electric telegraph that automatically prints the messages as received; also, a telegram so printed.

Telpher (te·lfəɹ), *a.* and *sb.* 1884. [contr. form (F. Jenkin) of **telephore*; see TELE-, -PHORE.] **A.** *adj.* or *attrib. sb.* Of or relating to a system of telpherage. **B.** *sb.* Any travelling unit on a telpher line; also, the plant and rolling stock of a system of telpherage.

a. *T. line, railway*, a light overhead line on which the haulage is worked by electric power; so *t. train*. Hence **Te·lpher** *v. trans.* to transport (goods, etc.) by means of telpherage.

Telpherage (te·lfərédʒ). 1883. [f. as prec. + -AGE.] Transport effected automatically by the aid of electricity.

Telson (te·lsən). 1855. [– Gr. τέλσον limit.] *Zool.* The last segment of the abdomen or its median axis in certain crustaceans and arachnidans, as the middle flipper of a lobster's tail-fin, the sting of the scorpion, etc.

‖**Telugu, Teloogoo** (te·lugū), *sb., a.* 1789. [Native name of the language, and of a man of the race. Origin and deriv. unkn.] **1.** The name of a Dravidian language, spoken on the Coromandel coast of India, north of Madras 1813. **2.** One of the Dravidian people or race who speak this language 1789. **3.** *attrib.* or as *adj.* Of or pertaining to this language, people, or country 1888.

‖**Temenos** (te·mėnǫs). 1820. [– Gr. τέμενος, f. τεμ-, stem of τέμνειν cut off, sever. Cf. TEMPLE *sb.*[1]] *Gr. Antiq.* A piece of ground surrounding or adjacent to a temple; a sacred enclosure or precinct.

Temerarious (temĕrēə·riəs), *a.* Now only *literary*. 1532. [f. L. *temerarius* fortuitous, rash (f. *temere* blindly, rashly + *-arius* -ARY[1]) + -OUS.] **1.** Characterized by temerity; reckless, heedless, rash. †**2.** Fortuitous, casual, haphazard –1775.

1. Your resolves are t. and presumptuous 1645. Hence **Temera·rious-ly** *adv.*, **-ness.**

Temerity (tĭme·rĭti). late ME. [– L. *temeritas, -tat-*, f. *temere*; see prec., -ITY. Cf. Fr. *témérité*.] Excessive boldness, rashness; foolhardiness, recklessness; an instance of this.

Marlborough might have been made to repent his t. at Blenheim JOHNSON.

Temerous (te·mĕrəs), *a.* Now *rare.* 1461. [f. L. *temere* rashly + -OUS, or f. as var. of †*temerary* (XV–XVII) by change of suffix.] Rash, foolhardy. **Te·merous-ly** *adv.*, **-ness.**

Temp., abbrev. of L. *tempore*, in the time of.

Tempe (te·mpi). 1567. [– L. *Tempe* – Gr. Τέμπη.] Proper name of a valley in Thessaly, watered by the Peneus, between Mounts Olympus and Ossa; used orig. in Latin literature as a general name for a beautiful valley; hence for any delightful rural spot.

The gay solitude of my own little T. 1770.

Temper (te·mpəɹ), *sb.* late ME. [f. next.] **I. 1.** The due or proportionate mixture or combination of elements or qualities; the condition or state resulting from such combination; proper or fit condition. Now *rare* or *Obs.* **2.** Proportionate arrangement of parts; regulation, adjustment; hence, mean or medium, a middle course; a compromise; a settlement. *arch.* 1523. **3.** Mental balance or composure, esp. under provocation of any kind; moderation in or command over the emotions, esp. anger; calmness, equanimity; now usu. in phr. *to keep* or *lose* (*one's*) *t.*, *to be out of t.* 1603.

2. The king..compiled a new body of laws, in order to find a t. between both BURKE. **3.** I keep my T., and win their Money STEELE. It would put me out of t., which is a state of mind I can't endure DICKENS.

II. †**1.** = TEMPERAMENT II. –1759. †**b.** Of things immaterial: Character, quality –1651. **2.** The particular degree of hardness and elasticity or resiliency imparted to steel by tempering 1470. †**3.** = CLIMATE *sb.* 3, TEMPERAMENT II. 2. –1705. †**4.** The relative condition of a body in respect of warmth or coldness –1884. †**5.** Bodily habit, constitution, or condition –1707. **6.** Mental constitution; habitual disposition 1595. **7.** Actual state of the mind or feelings; inclination, humour 1628. **8.** = *ill-temper*: Heat of mind or passion; explosive ill-humour 1828.

2. Between two blades, which beares the better t. SHAKS. *fig.* Intellectual implements of more ethereal t. 1866. **6.** The t. of the Puritan was eminently a t. of law GREEN. **7.** The Commons were in no t. to listen to such excuses MACAULAY. *Good t., ill t., bad t.* (cf. GOOD-TEMPERED, ILL-TEMPERED, *bad-tempered*). **8.** Johnson, when the first ebullition of t. had subsided, felt he had been unreasonably violent 1846. I can't tell you..what a t. I was in 1900.

III. Concr. senses. **a.** *Sugar-making.* A solution containing lime or some other alkaline substance serving to neutralize the acid in the raw cane-juice and clarify it 1657. **b.** An alloy of tin and copper 1875.

Comb.: **t.-screw**, a set-screw for adjustment; *esp.* in boring, a screw-connection for automatically adjusting the drill as the boring proceeds.

Temper (te·mpəɹ), *v.* [OE. *temprian* (= OS. *temperon*) – L. *temperare* mingle, restrain oneself. The sense-development of the Eng. verb was prob. infl. by the French (OFr. *temprer*, (O)Fr. *tremper*, mod. Fr. *tempérer*).] **I. 1.** *trans.* To bring (anything) to a proper or suitable condition, state, or quality, by mingling with something else; to qualify, alloy, or dilute by such mixture or combination. *arch.* **2.** To modify (some unsuitable or excessive state or quality, or some thing or person in respect of such), esp. by admixture of some other quality, etc.; to reduce to the suitable or desirable degree or condition free from excess in either direction; to moderate, mitigate, assuage, tone down OE. **3.** To mix, mingle, blend (ingredients) *together*, or (one ingredient) *with* another, in proper proportions. *arch.* late ME. **4.** To prepare by mingling; to make by due mixture or combination; to concoct, compound, make up, devise. *Obs.* or *arch.* late ME. †**5.** To restore the proper 'temper' or 'temperament' to; to cure, heal, refresh –1613. **6.** To bring into a suitable or desirable frame of mind; to dispose favourably; also, to appease, mollify, pacify. *Obs.* or *arch.* 1525.

1. As wine is tempered with water, so let discretion t. zeale 1591. **2.** T. sorow with mirth 1552. He..who tempers judgment with mercy 1871. **3.** Whan metalles be well tempered togyther they wyll be all as one 1530. **4.** Lo, thus I tempre mi diete 1390. **6.** The Lady so well tempered and reconciled them both, that she forced them to join Hands STEELE.

II. 1. To keep, conduct, or manage in just measure; to regulate; to control, guide, govern, overrule. *Obs.* exc. *dial.* OE. **2.** To restrain within due limits, or within the bounds of moderation; in later use often simply, to restrain, check, curb. Also †*refl.* OE. **3.** To regulate suitably to need or requirement; to fit, adapt, conform, accommodate, make suitable. Const. *to.* Now *rare* or *Obs.* 1450.

1. Supremest Jove Tempers the fates of human race above POPE. **2.** I wish that not onely Kings, but all other Persons..would so t. themselves as to commit no wrong HOBBES. Cortes..was more solicitous to t. than to inflame their ardour 1777. **3.** They were indeed not temper'd to his temper MILT.

III. Techn. uses. **1.** To bring (clay, mortar, etc.) to a proper consistence for use by mixing and working it up *with* water, etc. ME. †**2.** To moisten (a substance, usu. medicinal or culinary ingredients in a comminuted state) so as to form a paste or mixture –1674. **b.** *spec.* in *Painting.* To prepare (colours) for use by mixing them with oil, etc. 1531. †**3.** *trans.* To soften (iron, wax, etc.) by heating; to melt. Also *intr.* for *pass.* –1597. **4.** To bring (steel) to a suitable degree of hardness and elasticity or resiliency by heating it to the required temperature and immersing it, while hot, in some liquid, usu. cold water. Also *intr.* for *pass.* late ME. †**5.** To tune, adjust the pitch of (a musical instrument) –1593. **b.** *spec.* To tune (a note or instrument) according to some temperament; see TEMPERAMENT III. 3. 1727. **6.** To bring into harmony, attune. *Obs.* or *arch.* late ME.

3. 2 *Hen. IV*, IV. iii. 140. **4.** They have a great advauntage in Spayne, to t. their blades well, bycause of the nature of their ryvers PALSGR. **6.** Mean while the Rural ditties were not mute, Temper'd to th'Oaten Flute MILT.

‖**Tempera** (te·mperă). 1832. [It., in phr. *pingere a tempera* paint in distemper.] The method of painting in distemper: see DISTEMPER *sb.*[2]

Temperable (te·mpərăb'l), *a.* Now *rare.* late ME. [orig. prob. – med.L. *temperabilis*; later f. TEMPER *sb.* and *v.* + -ABLE.] †**a.** Of weather or climate: = TEMPERATE *a.* 3. †**b.** Of a person: = TEMPERATE *a.* 1. –1629. **c.** That may be tempered or made plastic 1841.

a. In somer he muste haue t. eir. late ME. **c.** The fusible, hard, and t. texture of metals EMERSON. Hence **Temperabi·lity.**

Temperality, joc. misused for *temper*. SHAKS.

Temperament (te·mpĕrămĕnt), *sb.* late ME. [– L. *temperamentum* due mixture, f. *temperare* TEMPER *v.*; see -MENT.] **I.** †**1.** A moderate and proportionable mixture of elements in a compound; the condition in which elements are combined in their due proportions –1684. †**2.** Consistence, composition; mixture –1673. **II.** †**1.** In the natural philosophy of the Middle Ages: The combination of supposed qualities (*hot* or *cold*, *moist* or *dry*), in a certain proportion, determining the nature of a plant or other body; characteristic nature; known *spec.* as *universal t.* –1677. **2.** The condition of the weather or climate as resulting from the different combinations of the qualities, heat or cold, dryness or humidity; climate. *Obs.* or *arch.* 1610. †**3.** Condition with regard to warmth or coldness –1799. **4.** In mediæval physiology: The combination of the four cardinal humours (see HUMOUR *sb.* 2 b) of the body, by the relative proportion of which the physical and mental constitution were held to be determined; known *spec.* as *animal t.*; also, the bodily habit attributed to this, as a *sanguine, choleric, phlegmatic*, or *melancholic t.* (see the adjs.) 1628. **5.** Constitution or habit of mind, esp. as depending upon or connected with physical constitution; natural disposition 1821.

2. The t. of their seasons is such that they have no disease JOWETT. **4.** Our minds are perpetually ..wrought on by the Temperament of our Bodies DRYDEN. **5.** The man of sanguine t. 1868.

III. 1. Moderating, moderation; lightening, alleviation, mitigation; due regulation. *Obs.* or *arch.* 1475. **2.** The action of duly combining or adjusting different principles, claims, etc.; adjustment, compromise. *Obs.* or *arch.* 1660. **b.** A middle course or state; a medium, mean. *Obs.* or *arch.* 1604. **3.** *Mus.* The adjustment of the intervals of the scale (in the tuning of instruments of fixed intonation, as keyboard instruments), so as to adapt them to purposes of practical harmony: consisting in slight variations of the pitch of the notes from true or 'just' intonation, in order to make them available in different keys; a particular system of doing this. (Sometimes extended to any system of tuning.) 1727.

2. These admit no t. and no compromise BURKE. **b.** The causes..of this t.—this *mezzo termino*—this middle course BENTHAM. **3.** The chief temperaments..are *mean-tone t.*..and *equal t.* (now almost universal), in which the octave is divided into twelve (theoretically) equal semitones, so that the variations of pitch are evenly distributed throughout all keys. O.E.D. Hence **Te·mperament** *v. rare. trans.* to endow with a t.

Temperamental (te:mpĕrăme·ntăl), *a.* 1646. [f. prec. + -AL[1] 1.] Of or relating to the temperament (chiefly in sense II. 5); in recent colloq. use, liable to or marked by variable or unaccountable moods. Hence **Tempera·me·ntally** *adv.*

Temperance (te·mpĕrăns). ME. [– AFr. *temperaunce* – L. *temperantia* moderation, f. *temperant-*, pr. ppl. stem of *temperare* TEMPER *v.*; see -ANCE.] **I. 1.** The practice or habit of restraining oneself in provocation, passion, desire, etc.; rational self-restraint. (One of the four cardinal virtues.) **2.** *spec.* The avoidance of excess in eating and drinking; *esp.*, in later use, moderation in regard to intoxicants; sobriety. Now often applied to teetotalism. 1542. **b.** *attrib.* Pertaining to, practising, or advocating total abstinence, as *t. association, drink, movement, society, work*; **t. hotel, inn,** one where no intoxicants are provided 1836.

1. He..calmd his wrath with goodly t. SPENSER. The secret of t. lies not in the scanty supply, but in the strong self-restraint 1846. **2.** With a delicate frame..I have been enabled, by t., to do the work of a strong man COBDEN. Where I can enjoy a stiff glass of grog with my feet on the hobs, and with nobody to preach t. 1887.

II. †1. a. = TEMPERAMENT III. 1, 2. –1596. **b.** = TEMPERAMENT I. 1, 2. –1638. **†2.** Moderate temperature; freedom from the extremes of heat and cold; mildness of weather or climate; temperateness –1610.

1. b. But were all Men of my T., and Wisdom too, You should woo us COWLEY. **2.** It [the island] must needs be of..tender, and delicate t. SHAKS. So **†Te·mperancy,** = TEMPERANCE, in senses I. 1, 2, II. 1 b.

Temperate (te·mpĕrĕt), *a.* late ME. [– L. *temperatus*, pa. pple. of *temperare*; see TEMPER *v.*, -ATE[2].] **1.** Of persons, their conduct, practices, etc.: Observing moderation, self-restrained, moderate. **2.** Of things, actions, qualities, conditions, etc.: Tempered; not excessive in degree; restrained. late ME. **3.** *spec.* Of the weather, season, climate, etc.: Moderate in respect of warmth: neither too hot nor too cold; of mild and equable temperature. late ME. **4.** Of monarchy or sovereignty, hence also of the sovereign: Restricted in extent of authority; not absolute; limited; constitutional. *Obs.* or *arch.* 1560.

1. This is a t. statement MILL. The t. life has gentle pains and pleasures JOWETT. That a young man of strictly t. habits should thus suddenly become a drunkard 1890. **2.** At the t. hour of nine, the bridal festivities closed 1855. **3.** So cleare the ayre, so t. the clime 1587. *T. zone*, each of the two zones or belts of the earth's surface lying between the torrid and frigid zones. **4.** That sober freedom out of which there springs Our loyal passion for our t. Kings TENNYSON. So **†Te·mperate** *v.* = TEMPER *v.* **Te·mperately** *adv.*, **-ness.**

Te·mperative, *a.* Now *rare* or *Obs.* late ME. [– late L. *temperativus*, f. *temperare* TEMPER *v.*; see -IVE.] Having the quality of tempering; alleviative, mitigating; tending to temperateness.

Temperature (te·mpĕrătiŭɹ, -tʃəɹ). 1531. [– Fr. *température* or L. *temperatura*, f. *temperat-*, pa. ppl. stem of *temperare* TEMPER *v.*; see -URE.] **†1.** The action or process of tempering; mixing or combination (of elements) –1677. **†2.** The fact or state of being tempered or mixed, mixture; also, the condition resulting from the mixture or combination in various proportions of ingredients or elements; the composition, consistence, or complexion so produced –1826. **†3.** Due measure or proportion in action, thought, etc.; freedom from excess or violence; moderation –1659. **†b.** A mean between opposites; a middle course, a compromise –1712. **†4.** = TEMPERAMENT II. 1. –1616. **†5.** = TEMPERAMENT II. 4. –1837. **†b.** = TEMPERAMENT II. 5. –1768. **†6.** A tempered or temperate condition of the weather or climate; also, a (specified) condition of these –1727. **7.** The state of a substance or body with regard to sensible warmth or coldness, referred to some standard of comparison; *spec.* that quality or condition of a body which in degree varies directly with the amount of heat contained in the body, and inversely with its heat-capacity; usu. measured by means of a thermometer or similar instrument 1670. **†8.** The temper of steel –1630.

3. b. His Constitution is a just T. between Indolence on one hand and Violence on the other 1712. **5.** There is no t. so exactly regulated but that some humour is fatally predominant JOHNSON. **b.** As touching the manners of learned men ..no doubt there be amongst them, as in other professions, of all temperatures BACON. **7.** A moderate Expence of Fire..serves to keep this large Room in a due T. STEELE. A comparison of the temperatures shown by the two thermometers HUXLEY. Phr. *To have a t.*, i.e. one higher than the normal, as in fever (*colloq.*).

Comb.: **t.-chart,** (*a*) a chart or card containing a *t.-curve* or its equivalent; (*b*) a chart of a region indicating temperatures at different points, as by isotherms; **-curve,** a curve showing variations of t., usu. in relation to equal periods of time, *esp.* in clinical use.

Tempered (te·mpəɹd), *a.* late ME. [f. TEMPER *v.* and *sb.* + -ED.] **1.** Brought to or having a proper or desired temper, quality, or consistence; hence, temperate. **b.** *Mus.* That has been tuned or adjusted in pitch according to some TEMPERAMENT (sense III. 3) 1727. **2.** Constituted or endowed with a specified temper or disposition (in various senses of *temper*). late ME. **3.** Modified by the admixture or influence of some other element; moderated, toned-down; limited 1654.

1. A court, open to the t. aire 1577. An excellently t. complexion 1638. T. steel 1655. **2.** A quiet and equally t. people 1628. Children, sweetly t. like their mother 1760. Hard at bargaining..and cross-tempered 1901. **3.** A t. monarchy BURKE. The t. wisdom of the Queen 1828.

Temperer (te·mpərəɹ). 1617. [f. TEMPER *v.* + -ER[1].] One who or that which tempers; *esp.* in senses III. 1 and 4 of the vb.

Te·mpersome, *a.* orig. *dial.* 1875. [f. TEMPER *sb.* + -SOME[1].] Quick-tempered. **Te·mpersomeness.**

Tempest (te·mpĕst), *sb.* ME. [– OFr. *tempeste* (mod. *tempête*) and *tempest* :– Rom. **tempesta* and **tempestum*, for L. *tempestas* season, weather, storm, f. *tempus* time, season.] **1.** A violent storm of wind, usu. accompanied by a downfall of rain, hail, or snow, or by thunder. **b.** A thunder-storm (*dial.*) 1532. **2.** *transf.* and *fig.* A violent commotion or disturbance; a tumult, rush; agitation, perturbation ME. **3.** A tumultuous throng; †a crowded assembly; a rushing crowd 1746.

1. A Station safe for Ships, when Tempests roar DRYDEN. **2.** In the midst of all this t. the ministers ..seem much at their ease BURKE. **3.** There are also drum-major, rout, t., and hurricane, differing only in degrees of multitude and uproar SMOLLETT.

Tempest (te·mpĕst), *v.* late ME. [– OFr. *tempester*, f. *tempeste*; see prec.] **1.** *trans.* To affect by or as by a tempest; to throw into violent commotion, to agitate violently. **2.** *fig.* To disturb violently (a person, the mind). late ME. **†3.** *intr.* Of the wind, weather, etc., and *impers.*: To be tempestuous, to blow tempestuously; to rage, storm –1615.

1. Fish..Wallowing unweildie, enormous in thir Gate, T. the Ocean MILT.

Tempestive (tempe·stiv), *a. arch.* 1611. [– L. *tempestivus* timely; see TEMPEST *sb.* and -IVE.] Timely, seasonable.

The chearefull and tempestiue showres HEYWOOD. Hence **Tempe·stively** *adv.*

†Tempesti·vity. 1569. [– L. *tempestivitas*, f. *tempestivus*; see prec., -ITY.] **1.** Seasonableness, timeliness –1656. **2.** A season, a time of a particular character –1683.

Te·mpest-to:ssed, -to:st, *a.* 1592. Tossed by, or as by, a tempest.

Tempestuous (tempe·stiŭəs), *a.* 1447. [– late L. *tempestuosus*; see TEMPEST, -UOUS. Earlier †*tempeste(v)ous, -ious*, after *plente(v)ous*, etc.; see PLENTEOUS.] **1.** Of, pertaining to, involving, or resembling a tempest; subject to or characterized by tempests; stormy, very rough or violent 1509. **2.** *transf.* and *fig.* Characterized by violent agitation or commotion; turbulent; passionate; agitated as by a tempest 1447.

1. A very blustering and a t. day LAUD. **2.** A winning wave (deserving note) In the t. petticote HERRICK. Cecilia was still in this t. state MISS BURNEY. Hence **Tempe·stuous-ly** *adv.*, **-ness.**

Templar (te·mplăɹ), *sb.* ME. [– AFr. *templer*, (O)Fr. *templier* – med.L. *templarius* or *templaris*, f. L. *templum* TEMPLE *sb.*[1]; see -ER[2] 2, -AR[2].] **1.** A member of a military and religious order, consisting of knights (*Knights Templars, Knights* or *Poor Soldiers of the Temple*), chaplains, and men-at-arms, founded *c*1118, chiefly for the protection of the Holy Sepulchre and of Christian pilgrims visiting the Holy Land; so called from their occupation of a building on or near the site of the Temple of Solomon at Jerusalem. They were suppressed in 1312. **2.** A barrister or other person who occupies chambers in the Inner or Middle Temple 1588. **3. a.** A member of an order of Freemasons calling themselves Knights Templars, extensively established in the United States 1859. **b.** Short for GOOD TEMPLAR –1874.

Templar (te·mplăɹ), *a.* 1728. [– late L. *templaris*, f. *templum* TEMPLE *sb.*[1]; see -AR[1].] Of, pertaining to, or characteristic of a (or the Jewish) temple.

Templary (te·mplări), *sb.* late ME. [– med.L. *templarius* TEMPLAR *sb.*; see -ARY[1].] **†1.** = TEMPLAR *sb.* 1. –1656. **2.** Templars collectively; *Hist.* the system or organization of the Templars; the Masonic and Temperance societies so called. 1661.

Template, var. of TEMPLET.

Temple (te·mp'l), *sb.*[1] [OE. *temp(e)l* (– L. *templum*), reinforced in ME. by (O)Fr. *temple* :– L. *templum* space marked out by an augur for taking observations, broad open space, consecrated space, sanctuary, prob. rel. to Gr. τέμενος; see TEMENOS.] **I. 1.** An edifice or place regarded primarily as the dwelling-place or 'house' of a deity or deities; hence, an edifice devoted to divine worship. **b.** *spec.* The sacred edifice at Jerusalem, the 'House of the Lord' and seat of the Jewish worship of Jehovah OE. **c.** *fig.* 1607. **2.** *transf.* A building dedicated to public Christian worship; a church; esp. applied to a large or grand edifice. late ME. **c.** *fig.* Any place regarded as occupied by the divine presence; *spec.* the person or body of a Christian (1 Cor. 3:16) OE.

1. But he that is hyest of all dweleth not in temples made with hondes TINDALE *Acts* 7:48. Tempilis & places of sacrifice to prophane Godis 1596. **c.** A t. of science now in ruins TYNDALL. **3.** Most sacrilegious Murther hath broke ope The Lords anoynted T., and stole thence The Life o' th' Building SHAKS.

II. †1. The head-quarters of the Knights Templars, on or contiguous to the site of the temple at Jerusalem; hence, the organization of the Templars –1656. **2.** *spec.* Name of two of the Inns of Court in London, known as the *Inner* and *Middle T.*, which stand on the site of the buildings once occupied by the Templars (of which the church alone remains) ME. **b.** Name of the place in Paris which formed the head-quarters of the Templars in Europe 1617.

Temple (te·mp'l), *sb.*[2] ME. [– OFr. *temple* (mod. *tempe*) :– Rom. **tempula*, alt. of L. *tempora*, pl. of *tempus* 'temple of the head'.] **1.** The flattened region on each side of the (human) forehead. (Chiefly in *pl.*) Also *transf.*, a corresponding part in lower animals. **2.** Each of the side-members or limbs of a pair of spectacles, which clasp the sides of the head of the wearer. *U.S.* 1877.

Temple (te·mp'l), *sb.*[3] 1483. [– Fr. *temple*, ult. identical with prec.] **1.** A contrivance for keeping cloth stretched to its proper width in the loom during the process of weaving. Usu. *pl.* **2.** = TEMPLET[1] 2 (*rare*) 1688.

Temple (te·mp'l), *v.* 1593. [f. TEMPLE *sb.*[1]] **1.** *trans.* To enclose in or as in a temple; to honour with a temple or temples, to build a temple to or for. **2.** To make or fashion into a temple 1839. **†3.** To dwell as in a temple. KEN.

1. The Heathen..Templed and adored this drunken god 1628. **2.** *ppl. a.* O'er which ye rise in templed majesty 1839.

Temple-bar. ME. [f. TEMPLE *sb.*[1] II. 2 (because of its proximity to the Temple buildings) + BAR *sb.*[1]] The name of the barrier or gateway closing the entrance into the City of London from the Strand; removed in 1878.

Templet[1] (te·mplėt). Also **template.** 1677. [prob. f. TEMPLE *sb.*[3]; see -ET.] **1.** *Building.* A horizontal piece of timber in a wall, or spanning a window or doorway, to take and distribute the pressure of a girder, or of joists or rafters; a plate. **2.** An instrument used as a gauge or guide in bringing any piece of work to the desired shape; usu. a flat piece of wood or metal having one edge shaped to correspond to the outline of the finished work; also, used as a tool in moulding, etc. 1819. **b.** A flat plate or strip perforated with holes used as a guide in marking out holes for riveting or drilling 1874.

Templet,[2] **-ette.** 1889. [Of unkn. origin.] Each of the four-sided facets which surround and 'support' the table of a brilliant.

‖**Tempo** (te·mpo). *Pl.* **tempi** (te·mpi). 1724. [It. :– L. *tempus* time.] *Mus.* Relative speed or rate of movement; pace; time; *spec.* the proper or characteristic speed and rhythm of a dance or other tune (in phr. *t. di marcia, t. di minuetto*, etc.).

T. primo, first or former time; a direction to resume the original speed after an alteration of it. *T. rubato*, robbed or stolen time; i.e. time occasionally slackened or hastened for the purposes of expression.

Temporal (te·mpŏrăl), *a.*[1] and *sb.*[1] ME. [– (O)Fr. *temporel* or L. *temporalis*, f. *tempus, tempor-* time; see -AL[1] 1. In B. 2 – eccl. L. *temporale.*] **A.** *adj.* **1.** Lasting or existing only for a time; passing, temporary. Now *rare* or merged in 2. late ME. **2.** Of or pertaining to time as the sphere of human life; terrestrial as opp. to heavenly; of man's present life; worldly, earthly. (Opp. to *eternal* or *spiritual.*) late ME. **3.** Secular as opp. to sacred; lay as dist. from clerical. Of law: civil or common as dist. from canon. Of rule, authority, or government: civil as dist. from ecclesiastical. (Opp. to *spiritual*) ME. **4. a.** *Gram.* and *Pros.* Relating to or depending on the quantity of syllables 1678. **b.** *Gram.* Of or pertaining to the tenses of a verb; of tense; also, expressing or denoting time, as an adv., a clause, etc. 1786. **5.** *gen.* Of, pertaining, or relating to time, the present time, or a particular time 1877.

1. For the things which are seene, are temporall, but the things which are not seene, are eternall 2 *Cor.* 4:18. **2.** The Jews. .expected. .a t. prince 1772. **3.** His Scepter shewes the force of temporall power, The attribute to awe and Maiestie SHAKS. *Lords t.*: see LORD *sb.* 9. **4.** *T. augment* (Gr. Gram.): see AUGMENT *sb.* 2.

B. *sb.* **1. a.** That which is temporal; esp. in *pl.* Temporal things or matters. late ME. **b.** Temporal power, possession, or estate; TEMPORALITY; chiefly in *pl.* = temporalities 1450. **2.** (Also in L. form **Temporale** (tempŏrēi·li, -ā·le).) That part of the breviary and the missal which contains the services in the order of the eccl. year, as dist. from those proper to saints' days. late ME.

1. b. The Pope commaundeth ouer the temporall of the Church called S. Peters patrimonie, as King 1594. Hence **Te·mporalism,** secularism, addiction to t. or mundane interests; also the principle of the t. power of the Pope. **Te·mporal-ly** *adv.*, **-ness** (*rare*).

Temporal (te·mpŏrăl), *a.*[2] and *sb.*[2] 1541. [– late L. *temporalis*, f. *tempora* the temples; see TEMPLE *sb.*[2], -AL[1] 1.] *Anat.* **A.** *adj.* Of, belonging to, or situated in the temples: esp. in names of structures, as *t. artery, bone, muscle, vein*, etc. 1597. **B.** *sb.* Ellipt. for *t. artery, bone, muscle*, etc.

A. *T. canals*, small passages for vessels and nerves through the malar bone to the t. surface; *t. fossa*, that in which the t. muscle originates.

Temporality (tempŏræ·lĭti). ME. [– late L. *temporalitas*, f. *temporalis* TEMPORAL *a.*[1]; see -ITY.] †**1.** = next 1. –1818. **b.** *pl.* Temporal or material possessions (esp. of the church or clergy) 1475. **2.** = next 2. 1456. **3.** The quality or condition of being t. or temporary; temporariness; relation to time 1634.

1. The Churches so great encrease of T. 1613.

Temporalty (te·mpŏrălti). *Obs.* or *arch.* late ME. [f. TEMPORAL *a.*[1] + -TY[1]. Superseded by prec. Cf. AFr. *temperautez* (pl. = 1 b).] **1.** Temporal or secular things, affairs, business; temporal authority. **b.** Chiefly *pl.* = prec. 1 b. late ME. **2.** The body of temporal persons or laymen, the laity; the temporal estate or estates of the realm, i.e. the temporal peers and the commons. late ME.

Temporaneous (tempŏrēi·nĭəs), *a.* Now *rare* or *Obs.* 1656. [f. late L. *temporaneus* timely (f. *tempus, tempor-* time) + -OUS.] †**1.** Lasting only for a time, temporary –1818. **2.** Pertaining or relating to time, temporal 1656. Hence **Tempora·neous-ly** *adv.*, **-ness.**

Temporary (te·mpŏrări), *a.* (*sb.*) 1547. [– L. *temporarius*, f. *tempus, tempor-* time; see -ARY.] **1.** Lasting for a limited time; existing or valid for a time (only); transient; made to supply a passing need. †**2.** = TEMPORAL *a.*[1] 2. –1751. †**3.** *Metaph.* Occurring or existing in time (not from eternity) –1701.

1. Inconveniences which they felt to be only t. J. H. NEWMAN. *T. star* (*Astron.*), a star which appears suddenly, shines for a time, and then disappears. *T. tooth*, a deciduous tooth, milk-tooth. **2.** *Meas. for M.* V. i. 145.

B. *sb.* †**1.** *pl.* Temporal goods –1665. **2.** A person employed or holding a post temporarily; a 'casual' 1848. Hence **Te·mporarily** *adv.* **Te·mporariness.**

†**Te·mporist.** 1596. [f. TEMPORIZE + -IST.] A temporizer, a time-server –1666.

Why, turne a t., row with the tide, Pursew the cut, the fashion of the age MARSTON.

Temporiza·tion. 1763. [f. next + -ATION.] The action of temporizing; time-serving; procrastination; gaining of time.

Temporize (te·mpŏrəiz), *v.* 1555. [– Fr. *temporiser* to pass one's time, wait one's time, = med.L. *temporizare* = *temporare* delay, f. L. *tempus, tempor-* time; see -IZE.] **1.** *intr.* To adopt some course for the time or occasion; hence, to adapt oneself or conform to the time and circumstances. †**2.** *intr.* To let time pass, spend time, 'mark time'; to procrastinate; to delay or wait for a more favourable moment. *Obs.* exc. as in 3. –1696. **3.** To act, parley, treat, deal (*with* a person, etc.) so as to gain time 1586. **4.** To negotiate, to discuss terms; to arrange or make terms, or effect a compromise (*with* a person, etc., *between* persons or parties) 1579.

1. The pope. .had privately advised Becket to avoid a quarrel with the king and to temporise FROUDE. **3.** William was still temporizing with Stigand; the time for his degradation was not yet come FREEMAN. Hence **Te·mporizer,** one who temporizes. **Te·mporizingly,** in a way designed to gain time, in a temporizing manner.

Temporo- (te·mpŏro), bef. a vowel occas. **tempor-,** used in *Anat.* as comb. form of L. *tempora* temples (of the head), forming adjs. in the sense 'pertaining to the temple or temples and (some other part)', as *t.-auricular, -facial, -malar, -mastoid, -maxillary.*

Tempt (tem^p^t), *v.* ME. [– OFr. *tempter*, learned form beside *tenter* :– L. *temptare* handle, feel, try the strength of, test, attempt.] **I.** To test, put to the test, try. †**1.** To try, make trial of, put to the test or proof. *Obs.* exc. as in 2. –1644. **2.** To make trial of, put to the proof or test, in a way that involves risk or peril ME. †**3.** = ATTEMPT *v.* 1. –1538. **b.** *with simple obj.* To attempt, try 1697.

2. *To t. God*, to experiment presumptuously upon His power, forbearance, etc.; to try how far one can go with Him; hence sometimes to provoke, defy; so *to t. providence, fate, fortune*, etc. *To t.* (*the storm, flood, sea*, etc.), to risk the perils of (chiefly *poet.*). **3. b.** Ere leave be giv'n to t. the nether skies DRYDEN.

II. To try to attract, allure, incite, induce. **1.** *trans.* To try to attract, to entice (a person) to do evil; to allure or incite to evil with the prospect of some pleasure or advantage. Const. *to* something, *to do* something. Also *absol.* ME. **b.** To try to draw (a person) to contradict, confute, or commit himself. *arch.* late ME. **2.** To attract or incite *to* some action or *to do* something; to allure, entice, invite, attract; to dispose, incline ME.

1. Idle men t. the devil to t. them 1869. **b.** Why tempte ye me? Brynge me a peny, that I maye se yt. TINDALE *Mark* 12:15. **2.** Unhappy land! whose blessings t. the sword COLLINS.

Temptable (te·m^p^tăb'l), *a.* 1628. [f. prec. + -ABLE.] That may be tempted; liable or open to temptation. Hence **Temptabi·lity, Te·mptableness,** accessibility to temptation.

Temptation (tem^p^tēi·ʃən). ME. [– OFr. *temptacion*, (also mod.) *tentation* – L. *temptatio, tent-, -ōn-*, f. *temptare*; see TEMPT *v.*, -ATION.] **1.** The action of tempting or fact of being tempted, esp. to evil. **b.** With *a* and *pl.* An instance of this ME. **c.** *transf.* A thing that tempts; a cause or source of temptation 1596. **2.** The action or process of testing or proving; trial, test. *Obs.* or *arch.* late ME.

1. Watche and praye that ye fall not into temptacion TINDALE *Matt.* 26:41. *The T.*, that of Jesus in the wilderness (*Matt.* 4, etc.). **c.** Dare to be great, without a guilty crown; View it, and lay the bright t. down DRYDEN. Hence **Tempta·tious** *a.* full of t.; tempting.

Tempter (te·m^p^təɹ). late ME. [– OFr. *tempteur* – eccl. L. *tem(p)tator, -ōr-* 'tempter', f. *tem(p)tare* TEMPT *v.*; see -ER[2] 3.] One who or that which tempts or entices to evil; *the t.*, (*spec.*) the devil.

The T., or the Tempted, who sins most? SHAKS.

Te·mpting, *ppl. a.* 1546. [f. TEMPT *v.* + -ING[2].] **1.** That entices to evil, or with evil design. **2.** Seductive, attractive, alluring, inviting 1596.

2. 'Tis such a t. offer 1818. Hence **Te·mptingly** *adv.*, **-ness.**

Temptress (te·m^p^trės). 1594. [f. TEMPTER + -ESS[1].] A female tempter.

Temse (tems, temz), *sb.* Now *dial.* late ME. [OE. **temes* (in *temespile, temesian*) = MLG. *temes, temse*, MDu. *temse* (Du. *teems*), G. dial. *zims*; WGmc., of unkn. origin.] A sieve, esp. one used for bolting meal; a searce, a strainer. In mod. local use *esp.* a sieve used in brewing.

Comb.: **t.-bread, -loaf,** bread or a loaf made of finely sifted flour.

Temse (tems, temz), *v.* Now *dial.* [OE. *temesian*; see prec. Cf. MLG. *temesen*, MDu. *temsen* (Du. *teemsen*).] *trans.* To sift or bolt (flour, etc.) with a temse. Hence **Temsed** *ppl. a.*; *temsed-bread* = *temse-bread* (see prec.).

Temulence (te·miŭlĕns). *rare.* 1803. [f. as next; see -ENCE.] = next.

Temulency (te·miŭlĕnsi). Now *rare.* 1623. [– L. *temulentia* drunkenness, f. *temulentus*; see next and -ENCY.] Drunkenness, inebriety.

Temulent (te·miŭlĕnt), *a.* Now *rare.* 1628. [– L. *temulentus*, from root *tem-* in *temetum* intoxicating drink, after *vinolentus* from *vinum* wine.] Drunken, intoxicated; given to, characterized by, or proceeding from drunkenness; intoxicating.

Ten (ten), *a.*, *sb.* (*adv.*). [OE. (Anglian) *tēn(e*, (WS.) *tīen(e* = OFris. *tiān, tēne, tine*, OS. *tehan* (Du. *tien*), OHG. *zehan* (G. *zehn*), ON. *tíu*, Goth. *taihun* :– Gmc. **teχan*, beside **teχun* :– IE. **dekm̥*, whence also L. *decem*, Gr. δέκα, Skr. *daśa*.] The cardinal numeral next higher than nine; the number of the digits on both hands or feet, and hence the basis of the ordinary or decimal numeration. **A.** *adj.* **1.** In concord with a sb. expressed. **b.** As multiple of another higher cardinal number, as in *ten hundred*, etc.; also in the ordinals of these, as *ten thousandth* OE. **c.** Used vaguely or hyperbolically, esp. in *t. times, tenfold*, etc. late ME. **2.** Absolutely or with ellipsis of sb. OE.

1. Which rage of water lasted tenne dayes 1513. *The T. Commandments*, the Mosaic decalogue; *slang*, the t. fingers. *T. tribes*, the lost tribes of Israel; *joc.* the Jews, as money-lenders. **b.** The guarantee for the ten-million loan 1905. **c.** A Iewell in a t. times barr'd vp Chest SHAKS. **2.** About t. at night 1843. Two girls of, perhaps, eight and t. 1891. A t.-and-sixpenny kettle 1908. Phr. *T. to one*, t. chances to one; odds of t. times the amount offered in a bet; hence, an expression of very strong probability. *Hart of t.*: see HART *sb.* *Upper t.* (= *upper t. thousand*): see UPPER *a.*

B. *sb.* (With pl. *tens*; and (less usu.) possessive *ten's*.) **1.** The abstract number; a symbol or the figures representing this, 10, X. OE. **b.** In a number expressed in decimal notation, the digit expressing the number of tens, e.g. in 1837 the figure 3. 1542. **c.** A person or thing distinguished by the number ten, usu. as the tenth of a series. Also *number ten.* 1888. **2.** A set of ten things or persons OE. **3.** *Coal-mining.* A measure of coal, locally varying between 48 and 50 tons, being the unit of calculation on which the lessor's rent or royalty is based. *n. dial.* 1590. **4.** A playing-card marked with ten pips 1593. **5.** Short for (*a*) ten-oared boat; (*b*) ten-pound note or ten-dollar bill. **6. a.** Short for *tenpenny nail* (i.e. costing

10*d.* a hundred); *double ten*, a nail costing the double of the tenpenny. 1572. **b.** A tallow candle weighing ten to a pound. 1802.

1. 12 tens, which do make 2 sixties 1594. **2.** I.. made them..captaines ouer tennes *Deut.* 1:15. *T. of rupees*, a unit of account in Indian money.

†**C.** *quasi*-adv. Ten times, tenfold. –late ME.

Comb.: **t.-foot** *a.*, measuring, or having, t. feet; *t.-foot coal*, in Yorkshire, a thick seam; **t.-hours act,** a law limiting the hours of work in factories; *spec.* the pop. name of the Act 10 & 11 Vict., c. 29; so, in the U.S.A., **t.-hour law; t. o'clock,** Amer. name for *Ornithogalum umbellatum*, the flowers of which open late in the morning; **-pointer,** a stag having antlers with t. points, a hart of t.; **-pound** *a.*, of or involving the amount or value of t. pounds; also, weighing t. pounds; spec. *t.-pound householder* = TEN-POUNDER 2 b; **-spot** (*U.S.*), a t.-dollar bill; also = TEN *sb.* 4; **-year** *a.*, of t. years' duration or standing.

Tenable (te·nă̆b'l, †tī·n-), *a.* 1579. [– (O)Fr. *tenable*, f. *tenir* hold; see -ABLE.] **1.** Capable of being held; that may be kept, kept in, kept back, retained, restrained, or held in control. Now *rare.* 1602. **2.** That may be held against attack; that may be successfully defended 1579. **3.** Capable of being held, occupied, possessed, or enjoyed 1840.

1. If you have hitherto concealed this sight Let it be t. in your silence still SHAKS. **2.** The City being not t...it yeelded 1579. *fig.* The letter of their theories is no longer t. 1837. **3.** Scholarships ..t. for three years 1883. Hence **Tenabi·lity, Te·nableness,** the quality of being t.

Tenace (te·nĕs). 1655. [– Fr. *tenace* – Sp. *tenaza* lit. pincers, tongs.] *Whist.* The combination of two cards of any suit, consisting of the next higher and the next lower in value than the highest card held by the other side, esp. when this combination is held by the fourth player. Used esp. in phr. *to have the t.*, formerly *tenaces.*

Tenacious (tĭnē¹·ʃəs), *a.* 1607. [f. L. *tenax, tenac-* holding fast (f. *tenēre* hold) + -OUS; see -ACIOUS.] **1. a.** Holding together, cohesive. **b.** Adhesive; viscous, glutinous; sticky 1641. **2.** Holding fast or inclined to hold fast; clinging tightly 1656. **3.** Keeping a firm hold; retentive *of* something 1645. **4.** *fig.* Strongly retaining, holding persistently, or inclined to retain, preserve, or maintain (a principle, method, secret, etc.); of memory, retentive. Const. *of.* 1640. **5.** Persistently continuing; resolute; perseveringly firm; obstinate, stubborn, pertinacious 1656. †**6.** *erron.* Persistently averse to any action –1811.

1. a. Gun-metal, or bronze, is a hard and t. alloy 1869. **b.** Female feet, Too weak to struggle with t. clay COWPER. **2.** T. hooked prickles 1869. **4.** T. of his Purpose once resolv'd 1708. **5.** He is..quick in opposition, and t. in defence JOHNSON. Hence **Tena·cious-ly** *adv.*, **-ness.**

Tenacity (tĭnæ·sĭti). 1526. [– (O)Fr. *ténacité* or L. *tenacitas*, f. as prec.; see -ITY.] The quality or property of being tenacious. **1.** Cohesiveness, toughness; viscosity, clamminess (of a liquid); also, adhesive quality, stickiness 1555. **2.** The quality of retaining what is held, physically or mentally; firmness of hold or attachment; firmness of purpose, persistence, obstinacy 1526. **b.** Retentiveness (of memory) 1814. †**3.** Miserliness, niggardliness, parsimony –1706.

2. The t. of Prejudice and Prescription SIR T. BROWNE. The t. of the English bull-dog 1878.

Tenacle (te·năk'l). Now *rare.* late ME. [– L. *tenaculum* holder; see next.] †**1.** *pl.* Forceps, pincers, nippers –1597. **2.** That by which a plant, a fruit, etc. is upheld or supported; in *pl.* the organs by which some climbing plants attach themselves 1500.

‖**Tenaculum** (tĭnæ·kiŭlŏm). *Pl.* **-ula.** 1693. [mod. uses of L. *tenaculum* holder, f. *tenēre* hold.] **1.** *Surg.* A kind of forceps. **b.** See quot. 1842. **2.** *Ent.* The abdominal process by which the springing organ is retained in the *Poduridæ* or spring-tails 1878.

1. b. *T.*, a surgical instrument, consisting of a fine sharp-pointed hook, by which the mouths of bleeding arteries are drawn out, so that in operations they may be secured by ligaments 1842.

‖**Tenaille** (tĭ-, tĕnē¹·l). 1589. [(O)Fr. :– L. *tenacula*, pl. of *tenaculum* holder; see prec.] †**1.** *pl.* Pincers, forceps –1727. **2.** *Fortif.* A small low work, consisting of one or two re-entering angles (*single* or *double t.*), placed before the curtain between two bastions 1589.

‖**Tenaillon** (tĕnæ·liŏn). 1842. [Fr., f. *tenaille* (prec.); see -OON.] *Fortif.* A work sometimes placed before each of the faces of a ravelin, leaving the salient angle exposed.

Tenancy (te·nănsi). 1579. [f. TENANT *sb.* + -ANCY; repr. med.L. *tenantia, tenentia* (XII).] **1.** *Law.* A holding or possession of lands or tenements, by any title of ownership 1590. **b.** Occupancy of lands or tenements under a lease. Also (contextually), the duration of a tenure; the period during which a tenement is held. 1598. **2.** Occupation or enjoyment of or residence in any place, position, or condition 1597. †**3.** That which is held by a tenant. **a.** A tenement. **b.** A post or office; occupation, employment. *rare.* –1670.

Tenant (te·nănt), *sb.* ME. [– (O)Fr. *tenant*, subst. use of pr. pple. of *tenir* hold – (with change of conjugation) L. *tenēre* hold; see -ANT.] **1.** *Law.* One who holds or possesses lands or tenements by any kind of title. (In English Law implying a *lord*, of whom the tenant holds.) **b.** With qualifications indicating the species of tenure, the relation between lord and tenant, etc. ME. **2.** One who holds a piece of land, a house, etc., by lease for a term of years or a set time. (Correl. of *landlord.*) late ME. **3.** *transf.* and *fig.* One who or that which inhabits or occupies any place; a denizen, inhabitant, occupant, dweller. late ME. **4.** *attrib.*, as *t.-farmer, -occupier* 1710.

1. b. *Customary, kindly, mesne, several, sole t.*: see the adjs. *T. in capite, in chief, in common, by courtesy*, etc.: see these words. *T. to the præcipe*, a t. against whom the writ præcipe was brought, being one to whom an entailed estate had been granted in order that it might be alienated by a recovery. **3.** That Frame [the gallows] outliues a thousand Tenants SHAKS. Sorrow..the t. of the soldier's bosom SCOTT. Tenants of our British waters 1879. Hence **Te·nantless** *a.* without a t.; untenanted, empty.

Tenant (te·nănt), *v.* 1634. [f. prec.] **1.** *trans.* To hold as tenant, to be the tenant of (land, a house, etc.); *esp.* to occupy, inhabit. **2.** *intr.* To reside, dwell, live *in* (*rare*) 1650.

1. We bought the farm we tenanted TENNYSON. Hence **Te·nantable** *a.* capable of being tenanted; fit for occupation; **-ness.**

Te·nant at wi·ll. 1500. *Law.* A tenant who holds at the will or pleasure of the lessor.

Te·nant-right. 1527. The right that a person has as a tenant (of any kind). *spec.* **a.** The right of a customary tenant; **b.** the right of a tenant at will or for a term of years to compensation for unexhausted improvements; **c.** the right of a tenant at will to sell his interest and goodwill to the incoming tenant.

Tenantry (te·năntri). late ME. [f. TENANT *sb.* + -RY.] **1.** The state or condition of being a tenant; occupancy as a tenant; tenancy; tenantship. **2.** Land held of a superior; land let out to tenants; also, the profits of such land. late ME. **3.** *spec.* That part of a manor or estate under common or open-field husbandry occupied by tenants, as dist. from the lord's demesne. Hence, locally applied to the condition or system of tenancy under open-field husbandry. 1794. **4.** The body of tenants on an estate or estates 1628.

Tenantship (te·nănt,ʃip). 1883. [f. TENANT *sb.* + -SHIP.] The condition or position of a tenant; tenancy, occupancy.

Tench (tenʃ). late ME. [– OFr. *tenche* (mod. *tanche*) :– late L. *tinca.*] A thick-bodied freshwater fish, *Tinca vulgaris*, allied to the carp, inhabiting still and deep waters; also, the flesh of this fish as food.

Tend (tend), *v.*¹ ME. [Aphetic f. ATTEND *v.*, and *entend* INTEND *v.*] †**1.** *intr.* and *trans.* = ATTEND *v.* I. 1. –1816. **2.** To turn the mind, attention, or energies; to apply oneself. **a.** *intr.* with *to, unto.* To attend to, look after. *Obs.* exc. *dial.* ME. †**b.** To apply oneself *to do* something –1688. **c.** *trans.* To attend to, mind (a thing). Now *rare.* 1549. **3.** To apply oneself to the care and service of (a person); now *esp.* to watch over and wait upon (the sick or helpless) 1489. **b.** To have the care and oversight of (a flock, herd, etc.) 1515. **c.** To attend to (*esp.* a plant, etc.); to work or mind (a pump, a machine, etc.) 1631. **4.** To wait upon as attendant or servant; to attend on. Now *dial.* late ME. **b.** *intr.* with *on, upon*; *spec.* to wait at table 1593. **5.** *trans.* To give one's presence at (a meeting, ceremony, etc.). Now *dial.* and *U.S.* 1460. †**6.** To wait for, await –1818. †**b.** *absol.* or *intr.* To wait in expectation or readiness. SHAKS. (Cf. TENDANCE 3.)

1. Take in the toppe-sale: T. to th' Masters whistle SHAKS. **2. c.** Tending the fire 1866. **3.** Nurses to t. those that were sick DE FOE. **b.** So many Houres, must I t. my Flocke SHAKS. **c.** He ..tended the graves hewn in the living stone KINGSLEY. **4.** Good Angels t. thee SHAKS. **b.** I t. on them, to fetch things for them DE FOE. **6.** By all the stars That t. thy bidding KEATS.

Tend (tend), *v.*² ME. [– (O)Fr. *tendre* :– L. *tendere* stretch.] **I.** To have a motion or disposition to move towards. **1.** *intr.* To direct one's course, make one's way, move or proceed towards something. **a.** Of persons or things. *Obs.* or *arch.* **b.** Of a road, course, journey, series of things 1574. **c.** To have a natural inclination to move (in some direction) 1641. **2.** *fig.* To have a disposition to advance, go on, come finally, or attain *to* (*unto, towards*) some point in time, degree, quality, state, or other non-material category; to be drawn *to* or *towards* in affection. late ME. **3.** To have a specified result, if allowed to act; to lead or conduce *to* some state or condition. Const. *to*, rarely *against.* 1560. **b.** To lead or conduce to some action 1565. **4.** *Naut.* Of a ship at anchor: To swing round with the turn of the tide or wind. Also *trans.* 1770.

1. a. Thither let us t. From off the tossing of these fiery waves MILT. **c.** As weighty bodies to the centre t. POPE. **2.** It is to this point all their speeches, writings, and intrigues of all sorts, t. BURKE. **3.** The labour of the righteous tendeth to life BIBLE (Genev.) *Prov.* 10:16. **b.** Acts tending to the conservation of the Peace HOBBES. To live in a society of equals tends..to make a man's spirits expand M. ARNOLD.

†**II.** *intr.* To extend, stretch, or reach (*to* a point, or in a particular direction) –1725.

The land tending to the west DE FOE.

†**III. 1.** *trans.* To stretch, make tense or taut; to set (a trap, snare, etc.) –1834. **2.** To bend (one's steps) –1644. **3.** *trans.*, or *intr.* with *to.* To relate or refer to; to concern –1654.

†**Te·ndable,** *a.* 1450. [f. TEND *v.*¹ + -ABLE.] Ready to give attention; attentive –1654.

Tendance (te·ndăns). 1573. [Aphetic f. ATTENDANCE, or occas. f. TEND *v.*¹ + -ANCE.] **1.** The attending to or looking after anything; tending, attention, care. **2.** The bestowal of personal attention and care; ministration to the sick or weak 1578. **b.** Attendants collectively; train or retinue 1607. †**3.** Waiting in expectation. SPENSER.

1. Hops dried in loft, aske t. oft 1573. They at her coming sprung And toucht by her fair t. gladlier grew MILT.

Tendence (te·ndĕns). Now *rare* and *literary.* 1627. [– (O)Fr. *tendance* – med.L. *tendentia*; see next, -ENCE.] = next 1.

Tendency (te·ndĕnsi). 1628. [– med.L. *tendentia*, f. L. *tendens, -ent-*, pr. pple. of *tendere* TEND *v.*²; see -ENCY.] **1.** The fact or quality of tending to something; constant disposition to move or act in some direction or toward some point, end, or purpose; leaning, inclination, bent, or bias toward some object, effect, or result. †**b.** A making toward something –1721. **c.** Drift, trend, or aim of a discourse; in recent use, conscious or designed purpose of a story, novel, or the like. (= G. *tendenz.*) 1732. **2.** *attrib. T. drama, novel, story*, one composed with an unexpressed but definite purpose. [After G.] 1838.

1. He seldom converses but with Men of his own T. 1680. A gouty t. 1806. **c.** The t. of all he said was to prove his own merits 1832.

Tendent (te·ndĕnt), *a.* Now *rare.* ME. [– OFr. *tendant*, pr. pple. of *tendre* TEND *v.*²; see -ENT.] Tending, having a tendency (*to* or *towards* some end). *Obs.* bef. 18th c.; revived late in 19th.

Tendential (tende·nʃăl), *a.* 1889. [f. TENDENCY, on the anal. of similar pairs, as *presidency/presidential, residency/residential*; see -IAL¹.] Of the nature of, or characterized by having, a tendency; *spec.* = next.

Tendentious (tende·nʃəs), *a.* 1900. [f. as prec.; see -IOUS.] Having a purposed tendency; composed or written with such a tendency.

A false and t. account of what had taken place 1909. Hence **Tende·ntious-ly** *adv.*, **-ness.**

Tender (te·ndəɹ), *sb.*[1] 1470. [f. TEND *v.*[1] + -ER[1], or aphet. f. ATTENDER.] **1.** †One who tends, or waits upon, another; an attendant, nurse, ministrant (*obs.*); a waiter; an assistant to a builder or other skilled workman (*dial.*). **2.** One who attends to, or has charge of, a machine, a business, etc., as *bar-tender* (a barman), *bridge-t.*, *machine-t.*; now esp. *U.S.* 1825. **3.** A ship or boat employed to attend a larger one. **a.** orig. A vessel commissioned to attend men-of-war, chiefly for supplying them with stores, conveying intelligence, dispatches, etc. Now, a vessel commissioned to act under the orders of another vessel. 1675. **b.** *gen.* A small steamer used to carry passengers, luggage, mails, goods, stores, etc., to or from a larger vessel 1853. **4.** A carriage specially constructed to carry fuel and water for a locomotive engine, to the rear of which it is attached 1825.

3. b. *fig.* Here she comes, i' faith, full sail, with.. a shoal of fools for tenders CONGREVE.

Tender (te·ndəɹ), *sb.*[2] 1542. [f. TENDER *v.*[1]] An act of tendering. **1.** *Law.* A formal offer duly made by one party to another 1562. **b.** *spec.* An offer of money, or the like, in discharge of a debt or liability, *esp.* an offer which thus fulfils the terms of the law and of the liability 1542. **2.** *gen.* An offer of anything for acceptance 1577. **3.** *Comm.* An offer made in writing by one party to another (freq. to a public body) to execute, at an inclusive price or uniform rate, an order for the supply or purchase of goods, or for the execution of work, the details of which have been submitted by the second party 1666. **4.** (esp. *legal, lawful,* or *common t.*) Money or other things that may be legally tendered or offered in payment; currency prescribed by law as that in which payment may be made 1740.

1. *T. of issue*, a plea which in effect invites the adverse party to join issue upon it. **2.** [He] made a t. of his sword and purse to the prince of Orange HUME. **3.** The lowest t. was accepted 1882.

Tender (te·ndəɹ), *a.* and *sb.*[3] ME. [– (O)Fr. *tendre* :– L. *tener* tender, delicate.] **A.** *adj.* **I. 1.** Soft or delicate in texture or consistence; fragile; easily broken, divided, compressed, or injured; of food, easily masticated, succulent. †**2.** Frail, thin, fine, slender (*rare*) –1703.

1. The t. Grass, and budding Flower DRYDEN. Many t. and fragile shells 1832. *fig.* There is Nothing of so t. a Nature..as the Reputation..of Ladies 1709. *T. porcelain*: soft porcelain.

II. Transf. from I. **1.** Of weak or delicate constitution; unable or unaccustomed to endure hardship, fatigue, or the like; delicately reared, effeminate ME. **b.** Of animals or plants: Delicate, easily injured by severe weather or unfavourable conditions; needing protection 1573. **2.** Having the weakness and delicacy of youth; youthful, immature ME. **3.** In ref. to colour or light (rarely, sound): Of fine or delicate quality or nature; soft, subdued 1503. **4.** Of things immaterial, subjects, topics, etc.: Easy to be injured by tactless treatment; needing cautious or delicate handling; delicate, ticklish 1625.

1. A tendre womman and a delicate WYCLIF *Deut.* 28:56. **2.** Boys and girls of a t. age 1844. **3.** The t. green of the young ferns 1894. **4.** A topic too t. to be tampered with SCOTT.

III. Tender toward or in regard to others. **1.** Of an action or instrument: Not forcible or rough; gentle, soft; acting or touching gently ME. **2.** Of persons, their feelings, or the expression of these: Characterized by, exhibiting, or expressing delicacy of feeling or susceptibility to the gentle emotions; kind, loving, gentle, mild, affectionate ME. †**b.** *transf.* Tenderly loved; dear, beloved, precious –1611. **3.** *T. of* (*for, on behalf of*, etc.): Careful of the welfare of; considerate of, thoughtful for; fond of ME. **b.** Chary *of*; scrupulous, cautious, circumspect; reluctant. Const. *of, in.* 1651.

1. Her other t. hand his faire cheeke feeles SHAKS. **2.** Call to remembrance, O Lorde, thy t. mercies & thy louing kindnesses COVERDALE *Ps.* 24[25]:6. *The t. passion* or *sentiment*, sexual love. **3.** So t. is the legislature of his interest 1868. **b.** I confess, I am sorry to find him so t. of appearing PEPYS.

IV. Easily affected, sensitive. **1.** Sensitive to, or easily affected by, external physical forces or impressions. late ME. **b.** *spec.* Acutely sensitive to pain; painful when touched; easily hurt 1709. **c.** Of a ship: Leaning over too easily under sail-pressure; crank, not 'stiff' 1722. **2.** Susceptible to moral or spiritual influence; impressionable, sympathetic; sensitive to pious emotions 1586. **3.** Sensitive to injury; ready to take offence; 'touchy'. *Obs.* exc. as *fig.* from 1 b. 1635.

1. b. The tumor being hard, and very t. 1799. **c.** The ship..was leaky and t. DE FOE. **2.** The form of words used, out of regard to t. consciences 1844. **3.** I am choleric by my nature and t. by my temper FULLER.

†**B.** *sb.* [the adj. used absol.] **1.** Tender state or condition (*rare*) –1691. **2.** Tender feeling, tenderness (*rare*) –1742. †**3.** Tender consideration; care, regard, concern. SHAKS.

2. To disengage my heart from this furious t., which I have for him DRYDEN. **3.** *Lear* I. iv. 230.

Comb.: chiefly parasynthetic adjs., as *t.-bodied, -minded, -natured*, etc.; **t.-dying** *a.*, dying young; **-foreheaded** *a.*, modest, ready to blush; †**-hefted** *a.*, set in a delicate 'haft' or bodily frame; hence, womanly, gentle; **-mouthed** *a.*, (*a*) of a horse: having a tender mouth, answering readily to the rein; †(*b*) dainty; (*c*) gentle in speaking. Hence **Te·nderize** *v. trans.* to make tender. **Te·nder-ly** *adv.*, **-ness.**

Tender (te·ndəɹ), *v.*[1] 1542. [– (O)Fr. *tendre* :– L. *tendere* stretch, hold forth (cf. TEND *v.*[2]). For the unusual retention of the infin. cf. RENDER *v.*] **1.** *trans. Law.* To offer or advance (a plea, issue, averment, evidence) in due and formal terms; *spec.* to offer (money) in discharge of a debt or liability, esp. in exact fulfilment of the requirements of the law and of the obligation. **2.** *gen.* To present (anything) for approval and acceptance; to offer, proffer 1587. **3.** [from TENDER *sb.*[2] 3.] *intr.* To offer by tender *for* a proposed contract, etc. 1865.

2. Several Aldermen..tendered their resignations 1849. *To t. an oath*, to offer or present an oath *to* a person, that he may take it; to put it *to* any one to take an oath.

Tender (te·ndəɹ), *v.*[2] *arch.* or *dial.* late ME. [f. TENDER *a.*] **1.** *trans.* To make tender. Now *dial.* and *techn.* **2.** To feel or act tenderly towards; to regard or treat with tenderness. late ME. **b.** To treat with proper regard 1490.

1. Deal with me, Omniscient Father! as thou judgest best And in thy season t. thou my heart LAMB. The fibre (of flax) tendered by excess of moisture 1880. **2.** He advised me, as I tendered my own safety, to keep aloof from his house 1786.

Te·nder, *v.*[3] 1905. [f. TENDER *sb.*[1]] *trans.* To ship (mails, luggage) on board a tender.

Tenderfoot (te·ndəɹfut). orig. *U.S.* and *Colonial. Pl.* **-foots, -feet.** 1881. A name given, orig. in the ranching and mining regions of the U.S., to a newly-arrived immigrant, unused to the hardships of pioneer life; a greenhorn; hence, a raw inexperienced person. Also, in the Boy Scout movement, a newly-joined recruit, until he has won his first 'badge' and become a 'Second Class Scout'.

Tender-hearted (stress var.), *a.* 1539. [f. *tender heart* + -ED[2].] Having a tender heart; pitiful, compassionate; loving; impressionable. Hence **Te:nder-hea·rtedness.**

Tenderling (te·ndəɹliŋ). 1541. [-LING[1].] **1.** A delicate person or creature; *contempt.*, an effeminate person. Now *rare.* **2.** A person of tender years; a young child 1587. †**3.** *pl.* The soft tops of a deer's horns when they are coming through –1688.

Te·nderloin. *U.S.* 1828. [f. TENDER *a.* + LOIN *sb.*] **1.** The tenderest or most juicy part of the loin of beef, pork, etc., lying under the short ribs in the hind quarter, and consisting of the psoas muscle; the fillet or 'undercut' of a sirloin. **2.** *slang.* In full *t. district*: applied to the police district of New York (and some other cities) which includes the great mass of theatres, hotels, and places of amusement 1895.

Tendinous (te·ndinəs), *a.* 1658. [– Fr. *tendineux* (Paré), f. med. or mod.L. *tendo, tendin-* (cf. It. *tendine*), which repl. *tendo, tendōn-*, on the model of L. words in *-do, -din-*.] Of the nature of a tendon; consisting of tendons.

‖**Tendo** (te·ndo). 1874. [med. or mod.L.; see next.] *Anat.* = next: freq. in *t. Achillis* (see next), and **t.-synovitis,** inflammation of the synovial membrane of a tendon.

Tendon (te·ndən). 1541. [– Fr. *tendon* or med.L. *tendo, tendon-* (also *tendin-*: see TENDINOUS); f. L. *tendere*, tr. Gr. τένων sinew (whence late L. *tenon*), subst. use of aorist pa. pple. of τείνειν stretch, TEND *v.*[2]] A band or cord of dense fibrous tissue forming the termination of a muscle, by which it is attached to a bone or other part; a sinew: usu. applied to such when rounded or cord-like, broad flat tendons being called *fasciæ* and *aponeuroses*.

T. of Achilles (L. *tendo Achillis*), the t. of the heel, by which the muscles of the calf of the leg are attached to the heel. So named because, when dipped in the Styx as an infant, Achilles was held by the heel, which thereby escaped dipping and remained vulnerable.

Tendonous (te·ndŏnəs), *a.* 1597. [f. prec. + -OUS; superseded by TENDINOUS.] = TENDINOUS.

‖**Tendre** (tāndr). Now *rare.* 1673. [Fr., from *tendre* TENDER *a.*] A tender feeling or regard; a fondness, an affection; a tenderness.

A pretty maid, who had a *t.* for me SMOLLETT.

‖**Tendresse** (tāndrẹs). *Obs.* exc. as Fr. late ME. [(O)Fr., f. *tendre* TENDER *a.*; cf. -ESS[2].] = TENDERNESS.

Tendril (te·ndril). 1538. [prob. alt., after Fr. dim. †*tendrillon*, of †*tendron* young shoot (AL. *tendro* XIV), (pl.) cartilages of the ribs (XIV) – (O)Fr. *tendron*, earlier *tendrum* tender part or shoot, cartilage = It. *tenerume* shoots :– Rom. **tenerumen* shoots, f. L. *tener* TENDER *a.*] A slender thread-like organ or appendage of a plant (consisting of a modified stem, branch, flower-stalk, leaf, or part of a leaf), often spiral in form, which stretches out and attaches itself to or twines round some other body so as to support the plant. (Dist. from a *twining stem* by not bearing leaves.)

transf. The glossy tendrils of his raven hair BYRON. *fig.* Inextricable seem to be the twinings and tendrils of this evil EMERSON. Hence **Te·ndrilled, -iled** (-ild) *a.* having a t. or tendrils.

Tendron (te·ndrən). late ME. [– (O)Fr. *tendron*; see prec.] **1.** A young tender shoot or sprout of a plant; a bud. Now *rare.* **2.** *pl.* The cartilages of the ribs (*esp.* in *Cookery*, of a deer or calf). late ME.

‖**Tenebræ** (te·nĕbrī). *R. C. Ch.* 1525. [L., 'darkness'; in med.L. in the eccl. sense.] The name given to the office of matins and lauds of the following day, usu. sung in the afternoon or the evening of Wednesday, Thursday, and Friday in Holy Week, at which the candles lighted at the beginning of the service are extinguished one by one after each psalm, in memory of the darkness at the time of the Crucifixion.

Tene·bricose, *a. rare.* 1730. [– L. *tenebricosus*, f. *tenebricus* dark, gloomy; see -OSE[1].] Full of darkness; dark, obscure; gloomy.

Tenebrific (tenĭbri·fik), *a.* 1785. [f. L. *tenebræ* darkness; see -FIC.] Causing or producing darkness; obscuring.

Books done by pedants and t. persons under the name of men CARLYLE. *T. stars*, 'by whose influence night is brought on, and which do ray out darkness and obscurity upon the earth as the sun does light'; also *fig.*

Tenebrious (tėne·briəs), *a.* 1594. [var. of TENEBROUS by substitution of suffix.] = TENEBROUS *a.*

Tenebrose (te·nĭbrōᵘs), *a.* 1490. [– L. *tenebrosus*, f. TENEBRÆ; see -OSE[1].] Dark. Also *fig.*, mentally or morally dark; gloomy, obscure. So **Tenebro·sity,** darkness, obscurity.

Tenebrous (te·nĭbrəs), *a.* late ME. [– OFr. *tenebrus* (mod. *ténébreux*) – L. *tenebrosus*; see prec., -OUS.] Full of darkness, dark. **b.** *fig.* Obscure, gloomy 1599.

The towering and t. boughs of the cypress LONGF. **b.** That t. philosophy 1849.

Tenement (te·nĭmĕnt). ME. [– OFr. *tenement* (mod. *tènement*) – med.L. *tenementum*, f. L. *tenēre* hold; see -MENT.] †**1.** The fact of holding as a possession; tenure –1651. **2.** Land or real property which is held of another by any tenure; a holding ME. **b.** *pl.* The technical expression for freehold interests in things immovable considered as subjects of property, they being not 'owned' but 'holden'; *esp.* in *lands and tenements*, i.e. lands and all other freehold interests ME. **3.**

gen. A building or house to dwell in; a dwelling-place, a habitation, residence, abode. late ME. **b.** *transf.* and *fig.* An abode; a dwelling-place, esp. applied to the body as the abode of the soul; also, the abode of any animal 1592. **4.** *spec.* **a.** In England, a portion of a house, tenanted as a separate dwelling; a flat; a suite of apartments, or a single room so let or occupied 1593. **b.** In Scotland, a large house let in portions to a number of tenants, each portion being called a 'house' (HOUSE *sb.*[1] 1 b) 1693.

1. *Free t.* = FREEHOLD. **2.** *T. at will*, a t. held at the will of the superior. **3.** The dingy t. inhabited by Miss Tox DICKENS. **b.** That spirit—now struggling to quit its material t. C. BRONTË. **4.** Almes-houses. .let out in Tenements 1593.

attrib. and *Comb.*: **t. house** (orig. U.S.), a house or edifice let out in flats or sets of apartments, or single rooms for separate tenants; **t. householder,** a tenant in a t. house. So **Teneme·ntal** *a.* of, pertaining to, or of the nature of a t.; let out to tenants. **Teneme·ntary** *a*, (*a*) leased to tenants; (*b*) consisting of tenements or dwelling-houses.

‖**Tenendum** (tĭne·ndŏm). 1628. [L., = 'to be held', n. gerundive of *tenēre* hold.] *Eng. Law.* That part of a deed which defines the tenure by which the things granted are to be held (cf. HABENDUM).

†**Tenent.** 1551. [– L. *tenent* they hold.] = TENET –1722.

Being so fickle in their Tenents FULLER.

Teneral (te·nĕrăl), *a.* 1891. [f. L. *tener* tender + -AL[1] 1.] *Ent.* Said of the imperfect imago of a neuropterous insect, when it has just emerged from the pupa state, and is still soft.

‖**Tenesmus** (tĭne·zmŏs). 1527. [med.L. *tenesmus*, *-asmus* = L. *tenesmos* (Pliny) – Gr. τειν-, τηνεσμός straining, f. τείνειν stretch, strain.] *Path.* A continual inclination to void the contents of the bowels or bladder, accompanied by straining, but with little or no discharge. Hence **Tene·smic** *a.* of, pertaining to, or of the nature of t.

Tenet (tī·net, te·net, -ĕt). 1619. [– L. *tenet* (he) holds, 3rd pres. sing. of *tenēre* hold; superseded earlier TENENT.] A doctrine, dogma, principle, or opinion, in religion, philosophy, politics, or the like, held by a school, sect, party, or person. **b.** *gen.* Any opinion held 1630.

The generall T., of all the Philosophers 1619. **b.** The Master of Benet Is of the like Tenet GRAY.

Tenfold (te·nfōᵘld), *a.* and *adv.* OE. [-FOLD.] **A.** *adj.* Ten times as great or as much; ten times increased or intensified; also *indefinitely*, many times as great. **b.** As predicate, passing into subst. use 1769.

1. Our t. griefe SHAKS. **b.** T. I'll give thee to preserve thy faith 1769.

B. *adv.* Ten times (in amount or degree) 1538.

False to himself, but ten-fold false to me! TENNYSON.

Tennantite (te·năntəit). 1839. [Named after Smithson *Tennant*; see -ITE[1] 2 b.] *Min.* A sulph-arsenide of copper and iron, closely related to tetrahedrite.

Tenné, tenny (te·ni), *a.* and *sb.* 1562. [– obs. Fr. *tenné*, var. of *tanné* TAWNY.] *Her.* 'Tawny' as a heraldic colour: variously described as 'orange-brown' or 'bright chestnut'; in engraving represented by diagonal lines from sinister to dexter, crossed by others, according to some authors, vertically, according to others, horizontally.

Tenner (te·nəɹ). *colloq.* 1861. [f. TEN + -ER[1].] A number or amount of ten; *spec.* A ten-pound note; in U.S. a ten-dollar bill.

Tennis (te·nis). [Late ME. *tenetz* (Gower), *teneys*, *tenes*, *tenyse*, usu. taken to be – (O)Fr. *tenez*, imper. of *tenir* hold, take, presumably the server's call to his opponent used as name of the game, which is recorded (XIV) as *tenes*, being introduced into Italy by French knights early in the year 1325. Cf. AL. *pila vocata tenes* (1375).] **1.** A game in which a ball is struck with a racket and driven to and fro by two players in an enclosed oblong court. **2.** Short for LAWN-TENNIS, a game played with a ball and rackets on an unenclosed rectangular space on a smooth grass lawn, or a floor of hard gravel, cement, etc., called a court 1888.

attrib. and *Comb.*: *t.-flannels*, *-lawn*, *-racket*; **t. -arm, elbow, -knee,** an arm, elbow, or knee sprained in playing lawn-t.

Te·nnis-ball. 1450. The small ball used in tennis or lawn-tennis. Also *fig.*; *esp.* a thing or person that is tossed or bandied about like a t.

The very tennisse-ball, in some sort, of fortune 1610.

Te·nnis-court. 1564. **1.** The enclosed quadrangular area, or building, in which the game of tennis is played. **2.** The plot of ground prepared and marked out for lawn-tennis 1881.

Te·nnis-play. 1440. The game of tennis; playing at tennis. So **Te·nnis-play:er,** one who plays at tennis; now, usu., at lawn-tennis.

Tennysonian (tenisōᵘ·niăn), *a.* and *sb.* 1853. [f. name of the poet Alfred (Lord) *Tennyson* (1809–1892) + -IAN.] **A.** *adj.* Of or pertaining to Tennyson, his works, or his style. **B.** *sb.* An admirer, imitator, disciple, or student of Tennyson. 1883.

Teno-, comb. element, arbitrarily formed from Gr. τένων TENDON. **Teno·logy** [-LOGY], that part of anatomy which relates to the tendons. **Te:no-synovi·tis** [see SYNOVIA and -ITIS], inflammation of a tendon and its sheath.

Tenon (te·nən), *sb.* late ME. [– Fr. *tenon*, f. *tenir* hold + *-on*; see -OON.] A projection fashioned on the end or side of a piece of wood or other material, to fit into a corresponding cavity or MORTISE in another piece, so as to form a close and secure joint.

Comb.: **t.-saw,** a fine saw for making tenons, etc., having a thin blade, a thick back, and small teeth very slightly 'set'.

Tenon (te·nən), *v.* 1596. [f. prec.] **1.** *trans.* To fix together with tenon and mortise. **2.** To furnish or fit with a tenon 1771. **b.** *intr.* To engage or fit in by or as by a tenon 1797.

Tenonian (tĕnōᵘ·niăn), *a.* 1890. [f. name of J. R. *Tenon*, a French anatomist (1724–1816) + -IAN.] *Anat.* Discovered or described by Tenon; as in *T. fascia* or *capsule* (*Tenon's capsule*), a delicate band of fascia with involuntary muscle fibres disposed round the eyeball. So **Tenoni·tis** inflammation of Tenon's capsule.

Tenonto-. 1860. [f. Gr. τένων, τενοντ- tendon.] A formative in technical terms relating to the tendons, as **Tenonto·logy** = TENOLOGY.

Tenor (te·nəɹ), *sb.* (*a.*) [ME. *tenur*, *-our* – AFr. *tenur*, OFr. *tenour* (mod. *teneur* course, import) – L. *tenor*, *-ōr-*, continuous course, substance, import of a law, etc., f. *tenēre* hold; see -OR 1.] **I. 1.** The course of meaning which holds on through something written or spoken; the general sense or meaning of a document, speech, etc.; substance, purport, effect, drift. (In techn. legal use implying the actual wording of a document; dist. from *effect.*) **b.** *concr.* An exact copy of a document, a transcript. Now *techn.* 1450. **c.** The value of a bank note or bill as stated on it: in phr. *old t.*, *middle t.*, *new t.*, referring to the successive issues of paper currency in the colonies of Massachusetts and Rhode Island in the 18th c. *Hist.* 1740. **2.** †**a.** The action or fact of holding on or continuing; continuance, duration –1694. **b.** Continuous progress, course, movement (*of* action, etc.); way of proceeding, procedure. late ME. **c.** The length of time that a bill is drawn to run before presentation for payment 1866. **3.** Quality, character, nature; condition, state. *Obs.* exc. in non-physical sense: the way in which a thing continues; *esp.* habitual condition of mind. *rare.* 1530.

1. *Merch. V.* IV. i. 235. **2. b.** Along the cool sequester'd vale of life They kept the noiseless tenour of their way GRAY. **3.** The senses, strongly affected in some one manner, cannot quickly change their tenour BURKE.

II. *Mus.* **a.** The adult male voice intermediate between the bass and the counter-tenor or alto, usu. ranging from the octave below middle C to the A above it; also, the part sung by such a voice, being the next above the bass in vocal part-music. (So called app. because the melody or *canto fermo* was formerly allotted to this part.) late ME. **b.** A singer with a tenor voice; one who sings the tenor part 1475. **c.** = *T. bell*: see B. *Second t.*, the next bell to the tenor. 1541. **d.** A name for the tenor violin or VIOLA 1836. **B.** *attrib.* or *adj.* Applied to a voice, part, instrument, string, etc. of the pitch described in II above, or intermediate between bass and alto 1522.

T. bell, the largest bell of a peal or set. *T. clef*, the C clef when placed upon the fourth line of the stave. *T. violin* (†*viol*), the viola.

Tenotomy (tĕnǫ·tŏmi). 1842. [– Fr. *ténotomie*; see TENO-, -TOMY.] *Surg.* Cutting or division of a tendon; also *attrib.*, as *t. knife*. So **Te·notome,** a surgeon's slender knife for (subcutaneous) division of tendons.

Tenpence (te·npĕns). 1592. A sum of money equal to ten pennies; a foreign coin of about this value.

Tenpenny (te·npĕni), *a.* (*sb.*) late ME. Valued at, costing, or amounting to ten pence; sold at tenpence the piece, dozen, pound, quart, yard, etc.; also in contempt; cf. *twopenny*.

T. piece = B. 1. *T.-worth*, the amount of anything to be bought for tenpence. *T. nail*, orig. a nail sold at tenpence a hundred; now, vaguely, a nail of large size.

B. *sb.* **1.** A piece of money: = TENPENCE 1824. **2.** A tenpenny nail 1820.

Ten-pins (te·npinz), *sb. pl.* Chiefly *U.S.* 1807. A game in which ten pins or 'men' are set up to be bowled at; cf. NINEPINS. Also, the pins, and in sing. *tenpin*, one of these.

Ten-pounder (te:npau·ndəɹ). 1695. [f. *ten pound(s* + -ER[1].] **1. a.** A thing (e.g. a ball, a fish) weighing ten pounds; *spec.* a fish, *Elops saurus*, inhabiting the warmer parts of the Pacific and Atlantic Oceans. **b.** A cannon throwing a ten-pound shot. **2.** Something of the value of, or rated at, ten pounds. **a.** A ten-pound note. **b.** A voter in a borough who was enfranchised in virtue of occupying property of the annual value of ten pounds. 1755.

Tenrec: see TANREC.

Tense (tens), *sb.* ME. [– OFr. *tens* (mod. *temps*) :– L. *tempus* time.] †**1.** Time –1509. **2.** *Gram.* Any one of the different forms or modifications (or word-groups) in the conjugation of a verb which indicate the different times (*past*, *present*, or *future*) at which the action or state denoted by it is viewed as happening or existing, and also (by extension) the different nature of such action or state, as continuing (*imperfect*) or completed (*perfect*); also *abstr.* that quality of a verb which depends on the expression of such differences. late ME.

Tense (tens), *a.* 1670. [– L. *tensus*, pa. pple. of *tendere* stretch; see TEND *v.*[2]] **1.** Drawn tight, stretched taut; strained to stiffness; tight, rigid: chiefly of cords, fibres, membranes. Opp. to *lax*, *flaccid*. **b.** *Phonetics.* Pronounced with tense muscles 1908. **2.** *fig.* In a state of nervous or mental strain or tension; highly strung; excited, or excitable 1821.

1. The skin was t. 1676. **2.** Gwendolen. .looked at her with t. expectancy, but was silent GEO. ELIOT. Hence **Te·nse-ly** *adv.*, **-ness. Te·nsity,** t. condition 1658.

Te·nseless, *a.* 1886. [f. TENSE *sb.* + -LESS.] Having no tenses or distinctions of tense (*loosely*, not expressing time).

Te·nser, -or. *Hist.* [– AFr. *tenser* (AL. *tensarius* XIII), f. OFr. *tense*, *tence* defence, protection, f. *tenser* = med.L. *tensare* protect (XII), exact payment for protection (XIII); ult. origin unknown. See -ER[2] 2, -OR 2 d.] A denizen of a city or borough.

Tensible (te·nsĭb'l), *a.* 1626. [– late L. *tensibilis*, f. *tens-*; see next, -IBLE.] = next 1. Hence **Tensibi·lity.**

Tensile (te·nsəil, -il), *a.* 1626. [– med.L. *tensilis*, f. *tens-*; see next, -ILE.] **1.** Capable of being stretched; susceptible of extension; ductile. **2.** Of, of the nature of, or pertaining to tension; exercising or sustaining tension 1841.

2. A. .t. strain 1841. A t. strength double that of good malleable iron 1868. Hence **Te·nsilely** *adv.* in relation to tension. **Tensi·lity.**

Tension (te·nʃən), *sb.* 1533. [– Fr. *tension* or L. *tensio*, *-ōn-*, f. *tens-*, pa. ppl. stem of L. *tendere* stretch; see -ION.] The action of stretching or condition of being stretched. **1.** *Physiol.* and *Path.* The condition, in any part of the body, of being stretched or strained; a sensation indicating or suggesting this; a feeling of tightness. **b.** *Bot.* Applied to a strain or pressure in the cells or tissues of plants arising from changes taking place in the course of growth 1875. **2.** *fig.* A straining, or strained condition, of the mind, feelings, or nerves 1763. **3.** *Physics.* A constrained condition of the particles of a body when subjected to forces acting in opposite directions away from each other (usu. along the body's greatest length), thus tending to draw them apart, balanced by forces of cohesion holding them together; the force or combination of forces acting in this way, esp. as a measurable quantity. (The opposite of *compression* or *pressure*.) 1685. **b.** Inexactly used for the expansive force of a gas or vapour, properly called *pressure* 1678. **c.** *transf.* A device in a sewing-machine for regulating the tightness of the stitch. Also *t.-device.* 1877. **4.** *Electr.* The stress along lines of force in a dielectric. Formerly applied also to surface density of electric charge, and until about 1882 used vaguely as a synonym for potential electromotive force, and mechanical force exerted by electricity: still so applied, in industrial and commercial use, in *high* and *low t.*; see sense 5. 1802. **5. High tension,** a high degree of tension (of any kind): **a.** *esp.* in *Electr.* a term for a high degree of electromotive force or difference of potential. So **Low t.** (See sense 4.) Chiefly *attrib.* as in *high* or *low t. system* (of electric lighting, etc.); also *high t.* or *low t. accumulator, battery, charge, current, fuse,* etc. 1889. **b.** Of the pulse 1898.

2. A t. of feeling which has had no parallel since the outbreak of the Crimean war 1885. **3. b.** The air..has a certain degree of elasticity or t. FARADAY. Hence **Te·nsion** *v. trans.* to subject to t., tighten, make taut (hence **Te·nsioned** *ppl. a.*). **Te·nsional** *a.* of, pertaining to, of the nature of, or affected with t.

Tensive (te·nsiv), *a.* 1702. [– Fr. *tensif* (Paré), f. L. *tens-*; see prec., -IVE.] Having the quality of stretching or straining; causing tension; in *Path.* applied to a sensation of tension or tightness in any part of the body.

‖**Tenson** (te·nsən, Fr. tãnsoṅ). 1840. [Fr. *tenson* = Pr. *tenso* poetical contest; in OFr. contention, contest.] A contest in verse between rival troubadours; a piece of verse or song composed for or sung in such a contest.

Tensor (te·nsǫɹ, -əɹ). 1704. [– mod.L. *tensor*, f. L. *tendere* stretch; see -OR 2.] **1.** *Anat.* (also *t. muscle*): A muscle that stretches or tightens some part. Opp. to *laxator.* **2.** *Math.* In Quaternions, a quantity expressing the ratio in which the length of a vector is increased 1853.

Tent (tent), *sb.*¹ ME. [– (O)Fr. *tente* :– Rom. **tenta*, n. pl. used as fem. of **tentum*, for L. *tentorium* tent, f. *tent-*, pa. ppl. stem of *tendere* stretch.] **1.** A portable shelter or dwelling of canvas (formerly of skins or cloth), supported by means of a pole or poles, and usu. extended and secured by ropes fastened to pegs which are driven into the ground; used by travellers, soldiers, nomads, and others; a pavilion. **2.** *transf.* Something likened to or resembling a tent; *spec.* **a.** in *Photogr.*, a curtained box serving as a portable dark-room; **b.** the silken web of a t.-caterpillar 1599. **3.** *fig.* An abode, residence, habitation, dwelling-place; esp. in phrases *to have, pitch one's tent(s.* late ME. **4.** *Sc.* (*Hist.*) A portable pulpit set up in the open air 1678.

1. To your tents, O Israel 1 *Kings* 12:16. **3.** To dwell in the tentes of the vngodly COVERDALE *Ps.* 83[4]:10.

Comb.; **t.-barge,** a barge having a t.-like canvas awning; **-bed,** (*a*) a camp bed; (*b*) a bed having an arched canopy and covered sides; **-caterpillar,** the gregarious larva of a N. Amer. bombycid moth, *Clisiocampa*, which spins a t.-like web; **-door,** the entrance or opening of a t.; **-fly,** see FLY *sb.*² 2 b; also, an exterior sheet stretched over the ridge-pole so as to cover the ordinary tent-roof with an air-space between; **-maker,** one who makes tents; **-pin** = TENT-PEG.

Tent (tent), *sb.*² Now *Sc.* and *n. dial.* ME. [Aphetic f. ATTENT and *entent* INTENT.] Attention, heed, care.

Phr. *Take t.*, to take heed, take care; with *to*, to pay attention to, take heed to.

Tent (tent), *sb.*³ late ME. [– (O)Fr. *tente*, f. *tenter* :– L. *temptare* touch, feel, try, TEMPT.] †**1.** A probe –1693. **2.** A roll or pledget, usu. of soft absorbent material, often medicated, formerly much used to search and cleanse a wound, or to keep open or distend a wound, sore, or natural orifice. late ME. †**3.** A paste which sets hard, used in setting precious stones –1656.

1. Modest Doubt is cal'd..the t. that searches To' th' bottome of the worst SHAKS.

Tent (tent), *sb.*⁴ 1542. [– Sp. *tinto* dark-coloured :– L. *tinctus*, pa. pple. of *tingere* dye, TINGE.] A Spanish wine of a deep red colour, and of low alcoholic content. Also *t. wine.* (Often used as a sacramental wine.)

Tent, *sb.*⁵ 1548. [f. TENT *v.*³; or shortened from TENTER *sb.*¹] A stretching frame for embroidery, etc.

Tent, *v.*¹ Now *Sc.* and *n. dial.* ME. [perh. short for *take tent*; see TENT *sb.*²] †**1.** *intr.* To give or pay attention *to*; to attend, take heed –1572. **b.** *trans.* To attend to, give heed to, take notice of (a person, his words, a matter) ME. **2.** To look after, attend to, tend (a person, flock, plant, machine, etc.). late ME. **3.** To take care to prevent or hinder (a person) *from* doing something 1781.

Tent (tent), *v.*² *arch.* 1597. [app. f. TENT *sb.*³] †**a.** *trans.* To probe. **b.** To treat by means of a tent; to apply a tent to (a wound, etc., also to a person); to plug with a tent.

I have a sword dares t. a wound as far As any SHIRLEY.

Tent (tent), *v.*³ 1553. [f. TENT *sb.*¹] **1.** *intr.* To abide or live in a tent; to encamp 1856. **b.** *fig.* To dwell temporarily; to tabernacle; of a thing, to have its seat, 'reside' 1607. **2.** *trans.* To cover or canopy as with a tent 1838. **3.** To accommodate, put up, or lodge in tents 1863. †**4.** To pitch or spread (a tent); to put up, as a tent or its canvas –1634.

1. b. The smiles of Knaues T. in my cheekes SHAKS. **3.** All officers are tented in the same manner as the men 1898.

Tentability (tentăbi·lĭti). *rare.* 1844. [f. *tentare* tempt, in Vulg., Matt. 4:1 *ut tentaretar a diabolo*; see -BILITY. Cf. med.L. *tentabilis* (XIV).] = TEMPTABILITY.

Tentacle (te·ntăk'l). 1762. [Anglicization of TENTACULUM.] *Zool.* A slender flexible process in animals, esp. invertebrates, serving as an organ of touch or feeling. **b.** *Bot.* Applied to a sensitive filament, as the viscous gland-tipped leaf-hairs of the Sundew 1875.

fig. The tentacles of the all-devouring Republic [Rome] 1895.

Comb.: **t.-sheath,** the sheath-like structure surrounding the base of the tentacles of many molluscs. Hence **Te·ntacled** *a.* having tentacles. So **Tenta·cular** *a.* of, pertaining to, or of the nature of a t. or tentacles.

Tentaculate (tentæ·kiŭlět), *a.* (*sb.*) 1846. [f. TENTACULUM + -ATE².] *Zool.* **1.** Furnished with tentacles or tentaculiform appendages; rarely = TENTACULIFORM; *spec.* of or pertaining to the *Tentaculata*, or stalked echinoderms; also *sb.* one of these, a pelmatozoan. So **Tenta·culated** *a.* (in sense 1). 1804.

Tentaculi- (tentæ·kiŭli). 1837. Combining form of mod.L. TENTACULUM, as in **Tenta:culi·ferous** *a.*, bearing tentacles: said of an animal or organ. **Tenta·culiform** *a.*, having the form or appearance of a tentacle.

Tentaculite (tentæ·kiŭləit). 1839. [– mod. L. *Tentaculites*; see TENTACULUM and -ITE¹ 2 a.] *Palæont.* A fossil mollusc of the genus *Tentaculites* or family *Tentaculitidæ* (thought by some to be allied to the pteropods) of which the conical usu. ringed shells abound in the Middle Devonian strata.

Tentaculocyst (tentæ·kiŭlo,si:st). 1880. [f. next + Gr. κύστις CYST.] *Zool.* One of the vesicular or cystic tentacles of a hydrozoan, representing a reduced and modified tentacle.

‖**Tentaculum** (tentæ·kiŭlŏm). *Pl.* **-a.** Also **tentacule.** 1752. [mod.L., f. L. *tentare* = *temptare* feel, try; see TEMPT, -CULE.] = TENTACLE.

Tentage (te·ntėdʒ). 1603. [f. TENT *sb.*¹ + -AGE.] Equipment of tents, tent accommodation.

‖**Tentamen** (tentē¹·měn). *Pl.* **tentamina** (-æ·mină). 1673. [L., f. *tentare* TEMPT.] An attempt, trial, experiment.

Tentation (tentē¹·ʃən). ME. [– L. *tentatio*, *-ōn-*; see TEMPTATION.] †**1.** Early f. TEMPTATION –1818. **2.** *techn.* A mode of working or adjusting by trial or experiment 1877.

Tentative (te·ntătiv), *a.* and *sb.* 1588. [– med.L. *tentativus* adj. (*tentativa* in schol. L.), f. *tentat-*, pa. ppl. stem of L. *tem(p)tare* try; see TEMPT, -IVE. So Fr. *tentative* sb. (XVI) examination, attempt; also as adj. experimental (*obs.*).] **A.** *adj.* Of the nature of an experiment, trial, or attempt; made or done provisionally as an experiment; experimental.

The interpretations must therefore be regarded as t. 1851.

B. *sb.* Something done as an experiment or trial; an essay, an attempt 1632.

Tentatives were made in both directions 1898. Hence **Te·ntative-ly** *adv.*, **-ness.**

Tented (te·ntėd), *a.* 1604. [f. TENT *sb.*¹ and *v.*³ + -ED.] **1.** Of a place: Covered with or full of tents. **2.** Formed or shaped like a tent 1747. **3.** Of persons: Lodged in, or furnished with, a tent or tents 1811.

1. The T. Field SHAKS. **3.** The t. Arabs 1811.

Tenter (te·ntəɹ), *sb.*¹ ME. [– AFr. **tentur* – med.L. *tentorium* (XIII), f. *tent-*, pa. ppl. stem of L. *tendere* stretch.] **1.** A wooden framework on which cloth is stretched after being milled, so that it may set or dry evenly and without shrinking. Also in pl. †**2.** = TENTER-HOOK 1. –1849. †**3.** *fig.* esp. in phr.: *To be on (the) tenter(s*, i.e. in a position of strain, difficulty, or uneasiness; to be in a state of anxious suspense; now *rare* or *Obs.*, repl. by *on tenter-hooks* 1533.

Comb.: †**t.-ground,** ground occupied by tenters for stretching cloth, etc.; †**-yard,** a yard or enclosure with tenters for stretching cloth, etc.

Tenter (te·ntəɹ), *sb.*² *dial.* 1828. [f. TENT *v.*¹ + -ER¹.] **1.** One who minds, or has charge of, anything requiring attention, as a machine, a flock, etc. **2.** An attendant on a skilled workman, who gives him unskilled help, supplies materials, etc. 1894.

Tenter (te·ntəɹ), *v.* late ME. [f. TENTER *sb.*¹] **1.** *trans.* To stretch (cloth) on a tenter or tenters. †**2.** *fig.* To set on the tenter, or on tenter-hooks. Also, to injure or pain as by stretching; to rack, torture (the feelings, etc.) –1734. †**3.** *intr.* Of cloth: To admit of being stretched on the tenter. BACON.

3. Woollen cloth will t., linen scarcely BACON.

Tenter-hook (te·ntəɹ,huk). 1480. [f. as prec. + HOOK *sb.*] **1.** One of the hooks or bent nails by which the edges of the cloth are firmly held on a tenter; a hooked or right-angled nail or spike. **b.** *transf.* A hooked organ or part 1665. **2.** *fig.* That on which something is stretched or strained; something that causes suffering or painful suspense 1532.

2. Phr. *To be on (the) tenter-hooks*, i.e. in a state of painful suspense or impatience.

Tenth (tenþ), *a.* and *sb.* OE. [ME. *tenþe* (XII), alt. by assim. to TEN of *tethe*, OE. *teogoþa*, *tēoþa*; see TITHE, -TH².] The ordinal numeral corresp. to the cardinal number TEN. **A.** *adj.* **1.** In concord with a sb. expressed or understood. **2.** The last of each row or series of ten; each or every tenth individual or part OE.

2. *T. wave*: every t. wave was formerly held to be larger than the nine preceding waves; hence *allus. T. part*, any one of the ten equal parts into which a whole may be divided.

B. *absol.* or *sb.* [orig. the adj. used ellipt. or absol., but from *c*1200 treated as sb. with pl.] **1.** A tenth part *of* anything ME. **b.** *spec.* A tenth part of produce or profits, or of the estimated value of personal property, appropriated as a religious or ecclesiastical due, a royal subsidy, etc. 1474. **2.** *Mus.* A note ten diatonic degrees above or below a given note (both notes being counted); the interval between, or the consonance of, two notes ten diatonic degrees apart 1597. **3.** The tenth day of the month 1580.

1. b. In the eccl. use *spec.*, the tenth part of the annual profit of every living in the kingdom, originally paid to the pope, but now forming a part of the fund known as Queen Anne's Bounty.

Comb.: **tenthmetre,** a metre divided by the t. power of ten (= one ten-millionth of a millimetre); **tenth-rate** *a.*, of the tenth relative quality, very inferior. Hence **Tenth** *v. trans.* to decimate, to tithe (*rare*). **Te·nthly** *adv.* in the t. place.

‖**Tenthredo** (tenþrī·do). 1658. [Latinized form of Gr. τενθρηδών, -δον- a kind of wasp.] *Ent.* A saw-fly: in mod. scientific use, a genus of hymenopterous insects, typical of the family *Tenthredinidæ*, comprising the large saw-flies called hornet-flies.

‖**Tentorium** (tentǭᵊ·riŏm). 1661. [L., = tent, f. *tent-*, pa. ppl. stem of *tendere* stretch; see TENT *sb.*[1], -ORIUM.] †**1.** A canopy. EVELYN. **2.** *Anat.* A membranous (sometimes ossified) partition between the cerebrum and cerebellum 1800. So **Tento·rial** *a. Anat.* of or pertaining to the t.

Te·nt-peg. 1869. One of the (usu. wooden) pegs, with a notch at the upper end, to which when stuck in the ground, the ropes of a tent are fastened. Hence **Te·nt-pe:gging,** an Indian cavalry sport, in which the player, riding at full speed, tries to transfix and carry off, on the point of his lance, a tent-peg fixed in the ground.

Te·nt-stitch. 1639. [First element unc.] A kind of embroidery or worsted-work stitch, in which the pattern is worked in series of parallel stitches arranged diagonally across the intersections of the threads.

Tentwort (te·ntwɒɹt). 1550. [perh. f. TAINT *sb.*] An old name for a small fern, *Asplenium ruta-muraria*.

‖**Tenue** (tənü). 1892. [Fr., deportment, subst. use of fem. pa. pple. of *tenir*.] Carriage, bearing, deportment; also, costume, 'rig'.

Tenui- (teniu,i), comb. form of L. *tenuis* thin, narrow, slender, in scientific use as in **te:nuifo·lious** [L. *folium* leaf] *a.*, having narrow or thin leaves.

Tenu·ious, *a.* Now *rare.* 1495. [f. L. *tenuis* thin + -OUS.] Thin, attenuated.

Tenuiroster (te:niu,irǫ·stəɹ). 1837. [– Fr. *tenuirostre* – mod.L. *tenuirostris*, f. *tenuis* thin + *rostrum* beak, bill.] *Ornith.* A member of the *Tenuirostres*, passerine or insessorial birds with slender bills; a slender-billed bird. So **Te:nuiro·stral** *a.* of or pertaining to the *Tenuirostres*.

‖**Tenuis** (te·nᵋu,is). 1650. [L., = thin, slender, fine; used in early Gr. Grammars as tr. Gr. ψιλόν bare, smooth, applied by Aristotle to the consonants κ, τ, π, as opp. to the *aspiratæ* (in Gr. δασέα, pl. of δασύ rough, thick).] *Phonetics.* An unvoiced, voiceless, or breath stop.

Tenuity (tĕniū·ĭti). 1535. [– L. *tenuitas*, f. *tenuis* thin; see -ITY. Cf. Fr. *ténuité*.] **1.** Thinness of form or size; slenderness 1578. **2.** Thinness of consistence; dilute or rarefied condition; rarity 1603. **b.** Faintness (of light); thinness (of voice) 1794. **3.** *fig.* Meagreness; slightness, slenderness, weakness, poverty 1535.

1. The t.—the thin part—behind, which a bull-dog ought to have JOHNSON. **2.** The t. and fineness of the mud 1802. **b.** A shrill, yet sweet, t. of voice 1858. **3.** The t. of the evidence 1867.

Tenuous (te·niu,əs), *a.* 1597. [irreg. f. L. *tenuis* thin + -OUS, superseding the regular etymol. form TENUIOUS.] **1.** Thin or slender in form; of small transverse measure or calibre; slim 1656. **2.** Thin in physical consistency; sparse; rare, rarefied, subtile; unsubstantial 1597. **3.** *fig.* Slender, of slight importance or significance; meagre, weak; flimsy, vague, unsubstantial 1817. Hence **Te·nuous-ly** *adv.*, **-ness.**

Tenure (te·niŭɹ). late ME. [– OFr. *tenure*, earlier *teneüre* (cf. med.L. *tena-*, *tene-*, *tenitura*), f. *tenir* hold; see -URE.] **1.** The action or fact of holding a tenement (esp. in *Eng. Law*) 1442. **b.** *gen.* and *fig.* The action or fact of holding anything material or non-material; hold upon something; maintaining a hold; occupation 1599. **2.** The condition of service, etc., under which a tenement is held of the superior; the title by which the property is held; the relations, rights, and duties of the tenant to the landlord. late ME. **b.** *transf.* Terms of holding; title; authority; hold over a person or thing; control 1871. **c.** *fig.* 1659. **3.** *concr.* A holding; = TENEMENT 2. Now *rare.* late ME.

1. We have not the mark system, but we have principle of common t. STUBBS. **b.** Their salary cannot be altered during their t. of office 1844. **2.** Those, who by their military tenures were bound to perform forty days service in the field BLACKSTONE. *T. at will*: cf. TENANT AT WILL. **c.** The office of a favourite hath a very uncertain t. SWIFT. **3.** Greenwich-park..is still a royal t. 1766.

Tenurial (teniūᵊ·riăl), *a.* 1896. [f. med.L. *tenura* or TENURE + -IAL.] Of, pertaining to, or of the nature of the tenure of land.

‖**Tenuto** (tenū·to), *a.* and *adv.* [It., = held.] *Mus.* Held, sustained: a direction to sustain a note its full length. Usu. abbrev. *ten.*

‖**Teocalli** (tī,okæ·li). 1578. [Mexican, f. *teotl* god + *calli* house.] A structure for purposes of worship among the ancient Mexicans and Central Americans, usu. a four-sided truncated pyramid built terrace-wise, and surmounted by a temple.

‖**Teosinte** (tī,osi·nti). 1877. [– Mexican *teocintli*, app. f. *teotl* god + *cintli* dry ear or cob of maize. Cf. Fr. *téosinté*.] An annual grass of Central America, *Euchlæna luxurians*, of large size, allied to maize; now widely cultivated as a fodder plant, occas. also as a cereal.

Tepee (tī·pi, tipī·). Also **teepee.** 1872. [Sioux or Dakota Indian *tī·pī* tent, house.] A tent or wigwam of the American Indians, formed of bark, mats, skins, or canvas stretched over a frame of poles converging to and fastened together at the top.

Tepefy (te·pĭfəi), *v.* Also **tepify.** 1656. [f. L. *tepefacere* make tepid, f. *tepēre* be lukewarm; see -FY.] *trans.* and *intr.* To make or become tepid or moderately warm.

‖**Tephillim, -in** (tĭfi·llīm, -īn), *sb. pl.* 1613. [Rabbinical Heb. *tᵉpillīm*, Aramaic *-īn*, heteroclite pl. of *tᵉpillāh* prayer.] A name for Jewish phylacteries, or for the texts inscribed on them.

Tephrite (te·frəit). 1879. [f. Gr. τεφρός ash-coloured (f. τέφρα ashes) + -ITE[1] 2 b.] *Min.* Name given to a class of volcanic rocks related to the basalts. Hence **Tephri·tic** *a.* pertaining to or consisting of t.

Tephroite (te·fro,əit). 1850. [– G. *tephroit* (Breithaupt, 1823), irreg. f. Gr. τεφρός; see prec., -ITE[1] 2 b.] *Min.* A silicate of manganese, occurring in crystalline masses of an ashy grey or reddish colour.

Tephromancy (te·fromænsi). 1652. [f. Gr. τέφρα ashes + -MANCY.] Divination by means of ashes.

Tepid (te·pid), *a.* late ME. [– L. *tepidus*, f. *tepēre* be warm; see -ID[1].] Moderately or slightly warm; lukewarm.

Let the Water stand in the Sun till it grow t. EVELYN. A t. assent H. SPENCER. Hence **Te·pidly** *adv.*, **-ness.**

‖**Tepidarium** (tepidēᵊ·riŏm). *Pl.* **-ia.** 1585. [L., f. *tepidus* TEPID; see -ARIUM.] The warm room in an ancient Roman bath, situated between the *frigidarium* and the *caldarium*.

Tepidity (tėpi·dĭti). 1656. [– late L. *tepiditas*, *-tat-*, f. *tepidus*; see TEPID, -ITY. Cf. (O)Fr. *tépidité*.] The quality or condition of being tepid; moderate or slight warmth; lukewarmness.

Ter- (təɹ), the L. adv. *ter* 'thrice', in comb. **1.** Prefixed to *adjs.*, in sense 'thrice, three times', as **ter-tri·nal** *a.*, consisting of three sets of three. **b.** Prefixed to *adjs.* and *sbs.*, as **ter-diu·rnal** *a.*, occurring or done thrice a day. **2.** *Chem.* With the names of classes of compounds, as *acetate*, *bromide*, expressing the presence of three atoms, molecules, or combining equivalents of the element or radical indicated by the rest of the word, as *nitrogen terchloride* NCl_3. Now mostly repl. by TRI-. **b.** In other compounds, as **ter-equi·valent, te·rvalent** *a.* = TRIVALENT; **te·rvalence** = TRIVALENCE.

‖**Terai** (tĕrai·, -rəi·). 1899. [From *Terai* (Hindi *tarāī* moist (land), f. *tar* moist, damp), name of a belt of marshy and jungly land between the lower foothills of the Himalayas and the plains, where this form of hat was first worn by hunters and travellers.] A wide-brimmed felt hat with double crown and special ventilation, worn by white men generally in sub-tropical regions.

Teraphim (te·răfĭm). late ME. [– Vulg. L. *theraphim*, LXX Gr. θεραφίν (Judges 17:5, Hosea 3:4), etc., – Heb. *ṯᵉrāpīm*, Aram. *-īn*.] A kind of idols or images, or an idol or image; app. *esp.* household gods; an object of reverence and means of divination among the ancient Hebrews and kindred peoples. As *pl.* or as *sing.* with pl. *teraphims*. Also sing. *teraph*, pl. *teraphs*.

‖**Terata** (te·rătă), *sb. pl.* 1902. [mod.L., = Gr. τέρατα, pl. of τέρας marvel, prodigy, monster.] *Biol.* and *Path.* Monstrous formations or births.

Teratical (tĕræ·tikăl), *a. rare.* 1722. [f. Gr. τέρας, τερατ- (see prec.) + -IC + -AL[1] 1.] Relating to marvels or prodigies.

‖**Teratogenesis** (te:răto,dʒe·nĕsis). 1857. [mod.L., f. Gr. τέρας, τερατ- (see TERATA) + GENESIS.] *Biol.* and *Path.* The production of monsters or misshapen organisms. So **Teratogeny** (-ǫ·dʒėni) in same sense.

Teratoid (te·rătoid), *a.* 1876. [f. Gr. τέρας, τερατ- (see TERATA) + -OID.] *Biol.* and *Path.* Having the appearance or character of a monster or monstrous formation; *t. tumour* = TERATOMA.

Teratological (te:rătolǫ·dʒikăl), *a.* 1857. [f. next + -IC + -AL[1] 1.] Of or pertaining to teratology; treating of monstrosities; involving monstrosity, monstrous.

Teratology (terătǫ·lŏdʒi). 1678. [f. Gr. τέρας, τερατ- (see TERATA) + -LOGY.] **1.** A discourse or narrative concerning prodigies; a marvellous tale, or a collection of such tales. **2.** *Biol.* The study of monstrosities or abnormal formations in animals or plants 1842. Hence **Terato·logist.**

‖**Teratoma** (terătōᵘ·mă). *Pl.* **-omata** (-ōᵘ·mătă). 1890. [mod.L., f. as prec.; see -OMA.] *Path.* See quot.

T., a tumor composed of various tissues or systems of tissue, as bone, teeth, etc., which do not normally exist at the place where the tumor grows 1890.

Terbium (tə̄·ɹbiŏm). 1843. [mod.L., from *Y*)*terby* in Sweden + -IUM; cf. ERBIUM.] *Chem.* One of the rare metallic elements found (together with yttrium and erbium) in gadolinite and other minerals.

Terce, variant of TIERCE.

Tercel, tiercel (tə̄·ɹs'l, tīᵊ·ɹs'l). late ME. [– OFr. *tercel*, also *terçuel* – Rom. **tertiolus*, dim. f. L. *tertius* third; perh. so named because it was believed that the third egg of a clutch produced a male bird.] The male of any kind of hawk; in Falconry esp. of the peregrine falcon (TERCEL-GENTLE) and the goshawk.

Tercelet, tiercelet (tə̄·ɹslėt, tīᵊ·ɹslėt). late ME. [– AFr. *tercelet* = (O)Fr. *tiercelet*, dim. (see -ET) of OFr. *tercel* TERCEL. Cf. med.L. *tercelettus* (1287).] = prec.

Tercel-ge·ntle. 1486. [f. TERCEL, after FALCON-GENTLE.] The male of the falcon.

fig. Hist Romeo hist, o for a falkners voyce, To lure this Tassel gentle back againe SHAKS.

Tercentenary (təɹse·ntĭnări, -sĕnti·nări), *a.* and *sb.* 1844. [f. TER- + CENTENARY.] **A.** *adj.* Of or belonging to the number of three hundred; usu., to a completed period of 300 years. **B.** *sb.* A duration of three hundred years; the three-hundredth anniversary of an event, or a celebration of it 1855.

Tercentennial (tə̄ɹ,sente·niăl), *a.* and *sb.* 1882. [f. TER- + CENTENNIAL.] **A.** *adj.* Of or belonging to a period of three hundred years; of or relating to the three-hundredth anniversary. **B.** *sb.* The three-hundredth anniversary *of* an event.

Terceroon (tə̄ɹserū·n). *rare.* 1760. [– Sp. **terceron*, f. *tercero* a third person, f. *tercio* third; cf. *cuarteron*, *quinteron*; see -OON.] The offspring of a white person and a mulatto, being third in descent from a negro; = QUADROON 1 a.

Tercet (tə̄·ɹsėt). 1598. [– Fr. *tercet* – It. *terzetto*, f. *terzo* (:– L. *tertius* third) + *-etto* -ET.] *Pros.* A set or group of three lines rhyming together, or bound by double or triple rhyme with the adjacent triplet or tripets; *spec.* **a.** each of the triplets of the Italian TERZA RIMA; **b.** each of the two triplets usu. forming the last six lines of a sonnet.

Tercine (tə̄·ɹsin). 1832. [– Fr. *tercine* (Mirbel, 1828), f. *tiers*, *tierce*, or L. *tertius* third; see -INE[1], and cf. PRIMINE.] *Bot.* A third integument supposed by some to occur in certain ovules.

Tercio, tertio (tə̄·ɹsio, tə̄·ɹʃio). Now *Hist.* 1583. [– Sp. *tercio*, It. †*tertio*, mod. It. *terzo*, Pg. *terço* a regiment :– L. *tertium* a third.] *orig.* A regiment of the Spanish infantry 16–17th c.; applied also to the Italian forces of that period; hence, a body of foot forming a main division of an army.

Terebene (te·rėbīn). 1857. [f. TEREBINTH + -ENE.] *Chem.* **1.** Used by Deville (1840) for a liquid obtained by the action of sulphuric acid on pinene, now known to be a mixture of terpenes together with cymene: one of the drugs of the British Pharmacopœia; also *attrib.* as *t. soap* 1898. †**2.** Sometimes a synonym of TERPENE –1871.

Terebenthene (te·rěbe·nþīn). 1857. [– Fr. *térébenthène*, f. *térébenthine* – L. *terebinthina* (*resina*); with suffix -ENE as in BENZENE.] *Chem.* Berthelot's name for the TERPENE which forms the chief constituent of French turpentine-oil, obtained from *Pinus pinaster* (*P. maritima*).

Terebic (tĕre·bik), *a.* 1857. [f. TEREBINTH + -IC.] *Chem.* Of, belonging to, or derived from turpentine, as in *t. acid*, $C_7H_{10}O_4$, a dibasic acid, a product of the action of nitric acid on turpentine-oil. Hence **Te·rebate**, a salt of t. acid.

Terebinth (te·rĕbinþ). late ME. [– OFr. *t(h)erebinte* (mod. *térébinthe*), corresp. to Sp., It. *terebinto*, or their source L. *terebinthus* – Gr. τερέβινθος, earlier τέρβινθος, τέρμινθος, of alien origin.] **1.** A tree of moderate size, *Pistacia terebinthus*, family *Anacardiaceæ*, the source of Chian turpentine; also called *turpentine tree.* †**2.** The resin of this tree; = TURPENTINE –1673.

‖**Terebinthina** (-i·nþină). 1693. [med.L., short for *terebinthina resina* (Celsius) terebinthine resin.] The pharmacopœial name of turpentine.

Terebinthinate (terĕbi·nþinĕt), *a.* and *sb.* 1680. [f. prec. or next + -ATE[1,2].] **A.** *adj.* Impregnated with turpentine; having the nature or quality of turpentine. **B.** *sb.* A terebinthine product; a medicinal preparation of turpentine 1750. So **Terebi·nthinate** *v. trans.* to impregnate with turpentine.

Terebinthine (terĕbi·nþin), *a.* and *sb.* 1513. [– L. *terebinthinus* (= Gr. τερεβίνθινος), f. *terebinthus*; see TEREBINTH, -INE.] **A.** *adj.* **1.** Of, pertaining to, of the nature of, or allied to the terebinth 1550. **2.** Of, pertaining to, or consisting of turpentine; turpentiny 1656. †**B.** *sb.* (the adj. used ellipt.) **1.** The terebinth –1513. **2.** Turpentine –1725.

‖**Terebra** (te·rībră). 1611. [L., a borer.] †**1.** An instrument for boring; *Surg.*, a trephine, or the boring part of it; also, a miner's drill –1787. **2.** *Ent.* The modified ovipositor of certain female insects, esp. terebrant Hymenoptera, with which they puncture leaves, fruit, etc., in order to insert their eggs 1713.

Terebrant (te·rībrănt), *a.* 1826. [– L. *terebrans, -ant-*, pr. pple. of *terebrare* bore, f. *terebra* borer; see -ANT.] Boring, or having the function of boring; belonging to the division *Terebrantia* of hymenopterous insects, having a boring ovipositor.

Terebrate (te·rībre[i]t), *v.* Now *rare.* 1623. [f. *terebrat-*, pa. ppl. stem of L. *terebrare*; see prec., -ATE[3].] *trans.* To bore, pierce, perforate; to penetrate by boring.

Terebration (terībrē[i]·ʃən). Now *rare* or *Obs.* late ME. [– L. *terebratio, -ōn-*, f. as prec.; see -ION. Cf. Fr. *térébration.*] The action of boring or perforating; †*spec.* in *Surg.* the operation of trephining.

‖**Terebratula** (terībræ·tiŭlă). *Pl.* **-æ** (-ī), or **-as** (-ăz). Also (after Fr.) **terebra·tule.** 1822. [mod.L. (Lhwyd, 1699), quasi-dim. of L. *terebratus*, pa. pple. of *terebrare* bore; see -ULE.] *Zool.* and *Palæont.* A genus of brachiopods, mostly extinct: so called from the perforated beak of the ventral valve. Formerly used to include any (esp. fossil) members of the *Terebratulidæ* and related families; the lamp-shells. Hence **Terebra·tular** *a.* of or pertaining to a t. **Terebra·tuliform** *a.* having the form of a t.

Teredo (tĕrī·do). *Pl.* **teredines** (-ī·dinīz), **teredos** (tĕrī·do[u]z). late ME. [– L. *teredo* – Gr. τερηδών, f. base *τερ- of τείρειν rub hard, wear away, bore.] **1.** *Zool.* A genus of lamellibranch boring molluscs; *esp.* the shipworm, *T. navalis*, well-known for its destruction of submerged timbers in ships, piers, sea-dikes, etc. by boring into the wood. **2.** *transf.* Any disease in plants produced by the boring of insects 1866.

Terentian (tĕre·nʃiăn), *a.* 1599. [– L. *Terentianus*, f. *Terentius* Terence; see -AN.] Pertaining to, or in the style of, the ancient Roman dramatic poet Terence.

Terephthalic (terĕfþæ·lik), *a.* 1857. [f. TEREBIC *a.* + PHTHALIC *a.*] *Chem.* Derived from or containing terebic and phthalic acids, as in *t. acid* (also called *insolinic acid*), $C_8H_6O_4 = C_6H_4(CO_2H)_2$, a dibasic acid produced as a white tasteless crystalline powder, nearly insoluble in water, alcohol, and ether. Hence **Tere·phthalate**, a salt of this acid.

Terete (tĕrī·t), *a.* 1619. [– L. *teres, teret-* rounded (off).] Rounded, smooth and round; in *Nat. Hist.*, having a cylindrical or slightly tapering form, circular in cross-section, and a surface free from furrows or ridges. Hence **Tere·tish** *a.* somewhat t.

Tereti- (te·rīti), comb. form of L. *teres, teret-* TERETE, as in **Te:reticau·date** *a.*, having a rounded tail, round-tailed.

Tereu (tīrū·). 1576. A feigned note of the nightingale. (*Tereu*, vocative of Gr.-L. *Tereus*, husband of Philomela's sister Progne; see Ovid *Met.* VI. viii.)

Tergal (tə̄·ɹgăl), *a.* 1860. [f. L. *tergum* back + -AL[1] 1.] *Zool.* Belonging to the tergum; dorsal.

Tergeminate (təɹˌdʒe·minĕt), *a.* 1793. [f. L. *tergeminus* (poet. var. of *trigeminus*) born three at a birth + -ATE[2].] *Bot.* Thrice-double; having three pairs of leaflets.

Tergite (tə̄·ɹdʒəit). 1885. [f. L. *tergum* back + -ITE[1] 3.] *Zool.* A back-plate, formed by the fusion of a pair of serial plates of one of the somites or segments of an arthropod or other articulated animal. Hence **Tergi·tic** *a.* of or pertaining to a t.

Tergiversate (tə̄·ɹdʒivəɹsē[i]t, -və̄:ɹse[i]t), *v.* 1654. [– *tergiversat-*, pa. ppl. stem of L. *tergiversari* turn one's back, practice evasion, f. *tergum* back + *vers-*, pa. ppl. stem of *vertere* turn; see -ATE[3].] **1.** *intr.* To practise tergiversation; to turn renegade, apostatize; to shuffle, use subterfuge; †to act the recusant. **2.** *lit.* To turn the back (for flight or retreat) 1875.

Tergiversation (tə̄:ɹdʒivəɹsē[i]·ʃən). 1570. [– L. *tergiversatio, -ōn-*, f. as prec.; see -ION.] **1.** The action of 'turning one's back on', i.e. forsaking, something in which one was previously engaged, interested or concerned; desertion or abandonment of a cause, party, etc.; apostasy, renegation. Also with *a* and *pl.*, an instance of this. 1583. **2.** Turning in a dishonourable manner from straightforward action or statement; shifting, shuffling, equivocation, prevarication. Also, an instance of this. 1570. **3.** The turning of the back for flight; flight, retreat (*lit.* and *fig.*). Now *rare* or *Obs.* 1652.

1. Their tergiuersation and backsliding from their duties 1583. **2.** The duplicity and t. of which he had been guilty SCOTT. His shifts and tergiversations G. MEREDITH.

Tergiversator (tə̄·ɹdʒivəɹsē[i]:təɹ). 1716. [f. TERGIVERSATE *v.* + -OR 2.] One who tergiversates; a renegade; a shuffler.

Tergo- (tə̄ɹgo), comb. form repr. L. *tergum* the back, used instead of the regular *tergi-*, as in **Tergola·teral** *a. Zool.*, pertaining to the tergum and the lateral plates of the shell in cirripeds.

‖**Tergum** (tə̄·ɹgŏm). *Pl.* **terga.** 1826. The L. word for 'back' (synon. w. DORSUM). **a.** The back of an arthropod or other articulated animal; more usu. the upper plate of each somite or segment of such an animal: opp. to *sternum.* **b.** Each of the two upper plates of the shell in cirripeds.

Term (tə̄ɹm), *sb.* ME. [– (O)Fr. *terme* :– L. TERMINUS.] **I.** A limit in space, duration, etc. **1.** That which limits the extent of anything; a limit, extremity, boundary, bound. Usu. in *pl.* Now *rare* or *arch.* late ME. **b.** Utmost or extreme limit, end. Now *rare* or *arch.* ME. **c.** That to which movement or action is directed or tends, as its object, end, or goal; (less commonly) that from which it begins, starting-point, origin. Now *rare* or *Obs.* late ME. **2.** *Astrol.* A certain portion of each sign of the zodiac, assigned to a particular planet. late ME.

1. Corruption is a Reciprocall to Generation: and they two, are as Natures two Terms or Boundaries BACON. **b.** He had now reached the t. of his prosperity GIBBON. **c.** Vehement actions without scope or t. M. ARNOLD.

II. A limit in time; a space of time. **1.** A definite point of time at which something is to be done, or which is the beginning or end of a period; a set or appointed time or date, esp. for payment of money due. *Obs.* or *arch.*, exc. in spec. uses. ME. **b.** *spec.* Each of the days in the year fixed for payment of rent, wages, and other dues, beginning and end of tenancy, etc. late ME. **2.** *transf.* A portion of time having definite limits; a period, *esp.* a set or appointed period; the space of time through which something lasts or is intended to last; duration, length of time ME. **3.** *spec.* Each of the periods (usu. three or four in the year) appointed for the sitting of certain courts of law, or for instruction and study in a university or school. Opp. to *vacation.* 1454. **4.** *Law.* An estate or interest in land, etc. for a certain period; in full, *t. of* or *for years.* late ME. **5. a.** The completion of the period of pregnancy; the (normal) time of childbirth 1844. †**b.** *pl.* The menstrual periods; the menstrual discharge, menses –1714.

2. Seven years (the usual t. of transportation) BYRON. Phr. *For t. of (one's) life*; The husbande hath Estate in the speciall tayle, and the wife but for terme of lyfe 1544. **3.** I am obliged to give up ..the hope of coming to Oxford this t. M. ARNOLD. Phr. *In t.*, during the t. *To keep terms*: see KEEP *v.* 4. **4.** Every estate which must expire at a period certain and prefixed..is an estate for years. And therefore this estate is frequently called a t. BLACKSTONE. *Outstanding t., satisfied t.*: when the purposes for which an estate was created were fulfilled (e.g. by the death of all beneficiaries) it was called a *satisfied t.*; but unless express provision had been made that it should then cease, it continued to exist for the period for which it was created, and was then known as an *outstanding* or *attendant t.*

III. Limiting conditions. **1.** *pl.* Conditions or stipulations limiting what is proposed to be granted or done. Rarely in *sing.* ME. **b.** *spec.* Stipulations for payment in return for goods or services; conditions with regard to price or wages; payment offered, or charges made 1670. **2.** *pl.* Standing, footing, mutual relation between two persons or parties 1543. †**3.** *pl.* Condition, state, situation, position, circumstances; (in Shaks.) vaguely or redundantly: relation, respect (rarely in *sing.*) –1656.

1. He was obliged..to offer terms of peace HUME. Phr. *On* or *upon terms*, (*a*) (advb.) on (such and such) conditions; also (without qualification) on certain conditions, conditionally; (*b*) (pred.) in treaty, negotiating. *To come to terms*, to agree upon conditions; so *to bring to terms. To keep terms*, to have or continue to have dealings *with*; also *fig.* to 'have to do *with*', be connected *with. To make terms = come to terms.* †*To stand on* or *upon terms*, to insist upon conditions; to stand upon one's rights or dignity. *Terms of reference*, the terms which define the scope of an inquiry. **2.** Phr. *On terms*, on friendly terms, friendly, sociable; in sporting slang, on terms of equality, on an equal footing *with. On* (*upon*) *equal terms, good terms, speaking terms, visiting terms*, etc. **3.** Be iudge..Whether I in any iust terme am Affin'd To loue the Moore? SHAKS.

IV. Uses leading up to the sense 'expression'. **1.** *Math.* (*a*) Each of the two quantities composing a ratio (antecedent and consequent), or a fraction (numerator and denominator). (*b*) Each of any number of quantities forming a series or progression. (*c*) Each of (two or more) quantities connected by the signs of addition (+) or subtraction (–) in an algebraical expression or equation. 1542. **b.** *In terms of*: (*Math.*) said of a series or expression stated in terms involving some particular quantity; hence *gen.*, by means of, or in reference to (some particular set of symbols, ideas, etc.); often used as if = in the phraseology of 1743. **c.** *transf.* A member or item of any series; each of the things constituting a series. Also more vaguely, an element of any complex whole. 1841. **2.** *Logic*, etc. Each of the two things or notions which are compared, or between which some relation is apprehended or stated, in an act of thought, or (more commonly) each of the words or phrases denoting these in a verbal statement; *spec.* the subject and predicate of a proposition; the *major, minor*, or *middle t.* of a syllogism, each of which occurs twice 1551. **3.** A word or phrase used in a definite or precise sense in some particular subject, as a science or art; a technical expression (more fully *t. of art*). late ME. **b.** More widely: Any word or group of words expressing a notion or conception, or denoting an object of thought; an expression (*for* something). Usu. with qualifying adj. or phr. (as *an abstract t., a t. of reproach*). 1477. **4.** Only in *pl.* Words or expressions collectively or generally (usu. of a specified kind); manner of expressing oneself, way of speaking, language. late ME. †**b.** *In terms*: in so many words –1667.

1. *Lowest terms* (*Math.*), the form of a fraction when the numerator and denominator are the least possible, i.e. have no common factor; hence *fig.* the simplest condition of anything; usu. in phr. *to bring* or *reduce to its lowest terms*. **3.** I ne kan no termes of Astrologye CHAUCER. The idea involved in the t. latent heat 1862. **4.** She in milde termes beg'd my patience SHAKS. **b.** He says in terms that the match..hath undone the nation PEPYS.

V. *Arch.* A statue or bust like those of the god TERMINUS, representing the upper part of the body, sometimes without the arms, and terminating below in a pillar or pedestal out of which it appears to spring; a terminal figure; the pillar or pedestal bearing such a figure 1604.

Term (tə̄ɹm), *v.* late ME. [In sense 1 prob. – OFr. *termer* bring to an end; in sense 2 f. prec.] †**1.** *trans.* To bring to an end or conclusion; to terminate –1570. **2.** To express or denote by a term or terms; to name, denominate, designate. Now only with compl. 1560.

2. The brain, which we tearme the seat of reason SIR T. BROWNE.

Termagant (tə̄·ɹmăgănt), *sb.* (*a.*) [In XIII *tervagaunt*, later *term-* (XIV) – OFr. *Tervagan(t* – It. *Trivigante, -vag-* (Ariosto), explained as if f. L. *tri-* TRI- + *vagans, -ant-*, pr. pple. of *vagari* wander.] **1.** (With capital T.) An imaginary deity held in mediæval Christendom to be worshipped by Moslems: in the mystery plays representing a violent overbearing personage. **2.** A savage, violent, boisterous, overbearing, or quarrelsome person (or thing personified); a blusterer, bully. Now *rare* exc. as in b. 1500. **b.** *spec.* A woman of this character; a virago, shrew 1659. **3.** *attrib.* or *adj.* Having the character of a termagant 1596.

1. I could haue such a Fellow whipt for o'redoing T.: it out-Herod's Herod SHAKS. **2.** Thys terryble termagaunt, thys Neroth, thys Pharao 1542. **b.** Yonder is Sarah Marlborough's palace, just as it stood when that t. occupied it THACKERAY. **3.** The most t. spirit that ever animated a female breast 1761. Hence **Te·rmagancy,** t. quality, violence of temper or disposition. †**Te·rmagantly** *adv.*

Termer (tə̄·ɹməɹ). 1556. [f. TERM *sb.* + -ER[1].] **1.** One who resorted to London in term, either for business at a court of law, or for amusements, intrigues, or dishonest practices. Now *Hist.* †**2.** Obs. form of TERMOR 1631.

‖**Termes** (tə̄·ɹmīz). *Pl.* **termites** (tə̄·ɹmitīz). 1800. [mod. use (Linn., 1748) of late L. *termes, termit-* wood-worm, alt. of earlier *tarmes* (Plautus) perh. by assim. to *terere* rub.] = TERMITE.

Terminable (tə̄·ɹmināb'l), *a.* late ME. [f. TERMINE *v.*, later f. TERMINATE *v.*, + -ABLE; in earliest use reflecting OFr. *terminable* and med.L. *terminabilis* (XIII).] †**1.** That may be or is to be terminated, determined, or finally decided –1450. **2.** Capable of being or liable to be terminated; limitable, finite; not lasting or perpetual 1581.

2. *T. annuity*, an annuity which comes to an end after a definite term; see ANNUITY 3. *T. annuitant*, one who holds a t. annuity. Hence **Terminabi·lity, Te·rminableness,** the quality of being t. **Te·rminably** *adv.*

Terminal (tə̄·ɹminăl), *a.* and *sb.* 1744. [– L. *terminalis*, f. *terminus* end, boundary; see -AL[1] 1. Cf. Fr. *terminal*, which may be partly the source.] **A.** *adj.* **1.** Belonging to or placed at the boundary of a region, as a landmark. **b.** Applied to a statue, bust, or figure terminating in and apparently springing from a pillar or pedestal; also to the pillar or pedestal itself 1857. **2.** Situated at or forming the end or extremity of something: chiefly in scientific use 1805. **b.** Situated at the end of a line of railway; forming, or belonging to, a railway terminus 1878. **3.** Occurring at the end of something (in time, or generally); forming the last member of a series; closing, concluding, final, ultimate 1831. **4.** Belonging to or lasting for a term or definite period; *esp.* pertaining to a university or law term; occurring every term or at fixed terms; termly 1827.

2. A prism with a six-sided t. pyramid 1869. *T. moraine* (Geol.), a moraine at the lower end of a glacier. **b.** T. stations 1878. **4.** The t. examinations called 'Collections' 1885.

B. *sb.* **1.** A terminal part or structure, i.e. one situated at or forming the end, or an end, of something; *spec.* in *Electr.* each of the free ends of an open circuit (by connecting which the circuit is closed), or any structure forming such an end, as the carbons in an arc-light, or the clamping-screws in a voltaic battery by which it is connected with the wire that completes the circuit 1850. **2.** A final syllable, letter, or word; a termination 1831. **3.** *pl.* Charges made by a railway company for the use of a terminus or other station, and for services rendered in loading or unloading goods, etc., there 1878. **4.** A terminus; a terminal point of a railway, a place or town at which it has a terminus. *U.S.* 1888. Hence **Te·rminally** *adv.*

Terminant (tə̄·ɹminănt), *a.* (*sb.*) Now *rare* or *Obs.* 1589. [– L. *terminans, -ant-*, pr. pple. of *terminare*; see TERMINATE *v.*, -ANT.] **1.** Terminating, concluding, final. Also as *sb.* A final syllable, termination, terminal. †**2.** Determining, defining –1610.

Terminate (tə̄·ɹminĕt), *ppl. a.* late ME. [– L. *terminatus*, pa. pple. of *terminare*; see next, ATE[2].] Terminated, in various senses; see the vb.

Terminate (tə̄·ɹmine[i]t), *v.* 1589. [– *terminat-*, pa. ppl. stem of L. *terminare* limit, end, f. *terminus* end, boundary; see -ATE[3].] **I.** *trans.* †**1.** To determine; to state definitely (*rare*) –1706. **2.** To direct (an action) to something as object or end 1599. †**b.** Of a thing: To be the object of (an action) –1704. **3.** To bring to an end, put an end to, cause to cease; to end (an action, condition, etc.) 1615. **b.** To come at the end of, form the conclusion of 1798. †**4.** To put a limit or limits to; to restrict, confine *to* (*in*) –1674. **5.** To bound or limit spatially; to be situated at the end of 1634. **6.** †**a.** To define (visual objects) –1762. **b.** To finish, complete (*rare*) 1825.

3. She had every hope that this..would t. every perplexity 1796. **5.** On another side, the great deep terminates the view 1746. **6. b.** During this interval of calm and prosperity, he terminated two figures of slaves..in an incomparable style of art 1857.

II. *intr.* **1.** To be directed to something as object or end 1699. **2.** To come to an end (in space); to end *at, in,* or *with* something 1644. **b.** Of a word: To end *in* (a letter or sound) 1824. **3.** To come to an end, so as to extend no further; to have its end or terminus *in* something 1613. **4.** To come to an end (in time); to end, cease, close 1815. **b.** To issue, result (*in* something) 1710.

1. My thoughts all t. in God 1856. **2.** The spot where the present gulf terminates 1862. **4.** The sweetest notes must t. and die WORDSW.

Termination (tə̄ɹminē[i]·ʃən). 1450. [– OFr. *termination*, (also mod.) *terminaison*, or L. *terminatio*. *-ōn-*, f. as prec.; see -ION.] **I.** †**1.** The action of determining; determination, decision –1660. **2.** The action of ending. †**a.** Bounding, limiting. **b.** Putting an end to; bringing to a close. 1604. **II.** The point or part in which anything ends. **1.** End (in time), cessation, close, conclusion 1500. **b.** Outcome, issue, result 1806. **2.** The ending of a word; the final syllable, letter, or group of letters; *spec.* in *Gram.* an (inflexional or derivative) ending, a suffix 1530. **3.** A limit, bound; an end, extremity 1755.

1. All human power has its t. sooner or later J. H. NEWMAN. **b.** Dissensions which could hardly have other than a hostile t. 1884. **3.** To improve the t. of the line at the Liverpool end 1830. Hence **Termina·tional** *a.* of, pertaining to, or forming a t. or terminations; closing, final (chiefly *Gram.*).

Terminative (tə̄·ɹmine[i]tiv, *-ĕtiv*), *a.* late ME. [– Fr. *terminatif, -ive* or med.L. *terminativus*, f. as prec.; see -IVE.] **1.** †Forming a boundary or limit, bounding; forming the termination or extremity of something. †**2.** Constituting an end, final, ultimate –1701. **3.** Bringing or coming to an end; finishing; conclusive 1680. Hence **Te·rminatively** *adv.*

Terminator (tə̄·ɹminē[i]təɹ). 1770. [In sense 2 mod. spec. use of late L. *terminator*; in sense 1 f. TERMINATE *v.* + -OR 2.] **1.** One who or that which terminates 1846. **2.** *Astron.* The line of separation between the illuminated and unilluminated parts of the disc of the moon or a planet 1770.

Te·rminatory, *a. rare.* 1756. [f. TERMINATE *v.* + -ORY[2].] Forming the end or extremity; terminal.

†**Te·rmine,** *v.* ME. [– (O)Fr. *terminer* – L. *terminare.*] = TERMINATE *v.* –1705.

Terminer, in *oyer and t.*: see OYER.

Terminism (tə̄·ɹminiz'm). 1882. [f. L. *terminus* end, limit + -ISM.] **a.** *Philos.* The doctrine that universals are mere terms or names: = NOMINALISM b. **b.** *Theol.* The doctrine (maintained by Reichenberg at Leipzig in the 17th c.) that God has appointed a definite term or limit in the life of each individual, after which the opportunity for salvation is lost. So **Te·rminist,** one who holds or maintains t. 1727.

Terminology (tə̄ɹminǫ·lŏdʒi). 1801. [– G. *terminologie* (C. G. Schütz, 1786) f. L. *terminus* in its med.L. sense 'term'; see -LOGY.] Etymologically, The doctrine or scientific study of terms; in use almost always, the system of terms belonging to any science or subject; technical terms collectively; nomenclature.

Kant, who..gave old ideas a novelty by giving them a new t. 1847. Every calling has its technical t. HUXLEY. Hence **Te·rminolo·gical** *a.* pertaining to t.; **-ly** *adv.* **Termino·logist,** one versed in t.

It could not..be classified as slavery..without some risk of terminological inexactitude W. S. CHURCHILL 1906.

Terminus (tə̄·ɹminŏs). *Pl.* **termini** (-əi). 1555. [– L. *terminus* end, limit, boundary, etc.] **1.** *Anc. Rom. Myth.* (With initial capital.) The deity who presided over boundaries or landmarks 1600. **2.** A statue or bust of, or resembling those of, the god Terminus; also, the pedestal of such a statue. Sometimes, a boundary post or stone. 1645. **3.** The point to which motion or action tends, goal, end; occas., starting-point 1555. **4.** A boundary, limit (*rare*) 1673. **5.** The end of a line of railway; also, the station at the end; the place at which a tram-line, etc. ends 1836. **b.** *transf.* or *gen.* An end, extremity; the point at which something comes to an end 1855.

3. Phr. (orig. scholastic L.) *T. a quo* 'term from which'. *T. ad quem* 'term to which'. **5. b.** The grey matter [of the brain] is a t.; to it the fibrous collections tend, or from it commence 1855.

Termite (tə̄·ɹməit). 1781. [– mod. use (Linn.) of late L. *termes, termit-*; see TERMES.] A pseudoneuropterous social insect of the genus *Termes* or family *Termitidæ*, chiefly tropical, and very destructive to timber; also called *white ant*.

Termless (tə̄·ɹmlės), *a.* 1586. [f. TERM *sb.* + -LESS.] **1.** Having no term or limit; boundless. †**2.** Inexpressible. SHAKS. **3.** Unconditional 1902.

1. Infinite and t. complication of detail RUSKIN.

Termly (tə̄·ɹmli), *a.* Now *rare.* 1598. [f. TERM *sb.* + -LY[1]; cf. *weekly*.] Occurring every term or at fixed terms; periodical; *esp.* paid or due every recurrent term or at fixed terms.

Te·rmly, *adv.* 1484. [f. as prec. + -LY[2].] Term by term; every term, or at fixed terms.

I would..put it in order for you t., or weekly, or daily SCOTT.

Termon (tə̄·ɹmən). 1533. [– OIr. *termonn*, mod. Ir. *tearmann*, anciently – L. *terminus* TERMINUS.] *Irish Hist.* Land belonging to a religious house.

Termor (tə̄·ɹmǫ̆ɹ). ME. [– AFr. *termer*, f. *terme* TERM *sb.*; see -ER[2] 2, -OR 2. Cf. AL. *terminarius.*] *Law.* One who holds lands or tenements for a term of years, or for life; one who has a term (TERM II. 4).

Te·rm-time. late ME. The period during which the law-courts are in session; the period of study at a university or school.

Tern (tɜ̄ɹn), *sb.*[1] 1678. [Of Scand. origin; cf. Da. *terne*, Norw. *terna*, Sw. *tärna* :- ON. *þerna*.] The common name of a group of sea-birds of the genus *Sterna*, or sub-family *Sterninæ*, akin to the gulls, but having generally a more slender body, long pointed wings, and a forked tail; a sea swallow.

Tern (tɜ̄ɹn), *a.* and *sb.*[2] ME. [As adj. – L. *terni* three each. As *sb.* app. – Fr. *terne*.] †**A.** adj. *Bot.* Arranged in threes; ternate –1828. **B.** *sb.* A set of three; a trio, triplet. *spec.* †**a.** *pl.* A double three in dicing. **b.** In a lottery, three winning numbers drawn together; a prize gained by such a drawing. **c.** A group of three stanzas. ME.

1. c. This late Poem composed of two Terns and an Envoy FURNIVALL.

Ternary (tɜ̄·ɹnări), *a.* and *sb.* late ME. [– L. *ternarius*, f. *terni* three at a time, three by three, f. *ter* thrice; see THREE, -ARY[1].] **A.** *adj.* **1.** Pertaining to, consisting of, compounded of, or characterized by a set (or sets) of three; three-fold, triple 1573. **b.** *Chem.* and *Min.* Compounded or consisting of three elements or constituents 1808. **c.** *Bot.* Arranged in threes around a common axis: usu. in ref. to the parts of a flower 1830. **d.** *Math.* Constructed on the number three as a base, as *t. scale* (of notation), etc.; involving three variables 1860. **2.** Third in subordination, rank, or order 1826.

1. *T. system* (of classification), one in which each division is into three parts. **b.** *Perfect granite* is a t. compound of quartz, felspar, and di-axial mica, universally diffused 1851.

†**B.** *sb.* A set or group of three; a ternion, a trio –1781.

I conclude this T. of Worthies with Cato 1654.

Ternate (tɜ̄·ɹnĕt), *a.* 1760. [– mod.L. *ternatus* (Linn., 1750), in form pa. pple. of med.L. *ternare* make threefold.] Produced or arranged in threes; *spec.* in *Bot.* applied to a compound leaf composed of three leaflets, or to leaves arranged in whorls of three; also to leaflets borne on secondary or tertiary similarly arranged petioles (*biternate*, *triternate*). Hence **Te·rnately** *adv.* in threes.

Tern(e)-plate (tɜ̄·ɹnplēⁱt). 1858. [prob. f. Fr. *terne* dull, lacking brilliancy.] Thin sheet-iron coated with an alloy of lead and tin; an inferior kind of tin-plate; a sheet or plate of this.

Ternion (tɜ̄·ɹniŏn). 1587. [– L. *ternio*, *-ōn-* company of three, triad.] **1.** A set of three (things or persons); a triad. **2.** A quire of three sheets, each folded in two 1609.

Terpene (tɜ̄·ɹpīn). 1873. [f. *terp-* in *terpentin*, obs. f. TURPENTINE, with suffix -ENE.] *Chem.* A general name of hydrocarbons having the formula $C_{10}H_{16}$, many of which occur in the volatile oils of plants, chiefly of the coniferous and aurantiaceous families. (Sometimes used to include hydrocarbons of formula C_5H_8 and its polymers.) Hence **Terpeny·lic** in *terpenylic acid*, $C_8H_{12}O_4$, obtained by oxidizing a t. with chromic acid.

Terpin (tɜ̄·ɹpin). 1848. [f. as prec. + -IN[1].] *Chem.* A derivative of pinene and other terpenes, $C_{10}H_{18}(OH)_2$, of which two modifications are known, *cisterpin*, melting at 103°C., and *transterpin*, at 156°C. Hence **Te·rpineol** (in Pharmacy **Terpinol**), a colourless oil formed by dehydrating t.

‖**Terpsichore** (təɹpsi·kŏri). 1711. [– Gr. Τερψιχόρη 'dance-enjoying', f. τέρπειν delight + χορός dance, CHORUS.] The Muse of dancing; hence, a female dancer; dancing as an art. Hence **Terpsichorean** (təɹpsikŏrī·an) *a.* of, pertaining to, or of the nature of dancing.

‖**Terra** (te·ră). 1871. L. (and It.) *terra* earth, used, with qualifying adjs., to form the names of medicinal and other earths, boles, and the like, as **t. alba**, pipe-clay; **t. cariosa**, tripoli or rotten-stone; **t. chia**, also *chia t.*, Chian earth, an astringent and cosmetic bole formerly obtained from the island of Chios; **t. merita** = TURMERIC; **t. ponderosa**, barium sulphate, heavy spar.

‖**Terra a terra.** Also (now always) ‖**terre à terre.** 1614. [It. *terra terra* level with the ground, infl. by Fr. *terre à terre*, Sp. *tierra a tierra*.] †**1.** An artificial gait formerly taught to horses, resembling a low curvet. **2.** Applied to a kind of dance. Also *fig.* and *attrib.* Without elevation of style. 1727.

Terrace (te·rĕs), *sb.* 1515. [– OFr. *terrace*, (also mod.) *-asse* †rubble, platform :- Rom. **terraceus*, *-acea*, f. L. *terra* earth; see -ACEOUS.] **1.** A raised level place for walking, with a vertical or sloping front or sides faced with masonry, turf, or the like, and sometimes having a balustrade; *esp.* a raised walk in a garden, or a level surface formed in front of a house on naturally sloping ground, or on the bank of a river 1575. †**b.** *Mil.* An earthwork thrown up by a besieging force –1816. **2.** A natural formation of this character: **a.** a tableland; **b.** *spec.* in *Geol.*, a horizontal shelf or bench on the side of a hill, or sloping ground 1674. †**3.** A gallery, open on one or both sides; a colonnade, a portico; a balcony on the outside of a building; a raised platform or balcony in a theatre or the like –1703. **4.** The flat roof of a house, resorted to for coolness in warm climates. Now *rare*. **5.** A row of houses on a level above the general surface, or on the face of a rising ground; now *freq.*, a row of houses of uniform style on a site slightly, if at all, raised above the level of the roadway; more recently often used arbitrarily 1769. **6.** A soft spot in marble, which is cleaned out and the cavity filled up with a paste 1877.

1. Gardens and marble terrases full of orange and cypress trees GRAY.

Comb.: **t.-cultivation**, the cultivation of hillsides in terraces; **-epoch** (*Geol.*), the epoch during which the river-terraces of N. America were formed.

Terrace (te·rĕs), *v.* 1615. [f. prec., or – Fr. *terrasser*.] **1.** *trans.* To form into a terrace or raised bank; to fashion or arrange in terraces 1650. †**2.** To furnish with a 'terrace' or balcony; to provide with a loggia or terrace-roof –1634. Hence **Te·rracing** *vbl. sb.*, also *concr.*

‖**Terra-cotta** (te:ră,kǫ·tă). 1722. [It., 'baked earth' :- L. *terra cocta*. So Fr. *terre cuite*.] **1.** A hard unglazed pottery of a fine quality, of which decorative tiles and bricks, architectural decorations, statuary, vases, and the like are made. **b.** With *a* and *pl.*: An object of art made of this substance 1810. **2.** The colour of this pottery, a brownish red of various shades 1882.

1. The Romans have left us numerous examples in bronze and *terra cotta* 1867. **b.** Ancient Terracottas in the British Museum 1810.

†‖**Te·rra damna·ta.** 1633. [L., = condemned or finally rejected earth.] = CAPUT MORTUUM 2. –1710.

‖**Terræ filius** (te:rī fi·liŏs). *Pl.* **terræ filii** (fi·li,əi). 1621. [L. *terræ filius* a son of the earth, a man of unknown origin.] **1.** A person of obscure parentage. **2.** Formerly, at the University of Oxford: An orator privileged to make humorous and satirical strictures in a speech at the public 'act' 1651.

‖**Terra firma** (te:ră fɜ̄·ɹmă). 1605. [L., 'firm land'.] †**1.** A mainland or continent, as dist. from portions of land partly or wholly isolated by water –1741. †**2.** *spec.* **a.** The territories on the Italian mainland which were subject to the state of Venice –1832. **b.** The northern coast-land of S. America (Colombia), as dist. from the West India Islands; also, in narrower sense, the Isthmus of Panama –1827. **3.** The land as dist. from the sea; dry or firm land 1693. †**4.** *joc.* Landed estate; land –1728.

3. They again got footing on terra firma 1779.

Terrain (terēⁱ·n), *sb.* (*a.*) 1727. [– Fr. *terrain* – pop.L. **terranum*, var. of L. *terrenum* TERRENE.] †**1.** 'The Manage-Ground upon which the Horse makes his Pist or Tread' (Bailey). †**b.** Standing-ground, position. –1832. **2.** A tract of country considered with regard to its natural features, configuration, etc.; in military use esp. as affecting its tactical advantages, fitness for manœuvring, etc.; also, an extent of ground, region, territory 1766. **3.** *Geol.* (Usu. spelt **terrane.**) A connected series, group, or system of rocks or formations; a stratigraphical subdivision 1823. **B.** *adj.* Of the earth, terrene, terrestrial 1882.

‖**Terra incognita** (te:ră inkǫ·gnită). *Pl.* **terræ incognitæ.** 1616. [L., 'unknown land'.] An unknown or unexplored region. Often *fig.*

‖**Terra japonica** (te:ră dʒăpǫ·nikă). 1654. [mod.L., 'Japanese earth'.] = CATECHU.

Terramare (terămā·ɹ, -mēᵊ·ɹ). *Pl.* **-ares.** Also in It. form **terrama·ra**, pl. **terrema·re.** 1866. [– Fr. *terramare* – It. dial. *terramara*, for *terra marna*, i.e. *terra* earth, *marna* MARL *sb.*] An ammoniacal earth found in the valley of the Po, in Italy, and collected as a fertilizer; it occurs in flat mounds, identified as the sites of dwellings of a people of the later neolithic period. Hence *transf.* (*pl.*) The prehistoric settlements themselves.

Terraneous (terēⁱ·nĭəs), *a. rare.* 1711. [f. L. *terra* earth, after †*mediterraneous*, *subterraneous* (XVII).] Of or pertaining to the earth; terrestrial. **b.** *Bot.* Growing upon land 1882.

Terrapin (te·răpin). 1613. [Of Algonquian origin; Abenaki *turepé*, Lenape *turupe* little turtle, with ending *-in* of obsc. origin.] A name orig. given to one or more species of N. Amer. turtles; thence extended to many allied species of the turtle and tortoise family, *Testudineæ*, widely distributed over America, the East Indies, China, N. Africa, etc. In N. America, *spec.* the Diamond-backed or Saltmarsh terrapin, *Malaclemmys palustris*, famous for its delicate flesh. **b.** The flesh of this animal as food 1867.

Terraqueous (terēⁱ·kwi,əs), *a.* 1658. [f. L. *terra* + AQUEOUS.] **1.** Consisting of, or formed of, land and water; usu. in *t. globe.* **2.** Living in land and water, as a plant; extending over land and water, as a journey 1694.

Terrar, terrer. *Obs.* exc. *Hist.* 1593. [– med.L. *terrarius*, subst. use of the adj., = pertaining to land or lands.] An officer of a religious house, who was orig. estates bursar for farms and manors belonging to the house; but whose office by the 16th c. at Durham was mainly connected with the entertainment of strangers.

†‖**Te·rra Sie·nna.** 1760. [– It. *terra di Siena* 'earth of Sienna'.] = SIENNA –1844.

‖**Terrazzo** (teræ·tso). 1902. [It., = terrace, balcony.] A proprietary name for a kind of flooring made of small chips of marble set irregularly in cement and polished. Chiefly *attrib.*

†‖**Terre·lla.** 1613. [– mod.L. *terrella* 'little earth', spherical magnet (1600, 1620), dim. f. L. *terra* earth + *-ella* -EL[2].] **1.** A little Earth; a small orb or planet –1682. **2.** A spherical loadstone or magnet –1837.

Terrene (tĕrī·n), *a.* ME. [– AFr. *terrene* – L. *terrenus*, f. *terra* earth; for the ending cf. *serene*.] **1.** = TERRESTRIAL 1. **2.** Of the nature of earth (the substance); earthy 1601. **3.** Occurring on or inhabiting the land as opp. to water 1661. **4.** = TERRESTRIAL 2. 1635. **5.** *absol.* or as *sb.* **a.** The earth, the world. **b.** A land or territory. 1667.

1. Alacke our T. Moone is now Eclipst SHAKS. **5.** Many a Province wide Tenfold the length of this t. MILT. Hence **Terre·ne-ly** *adv.*, **-ness** (*rare*).

‖**Terreno** (terre·no). 1740. [= It. (*piano*) *terreno* :- L. *terrenum* TERRENE.] A ground-floor; also, a parlour.

Terreplein (tēᵊ·ɹ,plēⁱn, ‖tęr(ə)plæṅ). 1591. [– Fr. *terre-plein* – It. *terrapieno*, f. *terrapienare* 'fill with earth', f. *terra* earth + *pieno* (:- L. *plenus*) full.] **1.** *orig.*, The talus or sloping bank of earth behind a wall or rampart; hence, the surface of a rampart behind the parapet; and strictly, the level space on which the guns are mounted, between the banquette and the inner talus. **2.** The level base (above, on, or below the natural surface of the ground) on which a battery is placed in field fortifications; sometimes, the natural surface of the ground 1669.

Terrestrial (tĕre·striăl, tĕ-), *a.* and *sb.* late ME. [f. L. *terrestris* (f. *terra* earth) + -AL[1] 1.] **1.** Of or pertaining to this world, or to earth as opp. to heaven; earthly; worldly; mundane. **2.** Of, pertaining or referring to, the earth; often in *t. ball, globe, sphere,* the earth 1593. **b.** *spec. T. globe,* a globe with a map of the earth on its surface; *t. telescope,* one used for observing terrestrial objects 1559. †**3.** Of the nature or character of earth, esp. as being dry and solid or pulverulent; possessing earth-like properties or qualities; earthy –1756. **4.** Of or pertaining to the land of the world, as dist. from the water 1628. **5.** *Nat. Hist.* Occurring on, or inhabiting, land: **a.** *Zool.* Living on the land as dist. from the waters, or on the ground as dist. from the air 1638. **b.** *Bot.* Growing in the soil; dist. from *aquatic, marine, parasitic,* or *epiphytic* 1831.

1. The happiest lot of t. existence JOHNSON. **2.** From vnder this Terrestriall Ball SHAKS. **4.** The t. and naval battailes here graven EVELYN. **5. a.** Fishes need lesse Refrigeration than Terrestriall Creatures 1638.

B. *sb.* (The adj. used absol.) **a.** A t. being; *esp.* a human being, a mortal 1598. **b.** The terrestrial world, the earth (*rare*) 1742. **c.** *pl.* Terrestrial animals, orders, or families 1842. Hence **Terre·strial-ly** *adv.*, **-ness** (*rare*).

†**Terre·strious,** *a.* 1600. [f. as prec. + -OUS.] **1.** Having the nature of earth, earthy –1741. **2.** Of or consisting of the land surface of the earth –1862. **3.** = prec. 5. SIR T. BROWNE.

Terret, -it (te·rĕt, -it). [Late ME. *tyret,* var. of *toret* – OFr. *toret, touret,* dim. of *tour* TOUR *sb.*; see -ET.] A round or circular loop or ring; *spec.* a ring on a dog's collar; each of the two rings by which the leash is attached to the jesses of a hawk; in horse-harness: one of the two (brass) rings fixed upright on the pad, or saddle, and on the hames, through which the driving reins pass. Hence **Te·rreted** *a.* provided or fitted with a t.

Terre-tenant (tēᵊ·ɹ,te:nănt). late ME. [– AFr. *terre tenaunt* 'holding land', f. *terre* land + *tenaunt* TENANT.] *Law.* One who has the actual possession of land; the occupant of land.

‖**Terre-verte** (tē̦r,vē̦rt). 1658. [Fr. *terre verte* 'green earth' (De Lisle, 1783).] A soft green earth of varying composition used as a pigment; esp. = CELADONITE or *green earth,* a variety of glauconite.

Terrible (te·rĭb'l), *a.* (*sb.*) late ME. [– (O)Fr. *terrible* – L. *terribilis,* f. *terrēre* frighten; see -BLE.] **1.** Exciting or fitted to excite terror; frightful, dreadful. **2.** Very violent, severe, painful, or bad; hence *colloq.* as a mere intensive: Very great, excessive 1596. **3.** quasi-*adv.* Terribly 1489. **B.** *sb.* A terrible thing or being; something that causes terror or dread. Usu. in *pl.* 1619.

A. 1. A foe more t. than the avalanches TYNDALL. **2.** The t. Bill against Conventicles MARVELL. She's a t. one to laugh DICKENS. **3.** I was in a t. bad way 1877. **B.** Job calls it the king of terrors.. or the most t. of terribles 1682. Hence **Te·rribleness. Te·rribly** *adv.* in a t. manner.

Terricole (te·rikoᵘl), *a.* (*sb.*) 1882. [– L. *terricola* earth-dweller, f. *terra* earth + *colere* inhabit.] **1.** *Bot.* Growing on the ground, as some lichens. **2.** *Zool.* Living on the ground or in the earth 1899. **B.** *sb.* An animal living on the ground, or burrowing in the earth; *spec.* a member of the *Terricolæ,* a group of annelids including the common earthworm 1896.

Terricolous (teri·kŏləs), *a.* 1835. [f. as prec. + -OUS.] *Zool.* Inhabiting the ground, not aquatic or aerial; living in the earth; *spec.* of or belonging to the *Terricolæ* or earthworms. So **Terri·coline** *a.*

Terrier[1] (te·riəɹ). 1477. [– OFr. *terrier,* subst. use of adj. (cf. Fr. *registre terrier*) :– med.L. *terrarius* (as in *liber terrarius*), *terrarium,* f. L. *terra* land.] A register of landed property, formerly including lists of vassals and tenants, with particulars of their holdings, services, and rents; a rent-roll; in later use, a book in which the lands of a private person, or of a corporation civil or ecclesiastical, are described by their site, boundaries, acreage, etc. Also, an inventory of property or goods.

Terrier[2] (te·riəɹ). 1440. [– early mod.Fr. (*chien*) *terrier* – med.L. *terrarius* (XIII), f. L. *terra* earth; see prec.] **1.** A small, active, intelligent variety of dog which pursues its quarry (the fox, badger, etc.) into its burrow or earth; the numerous breeds are dist. into two classes, the *short-* or *smooth-haired,* as the fox-t., black and tan t., etc., and the *long-* or *rough-haired,* as the Scotch t., Skye t., etc. Formerly also *t. dog.* **2.** A punning appellation for a territorial 1908.

Terrific (teri·fik, tĕ-), *a.* 1667. [– L. *terrificus,* f. *terrēre* frighten; see -FIC.] **1.** Causing terror, terrifying; fitted to terrify; dreadful, terrible, frightful. **2.** Applied intensively to anything very severe or excessive. *colloq.* 1809.

1. The Serpent..with brazen Eyes And hairie Main t. MILT. **2.** The crowd was immense, and the applause t. 1855. So **Terri·fical** *a.* (*rare*), **-ly** *adv.* **Terri·fic-ly** *adv.*, **-ness.**

Terrify (te·rifəi), *v.* 1575. [– L. *terrificare,* f. *terrificus*; see prec., -FY.] **1.** *trans.* To fill with terror; to frighten or alarm greatly. Also *absol.* 1578. **b.** To drive *from, out of, into,* etc. by terrifying 1575. **2.** To irritate, torment, harass, annoy, tease. Now only *dial.* 1641. †**3.** To make terrible. MILT.

1. Terrifi'd Hee fled, not hoping to escape, but shun The present MILT. **b.** It may t. her to death SCOTT. **3.** If the law, instead of aggravating and terrifying sin, shall give out licence, it foils itself MILT.

Terrigenous (teri·dʒĭnəs), *a. rare.* 1684. [f. L. *terrigenus* earth-born + -OUS.] **1.** Produced or sprung from the earth; earth-born. **2.** *Geol.* Land-derived: applied to marine deposits derived from the neighbouring land 1882.

Terrine (tĕrī·n). 1706. [Original form of TUREEN.] **1.** = TUREEN. *arch.* exc. as Fr. ‖**2.** *Cookery.* A French dish of game, meat, poultry, etc., stewed in a covered earthenware vessel 1706. **3.** A small earthenware vessel containing a table delicacy for sale; this with its contents 1911.

Territorial (teritōᵊ·riăl), *a.* (*sb.*) 1625. [– late L. *territorialis,* f. *territorium* TERRITORY. Cf. Fr. *territorial.*] **1.** Of, belonging or relating to, territory or land, or to the territory of any state, sovereign, or ruler 1768. **b.** Of or pertaining to landed property 1773. **c.** Owning or having an estate in land; landed 1832. **2.** Of or pertaining to a particular territory, district, or locality; local 1625. **3.** Of or belonging to one of the 'territories' of the United States 1812. **4.** *Mil. T. Army* or *Force,* the British Army of Home Defence instituted (on a territorial or local basis) in 1908. Also *Territorial* as *sb.* a member of the T. Army. 1907.

1. An actual Invasion of our t. rights WASHINGTON. **b.** The..t. revenue of India 1800. **c.** The t. aristocracy 1832. **2.** The gods..were local and t. divinities PRIESTLEY. Hence **Territoria·lity,** t. quality, condition, position, or status. **Terri·to·rially** *adv.*

Territorialism (teritōᵊ·riăliz'm). 1881. [f. prec. + -ISM.] A territorial system; landlordism; the organization of the Army on a t. or local basis; also applied, as tr. G. *Territorial-system,* to a theory of church government which places the supreme authority in the civil power. So **Territo·rialist,** a member or representative of the class of landowners.

Territorialize (teritōᵊ·riăləiz), *v.* 1818. [f. as prec. + -IZE.] *trans.* To make territorial; to place upon a territorial basis; to associate with or restrict to a particular territory or district.

Territory (te·ritŏri). late ME. [– L. *territorium,* f. *terra* land, after *dormitorium, prætorium.*] **1.** †**a.** The land or district lying round a city or town and under its jurisdiction. Chiefly as tr. L. *territorium.* –1651. **b.** The land or country belonging to or under the dominion of a ruler or state 1494. **c.** *transf.* Each half of a football ground considered as belonging to one of the teams: so in hockey, baseball, etc. 1896. **2.** A tract of land, or district of undefined boundaries; a region 1610. **3.** *fig.* The sphere, province or domain of a science, art, class, word, etc. 1640. **4.** In the U.S., One of certain regions in the West belonging to and under the government of the American Republic, and having some degree of self-government, but not yet admitted as a State into the Union 1799. **5.** orig. *U.S.* The district in which a commerical traveller operates 1925.

1. As they governed the City of Rome, and Territories adjacent HOBBES. **b.** A small port, still within the Neapolitan territories 1799. **2.** The most fertile territories of Anjou HOLLAND.

Terror (te·rəɹ). late ME. [First in Sc. (*terrour*) – OFr. *terrour* (mod. *terreur*) :– L. *terror, -ōr-,* f. *terrēre* frighten; see -OR 1.] **1.** The state of being terrified or greatly frightened; intense fear, fright, or dread. Also, with *a* and *pl.*, an instance of this. **2.** *transf.* The action or quality of causing dread; terrific quality, terribleness; also *concr.* a thing or person that excites terror or awe; something terrifying, awe-inspiring; *trivially,* a 'trying', embarrassing, or unruly person 1528.

1. The terrors of death are fallen vpon me BIBLE (Genev.) *Ps.* 55:4. **2.** So spake the grieslie terrour MILT. Phr. *King of Terrors,* Death personified. *Reign of terror,* a state of things in which the general community live in dread of death or outrage; esp. in *French Hist.* the period of the First Revolution from about March 1793 to July 1794, called also *the T., the Red T.* Hence **Te·rrorless** *a.* devoid of t.; exciting no dread.

Terrorism (te·rŏriz'm). 1795. [– Fr. *terrorisme,* f. L. *terror*; see -ISM.] A system of terror. **1.** Government by intimidation; the system of the 'Terror' (1793–4); see prec. **2.** *gen.* A policy intended to strike with terror those against whom it is adopted; the fact of terrorizing or condition of being terrorized 1798.

Terrorist (te·rŏrist). 1795. [– Fr. *terroriste,* f. L. *terror* TERROR; see -IST.] **1.** As a political term: **a.** Applied to the Jacobins and their agents and partisans in the French Revolution. **b.** Any one who attempts to further his views by a system of coercive intimidation; *spec.* applied to members of one of the extreme revolutionary societies in Russia 1866. **2.** An alarmist, a scaremonger 1803.

1. Thousands of those Hell-hounds called Terrorists..are let loose on the people BURKE. Hence **Terrori·stic, -ical** *adjs.* characterized by or practising terrorism.

Terrorize (te·rŏrəiz), *v.* 1823. [f. TERROR + -IZE.] **1.** *trans.* To fill or inspire with terror, reduce to a state of terror; *esp.* to coerce or deter by terror. **2.** *intr.* To rule, or maintain power, by terrorism; to practise intimidation 1856.

1. Superstitions which yet more or less..terrorise the ignorant 1885.

Terry (te·ri), *sb.* and *a.* 1784. [Of unkn. origin.] **A.** *sb.* The loop raised in pile-weaving left uncut; also short for *t. fabric, t. velvet,* etc. **B.** *adj.* Of pile-fabrics: Looped, having the loops that form the pile left uncut, as *t. pile, t. velvet.* Also, Of or pertaining to such a fabric. 1835.

‖**Ter-sanctus** (tə̄:ɹsæ·ŋktŏs). 1832. [L. *ter* thrice + *sanctus* holy; cf. SANCTUS, TRISAGION.] The Latin title of the hymn in the Liturgy beginning 'With Angels and Archangels'.

Terse (tə̄ɹs), *a.* 1601. [– L. *tersus,* pa. pple. of *tergēre* wipe.] †**1.** Wiped, brushed; smoothed; clean-cut, sharp-cut; polished, burnished; neat, trim, spruce –1824. †**2.** *fig.* Polite, polished, refined, cultured: esp. in ref. to language –1774. **3.** *spec.* Freed from verbal redundancy; neatly concise; compact and pithy in style or language 1777.

1. I am enamour'd of this street..'tis so polite and t. B. JONS. **2.** Pure, t., elegant Latin 1695. **3.** In eight t. lines has Phædrus told..A tale of goats 1777. Hence **Te·rse-ly** *adv.*, **-ness.**

Te·rtia. Now *Hist.* 1630. [app. altered f. TERCIO.] A division of infantry, a TERCIO.

Tertial (tə̄·ɹʃ'ăl), *a.* and *sb.* 1836. [f. L. *tertius* third + -AL[1] 1.] *Ornith.* **A.** *adj.* Of or pertaining to the third rank or row of quill- or flight-feathers in the wing of a bird. **B.** *sb.* A flight-feather of the third row.

Tertian (tə̄·ɹʃ'ăn), *a.* and *sb.* [Late ME. in *fever terciane,* or *terciane,* – L. *febris tertiana,* also *tertiana* sb., f. *tertius* third; see -AN.] **A.** *adj.* **1.** *Path.* Of a fever or ague: Characterized by the occurrence of a paroxysm every third (i.e. every alternate) day. **2.** *Mus.* Applied to the mean-tone temperament (in which the major thirds are perfectly in tune) 1875. **3.** *T. father:* a Jesuit in the third period of his probation 1855. Also as *sb.* Hence **Te·rtianship. B.** *sb.* **1.** Short for *t. ague* or *fever.* late ME. †**2.** A liquid measure for wine, oil, etc., the third of a tun, i.e. 84 wine gallons = 70 imperial gallons); also a large cask of this capacity; a puncheon –1749. **3.** A mixture stop on an organ, consisting of a tierce and larigot combined 1876.

Tertiary (tə̄·ɹʃ¹ări), *a.* and *sb.* 1550. [f. L. *tertiarius* of the third part or rank, f. *tertius* third; see -ARY¹.] **A.** *adj.* **1.** Of, in, or belonging to the third order, rank, degree, class, or category; third 1656. **b.** *Chem.* Applied to the substitution ammonias formed by the replacement of all three hydrogen atoms by an alcohol or acid radical 1857. **2.** *Geol.* Forming a third series in point of origin or age. **b.** In mod. geology, Of or pertaining to the third series of stratified formations: now restricted to the strata from the Eocene to the Pliocene, both inclusive. Also called CAINOZOIC. 1794. **3.** *Painting.* Applied to a colour formed by the mixture of two secondary colours 1848. **4.** *Path.* Of or belonging to the third or last stage of syphilis 1875. **5.** *R. C. Ch.* Of or belonging to the Third Order (i.e. an order of lay members not subject to the strict rule of the regulars, but retaining the secular life) in certain religious fraternities 1891. **6.** *Ornith.* Applied to certain feathers of the wing 1858.

1. I venture to assume that you will admit duty as at least a secondary or t. motive RUSKIN.

B. *sb.* **1.** *R. C. Ch.* A member of the Third Order of certain religious fraternities 1550. **2.** *Geol.* A stratum or formation belonging to the Tertiary system 1851. **3.** *Ornith.* (*pl.*) The quill- or flight-feathers that grow upon the humerus in the wing of a bird 1834. **4.** *Path.* (*pl.*) Tertiary syphilitic symptoms 1897. **5.** *Painting.* A tertiary colour 1854.

‖**Tertium quid** (tə̄·ɹʃ¹ŏm kwi·d). 1724. [Late L. *tertium quid* (Irenæus), tr. Gr. τριτόν τι 'some third thing'; n. of L. *tertius* third, *quid*, n. of *quis* somebody.] Something (indefinite or left undefined) related in some way to two (definite or known) things, but distinct from both.

‖**Tertius** (tə̄·ɹʃ¹ŏs). 1870. [L. *tertius* third.] In some public schools, appended to a surname to designate the youngest (in age or standing) of three boys of that name.

‖**Teru-tero** (te·ru,te·ro). 1839. [From its noisy cry.] The Cayenne lapwing or spur-winged plover, *Vanellus cayennensis.*

‖**Terza rima** (te·rtsă rī·mă). 1819. [It., fem. of *terzo* third, *rima* rhyme.] An Italian form of iambic verse, consisting of sets of three lines, the middle line of each set rhyming with the first and last of the succeeding (*a b a*, *b c b*, *c d c*, etc.).

‖**Terzetto** (tertse·tto). *Pl.* **-i** (-ī). 1724. [It.; see TERCET.] *Mus.* A (small) trio, esp. vocal.

Tesla (te·slă). 1902. The name of Nikola *Tesla* (born 1856), American electrician and physicist, used attrib. to denote apparatus invented by him and phenomena caused by this apparatus.

Tessara- (te·sără), also **tessera-**, – Gr. τέσσαρα, -ερα, n. pl. and comb. form of τέσσαρες, -ερες four, as in **Te·ssaraglo:t** *a.*, in, of, or pertaining to four languages.

‖**Tessella** (tese·lă). *Pl.* **-æ**; rarely **-as.** 1693. [L., dim of TESSERA.] A small tessera.

Tessellate (te·sĕle¹t), *v.* 1791. [– *tessellat-*, pa. ppl. stem of late L. *tessellare*, f. L. *tessella*; see prec., -ATE³.] **1.** *trans.* To make into a mosaic; to form a mosaic upon, adorn with mosaics; to construct (esp. a pavement) by combining variously coloured blocks so as to form a pattern. **2.** To combine so as to form a mosaic; to fit into its place in a mosaic 1838.

1. The floor is tesselated with great elegance 1826.

Tessellated (te·sĕlē¹tĕd), *ppl. a.* 1695. [f. L. *tessellatus* (or the derived It. *tessellato*), f. *tessella*; see prec., -ATE², -ED¹.] **1.** Composed of small blocks of variously coloured material arranged to form a pattern; formed of or ornamented with mosaic work 1712. **2.** Combined or arranged so as to form a mosaic 1838. **3.** *transf.* Consisting of or arranged in small cubes or squares; in *Bot.* and *Zool.* having colours or surface-divisions in regularly arranged squares or patches; chequered, reticulated 1695. Also **Te·ssellate** *a.* 1826.

1. The t. Pavement at Stansfield 1712. **3.** Fruit ..a fleshy t. berry 1829. *T. cells*, cells arranged in layers.

Tessellation (tesĕlē¹·ʃən). 1660. [f. TESSELLATE *v.* + -ATION.] **1.** The action or art of tessellating; tessellated condition; *concr.* a piece of tessellated work 1813. **2.** An arrangement or close fitting together of minute parts or distinct colours 1660.

Te·ssellite. 1819. [f. TESSELLA + -ITE¹ 2 b.] *Min.* A variety of apophyllite, exhibiting in polarized light a tessellated structure.

‖**Tessera** (te·sĕră). *Pl.* **-æ** (-ī). 1647. [L. *tessera* – Gr. τέσσερα, n. of τέσσερες, Ionic var. of τέσσαρες four.] **1.** *Anc. Hist.* A small quadrilateral tablet of wood, bone, ivory, or the like, used for various purposes, as a token, tally, ticket, label, etc. 1656. **b.** *fig.* A distinguishing sign or token; a watchword, a password 1647. **2.** *spec.* Each of the small square (usu. cubical) pieces of marble, glass, tile, etc. of which a mosaic pavement or the like is composed. Usu. in pl. 1797. **b.** *transf.* Any of the quadrilateral divisions into which a surface is divided by intersecting lines 1873. **c.** *Zool.* Each of the plates of which the carapace of an armadillo is composed 1909.

†**Tessera·ic** *a.* (*rare*) of, pertaining to, or composed of tesseræ; mosaic, tessellated.

Tesseral (te·sĕrăl), *a.* 1846. [f. prec. + -AL¹ 1.] **1.** Of, pertaining to, or resembling a tessera or tesseræ; composed of tesseræ. **2.** *Cryst.* = ISOMETRIC 3, CUBIC *a.* 1 b. 1854. **3.** *Math.* Relating to the tesseræ of a spherical surface 1873.

Tessular (te·siŭlăɹ), *a.* 1796. [f. mod.L. **tessula*, irreg. dim. of TESSERA + -AR¹.] *Cryst.* = ISOMETRIC 3.

Test (test), *sb.*¹ late ME. [– OFr. *test* pot, mod. *têt* cupel, etc. :– L. *testum*, *testu*, collateral form of *testa* tile, earthen vessel, pot. In mod. use, treated mainly as n. of action from TEST *v.*²] **1.** *orig.* The cupel used in treating gold or silver alloys or ore; now *esp.* the cupel, with the iron frame or basket which contains it, forming the movable hearth of a reverberatory furnace. **2.** That by which the existence, quality, or genuineness of anything is or may be determined; 'means of trial' (J.) 1594. **b.** *Cricket.* Short for *t.-match* 1908. **3.** That by which beliefs or opinions, esp. in religion, are tested or tried; *spec.* the oaths or declarations prescribed by the TEST ACT of 1673; also, either of the test acts 1665. **4. a.** *Chem.* The action or process of examining a substance under known conditions in order to determine its identity or that of one of its constituents; also, a substance by means of which this may be done 1800. **b.** *Mech.*, etc. The action by which the physical properties of substances, materials, machines, etc. are tested, in order to determine their ability to satisfy particular requirements 1877. **5.** *Microscopy.* A test object 1832. **6.** An apparatus for determining the flash-point of hydrocarbon oils 1877.

1. Of oure siluer citrinacion.. Oure yngottes testes and many mo CHAUCER. **2.** Phr. *To bring* or *put to the t.*, *to bear* or *stand the t.*; It is not madnesse That I have vttered; bring me to the Test SHAKS. **3.** The belief in tests ought to be as dead as the belief in witches 1906. Phr. *To take the t.*

Comb.: **t. case** (*Law*), a case the decision of which is taken as determining that of a number of others in which the same question of law is involved; **-frame,** the iron frame or basket in which a cupel is placed; **-furnace,** a reverberatory refining furnace in which silver-bearing alloys are treated; **-match** (*Cricket*), one of a series of matches played between representative teams to test the cricketing strength of the countries which they represent; **-meter,** a meter for testing the consumption of gas by burners; **t. object,** (*a*) a minute object used as a t. of the power of a microscope; (*b*) an object upon which a testing experiment is tried; **-paper,** (*a*) a paper impregnated with a chemical solution which changes colour in contact with certain other chemicals, and thus becomes a t. of the presence of the latter; (*b*) *U.S.* a document produced in court in determining a question of handwriting; (*c*) a paper set beforehand to try whether a student is fit and ready for an examination; **-roll,** the roll signed by a member of the House of Lords or Commons after having taken the oath or made the declaration required of him as such; **-type,** letters of graduated sizes used by opticians in testing sight.

Test (test), *sb.*² 1545. [– L. *testa*; see prec.] †**1.** A piece of earthenware, an earthenware vessel; a potsherd –1600. **2.** *Zool.* The shell of certain invertebrates 1842.

Test (test), *v.*¹ 1582. [orig. – OFr. *tester* bequeath – L. *testari* attest, make one's will, f. *testis* witness; but in 2 app. f. TESTE 2.] **1.** *intr.* To make a will. *Obs.* exc. *Sc.* **2.** *trans.* *Eng. Law.* To date and sign the teste of a writ, etc. 1727.

Test (test), *v.*² 1603. [f. TEST *sb.*¹] **1.** *trans.* To subject (gold or silver) to a process of separation and refining in a test or cupel; to assay. **2.** To subject to a test of any kind; to try, put to the proof 1748. **3.** *Chem.* To subject to a chemical test 1839.

2. Experience is the surest standard by which to t. the real tendency of the existing constitution WASHINGTON. They have not the means of testing the statements 1820.

‖**Testa** (te·stă). 1796. [L.; see TEST *sb.*²] *Bot.* The skin or coating of a seed.

‖**Testacea** (testē¹·ʃ¹ă), *sb. pl.* 1743. [L., n. pl. of *testaceus* adj. consisting of *testæ*, i.e. tiles, shells, etc.; also, covered with a shell; see -ACEA.] †**1.** Testaceous substances, as limestone, chalk (*rare*). **2.** *Zool.* A name for various groups of invertebrate animals having shells (excluding Crustacea); *spec.* in present use, (*a*) a suborder of pteropod molluscs including all having calcareous shells; (*b*) an order of Protozoa having shells, with apertures through which the pseudopodia are protrusible. 1816.

Testacean (testē¹·ʃ¹ăn), *a.* and *sb.* 1842. [f. prec.; see -ACEAN.] **A.** *adj.* Of or pertaining to the TESTACEA; shell-bearing: chiefly applied to molluscs 1846. **B.** *sb.* A member of the testacea; a shell-bearing invertebrate, *esp.* a mollusc 1842.

Testaceo- (testē¹·ʃio), comb. form of L. *testaceus*, as in **Testaceo·graphy,** descriptive testaceology; **Testaceo·logy,** the zoology of the testaceous animals.

Testaceous (testē¹·ʃəs), *a.* 1646. [f. L. *testaceus* consisting of tiles, shells, etc.; see TEST *sb.*², -ACEOUS.] †**1.** Made of baked clay; pertaining to or of the nature of earthenware or a potsherd (*rare*) –1675. **2.** Having a shell, esp. a hard, calcareous, unarticulated shell 1646. **3.** Of the nature or substance of shells; shelly; consisting of a shell or shelly material 1668. **4.** Of the colour of a tile, a flower-pot, unglazed pottery, etc.; dull red; in *Zool.* and *Bot.* applied to shades of brownish red, brownish yellow, and reddish brown 1688.

Te·st Act. 1708. [See TEST *sb.*¹ 3.] The name given in English History to various acts directed against Roman Catholics and Protestant Nonconformists; particularly, the act of 1673 (25 Chas. II. c. 2) by which the provisions of the Corporation Act of 1661 were extended to include all persons holding office under the Crown, and a declaration against transubstantiation was introduced. It was repealed 9 May, 1828.

Testacy (te·stăsi). 1864. [f. TESTATE *a.*, after INTESTACY.] *Law.* The state of being testate; the condition of leaving a valid will.

Testament (te·stămĕnt), *sb.* ME. [– L. *testamentum* will; also, in early Chr.L., used to render Gr. διαθήκη covenant; f. *testari* bear witness, make a will, f. *testes* witness; see -MENT.] **I.** *Law.* A formal declaration, usu. in writing, of a person's wishes as to the disposal of his property after his death; a will. Formerly, properly applied to a disposition of personal as dist. from real property. Now *rare* (chiefly in phr. *last will and t.*). **b.** *transf.* and *fig.* late ME.

b. The Gospels are Christ's T.; and the Epistles are the Codicils annex'd JER. TAYLOR.

II. In Christian L. use of *testamentum.* **1.** In Holy Scripture, a covenant between God and man. *arch.* ME. **2.** Hence **a.** Each of the two main divisions of the Sacred Scriptures or Bible, the *Old* and the *New T.*, consisting of the books of the old or Mosaic and the new or Christian covenant or dispensation respectively ME. **b.** The New Testament as dist. from the Old; a copy of the New Testament;

a volume containing this. Common in *Greek T.* 1500.

2. The coachman could..have taken his oath on the two Testaments DICKENS. **b.** Her little well-worn T. open on her knee 1888. Hence **Te·stament** *v. intr.* to make a will; *trans.* to leave by will, bequeath. **Testame·ntal** *a.* (now *rare*), of, pertaining to, or of the nature of a t.; **-ly** *adv.* by way of a t.

Testamentary (testăme·ntări), *a.* 1456. [– L. *testamentarius*, f. *testamentum*; see prec., -ARY¹.] **1.** Of, pertaining to, or having relation to a testament or will; of the nature of a will. **2.** Made or done by will; appointed by will 1547. **b.** Expressed or contained in a will 1762. **3.** Of or pertaining to the Old or New Testament 1849.

1. *T. capacity*, capacity to make a will. *T. estate*, estate subject to disposal by will. **2.** T. dispositions of land 1794. **b.** T. directions 1851.

†**Testamenta·tion.** 1765. [f. TESTAMENT *v.* + -ATION.] The disposal of one's property by will. BURKE.

‖**Testamur** (testēⁱ·mɒ̆ɹ). 1840. [f. L. *testamur* 'we testify', as used in the document.] In University use: A certificate from the examiners that a candidate has satisfied them. Also, a certificate generally.

Testate (te·stĕt), *a.* and *sb.* 1475. [– L. *testatus*, pa. pple. of *testari* (also *testare*) bear witness, attest, make one's will, etc., f. *testis* witness; see -ATE² and ¹.] **A.** *adj.* **1.** That has left a valid will at death. **2.** *transf.* Disposed of or settled by will 1792.

1. Persones diyng T. and Intestate 1475. **2.** His succession was partly intestate, partly t. 1875.

B. *sb.* †**1.** A witness; also, testimony –1652. †**2.** = TESTE 2. –1641. **3.** One who at death has left a valid will 1864.

Testate (te·steⁱt), *v. rare.* 1624. [– *testat-*, pa. ppl. stem of L. *testari*; see prec., -ATE³.] **1.** *intr.* To testify, to attest. **2.** To make one's will 1892.

Testation (testēⁱ·ʃən). 1642. [– L. *testatio*, *-ōn-*, f. as prec.; see -ION.] †**1.** Attestation, testimony –1656. **2.** The disposal of property by will 1832.

Testator (testēⁱ·tǫɹ). 1447. [In sense 1 – AFr. *testatour* – L. *testator*, *-ōr-*, f. *testari* make a will; in sense 2 direct from L.; see -OR 2.] **1.** One who makes a will; one who has died leaving a will. †**2.** A witness –1698.

Testatrix (testēⁱ·triks). 1591. Pl. **-trixes** (triksėz), **-trices** (trisīz). [– late L. *testatrix*, fem. of *testator*; see prec., -TRIX.] A female testator.

‖**Testatum** (testēⁱ·tŏm). 1607. [L., n. pa. pple. of *testari* (*-are*) attest, etc.] *Law.* †**1.** A writ formerly issued when a writ of capias was returned, the sheriff to whom it was first addressed testifying that the defendant was not to be found within his jurisdiction –1848. **2.** The witnessing-clause of a deed 1844.

Teste (te·sti). late ME. [– L. *teste* abl. of *testis* witness.] **1.** The L. word *teste* in abl. absol. constr. with a pronoun (e.g. *meipso* myself) or name of a person, as used in the authenticating clause of a writ, etc.: hence, in non-legal use, = (So-and-so) being witness, on the authority or evidence of (So-and-so); also as *sb.* 1654. **2.** The final clause in a royal writ naming the person who authorizes the affixing of the king's seal. late ME. †**b.** Hence, more gen., a clause stating the name of a witness (as to a charter in writ-form) –1617.

1. Many..commanders 'Swore terribly (*t.* T. Shandy) in Flanders' BARHAM.

Tester¹ (te·stəɹ). late ME. [– med.L. *testerium*, *testrum*, *testura*, f. Rom. ***testa* head (L. *testa* tile); cf. OFr. *testiere*, Fr. *têtière*, etc., having various applications with ref. to the head.] **1.** A canopy over a bed, supported on the posts of the bedstead or suspended from the ceiling; formerly also, a t.-bed's headboard and its fittings. **2.** *transf.* and *fig.* Something that overhangs; a shrine; a canopy carried over a dignitary; the sound-board of a pulpit, etc. late ME. **3.** *attrib.*, as *t.-bed* 1622.

1. A bedstead gilt, with a testor and counterpoint, with curtains belonging to the same 1548. **2.** A night under the starry t. of the heavens 1830.

†**Te·ster**². Also ‖**testiere.** late ME. [– OFr. *testiere* (mod. *têtière*), f. *teste* (*tête*) head; cf. med.L. *testera*, *testeria*. Cf. prec.] A piece of armour for the head; a head-piece, a casque; also, a piece of armour for the head of a horse –1484.

Tester³ (te·stəɹ). *arch.* 1546. [Obscure alt. of TESTON.] A name for the TESTON of Henry VIII, esp. as debased and depreciated; later a colloq. or slang term for a sixpence.

Tester⁴ (te·stəɹ). 1661. [f. TEST *v.*² or *sb.*¹; see -ER¹.] One who tests or proves; a device for testing.

‖**Testicardines** (testikā·ɹdinīz), *sb. pl.* 1878. [mod.L., f. L. *testa* shell + *cardo*, *cardin-* hinge.] *Zool.* A primary division of brachiopods having hinged shells; opp. to *Ecardines.* Hence **Testica·rdinate** *a.* having a hinged shell.

Testicle (te·stik'l). late ME. [– L. *testiculus*, dim. of *testis* witness (the organ being evidence of virility).] Each of the two ellipsoid glandular bodies constituting the sperm-secreting organs in male mammals and usu. enclosed in a scrotum. **b.** Rarely applied to the corresponding organs in non-mammals 1713. †**c.** *transf.* The ovary in females –1691.

Testicular (testi·kiŭlăɹ), *a.* 1656. [f. L. *testiculus* (see prec.) + -AR¹.] **1.** Of or pertaining to, containing, or having the nature or function of a testicle or testicles. **2.** Resembling a testicle in form; testiculate 1769.

Testiculate (testi·kiŭlĕt), *a.* 1760. [– late L. *testiculatus*; see TESTICLE, -ATE².] Formed like a testicle; also, applied to the twin tubers of certain species of Orchis. So **Testi·culated** *a.* 1725.

Testification (te:stifikēⁱ·ʃən). Now *rare.* 1450. [– Fr. †*testificacion* or L. *testificatio*, *-ōn-*, f. *testificat-*, pa. ppl. stem of *testificare*; see TESTIFY, -FICATION.] The action or an act of testifying; the testimony borne; a fact or object (as a document, etc.) serving as evidence or proof.

Testificator (te·stifikēⁱtəɹ). *rare.* 1730. [f. *testificat-*; see prec., -OR 2.] One who testifies or attests. So **Testifica·tory** *a.* of such a kind as to testify, or serve as evidence 1593.

Testifier (te·stifəi,əɹ). 1611. [f. TESTIFY *v.* + -ER¹.] One who testifies; a witness.

Testify (te·stifəi) *v.* late ME. [– L. *testificari* (later *-are*) bear witness, proclaim, f. *testis* witness; see -FY.] **1.** *trans.* To bear witness to, or give proof of (a fact); to assert the truth of (a statement); to attest. Also *intr.* (usu. with *of*) and *absol.* **2.** *transf.* of things: **a.** *trans.* To serve as evidence of; to constitute proof or testimony of 1445. **b.** *intr.* and *absol.* 1596. **3.** *trans.* To profess belief in; to proclaim as something that one knows or believes. Chiefly *biblical.* 1526. **b.** *intr.* To bear testimony 1784. **4.** *intr.* and *trans.* = PROTEST *v.* 1. *Obs.* exc. in biblical use. 1526. **5.** *trans.* To give evidence of, display (desire, emotion, etc.). *Obs.* or *arch.* 1560.

1. We speake that we knowe, and t. that we have sene TINDALE *John* 3:11. Those which take in hand to testifie of any matter whatsoever 1579. **2.** The brickes are aliue at this day to testifie it SHAKS. **3.** I testifie my sauioure openly COVERDALE 2 *Esdras* 2:36. **4.** At length a Reverend Sire among them came..And testifi'd against thir wayes MILT. **5.** He was the only person..who testified any real concern FIELDING.

Testimonial (testimōᵘ·niăl), *a.* and *sb.* late ME. [In XV also *tesmoignal* – OFr. *tesmoignal*, (also mod.) *testimonial* or late L. *testimonialis*, f. OFr. *tesmoin* (mod. *témoin*) L. *testimonium*; see TESTIMONY, -IAL.] **A.** *adj.* (now *arch.* or *techn.*) Of, pertaining to, or of the nature of testimony; serving as evidence; conducive to proof.

T. proof, proof by the testimony of a witness; parole evidence. †**Letter t.,** rarely **t. letter** (usu. pl. *letters testimonial(s)*, a letter testifying to the bona fides of the bearer; credentials.

B. *sb.* †**1.** = TESTIMONY *sb.* 1. –1707. †**2.** Something serving as proof or evidence; a token, record, manifestation –1803. †**3.** An affidavit, acknowledgement; a certificate; *spec.* an official warrant; a passport (as given to vagrants, labourers, discharged soldiers or sailors, etc.); a diploma; a credential or other authenticating document –1806. **4.** A writing testifying to one's qualifications and character, written usu. by a present or former employer, or by some responsible person who is competent to judge; a letter of recommendation of a person or thing 1571. **5.** A gift presented to some one by a number of persons as an expression of appreciation or acknowledgement of services or merit, or of admiration or respect 1838.

Testimonialize (testimōᵘ·niăləiz), *v.* 1852. [f. prec. + -IZE.] *trans.* To furnish with a letter of recommendation; also, to present with a public testimonial.

‖**Testimonium** (testimōᵘ·niŏm). 1692. [L., f. *testis* a witness + *-monium*; see -MONY.] **1.** A letter of recommendation given to a candidate for holy orders testifying to his piety and learning; also = TESTAMUR. **2.** *Law.* That concluding part of a document, usu. commencing 'In witness whereof', which states the manner of its execution; also *t. clause* 1852.

Testimony (te·stiməni), *sb.* late ME. [– L. *testimonium*; see prec.] **1.** Personal or documentary evidence or attestation in support of a fact or statement; hence, any form of evidence or proof. **b.** Any object serving as proof or evidence 1597. †**2.** A written certificate, a testimonial –1657. **3.** In Scriptural language (chiefly in O.T.). **a.** *sing.* The Mosaic law or decalogue as inscribed on the two tables of stone. late ME. **b.** *pl.* The precepts (of God), the divine law 1535. **4.** Open attestation or acknowledgement; confession, profession. *Obs.* or *arch.* 1550. **b.** *spec.* An expression or declaration of disapproval or condemnation of error; a protestation 1582.

1. Where a mans T. is not to be credited, he is not bound to give it HOBBES. **3. a.** *The two tables of t.* (Ex. 31:18); *Ark of (the) T.* = *Ark of the Covenant*, the chest containing the tables of the law and other sacred memorials; *tabernacle* or *tent of (the) t.*, the tabernacle containing the ark with its contents. **b.** So shall I kepe the testimonies of thy mouth COVERDALE *Ps.* 118[119]:88. **4.** Thou.. for the testimonie of Truth hast born Universal reproach MILT. **b.** Shake of the dust from your feete for a testimonie to them N. T. (Rhem.) *Mark* 6:11.

†**Te·stimony,** *v.* [Late ME. – ONFr. *testimoiner*, etc., – med.L. *testimoniare*, f. *testimonium* (see prec.); later, f. prec. sb.] **1.** *trans.* and *intr.* To bear witness, testify (to) –1642. **2.** *trans.* To test or prove by evidence. SHAKS.

†‖**Te·stis**¹. *Pl.* **testes** (te·stīz). 1483. The L. word for 'witness': from its legal use (cf. TESTE), occasional in Eng. context –1611.

‖**Testis**² (te·stis). Chiefly in pl. **testes** (te·stīz). 1681. [L., 'witness'; see TESTICLE.] *Anat.* **1.** = TESTICLE 1704. †**b.** *transf.* The ovary in females –1841. **2.** *transf. pl.* The posterior pair of the optic lobes or *corpora quadrigemina*, at the base of the brain in mammals 1681.

Teston, testoon (te·stən, testū·n). *Obs.* exc. *Hist.* 1543. [– Fr. †*teston*, It. †*testone*, f. *testa* head :– L. *testa* tile (in Rom. head); see -OON.] **1.** *orig.* The French name of a silver coin first struck at Milan by Galeazzo Maria Sforza (1468–76), bearing a portrait or head of the duke. Applied later to equivalent silver coins without a portrait, both in Italy and France. 1545. **2.** In England, a name first applied to the shilling of Henry VII, the first English coin bearing a true portrait; also to like coins of Henry VIII, and early pieces of Edward VI. It sank in value from 12 pence to 6*d.* and even lower, being of debased metal. 1543. †**b.** = TESTER³ –1598. **3.** The Portuguese silver *testão* or *tostão*; now = 100 reis, and worth about 2½*d.* 1598.

†**Te·stril.** [A dim. alteration of TESTER³.] A sixpence. SHAKS.

Te·st-tube. 1846. [f. TEST *sb.*¹ + TUBE.] A cylinder of thin transparent glass closed at one end, used to hold liquids under test. Also *attrib.* as *t. culture.*

Testudinarious (testiŭdinēᵊ·riəs), *a.* 1826. [f. L. *testudo*, *-in-* TESTUDO + -ARIOUS.] Having the character of a tortoise; marked or coloured like tortoise-shell.

Testudinate (testiū·dinĕt), *a.* (*sb.*) 1847. [f. as prec.; see -ATE²,¹.] **1.** Formed like a testudo; arched, vaulted. **2.** Of or pertaining to tortoises 1850. **B.** *sb.* A tortoise 1880. So **Testu·dinated** *ppl. a.* = 1.

Testudineous (testiudi·niəs), *a.* 1652. [f. L. *testudineus*, f. next; see -EOUS.] **1.** Resembling the shell of a tortoise, or a testudo 1656. **2.** Slow, dilatory, like the pace of a tortoise 1652.

Testudo (testiū·do). late ME. [– L. *testudo* tortoise, etc., f. *testa* pot, shell, etc., *testu* pot-lid.] **1.** *Path.* = TALPA 2. **2.** *Zool.* The typical genus of the tortoise family, *Testudinidæ*; a member of this genus 1520. **3.** *Rom. Antiq.* **a.** An engine of war used by besiegers, consisting of a screen or shelter with a strong arched roof, moved on wheels up to the walls, which could then be attacked in safety 1609. **b.** A shelter formed by a body of troops locking their shields together above their heads 1680. **4.** *Anc. Mus.* A lyre, said to have been made by Mercury of the shell of a tortoise 1702.

Testy (te·sti), *a.* [Late ME. *testif* – AFr. *testif*, f. OFr. *teste* (mod. *tête*) head :– L. *testa* shell, earthen vessel, tile, (Rom.) head; see -IVE. Cf. HASTY, JOLLY, TARDY.] †**1.** Of headstrong courage; impetuous; precipitate, rash; in later use, aggressive, contentious –1658. **2.** Prone to be irritated by small checks and annoyances; resentful of contradiction or opposition; irascible, short-tempered, peevish, tetchy, 'crusty' 1526. **b.** Of words, actions, personal qualities, etc. 1538.

2. A chollericke and testie Consull HOLLAND. **b.** Must I stand and crouch Vnder your Testie Humour? SHAKS. Hence **Te·sti-ly** *adv.*, **-ness.**

Tetanic (tĭtæ·nik), *a.* (*sb.*) 1727. [– L. *tetanicus*, – Gr. τετανικός; see TETANUS, -IC.] Of, pertaining to, or of the nature of tetanus; characterized by tetanus. Hence **Teta·nically** *adv.* by, or as by, tetanus.

Tetanine (te·tănin). 1857. [f. TETANUS + -INE[5].] †**a.** Strychnine. **b.** A ptomaine, $C_{13}H_{30}N_2O_4$, obtained from meat extract containing Rosenbach's microbe, the tetanus bacillus; occurring also in decaying corpses.

Tetanize (te·tănəiz), *v.* 1849. [f. TETANUS + -IZE.] *trans.* To produce tetanus or tetanic spasms in. Hence **Tetaniza·tion,** the production of tetanus or tetanic contraction in a muscle.

Tetano- (tetăno), comb. form of Gr. τέτανος TETANUS, as in **Tetano·lysin** [Gr. λύσις a loosening], a toxin produced by the tetanus bacillus; **Tetanomo·tor,** an instrument for producing muscular tetanus.

Tetanoid (te·tănoid), *a.* (*sb.*) 1856. [f. next + -OID.] Of the nature of, or resembling tetanus. **B.** *sb.* A tetanoid spasm or attack.

‖**Tetanus** (te·tănŏs). late ME. [L. – Gr. τέτανος muscular spasm, f. τείνειν stretch.] **1.** A disease characterized by tonic spasm and rigidity of some or all of the voluntary muscles, usu. occasioned by a wound or other injury. (Cf. LOCKJAW.) **2.** *Physiol.* A condition of prolonged contraction produced by rapidly repeated stimuli 1877.

Tetany (te·tăni). 1890. [– Fr. *tétanie* intermittent tetanus, f. prec.; see -Y[3].] A tetanoid affection characterized by intermittent muscular spasms.

Tetarto- (tĭtā·ɹto), comb. form of Gr. τέταρτος fourth (cf. TETRA-), in terms belonging chiefly to crystallography; as **Teta:rtohe·dral** [Gr. ἕδρα base] *a.*, having one fourth of the number of faces required by the highest or holohedral degree of symmetry belonging to its system; hence **Teta:rtohe·drally** *adv.*, in a tetartohedral manner. **Teta:rtohe·drism,** the property or quality of crystallizing in tetartohedral forms.

Tetch (tetʃ). Now *dial.* 1642. [Of unc. origin; perh. a back-formation from next.] A fit of petulance or anger; a tantrum.

Tetchy, techy (te·tʃi), *a.* 1592. [prob. f. *tecche*, var. of *tache* spot, blemish, fault – OFr. *teche*, (also mod.) *tache*, perh. of Gmc. origin; see -Y[1].] Easily irritated or made angry; quick to take offence; short-tempered; peevish, irritable; testy. **b.** Of qualities, actions, etc.: Characterized by or proceeding from irritability 1592. Hence **Te·tchily** *adv.* **Te·tchiness.**

‖**Tête** (tē̆t, Fr. tęt). *Obs.* exc. *Hist.* 1756. [Fr., 'head'.] A woman's head of hair, or wig, dressed high and elaborately ornamented, in the fashion of the second half of the 18th c.

‖**Tête-à-tête** (tē̆·tătē̆·t, Fr. tętatęt), *adv.*, *sb.*, and *a.* 1697. [Fr., lit. 'head to head'.] **A.** *adv.* Together without the presence of a third person; in private; face to face 1700.

The General and I. .moping together *t.* THACKERAY.

B. *sb.* (pl. *tête-à-têtes.*) **1.** A private conversation or interview between two persons; also *concr.* a party of two 1697. **2.** A form of sofa, of such a shape as to enable two persons to converse more or less face to face 1864. **C.** *adj.* (the sb. used *attrib.*) Pertaining to a *tête-à-tête*; consisting of or attended by two persons 1728.

A pretty cheerful *tête-à-tête* dinner 1728.

‖**Tête-bêche** (tęt bęʃ). 1882. [Fr., f. *tête* head + *bêche*, reduced from *béchevet* lit. double bed-head.] *Philately.* A term used to describe the printing of postage or other stamps upside down or sideways with reference to one another.

Tether (te·ðəɹ), *sb.* late ME. [– ON. *tjóðr*, corresp. to MLG., MDu. *tūder*, *tudder* (Du. *tuier*), OHG. *zeotar* fore-pole, repr. Gmc. **teudr-*, **tūdr-*; f. **teu-* fasten.] **1.** A rope, cord, or other fastening by which a horse, goat, or other beast is tied to a stake or the like, so as to confine it to the spot. **2.** *fig.* The cause or measure of one's limitation; the radius of one's field of action; scope, limit 1579. **b.** A bond or fetter 1609.

2. We soon find the shortness of our t. POPE. Phr. *The end* (*length*) *of one's t.*, the extreme limit of one's resources, endurance, etc. **b.** When weary of the matrimonial t. BYRON.

Tether (te·ðəɹ), *v.* 1470. [f. prec.] **1.** *trans.* To make fast or confine with a tether 1483. **2.** To fasten, make fast generally 1563. **3.** *fig.* To fasten or bind by conditions or circumstances; to bind so as to detain 1470.

1. The lamb. .by a slender cord was tethered to a stone WORDSW. **3.** All my life tethered to the law 1879.

Tetra- (tetră), bef. a vowel **tetr-**, – Gr. τετρα-, comb. form of τέτταρες, τέτταρα four.

1. *gen.* **Te·trabrach** (-bræk) [Gr. τετράβραχυς], *Anc. Pros.* a word or foot of four short syllables, as *facinora*; as a foot usu. called *proceleusmatic.* **Tetraca·rpellary** *a.*, *Bot.* of a compound fruit: having four carpels. **Tetracho·tomous** *a.*, *Zool.* and *Bot.* ramifying into four branches or divisions; doubly dichotomous. **Tetracoccous** (-kǫ·kəs) [Gr. κόκκος berry] *a.*, *Bot.* having four cocci or carpels; also, applied to bacteria when in four segments. ‖**Tetraco·lon**, *Gr. Pros.* a metrical period consisting of four cola or members. **Tetraco·ral,** one of the *Tetracoralla*, a division of corals (= *Rugosa*) in which the septa are in multiples of four. **Tetrada·ctyl(e** *a.*, having four fingers or toes; *sb.* a four-toed animal, esp. a vertebrate. **Tetrade·capod** *a.*, having fourteen feet; belonging to the *Tetradecapoda*, an order of Crustaceans; *sb.* a crustacean of this order. **Te·traglot** *a.*, speaking four languages; written or composed in four languages. **Tetrahexahe·dron,** *Geom.* a solid figure contained by twenty-four planes. **Tetrale·mma,** *Logic* a position presenting four alternatives. **Tetrano·mial** *a.*, *Math.* consisting of four (algebraic) terms; quadrinomial. **Tetrape·talous** *a.*, having four petals. **Tetraphy·llous** [Gr. φύλλον leaf] *a.*, *Bot.* having or consisting of four leaves; abbrev. 4-*phyllous.* **Tetrapneumo·nian** *a.*, *Zool.* of or pertaining to the *Tetrapneumones*, a division of spiders with two pairs of lung-sacs; *sb.*, a spider of this division. **Tetrapneu·monous** *a.*, *Zool.* having four lungs or respiratory organs; applied to the *Tetrapneumones* (see prec.) and to the *Tetrapneumona*, a group of holothurians (sea-cucumbers). ‖**Tetra·polis,** a district of four cities; a state or political division consisting of four towns. **Te·traptote** [Gr. τετράπτωτος], *Gram.* a noun with (only) four cases. **Te·trarch** *a.*, *Bot.* proceeding from four distinct points of origin. **Tetrase·palous** *a.*, *Bot.* having four sepals. **Tetraspe·rmous** [Gr. σπέρμα seed] *a.*, *Bot.* having four seeds, or seeds in fours. **Tetrathe·cal** [Gr. θήκη case, cell] *a.*, *Bot.* four-celled, as an ovary. **Tetra·xial** *a.*, having four axes, as some sponge-spicules; so **Tetra·xile** *a.* in same sense.

2. *Chem.* In the names of compounds and derivatives with the general sense of 'four-', 'four times'. **a.** In sbs.: (*a*) Prefixed to names of binary compounds of elements or radicals, names of salts, etc., to signify four atoms, groups, or equivalents of the element or radical in question; as *tetrachlo·ride*, a compound of four atoms of chlorine with some other element or radical; so *tetrasu·lphide*, TETROXIDE, etc. (*b*) Prefixed to names of elements or radicals (or the combining forms, as *bromo-*, *nitro-*, etc.) entering into the name of a compound, to signify that four atoms or groups of the element or radical are substituted in the substance designated by the rest of the name, as *te:trabromobe·nzene*, $C_6H_2Br_4$, in which four of the hydrogen atoms of benzene, C_6H_6, are replaced by four bromine atoms. (*c*) In some words used irregularly, as *te:trasa·licylide* $C_{28}H_{16}O_8$. **b.** Prefixed to adjs., in the names of acids, alcohols, aldehydes, ethers, salts, etc.; as *tetraso·dic*, containing four sodium atoms. **c.** In vbs. and their pples. derived from sbs. as in a., as *tetrahy·drated* (containing 4 molecules of water), etc.

Tetrabasic (tetrăbē̆i·sik), *a.* 1863. [f. TETRA- + BASIC.] *Chem.* Of an acid: Containing four atoms of hydrogen replaceable by more electropositive elements or radicals. Of a salt: Derived from such an acid.

Tetrabranchiate (tetrăbræ·ŋkiĕt), *a.* and *sb.* 1835. [– mod.L. *tetrabranchiatum*, f. TETRA- + Gr. βράγχια gills + -ATE[2] 2.] *Zool.* **A.** *adj.* Belonging to the *Tetrabranchiata*, an order of cephalopods (mostly extinct) having four branchiæ or gills. **B.** *sb.* A cephalopod belonging to this order. So **Te·trabranch** *sb.* and *a.*

Tetrachord (te·trăkǫɹd). 1603. [– Gr. τετράχορδον (*sc.* ὄργανον), a Greek musical instrument, f. τετρα- TETRA- + χορδή string.] **1.** An ancient musical instrument with four strings. **2.** *Mus.* A scale-series of four notes, being the half of an octave. †**b.** The interval between the first and last notes of this series; a perfect fourth. 1603. Hence **Tetracho·rdal** *a.*

‖**Tetractys** (tĭtræ·ktis). 1603. [– Gr. τετρακτύς.] A set of four; the number four; *esp.* the Pythagorean name for the sum of the first four numbers (1 + 2 + 3 + 4 = 10) regarded as the source of all things.

Tetrad (te·træd). 1653. [– Gr. τετράς, τετραδ- a group of four, the number four; see -AD.] **1.** A sum, group, or set of four; four (things, etc.) regarded as a single object of thought. **2. a.** *Chem.* An element, compound, or radical having a combining power of four units, i.e. of four atoms of hydrogen; a tetravalent element, etc. 1865. **b.** *Biol.* (*a*) A group of four cells, e.g. spores, pollen-grains. (*b*) A group of four chromosomes formed by the division of a single chromosome. (*c*) A quaternary unit of organization differentiated from a triad. 1876.

Te·tradeca:ne. 1877. [f. Gr. τετρα- TETRA- + δέκα ten + -ANE 2.] *Chem.* The saturated hydrocarbon or paraffin of the 14-carbon series, $C_{14}H_{30}$, = tetradecyl hydride; a waxy solid.

Tetradic (tĭtræ·dik), *a.* 1788. [f. TETRAD + -IC.] Of, pertaining to, or of the nature of a tetrad. **b.** *Chem.* That is a tetrad; tetravalent 1868. **c.** *Anc. Pros.* (*a*) Containing four different metres or rhythms. (*b*) Composed of groups of systems, each of which contains four unlike systems. 1891.

Tetradite (te·trădəit). 1727. [– late Gr. τετραδίτης, pl. -αι, f. τετράς, -αδ- TETRAD; see -ITE 1.] *pl.* The Manichees and others, who believed the Godhead to consist of four persons.

Tetradrachm (te·trădræm). 1579. [– Gr. τετράδραχμον; see TETRA- and DRACHM.] *Gr. Antiq.* A silver coin of ancient Greece, of the value of four drachms; see DRACHM 1. Hence **Tetradrachmal** (-dræ·kmăl) *a.* of or pertaining to a t.

Tetradymite (tĭtræ·diməit). 1850. [– G. *tetradymit* (W. Haidinger, 1831), f. Gr. τετράδυμος fourfold + -ITE[1] 2 b.] *Min.* Telluride of bismuth, found in pale steel-grey laminæ with a bright metallic lustre.

‖**Tetradynamia** (te:trădinæ·miă, -dəi-). 1760. [mod.L. (Linn. 1735), f. Gr. τετρα- TETRA- + δύναμις power, strength + -IA[1]; cf. DIDYNAMIA.] *Bot.* The fifteenth class in the Linnæan Sexual System comprising plants which bear hermaphrodite flowers with six stamens in pairs, four of which are longer than the others; corresponding to the family *Cruciferæ.* Hence **Tetradyna·mian** *a.* tetradynamous; *sb.* a plant of the class *Tetradynamia.* **Tetrady·namous** *a.* of or pertaining to this class; having four longer and two shorter stamens.

Tetragon (te·trăgǫn). 1626. [– late L. *tetragonum* – Gr. τετράγωνον quadrangle, subst. use of n. of adj. τετράγωνος; see TETRA-, -GON.] **1.** *Geom.* A figure having four angles and four sides; a quadrangle considered as one of the polygons. *Regular t.*, a square. 1630. **2.** A square fort; a quadrangular building or block of buildings 1669. **3.** *Astrol.* The aspect of two planets when they are 90° distant from one another relatively to the earth; the square or quadrate aspect 1626.

Tetragonal (tĭtræ·gŏnăl), *a.* 1571. [f. prec. + -AL[1] 1.] **1.** Of or pertaining to a tetragon; having four angles; quadrangular. **2.** *Bot.* and *Zool.* Quadrangular in section, like a 'square' rod; tetraquetrous 1753. **3.** *Cryst.* Applied to a system of crystallization in which the three axes are at right angles, the two lateral axes being equal, and the vertical of a different length 1868. Hence **Tetra·gonal-ly** *adv.*, **-ness.**

Tetragonous (tĭtræ·gŏnəs), *a.* 1760. [f. as prec. + -OUS.] *Bot.* = prec. 2.

Tetragram (te·trăgræm). 1870. [– Gr. τὸ τετράγραμμον (Clem. Alex.), the (word) of four letters, f. τετρα- TETRA- + γράμμα letter.] = next.

‖**Tetragrammaton** (tetrăgræ·mătǫn). *Pl.* **-ata.** late ME. [– Gr. (τὸ) τετραγράμματον (Philo) the (word) of four letters, neut. of τετραγράμματος, adj. f. τετρα- TETRA- + γραμματ- letter. So late and med.L. *tetragrammaton.*] A word of four letters; *spec.* the Hebrew word YHWH or JHVH (vocalized as YAHWEH, JAHVEH or JEHOVAH); often substituted for that word (regarded as ineffable), and treated as a mysterious symbol of the name of God; occas. used as a title of the Deity. **b.** *gen.* with *a* and *pl.* A word of four letters used as a symbol 1656.

‖**Tetragynia** (tetrădʒi·niă), *a.* 1760. [mod. L., f. TETRA- + Gr. γυνή, taken in sense 'female organ, pistil'; see -IA[1].] *Bot.* An order or division in many of the Linnæan classes of plants, comprising those having four pistils. Hence **Tetragy·nian, -ious, Tetra·gynous** *adjs.* belonging to this order of any class; having four pistils.

Tetrahedral (tetrăhī·drăl, -he·drăl), *a.* 1794. [f. late Gr. τετράεδρος (see TETRAHEDRON) + -AL[1] 1.] **1.** Having four sides (in addition to the base or ends); enclosed or contained laterally by four plane surfaces. **2.** Of, pertaining to, or having the form of a tetrahedron; *spec.* in *Cryst.*, belonging to a division of the isometric system of which the regular tetrahedron is the characteristic form 1805.

1. *T. quoin, angle,* one bounded by four planes meeting at a common apex. So **Tetrahe·drally** *adv.* **Tetrahe·dric, -al** *adjs.* **Tetrahe·droid** *a.* resembling a tetrahedron.

Tetrahedrite (tetrăhī·drəit, -he·drəit). 1868. [– G. *tetraëdrit* (W. Haidinger, 1845), f. as prec. + *-it* -ITE[1] 2 b.] *Min.* Native sulphide of antimony and copper, with various elements sometimes replacing one or other of these, often occurring in tetrahedral crystals.

Tetrahedron (tetrăhī·drǫn, -he·drǫn). *Pl.* **-a** or **-ons.** 1570. [– late Gr. τετράεδρον, subst. use of τετράεδρος four-sided, f. τετρα- TETRA- + ἕδρα base. In med.L. *tetrahedrum* (XIII).] *Geom.* A solid figure contained by four plane triangular faces, a triangular pyramid; *spec.* the *regular t.*, the first of the five regular solids, contained by four equilateral triangles. Hence, any solid body, esp. a crystal, of this form.

Tetra-icosane (tetră,əi·kosē[i]n). 1894. [f. Gr. τετρα- four + εἴκοσι twenty + -ANE 2 b.] *Chem.* The saturated hydrocarbon or paraffin of the 24-carbon series, $C_{24}H_{50}$ = $CH_3(CH_2)_{22}CH_3$, a solid waxy substance.

Te:trakis-hexahe·dron. 1878. [f. Gr. τετράκις four times + HEXAHEDRON.] A solid figure contained by twenty-four equal triangular planes, having the appearance of a cube with a low pyramid raised on each of its six faces. (In *Cryst.* belonging to the isometric system.)

Tetralogy (tĭtræ·lŏdʒi). 1656. [– Gr. τετραλογία, f. *tetra-* TETRA- + -λογία -LOGY.] **1.** *Gr. Antiq.* A series of four dramas, three tragic (the *trilogy*) and one satyric, exhibited at Athens at the festival of Dionysus. **b.** Hence, any series of four related dramatic or literary compositions 1742. **2.** A set of four speeches 1661. Hence **Tetralo·gic** *a.*

Tetramerous (tĭtræ·mĕrəs), *a.* 1826. [f. TETRA- + -MEROUS.] Having, consisting of, or characterized by four parts. *spec.* **a.** *Bot.* Having the parts of the flower-whorl in series of four. (Often written 4-*merous.*) **b.** *Ent.* Having the tarsi four-jointed, as the *Tetramera* among *Coleoptera.* **c.** Having four rays, as a star-fish. So **Tetra·meral** *a.* having parts in fours. **Tetra·merism,** t. condition.

Tetrameter (tĭtræ·mĭtəɹ). 1612. [– late L. *tetrametrus* – Gr. τετράμετρος, f. τετρα- TETRA- + μέτρον measure.] *Pros.* A verse or period consisting of four measures. Also *attrib.* or as *adj.*

Tetramorph (te·trămǭɹf). 1848. [– Gr. τετράμορφον, subst. use of n. of adj. -μορφος, f. τετρα- TETRA- + μορφή form.] *Christian Art.* A composite figure combining the symbols of the four evangelists (derived from Rev. 4:6–8 and Ezek. 1:5–10).

Tetramorphic (tetrămǭ·ɹfik), *a.* 1870. [f. as prec. + -IC.] **a.** *Nat. Hist.* Occurring in four different forms. **b.** Of or pertaining to a tetramorph.

‖**Tetrandria** (tetræ·ndriă). 1760. [mod.L. (Linn., 1735), f. Gr. τετρα- TETRA- + ἀνήρ, ἀνδρ- man, male; see -IA[1].] *Bot.* The fourth class in the Linnæan Sexual System comprising plants bearing hermaphrodite flowers with four equal stamens. Also an order in the classes Gynandria, Monœcia, and Diœcia, having four stamens. Hence **Tetra·ndrian** *a.* having four stamens. **Tetra·ndrious, Tetra·ndrous,** *adjs.* having four equal stamens; belonging to the class *T.*

Tetraonid (tĭtrē[i]·onid), *a.* (*sb.*) 1847. [f. mod.L. *Tetraonidæ*, f. L. *tetrao, -ōn-* – Gr. τετράων, applied to the Black Grouse, etc.; see -ID[3].] *Ornith.* Pertaining to the family *Tetraonidæ* of gallinaceous birds, including the grouse and allied forms; also as *sb.* a member of this family. (The term has also been used more widely to include the partridges, quails, and other birds.)

‖**Tetrapla** (te·trăplă). 1684. [– Gr. τετραπλᾶ, n. pl. of τετραπλοῦς fourfold, f. τετρα- TETRA- + -πλοος -fold.] A text consisting of four parallel versions, esp. that of the Old Testament made by Origen.

Tetrapod (te·trăpǫd), *a.* and *sb.* 1826. [– mod.L. *tetrapodus* – Gr. τετράπους, τετραποδ- four-footed, f. τετρα- TETRA- + πούς, ποδ- foot.] **A.** *adj.* Having four feet or four limbs; *spec.* in *Ent.*, belonging to the *Tetrapoda*, a division of butterflies having only four perfect legs, the anterior pair being unfitted for walking. **B.** *sb.* A four-footed animal; one of the *Tetrapoda.*

Tetrapody (tĭtræ·pŏdi). 1846. [– Gr. τετραποδία, f. τετραποδ-; see prec., -Y[3].] *Pros.* A group of four metrical feet; a verse of four feet. So **Tetrapo·dic** *a.*

Tetrapterous (tĭtræ·ptĕrəs), *a.* 1826. [f. mod.L. *tetrapterus* (– Gr. τετράπτερος four-winged) + -OUS.] Having four wings; *spec.* in *Ent.* applied to four-winged flies; in *Bot.* having four wing-like appendages, as certain fruits. So **Tetra·pteran** *a.* tetrapterous; *sb.* a four-winged insect.

Tetrarch (te·t-, tī·traɹk). late ME. [– late L. *tetrarcha*, cl.L. *tetrarches* – Gr. τετράρχης; see TETRA-, -ARCH.] **1.** *Rom. Hist.* The ruler of one of four divisions of a country or province; applied later to subordinate rulers generally, esp. in Syria. **2.** *transf.* and *fig.* **a.** A ruler of a fourth part, or of one of four parts, divisions, elements, etc.; also, a subordinate ruler generally 1610. **b.** One of four joint rulers or directors 1661. Hence **Te·trarchate,** the office or position of a t.

Tetrarchic (tĭtrā·ɹkik), *a.* 1818. [– Gr. τετραρχικός of a tetrarch; see -IC.] Of or pertaining to four rulers; pertaining to a tetrarch or to a tetrarchy. So **Tetra·rchical** *a.* (now *rare*) 1638.

Tetrarchy (te·traɹki). late ME. [– L. *tetrarchia* – Gr. τετραρχία, f. τετράρχης TETRARCH; see -Y[3].] **1.** The district, division, or part of a country or province ruled by a tetrarch; the government or jurisdiction of a tetrarch. **2.** *transf.* and *fig.* A government by four persons jointly; a set of four tetrarchs or rulers; a country divided into four petty governments.

Tetraspore (te·tră,spō[ə]ɹ). 1857. [f. TETRA- + SPORE.] *Bot.* A group (usu.) of four asexual spores, resulting from the division of a mother cell, in the *Florideæ*, a group of *Algæ.* Hence **Tetrasporic** (-spǫ·rik), **Tetrasporous** (tetră,spō[ə]·rəs, tĭtræ·spŏrəs) *adjs.* composed of or producing tetraspores.

Tetrastich (te·trăstik, tetræ·stik). 1580. [– L. *tetrastichon* (also used) – Gr. τετράστιχον, n. of τετράστιχος containing four rows, f. τετρα- TETRA- + στίχος row, line of verse.] *Pros.* A stanza of four lines.

Tetrastyle (te·trăstəil), *sb.* and *a.* 1704. [– L. *tetrastylos* adj., *tetrastylon* sb. – Gr. τετράστυλος (n. -ον) with four pillars, f. τετρα- TETRA- + στῦλος pillar.] *Arch.* **A.** *sb.* A structure having four pillars or columns; a group of four pillars. **B.** *adj.* Having or consisting of four columns 1837. Hence **Tetrastylic** (-sti·lik) *a.* = B.

Tetrasyllable (tetrăsi·lăb'l), *sb.* (*a.*) 1589. [f. TETRA- + SYLLABLE; cf. late L. *tetrasyllabus*, Gr. τετρασύλλαβος adjs.] **A.** *sb.* A word of four syllables. **B.** *adj.* Tetrasyllabic. So **Tetrasylla·bic, -al** *adjs.* consisting of four syllables.

Tetrathionic (tetră,þei,ǫ·nik), *a.* 1848. [f. TETRA- + THIONIC.] *Chem.* In *t. acid*, $H_2S_4O_6$, a colourless, inodorous, very acid liquid containing four atoms of sulphur in the molecule. Hence **Tetrathi·onate,** a salt of t. acid.

Tetratomic (tetrătǫ·mik), *a.* 1862. [f. TETR(A- + ATOMIC.] *Chem.* Containing four atoms in the molecule.

Tetravalent (tĭtræ·vălĕnt, tetrăvē[i]·lĕnt), *a.* 1868. [f. Gr. τετρα- TETRA- + *-valent*, deduced from VALENCY 2.] *Chem.* Combining with four atoms of hydrogen or other monovalent element, or with four monovalent radicals, or capable of replacing four atoms of monovalent elements in a compound. Also called *quadrivalent.* So **Tetravalence,** quadrivalence.

Tetrazone (te·trăzō[u]n). 1895. [f. TETRA- + AZ(O- + -ONE.] *Chem.* Name of a class of basic compounds containing four nitrogen atoms, with the formula $R_2NN:NNR_2$, in which R is any monovalent group.

†**Te·tric,** *a.* 1533. [– L. *tætricus, tetricus*, f. *tæter* foul; see -IC.] = next –1811.

Tetrical (te·trikăl), *a.* *Obs.* or *arch.* 1529. [f. as prec. + -AL[1] 1; see -ICAL.] Austere, severe, harsh, bitter, morose.

Tetrobol (te·trŏbǫl). 1693. [– late L. *tetrobolon*, Gr. τετρώβολον four-obolus piece, f. τετρα- four + ὀβολός OBOLUS.] A silver coin of ancient Greece of the value of four oboli.

‖**Tetrodon** (te·trŏdǫn). 1774. [mod.L. (Linn., 1766), f. Gr. τετρα- four + ὀδούς, ὀδοντ- tooth.] *Ichth.* A genus of plectognathic fishes, typical of the family *Tetrodontidæ*, in which the jaws are divided longitudinally by a groove, giving the appearance of four large teeth; a fish of this family, a globe-fish. So **Te·trodont** *a.* having (apparently) four teeth; belonging to the *Tetrodontidæ*; *sb.* a t. or globe-fish.

Tetrous (te·trəs), *a.* Now *rare.* 1637. [f. L. *tæter* foul + -OUS.] Offensive, foul.

Tetroxide (tetrǫ·ksəid). 1866. [f. TETRA- 2 a + OXIDE.] *Chem.* A binary compound containing four atoms of oxygen; e.g. nitrogen tetroxide, N_2O_4.

Tetryl (te·tril). 1857. [f. TETRA- 2 + -YL.] *Chem.* The monovalent radical of the tetracarbon series, C_4H_9, also called BUTYL; chiefly attrib. = *tetrylic.* Hence **Tetry·lic** *a.* of t., in *tetrylic acid*, etc.

Tetter (te·təɹ), *sb.* [OE. *teter*, cogn. with Skr. *dadru* skin disease, f. *dṝ* to crack; cf. Lith. *dedervinė* tetter; repr. in OHG. *zittaroh* and G. (dial.) *zitteroch*, etc.] **1.** A general name for any pustular herpiform eruption of the skin, as eczema, herpes, impetigo, ringworm, etc. **2.** A cutaneous disease in animals, esp. horses 1552.

1. *Crusted, pustular, running t.*, impetigo. *Eating t.*, lupus. *Honeycomb t.*, favus. *Humid* or *moist t.*, eczema. *Scaly t.*, psoriasis. Hence †**Te·tter** *v. trans.* to affect with, or as with, a t. SHAKS.

Tetter-berry (te·təɹberi). 1597. The common Bryony, *Bryonia dioica*; also, its berry. Variously said to cure and to produce tetter.

Tetterous (te·tərəs), *a.* 1719. [f. TETTER *sb.* + -OUS.] Of the nature of, proceeding from, or causing tetter.

Tetterworm (te·təɹwɒɹm). 1622. A cutaneous affection; a form of ringworm.

Tetterwort (te·təɹwɒɹt). late ME. The common Celandine, *Chelidonium majus*: so named because supposed to cure tetters.

‖**Tettix** (te·tiks). 1775. [Gr. τέττιξ.] **1.** The cicada or tree-cricket, a homopterous winged insect. **2.** *Ent.* A genus of *Acridiidæ*, or short-horned grasshoppers, typical of the orthopterous subfamily *Tettiginæ* 1891. **3.** *Golden t.* (Gr. χρυσοῦς τέττιξ), an ornament worn in the hair by Athenians before Solon's time, as an emblem of their being aboriginal 1874.

Teuto- (tiū*to*), bef. a vowel **Teut-**, comb. form irreg. f. TEUTON, TEUTONIC.

1. Combined with other ethnic sbs. or adjs. in the sense 'That is a Teuton, or Teutonic and..', as *Teut-Aryan, Teuto-Celt.* **2.** Formative of derivatives, as **Teutoma·nia,** a mania for what is Teutonic or German; **Teu·tophile, -phil** *sb.*, a lover or friend of Germany and the Germans; also as *adj.*

Teuton (tiū·tǫn, -t'n). 1727. [– L. *Teutoni, Teutones* (pl.), f. IE. base meaning 'people', 'country', 'land'.] **1.** In *pl.* (usu. in L. form *Teutones*) applied to an ancient people of unknown race, said to have inhabited the Cimbric Chersonesus in Jutland *c* 320 B.C., who, in company with the Cimbri, in 113–101 B.C. devastated Gaul and threatened the Roman Republic. **2.** A German; in extended ethnic sense, a member of the races or peoples speaking a Germanic or Teutonic language; now often used like 'Saxon' in opposition to 'Celt', and in avoidance of 'German' in its modern political sense 1833.

Teutonic (tiut*ǫ*·nik), *a.* and *sb.* 1605. [– Fr. *teutonique* – L. *Teutonicus*, f. *Teutones*; see prec., -IC.] **A.** *adj.* **1.** Of or pertaining to the Teutons; German, esp. High German 1645. †**b.** Of or pertaining to the ancient Teutones –1741. **2.** Of or pertaining to the group of languages allied to German (including Gothic, Scandinavian, Low German, and English), forming one of the great branches of the Indo-European, Indo-Germanic, or Aryan family, and to the peoples or tribes speaking these languages; now often called *Germanic* 1605. **3. T. Knights, T. Order** (of Knights): A military order of German Knights, orig. enrolled *c* 1191 as the Teutonic Knights of St. Mary of Jerusalem, for service in the Holy Land 1617. **4. T. cross,** a cross potent, being the badge of the Teutonic Order 1882. **B.** *sb.* **1.** †The language of any Teutonic race, *spec.* the German language (*obs.*); now applied by philologists only to the common or primitive speech, which afterwards broke up into the languages named in A. 2; also known as *Germanic* 1605. †**2.** *pl.* = Teutonic Knights –1796. Hence **Teuto·nicism,** T. (i.e. German) character or practice; a Teutonic expression; a Teutonism.

Teutonism (tiū·tǒnizm). 1854. [f. TEUTON + -ISM.] **1.** An idiom or mode of expression peculiar to or characteristic of the Teutonic languages, esp. German; a Germanism 1889. **2.** Teutonic or German character, type, constitution, system, or spirit; German feeling and action 1854. So **Teu·tonist,** one versed in the history, etc., of the Teutonic race or languages; one whose writings have a Teutonic character or style.

Teutonize (tiū·tǒnəiz), *v.* 1845. [f. TEUTON + -IZE.] *trans.* To make or render Teutonic or German. **b.** *intr.* To conform to Teutonism 1882.

Tew (tiū), *sb. Obs.* exc. *dial.* 1440. [f. TEW *v.*] †**1.** The tawing of leather. **2.** Constant work and bustling; a state of worry or excitement. *dial.* and *U.S.* 1825.

Tew (tiū), *v. Obs.* exc. *dial.* ME. [In branch I app. rel. to synon. TAW *v.* Branch II may be developed from branch I.] **I. 1.** *trans.* = TAW *v.* 2. **2.** To work (anything) into proper consistency by beating, etc.; to temper (mortar) 1641. †**3.** = TAW *v.* 3, 3 b. –1670. **II. 1.** *trans.* To fatigue or tire with hard work. *dial.* 1825. **2.** *intr.* To work hard, to toil; to bustle about. Now *dial.* and *U.S.* 1787.

Tewhit, tewit (tī·hwit, tī·wit, tiū·it; also tyū·χit, tyɒ·χit, tiū·fit). Now *local.* 1450. [orig. imit.; see PEWIT.] The common Lapwing or Pewit, *Vanellus cristatus.*

†**Tewtaw,** *sb.* 1649. [Goes with next.] An implement for breaking hemp or flax –1727.

Tewtaw, *v.* 1601. [Origin obsc.; cf. TAW *v.*] *trans.* To beat or dress (hemp or flax); = TAW *v.* Now *dial.*

Texan (te·ksăn), *a.* and *sb.* 1842. [f. next + -AN.] **A.** *adj.* Of or pertaining to the State of Texas; in some specific names of animals and plants 1860. **B.** *sb.* A person or animal native to or inhabiting Texas 1842.

Texas (te·ksăs). Name of one of the United States. **1.** *Western U.S.* The uppermost structure of a river-steamer, containing the pilot-house and officers' quarters 1872. **b.** The elevated gallery, resembling a louver or clear-story, in a grain-elevator 1909. **2.** In names of native Texan plants, animals, etc.: as *T. bead-tree, flax, snake-root* 1858.

Text (tekst), *sb.* [In XIV *text(e, tixt(e* – ONFr. *tixte*, (also mod.Fr.) *texte* – L. *textus* tissue, style of literary work (Quintilian), in med.L. the Gospel, written character, f. *text-*, pa. ppl. stem of L. *texere* weave.] **1.** The wording of anything written or printed; the structure formed by the words in their order; the very words, phrases, and sentences as written. **b.** The wording adopted by an editor as (in his opinion) most nearly representing the author's original work; a book or edition containing this; also, with qualification, any form in which a writing exists or is current, as a *good, bad, corrupt t.* 1841. **2.** *esp.* The very words and sentences as originally written: **a.** in the original language, as opp. to a translation or rendering; **b.** in the original form and order, as dist. from a commentary, or from annotations. Hence, in later use, the body of any treatise, the authoritative or formal part, as dist. from notes, appendices, etc. late ME. **c.** That portion of the contents of a manuscript or printed book, or of a page, which constitutes the original matter, as dist. from the notes, etc. late ME. †**3.** *spec.* The very words and sentences of Holy Scripture; hence, the Scriptures themselves; also, any single book of the Scriptures –1668. **b.** A copy of the Scriptures, or of a book of the Scriptures; *spec.* a volume containing the Gospels. *Obs.* exc. *Hist.* late ME. **4.** A short passage from the Scriptures, esp. one quoted as authoritative, as a motto, to point a moral, or as the subject of an exposition or sermon. late ME. **b.** A short passage from some book or writer considered as authoritative; a received maxim or axiom; a proverb; an adage; in later use, esp. one used as a copybook heading. Now *rare.* late ME. **c.** *fig.* The theme or subject on which any one speaks; the starting-point of a discussion 1605. **5.** Short for TEXT-HAND. See also CHURCH *t.*, GERMAN *t.* 1588.

1. Say, Stella, when you copy next, Will you keep strictly to the t.? SWIFT. **b.** The t. seems very corrupt FREEMAN. **2. b.** Coke upon Littleton, where the comment is of equal authority with the t. FIELDING. **4. b.** That t...That seith that hunters beth nat hooly men CHAUCER. **c.** No more; the t. is foolish SHAKS. **5.** Faire as a t. B. in a Coppie booke SHAKS.

attrib. and *Comb.*: **t.-blindness,** word-blindness; **-cut, -engraving, -picture,** an illustration occupying a space in the t. of a book; **-title,** a half-title, at the beginning of the t. of a book.

Text (tekst), *v.* Now *rare.* 1564. [f. prec.] †**1.** *trans.* To inscribe, write, or print in text-hand or in capital or large letters –1639. **b.** *intr.* To write in text-hand 1660. †**2. a.** To cite texts. **b.** *trans.* To cite a text at or against a person. –1615.

Text-book (te·kst,buk). 1779. A book used as a standard work for the study of a particular subject; a manual of instruction in a subject of study.

Te·xt-hand. 1542. [Cf. TEXT-LETTER.] A fine large hand in writing. *orig.* One of the larger and more formal hands in which the text of a book was often written, as dist. from the smaller and more cursive hand appropriate to the gloss, etc. **b.** In recent use, applied to a school-hand written in lines about half an inch wide.

Textile (te·kstəil, -il), *a.* and *sb.* 1626. [– L. *textilis*, f. *text-*; see TEXT *sb.*, -ILE.] **A.** *adj.* **1.** That has been or may be woven 1656. **b.** *Nat. Hist.* Having markings resembling a woven surface; e.g. *t. snake* 1802. **2.** Of or connected with weaving 1844.

1. Cotton and wool and other t. materials 1868. **b.** *T. cone*, a species of cone-shell, *Conus textilis*, having markings resembling a woven surface.

B. *sb.* **1.** A woven fabric; any kind of cloth. (Usu. in *pl.*) 1626. **b.** *attrib.* (or as *adj.*) Of or pertaining to weaving or to woven fabrics 1844. **2.** Fibrous material, as flax, cotton, silk, etc., suitable for being spun and woven into yarn, cloth, etc. 1641.

†**Te·xt-le:tter.** 1511. [repr. med.L. *littera textualis* (XIV).] A large or capital letter in handwriting –1706.

Textorial (tekstōᵊ·riăl), *a.* 1774. [f. L. *textor* weaver, *textorius* pertaining to weaving, f. *text-*; see TEXT *sb.*, -ORIAL.] Of or pertaining to weavers or weaving.

Textual (te·kstiu,ăl), *a.* [– med.L. *textualis* (XIV) (in Chaucer *textueel*); f. *textus* + *-alis*; see TEXT *sb.*, -AL[1] 1. Cf. Fr. *textuel* (XV).] †**1.** Of a person: Well acquainted with 'texts' or authors; well-read; literally exact in giving the text –1613. **2.** Of, pertaining to, or contained in the (or a) text, esp. of the Scriptures 1470. **3.** Based on, following, or conforming to the text, esp. of the Scriptures 1614.

1. But as I seyde I am noght textueel CHAUCER. **2.** The admitted principles of t. criticism 1859. His sagacity in t. emendations 1872. Hence **Te·xtually** *adv.* in or as regards the text; in the actual words of the text.

Textualism (te·kstiu,ăliz'm). 1863. [f. prec. + -ISM.] **1.** Strict adherence to the text, esp. of the Scriptures; the principles or method of a textualist. **2.** That department of scholarship which deals with the text of the Bible; textual criticism 1888.

Textualist (te·kstiu,ălist). 1629. [f. as prec. + -IST.] **a.** One learned in the text of the Bible. **b.** One who adheres strictly to, and bases his doctrine upon, the text of the Scriptures.

Textuary (te·kstiu,ări), *a.* and *sb.* 1608. [– med.L. *textuarius* (XV), f. *textus*; see TEXT *sb.*, -ARY[1]. Partly from Fr. *textuaire* (XVII).] **A.** *adj.* **1.** Of or belonging to the text; textual 1646. †**2.** That ranks as a text-book; regarded as an authority –1682.

1. The t. proofs of St. Peter's supremacy 1854.

B. *sb.* **1.** = prec. a; also, one ready at quoting texts 1608. †**2.** = prec. b. –1828.

†**Textuist.** 1631. [f. L. *textus* TEXT *sb.* + -IST.] A textual scholar –1700.

The crabbed textuists of his time MILT.

Textural (te·kstiūrăl), *a.* 1835. [f. TEXTURE + -AL[1] 1.] Of or belonging to texture. **b.** *Painting.* See TEXTURE *sb.* 6. 1859. Hence **Te·xturally** *adv.* in or as regards texture.

Texture (te·kstiŭɹ, -tʃəɹ), *sb.* 1447. [– L. *textura* weaving, f. *text-*; see TEXT *sb.*, -URE.] †**1.** The process or art of weaving –1726. **2.** The produce of the weaver's art; a woven fabric; a web. *arch.* 1656. **b.** *transf.* Any natural structure having an appearance or consistence as if woven; a tissue; a web, e.g. of a spider 1578. **3.** The character of a textile fabric, as to its being fine, close, coarse, ribbed, twilled, etc., resulting from the way in which it is woven 1685. **4.** The constitution, structure, or substance of anything with regard to its constituents, formative elements or physical character 1660. **5.** *fig.* Of immaterial things: Constitution; nature or quality, as resulting from composition. Of the mind: Disposition, as 'woven' of various qualities; temperament, character. 1611. **6.** In the fine arts: The representation of the structure and minute moulding of a surface (esp. of the skin), as dist. from its colour 1859.

2. Others..far in the grassy dale..their humble t. weave THOMSON. **3.** The t. that belongs to

Linen BOYLE. 4. Thou know'st the T. of my Heart, My Reins, and every vital Part WESLEY. The loose t. of snow HUXLEY. 5. An argument.. of so frail and brittle a t. BENTLEY. Hence †**Te·xture** *v. trans.* to construct by or as by weaving; to give a t. to.

‖**Textus** (te·kstŏs). 1856. [L., in med.L. sense; see TEXT *sb.*] **1.** = TEXT *sb.* 3 b. 1874. **2.** *Textus receptus*, lit., received text; *spec.* the received text of the Greek New Testament 1856.

Text-writer (te·kst,rəi:tə.ɹ). 1463. †**1.** A professional writer of text-hand –1491. **2.** *Law.* An author of a legal text-book 1845.

‖**Tezkere** (te·zkĕrĕ). 1612. [Turk. *tezkere* – Arab. *tadkira* lit. memorandum, record, note.] A Turkish official memorandum or certificate.

Th, in words of Old English or Old Norse origin, and in words from Greek, is a consonantal digraph representing one or other of a pair of simple sounds, one voiceless, the other voiced, denoted in this dictionary by the OE. letters (þ) and (ð); the former, as in *thin, bath* (þin, baþ), being the breath dental spirant akin to *t*, and the latter, as in *then, bathe* (ðen, bē¹ð), the voiced dental spirant akin to *d*.

Th-, th' (ME. þ-), a clipped form of some unstressed monosyllables, esp. when the following word begins with a vowel or *h*. **1.** = THE OE. †**2.** = THOU –1594. †**3.** = THEY –1707.

1. To th' shore SHAKS.

-th, *suffix*[1], a formative of sbs. **a.** from vbs.; in some words, as *bath, birth, death*, repr. the Indo-Eur. suffixes **-tos, -tâ, -tis, -tus*; in others, as *tilth*, going back to ON. or OE.; in others, as *growth, spilth, stealth*, of later analogical formation. **b.** from adjs. (rarely sbs.), repr. Indo-Eur. **itâ*, Gmc. **iþô*, OE. *-þu, -þo, -þ*, forming abstract nouns of state; as *filth, health, strength*, etc.; of later analogical formation, *breadth, sloth, wealth, width*. See also -T[2].

-th, *suffix*[2], forming ordinal numbers; in mod. literary Eng. used with all simple numbers from *fourth* onward; repr. OE. *-þa, -þe*, or *-oþa, -oþe*, from an original Indo-Eur. **-tos* (cf. Gr. πέμπτος, L. *quintus*), understood to be identical with one of the suffixes of the superlative degree.

In compound numerals *-th* is added only to the last, as $\frac{1}{1345}$, the *one thousand three hundred and forty-fifth part.*

Thack (þæk), *sb.* Now *dial.* [OE. *þæc* = MDu. *dac*, Du. *dak*, (O)HG. *dach* roof, ON. *þak* roof, thatch :– Gmc **þakam*, f. **þak-*; see THATCH *v.*] †**1.** The roof of a house or building –1526. **2.** = THATCH *sb.* 1. OE.

Thack (þæk), *v.* Now *dial.* ME. [app. partly f. OE. *þacian*, f. *þæc* (see prec.); or a later formation from the sb.] **1.** *intr.* = THATCH *v.* 5. **2.** *trans.* To cover (a roof) or roof (a house) with thatch, formerly also with lead, tiles, etc.; *spec.* to cover the top of a rick with straw or other material so laid as to carry off the rain 1440.

‖**Thakur, thakoor** (tʰā·kur). *India.* 1800. [– Hindi *ṭhākur*, Skr. *ṭhā·kkura* a deity.] A word meaning Lord, used as a title and term of respect; also applied to a chief or noble, esp. of the Rajput race.

‖**Thalamencephalon** (þæ:lămense·fălǫn). 1875. [f. THALAM(O- + ENCEPHALON.] *Anat.* That part of the brain which develops from the posterior part of the anterior cerebral vesicle, and includes the optic thalami, optic nerves, and parts about the third ventricle. Also called *diencephalon, middle brain*, etc.

Thalamic (þălæ·mik, þæ·lămik), *a.* 1860. [– mod.L. *thalamicus*; see THALAMUS, -IC.] Of or pertaining to a thalamus; in *Anat.*, pertaining to the optic thalamus.

Thalamifloral (þæ:lămiflōᵊ·răl), *a.* 1857. [f. mod.L. *Thalamifloræ* (f. THALAMUS + L. *flos, flor-* flower) + -AL[1] 1.] *Bot.* Belonging to the sub-class *Thalamifloræ* of dicotyledons, in which the stamens are inserted on the thalamus or receptacle; hypogynous. So **Thalamiflo·rous** *a.*

Thalamo- (þæ·lămo), bef. a vowel **thalam-**, comb. form of Gr. θάλαμος THALAMUS, in some anatomical terms, as **Thalamocœle** (þæ·lămosī:l) [Gr. κοιλία cavity, ventricle], the cavity of the thalamencephalon; the third ventricle of the brain.

‖**Thalamus** (þæ·lămŏs). *Pl.* **-mi** (-məi). 1753. [L. – Gr. θάλαμος an inner chamber.] **1.** *Anat.* A part of the brain at which a nerve originates or appears to originate; *spec.* the OPTIC thalamus 1756. **2.** *Bot.* **a.** The receptacle of a flower, on which the carpels are placed; the torus 1753. **b.** = THALLUS 1842. **3.** *Archæol.* An inner or secret chamber 1850.

Thalassian (þălæ·siăn), *a.* and *sb.* 1850. [f. Gr. θαλάσσιος marine, f. θάλασσα sea + -AN.] **A.** *adj.* Of or pertaining to the sea, marine; *spec.* applied to the marine tortoises and turtles. **B.** *sb.* A marine tortoise or turtle 1850.

Thalassic (þălæ·sik), *a.* 1860. [– Fr. *thalassique*, f. Gr. θάλασσα sea; see -IC.] **1.** Of or pertaining to the sea; marine. †In *Geol.* applied to strata supposed to be of marine formation. **2.** Pertaining to the (smaller or inland) seas as dist. from the pelagic waters or oceans 1883.

Thalassi·nian, *a.* and *sb.* 1842. [f. mod.L. *Thalassina* + -IAN.] **A.** *adj.* Of or pertaining to the *Thalassinidæ*, a family of long-tailed decapod crustaceans, the scorpion-lobsters. **B.** *sb.* A crustacean of this family.

Thalass(o- (þălæ·s(*o*), **Thala·ssi(o-,** from Gr. θάλασσα sea, and θαλάσσιος marine, formative elements of learned words, as in **Thalassa·rctine** *a.*, *Zool.* of or pertaining to the Polar Bear, *Thalassarctos*. **Thala·ssio-, Thala·ssophyte,** a plant of the *Thalassiophyta*; a seaweed, a marine alga. Also (after Attic Gr. θάλαττα) **Thalatto-.**

Thalassocracy (þælǣsǫ·krăsi). 1846. [– Gr. θαλασσοκρατία; see prec. and -CRACY.] Mastery at sea, sovereignty of the sea. So **Thala·ssocrat,** one who has the mastery of the sea.

Thalassography (þælǣsǫ·grăfi). 1888. [f. THALASSO- + -GRAPHY.] The branch of physical geography which treats of the sea, its configuration and phenomena; oceanography.

‖**Thaler** (tā·ləɹ). 1787. [G. *t(h)aler* DOLLAR.] A German silver coin; a dollar; see DOLLAR 1.

Thalerophagous (þælĕrǫ·făgəs), *a.* 1819. [f. Gr. θαλερός blooming, fresh; see -PHAGOUS.] *Ent.* Feeding on fresh vegetable substances.

‖**Thalia** (þăləi·ă). 1656. [– Gr. Θάλεια (blooming, f. θάλλειν bloom).] **1.** The eighth of the Muses, presiding over comedy and idyllic poetry; also, one of the three Graces, patroness of festive meetings. **2.** *Bot.* A genus of aquatic herbaceous plants, family *Marantaceæ*, natives of tropical America 1756. **3.** *Astron.* The twenty-third of the asteroids 1886.

Thaliacean (þæli,ē¹·ʃ¹ăn), *a.* and *sb.* 1888. [f. mod.L. *Thaliacea* (f. *Thalia*) + -AN.] *Zool.* **A.** *adj.* Of or pertaining to the *Thaliacea*, an order of tunicates, including the *Salpidæ*, etc. **B.** *sb.* A member of this order.

Thalian (þăləi·ăn, þē¹·liăn), *a.* 1864. [f. THALIA + -AN.] Of or pertaining to Thalia as the muse of pastoral and comic poetry; hence, of the nature of comedy, comic.

Thallic (þæ·lik), *a.* 1868. [f. THALLIUM + -IC.] *Chem.* Of, pertaining to, or derived from thallium; *spec.* applied to compounds containing thallium in greater proportion, relatively to oxygen, than *thallious* compounds. *T. oxide* = thallium trioxide, Tl_2O_3.

Thalline (þæ·ləin), *sb.* Also **-in.** 1885. [f. Gr. θάλλειν to flourish + -INE[5].] *Pharm.* A trade name for a colourless compound used as an antipyretic, obtained by the reduction of the corresponding chinoline derivative.

Thalline (þæ·ləin), *a.* 1856. [f. THALLUS + -INE[1].] *Bot.* Of or pertaining to a thallus.

Thallious (þæ·liəs), *a.* 1868. [f. next + -OUS.] *Chem.* Abounding in thallium; *spec.* containing thallium in greater proportion, relatively to oxygen, than *thallic* compounds.

Thallium (þæ·liŏm). 1861. [f. Gr. θαλλός green shoot (f. θάλλειν to bloom), from the brilliant green line distinguishing its spectrum + -IUM.] *Chem.* A rare metal, bluish white in colour with leaden lustre, extremely soft and almost devoid of tenacity or elasticity; occurring in small quantities in iron and copper pyrites. Atomic weight 204; symbol Tl.

Thallogen (þæ·lŏdʒen). 1846. [f. THALLUS + -GEN, after *exogen*, etc.] *Bot.* = THALLOPHYTE.

Thalloid (þæ·loid), *a.* 1857. [f. THALLUS + -OID.] *Bot.* Of the form of a thallus. So **Thalloi·dal** *a.*

Thallophyte (þæ·lŏfəit). 1854. [f. mod.L. *Thallophyta*, pl. f. Gr. θαλλός green twig; see -PHYTE.] *Bot.* A plant belonging to the lowest of the great groups in the vegetable kingdom, comprising those of which the vegetative body is a thallus, including Algæ, Fungi, and Lichens; a cellular cryptogam.

Thallous (þæ·ləs), *a.* 1888. [f. THALLIUM + -OUS.] *Chem.* = THALLIOUS.

‖**Thallus** (þæ·lŏs). 1829. [L. – Gr. θαλλός green shoot, f. θάλλειν to bloom.] *Bot.* A vegetable structure without vascular tissue, in which there is no differentiation into stem and leaves, and from which true roots are absent.

‖**T(h)alweg** (tā·lveg). 1862. [G., f. *t(h)al* valley + *weg* WAY *sb.*] *Physiog.* The line that follows the lowest part of a valley.

Thames (temz). [OE. *Temes(e* – L. *Tamesis, Tamesa*, med.L. *T(h)amisa* – British *Tamesā*.] The name of the river on which London is situated; also *attrib.* and *Comb.*

Phr. *To set the T. on fire*, to do something marvellous, to work wonders; usu. with neg. = to work no wonders, never to distinguish oneself.

‖**Thamin** (þămi·n). 1888. [Burmese *thă-min.*] A deer (*Cervus eldi*) of Burma and Siam, resembling the swamp deer.

‖**Thammuz, Tammuz** (tæ·mūz). 1535. [Heb. *tammūz.*] The tenth month of the Jewish civil year, and the fourth of the sacred, containing twenty-nine days, and corresponding to parts of June and July. Also, the name of a Syrian deity, identified with the Phœnician *Adôn* or Adonis, whose annual festival began with the new moon of this month.

Than (ðăn, ðən; *when quoted alone called* ðæn), *conj.* [OE. *þanne, þonne, þænne*, also *þan, þon*; orig. the same word as THEN, from which it was not finally differentiated in form until *c* 1700.] **1.** The conjunctive particle used after a comparative adj. or adv. to introduce the second member of the comparison; the conjunction expressing the comparative of inequality. In use it is always stressless, usu. joined accentually to the prec. word, e.g. *more than, other than* (mōᵊ·ɹ-ðən, ɒ·ðəɹðən). **b.** With a personal or relative pronoun in the objective case instead of the nominative (as if *than* were a prep.). Now considered incorrect, exc. with *whom.* 1560. **c.** Followed by *that*, or by *infin.* expressing a hypothetical result or consequence 1528. **2.** *Than* is regularly used after *other, else*, and their compounds (*otherwise, elsewhere*, etc.) ME. **b.** Hence sometimes after adjs. or advbs. of similar meaning to 'other', as *different, diverse*, etc., and after Latin comparatives, as *inferior, junior*: usu. with clause following. (Now mostly avoided.) late ME. **3.** Peculiar uses. **a.** = Except, besides, but. (perh. ellipsis for *other than, else than*, etc.) *Obs.* or *arch.* late ME. ¶**b.** After *hardly, scarcely*: = When (by confusion with *no sooner than*) 1864.

1. He is more to be feared then all goddes COVERDALE *Ps.* 95[6]:4. I had rather dye t. once to open my mouth 1566. Water, colder t. Ice, and clearer than Christal ADDISON. 'Tis better to have loved and lost, T. never to have loved at all TENNYSON. **b.** Bëëlzebub..then whom, Satan except, none higher sat MILT. He was much older t. me 1792. **c.** The bed is shorter, then that a man can stretch himselfe on it *Isa.* 28:20. He is more modest..to to deny it CONGREVE. Mr. Creech..knew his business better t. to satisfy their curiosity 1779. **2.** The acts or defaults of any person other t. himself 1896. **3. a.** There is almost nothing left then a shadow thereof 1585.

Than, þan, obs. and dial. f. THEN.

Thanage (þē¹·nédʒ). *Hist.* late ME. [= AFr. *thanage, thaynage*, in AL. *thanagium* (XII), f. THANE + -AGE.] The tenure by which lands were held by a thane; the land held by a thane, a thane-land; also, the rank, office, or jurisdiction of a thane.

Thanatism (þæ·nătiz'm). 1900. [f. Gr. θάνατος death + -ISM.] The belief or doctrine that at death the soul ceases to exist.

Thanato- (þæ·năto), bef. a vowel **thanat-**, comb. form of Gr. θάνατος death, chiefly in scientific words. **Thanato·graphy** (*nonce-wd.*) [after *biography*], an account of a person's death. ‖**Thanato·psis** [Gr. ὄψις sight], a contemplation of death.

Thanatology (þænătǫ·lŏdʒi). *rare*. 1842. [f. Gr. θάνατος death + -LOGY.] The scientific study of death, its causes and phenomena. So **Thanatolo·gical** *a.* of or pertaining to t.

Thane (þēⁱn). *Hist.* [OE. *þeġ(e)n* = OS. *thegan* man, OHG. *degan* boy, servant, warrior, hero (G. *degen* warrior), ON. *þegn* freeman, liegeman :- Gmc. **þeʒnaz* :- IE. **teknós* f. base **teq-* **toq-* repr. also by Gr. τέκνον child, τοκεύς parent. The sp. *thane* is derived from Sc. usage of XV–XVI; see THEGN.] †**1.** A servant, minister, attendant; in OE. often applied to (Christ's) disciples –1591. †**2.** A military attendant, follower, or retainer; a soldier. OE. only. **3.** One who in Anglo-Saxon times held land of the king or other superior by military service; orig. in the designation *cyninges þeġn*, 'king's thane, military servant or attendant'; in later times simply *þeġn*, as a term of rank, including several grades below that of an *ealdorman* or *eorl* (EARL *sb.* 2) and above that of the *ceorl* or ordinary freeman. (Superseded in the 12th c. by *baron* and *knight*.) OE. **4.** In *Sc. Hist.* A person, ranking with the son of an earl, holding lands of the king; the chief of a clan, who became one of the king's barons. late ME. **b.** *transf.* to modern persons, in various senses; e.g. a Scottish lord 1750.

3. Ecgulf the kings horse-thane 1853. **4.** By Sinells death, I know I am T. of Glamis, But how, of Cawdor? the T. of Cawdor liues SHAKS.

Comb.: **t.-land,** land held by a t., or by military tenure. Hence **Tha·nedom,** the domain or jurisdiction of a Scottish t. **Tha·nehood,** the condition or rank of a t. **Tha·neship,** the position or office of a t.; esp. in the Sc. sense.

Thank (þæŋk), *sb.* [OE. *þanc* = OFris. *thank, thonk*, OS. *thank*, MDu., OHG. *danc* (Du., G. *dank*), Goth. *þagks* :- Gmc. **þaŋkaz*, f. **þaŋk-* **þeŋk-* (see THINK).] †**1.** = THOUGHT –ME. †**2.** Good will; graciousness, favour –1609. †**3.** Grateful thought, gratitude. Rarely in *pl.* –1677. **4.** The expression of gratitude; the grateful acknowledgement of a benefit or favour. †**a.** in *sing.* –1642. **b.** in *pl.* †Formerly occas. const. as sing. ME.

4. a. Turning to god with lawde and thanke 1534. **b.** Else is his thanks too much SHAKS. Prayers precede, and Thanks succeed the benefit HOBBES. I return it to you with my sincere thanks 1805.

Phrases. *Thanks* (colloq.), = I give you my thanks, my thanks to you, or the like; also *many thanks, best thanks*. *Thanks to*, thanks be given to, or are due to; hence, owing to, as a result of (often ironical); so *no thanks to*, no credit to; not because or by reason of. *To give thanks*, to express gratitude; *spec.* = 'to give thanks to God'; now esp. of saying grace at a meal (*arch.*). *To return thanks*, to render thanks in return for a benefit or favour; now chiefly used of the formal or public expression of thanks, or of grace at a meal.

Thank (þæŋk) *v.* [OE. *þancian* = OS. *thankon*, OHG. *dankōn* (Du., G. *danken*) :- Gmc. **þaŋkōjan*, f. **þaŋkaz* THANK *sb.*] †**1.** *intr.* To give thanks. *Obs.* exc. as *absol.* of 2. –1500. **2.** *trans.* To give thanks to; to express gratitude or obligation to. (orig. *intr.* with *dat.*) Occas. const. *that*. ME. **b.** Const. *for* a thing 1591. **c.** *fig.* To make a return to a person in evidence of obligation or gratitude 1821. **d.** In the future tense, used to express a request 1843. **3.** With a thing as sole obj.: To return thanks for, express one's gratitude for (*rare*) 1470. **4.** To give the thanks or credit *for* something to; to consider or hold responsible: esp. in ironical use, = to blame 1560.

2. Yes I t. God, I am as honest as any man liuing, that is an old man, and no honester then I SHAKS. Sir Harry, you may t. your stars that conducted you to me FIELDING. That he has subjects in Scotland, I think he may t. God and his sword SCOTT. The young prince kissed his hand and thanked him 1841. **b.** *T. you for nothing*, an ironical expression indicating that the speaker thinks he has been offered nothing worth thanks. **3.** Charles forgot To t. his tale BYRON. **4.** She might t. herself for what happened 1794. The defendant had only himself to t. for it 1885.

Thankee (þæ·ŋki). 1824. Vulgar colloq. for *thank ye* THANK YOU.

Thankful (þæ·ŋkfŭl) *a.* OE. [f. THANK *sb.* + -FUL.] **1.** Feeling or expressing thanks or gratitude; grateful. †**2.** Worthy of thanks, gratitude, or credit; acceptable, grateful, agreeable –1611.

1. The thankfull songe of Anna COVERDALE 1 *Sam.* 2. Contents. Live ever in our t. hearts! DRYDEN. **2.** His good successe shall be most thankeful to your trust 1611. Hence **Tha·nkful-ly** *adv.*, **-ness.**

Tha·nkless, *a.* 1536. [f. THANK *sb.* + -LESS.] **1.** Not moved by or expressing gratitude; unthankful, ungrateful. Also *fig.* of things: Making no return, unresponsive. **2.** Of a task, or the like: Which brings no thanks; receiving or deserving no thanks 1547. **3.** Unthanked (*rare*) 1638.

1. And strictly meditate The thankles Muse MILT. **2.** A thancklesse office and displeasing SAVILE. **3.** To..send him thanklesse back againe 1638. Hence **Tha·nkless-ly** *adv.*, **-ness.**

Tha·nk-o:ffering. 1530. [f. THANK *sb.* + OFFERING *vbl. sb.*] In the Levitical law, An offering presented as an expression of gratitude to God; hence an offering or gift made by way of thanks or acknowledgement.

Tha·nksgi:ver. 1621. [f. as next + GIVER.] One who gives thanks.

Thanksgiving (stress var.). 1533. [f. *thanks*, pl. of THANK *sb.* + GIVING *vbl. sb.*] **1.** The giving of thanks; the expression of thankfulness or gratitude; *esp.* the act of giving thanks to God. **b.** A public celebration, with religious services, held as a solemn acknowledgement of Divine favours; a day set apart for this purpose, *spec.* in *U.S.* Thanksgiving Day 1641. **2.** An act or expression of thanks; *esp.* a form of words, a prayer or religious service used to render thanks for Divine benefits 1535.

1. For all the creatures of God are good, and nothing to be refused, yf it be receaued with thankesgeuynge BIBLE (Great) 1 *Tim.* 4:4. **2.** He hath put a new songe in my mouth, euen a thankesgeuynge vnto oure God COVERDALE *Ps.* 39[40]:3. *General T.*, the first of the forms of t. in the Book of Common Prayer, that for the blessings of life in general.

attrib.: **T. day,** a day set apart for public t. for Divine goodness; *spec.* in the U.S., an annual religious and social festival, now appointed by proclamation and held on the fourth Thursday of November.

Tha·nkwo:rthy, *a.* late ME. Worthy of thanks; deserving gratitude or credit.

For it is thankeworthye yf a man for conscience towarde god endure grefe, sufferinge wrongfully TINDALE 1 *Pet.* 2:19. Hence **Tha·nkwo:rthily** *adv.* **Tha·nkwo:rthiness.**

Tha·nk you. late ME. [Aphetic for *I thank you*.] A phrase used in courteous acknowledgement of a favour or service. **b.** as *sb.* An utterance of this phrase 1887.

She..said something meant for 'No, thank you'; but of which nothing was to be heard but 'q' 1862. **Thank-you-ma'am** *U.S. colloq.*, a hollow or ridge in a road. See O.E.D.

‖**Thar** (tʰăr). 1833. [Native name.] *Zool.* **1.** The native name in Nepal of a goat-antelope *Nemorhædus bubalina* belonging to the same genus as the Goral (*N. goral*). **2.** Also applied to the TEHR, or Himalayan wild goat (*Hemitragus jemlaicus*) 1896.

Tharf, *a. dial.* [OE.] Unleavened; e.g. *t-cake*.

Tharf, thar, *v. Obs.* exc. *Sc. dial.* [OE. **þurfan* = OFris. **thurva*, OS. *thurban*, ON. *þurfa*, OHG. *durfan* (G. *dürfen*), Goth. **þaurban*, pret.-pres. verbs :- Gmc. **þarf-* **þurb-*.] **1.** *intr.* To be under a necessity or obligation (*to do* something). **2.** *impers.* It is needful ME.

Tharm (þāɹm). Now *dial.* [OE. *þarm, þearm* = OFris. *therm*, (M)Du. *darm*, (O)HG. *darm*, ON. *þarmr* :- Gmc. **þarmaz* :- IE. **ter-* **tor-* **tr-* go through, repr. also by Gr. τρῆμα perforation.] **1.** An intestine; chiefly in *pl.* **2.** An intestine as cleansed and prepared for some purpose. Also in *sing.*, as a substance or material; catgut for fiddle-strings, etc. 1671.

That (ðæt), *dem. pron.*, *adj.*, and *adv.* [OE. *þæt* nom. and acc. sing. neut. of the simple dem. pron. and adj. *sĕ, sēo, þæt*, the adj. use of which has also produced the 'definite article' THE.] **A.** Demonstrative Pronoun. *Pl.* THOSE. **I.** As simple demonstrative pronoun. **1.** Denoting a thing or person pointed out or present, or that has just been mentioned or considered. **2.** Used emphatically, instead of repeating a previous word or phrase OE. **3.** In opposition to *this*: esp. in phr. *this and (or) that* = one thing and (or) another OE. **4.** As quasi-*sb.*, with pl. *thats* 1656.

1. The errur of Vibicus. And t. was this. 1579. The more fools they,—that's all RUSKIN. 'Bless us', cried the Mayor, 'what's t.?' BROWNING. Who's t. laughing? THACKERAY. **2.** The Moderator is full of Rhetorick and Oratory too, t. he is 1642. It was necessary..to act, and t. promptly 1833. 'They must be very curious creatures'. 'They are t.', said Humpty Dumpty. 'L. CARROLL.'

Phrases. *T. is* (more fully *t. is to say*, †*to wit*, etc.), introducing (or more rarely following) an explanation of the preceding word, phrase, or statement (or a modifying correction of it). *That's*, colloq. used in actual or anticipatory commendation, e.g. *that's a good lad, that's a dear*. *That's right*: a formula of approval: vulgarly used for 'It is so'. *That's t.* that is the end of the matter. *All t.*, that and everything of the kind. *And all t.*, and so forth, *et cetera*. *Not so..as all t.*, not so..as that amounts to; not quite so..as that. *For all t.*: see FOR VII. 4. *Like t.*, of that kind or in that manner. *After t.*, = after that time, or after that had happened. *At t.*: (*a*) immediately after that, upon that; (*b*) orig. *U.S. colloq.* or *slang*, even when that has been taken into consideration; estimated at that rate, at that standard, even in that capacity, in respect of that, too; 'into the bargain'. *By t.*, = by that time, or by the time that happened. *Upon t., with t.*, = as or immediately after that was said, done, etc. *Come out of t.!* (slang): clear out! *Take t.!* a phrase used in delivering a blow.

II. As antecedent pronoun. **1.** As antecedent to a relative (pron. or adv.) expressed or understood. late ME. **2.** With ellipsis of a following relative (subj. or obj. of the relative clause): = that person or thing (*sc.* 'that' or 'which'). Now only where *that* is demonstrative or emphatic as in I. 1. 1598. **3.** Followed by defining words (*of* or other prep. with a sb. or a pple. or other vbl. adj.) which serve to qualify or particularize *that* in the manner of a relative clause. late ME.

1. What the Mouth is, to an Animal; t. the Root is to a Plant 1674. Fine Art is t. in which the hand, the head, and the heart..go together RUSKIN. **2.** Be t. thou know'st thou art, and then thou art As great as t. thou fear'st SHAKS. **3.** So doth their Pearch exceed t. of other Countries 1602. T. in the mortar—you call it a gum? BROWNING.

B. Demonstrative Adjective. **1.** The simple demonstrative used (as adj. in concord with a sb.), to indicate a thing or person either as being actually pointed out or present, or as having just been mentioned and being thus mentally pointed out ME. **b.** Indicating a person or thing assumed to be known, or to be known to be such as is stated. Often (esp. before a person's name) implying censure, dislike, or scorn; but sometimes commendation or admiration. ME. **c.** Used with a plural sb. or numeral, instead of *those*; now only with plurals treated as singulars (e.g. *means, pains*) or taken in a collective sense ME. **2.** In opposition to *this*: prop. denoting the more distant of two things, but often vaguely indicating one thing as dist. from another ME. **3.** In concord with a sb. which is the antecedent to a relative (expressed or understood). Often interchangeable with *the*, but usu. more emphatic. 1470. **4.** Indicating quality or amount: Of that kind or degree; such, so great. Now chiefly *arch.* or *dial.* 1450. †**5.** As neut. sing. of the definite article. *Obs.* (exc. in *that ilk*: ILK *a.*¹) –1576.

1. Almost a yard broad, and twice t. length WALTON. **b.** T. Drug-damn'd Italy SHAKS. I hate that Andrew Jones WORDSW. **c.** T. ill manners.. I have been often guilty of SWIFT. **3.** A manne may saye 'the man that we spake of was here', or 't. man that we spake of was here' 1532. **4.** He blushed to t. degree that I felt quite shy 1865.

C. Demonstrative Adverb. To that extent or degree; so much, so; *esp.* with an adv. or adj. of quantity, e.g. *that far* (= as far as that), *that much, that high*: more definite than *so*, as indicating the precise amount. Now *dial.* and *U.S.* 1450.

I was on my guard for a blow, he was t. passionate DICKENS. I never liked anything t. long [= six weeks] MRS. STOWE.

That (ðăt, ðət), *relative pron.* OE. [The rel. pron. equiv. to *who* and *which*, in OE. a generalized use of the n. of THE (cf. THAT *dem. pron.*), repl. OE. and ME. indeclinable *þe*.] The general relative pronoun, referring to any antecedent, and used without inflexion irrespective of gender, number, and case. **I. 1.** Introducing a clause defining or restricting the antecedent, and thus completing its sense. (The ordinary use; referring to persons or things.) **b.** As obj. of a prep., which in this case stands at the end of the relative clause ME. **2.** Introducing a clause stating something additional about the antecedent (the sense of the principal clause being complete without the relative clause). Now only *poet.* or *rhet.*; usu. repl. by *who* (*whom*) of persons, and *which* of things. OE. **3.** As subj. or obj. of the relative clause, with ellipsis of the antecedent. **a.** Of things: = (the thing) that, that which, what. Now *arch.* and *poet.*; repl. by *what* in prose. OE. **b.** Of persons: = (the person) that, he (or him) that one that; *pl.* (persons) that, they (them), or those, who. Now only after *there are* and the like. ME.

1. O thou t. hearest prayer *Ps.* 65:2. This is about all t. he has to say JOWETT. **b.** The cuppe t. y shall drinke of TINDALE *Matt.* 20:22. All the cities t. they came to *Judges* 20:48. **2.** Smale foweles maken melodye, T. slepen al the nyght with open eye CHAUCER. **3. a.** I earne t. I eate: get t. I weare SHAKS. **b.** I am t. I am *Exod.* 3:14.

II. In various special or elliptical constructions, in some of which *that* passes into a relative or conjunctive adverb. (Cf. THAT *conj.*) **1.** After *same*: occas. = *as* ME. **2.** Preceded by a descriptive noun or adj., in a parenthetic exclamatory clause (e.g. *fool t. he is*): = As B. VI. 3. late ME. **3.** In *not t. I know*, and similar expressions: = According to what, as far as 1460. **4.** After the word *time*, or any sb. meaning a point or space of time: At, in, or on which; when OE. **5.** Connecting two clauses loosely or anacoluthically, the relative or dependent clause being imperfect (the part omitted being suggested by the principal clause). Now considered illiterate. late ME. **6.** *That* followed by a poss. pron. corresp. to the antecedent (e.g. *you t. your, the man t. his*) is an ancient mode of expressing the genitive of the relative = *whose*. Now *dial.* 1456. **¶7.** The relative is very frequently omitted by ellipsis ME.

1. They say Diana is the same t. the Moon is 1690. **2.** Stand still, true poet t. you are! I know you BROWNING. **3.** Nor was he there, t. I know of 1776. **4.** The night t. he went to the play 1802. **5.** Who riseth from a feast With that keene appetite t. he sits downe? SHAKS. **7.** I am monarch of all I survey COWPER. This is a spray the Bird clung to BROWNING.

That (ðăt, ðət), *conj.* OE. [A rel. or conjunctive particle in uses developed from those of THAT *dem. pron.* and THAT *rel. pron.* The development is CGmc., with differentiation of sp. (*dass*) in mod.G., and affix in Goth. *þatei*; for the evolution cf. Gr. ὅτι, from the n. of rel. pron. ὅστις, L. *quod*, n. of *qui* who.] **1.** Introducing a dependent substantive-clause, as subject, object, or other element of the principal clause, or as complement of a sb. or adj., or in apposition with a sb. therein. **b.** Introducing a clause in apposition to or exemplifying the statement in the principal clause: = in that, in the fact that. *Obs.* or *arch.* (now usu. expressed by *in* with gerund). OE. **†c.** Introducing a sb.-clause as obj. of a preceding preposition: = the fact that (*rare*) –1557. **d.** In periphrastic construction, following a clause of the form *it is* (*was*, etc.) + an adv. or advb. phr., to which emphasis is given by the periphrasis OE. **e.** Introducing an exclamatory clause expressing some emotion, usu. (now always) sorrow, indignation, or the like. (Now usu. with *should*.) OE. **2.** Introducing a clause expressing the cause, ground, or reason of what is stated in the principal clause ME. **b.** *Not that*..(ellipt.): = 'I do not say this because..'; or 'It is not the fact that..'; or 'One must not suppose that..': see NOT *adv.* 1601. **3.** Introducing a clause expressing purpose, end, aim, or desire OE. **b.** In exclams. of desire or longing ME. **c.** Introducing a clause expressing a hypothetical desired result: with vb. in subjunctive 1601. **4.** Introducing a clause expressing the result or consequence of what is stated in the principal clause: with verb. usu. in indicative OE. **b.** Introducing a clause expressing a fact or a supposition as a consequence attributed to the cause indicated by the principal clause (usu. interrog.): sometimes nearly = in consequence of which; or = since, seeing that OE. **5.** With a negative in the dependent clause (the principal clause having also a negative expressed or implied): = But that, but. (Now expressed by *without* with gerund.) OE. **6.** Added to relatives or dependent interrogatives (*who, which, what, why*, etc.). *Obs.* or *arch.* OE. **†b.** *That* alone had formerly the force of 'when that', 'when', after *hardly, scarcely*, etc. –1780. **7.** Formerly added with conjunctive force to various words that are now commonly used conjunctively without it; e.g. *because, if, lest, only, the* adv., *though*, etc. *arch.* or *Obs.* ME. **8.** Used (like Fr. *que*) as a substitute instead of repeating a previous conjunction, or conjunctive adv. or phr. Now *rare* or *arch.* ME. **¶9.** The conjunction *that* is very frequently omitted by ellipsis, esp. in sense 1. ME.

1. This shall be the token, y[t] I haue sent the COVERDALE *Exod.* 3:12. The story is as certain as t. Dr. Dodd was hung COLERIDGE. **b.** Thou hast well done, t. thou art come *Acts* 10:33. **d.** It was because he failed to prove this t. his case broke down 1890. **e.** T. a brother should Be so perfidious SHAKS. **2.** I wondered t. there was none to vphold *Isa.* 63:5. Neither should we censure Novalis t. he dries his tears CARLYLE. **b.** Where is she staying now? Not t. I care. T. HARDY. **3.** This is to Advertise all Persons, t. they do not lend her any Mony 1708. **b.** Oh t. those lips had language! COWPER. **c.** I would give all my goods that it had never happened 1861. **4.** He was a man of morals so bad t. his own relations shrank from him MACAULAY. A fire..scorch'd me t. I woke TENNYSON. **b.** Who is Silvia?..T. all our Swaines commend her? SHAKS. **5.** He never turned in his bed during that whole time t. she did not hear SOUTHEY. **6.** When t. the poore haue cry'de, Cæsar hath wept SHAKS. **b.** Until just t. we came CROMWELL. **8.** Although the rear was attacked..and t. 50 men..were captured SIR W. NAPIER. **9.** I think I do BUNYAN.

Thatch (þætʃ), *sb.* late ME. [A late collateral form of THACK *sb.*, conformed to next, which has superseded THACK *v.* in literary use.] **1.** Material used in thatching; straw or the like with which roofs are covered; esp. that actually forming a roof, the thatching. **b.** *transf.* A thatched dwelling. Now *rare.* 1693. **2.** *fig.* Covering; often *joc.* the hair of the head 1633. **3.** Name in the West Indies for several species of palm, the leaves of which are used for thatching. Also *thatch-palm.* 1866.

Thatch (þætʃ), *v.* [OE. *þeććan* = OFris. *thekka*, OS. *thekkian*, OHG. *decchen* (Du. *dekken*, G. *decken*), ON. *þekja* :– Gmc. **þakjan*, f. **þakam* THACK *sb.* The normal repr. of OE. *þeććan* is (dial.) *thetch*; the present form is due to assim. to THACK *sb.*] **†1.** *trans.* To cover. OE. only. **2.** *spec.* To cover or roof (a house) with straw, reeds, palm-leaves, heather, or the like, laid so as to protect from the weather; also, to cover the top of (a rick or wall) in a similar way. late ME. **3.** *fig.* To cover as with thatch 1589. **4.** Of a thing: To serve as a covering or roof to; to cover, to roof OE. **5.** *intr.* To do thatching; to thatch houses. late ME.

2. Many of the churches are thatched with heath 1774. Hence **Tha·tcher,** one who thatches.

Thatching (þæ·tʃiŋ), *vbl. sb.* late ME. [f. prec. + -ING[1].] The action of THATCH *v.*; also *concr.* = THATCH *sb.* 1.

Thatness (ðæ·tnės). 1643. [f. THAT *dem. pron.* + -NESS.] *Philos.* The quality or condition of being 'that', i.e. of existing as a definite thing.

Thaumato- (þǭmăto), comb. form of Gr. θαῦμα, θαυματ- wonder, marvel. **Thaumato·latry** [-LATRY], excessive reverence for the miraculous or marvellous. **Thaumato·logy** [-LOGY], an account of miracles; the description or discussion of the miraculous.

Thaumatrope (þǭ·mătroᵘp). 1827. [irreg. f. Gr. θαῦμα (see prec.) + -τροπος turning.] A scientific toy illustrating the persistence of visual impressions, consisting of a card or disc with two different figures drawn upon the two sides, which are apparently combined into one when the disc is rotated rapidly.

Thaumaturge (þǭ·mătɒ̆ɹdʒ). 1715. [– med.L. *thaumaturgus* (also used) – Gr. θαυματουργός, f. θαυματ- wonder + -εργος working. Orig. *-urg*; later assim. to Fr. *thaumaturge* (XVII).] A worker of marvels or miracles; a wonder-worker.

Thaumaturgic (þǭmătɒ̆·ɹdʒik), *a.* and *sb.* 1680. [f. as prec. + -IC.] **A.** *adj.* **1.** That works, or has the power of working, miracles or marvels; wonder-working. **2.** Of, pertaining to, or involving thaumaturgy 1825. **B.** *sb. pl.* **Thaumatu·rgics:** feats of magic, conjuring tricks 1730. So **Thaumatu·rgical** *a.* 1621.

Thaumaturgist (þǭ·mătɒ̆rdʒist). 1829. [f. THAUMATURGY + -IST.] = THAUMATURGE.

Thaumaturgy (þǭ·mătɒ̆ɹdʒi). 1727. [– Gr. θαυματουργία, f. THAUMATO- + -εργος working; see -Y[3].] The working of wonders; miracle-working; magic.

Thaw (þǭ), *sb.* late ME. [f. next.] **1.** The melting of ice and snow after a frost; the condition of the weather caused by the rise of temperature above the freezing point. **2.** *transf.* and *fig.* 1598.

1. The frost resolves into a trickling t. THOMSON. **2.** That t. Of rigid disapproval into dew Of sympathy BROWNING.

Thaw (þǭ), *v.* Pa. t. and pple. **thawed;** pa. pple. also **†thawn.** [OE. *þawian* = MLG. *dōien*, Du. *dooien*, OHG. *douwen* (cf. G. *verdauen* digest) :– WGmc. **þawōjan* (cf. ON. *þeyja* :– **þaujan*), of unkn. origin.] **1.** *trans.* To reduce (a frozen substance, as ice or snow) to a liquid state by raising its temperature above the freezing point; to melt (a frozen liquid). **b.** *fig.* 1591. **2.** *intr.* Of ice, snow, etc.: To pass from a frozen to a liquid or semi-liquid state; to melt under the influence of warmth; esp. by rise of temperature after frost ME. **b.** *transf.* and *fig.* 1602. **3.** *impers.* *It thaws*: said of the cessation of frost, when the ice, snow, etc. begin to melt ME. **4.** *trans.* To free from the physical effect of frost; to unfreeze 1596. **5.** *intr.* To become unfrozen; to become flexible or limp by rise of temperature 1596. **6.** *fig.* **a.** *trans.* To soften to sympathy or geniality 1582. **b.** *intr.* Of a person, his manner, etc.: To become softened; to throw off coldness and reserve 1598.

1. b. O, weep for Adonais! though our tears T. not the frost which binds so dear a head! SHELLEY. **2. b.** *Haml.* I. ii. 130. **4.** *Tam. Shr.* IV. i. 9. **6. a.** Tea even fails to t. completely their reserve 1883. **b.** Pride of rank..thawed into paternal love 1827.

Thawless (þǭ·lės), *a.* 1813. [f. THAW *sb.* or *v.* + -LESS.] That does not thaw; that never thaws.

Thawy (þǭ·i), *a.* 1728. [f. THAW *sb.* + -Y[1].] Characterized by thaw; of or pertaining to a thaw.

The (*bef. cons.* ðĕ, ðə; *bef. vowel* ði; *emphatic* ðī), *dem. adj.* ('*def. article*'). [Late OE. (Northumb. and North Mercian) *þĕ*, ME. *þe*, at first nom. m., but ult. superseding all cases of OE. m. *sĕ*, fem. *sēo, sīo*, n. *þæt*, corresp. to OFris. *thi, thiu, thet*, OS. *se, thĕ, thie, thiu, that* (Du. *de, dat*), OHG. *der, diu, daz* (G. *der, die, das*), ON. *sá, sú, þat*, Goth. *sa, sō, þata* (with suffix). The orig. CGmc. **sa*, **so*, **þat* = Gr. ὁ, ἡ (dial. ἁ), τό (:– *τόδ), Skr. *sa, sá, tat*; cf. L. *ip|se* same, self, Ir., Gael., Gaulish *so* this, L. *is|tud*; exc. in ON. and Gothic the original nom. m. and fem. were superseded by forms in *þ-* from the same stem as the n. *þæt* and the oblique cases.] **I.** Referring to an individual object (or objects). *Marking an object as before mentioned or already known, or contextually particularized. **1.** The ordinary use. **2.** Used before a word denoting time, as *the time, day, hour, moment*: the time (etc.) in question, or under consideration; the time (now or then) present OE. **b.** Used before numerals denoting years. (Now only in ref. to certain historical events or in expressions denoting a particular decade of a century or of a person's life.) ME. **3.** Before the name of a unique object, or one of which there is only one at a time OE. **b.** With names of rivers; of mountains, groups of islands, or regions, in the plural; of places or mountains, in the sing., now only when felt to be descriptive, as *the Land's End, the High Street, the Matterhorn*, or when *the* has come down traditionally, as *the Lennox, the Merse*; exceptionally in *the Tyrol* OE. **c.** With names of natural phenomena, seasons, etc.; of the points of the compass, as *the north, the east* OE. **4.** With a class-name, to indicate the individual example most familiar to one, or with which one is primarily or locally concerned, e.g. *the King, the Lord Mayor, the Tower; the Gospel, the Epistle* (for the day) ME. **5.** Formerly with names of branches of learning, arts, crafts, games, and pursuits. Now chiefly *dial.* ME. **6.** With names of literary or musical compositions; also of newspapers and periodicals ME. **7.** Formerly with names of languages; now only in conciously elliptical phrases, as *from the German* (sc. *language* or *original*) 1593. **8.** With names of diseases, ailments, etc. Now more often omitted. OE. **9.** Elliptically with the names of ships, as *the* (*ship*) *Swiftsure*, and of taverns, as *the Mermaid* (*tavern*), theatres, and other well-known buildings 1450. **10.** Before higher titles of rank, as *the King, Prince*, etc. (but not now when followed by the name, as *King George, Prince Edward*, etc.); also with some courtesy titles, as *the Right Honourable, the Reverend*, etc. ME. **b.** With the surnames of some Irish and Scottish chiefs of clans, as the O'Gorman Mahon, *the MacNab* 1561. **c.** Before names and titles of men; often in ME. a corruption of French *de*, as in *Robert the Bruce, the Mortimer*, etc. (*arch.*) ME. **d.** Before the names of well-known singers, actresses, etc., after French and Italian usage 1786. **11.** *spec.* Used emphatically, in the sense of 'the pre-eminent', 'the typical', or 'the only..worth mentioning'; *the* being usu. stressed in speech (ðī), and printed in italics 1824. **12.** With any part of the body of a person previously named or indicated, instead of the possessive pronoun; as 'he took him by the hand', i.e. *his* hand. So with *heart, soul*, used *fig.*; also with parts of personal attire. ME. **b.** Used colloq. with names of relatives, as *the wife, the mater* = my (your) wife, mother 1838. **13.** Used before names of weights and measures, in stating a rate: as (*so much*) *the pound*, etc. late ME.

1. What's the matter now? CONGREVE. *The one, the other*: see ONE, OTHER. **2.** At the moment, the bell rang DICKENS. On the morrow 1866. **b.** Ye have heard of a year they call the Forty-five SCOTT. It was in the early eighties (*mod.*). **3.** *The sun, the earth, the universe, the Almighty, the Saviour, the Bible, the Shah*, etc. **b.** *The Thames, the Alps, the Azores, the Indies*. **c.** *The spring, the day, the night; the wind, the cold*, etc. **5.** The Mathematickes, and the Metaphysickes Fall to them SHAKS. What was the use of my getting you taught the dress-making? 1824. **6.** The Edinburgh Review SCOTT. Plato, in the Timæus, gives the fullest account 1845. **8.** I..fell..ill of the measles 1671. **10. d.** The Guiccioli was present BYRON. **11.** His Commentary..is still *the* text-book on Corneille 1904.

Marking an object not before mentioned, but now identified by a clause, phrase, or word. **14. Where the object is defined by a relative clause, *the* stands before the object OE. **15.** Where the object is defined: **a.** by a following phrase with prep. (esp. *of*, repr. an OE. genitive) OE.; **b.** by an infinitive phrase with *to*. late ME. **c.** With an object particularized by a pple. 1658. **16.** *The* stands before a sb. defined by another sb. (usu. a proper name) in apposition, as *the poet Virgil* OE. **b.** More usu. the proper name precedes, as *William the Conqueror* OE. **17.** *The* is used with a sb. particularized or described by an adj. The adj. usu. precedes, but sometimes follows the sb.; in either case *the* stands first, as *the good man, the church militant*. OE. **b.** So with proper names of persons or places; e.g. *the judicious Hooker* OE. **c.** But when the adj. becomes a permanent epithet, *the* and the adj. usu. follow; e.g. *Alfred the Great*; so with ordinals following the names of sovereigns or popes, as *George the Fifth* OE. **18.** *spec.* When a sb. is particularized by a superlative, or by an ordinal number, the latter is regularly preceded by *the* OE. **b.** *The* also stands before the same adjs. when used absolutely OE.

14. The light that never was, on sea or land WORDSW. **15. a.** Like the poore Cat i' th' Addage SHAKS. **b.** The power To save th' Athenian Walls from ruine bare MILT. **c.** The privileges accorded ..to the merchants of the Hanse Towns 1876. **18.** This was the most vnkindest cut of all SHAKS. **b.** Your letter of Tuesday the 19th 1779.

II. Referring to a term used generically or universally. **1.** Before the name of an animal, plant, or precious stone, used generically OE. **b.** *gen.*, with the name of anything used as the type of its class; e.g. with the names of musical instruments, tools, etc. **c.** Before *body, mind, soul*, or parts, functions, and attributes of these OE. **d.** With names of days of the week, as *on the Monday*, i.e. on Monday of any or every week, on Mondays generally ME. **2.** Before a word of individual meaning used as the type of a class of persons OE. **3.** With an adj. used absol., usu. denoting an abstract notion; e.g. *the beautiful*, that which is beautiful. late ME. **4.** With a sb. in the plural, chiefly the name of a nation, class, or group of people, where *the* = 'those who are'; 'the..taken as a whole'. Also with family surnames, as 'the *Joneses* are of Welsh origin'. ME. **5.** Before an adj. or pple. having a plural reference (usu. of persons), as *the poor*, those who or such as are poor OE.

1. Burleigh..was of the willow, and not of the oak MACAULAY. It purrs like the Cat 1854. **b.** The pen is mightier than the sword 1839. **c.** [They] pall on the palate THACKERAY. **2.** 'Tis the voice of the Sluggard WATTS. Phr. *To act, be, play the man, the soldier*, etc. = to sustain the character of a man, a soldier, etc.; to do that which is manly, soldierlike, etc. **3.** A nose inclining to the aquiline SMOLLETT. **4.** The Tarquins were banished from Rome 1816. **5.** How low, how little are the Proud, How indigent the Great! GRAY. Thou knowest what a thing is Poverty Among the fallen on evil days SHELLEY.

The (ðĕ, ðə), *adv.* [repr. OE. *þē*, varying with *þȳ, þon*, instr. of THE *dem. adj.* and THAT *dem. pron.* (e.g. *þȳ māra* the greater, *þȳ mā* the more); cf. LEST.] **1.** Preceding an adj. or adv. in the compar. degree, the two words forming an advb. phrase modifying the predicate. (The radical meaning is 'in or by that', 'in or by so much'.) **2.** *The.. the..*: by how much..by so much; in what degree..in that degree..[= L. *quo..eo..*, Gr. ὅσῳ..τοσούτῳ..] denoting proportional dependence between the notions expressed by the two clauses, each having *the* + a comparative; one *the* being demonstrative, and the other relative in force OE.

1. Your fav'rite horse Will never look one hair the worse COWPER. And if others do not follow their example,—the more fools they RUSKIN. **2.** The bells must be removed, and the sooner the better 1771. The less said the sooner mended KINGSLEY.

Theandric (þiˌæ·ndrik), *a.* 1612. [– eccl. Gr. θεανδρικός, f. θέανδρος god-man (f. θεός god + ἀνήρ, ἀνδρ- man); see -IC.] Of or pertaining to both God and man; partaking of both the human and the divine.

Theanthropic (þiˌæ̆nþrǫ·pik), *a.* 1652. [f. eccl. Gr. θεάνθρωπος THEANTHROPOS + -IC.] Pertaining or relating to, having the nature of, both God and man; at once divine and human.

Theanthropism (þiˌæ·nþrŏpiz'm). 1817. [f. as prec. + -ISM.] **1.** *Theol.* The doctrine of the union of the divine and human natures, or of the manifestation of God as man, in Christ. **2.** *Mythol.* The attribution of human nature or character to the gods 1878. So **Thea·nthropist**, a believer in t. (also *attrib.* or as *adj.*).

†‖**Thea·nthropos.** 1635. [– eccl. Gr. θεάνθρωπος god-man, f. θεός God + ἄνθρωπος man.] A title given to Jesus Christ as being both God and man –1730. Hence **Thea·nthropy** [– eccl. Gr. θεανθρωπία], the union of the divine and human natures (in Christ).

Thearchic (þiˌā·ɹkik), *a.* 1855. [f. next + -IC.] Of or pertaining to thearchy.

Thearchy (þī·āɹki). 1643. [– eccl. Gr. θεαρχία, f. θεός God + -αρχια (see -ARCH).] **1.** The rule or government of God or of a god; a theocracy. **2.** An order or system of deities 1839.

Theatine (þī·ătəin), *sb.* (*a.*) 1581. [– mod. L. *Theatinus*, f. *Teate*, ancient name of *Chieti* in Italy; see -INE[1].] *R. C. Ch.* A member of a congregation of 'regular clerks' founded in 1524 by St. Cajetan in conjunction with John Peter Caraffa (till then Archbishop of Chieti, whence the name, and later Pope Paul IV); also, a corresponding congregation of nuns, founded *c* 1600. **b.** as *adj.* Of or pertaining to the Theatines 1693.

Theatral (þī·ătrăl), *a.* Now *rare.* 1594. [– L. *theatralis*, f. *theatrum*; see next, -AL[1] 1. Cf. Fr. *théâtral* (XVI).] Of, pertaining to, or connected with the theatre; theatrical; dramatic.

Theatre (þī·ătəɹ). Also *U.S.* **theater.** late ME. [– OFr. *t(h)eatre* (mod. *théâtre*) or L. *theatrum* – Gr. θέατρον 'place for viewing', f. θεᾶσθαι behold. From *c* 1550 to *c* 1700 the prevailing sp. was *theater*, now retained in U.S.A.] **1.** *Gr.* and *Rom. Antiq.* A place constructed in the open air, for viewing dramatic plays or other spectacles. †**b.** An amphitheatre –1548. **c.** A natural formation or place suggesting such a structure 1652. **2.** In mod. use, An edifice specially adapted to dramatic representations; a playhouse 1577. †**3.** *transf.* **a.** The stage or platform on which a play is acted –1774. **b.** A theatreful of spectators; the audience at a theatre 1602. **c.** Dramatic performances as a branch of art, or as an institution; the drama 1668. **d.** Dramatic works collectively 1640. **4.** A temporary platform, dais, or other raised stage, for any public ceremony 1517. **5.** A room or hall fitted with tiers of rising seats facing the platform, lecturer's table, etc. for lectures, scientific demonstrations, etc. 1613. **6.** *fig.* Something represented as a theatre in relation to a course of action performed or a spectacle displayed 1581. **b.** A place where some action proceeds; the scene of action 1615. †**7.** A book giving a 'view' or 'conspectus' of some subject; a text-book –1704.

1. High towers, faire temples, goodly theaters SPENSER. **c.** In Jura is a far retiring t. of rising terraces RUSKIN. **2.** *Patent t.*, a t. established or licensed by royal letters patent. *Picture t.*, a hall in which cinematographic pictures are exhibited. **3. c.** *Good* (etc.) *t.*, used predic. of a play, scene, etc., of specified dramatic quality, or that produces a good (etc.) effect on the stage. **6.** A t. on which he might display his great qualities 1769. **b.** The T. of a Civil War 1720.

Comb.: **t.-goer**, one who frequents theatres; so **-going** *sb.* and *adj.*

Theatric (þiˌæ·trik), *a.* 1656. [– late L. *theatricus* – Gr. θεατρικός, f. θέατρον THEATRE; see -IC.] **1.** = next 1. 1706. **b.** Resembling a theatre or amphitheatre in shape or formation 1764. **2.** Suggestive of the theatre; stagy 1656.

1. b. Its uplands sloping deck the mountain's side, Woods over woods in gay t. pride GOLDSM.

Theatrical (þiˌæ·trikăl), *a.* and *sb.* 1558. [f. as prec. + -AL[1] 1; see -ICAL.] **A.** *adj.* **1.** Pertaining to or connected with the theatre, or with scenic representations. **2.** That 'plays a part'; that simulates, or is simulated; artificial, affected, assumed 1649. **3.** Extravagantly or irrelevantly histrionic; 'stagy'; showy, spectacular 1709.

1. He..joins a t. company 1905. **3.** His T. Manner of making Love 1709.

B. *sb.* **1.** *pl.* The performance of stage plays; dramatic performance by amateurs (*amateur theatricals*), occas. in a private house (*private theatricals*). Also *fig.* doings of a theatrical character; 'acting', pretence. 1657. **2.** *pl.* Stage matters 1815. **3.** A professional actor 1859. Hence **Thea·tricalism**, t. style or character; 'staginess'. **Thea:trica·lity**, theatricalness; an instance of this. **Thea·trical-ly** *adv.*, **-ness.**

Theatricalize (þiˌæ·trikăləiz), *v.* 1778. [f. prec. + -IZE.] **1.** *trans.* To make or render theatrical. **2.** *intr.* **a.** To act on the stage. **b.** To attend or frequent theatrical performances. 1794.

Theatro- (þī·ătro, þiˌæ·tro), comb. form of Gr. θέατρον THEATRE, as in **Theatro·cracy**, absolute power exercised by the ancient

Athenian democracy, as exhibited at their assemblies in the theatre. **Thea:tropho·bia** [-PHOBIA], horror of theatres and theatre-going.

Theave, thaive (þīv, þēiv). *local.* 1465. [Of unkn. origin.] A female sheep of a particular age; usu. applied to a ewe of the first or second year that has not yet borne a lamb.

Thebaic (þibēi·ik), *a.*[1] 1687. [– L. *Thebaicus* – Gr. Θηβαϊκός, f. Θῆβαι, Θήβη Thebes.] Of or pertaining to the ancient city of Thebes on the Nile, formerly a centre of Egyptian civilization; *spec.* noting the Sahidic version of the Bible.

T. marble, stone, the syenite of Thebes and Upper Egypt.

Theba·ic, *a.*[2] 1746. [f. as prec., in ref. to the fact that Egypt is a chief source of the opium of commerce.] *Pharm. Chem.* Of or derived from opium; *t. extract, tincture*, laudanum. So **Thebaïne** (þī·beˌīn, -ain) [-INE[5]], a highly poisonous alkaloid, $C_{19}H_{21}NO_3$, obtained from opium.

Thebaïd (þī·beˌid), *a.* and *sb.* 1727. [– Gr. Θηβαΐς, -ιδ-, L. *Thebais, -id-*.] **A.** *adj.* Pertaining to Thebes; usually **B.** *sb.* the territory belonging to (*a*) Egyptian, or (*b*) Bœotian Thebes; the name of certain poems, esp. that of Statius relating to Bœotian Thebes.

Theban (þī·băn), *a.* and *sb.* late ME. [– L. *Thebanus*, f. *Thebæ*, Gr. Θῆβαι Thebes.] **A.** *adj.* **1.** Of or belonging to Thebes, capital of ancient Bœotia in Greece. **2.** = THEBAIC *a.*[1] 1645.

2. *T. drug*, opium or laudanum. *T. year*, the Egyptian year of 365¼ days.

B. *sb.* A native or inhabitant of Bœotian Thebes, a Bœotian. late ME.

Ile talke a word with this same lerned T. SHAKS.

‖**Theca** (þī·kă). *Pl.* **thecæ** (þī·si). 1662. [L. – Gr. θήκη case.] **1.** A receptacle, a cell. **2.** *Bot.* A part of a plant serving as a receptacle; a sac, cell, or capsule; *spec.* (*a*) an anther cell, containing pollen; (*b*) a vessel containing spores in various cryptogamous plants, as the capsule of a moss, the sporangium of a fern, etc. 1676. **3.** *Zool.* and *Anat.* A case or sheath enclosing some organ or part: as (*a*) the horny case of an insect pupa; (*b*) the loose sheath investing the spinal cord; (*c*) a cup-like or tubular structure in corals, containing a polyp 1665. Hence **The·cal** *a.* of, pertaining to, or of the nature of a t. **The·cate** *a.* having a t., sheathed.

Theclan (þe·klăn), *a.* 1884. [f. mod.L. *Thecla*, generic name + -AN.] *Ent.* Belonging to the genus *Thecla* of butterflies, comprising the Hair-streaks.

Theco- (þīko), erron. **theca-**, comb. form of Gr. θήκη case, receptacle.

Thecoda·ctyle [Gr. δάκτυλος digit] *a.*, having thick toes whose transverse scales furnish a sheath for the claw, as in some lizards; *sb.* a gecko of this type; so **Thecoda·ctylous** *a.* **The·codont** [Gr. ὀδούς, ὀδοντ- tooth] *a.*, of or belonging to the *Thecodontes*, an extinct family of saurians having the teeth fixed in sockets in the jaw-bone; *sb.*, a saurian having this character. **The·cophore** [-PHORE], (*a*) a surface or receptable bearing a theca or thecæ; (*b*) GYNOPHORE 1. **Theco·so·mate, The:cosoma·tous** [Gr. σῶμα body] *adjs.*, belonging to the *Thecosomata*, a group of pteropods having the body sheathed in a mantle-skirt. **The·cospore,** a spore produced in a theca, an ascospore; hence **Theco·sporous** *a.*, having thecospores.

Thé dansant (*te* daṅsaṅ). 1845. [Fr.] An afternoon dance at which tea is served.

Thee (ðī, ði, ðĭ), *pers. pron.* [OE. (i) acc. *þec, þeh*, later *þē* = OFris. *thi*, OS. *thic, thī*, OHG. *dih* (G. *dich*), ON. *þik*, Goth. *þuk* :- Gmc. **þeke* :- **tege*, f. **te* (repr. by L. *tē*, Gr. σέ, Doric τέ); (ii) dat. *þē* = OFris., OS. *thi*, (O)HG. *dir*, ON. *þér*, Goth. *þus* :- Gmc. **þez* :- **tes*. The vowel was orig. short, but was lengthened under stress. The acc. and dat. have been undistinguishable in form since IX (or, in late Northumb., X).] **1.** The objective case of the pronoun THOU, repr. the OE. accusative and dative. **2.** *Reflexive*: = thyself OE. **b.** After some intr. vbs. of motion and posture; esp. *sit* 1593. **3.** Used as *nom.*, instead of *thou*. (Often dial., and, in recent times, usu. by Quakers, esp. with vb. in 3rd pers. sing.) late ME. **4.** As *sb.* **a.** The person or 'self' of the individual addressed 1600. **b.** The word itself as used in addressing a person; esp. in phr. *thee and thou* 1694.

1. They haue not refused the, but me COVERDALE 1 *Sam.* 8:7. I haue..Told thee no lyes, made thee no mistakings SHAKS. To thee I call MILT. **2.** Get thee behinde me, Satan BIBLE (Genev.) *Matt.* 16:23. Thou wilt neuer get thee a husband, if thou be so shrewd of thy tongue SHAKS. **b.** Sit thee by our side SHAKS. **3.** How agrees the Diuell and thee about thy Soule? SHAKS. Friend, thee isn't wanted here 1852. **4. a.** That's for thy selfe to breed an other thee SHAKS. **b.** The Thee and Thou of the Quakers LONGF.

†**Thee,** *v.*[1] [OE. *þīon, þēon*, contr. f. **þīhan* = OS. *thīhan*, OHG. (*gi*)*dīhan* (G. *gedeihen*), Goth. *þeihan* :- Gmc. **þiŋx-*, earlier **þeŋx-* (**þaŋx-* **þuŋg-*).] *intr.* To grow; to thrive, prosper (*arch.* in 16th c. use) –1573. **b.** In imprecations and asseverations –1800.

He can not t. SKELTON. **b.** Full ill mought they both t. 1586.

Thee (ðī), *v.*[2] 1662. [f. THEE *pron.*] *trans.* and *intr.* (or *absol.*). To use the pronoun 'thee' to a person: see THOU *v.*

Though I Thee Thee and Thou Thee, I am no Quaker 1662.

Theft (þeft). [OE. (WS.) *þīefþ*, later *þȳfþ, þȳft*, non-WS. *þēofþ, þēoft* = OFris. *thiūfthe, thiūfte*, ON. *þýfð, þýft* :- Gmc. **þiubiþō*, f. **þeubaz* THIEF + *-*iþō* -T[2].] **1.** The action of a thief; the felonious taking away of the personal goods of another; larceny; also, with *a* and *pl.*, an instance of this. **2.** *concr.* That which is or has been stolen; the proceeds of thieving. Now *rare.* OE.

2. Yf the thefte be founde in his hande alyue..he shall restore double TINDALE *Exod.* 22:4.

Theft-boot, -bote. *Obs.* exc. *Hist.* ME. [orig. *thef-bote*, f. *thef* THIEF + *bote* BOOT *sb.*[1]] The taking of some payment from a thief to secure him from legal prosecution; either the receiving back by the owner of the stolen goods or of some compensation, or the taking of a bribe by a person who ought to have brought the thief to justice.

Thegn (þēⁱn). *Hist.* 1848. A form used by some recent historians to represent the OE. *þegn* THANE (sense 3), to distinguish the Anglo-Saxon from the Scottish use of THANE (sense 4), made familiar by Shakespeare. Hence **The·gnhood,** the condition or position of a t.; the order of thegns; thegns collectively.

Theine (þī·əin). 1838. [f. mod.L. *thea* TEA + -INE[5].] *Chem.* A vegetable alkaloid, orig. thought to be a principle peculiar to tea, but found to be identical with CAFFEINE.

Their (ðēᵊɹ), *poss. pron.* and *a.* ME. [– ON. *þeir*(*r*)*a*, gen. pl. of *sá, sú, þat* THE *dem. adj.*, THAT, used also as gen. pl. of the 3rd pers. pron. Cf. THEM, THEY.] **1.** Of, belonging or pertaining to them; also *refl.*, of or belonging to themselves. **b.** *obj. genit.* Of (for, to) them 1553. **c.** Coupled with genit. pl. of *all, bo, both*: †*t. aller, t. beyre, t. bother* (obs.); also *all t., t. both, both t., each of t.* (arch.): meaning 'of all of them, of both or each of them' ME. **2.** Used of a thing with which a number of persons have to do, or which is assumed to be the common possession of a class 1785. **3.** Often used in relation to a singular sb. or pronoun denoting a person, after *each, every, either, neither, no one, every one*, etc. Also so used instead of 'his or her', when the gender is inclusive or uncertain. (Regarded as ungrammatical.) ME. †**4.** After a sb. (usu. a proper name), instead of the genitive inflexion. –1681. **5.** As antecedent to a following relative. (Now usu. avoided.) 1574.

1. Vereley I saye vnto you they have there rewarde TINDALE *Matt.* 6:5. **b.** Shall..quite from off the earth t. memory be raste? SPENSER. **c.** Saying thus in all t. hearings PUTTENHAM. **2.** All those who love t. Devon 1905. **3.** A person can't help t. birth THACKERAY. It's enough to drive anyone out of t. senses G. B. SHAW. **4.** An answer to the parliament of England t. declaration 1642. **5.** Under t. obedience whome God hath set ouer us 1579.

Theirs (ðēᵊɹz), *poss. pron.* ME. [In form a double possessive, f. THEIR + *-es* (cf. *hers, ours*, etc.); see -S. Of northern origin.] The form of THEIR used when no sb. follows, i.e. either absol. or predic.: That or those belonging to them. **b.** *Of theirs.* late ME. †**c.** Used instead of THEIR (*rare*) –1774.

Their's not to make reply, Their's not to reason why, Their's but to do and die TENNYSON. **b.** An old acquaintance of t. 1831. **c.** Upon the importation..into t. or our country MARVELL.

Theism[1] (þī·iz'm). 1678. [f. Gr. θεός god + -ISM.] **a.** *gen.* Belief in a deity or deities, as opp. to *atheism*. **b.** Belief in one god, as opp. to *polytheism* or *pantheism*. **c.** Belief in the existence of God, with denial of revelation: = DEISM. **d.** *esp.* Belief in one God as creator and supreme ruler of the universe, without denial of revelation; in this use dist. from *deism*.

Theism[2] (þī·iz'm). 1886. [f. mod.L. *thea* TEA + -ISM.] *Path.* A morbid condition characterized by headache, sleeplessness, and palpitation of the heart, caused by excessive tea-drinking.

Theist (þī·ist). 1662. [f. Gr. θεός god + -IST.] One who holds the doctrine of theism: in earlier use = DEIST; in later use, esp. as dist. from this. Hence **Thei·stic, -al** *adjs.* of or pertaining to theists or theism; **-ly** *adv.*

Thelytokous (þili·tŏkəs), *a.* 1877. [f. Gr. θηλυτόκος bearing females + -OUS.] *Zool.* Producing only female offspring, as the parthenogenetic females of some species: opp. to *arrenotokous*. So **Thely·toky,** the production of females in parthenogenesis.

Them (ðem, ðĕm), *pers. pron.* [ME. *þeim, þeym* – ON. *þeim* to those, to them, dat. pl. of *sá, sú, þat*, pl. *þeir* THEY; properly a dat. form which was early used as a direct obj. The northern *tham*(*e* represents the equivalent OE. *þām, þǣm*.] **I.** Personal pronoun. **1.** As pronoun of the third person plural, objective, direct and indirect (accus. and dat.) of THEY. Also as antecedent pron. followed by relative or prepositional phrase, and having then a demonstrative function, equivalent to *those* but less emphatic. **b.** Sometimes *indefinitely*, as obj. case of THEY I. 3. *colloq.* or *dial.* **2.** Often used for 'him or her', referring to a singular person whose sex is not stated, or to *anybody, nobody, somebody, whoever*, etc. 1742. (Cf. THEIR 3.) **3.** Used for the nominative *they*. **a.** As antecedent or demons. pron.: = THOSE. Now only *dial.* or *illiterate*. 1489. **b.** As pers. pron. after *than, as*, and in the predicate after the vb. *to be*. Common *colloq.*, but considered grammatically incorrect. 1654.

1. T. that honour me, I wil honour BIBLE (Geneva) 1 *Sam.* 2:30. To show t. what they are to understand 1779. Too solemn for the comic touches in t. TENNYSON. **2.** Nobody else..has so little to plague t. 1853. **3. b.** It was not t. we wanted 1845.

II. As reflexive pron. = themselves.

They haue made t. a molten calfe COVERDALE *Exod.* 32:8.

III. As demonstr. adj. = THOSE. Now only *dial.* or *illiterate* 1596.

It was a rare rise we got out of t. chaps THACKERAY. T. ribbons of yours cost a trifle, Kitty S. LOVER.

‖**Thema** (þī·mă). *Pl.* **themata** (þī·mătă) *rare.* 1531. [L., THEME.] = THEME *sb.* I, 4, 5.

Thematic (þimæ·tik), *a.* 1861. [– Gr. θεματικός, f. θέμα THEME; see -IC.] Of or pertaining to a theme or themes. **1.** Of or pertaining to a subject or topic of discourse or writing (*rare*) 1871. **2.** *Mus.* Of, pertaining to, or constituting themes or subjects (see THEME 4); relating to themes and their contrapuntal development 1864. **3.** *Gram.* Of or pertaining to the theme or stem-form of a word: see THEME 5. 1861.

2. *T. catalogue, index, summary*, one containing the opening themes or passages of musical pieces. **3.** *T. vowel*, a vowel which comes between the root and the inflexion in a vb. or sb., as the ο and ε in φέρ-ο-μεν, φέρ-ε-τε. So **Thema·tical** *a.*, **-ly** *adv.*

Theme (þīm), *sb.* [ME. *teme* – OFr. **teme* (*tesme*) – L. *thema* (to which it was soon conformed in sp.) – Gr. θέμα proposition, f. θε-, base of τιθέναι place.] **1.** The subject of discourse, discussion, conversation, meditation, or composition; a topic. †**b.** *transf.* A subject treated by action (instead of by discourse, etc.); hence, matter, subject *of* or *for* specified action, feeling, etc. –1806. †**c.** *Logic.* That which is the subject of thought –1725. †**2.** *spec.* The text of a sermon; also, a proposition to be discussed –1618. **3.** An exercise written on a given subject, *esp.* a school essay. (The usual term in Jesuit schools.) 1545. **4.** *Mus.* The principal melody, plain-song, or *canto fermo* in a contrapuntal piece; hence, any one of the principal melodies or motives in a sonata, symphony, etc.; also, a simple tune on which variations are constructed 1674. **5.** *Philol.* The inflexional base or stem of a word, consisting of the 'root' with modification or addition; thus in Gr. λείπειν, the root is λιπ, the present theme or stem λειπ-; in τέκνον, the root is τεκ, the theme τεκνο- 1530. **6.** *Astrol.* The disposition of the heavenly bodies at a particular time, as at the moment of a person's birth 1652. **7.** *Anc. Hist.* Each of the twenty-nine provinces into which the Byzantine empire was divided 1788.

1. My t. is alwey oon and euere was Radix malorum est Cupiditas CHAUCER. His Highness's notorious treachery..the t. of all the public dispatches WELLINGTON. **b.** I must play my theame SHAKS. An infallible Theame of endlesse troubles SIR T. HERBERT. **3.** The theam of a Grammar lad MILT. Hence **Theme** *v. trans.* to furnish with a t. or subject.

‖**Themis** (þe·mis, þī·mis). 1656. [Gr. Θέμις.] **1.** Name of the ancient Greek goddess of law and justice; hence, Law or Justice personified. **2.** Name of the twenty-fourth of the asteroids 1886.

Themselves (ðĕmse·lvz), *pron. pl.* ME. [The original construction was nom., acc. *hī*, *hēo selfe*, dat. *heom selfum*, whence ME. *hemselve(n*. In XIV this was superseded in north. dial. by *þaim self(e*, *þaim selven*. *Themselfs*, *themselves* appears *c* 1500, and became the standard form *c* 1540.] **I.** Emphatic. = Those very persons or things. **1.** Standing in apposition with the pron. *they* (rarely *them*), or with a sb., or adj. used subst. **2.** Used alone for emphasis as a simple nominative. *arch.* ME. **b.** *To be t.*: to be in their normal condition of mind, body, or behaviour 1698. **3.** As emphatic objective. Now chiefly as object of a preposition. late ME.

1. Music-paper (which they mostly ruled themselves) T. HARDY. **2.** To remember how t. sate in fear of their persons SWIFT. **3.** You are one of t., you know—Middlemas of that Ilk SCOTT.

II. Reflexive: = L. *sibi*, *se*; Fr. *se*, *soi*; G. *sich*. **1.** As direct obj. (acc.), indirect obj. (dat.), or object of a preposition ME. **2.** In concord with a sing. pron. or sb. denoting a person, in cases where the meaning implies more than one, as when the sb. is qualified by a distributive, or refers to either sex: = himself or herself 1464. (Cf. THEIR 3.)

1. They..made themselues aprons *Gen.* 3:7. Not to make fools of t. 1779. **2.** Every one likes to keep it to t. as long as they can 1874.

III. From the 14th c. there has been a tendency to treat *self* as a sb. (= person, personality), and substitute *their* for *them*. (In literary Eng. this has place only where an adj. intervenes, as *their own*, *sweet*, *very selves*.)

Liking it well their selues ASCHAM. They their-selves stumbled and fell 1836.

Then (ðen), *adv.* (*conj.*, *adj.*, *sb.*) [ME. *þenne*, *þanne*, *þann* (XII), OE. *þænne*, *þanne*, *þonne* = OFris. *thenne*, *thanne*, *than*, OS. *thanna*, *than*, OHG. *danne*, *denne* (Du. *dan*, G. *dann*), f. demons. base **þa-* (see THAT, THE); see THAN.] **I.** Demonstrative adv. of time. **1.** At that time. Referring to a specified time, past or future: (opp. to NOW I. 1.) **b.** At the time defined by a relative or other clause (with vb. in pres. tense) ME. **2.** *Now and t.*, at one time and at another, at various times, at intervals, occasionally. *Now.. then..*, at one time..at another time. ME.

1. History, as it was t. written BUCKLE. Phr. *T. and there*, at that precise time and place; immediately and on the spot; also *there and t.* **b.** Yse which dissolueth, t. when it vanisheth away 1567. **2.** Restive, now sullen, t. in boisterous revolt 1894.

II. Of sequence in time, order, consequence, incidence, inference. **1.** At the moment immediately following the action, etc. just spoken of; upon that, thereupon, directly after that; also, next, after that, afterwards, subsequently (often in contrast to *first*) OE. **b.** In the next place, next (in a series of any kind, or esp. in order of narration); beyond that, more than that, in addition, besides ME. **2.** In that case; in those circumstances; if that be (or were) the fact; if so; when that happens. Often correl. to *if* or *when*. OE. **b.** *But t...*: but, that being so; but at the same time; but on the other hand, but: introducing a statement (rarely a phrase) in some way contrasted with or limiting the preceding 1445. **3.** (As a particle of inference, often unemphatic or enclitic.) That being the case; since that is so; on that account; therefore, consequently, as may be inferred; so. *Now t.*: see NOW II. b. OE.

1. First we Fast, and t. we Feast SELDEN. **b.** And t. she had such a fine head of hair C. BRONTË. **2.** Suppose you..had never a farthing but of your own getting; where would you be t.? MISS BURNEY. *What t.?* (ellipt.) what happens (or would happen) in that case? What of that? **b.** Pope knew next to no Greek, but t. he did not work upon the Greek text BIRRELL. **3.** Well t., take a good heart, and counterfeit to be a man SHAKS.

†**III.** As relative or conjunctive adv. of time: At the time that; when –1440.

IV. As *sb.* or *adj.* **1.** Preceded by a prep., as *by*, *since*, *till*, etc. (= by, etc. that time) ME. **2.** That time; the time referred to (esp. a past time): often contrasted with *now* 1549. **3. a.** In sense 1, followed by a pple. or adj. forming an adj. phrase, as *the t. existing system* = the system then existing 1653. **b.** *attrib.* or as *adj.* That existed or was so at that time; *the t. ruler* = the ruler that then was 1584.

1. Till t. who knew The force of those dire Arms? MILT. *By t. that*, by the time that; ellipt. *by t.* (as relative), by the time (*arch.* or *dial.*); By t. he had folded and addressed it, she returned READE. **2.** The tyme is tourned: t. was t., and now is now 1549.

Thenad (þe·n-, þī·næd), *adv.* 1803. [f. THENAR + -AD.] *Anat.* Towards the thenal aspect.

Then-a-days (ðe·nădēⁱz), *adv. rare.* 1688. [f. THEN *adv.*, after *nowadays*.] In those days, at that (past) time.

Thenal (þī·năl), *a.* 1803. [f. next + -AL[1] 1.] *Anat.* Of or pertaining to the thenar.

Thenar (þī·năɹ). 1672. [mod.L. – Gr. θέναρ palm of the hand, sole or flat of the foot.] *Anat.* The ball of muscle at the base of the thumb; the palm of the hand; the sole of the foot. Also *attrib.* or as *adj.* 1857.

T. muscles, the muscles which form the *t. eminence*, the ball at the base of the thumb.

Thenardite (þenā·ɹdəit, ten-). 1842. [f. name of L. J. *Thénard*, French chemist; see -ITE[1] 2 b.] *Min.* Anhydrous sodium sulphate occurring in white or brown translucent crystals.

Thence (ðens), *adv.* [ME. *þannes*, *þennes*, *þens*, f. *þanne*, *þenne* thence (see THENNE) + advb. gen. suff. *-es* (see -S). Spelt with *-ce* to express final voiceless *s*, as in *dice*, *mice*, *once*, *twice*, when final inflexional *s* became (z).] **1.** From that place; from there. (Now chiefly *literary*.) **b.** Preceded by redundant *from*. late ME. **2.** At a place distant or away from there; distant; absent. Now chiefly in stating distance. ME. **3.** From that time or date. Mostly with *from*. Now *rare* or *Obs.* late ME. **4.** From that, as a source, origin, or cause; from those premisses or data; therefrom. Also preceded by *from*. 1652.

1. If Sion hill Delight thee more..I t. Invoke thy aid MILT. **b.** Homeward from t. by easy stages GEO. ELIOT. **3.** From t. down to the present day 1751. **4.** It would t. follow, that [etc.] 1796.

Thenceforth (ðe·nsˌfōᵊɹþ, ðensˌfōᵊ·ɹþ), *adv.* late ME. [orig. two words.] **1.** From that time onward. Also with *from*. **2.** From that place or point onward (*rare*) 1449.

1. From thence forthe sought Pilate meanes to loose hym TINDALE *John* 19:12.

Thencefo·rward, *adv.* 1457. [orig. two words.] = prec. Also with *from*. So †**Thencefo·rwards** *adv.* –1727.

Thence-from, *adv. arch.* 1618. [Inversion of *from thence*.] From that place or source; thence.

†**Thenne, then**, *adv.* [ME. *þanne*, *þenne*, OE. *þanone*, *þanon* = OFris. *thana*, OS., OHG. *danana*, *danan* (Du. *dan*, G. *dannen*) :– WGmc. **þanana*.] = THENCE –1450.

Theo- (þīo), or, bef. a vowel, **the-**, repr. Gr. θεο-, stem of θεός God; in many compounds adopted from, or formed on the analogy of, Greek, or from Greek (rarely Latin or other) elements.

Theoce·ntric *a.*, centring or centred in God; having God as its centre. **Theochri·stic** [Gr. θεόχριστος] *a.*, anointed by God. **The:oˌphilo-so·phic** *a.*, that applies philosophy to theology.

‖**Theobroma** (þīobrōᵘ·mă). 1760. [mod. L., f. Gr. θεός god + βρῶμα food.] *Bot.* A genus of low trees, of which one species, *T. Cacao*, a native of tropical America, is the source of cocoa and chocolate. Hence **Theobro·mic** *a. Chem.* in *theobromic acid*, $C_{64}H_{128}O_2$, obtained from cacao-butter. **Theobromine** (þīobrōᵘməin), a bitter volatile alkaloid, $C_7H_8N_4O_2$, resembling caffeine, contained in the seeds of the cacao tree.

Theocracy (þīˌǫ·krăsi). 1622. [– Gr. θεοκρατία (Josephus); see THEO- and -CRACY.] A form of government in which God (or a deity) is recognized as the king or immediate ruler, and his laws are taken as the statute-book of the kingdom, these laws being usu. administered by a priestly order as his ministers and agents; hence (loosely) a system of government by a sacerdotal order, claiming a divine commission; also, a state so governed: esp. applied to the commonwealth of Israel from the exodus to the election of Saul as king. **b.** *transf.* A priestly order or religious body exercising political or civil power 1825.

Theocrasy (þī·oˌkrēⁱ:si, þiˌǫ·krăsi). 1816. [– Gr. θεοκρασία, f. θεός god + κρᾶσις mingling; see -Y[3].] *Anc. Myth.* A mingling of various deities or divine attributes into one personality; also, a mixture of the worship of different deities.

Theocrat (þī·okræt). 1827. [f. next; see -CRAT.] **1.** One who rules in a theocracy as the representative of the Deity; a divine or deified ruler. **2.** An advocate of theocracy 1843.

Theocratic (þīokræ·tik), *a.* 1741. [f. Gr. θεοκρατία THEOCRACY + -IC, after *aristocratic*, etc.] Of, pertaining to, or of the nature of theocracy. So **Theocra·tical** *a.* 1690, **-ly** *adv.*

Theodicy (þiˌǫ·disi). 1797. [– Fr. *Théodicée*, title of a work of Leibnitz (1710), f. Gr. θεός God + δίκη justice.] The, or a vindication of the divine attributes, esp. justice and holiness, in respect to the existence of evil; a writing, doctrine, or theory intended to 'justify the ways of God to men'.

Theodolite (þiˌǫ·dŏləit). 1571. [First in mod.L. form *theodelitus* (Leonard or Thomas Digges, its probable inventor); of unkn. origin.] A portable surveying instrument, orig. for measuring horizontal angles, and consisting essentially of a planisphere or horizontal graduated circular plate, with an alidad or index bearing sights; subsequently variously elaborated with a telescope instead of sights, a compass, level, vernier, micrometer, and other accessories, and now often with the addition of a vertical circle or arc for the measurement of angles of altitude or depression. Hence **Theodoli·tic** *a.* of, pertaining to, done, or made with a t.

Theodosian (þīdōᵘ·siăn, -dōᵘ·ʃⁱăn), *a.* and *sb.* 1765. [f. the name *Theodosius*; see -AN.] **A.** *adj.* Of or pertaining to one named Theodosius; *esp.* to the Roman emperor Theodosius II (A.D. 408–450).

T. code, a collection of laws made by direction of Theodosius II, and published A.D. 438.

B. *sb.* **1.** A follower of Theodosius, a rhetorician of Alexandria, who became (A.D. 535) the leader of a division of the Monophysites 1788. **2.** A member of a sect founded by Theodosius, a Russian monk 1860.

Theogony (þiˌǫ·gŏni). 1612. [– Gr. θεογονία generation or birth of the gods, f. θεός + -γονία a begetting.] The generation of the gods; *esp.* an account or theory, or the belief or study, of the genealogy or birth of the deities of heathen mythology. Hence **Theogo·nic** *a.* of, pertaining to, of the nature of t. **Theo·gonist**, one who is versed in or treats of t. **Theo·gonism**, a system or theory of t.

Theolatry (þiˌǫ·lătri). 1806. [f. THEO- + -LATRY.] The worship of a deity or deities.

Theologal (þiˌǫ·lŏgăl), *a.* and *sb.* 1484. [– (O)Fr. *théologal*, f. L. *theologus* (see

THEOLOGY) + *-al* -AL[1] 1.] †**A.** *adj.* in *t. virtues*; see THEOLOGICAL *a.* 1. –1610. **B.** *sb. R. C. Ch.* A lecturer on theology and Holy Scripture attached to a cathedral or collegiate church. Also called *theologus* and, more usually, *canon theologian* 1638.

Theologaster (þiˌǫlŏgæ·stəɹ). 1621. [– mod.L. (Luther 1518), f. *theologus* theologian; see -ASTER.] A shallow or paltry theologian; a smatterer or pretender in theology.

Theologer (þiˌǫ·lŏdʒəɹ). Now *rare.* 1588. [f. *theologus*, eccl. L. use of cl.L. (Cicero), – Gr. θεολόγος, or f. THEOLOGY + -ER[1]; see -LOGER.] = next (but now with less implication of scholarship). **a.** In ref. to Christianity or other monotheistic religions. **b.** In ref. to pagan religions 1609.

Theologian (þiŏlōᵘ·dʒ'ăn). 1483. [– (O)Fr. *théologien*, f. *théologie* or L. *theologia* THEOLOGY; see -IAN, -LOGIAN.] One who is versed in theology; *spec.* one who makes a study or profession of theology; a divine. **b.** = prec. b (*rare*) 1603. **c.** *Canon t.* (R. C. Ch.) = THEOLOGAL B. 1885.

The common gloss of Theologians MILTON.

Theologic (þiŏlǫ·dʒik), *a.* (*sb.*) 1477. [– (O)Fr. *théologique* – eccl. (med.) L. use of late L. *theologicus* (of pagan or non-Chr. systems) – Gr. θεολογικός, f. θεολογία THEOLOGY; see -IC.] **1.** = next 2. †**2.** = next 1. –1637. †**B.** *absol.* as *sb.* (*pl.*) Theological matters. YOUNG.

Theological (þiŏlǫ·dʒikăl), *a.* (*sb.*) 1484. [– med.L. *theologicalis* (Albertus Magnus), f. L. *theologus* (see THEOLOGER) + *-alis* -AL[1] 1; see -ICAL.] **1.** Of or pertaining to the word of God, i.e. the Bible; scriptural; in *t. virtues* [*virtutes theologicæ*], applied to faith, hope, and charity (1 Cor. 13:13), as dist. from the four *cardinal virtues* of Plato and the Stoics. **2.** Of, pertaining to, or of the nature of theology; treating of theology 1603.

2. The abolition of all t. tests 1904.

B. *sb.* †**1.** *pl.* The theological virtues –1600. †**2.** *pl.* Theological matters or principles –1774. **3.** A man trained at a theological college 1866. Hence **Theolo·gically** *adv.* in a t. manner; from a t. point of view; as regards theology.

Theologician (þiˌǫlodʒi·ʃăn). Now *rare.* 1560. [f. L. *theologicus* + -IAN; see -ICIAN.] = THEOLOGIAN.

Theologico- (þiŏlǫ·dʒiko), comb. form from Gr. θεολογικός THEOLOGICAL: 'theologically-, theological and..'; as in *t.-metaphysical.*

Theologism (þiˌǫ·lŏdʒiz'm). 1867. [f. next or THEOLOGIZE; see -ISM.] The action or product of theologizing; theological speculation or system: usu. in a derogatory sense.

Theologist (þiˌǫ·lŏdʒist). 1638. [– med.L. *theologista* (1483), f. *theologus*; see THEOLOGER, -IST.] A professed theologian. **a.** = THEOLOGER b. Now *rare.* **b.** = THEOLOGER a. 1641. **c.** In derogatory sense 1900.

Theologize (þiˌǫ·lŏdʒaiz), *v.* 1649. [In sense 1 – med.L. *theologizare* (Albertus Magnus), f. *theologia*; see -IZE. In 2 perh. formed directly from *theology.*] **1.** *intr.* To play the theologian; to speculate in theology 1656. **2.** *trans.* To render theological; to conform to theology; to treat theologically 1649.

1. My Design, which is not to T. in Philosophy 1662. Hence **Theo·logizer,** a theologer.

Theologo- (þiˌǫ·lŏgo), comb. form repr. Gr. θεολόγος a theologian; as in **t.-inquisito·rial** *a.*, of or pertaining to a theological inquisitor.

Theologue (þī·ŏlǫg). late ME. [– L. *theologus* – Gr. θεολόγος, f. θεός GOD + λέγειν to discourse; see -LOGUE. Before XVII only Sc.] **1.** = THEOLOGIAN. Now *rare.* **2.** [prob. after G. *theolog.*] A theological student. *U.S. colloq.* 1663.

Theology (þiˌǫ·lŏdʒi). late ME. [– (O)Fr. *théologie* – L. *theologia* (Varro ap. Aug.) – Gr. θεολογία, f. θεολόγος one who treats of the gods, f. θεός god; see -LOGY.] The study or science which treats of God, His nature and attributes, and His relations with man and the universe; 'the science of things divine' (Hooker); divinity. **b.** A particular theological system or theory 1669. **c.** Applied to pagan or non-Christian systems 1662.

Peter Lombard, the founder of systematic t. in the twelfth century 1837. *Dogmatic t.*, t. as authoritatively held and taught by the church; a scientific statement of Christian dogma. *Natural t.*, t. based upon reasoning from natural facts apart from revelation. *Pastoral t.*, that branch of t. which deals with religious truth in its relation to the spiritual needs of men, and the 'cure of souls'. **b.** Latest development of 'New T.' 1907.

Theomachy (þiˌǫ·măki). 1570. [– Gr. θεομαχία, f. θεός god; see -MACHY.] †**1.** A striving or warring against God; opposition to the will of God –1690. **2.** A battle or strife among the gods: esp. in ref. to that narrated in Homer's Iliad 1858. Hence **Theo·machist,** one who fights against God.

Theomancy (þī·omænsi). 1651. [– Gr. θεομαντεία spirit of prophecy, f. θεός + μαντεία; see -MANCY.] A kind of divination drawn from the responses of oracles or the predictions of sibyls and others supposed to be immediately inspired by some divinity.

Theomorphic (þīomǭ·ɹfik), *a.* 1870. [f. Gr. θεόμορφος of divine form (f. θεός god + μόρφη form) + -IC.] Having the form or likeness of God; of or pertaining to theomorphism. So **Theomo·rphism,** the doctrine that man has the form or likeness of God.

Theopaschite (þīopæ·skəit). 1585. [– eccl.L. *theopaschita* – eccl.Gr. θεοπασχίτης, f. θεός god + πάσχειν suffer; see -ITE[1] 1] *Eccl. Hist.* A member of a Monophysite sect of the 6th c., who held that the divine nature of Christ suffered on the Cross.

Theopathetic (þīoˌpăþe·tik), *a.* 1748. [f. next, after *pathetic.*] Of, pertaining to, or characterized by theopathy. So **Theopa·thic** *a.*

Theopathy (þiˌǫ·păþi). 1748. [– eccl. Gr. θεοπάθεια suffering of God; see THEO-, -PATHY.] Sympathetic passive feeling excited by the contemplation of God; susceptibility to this feeling; sensitiveness or responsiveness to divine influence; pious sentiment.

Theophany (þiˌǫ·făni). 1633. [– eccl.L. *theophania* (Rufinus) – Gr. θεοφάνεια and θεοφάνια (n. pl.) f. θεός + φαίνειν to show; see -PHANY.] A manifestation or appearance of God or a god to man.

Theophilanthropist (þī:oˌfilæ·nþrŏpist). 1797. [f. THEO- + PHILANTHROPIST, after Fr. *théophilanthrope*, erron. employed to express 'loving God and man'.] A member of a sect of Deists which appeared in France in 1796. So **The:ophila·nthropism** = next.

The:ophila·nthropy. 1798. [– Fr. *théophilanthropie*, intended to express 'love to God and man'; cf. prec.] The deistic system of the theophilanthropists, based on a belief in the existence of God and in the immortality of the soul.

‖**Theophobia** (þioˌfōᵘ·biă). 1870. [f. THEO- + -PHOBIA. Cf. Fr. *théophobie* (XVIII).] Anxious fear of God; dread of divine anger. So **Theo·phobist,** one who is affected with t.

Theopneust (þī·opniūst), *a.* 1647. [– Gr. θεόπνευστος, f. θεός god + -πνευστος inspired, f. stem πνευ- of πνεῖν breathe, blow.] Divinely inspired. So **Theopneu·stic** *a.* in same sense. **Theopneu·sty,** ‖**Theopneu·stia,** divine inspiration.

Theor (þī·ǫɹ). Also in L. form **theo·rus.** 1847. [– Gr. θεωρός spectator, envoy; see THEORY[2].] *Gr. Antiq.* An ambassador or envoy sent on behalf of a state, esp. to consult an oracle or perform a religious rite.

Theorbo (þiˌǭ·ɹbo). 1605. [– It. *tiorba*, with alt. of ending as in some words in -ADO; cf. Fr. *téorbe, théorbe*, also – It.] A large kind of lute with a double neck and two sets of tuning-pegs, the lower holding the melody strings and the upper the bass strings; much in vogue in the 17th c. Hence **Theo·rbist,** a player on the t.

Theorem (þī·ŏrĕm), *sb.* 1551. [– Fr. *théorème* or L. *theorema* = Gr. θεώρημα speculation, theory, (in Euclid) proposition to be proved, f. θεωρεῖν be a spectator, look at, f. θεωρός THEOR.] A universal or general proposition or statement, not self-evident (thus dist. from an AXIOM), but demonstrable by argument (in the strict sense, by necessary reasoning); 'a demonstrable theoretical judgement'. **a.** In Mathematics and Physics; *spec.* in Geometry, a proposition embodying merely something to be proved, as dist. from a PROBLEM, which embodies something to be done. **b.** *gen.*, or in ref. to any particular science or technical subject 1597.

a. Geometrical theorems grew out of empirical methods H. SPENCER. **b.** The..peaceful Theoremes of..a holy Religion JER. TAYLOR. Hence **The·orem** *v. trans.* to express in or by means of a t.

Theorematic (þī:ŏrĕmæ·tik), *a.* 1656. [– Gr. θεωρηματικός, f. θεώρημα, -ματ- THEOREM; see -IC.] Pertaining to, by means of, or of the nature of a theorem. So †**Theorema·tical** *a.*, **-ly** *adv.* †**Theore·mic** *a.*

Theoretic (þīŏre·tik), *a.* (*sb.*) 1656. [– late L. *theoreticus* – Gr. θεωρητικός, f. θεωρητός that may be seen, f. θεωρεῖν; see THEOREM, -IC.] †**1.** Speculative –1706. **2.** (tr. Gr. θεωρητικός in Aristotle.) Contemplative, as opp. to active or practical (πρακτικός). *rare.* 1907. **3.** = THEORETICAL 2. 2 b. 1661. **b.** Of persons, their minds, etc.: Versed in or proceeding by the scientific theory of the subject: opp. to *empirical*; also, Given to theories; speculative; theorizing: sometimes opp. to *practical* 1727.

3. I soon reduced my T. Knowledge to Practice 1773. Plots which cannot be executed; which are mostly t. CARLYLE. **b.** Distinguished..as a t. and practical farmer GEO. ELIOT.

B. *sb.* Usu. *pl.* Theory (as opp. to *practic*, practice); theoretical matters 1656.

Theoretical (þīŏre·tikăl), *a.* (*sb.*) 1616. [f. as prec. + -AL[1] 1; see -ICAL.] †**1.** Contemplative –1623. **2.** Of, pertaining or relating to theory; of the nature of or consisting in theory. Often opp. to *practical.* 1652. **b.** That is such according to theory; ideal, hypothetical 1826. **3. a.** Of the mind or intellectual faculties: Having the power of forming theories; speculative 1652. **b.** Of persons: Addicted to theory; constructing or dealing with theories; speculative 1840. **B.** *sb.* (*pl.*) Theoretical points or matters 1860.

2. These observations agree with the t. deductions 1860. **3. b.** Doubts have been thrown on this principle only by t. writers DARWIN. Hence **Theore·tically** *adv.*

‖**Theoria** (þiˌōᵊ·riă). *rare.* 1590. [Gr. θεωρία; see THEORY.] †**1.** Contemplation, survey. MARLOWE. **2.** The perception of beauty regarded as a moral faculty: dist. from *æsthesis.* RUSKIN.

Theoric (þī·ŏrik), *sb.* and *a.*[1] [In XIV *theorique* (Gower) – (O)Fr. *théorique* – med.L. *theorica* speculation, theory (XII), subst. use of fem. of late and med.L. *theoricus* contemplative; cf. Patristic Gr. θεωρικός learned in spiritual matters.] **A.** *sb.* **1.** = THEORY[1] 3 b, c, 4; chiefly in sense 3 b. *Obs.* or *arch.* †**b.** *pl.* **Theorics:** theoretical statements or notions; theory –1661. †**2.** A mechanical device theoretically representing or explaining a natural phenomenon –1657. †**3.** A man devoted to contemplation or speculation; a member of a contemplative sect of Essenes –1798.

1. So that the Art and Practique part of Life, Must be the Mistresse to this Theorique SHAKS.

†**B.** *adj.* = THEORETICAL *a.* –1804. So †**Theo·rical** *a.*, **-ly** *adv.*

Theoric (þiˌǫ·rik), *a.*[2] 1727. [– Gr. θεωρικός pertaining to spectacles, f. θεωρία viewing.] *Gr. Antiq.* Pertaining to or connected with public spectacles, religious functions, and solemn embassies: applied esp. to a fund provided for these purposes from the public treasury at Athens.

Theorician (þīori·ʃăn). 1841. [f. (after Fr. *théoricien*) on THEORIC sb. + -IAN. Cf. *logician*, etc.] A holder of a theory; = THEORIST.

‖**Theoricon** (þiˌōᵊ·rikǫn). 1828. [– Gr. θεωρικόν n. of θεωρικός THEORIC *a.*[2]] *Gr. Antiq.* The theoric fund in ancient Athens.

Theorist (þī·ŏrist). 1594. [f. THEORY + -IST.] **1.** An adept in the theory (as dist. from the practice) of a subject. Often with mixture of sense 2. **2.** One who theorizes; a theoretical investigator or writer; one who holds or maintains a theory; occas., a framer or maintainer of a mere hypothesis or speculation 1646.

2. It [gravitation] is lately demonstrated..by that very excellent and divine t. Mr. Isaac Newton 1692.

Theorize (þī·ŏrəiz), *v.* 1638. [f. as prec. + -IZE. Cf. med.L. *theorizare* (IX).] **1.** *intr.* To form or construct theories. **2.** *trans.* To construct a theory of or about 1848. **b.** To suppose, or assume, in the way of theory 1838. **c.** To bring *into* or *out of* some condition theoretically 1843.

2. [Mechanics] theorizes the forces and motions of the masses; [Chemistry] the intimate structure of each 1848. Hence **The:oriza·tion,** the action of theorizing. **The·orizer,** one who theorizes.

Theory[1] (þī·ŏri). 1597. [– late L. *theoria* – Gr. θεωρία contemplation, speculation, sight, f. θεωρός spectator (see THEOR), f. base of θεᾶσθαι look upon, contemplate; see -Y[3].] †**1.** Mental view, contemplation –1710. **2.** A conception or mental scheme of something to be done, or of the method of doing it; a systematic statement of rules or principles to be followed 1597. **3.** A scheme or system of ideas or statements held as an explanation or account of a group of facts or phenomena; a hypothesis that has been confirmed or established by observation or experiment, and is propounded or accepted as accounting for the known facts; a statement of what are held to be the general laws, principles, or causes of something known or observed 1638. **b.** That department of an art or technical subject which consists in the knowledge or statement of the facts on which it depends, or of its principles or methods, as dist. from the *practice* of it 1613. **c.** A systematic statement of the general principles or laws of some branch of mathematics; a set of theorems forming a connected system: as *the t. of equations, of numbers* 1799. **4.** Without article: Systematic conception or statement of the principles of something; abstract knowledge, or the formulation of it: often used as implying more or less unsupported hypothesis: dist. from or opp. to *practice* 1624. **5.** In loose or general sense: A hypothesis proposed as an explanation; hence, a mere hypothesis, speculation, conjecture; an idea or set of ideas about something; an individual view or notion 1792.

1. Nor can I thinke I have the true T. of death when I contemplate a skull, or behold a Skeleton with those vulgar imaginations it casts upon us SIR T. BROWNE. 2. The t. of the old Government of India was one which could not be defended BRIGHT. 3. Were a t. open to no objection it would cease to be a t., and would become a law 1850. The Copernican t., which placed the sun in the centre of our system 1879. b. Logic being concerned with the t. of Reasoning 1827. 4. Theorie without Practice will serve but for little 1692. 5. Whether I am right in the t. or not,..the fact is as I state it BURKE.

Theory[2] (þi,ōᵊ·ri). 1842. [– Gr. θεωρία, in a specialized sense.] *Gr. Antiq.* A body of theors sent by a state to perform some religious rite or duty; a solemn legation.

Theosoph (þī·ŏsǫf). 1822. [– Fr. *théosophe* – med.L. *theosophus* – late Gr. θεόσοφος wise concerning God, f. θεός God + σοφός wise.] One who pursues THEOSOPHY (sense 1).

Theosopher (þi,ǫ·sŏfəɹ). 1647. [f. THEOSOPHY + -ER[1].] = THEOSOPHIST. (Applied spec. to Jacob Boehme, 'the Teutonic T.', and his followers.)

Theosophic (þīosǫ·fik), *a.* 1649. [f. as prec. + -IC.] Of, pertaining to, or of the nature of theosophy; versed in theosophy. So **Theoso·phical** *a.* theosophic; also, of or belonging to THEOSOPHY (sense 2) 1642; **-ly** *adv.*

Theosophism (þi,ǫ·sŏfiz'm). 1791. [f. THEOSOPHY + -ISM.] The theory and practice of theosophy; theosophizing.

Theosophist (þi,ǫ·sŏfist). 1569. [f. as prec. + -IST.] **1.** One who professes or believes in THEOSOPHY (in sense 1). **a.** With specific ref. to Boehme. **b.** *gen.* 1814. **2.** A professor or adherent of THEOSOPHY (in sense 2); a member of the Theosophical Society; name of a magazine, the organ of that society 1881.

1. b. The t. is one who gives you a theory of God, or of the works of God, which has not reason, but an inspiration of his own for its basis 1856. Hence **Theosophi·stic, -al** *adjs.* of the nature of or pertaining to a t. or theosophy.

Theosophize (þi,ǫ·sŏfəiz), *v.* 1846. [f. THEOSOPHY + -IZE.] *intr.* To practise or pretend to theosophy; to reason or discourse theosophically.

Theosophy (þi,ǫ·sŏfi). 1650. [– med.L. *theosophia* – late Gr. θεοσοφία wisdom concerning God or things divine, abstr. sb. f. θεόσοφος; see THEOSOPH, -Y[3].] **1.** Any system of speculation which bases the knowledge of nature upon that of the divine nature: often with ref. to Boehme. **2.** Applied to a system of recent origin, resembling the above in its claim to a knowledge of nature profounder than is obtained from empirical science, and contained in an esoteric tradition of which the doctrines of the various historical religions are held to be only the exoteric expression. Sometimes called Esoteric Buddhism. 1881.

1. The Ancient, reall Theosophie of the Hebrewes and Egyptians 1650. 2. T. has no code of morals, being itself the embodiment of the highest morality MRS. BESANT.

Theotechny (þī·otekni). 1858. [f. Gr. θεός god + τέχνη art.] The introduction of divine or supernatural beings in the construction of a drama or epic; such beings collectively.

‖**Theotokos** (þi,ǫ·tŏkǫs). 1874. [– eccl. Gr. θεοτόκος (orig. adj.), f. θεός God + -τοκος bearing, bringing forth, f. τεκ-, τοκ-, base of τίκτειν bear. So late and med.L. *theotocos* (VI).] A title of the Virgin Mary as 'Mother of God'; = DEIPARA.

Theow, thew[1]. Now only *Hist.* or *arch.* [OE. *þīow, þēow, þēo* = OHG. *deo, dio,* ON. (Runic) *þewaR*, Goth. *þius* :– Gmc. **þewaz.*] A slave, bondman, thrall. Hence **The(o)w·dom,** slavery, bondage, thraldom (*Obs.* exc. *Hist.*).

-ther, *suffix*, repr. ult. Indo-Eur. compar. suffix *-tero-*, as in FURTHER; cf. AFTER.

‖**Therapeutæ** (þerăpiū·ti), *sb. pl.* 1681. [eccl.L. – Gr. θεραπευταί servants, attendants.] A sect of Jewish mystics residing in Egypt in the first century A.D., described in a book attributed to Philo.

Therapeutic (þerăpiū·tik), *sb.* 1541. [In sense 1 (orig. sing.) – Fr. *thérapeutique* or late L. *therapeutica* (pl.) – Gr. θεραπευτικά subst. use of n. pl. of θεραπευτικός, f. θεραπευτής minister, f. θεραπεύειν minister to, treat medically; in sense 2 absol. uses of the adj.] **1.** That branch of medicine which is concerned with the remedial treatment of disease; the art of healing. Now usu. in pl. **Therapeutics. 2. a.** A curative agent. **b.** A medical man. 1842.

Therapeu·tic, *a.* 1646. [In sense 1 attrib. use of prec.; in sense 2 f. THERAPEUTÆ + -IC.] **1.** Of or pertaining to the healing of disease. **2.** Of or pertaining to the Therapeutæ 1681. So **Therapeu·tical** *a.* (in sense 1) 1605; **-ly** *adv.*

Therapeutist (þerăpiū·tist) 1816. [f. THERAPEUTIC *sb.* + -IST.] One skilled in therapeutics; a physician.

Therapy (þe·răpi). 1846. [– mod.L. *therapia* – Gr. θεραπεία healing.] The medical treatment of disease; curative medical treatment.

-therapy (þe·răpi), terminal element (see prec.) of words denoting cure by means expressed by the first element, as *actino-, chemo-, psycho-, radio-, röntgentherapy.*

There (ðēᵊɹ, *unstressed,* ðĕr, ðəɹ), *adv.* (*sb.*) [OE. *þǣr, þēr* = OFris. *thēr*, OS. *thār*, OHG. *dār* (Du *daar*, G. *da*); cogn. with ON., Goth. *þar*; f. demons. base **þa-* (see THE, THAT) + advb. suffix *-r*, as in *here, where*; as in *these* and *ere* a final *e* was developed in early ME., whence the present sp.]

I. As demonstrative adv. **1.** In or at that place; in the place (country, region, etc.) pointed to, indicated, or referred to, and away from the speaker; the opposite of *here.* **2.** Appended, unstressed, to the name of a person or thing to whose presence attention is called: = who or that is there, whom or which you see there 1590. **b.** As a brusque mode of address to a person or persons in the place or direction indicated: = you (that are) there 1596. **c.** Emphatically appended to the demonstrative *that. dial.* and *vulgar.* 1742. **3.** Pointing to something as present to the sight or perception, chiefly in *there is, there are*; also calling attention to something offered (often *absol.*) 1535. **b.** Pointing out a person or object with approval or commendation, or the contrary. Also in anticipatory commendation of the person addressed. 1595. **4.** Used unemphatically to introduce a sentence or clause in which, for the sake of emphasis or preparing the hearer, the verb comes before its subject, as *t. comes a time when,* etc., *t. was heard a rumbling noise, breathes there the man..?* OE. **b.** esp. with the verb *to be* OE. **c.** (esp. with *to be*) as virtual antecedent of a rel. pron. (e.g. *there are who say..*) *arch.* late ME. **5.** At that point or stage in action, proceeding, speech, or thought; formerly sometimes referring to what immediately precedes or follows: at that juncture; on that; on that occasion; then. late ME. **6. a.** In that thing, matter, or business; in that fact or circumstance; in that respect, as to that. late ME. **b.** Referring to something said or done: In those words, in that act 1596. **7.** Used interjectionally, usu. to point (in a tone of vexation, derision, satisfaction, etc.) to some fact, condition, or consummation, presented to the sight or mind 1535. **8.** To that place: now taking in ordinary use the place of THITHER OE.

1. I have walked t., but have never walked thither COWPER. T. rolls the deep where grew the tree TENNYSON. 2. Hand me that book t., please (*mod.*). b. Silence t., hoe! 1596. Ball, you t. 1859. 3. T. is my hand, You shall be as a Father, to my Youth SHAKS. There's for you, dear Sir! 1742. T. was that lazy Mr. Lethbridge lounging in the doorway 1890. b. There's a Word for a Lady's Mouth! RICHARDSON. Have a cup of tea, there's a good soul DICKENS. There's glory for you! 'L. CARROLL'. 4. Lurk t. no hearts that throb with secret pain? BYRON. b. For many Miles about There's scarce a Bush SHAKS. c. T. was no knyȝt knewe from whens he came MALORY. 5. T. we are at this instant 1647. *And there('s) an end*, and that is the end of the matter; 'and that's all' (*Obs.* or *arch.*). 6. a. Thy Iuliet is aliue,..T. art thou happy SHAKS. T. is where the Japanese differ from us 1806. b. You have me t.! (*mod. colloq.*). 7. T.! I have put my foot in it! MRS. CARLYLE. 8. *T. and back,* to that place and back again. *To get t.* (colloq. or slang): see GET *v.* V. 1 b.

†**II.** As a relative or conjunctive adverb. **1.** In, on, at, or into which place; = WHERE –1594. **2.** In the very case or circumstances in which; where on the other hand, or on the contrary; whereas, while. –late ME.

1. It had been better for hym to haue taryed t. he was LD. BERNERS.

III. as *sb.* That place; the (or a) place yonder 1588.

He left. t. last night (*mod.*).

Phrases. *To be t.*, to be at or in the place in question; to be present or at hand. *To be all t.* (colloq.), to have all one's faculties or wits about one; to be smart or on the alert; hence, *not all t.* = not quite right in the head. *T. and then,* at that precise place and time; on the spot, forthwith. *Here and t., here, t., and everywhere, neither here nor t.*: see HERE *adv. T. or thereabouts,* primarily in the literal sense; hence also = that or very nearly that (amount); approximately. *T. he* (or *she*) *goes, t. you, they, go,* is primarily literal; but it also calls attention to the way in which a person goes on, acts, talks, etc., usu. expressing surprise or disapproval. *T. you are!* (colloq.) (*a*) = *t. you go!*; (*b*) = t. it is for you, t. you have it, the thing is done.

Thereabout (ðēᵊrăbau·t, ðēᵊ·răbaut), *adv.* [OE. *þǣr abūtan,* two words; see THERE and ABOUT.] **1.** = next 1. **2. a.** About or somewhere near a specified time or date. **b.** About a stated number, quantity, size, space of time, etc.; very nearly so; approximately so. (Chiefly after *or.*) ME. **3.** About, concerning, or with reference to that matter or business. Now *arch.* or *rare.* ME.

1. Quartered in the different villages t. 1864. 3. What wol ye dyne? I wol go ther-aboute. CHAUCER.

Thereabou·ts, *adv.* late ME. [f. prec. with advb. -S. Now more freq. than prec. in senses 1 and 2.] **1.** About, or in the neighbourhood of, that place; in the district, region, etc., round about there. **b.** *fig.* About that; near to that state or action. *Obs.* or *rare.* 1606. **2.** = prec. 2 a, b. late ME. †**3.** = prec. 3. –1657.

1. It is the best house t...in a broad street 1797. **b.** *Ant. & Cl.* III. x. 29. **2.** In three hours, or t. DE FOE. From the year 1660 or t. HUXLEY.

Thereafter (ðēᵊrɑ·ftəɹ), *adv.* [OE. *þær æfter*, two words; see THERE and AFTER.] **1.** After that in time, order, or sequence; subsequently; afterwards. (Now somewhat formal.) †**2.** Conformably thereto, accordingly –1727.

2. †*T. as*, according as: That, Madam, is t. as they be GAY. †*To be t.*, to be conformable or agreeable thereto. So **Therea·fterward** (*rare*) = sense 1.

Thereagainst (ðēᵊrăge·nst, -ăgēⁱ·nst), *adv.* Now *arch.* late ME. [f. THERE + *againes*, AGAINST *prep.*] **1.** Against or in opposition to that. †**2.** As a set-off thereto; contrariwise; on the other side –1558. **3.** In pressure or impact against that 1863.

1. Remedy provided there-against by an Act of Parliament 1647.

Thereanent (ðēᵊrăne·nt), *adv.* Orig. and chief *Sc.* and *north.* ME. [orig. two words, THERE and ANENT *prep.*] About, concerning, or in reference to that matter, business, etc.; relating thereto.

Thereat (ðeᵊræ·t), *adv.* Now *formal* or *arch.* [OE. *þæræt*, two words; see THERE and AT.] **1.** At the place, meeting, etc. mentioned; there. **b.** Expressing attachment to a thing 1566. **2.** On the occasion or occurrence of that, thereupon, because of that ME.

1. Many there be which goo yn there att TINDALE *Matt.* 7:13. **2.** T. the feend his gnashing teeth did grate SPENSER.

Therebesi·de, *adv.* Now only *arch.* and *poet.* ME. [orig. two words; see THERE and BESIDE *prep.*] By the side of that; next to that; near by.

Thereby (ðeᵊɹbəi·, ðēᵊ·ɹbəi), *adv.* [OE. *þærbī*, f. *þær* THERE + *bī* BY *prep.*] **1.** By that; by means of, or because of, that; through that. **2.** Beside, adjacent to, or near that. Now *arch.* and *dial.* ME. †**3.** Besides, together with, or in addition to that –1500. **4.** *Sc.* In ref. to a number or quantity. Very nearly so 1557. **5.** *T. hangs a tale*: see TALE *sb.* 2.

1. For fear of having my attention distracted.. and of my t. losing my bearings 1896. **2.** The twelve fountaines of Elim, and the seventy Palmes that grew t. 1641.

Therefore (ðēᵊ·ɹfǫɹ), **therefor** (ðeᵊɹfǭ·ɹ), *adv.* (*sb.*) [Early ME. *þerfore*, *þerefore*, f. OE. *þær-*, *þēr-* THERE + *fore*, OE. and early ME. collateral form of *for*; see FORE *adv.* and *prep.*] **I.** (Now stressed ðēᵊɹfǭ·ɹ, and usu. spelt *therefor* for distinction from II.) *formal* or *arch.* For that (thing, act, etc.); for that, for it. **b.** By reason of that; for that reason, on that account ME.

The love I had therefor MORRIS. **b.** They would all be..healthier men therefor HAWTHORNE.

II. (Now always spelt *therefore*, and stressed ðēᵊ·ɹfǫɹ.) In consequence of that; that being so; as a result or inference from what has been stated; consequently. Formerly sometimes unemphatic = THEN II. 3. late ME.

Things obscure are not t. sacred BERKELEY.

B. as *sb.* The word 'therefore' as marking a conclusion; an expressed conclusion or inference 1641.

Let him first answer our *Therefores*, and wee will quickly answer his *Wherefores* 1641.

Therefrom (ðeᵊɹfrǫ·m), *adv. arch.* or *formal.* ME. [orig. two words.] From that; from that place; away from there.

They took their name t. 1728.

Therein (ðeᵊri·n), *adv.* Now *formal*, *arch.*, or *dial.* [OE. *þærin*, f. *þær* THERE + IN *prep.*] **1.** In that place or (material) thing. **b.** In or during that time 1539. **2.** In that affair or matter; in that thing, circumstance, or particular ME. **3.** Into that place or (material) thing ME. **4. T. a·fter, t. befo·re, t. u·nder,** = after, before, below in that document, statute, etc. (Usu. written as single words.) 1818.

1. The compasse of the worlde, and all yᵗ dwell therin COVERDALE *Ps.* 24:2. **3.** Smell to a Spunge dipt there-in WESLEY.

Thereinto (ðeᵊri·ntu), *adv. arch.* ME. [f. THERE + INTO.] **1.** Into that place, matter, condition, etc. †**2.** = prec. 2. –1676.

1. Let not them..enter t. *Luke* 21:21.

Thereness (ðēᵊ·ɹnės). *rare.* 1674. [f. THERE + -NESS.] The quality or condition of being there; existence in a defined place. (Usu. opp. to *hereness.*)

Thereof (ðēᵊrǫv, *stress variable*; ðēᵊrǫ·f). Now *formal* or *arch.* [OE. *þær of*; see THERE, OF.] **1.** Of that or it. **b.** = *of it*, as obj. gen. ME. **c.** = *of it*, *its*, as possess. gen. late ME. **2.** From or out of that as source or origin ME.

1. Men makes þeroff gude glasse 1400. **b.** Disburse the summe, on the receit t. SHAKS. **c.** The chariot of Israel, and the horsemen t. 2 *Kings* 2:12. **2.** Much more good t. shall spring MILT.

Thereon (ðeᵊrǫ·n, ðēᵊ·rǫn), *adv.* Now *formal* or *arch.* [OE. *þæron*, f. *þær* THERE + ON *prep.*] **1.** Of position: On or upon that or it. **2.** Of motion or direction: On or upon that or it; onto that ME. **3.** = THEREUPON 2. ME.

1. If t. you relye. I'll take my leaue. SHAKS. To confer with him t. 1786. **2.** His hands t. to lay 1887. **3.** I care not greatly what succeed t. 1618.

Thereout (ðeᵊrau·t), *adv.* [OE. *þærūt*(*e*; see THERE, OUT.] **1.** Outside of that place, etc.; without. Now *rare.* **2.** Out of doors; in the open. Now *Sc.* ME. **3.** From or out of that (it, them), as source or origin; thence. *arch.* late ME.

3. As oft as he drank t. 1871.

Thereover (ðeᵊrōᵘ·vəɹ), *adv. arch.* [OE. *þærofer*; see THERE, OVER *prep.*] **1.** Over or above that, in position (or in transit; also in charge, rank, number, or amount). **2.** *fig.* In reference to that (which is under consideration or observation, or is the object of occupation, discourse, or attention) 1535.

1. In a dark blue kirtle was he clad, And a grey cloak t. MORRIS. **2.** I..came oft in parell of death therouer, tyll I was delyuered from it COVERDALE *Ecclus.* 34:12.

Therethrough (ðeᵊɹþrū·), *adv. arch.* [Early ME. *þer þurh*; see THERE, THROUGH *prep.*] **1.** Of place: Through that, it, or them. **2.** By means, or by reason, of that; thereby ME.

1. To make t. a navigable passage 1594. **2.** Winning renown and fame t. 1894.

Thereto (ðeᵊɹtū·, ðēᵊ·ɹtu), *adv.* Now *formal* or *arch.* [OE. *þær tō*, *þærtō*; see THERE, TO *prep.*] **1.** To that place, thing, affair, etc. **2.** (Belonging, pertinent, suitable, needful) to that matter or thing; (according) therewith; for that matter, purpose, etc. OE. **3.** In addition to that; besides, also, moreover. Now *arch.* and *poet.* OE.

1. He maketh it a grauen image, and falleth downe t. *Isa.* 44:15. **2.** Nothing more is needful t. 1748. **3.** Hir mouth ful smal, and ther to softe and reed CHAUCER.

Theretofore (ðēᵊ·ɹtufōᵊ·ɹ), *adv.* Now *formal.* [ME. *þer tofore*; see THERE, TOFORE *adv.*] Before that time; previously to that.

Thereunder (ðeᵊrʊ·ndəɹ), *adv.* Now *formal.* [OE. *þærunder*; see THERE, UNDER *prep.*] **1.** Under that or it; below or beneath that. **2.** Under that title, heading, etc.; under the provisions, or by authority, of that 1617.

2. Royalties paid t. were to be paid to the publishers 1908.

Thereunto (ðēᵊrʊntū·, ðeᵊrʊ·ntu), *adv. arch.* [ME., f. THERE + UNTO *prep.*] **1.** Unto or to that place; unto that thing, matter, subject, etc. †**2.** = THERETO 3. –1678.

Thereupon (ðēᵊrŭpǫ·n, ðēᵊ·rŭpǫn), *adv.* [In ME. two (or three) words.] **1.** Upon that or it (of position or motion). *arch.* or *formal.* **2.** Upon that (in time or order); on that being done or said; (directly) after that ME. **b.** On that ground; in consequence of that. *arch.* 1534. **3.** On that subject or matter; with reference to that (it, them). *arch.* or *formal.* late ME.

1. The Goods and Merchandizes laden t. 1716. **2.** For the purposes of the argument and the decision following t. 1891. **b.** *Com. Err.* v. i. 388.

Therewith (ðeᵊɹwi·ð, ðeᵊɹwi·þ), *adv.* Now *formal* or *arch.* [OE. *þær wiþ*, *þærwið*, f. *þær* THERE + *wið* WITH *prep.*] **1.** With that (or those) as accompaniment, adjunct, etc.; together or in company with that. **b.** In addition to that; besides ME. **c.** With that (word, act, or occurrence); that being said or done; thereat, thereupon, forthwith. late ME. **2.** With that as instrument; by means of that ME. **b.** With that as cause or occasion; on account of or because of that; in consequence of that 1440.

1. Every person connected t. 1886. **b.** Pagett, M.P., was a liar, and a fluent liar t. KIPLING. **2.** If you bathe the affected Part t. 1725. **b.** T. affrayd I ranne away SPENSER.

Therewithal (ðēᵊɹwiðǭ·l), *adv. arch.* ME. [orig. two words, THERE and WITHAL *adv.*] **1.** = prec. 1, 1 b. **2.** = prec. 1 c. ME. †**3.** = prec. 2. –1656.

1. Giue her that Ring, and therewithall This letter SHAKS. **2.** And t. to cover his intent A cause he found into the Town to go WORDSW.

Therewithin (ðēᵊɹwiði·n), *adv. arch.* [Early ME. *þer wiþinnen*, *wiþinne.*] Within or into that place; within there.

Theriac (þīᵊ·riæk), *sb.* (*a.*) *arch.* 1440. [– L. *theriaca*, *theriace* (med.L. *theriacum*) – Gr. θηριακή (ἀντίδοσις), θηριακὸν (φάρμακον), fem. and n. of θηριακός pertaining to wild beasts or poisonous reptiles, f. θηρίον, dim of θήρ wild beast. See TREACLE.] An antidote to poison, esp. to the bite of a venomous serpent. **B.** *adj.* Theriacal 1440. Hence **Theriacal** (þirəi·ăkăl) *a.* pertaining to or of the nature of **t.**; antidotal.

Thericlean (þeriklī·ăn), *a.* 1692. [f. L. *Thericleus* – Gr. Θηρίκλειος made by Thericles, a famous Corinthian potter; see -AN.] Of Thericles; of the form or kind made by Thericles, as a cup.

Therio- (þīᵊrio), bef. a vowel **theri-** (þīᵊri), repr. Gr. θηριο-, comb. form of θηρίον, dim. of θήρ wild beast.

The·riodont [Gr. ὀδούς, ὀδοντ- tooth], a fossil reptile with teeth of a mammalian type, *spec.* one of the order *Theriodontia*; also *attrib.* or as *adj.* †**Theriolo·gic**, †**-al** *adjs. rare*, zoological. **Therio·tomy** [Gr. τομή cutting], the dissection or anatomy of wild beasts; zootomy.

Theriomorphic (þīᵊrio,mǭ·ɹfik), *a.* 1882. [f. THERIO- + Gr. μορφή form + -IC.] Having the form of a beast; also *transf.* of or pertaining to a deity worshipped in the form of a beast.

Therm[1] (þəɹm). *arch.* 1549. [– (O)Fr. *therme* in pl. – L. *thermæ* – Gr. θέρμαι hot baths, f. θέρμη heat.] A public bath or bathing establishment.

Therm[2] (þəɹm). 1888. [f. Gr. θερμός hot, θέρμη heat.] *Physics.* A unit of heat: the quantity of heat required to raise the temperature of one gramme of water at its maximum density one degree centigrade. Also, a unit of heat adopted as a basis of the charge for the use of gas; = one hundred thousand British thermal units (see THERMAL *a.* 2).

‖**Thermæ** (þə̄·ɹmi), *sb. pl.* 1600. [L.; see THERM[1].] *Class. Antiq.* One of the public bathing establishments of the ancient Romans and Greeks.

Thermal (þə̄·ɹmăl), *a.* 1756. [– Fr. *thermal* (Buffon), f. Gr. θέρμη heat, θερμός hot; see -AL[1] 1.] **1.** Of, pertaining to, or of the nature of *thermæ* or hot springs; of a spring, etc., (naturally) hot or warm; also, having hot springs. **2.** Of or pertaining to heat; determined, measured, or operated by heat 1837. **3.** *fig.* Heated with passion; erotic, passionate, impassioned 1866.

1. The t. waters of Bath or Buxton 1800. **2.** *T. unit*, a unit of heat; the *British t. unit* (abbrev. *B.Th.U.*) is the amount of heat required to raise the temperature of a pound of water at its maximum density through one degree Fahrenheit. **3.** A t. school of poetry 1866. Hence **The·rmally** *adv.*

Thermantidote (þəɹmæ·ntidōᵘt). 1840. [f. Gr. θέρμη heat + ANTIDOTE.] An antidote to heat; *spec.* a rotating fan fitted in a window-opening and encased in wet tatties, used in India to drive in a current of cooled air.

Thermic (þə̄·ɹmik), *a.* 1846. [f. Gr. θέρμη heat + -IC.] = THERMAL 2.

T. balance = BOLOMETER. *T. fever*, fever resulting from external heat, e.g. heat-stroke, insolation.

Thermidor (þəɹmidǭ·ɹ, ‖tęrmidor). 1827. [– Fr. *Thermidor* (1793), f. Gr. θέρμη heat + δῶρον gift.] The eleventh month of the French revolutionary calendar, extending (in 1794) from July 19 to August 17.

Thermidorian (þəɹmidōᵊ·riăn), *sb.* and *a.* 1827. [– Fr. *thermidorien*, f. prec. + *-ien*

-IAN.] **A.** *sb. Fr. Hist.* One of those who took part in the overthrow of Robespierre on the 9th Thermidor (27 July) 1794. **B.** *adj.* Of or pertaining to Thermidor or to the Thermidorians 1891.

Thermion (þəɹmai·ǫn). 1920. [f. THERM(O- + ION.] An electrically charged particle emitted by an incandescent substance. Hence **Thermio·nic** *a.* freq. in *thermionic valve*. **Thermio·nically** *adv.*

Thermite (þə̄·ɹmait). 1900. [– G. *thermit*, f. Gr. θέρμη heat, θερμός hot + *-it* -ITE[1] 4 a.] A mixture of finely divided aluminium and oxide of iron or other metal, which produces on combustion a very high temperature (*c* 3000°C.). Used as a composition for incendiary bombs.

Thermo- (þə̄·ɹmo), bef. a vowel also **therm-**, repr. Gr. θερμο-, comb. form of θερμός hot, θέρμη heat (in some recent formations used as an abbreviation of THERMO-ELECTRIC).

Thermoba·rograph, an instrument which simultaneously records temperature and atmospheric pressure. **Thermobaro·meter,** a barometric instrument graduated for giving altitudes by the boiling point of water. **Thermo-ba·ttery,** short for *thermo-electric battery*. **Thermocau·tery,** any form of actual cautery; *spec.* a hollow platinum cautery in which heat is maintained by means of benzine or gasolene vapour. **The·rmocurrent,** the electric current produced in a thermo-electric battery. **The:rmo-electro·meter,** an instrument for measuring the heating power of an electric current, or for determining the strength of a current by the heat produced. **Thermoge·nesis,** generation of heat. **Thermokinema·tics,** the theory of the motion of heat. **Thermola·bile** *a.* liable to destruction at moderately high temperatures, as certain toxins and serums: opp. to *thermostable*. **Thermo-magne·tic** *a.*, pertaining to or of the nature of thermomagnetism. **Thermo-ma·gnetism,** magnetism caused or modified by the action of heat. **Thermo-mo·tive** *a.*, of, pertaining to, or caused by heat applied to produce motion. **Thermomu·ltiplier,** early name for a THERMOPILE. **The·rmophil, -phile** *a.* requiring a high temperature for development, as certain bacteria; *sb.* a thermophil organism. **The·rmophone,** an apparatus in which sonorous vibrations of a diaphragm are produced by heat-rays. **The·rmoscope,** an instrument for indicating changes of temperature; hence **Thermosco·pic** *a.* **Thermosta·ble** *a.* retaining its character or active quality at moderately high temperatures: opp. to *thermolabile*. **Thermosysta·ltic** *a.*, of or pertaining to systaltic motion due to heat. **Thermote·lephone,** a thermo-electric telephone. **Thermote·nsion,** tension or strain applied to material at a specified temperature to increase or test its tensile power. **Thermotro·pic** *a. Bot.* turning or bending under the influence of heat. **Thermo·tropism,** *Bot.* the property possessed by growing plant-organs of turning or bending towards or away from the sun or other source of heat. **Thermovolta·ic** *a.* of or pertaining to the thermal effects of voltaic electricity, or to heat and voltaic electricity.

Thermoche·mistry. 1844. [f. THERMO- + CHEMISTRY.] That branch of chemical science which deals with the quantities of heat evolved or absorbed when substances undergo chemical change or enter into solution. Also sometimes used to include all relations of heat to substances, such as conductivity, specific heat, etc. So **Thermoche·mic, -al** *adjs.* of or pertaining to t.; **-ly** *adv.* by means of or with reference to t.

Thermochrosy (þə̄·ɹmokrōᵘsi, þəɹmǫ·krǒsi). 1847. [f. THERMO- + Gr. χρῶσις colouring.] The 'coloration' of heat-rays; the property possessed by radiant heat of being composed of waves of different lengths and degrees of refrangibility (thus corresponding to the different colours of light-rays). So **Thermochro·ic** *a.* of or pertaining to t.

The:rmodyna·mic, *a.* 1849. [f. THERMO- + DYNAMIC.] Of or relating to thermodynamics; operating or operated by the transformation of heat into motive power. So **Thermodyna·mical** *a.*, **-ly** *adv.*

The:rmodyna·mics, *sb. pl.* 1854. [f. as prec. + DYNAMICS.] The theory of the relations between heat and mechanical energy, and of the conversion of either into the other.

The:rmo-ele·ctric, *a.* 1823. [f. THERMO- + ELECTRIC.] **1.** Of or pertaining to thermo-electricity; characterized or operated by an electric current produced by difference of temperature. **2.** Of or pertaining to heat and electricity; *t. alarm* or *call*, a device in which a rise or fall in temperature to a prearranged point closes an electric circuit so as to cause a bell to ring 1877.

1. A current of electricity will continue to flow so long as a difference of temperature is maintained between the junction and the extremities. This current is named a t. current, and the two metals form what is known as a t. pair; a combination of these pairs forms the t. pile or battery. 1876. So **Thermo-ele·ctrical** *a.*, **-ly** *adv.*

The:rmo-ele:ctri·city. 1823. [f. THERMO- + ELECTRICITY.] Electricity generated in a body by difference of temperature in its parts. Also, that branch of electrical science which treats of currents produced by means of heat.

Thermogram (þə̄·ɹmǒgræm). 1883. [f. THERMO- + -GRAM.] = next 2.

Thermograph (þə̄·ɹmǒgrɑf). 1840. [f. as prec. + -GRAPH.] **1.** A figure or tracing produced by the action of heat, esp. of the heat-rays of the spectrum upon a prepared surface. **2.** A graphic record of variations of temperature 1843. **3.** A self-registering thermometer 1881.

Thermography (þəɹmǫ·grăfi). 1840. [f. as prec. + -GRAPHY.] Any process of writing or drawing effected or developed by the influence of heat.

Thermology (þəɹmǫ·lǒdʒi). 1840. [– Fr. *thermologie*; see THERMO- and -LOGY.] The science of heat; that department of physics which treats of heat. Hence **Thermolo·gical** *a.*

Thermolysis (þəɹmǫ·lisis). 1875. [f. THERMO- + -LYSIS, after G. *thermolyse* (F. Mohr, 1874).] **1.** *Chem.* The separation of a compound into its elements by the action of heat; decomposition or dissociation by heat. **2.** *Physiol.* The dissipation or dispersion of heat from the body 1896. Hence **Thermoly·tic** *a.* pertaining to or producing t.; *sb.* a thermolytic agent or substance. **The·rmolyse** *v. trans.* to subject to t.; to decompose by the action of heat.

Thermometer (þəɹmǫ·mĭtəɹ). 1633. [– Fr. *thermomètre* (1624) or mod.L. *thermometrum*, f. Gr. θέρμη, θερμός; see THERMO-, -METER.] An instrument for measuring temperature by means of a substance whose expansion and contraction under different degrees of cold and heat are capable of accurate measurement.

Air-, Clinical, Differential, Register t., etc.: see the first elements. *Metallic* (or *bimetallic*) *t.*, a t. which indicates temperature by differential expansion and contraction of composite metal bars.

Thermometric (þə̄ɹmome·trik), *a.* 1784. [f. prec. + -IC.] = next.

Thermometrical (þə̄ɹmome·trikăl), *a.* 1664. [f. as prec. + -AL[1] 1; see -ICAL.] Of or pertaining to the thermometer or its use; made with or involving the use of the thermometer. Hence **Thermome·trically** *adv.* according to or by means of the thermometer or its indications.

Thermometrograph (þə̄ɹmome·trǒgrɑf). 1837. [f. THERMOMETER + -GRAPH.] A self-registering thermometer.

Thermometry (þəɹmǫ·mětri). 1669. [f. as prec.; see -METRY.] The department of science which deals with the construction of thermometers; the scientific use of the thermometer; the measurement of temperature.

Thermopile (þə̄·ɹmǒpəil). 1849. [f. THERMO- + PILE *sb.*[2] 5.] A thermo-electric battery, used in connection with a galvanometer for measuring minute quantities of radiant heat.

Thermos (þə̄·ɹmǫs). 1907. [– Gr. θερμός warm, hot.] A registered trade term noting a flask, bottle, or the like capable of being kept hot by the device (invented by Sir James Dewar) of surrounding the interior vessel with a vacuum jacket to prevent the conduction of heat.

Thermostat (þə̄·ɹmostæt). 1831. [f. THERMO- + Gr. στατός standing; cf. HELIOSTAT.] An automatic apparatus for regulating temperature; *esp.* a device in which the expansive force of metals or gas acts directly upon the source of heat, ventilation, or the like, or controls them indirectly by opening and closing an electric circuit. **b.** An apparatus which gives notice of undue increase of temperature; an automatic fire-alarm 1881. So **Thermosta·tic** *a.* of, pertaining to, or of the nature of a t. **Thermosta·tically** *adv.* by means of a t.

‖**Thermotaxis** (þə̄·ɹmotæksis). 1891. [mod. L., f. THERMO- + Gr τάξις arrangement.] **1.** *Physiol.* That function of the nervous system on which the normal temperature of the body depends; the regulation of the bodily heat. **2.** *Biol.* Movement or stimulation in a living body caused by heat 1900. Hence **Thermota·ctic, -ta·xic** *adjs.* of or pertaining to t. 1877.

Thermotic (þəɹmǫ·tik), *a.* 1837. [f. Gr. θερμωτικός warming, calorific; see THERMO-, -OTIC.] Of or pertaining to heat; *esp.* relating to thermotics. So **Thermo·tical** *a.*, **-ly** *adv.* **Thermo·tics** *sb. pl.* the science of heat, thermology.

Thero- (þīᵊro), repr. Gr. θηρο-, comb. form of θήρ wild beast, as in THEROPODOUS, etc.

Theroid (þīᵊ·roid), *a.* 1867. [f. Gr. θήρ (see prec.) + -OID.] Like or having the form of a brute; of bestial nature or character.

Theromorph (þīᵊ·romǭɹf). 1887. [f. mod. L. *Theromorpha* n. pl., f. Gr. θηρο- THERO- + μορφή form.] *Palæont.* A reptile of the extinct order *Theromorpha*, of Permian and Trias age, having certain mammalian characters.

Theropodous (þirǫ·pǒdəs), *a.* 1889. [f. mod.L. *Theropoda* n. pl. (f. Gr. θηρο- THERO- + -πούς, ποδ- foot) + -OUS.] *Palæont.* Of or belonging to the *Theropoda*, an order of carnivorous dinosaurs having feet like those of mammals. So **Theropod** (þīᵊ·ropǫd) *a.* theropodous; *sb.* a dinosaur of this order.

Thersitical (þəɹsi·tikăl), *a. rare.* 1650. [f. Gr. Θερσίτης Thersites ('the Audacious'), an ill-tongued Greek at the siege of Troy + -ICAL.] Like Thersites in language or address; abusive, reviling, scurrilous.

‖**Thesaurus** (þisǭ·rǒs). *Pl.* **-i.** 1736. [L. – Gr. θησαυρός store, treasure, storehouse.] **1.** *Archæol.* A treasury, as of a temple, etc. 1823. **2.** A 'treasury' or 'storehouse' of knowledge, as a dictionary, encyclopædia, or the like 1736.

These (ðīz), *dem. pron.* and *adj.* (*pl.*). [OE. *þās*, pl. of *þes*, *þēos*, *þis* THIS, ME. *þōs*, mod. THOSE, became ultimately the plural of THAT *a.* and *pron.*, its place as plural of *this* being taken first by *þes*, *þis*, and later by extended forms with the ending *-e* (on the analogy of *al*, *alle*, *sum*, *sume*), *þese*, *þise*, which are the immediate antecedents of the present form.] The pl. of THIS *pron.* and *adj.*, often in explicit or implied opposition to THOSE.

I haue ywedded bee Thise Monthes two CHAUCER When those went, t. went, and when those stood, t. stood *Ezek.* 1:21. T. are the wordes of S. Paule 1581. T. are diuels SHAKS. I'l give you another dish of fish one of t. dayes WALTON. Then was he glad, and that for t. reasons: First [etc.] BUNYAN. Some place the bliss in action, some in ease, Those call it Pleasure, and Contentment t. POPE. Though wedded we have been T. twice ten tedious years COOPER.

Thesis (þī·sis, þe·sis). *Pl.* **theses** (þī·sīz). late ME. [– late L. *thesis* (Br. I), med.L. (Br. II) – Gr. θέσις putting, placing; a proposition, affirmation, f. θε-, base of τιθέναι put, place.] **I.** In *Prosody*, etc.: opp. to ARSIS. **1.** orig. and properly, according to ancient writers, The setting down of the foot, or lowering of the hand in beating time, and hence (as marked by this) the stress or *ictus*; the stressed syllable of a foot in verse; a stressed note in music 1864. **2.** By later Latin writers used for the lowering of the voice on an unstressed syllable; hence in prevalent acceptation: The unaccented or weak part of a foot in verse (classical or modern), or an unaccented note in music. late ME. ‖**3.** *Mus. Per arsin et thesin* (= 'by raising and lowering'): used of a fugue, canon, etc. in which the subject or melody is inverted, so that the rising parts correspond to the falling ones in the original subject and *vice versa*: = *by inversion* 1597. **II.** In

Logic, *Rhetoric*, etc. **1.** A proposition laid down or stated, esp. as a theme to be discussed and proved, or to be maintained against attack (in *Logic* sometimes as dist. from HYPOTHESIS 2, in *Rhetoric* from ANTITHESIS 2); a statement, assertion, tenet 1579. **b.** *spec.* dist. from HYPOTHESIS 1. 1620. **c.** A theme for a school exercise, composition, or essay 1774. **2.** A dissertation to maintain and prove a thesis; esp. one written or delivered by a candidate for a university degree 1653.

2. Scott's t. was, in fact, on the Title of the Pandects, 'Concerning the disposal of the dead bodies of criminals' LOCKHART.

Thesmothete (þe·zmoþīt, -þet). Also in Gr. form **thesmothetes** (þezmǫ·þētīz), pl. **-thetæ.** 1603. [– Gr. θεσμοθέτης pl. -θέται, θεσμός law + -θετης 'one who lays down'.] Each of the six inferior archons in ancient Athens, who were judges and law-givers; *transf.* one who lays down the law.

Thespian (þe·spiǎn), *a.* and *sb.* 1599. [f. Gr. proper name Θέσπις + -AN.] **A.** *adj.* Of or pertaining to Thespis, the traditional father of Greek tragedy (6th c. B.C.); hence, of or pertaining to tragedy, or the dramatic art; tragic, dramatic. **B.** *sb.* A tragedian; an actor or actress 1827.

Theta (þī·tă). 1603. [– Gr. θῆτα.] The eighth letter of the Greek alphabet, Θ, θ TH. (In ancient Greece, on the ballots used in voting upon a sentence of life or death, θ stood for θάνατος death; hence *allus.*)

attrib. and *Comb.*: **t.-function**, *Math.* (*a*) the sum of a series from $n = -\infty$ to $n = +\infty$ of terms denoted by $\exp(n^2a+2na)$; also extended to a similar function of several variables; (*b*) a function occurring in probabilities, expressed by the integral $\int e^{-t^2}\,dt$.

Thete (þīt). 1652. [– Gr. θής, θητ-, orig. a villein, slave.] *Gr. Antiq.* In ancient Athens, by the constitution of Solon, a free man of the lowest class, whose property in land was assessed at less than 150 medimni.

Thetic (þe·tik), *a.* 1678. [– Gr. θετικός such as is placed, or is fit to be placed; positive, affirmative, f. θέτος placed, f. θε-; see THESIS, -IC.] **1.** Characterized by laying down or setting forth; involving positive statement. **2.** *Pros.* That bears the thesis; stressed 1815.

Thetical (þe·tikǎl), *a.* 1653. [f. as prec. + -AL[1] 1; see -ICAL.] Of the nature of or involving direct or positive statement; laid down positively or absolutely; dogmatic; arbitrary. Hence **The·tically** *adv.*

Thetis (þe·tis). late ME. [– Gr. Θέτις, proper name.] **1.** *Gr.* and *Rom. Myth.* One of the Nereids or sea-nymphs, the mother of Achilles; *poet.*, the sea personified. **2.** *Astron.* Name of the seventeenth asteroid 1886.

Theurgy (þī·ɒɹdʒi). 1569. [– late L. *theurgia* – Gr. θεουργία sorcery, f. θεός god + -εργος working; see -Y[3].] **1.** A system of magic, orig. practised by the Egyptian Platonists, to procure communication with beneficent spirits, and by their aid produce miraculous effects; in later times distinguished as 'white magic' from GOETY or 'black magic.' **2.** The operation of a divine or supernatural agency in human affairs; the effects produced among men by direct divine or spiritual action 1858.

1. There is yet another art, which is called Theurgie; wherein they worke by good angels 1584. Hence **Theu·rgic, -al** *adjs.* of or pertaining to t.; **-ly** *adv.* **The·urgist,** one who practises or believes in t.; a magician.

Thew *sb.*[1], see THEOW.

Thew (þiū), *sb.*[2] [OE. þēaw usage, conduct = OFris. *thāw*, OS. *thau*, OHG. *thau*, *dau* discipline; of unkn. origin.] †**1.** A custom, usage; *pl.* ordinances –1624. †**2.** A custom or habit of an individual; hence, a characteristic, attribute, trait –1805. †**b.** A good quality or habit; a virtue; courteous or gracious action –1575. **3.** *pl.* Physical good qualities, features, or personal endowments. †**a.** *gen.* –1567. **b.** The bodily powers or forces of a man (L. *vires*), might, strength, vigour; in Shaks., bodily proportions, lineaments, or parts, as indicating physical strength; in mod. use after Scott, muscular development, associated with *sinews*, and hence materialized as if = muscles or tendons 1566.

2. Forsoth yuele spechis corumpen (or distroyen) goode thewis (or vertues) WYCLIF 1 *Cor.* 15:33. **3. b.** Romans now Haue Thewes, and Limbes, like to their Ancestors SHAKS. Hence **Thew·y** *a.* muscular, brawny.

†**Thew,** *v.* ME. [app. f. OE. þēaw THEW *sb.*[2]] *trans.* To instruct in morals or manners; to discipline, train, instruct, chastise –1625.

Thewed (þiūd), *ppl. a.* ME. [orig. f. prec., but app. often treated as if f. THEW *sb.*[2] + -ED[2].] †**1.** Trained, instructed in morals or manners; having qualities or manners (of a specified kind) –1596. **2.** Having thews or muscles (of a specified kind) 1864.

1. Men..full of vicis, ryotous and evil thewit 1456.

They (ðē[i]), *pers. pron.* [ME. þei – ON. þeir (= OE. þā, ME. þā, þō THO), pl. of demons. *sá*, *sú*, *þat*; repl. OE. *hī*, *hīe*, pl. of *hē*, *hēo*, *hit*.] **I. 1.** As pron. of the 3rd pers. pl., nom. case; the pl. of *he*, *she*, or *it*: The persons or things in question, or last mentioned. **2.** Often used in ref. to a sing. noun made universal by *every*, *any*, *no*, etc., or applicable to either sex (= 'he or she') 1526. **3.** As indef. pron.: People in general; any persons, not including the speaker; people. Often in phr. *t. say* = people say, it is said. late ME.

1. They're Rogues, as sure as Light's in Heaven 1707. **2.** If a person is born of a..gloomy temper ..t. cannot help it CHESTERF. **3.** To strange sores strangely t. straine the cure SHAKS.

II. 1. As demonstr. pron., chiefly as antecedent: = THOSE I. 2, 4. Somewhat *arch.* late ME. **2.** As demonstr. adj. = THOSE II. 2, 4; but often in weaker sense, = THE (*pl.*). Now *dial.* ME.

1. The simple plan, That t. should take, who have the power, And t. should keep who can WORDSW.

‖**Thiasus** (þəi·ǎsɒs). 1850. [L. '– Gr. θίασος the Bacchic dance.] An assembly celebrating a festival of one of the gods.

Thick (þik), *a.* (*sb.*) [OE. þicce = OFris. *thikke*, OS. *thikki*, OHG. *dicki*, *dichi* (Du. *dik*, G. *dick*), ON. *þykkr* :– Gmc. *þeku-, *þekwia-, of unkn. origin.] **I. 1.** Having relatively great extension between the opposite surfaces or sides; of comparatively large measurement through. Opp. to *thin*; distinct from *long* and *broad*. †**b.** Extending far down from the surface; deep –1693. **c.** Of a person or animal: Thickset, stout, burly. *Obs.* exc. *dial.* ME. **2.** Used to express the third dimension of a solid, which has a direction at right angles at once to the length and the breadth: Having a (specified) thickness. (Sometimes = *deep*, but not now said of a body of water or other fluid.) In this sense not opp. to *thin*. OE. **3.** *fig.* Excessive in some disagreeable quality; too much to manage or to stand; *spec.* too gross or indelicate. *slang.* 1884.

1. My litle fynger shall be thicker then my fathers loynes COVERDALE 1 *Kings* 12:10. The Grapes.. have a t. skin 1687. T. lips 1809. (*To give one*) *a t. ear*, an ear swollen from a blow; hence freq. in threats (*vulg. slang*). *T. 'un*, a sovereign (*vulg. slang*). **b.** A t. Frost would kill the Roots, as well as the Head EVELYN. **c.** Vp on a thikke palfrey..Sit Dido CHAUCER. **2.** Let her paint an inch thicke, to this fauour she must come SHAKS. **3.** It's a bit t...when a man of my position is passed over for a beginner like young Merrick 1907.

II. In general sense of *dense*. **1.** Closely occupied, filled, or set with objects or individuals; crowded. Of hair: Bushy, luxuriant. OE. **b.** Often const. *with*. Also *transf.* Thickly covered (as in *t. with dust*). late ME. **2.** Of the individual things collectively: Densely arranged, crowded; hence, numerous, abundant, plentiful. (Usu. *predic.*) OE. †**b.** Of actions: Occurring in quick succession; rapid, frequent –1665. **3.** Having great or considerable density; dense, viscid; stiff. (Said of liquids and easily liquefiable solids.) OE. **b.** Of air: Foul from admixture of fumes, vapours, etc.; stuffy, close; also, dense, not rare or thin. Now *rare* or *Obs.* ME. **4.** Of mist, fog, smoke, etc.: Having the component particles densely aggregated, so as to intercept or hinder vision. Hence of the weather, etc.: Characterized by mist or haze; foggy, misty. OE. **b.** *transf.*, esp. of darkness: Difficult to penetrate; dense, deep, profound OE.

1. T. as the galaxy with stars is sown DRYDEN. A t. Forest ADDISON. Walls and towers..t. with defenders FREEMAN. **2.** His Legions..T. as autumnal leaves that strow the brooks In Vallombrosa MILT. **b.** He furnaces The thicke sighes from him SHAKS. **3.** Make the Grewell thicke, and slab SHAKS. It should solidify into a t. jelly 1893. *fig.* The people muddied, Thicke and vnwholsome in their thoughts SHAKS. **4.** The fogge..was so thicke, that we could not see two ships length before us 1654. **b.** Come t. Night, And pall thee in the dunnest smoake of Hell SHAKS.

III. *transf.* **1.** Of the voice, etc.: Not clear; hoarse; husky; indistinct, inarticulate; also, of low pitch; deep; guttural; throaty. late ME. **2. a.** Of or in ref. to hearing: Dull of perception; not quick or acute. Also of sight. Now *dial.* 1526. **b.** Of mental faculties or actions, or of persons: Slow of apprehension; dense, crass, thick-headed; stupid, obtuse. Now *dial.* 1597.

1. A t. confused cluttering Voice 1748. **2. a.** Their eares wexe thycke of hearinge TINDALE *Acts* 28:27. **b.** SHAKS. 2 *Hen. IV*, II. iv. 262.

IV. (*fig.* from II. 2.) Close in confidence and association; intimate, familiar 1756.

Colloq. phr. *As t. as glue, as peas in a shell, as* (*two*) *thieves, as three in a bed.*

Comb.: **t. ear**, a swollen or thickened external ear resulting from a blow or blows; **t. register,** the lowest register of the voice.

B. *absol.* use of *adj.*, passing into *sb.*: That which (rarely, one who) is thick, in any sense. **I.** Only in *sing.* **1.** The most densely occupied or crowded part (*of* a wood, an assemblage, etc.) ME. **b.** *fig.* The position, time, stage, or state in which activity is most intense; the midst, the height (of an action). Always *in the t. of* 1681. **2.** The thick part of a limb or of the body. late ME. **3.** So **thi·ckest:** the thickest part 1470.

1. In the t. of the dust and smoke presently entered his men 1610. **b.** We are now in the t. of a Cabinet crisis 1885. **3.** The t. of the fight 1868.

II. *sb.* with *pl.* **1.** = THICKET. Now *rare.* OE. **2.** *School slang.* A thick-headed or stupid person 1857.

1. Among the bushy thickes of bryar SURREY.

Thick (þik), *adv.* [OE. þicce = OS. *thikko*, OHG. *diccho*; see prec.] In a thick manner, thickly. **1.** So as to be thick; to a great depth. **2.** In a thick, dense, or crowded state; closely, densely, compactly; in crowds or throngs; numerously, abundantly OE. **3.** In close or rapid succession; frequently; quickly; fast. Often *t. and fast.* OE. **4.** With confused articulation; with a husky or hoarse voice 1556. **5.** With density or thick consistence; densely 1711.

1. The snow..lay t. upon the glacier TYNDALL. Phr. *To lay it on t.*, (*fig.*) to do something with vehemence or excess. **2.** Doubts came t. upon him 1855. **4.** 2 *Hen. IV*, II. iii. 24.

Phr. **T. and threefold,** *advb.* (*sb.*, *adj.*) *phr.* **a.** In large numbers; in quick succession; with rapid iteration. *arch.* and *dial.* †**b.** With vehemence. †**c.** as *adj.* Abundant and frequent.

Thick (þik), *v.* Now *rare* or *Obs.* [OE. þiccian, f. þicce THICK *a.*] **1.** *trans.* To make dense in consistence. *arch.* †**2.** To make (cloth, etc.) close in texture by fulling –1719. **3.** *intr.* To become thick, in various senses. Now *dial.* or *arch.* OE.

Thick and thin, thi·ck-and-thi·n, *phr.* late ME. **A.** as *sb.* **1.** Phr. *Through thick and thin*: through everything that is in the way; without regard to or in spite of obstacles or difficulties (app. orig. with ref. to 'thicket and thin wood'.) **2.** Adherence to some course, principle, or party, under all circumstances. **b.** *attrib.* or *adj.* (usu. hyphened): That adheres in all circumstances; constant, unwavering 1884.

1. And tag and rag through thick and thin came running DRAYTON. A thorough-paced liar, that will swear through thick and thin DRYDEN. **2.** The hidebound partisans of thick and thin 1884. **b.** A..thick-and-thin admirer 1886.

B. as *adj.* **1.** *Naut.* Of a tackle-block: Having one sheave larger than the other 1815. **2.** See A. 2 b.

Thicken (þi·k'n), *v.* late ME. [f. THICK *a.* + -EN[5].] To make or become thick or thicker. **1.** *trans.* To make dense in consistence; to coagulate, inspissate. **b.** *intr.* To increase in density or consistence; also, to become turbid, cloudy, indistinct, etc. 1598. **2.** To become dark, obscure, or opaque; of the weather, to become misty 1605. †3. *trans.* To make close or dense in disposition of parts or in texture –1812. 4. *intr.* To become crowded, numerous, or frequent; to gather thickly 1726. 5. a. *trans.* To increase the substance between opposite surfaces of; to make thicker in measure; *fig.* to make more substantial; to confirm 1604. b. *intr.* To become thicker in measurement 1763. 6. To become more complex or intricate (esp. said of a plot); to increase in intensity 1671.

1. Oatmeal was used scantily, but generally for thickening soup 1866. b. *fig.* There comes a time when..the speech thickens 1888. 2. Light thickens,..Good things of Day begin to droope, and drowse SHAKS. I'll face this Storm that thickens in the Wind DRYDEN. 4. The crowd every instant thickening 1789. 5. a. This may helpe to t. other proofes, That do demonstrate thinly SHAKS. b. Ice in the river thickening 1805. 6. Ay, now the Plot thickens very much upon us 1671. Hence **Thi·ckener,** that which (or one who) thickens; in *Dyeing*, a substance used to increase the consistence of the colours or mordants.

Thickening (þi·k'niŋ), *vbl. sb.* 1580. [f. prec. + -ING¹.] The action of THICKEN *v.*; *concr.* the result of this; a thickened substance or part. b. = THICKENER 1839.

Thicket (þi·kėt). [OE. *þiccet*, f. *þicce* THICK *a.* + *-et*, denominative suffix.] A dense growth of shrubs, underwood, and small trees; a place where low trees or bushes grow thickly together.

They sang like nightingales among the thickets 1855. *fig.* A t. of ever-growing problems 1866.

Thi·ck-head. 1837. One who or that which has a thick head. 1. One who is dull of intellect; a blockhead. Also *attrib.* or *adj.* 1871. 2. Any bird of the sub-family *Pachycephalinæ*, the Thick-headed Shrikes of the Australian region 1837.

Thick-headed (stress var.), *a.* 1707. [Parasynthetic f. as prec. + -ED².] Having a thick head; *fig.* dull of intellect; slow-witted, obtuse. Hence **Thickhea·dedness.**

Thickish (þi·kiʃ), *a.* 1545. [f. THICK *a.* + -ISH¹.] Somewhat thick.

Thick-knee (þi·kˌnī). Also **thicknee.** 1816. Any bird of the genus *Œdicnemus*, esp. the Stone Curlew, *Œ. scolopax*; so called from the enlargement of the tibio-tarsal joint. So **Thi·ck-knee:d** *a.* having thick knees 1776.

Thick-leaved (-līvd), **-leafed** (-līft), *a.* 1582. [See LEAVED, LEAFED.] a. Having or covered with dense foliage; thickly set with leaves. b. Having thick fleshy leaves 1707.

Thick-lipped (stress var.), *a.* Having thick or full lips. So **Thi·ck-lips,** one who has thick lips; a contemptuous appellation for a Negro.

Thickly (þi·kli), *adv.* late ME. [f. THICK *a.* + -LY².] In a thick manner; so as to be thick, in various senses.

Thickness. [OE. *þicness*, f. THICK *a.* + -NESS.] 1. The quality or condition of being thick. 2. That which is thick or has thickness; the part (of anything) which is thick; the space between opposite surfaces (e.g. a wall); a layer OE. Hence **Thi·cknessing** *vbl. sb.* the action of reducing (boards, etc.) to a given thickness.

Thick-set, *a.* and *sb.* late ME. [f. THICK *adv.* + *set*, pa. pple. of SET *v.*] A. *adj.* (Stress variable.) 1. Composed of individuals or parts arranged in close order; thickly studded or planted (*with* something). 2. Set or placed close together; closely arranged 1570. 3. Having a dense or close-grained nap 1709. 4. Of close compact build; *esp.* short and strongly made; square-built; stocky 1724.

1. T. with trees, a venerable wood DRYDEN. A t. underwood of bristling hair DRYDEN. 2. A..fence..with t. stakes 1848. 4. He was short and t. 1830.

B. *sb.* (þi·kˌset). 1. A thicket; a thick-set plantation 1766. 2. A stout twilled cotton cloth with a short very close nap; a kind of fustian; also, a garment of this. Now *rare* or *Obs.* 1756.

†**Thick-sighted,** *a.* 1592. Not seeing clearly; having obscure or dim vision –1863.

Thickskin (þi·kˌskin). 1582. One who has a thick skin; a person dull or slow of feeling.

Thick-skinned (stress var.), *a.* 1545. 1. Having a thick skin. 2. *fig.* Dull of sensation or feeling; obtuse, stolid; now *esp.* not sensitive to criticism or rebuff; the opposite of *thin-skinned* 1602.

2. He would be t. if he stands the clamour SCOTT.

Thick-skulled (stress var.), *a.* 1653. Having a thick skull; hence *fig.* = THICK-HEADED. So **Thi·ck-skull,** a thick-skulled person.

Thick-sown (stress variable), *a.* 1683. Sown thickly.

Metaphors are not so thick sown in Milton ADDISON.

Thick-witted (stress var.), *a.* 1634. Having 'thick' wits; dull of intellect, stupid.

Thief (þīf). *Pl.* **thieves** (þīvz). [OE. *þiof, þēof* = OFris. *thiāf*, OS. *thiof*, OHG. *diob* (Du. *dief*, G. *dieb*), ON. *þjófr*, Goth. *þiufs* :– Gmc. **þeubaz*, of which no further cogns. are known.] 1. One who takes portable property from another without the knowledge or consent of the latter, converting it to his own use; one who steals. a. *spec.* One who does this by stealth, esp. from the person; one who commits theft or larceny. b. One who robs with violence; a robber, free-booter, pirate, etc.; now *rare* exc. as a general designation of one who obtains goods by fraudulent means, over-reaching, deceit, etc. OE. c. *fig.* That which steals or furtively takes away 1742. 2. As a general term of reproach or opprobrium: Evil man, villain, scoundrel. *dial.* ME. 3. A horse that does not run up to form in a race. *slang.* 1896. 4. 'An excrescence in the snuff of a candle' (J.) which causes it to gutter and waste 1628.

1. A theef of venyson..Kan kepe a Forest best of any man CHAUCER. Provb. When theeues fall out, trewe men come to their goode 1562. Set a t. to take a t. 1670. A sort of honour may be found..even among thieves BENTHAM. b. The Story of Ali Baba, and the Forty Thieves 1712. *Border thieves*, the freebooters of the Scottish Border. c. Procrastination is the t. of time YOUNG.

attrib. and *Comb.*; **t.-catcher,** (*a*) = THIEF-TAKER; (*b*) a device used formerly in apprehending thieves; †**-leader,** a t.-taker; **-tube,** a tube for withdrawing liquids from casks, etc. Also with *thieves'*, as **thieves' Latin,** cant used by thieves; **thieves' vinegar,** an infusion of rosemary tops, sage leaves, etc., in vinegar, formerly esteemed as an antidote against the plague.

Thie·f-ta:ker. 1535. One who detects and captures a thief; *spec.* one of a company who undertook the detection and arrest of thieves.

Thieve (þīv), *v.* [OE. *þēofian*, f. *þēof* THIEF.] 1. *intr.* To act as a thief, commit theft, steal. 2. *trans.* To steal (a thing) 1695.

Thievery (þī·vəri). 1568. [f. THIEF, *thiev-*, or THIEVE *v.* + -ERY.] 1. The committing or practice of theft; stealing. With *a* and *pl.*, an act of thieving. 2. The result or produce of thieving; stolen property 1583.

1. They were whipped so for picking pockets, and other petty thieveries DE FOE. 3. *Tr. & Cr.* IV. ii. 45.

Thievish (þī·viʃ), *a.* 1450. [f. THIEF, *thiev-* + -ISH¹.] †1. Infested or frequented by thieves –1632. 2. Inclined or given to thieving; dishonest 1538. 3. Of, pertaining to, or characteristic of a thief or thieves; thief-like; furtive, stealthy 1450.

1. Or walke in theeuish waies SHAKS. 2. Their Magistrates are corrupt, their people t. 1748. 3. Times theeuish progresse to eternitie SHAKS. Hence **Thie·vish-ly** *adv.*, **-ness.**

Thigh (þəi). [OE. (Anglian) *þēh*, (WS.) *þēoh, þioh* = OFris. *thiāch*, ODu. *thio* (Du. *dij*), OHG. *dioh*, ON. *þjó* :– Gmc. **þeuxam*. OE. *þēh* is repr. by mod. north. *thee*; *thigh* descends from ME. *þīh* (XII), with ẹ̄ raised to ī, as in *die, high, nigh, shy*.] 1. The upper part of the leg, from the hip to the knee (in man). 2. In lower vertebrate animals, The part of the hind leg which is homologous with the human thigh, or which is regarded as corresponding to it in position or shape; in certain quadrupeds, as the horse, applied to the tibia; in birds to the tarsus; hence in insects, etc., the third section of the leg ME.

Comb.: **t.-bone,** the bone of the t., the femur; **-boot,** a boot with uppers reaching to the t.; **-piece,** a piece of armour for the t.

Thight, early and dial. f. TIGHT.

Thigmo-, used as comb. f. Gr. θίγμα touch, as in *thigmota·xis, thigmo·tropism.*

Thilk (ðilk), *dem. adj.* and *pron. arch.* or *dial.* [ME. *þilke*, f. *þe* THE + *ilca*, *-e* ILK, meaning 'that' or 'the same'.] A. *adj.* The very (thing, person, etc.) mentioned or indicated; the same; that; this. B. *pron.* That (or this) person or thing ME.

Thill[1] (þil). ME. [Of unkn. origin. Cf. FILL *sb.*²] The pole or shaft by which a wagon, cart, or other vehicle is attached to the animal drawing it, *esp.* one of the pair of shafts between which a single draught animal is placed.

Thill[2] (þil). ME. [Of unkn. origin. Cf. TILL *sb.*²] The thin stratum of fire-clay, etc. usu. underlying a coal-seam; under-clay; the floor or bottom of a seam of coal.

Thiller (þi·ləɹ). 1552. [f. THILL¹ + -ER¹.] = next.

Thill-horse (þi·lhǭɹs). ME. [f. THILL¹ + HORSE.] The shaft-horse or wheeler in a team.

Thimble (þi·mb'l), *sb.* [OE. *þȳmel*, f. *þūma* THUMB; see -LE.] †1. A fingerstall. OE. only. 2. A bell-shaped sheath of metal, etc. (formerly of leather) worn on the end of the finger to push the needle in sewing. late ME. b. A thimble or similar article as used by a thimblerigger 1716. 3. *Naut.* A broad ring of metal, having a concave outer surface, around which the end of a rope is spliced, so that the thimble forms an eye to the rope 1711. 4. *techn.* a. *Mech.* A ring, tube, or similar part, e.g. a sleeve, bushing, ferrule, etc. 1789. b. The outer casing of a rifle-ball 1860. 5. Applied (usu. in *pl.*) to certain flowers and plants, or parts of them, e.g. (*a*) the Foxglove, also known as *Fairy* or *Witches' Thimbles*; (*b*) the Sea Campion; (*c*) the Harebell; (*d*) the cup of an acorn 1873.

attrib. and *Comb.*: **t.-berry (t. blackberry),** the black raspberry of America, *Rubus occidentalis*, so called from the shape of its receptacle; **-eye,** (*a*) *Naut.* an eye in a plate through which a rope is rove without a sheave; (*b*) a fish, the Chub Mackerel, *Scomber colias*; **-plating,** the formation of a cylindrical boiler-shell or a flue by successive slightly overlapping rings of plate; **-weed,** any plant of the genus *Rudbeckia*, so called from the shape of its receptacle. Hence **Thi·mble** *v. intr.* to use a t., to sew.

Thimbleful (þi·mb'lful). 1607. [f. prec. + -FUL.] As much as a thimble will hold; hence, a small quantity; a dram.

Cordials were..on special occasions dealt out in thimblefuls 1889.

Thimblerig (þi·mb'lrig), *sb.* 1825. [f. THIMBLE *sb.* + RIG *sb.*³ 2; *lit.* 'thimble-trick'.] A swindling game usu. played with three thimbles and a pea which is ostensibly placed under one of them; the sharper then challenging the bystanders to guess under which thimble the pea has been placed, and to bet on their choice. Hence **Thi·mblerig** *v. intr.* to practise the cheat of the t.; *fig.* to cheat in a juggling manner; *trans.* to manipulate (a thing or matter) in this manner. **Thi·mblerigging** *vbl. sb.* and *ppl. a.*

Thimblerigger (þi·mb'lri:gəɹ). 1831. [f. prec. + -ER¹.] A professional sharper who cheats by thimblerigging; also *transf.*

Thin (þin), *a.* (*sb.*) and *adv.* [OE. *þynne* = OFris. *thenne*, OS. *thunni*, OHG. *dunni* (Du. *dun*, G. *dünn*), ON. *þunnr* :– Gmc. **þunnuz* (:– **þunw-*), based on IE. **tn-*, zero-grade of **ten-* **ton-* stretch, repr. in L. *tenuis*. Cf. TEND *v.*²] A. *adj.* I. Having relatively little extension between opposite surfaces; of little thickness or depth. b. Of small cross-section in proportion to length; slender, tenuous, attenuated. late ME. c. *spec.* Having little flesh; lean, spare. Also of ears of corn. OE. d. Penetrable by light or vision; *fig.* easily 'seen through', transparent, flimsy, as a pretext or excuse 1613.

1. Thyn skynne 1530. b. A very t. wire 1885. c. Seuen kyne,..thynne, euell fauoured, and leenfleshed COVERDALE *Gen.* 41:3. d. Under a t. disguise of name 1851. A t. veil of fog TYNDALL.

II. 1. Consisting of or characterized by individual constituents or parts placed at relatively large intervals; not thick, dense, or bushy. Opp. to THICK *a.* II. 1. OE. †b. Of the members of a collective group or class: Not numerous or abundant; scarce, rare, few, scanty –1725. †c. Of a place: Sparsely occupied or peopled; with *of*, sparsely furnished or supplied with; thinly occupied or attended by –1800. **d.** Of an assembly or body of people: Scantily furnished with members; thinly attended; not full 1637. **2.** Of a liquid or pasty substance: Of slight density or consistence; fluid; of air or vapour, not dense; rare, tenuous, subtile. Opp. to THICK *a.* II. 3. OE. **b.** *transf.* and *fig.* Wanting body or substance; unsubstantial; intangible 1610. **c.** Wanting depth or intensity; faint, weak, dim, pale 1649. **d.** Of sound: Wanting fullness, volume, or depth; weak and high pitched; shrill and feeble 1660. **3.** *fig.* Deficient in substance or quality; poor; unsubstantial; feeble; slight; scanty; not full or rich ME. **b.** *spec.* Of liquor: Without body; weak 1440.

1. [Lord Mountjoy's] haire was..thinne on his head 1617. **c.** The town being t., I am less pestered with company SWIFT. **d.** There I found but a t. congregation already PEPYS. **2.** Chalk, ground up with a little water into a t. paste 1850. **b.** These our actors..were all Spirits, and Are melted into Ayre, into t. Ayre SHAKS. **d.** I hear the groans of ghosts; T., hollow sounds DRYDEN. **3.** Yet was her wit but t. 1580. A t. and slender pittance SHAKS. A t. Diet 1707. Slang phr. *A thin time*, an uncomfortable or distasteful experience. **b.** To forsweare thinne Potations, and to addict themselues to Sack SHAKS.

B. *absol.* as *sb.*: mostly ellipt. or nonce-uses. *T. and thick*: see THICK AND THIN. ME. **C.** *adv.* **1.** With little thickness or depth; with thin clothing. †*To go t.*: to be thinly clad. ME. **2.** Sparsely; not closely or thickly. late ME.

2. To sow something thinner than ordinary 1707.

Comb.: **t. coal**, coal found in shallow beds or seams; **t. miner**, a miner who gets coal from thin seams; **t. seam**, applied to coal seams less than 3 feet in thickness; **-sown** *a.*, sown or planted thinly; **-spun** *a.*, spun thinly; drawn out in spinning to a slender thread. Hence **Thi·n-ly** *adv.*, **-ness.**

Thin (þin), *v.* [OE. *þynnian*, f. *þynne* THIN *a.*] **1.** *trans.* To make thin; to reduce in thickness or depth; to spread or draw *out* in a thin layer or thread. **2.** *intr.* To become thin or thinner; to decrease in thickness or depth 1804. **b.** *spec.* To lose flesh; to become spare or lean 1870. **3.** *trans.* To render less crowded or close by removing individuals; hence, to reduce in number 1440. **4.** *intr.* Of a place: To become less full or crowded; of a crowd: to become less numerous 1779. **5.** *trans.* To dilute OE. **6.** *intr.* To become less dense or consistent; to grow fluid, tenuous, or rare 1834.

1. *To t. off, down*, to diminish gradually to vanishing point. **2.** *To t. out* (*off, away*), to become gradually thinner until it disappears, as a layer or stratum. **3.** To t. our population 1832. T. out superfluous shoots 1850. A head already thinned of hair 1905. **4.** The town begins to t., though Parliament is still sitting 1779. Hence **Thi·nner,** one who or that which thins; *spec.* a preparation for thinning paint.

Thine (ðəin), *poss. pron.* [OE. *þīn*, used as gen. case of *þū* THOU, and as poss. adj., = OFris., OS. *thīn*, OHG. *dīn* (Du. *dijn*, G. *dein*), ON. *þinn*, Goth. *þeins* :– Gmc. **þīnaz* :– IE. **t(w)einos*, f. *tū̆* THOU. Cf. MINE.] †**I.** Genitive case of THOU: = of thee –1500. **II.** The possess. adj. or pron. of the second person sing.: Belonging to thee. **1.** *attrib.* Now *arch.* or *poet.* bef. a vowel or *h*, or when following the sb.; otherwise superseded by THY. OE. **2.** *predic.* OE. **3.** *ellipt.* = THY with a sb. to be supplied from the previous context. late ME. **4.** *absol.* **a.** That which is thine; thy property OE. **b.** *pl.* Those who are thine; thy people, family, or kindred OE. **c.** *Of thine*: that is (or are) thine; belonging to thee. late ME.

I. *Maugre t.*, in spite of thee. **II. 1.** Drink to me only with t. eyes B. JONS. **2.** For thyne is the kyngedome and the power, and the glorye TINDALE *Matt.* 6:13. **3.** *S.* Tastes are different, you know... *E.* That's true; but thine's a devilish odd one. CHESTERF. **4. a.** Myne and Thyne (the seedes of all Myscheefe) 1555. **b.** Lasting shame On thee and thine..I will inflict SHAKS.

Thing (þiŋ), *sb.*[1] [OE. *þing* = OFris., OS. *thing*, OHG. *ding* asembly for deliberation and/or business (G. *ding* affair, matter, thing), ON. *þing* :– Gmc. **þiŋgam.*] **I.** †**1.** A meeting, assembly, *esp.* a deliberative or judicial assembly. OE. only. †**2.** A matter brought before a court of law; a legal process; a charge brought, a suit or cause pleaded before a court –1548. **3.** That with which one is concerned (in action, speech, or thought); *pl.* affairs, concerns, matters OE. **4.** That which is done or to be done; a doing, act, deed, transaction; an event, occurrence, incident; a fact, circumstance, experience OE. **5.** That which is said; a saying, utterance, expression, statement; with various connotations ME. **b.** That which is thought; an opinion, a notion, an idea 1765. †**6.** Used *absol.*, also *a t.*, in indefinite sense: = anything, something –1678.

3. You shall heare how things goe SHAKS. Things changed greatly in the course of a year 1867. **4.** The great t. was to get there 1902. *(The) first t.* (advb.), as that which is first done or to be done; in the first place, firstly. So *(the) next t.*, next; *(the) last t.*, in the last place, lastly; He often goes round the last t...to make sure that all is right 1871. **5.** I never heard a better T. SWIFT. The people who went about saying things 1859. **b.** Putting things in the poor girl's head 1885. **6.** Shall I tell you a t.? SHAKS.

II. An entity of any kind. **1.** That which exists individually (in the most general sense, in fact or in idea); that which is or may be in any way an object of perception, knowledge, or thought; a being, an entity. **a.** In unemphatic use OE. **b.** Applied to an attribute, quality, or property of an actual being or entity; hence sometimes = point, respect OE. **c.** Used indefinitely: a something, a somewhat 1602. **d.** In emphatic use: That which has separate or individual existence 1817. **2.** *spec.* That which is signified as dist. from a word, symbol, or idea by which it is represented; the actual being or entity as opp. to a symbol of it 1450. **b.** *esp.* A being without life or consciousness; an inanimate object 1689. **3.** Applied (usu. with qualifying word) to a living being or creature; occas. to a plant OE. **4.** Applied to a person, now only in contempt, reproach, pity, or affection; formerly also in commendation or honour ME. **5.** A material object, a body; a being or entity consisting of matter, or occupying space OE. **b.** A material substance (usu. of a specified kind); stuff, material; in mod. use chiefly applied to substances used as food, drink, or medicine OE. **6. a.** A piece of property, an individual possession; usu. in *pl.*, possessions, belongings, goods; *esp.* (*colloq.*), those which one has or carries with one at the time, e.g. on a journey ME. **b.** *spec.* (*pl.*) Articles of apparel; clothes, garments; *esp.* such as women put on to go out in, in addition to the indoor dress. *colloq.* 1634. **c.** *pl.* Implements or equipment for some special use; utensils. Chiefly *colloq.* 1698. **7.** An individual work of literature or art, a composition; a writing, piece of music, etc. late ME.

1. a. To compare Great things with small MILT. A man of parts is one t., and a pedant another BERKELEY. A t. of beauty is a joy for ever KEATS. The latest t. in tattooing GEO. ELIOT. **b.** I side in all things with the mob BERKELEY. Ignorance is an odious t. 1838. **c.** No Bird, but an invisible t., A voice, a mystery WORDSW. **d.** True words are things BYRON. **2.** The supposition that things are distinct from ideas takes away all real truth BERKELEY. **b.** Consideration of persons, things, times and places DICKENS. **3.** I wish no living t. to suffer pain SHELLEY. **4.** At a Play.. looking..at a young t. in a Box before us STEELE. To accept the sovereignty of a t. like Henry of Valois MOTLEY. **5.** Things perceivable by touch BERKELEY. Callest thou that t. a leg? TENNYSON. **6. a.** Busie in packing vp his things against his departure 1603. **b.** Take off your things—and we will order..tea 1833. **c.** The breakfast things 1844. **7.** I have a t. in prose, begun above twenty-eight years ago, and almost finished SWIFT.

Phrases, etc. ..*and things* (colloq., unstressed), and other things of the same kind; and the like, *et cetera. For one t.*, as one point to be noted; in the first place; so *for another t. To make a good t. of*, to turn to profit, make gain out of. *No great things* (used predic.), nothing great, nothing much (*colloq.* or *dial.*). *T. in itself* (tr. G. *ding an sich*, Kant), *Metaph.* a thing regarded apart from its attributes; a noumenon. *To know a t. or two*: see KNOW *v.* IV. 4; so *to learn, to show* (a person) *a t. or two. To be up to a t. or two* = to know a thing or two. **The t.** (colloq., emphatic). **a.** the correct thing; what is proper, befitting, or fashionable; also of a person, in good condition or 'form', 'up to the mark', fit (physically or otherwise); **b.** the special, important, or notable point; *esp.* what is specially required. *Any t., every t., no t., some t.* (in which *thing* is an unemphatic stressless use of sense II. 1 or II. 5), are now written each as one word (see ANYTHING, EVERYTHING, NOTHING, SOMETHING).

Thing (þiŋ), *sb.*[2] 1840. [– ON. *þing* (mod. Scand. *ting*); the same word as prec., but taken independently from ONorse.] In Scandinavian countries (or settlements, as in parts of England before the Conquest): A public meeting or assembly; *esp.* a legislative council, a parliament; a court of law. (Usu. with capital T.)

Thingman (þi·ŋmæ̆n). *Pl.* **-men.** 1870. [– ON. *þingmaðr*, in pl. *þingmenn.*] A member of a Scandinavian Thing; *spec.* = HOUSE-CARL.

Thingum (þi·ŋəm). *colloq. Obs.* exc. *dial.* 1680. [f. THING *sb.*[1], with meaningless suffix.] = THINGUMMY. So **Thingumajig** (þi·ŋəmădʒig) 1876.

Thingumbob (þi·ŋəmbǫb). Also **thingume-, thingummybob.** *colloq.* 1751. [Arbitrary extension of prec.] = next.

Thingummy (þi·ŋəmi). *colloq.* 1796. [f. THINGUM.] Used to indicate vaguely a thing (or person) of which the speaker cannot at the moment recall the name, or which he is at a loss or does not care to specify precisely; a 'what-you-may-call-it'.

Think (þiŋk), *sb. dial.* or *colloq.* 1834. [f. THINK *v.*[2]] **1.** An act of (continued) thinking; a meditation. **2.** What one thinks about something; an opinion 1835.

†**Think,** *v.*[1] *Obs.* exc. in METHINKS. [OE. *þynćan*, pa. t. *þūhte*, pa. pple. *ġeþūht* = OS. *thunkian*, OHG. *dunchen* (Du. *dunken*, G. *dünken*), ON. *þykkja*, Goth. *þugkjan* :– Gmc. **þuŋkjan* seem, appear, f. **þuŋk-*, wk. grade of **þiŋk-* (see next). In ME., owing to the fact that both OE. *þync-* and *þenc-* gave ME. *þink-*, and both *þūhte* and *pōhte* appeared in ME. as *pouȝt, thought*, the forms of this verb and THINK *v.*[2] became coincident.] *intr.* To seem, to appear –1635.

Think (þiŋk), *v.*[2] Pa. t. and pa. pple. **thought** (þǭt). [OE. *þenćan*, pa. t. *þōhte*, pa. pple. *ġeþōht* = OFris. *thenka*, etc., OS. *thenkian*, (O)HG. *denken*, ON. *þekkja*, Goth. *þagkjan*; factitive formation on Gmc. **þaŋk-*, str. grade of **þiŋk-* **þaŋk-* **þuŋk-* (see THINK *v.*[1]) :– IE. **teng-* **tong-* **tṇg-*.] **I.** To conceive in the mind, exercise the mind. **1.** *trans.* To form in the mind, conceive; to have in the mind as a notion, an idea, etc.; to do in the way of mental action. †**2.** (with simple obj.) To meditate on, ponder over, consider –1605. **b.** with indirect question as obj. OE. **c.** To have one's thoughts full of, imbued with, or influenced by; to think in terms of 1821. **3.** *intr.* To exercise the mind, esp. the understanding, in any active way; to form connected ideas of any kind; to meditate, cogitate OE. **4.** To form or have an idea of (a thing, action, or circumstance, real or imaginary) in one's mind; to imagine, conceive, fancy, picture. **a.** *trans.*; also *absol.* in colloq. phrases *only t.! you can't t.!* ME. **b.** *intr.* with *of* (*on* obs. or arch.), in same sense ME. **c.** *trans.* with simple obj. To picture in one's mind, apprehend clearly, cognize (with or without direct perception) 1864.

1. To thinke so base a thought SHAKS. I thought, He will surely come out to me 2 *Kings* 5:11. *To t. scorn* (*of* or *to do* something), to scorn (*arch.*); *to t. shame*, to be ashamed (now *dial.*). **2. b.** A-thinking what he should do 1778. **c.** Unless thou hast been drinking beer and thinking beer KINGSLEY. **3.** Who now thought of nothing but the pursuite of vanity EVELYN. Those who t. must govern those that toil GOLDSM. *T. aloud*, to express one's thoughts by audible speech as they pass through the mind. **4. a.** Thinke but this..That you haue but slumbred heere SHAKS. **b.** T. of me ever being rich! 1861. **c.** We t. the ocean as a whole by multiplying mentally the impression we get at any moment when at sea 1890.

II. To call to mind, take into consideration. **1. a.** *trans.* To call to mind; to consider, reflect upon; to recollect, remember, bear in mind OE. **b.** *intr.* To consider the matter; to reflect OE. **c.** *intr.* with *of* (arch. *on, upon*), or *inf.*: To call to mind, remember, bethink oneself (of), hit upon mentally ME. **2.** *intr.* with *of*, arch. *on* (*upon*): To take into consideration, have regard to, consider. ME. **3.** To bethink oneself of something in the way of a plan or purpose; to contrive, devise, plan, plot. **a.** *trans.* ME. **b.** *intr.* with *of* (*on, upon,* obs. or arch.) 1598. **4.** To conceive or entertain the notion of doing something; to intend, mean, 'have a mind', 'have thoughts (of)'. **a.** *trans.* OE. **b.** *intr.* with *of* 1698. **c.** *spec.* with *of*: To consider (a person) in view of some vacancy, or *esp.* of marriage; to cherish the notion or intention of marrying 1670:

1. a. I am afraid, to thinke what I haue done SHAKS. **b.** Pause here, and t. COWPER. **c.** The most conuenient place, that I can thinke of..is Black-Fryers SHAKS. *To t. better of*: see BETTER *adv.* **2.** Nothing was thought of, but how to save ourselves, and the little goods we had JOHNSON. **3. b.** His Majesty..hath thought of a way 1630. **4. a.** Peace is despaird, For who can t. Submission? MILT. He..thought he would send for his mother; and then he thought he would not T. HARDY. **b.** Each thought of taking to himself a wife CRABBE. **c.** I trust to your prudence, not to t. of Flora..; for you can't..marry a girl with so small a fortune MAR. EDGEWORTH.

III. To be of opinion, deem, judge, etc. **1.** *trans.* with *obj. cl.*, or parenthetic: To be of opinion, hold the opinion, believe, deem, judge, apprehend, consider; usu., to regard it as likely, to have the idea, to suppose; in ref. to a future event, to expect OE. **b.** *intr.* To hold the opinion (indicated by context) ME. **2.** *trans.* with complement: To believe, consider, or suppose (to be..); to look upon as ME. **3.** *intr.* To have a (good, bad, or other) opinion with regard to a person or thing; to value or esteem something (highly or otherwise). late ME. **4.** To believe possible or likely; to suspect; to expect, anticipate. **a.** *trans.* with simple obj. late ME. **b.** with *inf.* To expect. late ME. **c.** *intr.* with *of*, †*on* (*upon*), †*to*: To suspect; to expect, look for 1483. **d.** with *for*, after *as* or *than*, and with the prep. at the end of the clause: To expect, suppose 1530. **5.** *trans.* To judge or consider to exist; to believe in the existence of (*rare*) 1532.

1. Who would haue thought that our Uncle of Englande would haue made warre on vs? HALL. I t. that I understand him JOWETT. *Who do you t.? What do you t.?* (colloq.) phrases used, esp. parenthetically, to introduce a surprising statement. *I don't t.* (slang), used after an ironical statement, to indicate that the reverse is intended; 'You're a amiably-disposed young man, sir, I don't t.', resumed Mr. Weller DICKENS. **b.** He said he spake as he thought 1560. *To t. so*, to be of that opinion. *To t. with*, to be of the same opinion as. **2.** May I be bold To thinke these spirits? SHAKS. The little narrative which I thought proper to put forth in October SCOTT. *T.* (*it*) *long*, to grow weary with waiting; to be impatient; to long, yearn (*Obs.* exc. *dial.*). †*T.* (*it*) *much*, to think it a great or serious matter; to object, grudge; to be shy, hesitate; to be surprised, wonder (*that*..). **3.** I thinke nobly of the soule SHAKS. I didn't t. much of her 1813. Phr. *T. nothing of*, (*a*) to set no value upon, esteem as worthless; (*b*) to make light of, make no difficulty or scruple about. **4. a.** He, thinking no harm, agreed DE FOE. **b.** I thought to have seen you ere this SOUTHEY. **d.** Oh sir, the conceit is deeper than you t. for SHAKS. **5.** Unless there be who t. not God at all MILT.

Phr. **T. out** (*a*) to find out, devise, or elaborate by thinking, to construct intellectually; (*b*) to solve by a process of thought; (*c*) to think to the end, complete or finish in thought. **T.** (a thing) **over,** to give continued thought to (it) with the view of coming to a decision.

Thinkable (þi·ŋkăb'l), *a.* 1854. [f. prec. + -ABLE. Cf. *unthinkable* (1430).] **1.** Capable of being thought; such as one can form a notion or idea of; cogitable. **2.** Conceivable or imaginable as an existing fact 1865.

Thinker (þi·ŋkər). 1440. [f. as prec. + -ER¹.] One who thinks. **a.** *gen.* A person or being engaged in thinking, or having the power to think. **b.** with qualifying adj.: One who thinks in the way expressed by the adj. 1698. **c.** *spec.* One who has special or well-trained powers of thought, esp. abstract thought; also, a person who devotes himself to thinking, as dist. from action or practical affairs 1830.

Thinking (þi·ŋkiŋ), *vbl. sb.* ME. [f. THINK *v.*² + -ING¹.] The action of THINK *v.*² **1.** Thought, cogitation, meditation, mental action or activity, etc. **b.** *pl.* Thoughts; meditations. late ME. **2.** The holding of an opinion or opinions; judging, mental viewing; opinion, judgement, belief; colloq. phr. *to my t.* = in my opinion. late ME.

1. Plain living and high t. are no more WORDSW. **b.** I am wrap'd in dismall thinkings SHAKS. **2.** I heare a Bird so sing, Whose Musicke (to my t.) pleas'd the King SHAKS.

attrib. and *Comb.*: **t.-cap** (see CAP *sb.*¹); **t. part** (*Theatr. colloq.*), a part in which the actor has no words to speak.

Thi·nking, *ppl. a.* 1678. [f. as prec. + -ING².] **1.** That thinks; cogitative. **2.** Given to thinking; having special, or well-trained powers of thought; thoughtful, reflective, intellectual 1681.

1. What was the proper Employment of a t. Being? 1709.

Thi·nk-so. *dial.* 1666. [The phr. (*I*) *think so* used as a sb.] A mere opinion.

How if all our Faith, and Christ, and Scriptures should be but a Think-so too? BUNYAN.

Thinnish (þi·niʃ), *a.* 1545. [f. THIN *a.* + -ISH¹.] Somewhat thin; tending to thinness.

Thin-skinned (-skind; stress variable), *a.* 1598. **1.** Having a thin skin or rind. **2.** *fig.* Sensitive to criticism, ridicule, or abuse; easily hurt or offended; touchy 1680.

Thio- (þəi,o), also bef. a vowel **thi-,** repr. Gr. θεῖον sulphur; a formative element in names of substances containing or connected with sulphur.

1. *Chem.* In names of compounds containing sulphur = *sulpho-*. **Thia·ldine** [ALD(EHYDE + -INE⁵], a crystalline substance, $NH:2(CHCH_3.S):CHCH_3$, produced by passing hydrogen sulphide into a solution of aldehyde ammonia. **Thi·alol** [AL(COHOL + -OL 3], diethyl disulphide $(C_2H_5)_2S_2$, a colourless oily compound, having an odour like garlic. **Thi·enyl,** the radical C_4H_3S contained in *thiophene*, C_4H_4S. **Thi·o-acid,** an acid in which oxygen is replaced by sulphur. **Thioca·rbonate,** a salt of thiocarbonic acid. **Thiocarbo·nic** *a.*, in *t. acid*: in derivatives, as *mono-, di-, tri-thiocarbonic acid*: the last, H_2CS_3, is a dark yellow strongly smelling oil, very easily decomposed by heating into CS_2 and H_2S. **Thiocy·anate,** a salt of thiocyanic acid. **Thiocya·nic** *a.*, in *t. acid.* $N:C.SH$ = cyanic acid, $N:C.OH$, in which oxygen is replaced by sulphur; a liquid with a penetrating odour. **Thiona·phthene,** a colourless crystalline compound, C_8H_6S, consisting of benzene, C_6H_6, of which two atoms of H are replaced by $CH:CH.S$. **Thionic** (þəi·ǫnik) *a.*, in *t. acids*, group name for the acids represented by the formula $H_2S_nO_6$. **Thi·onine,** a brownish-black dye, $SC_{12}H_9N_3$, crystallizing in plates, called *phenylene violet* or *Lauth's violet*, and largely used to stain microscopic objects. **Thi·onyl** [-YL], the radical (SO)″. **Thi·ophene,** C_4H_4S, a colourless liquid with an odour like benzene, occurring in benzene from coal-tar to the extent of about 0·5 per cent.; hence **Thiophe·nic** *a.*, in *t. acid*, $C_4H_3S.CO_2H$, derived from thiophene. **Thiophe·nol,** a colourless liquid, C_6H_5SH (= PHENOL with S in place of O), with the odour of garlic. **Thiosu·lphide,** a salt of thiosulphuric acid; formerly called *hyposulphite*. **Thi:osulphu·ric** *a.*, in *t. acid*, $H_2S_2O_3$, an acid, the salts of which are applied in bleaching and photography; it is sulphuric acid, H_2SO_4, in which one atom of oxygen is replaced by sulphur; formerly called *hyposulphurous* acid. **Thioto·luene** [TOLUENE] = *methylthiophene*, $C_4H_3(CH_3)S$, a colourless oily compound, found as an impurity in crude toluene. **Thioxene** (þəi,ǫ·ksīn) = *dimethylthiophene*, $C_4H_2(CH_3)_2S$, found as an impurity in xylene.

2. In pharmaceutical and other terms, as **Thi·o-camph** [CAMPH(OR], a fluid disinfectant, used for fumigation, formed by the action of sulphur dioxide on camphor. **Thi·oform** [after *chloroform*], trade-name of a basic bismuth di-thiosalicylate, as an antiseptic for wounds.

Thiol- (þəi·ǫl). 1899. [Arbitrarily f. THIO-.] *Chem.* A name for the group SH in combination, analogous to hydroxyl, OH.

Thion- (þəi·ǫn). 1899. [– Gr. θεῖον sulphur; cf. THIO-.] *Chem.* A name for sulphur taking the place of oxygen in a compound and joined by two bonds to carbon. (Certain words beginning with *thion-* do not conform to this system; see THIONIC, etc.)

Third (þɔ̄ɹd), *a.* (*adv.*), *sb.* [OE. (late Northumb.) *þird(d)a, -e*, var. of *þridda* (whence ME. and Sc. till XVIII *thrid*) = OFris. *thredda*, OS. *thriddio*, OHG. *dritto* (Du. *derde*, G. *dritte*), ON. *þriði*, Goth. *þridja* :– Gmc. **þriðjaz* :– IE. **trit̯ós* (cf. L. *tertius*, Gr. τρίτος).] **A.** *adj.* **1.** The ordinal numeral corresponding to the cardinal three: last of three; that comes next after the second. **b.** *Gram.* In *t. person*: see PERSON *sb.* VI. Also in *t. declension, conjugation*, and in names of tenses, as *t. future* 1530. **2.** Additional to and distinct from two others already known or mentioned. *T. person* (in Law) = THIRD PARTY. ME. **3.** *T. part* = B. 1. ME. **4.** The last of each successive group of three; one in every three, i.e. one third of the whole. late ME.

1. The thryde day of Marche 1497. Pope Innocent the thred 1550. 'Hush! thou knave!' said a t. SCOTT. **3.** The t. part of the sea became blood *Rev.* 8:8. **4.** *T. penny*, one third of the whole sum.

Comb.: **t. best,** that is next inferior to the SECOND BEST; **t. degree,** in Freemasonry, the degree of Master Mason; *U.S.* applied to severe and prolonged cross-questioning of a suspected person by the police in order to extort an admission or confession of guilt; **t. estate,** the Commons; **t. floor,** (*a*) in England, the floor or storey of a building separated by two from the ground floor; (*b*) *Sc., U.S.*, etc., the t. storey, counting the ground floor as the first; **t. hour,** (*a*) among the Jews, the t. of the twelve equal divisions of time between morning and evening; the hour between 8 and 9 a.m.; (*b*) the hour of TIERCE; **t. order**: see TERTIARY A. 5; **t. rail,** in some systems of electric railways, an additional rail which conveys the current.

B. *sb.* **1.** A third part (A. 3) *of* anything; any one of three equal parts into which a whole may be divided. late ME. **2.** *Law.* (Mostly *pl.*) The third of the personal property of a deceased husband allowed to his widow. Also, the third of his real property to which the widow might be legally entitled for her life (*obs.* exc. *Hist.*). late ME. †**3.** A third of the proceeds of captures, or of certain fines, forfeitures, etc., of which two thirds were due to the king –1627. **4.** *Mus.* A note three diatonic degrees above or below a given note (both notes being reckoned); also (usu.) the interval between this and the given note, equivalent either to two tones (*major t.*), or to one tone and one diatonic semitone (*minor t.*); also, the harmonic combination of two such notes 1597. **5.** *Comm. pl.* Goods of the third degree of quality 1823. **6.** Ellipt. uses of the adj. passing into sb.: **a.** for third person (in Grammar); third day (of the month); third chapter (of a book of the Bible); third year (of a reign); third class (in an examination list) 1530. **b.** *T. of exchange*: the last of a set of three bills of exchange of even tenor and date.

4. We shall have the word In a minor t. There is none but the cuckoo knows BROWNING. *Diminished t.*, an interval equal to two diatonic semitones, being less by a chromatic semitone than a minor third. **6. a.** On Sunday the 3d of May. He only got a third in Modern Greats (*mod.*). Hence **Third** *v. trans.* to divide into three equal parts. **Thi·rdly** *adv.* in the t. place.

Thi·rdborough, thri·dborrow. *Obs.* exc. *Hist.* 1475. [prob. a ME. corruption of *friðborgh* :– OE. *friðborg* peace-pledge, peace-surety; see FRITHBORH, FRANK-PLEDGE.] Formerly, The head man of a frithborh or frank-pledge; hence, the conservator of peace or peace-officer of a tithing, the petty constable of a township or manor.

Third class, third-class (stress var.), *phr.* (*sb.* and *a.*) 1839. **1.** *sb.* The class next below the second; esp. of railway carriages; also in an examination list; hence, a place in the third class in an examination 1845. **2.** *attrib.* or *adj.* Of or belonging to the class next below the second 1839. **3.** quasi-*adv.* By a third-class conveyance 1864.

3. Natives almost invariably travel third-class 1864.

Third hand, third-hand. 1553. [After SECOND HAND.] **1.** In advb. phr. *at* (†*the*) *third hand*: from a second middleman or intermediary; at the second remove from the original source. **2.** *attrib.* or as *adj.* Obtained, copied, or imitated from a second-hand source 1599.

Thi·rd pa:rty. 1818. A party or person besides the two primarily concerned, as in a law case or the like. Also *attrib.*, as in *third-party insurance, risk*, etc.

Third-rate, *a.* and *sb.* 1649. [See RATE *sb.*¹] **A.** *adj.* †**1.** Of the third 'rate' (esp. of ships) –1693. **2.** Of the third class in point of quality; usu. *depreciative*, of decidedly poor or inferior quality 1838.

2. An actor of t. parts THIRLWALL.
B. *sb. Naut.* A war-vessel of the third rate 1666.
A Third Rate of 62 Guns 1695. Hence **Third-rater.**

Thirdsman (þɔ̄·ɹdzmæ̆n). 1818. A third person or party; *esp.* one called in as an intermediary, mediator, or arbiter.

Thirl (þɔ̄ɹl), *sb.* Now *dial.* [OE. *þyrel*, f. *þurh* THROUGH + -EL¹.] **1.** A hole, bore, perforation; an aperture. **b.** A nostril ME. **2.** An opening in a wall or the like. Also *fig.* OE.

Thirl (þɔ̄ɹl), *v. Obs.* exc. *dial.* and *local.* [OE. *þyrlian*, f. *þyrel* THIRL *sb.*; cf. THRILL *v.*] **1.** *trans.* To pierce, to run through or into (a body) as a sharp-pointed instrument does; to pierce (anything) with such an instrument; to perforate. **2.** *spec. Coal-mining.* To cut through (a wall of coal, etc.). Also *absol.* or *intr.* 1686. †**3.** *intr.* or *absol.* To pierce, penetrate (as a sharp instrument). Also *fig.* –1600.

Thirlage (þɔ̄·ɹlėdʒ). *Sc.* 1513. [f. *thirl*, metathetic var. of *thrill*, Sc. var. of THRALL *sb.*; see -AGE.] †**1.** Thraldom, bondage, servitude –1609. **2.** *Sc. Law.* A condition of servitude or state of obligation, in which the tenants of certain lands, or dwellers in certain districts are bound to restrict their custom to a particular mill, forge, or the like. In later times, spec. the obligation to grind their corn at a particular mill (orig. that of the lord or his assignee), and pay the recognized consideration (multure), or at least to pay the dues in lieu thereof. 1681. **b.** The multure exacted under this system 1799.

Thirst (þɔ̄ɹst), *sb.* [OE. *þurst* = OS. *thurst* (Du. *dorst*) :– WGmc. **þurstu* (cf. ON. *þorsti*, Goth. *þaurstei*); f. **þurs-* :– IE. **trs-* **tors-*, repr. also by L. *torrēre* dry, parch.] **1.** The uneasy or painful sensation caused by want of drink; also, the physical condition resulting from this want. **2.** *fig.* A vehement desire (*of* (arch.), *for*, *after* something, *to do* something) ME.
1. Þey deyde for hunger & þirst R. BRUNNE. The long t. of Tantalus allay GRAY. 2. Not in t. for Reuenge SHAKS. T. for money 1849. Hence **Thi·rstless** *a.* having no thirst; not thirsty.

Thirst (þɔ̄ɹst), *v.* [OE. *þyrstan* = OS. *thurstian*, OHG. *dursten* (Du. *dorsten*, G. *dürsten*), ON. *þyrsta.*] †**1.** *impers.*, as in *me thirsteth*, I am thirsty –1440. **2.** *intr.* To feel or suffer thirst; to be thirsty. Also *transf.*, e.g. of parched ground or plants. Somewhat *arch.* OE. **3.** *fig.* To have a longing, craving, or strong desire. Const. in OE. with gen., = of; later *after*, *for* something, *to do* something. OE. †**4.** *trans.* To desire vehemently; to long for –1718.
1. So thursted hym, that he Was well ny lorn CHAUCER. 2. Ho, euery one that thirsteth, come ye to the waters *Isa.* 55:1. 3. It is not necessary to teach men to t. after power BURKE. 4. Wicked men, that thursted the blud of all the senate Q. ELIZ. Hence **Thi·rster**, one who thirsts.

Thirsty (þɔ̄·ɹsti), *a.* [OE. *þurstiġ*, *þyrstiġ*, f. *þurst* THIRST *sb.* + *-iġ* -Y¹.] **1.** Having the sensation of thirst; feeling desire or craving for drink. **b.** *transf.* Of earth or plants; Greatly wanting moisture; dry, parched, arid. late ME. **2.** *fig.* Having or characterized by a vehement desire or craving; eager, greedy OE. **3.** *transf.* That causes thirst. Now *colloq.* 1599.
1. The Fountain being..very inviting to the t. Passenger 1703. **b.** The country was parched and t. 1878. 2. Refreshing to the t. curiosity of the traveller LAMB. 3. A t. walk up and down terrible bad roads 1897. Hence **Thi·rsti-ly** *adv.*, **-ness.**

Thirteen (þɔ̄ɹtī·n, þɔ̄·ɹtīn). [OE. *thrēotiene* = OS. *thriutein*, OHG. *drīzehan* (Du. *dertien*, G. *dreizehn*), ON. *þrettán*; f. *þrēo* THREE + *-tīene*, *-tēne* -TEEN.] The cardinal number composed of ten and three, represented by the symbols 13 or XIII. **A.** *adj.* **1.** In concord with a sb. expressed. Often *absol.* (with sb. implied in context) OE. †**2.** As ordinal: Thirteenth –1641.
1. Thirtine yeares past 1561. If t. sit down to sup, And thou first have risen up, Goodman, turn thy money! 1865. 2. He..died the t. of November, Anno 1142 KNOLLES.
B. *sb.* (With pl. *thirteens.*) **1.** The abstract number; a symbol or the figures representing this. late ME. **b.** A thing distinguished by the number thirteen, as an article of a certain size so called 1799. †**2.** An Irish silver shilling, as being worth thirteen pence of Irish copper currency –1830.
1. To shame the superstitious public out of their dread of the number 13. 1905. 2. Oft was his pocket without a t. 1810.

Thirteener (þɔ̄ɹtī·nəɹ). 1762. [f. prec. + -ER¹.] **1.** = prec. B. 2. **2. a.** *Cricket.* A hit for thirteen runs. **b.** The thirteenth of a series. 1891.

Thirteenth (þɔ̄ɹtī·nþ, þɔ̄·ɹtīnþ), *a.* and *sb.* [In OE. *þrīe-*, *þrēotēoþa*, etc. Northern ME. had *þrett-*, *þrittend(e* from ON. *þrettánde.* Hence *a*1400 *þrett-*, *þrittenþ(e*, and by metathesis *ther-*, *thyr- thirtenth*, and in XVI *thirteenth*, as if f. *thirteen* + -TH².] **A.** *adj.* The ordinal numeral belonging to the cardinal thirteen; the last of thirteen; that comes next after the twelfth.
The literature of the t. century 1878.
B. *sb.* **1.** A thirteenth part 1611. **b.** *Eng. Hist.* A thirteenth part of the value of movables, or of the rent of the year, formerly granted or levied as a tax 1893. **2.** *Mus.* A note thirteen diatonic degrees above or below a given note (both notes being counted); the interval between, or consonance of, two notes thirteen diatonic degrees apart; a chord containing this interval 1597. Hence **Thirtee·nthly** *adv.* in the thirteenth place.

Thirtieth (þɔ̄·ɹti,ėþ), *a.* and *sb.* [OE. *þrītigoþa*, *þritteogoþa*, ME. *thrittethe*, remodelled in the present form on the cardinal with metathesis; see -TH².] **A.** *adj.* The ordinal numeral belonging to the cardinal thirty; the last of thirty.
B. *sb.* A thirtieth part; in *Eng. Hist.* a thirtieth part of movable goods payable as an aid 1800.

Thirty (þɔ̄·ɹti), *a.* and *sb.* [OE. *þrītiġ*, f. *þrī* three + *-tiġ* -TY²; = OS. *thrītig*, OHG. *drīzzug* (Du. *dertig*, G. *dreissig*), ON. *þrirtegr*, Goth. (acc.) *þrins tiguns.*] The cardinal number equal to three tens, represented by the symbols 30, or XXX, xxx. **A.** *adj.* **1.** In concord with a sb. expressed or implied. **2.** *spec.* (*ellipt.*) **a.** The age of thirty; thirty years (of age, old, etc.). So *thirty-one*, etc. OE. **b.** In stating the time of day, thirty minutes; as in *six-thirty* = 6.30 o'clock, half-past six; also *attrib.* as *the* 6.30 *train* 1870. †**3.** As ordinal = THIRTIETH –1609.
1. Thirty per cent. interest 1837. *The T.* (*Tyrants*), the t. magistrates imposed by Sparta upon Athens at the end of the Peloponnesian War (403 B.C.). *The T. Years' War*, the religious wars of 1618–48 fought chiefly on German soil. 3. Ere the t. day of the next month 1594.
B. *sb.* **1.** The abstract number; also, a symbol representing this. So *thirty-one*, etc. OE. **2.** *The thirties*: the years of which the numbers begin with 30. 1880. **3.** *Thirty* and its compounds in elliptical uses 1802.
2. Some time in the early thirties 1892. 3. *T.-two*, a t.-two-pound gun; a flower-pot of which there are 32 in a 'cast'; see also THIRTYTWOMO.

Thirtytwomo (-tū·mo). 1771. [English reading of the symbol 32mo or XXXIImo, for L. (*in*) *tricesimo secundo.*] The size of a book, or of a leaf of a book, formed of sheets each folded five times, making thirty-two leaves; hence, a book of this size. Also **Thirty-twos.** So **Thirtysi·xmo (thirty-sixes).**

This (ðis), *dem. pron.* and *adj. Pl.* THESE. [The form *this* in generalized use dates from *c*1200 (Orm); it is identical with the OE. n. nom. and acc. and the stem of most of the inflected forms: *þes* masc., *þēos* fem., *þis* n. (cf. the masc. forms OFris. *this*, OS. **these*, OHG. *dese*(*r*, ON. *þessi*); WGmc. and ON. formation on **þa-* (see THE, THAT) and deictic **-se*, **-si.*] **I.** Demonstrative Pronoun. **1.** Indicating a thing or person near or present (actually in space or time, or ideally in thought); *spec.* as being nearer than some other (hence opp. to *that*). Of a person, now indicating a person actually present, and always as subj. of the vb. *to be* with the person as predicate. **b.** After various preps. (*after*, *before*, *by*, *ere*, etc.) = 'this time' OE. **c.** After a prep., or as obj. of a verb = 'this place'. Now (in colloq. use) more usu. *here.* 1460. **2.** In contrast to *that*: now almost always of things ME. **b.** *spec.* (after L. idiom.) The latter; in contrast to *that* = the former 1440. **c.** With *That*, as quasi-proper names (with capital), indefinitely denoting one person and another 1824.
1. O Stephano, ha'st any more of t.? SHAKS. T. is the wood they live in FLETCHER. T., t. is she To whom our vows and wishes bend MILT. Yet all of us hold this for true, No faith is to the Wicked due 1664. They said t. as a jeer to the Jews 1693. **b.** By t. the sun is setting KEATS. **c.** You filthy beast, get out of t. W. S. GILBERT. 2. T. is not fair; nor profitable that; Nor t'other Question proper for Debate DRYDEN. *T. and* (*or*) *that* = one thing (or person) and (or) another. **b.** Warm water..mixed with hot and cold, will lessen the heat in that, and the cold in t. BERKELEY. **c.** Miss That or This, or Lady T'other BYRON.
Phrases. *For all t.*, notwithstanding this. *Like t.*: of this kind; in this manner, thus. *T., that, and the other*: everything conceivable.
II. Demonstrative Adjective. **1.** Used in concord with a sb., to indicate a thing or person present or near (actually or in thought), esp. one just mentioned OE. **b.** Referring to something which is mentioned immediately after OE. **c.** In phrases denoting or referring to the present state or stage of existence; esp. *t. life*, THIS WORLD OE. **d.** Referring to something as known, talked about, or inferred; esp. to something now in vogue or recently introduced 1533. **e.** Used before a date, esp. (now only) in legal or formal documents 1503. **f.** Used instead of THESE in concord with a plural sb. or numeral; esp. (now only) with a plural treated as a singular (e.g. *means*, *odds*), or with a numeral expression denoting a period of time taken as a whole. late ME. **2.** In contrast to *that*; prop. denoting the nearer of two things, but often vaguely indicating one thing as distinct from another, esp. in phr. *this and* (*or*) *that*.. = one and (or) another 1460.
1. I have t. moment heard that Sheridan is returned 1772. *T. morning*, *t. afternoon*, *t. evening* now always mean the morning (etc.) of to-day. **b.** T. additional list..is larger than I expected THORESBY. **c.** For t. corruptible must putt on incorruptibilite TINDALE *I Cor.* 15:53. **d.** Oh t. learning, what a thing it is SHAKS. **e.** Given under my hand, this 20th September, 1648 CROMWELL. **f.** Within t. three houres will faire Iuliet wake SHAKS. The silence has kept my own heart heavy t. many a day RUSKIN. 2. T. way and that the impatient captives tend DRYDEN.

This (ðis), *adv.* late ME. [In I prob. OE. *þӯs*, *þīs*, instrumental case of THIS *dem. pron.*; in II app. advb. use of accus. sing. neut.] †**I.** In this way or manner; like this; thus –1592.
What am I that thou shouldst contemne me t.? SHAKS.
II. †**a.** To this extent or degree; as much as this; thus –1567. **b.** Qualifying an adj. or adv. of quantity, now chiefly in *t. much* 1460.
b. And t. far of the Iles called Hebrides 1596.

Thisness (ði·snės). 1643. [f. THIS + -NESS; tr. med. (scholastic) L. *hæcceitas.*] = HÆCCEITY.

Thistle (þi·s'l), *sb.* [OE. *þistel* (some mod. dials. authenticate *ī*, e.g. Somerset dai·sl) = OS. *thīstil*, OHG. *distil*, *distila* (LG. *diestel*, *dīstel*, Du. *distel*, G. *distel*, also *diestel*), ON. *þīstill* :– Gmc. **þīstilaz*, *-ilō*, of unkn. origin.] **1.** The common name of the prickly herbaceous plants of the composite genus *Carduus* and several closely allied genera (*Cnicus*, *Cirsium*, *Onopordum*, etc.), having the stems, leaves, and involucres thickly armed with prickles, the flower-heads usu. globular, and the flowers most commonly purple; many species are abundant as weeds. **b.** As the heraldic emblem of Scotland; also, a figure of a thistle as such 1488. **c.** As a part of the insignia of the *Order of the T.*, the distinctively Scottish order of knighthood; hence *transf.* the order itself, or membership in it 1687. **d.** *fig.* or in fig. context, with ref. to the thistle as a noxious or prickly weed 1563. †**2.** Applied (definitely) to other prickly plants, as artichoke, sea-holly (*Eryngium*), teasel, etc. –1578. **3.** With qualifying words, applied to various species of *Carduus* and allied genera, and to prickly plants of other families 1578.
1. **c.** The Duke of Argyll..received his T. from Lord Palmerston 1898. **d.** He snatcheth at the t. of a project, which first pricks his hands, and then breaks FULLER. 3. **Bull t.**, a local (Ireland and U.S.) name for *Carduus lanceolatus.* **Canada t.**

(*U.S.*), **Corn-t., Creeping t.,** *Carduus arvensis,* a troublesome weed with creeping root-stocks. **Gentle t.,** *Carduus anglicus.* **Holy t.,** (*a*) *Centaurea benedicta* (*Cnicus benedictus*), with yellow flowers and weak prickles on the leaves, formerly in repute as an antidote; also called *blessed t.*; (*b*) erron. applied to *Carduus marianus,* with white veins on the leaves; also called *Our Lady's t.* or *milk t.* **Russian t.** (*U.S.*), a species of saltwort, *Salsola tragus,* with prickly stems, introduced from Russia and now abundant as a weed in S. Dakota and neighbouring States. **Scotch t.,** a name for the species supposed to be that figured as the emblem of Scotland, variously identified as the spear-t. (*Carduus lanceolatus*), the musk t. (*Carduus nutans*), the milk t. (*Carduus marianus*), and the cotton-t. (*Onopordum acanthium*). **Silver t.,** a name for the cotton-t. **Yellow t.,** (*a*) a species of thistle with pale-yellow or purple flowers (*Cnicus horridulus*), found in the eastern U.S.; (*b*) the prickly poppy (*Argemone mexicana*).
attrib. and *Comb.*: **t.-ball,** the globular head of feathery seeds of the t.; **-bird,** a bird that feeds on t.-seeds; *spec.* the American goldfinch, *Chrysomitris* (*Spinus*) *tristis*; **-butterfly,** the 'painted lady', *Vanessa* (*Pyrameis*) *cardui,* whose larva feeds on the t.; **-cock** (*dial.*), the corn bunting, *Emberiza miliaria*; **-crown, -dollar,** names of Scottish coins having a thistle on the reverse; **t. funnel,** a funnel having a large bulb between the conical flaring part and the tube, so as to suggest the form of a thistle-head upon its stalk; **t. noble,** a Scottish gold half-merk of James VI, bearing the figure of a t. on the reverse. Hence **Thi·stle** *v. trans.* to clear of thistles. **Thistled** (þi·s'ld) *a.* covered with thistles; adorned with figures of thistles.

Thistle-down (ði·s'l,daun). 1561. [f. prec. + Down *sb.*²] The down or pappus which crowns the 'seeds' or achenes of the thistle, and by means of which they are carried along by the wind: either collectively, or that of a single 'seed'. **b.** As a type of lightness, flimsiness, or instability; hence *fig.* 1868.
b. The t. of sentiment hung about me all the time 1868.

Thi·stle-finch. 1589. [f. as prec. + Finch.] Any one of several species of finches which feed on the seeds of the thistle; *spec.* the goldfinch, *Carduelis elegans.*

†**Thi·stlewarp.** 1606. [f. as prec. + Warp *v.*] = prec. –1624.

Thistly (þi·s'li), *a.* 1598. [f. as prec. + -y¹.] **1.** Of the nature of or resembling a thistle; spiny, prickly; consisting of or constituted by thistles. **2.** Full of, abounding or overgrown with thistles 1710.
1. *fig.* A world, so thorny,..where none Finds happiness..Without some t. sorrow at it's side Cowper. **2.** The t. lawn Thomson.

This world. OE. The present world; the present stage or state of existence, as dist. from another, esp. a future one.
They alle shalle neuer mete more in thys world Malory. Hence **Thi·s-wo:rld-ly** *a.,* **-ness.**

Thither (ði·ðəɹ), *adv.* (*a.*) [OE. *þider,* alt. by assim. to *hider* Hither, of earlier *þæder,* corresp. to ON. *þaðra* there, thither, f. demons. base **þa* of The, That + suffix denoting 'towards' (IE. **trā*(*d,* as in L. *intrā* within, *extrā* outside, Skr. *tátra* there, then). For the change of d to ð cf. Father.] **1.** To or towards that place (with verb of motion expressed or implied). (Now almost exclusively literary; usu. repl. by There.) **b.** *Hither and t.*: see Hither *adv.* OE. †**2.** *transf.* To or towards that end, purpose, result, or action. Shaks. **B.** *adj.* Lying on that side or in that direction, i.e. the side or direction away from *this*; the farther or more remote (of two things) 1830.
These all came in..on the t. side of innocence Lamb.

Thitherto (ðiðəɹtū·, ði·ðəɹtu), *adv.* 1449. [f. prec. + To *prep.*; after *hitherto.*] **1.** Up to that time; until then. Now *rare.* †**2.** To that condition, point, or result –1662.

Thitherward (ði·ðəɹwǫɹd), *adv.* (*a.*) *arch.* [OE. *þiderweard*; see Thither and -ward.] **1.** Towards that place; in that direction; thither. †**2.** On the way thither; going thither –1634.
1. They shal aske the waye to Zion, with their faces thetherward Bible (Genev.) *Jer.* 50:5. So **Thi·therwards** *adv. arch.* (in sense 1).

‖**Thitsi, thitsee** (þi·tsī). *East Ind.* 1832. [Burmese *þitsī,* f. *þit* tree, wood + *asī,* in comb. *-sī* gum.] The 'black varnish tree', *Melanorrhœa usitatissima,* of the family *Anacardiaceæ,* of Burma and Pegu; also, the varnish obtained from it.

†**Tho,** *dem. pron.* and *adj.* (*rel. pron.*), *pl.* [OE. *þā,* nom. and acc. pl. of *sē, sēo, þæt* That, The.] **I.** Demonstrative pron. = Those I. (they, them) –1600. **II.** Demonstrative adj. **1.** = Those II. –1553. **2.** pl. of def. article The –ME. **III.** Relative pron., pl. of That *rel. pron.* –late ME.

Tho, *adv.* (*conj.*) *Obs.* exc. *dial.* [OE. *þā,* = ON. *þá* then, when; orig. a case-form of the demonstrative stem *þa-* of The, That; meaning 'that time', the sb. being omitted.] As dem. adv.: Then. **a.** At that time. †**b.** (Next) after that, upon that, thereupon –1642.
The queene..had herde ofte of Eneas er thoo Chaucer. **b.** Vn-to this Angel spak the frere tho Chaucer.

Tho, tho', abbrev. ff. Though.

Thole (þōᵘl, þaul), *sb.* [OE. *þol*(*l* = OFris. *tholl,* MLG., MDu. *dolle* (Du. *dol*), ON. *þollr* fir tree, tree, peg.] **1.** A vertical pin or peg in the side of a boat against which in rowing the oar presses as the fulcrum of its action; *esp.* one of a pair between which the oar works; hence, a rowlock. **2.** A pin or peg in general: *spec.* **a.** A pin by means of which the shafts are fastened to the carriage or axle of a cart, etc. **b.** The handle or 'nib' of a scythe-snathe (*local*) 1440.

Thole (þōᵘl), *v.* Now *n. dial.* or *arch.* [OE. *þolian* = OFris. *tholia,* OS. *tholon, tholian,* OHG. *dolōn, dolēn,* ON. *þola,* Goth. *þulan*; Gmc. f. **þul-* repr. wk. grade of IE. **tol-* **tel-* **tl̥-* raise, remove, as in Gr. τλῆναι endure, bear, L. *tollere* raise, *tuli* (pa. t.) bore.] **1.** *trans.* To be subjected or exposed to (something evil); to have to bear, suffer, endure, undergo. Also *absol.* **2.** To submit with patience to; to bear or put up with, 'abide', tolerate. Also *absol.* OE. †**3.** To allow, suffer, permit –1721.
2. He that has a good crop may t. some thistles 1800.

Tho·le-pin. 1440. [f. Thole *sb.* + Pin *sb.*] = Thole *sb.*

‖**Tholus** (þōᵘ·lǒs). *Pl.* **tholi** (-əi). Also in Gr. form **tholos** (þǫ·lǫs), *pl.* **tholoi** (-oi). 1644. [L. – Gr. θόλος a round building with a conical or vaulted roof.] *Arch.* A circular domed building or structure; a dome, cupola; a lantern. **b.** *Gr. Antiq.* An excavated circular tomb of the Mycenæan age, domed and lined with masonry 1885.

Thomæan (tomī·ǎn), *a.* and *sb.* 1727. [app. f. med.L. *Thomæus* (f. the name *Thomas*) + -an.] **A.** *adj.* Of or pertaining to the Christian church traditionally said to have been founded by St. Thomas the Apostle, which has existed from early times on the Malabar coast. **B.** *sb.* A member of this church.

Thomas (tǫ·măs). OE. [– late L. *Thomas,* eccl. Gr. Θωμᾶς.] **1.** A Greek, Latin, and common Christian name: well known as that of the 'doubting apostle' (see John 20:25), and hence used allus.; also used as a representative proper name for one of the populace taken at random. Abbrev. Tom, Tommy. **2.** Generic name for a footman or waiter 1846. **3. Thomas Atkins** (also *Thomas*): a familiar name for the typical private soldier in the British Army; arising out of the casual use of this name in the specimen forms of the official regulations. (Now more popularly Tommy Atkins or Tommy.) 1815.
1. Doubting Thomases, who will only believe what they see 1883.

Thomism (tōᵘ·miz'm). 1727. [f. prec. + -ism.] *Theol.* The doctrines of Thomas Aquinas or of the Thomists.

Thomist (tōᵘ·mist), *sb.* (*a.*) 1533. [– med.L. *Thomista* (Wyclif), f. *Thomas*; see -ist.] *Eccl.* A follower of Thomas Aquinas (known as 'The Angelical Doctor'), a scholastic philosopher and theologian of the 13th c. Also *attrib.* or as *adj.* Hence **Thomi·stic, -al** *adjs.* of or pertaining to the Thomists or their doctrines.

Thomite (tōᵘ·məit). *rare.* 1727. [f. Thomas + -ite¹ 1.] = Thomæan *sb.*

Thomsenolite (tǫ·msĕnolǝit). 1868. [Named after Dr. Julius *Thomsen* of Copenhagen; see -lite.] *Min.* Hydrous fluoride of aluminium, calcium, and sodium, found with pachnolite on the cryolite of Greenland.

Thomsen's (tǫ·msənz) **disease.** 1890. [Named after Dr. *Thomsen* of Schleswig-Holstein, who first described it.] *Path.* A peculiar congenital affection characterized by inability to relax the muscles immediately after contraction.

Thomsonian (tǫmsōᵘ·niǎn), *a.* (*sb.*) 1833. [f. the proper name *Thomson* + -ian.] **1.** Of or pertaining to the system of medicine practised by Dr. Samuel Thomson, of Massachusetts (1769–1843). Also as *sb.,* one who follows this system. **2.** Of, pertaining to, or characteristic of the poet James Thomson, author of 'The Seasons' 1890. Hence **Thomso·nianism,** the T. medical system.

Thomsonite (tǫ·msənəit). 1820. [Named after Dr. Thomas *Thomson* (1773–1852), professor of chemistry at Glasgow; see -ite¹ 2 b.] *Min.* Hydrous silicate of aluminium, calcium, and sodium, found often in fibrous radiated masses, white to reddish-brown in colour; = Comptonite.

Thong (þǫŋ). [OE. *þwang, þwong* = OFris. *thwang,* MLG. *dwank* constraint, OHG. *dwang* rein (G. *zwang* compulsion), f. Gmc. **þwaŋg-.*] A narrow strip of hide or leather, for use as a lace, cord, band, strap, or the like. **b.** Such a strip used as an instrument of flagellation; also as the lash of a whip; hence *spec.* a whip-lash of plaited hide 1592.
Thongs of raw hide 1867. **b.** Man's coltish disposition asks the t. Cowper.

Thong (þǫŋ), *v.* ME. [f. prec.] **1.** *trans.* To furnish with a thong; to fasten or secure with a thong or thongs; to bind with thongs. **2.** To flog or lash with a thong 1746.

Thooid (þōᵘ·oid), *a.* (*sb.*) 1880. [irreg. f. Thos or Thous + -oid.] *Zool.* Resembling in form, or related to, the sub-genus *Thous*; in an extended sense applied to a division of the genus *Canis* including the wolf, dog, and jackal; as dist. from the alopecoid, typified by the fox. **B.** *sb.* A beast of this division.

Thor (þǭɹ). OE. [– ON. *þórr*; see Thunder, Thursday.] The Scandinavian god of thunder, whose weapon was a hammer; his belt doubled his strength; hence in allusive use.

Thoraci- (þoræ·si), comb. form of L. *thorax, -ac-,* in same sense as Thoraco-; as in **Thora·ciform** *a.,* thorax-shaped.

Thoracic (þoræ·sik), *a.* (*sb.*) 1656. [– med.L. *thoracicus* – Gr. θωρακικός, f. θώραξ, θωρακ- Thorax; see -ic.] **1.** *Anat.* Of, pertaining to, or contained in the thorax; pectoral. **b.** Pertaining to, attached to, or forming part of the thorax (of an insect or crustacean) 1817. **2.** *Ichthyol.* Having the ventral fins situated directly beneath the pectoral; belonging to the *Thoracici,* the third order of fishes in the Linnæan system 1769. **3.** Having a thorax (as a distinguishing character); belonging to the *Thoracica,* a sub-order of cirripeds, in which the body consists of six thoracic segments, with a rudimentary abdomen 1891. **4.** As a specific distinction in *Nat. Hist.*: Having the thorax conspicuously marked or coloured 1812. **B.** *sb.* †**1.** A medicine acting on the thorax; a pectoral –1710. **2.** A thoracic fish: see 2 above 1828.

‖**Thoraco-** (þorēⁱ·ko), bef. a vowel **thorac-,** comb. form of Gr. θώραξ, θωρακ- Thorax.
Thoracente·sis, ‖**Thoracocentesis** (-sentī·sis) [Gr. κέντησις pricking], the perforation of the chest-wall to draw off morbid accumulations of fluid. **Thoracometer** (-kǫ·mĭtəɹ), an apparatus for measuring the movement of the chest-wall in respiration; a stethometer. **Thoraco·scopy,** the sounding or exploration of the chest. **Thoraco·stracous** [Gr. ὄστρακον hard shell] *a.,* of or pertaining to the *Thoracostraca,* a division of crustaceans, having a cephalothoracic shield and (usu.) stalked eyes. **Thoraco·tomy** [Gr. τομή cutting], incision into the thorax.

Thorax (þōᵊ·ræks). *Pl.* **tho·raxes** (*rare*), or in L. form **thoraces** (þorēⁱ·sīz). late ME. [– L. *thorax* – Gr. θώραξ breast-plate, breast, chest.] **1.** *Anat.* and *Zool.* That part of the body of a mammal between the neck and the abdomen, comprising the cavity enclosed by the ribs, breast-bone, and dorsal vertebræ, and containing the chief organs of circulation and respiration; the chest; also, the corresponding part in the lower vertebrates, as birds, serpents, and fishes. **2.** *Zool.* The middle region of the body of an arthropod, between the head and the abdomen 1750. ‖**3.** *Gr. Antiq.* A cuirass, corselet 1842.

‖**Thoria** (þōᵊ·riă). 1847. [f. as THORIUM + *-a*, after *alumina, silica*, etc.] *Chem.* An oxide of thorium, ThO_2, important in the manufacture of incandescent gas mantles.

Thorianite (þōᵊ·riănəit). 1904. [f. *thorian (f. THORIA) + -ITE¹ 2b.] The mineral consisting chiefly of the oxides of thorium, uranium, and other rare metals, found in the south-west of Ceylon in small brownish-black crystals having a resinous lustre; a variety of pitch-blende.

Thorite (þōᵊ·rəit). 1832. [– Sw. *thorit* (Berzelius 1828–9), f. *Thor* (as in *thorium*) + -ITE¹ 2b.] *Min.* Hydrous silicate of thorium, occurring crystalline, massive, and compact, orange-yellow (ORANGITE) to brownish-black or black, with a vitreous or resinous lustre.

‖**Thorium** (þōᵊ·riŏm). 1832. [– THOR, the Norse deity + -IUM (Berzelius, 1828–9).] *Chem.* A rare metallic element discovered by Berzelius in the mineral thorite, and subseq. found in small quantities in some other rare minerals. Symbol Th. (Now noted as one of the radio-active elements.)

Thorn (þǭɹn), *sb.* [OE. *þorn* = OS. *thorn* (Du. *doorn*), (O)HG. *dorn*, ON. *þorn*, Goth. *þaurnus* :– IE. **trnus*.] **I. 1.** A stiff, sharp-pointed, straight or curved woody process on the stem or other part of a plant; a spine, a prickle. **2.** *fig.* (or in fig. context): Anything that causes pain, grief, or trouble ME. **3.** A spine or spiny process in an animal ME.

1. Flours of all hue, and without T. the Rose MILT. **2.** Phr. *A t. in the flesh* or *side*, a source of continual grief, trouble, or annoyance. (*To be, sit, stand, walk*) *upon thorns*, (to be, etc.) in a painful state of anxiety or suspense.

II. 1. A plant which bears thorns or prickles; a bramble or brier; a prickly bush, shrub, or tree; a thorn-tree or thorn-bush; esp. any species of the genus *Cratægus*; in England, *spec.* the Hawthorn or White-thorn (*C. oxyacantha*) OE. **b.** (*without article*). Thorn bushes or branches collectively; also, the wood of a thorn-tree ME. **c.** *fig.* (occas. alluding to Matt. 13:7). ME. **2.** With qualifying words used to distinguish species and varieties of *Cratægus*, and to designate various other thorny plants. See BLACK-THORN, BOX-*t.*, WHITETHORN, etc. 1731.

1. Do briers bringe forth figges, and thorns grapes? 1545. **b.** It pricks like thorne SHAKS. **c.** I fall upon the thorns of life! I bleed! SHELLEY.

III. The name of the Old English and Icelandic runic letter þ (= th); named, like other runes, from the word of which it was the initial OE.

attrib. and *Comb.*: **t.-bill**, a humming bird of the S. Amer. genus *Rhamphomicron*; **-bird**, a S. Amer. bird, *Anumbius acuticaudatus*, which builds a large domed nest of thorny twigs; **-devil**, an Australian lizard, = MOLOCH 2; **-head, -headed worm** one of the *Acanthocephala*, intestinal parasitic worms having the proboscis furnished with hooks or spines; **-hopper**, a tree-hopper, *Thelia cratægi*, which frequents thorny shrubs; **-tail**, pop. name of the humming-birds of the S. Amer. genus *Gouldia*, distinguished by a long pointed tail.

Thorn (þǭɹn), *v.* Now *rare*. 1483. [f. prec.] **1.** *trans.* To make thorny, to furnish with thorns; *esp.* to protect (a newly planted quick-set hedge or the like) with dead thorn-bushes. **2.** To prick with or as with a thorn; to vex 1590.

2. I am the only rose of all the stock That never thorn'd him TENNYSON.

Tho·rn-a:pple. 1578. The common name of *Datura stramonium*, of the family *Solanaceæ*, a coarse annual plant bearing large four-celled capsules covered with prickly spines; also, the capsule or fruit itself.

Thornback (þǭ·ɹnbæk). ME. **1.** The common ray or skate (*Raia clavata*) of British seas, distinguished by having several rows of short sharp spines arranged along the back and tail. **2.** Short for *t. crab* 1891. †**3.** An old maid (*slang*) –1709.

attrib.: **t. crab**, a species of spider-crab or sea-spider, *Maia squinado*, called also in U.S. king-crab; **t. ray** = sense 1.

Tho·rn-bush. ME. Any bush that bears thorns; e.g. a hawthorn, a bramble.

Tho·rn-hedge. 1560. A hedge of thorny shrubs; *spec.* a hedge composed of hawthorn 'sets'.

Thornless (þǭ·ɹnlės), *a.* 1776. [f. THORN *sb.* + -LESS.] Free from thorns; without a thorn.

One of those Whose love has prov'd a t. rose! 1803.

Tho·rn-tree. 1483. A tree having or bearing thorns; in Great Britain, usu. a hawthorn tree.

attrib.: **t. fly**, a March trout-fly.

Thorny (þǭ·ɹni), *a.* [OE. *þorniġ*; see THORN *sb.*, -Y¹.] **1.** Abounding in, characterized by, or consisting of thorns or spines; spiny, prickly. **b.** Of an animal (or a part of one): Having thorn-like organs or appendages; spiny 1711. **2.** Overgrown with thorns or brambles OE. **3.** *fig.* Pricking or piercing to the mind; painful, distressing; harassing, vexatious, irritating ME. **b.** Full of points of contention or difficulty; delicate, ticklish 1653. **4.** In the names of species or varieties of plants, animals, or shells, characterized by having thorns or spines 1578.

1. Daphne roming through a thornie wood SHAKS. **2.** *T. ground*, fig. after the parable of the sower, *Matt.* 13:7, etc. **3.** The t. point Of bare distresse, hath tane from me the shew Of smooth ciuility SHAKS. **b.** I have finally arranged a t. transaction SCOTT. Hence **Tho·rnily** *adv.* **Tho·rniness.**

Thoro- (þōᵊ·ro), comb. form of THORIUM, in names of compound salts, minerals, etc., e.g. **Thorogu·mmite** *Min.*, a hydrated thoro-silicate of uranium.

Thorough (þɒ·rŏ, þɒ·rə), *prep.* and *adv.* Chiefly *arch.* or *Obs.* [Disyllabic development, *þuruh*, of OE. *þurh* THROUGH, paralleled in *borough, furrow, marrow, sorrow*.] **I.** *prep.* **1.** From side to side or end to end of. **2.** Along (to any distance) within. Without implication of traversing from end to end. OE. **3.** Over the whole extent of, in or to all parts of; throughout OE. **4.** From beginning to end of a space of time OE. **5.** Indicating intermediation, means, agency, instrumentality OE.

1. You ryde thorowe streetes, and townes 1540. **2.** He wente þorow a foreste fowre longe myle 1430. **3.** O'er hilly path and open Strath We'll wander Scotland t. WORDSW. **5.** Not thorow thy swerde, ner thorow thy bowe COVERDALE *Josh.* 24:12.

II. *adv.* (Now *arch.* or *dial.*) **1.** = THROUGH *adv.* 1, 2. *arch.* OE. **2.** Qualifying pa. pple. or adj.; = THROUGH *adv.* 4. a. *Obs.* or *dial.* ME.

1. The future hides in it Gladness and sorrow; We press still thorow CARLYLE. **2.** He had a t. good opinion of himself GOLDSM.

Thorough (þɒ·rŏ, þɒ·rə), *adj.* and *sb.* 1489. [attrib. use of prec. adv.] **A.** *adj.* **1.** Used chiefly with sbs. of action or position, being a kind of ellipt. use of the adv. = 'going, passing, or extending through'. *Obs.* exc. in special applications. **2. a.** Of an action, etc.: Carried out through the whole of something; thorough-going; fully executed; affecting every part or detail. Hence *gen.* That is fully what is expressed by the noun. 1489. **b.** of a person in ref. to his action or quality 1655.

2. a. A t. knowledge of the world GOLDSM. **b.** The . .most t. gentleman I ever saw LYTTON.

B. *sb.* [Ellipt. or absol. uses of THOROUGH *a.* or *adv.*] **1.** Thorough-going action or policy: in *Eng. Hist.* (with capital T) applied to that of Strafford and Laud in the reign of Charles I, and sometimes to that of Cromwell as Lord Protector 1634. **2.** *Agric.* A furrow; *water-t.*, a 'thorough' made for surface-draining; a water-furrow 1733.

1. And for the state, indeed, my lord, I am for T. LAUD.

Thorough- in combination.

1. With verbs, pples., or adjs.: **tho·rough-bind** *v., trans.* to bind or fasten (a wall, etc.) by a stone or iron, passing through from side to side; **-drain** *v., trans.* to drain (a field) by means of water-thoroughs; **-felt** *pa. pple.*, felt throughout; **-ripe (throu·gh-ripe)** *a.*, ripe throughout, thoroughly ripe. **2.** With sbs. or derived adjs.: **tho·rough-band (throu·gh-band)**, a stone, etc., extending through the breadth of a wall or dyke so as to bind the sides together; **-draught (throu·gh-draught)**, a draught or current of air passing through a room, etc.; **-edged** *a.*, thoroughly or perfectly edged; keen-edged; **-hearted** *a.*, whole-hearted; entirely devoted; **-winded** *a.* (of a horse) sound in 'wind'; not broken-winded.

Thoroughbass (þɒ·rŏbēˈs). 1662. [f. THOROUGH *prep.* or *adv.* + BASS *sb.*⁵] *Mus.* A bass part extending through a piece of music, and written by itself, with figures indicating the chords or harmonies to be played with it; a figured bass, *basso continuo*; *esp.* (formerly) an accompaniment thus written or played; hence *loosely*, an accompaniment in general. Also, the method of indicating harmonies by a figured bass, or the art of playing from it; *loosely*, the science of harmony in general. ¶**b.** *erron.* A loud or deep bass 1749.

Thoroughbrace (þɒ·rŏbrēˈs). *U.S.* 1837. [f. THOROUGH *prep.* or *adv.* + BRACE *sb.*²] Each of a pair of strong braces or bands of leather connecting the front and back C-springs and supporting the body of a coach or other vehicle. Hence **Tho·roughbraced** *a.*

Thoroughbred (þɒ·rŏbred), *a.* (*sb.*) [f. THOROUGH *adv.* + BRED *ppl. a.*] **1.** Thoroughly educated or accomplished; hence, complete, thorough, out-and-out. (Now regarded as *fig.* from 2.) **2.** Of a horse: Of pure breed or stock; *spec.* applied to a race-horse whose pedigree for a given number of generations is recorded in the stud-book. Also of a dog, bull, etc. 1796. **b.** *transf.* Applied to human beings or their attributes, usu. implying grace, distinction, or the like 1820.

2. b. More thorough-bred or fairer fingers BYRON.

B. *sb.* **1.** A thoroughbred animal, esp. a horse 1842. **2.** *transf.* and *fig.* A well-born, well-bred, or thoroughly trained person. Also, a first-rate motor-car, bicycle, etc. 1894.

1. I can't afford a t., and hate a cock-tail THACKERAY.

Thoroughfare (þɒ·rŏfēᵊɹ), *sb.* (*a.*) [In late ME. *thurghfare*, f. *þurh*, *þuruh* THROUGH + FARE *sb.*¹] **1.** A passage or way through. **a.** *gen.* †**b.** *spec.* A town through which traffic passes; a town on a highway or line of traffic –1829. **c.** A public way unobstructed and open at both ends; *esp.* a main road or street, a highway 1540. **d.** A piece of water, as a strait or river, affording passage for ships, etc.; an unobstructed channel 1699. **2.** The action of going or passing through, or the condition of being passed through or traversed; passage. Now *rare* or *Obs.* 1667. **3.** *attrib.* or *adj.* That is a t.; passed or travelled through by traffic; chiefly in *t. town* = sense 1 b. 1553.

1. a. This world nys but a thurghfare ful of wo, And we been pilgrymes, passynge to and fro CHAUCER. Phr. *No t.*, no public way through or right of way here. **c.** The Strand, that goodly thorow-fare betweene The Court and City 1658. **2.** Ye. .have. .made one Realm Hell and this World, one Realm, one Continent Of easie thorough-fare MILT.

Thoroughgoing (þɒ·rŏgōᵘ:iŋ), *a.* 1819. [f. THOROUGH *adv.* + *going*, pr. pple. of GO *v.*] Going the full length; doing things thoroughly; acting with completeness; uncompromising, thorough, extreme, out-and-out. (Of persons, actions, etc.) Hence **Tho·roughgo·ingly** *adv.*, **-ness.**

Tho·rough-light. Now *rare* or *Obs.* 1605. **a.** *pl.* Windows on opposite sides of a room, so that the light passes right through 1625. **b.** *fig.* (*sing.* and *pl.*) in ref. to the 'light' of knowledge or discovery. So **Tho·rough-lighted** *a.* having thorough-lights.

Thoroughly (þɒ·rŏli), *adv.* ME. [f. THOROUGH *adv.* or *adj.* + -LY².] †**1.** In a way that penetrates or goes through; right through, quite through (*rare*) –1703. **2.** In a thorough manner or degree; in every part or detail; fully, completely, entirely, perfectly 1473.

Thoroughness (þɒ·rŏnės). 1843. [f. THOROUGH *a.* + -NESS.] The quality of being thorough or of doing things thoroughly; the condition of being done thoroughly; completeness.

Thorough-paced (þɒ·rŏ,pēˈst), *a.* 1646. [f. THOROUGH *adv.* + PACED.] †**1.** *lit.* Of a horse: Thoroughly trained; having all his paces (*rare*) –1668. **2.** *fig.* Thoroughly trained or accomplished, perfectly skilled or versed (*in* something); hence, thoroughgoing, complete, perfect, thorough 1646.

2. A thoro'-pac'd villain 1710. A hearty t. liar LAMB.

Thorough-pin (þɒ·rŏ,pin). 1789. [f. THOROUGH- + PIN *sb.*¹] *Farriery.* A swelling in the sheath of the tendon of the flexor perforans muscle in a horse's hock, appearing on both sides so as to suggest a pin passing through; also a similar swelling in the carpal joint of the fore-leg.

Tho·rough-stitch, throu·gh-stitch, *sb.*, *adv.* and *adj.* *Obs.* exc. *dial.* 1569. [f. THOROUGH *adv.* + STITCH *sb.*] †**A.** *sb.* A stitch drawn right through the stuff; hence *fig.* in ref. to thoroughness of action (*rare*) –1663. **B.** *adv.* Right through, through to the end; thoroughly; completely 1579.

Phr. *To go t.* (*with*), to perform something thoroughly, go through with; 'a tailor's expression for finishing any thing once begun'; The..Cheif Justice Jefferies..went thorough stitch in that tribunal EVELYN.

†**C.** *adj.* Thoroughgoing, out-and-out –1828.

Thoroughwax (þʊ·rŏwæks). 1548. [f. THOROUGH *prep.* and *adv.* + WAX *v.* grow; from the branches appearing to grow through the leaves.] The umbelliferous herb *Bupleurum rotundifolium*, also called *hare's ear*, having roundish-oval perfoliate leaves, and small greenish-yellow flowers with conspicuous bracts.

Thoroughwort (þʊ·rŏwɒ̈ɹt). 1828. [f. THOROUGH *prep.* or *adv.* + WORT[1], after prec.] A N. Amer. composite plant, *Eupatorium perfoliatum*, having connate-perfoliate leaves and large corymbs of numerous white flowers; also called *boneset* or *crosswort*.

Thorp (þǭɹp). *arch.* and *Hist.* Also **thorpe.** [OE. *þrop*, occas. (prob. from ON.) *þorp* = OFris., OS. *thorp* (Du. *dorp*), (O)HG. *dorf* village, ON. *þorp* hamlet, farmstead, Goth. *þaurp* field, 'land' (ἀγρός) :- Gmc. **þurpam*; of unkn. origin.] A hamlet, village, or small town; in ME. *esp.* an agricultural village. (A frequent second element in place-names in the forms *-thorpe*, *-thrup*, *-trup*, chiefly in the Danelaw district.)

Within a little thorpe I staid at last 1600. I hurry down..By twenty thorps, a little town, And half a hundred bridges TENNYSON.

‖**Thos** (þōᵘs). *Pl.* **thoes** (þōᵘ·īz). 1601. [L. – Gr. θώς, pl. θῶες, beast of prey of the dog kind. Cf. THOUS, THOOID.] The Gr. and L. name of a beast of the canine group; probably a jackal of some species.

Those (ðōᵘz), *dem. pron.* and *adj.* (*pl.*) [OE. *þās*, ME. (southern) *þōs*, pl. of THIS; from XIV, first in northern and later in midland and southern speech, pl. of dem. pron. and adj. THAT; repl. THO *dem. pron.* and *adj.*, which remained in literary use till XVI, and survives in Sc. and north. dial. as *thae*.] **I.** Demonstrative pronoun. †**1.** = THESE *pron.* –ME. **2.** Pl. of THAT: indicating things or persons pointed to or already mentioned ME. **b.** Preceded by *and*, introducing an additional qualification of the things or persons mentioned in the previous clause 1545. **3.** In opposition to *these*; sometimes *spec.* = 'the former'. Also in contrast to (*the*) *others*. 1611. **4.** As antecedent pronoun, followed by a defining word or phrase ME. **II.** Demonstrative adjective. †**1.** Pl. of THIS II; = THESE *adj.* –ME. **2.** Pl. of THAT I. 1, 1 b. ME. **b.** Used instead of *that* with a sing. noun of multitude (now only with collectives in pl. sense, as *clergy*, *horse*, *vermin*); and esp. with *kind*, *sort*, followed by *of* with pl. sb. 1560. **3.** In opposition to *these*; pl. of THAT II. 2. 1641. **4.** In concord with a noun which is the antecedent to a relative, or which is further defined by a participle ME. **5.** = Such; pl. of THAT II. 4. Now *rare*. 1605.

2. Thy lips, t. kissing cherries SHAKS. Binde vp t. tresses SHAKS. A noted family in t. parts 1741. **b.** You, and t. poore number saued with you SHAKS. The little regard shown..to t. sort of things H. WALPOLE. **5.** He spoke of you in t. terms that make me glad that I have met the son DISRAELI.

Thou (þau), *sb.* 1869. A colloq. and familiar abbrev. of *thousand*, esp. = a thousand pounds (sterling).

Thou (ðau), *pers. pron.* 2nd *sing. nom.* [OE. *þū* = OFris., OS. *thū* (LG. *du*), OHG. *dū* (G. *du*), ON. *þú*, Goth. *þu* :- Gmc. repr. of IE. **tū*, whence also L., OIr., Av. *tū*, Gr. (Doric) τύ, Attic σύ, etc. See also THEE, THINE, THY.]

1. The pronoun by which a person (or thing) is addressed, in the nom. (or voc.) sing.; the pronoun denoting the person or thing spoken to.

Thou and its cases *thee, thine, thy* were in OE. used in ordinary speech; in ME. they were gradually superseded by the pl. *ye, you, your, yours*, in addressing a superior, and (later) an equal, but were long retained in addressing an inferior. Long retained by Quakers in addressing a single person, though now less general. In general English used in addressing God or Christ, also in homiletic language, and in poetry, apostrophe, and elevated prose.

b. Used in apposition to and preceding a sb. in the vocative; in reproach or contempt often emphasized by being placed or repeated after the sb. OE. **2.** as *sb.* **a.** The person or 'self' of the individual addressed 1693. **b.** The word itself; see also THEE *pron.* 4. 1655.

1. T., O God, art praysed in Sion COVERDALE *Ps.* 64[65]:1. Good t., saue mee a piece of Marchpane SHAKS. **b.** T. lyest, t. jesting Monkey t. SHAKS. **2. b.** They also used the plain language of T. and Thee to a single person PENN.

Thou (ðau), *v.* 1440. [f. prec. Cf. THEE *v.*[2]] *trans.* and *intr.* To use the pronoun 'thou' to a person: familiarly, to an inferior, in contempt or insult, or as done on principle by Quakers.

She [a Quakeress] thou'd him [the king] all along PEPYS. In this country 'thouing' is a lost art 1883.

Though (ðōᵘ), *adv.* and *conj.* [ME. *þōh* (in Orm. *þohh*) – **þóh*, prehistoric form of ON. *þó* (ON. *þau*), earlier **þauh* = OE. *þēah* (whence ME. *þeh*, etc., *þah*, *þauh*, which were obs. before 1500), OFris. *thāch*, OS. *thoh* (Du. *doch*), OHG. *doh* (G. *doch*), Goth. *þauh* or, yet; Gmc. advb. formation on base **þa-* THE, THAT + (in Goth. *-uh*) the particle repr. by L. *-que*, Gr. τέ, Skr. *ca* and.] An adversative particle expressing that relation of two opposed facts or circumstances (actual or hypothetical) in which the one is inadequate to prevent the other, and therefore both concur, contrary to what might be expected. **I.** *adv.* For all that; in spite of that; nevertheless, howbeit, however, yet. Now *colloq.*

Your hands then mine, are quicker for a fray, My legs are longer t. to runne away SHAKS. It did its duty, t. BROWNING.

II. *conj.* (or *conjunctive adv.*) **1.** Introducing a subordinate clause expressing a fact: Notwithstanding that; in spite of the fact that, although OE. **b.** With ellipsis of the subordinate clause 1592. **2.** Introducing a subordinate clause expressing a supposition or possibility: Even if; even supposing that; granting that OE. **b.** With ellipsis (as in 1 b) 1591. **3.** Introducing an additional statement restricting or modifying the preceding: And yet, but yet, but still, however ME. **4.** †**a.** After neg. or interrog. phrases with *wonder, marvel, be sorry, care*, etc., where *if* or *that* is now substituted –1637. **b.** In phr. *as though*: as if; as would or might be the case if; so as to suggest the supposition that ME. **5.** With special constructions (in sense 1, 2, or 3). †**a.** Followed by *that* –1711. **b.** Strengthened by *all*, following or preceding. *Obs.* exc. in comb. ALTHOUGH. Also by *even* preceding. ME.

1. The hone Gives edge to razors, t. itself has none 1746. The French..are very civil, thof I don't understand their lingo SMOLLETT. **b.** The base (t. bitter) disposition of Beatrice SHAKS. **2.** T. he slaye me, yet wyll I put my trust in hym BIBLE (Great) *Job* 13:15. **b.** T. nere so blacke, say they haue Angells faces SHAKS. **4. a.** He cares not t. the Church sinke 1637. **b.** I'faith, Ile eate nothing: I thanke you as much as t. I did SHAKS. **5. a.** *Lear* IV. vi. 219. **b.** Nor, even t. it be told to her, can she enter into it 1856.

Thought (þǭt), *sb.* [repr. OE. *þōht*, *ġeþōht* = OS. *githāht* (Du. *gedachte*), OHG. *gidāht* :- Gmc. **ȝaþanχt-*, f. **þaŋkjan* THINK; cf. synon. ON. *þótti, þóttr*, Goth. *þūhtus*, f. **þuŋχt-*.] **1.** The action or process of thinking; mental action or activity in general, esp. that of the intellect; exercise of the mental faculty; formation and arrangement of ideas in the mind. **b.** Thinking as a permanent characteristic or condition; the capacity of thinking; the thinking faculty OE. **c.** The product of mental action or effort; what one thinks; that which is in the mind ME. **d.** In a collective sense (with defining adj.): What is or has been thought by the thinkers of a specified class, time, or place 1853. **2.** (with *a* and *pl.*) A single act or product of thinking; an item of mental activity; something that one thinks or has thought; a thing that is in the mind; an idea, notion OE. **b.** *spec.* An idea suggested or recalled to the mind; a reflection, a consideration ME. **3.** In various specialized senses (from 1 and 2). **a.** Consideration, attention, heed, care, regard ME. **b.** Meditation, mental contemplation ME. **c.** Conception, imagination, fancy ME. **d.** The entertaining of some project in the mind; the idea or notion of doing something, as contemplated or entertained in the mind; hence, intention, purpose, design; *esp.* an imperfect or half-formed intention. Also in *pl.*, as *to have thoughts* (*of*). ME. **e.** Remembrance, 'mind'. *Obs.* or merged in general sense. ME. **f.** Mental anticipation, expectation ME. **g.** An opinion or judgement; a belief or supposition; what one thinks of or about a thing or person 1596. **4.** Anxiety or distress of mind; solicitude; grief, care, vexation. *Obs.* exc. *dial.* ME. **5.** A very small amount, a very little, a trifle. (Usu., now always, adverbial.) 1581.

1. Whether Brutes are capable of t.? 1704. **b.** Had he bin where he thought, By this had t. bin past SHAKS. **c.** Thus Bethel spoke, who always speaks his t. POPE. **d.** The leaders of scientific t. 1884. **2.** Good Thoughts in Bad Times FULLER. One scarce can say..That he even gave it a t. BROWNING. Phr. *Second thoughts*, ideas occurring subsequently; later and maturer consideration; so *first thoughts*. **b.** *Rich II*, V. v. 28. **3. a.** Evil is wrought by want of T., As well as want of Heart! HOOD. Phr. *To take t.*, to consider, meditate (how to do something, etc.). **b.** She was lost in t. (*mod.*). **c.** O change beyond report, t., or belief! MILT. **d.** I do begin to haue bloody thoughts SHAKS. **g.** My first t. was, he lied in every word BROWNING. **4.** Therfore take no t. saynge what shall we eate? TINDALE *Matt.* 6:31. **5.** I like the new tire ..if the haire were a t. browner SHAKS.

attrib. and *Comb.*: **t.-executing** *a.*, (*a*) in *Lear*, 'doing execution with the swiftness of t.'; (*b*) executing the t. or intention of a person; †**-sick** *a.*, sick with 't.' or thinking; **-transfer, -transference** (*Psychics*), transference or communication of t. from one mind to another apart from the ordinary channels of sense; telepathy; **-wave,** (*a*) *Psychics*, a 'wave' or undulation of a hypothetical medium of t.-transference; (*b*) a 'wave' or impulse of t. passing simultaneously through a crowd of persons or other living beings.

Thought (þǭt), pa. t. and pple. of THINK *v.*[1] and [2].

Thoughted (þǭ·tĕd), *a.* 1592. [f. THOUGHT *sb.* + -ED[2].] Having thoughts (of a specified kind).

Thoughtful (þǭ·tfŭl), *a.* ME. [f. THOUGHT *sb.* + -FUL.] **1.** Full of or characterized by thought; meditative, contemplative; preoccupied in mind. Also *transf.* of personal attributes, actions, etc. **b.** Disposed to think about or consider matters; reflective; †heedful or mindful *of*. Also *transf.* Characterized by thought or reflection. ME. †**2.** Full of mental trouble; anxious; sorrowful; melancholy, moody –1744. **3.** Showing thought or consideration for others; considerate 1851.

1. War, horrid war, your t. walks invades POPE. **b.** T. persons..had heard of these doings with uneasiness FROUDE. Not beyond the reach of t. enquiry 1884. **2.** The merry soul is freer from intended mischief than the t. man 1627. Hence **Thou·ghtful-ly** *adv.*, **-ness.**

Thoughtless (þǭ·tlĕs), *a.* 1592. [f. as prec. + -LESS.] **1.** Not taking thought; unreflecting, heedless, imprudent. **b.** With *of* or dependent clause: Not thinking; unmindful; heedless; unsuspecting. Now *rare*. 1615. †**c.** Free from care or anxiety –1789. **d.** Inconsiderate 1794. **2.** Deficient in or lacking thought; not given to thinking; stupid; destitute of ideas. Now *rare*. 1682. †**b.** Of inanimate things: Devoid of thought –1705.

1. Youth may be alleged as an excuse for rashness and folly, as being naturally t. 1736. **c.** The t. day, the easy night GRAY. **d.** Little fly, Thy summer's play My t. hand Has brush'd away BLAKE. **2.** An earnest thinker in a t. time 1879. Hence **Thou·ghtless-ly** *adv.*, **-ness.**

Thought-out (þǭt,aut; stress variable), *ppl. a.* 1870. [pa. pple. of *think out* used as adj.] Elaborated, constructed, or arrived at by thinking or mental labour; thoroughly considered.

Thou·ght-reading, *sb.* 1855. The reading of another person's thoughts; direct perception by one mind of what is passing in another, independent of ordinary means of expression or communication; a power alleged to be possessed by certain persons or by persons in certain psychic states. So **Thou·ght-rea:der. Thou·ght-rea:ding** *a.*

‖**Thous** (þōᵘ·ɒs). 1839. [mod.L., irreg. – Gr. θώς, θωός; see THOS.] *Zool.* A species or group of beasts of the extended genus *Canis*, canine beasts, natives of Africa and Asia; including *Thous* (or *Canis*) *anthus* (the North African Jackal), and *T. mesomelas, variegatus,* and *senegalensis*, African jackals.

Thousand (þau·zənd), *sb.* and *a.* [OE. *þūsend* = OFris. *thūsend*, OS. *thūsundig*, OHG. *thū-, dūsunt* (Du. *duizend*, G. *tausend*), ON. *þúsund*, Goth. *þūsundi* :– Gmc. **þūsundi*, cogn. with Balto-Sl. **tūssntjā*.] **1.** The cardinal number equal to ten times one hundred: denoted by the symbols 1000 or M (for L. *mille*), formerly often by m̄ or ᵐ, as xxxᵐ. **a.** As sb. or quasi-sb., with pl. (*a*) In sing. Usu. *a t.*, emphatically or precisely *one t.* OE. (*b*) In pl. *thousands* OE. (*c*) After another numeral the sing. is now commonly used as a collective pl. OE. (*d*) As a sb. it takes after it *of*, repr. the OE. genitive pl. Now after a numeral only as a unit of quantity by which things are sold. OE. **b.** As adj. or quasi-adj., followed immediately by a pl. (or collective) noun OE. **2.** Often used vaguely or hyperbolically for a large number OE. **3.** Ellipt. uses. **a.** A thousand of some weight, measure, or quantity OE. **b.** A thousand pounds sterling 1547. †**4.** As ordinal: = THOUSANDTH –1680.

1. a. (*a*) A t. to one, they have..some gnawing care 1668. *One in a t.*, a paragon. (*b*) They amounted in all to some thousands 1771. (*d*) Thousands of arrobas were..obtained 1880. **b.** So many t. Christians..murdered 1650. **2.** You may do good to thousands 1779. **3. a.** Instead of looking twenty, he looked a t. THACKERAY. The price of gas..was 3*s.* 9*d.* per t. 1901. **b.** A man of two t. a yeere B. JONS.

Thousandfold (þau·zəndfōᵘld), *a.*, *adv.*, and *sb.* [OE. *þūsendfeald*; see prec., -FOLD.] **A.** *adj.* One thousand times as much or as many; consisting of a thousand parts; a thousand times repeated or multiplied. **B.** *adv.* A thousand times (in amount); a thousand times as much ME. **C.** *sb.* A thousand times the amount or number 1711.

Thousandth (þau·zəndþ), *a.* and *sb.* 1552. [f. THOUSAND + -TH².] The ordinal number belonging to the cardinal THOUSAND. **A.** *adj.* **1.** Coming last in order of a thousand successive individuals. **2.** *T. part*: one of a thousand equal parts into which anything may be divided 1561. **B.** *sb.* A thousandth part 1793.

Thraldom (þrǭ·ldəm). ME. [f. next + -DOM.] The state or condition of being a thrall; bondage, servitude; captivity.

In the midst of my thraldome in Turkie 1590. This t. to their pleasures YOUNG.

Thrall (þrǭl), *sb.* (*a.*) Now *arch.* or *Hist.* [OE. *þræl* (first in late Northumb.) – ON. *þræll*, perh. :– **þrahilaz*, f. Gmc. **þrah-* **þreh-* run; cf. Goth. *þragjan* run, OHG. *dregil, drigil* servant, (prop.) 'runner'.] **1.** One who is in bondage to a lord or master; a villein, serf, bondman, slave; also, a servant, subject; *transf.* one whose liberty is forfeit; a captive, prisoner of war. **b.** *fig.* A slave (*to* something) OE. **2.** The condition of a thrall; thraldom, bondage, servitude; captivity ME. †**3.** Oppression, trouble, distress –1829.

1. Outcast of Nature, Man! the wretched t. Of bitter-dropping sweat THOMSON. **b.** Slaues of drinke, and thralles of sleepe SHAKS. **2.** To bring this noble Realme of England to thraule 1592.

B. *adj.* [The sb. used attrib.] **1.** That is a thrall; subject, captive, enslaved, in bondage ME. †**2.** Belonging to or characteristic of thraldom; slave-like, slavish, servile –1535.

1. To be t. to no vice UDALL. We now are captives that made others t. HAYWOOD.

Thrall (þrǭl), *v. arch.* [Early ME. *þrallen*, f. prec.] *trans.* To bring into bondage or subjection; to deprive of liberty; to hold in thraldom, enthrall, enslave; to take or hold captive.

Thranite (þrēⁱ·nəit). 1842. [– Gr. θρανίτης, f. θρᾶνος bench.] *Gr. Antiq.* In the ancient trireme, a rower in one of the tiers, prob. the uppermost tier, which had the longest oars and hardest work.

Thrash, thresh (þræʃ, þreʃ), *v.* [ME. *threshe(n* (XII), continuing metathetic alt. of OE. *þersćan* (late OE. *þrescan, þryscan*) = MLG., MDu. *derschen* (LG., Du. *dorschen*), OHG. *dreskan* (G. *dreschen*), ON. *þreskja*, Goth. *þriskan*, f. Gmc. **þersk-* :– IE. **tersk-*, repr. in Balto-Sl. by words denoting 'crackle', 'crash', 'rattle'.] **I.** To **thresh** or **thrash** corn, etc. and directly derived senses. **1.** To separate by any mechanical means, e.g. rubbing, shaking, trampling, stamping, beating, or intermittent pressure, the grains of any cereal from the husks and straw; esp. by beating with a flail; now also by the action of revolving mechanism in a mill or machine. Also, to shake out or separate in the same way the seed of any plant. *trans.* and *absol.* or *intr.* **2.** *fig.*: in earlier use sometimes with ref. to ancient modes of threshing ME. **3.** *transf.* To beat or strike as with a flail. *trans.* and *intr.* 1573.

1. Afftir hervest..men thresshe shevys LYDG. First thrash the Corne, then after burne the straw SHAKS. **2.** Phr. *To t. straw*, to work at what is unproductive or unprofitable. *To t. out* (*a subject*, etc.), to discuss (a matter) exhaustively; to get at the truth of (a question) by discussion or argument. **3.** The angler goes on threshing the water 1867.

II. To beat a person, an army, etc. (Now commonly **thrash.**) **1.** *trans.* To beat by way of punishment; to chastise by or as by beating; to flog, orig. with a stick, cudgel, whip, etc.; in mod. use also to pommel with the fists OE. **2.** To beat completely or thoroughly; to overcome with severe loss in war or fighting, or *at* a game or contest 1606.

1. Take a good cudgel, and thrash him with it FIELDING. **2.** The Colonel..has just been thrashing me at billiards 1890.

II. Transf. uses. (Usually **thrash.**) **1.** *intr. Naut.* To force or work one's way against opposing wind, tide, etc. Also *trans.* with *way*. 1830. **b.** *trans.* To force (a ship) forward, esp. against contrary wind or sea 1886. **2.** *intr.* To make wild movements like those of a flail or whip; to lash out; to throw oneself (or itself) to and fro with violence; to toss, plunge; of hair, branches, or anything free at one end: to flap, whip, lash 1850.

1. Hard labour to..thrash for an hour through blocks of ice before we could get out 1830. **b.** The screw began to thrash the ship along the Docks KIPLING. **2.** [A whale] blindly thrashed and rolled about in great agony 1850.

Thrasher¹, thresher (þræ·ʃəɹ, þre·ʃəɹ). late ME. [f. prec. + -ER.¹] **1.** One who or that which thrashes or threshes grain; a threshing-machine. (More usu. spelt *thresher*.) **2.** A sea-fox or fox-shark, *Alopias vulpes*; so called from the very long upper division of the tail, with which it lashes an enemy. Also called *thresher-* or *thrasher-fish, -shark*. 1609. **3.** One who thrashes or beats another 1907.

Comb.: **t.-whale**, a grampus or killer, as *Orca gladiator*.

Thrasher² (þræ·ʃəɹ). 1808. [perh. a survival of *thrusher, thresher*, an Eng. dial. name of the THRUSH (*Turdus musicus*).] A bird of the N. Amer. genus *Harporhynchus*, resembling the Song Thrush; esp. *H.* (*Turdus*) *fuscus*, the best known of the species, of the north-eastern U.S., called also *brown t., brown thrush*.

Thra·shing-, thre·shing-floor. late ME. A prepared hard level surface on which corn is threshed.

Thra·shing-, thre·shing-machi:ne. 1797. A power-driven machine for separating grain or other seed from the straw or husk.

Thra·shing-, thre·shing-mill. 1797. A fixed threshing-machine; usually, one driven by water or wind power.

‖**Thraso** (þrēⁱ·so). *Pl.* **-os, -oes**, also as L., **Thrasones** (-ōᵘ·nīz). 1576. [L. *Thraso, -ōn-* – Gr. Θράσων, name of a braggart soldier in Terence's *Eunuchus*, f. θρασύς bold, spirited.] A braggart, a boaster.

Thrasonic (þrěsǫ·nik), *a.* 1657. [f. as next + -IC.] = next.

Thrasonical (þrěsǫ·nikăl), *a.* 1564. [f. L. *Thrason-*, THRASO + -ICAL.] Resembling Thraso or his behaviour; given to or marked by boasting; bragging, boastful, vainglorious.

Cesars Thrasonicall bragge of I came, saw, and ouercame SHAKS. Hence **Thraso·nically** *adv.*

Thrave, threave (þrēⁱv, þrīv). Chiefly *Sc.* and *north.* OE. [Of Scand. origin; cf. Icel. *þrefi*, MSw. *þrave*, Sw. *trafve*, Da. *trave*.] **1.** Two shocks or stooks of corn (or pulse), gen. containing twelve sheaves each, but varying in different localities; hence used as a measure of straw, fodder, etc. **2.** *transf.* and *fig.* A large number; a company; a multitude, a 'heap', a 'lot'. late ME.

2. Gallants..[have] beene seene to flock here In threaues B. JONS. Tidings..of a thrave of Jews newly converted 1656.

Thread (þred), *sb.* [OE. *þrǣd* = OS. *thrād*, OHG. *drāt* (Du. *draad*, G. *draht*), ON. *þráðr* :– Gmc. **þrǣðuz*, f. **þrǣ-* twist (see THROW).] **1.** A fine cord composed of the fibres or filaments of flax, cotton, wool, silk, etc. spun to a considerable length; *spec.* such a cord composed of two or more yarns, esp. of flax, twisted together; applied also to a similar product from glass, asbestos, a ductile metal, etc. **b.** The sacred thread with which Brahmins and Parsees are invested at initiation 1582. **2.** Each of the lengths of yarn which form the warp and woof of a woven fabric; hence, any one of these as an ultimate constituent of such a fabric, and thus of one's clothing; the least part of one's dress; esp. in the phr. *not a dry t. on one* ME. **b.** A lineal measure of yarn: the length of a coil of the reel, varying in amount according to the material, and also with the locality 1662. **c.** *fig.* A single element interwoven with others in any composite fabric, mental, moral, social, political, or the like 1836. **3.** Without *a*, as name of the substance of which the above-mentioned things are composed, or of these things taken in the mass; often with distinctive word, as *gold* or *silk t.*; sometimes *spec.* flaxen or linen thread as dist. from silk or cotton; in *pl.*, kinds of thread. late ME. †**b.** *fig.* The material or 'fibre' of which anything is composed; 'texture', quality, nature –1746. **4.** Something having the slenderness or fineness of a thread; e.g., a hair, a filament of a cobweb, etc. late ME. **b.** A 'string' of any viscid substance; a thin continuous stream of liquid, sand, etc.; a narrow strip of space; a fine line or streak of colour or light; a 'thin' continuity of sound 1593. **c.** A degree of stickiness reached in boiling clarified syrup for confectionery 1862. **5.** *transf.* The spiral ridge winding round the shank of a screw; also, each complete turn of this 1674.

1. From these little Threads..such strong Cables are form'd 1720. **2.** Till April's dead, change not a t. 1908. *T. and thrum*, each length of the warp-yarn, and the tuft where it is fastened to the loom; hence *fig.* the whole of anything; good and bad together. Also *threads and thrums*, ends of warp threads, miscellaneous scraps or waste fragments. **c.** The only threads of light in the dark web of his history are clerical and theurgic KINGSLEY. **3.** Linens and threads maintain the improvement lately reported 1887. **4. b.** The pale Aare..winds its white t. through the valley 1884.

II. 1. *fig.* Something figured as being spun or drawn out like a thread; esp. the continued course of life, represented in classical mythology as a thread which is spun and cut off by the Fates 1447. **2.** That which guides through a maze, perplexity, difficulty, or intricate investigation 1580. **3.** The sequence of events or ideas continuing through the whole course of anything; train of thought 1642. **4.** Some continuous feature which runs through the pattern of anything 1685. **5.** The central line of the current of a stream, esp. as a boundary line. [tr. L. *filum aquæ*.] 1691. **6.** That by which something is suspended, or upon which things hang OE. **7.** In ref. to other functions of a thread; esp. as a means of connecting or holding together 1818.

1. For my owne part, I would not..beginne againe the thred of my dayes SIR T. BROWNE. **3.** The matron..then Resumed the thrid of her discourse again DRYDEN. **6.** Phr. *To hang by a t.*, to be in a precarious condition. **7.** She kept in her hands the t. of many a political intrigue SCOTT.

attrib. and *Comb.*: **t.-animalcule**, a vibrionine animalcule; **-cell**, (*a*) a stinging cell in cœlenterates; a nematocyst; (*b*) a spermatozoon;

-drawing, the process of ornamenting a textile fabric by drawing out some of the threads so as to form a pattern; **-fin** = *thread-fish* (*a*); **-fish,** (*a*) a polynemoid fish; (*b*) the West Indian Cobbler-fish, *Blepharis crinitus*; (*c*) the cutlass-fish or silvery hair-tail, *Trichiurus lepturus*; **-gauge,** a gauge for ascertaining the number of turns to the inch in, or the accuracy of, a screw-t.; **-lace,** lace made with linen or cotton t., as dist. from silk lace; **-plant,** any plant from which fibre for t.-making is obtained; **t. rush,** *Juncus filiformis.*

Thread (þred), *v.* Also (now *arch.* and *dial.*) **thrid.** Pa. t. and pple. **threaded** (*arch.* and *dial.* **thrid, thridden**). late ME. [f. prec.] **1.** *trans.* To pass one end of a thread through the eye of (a needle) in order to use it in sewing; to furnish (a needle) with a thread. Also *transf.* and *fig.* **2.** To fix (anything) upon a string or wire that passes through it; *esp.* to string (a number of things) together on or as on a thread 1633. **3.** *fig.* To run or pass like a continuous thread through the whole length or course of; to pervade 1830. **4.** *trans.* To make one's way through (a narrow place, a forest, a crowd, or the like); to pass skilfully through the intricacies or difficulties of. Also to *t. one's way, course,* etc., also *intr.* 1593. **5.** *intr.* To creep, twine, wind 1611. **6.** *trans.* To interweave 1853. **b.** *pass.* To be penetrated, permeated, or interspersed as with threads 1861. **7.** To stretch threads across or over; to intersperse with threads so stretched 1884. **8.** To form a screw-thread on; to furnish (a bolt or the like) with a screw-thread 1858. **9.** *Cinematogr.* To feed (film) into a camera; feed (a camera) with film 1917.

1. The Girl can scarce t. a Needle STEELE. **2.** Amber..beads..Threaded 1705. **3.** One spirit and purpose threads the whole, and gives a sort of unity 1871. **4.** See where he thrids the thickets FLETCHER. **6. b.** His tawny hair..began to be threaded with silver 1891. **8.** The extreme end is threaded for a nut 1888.

Threadbare (þre·dbēᵊɹ), *a.* late ME. [f. THREAD *sb.* + BARE *a.*] **1.** Of a garment, etc.: Having the nap worn off, leaving bare the threads of the warp and woof; worn to the thread; shabby; worn-out. **2.** *fig.* Resembling a threadbare garment; hence meagre, scanty, poor, beggarly; 'sorry'. late ME. **b.** *esp.* Having lost its influence, freshness, or force by much use; trite; commonplace, stale, hackneyed 1598. **3.** Of persons: Wearing threadbare clothes; shabby, seedy; down-at-heel, out-at-elbows. Now *rare* or *Obs.* 1577.

1. Thread-bare cote, and cobled shoes, hee ware SPENSER. Hence **Threa·dbareness.**

Threaden (þre·d'n), *a.* Now *arch.* or *dial.* late ME. [f. THREAD *sb.* + -EN[4].] Composed or made of thread; *spec.* made of linen thread.

Threader (þre·dəɹ). late ME. [f. THREAD *v.* + -ER[1].] One who or that which threads; *spec.* **a.** a person who keeps the shuttles threaded in weaving; **b.** a bodkin for threading tape or ribbon through interstices in a garment, etc.

Threa·d-nee:dle. Also **thread-the-needle,** etc. 1751. [f. THREAD *v.* + NEEDLE.] **1.** A children's game in which, all joining hands, the player at one end of the string passes between the last two at the other end, the rest following. **2. Thread the needle,** as *verb. phr.*: in dancing, denoting the movement in which the lady passes under her partner's arm, their hands being joined 1844.

Threa·dneedle Street. A street in the City of London, the locality of the Bank of England; phr. *the Old Lady of* (or *in*), *the Old Woman of T.S.*, the Bank, its business, etc. (1797).

Threa·d-pa:per. 1746. A strip of folded paper serving to hold skeins of thread in its divisions 1761. **b.** *fig.* A person of slender or thin figure; also *attrib.* 1746.

Threadworm (þre·dwɔɹm). 1802. A worm of thread-like form, as the GUINEA WORM, HAIR-WORM, etc.; *esp.* the pin-worm, *Oxyuris* (*Ascaris*) *vermicularis*, parasitic in the human rectum, chiefly in children.

Thready (þre·di), *a.* ME. [f. THREAD *sb.* + -Y[1].] †**1.** Full of or covered with thread (*rare*) –1757. **2.** Of thread-like texture; composed of fine fibres; stringy, fibrous. late ME. **b.** Of liquid: Forming strings; viscid, ropy 1733. **3.** Of the nature of, consisting of, or resembling a thread or a mass of loose threads; thread-like, hair-like; of a root: fibrous 1597. **4.** Of the pulse (see quot.) 1753. **5.** Of the voice, etc.: Dry and thin; wanting in fullness 1860.

4. The pulse becomes quick,..and so t., it is not like a pulse at all, but like a string vibrating just underneath the skin FLOR. NIGHTINGALE.

Threap (þrīp), *v.* Now *Sc.* and *n. dial.* [OE. *þrēapian*, of unkn. origin.] **1.** *trans.* To rebuke, reprove, chide, scold, blame. **2.** *intr.* To contend in words; to inveigh *against*; to argue, dispute; to quarrel, bicker, disagree; to haggle ME. **3.** *trans.* (usu. with *obj. cl.*) To persist in asserting (something contradicted or doubted); to affirm positively or pertinaciously; to maintain obstinately or aggressively. late ME. Hence **Threap** *sb.* an act or the action of threaping.

Threat (þret), *sb.* [OE. *þrēat* masc., cogn. with ON. *þraut* fem. struggle, labour, f. Gmc. **þraut-* **þreut-* **þrut-*, base of OE. *þrēatian* THREATEN, *þrēotan* trouble, Du *ver|drieten* weary, OHG. *ir|driozan* vex (G. *ver|driessen* annoy), Goth. *us|þriutan* trouble; prob. cogn. with L. *trudere* thrust.] †**I.** A throng, press, crowd, multitude of people; a troop, band, body of men –ME. **II.** †**1.** Painful pressure, oppression, compulsion; vexation, torment; affliction, distress, misery; danger, peril –1450. **2.** A denunciation to a person of ill to befall him; *esp.* a declaration of hostile determination or of loss, pain, punishment or damage to be inflicted in retribution for or conditionally upon some course; a menace. Also *fig.* an indication of impending evil. OE.

2. There is no terror Cassius in your threats SHAKS. Clouds full of the t. of rain 1884. Hence **Threa·tful** *a.* (*rare*) full of threats, threatening; **-ly** *adv.*

Threat (þret), *v. arch.* and *dial.* [OE. *þrēatian*; see prec.] †**1.** *trans.* To press, urge, try to force or induce; esp. by means of menaces –1638. **2.** = next 2. OE. **b.** *fig.* Said of things. late ME. **3.** = next 3. ME. **4.** *absol.* or *intr.* = next 5. ME.

2. Sufficient..to t. the British fleets and islands with the most imminent danger 1781. **b.** The fate which threats kingdoms 1832. **3.** If ancient fabrics nod and t. to fall DRYDEN. Does haughty Gaul invasion t.? BURNS. **4.** Whiles I t., he liues SHAKS.

Threaten (þre·t'n), *v.* [OE. *þrēatnian*, superseding prec., f. THREAT *sb.* + -EN[5].] †**1.** = THREAT *v.* 1. OE. only. **2.** To try to influence (a person) by menaces; to utter or hold out a threat against; to declare (usu. conditionally) one's intention of inflicting injury upon; to menace ME. **b.** *fig.* To be likely to injure; to be a source of danger to; to endanger actively 1638. **3.** To hold out or offer (some injury) by way of a threat; to declare one's intention of inflicting ME. **4.** *fig.* Of things, conditions: To give ominous indication of (impending evil); to presage, portend 1611. **b.** With infin.: To appear likely *to do* some evil 1780. **5.** *absol.* or *intr.* To utter or use threats; to declare one's intention of injuring or punishing in order to influence ME. **b.** *fig.* To portend evil 1610.

2. Threatning them with Punishment HOBBES. **b.** The wind..blew very hard, threatening us with a storm DE FOE. **3.** Threatning to murder all who should oppose them 1748. The party that has lost the election threatens a petition BURKE. **4.** The skies look grimly, and t. present blusters SHAKS. **b.** It threatens to be wet to night DICKENS. **5.** An eye like Mars, to t. or command SHAKS. **b.** Though the Seas t. they are mercifull SHAKS. Hence **Threa·tener,** one who threatens. **Threa·tening** *ppl. a.*, **-ly** *adv.*

Three (þrī), *a.* and *sb.* [OE. *þrī*, *þrīe* masc., *þrīo*, *þrēo* fem., n. = OFris. *thrē*, *thriā*, *thriū*, OS. *thria*, *threa*, *thriu*, OHG. *drī*, *drīo*, *driu* (Du. *drie*, G. *drei*), ON. *þrír*, *þriár*, *þriú*, Goth. **þreis*, *þrija* :– Gmc. **þrijiz*, :– IE. **trejes* whence also L. *tres*, *tria*, Gr. τρεῖς, τρία, Skr. *tráyas*.] The cardinal number next above two, represented by the symbols 3, III, or iii. **A.** *adj.* **1.** In concord with a sb. expressed. **b.** Standing alone as predicate, or in concord with and following a pronoun, or pronominal adj. OE. †**c.** Rarely used for THIRD –1598. **2.** Used vaguely for a small or trifling number 1534. **3.** Absol. or with ellipsis of sb. (most often *persons*). late ME.

1. Like Cerberus, t. Gentlemen at once SHERIDAN. *T. fourths*, t. out of four equal parts into which a whole is or may be divided; t. quarters; often *loosely*, the greater part, most *of*. **b.** I galloped, Dirck galloped, we galloped all t. BROWNING. **c.** *Merry W.* I. i. 142. **2.** If they have but t. words of latin 1638. **3.** Sold in pots at two-and-three, and three-and-nine THACKERAY. The chubby, dirty-faced child of t. 1909.

Special collocations; *The t. kings, magi,* or *wise men* (MAGUS 2, WISE MAN 3); *the t. Persons* (PERSON *sb.* V. a); the *t. R's* (R II. 2 b); *t. sheets in the wind* (SHEET *sb.*[2] 1). *T. vowels* (slang), an I.O.U.

B *sb.* (With pl. *threes.*) **1.** The abstract number ME. **b.** The figure (3) denoting this number 1895. **2.** A group or set of three things or persons. *spec.* **a.** A card, a domino, or the side of a die marked with three pips or spots. **b.** *Cricket.* A hit for which three runs are obtained. 1540. **c.** In military drill, when each three men form a unit for the purpose of wheeling 1796. **3. a.** *ellipt.* for *t. parts* or *divisions*; as *to divide* (a thing) *in(to) t.* ME. **b.** With omission of *hours* (of the day): *t. o'-clock*, also simply *t.*; *half-past t.*; *t. fifteen*, 3.15 = a quarter past three 1460.

1. By Ioue, I alwaies tooke t. threes for nine SHAKS.

In phrases and specific uses. *T. in One* = the Trinity, the Triune God (also *One in T.*, and simply *T.*). *T. to one*, three chances to one. *T. times t.*, i.e. cheers. *Rule of T.*: see RULE *sb.* II. 2. *Threes*, short for three per cent stock, or THREE PER CENTS; for three-quarter-backs (in Football); for three-pennyworth (of liquor).

Comb. (unlimited in number). **a.** Adjs. formed of *three* and a sb. meaning 'of, pertaining to, consisting of, containing, measuring, etc. three of the things named', as *t.-act*, *-bushel*, *-cylinder*, *-fathom*, *-mile*, *-row*, *-volume*, etc. **b.** Parasynthetic adjs. in -ED[2], = 'having or characterized by three of the things named', as *t.-aisled*, *-angled*, *-handed*, *-storied*, *-syllabled*, etc.; spec. in bot. and zool. adjs., as *t.-capsuled*, *-celled*, *-nerved*, etc. **c.** Parasynthetic sbs. in *-er* [see -ER[1] 1], as *t.-miler*, *-tonner*, *-wheeler*, etc.

Special combs. and collocations: **t.-bottle** *a.*, applied to one who can drink t. bottles of wine at a sitting; **-card** *a.*, pertaining to or played with t. cards, as *t.-card trick*, a trick of race-course sharpers, also known as *find the lady*, in which a queen and two other cards are spread out face downwards, and bystanders invited to bet which is the queen; **-coat** *a.*, requiring t. coats, as work in plastering and painting; **-colour** *a.*, designating a photomechanical process of printing in which a coloured picture or letterpress is produced by the superposition of the three primary colours or their complementaries; also applied to a process of colour-photography; **-eight** (usu. $\frac{3}{8}$) *Mus.*, denoting a 'time' or rhythm with t. quavers in a bar; **t. estates** (see ESTATE *sb.*); **-field** *a.*, applied to a method of agriculture in which t. fields are worked on a t.-course system of two crops and a fallow; **-four** (usu. $\frac{3}{4}$) *Mus.*, denoting a 'time' or rhythm with t. crotchets in a bar; **-line, -lined** *a.*, having, consisting of, or marked with t. lines; in *Printing*, extended through t. lines, as a large capital letter; **-ply** *a.*, in *t.-ply wood*, also *absol.*: see PLYWOOD; **-pounder,** a thing weighing t. pounds: a gun firing a t.-pound ball; **-throw** *a.*, having t. throws (see THROW *sb.*[2]), as a *t.-throw crank*; hence, having such a crank, as *t.-throw pump* or *-engine*, one worked by a t.-throw crank-shaft; **-two** (usually $\frac{3}{2}$) *Mus.*, denoting a 'time' or rhythm with three minims in a bar; **-wire** *a.*, applied to a system of distributing electric power, involving t. mains and two dynamos, the two outer mains being joined to the free terminals of the dynamos, and the central main to a conductor joining the two.

Three-corner, *a.* 1548 = next, 1.

Three-cornered (þrīˌkǭ·ɹnəɹd; stress var.), *a.* late ME. **1.** Having three corners or angles; triangular. **b.** *transf.* Applied to a constituency represented by three members 1882. **c.** Applied to a contest, discussion, or the like, between three persons 1891. **2. a.** Of a horse; Awkwardly shaped. *colloq.* 1861. **b.** *fig.* Awkward, cross-grained, peevish 1850.

1. The old t. hat 1855. **c.** A t. fight 1894. **2. b.** A t., impracticable fellow GEO. ELIOT.

Three-·de·cker. 1795. [See DECKER[2].] **1.** A three-decked ship; formerly *spec.* a line-of-battle ship carrying guns on three decks. **b.** *fig.* Applied to a thing (or person) of great size or importance 1835. **2.** *transf.* Something consisting of three ranges or divisions; as, a three-volume novel, etc. 1874.

1. b. Some great t. of orthodoxy 1886.

Three·-fa·rthings. 1561. In the literal

sense: see FARTHING. Also, money of the value of three farthings; hence the name of a silver coin of that value issued by Queen Elizabeth. Hence **Three-fa·rthing** *a.* of the value of three farthings; hence, paltry, insignificant.

Threefold (þrī·fōuld), *a.* (*adv.*) [OE. *þrīfeald, þrȳfeald*; see THREE and -FOLD.] **A.** *adj.* **1.** Consisting of three combined in one, or one thrice repeated; comprising three kinds, parts, divisions, or branches; triple. **2.** Three times as great or as numerous ME.

1. His popish pride, and threefald crowne 1600.

B. *adv.* **1.** In a threefold manner, triply; in or into three parts (now *rare*) OE. **2.** Three times, thrice (in amount); three times or thrice as much. late ME.

Three·-foot, *a.* 1590. †**a.** Having three feet. **b.** Measuring three feet in length, breadth, or other dimension. So **Three·-foo:ted** *a.* (in sense a).

Three-halfpence (þrīhēi·pĕns). 1483. Money of the value of three halfpennies, or a penny and a halfpenny (1½*d.*); a silver coin of this value issued by Queen Elizabeth; also a silver coin of William IV and Victoria, issued for use in Ceylon.

Three-halfpenny (-hēi·pĕni), *a.* (*sb.*) 1552. That is worth, or costs, three-halfpence; often a depreciatory epithet of anything held in small esteem: paltry, contemptible. Also *sb.* a three-halfpenny piece. Hence **Three-halfpennyworth,** usu. contr. **-ha'-porth** (hēi·pəɹþ).

Three·-inch, *a.* 1596. Measuring three inches in length, thickness, etc.

Three·-legged (legd, le·gėd), *a.* 1596. Having three legs, as *a t. stool.*

T. race, a race run by couples, the right leg of one person being bound to the left leg of the other.

Three·-man, *a.* late ME. Requiring three men; managed, worked, or performed by three men; esp. in *three-man('s) song, glee,* a trio for male voices.

If I do, fillop me with a three-man-Beetle SHAKS.

Three·-mast, *a.* 1775. Having three masts. So **Three·-ma·sted** *a.* **Three·-ma·ster,** a three-masted ship.

Three·-pair, *a.* 1788. In full, *three pair of stairs.* Of or belonging to the third floor, as *three-pair room, back,* etc.

Three·-part, *a.* (*adv.*) 1840. Containing, consisting of, having, or involving three parts 1854. **b.** *adv.* (in comb.) = next 1840. So **Three-parted** *a.* tripartite 1553.

Three parts. 1711. Three out of four equal parts, three quarters. Hence as *advb. phr.,* To the extent of three quarters; well-nigh, almost.

Threepence (þri·pĕns, þre·pĕns, þrɒ·p-). 1589. [f. THREE + PENCE.] **1.** A sum of money equal in value to three pennies 1605. **2.** A silver coin of this value; a threepenny piece 1589.

Threepenny (þri·pĕni, þre·pĕni, þrɒ·p-), *a.* (*sb.*) late ME. **1.** Of the value or price of threepence. **b.** Costing or involving an outlay of threepence 1698. **c.** *transf.* Of or pertaining to threepence or to something worth threepence; able or willing to pay threepence 1630. **2.** *fig.* Of little worth; trifling, paltry, cheap, worthless 1613.

1. *T. bit, piece* = prec. 2; also *fig.* something very small. **b.** I play but t. ombre SWIFT. **2.** That threepenny baggage, Mistress Nelly SCOTT. So **Threepennyworth** (þri:pe·niwɒ̆ɹþ), contr. **threepenn'orth** (-pə·nəɹþ), the quantity that is worth, or costs, threepence.

Three per ce:nt, *adj.* and *sb. phr.* 1753. **A.** as *adj.* **a.** Yielding three per cent. interest. **b.** Containing three parts in every hundred.

b. A three-per-cent solution of carbolic acid 1880.

B. as *sb.* (*absol.* use of A. a.) In pl. **three: per ce·nts,** the Government securities of Great Britain, consolidated in 1751 into a single stock paying 3 per cent. interest (reduced in 1888 to 2¾ per cent., and in 1903 to 2½ per cent., so that the name ceased to be applicable) 1794.

Three·-pi·le, *a.* (*sb.*) 1607. [See PILE *sb.*[4]] Applied to velvet in which the loops of the pile-warp (which constitutes the nap) are formed by three threads, producing a pile of treble thickness; so of carpets; also *absol.* or as *sb.* = t. velvet.

I haue seru'd Prince Florizell, and in my time wore three pile SHAKS. Carpets of t. 1844.

Three·-piled (-pəild), *a.* 1588. [f. prec. + -ED[2].] **1.** = prec. 1603. †**2.** *fig.* Of the highest quality, refined, exquisite; also, of very great degree, excessive, extreme, intense –1690.

1. *Meas. for M.* I. ii. 35. **2.** Taffata phrases, silken tearmes precise, Three-pil'd Hyperboles SHAKS.

Three-qua·rter, -qua·rters, *sb., adj.,* and *advb. phr.* 1470. **A.** as *sb.* **1.** *Three quarters,* three of the four equal parts into which anything is or may be divided; *loosely,* the greater part of anything. **2.** *Three-quarter* (pl. *-quarters*), in *Football,* short for *three-quarter back* 1889. **B.** as *adj. Three-quarter* (rarely *-quarters*). Amounting to three quarters of the whole; three-fourths of the ordinary; also vaguely 1677. **b.** *spec.* Of portraits, etc. (*a*) orig. applied to a canvas 30 inches by 25 (about three-fourths of the area of a kitcat, 36 in. by 28). (*b*) Now usu. applied to a portrait showing three-fourths of the figure (in full *three-quarter(s length)*; also, to a lady's coat of similar length. (*c*) *Three-quarter-face* (esp. in *Photogr.*), the aspect intermediate between full face and profile. 1712. **c.** *ellipt.* Measuring or relating to three quarters (of a yard) in Cloth Measure, or three fourths of any quantity indicated by context; *spec.* of a coal seam, three quarters of a yard thick 1708. **C.** as *adv.* To the extent of three quarters 1584.

Comb.: **three-quarter back,** in *Rugby Football,* etc., one of two, three, or four players stationed between the half-backs and the full-backs; **three-quarter binding,** a style of bookbinding having more leather than half-binding; **three-quarters face,** *Mil.* three quarters of a full 'face' or turn.

Threescore (þrī·skōᵊɹ, þrī:skōᵊ·ɹ), *a.* (*sb.*) *arch.* late ME. [SCORE *sb.*] Three times twenty; sixty. [Formerly sometimes written in Roman numerals iij[xx].) **b.** *absol.* with ellipsis of *years,* in ref. to age 1605.

b. T. and ten I can remember well SHAKS.

Three-sided (stress var.), *a.* 1601. Trilateral; *fig.* having three parts or aspects.

T. stem..having three plane sides 1793. One of those t. tables 1878.

Threesome (þrī·sɒ̆m), *sb.* and *a.* Chiefly *Sc.* late ME. [f. THREE + -SOME[2].] **A.** *sb.* Three persons together, three forming a company. **b.** *Golf.* A game in which one person plays against two opponents 1899. **B.** *adj.* Consisting or composed of three; performed by three together 1839.

Three·-square, *a.* Now *dial.* or *techn.* 1440. [f. THREE, after *four-square.*] Having three equal sides; equilaterally triangular. Also *fig.* threefold, triple.

Take a triangular file, t. file it is called 1873.

Three·-way, *a.* 1587. Having, or connected with, three ways, roads, or channels; situated where three ways meet.

Three·-years, -year, *a.* 1617. **1.** Of or pertaining to, or lasting for, three years; of the age of three years 1665. **2. Three·-year-o:ld,** of the age of three years; *spec.* of horses; also, of three years' standing. Also *absol.* or as *sb.*; also *attrib.* 1617.

Thremmatology (þremătǫ·lŏdʒi). 1888. [f. Gr. θρέμμα, -ατ- nursling + -LOGY.] *Biol.* That part of biology which treats of the propagation or breeding of domestic animals and plants.

Threne (þrīn). Now *rare* or *Obs.* late ME. [– Gr. θρῆνος funeral lament.] A song of lamentation; a dirge, threnody; formerly *spec.* (in *pl.*) the Lamentations of Jeremiah. So **Threne·tic, -al** *adjs.* pertaining to a threnody; mournful.

Threnode (þrī·nōud). 1858. [Alteration of next, after *ode.*] = next.

Threnody (þre·nŏdi, þrī·n-). 1634. [– Gr. θρηνῳδία dirge, f. θρῆνος THRENE + ᾠδή song, ODE; see -Y[3].] A song of lamentation; *spec.* a lament for the dead, a dirge. So **Threno·-dial, -o·dian, -o·dic** *adjs.* of or pertaining to a t.; mournful. **Thre·nodist,** one who composes or utters a t.

‖**Threnos** (þrī·nǫs). 1601. [– Gr. θρῆνος.] = THRENE, THRENODY.

Thresh *v.,* see THRASH *v.*

Threshold (þre·ʃoᵘld). [OE. *þersċold, þresċold,* etc. = ON. *þreskǫldr, -kjǫldr*; OHG. *driscūfli* (G. dial. *drischaufel*); the first element is OE. *þersċan* THRASH, in the primitive sense of 'tread, trample', the second element is not identifiable.] **1.** The piece of timber or stone which lies below the bottom of a door, and has to be crossed in entering a house; the sill of a doorway; hence, the entrance to a house or building. ¶**b.** (*erron.*) The upper horizontal part of a door-case; the lintel (*rare*) 1821. **2.** *transf.* and *fig.* **a.** Border, limit (of a region); the line which one crosses in entering OE. **b.** In ref. to entrance, the beginning of a state or action, outset, opening 1586.

2. a. On what is known as 'the t. of England', the Sussex coast 1899. The t. of consciousness 1886.

Threw (þrū), pa. t. of THROW *v.*

Thrice (þrəis), *adv.* [ME. *þriȝes, þries,* f. (with *-es, -s*) *þrie* :– OE. *þrīga,* var. of *þrīwa* = OFris. *thria,* OS. *thriwo, thrio,* f. **þri-* THREE + advb. *-a,* with cons. glide intervening; cf. TWICE. Spelt with *-ce* to express final voiceless s, as in *dice, mice, once, twice,* etc.] **1.** Three times (in succession); on three successive occasions. **2.** Three times as much (in number, amount, or value). Often vaguely or hyperbolically: Many times (as much) ME. **3.** Combined with any adj., used vaguely (as in 2): Very, highly, greatly (L. *ter*) 1579.

1. Before the cocke crowe twise, thou shalt deny me thrise *Mark* 14:30. A Spoonful or two of Canary Wine twice or t. a day 1732. **2.** T. two hundred warriors GRAY. **3.** T. happy Iles MILT.

Thridace (þri·dės). 1831. [– Fr. *thridace* – late L. *thridax, -ac-,* Gr. θρίδαξ, -ακ- lettuce.] *Pharm.* The inspissated juice of lettuce, used as a sedative; = LACTUCARIUM.

Thrift (þrift), *sb.* ME. [– ON. *þrift,* f. *þrifask* THRIVE; see -T[1].] †**1.** The fact or condition of thriving; prosperity, success, good luck –1679. **b.** Means of thriving; industry, labour; profitable occupation. Now *dial.* 1580. **c.** Prosperous growth, physical thriving. (*rare*) ME. **2.** Savings, earnings, gains, profit; acquired wealth, estate, or substance (*arch.*) ME. **3.** Economical management, economy; frugality, saving; †*euphem.* parsimony, niggardliness 1553. **4.** A name given to various plants. **a.** The plant *Armeria maritima* (*vulgaris*), a sea-shore and alpine plant bearing rose-pink, white, or purple flowers on naked stems growing from a tuft of grass-like radical leaves; also called *sea-pink, sea gillyflower, sea-grass,* and *ladies' cushion* 1592. **b.** Hence, extended to other species of *Armeria*; also to plants of allied genera, or similar habit, as Lavender T., *Statice limonium,* etc. 1776.

1. b. With her distaff..and her spindle..she plied..the old fashioned Scottish t. SCOTT. **2.** He that drinks, or spends his t. at dice 1605. **3.** These people are well given to t. and good husbandry 1600. Hence **Thrift** *v. trans.* to save thriftily, to economize.

Thriftily (þri·ftili), *adv.* late ME. [f. THRIFTY + -LY[2].] †**1.** In a becoming or seemly manner, properly; handsomely; hence, thoroughly, well –1638. **2.** Frugally, carefully 1581. **3.** Thrivingly; vigorously 1865.

1. She toke here leue at hem ful þryftyly CHAUCER. **2.** They could neither order a household t., nor cut out a gown 1883.

Thriftiness (þri·ftinės). 1530. [f. as prec. + -NESS.] The state or quality of being thrifty.

Thriftless (þri·ftlės), *a.* late ME. [f. THRIFT + -LESS.] †**1.** Not thriving –1693. **2.** Unprofitable, worthless, useless. Now *rare.* 1568. **3.** Devoid of thrift; wasteful, improvident, spendthrift 1576. Hence **Thri·ftless-ly** *adv.,* **-ness.**

Thrifty (þri·fti), *a.* ME. [f. THRIFT *sb.* + -Y[1].] **1.** Characterized by success or prosperity; thriving, prosperous; fortunate. †**2.** Of a person: Worthy, worshipful, respectable –1596. **3.** Thriving physically; growing with vigour; in good or healthy condition; flourishing 1440. **4.** Characterized by thrift or frugality; economical; provident 1526. †**b.** Well-husbanded. SHAKS.

1. The family generally has been getting t. in the world 1860. **2.** The þriftieste and oon þe beste knyght That yn his tyme was CHAUCER. **3.** A small but t. specimen of the Sequoia, or California tree 1862. **4.** I told my wife she had been too t., for I found she had starved herself and her daughter SWIFT.

Thrill (þril), *sb.* 1680. [f. next.] **1.** A subtle nervous tremor caused by intense emotion or excitement (as pleasure, fear, etc.), producing a slight shudder or tingling through the body; a penetrating influx of feeling or emotion. **b.** Thrilling property (of a play, novel, narrative, speech, etc.); sensational quality; *transf.* (*slang*), a literary work having this quality, a 'thriller' 1886. **2.** The vibrating or quivering of anything tangible or visible; acute tremulousness, as of a sound; a vibration, throbbing, tremor 1817. **b.** *Phys.* and *Path.* A vibratory movement, resonance, or murmur, felt or heard in auscultation 1822.

1. Those communications..shot cold thrills through his frame 1799. **2.** The harplike t. of the breeze 1865. The electric nerve, whose instantaneous t. Makes next-door gossips of the antipodes LOWELL.

Thrill (þril), *v.* ME. [Metathetic form of THIRL *v.*] **I.** Of the action of material bodies. †**1.** *trans.* To bore, pierce, penetrate. Also *intr.* with *through*. –1661. †**2.** To cause (a lance, dart, etc.) to pass; to dart, hurl (a piercing weapon) –1646. **II.** Of the action of non-material forces. †**1.** *fig.* To pierce, penetrate (as a sound, or an emotion) –1642. **2.** *trans.* To affect or move with a sudden wave of emotion 1605. **b.** *intr.* To produce a thrill, as an emotion, or anything causing emotion; to pass with a thrill *through* 1592. **c.** To feel, or be moved by, a thrill of emotion 1595. **3.** To move tremulously or with vibration; to quiver, vibrate. (Said esp. of sound or light.) 1776. **b.** *trans.* To send forth tremulously 1647. **c.** To cause to quiver; to throw into vibration 1800.

1. Such sound..the Airy region thrilling MILT. **2.** A kind of pleasing dread thrilled her bosom MRS. RADCLIFFE. **b.** I haue a faint cold feare thrills through my veines SHAKS. **c.** Till the blood thrilled in his veins 1825. **3.** The great valley of purple heath thrilling silently in the sun T. HARDY.

†**Thrillant,** *a. rare.* 1590. [irreg. f. THRILL *v.* + -ANT.] = THRILLING *ppl. a.* 1.

Thriller (þri·ləɹ). 1889. [f. THRILL *v.* + -ER[1].] One who or that which thrills; *spec.* (*slang* or *colloq.*) a sensational play or story (cf. SHOCKER).

Thrilling (þri·liŋ), *ppl. a.* 1579. [f. THRILL *v.* + -ING[2].] That thrills. †**1.** Penetrating, piercing –1718. **b.** Piercing or penetrating, as cold 1603. **2.** Producing a sudden wave of excitement or emotion; piercing the feelings 1761. **3.** Quivering, vibrating 1850.

1. b. To recide In t. Region of thicke-ribbed Ice SHAKS. **2.** The t. verse that wakes the Dead GRAY. Hence **Thri·lling-ly** *adv.*, **-ness.**

Thri·msa, thry·msa. *Hist.* 1614. [repr. OE. *þrimsa, þrymsa*, late alt. of *trim(e)sa, trymesa*, gen. pl. of *trimes, trymes* – late L. *tremis*, third part of an aureus, f. *tres* three, after *semis* half (an as); also a weight, a drachma.] The OE. *trimes* or *trims*, a coin (or money of account) representing the Roman *tremis*, of uncertain value.

‖**Thrips** (þrips). Often erron. taken as pl., with a false sing. **thrip.** 1795. [L. *thrips* (Pliny) – Gr. θρίψ, pl. θρῖπες a wood-worm.] *Ent.* The typical genus of the *Thripsidæ* or *Thripidæ*, the sole family of the order *Thysanoptera*, comprising minute insects with four fringed wings, many of which are injurious to various plants; an insect of this genus or family.

Thrive (þrəiv), *v.* Pa. t. **throve** (þrōᵘv), **thrived** (þrəivd); pa. pple. **thriven** (þri·v'n), **thrived.** [ME. *þrive* – ON. *þrifask*, refl. of *þrífa* lay hold of suddenly, grasp.] **1.** *intr.* To grow or develop well and vigorously; to flourish, prosper. **2.** Of a person or community: To prosper, increase in wealth, be successful or fortunate ME. **b.** Of a thing: To be successful, turn out well 1587.

1. The young Prince continued there about twelve months, thriving apace 1697. *fig.* Thought thrives on conflict 1907. **2.** As I intend to thriue in this new World SHAKS. **b.** God is iust, iniustice will not t. 1587. Hence **Thri·veless** *a.* (*poet.*) not thriving; unsuccessful, profitless. **Thri·ver** (now *rare*), one who or that which thrives.

Thriving (þrəi·viŋ), *ppl. a.* late ME. [f. prec. + -ING[2].] That thrives. †**1.** Excelling, excellent, worthy –1470. **2.** Growing vigorously, flourishing 1645. **3.** Prosperous, doing well in business; successful, fortunate 1607. Hence **Thri·ving-ly** *adv.*, **-ness** (*rare*).

Throat (þrōᵘt), *sb.* [OE. *þrote, þrotu* = OHG. *drozza* (G. *drossel*; see THROTTLE), f. Gmc. **þrut-* **þrūt-*, repr. also by ON. *þroti* swelling, OE. *þrūtian*, ON. *þrutna* swell.] **I.** The part of the body. **1.** The front of the neck beneath the chin and above the collar-bones, containing the passages from the mouth and nose to the lungs and stomach. Also, the corresponding or analogous parts in vertebrates generally, and occas. the analogous part in insects, etc. **2.** The passage in the anterior part of the neck, leading from the mouth and nose to the gullet and wind-pipe; also, either of these passages considered separately OE. **3.** This part with its passages, considered in various capacities, e.g. as the entrance to the stomach, as containing the vocal organs, as a vital part, etc. ME. †**4.** *fig.* The devouring capacity of any destructive agency, as death, war, etc. (*rare*) –1746.

1. Her t. is well turned but seems to me somewhat thin 1878. **2.** Thou..choakst their throts with dust MARSTON. To clear the t. 1769. **3.** *To pour* (*send*) *down the t.*, to waste or squander (property or money) in eating and drinking. *To cram, ram, thrust down one's t.*, to force (an opinion or the like) upon one's acceptance. *To jump down one's throat*, to interrupt one in his speech sharply or roughly. *At the top of one's t.*, at the top of one's voice. (*To give*, etc. *one the lie*) *in one's t.*, regarded as the place of issue, to which the assertion is thrown back; also, with merely intensive force, *to lie in one's t.*, to lie foully or infamously. *To cut one's* (*own*) *t.*, to commit suicide by this method; hence, to adopt a self-destructive policy. *To cut one another's throats*, to engage in ruinous competition (*mod. colloq.*). **4.** He fights, Seeking for Richmond in the t. of death SHAKS.

II. *transf.* **1.** A narrow passage, esp. in or near the entrance of something; a narrow part in a passage 1584. **2.** *spec.* in technical use. **a.** *Arch.*, *Building*, etc. (*a*) The neck of an outwork. (*b*) The part in a chimney, furnace, or furnace-arch immediately above the fireplace, which narrows down to the neck or 'gathering'. (*c*) A groove on the underside of a coping or projecting moulding to keep the drip from reaching the wall. 1663. **b.** *Shipbuilding* and *Naut.* (*a*) The hollow of the bend of a knee-timber. (*b*) The outside curve of the jaws of a gaff; hence, the forward upper corner of a fore-and-aft sail. (*c*) The amidships part of a floor-timber. (*d*) The curve of the flukes of an anchor where they join the shank. 1711. **3.** *Bot.* The throat-like opening of a gamo-petalous corolla at which the tube and the petals unite 1847.

1. The..t. of Vesuvius EMERSON. Lang's Nek, the t. of the passage into the Transvaal 1899.

attrib. and *Comb.*: **t.-band,** *Saddlery* = THROAT-LATCH; **-deafness,** deafness caused by a diseased condition of the t.; **-halyards,** the ropes employed to hoist up a gaff; **-pipe,** the windpipe; also, the steam supply pipe in a steam-engine; **-register,** the lowest register of the voice.

Throat (þrōᵘt), *v.* 1611. [f. prec.] †**1.** *trans.* To utter in or from one's throat; to speak in a guttural tone (*rare*) –1622. **2.** *Building.* To furnish with a throat; to groove or channel. (Chiefly in *pa. pple.* and *vbl. sb.*) 1823. Hence **Throa·ting** *vbl. sb.*; *Building.* The cutting of a 'throat'; *concr.* the groove or channel thus cut.

Throat-latch, throat-lash. 1794. [f. THROAT *sb.* + LATCH *sb.*[1], LASH *sb.*[2] 1.] *Saddlery.* A strap passing under the horse's throat which helps to keep the bridle in position.

Throatwort (þrōᵘ·twɒɹt). 1578. [f. as prec. + WORT[1].] The Nettle-leaved Bell-flower (*Campanula trachelium*), so called because formerly considered to cure diseases of the throat; also extended to other species, and locally applied to the Foxglove, Fig-wort, and American Button Snake-root.

Throaty (þrōᵘ·ti), *a.* 1645. [f. as prec. + -Y[1].] **1.** Of vocal sounds, or of the voice: Guttural; hoarse. **2.** Of an animal: Having the skin about the throat loose and pendulous; having a prominent throat or capacious swallow 1778.

1. A wonderful mixture of the t. and the nasal 1876. Hence **Throa·tily** *adv.* **Throa·tiness.**

Throb (þrǫb), *sb.* 1579. [f. next.] An act of throbbing; a violent beat or pulsation of the heart or an artery. **b.** Applied to a (normal) pulsation 1653. **c.** *transf.* and *fig.* 1626.

The feverish t. of his pulsation was diminished SCOTT. **c.** Every t. of the locomotive 1892. Hence **Thro·bless** *a.*

Throb (þrǫb), *v.* late ME. [Presumably of imit. origin.] **1.** *intr.* Of the heart, etc.: To beat strongly, esp. as the result of emotion or excitement; to palpitate. **b.** To beat as the heart does normally; to pulsate (*rare*) 1725. **c.** *transf.* Said of the emotion or the like which affects the heart 1591. **d.** *transf.* Of a person, a body of people, etc.: To feel or exhibit emotion; to quiver 1841. **2.** *gen.* To be moved or move rhythmically; to pulsate, vibrate, beat 1847. **b.** Said esp. of a steamship with ref. to the beat of the engine 1864. **3.** *trans.* To cause to throb or beat violently (*rare*) 1606.

1. Your hearts will t. and weepe to hear him speake SHAKS. His temples throbbed—his head rang 1825. **c.** The simple affections of human nature throbbing under the ermine W. IRVING. **2.** The very air..Throbbed with sweet scent MORRIS. Hence **Thro·bbingly** *adv.*

Throe (þrōᵘ), *sb.* [ME. *þrowe*, north. *þrawe* (Sc. *þraw*), spelt *throe* (XVII) perh. by assoc. with *woe*; perh. repr. obscurely OE. *þrēa*, *þrawu* threat, calamity, with influence from *þrōwian* suffer.] **1.** A violent spasm or pang, such as convulses the body, limbs, or face. Also, a spasm of feeling; a paroxysm; agony of mind; anguish. **b.** *spec.* The pain and struggle of childbirth; *pl.* labour-pangs ME. **c.** The agony of death; the death-struggle, death-throe ME. **2.** *transf.* and *fig.* A violent convulsion or struggle preceding or accompanying the 'bringing forth' of something 1698.

Throe, *v. rare.* 1610. [f. prec.] †**1.** *trans.* To cause to suffer throes; to agonize as in childbirth; to torture (*rare*) –1683. **2.** *intr.* To suffer throes; to agonize; to 'labour' 1618.

Thro·gmo:rton Street. A street in the City of London, the locality of the Stock Exchange; hence the Stock Exchange, its operations, etc. (1900).

Thrombin (þrǫ·mbin). 1898. [f. Gr. θρόμβος THROMBUS + -IN[1].] *Phys. Chem.* The substance which by interaction with fibrinogen gives rise to fibrin, and is hence the immediate cause of the clotting of shed blood.

Thrombo- (þrǫ·mbo), bef. a vowel **thromb-,** comb. form of Gr. θρόμβος THROMBUS, as in **Thro:mbo-arteri·tis,** arterial inflammation producing thrombosis, etc.

‖**Thrombosis** (þrǫmbōᵘ·sis). 1706. [mod. L. – Gr. θρόμβωσις curdling, f. θρομβοῦσθαι, f. θρόμβος THROMBUS; see -OSIS.] †A coagulation or curdling (*rare*); *spec. Path.* a local coagulation of the blood in any part of the vascular system during life, the formation of a thrombus. Hence **Thrombo·tic** *a.* of, pertaining to, of the nature of, or caused by t.

‖**Thrombus** (þrǫ·mbŏs). 1693. [mod.L. – Gr. θρόμβος lump, piece, clot of blood, curd of milk.] †**a.** A small tumour occasioned by the escape of blood from a vein into the adjacent cellular tissue, and its coagulation there. **b.** A fibrinous clot which forms in a blood-vessel and obstructs the circulation.

Throne (þrōᵘn), *sb.* [ME. *trone* (assim. early to the L. form) – OFr. *trone* (mod. *trône*) – L. *thronus* – Gr. θρόνος elevated seat.] **1.** The seat of state of a potentate or dignitary; *esp.* the seat occupied by a sovereign on state occasions; now a more or less ornate chair, with a footstool, usu. placed on a dais and standing under a canopy. **b.** *Eccl.* (*a*) The seat occupied by a pope or a bishop on ceremonial occasions. late ME. (*b*) The rest on which the monstrance stands during the exposition of the Host. **c.** A seat provided by portrait-painters for their sitters 1838. **2.** As the seat of a deity, esp. of God or Christ ME. **3.** *fig.* A seat or position of dominion or supremacy 1548. **4.** *transf.* The position, office, or dignity of a sovereign; sovereign power or authority, dominion ME. **5.** *transf.* Put for: The occupant of the throne; the sovereign 1762. **6.** (With capital T.) *pl.* In mediæval angelology, The third of the nine orders of angels ME.

1. See where Salomon is set In royal throan DRAYTON. **2.** *The t. of grace* or *the t.*, the mercy-seat, the place where God is conceived as seated to answer prayer. **3.** The t. which Newton was destined to ascend 1855. **4.** To wade through slaughter to a t. GRAY. *T. and altar*, the civil and ecclesiastical systems as established. **6.** Thrones, Dominations, Princedoms, Vertues, Powers MILT. Hence **Thro·neless** *a.* without a t.; deposed from a t.

Throne (þrōᵘn), *v.* late ME. [f. prec.] **1.** *trans.* = ENTHRONE. **2.** *intr.* To be enthroned; to sit on or as on a throne; to sit in state 1607.

1. The seate Where loue is thron'd SHAKS. The Pope..Thrones and Unthrones Kings MILT. **2.** He wants nothing of a God but Eternity, and a Heauen to T. in SHAKS

Throng (þrǫŋ), *sb.* [ME. *þrang* (Cursor M.), *þrong*, shortened from OE. *ġeþrang* throng, crowd, tumult, f. verbal series *þring- þrang- þrung-*, repr. by dial. *thring* vb. press, crowd, throng, etc. Cf. ON. *þrǫng* throng, crowd.] **I.** Oppression; distress, straits; trouble, woe, affliction; danger. Now *dial.* (*rare*). **II. 1.** Pressing or crowding of people; an act of thronging or crowding; crowded condition ME. **2.** *concr.* A crowded mass of persons actually (or in idea) assembled together; a crowd ME. **b.** A great number of things crowded together; a multitude 1549. **3.** Pressure, or a pressing amount, *of* work or business. Now *dial.* 1642.

1. Went the summons forth Into all quarters and the t. began COWPER. **2.** The streets were filled with throngs of people DICKENS. **3.** This t. of Businesse CHAS. I.

Throng (þrǫŋ), *a.* (*adv.*) Now *Sc.* (in **thrang**) and *n. dial.* [ME. *þrang* (13..), *þrong*, from the same base as prec. Cf. ON. *þrǫngr* narrow, close, crowded.] **1.** Pressed or massed closely together as a crowd; crowded; †dense, close, thick. **2.** Crowded with people, etc., thronged 1660. **3.** Of times, seasons, places, etc.: Into which much is crowded; full of work; busy 1568. **4.** Of a person or persons: Closely engaged in work or business; pressed; busy 1623. **B.** *adv.* Earnestly; busily. late ME.

1. A t. congregation 1743. As t. as three in a bed 1770. **4.** When we're t., I help Hester 1863. As t. as Throp's wife (*local prov.*).

Throng (þrǫŋ), *v.* [ME. *þrange* (Cursor M.), *þronge*, in form a derivative of *thring* vb. (see THRONG *sb.*), with which it agrees in sense. It may continue an unrecorded OE. **þrongian*, or may be f. THRONG *sb.*] **†1.** *trans.* To press or compress violently; to squeeze, crush –1825. **†2.** *intr.* To push or force one's way; to press –1625. **3.** To assemble in a crowd or group; to crowd; also, to go in large numbers 1550. **4.** *trans.* To crowd round and press upon; to press upon as in a crowd, to jostle 1534. **5.** To bring or drive into a crowd, or into one place; to collect closely, to crowd. Chiefly in *pa. pple.* 1578. **6.** To fill or occupy (a place) *with* a large number of things or persons, or a quantity of something; to crowd, cram, stuff 1607. **b.** Of a multitude of persons or things: To occupy completely, fill, crowd (a place, etc.) 1819. **c.** *pa. pple.* Occupied by a crowd or multitude; crowded, crammed.

3. Childe Harold saw them..Thronging to war BYRON. *fig.* I hear the Echoes through the mountains t. WORDSW. **4.** Moche people followed him, and thronged him TINDALE *Mark* 5:24. **6.** Thronging the Seas with spawn innumerable MILT. **c.** The streets were thronged 1894.

Thropple, thrapple (þrǫ·p'l, þra·p'l). *Sc.* and *n. dial.* ME. [Of unkn. origin; its date is against its being an altered form of throttle.] The throat; now *esp.* the windpipe or gullet.

Throstle (þrǫ·s'l). [OE. *þrostle* = OS. *throsla*, OHG. *drōscala* (G. *drossel*), f. Gmc. **þrau(d)st-, -sk-*, based on IE. formations repr. by L. *turdus*. See THRUSH¹.] **1.** A thrush; *esp.* the song-thrush or mavis, *Turdus musicus*. Now only *literary* and *dial.* **2.** A spinning-machine for cotton, wool, etc., a modification of that orig. called a *water-frame*; differing from a *mule* in having a continuous action, the processes of drawing, twisting, and winding being carried on simultaneously 1825.

Thro·stle-cock. ME. The male throstle or song-thrush; *dial.* the male missel-thrush.

Throttle (þrǫ·t'l), *sb.* 1547. [Has the form of a dim. of *throte* THROAT, like synon. G. *drossel* (f. MHG. *drozze*, OHG. *drozza*).] **1.** The throat. Now chiefly *dial.* **b.** The larynx. Now *rare.* 1615. **2.** Short for *t.-valve*; also a similar valve in a motor engine 1877.

attrib. and *Comb.*: **t.-lever,** a lever for opening or closing a t. or t.-valve; **-valve** (prob. from the vb.), a valve for regulating the supply of steam, esp. to the cylinder of a steam-engine.

Throttle (þrǫ·t'l), *v.* [Late ME. *throtel, -il*, perh. f. THROAT + -LE. Not f. prec., which appears 150 years later.] **1.** *trans.* To stop the breath of by compressing the throat, to strangle; to kill in this way; *loosely*, to stop the breath of in any way, to choke, suffocate. **b.** *transf.* To compress by fastening something round 1863. **2. a.** To check or break off (utterance) as if choking 1582. **b.** *fig.* To stop forcibly the utterance of (a person or thing) 1641. **3.** *intr.* To undergo suffocation; to choke 1566. **4.** *trans.* To check or stop the flow of (a fluid in a tube, etc.) esp. by means of a valve, or by compression; to regulate the supply of steam or gas to (an engine) in this way 1875.

1. Then t. thy self with an Ell of strong Tape SWIFT. **2.** I haue seene them shiuer and looke pale..T. their practiz'd accent in their feares SHAKS. **b.** And thus you t. your selfe with your owne Similies MILT.

Through (þrū), *a.* 1523. [attrib. use of THROUGH *adv.*] That passes, extends, or affords passage through something. **b.** That goes, extends, or conveys through the whole of a long distance or journey without interruption, or without change; as a *t. train, passenger, fare, ticket, traffic* 1845.

Through (þrū, þru), *prep.* and *adv.* Also **thro', thro.** [OE. *þurh* = OFris. *thruch*, OS. *thurh, thuru*, (M)Du. *door*, OHG. *duruh, -ih, dur* (G. *durch*, dial. *dur*) :– WGmc. **þurχ*. The metathetic forms (*þruh*, etc.) appear *c* 1300 and became universal in XV. Cf. THOROUGH, THRILL *v.*] **A.** *prep.* The preposition expressing the relation of transition or direction within something from one limit of it to the other; primarily in ref. to motion in space. **1.** From one end, side, or surface to the other or opposite end, side, or surface of (a body or a space) by passing within it; usu. implying into, at one end, side, etc. and out of at the other. **b.** Denoting transmission of light, or of sight, by an aperture or a transparent medium ME. **c.** In ref. to a (more distant or fainter) sound heard simultaneously with another which does not 'drown' it or prevent it from reaching the ear 1819. **d.** With pl. (or collective) sb., expressing passage between or among things so as to penetrate the whole mass or body of them 1535. **2.** Of motion or direction within the limits of; along within OE. **3.** Over or about the whole extent of, all over (a surface); so as to traverse or penetrate every part or district of; in or to all parts of; throughout; everywhere in OE. **4.** During the whole of (a period of time, or an action, etc., with ref. to the time it occupies from beginning to end) OE. **5.** From beginning to end of; in or along the whole length or course of (an action, an experience, a piece of work, etc.; also of a discourse, a book, etc.) 1449. **b.** with emphasis on the intervening or intermediate stage or condition 1671. **c.** with emphasis laid upon the completion: To the end of 1628. **6.** Indicating a point or position ultimately reached. (Usu. in predicate, after verb *to be.*) 1791. **7.** Indicating medium, means, agency, or instrument: By means of; by the action of, by (*obs.* or *arch.*). Now *spec.* by the instrumentality of. OE. **8.** Indicating cause, reason, or motive: In consequence of, by reason of, on account of, owing to OE.

1. George..was lying..dead, with a bullet t. his heart THACKERAY. *To speak t. the throat, the nose* etc. *T. one's hands, t. a machine*, etc., referring to something being handled, manufactured, subjected to some process, or dealt with in any way. *To pay t. the nose*: see NOSE *sb.* *T. thick and thin*: see THICK AND THIN. *T. and t.*, repeatedly through; right through; entirely through. **b.** Thurgh a wyndow..He cast his eye vpon Emelya CHAUCER. **c.** Thy voice is heard thro' rolling drums TENNYSON. **d.** Bounding t. the trees 1890. **2.** The Night-Hag..riding t. the Air MILT. **3.** We will make thee famous t. the World SHAKS. **4.** T. the length of times he stands disgraced SHAKS. It will be like this all the night t. 1873. **5.** I had..put my horse t. all his paces GOLDSM. **b.** The..crisis t. which the world was to pass 1881. **c.** Seven children, who came all very well t. the smallpox 1744. **6.** I am half t. the poem SOUTHEY. **7.** The..Society..seeks to do t. him what it cannot otherwise do 1883. **8.** If he t. frailty err MILT.

B. *adv.* **1.** From end to end, side to side, or surface to surface (of a body or space) by passing or extending within; so as to penetrate OE. **b.** In ref. to travel or conveyance: Along the whole distance; all the way; to the end of the journey; to the destination 1617. **c.** In ref. to size: As measured from side to side; in diameter 1687. **2.** From beginning to end (of a time, course of action, life, trial, book, etc.; to the end or purposed accomplishment ME. **3.** Predicatively, after the verb *to be*, indicating a position, point, or condition ultimately arrived at 1481. **4.** Qualifying adjs. and pa. pples.: Throughout: hence, entirely, completely, thoroughly. **†a.** Standing before a pple. or adj. –1901. **b.** Now regularly after the adj. or pple., and only in ref. to physical condition 1766.

1. Huon..strake hym with his spere clene throwe 1533. **b.** The great bulk of our luggage had been registered t. to Paris 1858. **2.** Who now reads Bolingbroke? Who ever read him t.? BURKE. **3.** [He] did not arrive till the speech was half t. 1896. *To be t. with*, to have finished or completed; to have done with; also, to have arranged matters with (a person) (now *dial.*). *To be t.*: to have finished (*U.S.*). **4. a.** Once t.-hot long in cooling FULLER. **b.** It is of no use to put up your umbrella when you are wet t. 1825.

Phr. *T. and t.*, with repeated or complete penetration; completely from beginning to end; right through; entirely through; also, in all points or respects; thoroughly, wholly, out and out.

Through-, in combination.

1. Combinations of THROUGH *prep.* or *adv.* with verbs (pples., vbl. sbs.), or adjs. Chiefly *Obs.* **†Through-old** *a.*, extremely old; antiquated. **†Through-pierce** *v.*, *trans.* to pierce through, transfix. **†Through-swim** *v.*, *trans.* to swim through. **2.** Combinations with sbs. **Throu·gh-bo:lt,** a bolt passing through the objects fastened by it, and secured at each end. **†Throu·gh-co:ld,** a penetrating or deep-seated cold or chill. **Throu·gh-joi:nt,** a joint passing through the thickness of something. **Throu·gh-tang,** a method of hafting knives, forks, etc. by inserting the tang in a hole drilled right through the handle and riveting it at the end.

Throughly (þrū·li), *adv. arch.* 1440. [f. THROUGH *adv.* or *adj.* + -LY².] **1.** Fully, completely, perfectly. **2.** Through the whole thickness, substance, or extent; through, all through, quite through. *poet.* 1541. **†b.** Through, from beginning to end; for the whole length or time; all through –1692.

1. T. equipped from Head to Foot STEELE. **2.** When tis t. tosted..they eat it SIR T. HERBERT. **b.** Take this book; peruse it t. MARLOWE.

Throughout (þru,au·t), *prep., adv., adj.* [In OE. two words, *þurh* THROUGH, *ūt* OUT, later as one word or hyphened.] **A.** *prep.* **†1.** = THROUGH *prep.* 1, 2. –1629. **2.** Through the whole of (a space, region, etc.); in or to every part of; everywhere in ME. **b.** Through or during the whole of (a period of time or course of action); from beginning to end of 1540.

2. In euery parish t. the Realme STUBBES. **b.** T. my command in the Levant seas NELSON.

B. *adv.* **†1.** Right through, quite through –1660. **2.** Through the whole of a body, region, etc.; in or to every part, everywhere ME. **b.** Through the whole of a time or course of action; at every moment or point; all through 1766.

1. I never read a Romancy Book t. in all my life D'CHESS NEWCASTLE. **2.** A furde gowne lyned with foxe thorow-oute 1544. **b.** Act on these Principles t. 1766.

†C. *adj.* Thorough, out-and-out –1670. Such t. saints 1670.

Throu·gh-pa:ssage. 1566. A passage through; a thoroughfare.

Through-stone¹ (þrū·χʷstoᵘn, þrū·f-). Now only *Sc.* and *n. dial.* ME. [f. OE. *þrūh* tube, chest, trough + STONE *sb.*] A horizontal gravestone or slab over a tomb.

Through-stone[2] (þrū·stoun), **thorough-stone** (þʊ·rŏ,stoun). 1805. [f. THROUGH *prep.* + STONE *sb.*] *Building.* A stone placed so as to extend through the thickness of a wall; a bond-stone.

Throu·gh-toll. 1567. [See TOLL *sb.*[1]] A toll or duty levied on persons, animals, or goods passing through certain places, esp. through a town or territory. Also, a toll which passes one through two or more turnpike gates.

Throve, pa. t. of THRIVE *v.*

†**Throw,** *sb.*[1] [OE. *þrāg, þrāh*; not repr. in the cogn. languages.] **1.** The time at which anything happens; an occasion –1513. **2.** An instant, a moment –1590.

2. Downe himselfe he layd Upon the grassy ground to sleepe a t. SPENSER.

Throw (þrōu), *sb.*[2] 1530. [f. THROW *v.*] **I.** A twist, a turn. **1.** *Sc.*, in form **thraw.** An act of twisting or turning; the fact or condition of being twisted; a wrench, crook, warp; also, the act of turning a key or the like 1585. **2.** *Mech.* The action or motion of a slide-valve, or of a crank, eccentric, or cam; also, the extent of this measured on a straight line passing through the centre of motion; also, a crank-arm; a crank 1829. **3.** A machine by which a rotary motion is given to an object while being shaped; a lathe, esp. one worked by hand 1657.

1. Deil be wi' me if I do not give your craig [neck] a thraw SCOTT.

II. 1. An act of throwing a missile, etc.; a forcible propulsion from, or as from, the hand or arm; a cast 1530. **2.** The distance to which anything may or is to be thrown; often qualified, as a *stone's t.* 1582. **3.** *spec.* **a.** A cast at dice; the number cast 1577. **b.** A cast of a net, a fishing-line, etc. 1548. **c.** *Wrestling.* The throwing down of an opponent which finishes a bout or round 1819. **4.** *Geol.* and *Mining.* A dislocation in a vein or stratum, in which the part on one side of the fracture is displaced up or down; also, the amount of vertical displacement so caused 1796. **5.** A sudden angular movement of a galvanometer needle.

1. *To have a t. at (fig.)*, to attack, have an attempt at; to have a 'fling' at. He hewd, and lasht, and foynd, and thundred blowes..Ne plate, ne male, could ward so mighty throwes SPENSER. **3.** *fig.* This able general, who never risques his fortune on a single t., began to think of a retreat 1759.

Throw, *sb.*[3], earlier form of THROE *sb.*

Throw (þrōu), *v.* Pa. t. **threw** (þrū); pa. pple. **thrown** (þrōun). Also *Sc.* **thraw**; pa. pple. **thrawn.** [OE. *þrāwan* = OS. *thrāian*, OHG. *drāen* (Du. *draaien*, G. *drehen*); WGmc. based on IE. **ter-*, repr. by L. *terere* rub, Gr. *τείρειν* wear out, *τρῆμα* hole.] **I.** To twist, to turn, and derived uses. **1.** *trans.* To twist, to wring; to turn to one side; to twist about, twine, wreathe; to turn (a key or the like); in OE., to torture on the rack. Now *Sc.* and *n. dial.* **2.** *intr.* To turn, twist, curl, twine, writhe; of a moored boat, to swing, sway. Chiefly *Sc.* OE. **3.** *trans.* To form or fashion by means of a rotary or twisting motion. **a.** To turn (wood, etc.) in a lathe; to shape (pottery) on a potter's lathe or 'throwing-wheel'. Now *techn.* or *dial.* 1440. **b.** *Silk-manuf.* To prepare and twist (raw silk) into thread; *spec.* to form into thread by twisting two or more threads or 'singles' in the direction opposite to that of their component filaments 1455.

2. The empty boat thrawed i' the wind, Against the postern tied ROSSETTI. **3. a.** Balls thrown in a lathe JOHNSON. **b.** Silk is still 'thrown' at Derby 1897.

II. To project or propel through the air, and connected uses. **1.** *trans.* To project (anything) with a force of the nature of a jerk, from the hand or arm, so that it passes through the air or free space; to cast, hurl, fling; *spec.* to cast by a sudden jerk or straightening of the arm, esp. at the level of or over the shoulder (as dist. from *bowl, pitch, toss*) ME. **b.** *absol.* To hurl a missile, a weapon, etc. ME. **2.** *refl.* To fling or cast oneself; to precipitate oneself ME. **3.** *trans.* To cast (dice) from the dice-box; to make (a cast) at dice; also *absol.* or *intr.* to cast or throw dice; to play at dice 1587. **b.** To play (a card) out of one's hand; *esp.* to discard 1748. **c.** To cast (a die) 1844. **4.** To hurl, project, shoot, as a missile engine does; also of a person using such an engine. Often *absol.* late ME. **5.** To put forth with a throwing action (a fishing net, line, or bait); to cast, make a cast with. Also *absol.* 1841. **6.** Of the sea or wind: To drive or cast with violence (on rocks or a coast); to cast away, wreck 1659. **7.** To project (a ray, beam, light) *on, upon, over*, etc.; to emit (light); to project, cast (a shadow) 1598. **8.** To direct (words, an utterance) *towards*, etc., esp. in hostility or contempt; to hurl, cast; to cause (sound, or *fig.* a gesture) to pass or travel; to waft (a kiss), to cast (a nod) 1580. **9.** *To t. one's eye* or *eyes, a glance, a look*, to turn or direct one's gaze, to look; *esp.* to look hastily, rapidly or cursorily; to glance 1590. **10.** To perform, execute (a somersault or a leap, in which the body is thrown with force); also *to t. a fit*, to have a fit (*U.S. slang*) 1826.

1. When a man throweth his goods into the Sea for feare the ship should sink HOBBES. **2.** He threw himself upon his horse LEVER. Phr. *To t. oneself upon*, to attack with violence or vigour; to fall upon. **3.** That great day..on which a man is to t. his last cast for an eternity of joys JER. TAYLOR. **5.** Violet..learnt to t. a fly 1889. **6.** A billow..threw me..on dry land BURTON. **7.** Phr. *To t. (a) light on*, to contribute to the elucidation of, to make clearer or plainer. *To t. a shadow, cloud, gloom, lustre, over*: see the sbs. **8.** Not a word? *Ros.* Not one to t. at a dog. SHAKS. Throwing a kiss towards the boy SCOTT.

III. Pregnant uses. **1.** *trans.* To cause to fall to the ground; to cast down, knock down, prostrate, lay low; *spec.* in *Wrestling*, to bring (one's opponent) to the ground ME. **b.** *fig.* or in fig. context: To defeat in a contest; also, to be the cause of defeat to; to give or gain the verdict against in an action at law (*U.S.*) 1850. **2.** To cause forcibly (a tree or structure) to fall; to bring, knock, break, or cut down; to fell 1568. **3.** Of a horse, etc.: To cause (the rider) to fall off; to unseat, shake off; also in passive *to be thrown* (from a horse or vehicle) 1531. **4.** Of a snake, a bird, etc.: To cast (the skin); to moult (feathers). Of a horse: To cast or lose (a shoe). 1590. **5.** Of domestic animals: To produce as offspring; to give birth to, to drop. Also *absol.*, *to t. true*, to produce offspring true to the parent type. 1845. **6.** Of a fountain or pump: To eject or project (water); to discharge; also *absol.* 1644. **7.** Of a horse: *To t. the feet*, to lift them well in moving 1827.

1. b. The sceptic cannot t. his opponent if his own feet are in the air 1909. **3.** The untutored jade Threw me, and kicked me MASSINGER. **4.** There the snake throwes her enammel'd skinne SHAKS. **5.** You cannot possibly tell what sort of foal your mare may t. 1845. **6.** The pumps..t. daily 60,000 to 70,000 gallons 1864.

IV. *fig.* and *transf.* **1.** *trans.* To cause to pass, go, or come into some place or position by some action likened to throwing; to put or place with haste, suddenness, or force; e.g. to put (a garment) *on* or *off* hurriedly, hastily, or carelessly. late ME. **b.** In fig. uses of various phrases 1611. **c.** With immaterial object (e.g. blame, influence, power, obstacles, etc.) 1620. **d.** To put *into* as an addition; to add, incorporate 1676. **2.** *spec.* **a.** *To throw into prison*, etc. to imprison roughly or forcibly 1560. **b.** Troops, succour, supplies, etc. are said to be *thrown* into a besieged place, or a strategic position. Also *refl.* 1617. **c.** A bridge or arch is said to be *thrown* from one side to another of, or *over*, a river, passage, or space 1751. **3.** To cause to fall, pass, or come into or out of some condition or relation (or place or thing implying this); properly, with the connotation of abruptness, suddenness, or force; to cast, force, drive, plunge, thrust. Usu. with *prep.* 1560. **b.** To put deftly into a particular form or shape; to express in a specified form (in speech or writing); to convert, change, or translate *into* some other form, or another language 1723.

1. Her arms Round Ellen's neck she threw COLERIDGE. T. the rifle smartly to the front of the right shoulder 1859. **b.** Phr. *To t. a veil over. To t. good money after bad*, to incur a further loss in trying to make good a previous one. *To t. oneself* or *be thrown at* or *at the head of* (a man), of a woman, to put herself or be put designedly in the way of, so as to invite the attention of. *To t. oneself into the arms of*, to become the wife or mistress of. **d.** The saddle being thrown into the bargain 1862. **3.** The fatigues I had undergone threw me into a fever GOLDSMITH. Easily thrown off its balance SCOTT. Phr. *To t. open (apart, asunder)*, to set open (separate, break asunder) with a sudden or energetic impulse; hence *fig.* to make publicly accessible or available. *To t. open one's doors to*, to receive as a guest. *To t. oneself on* or *upon*, to have urgent recourse to (some one) for succour, etc.; to commit oneself entirely to; also, *pass.*, to be made or become dependent upon. *To t. oneself into*, to engage in with zeal or earnestness; so *to t. one's soul, heart, spirit, energy, efforts*, etc., *into* a thing or action. **b.** Two dress boxes.. were thrown into one 1824. Cædmon..throws Scripture into metrical paraphrase 1893.

With adverbs. **T. about. a.** *trans.* See simple senses and ABOUT. **b.** *Naut. absol.* or *intr.* To turn about at once; to go about, put about. **T. aside. a.** *trans.* See simple senses and ASIDE. **b.** *spec.* To cast aside out of use, or as useless; *fig.* to discard, cease to use. **T. away. a.** *trans.* To cast away out of one's hands or possession as useless or unneeded. **b.** To spend or use without adequate return; to squander, waste; to bestow upon an unworthy object; also, to neglect to take advantage of (an opportunity, etc.); *spec.* at *Cards*, to play (a losing card) when one cannot follow suit, to discard. **c.** refl. *To t. oneself away*: chiefly said of a woman in ref. to an unsuitable marriage. **T. back. a.** *trans.* See simple senses and BACK *adv.* **b.** To put back in time or condition; to delay, make late; to retard or check in expected or desired progress. **c.** With *upon*: to compel to fall back upon. **d.** *intr.* To revert to an ancestral type or character not present in recent generations, to exhibit atavism (*colloq.*). **e.** *intr.* To go back in date *to*. †**T. by.** *trans.* To put aside with decision; discard. **T. down. a.** *trans.* See simple senses and DOWN *adv.* **b.** Expressing a symbolic action; as *to t. down one's arms*, to surrender; *to t. down one's brief* (of a barrister), to decline to go on with a case; *to t. down one's tools*, (of a workman) to 'strike'. **c.** To cause to fall; to demolish (a building, etc.). **d.** To deposit or cause to be deposited from solution; to precipitate. **e.** *fig.* To put down with force; to lower in rank or station; to degrade; also, to bring to nought. **T. in. a.** *trans.* See simple senses and IN. **b.** To put in as a supplement or addition; to add esp. to a bargain. **c.** To introduce, insert, or interject in the course or process of something; *esp.* to interpose or contribute (a remark). **d.** In techn. uses (often *absol.*). (*a*) *Fishing.* To make a cast. (*b*) *Hunting.* To start (hounds) upon the scent. (*c*) *Wrestling* and *Pugilism.* To toss one's hat into the ring as a challenge or acceptance; hence *fig.* to become a candidate, put in *for*. (*d*) *Football* and *Cricket.* cf. *throw-in* sb. (THROW- 2). **e.** *To t. in one's lot with*, to enter into association with, so as to share the fortunes of. **f.** *To t. in one's hand*, in Poker, etc., to give up one's cards without betting, or without finishing the game; hence *fig.* **T. off. a.** *trans.* See simple senses and OFF. **b.** To rid oneself by force from, shake off (a yoke, restraint, burden, etc.); also, to cast off, disown (an associate). **c.** To cast off, put off energetically (something put on or assumed, as a garment); to divest oneself of (a quality, illness, habit, feeling, etc.); to lay aside quickly or decisively; to discard. **d.** To shake off (a pursuer or competitor in a race); also, to put off the scent. **e.** *Hunting.* To free from the leashes, to start (hounds) in the chase; to let fly (a hawk, etc.). Now esp. *absol.* or *intr.*, of foxhunters or hounds: To begin hunting; hence *fig.* to begin. **f.** To eject, emit, give off, esp. from the body or system; *esp.* to expel or discharge (waste or morbid products). **g.** To produce and send forth (as offspring or the like); *esp.* of a hive of bees: to send forth (a swarm). **h.** To produce with speed and facility (a literary or artistic work or sketch). **i.** *Printing.* To print off. **T. on. a.** *trans.* See simple senses and ON. **b.** To put on (apparel) hastily or carelessly; the opposite of *throw off.* **c.** To put (hounds) on the scent. **T. out. a.** *trans.* See simple senses and OUT; *spec.* of frost, etc.: to force (young plants) out of the ground. **b.** To eject, expel, turn out. **c.** *transf.* and *fig.* To put forth vigorously from within; to emit, radiate (heat or light); to exude; to produce, be the source of; to send out, put forth (buds, shoots, etc.). **d.** To cause to project, protrude, stretch out, or extend. **e.** To cause to 'stand out'. **f.** *Mil.* To send out (skirmishers, etc.) to a distance from the main body. **g.** To put forward tentatively, give (a hint or suggestion); also with obj. clause, to suggest. **h.** To dismiss from acceptance, use, or consideration; to reject; to leave out of a reckoning; in *Écarté*, to discard. **i.** Of a legislative assembly or a grand jury: To reject (a bill, etc.). **j.** *Sporting.* To put out of place or order by leaving behind in a chase or race; to distance, outpace. **k.** = PUT *out.* **l.**

Cricket. Of a fieldsman: To put (the batsman) 'out' by throwing the ball so as to hit his wicket. **m.** *intr.* for *refl.* To move outwards from a centre; to strike out with hands or feet; to let oneself go; to push out (as a root). **n.** *intr.* or *absol.* Of a printing machine: To fail to register. **T. over. a.** See simple senses and OVER. **b.** To throw overboard (in *fig.* sense); to cast off (a lover, associate, or ally); to abandon. **T. together. a.** *trans.* See simple senses and TOGETHER. **b.** To put together hastily or roughly. (Said *esp.* in relation to literary work.) **c.** To bring (persons) casually into contact or association. **T. up. a.** *trans.* See simple senses and UP. **b.** To discharge by vomiting; to vomit. **c.** To raise (the hands, eyes, etc.) quickly or suddenly; *spec.* in *T. up your hands,* as a command to surrender. *To t. up the sponge*: see SPONGE *sb.* I. 1. **d.** To cast up (a heap or earthwork) with or as with the spade; to construct hastily. **e.** To render prominent or distinct; to cause to 'stand out'. **f.** *Naut. To t.* (a ship) *up in* (*into, on*) *the wind,* to turn the vessel into the wind till she points almost directly to windward; also *absol.* said of the navigator. **g.** To cease definitely to do, use, or practise; to relinquish, abandon, quit, give up (a project, associate, etc.); orig. in the phr. *to t. up the game* or *one's cards,* i.e. to place one's cards face upwards on the table on withdrawing from the game. **h.** Of hounds: To lift the head from the ground, the scent having been lost.

Throw- in Comb. [THROW *sb.*[2] or stem of THROW *v.*, in comb. with sbs. or advbs., forming sbs. or adjs.]

1. In comb. with sbs. **a. t.-crank,** a crank which converts rotary into reciprocating motion; **-disc, -lever,** a disc-crank or a lever having a specified or adjustable throw; **-lathe,** a lathe driven by hand; **-wheel,** the driving-wheel of a throw or lathe. **b. t.-line,** a fishing-line thrown out by hand, a hand-line.

2. In comb. with advbs., forming sbs. expressing the action of the corresponding vbl. phrases; as *t.-in, -up* (an act of throwing in or up); **t.-in,** in Football, an act of throwing the ball into play again after it has crossed one of the touch-lines; in Cricket, an act of throwing in the ball from the field to the wicket-keeper or bowler; **-out,** an act of throwing-out, or a thing thrown out; anything discarded or rejected.

Throw·-back. 1856. [f. phr. *to throw back.*] An act of throwing back; a check, reverse; *spec.* reversion to an earlier ancestral type or character; an example of this.

Throw·-crook. *Sc.* and *n. dial.* **thraw·-crook.** 1568. [f. THROW *v.* + CROOK *sb.*] A hooked implement for 'throwing' or twisting coarse rope from hay, straw, or hair.

Thrower (þrōᵘ·əɹ). 1450. [f. THROW *v.* + -ER[1].] One who throws, in various senses. *spec.* **a.** One who shapes pottery on a potter's wheel or throw; a potter 1604. **†b.** One who twists filaments of silk into silk thread; a throwster –1688.

Throwing (þrōᵘ·iŋ), *vbl. sb.* ME. [f. as prec. + -ING[1].] The action of THROW *v.*

attrib. and *Comb.*: **t.-balls,** the S. Amer. BOLAS; **-iron,** a knife-like missile used by some African savages; **-mill,** (*a*) a building in which silk-throwing is carried on; (*b*) a machine for twisting raw silk into thread; **-wheel,** a potter's wheel.

Throw·ing-stick. 1770. **a.** A short wooden implement by which a dart or spear is thrown, in order to give increased velocity to it. **b.** A short club used as a missile.

Thrown (þrōᵘn), *ppl. a.* 1463. [pa. pple. of THROW *v.*] **I. 1. a.** Turned on a lathe, as woodwork. Now *dial.* **b.** Shaped on the potter's wheel 1483. **2.** Of silk: Twisted into thread 1463.

2. *T. silk,* silk thread consisting of two or more singles twisted together. *T. singles,* silk thread consisting of a single strand of raw silk which has been cleaned, wound, and twisted.

II. Cast, pitched, hurled; unseated from a horse 1833.

Throw-off. 1859. [f. the vbl. phr. *to throw off.*] **a.** *Fox-hunting.* The throwing-off of the hounds, the start of a hunt; by extension, of a race; hence, a start generally. **b.** A mechanism by which some part of a machine is disconnected, or its action suspended. **c.** That which is thrown off; something produced or given off, an offshoot.

Throw·-o:ver. 1819. [f. the vbl. phr. *to throw over.*] The act or result of throwing over; also, *concr.*, a wrap to throw over the shoulders; a loose outer garment.

Throwster (þrōᵘ·stəɹ). 1455. [f. THROW *v.* + -STER.] One who twists silk fibres into raw silk or raw silk into thread, a silk-thrower; orig. a woman who did this.

Throw·-stick. 1837. [f. THROW *v.* + STICK *sb.*] **a.** An ancient kind of boomerang. **b.** = THROWING-STICK a.

Thrum (þrɒm), *sb.*[1] [OE. *þrum* in (*under*)*tunge þrum* ligament of the tongue = MDu. *drom, drum* (mod.Du. has *dreum* thrum), OHG. *drum* end-piece, remnant (G. *trumm* end-piece, *trümmer* remnants, ruins), f. Gmc. **þrum-* **þram-*; the IE. base **trm-* is repr. also by L. *terminus, termo,* Gr. τέρμα end, TERM.] **1.** *Weaving.* Each of the ends of the warp-threads left unwoven and remaining attached to the loom when the web is cut off; usu. in *pl.* (also *collect. sing.*) the row or fringe of such threads. late ME. **2.** A short piece of waste thread or yarn (including the unwoven ends of the warp); *pl.* or *collect. sing.* odds and ends of thread; also, a tuft, tassel, or fringe of threads at the edge of a piece of cloth, etc. ME. **b.** *Naut.* (*pl.*, also *collect. sing.*) Short pieces of coarse woollen or hempen yarn, used for mops, etc. 1466. **c.** *fig.*: *pl.* (or *collect. sing.*) Odds and ends, scraps 1648. **†3.** Applied to various structures in plants or animals resembling small threads, or a tuft of these –1812. **†4.** Applied *joc.* or contemptuously to a person –1727.

attrib. and *Comb.*: **†t.-cap,** a cap made of thrums; *transf.* a person wearing a t. cap; **-eyed** (-əid) *a.*, applied by florists to the short-styled form of a flower (esp. of the genus *Primula*), which shows the boss of 'thrums' or anthers at the top of the corolla-tube (opp. to PIN-EYED); so **t. eye; †-stone,** a name for asbestos, as being a fibrous mineral.

Thrum (þrɒm), *sb.*[2] 1553. [imit.; cf. THRUM *v.*[2]] A word representing various sounds, esp. those produced by 'thrumming' a guitar or similar instrument; also *dial.* the purring of a cat.

Thrum, *v.*[1] 1525. [f. THRUM *sb.*[1]] *trans.* To furnish or adorn with thrums or ends of thread (or something similar); to cover with thrums or small tufts, raise a pile upon (cloth); to make shaggy. Now *dial.* **†b.** *transf.* and *fig.* To fringe or clothe –1630. **c.** *Naut.* To sew or fasten bunches of rope-yarn over (a mat or sail) so as to produce a shaggy surface, suitable to prevent chafing or stop a leak 1711.

b. A craggy Rocks steep-hanging boss (Thrumm'd half with Ivie, half with crisped Moss) SYLVESTER.

Thrum, *v.*[2] 1592. [imit.; cf. THRUM *sb.*[2]] **1. a.** *intr.* To play on a stringed instrument, as a guitar, harp, etc. by plucking the strings; to play on any stringed instrument in an idle, mechanical, or unskilful way; to strum. **b.** *trans.* To play (a stringed instrument, or a tune on it) idly, monotonously, or unskilfully; to strum upon; also, to pluck, twang (a string) 1625. **2.** *intr.* To sound as an instrument or string when thrummed; to sound monotonously; to hum 1763. **†3. a.** *trans.* To recite or tell in a 'sing-song' or monotonous way; also, to hum over (a melody) 1710. **b.** *intr.* To speak or read monotonously; to 'drone', mumble 1774. **4.** To strike something with the fingers as if playing on a musical instrument; to drum upon (a table, etc.). **a.** *trans.* 1750. **b.** *intr.* with *on* or *upon* 1820.

3. b. Boswell..has thrummed upon this topic till it is threadbare SCOTT. **4. b.** The squire was thrumming on the back of his chair 1865.

Thrummy (þrɒ·mi), *a.* Now *rare.* 1597. [f. THRUM *sb.*[1] + -Y[1].] Consisting of, characterized by, or resembling thrums; covered with thrums; shaggy, downy, velvety. Formerly of flowers with conspicuous anthers, of fibrous roots, etc.

Thrumwort (þrɒ·mˌwɒɹt). 1829. [f. as prec. + WORT[1].] A name for plants having parts resembling thrums. **a.** The water-plantain, *Alisma plantago*; also, the allied star-fruit, *Actinocarpus damasonium.* **b.** 'Love-lies-bleeding', *Amarantus caudatus.*

Thrush[1] (þrɒʃ). [OE. *þrysće* (:– **þruskjōn*), rel. to synon. OE. *þrǣsće,* **þrēasće* = OHG. *drōsca* (:– **þrauskōn*); cf. THROSTLE.] Historically, a name of two British and general European birds; (1) that also called *Throstle* and *Mavis,* distinctively Song-thrush (*Turdus musicus*); (2) the Mistletoe thrush, Mistle- or Missel-thrush, (*T. viscivorus*) a larger and less musical species. Thence extended (with qualifications) by ornithologists to other species of the genus *Turdus,* or more widely, to all members of the family *Turdidæ.* **b.** With qualifying words applied to various species of the genus *Turdus* or family *Turdidæ*; also, popularly, to numerous species of other families (starlings, warblers, shrikes, etc.) more or less resembling the true thrushes.

b. Migratory t., the American robin. **New York t.,** an American water-t., *Seiurus nævius.* **Pacific t.,** a Polynesian bird, *Lalage pacifica.* **Shrike-t.:** see SHRIKE. **Wilson's t.,** the Veery of N. America. See also ANT-THRUSH, GROUND-THRUSH, HERMIT-THRUSH, etc.

Comb.: **t.-nightingale,** a nightingale (*Daulias philomela*) with a slightly speckled breast, found in central and eastern Europe; **-tit,** a book-name for birds of the genus *Cochoa* (or *Xanthogenys*) inhabiting the Himalayas, China, and Java.

Thrush[2] (þrɒʃ). 1665. [Of unkn. origin; but in sense 1 cf. Sw., ODa. *torsk,* Da. *troske,* in sense 2 FRUSH *sb.*[2]] **1.** A disease, chiefly of infants, characterized by white vesicular specks on the inside of the mouth and throat, and on the lips and tongue, caused by a parasitic fungus; scientifically called *aphtha* or *parasitic stomatitis.* **2.** In the horse, an inflammation of the lower surface of the frog of the hoof, accompanied with a fetid discharge 1753.

1. He hath a fever, a t. and a hickup PEPYS.

Comb.: **t.-fungus,** the parasitic fungus *Saccharomyces albicans,* which causes thrush (sense 1).

Thrust (þrɒst), *sb.* 1513. [f. next.] **I. †1.** An act of pressing or pressure; chiefly *fig.* 'pinch', hardship –1670. **†2.** Pressure or pushing of a crowd, jostling, crowding; a crowd, throng, 'press' –1620. **3.** *Mech.*, etc. A pushing force exerted by one part of a structure, etc. upon another contiguous part; *spec.* (*a*) *Arch.*, etc. Such a force exerted laterally by an arch or other part of a building or structure against an abutment or support; (*b*) the driving force exerted by a paddle or propeller-shaft in a ship or aeroplane; (*c*) *Mining,* the breaking down or the slow descent of the roof of a gangway; (*d*) *Geol.* a compressive strain in the earth's crust. 1708. **b.** Short for *t.-bearing* 1875. **II. 1.** An act or the action of thrusting (in sense I. 1. of the vb.); a forcible push or pushing 1823. **2.** An act of thrusting (in sense II. 1 of the vb.); a lunge or stab made with a weapon 1586. **b.** *transf.* and *fig.* 1668.

1. The t. of the descending glacier TYNDALL. 2. While we were enterchanging thrusts and blowes SHAKS. Phr. *Cut and t.*: CUT *sb.*[2]; *t. and parry* (*lit.* and *fig.*).

Comb.: **†t.-bearer, t.-bearing,** a bearing designed to receive a t. in machinery; *spec.* the bearing in which revolves the foremost length of propeller-shafting in a screw steamer, its function being to transmit the t. of the shaft to the hull of the ship; **-fault** *Geol.* = OVERFAULT; **-plane** *Geol.*, the plane of dislocation in an overfault, along which the dislocated strata have been driven; **-shaft,** a propeller-shaft.

Thrust (þrɒst), *v.* Pa. t. and pa. pple. **thrust.** [Early ME. *þrüste,* e. midl. *þriste, þreste* – ON. *þrýsta* (:– **þrūstjan*), which has been referred to IE. **trŭd-,* whence L. *trūdere* thrust.] **I. 1.** *trans.* To exert the force of impact upon or against (a body) so as to move it away; to push, shove, drive. Now chiefly *literary.* **b.** *transf.* and *fig.* Applied to action of any kind having an effect analogous to that of physical pushing or moving ME. **c.** *absol.* or *intr.* To push against something; to make a thrust ME. **2.** To push or force one's way, as through a crowd; to crowd *in*; to press onwards or into a place, etc. ME. **3.** *trans.* To press, compress, squeeze. *Obs.* exc. in spec. ref. to cheese-making. late ME.

1. T. him downe stayres SHAKS. **b.** Thrusting aside all authority but that of Reason 1854. **c.** They thrust at me, that I might fall COVERDALE *Ps.* 117[8]:13. **2.** She thrust in between them SCOTT.

II. †1. To strike with a pushing action; to stab or pierce *with* a pointed instrument –1770. **b.** *intr.* To make a thrust, stab, or lunge with a pointed weapon; *spec.* in *Fencing* 1596. **2.** *trans.* To cause (anything, esp. something grasped in the hand) to enter, pierce, or penetrate something or place by or as by pushing; to put, drive, or force into some place or position ME. **b.** To put forth, extend (a limb or member) into some place or in some direction; to put forth as in the process of growth (a root, branch, or connected part) so as to project. late ME. **c.** *transf.* and *fig.* 1588.

1. b. These foure..thrust at me; I..tooke all their seuen points in my target SHAKS. **2.** You should have..thrust The dagger thro' her side TENNYSON. **b.** I perceived him t. his tongue in his cheek SMOLLETT. **c.** Thrusting this report Into his eares SHAKS.

III. 1. *fig.* To put a person forcibly *into* some condition or course of action (usu. against his own will). late ME. **b.** To put (something) improperly *into* some position; esp. in phr. *t. in*, to interpolate 1574. **2.** To put (a person) forcibly *into* some position (against the will of others concerned); to intrude (some one) *upon* (a person or persons) 1559. **b.** *refl.* To intrude oneself *into* any position, condition or circumstances, or *upon* another person; to push oneself forward 1530. **c.** To press, force, or impose the acceptance of something (*upon* some one) 1593.

1. I will not willfully t. myself in danger 1639. **2.** Stephen Langhton, thrust into the archebisshopp-ricke of Canterbury by the pope 1559. **b.** They would t. themselves into my company 1797. **c.** Some are born great, some atcheeue greatnesse, and some haue greatnesse thrust vppon em SHAKS.

Thruster (þrɒ·stəɹ). 1597. [f. prec. + -ER[1].] **1.** One who or that which thrusts. **2.** *Hunting slang.* One who thrusts himself forward in the field, or rides too close to the hounds 1886.

Thru·sting, *vbl. sb.* late ME. [f. as prec. + -ING[1].] **1.** The action of THRUST *v.* **2.** *concr.* in pl. *thrustings* = *thrutchings*, whey which is squeezed out while the cheese is under pressure 1794.

Comb.: **t.-screw,** a screw by which a press, esp. a cheese-press, is actuated and regulated.

Thrutch (þrɒtʃ), *v.* Now *dial.* [OE. *þryććan* = OHG. *drucchen* press :- WGmc. **þrukkjan.*] **1.** *trans.* To press, squeeze, crush; to crowd, throng; *fig.* to oppress. **b.** *spec.* To press (cheese) 1688. **2.** To thrust, push ME. **3.** *intr.* To push or press into a place; to jostle 1837.

Thud (þɒd), *sb.* orig. *Sc.* or *n. dial.* 1513. [f. next.] **1.** A blast of wind or tempest; a gust; a squall. *Sc.* **2.** A heavy blow; a thump with the fist. Also *fig.* a severe affliction, a 'blow'. *Sc.* and *n. dial.* 1787. **3.** A dull heavy sound without resonance, such as is produced when a heavy stone strikes the ground. 1825. **b.** As interj. or adv.: With a thud 1880.

2. The heavy t. of the steam-hammer 1878.

Thud (þɒd), *v.* orig. *Sc.* 1513. [prob. identical with OE. *þyddan* (:- **þudjan*), ME. *thüdde* thrust, push, rel. to OE. *þoddettan* push, beat (:- **þudatjan*) and *þoden*, ME. *þode*, early mod. *thode* (Bunyan) violent wind.] **1.** *intr.* To come with a blast or gust, as the wind; sometimes including the notion of sound. *Sc.* **2.** To produce a thud or dull heavy sound; to fall or impinge with a thud; also said of the body or surface struck 1796.

2. A bullet thudded into the wall above me 1908.

Thug (þɒg), *sb.* 1810. [- Hindi, Marathi *ṭhag* cheat, swindler.] (With capital T.) One of an association of professional robbers and murderers in India, who strangled their victims. **b.** *transf.* A cutthroat, ruffian, rough. Now *U.S.* 1839. Hence **Thug** *v. trans.* to assassinate by thuggee. **Thu·ggery, Thu·ggism** = next.

Thuggee (þɒgī·). 1837. [- Hindi *ṭhagī*, abstr. sb. f. *ṭhag* THUG.] The system of robbery and murder practised by the Thugs.

‖**Thuja** (þiū·dʒă). 1760. [mod.L. (Linn.); see THUYA.] The more common English form of the name of trees or shrubs of the botanical genus now called THUYA, also of the wood of *T. occidentalis*, and of drugs derived from it.

Oil of t., an essential oil obtained by distilling the ends of the branches and leaves of *T. occidentalis* with water.

‖**Thule** (þiū·li). [OE., ME. *Tyle, Tile*, mod. *Thule* (XVI) – L. *Thule, Thyle* – Gr. Θούλη, Θύλη, of unkn. origin.] The ancient Gr. and L. name for a land six days' sail north of Britain, which Polybius supposed to be the most northerly region of the world. (Variously identified with the Shetland Islands (so app. in Pliny and Tacitus), Iceland, the northern point of Denmark, or some point on the coast of Norway). **b.** *transf.* As the type of the extreme limit of travel and discovery, chiefly in the phr. *ultima Thule* (farthest Thule); hence *fig.* the highest or uttermost point or degree attained or attainable; the acme 1771.

Thumb (þɒm), *sb.* [OE. *þūma* = OFris., OS. *thūma*, MLG., MDu. *dūme* (Du. *duim*), OHG. *dūmo* (G. *daumen*) :- WGmc. **þūmo*, repr. IE. **tum-*, whence L. *tumēre* swell.] **1.** The short thick inner digit of the human hand, opposable to the fingers, and distinguished from them by having only two phalanges; hence, *gen.*, the inner digit of a limb when opposable to and set apart from the other digits (as in the *Quadrumana* and opossums). †**b.** The great toe –1643. **c.** In the lower animals generally: The inmost digit of the fore-foot; in a bird, the first digit of the wing, bearing the bastard-wing or alula; also the hind toe, inner hind toe, or hallux 1607. **2.** *transf.* The part of a glove or mitten which covers the thumb 1888. **3.** A part or thing analogous to or in some way resembling a thumb 1745. **4.** As a measure: The breadth of the thumb, taken as equal to an inch 1622.

1. 'Twixt his Finger and his Thumbe, he held A Pouncet-box SHAKS. **3.** 'Tot', a small mug, that held a quartern, also called a t. 1901.

Phrases. *T. of gold, a golden t., miller's t.*, in ref. either to the alleged dishonesty of millers or the lucrativeness of their trade. *One's fingers all thumbs* (etc.), said of a person who is clumsy or wanting in dexterity. *To bite one's thumbs*, as an indication of anger or vexation; *to bite the t. at*, as an insult: see BITE *v.* *Under the t. of*, entirely at the disposal or direction of, completely subservient to. *To turn up (down) the thumb(s*, in ref. to the use of the t. by the spectators in the ancient amphitheatre, to indicate approbation or the opposite. *(Put your) thumbs up!* (mod. slang), be cheerful, 'keep smiling'.

Comb.: **t.-bird,** a local name for the Goldcrest; **-index,** a reference-index consisting of grooves cut in the front edges of the leaves, or formerly of projecting tabs, or margins so cut as to show initial letters or titles, so that any division may be turned to by placing the t. or finger on the proper initial, etc.; **-latch,** a door-latch which is operated by pressing with the thumb; **-nut,** a nut for a screw, having wings to grasp between the thumb and fingers in turning it; **-pot,** a flower-pot of the smallest size; **-print,** an impression made with the inner surface of the top joint of the t.; **-rule** = RULE OF THUMB; **-tack,** a tack with a broad head, which may be pushed in with the t.

Thumb (þɒm), *v.* 1593. [f. prec.] **1.** *trans.* To feel with or as with the thumb; to handle 1623. **2.** To play (a wind instrument, an air) with or as with the thumbs; to perform or manipulate clumsily. Also *intr.* with *it*. 1593. **3.** To soil or wear (esp. a book) with the thumbs in using or handling; hence, to read much or often 1644. **4. a.** To press, smooth, clean, spread, or smear with the thumb. **b.** To cover (the touchhole of a cannon) with the thumb 1768.

2. One winds a Horn..Another thumbs it on a Tabor COTTON. **3.** These early editions were thumbed out of existence ARBER. **4. a.** To t. down the tobacco in his pipe 1904.

Thumbed (þɒmd), *a.* 1529. [f. THUMB *sb.* and *v.* + -ED.] **1.** *adj.* Provided with or having thumbs (of a certain kind); chiefly in comb. **2.** *ppl. a.* Of a book or the like: Having the pages soiled or worn by the thumbs of readers; showing signs of much use 1800.

Thumbikins, thumbkins (þɒ·mikinz, þɒ·mkinz), *sb. pl. Sc.* 1684. [f. THUMB *sb.* + -(*i*)KIN dim. suffix. Cf. CUTIKIN.] = THUMB-SCREW 2.

Thumbless (þɒ·mlės), *a.* 1720. [-LESS.] Having no thumb or thumbs; destitute or deprived of thumbs; *spec.* applied to the African *Colobus* and to the Amer. Spider-monkeys (*Ateles*) in which the thumb is rudimentary or functionless.

Thu·mb-mark, *sb.* 1845. A mark made with the thumb, esp. on the page of a book in turning the leaves; also, such a mark made with the inked thumb for identification of a person. Hence **Thu·mb-mark** *v. trans.* to mark with the thumb.

Thu·mb-nail. 1604. **1.** The nail of the thumb. Often *allus.* **2.** *transf.* A drawing or sketch of the size of the thumb-nail; hence *fig.* a description on a small scale; a brief word-picture. Chiefly *attrib.*, as *t. sketch*. 1900.

1. The whole code..may be written on the t. 1841.

Thu·mb-ring. 1596. **a.** A ring formerly worn on the thumb. **b.** A ring for the thumb on the guard of a sword or dagger 1891.

Thu·mb-rope. Now *dial.* 1601. A rope made by twisting hay or straw on the thumb.

Thu·mb-screw, thu·mbscrew, *sb.* 1794. [f. THUMB *sb.* + SCREW *sb.*] **1.** A screw with a flattened or winged head, for turning with the thumb and fingers; a butterfly screw; also, a small clamp adjusted by such a screw. **2.** An instrument of torture by which one or both thumbs were compressed; also called 'the screws' 1817. Hence **Thu·mb-screw, thu·mbscrew** *v. trans.* to torture by screwing the thumbs; to torture with or as with thumb-screws.

Thu·mb-stall. 1589. [STALL *sb.*[1] 6.] **a.** A shoemaker's or sailmaker's thimble. **b.** A sheath worn on the thumb to protect it when injured 1654.

‖**Thummim** (þɒ·mim). 1539. [Heb. *tummīm*, pl. of *tōm* completeness.] Used in the collocation *Urim and T.*, rarely *T. and Urim*; see URIM.

Thump (þɒmp), *sb.* 1552. [Goes with next.] **1.** 'A hard heavy dead dull blow with something blunt' (J.), as with a club or the fist; also, the heavy sound of such a blow (not so dull as a *thud*). **b.** Repeated, expressing a series of thumps 1850. **c.** *advb.* With a thump 1704. **2.** *spec.* **a.** A knocking or pounding of machinery arising from slackness at a joint where there is reciprocal motion. **b.** *pl.* A beating of the chest in the horse due to spasmodic contractions of the diaphragm, analogous to the hiccup in man. 1903.

1. Down with a t. he falls upon his face HOBBES. **b.** The t.-t. and shriek-shriek Of the train BROWNING.

Thump (þɒmp), *v.* 1537. [imit.; similar forms are EFris. *dump* knock, Icel., Sw. dial. *dumpa* vb. thump.] **1.** *trans.* To strike or beat heavily, as with the fist, a club, or any blunt instrument, producing a dead, dull, somewhat hard sound; also, to hammer, pound, knock forcibly. **b.** Of the feet, etc.: To beat or strike (the ground, etc.) heavily and noisily; also of a body: to impinge upon with a thump; to strike violently 1582. **2.** *fig.* To 'beat' (in a fight), to drub, lick, thrash severely. *colloq.* 1594. **3.** *intr.* To strike or beat with force or violence, with an abrupt dull noise 1565. **b.** To walk with heavy sounding steps; also, of a thing, to move with thumps or noisy jolts 1604. **c.** Of the heart, etc.: To beat violently or audibly 1784.

1. The sturdy Pavior thumps the ground GAY. *To t. a cushion, the pulpit*, etc., said of a preacher who uses violent gestures. **2.** These bastard Britaines, whom our Fathers Haue in their owne Land beaten, bobb'd and thump'd SHAKS. **3.** I heard the boat thumping under the main channels MARRYAT. **c.** How my heart thumps 1880.

Thumper (þɒ·mpəɹ). 1537. [f. prec. + -ER[1].] **1.** One who or that which thumps. **2.** Anything 'thumping' or strikingly big of its kind; *esp.* a 'thumping' lie; a 'whopper', 'whacker'. *colloq.* 1660.

Thu·mping, *ppl. a.* 1576. [f. as prec. + -ING[2].] **1.** That thumps; beating, banging, throbbing 1581. **2.** *fig.* Exceptionally large or heavy; 'whacking', 'whopping'. *colloq.* 1576.

Thunder (þɒ·ndəɹ), *sb.* [OE. *þunor* = OFris. *thuner*, OS. *thunar*, OHG. *donar* (Du. *donder*, G. *donner*), ON. *þórr* (see THOR) :- Gmc. base repr. IE. **tn-* **ton-*, as in L. *tonare* thunder.] **1.** The loud noise accompanying a flash of lightning (apparently following it, being heard after it at an interval depending on distance), varying from a sharp report or crash to a prolonged roll or reverberation. Also, the meteorological condition or action from which the loud noise proceeds. **b.** Regarded as the destructive agent producing the effects usu. attributed to the lightning; (with *a* and *pl.*) a thunderstroke or 'thunderbolt'. Now only *poet.* or *rhet.* (exc. *fig.*). OE. **c.** (with *a* and *pl.*) A peal of thunder, a thunderclap. Now only *poet.* or *rhet.* OE. **d.** (with *a* and *pl.*) A thunderstorm. *Obs.* exc. *dial.* ME. **2.** *transf.* Any loud deep rumbling or resounding noise. (Also with *a* and *pl.*) 1590. **3.** *fig.* **a.** Threatening, terrifying, or strongly impressive utterance; awful denunciation, menace, censure, or invective; vehement or powerful eloquence. (*sing.* and *pl.*) late ME. **b.** In phrases denoting great force or energy 1535. **4.** *slang.* or *colloq.* Used vaguely in exclams., intensive phrases, etc. 1709.

1. A drumme..That shall..mocke the deepe mouth'd T. SHAKS. **b.** Let thy blowes..Fall like amazing t. on the Caske Of thy amaz'd pernicious enemy SHAKS. **c.** Low thunders bring the mellow rain TENNYSON. **2.** The t. of my Cannon shall be heard SHAKS. Thunders of applause 1807. The t. of surf on the shore 1887. **3.** Phr. *To steal (a person's) t.*, to use his weapons or equipment so as to reduce or annul the effect of his words or actions (see O.E.D., Suppl.).

Comb.: **t.-bird,** (*a*) a species of Australian shrike or thickhead (*Pachycephala gutturalis*); (*b*) a mythical bird thought by some savage tribes to cause t.; **-dint** (*arch.*), a t.-stroke; **-drop,** one of the large scattered drops of rain which fall at the beginning of a t.-shower; **-fish,** (*a*) a siluroid fish of African rivers, *Malapterurus electricus*, capable of inflicting electric shocks; (*b*) a European cyprinoid fish, *Misgurnus fossilis*, which burrows in mud, and comes to the surface before bad weather; also called *weather-fish*; **-hammer,** pop. name for a celt or other prehistoric implement; **-head,** a rounded mass of cumulus cloud seen near the horizon projecting above the general body of cloud, and portending a t.-storm; **-pumper,** (*a*) the Amer. bittern, also called *pump-t.*; (*b*) the Amer. fish *Haplodinotus grunniens*, also called *freshwater drum, croaker*, or *sheepshead*; in both cases from the sounds they emit; **-shower,** a shower of rain accompanied by t. and lightning, or one of similar violence; **-snake,** (*a*) a snake of the genus *Ophibolus*, (*b*) the common little worm-snake, *Carphiophis amœna*, of the U.S.; **-tube** = FULGURITE 1.

Thunder (þʊ·ndəɹ), *v.* [OE. *þunrian*, in XIII *þondren*, f. *þunor* THUNDER *sb.*] **I.** *intr.* **a.** Impersonally: *it thunders*, thunder sounds, there is thunder. **b.** With subject (the or a deity, heaven, the clouds, the sky, etc.): To cause or give forth thunder; to sound with thunder OE. **c.** *trans.* To deal *out* or inflict by thunder; to strike *down* by thunder; to utter in thunder. *arch. rare.* 1579. **2.** *transf. intr.* To make a loud resounding noise like thunder; to sound very loudly; to roar. Occas. connoting violent movement: To rush or fall with great noise and commotion. late ME. **b.** *trans.* To deal or inflict, drive or impel, sound or give forth, strike, attack, or bombard, put *down* or overwhelm, etc. with a loud noise or other action like thunder 1590. **3.** *fig.* **a.** *intr.* To speak in the way of vehement threatening or reproof; to 'fulminate', to inveigh powerfully *against*; occas., to speak bombastically, or with powerful eloquence. Also simply, to shout loudly, to vociferate. ME. **b.** *trans.* To utter or publish in the way of terrible threatening, denunciation, or invective; also, to shout out, roar. late ME.

1. b. He would not flatter..Ioue, for's power to T. SHAKS. **2.** The great artillary began to t. from either side 1568. Avalanches thundered incessantly from the Aiguille Verte TYNDALL. **3. a.** The Ministers..thundered against these, and other wicked Practices DE FOE. **b.** Fearful echoes t. in mine ears, 'Faustus, thou art damned!' MARLOWE.

Thu·nder and li·ghtning. 1460. **1.** *lit.* **2.** *fig.* Denunciation, invective 1638. **3.** *transf.* †**a.** Applied to a cloth, app. of glaring colours, worn in 18th c. 1766. **b.** *attrib.* Applied to articles of apparel of a 'loud' or 'flashy' style, or combining two strongly contrasted colours 1837.

3. b. A tall fellow, in thunder-and-lightning waistcoat HUGHES.

Thu·nder-bea:rer. 1605. The bearer of thunder or of thunderbolts, i.e. Jupiter.

Thu·nder-blast. Chiefly *poet.* ME. **a.** A peal or clap of thunder. **b.** A stroke of 'thunder'. So **Thu·nder-bla:sted** *a.* blasted with 'thunder', struck by lightning.

Thunderbolt (þʊ·ndəɹbōᵘlt). 1440. **1.** A supposed bolt (BOLT *sb.*[1]) or dart formerly (and still vulgarly) believed to be the destructive agent in a lightning-flash when it 'strikes' anything; *Myth.* an attribute of Jove, Thor, or other deity. **b.** An imaginary or conventional representation of the above as an emblem of a deity, a heraldic bearing, etc. 1727. **2.** *fig.* Something very destructive, terrible, or startling 1559. **b.** Applied to a person noted for violent or destructive action 1593. **3.** Locally applied to: **a.** a belemnite or other fossil cephalopod; **b.** A flint celt or similar prehistoric implement; **c.** a mass or nodule of iron pyrites occurring in chalk 1618. **d.** *erron.* Applied to a meteoric stone or meteorite 1802.

2. This information was a t. to her 1787. **b.** Prince Edward the t. of warre in his time 1599.

attrib.: **t. beetle,** a species of beetle, *Arhopalus fulminans*, with dark wing-cases crossed with zigzag grey lines.

Thu·nder-clap. late ME. [f. THUNDER *sb.* + CLAP *sb.*[1]] A clap or loud crash of thunder; formerly also, a thunderstroke. **b.** *transf.* of other loud noises 1610. **c.** *fig.* A sudden startling or terrifying occurrence, act, utterance, or piece of news 1610.

This Answer was like a T. 1686. **b.** Thunder-claps of Applause ADDISON.

Thu·nder-cloud. 1697. A storm-cloud charged with electricity, that sends forth thunder and lightning.

Thunderer (þʊ·ndərəɹ). late ME. [f. THUNDER *v.* + -ER[1].] One who or that which thunders. **1.** He who thunders or causes thunder: applied to God, or to a deity, as Jupiter or Thor. **2.** *fig.* A resistless warrior; a powerful declaimer, an utterer of violent invective or the like; *spec.* as a sobriquet of the London *Times* newspaper 1586.

Thu·nder-gust. Chiefly *U.S.* 1748. [GUST *sb.*[1]] A strong gust of wind accompanying a thunder-storm.

Thundering (þʊ·ndəriŋ), *vbl. sb.* OE. [f. THUNDER *v.* + -ING[1].] The action of the vb. THUNDER. **1.** *lit.*; also in *pl.*: = THUNDER *sb.* 1, 1 c (now *rare* or *arch.*). **2.** *transf.* = THUNDER *sb.* 2. 1560. **3.** *fig.* = THUNDER *sb.* 3. 1564.

Thu·ndering, *ppl. a.* (*adv.*) 1530. [f. as prec. + -ING[2].] That thunders. **b.** Very energetic or forcible; freq. as a mere intensive: Very great or big, 'tremendous', 'terrific'. *colloq.* or *slang.* 1618. **c.** as *adv.* Excessively, immensely, 'tremendously'. *colloq.* or *slang.* 1852.

The double, double, double beat of the thundring Drum DRYDEN. T. letters came from the Parliament, with great menaces what they would do CLARENDON. **b.** Such a t. lie 1900. Hence **Thu·nderingly** *adv.*

Thunderous (þʊ·ndərəs), *a.* 1582. [f. THUNDER *sb.* + -OUS.] **1.** Full of or charged with thunder; of or pertaining to thunder; thundery. **2.** Resembling thunder in its loudness 1606. **3.** *fig.* Suggestive of thunder; of threatening aspect, or charged with latent energy, like a thunder-cloud; violent, destructive, or terrifying like thunder 1844.

1. Notus and Afer black with thundrous Clouds MILT. **3.** Homer, with the broad suspense Of t. brows E. B. BROWNING. Hence **Thu·nderous-ly** *adv.*, **-ness.**

Thunder-stone (þʊ·ndəɹ,stōᵘn). 1598. **1.** = THUNDERBOLT 1. *arch.* **2.** = THUNDERBOLT 3. 1681.

1. I..Haue bar'd my Bosome to the Thunder-stone SHAKS.

Thu·nder-storm. 1598. A storm of thunder and lightning, usu. accompanied with heavy rain.

Thunderstricken (þʊ·ndəɹ,stri:k'n), *a.* 1586. [f. THUNDER *sb.* + STRICKEN.] = THUNDERSTRUCK 1, 2.

Thunderstrike (þʊ·ndəɹ,strəik), *v.* Pa. t. and pple. **thunderstruck.** 1613. [Back-formation from prec., that being taken as a pa. pple.] **1.** *trans.* (*lit.*) To strike with 'thunder' or lightning. **2.** *fig.* To strike as with 'thunder'. **a.** To strike with amazement. *Obs.* exc. as in *thunderstricken, thunderstruck.* 1613. **b.** To inflict severe or terrible vengeance, reproof, or the like, upon 1638.

2. b. He had..thunder struck him, with a storme of mighty words SIR T. HERBERT.

Thunderstroke (þʊ·ndəɹ,strōᵘk). 1600. A stroke of 'thunder'; the impact of a lightning flash.

They fell together..as by a Thunder-stroke SHAKS.

Thunderstruck (þʊ·ndəɹ,strʊk), *ppl. a.* 1613. [orig. a later equivalent of *thunderstricken.*] **1.** *lit.* Struck by lightning. Now *rare* or *Obs.* 1638. **2.** *fig.* Struck with amazement, terror, or the like 1613.

2. Thunder-struck with this unexpected answer 1687.

Thundery (þʊ·ndəri), *a.* 1598. [f. THUNDER *sb.* + -Y[1].] **1.** Of or pertaining to thunder; characterized by or betokening thunder. **2.** *fig.* Threatening an explosion of anger or passion; gloomy, frowning 1824.

1. In sultry, thundry weather 1774. **2.** That t. countenance of yours CARLYLE.

Thurible (þiūᵊ·rib'l). 1440. [– (O)Fr. *thurible* or L. *t(h)uribulum*, f. *t(h)us, t(h)ur-* incense; see THUS *sb.*] A vessel in which incense is burnt in religious ceremonies; a censer. (Now usu. a metal vase with pierced cover, containing combustible material to burn the gums used as incense, which is swung in the hand or suspended by chains.)

Thurifer (þiūᵊ·rifəɹ). 1853. [mod. application of late L. *thurifer* one who offers incense to the gods (Augustine), f. L. *thus, thur-* (THUS *sb.*) + *-fer* bearing.] An acolyte who carries the thurible. So **Thuri·ferous** *a.* that produces frankincense.

Thurification (þiūᵊ:rifikē[i]·ʃən). 1496. [– late L. *thurificatio, -ōn-*, f. *thurificare* THURIFY; see -ATION. Cf. Fr. †*thurification* (XV–XVI).] The action of thurifying; the burning or offering of, or perfuming with incense.

Thurify (þiūᵊ·rifəi), *v.* late ME. [– Fr. †*thurifier* (XV–XVI) or late L. *thurificare* offer incense to the gods (Augustine), f. L. *thus, thur-*; see THUS *sb.*, -FY.] †**1.** *intr.* = CENSE *v.*[1] 2 (*rare*) –1460. **2.** *trans.* To perfume with incense; to burn incense before, offer incense to 1570.

Thuringite (þiuri·ndʒəit, -iŋgəit). 1844. [– G. *thuringit* (Breithaupt, 1832), f. Thuringia, in Central Germany, where found; see -ITE[1] 2 b.] *Min.* A hydrous silicate of aluminium and iron, occurring as an aggregation of minute dark-green scales.

Thursday (þɔ̄·ɹzdei, -di). [OE. *þur(e)sdæġ*, for *þunresdæġ*, f. gen. of *þunor* THUNDER; partly assoc. with ON. *þórsdagr*; corresp. to (M)Du. *donderdag*, OHG. *donarestac* (G. *donnerstag*); rendering late L. *Jovis dies* Jupiter's day.] **1.** The fifth day of the week. **2. Holy Thursday. a.** Thursday in Rogation Week, Ascension Day ME. **b.** Maundy Thursday, Sheer Thursday 1645.

Thus (þʊs, þūs), *sb.* late ME. [– L. *t(h)us, t(h)ur-* incense – Gr. θύος sacrifice, offering, incense.] Frankincense. **a.** Olibanum. **b.** Resin obtained from the spruce-fir, and from various species of pine.

Thus (ðʊs), *adv.* Now chiefly *literary* or *formal.* [OE. *þus* = OS. *thus*, (M)Du. *dus*, of unkn. origin.] **1.** In this way, like this. **b.** Ellipt. for *thus says* or *said* (referring to either a preceding or a subsequent speech). *poet.* or *arch.* 1568. **2.** In accordance with this; accordingly, and so; consequently; therefore ME. **3.** Qualifying an adj. or adv.: To this extent, number, or degree; as..as this; esp. *thus far*, to this point; *thus much*, as much as this OE.

1. T. the Hogen-Dutchman got Money 1689. After tea..she began t. GOLDSM. **b.** Cassandra t.; and t. the Paphian maid: Your gen'rous love [etc.] 1757. **c.** *U.S.* = So; esp. in *thus and so*, var. of *so and so* (cf. SO-AND-SO C. 2) 1873. **3.** But t. moche dar I sayn CHAUCER. T. farre..Our bending Author hath pursu'd the Story SHAKS.

Thusness (ðʊ·snės). *colloq.* 1867. [f. THUS + -NESS.] The condition of being thus. Chiefly *joc.* So **Thu·sly** *adv.*

What is the reason of this t.? 'A. WARD.'

Thuswise (ðʊ·swəiz), *adv.* ME. [f. THUS + *-wise* (WISE *sb.*[1] II).] = THUS.

‖**Thuya** (þ[i]ū·yă). 1707. [An irregular repr. of Gr. θύια, more correctly θύα, name of an African tree (*Thuja articulata* Linn., now *Callitris quadrivalvis*). See THUJA.] *Bot.* Name of a genus of coniferous trees, consisting of about ten species, of which the N. Amer. *T. occidentalis* and the Chinese *T. orientalis* are commonly cultivated under the name Arbor Vitæ. Also *attrib.*, as *thuya-wood.*

Thwack (þwæk), *sb.* 1587. [f. next.] A vigorous stroke with a stick or the like; a whack.

But Talgol first with hardy T. Twice bruis'd his head, and twice his back BUTLER.

Thwack (þwæk), *v.* 1530. [imit.; cf. (dial.) *thack*, OE. *þaccian*, ME. *thakke.*] **1.** *trans.* To beat or strike vigorously, as with a stick; to bang, thrash, whack. **2.** To drive or force by or as by thwacking; to knock (*down, in,* *out*, etc.) 1566. **3. a.** To clap; to clap *together*, to pack or crowd together (things or persons); to clap *down* 1589. **†b.** To pack or crowd (a thing or place) –1698.

1. Take all my cushions down and t. them soundly MIDDLETON. *fig.* Here's he that was wont to thwacke our Generall, Caius Martius SHAKS. **2.** Wee'l t. him hence with Distaffes SHAKS.

Thwait(e (þwēⁱt). *dial.* 1628. [– ON. *þveit, þveiti* piece of land, paddock, lit. cutting, cut-piece, f. **þvita* = OE. *þwītan* cut, cut off.] A piece of ground; *esp.* one cleared from forest or reclaimed from waste. Now *rare* or *Obs.* as a separate word. (Entering into numerous place-names, as *Applethwaite, Crosthwaite, Seathwaite*, etc.).

Thwart (þwǭɹt), *sb.*[1] Now *rare*. 1611. [f. THWART *v.*] An act or instance of thwarting; a check, hindrance, obstruction, frustration.

Thwart (þwǭɹt), *sb.*[2] 1736. [Appears in Bailey as a var. of *thought* (Sandahl XIV), which is a var. of earlier n. dial. *thoft*, OE. *þofte* = MDu. *dofte, dochte* (Du. *doft*), OHG. *dofta* (G. *ducht, duft* is from LG.), ON. *þopta*. The present form is presumably due to assoc. with next.] A seat across a boat, on which the rower sits; a rower's bench.

Thwart (þwǭɹt), *adv., prep.*, and *adj.* [Early ME. *þwert* – ON. *þvert*, orig. n. of *þverr* transverse, cross = OE. *þwe(o)rh* crooked, cross, perverse, OHG. *dwerh, twerh* (G. *zwerch*, in *zwerchfell* diaphragm), Goth. *þwairhs* cross, angry :– Gmc. **þwerχwaz*, f. IE. **twerk-* **twork-*, as in L. *torquēre* twist.] **A.** *adv.* **†1.** Across or transversely to the length, direction, or course of anything; athwart –1664. **2.** From one side to the other of anything (with motion implied); across. *arch.* 1511. **†3.** *T. of.* **a.** *Naut.* Opposite to, over against (a place on the coast) –1670. **†b.** Transversely to, across the direction of. MILT.

3. a. Being t. of the Shoals of Brazil 1670.

B. *prep.* **1.** From side to side of, across. *arch.* or *poet.* 1470. **2.** = Across the course or direction of. *T. the hawse*, across the stem of a ship. Chiefly *Naut.* 1495. **†3.** Across the course of, so as to obstruct. MILT. **C.** *adj.* **1.** Lying, extending, or passing across; transverse, cross. late ME. **2.** *fig.* **a.** Of persons or their attributes: Disposed to resist, oppose, or obstruct; cross-grained; perverse, froward, obstinate, stubborn, awkward ME. **b.** Of things: Adverse, unfavourable, untoward, unpropitious; esp. applied (with mixture of literal sense) to a wind or current: cross 1610. **†3.** Opposed, contrary (*to*) –1624.

1. The Diagonal or T.-walk 1712. **2. a.** Ignorance makes them churlish t., and mutinous BACON. **b.** A t. sea-wind full of rain and foam SWINBURNE. Hence **Thwa·rt-ly** *adv.*, **†-ness.**

Thwart (þwǭɹt), *v.* late ME. [f. prec. adv.] **I. 1.** *trans.* To pass or extend across from side to side of; to traverse, cross; also, to cross the direction of, to run at an angle to. *Obs.* or *arch.* **b.** *intr.* To pass or extend across, to cross. *Obs.* or *arch.* 1552. **†c.** *trans.* To cross the path of; to meet –1812. **†d.** *Naut.* Of a ship, etc.: To get athwart so as to be foul of. Also *intr.* –1813. **†2.** To lay (a thing) athwart or across; to place crosswise; to set or put (things) across each other –1632. **3.** To cross *with* a line, streak, band, etc. (Only in pa. pple.) *Obs.* or *arch.* 1610. **b.** To cross-plough; also, to cut crosswise 1847. **4.** To obstruct (a road, course, or passage) with something placed across; to block. *Obs.* exc. *fig.* 1630.

1. The current thwarts the course of a ship 1769. **3.** I saw Vesuvius..thwarted by a golden cloud 1861.

II. 1. To act or operate in opposition to; to oppose, hinder. Also *absol.* Now *rare.* ME. **b.** *intr.* To speak or act in contradiction or opposition; to be adverse or at variance; to conflict. Const. *with.* Now *rare* or *Obs.* late ME. **2.** *trans.* To oppose successfully; to prevent (a person, etc.) from accomplishing a purpose; to prevent the accomplishment of (a purpose); to foil, frustrate, balk, defeat 1581.

1. General laws, however well set and constituted, often t. and cross one another PALEY. **2.** Thus are all our best plans thwarted WELLINGTON. The party which had long thwarted him had been beaten down MACAULAY. Hence **Thwa·rter,** one who or that which thwarts. **Thwa·rtingly** *adv.*

Thwart-ship, thwartship (þwǭ·ɹtˌʃip), *a.* and *adv.* 1829. [f. THWART *prep.* + SHIP *sb.*] *Naut.* **A.** *adj.* Placed or fixed across the ship's length. **B.** *adv.* (þwǭ·ɹtˌʃi:p). From side to side of the ship; across the length of the ship 1882. So **Thwa·rt-shi:ps** *adv.* 1625.

Thwartwise (þwǭ·ɹtwəiz), *adv.* and *a.* 1589. [f. THWART *a.*] **A.** *adv.* Crosswise, transversely. **B.** *adj.* Situated or extending transversely; cross, transverse 1890.

Thy (ðəi), *poss. adj.* [Early ME. *þī*, reduced form of *þīn* THINE, used in ME. bef. consonants exc. *h*, but occurring before vowels in XV, and ult. universal in prose use as the poss. adj. preceding its sb.] Of or belonging to thee, that thou hast.

Turn, Fortune, turn t. wheel and lower the proud TENNYSON.

Thyestean (þəiˌestī·ăn, þəiˌe·stiăn), *a.* 1667. [f. L. *Thyesteus* – Gr. Θυέστειος (f. Θυέστης, prop. name) + -AN.] Of or belonging to Thyestes, in ancient Gr. legend brother of Atreus, who at a banquet made him eat of the flesh of his own two sons; hence *allus.*

Thyiad (þəi·iˌæd), **Thyad** (þəi·æd). 1846. [– Gr. θυιάς, θυιαδ- a frenzied woman.] A Bacchante.

Thyine (þəi·in), *a.* ME. [– L. *thyinus* – Gr. θύϊνος of the tree θύα THUYA; see -INE[1].] Epithet of a tree and its wood, mentioned in Rev. 18:12; supposed to be the African coniferous tree *Callitris quadrivalvis*, which yields gum sandarac.

Thylacine (þəi·lăsəin). 1838. [– Fr. *thylacine*, mod.L. *thylacinus*, f. Gr. θύλακος pouch; see -INE[1].] The native Tasmanian 'wolf' or 'zebra-wolf', *Thylacinus cynocephalus*, the largest of existing carnivorous marsupials (now very scarce).

Thyme (təim). late ME. [– (O)Fr. *thym* – L. *thymum* – Gr. θύμον (also -ος), f. θύειν burn sacrifice.] **1.** A plant of the genus *Thymus*, family *Labiatæ*, comprising shrubby herbs with fragrant aromatic leaves, found chiefly in the Mediterranean region; esp. *T. vulgaris* (Garden T.), cultivated as a pot-herb, and *T. serpyllum* (Wild T.), occurring on dry banks and pastures in Britain and throughout Europe. **b.** With qualifying words, denoting various species or varieties. Also applied to plants of other genera, as BASIL *t.*, CAT-*thyme*, HORSE-*thyme* 1558. **2.** *Oil of t.*: a fragrant volatile oil obtained from the common thyme, used as an antiseptic 1753.

1. I knowe a banke where the wilde time blowes SHAKS. Desert Caves, With wilde T. and the Gadding Vine o'ergrown MILT. **b. Creeping t., mother of t., running t.** = *wild t.*; **lemon t.,** a cultivated variety of *T. serpyllum*, having a scent like that of lemons

‖**Thymele** (þi·mĭlī). 1753. [– Gr. θυμέλη altar, f. θύειν to sacrifice.] *Gr. Antiq.* The altar of Dionysus in the centre of the orchestra in an ancient Greek theatre.

Thymene (þəi·mīn). 1857. [f. THYME + -ENE.] *Chem.* A clear oily hydrocarbon, $C_{10}H_{16}$, of the terpene group, contained in the oil of thyme.

Thymic (þəi·mik), *a.*[1] 1656. [f. Gr. θύμος THYMUS + -IC.] **1.** *Anat.* and *Path.* Of, pertaining to, or connected with the thymus gland. **2.** *Phys. Chem.* In *t. acid*, $C_{16}H_{25}N_3P_2O_{12}$, a colourless acid obtained from the thymus gland. Its salts are **Thymates** (þəi·meⁱts). 1894.

Thymic (þəi-, təi·mik), *a.*[2] 1868. [f. Gr. θύμον THYME + -IC.] *Chem.* Of, pertaining to, or derived from thyme; in *t. acid* = THYMOL.

Thymin (þəi·min). 1894. [f. THYMIC *a.*[1] + -IN[1].] *Chem.* A colourless crystalline alloxur base, $C_5H_6N_2O_2$, obtained by the action of dilute sulphuric acid on thymic acid.

Thymo-, comb. form from Gr. θύμον THYME, as in **Thy·moform** *Pharm.*, a yellowish antiseptic powder prepared from formaldehyde and thymol.

Thymol (þəi·mǫl). 1857. [f. Gr. θύμον THYME + -OL.] *Chem.* The phenol of cymene, $C_{10}H_{13}.OH$, obtained from oil of thyme, also from the volatile oil of horse-mint, crystallizing in transparent rhomboidal plates; a powerful antiseptic.

‖**Thymus** (þəi·mŏs). *Pl.* **thymi** (þəi·məi). 1693. [mod.L. – Gr. θύμος a warty excrescence; also the thymus gland (Galen).] *Anat.* A glandular body (one of the so-called 'ductless glands') situated near the base of the neck in vertebrate animals; in man usu. disappearing after the period of childhood. **b.** Now usu. *t. gland* (rarely *body*) 1776.

Thymy (təi·mi), *a.* 1727. [f. THYME + -Y[1].] **1.** Abounding in or overgrown with thyme. **2.** Pertaining to or of the nature of thyme; *esp.* having the scent of thyme 1747.

1. Lingering about the t. promontories TENNYSON. **2.** The t. sweetness of the fell breeze 1880.

Thyro- (þəiᵊ·ro), also (more correctly but less commonly) **thyreo-** (þəiᵊ·rio), used as comb. form of THYROID, in ref. to the thyroid cartilage or the thyroid gland.

1. In ref. to the thyroid cartilage. **Thyro-arytenoid** (æritī·noid) *a.*, pertaining to or connecting the thyroid and arytenoid cartilages of the larynx. **Thyro-hyal** (həi·ăl) *a.* = next; usu. as *sb.* applied to the greater cornu of the hyoid bone in mammals, or to each of the long horns of the same bone in birds. **Thyro-hyoid** (həi·oid) *a.*, pertaining to or connecting the thyroid cartilage and the hyoid bone; *sb.* = thyro-hyoid muscle. **Thyro·tomy** (also **thyreo-**) [Gr. τομή cutting], incision or division of the thyroid cartilage.

2. In ref. to the thyroid gland. (Often **thyreo-.**) **Thyro-antito·xin,** an antitoxin developed in thyroid poisoning; trade-name of a thyroid preparation used as a therapeutic. **Thy·rocele,** a tumour of the thyroid gland; goitre. **Thyro-the·rapy,** treatment of disease by a preparation of the thyroid glands of sheep.

Thyroid (þəiᵊ·roid), *a.* (*sb.*) 1726. [– Fr. †*thyroïde* (Paré; mod. *thyréoïde*) or mod.L. *thyroides* (Blancard), irreg. – Gr. θυρεοειδής shield-shaped (χόνδρος θ. thyroid cartilage, Galen), f. θυρεός oblong shield + -ειδής -OID.] Having the form of a shield, shield-shaped. *Anat.* **a.** *T. cartilage*: the largest of the cartilages of the larynx, consisting of two broad quadrilateral plates united in front at an angle, forming the projection in front of the throat known (in men) as 'Adam's apple'; within the angle are attached the vocal chords. **b.** *T. gland* (also called *t. body*): one of the so-called 'ductless glands', a very vascular body adjacent to the larynx and upper part of the trachea in vertebrates 1726. **c.** Applied to various structures connected with the thyroid cartilage or gland, as the *t. arteries, nerves, veins*, etc. 1831. **d.** *T. foramen, membrane*: names for the obturator foramen and membrane of the hip-bone, from their shield-like shape 1890. **B.** as *sb.* **1.** Short for *t. cartilage* 1840. **2.** Short for *t. gland*; also for *t. extract* or *product* 1849. So **Thyroi·dal, Thyroi·deal, Thyroi·dean,** *adjs.* pertaining to the thyroid cartilage or gland. **Thyro·xin,** a product secreted by the thyroid gland.

Thyrse (þɔ̄ɹs). 1603. [– Fr. *thyrse*, in same senses, – L. THYRSUS Bacchic staff.] **1.** *Gr.* and *Rom. Antiq.* = THYRSUS 1. **2. †a.** A stem or shoot of a plant. **b.** *Bot.* = THYRSUS 2. 1658.

Thyrsoid (þɔ̄·ɹsoid), *a.* 1829. [f. THYRSUS + -OID.] *Bot.* Of the form of, or resembling, a thyrsus or contracted panicle. So **Thyrsoi·dal** *a.*

‖**Thyrsus** (þɔ̄·ɹsŏs). *Pl.* **thyrsi** (þɔ̄·ɹsəi). 1591. [L. *thyrsus* – Gr. θύρσος stalk of a plant, the Bacchic staff.] **1.** *Gr.* and *Rom. Antiq.* A staff or spear tipped with an ornament like a pine-cone, and sometimes wreathed with ivy or wine branches; borne by Dionysus (Bacchus) and his votaries. **2.** *Bot.*, etc. A form of inflorescence: a contracted kind of panicle, esp. one in which the primary branching is centripetal (racemose) and the secondary centrifugal (cymose), as in lilac and horse-chestnut 1744.

Thysanopter (þisănǫ·ptəɹ). 1864. [– mod. L. *Thysanoptera* (Haliday, 1836), f. Gr. θύσανος tassel, fringe + πτερόν wing.] *Ent.* An insect of the order *Thysanoptera*, comprising *Thrips* and allied genera, characterized by long fringes on the wings. So **Thysano·pteran** *a.* = *thysanopterous*; *sb.* = *thysanopter*. **Thysano·pterous** *a.* belonging to the order *Thysanoptera*.

Thysanuran (þisăniūᵊ·răn), *a.* and *sb.* 1835. [f. mod.L. *Thysanura* Cuvier (f. Gr. θύσανος + οὐρά tail) + -AN.] *Ent.* **A.** *adj.* Belonging to the *Thysanura*, a wingless order of insects, comprising springtails, bristletails, etc., having filamentous appendages at the posterior end of the body. **B.** *sb.* An insect of this order. So **Thysanu·rous** *a.* belonging to or having the characters of the *Thysanura*.

Thyself (ðəise·lf), *pron.* [ME. *þi sülf, þi self* (XIII), repl. *þē self* (OE. to XIV), i.e. THEE and SELF; cf. MYSELF.] **I.** Emphatic uses. **1.** Accompanying the subject-pronoun *thou* (or, after a vb. in the imperative, without *thou*). **2.** By ellipsis of *thou*, used as a simple subject (with vb. usu. in 2nd person; occas. in 3rd, *self* being treated as a sb.) ME. **b.** Used as predicate, or after *as* or *than* 1535. **3.** Used instead of *thee* as object of a vb. or prep. late ME.

1. Then get thee gone, and digge my graue thy selfe SHAKS. **2.** T. hast called me by my name WESLEY. **b.** Thou art Dromio, thou art my man, thou art thy selfe SHAKS. **3.** He, whom next thy selfe Of all the world I lou'd SHAKS.

II. Reflexive uses. As direct or indirect object of a vb., or in dependence on a prep. (orig. only emphatic reflective; later in general use, taking the place of *thee* reflexive, which is more decidedly archaic.) OE.

Learn Solons saying, 'Mortall know thy selfe' 1616.

Tiar (təi·ăɹ). Chiefly *poet.* 1513. [Anglicized f. next, partly due to (O)Fr. *tiare.*] **1.** = next 1. **2.** = next 2. 1616. **3.** = next 4. 1660.

Tiara (tī,ā·ră, *U.S.* təi,ēᵊ·ră). 1555. [– L. *tiara* – Gr. τιάρα, τιάρας, partly through It. *tiara.*] **1.** The raised head-dress or high-peaked cap worn by the Persians and some other eastern peoples, varying in shape according to the rank of the wearer; a kind of turban. **2.** A high ovate-cylindrical or dome-shaped diadem worn by the Pope, surmounted by the orb and cross of sovereignty, and encircled with three crowns symbolic of triple dignity, and usu. richly wrought with jewels; often called the *triplet*, or *triple crown*. Hence *transf.* the position or dignity of pope; the papacy. 1645. **3.** The head-dress of the Jewish High Priest 1868. **4.** An ornamental frontal, coronet, or head-band. (In mod. use, a jewelled or profusely decorated ornament worn by women above the forehead.) 1718. **5.** *Zool.* A mitre shell, or a genus of mitre-shells 1835.

4. *fig.* She [Venice] looks a sea Cybele . . with her t. of proud towers BYRON. Hence **Tia·raed, -ra'd** (-ăd) *ppl. a.* adorned with a t.

†**Tib** (tib). 1533. [perh. the same as *Tib*, pet form of *Isabel.*] Formerly, a typical name for a woman of the lower classes, as in *T. and Tom*. Also, a girl or lass, a sweetheart, a mistress; *dyslogistically*, a strumpet. –1700.

Comb.: **t.-cat,** *dial.*, a female cat.

Tibet, Thibet (tibe·t). 1827. Name of a country in central Asia; used *attrib.* of wool obtained thence, or of cloth or garments made from this. *absol.* Tibet cloth, or a gown or shawl made of it. Hence **Tibetan** (tibe·tăn) *a.* of, belonging to, or characteristic of T.

‖**Tibia** (ti·biă). *Pl.* **-æ** (*i*). 1548. [L., shin-bone, pipe or flute.] **1.** *Anat.* and *Zool.* The inner and usu. larger of the two bones (*tibia* and *fibula*) of the lower leg, from the knee to the ankle; the shin-bone. **b.** *Ent.* The fourth of the five joints of the leg of an insect, that between the femur and the tarsus 1815. **2.** *Antiq.* An ancient (single or double) flute or flageolet 1705.

Tibial (ti·biăl), *a.* (*sb.*) 1599. [– L. *tibialis*, f. *tibia*; see prec., -AL[1] 1.] **1.** *Anat.* and *Zool.* Of or pertaining to the tibia. Also as *sb.*, ellipt. for *t. artery, muscle*, etc. **2.** Of or pertaining to a tibia or ancient flute 1656.

Tibio- (tibio), used as comb. form of TIBIA, as in **Tibiota·rsal** *a.*, of or pertaining to the tibia and the tarsus; pertaining to the tibiotarsus; **Tibiota·rsus,** *Ornith.* the tibia of a bird's leg with the condyles formed by its fusion with the proximal bones of the tarsus.

Tiburtine (təi·bɒɹtəin), *a.* 1440. [– L. *Tiburtinus*, f. *Tiburs, Tiburt-* Tibur; see -INE[1].] Of or pertaining to the region or district of Tibur (now Tivoli) in ancient Latium. *T. stone* = TRAVERTINE.

Tic (tik). 1800. [– Fr. *tic* (XVII) – It. *ticchio.*] **1.** A disease or affection characterized by spasmodic twitching of certain muscles, esp. of the face; nearly always short for *tic douloureux*: see 2. 1822. **2.** *Tic douloureux* (*dulurö*) [Fr., = painful twitching], severe facial neuralgia with twitching of the facial muscles 1800.

‖**Tical** (*in Siam* tikā·l, *in Burma* ti·k'l). 1662. [– Pg. *tical*, repr. *ṭaṅkā* in various Indian vernaculars; see TANGA.] A term in use by foreign traders in Siam and Burma, applied to a silver coin and its weight, repr. roughly the Indian rupee (orig. the same as the *ṭaṅkā*), which has varied in value from 2*s.* 6*d.* to 1*s.* 2*d.*

‖**Ticca** (ti·kă, tī·kā). *India.* 1827. [– Hindi *ṭhīkā* or *ṭhīkah* hire, fare, fixed price (Yule).] *attrib.* Engaged on contract, hired; esp. in *t. gharry*, hired carriage.

Tice (təis), *sb.* 1874. [f. next.] An act of enticing, an enticement; *spec.* a stroke at croquet, or 'ball' (bowled) at cricket, which tempts or entices the opponent to take aim.

Tice (təis), *v. Obs.* exc. *dial.* ME. [Aphetic f. ATTICE or ENTICE, but earlier than these forms and prob. immed. – OFr. *atisier.*] *trans.* To entice; to induce or attract by the offer of pleasure or advantage. Also *absol.*

Tichorhine (təi·korəin), *a.* Also **-orrhine, -orine.** 1851. [– mod.L. *tichorrhinus*, f. Gr. τεῖχος wall + ῥίς (ῥιν-) nose.] *Palæont.* Having an ossified nasal septum; the English form of the specific name of the Woolly Rhinoceros.

Tick (tik), *sb.*[1] [OE. **ticca* or **tīca*, ME. *tyke, teke*, later *ticke* (XVI), corresp., with variation of vowel and cons., to MLG., MDu. *tēke* (Du. *teek*), OHG. *zēcho* (G. *zecke*), f. WGmc. **tīk-, *tikk-*; the ME. forms may be partly due to MLG. or MDu.] **1.** The common name for several kinds of mites or acarids, esp. of the genus *Ixodes* or family *Ixodidæ*, which infest the hair or fur of various animals, as dogs, cattle, etc., and attach themselves to the skin as temporary parasites; also, for the similarly parasitic dipterous insects of the families *Hippoboscidæ* (bird-ticks, horse-ticks, sheep-ticks) and *Nycteribiidæ* (bat-ticks). **2.** Short for *t.-bean* 1765.

Comb.: **t.-bean,** a small-seeded variety of the common bean, *Vicia faba*, so called from the resemblance of the seed to a dog-t.; **-bird,** any bird, e.g. the African *Buphaga* (rhinoceros-bird), which feeds on the ticks that infest large quadrupeds; **-fly,** any of the dipterous insects called ticks (see 1); **-seed,** name for various plants having seeds resembling ticks; **-trefoil,** a plant of the genus *Desmodium*, so named from the joints of the pods adhering like ticks to the fur of animals.

Tick (tik), *sb.*[2] 1466. [In XV *tikke, tēke, tyke*, corresp. to and prob. immed. – MLG., MDu. *tēke* and MDu. *tīke* (Du. *tijk*), rel. to OHG. *ziahha, ziehha* (G. *zieche* bed-tick, pillow-case); WGmc. – L. *theca* – Gr. θήκη case.] The case or cover containing feathers, flocks, or the like, forming a mattress or pillow; also, applied to the strong hard linen or cotton material used for making such cases.

Tick (tik), *sb.*[3] 1440. [Goes with TICK *v.*[1] The parallel LG. *tikk* touch, moment, instant, Du. *tik* pat, touch, MHG. *zic* slight touch, may point to a WGmc. base, or the various forms may be independent expressive formations.] **1.** A light but distinct touch; a pat, a tap. *Obs.* exc. *dial.* **b.** = TIG *sb.*[1] 2. (*rare*) 1622. **2.** A quick light dry sound, distinct but not loud; *esp.* the sound produced by the alternate check and release of the train in the escapement of a watch or clock; also the similar sound made by the death-watch beetle 1680. **b.** A beat of the heart or of the pulse 1823. **3.** A small dot or dash (often formed by two strokes at an acute angle) made with a pen or pencil, to draw attention to something or to mark a name, figure, etc., in a list as having been noted or checked 1844. **4.** *transf.* (from 2). The time between two ticks of the clock; a moment, second, instant. *colloq.* 1879.

4. It's all right. Can explain in two ticks 1904.

Tick, *sb.*[4] *colloq.* or *slang.* 1642. [app. abbrev. of TICKET *sb.* 7 in the phr. *on the ticket.*] **1.** Phr. *On* or *upon* (†*the*) *t.*, on credit, on trust; *to go on t.* (also *go t.*), *run on, upon t.*, to buy on credit, run into debt. **2.** Hence, credit, trust; reputation of solvency and probity 1668. **3.** A debit account; a score, reckoning 1681.

1. This villainous habit of living upon t. STEVENSON. **3.** He . . had a long t. at the tavern 1755.

Tick (tik), *v.*[1] 1546. [Goes with TICK *sb.*[3] Cf. Du. *tikken* pat, tick, OHG. *zekōn* pluck, MHG. *zicken* push; see TICK *sb.*[3]] **1.** *intr.* To touch or tap a thing or person lightly. *Obs.* exc. *dial.* **2.** Of a clock, watch, etc.: To make the light quick sound described under TICK *sb.*[3] 2. 1721. **b.** *trans.* With complement: To wear *away* or *out*, bring to an end, in ticking; to throw *off* or deliver by ticking 1870. **3.** To mark (a name, an item in a list, etc.) with a tick; to mark *off* with a tick, as noted, passed, or done with 1861. **b.** *slang. To t. off*, to reprimand, scold, 'tell off' 1919.

1. Stand not ticking and toying at the braunches . . but strike at the roote LATIMER. **3.** I compared each with the bill, and ticked it off DICKENS.

Tick (tik), *v.*[2] *colloq.* or *slang.* 1648. [f. TICK *sb.*[4]] **1.** *intr.* To 'go on tick' (see TICK *sb.*[4] 1); to deal with a tradesman, or the like on credit; to run into debt. **b.** *trans.* To leave (an amount) owing to be entered to one's debit 1674. **2.** *intr.* To give credit 1712. **b.** *trans.* To give (a person) credit 1842.

Ticken (ti·k'n). 1701. Local f. TICKING.

Ticker (ti·kəɹ). 1828. [f. TICK *v.*[1] + -ER[1].] Something that ticks. **a.** The pendulum or escapement of a clock or watch; also (*slang*) a watch. **b.** A telegraphic recording instrument, a tape-machine; a stock-indicator 1883.

Ticket (ti·kėt), *sb.* 1528. [Aphetic – Fr. †*étiquet* (cf. ETIQUETTE), OFr. *estiquet(te*, f. *estiquier, estequier* fix, stick, var. of *estichier, estechier* – MDu. *steken*; see -ET.] †**1.** A short written notice or document; a memorandum, a note, a billet. *Obs.* exc. as in b, c. –1760. **b.** *spec.* A written tender for ore, made by the smelter (*local*) 1778. **c.** *Stock Exch.* see quot. 1882. **2.** A written notice for public information; formerly, a notice posted in a public place, a placard; now *esp.* a slip of cardboard, etc. attached to an object and bearing its name, description, price, or the like; a label, show-card 1567. **3.** A visiting-card. Now *Obs.* or *dial.*; also *Anglo-Ind.* 1673. †**4.** A certificate or voucher; a warrant, licence, permit –1675. **5.** A slip, usu. of paper or card-board, bearing the evidence of the holder's title to some service or privilege, to which it admits him; as a *railway, tram* or *bus t., lottery-t., member's t., luncheon-t., soup-t.*, etc. 1673. **6.** A pay-warrant; *esp.* a discharge warrant in which the amount of pay due to a soldier or sailor is certified 1596. **b.** Short for TICKET OF LEAVE 1904. †**7.** An I O U; a promise to pay; a note or memorandum of money or goods received on credit; a debit account, a score; hence phr. *on, upon (the) t.*, on credit, on TICK –1656. **8.** In U.S. politics, the list of candidates for election nominated or put forward by a party or faction 1711. **9.** *slang.* **a.** The correct thing; what is wanted, expected, or fashionable; esp. in phr. *that's the t.* 1838. **b.** The program or plan of action; that which is to be done; the thing on hand 1842.

1. c. *T. Day*, The day for the passing of tickets between brokers and jobbers, by means of which they learn the amount of stocks and shares they have respectively to deliver or receive on the day following 1882. **2.** The t. in the window which announced 'Apartments to Let' THACKERAY. **5.** *fig.* Your Approbation is the T. by which they gain Admittance into your Paper STEELE. **8.** According to circumstances a man is said to vote the *straight t.*, i.e. the t. containing the 'regular nomination' of his party without change; a *scratch t.*, a t. from which the names of one or more of the candidates are erased; a *split t.*, a t. representing different divisions of his party; or a *mixed t.*, a t. in which the nominations of different parties are blended into one 1859.

Comb.: **t.-day** (see quot., sense 1 c); **-porter,** a member of a body of porters in the City of London who were licensed by the Corporation (now *Hist.*).

Ticket (ti·kėt), *v.* 1611. [f. prec.] **1.** *trans.* To attach a ticket to; to distinguish by means of a ticket; to label. Chiefly in *pa. pple.* **b.** *fig.* To describe or mark as by a ticket; to designate, set down (*as* so and so) 1654. **2.** To furnish with a ticket; to 'book'; also *absol.*, to issue tickets. *U.S.* 1842. **3.** *intr.* To make a tender *for* tin or copper ore by means of a 'ticket' or written tender (*local*) 1778.

1. Pictures which are sold during the exhibition will be ticketed as such 1810. **2.** We were 'ticketed through to the depot' LONGF.

Ticket of leave. 1732. A ticket or document giving leave or permission; an order, a permit (*rare*). Now, 'an order of licence' giving a convict his liberty under certain restrictions before his sentence has expired. Also *attrib.*, as *ticket-of-leave man*, etc.

Ticking (ti·kiŋ). 1649. [f. TICK *sb.*[2] + -ING[1].] The material of which bed-ticks are made; see TICK *sb.*[2]

Tickle (ti·k'l), *sb.*[1] 1770. [Of unkn. origin.] A name given on the coasts of Newfoundland and Labrador to a narrow difficult strait or passage.

Tickle (ti·k'l), *sb.*[2] 1801. [f. TICKLE *v.*] An act of tickling; a touch that tickles; a tickling sensation; a tickled or pleasantly excited feeling.

Tickle (ti·k'l), *a.* (*adv.*) late ME. [Goes with TICKLE *v.*; the use of the vb.-stem as adj. is unusual, but cf. KITTLE *a.* beside KITTLE *v.*[1], in same senses.] †**1.** Easily affected in any way; not firm or steadfast; loose; also, susceptible to tickling –1563. **2.** Not to be depended upon; uncertain; unreliable; changeable, capricious, fickle. Now *dial.* late ME. **3.** In unstable equilibrium, easily upset or overthrown, insecure, tottering, crazy; also, easily set in motion; nicely poised; delicate, sensitive. Now *dial.* 1515. **b.** *transf.* Of a place, condition, etc.: Insecure; precarious; risky. *Obs.* or *arch.* 1579. **4.** = TICKLISH *a.* 5. Now *dial.* 1569. **b.** Fastidious, dainty, squeamish; easily upset or disordered. Now *dial.* 1456. **c.** Difficult to deal with 1570. **d.** Of an animal: Easily scared; shy, wild. *dial.* 1876.

2. This world is now ful tikel sikerly CHAUCER. **3.** *T. of the sear*: see SEAR *sb.* **b.** Footing..still more t., and unsafe COTTON. **4.** Tell wit how much it wrangles In t. points of niceness RALEGH. Hence †**Ti·ckle-ly** *adv.* (*rare*), **-ness.**

Tickle (ti·k'l), *v.* ME. [prob. frequent. of TICK *sb.*[3]; see -LE.] **I.** *intr.* †**1.** To be affected or excited by a pleasantly tingling or thrilling sensation: said of the heart, lungs, blood, 'spirits', etc., also of the person –1647. **2.** To tingle; to itch; also *fig.* (*dial.*) to have an uneasy desire (usu. *to do* something); to be eager. Now *rare.* 1542.

1. Oh how my lungs do t.! ha, ha, ha! FLETCHER. **2.** Whose eares euer tickled to heare newes 1557.

II. *trans.* (= L. *titillare*). **1.** Said of a thing, or impersonally with *it*: To excite agreeably (a person, his ears, palate, etc.); to please, gratify. late ME. **2.** To touch or stroke lightly with or as with the finger-tips, a straw, a feather, a hair, or the like; to irritate lightly, so as to cause a peculiar uneasy sensation. Also *absol.* 1450. **b.** To touch or poke (a person) lightly in a sensitive part so as to excite spasmodic laughter. Also *absol.* 1530. **c.** Applied to a method of catching trout or other fish: see TICKLING *vbl. sb.* b. Often *allus.* 1601. **3.** *fig.* To excite amusement in; to divert; often in the phr. *to t. the fancy.* Also *absol.* 1688. **4.** To touch (a stringed instrument, etc.) lightly; to stir (a fire, etc.) slightly 1589. **b.** *iron.* To beat, chastise 1592. †**5.** To excite, affect, move; also, to vex, irritate, provoke –1698. †**b.** To arouse by or as by tickling; to stir up, incite, provoke; to prompt or impel *to do* something –1592. **c.** With *up*: To stir up, arouse by tickling, excite to action 1567. **d.** To get or move (a thing) *into* or *out of* some place, position, or state, by action likened to tickling 1677.

1. Elements that..tickled..curiosity GEO. ELIOT. Phr. *To t. to death*, to divert greatly. **2.** If my haire do but t. me, I must scratch SHAKS. **b.** If you t. vs, doe we not laugh? SHAKS. Phr. *To t.* (*a person's*) *palm*, to tip him. **c.** *Twel. N.* II. v. 26. **4.** To t. a Cittern, or have a sweete stroke on the Lute NASHE. **b.** These little rogues..should be well tickled with the birch 1800. **5.** Shee's tickled now, her Fume needs no spurres SHAKS.

Comb.: †**t.-brain**, potent liquor; hence *transf.* one who supplies it; †**-toby**, a birch, rod, switch.

Ticklenburgs (ti·klənbɒ̄ɹgz), *sb. pl.* 1696. [f. *Tecklenburg*, Westphalia, noted for its manufactures of linen.] A coarse mixed linen fabric made for the West India market.

Tickler (ti·kləɹ). 1680. [f. TICKLE *v.* + -ER[1].] One who or that which tickles, in various senses. **1.** One who tickles by touching or stroking lightly 1715. **2.** Something that tickles or is used for tickling; e.g. an instrument for extracting bungs from casks; a rod or birch used in castigation; a slender steel rod used for stirring the fire; an implement for tickling a person, with the purpose of irritating or teasing; (*US.*) a book in which a register of notes or debts is kept for reference 1680. **3.** *U.S.* A large Amer. longicorn beetle. *Monohammus titillator*, with very long antennæ 1841.

Tickling (ti·kliŋ), *vbl. sb.* late ME. [f. TICKLE *v.* + -ING[1].] The action or condition denoted by TICKLE *v.*; slight nervous irritation akin to itching; uneasy desire, hankering, craving; pleasing excitement, gratification; etc. **b.** *spec.* The taking of trout, etc., by the method described in the quot. 1616.

Woman haue in them selues a t. and studie of vaine glorie KNOX. He had some t. in his throat 1898. **b.** Groping for trout (or tickling)—is tracing it to the stone it lies under, then rubbing it gently beneath, which causes the fish to gradually move backwards into the hand, till the fingers suddenly close in the gills JEFFERIES.

Ticklish (ti·kliʃ), *a.* 1581. [f. TICKLE *a.* or *v.* + -ISH[1].] **1.** Easily tickled; sensitive to tickling 1598. **2.** Unstably balanced or poised; easily upset; unsteady; of a boat, easily capsized 1601. **3.** *fig.* Easily upset in temper; apt to be offended, sensitive, touchy 1581. **4.** Unstable, unsteady, unsettled, uncertain, fickle 1606. **5.** Needing cautious handling or action; delicate, precarious, risky, hazardous 1591. **6.** quasi-*adv.* Ticklishly. Now *rare.* 1661.

1. Some part of the skin is..thin, as in the..soales of the feete, which is the reason that there men are t. 1615. **2.** So t. are the scales of victory, a very mote will turn them FULLER. **3.** You are t. on such points BYRON. **4.** But foreign friendship is t., temporary, and lasteth no longer than it is advantaged with mutual interest FULLER. **5.** A very t. predicament 1809. Hence **Ti·cklish-ly** *adv.*, **-ness.**

Tickly (ti·kli), *a.* 1530. [f. TICKLE *a.* + -Y[1].] Ticklish.

Tick-tack (ti·kˌtæ·k). 1549. [imit. Cf. Du. *tiktak*, G. *ticktack*, Fr. *tic-tac.*] **1.** An imitation of a reduplicated or alternating ticking sound, esp. that made by a clock; also that of the firing of small artillery. (Used as *adv.* or *int.*, and hence as *sb.* to denote the sound.) **b)** (usu. in Fr. form *tic-tac.*) In auscultation, the sound of the heart-beat 1853. †**2.** An old variety of backgammon, played on a board with holes along the edge, in which pegs were placed for scoring. (Also called TRIC-TRAC.) –1740. **3.** A system of signalling used by bookmakers, hence the men who practise this 1899. **4. Tick-tack-toe,** a children's game played with a pencil on a slate 1884. Hence **Tick-tack** *v.* to signal (cf. 3 above).

Tick-tick (ti·kˌti·k). 1774. [imit.] An imitation of the ticking of a clock or watch, or a similar sound; hence, a child's name for a clock or watch. Also **Ti·ck-to·ck** 1848.

‖**Tic-polonga** (tikˌpolǫ·ŋgă). 1825. [– Sinhalese *tit-polongā*, f. *tita*, in comb. *tit-* speck, freckle, spot, mark + *polongā* viper. *Tik* spot, freckle, etc. has app. been substituted for *tit-*.] *Zool.* A venomous snake of India and Ceylon; the chain viper or necklace-snake, *Daboia russelli*.

Tidal (təi·dăl), *a.* 1807. [f. TIDE *sb.* II. -AL[1] 1.] **1.** Of, pertaining to, or affected by tides; ebbing and flowing periodically. **b.** *T. wave*: the high water wave caused by the movement of the tide; *erron.* an exceptionally large ocean wave caused by an earthquake or other local commotion 1830. (*b*) *fig.* A great progressive movement or manifestation of feeling, opinion, or the like 1884. (*c*) *Physiol.* The main or primary height of flow in a beat of the pulse 1896. **2.** *transf.* and *fig.* That 'ebbs and flows'; periodic, intermittent; alternating, varying 1872. **3.** Dependent upon or regulated by the state of the tide or time of high water 1858.

1. *T. river*, a river which is affected by the tides for some distance from its mouth; Up to Teddington..the Thames is a t. river HUXLEY. **2.** *T. air* (*Physiol.*), the air passing in and out of the lungs at each ordinary respiration. **3.** *T. basin, harbour*, a basin or harbour which is accessible or navigable only at high tide. *T. boat, steamer*, a vessel the sailings of which depend on the time of the tide. *T. train*, a train running in connection with a t. steamer. Hence **Ti·dally** *adv.* in a t. manner; by or in respect of the tides.

Tiddle (tid'l), *v. Obs.* exc. *dial.* or *slang.* 1560. [With sense 1 cf. TIDLING.] **1.** *trans.* To fondle or indulge to excess; to tend carefully, nurse, cherish. **2.** *intr.* To potter, trifle, 'fiddle'; to fidget, fuss 1747.

Ti·ddler. 1885. [perh. rel. to TITTLEBAT and *tiddly* 'little'.] Nursery name for a small minnow or a stickleback.

Tiddlywink (ti·dliwiŋk). 1870. [Of unkn. origin.] **a.** A game played with dominoes. **b.** *pl.* A game in which small counters are caused to spring from the table into a receptacle, by pressing upon their edges with larger counters.

Tide (təid), *sb.* [OE. *tīd* = OS. *tīd* (Du. *tijd*), OHG. *zīt* (G. *zeit*), ON. *tīð* :- Gmc. **tīdiz*, f. **tī-* (cf. TIME). In Branch II. prob. after MLG. (*ge*)*tīde*, *tīe*, MDu. *ghetīde* (Du. *tij*, *getij*), a special development of the sense 'fixed time'.] **I.** Time. †**1.** A portion, extent, or space of time; an age, a season, a while –1871. **2.** A point in the duration of the day, month, or year, of human life, or of other period. *arch.* or *poet.* OE. **b.** A suitable, favourable, or proper time or occasion; opportunity. *arch.* OE. **3.** Any definite time in the course of the day; *Obs.* exc. as EVEN-TIDE, NOON-TIDE OE. **b.** A more or less definite point or season in the course of the year, of life, etc.; as *New-Year's tide*, SPRING-TIDE, etc. *arch.* or *poet.* OE. **4.** An anniversary, or festival of the church. See EASTER-TIDE, LAMMAS-TIDE, WHITSUNTIDE, etc. OE.

2. He, who, from ill death Saved me that t. MORRIS. **3. b.** High over all the yellowing Autumn-tide TENNYSON. **4.** What hath this day deseru'd.. That it..should be set Among the high tides in the Kalendar? SHAKS.

II. Tide of the sea. [prob. – MLG. (*ge*)*tīde.*] **1.** The flowing or swelling of the sea, or its alternate rising and falling, twice in each lunar day, due to the attraction of the moon and, in a less degree, of the sun; the alternate inflow and outflow produced by this on a coast, the flood and ebb. late ME. **b.** *transf.* A recurrent flow, alternate rise and fall or increase and decrease, other than of the sea 1604. **2.** The space of time between two successive points of high water, or between low water and high water, in the sea; also, that portion of this time during which the height of the water ('state of the tide') allows of work being done, as in *tide's work*. So, in *Mining* a period of twelve hours. 1495. **3.** *fig.* Applied to that which is like the tide of the sea in some way; as in ebbing or flowing, rising or falling, or 'turning' at a certain time. late ME. **4.** *spec.* = FLOOD-TIDE. Also *fig.* 1570. **5.** *transf.* A body of flowing water or other liquid; a stream, a current. *poet.* and *rhet.* 1585. **b.** *transf.* and *fig.* 1601. **6.** The water of the sea; the sea (esp. when the tide is flowing). *poet.* 1791.

1. Both winde and t. stayes for this Gentleman SHAKS. Phr. **Cross t.,** a tide running across the direction of another; **high t.,** (*a*) = HIGH WATER; (*b*) = SPRING-TIDE; **low t.** = LOW WATER; **leeward, neap, windward t.**: see the defining words; also FLOOD-TIDE, SPRING-TIDE. **b.** Swayed by the sweeping of the tides of air 1856. **2.** *Tide's work*, the amount of progress a ship has made during a favourable t. Also, a period of necessary labour on a ship during the ebbing and slack water of a t. 1867. **3.** *Jul. C.* IV. iii. 218. From that moment the t. of battle turned MACAULAY. **4.** I haue important businesse The t. whereof is now SHAKS. **5.** Deep in the roaring t. he plung'd GRAY. **b.** Thou art the Ruines of the Noblest man That euer liued in the T. of Times SHAKS. **b.** Bounding o'er yon blue t. BYRON.

Phrases. †*T. and* (or) *time* (also *time and t.*), an alliterative reduplication, in which the two words were more or less synonyms, or = time and (or) season. *Time and t. wait for no man* (here *tide* orig. meant 'time', but from the 16th c. has usually meant the tide of the sea). (*In*) *double tides*, perh. = as if taking advantage of both the tides in one day; esp. *to work double tides*, to work as hard as possible.

Comb.: **t.-boat**, a boat or small vessel which travels with or by means of the t.; **-gate**, a gate through which the water passes into a dock or the like at flood t., and by which it is retained during the ebb; **-lock**, a double lock between tidal water and a canal or the like; a guard-lock; **-river**, tidal river; **-rode** *a.*, *Naut.* (for *tide-ridden*), swung by the tide, as a ship at anchor; opp. to *wind-rode*; **-surveyor**, a customs official who supervised the t.-waiters; **-table**, a table, or tabular list showing the times of high water at a place or places during some period; **-wave**, the undulation which passes over the surface of the ocean, and causes high or low tide as its highest or lowest point reaches any place; **-work**, work which can be carried on only during hours when the tide is low, or that is paid for by the tide.

Tide (təid), *v.*[1] [OE. *tīdan* (oftener *ġetīdan*) happen, come about, f. *tīd* TIDE *sb.*] *intr.* To happen, befall. Often impersonal. *arch.*

Tide (təid), *v.*[2] 1593. [f. TIDE *sb.* II.] **1.** *trans.* **a.** To carry, as the tide does 1640. **b.** To enable (a person) to surmount (a difficulty) as on a swelling tide 1860. **2.** *intr.* To flow or surge, as does the tide; to flow to and fro; sometimes = 'flow' as opp. to 'ebb' 1593. **3.** To float or drift on the tide; *spec. Naut.* to navigate a ship by taking advantage of favouring tides, and anchoring when the tide turns; usu. with adv. of direction. Often *to t. it.* 1627. **b.** *fig.* To pass or be carried as on the tide; to drift 1835. **4.** *intr. fig. To t. over*: To get over or surmount (a difficulty, etc.) as if by rising on the flowing tide, or by taking advantage of a favourable tide 1659.

1. The Relicks of the Wrack..are tided back By the wild Waves, and rudely thrown ashore DRYDEN. **2.** The seas, Whose equal valour neither ebbs nor tides 1661. **3.** Hither there tided The loose-limbed Briton 1896. **4.** For the moment the difficulty is tided over 1884.

Tideless (təi·dlės), *a.* 1779. [f. TIDE *sb.* + -LESS.] Having no tide; unaffected by tides; not washed or covered by a tide.

The waters of the t. Mediterranean 1886. Hence **Ti·delessness.**

Tideling, -lynge, var. TIDLING.

Ti·de-mark. 1799. The mark left or reached by the tide at high or (rarely) low water; by extension, the mark left by a river-flood. Also, a post or the like set up to mark the rise or fall of, or the point reached by the tide.

Ti·de-mill. 1796. **1.** A mill driven by the flux and reflux of the tide acting on a water-wheel. **2.** A mill for clearing lands from tide-water 1828.

Ti·de-rip. 1830. [RIP *sb.*[3] 1.] **1.** A commotion of the sea caused by opposing currents, or by a rapid current passing over an uneven bottom. **2.** A tidal wave or current 1903.

Tidesman (təi·dzmǣn). 1667. †**1.** = TIDE-WAITER 1. –1809. **2.** One whose work depends on the tide 1882.

Ti·de-wai:ter. 1699. **1.** A customs officer who awaited the arrival of ships (formerly coming in with the tide), and boarded them to prevent the evasion of custom-house regulations. Now *Hist.* **2.** *fig.* One who waits for a favourable season 1841.

Ti·de-wa:ter. 1799. **1.** Water brought by the flood-tide. **2.** *U.S.* Water affected by the ordinary ebb and flow of the tide; tidal water 1789. **b.** *attrib.* as *t.-w. country* 1829.

Tideway (təi·dˌweⁱ). 1627. A channel in which a tidal current runs; also, the tidal part of a river; *transf.* a strong current running in such a channel.

Ti·dily, *adv.* ME. [f. TIDY *a.* + -LY[2].] In a tidy manner. So **Ti·diness,** the quality of being tidy.

Tiding (təi·diŋ); pl. **tidings** (təi·diŋz). [Late OE. *tīdung*, early ME. *tiding*, as if f. OE. *tīdan* happen, befall + -ING[1]; but prob. – ON. *tíðendi, -indi* events, occurrences, the reports of these, f. *tíðr* occurring + *-endi, -indi* nominal suffix.] **1.** Something that happens; an event, incident, occurrence. *Obs.* or *arch.* **2.** The announcement of an event or occurrence; a piece of news (*obs.* or *arch.*); usu. in pl. *tidings*, reports, news, intelligence, information OE.

1. How that this blisful tidyng is bifalle CHAUCER. **2.** To me þis is a Ioyfull tydyng 1485. Her Son.. left at Jordan, tydings of him none MILT. The tidings was world-old, or older CARLYLE.

Tidling (ti·dliŋ). Now *dial.* (**tiddling**). 1520. [perh. f. TIDDLE *v.* 1: see -LING[1].] A child or animal reared with special care; a pampered pet.

Tidy (təi·di), *a.* (*sb.*, *adv.*) [ME. *tidi*, f. *tīd* time, TIDE *sb.* + -Y[1].] †**1.** Timely, seasonable, opportune; in season –1721. **2.** In good condition, or of good appearance; fair, well-favoured; fat, plump, healthy. Now *dial.* ME. **3.** As an indefinite epithet of admiration or commendation. †**a.** Good, excellent, satisfactory, useful –1625. **b.** Fairly satisfactory, 'pretty good'; decent; 'nice' (*colloq.*) 1844. **c.** Considerable (in amount or degree); 'pretty big'. *colloq.* 1838. **4. a.** Of persons: Orderly in habits, or in personal appearance; disposed to keep things neat and in order 1706. **b.** Of things, esp. of a house, room, receptacle, etc.: Neatly arranged; orderly, neat, trim 1828.

2. Thou whorson little tydie Bartholmew Borepigge SHAKS. A t. girl 1881. **3. b.** He was a t. chap, though queer 1899. **c.** They do swear a t. bit 1903. *A t. penny* = 'a pretty penny' (PRETTY *a.* 5). **4. a.** A t. Servant 1706. The tidiest woman in the world 1849.

B. *sb.* **a.** A pinafore or overall. *dial.* 1825. **b.** *U.S.* An ornamental loose covering for the back of a chair or the like; an antimacassar 1850. **c.** A bag in which to keep scraps, odds and ends, etc.; a work-bag, toilet-tidy, hair-tidy 1828. **C.** *adv.* Tidily; pretty well; nicely, finely; also *iron.*, *dial.*, or *vulgar.* 1824.

Ti·dy, *v.* Chiefly *colloq.* 1821. [f. TIDY *a.*] *trans.* To make tidy or orderly; to arrange neatly; *refl.* to put one's hair, dress, etc. in order; to make oneself neat. Often with *up.* Also *absol.* **b.** To stow *away* or clear *up* for the sake of tidiness 1867.

b. It..had been 'tidied up' by one of those.. housemaids who are the bane of every busy man 1884.

Tie (təi), *sb.* [OE. *tēah* (*tēag-*), *tēġ* = ON. *taug* rope :– Gmc. *tauʒō, f. *tauχ- (cf. TEAM, TOW *v.*).] **1.** That with which anything is tied; *esp.* an ornamental knot or bow of ribbon, etc. **2.** *Naut.* **a.** A rope or chain by which a yard is suspended 1465. **b.** A mooring-bridle 1867. †**3.** A knot of hair; a pig-tail; also short for TIE-WIG –1817. **4.** A neck-tie, a cravat. Also, a woman's fur necklet. 1761. **5.** A kind of low shoe fastened with a tie or lace 1826. **6.** *gen.* Something that connects or unites two or more things in some way; a link 1711. **b.** *Mus.* A curved line placed over or under two notes of the same pitch, to indicate that the sound is to be sustained (not repeated) 1656. **7.** *Arch.*, etc. A beam or rod used to 'tie' or bind together two parts of a building or other structure by counteracting a tensile strain which tends to draw them apart 1793. **b.** *U.S.* A (transverse) railway sleeper 1857. **8.** *fig.* Something that ties or binds in an abstract or fig. sense 1555. **9.** The fact or method of tying; the condition of being tied, bound, or united 1718. **10.** Equality between two or more competitors or the sides in a match or contest; a match in which this occurs, a drawn match; a dead heat. Hence, *to play off, shoot off*, etc. *a tie*, to determine a tie by playing another match 1680. Hence **b.** A deciding match played after a draw; also, a match played between the victors in previous matches or heats 1895.

1. Great formal wigs, with a t. behind DICKENS. **4.** He'll come down to dinner in a flannel shirt and no t. 1895. **8.** They haue charitie in such sure t. that they cannot lose it LATIMER. I was..under tye of Secrecy 1641. Bound..by..the Ties of Moral Duty 1754. The ties of a common blood, and a common speech 1874. **10. b.** *Cup.-t.*, a match between two sides in a knockout competition for a cup.

Tie (təi), *v.* Infl. **tied, tying.** [OE. *tīġan*, late form of WS. *tīeġan*, Anglian *tēġan* (ME. *teʒen*) :– Gmc. *tauʒian (cf. ON. *teygja* draw). For the vocalism cf. DIE *v.*[1], EYE *sb.*, etc.] **1.** *trans.* To bind, fasten, make fast (one thing to another, or two or more things together) with a cord, rope, band, or the like, drawn together and knotted; to confine (a person or animal) by fastening to something. **b.** To draw together the parts of (a single thing) with a knotted cord or the like; to fasten (a part of dress, etc.) in this way, esp. with strings already attached to it (as a bonnet, a shoe); also, to draw together (a cord or the like) into a knot, esp. for the purpose of fastening something. late ME. **c.** *Surg.* To bind and constrict (an artery or vein) with a ligature, so as to prevent the flow of blood through it 1597. **d.** To make or form by tying (a knot, etc.) 1647. **2.** To fasten together, connect, join (material things) in any way; *spec.* in *Arch.* to connect and make fast by a rod or beam, or by other means 1585. **b.** To check the free movement or working of 1597. **c.** *Mus.* To connect (notes) by a tie or ligature 1597. **d.** *U.S.* To furnish (a railway line) with 'ties' or sleepers 1883. **3.** *fig.* To join closely or firmly; *esp.* to unite in marriage (now *dial.*) OE. **b.** *intr.* for *refl.* To attach oneself *to*. *U.S. colloq.* 1879. **4.** To bind, oblige, restrain, constrain *to* (also *from*) some course of action, etc.; to limit, confine, restrict ME. **b.** To bind, oblige (*to do* something): usu. in *pass.* Now only *dial.* 1596. †**c.** To bring into bondage –1613. **d.** To bind by favour or service rendered: usu. in *pass.* 1576. **e.** To restrict (a dealer or firm) to a particular source for articles sold; only in *pa. pple.*, usu. applied to a public house so restricted as to liquor 1817. †**5.** *fig.* To confirm, ratify; to 'knit', 'cement' –1697. **6.** *intr.* To be equal (*with*) in a contest, etc. 1680.

1. Such bells were also tyed to Hawks 1816. Phr. *Ride and t.*: see RIDE *v.* Phr. *To t. the hands of*, to deprive of freedom of action. *Tied to* a woman's *apron-strings*: see APRON-STRING. **b.** They tye their Garments about with a Girdle 1662. **d.** *To t. the knot*, to perform the ceremony of marriage. **3.** How could you think of tying yourself to such a family? DE FOE. **4.** Phr. *To be tied to* (or *for*) *time*, to be limited to a certain time for doing something. **b.** *Tam. Shr.* I. i. 217. **c.** *Hen. VIII*, IV. ii. 36. **d.** *Cymb.* I. vi. 23.

With advbs. **Tie down. a.** To fasten down or confine by tying. **b.** *fig.* To confine stringently (*to* some thing or action). **T. up. a.** *trans.* To fasten (a thing) with a cord or band tied round it; to bind up, wrap up. **b.** To tie (a person or animal) to some fixed object or in some confined space, so as to prevent from escaping. **c.** *fig.* To bind, restrain, or confine strictly; to oblige to act in a particular way. **d.** To moor (a ship or boat); also *absol.* or *intr.* for *pass.* **e.** *fig.* To invest or place (money or property) in such a way as to prevent it from being spent or alienated. **f.** To join in marriage (*colloq.* or *slang*). **g.** To associate oneself *with* (orig. *U.S.*).

Tie- in comb. [f. TIE *sb.* or *v.*]

1. attrib. or obj. combs. of TIE *sb.*; **tie-block** *Naut.*, the block on the yard through which the tie passes (see TIE *sb.* 2 a); **-maker; -pin,** a pin, usu. ornamental, worn in a neck-tie; **-shooting,** the shooting off of a tie (TIE *sb.* 10) in rifle practice.

2. *Comb.* with sbs., in which the first element may be either TIE *sb.* or *v.*: **tie·-bar,** a bar which ties or acts as a tie, in a building, etc.; **-beam,** a horizontal beam which acts as a tie; **-bolt,** *sb.*, a bolt which ties together the component parts of a structure; hence as *vb.*; †**-dog,** a dog kept tied or chained up, either to guard a house, or because of its fierceness; **-knot,** a knot with which something is tied; **-post,** a post to with a horse, etc. may be tied; **-rod,** a long tie-bolt or iron rod which acts as a tie in a building, etc.; **-string,** a string for tying something, e.g. a bonnet or other part of costume; **-vote,** a vote resulting in a tie, the numbers on each side being equal.

Tier[1] (tīᵊɹ). 1569. [*Tier, tire* (XVI) – (O)Fr. *tire* sequence, rank, order, f. *tirer* draw, draw out :– Rom. **tirare*, of unkn. origin.] **1.** A row, rank, range, course; usu. one of a series of rows placed one above another, or rising each above the preceding one. **b.** A row of guns or gun-ports in a man-of-war or a fort 1573. **c.** A rank of pipes in an organ controlled by one stop 1828. **d.** *transf.* and *fig.* Rank, grade; stratum 1590. **2.** *Naut.* **a.** A row of ships moored or anchored at a particular place; hence, an anchorage or mooring-place where ships lie in rows or columns 1732. **b.** A large rack, in which the cables, anchor gear, runners and tackles, etc. are stowed 1797.

1. e. *U.S.* A range of counties, etc. 1693.

Tier[2] (təi·əɹ). Also **tyer.** 1633. [f. TIE *v.* + -ER[1].] **1.** One who ties; *spec.* a person employed to tie something. Also *t. up.* **2.** Something that ties or is used for tying; a band 1844. **3.** *U.S.* A pinafore or apron covering the whole front of the dress 1846.

Tierce (tīᵊɹs). late ME. [– (O)Fr. *tierce*, *terce* :– L. *tertia*, subst. use of fem. of *tertius* THIRD.] †**1.** A third part –1651. **2.** *Eccl.* **a.** The third hour of the canonical day, ending at 9 a.m.; also, the period from 9 a.m. till noon. *Obs.* exc. *Hist.* late ME. **b.** (Now usu. spelt **terce.**) The office said at this hour. late ME. **3.** An old measure of capacity equivalent to one third of a pipe (usu. 42 gallons old wine measure); also, a cask or vessel holding this quantity, usu. of wine, but also of various kinds of provisions or other goods; also, such a cask with its contents 1531. **4.** One of the positions in fencing; the third of the eight parries in sword-play, or the corresponding thrust 1692. **5.** In piquet and other card games, a sequence of three cards in any suit 1659. **6.** *Mus.* **a.** The interval of a third; the note at this interval above a given note. Now *rare* or *Obs.* **b.** The note two octaves and a major third (= a major 17th) above a fundamental note; hence, a mutation stop in an organ giving tones at this interval above the normal pitch 1606. **7.** *Her.* The division of a shield by lines into three equal parts: see next 1847.

5. *T. major*, the highest three cards of a suit; *t. minor*, the lowest three, i.e. seven, eight, and nine; *t. to a king, queen*, etc., a t. of which the king, queen, etc. is the highest.

‖**Tiercé** (tyęrse, tīᵊ·ɹse), *a.* 1725. [Fr., pa. pple. of (O)Fr. *tiercer* divide into three parts.] *Her.* Said of a field divided *en tierce*, i.e. into three equal parts all of different tinctures. Also anglicized as **Tierced** (tīᵊɹst).

Tierceron (tīᵊ·ɹsěrǫn). 1842. [– Fr. *tierceron* (XVI), f. *tiers* third + *-on* -OON, with intercalated *-er-*.] *Arch.* A subordinate arch springing from the point of intersection of two main arches of a vault.

‖**Tierras** (tye·ras), *sb. pl. U.S.* 1874. [Sp., pl. of *tierra* earth :– L. *terra*.] *Mining.* Pulverulent ore, *spec.* of quicksilver, mingled with sand and earthy matter; in Mexico, inferior pulverulent ores generally.

‖**Tiers état** (tyęrzeta). 1783. [Fr., = third estate; see TIERCE and ESTATE *sb.*] A third estate or class; *esp.* the third estate, the body of commons or their representatives in the French National Assembly before the Revolution; occas. also, the corresponding body in other countries.

Tie·-wig. 1713. [Cf. TIE- 2.] A wig having the hair gathered together behind and tied with a knot of ribbon. Now *arch.*

Tiff (tif), *sb.*¹ *colloq.* or *slang.* Now *rare* or *Obs.* 1635. [Of unkn. origin; goes with TIFF *v.*² (also *tift* vb., Sc. and dial. XVIII).] **1.** Liquor, *esp.* poor, weak, or 'small' liquor, 'tipple'. **2.** A sip or little drink of punch or other diluted liquor 1727.

Tiff (tif), *sb.*² *colloq.* 1727. [Of unkn., prob. dial., origin.] **1.** A slight outburst or fit of temper, pettishness, or ill-humour. Now *rare.* **2.** A slight or petty quarrel; a 'breeze'; occas. applied to a more serious quarrel 1754.

†**Tiff,** *v.*¹ ME. [– OFr. *tifer, tiffer*, (mod. *attifer*) adorn.] *trans.* To attire, deck out, 'titivate' (one's person, hair, etc.). Also *absol.* or *intr.* –1768.

Tiff, *v.*² *colloq.* or *slang.* Now *rare* or *Obs.* 1769. [See TIFF *sb.*¹] *trans.* To drink; *esp.* to drink slowly or in small portions, to sip.

Tiff, *v.*³ 1727. [f. TIFF *sb.*²] *intr.* To be in a tiff or pet; to have a tiff, or petty quarrel.

Tiff, *v.*⁴ *India.* 1803. [app. back-formation from or abbrev. of *tiffing* TIFFIN.] *intr.* = TIFFIN *v.*

Tiffany (ti·fǎni). ME. [– OFr. *tifanie* :– eccl. L. *theophania* (IV) – Gr. θεοφάνεια; see THEOPHANY. Sense 2 is found only in English, and the origin of this sense is obsc.] †**1.** The festival of the Epiphany or Twelfth Day (Jan. 6) –1633. **2.** A kind of thin transparent silk; also, a transparent gauze muslin, cobweb lawn 1601. **b.** An article made of tiffany, as a head-dress, a sieve, etc. 1606. **c.** *attrib.* or as *adj.* Made of tiffany; *fig.* 'transparent', flimsy 1608.

2. Their sleeves..shewing their naked armes, thro' false sleeves of t. EVELYN.

Tiffin (ti·fin), *sb. India.* †Also **tiffing.** 1785. [app. f. *tiffing*, f. TIFF *v.*² take a little drink or sip; specialized in Anglo-Ind. use.] In India and neighbouring eastern countries: A light midday meal; luncheon. Hence **Ti·ffin** *v. intr.* to take t., to lunch.

Tift. *dial.* 1751. [app. var. of TIFF *sb.*²] = TIFF *sb.*²

Tig (tig), *sb.* 1721. [f. next. Cf. TICK *sb.*³] **1.** A touch, usu. a light but significant touch, a tap or pat. **2.** A children's game, in which one of the players pursues the others until he overtakes and touches or 'tigs' one 1816.

Tig (tig), *v.* 1821. [var. of TICK *v.*¹] *trans.* To touch in the game of tig. Also *absol.*

‖**Tige** (tīʒ). 1664. [Fr., 'stalk' :– L. *tibia* shank, pipe.] The shaft of a column; also *transf.*; in *Bot.* a stem.

Tigelle (tiʒe·l). Also **tigel,** and in L. form **tigella.** 1860. [– Fr. *tigelle*, dim. of *tige*; see prec., -EL².] *Bot.* The embryonic axis or primitive stem, which bears the cotyledons; the caulicle or radicle. Sometimes applied to the plumule. Hence **Tigellate** (ti·dʒeleᶦt) *a.* having a t.

Tiger (təi·gəɹ). [ME. *tygre* – (O)Fr. *tigre* – L. *tigris* – Gr. τίγρις.] **1.** A large carnivorous quadruped, *Panthera tigris*, one of the two largest living felines, a cat-like maneless animal, in colour tawny yellow with blackish transverse stripes and white belly; widely distributed in Asia, and proverbial for its ferocity and cunning. **2.** Applied to other animals of the same genus, as in America to the Jaguar, *Felis onca*, and the Puma or Cougar, *F. concolor* (rare); and esp. in S. Africa, to the Leopard or Panther, *F. pardus* 1604. **b.** esp. with qualifications 1774. **c.** Applied to other than feline beasts 1832. **3.** The figure or representation of a tiger, *esp.* one used as a badge or crest; hence, pop. applied to an organization or society having this badge; also, a member of such a society; *spec.* (*Tammany T.*), the Tammany organization (*U.S.*) 1475. **4.** *transf.* and *fig.* Applied to one who or that which in some way resembles or suggests a tiger 1500. **5.** A smartly-liveried boy acting as groom or footman; less strictly, an outdoor boy-servant. *slang. Hist.* 1817. †**6.** A vulgarly or obtrusively overdressed person; also, a hanger-on, parasite; a roué, rake, swell-mobsman. *slang.* –1849. **7.** *U.S. slang.* A shriek or howl (often the word 'tiger') terminating a prolonged and enthusiastic cheer 1856. **8.** Short for *t.-moth*, *-shark*, etc. 1797.

1. Tyger, tyger, burning bright, In the forests of the night BLAKE. *Bengal t.*, *Royal t.*, the tiger of Bengal, where it attains its typical development. **2. b.** †*American t.*, †*Mexican t.*, the jaguar; *clouded t.*, *marbled t.*, *tortoiseshell t.*, species of TIGER-CAT. **c.** *Tasmanian* or *native t.*, the striped wolf or zebra-wolf of Tasmania. *Sabre-toothed t.*, see SABRE *sb.* **3.** The 17ᵗʰ [foot]..the Bengal Tigers, from their badge—a t. 1874. **4.** The blood-thirsty tygers of the French revolution 1806. 'The tigers of the sea' [sharks] 1885. **6.** That man is a t...a low man THACKERAY. **7.** The scamp.. proposes three cheers and a t. for Mr. Gordon 1869.

Comb.: **t.-beetle,** any species of the family *Cicindelidæ*, characterized by variegated colouring, activity, and voracity; **-bird,** (*a*) a S. Amer. scansorial barbet; (*b*) = *t.-bittern*; **-bittern,** a S. Amer. bittern of the genus *Tigrosoma*, with striped plumage; **-eye** = *tiger's eye*; **-flower,** any plant or species of *Tigridia*, a genus of tropical Amer. bulbous plants bearing large purple, yellow, or white spotted flowers; esp. *T. pavonia* with brilliant orange blooms; **-foot** = *tiger's foot*; **-grass (palm),** a dwarf fan-palm, *Nannorhops* (*Chamærops*) *ritchieana*, of Western India and Persia; **-lily,** a tall garden lily, *Lilium tigrinum*, with bell-like orange flowers marked with black or purplish spots; **-moth,** a moth of the family *Arctiidæ*, esp. the British species *Arctia caja*, a large scarlet and brown moth spotted and streaked with white; **-shark,** any of various voracious sharks, as *Galeocerdo maculatus* of warm seas, *Stegostoma tigrinum* of the Indian Ocean; in New Zealand, the Porbeagle, *Lamna cornubica*; **-ware,** an old English stoneware with a spotted glaze; **-wolf,** (*a*) the Spotted Hyena (*Hyæna crocuta*); (*b*) the striped wolf or zebra-wolf of Tasmania; **-wood,** a streaked black and brown cabinet-maker's wood; also, a variety of citron-wood.

b. *Comb.* with *tiger's*: **tiger's eye,** a yellowish brown quartz with brilliant lustre, used as a gem; **tiger's-foot,** a convolvulaceous plant, *Ipomœa pestigridis*, common in India, with hairy palmate leaves; **tiger's horn, tiger's tooth,** old names for species of *Strombus* or wing-shell; **tiger's mouth,** a local name for the Snapdragon, Foxglove, and various species of Toad-flax.

Ti·ger-cat. 1699. Any of the feline beasts of moderate or small size which resemble the tiger in their markings or otherwise; including the Margay, Ocelot, Serval, etc. **b.** In Australasia applied to two carnivorous marsupials, *Dasyurus viverrinus* and *D. maculatus* 1832.

Tigerish (təi·gəriʃ), *a.* 1573. [f. TIGER + -ISH¹.] **1.** Like, or like that of, a tiger; *esp.* cruel, bloodthirsty, fierce, relentless. †**b.** Loud, flashy (*slang*) –1853. **2.** Abounding in or infested with tigers 1819. Hence **Ti·gerishly** *adv.*, **-ness.**

Tight (təit), *a.* (*adv.*) late ME. [prob. alt. of *thight* (surviving dial. in *thite, theat* impervious, dense, close), perh. orig. in †*tonnet(h)ight* XIV (see sense 13) – ON. **þehtr*, *þéttr* watertight, of close texture = OE. *þiht* firm, solid, MLG., MDu. (whence G.) *dicht* dense, close.] †**1.** Dense, as a wood or thicket. late ME. only. †**b.** Close or compact in texture or consistency; dense, solid (*rare*) –1797. **2.** Of such close texture or construction as to be impervious to a fluid, etc. 1501. **b.** *esp.* Of a ship: Water-tight; not leaky 1568. **c.** *transf.* and *fig.* 1661. **3.** *fig.* of a person, expressing somewhat indefinite commendation: Competent, able, skilful; smart; lively, vigorous; also in ironical use. *Obs.* exc. *dial.* 1598. **4.** Neat in appearance; trim, tidy, smart; also, well-made, shapely. *arch.* or *dial.* 1697. **b.** Of things: Neatly constructed or arranged; tidy, snug, compact. Now *dial.* 1720. **5.** Firmly fixed or bound in its place; also *fig.* faithful, constant. Now *rare.* 1513. **6.** Drawn or stretched so as to be tense; not loose or slack; taut 1576. **b.** *fig.* Strict, stringent; severe 1872. **7.** Drunk; tipsy (*slang*) 1853. **8.** Of a garment, etc.: Fitting closely; often = *too t.*, closely fitting because not large enough 1779. **9.** Difficult to deal with or manage; hard, severe, 'tough', 'stiff'; esp. in phr. a *t. place, corner, squeeze*, etc. (*colloq.*) 1764. **10.** *colloq.* or *techn.* **a.** Said of a contest in which the combatants are evenly matched; close; so of a bargain: with little margin of profit. *orig. U.S.* 1828. **b.** Of a person: Close-fisted. **c.** *Finance.* Of money: Difficult to obtain except on high terms; also *transf.* of the money-market when money is scarce. 1828. **11. a.** Closely packed 1856. **b.** Of language: Terse, concise, condensed 1870. **c.** *Art slang.* Lacking freedom or breadth of treatment; restricted 1891. **12.** The adj. used absol. (See also TIGHTS.) *Rugby Football.* = SCRIMMAGE *sb.* 3. *rare.* 1904. †**13.** Formerly appended to *ton, pipe, hogshead*, etc. as measures of capacity, orig. and esp. in stating the number of tons burden (*i.e.* the tonnage) of a ship –1603.

2. A t. house, warm apparel, and wholesome food BERKELEY. *Air-, water-, wind-tight*, etc., the first element denoting that which the vessel keeps in or out. **c.** O, 'tis a snug little island! A right little, t. little island! DIBDIN. **3.** *Ant. & Cl.* IV. iv. 16. **4.** A t. clever wench 1712. **6.** The belt..was drawn t. 1885. **8.** *A. t. fit*, a garment, etc. which fits tightly; hence *transf.* (*colloq.*). **10. c.** Money was 'tight' being the text of all he said 1868.

B. *adv.* (The adj. used advb.) **1.** Soundly, roundly. Now *dial.* and *U.S.* 1790. **2.** Firmly, closely, securely; so as not to allow any movement 1680. **3.** With close constriction or pressure; closely, tensely 1818.

2. Phr. *To sit t.*, to maintain one's position firmly in reference to something; also, to sit close, to remain under cover (*colloq.*); No money is forthcoming, and banks sit t. 1898.

Comb.: **t. barrel** or **cask,** a barrel for liquids; also called *wet barrel* or *cask*; so **t. cooper,** a cooper who makes casks for liquids; **-fisted** *a.*, parsimonious, close-fisted.

Tighten (təi·t'n), *v.* 1725. [f. TIGHT *a.* + -EN⁵.] **1.** *trans.* To draw tight or tighter; to make taut or tense, to draw close; hence, to fix tightly, to make strict or rigid; to secure. **2.** *intr.* To grow tight or tense; to be stretched tight or drawn close 1846.

1. What reins were tightened in despair SCOTT. *To t. one's belt*: orig. as a device to mitigate the pangs of hunger; *fig.* to reduce one's consumption of food or one's expenditure. **2.** As the market tightens the rate of discount rises 1868. Hence **Ti·ghtener,** one who or that which tightens.

Tight-laced (-lēᶦst; stress var.), *a.* 1741. That is laced tightly; wearing stays tightly laced; constricted or compressed by tight-lacing. **b.** *fig.* Strict in the observance of rules or usages of morality or propriety. (Usu. dyslogistic.) So **Ti·ght-la·cing** *vbl. sb.* the action or process of lacing tightly; *spec.* the practice of wearing tightly-laced stays in order to reduce or preserve the form of the waist.

Tightly (təi·tli), *adv.* 1598. [f. TIGHT *a.* + -LY².] In a tight manner. **1.** Soundly, properly, well; stoutly, vigorously. Now *dial.* **2.** With constriction, tension, or compression; closely; strictly 1758. **3.** Firmly, securely 1866. **4.** Neatly, tidily, smartly (*rare*) 1825. So **Ti·ghtness,** the quality or condition of being tight.

Tight rope, ti·ght-rope. 1801. A tightly stretched rope, wire, or wire cable, on which rope-dancers and acrobats perform feats of equilibristic skill. Also *attrib.* as *t. dancer.*

Tights (təits), *sb. pl.* 1833. [ellipt. use of TIGHT *a.*] **a.** Tight-fitting breeches, worn by men in the 18th and early 19th c. and still forming part of court dress. **b.** Garments of thin elastic material, fitting tight to the skin, worn by dancers, acrobats, and others to facilitate their movements or display the form. Sometimes covering the whole body, but usu. the legs only. 1836.

Tiglic (ti·glik), *a.* 1875. [f. mod.L. *Tiglium*, specific name of the croton oil plant, *Croton tiglium* (Linn.); see -IC.] *Chem.* Contained in or derived from croton oil; *t. acid*, a colourless crystalline compound, crystallizing in triclinic plates or rods, obtained from croton and other oils. So **Ti·glate**, a salt of this acid.

Tigress (təi·grės). 1611. [f. TIGER + -ESS[1], after Fr. *tigresse*.] **1.** A female tiger. **2.** *fig.* A fierce, cruel, or tiger-like woman 1700.

Tigrine (təi·grəin), *a.* 1656. [– L. *tigrinus*; see -INE[1].] Of, pertaining to, or resembling a tiger, esp. in marking or colouring; in specific names of animals tr. L. *tigrinus*.

Carpet, diamond, and t. snakes 1908. So **Ti·groid** *a.* 1901.

Tigurine (ti·giurəin), *a.* and *sb.* 1651. [– L. *Tigurinus* in *Tigurinus pagus*, a district of ancient Helvetia.] **A.** *adj.* Of or pertaining to Zürich; hence = ZWINGLIAN. **B.** *sb.* A Zwinglian.

‖**Til**[1] (til). *India.* 1840. [Hindi *til* :– Skr. *tilá*.] The plant *Sesamum indicum*; esp. in *t.-seed (oil)*.

‖**Til**[2]. 1858. [Native name in Madeira; perh. a use of Pg. *til* linden.] A lauraceous tree, *Oreodaphne fetens*, of the Canary Islands and Madeira; also its wood, which has a fetid smell. Chiefly *attrib.*, as *t.-tree, -wood.*

Tilbury (ti·lbŏri). 1796. [f. *Tilbury*, name of the inventor.] A light open two-wheeled carriage, fashionable in the first half of the 19th c.

‖**Tilde** (ti·lde). 1864. [Sp., metathetic form of *tidlo – L. *titulus* TITLE.] The diacritic mark ˜ placed in Spanish above the letter *n* to indicate the *mouillé* or palatalized sound (nʸ), as in *señor* (senʸor).

Tile (təil), *sb.* [OE. *tiġele* (*tiġule*), corresp. to OS. *tiegla* (Du. *tegel*), OHG. *ziagal, -ala* (G. *ziegel*), ON. *tigl* – L. *tēgula*, f. IE. *tĕg-* cover; see THATCH *v.*] **1.** A thin slab of burnt clay; usu. unglazed and flat or curved for covering the roofs of buildings, flat for lining ovens, etc.; flat, usu. glazed and often ornamented when used to pave floors or line walls, fireplaces, etc.; of semi-cylindrical, tunnel or tube shape when used for purposes of drainage. **b.** *Metall.* A small flat piece of baked earth or earthenware used to cover vessels in which metals are fused 1741. **2.** The material of which tiles or bricks consist, burnt clay; tiles collectively (in early use const. as pl.) ME. **3.** *slang.* A hat 1823.

1. The house..is couered with Tiles of siluer PURCHAS. The better houses..have red tiles upon the roofs 1840. The fireplace..paved..with quaint Dutch tiles DICKENS. Phr. *To have a t. loose*, to be slightly crazy or not quite right in the head (*slang*). **3.** Afore the brim went, it was a wery handsome t. DICKENS.

attrib. and *Comb.*: **t.-drain** *sb.*, a drain constructed of tiles; so **t.-drain** *v. trans.*, to drain (a field, etc.) by means of tiles; **-earth**, a kind of clay adapted for making tiles; **-kiln**, a kiln in which tiles are baked; **-ore**, an earthy variety of cuprite or copper ore, usu. of a reddish colour; **-pipe**, a hollow cylindrical t. for drainage; **-red** *a.* and *sb.*, (of) a red colour like that of tiles; **-tea**, an inferior kind of brick-tea; **-yard**, a yard or enclosure where tiles are made.

Tile (təil), *v.* late ME. [f. prec.; in sense 2, back-formation from TILER 2.] **1.** *trans.* To cover with tiles; to overlay (a floor or roof) or line (a wall, fire-place, etc.) with tiles. **b.** *transf.* and *fig.* 1512. **2.** *Freemasonry.* (Usu. with spelling **tyle.**) To protect (a lodge or meeting) from interruption or intrusion, so as to keep its proceedings secret, by posting a tyler at the door. Also *transf.* to bind (a person) to secrecy; to keep (any meeting or proceeding) strictly secret. 1762.

1. b. God..hath..tyled one favour upon another 1641. **2.** Come, come, Snob my boy, we are all tiled, you know THACKERAY. Hence **Tiled** (təild) *a.*

Ti·le-fish. 1881. [Suggested by the termination of the generic name *Lophalotilus*, and by the brilliant colouring resembling ornamental tiles.] The fish *Lophalotilus chamæleonticeps*, found in abundance in 1879 off the coast of New England, and valued as food; supposed to be extinct from 1882 till 1892, since which year its numbers have again increased.

Ti·le-pin. ME. A 'pin' or peg of hard wood used to fasten the tiles to the laths of a roof.

Tiler (təi·ləɹ). ME. [f. TILE *sb.* and *v.* + -ER[1].] **1.** One who covers the roofs of buildings with tiles, a tile-layer; also formerly, a tile-maker. **2.** *Freemasonry.* (Usually **tyler.**) The door-keeper who keeps the uninitiated from intruding upon the secrecy of the lodge or meeting 1742.

Tilery (təi·ləri). 1846. [f. TILE *sb.*, TILER; see -ERY.] A place where tiles are made; a tile-field or -kiln.

Tilestone (təi·lˌstōᵘn). [OE. *tiġelstān*, f. *tiġele* TILE *sb.* + *stān* STONE *sb.*] †**1.** = TILE *sb.* 1, 2. –1681. **2.** *Geol.* Any laminated flagstone, splitting into layers thicker than *slate*, suitable for roofing-tiles; *spec.* a group of sand-stones forming the transition beds between the Silurian and Devonian systems 1668.

Tiliaceous (tiliˌēⁱ·ʃəs), *a.* 1891. [f. *Tiliaceæ* + -OUS; see -ACEOUS.] *Bot.* Belonging to the family *Tiliaceæ*, typified by the genus *Tilia*, the lime or linden tree.

Tiling (təi·liŋ), *vbl. sb.* 1440. [f. TILE *v.* and *sb.* + -ING[1].] **1.** The action of TILE *v.*; the covering (of a roof, etc.) with or as with tiles. **b.** *Freemasonry.* (Usually **tyling.**) The proper guarding of a lodge 1888. **2.** *concr.* Work consisting of tiles; the tiles forming the covering of a roof, floor, etc., collectively 1526.

Till (til), *sb.*[1] 1452. [Of unkn. origin.] †**1.** A small box, casket, or closed compartment, contained within or forming part of a larger box, chest, or cabinet; sometimes one that could be lifted out, sometimes a drawer in a cabinet or chest of drawers; used for keeping valuables, etc., more safely –1737. **2.** *spec.* A drawer, money-box, etc. in a shop or bank, in which cash for daily transactions is temporarily kept 1698.

Comb.: **t.-alarm**, a device by which a bell is automatically rung when the till is opened.

Till, *sb.*[2] orig. and chiefly *Sc.* 1672. [Of unkn. origin. Cf. THILL[2].] **1.** A stiff clay, more or less impervious to water, usu. occurring in unstratified deposits, and forming an ungenial subsoil 1765. **b.** In the majority of cases this clay belongs to the Glacial or Drift period, and in geological use 'till' has the specific sense 'boulder clay' 1842. **2.** Hard or soft shale; app. = THILL[2]. *dial.* 1672.

Till, *sb.*[3] *Printing.* 1611. [Of unkn. origin.] In early hand-presses, a board or shelf through which the sleeve and spindle pass.

Till (til), *v.*[1] [OE. *tilian* strive after, etc., (late) cultivate = OFris. *tilia* get, cultivate, OS. *tilian, tilon* obtain (Du. *telen* produce, cultivate), OHG. *zilōn, zilēn* (G. *zielen* aim, strive), Goth. *gatilon* :– Gmc. **tilōjan*, **tilējan*, f. **tilam* aim, goal (see TILL *prep.*).] **I.** †**1.** *intr.* To labour, work –ME. **2.** *trans.* To bestow labour and attention, such as ploughing, harrowing, manuring, etc., upon (land) so as to fit it for raising crops; to cultivate. Also *absol.* ME. **b.** *spec.* To plough (land). Also *absol.* late ME. **3.** *fig.* To cultivate (the mind, a 'field' of knowledge, a virtue, etc.). late ME.

2. The prisoners were forced to t. the enemy's land 1835. **b.** They drained, they tilled, they planted 1850.

II. 1. *trans.* To spread (a net), set (a trap or snare). Also, to set in any position. Now *s.w. dial.* Also *absol.* ME. †**2.** To pitch (a tent) –1628.

Till (til), *v.*[2] 1841. [f. TILL *sb.*[1]] *trans.* To put (money) into a till.

Till (til), *prep., conj.* [OE. (Northumb.) *til*, prep. with dat. = OFris. *til* (with dat.), ON. *til* (with gen.); prob. from advb. use of Gmc. sb. **tilam* (cf. TILL *v.*[1]), repr. by OE. *till* fixed point, station, MLG. *til* aim, point of time, OHG. *zil* (G. *ziel* end, limit, goal), ON. *aldr|tili* 'end of life', Goth. *til* opportunity. In ME. (and later) use due to adoption of the ON. word.] **A.** *prep.* **I.** Local and datival. Now *n. dial.* and *Sc.*, where normally used instead of *to* before a vowel or *h*. **1.** = To *prep.* **2.** Expressing the indirect object or dative relation OE. **II.** Of time: Onward to (a specified time); until ME. **b.** After a neg., denoting the continuance of the negative condition up to the time indicated (and implying its cessation then); thus nearly = *before* 1590.

Fight t. the last gaspe SHAKS. 'Till then farewel 1746. **b.** [He] begged of me not to go on shore t. day DE FOE.

III. = *To* with inf. Now only *Sc.* ME.

B. *conj.* (orig. the prep. governing the dem. pron. *that*, in apposition with the following clause). **1.** To the time that; up to (the point) when; until OE. **b.** So long or so far that; so that at length ME. †**2.** During the time that; so long as; while –1604.

1. I shall count the hours t. I return 1796. We shall never prosper..t. the system is wholly changed 1832. **b.** Blow t. thou burst thy winde SHAKS.

Tillable (ti·lăb'l), *a.* 1573. [f. TILL *v.*[1] + -ABLE.] Capable of being tilled or cultivated; usu., capable of being ploughed, arable.

Tillage (ti·lėdʒ). 1488. [f. TILL *v.*[1] + -AGE.] **1.** The act, operation, or art of tilling or cultivating land so as to fit it for raising crops; agriculture, husbandry 1538. **b.** The state or condition of being tilled or cultivated 1488. **c.** *fig.* The culture of the mind or spirit 1555. **2.** *concr.* Tilled or ploughed land; land under crops as dist. from pasturage; the crops growing on tilled land 1543.

‖**Tillandsia** (tilæ·ndziă). 1759. [mod.L., named after Elias *Tillands*, a Swedish botanist; see -IA[1].] *Bot.* A large genus of herbaceous plants of the pine-apple family (*Bromeliaceæ*), found in tropical and subtropical America and the West Indies, chiefly epiphytic on trees.

Tiller (tiləɹ), *sb.*[1] Now *literary* or *arch.* [ME. *tiliere*, repl. OE. *tilia*, f. *tilian* TILL *v.*[1] + *-ere* -ER[1]; subseq. spelt after the vb.] One who tills the soil; a husbandman, cultivator; a farmer or farm labourer.

Ti·ller, *sb.*[2] [Late ME. *tiler, telor* – AFr. *telier* weaver's beam :– med.L. *telarium*, f. L. *tela* web; see -ER[2] 2.] †**1.** *Archery*, etc.: In a cross-bow: The wooden beam which is grooved for reception of the arrow, or drilled for the bolt or quarrel –1618. †**b.** *transf.* A bow fitted with a tiller –1688. **2.** *Naut.* A horizontal bar or beam attached to the rudder-head, acting as a lever by means of which the rudder is moved in the act of steering 1625.

Comb.: **t.-head**, the extremity of the t. to which are secured the two ends of the t.-rope or -chain; **-rope**, (*a*) the rope (now usu. a chain) connecting the t.-head with the drum or barrel of a ship's steering-gear; (*b*) a rope leading from the t.-head to each side of the deck, to assist in steering in rough weather; **-steerage, -steering**, the arrangement for steering a motor-car by means of a lever (as dist. from wheel-steerage).

Ti·ller, *sb.*[3] Now *dial.* [app. repr. OE. *telgor, tealgor, telgra*, extended f. *telga* branch, bough, twig.] †**1.** (In OE.) A plant, a shoot, a twig; *esp.* a shoot or sucker from the root. **2.** A young tree, a sapling; *esp.* a stock-shoot, rising from the stock or stool of a felled tree 1664. **3.** One of the lateral shoots from the base of the stalk of corn or grass or other herbaceous plant 1733.

Tiller (ti·ləɹ), *v.* 1677. [f. prec.] *intr.* Of corn or other plants: To produce 'tillers' or side shoots from the root or base of the stem; also said of the shoots thus arising.

Tillet (ti·lėt), **tillot** (ti·lət). 1466. [app. – OFr. *tellette*, collateral form of *teilete, toilete* a wrapper of cloth; see also TOILET.] A kind of coarse cloth, used for wrapping up textile fabrics and (formerly) garments; also for making awnings. **b.** A bag of thin glazed muslin, used as a covering for dress-goods 1871.

Tilly (ti·li). 1712. [– Fr. *tilli* (It. *tiglia*) – mod.L. *tiglium*; see TIGLIO.] In *t.-seed*, the seed of a species of *Croton* (formerly called *C. pavana*, now identified with *C. tiglium*), which yields croton oil.

Tilly-vally, *int.* *Obs.* or *arch.* 1529. [Of unkn. origin.] An exclam. of impatience: Nonsense! Fiddlesticks!

Tilt (tilt), *sb.*[1] 1440. [In XV *till*, var. of OE. *teld* = (O)HG. *zelt* tent), ME. *telde, tilde*, perh. infl. by TENT *sb.*[1]] **1.** A covering of coarse cloth; an awning; a booth, tent, or tabernacle. **2.** *spec.* An awning over a boat 1611. **3.** An awning or cover for a cart or wagon, usu. of canvas or tarpaulin 1620. **4.** In Labrador and Newfoundland: a fisherman's or wood-cutter's hut 1895.

Comb.: **t.-bonnet,** a woman's or girl's bonnet in the form of a wagon-tilt; **-roof,** a round-topped roof, shaped like a t. or wagon-cover.

Tilt (tilt), *sb.*[2] 1510. [In branch I of unkn. origin; in branch II f. TILT *v.*[1]] **I. 1.** The barrier which separated the combatants in a tilt (sense 2). Hence, a tilting ground or yard; the lists. **2.** A combat for exercise or sport between two armed men on horseback with lances, riding on opposite sides of a barrier and scoring by attaints and lances broken; also, the exercise of riding with a lance or the like at a mark, as the quintain 1511. **b.** *transf.* and *fig.* An encounter, a combat; a debate 1567. **c.** A thrust of a weapon, as at a tilt. Now only *fig.* 1716.

1. *To run at (the) t.* = TILT *v.*[2] III. 1. **2.** *Full t.* (advb. phr.), at full speed and with direct thrust; with the utmost adverse force or impetus.

II. 1. The act of tilting or the fact or condition of being tilted; inclination upward or downward 1562. **b.** *Geol.* An abrupt upheaval of strata to a considerable angle from the horizontal. **c.** *gen.* A slope, or sloping portion, of the surface of the ground. 1859. **2.** Short for TILT-HAMMER 1831.

1. Phr. *On* or *upon the t.*, in a tilted position, like a cask or vessel raised on one end or side when nearly empty.

III. The Stilt or Long-legged Plover of North America 1813.

attrib. and *Comb.*: **t.-cart,** a cart of which the body can be tilted so as to empty out the contents; **-mill,** (*a*) the machinery for working a t.-hammer; (*b*) a building in which a t.-hammer is worked.

Tilt (tilt), *v.*[1] [Late ME. *tilte, tylte* may represent OE. **tyltan*, later form of **tieltan* :- **taltjan*, f. **taltaz* (OE. *tealt* unsteady, whence *tealtian* totter); but perh. of Scand. origin (cf. Norw. *tylten* unsteady, Sw. *tulta* totter). Branch III is from TILT *sb.*[2] I 1; branch IV from TILT-HAMMER.] **I. †1.** *trans.* To cause to fall; to thrust, push, throw down or over; to overturn, upset -1587. **2.** *intr.* To move unsteadily up and down; *esp.* of waves or a ship at sea, to pitch 1590.

2. The floating Vessel..with beaked prow Rode tilting o're the Waves MILT.

II. *trans.* To cause to lean abruptly from the vertical or incline abruptly from the horizontal; to slope, slant; *to t. up*, to raise one end or side above the other, to tip up 1594. **b.** *intr.* To move into a slanted position or direction; to incline, slope, slant, heel over, tip *up* 1626. **c.** *trans.* To pour or empty out (the contents of a vessel), or cause them to flow to one side, by tilting the vessel 1613.

His helmet tilted well to the rear to screen his neck 1908. **c.** To tumble out their sentences as they would t. stones from a cart 1865.

III. [orig. for *run at tilt*: see prec. I. 1.] **1.** *intr.* To engage in a 'tilt' 1595. **b.** *transf.* and *fig.* To engage in a contest; to combat, encounter, contend (*with*); to strike or thrust *at* with a weapon, to charge or impinge *against* 1588. **2.** *trans.* **a.** To poise (the lance) for a thrust 1708. **b.** To tilt at; to rush at, charge; to drive or thrust by tilting 1796.

1. He ran at the ring, and tilted with the Lord Montjoy 1622. **b.** He Tilts With Peircing steele at bold Mercutio's breast SHAKS.

IV. To forge or work with a tilt-hammer 1825.

Tilt (tilt), *v.*[2] 1499. [f. TILT *sb.*[1]] *trans.* To cover with a tilt or awning. (Chiefly in *pa. pple.*)

Ti·lt-boat. 1463. [f. TILT *sb.*[1] (or short for *tilted*) + BOAT *sb.*] A large rowing boat having a tilt or awning, formerly used on the Thames, esp. as a passenger boat between London and Gravesend.

Tilter (ti·ltəɹ), *sb.* 1611. [f. TILT *v.*[1] + -ER[1].] **1.** One who tilts or jousts; a combatant in a tilt. **†b.** A rapier or sword. *slang.* -1713. **2.** One who or that which tilts, inclines, or slopes (something) up or down; *spec.* an apparatus for tilting a cask so as to empty it without stirring up the dregs 1630. **3.** One who works with a tilt-hammer 1829.

1. *fig.* I was always a t. at windmills 1898.

Tilth (tilþ). [OE. *tilþ, tilþe*, f. *tilian* TILL *v.*[1] + -TH *suffix*[1].] **†1.** Labour, work, or effort directed to useful or profitable ends. OE. only. **2.** *esp.* Labour or work in the cultivation of the soil; tillage, agricultural work, husbandry OE. **b.** *fig.* The cultivation of knowledge, religion, the mind. *arch.* ME. **c.** (with *pl.*) An act of tilling; a ploughing, harrowing, or other agricultural operation 1565. **d.** The condition of being under tillage; hence (good or bad) condition (of land under tillage) 1488. **†3.** *transf.* Crop, harvest -1781. **4.** Land under cultivation, as dist. from pasture, forest, or waste land; tilled or arable land; a piece of tilled land, a ploughed field. late ME. **b.** The prepared surface soil; the crumb, or depth of soil dug or cultivated 1743.

2. After four year's t., lay down your land 1660. **4.** Vineyard and t., Green meadow-ground, and many-coloured woods WORDSW.

Ti·lt-ha:mmer. 1773. [f. TILT *sb.*[2] or *v.*[1]] A heavy hammer used in forging, fixed on a pivot and acted upon by a cam-wheel or an eccentric, which alternately tilts it up and allows it to drop.

Tilting (ti·ltiŋ), *vbl. sb.* 1610. [f. TILT *v.*[1] + -ING[1].] **1.** The action of TILT *v.*[1]; justing. **b.** With *a* and *pl.* A tilt. Now *rare* or *Obs.* 1618. **2.** Inclination from the vertical or horizontal 1658. **3.** Working with a tilt-hammer 1839.

attrib. and *Comb.*: **t.-helm, -helmet,** a large heavy helmet worn over the ordinary one in tilting, completely covering head and face, with slits for breathing and vision; **-mill** = *tilt-mill*; **-yard** = TILT-YARD.

Ti·lt-up, *sb.* and *a.* 1848. [f. phr. *to tilt up* (TILT *v.*[1] II).] **A.** *sb.* Something that tilts up; *spec.* the American sandpiper (*U.S.*) **B.** *adj.* That tilts up 1891.

Tilt-yard (ti·lt,yāɹd). 1528. [f. TILT *sb.*[2] + YARD.] A yard or enclosed space for tilts and tournaments; a (permanent) tilting-ground.

‖**Timar** (tĭmā·r). 1601. *Hist.* [Turk. *tımar* – Pers. *timār* attendance, watching.] Formerly, in the feudal system of Turkey, a fief held by military service.

Timariot (timā·riǫt). 1601. [– Fr. *timariot* – It. *timariotto*, f. Pers. *timār*; see prec., -OT[2].] The holder of a timar.

Timbal, tymbal (ti·mbăl). Now *Hist.* or *arch.* 1680. [– Fr. *timbale*, alt. after *cymbale* cymbal of †*tamballe* – (with assim. to *tambour* drum) Sp. *atabal*; see ATABAL.] A kettledrum.

Timbale (tæṅbal). 1854. [Fr.; see prec.] **1.** *Ent.* A membrane (resembling a drum-head) in certain insects, as the cicada, by means of which a shrill chirping sound is produced. **2.** *Cookery.* A dish made of finely minced meat, fish, or other ingredients, cooked in a crust of paste or in a mould; so called from its shape 1880.

Timber (ti·mbəɹ), *sb.*[1] [OE. *timber* = OFris. *timber*, OS. *timbar*, OHG. *zimbar* (G. *zimmer* room), ON. *timbr* :- Gmc. **timram* (cf. Goth. *timrjan* build, *timrja* builder) :- IE. **dĕm-* **dŏm-* **dm-* build.] **†1.** A building, edifice, house. OE. only. **†2.** Building material generally; the matter or substance of which anything is built up or composed; matter, material, stuff -1840. **3.** *spec.* Wood used for the building of houses, ships, etc., or for the use of the carpenter, joiner, or other artisan; wood in general as a material OE. **b.** Wood as a substance. Now *dial.* 1530. **4.** Applied to the wood of growing trees capable of being used for structural purposes; hence collectively to the trees themselves; *standing t.*, trees, woods. Rarely in *pl.* OE. **b.** *spec.* in *English Law*, Trees growing upon land, and forming part of the freehold inheritance; embracing usu. the oak, ash, and elm, of the age of twenty years and more; in particular districts, by local custom, including other trees 1766. **5.** *transf.* Applied to any object familiar to the speaker, composed wholly or chiefly of wood, as a ship; the stocks (*slang*); wooden gates and fences (*Hunting slang*); a wicket (*Cricket slang*). late ME. **6.** A single beam or piece of wood forming or capable of forming part of any structure. Also collectively in *pl.* **a.** *gen.* 1555. **b.** *pl. spec. Naut.* The pieces of wood composing the ribs, bends, or frames of a ship's hull 1748. **7.** *fig.* Bodily structure, frame, build; also in later use, the 'stuff' of which a person is made 1612. **8.** *attrib.* or *adj.* Made or consisting of wood; wooden 1529.

2. Such disposicions are..the fittest tymber to make great Politiques of BACON. **3.** Their Boats of T. without any Iron in them MILT. **4.** A forest of grand t. 1880. **b.** By the custom of the county of Buckingham beech trees are t. 1891. **6. b.** Her timbers yet are sound COWPER. *My timbers! Shiver my timbers!* meaningless exclams. (*Naut. slang*).

Comb.: **t.-beetle,** any beetle which, in the larval or the perfect state, is destructive to t.; **-doodle** *U.S. local*, the Amer. woodcock, *Philohela minor*; *slang*, spirituous liquor; **-grouse** *U.S.*, any species of grouse frequenting woodlands; **-head** *Naut.*, the head or end of any t.; *spec.* such an end rising above the deck and serving as a bollard; **-hitch** *sb.*, a knot used in attaching a rope to a log or spar for hoisting or towing it; hence **-hitch** *v. trans.*, to make fast with a t.-hitch; **-jumper** *Hunting slang*, a horse good at jumping over gates and fences; **-mare,** a kind of wooden horse on which offending soldiers and others were made to ride as a punishment; **-sow,** a wood-louse or sow-bug, *Oniscus*; **-toe** *slang*, a wooden leg; hence **-toe, -toes,** a wooden-legged man; so **-toed** *a.*; **-worm,** a 'worm' or larva injurious to t.

Timber (ti·mbəɹ), *sb.*[2] ME. [– OFr. *timbre*, in med.L. *timber* (1086), *timbra, -ia, -ium*, MLG. *timber* (XIII); supposed to be ult. a special use of TIMBER *sb.*[1]] A definite quantity of furs, a package containing 40 skins (i.e. half-skins, 20 pair) or ermine, sable, marten, and the like. (After a numeral commonly *timber*, less usu. *timbers*.)

Timber (ti·mbəɹ), *v.* [OE. *timbran* and *timbrian*; see TIMBER *sb.*[1]] **1.** *trans.* To build, construct, make (as a house, ship, etc.); *spec.* (in later use) to build or construct of wood. *Obs.* or *arch.* **b.** *absol.*; *spec.* of a bird, to build (*sc.* its nest) OE. **†2.** To construct, frame, effect, do, form, cause, bring about, bring into existence or operation (any action, condition, etc.) -1646. **3.** To furnish with timber; to put in or apply timber to support the roof of a mine, the sides of a shaft, etc. 1548.

2. Heads that were never timber'd for it SIR T. BROWNE. **3.** The new shaft..has been sunk, timbered, and centred to a depth of 260 feet 1872.

Timbered (ti·mbəɹd), *ppl. a.* late ME. [f. TIMBER *sb.*[1] and *v.* + -ED.] **1.** Constructed of timber; built or made of wood; wooden. **2. †a.** Of a thing: Having a structure (of a specified kind); constructed, framed, built, made -1771. **b.** Of a person or animal: Having (such and such) a bodily structure or constitution 1581. **3.** Furnished with growing trees; wooded 1701.

A low t. House 1699. **2. a.** *Haml.* IV. vii. 22. **b.** A fine straite timber'd man and a brave soldier 1622. **3.** A very ill-t. estate FIELDING.

Timbering (ti·mbəriŋ), *vbl. sb.* ME. [f. TIMBER *v.* + -ING[1].] **1.** The action of TIMBER *v.* **2.** *concr.* Building material (esp. of wood); timber-work; *spec.* in *Mining*, the timber used to support the sides of a shaft or the roof of a working 1486.

Timberling (ti·mbəɹliŋ). 1787. [f. TIMBER *sb.*[1] + -LING[1].] A young timber-tree; a sapling.

Timberman (ti·mbəɹmæ̆n). late ME. [f. TIMBER *sb.*[1] + MAN *sb.*] **†1.** A man who supplies or deals in timber -1656. **b.** A man employed in handling timber 1890. **2.** A man employed in timbering the shafts or roofs of a mine, the sides of a trench, or any other excavation 1849.

Ti·mber-tree. 1505. A tree yielding timber fit for building or construction.

Ti·mber-wood. Now *rare.* 1483. = TIMBER *sb.*[1] 3.

Ti·mber-work. late ME. **1.** Work executed in timber; the wooden part of any structure. **2.** *pl.* An establishment where timber is prepared or worked up 1875.

Ti·mber-yard. 1482. An open yard or place where timber is stacked or stored.

†Ti·mbre, *sb.*[1] ME. [– OFr. *timbre* :- Rom. **timbano* – med. Gr. τίμβανον timbrel, kettledrum = Gr. τύμπανον TYMPANUM.] = TIMBREL *sb.* –1516.

Timbre, tymber (ti·mbəɹ), *sb.*² *Obs.* exc. *Hist.* late ME. [– (O)Fr. *timbre*, the same wd. as prec., in transf. sense.] The crest of a helmet; hence, the crest or exterior additions placed over the shield in heraldic arms. Hence **Ti·mbre** *v. trans.* to furnish or adorn with a crest; to surmount as a crest.

‖**Timbre** (tæ̃ṅbr), *sb.*³ 1849. [Fr., the same word as TIMBRE *sb.*¹] The character or quality of a musical or vocal sound (distinct from its pitch and intensity) depending upon the particular voice or instrument producing it; caused by the proportion in which the fundamental tone is combined with the harmonics or overtones (= G. *klangfarbe*).

Timbrel (ti·mbrĕl), *sb.* Now chiefly *biblical.* 1500. [perh. dim. of TIMBRE *sb.*¹; see -EL.] A musical instrument of percussion; a tambourine or the like that could be held up in the hand.

Miriam the prophetisse..toke a tymbrell in hir hande, and all the women folowed out after her with timbrels in a daunse COVERDALE *Exod.* 15:20. Hence **Ti·mbrel** *v. intr.* to play upon a t.; *trans.* to accompany with a t.

Time (təim), *sb.* [OE. *tīma* = ON. *tími* time, good time, prosperity :– Gmc. **tīmon*, f. **tī-* stretch, extend + *-mon-*. The notion is also expressed in OE. and other Gmc. languages by another derivative of the same base, viz. TIDE *sb.*, which was superseded by *time* in the strictly temporal senses.] **I.** A space or extent of time. **1.** A limited stretch or space of continued existence, as the interval between two successive events or acts, or the period through which an action, condition, or state continues; as *a long t.*, *a short t.*, *some t.*, *for a t.* **2.** A particular period indicated or characterized in some way OE. **3.** A period in the existence or history of the world; an age, an era. In later use more indefinite, esp. in *pl.* OE. **4.** With possessive or *of*: The period contemporary with the life, occupancy, or activity of some one; (his) age, era, or generation. Often *pl.* OE. **5.** A period considered with ref. to its prevailing conditions; the general state of affairs at a particular period. Chiefly *pl.* 1484. **b.** *pl.* Used as the name of a newspaper 1788. **6.** A period considered with ref. to one's personal experience; hence, an experience of a specified nature lasting some time 1529. **7.** Period of duration; prescribed or allotted term. **a.** Period of existence or action; period of one's life OE. **b.** *spec.* (*a*) The period of gestation OE. (*b*) (One's) term of apprenticeship 1645. (*c*) The duration of a term of imprisonment; usu. in phr. *to do t.* (slang) 1865. (*d*) The prescribed duration of the interval between two rounds in boxing, or the like, or the moment at which this begins or ends; also *ellipt.* as the signal to begin or end a bout, as in *to call t.* 1812. **8.** The length of time sufficient, necessary, or desirable for some purpose; also, time available for employment; leisure or spare time ME. **b.** The (shortest) period in which a given course of action is completed 1894. **9.** *spec.* The amount of time worked under a specific contract; hence, in workmen's speech, pay equivalent to the period worked 1795. **10.** *Anc. Prosody.* A unit or group of units in metrical measurement 1589. **11.** *Mil.* The rate of marching, calculated on the number of paces taken per minute 1802. **12.** *Mus.* **a.** †The duration of the breve in relation to the semibreve; hence, the rhythm or measure of a piece of music, now marked by division of the music into bars, and usu. denoted by a fraction expressing the number of aliquot parts of a semibreve in each bar (*t.-signature*). 1531. **b.** The rate at which a piece is performed; hence, the characteristic tempo, rhythm, form, and style of a particular class of compositions, usu. in comb. as *dance-t.*, *march-t.* 1887.

1. *In no t.*, *in less than no t.* (colloq.), immediately, very quickly or soon; In less than no t. you shall hear JOWETT. *Absolute t.*, t. considered in itself without ref. to that portion of duration to which it belongs. **2.** You can fool all the people some of the t., and some of the people all the t., but you cannot fool all the people all the t. (*attributed to President Lincoln*). *At* or *for the t.*, *for the t. being*, during the period under consideration. **3.** A superstition of these modern times 1884. *Time(s past, past time(s*; *old, olden*, or *ancient time(s*, etc. *Time(s to come, times to be* (arch.), future time; esp. future ages, the future. *The t.* (*the times*), the age now or then present. **4.** The spacious times of great Elizabeth TENNYSON. **5.** When times grew cold and unbelieving J. H. NEWMAN. Colloq. phrases. *As times go*, as things go in these times. *Behind the times*, behind the modes or methods of these times. **6.** I went and had as good a t. as heart could wish PEPYS. Phr. (*To have*) *a* (*good, bad*, etc.) *t.* (*of it*). *To have the t. of one's life*, i.e. the best one has ever had. **7. a.** One man in his t. playes many parts SHAKS. It will last my t. CARLYLE. **8.** Pray take your own t. 1796. **9.** Phr. *T. and lime*, in the shipbuilding trade, applied to a contract to build at cost plus an agreed percentage. **11.** See also QUICK TIME. **12. a.** *In t.*, *out of t.*, in or out of correct rhythm. *To beat t.*: see BEAT *v.*¹ II. 9.

II. Time when: a point of time; a space of time treated without ref. to its duration. **1.** A point in the course of time or of a period. In mod. Eng. *What is the t.?* i.e. the hour and minute as shown by the clock. (*At*) *what t.*, = when, at the time that: see WHAT *a.* ME. **b.** A point or fixed part of the year, a season; also, of a day, as *t. of day*, *t. of night*, *dinner-t.*, *bed-t.* OE. **2.** A point in duration marking or marked by some event or condition; a point of time at which something happens; an occasion OE. **3.** Appointed, due, or proper time OE. **b.** Qualified by poss. pron., as *his*, *her*, *its*; often ellipt. for *t. of death*, *of childbirth*, etc.; *before* (*his*, etc.), *t.*, prematurely OE. **4.** A or the favourable, convenient, or fitting point of time for doing something; the right moment; opportunity. (Often with *his*, *her*, etc.) OE. **5.** Any one of the occasions on which something is done or happens. Often qualified by a numeral. ME. **6.** Preceded by a cardinal numeral and followed by a number or expression of quantity: used to express the multiplication of the number, etc. late ME. **b.** Also followed by an adj. or adv. in the comparative degree, or in the positive by *as* with an adj. or adv., expressing comparison 1551. **7.** *pl.* orig. The fixed hours of the day at which an omnibus started from its various stations; hence, the established business enterprise of running an omnibus on a given route at such times, and the 'goodwill' thus created by the owners of public service vehicles over particular routes as a recognized vendible asset 1863.

1. To knowe..euery tyme of the nyht by the sterres fixe CHAUCER. **b.** Fleeting showers..unseasonable at the t. of year 1825. **2.** This..trick escaped detection at the t. 1845. Phr. *At no t.*, on no occasion. *Once upon a t.*: at a certain (undefined) period. *At one t.*: = ONCE 4. **3.** It was tyme to go to bed CAXTON. *No t. for*: not a fitting occasion for. **b.** Yᵉ Quene..was with childe, and nere her t. 1560. **4.** When he sawe his tyme, he cryed his worde & token 1533. It is the T. to buy STEELE. The devil bides his t. 1722. **5.** He did it fifty times, at the very least LANDOR. Phr. *At a t.*, *at one t.*, *at the same t.*, at once, simultaneously. *Many a t.*, *many times*, ellipt. *times*, also *times without* or *out of number*, *many a t. and oft* (*often*), on many occasions, in many instances; often, frequently. **6.** Four times fifty living men COLERIDGE. **b.** Men who had ten or twenty times less to remember GLADSTONE.

III. *gen.* **1.** Indefinite continuous duration regarded as that in which the sequence of events takes place. late ME. **2.** Personified as an aged man, bald, but having a forelock, and carrying a scythe and an hour-glass 1509. **3.** In restricted sense, duration conceived as beginning and ending with the present life or material universe; finite duration as dist. from eternity. late ME. **4.** A system of measuring or reckoning the passage of time 1706.

1. Remember that t. is money B. FRANKLIN. Add event to event, still T. is recognised as stretching forth, and still there is room for more 1854. **2.** *To take T. by the forelock*, to seize one's opportunity, to act promptly. **3.** All t. compared with eternitie is but short t., yea indeed as no t. 1635. **4.** Common watches and clocks, are made to show the hour of mean t. 1834.

Phrases. **1. Time of day. a.** The hour as shown by the clock; hence, a point or stage in any course or period (somewhat *colloq.*). **b.** In salutations, as *to give one*, or *pass*, *the t. of day* (now *dial.* and *colloq.*), to greet, salute, exchange salutations. **c.** *colloq.* or *slang*. The state of the case; (to know) 'what's what'; also, the right way of doing anything; the latest dodge. **T. out of mind,** from a time or during a period beyond human memory; so *t.* (also *for*, *from t.*) *immemorial*. **T. and tide,** an alliterative reduplication; now only or mainly in proverbial phrases, as *t. and tide wait* (or *stay*) *for no man*. **T. after t.,** repeatedly. **T. and again,** with frequent recurrence; repeatedly, very often. **T. enough,** soon enough, in time, sufficiently early.

2. Against t., in competition with the passage of time; so as to finish one's task before the expiry of a certain period. **At time(s,** at one time and another, at various times, occasionally. **b.** (*At*) *one t. with* (*and*) *another*, during various detached periods, on various occasions. **c.** *At the same t.*, during the same period, at the same moment, not before or after. Also, used in introducing a reservation, explanation, or contrast, = 'while saying this, nevertheless, however, yet, still'. **Between times,** in the intervals between other actions; betweenwhiles. **From t. to t. a.** At more or less regular intervals; now and again, occasionally. †**b.** Continuously, at all times. **In t. a.** In the course of time, sooner or later. **b.** Soon or early enough, not too late. **c.** *In good t.* (*a*) After the lapse of a suitable interval; in due course; at a proper time. (*b*) Soon or early; quickly. †(*c*) As an expression of ironical acquiescence, incredulity, or the like: To be sure! indeed! very well! (Cf. Fr. *à la bonne heure.*) **On t.,** punctually; also *pred.* punctual. Chiefly *U.S. colloq.* **Out of t. a.** *adv. phr.* After the prescribed period has elapsed; too late. **b.** *adj. phr.* Unseasonable. **With t.,** with the lapse of time, in the course of time.

3. (The) t. was (hath been, shall be), inversion of *there was* (etc.) *a time* (*when*). **To keep t.: a.** *Mus.* To mark the rhythm by movements of the hands or baton; to beat time; also, of a performer, to adhere to the correct rhythm and rate of the music, to keep pace *with* a measure or another performer, etc. **b.** Of a timepiece: To register the passage of time correctly.

Comb.: **t.-bill,** (*a*) a t.-table of trains, etc.; (*b*) a record kept by the guard of a train of the t. it leaves each station; **-book,** (*a*) a book in which an entry is made of the t. worked by employees; (*b*) = *t.-bill* (*a*); **-card,** a card on which a record is kept of t. worked; **-clock,** a clock which records the t. at which a workman arrives or departs, or punches a t.-card; **-course** *Naut.*, a ship's run, as on a fog, calculated by the vessel's speed, the t. occupied and the direction; **-detector,** a clock (stationary at a point) or watch (carried by the watchman) having additional mechanism, operated by the watchman, to show the times at which he was at certain points of his round; also called *t.-watch*; **-expired** *a.*, whose term of engagement has expired; **-exposure** *Photogr.*, exposure for a regulated time, as dist. from instantaneous exposure; **-lag,** the length of t. separating two correlated physical phenomena; **-lock,** a lock with clockwork attachment which prevents its being unlocked until a set t.; **-sheet,** a t.-table (on a sheet); the paper on which are entered the names of workmen and the hours worked by them; **-shutter** *Photogr.*, a shutter for t.-exposures; **-signal,** a visible or audible signal made at an observatory, etc., to announce the exact t.; **-signature** *Mus.*, a sign placed at the beginning of a piece of music, or where the t. changes, to show the measure or rhythm; **-value** *Mus.*, the relative duration of a note; **-watch** = *t.-detector*; **-work,** work paid for on the basis of the t. occupied; dist. from *piecework*.

Time (təim), *v.* Pa. t. and pa. pple. **timed** (təimd). late ME. [f. prec.] **1.** *trans.* To appoint or arrange the time of (an action or event); to choose the moment for. Usu. (in context) to do (a thing) at the right time; 'to adapt to the time' (J.). **b.** To arrange the time of arrival of (a train, etc.); hence, to regulate the rate of travelling of; also, to calculate the pace and moment of impact of (a ball or moving body) 1861. **c.** To adjust (a clock, etc.) to keep accurate time 1825. **2.** To mark the rhythm or measure of, as in music; to sing or play (an air or instrument) in (good or bad) time 1500. **b.** To set the time of; to cause to coincide in time with something 1655. **c.** *intr.* To keep time *to*; to sound or move in unison or harmony *with* 1850. **3.** To fix the duration of; to assign the metrical quantity of (a syllable) or the duration of (a note); also, to regulate the action of (a mechanism, etc.) as to duration 1589. **4.** To ascertain or note the time at which (something) is done or happens; to note the time occupied by (a person) or the duration of (an action, etc.) 1670. **5.** *Mech.* To adjust the parts of (a mechanism) so that a succession of movements or operations takes place at the required intervals and in the desired sequence 1895.

1. There is surely no greater Wisedome, then well to t. the Beginnings, and Onsets of Things BACON. **b.** The Royal train was timed to reach

Leamington at 1.17 p.m. 1861. **2.** He was a thing of Blood, whose euery motion Was tim'd with dying Cryes SHAKS. **b.** Old Epopeus..Who overlook'd the oars, and tim'd the stroke ADDISON. **c.** Beat, happy stars, timing with things below TENNYSON. **3.** Phr. †*To t. it out* to procrastinate, delay, spin out the time (*rare*). **4.** Slowly as he read, it was over in twelve minutes, for I timed him 1859. Hence **Timed** *ppl. a.* esp. in comb., as *well-timed.*

Ti·me-ball. 1858. A ball moving on a vertical rod or pole, placed in some prominent position, for the purpose of indicating mean time, which it does by dropping at a certain moment each day from the top to the bottom of the rod.

Ti·me-ba:rgain. 1775. A contract for the sale or purchase of goods or stock at a stipulated price on a certain future day; in Stock Exchange parlance, a transaction in which one accepts the liability to profit or lose by the amount of the difference between the prices of the stock involved on the day of dealing and on the settling-day.

Timeful (təi·mfŭl), *a. rare.* ME. [f. TIME *sb.* + -FUL.] Seasonable, due. Hence **Ti·mefully** *adv.* with timely action CARLYLE.

Ti·me-ho:noured, *a.* 1593. Honoured or made honourable by length of time; respected on account of long existence or old establishment.

Old Iohn of Gaunt, time-honoured Lancaster SHAKS.

Ti·me-kee:per, timekeeper. 1686. **1.** An instrument for registering the passage of time; a timepiece; formerly, a chronometer. **2.** One who notes, measures, or records time; *spec.* **a.** one who is employed in keeping account of workmen's hours of labour; **b.** one who beats time in music; **c.** one who marks the time occupied by a race, the rounds in a pugilistic encounter, etc. 1795. **3.** A person or thing that keeps (good or bad) time 1899.

Timeless (təi·mlés), *a.* (*adv.*) 1560. [-LESS.] **1.** That is out of its proper time; untimely; ill-timed. Chiefly *poet.*, now *arch.* or *Obs.* **b.** as *adv.* Out of due time 1586. **2.** Not subject to time; not affected by the lapse of time; eternal. Chiefly *poet.* and *rhet.* 1628. **3.** *Gram.* Not expressing time or a temporal aspect.

1. Let earth and heaven his t. death deplore MARLOWE. **2.** When worlds..headlong rush To t. night, and chaos, whence they rose YOUNG. Hence **Ti·melessly** *adv.* out of due time (*arch.* or *Obs.*); without reference to time, independently of the passage of time.

‖**Timelia** (təimī·liă). 1896. [alt. by Sundevall (1872) from Horsfield's name *Timalia* (1820), said to be from an EInd. name; see -IA¹.] *Ornith.* A genus of East Indian oscine birds, the type of which is *T. pileata*, a small bird found from Nepal to Cochin China and Java. Hence **Time·lian** *a.* **Timeliine** (təimī·liˌəin) *a.* allied, or assumed to be allied, to *T.*

Ti·me-li:mit. 1880. A limit in time, or to the duration of some action or condition; also, a limit to the duration of a licence or privilege.

Timeliness (təi·mlinės). 1599. [f. next + -NESS.] The quality of being timely; †early maturity (*rare*); seasonableness, suitableness to the time.

Timely (təi·mli), *a.* ME. [f. TIME *sb.* + -LY¹.] **1.** Occurring or appearing in good time; early. Now *rare* or *Obs.* late ME. **2.** Seasonable, opportune, well-timed ME.

2. Now Gilpin had a pleasant wit, And loved a t. joke COWPER.

Timely (təi·mli), *adv.* [Late OE. *tīmlīće*; see TIME *sb.*, -LY².] **1.** Early, betimes; soon, quickly. Now *arch.* or *poet.* **2.** †Soon enough, in time; hence, in due season, seasonably; opportunely as regards time ME. **3.** Usu. hyphened to an adj. or pple. when used attrib. 1593.

1. The Spring visiteth not these quarters so t., as the Eastern parts 1602. **2.** All requisite materials t. provided 1715. **3.** Our t.-repented and often-forsaken habits of sin JER. TAYLOR.

Timenoguy (ti·mənǫgi). *Naut.* 1794. [prob. ult. based on (O)Fr. *timon* wagon-pole, tiller and GUY *sb.*¹] A rope passing from the fore-rigging to the anchor-stock to prevent the fouling of the fore-sheet.

Timeous, timous (təi·məs), *a.* (*adv.*) Chiefly *Sc.* 1470. [f. TIME *sb.* + -OUS. Occas. pronounced (təi·mīəs) or (ti·myəs), from the spelling.] **1.** = TIMELY *a.* 1. **b.** as *adv.* Early, betimes. Now *dial.* 1578. **2.** = TIMELY *a.* 2. 1626. Hence **Ti·meously** *adv.* in a t. manner.

Timepiece (təi·mˌpīs). 1765. [PIECE *sb.* II. 8 ('pieces made at Augsburgh, that moved by the help of Clock-work', 1698).] An instrument for measuring and registering the passage of time.

Timer (təi·məɹ). 1841. [f. TIME *sb.* and *v.* + -ER¹.] **1.** One who appoints the time for an action event, etc. **2. a.** A (good or bad) time-keeper. **b.** One who times clocks, etc. **c.** = TIME-KEEPER 2 c. 1884. **3.** In comb., as FULL-TIMER, HALF-TIMER, etc.; **fast t.,** one who or that which completes a race, etc. in fast time 1891.

Ti·me-se:rver. 1584. [f. phr. *to serve the time*; see SERVE *v.* I. 10.] One who adapts his conduct to the time or season; usu., one who on grounds of self-interest shapes his conduct in conformity to the views that are in favour at the time; a 'trimmer'.

Ti·me-se:rving, *vbl. sb.* 1621. [f. as prec. + -ING¹.] The action or conduct of a time-server; 'trimming'.

Ti·me-se:rving, *ppl. a.* 1630. [f. as prec. + -ING².] Characterized by interested compliance; 'trimming', temporizing.

Ti·me-spi:rit. 1831. [tr. G. *zeitgeist.*] The spirit of the time, the genius of the age.

Ti·me-ta:ble. 1838. A tabular list or schedule of the times at which successive things are to be done or happen, or of the times occupied in the parts of some process. *spec.* **a.** A printed table or book of tables showing the times of arrival and departure of railway trains at and from the stations; also, a similar table of times of arrival and departure of steam-boats, etc. **b.** A chart used in railway traffic offices, showing by means of cross lines, in one direction representing hours and minutes and in the other miles, the position of the various trains at any given moment. **c.** A table showing how the time of a school, etc., for any day, or for a week, is allotted to classes and subjects.

a. Bradshaw's Railway Time Tables 1839.

Ti·me-worn, *a.* 1729. Worn by process of time; impaired by age.

Timid (ti·mid), *a.* 1549. [– Fr. *timide* or L. *timidus*, f. *timēre* fear; see -ID¹.] Subject to fear; easily frightened; wanting boldness or courage; fearful, timorous. **b.** Characterized by or indicating fear 1741.

Poor is the triumph o'er the t. hare THOMSON. **b.** Carry to him thy t. counsels GRAY. **Ti·mid-ly** *adv.*, **-ness** (*rare*).

Timidity (timi·dĭti). 1598. [– Fr. *timidité* or L. *timiditas*, f. *timidus* TIMID; see -ITY.] The quality of being timid; fearfulness.

Timist (təi·mist). 1613. [-IST] †**1.** A time-server –1658. **2.** One who keeps correct time in music 1765. **3.** *Cricket.* One who times the ball (well or badly) 1893.

Timocracy (təimǫ·krăsi). 1586. [– (O)Fr. *timocratie* – med.L. *timocratia* – Gr. τιμοκρατία, f. τιμή honour, value + -κρατια -CRACY.] **1.** In the Aristotelian sense: A polity with a property qualification for the ruling class. **2.** In the Platonic sense: A polity (like that of Sparta) in which love of honour is said to be the dominant motive with the rulers 1656. Hence **Timocra·tic, -al** *adjs.*

Timon (təi·mǫn). 1588. [Gr. Τίμων, personal name.] The name of a noted misanthrope of Athens, the hero of Shakespeare's *Timon of Athens*; hence, one like Timon, a misanthrope.

Timoneer (təimŏnī^ə·ɹ). *rare.* 1762. [– (O)Fr. *timonier*, f. *timon* helm :– L. *temo*, *-ōn-*; see -EER.] A helmsman, steersman.

Timorous (ti·mŏrəs), *a.* 1450. [– OFr. *temoros*, *-eus* – med.L. *timorosus*, f. L. *timor* fear, f. *timēre*; see TIMID, -OUS.] **1.** Full of or affected by fear (either for the time or habitually); fearful. **b.** Indicating or proceeding from fear; characterized by timidity 1581. †**2.** Causing fear or dread; dreadful, terrible –1632.

1. Timerous of death 1613. Animals of the hare kind..are inoffensive and t. GOLDSM. **b.** This t. policy 1838. Hence **Ti·morous-ly** *adv.*, **-ness.**

Timorsome (ti·məɹsŏm), *a.* Now *dial.* 1599. [f. TIMOROUS, with substitution of -SOME¹ for -OUS.] Subject to or characterized by fear; timorous, timid.

Timothy (ti·mŏþi). 1747. Short for next. Also *attrib.* as *t. field, hay.*

Ti·mothy grass. 1736. [Said to be f. name of *Timothy* Hanson, who was the first to cultivate it as an agricultural plant.] A name (orig. Amer.) for Meadow Cat's-tail Grass, *Phleum pratense*, a native British grass, introduced into cultivation under this name in the N. Amer. colonies in the 18th c.

†**Timwhi·sky.** 1764. [f. WHISKY *sb.*²; first element unkn.] A kind of high light carriage, seated for one or two, drawn by a single horse or by two horses driven 'tandem'; a gig; a whisky –1837.

Tin (tin), *sb.* [OE. *tin* = OFris., (M)LG., (M)Du. *tin*, OHG. *zin* (G. *zinn*), ON. *tin* :– Gmc. **tinam*, of unkn. origin, perh. a pre-IE. word of western Europe.] **1.** A well-known metal, nearly approaching silver in whiteness and lustre, highly malleable, and taking a high polish; used in the manufacture of articles of block tin, in the formation of alloys, as bronze, pewter, etc., and, on account of its resistance to oxidation, for making tin-plate and lining culinary and other iron vessels. As a chemical element, symbol Sn (*stannum*), atomic weight 119. **b.** With defining attribute 1610. **2.** A vessel made of tin, or more usu. of tinned iron; *spec.* a vessel in which meat, fish, fruit, etc., is hermetically sealed for preservation; locally, a small cylindrical drinking vessel or mug with a handle 1821. **b.** Tin-plate as the material of such vessels 1879. **3.** *slang.* Money, cash 1836.

1. b. Bar-t. = *block t.*; **black t.,** t. ore (the dioxide, SnO_2) prepared for smelting; **block t.,** metallic t. refined and cast into blocks; **grain t.,** a very pure t. obtained by fusing stream t. in a blast furnace supplied with charcoal and breaking it into small pieces; **phosphor t.,** an artificial compound of t. and phosphorus; **stream t.,** t. ore washed from the sand or gravel in which it occurs; **white t.,** refined metallic t.

attrib. and *Comb.*: as *t. box, -mine, -ore, -whistle, -works*; also *fig.* with ref. to t. as a base metal; also, made of corrugated iron; **t.-bath,** the mass of melted t. in a t.-furnace; **-can** = sense 2; **t. hat** (*Mil. slang*), a shrapnel helmet; *to put the t. hat on*, to 'finish', 'put the lid on'; **t. god** *fig.*, a base or unworthy object of veneration; **-liquor,** a solution of t. in strong acid mixed with common salt, used as a mordant in dyeing; **-mordant,** a mordant consisting of a solution of t. in acid, as *t.-liquor*; **-opener,** an instrument for opening soldered tins; **-pyrites,** a sulphide of t.; **-stuff,** a miner's name for tin ore.

Tin (tin), *v.* late ME. [f. prec.] **1.** *trans.* To cover with a thin deposit of tin; to coat or plate with tin. **2.** In soldering iron, brass, etc.: To perform the preliminary processes of heating the surfaces and covering them with a thin coating of the solder 1873. **3.** To put up or seal (provisions) in a tin for preservation; to can 1887.

‖**Tinamou** (ti·nămū). 1783. [– Fr. *tinamou* – Galibi *tinamu.*] A bird of the genus *Tinamus* or family *Tinamidæ* of dromæognathous birds, having an external resemblance to partridges or quails.

Tincal (ti·ŋkăl), **tincar** (ti·ŋkăɹ). 1635. [In form *tincal* – Malay *tingkal* :– Skr. *ṭaṅkaṇa*; in Pers., Urdu *tankār, tinkār*, whence the form *tincar*; cf. med.L. *tincar* (XII). Cf. ALTINCAR.] Crude borax, found in lake-deposits in Tibet, Persia, and other Asiatic countries.

Tinchel (ti·nxʸĕl, ti·ŋkĕl). *Sc.* 1549. [– Gael. *timchioll* (tʃi·mxʸŏl) circuit, compass, round.] In Scotland, a wide circle of hunters driving together a number of deer by gradually closing in on them.

Tinct (tiŋkt), *sb.* Now *poet.* 1471. [– L. *tinctus* a dyeing, f. *tingere* to stain.] **1.** = TINCTURE *sb.* 1, 2, 4. 1602. †**2.** *Alch.* A transmuting elixir –1606.

1. White and Azure lac'd With Blew of Heauens owne t. SHAKS. **2.** *Ant. & Cl.* I. v. 37.

Tinct, *ppl. a. poet.* 1579. [– L. *tinctus* pa. pple. of *tingere*; see next.] Coloured, tinted; dyed, tinged; imbued. Const. as *pa. pple.*

Lucent syrops, t. with cinnamon KEATS.

†**Tinct**, *v.* 1594. [– *tinct-*, pa. ppl. stem of L. *tingere* dye, colour.] **1.** *trans.* To colour; to dye; to tinge, tint –1686. **2.** *transf.* and *fig.* = TINCTURE *v.* 2 a, b. –1734. **3.** *Alch.* To subject to a transmuting elixir –1655.

Tinctorial (tiŋktōᵊ·riăl), *a.* 1655. [f. L. *tinctorius* (f. *tinctor* dyer) + -AL¹ 1.] Of, pertaining to, or used in dyeing; yielding or using dye or colouring matter. Hence **Tincto·rially** *adv.*

Tincture (ti·ŋktiŭɹ, -tʃəɹ), *sb.* late ME. [– L. *tinctura* dyeing, f. *tinct-*; see TINCT *v.*, -URE.] †**1.** A dye, pigment; *spec.* a dye used as a cosmetic –1825. **2.** Hue, colour; a tinge, tint. Now *rare*. 1477. **b.** *Her.* Inclusive term for the metals, colours, and furs used in coats of arms, etc. 1610. †**3.** The action of dyeing, staining, or colouring –1681. †**b.** *fig* A stain, blemish –1658. †**4.** *fig.* An imparted quality likened to a colour or dye; a specious or 'colourable' appearance; a tinge –1806. †**5.** A physical quality (other than colour) communicated to something; *esp.* a taste or flavour, a taint –1727. **b.** A slight infusion (*of* some element, quality, etc.); a tinge, shade, flavour, trace; a smattering (*of* knowledge, etc.) 1612. †**6.** *Alch.* A supposed spiritual principle or immaterial substance whose character or quality may be infused into material things, which are then said to be tinctured; the quintessence, spirit, or soul of a thing. *Universal t.*, the Elixir. –1693. †**b.** An active principle, of a physical nature, emanating or derivable from any body or substance; a liquid or volatile principle –1677. **7.** *Chem.* and *Pharm.* †**a.** The (supposed) essential principle of any substance obtained in solution. Also, the extraction of this essential principle. 1610. **b.** *Mod. Pharmacy.* A solution, usu. in a menstruum of alcohol, of some principle used in medicine, chiefly vegetable, as t. of opium (laudanum), but occas. animal, as t. of cantharides, or mineral, as t. of ferric chloride 1648.

More particularly called an *alcoholic tincture*. But the menstruum may also be sulphuric ether or spirit of ammonia (both mainly alcohol), which give *ethereal* and *ammoniated* tinctures respectively; when wine is used they are called *medicated wines*.

2. 'Tis not..The t. of a skin, that I admire ADDISON. **b.** *Tinctures*, in Heraldry are of three descriptions: metals, colours, and furs. The former are or, argent; the second gules, azure, sable, vert, purpure, sanguine, and tenny. The chief furs are ermine and vair; but there are several varieties of both, distinguished by different names. 1842. **4.** The Saxon language received little or no t. from the Welsh BURKE. **5. b.** This, perhaps, cannot be called Affectation; but it has some T. of it STEELE.

Ti·ncture, *v.* 1616. [f. prec.] **1.** *trans.* To impart a tincture or dye to; to dye; to colour, tinge, imbue. (Chiefly in pa. pple.) **2.** *transf.* and *fig.* To imbue or impregnate with a quality; to communicate some quality to; to affect, tinge, taint. (Chiefly in pa. pple., const. *with.*) †**a.** with a physical quality, as smell or taste –1820. **b.** with a mental or moral quality or character 1636.

1. Cheekes tinctured with Vermillion SIR T. HERBERT. **2. b.** His Conversation was tinctured throughout with the Ancient Mythology 1718.

Tind (tind), *v. Obs.* exc. *dial.* ME. [repr. OE. causative *-tendan* :– Gmc. **tandjan* (whence Goth. *tandjan* kindle), f. **tend-* **tand-* **tund-* kindle; see TINDER.] **1.** *trans.* To set fire to, light, kindle (a fire, torch, flame.). **2.** *intr.* To catch fire, kindle, become ignited, begin to burn ME. **3.** *fig. trans.* To inflame, excite, arouse, inspire ME.

1. As one candle tindeth a thousand 1663. **2.** Wash your hands, or else the fire Will not teend to your desire HERRICK. **3.** Shop-consciences,.. Preach'd up, and ready tined for a rebellion DRYDEN.

‖**Tindal** (ti·ndăl). *India.* 1698. [– Hind. *tandel* – Malayalam *tandal*, Telugu *tandelu.*] **1.** A native petty officer of lascars, on board ship, or in the ordnance department; also, the foreman of a gang of labourers on public works (Yule); a boatswain; a foreman. **2.** A personal attendant 1859.

Tinder (ti·ndəɹ). [OE. *tynder, tyndre*, corresp. (with variation in suffix and gender) to (M)LG. *tunder* (Du. *tonder*), OHG. *zuntara* (G. *zunder*), ON. *tundr*, f. Gmc. **tund-*; see TIND *v.*] Any dry inflammable substance that readily takes fire from a spark and burns or smoulders; esp. that prepared from partially charred linen and from species of *Polyporus* or corkwood fungus (AGARIC 1), formerly in common use to catch the spark struck from a flint with a steel, as the means of kindling a fire or 'striking' a light.

attrib. and *Comb.*: **t.-box**, a box containing t. (also usu. the flint and steel with which the spark was struck); **-fungus**, a fungus from which t. is made, as **t.-polypore**, *Polyporus fomentarius*.

Tindery (ti·ndəri), *a.* 1754. [f. prec. + -Y¹.] Of the nature of or resembling tinder, tinder-like, also *fig.* 'inflammable', passionate.

Tine (təin), *sb.*¹ [OE. *tind* (whence AL. *tinda* XIII) = MLG. *tind*, OHG. *zint*, ON. *tindr*, rel. to synon. MLG. *tinne*, OHG. *zinna* (G. *zinne* pinnacle). For the loss of final *d* cf. *groin, lawn, woodbine.*] **1.** Each of a series of projecting sharp points on some weapon or implement, as a harrow, fork, etc.; a prong, spike, tooth. **2.** Each of the pointed branches of a deer's horn. late ME.

†**Tine**, *sb.*² (Only in and after Spenser.) 1590. [By-form of TEEN *sb.* Perh. from Norse: cf. Norw. dial. *týne* injury.] Affliction, trouble, sorrow –1610.

To seek her out with labor and long tyne SPENSER.

†**Tine**, *a.* and *sb.*³ late ME. [Of unkn. origin. Cf. TINY.] **A.** *adj.* = TINY *a.* –1605. A ioynt of Mutton, and any pretty little t. Kickshawes SHAKS.

B. *sb.* or quasi-*sb.* A very little space, time, or amount; a very little; 'a bit' –1556.

Tine, tyne (təin), *v.*¹ *Obs.* exc. *dial.* [OE. *tȳnan* = OFris. *tēna*, MDu. *tūnen* (Du. *tuinen*), OHG. *zūnen* (G. *zäunen*) :– WGmc. **tūnjan*, f. *tūn-* enclosure; see TOWN.] **1.** *trans.* To close, shut (a door, gate, or window; a house, one's mouth, eyes, etc.). Also with *to* adv. and *absol.* **2. a.** To enclose or shut (a thing) up *in* something. late ME. **b.** To fence, hedge in OE.

Tine, tyne (təin), *v.*² Now *n. dial.* and *Sc.* Pa. t. and pa. pple. **tint** (tint). ME. [– ON. *týna* (:– **tiunjan*) destroy, lose, perish, f. *tjón* loss, damage, cogn. with OE. *tēon*; see TEEN *sb.* and *v.*] = LOSE *v.*¹

Tine, var. of TIND *v.*

‖**Tinea** (ti·niă). late ME. [L., a gnawing worm, a moth, bookworm.] **1.** *Path.* Technical name of the disease RINGWORM. **2.** *Ent.* A genus of small moths (*Microlepidoptera*), including *T. tapetzella* and *T. pellionella*, and *T. destructor*, the larvæ of which are very destructive to cloth, feathers, soft paper, stuffed birds, etc. In earlier times the word was applied to other destructive insects and worms. Hence **Ti·nean, Ti·neid** *a.* of or belonging to the genus *T.* or family *Tineidæ*; *sb.* a member of this genus or family.

Tined (təind), *a.* late ME. [f. TINE *sb.*¹ + -ED².] Furnished with or having tines.

Tinfoil (ti·nfoil), *sb.* late ME. [f. TIN *sb.* + FOIL *sb.*¹] Tin hammered or rolled into a thin sheet; also, a sheet of the same rubbed with quicksilver, used for backing mirrors and precious stones; a similar sheet of an alloy of tin and lead, used as a wrapping to protect comfits, etc., from moisture or air. Hence **Ti·nfoil** *v. trans.* to cover or coat with t.; **Ti·nfoiled** *ppl. a.* esp. *fig.*

Ting (tiŋ), *sb.* 1602. [f. next.] The sound emitted by a small bell, or other resonant body, as the result of a single stroke. Also *advb.*, or without grammatical construction, esp. when repeated. **b.** *T.-a-ling, t.-a-ring*, the sound of the ringing of a small bell, or the like 1833. Also **Ting-tang** 1680.

The sharp t. of a hand-bell 1895. **b.** Ting-a-ling. Telephone again. 1906.

Ting (tiŋ), *v.* 1495. [imit.] **1.** *trans.* To cause (a small bell or the like) to emit a ringing note. **2.** *intr.* Of a bell, a metal or glass vessel, or the like: To emit a high-pitched ringing note when struck, to ring 1562. **3.** To make a ringing sound *with* a bell, etc. 1605.

Tinge (tinᵈʒ), *sb.* 1752. [f. TINGE *v.*] **1.** A slight shade of colouring, *esp.* one modifying a tint or colour. **2.** *fig.* A modifying infusion or intermixture; a touch or flavour of some quality 1797.

2. His political opinions had a t. of Whiggism MACAULAY.

Tinge (tinᵈʒ), *v.* 1477. [– L. *tingere* to dye, colour.] **1.** *trans.* To impart a trace or slight shade of some colour to; to tint; to modify the tint or colour of (const. *with*). Also *absol.* **b.** *transf.* To impart a slight taste or smell to; to affect slightly by admixture 1690. **2.** *intr.* To become modified in colour; to take a (specified or implied) tinge 1662. **3.** *fig.* To qualify, modify, or slightly vary the tone of 1674.

3. This grief tinged the whole of Mr. Croker's subsequent life 1884.

Tingent (ti·ndʒĕnt), *a.* Now *rare* or *Obs.* 1650. [– L. *tingens, -ent-*, pr. pple. of *tingere*; see prec., -ENT.] That tinges or colours, colouring, dyeing.

Tin-glass. Now *rare.* 1478. [f. TIN *sb.* + GLASS.] An old name for: Bismuth.

Tingle (ti·ŋg'l), *sb.* 1700. [f. next.] An instance, act, or condition of tingling. Also advb. or without constr.

The t. of the morning air 1908.

Tingle (ti·ŋg'l), *v.* late ME. [perh. modification of TINKLE *v.*¹ by assoc. with RING *v.*²] **I. 1.** *intr.* Said of the ears: To be affected with a ringing or thrilling sensation at the hearing of anything. **b.** Said also of the cheeks under the influence of shame, indignation, etc. 1555. **2.** Of other parts of the body: To be thrilled by a peculiar stinging or smarting sensation, physical or emotional; to smart, thrill, vibrate; also *fig.* of inanimate things, companies of persons, etc. late ME. **b.** Predicated of that which causes the sensation: To thrill, vibrate; to pass with a thrill 1819. **3.** *trans.* To cause to tingle; to sting, excite, stimulate 1572. **b.** *absol.* or *intr.* 1872.

1. Least I cause good and learned mens eares to t. at his leud and vnseemely rimes HAKLUYT. **2.** Wounds t. most when they are about to heal THACKERAY. **b.** The lust of battle tingling in him from head to heel KINGSLEY. **3.** The cold, inconsiderate of persons, tingles your blood EMERSON.

II. 1. *intr.* To make a continued light ringing sound. Now *rare.* late ME. **2.** *trans.* To cause (a bell) to ring lightly; to ring (a bell, a chime, etc.). Now *rare.* 1649. Hence **Ti·ngler**, something that causes tingling, as a blow; a 'stinger'. **Ti·nglingly** *adv.*

Tink (tiŋk), *int.* and *sb.* 1609. [imit.] A representation of the abrupt sound made by striking resonant metal with something hard and light; often reduplicated; also with such variations as *t.-tank, t.-a-t.*, etc. Hence as *sb.* a single sound of this kind; also *fig.* in ref. to rhyme or verse.

Tink (tiŋk), *v.*¹ Now *rare* or *Obs.* late ME. [imit. (Wyclif). See TINKLE *v.*¹] **1.** *intr.* To emit a metallic sound with very short resonance, e.g. as is done by a cracked bell, but occas. used as = TINKLE, to chink, clink. **2.** Of a person: To make such a sound by striking upon metal or other resonant substance 1533. **3.** *trans.* To cause to emit an abrupt metallic sound 1495.

1. Prov. *As the fool thinketh, the bell tinketh*, i.e. to the fool the bell seems to say what he wants it to say; in ref. to a superstitious notion that the tinkling of a bell sometimes gives an oracular monition or answer.

Tink, *v.*² Now *rare* or *Obs.* ME. [Goes with TINKER *sb.*, of which, if its history could be traced further back, it may be the source; but it may also be a back-formation from *tinker*. See also TINKLER.] *trans.* To mend, solder, rivet (rarely, to make) pots and pans, as a tinker.

Tinker (ti·ŋkəɹ), *sb.* ME. [Earliest in AL. *Editha le Tynekere* (c1265), then *Tomkyn þe Tinkere* (Langland). The corresp. verb TINK *v.*² is not recorded until XV. See TINKLER.] **1.** A craftsman (usu. itinerant) who mends pots, kettles, and other metal household utensils. **b.** In Scotland and north of Ireland, a gipsy. Also applied to itinerant beggars, traders, and performers generally. 1561. **c.** A clumsy or inefficient mender; a botcher; also *fig.* In U.S. also applied to a 'jack-of-all-trades'. 1644. **2.** [f. next.] An act or bout of tinkering; *fig.* a bungling or unskilful attempt at mending something 1857. **3.** Local name for: **a.** The skate. **b.** The stickleback. **c.** *U.S.* A small or young mackerel. **d.** The guillemot 1836. (Cf. TINKERSHERE.) **4.** *Ordnance.* A small mortar fixed on the end of a staff, and fired by a trigger and lanyard. *U.S.* 1877.

1. Phr. *Not to care*, or *be worth, a tinker's curse* or *damn*, an intensification of 'not to care a curse or damn', with ref. to the reputed addiction of tinkers to profane swearing.

Tinker (ti·ŋkəɹ), *v.* 1592. [f. prec.] **1.** *intr.* To work as a tinker; to mend metal utensils (and hence *gen.* any material objects), esp. in a clumsy or bungling way. **b.** *fig.* To work at something (immaterial) clumsily or imperfectly; also, to occupy oneself about something in a trifling or aimless way; to potter 1658. **2.** *trans.* To mend as a tinker; to patch *up* 1753.

1. b. The public were tired of government which merely tinkered at legislation 1880. **2.** *fig.* Men are prone to be tinkering the work of their own hands LOWELL.

†**Ti·nkerly,** *a.* 1586. [f. TINKER *sb.* + -LY[1].] Having the character of a tinker or of tinker's work; clumsy, bungling, unskilful; of poor quality; mean, low, disreputable –1681.

Tinkershere, -shire (ti·ŋkəɹʃīᵊɹ). *local.* 1799. [f. TINKER *sb.*; second element of unkn. origin.] The common guillemot; the black guillemot.

Tin-kettle. 1775. A kettle of tinned iron. (Often *fig.* with allusion to its being fastened to a dog's tail to tease and frighten it, or to the noise made by beating it.)

Tinkle (ti·ŋk'l), *sb.* 1682. [f. next.] The act or action of tinkling; a sharp light ringing sound, such as that made by a small bell, etc. 1804. **b.** *fig.* in ref. to speech or verse 1725. **c.** Reduplicated, expressing repetition of such sounds; also as *adv.* 1682.

Of ice and glass the t., Pellucid, silver-shrill HENLEY.

Tinkle (ti·ŋk'l), *v.*[1] late ME. [In form, a frequent. of TINK *v.*[1] (see -LE 3), which also suits the chronology, both being used by Wyclif.] **I.** *intr.* Of the ears: = TINGLE *v.* 1. Now *rare.*

His Ears tinckled, and his Colour fled DRYDEN.

II. 1. To give forth a series of short light sharp ringing sounds. Said of bells, musical instruments, and other resonant objects. late ME. **b.** To flow or move with a tinkling sound 1822. **c.** *transf.* To rhyme or jingle 1626. **2.** Of a person: To produce such a sound 1750. **b.** *fig.* To utter empty sounds or senseless words, talk idly, prate 1641. **3.** *trans.* **a.** To make known, call attention to, or express by tinkling (*lit.* or *fig.*) 1562. **b.** To affect, attract, or summon by tinkling 1582. **4.** To cause (something) to tinkle or make a short light ringing sound 1582.

1. A sheepbell tinkles on the heath 1819. **b.** A small rill tinkled along close by W. IRVING. **2.** We are but crackt cimbals, we do but tinckle, we know nothing MILTON.

†**Tinkle,** *v.*[2] 1599. [Back-formation from next.] = TINKER *v.* 1 –1630.

Tinkler (ti·ŋkləɹ). *Sc.* and *dial.* ME. [Earliest in AL. *Jacobi tinkler* (c1175), *Christoferus Tynkeler* (1484); in Eng. context from 1570. Earlier by a century than TINKER *sb.*, its relation to this, and to TINK *v.*[2], cannot be determined.] A tinker, a worker in metal; in Scotland, etc., usu. a gipsy, or other itinerant mender of pots, pans, and metal-work.

Tinkling (ti·ŋkliŋ), *vbl. sb.* 1495. [f. TINKLE *v.*[1] + -ING[1].] **1.** The action of TINKLE *v.*[1] **2.** Short for *tinkling grackle*; see next. 1847.

1. Drowsy tinklings lull the distant folds GRAY.

Tinkling (ti·ŋkliŋ), *ppl. a.* 1440. [f. as prec. + -ING[2].] That tinkles. **b.** *T. grackle*, also simply *tinkling*: a bird, a species of grackle (*Quiscalus crassirostris*) found in Jamaica; so called from its note 1847. Hence **Ti·nklingly** *adv.*

Tinkly (ti·ŋkli), *a.* 1892. [f. TINKLE *v.*[1] or *sb.* + -Y[1].] Characterized by tinkling.

The t. piano 1894.

Tinman (ti·nmæ̆n). 1611. [f. TIN *sb.* + MAN *sb.*] A man who works in or with tin; a tinsmith. In Cornwall, a man employed in dressing tin ore.

Tinned (tind), *ppl. a.* late ME. [f. TIN *sb.* or *v.* + -ED.] **1.** Coated or plated with tin. **2.** Preserved in air-tight tins; canned 1879. **3.** Of music: Produced by mechanical means, as in a cinema 1929.

Tinner (ti·nəɹ). 1512. [f. TIN *sb.* or *v.* + -ER[1].] **1.** A tin-miner. **2.** One who works in tin; a tin-plater, tinman, tinsmith 1611. **3.** One who tins meat, fruit, etc.; a canner 1906.

Tinnery (ti·nəri). 1769. [f. TINNER + -Y[3], or f. TIN + -ERY.] Tin-mining; *pl.* tin-mines or tin-works.

Tinning (ti·niŋ), *vbl. sb.* 1440. [f. TIN *v.* or *sb.* + -ING[1].] **1.** Coating, lining, or plating with tin; working at tin-ware. **b.** *concr.* A tin coating or lining 1761. **2.** The putting up and sealing of meat, fish, fruit, etc., in tins for preservation 1903. **3.** Tin-mining 1855.

‖**Tinnitus** (tinəi·tŭs). 1843. [L., f. *tinnire* ring, tinkle, of imit. origin.] *Med.* A sensation of ringing in the ears.

Tinny (ti·ni), *a.* 1552. [f. TIN *sb.* + -Y[1].] **1.** Consisting of, abounding in, or yielding tin; formerly also, of tin, made of tin. **2.** Like or resembling tin or that of tin; *esp.* of sounds; in *Painting*, hard, crude, metallic 1877. **3.** *slang.* Having plenty of 'tin'; wealthy 1871.

1. Dart, nigh chockt with sands of t. mines SPENSER. **2.** The old t.-sounding spinnet 1904.

Tinoceratid (təinose·rătid), *a.* and *sb.* 1889. [irreg. f. Gr. τείνειν stretch, as if = stretching out + κέρας, κερατ- horn + -ID[3].] *Palæont.* **A.** *adj.* Of, pertaining to, or having the characters of the *Tinoceras*, a very large fossil mammal. **B.** *sb.* A fossil of this genus 1891.

Tin-plate. 1677. Sheet-iron or, in recent use, often sheet-steel, coated with tin; a plate of this. So **Ti·n-pla·ted** *ppl. a.* **Ti·n-pla·ter.**

Tin-pot (ti·n,pǫ·t, ti·npǫt). 1772. **1.** (as two words) A pot made of tin or tin-plate. **2.** The pot of molten tin into which the sheet of iron is dipped in the manufacture of tin-plate 1839. **3.** *attrib.* Resembling or suggesting a tin pot in quality or sound; hence *contempt.*, of inferior quality, shabby, poor, cheap 1865.

3. Miserable t. politicians 1897.

Tinsel (ti·nsĕl, -s'l), *sb.* and *a.* 1502. [First in *tinsell(e saten*, prob. repr. AFr. **satin estincelé*, with loss of final -*é* as in *costive*; hence, by ellipsis, used subst. OFr. *estincelé* (in which the *s* had become mute in XIV), f. *estincele* (mod. *étincelle* spark), repr. pop. L. **stincilla*, for L. SCINTILLA.] **1.** *adj.* passing into *sb.* used *attrib.* Of satin, etc.: Made to sparkle or glitter by the interweaving of gold or silver thread, by brocading with such thread, or by overlaying with a thin coating of gold or silver. †**2.** A kind of cloth or tissue; tinselled cloth; a rich material of silk or wool interwoven with gold or silver thread; occas., a thin net or gauze thus made; later, a cheap imitation of this –1755. **3.** Very thin plates or sheets, spangles, strips, or threads, orig. of gold or silver, later of copper, brass, etc., used chiefly for ornament; now esp. for cheap and showy ornamentation, gaudy stage costumes, and the like 1593. **4.** *fig.* Anything showy or attractive with little or no intrinsic worth 1660. **5.** *attrib.* passing into *adj.* †Glittering, splendid. Chiefly in disparagement: Showy with little real worth; cheaply gaudy, tawdry 1595.

3. As twinckling starres, the tinsell of the night 1593. **4.** That poverty of ideas which had been hitherto concealed under the t. of politeness JOHNSON. **5.** Neither their t. wit, nor superficial learning will hold them up then 1680.

Ti·nsel, *v.* 1594. [f. prec.] **1.** *trans.* To make glittering with gold or silver (or imitations thereof) interwoven, brocaded, or laid on. **2.** To give a speciously attractive or showy appearance to; to cover the defects of with or as with tinsel 1748. Hence **Ti·nselled** *ppl. a.* = prec. 1; also, embellished with gold or silver leaf.

Tinselly (ti·nsĕli), *a.* 1811. [f. as prec. + -Y[1].] Of the nature of, characterized by, or abounding in tinsel; hence, cheaply splendid or sparkling, 'pinchbeck'.

Tinsmith (ti·n,smiþ). 1858. [f. TIN + SMITH.] A worker in tin; a maker of tin utensils; a whitesmith.

Ti·n-stone. 1602. The most commonly occurring form of tin ore; cassiterite, native tin dioxide (peroxide).

Tint (tint), *sb.* 1717. [alt. (perh. by assim. to It. *tinta*) of TINCT *sb.*] **1.** A colour, hue, usu. slight or delicate; a tinge; *esp.* one of the several lighter or deeper shades or varieties, or degrees of intensity, of the same colour. **b.** *fig.*; *esp.* Quality, kind; a slight imparted or modifying character 1760. **2.** *spec.* **a.** *Painting.* A grade of colour; *spec.* a mixture of a colour with white 1753. **b.** *Engraving.* The effect produced by a series of fine parallel lines more or less closely drawn so as to produce an even and uniform shading 1880.

1. Autumn tints of brown and gold 1878. **b.** Our inborn spirits have a t. of thee BYRON.

Comb.: **t.-block,** a block of wood or metal hatched with fine parallel lines suitable for printing tints; **-tool,** an implement used for hatching a t.-block.

Tint (tint), *v.* 1791. [f. prec.] *trans.* To impart a tint to; to colour, esp. slightly or with delicate shades; to tinge. Also *absol.* **b.** *intr.* for *pass.* To become tinted or coloured 1892.

Tint, pa. pple. of TINE *v.*[2]

Ti·n-tack. 1840. [TACK *sb.*[1]] A tack, or short light iron nail, coated with tin.

Phr. *To come down to tin-tacks*: cf. TACK *sb.*[1] I. 2.

Tintamarre (tintămā·r). Now *rare.* 1567. [– Fr. *tintamarre*, of unkn. origin.] A confused noise, uproar, clamour, racket, hubbub, clatter.

†**Tint for tant.** 1620. [alt. of *taunt for taunt* (see TAUNT *sb.*), perh. after the earlier *tit for tat.*] = *tit for tat* (TIT *sb.*[1]). –1828.

Tintinnabulant (tintinæ·biŭlănt), *a.* 1812. [f. as next + -ANT.] Ringing or tinkling as a small bell; jingling. (This and the allied words are all pedantic.)

Tintinnabular (tintinæ·biŭlăɹ), *a.* 1767. [f. L. *tintinnabulum* bell + -AR[1].] = next.

Tintinnabulary (tintinæ·biŭlări), *a.* 1787. [f. as prec. + -ARY[1].] Of or pertaining to bells or bell-ringing; of the nature of a bell; characterized by bell-ringing.

Tintinnabulation (ti:ntinæbiŭlēi·ʃən). 1831. [f. as prec.; see -ATION.] Bell-ringing; the sound or music so produced.

Tintinnabulous (tintinæ·biŭləs), *a.* 1791. [f. as prec.; see -OUS.] Characterized by or pertaining to bell-ringing.

‖**Tintinnabulum** (tintinæ·biŭlŏm). *Pl.* **-a.** 1597. [L., bell, f. *tintinnare* to ring + *-bulum*, suffix of instrument.] A small tinkling bell.

Tintometer (tintǫ·mĭtəɹ). 1889. [f. TINT *sb.* + -METER.] Proprietary name of an apparatus for the determination of colour by comparison with standard shades.

Tin-type (ti·n,təip). 1875. [f. TIN *sb.* + TYPE.] *Photogr.* A photograph taken as a positive on a thin tin plate.

Tiny (təi·ni), *a.* (*sb.*) 1598. [In the earliest examples always preceded by *little*; extension with -Y[1] of synon. TINE *a.* and *sb.*[3]] Very small, little, or slight; minute.

This Cupid was a little tyny, Cogging, Lying Peevish Nynny COTTON.

B. as *sb.* A tiny one, a very small child, an infant. Usu. in pl. *tinies.* 1863.

-tion, a compound suffix, repr. (orig. through Fr. *-tion*) L. *-tio, -tion-*, which consists of the suffix *-io, -ion-* added to the *-t-* of a L. ppl. stem, as in *rela-t-ion, deten-t-ion, op-t-ion.* The etymological meaning was primarily 'the state or condition of being (what the pa. pple. imports)'. But already in L. *-tio* was used for action or process, and also concretely or quasi-concretely, as in *dictio, natio, oratio.* In Eng. the most usual sense is that of a noun of action, = -ING[1].

-tious, compound suffix, repr. L. *-t-iosus*, which consists of *-iosus* -IOUS, added to the *-t-* of a L. ppl. stem. It thus serves to form adjs. belonging to sbs. in *-tion*, as in *ambition, ambitious, caution, cautious*, etc.

Tip (tip), *sb.*[1] late ME. [– ON. *typpa* sb. (*typpa* vb., *typptr* tipped, topped, edged, *typpingr* edging), f. Gmc. **tupp-* TOP *sb.*[1]; prob. reinforced by (M)LG., (M)Du. *tip* apex, extremity.] **1.** The slender extremity or top of a thing; *esp.* the pointed or rounded end of anything long and slender; the top, summit, apex, very end 1440. †**b.** *fig.* Utmost point; highest point –1626. **2.** A small piece of metal, leather, etc., attached or fitted on to something so as to form a serviceable end; as a ferrule, the leather pad on the point of a billiard-cue, a protecting cap or plate for the toe of a shoe, etc. 1440. **b.** *Costume.* The end of a tail of fur, or of a feather, as used in trimming, etc. 1681. **c.** *Angling.* The topmost joint of a fishing-rod 1891. **d.** *Hat-making.* The upper part of the crown of a hat; a stiff lining pasted in this part 1864. **3.** A thin flat brush of camel's or squirrel's hair (orig. the tip of a squirrel's tail), used for laying gold-leaf, as in bookbinding 1815.

1. The Pole-star. . in the t. of the little Beares taile 1634. The t. of a root DARWIN.

Phrases. *From t. to toe*, from head to foot. *On* (or *at*) *the t. of one's tongue*, on the point of being, or ready to be, uttered. So *at the tips of one's fingers*, ready to be performed or executed.

Tip, *sb.*[2] 1466. [Earliest in *tip for tap* (XV–XVII); app. f. TIP *v.*[1] See TIT *sb.*[1]] An act of tipping; a light but distinct impact, blow, stroke, or hit; a noiseless tap; a significant touch.

Tip, *sb.*[3] 1755. [f. TIP *v.*[4]; cf. next.] A small present of money given to an inferior; a gratuity, a douceur. Also *attrib.*

A schoolboy's t. THACKERAY. The porter will expect a t. (*mod.*).

Tip, *sb.*[4] *colloq.* or *slang.* 1845. [f. TIP *v.*[5]] A piece of useful private or special information communicated by an expert; a friendly hint; *spec.* 'an advice concerning betting or a Stock-Exchange speculation intended to benefit the recipient'; also, a hint as to points thought likely to come up in an examination; hence *transf.* a 'wrinkle', 'dodge'.

Phr. *The straight t.*, orig. a t. coming direct from the owner or trainer of a horse; now often, a direct hint on any subject. *To miss one's t.*, to fail in one's aim or object.

Tip, *sb.*[5] 1673. [f. TIP *v.*[2]] †**I.** *Skittles.* The knocking over of a pin by another which falls or rolls against it –1819. **II. 1.** An act of tipping up or tilting, or the fact of being tilted; inclination 1849. **2.** A place or erection where wagons or trucks of coal, etc. are tipped and their contents discharged into the hold of a vessel, or into a cart, etc. **b.** A wagon or truck from which coal, etc. is tipped. 1862. **3. a.** The mound or mass of rubbish, etc. that is tipped. **b.** A dumping-ground. 1863.

Tip, *v.*[1] ME. [First in *Ancrene Riwle* (*a*1225) and thereafter not till XVI (thence prob. TIP *v.*[4]); perh. orig. identical with TIP *sb.*[1], as if 'touch the point of', or 'touch as with a point'; cf. LG., Du. *tippen.*] **1.** *trans.* To strike or hit smartly but lightly; to tap noiselessly. **b.** *Cricket.* To hit (a ball) with the edge of the bat so that it glances off. **2.** *intr.* To step lightly; to trip; to walk mincingly, or on tiptoe 1819.

1. [He] felt himself suddenly tipped on the shoulder THACKERAY. **b.** *T.-and-run*, a form of cricket in which the batsman is obliged to run if he touches the ball with the bat.

Tip, *v.*[2] late ME. [orig. *tipe*, in literary use till XVI and still dial., the distribution suggesting Scand. origin. The present form may be due to the pa. pple. (*tipt*), and contact with TIP *v.*[1]] **I.** *trans.* 1. To overthrow, knock, or cast down, cause to fall or tumble; to overturn, upset; to throw down by effort or accidentally. **b.** *Skittles.* Applied to various modes of knocking down a pin 1679. **2.** To raise, push, or move into a slanting or sloping position; to incline, tilt. Often with *up*. 1624. **3.** To empty out (a wagon, cart, or the like, or its contents) by tilting it up; to dump 1838.

1. I tipp'd my nag over a broken place in the wall 1791. **2.** Phr. *To t. the scales*: to turn the scale; also *fig.* **3.** A piece of land. . used for the purpose of tipping rubbish 1910.

II. *intr.* **1.** To fall by overbalancing; to tumble or topple over 1530. **2.** To assume a slanting or sloping position; to incline, tilt, now *esp.* of a cart, a plank, etc. (usu. with *up*), to tilt up at one end and down at the other 1666. **3** *To t. off*, also simply *to t.*, or *t.* (*over*) *the perch*: to die. *slang or dial.* 1700.

1. Over tips table, candle, and cloth and all 1890. Hence **Ti·pper**[1], a workman engaged in tipping; a device for tipping.

Tip, *v.*[3] late ME. [f. TIP *sb.*[1], partly repr. ON. *typpa* (see TIP *sb.*[1]).] *trans.* To furnish with a tip; to put a tip on, or put something on at the tip (const. *with*); to form the tip of, or adorn at the tip. Usu. in pa. pple.

Flowers. . white tipped with green 1776.

Tip, *v.*[4] 1610. [orig. Rogues' Cant, prob. f. TIP *v.*[1], q.v.] **1.** *trans.* (*Rogues' Cant*, and *slang.*) To give; to hand, pass; to let one have; to present or exhibit the character of: usu. with dat. of person. **2.** *colloq.* (orig. *slang*). To give a gratuity to (an inferior), esp. a servant or employee of another; also to a child or schoolboy 1706. **b.** *absol.* To give a tip or tips 1727.

1. 'T. me your fin, my heart of oak', said Joe 1884. Come, t. me a shilling 1884. **2.** T'wou'd have paid The reck'ning clean, and tipp'd the maid 1747. You. . used to t. me when I was a boy at school THACKERAY.

Phr. *To t. the* (or *a*) *wink*, to give (a person) a private signal or warning.

Tip, *v.*[5] *colloq.* 1883. [prob. f. TIP *v.*[1], q.v.] **1.** *trans.* To give a 'tip' or piece of private information about. **2.** To give a 'tip' to; to furnish (a person) with private information as to the chances of some event 1891. **3.** *intr.* To furnish 'tips'; to carry on the business of a tipster 1903.

1. Florio Rubattino. . has been 'tipped' by some of the papers for this race 1897.

Tip-, the stem of TIP *v.*[2] (or TIP *sb.*[5]), in comb., as in *t.-cart, -truck, -wagon*, etc., vehicles constructed to tip or tilt for the purpose of emptying out the contents; also **t.-head,** the top of the slope over which material or rubbish is tipped; **-horse,** the horse which runs out the wagons to the tip-head.

Tip-cat. 1676. [f. TIP *v.*[2] + CAT *sb.*[1] II. 5.] **1.** A short piece of wood tapering at both ends, used in the game described in 2. **2.** A game in which the tip-cat (see 1) is struck or 'tipped' at one end with a stick so as to spring up, and then knocked to a distance by the same player 1801.

†**Tipe, type.** 1530. [Origin and history obscure. Sense 2 is app. synon. with TIP *sb.*[1] 1.] **1.** A small cupola or dome –1708. **2.** *fig.* The summit, acme, or highest point (*of* honour, dignity, etc.) –1603.

Ti·p-it, ti·ppit. 1889. [f. phr. *to tip it.*] A game of chance in which an object hidden in a player's hand is to be detected.

Tipper[2] (ti·pəɹ). 1844. [From name of Thomas *Tipper* (d. 1785), who first brewed it.] A kind of ale brewed in Sussex.

Tippet (ti·pėt). ME. [Of unkn. origin; prob. – AFr. deriv. of TIP *sb.*[1]; see -ET.] **1. a.** A long narrow slip of cloth or hanging part of dress, formerly worn, either attached to and forming part of the hood, head-dress, or sleeve, or loose, as a scarf or the like. *Obs.* exc. *Hist.* **b.** A garment, usu. of fur or wool, covering the shoulders, or the neck and shoulders; a cape or short cloak 1481. **c.** *Eccl.* A band of silk or other material worn round the neck, with the two ends pendent from the shoulders in front 1530. **d.** = CAMAIL 1 (*rare*). late ME. †**2.** *joc.* A hangman's rope: usu. *Tyburn t.* –1823. **3.** An organ or formation in animals resembling or suggesting a tippet: in birds, dogs, etc. = RUFF *sb.*[2] 3. 1815. **4.** *Angling.* **a.** A length of twisted hair or gut forming part of a fishing-line. *Sc.* **b.** Part of an artificial fly. 1825.

1. Phr. †*To turn* (*one's*) *t.*, to change one's course or behaviour completely; in bad sense, to act the turncoat or renegade. **b.** She had furry articles for winter wear, as tippets, boas, and muffs DICKENS.

attrib. and *Comb.*: **t. cuckoo, grouse,** names for species of these birds having a t. or ruff; **-grebe,** a species of grebe, of which the skin, with the feathers on, is used for tippets.

Ti·pping, *vbl. sb.* 1819. [f. TIP *v.*[1] + -ING[1].] The action of TIP *v.*[1] *spec.* **b.** *Mus.* The action of striking the tongue against the palate: = TONGUING 1898.

Tipple (ti·p'l), *sb.*[1] *colloq.* or *slang.* 1581. [f. TIPPLE *v.*[1]] Drink; *esp.* strong drink.

Ti·pple, *sb.*[2] *U.S.* 1886. [f. TIPPLE *v.*[2]] = TIP *sb.*[5] 2.

Tipple (ti·p'l), *v.*[1] 1500. [Back-formation from TIPPLER[2].] †**1. a.** *trans.* To sell (ale or other strong drink) by retail. **b.** *absol.* or *intr.* To carry on the trade of a 'tippler'; to sell from the tap. –1662. **2.** *intr.* To drink of intoxicating liquor: in earlier use, to drink freely or hard; to booze; now *esp.*, to indulge habitually to some excess in taking strong drink 1560. **b.** *trans.* To drink (intoxicating liquor), esp. to take (drink) constantly in small quantities 1581. **c.** *transf.* and *poet.* To drink, sip. *intr.* and *trans.* Now *rare* or *Obs.* 1648. †**3.** *trans.* To intoxicate, make drunk –1648.

2. I wondered to see how the ladies did t. PEPYS. **c.** Fishes that t. in the deep Know no such liberty LOVELACE. **3.** Opium,. . which tipples, intoxicates and duls them PURCHAS.

Ti·pple, *v.*[2] *dial.* 1847. [frequent. of TIP *v.*[2]; see -LE.] **1.** *intr.* To tumble or topple over. **2.** *trans.* To throw, pitch 1887. Hence **Ti·ppler**[1], a tipping contrivance; a tumbler pigeon 1831.

Tippler[2] (ti·pləɹ). late ME. [Of unkn. origin; connection with Norw. dial. *tipla* drip slowly, *tippa* drink in small quantities, cannot be established.] †**1.** A tapster; a tavern-keeper –1642. **2.** One who tipples; a habitual drinker of intoxicating liquor (implying some excess, but usu. short of positive drunkenness) 1580.

Ti·ppling-house. *Obs.* exc. *Hist.* 1547. [f. *tippling*, vbl. sb. f. TIPPLE *v.*[1] + HOUSE *sb.*] A house where intoxicating liquor is sold and drunk; an ale-house, a tavern.

Tippy (ti·pi), *a.* 1892. [f. TIP *sb.*[1] + -Y[1].] Of tea: Containing a large proportion of the 'tips' or leaf-buds of the shoot.

Tipsify (ti·psifəi), *v.* 1830. [f. TIPSY *a.* + -FY.] *trans.* To make tipsy; to intoxicate.

Tipstaff (ti·pˌstɑf). *Pl.* **-staffs** (-stɑfs), or **-staves** (stēivz). 1541. [contr. of *tipped* or *tipt staff.*] †**1.** A staff with a tip or cap of metal, carried as a badge by certain officials –1695. **2.** An official carrying a tipped staff; *spec.* **a.** A sheriff's officer, bailiff, constable; **b.** A court crier or usher. *arch.* 1570.

Tipster (ti·pstəɹ). 1862. [f. TIP *sb.*[4] + -STER.] A man who makes a business of furnishing 'tips' or confidential information as to the probable chances of an event on which betting depends, esp. in horse-racing. **b.** *transf.* One who furnishes 'tips' in general 1884.

Tipsy (ti·psi), *a.* 1577. [f. TIP *v.*[2] + -SY.] Affected with liquor so as to be unable to walk or stand steadily; partly intoxicated: often *euphem.* for: Intoxicated, drunk. **b.** *transf.* Characterized or accompanied by intoxication; arising from or causing tipsiness 1634. **c.** *fig.* Unsteady as if from drink; inclined to tip or tilt 1754.

The riot of the tipsie Bachanals SHAKS. **b.** Tipsie dance, and Jollity MILT. **c.** He was t. poor man with his joy RICHARDSON. Hence **Ti·psily** *adv.* **Ti·psiness.**

Ti·psy-cake. 1806. A cake saturated with wine or spirit, stuck with almonds, and served with custard.

Ti·p-ti:lted, *a.* 1872. [f. TIP *sb.*[1] + pa. pple. of TILT *v.*[1] II.] Having the tip 'tilted', i.e. turned up.

Her slender nose T. like the petal of a flower TENNYSON.

Tiptoe, tip-toe (ti·pˌtōᵘ), *sb. adv., a.* late ME. [f. TIP *sb.*[1] + TOE *sb.*] **1.** *pl.* The tips of the toes. **b.** *fig.*: usu. with ref. to expectation or eagerness (formerly to pretension or haughtiness) 1579. **2.** *sing.* The tips of the toes collectively; almost always in phr. *on* or *upon tiptoe* 1440.

1. To go soft and faire on his tippetoes 1573. **b.** All stood on the tiptoes of expectation FULLER. **2.** Standing on tiptoe, [he] looked into one of the windows 1833. *fig.* Your eyes should sparkle joy, Your bosome rise on t. at this news MARSTON.

B. *adv.* Short for *on* or *a-tiptoe* 1592.

Iocond day Stands tipto on the mistie Mountaines tops SHAKS.

C. *adj.* Standing or walking, or characterized by standing or walking, on tiptoe 1744. **b.** *transf.* and *fig.* in various senses: e.g. straining upwards, ambitious; eagerly expectant; tripping, dancing; silent, stealthy 1593.

b. How tiptoe Night holds back her dark-grey hood KEATS.

Ti·ptoe, *v.* 1661. [f. prec.] **1.** *intr.* To raise oneself or stand on tiptoe. **2.** To go or walk on tiptoe; to step or trip lightly 1748.

Tip-top, *sb., a., adv. colloq.* 1702. [redupl. of TOP *sb.*[1], prob. with assoc. of TIP *sb.*[1]] **A.** *sb.* **1.** The very top; the highest point or part. **2.** *fig.* **a.** Highest pitch or degree; extreme height; acme 1702. †**b.** *sing.* and *pl.* People of the highest quality or rank (collectively); 'swells' –1849.

2. b. We go here to the best houses, the tiptops, I tell you THACKERAY.

B. *adj.* Situated at the very top; very highest; almost always *fig.* first-rate, superlatively good; of persons, belonging to the highest rank or class 1722.

A t. price 1825. The t. nobility THACKERAY.

C. *adv.* In the highest degree, superlatively, extremely well 1888.

‖**Tipula** (ti·piŭlă). *Pl.* **tipulæ** (-lī). 1752. [L. *tippula* water-spider, water-bug.] *Ent.* A genus of dipterous insects, typical of the family *Tipulidæ* or crane-flies. Hence **Ti·pulary** *a.* belonging or allied to the genus *T.* or family *Tipulidæ*.

Ti·p-up, *sb.* and *a.* 1848. [f. phr. *tip up*; TIP *v.*[2]] **A.** *sb.* A name for the Amer. sandpiper. **B.** *adj.* Constructed to tip or tilt up, as a receptacle, for the purpose of emptying out its contents, a seat (in a theatre, etc.) when not occupied 1884.

Tirade (ti-, təirēⁱ·d). 1801. [– Fr. *tirade* – It. *tirata* volley, f. *tirare* :– Rom. **tirare* draw; see TIRE *v.*[2]] **1.** A volley of words; a long and vehement speech on some subject; a declamation; a protracted harangue, *esp.* of denunciation, abuse, or invective. **2.** *spec.* A passage or section of verse, of varying length, treating of a single theme or idea 1878.

1. The King..had..to impose silence on the tirades which were delivered from the University pulpit GREEN.

‖**Tirailleur** (tira·lʸör). 1796. [Fr., f. *tirailler* shoot in independent firing, f. *tirer* draw, shoot; see TIRE *v.*[2]] One of a body of skirmishers employed in the wars of the French Revolution (1792); a skirmisher, a sharp-shooter; a soldier (usu. of infantry) trained for independent action.

Tire (təiᵊɹ), *sb.*[1] ME. [aphet. f. *atir* ATTIRE *sb.*] †**1.** Apparatus, equipment, accoutrement –1705. **2.** Dress, apparel, raiment. *arch.* ME. **3.** *spec.* A woman's head-dress; occas. perh. confused with TIAR, tiara. *arch.* late ME. **4.** A pinafore or apron to protect the dress; also written *tier. U.S.* 1846.

1. *Per.* III. ii. 22. **2.** You in Grecian tires are painted new SHAKS. **3.** And on her head she wore a tyre of gold SPENSER.

attrib. and *Comb.* (*Obs.* or *arch.*): **t.-glass,** a toilet-glass; **-room,** a dressing-room, tiring-room.

Tire (təiᵊɹ), *sb.*[2] See also TYRE. 1485. [perh. a use of TIRE *sb.*[1]] †**1.** *collect. sing.* The curved pieces of iron plate, called strakes or streaks, placed end to end or overlapping, with which cart and carriage wheels were formerly shod –1827. **2.** A rim of metal encompassing the wheel of a vehicle, consisting of a hoop of iron or steel 1782. **b.** An endless cushion of rubber, solid, hollow, or tubular, fitted (usu. in combination with an inner tube filled with compressed air) on the rim of a bicycle, tricycle, motor-car, etc., wheel. In this sense now usu. spelt *tyre* in Great Britain, *tire* in America. 1877.

2. b. Rubber tires, in place of iron ones, appeared in 1868. 1910.

†**Tire,** *sb.*[3] 1575. [– Fr. *tir* in sense 'shot, volley', f. *tirer*; see TIRE *v.*[2]] The simultaneous discharge of a battery of ordnance; a volley or broadside –1687.

In posture to displode thir second t. Of Thunder MILT.

Tire (təiᵊɹ), *v.*[1] [OE. *tēorian*, freq. in comps. *ātēorian*, *ġetēorian*, of unkn. origin. The development of vowel (*tēre* to *tīre*) is paralleled in *briar, friar, quire.*] **I.** *intr.* †**1.** To fail, cease (as a supply, etc.); to give out –ME. **2.** To become weak or exhausted from exertion; to become fatigued OE. **3.** To have one's appreciation, power of attention, or patience exhausted by excess; to become or be weary or sick *of*, to 'have enough' *of* 1500.

2. A merry heart goes all the day, Your sad tyres in a Mile-a SHAKS. **3.** Unwearied himself, he supposed his readers could never t. GOLDSM.

II. *trans.* **1.** To wear down or exhaust the strength of by exertion; to fatigue, weary. Also *absol.* OE. **2.** To weary or exhaust the patience, interest, or appreciation of (a person, etc.) by long continuance, sameness, or want of interest; to satiate, make sick of something; to bore. Also *absol.* 1500. **b.** *fig.* To exhaust (another's patience, bounty, efforts, etc.); †to wear out, spend (time) 1589.

1. The same work tires, but different works relieve BERKELEY. **2.** I hope I have not tired your Lordship with my long tale GOLDSM. **b.** Till tiring all his Arts, he turns agen To his true Shape DRYDEN.

Phr. *To t. out, t. to death,* to tire to utter exhaustion (*colloq.*). *To t. down,* to exhaust (a hunted animal) by persistent pursuit.

Tire (təiᵊɹ), *v.*[2] *arch.* ME. [– Fr. *tirer* :– Rom. **tirare* draw, of unkn. origin.] †**I.** *intr.* and *trans.* To draw, pull, tug –1580. **II.** *Falconry. intr.* Of a hawk: To pull or tear with the beak at a tough morsel given to it that it may exercise itself in this way; also, to tear flesh in feeding, as a bird of prey. *arch.* or *Obs.* ME. †**b.** *fig.* To prey *upon* –1624. **c.** To exercise oneself *upon* SHAKS.

b. The grief that tires upon thine inward soul 1594. **c.** *Timon* III. vi. 4.

Tire (təiᵊɹ), *v.*[3] ME. [Aphetic f. ATTIRE *v.*] **1.** *trans.* †**a.** To attire, clothe duly, dress, adorn –1706. **b.** To dress (the hair or head), esp. with a tire or head-dress. *arch.* 1539. **2.** To plaster or decorate (a building). Now *dial.* late ME.

1. b. Iezabel..starched her face, and tired her heed BIBLE (Great) 2 *Kings* 9:30.

Tire (təiᵊɹ), *v.*[4] 1891. [f. TIRE *sb.*[2]] *trans.* To furnish with a tire or tires.

Tired (təiᵊɹd), *ppl. a.* late ME. [f. TIRE *v.*[1] + -ED[1].] **1.** Fatigued, wearied; also, sick or weary *of*, impatient *with* (something); *slang*, habitually disinclined to exertion, incorrigibly lazy. **2.** *transf.* and *fig.* Exhausted, worked out, used up 1548. Hence **Ti·red-ly** *adv.*, **-ness.**

1. *T. Tim*, usu. associated with *Weary Willie*, both being taken as symbolical names of men who are disinclined to work. *To make* (a person) *t.* (U.S. slang), to annoy and bore 1896.

Tireless (təiᵊ·ɹlės), *a.* 1591. [f. TIRE *v.*[1] + -LESS.] Untiring, indefatigable. Hence **Ti·reless-ly** *adv.*, **-ness.**

†**Tireling** (təiᵊ·ɹliŋ), *sb.* (*a.*) 1590. [f. TIRE *v.*[1] + -LING[1]; cf. *hireling, shaveling.*] A tired person or animal; only *attrib.* or as *adj.* –1613.

Tiresome (təiᵊ·ɹsŏm), *a.* 1500. [f. TIRE *v.*[1] + -SOME[1].] **1.** Having the property of tiring by continuance, sameness, or lack of interest; wearisome, tedious. **b.** *loosely.* Troublesome, disagreeable, unpleasant; annoying, vexatious. *colloq.* 1798. †**2.** Causing physical fatigue. (Now merged in 1.) –1728.

1. It is slow, t. work 1854. **b.** A t. fidgety schoolboy as a travelling companion 1898. Hence **Ti·resome-ly** *adv.*, **-ness.**

Ti·re-wo:man. 1615. [f. TIRE *sb.*[1] + WOMAN.] A woman who assists at a lady's toilet; a lady's maid (*arch.*); †also, a dressmaker, costumier.

To Mrs. Grotier's, the Queen's t., for a pair of locks for my wife PEPYS.

Tiring (təiᵊ·riŋ), *vbl. sb.* c1552. [f. TIRE *v.*[3] + -ING[1].] The action of TIRE *v.*[3]; also *concr.* attire, apparel, head-dress (*arch.*).

Comb.: **t.-house** = TIRING-ROOM; **-woman,** a lady's maid (*Obs.* or *arch.*).

Tiring-irons (təiᵊ·riŋ,əi:əɹnz), *sb. pl.* 1601. Also (contemp.) †**tarr(y)ing-.** [f. TIRE *v.*[1], TARRY *v.*] A ring-puzzle.

Tiring-room (təiᵊ·riŋ,rūm). 1623. [f. TIRING *vbl. sb.* + ROOM.] A dressing-room (*arch.*); *spec.* the dressing-room of a theatre.

Tiro, tyro (təiᵊ·ro). *Pl.* **-oes, -os** (-oz). 1611. [– L. *tiro*, pl. *tirones* (in med.L. often spelt *tyro, tyrones*) young soldier, recruit, beginner. Commonly spelt *tyro.*] A beginner or learner in anything; one who is learning or who has mastered the rudiments only of any branch of knowledge; a novice.

The management of tiroes of eighteen Is difficult COWPER.

‖**Tirocinium** (təirosi·niŏm). Also (less correctly) **tyro-.** 1651. [L., first military service on campaign, young troops, f. TIRO.] **a.** First experience of or training in anything; apprenticeship, pupilage, novitiate; hence, inexperience, rawness. **b.** *concr.* A band of novices or recruits.

Tironian (təirōᵘ·niăn), *a.* 1828. [– L. *Tironianus*, in *notæ Tironianæ* Tironian notes; see -IAN.] Of or pertaining to Tiro, the freedman and secretary of Cicero: *T. notes*, a system of shorthand in use in ancient Rome, said to have been invented or introduced by Tiro.

Tirra-lirra (ti·ră,li·ră). 1611. [imit.] A representation of the note of the skylark, or of a similar sound uttered as an exclam. of delight or gaiety, or as a refrain.

The Larke, that tirra-Lyra chaunts SHAKS.

Tirrit (ti·rit). *rare.* 1597. [perh. illiterate for *terror.*] A fit of fear or temper; an 'upset'.

‖**Tirshatha** (tirʃā·þă). late ME. [Heb. *tiršāṯa* – Pers. *taršta* his reverence.] The title of an ancient Persian viceroy or prefect: applied in O.T. to Nehemiah.

'Tis (tiz), aphetic abbrev. of *it is*, now *poet.* or *arch.* exc. in *'tisn't.*

‖**Tishri** (ti·ʃri), **Tisri** (ti·zri). 1833. [– late Heb. *tišrī*, f. Aram. *šᵉrā* begin.] The first month of the Jewish civil year, or the seventh of the ecclesiastical, corresponding to parts of September and October.

Tisic, -ical, obs. and dial. ff. PHTHISIC, -AL.

Tissue (ti·ʃu, ti·siu), *sb.* late ME. [– OFr. *tissu*, subst. use of pa. pple. of *tistre* :– L. *texere* weave.] **1. a.** A rich kind of cloth, often interwoven with gold and silver. *Obs.* exc. *Hist.* **b.** Now applied to various rich or fine stuffs of delicate or gauzy texture 1730. †**2.** A band or girdle of rich stuff –1603. **3.** Any woven stuff or fabric 1565. **4.** *fig.* Something likened to a woven fabric; a 'fabric', 'network', 'web' (*of* things abstract, usu. of a bad kind, as absurdities, lies, etc.). Also the structure or contexture of such a 'fabric'. 1711. **5.** *Biol.* The substance, structure, or texture of which an animal or plant body, or any part or organ of it, is composed; *esp.* any one of the various structures, each consisting of an aggregation of similar cell or modifications of cells, which make up the organism 1831. **6.** Short for TISSUE-PAPER 1780. **7.** *Photogr.* Paper made in strips coated with a film of gelatine containing a pigment, used in carbon printing 1873.

1. The quene..clothed in a riche mantell of t. GRAFTON. **3.** They..weave with bloody hands the t. of thy line GRAY. **4.** The t. of misrepresentations..woven round us 1820. **5.** The chief forms of t. in the higher animals are the *epithelial* (incl. *glandular*), *connective* (incl. *cartilaginous* and *osseous*), *muscular*, and *nervous* tissues. In the higher plants there are three systems of tissues, the *epidermal*, *fundamental*, and *fibro-vascular.* O.E.D.

Tissue, *v.* Now *rare.* 1483. [f. prec.] *trans.* To make into a tissue, to weave; *spec.* to weave with gold or silver threads, to work or form in tissue; to adorn or cover with tissue.

The Charriot was covered with cloth of Gold tissued upon Blew BACON.

Tissued (ti·ʃ,ud, ti·siud), *ppl. a.* 1584. [f. TISSUE *v.* (or *sb.*) + -ED.] Woven, *spec.* woven with gold or silver thread (cf. Fr. *or tissu*).

Ti·ssue-pa:per. 1777. A very thin soft gauze-like unsized paper, used for wrapping delicate articles, for covering illustrations in books, as copying-paper, etc.

Tit, *sb.*[1] 1556. [Goes with TIT *v.* In phr. *tit for tat* a var. of †*tip for tap*, known a century earlier; see TIP *sb.*[2]] **1.** In phr. **tit for tat.** One blow or stroke in return for another; retaliation. **2.** *dial.* A light stroke or tap; a slap 1808.

Tit, *sb.*[2] 1548. [Occurs much earlier (XIV) in comps. TITLING and TITMOUSE; prob. of Scand. origin (cf. Icel. *tittlingr* sparrow, Norw. dial. *titling*, small size of stockfish).] **I. 1.** A small horse; later often applied in depreciation or meiosis to any horse; a nag. Now *rare.* †**b.** *fig.* of a person, etc. –1734. **2.** A girl or young woman. Usu. in depreciation: a hussy, a minx. (Now *low slang.*) 1599. **II.** Used in comb. in the names of various small birds as TITLARK, TITMOUSE, TOMTIT, etc. Used alone, as a shortened form of TITMOUSE, applied to: **a.** any bird of the genus *Parus*, and, more widely, any member of the family *Paridæ*. **b.** with qualification, to certain birds of other families, as the *Bearded t.* 1706.

attrib. and *Comb.*: **t.-babbler,** one of several species of hill-tits, esp. *Trichostoma rostratum*; **-pipit,** the TITLARK or meadow pipit, *Anthus pratensis*; **-warbler,** a bird of the sub-family *Parinæ*.

Tit, *sb.*[3] *dial.* and *vulgar*. [OE. *tit*, corresp. to (M)LG. *titte*, Du. *tit*, (M)HG. *zitze*.] = TEAT.

Tit, *v.* Now *dial.* 1589. [Goes with TIT *sb.*[1]; of unkn. origin.] *trans.* and *intr.* To strike or tap lightly.

Titan (təi·tăn). late ME. [– L. *Titan, -ān-*, elder brother of Chronos; – Gr. Τιτάν, pl. Τιτᾶνες.] **1.** Used (chiefly in poetry) as a name for the Sun-god, the grandson of Titan, or for the sun personified. **2. a.** *Gr. Myth.* In *sing.* The ancestor of the Titans, the elder brother of Chronos. In *pl.* a family of giants, the children of Uranus (Heaven) and Gæa (Earth), who contended for the sovereignty of heaven, and were overthrown by Zeus 1667. **b.** *transf.* and *allus.* 1828. **c.** Applied descriptively to machines of great size and power; e.g. a dredger, crane, etc. 1876. **3.** *Astron.* Name of the sixth and largest of Saturn's eight satellites 1868. **4.** *attrib.* or as *adj.*; *transf.* titanic, gigantic 1697.

1. Let T. rise as early as he dare SHAKS. **2. a.** T. Heav'ns first born With his enormous brood MILT. **b.** *Weary T.*, Atlas, who held up the world on his shoulders; *fig.* a state or empire that has heavy responsibilities; The weary T. need not complain too much 1903. **4.** The T. obelisk of the Matterhorn TYNDALL. So **Titane·sque** *a.* colossal, gigantic. **Ti·taness,** a female T.; a giantess. **Tita·nian** *a.* Titanic.

Titanate (təi·tănēˈt). 1839. [f. TITANIC *a.*[2] + -ATE[4].] *Chem.* A salt of titanic acid.

Titanic (təitæ·nik), *a.*[1] 1656. [– Gr. τιτανικός, f. Τιτᾶνες; see TITAN, -IC.] †**1.** Of or pertaining to the sun (*rare*) –1658. **2.** Pertaining to, resembling, or characteristic of the Titans of mythology; gigantic, colossal; also, of the nature or character of the Titans 1709.

2. The figure of Napoleon was t. CARLYLE. So †**Tita·nical** *a.* (in sense 2).

Tita·nic, *a.*[2] 1826. [f. TITANIUM + -IC b.] Of, pertaining to, or derived from titanium; in *Chem.* applied to compounds in which titanium has its higher valency as *t. oxide* (*t. acid*), a white tasteless powder, TiO_2. In *Min.*, *t. iron-ore* = ILMENITE; *t. schorl* = RUTILE.

Titaniferous (təităni·fĕrəs), *a.* 1828. [f. TITANIUM + -FEROUS.] Containing or yielding titanium.

Titanism (təi·tăniz'm). 1867. [– Fr. *titanisme*; see TITAN, -ISM.] The character of a Titan. **a.** Revolt against the order of the universe **b.** Titanic force or power.

Titanite (təi·tăneit). 1858. [– G. *titanit* (Klaproth, 1795), f. TITANIUM + *-it* -ITE[1] 2 b.] *Min.* A mineral composed chiefly of calcium titano-silicate, $CaO.TiO_2.SiO_2$; also called *sphene*.

Titanium (təitēˈ·niəm). 1796. [f. Gr. Τιτάν TITAN, named by Klaproth, 1795, after *uranium*, also named by him; see -IUM and cf. TELLURIUM.] *Chem.* A metallic element, never found free in nature, but obtainable as an iron-grey powder with a metallic lustre. It belongs to the same group as zirconium, cerium, and thorium. Symbol Ti; atomic weight 48·1.

Titano-[1], – Gr. τιτανο-, comb. form of Τιτάν TITAN, as in **Titano·machy** [-MACHY], the warfare of the Titans. ‖**Ti:tano-, ti:tano,the·rium** [mod.L. f. Gr. θηρίον beast], also anglicized **ti·tanothe:re,** an extinct genus of ungulates from the Tertiary formation, resembling gigantic rhinoceroses.

Titano-[2] (təi·tăno), comb. form of TITANIUM (and TITANITE), used in the names of chemical and mineral compounds, as *t.-cyanide, -ferrite, -fluorite, -silicate*.

Titanous (təi·tănəs), *a.* 1866. [f. TITANIUM + -OUS.] *Chem.* Containing titanium, spec. in its lower valency, as *t. oxide*, sesquioxide of titanium, Ti_2O_3; contrasted with TITANIC *a.*[2]

Tit-bit (ti·t,bi·t), **tid-bit** (ti·d,bi·t). 1640. [In XVI *tyd bit*, perh. f. dial. *tid* adj. 'tender, soft, nice' (Johnson) + BIT *sb.*[2]; later mainly *tit-bit*.] A small and delicate or appetizing piece of food; a toothsome morsel. **b.** *fig.*; *spec.* a brief and isolated interesting item of news or information; hence in *pl.*, name of a periodical consisting of such items 1708.

Tithable (təi·ðăb'l) *a.* 1440. [f. TITHE *v.* + -ABLE.] **1.** Of produce: Subject to the payment of tithes. **2.** Liable to pay tithes (*rare*) 1722.

Tithe (təið), *a.* and *sb.* [OE. *tēoþa*, contr. of *teogoþa*, ME. *tiȝ(e)þe, tiþe*; see TENTH.] **A.** *adj.* Tenth.

One good woman in ten Madam..Weed finde no fault with the t. woman SHAKS.

B. *sb.* Absolute use of the adj. **1.** The tenth part of the annual produce of agriculture, etc., being a due or payment (orig. in kind, for the support of the priesthood, religious establishments, etc.; *spec.* applied to that ordained by the Mosaic law, and to that introduced in conformity therewith in England and other Christian lands ME. **b.** chiefly in *pl.*, including the various amounts thus due or received ME. **2.** Any levy, tax, or tribute of one tenth 1600. **3.** A tenth part (of anything); now chiefly hyperbolical: a very small part 1494.

1. Half the cultivated land of Great Britain is unaffected by t. 1845. *Great t.*, the chief predial tithes, as corn, hay, wood, and fruit. *Mixed t.*: (partly personal, partly predial). *Personal t.*, t. of the produce of labour or occupation. *Predial t.*: see PREDIAL *a.* *Rectorial t.*, tithes pertaining to the rector of the parish, the great tithes. *Small t.*, such predial tithes as are not great tithes, together with the personal and mixed tithes. *Vicarial t.*, tithes pertaining to the vicar of the parish; the small tithes. **2.** The admirals took t. on every ship and cargo seized at sea 1871. **3.** I cannot tell you a t. of what he said 1872.

attrib. and *Comb.*: **t.-barn,** a barn for holding the parson's t.-corn; **-man,** a collector of tithes (now only *Hist.*); **-pig,** a pig due or taken as t.; **-proctor,** an agent employed to collect a parson's tithes, or one who farmed the t.

Tithe (təið), *v.* [OE. *tēoþian, teogoþian*, f. prec.] *gen.* To take the tenth of, to decimate. **1.** *trans.* To grant or pay one tenth of (one's goods, earnings, etc.), esp. to the support of the church; to pay tithes on. †**2.** *intr.* To pay tithe; to pay the tenth, esp. to the church –1606. **3.** *trans.* To impose the payment of a tenth upon (a person, etc.); to exact tithe from. late ME. **b.** To exact or collect one tenth from (goods or produce) by way of tithe; to take tithe of (goods) 1591. †**4. a.** *trans.* To take every tenth thing or person from (the whole number); to take one tenth (of the whole); to divide into tenths –1641. †**b.** *spec.* To reduce (a multitude) to one tenth of its numbers by keeping only every tenth man alive (always with ref. to the sacking of Canterbury by the Danes in 1011) –1670.

1. *To t. mint (and anise) and cummin* (*Matt.* 23:23), to be conspicuously scrupulous in minutiæ while neglecting important matters of duty. **4. b.** The multitude are tith'd, and every tenth only spar'd MILT.

Tither (təi·ðəɹ). late ME. [f. TITHE *v.* + -ER[1].] **a.** One who pays tithes. Now *rare*. **b.** An exactor or receiver of tithes; also, a supporter of the system of ecclesiastical tithes 1591.

Tithing (təi·ðiŋ). [OE. *tēoþung*, f. *tēoþa* TITHE *sb.* or *tēoþian* TITHE *v.*; see -ING[1], [3].] **1.** = TITHE *sb.* 1. †**2.** A tenth part of anything –1609. **3.** A company *orig.* of ten householders in the system of FRANKPLEDGE; now only as a rural division (orig. regarded as one tenth of a hundred) to which this system gave its name OE.

Tithingman[1] (təi·ðiŋmæn). OE. [f. prec. + MAN *sb.*] **a.** Anciently, The chief man of a tithing, a headborough; in later use, a parish peace-officer, or petty constable. Now *Hist.* **b.** In Maryland and New England: A former elective officer of a township, whose functions were derived from those of the English tithingman; in particular he was charged with the prevention of disorderly conduct, and, in New England in later times, chiefly with enforcing the observance of the Sabbath and of order during divine service. Now *Hist.* 1638.

Ti·thing-man[2]. 1625. [f. *tithing* vbl. sb., f. TITHE *v.*] A collector of tithes; a tithe-proctor.

Titian (ti·ʃ'ăn). 1824. [Anglicization of *Tiziano* Vecellio, Venetian painter, died 1576.] With capital T: A picture by Titian Also *attrib.* or *adj.* denoting a 'bright golden auburn' colour of the hair favoured by Titian in his pictures; also more loosely as an appreciative word for 'red'. Hence **Titia·nic** *a.* of or belonging to T. **Titiane·sque** *a.* in the style of T.

Titillate (ti·tilēˈt), *v.* 1620. [– *titillat-*, pa. ppl. stem of L. *titillare* tickle; see -ATE[3].] **1.** *trans.* = TICKLE *v.* 3. **2.** = TICKLE *v.* 4. Also *absol.* 1837.

1. Not to t. his palate but to keep up his character for hospitality MACAULAY.

Titillation (titilēˈ·ʃən). late ME. [– (O)Fr. *titillation* or L. *titillatio*, f. as prec.; see -ION.] **1.** Excitation or stimulation of the mind or senses; *esp.* pleasing excitement, gratification. **2.** A sensation of being tickled; a tingling, an itching 1621. **3.** The action of tickling, or touching lightly so as to tickle 1623. †**4.** *transf.* A means of titillating –1610.

1. Thrills and titillations from games of hazard T. HARDY. **3.** Laughter provok'd by T., grows an excessive Pain SHAFTESB.

Titivate, tittivate (ti·tiveˈt), *v.* *colloq.* 1805. [In early examples *tidi-* or *tiddivate*, perh. f. TIDY, after *cultivate*.] *trans.* To make small alterations or additions to one's toilet, etc. so as to add to one's attractions; to make smart or spruce; to put the finishing touches to. Also with *off, up*. Also *intr.* for *refl.* Hence **Titi-, tittiva·tion.**

Titlark (ti·t,lāɹk). 1668. [f. TIT *sb.*[2] + LARK *sb.*[1]] A bird of the genus *Anthus* or some allied genus, resembling a lark; a pipit; *esp.* in England, the meadow pipit, *A. pratensis*; in U.S., *A. ludovicianus* (American t.).

Title (təi·t'l), *sb.* ME. [– OFr. *title* (mod. *titre*) – L. *titulus* placard, inscription, title.] †**1.** An inscription placed on or over an object, giving its name or describing it; a legend –1645. **2.** The descriptive heading of each section or subdivision of a book (now only in law-books); the formal heading of a legal document ME. **3.** The name of a book, poem, or other (written) composition; an inscription at the beginning of a book, describing or indicating its subject, contents, or nature, and usu. giving also the name of the author, compiler, or editor, and of the publisher, and the place and date of publication; also = TITLE-PAGE. Also, the designation of a picture or statue. ME. **b.** *Bookbinding.* The label or panel on the back of a book giving a brief title (*binder's t.*) 1891. **4.** A descriptive or distinctive appellation; a name, denomination, style. late ME. **5.** An appellation attaching to an individual or family in virtue of rank, function, office, or attainment, or the possession of or association with certain lands, etc.; *esp.* an appellation of honour pertaining to a person of high rank; also *transf.* (colloq.) a person of title 1590. **6.** That which justifies or substantiates a claim; a ground of right; hence, an alleged or recognized right. Const. with *inf.*, or *to, in*, or *of* the thing claimed. ME. **7.** *spec. Law.* Legal right to the possession of property (esp. real property); the evidence of such right; title-deeds. late ME. †**b.** An assertion of right; a claim –1701. **8.** *Eccl.* A certificate of presentment to a benefice, or a guarantee of support, required (in ordinary cases) by the bishop from a candidate for ordination. late ME. **9.** *Eccl.* Each of the principal or parish churches in Rome, the incumbents of which are cardinal priests; a cardinal church 1460. **10.** *Assaying*, etc. The expression in carats of the degree of purity of gold (= Fr. *titre*) 1873.

1. An aulter..with this t. ther by: Vnto the Lorde COVERDALE *Isa.* 19:19. **3.** The fifth t. of the fifth book *De Magistris* 1581. **5.** From the death of this young Earle of Warwicke this t. lay asleepe 1610. A gay young Gentleman, who has lately succeeded to a T. and an Estate STEELE. If you retain any Curate, to whom you did not give a T. for Orders 1720.

attrib. and *Comb.*: **t.-part, -rôle,** the part in a play, etc., from which the t. of the piece is taken; **-sheet,** the first sheet of a book, one page of which bears the t.

Title (təi·t'l), *v.* ME. [f. TITLE *sb.*; cf. OFr. *titler*, which may be partly the source.]

I. †**1.** *trans.* To write, set down, or arrange under titles or headings; to make a list of; to set down in writing –1552. **2.** To furnish with a (specified) title; also, to inscribe the title on (a book or the like); to write the headings to or in (a manuscript book or account). late ME. †**3.** To dedicate (by name); to assign, ascribe –1584. †**4.** To inscribe as a title, attach as a label –1642.

2. In the Order of the Day these questions now appear numbered and titled 1894. **4.** By the intrapping autority of great names titl'd to false opinions MILT.

II. To designate by a certain name, indication of relationship, character, office, etc.; to term style, name, call 1590. **b.** To endow or dignify with a title of rank; to speak of by a title of dignity 1746.

That sober Race of Men, whose lives Religious titl'd them the Sons of God MILT.

Titled (təi·t'ld), *ppl. a.* 1746. [f. prec. + -ED[1].] Having or furnished with a title, esp. a title of rank.

A younger scion of a t. family 1909.

Title-deed (təi·t'l,dīd). 1768. A deed or document containing or constituting evidence of ownership. (Most common in *pl.*)

Titleless (təi·t'l,lės), *a.* late ME. [f. TITLE *sb.* + -LESS.] Having no title, destitute of a title; untitled.

Ti·tle-page. 1613. The page at (or near) the beginning of a book which bears the title.

The world's all t., there's no contents YOUNG.

Titler (təi·tləɹ). 1594. [app. f. TITLE *sb.* + -ER[1].] †**1.** One who claims or asserts a legal title –1634. **2.** Trade name for a truncated cone of refined sugar 1858.

Titling (ti·tliŋ). ME. [f. TIT *sb.*[2] + -LING[1].] †**1.** A small size of stockfish –1858. **2. a.** The hedge-sparrow. Now only *Sc.* and *n. dial.* **b.** = TITLARK. **c.** = TITMOUSE (*rare*) 1549.

2. He had frequently..watched young cuckoos while being fed by titlings (*Anthus pratensis*) 1882.

Titmouse (ti·t,maus). *Pl.* **titmice** (-məis). [ME. *titmōse*, f. TIT *sb.*[2] + *mōse*, OE. *māse* = MLG., MDu. *mēse* (Du. *mees*), OHG. *meisa* (G. *meise*) :- WGmc. **maisō*. In XVI assim. to *mouse*.] **1.** A bird of the genus *Parus* or family *Paridæ*, comprising numerous species of small active birds. (Now commonly shortened to *tit*.) **2.** With qualification, denoting various species of *Parus* or of the family *Paridæ* 1609. **3.** *fig.* A small, petty, or insignificant person or thing 1596.

2. Blue t., *P. cæruleus*; **coal t.**, *P. ater*; **crested t.**, *Parus* (*Lophophanes*) *cristatus*, or any species of the subgenus *Lophophanes*; **great t.**, *P. major*, also called OX-EYE; **long-tailed t.**, *Acredula caudata*; **marsh t.**, *P. palustris*.

Titrate (ti·tre[i]t), *v.* 1870. [f. Fr. *titrer*, f. *titre* title, qualification, fineness of alloyed gold or silver, etc.; see -ATE[3].] *Chem. trans.* To ascertain the amount of a constituent in (a mixture, or (less usu.) a compound) by volumetric analysis; i.e. by adding to a solution thereof of known proportion, a suitable reagent of known strength, until a point is reached at which reaction occurs or ceases. So **Ti·trated** *ppl. a.* (= Fr. *titré*) of a solution, having a known strength, and thus being suitable for use in titration.

Titration (titrē[i]·ʃən). 1864. [f. prec.; see -ATION.] The action or process of titrating; volumetric analysis.

‖**Titre, titer** (tī·təɹ). 1839. [– Fr. *titre*; see TITRATE.] The fineness of gold or silver; *Chem.* the strength of a solution as determined by titration.

Titrimetry (titri·mǐtri). 1891. [f. Fr. *titre*; see TITRATE *v.* and -METRY.] *Chem.* = TITRATION.

Titter (ti·təɹ), *sb.* 1728. [f. next.] The act of tittering; a stifled laugh, a giggle.

A continual t. among the young ladies MME. D'ARBLAY.

Titter (ti·təɹ), *v.*[1] 1619. [imit.] *intr.* To laugh in a suppressed or covert way (often as a result of nervousness, or in affectation or ridicule); to giggle. **b.** *trans.* To utter or say with suppressed laughter 1787.

Upon which Mrs. Nickleby tittered, and Sir Mulberry laughed, and Pyke and Pluck roared DICKENS.

Titter (ti·təɹ), *v.*[2] Now *dial.* [In XIV *titer* (*titeryng* Chaucer) = ON. *titra* shake, shiver, cogn. with OHG. *zittarōn* (G. *zittern* tremble). Cf. TEETER.] **1.** *intr.* To move unsteadily, totter, reel, sway to and fro. **2.** To see-saw 1825.

Titter-totter (ti·təɹ,tǫ·təɹ), *sb.* (*adv.*) Now *dial.* 1530. [Reduplication from stem of prec. or TOTTER *v.*] **A.** *sb.* = SEE-SAW. **B.** *adv.* Totteringly; *fig.* hesitatingly, waveringly 1725. Hence **Ti·tter-to·tter** *v. intr.* to see-saw.

Tittle (ti·t'l), *sb.* [Late ME. *titel*, *-il* – L. *titulus* TITLE, in mediæval sense of 'little stroke', 'accent'.] **1.** A small stroke or point in writing or printing. **a.** orig. tr. L. *apex*, applied to any minute point or part of a letter, also to the mark over a long vowel, as *á*, later to a line indicating an abbreviation, etc. By extension, any stroke or tick with a pen. **b.** The dot over the letter *i*; a punctuation mark; a diacritic point over a letter; any Hebrew or Arabic vowel-point or accent; also, a pip on dice 1538. **2.** *fig.* The smallest or a very small part of something; a minute amount. Often in phr. *jot or t.*; see JOT *sb.*[1] late ME.

2. I owe much more to his father's memory than ever I can pay a t. of SCOTT. Phr. *To a t.*, with minute exactness, to a T.

Tittle (ti·t'l), *v.* Now *dial.* or *colloq.* late ME. [imit.; somewhat earlier than TATTLE, but app. treated as a parallel form of that vb. with lighter vowel expressing lighter sound; see TITTLE-TATTLE.] *intr.* and *trans.* To speak in a whisper or in a low voice, to whisper; also, to tell or utter by way of tattle or gossip.

Tittlebat (ti·t'lbæt). Also **-back.** 1820. A variant of STICKLEBACK, of childish origin.

Tittle-tattle (ti·t'l,tæ·t'l), *sb.* 1529. [redupl. formation on TATTLE *v.*, or combination of this with TITTLE *v.* Cf. LG. *titel-tateln* and PRITTLE-PRATTLE.] **1.** Talk, chatter, prattle; *esp.* petty gossip. †**2.** A habitual tattler, one given up to gossip; esp. a woman so addicted –1710. **3.** *attrib.* or as *adj.* Characterized by or addicted to tattling; gossiping 1719.

3. Bath is as t. a town as Lynn MME. D'ARBLAY. So **Ti·ttle-ta·ttle** *v. intr.* to chatter, talk idly; to gossip. **Ti·ttle-ta·ttling** *vbl. sb.* and *ppl. a.*

Tittup (ti·tŏp), *sb.* Chiefly *dial.* 1703. [app. echoic, from the sound of the horse's feet.] **1.** A horse's canter; a hand-gallop; also, a curvet. **2.** An impudent or forward woman or girl; a hussy, minx 1762.

Tittup (ti·tŏp), *v.* 1785. [Goes with prec.] *intr.* To walk or go with an up-and-down movement; to walk in an affected manner; to mince or prance in one's gait; of a horse or other animal, to canter, gallop easily; also, to prance; hence of a rider, or one driving a vehicle. **b.** *Naut. slang.* To toss for drinks.

Tittupy (ti·tŏpi), *a. colloq.* 1798. [f. TITTUP *sb.* or *v.* + -Y[1].] Apt to tittup or tip up; unsteady, shaky.

Ti·tty. 1746. A dial. and nursery dim. of TEAT, the breast, esp. the mother's breast.

Titubancy (ti·tiŭbănsi). *rare.* 1800. [– L. *titubantia*, f. *titubans*, *-ant-*; see next, -ANCY.] The condition of being titubant; unsteadiness, tipsiness. (This and allied words all more or less affected.)

Titubant (ti·tiŭbănt), *a. rare.* 1724. [– L. *titubans*, *-ant-*, pr. pple. of *titubare*; see next, -ANT.] Staggering, reeling, unsteady; *transf.* and *fig.* stammering; tipsy; hesitating, wavering.

Titubate (ti·tiŭbe[i]t), *v. rare.* 1575. [– *titubat-*, pa. ppl. stem of L. *titubare* stagger, expressive reduplicating formation; see -ATE[3].] **1.** *intr.* To stagger, reel, totter, stumble; to rock, roll. **2.** *fig.* To stammer 1623.

Titubation (titiŭbē[i]·ʃən). *rare.* 1641. [– L. *titubatio*, *-ōn-*, f. as prec.; see -ION. Cf. Fr. *titubation* (XVI).] The action of titubating; staggering, reeling, tottering; unsteadiness in gait or carriage, *spec.* in *Path.*; *fig.* faltering, perplexity, embarrassment.

Titular (ti·tiŭlăɹ), *a.* and *sb.* 1591. [– Fr. *titulaire* or mod.L. *titularis*, f. *titulus* TITLE; see -AR[1].] **A.** *adj.* **1.** That exists or is such only in title or name, as dist. from *real* or *actual*; nominal, so-styled 1611. **2.** Of, pertaining to, consisting of, or denoted by a title of dignity; also, having a title of rank, titled; bearing, or conferring, the appropriate title 1611. **3.** Of or pertaining to a title or name; of the nature of or constituting a title. *T. character*, title-rôle. 1656. **4.** From whom or which a title or name is taken; *spec.* noting the parish churches of Rome from which the titles of the cardinals are derived; hence *transf.* of a cardinal 1664.

1. Her mother the t. queen of Naples and Jerusalem H. WALPOLE. *T. bishop*, in R. C. Ch., a bishop deriving his title from an ancient see lost (esp. by Moslem conquest) to the control of the Roman pontificate.

B. *sb.* **1.** One who holds a title to an office, benefice, or possession, irrespective of the functions, duties, or rights attaching to it; *spec.* a cleric who bears a title whether he performs the duties or not; esp. short for *t. bishop* 1620. **b.** *transf.* One who has a title or appellation of some kind 1824. **2.** A titled person 1757. Hence **Titula·rity** (*rare*), the quality or state of being t., or merely t. **Ti·tularly** *adv.* in respect of title, name, or style; *esp.* in name only, nominally.

Titulary (ti·tiŭlări), *a.* (*sb.*) Now *rare.* 1603. [var. of TITULAR by substitution of suffix -ARY[1], [2].] = prec., in various senses.

Titule (ti·tiul), *v.* 1569. [– late L. *titulare* give a title to, f. *titulus* TITLE *sb.*] Occasional var. of TITLE *v.*, esp. in pa. pple. or ppl. adj. **Tituled.**

†**Tityre-tu** (ti·tire,t[i]ū·). 1623. [The first two words of Virgil's first eclogue.] One of an association of well-to-do roughs who infested London streets in the 17th c.

Tiver (ti·vəɹ), *sb. dial.* 1792. [mod., app. repr. OE. *tēafor*, glossing 'minium' (red lead).] A red colouring matter, used esp. for marking sheep. Hence **Ti·ver** *v. dial. trans.* to mark or colour with t.

Tivy (ti·vi), *int.* and *v. rare.* 1669. [See TANTIVY.] = TANTIVY *int.* and *v.* 1.

‖**Tiza** (tī·ză). 1865. [– Quichua (Peruvian) *t'isa* card wool; from its fibrous appearance.] *Min.* Ulexite or hayesine.

Tizzy (ti·zi). *slang.* 1804. [Of unkn. origin.] A sixpenny-piece.

‖**Tmesis** (tmī·sis). 1577. [– Gr. τμῆσις a cutting.] *Gram.* and *Rhet.* The separation of the elements of a compound word by the interposition of another word or words.

T.N.T. (tī·,en,tī·). = TRINITROTOLUENE, -TOLUOL.

To (tū, *tu*, tu, tŭ, tə), *prep.*, *conj.*, *adv.* [OE. *tō* adv. and prep. (mainly with dat.) = OFris., OS. *tō* (Du. *toe* adv.), OHG. *zō*, *zuo* (G. *zu*) :- WGmc. **tō* (essentially adv.), alongside OE. (ME.) *te* = OFris., OS. *te*, *ti* (Du. *te*), OHG. *ze*, *zi*, *za* :- WGmc. **ta* prep. (ON. has *til* TILL prep., conj., Goth. *du*), perh. a proclitic form of **tō*.] **A.** *prep.* **I.** Expressing a spatial or local relation. **1.** Expressing motion directed towards and reaching. (The opposite of FROM.) **b.** In fig. expressions of motion; the following sb. denoting (*a*) a state or condition attained, or (*b*) a thing or person reached by some action figured as movement OE. **c.** Elliptical uses, (*a*) with ellipsis of *go* or other verb of motion, esp. in commands, or (*arch.*) after an auxiliary verb. late ME. (*b*) = Gone to; in going to, on the way to. (Chiefly *dial.*) 1451. (*c*) after a sb. implying or suggesting motion: = That goes, or takes one, or causes one to go, to OE. **2.** Expressing direction: In the direction of, towards OE. **b.** In expressing the position of something lying in a specified direction OE. **c.** In fig. expressions of direction (inclination, tendency, etc.). Also *fig.* from b, in phr. *to the bad*, *to the good* (= on the wrong, or right, side of the account), *to the fore*; in *to the contrary* with both senses (2 and 2 b). ME. **3.** Indicating the limit of a movement or extension in space: As far as (to) OE. **b.** After expressions of distance, indicating the remote limit OE. **4.** Expressing simple position: At, in (a place, also *fig.* a condition, etc.). Now only *dial.* and *U.S. colloq.* OE. **5.** Expressing the relation of contact or the like. **a.** Into (or in) contact with; on, against OE. **b.** By, beside. Also *fig.* or with additional implication, as in *to one's face*, *teeth*, etc. = in presence and defiance of. OE.

1. When the poore man might turne out a cow, or two..to the commons 1583. **b.** When he came to the crown LAUD. To reclaim a lost child to virtue GOLDSM. **c.** (*a*) To youre tentes, O Israel! BIBLE (Great) 1 *Kings* 12:16. (*b*) For now the sonne is to his rest 1500. (*c*) The path of duty was the way to glory TENNYSON. **2.** As pilot..That to a stedfast starre his course hath bent SPENSER. **b.** Cannon to right of them, Cannon to left of them TENNYSON. **3.** Wet to the skin 1873. **5. a.** Applying plenty of yellow soap to the towel DICKENS. **c.** Phr. *To hand*: see HAND *sb.*

II. Expressing a relation in time. **1.** Indicating a final limit in time, or the end of a period: Till, until; often correl. to *from* OE. **b.** (So long) before (a definite future time); *esp.* in stating the time of day: (so many minutes) before (an hour). Opp. to *past.* OE. **c.** *from..to*, with repeated sb. of time, denoting regular recurrence; as *from day to day*, etc. OE. **2.** Indicating the precise time at which something is to be done, or at which one is to arrive: At and not after (an appointed time), precisely or punctually at or on 1722.

1. The business hours..were from ten to six DICKENS. **b.** It was exactly a quarter to four o'clock 1843. We shall be late..it's..ten *to* now 1852. **2.** Unable to pay their hearth money to the day MACAULAY.

III. Expressing the relation of purpose, destination, result, effect, resulting condition or status. **1.** Indicating aim, purpose, intention, or design: For; for the purpose of; with the view or end of; in order to. (Now often repl. by *for*.) OE. **b.** *spec.* Towards or for the making of; as a contributory element or constituent of 1450. **2.** Indicating destination, or an appointed or expected end or event ME. **3.** Indicating result, effect, or consequence: So as to produce, cause, or result in OE. **4.** Indicating a state or condition resulting from some process: So as to become OE. **b.** Indicating resulting position, status, or capacity: For, as, by way of, in the capacity of. *Obs.* or *arch.* exc. in certain phrases, as *to take to wife, to call to witness*, etc. OE. **5. a.** Indicating the object of inclination, desire, or need: For. Also (after *to drink*, etc.), as an expression of desire for (one's health, success, etc.). ME. **b.** Indicating the object of a right or claim ME.

1. He was bred up to Joynery 1683. We were out..to breakfast 1838. The captain..came to our rescue 1843. **b.** Whole gardens of roses go to one drop of the attar 1890. *That's all there is to it* (colloq. phr., orig. U.S.), there is no more to add or to do. **2.** Born to bitter Fate DRYDEN. He was..sentenced to transportation 1887. **3.** To his ..astonishment 1802. **4.** Forester..took the flowers..and pulled them to pieces 1802. **b.** Who had Canace to wife? MILT. **5. a.** Instead of marrying Torfrida..I have more mind to her niece KINGSLEY. **b.** This lease..is a document of title to land 1890.

IV. Followed by a word or phrase expressing a limit in extent, amount, or degree. **1.** Indicating a limit or point attained in degree or amount, or in division or analysis: As far as; to the point of; down to (an ultimate element or item), as in phr. *to a hair, to the last man, to a man* (including every man, without exception); within (a limit of variation or error), as *to an inch, to a day* OE. **b.** Indicating the final point or second limit of a series, or of the extent of a variable quantity or quality; correl. to *from* 1699. **2.** Indicating the full extent, degree, or amount: So as to reach, complete, or constitute OE. **b.** So far or so much as to cause ME. **c.** Before a sb. expressing the amount, extent, space, etc. to which something is restricted 1518.

1. He was generally punctual to a minute 1779. **b.** Every style from early Norman to late perpendicular 1891. **2.** Phr. *To a certainty, to a degree, to* (*that*, etc.) *extent, to a fault, to the full*, etc. **b.** The schoolroom was hot to suffocation 1890. **c.** To cut down the widow's absolute interest to a life estate 1885.

V. Indicating addition, attachment, accompaniment, appurtenance, possession. **1.** In addition to, besides, with OE. **b.** To the accompaniment of; as an accompaniment to 1561. **2.** After words denoting attachment or adherence; hence, occas. = Attached, fastened, or joined to OE. **3.** After *belong* and similar verbs; also after *be* with the sense of *belong*; also after a sb., in the sense 'appertaining or belonging to'; sometimes = 'of' or the possessive case of the sb. OE.

1. He can't have cream to his tea RUSKIN. **b.** Phr. *To ride to hounds*: see HOUND *sb.*¹ 2. **2.** Sincerely attached to the Established Church MACAULAY. **3.** Clerk to an attorney DE FOE. Without clothing to his back, or shoes to his feet 1840.

VI. Expressing relation to a standard or to a stated term or point. **1.** Expressing comparison: In comparison with, as compared with OE. **2. a.** Connecting the names of two things compared or opposed to each other in respect of amount or value: Against, as against 1530. **b.** Connecting two expressions of number or quantity which correspond to each other, or of which one constitutes the amount or value of the other: In; making up. (*To the* = in every.) OE. †**c.** Introducing an expression denoting price or cost: For, at. *Obs.* (exc. as coinciding with b). –1862. **3.** Expressing agreement or adaptation: In accordance with, according to, after, by OE. **4.** After words expressing comparison, proportion, correspondence, agreement or disagreement, and the like ME. **5.** Expressing relation: In respect of, concerning, about, of, as to. Now only in special collocations. ME. **6.** Expressing relative position; esp. *Geom.* 1570.

1. The men are noodles to her 1863. **2. a.** Their enemies..wer foure to one HALL. **b.** He..made vs pay..one shilling to the pound SHAKS. Thirteen to the dozen 1801. **3.** Temple is not a man to our taste MACAULAY. They were to all appearances distinct bills 1885. *To my knowledge*, qualifying a positive statement = 'as I actually know'; qualifying a negative statement = 'as far as I know'. **4.** I can finde out no rime to Ladie but babie, an innocent rime SHAKS. **5.** What will Doris say to it? 1884. Asking questions intended to show the untrustworthy character of a witness, or..'cross-examining to credit' 1892. **6.** Unable to see how they lie to each other 1848.

VII. Expressing relations in which the sense of direction tends to blend with that of the dative. **1.** After words denoting application, attention, or the like, indicating the object of this. Also (*arch.* or *rhet.*) with ellipsis of *go, betake oneself*, etc. (in imper., or after an auxiliary). ME. **2.** Expressing impact or attack: At, against, upon ME. **b.** After words denoting opposition or hostility: Against; towards (*obs.* or *arch.*). late ME. **3.** Indicating the object of speech, address, or the like OE. **b.** In honour of; for the worship of; in salutation of and expression of good wishes for (as *to drink to*). late ME. **4.** Expressing response or the like (of a voluntary agent); e.g. reply (*to* a statement, question, etc.) obedience (*to* a command, etc.) ME. **b.** Expressing reaction or responsive action (of an involuntary or inanimate agent). *poet.* 1682. **5.** Expressing exposure (of a thing *to* some physical agent). *rare.* 1460.

1. I'll to my own Art WALTON. Come, lads, all hands to work! 1843. **2.** His father's unmerciful use of the whip to him 1882. **3.** Hail to thee, blithe Spirit! SHELLEY. **b.** An auter, in which was writun, To the vnknowun God WYCLIF *Acts* 17:23. Drink to me, only with thine eyes B. JONSON. **4.** Disobedience to his orders 1766. **b.** Little waves..sparkling to the moonbeams SCOTT. **5.** That tower of strength Which stood four-square to all the winds that blew TENNYSON.

VII. Supplying the place of the dative in various other languages and in the earlier stages of English itself. **1.** Introducing the recipient of anything given, or the person or thing upon whom or which an event acts or operates ME. **2.** For; for the use or benefit of; for (some one) to deal with (esp. after *leave* vb.); at the disposal of ME. **b.** Indicating the person or thing towards which an action, feeling, etc., is directed; esp. as the object of conduct, behaviour, or demeanour OE. **3.** Used in the syntactical constr. of many intr. verbs, as *yield, trust, allude*, etc. (See the verbs themselves.) ME. **b.** After, *testify, witness, confess, swear*, etc.: In support of; in assertion or acknowledgement of 1630. **4.** In the syntactical const. of many trans. verbs, introducing the indirect or dative object. (See the verbs themselves.) ME. **5.** Expressing the relation of an adj. (or derived adv. or sb.) to a sb. denoting a person or thing to which its application is directed or limited OE. **b.** After pa. pples. of verbs of perception (now only with *known, unknown*; nearly = by) ME.

1. Having a Son born to him ADDISON. Phr. *To be* (something) *to*, to be (something) in the eyes, view, apprehension, or opinion of; also, to be of importance or concern to. *What is that to you?* How does that concern you? **2.** The rest is left to the imagination DRYDEN. Phr. *To oneself* (as pred.), to or at one's own disposal, free from the approaches or action of others; I'll first assay To get the Persian kingdom to myself MARLOWE. **b.** Bacchus is a friend to Love 1758. Phr. *To you*, an elliptical formula of courtesy, = 'my service to you'. **3. b.** That is a fact to which I can speak 1776. **4.** We fought them and put them to the run PEPYS. **5.** This..is new to me 1777. True to nature 1843. Comte..lays himself specially open to attack 1886. Alive to the value of his wares 1887.

B. To before an infinitive (or gerund). **I.** with infinitive in advb. relation. **Indicating purpose or intention.* **1. a.** Dependent on a vb., *to* with inf. = *in order to* OE. **b.** Dependent on an adj.; indicating the purpose or function to which the adj. refers OE. **c.** Dependent on a sb.; the inf. expressing the use or function of that which is denoted by the sb. OE. (*b*) After *time, room*, etc.: equivalent to *for* with gerund, or = at or in which (one) can or should..ME. **2.** In absol. or independent construction, usu. introductory or parenthetic ME.

1. I gave a soldier five dollars to carry them news DE FOE. Fools, who came to scoff, remained to pray GOLDSM. **c.** A light to lighten the gentyls TINDALE *Luke* 2:32. (*b*) The time to learn is when you're young 1887. **2.** But to return to our Subject ADDISON.

***Indicating objectivity.* **3.** Dependent on various verbs chiefly trans., pass., or refl.: indicating an action, etc. to which that of the principal verb is in some way directed. (See also the verbs themselves.) OE. **b.** In obsolete, arch., or dial. uses; now replaced by various prepositions with the gerund, or by other constructions 1525. **4.** Dependent on various adjs. (also pples. and adjectival or predicative phrases): usu. indicating the application of the adj., etc. OE. **b.** With inf. passive. *arch.* 1460. **5.** Dependent on various abstract sbs.: usu. indicating object or application; also (after *favour, honour, pleasure*, etc.) indicating an action which is the substance or form of that which is denoted by the sb., i.e. in which it consists; often replaceable by *of* with gerund OE.

3. I strive to be concise 1746. **b.** Abstaining to write to her G. MEREDITH. **4.** Careless their merits or their faults to scan GOLDSM. At liberty to enforce her claims 1838. **b.** The fittest to be chosen EVELYN. **5.** I had the Honour to be a Member of it SWIFT. As though in act to spring 1842. *Going to*: see GO *v.* V.

****Indicating appointment or destination.* **6.** Indicating destiny, or (expected or actual) event or outcome. late ME.

When we two parted..To sever for years BYRON.

*****Indicating result or consequence.* **7.** Expressing result or consequence (potential or actual); esp. after *so* or *such* (now always with *as* before *to* = *that* with finite vb.), or *enough* ME. **b.** After *too*, with neg. implication (*too..to..* = *so..as not to*, or *so..that.. not..*) ME.

The man is become as one of us, to know good & euill *Gen.* 2:22. **b.** Too proud to care from whence I came TENNYSON.

******Indicating occasion or condition.* **8.** Indicating occasion (passing into ground, reason, or cause): = *at, in, on, for, of, by*, etc. with gerund, or *because* with finite vb. late ME. **9.** With inf. after an adj. or (predicate) sb., in passive sense, the main sb. of the principal clause being the implied object of the inf., or of a preposition following OE. **10.** With inf. expressing a fact or supposition which forms the ground of the statement in the principal clause, or is considered in connection with it ME. †**b.** With inf. equivalent to a conditional clause with indef. subject (= *if one were to..*) –1611.

8. I blusht to heare his monstrous deuices SHAKS. **9.** A flour, þat es fayre to se HAMPOLE. **10.** Thou art a rustic to call me so ADDISON. **b.** To keepe them here, they would but stinke SHAKS.

II. With infinitive in adjectival relation. **1.** With inf. in adjectival relation to a sb.; either as predicate after the vb. *to be*, or immediately qualifying the sb. **a.** Expressing intention or appointment, and hence simply futurity (thus equivalent to a future pple.) OE. **b.** Expressing duty, obligation, or necessity OE. **c.** Expressing possibility or potential action OE. **d.** Expressing quality or character: = such as to.., such as would...late ME. **2.** With inf. equivalent to a relative clause with indicative; chiefly after *first, last*, or the like; as *the first to come* = 'the first in coming', 'the first who comes or came' 1535.

1. a. The best is yet to be BROWNING. This house to let or for sale (*mod.*). **b.** Unprofitable questions are to be avoided 1560. They had no time to lose 1794. What, then, are you to do? 1887. **c.** There was no man to saye hym naye 1533. Not a sound was to be heard 1818. The gates are mine to open, As the gates are mine to close KIPLING. **d.** A sight to gladden Heav'n! THOMSON. **2.** Not an eye that sees you, but is a Physician to comment on your Malady SHAKS.

III. With infinitive in substantival relation. Equivalent to a noun or gerund; *to* being ult. reduced to a mere 'sign' of the inf. without any meaning of its own. **1. a.** with inf. as subj., or as obj. with complement, introduced by *it* or an impersonal vb. OE. **b.** with inf. as direct subj. or predicate, or in apposition with a sb. or pron., or after *than* ME. **2.** with inf. as direct obj. of a trans. vb. OE. **b.** rarely as object of another preposition, instead of the vbl. sb. or gerund 1485.

1. a. God hath pronounc't it death to taste that Tree MILT. **b.** Talking is not always to converse COWPER. **2.** I love not to be idle B. JONS. **b.** Not to affirm is a very different thing from to deny 1879.

IV. With infinitive equivalent to a finite vb. or clause. **1.** With inf. as complement to a sb. or pron., forming a compound obj. or sb. phrase, corresponding to the 'accusative and infinitive' construction in Latin and Greek OE. **2.** With inf. after a dependent interrogative or relative; equivalent to a clause with *may, should*, etc. ME. **b.** In absolute or independent const. after an interrogative, forming an elliptical question 1713. **3.** In absolute or independent constr., with subject expressed (in nom.) or omitted; in exclams. expressing astonishment, indignation, sorrow, or (after *O* or other interj.) longing 1450. †**4.** With inf. immediately following the subject, in vivid narrative, equivalent to a past tense indic.; almost always with *go* and vbs. of like meaning –1668.

1. Shee will..cause thy throate to be cut CORYAT. **b.** The Houyhnhnms..could hardly believe me to be a right Yahoo SWIFT. **2.** He.. wyst not what to do MALORY. **b.** But..how to hinder vexatious prosecutions? J. H. NEWMAN. **3.** My owne flesh and blood to rebell SHAKS. Oh, to be in England! BROWNING. **4.** I..away home ..and there to read again and sup with Gibson PEPYS.

V. Peculiar constructions. †**1.** *To* was formerly often used with the second of two infinitives when the first was without it –1803. **2.** Occasionally an adv. or advb. phr. (formerly sometimes an object or predicate) is inserted between *to* and the infinitive, forming the construction now usu. (but loosely) called 'split infinitive' ME. **3.** Used absol. at the end of a clause, with ellipsis of the inf. *rare* bef. 19th c.; now a frequent colloquialism. ME.

1. *Merry W.* IV. iv. 57. **2.** Milton was too busy to much miss his wife JOHNSON. This answer seemed to seriously offend him 1805. **3.** I kept on ..I had to 1883.

†**C. To** *conj.* **a.** To the time that; till, until –1575. **b.** followed by *that* –1626.

D. To (tŭ) *adv.* †**1.** Expressing motion resulting in arrival: To a place, etc. implied or indicated by the context –1450. **2.** Expressing direction: Towards a thing or person implied, after *end, head*, etc., forming advb. phrases 1889. **b.** In conjunction with other advs. of direction: In one direction (as contrasted with the opposite one). Now only in TO AND FRO. late ME. **3.** Expressing contact: So as to come close against something; *esp.* with vbs. forming phrases denoting shutting or closing. Now *arch.* and *colloq.* ME. **4.** Expressing attachment, application, or addition; also predic., *spec.* of a horse: = harnessed to a vehicle. Now *dial.* or *colloq.* late ME. **b.** In the senses 'in addition, besides, also', and 'in excess', now written TOO. **5.** Expressing attention or application; after vbs., as *fall, go, set.* †Also *absol.* (with ellipsis of vb. in imper.). ME. **6.** Used idiomatically with many vbs., as *bring, come, go, lay, lie*, etc.: see the vbs. **7. To and again. a.** = TO AND FRO A. 1. *Obs.* exc. *dial.* 1627. †**b.** For and against a question –1666. †**c.** Again and again –1666.

2. Three young owls with their feathers turned wrong end to 1889. **b.** *Ant. & Cl.* I. iv. 46. **3.** She ..clapte the wyndow to CHAUCER. **4.** Can Honour set too a legge? SHAKS. **5.** To Achilles, to Aiax, to SHAKS. **7. c.** Sent him to and again to get me 1000 *l.* PEPYS.

To-, *prefix*[1], the prep. and adv. To used in combination with vbs., sbs., adjs., and advs. in the sense of motion, direction, or addition to, or as the mark of the infinitive.

To-, *prefix*[2]. *Obs.* exc. in rare *arch.* or *dial.* use. [OE. *to-*, ME. *to-* (*te-*) = OFris. *ti-, te-*, OS. *ti-* (*te-*), OHG. *zi-, za-, ze-* and *zir-, zar-* (G. *zer-*) :– WGmc. **ti-* :– Gmc. **tiz-* = L. *dis-*, a particle expressing separation, 'asunder, apart, in pieces'.] **1.** With separative force: Asunder, apart, to or in pieces; also, away, about, abroad, here and there. **2.** Used as a mere intensive: Completely, entirely, soundly, greatly, severely, etc. **3.** Hence **all to-, all to, all-to,** †**alto,** employed in middle and early modern Eng. as an intensive to any vb.

Toad (tōᵘd), *sb.* [OE. *tāda, tādde*, shortening of *tādiġe, tādie*, early ME. also *tadde* (XII); of unkn. origin and unusual formation.] **1.** A tailless amphibian of the genus *Bufo*; primarily the common European species *B. vulgaris*; thence extended to many foreign species of the genus or of the family *Bufonidæ*. **b.** As a type of anything hateful or loathsome 1548. **c.** *fig.* and *provb.* 1649. **2.** Applied to allied animals, as *Surinam t.* = PIPA; *midwife, obstetrical t.*, the nurse-frog: see OBSTETRICAL 1757. **3.** Applied opprobriously to human beings and animals 1568. **4.** = TOADY *sb.* 2. 1831. **5.** Cookery. *Toad in a hole*: meat (usu. sausage-meat) baked in a batter pudding 1787.

1. The t., ougly and venemous SHAKS. Him there they found Squat like a T., close at the eare of Eve MILT. *Running t.*, the natterjack. **b.** *Tr. & Cr.* II. iii. 170. **c.** *To eat (any one's) toads*, to toady. *T. under a harrow*, a simile for a person under constant persecution or oppression. **3.** What a miserable poor t. is a husband, whose misfortunes not even death can relieve! 1771.

Comb.: **t.-cheese**, a poisonous fungus; **-head**, the Amer. golden plover (*local U.S.*); **-lizard** (*a*) the horned t.; (*b*) the labyrinthodon; **-pipe**, any one of various species of *Equisetum*; **-rush**, *Juncus bufonius*; **toad's mouth**, the snapdragon, *Antirrhinum majus*; **-snatcher**, the reed-bunting; **-spit, -spittle** = CUCKOO-SPIT[2] I. Hence **Toad** *v. trans.* to act as a toady to; to toady; also *intr.* **Toa·dish** *a. rare*, of the nature of a t.; like a t. **Toa·dlet, Toa·dling**, a young or little t.

Toad-eat (tōᵘ·dᵢīt), *v. rare.* 1766. [Back-formation from next.] *trans.* To flatter, fawn upon (a person); to toady. Also *intr.* So **Toa·d-ea:ting** *vbl. sb.* and *ppl. a.*

Toad-eater (tōᵘ·dᵢī:təɹ). 1629. **1.** One who eats toads; *orig.* the attendant of a charlatan, employed to eat toads (held to be poisonous) to enable his master to exhibit his skill in expelling poison. **2.** *fig.* A fawning flatterer, parasite, sycophant 1742. **b.** A humble friend or dependant; *spec.* a female companion or attendant. *contempt.* Now *rare.* 1744.

2. Lord Edgcumbe's [place]..is destined to Harry Vane, Pulteney's toad-eater H. WALPOLE.

Toad-fish (tōᵘ·dᵢfiʃ). 1612. A name applied, from their appearance, to several fishes; *esp.* **a.** A swell-fish, or puffer, spec. *Tetrodon turgidus.* **b.** The sea-devil, fishing frog, angler, or wide-gab, *Lophius piscatorius.* **c.** *American t.*, the oyster-fish, *Batrachus tau*, of the Atlantic coast of U.S.A.

Toad-flax (tōᵘ·dᵢflæks). 1578. [From the flax-like appearance of the foliage.] The European plant *Linaria vulgaris*; hence extended as a generic name to other species of *Linaria*.

Toadstone[1] (tōᵘ·dstoᵘn). 1558. [tr. L. *batrachites*, Gr. βατραχίτης, or med.L. *bufonitis, crapaudinus*, Fr. *crapaudine* (XIII).] Formerly, any of various stones likened to a toad in colour or shape, or supposed to be produced by a toad; often worn as jewels or amulets, or set in rings. The most valued kind was fabled to be found in the head of the toad; cf. *A.Y.L.* II. i. 13.

Toadstone[2] (tōᵘ·dstoᵘn). *local.* 1784. [perh. repr. G. *todtes gestein* 'dead rock'.] A name given by the Derbyshire lead-miners to an igneous rock, occurring as irregular sheets of contemporaneous lava, interstratified with, or in connection with the metalliferous mountain limestone.

Toadstool (tōᵘ·dstūl). late ME. [f. TOAD *sb.* + STOOL, a fanciful name.] A fungus having a round disc-like top and a slender stalk, a mushroom. **b.** Popularly restricted to poisonous or inedible fungi, as distinct from edible 'mushrooms' 1607.

Toady (tōᵘ·di), *sb.* 1826. [f. TOAD-EATER + -Y[6].] A servile dependant or parasite; = TOAD-EATER 2, 2 b.

Toady (tōᵘ·di), *a. rare.* 1628. [f. TOAD *sb.* + -Y[1].] **1.** Toad-like, repulsive. **2.** Infested with toads 1882.

Toady (tōᵘ·di), *v.* 1827. [f. TOADY *sb.*] **1.** *trans.* To play the toady to; to flatter or attend to with servility from interested motives. **2.** *intr.* To play the servile dependant; to pay deference from interested motives 1861.

Toadyism (tōᵘ·diᵢiz'm). 1840. [f. TOADY *sb.* + -ISM.] The action or behaviour of a parasite or sycophant; mean and interested servility.

To and fro (tūənᵈfrōᵘ·), *phr.* ME. [TO, FRO *advs.* and *preps.*] **A.** *adv.* **1.** Successively to and from some place, etc.; hence more vaguely: In opposite or different directions alternately; from side to side; backwards and forwards; hither and thither; up and down. †**2.** In places lying in opposite or different directions; here and there –1697. †**3.** To or on opposite sides alternately; for and against a question; pro- and con –1690.

1. Idle children, wandering to and fro CRABBE. **3.** Thus shall they be too and fro, doubtfull and ambiguous in all thir doings MILT.

B. *prep.* To and from (a place); alternately to and from each of (two places): the latter now commonly expressed by *between.* Now *rare.* 1574. **C.** *sb.* (now with hyphens; but pl. *tos and fros*). **1.** Alternating or reciprocating movement; the action of walking or passing to and fro 1847. **2.** *fig.* Alternation generally; vacillation 1553.

1. Watching the to-and-fro of a shuttle 1906.

D. *adj.* (usu. with hyphens). Executed, as movement, in opposite directions alternately; alternating, reciprocating; characterized by, or characterizing, such movement; passing to and fro 1839.

The regular to-and-fro motion of the water in its estuary HUXLEY.

E. as *vb. phr.* (only in pres. pple. and vbl. sb.) **a.** *intr.* To pass to and fro, to go hither and thither 1847. **b.** *trans.* To lead to and fro 1852.

a. There were clerks to-ing and fro-ing 1872.

Toarcian (toᵢā·ɹsiăn), *a.* (*sb.*) 1885. [– Fr. *Toarcien*, f. L. *Toarcium* (Fr. *Thouars*), in western France.] *Geol.* Applied to a series of strata corresponding in position to the Upper Lias of England, which are extensively developed in Central and Southern France.

Toast (tōᵘst), *sb.*[1] late ME. [f. TOAST *v.*[1]] **1.** (with *a* and *pl.*) A slice or piece of bread browned at the fire: often put in wine, water, or other beverage. Now *rare* or *Obs.* exc. as in b. **b.** As the type of what is hot or dry. late ME. **2.** As a substance (without *a* or *pl.*): Bread so browned by fire 1730. †**3.** *fig.* (usu. *old t.*) One who drinks to excess, a soaker, a boon companion; a brisk old fellow fond of his glass. *slang.* –1709.

1. b. It keeps this end of the valley as warm as a t. STEVENSON. **2.** *Ale and t., t. and ale, t. and water. On t.*, served up on a slice of toast; fig. *to have* (a person) *on t.*, to have at one's mercy (*slang*).

Comb.: **t.-rack**, a contrivance for holding toast, keeping each piece on edge and separate; **-water**, water in which toasted bread has been steeped, used as a drink for invalids, etc.

Toast *sb.*[2] 1674. [A fig. application of prec., the name of a lady being supposed to flavour a bumper like a spiced toast in the drink.] **1.** A lady who is named as the person to whom a company is requested to drink; often one who is the reigning belle of the season. Now only *Hist.* **2.** Any person, male or female, whose health is proposed and drunk to; also any event, institution, or sentiment, in memory or in honour of which a company is requested to drink; also, the call or act of proposing such a health 1746.

1. The present beauty,..a Mrs. Musters,..the reigning t. of the season MME. D'ARBLAY. **2.** He then gave as a t., 'Success to Scotland, and its worthy inhabitants' 1831.

Comb.: **t-master,** one who at a public dinner or the like is appointed to propose or announce the toasts.

Toast (tō^{u}st), *v.*[1] late ME. [– OFr. *toster* roast, grill :– Rom. **tostare*, f. *tost-*, pa. ppl. stem of L. *torrēre* parch.] **1.** *trans.* To burn as the sun does, to parch; to heat thoroughly; now *spec.* as in technical operations. **b.** *intr.* for *refl.* To warm oneself thoroughly 1614. **2.** To brown (bread, cheese, etc.) by exposure to the heat of a fire. late ME. **b.** *transf.* To warm (one's feet or toes) at a fire 1860. Hence **Toa·sting** *vbl. sb.*; **toa·sting-fork,** a fork used for toasting bread, etc.; *fig.* a rapier or sword.

Toast, *v.*[2] 1700. [f. TOAST *sb.*[2]] **1.** *intr.* To name a person to whose health or in whose honour, or a thing or sentiment to the success of which or in honour of which, the company is requested to drink; to propose or drink a toast. Const. *to.* **2.** *trans.* To name when a toast is drunk; to drink in honour of (a person or thing) 1700.

2. Times without number did he t. 'The Liberty of the Press' 1836.

Toaster (tō^{u}·stəɹ). 1582. [f. TOAST *v.*[1] + -ER[1].] **1.** One who toasts anything by the fire. **2.** A toasting-fork, *joc.* a rapier or similar weapon 1695. **b.** A kind of cheese, bread, etc., that toasts (well or otherwise) 1845.

Tobacco (tŏbæ·ko). 1577. Also (orig.) **†tabaco, †tabacco.** [Altered from Sp. *tabaco*, according to Oviedo (1535) the native name of the tube or pipe through which the Indians inhaled the smoke; but according to Las Casas (1552) applied to a tubular roll of leaves used by the Indians like a rude cigar. Taken by the Spaniards as the name of the herb or leaf, in which sense it passed into the other European langs.] **1.** The leaves of the tobacco-plant dried and variously prepared, forming a narcotic and sedative substance widely used for smoking, also for chewing, or in the form of SNUFF, and to a slight extent in medicine 1588. **2.** The plant whose leaves are so used: Any one of various species of *Nicotiana* (family *Solanaceæ*), esp. *N. tabacum*, a native of tropical America, or *N. rustica* (*green* or *wild t.*), now widely cultivated 1577. **b.** With defining words, applied to plants of other genera, as **Indian t.,** (*a*) *Lobelia inflata* of N. America, used medicinally; (*b*) Indian hemp, *Cannabis indica*; **mountain t.,** *Arnica montana*; **wild t.** = *Indian t.* (*a*) 1597.

Comb., as *t.-ash, -jar, -smoke*: **t.-cutter,** (*a*), a person employed in cutting t.; (*b*) a machine or knife for this purpose; **t. heart,** *Path.*, a heart functionally disordered by excessive use of t., characterized by a rapid and irregular pulse; **-man,** a tobacconist (now *rare* or *Obs.*); **-pouch,** a pouch for carrying t. for smoking or chewing; **-stopper,** a contrivance for pressing down the t. in the bowl of a pipe while smoking; **-worm,** the larva of a sphinx-moth, *Protoparce carolina*, which feeds on the leaves of the t.-plant.

Toba·cco-box. 1599. **1.** A box for holding tobacco, *esp.* a small flat box to be carried in the pocket. **2.** Local name for two N. Amer. fishes, from their flattened shape: (*a*) a species of skate or ray, *Raia erinacea*; (*b*) the common sunfish, *Pomotis gibbosus* 1891.

Tobacconist (tŏbæ·kŏnist). 1599. [f. TOBACCO + -IST, with inserted euphonic *-n-*.] **†1.** A person addicted to the use of tobacco –1757. **2.** A dealer in, or manufacturer of, tobacco 1657.

Toba·cco-pipe. 1596. **1.** A pipe for smoking tobacco, consisting of a bowl in which the tobacco is placed and ignited, with a slender tube through which the smoke of it is drawn into the mouth. **2.** *U.S.* Local name for a parasitic plant, also called *Indian pipe* 1845.

1. *King's* (*Queen's*) *tobacco-pipe*: see PIPE *sb.*[1] III.

Comb.: **t. clay** = PIPE-CLAY.

Toba·cco-plant. 1761. = TOBACCO 2. **b.** A name for species of *Nicotiana* 1884.

Tobe (tō^{u}b). 1835. [– Arab. *ṭawb* (locally pron. *tōb, sōb*) a garment.] A length of cotton cloth used as a garment in Northern and Central Africa.

To-be (tŭ₁bī·), *a.* and *sb.* 1600. [inf. of vb. BE.] That, that which, is to be; future.

Tobin's tube. Also **Tobin tube.** 1884. A device for admitting fresh air into a room in an upward direction, invented by Martin Tobin of Leeds in 1873.

Toboggan (tŏbǫ·găn). 1829. [– Canadian Fr. *tabaganne* – Algonquian word of which closely similar vars. are Micmac *tobākun*, Abnaki *udābāgan*.] **1.** orig., A light sledge consisting of a thin strip of wood turned up in front, used by the Canadian Indians for transport over snow; now, a similar vehicle, sometimes with low runners, used in the sport of coasting (esp. down prepared slopes of snow or ice). **2.** [f. next.] The sport of tobogganing 1879.

Tobo·ggan, *v.* 1856. [f. prec.] *intr.* To ride on a toboggan or sleigh; *esp.* to 'coast' or slide down a snowy (or other) slope on a toboggan. Hence **Tobo·gganer, Tobo·gganist.**

†To-brea·k, *v.* [OE. *tobrecan*, f. TO-[2] + *brecan* BREAK.] **1.** *trans.* To break to pieces; to shatter, rupture; to break down, demolish –1688. **2.** *intr.* To break into pieces; to burst asunder; to be ruptured, shattered, or fractured –1520.

1. This was it, that all to-brake his heart BUNYAN.

Toby (tō^{u}·bi). 1681. [Familiar form of Christian name *Tobias.*] **1.** The posteriors, the buttocks. **2.** (With capital T.) A jug or mug in the form of a stout old man in a long and full skirted coat and a three-cornered hat (18th c. costume). Also *attrib.* as *T. jug.* 1840. **3.** The name of the trained dog introduced (in the first half of the 19th c.) into the Punch and Judy show 1840.

3. *T. collar, frill*: a turndown pleated frill like that of dog Toby.

‖**Toccata** (tokkā·tă). 1724. [It., subst. use of fem. pa. pple. of *toccare* touch.] *Mus.* A composition for a keyboard instrument, intended to exhibit the touch and technique of the performer, and having the air of an improvisation; in later times loosely applied.

Toc H (tǫk ē^{i}tʃ). [Signaller's name for T + H, denoting Talbot House, Poperinghe, founded 1915 in memory of Gilbert Talbot (killed July 1915).] A society for the maintenance of comradeship since the war of 1914–18.

Tocher (tǫ·χər). *Sc.* and *n. dial.* 1485. [– Ir. and OGael. *tochar.*] The marriage portion which a wife brings to her husband; dowry, *dot.*

‖**Toco**[1] (tō^{u}·kŏ). 1781. [Native name in Guiana.] *Ornith.* The typical species of TOUCAN, *Rhamphastos toco*, a native of Guiana.

Toco[2] (tō^{u}·ko). *slang.* Also **toko.** 1823. [– Hind. *ṭhōkō*, imper. of *ṭhoknā* thrash, hit.] Chastisement, corporal punishment.

Toco- (tǫko), comb. form of Gr. τόκος offspring, as in **Toco·logist,** one versed in tocology; **Toco·logy,** the science of parturition or of midwifery, obstetrics.

Tocsin (tǫ·ksin). 1586. [– Fr. *tocsin*, OFr. *touquesain, toquassen* – Pr. *tocasenh*, f. *tocar* strike, TOUCH + *senh* bell.] **1.** A signal, esp. an alarm-signal, sounded by ringing a bell or bells: used orig. and esp. in ref. to France. **2.** *transf.* A bell used to sound an alarm 1842.

1. The t...is pealing madly from all steeples CARLYLE. **2.** The great bell of St. Paul's was the t. which summoned the citizens to arms 1868.

Tod (tǫd), *sb.*[1] *Sc.* and *n. dial.* ME. [Northern word of unkn. origin.] **1.** A fox. **2.** *fig.* A person likened to a fox; a crafty person 1500. **†3.** *ellipt.* Foxskin –1564.

2. Take care of the old t.; he means mischief STEVENSON.

Tod (tǫd), *sb.*[2] late ME. [prob. of LDu. origin (cf. LG. *todde* bundle, pack); cf. ON. *toddi* bit, piece, OHG. *zot(t)a, zata*, MHG. *zotte* tuft of wool.] **1.** A weight used in the wool trade, usu. 28 pounds or 2 stone, but varying locally. **b.** A load, either generally, or of a definite weight 1479. **2.** A bushy mass (esp. of ivy; also *ivy-tod*: see IVY) 1553.

Tod (tǫd), *v. dial.* Now *rare* or *Obs.* 1611. [f. prec.] *intr.* Of (so many) sheep or fleeces: To produce a tod of wool; *to t. threes* (etc.), to produce a tod from every three (etc.) sheep; hence, To obtain a tod of wool from a specified number of sheep.

To-day (tŭdē^{i}·), *adv.* and *sb.* [OE. *tō dæġ*, TO + DAY.] **A.** *adv.* **1.** On this very day. **2.** *transf.* At the present time, in the present age; in these times; nowadays ME.

1. To day they chas'd the Boar OTWAY.

B. *sb.* **1.** This day; also, any day considered as present 1535. **2.** *transf.* This present time or age 1848.

2. The fad of today is the orthodoxy of tomorrow 1910.

Toddle (tǫ·d'l), *sb.* 1825. [f. next.] **1.** An act or the action of toddling; *transf.* a leisurely walk, a stroll. **2.** (Also toddles.) A toddling child 1825.

Toddle (tǫ·d'l), *v.* 1600. [orig. *todle*, Sc. and north. Eng.; of unkn. origin.] *intr.* To walk or run with short unsteady steps, as a child just beginning to walk, an aged or invalid person. **b.** Hence, To walk or move with short easy steps; to saunter, stroll; by meiosis, simply = walk, go 1724.

When his strength enabled him to t. abroad THACKERAY. Hence **To·ddler,** one who toddles; *esp.* a toddling child.

Toddy (tǫ·di). 1609. [– Hind. *tāṛī* (with cerebral *r*, approaching Eng. *d*), f. Hind. *tāṛ* palm-tree :– Skr. *tāla* palmyra.] **1.** The sap obtained from the incised spathes of various species of palm, esp. *Caryota urens*, the wild date, the coco-nut, and the palmyra, used as a beverage in tropical countries; also, the intoxicating liquor produced by its fermentation. **2.** A beverage composed of whisky or other spirituous liquor with hot water and sugar 1786.

Comb.: **t.-bird,** any of various E. Indian birds, as *Ploceus baya*, which feed on the sap of palms; **-cat** = *palm-cat* a.; **-palm,** any palm that yields t.; spec. *Caryota urens*, and the wild date-tree of India, *Phœnix sylvestris*.

To do, to-do: see DO *v.* IV. 2.

Tody (tō^{u}·di). 1773. [– Fr. *todier* (XVIII) – L. *todus*, name of some small bird, adopted by Linnæus as a generic name.] *Ornith.* Any member or species of the genus *Todus* or family *Todidæ* of small insectivorous birds, resembling and allied to the kingfisher; of which four species are found in the Greater Antilles.

Toe (tō^{u}), *sb.* [OE. *tā*, pl. *tān* (ME. *tō*, pl. *to(o)n, to(o)s*) = MLG. *tē*, (M)Du. *tee*, OHG. *zēha* (G. *zeh, zehe*), ON. *tá* :– Gmc. **taix(w)ōn*, of unkn. origin.] **1.** Each of the five digits of the human foot. **2.** Each of the digits of the foot of a beast or bird. late ME. **b.** The front part of the hoof (or shoe) of a horse 1566. **3.** *transf.* The part of a shoe or stocking which covers the toes; the hood or cap for the toe sometimes attached to a stirrup; a toe-piece 1600. **4.** A part resembling a toe or the toes, in shape or position; (usu.) the lower extremity or projection of anything; a point, tip; often identical with *foot.* **a.** *gen.* 1440. **b.** The lower extremity of a spindle or screw, as in a press: the projection on a lock-bolt or the like, against which the key or a cam presses 1677. **c.** The lower extremity of a gun-stock, rafter, organ-pipe, etc. 1860. **d.** The thin end of a hammer-head, the peen; the tip of the 'head' of a golf or hockey club 1873.

1. *Big* or *great t.*, the thick inner toe; *little t.*, the short outer toe. *fig.* What do you thinke? You, the great T. of this Assembly? SHAKS. **3.** Place thy foot on the t. of my boot SCOTT.

Phrases (chiefly *colloq.* and *slang*). *T. and heel*, (*a*) a style of dancing, in which the toe and heel tap rhythmically on the ground; also *attrib.*; (*b*) a manner of walking in which the heel of one foot and the toe of the other are always upon the ground together. *To kiss the pope's t.*: to kiss the golden cross of the sandal on the pope's right foot, as a mark of respect: the customary salutation of those (excepting sovereigns) to whom audience is granted. *To step* or *tread on the toes of*; also *fig.* to give offence to, to vex. *To turn one's toes up*, to die.

Comb.: **t.-ball**, the thickened fleshy pad under the t.; **-cap**, a cap of leather covering the t. of a boot or shoe; **-clip**, (*a*) an attachment to a bicycle-pedal in which the t. of the shoe is placed to prevent the foot slipping; (*b*) a tip turned up at the t. of a horse-shoe, to keep the shoe in position; **-crack** *Farriery*, a sand-crack in the front of the hoof; **-dancer**, one who dances on the extreme tips of the toes; **-hardy**, a half-round hardy or cold-chisel; **-hold**, in *Wrestling*, a hold in which the t. is seized and the leg forced backwards; **-nail** *sb.*, the nail of a t.; **-nail** *v.*, to fasten with toed nails: see TOED 2; **-step** *Mech.*, the socket in which the end of a spindle works.

Toe (tō^u), *v.* 1607. [f. prec.] **1.** *trans.* To furnish with a toe or toes; to make or put a new toe on (a stocking, etc.). **2.** To touch or reach with the toes 1833. **3. a.** To kick with the toe. **b.** *Golf.* To strike (a ball) with the tip of the club. 1865. **4.** *intr.* To move the toe, to tap rhythmically with the toe in dancing; *to t. and heel (it)*, to dance 1828. **5.** *trans. Carpentry.* To secure or join together by nails driven obliquely: see TOED 2. 1877.

2. Phr. *To t. a* or *the line, mark, scratch, crack*: to stand with the tips of one's toes exactly touching a line; to stand in a row; hence *fig.* to present oneself in readiness for a race, contest, or undertaking; also, to conform to the defined standard or platform of a party.

Toed (tō^ud), *ppl. a.* 1611. [f. TOE *sb.* and *v.* + -ED.] **1.** Having a toe or toes, as *three-t.*, *black-t.* Of a stocking, Having separate divisions for the toes; of a clog, or the like, Having a (leather) toe-piece. **2.** *Carpentry.* Secured or joined by nails driven obliquely; also of a nail, driven obliquely 1877.

To-fall (tū-fǭl). *Sc.* and *n. dial.* late ME. [f. TO *prep.* + FALL *v.* or *sb.*] **1.** A lean-to; a penthouse; a shed. **2.** The act of falling to; *t. of the day* or *night*, the close of day 1749.

Toff (tǫf). *vulgar.* 1851. [perh. alt. of TUFT *sb.* 5 b.] One who is stylishly dressed or who has a smart appearance; a swell; hence, one of the well-to-do, a 'nob'. **b.** Sometimes applied in compliment to a person who behaves 'handsomely'; a 'gent' 1898.

Toffee, toffy (tǫ·fi). 1825. [alt. of TAFFY[1]; vars. *tuffy, toughy* show assoc. with TOUGH; of unkn. origin.] A sweetmeat made from sugar or treacle, butter, and sometimes a little flour, boiled together; often mixed with bruised nuts, as *almond* or *walnut t.* Also, with *a* and *pl.*: A piece of toffee.

Not for t. (vulgar phr.): not under any circumstances. *Not to be able to do* a thing *for t.* (slang): to be incompetent at it.

†**Tofo·re**, *prep.*, *adv.*, and *conj.* [OE. *tōforan*, f. TO *prep.* + *foran* adv.; cf. BEFORE.] = BEFORE, in various senses.

Toft (tǫft). [OE. *toft* – ON. *topt*, beside *tomt* :– **tumft-*, with which cf. Gr. δάπεδον (:– **dmpedom*) level surface, building site.] **1.** *orig.* A homestead, the site of a house and its outbuildings; a house site. Often in *t. and croft*, the whole holding, consisting of the homestead and attached piece of arable land. **2.** Apparently including the croft, or applied to a field or piece of land larger than the site of a house 1440. **3.** An eminence, knoll, or hillock in a flat region. Now *local.* late ME.

3. I sauh a Tour on A T...; A Deop Dale binepþe LANGL.

Comb.: **toftman**, the owner and occupier of a t.

Tog (tǫg), *sb.*; usu. *pl.* **togs.** *slang* or *colloq.* 1798. [app. a shortening of TOGEMAN(S, TOGMAN.] **1.** *Cant* and *slang.* A coat; any outer garment. **2.** *pl.* Clothes. *slang* and *joc. colloq.* 1809.

2. *Long togs* (Naut.), landsmen's clothes.

Tog, *v.* 1793. [Occurs chiefly as *togged* (tǫgd), prob. orig. from prec.] *trans.* To clothe, to dress: often with *up*. Also *intr.* for *refl.*

‖**Toga** (tō^u·gă). 1600. [L. *toga*, rel. to *tegere* to cover.] *Rom. Antiq.* The outer garment of a Roman citizen in time of peace, consisting of a single piece of stuff, long, broad, and flowing, without sleeves or armholes, and covering the whole body with the exception of the right arm. **b.** *transf.* and *fig.* A robe of office; a professional gown, a cloak, a 'mantle'; a dress coat 1738.

T. prætexta, a toga with a broad purple border worn by children, magistrates, persons engaged in sacred rites, and later by emperors. *T. virilis*, the toga of manhood, assumed by boys at puberty. Hence **To·gaed, to·ga'd** (tō^u·găd): clad in a t.; togated.

Togate (tō^u·ge^it), *a.* 1851. [– L. *togatus*, f. prec.; see -ATE[2].] = TOGAED.

Togated (tō^u·ge^itėd), *a.* 1634. [f. as prec. + -ED[1].] **1.** Clad in a toga; wearing the toga; hence, associated with the idea of peace, peaceful. **2.** Of words: Latinized; stately, majestic 1868.

2. Such t. words as 'The multitudinous sea incarnadine' 1868.

†**To·ged,** *a.* 1604. [f. †*toge* toga (f. as next) + -ED[2].] Clad in a toga, togated; hence, robed –1862.

†**To·geman(s, to·gman.** *Vagabonds' Cant. rare.* 1567. [f. Fr. *toge* or L. TOGA + *-man(s*, as in DARKMAN(S night, LIGHTMAN(S day.] A cloak or loose coat –1785.

Together (tŭge·ðəɹ), *adv.* (*prep.*) OE. [ME. *togedere*, repl. *togadere*, OE. *tōgædere* = OFris. *togadera, -ere*, MDu. *tegadere* (Du. *-er*); LDu. formation on **tō* TO + **gad-*, as in OE. *gæd* fellowship, *ġegada* associate, Du. *gade*, MDu. *ghegade* comrade; see GATHER *v.* For (ð) from *d* cf. *father.*] **1.** Into one gathering, company, mass, or body. **b.** Of two persons or things: Into companionship, union, proximity, contact, or collision OE. **2.** In one assembly, company, or body; in one place ME. **b.** Of two persons or things: In each other's company; in union or contact ME. **c.** In ideal combination; considered collectively 1796. **3.** In ref. to a single thing. **a.** With union or combination of parts or elements; into or in a condition of unity; so as to form a connected whole ME. **b.** After *fold, roll*, etc.: Of different parts (sides, ends, etc.): Into or in contact or junction, so as to form a compact body 1480. **4.** At the same time, at once, simultaneously ME. **5.** Without intermission, continuously, consecutively, uninterruptedly, 'running', 'on end'. (Usu. in ref. to time.) ME. **6.** In concert or co-operation; unitedly; conjointly ME. **7.** In the way of, into, or in mutual action; with or against each other; mutually, reciprocally ME. **b.** After *multiply*: By or into one another 1709. **c.** After *belong*: To one another; hence, to one or the same whole, company, or set 1897. **8. Together with:** Along with; in combination with, in addition to, or with the addition of; in company or co-operation with; at the same time as 1478.

1. My next care was to get t. the wrecks of my fortune GOLDSM. **b.** Two flints struck t. yielded fire 1894. **2. b.** You and I have eaten a great deal of salt t. 1645. **3. a.** While society holds t. 1832. **5.** He..never slept twice t. in the same apartment 1840. **6.** The contract and the label t. constituted a written warranty 1891. **7.** I could perceive.. my wife and daughters in close conference t. GOLDSM.

†**B.** *prep.* Along with, in addition to, with the addition of, with (*rare*) –1657.

Togger (tǫ·gəɹ). *slang.* 1897. [Perversion of TORPID.] A boat rowing in the Oxford college races called 'Torpids'; *pl.* the Torpids.

Toggery (tǫ·gəri). *slang* or *colloq.* 1812. [f. TOG *sb.* + -ERY.] **1.** Garments; clothes collectively. **b.** *esp.* Professional or official dress 1826. **2.** The trappings of a horse 1877.

1. b. *Long t.* = long togs.

Toggle (tǫ·g'l), *sb.* 1769. [Of unkn. origin.] **1.** *Naut.* A short pin passing through a loop or the eye of a rope, or a link of a chain, or through a bolt, to keep it in place, or for the attachment of another line. **2.** *transf.* **a.** A cross-piece attached to the end of a line or chain (e.g. a watch-chain), or fixed in a belt or strap for attaching a weapon, etc. by a loop or ring; also, a cross-piece put through a loop to effect compression by twisting. **b.** A movable pivoted cross-piece serving as a barb in a harpoon. **c.** *Mech.* A toggle-joint. 1873.

Comb.: **t.-bolt**, a bolt having a hole through the head to receive a t.; **-harpoon, -iron**, a harpoon with a pivoted t. instead of barbs; **-joint**, a joint consisting of two pieces hinged endwise, operated by applying pressure at the elbow. Hence **To·ggle** *v. trans.* to secure or make fast by means of a t. or toggles; to furnish with a t. or toggles.

Togue (tō^ug). 1877. [Adaptation of Indian name.] The great lake trout (*Salvelinus namaycush*) of N. America; also called *lunge* or *longe* and *namaycush.*

‖**Tohu-bohu** (tō·hū,bō·hū). 1619. [In XIX – Fr. *tohu-bohu* (Voltaire) – Heb. *tōhû wa-bōhû* emptiness and desolation (Gen. 1:2). Earlier (XVII) repr. by †*tohu and bohu* (cf. *thohu et bohu* Rabelais), †*tohuvabohu.*] That which is empty and formless; chaos; utter confusion.

‖**Tohunga** (tohū·ŋgă). 1872. [Maori *tóhunga*, lit. one skilled in signs and marks, f. *tohu* sign, omen.] A Maori priest or doctor.

Toil (toil), *sb.*[1] ME. [– AFr. *toil* = OFr. *tooil, touil, tueil* bloody mêlée, trouble, confusion, f. *tooillier* TOIL *v.*[1]] **1.** †Verbal contention, argument; also, battle, strife, mêlée, turmoil (*arch.* or merged in 2). **2.** With *a* and *pl.* A struggle, a 'fight' (with difficulties); hence, a spell of severe labour; a laborious task or operation 1576. **3.** Without *a* or *pl.* Severe labour; hard and continuous work or exertion which taxes the bodily or mental powers 1594.

1. To toils of battle bred POPE. **2.** I doo not loue so to make a toyle of a pleasure 1603. **3.** The t. of man is irksome to him, and he earns his subsistence with pain GOLDSM.

Toil (toil), *sb.*[2] 1529. [– OFr. *toile, teile* (mod. *toile* cloth, linen, web) :– L. *tēla* :– **texla*, f. **tex-* weave.] **1.** A net or nets set so as to enclose a space into which the quarry is driven, or within which the game is known to be. In later use usu. *pl.* †**2.** A trap or snare for wild beasts (*rare*) –1727. **3.** *fig.* or in fig. context (*sing.* and *pl.*) 1548.

1. He drives into a T. the foaming Boar COWLEY. The Toiles are already set round a large Lake 1707. **3.** Extol not Riches then, the toyl of Fools MILT.

Toil (toil), *v.*[1] ME. [– AFr. *toiler* dispute, wrangle = OFr. *tooillier* (mod. *touiller* mix, stir up) :– L. *tudiculare* stir about, f. *tudicula* machine for bruising olives, f. **tud-*, base of *tundere* beat, crush.] †**I. 1.** *intr.* To dispute, argue; also, to contend in battle; to fight, struggle. –late ME. **2.** *trans.* To pull, drag, tug about –1440. **II. 1.** *intr.* To struggle for some object, or for a living; to labour arduously. late ME. **b.** *fig.* To struggle mentally 1788. **c.** *intr.* With advb. extension: To move or advance toilsomely or with struggling and labour 1781. **2.** *trans.* To bring into some condition or position, or to procure, by toil; *t. out*, to accomplish by toil 1667. **3.** To subject to toil; to weary, tire, fatigue, esp. with work. *arch.* and *dial.* 1549.

1. For worldlie wealth, men can t. and moil all the week long 1654. **c.** The women and children weeping, famished, and toiling through the mud up to their knees MACAULAY. **2.** I Toild out my uncouth passage MILT. **3.** *T. out*, to tire out or exhaust with toil; The army was toiled out with cruell tempests HOLLAND.

Toil (toil), *v.*[2] 1592. [f. TOIL *sb.*[2]] *trans.* To trap or enclose in a toil; to drive (game) into a toil; *fig.* to entangle; *dial.* to set (a trap).

‖**Toile** (twal). 1858. [Fr.; see TOIL *sb.*[2]] A dress material: linen cloth or a mixture of silk and linen.

Toiler (toi·ləɹ). 1549. [f. TOIL *v.*[1] + -ER[1].] One who toils, a hard worker.

Toilet (toi·lėt). Also †**toilette, toy-.** 1540. [– Fr. *toilette*, dim. of TOILE; see -ET, -ETTE.] †**1.** A piece of stuff used as a wrapper for clothes –1611. †**b.** A towel or cloth thrown over the shoulders during hairdressing –1687. **2.** A cloth cover for a dressing-table; now usu. called a *t.-cover* 1682. **3.** *collective.* The articles required or used in dressing; the furniture of the toilet-table; †a case containing these 1662. †**4.** The table on which these articles are placed; a toilet-table –1838. **5.** The action or process of dressing 1681. **b.** The reception of visitors by a lady during the concluding stages of her toilet; very fashionable in the 18th c. Now *Hist.* 1703. **6.** Manner or style of dressing; dress, costume, 'get-up'; also, a dress or costume, a gown 1821. **7.** A dressing-room; in *U.S. esp.*, a dressing-room furnished with bathing facilities; also, a bathroom, a lavatory 1819. **8.** *transf.* from 5. **a.** *Surg.* The cleansing of a part after an operation 1879. **b.** The cleaning up of a street, a ship, etc. 1901. **c.** Preparation for execution (in Fr. form *toilette*) 1885.

5. The long labours of the T. cease POPE. **6.** Lady Dudley's black toilette was much admired 1883.

Comb.: **t.-case,** a dressing-case; **-cloth, -cover,** a cloth for the t.-table; **-glass,** a looking-glass for dressing; **-paper,** soft paper prepared for shaving, hair-curling, use in lavatories, etc.; **-room,** a dressing-room; in U.S. *spec.* a lavatory or bath-room; **-table,** a dressing-table furnished with the utensils and materials of the t.; **-vinegar,** aromatic vinegar used as an emollient. Hence **Toi·leted** *ppl. a.*, dressed, 'got up'.

Toilful (toi·lfŭl), *a.* 1596. [f. TOIL *sb.*[1] + -FUL.] **1.** Characterized by toiling; labouring; hard-working. **2.** Of an action, condition, etc.: = TOILSOME 1. 1614.

1. The fruitful lawns confess his t. care 1789. **2.** Long trauell, tyrings, and toylefull labours 1621. Hence **Toi·lfully** *adv.*

Toi·linet, -ette, toilene·tte. 1799. [app. f. Fr. *toile* linen, after *satinet, -ette*, etc.] A kind of fine woollen cloth; used formerly for waistcoats of grooms, huntsmen, etc.; see also quot.

Toilinet, a kind of German quilting; silk and cotton warp with woollen weft 1858.

Toilless (toi·l,lĕs), *a.* 1606. [f. TOIL *sb.*[1] + -LESS.] Without toil. †**a.** Entailing no toil. **b.** That is or acts without labour or exertion.

Toilsome (toi·lsŏm), *a.* 1581. [f. TOIL *sb.*[1] + -SOME[1].] **1.** Of actions, conditions, etc.: Characterized by or involving toil; laborious, tiring. **b.** Of concrete things: Entailing toil 1609. **2.** Of an agent = TOILFUL 1. 1655. †**3.** Caused by toil. SPENSER.

1. What can be toilsom in these pleasant Walkes? MILT. **b.** The t. oar COWPER. **3.** Toylsom sweat SPENSER. Hence **Toi·lsome-ly** *adv.*, **-ness.**

Toil-worn (toi·lwō̆ɹn), *a.* 1751. [f. TOIL *sb.*[1] + WORN *ppl. a.*] Worn by toil; showing marks of toil.

Toise (toiz), *sb.* 1598. [– Fr. *toise* :– OFr. *teise* :– Rom. **tēsa*, for *tensa*, subst. use (sc. *bracchia* arms) of n. pa. pple. (taken as fem.) of L. *tendere* stretch.] A French lineal measure of 6 French feet, roughly = 1·949 metres, or 6⅜ English feet. Chiefly in military use. So **Toise** *v.* (*rare*) *trans.* to measure with the eye, to eye from head to foot.

‖**Toison d'or** (twazoṅdǭr). 1623. [Fr., = fleece of gold.] **a.** The golden fleece; see GOLDEN *a.* 1. **b.** *Her.* The figure of this, giving name to an order of knighthood (see FLEECE *sb.* 1 b), and afterwards borne by certain families.

Tokay[1] (tokē[i]·). 1710. [Name of a town in Upper Hungary.] A rich sweet wine of aromatic flavour, made near Tokay in Hungary. (Also *T. wine.*) **b.** *T. grape*, the variety of grape from which this wine is made 1896.

‖**Tokay**[2] (tō[u]·ke). 1753. [– Malay *tŏkē.*] A species of gecko, or lizard of the family *Geckonidæ*, app. *G. verticillatus*, of Burma, Siam, and the Malay region.

Token (tō[u]·kĕn), *sb.* [OE. *tāc(e)n* = OFris. *tēk(e)n*, OS. *tēcan*, OHG. *zeihhan* (Du. *teeken*, G. *zeichen*), ON. *teikn* :– Gmc. **taiknam* (Goth. *taikns* :– **taikniz*), rel. to **taikjan* show, TEACH.] **1.** Something that serves to indicate a fact, event, object, feeling, etc.; a sign, a symbol. **2.** A sign or mark indicating some quality, or distinguishing one object from others; a characteristic mark OE. **b.** A spot on the body indicating disease, esp. the plague. Now *rare* or *Obs.* 1603. **3.** Something serving as proof of a fact or statement; an evidence OE. **4.** In biblical use: An act serving to demonstrate divine power or authority. *Obs.* or *arch.* OE. **5.** A sign or presage of something to come; an omen, portent, prodigy. *Obs.* (exc. as included in 1). OE. **6.** A signal given; a sign to attract attention or give notice. Now *rare* or *Obs.* OE. **7.** A sign arranged or given to indicate a person; a word or material object employed to authenticate a person, message, or communication; a mark giving security to those who possess it; a password. late ME. **8.** Something given as an expression of affection, or to be kept as a memorial; a keepsake. late ME. **9.** A stamped piece of lead or other metal given (orig. after confession) as a voucher of fitness to be admitted to the communion: in recent times used in Scotland in connection with the Presbyterian Communion service, but now usually represented by a 'communion card' 1534. **10.** A stamped piece of metal, issued as a medium of exchange by a private person or company, who engage to take it back at its nominal value, giving goods or legal currency for it 1598. **11.** *Printing.* A measure or quantity of press-work; a certain number of sheets of paper (usu. 250 pulls on a hand-press) passed through the press 1683.

1. Charlemayne..kyssyd Huon in t. of peace 1533. **2.** The tokens on his helmet tell The Bruce SCOTT. **3.** These..were brought as tokens of peace and amity COOK. **4.** They also that dwell in the vttermost parts are afraid at thy tokens *Ps.* 65:8. **10.** Buy a tokens worth of great pinnes B. JONS.

Phrases. *By the same t., by this* (or *that*) *t.*, (*a*) in the 15th c. app.: on the same ground; for the same reason; in the same way; (*b*) since 1600 (= Fr. *à telles enseignes que*), 'the proof of this being that'; introducing a corroborating circumstance, often weakened down to a mere associated fact that helps the memory or is recalled to mind by the main fact (*arch.* or *dial.*). *More by t.*, still more, the more so (*dial.*).

Comb.: **t. coin, coinage, currency:** see TOKEN-MONEY; **-payment,** payment of a small proportion of the sum due as indication that a debt is not repudiated; **-sheet,** *Printing*, the last sheet of each t. (see 11), turned down to facilitate counting the whole number.

Token (tō[u]·kĕn), *v.* Now *rare.* [OE. *tācnian* = MLG. *tēkenen*, OHG. *zeihhanen, -ōn* (G. *zeichnen*), Goth. *taiknjan.*] **1.** *trans.* To be a token or sign of; to signify. **2.** To typify, symbolize OE.

To·ken-mo:ney. 1546. **a.** *Eccl.* The payment made or contribution given (by way of Easter Offering) by persons on receiving their token that they were duly prepared to make their Easter communion. **b.** Private tokens issued by a trader or company to serve as a fractional currency and temporary medium of exchange between trader and customer 1890. **c.** State coinage of money not having the intrinsic value for which it is current, but bearing a fixed value relative to gold coin, for which it is exchangeable 1889.

Toko: see TOCO[2].

‖**Tola** (tō[u]·lā). *India.* 1614. [Hindi *tola* :– Skr. *tulā* balance, scale, weight, f. *tul* weigh.] An E. Indian weight, since 1833, in the British dominions fixed at 180 grains (the weight of the rupee); a coin of this weight.

Tolbooth, toll-booth (tō[u]·lbūð, -būþ, tǫ·lbūþ). Chiefly *Sc.* ME. [f. TOLL *sb.*[1] + BOOTH, *lit.* the booth, stall, or shed of the tax-collector.] †**1.** A booth, stall, or office at which tolls, duties, or customs are collected; a custom-house –1756. **2.** A town hall or guildhall. (Often comprehending senses 1 and 3.) 1440. **3.** A town prison, a jail. (Formerly usu. consisting of cells under the town hall.) 1470.

1. He seiȝ a man sittynge in a tolbothe, Matheu by name WYCLIF *Matt.* 9:9.

Told (tō[u]ld), *ppl. a. rare.* ME. [pa. pple. of TELL *v.*] Related, narrated, recounted; counted, reckoned; †esteemed. Chiefly in comb., as *oft-t., twice-t.*

Tol de rol. 1765. A song refrain.

Toledo (tolī·do). 1598. [Name of a city in Spain, long famous for its finely tempered sword-blades.] Short for *T. blade* or *sword*: A sword or sword-blade made at Toledo, or of the kind made there.

Tolerable (tǫ·lĕrăb'l), *a.* (*adv.*) late ME. [– (O)Fr. *tolérable* – L. *tolerabilis*, f. *tolerare* bear, endure; see -ABLE.] **1.** Capable of being borne or endured; supportable; bearable. **2.** Such as to be tolerated, allowed, or countenanced; sufferable, allowable. Now *rare.* 1531. **3.** Moderate in degree, quality, or character; mediocre, passable; now *esp.* moderately good, fairly good or agreeable, not bad 1548. **4.** as *adv.* **a.** Tolerably 1673. **b.** *pred.* In fair health. *colloq.* 1847.

1. He did not know how to maintain himself and his Family in any t. sort 1704. **3.** Found a t. road 1835. He had eaten a very t. lunch 1866. **4. b.** We're t., sir, I thank you C. BRONTË. Hence **To:lerabi·lity, To·lerableness. To·lerably** *adv.*

Tolerance (tǫ·lĕrăns). late ME. [– (O)Fr. *tolérance* – L. *tolerantia*, f. *tolerans, -ant-*; see next, -ANCE.] †**1.** The action or practice of enduring or sustaining pain or hardship; the power or capacity of enduring; endurance –1814. **b.** *Phys.* The power, constitutional or acquired, of enduring large doses of active drugs, or of resisting the action of poison, etc. 1875. **2.** The action or practice of tolerating; toleration; the disposition to be patient with the opinions or practices of others; forbearance; catholicity of spirit 1765. **3.** *techn.* **a.** *Coining.* The small margin within which coins, when minted, are allowed to deviate from the standard fineness and weight; also called *allowance* 1868. **b.** *Mech.* An allowable amount of variation in the dimensions of a machine or part 1909.

1. Diogenes, one terrible frosty Morning, came into the Market-place; And stood Naked shaking to show his T. BACON. So **To·lerancy** (*rare*), the quality or habit of being tolerant.

Tolerant (tǫ·lĕrănt), *a.* (*sb.*) 1780. [– Fr. *tolérant*, pr. pple. of *tolérer* – L. *tolerare*; see next, -ANT.] **A.** *adj.* Disposed or inclined to tolerate or bear with something; practising or favouring toleration 1784. **b.** *transf.* Of a thing: Capable of bearing or sustaining. Const. *of.* 1864. **c.** *Phys.* Able to endure the action of a drug, an irritant, etc., without being affected; capable of resisting. Const. *of.* 1879. **B.** *sb.* (sb. use of the adj.; so in Fr.) One who tolerates opinions or practices different from his own; one free from bigotry 1780.

A. b. How far the Articles were t. of a Catholic, or even of a Roman interpretation J. H. NEWMAN. Hence **To·lerantly** *adv.*

Tolerate (tǫ·lĕre[i]t), *v.* 1531. [– *tolerat-*, pa. ppl. stem of L. *tolerare* bear, endure; see -ATE[3].] †**1.** *trans.* To endure, sustain (pain or hardship) –1616. **b.** *Phys.* To endure with impunity the action of (a poison or strong drug) 1895. **2.** To allow to exist or to be done or practised without authoritative interference or molestation; also *gen.* to allow, permit 1533. **3.** To bear without repugnance; to allow intellectually, or in taste, sentiment, or principle; to put up with 1646.

2. England..was in no humour to t. treason FROUDE. **3.** By discipline of Time made wise, We learn to t. the infirmities And faults of others WORDSW.

Toleration (tǫlĕrē[i]·ʃən). 1517. [– Fr. *tolération* – L. *toleratio, -ōn-*, f. as prec.; see -ION.] †**1.** The action of sustaining or enduring; endurance (of evil, suffering, etc.) –1623. **b.** *Phys.* = TOLERANCE 1 b (*rare*) 1877. †**2.** The action of allowing; permission granted by authority, licence –1727. **3.** The action or practice of tolerating or allowing what is not actually approved; forbearance, sufferance 1582. **4.** *spec.* Allowance (with or without limitations), by the ruling power, of the exercise of religion otherwise than in the form officially established or recognized 1609. **b.** *Act of T., T. Act*, an act or statute granting such toleration; esp. in *Eng. Hist.* Act 1 Will. & Mary (1689) cap. 18, by which freedom of religious worship was granted, on certain conditions, to Dissenting Protestants 1692. **5.** *Coining.* = TOLERANCE 3 a. 1887. Hence **Tolera·tionism,** toleration of religious differences as a principle or system. **Tolera·tionist,** one who advocates or supports t.

Toll (tō[u]l), *sb.*[1] [OE. *toll* = OHG. *zol* (G. *zoll*), ON. *tollr* masc., with by-forms OE. *toln*, OFris. *tol(e)ne*, OS. *tolna* fem. – med.L. *toloneum*, alt. of late L. *teloneum* – Gr. τελώνιον toll-house, f. τελώνης collector of taxes, f. τέλος toll, tax.] **1.** orig., A general term for (*a*) a definite payment exacted by a king, ruler, or lord, or by the state or the local authority, by virtue of sovereignty or lordship, or in return for protection (*Obs.* exc. *Hist.*); more especially, (*b*) for permission to pass somewhere, do some act, or perform some function; or (*c*) as a share of the money passing, or profit accruing, in a transaction; a tax, tribute, impost, custom, duty. **b.** In the obsolete law phrase *sac and sóc, t. and team*, etc.: The right to 'toll' included (among others) in the grant of a manor by the Crown OE. **2.** *spec. uses.* **a.** A proportion of the grain or flour taken by the miller in payment for grinding. *Obs.* or *rare dial.* late ME. **b.** A charge for the privilege of bringing goods for sale to a market or fair, or of setting up a stall ME. **c.** A charge for the right of passage along a road (at a turnpike or toll-gate: now abolished in Great Britain), along a river or channel, over a bridge or ferry 1477. **d.** A charge for the right of landing or shipping goods at a port; formerly also, a customs duty. *Obs.* exc. *Hist.* 1680. **e.** A charge made for transport of goods, esp. by railway or canal. (Arising out of c.) 1889. **f.** *fig.* (Cf. *tribute*, similarly used.) late ME. **g.** with defining words: **through t.** (also *t. through, thorough*), **t. traverse, turn t.** (also *t. turn*): see quots. 1567. **h.** A short-distance telephone trunk-call: freq. *attrib.* 1927.

1. The Graunte of the Tolle of oure Towne of Knyghton 1485. Phr. *To take t. of.* **b.** *T.* is sometimes the right to take toll, sometimes the right to be free of toll; but often it is merely the right to tallage one's villeins POLLOCK & MAITLAND. **2. f.** Nott's gallant division..paid its t. of killed and wounded 1909. **g.** *Through tolle*, is where a Towne prescribes to haue tol for euery beast that goeth through their Towne. *Tolle trauers*, that is where one claimeth to haue a halfepeny, or such like toll of euery beast that is driuen ouer his ground. 1567. *Toll-turn*, which is Toll paid at the return of Beasts from Fair or Market, though they were not sold BLOUNT.

Comb.: **t.-bar**, a barrier (usu. a gate) across a road or bridge, where t. is taken; **-bridge**, a bridge at which t. is charged for passage; **-corn**, corn retained by a miller as t.; **-farmer**, one who farms the t. at a certain place; **-road**, a turnpike road (*Sc.* and *U.S.*).

Toll (tōᵘl), *sb.*[2] 1452. [f. TOLL *v.*[2]] The act of tolling a bell, or the sound made by a bell when tolled; (with *pl.*) a single stroke made in tolling, or the sound made by such stroke.

Toll, tole (tōᵘl), *v.*[1] Now *dial.* and *U.S.* [ME. *tolle, tulle*, repr. OE. **tollian*, **tullian*, rel. to *for|tyllan* seduce; cf. †*till* draw, entice.] **1.** *trans.* To attract, entice, allure, decoy. **2.** *spec. U.S.* To lure or decoy (wild animals) for the purpose of capture. Also *absol.* or *intr.* 1858. †**3.** To pull, drag, draw physically –1654.

1. Whatever you observe him to be more frighted at..be sure to tole him on to by..Degrees LOCKE.

Toll (tōᵘl), *v.*[2] 1452. [prob. orig. a particular use of prec. 3.] **1.** *trans.* To cause (a great bell) to sound by pulling the rope, esp. in order to give an alarm or signal: to ring (a great bell). *arch.* or *rhet.* 1494. **2.** *spec.* To cause (a large or deep-toned bell) to give forth a sound repeated at regular intervals by pulling the rope so that the bell swings through a short arc (in contrast to *ringing* it in full swing), or by striking it with a hammer or the like, or pulling the clapper; esp. for summoning a congregation to church, and **b.** (now) on the occasion of a death (the passing-bell) or funeral. Also *absol.* or *intr.* 1526. **3.** Said of a bell (also of the ringer): To sound (esp. a knell, etc.) by ringing as in sense 2; also of a clock, to strike (the hour) in a deep tone with slow measured strokes 1452. **4.** *intr.* Of a bell: To give forth sounds of this character by being tolled. Also said of a clock striking the hour on a deep-toned bell. 1551. **b.** *transf.* and *fig.* To make a sound like the tolling of a bell 1747. **5.** *trans.* To announce (a death, etc.) by tolling; to toll for (a dying or dead person) 1597. **6.** To summon or dismiss by tolling 1611.

1. Let the Bell of the Church of S. German be touled 1684. **2.** A large bell may be tolled easily by one man, if it is properly hung 1868. **b.** T. for the brave! The brave that are no more! COWPER. **3.** Slow tolls the village-clock the drowsy hour 1771. **4.** If I heard the Bell Toull for some that were dead BUNYAN. **b.** Sullen tolls the far-off river's flow 1849. **5.** Groning like a bell, That towles departing soules MARSTON.

Toll (tōᵘl), *v.*[3] Now *rare.* ME. [f. TOLL *sb.*[1]] **1.** *intr.* To take or collect toll; to exact or levy toll. **2.** *trans.* To take toll of (something); to exact a part of by way of toll. late ME. **b.** To charge (a person, etc.) with a toll, impose a toll upon 1583. **c.** To take or gather (something) as toll 1597. †**3.** *intr.* To pay toll; *to t. for* (*spec.*), to enter (a horse, etc.) for sale in the toll-book of a market –1664.

1. No Italian priest Shall tythe or t. in our dominions SHAKS. **2. c.** Like the bee toling from euery flower The vertuous Sweetes SHAKS.

Toll (tōᵘl), *v.*[4] 1467. [– AFr. *toller, toler, touller* – L. *tollere* take away.] *Law. trans.* To take away, bar, defeat, annul. *To t. an entry*, to take away the right of, or bar entry.

Tollage (tōᵘ·lėdʒ). 1494. [perh. f. TOLL *v.*[3] + -AGE; confounded with TALLAGE *sb.*] **1.** = TOLL *sb.*[1] †**2.** = TALLAGE *sb.* –1634.

†**To·ll-book.** 1596. [TOLL *sb.*[1]] A book containing a register of beasts or goods to be sold at a market or fair, and the tolls payable for them; also, a tax-collector's register or assessment-book –1679.

To·ll-dish. 1550. [TOLL *sb.*[1]] A dish or bowl of stated dimensions for measuring the toll of grain at a mill; a multure-dish.

Tollent (tǫ·lĕnt), *a. rare.* 1837. [– L. *tollens, -ent-*, pr. pple. of *tollere* lift, take away; see -ENT.] *Logic.* That 'takes away' or negatives; opp. to PONENT.

Toller[1] (tōᵘ·ləɹ). Now *rare.* [OE. *tollere*, f. TOLL *sb.*[1] + -ER[1].] One who takes toll, a toll-collector.

Toller[2], **toler** (tōᵘ·ləɹ). 1440. [f. TOLL *v.*[1] + -ER[1].] †**1.** One who 'tolls', entices, or instigates. **2.** A decoy; *spec.* a dog of a small breed used in decoying ducks. *U.S.* 1874.

Toller[3] (tōᵘ·ləɹ). 1562. [f. TOLL *v.*[2] + -ER[1].] One who tolls a bell.

To·ll-free, *a.* OE. Exempt from payment of toll.

To·ll-ga:therer. Now *rare.* late ME. [f. TOLL *sb.*[1] + GATHERER.] A tax-gatherer.

To·ll-house. 1440. [f. TOLL *sb.*[1] + HOUSE.] A house or building at which tolls or dues are collected. **1.** = TOLBOOTH 1 (*obs.*) or 2 (now *local*). **2.** A house by a toll-gate or toll-bridge, occupied by the toll-taker 1763.

Tollman (tōᵘ·lmæn). *Pl.* **-men.** 1743. [f. TOLL *sb.*[1]] A man who collects tolls; the keeper of a toll-gate.

Tol-lol (tǫ·lˌlǫ·l), *a. slang.* 1797. [f. the first syllable of TOLERABLE, with rhyming extension.] Tolerable, passable, 'middling'.

Tolsel (tōᵘ·lsĕl). Also **tolzey.** *local.* ME. [f. TOLL *sb.*[1] + *seld* seat, or *sele* hall; cf. OE. *tollsetl* 'toll-booth, custom-house'.] = TOLBOOTH 2.

Tolstoyan (tǫ·lstoiˌăn), *a.* and *sb.* Also **Tolstoian.** 1894. [f. proper name *Tolstoy* + -AN.] Of or pertaining to, a follower of, Count Leo N. Tolstoy a famous Russian writer and social reformer (1828–1910).

Tolt (tōᵘlt). 1607. [– AFr. *tolte, toulte* = AL. *tolta*, f. L. *tollere* in sense 'take away', with the form of a sb. from pa. pple.] *Old Law.* A writ by which a cause was removed from a court-baron to the county court.

Tolu (tǫlˈū·, tōᵘ·lˈu). 1671. [f. *Tolu* (now *Santiago de Tolu*) in the United States of Colombia, whence obtained.] In **T. balsam, balsam of T.:** A balsam obtained by incision from the bark of the **T.-tree,** *Myrospermum* (*Myroxylon*) *toluiferum*, a leguminous tree of tropical S. America; used in medicine and perfumery.

Tolu-, the prec. word as a formative element in chemical terms. **To·luate,** a salt of toluic acid, as toluate of calcium, $C_{16}H_{14}CaO_4$. **Toluene** (tōᵘ·liuˌīn), [so named because first obtained by the dry distillation of tolu balsam], C_7H_8 = Benzylic hydride, $C_7H_7.H$, a colourless very mobile strongly refracting liquid, with a smell like benzene and a burning taste. **Toluic** (tōᵘliū·ik) *a.* [*toluene* + -IC], in *toluic* or *tolulic acid*, $C_8H_8O_2$, an aromatic acid, homologous with benzoic acid, prepared from toluene, cymene, or xylene. **To·luides,** compounds homologous with the anilides, derived from toluidine salts by abstraction of water, e.g., *aceto-toluide.* **Tolu·idine,** also called *amidoto·luene*, and formerly *toluylia*, $C_7H_7(NH_2)$, a crystalline base, produced by the action of sulphydric acid on nitrotoluene, solidifying in snow-white crystals, which gradually turn brown on contact with the air. **To·luol,** earlier name of *toluene.* **Toluo·xyl,** C_8H_7O, the radical of toluic acid and its derivatives. **Tolu·ric** *a.*, in *toluric acid*, $C_{10}H_{11}NO_3$, also called *toluglycic acid*, homologous with hippuric acid, produced in the passage of toluic acid through the animal body; its salts are **Tolu·rates. Toluyl** (tōᵘ·liuˌil, -əil), the radical C_8H_9; hence **To·luylene** = STILBENE; **Toluy·lic** *a.*, of or belonging to toluyl.

†**Toluta·tion.** *rare.* 1646. [f. stem of L. *tolutim* adv. 'at a trot' + -ATION.] *prop.* Trotting; but used by Sir T. Browne and others for 'ambling'; in later use only a humorous pedantry –1803.

Tolyl (tǫ·lil, -əil). *Chem.* 1868. [f. TOLU + -YL.] A hypothetical monatomic radical, C_7H_7.

Tolypeutine (tǫlipiū·təin), *a.* and *sb.* 1885. [f. mod.L. *Tolypeutes* + -INE[1].] *Zool.* **A.** *adj.* Belonging to the genus *Tolypeutes* of armadillos. **B.** *sb.* An armadillo of this genus.

Tom (tǫm). late ME. **1.** (With capital T.) A familiar shortening of the Christian name *Thomas*; often a generic name for any male representative of the common people; esp. in *T., Dick,* and *Harry*, any men taken at random from the common run; *Blind T.*, blindman's-buff. †**b.** = *T. o' Bedlam* –1683. **2.** As the name of some exceptionally large bells, esp. in *great, mighty T., T. of Lincoln, T. of Christ Church, of Oxford*, etc. 1630. **3. a.** (usu. *long t.*) A long trough formerly used in gold-washing 1855. **b.** *Long T.*: a long gun; *esp.* a naval gun mounted amidships, as dist. from the shorter guns of the broadside 1867. **4.** *Old T.*: gin (*slang*) 1823. **5.** The male of various beasts and birds; perh. first for a male cat 1791.

Phrases: **T. tower,** a tower in which a great bell hangs; *spec.* at Oxford, the western tower of Christ Church. (*b*) As the first element in a personal name, allus.: **T. Farthing,** a fool, simpleton; **T. Tyler, Tiler,** any ordinary man; also, a hen-pecked husband. (*c*) Followed by another word, forming a *quasi*-proper name or nickname: **T. Long,** one who takes a long time in coming, or in finishing his tale; **T. o' Bedlam,** a madman; a deranged person discharged from Bedlam and licensed to beg.

Tomahawk (tǫ·măhǭk), *sb.* 1634. [– Renâpe (N. Amer. Indian of Virginia) *tämähāk* (given by Capt. J. Smith as *tomahack*), apocopated form of *tämähākan* 'what is used for cutting', from *tämähāken* 'he uses for cutting', from *tämäham* 'he cuts'.] The axe of the N. Amer. Indians, used as a weapon of war and the chase, and also as a tool and agricultural implement; in Eng. use usu. applied to it as the war-axe. **b.** erron. applied to a war-club or knobkerry 1674. **c.** *transf.* Applied to similar weapons used by savages elsewhere; also *Naut.* a pole-axe used by sailors; in Australia, the usual word for *hatchet* 1670.

fig. That age of fierce and savage controversy, of the t. and scalping-knife 1836.

Phrases. *To bury* or *lay aside the t.*, to lay down one's arms, to cease from hostilities. *To dig up, raise*, or *take up the t.*, to commence hostilities.

Tomahawk (tǫ·măhǭk), *v.* 1755. [f. prec.] **1.** *trans.* To strike, cut, or kill with a tomahawk. **2.** *Australia.* To cut (a sheep) in shearing it 1859.

1. *fig.* The book which Thackeray tomahawked 1895.

‖**Tomalley** (tǫmæ·li, tǫmæ·li). 1666. [Said to be a Carib word; cf. Fr. *taumalin.*] The fat or 'liver' of the N. Amer. lobster, which becomes green when cooked, and is then known as *t. sauce.*

‖**Toman**[1] (tomā·n, tu·măn, tǫ·măn). 1566. [– Pers. *tūmān, tumān, tuman*, a Yuzbeg Tartar word, lit. 'ten thousand'.] **1.** Formerly among the Mongols, Tartars, etc., and thence in Persia and Turkey: The sum of ten thousand; also, a military division consisting of 10,000 men. Now *rare.* 1599. **2.** A Persian gold coin, nominally worth 10 silver krans or 10,000 dinars; formerly a money of account, which was constantly depreciated in value 1566.

‖**Toman**[2] (tǫ·măn). 1811. [Gaelic, dim. of *tom* hill.] A hillock; a mound of earth. Often applied to mounds representing ancient glacial moraines, found in the heads of valleys in the Highlands.

Tom and Jerry. 1828. Names of the two chief characters in Egan's *Life in London*, 1821, and its continuation, 1828: whence in various allus. and attrib. uses, esp. as name of a kind of highly-spiced punch (U.S.); and *attrib.* in *Tom and Jerry shop*, a low beer-house.

Tomato (tŏmā·to, U.S. -ēˈ·to). 1604. [Earliest form *tomate* – Fr. *tomate* or Sp., Pg. *tomate* – Mex. *tomatl*; *tomato, tomata*, and *tomatum* were pseudo-Sp. and L. modifications (XVIII).] The glossy fleshy fruit of a solanaceous plant (*Solanum lycopersicum* or *Lycopersicum esculentum*), a native of tropical America, now widely cultivated. It varies when ripe from red to yellow in colour, and greatly in size and shape, the common form being irregularly spheroidal. Formerly called *love-apple*, from supposed aphrodisiac qualities. Also, the plant, an annual with a weak trailing or climbing stem, irregularly pinnate leaves, and yellow flowers resembling those of the potato.

attrib. and *Comb.*, as *t.-ketchup, sauce*; **t. hawk-moth** or **sphinx,** an American sphingid moth, *Protoparce celeus*; **-worm,** the caterpillar of this, which feeds on t. leaves.

Tomb (tūm), *sb.* [ME. *toumbe, tumbe*, – AFr. *tumbe*, (O)Fr. *tombe* :– late L. *tumba* – Gr. τύμβος mound, tomb.] **1.** A place of burial; an excavation in earth or rock for the reception of a dead body, a grave. Also, a chamber or vault formed wholly or partly in the earth, and, in early times, a tumulus or mound raised over the body. **b.** *transf.* and *fig.* 1812. **2.** A monument erected to enclose or cover the body and preserve the memory of the dead; a sepulchral structure raised above the earth. Hence sometimes a cenotaph. Also formerly, a tombstone erected over a grave. ME. **3.** Regarded as the final resting-place of every one; hence occas. used for the state of death 1559. **4.** *R.C.Ch.* A cavity in an altar, where relics are deposited 1886.

1. A t... which was.. believed to contain his bones 1838. **b.** The t. of thy dead self SHELLEY. **2.** To make a Toombe ouer his wiues Graue 1657. **3.** Charity, that glows beyond the t. GRAY.

Tomb (tūm), *v.* Now *rare.* ME. [f. prec.] **1.** *trans.* To deposit (a body) in the tomb; to bury, inter, entomb. **2.** To enclose or contain as a tomb; to serve as a tomb for 1586.

1. In the Atlantic's bed Tombed ten leagues deep 1899. **2.** The Stone that tombs the Two SIDNEY.

Tombac (tǫ·mbæk). 1602. [– Fr. *tombac*, with early variations from Sp. *tumbaga*, Pg. *tambaca* – Malay *tambāga* copper.] An alloy of copper and zinc, in various proportions, containing from 82 to 99 per cent. of copper. Used in the East for gongs or bells; in Europe, under various names, as Prince's metal, Mannheim gold, etc., as a material for cheap jewellery.

To·mb-bat. 1883. A bat of the genus *Taphozous*, family *Emballonuridæ*, which frequent tombs as their dwelling-places.

Tombless (tū·mlės), *a.* 1594. [f. TOMB *sb.* + -LESS.] Having no tomb, destitute of a grave; unburied.

Tombola (tǫ·mbŏlă). 1880. [– Fr. *tombola* or its source It. *tombola*, f. *tombolare* turn a somersault, tumble.] A kind of lottery, esp. for charity.

Tomboy (tǫ·mboi). 1553. [f. TOM *sb.* + BOY *sb.*] †**1.** A rude, boisterous, or forward boy –1599. †**2.** A bold or immodest woman –1700. **3.** A girl who behaves like a spirited or boisterous boy; a wild romping girl 1592.

Tombstone, tomb-stone (tū·mstoᵘn). 1565. A horizontal stone covering a grave; in early use, the cover of a stone coffin, or the stone coffin itself. **b.** A stone or monument of any kind placed over a grave to preserve the memory of the dead; a gravestone; including a headstone. Also *fig.* 1611.

To·mca·t. 1809. [TOM 5.] A male cat.

Tom-cod (tǫ·mˌkǫ·d). 1795. Name for several small fishes. In U.S.: **a.** The frost-fish; also, loosely, one of various small fishes confused with this. **b.** In California, the Jack-fish (*Sebastodes paucispinis*), a rock-fish. **c.** = KINGFISH d. In Great Britain: **d.** A young codfish.

Tome (tōᵘm). 1519. [– Fr. *tome* – L. *tomus* – Gr. τόμος slice, piece, roll of papyrus, volume, rel. to τέμνειν cut.] †**1.** Each of the separate volumes which compose a literary work or book; rarely, one of the largest parts or sections of a single volume –1731. **2.** A book, a volume; now usu. suggesting a large, heavy, old-fashioned book 1573. **3.** A papal letter or epistle. *Hist.* 1788.

-tome[1] (tōᵘm), terminal element (= Fr. *-tome*) repr. Gr. -τόμον, neut. of -τόμος -cutting, in designations of instruments used in the surgical operation expressed by the corresp. word in -TOMY.

-tome[2], terminal element repr. Gr. τομή a cutting, with the meaning 'section', 'segment'.

Tomentose (tōᵘme·ntōᵘs), *a.* 1698. [f. next + -OSE[1].] **1.** *Bot.* Closely covered with down or short hairs; pubescent, downy. **2.** *Ent.* and *Anat.* Flocculent, flossy, woolly 1826. So **Tome·ntous** *a.*

‖**Tomentum** (tome·ntŏm). 1699. [L., stuffing for cushions.] **1.** *Bot.* The soft down or pubescence growing on the stems, leaves, or seeds of certain plants. **2.** *Anat.* A downy covering or investment; *spec.* the flocculent inner surface of the pia mater 1811.

To·m-foo·l. ME. [f. TOM + FOOL *sb.*[1]] **a.** As quasi-proper name, *Tom Fool*: a half-witted man. **b.** One who enacts the part of a fool in the drama, etc.; a buffoon; *spec.* a buffoon who accompanies morris-dancers; also, a butt, laughing-stock 1650. **c.** A foolish or stupid person. (More emphatic than *fool.*) 1721. **d.** *attrib.* (in senses b and c) 1819.

More folks know Tom Fool, than Tom Fool knows 1865. **d.** You may..wear whatever tom-fool costume you like to assume 1879. Hence **Tomfoo·lery,** the action or behaviour of a t.; foolish action; silly trifling; an instance of this.

‖**Tomin** (tomī·n). 1600. [Sp.] A Spanish measure of weight for silver, = 9.26 grains; also, **b.** in Spain and Sp. America, the name of various small silver coins.

‖**Tomium** (tōᵘ·miŏm). *Pl.* **tomia** (-iă). 1834. [mod.L., app. irreg. f. Gr. τομός cutting, sharp, after *cranium*.] *Ornith.* Each of the cutting edges of a bird's bill. Hence **To·mial** *a.* of or pertaining to the tomia or to a t.

Tommy (tǫ·mi). 1783. [dim. or pet form of TOM; see -Y[6].] **1.** With capital T: Familiar form of *Thomas.* **b.** A simpleton. *dial.* 1829. **c.** Short for *T. Atkins* 1893. **2.** A soldiers' name for the brown bread formerly supplied as rations (also *brown t.*); with *a* and *pl.*, a loaf of bread (*dial.*); among workmen, Food, provisions generally, *esp.* those carried with them to work each day 1783. **b.** Goods; *esp.* provisions supplied to workmen under the truck system; also, short for *t.-shop*, and for the truck system 1830.

1. c. A group of Tommies in uniform 1907. **2.** Soft T., or white T.; bread is so called by sailors, to distinguish it from biscuit GROSE.

attrib. and *Comb.*: **T. Atkins,** familiar form of *Thomas Atkins*, as a name for the typical private soldier; see THOMAS 3; hence, *transf.* a private in any army; **T. Dod(d,** the 'odd man' in odd-man-out; **t.-ro·t,** nonsense, bosh, twaddle; **-shop,** a store (esp. one run by the employer) at which vouchers given to employees instead of money wages may be exchanged for goods.

Tom-noddy (tǫmˌnǫ·di). 1702. [f. TOM + NODDY *sb.*[1]] **1.** *local.* The Puffin (*Fratercula arctica*). **2.** A foolish or stupid person 1828.

To-morn (tŭmǭ·ɹn), *adv.* and *sb.* Now *dial.* or *arch.* [ME. *to morwen*, OE. *to morȝenne*, i.e. TO + dat. of *morȝen* MORN, MORROW.] **A.** *adv.* = next A. Revived as poetical archaism *c*1850. **B.** *sb.* = next B. 1. ME.

To-morrow (tŭmǫ·roᵘ), *adv.* and *sb.* [ME. *to mor(e)we*, earlier *to morwen*; see prec. and MORROW.] **A.** *adv.* For or on the day after to-day; for or on the morrow.

Euery day in the weeke it was sayde, he departeth to morwe GRAFTON.

B. *sb.* **1.** The day after this day; the next succeeding day; the morrow. late ME. **2.** *attrib.* with times of the day: *to-morrow morning, afternoon*, etc. The comb. is used both as *sb.* and as *adv.* ME.

1. One to-day is worth two to-morrows FRANKLIN. Phr. *To-morrow come never*, a day that will never arrive; 'on the Greek Kalends'.

†**Tompion** (tǫ·mpiən). 1727. [f. name of Thomas *Tompion* (1639–1713) a noted watch-maker in the reign of Queen Anne.] A watch made by Tompion or of the same type –1871.

Tompion, variant of TAMPION.

Tom Thumb. 1579. [In ref. to diminutive stature.] **1.** A dwarf or pigmy of popular tradition, whose history was common as a chapbook; hence, a name for a dwarf or diminutive male person; also *contempt.* a petty or insignificant person, a pigmy holder of a high position. **2.** *attrib.* Applied to dwarf varieties of animals or plants; also, *ellipt.* or *absol.* as *sb.* **a.** A kind of dwarf oyster. **b.** A dwarf variety of cabbage, lettuce, or other vegetable, of antirrhinum, nasturtium, or other flower. 1876.

Tom Tiddler's ground. Also *dial.* 1823. Name of a children's game, in which one of the players is 'Tom Tiddler', his territory being marked by a line drawn on the ground; over this the other players run, crying 'We're on Tom Tiddler's ground, picking up gold and silver'. **b.** *transf.* Any place where money, etc., is 'picked up' or acquired readily; also, a 'debatable territory, a no man's land between two states' 1848.

Tom-tit, tomtit (tǫmˌti·t). 1709. [See TIT *sb.*[2]] A common name of the Blue Titmouse (*Parus cæruleus*); also *locally* of the Coal Titmouse (*P. ater*), and the American *P. atricapillus*; incorrectly of other small birds, as the Wren, and the Tree-creeper. **b.** *transf.* applied to a little man or boy 1741.

Tom-tom (tǫ·mˌtǫm), *sb.* 1693. [– Hind. *tam tam* (so Fr.); cf. Sinhalese *tamaṭṭama*, Malay *tong tong.*] **1.** A native E. Indian drum; extended also to the drums of barbarous peoples generally. **2.** The beating of a drum; an imitation of the sound of this 1898.

To·m-tom, *v.* 1857. [Partly f. prec., partly imit.] **a.** *intr.* To beat a tom-tom or drum; to drum. **b.** *trans.* To call attention to by beating a tom-tom. **c.** To perform on a tom-tom or drum; *transf.* to play in a monotonous way, to strum.

-tomy, – Gr. -τομια, often through mod.L. *-tomia*, used to form abstract sbs. from adjs. in -τομος cutting; f. ablaut-series τεμ-, τομ-, τμ- in τέμνειν to cut, τομή, τμῆσις cutting.

Ton[1] (tɒn). late ME. [In origin the same word as TUN. Differentiated from *tun c*1688 in the senses hereunder.] †**1.** A large wine-vessel, a cask; hence, a measure of capacity used for wine; now spelt TUN. **2.** A unit used in measuring the carrying capacity or burden of a ship, the amount of cargo, freight, etc. Orig. the space occupied by a tun cask of wine. Now, for the purposes of registered tonnage, the space of 100 cubic feet. For purposes of freight, usu. the space of 40 cubic feet, unless that bulk would weigh more than 20 cwt., in which case freight is charged by weight. late ME. **3.** A measure of capacity: **a.** for timber; usu. = 40 cubic feet (or for hewn timber, 50) 1521. **b.** for various solid commodities, as stone, gravel, lime, plaster, wheat, cheese, etc. late ME. **4.** A measure of weight, now generally 20 cwt.; in Great Britain legally 2240 lbs.; in the United States, for most purposes 2000 lb. *Metric t.* (Fr. *tonne*) = 1000 kilogrammes (2204.6 lbs. avoirdupois). 1485. **b.** *colloq.* A very large amount. Mostly in *pl.* 1895.

3. A pound of goold is worth a tunne of leade 1588. **4. b.** 'Is there any culture at Chicago?'.. 'You bet your sweet life!..Tons of it. 1895.

attrib. and *Comb.*: **t.-fathom,** the equivalent of the work done in raising a t. through the depth of a fathom, as in the shaft of a mine; **-mile,** the same in carrying a t. the distance of a mile, as by a railway-train; **-mileage,** amount of or reckoning in ton-miles, or charge per ton-mile; **t. tight:** see TIGHT *a.* 14.

‖**Ton**[2] (toṅ, †tǫn). Now *rare.* 1769. [Fr., :– L. *tonus* TONE.] The fashion, the vogue, the mode; fashionable air or style. **b.** *transf.* People of fashion; the fashionable world 1815.

None of the London whips of any degree of t. wear wigs now SHERIDAN.

-ton (tən), terminal element of many town-names (repr. unstressed development of OE. *tūn* TOWN), and consequently in many surnames, e.g. *Longton, Somerton*, whence extended to form designations of persons and things, as *simpleton, singleton.* Cf. -BY *suffix* 2 and RUDESBY.

Tonal (tōᵘ·năl), *a.* 1776. [– med.L. *tonalis*, f. L. *tonus* TONE; see -AL[1] 1.] **1.** *Mus.* †**a.** Pertaining to the eccl. modes. **b.** Applied to a fugue or a sequence, in which the repetitions of the subject in different positions are all in the same key, and therefore vary in their intervals 1869. **2.** Of, pertaining to, or relating to the tone or tones. Of speech or a language: expressing difference of meaning by variation of tone 1866. Hence **To·nally** *adv.* in respect of tone.

Tonality (tonæ·līti). 1838. [f. TONAL *a.* + -ITY.] Tonal quality. **1.** *Mus.* The relation, or sum of relations, between the tones or notes of a scale or musical system; *spec.* in modern music, = KEY *sb.* II. 5 c; hence *transf.* a particular scale or system of tones; in modern music = KEY *sb.* II. 5 b. **2.** *Painting.* The quality of a painting in respect of tone; the general tone or colour-scheme of a picture 1866.

To-name (tū·nēᶦm). Now *dial.* [OE. *tōnama*, f. To-¹ + NAME *sb.*] A name or epithet added to an original name; a cognomen, surname, nickname; now in *Sc.* a name added to distinguish one individual from another having the same Christian name and surname.

‖**Tondo** (to·ndo). *Pl.* **tondi** (to·ndi). 1890. [It. 'a round, circle, compass'; shortened from *rotondo* round.] An easel painting of circular form; also, a carving in relief within a circular space.

Tone (tōᵘn), *sb.* ME. [repr. various adoptions of (O)Fr. *ton* or its source L. *tonos* tension, sound, tone – Gr. τόνος with the same senses.] **I. 1.** A musical or vocal sound considered with ref. to its quality, as acute or grave, sweet or harsh, loud or soft, clear or dull. **b.** (without *a* or *pl.*) Quality of sound 1663. **2.** *Mus.* and *Acoustics.* A sound of definite pitch and character produced by regular vibration of a sounding body; a musical note. late ME. †**b.** (without *a* or *pl.*) Pitch of a musical note; correct pitch, 'tune' –1704. **3.** *Mus.* In plainsong, any of the nine psalm-tunes (including the *peregrine t.*), each of which has a particular 'intonation' and 'mediation' and a number of different 'endings'; commonly called *Gregorian tones* 1776. **4.** *Mus.* One of the larger intervals between successive notes of the diatonic scale; a major second; sometimes called *whole t.*, as opp. to *semitone* 1609. **5.** A particular quality, pitch, modulation, or inflexion of the voice expressing or indicating affirmation, interrogation, hesitation, decision, or some feeling or emotion; vocal expression 1610. **b.** The distinctive quality of voice in the pronunciation of words, peculiar to an individual, locality, or nation; an 'accent' 1680. **c.** Intonation; †*esp.* a special, affected, or artificial intonation in speaking 1687. **d.** *transf.* A particular style in discourse or writing, which expresses the person's sentiment or reveals his character 1765. **6.** *Phonetics.* **a.** A word-accent; a rising, falling, or compound inflexion, by which words otherwise of the same sound are distinguished, as in ancient Greek, modern Chinese, and other languages 1763. **b.** The stress accent (Fr. *accent tonique*) on a syllable of a word; the stressed or accented syllable 1874.

1. Harmonie Divine So smooths her charming tones, that Gods own ear Listens delighted MILT. **2.** *Difference-t.* (or *differential t.*), *summation-t.* (or *summational t.*), the secondary or resultant tones produced when two notes of different pitch are sounded together with sufficient force, having rates of vibration equal respectively to the difference and the sum of those of the primary tones. *Fundamental, partial,* (etc.) *t.*: see the adjs. **5.** She asked in a t. of displeasure, who was there? 1796. **b.** The t. and accent remained broadly Scotch LOCKHART. **d.** His book..is bright and joyous in t. 1866.

II. 1. *Physiol.* The degree of firmness or tension proper to the organs or tissues of the body in a strong and healthy condition 1669. †**2.** A state or temper of mind; mood, disposition –1820. **3.** A special or characteristic style or tendency of thought, feeling, action, etc.; *esp.* the character of the prevailing state of morals or manners in a society or community 1635.

1. Of sovereign efficacy in restoring debilitated stomachs to their proper t. 1780. **2.** A philosophical t., or temper 1744. A healthful t. of mind and spirits W. IRVING. **3.** The t. of the market is..dull 1884.

III. The prevailing effect of the combination of light and shade, and of the general scheme of colouring, in a painting, building, etc. 1816. **b.** A quality of colour; a tint; *spec.* the degree of luminosity of a colour; shade 1821.

attrib. and *Comb.*: **t.-arm,** the tubular arm connecting the sound-box of a gramophone to the horn; **-colour** (after G. *tonfarbe*), timbre; **-painting,** the employment of tone and esp. tone-colours in creating musical effects; so **-painter**; **-picture,** a musical composition, usu. for orchestra, characterized by pictorial suggestion; **-poem** [G. *tondichtung*], (*a*) an orchestral composition illustrating or translating a poetic idea; (*b*) a painting in which the tones are harmonized poetically; so **-poet, -poetry; -syllable,** the stressed syllable.

Tone (tōᵘn), *v.* ME. [f. prec.] **I.** †**1.** *trans. Mus.* To sound with the proper tone or musical quality –1570. **2.** *intr.* To issue forth in musical tones (*rare*) 1447. **3.** *trans.* To utter with a musical sound, or in a special or affected tone; to intone 1660.

II. To alter or modify the tone or general colouring of; to give the desired tone to; *spec.* to cover (a painting) with oil or varnish so as to soften the colouring; to alter the tint of (a photograph) in the process of finishing it. Also *absol.* 1859. **b.** *intr.* To receive or assume a tone, tint, or shade of colour; *esp.* in *Photogr.* 1868. **c.** To harmonize *with* in colouring 1880.

III. *trans.* To impart a tone to (in various senses of the sb.); to modify, regulate, or adjust the tone or quality of; to give physical or mental tone to, to brace 1811. **b.** *T. down,* to lower the tone, quality, or character of; to soften. *T. up,* to raise or improve the tone of, to give a higher or stronger tone to. 1860. **c.** *intr.* for *pass. T. down,* to become lowered, weakened, or softened in tone; *t. up,* to rise or improve in tone 1850.

Your mind is properly toned by these influences 1871. **b.** Some remedy that will tone-up the nervous system 1896. **c.** Public excitement with respect to Russia has considerably toned down 1885.

Toned (tōᵘnd), *ppl. a.* and *adj.* 1460. **A.** *ppl. a.* [f. prec. + -ED¹.] **1. a.** Sounded with the proper, or a specified, tone. **b.** Of body or mind: Brought into tone; braced, strung 1742. **2.** Slightly or finely coloured or shaded; tinted 1864. **b.** *Photogr.* Treated with chemicals so as to acquire the desired tone or shade of colour 1861.

1. b. A human being whose mind was quite as firmly toned at eighty as at forty MACAULAY. **2.** *T. paper,* paper which is not quite white, but cream-coloured or slightly buff.

B. *adj.* [f. TONE *sb.* + -ED².] In comb.: Having a tone (in various senses) of a specified kind or quality; e.g. *deep-, high-, low-t.* 1790.

Toneless (tōᵘ·nlės), *a.* 1773. [f. TONE *sb.* + -LESS.] Destitute of tone, in various senses. Hence **To·neless-ly** *adv.*, **-ness.**

Tong (tǫŋ). 1918. [Chinese *t'ang* hall, meeting-place.] A Chinese secret society. Murder by order of a t. 1928.

‖**Tonga**¹ (tǫ·ŋgă). India. 1874. [– Hindi *tāngā.*] A light and small two-wheeled carriage or cart used in India.

‖**Tonga**² (tǫ·ŋgă). 1880. [Arbitrary.] A drug extracted from the root of the Fijian plant *Epipremnum pinnatum,* used by the natives of Fiji as a remedy for neuralgia; also known in England and America.

Tongrian (tǫ·ŋgriăn), *a.* 1883. [f. *Tongres,* in Belgium, where developed + -IAN.] *Geol.* Name for marine strata of the Lower Oligocene of Belgium.

Tongs (tǫŋz), *sb. pl.* [OE. *tang* and *tange,* corresp. to OFris. *tange,* OS. *tanga,* OHG. *zanga* (Du. *tang,* G. *zange*), ON. *tǫng* (:– **tanguz*) :– Gmc. **tang* :– IE. **dank-,* repr. also by Gr. δάκνειν bite, Skr. *daṃś.*] An implement consisting of two limbs or 'legs' connected by a hinge, pivot, or spring, by means of which their lower ends are brought together, so as to grasp and take up objects which it is impossible or inconvenient to lift with the hand. Used formerly in sing., now always in pl. with pl. or (chiefly Sc.) sing. concord. *Pair of t.* is used when qualification by a numeral or an indef. article is necessary. **b.** Used in burlesque music 1590. **c.** Often short for *curling-t., sugar-t.,* etc. 1713. **d.** In various transf. and techn. applications. late ME.

Phr. *Not to touch with a pair of t.,* expressing repugnance to have anything to do with. **b.** I haue a reasonable good eare in musicke. Let us haue the tongs and the bones. SHAKS.

Tongue (tʊŋ), *sb.* [OE. *tunge* = OFris. *tunge,* OS. *tunga,* OHG. *zunga* (Du. *tong,* G. *zunge*), ON. *tunga,* Goth. *tuggō* :– Gmc. **tuŋgōn,* rel. to L. *lingua* – **dingua.*] **I. 1.** An organ, possessed by man and most vertebrates, occupying the floor of the mouth, and attached at its base to the hyoid bone; often protrusible and freely movable. In its development in man and the higher mammals, it is tapering, blunt-tipped, muscular, soft and fleshy, important in taking in and swallowing food, also as the principal organ of taste, and in man of articulate speech. **b.** In ref. to invertebrate animals, applied to organs or parts of the mouth having some analogy to the tongue of vertebrates 1753. **c.** Erron. regarded as the 'stinging organ' 1581. **2.** A figure or representation of this organ ME. **3.** The tongue of an animal as an article of food; *esp.* an OX-TONGUE or NEAT'S TONGUE. late ME.

1. I had rather haue this t. cut from my mouth SHAKS. Phr. *To put one's t. out,* to protrude the tongue either for medical inspection or as a grimace. **c.** *Much Ado* V. i. 90. **2.** And tungis dyuersely partid as fyer apperiden to hem WYCLIF *Acts* 2:3. The classical 'egg and t.' and 't. and dart' patterns 1886.

II. In ref. to speech. **1.** Considered as the principal organ of speech; hence, the faculty of speech; voice, speech; words, language OE. **2.** The action of speaking; speech, talking, utterance, voice; also, what is spoken or uttered; words, talk, discourse OE. **b.** Speech as dist. from or contrasted with thought, action, or fact. late ME. †**c.** A 'voice', vote, suffrage. SHAKS. †**d.** Eulogy, fame. FLETCHER. **3.** Manner of speaking or talking, with regard to the sense or import of what is said, the mode of expression or form of words used, or the sound of the voice 1460. **4.** Of a dog. **a.** In phrases: *To give t., to throw (its) t.,* prop. of a hound: to give forth its voice when on the scent or in sight of the quarry. Also *transf.* of persons. 1737. **b.** Hence, the hunting-cry or 'music' of a hound in pursuit of game 1787. **5.** The speech or language of a people or race; also, that of a particular class or locality OE. **b.** *The tongues,* foreign languages; often *spec.* the classical or learned languages 1535. **c.** The knowledge or use of a language; esp. in phrases *gift of tongues, to speak with a t.* (*tongues*), in ref. to the Pentecostal miracle and the miraculous gift in the early Church 1526. **6.** *transf.* in biblical use: A people or nation having a language of their own. Usu. in pl.: *all tongues,* people of every tongue. late ME.

1. This our life..Findes tongues in trees, bookes in the running brookes SHAKS. I would..give him a lick with the rough side of my t. SCOTT. Vather'll..call ee everything he can lay his t. to 1899. Phr. *To hold one's t.,* to refrain from speech, keep silence, say nothing. *To put,* or *speak with, one's t. in one's cheek,* to speak insincerely. So, *to stick* (or *thrust*) *one's t. in one's cheek,* as a gesture of contemptuous or sly humour. *To keep a civil t. in one's head,* to avoid rudeness. *To have lost one's t.,* to be too bashful or sulky to speak; Have you lost your t., Jack? DICKENS. So *to find one's t.,* to speak after a period of shyness or sullenness. **5.** To speak all Tongues, and do all Miracles MILT. **6.** I wil come to gather all people and tonges COVERDALE *Isa.* 66:18.

III. Anything that resembles or suggests the human or animal tongue by its shape, position, function, or use; a tapering, projecting, or elongated object or part, esp. when mobile, or attached at one end or side. **1.** Any tongue-like part or organ of the human or animal body. †*T. of the throat,* the uvula. late ME. **2.** (Cf. *t.-fish.*) A young or small-sized sole 1825. **3.** A tongue-like projecting piece of anything. **a.** A narrow strip of land, running into the sea, or between two branches of a river, or two other lands; also, a narrow inlet of water running into the land, etc. 1566. **b.** A narrow and deep part of the current of a river, running smoothly and rapidly between rocks 1891. **c.** A tapering jet of flame 1797. **4.** *techn.* **a.** The pin of a buckle or brooch ME. **b.** The pointer of a balance; also of a dial. late ME. **c.** = REED II. 3 a. c. 1551. **d.** The clapper of a bell; hence, the pistil or a stamen of a bell-flower 1577. **e.** The pole of a wagon or other vehicle

1591. **f.** A projecting tenon along the edge of a board, to be inserted into a groove or mortise in the edge of another board; in *Mech.* a projecting flange, rib, or strip for any purpose 1842. **g.** A short piece of rope spliced into the upper part of the standing backstays, etc. 1815. **h.** The wedge-shaped or tapered end of a scion in grafting 1832. **i.** The tapered end of a pole, etc., by which it is fixed in a socket 1815. **j.** A projecting piece of leather or the like forming a tab or flap; the strip of thin leather closing the opening in a laced or buttoned shoe or boot 1597. **k.** The movable tapered piece of rail in a railway switch 1841.

Comb.: **t.-bird,** local name of the wryneck, from its long retractile t.; **-bit,** a bridle bit having a plate attached so as to prevent the horse from putting his t. over the mouthpiece; **-bone,** the hyoid bone; **-fence,** argument, debate; **-fish,** the sole; **-grafting,** whip or splice grafting, in which a thin wedge-shaped t. of the scion is fitted into a cleft in the stock; **-pipe,** a reed-pipe in an organ or similar instrument; **-shaped,** *a.* shaped like a t.; linguiform; **-shell,** a brachiopod of the family *Lingulidæ*; **-test,** a test of the existence or strength of an electric current by applying the t. to a break in the circuit; **-twister,** something said to twist the t.; *spec.* a sequence of words, often alliterative, difficult to articulate quickly; **-worm,** *(a)* a pentastom; *(b)* the 'worm' of the t. in dogs; = LYTTA.

Tongue (tɒŋ), *v.* late ME. [f. prec.] **1.** *trans.* To assail with words; to reproach, scold; to discuss or talk about injuriously. **2.** *intr.* To use the tongue, talk, speak; *esp.* to talk volubly, to prate 1624. **b.** Of a hound: To give tongue 1832. **3.** *trans.* To utter or turn *over* with the tongue; to say 1611. **4.** To touch with the tongue 1687. **5.** *intr.* To project as a protruding tongue (of ice); to throw out tongues (of flame) 1814. **6.** *trans.* To furnish with a tongue (*lit.* or *fig.*) **a.** To give a speaking tongue or utterance to 1602. **b.** *(a)* To cut a tongue on (a plank, etc.). *(b)* To slit or shape a tongue in (a plant-stem or shoot) for grafting or layering 1733. **c.** To join or fit together by means of a tongue and groove or tongue and socket 1823.

1. *Meas. for M.* IV. iv. 28. **3.** 'Tis still a Dreame; or else such stuffe as Madmen T., and braine not SHAKS.

Tongued (tɒŋd), *a.* (*ppl. a.*) late ME. [f. TONGUE *sb.* or *v.* + -ED.] Having or furnished with a tongue or tongues (in various senses).

Nosd like a Goose, and toungd like a woman 1611. Reeded and t. instruments 1854. Grooved and T. Flooring Boards 1883.

Tongueless (tɒ·ŋlės), *a.* late ME. [See -LESS.] **1.** Having no tongue, without a tongue. **2.** Without the faculty of voice or speech, dumb, mute; also, without speaking, speechless, silent 1447. **b.** Said of things 1593. †**3.** Not spoken of. SHAKS.

2. b. Euen from the toonglesse cauernes of the earth SHAKS. **3.** One good deed, dying tonguelesse, Slaughters a thousand, wayting vpon that SHAKS.

Tonguelet (tɒ·ŋlėt). 1840. [f. TONGUE *sb.* + -LET.] A little tongue or tongue-like object; *spec.* **a.** = LIGULA 1 b.; **b.** = *tongue-worm (a).*

Tongue-tie (tɒ·ŋtəi), *sb.* 1641. [f. TONGUE *sb.* + TIE *sb.*] That which ties the tongue, or restrains speech; also, the condition of being tongue-tied (*lit.* and *fig.*).

Tongue-tie, abnormal shortness of the frænum linguæ, or adhesion of the tongue to the floor of the mouth 1890.

Tongue-tie (tɒ·ŋtəi), *v.* 1555. [prob. a back-formation from next.] *trans.* To tie or confine the tongue of; to restrain or debar from speaking; to render speechless.

Tongue-tied (tɒ·ŋtəid), *ppl. a.* 1529. [f. TONGUE *sb.* + TIED *ppl. a.*] Tied as to or in the tongue. **1.** Having the frænum of the tongue too short, so that its movement is impeded or confined; incapable of distinct utterance from this cause; also, unable to speak, dumb (*poet.*) 1530. **2.** *fig.* Restrained or debarred from speaking or free expression from any cause; dumb, silent; also, reticent, reserved 1529.

2. Criticks be tongue-ti'd, stand, admire 1640.

Tonguey (tɒ·ŋi), *a.* late ME. [f. TONGUE *sb.* + -Y[1].] **1.** Full of 'tongue' or talk; loquacious (now *U.S.* and *dial.*); of hounds, 'giving tongue'. **2.** Of the nature of the tongue; produced or modified by the tongue; lingual 1859.

1. A very t. Yankee lawyer 1836.

Tonguing (tɒ·ŋiŋ), *vbl. sb.* 1682. [f. TONGUE *v.* + -ING[1].] The action of TONGUE *v.*; *spec.* in playing the flute and other wind instruments: the use of the tongue to produce certain effects.

Tonic (tǫ·nik), *a.* and *sb.* 1649. [– Fr. *tonique* (XVI) – Gr. τονικός of or for stretching, f. τόνος TONE; see -IC.] **A.** *adj.* **1.** *Phys.* and *Path.* Pertaining to, consisting in, or producing tension; *esp.* in relation to the muscles. **b.** Pertaining to, or maintaining, the tone or normal healthy condition of the tissues or organs 1684. **2.** *Med.*, etc. Having the property of increasing or restoring the tone or healthy condition and activity of the system or organs; strengthening, invigorating, bracing 1756. **3.** *Mus.* Formerly applied to the key-note of a composition (*t. note*), now called simply *tonic* (see B. 2); now, Pertaining to or founded upon the tonic or key-note 1760. **4.** Pertaining or relating to tone or accent in speech; indicating or bearing the tone or accent of spoken words or syllables; characterized by distinctions of tone or accent 1859.

1. *T. contraction,* continuous muscular contraction without relaxation. *T. convulsion* or *spasm,* one characterized by such contraction (opp. to CLONIC). **2.** T. bitters 1800. **3.** *T. chord,* a chord having the tonic for its root. *T. pedal,* the tonic sustained as a PEDAL. *T. sol-fa,* a system of teaching music, esp. vocal music, in which the seven notes of the ordinary major scale in any key are sung to syllables written *doh, ray, me, fah, soh, la, te* (modification of the older *do, re, mi, fa, sol, la, si*), and indicated in the notation by the initials d, r, m, etc.; *doh* always denoting the tonic or key-note, and the remaining syllables indicating the relation to it of the other notes of the scale. **4.** *T. accent* (= Fr. *accent tonique*), the stress-accent of a word.

B. *sb.* **1.** *Med.* A tonic medicine, application, or agent 1799. **b.** *fig.* A bracing influence 1840. **2.** *Mus.* = KEY-NOTE 1. 1806.

1. b. The t. of a wholesome pride CLOUGH. **2.** *T. major* or *minor,* that key (major or minor) which has the same key-note as a given key (minor or major). Hence **To·nic,** *v. trans.* to act as a t. upon, to 'brace up'; to administer a t. to. So †**To·nical** *a.* in senses 1, 1 b, 4; **-ally** *adv.*

Tonicity (toni·sĭti). 1824. [f. prec. + -ITY.] Tonic quality or condition; the property of possessing tone; the normal state of elastic tension of living muscles, arteries, etc., by which the tone of the organs is maintained. **b.** Of spasm: see TONIC *a.* 1. 1897.

To-night (tŭnəi·t), *adv.* and *sb.* [OE. *tō niht,* TO + NIGHT.] **A.** *adv.* **1.** On this very night (i.e. the night now present) ME. **b.** On any night (as contrasted with the next day) 1500. **2.** On the night following this day OE. **3.** Last night. *Obs.* exc. *dial.* ME.

1. T. I saw the sun set TENNYSON. **2.** Duncan comes here to Night SHAKS. **3.** I dreampt a dreame to night SHAKS.

B. *sb.* This night, or the night after this day ME.

Tonish, tonnish (tǫ·niʃ), *a.* Now *rare.* 1778. [f. TON[2] + -ISH[1].] Having 'ton'; fashionable, modish, stylish.

Tonite (tōᵘ·nəit). 1881. [f. L. *tonare* to thunder + -ITE[1] 4a.] A high explosive composed of pulverized gun-cotton impregnated with barium nitrate; cotton powder.

Tonitrual (toni·tru,ăl), *a. rare.* 1693. [– L. *tonitrualis,* f. *tonitrus* thunder; see -AL[1] 1.] Pertaining to, or loaded with, thunder. So **Toni·truous** *a.* thundery (*lit.* and *fig.*).

Tonk (tǫŋk), *v.* 1910. [imit.] *trans.* To strike vigorously. So **Tonk** *sb.*

‖**Tonka** (tǫ·ŋkă). 1796. [Negro name in Guiana of the bean.] **1. Tonka bean:** the black, fragrant, almond-shaped seed of a large leguminous tree, *Dipterix odorata,* of Brazil, Guiana, and adjacent regions, used for scenting snuff, and as an ingredient in perfumes. Also the tree itself. **2. Tonka-bean** (or *Tonga-bean*) **wood,** the wood of *Alyxia buxifolia,* a Tasmanian evergreen shrub, also called *Tonquin Bean-tree*; scent-wood 1862.

Tonnage (tɒ·nėdʒ), *sb.* Also **tunnage.** late ME. [In sense 1 – OFr. *tonnage,* AL. *tonnagium* (XIII), f. *tonne* TUN; in other senses f. TON *sb.*[1] + -AGE.] **I.** Charge, duty, or payment of so much per ton or tun. **1.** *Eng. Hist.* A tax or duty formerly levied upon wine imported in tuns or casks, at the rate of so much for every tun. Commonly in association with *poundage.* †**2.** A charge for the hire of a ship of so much a ton (of her burden) per week or month –1587. **3.** A charge or payment per ton on cargo or freight; e.g. that payable at any port or wharf, or on a canal 1617. **II.** Carrying capacity, weight, etc., in tons. **1.** The carrying capacity of a ship expressed in tons of 100 cubic feet (see TON[1] 2) 1718. **2.** *transf.* Ships collectively, shipping (in relation to their carrying capacity, or together with the merchandise carried by them) 1633. **3. a.** Weight in tons (*rare*) 1793. **b.** Weight of (iron or other heavy merchandise) in the market 1898. **4.** Mode of reckoning the ton of cargo for freightage 1913.

1. *Under-deck t.* the cubic content of the space under the t.-deck; this with the addition of the contents of all enclosed spaces above this deck gives the *gross t.*; the deduction from the latter of the space occupied by the quarters of the crew, and that taken up in a steamer by the engines, boilers, etc., gives the *register t.*, for which vessels are registered, and on which the assessment of dues and charges on shipping is based. *Dead-weight t.* (or *carrying capacity*), occas. applied to the number of tons of 20 cwt. that a ship will carry laden to her load-line. *Displacement t.*, the number of tons of water displaced by a ship when thus loaded, used in England in stating the tonnage of men-of-war since *c* 1870. **2.** If the additional T. does not arrive tomorrow, I shall settle to leave behind the veteran battalion or the 36th WELLINGTON.

attrib. and *Comb.*: **t.-deck,** in a ship, the second deck from below in all vessels of two or more decks; the only deck in a vessel of one deck; **t.-displacement** = displacement t. Hence **To·nnage** *v. trans.* to impose t. upon; to have a t. of (so much).

‖**Tonneau** (tǫ·nōᵘ). 1901. [Fr., spec. application of *tonneau* cask, tun.] Name for the rounded rear body of a motor-car (orig. with the door at the back).

Tonner (tɒ·nəɹ). 1883. [f. TON[1] + -ER[1].] In comb. with prefixed numeral: A vessel of (so many) tons burden.

Tono- (tǫno), repr. Gr. τονο-, comb. form of τόνος stretching, tension, TONE, as in **To·nograph** [-GRAPH], a recording tonometer. **To·nophant** [Gr. -φάντης one who shows], a device whereby acoustic vibrations are rendered visible.

Tonometer (tonǫ·mĭtəɹ). 1725. [f. TONO- + -METER.] **1.** *Mus.* An instrument for determining the pitch of tones; *spec.* a tuning-fork, or a graduated set of tuning-forks, for determining the exact number of vibrations per second which produce a given tone. **2.** An instrument for measuring *(a)* tension of the eyeball in glaucoma 1876, *(b)* intravascular blood-pressure 1898, *(c)* strains within a liquid 1909. Hence **Tonome·tric** *a.* of or pertaining to tonometry. **Tono·metry,** the using of a t.; measurement of vibrations of sound or of tension.

Tonsil (tǫ·nsĭl), usu. in pl. **tonsils** (tǫ·nsĭlz). 1601. [– Fr. *tonsilles* (Paré) or L. *tonsillæ* pl.] **1.** Each of two oval lymphoid glands situated one on each side of the fauces between the anterior and posterior arches. **2.** Each of the two lobes of the cerebellum; also called *amygdala* 1891.

†**To·nsile,** *a.* 1664. [– L. *tonsilis,* f. *tons-,* pa. ppl. stem of *tondere* shear; see -ILE.] That may be clipped or shorn –1878.

Tonsillar (tǫ·nsilăɹ), *a.* 1831. [f. TONSIL + -AR[1].] Of or pertaining to the tonsils; affected by the tonsils, as a *t. voice.* So **To·nsillary** *a.*

Tonsillectomy (tǫnsil,e·ktŏmi). 1901. [f. as next + -ECTOMY.] Surgical excision of the tonsils. So **Tonsille·ctome** (see -TOME[1]).

Tonsillitis (tǫnsiləi·tis). 1801. [f. L. *tonsilla* + -ITIS.] *Path.* Inflammation of the tonsils. Hence **Tonsilli·tic** *a.* affected with t.

Tonsillo·tomy. 1881. [f. as prec. + -TOMY.] = TONSILLECTOMY. **Tonsi·llotome.**

Tonsor (tǫ·nsǫɹ). 1656. [– L. *tonsor,* f. *tons-*; see next, -OR 2.] A barber.

Tonsorial (tǫnsōᵊ·riăl), *a.* 1813. [f. L. *tonsorius,* f. *tonsor* barber, f. *tons-*; see next,

-AL¹ 1.] Of or pertaining to a barber or his work; often used joc., as a 't. artist'.

Tonsure (tǫ·nʃəɹ, tǫ·nsiŭɹ), *sb.* late ME. [– (O)Fr. *tonsure* or L. *tonsura*, f. *tons-*, pa. ppl. stem of *tondere* shear, clip.] **1.** *gen.* The action or process of clipping the hair or shaving the head; the state of being shorn. **2.** *spec.* The shaving of the head or part of it as a religious practice or rite, esp. as a preparation to entering the priesthood or a monastic order. late ME. **b.** The part of a priest's or monk's head left bare by shaving the hair. late ME. †**3.** The clipping (*a*) of coin; (*b*) of shrubs or hedges (*rare*) –1691. Hence **To·nsure** *v. trans.* to clip or shave the hair of; to confer the ecclesiastical t. upon.

Tonsured (tǫ·nʃəɹd, tǫ·nsiŭɹd), *ppl. a.* 1706. [f. TONSURE *v.* + -ED¹.] **1.** That has received tonsure; hence, in orders. **b.** *fig.* Bald or partially bald 1855. **2.** Clipped, as a yew or box (*rare*) 1837.

1. The cowled and t. Middle Age M. ARNOLD.

Tontine (tǫntī·n), *sb.* (*a.*) 1765. [– Fr. *tontine*, f. name of Lorenzo *Tonti*, a Neapolitan banker, who initiated the scheme in France *c* 1653.] A financial scheme by which the subscribers to a loan or common fund receive each an annuity during his life, which increases as their number is diminished by death, till the last survivor enjoys the whole income; also applied to the share or right of each survivor.

This gentlewoman had ventured 300 livres in each T. and in the last year of her life she had for her annuity..about 3600 *l.* a year 1791.

B. *adj.* (or *attrib.* use of the sb.) Of, pertaining to, or of the nature of a tontine 1824.

‖**Tonus** (tōᵘ·nɒs). 1876. [L. – Gr. τόνος TONE.] *Physiol.* and *Path.* **1.** The condition or state of muscular tone; tonicity. **2.** A tonic spasm 1891.

†**To·ny,** *sb. slang.* 1654. [A particular application of *Tony*, short for *Antony*.] A foolish person; a simpleton –1784.

Tony (tōᵘ·ni), *a.* orig. *U.S.* and *Colonial. colloq.* 1886. [f. TONE *sb.* + -Y¹.] High-toned, stylish; 'swell'.

Too (tū), *adv.* OE. [Stressed form of To *prep.*, which in XVI began to be spelt *too.*] **1.** In addition; furthermore, besides, also. (Not now used, exc. in U.S., at the beginning of a clause.) **2.** In excess; more than enough; overmuch, superfluously, superabundantly OE. **3.** As a mere intensive: Excessively, extremely, exceedingly, very. (Now chiefly an emotional colloquialism.) ME. **4.** Reduplicated for emphasis: *too too* 1489. **b.** as *adj.* Excessive, extreme; extremely good, highly exquisite. (*affected.*) 1891.

1. Prettie and wittie; wilde, and yet t. gentle SHAKS. **2.** One that lou'd not wisely, but t. well SHAKS. Men of Letters know t. much to make good Husbands STEELE. At best a blunderer and t. probably a traitor MACAULAY. **3.** 'We shall see you at dinner perhaps'..'I shall be too happy', replied Noel 1825. **4.** Oh that this t. t. solid Flesh would melt SHAKS. **b.** My frocks are too too! 1893.

Special collocations. *T. much* (as predicate), more than can be endured, intolerable; also *t. much of a good thing. T. much for*, more than a match for; so *t. many for, t. hard for*, etc. (chiefly *colloq.*). *But t..., only t.*: here *t.* is app. = 'more than is desirable', or 'more than is or might be expected', while *but* or *only* app. emphasizes the exclusion of any different quality or state of things such as might be desired or expected. *Only t.* in recent use, is often a mere intensive, = 'extremely'. *None too*..is used by meiosis for 'not quite..enough', 'somewhat insufficiently'. *Quite t...*: see QUITE 4.

Tool (tūl), *sb.* [OE. *tōl* = ON. *tól* (n. pl.) :– Gmc. **tōwlam*, f. **tōw-* **tāw-*, whence **tāwjan* prepare; see TAW *v.*, -EL¹.] **1.** 'Any instrument of manual operation' (J.); a mechanical implement for working upon something, as by cutting, striking, rubbing, or other process, in any manual art or industry; usu., one held in and operated directly by the hand, but including also certain simple machines, as the lathe. See also EDGE-TOOL. **b.** A weapon of war, *esp.* a sword. *arch.* late ME. **c.** *spec.* in techn. use: (*a*) *Bookbinding.* A small stamp or roller used for impressing an ornamental design upon leather book-covers 1727. (*b*). A large kind of chisel 1815. (*c*) A generic name for any kind of paint-brush used by house-painters or decorators 1859. **2.** *fig.* Anything used in the manner of a tool; a means of effecting something; an instrument OE. **b.** A bodily organ; *spec.* the male generative organ. Now *arch.* or *slang.* 1553. **3.** *fig.* A person who is, or allows himself to be, made a mere instrument by another; a cat's-paw 1663. **b.** (esp. qualified by *poor* or the like.) An unskilful workman; a shiftless person. *slang* or *dial.* 1700. **4.** *Bookbinding.* (*transf.* from 1 c (*a*).) A tooled design on a book-cover 1881.

1. b. Draw thy toole, here comes of the house of Mountagues SHAKS. **2.** They..make use of Similitudes..and other tooles of Oratory HOBBES. **3.** The sheriffs were the tools of the government MACAULAY.

Comb.: **t.-box,** *spec.* the steel box in which the cutting t. of a planing or other machine is clamped; **-post,** an upright piece in the t.-rest of a lathe, with a slot and a screw for holding the cutting-t.; **-rest,** a part of a lathe serving to support a hand-t., or to hold a mechanical t. in place; **-stock** = *t.-post.*

Tool, *v.* 1812. [f. prec.] **1.** *trans.* To work or shape with a tool; *spec.* to smooth the surface of a building stone with the chisels called 'tools' 1815. **b.** *Bookbinding.* To impress an ornamental design upon the binding of (a book) with a special tool 1836. **c.** *intr.* To work with a tool or tools 1890. **2.** *slang.* **a.** *trans.* To drive (a team of horses, a vehicle, or a person in a vehicle); of a horse, to draw (a person) in a vehicle 1812. **b.** *intr.* To drive, to travel in a horse-drawn vehicle; also said of the vehicle or team; hence, to travel, go *along* 1839.

1. Aluminium..is ductile, but difficult to t. 1895. **2. a.** He could t. a coach LYTTON. **b.** Went to Ascot..and we 'tooled' down in very good style 1893.

Tooled (tūld), *ppl. a.* 1815. [f. prec. + -ED¹.] Worked or shaped with a t.; *spec.* in *Bookbinding.*

Tooling (tū·liŋ), *vbl. sb.* 1815. [f. as prec. + -ING¹.] The action of TOOL *v.*; *spec.* **a.** The dressing of stone with a broad chisel. **b.** *Bookbinding.* The impressing of ornamental designs upon the covers of books by means of heated tools or stamps; also applied to the designs so formed: either with gilding (*gold-* or *gilt-t.*) or without it (*blind-t.*) 1821.

Toom (tūm; in mod. Sc. tōm, tüm), *a.* Now only *Sc.* and *n. dial.* [OE. *tōm* = ON. *tómr*; also OS. *tōm(i*, OHG. *zuomig*; f. Gmc. **tōm-*, see TEEM *v.*²] Empty (*lit.* and *fig.*); destitute (*of* something).

Toom, *v. Sc.* and *n. dial.* 1500. [f. prec., repl. earlier TEEM *v.*²] **1.** *trans.* To empty (a vessel, etc.); *esp.* to drink off the contents of. **2.** To empty out (water, the contents of a vessel, etc.) 1535.

‖**Toon, tun** (tūn). *India.* 1810. [– Hindi *tun, tūn*, Skr. *tunna.*] An E. Indian tree, *Cedrela toona*, which yields a timber resembling mahogany but softer and lighter; the wood of this tree, also called *Indian mahogany.*

Toon, obs. f. TONE, TUN; dial. f. TOWN.

Toot (tūt), *sb.* 1461. [f. TOOT *v.*²] An act of tooting; a note or short blast of a horn, trumpet, etc.

Toot (tūt), *v.*¹ Now *dial.* [OE. *tōtian* (once, K. Ælfred).] **1.** *intr.* To protrude, stick *out*, 'peep *out*', so as to be seen. **2.** *intr.* To peep, peer, look out; to gaze ME. **b.** To pry. late ME.

2. b. With bowe and bolts..For birds in bushes tooting SPENSER.

Toot (tūt), *v.*² 1510. [prob. – MLG. *tūten*, unless a parallel imit. formation.] **I.** *intr.* **1.** To sound or blow a horn or the like 1549. **2.** Of a wind-instrument: To give forth its characteristic sound; to sound 1510. **3.** Of an animal: To make a sound likened to that of a horn, etc.; to trumpet as an elephant, bray as an ass; *spec.* of grouse, to 'call' 1817.

1. Tooting with their Trumpets, and beating with their Drums 1698. **3.** The storm-cock touts on his towering pine HOGG.

II. *trans.* **1.** To cause (a horn, etc.) to sound by blowing it. Also *transf.* of an animal. 1682. **2.** To sound (notes, a tune, etc.) on a horn, pipe, or the like 1614. **3.** To call out aloud, to shout (something) 1582.

2. With eight Trumpeters tooting the Dead March in Saul BARHAM. Hence **Too·ter,** one who or that which toots.

Tooth (tūþ), *sb. Pl.* **teeth** (tīþ). [OE. *tōþ*, pl. *tēþ* = OFris. *tōth*, OS. (Du.) *tand*, OHG. *zan* (G. *zahn*), also *zand*, ON. *tǫnn* :– Gmc. **tanþuz*, beside Goth. *tunþus*; CIE. **dont-* **dent-* **dn̥t* is repr. by L. *dens, dent-*, Gr. ὀδών, ὀδούς, ὀδοντ-, Skr. *dán, dánt-.*] **1.** *pl.* The hard processes within the mouth, attached in a row to each jaw in most vertebrates except birds, having points, edges, or grinding surfaces, and serving primarily for the biting, tearing, or trituration of solid food, and secondarily as weapons of attack or defence, and for other purposes; in *sing.* each of these individually. Also applied to similar analogous structures occurring in the mouth or alimentary canal in some invertebrates. **b.** *spec.* An elephant's tusk (projecting upper incisor tooth), as a source of ivory OE. **c.** In expressions referring to speech (now esp. biting or angry speech) ME. **2.** *fig.* or in fig. expressions: **a.** referring to eating, esp. to the sense of taste; hence often = taste, liking. late ME. **b.** referring to biting or gnawing 1546.

1. She has not a T. in her Head STEELE. **2. a.** What a t. for fruit has a monkey! 1851. **b.** It is impossible to auoide the teethe of malicious enuy 1546.

II. *transf.* A projecting part or point resembling an animal's tooth; esp. one of a row or series of such. **a.** As an artificial structure, in an implement, machine, etc.; e.g. one of the pointed projections of a comb, saw, file, rake, harrow, fork, etc.; a prong, tine; a cog 1523. **b.** As a natural structure, in animals, plants, etc.; e.g. the odontoid process of the axis vertebra; each of a row of small projections on the edge of one valve of the shell in some bivalve molluscs; each of the pointed processes on the margin of leaves or other parts in many plants, or of those forming the peristome of the capsule in mosses; also, gen., a projecting point of rock, etc. 1694. **c.** *pl.* The lower zone of facets in a rose-diamond 1877. **d.** *pl. fig.* A ship's guns. *Naut. slang.* 1810.

d. They were..large schooners..showing a very good set of teeth MARRYAT.

Phrases. **In the teeth, in** (one's) **teeth. a.** *In the teeth of*, in direct opposition to, so as to face or confront. **b.** *In the teeth of*, in defiance of, in spite of. **c.** *In the teeth of*, in the presence of, in the face of; threateningly confronted by. **d.** *To cast* (a thing) *in* a person's *teeth, to throw in* a person's *teeth*, to reproach, upbraid, or censure with; to bring up in reproach against; also in similar phrases expressing reproachful or defiant utterance. **In spite of** (*despite, maugre*, etc.) one's **teeth**: notwithstanding one's opposition; in spite of one, in defiance of one. Now *rare* exc. *dial.* **To the teeth. a.** So as to be completely equipped; very fully or completely: in *armed to the teeth.* **b.** *To* (one's) *teeth, to the teeth of*, intensive of 'to one's face'; directly and openly; defiantly. **Tooth and nail** (orig. *with tooth and nail*), advb. phr. *lit.* With the use of one's teeth and nails as weapons; by biting and scratching: almost always *fig.*, vigorously, fiercely, with one's utmost efforts, with all one's might. **From the teeth forward(s** or **outward(s** (also *simply* **from one's teeth**), in profession but not in reality (opp. to *from the heart*). **To set one's teeth,** to press or clench one's teeth firmly together from indignation or fixed resolution; hence *fig.* and *allus.* **To show one's teeth,** *lit.* to uncover the teeth by withdrawing the lips from them: see SHOW *v.* II. 6. **b.** *Long in the t.*, old (orig. of horses, from recession of gums with age) 1852 (THACKERAY).

attrib. and *Comb.*: **t.-back,** a moth of the family *Notodontidæ*, or its larva, which has a t.-like prominence on the back; **-bone,** (*a*) = DENTINE; (*b*) the bony substance or 'cement' of the teeth; **-comb,** a small-t. comb; **-coralline** = SERTULARIA; **-ivory** = DENTINE; **-mark,** a mark made by a t. in biting; **t. ornament,** *Arch.* a kind of ornament or moulding suggesting a t. or teeth; **-paste,** a paste used for cleaning the teeth; **-powder,** a powder used for cleaning the teeth, a dentifrice; **-rail,** a tramway rail having teeth or cogs; **-rash,** an eruptive disease incident to infants when teething; **-sac,** a sac or hollow structure of connective tissue, within which a tooth is developed; **-wheel,** a toothed wheel, cog-wheel.

Tooth (tūþ), *v.* late ME. [f. prec.] †**1.** *intr.* To develop, grow, or 'cut' teeth; to teethe –1796. **2.** *trans.* To supply or furnish with teeth; to fit or fix teeth into; to cut teeth in or upon; to indent 1483. **3.** To exercise the teeth upon; to bite, gnaw 1579. **4.** To fit or fix into something by projections like teeth, or in the manner of teeth. **a.** *trans.* 1672. **b.** *intr.* for *pass.* To interlock 1703.

2. I toothed two Pieces of Brass..to fit each other 1745.

Toothache (tū·þ,ēⁱk). late ME. [TOOTH *sb.*, ACHE *sb.*] An ache or continuous pain in a tooth or the teeth. (As a malady, commonly *the tooth ache* down to 19th c.)

Comb.: **t.-grass,** a. N. Amer. grass (*Ctenium americanum*) having a very pungent taste; **-tree,** (*a*) name for N. Amer. species of *Xanthoxylon*, having pungent aromatic fruit, esp. *X. fraxineum*, also called *prickly ash*; (*b*) the similar N. Amer. *Aralia spinosa*, also called *angelica-tree*.

Tooth-billed (tū·þ,bild), *a.* 1862. *Ornith.* Having one or more tooth-like projections on the edge of the bill; dentirostral or serratirostral. So **Too·thbill,** the t. pigeon.

Too·th-brush. 1651. A small brush with a long handle, used for cleansing the teeth. **b.** *attrib.* **t. moustache,** a short bristly moustache 1904.

Too·th-drawer. late ME. **1.** One who 'draws' or extracts teeth; a dentist. Now *contemptuous.* †**2.** A dentist's instrument for extracting teeth –1694.

Toothed (tūþt, *poet.* tū·þėd), *a.* ME. [f. TOOTH *sb.* or *v.* + -ED.] **1.** *lit.* Having teeth; having teeth of a specified kind. †**b.** *fig.* 'Biting', pungent, corrosive –1675. **2.** Having natural projections or processes like teeth; dentate, indented; jagged: *esp.* of leaves or other parts of plants; also of the bill of birds, the margin of shells, etc. late ME. **3.** Made or fitted artificially with teeth or tooth-like projections; *spec.* of a wheel, cogged, late ME.

2. *T. vertebra*, the axis vertebra, from its tooth or odontoid process. **3.** *T. ornament* (Arch.) = *tooth ornament*.

Toothful (tū·þful), *sb.* 1774. [f. TOOTH *sb.* + -FUL 2.] *lit.* As much as would fill a tooth; a small mouthful, esp. of liquor.

Toothful (tū·þfŭl), *a.* 1591. [f. TOOTH *sb.* + -FUL 1.] **1.** Full of teeth; having many teeth (*rare*), †**2.** = TOOTHSOME –1622.

Toothing (tū·þiŋ), *vbl. sb.* 1440. [f. TOOTH *sb.* or *v.* + -ING¹.] **1.** = TEETHING *vbl. sb.* 1. *Obs.* or *rare.* **2.** A structure or formation consisting of teeth or tooth-like projections; such teeth collectively; dentation, serration 1611. **b.** *spec.* in *Building.* Bricks or stones left projecting from a wall to form a bond for additional work to be built on; the bond or attachment thus formed; the construction of this 1672. **3.** The process of forming teeth or serrations; the furnishing (of a saw, etc.) with teeth 1833.

Comb.: **t.-plane,** a plane having the iron almost upright, with a serrated edge, used to score and roughen a surface.

Toothless (tū·þlės), *a.* late ME. [-LESS.] Having no teeth; destitute of teeth. **1. a.** That is naturally without teeth. **b.** That has not yet cut its teeth. **c.** Having lost the teeth, as from age. **2.** *transf.* Destitute of tooth-like formations or projections; not jagged or serrated 1812. **3.** *fig.* Destitute of keenness or 'edge'; not biting or corrosive 1592.

Toothpick (tū·þpik). 1488. [See PICK *sb.*¹ II. 3.] **1.** An instrument for picking the teeth: usu. a pointed quill or small piece of wood. **2.** *pl.* Splinters, small elongated fragments, 'matchwood'; in hyperbolical phr. *smashed* (etc.) *into toothpicks* 1839. **3.** *U.S. slang.* A bowie-knife; also *Arkansas t.* 1867. **4.** A very narrow pointed boat. *slang.* 1897.

Too·th-shell. 1711. The long tubular shell, in shape like a tooth or tusk, of any gasteropod mollusc of *Dentalium* or other allied genus; also, the mollusc itself.

Toothsome (tū·þsŏm), *a.* 1551. [-SOME¹.] **1.** Pleasant to the taste, savoury, palatable. **2.** Having a 'dainty tooth' 1837.

1. The Patattoes, which they eate as a delicate and t. meate 1604. Hence **Too·thsome-ly** *adv.*, **-ness.**

Toothwort (tū·þwɒɹt). 1597. [f. TOOTH *sb.* + WORT¹.] **1.** *Lathræa squamaria* (family *Orobanchaceæ*), a leafless fleshy herb, parasitic on the roots of hazel and other trees, having tooth-like scales upon the root-stock. **2.** A plant of the cruciferous genus *Dentaria*, characterized by tooth-like projections upon the creeping root-stock; *esp.* the British species *D. bulbifera*, occurring locally in woods 1668.

Toothy (tū·þi), *a.* 1530. [f. TOOTH *sb.* + -Y¹.] **1.** Having numerous, large, or prominent teeth. **2.** Furnished with or full of teeth or tooth-like projections; toothed 1611. **3.** *fig.* 'Biting', ill-natured, peevish. *n. dial.* and *Sc.* 1691.

3. T. critics by the score BURNS.

Too·thy-peg. 1828. [f. TOOTH *sb.* + -Y⁶ + PEG *sb.*¹ Cf. local *toossie-*, *tushypeg* (f. *tush* tooth).] Nursery name for a tooth.

Tootle (tū·t'l), *sb.* 1852. [f. next.] **1.** An act or the action of tootling or sounding a horn or similar wind-instrument. **2.** Speech or writing of more sound than sense; twaddle 1883. So **Too·tle-te-too·tle,** a piece of continuous tootling.

Tootle (tū·t'l), *v.* 1820. [f. TOOT *v.*² + -LE 3.] *intr.* To toot continuously; to produce a succession of modulated notes on a wind-instrument 1842. **b.** Of birds: To make a similar noise 1820. **c.** *fig.* To write twaddle or mere verbiage 1883.

Tootling on the sentimental flute STEVENSON.

Too-too (tū,tū·), *v.* 1828. [imit.; usu. depreciatory.] *intr.* To make an instrumental or vocal sound resembling these syllables.

The singers..begin too-tooing most dismally DICKENS.

Tootsy, tootsy-wootsy (tu·tsi, wu·tsi). *colloq.* 1854. [Playful alt. of FOOT + -SY.] A playful or endearing name for a child's or a woman's small foot.

Top (tǫp), *sb.*¹ [Late OE. *topp* = OFris. *topp* tuft, (M)Du. *top* crest, summit, tip, (O)HG. *zopf* plait, tress, ON. *toppr* top, tuft :- Gmc. **toppaz.*] **I.** A tuft, crest, or bush of hair, etc. **1.** The hair on the summit or crown of the head; the hair of the head. *Obs.* exc. *Sc.* **2.** A tuft or handful of hair, wool, fibre, etc.; *esp.* the portion of flax or tow put on the distaff. Now only *Sc.* and *n. dial.* ME. **b.** *spec.* A bundle of combed wool prepared for spinning. Chiefly *pl.* (also *collect. sing.*). 1637.

1. Let's take the instant by the forward t.: For we are old SHAKS.

II. The highest or uppermost part. **1.** The highest point or part of anything; the highest place or limit *of* something OE. **b.** That part of anything portable which, when it is in use, occupies the highest place; e.g. the t. of a page, map, etc. 1593. **c.** The higher end of anything on a slope; also, that end of anything which is conventionally considered the higher, as of a room or dining-table; the end of a billiard-table opposite the baulk 1624. **2.** The uppermost division of the body; the head; *esp.* the crown of the head ME. **3.** Usu. *pl.* The part of a plant growing above ground as dist. from the root; esp. of a vegetable grown for the 'root', as *turnip-tops* 1523. **4.** *pl.* (also *collect. sing.*) The smaller branches and twigs of trees as dist. from the timber 1485. **5.** The extremity of a growing part; hence the narrower end (of anything tapering), the point, tip 1538.

1. From Sinai's t. Jehovah gave the law COWPER. *To go over the t.*, to scale the parapet of a trench, for an attack or raid. **c.** In the omnibus to the t. of Sloane Street 1849. **2.** Soft hoa, what truncke is heere? Without his t.? SHAKS. **4.** In a sale of standing timber trees they are advertised with their 'lop, t., and bark' 1858. **5.** *T. and butt* (Shipbuilding), a method of working long tapering planks together in pairs with the t. of one to the butt of another, so as to maintain a constant width.

III. A piece or part placed upon or fitted to anything, and forming its upper part or covering. **1.** A platform near the head of each of the lower masts of a ship. In a modern warship, an armoured platform on a short mast, for machine-guns, signalling, etc.; more fully *fighting t.*, *military t.* In a sailing ship, a framework and platform serving to extend the rigging, and for convenience in making sail. late ME. **b.** *Naut.* Short for *topsail* 1513. **c.** *T. and topgallant*, short for *topsail and topgallant sail*; hence *fig.*; as *advb.* with all sail set, in full array or career 1593. **2.** The uppermost part of the leg of a high boot or riding-boot, *spec.* when widened out or turned over; now, a broad band of material (simulating the turned-over part), white, light-coloured, or brown. Also *pl.* short for TOPBOOTS. 1629. **b.** The gauntlet part of a glove; the turned-down top part of men's hose 1819. **3.** In various techn. uses, e.g. the stopper of a scent-bottle or the like; the part of an earring worn in the lobe of the ear; the hood or cover of a carriage 1453. **b.** Short for *t.-button* 1852.

IV. *fig.* and *transf.* The part of anything which has the first place in time, order, or precedence. **1.** Of time: The earliest part of a period 1440. **2.** The highest or chief position, place, or rank; the head, forefront; now esp. in *the t. of the tree* (fig.) 1627. **b.** One who or that which occupies the highest or chief position; the head (of a clan, family, etc.) 1612. **3.** The highest pitch or degree; the height, summit, zenith, pinnacle 1552. **b.** The most perfect example or type of something 1593. **c.** *Motoring slang.* The top or highest gear; usu. *on* (*the*) *t.* 1906. **4.** The highest point reached in a progression or series; the culminating point 1670. **5.** The best or choicest part; the cream, flower, pick. Now esp. in *the t. of the morning*, as an Irish morning greeting. 1663.

3. By how much from the t. of wondrous glory,.. To lowest pitch of abject fortune thou art fall'n MILT. Phr. *The t. of one's bent* (see BENT *sb.*²); *the t. of one's voice.* **b.** If he, which is the t. of Iudgement, should But iudge you, as you are SHAKS. **4.** Phr. *The t. of the tide. The t. of the market*, the moment at which prices are highest. **5.** A 't. of the basket' young lady 1894.

V. Forward spin imparted to a ball by the mode of its impulsion or delivery (in billiards, by striking it above the centre; hence in cricket and tennis) 1901.

VI. *attrib.* passing into *adj.* **1.** Having a top, as *t.-buggy*, *-wagon*, *ship* 1686. **2.** Of or pertaining to the top; upper, uppermost. Now usu. written separate as *adj.* 1593. **3.** Forming the top, or the exterior surface or layer; upper, outer. Now usu. separate. 1603. **4.** First in rank, order, or quality 1647. **5.** Highest (in degree), greatest (in amount); very high, very great; also in weakened sense, first-rate, tip-top, excellent 1714.

2. There were two doors on the t. landing 1888. **3.** A foot-and-a-half of blackish t.-soil 1904. **4.** The t. wits of the Court SWIFT. **5.** His common trot is just a match for your t. speed 1806.

Phrases. **At t., on t.** (see prec. senses); *fig.* supreme, dominant; **on** or **upon** (*the*) **t. of,** above, upon, close upon, following upon. **T... bottom. a.** *T. to bottom*, so that the highest part becomes the lowest; with complete inversion. **b.** *From t. to bottom* = *from t. to toe.* **T... tail. a.** *T. and tail.* (*a*) The whole, every part. (*b*) The long and short of it, the substance, upshot. (*c*) *advb.* From head to foot; all over. **b.** *T. or tail*, (in neg. statements), any part; anything definite or intelligible; head or tail. **c.** *From t. to tail* = a (*c*); also *fig.* wholly, absolutely. **T...toe.** *From t. to toe*, from head to foot, in every part.

Comb.: **t.-button,** †(*a*) a metal button of which the t. or face is gilt or silvered; (*b*) an ornamental knob on the top of a mast; **-card** *Spinning*, a flat strip of wood covered with hooked teeth set over the drum of a carding-engine; **-coat,** overcoat, great-coat, outer-coat; hence **-coated** *a.*; **t. dog,** *lit.* the dog uppermost or 'on top' in a fight; *fig.* the victorious or dominant party; **t. drawer,** the uppermost drawer of a chest, etc.; *to come out of the t. drawer*, to be well bred; **-gear,** (*a*) the rigging, sails, and spars of a ship; (*b*) (without hyphen) in power transmission, the alternative gearing which produces the highest speed in proportion to that of the motor; **-heat** *Hortic.*, heat generated in a frame or greenhouse; **-hole, t. notch,** the highest hole or notch; *fig.* the highest point attainable; also *attrib.* first-rate, 'tip-top' (*slang*); hence **t.-notcher; t. note,** the highest note in a singer's compass; **-proud** *a.*, proud to the highest degree; **t. sergeant** (*U.S. colloq.*), the first sergeant; **t. story,** the uppermost story of a house; *fig.* the head as the seat of intellect; **-tool,** any smith's tool which is held upon the work while being struck, as dist. from a *bottom-tool*, which is socketed in the anvil; **-weight,** the heaviest weight carried by a horse in a race; *transf.* a horse carrying this weight.

b. From sense III. 1; (*top* being also short for *topsail* or *topmast*): **t.-block,** a large block suspended below the cap of the lower mast, used in hoisting or lowering topmasts; **-chain,** a chain used to sling the yards in action, in case the ropes by which they are hung should be shot away; **-lantern, -light,** a signal-light carried in the top of a vessel; **-rope**, a rope used for hoisting or lowering topmasts; *to sway* (erron. *swing*) *on all top-ropes*, to go to great lengths; **-tackle**, a tackle used in raising or lowering topmasts.

Top (tǫp), *sb.*² [Late OE. *top* (once); further evidence is not frequent until after 1400; the origin is unkn.; words similar in form and meaning in G. and Fr., but their relations are obscure; perh. the word is to be identified with prec.] **1.** A toy of various shapes (cylindrical, obconic, etc.), but always of a circular section, with a point on which it is made to spin, usu. by the sudden pulling of a string wound round it; the common *whip-* or *whipping-top* is kept spinning by lashing it with a whip. **b.** As the type of a sound sleeper, in ref. to the apparent stillness of a spinning top when its axis of rotation is vertical 1616. **2.** A marine gasteropod having a short conical shell; any species of the genus *Trochus* or family *Trochidæ*; a top-shell. In earliest use, *sea t.* 1682. **3.** *Rope-making.* (Also *laying-t.*) A conical piece of wood, with three or four grooves for the strands 1794.

1. *Parish t., town t.*, a large t. kept for public use, which two players or parties whipped in opposite directions. **b.** Phr. *To sleep like* (*as sound* or *as fast as*) *a t. Old t.* (slang), old fellow, old girl.

Comb.: **t.-shell** = sense 2.

Top (tǫp), *v.*¹ ME. [f. TOP *sb.*¹] **I.** To deprive of the top. †**1.** *trans.* To cut *off* (the hair of the head), poll (the head), crop (a person) –1632. **2.** To cut off the top of (a growing tree, a plant, or the like); to poll or pollard (a tree); to cut or break off the head, flower, or ear of (a plant), the withered calyx from (a gooseberry or other fruit); often in phr. *to t. and lop, t. and tail* 1509. †**3.** To snuff (a candle) –1840.

2. *fig.* Topping rank desires which vain exceed 1633.

II. To put a top on or form a top to. **1.** To furnish with a top; to cover or surmount, crown, cap (*with*) 1581. **2.** To complete by putting the top on, or forming the top of (a stack, etc.); often *to t. up*; hence (*colloq.*) to finish *off*, round *off*, crown 1504. **b.** *absol.* or *intr.* To finish *up* or *off* (with something). *colloq.* 1836. **3.** *trans.* **a.** *Dyeing.* To give a final bath of colour to; to finish *off* (a dyeing process) with a certain dye. **b.** To top-dress (land). **c.** To stain the tips of the hair of (fur). 1856. †**4.** To 'cover', copulate with (*rare*)–1633.

2. *To t. up* (Electr.): to maintain the acid level in an accumulator, by adding distilled water. **b.** Then you..find the inmates of another room topping off with chocolate or coffee 1870. Everything went wrong.., and to t. up with I got the fever badly 1885. **4.** *Oth.* III. iii. 396.

III. To exceed or come up to in height. **1.** *trans.* To exceed in height; to overtop; also, to exceed in weight, amount, number, etc. 1582. **b.** To surpass, excel, outdo; to cap 1586. **2.** To rise above; to mount beyond the level of 1773. **b.** To get or leap over the top of 1735. **3.** To ascend to the top of 1600. **4.** *Theatr. To t. one's part*, to play one's part to its utmost possibilities; also, to transcend the character assigned to one; *transf.* to sustain (a character) with success 1672. **5.** To be at the top of, constitute the top of 1615. **b.** To get the better of 1633.

1. She was so tall that she topped her father..by a head 1887. **b.** Topping all others in boasting SHAKS. **3.** Wind about, till thou have topp'd the Hill DENHAM. **5.** The decent church that topt the neighbouring hill GOLDSM. In character as in intellect Bacon tops the list 1861.

Phrases. *To t. a ball* (Golf), to hit the ball above its centre; so *to t. one's drive. To t. a saw* (*U.S.*), to fix a stiffening piece or a gauge for limiting the depth of the cut.

Top (tǫp), *v.*² 1549. [– Du. (whence LG./G. naut.) *toppen* top or peak (a yard; see PEAK *v.*³). So Du. (LG./G.) *toppenant* (pl. *-en*) topping-lift. Branch II is prob. a distinct word.] **I.** *Naut.* **1.** *trans.* To tip *up* or slant (a yard) by tilting up one arm and depressing the other. **2.** *intr.* To assume a slanting position, tip *up*, tilt *up* 1860. **II.** †**1.** *intr.* = TOPPLE *v.* 1. –1620. **2.** *trans.* = TOPPLE *v.* 3. *Obs.* exc. *dial.* 1662.

Toparch (tǫ·pąɹk). 1640. [– Gr. τοπάρχης ruler of a small district, f. τόπος place + -αρχης -ARCH; hence late L. *toparcha*.] The ruler or prince of a small district, city, or petty state; a petty 'king'. So **Topa·rchical** *a.* of or pertaining to a t. or toparchy.

Toparchy (tǫ·pąɹki). 1601. [– L. *toparchia* (Pliny) and its source Gr. τοπαρχία, f. τοπάρχης; see prec., -Y³.] The small district or territory under the rule of a toparch.

Topass (tōᵘ·pǎs). *India.* 1680. [– Pg. *topaz*, app. – *tōpāshé*, Malayalam form of Hindi *dōbāshī* man of two languages, interpreter. See DUBASH.] A dark-skinned half-breed of Portuguese descent; often applied to a soldier, or a ship's scavenger or bath-attendant, who is of this class.

Topaz (tōᵘ·pæz). [ME. *topace* – OFr. *topace*, (also mod.) *topaze* – L. *topazus, -azius, -ion* – Gr. τόπαζος, -αζιον.] **1. a.** The name given by the Greeks and Romans to the *yellow* or *oriental t.*, a yellow sapphire or corundum; by Pliny also to the modern chrysolite. **b.** In mod. use (*true* or *occidental t.*), a fluosilicate of aluminium, transparent and lustrous, yellow, white, pale blue, or pale green, found in Brazil, Mexico, Saxony, Scotland, the Ural Mountains, etc. **2.** *Her.* In blazoning by precious stones, the tincture Or 1562.

1. *False t.*, a transparent pale yellow variety of quartz. *Pink t.*, pink or rose-coloured t., artificially produced by exposing the yellow Brazilian stone to strong heat.

Comb.: **t. humming-bird**, two S. Amer. species of humming-bird of brilliant colours, *Topaza pella* and *T. pyra*.

Topazolite (topæ·zolǝit). 1819. [f. TOPAZ + -LITE.] *Min.* A variety of garnet resembling topaz in colour.

Top-boot (tǫ·pˌbū·t). 1813. [f. TOP *sb.*¹ + BOOT *sb.*³] **1.** *prop.* A high boot, having a top of white, light-coloured, or brown leather or the like (TOP *sb.*¹ III. 2); now worn by hunting men, jockeys, grooms, and coachmen. Usu. in *pl.* **2.** Improperly applied to any long or high boots which partly cover the leg 1891.

†**Top-castle.** ME. [Cf. TOP *sb.*¹ III. 1, CASTLE *sb.* II. 1.] An embattled platform at the head of a ship's masts, from which missiles were discharged –1688.

To·p-dre:ss, *v.* 1733. [f. TOP *sb.*¹ + DRESS *v.*] *trans.* To manure on the surface, as land, grass, or any crop. Also *absol.*

To·p-dressing, *vbl. sb.* 1764. [f. prec. + -ING¹.] The application of manure to the surface of the soil; *concr.* the manure or fertilizer so applied. Also *transf.* and *fig.*

Tope (tōᵘp), *sb.*¹ 1686. [Of unkn. origin; perh. Cornish.] A small species of shark, *Galeus galeorhinus* or *G. canis*, native to British seas, esp. off the coast of Cornwall. Called also *dog-fish, penny-dog, miller's-dog*. **b.** The Australasian species. *Galeus australis* 1898.

Tope (tōᵘp), *sb.*² 1813. A local name for the wren.

‖**Tope** (tōᵘp), *sb.*³ *India.* 1698. [– Telugu *tōpu*, Tamil *tōppu*.] A clump, grove, or plantation of trees; in Upper India, chiefly of fruit-trees; *esp.* a mango grove or orchard.

‖**Tope** (tōᵘp), *sb.*⁴ *India.* 1815. [– Hind. (Panjabi) *tōp* :– Prakrit, Pali *thūpo* :– Skr. *stūpa*.] In India and south-eastern Asia: An ancient structure, in the form of a dome or tumulus of masonry, for the preservation of relics or in commemoration of some fact; usu. of Buddhist or Jain origin.

Tope, *v.* Now only *literary* or *arch.* 1654. perh. alt. of †*top* (XVI) drink off, quaff, by assoc. with TOPE *int.*] **1.** *trans.* To drink, *esp.* to drink copiously and habitually. **2.** *intr.* To drink largely or in large draughts 1667.

2. I'll T. with you, I'll Sing with you, I'll Dance with you DRYDEN.

†**Tope,** *int.* 1651. [– Fr. *top, tope, tôpe*, ellipt. for *je tope* I accept the wager; orig. a word of dice-play; = It. *toppa* 'done!' Used also in drinking.] An exclam. used in drinking; app. = I pledge you –1664.

Toper (tōᵘ·pǝɹ). Now chiefly *literary.* 1673. [f. TOPE *v.* + -ER¹.] One who topes or drinks a great deal; a hard drinker; a drunkard.

Top-full (tǫ·pfu·l), *a.* Now *rare.* 1553. [f. TOP *sb.*¹ + FULL *a.*] Full to the top; brimfull. †**b.** *transf.* Said of that which fills (to the top): Brimming (*rare*) –1608.

A huge great purse top full of gold 1617. *fig.* Top-full of busines as I am 1648.

Topgallant (tǫpgæ·lǎnt, tǝgæ·lǎnt), *sb.* and *a.* 1514. [f. TOP *sb.*¹ III. 1 + GALLANT *a.*, as making a gallant show in comparison with the lower tops.] **A.** *sb.* †**1.** *Naut.* A 'top' at the head of the topmast, and thus in a loftier position than the original top-castle or top 1590. **2.** *pl.* Short for *t. sails*, the sails above the topsail and topgallant 1599. **3. a.** *transf.* (from 1 and 2) The most elevated (*lit.* or *fig.*) part or member *of* anything 1581. **b.** *fig.* The highest point or pitch; summit 1592.

2. She had..got up..jury-masts, with topgallants for topsails MARRYAT. **3. b.** Which to the high top gallant of my ioy, Must be my conuoy in the secret night SHAKS.

B. *attrib.* or *adj.* **1.** Of, pertaining to, or having the position of topgallant 1514. **2.** Allowing topgallant sails to be used, as *t. weather* 1697. **3.** *fig.* Lofty, grand, topping 1613.

1. *T. mast, sail, yard*, the mast, sail, or yard above the topmast and topsail; the third mast, sail, or yard above the deck. **2.** The wind..blew what seamen call a top-gallant breeze 1806.

Toph(e (tōᵘf). Now *rare.* 1552. [– L. TOPHUS.] **1.** usu. *toph stone*: = TOPHUS 1. **2.** *Path.* = TOPHUS 2. 1584.

Tophaceous (tofēⁱ·ʃǝs), *a.* 1672. [– L. *tof-, tophaceus*, f. TOPHUS; see -ACEOUS.] **1.** Of the nature of tophus; sandy, gritty; rough, stony. **2.** *Path.* Gritty or calcareous, as the matter deposited in gout 1687.

To·p-ha·mper. 1791. [f. TOP *sb.*¹ + HAMPER *sb.*²] *Naut.* Weight or encumbrance aloft: orig. said of the upper masts, sails, and rigging of a ship; later, also, weight or encumbrance on the deck, as in a steamer, ironclad, etc.

To·p-ha·t. *colloq.* 1881. A man's silk or beaver hat with high cylindrical crown; a tall or high hat.

Top-heavy (stress var.), *a.* 1533. Disproportionately heavy at the top; having the upper part so heavy as to overbalance the lower; hence, unstable and inclined to topple. **b.** Said of an intoxicated person: Tipsy 1687.

Tophet (tōᵘ·fėt). late ME. [– Heb. *tōpeṯ*; etym. uncertain.] **1.** *orig.* Proper name of a place near Gehenna or the Valley of the Son or Children of Hinnom, south of Jerusalem, where the Jews made human sacrifices to strange gods (Jer. 19:4). Later, it was used as a place for the deposit of refuse, and became symbolic of the torments of hell. **2.** The place of punishment for the wicked after death; hell, Gehenna. late ME. **3.** *fig.* A place, state, condition, or company likened to hell 1618.

1. [Moloch] made his Grove The pleasant valley of Hinnom, Tophet thence And black Gehenna call'd, the Type of Hell MILT. **2.** *Isa.* 30:33.

†**To·phous,** *a.* 1634. [f. next + -OUS.] Of the nature of a stony or calcareous concretion –1756.

‖**Tophus** (tōᵘ·fǒs). *Pl.* ‖**tophi** (ǝi). 1555. [L. *tophus*, better *tofus*, a general name for loose porous stones of various kinds, whence It. *tufo*, Fr. *tuf*; see also TUFF, TUFA.] **1.** A soft porous stone, arenaceous, calcareous, or volcanic; *esp.* a stony substance deposited by calcareous springs. **2.** *Path.* A concretion which forms on the surface of the joints, the pinna of the ear, etc. in gout; a gouty deposit; also gravel, or a stone or calculus, formed within the body 1607.

Comb.: **t.-stone** = TRAVERTINE.

‖**Topi, topee** (topī·). *India.* 1826. [– Hindi *ṭopī* hat.] Orig. applied by Indian natives to the European hat; now *spec.* in Anglo-Indian, as a name for the *sola topi*, sola hat or helmet: see SOLA *sb.*

Topiarian (tōᵘpiˌēᵊ·riǎn), *a.* 1694. [f. L. *topiarius*; see next, -AN.] = TOPIARY.

‖**Topiarius** (tōᵘpiˌēᵊ·riǒs). 1706. [L. *topiarius* 'of or pertaining to ornamental gardening' (Pliny); sb. 'ornamental gardener' (Cicero), f. *topia* (sc. *opera* work) fancy or landscape gardening – Gr. τοπία, pl. of τοπίον, dim. of τόπος place.] One skilled in fanciful landscape-gardening.

Topiary (tōᵘ·piǎri), *a.* (*sb.*) 1592. [– Fr. *topiaire* (Rabelais) – L. *topiarius* adj.; see prec., -ARY.] *Gardening.* Consisting in clipping and trimming shrubs, etc., into ornamental or fantastic shapes. **B.** *sb.* The topiary art 1908.

Topic (tǫ·pik), *a.* and *sb.* 1568. [As adj. – Gr. τοπικός of or pertaining to τόπος a place; local, or concerning τόποι commonplaces; see -IC. As *sb.* – L. *topica* – Gr., in τὰ τοπικά, title of a work of Aristotle, lit. matters concerning τόποι.] †**A.** *adj.* **1.** Pertaining to or of the nature of a 'commonplace' (COMMONPLACE A. 1) or general maxim –1653. **b.** Containing 'commonplaces'; *t. folio*, a commonplace-book –1644. **2.** Of or pertaining to a particular place or locality; local –1793. **b.** *Med.* Of or pertaining to a particular part of the body; designed for external local application –1671.

B. 1. *pl.* As title of the treatise of Aristotle, or as name for a work of the same nature, or for a set of general rules or maxims 1568. †**2.** A kind or class of considerations suitable to the purpose of a rhetorician or disputant, passing into the sense 'consideration', 'argument' –1840. †**b.** A head under which arguments or subjects may be arranged –1806. **3.** The subject of a discourse, argument, or literary composition; a theme; also, a subject of admiration, animadversion, satire, mockery, or other treatment 1720. †**4.** *Med.* An external remedy locally applied, as a plaster or blister –1758.

1. These Topics or Loci, were no other than general ideas applicable to a great many different subjects, which the Orator was directed to consult, in order to find out materials for his Speech 1783. **2.** These strong topics, in favour of the house of Lancaster, were opposed by arguments no less convincing on the side of the house of York HUME. **3.** He had exhausted every t. of conversation 1797.

Topical (tǫ·pikăl), *a.* 1588. [f. as prec. + -AL¹ 1; see -ICAL.] **1.** Of or pertaining to a place or locality; local. **b.** *Med.* That belongs or is applied to a particular part of the body 1608. †**2.** Pertaining to a topic or general maxim; hence, not demonstrative but merely probable –1710. **3.** Of or pertaining to a general heading, a topic or subject of discourse, composition, etc. 1856. **b.** Of or pertaining to the topics of the day; containing local or temporary allusions 1873.

1. Their truth is not t. and transitory, but of universal acceptation 1870. **2.** This Argument is ..but Topicall and probable 1624. **3. b.** A great many 't.' allusions to events of the hour, and rough political hits 1881. As *sb.*, a film dealing with t. events. **To·pically** *adv.* in a t. manner; in reference to topics.

Topknot (tǫ·pₗnǫt). 1686. [f. TOP *sb.*¹ + KNOT *sb.*¹] **1. a.** A knot or bow of ribbon worn on the top of the head by ladies towards the end of the 17th and in the 18th century; later, a bow of ribbon worn in a lace cap. **b.** A tuft of hair on the top or crown of the head of a person or animal; also, a plume or crest of feathers or filaments on the head of a bird 1700. **c.** The head. *slang.* 1869. **2.** *transf.* **a.** One who wears a topknot 1697. **b.** One of several species of small European flatfish, with a tapering filament on the head 1832. Hence **To·p-knotted** *a.* having a t.

Topless (tǫ·plės), *a.* 1589. [f. TOP *sb.*¹ + -LESS.] **1.** Having no top (*rare*) 1596. **2.** *fig.* Seeming to have no top or summit; immensely or immeasurably high; unbounded 1589.

2. The glister of the Sunne vpon the toplesse Promontorie of Sicilia GREENE. My toplesse villany 1602.

Topman (tǫ·pmæ̆n). 1513. [f. TOP *sb.*¹ + MAN *sb.*] †**1.** A ship with a top on its mast –1577. **2.** *Naut.* A seaman stationed in one of the tops, to attend to the upper sails, or in a fighting ship as a marksman 1748. **3. a.** The upper man in a saw-pit 1678. **b.** A miner or pitman working at the top of the shaft 1890.

Topmast (tǫ·pₗmɑst, -məst). 1485. A smaller mast fixed on the top of a lower mast; *spec.* the second section of a mast above the deck, which was formerly the uppermost mast, but is now surmounted by the top-gallant mast.

Topmost (tǫ·pmoᵘst, -mŏst), *a.* 1697. [f. TOP *sb.*¹ + -MOST.] Uppermost, highest. Also *absol.*, highest part.

The..spear..shore away the t. of his crest MORRIS.

Topo-, bef. a vowel **top-** – Gr. τοπο-, comb. f. τόπος place, as in τοπο-γράφος (see next).

Topographer (tŏpǫ·grăfəɹ). 1603. [f. Gr. τοπογράφος + -ER¹ 4; see -GRAPHER.] One who is skilled in topography; one who describes or delineates a particular locality.

Topographic (tǫpŏgræ·fik), *a.* 1632. [– Gr. τοπογραφικός, f. stem of τοπογραφία TOPOGRAPHY: see -IC. Cf. Fr. *topographique* (XVI).] = next.

Topographical (tǫpŏgræ·fikăl), *a.* 1570. [f. as prec. + -AL¹ 1; see -ICAL.] Of, pertaining to, or dealing with topography. Hence **Topogra·phically** *adv.*

Topo·graphize, *v.* 1810. [f. TOPOGRAPHY + -IZE.] **a.** *trans.* To describe or treat topographically. **b.** *intr.* To make topographical researches.

Topography (tŏpǫ·grăfi). late ME. [– late L. *topographia* – Gr. τοπογραφία, f. τοπογράφος; see above, -GRAPHY. Cf. Fr. *topographie* (XVI).] **1.** The science or practice of describing a particular place, city, town, manor, parish, or tract of land; the accurate and detailed delineation and description of any locality 1549. **b.** A detailed description or delineation of the features of a locality. late ME. **c.** Localization, local distribution; the study of this 1658. **2.** The features of a region or locality collectively 1847.

2. *fig.* I am not so well acquainted with the t. of the mind 1764.

Topology (tŏpǫ·lŏdʒi). 1659. [f. TOPO- + -LOGY.] **1.** †**a.** The department of botany which treats of the localities where plants are found. **2.** The scientific study of a particular locality 1850.

2. The comparatively new study of topology, the science by which, from the consideration of geographical facts about a locality, one can draw deductions as to its history 1905.

Toponymy (tŏpǫ·nĭmi). 1876. [f. TOPO- + Gr. -ωνυμια, f. ὄνομα name.] The place-names of a country or district as a subject of study. Also **Topony·mic, -ical** *adjs.*

Topped (tǫpt), *ppl. a.* 1459. [f. TOP *sb.*¹ and *v.*¹ + -ED.] **1.** Having or furnished with a top or tops. **2.** Having the top removed; of a tree: polled, pollarded 1712.

Topper (tǫ·pəɹ). Chiefly *slang* or *low colloq.* 1709. [f. TOP *sb.*¹ + -ER¹.] **1.** A 'top' thing or person; the best or one of the best of the kind. *colloq.* **2.** A top-hat, a tall hat. *slang* and *colloq.* 1820. **3.** *pl.* The largest and finest fruit (orig. esp. strawberries) displayed at the top of a punnet, package, or pile. *slang.* 1839.

To·p-piece. 1682. The piece that forms or is at the top of anything; *spec.* †**a.** The *chef-d'œuvre*, masterpiece. BUNYAN. **b.** The head. *colloq.* 1838. **c.** *Shoe-making.* The piece put on and nailed down to the lifts of the heels 1911.

To·pping, *vbl. sb.*¹ late ME. [f. TOP *v.*¹ + -ING¹.] **1.** The action of TOP *v.*¹ in various senses 1504. **2.** A distinct part or appendage which forms a top to anything; a crest; as a forelock of the hair, the crest of a bird; also *joc.* the head. late ME. **3.** That which is put on the top of anything to complete it; a top layer 1839. **4.** *pl.* **a.** Cuttings from the tops of trees; also, the tops of hemp removed in hatchelling. **b.** The second skimmings of milk. *dial.* **c.** The best bran. *dial.* 1531.

To·pping, *vbl. sb.*² 1743. [f. TOP *v.*² + -ING¹.] The action of TOP *v.*²

T.-lift (Naut.), each of a pair of lifts by which a yard may be topped.

To·pping, *ppl. a.* 1681. [f. TOP *v.*¹ + -ING².] That tops, in various senses of TOP *v.*¹ †**1.** *lit.* That exceeds in height; very high (*rare*) –1705. **2.** *fig.* Very high or superior in position, rank, estimation, etc.; chief, principal; preeminent, distinguished; overhanging; 'towering' 1674. **3.** Of high quality; very fine, excellent; tip-top, first-rate. *colloq.* and *slang.* 1822. **4.** Domineering; confident, boastful. *U.S.* 1885.

2. Some of the t. Sinners of the World 1716. **3.** We came on at a t. pace 1841. Hence **To·ppingly** *adv.* (*slang* or *dial.*), **-ness.**

Topple (tǫ·p'l), *v.* 1590. [f. TOP *v.*¹ + -LE 3.] **1.** *intr.* To fall top foremost, or as if top-heavy; to fall headlong, tumble or pitch over. **2.** To lean over unsteadily, as if on the point of falling; to overhang threateningly 1827. **3.** *trans.* To cause to tumble over or fall headlong; to thrust over, overturn, throw down 1596. **4.** To cause to tip or tilt so as to be in danger of being upset (*rare*) 1656.

1. Though castles t. on their Warders heads SHAKS. **2.** Masses of granite..toppling above the terminal face of the glacier TYNDALL. **3.** They t. over the biggest trees in this way 1907.

Topsail (tǫ·psēᵊl, tǫ·ps'l). late ME. [f. TOP *sb.*¹ III. 1 + SAIL *sb.* Cf. LG. *toppseil*, Du. *topzeil.*] A sail set above the lower course, orig. the uppermost sail. In a square-rigged vessel, orig. a single square sail set next above the lower sail or yard; now, in larger ships, divided into an *upper* and a *lower t.* (*double topsails*). In a fore-and-aft rig, a square or triangular sail set above the gaff.

fig. You may tell Your Pope, that..I shall not strike a t. for the breath Of all his maledictions! SOUTHEY.

To·p-saw·yer. 1823. **a.** The sawyer who works the upper handle of a pit-saw. Hence, **b.** *fig.* One who holds a superior position; the best man 1826. **c.** *loosely.* A first-rate hand at something; a distinguished person 1823.

Topside (tǫ·psəid), *sb.* (*adv.*) 1677. [f. TOP *sb.*¹ + SIDE *sb.*¹] **a.** *gen.* The upper side of anything. **b.** *Shipbuilding.* The upper part of a ship's side 1815. **c.** *Butchering.* The outer side of a round of beef, cut from the haunch between the 'leg' and the 'aitch-bone'; the bottom of this is the 'silver-side' 1898. **B.** *adv.* On the top. Also *fig.* (*colloq.*) 1873.

To·psman. *dial.* and *slang.* 1825. [f. *top's*, genitive of TOP *sb.*¹ + MAN *sb.*] **1.** *Sc.* and *n. dial.* A head man, bailiff, or principal servant; *esp.* the chief drover in charge of a herd of cattle on the road. **2.** *slang.* A hangman 1825.

To·p-stone. 1658. A stone which is placed upon or forms the top of something; a capstone: chiefly *fig.* Also, the upper end-stone or jewel in a chronometer.

To·psy-tu·rn, *v.* Now *rare.* 1573. [f. *topsy* as in next + TURN *v.*] *trans.* To turn topsy-turvy, turn upside down; *fig.* to throw into confusion.

Topsy-turvy (tǫ·psiₗtō̆·ɹvi), *adv.* (*a.*, *sb.*, and *v.*) 1528. [The first element is almost certainly *top* (or *tops*), and prob. the second is related to *terve* vb. turn, turn over, overturn (cf. prec.); for the terminal elements *-sy* and *-y* cf. ARSY-VERSY.] With the top where the bottom should be; in or into an inverted position; upside down, bottom upwards.

A chaos of carts, overthrown and jumbled together, lay t. at the bottom of a..hill DICKENS. *fig.* I found nature turned topsy-turvey, women changed into men, and men into women ADDISON.

B. *adj.* Turned upside down; inverted, reversed; *fig.* utterly confused or disorderly 1618.

A very t. way of reasoning 1887.

C. *sb.* The act of turning or fact of being turned upside down; state of utter confusion or disorder 1655. **D.** as *vb. trans.* To turn topsy-turvy or upside down; to invert; *fig.* to reverse; to throw into utter confusion 1626.

My poor mind is all topsy-turvied RICHARDSON.

To·p-ti:mber. 1626. *Shipbuilding.* One of the uppermost timbers in the side of a ship, one of the timbers forming the topside.

Toque (tōᵘk, ‖tok). 1505. [– Fr. *toque*, corresp. obscurely to It. *tocca, tocco*, Sp. *toca*, Pg. *touca* cap, woman's head-dress; of unkn. origin.] **1. a.** A kind of small cap or bonnet worn by men and women in various countries. **b.** A kind of bonnet, cap, or, as now worn by women, a small hat without a brim, or with a very small or closely turned-up brim 1817. **2.** *T. monkey*, also simply *t.*: the bonnet-monkey or bonnet-macaque, *Macacus pileatus*, a native of Ceylon 1840.

Tor (tǭɹ). [OE. *torr*, of British origin (cf. OW. *twrr* bulge, belly, Gael. *tòrr* bulging hill).] **1.** A high rock; a pile of rocks, *gen.* on the top of a hill; a rocky peak; a hill. **2.** *attrib.* **T. ouzel**, local name of the ring ouzel, *Turdus torquatus* 1770.

1. Mount St. Michaells a Steepe and most craggie torr 1610.

‖**Torah** (tōᵊ·rā). 1577. [– Heb. *tōrāh* direction, instruction, doctrine, law, f. *yārāh* throw, (in Hiphil) show, direct, instruct.] The teaching or instruction, and judicial decisions, given by the ancient Hebrew priests as a revelation of the divine will; the

Mosaic or Jewish law; hence, a name for the five books of the law, the Pentateuch.

Torbanite (tǭ·ɹbănəit). 1858. [f. *Torbane* Hill in Linlithgowshire, where found; see -ITE[1] 2b.] *Min.* A deep brown shale, allied to cannel coal, valuable for the production of petroleum and gas.

Torbernite (tǭ·ɹbəɹnəit). 1852. [– G. *torbernit* (Werner, 1792), f. *Torbernus*, latinized form of the name of the chemist *Torber* Bergmann. See -ITE[1] 2b.] *Min.* A native phosphate of uranium and copper, found in bright green tubular crystals; also called *copper-uranite*.

Torch (tǭɹtʃ), *sb.* ME. [– (O)Fr. *torche* :– Rom. **torca*, for L. *torqua* (Varro), var. of *torques* necklace, wreath, f. *torquēre* twist.] **1.** A light to be carried in the hand or upon a pole or the like, consisting of a stick of resinous wood, or of twisted hemp or the like soaked with tallow, resin, or other inflammable substance. In church use, a large candle for carrying. **b.** *fig.* or *allus.* Something figured as a source of illumination, enlightenment, or guidance, or of heat or 'conflagration' 1621. **2.** *transf.* **a.** A spike composed of spikelets; also *fig.* said of a red or flame-coloured flower 1578. **b.** (Usu. in *pl.* **Torches.**) The Great Mullein, *Verbascum thapsus* (or other species): from its tall spike of yellow flowers 1552.

1. *Electric t.*, a contrivance consisting essentially of an electric lamp enclosed in a portable case containing a battery. **b.** The t. of Greek learning and civilisation was to be extinguished 1878. *To hand on the t.*, to preserve the knowledge of a subject.

attrib. and *Comb.*: **t.-fishing,** fishing by t.-light at night; **-lily,** the liliaceous genus *Tritoma*, having spikes of bright scarlet flowers; also called 'red-hot poker'; **-race** = LAMPADEDROMY; **-thistle,** a name for a columnar cactus of the genus *Cereus*. Hence **Torch** *v. trans.* to furnish, or light, with a t. or torches. †**To·rcher,** = next SHAKS.

To·rch-bea:rer. 1538. One who carries a torch.

To·rch-light. late ME. The light of a torch; illumination by a torch or torches. **b.** The time when torches are lighted; dusk 1656. **c.** *attrib.* Performed or carried on by torch-light 1876.

c. In the evening, a t. procession 1876.

‖**Torchon** (torʃoṅ). 1879. [Fr., duster, dish-cloth; f. *torcher* wipe.] Used *attrib.* in **t. board,** a board covered with *t. paper*, used in water-colour drawing; **t. lace** (also abbrev. *torchon*, pl. *-ons*), a coarse bobbin lace, of loose texture; **t. paper,** a kind of paper with a rough surface, used for water-colour drawing, etc.

To·rch-wood. 1601. **1.** Resinous wood of which torches are made. **2. a.** A tree of the genus *Amyris*, family *Rutaceæ*, having resinous wood, as *A. sylvatica* and *A. balsamifera*. **b.** A W. Indian shrub, *Casearia* (*Thiodia*) *serrata*. **c.** A species of cactus, *Cereus heptagonus*.

‖**Torcular** (tǭ·ɹkiulăɹ). 1621. [L., a press for wine or oil.] **1.** *Anat.* (in full *t. Herophili*) = †*Press of Herophilus*: a depression in the occipital bone at the confluence of a number of venous sinuses. **2.** *Surg.* A tourniquet 1727. So **To·rcular** *a.* pertaining to the *t. Herophili*.

Tore (tōᵊɹ), *sb.* 1664. [– Fr. *tore* (XVII) – L. TORUS.] = TORUS 1, 4.

Tore: see TEAR *v.*

Toreador (tǫriădōᵊɹ). 1618. [– Sp. *toreador*, f. *torear* fight (bulls) in the ring, f. *toro* bull :– L. *taurus*.] A Spanish (usu. mounted) bull-fighter.

†**To-re·nd,** *v.* [OE. *torendan*, f. TO-[2] + *rendan* REND *v.*] *trans.* To rend in pieces –1631.

‖**Torero** (torē·ro). 1728. [Sp.: see TOREADOR.] A (Spanish) bull-fighter (on foot).

Toreutic (torū·tik), *a.* and *sb.* 1837. [– Gr. τορευτικός, f. τορεύειν to work in relief, etc.] **A.** *adj.* Of or pertaining to toreutics; chiefly in phr. *t. art* = toreutics; also, of figures, etc., executed according to the toreutic art; of an artist, working in toreutics. **B.** *sb.* [tr. Gr. τορευτική (sc. τέχνη).] Chiefly in pl. **Toreutics:** The art of chasing, carving, and embossing, esp. metal.

‖**Torgoch** (tǭ·ɹgǫχ). Also †**torcoch.** 1611. [Welsh, f. *tor* belly + *coch* red.] The red-bellied char, found in the Welsh lakes.

Toric (tōᵊ·rik), *a.* 1900. [f. TOR(US + -IC.] Of or pertaining to a torus (see TORUS 4).

T. lens, a spectacle lens having for one of its surfaces a segment of an equilateral zone of a torus. Also *ellipt.* as *sb.*

Torment (tǭ·ɹmĕnt), *sb.* ME. [– OFr. *torment*, (also mod.) *tourment* :– L. *tormentum* engine for throwing missiles, cord, cable, instrument of torture, f. *torquēre* twist.] †**1.** An engine of war worked by torsion, for hurling stones, darts, etc. –1531. **2.** An instrument of torture; hence, the infliction of torture by such an instrument; torture inflicted or suffered ME. **b.** *spec.* The punishment of hell 1852. **3.** A state of great suffering, bodily or mental; agony; severe pain felt or endured ME. **4.** An action, circumstance, or condition which causes extreme pain or suffering of body or mind; a source of pain, trouble, or anguish, or in weakened sense, of worry or annoyance 1599. **b.** Applied to a person who causes trouble 1784. **5.** A violent storm; a tempest, tornado. *Obs.* exc. in Fr. form *tourmente*. ME.

2. It was a t. To lay upon the damn'd SHAKS. **3.** That doubleth al my t. and my wo CHAUCER. **4.** Why, death's the end of evils, and a rest Rather than t. B. JONS. The conviction that he had made himself absurd..was his t. 1825.

Torment (tǫɹme·nt), *v.* ME. [– OFr. *tormenter*, (also mod.) *tourmenter*, f. *to*(*u*)*rment* (see prec.). Cf. late L. *tormentare*.] **1.** *trans.* To put to torment or torture; to inflict torture upon. **2.** To afflict or vex with great suffering or misery, physical or mental; to pain, distress, plague ME. **b.** To tease or worry excessively; to trouble, 'plague' 1718. **3.** To throw into agitation; to toss, disturb, shake up, or stir physically. *Obs.* exc. as a Gallicism. 1491. **b.** *fig.* To twist, distort (sense, style, etc.) 1647.

1. For what offences..men are to be Eternally tormented HOBBES. **2. b.** We are tormenting our brains with some scheme of politics 1718. **3.** That warr..soaring on main wing Tormented all the Air MILT.

Tormentil (tǭ·ɹmĕntil). late ME. [–(O)Fr. *tormentille* – med.L. *tormentilla*, of unkn. origin.] A low-growing rosaceous herb, *Potentilla tormentilla* (*T. repens*), of trailing habit, common on heaths and dry pastures, and having strongly astringent roots; in use from early times in medicine, and in tanning. Also called *septfoil*.

Torme·nting, *ppl. a.* 1575. [f. TORMENT *v.* + -ING[2].] That torments, in various senses.

Sight hateful, sight t.! MILT. Hence **Torme·nting-ly** *adv.*, **-ness.**

Tormentor (tǫɹme·ntǭɹ). [ME. and AFr. *tormentour* = OFr. *tormentēor*, f. *tormenter*; see TORMENT *v.*, -ER[2] 3.] **1.** An officer who inflicts torture or cruelty; an official torturer; an executioner. **2.** One who or that which persistently inflicts intense pain, suffering, vexation, or annoyance 1553. **3.** An instrument that torments in some way, as a wheel-harrow for breaking up stiff soil; *pl.* riding spurs (*slang*), etc. 1609.

2. These words heereafter, thy tormentors bee SHAKS.

Tormentress (tǫɹme·ntrĕs). late ME. [– AFr. *tormenteresse*, fem. of *tormentour*; see -ESS[1].] A female tormentor.

To·rmentry. Now *rare.* late ME. [– OFr. *tormenterie*, f. *tormentēor*; see TORMENTOR, -RY.] †**1.** The infliction or suffering of torture or torment, as by executioners or fiends –1534. **2.** Tormenting feeling; severe suffering, pain, or vexation. Now *rare.* late ME.

‖**Tormina** (tǭ·ɹmină), *sb. pl.* 1656. [L. *tormina* griping of the bowels, ult. f. *torquēre* twist.] *Path.* Acute griping or wringing pains in the bowels; gripes. Hence **To·rminal,** †**To·rminous** *adjs.* of the nature of or characterized by t.

Torn (tǭɹn), pa. pple. of TEAR *v.*[1]

‖**Tornada** (tǫrnā·dă). 1823. [Prov., f. pa. pple. of *tornar* turn.] An envoy of three lines, in which the verse-endings of the preceding stanzas recur.

Tornado (tǫɹnē[i]·do). 1556. [Earliest form *ternado*, later *turnado*, *tournado*, *tornado*; perh. orig. altered – Sp. *tronada* thunderstorm (f. *tronar* to thunder), later assim. to *tornar* TURN; see -ADO.] **1.** A term applied by 16th c. navigators to violent thunderstorms of the tropical Atlantic, with torrential rain, and often with sudden and violent gusts of wind. Now *rare.* **2.** A very violent storm affecting a limited area, in which the wind is constantly changing its direction or rotating; a whirling wind, whirlwind; loosely, any very violent storm of wind, a hurricane 1626.

2. *fig.* One of Turner's magnificent tornadoes of colour THACKERAY. On this passage followed a great t. of cheering 1849. Hence **Tornadic** (tǫɹnæ·dik) *a.* of, pertaining to, or of the nature of a t.

‖**Tornaria** (tǫɹnēᵊ·riă). 1888. [mod.L., f. Gr. τόρνος or L. *tornus* a turner's wheel, in ref. to the shape of the larva.] *Zool.* The larval form of species of the Sea-acorn, *Balanoglossus*.

‖**Tornus** (tǭ·ɹnŏs). *Pl.* **-i** (-əi). 1897. [L., – Gr. τόρνος; see prec.] *Ent.* The inner or anal angle of the wing of an insect, esp. of the secondary wing of a tineid moth. Hence **To·rnal** *a.* of or pertaining to the t.

Torose (torōᵘ·s), *a.* 1760. [– L. *torosus*, f. *torus* bulge, brawn; see -OSE[1].] *Nat. Hist.* Bulging, swollen, protuberant: said of an approximately cylindrical body swollen here and there. So **To·rous** *a.* 1657.

Torpedinous (tǫɹpi·dinəs), *a. rare* or *Obs.* 1774. [f. L. *torpedo*, *-din-*, TORPEDO + -OUS.] Having the quality of a torpedo; benumbing, paralysing; also, of or pertaining to the torpedo or electric ray.

Fishy were his eyes; t. was his manner DE QUINCEY.

Torpedo (tǫɹpī·do), *sb. Pl.* **-oes.** 1520. [– L. *torpedo* stiffness, numbness, also the cramp-fish or electric ray, f. *torpēre* be stiff or numb.] **1.** A flat fish of the genus *Torpedo* or family *Torpedinidæ*, having an almost circular body with tapering tail, and characterized by the faculty of emitting electric discharges; the electric ray; also called *cramp-fish*, *cramp-ray*, *numb-fish*. **b.** *fig.* One who or that which has a benumbing influence 1590. **2.** *orig.* A case charged with gunpowder designed to explode under water after a given interval so as to destroy any vessel in its immediate vicinity; later also, a self-propelled submarine missile, usu. cigar-shaped, carrying an explosive which is fired by impact with its objective 1775. **b.** A type of car-body shaped like a torpedo 1909.

The original torpedo was a towed or drifting submarine mine, still used to defend channels, harbours, and the like (*drifting* or *moored t.*); it was towed at an angle by means of a spar extending at right angles (*otter* or *towing t.*), or carried on a ram or projecting pole (*boom-*, *outrigger-*, *spar-t.*).

3. a. *Mil.* A shell furnished with a percussion or friction device buried in the ground, which explodes when the ground above the device is trodden upon; a petard. *U.S.* **b.** A toy which explodes when thrown on a hard surface. **c.** A cartridge exploded in an oil-well to cause a renewal or increase of the flow. *U.S.* **d.** = FOG-SIGNAL 2 (*U.S.*). **e.** *Aerial t.*, a torpedo discharged from aircraft. 1786.

attrib. and *Comb.*: **t.-anchor,** an anchor for mooring a stationary t.; **-beard,** a pointed beard; **-body,** a motor-car body tapered at the ends; **-boom,** a spar bearing a t. on its upper end, the lower end swivelled and anchored to the bottom of the channel; **t. destroyer,** a torpedo-boat destroyer (officially called simply 'a destroyer'); **t. gun** = *t.-tube*; **-net,** a steel-wire netting suspended round a ship on projecting booms as a protection against torpedoes; **-ram,** a ram provided with t.-tubes; **-spar,** a spar rigged to a t. boat, to which a t. is attached; **-tube,** a kind of gun from which torpedoes are discharged by compressed air or gunpowder.

Torpe·do, *v.* 1873. [f. prec.] **1.** *trans.* To destroy or damage by means of a torpedo; to attack with a torpedo 1879. **b.** To lay (a channel, etc.) with torpedoes or submarine mines; to defend with torpedoes 1877. **2.** To explode a 'torpedo' at the bottom of (an oil-well) to increase the flow by shattering the rock or clearing the passage. Also *intr. U.S.* 1873.

Torpe·do boat. 1810. A vessel carrying one or more torpedoes; now, a small, fast warship from which torpedoes are discharged.

Comb.: **torpedo-boat catcher, torpedo-boat destroyer** (abbrev. *t.b.d.*), two types of small fast war-ships, orig. designed to prevent torpedo-boats from operating against a fleet.

Torpid (tǭ·ɹpid), *a.* (*sb.*) 1613. [– L. *torpidus* benumbed, f. *torpēre* be sluggish; see -ID¹.] **1.** Benumbed; deprived or devoid of the power of motion or feeling; dormant. **b.** *Path.* Sluggish in action or function 1807. **2.** *fig.* Wanting in animation or vigour; inactive; slow, sluggish; dull; stupefied; apathetic 1656.

1. Some animals became t. in winter, others were t. in summer EMERSON. **b.** Tendency to t. liver 1899. **2.** It is a man's own fault..if his mind grows t. in old age JOHNSON.

B. *sb.* At Oxford: usu. *pl.* The races rowed in Lent term in eight-oared clinker-built open boats; orig. designating the boats; later also the crews 1838. Hence **To·rpid-ly** *adv.*, **-ness.**

Torpidity (tǫɹpi·dĭti). 1614. [f. prec. + -ITY.] The condition or quality of being torpid; torpor, sluggishness, numbness.

Torpitude (tǭ·ɹpitiūd). Now *rare.* 1713. [irreg. for *torpetude, f. L. *torpēre* + -TUDE.] = prec.

Torpor (tǭ·ɹpǫɹ). 1607. [– L. *torpor*, f. *torpēre* be sluggish; see -OR 1.] Torpid condition or quality. **a.** Absence or suspension of motive power, activity, or feeling; †inertia; suspended animation or development; *Path.* morbid inertia or insensibility, stupor 1626. **b.** *transf.* Intellectual or spiritual lethargy; apathy; dullness; indifference 1607.

b. A universal t. of the mental faculties 1789.

Torporific (tǭɹpŏri·fik), *a.* (*sb.*) 1769. [f. stem of L. *torpor* (see prec.) + -FIC.] Causing torpor; also *fig.* stupefying, deadening. **b.** *absol.* as *sb.* Something causing torpor 1840.

Torquate (tǭ·ɹkweˡt), *a.* 1661. [– L. *torquatus* wearing a TORQUES; see -ATE².] *Zool.* Having a ring-like marking, formed by hairs or feathers of special colour or texture, round the neck; collared.

To·rquated, *a.* 1623. [f. as prec. + -ED¹.] **1.** Wearing a torque. **2.** Formed as or like a torque; twisted from a narrow strip or band 1851. **3.** *Zool.* = prec. 1891.

Torque¹, torc (tǭɹk). 1834. [– Fr. *torque* – L. TORQUES.] A collar, necklace, bracelet, or similar ornament, consisting of a twisted narrow band or strip, usu. of precious metal, worn especially by the ancient Gauls and Britons.

Torque² (tǭɹk). 1884. [f. L. *torquēre* twist.] *Physics.* The twisting or rotary force in a piece of mechanism (as a measurable quantity); the moment of a system of forces producing rotation. **b.** *attrib.*, as *t. rod, tube.*

Torqued (tǭɹkt), *a.* 1572. [After Fr. †*torqué*, pa. pple. of †*torquer* – L. *torquēre* twist.] **1.** Twisted, convoluted; formed like a torque 1577. **2.** *Her.* Twisted or bent into a double curve like the letter S: said of a serpent or dolphin used as a bearing 1572.

‖**Torques** (tǭ·ɹkwīz). 1693. [L., f. *torquēre* twist.] **1.** = TORQUE¹. **2.** *Zool.* A collar or ring-like marking round the neck of an animal, formed by hair, feathers, etc. of special colour or texture 1891.

Torrefaction (tǫrĭfæ·kʃən). 1612. [f. TORREFY, after similar pairs; see -FACTION.] The process of drying or roasting by fire; the state or condition of being roasted.

Torrefy (tǫ·rĭfəi), *v.* 1601. [– Fr. *torréfier* – L. *torrefacere* dry by heat, f. *torrēre* scorch; see -FY.] **1.** *trans.* To roast, scorch, or dry by fire. **b.** To deprive of all moisture by heating, as a chemical or drug 1601. **c.** *Metall.* To roast, as ores, in order to deprive of sulphur, arsenic, or other volatile substance 1686. **2.** *intr.* To become reduced to a cinder or ash 1615.

Torrent (tǫ·rĕnt), *sb.* (*a.*) 1601. [– Fr. *torrent* – It. *torrente* – L. *torrens, -ent-*, subst. use of pr. pple. (scorching, (of streams) boiling, roaring, rushing) of *torrēre* scorch; see -ENT.] **1.** A stream of water flowing with great swiftness and impetuosity, whether from the steepness of its course, or from being temporarily flooded; more esp. applied (as in Fr.) to a mountain stream which at times is swollen and at other times more or less dry. **2. a.** *fig.* A violent or tumultuous flow or 'stream', e.g. of words, feelings, opposition, etc. 1647. **b.** *transf.* A forcible stream, e.g. of lava, loose stones, wind, light; also, a violent downpour of rain 1781.

1. The dry beds of mountain torrents, which had lived too fierce a life to let it be a long one HAWTHORNE. **2. a.** A t. of abuse 1784. **b.** A soaking t. of rain 1806.

B. *adj.* Rushing like a torrent 1667.

A t. mountain-brook TENNYSON.

Torrential (tǫre·nʃăl), *a.* 1849. [f. TORRENT *sb.* + -IAL.] **1.** Of, pertaining to, or of the nature of a torrent; produced by the action of a torrent 1861. **2.** Like a torrent in rapidity or violence; rushing; falling in torrents, as rain 1849. **b.** *fig.* As copious or impetuous as a torrent 1877.

2. To the intense heat,..has succeeded t. rain 1865.

Torricellian (tǫritʃe·liăn, tǫrise·liăn), *a.* 1660. [f. name of *Torricelli*, an Italian physicist (1608–1647) + -AN.] Of or belonging to Torricelli.

T. experiment, that by which, in 1643, Torricelli proved that the column of mercury in a closed tube inverted in a vessel of mercury is supported by the pressure of the atmosphere on the mercury in the vessel, and that the height of the column corresponds exactly to the atmospheric pressure. *T. tube*, early name for the tube of the mercurial barometer. *T. vacuum*, the vacuum above the mercurial column in the barometer, produced by filling the tube with mercury and then inverting it in a cup of mercury.

Torrid (tǫ·rid), *a.* 1586. [– Fr. *torride* or L. *torridus*, f. *torrēre* scorch; see -ID¹.] **1.** Scorched, burned, exposed to great heat; also, intensely hot, burning, scorching 1611. **b.** *esp.* in *t. zone*, the region of the earth between the tropics 1586. **2.** *fig.* **a.** In ref. to the 'heat' of persecution 1635. **b.** Hot in temper or passion; ardent, zealous 1646.

1. A t. and scorched earth PURCHAS. **2. a.** In Maryes t. dayes.., when Cruelty was witty 1635. **b.** Temper'd 'twixt cold despair and t. joy CRASHAW. Hence **To·rrid-ly** *adv.*, **-ness.** **Torri·dity**, the state, condition, or quality of being t.

Torse¹ (tǭɹs). 1572. [– obs. Fr. *torse, torce* wreath :– Rom. **torsa* = L. *torta*, fem. pa. pple. of *torquēre* twist.] *Her.* The twisted band or wreath by which the crest is joined to the helmet.

Torse² (tǭɹs). 1622. [– Fr. *torse* – It. *torso* TORSO.] = TORSO.

Torse³ (tǭɹs). 1863. [app. arbitrarily f. *tors-* in TORSION.] *Geom.* A developable surface; a surface generated by a moving straight line which at every instant is turning, in some plane or other through it, about some point or other in its length. Hence **To·rsal** *a.* of or pertaining to a t.

Torsibi·lity. 1864. [f. **torsible* (f. as prec. + -IBLE) + -ITY.] Capability of being twisted; esp. in ref. to degree or amount.

Torsile (tǭ·ɹsəil, -il), *a.* 1882. [f. *torsion*, after *tension*/*tensile*; see -ILE.] Of the nature of torsion.

Torsion (tǭ·ɹʃən). late ME. [– (O)Fr. *torsion* – late L. *torsio, -ōn-*, by-form of L. *tortio*, f. *tort-*, pa. ppl. stem of *torquēre* twist; see -ION.] **1.** The action of twisting, or turning a body spirally by the operation of contrary forces acting at right angles to its axis; also, the twisted condition produced by this action; twist 1543. **b.** A twisting of the body or a part of it (*rare*) 1660. **c.** *Surg.* The twisting of the cut end of an artery to stop hæmorrhage 1835. †**2.** *Path.* A wringing or griping of the bowels; tormina –1689.

1. *Angle of t.*, (*a*) the angle through which one end of a rod or other body is twisted while the other end is held fast; (*b*) *Geom.* the infinitesimal angle between two consecutive osculating planes of a tortuous curve. *Balance of t.* = t.-balance.

attrib. and *Comb.*: **t.-balance,** an instrument for measuring minute horizontal forces, consisting of a wire or filament having a horizontal arm to the end of which the force is applied so as to make it revolve and twist the wire, etc., through an angle proportional to the twisting moment of the force; **-curve,** a curve caused by t. Hence **To·rsional** *a.* of, pertaining or relating to, caused by or resulting from t.; **-ly** *adv.*

Torsk (tǭɹsk). 1680. [– Norw. *torsk, tosk*, Sw., Da. *torsk* :– ON. *þorskr, þoskr*; prob. f. root of ON. *þurr* dry.] A gadoid fish, *Brosmius brosme*, much used for food in the dried form of *stockfish*.

Torso (tǭ·ɹso). *Pl.* **torsos.** 1797. [– It. *torso* stalk, stump, core, trunk of a statue :– L. *thyrsus*; see THYRSUS.] **1.** *Sculpture.* The trunk of a statue, without or considered independently of head and limbs; also, the trunk of the human body. **2.** *fig.* Something left mutilated or unfinished 1852.

1. The T. of the Belvedere, a colossal fragment of Herculean stature 1875. Clad only in a waist-cloth, his t. was fully revealed 1899.

Tort (tǭɹt). ME. [– OFr. *tort* :– med.L. *tortum* (IX), subst. use of n. of L. *tortus*, pa. pple. of *torquēre* twist.] †**1.** Injury, wrong –1748. **2.** *Eng. Law.* The breach of a duty imposed by law, whereby some person acquires a right of action for damages 1586.

1. No wild beasts should do them any torte SPENSER.

‖**Torta** (tǭ·ɹtă). 1839. [Sp. :– late L. *torta* cake.] *Mining.* One of the large flat circular heaps or 'cakes' of ore spread upon the floor or *patio* in the Mexican amalgamation process.

‖**Torteau** (torto). *Pl.* **torteaux** (tortōᵘz, Fr. -o). 1486. [Earliest *tortellis* pl. (XV) – OFr. *tortel*; later *torteau(x* – Fr. *tourteau* 'large round cake, etc.' deriv. of *tourte* :– late L. *torta* (see prec.). Cf. AL. *tortella* XIV/XV.] **1.** *Her.* A roundle gules; the specific name of a small red circular figure charged upon a shield, supposed to represent a cake of bread. †**2.** A flat cake, a pancake. PURCHAS.

Tortfeasor (tǭ·ɹtˌfī:zǭɹ). 1659. [– OFr. *tort-fesor, -faiseur*, etc., f. *tort* wrong, evil + *-fesor, faiseur* doer.] *Law.* One who is guilty of a tort; a wrong-doer, trespasser.

‖**Torticollis** (tǭɹtikǫ·lis). 1811. [mod.L., f. L. *tortus* crooked, twisted + *collum* neck.] *Path.* A rheumatic or other affection of the muscles of the neck, in which it is so twisted as to keep the head turned to one side; wry-neck.

Tortile (tǭ·ɹtəil, -il), *a. rare.* 1658. [– L. *tortilis*, f. *tort-*, pa. ppl. stem of *torquēre* twist; see -ILE.] Twisted, coiled; winding; capable of being twisted. Hence **Torti·lity,** the quality of being t.

‖**Tortilla** (tortī·lʸa). 1699. [Sp. dim. of *torta* cake; see TORTA.] In Mexico, A thin round cake made of maize-flour, baked on a flat plate of iron, earthenware, etc. and eaten hot.

Tortious (tǭ·ɹʃəs), *a.* late ME. [– AFr. *torcious* (XIV), f. stem of *torcion, tortion* extortion, violence :– late L. *tortio, -ōn-* torture; see -OUS.] †**1.** Wrongful, injurious, hurtful; illegal –1742. **2.** *Law.* Pertaining to or of the nature of a tort 1544.

1. A torcious vsurper HALL. Hence **To·rtiously** *adv.*

Tortive (tǭ·ɹtiv), *a. rare.* 1606. [– Fr. †*tortif*, or suffix-var. of TORTILE. L. *tortivus* = pressed or squeezed out.] Twisting, twisted, tortuous.

Tortoise (tǭ·ɹtəs). late ME. [The earliest examples show a variety of forms reflecting med.L. *tortuca*, (O)Fr. *tortue*, and (occas.) Sp. *tortuga*; the present form (of obscure origin) appears in XVI.] **1.** A four-footed reptile of the order *Chelonia*, in which the trunk is enclosed between a carapace and plastron, formed by the dorsal vertebræ, ribs, and sternum; the skin being covered with large horny plates, commonly called the shell.

The *Chelonia* are usually divided into Land tortoises (*Testudinidæ*), Marsh-tortoises (*Emydæ*), River-tortoises (*Trionycidæ*), and Marine tortoises (*Chelonidæ*). The last are now commonly distinguished as *turtles*. By some zoologists the name 'tortoise' is confined to the terrestrial genus *Testudo* and its immediate congeners; see also TERRAPIN.

b. A figure or image of a tortoise 1648. **c.** Taken as a type of slowness of motion; hence, applied to a very slow person or thing 1825. **2.** = TESTUDO 3 a, b. 1569. **3.** Short for TORTOISE-SHELL. Usu. *attrib.* or as *adj.* 1654.

2. His soldiers, protected from missiles by moveable penthouses (called Tortoises) GROTE. **3.** A Gold Snuff-box,..the bottom T. 1702.

attrib. and *Comb.*: **t.-beetle,** a leaf-beetle of the family *Cassididæ*, from the resemblance of the wing-cases and prothorax to the carapace of a t.; **-lyre,** a lyre made of a t.-shell; **-plant,** a S. African plant, *Testudinaria elephantipes*, allied to the yam, having a large fleshy root-stock growing above ground, the surface of which becomes deeply cracked so as to suggest the carapace of a t.

Tortoise-shell (tǭ·ɹtəs,ʃəːl, *usu.* tǭ·ɹtəʃel). 1601. **1.** The shell, esp. the upper shell or carapace, of a tortoise, consisting of horny scales covering the dermal skeleton. **b.** As a material (without *a* or *pl.*): The shell of certain tortoises, esp. that of the hawk's-bill turtle, *Chelone imbricata*, which is semi-transparent, with a mottled or clouded coloration, and is much used in ornamental work, as inlaying, etc. 1632. †**2.** Short for (*a*) *t. cat*, (*b*) *t. butterfly* 1840. **3.** *attrib.* or as *adj.* **a.** Made of tortoise-shell 1651. **b.** Having the colouring or appearance of tortoise-shell; mottled or variegated with black, red, and yellow, etc. 1782. **c.** Producing tortoise-shell 1886.

3. b. T. butterfly, one of several butterflies, esp. the European *Vanessa urticæ* and *V. polychlorus*, and the Amer. *Aglais milberti*; **t. cat,** a domestic cat of this colour. **c. T. turtle,** the hawk's-bill turtle, or other species from which t. is obtained.

Tortricid (tǭ·ɹtrisid), *a.* and *sb.* 1889. [f. mod.L. *Tortricidæ* pl., f. TORTRIX; see -ID³.] **a.** *Ent. adj.* Belonging to the family *Tortricidæ* of *Lepidoptera*, comprising the leaf-roller moths, typified by the genus *Tortrix*; *sb.* a moth of this family. **b.** *Zool. adj.* Belonging to the family *Tortricidæ* of snakes, typified by the genus *Tortrix* or *Ilysia*; *sb.* a snake of this family.

‖**Tortrix** (tǭ·ɹtriks). *Pl.* **tortrices** (-əi·sīz). 1797. [mod.L. *tortrix*, *-ic-*, fem. of *tortor* in sense 'twister', in ref. to the leaf-rolling habits of the larvæ.] **1.** *Ent.* A genus of moths, typical of the family *Tortricidæ* (see prec. a); a moth of this genus or family, a leaf-roller moth. **2.** *Zool.* A genus of snakes, also called *Ilysia*, including the coral-snake of Guiana, *T.* (*I.*) *scytale* 1843.

Tortuosity (tǭɹtiu,ǫ·sīti). 1603. [– late L. *tortuositas*, f. L. *tortuosus*; see next, -ITY.] The quality or condition of being tortuous; twistedness, crookedness, sinuosity; an instance of this.

Tortuous (tǭ·ɹtiu,əs), *a.* late ME. [– OFr. *tortuous* (mod. *tortueux*) – L. *tortuosus*, f. *tortus* twisting, f. *tort-*, pa. ppl. stem of *torquēre* twist; see -UOUS.] **1.** Full of twists, turns, or bends; winding, crooked, sinuous. **b.** *Geom.* Applied to a curve of which no two successive portions are in the same plane 1867. **2.** *fig.* Not direct or straightforward; devious, circuitous, crooked: esp. in a moral sense 1682.

1. We found the river-course very t. DARWIN. **2.** A more t. way of trying to get possession of goods he had never heard of 1911. Hence **To·rtuous-ly** *adv.*, **-ness.**

Torturable (tǭ·ɹtiŭrăb'l, -tʃər-), *a. rare.* 1655. [f. TORTURE *v.* + -ABLE.] Capable of being tortured.

Torture (tǭ·ɹtiŭɹ, -tʃəɹ), *sb.* 1540. [– (O)Fr. *torture* or late L. *tortura* twisting, writhing, torment, f. *tort-*; see TORTUOUS, -URE.] **1.** The infliction of excruciating pain, as practised by cruel tyrants, savages, brigands, etc., in hatred or revenge, or as a means of extortion, etc.; spec. *judicial t.*, inflicted by a judicial or quasi-judicial authority, for the purpose of forcing an accused or suspected person to confess, or an unwilling witness to give evidence or information; a form of this (often in *pl.*) 1551. †**b.** *transf.* An instrument or means of torture –1722. **2.** Severe or excruciating pain or suffering (of body or mind); anguish, agony, torment; the infliction of such 1540. **b.** *transf.* A cause of severe pain or anguish 1612. **3.** *transf.* and *fig.* Severe pressure; violent perversion or 'wresting'; violent action or operation; severe testing or examination 1605.

1. *To put to* (*the*) *t.*, to inflict t. upon, to torture. **2.** The tortures of suspense 1797. **b.** An ugly picture was t. to his cultivated eye 1873. **3.** Much so-called wit..is nothing more than the systematic t. of words 1887.

To·rture, *v.* 1588. [f. prec.] **1.** *trans.* To inflict torture upon; *spec.* to subject to judicial torture; to put to the torture 1593. **2.** To inflict severe pain or suffering upon; to torment; to distress or afflict grievously; also, to puzzle or perplex greatly. Also *absol.* to cause extreme pain. 1588. **3.** *fig.* **a.** To act upon violently in some way, so as to strain, twist, distort, etc. 1626. **b.** To 'twist' (language, etc.) from the proper meaning or form; to distort 1648. **4.** To extract by torture; to extort (*rare*) 1687.

1. Slowly tortured to death by the Turks 1847. **2.** Jeffreys was..tortured by a cruel internal malady MACAULAY. **3.** The Bow tortureth the String continually, and thereby holdeth it in a Continuall Trepidation BACON. **b.** To t. Scripture for the defending of his errors 1648. Hence **To·rturer,** one who or that which inflicts or causes torture; a tormentor; *spec.* one who executes judicial torture. **To·rturingly** *adv.*

Torturous (tǭ·ɹtiŭrəs, -tʃər-), *a.* 1495. [– AFr. *torturous* = OFr. *-eux*, f. *torture* TORTURE *sb.*; see -OUS. In mod. use direct f. TORTURE *sb.*] Full of, involving, or causing torture.

The torterous inventions of hard snaffles 1618.

‖**Torula** (tǫ·rˈulă). *Pl.* **-æ** (*-i*). 1833. [mod.L. dim. (with change of gender) of TORUS (sense 3); see -ULE.] *Biol.* lit. A small rounded swelling or bulge. **a.** Each of the small rounded cells of various fungi or microbes, as the yeast-plant, etc.; also, a chain of such cells. **b.** (With capital.) A genus of fungi, chiefly fermentative. Hence **To·rulifo:rm** *a.* having the form of a t. or chain of rounded cells, moniliform. **To·rulose** (1806), **To·rulous** (1752) *adjs.* (*Nat. Hist.*) having at intervals small rounded swollen parts, as a stem, pod, tube, antenna.

‖**Torus** (tōᵊ·rǫs). *Pl.* **tori** (tōᵊ·rəi). 1563. [L., swelling, bolster, round moulding.] **1.** *Arch.* A large convex moulding, of semi-circular or similar section, used esp. at the base of a column. **2.** *Bot.* The swollen summit of the flower-stalk, which supports the floral organs 1829. **3. a.** *Zool.* A protuberant part or organ, as the ventral parapodia in some annelids. **b.** *Anat.* A smooth rounded ridge or elongated protuberance, as of a muscle; *spec.* the *tuber cinereum* of the brain. 1877. **4.** *Geom.* A surface or solid generated by the revolution of a circle or other conic about any axis; e.g. a solid ring of circular or elliptic section 1870.

Torve (tǭɹv), *a. rare.* 1650. [– L. *torvus* grim.] Stern in aspect; grim, fierce-looking. So **To·rvid, To·rvous** *adjs.* in same sense. **To·rvity,** grimness.

Tory (tōᵊ·ri), *sb.* and *a.* 1646. [Presumably – Ir. **tóraighe* (tō·rīye) pursuer, implied in *tóraighheachd* pursuit, f. *tóir* pursue.] **A.** *sb.* **1.** In the 17th c., one of the dispossessed Irish, who became outlaws, subsisting by plundering and killing the English settlers and soldiers; a bog-trotter, a rapparee; later, often applied to any Irish Papist or Royalist in arms. *Obs.* exc. *Hist.* **2.** With capital T: A nickname given 1679–80 by the Exclusionists to those who opposed the exclusion of James, Duke of York (a Roman Catholic) from the succession to the Crown 1681. **3.** Hence, from 1689, the name of one of the two great parliamentary and political parties in England, and (at length) in Great Britain. (The party sprang from the 17th c. Royalists and Cavaliers, and its members at first were more or less identical with the Anti-Exclusionists or 'Tories' in sense 2.) Opp. orig. and during the 18th c. to WHIG; later to LIBERAL, RADICAL, or LABOUR; superseded officially *c*1830 by CONSERVATIVE, which was partly eclipsed by UNIONIST after 1886; retained colloq. and in hostile use. O.E.D. **4.** *U.S. Hist.* A member of the British party during the Revolutionary period; a loyal colonist 1775. **5.** *transf.* Applied to any one in foreign countries or former ages holding views analogous to those of the English Tories; also, one who is by temperament or sentiment inclined to conservative principles 1797. **B.** *adj.* **1.** That is a Tory; of, pertaining to, or characteristic of a Tory or Tories; consisting of or constituted by Tories; also, having the principles or aims of a Tory; supported or recognized by the Tory party; Conservative 1682. **2.** In extended or transf. senses: see A. 5. 1832.

1. We drank 'Church and King' after dinner with true T. cordiality BOSWELL. **2.** The still orthodox and t. view found in the Old Testament 1899.

Comb.: **T. Democracy,** combination of Toryism with democracy; democracy under T. leadership; new or democratic Toryism; progressive Conservatism; so **T. democrat,** one who professes T. democracy. Hence **To·ryish** *a.*

Toryism (tōᵊ·ri,iz'm). 1682. [f. prec. + -ISM.] The principles, practices, and methods of Tories.

‖**Tosca** (tǫ·skă). 1818. [Sp., fem. of *tosco* coarse.] A soft dark-brown limestone occurring embedded and sometimes stratified in the surface formation of the Pampas.

Tosh. *slang.* 1892. [Of unkn. origin.] Bosh, nonsense, twaddle.

Tosher (tǫ·ʃəɹ). *Undergraduates' slang.* 1889. [joc. deformation of *unattached* + -ER¹.] An unattached or non-collegiate student at a university having residential colleges.

Toss (tǫs), *sb.* 1634. [f. next.] An act of tossing. **1.** A pitching up and down or to and fro. †**2.** A state of agitation or commotion –1837. **3.** An act of casting, pitching, throwing, or hurling; a throw, a pitch 1660. **4.** A sudden jerk; *esp.* a quick upward or backward movement of the head 1676. **5.** An act of tossing a coin; a decision arrived at thus 1798. *T. and catch* (U.S.) = PITCH-AND-TOSS 1904. **6.** The throwing off of homing pigeons in a trial of their flight and homing powers 1897.

2. Lord! what a tosse I was for some time in PEPYS. **3.** *Full t.*, in *Cricket*, the delivery of a ball which does not touch the ground in its flight between the wickets. **b.** A throw from a horse 1917; phr. *to take a t.* (lit. and fig.). **4.** She throws up her Head with a scornful T. 1718.

Comb.: **t.-up,** the throwing up of a coin to arrive at a decision; *fig.* an even chance (*colloq.*).

Toss (tǫs), *v.* Pa. t. and pa. pple. **tossed** (tǫst), also **tost.** 1506. [Of unkn. origin.] **I.** *trans.* **1.** To throw, pitch, or fling about, here and there, or to and fro: expressing the action of wind or wave, or the light, careless, or disdainful action of a person, on something easily moved. **2.** To shake, shake up, stir up 1557. **3.** *fig.* To disturb or agitate; to disorder, disquiet 1526.

1. The shippe was in the middes of the see, and was toost with waves TINDALE *Matt.* 14 : 24. *fig.* Here, there, by various fortune tost GAY. **3.** Thus was I tost..With strugling doubts 1672.

II. *intr.* †**1.** To be in mental agitation or distraction; to be disquieted in mind or circumstances –1582. **2. a.** for *refl.* To fling or jerk oneself about; to move about restlessly 1560. **b.** for *pass.* To be flung or rocked about; to be kept in motion; to be agitated 1582.

2. a. Wretch, that long has tost On the thorny bed of Pain GRAY. **b.** A fleet of merchantmen tossing on the waves MACAULAY.

III. *trans.* **1.** To throw, cast, pitch, fling, hurl (without any notion of agitation) 1570. **b.** *absol.* To fling oneself (like a body tossed) 1728. **2.** *esp.* Of two players: To throw, or impel by hitting (a ball, etc.) to and fro between them. Often *fig.* or in fig. context. 1514. **b.** *fig. spec.* To bandy (a subject or question) from one side to the other in debate; to discuss; to make the subject of talk 1540. **3.** To throw up, throw into the air; *esp.* to throw (a coin, etc.) up, to see how it falls; = *toss up.* Also *absol.* 1526. **4.** To throw or jerk up suddenly without letting go 1590. †**b.** To drink out of (a cup, etc.), tilting it up; hence, to empty by drinking; = *toss off* –1708. **5.** To lift, jerk, or throw up (the head, etc.) with a sudden, impatient, or spirited movement 1591.

1. The governor's daughter..tossed a note to him over the wall 1718. **b.** She tossed out of the room THACKERAY. **2.** Phr. *To t. from pillar to post* (PILLAR *sb.*). **b.** If we were to t. the matter about..for twenty days, we could only end as we began BURKE. **3.** Phr. *To t. in a blanket*, to throw (a person) upward repeatedly from a blanket held slackly at each corner. *To t. a pancake*, to throw it up so that it falls back into the pan with the other side up. **4.** Phr. *T. t. oars*, 'to throw them up out of the rowlocks, and raise them perpendicularly an-end' (Adm. Smyth).

With advs. **T. off. a.** To drink off with energetic action. **b.** To dispose of in an off-hand manner. **T. up. a.** See prec. senses and UP. **b.** *absol.* To t. a coin, etc., in the air to wager on which side it will fall, or to determine a question by this. †**c.** To prepare, serve up, hastily. Hence **To·sser,** one who or that which tosses.

Tosspot (tǫ̀spǫt). 1568. [f. phr. *to toss a pot*, Toss *v.* III. 4 b.] One accustomed to toss off his pot; a heavy drinker; a toper.

Tost, var. TOSSED, pa. t. and pa. pple. of Toss *v.*, also *ppl. a.* Still freq. in poetry and combs. as *tempest-t.*

Tosticate (tǫ·stikeⁱt), *v.* Now *dial.* 1650. Usu. in pa. pple. *tosticated*, app. orig. for *intoxicated*, but later also assoc. w. *tossed*, *tost*, and used as = tossed about, distracted.

I have been so tosticated about since my last SWIFT.

Tot (tǫt), *sb.*[1] 1690. [Short for *total* or L. *totum*. See TOTE *sb.*] The total of an addition; hence, an addition sum; also (*t.-up*), adding up, totalling.

Tot, *sb.*[2] *colloq.* or *local*. 1725. [Of dial. origin.] **1.** A very small or tiny child. **2.** A very small drinking-vessel; a child's mug. Chiefly *dial.* 1828. **3.** A minute quantity, esp. of drink; a dram; also, anything very small 1828.

Tot (tǫt), *v. colloq.* 1760. [f. TOT *sb.*[1]] *trans.* To add *together* and bring out the total of; to sum *up*. **b.** *intr. To t. up*: to amount, 'come' (*to*) 1882.

b. Three stalls a week t. up frightfully in a year 1892.

Total (tōᵘ·tăl), *a.* and *sb.* late ME. [– (O)Fr. *total* – schol. L. *totalis*, f. *totum* the whole, subst. use of n. of L. *totus* entire, whole.] **A.** *adj.* **1.** Of, pertaining to, or relating to the whole of something. Now *rare* exc. in *t. eclipse*, an eclipse of the sun or moon in which the whole of the disc is obscured. **2.** Constituting or comprising a whole; whole, entire. late ME. **3.** Complete in extent or degree; absolute, utter 1647.

2. Its t. revenue does not pay its expenses 1833. **3.** A t. absence of self-respect 1838. *T. abstinence*, *spec.* entire abstinence from alcoholic drinks; so *t. abstainer*.

B. *sb.* (the adj. used absol.) The aggregate; the whole sum or amount; a whole 1557. Hence **To·tally** *adv.*

Total (tōᵘ·tăl), *v.* 1716. [f. prec.] **1. a.** *trans.* To reach the total of, amount to 1859. **b.** *intr.* To amount *to*, mount *up to* 1880. **2.** *trans.* To bring to a total, add up, complete 1716.

Totality (totæ·lĭti). 1598. [– schol. L. *totalitas*, f. *totalis* TOTAL *a.*; see -ITY. Cf. (O)Fr. *totalité*.] **1.** The quality of being total; entirety 1627. **b.** *Astron.* Total obscuration of the sun or moon in an eclipse; the moment of occurrence or time of duration of this 1842. **2.** That which is total; a whole; the total number or amount 1598.

Hence **Totalita·rian** *a. Civics*, of or pertaining to a polity which permits no rival loyalties or parties.

Totaliza·tion. 1888. [f. TOTALIZE *v.*; see -ATION.] The action or process of totalizing, or the condition of being totalized; calculation of the total.

Totalizator (tōᵘ·tăləizēⁱ:təɹ). 1879. [f. TOTALIZE + -ATOR, after Fr. *totalisateur*.] A machine or apparatus for registering and showing the total of operations, measurements, etc.; *spec.* an apparatus for registering and indicating the number of tickets sold to betters on each horse in a race.

Totalize (tōᵘ·tăləiz), *v.* 1818. [f. TOTAL *a.* + -IZE. Cf. Fr. *totaliser*.] *trans.* To make total; to combine into a total or aggregate.

‖**Totara** (tōᵘ·tără, totā·rā). 1832. [Maori *tótăra*.] A large New Zealand coniferous tree, *Podocarpus totara*, producing light, durable, tough timber of a dark red colour, highly valued for building, piles, cabinet work, etc.

Tote (tōᵘt), *sb.* 1771. **1.** [Short for *total*; cf. TOT *sb.*[1]] The total amount, number, or sum. Chiefly in pleonastic phr. *the whole t.* Now *dial.* **2.** Abbreviation of *total abstainer* (*dial.* or low *colloq.*) 1870; and (orig. *Australian*) of TOTALIZATOR (*colloq.*) 1891. attrib. *tote club*, *-house*.

Tote (tōᵘt), *v. U.S. colloq.* 1676. [In English use in XVII; prob. of dial. origin.] *trans.* To carry as a burden or load; also, to transport, esp. supplies to, or timber, etc. from, a logging-camp or the like.

At Baltimore I made a stay of two days, during which I was toted about town W. IRVING.

†**To-tea·r**, *v.* [OE. *to-teran*, f. TO-[2] + *teran* TEAR *v.*] *trans.* To tear to pieces –1605.

Totem (tōᵘ·tĕm). 1760. [From Ojibwa, or some kindred Algonquian di[alect.]] Among the Amer. Indians: The hereditary mark, emblem, or badge of a tribe, clan, or group of Indians, consisting of a figure or representation of some animal, less commonly a plant or other natural object, after which the group is named; also applied to the animal or natural object itself, sometimes considered to be ancestrally or fraternally related to the clan. **b.** By anthropologists the name has been extended to refer to other savage peoples or tribes, which (though they may not use totem marks) are similarly divided into groups or clans named after animals, etc. 1874.

Twelve of these placed their totems opposite my signature; each t. consisting of the rude representation of a bear, a deer, an otter, a rat, or some other wild animal 1887.

Comb.: **t.-exogamy**, the custom of marrying only one of a different t. or totem-clan; **-pole**, **-post**, a post carved and painted with totem figures, erected by the Indians of the north-west of North America in front of their houses. Hence **Tote·mic** *a.* of, pertaining to, or of the nature of a t. or totems; characterized by or having totems.

Totemism (tōᵘ·tĕmiz'm). 1791. [f. prec. + -ISM.] The use of totems, with the clan division, and the social, marriage, and religious customs connected with it.

To·temist. 1881. [f. as prec. + -IST.] **1.** One who belongs to a totem clan, or has a totem. **2.** One who is versed in the history of totemism 1897. So **Totemi·stic** *a.* of, pertaining to, or characterized by totemism.

Tother (tʊ·ðəɹ), *pron.* and *a.* Also **t'other.** Now *dial.* [ME. *þe toþer*, for earlier *þet oþer*, *þat oþer* the other, *þet*, *þat* being orig. n. of the def. art.] **A.** *pron.* or *adj.* used absol. **1.** The other (of two). †**2.** The second (of two or more) –1450. **3.** *pl.* (†*the tother, tothers* rare): The others, the rest ME.

1. Thei crieden the t. to the t. WYCLIF *Isa.* 6:3. You cannot tell one from t. 1870. ¶ *To tell t. from which* (= to distinguish between a number of things), joc. phr. in gen. colloq. use.

B. as *adj.* preceding a sb. **1.** The other (of two) ME. †**b.** After a possessive: Other –1721. **2.** The second, another, one more. *Obs.* exc. *Sc.* 1600. **3.** (*The*) *t.* (*day*, etc.), the other (day, night, etc.); a few (days, etc.) ago 1575.

‖**Toties quoties** (tōᵘ·ʃiiz kwōᵘ·ʃiiz), *adv.* Also **totiens quotiens.** 1525. [L. 'so often as often'.] As often as something happens or occasion demands; repeatedly.

Totipalmate (tōᵘtipæ·lmeⁱt), *a.* (*sb.*) 1872. [f. *toti-*, comb. form of L. *totus* whole + PALMATE *a.*] *Ornith.* Wholly webbed; having all the toes connected by membrane which reaches to the extremities; steganopodous. **B.** *sb.* A totipalmate bird. Hence **To:tipalma·tion,** the condition of being t.

Totipotent (toti·pŏtĕnt), *a.* 1901. [f. L. *toti-* (see prec.) + POTENT *a.*] *Biol.* Capable of developing into or generating a complete organism: said of a cell.

‖**Toto** (tōᵘ·to), abl. sing. masc. and neut. of L. *totus* all, whole, entire (cf. IN TOTO): occurring in a few phrases, as **Toto cælo** (tōᵘ·to sī·lo), 'by the whole heaven', by as much as the distance between the poles, diametrically.

Toto-, used as comb. form of L. *totus* whole, in certain cases, instead of *toti-* (see -O-), forming compound adjs., **a.** in sense 'wholly' (see -O- 1), as **to:to-conge·nital, to:to-mu·te; b.** in sense 'total and..' (see -O- 2), as **To:to-pa·rtial** *Logic*, of a proposition: of which one term is universal and the other particular; so **To:to-to·tal,** having both terms universal.

Totter (tǫ·təɹ), *sb.* 1747. [f. TOTTER *v.*] The action, or an act, of tottering; wavering, oscillation; an unsteady or shaky movement or gait as of one ready to fall.

I..had his bend in my shoulders, and his t. in my gait JOHNSON.

Comb.: **t.-grass**, quaking-grass, *Briza media.*

Totter (tǫ·təɹ), *v.* [ME. *toter* swing – MDu. *touteren* swing (so Eng. dial. *totter* sb. XIV, Du. *touter* sb.) :- OS. **taltron* = OE. *tealtrian* totter, stagger, whence dial. *tolter* adj. XV, *tolter* vb. XVI.] †**1.** *intr.* To swing to and fro, esp. at the end of a rope; *fig.* to waver, vacillate –1633. **2.** To rock or shake to and fro on its base, as if about to overbalance or collapse. late ME. **3.** To walk or move with unsteady steps; to go shakily or feebly; to toddle; also, to walk with difficulty; to reel, stagger 1602. †**4.** *trans.* To cause to shake to and fro, to rock; to render unstable –1693.

1. *All's Well* I. iii. 129. **2.** Troy nods from high, and totters to her fall DRYDEN. *fig.* If th' other two be brain'd like vs, the State totters SHAKS. **3.** He totterd from the reeling decke MARSTON. Hence **To·tterer. To·tteringly** *adv.*

Tottery (tǫ·təri), *a.* 1861. [f. prec. + -Y[1].] Given to tottering; shaky; unsteady.

Totty (tǫ·ti), *a.* Now *dial.* late ME. [app. f. *tot-* as in *totter* + -Y[1].] Unsteady, shaky, tottery (physically or mentally); dizzy, dazed; tipsy, fuddled.

Myn heed is toty of my swynk to nyght CHAUCER.

Toucan (tukā·n, tū·kăn). 1568. [– Tupi *tucana*, Guarani *tucă*, *tucã*, whence also Fr. *toucan* (XVI), Sp. *tucan*, Pg., It. *tucano*, G. *tukan*.] **1.** A Neotropical bird of the genus *Rhamphastos* or the family *Rhamphastidæ*, inhabiting the tropical parts of South America, etc. They are noted for the enormous size of the beak and their striking colouring. The species orig. so named was app. *R. toco*. **b.** Misapplied to other birds; esp. in the East Indies to species of Hornbill (*Buceros*) 1816. **2.** *Astron.* Name of a southern constellation 1669. Hence **Toucanet** (tū·kăne:t), any of the smaller kinds of t.

Touch (tʊtʃ), *sb.* ME. [orig. – (O)Fr. *touche*, f. *toucher* TOUCH *v.* In some later uses, f. TOUCH *v.*] **I. 1.** The action or an act of touching; exercise of the faculty of feeling upon a material object. **b.** *euphem.* Sexual contact ME. **c.** *Med.* Examination by feeling, esp. of a cavity of the body; palpation 1805. **d.** *Mil.* Contact between the elbows of a rank of soldiers 1877. **e.** A children's game, in which one player touches another, who then chases and tries to touch any of the other players; in full *t.-and-run* 1815. **2.** The act, fact, or state of touching or being touched; contact. late ME. **b.** A small quantity of some substance brought into contact with a surface so as to leave its mark or effect; a dash, as of paint; a mark or stain so produced 1581. **3.** That sense by which a material object is perceived by means of the contact with it of some part of the body; the most general of the bodily senses, diffused through all parts of the skin, but (in man) specially developed in the tips of the fingers and the lips. late ME. **b.** The sensation caused by touching something (considered as an attribute of the thing); tactile quality, feel 1674. **4.** A hit, knock, stroke, blow; *esp.* a very slight blow or stroke ME. **b.** *fig.* A 'hit', stroke (of wit, satire, etc.); a 'knock', a 'blow' 1522.

1. He toucheth the face and breast with cold touches PURCHAS. A submissive t. to his cap 1898. Phr. *Within* or *in t.*, near enough to touch or be touched; within reach (*of*); accessible. **b.** *Meas. for M.* V. i. 141. **2.** The t. of the cold water made a prettie kinde of shrugging come ouer her bodie SIDNEY. **b.** Phr. *A t. of the tar-brush*, a small amount of Negro blood. **3.** By t. the first pure qualities we learn Which quicken all things, hot, cold, moist, and dry 1599. **b.** A Country Lip may have the Velvet t. DRYDEN. **4. b.** To whom soon mov'd with t. of blame thus Eve MILT.

II. Technical and allied senses. **1.** The action or process of testing the quality of gold or silver by rubbing it upon a touchstone. late ME. **b.** An official mark or stamp upon gold or silver indicating that it has been tested, and is of standard fineness; also, a die, punch, or stamp for impressing this. Also, an official mark stamped upon pewter. late ME. **c.** The quality or fineness of gold or silver (or other metal) as tested with the touchstone and indicated by the official mark ME. **d.** *fig.* Quality, kind, sort, 'stamp'. late ME. †**2.** Short for *touchstone* (see TOUCHSTONE 2) 1485. **3.** *fig.* An act of, or thing that serves for, testing; a test, trial, proof; a criterion, 'touchstone'. Now chiefly in phr. *to put to the t.* 1581. **4.** *Mus.* The act or manner of touching or handling a musical instrument, so as to bring out its tones; now *esp.* the manner of striking or pressing the keys of a keyboard instrument so as to produce special varieties of tone or effect. Hence *transf.* (chiefly *poet.*) a note or brief strain of instrumental music. late ME. **b.** As an attribute of the performer: capacity, skill, or style of playing 1601. **c.** As an attribute of a keyboard instrument, referring to the manner in which its keys and action respond to the touch of the player 1884. **5.** *Bell-ringing.* Any series of changes less than a peal 1872. **6.** An act of touching a surface with the proper tool in painting, writing, carving, etc.; a stroke or dash of a brush, chisel, or the like; a slight act or effort added in doing or completing a piece of work of any kind 1607. **b.** Artistic skill or faculty; style or quality of artistic work; method of handling, execution 1815. **7.** *Magnetism.* The action or process of magnetizing a steel bar or needle by contact with one or more magnets 1705. **8.** *Football.* The act (in the Rugby game) of touching the ground with the ball behind the goal, usu. the opponents' goal; *transf.* (esp. in phr. *in* or *into t.*), that part of the ground outside the boundary lines of the field of play (*t.-lines* and *goal-lines*); *t.-in-goal*, that part of this behind the goal-line 1864.

1. Good metall bides the t. that trieth out the gold 1587. **d.** My Friends of Noble t. SHAKS. **2.** Gates all like Masonrie, of White and Blacke, Like Touche and White Merbell HALL. **4.** Orpheus Lute,..Whose golden t..could soften steele and stones SHAKS. **6.** It [a picture] tutors Nature, Artificiall strife Liues in these toutches, liuelier then life SHAKS.

III. *fig.* **1.** The act of touching or fact of being touched (in *fig.* senses of the vb.) 1586. **b.** *spec.*, An impression upon the mind or soul; a feeling, sense (*of* some emotion, etc.) 1586. **2.** A faculty or capacity of the mind analogous or likened to the sense of touch; mental or moral perception or feeling 1656. **3.** A stroke of action, an act; a brief turn or 'go' *at* some occupation; †in early use, a sly, mean, or deceitful trick. Now *rare.* 1481. **4.** An act of touching upon or mentioning something; a mention, slight notice, hint. Now *rare* or *Obs.* late ME. †**b.** The fact or quality of touching, affecting, concerning, or relating to something. BACON. †**5.** The quality or fact of affecting injuriously; reproach, blemish, stain, taint –1616. **6.** A distinguishing quality, characteristic, trait 1539. **7.** 'A small quantity intermingled' (J.); a trace, spice, smack 1594. **b.** *spec.* A slight affection or attack *of* illness or disease; a twinge 1662. **8.** *slang.* or *colloq.* An article or 'affair' that will touch or move purchasers to the extent of a certain price 1712.

1. Free From all t. of age 1586. Phr. *In* or *out of t. with*, *to keep* or *lose t. with*; To bring religion into t. with conduct 1887. **b.** Didst thou but know the inly t. of Loue SHAKS. **2.** An accuracy and delicacy of intellectual t. 1872. **4. b.** Speech of t. toward others, should bee sparingly vsed BACON. **6.** One t. of nature makes the whole world kin: That all with one consent praise new borne gaudes SHAKS. But cared greatly to..keep the Nelson t. 1897. **7.** Madam, I haue a t. of your condition, That cannot brooke the accent of reproofe SHAKS. **b.** A t. of sore throat 1890. **8.** At night went to the Ball at the Angel. A guinea t. 1720.

IV. Concrete senses. **1.** Short for TOUCH-POWDER, TOUCHWOOD, or the like. *Obs.* exc. *dial.* 1541. **2.** *Shipbuilding.* In a plank tapering both ways, the projecting angle at the broadest part (near one end if worked top-and-butt, in the middle if worked anchor-stock fashion); also, each of the angles of the stern-timbers at the counters 1711.

Phrases. †*To keep t.* **a.** To keep covenant, act faithfully; so *to break t.* **b.** To keep up communication, keep in touch *with. Rum t.*: an odd or queer fellow or affair (*slang*). *In* or *out of t. with*: see III. 1. *In* or *within t.*: see I. 1. *To put to the t.*: see II. 3.

Touch (tʊtʃ), *v.* [ME. *toche, touche, tuche* – OFr. *tochier, tuchier* (mod. *toucher*) :- Rom. **toccare* make a sound like *toc*, of imit. origin.] **I. 1.** *trans.* To put the hand or finger or some other part of the body upon, or into contact with (something) so as to feel it; 'to exercise the sense of feeling upon' (Phillips, 1696). Also with the hand, etc., as subject, and in other constrs.; rarely *absol.* **2.** *spec.* **a.** To have sexual contact with. *trans.* or †*intr.* with *to. Obs.* exc. as in II. 1. ME. **b.** To lay the hand upon (a diseased person) for the cure of the 'king's evil' or scrofula, as formerly practised by French and English sovereigns. Also *absol.* 1600. **c.** *Med.* To examine by touch or feeling. Also *absol.* 1734. **d.** To bring by touching *into* some condition 1813. **e.** *Football.* = T. down 1864. **f.** *absol.* or *intr.* Of soldiers in the rank: To close up until the elbows are in contact 1803. **3.** *trans.* To come into or be in contact with. Also *intr.* or *absol.* ME. **4.** To adjoin, border on; to skirt. late ME. **b.** *Geom.* Of a line (straight or curved) or a surface: To meet (another line or surface) at a point so that when produced it does not (ordinarily) intersect or 'cut' it at that point; to be tangent to. Also *absol.* or *intr.* in reciprocal sense. 1570. **5.** To strike or hit lightly (esp. with the spur, or in *Fencing*) ME. **6.** To affect physically in some way by contact. **a.** To make an impression upon; to stain, scratch, abrade, corrode, decompose, etc. 1440. **b.** To magnetize by contact or rubbing with a magnet. Now *rare* or *Obs.* 1627. **c.** To apply some substance lightly to (a part of the body, etc.) by contact, esp. for medicinal purposes; const. *with* 1602. **7.** To affect injuriously in some physical way, (e.g. by fire or frost), esp. in a slight degree. (Usu. in *pa. pple.*) 1595. **8.** To test the fineness of (gold or silver) by rubbing it upon a touchstone 1548. **b.** To mark (metal) with an official stamp, after it has been tested. late ME. **9.** To strike the strings, keys, etc. of (a musical instrument) so as to make it sound; to play on, esp. to play a few notes on; to sound (a horn, a bell) 1470. **b.** *transf.* To produce (musical sounds) by 'touching' an instrument; to play (an air) 1823. **10.** In drawing, painting, etc.: To mark, draw, delineate (a detail of the work) by touching the surface with the pencil, brush, etc.; also, to modify or alter by such touches. Hence *transf.* in literary composition. 1675. **b.** *fig.* To mark slightly or superficially *with* some colour or aspect: chiefly in *pa. pple.* 1600. **11.** *intr.* Of a ship or those on board: To arrive and make a short stay in passing at a port or place on the way. Also *transf.* of a traveller. Usu. with *at.* 1517. **b.** *trans.* with the port or place as obj.: To land upon; to visit in passing 1593.

1. Jesus sayde vnto her: touche me not TINDALE *John* 20:17. Him thus intent Ithuriel with his Spear Touch'd lightly MILT. T. a match to it, and you will presently have a fire 1897. **2. b.** His Majestie began first to t. for the evil, according to costome EVELYN. **3.** Loose shingle..falls upon the ice where it touches the rocks TYNDALL. *absol.* Those spheres..T., mingle, are transfigured SHELLEY. **6. a.** The Aqua Regalis, which dissolves Gold, will not t. Silver 1725. **c.** Phr. *To t. the gums* (Med.), to induce salivation, as by the use of mercury. **7.** A horse which was touched in the wind 1772. The plants that were touched with frost 1884. **8.** They haue all bin touch'd, and found Base-Mettle SHAKS. **9.** Timotheus.. With flying fingers touched the lyre DRYDEN. **b.** [He] touched a light and lively air on the flageolet SCOTT. **10.** The lines, tho' touch'd but faintly, are drawn right POPE. **b.** The rock on the woody promontory..is touched with rose-colour 1847. **11.** We touched at Panaria 1828. **b.** Shall we t. the continent? JOHNSON.

II. 1. To handle or have to do with in any or the slightest degree; to 'lay a finger on'. (Usu. with neg.) late ME. **b.** *spec.* To lay hands on or meddle with so as to harm; to injure, hurt, in any or the least degree ME. **c.** To take (food or drink); usu. (with neg.), not to take any at all. late ME. **2.** *trans.* To get or go as far as; to reach, attain (*lit.* and *fig.*); *fig.* to attain equality with, compare with. late ME. **3.** *intr.* with *at, to, on, upon* (also *absol.*): To approach closely; to verge upon 1451. **b.** *Naut.* (*trans.*) To keep as close to (the wind) as the vessel will sail. Also *absol.* 1568. **4.** *trans.* To take in the hand, take, receive, draw (money) = Fr. *toucher de l'argent*; sometimes, to get by underhand means. Also *absol.* Now chiefly *slang* or *colloq.* 1654. **5.** To 'come down upon' (a person) *for* money, to succeed in getting money from. *colloq.* 1760.

1. I had never touched a card RUSKIN. **b.** The Lion will not t. the true Prince SHAKS. **c.** I never t. a drop GOLDSM. **2.** I haue touch'd the highest point of all my Greatnesse SHAKS. *fig.* Is there one of you that could t. him? DICKENS. **3.** During the course of a political life just touching to its close BURKE. **4.** The..matrimonial arrangement is concluded (the agent touching his percentage) THACKERAY. **5.** I could t. Dad for a few hundreds 1809.

III. †**1.** *trans.* To succeed in getting at, 'hit'; to guess or state correctly –1797. **2.** To treat of, mention; now always, to mention briefly, casually, or in passing; to allude to. Now *rare* or *arch.* late ME. **b.** *intr.*, usu. with *on, upon*, etc., in same sense ME. **3.** *trans.* To say something apt or telling about, esp. in censure. Also *to t. to the quick.* 1529. **4.** To pertain or relate to; to be the business of; to concern. *Obs.* or *arch.* ME. **b.** To have affinity with. *Obs.* or *arch.* 1611. **5.** To be a matter of moment to; to affect, make a difference to 1470. †**6.** To strike, impress (the senses, or organs of sense) –1667. **7.** To affect mentally or morally, to imbue *with* some quality; in bad sense, to infect, taint. Also predicated of the quality. Usu. in *pa. pple.* ME. **b.** *pass.* To be deranged mentally in a slight degree; in *pa. pple.* slightly insane or crazy, 'cracked' 1704. **8.** To affect *with* some feeling or emotion; *spec.* to affect with tender feeling, as pity or gratitude ME. **b.** To influence, move (in mind or will) 1570. **9.** To hurt or wound in mind or feelings, as if by touching a sore or tender part; to irritate, sting, nettle. Often in *fig.* phrases, as *t. to the quick.* 1589.

1. There you toucht the life of our designe SHAKS. **2. b.** He touches on the same difficulties and he gives no answer to them JOWETT. **3.** Ev'n those you t. not, hate you POPE. **4.** This.. touches us not as Liberals or Conservatives, but as citizens 1883. **5.** His Curses and his blessings T. me alike: th' are breath I not beleeue in SHAKS. **7.** High nature amorous of the good, But touch'd with no ascetic gloom TENNYSON. **b.** You see master's a little—touched, that's all VANBRUGH. **8.** I can't say how much the thought of that fidelity has touched me THACKERAY. **9.** It touched..scores of labourers on the raw 1898.

Phrases. *To t. and go*, to touch for an instant and immediately go away or pass on; to deal with momentarily or slightly. *To t. one's cap, hat*, to raise the hand to the cap or hat and touch it in token of salutation; const. *to*. *To t. wood*, in folk-lore or *quasi*-superstitious use: to t. wood as a charm to avert apprehended misfortune. esp. that apt to follow untimely boasting or self-gratulation.

With adverbs. **Touch down.** *Rugby Football. trans.* To t. the ground with (the ball) behind the goal, usu. that of the opponents; also *absol.* **T. in.** *trans.* In drawing, etc.: To insert (a detail) by touching with the pencil, brush, etc. **T. off.** *trans.* **a.** To represent exactly, to 'hit off'. **b.** To fire off (a cannon, etc.), orig. by putting a match to the touch-hole. **c.** To break off a telephone interview. **T. up. a.** *trans.* To improve, finish, or modify, by adding touches or light strokes. **b.** To stimulate by striking lightly or sharply, as with a whip.

Touch- *sb.* or *vb.* in comb.

1. a. t.-judge, in *Rugby Football*, an umpire who marks when and where the ball goes 'into touch'; **-needle**, a slender bar or rod of gold or silver, one of a set of different standards of fineness, used in conjunction with a touchstone for testing the fineness of gold or silver; **-plate**, one of a set of plates bearing the 'touches' or official marks of the company of pewterers; **-watch**, a watch so contrived that the time by it can be ascertained by touch, e.g. in the dark. **b.** Connected with the notion of ready ignition; cf. TOUCH-POWDER; **t.-pan**, the pan of an old-fashioned gun, into which the touch-powder was put; **-string**, string steeped in nitre used as a fuse.

2. t.-back (*Rugby Football*), the act of touching the ground with the ball on or behind the player's own goal-line after it has been driven there by the opposing side; **-down** (*Rugby Football*), the act of touching the ground with the ball behind the goal-line, usu. that of the opposing side; *safety touch-down*, the same done behind the player's own goal-line after it has been driven there by his own side, in order to prevent the opposing side from making a touch-down; **-up**, an act of touching up; a stroke added by way of improvement or finish; also, a slight reminder.

Touchable (tʊ·tʃăb'l), *a.* late ME. [f. TOUCH *v.* + -ABLE.] Capable of being touched. Hence **Tou·chableness.**

Tou·ch and go·, *sb.* and *adj. phr.* (Also with hyphens.) 1655. [The vbl. phr. *touch and go* used as sb. or adj.] **A.** *sb.* **1.** The act of touching for an instant and quitting immediately; something done quickly or instantaneously. **2.** A risky, precarious, or ticklish case or state of things (such that a mere touch may cause disaster); a narrow escape, 'near shave' 1815.

2. Though it was touch and go she managed to retain her seat 1887.

B. *adj.* **1.** Involving or characterized by rapid, slight, or superficial execution; sketchy; casual; instantaneous; expeditious 1812. **2.** Risky, of the nature of a narrow escape 1856.

1. 'Touch-and-go' sketches 1891.

Tou·ch-box. *Obs.* exc. *Hist.* 1549. [For *touch-powder box*; see TOUCH-POWDER.] A box for 'touch-powder' or priming-powder, formerly forming part of a musketeer's equipment.

Touched (tɒtʃt), *ppl. a.* late ME. [f. TOUCH *v.* + -ED¹.] In various senses of TOUCH *v.*

T. proof, a 'proof' from an engraved or etched plate approaching completion, submitted to the artist of the picture copied, for his approval or criticism.

Toucher (tɒ·tʃəɹ). late ME. [f. as prec. + -ER¹.] One who or that which touches, in senses of the vb.; *esp.* in *Bowls*, a bowl which touches the jack. **b.** *colloq.* or *slang.* (*a*) A case of close contact, an exact fit. (*b*) A very near approach; in phr. *as near as a t.*, very nearly, all but. 1828.

Tou·ch-hole. 1501. [f. TOUCH- in *touch-powder* + HOLE.] A small tubular hole in the breech of a fire-arm, through which the charge is ignited; the vent.

Touching (tɒ·tʃiŋ), *vbl. sb.* ME. [f. TOUCH *v.* + -ING¹.] The action of TOUCH *v.* **1.** The action, or an act, of feeling something with the hand, etc.; the fact or state of being contiguous; touch, contact; a touch; *spec.* for the 'king's evil'. **2.** In various *fig.* senses: Mention, treatment or discussion; affecting or injuring, etc. late ME.

Tou·ching, *ppl. a.* 1508. [f. as prec. + -ING².] That touches: esp. *fig.* that touches the feelings or emotions; such as to excite tender feeling or sympathy; affecting, pathetic.

O insupportable, and t. losse! SHAKS. A t. faith in the efficacy of acts of parliament 1870. Hence **Tou·ching-ly** *adv.*, **-ness.**

Tou·ching, *prep.* Now somewhat *arch.* ME. [– (O)Fr. *touchant*, pr. pple. of *toucher* TOUCH *v.*; see -ANT. The Fr. form was current in Eng. XIV–XV.] **1.** Where *touching* is in concord with a prec. sb. or pron., and may be rendered 'that refers or relates to'. (Cf. CONCERNING *prep.* 1.) **2.** Without concord: In reference or relation to; as to, respecting, regarding; in the way of mentioning or treating of; concerning, about. late ME. **3.** Preceded by *as.* late ME.

1. A late Request..t. the Care of a young Daughter STEELE. **2.** T. the bargain, your.. mother was a little too calm DICKENS. **3.** As t. the Guls or Sea-cobs, they build in rockes 1601.

Tou·ch-line. 1551. [f. TOUCH- + LINE *sb.*²] †**1.** *Geom.* A tangent –1675. **2.** (*touch line.*) A line in a diagram representing the touch of the counter of a ship 1797. **3.** *Football*, etc. The boundary line on each side of the field of play, extending from goal-line to goal-line 1868.

Tou·ch-me-no:t, *sb.* (*a.*) 1597. [Phrase used as sb.; transl. of NOLI-ME-TANGERE.] **1.** Name for two different kinds of plants with seed-vessels which burst at a touch. †**a.** The Squirting Cucumber –1760. **b.** The Yellow Balsam (*Impatiens noli-tangere*), or other species of *Impatiens* 1659. **2.** *gen.* A person or thing that must not be touched 1893. **b.** *attrib.* or as *adj.* 1852.

2. b. The saucy little beauty carried her head with a toss..and assumed a t. air THACKERAY.

Tou·ch-pa:per. 1750. [TOUCH- 1 b.] Paper steeped in nitre so as to burn slowly on being touched by a spark, used for firing gunpowder, etc.

Tou·ch-piece. 1844. [f. TOUCH- + PIECE *sb.*] **1.** A coin or medal given by the sovereign to each person touched for the 'king's evil'. **2.** A piece of mechanism operated by a touch 1897.

†**Tou·ch-pow:der.** 1497. [app. the earliest of a series of compounds (see TOUCH- 1 b) in which *touch-* signifies the ready setting fire to something; app. f. OFr. *tochier* (*le feu*), *touchier* to set fire; prob. repr. an OFr. **poudre-à-toucher* (*le feu*).] A fine kind of gunpowder placed in the pan over the touch-hole in an old-fashioned fire-arm; priming powder.

Touchstone (tɒ·tʃ,stoᵘn). 1481. [f. TOUCH- 1 + STONE *sb.*, based on OFr. *touchepierre* (mod. *pierre de touche*).] **1.** A smooth, fine-grained, black or dark-coloured variety of quartz or jasper (also called BASANITE), used for testing the quality of gold and silver alloys by the colour of the streak produced by rubbing them upon it; a piece of such stone used for this purpose 1530. **b.** *fig.* That which serves to test or try the genuineness or value of anything; a test, criterion 1533. **2.** Applied to other stones of similar texture and colour, as black marble or basalt 1481.

1. b. Time..is the only true t. of merit 1720.

Touchwood (tɒ·tʃ,wud). 1579. [f. TOUCH- 1 b + WOOD *sb.*] Wood or anything of woody nature, in such a state as to catch fire readily, and which can be used as tinder. **a.** The soft white substance into which wood is converted by the action of certain fungi, esp. of *Polyporus squamosus*, and which has the property of burning for many hours when once ignited, and is occas. self-luminous. **b.** A name given to various fungi, esp. two species of *Polyporus* (*P.* or *Fomes fomentarius* and *P.* or *F. igniarius*), or to the tinder called 'amadou' made from them 1598. **c.** *fig.* Said of a thing or person that easily 'takes fire'; *esp.* an irascible or passionate person, one easily incensed. Now *rare.* 1617.

Touchy (tɒ·tʃi), *a.* 1605. [f. TOUCH *sb.* or *v.* + -Y¹; in sense 1 perh. an alteration of TETCHY.] **1.** Easily moved to anger; apt to take offence on slight cause; irascible, irritable, testy, tetchy. **2.** Sensitive to touch; physically irritable 1618. **b.** Easily ignited 1660. **3.** Ticklish, risky; not to be touched without danger 1620.

1. She was most t. upon the subject of age 1843. Hence **Tou·chily** *adv.* **Tou·chiness.**

Tough (tɒf), *a.* (*sb.*) [OE. *tōh* = OHG. *zāh*, MLG. *tā* :– **taŋxuz*, f. base repr. also (with *-ja* suffix) by MLG. *tei*, Du. *taai*, OHG. *zāhi* (G. *zäh*).] **1.** Of close tenacious substance or texture; not easily broken, divided, or disintegrated; not fragile, brittle, or tender; of food, difficult to masticate. **2.** Of viscous consistence or nature; sticky, adhesive, tenacious; glutinous OE. **3.** *fig.* Stiff, severe, violent; of a contest, etc.: stoutly maintained, strenuous, vigorous and stubborn ME. **4.** Capable of great physical endurance; hardy, stout, sturdy ME. **5.** Having great intellectual or moral endurance; difficult to influence, affect, or impress; firm, persistent; also, stubborn, hardened. late ME. **6.** Difficult to do, perform, or deal with 1619. **b.** Taxing credulity or comprehension 1820. **7.** *U.S.* Of criminal or vicious propensities; also, rowdy, disorderly 1884.

1. The pure parts of metals are of themselves very flexible and tuff 1665. The 'cold fowl' was.. as t. as leather 1843. **2.** T. viscid saliva 1789. **3.** A t. breeze from the westward 1865. **4.** That was what t. old Sir Evan Dhu used to say SCOTT. **5.** A man of ripe yeares, but..t. in opinion 1603. **6.** A t. job SCOTT. **b.** Tell us t. yarns, and then swear they are true BARHAM.

B. *sb. U.S.* A street ruffian 1866.

Comb.: **t.-cake, -pitch,** refined or commercial copper. Hence **Tou·gh-ly** *adv.*, **-ness.**

Toughen (tɒ·f'n), *v.* 1582. [f. prec. + -EN⁵.] *trans.* and *intr.* To make or become tough.

Toughish (tɒ·fiʃ), *a.* 1776. [f. as prec. + -ISH¹.] Somewhat tough.

Toupee (tū·pi). Now *rare.* 1727. [– Fr. *toupet*; see next.] A curl or artificial lock of hair on the top of the head, esp. as a crowning feature of a periwig; a periwig in which the front hair was combed up, over a pad, into such a top-knot; also, the natural hair dressed in this mode; a patch of false hair or a small wig to cover a bald place 1731. †**b.** One who wears a toupee; a beau –1747.

‖**Toupet** (tū·pe, Fr. tupę). 1728. [Fr. *toupet* tuft of hair, esp. over the forehead, f. OFr. *toup, top*; see TOP *sb.*¹, -ET.] **1.** = prec. **2.** †The forelock of a horse, etc.; a thick head of hair 1797. **3.** *attrib.*, as **t.-titmouse,** the Crested Titmouse 1731.

Tour (tūᵊɹ), *sb.* ME. [– (O)Fr. *tour*, earlier *tor, torn* :– L. *tornus* – Gr. τόρνος lathe (cf. TURN *sb.*).] **I. 1.** One's turn or order (to do something); also, a spell of work or duty; a shift. In later use *Mil.* †**2.** A turning round, revolution (*rare*) –1719. **3.** A going or travelling from place to place, a round; an excursion or journey including the visiting of a number of places in a circuit or sequence 1643. **b.** *transf.* and *fig.* A round 1704. †**c.** A short outing; also, the route taken; in 17th c., in London, the drive round Hyde Park –1773. **d.** The circuit *of* an island, etc.; a round 1719. **4.** A crescent front of false hair. *Obs.* exc. *Hist.* 1674.

2. He made so many Tours..and led us by such winding Ways DE FOE. **3.** *The* (*grand*) *t.*: see GRAND TOUR. *On t.*, touring: see TOUR *v.* 2. **c.** Mr. Povy and I in his coach to Hyde Parke, being the first day of the t. there PEPYS.

II. Fig. uses (mostly from French). †**1.** A shift, expedient –1699. †**2.** A 'turn' given to a phrase or sentence, etc. –1751. †**3.** Manner of presenting or exhibiting anything –1734. †**4.** Range, scope –1737. †**5.** A round, a course (of engagements, etc.). STEELE. **6.** One of the several trills, variations, or changes in the song of a trained canary 1906.

Tour (tūᵊɹ), *v.* 1746. [f. prec.] †**1.** *intr.* To 'take a turn' in or about a place, esp. riding or driving –1760. **2.** *intr.* To make a tour or circuitous journey, in which many places are visited, for recreation or business; *spec.* of an actor, a theatrical company, or the like: to go 'on tour', to travel from town to town fulfilling engagements 1789. **3.** *trans.* To make the tour or round of (a country or district) 1885. **4.** *spec. Theatr.* To take (a play or entertainment) on tour; to tour with 1897.

3. Mr. R. is this week touring his constituency 1898. **4.** The American drama..now being toured in the provinces 1897. Hence **Tou·rer** one who tours; a touring-car. **Tou·ring** *vbl. sb.* (*attrib.* in *touring-car*).

‖**Touraco** (tūᵊ·răko). 1743. [= Fr. *touraco*; native name in W. Africa of *Turacus persa.*] Any bird of the family *Musophagidæ* (plantain-eaters), natives of southern, western, and central Africa, and esp. of the genus *Turacus*, large birds with brilliant purple, green, and crimson plumage and prominent crest (hence formerly called *crown-birds*); also of the genus *Schizorrhis*, with plumage of a plainer character.

Tourbillion (tuᵊɹbi·lyən), ‖**tourbillon** (turbiˈyoṅ). 1477. [– Fr. *tourbillon*, OFr. *torbeillon* :– pop. L. **turbellio, -ōn-*, dim. of L. *turbellæ* bustle, stir, blended with *turbo* whirlwind.] **1.** A whirlwind; a whirling storm. Now *rare* or *Obs.* **2.** *transf.* A whirling mass or system; a vortex; a whirl. *Obs.* exc. as Fr. 1712. **3.** A kind of firework which spins as it rises, describing a spiral 1765.

2. The *t.* of Ranelagh surrounds you H. WALPOLE.

‖**Tour de force** (turdəfors). 1805. [Fr. *tour* turn, feat, *de* of, *force* strength.] A feat of strength, power, or skill.

Tourism (tūᵊ·riz'm). 1811. [f. TOUR *sb.* + -ISM.] The theory and practice of touring; travelling for pleasure.

Tourist (tūᵊ·rist). 1800. [f. TOUR *sb.* + -IST.] One who makes a tour or tours; *esp.* one who does this for recreation; one who travels for pleasure or culture, visiting a number of places for their objects of interest, scenery, or the like. Also *attrib.*, as *t. agency, ticket*; **t.-car,** a railway carriage with special accommodation for tourists.

Tourmaline (tūᵊ·ɹmălin, *-in*). 1759. [– Fr. *tourmaline* 1771, G. *turmalin* 1707, Du. *toermalijn* 1778, Sp., It. *turmalina*, ult. f. Sinhalese *toramalli* cornelian.] *Min.* A brittle pyro-electric mineral, occurring in crystals, also massive, compact, and columnar, orig. obtained from Ceylon; a complex silicoborate with a vitreous lustre, usu. black or blackish and opaque (SCHORL), but also blue (INDICOLITE), red (RUBELLITE), green, or colourless, and in various rich transparent or semi-transparent shades, known as *precious t.*, and much used as a gem. **b.** With *a* and *pl.* A specimen or gem of this mineral; also, a transparent plate of tourmaline cut parallel to the vertical crystal axis, used in polariscopes, etc.

Tourmente (turmänt). 1847. See TORMENT *sb.* 5.

Tourn (tūᵊɹn). late ME. [– AFr. *tourn* (whence AL. *turnus, tornus*, XII), f. *tourner* turn, go round; see TURN *v.*] *Eng. Hist.* The tour, turn, or circuit formerly made by the sheriff of a county twice in the year, in which he presided at the hundred-court in each hundred of the county; the great court leet of the county, held on these occasions: it was a court of record.

Tournament (tūᵊ·ɹnămĕnt). [ME. *turne-, tornement* – AFr. vars. of OFr. *tur-, torneiement*, f. *torneier*; see TOURNEY *v.*, -MENT.] **1.** *orig.* A martial sport or exercise of the middle ages, in which two parties of combatants, mounted and in armour, fought with blunted weapons for the prize of valour; later, a meeting at an appointed time and place for knightly sports and exercises. **2.** *fig.* An encounter or trial of strength 1638. **3.** *transf.* A contest in any game of skill in which a number of competitors play a series of selective games, e.g. a *chess* or *lawn tennis t.* 1761.

1. After they be-gonne a turnemente, and departed hem in two partyes 1450.

Tourney (tūᵊ·ɹni, tǭ·ɹni), *sb.* [ME. *tornei*, etc. – OFr. *tornei* (mod. *tournoi*), f. *torneier*; see next.] = prec. 1.

I. .hauntyd the iustes & tornoys 1533. Great Bards. .have sung, Of Turneys and of Trophies hung MILT.

Tourney (tūᵊ·ɹni, tǭ·ɹni), *v.* ME. [– OFr. *torneier* :– Rom. **tornidiare*, f. L. *tornus* TURN *sb.*] *intr.* To take part in a tourney; to contend or engage in a tournament.

They justyd and turneyd there 1435. Hence **Tou·rneyer,** one who engages in a tourney.

Tourniquet (tūᵊ·ɹniket, ‖turnike). 1695. [– Fr. *tourniquet* (XVI), taken to be alt. of OFr. *tournicle*, var. of *tounicle, tunicle* coat of mail, TUNICLE, by assoc. with *tourner* TURN *v.*] **1.** A surgical instrument, consisting essentially of a bandage, a pad, and a screw, for stopping or checking by compression the flow of blood through an artery; also, a bandage tightened by twisting a rigid bar put through it. **2.** A turnstile (*rare*) 1706.

‖**Tournois** (turnwa), *a.* (*sb.*) *Hist.* ME. [Fr. :– L. *Turonensis* of Tours, *Turones*, a city of France.] Of or pertaining to Tours: esp. said of the money coined at Tours, one-fifth less in value than that struck at Paris 1475. **B.** *sb.* Money or a coin of Tours ME.

‖**Tournure** (turnūr). 1748. [Fr. *tournure*, OFr. *torneure* :– pop. L. *tornatura* (Reichenau, VIII), f. L. *tornare* TURN *v.*; see -URE.] **1.** (Graceful) manner or bearing; cultivated address. **2.** The turning of a phrase (*rare*) 1816. **3.** Contour, shape (of a limb, etc.) 1841. **4.** A pad formerly worn round the waist or hips to give shapeliness to a woman's figure; also = BUSTLE *sb.*² 1874.

Touse (tauz, taus), *sb. dial.* 1795. [f. next.] Horse-play; a 'row', commotion; a fuss.

Touse (tauz), *v.* Now *rare*. 1509. [ME. *-tuse, -touse* in *to*|*tuse* (XIII), *be*|*touse* (XIV), repr. OE. **tūsian* = LG. *tūsen* pull or shake about, OHG. *zir*|*zusōn, er*|*zūsen* tear to pieces, G. *zausen*.] **1.** *trans.* To pull roughly about; to handle roughly; of a dog: to tear at, worry. †**b.** To pull out of joint, to rack. SHAKS. **2.** To disorder, dishevel (the hair, dress, etc.); to tumble, rumple (bed-clothes, sheets, etc.) 1598. **3.** *fig.* To abuse or maltreat in some way. Now *rare* or *Obs.* 1530. †**4.** To tease (wool) –1706. †**5.** *intr.* To touse each other, tussle –1681.

1. As a Beare, whom angry curres have touzd SPENSER. **3.** Fortune, the World that towzes to and fro DRAYTON.

Tou·sle, tou·zle (see next), *sb.* 1738. [f. next.] **1.** A struggle, a tussle. *Sc.* **2.** A tousled mass or mop (of hair) 1880.

Tousle, touzle (tau·z'l, *Sc.* tū·z'l), *v.* 1440. [frequent. of TOUSE *v.*; see -LE 3 and cf. TUSSLE.] **1.** To pull about roughly; to handle (esp. a woman) rudely or indelicately; to disorder, dishevel (the hair, clothes, etc.). **2.** *intr.* To toss oneself about; also, to rout, rummage 1852. Hence **Tou·sled** *ppl. a.*

‖**Tous-les-mois** (tulęmwa). 1839. [Fr., = 'all the months, every month'; but prob. a popular perversion of *toloman*, the name in the French Antilles.] The name in St. Kitts, etc., of species of *Canna*, esp. *C. edulis*, and of the starch obtained from its root-stocks.

Tousy, towsy (tau·zi, tū·zi), *a.* Chiefly *Sc.* and *n. dial.* 1786. [f. TOUSE *v.* + -Y¹.] Dishevelled, unkempt, tousled; shaggy, rough.

Tout (taut), *sb.*¹ 1718. [f. TOUT *v.*] **1.** A thieves' scout. *slang.* **2.** One who solicits custom 1853. **3.** (More fully *racing t.*) One who surreptitiously watches the trials of race-horses, so as to gain information for betting purposes 1865.

Tout (tū), *sb.*² 1678. [perh. – Fr. *tout* all.] A specially successful result in certain games.

Tout (taut), *v.* [ME. *tūte* :– OE. **tūtian*, f. **tūt-* project, stick out, repr. by OE. *tȳtan* (once) peep out, become visible, MLG. *tūte* horn, funnel (LG. *tūte, tūt* spout), MDu. *tūte* nipple (Du. *tuit* spout, nozzle), ON. *túta* teat-like prominence. See TOOT *v.*¹] †**1.** *intr.* To peep, peer, look out; to gaze –1676. **b.** To keep a sharp look-out. *Thieves' cant.* 1700. **2.** *trans.* To watch, spy on. *slang.* 1700. **b.** To watch furtively or spy upon (a race-horse or its trainer) with a view to using or disposing of the information for betting purposes 1812. **3.** *intr.* To solicit custom, employment, etc. importunately; also, *Colonial* and *U.S.*, to canvass for votes 1731. Also *trans.* with the person or thing as object 1928.

‖**Tout court** (tu kūr). [Fr. = quite short.] Without further addition or explanation.

Tout ensemble: see ENSEMBLE B.

Touter (tau·təɹ). 1754. [f. TOUT *v.* + -ER¹.] = TOUT *sb.*¹

Tow (tōᵘ), *sb.*¹ late ME. [– MLG. *touw* :– OS. *tou* = ON. *tó* wool, tow, rel. to **tōw-* in OE. *towcræft* spinning, *towhūs* spinning-house :– **tāw-* (see TOOL *sb.*).] †**1.** *app.* The unworked stem or fibre of flax, before it is heckled. late ME. only. **2.** The fibre of flax, hemp, or jute prepared for spinning by some process of scutching. late ME. **3.** More strictly, the shorter fibres of flax or hemp, which are separated by heckling from the fine and long-stapled, called *line* 1530. **4.** *attrib.* 1601.

Tow (tōᵘ), *sb.*² 1600. [f. TOW *v.*¹] **1.** A rope used for towing, a tow-line. **2.** The action of towing or fact of being towed 1622. **3.** A vessel taken in tow; also, a string of barges, boats, etc., being towed 1805. **b.** A vessel that tows; a tug 1874.

2. Phr. *In t.*, in the condition of being towed (*of* or *by* the towing vessel). *To take in t.* (said of a ship, etc.), to begin and continue to tow, to tow; *fig.* to take under one's guidance or patronage; to take charge of.

Comb.: **t.-boat,** a boat used in towing; *spec.* a tug; **-post,** a towing-post.

Tow (tōᵘ), *v.*¹ [OE. *togian* = OFris. *togia*, MLG. *togen*, OHG. *zogōn*, ON. *toga* :– Gmc. **toȝōjan*, f. **toȝ-* (**tuȝ-*), wk. grade of **teux-* **taux-* **tuȝ-* draw; see TEE *v.*¹] †**1.** *trans.* To draw by force; to pull, drag –1583. **2.** *spec.* To draw or drag (a vessel, etc.) on the water by a rope. late ME. **3.** To drag by or as by a line. *joc.* 1663. **4.** *intr.* or *absol.* To proceed by towing or being towed 1612.

3. A mounted Mexican towing a bull 1883.

Tow (tōᵘ), *v.*² 1615. [f. TOW *sb.*¹] *trans.* To comb or card flax; also, to reduce to the state of tow or fibre.

Towage (tōᵘ·ėdʒ). ME. [orig. – AFr. *towage*, AL. *towagium* (XIII in both senses), f. ME. *towe* TOW *v.*¹ In mod. use apprehended as f. TOW *v.*¹] **1.** The charge or payment for towing a vessel 1562. **2.** The action or process of towing or being towed ME.

Towan (tau·ăn). *Cornw.* 1803. [Cornish.] A coast sand-hill.

Toward (tōᵘ·(w)əɹd), *a.* and *adv.* [OE. *tōweard* = OS. *tōward*, OHG. *zuowart, -wert* 'directed forwards'; see TO *prep.*, -WARD.] **A.** *adj.* †**1.** That is to come, coming, future –1613. †**2.** Approaching, imminent, impending –1586. **b.** *pred.* Now *rare* or *Obs.* OE. **c.** In progress, going on; being done 1838. **3.** Of young persons: Promising, 'hopeful', forward; making good progress; disposed, willing or apt to learn; docile. *Obs.* or *arch.* ME. **4.** Willing, compliant, obliging, docile. *Obs.* or *arch.* 1440. **b.** Of things: Favourable, propitious; the opposite of *untoward* (rare) 1850.

2. b. There is sure another flood t., and these couples are comming to the Arke SHAKS. **3.** There was neuer mother had a towarder son HEYWOOD. **4. b.** A t. breeze GLADSTONE.

B. *adv.* **1.** In a direction toward oneself, or toward something aimed at. *Obs.* or *arch.* ME. **2.** Onward (in a course), forward. late ME.

Toward (tŭwǭ·ɹd, tōᵘ·əɹd, tōᵊɹd), *prep.* [OE. *tōweard*, n. of the adj., orig. construed with gen., later with dat.] **1.** Of motion (or action figured as motion): In the direction of; so as to approach (but not necessarily reach). †**b.** With implication of reaching; to –1611. **2.** Of position: In the direction of; on the side next to; facing ME. **3.** In the direction of (in *fig.* senses) ME. **4.** Of time: So as to approach; at the approach of, shortly before, near. late ME. **5.** Nearly as much as, nearly 1449. **6.** In the way of a contribution to; as a help to; for 1468.

1. I presse t. the marke *Phil.* 3:14. **b.** Pilgrimes were they alle That t. Caunterbury wolden ryde CHAUCER. **2.** Under Suth-rey t. the South lieth. . Suth-sex HOLLAND. **3.** This is the way in which I act t. my own children 1867. **4.** At dates well t. the middle of this century 1876. **5.** They rise. . t. a hundred feet above the plain 1879. **6.** Here is two and eightpence halfpenny t. your loss SWIFT. A fund. . t. the expenses of removing paupers by emigration SOUTHEY.

Towardly (tōᵘ·(w)əɹdli, tō·əɹd-), *a. arch.* 1520. [f. TOWARD *a.* + -LY¹.] **1.** Likely to lead to a desired result; propitious; favourable; seasonable, befitting. **2.** = TOWARD *a.* 3. 1528. **3.** Well-disposed, dutiful, tractable 1513. **b.** Favourably disposed, friendly, affable 1550.

1. He must choose a t. hour 1884. **2.** He was my Pupil at Oxford, and a very t. one 1627. **3. b.** England proved not yet so t. as he expected CLARENDON. **To·wardliness** (now *dial.* or *arch.*). So **To·wardly** *adv.* in a toward or t. manner.

Towardness (tōᵘ·(w)əɹdnės, tō·əɹd-). Now *Obs.* or *arch.* 1461. [f. as prec. + -NESS.] The quality or condition of being 'toward'.

Towards (tŭwǭ·ɹdz, tōᵘ·əɹdz, tōᵊɹdz), *prep.* and *adv.* [OE. *tōweardes*, f. *tōweard* TOWARD *a.* + -S; see -WARDS.] **A.** *prep.* = TOWARD *prep.* **B.** *adv.* or predicative *adj.* †**1.** In preparation, at hand, imminent –1697. **2.** In the direction of some person or thing indicated by the context. *Obs.* or *arch.* 1590.

Towel (tau·ĕl), *sb.* [ME. *towaile, towel, touel* – OFr. *toail(l)e* (mod. *touaille*) :– Gmc. **þwaxljō* (OHG. *dwahila*, G. dial. *zwehle* napkin), f. **þwaxan* wash, whence OE. *þwēan*, OS. *thwahan*, OHG. *dwahan*, ON. *þvá*, Goth. *þwahan*.] **1.** A cloth for wiping something dry, esp. for wiping the hands, face, or person after washing or bathing. Also formerly a table-napkin or other cloth used at meals. **b.** Phr. *To throw* (or *toss*) *in the t.*: cf. SPONGE *sb.*¹ I. 1. Phr. †**2.** *Eccl.* Applied to an altar-cloth; also, a communion-cloth –1737. **3.** slang. *Oaken t.*, a stick, cudgel; *lead t.*, a bullet 1709.

1. *Bath-, face-, glass-t.*

Comb.: **t.-horse,** a wooden frame on which towels are hung; **-roller,** a horizontal roller on which an 'endless' t. (*roller-* or *round-t.*) is hung.

Tow·el, *v.* 1705. [f. prec.] **1.** *trans.* To apply a towel to; to rub or dry with a towel 1836. **b.** *intr.* with *at* 1861. **2.** *slang.* To beat, cudgel, thrash 1705.

Towelling, toweling (tau·ĕliŋ). 1583. [f. TOWEL *sb.* and *v.* + -ING¹.] **1.** Material for or of towels. **2.** Rubbing with, or application of, a towel 1859. **3.** *slang.* A drubbing, thrashing 1851.

Tower (tauᵊɹ, tau·əɹ), *sb.*¹ [OE. *torr* – L. *turris*; early ME. *tūr*, later *tour, towr* – AFr., OFr. *tur, tor*, (also mod.) *tour* :– stem of L. *turris* – Gr. τύρρις τύρσις.] **I. 1.** A building lofty in proportion to the size of its base, either isolated, or forming part of a castle, church, or other edifice, or of the walls of a town. **2.** Such a structure used as a stronghold, fortress, or prison, or built primarily for purposes of defence. (In this sense often used to include the whole stronghold of which the tower was the nucleus.) ME. **3.** *fig.* ME. **4.** *transf.* A lofty pile or material mass ME. **5.** The gun-turret on an ironclad 1889. **6.** Applied to things having the form of or likened to a tower. †**a.** *Chess.* The castle or rook –1649. **b.** A very high head-dress worn by women in the reigns of William III and Anne. *Hist.* 1612. **c.** Applied to various technical structures and devices, now only descriptively 1662. **d.** *U.S.* A railway signal-box 1904.

1. *Bell-, church-, watch-, water-t. Round t.*: see ROUND *a. T. of silence*, the structure on which the Parsees expose their dead. **2.** The Bastile is but another word for a t. STERNE. *T. of London*, also called *His Majesty's T.*, and often simply *The T.*, is the entire fortress surrounding the original *White T.* of William Rufus. **3.** He is my goodnes and my fortres, my t. and my deliuerer BIBLE (Genev.) *Ps.* 144 : 2.

II. a. Lofty flight; soaring 1486. **b.** The vertical ascent of a wounded bird 1890.

Phr. *T. and town* (also *town and t.*), an alliterative phrase for the inhabited places of a country or region generally.

Comb.: **t.-cress,** the cruciferous plant *Arabis turrita*; **t. hill,** a hill near or on which a t. is built; *spec.* (with caps.) the rising ground by the T. of London; **-man** *U.S.*, a railway signalman; **-stamp,** the official mark on gold and silver articles; hall-mark.

Tower (tōᵘ·əɹ), *sb.*² 1611. [f. TOW *v.*¹ + -ER¹.] One who tows or draws with a rope; *esp.* one who tows a boat on a river or canal.

Tower (tauᵊɹ, tau·əɹ), *v.* 1582. [f. TOWER *sb.*¹] **1. a.** *intr.* To rise to a great height like a tower; to rise aloft, stand high. **b.** *fig.* Usu. const. *above.* 1776. **2.** *trans.* To raise or uplift to a height; to exalt 1596. **3.** *intr.* **a.** *Hawking.* To mount up, as a hawk, so as to be able to swoop down on the quarry 1593. **b.** To soar aloft, as a bird 1647. **c.** To rise vertically, as a bird when wounded 1812. †**4.** *fig.* To rise on high, to soar –1748. †**5.** *trans.* To soar aloft in or into; to rise to –1667.

1. a. On th' other side an high rocke toured still SPENSER. **b.** Does not Gray's poetry, sir, t. above the common mark? BOSWELL. **2.** Where hills tower'd high their crowns CLARE. **3. a.** My Lord Protectours Hawkes do towre so well SHAKS. **b.** The Eagle had cast its Feathers, and could towre no more 1647. **5.** Yet oft they..towre The mid Aereal Skie MILT.

Towered (tau·əɹd), *a.* late ME. [f. TOWER *sb.*¹ and *v.* + -ED.] **1.** Having a tower or towers, adorned or defended by towers; raised or rising on high like a tower. †**2.** Immured in a tower –1750.

1. Towred Cities please us then MILT.

Tow·ering, *ppl. a.* 1598. [f. TOWER *v.* + -ING².] **1.** That towers, in various senses. **2.** Rising to a high pitch of violence or intensity 1602.

1. The towring Ash is fairest in the Woods DRYDEN. A man..of t. ambition 1840. **2.** The brauery of his griefe did put me Into a Towring passion SHAKS. Hence **Tow·eringly** *adv.*

Tower mustard. 1597. [So named from its habit of growth.] A cruciferous plant *Turritis glabra*, found on banks and cliffs. **b.** Sometimes applied to *Arabis turrita*, the tower-cress 1760.

Tower pound. Also †**pound Tower.** 1469. [So called from the standard pound which was kept in the Tower of London.] A pound weight of 5400 grains (= 11¼ Troy ounces), which was the legal mint pound of England prior to the adoption of the Troy pound of 5760 grains in 1526. So **Tower weight,** weight expressed in terms of the Tower pound.

Towery (tauᵊ·ri), *a.* 1611. [f. TOWER *sb.*¹ + -Y¹.] **1.** Having towers; adorned or defended with towers. **2.** Rising to a lofty height; tower-like; also *fig.* aspiring; exalted 1731.

1. Windsor's tow'ry pride POPE. **2.** T. trees 1870.

Towhee (tau·hī, tau·ī). *U.S.* 1730. ['From one of its notes' (Newton).] The ground-robin or CHEEWINK of N. America.

Towing (tōᵘ·iŋ), *vbl. sb.* 1494. [f. TOW *v.*¹ + -ING¹.] The action of TOW *v.*¹

attrib.: **t.-lights** *sb. pl.* white lights carried one above another by a vessel which has another or others in tow; **-path** = TOW-PATH; **-post,** a post to make a tow-rope fast to.

Tow-line (tōᵘ·ləin). 1719. [f. TOW *v.*¹ or *sb.*² + LINE *sb.*²] A line, rope, or hawser by which anything is towed; *spec.* in *Whaling*, the whale-line.

Town (taun), *sb.* [OE. *tūn* = OFris., OS. *tūn*, OHG. *zūn* (Du. *tuin* garden, G. *zaun*) fence, hedge, ON. *tún* :– Gmc. **tunaz, *tunam*, rel. to Celtic **dun-* in the place names (e.g. *Lugdunum* Leiden, Lyons), OIr. *dūn*, W. *din* fort, castle, camp, fortified place.] †**1.** An enclosed place or piece of ground, an enclosure; a field, garden, yard, court. –late ME. †**b.** *spec.* The enclosed land surrounding or belonging to a single dwelling; a farm with its farmhouse; a manor; the enclosed land of a village community; sometimes also = parish, when this was coextensive with a manor –1785. **2.** The house or group of houses or buildings upon this enclosed land; the farmstead or homestead on a farm or holding. Now esp. *Sc.* OE. **3.** A (small) group of dwellings or buildings; a village or hamlet with little or no local organization. (Often = L. *vicus.*) Now *dial.* OE. **4.** Now commonly designating an assemblage of buildings, public and private, larger than a village, and having more complete and independent local government; applied not only to a 'borough', and a 'city', but also to an 'urban district', and sometimes also to small inhabited places below the rank of an 'urban district' ME. **b.** Without article, after preps. and verbs, as *in, out of, to t., to leave t.*, etc.: i.e. the particular town under consideration, or that with which one has to do; the chief town of the district or province, the capital; in England since *c*1700 *spec.* said of London ME. **c.** With def. art., opp. to *the country.* late ME. **d.** In ME., and later in ballad poetry, etc., often added after the name of a town, in apposition. *arch.* ME. **5.** As a collective sing. **a.** The community of a town in its corporate capacity; the corporation; **b.** The townspeople; **c.** *spec.* The fashionable society of London (or other leading city thought of); 'society'. *arch.* ME. **d.** *absol.* at Oxford and Cambridge: The body of citizens or townsmen as dist. from members of the university; esp. in phr. *t. and gown* 1647. **6.** *U.S.* A geographical division for local or state government. **a.** A township; also, its inhabitants. (Esp. in the New England States.) **b.** A municipal corporation, having its own geographical boundaries (as dist. from a.). 1808. **7.** *transf.* An assemblage of burrows of prairie-dogs, nests of penguins, etc. 1808.

2. Waverley learned..from this colloquy that in Scotland a single house was called a *town* SCOTT. **4. b.** When he is in T., he lives in Soho-Square STEELE. **c.** You say I love the t. 1712. Land in the town seems to be let by the grain as if it was radium 1909. **d.** A trainband captain eke was he Of famous London t. COWPER. **5. a.** I find all the t. almost going out of t. PEPYS.

Phrases. *To come to t.*, to make one's appearance, arrive, come in. *Man about t.*, one who is in the round of social functions, fashionable dissipations, etc. in 'town'. *Man* or *woman* (*girl*) *of the t.*, one belonging to the shady or 'fast' side of t. life. *On the t.*, (*a*) in the swing of fashionable life; (*b*) getting a living by prostitution, thieving, or the like; cf. *on the streets*; (*c*) chargeable to the parish (*dial.*); so *to come upon the t.*

attrib. and *Comb.*: **t.-bull,** a bull formerly kept in turn by the cow-keepers of a village; hence *fig.* of a man; **-council,** the elective, deliberative, and administrative body of a t.; hence **t.-councillor; -crier,** a public crier; **-cross,** the market cross of a t.; **-ditch** (now *Hist.*), the ditch or moat surrounding a walled t.; **-dweller,** one who dwells in a t., a townsman; **-living,** town-life; also, an eccl. benefice in a t.; **-mouse,** *fig.* a dweller in a t., esp. as unfamiliar with country life (in allusion to Æsop's fable); **-reeve** (now *Hist.*), the bailiff or steward of a *tūn*. **b.** Combs. with *town's*: **townsfolk** = TOWNSPEOPLE; †**town's husband,** a borough official having charge of the accounts, etc.; **townswoman,** a woman inhabitant of the t.; with possessive, a woman of the same t.

Town, *v. rare.* (Only in *pa. pple.* **Towned.**) 1585. [f. prec.] *trans.* **a.** To furnish with towns. **b.** To make into a town.

Town-clerk. ME. The clerk or secretary to the corporation of a town, who has charge of the records, correspondence, and legal business, the conduct of municipal elections, etc.

†**Tow·n-cress.** [OE. *tūncressa*, f. *tūn* garden, TOWN + CRESS.] Garden cress (*Lepidium sativum*).

Townee (taunī·). 1897. [f. TOWN *sb.* + -EE¹ (Oxford); earlier in U.S. *towny.*] A townsman, esp. as dist. from a member of the university.

Town-end. Now *dial.* Also **town's end.** late ME. The end of the main street of a town or village; one of the extremities of a town.

Tow-net (tōᵘ·net). 1816. [f. TOW *sb.*² or *v.*¹ + NET *sb.*¹] A drag-net or dredge used for the collection of natural specimens.

Town hall. 1481. A large hall used for the transaction of the public business of a town, the holding of a court of justice, assemblies, entertainments, etc.; the great hall of the town-house; now commonly applied to the whole building.

Town-house, town house. 1530. **1.** A municipal building containing the public offices, court-house, and town hall; now usu. called TOWN HALL. **b.** *U.S.* (*a*) An almshouse, workhouse. (*b*) A town prison. 1889. **2.** (**Town house.**) A house in a town; a residence in town, as dist. from a country house 1825.

Townish (tau·niʃ), *a.* late ME. [f. TOWN *sb.* + -ISH¹.] †**1.** Of or pertaining to a town; urban –1674. **2.** Pertaining to or characteristic of the town or town life, esp. as dist. from the country; having the manners or habits of town-dwellers 1500.

Townlet (tau·nlėt). 1552. [f. as prec. + -LET.] A tiny or diminutive town.

Townly (tau·nli), *a.* 1749. [-LY¹.] = TOWNISH 2.

Town-made (stress var.), *a.* 1809. Made or manufactured in a town; spec. in the town of the district. Also as *sb.*

Town-major. *Obs.* or *Hist.* 1676. **a.** The major of a town-guard, as formerly in Edinburgh. **b.** The chief executive officer in a garrison-town or fortress 1702. **c.** Applied vaguely to the chief magistrate or administrative officer of a foreign town 1748.

Town-meeting. 1636. A general assembly of the inhabitants of a town; *spec.* in *U.S.* a legal meeting of the qualified voters of a 'town' for the transaction of public business, having certain powers of local government.

To·wn-pla:nning. 1906. The preparation and construction of plans in accordance with which the growth and extension of a town is to be regulated, so as to make the most of the natural advantages of the site, and to secure the most advantageous conditions of housing and traffic, etc.

Township (tau·nʃip). [OE. *tūnscipe*; see TOWN, -SHIP.] †**1.** In OE., The inhabitants or population of a *tūn* or village collectively. **2.** The inhabitants of a particular manor, parish, or division of a hundred, as a community, or in their corporate capacity. Now chiefly *Hist.* 1444. **b.** Applied to the manor, parish, etc. itself, as a territorial division. Now chiefly *Hist.* late ME. **c.** *spec.* Each of the local divisions of, or districts comprised in, a large original parish, each containing a village or small town, usu. having its own church 1540. **3.** *transf.* Often rendering L. *pagus*, Gr. δῆμος, and thus applied to independent or self-governing towns of ancient Greece, Italy, and other lands, etc. 1602. **4.** *Sc.* A farm held in joint tenancy 1813. **5.** *U.S.* and *Canada.* A division of a county having certain corporate powers of local administration (in the newer states, a division six miles square, and so called even when still unsettled); the same that in New England is called a town 1685. **6.** In Australia, A site laid our prospectively for a town 1802. **7.** By some 19th c. historical writers, adopted to designate what they consider to have been the simplest form of local or social organization in primitive OE. times 1832.

Townsman (tau·nzmӑn). OE. [f. *town's* genitive of TOWN + MAN *sb.*] †**1.** OE. (*tūnesman*). One who lives in a *tūn*; a villager, a villein. **2.** A man who lives in a town or city; a citizen. late ME. **b.** A man of one's own or the same town; a fellow-townsman ME. **c.** An ordinary citizen or resident of a university town as dist. from a GOWNSMAN (3 c) 1768. **3.** *New England.* = SELECTMAN 1656.

Townspeople (tau·nz,pī:p'l). 1648. [f. as prec.] People or inhabitants of a town or towns; townsmen and townswomen; townsfolk. (Usu. const. as *pl.*)

Town-talk. 1654. The common talk or gossip of the people of a town; the subject or matter of such talk.

Townward (tau·nwǭɹd), *adv.* (*a.*) late ME. [f. TOWN *sb.* + -WARD.] Towards or in the direction of the town. **B.** *adj.* Going or directed toward the town 1806.

The t. drift of the people 1893. So **Tow·nwards** *adv.*

Tow-path (tōᵘ·pɑþ). 1846. [f. TOW *v.*¹ + PATH.] A path by the side of a canal or navigable river for use in towing.

Tow-rope (tōᵘ·rōᵘp). ME. [f. TOW *v.*¹ + ROPE *sb.*¹] A rope (hawser, cable, or the like) used in towing.

Tow-row (tau·rau), *sb.* and *a.* 1709. [Redupl. form of ROW *sb.*³; orig. *dial.*] **A.** *sb.* An uproar, hubbub, din 1877. †**B.** *adj.* Intoxicated.

Towser (tau·zəɹ). 1678. [f. TOUSE *v.* + -ER¹.] (With capital T.) A common name for a large dog, such as was used to bait bears or bulls; also *transf.* of a person.

Towy (tōᵘ·i), *a.* 1601. [f. TOW *sb.*¹ + -Y¹.] Like or of the nature of tow.

Tox-¹, comb. form, repr. TOXI- or TOXO-² bef. a vowel.

‖**Toxæmia** (tǫksī·miă), [Gr. αἷμα blood, after *anæmia*, etc.], a morbid condition of the blood caused by a toxin; blood-poisoning; hence **Toxæmic** (-ī·mik) *a.*, pertaining to or affected with toxæmia. **Toxanæmia** (-ănī·miă), anæmia caused by the action of a poison, usu. a ptomaine.

Tox-²: see TOXO-¹.

Toxi- (tǫksi), comb. form arbitrarily repr. TOXIC or TOXIN, as in **Toxidermic** (-dɔ̄·ɹmik) *a.* [Gr. δέρμα skin], pertaining to skin-disease produced by a poison. ‖**Toxipho·bia** [-PHOBIA] fear of being poisoned, as a form of insanity or monomania.

Toxic (tǫ·ksik), *a.* (*sb.*) 1664. [f. med.L. *toxicus* poisoned, imbued with poison, adj. of which the neut. *toxicum* was already in cl.L., = poison – Gr. τοξικὸν φάρμακον poison for smearing arrows (τοξικός orig. meaning 'of or pertaining to the bow', τόξον).] **1.** Of the nature of a poison; poisonous. **2.** Caused or produced by a poison; due to poisoning 1872. **B.** *sb.* A toxic substance, a poison 1890.

1. The introduction into the torrent of the circulation of t. substances 1876. **2.** T. Insanity 1874. So **To·xical** *a.* of t. nature or character 1607.

Toxicant (tǫ·ksikănt), *a.* and *sb. rare.* 1882. [var. of INTOXICANT with differentiation of meaning; cf. next.] **A.** *adj.* Acting as a poison; poisonous, toxic 1891. **B.** *sb.* A poisonous substance, a poison 1882.

Toxication (tǫksikēⁱ·ʃən). 1821. [var. of INTOXICATION 'the action of poisoning' (obs. exc. *Med.*).] Poisoning: esp. by toxic substances produced by disease-germs.

Toxicity (tǫksi·sĭti). 1881. [f. TOXIC + -ITY.] Toxic or poisonous quality, esp. in relation to its degree or strength.

Toxico- (tǫ·ksiko), bef. a vowel **toxic-**, repr. Gr. τοξικόν in sense 'poison' (see TOXIC), but mostly used as comb. form of TOXIC, as in ‖**Toxicoderma** (-dɔ̄·ɹmă), **-dermati·tis**, **-dermi·tis** [Gr. δέρμα skin; see -ITIS], inflammation of the skin caused by an irritant poison. ‖**Toxicoma·nia** [MANIA], a morbid craving for poisons. **Toxicopho·bia** = *toxiphobia*.

Toxicology (tǫksikǫ·lŏdʒi). 1799. [f. TOXICO- + -LOGY. Cf. Fr. *toxicologie*.] The science of poisons; that department of pathology or medicine which deals with the nature and effects of poisons. So **To:xicolo·gical** *a.* belonging or relating to t. (sometimes erron. used for *toxical*). **To:xicolo·gically** *adv.* in relation to t. **Toxico·logist**, a person versed in t.

‖**Toxicosis** (tǫksikōᵘ·sis). *Pl.* **-oses** (-ōᵘ·sīz). 1857. [mod.L., f. as prec. + -OSIS.] *Path.* A disease or morbid condition produced by the action of a poison.

To·xifer. 1853. [– mod.L. *Toxifera*, f. Gr. τόξα arrows + L. *-fer* bearing.] *Zool.* A mollusc of the sub-order *Toxifera*.

Toxin (tǫ·ksin). 1886. [f. TOXIC + -IN¹.] A specific poison, usu. of an albuminous nature, esp. one produced by a microbe, which causes a particular disease when present in the system of a human or animal body.

Toxo-¹ (tǫkso), bef. a vowel **tox-**, comb. form repr. Gr. τόξον bow, in TOXODON, TOXOPHILITE, etc.

Toxo-², used as comb. form of TOXIN (cf. TOXI-) or instead of TOXICO-, as in **To·xophil** (-fil) *a.* [Gr. -φιλος loving], having affinity for a toxin. **To·xophore** (-fōᵊɹ), **Toxophoric** (-fǫ·rik), **Toxophorous** (-ǫ·fŏrəs) *adjs.* [Gr. -φορος bearing, carrying], poison-bearing; applied to a particular group of atoms in the molecule of a toxin to which its toxic properties are due.

Toxodon (tǫ·ksŏdǫn). 1837. [mod.L., f. Gr. τόξον bow + ὀδούς, ὀδοντ- tooth.] *Palæont.* A genus of large extinct quadrupeds, having strongly curved molar teeth, whose remains are found in Pleistocene deposits in S. America. Hence **To·xodont** *adj.* belonging to or having the characters of the order *Toxodonta*, typified by this genus; *sb.* a quadruped of this order.

Toxoglossate (tǫksoglǫ·seⁱt), *a.* 1853. [f. mod.L. *Toxoglossa* (Troschel, 1848), f. Gr. τόξα arrows, darts + γλῶσσα tongue; see -ATE² 2.] *Zool.* Having the characters of the *Toxoglossa* of Troschel, a group of gasteropod molluscs; the same as Gray's *Toxifera*.

Toxophilite (tǫksǫ·filəit). 1794. [f. *Toxophilus*, title of Ascham's book (1545) intended to mean 'lover of the bow' (f. Gr. τόξον bow + φίλος -PHIL) + -ITE¹; *quasi* 'a follower of Toxophilus'.] A lover or devotee of archery, an archer 1812. **b.** *attrib.* Of or pertaining to archers or archery 1794. Hence **Toxo·phily**, the practice of, or addiction to, archery.

Toy (toi), *sb.* 1500. [Of unkn. origin; there are serious gaps in the early evidence; MDu. *toi* (Du. *tooi*) attire, finery, agrees in form but not in sense.] **I.** Abstract senses. †**1.** Amorous sport, dallying, toying; with *pl.*, an act or piece of this, a light caress –1707. †**2.** A sportive or frisky movement; an antic, a trick –1777. **3.** A fantastic or trifling speech or piece of writing; a foolish or idle tale; a jest, joke, pun; a light or facetious composition. *arch.* 1542. †**4.** A whim, crotchet, caprice –1699. †**b.** *spec.* A foolish or unreasoning aversion; esp. in phr. *to take (a) t. at* something –1697.

1. So said he, and forbore not glance or t. Of amorous intent, well understood Of Eve MILT. **3.** I neuer may beleeue These anticke fables, nor these Fairy toyes SHAKS.

II. Concrete senses. **1.** *gen.* A thing of little or no value or importance, a trifle; a foolish or senseless affair, a piece of nonsense; *pl.* trumpery, rubbish 1530. **2.** A plaything for children or others; also, something contrived for amusement rather than for practical use (esp. in phr. *a mere t.*) 1586. **3.** A small article of little intrinsic value; a knick-knack, trinket, gewgaw; hence applied to anything small, flimsy, or inferior of its kind (now chiefly *attrib.*) 1596. **4.** *fig.* Applied to a person 1598. **5.** Applied to a diminutive breed or variety of animals 1877. **6.** *Sc.* A close cap or head-dress, of linen or wool, with flaps coming down to the shoulders, formerly worn by women of the lower classes in Scotland. Now *rare* or *Obs.* 1724. **7.** *attrib.*: **a.** That is a toy (in sense II. 2); applied to small models or imitations of ordinary objects used as playthings, as *t. cannon, train*, etc. 1836. **b.** *transf.* and *fig.* Applied to things of diminutive size, flimsy construction, or petty character 1821. **c.** Applied to an animal, esp. a dog of a diminutive breed or variety, kept as a pet 1863.

1. From this instant, There's nothing serious in Mortalitie: All is but Toyes SHAKS. **2.** Lead soldiers, dolls, all toys. .are in the same category 1881. **3.** A conspicuous t. of a church 1888. **4.** Elues, list your names: Silence, you aiery toyes SHAKS. A Russian. .being a mere t. in the hands of the commonest policeman 1883. Hence **Toy·ful** *a.*; amusing (now *rare* or *Obs.*).

Toy, *v.* 1529. [Goes with TOY *sb.*] **1.** *intr.* To act idly; to trifle, 'play' (*with* a person or thing). **2.** To sport amorously; to dally, flirt. Usu. const. *with.* 1550. **3.** To play, sport; to frisk about 1530.

2. To t., to wanton, dallie, smile, and iest SHAKS. *fig.* He had. .toyed a little with the muses 1842. **3.** *T. with*, to play with (a material object), to handle or finger idly; hence, to work idly or carelessly with or at. Hence **Toy·er,** one who toys; a trifler.

To-year (tŭ,yīᵊ·ɹ), *adv.* Now *dial.* ME. [f. TO *prep.* A. II. 2 + YEAR; cf. *to-day*, etc.] This year.

Toy·ing, *ppl. a.* 1566. [f. TOY *v.* + -ING².] That toys; *esp.* amorously sportive. Hence **Toy·ingly** *adv.*

Toyish (toi·iʃ), *a.* Now *rare.* 1563. [f. TOY *sb.* + -ISH¹.] Having the character of a toy, or addicted to toys. **1.** Trifling; foolish, nonsensical 1574. †**2.** Sportive, frisky, skittish; amorously sportive, wanton –1680. **3.** Of the nature of, or fit for, a plaything; of a sportive character, as a writing 1699. Hence **Toy·ish-ly** *adv.*, **-ness.**

Toyman (toi·mæ̆n). 1707. [f. TOY *sb.* + MAN *sb.*] A man who sells toys, or who keeps a toy-shop.

Toy·-shop. 1693. **1.** A shop for the sale of trinkets, knick-knacks, or small ornamental articles. *arch.* **2.** A shop for the sale of toys or playthings 1818.

†**Toy·some,** *a. rare.* 1638. [f. TOY *sb.* + -SOME¹.] Full of 'toys', or having the character of a 'toy'; fantastic; playful; amorously sportive –1754.

Toze, tose (tōᵘz), *v.*¹ *Obs.* exc. *dial.* [ME. *tose* repr. OE. *tasian :– *taisōjan, f. WGmc. *tais-; see TEASE.] *trans.* = TEASE *v.* 1. Also *fig.*

Toze (tōᵘz), *v.*² 1758. [Possibly same word as prec.] *Tin-mining.* (*trans.*) To separate tin ore from the gangue or rough ore by stirring the slimes in a keeve, and allowing the heavier particles to settle.

‖**Trabea** (trēⁱ·bĭă). *Pl.* **-eæ** (-i,ī). 1600. [L.] *Rom. Antiq.* A toga ornamented with horizontal purple stripes, worn as a state robe by kings, consuls, and other men of rank in ancient Rome.

Trabeate (trēⁱ·bĭeⁱt), *a.* 1890. [irreg. f. L. *trabs, trab-* beam + -ATE², presumably confused with L. *trabeatus* 'wearing a trabea'.] *Arch.* = next.

Trabeated (trēⁱ·bi,eⁱtėd), *a.* 1843. [f. as prec. + -ED¹.] *Arch.* Constructed with beams; having beams or long squared stones as lintels and entablatures, instead of using the arch; covered with a beam or entablature, as a doorway.

Trabeation (trēⁱbi,ēⁱ·ʃən). 1563. [irreg. f. L. *trabs, trab-* beam; see -ATION, and cf. TRABEATE.] *Arch.* †**a.** An entablature. **b.** Trabeated structure.

‖**Trabecula** (trăbe·kiŭlă). *Pl.* **-æ** (-ī). 1886. [L., dim. of *trabs, trab-* beam; see -CULE.] A structure in an animal or plant resembling a small beam or bar. So **Trabe·cular** *a.* pertaining to or of the nature of a t.; composed of or furnished with trabeculæ 1822. **Trabe·culate** (1866), **-ated** (1876) *adjs.* furnished with or having trabeculæ.

Trabuch (trăbu·k). *Obs.* or *arch.* 1482. [– OFr. *trabuc*, f. *tra-, tres-* (:– L. *trans*, expressing displacement) + *buc* trunk (of the body), bulk – Frankish *būk* belly. Cf. TREBUCHET.] A mediæval engine of war for throwing great stones against walls, etc.

‖**Tracasserie** (trakasri). 1656. [Fr., f. *tracasser* bustle, worry oneself; see -ERY.] A state of disturbance or annoyance; a turmoil, bother, fuss; a petty quarrel. (Chiefly in *pl.*)

Trace (trēⁱs), *sb.*¹ ME. [– (O)Fr. *trace*, f. *tracier* (mod. *tracer*); see TRACE *v.*] †**1.** The way or path which anything takes; course, road –1768. †**2.** A line, file, or train of persons –1598. †**3.** *pl.* The series or line of footprints left by an animal; hence in *sing.* a footprint –1706. **4.** The track made by the passage of any person or thing, whether beaten by feet or indicated in any other way. late ME. **b.** *spec.* A beaten path through a wild or unenclosed region, made by the passage of men or beasts; a track, a trail. *U.S.* 1807. **5.** *pl.* Vestiges or marks remaining and indicating the former presence, existence, or action of something; *sing.* a vestige, an indication. late ME. **b.** An indication of the presence of a minute amount of some constituent in a compound; a quantity so minute as to be inferred but not actually measured; esp. in *Chem.*;

transf. a very little 1827. **6.** *fig.* A non-material indication or evidence of the presence or existence of something, or of a former event or condition; a sign, mark 1656. **7.** A line or figure drawn; a tracing, drawing, or sketch; the traced record of a self-recording instrument; in *Fortif.* the ground-plan of a work 1744. **8.** *Geom.* **a.** The track described by a moving point, line, or surface. **b.** The intersection of a line or surface with a surface; *spec.* the intersection of a plane with one of the co-ordinate planes, or with one of the planes of projection. 1834.

4. Phr. *On one's trace(s*, in pursuit of one. **5.** My niece..saw the traces of the ditch at once SCOTT. **b.** Traces of oxalic acid can be detected 1838. **6.** The shady empire shall retain no t. Of war or blood, but in the sylvan chase POPE.

Trace (trēis), *sb.*[2] [ME. *trais*, first as collect. pl., later as sing. – OFr. *trais*, pl. of *trait* draught, harness-strap :– L. *tractus* draught, f. pa. ppl. stem of *trahere* draw. Cf. TRACT *sb.*[3], TRAIT.] †**1.** as *pl.* The pair of ropes, chains, or (now usu.) leather straps by which the collar of a draught-animal is connected with the splinter-bar or swingletree. (Usu. *collective.*) –1807. **2.** as *sing.* Each of the individual ropes or leather straps mentioned above; in *pl.* = sense 1. late ME. Also *attrib.*, as *t.-horse*.

2. Phr. (*fig.*) *Into the traces*, into regular work; He was too fond of my genius to force it into the traces 1824. *To kick over the traces*: see KICK *v.*[1] I. 1.

Trace (trēis), *v.* ME. [– OFr. *tracier* (mod. *tracer*) :– Rom. **tractiare*, f. L. *tractus*; see TRACT *sb.*[3]] †**I. 1.** *intr.* To take one's course, make one's way; to proceed, pass, go, travel, tread –1793. **2.** To pace or step in dancing; to dance –1808. **3.** *trans.* To tread (a path, way, street, etc.) –1794. **4.** To travel or range over; to traverse –1807.

3. The passage..commonly called the dolorous way,..traced with the blessed feet of our Saviour FULLER.

II. 1. To follow the footprints or traces of; *esp.* to track by the footprints; also with the traces as object; hence, to pursue, to dog 1440. **2.** *fig.* To follow the course, development, or history of. Also with the course, etc. as object. 1654. **b.** *intr.* for *pass.* To go *back* in time, to date *back* 1886. **3.** *trans.* To make out and follow the course or line of 1703. **b.** To make out, decipher (worn or obscure writing) 1761. **4.** To ascertain by investigation; to search out 1642. **b.** To find traces of 1697.

1. It is forbydden to t. hares in snowe tyme 1530. **2.** No libel on the government had ever been traced to a Quaker MACAULAY. **3.** The form of the ancient manor house may still be traced 1907. **b.** Thrice he traced the runic rhyme GRAY. **4.** Tracing a connection..where in reality none exists 1869. **b.** He observes no Method that I can t. DRYDEN.

III. 1. *trans.* To mark, make marks upon; *esp.* to ornament with lines, figures, or characters. late ME. **2.** To make a plan, diagram, or chart of (something existing or to be constructed); to mark out the course of (a road, etc.) on, or by means of, a plan or map; to set out (the lines of a work or road) on the ground itself. Also *fig.* to devise (a plan of action), map out (a policy). late ME. **3.** To draw; to draw an outline or figure of; also, to put down in writing, to pen. late ME. **b.** To copy (a drawing, plan, etc.) by following the lines of the original drawing on a transparent sheet placed upon it; to make a tracing of 1762.

1. The deep-set windows, stain'd and traced TENNYSON. **2.** The castle [in Milan], by which the citadel of Antwerp was traced 1645.

Traceable (trēi·săb'l), *a.* 1748. [f. prec. + -ABLE.] Capable of being traced. Hence **Traceabi·lity, Tra·ceableness. Tra·ceably** *adv.*

Traceless (trēi·slės), *a.* 1651. [f. TRACE *sb.*[1] + -LESS.] Leaving no trace or track; that cannot be traced; of a surface, that shows no traces or lines.

Tracer (trēi·səɹ). 1552. [f. TRACE *v.* + -ER[1].] One who or that which traces. **1.** One who follows the track of anything; one who tracks, investigates, or searches out. **2.** A thing used for tracing; *spec.* in *Anat.* a slender probe used in tracing the course of a nerve or vessel 1882. **3.** *gen.* Something which traces lines or makes tracings, in various spec. uses 1790. **4.** = *t. bullet, shell*; also, the smoke emitted 1910.

attrib.: **t. bullet**, etc., a bullet, etc., whose trajectory is made visible by smoke or a luminous glow.

Tracery (trēi·səri). 1464. [An Eng. formation f. TRACE *v.* or TRACER; see -ERY.] †**1.** A place for tracing or drawing (*rare*). **2.** *Arch.* The term given to the intersecting rib-work in the upper part of a Gothic window, formed by the elaboration of the mullion, and to the interlaced work of a vault, and that on walls, in panels, and in tabernacle work or screens 1699. **3.** *transf.* and *fig.* Any delicate interweaving of lines or threads, as in embroidery, carving, etc.; also, an interlacing of boughs or foliage; network, open-work 1827.

‖**Trachea** (trēi·kiă, trăkī·ă). *Pl.* **-eæ.** late ME. [med.L., = late L. *trachia* – Gr. τραχεῖα (fem. of τραχύς rough), short for ἀρτηρία τραχεῖα 'rough artery', in med.L. *arteria trachea* (XIII).] **1.** *Anat.* and *Zool.* **a.** The musculo-membranous tube extending from the larynx to the bronchi, and surrounded by gristly (or in birds often bony) rings, which conveys the air to the lungs in air-breathing vertebrates; the windpipe. **b.** Each of the tubes which constitute the respiratory organ in insects and other arthropods 1826. **2.** *Bot.* One of the ducts or vessels in the woody tissue of plants, formed from the coalescence of series of cells by disappearance of the partitions between them, formerly supposed to serve for the passage of air; a wood-vessel 1744. So **Tracheal** (trēi·kiăl, trăkī·ăl) *a.* pertaining to or of the nature of a t.; connected with, composed of, tracheæ. **Trachean** (trēi·kiăn, trăkī·ăn) *a. Zool.* pertaining to or of the nature of a t.; having tracheæ; *sb.* a tracheate arachnid.

Tracheary (trēi·kiări), *a.* (*sb.*) 1835. [– mod.L. *trachearius*; see -ARY and cf. next.] **1.** *Zool.* Belonging to the order *Trachearia* of arachnids. **2.** *Bot.* Of the nature of, or composed of, tracheæ; esp. applied to tissue containing both tracheæ and tracheides 1885. **B.** *sb.* A tracheate arachnid 1835.

Tracheate (trēi·ki,ėit), *a.* (*sb.*) 1877. [– mod.L. *Tracheata*, f. *trachea*; see -ATE[2] 2.] *Zool.* Furnished with or having tracheæ, as an arthropod; belonging to the group *Tracheata*, in some classifications comprising the insects, myriapods, arachnids, and the genus *Peripatus*, or *spec.* to the order *Tracheata* or *Trachearia* of arachnids, which breathe by tracheæ alone. **B.** *sb.* A tracheate arthropod. So **Tra·cheated** *a.*

Tracheide (trēi·ki-, trăkī·,əid). 1875. [– G. *tracheïde*, f. TRACHEA + -IDE, -ID[2].] *Bot.* A vascular cell, with pitted lignified wall, which serves for the conduction of water; a vascular wood-cell. Hence **Tracheidal** *a.* pertaining to or of the nature of a t.

‖**Tracheitis** (trēiki,əi·tis, træk-). 1859. [mod.L., f. TRACHEA + -ITIS.] *Path.* Inflammation of the trachea.

Trachelate (træ·kīlėit), *a.* 1826. [f. Gr. τράχηλος neck; see -ATE[2].] *Entom.* Having a neck, or a constriction like a neck: said of the prosternum in certain hymenopterous insects. So **Tracheliate** (trăkī·li,ėit) *a.* belonging to the division *Trachelia* or *Trachelida* of beetles, which have a neck-like constriction behind the eyes. **Trachelidan** (trăke·lidăn) *a.* = *tracheliate*; *sb.* a member of the *Trachelida*.

Trachelo- (trăkī·lo), comb. form repr. Gr. τράχηλος neck.

Trache:lobra·nchiate *a.*, *Zool.* having branchia or gills on the neck, as the division *Trachelobranchia* of gasteropod molluscs. **Trache·lo·rrhaphy** [Gr. ῥαφή sewing], *Surg.* repair or suture of a laceration of the neck of the womb. **Trachelo·tomy** [Gr. τομή cutting], *Surg.* amputation of the neck of the womb.

‖**Trachenchyma** (trăke·ŋkimă). 1848. [f. TRACHEA + Gr. ἔγχυμα infusion, after PARENCHYMA.] *Bot.* Tracheary tissue.

Tracheo- (trēi·kio, trăkī·o), used as comb. form of TRACHEA.

‖**Tracheobranchia** (-bræ·ŋkiă), pl. **-æ**, a respiratory organ in certain insect larvæ, combing the characters of a trachea and a branchia or gill. **Tracheobronchial** (-brǫ·ŋkiăl) *a.*, pertaining to the trachea and the bronchi; also as *sb.* a tracheobronchial muscle (in birds). **Trache·ocele** (-sīl) [Gr. κήλη tumour], a tumour in or upon the trachea; also loosely applied to goitre. **Trache·ophone** (-fōun) [Gr. φωνή voice], *sb.* a member of the *Tracheophonæ* or *Tracheophones*, a group of S. American passerine birds, having the syrinx or vocal organ situated wholly or chiefly in the trachea; *adj.* belonging to this group. **Tracheo·scopy** [Gr. -σκοπία, f. σκοπεῖν to view], inspection of the trachea, as with a laryngoscope.

Tracheotomy (trēiki,ǫ·tŏmi, træ·k-). 1726. [f. TRACHEO- + -TOMY.] *Surg.* Incision of the trachea or windpipe.

Trachinoid (træ·kinoid), *a.* and *sb.* 1889. [f. mod.L. *Trachinus* (Linn., 1758), the typical genus + -OID; f. med.L. *trachina*, local name of a fish.] **A.** *adj.* Resembling, allied to, or having the characters of, the *Trachinidæ* or weevers, a family of spiny-finned fishes. **B.** *sb.* A fish of this family.

‖**Trachoma** (trăkōu·mă). 1693. [mod.L. – Gr. τράχωμα roughness, f. τραχύς rough.] *Path.* An infectious disease of the eyes, characterized by roughness or granulation of the inner surface of the eyelids, often supervening upon purulent ophthalmia; also called *granular lids*. **b.** Also, an affection of the larynx characterized by nodular swellings on the vocal chords.

Trachomedusan (trēi:komĭdiū·săn), *a.* and *sb.* 1907. [f. mod.L. *Trachomedusæ*, pl. f. *tracho-*, var. of TRACHY- + MEDUSA; see -AN.] *Zool.* **A.** *adj.* Belonging to the sub-order *Trachomedusæ* of the order *Trachymedusæ* of craspedote Hydrozoa. **B.** *sb.* A hydrozoan of this sub-order.

Trachy- (trēiki, træki-), combining form repr. Gr. τραχύς rough.

Trachyca·rpous [Gr. καρπός fruit] *a.*, *Bot.* rough-fruited. **Tra:chymedu·san**, *Zool.*, *a.* belonging to the family *Trachymedusæ* of Craspedote Hydrozoa; *sb.* a hydrozoan of this family. **Trachyspe·rmous** [Gr. σπέρμα seed] *a.*, *Bot.* rough-seeded. **b.** *Min.* In names of rocks, taken as comb. form of TRACHYTE, and denoting an igneous rock or lava intermediate between trachyte and that denoted by the second element, as **trachyba·salt**, etc.

Trachyte (trēi·kəit, træ·kəit). 1821. [– Fr. *trachyte* (Haüy), f. Gr. τραχύς rough or τραχύτης roughness; see -ITE[1] 2 b.] *Geol.* and *Min.* A group of volcanic rocks, having a characteristically rough or gritty surface. Now confined to rocks mainly consisting of sanidine (or glassy orthoclase) feldspar. Hence **Trachy·tic** *a.* consisting or of the nature of t.; containing or abounding in trachyte. **Tra·chytoid** *a.* resembling or allied to trachyte.

Tracing (trēi·siŋ), *vbl. sb.* 1440. [f. TRACE *v.*[1] + -ING[1].] **1.** The following of traces, tracking, *esp.* **2.** Drawing, delineating, marking out; the copying of a drawing, etc., by means of a transparent sheet placed over it 1440. **b.** *concr.* That which is produced by tracing or drawing; a drawing; *spec.* a copy made by tracing; also, the record of a self-registering instrument 1811.

Comb.: **t.-cloth, -linen,** smooth transparent linen sized on one side, used for making tracings; **-paper,** (*a*) transparent paper for copying drawings, etc. by tracing; (*b*) lithographic transfer paper; **-wheel,** a toothed wheel or roulette for marking out patterns.

Track (træk), *sb.* 1470. [– (O)Fr. *trac*, perh. – LDu. (MDu., LG.) *tre(c)k* drawing, draught, pull (cf. TREK *sb.*), but the phonology is difficult.] **I. 1.** The mark or series of marks left by the passage of anything; a trail; a wheel-rut; the wake of a ship; a series of footprints; the scent followed by hounds; *spec.* in *Geol.* a series of fossilized footprints of an animal. **b.** *Zool.* The sole of the foot, esp. in birds 1891. †**2.** *fig.* = TRACE *sb.*[1] 5, 6. –1694. **3.** A way made or beaten by the feet of men or animals; a path; a rough unmade road 1643. **4.** A line of travel, passage, or motion; the actual course or route followed 1570. **b.** The course of a nerve or blood-vessel, or the like; the course of a wound 1807. **5.** *fig.* **a.** A course of action or conduct; a method of proceeding. The *beaten t.*, the ordinary (*quasi* well-worn) way. 1638. **b.** A train or sequence of events, thoughts, etc. 1681. **6.** A path made or laid down for a special purpose; *spec.* **a.** (now *U.S.*) A continuous line of a pair of rails and the space between them, on which railway vehicles travel. *Off the t.*, off the line, derailed; also *fig.* 1805. **b.** A course prepared or laid out for racing, or the like 1887. **c.** Each of the bands of a caterpillar tractor 1927. **7.** [f. TRACK *v.*[1]] The action of tracking; the pursuit of a criminal or fugitive 1542.

1. They came on the trakkys of there enmyes 1500. The tracks of snails and slugs DICKENS. 3. An Indian t., newly made 1675. The road was only a slight t. upon the grass 1791. 4. Far from t. of men MILT.

Phrases. *In one's tracks* (U.S.), on the spot where one is at the moment; instantly, immediately. *On the t.* (*of*), in pursuit of; also, having a trace of or clue to. *To cover* (*up*) *a person's tracks*, to conceal or screen his motions or measures. *To make tracks* (*for*), to make off, to make *for*; to go off quickly (orig. *U.S.*). *To keep t.*, to follow or grasp the course, progress, or sequence *of*; so *to lose t. of*.

II. [Used by confusion for TRACT *sb.*[3]] An extent of land; also, a space of time, a period; also, †a sequence or succession of actions or events 1687.

attrib. and *Comb.*: **t.-brake**, a railway brake which acts by pressure directly against the rail; **-clearer**, a cross-bar carried immediately in front of the wheels of a locomotive or tram-car to push obstructions off the rails; also, a cow-catcher or snow-sweeper fixed in front of a locomotive; **-mile**, a mile of 't.' or single line; hence **-mileage**; **-scale**, a weigh-bridge for railway vehicles.

Track, *v.*[1] 1565. [f. prec., or – Fr. *traquer* (XV).] **1.** *trans.* To follow up the track of; to pursue by or as by the track left. **b.** To find out and follow (a track, trail) 1681. **c.** *intr.* Of the wheels of a vehicle: To run in the same track; of a gear-wheel, To be in alinement (*with* another wheel). **2.** *trans.* To mark out, trace (a path); to indicate the path or course of; *esp.* to mark out (a path) by repeatedly traversing it; to mark (a way) with tracks; to tread, beat 1589. **b.** To lay a track on or for (a railway); to furnish with a line of rails. Only in compounds, as *to double-t.*, *single-t.* *U.S.* 1874. **3.** *intr.* To follow a track or path; to make one's way, pass, go, travel. Now *U.S. slang.* 1590. **b.** *Path.* To make a track for itself; to find its way 1903.

1. The first point was to t. the lion to his covert 1834. 2. The way was smooth and well tracked 1815.

Track, *v.*[2] 1727. [app. – Du. *trekken* draw, pull, etc. (see TREK), assimilated in form to prec.] *trans.* To tow (a vessel), esp. from the bank or tow-path. Also *absol.* **b.** *intr.* To proceed by towing. Said of a boat or of those in it. 1854.

Track-, stem of TRACK *v.*[2], in comb., as *t.-barge, -boat, -road.*

Trackage[1] (træ·kėdʒ). 1820. [f. TRACK *v.*[2] + -AGE.] The action or process of tracking or towing, or fact of being tracked; towage, haulage.

Tra·ckage[2]. *U.S.* 1884. [f. TRACK *sb.* 6 a + -AGE.] The tracks or lines of a railway system collectively. Also *attrib.* **t. charge**, charge made for the use of a railway line by another company.

Tracker[1] (træ·kəɹ). 1617. [f. TRACK *v.*[1] + -ER[1].] One who or that which tracks; one skilled in following a track or trail.

Black t., an Australian native employed by the government to track criminals.

Tra·cker[2]. 1791. [f. TRACK *v.*[2]; cf. Du. *trekker.*] **1.** One who tracks or tows a vessel; a tower; also, a tugboat. **2.** *Organ-building.* A strip or rod of wood forming part of the connection between the key and the pallet, and exerting a pulling action 1843.

Trackless (træ·klės), *a.* 1656. [f. TRACK *sb.* + -LESS.] Without a track or path; pathless; untrodden. **b.** Leaving no track or trace 1695. **c.** Not running on a track or line of rails, while propelled by electric power from overhead conductors 1909.

The recesses of a t. wilderness. Hence **Tra·ckless-ly** *adv.*, **-ness.**

Trackway (træ·kwēⁱ). 1818. [f. TRACK *sb.* + WAY.] A path beaten by the feet of passers, a track; also, an ancient British roadway, a ridgeway.

Tract (trækt), *sb.*[1] late ME. [app. abbrev. of L. *tractatus* TRACTATE; not in any other lang.] †**1.** Literary treatment or discussion (*rare*) –1659. **2.** A book or written work treating of some particular topic; a treatise; a written or printed discourse or dissertation. Now *rare* in *gen.* sense. **b.** A division of a book or literary work treating of a separate subject or branch (*rare*) 1662. **3.** In later use: A short pamphlet on some religious, political, or other topic, suitable for distribution or for purposes of propaganda 1806.

3. Am I really as dull as a t., my dear? G. MEREDITH. *Tracts for the Times*, a series of pamphlets on theological and ecclesiastical topics (known also as the *Oxford Tracts*), started by J. H. Newman, and published at Oxford 1833–41, on the doctrines of which the Tractarian movement was based.

Tract, *sb.*[2] late ME. [– med.L. TRACTUS.] *Liturg.* An anthem consisting of verses of Scripture, usu. from the Psalms, sung instead of the Alleluia in the Mass from Septuagesima till Easter Eve.

Tract (trækt), *sb.*[3] 1486. [– L. *tractus* drawing, etc., f. pa. ppl. stem of *trahere* to draw, drag.] **I.** †**1.** The drawing out, duration, process, or lapse *of time*; the course *of time* –1734. †**b.** Protraction (of time), delay –1600. **c.** An extent of time, a period 1494. **2.** The continuance or continued duration *of* some action or state; the course or continuity *of* a narrative, etc.; a continued series. Now *rare* or *Obs.* 1581. **3.** A stretch or extent *of* territory, etc.; a space or expanse of land (more rarely, of water, air, etc.); a region, district 1553. **b.** *Nat. Hist.*, etc. A region or area of some natural structure, as a mineral formation, or the body of an animal or plant 1811.

1. We conclude this art..to be very ancient, and derived to us by long t. of time 1658. c. A long t. of serene weather 1799. 3. This vast t. of land DE FOE. A t. of water..which..boiled white all over 1886.

†**II.** The action of drawing or pulling; attraction (*rare*) –1620. †**III.** = Fr. *trait* (see TRAIT). A lineament, a feature –1775. **IV.** Senses coinciding with those of TRACK and TRACE. Now chiefly *rare* or *Obs.*, being in the main superseded by these words. **1.** = TRACK *sb.* I. 3, 4. 1555. **2.** *fig.* = TRACK *sb.* I. 5. 1566. **3.** = TRACE *sb.*[1] 3, 4. 1547.

1. In the t. of the Manila ship 1726. 2. Any particular thought which breaks in upon the regular t. or chain of ideas HUME. 3. But flies an Eagle flight..Leauing no T. behinde SHAKS.

†**Tract**, *v.*[1] 1508. [– L. *tractare* handle, etc., frequent. of *trahere* draw; cf. TREAT *v.*] **1.** *trans.* To negotiate. **2.** To deal with in speech or writing; to discuss or discourse (*trans.*, or *intr.* with *of*) –1637.

†**Tract**, *v.*[2] 1523. [f. *tract-*, pa. ppl. stem of L. *trahere* draw.] **I. 1.** *trans.* To draw, pull along, haul, tow –1769. **2.** To lengthen out, prolong, protract (time); to spend or waste in delay; to delay, put off –1647. **3.** *fig.* To draw on, draw out; to induce 1615. **II. 1.** = TRACE *v.* I. 3. –1613. **2.** = TRACE *v.* II. 1. –1654.

Tractable (træ·ktăb'l), *a.* 1502. [– L. *tractabilis*, f. *tractare*; see TRACT *v.*[1], -ABLE.] **1.** That can be easily managed; docile, compliant, governable. **b.** Const. *to* with sb. or inf. 1509. **2.** Of things (usu. concrete): Easy to deal with, handle, or work; manageable 1555. †**3.** That can be handled; palpable, tangible –1694.

1. A large wolf-dog, ..as t. as he was strong and bold SCOTT. Hence **Tractabi·lity, Tra·ctableness. Tra·ctably** *adv.*

Tractarian (træktēə·riăn), *sb.* and *a.* 1824. [f. TRACT *sb.*[1] + -ARIAN.] **A.** *sb.* **1.** A writer, publisher, or distributor of tracts (*nonce-uses*). **2.** A member of that school of High Churchmen which maintains the doctrines and practices set forth in 'Tracts for the Times' (see TRACT *sb.*[1] 3) 1839. **B.** *adj.* Of or belonging to the Tractarians 1840. **2.** Distributing tracts (*nonce-use*) 1885. Hence **Tracta·rianism**, the tenets or principles of the Tractarians, the T. system; adherence to or maintenance of this.

Tractate (træ·kteⁱt). 1474. [– L. *tractatus*, f. *tractare* TREAT; see TRACT *v.*[1], -ATE[1].] **1.** A book or literary work treating of a particular subject; a treatise. †**2.** Negotiation, dealing, transaction –1630.

1. In the Rabbinic t. on the Samaritans 1883.

†**Tracta·tor.** 1638. [– late L. *tractator*, f. L. *tractare*; see TRACT *v.*[1], -OR 2.] One who treats of a subject; the writer of a tractate –1725. **b.** *spec.* Any one of the writers of 'Tracts for the Times' –1844.

Tractile (træ·ktəil, -il), *a. rare.* 1626. [f. *tract-*, pa. ppl. stem of L. *trahere* draw + -ILE, after *ductile.*] †**1.** Capable of being drawn out to a thread. BACON. **2.** That may be drawn, as money from a bank 1892. Hence **Tracti·lity,** the quality of being t.

Traction (træ·kʃən). 1615. [– Fr. *traction* or med. L. *tractio, -ōn-*, f. as prec.; see -ION.] **1.** The action of drawing or pulling; draught; opp. to *pulsion* or pushing, and (in *Dynamics*) to *pressure* 1656. **b.** *Phys.* and *Path.* A drawing or pulling of a part or organ (in an animal or plant) by some vital process, as the contraction of a muscle, etc. 1615. **c.** A drawing or pulling movement used in massage, etc. 1841. **d.** *fig.* Drawing, attraction, attractive power 1649. **2.** *spec.* The drawing of vehicles or loads along a road or track; esp. in ref. to the power by which this is done 1822. **3.** Short for *force of t.* (as a measurable quantity); the amount of rolling friction (also *t. of adhesion*) as measuring this 1825.

1. *Force of t.*, the force exerted in or required for t. *Line of t.*, the line along which this force acts. *Angle of t.*, the angle between the line of t. and the surface along which the body is drawn. b. There was..a slight..t. of face to the right side when the patient laughed 1876. d. He feels the resistless t. of fate 1883. 2. The three stages are horse-t., steam t., and electric t. 1902.

Comb.: **t.-wheel**, a driving-wheel.

Tra·ction-e:ngine. 1859. A steam-engine used for drawing heavy loads along an ordinary road; also, a similar engine used in agricultural work.

†**Tra·ctism.** 1834. [f. TRACT *sb.*[1] + -ISM.] = TRACTARIANISM –1844.

Tractive (træ·ktiv), *a.* 1615. [f. *tract-*, pa. ppl. stem of L. *trahere* draw + -IVE; cf. TRACTILE, and TRACT *v.*[2]] Having the property of drawing or pulling; used for traction.

Tractor (træ·ktǫɹ, -əɹ). 1798. [f. as prec. + -OR 2.] **1.** *pl.* (in full (*Perkins's*) *metallic tractors*): A device consisting of a pair of pointed rods of different metals, as brass and steel, which were believed to relieve rheumatic or other pain by being drawn or rubbed over the skin: see PERKINISM. *Obs.* exc. *Hist.* **2.** One who or that which draws or pulls something; *esp.* a traction-engine 1856. **3.** An aeroplane with one or more propellers or screws in front: opp. to *pusher*. Also *t.-aeroplane* 1912. Hence **Tractora·tion,** the use of metallic tractors (see 1).

Tractory (træ·ktŏri), *a.* and *sb. rare.* 1684. [– L. *tractorius* of or for drawing, f. as prec.; see -ORY.] †**A.** *adj.* Serving for traction; tractive. **B.** *sb. Geom.* = next 1820.

‖**Tractrix** (træ·ktriks). *Pl.* **tra·ctrices** (-isīz). 1727. [mod. L. (Huygens), fem. (see -TRIX) of *tractor* TRACTOR; cf. DIRECTRIX.] *Geom.* A curve such that the intercept on the tangent between its point of contact and a fixed straight line is constant; so called as being traced by the centre of gyration of a rigid rod of which one end is moved along the fixed straight line. Also, one of a class of curves similarly traced, e.g. by movement along a fixed curve.

‖**Tractus** (træ·ktŏs). 1450. [med.L., sc. *cantus*, lit. drawn-out song; see TRACT *sb.*[2]] = TRACT *sb.*[2]

Tradable (trēⁱ·dăb'l), *a.* Also **tradeable.** 1599. [f. TRADE *sb.* or *v.* + -ABLE.] That may be dealt with in the way of trade; marketable.

Trade (trēⁱd), *sb.* ME. [– MLG. *trade* track, corresp. to OS. *trada*, OHG. *trata*, f. *trad- *tred- TREAD *v.*] **I.** †**1.** A course, way, path –1564. †**2.** The track or trail of a man or beast; footprints –1596. **3.** Course, way, or manner of life; course of action; mode of procedure, method. *Obs.* or *dial.* 1456. **b.** A regular or habitual course of action. *Obs.* exc. *dial.* 1586. **4.** The practice of some occupation, business, or profession habitually carried on, esp. when practised as a means of livelihood or gain; a calling; now usu. applied to a mercantile occupation and to a skilled handicraft, as dist. from a profession, and *spec.* restricted to a skilled handicraft, as dist. from a professional or mercantile occupation on the one hand, and from unskilled labour on the other 1546. **b.** Anything practised for a livelihood 1650. **5.** *The t.*: those concerned in the particular business or industry in question; *spec.* the publishers and booksellers; now more commonly, those engaged in the liquor trade 1697.

1. A postern..there was, A common t. to passe through Priams house SURREY. *fig. Hen. VIII*, v. i. 36. **2.** As Shepheardes curre, that..Hath tracted forth some salvage beastes t. SPENSER. **3.** Teache a childe in the t. of his way, and when he is olde, he shal not departe from it BIBLE (Genev.) *Prov.* 22:6. **b.** Thy sinn's not accidentall, but a T. SHAKS. Phr. †*To blow t.*, of the wind, to blow in a regular or habitual course, or constantly in the same direction (cf. TRADE-WIND). **4.** A Potter, Sir, he was by t. WORDSW. His being in t. was an obstacle 1813. *The t.* (Navy colloq.), the submarine service 1916.

II. 1. a. *lit.* Passage to and fro; coming and going; resort. Now *dial.* 1591. †**b.** *fig.* Intercourse, 'commerce', dealings –1708. **2.** Passage or resort for the purpose of commerce; hence, the buying and selling or exchange of commodities for profit; commerce, traffic, trading 1555. **3.** With *a* and *pl.* An act of trading, a transaction, a bargain; *spec.* in politics, a 'deal' or 'job'. orig. *U.S. slang.* 1829. †**4.** A fleet of trading ships under convoy –1803. **5.** Stuff, goods, materials, commodities; now *dial.*, usu. = rubbish, trash 1645. **6.** Commodities for use in bartering with savages; also, native produce for barter 1847. **7.** Abbrev. of TRADE-WIND; chiefly in *pl.* 1796.

1. a. Ile be buryed in the Kings high-way, Some way of common T., where Subjects feet May howrely trample on their Soueraignes Head SHAKS. **b.** Haue you any further T. with vs? SHAKS. **2.** The balance of t...is the difference between the aggregate amount of a nation's exports or imports, or the balance of the particular account of the nation's trade with another nation 1835. **4.** This squadron,..and the t. under their convoy,..tided it down the Channel 1748.

Comb.: **t. allowance,** a wholesale discount, allowed to dealers or retailers on articles to be sold again; **t. board,** a council regulating conditions of employment in certain trades; **t. dollar,** a dollar issued by the U.S.A. for Asiatic t.; **-name,** (*a*) a descriptive or fancy name used to designate some proprietary article of t.; (*b*) the name by which an article or substance is known to the trade; (*c*) the name or style under which a business is carried on; **t. price,** the price at which the wholesale dealer sells to the retailer; **-route,** a route followed by traders or caravans, or by trading-ships; **-sale,** an auction held by and for a particular t.; **t. school,** a school in which handicrafts are taught; **-show,** the performance of a cinematograph picture for 'exhibitors'; hence **-show** *v. trans.* Hence **Tra·deful** *a.* full of t.; †full of traffic. **Tra·deless** *a.* without a t.; destitute of t. or commerce.

Trade (trēid), *v.* 1548. [f. prec.] †**1.** *trans.* To tread (a path); to traverse (the sea); *fig.* to go through, lead (one's life) –1649. †**2.** *intr.* To tread, step, walk, go in a course –1651. †**3.** *trans.* To follow (a course) habitually; to practise –1631. †**4.** To familiarize with the use, practice, or knowledge of something; to accustom *to* or *to do* something; to school, exercise –1652. **5.** *intr.* †**a.** To have dealings; to treat, negotiate (*with* a person) –1676. **b.** To occupy oneself *in* something; to deal, have dealings *in*. *Obs.* exc. as *fig.* from 6 b. 1606. **6. a.** To resort *to* a place for purposes of trade 1570. Hence, **b.** to engage in or carry on trade (*with* a person, *in* a commodity) 1570. **c.** With sinister implication: To traffic *in* something which should not be bought or sold 1663. **d.** *To t. on* or *upon*: to make use of for one's own ends; to take advantage of 1884. †**7.** *trans.* To frequent for purposes of trade –1707. **8.** †To employ (money) in trade (*rare*); to make (anything) the subject of trade, to trade in; to acquire or dispose of (also *to t. off*) by barter (*U.S.*); to buy and sell, to barter, to exchange 1628. *To t. in* (U.S.), to give used articles in part payment for new ones 1927.

2. By the labour of trading from one place to another HOBBES. **4.** Being..traded in wel doing, from the cradle 1603. **5. a.** How did you dare To T. and Trafficke with Macbeth, In Riddles, and Affaires of death SHAKS. **b.** Musicke, moody foode of vs that t. in Loue SHAKS. **6. a.** They traded with profit only to China 1844. **b.** I used..to t. in salt 1776. **d.** They..still t. on the fears and fancies of their fellows 1885.

†**Traded** (trēi·dėd), *ppl. a.* and *a.* 1548. [f. TRADE *v.* and *sb.* + -ED.] **1.** Of a road: Much used or trodden; frequented; also *gen.* habitually used –1631. **2.** Versed, practised; experienced; conversant –1654. **3.** Of a place: Frequented for the purpose of trading. (Usu. with *well*, etc.) –1707. **4.** Having a trade (of such a kind) –1656.

†**Tra·de-fa:llen,** *a.* 1596. Fallen or broken in trade, bankrupt –1632.

Trade-mark (trēi·dmāɹk), *sb.* 1838. [f. TRADE *sb.* + MARK *sb.*[1]] A mark (now, one secured by legal registration) used by a manufacturer or trader to distinguish his goods from similar wares of other firms. **b.** *fig.* A distinctive mark or token 1873. Hence **Tra·de-mark** *v. trans.* to affix or imprint a t. upon.

Trader (trēi·dəɹ). 1585. [f. TRADE *v.* + -ER[1].] **1.** One whose business is trade or commerce, or who is engaged in trading; a dealer or trafficker. **b.** A vessel engaged in trading 1712. †**2.** One who is occupied or concerned *in* something; a dealer –1800.

1. Great traders, with merchandise & ready monie 1585. **2.** The nonconformists were great traders in Scripture 1673.

‖**Tradescantia** (trædėskæ·ntiă). 1766. [mod.L. (Ruppius, 1718), f. name of John *Tradescant* (the elder), a 17th c. naturalist + -IA[1].] *Bot.* An Amer. genus of perennial herbs of the family *Commelynaceæ*; spiderwort.

Tradesfolk (trēi·dzfoᵘk). 1760. [f. as next + FOLK.] People in trade; tradespeople. **a.** Artisans; **b.** Shopkeepers.

Tradesman (trēi·dzmǣn). *Pl.* **-men.** 1597. [f. *trade's*, gen. of TRADE + MAN *sb.*] **1.** One who is skilled in and follows one of the industrial arts; an artisan, a craftsman. Now *Sc.*, *local Eng.*, *U.S.*, and *Colonial.* **2.** One who is engaged in trade or the sale of commodities; *esp.* a shopkeeper 1601.

Tra·despeo:ple. 1728. [f. as prec. + PEOPLE *sb.*] People engaged in trade; tradesmen, and their families and employees.

Tra·deswo:man. *Pl.* **-women.** 1707. [f. as prec. + WOMAN.] A woman engaged in trade, or in a particular trade or calling.

Trade-u·nion, trades-u·nion. 1831. [f. TRADE or pl. *trades* + UNION.] An association of the workers in any trade or in allied trades for the protection and furtherance of their interests in regard to wages, hours, and conditions of labour, and for the provision, from their common funds, of pecuniary assistance to the members during strikes, sickness, unemployment, old age, etc. Hence **Trade-, trades-u·nionism,** the system, principles, or practice of trade-unions. **Trade-, trades-u·nionist,** a member of a t.

Tra·de-wind. 1650. [f. TRADE *sb.* + WIND *sb.* App. originating in the phr. *to blow trade*; see TRADE *sb.* I. 3 b. Often shortened in naut. use to *trade*, pl. *the trades.*] †**1.** Any wind that 'blows trade', i.e. in a constant course or way; a wind that blows steadily in the same direction –1807. †**2.** Applied to the seasonal winds of the Indian Ocean; = MONSOON 1, 2. –1840. **3.** Now *spec.* The wind that blows constantly towards the equator from about the thirtieth parallels, north and south; its main direction in the northern hemisphere being from the north-east, and in the southern hemisphere from the south-east 1712.

3. The heat of the torrid zone and its velocity of rotation produce the trade winds which blow constantly in the same directions in the same latitudes on the great oceans 1867.

attrib.: **t.-cloud,** the cumulus which collects in the t. regions in the day-time.

Trading (trēi·diŋ), *vbl. sb.* 1590. [f. TRADE *v.* + -ING[1].] The action of TRADE *v.*; *esp.* the carrying on of trade; buying and selling; commerce, trade, traffic. **b.** *attrib.*, esp. in sense 'frequented for, employed in, made or done for trading', as *t. craft, house, post, station, vessel, voyage*, etc. 1590; **t. stamp** (*U.S.*), a coupon given as a voucher by a trader to a customer.

Tra·ding, *ppl. a.* 1690. [f. TRADE *v.* + -ING[2].] That trades; *esp.* engaged in trade, commercial. †**b.** That trades in or makes a trade of something (e.g. a public office) –1839.

b. The common herd of t. politicians 1839.

Tradition (trădi·ʃən), *sb.* late ME. [– (O)Fr. *tradicion*, (also mod.) *-tion*, or L. *traditio*, *-ōn-*, f. *tradere* hand over, deliver, f. *trans* TRANS- + *dare* give; see -ITION.] **1.** The action of handing over (something material) to another; delivery, transfer. (Chiefly in *Law.*) 1540. †**2.** A giving up, surrender; betrayal –1653. **b.** *spec.* in *Ch. Hist.* Surrender of sacred books in times of persecution 1840. **3.** Delivery, *esp.* oral delivery, of information or instruction. Now *rare.* 1500. **b.** *T. of the Creed* (Ch. Hist.): oral instruction upon the Creed given to catechumens 1888. **4.** The act of transmitting or handing down or fact of being handed down, from one to another, or from generation to generation; transmission of statements, beliefs, rules, customs, or the like, esp. by word of mouth, or by practice without writing. Chiefly in phr. *by t.* 1591. **5. a.** That which is thus handed down; a statement, belief, or practice transmitted (esp. orally) from generation to generation. late ME. **b.** More vaguely: A long established and generally accepted custom, or method of procedure, having almost the force of a law; an immemorial usage 1593. **6.** *spec.* (*Theol.* and *Eccl.*) **a.** Among the Jews, Any one, or the whole, of an unwritten code of regulations, etc. held to have been received from Moses, and handed down orally from generation to generation and embodied in the MISHNAH. late ME. **b.** In the Christian Church, Any one, or the whole, of a body of teachings transmitted orally from generation to generation since early times; held by Roman Catholics to comprise teaching derived from Christ and the aspostles, together with that subsequently communicated to the church by the Holy Spirit, and to be of equal authority with Scripture. Also, (as in 4) the transmission of such teaching. 1551. **c.** Among Moslems, An account of sayings and doings of Mohammed transmitted at first orally, and afterwards recorded; esp. = SUNNA 1718.

1. A deed takes effect only from this t. or delivery BLACKSTONE. **4.** Old songs delivered to them, by t., from their fathers 1591. Wolves, so says t., first took gold to Delphi 1863. **5. a.** The traditions associated with these..monuments 1851. **b.** The t. is that a President may be re-elected once and once only 1882. **6. a.** But whi breken ȝe Goddis maundement, for ȝoure veyn tradicioun? WYCLIF. **b.** The Sunday, or the Lord's-Day, which we observe by Apostolical T. instead of the Sabbath 1737.

Comb.: **T. Sunday** (*Ch. Hist.*), a name for Palm Sunday, as the day of 't. of the creed' (see 3 b) in some churches.

Tradition, *v. rare.* 1640. [f. prec.] *trans.* To transmit by tradition, relate as a tradition.

Traditional (trădi·ʃənăl), *a.* 1594. [f. TRADITION *sb.* + -AL[1] 1.] **1.** Belonging to, consisting in, or of the nature of tradition; handed down by or derived from tradition 1600. **b.** That is such according to tradition 1856. †**2.** Observant of, bound by tradition (*rare*) –1644.

1. The t. records of the respectable and ingenious Mrs. Grant of Laggan SCOTT. **b.** The heirlooms of a t. past 1874. **2.** *Rich. III*, III. i. 45. Hence **Tradi·tionally** *adv.*

Tradi·tionalism. 1860. [– Fr. *traditionalisme*, or f. prec. + -ISM.] **1.** A system of philosophy which arose in the Roman Church *c*1840, according to which all human knowledge is derived by traditional instruction from an original divine revelation 1885. **2.** Adherence to traditional doctrine or theory; maintenance of, or submission to, the authority of tradition; excessive reverence for tradition: esp. in matters of religion 1860. So **Tradi·tionalist,** an adherent of t.; one who upholds the authority of tradition.

Traditionary (trădi·ʃənări), *a.* (*sb.*) 1613. [f. TRADITION + -ARY[1].] **1.** = TRADITIONAL *a.* 1, 1b. 1661. †**2.** = TRADITIONAL *a.* 2. –1666.

1. The Corrupted Remains of some t. Revelation 1748.

B. *sb.* One who maintains or accepts the authority of tradition; a traditionalist (*rare*) 1727.

Traditioner (trădi·ʃənəɹ). *rare*. 1646. [f. as prec. + -ER¹.] = next.

Traditionist (trădi·ʃənist). 1666. [f. as prec. + -IST.] **1.** One who accepts, adheres to, or maintains the authority of tradition. **2.** One who gives vogue to, hands on, or records a tradition 1759.

Traditive (træ·dĭtiv), *a*. Now *rare*. 1611. [– Fr. †*traditif* (xv) traditional, f. late L. *traditus* oral transmission; see -IVE.] Characterized by, belonging to, or being transmitted by, tradition; traditional.

The question lay between t. and private interpretation KEBLE.

Traditor (træ·ditǫɹ). late ME. [– L. *traditor*; see TRAITOR.] †**1.** A betrayer, traitor. *Obs.* in general sense. –1711. **2.** *Ch. Hist.* One of those early Christians who, in the great persecution under Diocletian, in order to save their own lives, delivered up their sacred books, vessels, etc., or betrayed their fellow-Christians 1597.

Traduce (trădiū·s), *v*. 1533. [– L. *traducere*, f. *trans* TRANS- + *ducere* lead.] †**1.** *trans.* To convey from one place to another; to transport –1678. †**b.** To translate, render; to alter, modify, reduce –1850. †**c.** To transfer from one use, sense, ownership, or employment to another –1640. †**2.** To transmit, esp. by generation –1733. †**b.** *transf.* To propagate –1711. †**c.** To derive, deduce, obtain *from* a source –1709. **3.** To speak evil of, esp. (now always) falsely or maliciously; to defame, malign, slander, calumniate, misrepresent 1586. †**b.** To expose (to contempt); to dishonour, disgrace (*rare*) –1661. †**4.** To falsify, misrepresent, pervert –1674.

1. b. Milton has been traduced into French and overturned into Dutch SOUTHEY. **2.** Vertue is not traduced in propagation, nor learning bequeathed by our will, to our heires 1606. **3.** The man that dares t., because he can With safety to himself, is not a man COWPER. **b.** By their own ignoble actions they t., that is, disgrace their ancestors 1661. **4.** Who taking Texts..traduced the Sense thereof 1648. Hence **Tradu·cement**, the, or an, action of traducing; defamation, calumny, slander. **Tradu·cingly** *adv.*

Traducer (trădiū·səɹ). 1614. [f. prec. + -ER¹.] One who traduces; a slanderer, calumniator.

Traducian (trădiū·siăn, -diū·ʃ'ăn), *sb.* and *a*. 1727. [– eccl. L. *Traduciani* (Augustine), subst. use of *traducianus* transmitting, transmitter, deriv. of L. *tradux* vine-shoot for propagation, later in transf. sense; see -IAN.] **A.** *sb.* (*a*) One who holds that the soul of a child, like the body, is propagated by or inherited from the parents. (*b*) *less commonly*, One who holds the doctrine of the transmission of original sin from parent to child. **B.** *adj.* Applied to such doctrine or theory. Hence **Tradu·cianism,** the doctrine of the Traducians.

Traduction (trădɒ·kʃən). 1501. [– (O)Fr. *traduction* or L. *traductio*, *-ōn-* leading across, transference, in Chr. L. also in sense 3, f. *traduct-*, pa. ppl. stem of *traducere* TRADUCE; see -ION.] †**1.** Conveyance from one place to another; transportation, transference –1677. †**2.** Translation into another language; *concr.* a translation –1823. **3.** Transmission by generation to offspring or posterity; propagation; derivation from ancestry, descent. Now *rare* or *Obs.* 1593. †**b.** *gen.* Transmission; derivation; handing down, tradition –1827. †**c.** *transf.* Something transmitted or derived –1794. **4.** The action of traducing or defaming; calumny, slander (*rare*) 1656. **5.** *Logic.* Transference or transition from one classification or order of reasoning to another 1847.

1. T. of the Brutes into America from the known World 1677. **3.** A great question,.. touching the t. of the soule 1617. **b.** Arts have their successive invention and perfection and t. from one People to another 1677. **4.** I left t. to its perjuries 1881.

Traductive (trădɒ·ktiv), *a*. 1657. [f. prec. 3 (cf. also TRADUCE 2) + -IVE.] **1.** Having the property of being 'traduced' or transmitted; hereditary; derivative. Now *rare* or *Obs.* **2.** *Logic.* Involving 'traduction' 1847.

Traffic (træ·fik), *sb*. 1506. [Early forms are *traffigo*, *-ico*, *trafficque* – Fr. *traf(f)ique* (mod. *trafic*), Sp. *tráfico*, It. *traffico* (usu. taken to be the source of the Fr.); of unkn. origin.] **1.** The transportation of merchandise for the purpose of trade; hence, trade between distant or distinct communities; commerce. **2.** In wider sense: The buying and selling or exchange of goods for profit; bargaining; trade. Also with *a* and *pl.* 1568. **b.** With evil connotation: Dealing or bargaining in something which should not be made the subject of trade 1663. **3.** *fig.* Intercourse, communication; dealings, business. Now *rare*. 1548. †**4.** *transf.* Saleable commodities. Also *pl.* in same sense. –1778. **5.** The passing to and fro of persons, or of vehicles or vessels, along a road, railway, canal, or other route of transport 1825. **b.** The amount of business done by a railway, etc., in the transport of passengers and goods; the account of or revenue from this 1858.

1. It was not in the Way to or from any Part of the World, where the English had any Traffick DE FOE. **2.** Engaged in a low clandestine traffick, prohibited by the laws of the Country BURKE. **3.** The two hours' t. of our stage SHAKS. **4.** You'll see a draggled damsel, here and there From Billingsgate her fishy t. bear GAY. **5.** We have long since agreed to call street movement 't.' 1894. **b.** This week's batch of Home Railway traffics 1905.

attrib. and *Comb.*: as *t. signal*; **t. density,** the number of passengers and of tons of freight carried over any section of a railway or highway in a given period; **t.-taker,** a railway official whose business is to compile t. returns. Hence **Tra·fficless** *a.* devoid of t.

Traffic (træ·fik), *v*. Infl. **trafficked** (-ikt), **trafficking.** 1542. [– Fr. *traf(f)iquer*, Sp. *traficar*, It. *trafficare*; see prec.] **I.** *intr.* **1.** To carry on trade, to trade, to buy and sell; to have commercial dealings *with* any one; to deal *for* a commodity. Occas., To resort *to* a place for the purpose of trade. **b.** In a disparaging sense, or said of dealing considered improper 1657. †**2.** *fig.* To be concerned, to busy or exercise oneself (*in* some matter) –1882. **b.** To deal, intrigue, conspire (*with* some one, *in*, *for*, or *to do* something); to practise 1567.

1. He was..A thriving man, and trafficked on the seas WORDSW. **b.** Beautiful and dissolute females..trafficking in their charms 1854. **2.** On no pretence I trafick in any tainting politique 1721. **b.** He was trafficking with her enemies and tampering with her friends 1852.

II. *trans.* †**1.** To frequent for the purpose of trading; to carry on trade in (a place) –1611. **b.** To pass to and fro upon (a road, etc.); to traverse 1825. **2.** To carry on a trade in, to buy and sell; to deal in; often with sinister implication. Now *rare*. 1597.

2. The honour of the proud house of Este was being basely trafficked away 1879.

Trafficable (træ·fikăb'l), *a*. 1649. [f. prec. + -ABLE.] **1.** That may be bought or sold; marketable. **2.** Suitable for passage to and fro 1890.

Trafficker (træ·fikəɹ). 1570. [f. TRAFFIC *v.* + -ER¹.] **1.** One who is engaged in traffic or trade; a trader, merchant, dealer 1580. **b.** With opprobrious force 1785. **2.** A go-between, a negotiator; an intriguer; a schemer 1570.

1. b. Some fell traficker in slaves 1785. **2.** The whole clan of old Jacobite spies and traffickers STEVENSON.

Tragacanth (træ·găkænþ). 1573. [– Fr. *tragacante* – L. *tragacantha* – Gr. τραγάκανθα goat's-thorn, tragacanth-shrub, f. τράγος he-goat + ἄκανθα thorn.] **1.** A 'gum' or mucilaginous substance obtained from several species of *Astragalus*, by natural exudation or incision, in the form of whitish strings or flakes, only partially soluble in water. Used in medicine (chiefly as a vehicle for drugs) and in the industrial arts. Commonly called *gum t.* †**2.** Any one of several low-growing spiny leguminous shrubs of the genus *Astragalus*, found in Persia, etc., which yield gum t. (*rare*) –1741. Hence **Tragaca·nthin** (also contr. **traga·nthin**), *Chem.* = BASSORIN.

Tragedian (trădʒī·diăn). late ME. [– OFr. *tragediane*, Fr. *tragédien*, f. (O)Fr. *tragédie* TRAGEDY; see -IAN.] **1.** A tragic poet or author. **2.** A tragic actor 1592. †**3.** *fig.* The victim, or inflicter, of a tragic fate –1635.

1. Under this curled marble..Sleepe rare T. Shakespeare, sleepe alone DONNE. **2.** The well-lung'd Tragedians Rage DRYDEN.

‖**Tragédienne** (traʒedyɛn). 1851. [Fr., fem. of *tragédien* TRAGEDIAN.] A female tragedian; a tragic actress.

†**Trage·dious,** *a*. 1494. [f. L. *tragœdia* TRAGEDY + -OUS.] Full of, or having the character of, tragedy; calamitous, tragic –1691.

Tragedize (træ·dʒĭdəiz), *v*. 1593. [f. TRAGEDY + -IZE.] **1.** *trans.* To act or perform as a tragedy; *fig.* to do or carry on tragically. **2.** *intr.* To perform as a tragedian; *fig.* to act or speak in tragic style 1756. **3.** *trans.* To dramatize in tragic form 1811.

Tragedy (træ·dʒĭdi). late ME. [– (O)Fr. *tragédie* – L. *tragœdia* – Gr. τραγῳδία, usu. taken to be f. τράγος he-goat + ᾠδή ODE (but the history is disputed).] **1.** A play or other literary work of a serious or sorrowful character, with a fatal or disastrous conclusion: opp. to COMEDY 1. †**a.** In mediæval use: A tale or narrative poem of this character –1593. **b.** Applied to ancient Greek and Latin works, the earlier (Dorian) being lyric songs, the later (Attic and Latin) dramatic pieces. late ME. **c.** Applied to a modern stage-play 1538. **2.** That branch of dramatic art which treats of sorrowful or terrible events, in a serious and dignified style: opp. to COMEDY 2. late ME. **3.** *fig.* An unhappy or fatal event or series of events in real life; a dreadful calamity or disaster 1509. †**b.** A doleful or dreadful tale –1664. †**c.** With *of* or possessive: Sad story, unhappy fate; *esp.* sorrowful end, violent death –1738.

1. a. Tragedye is to seyn, a dite of a prosperite for a tyme þat endith in wrecchydnesse CHAUCER. **c.** Five of his sixteen plays are tragedies, that is, are concluded in death 1838. **2.** Som time let Gorgeous T. In Scepter'd Pall com sweeping by MILT. *attrib.* She bowed me out of the room like a t. queen THACKERAY. **3. c.** Thou..shalt look on and see The Wicked's dismal T. WESLEY.

Tragelaph (træ·gĭlæf). Also in L. form **tragelaphus** (trăge·lăfɒs), pl. **-i.** late ME. [– L. *tragelaphus* – Gr. τραγέλαφος, f. τράγος he-goat + ἔλαφος deer.] **1.** (tr. Gr. τραγέλαφος.) **a.** A name for some foreign species of capriform antelope or other horned beast, vaguely known to the ancients. **b.** *Myth.* A fabulous or fictitious beast compounded of a goat and a stag; hence *allus.* 1644. **2.** *Zool.* Any antelope of the modern genus *Tragelaphus*, as the S. African boschbok, *T. sylvaticus* 1888. So **Trage·laphine** *a.* belonging to the group *Tragelaphinæ* of antelopes, typified by the genus *Tragelaphus*; *sb.* an antelope of this group.

Tragi- (trædʒi), comb. form repr. TRAGIC, in a few nonce-words on the model of TRAGI-COMEDY, as *tragi-farce*.

Tragic (træ·dʒik), *a.* and *sb*. 1545. [– Fr. *tragique* – L. *tragicus* – Gr. τραγικός, f. τράγος he-goat, but assoc. with τραγῳδία TRAGEDY.] **A.** *adj.* **1.** Of, pertaining, or proper to tragedy as a branch of the drama; composing, or acting in, tragedy; opp. to COMIC *a.* 1. **b.** Befitting, or having the style of, tragedy 1684. **2.** Resembling tragedy in respect of its matter; relating to or expressing fatal or dreadful events; sad, gloomy 1593. **3.** Resembling the action or conclusion of a tragedy; characterized by or involving 'tragedy' in real life; calamitous, disastrous, terrible, fatal 1545.

1. Yclad in costly garments fit for tragicke Stage SPENSER. **b.** Never any exprest a more lofty and Tragick height 1684. **2.** The t. story that you are well acquainted with 1718. **3.** Swift ..is the most t. figure in our literature 1876.

B. *sb.* **1.** = TRAGEDIAN 1, 2. 1587. †**2.** A tragic poem or drama –1750. †**3.** quasi-*sb.* *The t.*: that which is t.; the tragic side of the drama, or of life; tragic style or manner 1872. So **Tra·gical** *a.* 1489; hence **-ally** *adv.*, **-ness.**

Tragi-comedy (trædʒiˌkǫ·mĭdi). 1579. [– Fr. *tragicomédie* or It. *tragicomedia* – late L. *tragicomœdia*, for *tragicocomœdia* (Plautus); see TRAGEDY, COMEDY.] **1.** A play (or, *rarely*, a story) combining the qualities of a tragedy and a comedy, or containing both tragic and comic elements; occas. *spec.* a play mainly of tragic character, but with a happy ending 1581. **2.** *fig.* A combination of pathetic and humorous elements in real life 1579.

1. The noble tragicomedy of Measure for Measure MACAULAY. **2.** This t., called life 1649. Hence **Tra:gi-come·dian,** an actor who performs in t.

Tragi-comic (træ:dʒiˌkǫ·mik), *a.* 1683. [f. TRAGI- + COMIC.] Having the character of a tragi-comedy; combining tragic with comic elements. So **Tra:gi-co·mical** *a.* 1567, **-ly** *adv.* Also **Tra:gi-co:mi-pa·storal** *a.* (*nonce-wd.*), combining the qualities of tragi-comedy and pastoral.

Tragopan (træ·gopæn). 1831. [– L. *tragopan* – Gr. τραγόπαν, f. τράγος he-goat + Πάν Pan.] *Ornith.* A pheasant of the genus *Ceriornis* (formerly *T.*), having a pair of erectile fleshy horns on the head.

‖**Tragus** (trēⁱ·gǒs). *Pl.* **tragi** (-dʒəi). 1693. [Late L. – L. *tragus* – Gr. τράγος he-goat, so named on account of the bunch of hairs which it bears. Cf. ANTITRAGUS.] *Anat.* A prominence at the entrance of the external ear, in front of and partly closing the orifice, and in men usu. bearing a tuft of hairs.

Trail (trēⁱl), *sb.*[1] late ME. [app. f. TRAIL *v.*] **I.** Something that trails or hangs trailing. **1.** A long-trailing or loose-hanging slender mass of hair, fibres, or the like; 'any thing drawn to length' (J.) 1844. **2.** A trailing ornament in the form of a wreath or spray of leaves or tendrils; a wreathed or foliated ornament. late ME. **b.** A trailing tendril or branch 1598.

1. A t. of golden hair E. B. BROWNING. **2. b.** Trails of tangled eglantine 1861.

II. Something trailed or made by trailing. †**1.** A sledge [= L. *tragula*] –1600. **2.** A drag-net [= L. *tragula*] 1711. **3.** The hinder end of the stock of a gun-carriage, which rests or slides on the ground when the gun is unlimbered 1768. **4.** Anything drawn behind as an appendage; a train 1621. **5.** A mark left where something has been trailed or has passed along; a trace, track 1610. **b.** *spec.* in astronomical photography, The trace produced by the motion of the image of a star across the plate during exposure 1889. **6.** *spec.* The track or other indication, as scent, left by a person or animal, esp. as followed by a huntsman or hound, or by any pursuer 1590. **7.** A path or track worn by the passage of persons travelling in a wild or uninhabited region. (Chiefly in U.S. and Canada.) 1807. **8.** *Geol.* A name for certain mixed glacial or other deposits resting upon older formations 1866.

4. Seeming Stars..shooting through the Darkness..with..long Trails of Light DRYDEN. **5.** But the t. of the serpent is over them all MOORE. **6.** How cheerefully on the false Traile they cry SHAKS. **7.** Indian Paths—which were narrow trails worn by the feet in marching single file 1875.

III. Action of trailing. **1.** The action of dragging oneself or something along, or of creeping or crawling (*rare*) 1547. **2.** The action of hunting by the trail; chase by the track or scent 1669. **3.** *Mil.* The act of trailing a rifle, or the position of it when trailed 1833. **4.** An act of drawing out, enticing, befooling (*rare*) 1847.

Comb.: **t.-board,** a carved piece in a ship, reaching from the main stem to the figure, or to the brackets; **-net** = sense II. 2.

†**Trail,** *sb.*[2] [Late ME. *treylle, trayle* – (O)Fr. *treille* :– L. *trichila* bower, arbour.] **1.** A trellis for training climbing plants upon –1727. **2.** A lattice; a grating; a grill –1552.

†**Trail,** *sb.*[3] 1764. [Aphetic f. ENTRAIL.] Entrails, intestines, collectively; *esp.* those of certain birds, as woodcock and snipe, and fishes, as red mullet, which are cooked and eaten with the rest of the flesh –1846.

Trail (trēⁱl), *v.* ME. [prob. of mixed origin; – OFr. *traillier* or MLG., MFlem. *treilen* haul (a boat), which point to Rom. or pop.L. **tragulare,* f. L. *tragula* drag-net, etc. Cf. TRAWL.] **I.** *trans.* **1.** To draw behind one; to drag along upon the ground or other surface (esp. something hanging loosely, as a long garment); also, to drag (a person) roughly, to hale; to haul. late ME. **b.** To carry or convey by drawing or dragging, as in a vehicle or ship. late ME. **c.** To draw (the body or limbs) along wearily or with difficulty in walking, etc., esp. from disablement or exhaustion. Also *refl.* 1562. **2.** *Mil.* orig. To carry (a pike, etc.) in the right hand in an oblique position with the head forward and the butt nearly touching the ground; later *spec.* to carry (a lance or rifle) in a horizontal position in the right hand with the arm fully extended downward. Phr. †*To t. a pike,* to serve as a soldier. 1549. **3.** *fig.* or in fig. context 1604. **b.** To draw as by persuasion or art; to draw on; hence *colloq.* 'to quiz, befool' 1717.

1. They shall not t. me through thir streets Like a wild Beast MILT. What boots..That long behind he trails his pompous robe? POPE. **b.** The yacht is not big enough to convey all the tables and chairs and conveniences that he trails along with him H. WALPOLE. **c.** He trailed himself, a broken-hearted man, to Falkland Palace 1908. **2.** How proud..should I be To t. a pike under your brave command FLETCHER & MASSINGER. **3.** Not in utter nakedness, But trailing clouds of glory do we come From God WORDSW. **b.** I..perceived she was (what is vernacularly termed) trailing Mrs. Dent; that is, playing on her ignorance C. BRONTË.

II. *intr.* **1.** (*intr.* for *pass.*) To hang down so as to drag along the ground or other surface; to be drawn loosely behind (by a person, animal, or thing in motion) ME. **2.** To hang down or float loosely from its attachment, as dress, hair, etc.; of a plant: to grow decumbently and stragglingly to a considerable length, so as to rest upon the ground or other support; to 'creep'. late ME. **3.** To drag one's limbs, walk slowly or wearily as if dragged along; to move or go in extended order; to creep, crawl, as a serpent or other reptile 1608. **b.** Of inanimate things: To move along slowly; to form a trail 1470. **4.** To extend in a straggling line, to straggle 1600.

1. The sound Of silken dresses trailing o'er the ground MORRIS. **2.** In open sunny situations it grows trailing,..but in woods it is upright 1776. **3.** The camels that trailed away from the city 1905.

III. 1. *trans.* To decorate or cover *with* a trailing pattern or ornament. late ME. **2.** To follow the trail of, to track 1590. **3.** To mark out (a trail or track) 1586. **4.** *intr.* To follow the trail of game 1741.

2. The ranchman is away..trailing horse thieves 1910.

IV. *intr.* To fish by trailing a bait from a moving boat 1857.

Trailer (trēⁱ·lər). 1590. [f. prec. + -ER[1].] **1.** One who, or that which trails. **2.** *spec.* **a.** A rail or road car designed to be drawn along by a motor vehicle. **b.** A small carriage, usu. a light chair on wheels, drawn along by a bicycle or tricycle. 1890. **c.** The rear-wheel of a front-driven bicycle, or one of the rear wheels of a locomotive, as opp. to the *driver* or driving-wheel 1884.

Trailing (trēⁱ·liŋ), *ppl. a.* ME. [f. as prec. + -ING[2].] **1.** That trails (almost always in *intr.* sense). **2.** techn. *T. wheel,* a wheel to which the motive force is not directly applied (opp. to *driving-wheel*), as one of the hinder wheels of a locomotive. Also applied to parts connected with this, as *t. axle, spring* 1849. **b.** *T. points,* points directed away from an oncoming railway train (opp. to *facing points*) 1889. Hence **Trai·lingly** *adv.*

Train (trēⁱn), *sb.*[1] ME. [– (O)Fr. *train* masc., *traine* (mod. *traîne*) fem., f. OFr. (orig.) *trahiner, traïner* (mod. *traîner*) :– Rom. **traginare,* f. **tragere,* f. L. *trahere* draw.] **I.** †**1.** Tarrying, delay –1553. †**2.** Course or manner of running (of a horse); a course of riding –1677. **II.** That which drags or trails, or is trailed. **1.** An elongated part of a robe or skirt trailing behind on the ground 1440. **b.** The tail or tail-feathers of a bird, esp. when long and trailing, as in the peacock; in *Falconry,* the technical name for the tail of a hawk 1579. **c.** The tail of a comet; a luminous trail, such as that following a meteor 1602. **2.** *poet.* Applied to the current of a river, etc., also to the elongated body of a serpent 1667. †**3.** Something dragged along the ground to make a scent or trail; a drag; also pieces of carrion, etc. laid in a line or trail for luring certain wild beasts, as wolves, foxes, etc. into a trap –1727.

1. A Baronesse may haue no trayne borne; but haueing a goune with a trayne, she ought to beare it her selfe 1600. They..pinned up each other's trains for the dance J. AUSTEN. **b.** A splendid goshawk,..with a..queenly t. 1852. **2.** Within those banks, where Rivers now Stream, and perpetual draw thir humid traine MILT.

III. 1. A number of persons following or attending on some one, usu. a person of rank; a retinue, suite 1440. **b.** *Mil.* The artillery and other apparatus for battle or siege, with the vehicles conveying them, and the men in attendance, following an army 1523. **2.** *fig.* A set of attendant things, circumstances, or conditions; a series of consequences. Often in phr. *in the t. of,* as a sequel to. 1570. **3.** A body of persons, animals, vehicles, etc., travelling together in order, esp. in a long line or procession; *fig.* (chiefly *poet.*) a set or class of persons 1489. **4.** A series or course of actions, events, etc. 1530. **b.** Proper sequence, order, or arrangement for some result; connected order 1528. **5.** A line of gunpowder or other combustible substance laid so as to convey fire to a mine or charge for the purpose of exploding it 1548. **6.** An extended series of material objects or the like; a row, rank 1610. **7.** A set of connected parts of mechanism which actuate one another in series 1797. **8.** (orig. *t. of carriages,* etc.) A number of railway carriages, vans, or trucks coupled together (usu. including the locomotive by which they are drawn) 1824.

1. A t. of listeners followed him JOWETT. **2.** This vice draweth after it a t. of evils BERKELEY. **3.** The best Hawks..fly in Trains like Wild Geese 1698. **4.** He that leads of life an uncorrupted traine SIDNEY. A t. of Ideas, which constantly succeed one another in his Understanding LOCKE. Long..trains of reasoning 1764. **b.** Putting matters in t. for the election 1885. **5.** *fig.* He..had already laid his t...for revolt GROTE. **8.** A t. left Warsaw early in the morning 1885. Comb. (*U.S.*) *t.-man, -master, -porter.*

IV. Applied to various material objects that are dragged. **a.** The trail of a gun-carriage 1769. **b.** A rough kind of sledge or sleigh used in Canada for transport 1835. †**c.** A drag-net, a seine –1609.

attrib. and *Comb.*: **t.-bearer,** an attendant who carries the t. of a sovereign or other person; **-ferry,** a ferry for conveying trains across a piece of water from one railway to another; **-mile,** each mile of the aggregate distance run by all the trains on a railway in a given period, as a unit in estimating amount of traffic, working expenses, etc.; so *t.-mileage*; **-net** = sense IV. c; **-rope, -tackle,** a tackle hooked to the trail of a gun-carriage on board ship; **-sickness,** sickness or nausea induced by travelling in a t.; **-stop,** an automatic apparatus, in connection with a railway signal, for stopping a t.; **-way,** (*a*) a temporary line of rails for the conveyance of small loads; (*b*) a platform hinged to a wharf, with a line of rails upon which railway cars or trucks may run to and from a ferry-boat (*U.S.*).

†**Train,** *sb.*[2] late ME. [– OFr. *traïne* guile, deceit, ruse, f. *traïr* (mod. *trahir*). See BETRAY.] **1.** Treachery, guile, deceit, trickery –1600. **b.** With *a* and *pl.* A trick, stratagem, artifice, wile –1767. **2.** A trap or snare for catching wild animals. (In phr. *to lay a t.,* assoc. with or merged in senses of TRAIN *sb.*[1]) –1697. **3.** A lure, bait, decoy –1602.

1. **b.** *Macb.* IV. iii. 118. **2.** Caught in the T. which thou thyself hast laid DRYDEN.

†**Train,** *sb.*[3] 1497. [Earliest form *trane* (XV) – (M)LG. *trān,* MDu. *traen* (Du. *traan*) = G. *tran,* rel. to *träne* TEAR *sb.*[1]] = TRAIN-OIL –1802. Hence †**Trai·ny** *a.* having the quality of train-oil. GAY.

Train, *v.* late ME. [– OFr. *trahiner, traïner* (mod. *traîner*); see TRAIN *sb.*[1]] **I. 1.** *trans.* To draw or pull along after one; to drag, haul, trail. *Obs.* or *arch.* 1450. **b.** *intr.* (for *pass.*) Of a garment: To hang down, esp. so as to drag or trail. Now *rare.* 1590. †**2.** *fig.* (*trans.*) To draw out, protract, spin out. Also *intr.* –1652. †**3.** To lead, conduct, bring –1642.

1. Behold..the Foe Approaching..; in hollow Cube Training his devilish Enginrie MILT.

II. *fig.* To draw by art or inducement; to draw *on*; to allure, entice, decoy; to lead astray, take in. *arch.* late ME. †**b.** To draw by persuasion; to persuade, convert –1612.

Being trained into a well-laid ambush 1781.

III. 1. To treat so as to bring to the proper or desired form; *spec.* in *Gardening*, to manage (a plant or branch) so as to cause it to grow in some desired form or direction, esp. against a wall, or upon a trellis or the like 1440. **2. a.** To instruct and discipline generally; to educate, rear, bring up 1542. **b.** To instruct and discipline in or for some particular art, profession, occupation, or practice; to exercise, practise, drill. Const. *in, to, for.* 1555. **c.** To discipline and instruct (an animal) so as to make it obedient to orders, or capable of performing tricks; to prepare a race-horse for its work 1609. **d.** To bring by diet and exercise to the required state of physical efficiency for a race or other athletic feat 1835. **3.** *intr.* for *pass.* To undergo or follow a course of instruction and discipline 1605.

1. The vines are trained and supported by poles 1792. **2. a.** Traine vp a childe in the way he should goe *Prov.* 22 : 6. **b.** Bandsmen..fully trained to the use of the rifle 1859. **c.** The present Robert Sherwood, who now trains at Newmarket 1894. **3.** Phr. *T. on,* to improve by training; †*t. off,* to lose one's vigour or skill as by over-training; *t. down,* to reduce one's weight by training; *t. with* (fig., U.S. colloq.), to associate with, ally oneself with.

IV. 1. *trans. Mining.* To trace (a vein, etc.) 1710. **2.** To direct, point, or aim (a cannon or other fire-arm, or *transf.* a photographic camera); to bring by horizontal movement to bear (*on, upon,* the thing aimed at) 1841. **3.** To convey by a railway train (*rare*) 1886. **b.** *intr.* To go by train, travel by railway 1888. Hence **Trai·nable** *a.* capable of being trained; educable.

Trai·nba:nd, train-band. Now *Hist.* 1630. [Clipped f. *trained band.*] A trained company of citizen soldiery, organized in London and other parts in the 16th, 17th, and 18th centuries.

The Country Captains of the Train-bands were.. very unskilful..in the use of their Armes 1654. *attrib.* A train-band captain eke was he Of famous London town COWPER.

‖**Traineau** (trēinōu·, ‖trenọ). 1715. [Fr., f. *traîner* TRAIN *v.*] A sledge, sleigh; esp. one drawn by one or more horses over snow or ice.

Trained (trēind, *poet.* trēi·nėd), *ppl. a.* 1570. [f. TRAIN *v.* + -ED[1].] In the senses of TRAIN *v.* **b.** *spec.* Subjected to military discipline and instruction, drilled; esp. in *t. band* = TRAIN-BAND (now *Hist.*).

Trainer (trēi·nəɹ). 1581. [f. TRAIN *v.* + -ER[1].] One who trains; an instructor; *spec.* †(*a*) one who trains or drills soldiers, a drill-sergeant; (*b*) one who trains persons or animals for some athletic performance, as a race; *spec.* one who trains race-horses 1598. **b.** A member of a train-band, esp. when assembled for 'training' or drill; a militia-man. (In later use *U.S.*) 1581.

Training (trēi·niŋ), *vbl. sb.* 1440. [f. TRAIN *v.* + -ING[1].] The action of TRAIN *v.*; *spec.* Military drill; *esp.* in former use, a public meeting or muster at a stated time for drill of militia and volunteer forces; now much used for the periodical camp work of the Territorials.

Phr. *In t.*, in a state of athletic 'fitness' induced by training; so *out of t.*

attrib. and *Comb.*: **t.-college,** a college for training persons for some particular profession; *spec.* a college for training teachers; **-day,** a day devoted to training; *spec.* in former use, a stated or legally appointed day for the drilling of militia and volunteer forces; **-ship, -vessel,** a ship on which boys are trained for naval service.

Trainless (trēi·nlės), *a.* 1859. [f. TRAIN *sb.*[1] + -LESS.] **1.** Devoid of a train (as a robe, a meteor, etc.) 1868. **2.** Devoid of (railway) trains 1859.

Trai·n oi·l, trai·n-oil. 1553. [f. TRAIN *sb.*[3] + OIL *sb.*] Oil obtained by boiling from the blubber of whales, esp. of the right whale; also, formerly, that obtained from seals, and from various fishes.

Traipse: see TRAPES.

Trait (trē, *U.S.* trēit). 1477. [– Fr. *trait* :– L. *tractus* drawing, draught; see TRACT *sb.*[3]] †**1.** 'Shot' of any kind, missiles; *orig.* arrows. CAXTON. **2.** A stroke made with pen or pencil; a short line; a touch (in a picture) 1589. **3.** A line or lineament of the face; a feature 1773. **4.** A distinguishing quality; a characteristic 1752. **b.** A 'touch' *of* some quality. Now *rare.* 1815. †**5.** A stroke or flash of wit, sarcasm, or pleasantry –1859.

3. Her face is somewhat altered. The traits have become more delicate. SHELLEY. **4.** Who have no national t. about them but their language W. IRVING.

‖**Traiteur** (trẹtör.) 1751. [Fr., f. *traiter* treat, supply with food for money.] A keeper of an eating-house (in France, Italy, etc.) who supplies or sends out meals to order.

Traitor (trēi·təɹ). ME. [– OFr. *traïtour, -ur* :– L. *trāditō·r-*, stem of *trā·ditor* (whence OFr. *traitre,* mod. *traître*), f. *tradere* deliver, betray, f. *trans* TRANS- + *dare* give; see -OR 2.] **1.** One who betrays any person that trusts him, or any duty entrusted to him; a betrayer. In early use often, and still traditionally, applied to Judas Iscariot. **2.** *spec.* One who is false to his allegiance to his sovereign or to the government of his country; one adjudged guilty of treason or of any crime so regarded ME. **3.** *attrib.* or as *adj.* That is a traitor, traitorous ME.

2. Vnlesse I proue false t. to my selfe SHAKS. He is a t., and betray'd the state BYRON. *Traitor's Gate,* the river gate of the Tower of London by which traitors, and state prisoners generally, were committed to the Tower.

†**Trai·torly,** *a.* 1586. [f. prec. + -LY[1].] = prec. –1668.

Traitorous (trēi·tərəs), *a.* late ME. [– (O)Fr. *traîtreux,* f. *traître* TRAITOR; see -OUS.] Having the character of, or characteristic of, a traitor; treacherous; perfidious.

A t. Crew of villanous Phanaticks 1683. Hence **Trai·torous-ly** *adv.*, **-ness.**

Traitress (trēi·trės), **trai·toress.** late ME. [– (O)Fr. *traîtresse,* fem. of *traître* TRAITOR; see -ESS[1]. In form *traitoress* f. TRAITOR + -ESS[1].] A female traitor; a traitorous or treacherous woman (or being personified as a woman).

Traject (træ·dʒekt), *sb.* 1552. [– L. *trajectus* passing over, place for crossing, f. *traicere* throw across, f. *trans* TRANS- + *jacere* throw.] **1.** A way or place of crossing over; *esp.* a ferry. **2.** The action or an act of crossing over water, land, a chasm, etc.; passage 1774.

Traject (trădʒe·kt), *v.* 1624. [– *traject-,* pa. ppl. stem of L. *traicere*; see prec.] †**1.** *trans.* To pass across (a river, sea, etc.). Also *intr.* –1711. **2.** To carry or convey across or over; to transport. †**a.** (something material) –1684. **b.** To transmit (light, shadow, or colour) 1657. **c.** To transmit (thought, words, etc.) 1711.

2. b. A Prism, by which the trajected Light might be refracted either upwards or sideways NEWTON.

Trajection (trădʒe·kʃən). 1594. [– L. *trajectio, -ōn-*, f. as prec.; see -ION.] **1.** The action of trajecting or fact of being trajected; a throwing or carrying across; passage through 1633. †**2.** A perception transmitted to the mind; an impression, a mental image –1646. **3.** Transposition; metathesis 1612.

Trajectory (træ·dʒektəri, trădʒe·ktəri). 1668. [– med.L. *trajectorius* pertaining to trajection, f. as prec.; see -ORY.] **A.** *adj. Physics.* Of or pertaining to that which is thrown or hurled through the air or space. **B.** *sb.* **1.** *Physics.* The path of any body moving under the action of given forces; *esp.* the curve described by a projectile in its flight through the air 1696. **2.** *Geom.* A curve or surface passing through a given set of points, or intersecting each of a given series of curves or surfaces according to a given law, e.g. at a constant angle 1795.

‖**Trajet** (Fr. traʒẹ, træ·dʒėt). 1741. [Fr. – L. *trajectus* TRAJECT *sb.*] A crossing, passage.

Tra-la, Tra-la-la (trălā·, trălālā·), *int.* 1823. Phrase expressive of joy or gaiety, sometimes used as a refrain; also used to symbolize the flourish of a horn, etc.

The flowers that bloom in the spring tra-la, Have nothing to do with the case W. S. GILBERT.

Tralatitious (trælăti·ʃəs), *a.* 1645. [– L. *tralaticius, trans-,* f. *translat-,* pa. ppl. stem of *transferre* TRANSFER; see -ITIOUS[1].] **1.** Characterized by transference; *esp.* of words or phrases, metaphorical, figurative. **2.** Handed down from generation to generation; traditional; also, repeated by one from another, as a statement 1795.

1. A secondary and t. Association 1748. Hence **Tralati·tiously** *adv.* metaphorically.

†**Trali·neate,** *v. rare.* 1700. [f. It. *tralignare* degenerate, †deviate.] *intr.* To go out of the direct line; to deviate –1745.

†**Tralu·cency.** 1599. [f. as next; see -ENCY.] = TRANSLUCENCY –1649.

†**Tralu·cent,** *a.* 1592. [– *tralucent-,* pr. ppl. stem of L. *tralucēre, trans-,* shine across or through; see -ENT.] = TRANSLUCENT –1664.

Tram, *sb.*[1] 1679. [– (O)Fr. *trame* :– L. *trama* woof.] Woof or weft; *spec.* silk thread consisting of two or more single strands loosely twisted together; used for the weft or cross threads of the best silk goods. Also *t. silk.*

Tram (træm), *sb.*[2] 1500. [– MLG., MDu. *trame* balk, beam, rung of a ladder, of unkn. origin; the sense-development is obscure and is not paralleled in LG. or Du.] **1.** Each of the two shafts of a cart or wagon, a hand-barrow, or a wheelbarrow. *Sc.* **2.** *Coal-mining.* A quadrilateral frame or skeleton truck on which the corves were formerly carried; now in some colliery districts applied to the small iron truck which supplies the place of the earlier 'tram' and corve 1516. **3.** A continuous line or track of timber beams or 'rails', or later of stone blocks or slabs, a parallel pair of which lines formed a tram-way, orig. in or from a mine. Hence, each 'rail' of a tramroad of an early type, or of a tramway or railway. 1826. **4.** A road laid with such wooden planks or rails, or with parallel rows of stone slabs or of iron plates or 'rails'; a tram-road of an early type 1850. **5.** (Short for *tram-car.*) A passenger car on a street tramway; a tram-car 1879.

5. The discordant clanging of the gongs of electric trams 1902.

attrib. and *Comb.*, as *t.-conductor, -driver, -ticket*; **t.-man,** a man employed on a tramway, esp. a t.-conductor or driver.

Tram (træm), *v.* 1826. [f. prec.] **1.** *intr.* To travel by a tramway or on a tram-car. *colloq.* **2.** trans. *Mining.* To convey (coal, ore, etc.) by a tram or trams 1874. **b.** To push (a tram, etc.) to and from the shaft in a mine 1883.

Tram-car (træ·m₁kāɹ). 1873. [f. TRAM *sb.*[2] 3 + CAR.] A public car or carriage running on a tramway for the conveyance of passengers; also simply *tram.*

Tra·m-line. 1886. [f. TRAM *sb.*[2] 4 or 5 + LINE *sb.*[2]] A tramway; also, a tram-rail.

Trammel (træ·mĕl), *sb.* late ME. [In sense 1 – (O)Fr. *tramail,* mod. *trémail* – med.L. *tramaculum,* var. of *tremaculum, tri-* (Salic Law), perh. f. L. *tri-* three, TRI- + L. *macula* mesh (cf. MAIL *sb.*[1]). The history of the later senses is obscure.] **1.** In full *t.-net*: A long narrow fishing-net, set vertically with floats and sinkers; consisting of two 'walls' of large-meshed netting, between which is a net of fine mesh, loosely hung. **b.** A fowling-net 1530. †**2.** A hobble to prevent a horse from straying or kicking; also, a contrivance for teaching a horse to amble –1766. **3.** *transf.* and *fig.* Anything that confines, restrains, fetters, or shackles. Chiefly *pl.* 1653. **4.** *Mech.* An instrument for describing ellipses, consisting of a cross with two grooves at right angles, in which slide pins carrying a beam or ruler with a pencil; also applied to the *beam-compass.* Also *pl.* 1725. **5.** A series of rings or links, or other device, to bear a crook at different heights over the fire. Now *local Eng.* and *U.S.* 1537. †**6.** *pl.* The plaits, braids, or tresses of a woman's hair –1673.

3. She, for the most part, refused to bind herself by conventional trammels 1889.

Tra·mmel, *v.* 1588. [f. prec.] **1.** *intr.* To use a trammel-net; *trans.* to take (fish or birds) with a trammel-net. †**2.** *trans.* To fasten together (the legs of a horse) with trammels –1639. **3.** *fig.* To entangle or fasten *up* as in a trammel 1605. **4.** *fig.* To put restraint upon, hamper, impede, confine 1727.

3. If th' Assassination Could trammell vp the Consequence, and catch. . Successe SHAKS. Hence **Tra·mmeller,** one who or that which trammels.

Tra·mmel-net. 1516. [f. TRAMMEL *sb.* + NET *sb.*[1]] = TRAMMEL *sb.* 1, 1 b.

Trammer (træ·mər). 1839. [f. TRAM *sb.*[2] or *v.* + -ER[1].] **1.** *Coal-mining,* etc. A man or boy who removes the trams of coal, etc. from the workings; a putter. **2.** One who is employed on a tramway; also, a horse used to draw a tramcar 1889.

Tramontane (trămǫ·ntēⁱn, træmǫntēⁱ·n), *a.* and *sb.* late ME. [– It. *tramontana* north wind, pole star, *tramontani* dwellers beyond the mountains – L. *transmontanus,* f. *trans* TRANS- + *mons, mont-* MOUNT *sb.*[1]; see -ANE.] **A.** *adj.* **1.** Dwelling or situated beyond, or pertaining to the far side of, the mountains (orig. and in ref. to Italy, the Alps); hence, foreign 1596. **b.** With the connotation 'uncouth, unpolished, barbarous'. Now *rare.* 1739. **2.** Of the wind: Coming across or from beyond the mountains; *spec.* in ref. to Italy, blowing from beyond the Alps 1705.

1. A t. ecclesiastic 1884.

B. *sb.* †**1.** The north pole-star: orig. so called in Italy and Provence, because visible beyond the Alps –1633. **2.** In the Mediterranean and esp. in Italy, The north wind, as coming from beyond the Alps; hence *gen.*, a cold wind from a mountain range. (Now usu. in It. form *tramontana.*) 1615. **3.** One who dwells beyond the mountains: orig. applied in Italy to foreigners beyond the Alps; also by these to the Italians; hence, a stranger, a foreigner; an outsider, barbarian 1593.

3. Yet was it a great labour for a Tramountain to climb over the Alps to S. Peters Chair FULLER.

Tramp (træmp), *sb.* 1664. [f. next.] **1.** An act of tramping; a heavy or forcible tread; a stamp 1808. **2.** The measured and continuous tread of a body of persons or animals; hence, the sound of heavy footfalls 1817. **3.** A bout of tramping on foot; a trudge; a walking excursion. *colloq.* 1786. **4.** A person on the tramp; one who travels from place to place on foot, esp. in search of employment, as a vagrant 1664. **5.** In full, *ocean t.*: A cargo vessel, esp. a steamship, which takes cargoes wherever obtainable and for any port 1880. **6. a.** A plate of iron worn under the hollow of the boot to protect it in digging; also, the part of the spade, etc., which is pressed upon by the foot 1825. **b.** A piece of spiked iron fastened to the sole of the shoe to give a firm foothold on the ice 1830.

3. Phr. *On* (*the*) *t.*, on one's way from place to place on foot, esp. in search of employment, or wandering as a vagrant.

Tramp (træmp), *v.* late ME. [XIV in Wyclif, prob. of LDu. origin and based on Gmc. stem **tramp-*; cf. MLG. *trampen.*] **1.** *intr.* To tread or walk with a firm, heavy, resonant step; to stamp. **2.** = TRAMPLE *v.* 3. 1596. **3.** *trans.* To press or compress by treading; to tread or trample upon 1533. **b.** *refl.* Of a horse: To injure itself by setting one foot on another 1844. **4.** *intr.* To walk; *esp.* to walk steadily or heavily; to trudge; to go on a walking expedition. *colloq.* 1643. **b.** To go about or travel as a tramp. *colloq.* 1891. **5.** *trans.* To walk through or over with heavy or weary tread; to traverse on foot, *spec.* as a tramp 1774. **6.** *intr.* To make a voyage on a tramp steamer; also *trans.* to run (a tramp steamer). *colloq.* 1899. **7.** The vb.-stem used *advb.* 1796.

4. **b.** I'd rather have tramped it than gone in for any top-hatted occupation 1909. **5.** He tramped the island in pursuit of his calling 1894. Hence **Tramping-card,** a certificate issued to a member of a trade organization, entitling him to maintenance while tramping in search of employment.

Tramper (træ·mpər). 1725. [f. prec. + -ER[1].] **1.** One who or that which tramps. **2.** A person who tramps or travels on foot, a pedestrian; *spec.* a tramp, a vagrant 1760.

Trample (træ·mp'l), *sb.* 1604. [f. the vb.] An act or the action of trampling.

Trample (træ·mp'l), *v.* late ME. [XIV in Wyclif, f. TRAMP *v.* + -LE 3. Cf. (M)HG., LG. *trampeln.*] **1.** *intr.* To tread or walk heavily; to stamp. †**2.** = TRAMP *v.* 4 (*rare*) –1631. **3.** With *on, upon, over.* **a.** *lit.* To tread repeatedly upon with heavy or crushing steps 1577. **b.** *fig.* To treat with contempt; to domineer over 1646. **4.** *trans.* To tread heavily and (esp.) injuriously upon; to crush, break down or destroy by heavy treading; also *to t. down, t. under foot* 1530.

3. An elephant trampling upon a snake 1879. **b.** Wit tramples upon rules JOHNSON. **4.** Neither cast yee your pearles before swine: lest they t. them vnder their feet *Matt.* 7 : 6. *fig.* Thus they t. all Learning under foot 1675. Hence **Tra·mpler,** one who tramples.

Tram-road (træ·m,rōᵘd). 1800. [f. TRAM *sb.*[2] + ROAD.] **a.** In mining districts, a road having 'trams' (see TRAM *sb.*[2] 3) laid in parallel lines, to form wheel-tracks for the easier transport of minerals in 'trams' or wagons; hence, *gen.*, a track thus made for vehicles. **b.** A special track or narrow railroad for wagons or cars, as dist. from a *tramway* laid down for tramcars on an ordinary road or street.

Tramway (træ·mwēⁱ). 1825. [f. TRAM *sb.*[2] + WAY.] **1.** = prec. **b.** Now *spec.* A track with rails flush with the road surface, laid in a street or road, on which tram-cars are run, for the conveyance of passengers 1860. **2.** *transf.* A cable or system of cables on which suspended cars can travel. *U.S.* 1872.

Trance (trɑns), *sb.* late ME. [– OFr. *transe* (mod. *trance*), f. *transir* depart, be benumbed – L. *transire*; see TRANSIT.] †**1.** A state of extreme apprehension or dread; a state of doubt or suspense –1577. **2.** An unconscious or insensible condition; a swoon, a faint; in mod. use, a state characterized by a more or less prolonged suspension of consciousness and inertness to stimulus; a cataleptic or hypnotic condition. late ME. **3.** An intermediate state between sleeping and waking; a stunned or dazed state. late ME. **b.** A state of mental abstraction from external things; absorption, exaltation, ecstasy. late ME.

2. Most of the night he had lien in a t. 1617. **3.** All thys I saw as I lay in a traunce 1420. **b.** As, in a kind of holy t., She hung above those fragrant treasures MOORE.

Trance (trɑns), *v.* ME. [In sense 1 – OFr. *transir* pass away, die; in sense 2 f. prec.] †**1.** *intr.* **a.** To pass away, to die. **b.** To swoon, faint. **c.** To be in great dread, doubt, or suspense. –1632. **2.** *trans.* To throw into a trance or a similar state; †to stupefy; to entrance, enrapture. Chiefly *poet.* 1597.

2. I trod as one tranced in some rapturous vision SHELLEY. *fig.* When thickest dark did t. the sky TENNYSON.

‖**Tranché** (trañʃe), *a.* 1661. [Fr., pa. pple. of *trancher* cut, TRENCH *v.*] *Her.* Party per bend.

†**Tra·ngam.** 1658. [Of unkn. origin. Not connected with TANGRAM.] An odd or intricate contrivance of some kind; a knick-knack, a puzzle: used with contempt. –1820.

Tranquil (træ·ŋkwil), *a.* 1604. [– Fr. *tranquille* or L. *tranquillus.*] Free from agitation or disturbance; calm, serene, placid, quiet, peaceful. **b.** Of things or actions: Steady, regular, even 1769.

Farewell the Tranquill minde; farewell Content SHAKS. The treasures of this t. scene CRABBE. **b.** The heating power of the t. flame FARADAY. So **Tranqui·llity** [– (O)Fr. *tranquillité* (XII)], the quality or state of being t.; serenity, calmness. late ME. **Tra·nquil-ly** *adv.*, **-ness.**

Tranquillize (træ·ŋkwiləiz), *v.* 1623. [f. TRANQUIL *a.* + -IZE.] *trans.* and *intr.* To make or become tranquil or quiet.

It tranquillises the mind as well as the body 1835. Hence **Tra:nquilliza·tion. Tra·nquillizer.**

‖**Tranquillo** (traŋkwi·llo), *adv.* 1854. [It.] *Mus.* In a tranquil style or tempo.

Trans- (trɑns, trɑnz), *prefix.* The Latin preposition *trans* across, to or on the farther side of, beyond, over; also used in comb. In English *trans-* occurs in compounds representing those already used in Latin, and in others formed analogously from L. elements, or in which the second element is an English or other non-Latin word.

1. With the sense 'across, through, over, to or on the other side of, beyond, outside of, from one place, person, thing, or state to another': in vbs. and their derivative sbs. and adjs. representing L. compounds, or formed on L. elements; e.g. *transcribe, transcript, transport, transportation.* **2.** in vbs., etc. formed on Eng. vbs., adjs., or sbs., as *transfashion, tranship, trans-shape.* **3.** in adjs. and their derivs., repr. L. adjs. or formed on L. words, as *transmarine, transmural,* also on Eng. sbs. or adjs., as *trans-border, -frontier, -oceanic.* Special groups are: **4.** in adjs. with the sense 'beyond, surpassing, transcending', as *transhuman, -material.* **5.** in adjs., scientific terms (chiefly anatomical), with the sense 'through, across' (the thing denoted by the sb. implied), as *transfrontal, -ocular, -uterine.* **6.** in sbs. with the sense 'transverse', as *trans-muscle, trans-stroke* (rare). **7.** in geographical adjs. (unlimited in number), formed on the names of rivers, seas, mountains, territories, etc., with the sense 'situated or lying beyond or on the other side of', as TRANSATLANTIC, TRANS-PACIFIC. **8.** in geographical adjs., formed as in 7, with the sense 'passing across, crossing', as in *trans-African, -Andean,-Balkan,-Manchurian, -Siberian.*

Transaccidentation (trɑns,æ:ksidentēⁱ·ʃən, -z-). 1581. [– schol.L. *transaccidentatio* (Duns Scotus); after *transubstantiatio.*] A transmutation of the accidents of the bread and wine in the Eucharist, as dist. from *transubstantiation,* in which the substance alone is changed.

Transact (trɑnzæ·kt, trɑns-), *v.* 1584. [– *transact-*, pa. ppl. stem of L. *transigere* drive through, accomplish, f. *trans* TRANS- + *agere* drive, do.] **1.** *intr.* To carry through negotiations; to have dealings, do business; to treat; also, to manage or settle affairs. Now *rare.* **b.** *fig.* (usu. *dyslogistic.*) To have to do, to compromise 1888. **2.** *trans.* To carry through, perform (an action, etc.); to manage (an affair); now *esp.* to carry on, do (business) 1635. **3.** To deal in or with; to traffic in, negotiate about; to handle, treat; to discuss. *arch.* 1654. †**4.** To transfer –1889.

1. **b.** In his criticism. . he seems to us a little to 't.' with cant 1890. **2.** A country fully stocked in proportion to all the business it had to t. ADAM SMITH.

Transaction (trɑnzæ·kʃən, trɑns-). 1460. [– late L. *transactio, -ōn-*, f. as prec.; see -ION. Cf. (O)Fr. *transaction.*] **1.** *Roman* and *Civil Law.* The adjustment of a dispute between parties by mutual concession; compromise; hence *gen.* an arrangement, an agreement, a covenant. Now *Hist.* exc. as in 3 b. **2.** The action of transacting or fact of being transacted 1655. **3.** That which is or has been transacted; a piece of business; in *pl.* doings, proceedings, dealings 1647. **b.** *Theol.* In ref. to the Atonement, 'transaction' has senses ranging from 1 to 3. (In sense 1 chiefly in deprecation.) 1861. †**4.** The action of passing or making over a thing from one person, thing, or state to another –1691. **5.** *pl.* The record of its proceedings published by a learned society. Rarely in *sing.* 1665.

3. Discoursing of the Court of France, and the transactions there CLARENDON. Hence **Transa·ctional** *a.*, **-ly** *adv.*

Transactor (trɑnzæ·ktər, trɑns-). 1611. [f. TRANSACT *v.* + -OR 2.] One who transacts; a negotiator or intermediary; a manager, conductor, doer.

Transalpine (trɑns,æ·lpəin, -z-), *a.* (*sb.*) 1590. [– L. *transalpinus,* f. *trans-* TRANS- + *alpinus* Alpine, f. *Alpes* the Alps.] **1.** That is situated beyond the Alps: **a.** orig. beyond the Alps from Rome or Italy, i.e. north of the Alps; also, belonging to a region beyond the Alps; also †*transf.* rude, uncultured. **b.** Beyond the Alps from England, or from Europe generally; Italian 1624. **c.** Of or pertaining to the party in the Roman Church opposed to the Ultramontanes 1794. **2.** (Passing) across the Alps (*rare*) 1654. **B.** *sb.* A native or inhabitant of a country beyond or across the Alps (*rare*) 1617.

1. The first t. garden of this kind arose at Leyden 1837. **2.** In his Trans-Alpine Expedition 1654.

Tra:ns,anima·tion. Now *rare.* 1574. [– eccl.L. *transanimatio, -ōn-* (Jerome), f. *trans* TRANS- + *anima* soul; see -ATION.] = METEMPSYCHOSIS.

Tra:nsatla·ntic (trɑns,-, trɑnz,-), *a.* (*sb.*) 1779. [f. TRANS- + ATLANTIC.] **1.** Passing or extending across the Atlantic Ocean. **2.** Situated or resident in, or pertaining to a region beyond the Atlantic; chiefly in

European use: = American 1782. **B.** *sb.* (the adj. used absol.): One who or that which is across the Atlantic; *spec.* an American; also short for 't. steamer' 1826.

Trans-bo·rder, *a.* 1807. [f. TRANS- 3 + BORDER *sb.*] Lying or living beyond a (or the) border; occupying territory outside the border.

Transcalent (transˌkēⁱ·lĕnt, traˑnsˌkălĕnt), *a.* 1834. [f. TRANS- + *calens, -ent-*, pr. pple. of L. *calēre* be hot, glow; see -ENT.] Having the property of freely transmitting radiant heat; diathermanous. Hence **Traˑnsˌcalency,** the property of being t.

Transcend (transe·nd), *v.* ME. [– OFr. *transcendre* or L. *tran(s)scendere* climb over, surmount, f. *trans* TRANS + *scandere* climb.] †**1.** *trans.* To pass over or go beyond (a physical obstacle or limit); to climb or get over the top of (a wall, mountain, etc.) –1695. **2.** To pass or extend beyond or above (a non-physical limit); to go beyond the limits of (something immaterial); to exceed ME. **b.** *Theol.* To be above and independent of: esp. said of the Deity in relation to the universe 1898. **3.** To rise above, surpass, excel, exceed. late ME. †**4.** *intr.* To ascend, go up, rise –1613. **5.** To be tran-scendent; to excel. *arch.* 1635.

1. Nimble Wings which can T. the Polar Height 1695. **2.** Unable as we are to t. consciousness H. SPENCER. **3.** Electro-magnets far t. permanent magnets in power 1866.

Transcendence (transe·ndĕns). 1601. [– late L. *transcendentia*, f. *transcendent-*, pr. ppl. stem of *transcendere*; see prec., -ENCE.] **1.** The action or fact of transcending, surmounting, or rising above; also, the condition or quality of being transcendent. **b.** *spec.* Of the Deity: The attribute of being above and independent of the universe; dist. from *immanence* 1848. †**2.** Exaggeration, hyperbole (*rare*) –1645.

2. This would have done better in Poesy; where Transcendences are more allowed BACON.

Transcendency (transe·ndĕnsi). 1615. [f. as prec.; see -ENCY.] The condition or quality of being transcendent; excess; surpassing excellency; with *pl.* a transcendent quality. **b.** The fact of transcending; an instance of this 1907.

Transcendent (transe·ndĕnt), *a.* and *sb.* 1581. [– L. *transcendens, -ent-*, pr. pple. of *transcendere* TRANSCEND; see -ENT.] **A.** *adj.* **1.** Surpassing or excelling others of its kind; pre-eminent; extraordinary. Also, loosely, Eminently great or good. 1598. †**2.** Of an idea or conception: Transcending comprehension; hence, obscure or abstruse –1646. **3.** *Philos.* **a.** Applied by the Schoolmen to predicates which were considered to transcend the Aristotelian categories or predicaments 1706. **b.** By Kant applied to that which transcends his own list of categories; hence, not an object of possible experience 1803. **4.** *Theol.* Of the Deity: In His being, exalted above and distinct from the universe; dist. from *immanent* 1877.

1. That t. Apostle Saint Paul MILT. Such t. goodness of heart RICHARDSON.

B. *sb.* [the adj. used *absol.*] **1.** *Philos.* †**a.** A predicate that transcends, or cannot be classed under, any of the Aristotelian categories or predicaments –1697. **b.** *transf.* A person or thing that transcends classification 1591. **c.** In Kantian philosophy: That which is beyond the bounds of human cognition and thought 1810. †**2.** One who or that which transcends the ordinary rank of persons or things –1679. **3.** *Math.* A transcendental expression or function; see next 4. 1809. Hence **Transce·ndent-ly** *adv.*, **-ness** (*rare*).

Transcendental (transende·ntăl), *a.* (*sb.*) 1668. [– med.L. *transcendentalis* (Wyclif), f. as prec. + *-alis* -AL[1] 1.] **1.** = prec. A. 1. 1701. **2.** *Philos.* **a.** *orig.* in Aristotelian philosophy: Transcending or extending beyond the bounds of any single category. In 17th c. often synonymous with *metaphysical.* 1668. **b.** In Kant (1724–1804): Not derived from experience, but concerned with the presuppositions of experience; *a priori*; critical 1798. **c.** Used of any philosophy which resembles Kant's in being based upon the recognition of an *a priori* element in experience 1829. **d.** By Schelling 't. philosophy' was used for the philosophy of mind as dist. from that of nature 1903. **3.** Hence, **a.** Beyond the limits of ordinary experience, extraordinary 1831. **b.** Super-rational, superhuman, supernatural 1826. **c.** *Vaguely*, Abstract, metaphysical, *a priori* 1835. **d.** Applied to the movement of thought in New England of which Emerson was the principal figure 1844. **4.** *Math.* Not capable of being produced by (a finite number of) the ordinary algebraical operations of addition, multiplication, involution, or their inverse operations; expressible in terms of the variable only in the form of an infinite series 1706. **B.** *sb.* [the adj. used *absol.*] A transcendental term, conception, or quantity 1668.

3. a. Very frightful it is when a Nation. . becomes t. CARLYLE. **c.** An unmeaning and t. conception JOWETT. **4.** The. . t. functions,. . sin x, cos x, &c., . . e^x, and log x 1882. Hence **Transcende·ntal-ly** *adv.*, **-ness** (*rare*).

Transcendentalism (transende·ntăliz'm). 1803. [f. prec. + -ISM.] **1.** Transcendental philosophy; a system of this; applied to that taught by Kant and others; also, to the idealism of Schelling. **b.** The religio-philosophical teaching of the New England school of thought represented by Emerson and others 1842. **2.** Exalted character, thought, or language; also, that which is extravagant, vague, or visionary in philosophy or language; idealism 1831. So **Transcende·ntalist,** an adherent of some form of t.

Transcendentalize (transende·ntăləiz), *v.* 1846. [f. as prec. + -IZE.] *trans.* **a.** To render transcendent. **b.** To idealize.

Transcension (transe·nʃən). *rare.* 1611. [f. TRANSCEND, after *ascend/ascension.*] A passing beyond or above; transcendence.

Transˌcolora·tion, -coloura·tion. Now *rare* or *Obs.* 1664. [f. TRANS- + COLORATION.] The action or process of transcolouring; change of colour.

†**Transˌco·lour,** *v. rare.* 1664. [f. TRANS- + COLOUR *v.*] *trans.* To change the colour of; to cause to change colour –1837.

Traˑns-contine·ntal, *a.* 1869. [f. TRANS- 3 + CONTINENTAL.] That extends or passes across a continent.

Tranˌscri·bble, *v. rare.* 1750. [f. TRANS- + SCRIBBLE *v.*, after next.] *trans.* To transcribe carelessly. So **Transcri·bbler** 1746.

Transcribe (tranˌskrəi·b), *v.* 1552. [– L. *transcribere*, f. *trans* TRANS- + *scribere* write.] **1.** *trans.* To make a copy of (something) in writing; to copy out from an original; to write (a copy). Also *absol.* **b.** Less exactly: To copy or reproduce the matter or statements of (a writing or book) without regard to the wording. Now *rare.* 1633. **2.** To write out in other characters, to transliterate; to write out (a shorthand account) in ordinary 'long-hand'; formerly also, to translate 1639. **b.** *Mus.* To adapt (a composition) for a voice or instrument other than that for which it was originally written 1891. †**3.** *fig.* To copy or imitate (a person, his qualities, etc.); to reproduce –1729. †**4.** To ascribe *to* another by transference –1651. **5.** *Rom. Law.* To transfer *to* another 1880.

1. The primitive Christians were careful to t. copies of the gospels BERKELEY. **b.** A few plain, easy rules. Chiefly transcribed from Dr. Cheyne. WESLEY. **2.** The Agamemnon of Æschylus transcribed by Robert Browning 1877. Hence **Tranˌscri·ber.**

Transcript (tra·nˌskript). [ME. *transcrit* – (O)Fr. *transcrit*, later (XV) assim. to L. *transcriptum*, subst. use of n. pa. pple. of *transcribere* TRANSCRIBE.] **1.** A written copy; also *transf.* a printed reproduction of this; *spec.* in *Law*, a copy of a legal record. **2.** *transf.* and *fig.* A copy, reproduction; a rendering 1646.

1. A t. of which lettre hereaftur ensueth 1481. **2.** Let our lives be a true t. of our Sermons 1657.

Transcription (tranˌskri·pʃən). 1598. [– Fr. *transcription* or late L. *transcriptio, -ōn-*, f. *transcript-*, pa. ppl. stem of L. *transcribere* TRANSCRIBE; see -ION.] **1.** The action or process of transcribing or copying. **2.** A transcript; a copy 1650. **3.** *Mus.* The arrangement, or (less properly) modification, of a composition for some voice or instrument other than that for which it was originally written; a transcribed piece 1864. **4.** *Rom. Law.* A transfer, assignment (of a debt or obligation) 1677.

1. The error was committed in the t. of the copy from Ptolomies library 1610.

Transcriptive (tranˌskri·ptiv), *a.* 1646. [f. TRANSCRIPTION, after *description/descriptive.*] **1.** Having the quality or habit of transcribing; given to transcription. **2.** *Rom. Law.* Transferring obligation 1875. Hence **Tranˌscri·ptively** *adv.*

†**Transˌcu·rsion.** 1624. [– late L. *transcursio, -ōn-* lapse of a period of time; hasty treatment, f. pa. ppl. stem of L. *transcurrere* run across; see -ION.] The action of running or passing across or through; transition, penetration; also, a journey or passage through a country, etc. –1665.

Transdialect (transdəi·ălekt, -z-), *v. rare.* 1698. [f. TRANS- + DIALECT.] *trans.* To translate from one dialect into another.

Transduction (transˌdʌ·kʃən). *rare.* 1656. [f. TRADUCTION by subst. of the more familiar prefix TRANS-.] The action of leading or bringing across.

Transect (transe·kt), *v.* 1634. [f. TRANS- + *sect-*, pa. ppl. stem of L. *secare* cut.] *trans.* To cut across; in *Anat.* to dissect transversely. So **Transe·ction,** the action of transecting; a transverse section.

Transelement (tranzˌe·lĭment), *v.* 1567. [– med.L. *transelementare (tr. Patr. Gr. μεταστοιχοῦν), f. *trans* TRANS- + *elementa* (pl.) elements, *στοιχεῖα.*] *trans.* To change or transmute the elements of. So **Transˌ-eˌlementa·tion,** the action or process of changing the elements of something 1550.

Transept (tra·nsept). 1538. [– mod.L. (AL.) *transeptum* 'cross division'; see TRANS-, SEPTUM.] The transverse part of a cruciform church considered apart from the nave; also, each of the two arms of this (the *north* and *south transepts*).

Transfashion (transfæ·ʃən), *v.* 1601. [TRANS- 2.] *trans.* To change the fashion of, to transform.

Transfer (tra·nsfəɹ), *sb.* 1674. [f. next.] **1.** *Law.* Conveyance from one person to another of property, *spec.* of shares or stock. **2.** *gen.* The act of transferring or fact of being transferred; conveyance or removal from one place, person, etc. to another; transmission; transference 1785. **3.** A thing (*rarely*, a person) that is transferred; *spec.* writing, drawing, or a design, transferred or to be transferred in reverse, from one surface to another, as by copying-ink, or by pressure in lithography, photography, etc. 1839. **4.** A means or place of transfer. Chiefly U.S. *spec.* **a.** *U.S. Post Office.* A telegraphic money-order. **b.** On a railway, etc.: (*a*) A siding connecting tracks at a crossing or on different levels; (*b*) a t.-ticket; (*c*) the conveyance of passengers and luggage from one railway station to another, when these are not contiguous (attrib. *t.-man, -porter*) 1891.

2. b. The transference of a worker or player from one sphere to another; also, one transferred (attrib. *t. fee, money*) 1911.

attrib. and *Comb.*: **t.-book,** a register of transfers of property, esp. that of its shares or stock, kept by a joint-stock company; **-day,** at the Bank of England, a day for the register of transfers of bank-stock; **-ink,** ink used in lithography; **-paper,** paper used in making transfers in lithography, etc.; **-printing,** a process by which designs are printed on fictile, etc. ware; **-table** (*U.S.*), a railway traverse-table; **-ticket,** a ticket entitling a passenger to change from a conveyance to one on another line or route without re-booking or further payment.

Transfer (transfə̄·ɹ), *v.* Infl. **transferred, -ing.** late ME. [– Fr. *transférer* or L. *transferre*, f. TRANS- + *ferre* bear, carry.] **1.** *trans.* To convey or take from one place, person, etc. to another; to transmit, transport; to give or hand over from one to another. **b.** *intr.* for *refl.* or *pass.* 1646. **2.** *Law.* To convey or make over (title, right, or property) by deed or legal process 1598. **3.** To convey (a drawing or design) from one surface to another, esp. to a lithographic stone 1839.

1. For transferring £5690 Reduced Stock into the Four per Cents 1809. **b.** He transferred later to the 19th Hussars 1901. **2.** A grant only transfers what the grantor may lawfully give 1818. Hence **Transfe·rrer,** one who or that which transfers.

Transferable (tra·nsfĕrăb'l, transfǭ·răb'l), *a.* 1646. [f. prec. + -ABLE.] Capable of being transferred or legally made over to another; *spec.* of bills, drafts, cheques, etc.: Assignable in the course of business from one person to another. Hence **Tra:nsferabi·lity,** the quality of being t.

Transferee (transfĕrī·). 1736. [f. as prec. + -EE[1].] **1.** One to whom a transfer is made. **2.** One who is transferred or removed 1892.

Transference (tra·nsfĕrĕns). 1760. [f. TRANSFER *v.* + -ENCE.] The action or process of transferring; transfer. **b.** *Psychoanalysis.* [tr. G. *übertragung.*] Direction of feelings and desires toward a new object 1916.

Transferor (tra·nsfĕrǭɹ, -ǭɹ). 1875. [f. TRANSFER *v.* or *sb.* + -OR 2.] One who makes a transfer or conveyance of property, etc.

Transfe·rrable, *a.* Also **-ible.** 1660. [f. TRANSFER *v.* + -ABLE.] = TRANSFERABLE.

Transfigurate (transfi·giŭrēit), *v.* Now *rare.* late ME. [– *transfigurat-*, pa. ppl. stem of L. *transfigurare*; see TRANSFIGURE, -ATE[3].] *trans.* = TRANSFIGURE.

High heaven is there Transfused, transfigurated BYRON.

Transfiguration (tra:nsfigiŭrē·ʃən, -figər-, tranz-). late ME. [– (O)Fr. *transfiguration* or L. *transfiguratio, -ōn-* (Pliny), f. as prec.; see -ION.] **1.** The action of transfiguring or state of being transfigured; metamorphosis 1548. **2.** The change in the appearance of Jesus Christ on the mountain (Matt. 17:2; Mark 9:2, 3). late ME. **b.** *Eccl.* The church festival commemorating this event, observed on the 6th of August. 1460. **c.** A picture of this event 1712.

Transfigure (transfi·giŭɹ, -fi·gəɹ, -z-), *v.* ME. [– (O)Fr. *transfigurer* or L. *transfigurare* (Pliny), f. *trans* TRANS- + *figura* FIGURE.] **1.** *trans.* To alter the figure or appearance of; to transform. **2.** *trans. fig.* (in allusion to the Transfiguration of Christ): To elevate, glorify, idealize, spiritualize. late ME.

1. They saw Jesus transfigured in a radiance of glory 1911. **2.** His morality is transfigured into Religion 1841.

Transfission (transfi·ʃən). 1891. [f. TRANS- 1 or 6 + FISSION 2.] *Biol.* The transverse splitting of a cell or organism as a mode of reproduction.

Transfix (transfi·ks), *v.* 1590. [– *transfix-*, pa. ppl. stem of L. *transfigere*; see TRANS-, FIX *v.* Cf. Fr. *transfixer.*] *trans.* To pierce through with, or impale upon, a sharp-pointed instrument (also said of the instrument); to fix or fasten by piercing.

fig. His heart transfixt With anguish COWPER.

Transfixion (transfi·kʃən). 1609. [f. prec.; see -ION.] The action of transfixing or state of being transfixed. **b.** *Surg.* The process of piercing the limb transversely, and cutting from within outward, in amputation 1872.

Transfluent (tra·nsflu,ĕnt), *a. rare.* 1828. [– L. *transfluens, -ent-*, pr. pple. of *transfluere* (Pliny); see TRANS-, FLUENT.] Flowing across or through; in *Her.* said of a stream represented as flowing through a bridge.

Transfluvial (transflū·viăl), *a.* 1806. [– eccl. L. *transfluvialis*, tr. Heb. *'ibrī* 'one from the other side' see TRANS-, FLUVIAL. Cf. HEBREW.] Situated or dwelling across or beyond a river.

Transform (transfǭ·ɹm), *v.* ME. [– (O)Fr. *transformer* or L. *transformare*; see TRANS-, FORM *v.*] **1.** *trans.* To change the form of; to metamorphose. **b.** *transf.* To change in character or condition; to alter in function or nature 1556. **c.** *Math.* To alter (a figure, expression, etc.) to another differing in form, but equal in quantity or value 1743. **d.** *Physics.* To change (one form of energy) into another 1871. **e.** *Electr.* To change a current in potential or in type 1883. **2.** *intr.* To undergo a change in form or nature; to change. Now *rare.* 1597.

1. To Samarcand..we owe the art of transforming linen into paper J. H. NEWMAN. **b.** He transformed an undisciplined body of peasantry into a regular army of soldiers 1796. **2.** Then did this iolly feast, to fast transforme 1597. Hence **Transfo·rmable** *a.* capable of transformation.

Transformation (transfǫɹmēi·ʃən). late ME. [– (O)Fr. *transformation* or late L. *transformatio, -ōn-*, f. *transformat-*, pa. ppl. stem of L. *transformare*; see prec., -ION.] **1.** The action of changing in form, shape, or appearance; metamorphosis. **†b.** A changed form; a person or thing transformed. SHAKS. **c.** *Theatr.* More fully *t. scene*: A mechanical disclosing scene in a pantomime; *spec.* the scene in which the principal performers were transformed in view of the audience into the players of the ensuing harlequinade 1859. **2.** *transf.* A complete change in character, condition, etc. 1581. **3. a.** *Zool.* Change of form in animal life; metamorphosis 1638. **b.** *Physiol.* and *Path.* Change of form or substance in an organ, tissue, vital fluid, etc. 1834. **c.** *Math.* Change of form without alteration of quantity or value; substitution of one geometrical figure for another of equal magnitude but different form 1571. **d.** *Physics.* Change of form of a substance from solid to liquid, from liquid or solid to gaseous, or the reverse; *Chem.* change of chemical composition, as by replacement of one constituent of a compound by another 1857. **e.** Change of energy from one form into another 1877. **f.** *Electr.* Change of a current into one of different potential, or different type, or both, as by a transformer 1884. **4.** An artificial head of hair worn by women 1901.

Transformative (transfǭ·ɹmătiv), *a.* 1671. [– med.L. *transformativus*, f. as prec.; see -IVE.] Having the faculty of transforming; fitted or tending to transform.

Transfo·rmer. 1601. [f. TRANSFORM *v.* + -ER[1].] **1.** One who or that which transforms. **2.** *Electr.* An apparatus for transforming electric energy; now *spec.* a static apparatus for transforming alternating currents, and consisting essentially of two coils of wire wound round an iron core 1883. *Rotary t.*, also called *dynamotor.*

Transformism (transfǭ·ɹmiz'm). 1878. [– Fr. *transformisme* (Broca, 1867), f. *transformer* TRANSFORM; see -ISM.] **1.** *Biol.* The hypothesis that existing species are the product of the gradual transformation of other forms of living beings (*loosely*, such transformation itself); any form of the doctrine of evolution of species. **2.** The doctrine of gradual evolution of moral and social relations; *loosely*, such evolution itself 1885. Hence **Transfo·rmist.**

†Transfreta·tion. 1612. [– L. *transfretatio, -ōn-*, f. *transfretare*, f. *trans* TRANS- + *fretum* strait; see -ATION.] The action of crossing or passing over a strait, channel, or narrow sea –1782.

Transfro·ntal, *a.* 1889. [TRANS- 5.] *Anat.* Crossing the forehead or the frontal lobe of the brain.

Trans-fro·ntier, *a.* 1877. [TRANS- 3.] Lying, living or done beyond the frontier of a country.

Transfuse (transfiū·z), *v.* late ME. [– *transfus-*, pa. ppl. stem of L. *transfundere*; see TRANS-, FUSE *v.*[1]] **1.** *trans.* To pour (a liquid) from one vessel or receptacle into another 1601. **2.** *transf.* and *fig.* To cause to 'flow' from one to another; to diffuse into or through something; to cause to permeate; to instil. late ME. **3.** *Med.*, etc. To transfer (the blood of a person or animal) into the veins of another 1666. **b.** To treat (a person) with transfusion of blood (or of some solution) 1897.

2. The sole way of transfusing the principles of Christianity into men 1618. It's..Influence is transfus'd thro' several..Channels 1709. So **Transfu·sible** *a.* (*rare*) capable of being transfused.

Transfusion (transfiū·ʒən). 1578. [– L. *transfusio, -ōn-*, f. as prec.; see -ION.] **1.** The action of pouring a liquid from one vessel into another; also *fig.* transference; translation. **2.** *Med.*, etc. The process of transferring the blood of a person or animal into the veins of another; the injection of blood or other fluid into the veins 1643.

1. I grant that something must be lost in all t., that is, in all translations DRYDEN.

Transfusive (transfiū·siv), *a.* 1677. [In XVII perh. – med.L. *transfusivus* (Albertus Magnus), f. as prec.; see -IVE. In mod. use f. TRANSFUSE 2.] Having the quality of or a tendency to transfusion.

†Tra·nsgress, *sb. rare.* 1578. [– Fr. †*transgrès* (XV); in mod. use f. the vb.] Transgression, trespass –1839.

Transgress (transgre·s, -z-), *v.* 1526. [– (O)Fr. *transgresser* or *transgress-*, pa. pple. stem of L. *transgredi*, f. *trans* TRANS- + *gradi* step, go.] **1.** *trans.* To go beyond the limits prescribed by (a law, command, etc.); to break, violate, infringe, trespass against. **b.** *absol.* or *intr.* (const. *against*): To trespass, offend, sin 1526. **†c.** *trans.* To offend against (a person); to disobey (*rare*) –1625. **2.** To go or pass beyond (any limit or bounds) 1619.

1. So they transgresse & breke the commaundement of god 1526. **b.** I would not marry her, though she were indowed with all that Adam had left him before he transgrest SHAKS. **c.** I never Blasphemed 'em, uncle, nor transgrest my parents FLETCHER. **2.** Hard mouthed coursers..Apt to run riot, and t. the goal DRYDEN.

Transgression (transgre·ʃən, -z-). late ME. [– (O)Fr. *transgression* – L. *transgressio, -ōn-*, f. as prec.; see -ION.] **1.** The action of transgressing or passing beyond the bounds of legality or right; a violation of law, duty, or command; disobedience, trespass, sin. **b.** The action of passing over or beyond (due bounds) 1623. **2.** *Geol.* The spread of the sea over the land along a subsiding shore-line, producing an overlap by deposition of new strata upon old 1882.

1. Heauen lay not my t. to my charge SHAKS. Punishments ordained beforehand for their t. HOBBES. Hence **Transgre·ssional** *a.* of or pertaining to t.; of the nature of a t.

Transgressive (transgre·siv, -z-), *a.* 1646. [f. TRANSGRESS + -IVE.] **1.** Having the character or quality of transgressing; sinful; passing beyond some limit (*rare*). **2.** *Geol.* Overlapping; cf. TRANSGRESSION 2. 1854.

1. Adam..from the t. infirmities of himselfe might have erred alone, as well as the Angels before him SIR T. BROWNE. Hence **Transgre·ssively** *adv.*

Transgressor (transgre·səɹ, -z-). late ME. [– Chr. L. *transgressor*; see TRANSGRESS, -OR 2.] One who transgresses; a law-breaker; a sinner.

To committe the transgressours..to the next Gaole 1463. A t. of the laws 1875.

Tranship (tran,ʃi·p), *less commonly* **transship** (trans,ʃi·p), *v.* 1792. [f. TRANS- + SHIP *v.*] **1.** *trans.* To transfer from one ship (or *transf.* from one railway train or other conveyance) to another. Also *absol.* **2.** *intr.* Of a passenger: To change from one ship or other conveyance to another 1879. **Trans(-)shi·pment.**

Transhuman (trans,hiū·măn, -z-), *a.* 1812. [f. TRANS- 4 + HUMAN; after It. *trasumanar* in Dante.] Beyond the human; superhuman. So **Transhu·manize** *v. trans.* to make t. **Transhumana·tion.**

Transhumance (transhiū·măns). 1911. [– Fr. *transhumance* (see -ANCE), f. *transhumer* (ult. f. L. *trans* across + *humus* ground).] The seasonal moving of live stock to regions of different climate. **Transhu·mant** *a.*, **-hu·me** *v.*

Transience (tra·nsiĕns, -z-; tra·nʃĕns, -ʒ-). 1745. [f. as TRANSIENT; see -ENCE.] **1.** The action or fact of being transient, transiency. **2.** = TRANSCENDENCE 1 b. 1882.

Transiency (cf. prec.). 1652. [f. as prec.; see -ENCY.] **1.** The quality or condition of being transient; transitoriness. **2.** A transient thing or being 1866.

Transient (tra·nsiĕnt, -z-), *a.* (*sb.*) 1607. [– L. *transiens* (obl. *transeunt-*, whence the form *transeunt* in sense 2), pr. pple. of *transire* pass over, f. *trans* TRANS- + *-ire* go. Cf. AMBIENT.] **1.** Passing by or away with time; not durable or permanent; temporary, transitory; *esp.* passing away quickly or soon, brief, momentary, fleeting. **2.** Passing out or operating beyond itself; transitive; opp. to *immanent.* (Often spelt *transeunt.*) 1613. **3.** Passing or flowing through; passing from one thing or person to another. Now *rare.* 1619. **4.** Passing through a place without staying in it, or staying only for a short time; *spec.* (*U.S. colloq.*) applied to a guest at a hotel, etc. 1685.

1. b. *U.S.* Of a newspaper advertisement: appearing only once 1857. **4.** Love, hitherto a t. guest SWIFT.

B. *sb.* **1.** A transient thing or being 1652. **2.** *U.S. colloq.* A person who passes through a place, or stays in it only for a short time; *spec.* a 'transient guest' at a hotel or boarding-house 1880. Hence **Tra·nsient-ly** *adv.*, **-ness.**

Transilience (trɑnsi·liĕns). *rare.* 1657. [f. as next; see -ENCE.] A leaping from one thing to another, an abrupt transition; *spec.* in *Min.* abrupt transition of one mineral or rock into another.

Transilient (trɑnsi·liĕnt), *a.* 1811. [– L. *trans(s)iliens, -ent-*, pr. pple. of *trans(s)ilire* leap across, f. *trans* TRANS- + *salire* leap; see -ENT.] Leaping or passing from one thing or condition to another; in *Min.* said of one rock substance passing abruptly into another.

Transilluminate (trans,ilⁱū·mineⁱt, -z-). *v.* 1900. [f. TRANS- + ILLUMINATE *v.*] *trans.* To cause light to pass through; *spec.* in *Med.* to throw a strong light through (an organ or part) to discover the presence or cause of disease. So **Transillumina·tion** 1890.

‖**Transire** (trɑns,əiᵊ·ri, -z-). 1599. [L., f. *trans* TRANS- + *ire* go.] *Law.* A warrant issued by the custom-house, permitting the passage of merchandise.

Transit (tra·nsit, -z-), *sb.* 1440. [– L. *transitus*, f. *transire*; see prec.] **1.** The action or fact of passing across or through; passage or journey from one place or point to another. **b.** The passage or carriage of persons or goods from one place to another 1800. **2.** *fig.* A passing across; a transition or change; *esp.* the passage from this life to the next by death 1657. **3.** *Astrol.* The passage of a planet across some special point or region of the zodiac 1671. **4.** *Astron.* **a.** The passage of an inferior planet (Mercury or Venus) across the sun's disc, or of a satellite or its shadow across the disc of a planet 1669. **b.** The passage of a star or other celestial body across the meridian at its culmination 1812. **c.** Short for *t.-circle, -compass, -instrument, -theodolite* 1793.

1. Sometimes..the t. from Nantes to Orleans takes two months! 1833. Phr. *In t.* **b.** The means of t. are so bad, that much good corn is left to rot upon the ground 1870.

attrib. and *Comb.*: **t.-circle,** an astronomical instrument consisting of a telescope carrying a large graduated circle, by which the right ascension and declination of a star may be determined by observation of it in t.; a meridian-circle; **-compass,** an instrument, resembling a theodolite, used in surveying for the measurement of horizontal angles; **-duty,** a duty paid on goods passing through a country; **-instrument,** an astronomical telescope mounted on a fixed east-and-west axis, by which the time of the passage of a celestial body across the meridian may be determined; usu. applied to one without a circle; **-theodolite,** = *t.-compass*; **-trade,** trade arising out of the passage of foreign goods through a country.

Transit (tra·nsit, -z-), *v.* 1440. [– *transit-*, pa. ppl. stem of L. *transire*; see prec.] **1.** *intr.* To pass through or over; to pass away. **2.** *trans. Astrol.* To pass across (a sign, 'house', or special point of the zodiac). Also *absol.* or *intr.* 1647. **3.** *Astron.* To pass across (the disc of a celestial body, the meridian of a place, or the field of view of a telescope). Also *absol.* or *intr.* 1686.

Transition (trɑnsi·ʒən, -si·ʃən, -zi·ʃən). 1551. [– (O)Fr. *transition* or L. *transitio, -ōn-*, f. as prec.; see -ION.] **1.** A passing or passage from one condition, action, or (rarely) place, to another; change. **2.** Passage in thought, speech, or writing from one subject to another 1592. **3.** *Mus.* The passing from one key to another, modulation; *spec.* a passing or brief modulation; also, modulation into a remote key 1877. **4.** The passage from an earlier to a later stage of development or formation. **a.** *Geol.* Formerly *spec.* applied *attrib.* to certain early stratified rocks believed to contain the oldest remains of living organisms; now classified as Silurian 1813. **b.** *Arch.* Change from an earlier style to a later; a style of mixed character 1835. **c.** *Philol.* The historical passage of language from one well-defined stage to another; hence, applied to the interval occupied by this, and to the transitional form of the language during this interval 1873.

1. A quick t. from poverty to abundance can seldom be made with safety JOHNSON. **2.** Heer the Archangel paus'd..Then with t. sweet new Speech resumes MILT. Hence **Transi·tional** *a.* of or pertaining to t.; characterized by or involving t.; intermediate; **-ly** *adv.* **Transi·tionary** *a.* transitional.

Transitive (tra·nsitiv, -z-), *a.* (*sb.*) 1560. [– late L. *transitivus* (Priscian), f. as prec.; see -IVE. In sense 1 app. – OFr. *transitif* transient.] †**1.** Transient, transitory (*rare*) –1845. **2.** *Gram.* Of verbs and their construction: Expressing an action which passes over to an object; taking a direct object to complete the sense 1571. **b.** as *sb.* A transitive verb 1612. **3.** *Philos.* Passing out of itself; passing over to or affecting something else; operating beyond itself; opp. to *immanent* 1613. **4.** Characterized by or involving transition, in various senses. Now *rare* or *Obs.* 1660.

3. Cold is Active and T. into Bodies Adjacent, as well as Heat BACON. Hence **Tra·nsitive-ly** *adv.*, **-ness.**

Transitory (tra·nsitəri, -z-), *a.* late ME. [– AFr. *transitorie*, (O)Fr. *transitoire* – Chr. L. *transitorius*, f. as prec.; see -ORY².] **1.** Having the quality of passing away; fleeting, momentary, brief; transient. **2.** *Law. T. action*, an action in which the venue might be laid in any county 1665. †**3.** (app.) Trifling, of little moment. DRYDEN.

1. This world is not but a vayn thinge and transitoire CAXTON. Hence **Tra·nsitorily** *adv.* **Tra·nsitoriness.**

Translatable (trɑns,lēⁱ·tăb'l), *a.* 1745. [f. TRANSLATE *v.* + -ABLE.] Capable of being translated.

Translate (trɑns,lēⁱ·t), *v.* Pa. t. and pple. **translated.** ME. [prob. first in pa. pple. *translate* – L. *translatus*, functioning as pa. pple. of *transferre* TRANSFER *v.*; but perh. reinforced by OFr. *translater*, med.L. *translatare*; see -ATE³.] **I.** *trans.* To bear, convey, or remove from one person, place or condition to another; to transfer, transport; *spec.* to remove a bishop from one see to another, or a bishop's seat from one place to another; also, to remove the body or relics of a saint (or a hero) from one place of interment or repose to another. **b.** To carry or convey to heaven without death; also, in later use, said of the death of the righteous. late ME. **c.** *Med.* To remove the seat of (a disease) from one person, or part of the body, to another. Now *rare* or *Obs.* 1732. **d.** *Physics.* To move (a body) from one place or point to another without rotation.

Hys body was translat to Rome 1517. Morley, made at first bishop of Worcester, and soon after..translated to Winchester BURNET. **b.** Bi feith Enok is translatid, that he schulde not se deeth; and he was not founden, for the Lord translatide him WYCLIF *Heb.* 11:5.

II. 1. To turn from one language into another; 'to change into another language retaining the sense' (J.); to render; also, to paraphrase ME. **b.** *absol.* To practise translation; also *intr.* for *pass.*, of a language, speech, or writing: To bear or admit of translation 1440. **2.** *fig.* To interpret, explain; also, to express (one thing) in terms of another 1598.

1. It was translated out of latyn in to frenshe 1477. **b.** Sometimes Johnson translated aloud MACAULAY. **2.** There's matters in these sighes.. These profound heaues You must t. SHAKS.

III. 1. To change in form, appearance, or substance; to transmute; to transform. late ME. **2.** To re-transmit (a telegraphic message) by means of an automatic repeater 1855. **3.** To transport with the strength of some feeling, to enrapture, entrance. *arch.* 1643.

1. Nabuchadnezar was really translated into a beast BURTON. **3.** Their souls, with devotion translated LONGF.

Translating (trɑns,lēⁱ·tiŋ), *vbl. sb.* 1460. [f. prec. + -ING¹.] The action of TRANSLATE *v.*

attrib.: **t.-relay** (*Telegr.*): see RELAY *sb.* 4.; **-roller, -screw** (*Mech.*), a screw which moves a part of a mechanism in relation to the other parts; **-station** (*Telegr.*) a station at which an automatic repeater is introduced.

Translation (trɑns,lēⁱ·ʃən). ME. [– (O)Fr. *translation* or L. *translatio*, f. *translat-*, pa. ppl. stem of *transferre*; see TRANSLATE *v.*, -ION.] **I.** Transference; removal or conveyance from one person, place, or condition to another. **b.** Removal from earth to heaven, *orig.* without death, as the translation of Enoch; but in later use also said *fig.* of the death of the righteous. late ME. **c.** *Med.* Transference of a disease from one person or part of the body to another. Now *rare* or *Obs.* 1665. **d.** *Physics.* Transference of a body, or form of energy, from one point of space to another 1715.

The Feast of the T. of Saint Eadward 1869. *T. of a feast* (Eccl.), its transference from the usual date to another, to avoid its clashing with another (movable) feast of superior rank. **b.** The news of dear Mr. Polhill's sudden t. 1760. **d.** *Motion* or *movement of t.*, onward movement without (or considered apart from) rotation.

II. 1. The action or process of turning from one language into another; also, the product of this; a version in a different language ME. **b.** *transf.* and *fig.* The expression or rendering of something in another medium or form 1588. **2.** Transformation, alteration, change; changing or adapting to another use; renovation. late ME.

1. Nor ought a genius less than his that writ, Attempt t. DENHAM. **b.** His translations on copper, to compare them with..verbal translations..display much of the elegance of Pope 1812.

III. 1. *Law.* A transfer of property; *spec.* alteration of a bequest by transferring the legacy to another person 1590. **2.** In long distance telegraphy, the automatic re-transmission of a message by means of a relay 1866.

1. All Contract is mutuall t., or change of Right HOBBES.

attrib.: **t.-wave,** an ocean wave with a propelling or forward impulse; a forced wave. Hence **Transla·tional** *a.* of or pertaining to t.; in *Physics*, consisting in onward motion, as dist. from rotation, vibration, oscillation, etc.

Translative (trɑns,lēⁱ·tiv, tra·ns,lătiv), *a.* 1589. [– L. *translativus* pertaining to transfer (sense 1 in Isidore), f. as prec.; see -IVE.] †**1.** Involving transference of meaning. PUTTENHAM. **2.** Involving transference from one place to another; in *Physics*, of the nature of onward movement without rotation or reciprocation 1682. **3.** Relating to translation 1748. **4.** *Law.* Expressing or constituting transference of property, etc. 1875.

Translator (trɑns,lēⁱ·təɹ). ME. [In sense 1 orig. – OFr. *translator, -our* (mod. *-eur*) or late L. *translator* (Jerome); later f. the Eng. vb.] One who (rarely, that which) translates. **1.** The author of a translation. **b.** One who renders a painting by engraving, or the like 1855. **2.** One who transforms, changes, or alters; *spec.* a cobbler who renovates old shoes 1594. †**3.** One who transfers or transports –1633. **4.** An automatic repeater in long-distance telegraphy 1855.

1. The symple..translatore of this litel book 1413. Mr. Cary, the t. of Dante 1837. Hence **Transla·torship,** the function of a t. **Transla·tory** *a.* of or pertaining to (physical) translation. **Transla·tress, -trix,** a female t.

Transliterate (trɑns,li·tĕreⁱt, -z-), *v.* 1861. [f. TRANS- 1 + L. *littera* letter + -ATE³.] *trans.* To replace (letters or characters of one language) by those of another used to represent the same sounds; to write (a word, etc.) in the characters of another alphabet.

Transliteration (trɑns,litĕrēⁱ·ʃən, -z-). 1861. [f. as prec. + -ATION.] The action or process of transliterating; the rendering of the letters or characters of one alphabet in those of another; *concr.* a word or character thus rendered.

Translocation (trɑns,lokēⁱ·ʃən). 1624. [f. TRANS- + LOCATION, orig. perh. after *translation*. Cf. med.L. *translocare* transfer (XIII).] Removal from one place to another; displacement; dislocation; †transmigration. **b.** *Vegetable Phys.* The transference of reserve material from one part to another. 1900. So **Tra·nslocate** *v. trans.* to remove from one place to another; to displace (*rare*).

Translucence (trɑns,lⁱū·sĕns, -z-). 1755. [f. as next; see -ENCE.] **1.** The action or fact of shining through 1826. **2.** = next 1755.

Translucency (trɑns,lⁱū·sĕnsi, -z-). 1630. [f. next; see -ENCY.] The quality or condition of being translucent; partial transparency.

Translucent (trans,l'ū·sĕnt, -z-), *a.* 1596. [– L. *translucens, -ent-*, pr. pple. of *translucēre*; see TRANS-, LUCENT.] †**1.** That shines through; emitting penetrating rays –1791. **2.** Through which light passes; transparent 1607. **b.** Now, allowing the passage of light, yet diffusing it so as not to render bodies lying beyond clearly visible; semi-transparent 1784.

2. Sabrina fair..sitting Under the glassie, cool, t. wave MILT. **b.** A pane of thin t. horn COWPER. Hence **Trans,lu·cently** *adv.*

Translucid (trans,l'ū·sid), *a.* 1626. [– L. *translucidus* translucent; see TRANS-, LUCID.] = prec. 2, 2 b.

Translunary (trans,l'ū·nări, -z-), *a.* 1627. [f. TRANS- 3 after *sublunary.*] Lying beyond or above the moon: the opposite of *sublunary*; chiefly *fig.*, etherial, insubstantial, visionary.

Neat Marlow bathed in the Thespian springs Had in him those braue t. things DRAYTON.

Trans,ma·ke, *v.* 1844. [f. TRANS- 2 + MAKE *v.*, rendering Gr. μεταποιεῖν.] *trans.* To make into something different.

Transmarine (trans,mărī·n, -z-), *a.* 1583. [– L. *transmarinus*; see TRANS-, MARINE. Cf. (O)Fr. *transmarin.*] **1.** Born, existing, situated, or found on the other side of the sea; over-sea. **2.** Crossing or extending across the sea 1860.

1. An aliaunt, or a t. straunger 1583. The King's other T. Dominions 1700. **2.** Long t. migrations 1860.

Transmeridional (trans,mĕri·diŏnăl), *a.* 1883. [f. TRANS- 3 + MERIDIONAL 4.] Crossing or traversing the meridian lines; running east and west.

Transmew, transmue (trans,miū·), *v.* *Obs.* or *arch.* late ME. [– (O)Fr. *transmuer* – L. *transmutare*; see TRANSMUTE.] = TRANSMUTE 1.

Transmigrant (tra·ns,migrănt, -z-), *a.* and *sb.* 1622. [– L. *transmigrans, -ant-*, pr. pple. of *transmigrare*; see next, -ANT.] **A.** *adj.* That transmigrates (*rare*) 1654. **B.** *sb.* †**1.** *orig.* One who leaves his own land and dwells in another. BACON. **2.** A person passing through a country or place on his way from the country from which he is an emigrant to that in which he will be an immigrant 1894.

Transmigrate (tra·ns,məigrē'ɪt, -migrē'ɪt, -z-), *v.* late ME. [– *transmigrat-*, pa. ppl. stem of L. *transmigrare*; see TRANS-, MIGRATE *v.*] **1.** *intr.* To remove or pass from one place to another; *esp.* of persons, or a tribe; to migrate 1611. **b.** *trans.* in causal sense: To transfer. late ME. **2.** *intr. spec.* Of the soul: To pass after death into another body 1606. **b.** *trans.* To cause to pass 1559.

2. I think my soul would transmigrat into some tree, when she bids this body farewell 1645. Hence **Tra·nsmigrator,** one who or that which transmigrates.

Transmigration (trans,məigrē'ɪ·ʃən, -mi-, -z-). ME. [– eccl. L. *transmigratio, -ōn-* (in Vulg., 1 Esd. 6:16, the Babylonian Captivity), f. L. *transmigrare*; see TRANS-, MIGRATION.] †**1.** The removal of the Jews into captivity at Babylon; sometimes used for the Captivity –1609. **2.** Passage or removal from one place to another, esp. from one country to another. late ME. †**3.** Transition from one state or condition to another; *esp.* passage from this life, by death; also *absol.* death –1675. Also, loosely, transformation –1643. **4.** *spec.* Passage of the soul at death into another body; metempsychosis 1594.

4. Imagining as did Pythagoras, the t. of mens soules into other creatures 1634.

Transmigratory (trans,məi·grătəri, -z-), *a.* 1816. [f. TRANSMIGRATE + -ORY².] Having the quality of transmigrating; of or pertaining to transmigration.

Transmissible (trans,mi·sĭb'l, -z-), *a.* 1644. [f. TRANSMIT, after *admit/admissible*, etc., perh. after Fr. *transmissible* (XVI).] Capable of being transmitted. Hence **Trans,missibi·lity,** t. quality.

Transmission (trans,mi·ʃən, -z-). 1611. [– L. *transmissio, -ōn-*; see TRANS-, MISSION. Cf. (O)Fr. *transmission.*] The action of transmitting or fact of being transmitted; conveyance from one person or place to another; transference. **b.** *Physics.* Conveyance or passage through a medium, as of light, heat, sound, etc. 1704. **c.** *Biol.* The transmitting of the peculiar nature, or of some character, of an organism to its descendants 1871. **d.** *Mech.* Transference of motive force from one place to another; *concr.* a device for effecting this 1906.

Alphabetical writing made..the t. of events more easy and certain JOHNSON. **b.** *spec.* in *Wireless.*

Transmissive (trans,mi·siv, -z-), *a.* 1649. [f. TRANSMIT, after *permit/permissive*, etc.] **1.** Having the quality or action of transmitting. **2.** Having the quality of being transmitted 1700.

2. The Sire [may] inculcate to his Son T. Lessons of the King's Renown PRIOR.

Transmit (trans,mi·t, -z-), *v.* late ME. [– L. *transmittere*, f. *trans* TRANS- + *mittere* send.] **1.** *trans.* To cause (a thing) to pass, go, or be conveyed to another person, place, or thing; to send across an intervening space; to convey, transfer. **2.** *fig.* To convey or communicate (usu. something immaterial) *to* another or others; to pass on, esp. by inheritance or heredity; to hand down 1629. **3.** *Physics* and *Mech.* To cause (light, heat, sound, etc.) to pass through a medium; also, of a medium, to allow (light, etc.) to pass through; to conduct. Also, to convey (force or movement) from one part of a body, or of mechanism, to another. 1664.

1. Hasten in my rents and debts, and t. them with all possible speed PENN. **2.** His Apostles.. transmitted the same Spirit by Imposition of hands HOBBES. **3.** *spec.* in *Wireless.* Hence **Trans,mi·ttable, -ible** *a.* (*rare*) transmissible.

Transmittal (trans,mi·tăl). *rare.* 1724. [f. prec. + -AL¹ 2.] The action of transmitting; transmission.

Transmitter (trans,mi·təɹ, -z-). 1727. [f. as prec. + -ER¹.] One who or that which transmits. **b.** *spec.* That part of a telegraphic or telephonic apparatus by means of which messages are transmitted or dispatched; a transmitting instrument; opp. to RECEIVER 6. 1876.

b. Also, the transmitting apparatus used in wireless telegraphy 1898.

Transmogrify (trans,mǫ·grifəi, -z-), *v.* Chiefly *joc.* 1656. [Of obscure origin; if the orig. form was, as has been suggested, *transmigrafy*, this may have been a vulgar or uneducated formation in *-fy* from TRANSMIGRATE *v.*; cf. TRANSMIGRATION 3. App. it was orig. *persons* that were 'transmografied' or metamorphosed.] *trans.* To alter or change in form or appearance; to transform (utterly, grotesquely, or strangely). Hence **Transmo:grifica·tion,** (strange or grotesque) transformation.

Transmontane (trans,mǫ·ntē'ɪn, -mǫntē'ɪ·n), *a.* 1727. [– L. *transmontanus*; see TRAMONTANE.] **1.** = TRAMONTANE A. 1. **b.** In ref. to mountains other than the Alps, e.g. the Grampians in Scotland, the Rocky Mountains in N. Africa 1884.

Transmundane (trans,mʊ·ndē'ɪn), *a.* 1777. [f. TRANS- 3 + L. *mundus* world. Cf. MUNDANE.] That is or lies beyond the world.

Transmutable (trans,miū·tăb'l, -z-), *a.* 1460. [– med.L. *transmutabilis* (Albertus Magnus), f. L. *transmutare* TRANSMUTE; see -ABLE.] Capable of being transmuted or changed into something else. †**b.** Liable to change, mutable –1509. Hence **Transmutabi·lity,** t. quality. **Transmu·tably** *adv.*

Transmutation (trans,miutē'ɪ·ʃən, -z-). late ME. [– (O)Fr. *transmutation* or late L. *transmutatio, -ōn-*, f. L. *transmutare*; see TRANSMUTE, -ATION.] **1.** Change of condition; mutation. *Obs.* or *arch.* **2.** Change of one thing into another; alteration, transformation. Also with *a* and *pl.* an instance of this. late ME. **3.** *spec.* **a.** *Alch.* The (supposed or alleged) conversion of one element or substance into another, esp. of a baser metal into gold or silver 1478. **b.** *Law.* Transfer: usu. *t. of possession*, transfer or change of ownership 1488. **c.** *Biol.* Conversion or transformation of one species into another; *spec.* applied to the form of evolution or development propounded by Lamarck (1815–1822) 1626. †**d.** *Math.* = TRANSFORMATION 3 c –1743.

2. The supposed change of Worms into Flies is no real t. 1692. Hence **Trans,muta·tionist,** one who believes in or advocates a theory of t., e.g. in sense 3 c.

Transmutative (trans,miū·tătiv, -z-), *a.* 1611. [– med.L. *transmutativus* (Albertus Magnus), f. L. *transmutare*; see next, -ATIVE.] Having the quality of transmuting; tending to transmute.

Transmute (trans,miū·t, -z-), *v.* late ME. [– L. *transmutare*, f. *trans* TRANS- + *mutare* change. Replaced TRANSMEW.] **1.** *trans.* To alter or change in nature, properties, appearance, or form; to transform, convert, turn. **b.** *Alch.* To change (one substance) into another, esp. a baser metal into gold or silver. Also *absol.* †**2.** To remove from one place to another (*rare*) –1817.

1. To t. its energy..into vibratory motion TYNDALL. **2.** I was transmuted to Dublin, to be.. lodged in Kilmainham MAR. EDGEWORTH. Hence **Transmu·ter.**

Trans,na·ture, *v.* Now *rare.* 1567. [f. TRANS- 2 + NATURE *sb.*] *trans.* To change the nature of.

Trans,no·rmal, *a.* 1860. [f. TRANS- 4 + NORMAL *a.*] Beyond or above the normal.

Trans-oceanic (tranz,ōᵘʃi,æ·nik, -s-), *a.* 1827. [f. TRANS- + OCEANIC.] **1.** Existing or situated beyond the ocean; *transf.* pertaining to a region beyond the ocean. **2.** Passing or extending across the ocean 1868.

1. A t. world 1899.

Transom (træ·nsəm). ME. [Early forms *traversayn, transyn, -ing* (Sandahl XIII–XV) – (O)Fr. *traversin* in same sense, f. *traverse* TRAVERSE *sb.*] **1.** In building, etc.: A cross-beam or cross-piece, esp. one spanning an opening to carry a superstructure; a lintel 1487. **b.** A beam resting across a saw-pit to support the log. *dial.* 1885. **2.** A horizontal bar of wood or stone across a mullioned window 1502. **b.** Short for *t. window*: A window divided by a transom; also, a small window above the lintel of a door. *U.S. colloq.* 1844. **3.** *techn.* †**a.** The vane of a cross-staff –1696. †**b.** The transverse member in a cross –1864. **c.** A cross-piece connecting the cheeks of a gun-carriage 1688. **d.** *pl.* On a railway: Cross-timbers laid between (or, formerly, beneath) longitudinal sleepers 1838. **e.** The seat of a throne; also, a couch or seat built at the side of a cabin or state-room on board ship 1883. **4.** *Shipbuilding.* †A cross-beam in the frame of a ship; *spec.* each of several transverse beams bolted to the stern-post, which support the ends of the decks and determine the breadth of the stern at the buttocks 1545.

attrib. and *Comb.*: **t.-bar,** the cross-bar over a door having a fan-light above it (*U.S.*); **-knee** (*Shipbuilding*), each of the curved timbers or angle-irons by which the transoms are fastened to the stern-timbers; **-window** = 2 b. Hence **Tra·nsomed** (-səmd) *a.* divided by or having a t. or transoms.

Tra:ns-Paci·fic, *a.* 1891. [TRANS- 7, 8.] **a.** Across or crossing the Pacific Ocean. **b.** On the other side of the Pacific.

Transpadane (tra·ns,pădē'ɪn), *a.* (*sb.*) 1617. [– L. *transpadanus*, f. *trans-* TRANS- + *padanus* of the Po (*Padus*); see -ANE.] That is beyond the river Po (from Rome); opp. to *cispadane.* **B.** *sb.* One living north of the Po.

Transparence (trans,pē°·rĕns). *rare.* 1594. [f. as next; see -ENCE. Cf. (O)Fr. *transparence.*] = next 1.

Transparency (trans,pē°·rĕnsi, -pæ·rĕnsi). 1591. [– med.L. *transparentia*, f. *transparent-*; see next, -Y³, -ENCY.] **1.** The quality or condition of being transparent; diaphaneity, pellucidity 1615. **2.** That which is transparent 1591. **b.** *spec.* A picture, print, inscription, or device on some translucent substance, made visible by means of a light behind 1807. **c.** A photograph or picture on glass or other transparent substance, intended to be seen by transmitted light 1874. **3.** A burlesque translation of the German title of address *Durchlaucht* 1844.

Transparent (trans,pē°·rĕnt, -pæ·rĕnt), *a.* (*sb.*) late ME. [– (O)Fr. *transparent* – med.L. *transparens, -ent-*, pr. pple. of *transparēre* shine through, f. *trans* TRANS- + *parēre* APPEAR.] **1.** Having the property of transmitting light, so as to render bodies lying beyond completely visible; that can be seen through. †**b.** Penetrating, as light –1593. †**c.** Admitting the passage of light through interstices (*rare*) –1693. **2.** *fig.* **a.** Open, candid, ingenuous 1590. **b.** Easily seen through, recognized, or detected; manifest, obvious 1592.

1. The Firmament, expanse of liquid, pure, T., Elemental Air MILT. **b.** Like to the glorious Sunnes transparant Beames SHAKS. **2. a.** An ingenuous, t. life HARDY. **b.** A t. fallacy 1638. The t. sincerity of his purpose 1879. Hence **Trans,pa·rent-ly** *adv.*, **-ness** (*rare*).

†**Trans,pa·ss,** *v. rare.* 1592. [– Fr. †*transpasser* or med.L. *transpassare*; see TRESPASS *v.*] **1.** *intr.* To pass away, depart, die. DANIEL. **2.** To pass across or through; also *trans.* to pass beyond (a boundary or limit) –1646.

Transpeciate (tran,spī·ʃi,eⁱt), *v.* Now *rare.* 1643. [f. TRANS- + L. *species* look, form, kind + -ATE³.] *trans.* To change into a different form or species; to transform.

Transpicuous (tran,spi·kiu,əs), *a.* 1638. [f. mod.L. *transpicuus* (cf. PERSPICUOUS) + -OUS. In sense b, blending of TRANSPARENT and PERSPICUOUS.] That can be seen through; pervious to vision. **b.** *fig.* Of language, etc.: Plain, clear in meaning; also *gen.* easily detected, manifest 1877.

Transpierce (trans,pīᵊ·ɹs), *v.* 1594. [f. TRANS- + PIERCE, after (O)Fr. *transpercer.*] **1.** *trans.* To pierce through from side to side (with the agent or the instrument as subject). Also *transf.* and *fig.* **2.** To pass through, to penetrate 1604.

Transpirable (tran,spəiᵊ·răb'l), *a.* 1578. [– Fr. *transpirable* (Paré), f. *transpirer*; see TRANSPIRE, -ABLE.] Admitting of transpiration; capable of being breathed through.

Transpiration (tran,spirēⁱ·ʃən). 1551. [– Fr. *transpiration* (Paré), f. *transpirer*; see next, -ATION, and cf. prec.] The action or process of transpiring. **1.** Exhalation through the skin or surface of the body; formerly, also, evaporation. Also *concr.* matter transpired. 1562. **2.** *Bot.* The exhalation of watery vapour from the surface of the leaves and other parts of plants, in connection with the passage of water or sap through the tissues 1551. **3.** *Physics.* The passage of a gas or liquid under pressure through a capillary tube or porous substance 1867. **4.** The action or fact of something transpiring or becoming indirectly known (*rare*) 1802.

Transpire (tran,spəiᵊ·ɹ), *v.* 1597. [– Fr. *transpirer* (Paré) or med.L. *transpirare*, f. L. *trans-* TRANS- + *spirare* breathe.] **1.** *trans.* To emit or cause to pass in the state of vapour through the walls or surface of a body; also, to exhale (an odour); to breathe forth (vapour or fire). **b.** To cause (a gas or liquid) to pass through the pores or walls of a vessel 1864. **2.** *intr.* Of a body: †To emit vapour or perfume; of the animal body (or a person): to give off moisture through the skin (*obs.* exc. as tr. Fr. *transpirer*); now only of plants: to give off watery vapour from the surface of leaves, etc. 1648. **3.** Of a volatile substance: To pass out as vapour through pores, to exhale; of a liquid: to escape by evaporation 1643. **4.** *fig.* 'To escape from secrecy to notice' (J.); to 'leak out' 1741. ¶**b.** Misused for: To occur, happen. *orig. U.S.* 1804.

4. Yesterday's quarrel may t. 1741. **b.** An event..which we believe transpired eighteen hundred years ago 1841.

Transplace (trans,plēⁱ·s), *v. rare.* 1615. [f. TRANS- + PLACE *v.*] *trans.* To change the place of, transpose; to oust from its position in favour of something else.

Transplant (trɑ·ns,plɑnt), *sb.* 1756. [f. next.] That which is transplanted; *spec.* in forestry, a seedling transplanted once or several times.

Transplant (trans,plɑ·nt), *v.* 1440. [– late L. *transplantare*; see TRANS-, PLANT *v.* Cf. Fr. *transplanter* (XVI).] **1.** *trans.* To remove (a plant) from one place or soil and plant it in another. **2.** To remove from one place to another; to transport; *esp.* to bring (people, a colony, etc.) from one country to settle in another 1555. **3.** *Surg.* To transfer (an organ or portion of tissue) from one part of the body, or from one person or animal, to another 1786. **4.** *intr.* (for *pass.*) To bear transplanting 1796.

2. The policy of transplanting nations..was adopted, as a regular part of Assyrian, Babylonian, and Persian policy PUSEY. Hence **Transpla·nter,** one who transplants; an implement or contrivance for transplanting.

Transplantation (trans,plantēⁱ·ʃən). 1601. [f. prec. + -ATION. Cf. Fr. *transplantation* (XVI), and med. and mod.L. *transplantatio.*] **1.** The action of transplanting, in senses of the verb. **2.** *Surg.* The operation of transferring an organ or a portion of tissue from one part of the body, or from one person or animal, to another 1813. **3.** That which has been transplanted; a transplanted company or body. *rare.* 1641.

1. The T. of the Plague from Turkey to Holland 1720.

Tran,sple·ndent, *a. rare.* 1541. [f. TRANS- + SPLENDENT; cf. *resplendent.*] Brilliantly translucent; resplendent in the highest degree. Hence **Tran,sple·ndently** *adv.*

Transpontine (trans,pǫ·ntəin), *a.* 1844. [f. TRANS- 3 + L. *pons, pont-* bridge + -INE¹.] That is across or over a bridge; *spec.* on the other side of the bridges in London, i.e. south of the Thames; *transf.* (from the style of drama in vogue in the 19th c. at the 'Surreyside' theatres), melodramatic, sensational.

Transport (trɑ·ns,poɹt), *sb.* 1456. [f. next, or – (O)Fr. *transport* (cf. med.L. *transportus* transferment).] **1.** The action of transporting; conveyance 1611. †**b.** Transfer or conveyance of property –1682. **2.** The state of being 'carried out of oneself'; vehement emotion (now usu. of a pleasurable kind); rapture, ecstasy. Also with *a* and *pl.*, an instance of this. 1658. **3.** A means of transportation or conveyance; orig. a vessel employed in transporting soldiers, military stores, or convicts; later also, the horses, wagons, etc. employed in transporting the ammunition and supplies of an army 1694. †**4.** A person sentenced to transportation. –1851.

1. The Bill against t. of golde aud sylver 1621. 2. An unheard-of T. of Fury 1686. The letter was received with transports of joy BURNET. Moderate your transports DICKENS. 3. The Dee was crowded with men of war and transports 1855. *Comb.*: **t.-buoy,** a buoy used for the mooring and warping of vessels; **-rider** (*S. Afr.*), a goods carrier; **-ship, -vessel:** see 4.

Transport (trans,pōᵊ·ɹt), *v.* late ME. [– (O)Fr. *transporter* or L. *transportare*, f. *trans-* TRANS- + *portare* carry.] **1.** *trans.* To carry, convey, or remove from one person or place to another; to convey across 1483. **b.** *fig.* late ME. †**c.** To remove from this world to the next. SHAKS. **2.** *Sc. Ch.* To translate (a minister); to remove (the site of a church) 1637. **3.** To carry away or convey into banishment, as a criminal or a slave; to deport 1666. **4.** *fig.* To 'carry away' with the strength of some emotion; to cause to be beside oneself, to enrapture 1509.

1. Mules to t. his Provisions and Ammunition STEELE. **c.** *Meas. for M.* IV. iii. 72. **4.** Transported with celestiall desyre Of those faire formes SPENSER. Seest thou what rage Transports our adversarie? MILT. Hence **Transpo·rtable** *a.* capable of being transported; involving or liable to transportation. **Trans,portabi·lity, Trans,po·rtableness,** transportable quality. **Transpo·rtal, Transpo·rtance,** transport, conveyance. †**Transpo·rtment,** transportation (*rare*); vehement emotion, rapture, ecstasy.

Transportation (trans,poɹtēⁱ·ʃən). 1540. [f. prec. + -ATION. Cf. Fr. *transportation* (XVI).] **1.** The action or process of transporting; conveyance (of things or persons) from one place to another. (After 1660 gradually repl. by *transport.*) **b.** *Geol.* The movement of land-waste by rivers, ocean-currents, glaciers, winds, etc. 1830. **2.** *spec.* Removal or banishment, as of a criminal to a penal settlement; deportation 1669. **3.** *transf.* Means of transport or conveyance. *U.S.* 1861. **b.** A ticket or pass for travelling by a public conveyance. *U.S.* 1909. †**4.** Transport (of feeling), rapture, ecstasy –1690.

1. The t. of the troops was going..on PRESCOTT. 2. Were you sentenc'd to T.? GAY.

Transported (trans,pōᵊ·ɹtėd) *ppl. a.* 1600. [f. TRANSPORT *v.* + -ED¹.] **1.** Conveyed from one place to another 1693. **b.** Compulsorily carried to a distant country 1728. **2.** 'Carried away' by excitement or vehement emotion; excited beyond self-control; enraptured 1600. Hence **Transpo·rted-ly** *adv.*, **-ness.**

Transporter (trans,pōᵊ·ɹtəɹ). 1535. [f. as prec. + -ER¹.] **1.** One who transports. **2.** Any carrying apparatus; *esp.* a device for transporting coal from a quay or from one vessel to another 1893.

2. *T.-bridge*, a bridge over a navigable waterway, high enough not to interfere with navigation, carrying a suspended platform or car which travels from bank to bank and conveys the traffic.

Transposable (trans,pōᵘ·zăb'l), *a.* 1879. [f. TRANSPOSE *v.* + -ABLE.] Capable of being transposed; interchangeable.

Transposal (trans,pōᵘ·zăl). *rare.* 1695. [f. as prec. + -AL¹ 2.] Transposition.

Transpose (trans,pōᵘ·z), *v.* late ME. [– (O)Fr. *transposer*, f. *trans-* TRANS- + *poser* place, POSE.] †**1.** *trans.* To transform, transmute, convert –1605. †**2.** To change the purport, application, or use of; in bad sense, to corrupt, pervert, misapply –1644. **3.** To remove from one place or time to another; to transfer, shift (*lit.* and *fig.*; now *rare* exc. as in 4) 1510. **4.** To alter the order of (a set or series of things), or the position of (a thing) in a series; to interchange; *esp.* to alter the order of letters in a word or of words in a sentence 1538. **b.** *Algebra.* To transfer (a quantity) from one side of an equation to the other, with change of sign 1810. **5.** *Mus.* To alter the key of; to put into a different key 1609.

1. That which you are, my thoughts cannot t.; Angels are bright still, though the brightest fell SHAKS. Hence **Trans,po·ser,** one who transposes.

Transposition (trans,pŏzi·ʃən). 1538. [– Fr. *transposition* or late L. *transpositio, -ōn-*; see TRANS-, POSITION.] **1.** *gen.* Removal from one position to another; transference. **2.** Alteration of order, or interchange of position, esp. of letters in a word, or words in a sentence; the result of such action; a word or sentence transposed 1582. **3.** *Mus.* **a.** Alteration of key; also *transf.* a transposed piece. †**b.** Inversion of parts in counterpoint. 1609. **4.** *Algebra.* Transference of a quantity from one side of an equation (or one member of a proportion) to the other 1664. **5.** *Anat.* Abnormal position of the organs of the body; heterotaxy 1857.

2. For in an Anagram Iskariott is, By letters t., Traitor kis 1630. So **Trans,po·sitive** *a.* characterized by or given to t.

Transprose (trans,prōᵘ·z), *v.* 1671. [f. TRANS- 2 + PROSE *sb.*] *trans.* To turn into prose; to render in prose. (Chiefly *joc.*)

Transrhenane (transrī·neⁱn), *a.* 1727. [– L. *transrhenanus*, f. *trans* across + *Rhenus* the Rhine; see -ANE.] That is across or beyond the Rhine; hence, German as opp. to Roman or to French.

Trans-shape (trans,ʃēⁱ·p), †**transha·pe,** *v.* Now *rare. arch.* 1575. [f. TRANS- + SHAPE *v.*] *trans.* To alter the shape or form of; to transform.

†**Trans-shi·ft,** *v.* [TRANS- 2.] *trans.* and *intr.* To shift across or away. HERRICK.

Trans-subje·ctive, *a.* 1887. [TRANS- 4.] That transcends or is beyond subjective or individual experience as such.

Transubstantial (tran,sŏbstæ·nʃăl), *a.* 1567. [– med.L. *transubstantialis* (XV), f. *trans* TRANS- + Chr. L. *substantialis* SUBSTANTIAL.] **a.** Changed or changeable from one substance into another; of or pertaining to transubstantiation. **b.** Made of something beyond substance; non-material, incorporeal.

Transubstantiate (tran,sŏbstæ·nʃi,eⁱt), *v.* 1533. [–*transubstantiat-*, pa. ppl. stem of med. L. *transubstantiare*, f. *trans* TRANS- + *substantia* SUBSTANCE; see -ATE³. Cf. (O)Fr. *transubstantier.*] *trans.* To change from one substance into another; to transform, transmute. Also *absol.* 1584. **b.** *spec.* in *Theol.*: see next 2. 1533.

The Philosophers stone..which would..t. other Metals into..Gold and Silver 1670. So **Tran,substa·ntiate** *ppl. a.* transubstantiated 1450.

Transubstantiation (trɑ·n,sŏbstænʃi,ēⁱ·ʃən, -stænsi,ēⁱ·ʃən). late ME. [– med.L. *tran(s)substantiatio, -ōn-* (XI), f. as prec.; see -ION. Cf. (O)Fr. *transubstantiation.*] **1.** The changing of one substance into another. **2.** The conversion in the Eucharist of the whole substance of the bread into the body and of the wine into the blood of Christ, only the appearances (and other 'accidents') of bread and wine remaining: according to the doctrine of the Roman Catholic Church 1533.

Transudation (trɑnˌsiudēⁱ·ʃən). 1612. [– Fr. *transsudation*, f. *transsuder*; see TRANSUDE, -ATION.] The action or process of transuding. **b.** *concr.* Something which is transuded 1650.

Transˌsu·datory, *a.* 1752. [f. †*transudate* vb. (Boyle) + -ORY².] Having the quality of transuding; characterized by transudation.

Transude (trɑnˌsiū·d), *v.* 1664. [– Fr. *transsuder* (XVII), refash. of OFr. *tressuer* :– Gallo-Rom. **transsudare*, f. *trans* TRANS- + L. *sudare* sweat.] **a.** *intr.* To ooze through or out like sweat; to exude through pores (in the human body or anything permeable). **b.** *trans.* To ooze through (something) like sweat 1781. **c.** To cause (something) to ooze through 1861.

Transume (trɑnˌsiū·m), *v.* *Obs.* exc. *Hist.* 1482. [– L. *tran(s)sumere*, in med.L. sense 'transcribe, copy'; f. L. *trans* TRANS- + *sumere* take, seize.] **1.** *trans.* To make an official copy of a (legal) document. †**2.** To take over; to transfer, transport –1656. †**3.** To transmute (*into* something else) –1652.

Transumpt (trɑnˌsɒ·mᵖt). 1480. [– med.L. *tran(s)sumptum*, subst. use of n. pa. pple. of *tran(s)sumere*; see prec. Cf. Fr. †*transumpt* (XV).] A copy, transcript; *spec.* a copy of a record, deed, or other legal document; an exemplification.

†**Tranˌsu·mption.** late ME. [In sense 3 – L. *transumptio*, *-ōn-* (Quintilian, tr. Gr. μετάληψις); in sense 1 in med.L. sense 'copying'; f. *transumpt-*, pa. ppl. stem of *transumere*; see prec., -ION. Cf. Fr. †*transumption* (XV).] **1.** Transcription, copying; a passage copied from any author; a quotation –1716. **2.** Transference or translation to another part or place –1684. **3.** *Rhet.* Transfer of terms; metaphor –1677.

Tranˌsu·mptive, *a.* *Obs.* or *arch.* 1597.; [– *transumptivus* (Quintilian), f. as prec.; see -IVE.] Characterized by transumption metaphorical.

Transvaal (trɑ·nzvāl, -s-). [f. TRANS- 7 + *Vaal*, a tributary of the Orange River in S. Africa.] A former S. African republic, now a state of the Union of S. Africa, lying north of the Orange Free State, from which it is separated by the River Vaal.

Transvase (trɑnsvēⁱ·s), *v.* *rare.* 1839. [– (O)Fr. *transvaser*, f. *trans* TRANS- + L. *vas* vessel.] *trans.* To pour out of one vessel into another.

Transversal (trɑnzvə̄·ɹsăl, -s-), *a.* and *sb.* 1440. [– med.L. *transversalis*, f. L. *transversus*; see next, -AL¹ 1.] **A.** *adj.* **1.** = next A. 1. †**2.** *Genealogy.* Collateral –1594. **B.** *sb.* †**1.** Something transversal, a transverse line; *fig.* a deviation, digression (*rare*) –1620. **2.** *Geom.* A line intersecting two or more lines, or a system of lines 1881. **3.** *Roulette.* A bet placed at the end of any three numbers taking them horizontally 1895. Hence **Transve·rsally** *adv.*

Transverse (trɑnzvə̄·ɹs, trɑ·nzvəɹs, -s-), *a.* (*sb.*, *adv.*) 1596. [– L. *transversus*, pa. pple. of *transvertere* turn across; see TRANSVERT *v.* Cf. Fr. *transverse* (XVI).] **A.** *adj.* **1.** Lying across; situated or lying crosswise or athwart; *esp.* situated or extending across the length of something, *spec.* at right angles 1621. †**2.** Of kindred: Collateral, as between brothers, cousins-german, etc. (*rare*) –1660.

1. A kettle slung Between two poles upon a stick t. COWPER. **T. axis,** (*a*) an axis transverse to the main axis, as in a crystal; (*b*) *Geom.* the axis passing through the foci of a conic section (in an ellipse, the major axis); **t. muscle,** *Anat.* any one of various muscles extending across other parts; **t. process,** a lateral process of a vertebra; **t. suture,** the suture between the frontal and facial bones.

B. *sb.* [The adj. used *absol.*] **1.** Something that is transverse; e.g. the transverse axis of a conic section, a transverse muscle, etc. 1633. †**2.** *By t.* [L. *per transversum*], crosswise; athwart. SPENSER. **C.** *adv.* In a transverse direction or position; transversely, across, athwart. Now *rare* or *poet.* 1660.

These two proportioned ill drove me t. MILT. Hence **Transve·rsely** *adv.*

Transverse (trɑnsvə̄·ɹs, -z-), *v.*¹ Now *rare.* late ME. [– OFr. *transverser* (mod. *traverser*) – med.L. *transversare*, f. *transvers-*, pa. ppl. stem of L. *transvertere* TRANSVERT.] **1.** *trans.* To pass or lie athwart or across; to cross, traverse (*rare*). **2.** To turn upside down or backwards; to overturn, turn topsy-turvy. Now *rare* or *Obs.* 1520. **b.** To convert into something different 1687.

Transve·rse, *v.*² 1672. [f. TRANS- 2 + VERSE *sb.* (orig. as a pun on prec.).] *trans.* To turn into verse; to translate or render in verse. Hence **Transve·rsion²**, a turning into verse; *concr.* a metrical version of something.

Transversion¹ (trɑnsvə̄·ɹʃən, -z-). *rare.* 1656. [f. TRANSVERT *v.*, after *convert*/*conversion*, etc.] The action of turning across or athwart; intersection; a turning into something else; transposition.

†**Transve·rt,** *v.* late ME. [– L. *transvertere* turn across, f. *trans* TRANS- + *vertere* turn.] *trans.* To turn across or athwart; to turn *into* something else, transform, convert; to turn about, reverse, overturn –1660.

Tranter (trɑ·ntəɹ). Now *dial.* 1500. [app. syncopated from AFr. *traventer* (*a*1400) = AL. *traventarius* (1300), *travetarius* (1215), of unkn. origin.] In various local uses: chiefly, a man who does jobs with his horse and cart. Hence **Trant** *v.* to follow the occupation of a tranter 1597.

Trap (træp), *sb.*¹ [OE. *træppe* (in *coltetræppe* Christ's thorn), *treppe*, corresp. in form and sense to MDu. *trappe*, Flem. *trape*, med.L. *trappa*, OFr. *trape* (mod. *trappe*), Pr., Pg. *trapa*, Sp. *trampa*, but the mutual relations are obscure.] **1.** A contrivance set for catching game or noxious animals; a gin, snare, pitfall. **b.** *transf.* and *fig.* ME. **c.** Popularly applied to a police arrangement for the timing of motorists over a measured distance, in order to secure the conviction of such as exceed the legal speed-limit. Also *police-*, *speed-t.* 1906. **2.** A movable covering of a pit, or of an opening in a floor, designed to fall when stepped upon; hence applied to any similar door flush with the surface in a floor, ceiling, roof, the top of a cab, or the like ME. **3.** The pivoted wooden instrument with which the ball is thrown up in the game of TRAP-BALL; hence, the game itself 1591. **4.** A device for suddenly releasing or throwing into the air an object to be shot at, as a clay pigeon 1812. **5.** *colloq.* or *slang.* Deceitful practice; trickery; fraud 1681. **6.** *slang.* One whose business is to 'trap' or catch offenders; a thief-taker; a detective or policeman; a sheriff's officer 1705. **7.** *colloq.* A small carriage on springs; usu., a two-wheeled spring carriage, a gig 1806. **8.** A device for preventing the upward escape of noxious gases from a pipe, as a double curve in or U-shaped section of the pipe, in which water stands 1833. **b.** Applied to various contrivances for preventing the passage of steam, water, silt, etc. Also, a ventilation door in a mine. 1877. **9.** A recess in the butt of a musket or rifle in which accessories are carried 1844.

1. See also MAN-TRAP, MOUSE-TRAP, RAT-TRAP, etc. **b.** Let her lay traps for admiration 1765. **4. b.** In greyhound racing, a compartment in which a greyhound is placed and from which it is released at the start of a race 1928. **5.** *To understand t.*, to know one's own interest; *to be up to t.*, to be knowing or cunning.

attrib. and *Comb.*: **t.-bat,** a bat used in playing t. or t.-ball; also, the game itself; **-creel,** a basket used for catching lobsters, etc.; **-drummer,** one who plays a drum and other instruments at once; **-hole,** a hole closed by a t.-door; also (*pl.*) pits dug in the ground to serve as obstacles to an enemy, *trous-de-loup*; **-nest,** a nesting-box which a hen can get into but cannot leave until released; **-net,** a large net with a device for trapping fish; **-point,** on railways, a safety-point which prevents an unauthorized movement of a train or vehicle from a siding on to the main line by derailing it; **-shooting,** the sport of shooting clay pigeons, glass balls, etc., released from a spring t.; **-tree,** the jack-tree, *Artocarpus integrifolia*, which provides gum for bird-lime.

Trap, *sb.*² 1794. [– Swed. *trapp* (Bergman, 1766) so named from the stair-like appearance often presented by the rock, f. *trappa* stair.] *Min.* A dark-coloured igneous rock more or less columnar in structure: now extended to include all igneous rocks which are neither granitic nor of recent volcanic formation. Also *attrib.*, as *t.-rock*, *-shale*.

Trap, *v.*¹ [ME. *trappen* :– OE. **træppan* in *betræppan*, f. *træp* TRAP *sb.*¹] **I.** *trans.* **1.** To catch in or as in a trap, entrap, ensnare. **2.** To furnish with traps; to set (a place) with a trap or traps 1841. **3.** To furnish (a drain, etc.) with a trap or traps 1862. **4.** Chiefly *Mech.* To stop and hold or retain by a trap or contrivance for the purpose; to separate or remove by a trap.

1. *fig.* With ambush'd arms I trapp'd the foe DRYDEN. **2.** The right of hunting and trapping the streams and lakes 1841.

II. *intr.* **1.** To practise catching wild animals in traps for their furs; also *gen.* to set traps for game 1807. **2.** To use, handle, or work a trap or traps 1842.

1. I should like to come and t. on these waters all winter 1835.

Trap, *v.*² ME. [f. †*trap* (XIV), altered form of (O)Fr. *drap* cloth, covering (see DRAPE *sb.*); cf. TRAPPER¹.] *trans.* To adorn (a horse, mule, etc.) with trappings; to caparison.

fig. A Prophecy so trapped with the ornaments of speech 1641.

Trap-ball (træ·pˌbǭl). 1658. [f. TRAP *sb.*¹ + BALL *sb.*¹] A game in which a ball, placed upon one end (slightly hollowed) of a trap (TRAP *sb.*¹ 3), is thrown into the air by the batsman striking the other end with his bat, with which he then hits the ball away.

Trap-cut. 1850. [app. f. Du. *trap* step, stair + CUT *sb.*] A mode of cutting gems with the facets in parallel planes round the centre of the stone; also *step-cut*, *degree-cut*.

Trap-door (træ·pˌdōᵊ·ɹ, træ·pˌdōᵊɹ). late ME. [TRAP *sb.*¹] A door, either sliding or moving on hinges, and flush with the surface, in a floor, roof, or ceiling, or in the stage of a theatre. **b.** *Mining.* A door in a level for directing the ventilating current; a weather-door 1851. **c.** An L-shaped tear in cloth, etc.

Comb.: **t. spider,** one of a group of large spiders, which make a nest in the shape of a tube with a hinged lid which opens and shuts like a t.

Trapes, traipse (trēⁱps), *sb.* 1676. [Goes with next.] **1.** An opprobrious name for a slovenly woman or girl; 'a dangling slattern'. *dial.* **2.** An act or course of 'trapesing'; a tiresome or disagreeable tramp. *colloq.* 1862.

Trapes, traipse (trēⁱps), *v.* *colloq.* and *dial.* 1593. [Origin unkn.; related to obs. *trape* vb. In many dialects a disyllable.] **1.** *intr.* To walk in a trailing or untidy way; to walk with the dress trailing or bedraggled; to walk about aimlessly or needlessly (usu. said of a woman or child.) **2.** *trans.* To walk or tramp over; to tread, tramp (the fields, streets, etc.) 1885.

Trapeze (trăpī·z). 1861. [– Fr. *trapèze*, – late L. TRAPEZIUM.] A gymnastic apparatus, consisting of a horizontal cross-bar suspended by two ropes in the manner of a swing.

Trapeziform (trăpī·zifǭɹm), *a.* 1776. [f. next + -FORM.] Having the form of a trapezium.

Trapezium (trăpī·ziǒm). *Pl.* **-ia, -iums.** 1570. [– late L. *trapezium* – Gr. τραπέζιον, f. τράπεζα table.] **1.** *Geom.* Any four-sided plane rectilineal figure that is not a parallelogram; any irregular quadrilateral. (The Euclidean sense.) **b.** *spec.* A quadrilateral having only one pair of its opposite sides parallel 1570. **c.** = TRAPEZOID A. 1 a. Now *U.S.* 1795. **2.** *Anat.* **a.** A bone of the wrist, articulating with the metacarpal bone of the thumb (so called from its shape); also, the corresponding bone in the lower animals. Also *t. bone.* 1840. **b.** (in full, *t. cerebri.*) A band of nerve-fibres in the *pons Varolii* of the brain 1890. **3.** = TRAPEZE (*rare*) 1856.

‖**Trapezius** (trăpī·ziǒs). *Pl.* **-ii** (-iˌəi). 1704. [mod.L. *trapezius* (*musculus*), f. *trapezium*; see prec.] *Anat.* Each of a pair of large flat triangular muscles (together forming the figure of a trapezium) extending over the back of the neck and adjacent parts. Also *t. muscle*.

Trapezohedron (træ:pĭzohī·drǫn, -he·d-rǫn). *Pl.* **-hedra, -hedrons.** 1816. [f. *trapezo-*, as comb. form of TRAPEZIUM, after *tetrahedron*, etc.] *Geom.* and *Cryst.* A solid figure whose faces are trapeziums or trapezoids; as the icositetrahedron or deltohedron, with 24 faces, etc. Hence **Tra:pezohe·dral** *a.* pertaining to or of the form of a t.

Trapezoid (træ·pĭzoid, trăpī·zoˌid), *sb.* and *a.* 1706. [– mod.L. *trapezoides* – late Gr. τραπεζοειδής, f. τράπεζα table; see -OID. Cf. Fr. *trapézoïde* (XVII).] **A.** *sb.* **1.** *Geom.* **a.** A quadrilateral figure no two of whose sides are parallel. **b.** = TRAPEZIUM 1 b. *U.S.* 1795. **2.** *Anat.* A bone of the wrist, the second of the distal row of the carpus: so called from its shape 1831. **B.** *adj.* = next 1819. **b.** Anat. *T. body* = TRAPEZIUM 2 b. *T. bone* = A. 2. *T. ligament*, the CORACO-CLAVICULAR ligament. 1890.

Trapezoidal (træpĭzoi·dăl), *a.* 1796. [f. prec. + -AL[1] 1.] Having the form of a trapezoid; irregularly quadrilateral. **b.** Having trapezoidal faces; trapezohedral 1796.

Trapfall (træ·pfǭl). 1596. [f. TRAP *sb.*[1] + FALL *sb.*[2] Cf. PITFALL.] A trap consisting of a trap-door or covering over a pit or cellar arranged so as to give way beneath the feet.

‖**Trapiche** (trapi·tʃe). 1648. [Amer. Sp.] A mill for grinding sugar-cane or ore.

Trappean (træ·piăn), *a.* 1813. [f. TRAP *sb.*[2] + -EAN.] *Min.* Pertaining to, of the nature of, or consisting of trap-rock.

Tra·pper[1]. *Obs.* exc. *Hist.* [ME. *trappo(u)r* (XIV) – AFr. **trapour* (cf. AL. *trappatura*), var. of OFr. *drapure*, f. *drap* cloth (see DRAPE *sb.*).] A covering put over a beast of burden, made of metal or leather for defence or of cloth for shelter and adornment.

Trapper[2] (træ·pəɹ). 1768. [f. TRAP *v.*[1] and *sb.*[1] + -ER[1].] **1.** One who sets traps or snares; *spec.* one engaged in trapping wild animals for their furs. **2.** A boy stationed to open and shut a trap door for the passage of trams in a coal-mine 1815. **3.** One who manages a trap in trap-shooting 1892.

Trapping (træ·piŋ), *vbl. sb.* Chiefly in pl. **trappings.** late ME. [f. base of synon. *trappo(u)r* TRAPPER[1], with substitution of -ING[1].] A cloth or covering spread over the harness or saddle of a horse or other beast of burden; a caparison. **b.** *transf.* 'Ornaments; dress; embellishments; external, superficial, and trifling decoration' (J.) 1596.

The embroidered trappings of the elephants 1817. **b.** These, but the Trappings, and the Suites of woe SHAKS. He needs no Trappings of fictitious Fame DRYDEN.

Trappist (træ·pist) *sb.* (*a.*) 1814. [– Fr. *trappiste*, from *La Trappe*, name of the convent.] A monk of the branch of the Cistercian order observing the reformed rule established in 1664 by De Rancé, abbot of La Trappe, in Normandy. **b.** *attrib.* or as *adj.* Of or pertaining to this branch of the Cistercian order 1836.

Trappose (træ·pōᵘs), *a.* 1796. [f. TRAP *sb.*[2] + -OSE[1].] *Min.* Of, pertaining to, or of the nature of trap or trap-rock; trappean.

Traps (træps), *sb. pl. colloq.* 1813. [Of unc. origin; perh. contr. of TRAPPINGS.] Portable articles for dress, furniture, or use; personal effects; baggage; belongings.

Tra·pˌstick. 1591. [f. TRAP *sb.*[1] + STICK *sb.*] A stick used in the game of trap or trap-ball.

Trash (træʃ), *sb.*[1] 1518. [Of unkn. origin.] **1.** That which is broken, snapped, or lopped off anything in preparing it for use; e.g. twigs, splinters, 'cuttings from a hedge, small wood from a copse', straw, rags; refuse 1555. **b.** Broken ice mixed with water 1856. **2.** *spec.* The refuse of sugar-canes after the juice has been expressed; cane-trash; also, the dried leaves and tops of the canes, stripped off while still growing, to allow them to ripen; field-trash 1707. **3.** Worthless stuff; dross; rubbish 1518. **b.** Worthless notions, talk, or writing; nonsense; 'rubbish', 'stuff' 1542. †**c.** Contemptuously applied to money or cash; 'dross'. *slang.* –1809. **4.** A worthless or disreputable person; now usu., such persons collectively 1604.

1. Who steales my purse, steales t. SHAKS. **b.** Those Theological Disputations..leven pure Doctrin with scholastical T. MILT. **4.** I do suspect this T. To be a party in this Iniurie SHAKS. *White t.*, the poor white population in the southern U.S. *Comb.*: **t.-ice** = sense 1 b.

Trash, *sb.*[2] Now *dial.* 1611. [Goes with next.] In full *t.-cord*: a cord used to check dogs in breaking or training them; a leash.

Trash (træʃ), *v.*[1] 1610. [Origin obsc.] †**1.** *trans.* To check (a hound) by a cord or leash; hence *gen.* to hold back, retard, encumber, hinder –1837. **2.** *West. U.S.* To efface 1859.

1. Who t'aduance, and who To t. for ouertopping SHAKS.

Trash, *v.*[2] *Obs.* exc. *dial.* 1607. [app. f. Norse; cf. Sw. *traska*, Norw. *traske* in the same sense.] **1.** *intr.* To walk or run with exertion and fatigue, esp. through mud or mire. **2.** *trans.* To fatigue (with walking, running, etc.); to wear out 1650.

Trash, *v.*[3] 1793. [f. TRASH *sb.*[1]] **1.** *trans.* To free from trash or refuse; *spec.* to strip the outer leaves from (growing sugar-canes) so that they may ripen more quickly. **2.** To treat as trash; hence, to discard as worthless 1909.

Trashy (træ·ʃi), *a.* 1620. [f. TRASH *sb.*[1] + -Y[1].] Of the nature of trash; rubbishy; worthless. Hence **Tra·shily** *adv.* **Tra·shiness.**

Trass (tras). 1796. [– Du. *trass*, G. *trass*; see TARRAS.] = TARRAS.

‖**Trattoria** (tratorī·a). 1832. [It.] In Italy, an eating-house and cook-shop.

Traulism (trǭ·liz'm). *rare.* Also in L. form **traulismus.** 1678. [– Gr. τραυλισμός, f. τραυλίζειν to lisp.] A stammering, stuttering.

‖**Trauma** (trǭ·mă). 1693. Pl. **traumata** (trǭ·mătă), also **traumas.** [– Gr. τραῦμα wound.] *Path.* A wound, or external bodily injury in general; also, the condition caused by this; traumatism. **b.** *Psychoanalysis.* A disturbing experience which affects the mind or nerves of a person so as to induce hysteria or 'psychic' conditions; a mental shock 1916.

Traumatic (trǫmæ·tik), *a.* 1656. [– late L. *traumaticus* – Gr. τραυματικός, f. τραῦμα, -ματ- wound; see -IC.] Of, pertaining to, or caused by a wound, injury, or shock.

Traumatism (trǭ·mătiz'm). 1857. [f. Gr. τραῦμα, -ματ- wound + -ISM.] *Path.* The morbid condition of the system due to a trauma.

Traumato- (trǭmăto), repr. Gr. τραυματο-, comb. f. τραῦμα wound, as in **Traumato·logy**, the scientific description of wounds.

Travail (træ·veⁱl), *sb.* ME. [– (O)Fr. *travail* painful effort, trouble, work, f. *travailler*; see next, and TRAVEL *sb.*] **1.** Bodily or mental labour or toil, esp. of a painful or oppressive nature; exertion; trouble; hardship; suffering. *arch.* †**2.** With *a* and *pl.* A work, a task; *pl.* labours –1724. †**3.** The outcome of toil or labour; a (finished) 'work'; *esp.* a literary work –1624. **4.** The labour and pain of child-birth. Now freq. *fig.* ME. **5.** Journeying, a journey. Now differentiated under the spelling TRAVEL, q.v.

1. Faint and sick with travaile and fear JER. TAYLOR. **4.** Phr. *In t.*: A woman, when shee is in trauaile, hath sorrow, because her houre is come *John* 16:21.

Travail (træ·veⁱl), *v.* ME. [– (O)Fr. *travailler* :– Rom. **trepaliare*, f. med.L. *trepalium* instrument of torture, presumably f. L. *tres* three + *palus* stake.] **1.** *trans.* To torment, distress, afflict, trouble; to weary, tire. *Obs.* or *arch.* †**b.** To put to work, cause to work; to exert, employ –1630. **2.** *intr.* (for *refl.*) To exert oneself, labour, toil, work hard. *arch.* ME. **3.** Of a woman: To suffer the pains of child-birth; to be in labour ME. †**4.** To journey, etc.: see TRAVEL *v.*

1. They were wery and sore traueyled by the waye which was longe CAXTON. **2.** Trauell not too much to be rich 1612. **3.** Flowres which only Dame Nature trauels with 1634.

Tra·vailous, *a.* *Obs.* or *arch.* ME. [– OFr. *travaillos, -eus* toilsome, f. *travail* TRAVAIL *sb.*; see -OUS.] Full of or characterized by 'travail' or hard labour; toilsome; wearisome.

Trave. *Obs.* exc. *dial.* late ME. [In sense 1 – OFr. *trave* beam. With sense 2 cf. Fr. *entrave* clog, restraint, etc.] **1.** A (timber or wooden) beam. **2.** A frame or enclosure of bars in which a restive horse is placed to be shod. late ME.

Travel (træ·vĕl, -v'l), *sb.* ME. [orig. the same word as TRAVAIL *sb.*, in a specialized sense and form, the latter due to shifting of stress.] †**1.** = TRAVAIL *sb.* **2.** The action of travelling or journeying. late ME. **b.** With *a* and *pl.* An act of travelling; a journey. Now only *pl.*, exc. *dial.* 1559. **c.** *pl.* (*ellipt.*) 'Account of occurrences and observations of a journey into foreign parts' (J.) 1706. **d.** *transf.* Passage of anything in its course or path, or over a distance 1742. **3.** A single movement of some part of mechanism, as a piston, etc.; also, the distance through which it moves 1841. **4.** Capacity or force of movement 1816.

2. The wayes are everywhere unsafe for travell 1650. **b.** His travels ended at his country seat DRYDEN.

Comb., as *travel-stained*, *-worn* adjs.

Travel (træ·vĕl, -v'l), *v.* ME. [orig. the same word as TRAVAIL *v.* Derivs., as *travelled*, *-er*, *-ing*, etc. are usu. spelt with *ll* in Great Britain, with single *l* in America.] †**1.** = TRAVAIL *v.* **2.** *intr.* To make a journey; to go from one place to another; to journey ME. **b.** To journey from place to place as a commercial traveller. Const. *in* a commodity. 1830. **c.** Of an animal: To walk or run; *spec.* of deer, to move on while browsing 1877. **3.** *transf.* To move, go; to pass from one point or place to another; *esp.* in mod. scientific use, to pass, be transmitted 1662. **b.** *fig.* of some action figured as movement 1600. **c.** Of a piece of mechanism: To move, or be capable of movement, along a fixed course 1815. **d.** *colloq.* To bear transportation 1852. **e.** To move on, esp. with speed. *colloq.* or *slang.* 1884. **4.** *trans.* (or with advb. accus.) To journey through (a country, district, space, etc.); to traverse (a road, etc.); to follow (a course or path) ME. **b.** To traverse, cover (a specified distance) 1660. **5.** To cause to journey, to drive or lead from one place to another 1598.

2. To preserue all that trauayle by lande or by water *Bk. Com. Prayer.* **b.** Mr. Bingle travelled in whisky 1906. **3.** Thy thunders t. over earth and seas COWPER. Phr. *To t. out of the record*: see RECORD *sb.* II. 1. **4.** The senior judge..who actually travels that circuit 1885. Phr. †*To t. the road*, to practise highway robbery. **b.** Their number is..greater than that of the miles you t. 1804. **5.** It would be advisable..not..to t. any stock at present 1891.

Travelled (træ·vĕld), *ppl. a.* Also (chiefly *U.S.*) **traveled.** late ME. [f. prec. + -ED[1].] **1.** That has travelled, esp. to distant countries; experienced in travel. Also with adv. as *far-t.* **2.** *Geol.* Of blocks, boulders, etc.: Transported to a distance from their original site, as by glacial action; erratic 1830. **3.** Of a road, etc.: Frequented by travellers 1882.

1. A well trauelled knight and well knowen LD. BERNERS.

Traveller (træ·vĕləɹ). Also (chiefly *U.S.*) **traveler.** late ME. [f. TRAVEL *v.*; in XIV *travaillour*, *travellour*, + -ER[2] 3; from XVI *traveller*, + -ER[1].] One who or that which travels. **1.** One who is travelling from place to place, or along a road or path; one who is on a journey; a wayfarer; a passenger. **b.** = TRAMP *sb.*[1] 4. Now *dial.* 1763. **2.** *spec.* One who travels abroad; one who journeys or has journeyed through foreign countries or strange places 1556. **3.** *spec.* (in full, *commercial t.*): An agent employed by a commercial firm to travel from place to place showing samples of goods and soliciting custom 1800. **4. a.** A horse, a vehicle, etc., that travels or goes along (fast, well, etc.).

b. Applied to birds making a long flight, or migrating. 1660. **5.** A piece of mechanism constructed to 'travel', run, or slide along a support; as a travelling crane, etc. 1842. **b.** *Naut.* An iron ring or thimble running freely on a rope, rod, or spar 1762. **c.** In ring-spinning, a metal ring or loop used to guide the yarn in winding it on the spindle 1853. **d.** *Angling.* A tackle which permits the bait to travel or move down the swim 1867.

Comb. with *traveller's*: **traveller's joy,** the wild shrub *Clematis vitalba*, from its trailing over and adorning hedges by the wayside; **traveller's palm, tree,** names for certain trees which yield water or sap sought after by travellers to allay thirst, as *Ravenala madagascariensis*, a palm-like tree of Madagascar whose hollow leaf-sheaths contain a store of water.

Tra·velling, *vbl. sb.* Also (chiefly *U.S.*) **traveling.** late ME. [f. TRAVEL *v.* + -ING[1].] The action of TRAVEL *v.*

attrib., as *t. clock, expenses*; **t.-carriage,** a strong carriage used for t. before railways were introduced; **t. fellowship, scholarship,** one given to enable the holder to travel for purposes of study or research.

Travelogue (træ·vělǫg). 1903. [irreg. f. TRAVEL *sb.* + *-logue* of *monologue, dialogue.*] A lecture or talk on travel, often illustrated pictorially.

Traversable (træ·vəɹsăb'l), *a.* 1534. [f. TRAVERSE *v.* + -ABLE.] **1.** Capable of being traversed or crossed 1656. **2.** *Law.* Capable of being traversed or formally denied 1534.

1. Roads..t. at all seasons 1859.

Traverse (træ·vəɹs), *sb.* ME. [– OFr. *travers* masc. and *traverse* fem. partly f. *traverser*, partly repr. subst. uses of n. and fem. pa. pples.; cf. med.L. *tra(ns)versum* crossing, etc., *traversa* cross-road. See next and TRAVERSE *v.*] **I.** The action of TRAVERSE *v.* in a local sense. **1.** = PASSAGE 4. *Obs.* exc. *Hist.* **2.** The action of traversing, passing across, or going through (a region, etc.); passage, crossing: orig. from side to side 1599. **3.** *Surveying.* A single line of survey carried across a region or through a narrow strip of country, by measuring the lengths and azimuths of a connected series of straight lines. Also, a tract of country so surveyed. 1881. †**4.** *Fencing.* The action or an act of traversing –1706. **5.** *Mountaineering.* An act of traversing or making one's way in a horizontal direction across the face of a mountain or rock; also *concr.* a place where a traverse is made 1893.

5. Three o'clock found us still working westwards on the t. 1897.

II. 1. Something that crosses, thwarts, or obstructs; opposition; an obstacle; a mishap; *pl.* crosses. Now *rare.* late ME. **2.** *Law.* The traversing or formal denial in pleading of some matter of fact alleged by the other side; also, a plea consisting of this. late ME. †**3.** A dispute, controversy –1651. **III. 1.** A passage by which one may traverse or cross; a way, pass; a crossing 1678. **2.** *Naut.* The zigzag track of a vessel sailing against the wind; with *a* and *pl.*, each of the runs made by a ship in tacking 1594. **b.** *transf.* Each lap, length, or *pli* of a zigzag ascending road 1731.

2. b. We mounted by a military road cut in traverses JOHNSON.

IV. 1. A curtain or screen placed crosswise, or drawn across a room, hall, or theatre; also, a partition of wood, a screen of lattice-work, or the like. *Obs.* exc. *Hist.* late ME. **2.** A small compartment shut off or enclosed by a curtain or screen in a church, house, etc.; a closet. *arch.* 1494. †**3.** A bar or barrier across anything –1759. **4.** *Fortif.* A barrier or barricade thrown across an approach, the line of fire, etc. as a defence; *spec.* (*pl.*) parapets of earth raised at intervals across the terreplein of a rampart or the covered way of a fortress, to prevent its being enfiladed 1599. **5.** A natural structure forming a transverse partition, as the diaphragm; anything lying transversely or across 1604. **6.** Anything laid or fixed athwart or across; a cross-piece; a cross-beam in a timber roof; a rung of a ladder; etc. 1708.

attrib. and *Comb.*: **t.-board, travis-board,** *Naut.* a circular board marked with the points of the compass, and having holes and pegs by which to indicate the course of the ship; **-circle,** a circular or segmental track on which a gun-carriage is turned to point the gun in any required direction; **-drill,** a drill in which the boring tool has at the required depth a lateral motion; also, a drill in which the drill-stock is adjustable laterally on the bed; **t. jury,** a jury empanelled to adjudicate on an appeal from another jury; **-map,** a rough map, the main points on which have been determined by traversing.

Traverse (træ·vəɹs), *a. rare.* late ME. [– OFr. *travers* :– med.L. *tra(ns)versus*, f. L. *transversus* TRANSVERSE *a.*] **1.** Lying, passing, or extending across; cross, transverse. †**2.** Slanting; oblique –1649.

1. The t. part of the Cross 1703. The explosions at the Waltham Cordite Factory..the strong t. walls being blown to pieces 1894.

Traverse (træ·vəɹs), *v.* ME. [– (O)Fr. *traverser* :– late L. *traversare, trans-*, f. *transversus* TRANSVERSE *a.*] **I.** To run across or through; to cross. **1.** *trans.* †**a.** To run (something) through *with* a weapon; to pierce, stab. **b.** To pass through as a weapon, to penetrate, pierce. Now *rare.* late ME. **c.** To cross (a thing) with a line, stripe, bar, barrier, or anything that intersects. In *pass.*, To be crossed *with* lines, etc. Now *rare.* late ME. **2.** To cross (a mountain, river, sea) in travelling; now *esp.* to pass or journey across, over, or through; to pass through (a region) from side to side, or from end to end; also, to pass through (a space or solid body), as rays of light, etc. 1489. **b.** To trace (a geometrical figure, or part of one) continuously without lifting the pen or pencil. Also *intr.* or *absol.* 1905. **3.** *fig.*, etc. To 'go through' (life, time, or anything figured as an extended space or region); to read through or consider thoroughly (a subject, treatise, etc.) 1477. **4.** Of a thing: To lie, be situated, extend, stretch, or 'run' across (something); to cross, intersect 1481. **5.** To go to and fro over or along; to cross and recross 1590. **6.** *Surveying.* To make or execute a traverse (TRAVERSE *sb.* I. 3) of (a region); to delimit (an area) by thus determining the position of points on its boundaries; to trace the course of (a road, river, etc.) in this way 1874.

1. c. They traversed the streets with barricadoes 1748. **2.** What Experience Vlisses got by trauersing strange Countries GREENE. **3.** It was in the years which we are traversing that England became firmly Protestant GREEN. **4.** Deeply worn footpaths..traversing the country W. IRVING. **5.** Phr. *To t. one's ground*, to move from side to side, in fencing or fighting.

II. To turn, move, or bring (a thing) across. **1.** *trans.* To alter the position of (a gun, etc.) laterally, so as to take aim. Also *absol.* 1628. **b.** *intr.* To carry a gun so that it points at the head or body of another sportsman 1886. †**2.** To turn away, to divert; *fig.* to pervert (*rare*) –1689. **III.** To direct oneself or act against. **1.** *trans.* To act against, go counter to; to cross, thwart, oppose. late ME. **2.** *Law.* To contradict formally (a matter of fact alleged in the previous pleading); to deny at law. Also *absol.* ME. †**3.** To dispute; to discuss –1599.

1. He resolved to t. this new project ARBUTHNOT. **2.** Phr. *To t. an indictment*, to deny or take issue upon an indictment. *To t. an office*, to deny or impeach the validity of an inquest of office.

IV. *intr.* **1.** To move, pass, or go across; to cross, cross over; (of a ship) to tack. late ME. **2.** To move from side to side; to dodge. *Obs.* or *arch.* 1470. **3.** To run freely in its proper socket, ring, channel, or course (as a rope); to turn or move freely on a traverse-circle (as a gun); to turn about on a pivot (as the needle of the compass) 1829. **4. a.** *Falconry.* To move from side to side, to wriggle, as a hawk. **b.** *Manège.* To advance obliquely, as a horse. 1486. **5.** To advance or ascend in a zigzag line 1773. **6.** *Mountaineering.* To make one's way in a horizontal or transverse direction across the face of a mountain or rock 1893.

1. *fig.* His thoughts tossed and traversed like the inconstant clouds 1824. **2.** To see thee fight, to see thee foigne, to see thee trauerse SHAKS.

Traverser (træ·vəɹsəɹ). 1613. [f. prec. + -ER[1].] **1.** A person or thing that crosses or passes over. **2.** *Law.* One who traverses a plea 1812. **3.** On a railway: A platform, moving laterally on wheels, by which trucks or carriages may be shifted from one set of rails to another parallel to it 1851.

Tra·verse-ta:ble. 1669. [f. TRAVERSE *sb.*] **1.** *Naut.* A table from which the difference of latitude and departure corresponding to any given course and distance may be ascertained. **2.** On a railway: = prec. 3. *U.S.* 1864.

Travertine, -in (træ·vəɹtin). 1797. [– It. *travertino*, older *tivertino* :– L. *tiburtinus* TIBURTINE.] A white or light-coloured concretionary limestone, usu. hard and semi-crystalline, deposited from water holding lime in solution; also called *t. stone*; quarried in Italy for building.

Travesty (træ·vésti), *ppl. a.* and *sb.* 1662. [– Fr. *travesti*, pa. pple. of *travestir* (XVI) – It. *travestire* disguise, f. *tra-* TRANS- + *vestire* (:– L.) clothe.] **A.** *ppl. a.* Dressed so as to be made ridiculous; burlesqued. (Const. as pa. pple.) *Obs.* or only as Fr. **B.** *sb.* **1.** A burlesque or ludicrous imitation of a serious work; literary composition of this kind; hence, a grotesque or debased image or likeness 1674. **2.** In etym. sense: An alteration of dress or appearance; a disguise (*rare*) 1732.

1. It..has sometimes the effect of a ludicrous travesti of the Odyssey 1789. **2.** My design was to have travelled..*incognito*...But all my art and travestie was vain. 1732.

Travesty (træ·vésti), *v.* 1673. [app. first used in the pa. pple. *travestied* = Fr. *travesti* or It. *travestito.*] **1.** *trans.* To alter in dress or appearance; to disguise by such alteration 1686. **2.** To turn into ridicule by grotesque parody or imitation; to caricature, burlesque 1673.

1. Old Naturalism thus travestied under the name of Religion 1754. **2.** The comic poets.. travestied known characters so as to make them hardly recognisable 1874.

Travis: see TRAVERSE *sb.*

Trawl (trǭl), *sb.* 1759. [Short for TRAWL-NET.] **I.** A strong net or bag dragged along the bottom of fishing-banks, a drag-net; esp. that now often dist. as the *beam-t.*, a triangular purse-shaped net, the mouth of which is kept open by a beam supported on two upright frames (the *t-heads*). **2.** *U.S.* A buoyed line used in sea-fishing, having numerous short lines with baited hooks attached at intervals; a trawl-line 1864.

attrib. and *Comb.*: **t.-beam,** the beam which holds open the mouth of a t.-net; **-head,** see sense 1; **-warp,** the warp or rope of a t.-net.

Trawl (trǭl), *v.* 1561. [prob. – MDu. *traghelen* drag, rel. to *traghel* drag-net, perh. – L. *tragula* drag-net, obscurely f. *trahere* draw.] **1.** *intr.* To fish with a net the edge of which is dragged along the bottom of the sea to catch the fish living there, esp. flat-fish; to fish with a trawl-net or in a trawler. **2.** To drag a seine-net behind and about a shoal of herring, etc., in order to drive, enclose, and catch them. (Also *trans.* with the net as obj.) 1864. **3.** *trans.* To catch or take with a trawl or trawl-net 1864.

Trawler (trǭ·ləɹ). 1599. [f. TRAWL *v.* + -ER[1].] **1.** One who trawls. **2.** A vessel employed in fishing with a trawl-net; often more explicitly *steam-t.* 1847.

Traw·l-net. 1696. [f. TRAWL *sb.* or *v.* + NET *sb.*[1]] **1.** = TRAWL *sb.* 1. **2.** *Sc.* and *U.S.* Applied (erron.) to a kind of seine-net used to surround and enclose shoals of herring and other fish 1855.

Tray (trē[i]), *sb.*[1] [OE. *trēġ, *trīeġ, recorded only late as *trīġ* = OSw. *trø* corn-measure :– Gmc. *traujam, f. *trau- *treu- wood (see TREE).] **1.** A utensil of the form of a flat board with a raised rim, or of a shallow box without a lid, made of wood, metal, or other material, of various sizes and shapes; now used for carrying plates, dishes, cards, etc., for containing and exhibiting small articles, as jewellery, etc., and for various other purposes, as in mining, photography, chemistry, etc. **2.** Part of the life-guard used on tram-cars, etc., a flat grid on which obstructions are picked up 1910.

Comb.: **t.-cloth,** a cloth or napkin placed upon a tray on which dishes, etc. are carried. Hence **Tray·ful,** as much as a t. will hold.

Tray, *sb.*[2] 1812. [Same word as TREY, re-spelt after BAY *sb.*[6]] *Venery.* The third branch of a stag's horn.

†Trea·cher. ME. [– OFr. *trecheor, tricheor* (mod. *tricheur*), f. *trechier,* (also mod.) *tricher* cheat, trick; see TRICK *sb.*, -ER[2] 3.] A deceiver, cheat; *occas.* a traitor –1767.

Those same treachours vile SPENSER.

Treacherous (tre·tʃərəs), *a.* ME. [– OFr. *trecher-, tricherous,* f. *trecheor*; see prec., -OUS.] **1.** Of persons, etc.: Characterized by treachery; deceiving, perfidious, false; disloyal, traitorous. **2.** *fig.* Of things: Deceptive, untrustworthy, unreliable; of ground, ice, etc., unstable, insecure 1573.

1. A t., thievish, murderous cannibal 1897. **2.** I haue..One o' the treacherou'st memories, I doe thinke, Of all mankind B. JONS. Hence **Trea·cherous-ly** *adv.*, **-ness.**

Treachery (tre·tʃəri). ME. [– OFr. *trecherie,* (also mod.) *tricherie,* f. *trechier, trichier* cheat; see TRICK, -ERY.] Deceit, cheating, perfidy; violation of faith or betrayal of trust; perfidious conduct. **b.** *esp.* The deception or perfidy of a traitor; treason against a sovereign, lord, or master ME. **c.** With *a* and *pl.* An instance of this; an act of perfidy or treason ME.

But Talus usde..To keepe a nightly watch for dread of t. SPENSER. **b.** Iudas and his trecheri ME.

Treacle (trī·k'l), *sb.* [ME. *triacle* – OFr. *triacle* :– L. *theriaca* – Gr. θηριακή, subst. use (sc. ἀντίδοτος antidote) of fem. of adj. f. θηρίον wild beast, venomous animal, dim. of θήρ animal. For the parasitic *l* cf. *participle, principle, syllable.*] **I. †1.** *Old Pharm.* A medicinal compound, orig. a kind of salve, formerly in repute as an alexipharmic against, and an antidote to, venomous bites, poisons generally, and malignant diseases –1804. **†b.** *transf.* A sovereign remedy –1727. **†2.** *fig.* ME.

1. The chief Use of Vipers is for the making of T. 1693. **2.** With the sovran t. of sound doctrine.. to fortifie their hearts MILT.

II. The uncrystallized syrup produced in the process of refining sugar 1694. **b.** An inspissated saccharine juice obtained from various trees and plants 1731. **c.** *fig.* Something cloyingly sweet; *esp.* extravagant laudation, blandishment 1771.

attrib. and *Comb.*: **T. Bible,** a collector's name for any English version or edition of the Bible having 'triacle' or 'treacle' where others have 'balm', as in Jer. 8:22, etc.; **t.-mustard,** the plant *Thlaspi arvense,* so-called on account of its supposed medicinal virtue; by later writers applied to *Clypeola jonthlaspi,* also to *Erysimum cheiranthoides*; **-posset,** a hot drink made of cider or milk and treacle; **-vinegar, -water,** a cordial distilled with a spirituous menstruum from Venice treacle and various drugs and simples. Hence **Trea·cly** *a.* resembling t. in quality or appearance; *fig.* cloyingly sweet; honeyed.

Treacle (trī·k'l), *v.* 1838. [f. prec.] *trans.* To smear or spread with treacle; to dose with (brimstone and) treacle. **b.** To catch (moths) by attracting them with treacle or the like spread on trees. Also *intr.* 1905.

Tread (tred), *sb.* [Early ME. *trede,* f. next. Cf. TRADE *sb.*] **I. 1.** A footprint (*rare*). **†2.** A line of footsteps; the track or trail of a man or animal –1820. **†3.** A trodden or beaten way, a path, a track. *Obs.* exc. **b.** *fig.* path or way (of life or action). late ME. **4.** The action or an act of treading or trampling; a step. late ME. **b.** Manner of treading; hence, style of walking 1609. **c.** *transf.* The sensation produced by treading upon something (considered as an attribute of the thing). *rare.* 1819.

1. An Otter's T. is almost like that of a Badger 1727. **3. b.** Conditions which determine the t. and destiny of nations BUCKLE. **4.** That incessant t. of feet wearing the rough stones smooth DICKENS. **b.** She had the t. of an Empress 1881. **c.** A sloping green of mossy t. KEATS.

II. 1. a. *Farriery.* A bruise or wound of the coronet of a horse's foot, caused by setting one foot upon the other, or by over-reaching 1661. **b.** An act of treadling or pedalling a machine 1680. **2. a.** The action of the male bird in coition 1674. **b.** The cicatricula or chalaza 1593. **3.** The horizontal upper surface of a step in a stair; also, the width of this from front to back; also, each of the rungs of a ladder 1712. **4.** *Fortif.* A terrace at the back of a parapet, on which the defenders stand to fire over the parapet 1834. **5.** *techn.*, as a wheel track, a rut (*dial.*); the flat under side of the foot or of a shoe, the sole; the transverse distance between the two wheels of a cart or other vehicle; the outer surface of a wheel, tyre, or sledge runner; the rail surface on which the wheel bears, etc. 1735.

Tread (tred), *v.* Pa. t. **trod** (trǫd), *arch.* **trode** (trō^{u}d). Pa. pple. **trodden** (trǫ·d'n), **trod** (trǫd). [OE. *tredan* = OFris. *treda,* OS. *tredan,* OHG. *tretan* (Du. *treden,* G. *treten*) :– WGmc. **tređan.*] **1.** *trans.* To step upon; to pace or walk on (the ground, etc.); to walk in (a place); hence, to go about in (a place, etc.). **2.** To step or walk upon or along; to follow, pursue (a path, track, or road) OE. **3.** *intr.* To walk, go, pace; to set down the feet in walking; to step. Also said of the foot. OE. **4.** To step *on*; to put the foot down *upon,* esp. so as to press upon. late ME. **5.** *trans.* **†a.** To step or walk with pressure on (something) esp. so as to crush, beat down, injure or destroy it; to trample –1712. **b.** With advb. extension ME. **c.** *fig.* To crush, to oppress; to treat with contemptuous cruelty 1526. **6.** *intr.* To trample *on* or *upon* OE. **7.** *trans.* To press (something) downwards with the foot or feet in treadling or pedalling 1680. **8.** Of the male bird: To copulate with (the hen) ME. **b.** *absol.* Of birds: To copulate 1486. **9.** *trans.* To thresh (corn) by trampling it on a threshing-floor: said of the oxen, etc., or of one using them; also with *out.* **b.** To press out the juice of (grapes) by trampling them in a vat. **c.** To tramp (clothes) in washing. late ME. **10.** To make or form by the action of the feet in walking; *esp.* to beat *out* (a path or track). late ME. **11.** *Horticulture.* To beat down and consolidate (soil) by treading; also with plants, etc., as object 1440. **12.** *intr.* Of land (*t. loose,* hence ellipt. *t.*): To yield or give to the tread. *dial.* 1847. **13.** *trans.* With advs.: To get or put into or out of some position or condition by treading; *esp.* to put *out* (fire) by treading 1542.

1. 'Tis joy enough..to t. the grass of England once again WORDSW. *To t. the stage* (*the boards*), to act upon the stage, to follow the profession of an actor. *To t. this earth, shoe-leather,* to be alive, to live; A better man never trod shoe-leather 1828. *To t. the deck,* to be on board ship, be a sailor. *To t. the ground,* to walk; Methought she trod the ground with greater grace DRYDEN. **2.** The downward track he treads DRYDEN. *To t. a measure,* to go through a dance in a rhythmic or stately manner (*arch.* and *poet.*). **3.** As proper men as euer trod vpon Neats Leather SHAKS. fig. phr. *To t. on air,* to walk buoyantly or jubilantly. **4.** The poore Beetles that we treade upon SHAKS. Phr. *To t. on any one's heel* or *toes* (also *fig.*): see the sbs. **5. b.** *To t. down, under foot, to pieces,* etc. **6.** T. upon his neck, And treble all his father's slaveries MARLOWE. **7.** Phr. *To t. water,* in swimming, to move the feet as in walking upstairs, keeping the body erect, and the head above water. **9. b.** Who wine desires, let him the ripe grapes t. 1871. **c.** The clothes that they trod in the wash-tub CLOUGH. **10.** Paths trodden by the footsteps of ages FROUDE. **13.** The flame of civil war..was trodden out before it had time to spread MACAULAY. Phr. *To t. one's shoe awry,* to fall from chastity. Hence **Trea·der,** one who or that which treads.

Treadle (tre·d'l), *sb.* [OE. *tredel,* f. *tredan*; see prec., -LE.] **†1.** A step or stair (*rare*) –1878. **2.** A lever worked by the foot in machines and mechanical contrivances, usu. to produce reciprocating or rotary motion. late ME. **b.** A pedal of a bicycle or the like 1887. **3.** = TREAD *sb.* II. 2 b. Now *dial.* 1658.

Treadle (tre·d'l), *v.* 1891. [f. prec.] **1.** *intr.* To work a treadle; to move the feet as if doing this; also, of a cyclist: to make one's way by pedalling one's cycle: also *trans.* with *way.* **2.** *trans.* To operate (a machine) by working a treadle 1906.

Treadmill (tre·dmil). 1822. [f. TREAD *v.* + MILL *sb.*[1]] A horizontal cylinder made to revolve by the weight of persons treading on boards arranged as equidistant steps around its periphery. Formerly in use as an instrument of prison discipline.

A kind of mental tread-mill, where you are perpetually climbing, but can never rise an inch SCOTT.

Trea·d-wheel. 1573. [f. TREAD *v.* + WHEEL *sb.*] A wheel rotated by the treading of persons or animals to give motion to machinery, to raise water, etc.; *esp.* a wheel turned by the weight of a person or animal walking on the inside of its periphery; also = prec.

†Treague. *rare.* 1590. [– med.L. *trege, treuge* pl. (XII) = OE. *treowa,* Frankish **treuwa* (whence (O)Fr. *trève*), OS. *treuwa,* Goth. *triggwa*; see TRUCE.] A truce –1660.

Treason (trī·z'n). [ME. *treison, tresoun* – AFr. *treisoun, tres(o)un,* OFr. *traïson* (mod. *trahison*) :– L. *traditio, -ōn-,* f. *tradere* deliver up, BETRAY, f. *tra-* (*trans*) + *-dere* give; cf. -ISON.] **1.** The action of betraying; betrayal of the trust undertaken by or reposed in any one; breach of faith, treachery. **2.** *Law.* **a.** *High t.* or *treason* proper: Violation by a subject of his allegiance to his sovereign or to the state.

Defined 1350–51 by Act 25 Edw. III, Stat. 5, c. 2, as compassing or imagining the king's death, or that of his wife or eldest son, violating the wife of the king or of the heir apparent, or the king's eldest daughter being unmarried, levying war in the king's dominions, adhering to the king's enemies in his dominions, or aiding them in or out of the realm, or killing the chancellor or the judges in the execution of their offices. In 1795 the offence was extended to actual or contemplated use of force to make the king change his counsels, or to intimidate either or both of the Houses of Parliament.

b. *Petit* or *petty t.*, treason against a subject; *spec.* the murder of one to whom the murderer owes allegiance, as of a master by his servant, a husband by his wife, etc. Now only *Hist.* 1496. **c.** *Constructive t.*, action which though not actually or overtly coming under any of the acts specified in the Statute of Treason, was declared by law to be treason and punishable as such. *Misprision of t.*: see MISPRISION[1] 1. 1714. **†3.** With *a* and *pl.* An act of treason; also, a species of treason –1708.

1. Whas mouth is ful of weriynge & bitternes & treson HAMPOLE. **2. a.** Tell Bullingbroke.. That euery stride he makes vpon my Land, Is dangerous Treason SHAKS. T. doth never prosper, what's the reason? For if it prosper, none dare call it T. 1612. **b.** Joseph Armstrong was tried for petty t., in poisoning his master's lady 1777.

Comb.: **t.-fe·lony,** an offence, formerly included among acts of t., which by subsequent legislation has been removed from these, and is not punishable with death.

Treasonable (trī·z'năb'l), *a.* late ME. [f. prec. + -ABLE.] Of the nature of treason; characteristic of or involving treason; perfidious, treacherous. orig. *Sc.*

The t. packet had been found in his bosom MACAULAY. Hence **Trea·sonableness. Trea·sonably** *adv.*

Treasonous (trī·z'nəs), *a.* 1450. [f. as prec. + -OUS.] Full of or abounding in treason; treasonable.

To prohibit such and such pieces, that were blasphemous, libelleous or t. 1784. Hence **Trea·sonably** *adv.*

Treasure (tre·ʒŭɹ), *sb.* [ME. *tresor* – (O)Fr. *trésor* :– Rom. **tresaurus,* unexpl. alt. of L. THESAURUS.] **1.** Wealth stored or accumulated, esp. in the form of precious metals; gold or silver coin; hence *gen.*, money, riches, wealth. Usually without article or pl. **b.** *pl.* in same sense ME. **†c.** A store or stock *of* anything valuable (*rare*) –1707. **2.** *transf.* and *fig.* Anything valued and preserved as precious; also of a person, a 'jewel', 'gem'. *colloq.* ME. **†3.** A treasury; a treasure-house, a treasure-chest (*rare*) –1596.

1. Where a mans threasure ys there is his hart 1597. **b.** The last coin out of all their treasures RUSKIN. **2.** My..nurse, a t. and the most respectable of dames 1810. The fine house and its treasures 1907.

Comb.: **†t.-city,** a city in which supplies were stored.

Trea·sure, *v.* late ME. [f. prec.] **1.** *trans.* To put away or lay aside (anything of value) for preservation, security, or future use; to hoard or store up. Often *to t. up.* **2.** *fig.* To keep in store, lay up (e.g., in the mind, in memory). late ME. †**3.** To furnish with treasures; to enrich (*rare*) –1630. **4.** To hold or keep as precious; to cherish, prize 1907.

1. Wher ben the princes . . that siluer tresoren and gold? *Baruch* 3 : 16. **3.** T. thou some place, With beauties treasure SHAKS. **4.** Treasured as his most precious possessions 1907.

Trea·sure-hou:se. 1475. A house, building, or chamber in which treasure is kept; a treasury.

fig. The t. of literature 1895.

Treasurer (tre·ʒŭrəɹ). ME. [– AFr. *tresorer*, (O)Fr. *trésorier*, f. *trésor*, after late L. *thesaurarius*; see -ER^2 2.] **1.** One who has officially the charge of treasure; orig., a person entrusted with the receipt, care, and disbursement of the revenues of a king, noble, or other dignitary of a state, city, or church; now, one who is responsible for the funds of a public body, or of any corporation, association, society, or club. **b.** *U.S.* An officer of the Treasury Department, who receives and keeps the moneys, disbursing them only upon warrants drawn by the Secretary of the Treasury; also, an officer having the same function in each State 1790. **2.** *fig.* One who or that which is entrusted with the keeping of anything precious or valuable ME. **3.** [f. TREASURE *v.* + -ER^1.] One who treasures or hoards up; a preserver, keeper *of* something precious 1597.

1. *Lord High T. of England, of Great Britain*, also called *T., Lord T., High T., T. of the Exchequer*, formerly, the third great officer of the Crown, controlling the revenues of the sovereign (the duties of the office are now discharged by five Lords of the Treasury). Hence **Trea·surership,** the office of t.

Treasuress (tre·ʒŭrės). Now *rare.* 1450. [orig. *tresoresse* for *tresoreresse*, f. *tresorer* TREASURER; see -ESS^1.] A female treasurer.

Treasure-trove (tre:ʒŭɹ,trōᵘ·v). 1550. [– AFr. *tresor trové* (in AL. *thesaurus repertus* XI, *inventus* XII), i.e. *tresor* TREASURE, *trové*, pa. pple. of *trover* (mod. *trouver*) find. For the muting of final *é* cf. ASSIGN *sb.*^{2}; see -Y^5.] *lit.* 'Treasure found', i.e. anything of the nature of treasure which any one finds; *spec.* in *Eng. Law*: Treasure (gold or silver, money, plate, or bullion) found hidden in the ground or other place, the owner of which is unknown.

Treasury (tre·ʒŭri). ME. [– OFr. *tresorie*, for *tresorerie*, f. *tresor*, after med.L. *thesaur(ar)ia, -ium*; see -Y^3.] **1.** A room or building in which precious or valuable objects are preserved, *esp.* a place or receptacle for money or valuables (now *Hist.*); *transf.* the funds or revenue of a state or of a public or private corporation. **2.** *fig.* A repository of 'treasures'; a thesaurus. late ME. **3.** The department of State which controls the collection, management, and expenditure of the public revenue; *spec.* that of the United Kingdom. (This department is now managed by a T. Board of Commissioners, the First Lord of the T. (usu., the Prime Minister), the Chancellor of the Exchequer, and junior Lords not more than five in number, who act as party whips. The actual head of the department is the Chancellor of the Exchequer. late ME. **b.** The building where the Treasury Commissioners transact business; formerly also *T. Office* 1706. **4.** *Theatr. slang.* The weekly payment of a company of actors 1885. †**5.** = TREASURE *sb.* 1 –1672.

2. The Golden T. of English Songs PALGRAVE. **5.** As he, who hauing found great T. DANIEL.

Comb.: **t.-bench,** the front bench on the right hand of the Speaker in the House of Commons, occupied by the Leader of the House (usu. the First Lord of the T.), and other members of the Government; **-bill,** an instrument of credit, usu. drawn for 3 or 6 months, issued by authority of Parliament to the highest bidder, when money is temporarily needed by the Commissioners of the T.; **-bond,** an exchequer bond; **t. lord,** one of the commissioners of the T.; **t. department,** in the U.S. government, the finance department under the Secretary of the T.; **t. minute,** an administrative regulation for any department under the T.; **-note,** (*a*) *U.S.*, a demand note issued by the T. Department, receivable as legal tender for all debts; (*b*) English paper money used as currency, esp. a £1 or 10s. note; **-warrant,** a warrant or voucher issued by the T. for any sum disbursed by the exchequer.

Treat (trīt), *sb.* late ME. [f. next.] †**1.** The action or an act of treating, or discussing terms; parley; agreement; treaty –1645. †**2.** = TREATMENT 1; an instance of this –1711. **3.** *concr.* An entertainment *of* food and drink, esp. one given without expense to the recipient. *Obs.* or merged in b. 1651. **b.** Hence, an entertainment of any kind given gratuitously, esp. to children 1683. **c.** The action of treating or entertaining; one's part or turn to treat; an invitation to eat or drink 1690. **4.** Something highly enjoyable; a great pleasure, delight, or gratification. *colloq.* 1805.

1. [He] Bad that same boaster . . bide him batteill without further t. SPENSER. **3.** A very handsome table, covered with a cold t. of roasted mutton and beef DE FOE. Phr. *To stand t.*: see STAND *v.* IV. 7.

Treat (trīt), *v.* [ME. *trete* – AFr. *treter*, OFr. *tretier, traitier* (mod. *traiter*) :– L. *tractare* drag, manage, handle, etc., f. pa. ppl. stem of *trahere* draw.] **1. a.** *intr.* To deal or carry on negotiations (*with* another) with a view to settling terms; to bargain, negotiate. †**b.** *trans.* To negotiate, plan –1715. **2. a.** *intr.* To deal with some matter in speech or writing; to discourse. Const. *of*, formerly *on, upon.* late ME. **b.** *trans.* To deal with (a subject) in speech or writing; to discourse. In mod. use often: To deal with in the way of literary art. ME. **3.** To deal with, behave or act towards (a person, animal, etc.) in some specified way; to 'use' (well, ill, etc.). late ME. **b.** To consider or regard in a particular aspect and deal with accordingly. (Often with *as.*) 1456. **4.** To entertain, esp. with food and drink; to regale, feast, esp. at one's own expense, by way of kindness or compliment, or *spec.* of bribery, as at an election 1500. **b.** *absol.* or *intr.* To stand treat 1710. **5.** *trans.* To deal with in the way of art; to handle or represent artistically 1695. **6. a.** To deal with or operate upon (a disease or affection, a part of the body, or a person) in order to relieve or cure 1781. **b.** To subject to chemical or other physical action; to act upon *with* some agent 1816.

1. a. The governor beat a parley, desiring to t. 1647. **b.** He was treating a marriage with the archduchess BURNET. **2. a.** Certain writings of our divines that t. of grace BERKELEY. **b.** Questions which shall be treated under their proper heads TYNDALL. **3.** That Mahometan Custom . . of treating Women as if they had no Souls STEELE. **b.** The clergy are often treated as obstacles to the diffusion of knowledge 1868. **4.** Rebecca . . ordered a bottle of sherry and a bread cake . . to t. the enemy's lawyers THACKERAY. *To t.* (a person, etc.) *to*, to entertain with (food or drink, or any enjoyment or gratification); Dick had treated himself to two ices and a strawberry squash 1897. **5.** Familiar subjects . . treated with great lustre and fullness of colouring H. WALPOLE. **6. b.** Potato-starch when treated with sulphuric acid becomes sugar 1845.

Treatable (trī·tăb'l), *a.* [ME. *tretable* – (O)Fr. *traitable* :– L. *tractabilis* TRACTABLE. In some senses f. TREAT *v.* + -ABLE.] **1.** Easily handled or dealt with; tractable, docile; open to appeal or argument, affable. *Obs.* or *arch.* †**b.** Of or in ref. to actions, etc.: Gentle, easy, deliberate, not violent –1690. †**c.** Of utterance: Deliberate; distinct –1641. **2.** Capable of being or proper to be treated or dealt with 1570.

1. b. In France, and the Low Countries . . the Heats or the Colds, and Changes of Seasons, are less t. than they are with us 1690. **c.** [The parson's] voyce is humble, his words t. and slow G. HERBERT. Hence **Trea·tably** *adv.*

Treater (trī·təɹ). 1489. [In sense 1 – OFr. *traiteor, traiteur* ambassador; in other senses f. TREAT *v.* + -ER^1.] One who treats. **1.** One who negotiates terms of settlement; a negotiator. **2.** One who treats of or writes upon a subject 1594. **3.** One who gives a treat, or stands treat; an entertainer 1692.

Treatise (trī·tiz, -is). ME. [– AFr. *tretis*, OFr. **traitiz*, f. *traitier* TREAT *v.*] **1.** A book or writing which treats of some particular subject; now always, one containing a methodical discussion or exposition of the principles of the subject; formerly occas., a literary work in general. †**b.** A story, tale, narrative (spoken or written) –1605. †**2.** Negotiation, discussion of terms; arrangement of terms –1641.

1. I remember 'tis a letter, noe t., I have in hand 1633. **b.** The time ha's beene . . my Fell of haire Would at a dismall T. rowze, and stirre SHAKS. Hence †**Trea·tiser,** the writer of a t.

Treatment (trī·tmĕnt). 1560. [f. TREAT *v.* + -MENT. Cf. (O)Fr. *traitement.*] **1.** Conduct, behaviour; action or behaviour towards a person, etc.; usage. **2.** = TREAT *sb.* 3. *Obs.* exc. *dial.* 1656. **3.** Management in the application of remedies; medical or surgical application or service 1744. **4.** Subjection to the action of a chemical agent 1828. **5.** Action or manner of dealing with something in literature or art; literary or artistic handling esp. in ref. to style 1856.

Treaty (trī·ti). [ME. *trete(e* – AFr. *treté*, (O)Fr. *traité* :– L. *tractatus* TRACTATE; see -Y^5.] †**1. a.** The treatment of a subject in speech or writing; (literary) treatment; discussion –1663. **b.** A treatise, a dissertation; in early use, a story, narrative –1715. **2.** The treating of matters with a view to settlement; discussion of terms, conference, negotiation. Now *rare* or *Obs.* exc. in phr. *in t.* late ME. **3.** †**a.** A settlement arrived at by treating or negotiation; an agreement, covenant, compact, contract. *Obs.* exc. as in b. –1753. **b.** *spec.* A contract between states, relating to peace, truce, alliance, commerce, or other international relation; also, the document embodying such contract. late ME. †**4.** Entreaty, persuasion, request –1649. †**5.** Treatment, usage; behaviour (*rare*) –1654.

1. b. Sir Kenelme Digby in his excellent T. of bodies SIR T. BROWNE. **2.** It appears he is in t. for a place in the North 1881. **3. b.** A peace was concluded . . being in effect rather a bargain than a t. BACON. **4.** *Ant. & Cl.* III. xi. 62.

attrib. and *Comb.*: **t. coast, shore,** a coast on or along which some foreign nation has certain rights guaranteed by t.; **t.-port,** a port opened to foreign commerce by a t.

Treble (tre·b'l), *sb.* ME. [– OFr. *treble*, subst. use of the adj.; see next.] **I. 1.** Anything threefold; a sum or quantity three times as great as another. late ME. **2.** *techn.* and *ellipt.* **a.** A triple barrier; an obstacle consisting of three successive fences 1569. **b.** *Paper-making*, etc. A frame on which hand-made paper or printed sheets are hung to dry 1727. **c.** A kind of step-dance; the measure or music for this. *dial.* 1805. **d.** *Whist.* A game (at short whist) in which one side scores five and the other none, counting three points to the winners 1870. **e.** A method of crocheting in which three loops of thread are carried on the hook 1882.

1. Forfeiture . . of the t. of his seid wages 1463.

II. 1. *Mus.* The highest part in harmonized musical composition; the soprano part ME. **2.** A treble voice; also, a singer having a treble voice; one who sings the treble part 1475. **b.** *transf.* A high-pitched or shrill voice, sound, or note 1600. **3.** The string of treble pitch in a musical instrument; also, the chanter of a bagpipe 1562. **b.** = *t. bell* (see next A. 2 b.) 1598.

2. b. His bigge manly voice, Turning againe toward childish trebble, pipes And whistles SHAKS.

Treble (tre·b'l), *a.* and *adv.* ME. [– OFr. *treble* – L. *triplus*; see TRIPLE.] **A.** *adj.* **1.** = TRIPLE *a.* 1. late ME. **b.** Of threefold character or application; existing or occurring in three ways or relations; of three kinds. late ME. **c.** Three times as much or as many; triple. late ME. **2.** *Mus.* Of, pertaining to, or suited to the highest part in harmonized musical composition 1440. **b.** Hence in the names of musical instruments (or strings) of the highest pitch 1530. **c.** High-pitched; shrill 1562.

1. Thro' t. Plates it went Of solid Brass DRYDEN. **b.** A t. difficulty SCOTT. **2.** *T. voice*, a soprano voice. *T. clef*, the G clef when placed (as usually) upon the second line of the stave. **b.** *T. bell*, the smallest bell of a peal.

B. *adv.* **1.** In three ranks or rows, threefold; to three times the extent; three times over; trebly ME. **2.** In a high-pitched tone 1811.

Treble (tre·b'l), *v.* ME. [f. prec.] **1.** *trans.* To make three times as many or as great; to multiply by three. **b.** To be three times as many or as much as 1615. **2.** *intr.* (for *refl.*) To grow to three times the number, amount, or size; to become threefold 1625.

1. Double sixe thousand, and then t. that SHAKS. **b.** A body of the Carlists..whose numbers more than trebled his own BORROW. **2.** The circulation doubled, trebled, quadrupled 1882.

Trebly (tre·bli), *adv.* 1590. [f. TREBLE *a.* + -LY[2].] In a threefold degree or manner; triply.

Trebuchet (tre·bŭʃet, ‖ trebüʃe). ME. [– (O)Fr. *trébuchet* siege-engine (mod. trap, balance), in med.L. *tre-*, *trabuchetum*, f. *trébucher* overturn, overthrow, stumble, fall :– pop. L. **transbucare*, f. *trans* TRANS- + Frankish **buk* belly; see TRABUCH. In II, an application, in England, of med.L. *tre-buchetum* to the device known as the CUCKING-STOOL.] **I. 1.** A mediæval military engine for casting heavy missiles. *Hist.* **2.** A small delicately poised balance or pair of scales; an assay balance; a tilting scale 1550. **II.** = CUCKING-STOOL 1640.

‖**Trecento** (treˌtʃe·nto). 1841. [It., lit. 'three hundred', short for *mil trecento* 1300; cf. CINQUECENTO, SEICENTO.] The fourteenth century considered as a period of Italian art, architecture, etc. Hence **Trece·ntist**, ‖**Trecenti·sta** (It., pl. **-isti**), an Italian author, artist, etc., of the 14th c.

Treddle (tre·d'l). Now *dial.* [Metathetic f. ME. *tyrdyl*, etc., OE. *tyrdel*, dim. of *tord* TURD; see -LE.] A pellet of sheep's or goat's dung.

Treddle, var. of TREADLE.

Tredrille, tredille (tredri·l, -di·l). 1764. [f. QUADRILLE, with *tre-* three for *qua(d)-*.] A card-game played by three persons, usu. with thirty cards.

Tree (trī), *sb.* [OE. *trēo(w* = OFris. *trē*, OS. *trio, treo* (MDu. *-tere*), ON. *tré*, Goth. *triu* :– Gmc. **trewam*, f. wk. grade of IE. **deru-* **doru-*, repr. by Skr. *dâru*, *dru-* tree, Gr. δόρυ wood, spear, δρῦς tree, oak.] **1.** A perennial plant having a self-supporting woody main stem or *trunk* (which usu. develops woody branches at some distance from the ground), and growing to a considerable height and size. **b.** Extended to bushes or shrubs of erect growth and having a single stem; and even some perennial herbaceous plants which grow to a great height, as the banana and plantain ME. **2.** The substance of the trunk and boughs of a tree; wood; timber. *Obs.* or *arch.* OE. **3.** A piece of wood; a stem or branch of a tree, or a portion of one, usu. (now always) shaped for some purpose; a pole, post, stake, beam, wooden bar, etc.; *esp.* (now only) one forming part of some structure; usu. in comb., as AXLE-TREE, CROSS-TREE, †*door-tree*, ROOF-TREE, SWINGLETREE OE. **4. a.** The cross on which Christ was crucified. *arch.* and *poet.* OE. **b.** A gallows. Also *Tyburn t.* late ME. **5.** The wooden shaft of a spear, handle of an implement, etc.; hence, a spear, lance. Now *dial.* late ME. †**b.** A wooden structure; applied *poet.* or *rhet.* to a ship –1594. **c.** = SADDLE-TREE 1535. **d.** = BOOT-*tree*. late ME. **6.** Something resembling a tree with its branches: **a.** A diagram or table of a family, indicating its original ancestor as the root, and the various branches of descendants; in full *family* or *genealogical t.*; (*b*) *Porphyrian t.* (Logic): see PORPHYRIAN ME. **b.** Any structure or figure, natural or artificial, of branched form 1706.

1. *fig.* The Royall T. hath left vs Royall Fruit SHAKS. **2.** At Aberladie he shall light With hempen halters and hors of t. 1500. **4. a.** He..suffride oure synnes in his body on the t. WYCLIF 1 *Pet.* 2:24. **b.** Though it was thy luck to cheat the fatal t. 1704. **6. a.** Two genealogic trees H. WALPOLE.

Phrases. *At the top of the t.*, in the highest position. *Up a t.* (*colloq.*, orig. *U.S.*), debarred from escape, like a hunted animal driven to take refuge in a t.; entrapped; in a difficulty or 'fix'. *To bark up the wrong t.* (orig. *U.S.*), to make a mistake in one's object of pursuit. *T. of heaven* = AILANTO. *T. of Jesse*: see JESSE. *T. of knowledge*, (*a*) = next; (*b*) knowledge in general, or in all its 'branches'. *T. of the knowledge of good and evil*: see Gen. 2:9, etc. *T. of liberty*, a tree (or a pole) planted in celebration of a revolution or victory securing liberty (chiefly in ref. to the French Revolution). *T. of life*, (*a*) see Gen. 2:9, etc.; (*b*) = ARBOR VITÆ 1; (*c*) *Phys.* = ARBOR VITÆ 2.

Comb.: **a.** in names of plants, usu. denoting species or varieties that grow to the stature or in the form of a t., as *t. cabbage*, or those that grow on trees, as *t. orchis*; **t.-clover**, *Melilotus alba*; **t.-cotton**, *Gossypium arboreum*; **t. sorrel**, *Rumex lunaria*. **b.** In names of animals frequenting trees, as *t.-beetle*, *-kangaroo*, *-pipit*; **t.-bear** (*U.S. local*), the racoon; **-bug**, any one of various hemipterous insects which feed upon the juices of trees and shrubs; **-cat**, (*a*) a viverrine animal of the genus *Paradoxurus*, a palm-cat; (*b*) = *t.-fox*; **-crab**, a species of land-crab, *Birgus latro*, also called *palm-crab*; **-cricket**, a cricket of the genus *Œcanthus*; **-crow**, any one of various Oriental birds intermediate between crows and jays, as the genera *Crypsirhina*, *Dendrocitta*, etc.; **-dove**, any one of numerous arboreal species of pigeon of India, Australia, etc., belonging or allied to the genus *Macropygia*; **-duck**, a duck of the genus *Dendrocygna* or an allied genus; **-fox**, *Mustela pennanti*, also called *t.-cat*; **-frog**, any frog of arboreal habits; **-hopper**, any one of various homopterous insects which live on trees; sometimes *spec.* the cicada; **-lizard**, a lizard of the group *Dendrosaura*; **-lobster** = *t.-crab*; **-louse**, an aphis, a plant-louse; **-mouse**, any species of mouse of arboreal habits; **-oyster**, an oyster found upon the roots of the mangrove; **-pie**, a t.-crow of the genus *Dendrocitta*, found in India, China, and neighbouring countries; **-pigeon**, any one of various arboreal pigeons inhabiting Asia, Africa, and Australia; **-porcupine**, any porcupine of the subfamily *Sphingurinæ*, inhabiting America and the West Indies, living in trees, and having prehensile tails; **-rat**, an arboreal rodent, as those of the West Indian genera *Capromys* and *Plagiodon*; **-serpent**, **-snake**, any snake of arboreal habits, as those of the families *Dendrophidæ* and *Dipsadidæ*; **-tiger**, a name for the leopard; **-warbler**, a bird of the genus *Hypolais*.

c. Other Combs.: **t.-calf** *Bookbinding*, calf stained with acids in conventional imitation of the branches of a t.; **-coffin**, a prehistoric coffin made of a hollow t.-trunk; **-line**, the line or level on a mountain above which no trees grow (cf. *snow-line*); **-marble, marbling** *Bookbinding*, marbling or staining in a tree-like branching pattern (cf. *t.-calf*); **-nymph**, a nymph supposed to inhabit a t.; **-wool**, a woolly substance obtained from a t., as pine-wool.

Tree, *v.* 1650. [f. prec.] †**1.** *intr.* with *it*: To grow into a tree. FULLER. **2.** *trans.* To drive into or up a tree; to cause to take refuge in a tree, as a hunted animal. Also *fig.* to put into a difficulty or 'fix'. 1700. **3.** *intr.* To climb up or perch upon a tree; *esp.* to take refuge in a tree from a hunter or pursuer 1700. **4.** *techn.* **a.** *trans.* To furnish with an (axle-) tree. **b.** To stretch or shape upon a tree, as a boot or saddle. 1765.

3. Then the hunter must t. for his life 1902.

Tree·-cree:per. 1814. **1.** Any of various birds which creep on the trunks and branches of trees; *esp.* the common European *Certhia familiaris*, or other species of the family *Certhiidæ*. **2.** A plant that creeps or climbs upon trees; *spec.* the African rubber-plant, *Landolphia florida* 1887.

Tree·-fern. 1846. A fern with an upright stem, growing to the size and form of a tree; as those of the genera *Cyathea* and *Alsophila*, found in tropical regions, and in Australia and New Zealand.

Tree·-goose. *Obs.* exc. *Hist.* 1597. The barnacle-goose, formerly believed to be produced from a tree in the form of the barnacle (cirriped).

Treeless (trī·lės), *a.* 1814. [f. TREE *sb.* + -LESS.] Destitute of trees. Hence **Tree·lessness.**

Tree·-moss. 1611. **a.** Any moss or moss-like plant that grows on trees; applied esp. to certain lichens. **b.** A moss-like plant of branched form like a miniature tree, as club-moss (*Lycopodium*).

Treen (trī·ĕn, trīn), *a.* *Obs.* exc. *dial.* [OE. *trēowen*, etc., f. *trēow* TREE + -EN[4].] **1.** Made of 'tree'; wooden. †**2.** Of or belonging to, obtained or made from, a tree or trees –1670.

2. These T. Liquors; Especially, that of the Date EVELYN.

Treenail, trenail (trī·nēˡl, tre·n'l), *sb.* ME. [f. TREE *sb.* + NAIL *sb.*] A cylindrical pin of hard wood used in fastening timbers together, esp. in shipbuilding and other work where the materials are exposed to the action of water. Hence **Tree·-nail** *v. trans.* to fasten or secure (timbers) with treenails (chiefly in *pa. pple.*).

Tree·-spa:rrow. 1770. **a.** *Passer montanus*, a species of sparrow, widely distributed in Europe and Asia, and found locally in Britain. **b.** *Spizella monticola*, a bird (not of the sparrow family) common in N. America.

Tree·-toad. 1778. Any toad of arboreal habits, esp. those of the family *Hylidæ*, found chiefly in tropical America: often erron. called *t.-frogs*.

Tree·-top, tree top. 1530. The top of a tree; the uppermost branches of a tree.

Nursery rhyme. Hush-a-by, baby, On the t.

Trefa (trēˡ·fă). 1851. Also **trifa** (trəi·fă). [– Heb. *ṭ*ᵉ*rēpāh* flesh of an animal torn, f. *ṭārap* tear, rend.] Flesh meat forbidden to Jews because improperly killed.

Trefle (tre·f'l). 1510. [– (O)Fr. *trèfle* – Gr. τρίφυλλον or pop.L. **trifulum*. Cf. TREFOIL.] †**1.** = TREFOIL 1. –1527. **2.** *Mil.* A mine having three chambers 1756. **3.** = TREFOIL 2. 1877.

‖**Treflé, treflee** (trefle·, -ī·), *a.* 1725. [Fr. *tréflé* ending in trefoils, f. *trèfle* + *-é* (:– L. *-ata* -ATE[2]).] *Her.* Adorned with trefoils, either along one edge or at the end of each arm (of a cross).

Trefoil (trī·foil, tre·foil), *sb.* (*a.*) [Late ME. *treyfoyle, trifolie* – AFr. *trifoil* – L. *trifolium* (whence OFr. *trefueil*), f. *tri-* TRI- + *folium* leaf, FOIL *sb.*[1]] **1.** A plant of the genus *Trifolium*, having triple or trifoliate leaves; a clover: commonly applied to varieties other (esp. smaller) than those cultivated under the name of 'clover'; often to *T. inmus*, and also to *Medicago lupulina*. **b.** With defining words, applied to particular pecies of *Trifolium* or to plants of other genera having triple leaves (see e.g. BIRD'S-FOOT, HOP *sb.*[1], etc.) 1548. **2.** An ornamental figure representing or resembling a trifoliate leaf; *spec.* in *Arch.* an ornament with an opening divided by cusps so as to present or suggest the figure of a three-lobed leaf. late ME. **b.** *Her.* A bearing conventionally representing a clover-leaf with its stalk 1562. **3.** *fig.* A set of three closely united 1826. **4.** as *adj.* Three-leaved; having the figure of a trefoil or clover-leaf; furnished with such figures 1752. Hence **Tre·foiled** *a.* **a.** (chiefly *Arch.*) ornamented with a t. or trefoils; formed as a t. (sense 2); **b.** trifoliate; *transf.* three-lobed.

Tre·getour. *arch.* ME. [– OFr. *tre(s)geteo(u)r* juggler, f. *tre(s)geter* cast across or to and fro :– pop.L. **tra(ns)jectare*, f. TRANS- + *jactare* throw.] One who works magic or plays tricks by sleight of hand; a conjurer, juggler; hence, a trickster, a deceiver.

Trehala (trĭhā·lă). Also **tricala.** 1862. [– Turk. *tıgala*, native name.] The substance of the cocoons of a coleopterous insect, *Larinus maculatus*, found in Asia Minor; also called *t.-manna*, *Turkish* or *Syrian manna*. Hence **Trehalose** (trī·hălōᵘs, trĭhā·lōᵘs), *Chem.* a white crystalline sugar, $C_{12}H_{22}O_{11}.2H_2O$, obtained from t.

Treillage (trēˡ·lėdʒ, ‖trĕˡyāʒ). 1698. [– Fr. *treillage* (XVI), f. *treille* TRAIL *sb.*[2] + *-age* -AGE.] **1.** Latticework; a framework upon which vines or ornamental plants are trained; a trellis. **2.** A lattice or grill in a room 1836.

1. A walk under a t. of vines GREVILLE.

Trek (trek), *sb.* *S. Africa.* 1849. [– S. Afr. Du. *trek*, f. *trekken*; see next.] In travelling by ox-wagon, a stage of a journey between one stopping-place and the next; hence, a journey made in this way; also, travel by ox-wagon. **b.** An organized migration or expedition by ox-wagon 1890.

b. There has been a Boer t. into German South-west Africa 1901. **c.** Comb. as *t. Boer, sheep.*

Trek (trek), *v.* *S. Africa.* 1850. [– S. Afr. Du., (M)Du. *trekken* draw, pull, travel.] **1.** *intr.* To make a journey by ox-wagon; hence, to travel, migrate; also, to go, proceed; to go away, depart (*slang*). Also *transf.* of wild animals. **2.** *trans.* To draw or drag (a vehicle): said of oxen, etc. Also *absol.* 1863.

1. The wagons had been quietly treking along over an immense open country 1863. Hence **Tre·kker**, one who treks.

‖**Trekschuit, treck-** (tre·kskoit, Du. -sχœüt). 1696. [Du., f. *trek* sb. or *trek-* vb.-stem of *trekken* (see prec.) + *schuit*; see SCHUIT, SCOUT *sb.*[1]] A canal- or river-boat drawn by horses, carrying passengers and goods, as in common use in Holland; a track-boat.

Trellis (tre·lis), *sb.* [Late ME. *trelis* – OFr. *trelis, -ice* :– Rom. **trilicius, -ia*, f. L. *trilix, trilic-*, f. *tri-* TRI- + *licium* thread of a warp.] **1.** A structure of light bars of wood or metal crossing each other at intervals and fastened where they cross, having open square or diamond-shaped spaces between; a window, gate, screen, etc. so constructed; a lattice; a grating. Now *rare.* **b.** *Her.* The figure of a trellis used as a charge 1823. **2.** A similar framework used as a support upon which fruit-trees or climbing plants are trained 1513.

Trellis (tre·lis), *v.* late ME. [Almost always in pa. pple. *trellised* (tre·list), f. prec. + -ED.] **1.** *trans.* To furnish with a trellis; to enclose in a trellis or grating. **2.** To train (a plant) upon a trellis; to support on or as on a trellis 1818.

2. The vines..are trellissed upon..stakes SHELLEY.

Trellised (tre·list), *ppl. a.* 1472. [f. TRELLIS *sb.* or *v.* + -ED.] **1.** Furnished with a trellis or trellis-work; formed of trellis-work; trained upon a trellis. **2.** Shaped or arranged like a trellis; having a pattern or markings resembling a trellis 1664.

1. Trelliced vines SOUTHEY. The t. walls covered with honeysuckle and wild roses 1844.

Tre·llis-work. 1712. [f. TRELLIS *sb.* + WORK *sb.*] = TRELLIS *sb.* 1. Also, anything resembling this in structure or pattern.

Trematode (tre·mătōᵘd), *a.* and *sb.* 1836. [– mod.L. *Trematoda* n. pl., – Gr. τρηματώδης perforated, f. τρῆμα hole, orifice; see -ODE.] *Zool.* **A.** *adj.* Belonging to the class or order *Trematoda* or *Trematoidea* of parasitic worms, found in the bodies of various animals, having a flattish or cylindrical form, with skin often perforated by pores, and usu. furnished with adhesive suckers. **B.** *sb.* A trematode worm 1876. So **Tre·matoid** *a.* and *sb.*

Tremble (tre·mb'l), *sb.* 1609. [f. next.] **1.** An act or the action of trembling; a fit or state of trembling; a tremor; a vibration. **b.** Tremulousness or unsteadiness (of the voice) caused by emotion 1779. **2.** *pl. The trembles*: Any disease or condition characterized by an involuntary shaking, as ague or palsy (esp. in sheep); the tremor due to delirium tremens, etc.; the 'shakes' 1812.

1. Phr. *(All) in, all of a t., on the t.* (colloq.), trembling, esp. with agitation or excitement.

Tremble (tre·mb'l), *v.* ME. [– (O)Fr. *trembler* :– Rom., med.L. *tremulare*, rel. to L. *tremulus* TREMULOUS.] **1.** *intr.* Of persons (less commonly of animals), or of the body or a limb: To shake involuntarily as with fear, cold, or weakness; to quake, quiver, shiver. **b.** *fig.* and *rhet.* To be affected with dread or apprehension, or with any feeling that is accompanied by trembling. late ME. **2.** Of things: To be affected with vibratory motion; to shake, quake, quiver. late ME. **b.** Said of the tremulous or vibratory motion or effect of light, sound, speech, etc. late ME. **c.** *fig.* 1819. **3.** *trans.* To cause to tremble or shake 1591. **4.** *intr.* To pass tremulously. Chiefly *poet.* 1730.

1. I t. as doth a leef vpon a tree 1413. He trembled with anxiety 1797. **b.** The Grand Signior, with all his absolute power, trembles at a janissary's frown 1717. **2.** A little Harebell trembling in the breeze 1908. **b.** Tell how the Moon-beam trembling falls POPE. **c.** The liberties of Scotland ..were trembling in the balance BUCKLE. **3.** Thou art as a dove Trembling its closed eyes KEATS. **4.** A tear-drop trembled from its source TENNYSON.

Tremblement (tre·mb'lmĕnt). 1677. [– Fr. *tremblement*, f. *trembler*; see prec., -MENT.] **1.** The action or condition of trembling (*lit.* and *fig.*); also, an instance of this, a tremor. **2.** A cause of trembling; a terror (*rare*) 1677.

Trembler (tre·mbləɹ). 1552. [f. TREMBLE *v.* + -ER[1].] **1.** One who trembles, esp. with fear; a timorous or terrified person. **2.** = QUAKER. *Obs.* or *Hist.* 1689. **3.** *Electr.* A vibrating spring blade which alternately makes and breaks the circuit in an induction coil 1877.

attrib.: **t.-bell,** an electric bell rung by a hammer attached to a t.

Tre·mbling, *ppl. a.* late ME. [f. as prec. + -ING[2].] That trembles. **b.** *transf.* Characterized or accompanied by trembling. late ME.

Comb.: **t. bog,** bog-land formed over water or soft mud, which shakes at every tread, a quaking bog; **-grass,** quaking-grass (*Briza media*); **t. palsy,** paralysis characterized by trembling of the extremities or of the head; **-poplar,** the Aspen, *Populus tremula.* Hence **Tre·mblingly** *adv.*

Trembly (tre·mbli), *a.* *colloq.* 1848. [f. TREMBLE *v.* or *sb.* + -Y[1].] Full of trembling; tremulous.

‖**Tremella** (trĭme·lă). 1760. [mod.L. (Dillenius, 1741), dim. from L. *tremulus, -ula* shaking, shivering.] *Bot.* A genus of amorphous hymenomycetous fungi consisting of tremulous gelatinous substance, typical of the family *Tremellaceæ* or *Tremellineæ*, most species of which grow on decayed wood, but some on the ground. Hence **Tre·mellose** *a. Bot.* shaking, like *T.*, tremulous.

Tremendous (trĭme·ndəs), *a.* 1632. [f. L. *tremendus*, gerundive of *tremere* tremble, tremble at, rel. to TREMOR; see -OUS.] **1.** Such as to excite trembling, or awe; 'dreadful; horrible; astonishingly terrible' (J.). **2.** Hyperbolically, or as a mere intensive: Such as to excite wonder on account of its magnitude or violence; extraordinarily great; immense. *colloq.* 1812. **b.** Extraordinary in respect of some quality indicated in the context (*slang*) 1831.

1. Not blaspheming the t. name of God EVELYN. **2.** They..drive at a t. pace 1845. He..determined to smother his feelings in a t. dinner 1882. Hence **Treme·ndous-ly** *adv.*, **-ness.**

Tremogram (tre·mŏgræm). 1899. [f. Gr. τρέμειν tremble, quiver + -GRAM.] A tracing recording involuntary muscular motion. So **Tre·mograph** [-GRAPH], an instrument for recording such motion.

‖**Tremolando** (tremola·ndo), *a.* (*adv., sb.*) Also **tremulando.** 1852. [It., pr. pple. of *tremolare* TREMBLE.] *Mus.* **A.** *adj.* (or *attrib.*) Tremulous, shaking. **B.** *adv.* In a tremulous or quivering manner; with a tremolo. **C.** *ellipt.* as *sb.* = TREMOLO 1, 2.

Tremolite (tre·mŏləit). 1799. [f. *Tremola*, in Switzerland, where found + -ITE[1] 2 b.] *Min.* A white or grey (sometimes transparent) variety of AMPHIBOLE, occurring in fibrous masses or thin-bladed crystals. Also called *grammatite.*

‖**Tremolo** (tre·mŏlo). 1801. [It. *tremolo* adj. and sb.] *Mus.* **1.** A tremulous or vibrating effect produced on certain musical instruments or in the human voice in singing, esp. to express intensity of emotion; cf. VIBRATO. **2.** A mechanical contrivance in an organ by which such an effect is produced. Also *t. stop.* 1867.

Tremor (tre·mǫɹ, trĭ·mǫɹ). late ME. [– OFr. *tremour* and (later) L. *tremor*, rel. to *tremere*, Gr. τρέμειν; see TREMBLE *v.*, -OR 1.] †**1.** Terror –1490. **2.** Involuntary agitation of the body or limbs, resulting from physical infirmity or from fear or other strong emotion; trembling 1615. **b.** With *a* and *pl.* A fit of trembling 1616. **c.** *fig.* A nervous thrill caused by emotion or excitement; also, a state of tremulous agitation or excitement 1754. **3.** A vibration, shaking, quivering, caused by some external impulse 1635. **4.** A tremble or quaver in the voice; a tremulous note or sound 1797.

2. **c.** He went about all day in a t. of delight DICKENS. **3.** The peculiar t. of a cotton-factory 1853. *Earth-t.*, an earthquake. Hence **Tre·mor** *v.*

Tremulant (tre·miŭlănt), *a.* and *sb.* 1837. [In gen. use a var. of *tremulous* with substitution of suffix -ANT; in musical contexts reflecting the It. *tremolante* adj. and sb.] **A.** *adj.* Tremulous; trembling. **B.** *sb. Mus.* = TREMOLO 2. 1862.

Tremulous (tre·miŭləs), *a.* 1611. [f. L. *tremulus* (f. *tremere* tremble) + -OUS.] **1.** Of persons, their limbs, etc.: Characterized or affected by trembling or quivering; hence, fearful, timorous. Also said of writing, a line, or the like, done by a tremulous hand; hence, finely wavy. **2.** Of things: Characterized by trembling or vibration 1616. **b.** Ready to vibrate in response *to* some influence 1794.

1. His voice unstrung Grew t. COWPER. **2.** The t. ripple on the surface of the sea 1860. Hence **Tre·mulous-ly** *adv.*, **-ness.**

Trenail: see TREENAIL.

Trench (trenʹʃ), *sb.* late ME. [– OFr. *trenche* cutting, cut, ditch, slice, f. *trenchier* see TRENCH *v.*] †**1.** A path or track cut through a wood or forest; an alley; a hollow walk –1575. **2.** A long and narrow hollow cut out of the ground; a cutting; a ditch, fosse; a deep furrow 1489. **3.** *Mil.* An excavation of this kind, the earth from which is thrown up in front as a parapet, serving either to cover or to oppose the advance of a besieging force, or to give cover to fighting or supporting forces, etc. Chiefly in *pl.* 1500. **4.** Something resembling a trench. **a.** A cut, scar, or deep wrinkle in the face 1588. **b.** *Anat.* and *Zool.* A cavity, pit, fossa 1615.

1. And in a t. forth in the park gooth she CHAUCER. **3.** There are trenches too..In which to stand all night to the knees in water In gallants breeds the tooth-ache MASSINGER. Phr. *To open trenches*, to break ground for the purpose of making approaches towards a besieged place. *To mount, relieve the trenches*, to occupy them, relieve those who have been on duty there. **4. a.** Witnesse these Trenches made by griefe and care SHAKS.

Comb. as *t.-warfare*, etc.: **t.-cavalier** *Mil.*, a high parapet constructed by besiegers upon the glacis to command and enfilade the covered way of the fortress; **-coat,** a short rain-coat of the kind worn in the trenches in the war of 1914–18; **-foot, -feet,** a gangrenous disease of the feet caused by much standing in water; **-mortar,** a mortar used in trenches for throwing heavy charges of high explosive a short distance.

Trench (trenʃ), *v.* 1483. [– OFr. *trenchier* (mod. *trancher*) cut :– Rom. **trincare*, alt. f. L. *truncare*; see TRUNCATE *v.*] **I.** To cut, make a cutting. **1.** *trans.* To cut; to divide by cutting, slice, cut in pieces; to cut off, cut into; to cut *one's way.* Also *absol.* †**b.** To cut *in(to)* a surface –1665. †**c.** To make (a cut, gash, wound) *in(to)* something –1610. **2.** To cut or make a cutting through a ridge or raised surface 1601. **b.** *fig.* (with the surface furrowed or cut as obj.) 1624.

1. **b.** This weake impresse of Loue, is as a figure Trenched in ice SHAKS. **c.** The wide wound, that the boare had trencht In his soft flanke SHAKS. **2.** The ridge is deeply trenched with gullies and narrow glens 1865.

II. From TRENCH *sb.* **1.** To cut a trench or trenches in (the ground) 1530. **b.** *spec.* in *Agric.* and *Hortic.*: To make a series of trenches in digging or ploughing (a piece of ground), so as to bring the lower soil to the surface. Also *absol.* 1573. **c.** *intr.* or *absol.* To dig a trench or trenches 1786. **2.** *trans.* To furnish with, set, or place in a trench 1596. **3.** *Mil.* To surround or fortify with a trench; to cast a trench *about, around* (an army, town, etc.); to entrench 1548.

1. **b.** Thy garden plot latelie well trenched and muckt TUSSER. Phr. *To t. up*, to lay (land) in trenches and ridges alternately. **c.** T. deeply.. and as early in the winter as possible 1882. **3.** The place which they had trenched, dytched, and fortefied with ordenaunce HALL.

III. †**1.** *intr. To t. to* (*unto*): To extend in effect to; to extend so as to affect or touch –1633. †**b.** To extend or stretch (*rare*) –1775. **2.** †**a.** *To t. into* (*unto*): To 'cut' into, to enter into so as to affect or concern intimately –1641. **b.** *To t. on* or *upon*: To encroach (however slightly) *on* or *upon* a region which is the domain of another 1622. **c.** in vaguer use: To come in thought, speech, or action close *upon* (something); hence, to have a bearing *upon* or reference to (something) 1635.

2. **b.** To t. on the liberty of individuals 1799. **c.** He did t. a little too neare upon an untruth 1639. Some unlucky jest, trenching on treason 1841.

Trenchancy (tre·nʃănsi). 1866. [f. next; see -ANCY.] The quality of being trenchant.

Trenchant (tre·nʃănt), *a.* ME. [– OFr. *trenchant* (mod. *tranchant*), pr. pple. of *trenchier*; see TRENCH *v.*, -ANT.] **1.** Cutting, adapted for cutting; sharp. *arch.* and *poet.* **b.** *Zool.* Of a tooth, bill, etc.: Having a cutting edge; sectorial 1831. **c.** *transf.*, *fig.*, or *allus.* 1603. **2.** *fig.* esp. of language: Incisive; vigorous and clear; effective, energetic ME. **3.** *transf.* and *fig.* Clear-cut; distinct 1849.

1. The t. Blade, Toledo trusty 1663. **2.** Their Swords Were sharp and trencheant, not their Words 1663. **3.** The line of demarcation is seemingly most sharp and t. 1873. Hence **Tre·nchant-ly** *adv.*, **-ness.**

Trencher[1] (tre·nʃəɹ). ME. [– AFr. *trenchour*, OFr. *trencheoir*, f. *trenchier* TRENCH *v.*; see -ER[2] 3.] †**I.** A cutting or slicing instrument; a knife –1553. **II. 1.** A flat piece of wood, square or circular, on which meat was served and cut up; a plate or platter. *arch.* and *Hist.* ME. **2.** A trencher and that which it bears; a supply of food. *arch.* 1576. **3.** *transf.* A flat board, circular or otherwise 1511. **4.** *spec.* = TRENCHER-CAP 1834.

1. The first dinner which she ate on wooden trenchers delighted her MAR. EDGEWORTH. **2.** Phr. *To lick the t.*, to toady; to play the parasite. **4.** The girl students..in their red gowns and trenchers adorned with a red tassel 1906.

Trencher[2] (tre·nʃəɹ). 1871. [f. TRENCH *v.* + -ER[1].] One who cuts or digs trenches; one who trenches ground.

Tre·ncher-cap. 1721. [f. TRENCHER[1] + CAP *sb.*[1]] A popular name for the academic or college cap, in shape thought to resemble an inverted trencher with a basin upon it; a MORTAR-BOARD.

Tre·ncher-man. 1586. [f. TRENCHER[1] + MAN *sb.*] †**1.** A cook or caterer. SIDNEY. **2.** A feeder; an eater; usu. qualified, as *good*, *stout*, *valiant*, etc., one who has a hearty appetite 1590. **3.** One who frequents a patron's table; a dependent, hanger-on 1599.

Trenchmore (tre·nʃmōᵊɹ), *sb.* 1551. [Of unkn. origin.] An old English country dance of a lively or boisterous nature; also, the air to which it was danced.

Ile make him daunce a trenchmoor to my sword 1611. Hence **Tre·nchmore** *v. intr.* to dance the t.

Trench-plough, -plow (tre·nʃ,plau), *v.* 1731. [f. TRENCH *sb.* or *v.* + PLOUGH *v.*] *trans.* and *intr.* To plough to the depth of two furrows, bringing the lower soil to the surface. Hence **Tre·nch-plough** *sb.* a plough designed or adjusted for trench-ploughing.

Trend (trend), *sb.* 1777. [f. next.] **1.** *Naut.* **a.** That part of the shank of an anchor where it thickens towards the crown 1794. **b.** The angle between the direction of the anchor-cable and that of the ship's keel 1879. **2.** The way something trends or bends away; the general direction which a stream, coast, mountain-range, etc., tends to take 1777. **b.** *fig.* The general course, tendency, or drift (of action, thought, etc.) 1884.

2. The t. and character of the marine currents 1854. **b.** The general t. of affairs in Munster 1912.

Trend, *v.* Pa. t. and pa. pple. **trended.** [OE. *trendan*, f. Gmc. **trend*- **trand*- **trund*-, repr. also by OE. *trinda* round lump, ball, *ātrendlian* roll away. See TRENDLE, TRINDLE, TRUNDLE.] †**1.** *intr.* To turn round, revolve, rotate, roll; also *fig.* –1654. †**2.** *trans.* To cause (a thing) to turn round; to turn or roll (anything); *fig.* to revolve in one's mind –1616. **b.** To wind (wool, partly cleaned) into tops for spinning (*dial.*) 1777. †**3.** *intr.* To skirt, coast (*about*, *along*) –1622. †**b.** More vaguely: To turn or direct one's course –1846. **4.** To turn off in a specified direction; to run, stretch, incline, bend (in some direction) 1598. **b.** *fig.* To have a general tendency (as a discussion, events, etc.) 1863.

2. Not farre beneath i'th valley as she trends Her siluer streame 1613. **3. b.** The religion of blood, like the beasts of prey, will continue to t. northward LANDOR. **4.** Their path lay along the coast trending round to the west 1876.

Trendle (tre·nd'l), *sb.* [OE. *trendel* circle, ring, etc., = MLG. *trendel* round disc, MHG. *trendel* ball, circle :- Gmc. **trend*-; see prec., -LE.] †**1.** A circle, a ring, a coronet; a circular disc, orb; a ball, globe. –late ME. **2.** A wheel. *Obs.* exc. *dial.* ME. **3.** A bundle of (partly cleaned) wool 'trended'. *dial.* 1493. Hence †**Tre·ndle** *v.* = TRUNDLE *v.* 1a, b.

Trental (tre·ntăl). ME. [– OFr. *trentel* and med.L. *trentalis*, f. pop.L. **trenta*, for L. *triginta* thirty, f. *tres* TRI- + **gint*- ten; see -AL[1] 1.] **1.** A set of thirty requiem masses, said on the same day or on different days; also, the payment made for this. *arch.* and *Hist.* †**b.** *loosely.* An elegy or dirge. HERRICK. **2.** *Used as* = MONTH'S MIND, the commemoration service on the thirtieth day after burial. *arch.* 1659.

1. Obits, Trentals, and Services for the Dead 1694.

‖**Trente et quarante** (trãntekarãnt). 1671. [Fr. = thirty and forty.] Another name for the game of *rouge-et-noir* (in which thirty and forty are respectively winning and losing numbers).

Trentine (tre·ntəin), *a.* 1601. [f. *Trent*, a city of the Tyrol + -INE[1].] = TRIDENTINE.

Trenton (tre·ntən). 1854. *Geol.* (*attrib.*, or *ellipt.* as *sb.*) Applied to a limestone formation exemplified at Trenton Falls, New York, and hence to the series of Lower Silurian rocks to which it belongs.

Trepan (trĭpæ·n), *sb.*[1] late ME. [– med.L. *trepanum* – Gr. τρύπανον borer, f. τρυπᾶν pierce, bore, τρύπη hole.] **1.** A surgical instrument in the form of a crown-saw, for cutting out small pieces of bone, esp. from the skull. †**2.** A military engine formerly used in sieges –1610. **3.** A boring instrument for sinking shafts. (Usu. as Fr., *trépan.*) 1877.

Trepan, trapan (trĕ-, trăpæ·n), *sb.*[2] *Obs.* or *arch.* 1641. [orig. *trapan*, prob. formed in some way from TRAP *sb.*[1] or *v.*[1] Prob. a term of thieves' or rogues' slang.] **1.** A person who entraps or decoys others into actions or positions which may be to his advantage and to their ruin or loss. **2.** [f. TREPAN *v.*[2]] The action of entrapping; a stratagem, trick; a trap or snare 1665.

1. He was a Rogue, and a manifest T. of the Earl's NORTH. **2.** There being a Snare, and a Trapan almost in every Word we hear 1671.

Trepa·n, *v.*[1] ME. [– (O)Fr. *trépaner*, f. *trépan* TREPAN *sb.*[1]] *trans.* To operate upon with a trepan; to saw through with a trepan, as a bone of the skull. Also *absol.*

Trepan, trapan (trĕ-, trăpæ·n), *v.*[2] *Obs.* or *arch.* 1656. [f. TREPAN *sb.*[2]] *trans.* To catch in a trap; to entrap, ensnare, beguile. **b.** To lure, inveigle (*into* or *to* a place, course of action, etc., *to do* something, etc.) 1661. **c.** To cheat or beguile *out of* (a thing); to swindle 1662.

To lie upon the catch to t. his neighbour 1745. **c.** Ten of those Rogues had trapann'd him out of 500. Crowns 1662. Hence **Trepa·nner** = TREPAN *sb.*[2] 1.

‖**Trepang** (trĭpæ·ŋ). 1783. [Malay *trīpang.*] A marine animal, an echinoderm (*Holothuria edulis*), called also *sea-cucumber*, *sea-slug*, *sea-swallow*, or *bêche-de-mer*, eaten as a luxury by the Chinese.

Trephine (trĭfəi·n, -fī·n), *sb.* 1628. [orig. *trafine*, f. L. *tres fines* three ends, app. formed after TREPAN *sb.*[1]] An improved form of trepan, with a transverse handle, and a removable or adjustable sharp steel centre-pin which is fixed upon the bone to steady the movement in operating. Hence **Trephi·ne** *v. trans.* to operate upon with a t. **Trephina·tion.**

Trepid (tre·pid), *a. rare.* 1650. [– L. *trepidus* scared, alarmed.] Trembling; agitated; fearful.

Trepidate (tre·pideᴵt), *v. rare.* 1623. [– *trepidat*-, pa. ppl. stem of L. *trepidare*, f. *trepidus*; see prec., -ATE[3].] *intr.* To tremble with fear or agitation; also simply, †To shake.

Trepidation (trepidēᴵʃən). 1605. [– L. *trepidatio*, *-ōn*-, f. as prec.; see -ION.] **1.** Tremulous agitation; confused hurry or alarm; confusion; flurry; perturbation 1607. **2.** Tremulous, vibratory, or reciprocating movement; vibration; oscillation, rocking; an instance of this; also, tremor, as in paralytic affections 1605. **3.** *Astron.* A libration of the eighth (or ninth) sphere, added c950 to the system of Ptolemy, in order to account for certain phenomena, esp. precession, really due to motion of the earth's axis 1631.

1. They did their work at leisure..without t., as men lawfully employed JOHNSON. **2.** Earthquakes and trepidations of the earth 1696.

Trepidity (trĕpi·dĭti). 1721. [f. TREPID + -ITY. Cf. med.L. *trepiditas* (XIV).] Agitation, alarm, fearfulness.

Tresai·el, tresay·le. *Obs.* exc. *Hist.* 1491. [AFr., formed after BESAIEL; cf. Fr. *trisaïeul*, f. *tri*- TRI- + *aïeul* grandfather.] A grandfather's grandfather; a great-great-grandfather.

Trespass (tre·spăs), *sb.* ME. [– OFr. *trespas* passing across, etc. (mod. *trépas* death), f. *trespasser*; see next.] **1.** A transgression; a breach of law or duty; an offence, sin, wrong; a fault. **2.** *Law.* Any violation or transgression of the law; *spec.* one not amounting to treason, felony, or misprision of either ME. **3.** *Law. spec.* Any actionable wrong committed against the person or property of another; also short for *action of t.* ME. **4.** A passing beyond some limit (*rare*) 1650. **5.** An encroachment, intrusion *on* or *upon* 1769.

1. And ye wyll not forgeve men there trespases, no more shall youre father forgeve your treaspases TINDALE *Matt.* 6:12. **3.** *T. to land*, a wrongful entry upon the lands of another, with damage (however inconsiderable) to his real property. *T. on the case*, a form of action now obsolete in which the damage complained of is a result not immediate, but consequential of an unlawful act; so called from the L. name of the writs (*brevia de transgressione super casum*) under which it was brought; also the name of the writ itself. **5.** One t. more I must make on your patience GLADSTONE.

Tre·spass, *v.* ME. [– OFr. *trespasser* pass beyond, etc. (mod. *trépasser* die) – med.L. *transpassare*; see TRANS-, PASS *v.*] **1.** *intr.* To commit a transgression or offence; to offend; to sin. †**2.** *trans.* **a.** To transgress, violate (a law, etc.) –1613. †**b.** To offend against, wrong, violate (a person) –1556. **3.** *Law. intr.* To commit a trespass (see TRESPASS *sb.* 2); *spec.* to enter unlawfully on the land of another, or on that which is the property or right of another. Const. *on*, *upon.* 1455. **4.** *fig.* To make an improper or uninvited inroad on (a person's time, attention, patience, etc.); to intrude *on* or *upon* the rights or domain of; to encroach on, infringe 1652.

1. He trespasses against his duty who sleeps upon his watch BURKE. **2. a.** She had trespaced his commaundement CAXTON. **4.** I am afraid that I have trespassed a little upon the patience of the Reader 1652.

Trespasser (tre·spăsəɹ). [In XIV *trespas(s)our* (Langl.), – AFr. *trespassour* = OFr. *trespasseor*, f. *trespasser* TRESPASS *v.*; see -ER[2] 3.] **1.** A law-breaker; a wrong-doer, sinner, offender. **2.** *Law.* One who commits a trespass; *esp.* one who trespasses on the lands of another 1455.

Tress (tres), *sb.* ME. [– (O)Fr. *tresse*, †*tresce* ≐ Pr. *tressa*, It. *treccia*, in med.L. *trica*, *tricia*, *tricea*; referred by Diez to **trichea* f. Gr. τρίχα threefold.] A plait or braid of the hair of the head, usu. of a woman. **b.** (By extension) A long lock of hair (esp. that of a woman); mostly in pl. *tresses* ME. **c.** *transf.* and *fig.* Applied to long leafy shoots or tendrils, rays of the sun, etc. late ME.

Their beautiful hair [was] divided into many tresses, hanging on their shoulders 1717. **b.** Rose-checkt Adonis with his amber tresses 1595. **c.** Luxuriant tresses of maiden-hair fern 1875. Hence **Tre·ssful** *a.* full of or fully furnished with tresses.

Tress, *v.* Now *rare* exc. in *pa. pple.* late ME. [– (O)Fr. *tresser*, †*trecier* = It. *trecciare*, in med.L. *tricare* (XII); see prec.] *trans.* To arrange (hair) in tresses or (threads, etc.) in braids.

-tress, ending of feminines of agent-nouns in *-ter*, *-tor*, etc., usu. short for *-ter-ess*, *-tor-ess*; see -ESS[1].

Tressed (trest, *poet.* tre·sėd), *ppl. a.* and *a.* ME. [f. TRESS *sb.* and *v.* + -ED.] **1.** Of the hair: Arranged in tresses; braided. late ME. **2.** Having or furnished with tresses; often in comb., as *gold-t.*, etc. ME.

Tressure (tre·siūɹ, tre·ʃŭɹ). ME. [Earlier *tressour* – OFr. *tressour*; later *tressure* – OFr. *tress(e)ure*; see TRESS *sb.*, -OUR, -URE. These forms are reflected in AL. *tressatoria* tress, hair (in pl., XIII), *tressatura* interlacing, (XII), *tricatura* tress (XIII).] †**1.** A ribbon or band worn round the head; a net with which a woman's tresses are confined; a head-dress –1483. **2.** *Her.* A diminutive of the orle (ORLE 1 a), consisting of a narrow band of one-quarter the width of the bordure 1440. **3.** *Numism.* An ornamental enclosure, circular or of several arches, containing the type or distinctive device, found on many gold and silver coins of former centuries 1745.

Tressy (tre·si), *a.* 1614. [f. TRESS *sb.* + -Y[1].] Resembling, characterized by, or adorned with tresses.

Trestle (tre·s'l). ME. [– OFr. *trestel* (mod. *tréteau*) :– Rom. **transtellum*, dim. of L. *transtrum* beam; see -EL, -LE 2.] **1.** A support for something, consisting of a short horizontal beam or bar with diverging legs, usu. two at each end; *esp.* one of a pair or set used to support a board so as to form a table. **2.** *Her.* A low stool or bench used as a bearing: usu. represented with three legs 1610. **3.** *spec.* **a.** A framework consisting of upright (or more or less inclined) pieces with diagonal braces, used to support a bridge or other elevated structure 1796. **b.** One of the timber props or shores used to support a ship while being built 1860. **c.** = TRESTLE-TREE. **4.** *transf.* and *fig.*: esp. (*pl.*) applied to the legs 1610.

Comb.: **t.-bed,** a movable bed supported upon trestles, as used in a hospital tent, etc.; **-board,** a board laid upon trestles to form a table; **-bridge,** a bridge supported upon trestles or trestlework; **-table,** a table made of a board or boards laid upon trestles; **trestlework,** a framework composed of a series of trestles fastened together, for supporting a bridge or viaduct, esp. on a railway.

Trestle-tree. 1652. [f. TRESTLE + TREE *sb.* 3.] *Naut. pl.* Two strong pieces of timber fixed horizontally fore-and-aft on opposite sides of a mast-head, to support the cross-trees, the top, and the fid of the mast above.

Tret (tret). *Obs.* exc. *Hist.* 1500. [– AFr., OFr. *tret*, var. of *trait* draught (cf. TRAIT), but the sense development is obscure.] *Comm.* An allowance of 4 lb. in 104 lb. (= $\frac{1}{26}$) on goods sold by weight after the deduction for tare.

Trews (trūz), *sb. pl.* 1568. [– Ir. *trius*, Gael. *triubhas* (sing.); see TROUSE.] Close-fitting trousers, or breeches combined with stockings, formerly worn by Irishmen and Scottish Highlanders, and still by certain Scottish regiments.

Trey (trē[i]). late ME. [– OFr. *trei*, *treis* (mod. *trois*) :– L. *tres* THREE.] **1.** The three at dice or cards. **2.** *slang.* The number three; a set of three; a threepenny piece 1896.

Comb.: **t.-ace,** a throw that turns up trey with one die and ace with the other; so **t.-deuce.**

Tri- (trəi, *occas.* tri), *prefix*, – L. *tri-*, Gr. τρι-, comb. form of *tres*, τρεῖς three, τρίς thrice.

I. Forming adjs. (and derived sbs. and advbs.) with the senses: **1.** Having, characterized by, or consisting (*rarely*, belonging or relating to) three (of the things denoted by the second element). **a.** In comb. with adjs. derived from sbs., or with sbs. without adjectival termination. **Triade·lphous,** *Bot.* of stamens: united by the filaments into three bundles; of a plant: having such stamens. **Triarti·culate,** three-jointed. **Tribra·cteate,** *Bot.* having three bracts. **Trico·ccous,** *Bot.* composed of three *cocci* or carpels; of a plant: having fruit of this kind. **Tri:consona·ntal,** consisting of or containing three consonants: said chiefly of radical words of the Semitic langs. **Trico·rporal, -co·rporate,** three-bodied. **Tricro·tic** [after DICROTIC], *Physiol.* of the pulse, etc.: having or showing three undulations for each beat of the heart. **Trida·ctyl,** having three fingers or toes. **Tride·ntate,** *Bot.* and *Zool.* having three teeth or tooth-like processes. **Tridime·nsional,** having or exhibiting three dimensions, as a solid body. **Trifo·liolate,** *Bot.* consisting of three leaflets, or having leaves of this form. **Trifu·rcate,** divided into three branches like the prongs of a fork. **Trili·neal,** *Geom.* = TRILINEAR. **Trili·ngual,** speaking or using, written or expressed in, or relating to three languages. **Trilo·bate,** *Nat. Hist.* three-lobed. **Trilo·cular,** *Nat. Hist.* having three cells or compartments. **Trima·cular,** having or marked with three spots. **Trine·rvate,** *Nat. Hist.* having three nerves or veins. **Trino·ctial,** belonging to or lasting three nights. **Trino·dal,** having three nodes. **Trino·minal,** having three names. **Tri·ode,** of a thermionic valve, having three electrodes; also *absol.* as *sb.* **Tri·part** (*rare*), **-parted** = TRIPARTITE. **Tripedal** (stress var.), three-footed. **Tripe·talous,** *Bot.* having, or consisting of, three petals. **Triphy·llous,** *Bot.* three-leaved; *spec.* of a calyx or corolla, trisepalous or tripetalous. **Trirecta·ngular,** having three right angles, as a spherical triangle. **Trise·palous,** *Bot.* having or consisting of three sepals. **Trise·rial, Trise·riate,** arranged in three series or rows. **Trispe·rmous** [Gr. σπέρμα seed], *Bot.* containing three seeds. **Tristi·chous,** *Bot.* arranged in, or characterized by, three rows or ranks. **Tristigma·tic, Tristi·gmatose,** *Bot.* having three stigmas. **Trisu·lcate,** *Bot.* marked with three grooves; *Zool.* divided into three digits. **Tritube·rculate,** *Comp. Anat.* having three tubercles, as a tooth. **Tri·valve,** *Nat. Hist.* having three valves. **b.** With Eng. sbs. (without adj. ending); chiefly nonce-wds. as *tri-church*, *-party*, *-phase.* **c.** Occas. with sb. + -ED[2]; as *tri-bladed*, *-cornered*, *-faced*, etc.

2. Triply; three times; in three ways, directions, etc. **Tricli·nic,** *Cryst.* applied to that system of crystalline forms in which the three axes are unequal and obliquely inclined; belonging to this system. **Tricu·rvate,** 'curved in three directions, as a sponge-spicule.' **Trifa·cial,** *Anat.* applied to the fifth pair of cranial nerves, which divide into three branches supplying the face and some adjacent parts. **Triqua·drifid,** *Bot.* having three lobes each deeply divided into four segments. **Triqui·nate,** *Bot.* having three lobes each divided into five. **Trira·diate,** radiating in three ways from a central point. **Trite·rnate,** *Bot.* thrice ternate. **b.** *spec.* in *Cryst.* denoting forms having three ranges of facets, the number in each range being expressed by the second element; as **tri·octahe·dral** (8); also **tri-rhomboi·dal,** having eighteen faces occupying the positions of those of three different rhomboids.

3. In comb. with an adj. (usu. in *-ly*) derived from a sb. denoting a period of time: Comprising three —, lasting three —, occurring or appearing every three (days, etc.); also (*loosely*) occurring three times (a day, etc.); those in -LY are also used as advbs. = every three (days, etc.); as *tridai·ly*, *triwee·kly*, etc.

II. Forming sbs. with the senses: **a.** Something consisting of or equivalent to three (of the things denoted by the second element); a triple—. **Tri·phony,** in early mediæval music, diaphony for three voices. **b.** Something having, or related in some way to, three (of the things denoted or indicated by the second element). **Tri·phylite** [Gr. φυλή tribe], *Min.* a compound phosphate of iron, manganese, and lithium. **Tri·plane,** an aeroplane with three supporting planes. **Tri·pody,** *Pros.* a group or verse of three feet. **Tri:sacramenta·rian,** one who recognizes three and only three sacraments. **Tri·theism,** belief in three gods; *esp.* the doctrine that the three persons of the Trinity are three distinct gods; hence **Tri·theist, Tri·theite. Tri·tone,** *Mus.* an interval consisting of three whole tones; an augmented fourth. **Tri·valve,** a shell having three valves. **c.** Something (denoted by the second element) having three of some characteristic part, or related to three things. **Tri·car** (**-machine, -motor-car**), a motor-car with three wheels; a motor-tricycle with a seat for a person or a carrier for luggage in front. **Tri·coaster,** a combination of a three-speed gear with a 'coaster' brake on a cycle. **Tripy·ramid,** *Cryst.* a triangular pyramid, as a form in certain calcareous spars.

III. In Chemical nomenclature, in the names of compounds and derivatives, with general sense 'three', 'three times'. **a.** Prefixed to names of compounds of elements, radicals, or groups, names of salts, etc., to signify three atoms, groups, or equivalents of these elements or radicals in combination with another element or radical; e.g. **trichlo·ride,** a compound of three atoms of chlorine with another element or radical, as *arsenic trichloride.* So **tri-a·mide, -a·mine, -glyceride, -oxide, -saccharide, -silicate, -sulphate, -sulphide,** etc. Also in names of compound ethers or esters of glycerin with acids, as in **triolein, -palmitin, -stearin,** etc. **b.** Prefixed to adjs., or to sbs. used attrib., in the names or descriptions of acids, alcohols, compound ethers or esters, oxides, salts, etc.; e.g. *trisodic* or *trisodium*, (a salt) containing 3 atoms of sodium; *triethylic* or *triethyl* (a compound) containing 3 ethyl groups; so *trithionic*, etc. **c.** Prefixed to the names of elements or radicals, or their combining forms (as *azo-*, *bromo-*, etc.) entering into the name of a compound, to signify that three atoms or groups of the element or radical are present, or are substituted for hydrogen, in the substance designated by the rest of the name; so **triphen-, triphenyl-,** etc. **d.** In vbs. and their pples. derived from sbs. as in a, as *tribrominated*, *trichlorinated*, in which three hydrogen atoms have been replaced by atoms of bromine or chlorine; *trihydrated*, containing three molecules of water.

IV. Forming vbs. (and derivs.) as TRISECT, -SECTION.

Triable (trəi·ăb'l), *a.* late ME. [– AFr. *triable*, f. as TRY *v.* + -ABLE.] **1.** *Law.* Capable of being tried in a court of law; liable to judicial trial. **2.** That may be ascertained, tested, or proved 1612.

2. In our..first Experiment, and..others tryable in our Engine BOYLE.

Triacontad (trəi,ăkǫ·ntæd). 1621. [– Gr. τριακοντάς, -αδ-, f. τριάκοντα thirty; see -AD.] The number thirty, or a set of thirty. So **Triacontahedral** (-hī·drăl, -he·drăl) [Gr. ἕδρα base, side] *a.* contained by thirty faces, esp. by thirty rhombs, as a crystal.

Triaconter (trəi·ăkǫntəɹ) [– Gr. τριακοντήρης], an ancient Greek galley with thirty oars.

Triad (trəi·æd). 1546. [– Fr. *triade* or late L. *trias*, *triad-* – Gr. τριάς, τριαδ-, f. τρι- THREE; see -AD.] **1.** A group or set of three (persons, things, words, attributes, etc.); three collectively or in connection. **b.** The number three (in Pythagorean philosophy) 1660. **2.** *spec.* **a.** Applied to the Trinity 1661. **b.** A group of three associated or correlated deities, beings, or powers 1746. **c.** In Welsh literature: A form of composition characterized by an arrangement of subjects or statements in groups of three 1819. **d.** *Mus.* A chord of three notes consisting of a given note with the third and fifth above it; e.g. a common chord (without the octave) 1801. **e.** *Chem.* A trivalent element or radical 1865. **f.** *Math.* (*a*) A set of three things, esp. in *Geom.* of three points. (*b*) In Quaternions, an indeterminate product of three vectors. 1850.

1. Three triads of Lancet windows 1898. Hence **Tria·dic** *a.* of, pertaining to, or constituting a t., consisting of triads; so **Tria·dical** *a.*, **-ly** *adv.*

Triage (trəi·ėdʒ). 1727. [– (O)Fr. *triage*, f. *trier*; see TRY *v.* -AGE.] The action of assorting according to quality. Also *attrib.*; hence *concr.* coffee beans of the third or lowest quality.

Triakis- (trəi·ăkis), repr. Gr. τριάκις thrice, as in **Tri:akis,o:ctahe·dron** (pl. **-hedra**), *Geom.* and *Cryst.* a solid derived from the octahedron by erecting a triangular pyramid on each face, thus multiplying the original number of faces by three.

Trial (trəi·ăl), *sb.* 1526. [– AFr. *trial*, also *triel* (latinized *triallum*, perh. the immed. source), f. *trier* TRY *v.*; see -AL[1] 2.] The action or fact of trying or being tried, in various senses of TRY *v.* **1.** *Law.* The examination and determination of a cause by a judicial tribunal 1577. **b.** The determination of a person's guilt or innocence, or the righteousness of his cause, by a combat between the accuser and accused (*t. by battle*, *by* (*single*) *combat*, *by wager of battle*, *by the sword*); see also *t. by* ORDEAL 1593. **2.** The action of testing or putting to the proof the fitness, truth, strength, or other quality of anything; test, probation 1526. **b.** The fact or condition of being tried by suffering or temptation; probation 1550. **3.** Action, method, or treatment adopted in order to ascertain the result; experiment 1570. **4.** A testing of qualifications, attainments, or progress; examination 1672. **5.** An attempt to do something; an endeavour, effort 1614. **6.** That which puts one to the test; *esp.* a painful test of one's endurance, patience, or faith; hence, affliction, trouble, misfortune 1754. **7.** Something that serves as a sample or proof of a manufacture or material, the skill of an operator, etc.; *spec.* in *Pottery manuf.* a piece of clay or the like by which the progress of the firing process may be judged; a trial-piece 1608.

1. Phr. *To bring* (a person or cause) *to t.*; *to put* (a person) *on his t.*, *to stand* (*one's*) *t.*, etc.; also *t. by jury*, etc. **2.** The triall of mettall by fire 1604. **b.** That which purifies us is triall MILT. **3.** *Rule of t. and error*: see POSITION *sb.* 3. **5.** I proposed to make a t. for landing if the weather should suit SMEATON. **6.** All people have their trials DICKENS.

Phrases. *On t.* (sense 2) on the basis or condition

of being tried, as *to take* a person or thing *on t.*, to take subject to the condition of being satisfactory when tried. *To be on* (*his, her,* or *its*) *t.* (2, 4), to be in a state of probation until it is seen how he or it will succeed or work.

Comb.: **t. balance,** in book-keeping by double entry, an addition of the whole of the entries on each side of the ledger, when the sum of the debits ought to balance the sum of the credits; **t. eight,** *Boat-racing,* an eight-oared boat's provisional crew, from among whom some members of the final eight may be chosen; **-list,** the register of causes or prisoners to be tried; **-piece,** something made or taken as a specimen; *spec.* a coin or the like struck as a test of the die, or as a specimen of the design; **t. proof,** a proof taken from a plate during the process of engraving to show its state; **t. square** = try-square; **-trip,** a trip taken to test the speed, etc. of a vessel, etc.

Tri·al, *a.* 1886. [f. L. *tri-* + -AL[1] 1, after *dual.*] *Gram.* = TRINAL *a.* 2.

Triality (trəi,æ·lĭti). *rare.* 1529. [f. after earlier PLURALITY. Cf. DUALITY (AL. *dualitas*), and AL. *trialis* one holding three benefices (1577).] †**1.** The holding of three benefices at once –1637. **2.** The condition or quality of being threefold 1872.

Trialogue (trəi·ălǫg). 1532. [irreg. formation after *dialogue,* quasi *di-alogue.* Earliest as med.L. *trialogus, -ologius,* book by Wyclif.] A dialogue between three persons.

‖**Triandria** (trəi,æ·ndriă). 1748. [mod.L. (Linn., 1735), f. *triandrus,* f. Gr. τρεῖς three + ἀνήρ, ἀνδρ- man, taken as = stamen; see -ANDROUS.] *Bot.* The third class in the Linnæan Sexual System, comprising plants having hermaphrodite flowers with three stamens not cohering; also, an order in some classes, comprising plants having three stamens. So **Tria·ndrian, Tria·ndrious,** and (usu.) **Tria·ndrous** *adjs.* having three stamens; belonging to the *T.*

Triangle (trəi·æŋg'l). late ME. [– (O)Fr. *triangle* or L. *triangulum,* subst. use of n. of *triangulus* three-cornered, f. *tri-* TRI- + *angulus* ANGLE *sb.*[2]] **1.** *Geom.,* etc. A figure (usu. a plane rectilineal figure) having three angles and three sides. **b.** A figure of this form used symbolically (e.g. an equilateral triangle as a symbol of the Trinity), or in magic or necromancy 1584. **c.** *fig.* A group or set of three, a triad 1621. **2.** Something having the form of a triangle; any three-cornered body, object, or space 1618. **b.** *Astron.* The constellation *Triangulum,* north of *Aries* characterized by three stars in the positions of the angular points of an isosceles triangle 1551. **c.** A musical instrument of percussion, consisting of a steel rod bent into a triangular form, but open at one corner; it is struck with a small straight steel rod. Also, the player of this. 1801. **d.** *Mil.* (usu. *pl.*) A tripod, originally formed of three halberds stuck in the ground and joined at the top, to which soldiers were formerly bound to be flogged; a structure resembling this 1847. **e.** A drawing-instrument in the form of a right-angled triangle of wood, vulcanite, etc.; a set square 1877.

1. *Circular t.,* a plane triangle formed by three intersecting circular arcs. *Spherical t.,* a triangle formed by three arcs upon the surface of a sphere; see SPHERICAL. *T. of forces,* the theorem in statics that if three forces in one plane, acting at one point, be in equilibrium, three straight lines in that plane parallel to their directions will form a triangle whose sides are proportional to their magnitudes. **c.** Mrs. Dudeney's novel..deals with the eternal t., which, in this case, consists of two men and one woman 1907.

†**Triangled,** *a.* 1486. [f. prec. + -ED[1].] Three-cornered, triangular –1828.

Triangular (trəi,æ·ŋgiŭlăɹ), *a.* 1541. [– late L. *triangularis*; see TRIANGLE, -AR[1].] **1.** Having, or arranged in, the form of a triangle; contained by three sides and angles; three-cornered, three-sided. **b.** Having three edges, as a prism or pyramid; trihedral, triquetrous 1644. **c.** Contained by triangles, as a solid figure (*rare*) 1805. **2.** Pertaining or relating to a triangle 1701. **3.** *fig.* Relating to or taking place between three persons or parties, three-sided; also, constituting a triad, threefold, triple 1812.

2. *T. compasses,* a kind of compasses with three legs, used for taking off triangles. *T. numbers,* the first series of POLYGONAL numbers (1, 3, 6, 10, 15, 21, etc.) obtained by continued summation of the natural numbers 1, 2, 3, 4, 5, 6, etc. So **Tri-angula·rity,** the quality of being t. **Tria·ngularly** *adv.*

Triangulate (trəi,æ·ŋgiŭlět), *a.* 1610. [– med.L. *triangulatus* triangular, f. L. *triangulum* TRIANGLE; see -ATE[2].] Chiefly *Nat. Hist.* **1.** Having three angles, triangular. 1611. **2.** Made up or composed of triangles 1610. **3.** Having triangular markings 1891.

Triangulate (trəi,æ·ŋgiŭleᶦt), *v.* 1833. [f. L. *triangulum* + -ATE[3].] **1.** *trans. Surveying* (also *transf.,* as in *Astron.*). To measure and map out (a region or territory) by tracing a series or network of triangles from a base-line and measuring their sides and angles; to determine (e.g. a distance or altitude) in this way. Also *absol.* **b.** *gen.* To mark out into triangles 1853. **2.** To divide or convert into triangles 1864.

Triangulation (trəi,æŋgiŭlēᶦ·ʃən). 1818. [f. prec., or f. as prec., + -ATION.] The action or process of triangulating. **1.** The tracing and measurement of a series or network of triangles in order to survey and map out a territory or region. **2.** Division of a rectilinear figure into triangles 1891.

Triarch (trəi·aɹk). 1886. [f. TRI- + *-arch* in *tetrarch.*] The ruler of one of three divisions of a country or territory.

Triarchy (trəi·aɹki). 1601. [f. TRI- + Gr. -αρχία government (see -ARCH), or – Gr. τριαρχία triumvirate.] **1.** The government or jurisdiction of a triarch; one of three divisions of a country ruled by triarchs. **2.** Government by three rulers or powers jointly; a triumvirate 1656. **3.** A group of three districts or divisions each under its own ruler 1660.

Trias (trəi·æ̆s). 1610. [– late L. *trias*; see TRIAD. In sense 2 after G. *trias,* 1834.] **1.** The number three; a set of three, a triad. **2.** *Geol.* Name for the series of strata lying immediately beneath the Jurassic and above the Permian; so called because divisible, where typically developed (as in Germany), into three groups (*Keuper, Muschelkalk,* and *Bunter Sandstein*) 1841.

Triassic (trəi,æ·sik), *a.* 1841. [f. prec. + -IC, after G. *triassisch.*] *Geol.* Of or belonging to the Trias; *T. system* = TRIAS 2.

Triatic (trəi,æ tik), *a.* 1841. [Of unkn. origin.] *Naut.* In *t. stay*: 'a rope secured at each end to the heads of the fore and main masts, with thimbles spliced into its bight, to hook the stay tackles to' (Dana).

Triatomic (trəi,ătǫ·mik), *a.* 1862. [f. TRI- + ATOM + -IC.] *Chem.* **a.** Having three atoms in the molecule. †**b.** = TRIVALENT. **c.** Containing three hydroxyl groups (OH).

Tribade (tri·băd, ‖tribad). 1601. [– Fr. *tribade* (XVI), or its source L. *tribas, -ad-* – Gr. τριβάς, f. τρίβειν rub.] A woman who practises unnatural vice with other women. Hence **Tri·badism.**

Tribal (trəi·băl), *a.* 1632. [f. TRIBE + -AL[1] 1.] Of or pertaining to a tribe or tribes; characteristic of a tribe. Hence **Tri·bally** *adv.*

Tribalism (trəi·băliz'm). 1886. [f. prec. + -ISM.] The condition of existing as a separate tribe or tribes; tribal system, organization, or relations.

Tribasic (trəibēᶦ·sik), *a.* 1837. [f. TRI- + BASE + -IC; see BASIC.] *Chem.* Of an acid: Having the property of exchanging three atoms of hydrogen for three of potassium or sodium, and thus forming a salt. Of a salt: Containing three molecules of the basic oxide.

Tribble, obs. var. TREBLE.

Tribe (trəib), *sb.* ME. [First in pl. †*tribuz* (XIII), †*tribus* (XIV) – (O)Fr. *tribus,* pl. of *tribu* or L. *tribūs,* pl. of *tribus,* whence immed. *tribe* (XIV, Wyclif).] **1.** A group of persons forming a community and claiming descent from a common ancestor; *spec.* each of the twelve divisions of the people of Israel, claiming descent from the twelve sons of Jacob. **b.** A particular race of recognized ancestry; a family. late ME. **2.** *Rom. Hist.* One of the traditional three political divisions or patrician orders of ancient Rome in early times; later, one of the 30 political divisions of the Roman people instituted by Servius Tullius, and in B.C. 241 increased to 35. 1533. **b.** *Grecian Hist.* Rendering Gr. φυλή 1697. **c.** A division of some other nation or people 1693. **3.** A race of people; now applied esp. to a primary aggregate of people in a primitive or barbarous condition, under a headman or chief 1596. **4.** A class of persons; a fraternity, set, lot. Now often *contempt.* 1600. **5. a.** *Nat. Hist.* A group, usu. forming a subdivision of an order, and containing a number of genera; sometimes used as superior and sometimes as inferior to a family; also, loosely, any group or series of animals 1640. **b.** A class, group, sort, or kind of things 1731. **6.** A number or company of persons or animals; a 'troop'; in *pl.,* large numbers, flocks 1711.

1. The dukes were euer of the trybe of Iuda CAXTON. An Ebrew, as I guess, and of our T. MILT. **3.** Territory..occupied by numerous and warlike tribes of Indians 1823. **4.** The t. of vulgar politicians are the lowest of our species BURKE. *T. of Ben,* a name applied to themselves by literary associates and disciples of Ben Jonson in his later life. **6.** There were tribes of children in most of the cottages 1833. Hence **Tribe,** *v.* (*rare*), *trans.* to classify in tribes; also, to place in the same t. *with.* **Tri·beship,** the condition or position of being a t.; the members of a t. collectively, or their territory.

Tribesman (trəi·bzmæ̆n). 1798. [f. *tribe's,* genitive of TRIBE + MAN *sb.*] **a.** A member of a tribe. Chiefly *pl.* **b.** With possessive, a man of one's own tribe.

Triblet (tri·blėt). 1611. [– Fr. *triboulet,* of unkn. origin.] A cylindical rod or mandrel for forging rings, nuts, tubes, etc., or for drawing lead-pipe. Also *attrib.*: *t. tubes,* thin tubes which slide one upon the other, as in a telescope.

Tribometer (trəibǫ·mĭtəɹ). 1774. [– Fr. *tribomètre,* f. Gr. τρίβος rubbing + *-mètre* -METER.] An instrument for estimating sliding friction.

Tribrach (trəi·bræk, tri·-). 1589. [– L. *tribrachys* – Gr. τρίβραχυς, f. TRI- + βραχύς short.] *Prosody.* A metrical foot consisting of three short syllables. Hence **Tribra·chic** *a.* composed of tribrachs.

Tribrom-, tribromo- (trəi,brōᵘ m(o). 1852. [f. TRI- III. c + BROM(O-.] *Chem.* A formative signifying that three atoms of bromine are substituted for hydrogen in the substance designated by the rest of the name.

Tribual (trəi·biuăl), *a.* 1650. [f. L. *tribus* TRIBE + -AL[1].] Of, belonging or pertaining to a tribe; tribal.

Tribulate (tri·biŭleᶦt), *v.* 1637. [Back-formation from next.] *trans.* To afflict; to oppress; to trouble greatly.

Tribulation (tribiŭlēᶦ·ʃən). *arch.* ME. [– (O)Fr. *tribulation* – eccl. L. *tribulatio, -ōn-,* f. L. *tribulare* press (esp. pass. in Christian use) oppress, afflict, f. *tribulum* threshing-sledge, f. **trī-*, var. of **ter(e-* rub.] **1.** A condition of great affliction, oppression, or misery; 'persecution; distress; vexation; disturbance of life' (J.). **b.** With *a* and *pl.* An affliction ME. †**2.** The condition of being held in pawn (*slang*) –1764.

1. Tri'd in sharp t., and refin'd By Faith and faithful works MILT.

†‖**Tribu·na.** 1644. [It. *tribuna* – med.L. *tribuna,* for L. *tribunal*; see TRIBUNE[2].] An octagonal saloon in the Galleria degli Uffizi at Florence containing many famous paintings and statues –1757.

Tribunal (trəi-, tribiū·năl), *sb.* (*a.*) 1526. [– (O)Fr. *tribunal* or L. *tribunal, -ale* tribunal, judgement seat, f. *tribunus* TRIBUNE *sb.*[1]; see -AL[1] 1.] **1.** *orig.* A raised semicircular or square platform in a Roman basilica, on which the seats of the magistrates were placed; a dais; a raised throne or chair of state; a judgement seat (also *fig.*). **2.** A court of justice; a judicial assembly 1590. **b.** *fig.* Place of judgement or decision; judicial authority 1635. **c.** In the war of 1914–18, a local board set up to hear claims for exemption from military service 1916. †**3.** = TRIBUNE[2] 1, 2. –1797.

1. Those around the t. cried out against him 1833. **2. b.** Go up, my soul, into the t. of thy conscience

QUARLES. The t. of public opinion BENTHAM. *The t. of penance*, = the confessional.
B. *attrib.* or as *adj.* Pertaining to, of the nature of, or authorized by a tribunal 1554.

Tribunate (tri·biunĕt). 1546. [– L. *tribunatus*, f. *tribunus* TRIBUNE *sb.*[1]; see -ATE[1].] **1.** The office of tribune; tribuneship; government by tribunes. **2.** *Fr. Hist.* A representative body of legislators established under the constitution of the year 8 of the Revolutionary Calendar (1800–1). 1827.

Tribune[1] (tri·biun, trəi·-). late ME. [– L. *tribunus*, prob. orig. subst. use of adj. (sc. *magistratus*) 'magistrate of a tribe', f. *tribus* TRIBE.] **1.** A title designating one of several officers in the Roman administration: *spec.* **a.** *T. of the people* (L. *tribunus plebis*), one of two (later five, then ten) officers appointed to protect the interests and rights of the plebeians from the patricians. **b.** *Military t.* (L. *tribunus militaris*), one of six officers of a legion, each being in command for two months of the year. **2.** *transf.* and *fig.* An officer holding some position analogous to that of a Roman tribune; a judge; a popular leader, a demagogue 1587. Hence **Tri·buneship,** the office of a t.; the term of this office.

Tribune[2] (tri·biun, trəi·-). 1645. [– Fr. *tribune* – It. TRIBUNA.] **1.** = TRIBUNA. **2.** The semicircular or polygonal apse of a basilica or basilican church, usu. domed or vaulted 1771. **3.** A raised platform or dais; a rostrum; a pulpit; the throne or stall of a bishop 1762. **4.** A raised and seated area or gallery, esp. in a church; also applied to stands at continental race meetings 1865.

Tribunitial, -icial (tribiuni·ʃăl), *a.* 1598. [f. L. *tribunicius*, *-tius* + -AL[1] 1.] = next a.

Tribunitian, -ician (tribiuni·ʃăn), *a.* 1533. [f. as prec. + -AN.] Of, belonging or pertaining to a Roman tribune, or the office of tribune. **b.** *transf.* and *fig.* Having the power of veto like the Roman tribunes; popularly appointed; demagogic; factious 1637.
b. The t. fury of ecclesiastical demagogues 1854.

Tributary (tri·biŭtări), *a.* and *sb.* late ME. [– L. *tributarius*, f. *tributum*, *-us*; see next, -ARY[1].] **A.** *adj.* **1.** Paying tribute; subject to imposts. **2.** *transf.* and *fig.* Furnishing subsidiary supplies or aid; auxiliary, contributory; also said of a stream or river which flows into another 1611. **3.** Of the nature of tribute; contributory 1588.
1. At those dayes a great parte of y[e] worlde was trybutary to Rome 1494. **2.** For me your t. stores combine GOLDSM. The rivers t. to the Thames HUXLEY. **3.** Loe at this Tombe my tributarie teares, I render SHAKS.
B. *sb.* (The adj. used *absol.*) **1.** One who pays tribute. late ME. **2.** *transf.* and *fig.* One who or that which furnishes subsidiary supplies or aid; *spec.* a stream flowing into a larger stream or lake 1836.
2. What sedged brooks are Thames's tributaries M. ARNOLD.

Tribute (tri·biut), *sb.* ME. [– L. *tributum*, subst. use of n. of *tributus*, pa. pple. of *tribuere* assign, allot, grant, prop. divide among the tribes, f. *tribus* TRIBE.] **1.** A tax or impost paid by one prince or state to another in acknowledgement of submission or as the price of peace, security, and protection; rent or homage paid in money or an equivalent by a subject to his sovereign or a vassal to his lord. **b.** Hence contextually, The obligation or necessity of paying this; the condition of being tributary, as *to lay a t. on*. late ME. **2.** *transf.* and *fig.* Something paid or contributed as by a subordinate to a superior; an offering or gift rendered as a duty, or as an acknowledgement of affection or esteem 1585. **3.** In *Mining.* **a.** The proportion of the value of the ore raised, paid by the miners to the owners or lessors of the land or their representatives 1778. **b.** The proportion of ore raised or its value, paid to the miners by the owners of the mine or land, in payment of their labour 1832.
1. A large portion of the t. was paid in money GIBBON. **b.** *Under t.*, under obligation to pay t. **2.** Some frail memorial..Implores the passing t. of a sigh GRAY. **3.** Phr. *To work on t.*, or *on the t. system*, to work on the plan of paying or receiving certain proportions of the produce.
Comb.: **t.-money,** money paid as t. Hence **Tribute,** *v.* †*intr.* to yield t.; †*trans.* to pay as t.; *Mining, trans.* and *intr.* to work on t.

Trice (trəis), *sb.* 1440. [Found first in phrase *at a t.*, app. orig. 'at one pull', *trice* being vbl. sb. from TRICE *v.*; hence 'at once, immediately', whence later the simple sb. comes to be equal to 'instant, moment'.] **1.** †**a.** *At a t.*, lit. at a single pluck or pull; hence, in an instant –1635. **b.** *In a t.* in same sense 1508. †**2.** One single attempt or act; the time taken for this; an instant or moment –1668.

Trice (trəis), *v.* late ME. [– MDu. *trīsen* (Du. *trijsen* hoist) = MLG. *trīsen*, rel. to MDu. *trīse*, etc., windlass, pulley, of unkn. origin.] †**1.** *trans.* To pull; to pluck, snatch; rarely, to carry off (as plunder) –1618. **2.** To pull or haul with a rope; *spec.* (*Naut.*) usu. with *up*, to haul or hoist up and secure with a rope or lashing, to lash up. late ME.

-trice, *suffix*, – Fr. *-trice*, – L. *-trix*, *-tric-*, or It. *-trice*; in Latin forming feminines to agent-nouns in *-tor*. In modern Eng. -TRIX from the L. nominative is preferred.

Tricenary (trəisī·nări), *a.* and *sb.* 1482. [– L. *tricenarius* of, pertaining to, or consisting of thirty, f. *triceni* thirty each. As sb. – med.L. *tricenarium*.] **A.** *adj.* Of or pertaining to thirty; containing, or lasting, thirty days. Now *rare.* or *Obs.* 1655. **B.** *sb. R. C. Ch.* A series of masses said on thirty consecutive days 1482.

Tricentenary (trəise·ntĭnări, -sĕntī·nări), *a.* and *sb.* 1846. [f. TRI- + CENTENARY.] = TERCENTENARY.

Triceps (trəi·seps), *a.* and *sb.* 1704. [– L. *triceps*, f. *tri-* TRI- + *-ceps*, adj. comb. form corresp. to *caput* head.] *Anat.* **A.** *adj.* Of a muscle: Having three heads or points of origin. **B.** *sb.* A triceps muscle; *spec.* that of the thigh (*t. extensor cruris*) and that of the upper arm (*t. extensor cubiti*).

Trichi (tri·tʃi). *colloq.* or *slang.* 1877. Short for TRICHINOPOLI (cigar).

Trichiasis (triki͵ē·sis, trikəi·ăsis). 1661. [– late L. *trichiasis* – Gr. τριχίασις, f. τριχιᾶν be hairy.] *Path.* **a.** Introversion of the eyelashes. **b.** A disease in which small filamentous bodies are passed in the urine. **c.** A disease of the breasts in suckling women, in which the nipples crack into fine fissures.

‖**Trichina** (tri·kinā, trikəi·nă). *Pl.* **-æ.** 1835. [mod. L., f. Gr. τρίχινος adj. 'of hair', f. θρίξ, τριχ- hair.] *Zool.* A genus of minute parasitic nematoid worms; *esp.* the species *T. spiralis*, which infests man and various animals, the adult inhabiting the intestinal tract, and the larvæ migrating to and becoming encysted in the muscular tissue, causing TRICHINOSIS. Hence **Tri·chinal** *a.* of or pertaining to the t. ‖**Trichini·asis** = TRICHINOSIS. **Tri·chinize** *v. trans.* to infect with trichinæ. **Tri·chinous** *a.* infested with trichinæ; affected with, or of the nature of, trichinosis.

Trichinopoli (tritʃinǫ·pŏli). Also **-poly.** 1863. Name of a district and city in the Madras presidency; used *attrib.*, as *T. cigar*; also *absol.* a T. cigar.

Trichinosis (trikinō[u]·sis). 1866. [f. TRICHINA + -OSIS.] *Path.* A disease caused by the introduction of trichinæ into the alimentary canal, and the migration of their larvæ into the muscular tissue; characterized by digestive disturbance, slight fever, swelling, pain, and lameness in the muscles, etc.

Trichite (tri·kəit, trəi·-). 1868. [f. Gr. θρίξ, τριχ- hair + -ITE[1] 2 b; in 1 – G. *trichit* (Zirkel, 1867).] **1.** *Min.* A name for very minute dark-coloured hair-like bodies occurring in the substance of some vitreous rocks. **2.** *Zool.* A name for extremely fine siliceous fibres occurring in certain sponge-spicules, or for such spicules themselves 1887. Hence **Trichi·tic** *a.*

Trichiurid (triki͵yū[ə]·rid). 1819. [f. mod. L. *Trichiuridæ*, f. *Trichiurus*, prop. *Trichurus*, generic name, f. Gr. θρίξ, τριχ- hair + οὐρά tail; see -ID[3].] *Ichthyol.* A fish of the family *Trichiuridæ*, typified by the genus *Trichiurus*, characterized by a ribbon-like body and a long filament at the end of the tail. So **Trichi͵u·riform, Trichi͵u·roid** *adjs.* having the form of the fishes of this genus or family.

Trichlor-, trichloro- (trəi͵klō[ə]·ro). 1845. [f. TRI- III. c + CHLOR(O-.] *Chem.* A formative expressing the substitution of three atoms of chlorine for hydrogen, as in *trichlorobenzene*, $C_6H_3Cl_3$.

Tricho- (triko, trəiko), bef. a vowel **trich-** (trik, trəik), – Gr. τριχο-, τριχ-, comb. stem of θρίξ hair.
‖**Trichobranchia** (trikǫbræ·ŋkiă), **-æ,** *Zool.* name for the gills, set with filaments, of certain decapod crustaceans; hence **Trichobra·nchial, Trichobra·nchiate** *adjs.* **Tri·chocyst** (-sist), *Zool.* one of a number of minute rod-like bodies, each containing a coiled protrusible filament, found in the cuticle of many *Infusoria*, resembling the thread-cells of cœlenterates; hence **Tricho·cy·stic** *a.* **Trichogyne** (dʒəin) [Gr. γυνή], *Bot.* a hair-like process forming the receptive part of the female reproductive organ or procarp in certain algæ and fungi; hence **Trichogynial** (-dʒi·niăl), **Trichogynic** (-dʒi·nik) *adjs.* **Tricho·logy,** the study of the structure, functions, and diseases of the hair. ‖**Trichomanes** (trikǫ·mănīz), *Bot.* a genus of ferns having filamentous outgrowths from the margins of the fronds; the bristle-ferns. **Tri·chophore** (-fō[ə]ɹ) [see -PHORE], (*a*) *Bot.* the structure which bears the trichogyne in florideous algæ; (*b*) *Zool.* one of several projections of the integument in certain annelids, from which spring bundles of setæ or bristles; **Trichophoric** (-fǫ·rik) *a.*, pertaining to or of the nature of a trichophore. **Tri·chophyte** [Gr. φυτόν], a genus of minute fungi, parasitic on the skin; esp. the species *Trichophyton tonsurans*, which produces ringworm. **Tricho·pter** [Gr. πτέρον wing], *Ent.* a member of the group *Trichoptera* of neuropterous insects, characterized by specially hairy wings; a caddis-fly; so **Tricho·pteran** *a.* = *trichopterous*; *sb.* = *trichopter*; **Tricho·pterous** *a.*, belonging to or having the characters of the *Trichoptera*, hairy-winged.

‖**Trichoma** (trikō[u]·mă). 1799. [mod. L. – Gr. τρίχωμα growth of hair, f. τριχοῦν cover with hair; see -OMA.] **1.** *Path.* A disease of the hair; = PLICA 1. **2.** *Bot.* Each of the filaments composing the thallus in algæ of the order *Nostochineæ* 1866.

Trichome (tri·-, trəi·kō[u]m). 1875. [– Gr. τρίχωμα; see prec., -OME.] *Bot.* Any outgrowth of the epidermis or superficial tissue of a plant, as hairs, scales, prickles, etc.

Trichord (trəi·kǭɹd), *sb.* and *a.* 1776. [– Gr. τρίχορδος, f. τρι- TRI- + χορδή string.] **A.** *sb.* A musical instrument; of three strings; a three-stringed lyre or lute. **B.** *adj.* Having three strings to each note: applied to a pianoforte in which most of the keys have three strings each.

Trichotomize (tri-, trəikǫ·tŏməiz), *v.* 1651. [f. as next + -IZE; cf. DICHOTOMIZE.] *trans.* To divide into three parts; to arrange or classify in three divisions, or in groups of three.

Trichotomous (tri-, trəikǫ·tŏməs), *a.* 1800. [f. Gr. τρίχα triply + -τομος cut + -OUS; cf. DICHOTOMOUS.] **1.** *Bot.* Dividing into three branches. **2.** Making three divisions, classes, or categories; involving or of the nature of trichotomy 1855.

Trichotomy (tri-, trəikǫ·tŏmi). 1610. [f. Gr. τρίχα in three, triply, after DICHOTOMY; see -TOMY.] Division into three; arrangement or classification in three divisions, classes, or categories.

Trichroic (trəikrō[u]·ik), *a.* 1881. [f. Gr. τρίχροος, τρίχρους three-coloured + -IC.] Having or showing three colours; *spec.* of crystals, exhibiting three different colours when viewed in three different directions.

Trichroism (trəi·kro͵iz'm). 1847. [f. as prec. + -ISM.] The property of being trichroic; *spec.* in *Cryst.*: see prec.

Trichromatic (trəi͵kromæ·tik), *a.* 1891. [f. TRI- + CHROMATIC.] Having, showing, or pertaining to three colours; trichroic; *spec.* in *Optics*, having or relating to the three fundamental colour-sensations (red, green, violet) of normal vision. Applied also to lithographic printing in three colours. So **Trichro·matism. Trichro·mic** *a.* 1881.

Trick (trik), *sb.* late ME. [– OFr. *trique*, dial. var. of *triche*, f. *trichier* (mod. *tricher*) deceive, cheat, of unkn. origin.] **I. 1.** A crafty or fraudulent device of a mean or base kind; an artifice to deceive; a stratagem, ruse, wile. **b.** An illusory or deceptive appearance; a semblance, sham. *arch.* or *Obs.* 1592. **2.** A freakish or mischievous act; a roguish prank; a frolic; a hoax, practical joke 1590. **b.** A capricious, foolish, or stupid act. Usu. *contempt.* or *depreciative.* 1591. **3.** A clever or adroit expedient, device, or contrivance; a 'dexterous artifice' (J.); a 'dodge' 1573. **4.** The art, knack, or faculty of doing something successfully 1611. **5.** A feat of dexterity or skill, intended to surprise or amuse; a piece of jugglery or legerdemain 1606. **6.** *concr.* A trifling ornament or toy; a trinket, bauble, knick-knack; hence *pl.*, small and trifling articles; 'traps'. *U.S.* 1553.

1. He was again at his old tricks FREEMAN. Phr. *To play one a t., play* or *put a t.* or *tricks upon*: see PLAY *v.* I. 9, PUT *v.*[1] III. 13. **2.** Fortune has played me such a cruel t. this day MRS. CARLYLE. **b.** It were but a fool's t. to die for conscience CARLYLE. **3.** Rhetorical tricks HUME. The novelist..knows the tricks of his trade 1896. **5.** You have more Tricks than a Dancing Bear SWIFT.

II. 1. A particular habit, way, or mode of acting. (Usu., a bad or unpleasant habit.) 1576. **2. a.** A habit or fashion of dress. *arch.* 1543. **b.** A characteristic expression (of the face or voice) 1595. **c.** The mode of working a piece of mechanism, etc.; the system upon which a thing is constructed 1663. **3.** *Naut.* The time allotted to a man on duty at the helm; a turn; *esp.* in *to take* or *stand one's t.* (*at the wheel*, etc.) 1669.

1. The t. of laughing frivolously is by all means to be avoided 1754. **2. b.** The tricke of that voyce, I do well remember SHAKS.

III. *Her.* A sketch in pen and ink of a coat of arms. *In t.*, sketched in pen and ink. 1572. **IV.** *Card-playing.* The cards (usu. four) played, and won or 'taken' in one round, collectively; hence, *to take a* or *the t. Odd t.*: see ODD *a.* 1 1599.

Phrases. *A t. worth two of that*, a much better plan or expedient. *To do the t.*, to do what is wanted.

attrib. and *Comb.* (chiefly in sense I. 5): Of, pertaining to, or in the nature of a t. or tricks, skilled in or trained to perform tricks, as *t.-cycling, -cyclist, -riding, -writing*, etc.

Trick, *v.* 1500. [app. f. prec.; branch II perh. assoc. with Fr. †*s'estriquer* 'to tricke, decke, or trimme up himself' (Cotgr.); branch III with Du. *trekken* 'delineare' (Kilian), 'to delineate, to make a draught' (Hexham).] **I. 1.** *trans.* To deceive by a trick; to cheat 1595. **b.** *absol.* or *intr.* To practise trickery; to cheat 1700. **2.** To get or effect by trickery (*rare*) 1662. **3.** *intr.* To play tricks or trifle *with* 1881.

1. To t. a gauger was thought an excellent joke MAR. EDGEWORTH. **2.** The trick..of a tricked marriage is common in Congreve 1895.

II. 1. *trans.* To dress; to deck, prank; to adorn (usu. with the notion of artifice) 1500. **b.** *transf.* To dress *up*, to prepare (food). *rare.* 1824. †**2.** To adjust, arrange, trim –1810.

1. Till civil-suited Morn appeer, Not trickt and frounc't..But Cherchef't in a comly Cloud MILT. She was well tutored and tricked off for the occasion 1821.

III. To sketch or draw in outline; *spec.* in *Her.*, to draw (a coat of arms) in outline, the tinctures being denoted by initial letters (*o, a, s*, etc.) or by signs. Also with *out.* 1545.

The..shields of arms recorded in the MS. are..'tricked',..thus necessitating a description of the bearings 1859.

†**Trick,** *a.* and *adv.* 1542. [rel. in sense to TRIG *a.*] **A.** *adj.* **1.** Smart, clever, nimble, 'neat' (*rare*) –1593. **2.** Trim, neat, handsome; smart, 'fine' –1630.

2. A neighbour mine..That maried had a tricke and bonny lasse SIDNEY.

B. *adv.* **1.** Cleverly, 'neatly', 'finely' –1584. **2.** Neatly, smartly, elegantly, 'trigly' –1658.

2. Unless you coy it t. and trim 1594.

Tri·cker. 1629. Early and dial. form of TRIGGER[1].

Trickery (tri·kəri). 1800. [f. TRICK *sb.* + -ERY.] The practice of tricks; deceitful conduct or practice; deception, artifice; imposture.

Trickish (tri·kiʃ), *a.* 1705. [f. TRICK *sb.* + -ISH[1].] **1.** Given to tricks or trickery; rather tricky, crafty, or cunning. **2.** = TRICKY 2. 1900. Hence **Tri·ckish-ly** *adv.*, **-ness.**

Trickle (tri·k'l), *sb.* 1580. [f. next.] A falling or flowing drop; a tear; a small quantity of liquid; a small fitful stream.

Trickle (tri·k'l), *v.*[1] late ME. [Forms with variation of vowel and consonant have been current since XIV, intended to be imit. of the sound of falling drops, viz. *trygle, trikle, trekel, trigle, trinkle, tringle*; see -LE.] **1.** *intr.* To flow or fall in successive drops. Also, to flow in a very scanty and halting stream. **b.** *transf.* and *fig.* 1628. **2.** To emit falling or flowing drops; to drip or run (*with* tears, blood, etc.); to shed tears. late ME. **3.** *trans.* To give forth in successive drops or a thin fitful stream; also, to cause to trickle 1602.

1. Hise salte teeris trikled doun as reyn CHAUCER. A small glacier trickles into the desolate valley 1871. **b.** Fluent nonsense trickles from his tongue POPE. **2.** Mine eye trickleth downe and ceaseth not *Lam.* 3:49.

Comb.: **t.-charger**, a device for charging a low-tension accumulator from a supply of alternating high-tension current.

Tri·ckle, *v.*[2] orig. *dial.* 1825. [app. orig. East Anglian var. of TRUCKLE *v.*; in *Golf*, usu. assoc. w. prec.] *trans.* To trundle, to bowl. In *Golf*, to cause (the ball) to roll very slowly and gently. Also *intr.* of the ball.

Trickment (tri·kmĕnt). *rare.* 1619. [f. TRICK *v.* + -MENT.] Decoration, adornment.

Trickster (tri·kstəɹ). 1711. [f. TRICK *sb.* or *v.* + -STER.] One who practises trickery; a rogue, cheat, knave.

Tricksy (tri·ksi), *a.* 1552. [f. TRICK *sb.* and *v.* + -SY.] **1.** Artfully trimmed or decked; spruce, fine, smart. **2.** Full of or given to tricks or pranks 1596. **3.** Full of tricks or deception; crafty, cunning, cheating 1766. **4.** = TRICKY *a.* 2. 1835.

3. T. trout 1856. **4.** Kidderminster is a t. borough 1862. Hence **Tri·cksily** *adv.* **Tri·cksiness.**

Tricky (tri·ki), *a.* 1786. [f. TRICK *sb.* + -Y[1].] **1.** Given to or characterized by trickery. **b.** Skilled in performing clever tricks 1887. **2.** Having the deceptive character of a trick; needing cautious action or handling; risky, catchy, ticklish (*colloq.*) 1887.

2. Revolvers are t. things for young hands to deal with KIPLING. Hence **Tri·ckily** *adv.* **Tri·ckiness.**

‖**Triclinium** (trəikli·niŏm, triˌkləi·niŏm). *Pl.* **-ia.** 1646. [L. – Gr. τρικλίνιον, dim. of τρίκλινος dining room with three couches, f. τρι- TRI- + κλίνη couch, bed.] *Rom. Antiq.* A couch, running round three sides of a table, on which to recline at meals; also, a room for eating in; a dining-room. Hence **Tricli·nial** *a.* pertaining to a t.

Tricolour, tricolor (trəi·kɒləɹ), *a.* and *sb.* 1798. [– Fr. *tricolore* – late L. *tricolor, -ōr-*, f. *tri-* TRI- + *color* COLOUR.] **A.** *adj.* Having three colours; three-coloured 1815. **B.** *sb.* A tricolour flag, cockade, etc.; *esp.* the national flag of France adopted at the Revolution, consisting of equal vertical stripes of blue, white, and red 1798. So **Tri··coloured, -colored** *a.* (often with hyphen) 1795.

Tricorn (trəi·kɒɹn, tri··), *a.* and *sb.* Also (as Fr.) **tricorne.** 1760. [– Fr. *tricorne* or L. *tricornis*, f. *tri-* TRI- + L. *cornu* horn.] **A.** *adj.* Having three horns or horn-like projections; *spec.* applied to a cocked hat with the brim turned up on three sides 1844. **B.** *sb.* **1.** An (imaginary) creature with three horns 1760. **2.** A tricorn hat 1876.

Tri·cosane, tri·i·cosane. 1894. [f. Gr. τρία three + εἴκοσι twenty + -ANE.] *Chem.* A hydrocarbon belonging to the paraffin series, containing 23 atoms of carbon.

‖**Tricot** (trīko). 1872. [Fr., f. *tricoter* knit; of unkn. origin.] Knitting; knitted work or fabric; a woollen fabric, knitted by hand, or by machinery in imitation of hand-knitting.

Tric-trac (tri·kˌtræ·k). Also **trick-track.** 1687. [– Fr. *tric-trac*; so called from the clicking sound made by the pieces in playing the game.] An old variety of backgammon.

Tricuspid (trəikɒ·spid), *a.* (*sb.*) 1670. [– L. *tricuspis, -id-*, f. *tri-* TRI- + *cuspis* point.] Having three cusps or points. Also *absol.* or as *sb.*; hence *attrib.*

T. valve or **valves** (*Anat.*), the valve consisting of three triangular segments (or, as otherwise regarded, the set of three triangular valves) which guards the opening from the right auricle into the right ventricle of the heart. **Tricu·spidal, Tricu·spidate** *adjs.*

Tricycle (trəi·sik'l), *sb.* 1868. [f. TRI- + CYCLE; hence in Fr. Earlier in Fr. (1827), a three-wheeled coach.] A velocipede with three wheels (now usu. one in front and one on each side behind) driven by treadles actuated by the feet, or (*motor t.*) by a small motor attachment. Hence **Tri·cycle** *v. intr.* to ride a t.

‖**Tridacna** (trəi-, tridæ·knă). 1776. [mod. L. (Da Costa, 1776), f. Gr. τρίδακνος eaten at three bites, f. τρι- TRI- + δάκνειν bite.] *Zool.* A genus of bivalve molluscs, including the *T. gigas* or Giant Clam, the largest bivalve shell known.

Tridecane (trəi·dekēⁱn). 1894. [f. Gr. τρία three + δέκα ten + -ANE.] *Chem.* A colourless liquid hydrocarbon of the paraffin series, containing 13 atoms of carbon. So **Tridecyl** (trəi·disil) [-YL], the radical ($C_{13}H_{27}$) contained in t.

Trident (trəi·dĕnt), *sb.* (*a.*) 1599. [– L. *tridens, trident-*, f. *tri-* TRI- + *dens, dent-* tooth.] **1.** An instrument or weapon with three prongs. **a.** *esp.* A three-pronged fish-spear or sceptre as the attribute of the sea-god Poseidon or Neptune, also figured as borne by Britannia. **b.** A three-pronged spear used by the *retiarius* in ancient Roman gladiatorial combats (*rare*) 1693. **c.** *transf.* and *fig.* 1638. **2.** *Geom.* A plane cubic curve of a form suggesting a three-pronged weapon; also *t. curve* 1710. **3.** as *adj.* Having three prongs or forks; trident 1589. Hence **Tride·ntal** *a.* three-pronged, trifurcate. **Tri·dented** *a.* having a t.

Tridentine (tri·dĕntəin, trəide·ntəin), *a.* and *sb.* 1561. [– med.L. *Tridentinus*, f. *Tridentum* TRENT; see -INE[1].] **A.** *adj.* Of or pertaining to the city of Trent in Tyrol, or to the Council of the Roman Catholic Ch. held there (1545–63). **B.** *sb.* One who accepts and conforms to the decrees of the Council of Trent 1836.

Triduan (trəi·diuˌăn), *a.* 1597. [– L. *triduanus*, f. TRIDUUM; see -AN.] Lasting for three days; also, occurring every third day.

‖**Triduo** (trī·duo). 1848. [It. and Sp. :– L. TRIDUUM.] *Eccl.* = next.

‖**Triduum** (trəi·diuˌŏm). 1883. [L., prop. neut. of **triduus* adj. (sc. *spatium*), f. *tri-* TRI- + *dies* day.] A period of three days; *esp.* of religious observance.

Tridymite (tri·dimait). 1868. [– G. *tridymit* (vom Rath, 1866), f. Gr. τρίδυμος, f. τρι- TRI- + -δυμος, as in δίδυμος twin; named in allusion to its compound forms consisting of three individual crystals.] *Min.* A crystallized form of silica, occurring in small hexagonal tables, found in trachyte and other igneous rocks.

Tried (trəid), *ppl. a.* ME. [f. TRY *v.* + -ED[1].] †**1.** Separated from the dross or refuse; of fat: rendered, clarified; of flour, etc.: sifted, bolted, fine. –1639. **2.** Proved or tested by experience or examination. late ME.

2. Public men of t. abilities 1841.

Triennial (trəiˌe·niăl), *a.* and *sb.* 1620. [f. late L. *triennis* of three years, *triennium* period of three years, f. *tri-* TRI- + *annus* year; see -AL[1] 1.] **A.** *adj.* **1.** Existing or lasting for three years; changed every three years 1640. **2.** Recurring every three years 1620. **B.** *sb.* **1.** A period of three years 1661. **2.** An event recurring every three years; *spec.* the visitation of his diocese by a bishop every three years 1640.

A. 1. *T. Act.*, an act of 1640, limiting the duration of parliament in England to three years. **2.** There was a t. change of officers 1872. Hence **Triˌe·nnially** *adv.* every three years; once in three years.

‖**Triennium** (trəiˌe·niŏm). 1847. [L., prop. n. of **triennius* adj. (sc. *spatium*), f. *tri-* TRI- + *annus* year.] A space or period of three years.

‖**Triens** (trəi·enz). *Pl.* **trientes** (trəiˌe·ntīz). 1601. [L., = third part.] The third part of anything; *spec.* in *Rom. Antiq.* a copper coin worth one-third of the as; also, in later times, a gold coin, one-third of the aureus.

Trier (trəi·əɹ). ME. [f. TRY *v.* + -ER[1].] **1.** One who examines judicially; a judge. **2.** *pl.* Two persons appointed by a court of law to determine whether a challenge made to the panel of jurors, or to any of them, is well founded 1511. **3.** *Hist. pl.* A committee appointed by the King to determine to which court petitions should be referred, and, if necessary, to report them to the parliament 1844. **4.** *pl.* Members of the House of Lords sitting as a jury at the trial of a peer for treason or felony. In full, *lords triers*. 1539. **5.** One who or that which tests or proves something; a prover; a tester or test 1483. **6.** One who tries or attempts to do something; one who persists in trying *colloq.* 1891. **7.** Something devised to test or try quality; something trying or difficult 1797.

Trierarch (trəi·ĕrāɹk). 1656. [– L. *trierarchus* or Gr. τριήραρχος, -αρχης, f. τριήρης trireme + -αρχος -ARCH.] *Gr. Hist.* **a.** The commander of a trireme. **b.** A citizen who, singly or in conjunction with others, was charged with the duty of fitting out a trireme or galley for the public service. So **Tri·erarchal** *a.*

Trierarchy (trəi·ĕrāɹki). 1837. [– Gr. τριηραρχία, f. τριήραρχος TRIERARCH.] The position or office of a trierarch. **b.** The trierarchs collectively 1882.

Trieteric (trəi,ĭte·rik), *a.* and *sb.* 1592. [– Gr. τριετηρικός, L. *trietericus*, f. τριετηρίς a festival celebrated every third, i.e. alternate, year, f. τρι- three + ἔτος year.] **A.** *adj.* Taking place every alternate year, as the festivals of Bacchus and other divinities 1656. **B.** *sb.* (also *pl.*) A festival, esp. of Bacchus, celebrated every alternate year 1592.

Triethyl (trəi,ī·þəil, -e·þil). 1858. [f. TRI- III + ETHYL.] *Chem.* A formative denoting the presence of three ethyl groups, C_2H_5, in a compound. **b.** *spec.* denoting the substitution of three ethyl groups for three hydrogen atoms in the substance designated by the rest of the name.

Trifarious (trəifē^ə·riəs), *a. rare.* 1656. [f. L. *trifarius* + -OUS.] **1.** Of three sorts; facing three ways. **2.** *Bot.* Arranged in three rows 1846.

Trifid (trəi·fid), *a.* 1628. [– L. *trifidus*, f. *tri-* TRI- + *fid-*, stem of *findere* split.] Split into three by deep clefts or notches; *esp.* in *Bot.* and *Zool.* **b.** *gen.* Tripartite (*rare*) 1871.

Trifle (trəi·fl), *sb.* [ME. *truf(f)le* – OFr. *truf(f)le* by-form of *truf(f)e* deceit, gibe, corresp. to It. *truffa*, Sp., Pg. *trufa*; of unkn. origin.] †**1.** A false or idle tale, told (*a*) to deceive, cheat, or befool, (*b*) to divert; a lying story, a fiction; a jest or joke; a foolish, trivial, or nonsensical saying –1681. **2.** Hence, a matter of little value or importance; 'a thing of no moment' (J.); a trivial, paltry, or insignificant affair ME. †**b.** *transf.* A trifler –1716. **3.** *concr.* A small article of little intrinsic value; a toy, trinket, bauble. late ME. **4.** A literary work, piece of music, etc., light or trivial in style; a bagatelle. Often used in meiosis. 1579. **5.** A small sum of money, or a sum treated as of no moment; a slight 'consideration' 1595. **b.** An insignificant quantity or amount 1722. **c.** *A t.* (advb.): To a trifling extent; a little; somewhat, rather 1859. **6.** A light confection of sponge-cake or the like (freq. flavoured with wine or spirit), served with custard, whipped cream, etc. 1781. **7.** A kind of pewter of medium hardness; in *pl.* also, articles made of this 1610.

2. Trifles light as ayre, Are to the iealious, confirmations strong As proofes of holy Writ SHAKS. He's a mighty exact Man about Trifles 1706. **4.** Poems to Stella, and trifles to Dr. Sheridan, fill up a great part of that period 1751. **5. c.** Jehu is a t. below middle height 1887.

Trifle (trəi·f'l), *v.* [ME. – OFr. *truffler*, *truffer* make sport of, deceive = It. *truffare*; see prec.] †**1.** *trans.* To cheat, delude, befool; to mock (*rare*) –1533. †**2.** *intr.* To say what is untrue, to jest in order to cheat, mock, amuse, or make sport –1602. **b.** *T. with*: To treat with a lack of seriousness or respect; to 'play' or dally with 1523. **3.** *intr.* To toy, play (*with* a material object); to fiddle, fidget *with* 1460. **4.** To dally, loiter; to waste time. late ME. †**5.** *trans.* To waste (time). *Obs.* exc. as in b. –1742. **b.** esp. with *away* 1532. †**6.** To make a trifle of. SHAKS. **7.** *intr.* To act (or speak) idly or frivolously, esp. in serious circumstances 1736.

2. b. He shall not t. with your affections 1852. **2.** O'er cold coffee t. with the spoon POPE. **5.** We t. time, I pray thee pursue sentence SHAKS. **b.** Come Lords we t. time away SHAKS. **6.** *Macb.* II. iv. 4. Hence **Tri·fler,** one who trifles; one who is not serious or earnest in what he does.

Trifling (trəi·fliŋ), *vbl. sb.* late ME. [-ING[1].] The action of TRIFLE *v.*

Agreable t. or *badinage* CHESTERF. The solemn t. of the schools KINGSLEY.

Tri·fling, *ppl. a.* late ME. [-ING[2].] †**1.** Cheating, false, feigning –1560. **2.** Behaving idly or frivolously; frivolous; foolish 1535. **3.** Of little moment or value; trumpery; insignificant, petty 1538.

3. The worke of 10 years study for a t. reward EVELYN. Hence **Tri·fling-ly** *adv.*, **-ness.**

Trifoliate (trəifō^u·liĕt), *a.* 1753. [f. TRI- + FOLIATE *a.* 3.] Three-leaved; *esp.* in *Bot.* consisting of three leaflets, as a compound leaf; also of a plant, having such leaves; *transf.* having the form of such a leaf. Also **Trifo·liated** *a. Bot.* = prec.; *Arch.* having or consisting of trefoils 1698.

‖**Trifolium** (trifō^u·liŏm, trəi-). 1625. [L., f. *tri-* TRI- + *folium* leaf. Cf. TREFOIL.] *Bot.* A large genus of leguminous plants with trifoliate leaves, and flowers mostly in close heads; including many valuable fodder-plants, known as *clovers* or *trefoils*; *spec.* in recent agricultural use, applied to the genus *T. incarnatum*.

‖**Triforium** (trəifō^ə·riŏm). *Pl.* **-ia.** 1703. [AL. *triforium*, first found in Gervase of Canterbury (c1185), in ref. to Canterbury Cathedral; of unkn. origin.] *Arch.* A gallery or arcade in the wall over the arches at the sides of the nave and choir, and sometimes of the transepts, in some large churches: orig. applied to that in Canterbury Cathedral; in the 19th c. extended as a general term.

Triform (trəi·fǫɹm), *a.* 1450. [– L. *triformis*, f. *tri-* + *forma* FORM.] **1.** Having a triple form; combining three different forms; formed in three parts. **2.** Existing or appearing in three different forms 1623.

2. The neighbouring Moon..With borrowd light her countenance t. Hence fills and empties MILT. So **Tri·formity** (*rare*), the quality of being t.

Trig (trig), *sb.*[1] 1647. [Goes w. TRIG *v.*[1], the vb. being app. the source of the sb.] A wedge or block placed under a wheel or cask to prevent it from rolling; hence *gen.*, a brake.

Trig (trig), *a.* (*sb.*[2]) ME., orig. *north.* and *Sc.* [– ON. *tryggr* faithful, trusty, etc. = Goth. *triggws* true, faithful; see TRUE.] **1.** True, faithful, trusty. Now only *n. dial.* **2.** Trim or tight in person, shape, or appearance; of a place: neat, tidy. Chiefly *Sc.* and *dial.* 1513. **b.** Trim or neat in dress; spruce, smart 1725. **3.** Strong, sound, well; also, firm, steady 1704. **4.** Prim, precise, exact; cut and dried, smug (*rare*) 1793. †**B.** *sb.* A dandy, a coxcomb. B. JONS.

2. b. She really looked very smart and t. and jaunty 1893. **4.** Our system of t. and prig theology 1872. Hence **Tri·g-ly** *adv.*, **-ness.**

Trig, *v.*[1] 1591. [perh. – ON. *tryggja*, ODa. *trygge* make firm or secure, f. *tryggr* firm, sure, true; cf. prec.] **1.** *trans.* To make firm or fast; to prevent from moving; *esp.* to apply a wedge, block, etc. to (a wheel). **2.** To wedge up; to prop (*up*) 1711.

Trig, *v.*[2] Now *dial.* 1660. [f. TRIG *a.*] **1.** *trans.* To make trig or trim; now often, to dress smartly: freq. with *out*. 1696. **2.** To fill full, to stuff, cram 1660.

Trigamous (tri·gămǝs), *a.* 1842. [– Gr. τρίγαμος thrice married, f. τρι- TRI- + -γαμος married; see -OUS.] **1.** Characterized by, involving, or living in trigamy 1886. **2.** *Bot.* Having male, female, and hermaphrodite flowers in the same head 1842.

Trigamy (tri·gămi). 1615. [– late L. *trigamia* – eccl. Gr. τριγαμία, f. τρίγαμος; see prec., -Y[3].] **1.** *Eccl. Law.* Marriage for the third time after the death of former wives or husbands. *Obs.* or *arch.* **2.** The state of having three wives or husbands at the same time; the crime of contracting a third marriage while two previous spouses are alive 1634. So **Tri·gamist.**

Trigeminal (trəi,dʒe·minăl), *a.* (*sb.*) 1830. [f. L. *trigeminus* (see next) born three at a birth + -AL[1] 1.] *Anat.* Applied to the fifth pair of cranial nerves, from their dividing into three branches; also *absol.* as *sb.* **b.** Pertaining to, occurring in, or affecting the t. nerve 1874.

‖**Trigeminus** (trəi,dʒe·minŏs). 1706. [L., f. TRI- + L. *geminus* born at the same birth.] †**1.** The complexus muscle. **2.** The trigeminal nerve 1875.

Trigesimal (trəi,dʒe·simăl), *a. rare.* 1637. [f. L. *trigesimus* thirtieth + -AL[1] 1.] †**a.** Thirtieth. **b.** *loosely.* Consisting of thirty.

Trigger[1] (tri·gəɹ). 1621. [Earliest form *tricker* (which was usual till c1750 and is in widespread dial. use) – Du. *trekker*, f. *trekken* pull; see TREK *v.*, -ER[1]. For variation of *-gg-* from earlier *-ck-* cf. *smuggle*, *stagger*, etc.] **1.** A movable catch or lever the pulling or pressing of which releases a detent or spring, and sets some force or mechanism in action, e.g. springs a trap. **2.** *spec.* A small steel catch which on being 'drawn', 'pulled', or pressed by the finger, releases the hammer of a gunlock 1622.

Comb.: **t. finger,** the forefinger of the right hand, with which the t. is pulled; **-fish,** a fish of the genus *Balistes*; so named from the trigger-like second spine of the dorsal-fin. **b.** Also freq. *fig.* 'operating like a t.', as *t. action, question.*

Trigger[2] (tri·gəɹ). 1591. [f. TRIG *v.*[1] + -ER[1].] **1.** A device or appliance to retard or stop the motion of a vehicle descending a slope. Now *dial.* **2.** *Ship-building.* A support holding the dog-shore in position; also *transf.* the dog-shore itself 1867.

Trigintal (trəi,dʒi·ntăl). Now only *Hist.* 1491. [– med.L. *trigintale*, f. L. *triginta* thirty; see -AL[1] 1.] = TRENTAL.

Triglyph (trəi·glif). 1563. [– L. *triglyphus* – Gr. τρίγλυφος thrice-grooved, f. τρι- TRI- + γλυφή carving.] *Arch.* A member or ornament in the Doric order, consisting of a block or tablet with three vertical grooves or glyphs (strictly, two whole grooves, and a half-groove on each side), repeated at regular intervals along the frieze, usu. one over each column, and one in two between every two columns. Hence **Trigly·phic, -al** *adjs.* pertaining to or of the nature of a t.

Trigon (trəi·gǫn). 1563. [– L. *trigonum* – Gr. τρίγωνον triangle, n. of τρίγωνος, f. τρι- TRI- + -γωνος -angled, -cornered; see -GON.] **1.** A figure having three angles and three sides; a triangle. **2.** *Astrol.* **a.** A set of three signs of the zodiac, distant 120° from each other, as if at the angles of an equilateral triangle. **b.** = TRINE *sb.* 2. 1563. **3.** An ancient lyre or harp of triangular form 1727. **4.** An ancient game at ball, played by three persons 1842.

Trigonal (tri·gŏnăl), *a.* 1570. [– med.L. *trigonalis* triangular, f. L. *trigonum* triangle; see TRIGON, -AL[1] 1.] **1.** Of, pertaining, or relating to a trigon or triangle; triangular. **b.** *Geom.* and *Cryst.* Applied to a solid figure with triangular faces, or having some other relation to a triangle. Also, having a relation to three angles. 1878. **2.** Triangular in section, triquetrous: now *esp.* in *Zool.* and *Bot.* 1571.

Trigone (trigō^u·n, trəi·gō^u n). 1835. [– Fr. *trigone* – L. *trigonum* TRIGON.] *Anat.* The triangular area at the base of the urinary bladder, between the openings of the ureters and urethra.

Trigono- (tri·gŏno, trigō^u·no), comb. form repr. Gr. τρίγωνος adj. three-cornered, etc., neut. τρίγωνον as sb. a triangle; as in **Trigonocerous** (-ǫ·sĕrəs) *a.* [Gr. κέρας horn]. *Zool.* having horns of triangular section.

Trigonometric (tri:gŏno,me·trik), *a.* 1811. [f. TRIGONOMETRY + -IC; or the normal (later) var. of the orig. TRIGONOMETRICAL.] = next.

Trigonometrical (tri:gŏno,me·trikăl), *a.* 1666. [f. TRIGONOMETRY or mod.L. *trigonometria* + -ICAL. Cf. mod.L. *trigonometricus* (Newton).] Of, pertaining to, or performed by trigonometry.

T. functions, those functions of an angle, or of an abstract quantity, used in trigonometry, viz. the sine, tangent, secant, etc. *T. survey*, a survey of a country or region performed by triangulation and t. calculation. Hence **Tri:gonome·trically** *adv.*

Trigonometry (trigǒnǫ·mėtri). 1614. [– mod.L. *trigonometria* (B. Pitiscus, 1595), f. Gr. τρίγωνον triangle + -μετρία -METRY. So Fr. *trigonométrie* (1629).] That branch of mathematics which deals with the measurement of the sides and angles of triangles, particularly with certain functions of their angles, or of angles in general (the SINE, COSINE, TANGENT, COTANGENT, SECANT, and COSECANT), and hence with these functions as applied to abstract quantities; thus including the theory of triangles, of angles, and of (elementary) singly periodic functions. Hence **Trigono·meter,** a person versed in t.

‖**Trigonon** (trigōᵘ·nǫn). 1727. [– Gr. τρίγωνον.] *Antiq.* = TRIGON 3.

Trigonous (tri·gǒnəs), *a.* 1821. [f. Gr. τρίγωνος (see TRIGON) + -OUS.] *Nat. Hist.* = TRIGONAL 2.

Trigram (trəi·græm). 1606. [f. TRI- + -GRAM. Cf. MONOGRAM.] **a.** An inscription of three letters; also = TRIGRAPH. **b.** A figure or character formed of three strokes. **c.** *Geom.* A set of three lines; *spec.* the figure formed by three straight lines in one plane not intersecting in the same point. So **Trigramma·tic, Trigra·mmic** *adjs.* consisting of three letters or sets of letters. **Trigra·mmatism** = TRILITERALISM.

Trigraph (trəi·grɑf). 1836. [f. TRI- + -GRAPH.] A combination of three letters denoting a simple sound, as *eau* in Fr. *beau*, *sch* in G. *schaf*.

‖**Trigynia** (trəi,dʒi·niă). 1760. [mod.L. (Linn.), f. TRI- + Gr. γυνή woman, taken as = female organ, pistil; see -IA¹.] *Bot.* An order in many classes of the Linnæan system, comprising plants having three pistils. Hence **Tri·gyn,** a plant of the order *T.* **Trigy·nian, Trigy·nious** *adjs.* of or belonging to the order *T.* **Trigynous** (tri·dʒinəs) *a.* having three pistils.

Trihedral (trəihī·drăl, -he·drăl), *a.* (*sb.*) Also **triedral.** 1789. [f. Gr. τρι- TRI- + ἕδρα base + -AL¹ 1.] *Geom.*, etc. Of a solid figure or body: Having three sides or faces (in addition to the base or ends); triangular in section.

T. angle or *quoin*, a solid angle formed by three surfaces meeting at a point.

B. *sb. Geom.* A trihedral figure 1909. Also **Trihe·dron.** 1828.

Trike (trəik). Colloq. abbrev. of TRICYCLE.

Trilateral (trəilæ·tĕrăl), *a.* and *sb.* 1660. [f. late L. *trilaterus* three-sided + -AL¹ 1.] **A.** *adj.* Contained by three sides; three-sided. **B.** *sb.* A triangle 1766. **Trila·teral-ly** *adv.*, **-ness.**

Trilby (tri·lbi). 1895. [Name of the heroine of a novel (1893) of the same name by G. du Maurier.] (Usu. *attrib.*) Applied to various articles resembling those used or worn in the dramatized version of the novel; esp. a kind of soft felt hat worn by men; also *pl.* (*slang*) the feet (in allusion to the heroine's bare feet).

Trilemma (trəile·mă). 1672. [f. after DILEMMA; see TRI-] A situation, or (in *Logic*) a syllogism, of the nature of a DILEMMA, but involving three alternatives instead of two.

Trilinear (trəili·niăɹ), *a.* 1715. [f. TRI- + L. *linearis* LINEAR, f. *linea* line.] *Geom.* Of, contained by, or having some relation to, three lines.

T. co-ordinates, a system of co-ordinates determining a point in a plane by its distances, measured in three fixed directions, from three fixed straight lines forming a triangle.

Triliteral (trəili·tĕrăl), *a.* (*sb.*) 1751. [f. TRI- + L. *littera* + -AL¹ 1.] Consisting of three letters. **B.** *sb.* A triliteral word or root 1828. Hence **Trili·teralism,** the use of t. roots, as in Semitic languages. **Tri-litera·lity, Trili·teralness,** t. character. **Trili·terally** *adv.*

Trilith (trəi·liþ). Also in Gr. form **trilithon** (trəi·liþǫn). 1740. [– Gr. τρίλιθον, n. of τρίλιθος adj., of three stones, f. τρι- TRI- + λίθος stone.] A prehistoric structure or monument consisting of three large stones, two upright and one resting upon them as a lintel. Hence **Trili·thic** *a.* pertaining to or of the nature of a t.

Trill (tril), *sb.* 1649. [– It. *trillo*, †*triglio*, f. *trillare*; see TRILL *v.*³] **1.** *Mus.* **a.** A tremulous utterance of a note or notes as a 'grace'. **b.** A rapid alternation of two notes a degree apart; a shake. **2.** *transf.* A tremulous high-pitched sound or succession of notes, esp. in the singing of birds 1704. **3.** *Phonetics.* The pronunciation of a consonant, esp. *r*, with vibration of the tongue or other part of the vocal organs; a consonant so pronounced 1848.

Trill (tril), *v.*¹ Now *dial.* or *arch.* [ME. *trille*; cf. Sw. and Norw. *trilla*, Da. *trilde*, *trille* roll, trundle, wheel.] **1.** *trans.* To turn (a thing) round, to cause to revolve, rotate; to roll, bowl, trundle. †**2.** *intr.* Of a wheel, ball, etc.: To revolve, spin, roll, trundle –1681.

Trill, *v.*² *arch.* ME. [perh. developed from prec.] **1.** *intr.* Of tears, water, a stream: To roll, to flow in a slender stream, the particles of water being in constant revolution; to purl. **2.** *trans.* To cause to flow in this way 1485.

1. With many a teere trilling on my cheeke CHAUCER. A little dell, through which trilled a small rivulet SCOTT.

Trill, *v.*³ 1666. [– It. *trillare*; see TRILL *sb.*] **1.** *intr.* To sing with vibratory effect; to sing a trill or shake, to 'shake'; of a voice, etc.: To sound with tremulous vibration. **2.** *trans.* To utter or sing (a note, tune, etc.) with tremulous vibration of sound 1701. **b.** To cause (an instrument or the voice) to vibrate with a tremulous sound 1848. **3.** To pronounce (a consonant, esp. *r*) with a vibration of the tongue (or other vocal organ) and the corresponding auditory effect 1848.

1. My wife..proud that she shall come to t., and..I think she will PEPYS. **2.** The sober suited songstress trills her lay THOMSON.

Trilling (tri·liŋ). 1846. [= Da., Sw. *trilling*, Du. *drieling*; see TRI- and -LING¹.] One of a set of three. **a.** One of three children born at the same birth; a triplet. **b.** *Min.* A crystal composed of three individuals.

Trillion (tri·lyən). 1690. [– Fr. *trillion* or It. *trilione*, formed like BILLION on *million* with substitution of TRI-.] The third power of a million; a million billions, i.e. millions of millions. (In France and local U.S., a thousand 'billions', i.e. an English billion; see BILLION.)

‖**Trillium** (tri·liŏm). 1760. [mod.L. (Linn., 1753), in allusion to the triple leaves.] *Bot.* A genus of perennial endogenous herbs (family *Trilliaceæ*) bearing a whorl of three thin short-stalked or stalkless leaves at the summit of a simple stem, with a solitary flower in the middle. In America also called *wake-robin*. Also, a plant of this genus.

‖**Trillo** (tri·llo). 1651. [It.; see TRILL *sb.*] = TRILL *sb.*

Trilobite (trəi·lobəit, tri·-). 1832. [– mod.L. *Trilobites* (Walsh, 1771), f. Gr. τρι- TRI- + λόβος lobe (of the ear, etc.) + -ITE¹ 3.] *Palæont.* A member of a large group of extinct arthropodous animals, characterized by a three-lobed body; allied to the extinct Eurypterids and the existing King-crabs (*Limulus*); their remains are found abundantly in Palæozoic rocks, esp. the Silurian. Hence **Trilobi·tic** *a.* pertaining to, of the nature of, or containing trilobites.

Trilogy (tri·lŏdʒi). 1661. [– Gr. τριλογία, f. τρι- TRI- + λόγος discourse; see -LOGY.] **1.** *Gr. Antiq.* A series of three tragedies (orig. connected in subject) performed at Athens at the festival of Dionysus 1836. **2.** Any series or group of three related dramatic or other literary works 1661. **3.** *transf.* and *fig.* A group of three related utterances, subjects, etc. 1835.

1. All the plays of Æschylus, and the Henry VI of Shakespeare, are examples of a t. 1842. Hence **Trilo·gic, -al** *adjs.* of or pertaining to a t.

Trim (trim), *sb.* 1590. [f. TRIM *v.*] **1.** *Naut.* 1. The state of being trimmed or prepared for sailing; esp. the condition of being 'fully rigged and ready to sail'. **2. a.** The most advantageous set of a ship in the water on her fore and aft line. **b.** Adjustment of the sails with ref. to the direction of the wind and the ship's course. **c.** The condition of being properly balanced. **d.** The difference between the draught forward and the draught aft 1614. **e.** In vague use, the general appearance or look of a ship 1757.

2. e. In gallant t. the gilded Vessel goes GRAY.

II. 1. Adornment, array; equipment, outfit; dress: usu. in ref. to style or appearance; hence occas. nearly = guise, aspect 1596. **b.** The act of trimming or condition of being trimmed 1608. **2.** Condition, state, or order, esp. for work or action of any kind 1628. **3.** The nature, character, or manner of a person or thing; his or its 'way' 1706.

1. Bucklaw, in bridegroom t. SCOTT. *fig.* The Paint, and T. of Retorick 1650. **c.** *U.S.* The lighter woodwork of a building, esp. around openings 1884. **2.** Phr. *In t., into t.*, in or into proper condition or order.

Trim, *a.* (*adv.*) 1503. [Earliest in the adv. *trimly*, rel. to TRIM *v.*] **1.** In good condition or order; well prepared, furnished, or equipped; fit, proper, suitable; hence, sound, good, fine, beautiful. (Often a vague term of approval.) *arch.* **2.** Neatly or smartly made, prepared, or arranged; elegantly or finely dressed or 'got up'; having a neat, spruce, or tidy appearance or effect 1521. †**3.** In ironical use; cf. 'fine', 'nice', 'pretty', in similar use –1680. **B.** *adv.* Trimly 1529.

1. 'Twas t. sport for them that had the doing of it SHAKS. The ship was t. BYRON. **2.** Laurel hedges, but not so t. as ours BERKELEY. A t. and quiet girl came tripping to the door 1888. **3.** News quoth a? T. News truly OTWAY. Hence **Tri·m-ly** *adv.*, **-ness.**

Trim (trim), *v.* [Formally could repr. OE. *trymian*, *trymman* strengthen, confirm (= Branch I); but there is no connecting evidence of unequivocal character between the OE. period and 1500.] †**I.** (Only OE.) *trans.* To make firm or strong; to give as security; to arm or array (a force); to settle, arrange; to encourage, comfort, exhort. **II.** †**1.** To put into proper condition for some purpose or use; to prepare; to dress –1725. **2.** To fit out (a ship, etc.) for sea. *arch.* 1513. †**3.** To repair, restore, put right (something broken, worn or decayed) –1687. **4.** *spec.* To put (a lamp, fire, etc.) into proper order for burning, by removing any deposit or ash, and adding fresh fuel; also, to cleanse or cut level (a wick); by extension, to renew the burned-out carbons or electrodes of (an arc lamp) 1557. †**5.** To equip, supply –1667. **6.** To array, dress; to adorn, dress *up* 1516. **7.** *spec.* To decorate (a hat, garment, etc.) with ribbons, laces, embroideries, or the like; also, of a thing, to form the trimming of 1547. **8.** To dress (the hair or beard); to clip (the hair), or to clip the hair of (a person); also, to dub (a cock) 1530. **9.** *fig.* To beat, thrash, trounce; also, to reprimand, scold 1518. **10.** To cut off the excrescences or irregularities of; to reduce to a regular shape by doing this. Also with the part removed as object. Also with *up.* 1594. **11.** *Carpentry.* To bring (a piece of timber, etc.) to the required shape 1679. **12.** *Naut.* To distribute the load of (a ship or boat) so that she floats on an even keel 1580. **b.** *intr.* of a ship or boat 1861. **c.** *transf.* (*trans.*) To adjust (the balance) so as to equalize it 1817. **13.** *Naut.* To adjust (the sails or yards) with reference to the direction of the wind and the course of the ship 1624. Also *Aeronautics.* **b.** *absol.* or *intr.* 1697. **c.** *transf.* and *fig.* (*trans.*) To turn, adjust, adapt 1779. **14.** To stow or arrange (coal or cargo) in the hold of a ship, or carry it to the hatches when discharging; also, to shift (coal) in a ship's hold, etc.; also, to arrange (coal) as it is loaded on a truck 1797. **15.** *intr.* (Also with *it.*) To modify one's attitude in order to stand well with opposite parties; also, to accommodate oneself to the mood of the times 1685. **b.** *trans.* To modify according to expediency 1885.

1. *Rich. II*, III. iv. 56. **4.** Then all those virgins arose, & trymmed their lampes N.T. (Genev.) *Matt.* 25:7. **8. b.** *fig.* To cheat (a person) out of money; to fleece (*slang*) 1600. **9.** None of your jaw, you swab..else I shall t. your lac'd jacket for you SMOLLETT. **10.** No inclination..to t. the roadside hedges 1885. **11.** Phr. *To t. in.* to fit or frame (one piece) to or into another. **13.** The.. dexterous pilot..will t. his sails to every variation of wind 1836. **15.** Trimming it between God and the Devil 1685.

Trimelli·tic, *a.* 1872. [f. TRI- III + MELLITIC.] *Chem.* In *t. acid,* unsymmetrical benzene-tricarboxylic acid, obtained by the oxidation of colophony by means of nitric acid. (Named by Baeyer, 1870.)

Trimerous (tri·mĕrəs, trəi·-), *a.* 1826. [f. mod.L. *trimerus* – Gr. τριμερής, f. τρι- TRI- + μέρος part) + -OUS.] Having, consisting of, or characterized by three parts: *spec.* **a.** *Bot.* Having the parts of the flower, or the leaves, in series or whorls of three. **b.** *Ent.* Consisting of three segments or joints. So **Tri-meran** (tri·mĕrăn) *a. Ent.* belonging to the division *Trimera* of beetles, or of hymenopterous insects, characterized by t. tarsi; *sb.* an insect of either of these divisions.

Trimesic (trəimī·sik), *a.* 1889. [f. TRI- III + MES(ITYLENE + -IC.] *Chem.* In *t. acid,* $C_6H_3(CO_2H)_3$, symmetrical benzene-tricarboxylic acid. (So named by Fittig, 1867, when he obtained it from mesitylenic acid, and found it to be tribasic.)

Trimester (trəime·stəɹ). 1821. [– Fr. *trimestre* sb. – L. *trimestris* adj., f. TRI- + *mensis* month.] A period or term of three months.

Trimestrial (trəime·striăl), *a.* (*sb.*) 1693. [f. L. *trimestris* (see prec.) + -AL[1] 1.] Consisting of or containing three months; occurring or appearing every three months. **b.** as *sb.* A quarterly publication.

Trimeter (tri·mĭtəɹ, trəi·-), *sb.* and *a.* 1567. [– L. *trimetrus* adj. and sb. – Gr. τρίμετρος adj., f. τρι- TRI- + μέτρον METRE.] **A.** *sb.* A verse of three measures; i.e. in trochaics, iambics, or anapæstics, of three dipodies (= six feet); in other rhythms, of three feet. **B.** *adj.* Of a verse: Consisting of three measures 1706.

Trimethyl (trəimī·þəil, -me·þil). 1857. [f. TRI- III + METHYL.] *Chem.* **a.** A formative denoting the presence of three methyl groups, CH_3, in a compound. **b.** *spec.* denoting the substitution of 3 methyl groups for 3 hydrogen atoms in the substance denoted by the rest of the name. Hence **Trimethy·lic** *a.*

Trimetric (trəime·trik), *a.* 1837. [f. TRI- + Gr. μέτρον measure (or, in sense 2, f. as TRIMETER) + -IC.] **1.** *Cryst.* = ORTHORHOMBIC. **2.** *Pros.* Consisting of three measures 1889.

Trimmer (tri·məɹ). 1555. [f. TRIM *v.* + -ER[1].] **1.** One who trims, in the senses of the verb. **2.** One who or that which cuts, clips, prunes, etc.; *spec.* an implement or machine for trimming edges in industrial processes 1583. **3.** *Arch.* A short beam framed across an opening (as a stair-well or hearth) to carry the ends of those joists which cannot be extended across the opening 1654. **4.** One who trims between opposing parties in politics, etc.; hence, one who inclines to each of two opposite sides as interest dictates 1682. **5.** One who or that which trims or trounces; a stiff competitor, fighter, letter, bout, run, blow, etc. *colloq.* 1776. **6.** One whose business is to stow the cargo or coal in loading a ship; also, a mechanical contrivance for doing this; also, one who arranges the coal in loading trucks 1836. **7.** *Angling.* (*a*) A float, to which a line, with baited hook, is attached, used for taking pike; (*b*) a bank-runner, for the same purpose 1799.

4. One of the trimmers who went to church and chapel both T. HARDY. **5.** Mr. H. was clean bowled by a t. from Barnes 1882.

Trimming (tri·miŋ), *vbl. sb.* 1518. [-ING[1].] **1.** The action of TRIM *v.* 1519. **b.** *pl.* Pieces cut off in trimming 1805. **2.** *concr.* Adornment, array; *esp.* **a.** Any ornamental addition to the bare fabric of a dress, etc. Chiefly *pl.* 1625. **b.** *pl.* Accessories, usual accompaniments; e.g. to a joint of meat, etc. 1612. **3.** A beating; a drubbing; a sharp censure 1518.

2. b. A boiled leg of mutton with the usual trimmings DICKENS. **3.** He deserves a good t. for it 1787.

Comb.: **t.-joist,** a joist into which the end of a trimmer (sense 3) is fitted; **-tank,** a water-tank in the bow or stern of a ship which is filled or emptied as the trim of the ship demands.

Tri·mming, *ppl. a.* 1559. [f. TRIM *v.* + -ING[2].] That trims, in various senses of the verb; *colloq.* or *slang,* 'stunning', 'rattling', excellent. Hence **Tri·mmingly** *adv.*

Trimorphic (trəimǭ·ɹfik), *a.* 1866. [f. Gr. τρίμορφος (f. τρι- TRI- + μορφή form) + -IC.] Having, or existing in, three forms, as a plant, animal, or crystalline substance. So **Tri·morph,** *Cryst.* a t. substance, or each of its three different forms. **Trimo·rphism,** t. condition, occurrence in three different forms (of a plant, animal, or crystalline substance) 1860. **Trimo·rphous** *a.* = *tri-morphic.*

Trinacrian (trəinē[i]·kriăn), *a.* 1640. [f. L. *Trinacria* Sicily – Gr. Τρινακρία, taken as f. τρι- TRI- + ἄκρα point, cape; but orig. Θρινακίη, f. θρῖναξ trident; see -AN.] Of Sicily, Sicilian; hence, three-pointed.

Trinal (trəi·năl), *a.* 1590. [– med.L. *trinalis* (Adamnan), f. L. *trinus,* pl. *trini* three each, threefold; see -AL[1].] **1.** Threefold; triple; trine. **2.** *Gram.* Applied to a 'number' or inflected form expressing three 1853.

1. Wherwith he wont at Heav'ns high Councel-Table, To sit the midst of T. Unity MILT.

Trinary (trəi·nări), *a. rare.* 1474. [– late L. *trinarius,* f. as prec.; see -ARY[1].] Consisting or composed of a set of three; threefold; triple.

Trindle (tri·nd'l), *sb.* [Early ME. *trindel,* a parallel form to TRENDLE.] **1.** A wheel; *esp.* a 'trundle' or lantern-wheel in a mill; also, the wheel of a wheelbarrow. *Obs.* exc. *dial.* †**2.** Something of rounded form, as a pellet of sheep's or goat's dung –1660. **3.** *Book-binding.* Each of several flat pieces of thin wood or metal, shaped like toy horse-shoe magnets, by which (in pairs) the stitched, glued, and rounded back of a book is held flat while the front edge is ploughed 1818.

Tri·ndle, *v. Obs.* or *dial.* OE. [A parallel form to TRENDLE.] †**1.** *trans.* To make round, to round. OE. only. **2.** To cause (a wheel, etc.) to revolve; to cause to roll along a surface; to trundle 1595. **3.** *intr.* To revolve or turn round; to roll along a surface. late ME.

Trine (trəin), *a.* and *sb.* late ME. [– (O)Fr. *trin,* fem. *trine* :– L. *trinus* threefold, f. *tres, tria* THREE + multiplicative suffix.] **A.** *adj.* **1.** Threefold; triple. **2.** *Astrol.* Denoting the 'aspect' of two heavenly bodies which are a third part of the zodiac, i.e. 120°, distant from each other. Also, connected with or relating to a trine aspect. Also *fig.*: Favourable, benign. 1477.

1. *T. immersion,* the immersion of a person three times in baptism, in the name of the three Persons of the Trinity.

B. *sb.* **1.** A group of three; a triad 1552. **b.** *spec.* The Trinity 1568. **2.** *Astrol.* A trine aspect. Phr. *in t.* 1581. **3.** *pl.* Three children (or young) at a birth; triplets 1628.

1. O furyes! O Vindictive tryne 1614. **b.** Eternal One, Almighty T.! KEBLE. **2.** Fortunate aspects of T. and Sextile 1614. Hence **Trine** *v.* (*rare*) *trans.* to put or join in a t. aspect; to make a t. or triad of.

Tringle (tri·ŋg'l). 1696. [– Fr. *tringle* XVI (OFr. *tingle*).] **a.** *Arch.* A small square moulding or ornament. **b.** A curtain-rod, or any long slender rod.

‖**Trinidado** (trinidā·do). *Obs.* or *arch.* 1599. [Sp. adj. f. *Trinidad*; see -ADO.] A kind of tobacco from Trinidad.

Trinitarian (trinitē[ə]·riăn), *a.* and *sb.* 1628. [f. mod.L. *trinitarius* XVI (f. *trinitas* TRINITY) + -AN; see -ARIAN. Cf. Fr. *trinitaire* (Calvin).] **A.** *adj.* (In senses 1, 2 with capital T.) **1.** *Ch. Hist.* Belonging to the order of the Holy Trinity. **2.** *Theol.* Relating to the Trinity; holding the doctrine of the Trinity (opp. to *Unitarian*) 1656. **3.** Forming a trinity; triple, threefold 1812. **B.** *sb.* (With capital T.) **1.** A member of the religious order of the Holy Trinity; = MATHURIN 1628. **2.** *Theol.* One who holds the doctrine of the Trinity of the Godhead; a believer in the Trinity 1706. Hence **Trinita·rianism,** Trinitarian belief.

Trinitrate (trəi,nəi·trĕt). 1868. [f. TRI- III + NITRATE.] *Chem.* A compound formed from three molecules of nitric acid, HNO_3, by the replacement of the three hydrogen atoms by a trivalent element or radical.

Trini·trin. 1866. [f. TRI- III + NITR(IC + -IN[1].] *Chem.* = NITROGLYCERINE.

Trinitro- (trəinəi·tro), bef. a vowel **trinitr-.** 1851. [f. TRI- + NITRO-.] *Chem.* **a.** A formative denoting that three nitro-groups, NO_2, have replaced three hydrogen atoms in the substance designated by the rest of the name, the nitrogen atoms being directly joined to carbon atoms; e.g. **trinitro-phenol** or picric acid, $C_6H_2(NO_2)_3$-(OH); **trinitro-to·luene, -to·luol** (abbrev. *trotyl,* and T.N.T.), a high explosive (1916). **b.** In earlier nomenclature, *trinitro-* included cases in which the nitrogen atoms of the NO_2 groups were attached by oxygen atoms to the carbon atoms of the substance designated by the rest of the name; such compounds are now called TRINITRATES, e.g. **trinitro-ce·llulose,** gun-cotton.

Trinity (tri·nĭti). ME. [– (O)Fr. *trinité,* corresp. to Pr., Sp. *trinidad,* It. *trinità* :– L. *trinitas, trinitat-* (in Christian use (Tertullian) based on Gr. τριάς TRIAD) triad, trio, f. *trinus* TRINE; see -ITY.] **1.** The state of being threefold, threefoldness, threeness. **a.** *gen.* late ME. **b.** *spec.* In theological use: applied to the existence of one God in three persons. (In early use esp. in phr. 'God in t.', i.e. in threeness.) ME. **2.** The Father, Son, and Holy Spirit as constituting one God; the triune God. (Now always with capital T.) ME. **b.** *ellipt.* The festival of the Holy Trinity; Trinity Sunday ME. **3.** Any combination or set of three (persons, things, principles, etc.) forming a unity, or closely connected; a triad, trio 1542.

attrib.: **T. House,** shortened title of a guild or fraternity incorporated in the reign of Henry VIII and having the official regulation of British shipping, including the erection and maintenance of lighthouses and the licensing of pilots; hence *T. Brethren, high-water mark, pilot,* etc.; **T. Sunday,** the Sunday next after Whit-Sunday, observed as a festival in honour of the T.; **T. term,** the fourth of the terms or sessions of the High Court of Justice in England; since 1873 called officially *T. Sittings,* and now beginning on the Tuesday following T. Sunday; also, one of the university terms.

Trinket (tri·ŋkét), *sb.* 1533. [Of unkn. origin.] †**1.** Any small article forming part of an outfit; usu. *pl.* paraphernalia, accoutrements, 'traps'. –1787. **2.** A small ornament, usu. an article of jewellery for personal adornment 1533. †**3.** *fig.* Applied esp. to the decorations of worship, and to religious rites, beliefs, etc. –1655.

2. Trinkets, of which the girl was very fond SWIFT. Hence **Tri·nketry,** trinkets collectively; articles of personal decoration viewed as trinkets or toys.

†**Tri·nket,** *v.* Chiefly *Sc.* 1647. [Of unkn. origin.] *intr.* To intrigue *with*; to act in an underhand way, prevaricate –1821. Hence †**Tri·nketer,** a secret trafficker; an intriguer.

Trinomial (trəinō[u]·miăl) *a.* and *sb.* 1674. [Formed with TRI- after BINOMIAL.] **A.** *adj.* **1.** *Math.* Consisting of three terms, as an algebraical expression 1704. **2.** *Nat. Hist.* Consisting of three terms, viz. genus, species, and subspecies or variety, instead of the first two only; involving or characterized by three terms, as a system of nomenclature 1865. **B.** *sb.* **1.** *Math.* An expression consisting of three terms connected by + or −. 1674. **2.** *Nat. Hist.* The name of a subspecies or variety when composed of three terms (the names of the genus, species, and subspecies or variety) 1884.

Trio (trī·o, trəi·o). 1724. [– It. *trio* (partly through Fr.), f. L. *tres,* n. *tria* THREE, after *duo.*] **1.** *Mus.* A composition for three voices or instruments; also, a company of three performers singing or playing such a composition. **b.** Name for a second or subordinate division of a minuet or other dance movement, or of a scherzo or march; commonly in a different style (and occas., key) from the main part, which is repeated after it 1840. **2.** A group or set of three 1777. **b.** At piquet, a combination of three aces, kings, queens, or knaves in one hand 1891.

2. The t. of Kentucky hunters, Robinson, Rezner, and Hoback W. IRVING.

Triobol (trəi·obǫl, trəi,ō[u]·bǫl). Also **triobolus.** 1837. [– Gr. τριώβολον, f. τρι- TRI- + ὀβολός OBOL.] An ancient Greek coin of the value of three obols, or half a drachma. So †**Tri̦o·bolar**, †**Trio·bolary** *adjs. lit.* worth three obols; *fig.* of little value, paltry, mean.

Trioctile (trəi,ǫ·ktəil). 1727. [f. TRI- + L. *octo* eight, after *quartile*, etc.] *Astrol.* = *sesquiquadrate* (SESQUI- I c).

Triode (trəi·oᵘd). 1919. [f. TRI- + ELECTR)ODE.] *Wireless Telegr.* In full *triode valve*: Trade-name of a three-electrode valve.

‖**Triœcia** (trəi,ī·ʃiă). 1760. [mod.L. (Linn.), f. Gr. τρι- TRI- + οἶκος house; cf. DIŒCIA, etc., and see -IA[1].] *Bot.* The third order in the Linnæan class *Polygamia*, comprising plants having male, female, and hermaphrodite flowers on different individuals. Hence **Triœcious** (-ī·ʃ¹əs), **Tri,oi·cous** *adjs.* belonging to this order, or having the flowers thus distributed.

Triolet (trəi·ŏlėt, trī··). 1651. [– Fr. *triolet*, f. *trio*; see TRIO, -LET.] *Prosody.* A stanza of eight lines, constructed on two rhymes, in which the first line is repeated as the fourth and seventh, and the second as the eighth.

Trional (trəi·ŏnăl). 1889. [f. TRI- + *-onal* of *sulphonal*; see -AL[2].] *Pharm.* Trade-name of a synthetic narcotic drug resembling sulphonal.

‖**Triones** (trəi,ōᵘ·nīz), *sb. pl.* 1594. [L., ploughing-oxen, also as here.] *Astron.* The seven principal stars in *Ursa Major.*

Trionyx (trəi·ŏniks, trəi,ōᵘ·niks). 1835. [mod.L., f. Gr. τρι- TRI- + ὄνυξ nail.] *Zool.* A genus of chelonian reptiles, so called because only three of the five toes have nails. So **Trio·nychoid** *a.* belonging to the suborder *Trionychoidea* of *Chelonia*, typified by the genus *T.* of soft-shelled turtles; *sb.* a turtle of this suborder.

Trioxide (trəi,ǫ·ksəid). 1868. [f. TRI- III + OXIDE.] *Chem.* A compound of three atoms of oxygen with an element or radical.

Trip (trip), *sb.*[1] late ME. [f. TRIP *v.*] **I. 1.** The action or an act of tripping; a light lively movement of the feet; tripping gait or tread; the sound of this 1600. **2.** A short voyage or journey, a 'run'; *esp.* each of a series of journeys or runs over a particular route. App. orig. a sailor's term, but very soon extended to a journey on land. 1691. **b.** A short journey (by sea or land) for pleasure or health; later, often applied to such a journey whatever its length. Also, applied to a passage by rail provided at a fare lower than the usual; a *cheap t.*, an excursion; occas. short for 'party of trippers' or 'trip-train' 1749. **3.** *Naut.* A single board or reach in tacking; a tack 1700.

1. Yonder comes Dalinda; I know her by her t. DRYDEN. **2.** It will be what mariners call a *t.* to England RICHARDSON. The 'bus-driver..is paid by 't.', and anxious to get his trips done 1906.

II. 1. 'A stroke or catch by which the wrestler supplants his antagonist' (J.); a sudden catching of a person's foot with one's own so as to cause him to stumble or fall. late ME. **2.** A stumble or mis-step causing one to lose one's equilibrium 1681. **3.** A mistake, blunder, fault; a slip, lapse; a false step; a slip of the tongue 1548.

1. The Groom..watches with a T. his Foe to foil DRYDEN. *fig.* Or will not else thy craft so quickely grow, That thine owne t. shall be thine ouerthrow? SHAKS. **2.** The poor Animal being now almost tired, made a second T. STEELE. **3.** A t. in one point would have spoiled all 1773.

III. *Mech.* A contrivance that trips; a projecting part of some mechanism which comes into momentary contact with another part so as to cause or check some movement 1906.

attrib. and *Comb.*: **t. system,** a system of payment by the t. or journey; **-train,** a mineral train which is intended to make a certain number of trips, out and home, in the day; also, an excursion train.

Trip, *sb.*[2] ME. [Of unkn. origin.] †**1.** A troop or company of men –1578. **2. a.** A small flock (of goats, sheep, hares, etc.). *Obs.* exc. *local.* ME. **b.** A small flock of wild-fowl 1805.

Trip (trip), *v.* late ME. [– OFr. *treper, trip(p)er* = Pr. *trepar* – MDu. *trippen* skip, hop, rel. to OE. *treppan* tread, trample.] **I. 1.** *intr.* To move lightly and nimbly on the feet; to skip, caper; to dance. *arch.* **b.** *intr.* with *it* 1579. **2.** *trans.* To perform (a dance) with a light lively step (*rare*) 1627. **b.** To tread lightly and nimbly, dance upon 1749. **3.** *intr.* To go, walk, skip, or run with a light and lively motion; to move with a quick light tread; also with *it.* late ME. **4.** *trans.* To cause to trip or go nimbly 1598. **5.** *intr.* To make a trip or short excursion. Also with *it.* 1664.

1. b. Com, and t. it as ye go On the light fantastick toe MILT. **2. b.** The sportive graces t. the green SHENSTONE. **3.** T. and goe, my sweete, deliuer this Paper into the hand of the King SHAKS. **5.** I shall t. to Paris in about a fortnight H. WALPOLE.

II. 1. *trans.* To cause to stumble or fall by suddenly arresting or catching the foot; 'to throw by striking the feet from the ground by a sudden motion; to strike the feet from under the body' (J.). Also with *up.* Often with the heels, foot, etc. as object. late ME. **b.** *fig.* or in *fig.* context 1548. **2.** To overthrow by catching in a fault or blunder; to detect in an inconsistency or inaccuracy 1557. **3.** *intr.* To strike the foot against something, so as to hop, stagger, or fall; to stumble *over* an obstacle; to make a false step 1440. **b.** Said of the tongue: To stumble in articulation; to falter in speaking 1526. **4.** *intr.* To fall into an error; to make a mistake or false step; to commit a fault, inconsistency, or inaccuracy 1509.

1. The other following tript vp his heeles GREENE. **b.** To t. the course of Law, and blunt the Sword That guards the peace SHAKS. **2.** *Cymb.* V. v. 35. **3.** I tripped over my sword, and nearly fell on my nose MARRYAT. **b.** Drinking.. till his Tongue trips LOCKE. **4.** After many endeavours to catch me tripping in some part of my story SWIFT. Jenny had tript in her time TENNYSON.

III. 1. *Naut. trans.* To loose (an anchor) from its bed and raise it clear of the bottom by a cable or a buoy rope. Also *intr.* for *pass.* 1748. **2.** To tilt; *spec. Naut.* to give (a yard) the necessary cant in sending it down; also, to lift (an upper mast) in order that it may be lowered 1840. **3.** *intr.* To tilt or tip up 1869. **4.** *trans.* To release (a catch, etc.) by contact with a projection; to operate in this way 1897.

Tri·-pack. 1911. [f. TRI- II + PACK *sb.*[1]] In colour photography, a pack of three sensitive films.

Tripartite (trəi,pā·ɹtəit, tri·paɹtəit), *a.* late ME. [– L. *tripartitus*, f. *tri-* TRI- + pa. pple. of *partiri* divide, PART *v.*] **1.** Divided into or composed of three parts or kinds; threefold, triple. **b.** Involving, or of the nature of, division into three parts 1576. **2.** Made in three corresponding parts or copies, as an indenture drawn up between three parties, each of whom preserves one of the copies 1442. **3.** Engaged in by or concluded between three parties 1497. **4.** *Her.* **a.** = TIERCÉ. **b.** Applied to a cross or saltire when each of its members consists of three narrow bands with spaces between. 1796. **5.** Consisting of three parts or divisions 1658. **b.** *Bot. spec.* of a leaf, etc., divided into three segments nearly to the base. (Abbrev. *3-partite.*) 1753.

1. b. A t. division of that vast country BURKE. **3.** The t. treaty which..exists among three of the leading powers of the world 1857. Hence **Tripartitely** *adv.*

Tripartition (trəipaɹti·ʃən). 1652. [– late L. *tripartitio, -ōn-* (Augustine), f. *tripartire* divide into three; see prec., -ION.] Division into three parts; partition among three.

Tripe (trəip). ME. [– (O)Fr. *tripe* = Pr. *tripa*, It. *trippa*, of unkn. origin.] **1.** The first or second stomach of a ruminant, esp. of the ox, prepared as food. Now usu. *collect. sing.* **2.** The intestines, bowels, guts, as members of the body; hence, the paunch or belly including them. *arch.* or *low.* Commonly in *pl.* 1470. **b.** Applied *contempt.* to a person 1595. **3.** *transf.* and *fig.* Now freq.: Nonsensical rubbish, trash (*slang*) 1676.

1. *Plain t.*, the first stomach, paunch, or rumen; *honeycomb t.*, the second, or reticulum. **2. b.** Saist thou me so, thou T., thou hated scorne? 1595. **3.** A song..that would be worth a shopful of such 't.' 1895.

‖**Tripe de roche** (trip də roʃ). 1809. [Fr., 'rock tripe', from the appearance of the thallus.] A name orig. given in Canada to various edible lichens of the genera *Gyrophora* and *Umbilicaria*, which afford a slightly nutritious but bitter and purgative food.

Tri-personal (trəi,pə̄·ɹsənăl), *a.* 1641. [f. TRI- + PERSON *sb.* V a + -AL[1] 1.] *Theol.* Consisting of or existing in three persons: said of the Godhead; also, relating to the three persons of the Godhead. Hence **Tripe·rsonalist,** one who holds the doctrine of three persons in the Godhead. **Tri:persona·lity,** the condition of being t., existence in three persons.

Tripetalous (trəi,pe·tăləs), *a.* 1830. [f. TRI- + PETAL + -OUS.] *Bot.* Having, or consisting of, three petals. So **Tripe·taloid** *a.* (of a six-parted perianth) having three of the segments petaloid.

Tri·p-ha:mmer. 1809. [f. TRIP *sb.*[1] or *v.* + HAMMER.] A massive machine-hammer operated by a tripping device, as a wheel with projecting teeth, a cam, or the like, by which it is raised and then allowed to drop.

Triphane (trəi·feⁱn). 1816. [– Fr. *triphane* (Haüy, 1801) – Gr. τριφανής appearing threefold; so called from exhibiting three lustrous cleavages.] *Min.* = SPODUMENE.

Triphthong (tri·fþǫŋ). 1599. [– Fr. *triphtongue*, f. *tri-* TRI-, after DIPHTHONG.] A combination of three vowel sounds in one syllable; also, loosely, a combination of three vowel characters, a TRIGRAPH. Hence **Triphtho·ngal** *a.*

Tri·plane. 1912. See TRI- II.

Triple (tri·p'l), *sb.* late ME. [subst. use of next.] **1.** A triple quantity, sum, or number; thrice as much or as many. 1597. **2.** †**a.** *Mus.* Triple measure or rhythm 1597. **b.** A triple star 1890. **c.** A magic lantern having three optical tubes combined in one 1892. **3.** *Bell-ringing.* A peal rung on seven bells with the tenor, i.e. the eighth, behind; the bells interchanging in three sets of two 1798.

Triple (tri·p'l), *a.* (*adv.*) 1550. [– (O)Fr. *triple* or L. *triplus* – Gr. τριπλοῦς = L. *triplex.*] **1.** = TREBLE *a.* 1. 1551. **2.** = TREBLE *a.* 1 b. 1567. **3.** Three times as much or as many; multiplied by three 1550. †**4.** That is one of the three; third. SHAKS.

1. A t. thorn beneath the buds 1776. T. rows of chains 1874. **2.** A t. vse of fasting 1587. **4.** *All's Well* II. i. 111.

Special collocations. *T. alliance*, an alliance of three states or powers, e.g. that of Germany, Austria-Hungary, and Italy in 1883; also *transf. T. crown*, a threefold crown; *spec.* the papal tiara; also, a heraldic bearing representing this. *T. entente* (Fr.), an understanding as to political action between three powers. *T. line, plane* (*Geom.*), a line or plane formed by the coincidence of three lines or planes. *T. point* (*Geom.*), a point common to three branches of a curve, or at which the curve has three tangents. *T. ratio*, the ratio of three to one. *T. rhythm* (*Mus.*), a threefold rhythm consisting of one heavy and two light accents or beats. *T. salt* (*Chem.*), a salt containing three different bases. *T. star*, a treble star. *T. time* (*Mus.*), a rhythm of three beats in the bar. *Comb.*: **t.-expansion** (see EXPANSION 7); **-screw,** having three screw-propellers; **t. tree,** (*Cant*, now *Hist.* or *arch.*) a gallows (in ref. to its three parts).

B. *adv.* To three times the extent or amount; in a threefold manner 1606. **Tri·ply** *adv.*

Triple (tri·p'l), *v.* late ME. [– late and med.L. *triplare*, f. L. *triplus* TRIPLE *a.* Cf. Fr. *tripler* (XV).] **1.** *trans.* To make three times as great or as many; to multiply by three; to treble. **b.** *spec.* in *Mech.* To alter (a steam-engine) from single or double expansion to the triple-expansion type; also, to fit (a vessel, etc.) with triple-expansion engines 1891. **2.** *intr.* To grow to three times the former number or amount 1799.

1. The export of foreign commodities was tripled 1858.

Triplet (tri·plėt). 1656. [f. TRIPLE, after DOUBLET.] **1.** A set of three; three persons or things combined or united 1733. **2.** *spec.* **a.** Three successive lines of verse, esp. when rhyming together and of the same length 1656. **b.** *pl.* Three children at a birth; *sing.* one of three at a birth 1787. **c.** *Mus.* A group of three notes to be played in the time of two of the same time-value 1801. **d.** *Arch.* A window of three lights 1849. **e.** *Naut.* Three links between the cable and the anchor-ring 1891.

Triplex (trəi·-, tri·pleks), *a.* (*sb.*) 1601. [– L. *triplex*, *-plic-* threefold, f. *tri-* TRI- + *plic-* fold.] Triple, threefold. Also *absol.* as *sb.*

Triplicate (tri·plikĕt), *a.* and *sb.* late ME. [– L. *triplicatus*, pa. pple. of *triplicare*, f. *triplex*, *-ic-*; see prec., -ATE[2],[1].] **A.** *adj.* Threefold, triple; forming three exactly corresponding copies; consisting of or related to three corresponding parts.

T. bills of loading 1756. *T. proportion, ratio*, the proportion or ratio of cubes (third powers) in relation to that of the radical quantities.

B. *sb.* One of three things exactly alike, *esp.* one of three copies of a document; *pl.* three things exactly alike 1762.

In t., in three exactly corresponding copies or transcripts.

Triplicate (tri·plikeˈt), *v.* 1623. [– *triplicat-*, pa. ppl. stem of L. *triplicare*; see prec., -ATE[3].] **1.** *trans.* To multiply by three; to increase threefold; to triple. **2.** To make or provide in triplicate; to repeat a second time 1639.

Triplication (triplikēˈ·ʃən). 1577. [– AFr. *triplicacioun* or late L. *triplicatio*, *-ōn-* (also = surrejoinder), f. as prec.; see -ION.] **1.** The action or process of making threefold, or multiplying by three; also, the result of this 1610. **2.** *Civil* and *Canon Law.* The plaintiff's reply to the defendant's duplication, corresponding to the surrejoinder at common law 1577. So **Tri·plicature.**

‖**Triplice** (tripl*ī*·tʃe). 1896. [It., 'triple'.] The Triple Alliance between Germany, Austria, and Italy, formed 1882–3 against Russia and France.

Triplicity (tripli·sĭti). late ME. [– late L. *triplicitas*, *-tat-*, f. L. *triplex*, *-ic-*; see TRIPLEX, -ITY. Cf. (O)Fr. *triplicité*.] **1.** The quality or condition of being triple; threefold character or existence; tripleness 1555. **2.** A triad, trio, triplet 1585. **3.** *spec.* in *Astrol.* = TRIGON 2 a. late ME.

2. Many an Angels voice Singing before th' eternall majesty, In their trinall triplicities on hye SPENSER.

Triplite (tri·pləit). 1850. [– G. *triplit* (Hausmann, 1813), f. Gr. τριπλοῦς threefold; see -ITE[1] 2 b.] *Min.* A phosphate of iron and manganese, with cleavage in three directions mutually at right angles.

Triplo- (triplo), bef. a vowel **tripl-**, comb. form repr. Gr. τριπλόος, τριπλοῦς threefold, triple; as in **Triploblastic** (-blæ·stik) [Gr. βλαστός germ] *a.*, *Biol.* having three germinal layers in the embryo; belonging to the division *Triploblastica*, a synonym of CŒLOMATA.

Tri·p-madam. 1693. [= Fr. *tripe-madame*, alt. of earlier *trique-madame*, whence †*trick-madam*.] = PRICK-MADAM.

Tripod (trəi·pǫd, tri·pǫd), *sb.* and *a.* 1603. [– L. *tripus*, *tripod-* – Gr. τρίπους, τριποδ- (adj. and sb.), f. τρι- TRI- + πούς, ποδ- foot.] **A.** *sb.* **1.** *Gr.* and *Rom. Antiq.* A three-legged vessel; a pot or cauldron resting on three legs 1611. **2.** *spec.* A vessel of this kind at the shrine of Apollo at Delphi, on which the priestess seated herself to deliver oracles. Hence *allus.* the Delphic oracle; any oracle or oracular seat. 1603. **3.** A seat, table, stool, etc., with three legs 1656. **4.** A three-legged support of any kind; *esp.* a frame or stand with three (diverging) legs for supporting a camera, compass, or other apparatus 1825. **B.** *adj.* Having or resting upon three feet or legs; of the form of a tripod 1715. So **Tripodal** (tri·pŏdăl), **Tripo·dial, Tripo·dian** *adjs.* three-footed, three-legged; *Anat.* having three rays or processes, as a bone.

Tripoli (tri·pŏli). 1601. [– Fr. *tripoli*, f. *Tripoli*, a region in N. Africa or town in Syria, where found.] A fine earth used as a polishing-powder, consisting mainly of decomposed siliceous matter; called also *infusorial earth* or *rottenstone*. Hence **Tri·poline** *a.* of or pertaining to t.

Tripos (trəi·pǫs). 1589. [unexpl. alt. of L. *tripus*; see TRIPOD.] †**1.** = TRIPOD A. 1, 3, 4. –1827. †**b.** *spec.* = TRIPOD 2. –1780. **2.** *Cambridge University.* Formerly: **a.** A bachelor of arts appointed to dispute, in a humorous or satirical style, with the candidates for degrees at 'Commencement': so called from the three-legged stool on which he sat. **b.** A set of humorous verses, orig. composed by the 'Tripos', and (till 1894) published at Commencement after his office was abolished (in full *t. verses*). **c.** The list of candidates qualified for the honour degree in mathematics, orig. printed on the back of the paper containing these verses (in full, *t. list*). 1659. **d.** Hence, in current use: *orig.* The final honours examination for the B.A. degree in mathematics, consisting of two parts (formerly *first* and *second t.*, now the *Mathematical T.*, Parts I and II); later extended to the subsequently founded final honours examinations in other subjects (*Classical T.*, etc.) 1842.

attrib.: **t. list,** the list of successful candidates in a t.; **t. paper,** any one of the papers of questions set in a t. (examination); **t. speech,** the humorous or satirical speech delivered by the 'Tripos'; **t. verses** (see 2 b).

Trippant (tri·pănt), *a.* 1658. [– OFr. *trippant*, pr. pple. of *tripper*; see TRIP *v.*, -ANT.] *Her.* = TRIPPING *ppl. a.* 3.

Tripper (tri·pəɹ). late ME. [f. TRIP *v.* + -ER[1].] One who or that which trips. **1.** One who dances; one who moves with light sprightly steps. **2.** One who or that which causes to stumble 1605. **3.** One who goes on a 'trip'; an excursionist. *colloq.* 1813. (So **Tri·ppist** 1792.)

3. The modern t. leaves only desolation and dirty paper behind him 1899. *Cheap t.*, one who travels by a cheap trip. Hence **Tri·ppery** *a.*

Tripping (tri·piŋ), *vbl. sb.* 1591. [f. TRIP *v.* + -ING[1].] The action of TRIP *v.*

attrib. and *Comb.*: **t.-line** (*Naut.*), a light line for tilting the yards; also, a line for manipulating a drogue.

Tri·pping, *ppl. a.* 1562. [f. as prec. + -ING[2].] **1.** Moving quickly and lightly; light-footed; nimble 1567. **2.** Stumbling, erring, sinning 1577. **3.** *Her.* Of a buck, stag, etc.: walking, and looking toward the dexter side, with three paws on the ground and one fore-paw raised; the same as *passant* of other animals 1562. Hence **Tri·ppingly** *adv.*

Triptote (tri·ptōᵘt), *sb.* and *a.* 1612. [– L. *triptota* pl. – Gr. τρίπτωτα, pl. n. of τρίπτωτος with three case-endings, f. τρι- TRI- + πτωτός falling (πτῶσις case).] **A.** *sb.* A noun (or other word) used in three cases only. **B.** *adj.* Having only three cases 1886.

Triptych (tri·ptik). 1731. [f. TRI- after DIPTYCH.] **1. a.** *Antiq.* A set of three writing-tablets hinged or tied together. **b.** A card made to fold in three divisions. **2.** A picture or carving (or set of three such) in three compartments side by side, hinged so that the lateral ones fold over the central one; chiefly used as an altar-piece 1849.

Tripudiary (trəipiū·diări), *a. rare.* 1646. [f. L. *tripudium*; see next and -ARY[1].] **1.** *Rom. Antiq.* Denoting a species of divination (called *tripudium*) from the behaviour of birds, esp. of the sacred chickens, when fed. **2.** Of or pertaining to dancing (*affected*) 1819.

1. The conclusions of Southsayers in their Auguriall, and T. divinations SIR T. BROWNE.

Tripudiate (trəipiū·di,eˈt), *v.* Now *rare* and *affected.* 1623. [– *tripudiat-*, pa. ppl. stem of L. *tripudiare*, f. *tripudium* a beating the ground with the feet, a leaping or dancing, a religious dance (prob. f. *tri-* three + *pod-*).] **1.** *intr.* To dance for joy, or with excitement; to exult. **2.** To jump (*on* or *upon*) in contempt or triumph 1888. So **Tripu·diant** *a.* dancing; *fig.* exultant. **Tripudia·tion,** the action of dancing or leaping; exultation.

‖**Triquetra** (trəikwe·tră, -kwī·tră). 1586. [L., fem. of *triquetrus*; see TRIQUETROUS.] †**a.** A triangle. **b.** A triangular ornament, formed of three interlaced arcs or lobes.

Triquetral (trəikwe·trăl, -kwī·trăl), *a.* 1646. [f. as next + -AL[1] 1.] = next.

Triquetrous (trəikwe·trəs), *a.* 1658. [f. L. *triquetrus* three-cornered, triangular + -OUS.] Three-sided, triangular; in *Nat. Hist.* of triangular cross-section, three-edged, trihedral, triangularly prismatic or pyramidal.

Trireme (trəi·rīm), *sb.* and *a.* 1601. [– (O)Fr. *trirème* or L. *triremis*, f. *tri-* TRI- + *remus* oar.] **A.** *sb.* An ancient galley (orig. Greek, subseq. also Roman) with three ranks of oars one above another, used chiefly as a ship of war. **B.** *adj.* Having three ranks of oars 1697.

‖**Trisagion** (trisæ·giŏn, -ēˈ·giǫn). Also in L. form **trisagium.** late ME. [– Gr. (τὸ) τρισάγιον, n. of τρισάγιος thrice holy, f. τρίς thrice + ἅγιος holy.] An ancient hymn, used esp. in the Oriental Churches, beginning with a threefold invocation of God as holy. Also loosely applied to the TERSANCTUS.

Trisect (trəise·kt), *v.* 1672. [f. TRI- + *sect-*, pa. ppl. stem of L. *secare* cut, after BISECT.] *trans.* To divide into three equal parts (esp. in *Geom.*); sometimes *gen.* to divide into three parts. So **Trise·ction,** the action of trisecting; division into three (equal) parts 1664.

Triskele (tri·skīl). 1857. [f. Gr. τρι- TRI- + σκέλος leg.] A symbolic figure consisting of three legs radiating from a common centre.

‖**Trismus** (tri·zmŏs). 1693. [mod.L. – Gr. τρισμός = τριγμός scream, also a grinding, rasping.] *Path.* Lock-jaw. (Rarely extended to tetanus in general.)

Trisoctahedron (tri:sǫktăhī·drǫn, -he·drǫn). 1847. [f. Gr. τρίς thrice + OCTAHEDRON.] *Geom.* and *Cryst.* A solid figure having 24 faces, every three of which correspond to one face of an octahedron: either with triangular faces (= *triakisoctahedron*), or with trapezoidal faces (= *deltohedron*, *icositetrahedron*, or *trapezohedron*). So **Tri:stetrahe·dron.**

Trist, *a. Obs.* or *arch.*; in ordinary use now only as Fr. ‖**triste** (trīst). ME. [– (O)Fr. *triste* – L. *tristis*.] **1.** Sad, sorrowful; melancholy; lamentable. **2.** Dull, depressing, dreary (only as Fr.) 1756.

Tristesse. Now only as Fr. (tristęs). [In XIV *tristesce* (Gower) – OFr. *tristesce*, etc. (mod. *tristesse*) :– L. *tristitia* sadness, f. *tristis* sad; see -ESS[2].] Sadness, grief, melancholy.

Tristful (tri·stfŭl), *a. arch.* 1491. [f. TRIST *a.* + -FUL 1.] Full of sadness; sad, sorrowful; dreary, dismal. Hence **Tri·stfully** *adv.*

Tristich (tri·stik). 1813. [f. TRI-, after DISTICH.] *Pros.* A group of three lines of verse; a stanza of three lines.

Trisyllabic (trəi-, trisilæ·bik), *a.* 1637. [– Fr. *trissyllabique*, f. L. *trisyllabus* – Gr. τρισύλλαβος, f. τρι- three + συλλαβή syllable; see -IC.] Consisting of or involving three syllables. So **Trisylla·bical** *a.*, **-ly** *adv.*

Trisyllable (tri-, trəisi·lăb'l), *sb.* (*a.*) 1589. [f. TRI- + SYLLABLE.] A word, or a metrical foot, of three syllables. **B.** as *adj.* = prec. 1766.

Tritagonist (trəitæ·gŏnist). 1890. [– Gr. τριταγωνιστής, f. τρίτος third + ἀγωνιστής combatant, actor.] The third actor in a Greek tragedy.

Trite (trəit), *a.* 1548. [– L. *tritus*, pa. pple. of *terere* rub.] **1.** Worn out by constant use or repetition; devoid of freshness or novelty; hackneyed, commonplace, stale. **2.** Well worn; worn out by rubbing; frayed; (of a road or path) beaten, frequented 1599.

1. A t. observation 1762. **2.** Specimens of.. bronze coinage..mostly t. and faceless 1855. Hence **Tri·te-ly** *adv.*, **-ness.**

Trithing (trəi·ðiŋ), **thrithing** (þrəi·ðiŋ). [Late OE. **þriding*, **þriðing* (*treding*, *trethine*, *trithing* XI–XIII) – ON. *þriðjungr* third part, f. *þriði* THIRD; see -ING[3].] = RIDING *sb.* Now only *Hist.*

Tritical (tri·tikăl), *a.* 1709. [f. TRITE *a.*, with play on *critical*.] Of a trite or commonplace character. Hence **Tri·tical-ly** *adv.*, **-ness.** So **Tri·ticism** (after *criticism*).

Triticin (tri·tisin). 1838. [f. L. *triticum* wheat + -IN[1].] *Chem.* †**1.** Name given to the gluten of wheat by Hermbstaedt; also applied to a substance obtained from potato starch –1860. **2.** A carbohydrate obtained from the roots of couch-grass, *Triticum repens* 1874.

Trito- (trito, trəito), bef. a vowel **trit-**, comb. form repr. Gr. τρίτος third, occurring in technical terms (usu. corresp. to terms in PROTO- and DEUTERO-); as in **Trito·vum,** a third stage of an ovum, succeeding the deutovum. **Tritozooid** (-zōᵘ·oid), a tertiary zooid, produced from a deuterozooid.

Triton (trəi·tən). 1584. [- L. *Triton*, Gr. *Τρίτων*.] **1.** *Gr.* and *Rom. Myth.* Proper name of a sea-deity, son of Poseidon and Amphitrite, or of Neptune and Salacia, or otherwise of Nereus; also, one of a race of inferior sea-deities, or imaginary sea-monsters, of semi-human form. **b.** A figure of a Triton in painting, sculpture, etc.; in *Her.* represented as a bearded man with the hind quarters of a fish, and usu. holding a trident and a shell-trumpet 1601. **c.** *fig.* and *allus.*: esp. applied to a seaman, waterman, or the like. *T. of* or *among the minnows*: see MINNOW. 1589. **2.** *Zool.* **a.** A genus of marine gastropods with trumpet-shaped shells; an animal, or shell, of this genus, or of the family *Tritonidæ*. Also called *Triton's shell.* 1777. **b.** An extensive genus (now divided) of newts; an animal of this genus or group 1839.

1. So might I..hear old T. blow his wreathèd horn WORDSW. **c.** From their Lowzy Benches up started such a noizy multitude of old grizly Tritons 1704.

Triturate (tri·tiŭreᵗt), *v.* 1755. [- *triturat-*, pa. ppl. stem of L. *triturare* thresh corn, f. L. *tritura* rubbing, threshing, f. *trīt-*, pa. ppl. stem of *terere* rub; see TRITE, -URE, -ATE³.] *trans.* To reduce to fine particles or powder by rubbing, bruising, pounding, crushing, or grinding; to comminute, pulverize; also, to mix (solids, or a solid and a liquid) in this way. So **Tritura·tion,** the action or process of triturating; a mass produced, or medicine prepared, by trituration 1646.

†**Tri·ture.** 1657. [- L. *tritura*; see prec.] Pounding or grinding; comminution; trituration -1790.

Triumph (trəi·ŏmf), *sb.* [In XIV (Chaucer) - OFr. *triumphe* (mod. *triomphe*) - L. *triumphus*, earlier *triumpus*, prob. - Gr. *θρίαμβος* hymn to Bacchus (Dionysus).] **1.** *Rom. Hist.* The entrance of a victorious commander with his army and spoils in solemn procession into Rome, permission for which was granted by the senate in honour of an important achievement in war. **2.** *transf.* The action or fact of triumphing; victory, conquest, or the glory of this; also, a triumphal feat, signal achievement. late ME. †**b.** *transf.* The subject of triumph. MILT. †**3.** Pomp; splendour; glory; magnificence -1718. †**4.** A public festivity; a spectacle or pageant; *esp.* a tournament -1825. **5.** The exultation of victory or success; elation; rapturous delight 1582. **b.** *In t.*, triumphant; triumphantly 1593. †**6.** A triumphal arch (*rare*) -1658. †**7.** *Cards.* **a.** = TRUMP *sb.*² 1. -1606. †**b.** = TRUMP *sb.*² 1 b. -1626.

1. *transf.* That my sad looke, Should grace the T. of great Bullingbrooke SHAKS. **2.** It was the t. of civilization over brute force 1853. A dress is a t. of ugliness (*mod.*). **4.** What newes from Oxford? Hold those Iusts & Triumphs? SHAKS.

Triumph (trəi·ŏmf), *v.* 1483. [- OFr. *triumpher* (mod. *triompher*) - L. *triumphare*, f. *triumphus*; see prec.] **1.** *intr.* To celebrate a Roman triumph 1530. **2.** To be victorious; to prevail; to gain the mastery 1508. †**b.** *trans.* To triumph over; to conquer -1667. **c.** To live in pomp or splendour -1568. **3.** *intr.* To be elated at another's defeat, discomfiture, etc.; 'to insult upon an advantage gained' (J.); hence, to rejoice, be elated or glad; to glory 1535. †**4.** *intr. Cards.* To trump (*rare*) -1626.

1. He triumphed for his victories over the great Mithridates GIBBON. **2.** He shall ascend With victory, triumphing through the aire Over his foes and thine MILT. **b.** We, that..were born Free, equal lords of the triumphed world, And knew no masters, but affections B. JONS. **3.** France, t. in thy glorious Prophetesse SHAKS. *fig.* The blood of twentie thousand men Did t. in my face SHAKS. Hence **Tri·umpher. Tri·umphing** *ppl. a.* that triumphs; **-ly** *adv.* (now *rare*).

Triumphal (trəi,ɒ·mfăl), *a.* (*sb.*) late ME. [- OFr. *triumphal* (mod. *triomphal*) or L. *triumphalis*, f. *triumphus*; see TRIUMPH *sb.*, -AL¹ 1.] **1.** Of, pertaining to, or of the nature of a triumph; celebrating or commemorating a triumph or victory. †**2.** Victorious, triumphant -1618.

1. A t. ode in honour of Hercules 1835. *T. arch*, an arch erected in commemoration of a victory. *T. chaplet, garland, wreath*, the laurel wreath worn by the victor at a Roman triumph.

B. *sb.* †**1.** An ode of triumph or victory; a pæan -1589. †**2.** A token of triumph. MILT.

Triumphant (trəi,ɒ·mfănt), *a.* 1494. [- OFr. *triumphant* (mod. *triomphant*) or L. *triumphans, -ant-*, pr. pple. of *triumphare*; see TRIUMPH *v.*, -ANT.] **1.** Celebrating a triumph or victory; of, pertaining to, of the nature of, or befitting a triumph. Now *rare*. 1531. **2.** That has achieved victory or success; conquering; victorious 1494. †**b.** *transf.* Of or gained by conquest. SHAKS. †**3.** Splendid; glorious; magnificent; noble; notable -1696. **4.** Exulting or rejoicing for or as for victory; triumphing; exultant 1594.

1. Like Captiues bound to a T. Carre SHAKS. **2.** There is no reconciling..Goodness with t. evil BROWNING. *Church T.*: see CHURCH 4. **3.** She's a most t. Lady, if report be square to her SHAKS. **4.** The t. cries of an immense multitude 1907. Hence **Triu·mphancy,** the state or quality of being t. **Triu·mphantly** *adv.*

Triumvir (trəi,ɒ·mvəɹ). *Pl.* **-virs** (vəɹz), or in L. form **-viri** (-virəi). 1579. [- L. *triumvir*, sing. deduced from pl. *triumviri*, back-formation from *trium virorum*, gen. pl. of *tres viri* three men.] *Rom. Hist.* One of three magistrates or public officers forming a committee charged with one of the departments of the administration; also, a member of the coalition of Pompey, Cæsar, and Crassus, B.C. 60 (first triumvirate), or of the administration of Cæsar, Antony, and Lepidus, B.C. 43 (second triumvirate). **b.** *transf.* and *fig. pl.* Three persons (or things) associated in power or authority 1619. So **Triu·mviral** *a.* of or pertaining to a t. or a triumvirate 1579.

Triumvirate (trəi,ɒ·mvirĕt). 1584. [- L. *triumviratus*, f. *triumvir*; see -ATE¹.] **1.** *Rom. Hist.* The position, office, or function of the triumviri, or of a triumvir; an association of three magistrates for joint administration 1601. **2.** By extension: Any association of three joint rulers or powers 1584. **3.** Less exactly, A group or set of three persons (*rarely* things); *esp.* three persons of authority or distinction in any sphere 1654.

3. This plaguy t.! A parson, a milliner, and a mantua-maker! RICHARDSON.

†**Triu·mviry.** 1588. [perh. for L. *triumviri*, pl. of TRIUMVIR.] = prec. -1656.

Triunal (trəi,yū·năl), *a. poet. rare.* 1711. [f. as next + -AL¹ 1.] = next.

Triune (trəi·yūn, *occas.* trəiyū·n), *a.* (*sb.*) 1605. [f. TRI- + L. *unus* one.] Three in one; constituting a trinity in unity. **a.** of the Godhead 1635. **b.** *gen.* 1705. **B.** *sb.* A being that is three in one; a group of three things united; a trinity in unity 1605.

Triunity (trəi,yū·nĭti). 1621. [f. prec. + -ITY, or f. TRI- + UNITY.] **1.** The state or attribute of being three in one 1653. **2.** A set or group of three constituting a unity; the Godhead conceived as three persons 1621.

Trivalent (trəi·vēⁱlĕnt, tri·v-), *a.* 1868. [f. TRI- + *-valent*, deduced from VALENCY 2.] *Chem.* Having the combining power of three atoms of hydrogen or other univalent element; combining with three atoms of a univalent element or radical. Hence **Triva·lence, Triva·lency.**

Trivet (tri·vėt). [Late ME. *trevet*, repr. OE. *trefet* (recorded once in doubtful application) - L. *tripes, triped-*, f. *tri-* TRI- + *pes* foot, after Gr. *τρίπους* TRIPOD.] A three-footed stand or support. Now *rare* exc. *spec.* A stand for a pot, kettle, or other vessel placed over a fire for cooking or heating something; orig. and properly standing on three feet; now often with projections by which it may be secured on the top bar of a grate. late ME.

Phr. *As right as a t.*, thoroughly or perfectly right (in ref. to a trivet's always standing firm on its three feet).

Trivial (tri·viăl), *a.* (*sb.*) late ME. [- L. *trivialis*, f. TRIVIUM; see -AL¹ 1.] **I. 1.** Belonging to the trivium of mediæval university studies. †**2.** Threefold, triple. late ME. only. **II. 1.** Such as may be met with anywhere; common, everyday, familiar, trite. Now *rare*. 1589. **2.** Of small account, paltry, poor; trifling, inconsiderable, unimportant 1593. **3.** *Nat. Hist.* Applied to names of animals and plants: **a.** to a Latin name added to the generic name to distinguish the species: = SPECIFIC A. 5. 1759. **b.** Popular, vernacular, vulgar 1815.

1. The t. round, the common task KEBLE. **2.** The offence..could..be passed by as altogether t. FREEMAN. **3. b.** The t. name for the whole family of terns..is 'sea-swallow' 1901.

B. *sb.* **1.** *pl.* The three subjects of study constituting the trivium. Now only *Hist.* 1481. **2.** A trivial matter; a triviality, a trifle. Usu. *pl.* 1715. Hence **Tri·vialism** (*rare*) t. character; a triviality. **Tri·vialize** *v. trans.* to make t. **Tri·vial-ly** *adv.*, **-ness** (now *rare*).

Triviality (triviæ·lĭti). 1598. [f. TRIVIAL + -ITY. Cf. Fr. *trivialité*.] **1.** The quality of being trivial; commonplace or trifling character. **2.** With *a* or (commonly) in *pl.*: Something trivial; a trivial matter, remark, etc.; a trifle 1611.

2. I..find little but repetitions and trivialities 1664.

‖**Trivium** (tri·viŏm). 1804. [- med.L. use of L. *trivium* place where three roads meet, f. *tri-* TRI- + *via* way.] **1.** In the Middle Ages, the lower division of the seven liberal arts, comprising grammar, rhetoric, and logic. **2.** *Zool.* The three anterior ambulacra of an echinoderm 1870.

-trix, *suffix*, ending of L. feminine agent-nouns (with stems in *-tric-*, acc. *-tricem*, whence Fr. *-trice*: see -TRICE), corresp. to masculines in *-tor*, as *venatrix* huntress, etc. Used chiefly in legal terms, as ADMINISTRATRIX, EXECUTRIX, TESTATRIX, etc. In Geometry, words in *-trix* denote straight lines (*linea* being understood), as BISECTRIX, etc;. more rarely curves or surfaces, as INDICATRIX, TRACTRIX. The commoner suffix in Eng. is -TRESS; see also -TRICE.

Troat (trōᵘt), *v.* 1611. [Cf. OFr. *trout*, also *trut*, an interjection for urging on hunting dogs, asses, or sheep.] *Venery. intr.* To cry or bellow: said of a buck at rutting time.

Trocar (trōᵘ·kaɹ). 1706. [- Fr. *trocart*, also *trois-quarts*, f. *trois* three + *carre* (:- L. *quadra*) face of an instrument; so called from its triangular form.] A surgical instrument consisting of a perforator or stylet enclosed in a metal tube or cannula, used for withdrawing fluid from a cavity, as in dropsy, etc.

Trochaic (trokēⁱ·ik), *a.* and *sb.* 1589. [- L. *trochaicus* - Gr. *τροχαϊκός*, f. *τροχαῖος*; see TROCHEE, -IC. Cf. Fr. *trochaïque*.] *Pros.* **A.** *adj.* **1.** Of a verse, rhythm, etc.: Consisting of, characterized by, or based on trochees. **2.** Of a foot, etc.: Of the nature of a trochee 1756.

2. *T. spondee*, a spondee having the accent or *ictus* upon the first syllable.

B. *sb.* A trochaic verse or foot 1693.

Trochal (trǫ·kăl, trōᵘ·kăl), *a.* 1841. [f. Gr. *τροχός* wheel + -AL¹ 1.] *Zool.* Resembling a wheel; rotiform.

Trochanter (trokæ·ntəɹ). 1615. [- Fr. *trochanter* (Paré) - Gr. *τροχαντήρ* (in sense 1), f. *τρέχειν* run.] *Anat.* and *Zool.* **1.** A protuberance or process in the upper part of the thigh-bone, serving for the attachment of certain muscles; usu., as in man, two in number, the *great t.* (*t. major*), and the *lesser t.* (*t. minor*). **2.** *Ent.* The second joint of an insect's leg, next to the coxa 1816. Hence **Trochanteric** (-te·rik) *a.* pertaining to a t.

Troche (trōᵘtʃ, trōᵘʃ, trōᵘk). 1597. [An altered f. TROCHISK; sometimes written *trochee* (trōᵘ·ki).] *Pharm.* = TROCHISK.

Trochee (trōᵘ·ki). 1589. [- L. *trochæus* (also used) - Gr. *τροχαῖος*, prop. adj. (*sc.* *πούς* foot) running, tripping, f. *τρόχος*, f. *τρέχειν* run. Cf. Fr. *trochée*.] *Pros.* A metrical foot consisting of a long followed by a short syllable; in accentual verse, of an accented followed by an unaccented syllable.

Trochilic (troki·lik), *a.* and *sb. rare.* 1570. [f. Gr. *τροχίλος*, taken in sense of *τροχός* wheel + -IC.] **A.** *adj.* Of or pertaining to rotary motion; relating to wheels 1605. **B.** *sb.* The science or art of rotary motion 1570. Also **trochilics.**

Trochilidine (troki·lidəin), *a.* 1861. [f. mod.L. *Trochilidæ* (f. TROCHILUS[1], -ID[3]) + -INE[1].] *Ornith.* Belonging to or characteristic of the family *Trochilidæ* or humming-birds.

‖**Trochilus**[1] (trǫ·kilŏs). 1579. [L. – Gr. τροχίλος, f. τρέχειν run.] *Ornith.* **1.** A small Egyptian bird (not certainly identified) said by the ancients to pick the teeth of the crocodile. **2.** A Linnæan genus of Amer. birds, orig. including all the then known humming-birds: now greatly restricted 1752.

‖**Tro·chilus**[2]. 1563. [L., app. the same word as prec.; cf. Gr. τροχιλία sheaf of a pulley.] *Arch.* A concave moulding: esp. in classical architecture.

†**Tro·chisk.** late ME. [– Fr. *trochisque* – late L. *trochiscus* – Gr. τροχίσκος small wheel or globe, pill, lozenge, dim. of τροχός wheel.] A medicated tablet or disc; a (round or ovate) pastille or lozenge –1748.

Trochite (trǫ·kəit, trōᵘ·kəit). Now *rare* or *Obs.* 1676. [– mod.L. *trochites*, f. Gr. τροχός wheel; see -ITE[1] 2 a.] *Palæont.* = ENTROCHITE. Hence **Trochitic** (troki·tik) *a.*

‖**Trochlea** (trǫ·kliă). 1693. [L.; cf. Gr. τροχιλία sheaf of a pulley.] *Anat.* A pulley-like structure or arrangement of parts, with a smooth surface upon which some other part, as a bone or tendon, slides; *spec.* (*a*) the surface of the inner condyle of the humerus at the elbow-joint, with which the ulna articulates; (*b*) the cartilaginous loop through which the superior oblique muscle of the eye passes.

Trochlear (trǫ·kliăɹ), *a.* 1681. [In XVII – mod.L. *trochlearis*; in later use f. TROCHLEA + -AR[1].] **1.** *Anat.* Belonging to or connected with a trochlea, as a muscle, nerve, etc.; forming a trochlea, as a surface of a bone, etc. **2.** *Bot.* Pulley-shaped, as the embryo of *Commelynaceæ* 1830.

1. *T. muscle*, the superior oblique muscle of the eye. *T. nerve*, each of the fourth pair of cranial nerves, the motor nerves for the t. muscles.

Trocho- (trǫko), bef. a vowel **troch-** (trǫk), comb. form repr. Gr. τροχός wheel, disc; as in **Tro·chosphere,** a larval form constituting a stage in the development of most molluscs and of certain worms, esp. marine annelids, characterized by a spheroidal body with a ring of cilia.

Trochoid (trǫ·koid, trōᵘ·koid), *sb.* and *a.* 1704. [– Gr. τροχοειδής round like a wheel, f. τροχός wheel + εἶδος; see -OID.] **A.** *sb.* **1.** *Geom.* A curve traced by a point on or connected with a rolling circle; *orig.* = CYCLOID 1; now usu. restricted to the *curtate* and *prolate cycloids* traced respectively by points within and without the circle; also extended to the HYPOTROCHOID and the EPITROCHOID 1704. **2.** *Zool.* A gasteropod of the family *Trochidæ*; a top-shell 1839. **B.** *adj.* **1.** *Geom.* = next 1 (*rare*) 1882. **2.** *Conch.* Top-shaped, conical with flat base, as the shells of the genus *Trochus* or family *Trochidæ*; *Zool.* belonging to the family *Trochidæ* 1859. **3.** *Anat.* Applied to a pivot-joint, in which one bone turns upon another with a rotary motion 1857.

Trochoidal (trokoi·dăl), *a.* 1799. [f. prec. + -AL[1] 1.] **1.** *Geom.* Having the form or nature of a trochoid; pertaining or relating to trochoids. **2.** *Conch.* = prec. B. 2 (*rare*) 1891. **3.** *Anat.* = prec. B. 3 (*rare*) 1882.

‖**Trochus** (trōᵘ·kŏs, trǫ·kŏs). *Pl.* **trochi** (-kei), also **trochuses.** 1706. [L. – Gr. τροχός wheel, f. τρέχειν run.] **1.** *Gr.* and *Rom. Antiq.* A wheel or hoop, used in athletic exercises or as a plaything. **2.** *Zool.* **a.** A genus of gasteropod molluscs, having a top-shaped or conical shell; the type of the family *Trochidæ* or top-shells 1753. **b.** The internal ring of cilia in the trochal organ of a rotifer 1888.

Trod (trǫd), *sb.* Now *dial.* [OE. *trod* = ON. *troð* treading, trampling, f. ON. *troða*, Goth. *trudan* tread, f. grade-var. of **treð*, TREAD *v.*] †**1.** Tread, footprint, track, trace –1563. **2.** A trodden way; a footpath, path, way. *dial.* 1570.

2. Thus in the middle t. I safely went 1642.

Trod (trǫd), *ppl. a.* 1632. Shortened from TRODDEN: chiefly as second element of combs.

Trod (trǫd), pa. t. and pple. of TREAD *v.*

Trodden (trǫ·d'n), *ppl. a.* 1545. [Late ME. *troden*, repl. OE. and ME. *treden*, pa. pple. of TREAD *v.*] That has been walked, stepped, or trampled upon.

Troglodyte (trǫ·g-, trōᵘ·glŏdəit), *sb.* (*a.*) 1555. [– L. *troglodyta* – Gr. τρωγλοδύτης, corrupt form (as if = cave-dwellers) of τρωγοδύτης (-ται, name of an Ethiopian people in Herodotus), after τρώγλη hole.] **1.** One of various races or tribes of men (chiefly ancient or prehistoric) inhabiting caves or dens (natural or artificial); a cave-dweller, cave-man. **2.** Applied to: †**a.** A bird of the genus *Troglodytes*; a wren (*rare*). **b.** An anthropoid ape of the genus *Troglodytes*, as a gorilla or chimpanzee. 1706. **3.** *fig.* A person who lives in seclusion; one unacquainted with the ways of the world; a 'hermit'. Also, a dweller in a hovel or slum. 1854. **4.** *attrib.* or *adj.* That is a t.; of or belonging to a t. or troglodytes 1704.

1. They were Troglodites, and had no dwelling but in the hollowes of the rocks 1642. **3.** A belief worthy only of troglodytes inaccessible to Imperial..thought 1905. Hence **Tro·glody:tal** *a.*

Troglodytic (trǫg-, trōᵘglodi·tik), *a.* 1585. [– L. *troglodyticus* – Gr. τρωγλοδυτικός; see prec., -IC.] **1.** Inhabited or frequented by troglodytes; pertaining to or characteristic of a troglodyte. **2.** Having the habits of a troglodyte; cave-dwelling 1676. **3.** Resembling a troglodyte; of a degraded type; also *fig.* not interested in or conversant with affairs 1871.

3. A respectable t. peer 1910. So **Troglody·tical** *a.*

Trogon (trōᵘ·gǫn). 1792. [mod.L., Gr. τρώγων, pr. pple. of τρώγειν gnaw.] *Ornith.* A bird of the genus *Trogon* or family *Trogonidæ*, widely distributed in tropical and subtropical regions, esp. in the New World, and characterized by soft plumage of varied and usu. brilliant colouring.

Troic (trōᵘ·ik), *a.* 1831. [– Gr. τρωικός, f. Τρώς, name of the mythical founder of Troy.] Pertaining or related to ancient Troy; Trojan.

‖**Troika** (troi·kă). 1842. [Russ., f. *troe* three.] A Russian vehicle drawn by three horses abreast.

Troilite (trōᵘ·iləit). 1868. [f. the name of Dominico *Troili*, who described a meteorite containing this mineral which fell in 1766; see -ITE[1] 2 b.] *Min.* A sulphide of iron found in meteorites.

Trojan (trōᵘ·dʒăn), *a.* and *sb.* ME. [repl. earlier *Troian* (XIV, Chaucer) *Troyan* (XV) – L. *Troianus*, f. *Troia* Troy; see -AN.] **A.** *adj.* Of or pertaining to ancient Troy or its inhabitants. late ME. **B.** *sb.* **1.** An inhabitant or native of Troy ME. **2.** *colloq.* **a.** A merry or roystering fellow; a boon companion; a person of dissolute life; also (in later use only), a good fellow (often with *true* or *trusty*) 1600. **b.** A brave or plucky fellow; a person of great energy or endurance: usu in phr. *like a T.* 1846.

2. a. He was a kinde good fellow, a true Troyan 1600. **b.** Working like a T. 1846.

Troll (trōᵘl), *sb.*[1] 1663. [f. TROLL *v.*] **1.** The act of trolling; a going or moving round; routine or repetition 1705. **2.** A song the parts of which are sung in succession; a round, a catch 1820. **3.** *Angling.* The method of trolling in fishing for pike, etc. 1681. **4.** = TROLLEY *sb.* 1. *local.* 1663.

2. It is sad..to miss..the joyous t. of his ballads 1856.

Troll (trōᵘl), *sb.*[2] 1616. [– ON., Swed. *troll* (Da. *trold*); of unkn. origin.] In Scandinavian mythology, One of a race of supernatural beings formerly conceived as giants, now, in Denmark and Sweden, as dwarfs or imps, supposed to inhabit caves or subterranean dwellings.

Troll (trōᵘl), *v. arch.* and *dial.* late ME. [Of doubtful identity in all senses; Fr. *trôler* (†*troller*) wander casually, and (M)HG. *trollen* stroll, toddle, have been compared.] **I.** †**1.** *intr.* To ramble, saunter, stroll –1691. **2.** *trans.* To move (a ball, bowl, etc.) by or as by rolling; to roll, bowl, trundle; to roll (the eyes); to throw (dice). late ME. **3.** *intr.* To roll; also, to turn round and round; to spin, whirl 1581.

2. Shee trowled her angry eyes on euery side 1628. **3.** To t. it in a Coach and Six SWIFT.

II. *intr.* To move nimbly, as the tongue in speaking; to wag. Also said of a person. *Obs.* or *arch.* 1616. †**b.** *trans.* To move (the tongue) volubly –1747.

b. To sing, to dance, To dress, and troule the Tongue, and roule the Eye MILT.

†**III. 1.** To cause to pass from one to another; esp. in phr. *to t. the bowl* –1600. **2.** *intr.* Of the vessel or its contents: To circulate, be passed round –1808. **3.** To come *in* abundantly; to 'roll' in –1689.

1. Trowl the bowl, the jolly nut-brown bowl DEKKER.

IV. 1. *trans.* To sing (something) in the manner of a round or catch; to sing in a full rolling voice; to chant merrily 1575. **b.** *intr.* To sing in this way; to carol, warble 1879. **2.** Of bells: To give forth a recurring cadence of full, mellow tones; of a song: to be uttered in a full, rolling, or jovial voice; *transf.* of a tune: to 'run in one's head' 1607. **3.** *trans.* To utter nimbly or rapidly; to recite in a full rolling voice. Also *intr.* of speech. 1625.

1. Will you troule the Catch You taught me but whileare? SHAKS. **2.** I have had..a Tune trouling in my Head DRYDEN.

V. *Angling. intr.* To angle with a running line; also (*trans.*) to fish (water) in this way. *spec.* **a.** to fish for pike by working a dead bait by a sink-and-draw motion; **b.** to angle with a spinning bait; **c.** *U.S.* and *Sc.* to trail a baited line behind a boat 1606.

The peasant..With patient angle trolls the finny deep GOLDSM. Hence **Tro·ller.**

Trolley, trolly (trǫ·li). Also **trawley.** 1823. [Of dial. origin; cf. local *troll*, †*trole* (XVII), presumably f. TROLL *v.*, and the similar *lorry, rolly, rully.*] **1.** Locally applied to a low cart of various kinds, e.g. a costermonger's cart. **2.** A low truck without sides or ends, esp. one with flanged wheels for running on a railway, etc. 1858. **3.** A grooved metallic pulley which travels along, and receives current from, an overhead electric wire, the current being then conveyed by a *t.-pole* or other conductor to a motor, usu. that of a car on a street railroad; also called *t.-wheel.* Also applied to any pulley running along an overhead track. 1891. **b.** *U.S.* Short for *t. car* 1891.

Comb.: **t.-car** (*U.S.*), an electric car driven by means of a t.; **-pole,** a hinged pole on an electric car, supporting the t. and conveying the current from the overhead wire; **-wire,** an overhead electric wire supplying current to the trolleys of electric cars.

†**Tro·ll-ma:dam.** 1572. [app. an alteration of Fr. *trou-madame* (f. *trou* hole) by association with TROLL *v.*] A game played by ladies, resembling bagatelle –1819.

Trollop (trǫ·ləp). 1615. [Of unkn. origin; for form and sense cf. TRULL.] An untidy or slovenly woman; a slattern, slut; also, occas., a trull.

Hence **Tro·llop** *v.*, to act in a slovenly way.

Trolly (trǫ·li). 1700. [Cf. Flem. *tralje*, *traalje* trellis, lattice, mesh.] A kind of lace having the pattern outlined with a thick thread.

Tro·mbash. 1867. [Native name.] A Sudanese boomerang.

Trombone (trǫmbōᵘ·n, trǫ·mbōᵘn). 1724. [– Fr. *trombone* (earlier †*trombon*) or its source It. *trombone*, augm. of *tromba* TRUMP *sb.*[1]; cf. -OON.] **1.** *Mus.* A large loud-toned brass instrument of the trumpet kind, consisting of a long tube bent twice upon itself, and ending in a bell mouth; the U-shaped bend nearer the mouthpiece is of double telescoping tubes, sliding upon one another, so that the length of the sounding tube may be adjusted to produce the desired note. (It is also made with valves and pistons instead of the slide.) **b.** One who plays this instrument 1848. ‖**2.** (trombo·ne), pl. **tromboni** (-nī). = BLUNDERBUSS 1. 1754. **Trombo·nist** = 1 b.

Tromometer (tromǫ·mĭtəɹ). 1878. [f. Gr. τρόμος trembling + -METER.] An instrument for measuring or detecting faint earth-tremors. Hence **Tromome·tric, -al** *adjs.* **Tromo·metry,** the scientific use of the t.

‖**Trompe** (trõnp). 1828. [Fr.] An apparatus for producing a blast, in which water falling in a pipe carries air into a receiver, where it is compressed, and thence led to the blast-pipe.

Tron (trǫn). *Hist.* Chiefly *Sc.* 1449. [– OFr. *trone* :– L. *trutina* – Gr. τρυτάνη balance. Cf. AL. *trona* (XIII), *tronus*, *-um* (XII).] A public weighing apparatus in a city or (burgh) town; also, the post of this used as a pillory; a market-place.

Trona (trōᵘ·nă). 1799. [– Swed., app. f. North Afr. Arab. *ṭrūna*, apocopate f. *naṭrūn* NATRON – Gr. νίτρον soda.] *Min.* Native hydrous sodium carbonate, found in N. Africa and America.

Tronage (trōᵘ·nėdʒ). ME. [– AFr. *tronage* (whence AL. *tronagium* 1200); see TRON, -AGE.] The weighing of merchandise at the tron or public weighing machine; a charge or toll upon goods so weighed; the right of levying such charge.

Trone, obs. f. THRONE.

‖**Tronk** (trǫŋk). 1693. [S. Afr. Du. – Pg. *tronco* trunk, stock (of a tree), the stocks, prison.] A prison.

Troolie (trū·li). 1769. [Tupi *tururi*.] The leaf of the bussu palm. Also *t. hut*.

Troop (trūp), *sb.* 1545. [(Early also *troupe*, *trowpe*) – Fr. *troupe*, back-formation from *troupeau* flock, herd, dim. of med.L. *troppus* (sc. *de jumentis*) herd of mares, prob. of Gmc. origin.] **1. a.** A body of soldiers. **b.** A number of persons (or things) collected together; a party, company, band 1584. **c.** Of animals: A herd, flock, swarm 1587. **d.** Used to indicate a great number; a 'lot'; esp. in *pl.* 'flocks', 'swarms' 1590. †**e.** = TROUPE –1835. **2.** *pl.* Armed forces collectively 1598. **3.** *Mil. spec.* A subdivision of a cavalry regiment commanded by a captain, corresp. to a *company* of foot and a *battery* of artillery 1590. **b.** The command of a troop 1813. **c.** A company of boy scouts 1908. **4.** *Mil.* A signal on the drum for troops to assemble in readiness to march; the assembly 1672.

1. a. Amid the thickest troupes of his enemies in the battaile of Agincourt HOLLAND. **b.** At a little Distance..a T. of Gipsies ADDISON. **d.** Honor, Loue, Obedience, Troopes of Friends SHAKS. **2.** The courage displayed by our troops COBDEN.

attrib. and *Comb.*: **t.-bird** (*U.S.*), a troopial; **-boot** (*U.S.*), a cavalry boot; **-fowl** (*U.S.*), a scaup-duck; **-horse**, a cavalry horse.

Troop (trūp), *v.* 1565. [f. prec.] **1.** *intr.* To gather in a company; to come together; to flock, assemble. **2.** †**a.** *trans.* To assemble (individuals) into a troop or company –1620. **b.** *intr.* To associate *with* 1592. **3.** To walk, go, pass; *colloq.* (with *off*, *away*, etc.) to go away, 'be off', 'pack' 1590. **4.** To march in rank; to walk or pass in order. Now *colloq.* 1592. **5.** To come or go in great numbers; to flock (*in*, *out*) 1610. **6.** *trans.* (*Mil.*, from prec. 4) *To t. the colour* (or *colours*): to perform that portion of the ceremonial known as mounting guard in which the colour is received 1803. **7.** To transport (troops) 1882.

1. As Armies at the call Of Trumpet..T. to thir Standard MILT. **2. b.** So shewes a Snowy Doue trooping with Crowes SHAKS. **4.** Yᵉ verger troops before yᵉ Deane 1682. **5.** The flocking shadows pale T. to th' infernall jail MILT.

Trooper (trū·pəɹ). 1640. [f. TROOP *sb.* + -ER¹.] **1.** A soldier in a troop of cavalry. **2.** A horse ridden by a trooper; a troop-horse 1640. **3.** In Australia: A mounted policeman 1858. **4.** A troop-ship 1872.

1. Phr. *To lie, swear, like a t.*

Troopial, troupial (trū·piăl). 1825. [– Fr. *troupiale* (Brisson, 1760), f. *troupe* troop, from its living in flocks.] Any of various species of birds of the Amer. family *Icteridæ*; *esp.* the icteric oriole.

Troostite (trū·stəit). 1835. [f. name of Prof. G. *Troost* of Nashville, Tennessee; see -ITE¹ 2 b.] **1.** *Min.* A variety of WILLEMITE, with admixture of iron and manganese, occurring in reddish hexagonal crystals. **2.** *Metall.* A transitional constituent of steel 1902.

Tropæolin (tropī·ŏlin). 1880. [f. next + -IN¹; from the resemblance of the colour to that of the flowers of some species of *Tropæolum*.] Any of several orange dyes, of complex composition, belonging to the class of sulphonic acids.

‖**Tropæolum** (tropī·ŏlŏm). *Pl.* **-a, -ums.** 1785. [mod.L. (Linn., 1737), f. L. *tropæum* TROPHY; so called from the resemblance of the leaf to a shield and of the flower to a helmet.] *Bot.* A S. Amer. genus of herbs (family *Tropæolaceæ* or *Geraniaceæ*), mostly of trailing or climbing habit, with irregular spurred flowers, usu. deep orange or yellow.

Trope (trōᵘp). 1533. [– L. *tropus* figure of speech – Gr. τρόπος turn, rel. to τρέπειν turn.] **1.** *Rhet.* A figure of speech which consists in the use of a word or phrase in a sense other than that which is proper to it; also, in casual use, a figure of speech; figurative language. †**2.** In Gregorian Music, a short distinctive cadence at the close of a melody –1626. **3.** In the Western Church, a phrase, sentence, or verse introduced as an embellishment into part of the text of the mass or of the breviary office that is sung by the choir 1846. **4.** *Geom.* The reciprocal of a node on a curve or surface 1869.

1. [American] rhetoric is Rhodian rather than Attic, overloaded with tropes and figures BRYCE. Hence **Tro·pal** *a.* (*Geom.*) pertaining to or constituting a t.

‖**Trophi** (trōᵘ·fəi), *sb. pl.* 1826. [mod.L., pl. of *trophus* – Gr. τροφός feeder, f. τρέφειν nourish.] *Zool.* A collective name for the mouth-parts in insects, as organs for seizing and preparing the food. Also applied to the parts of the pharynx in rotifers, having a similar function.

Trophic (trǫ·fik), *a.* 1873. [– Gr. τροφικός, f. τροφή nourishment; see -IC.] *Biol.* Of or pertaining to nutrition; *spec.* of certain nerves and nerve-centres, Concerned with or regulating the nutrition of the tissues. So **Tro·phical** *a.* 1857, **-ly** *adv.*

Trophied (trōᵘ·fid), *a.* 1622. [f. TROPHY *sb.* or *v.* + -ED.] Adorned with a trophy or trophies.

Thro' t. tombs of heroes and of kings 1798.

Tropho- (trǫ·fo), comb. form repr. Gr. τροφή nourishment, f. τρέφειν nourish; as in **Tro·phoblast,** a layer of cells external to the embryo, and supplying it with nourishment; also applied to the morbid growth in cancer. ‖**Tro:phoneuro·sis,** any functional disorder due to derangement of the trophic action of the nerves. **Tro·phosome** [Gr. σῶμα body], the aggregate of nutritive zooids of a hydrozoan (dist. from *gonosome*).

Trophonian (trofōᵘ·niăn), *a.* 1792. [f. L. *Trophonius*, Gr. Τροφώνιος, proper name + -AN.] Pertaining to Trophonius, the mythical builder of the original temple of Apollo at Delphi, who after his death was worshipped as a god, and had an oracle in a cave in Bœotia, which was said to affect those who entered it with such awe that they never smiled again: hence *allus.*

Trophy (trōᵘ·fi), *sb.* 1513. [– Fr. *trophée* – L. *trophæum*, earlier *tropæum* – Gr. τρόπαιον, subst. use of n. of τροπαῖος, f. τροπή turning, putting to flight, defeat.] **1.** *Gr.* and *Rom. Antiq.* A structure erected (orig. on the field of battle, later in any public place) as a memorial of a victory in war, consisting of arms or other spoils taken from the enemy, hung upon a tree, pillar, etc. and dedicated to some divinity. Hence applied to similar monuments or memorials in later times. 1550. **b.** *transf.* A painted or carved figure of such a memorial; by extension, an ornamental or symbolic group of any objects, or a representation of such a group in decorative art 1634. **2. a.** *transf.* Anything taken in war, or in hunting, etc.; a spoil or prize, esp. if kept or displayed as a memorial 1513. **b.** *fig.* Anything serving as a token or evidence of victory, valour, skill, power, etc.; a monument, memorial 1569.

1. Around the posts hung helmets, darts, and spears, And captive chariots, axes, shields, and bars, And broken beaks of ships, the trophies of their wars DRYDEN. **2. a.** A defeat and a wound were the only trophies of his expedition GIBBON. **b.** The triumphs and trophies of intellect 1871.

Comb.: **t.-money, -tax** *Hist.*, a tax formerly levied on householders in each county, for incidental expenses connected with the militia. Hence **Tro·phy** *v. trans.* (chiefly *pass.*) †to transform into a t. (*rare*); to bestow a t. upon; to adorn with a t. or trophies.

Tropic (trǫ·pik), *sb.* and *a.*¹ late ME. [– L. *tropicus* – Gr. τροπικός pertaining to the 'turning' of the sun at the solstice, tropical, f. τροπή turning.] **A.** *sb.* **1.** *Astr.* †**a.** Each of the two solstitial points, the most northerly and southerly points of the ecliptic, at which the sun reaches its greatest distance north or south of the equator, and 'turns' or begins to move towards it again; also (*loosely*), each of the two signs (Cancer and Capricorn) at the beginning of which these points occur –1662. **b.** Each of two circles of the celestial sphere (*t. of* CANCER and *t. of* CAPRICORN), parallel to the equinoctial or celestial equator, and distant about 23° 28′ north and south of it, touching the ecliptic at the solstitial points 1503. **c.** *fig.* Turning-point; limit, boundary 1639. **2.** *Geog.* Each of two parallels of latitude on the earth's surface (corresp. to the celestial circles, 1 b, and called likewise *t. of Cancer* and *t. of Capricorn*), distant about 23° 28′ north and south of the equator, being the boundaries of the torrid zone 1527. **b.** *pl.* With *the*: The region between (and about) these parallels; the torrid zone and parts immediately adjacent 1837.

2. b. The tropics are one vast garden EMERSON.

B. *adj.* **1.** *Astr.* = TROPICAL *a.* 1. Now *rare* or *Obs.* 1551. **2.** *Geog.* = TROPICAL *a.* 2. 1799. **3. T. bird,** any bird of the family *Phaethontidæ*, comprising sea-birds resembling terns, widely found in tropical regions, and characterized by webbed feet, rapid flight, and varied coloration. **b.** *T. grape*, the gulf-weed 1850.

2. The rapid t. vegetation has reclaimed its old domains KINGSLEY.

Tro·pic, *a.*² 1881. [Arbitrarily f. ATROPIC; cf. TROPINE.] *Chem.* In *t. acid*, an acid forming a constituent of atropine.

Tropical (trǫ·pikăl), *a.* 1527. [f. as TROPIC *a.*¹; see -ICAL.] **1.** *Astr.* Pertaining or relating to the tropics, or either tropic (in sense A. 1 a or b). **2.** *Geog.* Pertaining to, occurring in, or inhabiting the tropics; belonging to the torrid zone 1698. **b.** *Path.* Applied to diseases to which one is liable in tropical regions 1828. **c.** *fig.* Very hot, ardent, or luxuriant 1834. **3.** Pertaining to, involving, or of the nature of a trope or tropes; metaphorical, figurative 1567.

1. *T. year*, the interval between two successive passages of the sun through the same 'tropic' or solstitial point (or, equivalently, through the same equinoctial point); the natural year of the seasons as reckoned from one solstice or equinox to the next. So *t. month*, the time taken by the moon in passing from either tropic (or either equinoctial point) to the same again. **2.** T. fruits 1700. The face of the desert..is scorched by the direct and intense rays of a t. sun GIBBON. **b.** T. Liver 1893. **c.** Home he came..in a hissing hot fit of t. rage 1834. **3.** A strict and literall acception of a loose and tropicall expression SIR T. BROWNE.

Tropically (trǫ·pikăli), *adv.* 1564. [f. prec. + -LY².] **1.** Metaphorically. **2.** With tropical heat, luxuriance, or violence 1852.

1. The Mouse-Trap: Marry how? T. *Ham.* III. ii. 247. **2.** The rain..continues, although not quite so t. 1886.

Tropicopolitan (trǫ:pikoˌpǫ·lităn), *a.* 1878. [f. TROPIC, after COSMOPOLITAN.] *Nat. Hist.* Belonging to or inhabiting the whole of the tropics, or tropical regions generally.

Tropidine (trǫ·pidīn, -əin). 1883. [Arbitrarily f. TROPINE.] *Chem.* A colourless oily alkaloid obtained from tropine by the action of acids. So **Tropi·lidine,** a liquid hydrocarbon, C_7H_8, obtained by the dry distillation of tropine with quicklime.

Tropine (trōᵘ·pīn, -əin). 1881. [Arbitrarily f. ATROPINE.] *Chem.* An alkaloid forming a constituent of atropine.

Tropism (trǫ·piz'm). 1899. [The second element of HELIOTROPISM, etc., used as an inclusive or generic term.] *Biol.* The turning of an organism, or part of one, in a particular direction in response to some special external stimulus.

Tropo-, comb. form repr. Gr. τρόπος turning, etc. (see TROPE); as in **Tropometer** (tropǫ·mĭtəɹ) [-METER], an instrument for measuring the angle of turning or torsion of some part of the body, as the eye-ball or a long bone.

Tropologic (trǫpǫlǫ·dʒik), *a.* late ME. [– late L. *tropologicus* = late Gr. τροπολογικός, f. τρόπος TROPE; see -IC.] = next.

Tropological (trǫpǫlǫ·dʒikăl), *a.* 1528. [f. as prec. + -AL¹ 1; see -ICAL.] Belonging to or involving tropology. **1.** Metaphorical, figurative 1555. **2.** Applied to a secondary sense or interpretation of Scripture, relating or applied to conduct or morals 1528. Hence **Tropolo·gically** *adv.*

Tropology (trǫpǫ·lŏdʒi). 1519. [– late L. *tropologia* – late Gr. τροπολογία, f. τρόπος TROPE; see -LOGY. Cf. (O)Fr. *tropologie.*] **1.** 'A speaking by tropes'; the use of metaphor in speech or writing. **2.** A moral discourse; a secondary sense or interpretation of Scripture relating to morals 1583. **3.** A treatise on tropes or figures of speech 1667.

Tropopause (trǫ·pǭpǭz). 1919. [f. as next + PAUSE *sb.*] The (imaginary) boundary between the troposphere and the stratosphere.

Troposphere (trǫ·pŏsfīᵊɹ). 1914. [f. TROPO- + SPHERE *sb.*] The lower stratum of the atmosphere, lying below the stratosphere, to which convective disturbances are confined.

Trot (trǫt), *sb.*¹ ME. [– (O)Fr. *trot*, f. *troter* (mod. *trotter*); see TROT *v.*¹] **I. 1.** A gait of a quadruped, orig. of a horse, between walking and running, in which the legs move in diagonal pairs almost together; hence applied to a similar gait of a man (or other biped) between a walk and a run. **b.** The sound of a horse, etc. trotting 1858. **2.** A trotting-race (*rare*) 1891. **3.** A toddling child; also, a small or young animal. *colloq.* 1854. **4.** *U.S. slang.* = CRIB *sb.* 17. 1891.

II. *Fishing.* (perh. a different word.) A long-line lightly anchored or buoyed, with baited hooks hung by short lines a few feet apart; a trawl-line; also, each of the short lines attached to this 1858. Hence **Trot** *v.*² 1864.

Trot (trǫt), *sb.*² [ME. *trat(t)e*, early mod. *trot* (XVI), obscurely rel. to AFr. *trote* (the second element in BAWDSTROT); of unkn. origin.] An old woman; usu. disparaging: an old beldame, a hag.

Trot (trǫt), *v.*¹ late ME. [– OFr. *troter* (mod. *trotter*) :– Rom., med.L. *trottare*, of Gmc. origin.] **1.** *intr.* Of a horse, etc.: To go at the gait called the trot. Also said of a person. **b.** *transf.* Of a rider, etc., or of a vehicle. late ME. **2.** To go or move quickly; to bustle; to run. Now *colloq.*, implying short, quick motion in a limited area. late ME. †**3.** *trans.* **a.** To trot upon (something). *rare.* **b.** To go through at a trot. **c.** To traverse (a path) as if by trotting (*rare*). –1638. **4.** To cause to trot; to lead or ride at the trot 1592. **b.** To conduct or escort (a person) *to* or *round* a place 1888. **c.** To jog a child on one's knee; to 'give a ride to' 1853.

1. b. I will t. to morrow a mile SHAKS. *transf.* We college poets t...on very easy nags THACKERAY. **2.** Wante makes the olde wyfe t. 1581. **3. a.** My horse..boundes from the Earth..he trots the ayre SHAKS. **4.** To trott the horses up and downe 1628. Phr. *To t. out*, to lead out and show off the paces of (a horse); hence *fig.* to bring forward (a person, an opinion, etc.) for or as for inspection or approval; to exhibit, show off (*colloq.*).

Troth (trōᵘþ, trǫþ), *sb. arch.* [Later form (XV) of ME. *trouth(e, trowth(e*, var. with stress-shifting and assim. to *trow* of *trēowþ* TRUTH.] **I. 1.** Faithfulness, good faith, honesty, loyalty. **2.** One's plighted word; the act of pledging one's faith, a promise, covenant. Chiefly in phr. *to plight one's troth*, to pledge one's faith; *spec.* to engage oneself to marry. ME.

1. I shall sweare that I will..true faith and t. beare to our soveraigne lord the king 1620. **2.** And therto I plight thee my trouth *Bk. Com. Prayer, Matrimony. By* (rarely *upon*) *my t.*, a form of asseveration.

II. Truth, in various senses –1663. **b.** *In t.* (arch.), †*of (a) t.*: truly, verily, indeed. late ME. **c.** Also *ellipt.* or as *int.* arch. 1603. Hence **Tro·thless** *a.* perfidious, disloyal.

Troth, *v. Obs.* or *arch.* late ME. [f. prec., or aphetic f. BETROTH *v.*] *trans.* To plight one's troth to; to engage in a contract, esp. of marriage.

Troth-plight (trōᵘ·þ,plait), *sb. arch.* 1513. [f. TROTH *sb.* + PLIGHT *sb.*¹] The act of plighting troth, or troth plighted; a solemn engagement, esp. of marriage; betrothal.

Tro·th-plight, *pa. pple.* and *ppl. a. arch.* ME. [f. as prec. + *plight*, pa. pple. of PLIGHT *v.*¹] Engaged by a 'troth' or covenant, esp. of marriage; betrothed.

Tro·th-plight, *v. arch.* 1440. [f. as prec. + PLIGHT *v.*¹] *trans.* = TROTH *v.*

Trotter (trǫ·təɹ). late ME. [f. TROT *v.* + -ER¹.] **1.** A horse, etc. which trots; *spec.* a horse especially bred and trained to the trot. **2.** One who moves or goes about briskly and constantly 1562. **3.** Usu. *pl.* The feet of a quadruped, esp. those of sheep and pigs as used for food; also *joc.*, the feet of a human being 1522.

‖**Trottoir** (trotwār). 1804. [Fr. (XVI), f. *trotter* TROT *v.*¹] A paved footway on each side of a street; a pavement.

Trotyl (trōᵘ·til). 1918. [f. *trot* of *trinitrotoluol* + -YL.] Trinitrotoluol.

Troubadour (trū·bădūᵊɹ, -dōᵊɹ). 1727. [– Fr. *troubadour* – Pr. *trobador* (= OFr. *troveor*; see TROUVÈRE), f. *trobar*, OFr. *trover*; see TROUVÈRE.] One of a class of lyric poets, living in southern France, eastern Spain, and northern Italy, from the 11th to the 13th cc., who sang in Provençal (*langue d'oc*), chiefly of chivalry and gallantry, sometimes including wandering minstrels and jongleurs. **b.** *transf.* One who composes or sings verses or ballads 1826.

Trouble (trɒ·b'l), *sb.* ME. [– OFr. *truble, turble* (mod. *trouble*), f. *tourbler*, etc.; see TROUBLE *v.*] **1.** Disturbance of mind or feelings; worry, vexation; affliction; grief; perplexity; distress. Now often also in lighter use. **b.** With *a* and *pl.*: An instance of this; a misfortune, calamity; a distressing circumstance, occurrence, or experience 1515. **c.** *transf.* A thing or person that gives trouble; a cause or occasion of affliction or distress 1591. **2.** Public disturbance, disorder, or confusion; with *a* and *pl.*, an instance of this. late ME. **3.** Pains or exertion; care, toil, labour. Phr. *To put to, to take (the) t.* 1577. **4. a.** A disease, ailment; a morbid affection 1726. **b.** A woman's travail. (Also of an animal.) *dial.* or *euphem.* 1825. **5.** *euphem., colloq.*, etc. **a.** Unpleasant relations with the authorities, esp. such as involve arrest, imprisonment, or punishment 1560. **b.** Said of the condition of an unmarried woman with child 1891. **6.** *Mining.* A dislocation in a stratum; a fault (usu. small) 1672. **b.** Faulty working of apparatus or machinery 1889.

1. In the tyme of my t. I call vpon the COVERDALE *Ps.* 85[6]:7. To prevent t. in case of a breakdown on the mains 1910. **b.** To take Armes against a Sea of troubles SHAKS. **2.** It maketh troble and rebellion in the realme LATIMER.

Trouble (trɒ·b'l), *v.* ME. [– OFr. *trubler, turbler* (mod. *troubler*) :– Rom. **turbulare*, f. **turbulus* (whence (O)Fr. *trouble* disturbed, turbid), for L. *turbidus* TURBID.] **I. 1.** *trans.* To disturb, agitate, ruffle (water, air, etc.); to make turbid, dim, or cloudy. Now *rare* or *arch.* **2.** To disturb, derange; to interrupt; to hinder, mar. *Obs.* or *arch.* ME.

1. Like a fountaine troubled, Muddie, ill seeming, thicke SHAKS. **2.** T. not the peace SHAKS.

II. 1. To put into a state of (mental) agitation or disquiet; to disturb, distress, perplex ME. **2.** To injure; to molest, oppress. late ME. **b.** Of disease or ailment: To afflict; sometimes in weakened sense, to affect. late ME. **3.** To vex, annoy; to tease, plague, worry, pester, bother 1538. **b.** In lighter sense: To put to inconvenience, incommode; 'to give occasion of labour to: a word of civility or slight regard' (J.) 1516. **c.** With *for*: To pester with requests, importune; hence, in a formula of polite request: to give (a person) the trouble of passing or handing something 1516. **d.** *refl.* To take the trouble, exert oneself (*to do* something) 1500. **e.** *intr.* for *refl.* = d. (*colloq.*) 1880.

1. Now my soule is troublid WYCLIF *John* 12:27. **2. b.** Being troubled with a raging tooth, I could not sleepe SHAKS. **3.** Take the Boy to you: he so troubles me, 'Tis past enduring SHAKS. **b.** Let me t. you with one more question JOWETT. **c.** The new pupil who 'troubled' Mr. Pecksniff for the loaf DICKENS. **d.** He had never troubled himself..to understand the question 1845. **e.** Do not t. to bring back the boat 1884. **Trou·bler,** one who or that which troubles; a disturber; an oppressor.

Troublesome (trɒ·b'lsŏm), *a.* 1548. [f. TROUBLE *sb.* + -SOME¹.] Full of, characterized by, or causing trouble.

Thys t. world *Bk. Com. Prayer.* He rather be vnmannerly, then t. SHAKS. The process is t. and dangerous 1836. Hence **Trou·blesome-ly** *adv.*, **-ness.**

Troublous (trɒ·bləs), *a.* Now only *literary* or *arch.* 1449. [– OFr. *troubleus*, f. *troble*, etc.; see TROUBLE *sb.*, -OUS.] **1.** Characterized by trouble, agitation, or disturbance; disordered, unsettled, confused. **b.** Causing disturbance; turbulent; restless, unquiet 1450. **2.** Causing trouble or grief; grievous; vexatious, troublesome 1463.

1. There are long t. periods, before matters come to a settlement CARLYLE. **b.** A sedicious fellow, and a t. preacher LATIMER. Hence **Trou·blously** *adv.*, **-ness.**

‖**Trou-de-loup** (trudlu). 1789. [Fr., lit. 'wolf-hole, wolf-pit'.] *Mil.* In field fortification, a conical pit with a pointed stake fixed vertically in the centre, rows of which are dug before a work to hinder an enemy's approach. Usu. *pl.* **trous-le-loup** (trudlu).

Trough (trǭf, trɒf), *sb.* [OE. *trog* = OFris., OS. *trog*, OHG. *troc* (Du., G. *trog*), ON. *trog* :– Gmc. **truʒaz* :– IE. **drukós*, f. **dru-* wood, TREE.] **1.** A narrow open box-like vessel, made of wood, stone, metal, or earthenware, to contain liquid; *esp.* a drinking-vessel for domestic animals; also, a tank or vat used for washing, kneading, brewing, and various other purposes. (Often with prefix, as *drinking-, hog-, horse-, kneading-t.*) **b.** A small vessel of similar shape used in chemistry, photography, etc. 1819. **2.** *spec.* **a.** An oblong vessel containing the water in which a grindstone runs 1725. **b.** An oblong box with divisions serving as the cells of a voltaic battery; also short for *t.-battery* 1806. **c.** *Mining.* An oblong tank in which ores are washed; a rocker or buddle 1877. **d.** *Typog.* A metal-lined box in which stones, etc. are washed 1891. †**3.** A small primitive boat –1633. **4.** A channel, pipe, or trunk for conveying water; a conduit; a gutter fixed under the eaves of a building. late ME. **5.** A hollow or valley resembling a trough; *spec.* in *Geol.* a basin-shaped depression (longer than broad) 1513. **b.** *Meteorol.* A line or elongated region of lower barometric pressure between two regions of higher pressure 1882.

5. The whole valley, or strath, or t. of the Clyde 1819. *T. of the sea*, the hollow on the surface between two waves.

attrib. and *Comb.*: **t. girder**, an iron girder shaped like a t.; **t. gutter**, a box-like channel for drainage; a rain-water pipe of this form; **t. shell**, a mollusc of the family *Mactridæ*. Hence **Trough** *v. trans.* (*a*) *Geol.* to form into a t. or into the shape of a t. (*b*) To treat in some way in a t.; to stain or mould in a t.

Trounce (trauns), *v.* 1551. [Of unkn. origin; connection with OFr. *troncer, troncher* cut, cut off a piece from, retrench, cannot be made out.] †**1.** *trans.* To trouble, afflict, distress; to discomfit, harass –1655. **2.** To beat, thrash, belabour, cudgel; to flog 1568. **3.** To punish; also, to get the better of, defeat 1657. **b.** To indict, to sue at law. Now *dial.* 1638. **4.** To censure; to scold severely 1607.

2. Flattered with the hopes of seeing a bailiff trounced SMOLLETT. Hence **Trou·ncer,** one who trounces; *spec.* an odd man (see ODD A. II. 4 d).

‖**Troupe** (trūp). 1825. [Fr., = TROOP.] A company of dancers, players, or the like. Hence **Troupe** *v.* **Trou·per.**

Trouse (trūz, trauz). Now *Hist.* and *arch.* 1578. [– Ir. (and Sc. Gael.) *triubhas*, orig. pronounced *trīvās* or *trīwās*, in mod. Ir. pronunc. *trius* (see TREWS). Ult. etym. obsc.] **1.** A close-fitting article of attire for the buttocks and thighs (divided below), to the lower extremities of which stockings were attached; *spec.* = TREWS. In later use, drawers or knee-breeches. †**2.** *pl.* = TROUSERS 2. –1820.

Trousers (trau·zəɹz), *sb. pl.* 1599. [Extension, after *drawers*, of prec.] †**1.** = prec. 1. –1834. **2.** A loose-fitting garment of cloth worn by men, covering the loins and legs to the ankles. (Also *a pair of t.*) 1681. **b.** The loose bag-like drawers or pantaloons worn by both sexes in Moslem countries 1775. **c.** Pantalettes 1821. **3.** In *sing.* form **trouser,** in various senses 1609. **b.** A single leg of a pair of trousers 1893.

Comb. (with *trouser-*): **trouser-press,** a contrivance for pressing the legs of t. so as to produce a crease; **trouser-stretcher,** a device for stretching t. so as to take out any 'bagginess'. Hence **Trou·ser** *v. slang, trans.* to put (money etc.) into the trouser-pocket, to pocket.

‖**Trousseau** (truso). ME. [Fr., dim. f. *trousse* TRUSS *sb.*] **1.** †**a.** A bundle. **b.** A bunch of keys. *rare.* (perh. only as Fr.) 1847. **2.** A bride's outfit of clothes, house-linen, etc. Also *attrib.* 1833.

Trout (traut). [Late OE. *truht* = late L. *tructa.*] **1.** A well-known freshwater fish of the genus *Salmo*, esp. *S. fario*, the common trout; it has numerous spots of red and black on its sides and head, and is greatly valued as a sporting fish and on account of its edible quality. **b.** *collect. sing.* 1602. **2.** Used as a name of various fish (chiefly *Salmonidæ*) resembling the trout in appearance or habits. Now *local.* 1604. **3.** With defining prefix, as the name of various species of the genus *Salmo* (or of the allied genus *Salvelinus*), and occas. of other genera 1661.

3. Bastard t. (*U.S.*), the squeteague, *Cynoscion nothus*; **brook t.,** *Salmo fario*; in *U.S.*, *S. fontinalis*, or *S. irideus*, the rainbow t.; **brown t.,** *S. fario*; **grey t.,** *Salmo trutta*; in *U.S.* the squeteague; **lake t.,** *S. ferox* (the great lake t.); in U.S. *S. confinis* (the N. Amer. lake t.), inhabiting the deepest waters of the Great Lakes; **rainbow t.,** *S. irideus*, a Californian species, now introduced in British t.-streams; **red-bellied t.,** the char, *S. salvelinus*; also *S.* or *Fario erythrogaster*, of the lakes of New York State and Pennsylvania; **rock t.,** *Chirus constellatus.*

attrib. and *Comb.*, as *t.-brook, -fishing, -preserve, -stream*; **t.-fly,** (*a*) the may-fly; (*b*) an artificial fly for t.-fishing; **-perch,** the black bass (*local U.S.*); also, a trout-like fish (*Percopsis guttatus*) of the rivers and Great Lakes of U.S., having the mouth and scales like those of a perch. Hence **Trou·ting,** t.-fishing. **Trou·tlet, Trou·tling,** a little or tiny t. **Trou·ty** *a.* full of, abounding in, or containing t.

‖**Trouvaille** (truvaⁱy). 1842. [Fr., f. *trouver* find.] A lucky find; a windfall.

‖**Trouvère** (truvęr), **trouveur** (truvör). 1795. [OFr. *trovere* (mod. *trouvère, trouveur*), obl. *troveor* (see TROUBADOUR), f. *trover* (mod. *trouver* find) compose, (later) invent, find, of much disputed origin.] One of a school of poets who flourished in Northern France from the 11th to the 14th c., whose works are chiefly epic in character. Cf. TROUBADOUR.

Trove: see TREASURE-TROVE. Also short for *treasure-trove*, in sense 'a valuable find' 1888.

Trover (trōᵘ·vəɹ). 1594. [– AFr. subst. use of OFr. *trover* (mod. *trouver* find); see TROUVÈRE, -ER⁴.] *Law.* The act of finding and assuming possession of any personal property; hence (in full, *action of t.*), an action at law to recover the value of personal property illegally converted by another to his own use.

Trow (trōᵘ, *locally* trōu, trau), *sb. local.* ME. [dial. var. of TROUGH 3.] A name for various kinds of boats or barges; *spec.* **a.** in the south of Scotland and north of England, a double canoe or boat used in spearing salmon by torchlight (also *pl.* const. as *sing.*); now *rare* or *Obs.*; **b.** on the south coast of England, a small flat-bottomed boat used in herring-fishing.

Trow (trōᵘ, trau), *v. arch.* [Of mixed origin; (1) OE. *trēowian, trēowan*, f. *trēow* TRUCE, with secondary stressing of the diphthong; (2) OE. *trūwian*; cf. TRUCE, TRUE, TRUST.] †**1.** *trans.* (orig. *intr.* with *dat.*). To trust, have confidence in, believe (a person or thing) –1829. **2.** *intr.* To believe *in* or *on*; to have confidence *in*; to trust *to*. *Obs.* or *rare arch.* OE. **3.** *trans.* To believe (a statement, etc.); to accept as true or trustworthy ME. **4.** with *obj. cl.* To believe, think, be of opinion, suppose, imagine; sometimes, to feel sure, be assured OE. **b.** Parenthetically or at the end of a sentence (often merely expletive), as *I t.* (in assertions) = 'I suppose, I ween'; †also rarely in questions (where the sense is not clear) ME. †**c.** Also simply *t.* (ellipt. for *I t.* or *t. you*) –1741.

3. Speake lesse then thou knowest,..Learne more then thou trowest SHAKS. **4.** Can anything be more clearly proved..? I t. not. 1872. **b.** Who's there, I troa? SHAKS. **c.** And haue you euer seene her, t.? 1620.

Trowel (trau·ĕl), *sb.* [ME. *truel, trowel* – OFr. *truele* (mod. *truelle*) – med.L. *truella*, alt. of L. *trulla* ladle, scoop, f. *trua* skimmer, spoon.] A flat-bladed tool of metal or wood, with a short handle; used by masons, bricklayers, and others, for spreading, moulding, or smoothing mortar, cement, and the like. **b.** A culinary ladle or slice of this shape 1773. **c.** A tool of this kind used in gardening, having a hollow, scoop-like, semi-cylindrical blade 1796.

To lay it on with a t., to express a thing coarsely or bluntly; now *spec.* to flatter excessively or grossly.

Comb.: **t.-bayonet,** a bayonet resembling a mason's trowel, which may be used as a light entrenchment tool, or, when detached from the rifle, as a hatchet. Hence **Trow·elful,** as much as can be taken up on a t.

Trowel (trau·ĕl), *v.* 1670. [f. prec.] **1.** *trans.* To spread, smooth, or dress (a surface) with or as with a trowel; to form or mould with a trowel. **2.** To put, place, or move (something) with or as with a trowel; to lay on with a trowel, i.e. thickly or clumsily; often *fig.* of flattery or laudation 1772.

Troy¹ (troi). 1520. Name of an ancient city in Asia Minor, besieged and taken by the Greeks; in comb. **Troy-fair, Troy-town,** *fig.* a scene of disorder or confusion (now *dial.*).

Troy² (troi). late ME. [app. named from a weight used at the fair of Troyes in France.] *T. weight*, also ellipt. *T.*: The standard system of weights used for the precious metals and precious stones; formerly also for bread. (The pound t. contains 5760 grains, and is divided into 12 ounces.) **b.** *fig.* in allusion to the pound troy being less than the pound avoirdupois 1599.

b. There was Cressid was T. weight, and Nell was avoirdupois 1599.

Trs., abbrev. of *transpose* (Typog.), *trustees.*

Tru·ancy. 1784. [f. next + -CY.] The action of playing truant; truant conduct or practice.

Truant (trū·ănt), *sb.* (*a.*) ME. [– OFr. *truant* (mod. *truand*) :– Gallo-Rom. **trugant-*, prob. of Celtic origin (cf. W. *truan*, Gael. *truaghan* wretched).] †**1.** One who begs without justification; a sturdy beggar; a vagabond; an idle rogue or knave. (Often a mere term of abuse.) –1656. **2.** A lazy, idle person; *esp.* a boy who absents himself from school without leave; hence *fig.*, one who wanders from an appointed place or neglects his duty or business 1449.

1. Hang him t., there's no true drop of bloud in him to be truly toucht with loue SHAKS. **2.** I haue a T. beene to Chiualry SHAKS. Phr. *To play t.*

B. *adj.* **1.** That is a truant, or plays truant; idle, lazy, loitering, *esp.* of a boy, staying from school without leave; hence, wandering, straying 1550. **b.** Marked by truancy or idleness; befitting a truant or idler 1602. †**2.** Trivial, trite; idle, vain (*rare*) –1682.

1. b. But what in faith make you from Wittemberge? *Hor.* A t. disposition, good my Lord. SHAKS. Hence **Tru·antly** *adv.* (now *rare*). **Tru·antry,** truancy. †**Tru·antship** (*rare*), truancy; also as a mock title.

Tru·ant, *v.* late ME. [f. prec.] †**1.** *intr.* To play the vagabond or rogue –1440. **2.** To idle, play truant (esp. from school); to wander, stray 1580. †**3.** *trans.* To waste or idle away (time); to spend in truanting –1708.

2. I must..truly study man, (A booke in which I yet have truanted) HEYWOOD. **3.** I dare not be the author Of truanting the time FORD.

Truce (trūs), *sb.* [ME. *trew(e)s, trues* (repl. OE. pl. *trēowa*, used as a sing.), pl. of *tru(w)e*, OE. *trēow*, corresp. to OFris. *trouwe*, etc., OS. *treuwa*, OHG. *triuwa* (Du. *trouw*, G. *treue*), Goth. *triggwa* covenant. Cf. TROW, TRUE, TRUST.] **1.** A suspension of hostilities for a specified period between armies at war; a temporary peace or cessation from arms; an armistice; also, an agreement or treaty effecting this. **b.** Loosely or vaguely: Cessation or absence of hostilities (without limitation of time); peace. late ME. **2.** Hence, Respite or intermission (more loosely, freedom or liberty) from something irksome, painful, or oppressive 1567. **b.** In interjectional phr. (*a*) *t. with*, now usu. (*a*) *t. to*, enough of, have done with 1700.

1. A t. which in the following November became a permanent peace STUBBS. *fig.* The Seas and Windes (old Wranglers) tooke a T. SHAKS. *T. of God*, a suspension of hostilities between armies, or of private feuds, ordered by the Church during certain days and seasons in mediæval times; hence *allus.* and *fig.* **2.** Where he may..find T. to his restless thoughts MILT. **b.** A t. to this light conversation 1835. Hence **Truce** *v.* (now *rare*) *intr.* to make a t.; *trans.* to bring to an end by or as by means of a t. **Tru·celess** *a.* that is without t.; unceasing in hostility.

†**Truchman.** 1485. [In XV *tourcheman* (Caxton) – med.L. *turchemannus* (whence also Fr. *trucheman*, etc.) – Arab. *tarjumān*. Cf. DRAGOMAN, TARGUM.] An interpreter.

fig. He is a Truch-Man, that interprets between learned Writers and gentle Readers 1680.

Trucial (trū·ʃăl), *a.* 1876. [f. TRUCE *sb.* + -IAL, app. after *fiducial*.] Of or pertaining to the maritime truce which regulated the relations of certain Arab Sheikhs to one another and to the British government: applied to (*a*) the sheikhs of the territories lying west of the Oman peninsula or the Arab littoral of the Persian Gulf, (*b*) the territories themselves.

Truck (trɒk), *sb.*¹ 1553. [f. TRUCK *v.*¹ Cf. AFr. *truke* (XIV).] **1.** The action or practice of trucking; trading by exchange of commodities; barter. **b.** with *a* and *pl.* A traffic, trade; an act of trading, a bargain or deal 1638. **2.** The payment of wages otherwise than in money; the system or practice of such payment, the *t. system*; occas., goods supplied in lieu of wages 1743. **3.** 'Traffic', intercourse, communication, dealings 1625. †**4.** Commodities for barter –1770. **b.** Small articles of a miscellaneous character; sundries; odds and ends; trash, rubbish. (Rarely *pl.*) 1785. **c.** *U.S.* Market-garden produce; hence, culinary vegetables 1784.

4. b. I can't smoke the t. the steward sells KIPLING.

attrib. and *Comb.*, as *t.-farm, -farmer, -garden, -produce*; **t.-shop, store,** a shop at which vouchers given instead of wages may be exchanged for goods, a tommy-shop; **-system,** the system of paying wages in vouchers for goods instead of in money.

Truck (trɒk), *sb.*² 1611. [perh. shortening of TRUCKLE *sb.*] **1.** A small solid wooden wheel or roller; *spec. Naut.* one of those on which the carriages of ships' guns were formerly mounted. **2.** *Naut.* A circular or square cap of wood fixed on the head of a mast or flagstaff, usu. with small holes or sheaves for halliards 1626. **b.** One of the small wooden blocks through which the rope of a parrel is threaded to prevent its being frayed against the mast. **c.** A similar block lashed to the shrouds to form a guide or fair-leader for running rigging. 1625. **3.** A wheeled vehicle for carrying heavy weights. **a.** A strong flat open trolley for carrying blocks of stone or the like; a lorry. **b.** A light two-wheeled hand-cart. **c.** An open railway wagon. **d.** = BOGIE 2. **e.** A low barrow of various types, with one to four wheels, as that used on railway platforms for moving luggage, etc. **f.** A small barrow, with two stout low wheels and a projecting plate or lip in front, used for moving sacks, etc. 1774.

3. f. Porters are hurrying to and fro with luggage on trucks 1866.

Truck (trɒk), *v.*¹ [ME. *trukie*, later *trukke* – AFr. **truquer*, OFr. **troquer* (reflected in med.L. *trocare*), of unkn. origin.] **1.** *trans.* To give in exchange *for* something else; to exchange (one thing) *for* another; also, to exchange (a thing) *with* a person (also *absol.*). **2.** To exchange (commodities) for profit; to barter 1440. **3.** To barter away (what should be sacred or precious) *for* something unworthy 1649. **4.** *intr.* To trade by exchange of commodities; to barter 1594. **5.** *fig.* or in fig. context: To bargain or deal *for* a commodity *with* a person; to negotiate; also, to have dealings *in*, to trade; esp. of dealings of an underhand or improper character: to traffic 1615. **b.** To have dealings or intercourse, be on familiar terms *with*. Now *dial.* 1622. **6.** *trans.* To pay (an employee) otherwise than in money; to pay or deal with on the truck-system (with the implication of profiting by the transaction). Also *intr.* 1871.

1. To t. the Latine for any other vulgar Language, is but an ill barter 1645. **3.** Liberty's too often truck'd for Gold DE FOE. **4.** Chinese.. tobacco, for which they t. with the Russians 1854. **6.** The very paupers used to be 'trucked', the inspectors..gave the paupers their relief in kind 1871. Hence †**Tru·ckage**,[1] the action of trucking; exchange, barter. MILT. **Tru·cker**, *spec.* (*U.S.*) one who grows 'truck' or garden produce for market; so **Tru·cking** *vbl. sb.*

Truck, *v.*[2] 1809. [f. TRUCK *sb.*[2]] *trans.* To put on or into a truck; to convey by means of a truck or trucks. Hence **Tru·ckage**,[2] conveyance by truck or trucks, or the cost of this; also, supply of trucks collectively.

Truckle (trɒ·k'l), *sb.* [Late ME. *trocle* – AFr. *trocle* – L. *trochlea* – Gr. τροχιλία, -εια sheaf of a pulley.] **1.** A small wheel with a groove in its circumference round which a cord passes; a pulley, a sheave. **2.** A small roller or wheel placed under or attached to a heavy object to facilitate moving it; a castor on a piece of furniture. Now *dial.* 1459. **3.** Short for TRUCKLE-BED 1637. **4.** A low-wheeled car; a truck. Chiefly *Irish.* 1689.

Truckle (trɒ·k'l), *v.* 1613. [f. *truckle* in TRUCKLE-BED.] †**1.** *intr.* To sleep in a truckle bed –1674. **2.** *fig.* †**a.** To be subservient, to submit, to give precedence *to* –1738. **b.** To submit from an unworthy motive; to act with servility 1680. **c.** To submit or give way timidly 1837. †**3.** To move on truckles or castors –1796.

2. a. Publick good is made to t. to private gain 1704. **b.** Too proud to t. to a Superior 1789. Hence **Truckler** (trɒ·kləɹ), one who truckles (in sense 2 b of the vb.).

Tru·ckle-bed. 1459. [TRUCKLE *sb.* 2.] A low bed running on truckles or castors, usu. pushed beneath a high or 'standing' bed when not in use. So **T. bedstead.**

Truculence (trɒ·k-, trū·kiŭlĕns). 1727. [– L. *truculentia*, f. *truculentus* TRUCULENT.] The condition or quality of being truculent; fierceness, savageness. So **Tru·culency** 1569.

Truculent (trɒ·kiŭlĕnt, trū·k-), *a.* 1540. [– L. *truculentus*, f. *trux*, *truc-* fierce, savage; see -ULENT.] **1.** Characterized by or exhibiting ferocity or cruelty; fierce, cruel, savage, barbarous. **b.** Of speech or writing: Hostile; aggressive; scathing; savage; harsh 1850. **2.** (In catachrestic use, assoc. w. TRUCK *sb.*[1], *v.*[1], TRUCKLE *v.*) Mean, base, mercenary 1825.

1. b. Voltaire is never either gross or t. MORLEY. **2.** A t. exchange not only of truth, but of sincerity, for money BENTHAM. Hence **Tru·culently** *adv.*, **-ness.**

Trudge (trɒdʒ), *sb.* 1748. [f. next.] †**1.** A person who trudges; a trudger –1775. **2.** An act or trudging; a 'tramp' 1835.

Trudge (trɒdʒ), *v.* 1547. [Early forms also †*tredge*, (dial.) *tridge*; of unkn. origin.] **1.** *intr.* To walk laboriously, wearily, or without spirit, but steadily and persistently; 'to jog on; to march heavily on' (J.). **b.** *spec.* To go away, be off, depart 1547. **2.** *trans.* To perform (a journey) or travel over (a distance) by trudging; to tramp 1635.

1. From house to house he trudges in the snow, visiting poor widows 1856. **b.** 'Tis time for me to t. 1623. Hence **Tru·dger**, one who trudges.

Trudgen (trɒ·dʒən). Also *erron.* **trudgeon.** 1893. [f. proper name *Trudgen.*] In full *t. stroke*: applied to a kind of hand-over-hand or double over-arm breast-stroke in swimming, with leg action resembling that of walking.

John Trudgen..in 1863..went to Buenos Ayres...While there he learnt 'to trudge' from the natives 1904.

True (trū), *a.* (*sb.*, *adv.*) [OE. *ġe*|*trīewe*, *trēowe*, later *trȳwe* (ME. *trewe*, *truwe*, *tru*) = OFris. *trīuwe*, OS. *triuwi*, OHG. *gi*|*triuwi* (Du. *getrouw*, G. *treu*), ON. *tryggr*, Goth. *triggws*, f. the Gmc. sb. repr. by TRUCE. The sp. *true* dates from XV.] **1.** Of persons: Steadfast in adherence *to* a commander or friend, *to* a principle or cause, *to* one's promises, faith, etc.; firm in allegiance; faithful, loyal, constant, trusty. Somewhat *arch.* **b.** *transf.* Of personal attributes or actions. Somewhat *arch.* OE. **c.** *fig.* of things: Reliable; constant ME. **2.** Honest, honourable, upright, virtuous, trustworthy (*arch.*); free from deceit, sincere, truthful; of actions, feelings, etc.: sincere, unfeigned OE. **3.** Of a statement or belief: Consistent with fact; agreeing with reality; representing the thing as it is ME. **b.** *transf.* Speaking truly, telling the truth; trustworthy in statement; veracious, truthful ME. **4.** Agreeing with a standard, pattern, or rule; exact, accurate, precise; correct, right 1550. **b.** In more general sense: Of the right kind, such as it should be, proper ME. **c.** That is rightly or lawfully such; rightful, legitimate. late ME. **d.** Accurately placed, fitted, or shaped; exact in position or form, as an instrument, etc. 1474. **e.** *T. to*: consistent with, exactly agreeing with, 'faithful to' 1735. **f.** Conformable to reality, natural 1870. **g.** Remaining constant to type 1839. **5.** Real, genuine; properly so called; not counterfeit, spurious, or imaginary; also, approaching or conforming to the ideal character of such. late ME. **b.** In scientific use: Conformable to the type, or to the accepted idea or character of the genus, class, or kind; properly or strictly so called 1578. **c.** *True bill*, (in *Law*) a bill of indictment found by a Grand Jury to be supported by sufficient evidence to justify the hearing of a case. Hence *allus.* a true statement or charge (*true* being loosely taken in sense 3). 1591.

1. Ye haue done as a trew subjet ought to do to his lorde 1533. T...to the cause of civil freedom 1855. **c.** T. as the Needle to the Pole 1733. **2.** Good Men and t. for a Petty Jury 1710. **3.** The truer opinion 1608. It is t., we were all but young in the War DE FOE. *To come t.*, to be verified or realized in actual experience, be fulfilled. **b.** This way the noise was, if mine ear be t. MILT. **4.** Apelles drew A Circle regularly t. PRIOR. **b.** Facts thus placed in their t. bearings 1911. **d.** Of the ground: Free from unevenness, level and smooth 1851. **e.** Be t. to your time in the morning DICKENS. **f.** I do not object to fiction provided it be t. 1894. **g.** This breed is very t. DARWIN. **5.** The time of t. noon 1854. **b.** T. nerve tumours are exceedingly rare 1899.

B. *sb.* (the adj. used absol.) †**1.** Nickname for a member of the Protestant or Whig party in the 17th c. NORTH. **2.** *The t.*: That which is true; truth, reality 1812. **3.** Accurate position or adjustment; in phr. *out of* (*the*) *t.* 1890. **C.** *adv.* = TRULY 1–4. ME. **b.** In accordance with the ancestral type; without variation; in phr. *to breed t.* 1859. Hence **True·ness.**

True, *v.* 1841. [f. prec.] *trans.* To make true, as a piece of mechanism; to place, adjust, or shape accurately; to make accurately or perfectly straight, level, round, smooth, sharp, etc. as required. Hence **Tru·er**, also *truer-up.*

True·-born, *a.* 1591. Born of a true or pure stock; legitimately born; having the sterling qualities associated with such descent.

Though banish'd, yet a true-borne Englishman SHAKS.

True·-bred, *a.* 1596. **a.** Bred of a true or pure stock; of the true breed; thoroughbred. **b.** Having or manifesting true breeding or education.

True-hearted (stress var.), *a.* 1471. Having a true heart; faithful, loyal; honest, sincere. Hence **True:hea·rtedness.**

True-love (trū·lɒv). ME. [TRUE *a.*, LOVE *sb.*] **1.** A faithful lover; one whose love is pledged; a sweetheart, beloved. late ME. †**2.** An ornament or symbol of true love; a TRUE-LOVE KNOT –1575. **3.** Herb Paris (*Paris quadrifolia*), the whorl of four leaves with the single flower or berry in the midst suggesting the figure of a true-love knot. late ME.

1. My true-love hath my heart, and I haue his SIDNEY. **3.** Vnder his tonge a trewe loue he beer For therby wende he to ben gracious CHAUCER.

True-love knot, true lover's knot. 1495. A kind of knot, of an ornamental form (usu. either a double-looped bow, or a knot formed of two loops intertwined), used as a symbol of true love; a figure of this. Also *fig.* or *allus.*

Truepenny (trū·peni). *arch.* 1519. A trusty person; an honest fellow (compared to a coin of genuine metal); *adj.* genuine *colloq.*

Art thou there t.? SHAKS.

Truffle (trɒ·f'l, tru·f'l). 1591. [prob. – Du *truffel*, †*truffele* – Fr. *truffle* (now *truffe*), perh. to be referred ult. to pop. L. **tufera*, for L. *tubera*, pl. of *tuber* TUBER.] Any one of various underground fungi of the family *Tuberaceæ*; *spec.* an edible fungus of the genus *Tuber*, a native of Central and Southern Europe, esteemed as a delicacy; esp. *T. æstivum*, or *cibarium*, the Common (English) Truffle, and *T. melanosporum*, the French Truffle, which have a black, warty exterior, and more or less resemble a potato in shape.

attrib. and *Comb.*: **t.-dog, -pig**, a dog or pig trained to discover truffles; **-worm**, the larva of an insect infesting the t. Hence **Truffled** (trɒ·f'ld) *a.* cooked, garnished, or stuffed with truffles.

Trug[1] (trɒg). *local.* 1580. [perh. dial. var. of TROUGH.] **1.** A wooden milk pan. **2.** A shallow oblong basket made of wood strips, chiefly used for carrying fruit, vegetables, etc. 1862.

Trug[2]. *Obs.* exc. *dial.* 1592. [perh. – It. *trucca* 'trull, whore or wench' (Florio); for *-g* from *-cc-* cf. SMUG.] A prostitute. †**b.** A catamite (*rare*) –1630.

Truism (trū·iz'm). 1708. [f. TRUE *a.* + -ISM.] A self-evident truth, esp. one of slight importance; a statement so obviously true as not to require discussion.

The fear of t. in our modern writers 1861. Hence **Trui·stic, -al** *adjs.* having the character of a t.; trivially self-evident.

Trull (trɒl). 1519. [One of a group of nearly synon. sbs. having initial *tr*, as TRAPES, TROLLOP, TROT *sb.*[2], TRUG[2]; cf. G. *trulle.*] **1.** A low prostitute or concubine; a drab, strumpet, trollop. †**2.** A girl, lass, wench (*rare*) –1600.

Truly (trū·li), *adv.* [OE. *trēowlīċe*; see TRUE, -LY[2].] **1.** Faithfully, loyally, steadfastly. *arch.* †**2.** Honestly, honourably, uprightly –1558. **3.** In accordance with the fact; truthfully; correctly (in ref. to a statement) ME. **4.** In accordance with a rule or standard; exactly, accurately, precisely, correctly. late ME. **b.** Rightly; as it ought to be, properly; often in phr. *well and t.* late ME. **c.** In accordance with nature; naturally 1600. **d.** Without cross-breeding; also, without variation from the ancestral type 1854. **5.** Genuinely, really, actually, in fact, in reality; sincerely, unfeignedly. late ME. **b.** Used to emphasize a statement: Indeed, forsooth, verily ME. **c.** In phr. *yours truly*, one of the more formal of the phrases used in subscribing a letter; hence joc. = 'myself' 1788.

1. *Cymb.* III. v. 110. **3.** Tell me truely how thou lik'st her SHAKS. **b.** His innocent Babe t. begotten SHAKS. **5.** A Mind t. virtuous STEELE. **b.** A wide freedom, t.! RUSKIN. **c.** Give the young one a glass,..and score it up to yours t. THACKERAY.

Trump (trɒmp), *sb.*[1] *arch.* and *poet.* [ME. *trompe* – (O)Fr. *trompe* (= Pg. *tromba*, *trompa*, Sp. *trompa*, It. *tromba*) – Frankish **trumpa* (cf. ON. *trumba* pipe, trumpet); prob. of imit. origin.] **1.** = TRUMPET *sb.* 1. **2.** *fig.* One who or that which proclaims, celebrates, or summons loudly like a trumpet; esp. in *t. of fame* and the like. 1531.

1. In the laste trumpe; forsoth the trumpe schal synge WYCLIF. 1 *Cor.* 15:52. **2.** Say we sound The t. of liberty GRAY.

Trump (trɒmp), *sb.*[2] 1529. [alt. of TRIUMPH *sb.* 7.] **1.** A playing-card of that suit which for the time being ranks above the other three, so that any one such card can 'take' any card of another suit; *spec.* the card, usu. that last turned up by the dealer, determining this suit; also, *pl.*, the suit thus determined. †**b.** An obsolete card-game, known also as ruff –1798. **c.** An act of trumping (*rare*) 1853. **2.** *fig.* and in fig. context 1595. **3.** *colloq.* A first-rate fellow; a 'brick' 1819.

2. *To turn up trumps*, to turn out well or successfully. *To put* (a person) *to his t.* or *trumps*, to oblige a card-player to play out his trumps; *fig.* 'to put to the last expedient' (J.). **3.** You're a t. DICKENS.

Trump (trɒmp), *v.*[1] Now *rare* or *Obs.* ME. [– (O)Fr. *tromper*, f. *trompe* TRUMP *sb.*[1]] **1.** *intr.* To blow or sound a trumpet. Also with *up*. **2.** *trans.* To proclaim, celebrate, or extol by, or as by, the sound of a trumpet. late ME.

Trump, *v.*[2] 1553. [f. TRUMP *sb.*[2]] **I. 1.** *Cards.* **a.** *trans.* To put a trump upon; to take with a trump 1598. **b.** *absol.* or *intr.* To play a trump 1680. **2.** *fig.* or in fig. context: now usu., to beat, to 'cap' 1586.

1. To T. a Card early in the Deal 1778. **2.** I trumped her old-world stories..with the latest.. intelligence THACKERAY.

II. *T. up* (trans.). †**a.** To bring up, allege –1772. **b.** To get up or devise in an unscrupulous way; to forge, fabricate, invent 1695.

Trumpery (trɒ·mpəri), *sb.* (*a.*) 1456. [– (O)Fr. *tromperie*, f. *tromper* deceive, of unkn. origin; see -ERY.] †**1.** Deceit, fraud, imposture, trickery –1847. **2.** 'Something of less value than it seems'; hence, 'something of no value; trifles' (J.); trash, rubbish 1456.

2. I haue sold all my Tromperie: not a counterfeit Stone, not a Ribbon, Glasse, Pomander, Browch..to keepe my Pack from fasting SHAKS. Embryos, and Idiots, Eremits and Friers White, Black and Grey, with all thir trumperie MILT. All the metaphysical t. of the schools DE FOE.

B. *attrib.* or *adj.* Of little or no value; paltry, insignificant; worthless, trashy 1576. It seems a t. quarrel 1869.

Trumpet (trɒ·mpėt), *sb.* ME. [– (O)Fr. *trompette*, dim. of *trompe* TRUMP *sb.*[1]; see -ET.] **1.** A musical wind-instrument (or one of a class of such) of bright, powerful, and penetrating tone, used from ancient times, esp. for military or other signals, and in modern times also in the orchestra; it consists of a cylindrical or conical tube, usu. of metal, straight or curved (or bent upon itself), with a cup-shaped mouthpiece and a flaring bell. (In modern forms of the instrument additional tones are obtained by means of slides, crooks, valves, or keys.) **2.** Something of the nature of or resembling a trumpet 1659. **b.** = EAR-T., SPEAKING-T. 1696. **3.** *fig.* A means or agent (real or imaginary) which proclaims, celebrates, or gives warning of something 1447. **4.** *transf.* A trumpeter. late ME. **b.** *fig.* = TRUMPETER 2. 1549. **5.** A sound like that of a trumpet; the loud cry of certain animals, esp. the elephant 1850. **6.** Something shaped like a trumpet 1668.

1. The general's t. gave the signal of departure GIBBON. *Feast of Trumpets*, a Jewish festival observed at the beginning of the month Tisri, blowing of trumpets being a prominent part of the solemnities. **2.** *Trumpet, Tromba*, a striking reed stop of clear penetrating tone 1876. *T. marine, marine t.* [tr. It. *tromba marina*, Fr. *trompette marine*], a large obsolete musical instrument of the viol kind, played with a bow, and having a single thick string passing over a bridge fastened at one end only, the other vibrating against the body, and producing a tone like that of a trumpet. **3.** The decree of Wormes was the trompet of this warre 1560. Phr. *To blow one's own t.*, to sound one's own praises, boast, brag. **4. b.** So hence: be thou the t. of our wrath SHAKS. **6.** The white and rosy trumpets of the bindweed 1883.

attrib. and *Comb.*: **t. animalcule,** an infusorian of the genus *Stentor* or family *Stentoridæ*, so called from its shape; **-call,** a call or summons sounded on the t.; **-conch** = *-shell*; **t. daffodil,** a variety of daffodil with a conspicuous 'trumpet' or tubular *corona*; **-fish,** any of various fishes with long tubular snout, *esp.* the bellows-fish or sea-snipe (*Centriscus scolopax*) and the tobacco-pipe fish (*Fistularia*); **-flower,** any of various plants with large or showy t.-shaped flowers, esp. of the genus *Tecoma* and *Bignonia*, also species of *Catalpa, Brunfelsia*, etc.; **-lily,** the white arum-lily; also some species of *Lilium*; **-major,** the chief trumpeter of a band or regiment; **-shaped** *a.*, *spec.* in *Nat. Hist.* tubular with one end dilated; **-shell,** a shell of the genus *Triton* or family *Tritonidæ*, or any other shell which can be blown like a t.; **-tongued** *a.*, 'having a tongue vociferous as a trumpet' (J.); loud-voiced; **-tree,** a W. Indian and S. Amer. tree *Cecropia peltata*, with hollow stem and branches which are used for wind-instruments; **-weed,** (*a*) = SEA-*trumpet*; (*b*) a N. Amer. species of hemp-agrimony, *Eupatorium purpureum*, with hollow stems which children blow through like trumpets; (*c*) a N. Amer. species of lettuce, *Lactuca canadensis*.

Tru·mpet, *v.* 1530. [f. prec., or – (O)Fr. *trompeter*.] **1.** *intr.* To blow or sound a trumpet. **b.** To emit a sound like that of a trumpet; esp. in ref. to the cry of an elephant when enraged or excited 1828. **2.** *trans.* **a.** To sound on a trumpet; to utter with a sound like that of a trumpet 1729. **b.** *fig.* To announce or publish as by sound of trumpet; to noise abroad 1604. **c.** To summon or denounce formally or to drive away, by sound of a trumpet 1680.

1. b. Anopheles, a mosquito that does not t. 1900. **2. b.** They trumpeted the story all over the town H. WALPOLE. **c.** They drummed and trumpeted the wretches out of their Hall BURKE.

Trumpeter (trɒ·mpėtəɹ). 1497. [f. TRUMPET *sb.* or *v.* + -ER[1], or – Fr. *trompeteur*.] **1.** One who sounds or plays upon a trumpet; *spec.* a soldier in a cavalry regiment who gives signals with a trumpet. **2.** *fig.* One who gives the signal for, proclaims, or extols something as by sound of trumpet 1581. **3.** *T.'s muscle*, †also simply *t.* = BUCCINATOR 1615. **4.** Any of various birds, from their loud note suggesting the sound of a trumpet. **a.** A variety of domestic pigeon 1725. **b.** Any species of the S. Amer. genus *Psophia* or family *Psophiidæ*, allied to the Cranes 1747. **c.** = *t.-swan* 1891. **5.** Any species of the genus *Latris*, comprising large food-fishes of Australia, Tasmania, and New Zealand; so called from the sound they utter when taken out of water 1834.

1. A t. was sent to summon the place MACAULAY. **2.** Subordinate instruments and trumpeters of sedition BURKE.

attrib.: **t. hornbill,** an African bird of the genus *Bycanistes*; **t. swan,** a large N. Amer. species of swan, *Cygnus* (*Olor*) *buccinator*.

Truncal (trɒ·ŋkăl), *a.* 1847. [f. TRUNK *sb.* + -AL[1] 1.] Pertaining to, or of the nature of, a trunk; situated in or affecting the trunk.

Truncate (trɒ·ŋke[i]t), *a.* 1716. [– L. *truncatus*, pa. pple. of *truncare* maim, etc.; see -ATE[2].] = TRUNCATED 2. So **Tru·ncately** *adv.* 1579.

Truncate (trɒ·ŋke[i]t), *v.* 1486. [– *truncat-*, pa. ppl. stem of L. *truncare*; see prec., -ATE[3].] *trans.* To shorten or diminish by cutting off a part; to cut short; to maim, mutilate. **b.** In scientific and technical use; *spec.* in *Cryst.* to 'cut off' or replace (an edge or solid angle) by a plane face, esp. so as to make equal angles with the adjacent faces. Chiefly in *pa. pple.* 1758. Hence **Truncature** (trɒ·ŋkătiŭɹ) = TRUNCATION 2.

Truncated (trɒ·ŋke[i]tėd), *ppl. a.* and *a.* 1486. [f. L. *truncatus* (see prec.) + -ED[1], or f. prec.] Cut short (actually or apparently); having a part cut off, or of such a form as if a part were cut off. **1.** *Her.* Of a cross or tree: Having the arms or boughs cut off; couped. Now *rare* or *Obs.* **2.** In scientific or techn. use. (Const. as *adj.* preceding, or as *pa. pple.* following, the noun.) **a.** *Geom.*, etc. Of a figure: Having one end cut off by a transverse line or plane; *esp.* of a cone or pyramid: Having the vertex cut off by a plane section, esp. one parallel to the base 1704. **b.** *Cryst.* and *Solid Geom.* Of an edge or solid angle: Cut off or replaced by a plane face; also said of a solid figure having its edges or angles thus cut off 1796. **c.** *Nat. Hist.* Appearing as if the tip or end were cut off transversely; terminating in a flat or broad edge or surface instead of a point 1752. **d.** So in *Arch.*, *Geol.*, etc. 1723. **3.** Maimed, mutilated 1731.

2. a. T. Pyramid or Cone 1704. **3.** *fig.* A t. and most imperfect friendship 1890.

Truncation (trɒŋkē[i]·ʃən). 1579. [– late L. *truncatio*, *-ōn-*, f. as TRUNCATE *v.*; see -ION.] **1.** The action of truncating; cutting short; maiming, mutilation. **2.** In scientific and techn. use: The process of truncating, or condition of being truncated; *spec.* in *Cryst.* replacement of an edge or solid angle by a plane face, esp. one equally inclined to the adjacent faces 1796. **b.** *transf.* The part or place where something is truncated 1805.

Truncheon (trɒ·nʃən), *sb.* ME. [– OFr. *tronchon* (mod. *tronçon*), repr. Rom. **truncio*, *-ōn-*, f. L. *truncus* TRUNK.] **1.** A piece broken or cut off, a fragment. *Obs.* or *arch.* **b.** *spec.* A fragment of a spear or lance. *Obs.* or *arch.* ME. **c.** The shaft of a spear. *Obs.* or *arch.* ME. **2.** A short thick staff; a club, a cudgel. *Obs.* or *arch.* exc. as in 3. ME. **3.** A staff carried as a symbol of office, command, or authority; a marshal's baton; now most freq., the short staff or club with which a police constable is armed 1573. **4.** A length cut from a plant, esp. one used for grafting or planting; a stout cutting. Now *rare.* 1572.

1. A huge t. of wreck half buried in the sands STEVENSON. **3.** Stones were thrown on the one side and truncheons used on the other 1880. Hence **Tru·ncheon** *v. trans.* to beat with a t. **Truncheoned** (trɒ·nʃənd) *a.* furnished or armed with a t. **Tru·ncheoner,** one who bears a t.

‖**Truncus** (trɒ·ŋkɒ̆s). 1693. [L.; see TRUNK.] **a.** *Anat.* The trunk or main stem of a vessel or nerve. **b.** *Zool.* The trunk or body of an animal, without the head, limbs, and tail; *Ent.* the thorax. **c.** *Bot.* The trunk or stem of a tree.

Trundle (trɒ·nd'l), *sb.* 1564. [Parallel form to TRENDLE, TRINDLE *sbs.*] **1.** A small wheel, roller, or revolving disc; *esp.* the wheel of a castor. **b.** In the draw-stop action of an organ, a roller by the rotation of which a slider is drawn or replaced 1876. **2.** A lantern-wheel (see LANTERN). Also, each of the staves of this device. 1611. †**3.** A low truck or carriage on small wheels –1766. **4.** An act of trundling 1675.

attrib. and *Comb.*: **t.-head,** (*a*) each of the discs of a trundle (sense 2); (*b*) *Naut.* 'the lower drum-head of a capstern, when it is double, and worked on one shaft both on an upper and lower deck' SMYTH.

Tru·ndle, *v.* 1598. [Parallel form to TRENDLE, TRINDLE *vbs.*] **1. a.** *trans.* To cause to roll along upon a surface, as a ball, hoop, etc.; to roll, bowl. **b.** *intr.* To move along on a surface by revolving; to roll 1629. **c.** *Cricket.* (*trans.* or *absol.*) To bowl. *colloq.* 1882. **2.** *trans.* To cause to rotate; to twirl, spin, whirl; *spec.* to twirl (a mop) so as to free it from water 1756. **3.** *intr.* To move or run on a wheel or wheels 1688. **b.** *trans.* To draw or push along on a wheel or wheels, as a wheelbarrow, vehicle, etc. 1825. **4.** To convey in a wheeled vehicle, to wheel 1773. **b.** *intr.* To go in a wheeled vehicle, on a bicycle, etc. 1840. **5.** *fig.* To go, walk, or run easily or rapidly; to go away, 'be off'; also, to walk unsteadily or with a rolling gait 1680. **b.** *trans.* To carry or send off, turn out, dismiss 1794.

3. Such are termed Truckle beds, because they t. under other beds 1688. **b.** Trundling a wheelbarrow full of sand 1862. **5. b.** The women.. always contrived to t. me out of favour before the honeymoon was over SCOTT. Hence **Tru·ndler.**

Tru·ndle-bed. Now *rare.* 1542. [TRUNDLE *sb.* 1.] = TRUCKLE-BED.

Tru·ndle-tail. *Obs.* or *arch.* 1486. **1.** A dog with a curly tail; a low-bred dog, a cur. Also *attrib.* †**2.** (as two words) A curly tail (of a dog). *rare.* 1625.

Trunk (trɒŋk), *sb.* [Late ME. *tron*(*c*)*k* – (O)Fr. *tronc* :– L. *truncus*. In branch III app. assoc. with TRUMP *sb.*[1]] **I.** The main part of something. **1.** The main stem of a tree, as distinct from the roots and branches; the bole or stock 1490. **b.** *transf.* The shaft of a column; also, the dado or die of a pedestal 1563. **2.** The human body, or that of an animal, without the head, or esp. without the head and limbs, or considered apart from these; in *Ent.* the thorax 1494. †**3.** A dead body, a corpse; also, the body considered apart from the soul or life –1709. **4.** *Anat.* The main body or line of a blood-vessel, nerve, etc., as distinct from its branches; also *transf.* the main line of a river, railway, telegraph or telephone, road or canal system 1615. **b.** *pl*, Short for Grand Trunk Railway of Canada, or its stock 1892.

1. With Trunks of Elms and Oaks the Hearth they load DRYDEN. **2.** 2 *Hen. VI*, IV. x. 90. **3.** *Lear* I. i. 180.

II. A chest, box, case, etc. (supposed to have been orig. made out of a tree-trunk).

†**1.** A chest, coffer, box. *Obs.* in *gen.* sense. –1726. **2.** A box, usu. lined with paper or linen and with a rounded top, for carrying clothes and other personal necessaries esp. when travelling; orig. covered with leather, now often of fibre, painted metal, etc. 1609. **3.** A perforated floating box in which live fish are kept 1440. **b.** An open box or case (containing from 80 to 90 lb.) in which fresh fish are sold wholesale 1883. **4.** *Mining.* A long shallow trough in which lead or tin ore is dressed 1653. **5.** A box-like passage for light, water, etc., usu. made of boards; a shaft, conduit; a chute. Now chiefly *techn.* 1610. **b.** In a steam-engine, a tubular piston-rod large enough to allow of the lateral movement of the connecting-rod when jointed directly to the piston 1859. **c.** *Naut.* A water-tight shaft passing through the decks of a vessel, for loading, coaling, etc. 1862. **d.** *Salt-making.* A box-like cover placed over an evaporating-pan 1885.

2. We were forced to send for a smith, to break open her t. PEPYS. Have your trunks packed 1859.

III. A pipe or tube. †**1.** A pipe used as a speaking-tube or ear-trumpet –1704. †**2.** A blow-gun, a pea-shooter –1801. **3.** The elongated proboscis of the elephant; also *transf.* the prolonged flexible snout of the tapir, etc. 1565. **b.** The proboscis of some molluscs; also the proboscis of various insects. Now *rare* or *Obs.* 1661. †**3.** *pl.* Also *small trunks*: = TROLL-MADAM –1854. **IV.** *pl.* †**a.** = TRUNK-HOSE –1672. **b.** Short breeches of silk or other thin material; in theatrical use, often worn over tights 1825. **c.** Short tight-fitting drawers worn by swimmers and athletes 1883.

attrib. and *Comb.*: (sense I. 4) *t. line, road*; **t.-call,** a call from one telephone exchange to another; **-engine,** an engine having a tubular piston-rod; see sense II. 5 b; **t. main,** a large pipe for the conveyance of water, etc. under pressure, as dist. from the reticulation of smaller mains fed therefrom; **-nail,** a short nail with broad convex brass head used for ornamenting trunks, etc.; †**-work,** secret or clandestine action, as by means of a t. Hence **Trunk** *v. trans. Mining,* to dress (lead or tin ore) by agitating it in water; to cover or enclose as with a casing. **Tru·nkful,** as much or as many as a t. will hold.

Tru·nk-bree:ches, *sb. pl.* Now only *Hist.* 1662. = TRUNK-HOSE.

Trunked (trɒŋkt), *a.* 1640. [f. TRUNK *sb.* + -ED².] **1.** Having a trunk, as a tree; usu. in comb., as *straight-t.*, etc. **b.** *Her.* Having the trunk of a tincture different from the rest of the tree 1678. **2.** Having a trunk or proboscis 1794.

Tru·nk-fish. 1804. Any fish of the genus *Ostracion* or family *Ostraciontidæ*, inhabiting tropical seas, and having the body of angular cross-section and covered with bony hexagonal plates; a coffer-fish.

Tru·nk-hose. Now only *Hist.* 1637. [f. TRUNK *sb.* (or obs. *trunk* vb. truncate) + HOSE.] Full bag-like breeches covering the hips and upper thighs, and sometimes stuffed with wool or the like; worn in the 16th and early 17th c. **b.** *attrib.*, in sense 'wearing trunk-hose'; hence, old-fashioned, out-of-date 1643.

Tru·nk-ma:ker. 1704. One who business is the making of trunks; often with allusion to the use of the sheets of unsaleable books for trunk-linings.

Trunnion (trɒ·nyən). Chiefly in *pl.* 1625. [– (O)Fr. *trognon* core of fruit, trunk of a tree, of unkn. origin.] Each of a pair of opposite gudgeons on the sides of a cannon, upon which it is pivoted upon its carriage. (Disused in large modern guns.) **b.** Each of any similar pair of opposite pins or pivots on which anything is supported; *spec.* in the oscillating steam-engine, a hollow gudgeon on each side of the cylinder, upon which it is pivoted, and through which steam passes into and out of the cylinder; also, a single projecting pivot 1727.

attrib. and *Comb.*: **t.-box,** a metal case fixed over the t. to prevent the gun leaving the carriage; **-carriage,** the top carriage of a mortar; **-plate,** an iron plate on the cheek of a wooden gun-carriage, on which the t. plays; also, a strengthening shoulder reinforcing the t.; **-ring,** the raised band or moulding encircling a cannon a little in front of the trunnions.

Trusion (trū·ʒən). Now *rare* or *Obs.* 1604. [– med.L. *trusio*, *-ōn-*, f. pa. ppl. stem of L. *trudere* push, thrust; see -ION.] **1.** *Law.* = INTRUSION 2. **2.** The action of pushing or thrusting 1656.

Truss (trɒs), *sb.* ME. [– OFr. *trusse, torse* (mod. *trousse*), perh. f. correl. OFr. *trusser* (mod. *trousser*); see TRUSS *v.*] **1.** A bundle, pack. Now chiefly *techn.* **b.** *spec.* A bundle of hay or straw; in techn. use, of a definite weight, varying at different times and places. (Now generally, in England, of old hay, 56 lbs.; of new hay, 60 lbs.; of straw 36 lbs.) 1483. **2.** *Naut.* A tackle by which the centre of the yard was hauled back and secured to the mast; in mod. use extended to an iron fitting consisting of a ring encircling the mast, with a gooseneck by which the yard is secured ME. †**3. a.** A close-fitting body-garment or jacket formerly worn by men and women –1612. †**b.** *pl.* = TROUSE² –1631. **4.** A surgical appliance serving for support in cases of rupture, etc., now usu. consisting of a pad with a belt or spring to produce equable pressure on the part 1543. **5.** *Gardening.* A compact cluster of flowers growing on one stalk 1688. **6.** *Building,* etc. A framework of timber or iron, or both, so constructed as to form a firm support for a superincumbent weight, as that of a roof or bridge 1654. **b.** *Arch.* A projection from the face of a wall, often serving to support a cornice, etc.; a kind of large corbel or modillion 1519. **c.** *Ship-building.* Any one of the diagonal shores crossing each other and resting against the abutments 1860.

1. Undir his heed no pilowe was, But in the stede a trusse of gras 1400. **3. a.** Puts off his Palmer's weede vnto his trusse, which bore The staines of ancient Armes DRAYTON.

Comb.: **t.-beam,** a beam forming part of a t.; also, a beam or iron frame used as a beam, strengthened with a tie-rod or struts, so as to form a t.; **-rod,** a tie-rod forming part of a t.

†**Truss,** *a.* 1674. [attrib. use of prec. in similative sense.] Of a thick rounded form, like a bundle or parcel; tight, compact –1825.

Truss (trɒs), *v.* [ME. *trusse* (XIII) – OFr. *trusser* (mod. *trousser*), of unkn. origin; see TRUSS *sb.*] **1.** *trans.* To tie in a bundle, or stow away closely in a receptacle; to bundle, pack. Also with *up.* Now *rare* or *Obs.* **b.** *Naut.* To furl (a sail). Also *absol.* late ME. **2.** To make fast to something with or as with a cord, band, or the like; to bind, tie, fasten. Now *rare.* ME. **b.** *spec.* To tie the 'points' or laces with which the hose were fastened to the doublet. *Obs.* exc. *Hist.* 1460. **3.** To confine or enclose (the body, or some part of it) by something fastened closely round; to bind or tie up; to gird; to fasten up (the hair) with ribbon, pins, combs, etc.; to adjust and draw close the garments of (a person); hence contemptuously in ref. to dress. Also with *up.* Now *rare* or *Obs.* ME. **4.** To fasten *up* on a gallows or cross; to 'string up'. *arch.* 1536. **5.** To fasten the wings or legs of (a fowl, etc.) to the body with skewers or otherwise, in preparation for cooking 1450. **6.** Of a bird of prey: To seize or clutch (the prey) in its talons; *spec.* to seize (the quarry) in the air and carry it off. *arch.* (and *Her.*) 1567. **7.** To compress the staves of (a cask) into the required shape and position by means of a *trussing-hoop* 1535. **8.** *Building,* etc. To support or strengthen with a truss 1823.

1. But hood..wered he noon, For it was trussed vp in his walet CHAUCER. **6.** So—at last he has trussed his Quarry DRYDEN. Hence **Tru·ssing** *vbl. sb.* the action of the vb.; *concr.* the timber or other material forming a truss; a work or structure consisting of trusses; also *attrib.* adapted or used for trussing or adapted for being trussed, as *t.-hoop, -needle, -rope,* etc.

Trust (trɒst), *sb.* [Early ME. *trost(e, truste* – ON. *traust*; see next.] **1.** Confidence in or reliance on some quality or attribute of a person or thing, or the truth of a statement. **b.** *transf.* with possessive: That in which one's confidence is put; an object of trust 1526. **2.** Confident expectation of something; hope. late ME. **3.** = CREDIT *sb.* 9 a. Chiefly in phrases *on, upon t.* 1573. **4.** The quality of being trustworthy; fidelity; loyalty, trustiness. Now *rare.* 1470. **5. a.** The condition of having confidence reposed in one, or of being entrusted *with* something 1548. **b.** The obligation or responsibility imposed on one in whom confidence is placed or authority is vested, or who has given an undertaking of fidelity 1535. **c.** The condition of that which is entrusted to some one. Only in phr. *in t.* late ME. **d.** (with *pl.*) A duty or office, also a thing or person, entrusted to one 1643. **6.** *Law.* The confidence reposed in a person in whom the legal ownership of property is vested to hold or use for the benefit of another; hence, an estate committed to the charge of trustees; also *transf.* a trustee; a body of persons appointed as trustees 1442. **7.** *Commerce.* A body of producers or traders in some class of business, organized to reduce or defeat competition, lessen expenses, and control production and distribution for their common advantage; *spec.* such a combination of companies, with a central governing body of trustees which holds a majority or the whole of the stock of each of the combining firms, thus controlling each 1887.

1. To see and know and feel that our t. was not vain 1729. Phr. *To take on* or *upon t.*, to accept without investigation or evidence. **2.** His t. was with th' Eternal to be deem'd Equal in strength MILT. **3.** My master lived on t. at an ale-house JOHNSON. **5. a.** As we were allowed of God to bee put in t. with the Gospel 1 *Thess.* 2:4. **b.** A breach of t. 1907. **c.** A gift to a college, in t. for another charitable object 1827. **7.** A distiller's 'trust' 1887. A t. is defined..as a combination to destroy competition and to restrain trade G. B. SHAW.

Comb.: **t.-certificate** (in full *t.-share certificate*) a negotiable certificate issued by the controlling board of a t. (sense 7), which entitles the holder to all dividends declared upon the surrendered shares which it represents, but gives him no voting power; **t. company,** a company formed (orig. in *U.S.*) for the purpose of exercising the functions of a trustee, with which other financial activities were later combined; **t. deed,** a deed of conveyance by which a t. (sense 6) is created, and its conditions set out; **t. house,** a public house or hotel owned and managed by a trust company, instead of by brewers or private individuals; **-investment,** the investment of t.-money; also trustee stock.

†**Trust,** *a.* [Early ME. *trust, trost* – ON. *traustr.*] **1.** Confident, safe, secure. –late ME. **2.** Faithful, trusty; reliable –1440.

Trust (trɒst), *v.* [ME. *traiste* (XIII) – ON. *treÿsta*, assim. to TRUST *a.* and *sb.*] **1.** *intr.* To have faith or confidence; to place reliance; to confide. Const. *in, to* (†*of, on, upon*). **2.** *trans.* To have faith or confidence in; to rely or depend upon. late ME. **b.** Imperative, used sarcastically or ironically to express one's assurance that a person will or will not do something. *colloq.* 1834. **3.** To have faith or confidence *that* something desired is, or will be, the case; also const. with *infin.* or *for*; to hope 1482. **4.** To give credence to (a statement); to rely upon the veracity or evidence of (a person, etc.). late ME. **5.** To commit the safety of (something) with confidence *to* a place, etc., *to* or *with* a person; to entrust; to place or allow (a person or thing) to be *in* a place or condition, or *to do* some action, with expectation of safety, or without fear of the consequences ME. **6.** To invest *with* a charge; to confide or entrust something to the care or disposal of 1548. **7.** To give (a person) credit *for* goods supplied; †to supply *with* goods on credit 1530.

1. Each had to t. to himself TYNDALL. **2.** I cannot t. other people, without perpetual looking after them RUSKIN. **b.** T. a religious old maid for scenting out love! 1902. **3.** I t. that these things are wholly repugnant to my nature BURKE. **4.** T. me I am vnused to these deuices 1586. **5.** My ventures are not in one bottome trusted SHAKS. He trusted the event to valour and to fortune GIBBON. **6.** I will rather t. a Fleming with my butter..then my wife with her selfe SHAKS. **7.** Without money the stubborn townspeople will not t. them for the worth of a penny CROMWELL. Hence **Tru·sting** *ppl. a.* that trusts; **-ly** *adv.*, **-ness.**

Trustee (trɒsti·), *sb.* 1647. [f. TRUST *v.* + -EE¹.] **1.** One who is trusted, or to whom something is entrusted (*rare*). *Obs.* or merged in 3. **2.** *Law. spec.* One to whom property is entrusted to be administered for the benefit of another; often *loosely*, one of a number of persons appointed to manage the affairs of an institution 1653. **b.** In *U.S.* by extension, One in whose hands the property of a debtor is attached in a *t. process* 1794. **3.** *transf.* One who is held responsible for the preservation and administration of anything 1655.

Comb.: **t. process,** in *U.S.*, a judicial process by which the goods, effects, and credits (but not the real estate) of a debtor may be attached while in the hands of a third person; in Eng. Law called *foreign attachment*; **t. security, t. stock,** a high-class stock in which trust-funds are or may legally be invested.

Trustee (trɒstī·), *v.* 1818. [f. prec.] **1. a.** *trans.* To place (a person or his property) in the hands of a trustee or trustees. **b.** *intr.* To act as a trustee. **2.** *U.S.* **a.** To appoint (a person) trustee in the *trustee process* (see prec.), in order to restrain a debtor from collecting moneys due to him. **b.** To attach (effects of a debtor) in the hands of a third person. 1883.

Trusteeship (trɒstī·ʃip). 1730. [f. TRUSTEE + -SHIP.] The office or function of a trustee; also, a body of trustees.

Truster (trɒ·stəɹ). 1537. [f. TRUST *v.* + -ER[1].] One who trusts, confides, or relies; one who believes or credits; one who gives credit, a creditor.

Trustful (trɒ·stfŭl), *a.* 1580. [f. TRUST *sb.* + -FUL.] †**1.** Trustworthy, trusty, faithful –1674. **2.** Full of or exercising trust; trusting, confiding 1832. Hence **Tru·stful-ly** *adv.*, **-ness.**

Trustify (trɒ·stifəi), *v.* 1902. *Commerce.* [f. TRUST *sb.* + -FY.] *trans.* To convert into a trust. Hence **Tru:stifica·tion.**

Trustless (trɒ·stlės), *a.* 1530. [f. TRUST *sb.* + -LESS.] **1.** Not to be trusted; unreliable, treacherous, untrustworthy. **2.** Having no trust or confidence; unbelieving, distrustful 1598. Hence **Tru·stlessness.**

Trustworthy (trɒ·stˌwɒ̄:ɹði), *a.* 1808. [f. TRUST *sb.* + WORTHY *a.*] Worthy of trust; reliable. Hence **Tru·stwo:rthily** *adv.* **Tru·stwo:rthiness.**

Trusty (trɒ·sti), *a.* (*sb.*) ME. [f. TRUST *sb.* + -Y[1].] **1.** Characterized by trust; having faith, confidence, or assurance; trustful, confident. Now *rare.* **2.** Characterized by faithfulness or reliability; that may be relied upon; trustworthy. (Privy Councillors are in letters addressed by the sovereign as Right t. and well-beloved.) ME. **b.** *transf.* and *fig.* of things 1596.

2. Our right t. and welbeloved George baron Keith 1803. **b.** His trustie sword, the servant of his might SPENSER.

B. *sb.* One who (or that which) is trusty; *spec.* in *U.S.*, a well-conducted convict to whom special privileges are granted 1573. Hence **Tru·stily** *adv.* **Tru·stiness.**

Truth (trūþ). [OE. *triewþ*, *trēowþ*, corresp. to OHG. *triuwida*, ON. (pl.) *trygðir* plighted faith; f. TRUE; see -TH[1] and cf. TROTH.] **I.** The quality of being true (and allied senses). **1.** The character of being, or disposition to be, true to a person, principle, cause, etc.; fidelity, loyalty, constancy, steadfast allegiance. Now *rare* or *arch.* †**2.** = TROTH 2. –1650. **3.** Disposition to speak or act truly or without deceit; truthfulness, veracity, sincerity; formerly sometimes in wider sense: Honesty, uprightness, righteousness, virtue, integrity ME.

1. Alas! they had been friends in youth: But whispering tongues can poison t. COLERIDGE. **3.** Loue is all t., lust full of forged lies SHAKS.

II. 1. Conformity with fact; agreement with reality; accuracy, correctness (of statement or thought) 1570. **b.** Agreement with the thing represented, in art or literature; the quality of being 'true to life'. Also, in *Arch.*, absence of deceit, pretence, or counterfeit, e.g. of imitation of stone in paint or plaster 1828. **2.** Agreement with a standard or rule; accuracy, correctness; *spec.* accuracy of position or adjustment; often in phr. *out of t.* 1669. **3.** Genuineness, reality, actual existence 1599.

1. There is some t. in what you say 1849. **2.** Otherwise the door, when put together, will be out of t. 1825. **3.** On to dawn, when dreams Begin to feel the t. and stir of day TENNYSON.

III. Something that is true. **1.** True statement or account; that which is in accordance with the fact. late ME. **b.** *loosely.* Mental apprehension of truth; knowledge 1644. **2.** True religious belief or doctrine; orthodoxy. Often with *the*, esp. in Quaker language. late ME. **b.** Conduct in accordance with the divine standard. late ME. **3.** That which is true (in a general or abstract sense); reality; *spec.* in religious use, spiritual reality as the subject of revelation or object of faith. late ME. **b.** Personified; *spec.* each of the two goddesses of truth in ancient Egyptian mythology. late ME. **4.** The fact or facts; the actual state of the case; the matter or circumstance as it really is ME. **b.** The real thing, as dist. from an imitation; the genuine article; the reality corresponding to a type or symbol, the antitype. Now *rare* or *Obs.* 1531. **5.** With *a* and *pl.* A true statement or proposition; a point of true belief, a true doctrine; a fixed or established principle; a verified fact; a reality. late ME.

1. The t. you speake doth lacke some gentlenesse SHAKS. T. is always strange; Stranger than fiction BYRON. Phr. *To say, speak,* or *tell the t.* (also *arch.* without *the*), to speak truly, to report the matter as it really is. Prov. *Tell* (*speak*) *the t. and shame the devil*: see SHAME *v.* **2.** Them who kept thy t. so pure of old When all our Fathers worship't Stocks and Stones MILT. The Friend was declaring the T., when the Priest..came in 1710. **b.** He that doth the trueth commeth to the light TINDALE *John* 3:21. **3.** T. has no greater enemy than its unwise defenders 1855. **b.** So T. be in the field, we do injuriously by licencing and prohibiting to misdoubt her strength MILT. **4.** We judge the Distances to be less than the T. 1748. **5.** Leave your friend to learn unpleasant truths from his enemies 1858.

Phrases. *In t., of a t.* (arch.), in fact, as a fact; really, indeed: mostly used to strengthen or emphasize a statement. *Truth!* either as an expression of assent, or as intensive (= *in t.*). *arch.* Hence **Tru·thless** *a.* destitute of t.; faithless (*obs.* or *arch.*); untrue, false, mendacious. **Tru·thy** *a.* (*rare* or *dial.*) truthful, true.

Truthful (trū·þfŭl), *a.* 1596. [f. TRUTH *sb.* + -FUL.] **1.** Of statements, etc.: Full of truth; sincere. (Now only as *transf.* from 2.) **2.** Of persons (or their attributes): Disposed to tell, or habitually telling, the truth; veracious. Also *fig.*: Not deceptive. 1787. **3.** Of ideas, artistic representation, etc. Characterized by truth; corresponding with fact or reality; true, accurate, exact 1859.

2. A singularly t. person 1866. **3.** A..t. portrait 1871. Hence **Tru·thful-ly** *adv.*, **-ness.**

Try (trəi), *sb.* 1475. [f. TRY *v.*] **1.** An act of trying; an experiment (*rare*), attempt, effort (chiefly *colloq.*); †a trial, test 1556. **b.** *Rugby Football.* The right of attempting to kick a goal, obtained by carrying the ball behind the opponent's goal-line and touching it on the ground; the points scored when the try is not 'converted' into a goal 1845. †**2.** A sieve or sifting screen –1804.

1. Then this breaking of his, Ha's beene but a T. for his Friends? SHAKS. I should have had a t. at it 1832. †*At try*: see A-TRY.

†**Try, trie,** *a.* [ME. *trie*, prob. = OFr. *trié*, pa. pple. of *trier* (see TRY *v.*), or – OFr. *trie* sb. choice, 'élite', used attrib.] **1.** Choice, excellent, good –1596. **2.** *Joinery.* Quite true, correctly wrought –1678.

1. Those hands of gold..those feete of silver trye SPENSER.

Try (trəi), *v.* Pa. t. and pple. **tried.** ME. [– OFr. *trier* sift, pick out = Pr., Cat. *triar*, a Gallo-Rom. vb. of unkn. (perh. Gaulish) origin.] **1.** *trans.* To separate (one thing) from another or others; to set apart; to distinguish. Often with *out. Obs.* or *arch.* †**2.** To separate the good part of a thing from the rest, esp. by sifting or straining; hence, to sift or strain. Usu. with *out.* –1790. †**3.** *spec.* To separate (metal) from the ore or dross by melting; to refine, purify by fire; also, to remove (the dross or impurity) from metal by fire. Usu. with *out.* –1686. **4.** To extract (oil) from blubber or fat by heat; to melt down (blubber, etc.) to obtain the oil; to render; also, to extract (wax) from a honeycomb. Usu. with *out.* 1582. †**5.** To ascertain, find *out* (something doubtful, obscure, or secret) by search or examination –1761. **b.** To ascertain the truth or right of (a matter, a quarrel, etc.) by test or endeavour; with *out,* to thrash or fight out; to determine 1542. **6.** *Law.* To examine and determine (a cause or question) judicially; to determine the guilt or otherwise of (an accused person) by consideration of the evidence; to judge. Also *fig.* ME. **7.** To put to the proof, test, prove. late ME. **8.** *Joinery.* To bring (a piece of timber) to a perfectly flat surface by repeatedly testing it and planing off the projecting parts; to plane with the trying-plane; also, to test the straightness or correspondence of (a planed surface, adjoining surfaces); also *intr.* (of a surface) to prove accurate or straight when tested 1593. **9.** *T. on*: to test the fit or style of (a garment) by putting it on. Also *absol.* 1693. **10.** To subject to a severe test or strain; to put to straits, afflict 1539. **11.** To test the effect or operation of; to experiment with 1545. **b.** To experiment upon (*with* something); to test the effect of something upon 1784. **12.** To endeavour to ascertain by experiment or effort; to attempt to find out; sometimes nearly = sense 11. 1573. **13.** To show or find to be so by test or experience. Now *rare* or *Obs.* late ME. †**14.** To undergo, go through –1738. **15.** To test one's ability to deal with (something); to venture upon, to essay. *To t. over*, to go through (a performance, etc.) experimentally. ME. **16.** *intr.* To make an effort, endeavour, attempt. (With *inf.* or *absol.*) 1638. **b.** Followed by *and* and a co-ordinated verb (instead of *to* with inf.) expressing the action attempted. *colloq.* 1686. **c.** *intr.* and *trans.* To search a place in order to find something, esp. game, or its scent. *colloq.* 1810. †**17.** *Naut. intr.* Of a vessel: To lie to –1867.

3. I..will..trye them, like as golde is tryed COVERDALE *Zech.* 13:9. **5. b.** He was enforced by them to t. it out in battel with them 1654. **c.** *To t. out* (orig. *U.S.*), to test the possibilities, etc. (of a thing); to test (a person). **7.** The friends thou hast, and their adoption tride, Grapple them to thy Soule, with hoopes of Steele SHAKS. *To t. a door, window,* etc., to ascertain by attempting to open it whether it is fastened or locked. **11.** *To t. an experiment*, to make an experiment; to do something in order to see what will come of it, or whether it produces the expected result. *To t.* (*one's*) *hand*, to attempt to do something for the first time; to test one's ability or aptitude *at* something. **c.** To test the effect of (a thing) *on* (a person, thing, etc.). *To t. it on the dog*: to experiment so that any harm will fall only upon an inferior person or thing; to test (a theatrical production) by provincial performance (orig. *U.S.*). **12.** *Tam. Shr.* I. ii. 17. They think they are *trying their luck*, as the phrase is 1838. **13.** He hath still beene tried a holy man SHAKS. **15.** Phr. *T. it on*, (*slang*) to attempt an imposition; *spec.* in *Thieves' Cant*, to live by thieving; also, to attempt something knowing that one is likely to be unsuccessful. **16.** You will have to t. and t. again 1847. *T. for*, to attempt to obtain or find (an object), or to reach (a place). *T. at*, to make an attempt upon; to attempt to do or accomplish. **c.** Phr. *T. back* (intr.), to go back (*lit.* or *fig.*) so as to cover ground afresh where something has previously been missed.

Try-, the vb.-stem in comb., as in **t.-cock,** = gauge-cock; **-pit,** a testing pit for trying new engines; **-square,** a carpenter's square for laying off short perpendiculars; also with advs. as **t.-on,** (*a*) (*slang*) an attempt, *esp.* an attempt at imposition or deceit; also *transf.* the subject of an attempt; (*b*) the act of trying on a garment; **-out,** a selective trial (*U.S. slang* or *colloq.*); also, a test of efficiency, fitness, etc.

‖**Trygon** (trəi·gɒn). 1749. [L. – Gr. τρυγών dove, also the fish.] A fish with a sharp spine in its tail, a sting-ray.

Trying (trəi·iŋ), *vbl. sb.* 1440. [f. TRY *v.* + -ING[1].] The action of TRY *v.*

attrib.: **t.-plane,** a long heavy plane used after the jack-plane for the accurate squaring of timber.

Trying (trəi·iŋ), *ppl. a.* 1577. [f. TRY *v.* + -ING[2].] That tries. **1.** That tests severely; that is a trial; that tries one's endurance or patience 1718. **2.** Attempting, endeavouring (*rare*) 1577.

1. The month of May is..a 't.' month HONE. Hence **Try·ing-ly** *adv.*, **-ness.**

‖**Tryma** (trəi·mă). 1857. [mod.L. (Necker), – Gr. τρῦμα or τρύμη hole, f. τρύειν rub down, wear out.] *Bot.* A fruit resembling a drupe, but formed from an originally compound ovary, and having an ultimately dehiscent fleshy or fibrous exocarp, as the walnut and coco-nut.

||**Trypanosoma** (triːpănoˌsōᵘ·mă). 1880. [mod.L., f. Gr. τρύπανον borer + σῶμα body.] *Zool.* A genus of flagellate infusorian protozoa, species of which are parasitic in the blood of man and other animals, causing specific diseases, such as sleeping-sickness; an infusorian of this genus.

Trypsin (tri·psin). 1876. [perh. for *tripsin, f. Gr. τρῖψις rubbing, f. τρίβειν rub; so named because first obtained by rubbing down the pancreas with glycerin; see -IN[1].] *Physiol. Chem.* The chief digestive ferment of the pancreatic juice, which converts proteins into peptones. Hence **Trypsi·nogen** (-dʒən) [-GEN 1], a granular substance occurring in the pancreas, from which t. is formed.

Tryptic (tri·ptik), *a.* 1888. [f. prec. after *pepsin, peptic.*] Pertaining to or of the nature of trypsin. So **Tryptone** (tri·ptoᵘn) a peptone formed by the action of trypsin upon a protein.

Trysail (trəi·sēⁱl, trəi·s'l). 1769. [f. TRY *sb.* + SAIL.] *Naut.* A small fore-and-aft sail, set with a gaff, and sometimes with a boom, on the fore- or mainmast, or on a small supplementary mast abaft either of these.

Tryst (trist, trəist), *sb.* Chiefly *Sc.* bef. 19th c. late ME. [spec. use of †*trist* (var. of TRUST *sb.*), at first prob. extension of the sense 'appointed station in hunting', var. of †*tristre* – OFr. *triste, tristre* (cf. AL. *trista, tristra,* perh. – ME. *trist*); see TRUST *sb.*] **1.** A mutual appointment, agreement, covenant. Now *rare* or *Obs.* exc. as in 2. **2.** *spec.* An appointment or engagement to meet at a specified time and place. late ME. **3.** = RENDEZVOUS 4. late ME.

2. Phr. *To make t.*; *to hold, keep t.*; *to break t. To bide t.*, to wait at the appointed place for the person with whom the appointment is made; 'You walk late, sir', said I...'I byde tryste', was the reply. SCOTT.

Tryst (trist, trəist), *v.* orig. and chiefly *Sc.* late ME. [f. prec.] **1.** *intr.* To make an agreement *to do* something, *with* a person; *esp.* to fix time and place of meeting *with* some one. **2.** *trans.* To engage (a person) to meet one at a given time and place; to appoint or agree to meet 1643. **3.** *intr.* To keep tryst; to meet at the appointed time and place 1842. Hence **Try·ster. Try·sting** *vbl. sb., attrib.* in *t. day,* etc.

Tsar (tsāɹ, zāɹ). 1670. [Russ.] See CZAR.

Tsetse (tse·tsi). 1849. [Tswana (language of Bechuanaland).] In full *t.-fly*: A dipterous insect (*Glossina morsitans,* of the family *Tabanidæ*), abundant in parts of tropical and southern Africa; its bite is often fatal to horses and other domestic animals. Also applied to other species of *Glossina.*

T square: see T 3 b.

||**Tuan**[1] (tū·ăn). 1846. Australian name for the Flying Squirrel.

||**Tuan**[2] (tuā·n). 1895. [Malay, 'lord, master'.] Respectful form of address; 'Sir'.

||**Tuatara** (tūatā·ra). 1890. [Maori, f. *tua* on the back + *tara* spine.] A large lizard, *Sphenodon punctatum,* having a dorsal row of yellow spines; formerly common in N. Zealand.

||**Tuath** (tū·ăh). *Irish Hist.* 1873. [Ir. *tūath* people.] A 'tribe' or 'people' in Ireland; hence, the territory occupied by a tuath.

Tub (tɒb), *sb.* late ME. [prob. – LDu. (cf. MLG., MDu. *tubbe,* also MFlem., Du. *tobbe*); of unkn. origin. In AL. *tubba, tobba.*] **1.** An open wooden vessel, wide in proportion to its height, usu. formed of staves and hoops, of cylindrical or slightly concave form, with a flat bottom. †**b.** A sweating-tub formerly used in the treatment of venereal disease; hence, the use of this –1688. **2.** A bathing-tub, bath-tub (of any shape); *colloq.* or *joc.* a bath; hence, the action or practice of taking a bath, esp. on rising 1849. **3.** Applied to a slow clumsy ship, esp. one which is too broad in proportion to its length; often *joc.* or *contempt.*; also, a short, broad boat; *spec.* a stout roomy boat used for rowing practice, as dist. from a racing-boat 1618. **4.** Applied *contempt.* or *joc.* to a pulpit, esp. of a nonconformist preacher 1643. **5.** *Coal-mining.* Orig. a mining bucket, now specially applied to the open-topped box of wood or iron, mounted on wheels, in which coal is brought from the face to the surface 1851. **b.** The lining of a pit-shaft 1839.

1. b. *Meas. for M.* III. ii. 60.

Provb. phrases. †*A tale of a t.*, an apocryphal tale; a 'cock and bull' story. (*To throw out*) *a t. to the whale,* to create a diversion, esp. in order to escape a threatened danger. *Every t. must stand on its own bottom*: cf. BOTTOM *sb.* 9.

attrib. and *Comb.*: **t.-butter,** butter packed in tubs for keeping or export; †**-fast,** abstinence during treatment in the sweating-tub; **-frock,** a dress of washing material; **-gig,** (*a*) a governess car; (*b*) = **t.-pair,** a pair-oared practice boat; **-wheel,** (*a*) the wheel of a colliery 'tub'; (*b*) a horizontal water-wheel with spiral floats.

Tub (tɒb), *v.* 1610. [f. prec.] **1.** *trans.* To bathe or wash in a tub or bath. *colloq.* **b.** *intr.* To wash oneself in a tub or bath; to take a tub or bath, esp. on rising. *colloq.* 1867. **2.** *trans.* To line (a pit-shaft) with a watertight casing of timber, masonry, or iron; to dam *back* (water) in a shaft or tunnel in this way; to shut *off* (watery strata or seams) from the shaft with tubbing 1812. **3.** To put or pack in a tub; to plant in a tub 1828. **4.** *trans.* and *intr.* To coach (oarsmen) in a 'tub'; to practise rowing in a 'tub'. *Rowing slang.* 1882.

1. b. Gentlemen who didn't t. of a morning 1867. **4.** An hour and a half was then spent in tubbing the men 1883.

||**Tuba**[1] (tiū·bă). 1852. [It. – L. *tuba.*] **1.** (*pl.* **tubæ.**) The straight bronze war-trumpet of the ancient Romans 1882. **2.** *Mus.* (*pl.* **tubas.**) A bass wind-instrument of the sax-horn family; a sax-tuba or bombardon; also, one who plays this instrument 1852. **b.** An 8-foot high-pressure reed-stop in an organ 1876.

||**Tuba**[2] (tū·ba). 1817. [Arab. *ṭūbā.*] A mythical tree growing in the Moslem paradise.

Tubal (tiū·băl), *a.* 1735. [– mod.L. *tubalis,* f. L. *tubus* TUBE; see -AL[1] 1. Later, f. TUBE + -AL[1] 1.] **1.** Of, pertaining to, or of the nature of a tube; consisting of tubes; tubular (*rare*). **2.** *Anat.* and *Path.* Pertaining to, occurring in, or affecting the Fallopian tube, as *t. dropsy,* the bronchial tubes, as *t. cough,* or the renal tubules, as *t. nephritis* 1822.

Tubbing (tɒ·biŋ), *vbl. sb.* 1657. [f. TUB *v.* (or *sb.*) + -ING[1].] **1.** The action of TUB *v.* **2.** The lining of a pit-shaft or tunnel with a watertight casing; *concr.* the casing of timber, masonry, or metal sections used for this 1839. **3.** Rowing or training in a 'tub' 1884.

Tubby (tɒ·bi), *a.* 1806. [f. TUB *sb.* + -Y[1].] **1.** Tub-shaped, tub-like; of rounded outline, and stout or broad in proportion to the length; of a person, corpulent 1835. **2.** Sounding like a tub when struck; dull or wooden in sound. (Said of stringed instruments.) 1806. Hence **Tu·bbiness.**

Tube (tiūb), *sb.* 1651. [– Fr. *tube* or L. *tubus,* rel. to TUBA[1].] **I. 1.** A hollow body, usu. cylindrical, and long in proportion to its diameter, of wood, metal, glass, etc., used to convey or contain a liquid, or for other purposes; a pipe 1658. **b.** = TUBING, material of a tubular form 1823. **2.** In specific applications usu. indicated by context; *esp.* = TEST-TUBE 1800. **3.** An optical instrument of tubular form, *esp.* a telescope; more fully *optic t.* Now *arch.* 1651. †**4.** A cannon; also, a rifle or hand-gun. *poet.* –1816. **b.** A small pipe introduced through the vent, formerly used in firing cannon; a *friction-t., quill-t.*, or *priming-t.* 1797. **c.** The inner cylinder of a built-up gun, upon which the outer case is shrunk 1895. **5.** A musical wind-instrument, a pipe. *poet. rare.* 1820. **6. a.** A pneumatic dispatch-tube 1860. **b.** The cylindrical tunnel in which an underground electric railway runs; also short for *t.-railway* (*colloq.*) 1900. **7.** *Physics.* A tubular figure conceived as being formed by lines of force or action passing through every point of a closed curve 1878.

2. Collapsible tin tubes for artists' colours 1877. Owing to the depth of the wound two drainage tubes were introduced 1902. *Wireless* (*U.S.*) A valve. **6. b.** *Twopenny T.*: see TWOPENNY.

II. 1. *Anat.* and *Zool.* A hollow cylindrical vessel or organ in the animal body; a canal, duct, passage, or pipe; often preceded by a defining word, as *Eustachian, Fallopian, intestinal t.*, etc.; see the qualifying words 1661. **b.** One of the siphons of a mollusc 1839. **2.** A hollow cylindrical channel in a plant; *spec.* in *Bot.* the lower united portion of a gamopetalous corolla or gamosepalous calyx; also, a united circle of stamens 1704. **3.** Applied to other tubular or cylindrical objects or formations of natural origin 1831.

Comb.: **t.-case,** in a steam-engine, the chamber containing the tubes of a surface-condenser; **-colour,** paint packed in a collapsible t.; **-condenser,** in a steam-engine, a condenser in which the cooling surface consists of tubes; **-coral,** organ-pipe coral, or its polyp; **-culture,** culture of a microbe in a test-t.; **-foot,** one of the numerous ambulacral tubes of an echinoderm; **-medusa,** a siphonophore; **-nosed** *a.*, tubinarial; **-plate,** the plate in which the ends of the boiler-tubes are set; **-shell,** a bivalve mollusc of the family *Tubicolæ* or *Gastrochænidæ,* distinguished by having a shelly t. enclosing the siphons, in addition to the ordinary valves of the shell; **-spinner, -weaver,** a spider which spins a tubular nest or lair; **-worm,** a tubicolous worm; a pipe-worm; **-wrench,** a wrench for gripping pipes or tubes.

Tube, *v.* 1828. [f. prec.; cf. Fr. *tuber.*] **1.** *trans.* To furnish or fit with a tube or tubes; to insert a tube in. **2.** To pass through or enclose in a tube 1863. **3.** *intr.* To travel by tube railway; also, *to t. it* (*colloq.*) 1902. Hence **Tubed** *ppl. a. spec.* of a horse: having a tube introduced into the throat to enable it to breathe easily.

Tuber (tiū·bəɹ). 1668. [– L. *tuber* hump, swelling.] **1.** *Bot.* An underground structure consisting of a solid thickened rounded outgrowth of a stem or rhizome, bearing 'eyes' or buds from which new plants may arise; a familiar example is the potato. Also applied to other underground structures resembling this but of different origin. ||**b.** A genus of underground discomycetous fungi, comprising the truffles 1704. **2. a.** *Path.* A morbid swelling, as of a gland, etc. 1706. **b.** *Anat.* A tuberosity 1741. **3.** *gen.* A protuberance (*rare*) 1888.

Tubercle (tiū·bəɹk'l). 1578. [– L. *tuberculum,* dim. of *tuber* TUBER; see -CULE.] **1.** *Anat.* and *Zool.* A small rounded projection or protuberance, as on a bone, or on the surface of the body in various animals. **2.** *Path.* A small firm rounded swelling or nodule on the surface of the body or in a part or organ; *spec.* a mass of granulation-cells characteristic of *tuberculosis*; *transf.* tuberculosis 1661. **3.** *Bot.* **a.** A small tuber, or a root-growth resembling a tuber, as in many orchids. **b.** A small wart-like swelling or protuberance on a plant. 1727.

Comb.: **t. bacillus,** the species of bacillus which causes tuberculosis. Hence **Tubercled** (tiū·bəɹk'ld) *a. Nat. Hist.* and *Path.* furnished or affected with tubercules; tuberculate.

Tubercular (tiubə̄·ɹkiŭlăɹ), *a.* 1799. [f. L. *tuberculum* TUBERCLE + -AR[1].] **1.** *Nat. Hist.*, etc. **a.** Of the nature or form of a tubercle; consisting of or constituting a tubercle. **b.** Having or covered with tubercles, tuberculate. 1817. **2.** *Path.* Of, pertaining to, caused or characterized by, or affected with tubercles 1799. **b.** *spec.* In ref. to tuberculosis or the tubercle-bacillus; now techn. replaced by TUBERCULOUS 1799. Hence **Tube·rcularize** *v. trans.* to make t.; to infect with tubercles, *spec.* with tuberculosis. **Tubeːrculariza·tion.**

Tuberculate (tiubə̄·ɹkiŭlĕt), *a.* 1785. [f. as prec. + -ATE[2].] *Nat. Hist.* and *Path.* Furnished or affected with tubercles; tubercled. So **Tube·rculated** *a.* 1771.

Tuberculation (tiubə̄ɹkiŭlēⁱ·ʃən). 1835. [f. L. *tuberculum* TUBERCLE + -ATION.] **1.** *Nat. Hist.* Formation of tubercles; *concr.* a growth or set of tubercles. **2.** *Path.* Formation of tubercles as a sympton of disease; tubercular or tuberculous affection 1861.

Tubercule (tiū·bəɹkiul). 1678. [– Fr. *tubercule* (Paré) – L. *tuberculum* TUBERCLE; see -CULE.] = TUBERCLE.

Tuberculin (tiubə̄·ɹkiŭlin), *a.* 1891. [f. L. *tuberculum* TUBERCLE + -IN[1].] *Med.* A liquid prepared from cultures of tubercle-bacillus, used by hypodermic injection as a remedy, or (now esp.) as a test, for tuberculosis.

Tuberculize (tiubɔ̄·ɹkiŭləiz), *v.* 1847. [f. as prec. + -IZE.] *trans.* and *intr.* To affect or infect with tubercle or tuberculosis; to become tuberculous. Hence **Tube:rculiza·tion** 1843.

Tuberculo- (tiubɔ̄·ɹkiŭlo), comb. form of L. *tuberculum* TUBERCLE, prop. used advb.; also attrib. or objectively, in several technical terms, chiefly of pathology and medicine: **Tube:rculo-fi·broid** *a.*, 'characterized by tubercle that has undergone a fibroid degeneration'. **Tube:rculopho·bia,** morbid dread of tuberculosis.

Tuberculose (tiubɔ̄·ɹkiŭlōᵘs), *a.* 1752. [f. L. *tuberculum* TUBERCLE + -OSE¹.] = TUBERCULATE.

‖**Tuberculosis** (tiubɔ̄ɹkiŭlōᵘ·sis). 1860. [mod.L., f. L. *tuberculum* TUBERCLE; see -OSIS.] *Path.* orig. Any disease characterized by the formation of tubercles; now *spec.* restricted to disease caused by the tubercle bacillus in any of the bodily tissues; examples are pulmonary consumption or phthisis (t. of the lungs), and scrofula (t. of the lymphatic glands).

Tuberculous (tiubɔ̄·ɹkiŭləs), *a.* 1747. [f. as prec. + -OUS.] **1.** *Path.* Pertaining to or produced by tubercles; consisting or of the nature of tubercles; affected with tubercles. **b.** Since the discovery of the tubercle bacillus in 1882, usu. *spec.* in ref. to the tubercle bacillus or to tuberculosis, and thus techn. dist. from *tubercular* in the general sense 1891. **2.** *Nat. Hist.* Full of or covered with tubercles; tuberculate, tubercular. (Now disused.) 1828.

Tuberiferous (tiŭbəri·fĕrəs), *a.* 1846. [f. L. *tuber* TUBER + -FEROUS.] *Bot.* Producing or bearing tubers.

Tuberiform (tiŭ·bərifǭːɹm), *a.* 1822. [f. as prec. + -FORM.] *Nat. Hist.* and *Path.* Having the form of a tuber; also characterized, as a disease, by growths of this form.

Tuberose (tiŭ·bərōᵘs, often *erron.* tiŭ·bɪrōᵘz), *sb.* 1664. [– L. *tuberosa*, specific name of the plant, fem. of *tuberosus* (see next); corrupted by pop. etym. into a disyllable, as if f. *tube* + *rose*.] A liliaceous plant, *Polianthes tuberosa*, with creamy white, funnel-shaped, very fragrant flowers, and a tuberous root.

Tuberose (tiŭ·bərōᵘs), *a.* 1704. [– L. *tuberosus*, f. *tuber* TUBER; see -OSE¹.] = TUBEROUS.

Tuberosity (tiŭbərǫ·sĭti). 1541. [– Fr. *tubérosité* (Paré) – med.L. *tuberositas*, f. L. *tuberosus*; see prec., -OSITY.] **1.** The quality or condition of being tuberous; bulging; gibbosity. Now *rare* or *Obs.* **2.** *concr.* A tuberous formation or part; a swelling, protuberance 1611.

Tuberous (tiŭ·bərəs), *a.* 1650. [– Fr. *tubéreux* or L. *tuberosus*, f. *tuber* TUBER; see -OUS.] **1.** *Anat.*, *Zool.*, etc. Of the form of, or constituting, a tuber or rounded projection; covered with such projections; knobbed, knobby. Now *rare.* **2.** *Path.* Affected with tubers or morbid swellings; of the nature of such a swelling; characterized, as a disease, by such swellings 1656. **3.** *Bot.* **a.** Of the nature of a tuber 1668. **b.** Of a plant: Producing or bearing tubers 1664. Hence **Tu·berous-ly** *adv.*, **-ness.**

Tubful (tɒ·bful). 1788. [f. TUB *sb.* + -FUL.] As much as a tub will hold.

Tubi- (tiŭbi), comb. form of L. *tubus* TUBE; as in **Tubicolar** (tiubi·kŏlăɹ), **Tubicolous** (tiubi·kŏləs) *adjs.* [mod.L. *tubicola*, f. *colere* cultivate, inhabit], inhabiting a tube; applied to annelids and rotifers that secrete tubular cases, spiders that spin tubular webs, and molluscs with shelly tubes; so **Tubicole** (tiŭ·bikōᵘl) *a.* = prec.; *sb.* a tubicolar annelid or mollusc. **Tu·bicorn** [L. *cornu* horn], *sb.* a hollow-horned ruminant; *adj.* hollow-horned, as a ruminant; also **Tubico·rnous** *a.* **Tu·biform,** *a.* having the form of a tube; tube-shaped, tubular. **Tubinarial** (-nēᵊ·riăl), **Tubinarine** (-nēᵊ·rəin) [L. *naris* nostril], *adjs.* belonging to the order *Tubinares* of water-birds, comprising the albatrosses and petrels, having nostrils of tubular form. **Tu·bipore** (-pōᵊɹ), *sb.* a member of the genus *Tubipora*, family *Tubiporidæ*, or order *Tubiporaceæ*, of alcyonarians (the organ-pipe corals), in which each polyp has a tubular corallet opening by a pore; *adj.* belonging to or having the characters of this genus, family, or order; so **Tubi·porite** [-ITE¹ 2 a], a fossil tubipore. **Tu·bivalve,** *sb.* a bivalve mollusc having a shelly tube in addition to the valves of the shell; a tube-shell; *adj.* having such a tube.

Tubing (tiŭ·biŋ), *vbl. sb.* 1845. [f. TUBE *v.* or *sb.* + -ING¹.] The action of furnishing with a tube or tubes; also *concr.* tubes collectively, or as a material; a length or piece of tube.

Tubman, tub-man (tɒ·bmæn). 1642. [f. TUB *sb.* + MAN *sb.*] †**1.** = TUB-PREACHER –1651. **2.** A barrister in the Court of Exchequer whose place was beside the tub used as a measure of capacity in excise cases; the position conferred the right of precedence in motions, except over the 'postman' and in Crown business. *Obs.* exc. *Hist.* 1768.

Tubo- (tiŭbo), used in certain cases as comb. form of L. *tubus* TUBE, instead of TUBI-.

Tu·b-prea:cher. *contempt.* 1643. [See TUB *sb.* 4.] One who preaches from a 'tub'; a dissenting preacher or minister.

Tu·b-thu:mper. *contempt.* 1662. [TUB *sb.* 4.] A speaker or preacher who for emphasis thumps the pulpit; a violent or declamatory preacher or orator; a ranter.

Tubular (tiŭ·biŭlăɹ), *a.* 1673. [f. L. *tubulus* small tube + -AR¹.] **1.** Tube-shaped; constituting or consisting of a tube; cylindrical, hollow, and open at one or both ends. **b.** *Bot.*: *esp.* applied to a flower or floret consisting mainly of a tube, with small or inconspicuous limb 1776. **2.** Constructed with or consisting of a number of tubes; as a *t. boiler* 1804. **3.** *Phys.* and *Path.* Applied to a high-pitched respiratory murmur, like the sound made by blowing through a tube, heard normally over the trachea and bronchial tubes, and in diseased conditions over the lung 1834.

1. *T. bridge*, a bridge formed of a great tube or hollow beam, usu. of wrought iron, through which the road or railway passes. Hence **Tu·bularly** *adv.*

Tubularian (tiŭbiŭlēᵊ·riăn), *a.* and *sb.* 1859. [f. mod.L. *Tubularia* (Linnæus 1775, f. L. *tubulus* TUBULE); see -ARY¹ 3, -AN.] *Zool.* **A.** *adj.* Belonging to the Linnæan genus *Tubularia*, the group *Tubulariæ*, or the family *Tubulariidæ*, of gymnoblastic Hydrozoa, in which the polyps are of tubular form, protected by a perisarc, with naked hydranths. **B.** *sb.* A tubularian hydroid.

Tubulate (tiŭ·biŭlĕt), *a.* 1753. [– L. *tubulatus*, f. *tubulus* TUBULE; see -ATE².] *Nat. Hist.* Formed into or like a tube; tubular.

Tubulated (tiŭ·biŭleᵗtėd), *a.* 1663. [f. L. *tubulatus* TUBULATE *a.* + -ED¹.] **1.** Furnished with a tube; *esp.* of a retort or receiver: Having a short tube with a stopper (*tubulature* or *tubulure*), through which substances can be introduced. **2.** Formed into, or like, a tube; longitudinally perforated; tubular 1713. So **Tubula·tion,** the process of making or becoming tubular. **Tu·bulature** [see -URE]: = TUBULURE.

Tubule (tiŭ·biul). 1677. [– L. TUBULUS; see -ULE.] A small tube; a minute tubular structure in an animal or plant body, as the *Malpighian* or *uriniferous tubules* of the kidney, etc.

Tubuli- (tiŭ·biŭli), comb. form of mod.L. *tubulus* TUBULE, as in **Tu:bulide·ntate** [L. *dentatus* toothed], *a.* *Zool.* belonging to the *Tubulidentata*, a group of edentates having compound teeth traversed by parallel vertical tubules. **Tubuli·ferous,** *a.* *Nat. Hist.* bearing tubules; *spec.* having a tubular ovipositor, as the females of certain insects. **Tu·bulifo:rm,** *a.* having the form of a tubule, tubular. **Tu·bulipo:re** [L. *porus* PORE], *Zool.* a polyzoan of the genus *Tubulipora* or family *Tubuliporidæ*, having tubular calcareous calicles.

Tubulose (tiŭ·biŭlōᵘs), *a.* Now *rare.* 1713. [f. TUBULE + -OSE¹.] = next 1. Now *rare.*

Tubulous (tiŭ·biŭləs), *a.* 1664. [f. TUBULE + -OUS.] **1.** = TUBULAR 1. **2.** Containing or composed of tubes 1864. **b.** Of a steam-boiler: Having either fire-tubes or water-tubes 1860.

Tubulure (tiŭ·biŭliŭɹ). 1800. [– Fr. *tubulure* (XVIII), f. *tubule* (XVII) TUBULE; see -URE.] A short tube, or projecting opening for the insertion of a tube, in a retort or receiver.

‖**Tubulus** (tiŭ·biŭlɒs). *Pl.* **-i** (-əi). 1826. [L., dim. of *tubus* TUBE; see -ULE.] = TUBULE; in *Ent.* a tubular ovipositor.

Tuchun (tū·tʃɒn). 1920. [Chinese]. The military governor of a province in China. Hence **Tu·chunate. Tu·chunism.**

Tuck (tɒk), *sb.*¹ late ME. [f. TUCK *v.*¹] **1.** A fold or pleat in drapery; now *spec.* a flattened fold (or one of several parallel folds) in a garment, secured by stitching, either to shorten the garment or for ornamentation. **2.** The gathering of the ends of the bottom planks of a ship under the stern; that part of the hull where the bottom planks are collected and terminated by the *t.-rail* 1625. **3.** *Fishing.* Short for TUCK-NET. 1602. **4.** The thrusting in of the ends or edges of anything so as to secure them in position. Also with *in.* 1852. **5.** *slang.* Usu. *t.-in* (also *t.-out*): A hearty meal; esp. in school use, a feast of delicacies 1823. **b.** Food, eatables; *esp.* delicacies, as sweet-stuff, pastry, jam, etc. (*school slang*) 1857.

Phr. *Nip and t.*: see NIP *sb.*¹ 4.

attrib. and *Comb.*: **t.-boat,** in seine-fishing, a boat which carries the t.-net; **-rail,** the rail which forms a rabbet for the purpose of caulking the butt ends of the planks of the bottom; **-seine** = TUCK-NET.

Tuck (tɒk), *sb.*² *arch.* and *dial.* Chiefly *Sc.* 1500. [f. TUCK *v.*²; cf. It. *tocco* stroke, knock, f. *toccare* to touch, strike.] A blow, a stroke, a tap; esp. in *t. of drum.*

Tuck (tɒk), *sb.*³ *arch.* 1508. [Early forms *toke*, *tocke*, *touke*, prob. – Fr. dial. *étoc*, OFr., Pr. *estoc* = It. *stocco*, of Gmc. origin (cf. G. *stock* stick).] A slender, pointed, straight, thrusting sword; a rapier.

Tuck (tɒk), *v.*¹ OE. [Senses 1–2 app. repr. OE. *tūcian*, ME. *tūke*. The later forms *tokke*, *tukke* (XV) – MLG., MDu. *tucken* draw, pull sharply or forcibly (= OHG. *zucchen*, G. *zucken* twitch, snatch), f. base of Gmc. **teux-* (cf. TUG).] †**1.** *trans.* To punish; to ill-treat, torment –ME. †**b.** *fig.* To reprove, check, rebuke, reproach –1651. **2.** To dress or finish (cloth) after it comes from the weaver, esp. to stretch on tenters; also *intr.* to work as a tucker. Now *local.* late ME. **3.** *Fishing.* To take the fish from (the seine) by means of a *tuck-net*; also with the fish as object 1786. **4.** To pull or gather up in a fold or folds; *esp.* to gird up (a garment, etc.). Usu. const. *up.* 1440. **b.** To put a tuck or tucks in 1626. **5.** To pull or gather up and confine the loose garments of; to gird (a person) *up.* Chiefly in *pa. pple.* Now *rare.* late ME. **b.** *fig.* To cramp or hamper by lack of space, time, or means 1886. **6.** To thrust or put away (an object) into a close place where it is snugly held or concealed 1587. **7.** To thrust in the edge or end of (anything pendent or loose) so as to retain or confine it; now *esp.* to turn in the edges of (bed-coverings or the like) under the bed or its occupant. With advs., esp. *in*, *up.* 1635. **b.** With the person as obj. 1692. **c.** *intr.* To draw together, contract, pucker 1797. **8.** *slang.* **a.** *trans.* To 'put away' (food or drink) 1784. **b.** *intr.* To feed heartily or greedily; esp. with *in*, *into* 1810. **9.** *slang.* To hang (a criminal); usu. with *up* 1700.

4. He tucked up his sleeves and squared his elbows DICKENS. 6. He tucked his wife's arm under his own 1874. 7. A nymph that can t. my bed-clothes up THACKERAY. 8. b. There is Rasherwell 'tucking' away in the coffee-room THACKERAY.

Tuck (tɒk), *v.*² Now *dial.* Chiefly *Sc.* late ME. [– ONFr. *toquer* touch, strike, northern form of *toucher* TOUCH *v.*] *trans.* and *intr.* To touch (*rare*); to beat the drum; also *intr.* of a drum: To sound.

Tuckahoe (tɒ·kăho). *U.S.* 1612. [– Powhatan or Virginian (N. Amer. Indian) *tockawhoughe.*] A name applied by N. Amer. Indians (esp. of Virginia) to edible roots of various plants. Now app. restricted to an underground tuber-like production (*Pachyma cocos* or *Lycoperdon solidum*), prob. the sclerotium of some fungus, parasitic on tree-roots in the southern parts of North America, the affinities of which are uncertain. Also called *Indian bread, Indian loaf, Indian head,* and *t. truffle.*

Tucker (tɒ·kəɹ), *sb.* late ME. [f. TUCK *v.*[1] + -ER[1].] **1.** A fuller; a cloth-finisher. *Obs.* exc. *dial.* **2.** A piece of lace or the like, worn by women within or around the top of the bodice in the 17–18th c.; a frill of lace worn round the neck 1688. **3.** One who makes or 'runs' tucks; the device in a sewing-machine which does this 1905. **4.** *Australian slang.* The daily supply of food of a gold-digger or station-hand; rations, meals; also, food generally, victuals 1858.

2. *Best bib and t.*: see BIB *sb.*[1] **4.** *To earn* or *make one's t.*, to earn merely enough to pay for one's keep.

Tucker (tɒ·kəɹ), *v. New England. colloq.* 1840. [f. TUCK *v.*[1]; see -ER[5].] *trans.* To tire, to weary; usu. *t. out*; esp. in pa. pple, *tuckered out*, worn out, exhausted.

Tucket (tɒ·kėt). *arch.* 1593. [f. TUCK *v.*[2]; see -ET.] A flourish on a trumpet; a signal for marching used by cavalry troops.

Tu·ck-net. 1520. [f. TUCK *v.*[1]] A smaller net used within the great seine to gather and bring the fish to the surface.

Tu·ck-shop. *slang.* 1857. [f. TUCK *sb.*[1]] A pastry-cook's shop for the sale of pastry, sweets, fruit, and the like, chiefly to schoolboys.

‖**Tucum** (tū·kǒm). 1810. [– Tupi *tucumá.*] Any of several Brazilian palms, esp. *Astrocaryum vulgare*, from the young leaves of which the natives obtain a fibre which they make into cordage, nets, hats, etc.; also, the fibre itself.

‖**Tucuma** (tū·kumă). 1824. [Tupi *tucumá.*] A Brazilian palm, *Astrocaryum tucuma*, which produces a fleshy fruit used by the natives as food, and a fibre like that of tucum.

‖**Tucutucu** (tū·kuˌtū·ku). 1833. [Native name, imitating the sound made by the animal when in its burrow.] A rat-like burrowing rodent of the genus *Ctenomys*, esp. *C. magellanica* and *C. brasiliensis*; found in Patagonia and La Plata. Also, the sound made by this animal.

-tude (tiud), *suffix*, repr. L. *-tudo, -tudin-* (Fr. *-tude*), a suffix of abstract nouns, chiefly from adjs., as *altitudo* height, f. *altus* high, etc., less commonly from pa. pples., as *consuetudo* custom, f. *consuetus*, or verb-stems, as *valetudo*, f. *valere*; occurring in words derived directly from L., as *altitude*, etc., or through Fr., as *consuetude, solitude*, etc., or formed (in Fr. or Eng.) on L. analogies, as *decrepitude, exactitude.*

Tudor (tiū·dǫɹ), *a.* 1779. [attrib. use of the Welsh surname (*Tewdwr*).] **1.** Belonging to the line of English sovereigns (from Henry VII to Elizabeth) descended from Owen Tudor, who married Catherine, the widowed queen of Henry V. **2.** Applied to the style of architecture (the latest form of Perpendicular) which prevailed in England during the reigns of the Tudors; belonging to or characteristic of this 1815.

2. *T. flower*, an upright stalked trefoil ornament used in long rows on cornices, etc., in T. architecture. *T. rose*, a conventional figure of a rose adopted as a badge by Henry VII, occurring in decoration of the T. period; in *Her.* figured as a combination of a red and a white rose.

Tuedian (twī·diăn), *a.* 1856. [f. med.L. *Tueda* the river Tweed + -IAN.] *Geol.* Applied to the lowest beds of the Carboniferous.

Tuesday (tiū·zde[i], -di). [OE. *Tīwesdæġ* = OFris. *tiesdei*, OHG. *zīostag* (G. dial. *zistig*), ON. *týsdagr, týrsdagr*; f. gen. of *Tīw* (= OHG. *Zio*, ON. *Týr*, name of a Teutonic deity identified with Mars :– Gmc. **Tīwaz*, cogn. with L. *deus*) + *dæġ* DAY; tr. L. *dies Martis* day of Mars (whence Fr. *mardi*, It. *martedì*).] The third day of the week.

Tufa (tū·fă, tiū·fă). Also **tufo.** 1770. [– It. †*tufa*, local var. of *tufo* – late L. *tofus, tophus*; see TOPHUS, TUFF.] *Geol.* A generic name for porous stones, formed of pulverulent matter consolidated and often stratified. *spec.* **a.** *Calcareous t.*: a porous or vesicular carbonate of lime, generally deposited near the sources and along the courses of calcareous springs 1811. **b.** *Volcanic t.*: see next 1 b. 1770. Hence **Tufaceous** (-ē·ʃəs) *a.* having the nature or texture of t.; consisting of t.

Tuff (tɒf). 1569. [– Fr. *tuffe, tufe, tuf* (XVI) – It. *tufo*; see prec.] *Geol.* = prec. (But there is a recent tendency to restrict *tuff* to 'volcanic t.'.) **a.** *Calcareous* (or *calc*) *t.*: see prec. a. **b.** *Volcanic t.*, a tuff produced by the consolidation of volcanic ashes and other erupted material 1815. Hence **Tuffa·ceous** *a.* having the properties of or composed of volcanic t.

Tuft (tɒft), *sb.* late ME. [In XIV *toft*, presumably – OFr. *tofe, toffe* (mod. *touffe*), of unkn. origin; for the parasitic *t* cf. CLIFT *sb.*[2], GRAFT *sb.*[1]] **1.** A bunch (natural or artificial) of small things, usu. soft and flexible, as hairs, feathers, etc., fixed or attached at the base. **b.** *Bot.*, etc. A cluster of short-stalked leaves or flowers growing from a common point, of stems growing from a common root, etc.; an umbel or fascicle; also, a clump of small herbs growing closely together 1523. **2.** A small tufted patch of hair on the head or chin; a lock; an imperial 1601. **3.** A clump of trees or bushes 1555. **4.** *Anat.* A small cluster or plexus of capillary blood-vessels; a glomerule 1841. **5.** *Hist.* An ornamental tassel on a cap; *spec.* the gold tassel formerly worn by titled undergraduates at Oxford and Cambridge 1670. **b.** *transf.* in *Univ. slang*, One who wore a tuft; a titled undergraduate 1755.

1. b. A t. of deep purple, the beautiful Alpine saxifrage 1853. **2.** On his Chin 2 thin forked Tuffs 1711. **3.** Behind the t. of Pines I met them SHAKS.

Tuft, *v.* 1535. [f. prec.] **1.** *trans.* To furnish with a tuft or tufts. **2.** *intr.* To form a tuft or tufts; to grow in tufts 1598. **3.** *trans.* To beat (a covert) in stag-hunting. Also *absol.* 1590. **b.** To dislodge (the game) by 'tufting' 1640.

Tuftaffeta, -taffety (tɒfˌtæ·fėtă, -tæ·fėti). *Obs.* or *arch.* 1572. [f. *tuff*, TUFT *sb.* + TAFFETA, TAFFETY.] **1.** A kind of taffeta with a pile or nap arranged in tufts. **2.** *attrib.* **a.** Made of tuftaffeta 1587. **b.** Clothed in tuftaffeta; luxuriously dressed 1598.

2. a. I'll help to fit her With a tuft-taffeta cloak B. JONS.

Tufted (tɒ·ftėd), *a.* 1606. [f. TUFT *sb.* and *v.* + -ED.] **1.** Having or adorned with a tuft or tufts. **2.** Formed into or forming a tuft; growing in a tuft or tufts; clustered 1632. **3.** *Nat. Hist.* **a.** *Bot.* Bearing flowers in tufts or fascicles. **b.** *Bot.* and *Zool.* Growing in tufts, cæspitose. 1629. **c.** Of a bird: Having a tuft of feathers upon the head; crested: *esp.* in *Ornith.* as the epithet of a particular species 1768.

1. Tall rocks and t. knolls SCOTT. **2.** Towers and Battlements..Boosom'd high in t. Trees MILT. **3.** T. Loosestrife 1857. **c.** The t. plover [will] pipe along the fallow lea TENNYSON.

Tufter (tɒ·ftəɹ). 1856. [f. TUFT *v.* 3 + -ER[1].] *Stag-hunting.* A hound trained to drive the deer out of cover.

Tu·ft-hu:nter. 1755. [f. TUFT *sb.* + HUNTER.] One who meanly or obsequiously courts the acquaintance of persons of rank and title (orig. at the universities: see TUFT *sb.* 5, 5b); a toady, sycophant. So **Tu·ft-hu:nting** *sb.* and *a.*

Tufty (tɒ·fti), *a.* 1611. [f. TUFT *sb.* + -Y[1].] **1.** Full of or abounding in tufts; covered or adorned with tufts 1612. **2.** Forming a tuft or tufts; consisting of or growing in tufts 1611.

1. Vallies..Deckt with t. woods 1638. **2.** An humble dale, Where t. daizies nod at every gale 1613.

Tug (tɒg), *sb.* late ME. [f. next.] **1.** An act or the action of tugging; a forcible pull; a severe strain or drag 1500. **2.** A hard try; a struggle; a 'go' 1673. **3.** A strenuous contest between two forces or persons 1660. **4.** In harness; **a.** (Chiefly *pl.*) A pair of short chains attached to the hames, by which the collar is connected with the shafts. **b.** A trace. **c.** A short strap sewn on various parts of the harness and serving to keep it in position. **d.** A metal stud or pin on the shaft to prevent it running too far through the loops of the back-strap. Also *locally* applied to other parts of harness. late ME. **e.** *Mining.* The iron hoop of a corf or hoisting bucket 1858. **5.** A small, stoutly-built, powerful steamer used to tow other vessels; a tug-boat 1817.

1. Downward by the feet he drew The trembling dastard: at the t. he falls DRYDEN. **3.** *T. of war*: (*a*) the decisive contest; the real struggle or tussle; (*b*) an athletic contest between two teams who haul at the opposite ends of a rope, each trying to drag the other over a line marked between them.

Tug (tɒg), *v.* [Earliest form *togge*, f. weak grade of Gmc. **teux-*; see TEE *v.*[1]] **1.** *intr.* To contend, strive in opposition. Now *rare.* **2.** To toil, labour, struggle; to go toilsomely 1619. **b.** *trans.* To lug, drag. *colloq.* 1710. **3.** To pull at with force; to strain or haul at ME. †**b.** To pull about roughly; to maul –1611. **4.** To move by pulling forcibly; to drag, haul ME. **5.** *intr.* To pull with great effort or force; to drag, haul. Often with *at.* ME. **6.** *trans.* To tow by means of a steam-tug 1839.

1. Let us tugge, till one the mastrie winne 1598. **2.** All for which you tugge thus diligently, shall perish 1634. **3.** Those two massie Pillars..He tugg'd, he shook, till down they came MILT. Each oar was tugged by five or six slaves MACAULAY. **b.** *Macb.* III. i. 112. **4.** Haled and tugged from place to place 1526. **5.** *fig.* How many recollections tugged at his heart as he went on! 1833. Phr. *To t. at the* (*an*) *oar*: to row as a galley-slave; hence *fig.* to toil unremittingly; to do the drudgery. Hence **Tu·gger,** one who tugs. **Tu·ggingly** *adv.*

‖**Tui** (tū·i). 1835. [Maori.] = PARSON-BIRD 1.

Tuille, tuile (twīl). late ME. [– Fr. *tuile*, OFr. *tieule* :– L. *tegula* TILE.] In mediæval armour, one of two or more plates of steel hanging below or forming the lowest part of the tasses, and covering the front of the thighs.

Tuism (tiū·iz'm). *rare.* 1796. [f. L. *tu* thou + -ISM, after *egoism.*] A form of expression involving the use of the pronoun *thou*, or implying reference to a second person; also, in *Ethics*, primary regard to the interests of another person or persons; in *Philos.*, the doctrine that all thought is addressed to a second person, or to one's future self as a second person. Hence **Tui·stic** *a.* of the nature of t.

Tuition (tiuˌi·ʃən). late ME. [– OFr. *tuition* – L. *tuitio, -ōn-* protection (Cicero), f. *tueri* look after; see -ITION.] †**1.** The action of looking after or taking care of, or condition of being taken care of; protection, defence, custody, care, tutelage –1790. †**b.** *spec.* Guardianship –1690. **2.** The action or business of teaching a pupil or pupils, esp. in private; tutorial instruction 1582.

1. For the tuicion and defence of this owr Realme 1462. **2.** T. on the violin and clavier 1845. Hence **Tui·tional, Tui·tionary** *adjs.* pertaining or relating to t.

Tula (tū·lă). 1839. In full *t. metal*: Niello made at Tula in Russia.

‖**Tule** (tū·le). *U.S.* Also **tula.** 1850. [– Aztec *tullin*, the final *n* being dropped by the Spaniards as in *Guatemala*, etc.] Either of two species of bulrush (*Scirpus lacustris* var. *occidentalis*, and *S. tatora*) abundant in low lands along riversides in California; hence, a thicket of this, or a flat tract of land on which it grows.

Tulip (tiū·lip). 1578. [Earliest in forms *tulip*(*p*)*a, -ipan*(*t, tulpia*; – mod.L. *tulipa*, Fr. †*tulipan, tulipe* – Turk. *tul*(*i*)*band* (now *tülbend*) – Pers. *dulband* TURBAN. The expanded flower was thought to resemble a turban.] **1.** A bulbous plant of the liliaceous genus *Tulipa*, esp. the species *T. gesneriana*, introduced from Turkey into western

Europe in the 16th c., blooming in spring, with broad bell-shaped or cup-shaped, usu. erect, showy flowers, of various colours and markings; also, the flower itself. **b.** Applied, with defining word, to species of this, and various plants or flowers more or less resembling it; also to the flowers of the TULIP-TREE 1759. **2.** *fig.* A showy person or thing, or one greatly admired 1647. **3.** A tulip-like object: a bishop's mitre; a bell-shaped outward swell in the muzzle of a gun, now generally disused 1879.

1. The bloud-red T. with a yellow bottome 1633. **2.** Morgiana was a t. among women, and the t. fanciers all came flocking round her THACKERAY. *Comb.*: **t.-grass,** any of several S. African poisonous herbs of the genus *Homeria*; **-root,** (*a*) the root or bulb of a t.; (*b*) a disease of oats, characterized by a swelling at the base of the stem, caused by a minute nematoid worm; **-shell,** (*a*) a bivalve of the genus *Tellina*; (*b*) any gasteropod of the family *Fasciolariadæ*, as *Fasciolaria tulipa*.

Tu·lip-tree. 1705. **a.** A large N. Amer. tree, *Liriodendron tulipifera* (family *Magnoliaceæ*), bearing flowers resembling large tulips, of a greenish colour variegated with yellow and orange; also called *tulip poplar*, *saddle-tree* (from the shape of its truncated leaves), and *whitewood*. **b.** Applied to other trees with tulip-like flowers, as species of *Magnolia*, and the mountain mahoe (*Paritium elatum* or *Hibiscus elatus*, family *Malvaceæ*) of the West Indies 1751.

Tu·lip-wood. 1843. **a.** The wood of the tulip-tree (see prec. a), a light ornamental wood used by cabinet-makers, etc. **b.** Any of various coloured and striped woods, or the trees producing them, as *Physocalymma floribundum* of Brazil, and species of *Owenia* and *Harpullia*, of Australia.

‖**Tulle** (tiul, tul, Fr. tül). 1818. [Fr., named from *Tulle*, in Corrèze, France, where it was first made.] A fine silk bobbin-net used for women's dresses, veils, hats, etc.

Tulle, obs. f. TOLL *v.*[1]

Tullibee (tɒ·libī). Also **tulibbi.** 1888. [– N. Amer. Indian (Cree and Ojibwa) *toonie-bee*.] A species of whitefish (*Coregonus tullibee*) found in the Great Lakes of N. America.

‖**Tulsi** (tū·lsi). *India.* 1698. [Hindi *tūlsī*.] A species of basil sacred to Vishnu.

‖**Tulwar** (tɒ·lwāɹ). Also **tal-.** 1834. [Hindi *talwār* (also *tarwār*).] An (Indian) sabre.

Tum (tɒm), *sb.* and *v.* 1830. [imit. Cf. TUM-TUM *sb.*[1]] An imitation of the sound made by plucking a tense string, striking a drum, or the like. As *v. trans.* and *intr.*, to produce this sound.

Tumble (tɒ·mb'l), *sb.* 1634. [f. next.] **1.** An act of acrobatic tumbling (*rare*) 1824. **2.** An accidental fall; also *fig.*, a fall, downfall 1716. **3.** Tumbled condition; disorder, confusion; a confused heap 1634.

2. A t. in the deeper snow 1860. *fig.* The.. Baronet had a bloody T. 1728.

Tumble (tɒ·mb'l), *v.* [ME. *tumbel*, Sc. *tummyll* – MLG. *tummelen*, = OHG. *tumalōn* (G. *tummeln*), frequent. (see -LE) f. base of OHG. *tūmōn*, *tūmalōn* (G. *taumeln*); cf. OE. *tumbian* dance, MHG. *tumben*, ON. *tumba* tumble.] **I. 1.** *intr.* †To dance with posturing, balancing, contortions, and the like; to perform as an acrobat; *esp.* to execute leaps, springs, somersaults, etc. **2.** To roll about on the ground, or in the water or air; to wallow; also, to throw oneself about in a restless way on a bed or couch; to toss. late ME. **b.** *spec.* of a pigeon: To throw itself over backwards during its flight; in gunnery, of a projectile, to turn end over end in its flight 1698.

1. A man who is paid for tumbling upon his hands JOHNSON. **2.** I saw the Porpas how he bounst and tumbled SHAKS. **b.** Pigeons tumbling in the Air 1698.

II. 1. To fall; *esp.* to fall in a helpless way, as from stumbling or violence; to be precipitated, fall headlong ME. **b.** To fall prone, fall to the ground; freq. const. *down*, *over*. Also, to stumble by tripping *over* an object. ME. **c.** Of a building, etc.: To collapse. late ME. **d.** *Commercial slang.* To fall rapidly in value, amount, or price 1886. **2.** *trans.* To cause to fall suddenly or violently; to throw or cast down. late ME. **3.** To cause to fall in a confused heap; to throw *down, in, out*, etc. without order or regularity; to jumble *together* 1562. **4.** To propel or drive headlong or with a falling, stumbling, or rolling movement; to precipitate; to toss, pitch, bundle 1509. **5.** *intr.* To move or pass with a motion as if falling or stumbling; to proceed hastily; to bowl, bundle, roll, rush. Now *colloq.* 1590. **6.** *trans.* To turn over as in examination or search. Now *rare*. 1597. **7.** To handle roughly or indelicately; to disorder, rumple; to disarrange by tossing 1602. **8.** *intr. fig.* or in fig. context; *esp.* To come by chance, stumble, blunder *into, on, upon* 1565. **b.** *fig.* const. *to*: To understand something not clearly expressed; to apprehend a hidden design or signal. *slang.* 1851.

1. One of the gang tumbled off of his mule 1687. **c.** Obelisks have their term, and Pyramids will t. SIR T. BROWNE. **2.** Vnruly Winde..which.. tombles downe Steeples, and mosse-growne Towers SHAKS. T. her out at window 1623. **4.** To be tossed and tumbled about like a football SMOLLETT. **5.** T. into bed and go to sleep LEVER. **7.** *Haml.* IV. v. 62. **8. b.** I didn't t. to this for a long time 1889.

III. *intr.* Of the sides of a ship: To incline or slope inwards, to contract above the point of extreme breadth; to batter. Usu. *t. home.* Opp. to FLARE *v.* 3. 1687.

Tumble-, the vb.-stem in combination:

1. With sbs.: **t.-bug, -dung,** *U.S.* a scarabæid beetle which rolls up balls of dung, in which it deposits its eggs and in which the larvæ go through their transformations; a dung-beetle; **-weed,** *U.S.* any of various plants which form a globular bush which in late summer is broken off and rolled about by the wind; a rolling weed. **2.** with advs.: **t. home,** in a ship, the inward inclination of the upper part of a ship's sides; opp. to FLARE *sb.*[1] 4.

Tu·mble-down, *a.* 1818. [The phr. *tumble down* used attrib.] That is in a tumbling condition; dilapidated, ruinous.

Tumbler (tɒ·mblәɹ). ME. [f. TUMBLE *v.* + -ER[1].] **1.** One who performs feats of agility and strength, somersaults, leaps, and gymnastics; an acrobat. **2.** A dog like a small greyhound, formerly used to catch rabbits; a lurcher: so called from its action in taking its quarry. *Obs.* exc. *Hist.* 1519. **3.** A variety of domestic pigeon characterized by the habit or faculty of turning over and over backwards during its flight 1678. **4.** One who tumbles or falls 1904. **5.** A drinking cup, orig. having a rounded or pointed bottom, so that it could not be set down until emptied; often of silver or gold; now, a tapering cylindrical or barrel-shaped glass cup without a handle or foot, having a heavy flat bottom 1664. **b.** A tumblerful 1831. **6.** = TUMBREL 2, 2 b. *slang* and *dial.* 1673. **7.** *U.S.* = TUMBLE-*dung*. 1807. **8.** In mechanical applications. **a.** In a gun-lock, a pivoted plate through which the mainspring acts on the hammer and in the notches of which the sear engages 1624. **b.** In a lock: †A pivoted piece through which the pressure of a spring was transmitted to the tail of the bolt, tending to keep it pushed forwards; now, a pivoted piece kept in position by a spring, with projections which drop into notches in the bolt and hold it until lifted by the proper key 1677.

attrib. and *Comb.*, as *t. lock, pigeon, screw*; **t. switch,** an electric switch operated by pushing over a small spring t. or thumb-piece. Hence **Tu·mblerful,** the quantity that fills a t.

Tumbling (tɒ·mbliŋ), *vbl. sb.* late ME. [f. TUMBLE *v.* + -ING[1].] The action of TUMBLE *v.* **b.** *T. home* = TUMBLE *home.* 1664.

Tumbling-. The vbl. sb. and ppl. adj. in combs. and special collocations: **t.-barrel** = *t.-box*; **-bay,** an outfall from a river, canal, or reservoir; a weir; also, the pool into which the water falls from this; **-box,** a rotating drum in which small articles (usu. of metal) are cleaned and polished by attrition; also used in dissolving and mixing paints, varnishes, etc.

Tumbrel, tumbril (tɒ·mbrĕl, -ɪl). 1440. [– OFr. *tomb-*, *tumberel* (mod. *tombereau*), in AL. *tumb(e)rellus, -um*, f. *tomber* fall; see TUMBLE, -EL.] **1.** An instrument of punishment; from 16th c. usu. identified with CUCKING-STOOL 1494. **2.** A cart so constructed that the body tilts backward so as to empty out the load; *esp.* a dung-cart 1440. †**b.** app. *transf.* to a lumbering cart –1800. †**3.** *transf.* A flat-bottomed boat or barge –1676. **4.** *Mil.* A two-wheeled covered cart which carries ammunition, tools, or sometimes money for an army 1715.

Tumefaction (tiūmĭfæ·kʃәn). 1597. [– Fr. *tuméfaction* (XVI), f. L. *tumefacere*; see next, -FACTION.] **1.** The action or process of tumefying or state of being tumefied; swollen condition. **2.** *concr.* A swollen part; a swelling, a tumour 1802.

Tumefy (tiū·mĭfәi), *v.* 1597. [– Fr. *tuméfier* – L. *tumefacere*, pass. *-fieri*, f. *tumēre* swell; see -FY.] **1.** *trans.* To cause to swell; to swell, make tumid. **2.** *intr.* To swell, swell up, become tumid 1615.

1. *fig.* To swell, t., stiffen, not the diction only, but the tenor of the thought DE QUINCEY.

Tumescence (tiume·sĕns). 1859. [f. next; see -ENCE.] A becoming tumid, swelling up; a tendency to tumidity; also *concr.* a tumid part, a swelling.

Tumescent (tiume·sĕnt), *a.* 1882. [– L. *tumescens, -ent-*, pr. pple. of *tumescere*, f. *tumēre* swell; see -ESCENT.] Becoming tumid, swelling; somewhat tumid.

Tumid (tiū·mid), *a.* 1541. [– L. *tumidus*, f. *tumēre* swell; see -ID[1].] **1.** Swollen; characterized by swelling. **b.** Morbidly affected with swelling, as a part of the body. **c.** Of a swollen or protuberant form; swelling, bulging. In later use chiefly *Nat. Hist.* 1621. **2.** *fig.* esp. of language or literary style: 'Swelling', inflated, turgid, bombastic 1648. **b.** 'Big', pregnant, teeming (*rare*) 1840.

1. My thighs grow very t. JOHNSON. **2.** Turgid ode and t. stanza BYRON. Hence **Tumi·dity,** the quality or condition of being t.; swollenness. **Tu·mid-ly** *adv.*, **-ness.**

Tummy (tɒ·mi), *colloq.* (orig. infantile) alteration of STOMACH; also *attrib.*, in *t.-ache.*

Tumorous (tiū·mŏrәs), *a.* 1547. [– late and med. L. *tumorosus*, f. *tumor*; see next, -OUS. In mod. use f. next + -OUS.] †**1.** Swollen, protuberant, bulging, tumid. *Obs.* exc. as in b. –1678. **b.** Pertaining to or of the nature of a (morbid) tumour; affected with tumours 1863. †**2.** *fig.* Vainglorious, puffed up, haughty; also, = TUMID 2. –1676.

Tumour, tumor (tiū·mәɹ). 1541. [– L. *tumor, -ōr-*, f. *tumēre* swell; see -OR 1.] †**1.** The action or an act of swelling; swollen condition –1693. **2.** *concr.* A part rising above or projecting beyond the general level or surface; a swollen part or object; a swelling. Now *rare* or *Obs.* exc. as in 3. 1601. **3.** An abnormal or morbid swelling or enlargement in any part of the body of an animal or plant; an excrescence; a tumefaction 1597. **b.** *spec.* A permanent circumscribed morbid swelling, consisting in a new growth of tissue, without inflammation 1804. †**4.** *fig.* 'Swelling' of passion, pride, or the like –1778. †**b.** Turgidity of language, style, or deportment; bombast –1840.

4. The tumour of insolence, or petulance of contempt JOHNSON.

Tump (tɒmp), *sb. local.* 1589. [Chiefly a western and w. midl. word; origin unkn.] **1.** A hillock, mound; a mole-hill, or ant-hill; a barrow, tumulus. **2.** A clump of trees, shrubs, or grass 1802.

Tump, *v.*[1] *local.* 1721. [f. prec.] To make a 'tump' or mound about the root of a tree.

Tump, *v.*[2] *U.S.* 1855. [Of unkn. origin; cf. next.] *trans.* To drag or carry by means of a tump-line.

Tu·mp-line. *local U.S.* 1860. [Cf. prec.] A strap placed across the forehead to assist in carrying a pack on the back.

Tum-tum (tɒ·m,tɒ·m), *sb.*[1] and *adv.* Also in extended forms, as **tum-ti-tum.** 1859. [Reduplication of TUM.] An imitation of the sound of a stringed instrument or instruments, esp. when monotonously played; strumming; a monotonous air. So **Tum-tum** *v. intr.* to play monotonously; to strum.

Tum-tum, *sb.*[2] *India.* 1863. [Of unkn. origin.] A dog-cart.

Tum-tu·m, *sb.*[3] *colloq.* Reduplicated f. *tum* in TUMMY.

Tumular (tiū·miŭlăɹ), *a.* 1828. [f. L. *tumulus* (see TUMULUS) + -AR¹.] Pertaining to or consisting of a mound or tumulus.

Tumulate (tiū·miŭleᶦt), *v. rare.* 1623. [– *tumulat-*, pa. ppl. stem of L. *tumulare*, f. *tumulus*; see TUMULUS, -ATE³.] *trans.* To bury, entomb.

Tumult (tiū·mɒlt), *sb.* late ME. [– (O)Fr. *tumulte* or L. *tumultus* (cf. Skr. *tumulaḥ* tumult, noisy).] **1.** Commotion of a multitude, usu. with confused speech or uproar; public disturbance; disorderly or riotous proceeding. **b.** (with *pl.*) An instance of this: a popular commotion or disturbance 1560. **2.** *gen.* Commotion, agitation, disturbance; disorderly or noisy movement or action. Also *pl.* 1580. **3.** *fig.* Great disturbance or agitation of mind or feeling; confused and violent emotion 1663.

1. When the loud T. speaks the Battel nigh PRIOR. **b.** The late tumults in Belgia EVELYN. **2.** It Thunders and Lightens..What tumult's in the Heauens? SHAKS. **3.** A t. of grief and indignation 1844.

Tu·mult, *v.* 1570. [f. prec.] †**1.** *intr.* To make a tumult, commotion, or disturbance; to riot –1864. **2.** *trans.* To put into tumult; to agitate violently 1819.

1. Why do the Gentiles t.? MILT. Hence †**Tu·multer,** one who stirs up a tumult; a rioter.

Tumultuary (tiumɒ·ltiuˌări), *a.* (*sb.*) 1590. [– L. *tumultuarius* of or belonging to hurry or tumult, (of troops) raised hastily, f. *tumultus*; see TUMULT, -ARY¹.] **1.** Of troops: Gathered hastily and promiscuously, without order or system; irregular, undisciplined. Also of warfare, etc. carried on by such troops, or in an irregular way. **2.** Hurriedly done; disorderly, confused; haphazard, unsystematic 1609. †**b.** Of a person: Acting, speaking, or writing hastily and at random –1648. **3.** Disposed to, marked by, or of the nature of tumult; tumultuous, turbulent 1650. **B.** *sb.* in *pl.* Tumultuary forces 1654.

1. A tumultuarie armie in great hast levied..out of all quarters HOLLAND. **2.** Ashamed of their t. injustice 1879. **3.** The t. disorders of our passions 1661. Hence **Tumu·ltuarily** *adv.* **Tumu·ltuariness.**

Tumultuate (tiumɒ·ltiuˌeᶦt), *v.* Now *rare.* 1611. [– *tumultuat-*, pa. ppl. stem of L. *tumultuari* make a bustle or disturbance, f. *tumultus*; see -ATE³.] **1.** *intr.* To stir up a tumult; to become or be tumultuous, turbulent, agitated, or restless. **2.** *trans.* To excite to tumult; to disorder or disturb violently 1616.

1. Noise of Winds, that..t. 1671. So **Tumultua·tion** (now *rare*), the action of making a tumult; a condition of tumult; commotion.

Tumultuous (tiumɒ·ltiuˌəs), *a.* 1548. [– OFr. *tumultuous* (mod. *-ueux*) or L. *tumultus* TUMULT; see -OUS.] **1.** Full of tumult or commotion; disorderly and noisy; turbulent. **2.** Making a tumult or commotion; turbulent; riotous 1576. **3.** Of physical actions or agents: Marked by disorderly commotion; confusedly agitated 1667. **4.** *fig.* of, or in ref. to, emotion or thought 1667.

1. The t. advance of the conquering army 1840. **2.** His house was beset by a t. crowd 1868. **3.** A roaring and t. river 1856. **4.** A t. dream 1822. Hence **Tumu·ltuous-ly** *adv.*, **-ness.**

‖**Tumulus** (tiū·miŭlɒs). *Pl.* **-li** (-ləi). 1686. [L., rel. to *tumēre* swell.] An ancient sepulchral mound, a barrow.

Tun (tɒn), *sb.* [OE. *tunne*, corresp. to OFris., MLG., MDu. *tunne*, *tonne* (Du. *ton*), OHG. *tunna* (G. *tonne*), late ON. *tunna* – med. L. *tunna* (whence Fr. *tonne*, etc.), prob. of Gaulish origin. Cf. TON¹.] **1.** A large cask or barrel, usu. for liquids, esp. wine, ale, or beer, or for various provisions. Now less common than *cask.* †**b.** A large vessel in general; a tub or vat; a chest –1601. **c.** *Brewing.* A mashing-vat (*mash-t.*) or fermenting-vat (*gyle-t.*) 1713. **2.** A cask of definite capacity; hence, a measure of capacity for wine and other liquids (formerly also for other commodities), usu. equivalent to 2 pipes or 4 hogsheads, containing 252 old wine-gallons. late ME. **3.** A measure of capacity or weight: see TON¹ 3, 4. **4.** *Conch.* = *t.-shell* 1837.

1. A vast T. (as big as that at Heidelberg) EVELYN. *fig.* A fat old Man; a Tunne of Man is thy Companion SHAKS.

Comb.: **t.-shell,** *Conch.* a shell of the genus *Dolium.*

Tun, *v.* late ME. [f. prec., but cf. AL. *tunnare* put into tuns (XV).] **1.** *trans.* To put into or store in a tun or tuns. Also *absol.* †**2.** To fill as, or like, a cask –1664.

1. *fig.* He used to t. down beer..during dinner 1841.

‖**Tuna**¹ (tū·na). 1555. [Haytian, through Sp.] = INDIAN FIG 1, PRICKLY PEAR; esp. *Opuntia tuna*, a tall-growing species found in Central America and the West Indies.

‖**Tuna**² (tū·na). 1900. [Amer.-Sp.; perh. related to L. *thunnus, tunnus* TUNNY.] Name in California for the tunny.

Tunable, tuneable (tiū·năb'l), *a. arch.* 1500. [f. TUNE *sb.* or *v.* + -ABLE.] Tuneful, musical, harmonious, sweet-sounding.

The tunable voyces of men LODGE. *Mids. N.* IV. i. 130. *fig.* This counsel, harsh at first, grew tunable in the ears of the Hospitallers FULLER. Hence **Tu·n(e)ableness. Tu·n(e)ably** *adv.*

‖**Tunal** (tunā·l). 1613. [Sp., f. TUNA¹ + *-al* (cf. CHAPARRAL).] A grove or thicket of tunas.

Tun-bellied (tɒ·nˌbeːlid), *a.* 1550. Having a belly rounded like a tun; pot-bellied.

Tund (tɒnd), *v.* 1871. [– L. *tundere* beat.] **1.** *Winchester School slang. trans.* To beat with a stick, esp. an ash rod, by way of punishment. **2.** *gen.* To beat, thump (*trans.* and *intr.*) 1885.

Tun-dish, tundish (tɒ·nˌdiʃ). Now *local.* late ME. [f. TUN *sb.* + DISH *sb.*] A wooden dish or shallow vessel with a tube at the bottom fitting into the bung-hole of a tun or cask, forming a kind of funnel used in brewing; hence *gen.* = FUNNEL *sb.*¹ 1.

‖**Tundra** (tu·ndră, tɒ·n-). 1841. [Lappish.] One of the vast, nearly level, treeless regions which make up the greater part of the north of Russia, resembling the *steppes*, but with arctic climate and vegetation. Also applied to similar regions in Siberia and Alaska.

Tune (tiūn), *sb.* [Late ME. *tune, tewne*, unexpl. var. of TONE *sb.*] †**1.** = TONE *sb.* I. 1. –1849. **2.** A rhythmical succession of musical tones produced by (or composed for) an instrument or voice; an air, melody (with or without the harmony which accompanies it). late ME. **b.** *spec.* A musical setting of a hymn or psalm, usu. in four-part harmony, intended for use in public worship; a hymn-tune 1450. **3.** The state of being in the proper pitch; correct intonation in singing, or in instrumental music; agreement in pitch, unison, or harmony (*with* something); mostly in phr. *in* or *out of t.* 1440. **b.** *transf.* Harmony or accordance in respect of vibrations other than those of sound; *spec.* between the receiver and transmitter in wireless telegraphy or telephony 1909. †**4.** Style, manner, or 'tone' (of discourse or writing) –1610. **b.** *To change one's t., sing another t.* (etc.); *fig.* to change one's tone, speak in a different strain 1524. **5.** *fig.* Frame of mind, temper, mood, disposition, humour 1599.

1. Melodious discord, heauenly t. harsh sounding SHAKS. **2.** Best sing it to the t. of *Light o' Loue* SHAKS. *Prov.* He who pays the piper, calls the t. *The t. the (old) cow died of*, joc. applied to a grotesque or unmusical succession of sounds, or a tedious ill-played piece of music. **3.** My voice is harsh here, not in t. TENNYSON. *In t., out of t.* (fig.), in or out of order or proper condition; in or out of harmony *with* some person or thing. **4.** I must nedes now..write unto you in an other t. CROMWELL. **5.** This is the tone and t. of men in distress 1647.

Phrases. *To the t. of* (*fig.* from 2): †**a.** According to the gist of, in accordance with. **b.** To the amount or sum of. So *to some t.*, to a considerable extent.

Tune, *v.* 1500. [f. prec.; earlier in ENTUNE (Chaucer).] **1.** *trans.* To adjust the tones of (a musical instrument, etc.) to a standard of pitch; to bring into condition for producing the required sounds correctly; to put in tune. Also *absol.* 1505. **b.** To adapt (the voice, song, etc.) to a particular tone, or to the expression of a particular feeling or subject; to modify or modulate the tones of, according to the purpose in view 1596. **c.** *transf.* To adapt, put in accordance, or make responsive, in respect of some physical quality or condition 1887. **d.** *Wireless.* To adjust to a desired frequency. (See also *t. in* below.) **2.** *fig.* To 'put in tune' (with various shades of meaning) 1530. **3.** *intr.* To give forth a musical sound; to sound; to sing 1500. **4.** *trans.* To utter or express (something) musically, to sing; to celebrate in music. *poet.* or *arch.* 1593. †**b.** To set or start the tune for (a hymn, etc. in public worship), as a precentor –1895. **5.** To produce music from, to play upon (an instrument, esp. the lyre). *poet.* 1701.

1. Letts t. our instruments 1597. **b.** For now to sorrow must I t. my song MILT. **2.** All his life was religiously tuned FULLER. The most effective way..of tuning public opinion 1868. **3.** Last week..I heard a blackbird tuning 1906. **4.** To Bacchus..let us t. our Lays DRYDEN. **5.** When Orpheus tun'd his lyre..Rivers forgot to run, and winds to blow ADDISON.

With advs. **T. in.** *trans.* To adjust (a wireless receiver) to receive a message, etc.; to adjust a receiver to the 'wave-length' of (a wireless station, etc.); also *absol.*; so **T. off, out. T. up. a.** *trans.* and *intr.* To raise one's voice, to sing out. **b.** *trans.* To bring (an instrument) up to the proper pitch, to put in tune; also *absol.* **c.** To put (a machine, a racing vessel, etc.) into the most efficient working order.

Tuneful (tiū·nfŭl), *a.* 1591. [f. TUNE *sb.* + -FUL.] **1.** Full of 'tune' or musical sound; musical, sweet-sounding 1598. **2.** Producing or yielding musical sounds; performing or skilled in music; musical (as a person, instrument, etc.) 1591. **3.** Relating or adapted to music 1697.

1. In tunefull numbers keeping musicks time MARSTON. **2.** Chaunt of t. Birds MILT. **3.** Milton's t. ear 1842. Hence **Tu·neful-ly** *adv.*, **-ness.**

Tuneless (tiū·nlės), *a.* 1594. [f. as prec. + -LESS.] **1.** Having no sweetness of tone; untuneful, unmusical, unmelodious. **2.** Giving no 'tune' or sound; songless; silent 1728.

1. My tuneless harp SPENSER. **2.** The heroic lay is t. now BYRON. Hence **Tu·neless-ly** *adv.*, **-ness.**

Tuner (tiū·nəɹ). 1580. [f. TUNE *v.* + -ER¹.] One who or that which tunes; *spec.* one whose occupation is to tune pianos or organs. **b.** *Electr.* An instrument for tuning an electric circuit. **c.** *Wireless.* The part of a receiving set consisting of the circuit or circuits used to tune in.

Tung-oil, -tree: see WOOD-OIL (*c*).

Tungstate (tɒ·ŋstĕt). 1800. [f. TUNGSTIC + -ATE⁴.] *Chem.* A salt of tungstic acid.

Tungsten (tɒ·ŋstĕn). 1770. [– Sw. *tungsten*, f. *tung* heavy + *sten* stone.] †**1.** *Min* = SCHEELITE, native calcium tungstate –1822. **2.** *Chem.* A heavy, steel-grey, ductile, very infusible metal, contained in the above mineral and in wolfram and other minerals; used for wire in incandescent electric lamps. Symbol W (= *wolframium*); atomic weight 184.

Tungstic (tɒ·ŋstik), *a.* 1796. [f. prec. + -IC 1 b.] *Chem.* Pertaining to or formed from tungsten; applied to compounds in which tungsten combines as a hexad, as *t. oxide*, WO_3, etc.; also to minerals containing tungsten, as *t. ochre*, native tungstic oxide, called also **Tu·ngstite.**

Tungstous (tɒ·ŋstəs), *a.* 1860. [f. as prec. + -OUS c.] *Chem.* Applied to compounds in which tungsten combines as a tetrad, as *t. chloride*, WCl_4, *t. oxide*, WO_2.

Tunhoof (tɒ·nhūf). Now *dial.* [OE. *tunhōfe*, f. TUN *sb.* + *hōfe*: cf. ALE-HOOF.] The herb Ground Ivy (*Nepeta glechoma*).

Tunic (tiū·nik). OE. [– (O)Fr. *tunique* or L. *tunica.*] **1.** A garment resembling a shirt, worn by both sexes among the Greeks and Romans; in OE. and mediæval times, a body-garment over which a loose mantle or cloak was worn. **2.** *Eccl.* = TUNICLE 2. *Hist.* 1696. **3.** In modern costume. **a.** A close, usu. plain, body-coat; now *spec.* that forming part of the uniform of soldiers and policemen 1667. **b.** A garment worn by women, consisting of a bodice and an upper skirt, belted or drawn in at (or fitted to) the waist, worn over and displaying a longer skirt. Also, a kind of belted frock or smock worn by children and by women at games 1762. **4.** *transf.* **a.** *Anat.* A membranous sheath lining an organ of the body 1661. **b.** The integument of a part or organ in a plant; *spec.* in *Bot.* any loose membranous skin not formed from the epidermis; also, each layer or coating of a tunicate bulb 1760.

3. a. Put on my new tunique of velvett; which is very plain, but good PEPYS. **4. b.** The tunics of the onion 1832.

Tunicary (tiū·nikări), *a.* and *sb.* 1835. [f. L. *tunica* TUNIC + -ARY[1].] **A.** *adj.* Of or pertaining to a tunic or membrane 1900. **B.** *sb. Zool.* A member of the *Tunicata*; a tunicated mollusc 1835.

‖**Tunicata** (tiūnikēi·tă), *sb. pl.* 1828. [mod. L. (sc. *animalia*), n. pl. of *tunicatus* TUNICATE.] *Zool.* A division of animals, now regarded as a sub-phylum of the *Chordata*; also called *Urochorda*: see next, B.

Tunicate (tiū·nikeit), *a.* and *sb.* 1760. [– L. *tunicatus*, pa. pple. of *tunicare* clothe with a tunic, f. *tunica* TUNIC; see -ATE.] **A.** *adj.* Having or enclosed in a tunic or covering; *spec. Bot.* having or consisting of a series of concentric layers, as a bulb; *Ent.* sheathed in or issuing from one another, as the joints of antennæ; *Zool.* having a tunic or mantle; belonging to the *Tunicata*. **B.** *sb.* One of a class of marine animals, formerly regarded as molluscs, but now classified as a degenerate branch of *Chordata*, comprising the ascidians and allied forms, characterized by a pouch-like body enclosed in a tough leathery integument, with a single or double aperture through which the water enters and leaves the pharynx 1848.

Tunicated (tiū·nikeitėd), *a.* 1744. [f. as prec. + -ED[1].] = prec. A.

Tunicin (tiū·nisin). 1862. [f. TUNIC + -IN[1].] *Chem.* A kind of animal cellulose, or chitin, occurring in the mantles of tunicates.

Tunicle (tiū·nik'l). late ME. [– OFr. *tunicle* (alt. of *tunique*) or L. *tunicula*, dim. of *tunica*; see -CLE.] †**1.** A small tunic; also *fig.* a wrapping, covering, integument –1744. **2.** *Eccl.* A vestment resembling the dalmatic, worn by a subdeacon over the alb (and also by bishops between the alb and the dalmatic) at a solemn celebration of the Eucharist. late ME. **3.** = TUNIC 4 a, b. *Obs.* (or *rare arch.*) late ME.

3. The stomach had a very thick inward t. 1725.

Tuning (tiū·niŋ), *vbl. sb.* 1554. [f. TUNE *v.* + -ING[1].] The action of TUNE *v.*

attrib. and *Comb.*: **t.-crook,** (*a*) an implement used in tuning the reed-pipes of an organ; (*b*) in brass wind-instruments = CROOK *sb.* 5; **-hammer,** a tuning-key for a piano, prop. one with a double head like that of a hammer, used for driving in the wrest-pins when new strings are fitted in; **-peg, -pin,** one of the pegs round which the strings of a stringed instrument are passed, and by turning which they are tuned; **-slide,** a slide in a metal wind-instrument, used to bring it into tune with other instruments in an orchestra. Also in *Wireless*, as *t. coil, condenser, inductance.*

Tu·ning-fork. 1799. **1.** A small steel instrument (invented in 1711) consisting of a stem with two stout flat prongs which on being caused to vibrate produce a definite musical note of constant pitch. **2.** An instrument used for turning the pins in tuning a pianoforte 1877.

Tunnel (tʊ·nĕl), *sb.* 1440. [– OFr. *tonel* (mod. *tonneau* tun, cask), f. *tonne* TUN; see -EL[2].] **1.** A net for catching partridges or waterfowl, having a pipe-like passage with a wide opening, and narrowing towards the end; a t.-net. Now *rare* or *Obs.* †**2.** The shaft or flue of a chimney –1818. **b.** A pipe or tube in general. Now *rare.* 1545. **3.** A funnel. *Obs.* exc. *dial.* 1529. **4.** A subterranean passage; a road-way excavated under ground, esp. under a hill or mountain, or beneath the bed of a river: now most commonly on a railway; also, on a canal, in a mine, etc. 1782. **b.** *transf.* The burrow of an animal 1873. **c.** A canal in an animal body resembling a tunnel, as that of the organ of Corti in the internal ear 1882. **d.** A working-hole in the wall of a glass-furnace 1839.

2. The Chimney is just under the window and the Tunnells runnes upon each side 1710. **4.** The vein has been attacked by various tunnels and shafts 1872.

attrib. and *Comb.*: **t.-head,** (*a*) the top of a shaft- or blast-furnace; (*b*) the point to which the construction of a t. has progressed; **-hole,** the throat of a blast-furnace; **-kiln,** a lime-kiln in which coal is burnt, as dist. from a flame-kiln in which wood or peat is used; **-net** = sense 1; also, a similar net for fishing; **-pit, -shaft,** a shaft sunk to the level of a t.

Tu·nnel, *v.* 1687. [f. prec.] **1.** *trans.* To catch (partridges) with a tunnel-net. Also *absol.* **2.** *intr.* To make a tunnel; to excavate a passage under ground, or through some body or substance 1795. **b.** *trans.* To excavate, as a tunnel; to make (one's way) by boring or excavating 1856. **c.** To make a tunnel through 1865.

2. As some great earth-monster, Johnson tunnels under ground, and heaves out rocks and tons of soil 1839. **c.** You have tunnelled the cliffs of Lucerne by Tell's chapel RUSKIN. Hence **Tunne(l)led** (tʊ·nĕld) *ppl. a.* **Tu·nnel(l)er.**

Tunny (tʊ·ni). 1480. [In XVI also *ton(n)y*; – (O)Fr. *thon* – Pr. *ton* = It. *tonno* :– L. *thunnus* – Gr. θύννος; the ending *-y* is unexplained.] A scombroid fish of the genus *Orcynus*, esp. the common tunny, *O. thynnus*, which has been fished from ancient times in the Mediterranean and Atlantic; it is one of the largest of food-fishes.

Tunu (tū·nu). 1883. [Carib name in Honduras.] The Central Amer. tree *Castilloa tunu*, yielding *t. gum.*

Tup (tʊp), *sb.* ME. [Chiefly north. and Sc.; in earliest use *tope, toupe*; of unkn. origin.] **1.** A male sheep; a ram. **b.** *transf.* Applied to a person 1652. **c.** *transf.* The head of a forge-hammer or steam-hammer 1873.

Tup (tʊp), *v.* 1549. [f. prec.] **1.** *trans.* Of the ram: To copulate with (the ewe); also *transf.* 1604. **2.** *intr.* **a.** Of the ewe: To admit the ram. **b.** Of the ram: To copulate. Also *transf.* 1549.

‖**Tupaia** (tupai·ă). 1820. [mod.L. – Malay *tūpai* squirrel.] *Zool.* An animal of the genus of insectivorous mammals, typical of the family *Tupaiidæ*, including the Banxring, *T. peguana*, of Burma and Pegu, and the Tana T., *T. tana*, of Borneo, etc.

‖**Tupelo** (tū·pėlo). 1730. [Creek Indian; *ito* tree, *opilwa* swamp.] Native name of trees of the N. Amer. genus *Nyssa* (family *Alangiaceæ* or *Nyssaceæ*), large trees growing in swamps or on river banks in the southern States; esp. *N. villosa* or *multiflora* (also called Black or Sour Gum, and Pepperidge), and the large t. or t. gum (*N. uniflora*), which produces a light tough timber.

‖**Tupi** (tū·pī). 1882. A native language widely spoken in Brazil.

Tuque (tiūk, tūk). *Canadian.* 1871. [– Canadian Fr., f. Fr. *toque* TOQUE.] A knitted stocking-cap tapered and closed at both ends, one end being tucked into the other to form the cap; formerly the characteristic winter head-dress of the Canadian 'habitant'.

‖**Tu quoque** (tiū₁kwōu·kwī). 1671. [L., lit. 'thou also', = Eng. slang 'you're another!'] An argument which consists in retorting a charge upon one's accuser. Also *attrib.*

The t. rejoinder, 'Physician, heal thyself' 1874. I leave myself open to a *t.*, I know 1903.

Turacin (tiūə·răsin). 1868. [f. mod.L. *Turacus* TOURACO + -IN[1].] *Chem.* A crimson animal pigment, found in the wing-feathers of several species of birds of the genera *Turacus, Gallirex,* and *Musophaga*; closely allied to hæmoglobin, but free from iron, and containing over 7 per cent. of copper.

Turacoverdin (tiūə:răko₁vō·ɹdin). 1885. [f. TOURACO + *verd-* (as in *verdure*) + -IN[1].] *Chem.* A green colouring-matter occurring in the feathers of some touracos.

Turanian (tiurēi·niăn), *sb.* and *a.* 1777. [f. Pers. *Tūrān*, name of the realm beyond the Oxus, used by Firdawsi c1000 in opposition to *Īrān* or Persia; see -IAN.] **A.** *sb.* **1.** A member of any of the races speaking the 'Turanian' or Ural-Altaic languages. **2.** The so-called Turanian languages collectively 1908. **B.** *adj.* **1.** Applied loosely to a group or supposed 'family' of languages, orig. applied to all or nearly all of Asiatic origin that are neither Aryan or Semitic; in later use nearly = URAL[1]-*Altaic* 1854. **2.** Applied to the peoples speaking these languages 1859.

Turban (tō·ɹbăn), *sb.* 1561. [Three main types are repr. by *tolibant, tulipan, turban(t* – Fr. †*tolliban,* †*tulban,* †*turbant* (mod. *turban*), It. †*tolipano, -ante,* Sp., Pg., It. *turbante* – Turk. *tülbend* – Pers. *dulband.* Cf. TULIP.] **1.** A head-dress of Moslem origin worn by men of Eastern nations, consisting of a cap round which is wound a long piece of linen, cotton, or silk. **b.** As the symbol of Islam, or of those who profess it 1610. **c.** A figure of a turban, e.g. on Moslem funeral monuments. Also in *Her.* 1687. **d.** *transf.* and *fig.* Applied to a head-dress, or a head of hair, likened to a turban 1609. **2.** A head-dress made to resemble or suggest the Oriental turban, worn by ladies during the late 18th and early 19th c., and temporarily revived in 1908. 1776. **3.** A bright-coloured cloth worn as a head-dress by Negroes (esp. women) in the West Indies and Southern U.S. 1839. **4.** A small brimless hat, or round cap with closely turned up brim, worn, chiefly by women and children, since about 1850. 1862. **5. a.** The spire or whorl of a twisted univalve shell (*rare*). **b.** A mollusc of the genus *Turbo*. 1681. **6.** *Zool.* Any of certain species of echinoderms, esp. the genus *Cidaris* 1713.

1. b. Though turbans now pollute Sophia's shrine BYRON. **2.** Went to the Opera: wore my tissue t. 1823.

attrib. and *Comb.*: **t.-shell,** = 5 b, 6; **-squash,** a variety of squash or pumpkin in which the fleshy receptacle does not extend over the ovary, which therefore protrudes so as to resemble a t.; **-stone,** a Moslem tombstone, a pillar having at the head the carved representation of a t. Hence **Tu·rban** *v. trans.* to envelop as or with a t.; also, to wind a cloth round (a cap).

Turbaned (tō·ɹbănd), *a.* 1591. [f. TURBAN *sb.* + -ED[2].] Wearing a turban. **b.** Of a Moslem tombstone: Surmounted by a carved turban 1835.

A malignant, and a Turbond-Turke SHAKS.

Turbary (tō·ɹbări). late ME. [– AFr. *turberie*, OFr. *tourberie* (med.L. *turbaria* XII), f. *tourbe* TURF; see -ARY[1].] **1.** Land, or a piece of land, where turf or peat may be dug for fuel; a peat-bog or peat-moss. **2.** *Law.* In full *common of t.*: The right to cut turf or peat for fuel on a common or on another person's land 1567.

Turbellarian (tōɹbelēə·riăn), *a.* and *sb.* 1879. [f. mod.L. *Turbellaria*, n. pl. (f. L. *turbella*, dim. of *turba* crowd) + -AN.] *Zool.* **A.** *adj.* Of or belonging to the *Turbellaria*, a class of worms inhabiting fresh or salt water or damp earth, having the body covered with vibratile cilia producing minute whirls in the water. **B.** *sb.* A worm of this class; a whirl-worm 1883.

Turbid (tō·ɹbid), *a.* 1626. [– L. *turbidus* full of confusion, troubled, muddy, etc., f. *turba* crowd, disturbance; see -ID[1].] **1.** Of liquid: Thick or opaque with suspended matter; not clear; cloudy, muddy. **b.** Of air, smoke, clouds, etc.: Thick, dense; dark 1705. **2.** *fig.* Characterized by or producing confusion or obscurity of thought, feeling, etc.; mentally confused, perplexed, muddled; disturbed, troubled 1645.

1. The Lees doe make the Liquour turbide BACON. **b.** T. streaming Clouds Of Smoak sulphureous 1705. **2.** The t. utterances and twisted language of Carlyle 1896. So **Turbi·dity, Tu·rbidness,** t. quality or condition. **Tu·rbidly** *adv.*

Turbinal (tō·ɹbinăl), *a.* and *sb.* 1584. [f. L. *turbo*, *-in-* (see TURBO) + -AL[1] 1.] **A.** *adj.* Turbinated, top-shaped; in *Anat.* = TURBINATE *a.* **B.** *sb. Anat.* A turbinal or turbinate bone; the ethmo-, the maxillo-, or the spheno-turbinal 1848.

Turbinate (tō·ɹbinĕt), *a.* and *sb.* 1661. [– L. *turbinatus*, f. as prec.; see -ATE[2].] **A.** *adj. Nat. Hist.* Resembling a spinning-top in shape; of a mollusc, having a spiral shell; *Bot.* inversely conical; having a narrow tapering base and broad rounded apex; *Anat.* applied to the scroll-like spongy bones of the nasal fossæ in the higher vertebrates. **B.** *sb.* **a.** A turbinate shell. **b.** A turbinate bone. 1802.

Turbinated (tō·ɹbineitėd), *a.* 1615. [f. as prec. *a.* + -ED[1].] **1.** = prec. A. †**2.** Of motion: Like that of a top; rotary, whirling –1692.

Turbination (tōɹbinēi·ʃən). 1623. [– L. *turbinatio*, *-ōn-* a pointing in the form of a cone, f. *turbinatus* TURBINATE; see -ION.] **1.** †The action of making top-shaped; top-like or turbinate form; formation of a whorl. †**2.**

The action of spinning or whirling round like a top –1680.

Turbine (tə̄·ɹbin, -əin). 1842. [– Fr. *turbine* – L. *turbo, turbin-*; see TURBO.] **1.** Applied orig. to a wheel revolving on a vertical axis, and driven by a column of water falling into its interior, and escaping by pipes or apertures, so arranged as to press by reaction on the periphery of the wheel, and cause it to revolve in the direction opposite to that of the escaping water. Now applied to any kind of machine in which this principle is used or developed. **2.** More fully *steam-t.*: A steam motor in which rotatory motion is produced by steam impinging directly upon a series of vanes upon the circumference of a revolving cylinder or disc (or, in some types, acting and reacting alternately on moving and stationary elements) 1900. **c.** A centrifugal separator used in sugar manufacture 1873.

attrib. and *Comb.*, as *t. boat, destroyer, steamer, yacht*, etc., one driven by a steam t.; **t.-alternator, -generator** (see TURBO-); **-pump,** a t. water wheel used to raise water by being driven by external power in the direction opposite to that in which it turns when used as a motor.

Turbiniform (tɒɹbi·nifǭɹm), *a.* 1826. [f. L. *turbo, turbin-*; see TURBO, -FORM.] *Nat. Hist.* Top-shaped, turbinate; also, having the form of the genus *Turbo* of gasteropods; turbinoid, spiral.

Turbinite (tə̄·ɹbinəit). 1828. [f. as prec. + -ITE[1] 2 a, as Fr. *turbinite* (XVIII), perh. the immediate source.] *Zool.* A fossil turbinate shell.

Turbinoid (tə̄·ɹbinoid), *a.* 1861. [f. as prec. + -OID.] *Zool.* Resembling the genus *Turbo* or family *Turbinidæ* of gasteropod molluscs.

Turbit (tə̄·ɹbit). 1688. [app. f. L. *turbo* top, from its figure.] A small fancy variety of the domestic pigeon, dist. by its stout rounded build, a short beak, the ruffle or frill on its neck and breast, and a small crest.

Turbo (tə̄·ɹbo). 1661. [– L. *turbo* (also *turben*), *turbin-* 'that which spins or twirls round', spec. whirlwind, spinning-top.] ‖**1.** (mod.L., pl. *turbines* (-nīz).) A genus of gasteropod molluscs, typical of the family *Turbinidæ*, having a regularly turbinate or whorled shell, with a rounded aperture and a calcareous operculum; also loosely, any member of the *Turbinidæ*; any turbinate or wreathed shell. **2.** *Mech.* = TURBINE. *colloq.* 1904.

Turbo- (tə̄·ɹbo), used as combining form of TURBINE, in compounds forming the names of machines driven by and directly coupled to a turbine, or which are themselves turbines; as *t.-alternator, -dynamo, -generator*, etc.

Turbot (tə̄·ɹbət). ME. [– OFr. *turbot* – OSw. *törnbut* (= early mod. Eng. *thornbut*), f. *törn* thorn + *but* BUTT *sb.*[1]] **1.** A large flat fish (*Rhombus maximus* or *Psetta maxima*), having a wide scaleless body covered with conical bony tubercles, with the eyes normally on the left side, found on the European coasts and much esteemed as food. **2.** Applied to other fish more or less resembling the turbot. **a.** The halibut *Sc.* and *north.* **b.** In U.S., any of various large flat fishes, as the diamond flounder of California (*Hypopsetta guttulata*), or the spotted flounder of the Pacific coast (*Bothus maculatus*). **c.** Locally, any of various species of *Balistes*, the file-fishes and trigger-fishes. 1555.

Turbulence (tə̄·ɹbiŭlĕns). 1490. [– (O)Fr. *turbulence* or late L. *turbulentia*, f. *turbulent, turbulentus*; see TURBULENT, -ENCE.] The state or quality of being turbulent; violent commotion, agitation, or disturbance; disorderly character or conduct; with *a* and *pl.*, an instance of this. **b.** Of natural conditions: Stormy or tempestuous state or action. **c.** The spirally curved path given to the gas entering the cylinders under pressure in supercharged internal-combustion engines 1928.

The t. of ecclesiastical politics NEWMAN.

Tu·rbulency. Now *rare.* 1607. [f. as prec.; see -ENCY.] Turbulent state, disturbed condition.

Turbulent (tə̄·ɹbiŭlĕnt), *a.* 1538. [– L. *turbulentus*, f. *turba* crowd, *turbare* disturb, agitate; see -ULENT. Cf. (O)Fr. *turbulent.*] **1.** Of persons, etc.: Causing disturbance or commotion; inclined to disorder; tumultuous; unruly; violent. †**b.** Of things: Having a disturbing effect –1671. **c.** Violent in action or effect (*rare*) 1656. **2.** Characterized by violent disturbance or commotion; violently disturbed; disorderly, troubled 1573. **3.** *Meteorol.* and *Aviation.* Of wind: Characterized by eddies 1907.

1. These t. and stormy assaultes of the wicked COVERDALE. **b.** Whose heads that t. liquor fills with fumes MILT. **2.** T'as been a t. and stormie night SHAKS. Thir inward State of Mind, calme Region once And full of Peace, now tost and t. MILT. The City of London lately so t. MACAULAY. Hence **Tu·rbulent-ly** *adv.*, **-ness** (*rare*).

†**Turcism** (tə̄·ɹsiz'm). 1566. [f. med.L. *Turcus* TURK + -ISM.] The religion or system of the Turks; Islam –1721. **b.** Turkish principles or practice –1705.

Turco (tə̄·ɹko). 1839. [– Sp., Pg., It. *Turco* TURK.] **1.** A Chilian bird, *Hylactes megapodius.* **2.** One of a body of native Algerian light infantry in the French Army; a Zouave soldier 1860.

Turco-, Turko- (tə̄·ɹko), comb. form repr. med.L. *Turcus* or TURK; as in *T.-Bulgarian*; also **Turcoma·nia,** a rage for Turkish manners or customs; excessive favour for Turkish policy; **Tu·rcophil, -e** *a.*, tending to favour Turkey or the Turks; also *sb.*

Turcoman (tə̄·ɹkomæ̆n). 1600. [– Pers. *turkumān* (partly through med.L. *turcomannus*, Fr. *turcoman*) f. *turk* TURK + *mānistan* resemble.] **1.** A member of a branch of the Turkish race, consisting of a number of tribes inhabiting the region lying east of the Caspian Sea and about the Sea of Aral, formerly known as Turkestan and parts of Persia and Afghanistan. **2.** A Turcoman horse 1831. **3.** *attrib.* or as *adj.* Of or pertaining to the Turcoman people, their language, or the region they inhabit 1613.

3. *T. carpet* or *rug*, a soft rich-coloured carpet made by the Turcomans.

Turd (tə̄ɹd). Not now in polite use. [OE. *tord* = MDu. *tort, torde* (also in OE. *tordwifel*, †Du. *tortwevel*, ON. *tordýfill* 'turd-weavil', dung-beetle) :– Gmc. **turdam*; a mutated form OE. *tyrdel* (see -EL[1]) is repr. by TREDDLE.] A lump or piece of excrement; also, excrement, ordure.

Turdiform (tə̄·ɹdifǭɹm), *a.* 1874. [f. L. *turdus* thrush + -FORM.] *Ornith.* Having the form or appearance of a thrush; thrush-like.

Tureen (tiurī·n, tərī·n). 1706. [Earliest forms *terrene, -ine* – Fr. *terrine* large circular flat-bottomed eathenware dish, subst. use of fem. of OFr. *terrin* earthen :– Rom. **terrinus*, f. L. *terra* earth.] A deep earthenware or plated vessel (often oval) with a lid, from which soup is served. Also, a smaller vessel of similar shape for sauce or gravy.

Turf (tə̄ɹf), *sb.* *Pl.* **turves, turfs.** [OE. *turf*, corresp., with variation of gender and declension, to OFris., OS. (Du.) *turf* (LG., whence G., *torf*), OHG. *zurba, zurf*, ON. *torf, torfa*; Gmc. sb. f. **turƀ-* (whence med.L. *turba*, OFr. *tourbe*; cf. TURBARY) :– IE. **drbh-*, the base of Skr. *darbhá* tuft of grass.] **1.** A slab pared from the surface of the soil with the grass and herbage growing on it; a sod of grass, with the roots and earth adhering. **b.** *collect.* as a substance or material. *arch.* 1565. **2.** *collect. sing.* The covering of grass and other plants, with its matted roots, forming the surface of grass land; the greensward; growing grass OE. **3.** A slab or block of peat dug for use as fuel ME. **b.** *collect.* as a substance; peat 1510. **4.** *The turf* (often with capital T): the grassy track or course over which horse-racing takes place; hence, the institution, action, or practice of horse-racing; the racing world 1755.

1. A bench of turues fressh and grene CHAUCER. **2.** The Shepheard. . Who you saw sitting by me on the Turph SHAKS. **3. b.** Abundance of turfe. . for fewell 1610. **4.** If you are a true sportsman and have the honour of the t. at heart 1755.

Comb.: **t.-ant,** a small yellow European ant (*Formica flava*, or *Lasius flavus*), living in dry heathy t.; **-drain,** a drain in which the channel is covered by turves placed over it; a sod-drain; **-man,** a devotee of the t., a racing man; **-spade,** a spade for cutting t. or peats; also, a turfing-iron; **-worm,** the sod-worm. Hence **Tu·rfen** *a.* made or covered with t.; turfy. **Tu·rfite,** a devotee of the t., a racing-man. **Tu·rfless** *a.* devoid of t., bare.

Turf, *v.* ME. [f. prec.] **1.** *trans.* To cover with turf; to lay with turf. **b.** *transf.* To place or lay under the turf; to cover with turf, or as turf does; to bury; also *intr.* with *it*, to die and be buried 1628. **2.** To dig up or excavate for turf or peat 1780. **3.** *intr.* To get turf or peat for fuel. *dial.* 1876.

1. b. That you may not think I have turfed it, to speak in the New market phrase. . I send you this letter COWPER.

Turfing (tə̄·ɹfiŋ), *vbl. sb.* 1649. [f. TURF *v.* or *sb.* + -ING[1].] The action of TURF *v.*

attrib.: **t.-iron,** a tool for raising turf; **-spade,** a peat-spade.

Turfy (tə̄·ɹfi), *a.* 1552. [f. TURF *sb.* + -Y[1].] **1.** Covered with or consisting of turf; grassy; turfen. **2.** Of the nature of or abounding in turf or peat; peaty 1660. **3.** Pertaining to or characteristic of the turf; suggestive of horse-racing; horsy 1844.

1. Thy Turphie-Mountaines, where liue nibling Sheepe SHAKS. Hence **Tu·rfiness.**

Turgent (tə̄·ɹdʒĕnt), *a.* Now *rare* or *Obs.* 1440. [– L. *turgens, -ent-*, pr. pple. of *turgēre* swell out; see -ENT.] **1.** Physically swelling or swollen; distended, turgid. **2.** *fig.* Swollen or inflated with pride or conceit; bumptious; also, using inflated language 1621.

2. Puffed vp with t. titles BURTON. Hence **Tu·rgency** (now *rare* or *Obs.*)

Turgescence (tɒɹdʒe·sĕns). 1631. [– mod.L. *turgescentia*; see TURGESCENT, -ENCE.] **1.** The action or condition of swelling up; the fact or state of being swollen. **2.** *fig.* **a.** Progressive swelling or increase. **b.** Inflation, pomposity, bombast. 1806.

Turgescency (tɒɹdʒe·sĕnsi). 1666. [f. as prec.; see -ENCY.] The quality or state of being turgescent; swelling or swollen condition.

Turgescent (tɒɹdʒe·sĕnt), *a.* 1727. [– L. *turgescens, -ent-*, pr. pple. of *turgescere*, inceptive of *turgēre* swell; see -ESCENT.] Becoming swollen; swelling, growing bigger.

Turgid (tə̄·ɹdʒid), *a.* 1620. [– L. *turgidus*, f. *turgēre* swell; see -ID[1].] **1.** Swollen, distended, puffed out. **2.** *fig.* in ref. to language: Inflated, grandiloquent, pompous, bombastic 1725.

1. Proud and t. buds 1669. Bladders. . t. with Sap 1674. **2.** Their t. and loquacious rhetoric GIBBON. Hence **Tu·rgid-ly** *adv.*, **-ness.**

Turgidity (tɒɹdʒi·dĭti). 1732. [f. L. *turgidus* (see prec.) + -ITY.] **1.** The state of being turgid or swollen. **2.** Inflation of language; grandiloquence, pomposity, bombast; also with *a* and *pl.* an example of this 1756.

2. T., and a false grandeur of diction WARTON.

Turion (tiū̆ə·riǭn). 1725. [– Fr. *turion* – L. *turio*, pl. **turiōnes,** formerly also in Eng. use.] *Bot.* A young shoot rising from the ground, produced from a subterranean bud.

Turk[1] (tə̄ɹk). ME. [= Fr. *Turc*, It., Sp., Pg. *Turco*, med.L. *Turcus*, Byz. Gr. Τοῦρκος, Pers. (and Arab.) *turk*. A national name of unkn. origin.] **1.** *Ethnology.* Pl. *Turks.* A numerous and widely spread family of the human race, occupying from prehistoric times large parts of Central Asia, and speaking a language belonging to the TURKIC branch of the Ural-Altaic linguistic family 1500. **2.** *Politics.* A member of the dominant race of the Ottoman empire; in earlier times, a Seljúk; since 1300, an Osmanli or Ottoman. Sometimes, any subject of the Grand Turk or Turkish Sultan; but usu. restricted to Moslems. Pl. *The Turks*, the Ottomans, the Turkish people. ME. **b.** *The T.*: the Turks; the Turkish power; also, the Turkish Sultan. 1482. **c.** *The Grand* or *Great T.*, the Ottoman Sultan 1482. **3.** Often used as = Moslem 1548. **4.** *transf.* Applied to any one having qualities attributed to the Turks; a cruel, savage, rigorous, or tyrannical man 1536. **5.** *attrib.* or as *adj.* = TURKISH. late ME.

2. *Young Turk*: a member of a twentieth-century

political group of Ottomans having for its object the rejuvenation of the Turkish Empire. **3.** He is a Christian at Rome, a Heathen at Japan, and a T. at Constantinople 1697. Phr. *To turn T.*, *become T.*; If the restc of my Fortunes turne Turke with me SHAKS. **4.** The man who has been a T. all his life lives long to plague all about him 1875. *Young* or *little T.*: an unmanageable or violent child or youth.

Turk[2]. 1712. [– Fr. *turc* (XVII), supposed to be rel. to Breton *teurk* tick.] The larva of an insect noted for the destruction of pear-trees by mining under their bark.

Turkey[1] (tɔ̄·ɹki). ME. [– Fr. *Turquie*, med.L. *Turchia*, *Turquia*, f. *Turc*, *Turcus* TURK[1]; cf. -Y[3].] **1.** The land of the Turks, 'Turkey in Asia' and 'Turkey in Europe'; formerly occas. Turkestan or Tartary. **†2.** Short for: **a.** TURKEY STONE. –1680. **b.** *T. leather* –1835.

Comb.: **T. corn,** an old name for Indian corn; **T. leather,** leather tawed with oil, the hair side not being removed until after the tawing; **T. oak,** the mossy-cup oak of southern Europe, *Quercus cerris*; **T. rhubarb,** medicinal RHUBARB (1); **T. wheat,** maize, called also †*Guinea corn* and *Indian corn*.

Turkey[2] (tɔ̄·ɹki). 1555. [Short for TURKEY-COCK, -HEN, app. applied orig. to the Guinea-fowl, a native of Africa.] **†1.** The Guinea-fowl –1655. **2.** A well-known large gallinaceous bird of the Linnæan genus *Meleagris*, the species of which are all American; esp. *M. gallopavo*, which was found domesticated in Mexico at the discovery of that country in 1518, and is now valued as a table-fowl in all civilized lands 1555. **b.** *Wild t.*, the wild original of the domestic fowl 1613. **c.** The flesh of this bird, esp. the domestic turkey, as food 1573. **3.** Applied with qualification to other birds: A local name of the Bustard; now usu. applied to the Australian Bustard, also called *Native*, *Plain*, or *Wild T.* (*Eupodotis* (*Otis*) *australis*); also in Australia, the *Brush-* or *Wattled T.*; etc. 1848.

2. c. Cold t. and ham, or roast chicken 1886.

attrib. and *Comb.*; **t.-beard,** also **turkey's beard,** a N. Amer. liliaceous herb, *Xerophyllum asphodeloides*, having a tuft of wiry root-leaves, and an erect stem with a raceme of white flowers; **-berry,** (*a*) *Solanum mammosum* and *S. torvum* of the West Indies; (*b*) the fruit of a W. Indian tree, *Cordia collococca* (*t.-berry tree*); **-buzzard,** an Amer. carrion vulture, *Cathartes aura*, so called from its bare reddish head and neck and dark plumage; in W. Africa, the Vulturine Pic, *Picathartes gymnocephalus*; **-trot,** a kind of ball-room dance introduced from U.S. *c*1912; **-vulture** = *t. buzzard*.

Tu·rkey ca·rpet. 1546. [f. TURKEY[1] + CARPET.] A carpet made in or imported from Turkey, or of a style in imitation of this; woven in one piece of richly-coloured wools, and having a deep pile, cut so as to resemble velvet.

Turkey-cock (tɔ̄·ɹki kǫ:k). 1541. [f. TURKEY[1] + COCK *sb.*[1] In XVI synonymous with *Guinea-cock* or *Guinea-fowl*, the Amer. bird being at first identified with or treated as a species of this.] **†1.** The male of the Guinea-fowl, *Numida meleagris* –1601. **2.** The male of the turkey 1578.

2. *fig. Twel. N.* II. v. 36.

Tu·rkey-hen. 1552. [Cf. prec.] **†1.** The guinea-hen –1601. **2.** The female of the turkey 1555.

Turkey red. 1789. [TURKEY[1].] A brilliant and permanent red colour produced on cotton goods, essentially a madder red in combination with oil or fat, with an aluminous mordant. Also called *Adrianople* or *Levant red*. **b.** Cotton cloth of this colour 1880.

Turkey stone. 1607. [TURKEY[1].] **1.** = TURQOISE. **2.** A hard, fine-grained, siliceous rock imported from the Levant for whetstones; novaculite; a whetstone made of this 1816.

Turki (tu·ɹki), *a.* (*sb.*) 1782. [– Pers. *turkī*, adj. deriv. of *turk* TURK[1].] Turkish; belonging to the typical Turkic languages, *East* and *West T.*, and to the peoples speaking them. **B.** *sb.* A member of the Turkish race; also, a Turkish horse.

Turkic (tɔ̄·ɹkik), *a.* 1859. [f. TURK[1] + -IC.] Applied to one of the branches of the Ural-Altaic or Turanian family of languages, comprising Eastern Turki or Uigur, West Turki or Seljûk and Osmanli, Kazan Tartar, Kirghiz, Nogai, Yakut, etc., the languages of the Turks (in the wide sense); also applied to the peoples using these.

Turkish (tɔ̄·ɹkiʃ), *a.* (*sb.*) 1545. [f. TURK[1] + -ISH[1], repl. earlier *Turkes* (XIV), *Turkeys* – OFr. *turqueis*.] Of, pertaining or belonging to the Turks or to Turkey; now commonly = Ottoman. **b.** Resembling the Turks or their character; cruel, savage, barbarous 1600.

Collocations. **T. bath,** a hot steam bath introduced from the East, inducing copious perspiration, followed by soaping, washing, shampooing, massage, and cooling. **T. delight,** a sweetmeat of T. origin usu. made of jelly of tough consistence and sugar-coated; **T. music,** the noisy percussion instruments in an orchestra; **T. towel,** a cotton towel having a long nap, cut or uncut; hence **T. towelling.**

B. *sb.* **1.** The Turkish or Turk's language 1718. **2.** *ellipt.* for *T. delight*, *T. tobacco* (colloq.) 1898. Hence **Tu·rkish-ly** *adv.*, **-ness.**

Turkism (tɔ̄·ɹkiz'm). 1595. [f. TURK[1] + -ISM.] = TURCISM.

Turkize (tɔ̄·ɹkəiz), *v.* 1599. [f. TURK[1] + -IZE.] **1.** *trans.* To render Turkish. **2.** *intr.* To play the Turk; †to tyrannize *over* 1599.

Turk's cap. 1597. [TURK[1].] **†1.** Early name for the tulip –1629. **2.** The Martagon lily; also *Turk's-cap lily* 1672. **3.** The Melon-thistle, *Cactus melocactus*; also †*Turk's head* 1829.

Turk's head. 1725. [TURK[1].] **†1.** = prec. 3. –1760. **2.** *Naut.* An ornamental knot resembling a turban 1833. **3.** A round long-handled broom or brush; = POPE'S HEAD 2. 1859.

Turm (tɔ̄ɹm). 1483. [– Fr. †*turme* or L. *turma* troop, squadron.] A body or band of people, *esp.* a troop of horsemen; *spec.* a troop of thirty or thirty-two horsemen.

Legions and Cohorts, turmes of horse and wings MILT.

Turmeric (tɔ̄·ɹmərik), *sb.* (*a.*) 1538. [Early forms also *tarmaret*, *tormarith*, which appear to be – Fr. *terre mérite*, mod.L. *terra merita* (XVI), perh. alt. of some native form; the ending shows assim. to -IC.] **1.** The aromatic and pungent root-stock of an E. Indian plant (see 2); the powder made from this, the chief ingredient in curry powder, used also as a dye, as a chemical test, and in the East as a condiment, as well as medicinally. **2.** The plant *Curcuma longa*, family *Zingiberaceæ* 1601.

attrib. and *Comb.*: **t.-oil** = TURMEROL; **t. paper,** unsized paper tinged with a solution of t., used as a test for alkalis.

B. *adj. Chem.* Obtained from t.; in *t. acid*, an acid, $C_{11}H_{14}O_2$, formed by the oxidation of turmerol.

Turmerol (tɔ̄·ɹmərǫl). 1890. [f. prec. + -OL 3.] *Chem.* An aromatic volatile oil obtained from turmeric.

Turmoil (tɔ̄·ɹmoil), *sb.* 1526. [f. next.] A state of agitation or commotion; disturbance, tumult; trouble, disquiet. **†b.** Harassing labour, toil (*rare*) –1591.

b. And there Ile rest, as after much turmoile, A blessed soule doth in Elizium SHAKS.

Turmoil (tɔ̄·ɹmoil), *v.* 1511. [The senses correspond to the transf. senses of MOIL *v.*, and, like these, are first recorded in pass. and refl. use; of unkn. origin.] **1.** *trans.* To agitate, disquiet, disturb; to trouble, worry, torment. Now somewhat *rare*. **b.** To disorder or distress physically. *arch.* 1542. **†2.** *intr.* To be or live in turmoil, agitation, or commotion –1681. **3.** *intr.* To toil, drudge. Now *dial.* 1548.

1. I was so turmoyled in the contre where I was that I coude no lenger there dwell TINDALE.

Turn (tɔ̄ɹn), *sb.* ME. [Partly – AFr. **torn*, *turn*, *tourn* = OFr. *torn* (mod. *tour*) :– L. *tornus*; see next.] **I.** Rotation, and connected senses. **1.** The action of turning about an axis or centre, as a wheel; rotation, revolution. Now *rare*. **2.** An act of turning; a movement of rotation (complete or partial); *esp.* a single revolution, as of a wheel 1481. **3.** = GID[1]. 1523. **4.** A movement round something, a twist; *spec. Naut.* an act of passing a rope once round a mast or other object 1743. **5.** *Mus.* A melodic ornament consisting of a group of three (four, or five) notes, viz. the principal note (*on* which it is performed) and the notes one degree above and below it 1801. **6.** The condition of being or direction in which something is twisted or convoluted; hence, a portion of something of a convoluted or twisted form, corresponding to one whole revolution; a (single) coil or twist 1669. **7.** A lathe; now only applied to a watchmaker's lathe, also called a *pair of turns* 1483.

1. Fortune's-wheel..is always..upon the T. 1680. **2.** In a few turns of the hands of the.. clock RUSKIN. Phr. (*Roasted, done*, etc.) *to a t.*, i.e. precisely right: orig. in ref. to the turns of the spit. *T. of the scale(s*, the slight advantage given to the buyer by which the article sold overbalances the weight and brings down the scale-pan; hence, a very little (just enough to *turn the scale*).

II. Change of direction or course, etc. **1.** An act of turning or facing another way; a change of direction or posture. late ME. **b.** 'A step off the ladder at the gallows' (J.); hanging. Now *rare* or *Obs.* 1631. **c.** Change of position (by a rotatory movement) of something inanimate, as a die when thrown 1801. **2.** *Printing.* A reversal of type in composing 1888. **3.** An act (or, rarely, the action) of turning aside from one's course; deflection, deviation; a roundabout course, a detour ME. **4.** A place or point at which a road, river, or the like turns, or turns off; a bend, curve, or angle. late ME. **5.** The act of turning so as to face about or go in the opposite direction; reversal of position or course; turning back. Also *fig.*, esp. in *t. of the tide*, etc. 1669. **6.** *Coursing.* The act of suddenly turning, as of a hare when closely pursued, and making off more or less in the opposite direction, or at a considerable angle from the direction of pursuit. Usu. in phr. *to give the hare* (etc.) *a t.*, said of the hound. 1575. **†7.** A journey, tour, course –1734. **b.** A sheriff's tour or court; see TOURN. **8.** An act of walking or pacing around or about a limited area; a short walk (or ride) forth and back, esp. by a different route; a stroll 1591.

1. She..made a sudden t. As if to speak TENNYSON. **c.** Stake their liberty upon the t. of the dice 1801. **3.** The river nobly..flows..And all its thousand turns disclose Some fresher beauty BYRON. **5.** Phr. *At every t.*, usu. *fig.* at every change of circumstance; hence, on every occasion, constantly. Phr. *On the t.*, in or close upon the act of turning, at the turning-point. **7.** His design to take a t. into England H. WALPOLE. **8.** A turne or two Ile walke To still my beating minde SHAKS. I took several Turns about my Chamber STEELE.

III. Change in general. **1.** The action, or an act, of turning or changing; change, alteration (*rare* exc. as in 2.) 1597. **2.** *spec.* A change in affairs, conditions, or circumstances; vicissitude; revolution; *esp.* a change for better or worse, or the like, at a crisis; hence, sometimes, the time at which such a change takes place 1607. **3.** A momentary shock caused by sudden alarm, fright, or the like. *colloq.* 1846.

1. The t. of the leaf was very brilliant 1901. Phr. *On the t.*, turning sour, as food; of the weather or the season, changing. **2.** Some t. this sickness yet might take TENNYSON. Phr. *T. of life*: = *change of life* (CHANGE *sb.* 3). **3.** It was only a dream.. But it gave me a terrible t. 1886.

IV. Senses denoting actions of various kinds. **†1.** A movement, device, or trick, by which a wrestler attempts to throw his antagonist; = Fr. *tour* –1562. **†2.** A subtle device of any kind; a trick, wile, artifice, stratagem –1735. **3.** An act of good or ill will, or that does good or harm to another; usu. qualified, as *good t.*, a benefit, etc. ME. **4.** A stroke or spell of work; a task, job. *north.* and *Sc. Obs.* exc. in *hand's t.* late ME. **5.** A spell or bout of action, a 'go'; *spec.* a spell of wrestling; hence, a contest. late ME. **b.** An attack of illness, faintness, or the like; also, a fit of passion or excitement 1775. **†6.** An event, circumstance, trap. *Obs.* or merged in other senses. –1719.

2. A variety of artifices and turns H. WALPOLE. **3.** One good t. deserves another 1654. **5. b.** Some wild t. of anger TENNYSON.

V. Occasion, etc. **1.** (Each or any one's) recurring occasion of action, etc. in a series of acts done, or to be done, by (or to) a number in rotation. late ME. **2.** *spec.* **a.** A shift

1793. **b.** *Theatr.* A public appearance on the stage, preceding or following others; an item in a variety entertainment; also *transf.* applied to the performer 1890. **3.** Requirement, need, exigency; purpose, use, convenience. *arch.* (Chiefly in special phrases.) 1573.

1. Phr. *By turns*, one after another in regular succession. *In t., in turns*, each in due succession. *In one's t.*, in one's due order in the series; so *out of one's t.*, out of one's due order in the series. *T. about, t. and t. about*: *advb.* in t., by turns, alternately; *adj.* performed in t., mutual, reciprocal (*rare*); *sb.* the action of doing something in t. **3.** You will answer my t...as well as another 1881. Phr. *To serve one's t.*, to answer one's purpose or requirement; to suit, answer, serve, avail, 'do'. So *To serve the t. To serve one's (one's own, or a) t.* (said of a person): to compass one's own purpose, consult one's own need.

VI. 1. Style, character, quality; *esp.* style of language, arrangement of words in a sentence 1601. **2.** (with *a* and *pl.*) A modification of phraseology for a particular effect, or as a grace or embellishment; a special point or detail of style or expression 1693. **3.** Form, make, mould, cast (of a material object). Now *rare* or *Obs.* 1702. **4.** Natural inclination, disposition, bent; aptitude, capacity *for* something 1702. †**b.** A characteristic –1764. **5.** Direction, tendency, drift, trend 1704. **6.** A change from the original intention; a particular construction or interpretation put upon something: usu. with *give* 1710.

1. Her T. of Wit was gentle, polite, and insinuating 1718. **2.** His felicitous turns of expression 1868. **3.** The T. of his Neck and Arms ADDISON. **4.** Mr. Ledbury was of an enquiring t. of mind 1844. Persons of a dyspeptic t. 1871. Phr. *T. of speed*, capacity for speed, ability to run or go fast. **5.** I discovered what gave my thoughts a new t. 1845. **6.** Do not give so cruel a t. to my silence FIELDING.

VII. Techn. senses. **1.** A measure of various commodities, as of haddocks, wood, furskins, etc. 1674. **2.** *Comm.* (in full, *t. of the market*): A change in price, or the difference between the buying and selling prices, of a stock or commodity; the profit made by this 1882.

Turn (tɒ̃ɹn), *v.* [OE. *tyrnan* and *turnian*, both – L. *tornare* turn in a lathe, round off, f. *tornus* lathe – Gr. τόρνος lathe, circular movement; prob. reinforced from OFr. *turner, torner* (mod. *tourner*) from the same source.] **I.** To rotate or revolve, and derived senses. **1.** *trans.* To cause to move round on an axis or about a centre; to cause to rotate or revolve, as a wheel. **b.** To cause to move round, or (usu.) partly round, in this way, esp. for opening or closing something: as a key, tap, door-handle, screw, etc. ME. **c.** To perform by revolving, as a somersault 1860. **2.** *intr.* To move round on an axis or about a centre; to move partly round in this way OE. **b.** *fig.* To revolve (as time, etc.). In later use said chiefly of the head or brain: To reel, swim, be in a whirl. OE. **3.** *To t. on* or *upon* (fig.): **a.** To hinge upon, depend on, have as the centre or pivot of movement or action 1661. **b.** To have as its subject, be about, relate to; usu. said of conversation or debate 1711.

1. Waters turning busy mills COWPER. **b.** The lamp was turned very low 1880. **2.** As the dore turneth vpon his henges BIBLE (Genev.) *Prov.* 26:14. A little boy..turning head over heels MME. D'ARBLAY. **b.** I looked at the handbill and my head turned 1892. **3. a.** Great Events often t. upon very small Circumstances SWIFT. **b.** The debate..did not t. upon any..practical proposition 1884.

II. To form or shape by rotation, etc. **1.** *trans.* To shape, esp. into a rounded form, by cutting with a chisel or similar tool while rotating in a lathe; to form, work, or make by means of a lathe. Also *absol.* to work with a lathe. ME. **b.** *Building.* To form, construct, build (an arched or vaulted structure) 1703. **c.** *Cookery.* To pare off the rind or peel of (an orange, lemon, etc.) round and round in a long narrow thin strip; to stone (an olive) in this way 1706. **d.** *Knitting* and *Lace-making.* To make in a curved form 1882. **2.** *fig.* To shape, form, or fashion artistically or gracefully 1616. †**b.** *pa. pple.* Of a person (or the mind, etc.): Naturally adapted, fitted, or 'cut out' for some pursuit –1728.

1. Such as turne wooden vessels 1600. **d.** She.. appeared to be in a perpetual state of turning the heel of a stocking 1902. **2.** Some studied compliments..finely turned BOSWELL. The hand long, delicate, and well turned 1847. **b.** By nature turn'd to play the rake SWIFT.

III. To change or reverse position. **1.** *intr.* To move or shift (by a rotary motion, or through an angle) so as to change one's posture or position; *esp.* to shift the body (as on an axis) from side to side; to twist or writhe about OE. **b.** Said of the scale or beam of a balance, or of the balance itself: To move up or down from the horizontal position 1596. **2.** *trans.* To alter the position or posture of (an object) by moving it through an angle; to move (a thing or person) into a different posture. late ME. **3.** *fig.* To revolve in the mind 1725. **4.** To give a curved or crooked form to; to bend or twist; to form by bending ME. **b.** *spec.* To bend back (the edge of a sharp instrument) so as to make it useless for cutting; to blunt in this way 1568. **c.** *intr.* for *pass.* To assume a curved form, to bend; to become blunted by bending 1579. **5.** *trans.* To reverse the position or posture of; to move into the contrary position, so that the upper side becomes the under, or the front the back ME. **6.** *spec.* **a.** To reverse (a leaf of a book) in order to read (or write) on the other side or on the next leaf; to do this with the leaves of (a book) in succession so as to read or search through ME. **b.** To reverse the position of the turf, or of the soil, in ploughing or digging, so as to bring the under parts to the surface. Also *absol.* 1477. **c.** To reverse (a garment, etc.) so that the inner side becomes the outer; hence, to alter or remake by putting the inner side outward 1483. **7.** To cause (the stomach) to reject or revolt against food 1622. **b.** *intr.* Of the stomach: To be affected with nausea 1719.

1. Phr. *To make* (a person) *t. in his grave*: see GRAVE *sb.*[1] 1. **b.** If the scale doe turne But in the estimation of a hayre SHAKS. **3.** T. these things in your mind 1825. **4.** His mustaches were turned and curled SCOTT. Phr. *To t.* (a person) *round one's (little) finger*, to be able to do what one likes with him. **b.** *fig.* A difficulty sufficient to t. the edge of the finest wit 1714. **5.** Her..fine legerdemain in turning pancakes RUSKIN. *To t. turtle*; see TURTLE *sb.*[2] 1. **6. b.** The first sod of the.. Railway was turned on Tuesday 1892. **c.** A way of turning an old frock 1893. **7.** This filthy simile..Quite turns my stomach POPE. **b.** Their stomachs turned at this sight DE FOE.

IV. To change or reverse course. **1.** *trans.* To alter the course of; to divert, deflect ME. **b.** To check the course of; to cause to go aside or retreat; to throw off, keep out (wet) 1620. **2.** *fig.* To divert or deflect from a course of action, purpose, thought, etc.; to alter the course of (something immaterial) ME. **3.** 'To keep passing in a course of exchange or traffick' (J.); to cause (money or commodities) to circulate 1605. **4.** *intr.* To change one's course so as to go in a different direction; to deviate ME. **b.** *Naut.* To beat to windward; to tack 1569. **c.** Of the wind: To shift 1610. **d.** Of a road, path, line, etc.: To change direction; also, to branch off from the main road or line 1535. **5.** *trans.* To go or pass round (a corner, etc.) 1687. **b.** *Mil.* To get round (an enemy's position, etc.) 1845. **6.** To pass, get beyond (a particular age, time or amount) 1789. **b.** *pa. pple.* (in active sense): Having passed (a particular age or time); more than, past 1700. **7.** To reverse the course of; to cause to go in the opposite direction ME. **8.** *intr.* To reverse one's, or its course; to begin to go, or to tend, in the opposite direction ME. †**9.** *intr.* and *trans.* To give or send back; to return –1637.

1. They turn'd the winding rivulet's course CLARE. **b.** Horatius Right deftly turned the blow MACAULAY. **2.** She turn'd the talk DRYDEN. **3.** Phr. *To t. the penny, to t. an honest penny*: see PENNY III, HONEST *a.* 4 b. **4. e.** *Cricket.* Of a ball: To break 1911. **5.** Before Gama had turned the Cape MACAULAY. **6.** It had turned a quarter past one 1893. **b.** I'm nineteen..and you are turned twenty 1890. **7.** Phr. *To t. the dice, t. the tide*, to reverse the luck, the progress of circumstances. **8.** Stocks fell..the exchange turned, money became scarce DISRAELI. **9.** Ere from this warre thou turne a Conqueror SHAKS.

V. 1. a. *trans.* To change the direction of; to direct another way, or different ways alternately (esp. the eyes or face) ME. **b.** *refl.* = c. *arch.* ME. **c.** *intr.* To face about ME. **2. a.** *trans.* To direct, present, point (towards or away from some specified person or thing, or in some specified direction) ME. **b.** *refl.* = c. *arch.* late ME. **c.** *intr.* To direct oneself; to face (with implied change of direction) ME. **3. a.** *trans.* To set going in a particular direction; to bend the course of ME. **b.** *refl.* = c. *arch.* ME. **c.** *intr.* To direct one's course; to set oneself to go in a particular direction: usu. with implied change of course ME. **4.** *trans.* To cause or command to go away from a place or one's presence; *esp.* to send or order away 1526. **b.** *spec.* To drive or put forth (beasts) to pasture 1602. **c.** To put, cast, or convey into a receptacle or the like; now esp. by inverting the containing vessel, or diverting into a new channel 1594. **5.** *fig. trans.* To direct or set (thought, desire, speech, action, etc.) towards (or away from) something. Usu. const. *to*, rarely *on, upon.* ME. **b.** To cause or induce (a person, etc.) to take a particular course; to direct the course of (events, etc.) *arch.* late ME. **6.** *refl.* = 7, 7 b, c. Now *rare* or *arch.* ME. **7.** *intr.* To direct one's mind, desire, or will to or from some person, thing, or action ME. **b.** *spec.* To direct one's attention *to* a different subject. late ME. **c.** To direct one's attention *to* something practically; to apply oneself *to* an occupation or pursuit 1667. **d.** *To t. to*: to refer to, look up, consult (a book, list, etc.) 1631. **e.** To have recourse *to* (a person, etc.); to appeal *to* for help or support 1821. †**8.** *trans.* To convert; less commonly in bad sense, to pervert. *Obs.* or merged in other senses. ME. **9.** *intr.* To adopt a different (esp. the true) religion, or a godly life; to be converted ME. **b.** To go over to another side or party; to revolt, desert. Const. *to. Obs.* or *arch.* ME. **10.** *trans.* To direct or bring to bear in the way of (active) opposition; to retort or cause to recoil *upon*; to proceed to use *against* ME. **b.** To direct *against* in feeling; to imbue with hatred or dislike 1831. **11.** *intr.* To recoil *upon*; to have an adverse tendency or result. Now *rare* or *Obs.* or merged in next. late ME. **12.** To change one's position in order to attack or resist some one; to take up an attitude of opposition; with *on* or *upon*, to assail suddenly or violently (in act or word); with *against.* usu. implying a change from previous friendliness ME. **13.** *trans.* To apply *to* some use or purpose; to make use of, employ ME. **b.** To set (a person) to some work or employment 1781.

1. b. Turne thee Benuolio, looke vpon thy death SHAKS. **c.** *Right t.! Left t.!*, as military words of command = turn (through a right angle), to the right, to the left. *(Right) about t.!* = turn (by a movement to the right) so as to face in the opposite direction. **2. a.** A soured man prefers to t. his worst side outwards 1880. **c.** Where'er she turns the Graces homage pay GRAY. Phr. *Not to know which way to t.*, etc., not to know what course to take, what to do. **3. c.** Thither their footsteps t. 1893. **4.** You will not..t. me from your door MISS BURNEY. **b.** The privilege of turning stock into the park 1847. **5.** We..turned our attention to poor Tom. STEVENSON. **b.** Great Apollo Turne all to th' best SHAKS. **6.** Turne the vnto me, and haue mercy vpon me *Bible* (Great) *Ps.* 25:16. **7.** Where'er I roam.. My heart untravell'd fondly turns to thee GOLDSM. **c.** He turned next to log-splitting 1891. **9.** So would they say to all Protestants..T., or burn 1679. **10.** To wrest his weapon out of his hands, and turne it upon himselfe 1641. **b.** The hearts of the poor were turned in bitterness against the rich 1831. **12.** His adulators of yesterday are prepared to t. and rend him 1892. **13.** Virgil, turning his pen to the advantage of his country BACON.

VI. To change, alter. **1.** *trans.* To change, transmute; to alter, make different, or substitute something else (of the same kind) for. Now *rare* or *Obs.* ME. **2.** *intr.* To undergo change or alteration; to change (*rare*) ME. **3.** *trans.* with *into* or *to*: To change, transform, or convert into ME. **b.** *transf.* To exchange for; also, to substitute something else for 1449. **4.** *intr.* with *into* or *to*: To change into; to become ME. **5.** with *compl.* To change so as to be, to become ME. **6.**

trans. with *compl.* (usu. *adj.*) To change so as to make..; to make (so) by alteration; to render 1607. **7.** With *into* or *to*: To make the subject of (praise, mockery, etc.) late ME. **8.** *intr.* with *to*: To lead to as a consequence; to result in, bring about. *Obs.* or merged in other senses. ME. †**b.** *To t.* (a person) *to* (something): to result in or bring about for the person; to put him to (trouble, etc.); to be for (his advantage, etc.) –1610. **9.** *trans.* To translate or paraphrase; to render. Also *absol.* ME. **b.** To alter the phrasing of (a sentence); to give another turn to 1593. **10.** To disturb or overthrow the mental balance of; to make mad or crazy, to distract, dement, infatuate ME. **b.** *intr.* for *pass.* of the head (*rare*) 1852. **11.** *trans.* To make sour, taint (milk, etc.) 1548. **b.** *intr.* To become sour or tainted 1577. **12.** To change colour, become of a different colour (as ripening fruit, fading leaves, etc.) 1578. **b.** *trans.* To change the colour of 1791.

1. *Merch. V.* III. ii. 249. **2.** Things change their titles, as our manners t. POPE. **3.** May not honey's self be turn'd to gall? GRAY. **b.** [They] turned their little stock into Cash 1855. **4.** These rocks, by custom, t. to beds of down GOLDSM. **5.** Vnlesse the diuell himselfe turne Iew SHAKS. Cygnets from Gray turne White BACON. **7.** Phr. *To t.* (a thing) *into ridicule* (see RIDICULE *sb.*[1]). **8. b.** All the trouble thou hast turn'd me to SHAKS. **9.** In 1648 he turned nine psalms, and.. in 1653, 'did into verse' eight more 1879. **10.** The Prince's head was a little turned 1683. **12.** When her hair had begun to t. 1888.

Phrases. **Turn the** (or **one's**) **back,** to turn away, go away; *t. the back upon*, to depart from, abandon. **T. the balance** or **beam,** = *t. the scale*. **T. bridle,** to turn one's horse and ride back; to retreat, as a rider. **T. one's coat,** to change one's principles or party (see COAT *sb.*). **T. (one's) colour,** to change colour; of a person, to become pale or red in the face (now *rare*). **T. a deaf ear,** to refuse to listen. **T. edge**: see III. 4 b. **Turn..flank,** *Mil.* to get round an enemy's flank, so as to make an attack in flank or rear; hence *fig.* to 'get round', circumvent, or outwit a person. **T. one's hand. a.** To make an attack *upon* (*arch.*). **b.** with *to*: To apply oneself to, set to work at, take up as an occupation. †**T. head,** to turn and face an enemy; to show a bold opposing front; opp. to *t. tail*. **T. the scale,** to cause one scale of a balance to descend: said of an additional weight, usu. a slight or just sufficient one; hence *fig.* to preponderate so as to determine the success or superiority of one of two opposing parties. **b.** with *at*, To weigh slightly more than. **T. tail. a.** (orig. in *Falconry*) To turn the back and flee; to run away. **b.** with *on* or *upon*: To abandon, forsake. **T. loose.** *trans.* To set free (an animal) and allow to go loose; *transf.* and *fig.* to leave to oneself or one's own devices. **T. to account.** †**a.** *intr.* To be profitable, to 'pay'. **b.** *trans.* To employ profitably. **T. to bay,** to turn and defend oneself as a hunted animal at bay; also *fig.* †**T. and wind. a.** *intr. and refl.* To turn this way and that; to go or move in a winding course. **b.** *trans.* To turn this way and that, as a rider his horse; *fig.* to do what one will with.

With advs. **T. about.** (See simple senses and ABOUT *adv.*) †**a.** *intr.* To move circularly on an axis; to rotate, revolve. **b.** To t. so as to face or go in the opposite direction. Now *rare*. †**c.** *trans.* To cause to rotate or revolve. **d.** To put into a different or the opposite position (by a rotary motion). Now *rare* or *Obs.* **e.** To turn this way and that; to move or push about; also *fig.* = *t. over*. **T. again.** (See simple senses and AGAIN *adv.*) *intr.* †To face round the other way, return, go back. **T. aside**: see simple senses and ASIDE *adv.* **T. away.** (See simple senses and AWAY *adv.*) **a.** *trans.* To avert (one's face, etc.). **b.** *fig.* To divert; to avert (calamity, etc.). **c.** To send away, dismiss; *spec.* to dismiss from service. **d.** *intr.* To turn so as to face away from some person or thing; to avert one's face. **e.** To leave the straight course, deviate; to be averted. *Obs.* or *arch.* **T. back.** (See simple senses and BACK *adv.*) **a.** *trans.* To reverse the course of, drive back, cause to retreat. †**b.** To send or give back, return. **c.** To reverse the direction of; to direct backwards. **d.** To fold or double back or over (part of a garment, etc.). **e.** *intr.* To turn and go back. †**f.** To come or go back. **T. down.** (See simple senses and DOWN *adv.*) **a.** *trans.* To fold or double down; to bend downwards. **b.** To turn upside down; to turn (a card) face downwards. **c.** To put down, send to a lower position (as in a class at school). **d.** *slang.* orig. *U.S.* To rebuke, snub; to reject. **e.** *Sporting*, etc. To put (game, etc.) in a place to stock it. **f.** To lower (a lamp, gas, etc.) by turning the wick, tap, or stop-cock. **g.** *intr.* To turn aside and go down. **h.** To bend downwards. **T. in.** (See simple senses and IN *adv.*) **a.** *trans.* To send, drive, put, or take in. **b.** *Agric.* To dig or plough (weeds, stubble, manure) into the ground. Also with the ground as obj. **c.** To bend or fold inwards. **d.** To cause to point or face inwards. **e.** To hand in, bring in, deliver (*U.S.*). **f.** *intr.* To turn aside and go in (to a place, house, room, etc.). **g.** (orig. *Naut.*) To go to bed. *colloq.* **h.** To have an inward direction, point inwards. **T. off.** (See simple senses and OFF *adv.*) **a.** *trans.* To dismiss, send away; *spec.* to discharge from service or employment. **b.** To hang (on a gallows); orig. *to t. off the ladder*. Now *rare* or *Obs.* **c.** *joc.* (perh. *fig.* from prec.) To marry, join in marriage. **d.** To deflect, divert. **e.** *spec.* To divert attention from, or alter the effect of (a remark, etc.). **f.** To stop the flow of (water, gas, etc.) by turning a tap or the like, or by closing a sluice; to shut off; to turn out (a light). Also with the tap, etc. as obj. **g.** To complete and get off one's hands; to produce (with skill or facility). **h.** *intr.* To deviate from the direct road; also *transf.* of a road or path, to branch off. **i.** To fall in quality, 'go off'; to wither and fall off; also, of food, etc., to become sour or bad. **T. on. a.** *trans.* To induce a flow of (water, steam, gas, etc.) by turning a tap or stop-cock, or by opening a sluice; also with the tap, etc. as obj.; also *intr.* for *pass.* **b.** To set (a person) *to do* something. *colloq.* **T. out.** (See simple senses and OUT *adv.*) **a.** *trans.* To cause to go or come out; to expel; also, to fetch or summon out. **b.** To drive or put out (beasts) to pasture or to the open, or (pheasants, etc.) into a covert. **c.** To dismiss or eject from office or employment. **d.** To put (things) out of a house, room, or receptacle; to empty out by sloping or inverting the containing vessel. **e.** (*transf.* from d.) To clear (a receptacle or room) of its contents; to empty (usu. for the sake of examining or re-arranging the contents). **f.** To put out (a lamp, gas) by turning a tap or the like. **g.** To finish making and get off one's hands; to produce (usu. implying rapidity, facility, or skill). **h.** To equip, 'rig out', 'get up'. **i.** To alter the position of so as to bring it to the outside. **j.** To direct or cause to point outwards. **k.** *intr.* To turn aside and go out; to 'clear out'; to go forth, sally forth (usu. with the notion of some compelling force, or of leaving a place of safety or comfort for one of danger or discomfort). **l.** To get out of bed. *colloq.* **m.** To leave one's abode and betake oneself to some outside occupation. **n.** To abandon one's work; to go out on strike. **o.** To bend or be directed outwards. **p.** (*a*) To result, eventuate. (*b*) with *compl.* To come to be, become ultimately (and so be found or known to be). (*c*) To prove *to be* (without implication of becoming). **T. out of.** (See simple senses and OUT OF.) **a.** *trans.* To drive, send, or put out of (a place) or dismiss from (a position or office) forcibly or peremptorily; to expel or eject from. **b.** *intr.* To get out of, leave, quit. **T. over.** (See simple senses and OVER *adv.*) **a.** *trans.* To turn (something) from its position on to one side, or from one side to the other, or upside down; to invert, reverse; to overturn, upset. **b.** To reverse (a leaf, or the successive leaves, of a book) in order to read (or write) on further; to read or search through (a book) by doing this. **c.** To reverse or shift (soil, hay, etc.) so as to expose the under parts, or different parts successively. **d.** To reverse and shift successively (papers or other articles lying flat in a heap) for the purpose of examining those that are beneath. **e.** *fig.* To agitate or revolve *in the mind*, consider and reconsider. **f.** To turn off the ladder in hanging. **g.** To transfer, hand over, make over, deliver, commit (*to*); *spec.* to transfer (an apprentice) to another master, (a sailor) to another ship. **h.** *Comm.* To pass or hand over in the way of exchange; to employ in business; to sell or dispose of goods to the amount of (a specified sum). **i.** *intr.* To turn on to one side, or from one side to the other, or upside down; to reverse itself; to capsize; to roll about. **T. round.** (See simple senses and ROUND *adv.*) **a.** *intr.* To move round on an axis or centre; to rotate, revolve. Also *fig.* of the brain or head. **b.** To turn so as to face in the opposite direction; to face about; to turn from one side to the other. **c.** *fig.* To change to the opposite opinion, state of mind, etc.; *esp.* to change from a friendly to a hostile attitude; with *on* or *upon*, to assail suddenly. **d.** *trans.* To cause to revolve or rotate; also, to cause to face in all directions successively. **e.** To reverse (*lit.* and *fig.*). **f.** To cause to face in a different direction. Also *fig.* to induce (a person) to take an opposite course or view. **T. to. a.** *intr.* To apply oneself to some task or occupation; to set to work. **b.** *trans.* To set (a person) to work. **T. up.** (See simple senses and UP *adv.*) **a.** *trans.* To direct or bend upwards. **b.** esp. in phr. *to t. up one's nose* (as an expression of contempt): usu. *fig.* **c.** To turn upside down, invert (now esp. in order to examine what is beneath). **d.** To fold over (a garment or part of one) so as to shorten it: also *transf.* with the person as obj. **e.** In *pa. pple.* of a garment: Having the border turned or folded over (and covered *with* some ornamental material). **f.** To turn (soil, etc.) so as to bring up the under parts to the surface; to dig or plough up; also, to bring to the surface (something buried) by digging, etc. **g.** To turn (a card) face upwards; *esp.* to do this in dealing to determine the trump suit. **h.** To find in a book, a set of papers, etc. some passage or document; to look up, refer to. (With the book, etc., or the passage, as obj.) **i.** To lay (a person or animal) on the back; hence, to kill. **j.** *To t. up one's heels* (or *toes*), to die; *to t. up* (a person's) *heels*, to lay low, kill. **k.** To turn the stomach of; also *fig.* **l.** To turn the regulator or tap of (a lamp or gas-jet) so as to raise the wick or increase the flow of gas, and thus make it burn more brightly. **m.** *Naut.* To cause to appear above the horizon, come in sight of. **n.** *Naut.* To summon (the crew) on deck. **o.** *intr.* To bend or point upwards. **p.** *Naut.* To beat up to windward; to tack. Also with *it*. **q.** To make its (or one's) appearance; to present (itself or oneself) casually or unexpectedly; to occur, appear, be discovered or encountered. **r.** with *compl.* To appear or present itself in a specified character, to be found to be. †**s.** *trans.* and *intr.* (for *refl.*): app. to prostitute; to prostitute oneself.

Turn-, the vb.-stem in comb. with a sb. adv., or adj., forming sbs. and adjs., in the sense 'that turns or is turned', 'for turning', in various uses of the vb.

T. bridge, a bridge turning horizontally on a pivot; **-broach** = TURNSPIT 2, 3; **-plate,** †(*a*) a curved plate-rail; (*b*) = TURN-TABLE 1; **-rail** = TURN-TABLE 1; also, a point or switch for directing railway vehicles from one line to another; **-screw,** a screwdriver; **-stone,** a limicoline bird, *Strepsilas interpres*, which turns over stones to get at the crustacea and other small animals to be found under them; also, a wrench; **-to,** a tussle, a set-to.

Turnback (tǝ̄·ɹnbæk), *sb.* and *a.* 1847. [f. the vbl. phr. *turn back.*] One who or that which turns back or is turned back. **A.** *sb.* **a.** One who faintheartedly retreats, or gives up. **b.** That part of anything which is folded back. **B.** *attrib.* or *adj.* That is folded back.

Tu·rn-bu:ckle. 1703. [f. TURN *v.* + BUCKLE *sb.*] **1.** A catch or fastening for window casements, shutters, etc., consisting of a thin flat bar pivoted so that it falls by its weight into a slit or groove. **2.** A coupling with internal screw threads for connecting metal rods lengthwise or for regulating their length or tension; *transf.* a device for coupling electric wires 1877.

Turncoat (tǝ̄·ɹnko^{u}t), *sb.* and *a.* 1557. [f. TURN *v.* + COAT *sb.*, lit. one who turns his coat.] **A.** *sb.* One who changes his principles or party; a renegade; an apostate. †**b.** *transf.* applied to anything that changes in appearance or colour –1608. **B.** *adj.* Of, pertaining to, or that is a turncoat 1571.

A. Wine is a turne-coate (first a friend, then an enemy) 1632.

Tu·rncock. 1702. [f. TURN *v.* + COCK *sb.*[1]] †**1.** A stop-cock of which the plug is turned to open or close it –1755. **2.** A waterworks official who turns on the water from the mains to supply-pipes, etc. 1711.

Tu·rn-down, *a.* and *sb.* 1840. [f. the vbl. phr. *turn down.*] **A.** *adj.* **1.** That turns down or may be turned down, esp. said of a collar worn with the upper part turned down over the neck-band; *t. bed*, a folding bed. **2** *Electr.* Designating an incandescent lamp of which one small filament only is used when little light is wanted 1911. **B.** *sb.* **1.** The turned-down part of anything; also, something worn turned down; *spec.* a turn-down collar 1849. **2.** *slang.* Rejection (cf. *turn down* d, TURN *v.*) 1902.

Turner (tǝ̄·ɹnəɹ). ME. [– OFr. *tornere*, obl. *torneor* – late L. *tornator*, *-ōr-*, f. *tornare*; see TURN *v.*, -ER[2] 3.] **1.** One who turns or fashions objects of wood, metal, bone, etc. on a lathe. **b.** A potter, *esp.* one who finishes and smooths the ware before it is fired 1601. **2.** In general senses: see TURN *v.* 1440. †**3.** A variety of fancy pigeon –1735. **4.** [– G. *turner*, f. *turnen* to perform gymnastic exercises.] A member of one of the gymnastic societies instituted in Germany by F. L. Jahn (1778–1852) 1860.

Turneresque (-e·sk), *a.* 1851. [f. name of J. M. W. *Turner* (1775–1851), landscape painter + -ESQUE.] Resembling in some respect the pictures of Turner.

The T. splendour of sunset in a great city 1877.

Turnerite (tǝ̄·ɹnərəit). 1823. [f. name of C. H. *Turner* + -ITE[1] 2 b.] *Min.* A variety of monazite, occurring in yellow or brown crystals.

Turnery (tɔ̄·ɹnəri). 1644. [f. TURNER + -Y³.] **1.** The art of the turner; the fashioning of objects or designs by means of a lathe 1662. **2.** *collect.* Turner's work; turnery ware 1644. **3.** A turner's workshop 1863.

2. [Some old chairs] the backs, arms, and legs loaded with t. H. WALPOLE.

Turning (tɔ̄·ɹniŋ), *vbl. sb.* ME. [f. TURN *v.* + -ING¹.] The action of TURN *v.* in various senses (also concretely). **1.** Movement about an axis or centre; rotation, revolution. late ME. **2.** The action of shaping or working something on a lathe; the art of shaping things by means of a lathe; the work of a turner 1440. **b.** *pl.* (*concr.*) Chips or shavings of some substance produced by turning in a lathe 1800. **3.** *fig.* Shaping, moulding, fashioning (of literary work, etc.) 1586. **4.** The action, or an act, of changing posture or direction by moving as on a pivot; movement so as to face or point in a different, or in some particular, direction ME. **b.** The practice of gymnastics according to the system of F. L. Jahn: cf. TURNER 4. 1888. **5.** Reversal, inversion 1536. **6.** The action of bending or folding over, or condition of being folded over; a fold 1631. **7.** A change in the direction of movement or course; deflexion, deviation; winding, tortuous course. late ME. **8.** A place or point where a road, path, etc. turns, or turns off. late ME. **9.** Reversal of movement or course 1440. **10.** *fig.* Conversion; perversion; desertion to another side. *arch.* ME. **11.** Change; vicissitude; alteration 1548.

3. Skill in the t. of phrases LONGF. **8.** Turne vpon your right hand at the next t., but at the next t. of all on your left SHAKS. **9.** I abhor even the shadow of changing or t. with the tide SCOTT.

attrib. and *Comb.*: **t. engine,** (*a*) a lathe; (*b*) a small engine for turning over a large one slowly for inspection or adjustment.

Tu·rning, *ppl. a.* 1450. [f. as prec. + -ING².] That turns, in various senses of the vb.

Comb.: **t. bridge,** = *turn-bridge* (see TURN-); †**-stile,** = TURNSTILE; **-table,** = TURN-TABLE.

Tu·rning-point. 1851. [f. TURNING *vbl. sb.* + POINT *sb.*] **1.** *lit.* A point at which something turns, or changes its direction of motion 1856. **2.** *fig.* A point at which a decisive change of any kind takes place; a critical point, crisis 1851.

Turnip (tɔ̄·ɹnip), *sb.* 1533. [Early forms *turnepe, -nep*; the first element is indeterminable; the second is NEEP.] **1.** The fleshy, globular or spheroidal root of a biennial cruciferous plant, *Brassica rapa*, var. *depressa*, cultivated from ancient times as a culinary vegetable, and for feeding sheep and cattle; also, the plant itself, of which the young shoots (*t.-tops*) are freq. boiled as greens. **2.** Applied to other species or varieties of *Brassica*; as **French t.** (*a*) the rape *B. napus* (or *campestris*); (*b*) a variety of *B. napus* extensively cultivated in France and Germany, and used to flavour soups; **Swedish t.,** *B. campestris rutabaga* 1548. **3.** Slang term for an old-fashioned thick silver watch 1840.

Comb.: **t.-aphid, -aphis,** the plant-louse of the t., *Aphis rapæ*; **-beetle, -flea** (also **t. flea beetle**), a minute shiny black leaping beetle, *Haltica nemorum*, which feeds on the young leaves of the t. and other crucifers; its larva mines in the full-grown leaf; **-fly,** (*a*) = *t.-flea*; (*b*) the t.-sawfly, *Athalia centifoliæ*, the larva of which feeds on t.-leaves; (*c*) a dipterous insect, *Anthomyia radicum*, whose larva lives in the root of the t.; **-lantern,** the hollowed rind of a t. employed as a lantern; **-shell,** a shell of the family *Turbinellidæ*, esp. of the genus *Rapa*; **-top** (usu. *pl.*), the sprouting leaves of the second year's growth of the t., used as a vegetable.

‖**Turnix** (tɔ̄·ɹniks). 1819. [mod.L. (Bonnaterre, 1790), app. shortened from L. *coturnix* quail.] *Ornith.* A genus of quail-like birds (also called *Hemipodius*); the bush-quails.

Turnkey (tɔ̄·ɹnkī). 1654. [f. TURN *v.* + KEY *sb.*¹] **1.** One who has charge of the keys of a prison; a jailer, *esp.* a subordinate. **2.** A tooth-key, formerly used in dentistry; a tooth-wrest 1877.

Turn-out (tɔ̄·ɹn,aut), *sb.* (*a.*) 1688. [f. the vbl. phr. *turn out.*] **1.** A turning out or getting out (of bed, etc.); hence, a call to duty, esp. during one's period of rest; *spec. Mil.* a signal to rise (now *rare* or *obs.*). **2.** A strike 1806. **3.** Those who turn out or assemble for any purpose; an assemblage, muster; also, a turning out or assembling of persons 1816. **4.** A loop-line or siding in a railway or tramway; also, in a narrow road, a part wider than the rest, or a short side road, to enable vehicles to pass each other; a similar place in a canal 1824. **5.** A turning or clearing out; a clearance 1856. **6.** The manner in which anything is turned out or equipped; 'get-up'; also *concr.* equipment, outfit, array 1812. **7.** A driving equipage 1817. **8.** The quantity of anything turned out in an industry, etc.; the total product; output 1879. **B.** *attrib.* or as *adj.* That turns out, or is turned out, in various senses 1899.

1. The bugles were sounding the t. THACKERAY. **5.** A t. of the den HUGHES. **7.** A special prize.. for the best t. of donkey and barrow 1895.

Turn-over (tɔ̄·ɹn,ōᵘ:vəɹ), *sb.* and *a.* 1611. [f. the vbl. phr. *turn over.*] **1.** The action of turning over; *spec.* in *Polit. slang*, a transference of votes from one party to another 1660. **2.** An apprentice whose indentures are transferred to another master on the retirement or failure of his original one; also, the action or process of turning over an apprentice. Now *dial.* 1631. **3.** Any part or thing which is turned or folded over; e.g. the flap of an envelope, etc. 1611. **b.** An article that begins in the last column of a newspaper page and continues overleaf 1842. **4.** A kind of tart in which fruit or jam is laid on one half of the rolled out paste, and has the other half turned over it 1798. **5.** The total amount of business done in a given time; also, the amount of goods produced and disposed of by a manufacturer; also, the 'turning over' of the capital involved in a business; also, the net profit derived from a business in a given time 1879. **B.** *adj.* That turns or is turned over, as *t. collar, majority* 1849.

Turnpike (tɔ̄·ɹnpəik). late ME. [f. TURN- + PIKE *sb.*¹] **1.** *Hist.* A spiked barrier fixed in or across a road or passage, as a defence against sudden attack, esp. of men on horseback. †**2.** A turnstile –1755. †**3.** A barrier across a water-course or stream; a water-gate; also, a lock on a navigable stream –1751. **4.** A barrier placed across a road to stop passage till the toll is paid; a toll-gate. Now chiefly *Hist.* 1678. **5.** *ellipt.* for TURNPIKE ROAD 1748. **6.** *Sc.* A spiral or winding stair 1501.

2. I moue vpon my axell, like a turne-pike B. JONS.

Tu·rnpike road. 1745. A road on which turnpikes are or were erected for the collection of tolls; hence, a main road or highway, formerly maintained by a toll levied on cattle and wheeled vehicles.

Turn-sick (tɔ̄·ɹnsik), *a.* and *sb. Obs.* exc. *dial.* 1440. [f. TURN *v.* + SICK *a.*] †**A.** *adj.* Affected with vertigo; giddy; dizzy –1664. **B.** *sb.* †**1.** Vertigo; also staggers in the horse –1592. **2.** The gid or sturdy in sheep. *dial.* 1834.

Turnsole (tɔ̄·ɹnsoᵘl). late ME. [– (O)Fr. *tournesole* – It. *tornasole* or Sp. *tornasol*, f. L. *tornare* TURN *v.* + *sol* sun.] **1.** A violet-blue or purple colouring matter, obtained from the plant *Crozophora tinctoria*. **b.** *transf.* = LITMUS 1839. **2.** A plant of which the flowers or leaves turn so as to follow the sun. **a.** An annual euphorbiaceous plant, *Crozophora tinctoria*, cultivated in the south of France for its colouring juice (see 1) 1578. **b.** The plant *Heliotropium europæum* 1578. **c.** Formerly applied to the Sunflower; also to the Sun-spurge or Wartwort, *Euphorbia helioscopia* 1725.

Turnspit (tɔ̄·ɹnspit). 1576. [f. TURN *v.* + SPIT *sb.*¹] **1.** A dog kept to turn the roasting-spit by running within a kind of tread-wheel connected with it; a *t. dog.* **2.** A boy or man whose office was to turn the spit. Also as a term of contempt. 1607. **3.** A roasting-jack (*rare*) 1606.

Turnstile (tɔ̄·ɹnstəil). 1643. [f. TURN *v.* + STILE¹.] A gateway formed of four radiating arms of timber or iron at right angles to each other, revolving horizontally on a fixed vertical post, set up in a passage or entrance, orig. to exclude any but foot-passengers, now often to prevent the passage of more than one person at a time at a place where fees, fares, or tickets are collected.

Turn-table (tɔ̄·ɹntēⁱb'l). 1835. [f. TURN *v.* + TABLE *sb.*] **1.** On a railway: A revolving platform turning on a central pivot, laid with rails connecting with adjacent tracks, for turning railway vehicles; a turn-plate. **2.** A revolving platform, table, stand, or disc of various kinds; e.g. for carrying heavy guns in fixed armoured redoubts or barbettes, etc., or for carrying the record disc in a gramophone 1865.

Turn-up (tɔ̄·ɹn,ɒp), *sb.* and *a.* 1685. [f. the vbl. phr. *turn up.*] **1.** The turned up part of anything, esp. of a garment 1688. **b.** *pl.* The turned-up part at the bottom of trouser-legs. **2.** The turning up of a particular card or die in games of chance; the card or die turned up; hence *fig.*, a mere chance, a 'toss-up'; a result which is purely a matter of chance 1810. **3.** A boxing contest; hence, *loosely*, a set-to, esp. with the fists; also, a tussle; a disturbance, row 1810. **B.** *attrib.* or *adj.* That is turned up, or turns up, in various senses 1685.

Turnwrest (tɔ̄·ɹnrest), *a.* (*sb.*) 1653. [f. TURN- + WREST *sb.*²] *T. plough*, a plough in which the mould-board may be shifted from one side to the other at the end of each furrow, so that the furrow-slice is always thrown the same way; a one-way plough. (In the 18th c. freq. called the *Kentish plough.*) **b.** *ellipt.* as *sb.* 1778.

Turonian (tiurōᵘ·niăn), *a.* 1850. [– Fr. *turonien*, f. L. *Turones*, a people of ancient Gaul, whence Tours on the Loire took its name; see -IAN.] *Geol.* Denoting a subdivision of the Cretaceous or Chalk period and series of strata, answering to the 'Lower White Chalk without flints' of English geologists.

Turpentine (tɔ̄·ɹpĕntəin), *sb.* late ME. [Forms *ter(e)bentine, turbentyne, terpentine* – OFr. *ter(e)bentine* – L. *ter(e)benthina* (sc. *resina* resin), f. *terebinthus* TEREBINTH; see -INE¹.] **1.** A term applied orig. (as in Gr. and L.) to the semifluid resin of the terebinth tree, *Pistacia terebinthus* (Chian or Cyprian t.); now chiefly to the various oleoresins which exude from coniferous trees, consisting of more or less viscid solutions of resin in a volatile oil. **b.** With qualification, indicating different varieties 1577. **c.** *pl.* Varieties of turpentine 1605. **d.** = *Oil of t.* (see 3) 1876. **2.** †**a.** The fruit of the terebinth tree. **b.** A terebinth tree. Also, any tree that yields turpentine, as the larch. 1562. **3.** In full: **Oil of t.** (also vulgarly known as *spirit of t.*), a volatile oil, contained in the wood, bark, leaves, etc. of coniferous trees, and usu. prepared by distilling crude turpentine. There are many varieties according to the source, which, though all having the same formula, $C_{10}H_{16}$, vary in their physical, and, more especially, in their optical properties. 1597.

Comb.: **t. moth,** a leaf-roller moth of the genus *Retinia*, of which the larvæ bore into the twigs of conifers; **t. oil** = *oil of t.*; **T. State** (U.S.), North Carolina, so called from the quantity of t. obtained from its pine forests; **t. tree,** *orig.* the Terebinth, *Pistacia terebinthus* (see 1); any tree yielding t., esp. species of pine and fir, as the Larch, which yields Venice t. Hence **Tu·rpentine** *v.* to treat, rub, or smear with t. or t. oil.

Turpeth, turbith (tɔ̄·ɹpĕþ, -biþ). [In XV *turbit* – med.L. *turbit(h)um, turpetum* – Pers., Arab. *turbid*, whence also Fr. *turbith*, †*-bit.*] **1.** A cathartic drug prepared from the root of East Indian jalap, *Ipomœa turpethum*, an Indian and Australian plant; also, the plant itself, or its root. **2.** *T. mineral*, basic sulphate of mercury ($HgSO_4$. 2 HgO), obtained as a lemon-yellow powder from the normal sulphate by washing with hot water 1616.

Turpinite (tɔ̄·ɹpinəit). 1895. [– Fr. *turpinite*, f. *Turpin*, name of the inventor + -ITE¹ 4 a.] An explosive, used in making shells.

Turpitude (tǭ·ɹpitiūd). 1490. [– Fr. *turpitude* or L. *turpitudo*, f. *turpis* base, disgraceful; see -TUDE.] Base or shameful character; vileness; depravity, wickedness. **b.** With *a* and *pl.* An instance of this 1597.

Turps (tǭɹps). 1823. *colloq.* = TURPENTINE 3.

Turquoise (tǭ·ɹkoiz, tǭ·ɹkwoiz, tǭ·ɹkwāz, *arch.* tǭɹki·z, tǭ·ɹkiz), *sb.* (*a.*) [Late ME. *turkeis*, later *turkes*, *turques* (XV), *turkoise*, *turquoise* (XVI) – OFr. *turqueise*, later *-oise*, for *pierre turqueise*, etc. 'Turkish stone', so called from being first known in Turkestan or conveyed through Turkish dominions.] **1.** A precious stone found in Persia (the *true* or *Oriental t.*), much prized as a gem, of a sky-blue to apple-green colour, almost opaque or sometimes translucent, consisting of hydrous phosphate of aluminium. **b.** In *collect. sing.*, esp. as a substance 1607. **2.** More fully **t. stone.** Now *rare.* 1556. **3.** As name for a colour (short for *t. blue*) 1853. **4.** Lapidaries' name for odontolite 1796. **B.** as *adj.* Of the colour of the turquoise; turquoise-blue 1573.

1. The azurn sheen Of Turkis blew and Emrauld green MILT. 3. The..t. of the heavens 1876.

Turret (tʊ·rėt), *sb.* [ME. *turet*, *touret* – OFr. *torete*, *tourete*, dim. of *tur*, *tor*, *tour* TOWER; see -ET.] **1.** A small or subordinate tower, usu. one forming part of a larger structure; *esp.* a rounded addition to an angle of a building, sometimes commencing at some height above the ground, and freq. containing a spiral staircase. **2.** *Mil.* A low flat armour-plated tower, commonly cylindrical or conical, on a ship of war or a fort, made to contain a gun and gunners, and usu. to revolve horizontally 1862. **3.** *U.S.* A raised central portion in the roof of a railway passenger carriage 1875. **4.** An attachment to a lathe, drill, etc., consisting of a round or polygonal block with sockets for various dies or cutting tools, and capable of being rotated, so as to present the required tool to the work 1875.

1. He perceived the turrets of an ancient chateau rising out of the trees W. IRVING.

attrib. and *Comb.*: **t. deck,** an upper deck of a cargo steamer to which the sides of the vessel curve upward convexly from the main deck; **t. head** = sense 4; **-lathe,** a lathe fitted with a t.; **-ship,** a ship of war with a t. Hence **Tu·rret** *v. trans.* to fortify, or adorn with or as with a t. or turrets; usu. in *pa. pple.*

Turreted (tʊ·rėtėd), *a.* 1550. [f. TURRET *sb.* or *v.* + -ED.] **1.** Furnished with or having a turret or turrets. **2.** Furnished with something resembling a turret 1610. **b.** *spec.* = TURRITED 1826.

2. Turretted ships 1837. Head of Kybele.., wearing t. crown 1872.

Turriculated (tʊri·kiŭlėʹtėd), *ppl. a.* 1822. [f. L. *turricula* (dim. of *turris* tower) + -ATE[3] + -ED[1].] Furnished with a turret or turrets, turreted; *spec.* in *Conch.* = TURRITED. Also **Turri·culate** *a.*

Turrilite (tʊ·riləit). 1828. [– mod.L. *Turrilites* (Lamarck, 1801), f. *turris* tower + Gr. λίθος stone; see -LITE.] *Palæont.* A fossil cephalopod belonging or related to the genus *Turrilites*, allied to the ammonites, but having a long spiral (turreted) shell, found in the Cretaceous formations.

Turrited (tʊ·rəitėd), *a.* 1758. [f. L. *turritus* towered (f. *turris* tower) + -ED[1].] = TURRETED 2: *spec.* of a shell, having a long spire resembling a tower or turret. Also **Tu·rrite** *a.*

Turritellid (tʊrite·lid). 1860. [– mod.L. *Turritellidæ* pl., f. *Turritella* (Lamarck, 1799), name of the typical genus, f. *turris* tower; see -ID[3].] *Zool.* A gasteropod of the family *Turritellidæ*, characterized by long turreted shells with spiral striations; a screw-shell. So **Turrite·lloid** *a.* resembling a screw-shell; having the characters of the *Turritellidæ.*

Turtle[1] (tǭ·ɹt'l). Now *rare* or *arch.* [OE. *turtla*, *turtle* = OHG. *turtulo*, *-ula*; OE., ME. also *turtur*, ME. *turture*, partly – OFr. *turtre* (mod. *tourtre*) or ON. *turturi*; all – L. *turtur*, of imit. origin (for change of *r* to *l* cf. PURPLE.] **1.** = TURTLE-DOVE 1. **b.** *Greenland t.*, *Sea-turtle*, the Black Guillemot 1678. **2.** *fig.* Applied to a person, as a term of endearment, etc., or esp. to lovers or married folk, in allusion to the turtle-dove's affection for its mate. late ME.

Turtle[2] (tǭ·ɹt'l). 1657. [perh. alt. of Fr. *tortue* TORTOISE, but the existence of a var. *turckle* (Purchas) may point to a native (Bermudan) name.] **1.** Any species of marine tortoise; also extended to various other tortoises. (Pl. *turtles*, collectively usu. *turtle.*) **b.** The flesh of various species of turtle used as food; also short for *t.-soup.* (See also MOCK TURTLE.) 1755. **2.** *Typog.* A curved bed in which types or stereotypes are secured, and which is mounted on one of the cylinders of a rotary printing-press: so called from a fancied resemblance of the bed to the back of a turtle 1860.

1. **Alligator-t.,** the snapping-t., also called *alligator-tortoise*; **chicken-t.,** *Chrysemys reticulata*, also called *chicken-tortoise*; **green t.,** various species of *Chelonia*, having green shells, as *C. midas* of the West Indies and *C. virgata* of the Pacific, both much esteemed as food. Phr. *To turn t.*: **a.** *lit.* to catch t. by throwing them on their backs; **b.** *fig.* to turn over, capsize, be upset.

attrib. and *Comb.*, as *t.-catcher*, *-fishing*, *-soup*; **t. cowry,** a large species of cowry, *Cypræa testudinaria*; **-grass,** either of two marine plants with long narrow grass-like leaves: (*a*) *Thalassia testudinum*, of the W. Indies, etc.; (*b*) the grass-wrack, *Zostera marina*; **-head,** a N. Amer. scrophulariaceous plant, *Chelone glabra*, so called from the shape of the flower; **-shell,** (*a*) the shell of a t.; the material of this, tortoise-shell; (*b*) = *t.-cowry.* Hence **Tu·rtler,** a person, or a vessel, engaged in turtling; a t.-catcher. **Tu·rtling,** the action of 'fishing' for or catching t.

Tu·rtle-back. 1881. [f. prec.] **1.** An arched structure over the deck of a steamer at the bow, and often also at the stern, to protect it from damage by a heavy sea. **2.** *Archæol.* A roughly chipped stone implement, having one or both faces slightly convex 1890. Hence **Tu·rtle-ba:cked** *a.* having a back like a turtle's; furnished with a t. (sense 1).

Turtle-dove (tǭ·ɹt'l,dʊv). ME. [f. TURTLE *sb.*[1] + DOVE. Cf. OHG. *turtulatuba* (G. *turteltaube*) = MLG. *tortelduve*, MSw. *turturdufva.*] **1.** A dove of the genus *Turtur*, esp. the common European species *T. communis*, noted for its graceful form, harmonious colouring, and affection for its mate. **2.** *fig.* applied to a person 1535.

2. My darling and my harts desyre, my onely Turtle Doue 1575.

†**Turtur.** [OE., ME. *turtur*; see TURTLE[1].] = TURTLE.[1] –1649.

Tuscan (tʊ·skăn), *a.* and *sb.* late ME. [– Fr. *tuscan*, It. *toscano* – L. *Tuscanus*, f. *Tusci*, pl. of *Tuscus*, called also *Etrusci* (see ETRUSCAN); see -AN.] **A.** *adj.* **a.** = ETRUSCAN *a.* 1513. **b.** Of or pertaining to Tuscany, formerly a grand duchy, having Florence as its capital; now a part of the kingdom of Italy 1588. **c.** *Arch.* Applied to the simplest and rudest of the five classical orders of architecture; allied to the Doric, but devoid of all ornament; belonging to this order, as *a T. pillar* 1563. **d.** Applied to a method of plaiting the fine wheaten straw grown in Tuscany for hats, etc.; also to the golden yellow colour of this 1834. **B.** *sb.* **a.** = ETRUSCAN *sb.* late ME. **b.** A native or inhabitant of Tuscany 1633. **c.** The language of Tuscany, regarded as the classical form of Italian 1568.

Tush (tʊʃ), *sb.*[1] [ME. *tus(s)ch*, *tos(s)ch*, normal repr. of OE. *tusć*; see TUSK.] **1.** = TUSK *sb.* 1. Now chiefly *arch.* or *dial.* **b.** *spec.* A canine tooth, esp. of a horse 1607. **c.** A stunted tusk in some Indian elephants 1859. **2.** In a plough: = FIN *sb.* 3 b. *Obs.* exc. *dial.* 1649.

Tush (tʊʃ), *int.* (*sb.*[2]) *arch.* 1440. [A natural utterance; cf. rare †*twish* (XVI), PISH.] An exclam. of impatient contempt or disparagement.

T., said Obstinate, away with your book BUNYAN.

B. *sb.* as a name for this utterance 1600. Hence **Tush** *v. intr.* to say 't.!', to scoff or express impatience *at.* **Tu·shery,** R. L. Stevenson's name for a style of romance characterized by excessive use of affected archaisms such as 't.!'.

Tusk (tʊsk), *sb.* [Metathetic alt. of OE. *tux* (var. of *tusć* TUSH *sb.*[1]) = OFris. *tusk*, *tosk*; not certainly known outside the Anglo-Frisian area.] **1.** A long pointed tooth; *esp.* a (canine or incisor) tooth specially developed so as to project beyond the mouth, as in the elephant, wild boar, etc. **b.** Applied *spec.* to the permanent canine teeth of the horse. More usu. called *tush.* 1808. **2.** A projecting part or object resembling the tusk of an animal, as (*Carpentry*), a bevel or sloping shoulder on a tenon, for additional strength 1679.

Comb.: **t.-shell** = TOOTH-SHELL; **t. tenon,** a tenon made with a t.

Tusk, *v.* 1614. [f. TUSK *sb.*] **1.** *intr.* †**a.** app., To show the teeth. B. JONS. **b.** To use, or thrust with, the tusks; of a horse, to pull roughly with the teeth *at* 1825. **2.** *trans.* To root or dig *up*, or to tear *off* with the tusks; to wound with the tusk 1629.

Tusker (tʊ·skəɹ). 1859. [f. TUSK *sb.* + -ER[1].] A beast having tusks, esp. an elephant or wild boar.

Tusky (tʊ·ski), *a.* 1620. [f. as prec. + -Y[1].] Characterized by tusks; tusked: chiefly as a poetic epithet of the wild boar.

On Mountain tops to chace the t. Boar DRYDEN.

Tusseh, -er: see TUSSORE.

Tussive (tʊ·siv), *a.* 1857. [f. L. *tussis* cough + -IVE.] Pertaining to or caused by cough.

Tussle (tʊ·s'l), *sb.* 1629. [f. TUSSLE *v.*] A vigorous or disorderly conflict; a severe struggle, a hard contest; a scuffle. **b.** fig.; *esp.* a sharp and determined contention or dispute 1857.

b. The t. of life 1883.

Tussle (tʊ·s'l), *v.* 1470. [orig. app. Sc. and north., perh. f. TOUSE *v.* Cf. TOUSLE.] **1.** *trans.* To push or pull about roughly, to hustle; to engage in a tussle with. Now *rare.* **2.** *intr.* To struggle or contend in a vigorous and determined way; to wrestle confusedly; to scuffle 1638. **b.** in *fig.* use 1862.

Tussock (tʊ·sək). 1550. [contemp. with synon. (dial.) *tusk* (of unkn. origin), of which it is prob. an alt. form with assim. to -OCK.] **1.** A tuft or bunch of hair. Now *rare.* **2.** A tuft, clump, or matted growth, forming a small hillock, of grass, sedge, or the like 1607. **3.** Short for *t.-moth* or *caterpillar* 1819. **4.** Short for TUSSOCK-GRASS. Also in *pl.* 1832.

1. Bushy tussocks of grey eyebrow 1893.

Comb.: **t.-caterpillar,** the larva of the **t.-moth,** any of various kinds of moth, as those of the genus *Orgyia*, the larvæ of which have long tufts of hairs. Hence **Tu·ssocky** *a.* abounding in or forming tussocks.

Tu·ssock-grass. 1842. **1.** Any of several grasses of the Southern Hemisphere; esp. (*a*) *Poa flabellata* (formerly *Dactylis cæspitosa*), a tall-growing valuable grass of the Falkland Islands and Patagonia; (*b*) various New Zealand species of *Arundo* and *Poa.* **2.** The tufted hair-grass, *Aira cæspitosa*, or other native grass growing in tussocks 1860.

Tussore (tʊsǭᵊ·ɹ, tʊ·soᵊɹ). Formerly **tusser** (tʊ·səɹ); also **tusseh, tussah.** 1619. [– Urdu – Hindi *ta·sar* (:– Skr. *tasara*) shuttle, assim. to SALEMPORE, etc.] **1.** In full *t. silk*: A coarse brown silk (furnished by *Antheræa mylitta* and other species of silkworm) made in and imported from India. Also *ellipt.* a dress made of this. **2.** = *t.-worm* 1796.

Comb.: **t.-moth,** any moth of which the larva (*t.-worm*) yields t.; **t.-(silk)worm,** any silkworm yielding t.; the larva of a tusser-moth.

Tut (tʊt), *sb.*[1] 1553. [Of unkn. origin.] **1.** *western dial.* A small seat or hassock made of straw; a cushion or hassock for kneeling upon. †**2.** The orb borne as an emblem of sovereignty (*rare*) –1706.

Tut (tʊt), *sb.*[2] *local.* 1702. [Of unkn. origin.] Originally in Cornish tin-mines, and in s.w. agricultural areas, now also in Derbyshire lead-mining: in the phr. *upon t.* (also *by the t.*), and *attrib.* as *t.-work*, *-workman*: denoting a system of payment by measurement or by the piece, adopted in paying for work which brings no immediate returns; hence, work of this character; dead-work.

Tut (tʊt), *int.* (*sb.*[3]) 1529. [A natural utterance.] An ejaculation (often reduplicated) expressing impatience, dissatisfaction, or contempt. **B.** *sb.* The (or an) utterance of this exclam. 1676.

I come..once more, to ask pardon...T., boy, a trifle GOLDSM. Hence **Tut** *v. intr.* to utter the exclam. 'tut'.

Tutania (tiutēⁱ·niă). 1790. [f. *Tutin*, name of the maker or inventor.] An earlier name for Britannia-metal.

Tutelage (tiū·tĭlėdʒ). 1605. [f. L. *tutela* keeping (f. *tut-*, pa. ppl. stem of *tueri* watch, look after) + -AGE.] **1.** The office or function of a guardian; protection, care, guardianship; governorship of a ward. **b.** Instruction, tuition 1857. **2.** The condition of being under protection or guardianship 1650.

1. Under the t. of a patron saint 1879. **b.** Under the t. of several different masters 1863.

Tutelar (tiū·tĭlăɹ), *a.* and *sb.* 1600. [– late L. *tutelaris* adj. and sb., f. as prec.; see -AR¹.] **A.** *adj.* = next A. **B.** *sb.* A tutelary deity, angel, or saint 1603.

Tutelary (tiū·tĭlări), *a.* and *sb.* 1611. [– L. *tutelarius* guardian, f. as prec.; see -ARY¹. Cf. Fr. *tutélaire* adj.] **A.** *adj.* **1.** Of supernatural powers: Having the position of protector, guardian, or patron; *esp.* protecting or watching over a particular person, place, or thing. **2.** *transf.* Of or pertaining to protection or a protector or guardian 1651.

1. The patron and t. genius of liberty 1806. **2.** Great acts of t. friendship GLADSTONE.

B. *sb.* = prec. B. 1652.

Tutenag (tiū·tĕnæg). 1622. [– Marathi *tuttināg*, said to be f. Skr. *tuttha* copper sulphate + *nāga* tin, lead.] A whitish alloy of copper, zinc, and nickel, with a little iron, silver, or arsenic, resembling German silver; also used loosely in the Indian trade for zinc.

Tutiorist (tiū·ʃiŏrist). 1845. [f. L. *tutior* safer, compar. of *tutus* safe; see next. -IST.] One who holds that in cases of conscience the course of greater moral safety should be chosen.

Tutor (tiū·təɹ), *sb.* [In XIV (Langland) *tutour* – AFr., OFr. *tutour* (mod. *tuteur*), or L. *tutor*, f. *tut-*, pa. ppl. stem of *tueri* look at or after, protect; see -OR 2.] †**1.** A guardian; a protector, defender –1602. **2.** One who has the custody of a ward; a guardian. †**a.** *gen.* –1690. **b.** *spec.* in *Rom.* and *Sc. Law*: The guardian and representative, and administrator of the estate, of a person legally incapable, failing the father. late ME. **3.** One employed in the supervision and instruction of a youth in a private household. Also one engaged to travel abroad with one or more pupils, a *travelling* or *foreign t.* late ME. **4.** In the Universities of Oxford, Cambridge, and Dublin: A graduate (most often a fellow of a college), to whom the special supervision of an undergraduate (called his pupil) is assigned 1610. **b.** In U.S. universities and colleges: A teacher subordinate to a professor 1828.

4. *Private t.* (at the Eng. Universities), a person engaged by students to assist them in their studies and preparation for the examinations, but not appointed or recognized by their University or College; also, a person who makes it his business to 'coach' students for professional examinations apart from the universities.

Tu·tor, *v.* 1592. [f. prec.] **1.** *trans.* To act the part of a tutor towards; to give special or individual instruction to; to teach, instruct (*in* a subject). Also *absol.* **2.** To instruct under discipline; to subject to discipline, control, or correction; to school; also to admonish or reprove 1592. **3.** To tell (a person) what to do or say; often in sinister sense: to sophisticate or tamper with (a witness or his evidence) 1757. **4.** *intr.* (*U.S.*) To study under a tutor 1921.

2. The World however it may be taught will not be tutor'd SHAFTESB.

Tutorage (tiū·tərėdʒ). 1617. [f. as prec. + -AGE.] **1.** The office, authority, or action of a tutor or guardian; tutorship, guardianship, custody; tutorial control, direction, or supervision; instruction. **b.** *spec.* at a university; also, the charge for or cost of this 1638. **c.** A tutorship 1796. †**2.** = TUTELAGE 2. –1768.

Tu·toress. 1614. [f. as prec.; see -ESS¹.] **a.** An instructress. **b.** A female guardian 1759.

Tutorial (tiutōᵊ·riăl), *a.* (*sb.*) 1742. [f. L. *tutorius* (f. *tutor* TUTOR) + -AL¹ 1.] Of or pertaining to a tutor. **1.** *Rom.* and *Sc. Law.* Of or pertaining to a legal guardian. **2.** Of or pertaining to a teacher or instructor; *esp.* pertaining to a college tutor 1822. **B.** *sb.* [app. short for *t. hour.*] A period of individual instruction given by a college tutor 1923. Hence **Tuto·rially** *adv.*

Tutorize (tiū·tərəiz), *v.* 1611. [f. TUTOR *sb.* + -IZE.] **a.** *intr.* To act as a tutor. (Also with *it.*) **b.** *trans.* To be tutor to; to instruct as a tutor.

Tutorly (tiū·təɹli), *a. rare.* 1611. [f. as prec. + -LY¹.] Like a tutor; dictatorial, pedagogic.

Tutorship (tiū·təɹʃip). 1559. [f. as prec. + -SHIP.] †**1.** The office of guardian or protector; guardianship –1665. **2.** The position or office of an instructor or teacher 1581.

Tutory (tiū·təri). late ME. [f. as prec.; see -ORY¹.] **1.** Guardianship, charge, protection; *spec.* the custody of a ward. *Obs.* exc. in *Law.* †**2.** Tuition (*rare*) –1764.

‖**Tutoy·er**, *v.* 1697. [Fr. *tutoyer*, f. the sing. pronoun *tu, toi*, as used in speaking to a person instead of the pl. *vous.*] *trans.* To use the sing. pron. *tu, toi, te* ('thou' and 'thee') to; to treat as an intimate; to address with familiarity, or as an inferior in rank or order. Also *intr.*

Tutress (tiū·trės). 1599. [– OFr. *tutresse, tuteresse*, or f. L. *tutrix* by change of ending.] = TUTORESS.

†**Tutrix** (tiū·triks). 1515. [– L. *tutrix*, fem. of *tutor* TUTOR.] = TUTORESS –1703.

Tutsan (tɒ·tsăn). late ME. [– AFr. †*tutsaine*, Fr. *toute-saine*, f. *toute*, fem. of *tout* all + *saine*, fem. of *sain* wholesome.] A name applied to various plants on account of their healing virtues; formerly to Agnus Castus; now, in Eng., to a shrubby species of St. John's-wort, *Hypericum androsæmum*, with strongly aromatic foliage and berry-like fruit; formerly esteemed as a vulnerary.

‖**Tutti** (tu·tti). 1724. [It., = 'all'; pl. of *tutto.*] *Mus.* In concerted music, a direction that all the performers are to take part; also, a passage or movement rendered by all the performers together.

Tutty (tɒ·ti). late ME. [– OFr. *tutie* – med. L. *tutia* – Arab. *tūtiyā.*] A crude oxide of zinc found adhering in grey or brownish flakes to the flues of furnaces in which brass is melted; also occurring in some countries as a native mineral; formerly used medically, and now as a polishing powder.

‖**Tutulus** (tiū·tiŭlɒs). *Rom. Antiq.* 1753. [L.] A head-dress worn by the flamen and his wife.

Tu-whit, tu-whoo (tuʰwi·t tu·ʰwū·), *int.* (*sb.*) 1588. [Imitative.] An imitation of the call of an owl. **B.** *sb.* The utterance of this cry; the hoot of an owl 1830.

Then nightly sings the staring Owle Tu-whit to-who. A merrie note. SHAKS.

Tu-whoo (tuʰwū·), *int.* (*sb.*) 1797. [Cf. prec.] = prec. Hence **Tu-whoo·** *v. intr.*

Tuxedo (tɒksī·do). 1899. [Name of a club at T. Park, New York.] A dinner jacket.

Tuyere (twīᵊɹ, twəiᵊɹ, ‖tüiyę̄r, tüyę̄r). 1781. [– Fr. *tuyère*, f. *tuyau* pipe, with substitution of suffix.] The nozzle through which the blast is forced into a forge or furnace.

Comb.: **t. arch**, in a blast furnace, an arch through which a t. is admitted.

Tuza (tū·ză). 1787. [– Sp. – Mexican *tuçan* or *tozan*, native name.] A Mexican pocket-gopher or pouched rat.

Tw-, obs. and dial. var. QU-.

Twaddell (twǫ·d'l). 1860. [Short for *Twaddell's hydrometer*, from the inventor's name.] A form of hydrometer or hydrometric scale in which 200 degrees correspond to a unit of specific gravity, that of distilled water being denoted by zero.

Twaddle (twǫ·d'l), *sb.* (*a.*) 1782. [alt. of *twattle* (XVII) and †*twittle-twattle* (XVI); the corresp. vb. (dial. *twattle*) is earlier (XVI) and varied formerly with †*twittle*, itself alt. of TITTLE *v.* (see TITTLE-TATTLE); *w* of the altered forms is unexplained.] **1.** Senseless, silly, or trifling talk or writing; empty verbosity; prosy nonsense. †**2.** A twaddler –1838. **3.** *attrib.* or as *adj.* Of the nature of twaddle 1830.

1. No need to talk a lot of t. and nonsense to a woman with brains 1878. Hence **Twa·ddly** *a.*

Twa·ddle, *v.* 1825. [f. prec.; or perh. alt. f. *twattle* vb.] **1.** *intr.* To utter twaddle; to talk or write in a silly, empty, or trashy style. **2.** *trans.* To utter as twaddle, or in a trashy and prosy way 1837. So **Twa·ddler**, one who twaddles; one who talks or writes twaddle 1787.

Twain (twēⁱn), *numeral a.* and *sb. arch.* [OE. *twēġen*, corresp. to OFris., OS. *twēne*, OHG. *zwēne* (G. arch. *zween*), nom. and acc. masc. of the numeral of which fem. and n. are repr. by TWO.] = TWO. **A.** *adj.* **1.** In concord with a sb., etc. **2.** Absolutely with ellipsis of sb., or following a pron. or pronominal adj. OE. **3. a.** Separate, parted asunder; disunited, estranged, at variance. (Only *predic.*) 1472. **b.** Double, twofold (*rare*). late ME.

1. The bottles t...Were shatter'd at a blow COWPER. **2.** To tarry a day or t. SCOTT. Phr. *In t.*, in two, asunder. **3. a.** Thou and I long since are t. MILT.

B. *sb.* †**1.** The abstract number two –1483. **2.** A group of two; a pair, couple 1607. **3.** *pl.* Twins. *dial.* 1580.

2. To blesse this twaine, that they may prosperous be SHAKS.

Twain, *v. Obs.* or *arch.* late ME. [f. prec.] *trans.* To part or divide in twain; to put apart, separate. late ME.

Twait(e (twēⁱt). *local.* 1613. [Of unkn. origin.] A European species of shad, *Alosa finta.*

Twang (twæŋ), *sb.*¹ 1553. [imit., the *tw-* expressing the sound of plucking, the *-ang* resonance.] **1.** A vocal imitation of the resonant sound produced when a tense string is sharply plucked or suddenly released; used as interj. or advb. **b.** A sound of the above character; also, any sharp ringing sound resembling this 1565. **c.** *transf.* and *fig.* Ringing sound or tone 1646. **2. a.** Nasal intonation; now esp. as characterizing an individual, a country, or locality. More fully *nasal t.* 1661. **b.** A distinctive manner of pronunciation or intonation; esp. one associated with a particular district or locality 1697. **3.** *transf.* A ringing or resounding blow (*rare*) 1712. **4.** *transf.* A sharp pluck or twitch; a tweak; also, the effect of this; a twinge, a sharp pang. Now *dial.* 1720.

1. b. The t. of a bow-string 1853. **2. a.** Odious as the nasal t. Heard at conventicle COWPER. The true Kentucky t. through the nose 1839. **b.** A grating voice that had an Irish t. THACKERAY.

Twang, *sb.*² 1611. [Alteration of TANG *sb.*¹; but often assoc. w. prec.] **1.** A penetrating or persistent taste, flavour, or odour, usu. disagreeable. **2.** *fig.* A 'smack', touch, tinge; a taint 1633.

Twang, *v.* 1542. [Goes with TWANG *sb.*¹] **I.** Of sound. **1.** *intr.* To give forth a ringing note, as a tense string when plucked. Said also of the sound produced. 1567. **2.** *trans.* To cause to make a ringing note, as by plucking or twitching a tense string or strings of a bow or of a musical instrument; hence, to play on (an instrument). 1579. **3.** *intr.* To produce a ringing note by or as by plucking a string or stringed instrument; hence (in depreciative sense) to play *on* a stringed instrument 1594. **4.** *trans.* To play (a melody or the like) on a stringed instrument; to sound forth on a twanging instrument. Also said of the instrument or its strings. 1542. †**5.** *trans.* To utter with a sharp ringing tone. SHAKS. **6.** *intr.* To speak with a nasal intonation or twang. Also *trans.* with *nose* as obj. (*rare*) 1615. **b.** *trans.* To utter or pronounce with a nasal or other twang 1748.

1. This said, the bow-string twangs 1621. **2.** Musicians came and twanged guitars to her THACKERAY. **4.** She twanged off a rattling piece of Liszt THACKERAY.

II. Of the action (without special ref. to the sound). **1.** *trans.* To pull or pluck (the string of a bow) so as to shoot 1600. **2.** To discharge (an arrow) with a twang of the bow-string; to let fly (an arrow) 1751. **b.** *intr.* Of an arrow: To leave the bow-string with a twang 1795.

1. He..Twanged the string, out flew the quarell

long 1600. **2. b.** When twanged an arrow from Love's mystic string COLERIDGE.

Twangle (twæ·ng'l), *sb.* 1812. [Cf. next.] A twangling sound; a continuous or repeated resonant sound, usu. lighter or thinner than a twang; a jingle.

Twangle (twæ·ng'l), *v.* 1558. [dim. and frequent. of TWANG *v.* (see -LE).] **1.** *intr.* Of a stringed instrument or one who plays it: To twang lightly and continuously or frequently; to jingle. **2.** *trans.* To twang (a stringed instrument) lightly; to play upon in a petty or trifling manner. Also, to play (a melody) in this way. 1607.

Twankay (twæ·ŋke). 1840. [– Chinese *Tong* (or *Taung*) *-ké* (or *-kei*), dial. form of *Tun-ki* or *Tun-chi*, name of two streams (and a town) in An-hui and Chi-kiang, China.] A variety of green tea (in full *T. tea*), properly that from one of the places so called, but also applied to blends of this with other growths.

'twas (twǫz, twəz), abbrev. of *it was*, now poet. or arch., and dial.

Tway (twēⁱ), *numeral a.* Now *rare arch.* [Apocopate form, orig. Northumb. and Anglian, of OE. *tweġen* TWAIN.] = TWO.

Twayblade (twēⁱ·blēⁱd). 1578. [f. prec. + BLADE leaf, tr. med.L. *bifolium*.] **a.** An orchidaceous plant of the genus *Listera*, characterized by two nearly opposite broad leaves springing from the stem; esp. the Common T., *L. ovata*, and Mountain or Heart-leaved T., *L. cordata*. **b.** Applied to N. Amer. species of the orchidaceous genus *Liparis*, with two leaves springing from the root.

Tweak (twīk), *sb.* 1609. [f. next.] **1.** An act of tweaking; a sharp wringing pull; a twitch, a pluck. †**2.** *fig.* In phr. *in a t.*, in a state of excitement or agitation, in a 'taking' –1841.

Tweak (twīk), *v.* 1601. [prob. alt. of (dial.) *twick*, OE. *twiććian* = OHG. *zwicken*, rel. to TWITCH.] *trans.* To seize and pull sharply with a twisting movement; to twitch, wring, pluck; *esp.* to pull (a person) *by* the nose (or a person's nose) as a mark of contempt or insult.

Twee (twī), *a. colloq.* 1905. [For *tweet*, minced pronunc. of *sweet*.] 'Sweet', dainty, chic.

Tweed (twīd). 1847. [A trade name originating in a misreading of *tweel*, Sc. form of TWILL, helped by association with the river *Tweed*.] A twilled woollen cloth of somewhat rough surface, orig. and still chiefly made in the south of Scotland (usu. of two or more colours combined in the same yarn); inferior kinds are made of wool with a mixture of shoddy or cotton. In *pl.*, cloths or garments of this kind. Hence **Twee·dy** *a. attrib.* A young gentleman in t. suit and wide-awake 1864.

Tweedle (twī·d'l), *v.* 1684. [imit.] **1.** *intr.* Of a musical instrument or one who plays it: To produce a succession of shrill modulated sounds; also, to play triflingly or carelessly *upon* an instrument. **2.** *trans.* To entice by or as by music; to wheedle, cajole 1719.

2. A fiddler brought in with him a body of lusty young fellows, whom he had tweedled into the service ADDISON.

Tweedle- (twī·d'l), the stem of TWEEDLE *v.*, used in comb. to denote the action of the vb., or a high-pitched musical sound; chiefly in the humorous phrase **Tweedledu·m and tweedledee·**, used orig. in ref. to two rival musicians; hence **b.** *fig.* usu. in phr. *tweedledee and tweedledum*, two things or parties the difference between which is held to be insignificant 1851. **Tweedle-dee·** *v. intr.*, to play or sing in a high-pitched tone; also, to play idly; to tweedle.

'Tween, †tween (twīn), *prep.* ME. Aphetic form of ATWEEN, BETWEEN.

'Tween-decks (twī·nˌdeks). 1816. The usual sailors' abbrev. of BETWEEN-DECKS.

Tweeny (twī·ni). 1888. [f. 'TWEEN + -Y⁶.] A maid-servant who assists both the cook and the housemaid; a between-maid. **b.** A small cigar.

Tweet (twīt), *sb.* and *int.* 1845. [imit.] An imitation of the sound made by a small bird. Also reduplicated. Hence **Tweet** *v. trans.* and *intr.* to twitter.

†Tweeze. 1622. [Aphetic f. *etweese* = *etuys, etuis*, pl. of ETUI.] A case of small instruments, an etui; also *pl.*, instruments kept or carried in a small case. Occas. *a pair* (= set) *of tweezes*. –1681.

Twee·zer, *sb.* 1654. [Back-formation from TWEEZERS.] †**1.** A case of small instruments; an etui, a tweezer-case –1746. **2.** = TWEEZERS 2; also *attrib.* formed like tweezers 1904.

Twee·zer, *v.* 1806. [f. prec.] *intr.* To use tweezers; *trans.* to pull out with tweezers.

Twee·zer-case. 1686. [f. TWEEZER(S + CASE *sb.*²] A case in which tweezers and other small instruments are carried; an etui or 'tweeze'.

Tweezers (twī·zəɹz), *sb. pl.* 1654. [alt., by assoc. with *nippers, pincers, pliers*, or *scissors*, of *tweezes*, pl. of TWEEZE.] Also *a pair of t.* †**1.** A set or case of small instruments (*rare*) –1742. **2.** Small pincers or nippers (orig. as included in the contents of an etui) used for plucking out hairs from the face or for grasping minute objects 1654.

1. Bought me a pair of t., cost me 14/- PEPYS.

Twelfth (twelfþ), *a.* and *sb.* [OE. *twelfta* = OFris. *twil(i)fta*, MDu. *twalefde*, OHG. *zwelifto* (Du. *twaalfde*, G. *zwölfte*), ON. *tólfti*, f. *twelf*, etc.; the new formation with *-th* (XIV) became general from XVI. See -TH².] **A.** *adj.* **1.** The ordinal numeral corresponding to the cardinal TWELVE; the last of twelve; that comes next after the eleventh. **a.** In concord with a sb., expressed or understood; also with ellipsis of *day* (of the month), or *chapter* (of a book of Scripture). **b.** *spec.* The 12th of August, on which grouse-shooting legally begins 1868. **2.** *T. part*, any one of twelve equal parts of a whole 1590. **B.** *sb.* **1.** A twelfth part 1557. **2.** *Mus.* A note twelve diatonic degrees above or below a given note (both notes being counted); the octave of a fifth; hence (usu.) the interval between two such notes 1597.

Twe·lfth-cake. 1774. [Short for *Twelfth-night* or *Twelfth-tide cake*.] A large cake used at the festivities of Twelfth-night, usu. frosted and otherwise ornamented, and with a bean or coin introduced to determine the 'king' or 'queen' of the feast.

Twe·lfth-day. OE. The twelfth day after Christmas; the sixth of January, on which the festival of the Epiphany is celebrated; formerly observed as the closing day of the Christmas festivities.

Twe·lfth-night. OE. The night of the twelfth day after Christmas (6 January) marked by merrymaking (cf. TWELFTH-CAKE and prec.).

†Twe·lfthtide. 1530. [See TIDE *sb.*] The season including Twelfth-night and Twelfth-day; the season of Epiphany –1687.

Twelve (twelv), *numeral a.* and *sb.* [OE. *twelf*, inflected *twelfe* = OFris. *twel(e)f*, OS. *twelif*, OHG. *zwelif* (Du. *twaalf*, G. *zwölf*). ON. *tólf*, Goth. *twalif*; Gmc. prob. f. **twa-* TWO + **lif-* as in ELEVEN.] The cardinal number composed of ten and two; represented by the symbols 12 or XII. **A.** *adj.* **1.** In concord with a sb. expressed. **b.** As multiplier before a higher numeral (*hundred, thousand*, etc.). ME. **2.** *absol.* with ellipsis of sb., preceded by a pronoun or demonstrative, or as predicate OE. *spec.* **b.** with ellipsis of *hours* (of the day); also *t. o'clock* 1482. **c.** with ellipsis of *years* (of age) 1607. **d.** *The t.* (spec.): applied to various bodies of twelve men having some special office, as the twelve apostles, etc.; also, the books of the twelve 'minor prophets' in the Old Testament OE. **3.** Used for the ordinal TWELFTH. *Obs.* (exc. after the sb. in *page t., chapter t.*, etc.). late ME.

1. b. *T. score*, t. twenties, two hundred and forty. **2. b.** Phr. *To strike t. the first time* (or *all at once*), *fig.* to display all one's capacities in one's first performance. **c.** At t. he was a..quiet boy BYRON.

B. *sb.* (with pl. *twelves*). **1.** The abstract number. late ME. **2.** A set or group of twelve persons or things; *esp.* a company of twelve players forming a 'side' at some game 1573. **3. a.** A thing or person distinguished by the number twelve; also *number t.* (see NUMBER *sb.* 4). **b.** A shoe, glove, etc. of size twelve. 1607. **4.** A thing characterized in some way by the number twelve; e.g. a t.-pounder gun, a candle weighing t. to the pound 1804. **5.** (Always in *pl.*) **a.** A sheet of a book folded into twelve leaves (usu. in phr. *in twelves*) 1670. **b.** A book (or books) of which each sheet is folded into twelve leaves 1683.

4. A Ship Privateer, carrying sixteen twelves and sixes 1804. **5. b.** Shelves..charged with octavos and twelves COWPER.

Comb.: **t. bore** *a.* (of a gun) having a bore corresponding to the diameter of spherical bullets of twelve to the pound; *sb.* a t.-bore gun; **-eight** (usu. $\frac{12}{8}$), *Mus.*, applied to a 'time' with t. quavers in a bar; **-pounder,** a cannon which discharges shot weighing t. pounds.

Twelvefold (twe·lvfōᵘld), *a.* and *adv.* 1557. [f. TWELVE + -FOLD.] **A.** *adj.* **a.** Twelve times as great or as much. **b.** Composed of twelve parts or divisions. **B.** *adv.* Twelve times in amount 1660.

Twelvemo (twe·lvmo). 1819. English reading of the abbreviation 12mo or XIImo for DUODECIMO.

Twelvemonth (twe·lvmɒnþ). [f. OE. *twelf* TWELVE + *mōnað* pl., MONTH.] **1.** A period of twelve months; a year. **2.** *Twelvemonth('s mind*: a commemoration of a deceased person by celebration of masses, etc. a year after (or annually on the anniversary of) the day of his death or funeral. *Obs.* exc. *Hist.* late ME.

In phr., as *That day t., Michaelmas was a t., Easter come t.*: = a year before or after. Hence **Twe·lvemonthly** *adv.* every twelve months, annually.

Twelvepence (twe·lvpĕns). late ME. **a.** A sum of money equal to twelve pennies. Now *rare.* †**b.** A coin of this value, a shilling. Formerly abbrev. xijd.

Twelvepenny (twe·lvpĕni), *a.* Now *rare.* 1594. **1.** Of the value of, or amounting to, twelvepence. **2.** Costing or priced at twelvepence 1609. **3.** That may be hired for twelvepence; paying, or receiving, twelvepence 1614.

Twentieth (twe·ntiėþ), *a.* and *sb.* [OE. *twentiġoða*, f. *twentiġ* TWENTY + *-oða* (see -TH²); becoming in ME. *twentiþe, -ythe*, from XVI *twentieth*.] **A.** *adj.* **1.** The ordinal numeral corresponding to the cardinal TWENTY; last of twenty; next after the nineteenth. **2.** *T. part*: any one of twenty equal parts into which a whole may be divided ME. **B.** *sb.* A twentieth part ME.

Twenty (twe·nti), *numeral a.* and *sb.* [OE. *twentiġ* = OFris. *twintich*, OS. *twēntig*, OHG. *zweinzug* (G. *zwanzig*); the first element is variously explained; cf. ON. *tuttugu*, Goth. *twai tigjus*; see -TY².] The cardinal number equal to twice ten: represented by the symbols 20 or XX (formerly occas. xxᵗⁱ = L. *viginti*). **A.** *adj.* **1.** In concord with a sb. expressed (or in OE. in pl. form with implied sb.). **b.** Combined with the numerals below ten to express the numbers between twenty and thirty OE. **c.** As multiplier before a numeral, as *t. thousand*, etc. (often hyperbolically) OE. **d.** Used vaguely or hyperbolically for a large number 1470. **2.** With ellipsis of sb. OE. **b.** *spec.* with ellipsis of *years* (of age); so *t.-one*, etc. 1773. **3.** Used for the ordinal TWENTIETH. Now only after a sb. as in *chapter t.* OE.

2. His thermometer..registered t. below zero 1902. Phr. *T. to one*, twenty chances to one; an expression of strong probability.

B. *sb.* (with pl. *twenties*). **1.** The abstract number 20; a symbol representing this. late ME. **b.** A person or thing distinguished by this number 1888. **2.** A group or set of twenty persons or things 1637. **b.** Something equivalent to twenty of some unit, e.g. a t.-pound bank-note 1850. **c.** A sheet (of a book) folded into twenty leaves (4 × 5), or each leaf of such a sheet 1771. **3.** Something characterized in some way by the number twenty 1842. **4.** *pl.* The numbers from 20 to 29; the years in a century or of one's life, or the degrees of any scale (e.g. of a thermometer) so numbered 1874.

1. Five Twenties make a Hundred WATTS. **4.** In their twenties girls feel differently from what they do in their teens 1874.

Twenty-five. 1877. *Rugby Football*, etc. The line drawn across the ground twenty-five yards from each goal; also, the space enclosed by this, and (in hockey) a bully on the twenty-five line.

Twentyfold (twe·ntifōᵘld), *a.* and *adv.* 1610. [f. TWENTY + -FOLD.] **A.** *adj.* Twenty times as many or as great; multiplied by twenty; twenty times repeated. **B.** *adv.* Twenty times (in amount); twenty times as much 1872.

Twenty-fou·r. 1673. A sheet folded into 24 leaves; a book in which the sheets are thus folded. (Always in *pl.*; usu. in phr. *in twenty-fours.*)

Twentyfou·rmo. 1841. [English reading of 24mo or xxivmo, used as abbrev. of L. *vicesimo quarto*, after 12mo = *duodecimo*.] The size of a book in which each sheet is folded into 24 leaves. So **Twe·ntymo** [= 20mo or xxmo, for L. *vicesimo*], the size of a book in which each sheet is folded into 20 leaves.

'twere (twēᵊɹ, twəɹ). 1605. Abbreviation of *it were*, now poet. or arch; see IT.

Twi-, twy- (twəi), *prefix.* [OE. *twi-*, *twy-* = OFris. *twi-*, OHG. *zwi-*, ON. *tvi-*, cogn. with L. *bi-*, Gr. δι-, Skr. *dvi-*, f. base akin to that of TWO. In mod. Eng. gen. repl. by *two-*, as *twofold* (ME. *twafald* XII, OE. *twifeald*).] In OE. the regular comb. form expressing *two*, sometimes *twice*.

Twibill, twybill (twəi·bil). *arch.* [OE. *twibil(l* and *twibile*, f. TWI- + BILL *sb.*[1] and *sb.*[2]] †**1.** A kind of axe with two cutting edges; formerly used for cutting mortises –1686. **2.** A mattock; also, a similar tool used in mining. Now *local.* 1440. **b.** A reaping-hook used in cutting beans and peas; a pea-hook. *dial.* 1763. **3.** A double-bladed battle-axe or bill. *poet.* 1558.

Twice (twəis), *adv.* (*sb.*, *a.*) [Early ME. *twiġes* (XII), f. OE. *twiġe*, earlier *twiġ(e)a* = OFris. *twia*, OS. *twio* (f. **twi-* Two) + *-es*, -S. Cf. THRICE.] **1.** Two (successive) times; on two occasions. **b.** Contextually: A second time; for the second time ME. **2.** Expressing multiplication by two: Two times in number, amount, or value; doubly ME. **3.** quasi-*sb.*, preceded by a prep. or demonstrative: Two times 1494. **4.** quasi-*adj.* Performed, occurring, given, etc. twice; doing something (implied by the sb.) twice 1577.

1. Wouldst thou haue a Serpent sting thee t.? SHAKS. *Once or t.*, *t. or thrice*, a few times. **b.** They say, an old man is t. a childe SHAKS. *To think t.*, to consider a matter a second time (before deciding or acting). **2.** Two is t. one 1875. **3.** I have written this at t. H. WALPOLE. **4.** His t. Imprisonment in the Tower 1683.

Comb. with pples., forming compound adjs., as *t.-baked*, *-boiled*, *-married*; **t.-laid**, of rope, made from the yarns of old rope; **-told**, counted or reckoned t.; t. as much as; narrated or related t.

Twi·ce-born, *a.* late ME. **1.** Born twice; esp. as an epithet of Bacchus (also *absol.*). **2.** An epithet of the three higher castes of Hindus. Also *absol.* 1794. **3.** *Theol.* That has experienced the second birth; born again, regenerate. Also *absol.* 1849.

Twiddle (twi·d'l), *sb.* 1774. [f. next.] An act of twiddling; a twirl or twist; also, a twirled mark or sign.

Twiddle (twi·d'l), *v.* 1540. [prob. intended to combine the notions of TWIRL *v.* and FIDDLE *v.*] **1.** *intr.* To be busy about trifles; to trifle; also *to t. with* or *at* = sense 2. **2.** *trans.* To turn (anything) about, esp. with the fingers; to twirl; to play with idly or absently 1676. **3.** *intr.* To move in a twirling manner; to turn about in a light or trifling way 1812.

2. Phr. *To t. one's thumbs*, or *fingers*, to keep turning them idly around each other; *fig.* to have nothing to do.

†**Twie, twye**, *adv.* [OE. *twiġa*, etc.; see TWICE.] = TWICE –1450.

†**Twifa·llow, twy-**, *v.* 1557. [f. TWI- + FALLOW *v.*[2]] *trans.* To fallow twice; to fallow a second time; to plough up (land) a second time in the course of its lying fallow –1733.

Twifold, twyfold (twəi·fōᵘld), *a.* and *adv.* *arch.* [OE. *twifeald*, *twyfeald*; see TWI- and -FOLD.] **A** *adj.* **1.** Twofold, double. †**2.** *fig.* **a.** Double-dealing, deceitful, insincere. **b.** Double-minded, irresolute. –ME.

1. Within those orbs the twyfold being shone CARY.

†**B.** *adv.* In two parts or divisions; (folded) double; doubly (*rare*) –1619.

Twig (twig), *sb.*[1] [OE. (late Northumb.) *twigge*, obscurely rel. to *twiġ*, *twi*, corresp. to ODa. *tvige* fork and (with long vowel) MLG. *twīch* (*-g-*), Du. *twijg*, OHG. *zwīg* (G. *zweig*); all based on Gmc. **twi-* (:– IE. **dwi-*); cf. TWAIN, TWIN, TWINE, TWO.] **1.** A slender shoot issuing from a branch or stem. **2.** *spec.* Short for LIME-TWIG (*obs.*); also, in *pl.*, the twigs forming a birch-rod 1601. **3.** transf. *Anat.* A small ramification of a blood-vessel or nerve 1683.

1. Just as the T. is bent, the Tree's inclin'd POPE.

Comb.: **t.-beetle**, **-borer** (*U.S.*), any of various small beetles which bore into the twigs of trees; **-girdler** (*U.S.*), an Amer. beetle, *Oncideres cingulatus*, which deposits its eggs in the tips of twigs, which it then girdles below the eggs; **t. insect**, the stick-insect or 'walking-stick'; **-rush**, a tall marsh-plant, *Cladium mariscus*, family *Cyperaceæ*, having very long narrow rigid leaves.

Twig, *sb.*[2] *slang.* Now *rare* or *Obs.* 1811. [Of unkn. origin.] Style, fashion; also, condition, state, fettle; esp. in the phrases *in* (*prime*, *good*) *t.*

Twig, *v.*[1] *Obs.* or *dial.* 1550. [f. TWIG *sb.*[1]] *trans.* To beat with or as with a twig; *fig.* to reprove.

Twig, *v.*[2] *slang* or *colloq.* 1764. [Of unkn. origin; perh. an application of *twig* pull (XVII; cf. *twick*, TWEAK *v.*).] **1.** *trans.* **a.** To watch; to look at; to inspect. **b.** To become aware of by seeing; to perceive, catch sight of; to recognize 1796. **2.** *fig.* To understand, comprehend. Also *intr.* 1815.

1. 'T. the old connoisseur', said the squire to the knight SCOTT. **b.** I twigged the tigress creeping away in front of us 1879. **2.** I twigged what you were after, and kept him up in talk SURTEES.

Twiggen (twi·g'n), *a.* *arch.* 1549. [f. TWIG *sb.*[1] + -EN[4].] **a.** Made of twigs or wicker-work; also, having a wickerwork covering. **b.** Arising from burning twigs or brushwood.

Twiggy (twi·gi), *a.* 1562. [f. TWIG *sb.*[1] + -Y[1].] **1.** Like a twig; slender, as a shoot or branch. **2.** Full of or abounding in twigs; bushy, shrubby 1600.

2. Masses of t. growth at the bottom 1882.

Twilight (twəi·ləit). [In XV *twyliȝt*, etc., f. TWI- + LIGHT *sb.* The exact force of *twi-* here is doubtful; cf. Du. †*tweelicht*, LG. *twelecht*.] **1.** The light diffused by the reflection of the sun's rays from the atmosphere before sunrise, and after sunset; the period during which this prevails between daylight and darkness 1440. **b.** *spec.* Most commonly applied to the evening twilight, from sunset to dark night. late ME. **c.** Morning twilight, which lasts from daybreak to sunrise 1440. **2.** *transf.* A dim light resembling twilight; partial illumination 1667. **3.** *fig.* An intermediate condition or period; a condition before or after full development 1600. **4.** *attrib.* or as *adj.* **a.** Of, pertaining to, or resembling twilight; seen or done in the twilight 1633. **b.** *fig.* Having an intermediate character 1730. **c.** Lighted as by twilight; dim, obscure, shadowy; also *fig.* of early times 1629. **d.** *fig.* Of the nature of or pertaining to imperfect mental light 1677.

1. b. Now came still Eevning on, and T. gray Had in her sober Liverie all things clad MILT. **2.** As when the Sun..In dim Eclips disastrous t. sheds MILT. **3.** *T. of the gods* [tr. Icel. *ragna rökkr*, altered from *ragna rök* history or judgement of the gods], in Scandinavian mythology, the destruction of the gods and of the world in conflict with the powers of evil. **4.** When the lingering t. hour was past BYRON. **c.** Arched walks of t. groves MILT. **d.** A doubtful, uncertain, and t. sort of rationality SCOTT. **e. T. sleep** [tr. G. *dämmerschlaf*], a method of making childbirth painless by inducing a comatose condition in the mother. So **Twi·lit** *ppl. a.* lit by or as by t. 1869.

Twill (twil), **tweel** (twīl), *sb.* ME. [north. and Sc. forms of ME. *twile* TWILLY *sb.*[1]] A woven fabric characterized by parallel diagonal ridges or ribs, produced by causing the weft threads to pass over one and under two or more threads of the warp, instead of over and under in regular succession, as in plain weaving. **b.** The, or a, method or process of weaving this fabric; also, the ribbed appearance or diagonal pattern of the material so woven 1779.

Twill (twil), **tweel** (twīl), *v.* 1808. [f. prec.] *trans.* To weave so as to produce diagonal ridges on the surface of the cloth.

†**Twi·lly**, *a.* and *sb.*[1] [OE. *twili* = OHG. *zwilih* (G. *zwillich*), semi-tr. of L. *bilix*, *bilic-* two-threaded, f. *bi-* BI- + base of *licium* thrum, thread. The Sc. form is *tweel*; see TWEED.] **A.** *adj.* Twilled. **B.** *sb.* A twilled cloth –1714.

Twilly (twi·li), *sb.*[2] Also **twilley.** 1858. [Altered f. *willy* WILLOW.] A willowing machine; also called *t. devil* (see DEVIL *sb.* 8). Hence **Twi·lly** *v. trans.* to willow.

Twin (twin), *a.* and *sb.* [Late OE. *twinn*, earlier *ġetwinn* adj. and sb., corresp. to ON. *tvinnr*, *tvennr* two-fold, double :– Gmc. **twisnaz*; f. same base as TWI-.] **A.** *adj.* †**1.** Consisting of two; double. –late ME. **2.** (attrib. use of B. 1.) Born at the same birth, as two children or animals, or one of such 1590. **3.** Forming a pair or couple; two closely associated, connected, or related, and (usu.) alike or equal 1591. **b.** Composed of, or having, two similar and equal (or closely connected or related) parts or constituents 1585. **c.** *Nat. Hist.* Germinate 1812. **4.** Forming one of a pair or couple; closely associated with or related to another 1605.

2. He, and I, And the t. Dromio SHAKS. **3.** T. truths COLERIDGE. **b.** *T. crystal.* = B. 3 b. **4.** Yesterday's face t. image of to-day COWPER.

B. *sb.* **1.** *pl.* Two children or young brought forth at one birth ME. **b.** *sing.* One of two children or young brought forth at a birth; with possessive or *of* = twin brother or sister 1440. **c.** *Astron.* (pl.) The zodiacal constellation and sign GEMINI. late ME. **2.** *fig.* **a.** *pl.* Two persons or things intimately associated, connected, or related; two forming a pair or couple 1589. **b.** *sing.* One of two thus related; now usu. with *of*, *to*, or possessive: a fellow, counterpart 1540. **3.** A pair of twin children or young; also *fig.* or *gen.* a pair, couple, brace. *Obs.* exc. *dial.* 1569. **b.** *Cryst.* A composite crystal consisting of two (usu. equal and similar) crystals united in reversed positions with respect to each other, either by juxtaposition, embedding, or interpenetration 1845.

2. a. Two were never found Twins at all points COWPER. **b.** All who joy would win Must share it—Happiness was born a t. BYRON.

Comb.: **t.-axis** *Cryst.*, the axis of twinning in a t. crystal, i.e. the line about which either of the constituent crystals would have to revolve to come into the position of the other; **-birth**, the birth of twins; a pair born or produced as twins, or one of such in relation to the other (usu. *fig.*); **-law** *Cryst.*, the law or principle of twinning of a t. crystal; **-plane** *Cryst.*, a plane perpendicular to the t.-axis of a t. crystal; **-screw**, *a.* having twin screws; *spec.* of a steamer, having two screw propellers on separate shafts, which turn in opposite directions so as to counteract the tendency to lateral vibration; also *ellipt.* as *sb.* a t.-screw steamer.

Twin, *v.*[1] *Obs.* exc. *Sc.* [ME. *twinnen*, f. prec. Cf. TWINE *v.*[2]] **1.** *trans.* To put asunder (*prop.* two things or persons, or one *from* the other); to separate, disjoin, disunite, sunder, sever, part, divide; *fig.* to distinguish. **2.** *intr.* To go asunder; to separate, part ME.

2. We twa will never t. 1790.

Twin, *v.*[2] late ME. [f. TWIN *a.* and *sb.*] **1.** *intr.* To bring forth two children or young at a birth; to bear twins 1573. **b.** *trans.* To conceive or bring forth as twins, or as a twin *with* another 1607. **c.** *intr.* in passive sense: To be born at the same time *with*. Now *rare* or *Obs.* 1604. **2.** *trans.* To couple, join, unite, combine (two things or persons) closely or intimately. late ME. **b.** *intr.* To be coupled; to join, combine, unite (*rare*) 1621. **c.** *Cryst.* (*trans.*) To unite (two crystals) according to some definite law so as to form a twin crystal. Only in passive, and in vbl. sb. 1845. **3.** To be, or furnish, a 'twin' or counterpart to; to match, parallel 1605.

1. Two more ewes have twinned HARDY. **c.** *Oth.* II. iii. 212. **2.** Still we moved Together, twinn'd as horse's ear and eye TENNYSON.

Twin-born, *a.* 1599. Born a twin or twins; born at the same birth, as two, or one of two.

Latona's twin-born progenie MILT.

Twin-brother. (Also as two words.) 1598. [TWIN *a.* 2.] A brother born at the same birth, as one of twins.

fig. Sleep, Death's twin-brother TENNYSON.

Twine (twəin), *sb.* (*a.*) [OE. *twin, twiġin* linen = Du. *twijn* twine, twist, f. Gmc. **twi*- TWI- with *n*-formative.] **1.** Thread or string composed of two or more yarns or strands twisted together; now *spec.* string or strong thread, made of hemp, cotton, or other fibre, used for sewing coarse materials, tying packages, netting, and the like; with *a* and *pl.* a piece or kind of this. **2.** A twined or twisted object or part. **a.** A twining stem or spray of a plant 1579. **b.** A fold; a coil; a convolution 1600. **c.** A tangle, knot 1865. **3.** The action or an act of twining. Now *rare* or *Obs.* 1602.

1. *fig.* Destiny..Spinn's all their fortunes in a silken t. DRYDEN. **2. b.** Typhon huge ending in snaky t. MILT.

Twine (twəin), *v.*[1] [ME. *twinen*, related to TWINE *sb.*] **I.** *trans.* **1.** To twist (two or more strands or filaments) together so as to form a thread or cord; to twist (one thread, etc.) *with* another; to form (thread or cord) by twisting or spinning; to spin (yarn, etc.) into thread or cord; also *gen.* to combine or make compact by twisting. **b.** *transf.* To form by interlacing; to weave, to wreathe 1612. **c.** *transf.* To interlace, entwine 1679. **2.** To cause (one thing) to encircle or embrace another; to twist, wreathe, clasp, or wrap (a thing) *about* or *around* another 1585. **3.** To enfold, wreathe, or encircle (one thing) *with* another; also of a plant, wreath, etc.: to encircle, enwrap 1602.

1. We'll t. a double strong halter for the Captain KINGSLEY. *fig.* Our fortunes Were twyn'd together 1612. **2.** Let me t. Mine armes about that body SHAKS. **3.** Let wreaths of triumph now my temples t. POPE.

II. *intr.* **1.** To wind or twist (*about, over,* or *round* something): almost always of a plant: to grow in a twisting or spiral manner. late ME. **2.** To extend or proceed in a winding manner; to bend, incline circuitously; to wind about, meander; of a serpent, etc., to crawl sinuously 1553. **3.** To contort the body; to writhe, wriggle, squirm. Now *dial.* 1666.

1. Amidst thy Laurels let this Ivy t. DRYDEN. **2.** The little brown river..twined to the sea 1902. Hence **Twi·ner,** one who or that which twines; a plant of twining habit.

Twine, *v.*[2] *Sc.* 1621. [Later form of TWIN *v.*[1]] *intr.* and *trans.* = TWIN *v.*[1]

Twinge (twinᵈʒ), *sb.* 1548. [f. next.] †**1.** An act of tweaking or pinching; a tweak or pinch –1692. **2.** A sharp pinching or wringing pain; often, a momentary local pain; *esp.* applied to that of gout and rheumatism 1608. **3.** *fig.* A sharp mental pain; a pang of shame, remorse, sorrow, or the like; a prick of conscience 1622.

1. For the twindge by th' nose, 'Tis certainly unsightly 1625. **2.** The gout..gave him such severe twinges 1863. **3.** It cost the Vicar some twinges of conscience HUGHES.

Twinge (twinᵈʒ), *v.* [OE. *twenġan* = MLG. *twengen*, OHG. *zwengen*, f. Gmc. **twaŋg*-, repr. by MHG. *zwange* tongs, *zwangen* pinch, OHG. *zwangōn, zwengen.*] **1.** *trans.* To pinch, wring, tweak, twitch. Also *intr. Obs.* exc. *dial.* **2.** †To cause to smart or tingle, to irritate; to affect (the body or mind) with a twinge or sharp pain; to prick (the conscience) 1647. **b.** *intr.* To experience a twinge or smart 1640.

1. Twindging him by th' Ears or Nose 1678. **2.** Nothing did t. my Conscience like this BUNYAN.

Twingle-twangle (twi·ŋg'l,twæ·ŋg'l). 1634. [Reduplication of TWANGLE.] A representation of the sound of the harp, or other such instrument.

Twining (twəi·niŋ), *ppl. a.* 1593. [f. TWINE *v.*[1] + -ING[2].] That twines, in various senses; *spec.* of a plant growing spirally round a support.

Twink (twiŋk), *sb.* late ME. [f. next.] A winking of the eye; *transf.* the time taken by this; a twinkling; now always in phr. *in a t.*

Twink (twiŋk), *v.* [Late ME. *twinken*, corresp. to MHG. *zwinken* (cf. G. *zwinkern* blink, wink, twinkle); repr. the simple stem from which TWINKLE *v.* is formed.] †**1.** *intr.* To wink, to blink –1681. **2.** To twinkle, sparkle 1637.

Twinkle (twi·ŋk'l), *sb.* 1548. [f. next.] **1.** A winking of the eye; a wink, blink; also, a momentary glance. **b.** *transf.* A twitch, flicker, quiver 1733. **2.** = TWINKLING *vbl. sb.* 3; now only in phr. *in a t., in the t. of an eye* 1592. **3.** A sparkle, a scintillation; also, a faint or momentary gleam, a glimmer 1663.

1. Suddenly, with twincle of her eye, The Damzell broke his misintended dart SPENSER. **3.** He had a roguish t. in his eye THOMSON.

Twinkle (twi·ŋk'l), *v.* [OE. *twinclian*, f. base of TWINK *v.*; see -LE.] **1.** *intr.* To shine with rapidly intermittent light; to sparkle; to glitter; †to shine dimly, to flicker. **b.** *trans.* To emit (radiance, flashes, or beams) rapidly and intermittently; to communicate (a message or signal) in this way 1547. **c.** *poet.* To guide or light *to* some place by twinkling 1690. **2.** *intr.* To close and open the eye or eyes quickly; to make a signal by this means; to wink, blink; also said of the eye or eyes. *Obs.* or *arch.* ME. **b.** *trans.* With the eyes, eyelids, etc. as obj. 1591. **3.** *intr.* To move to and fro, or in and out, with rapid alternation; to appear and disappear in quick succession; to flutter, flit, flicker 1616.

1. Hise eyen twynkled..As doon the sterres in the frosty nyght CHAUCER. **b.** The challenge-word..was twinkled..by the luminous dots and dashes from her masthead 1899. **2.** The old Justice twinkles, hems, coughs, and chuckles 1784. **3.** The open space..twinkles, is alive With heads WORDSW.

Twinkler (twi·ŋklər). 1591. [f. TWINKLE *v.* + -ER[1].] Anything which emits intermittent, transient, or faint radiance; sometimes applied to eyes.

Such tiny twinklers as the planet orbs SHELLEY.

Twinkling (twi·ŋkliŋ), *vbl. sb.* ME. [f. TWINKLE *v.* + -ING[1].] The action of the vb. TWINKLE. **1.** The action of shining with tremulous or faint radiance; scintillation. late ME. **2.** The action or an act of winking; nictitation. *Obs.* exc. as in 3. ME. **3.** The time taken in winking the eye; a moment, an instant ME.

1. The t. of the starres is the vibration or trembling of their light 1635. **3.** Phr. *In the t. of an eye*, in an instant; In a moment, in the t. of an eye, at the last trump;..the dead shall be raised incorruptible 1 *Cor.* 15:52. *In a t.*; I'll.. be with you again in a t. DRYDEN.

Twinned (twind, *poet.* twi·nėd), *ppl. a.* 1607. [f. TWIN *sb.* or *v.*[2] + -ED.] **1.** Born two at one birth; twin. **2.** Intimately joined or united, as two things; coupled (usu. also implying close similarity) 1611. **b.** *Cryst.* United, as two crystals, or consisting of two crystals united, so as to form a 'twin' 1879.

Twi·nning, *vbl. sb.* 1573. [f. TWIN *v.*[2] + -ING[1].] The action of TWIN *v.*[2] *attrib.*: **t.-axis, -law, -plane,** *Cryst.* = *twin-axis, -law, -plane.*

Twinship (twi·nʃip). 1674. [f. TWIN *a.* or *sb.* + -SHIP.] The condition of being twin, or a twin; the relation of a twin or twins.

Twin-sister. (Also as two words.) 1707. [TWIN *a.* 2.] A sister born at the same birth, as one of twins.

Twire (twəiᵊɹ), *v. arch.* and *dial.* 1568. [Of unkn. origin, but corresp. in form to MHG. *zwieren* (now Bavarian dial.) blink, peer.] **1.** *intr.* To look narrowly or covertly; to peer; to peep. Also *fig.* of a light, etc. †**2.** *intr.* To wink. HOLLAND. Hence †**Twire** *sb.* (*rare*) a glance, a leer (*slang*).

Twirl (twɔ̄ɹl), *sb.* 1598. [f. next.] The action or an act of twirling, or the condition of being twirled; a rapid whirling or spinning; a twist; a spin; a whirl. **b.** Anything that twirls or is twirled; †a winch; each of the whorls of a shell; a curved line 1688. Hence **Twi·rly** *a.* full of or characterized by twirls or curves.

Twirl (twɔ̄ɹl), *v.* 1598. [prob. alt., by assoc. with *whirl*, of †*tirl* (XVI), metathetic var. of TRILL *v.*[3]] **1.** *intr.* To rotate rapidly, to spin; to be whirled round or about; also *fig.* of the mind or head: to be in a whirl. **2.** *trans.* To cause to rotate or spin; to turn (an object) round rapidly; to turn about with the fingers; to twiddle idly or playfully 1623. **b.** To turn (one's fingers or thumbs) rapidly about one another 1777. **3.** To twist spirally (threads, etc.); now *esp.* to twist (the moustache) 1614. **4.** To whirl. Now *rare.* 1646. **5.** *intr.* To twine, coil, curl (*rare*) 1706.

1. The [compass] needle..sometimes twirling swiftly round TYNDALL. **2.** When..dexterous Damsels twirle the sprinkling Mop GAY. **b.** Phr. *To t. one's thumbs*, as an idle occupation when one has nothing to do. **3.** He twirled his long moustache 1894. **5.** The monster's hideous tail.. writhing and twirling THACKERAY.

Twist (twist), *sb.* ME. [Of complicated history; partly dependent on OE. *twist*, in comps. denoting a hinged or branched object, viz. *candeltwist* snuffers, *mæst twist* mast rope, stay, *yltwist* bird-trap, and in place-names prob. denoting 'fork'; presumably f. the base **twis*-, identical with that of TWIN, TWINE.] **I.** A divided object or part. †**1.** The flat part of a hinge, fastened on a door or gate, and turning on a hook or pintle fixed in the post –1805. †**2.** A twig; a branch –1622. **3.** The part of anything at which it divides or branches; *spec.* the junction of the thighs, the fork; now (exc. *arch.*) only that of sheep and cattle. late ME. **II.** The twisting of threads into a cord, etc. **1.** Thread or cord composed of two or more fibres or filaments of hemp, silk, wool, cotton, or the like, wound round one another 1555. **b.** *spec.* (*a*) in *Cotton-spinning*, warp yarn, which is more twisted in spinning, and stronger than weft; (*b*) fine silk thread used by tailors, hatters, etc. With *pl.*, a kind of this. 1805. **2.** A cord, thread, or the like, formed by twisting, spinning, or plaiting; also, a conical bag or wrapper made by twisting a piece of paper, etc., a 'screw' 1598. **b.** *Naut.* Each of the strands of which a rope consists 1635. †**3.** *fig.* The course of life figured as a thread –1638. **4.** A beverage consisting of a mixture of two liquors or ingredients, as tea and coffee, gin and brandy, etc. *slang.* 1700. **5.** Tobacco made into a thick cord; a piece or 'length' of this 1791. **6.** A loaf made of one or more twisted rolls of dough; a small twisted roll of bread 1845.

3. Cruell Atropos..cutting the t. in twaine SPENSER. **5.** The prize..was..a t. of tobacco 1808. **6.** Dainty new bread, crusty twists, cool fresh butter DICKENS.

III. Senses denoting chiefly the action of the verb. **1.** An act or the action of turning on or as on an axis; a turn; a twirl; the condition of being twisted or turned in this way; rotary motion, spin 1576. **2. a.** In *Tennis, Cricket, Billiards*, etc.: Lateral spin imparted to a ball in striking or delivery, causing it to diverge on rebounding; 'screw'; a stroke by which such spin is given; the action or knack of giving this spin to a ball; also, a ball having such spin 1699. **b.** *Physics.* Movement parallel to, combined with rotation about, an axis (as in the motion of a screw); also, the velocity of such movement (= *t.-velocity*) 1891. **3.** The amount or direction of twisting given to the strands of a rope (*rare*); also, the twisting given to yarn in spinning 1712. **4.** The condition of being twisted spirally; the amount or degree of this; *spec.* the angle of torsion; also, a spirally twisted object or figure; a spiral line or pattern; *spec.* the rifling in the bore of a gun, etc.; a spiral ornament in the stem of a wine-glass 1711. **b.** *Dynamics.* Twisting strain or force; torque 1891. **5. a.** A twisting or screwing of the body or features; a contortion or screw 1865. **b.** A strain or wrench (of a limb or joint) 1865. **6.** A hearty appetite. *slang.* 1785. **7.** An irregular bend; a crook, a kink; also, a tangle 1776. **8.** A turning aside, a deviation; also *fig.* a change of circumstances, vicissitude; also, a point or place at which a road alters its direction; a bend, turn 1798. **9.** *fig.* **a.** An eccentric or perverted inclination or attitude; *esp.* a peculiar mental turn or bent; an intellectual or moral bias or obliquity; a craze, whim, crotchet 1811. **b.** A wresting, perversion, distortion 1862.

7. Phr. *A t. in one's tongue*, inability to articulate clearly. **8.** Phr. *Twists and turns*, intricate windings, ins and outs; The twists and turns of the law 1875. **9. a.** He has a t., or, as the Scotch say, a 'craze' on the subject of dress 1813. **b.** The most curious t. of meaning 1875.

Comb.: **t. barrel,** a gun-barrel formed of a spirally twisted strip or strips of iron; **-drill,** one having a twisted body like that of an auger; **-yarn** = sense II. 1 b (*a*).

Twist (twist), *v.* ME. [Of mixed origin;

partly f. the sb.] **I.** To divide, separate. †**1.** *intr.* To divide into branches; to branch (*rare*). –late ME. **2.** *trans.* To prune, clip. *Obs.* or *dial.* 1483. **II.** To combine, unite, etc. **1.** *trans.* To combine two or more yarns or fibres of (any suitable material) into a thread or cord by spinning; to form (a thread or cord) by spinning the yarns or strands. Also *absol.* 1471. **2.** To join or unite by twining or interlacing; to twine *together*; to entwine (one thing) *with* another; to intertwine, interweave 1563. **3.** *fig.* To unite, combine, connect, associate intimately, like strands in a cord 1573. **4.** To wind or coil (a thread or the like) *on* or *round* something; to attach in this way; to encircle (an object) *with* or as with a thread, etc.; to entwine *in* something else 1582. **5.** *intr.* and *refl.* To pass or move in a tortuous manner; to coil or twine *about* or *round*; to penetrate *into* something with a tortuous movement or action 1635.

1. Tow-lines..they supplied by twisting a strong tough kind of flag or rush DE FOE. *fig.* He a rope of sand could t. As tough as learned Sorbonist 1663. **2.** A Pillar made of three brazen Serpents twisted together 1687. **3.** Our Monarch's Fate Was twist in his 1646. **4.** A few wild flowers were twisted in her fine hair 1820. **5.** The weeds..have twisted themselves into its crannies RUSKIN.

III. To wring, wrench. †**1.** *trans.* To compress with a turning movement; to wring; also *fig.* to torment, harass. late ME. only. **2.** To wring out of place or shape, or so as to change the shape; *esp.* to force (a limb, etc.) round so as to sprain it; to wrench 1530. **3.** To turn awry; to screw up or contract (the features, etc.); to contort, distort 1789. **b.** *fig.* To wrest the form or meaning of; to pervert; to distort; to force a meaning from 1821. **4.** To force *down*, pull *off* or *out* with a turning strain; to wrench or wring *off*, etc. 1784. **5.** To form into a spiral; to bend, curve, or coil spirally; to screw *up*. Also *intr.* for *refl.* or *pass.* 1744. **b.** *Insurance.* (*U.S.*) To induce (a person) to drop a policy in one company and take out a new one, usu. in another company 1906. **6.** *intr.* and *trans.* To eat heartily; also *to t.* (food) *down. slang.* 1694.

3. b. Twisting my opinions into accordance with a party 1883. **5.** Phr. *To t.* (a person) *round one's finger*, to have completely under one's influence; so *to turn, t., and wind* (a person).

IV. To rotate, etc. **1.** *trans.* To cause to rotate as on an axis; to turn (anything) round so as to alter its position or aspect 1789. **b.** *Cricket.* In bowling, to give a lateral spin to (the ball), so that it 'breaks' or turns aside on rebounding 1833. **2.** *intr.* To rotate, revolve; also, to turn so as to face another way 1680. **3.** To turn aside and proceed in a new direction; *spec.* of a ball (at cricket, etc.): to turn aside or 'break' on rebounding; also, to proceed with frequent turns; to follow a circuitous route; to wind, meander 1833.

3. He..twisted from side to side 1863.

Twi·sted, *ppl. a.* 1548. [f. prec. + -ED[1].] **1.** Consisting of two or more threads, strands, or the like twined together; formed into a cord by being intertwined with another or others; made of spun or doubled thread, or by spinning; also *transf.* wreathed, plaited, interwoven. **2.** Wrung out of shape; distorted; contorted; turned or bent awry; *spec.* in *Bot.* = CONTORTED 2; crooked, tortuous, winding; turned or wrung spirally, of coiled or screw-like form, spiral or helical; also, involved, tangled, confused 1725.

Special collocations: **t. bit**, a bit of which the mouthpiece consists of a square bar spirally twisted; **t. drill** = *twist-drill*.

Twister (twi·stəɹ), *sb.* 1579. [f. as prec. + -ER[1].] **1.** A girder 1875. **2.** One who (or that which) spins thread, cord, or the like; *spec.* one whose occupation is to twist together the ends of the yarns of the new warp to those of that already woven 1579. **b.** A mechanical device for spinning yarns, etc. 1703. **3.** One who or that which turns about, turns from side to side, rotates, etc. **a.** One who turns this way and that; *fig.* one who shuffles or cheats 1834. **b.** *Cricket*, etc. A delivery in which the ball twists or 'breaks'; a break 1857. **4.** One who curves, bends, or rolls something 1879. **5.** That which (or one who) wrings or causes contortion; esp. *fig.* something that confounds, nonplusses, or 'doubles up'; a 'staggerer' (*slang*) 1873.

Twisty (twi·sti), *a.* 1857. [f. TWIST *sb.* or *v.* + -Y[1].] Full of twists or turns; also *fig.* dishonest, not straightforward.

Twit (twit), *sb.* 1528. [f. next.] An act of twitting; a (light) censure or reproach; a taunt.

Twit (twit), *v.* 1530. [orig. *twite*, aphet. f. ATWITE.] **1.** *trans.* To blame, find fault with, censure, reproach, upbraid (a person), esp. in a light or annoying way; to cast an imputation upon; to taunt. **2.** To condemn as a fault, blame, reprove, rebuke (an act, etc.); to cavil at, disparage. Now *rare.* 1571.

1. My friend..now twitting me with all his kindness,..discarded me for ever FIELDING.

Twitch (twitʃ), *sb.*[1] 1523. [f. TWITCH *v.*[1]] **1.** An act of twitching; a sudden sharp pull or tug; a jerk; a pluck; a snatch. **2.** A sharp pain; a pinch, pang, twinge. Freq. of mental pain. 1532. **3.** A noose or loop; *spec.* a noose which may be tightened by twisting the stick to the end of which it is attached, used to compress the lip or muzzle of a horse to restrain him during a painful operation 1623. **4.** *Mining.* A place in, or part of, a vein where it is compressed and narrowed 1653. **5.** A quick, involuntary, usu. slight movement of a muscle, etc., esp. of nervous origin; a convulsive or spasmodic jerk or quiver 1718.

2. My conscience..beginning to give some twitches LAMB. **5.** That side of his face was affected with a nervous t. 1897.

Twitch (twitʃ), *sb.*[2] 1595. [Altered f. QUITCH.] Couch-grass, *Triticum repens*.

Comb.: **t.-grass**, (*a*) *Triticum repens*; (*b*) a species of fox-tail grass, *Alopecurus agrestis*.

Twitch, *v.*[1] ME. [First in *to|twićće* (XII–XIV) pull apart, corresp. to LG. *twikken*, OHG. *gizwickan*, (M)HG. *zwicken*, f. Gmc. **twik-*, repr. also by OE. *twiććian* (dial. *twick*) pluck.] **1.** *trans.* To give a sudden abrupt pull at; to pluck; to jerk. **2.** *intr.* To pull or pluck sharply or forcibly (*at* something); to tug ME. **3.** *trans.* To pull, draw, or take suddenly or with a jerk; to pluck, snatch ME. **4.** To pinch and pull at with or as with pincers or the like; to nip; to hurt or pain, as by doing this. late ME. **5.** *intr. Mining.* Of a vein of ore: To contract; with *out*, to come to an end; also *trans.* of the containing rock; to converge upon and contract or close (a vein of ore) 1709. **6.** *trans.* To draw tight by means of a cord or the like; to tie, fasten, secure tightly or firmly. Also with the cord as obj. Now *dial.* 1615. **7.** *intr.* To proceed in a jerking or irregular way (*obs. rare*); now always in ref. to involuntary bodily movements; to move in a jerky, spasmodic, or convulsive manner; to jerk, jump, start 1592.

1. She..twitch'd her fragrant robe COWPER. **2.** It seemed as if a legion of imps were twitching at him W. IRVING. **7.** I tried to keep my countenance,..but it would not do. My muscles began to t. W. IRVING.

Twitch (twitʃ), *v.*[2] *dial.* 1795. [f. TWITCH *sb.*[2]] *intr.* To gather and destroy twitch or couch-grass; also *trans.* to clean (land) from twitch.

Twite (twəit). 1562. [Imitative, from the note of the bird.] A species of linnet, *Linota flavirostris* or *L. montium* found in hilly and moorland districts in the northern parts of Britain and in Scandinavia, and elsewhere as a winter visitant; also **t.-finch.**

Twitter (twi·təɹ), *sb.* 1678. [f. TWITTER *v.*] **1.** A condition of twittering or tremulous excitement; a state of agitation; a flutter; a tremble. Now chiefly *dial.* **2.** An act or the action of twittering, as a bird; light tremulous chirping. Also *transf.* a sound resembling this. 1842.

1. In a t. of indignation THACKERAY. **2.** The hesitating t. of sleepy birds 1849.

Twitter (twi·təɹ), *v.* late ME. [imit.; see -ER[5].] **1.** *intr.* Of a bird: To utter a succession of light tremulous notes; to chirp continuously with a tremulous effect. **b.** *transf.* Of a person: To sing or chatter after the above manner 1829. **2.** *trans.* Of a bird: To utter or express by twittering. late ME. **b.** *transf.* Of a person 1864. **3.** *intr.* To move tremulously, tremble, shake, shiver; *esp.* to tremble with excitement, eagerness, fear, etc.; to be in a flutter. Now *dial.* 1616.

1. The swallow twittring from the straw-built shed GRAY. **2.** The Squallid owle Twitters a mid-night note 1645. **3.** I was..twittering with cold STEVENSON. Hence **Twi·tterer. Twi·ttering** *vbl. sb.* the light tremulous chirping of a bird or birds; a sound resembling or likened to this.

'Twixt, †twixt (twikst), *prep.* ME. Aphetic form of ATWIXT, BETWIXT.

Two (tū), *numeral a., sb.* (*adv.*) [OE. *twā* fem., *twā*, *tū* n. = OFris. *twā*, OS. *twā*, *twō*, OHG. *zwā*, *zwō*, ON. *tvær*, Goth. *twōs*; cogn. with Gr. *δύο* (*δω-*), L. *duo*, Skr. *dwau* masc., *dwe* fem. and n.] The cardinal number next after one; one added to one; denoted by the symbols 2 or II. **A.** *adj.* **1.** In concord with a sb. expressed. **b.** As ordinal: = SECOND *a.* Now only after the sb. (also *number t.*) 1586. **2.** *absol.* with ellipsis of sb., or after a pronoun or demonstrative, or as predicate OE. **b.** *spec.* with ellipsis of *hours* or *years* (of age) 1485. **3.** Forming compound numerals OE. **4.** In pregnant sense: = Two different, two distinct 1570. †**b.** *predic.*: At variance –1738. **5.** *A..or t.*: an indefinite small number of.. So *two or three*. ME.

1. To conquer Sin and Death the t. grand foes MILT. The t. best ships in the navy 1805. Phr. *T. parts*, t. out of three equal parts, t. thirds. Chiefly *Sc.* **b.** Column t. 1824. **2.** The Ministry carried it t. to one 1779. Phr. *In t.*, into or in t. pieces or parts. *T. and t.*, *t. by t.*, in groups or sets of t.; t. at a time; by twos. **b.** The minster-clock has just struck t. WORDSW. **3.** *T.-and-thirty*, now usu. *thirty-t.*; *a hundred and t. T.-thirds*; also *attrib.* as a *t.-thirds majority*. *Comb.* A t.-hundred-pound buck 1897. **4.** To say and to do are t. things 1570. *To be in t. minds*: see MIND *sb.* II. 3.

B. *sb.* **1.** The abstract number equal to one and one 1697. **b.** The figure (2) denoting this number 1877. **c.** A person or thing denoted by this number. Also *number t.* 1890. **2.** A group or set of two persons or things; a pair, couple. Usu. in *pl.* 1585. **b.** A card or domino, or the side of a die, marked with two pips or spots 1500. **c.** In military drill, a set of two men forming a unit in wheeling 1796. **d.** *Cricket.* A hit for which two runs are scored 1881. **e.** *In t. twos*: in a very short time. *slang* or *colloq.* 1838. †**C.** *adv.* = TWICE 2. –1420.

1. Phr. *To put t. and t. together*, to consider several facts together and draw an inference. *T. and t. make four*, used as a typically obvious or undeniable statement. *T. of a trade*, two rival experts. **c.** Smith who rowed t. in the last University race 1890. **2.** The people dispersed in twos and threes 1902. **e.** The business was over in t. twos 1882.

Comb. **a.** Adjs. formed of *two* with a sb. in sense 'of, pertaining to, consisting of, having, containing, measuring, etc. two of the things named', as *t.-bushel*, *-cylinder*, *-hour*, *-ounce*, *-party*, *-phase*, *-ply*, *-story*, *-syllable*. **b.** Parasynthetic adjs. formed on similar collocations, usu. with -ED[2], in sense 'having or characterized by two of the things named', as *t.-arched*, *-coloured*, *-handled*, *-storied*, *-toed*; also *t.-dimensional*, *-monthly*. **c.** Parasynthetic sbs. in -ER[1], as *t.-master* (a t.-masted vessel), *-pounder*. **d.** In sense 'in two, doubly', as *t.-cleft*, *-ploughed*, etc. **e.** Special combs.: **t.-bill** = TWIBILL; **-bottle** *a.*, applied to one who can drink t. bottles of wine at a sitting; **-ended** *a.*, having t. ends, *spec.* with different properties, as a magnet; **-eyed** *a.*, having t. eyes; involving or adapted for the use of both eyes; **-field** *a.*, denoting a system of agriculture in which t. fields are cropped and fallowed alternately; **-four,** (usu. ²⁄₄) *Mus.*, denoting a 'time' or rhythm with t. crotchets in a bar; **-lipped** (-lipt) *a.*, having t. lips; *esp.* in *Bot.* of a corolla, calyx, etc.; bilabiate; **-monthly** *a.*, occurring every t. months; **-oar**, a t.-oared boat; **-pair** *a.* (in full *t.-pair-of-stairs*), situated above t. 'pairs' or flights of stairs, i.e. on the second floor; also *ellipt.* as *sb.* (sc. room); **-shear**, *a.* of a sheep, that has been shorn twice; *sb.* a t.-shear sheep; **-step**, a round dance characterized by sliding steps in duple rhythm; also, the music for this; **-throw** *a.*, having t. throws, as a crank (see CRANK *sb.*[1]); **-tongued** *a.*, having t. tongues; *fig.* double-tongued, deceitful.

Two:-de·cker. 1790. [f. TWO + DECK *sb.* + -ER[1].] **1.** A two-decked ship or boat; formerly *spec.* a line-of-battle ship carrying guns on two decks. **2.** *transf.* and *fig.* Something consisting of two ranges or divisions, as a tram-car with seats on the roof and an additional roof over them 1884.

Two-edged (-edʒd, *poet.* -edʒėd), *a.* 1526.

[See -ED².] Having two edges; esp. of a sword, axe, etc., having two cutting edges, one on each side of the blade. Also *fig.* of a remark, etc.

Alashtar..wielded a t. sword 1850.

Two-faced (-fē¹st; stress var.), *a.* 1619. = DOUBLE-FACED *a.*

Twofold (tū·fōᵘld), *a., adv.* [ME. *twafald*, repl. *twifald* TWIFOLD; see TWI-.] **A.** *adj.* †**1.** Double (in *fig.* sense); double-minded, wavering. ME. only. **2.** Consisting of two combined; composed of two parts or elements; existing in two relations or manners; of two kinds; double, dual 1559. **3.** Double in amount; twice as great 1812. **4.** Of yarn: Consisting of two strands twisted into one 1880.

2. A t. victorie HOLLAND. Two t. blocks NELSON.

B. *adv.* **1.** In two folds; so as to be folded or doubled. Chiefly *Sc.* of persons. late ME. **2.** To twice the amount, doubly 1526.

Two-foot (tū·fut), *a.* 1620. **1.** †**a.** Two-footed. **b.** Performed with both feet (*rare*). **2.** Measuring two feet; two feet long, wide, or thick 1664.

2. *T. rule*, a measuring rule two feet long.

Two-footed (stress var.), *a.* late ME. Having two feet; biped; two-legged; standing on two feet.

Two·-hand, *a.* late ME. = next 1.

Two-handed (stress var.), *a.* ME. **1.** Wielded with both hands, as a sword, etc.; involving the use of both hands. **2.** Wielded or worked by the hands of two persons, as a saw; engaged in by two persons, as a card-game, etc. 1657. **3.** Big, bulky, strapping. *colloq.* Now *rare* or *Obs.* 1687. **4.** Having two hands 1847. **5.** Ambidextrous; handy, efficient 1861.

1. That t. engine..Stands ready to smite MILT. **3.** A huge two-handed lubber 1687.

Two-headed (stress var.), *a.* 1596. **1.** Having, or represented with, two heads. **2.** *fig.* Having or governed by two chiefs or rulers 1885.

1. By two-headed Ianus SHAKS.

Two-leaved (līvd), *a.* 1610. Having or consisting of two leaves. **a.** Having two hinged or folding parts, as a door, table, etc. **b.** Having two foliage-leaves or two petals or sepals; having leaves growing in pairs 1688.

Two-legged (legd, le·gėd), *a.* 1561. Having two legs; usu. as an epithet suggestive of a human being having the qualities of the animal named.

The neighbours hens yᵘ takest, and playes the two legged fox 1575.

Twoness (tū·nės). 1648. [f. TWO + -NESS.] The fact or condition of being two; duality, doubleness.

Two·-part, *a.* 1854. Containing, consisting of, having, or involving two parts; composed in two parts, as a piece of music, or for two actors, as a play. So **Two-parted** *a.* divided into two parts, bipartite.

Twopence (tv·pėns). 1450. **1.** A sum of money equal to two pennies 1477. **2.** An English silver coin of the value of two pennies; = *half*-GROAT (since 1662 coined only as Maundy money). **b.** A copper coin of this value issued in the reign of George III. 1450. **3.** As type of a very small amount; now esp. in phr. (*not*) *to care t.* 1691.

Twopenny (tv·pěni), *a.* and *sb.* 1532. **A.** *adj.* **1.** Of the value of, amounting to, or costing twopence. **b.** Involving an outlay of twopence; for the use of or admission to which there is a charge of twopence 1599. **2.** *fig.* Of very little value; paltry, trumpery, trifling, worthless 1560.

1. *T. ale*, a quality of ale orig. sold at twopence per quart 1710. **b.** *T. tube*, former pop. name for the Central London Railway, opened in 1900, on which the fare was orig. twopence for any distance. **2.** This woman, with her t. gentility THACKERAY.

B. *sb.* (the adj. used ellipt.). **1.** Short for *t. ale* 1711. **2.** A form of address to a child or young or small person 1844. **3.** *colloq.* (with poss. adj.) One's head 1859. So **T.-halfpenny** (tv·pěni,hē¹·pěni) *a.* of the value of two pennies and a halfpenny; usu. *fig.* as an epithet of disparagement. **Two-pe·nny-worth,** as much as is worth or costs two pence; *fig.* a small amount.

Two-pile (tū·pəil), *a.* 1611. Applied to velvet in which the loops of the pile-warp are formed by two threads, producing a pile of double thickness. Also **Two-piled** *a.*

Two-seater (tū:sī·təɹ). 1906. [See TWO *Comb.* c.] A motor car or aeroplane having seats for two persons.

Two-sided, *a.* 1863. Having two sides, bilateral; *fig.* having two parts or aspects.

Twosome (tū·səm). Chiefly *Sc.* [f. TWO + -SOME².] Two persons together.

Two-way (stress var.), *a.* 1571. **1.** Having, or connected with, two ways, roads, or channels; situated where two ways meet. **2.** *Math.* Extending in two directions or dimensions, or having two modes of variation 1891.

1. *T. switch*, one by which electric current may be switched on or off from either of two points.

Two·-year-old, *a.* and *sb.* 1594. **A.** *adj.* Of the age of two years. Chiefly of animals, *esp.* colts 1601. **B.** *sb.* An animal (*esp.* a colt) or child of two years of age 1594.

-ty, *suffix*¹, denoting quality or condition, repr. ME. *-tie, -tee, -te*, from OFr. *-te* (mod.Fr. *-té*), earlier *-tet* (*-ted*) :– L. *-itat-*, nom. *-itas*. Such L. types as *bonitat-*, *feritat-*, were in OFr. normally reduced to two syllables (*bontet, fertet*) by elision of the *-i-* between the two stresses, so that *-tet*, later *-te*, became the regular form of the suffix. From the types *lealte*, *realte*, the ending *-alte* (mod.Fr. *-auté*) was in OFr. extended to formations from different stems, and many words of this form (ult. written with *-alty*) established themselves in English, as *admiralty, casualty, commonalty, mayoralty*, etc. Although occurring in a large number of words the suffix has been very little used as a formative element in English; *shrievalty, sheriffalty* are among the very small number of words from English stems with this suffix. Such words as *faculty, honesty, modesty* represent Latin formations in which *-tas* is directly added to a consonantal stem. The AFr. form *-teth* survives in Sc. *bountith, poortith*.

-ty, *suffix*², denoting 'ten', forming the second element of the decade numerals from 20 to 90, as *twenty, thirty* (OE. *twentig, þrītiġ*), etc. OE. *-tiġ* corresponds to OFris. *-tich*, OS. *-tig*, OHG. *-zug* (G. *-zig*), and is the same as ON. *tigr* and Goth. *tigus*, which were independent words.

Tyburn (təi·bɒɹn). late ME. The place of public execution for Middlesex until 1783, situated at the junction of the present Oxford Street, Bayswater Road, and Edgware Road.

attrib. †**T. ticket,** a certificate granted to one who secured the conviction of a felon, exempting the holder from all parochial duties in the parish where the offence was committed. **T. tree,** the gallows.

transf. Executed at T. near York, Colonel John Morrice 1736.

Tychonian (təikōᵘ·niăn), *a.* and *sb.* 1647. [f. mod.L. *Tychon-*, stem of *Tycho*, latinized form of Da. *Tyge* + -IAN.] **A.** *adj.* = next 1710. **B.** *sb.* A disciple or adherent of Tycho Brahe or of his his system of astronomy (*rare*) 1647.

Tychonic (təikǫ·nik), *a.* 1670. [f. as prec. + -IC.] Of or pertaining to the Danish astronomer Tycho Brahe (died 1601), or to his system of astronomy.

‖**Tycoon** (təikū·n). 1861. [– Jap. *taikun* great lord or prince, f. Chinese *ta* great + *kiun* prince.] The title by which the shogun of Japan was described to foreigners. **b.** *U.S.* A 'big bug'.

Tyg, tig (tig). 1855. [Of unkn. origin.] A drinking-cup with two or more handles, attributed to the 17th and 18th c.

Tying (təi·iŋ), *vbl. sb.* 1480. [f. TIE *v.* + -ING¹.] **1.** The action of TIE *v.* †**2.** *concr.* Something used for tying; a tie –1844.

Tyke (təik). Chiefly *Sc.* and *n. dial.* late ME. [– ON. *tik* bitch (Norw. *tik* bitch, vixen); cf. MLG. *tike* bitch.] **1.** A dog; usu. in depreciation, a low-bred, or coarse dog, a cur, a mongrel. **2.** *transf.* A low-bred, lazy, mean, surly, or ill-mannered fellow; a boor. late ME. **3.** A nickname for a Yorkshireman; in full *Yorkshire t.* 1700.

1. Toby was the most utterly shabby, vulgar, mean-looking cur I ever beheld—in one word, a t. 1861. **3.** Give a t. a bridle and he'll soon have a horse 1820.

Tylo- (təilo), bef. a vowel or *h* **tyl-** (til), comb. form repr. Gr. τύλος knob or τύλη callus, cushion, used in a few terms of zoology; as in **Ty·lopod** [Gr. πούς, ποδ- foot], *a.* having pads on the digits instead of hoofs; belonging to the *Tylopoda*, a group of ruminants comprising the camels and llamas (synonymous with *Camelidæ*); *sb.* a member of the *Tylopoda*, so **Tylo·podous** *a.*

‖**Tylosis** (təilōᵘ·sis). 1876. [mod.L., in sense 1 – Gr. τύλωσις, f. τύλος or τύλη; see TYLO- and -OSIS.] **1.** *Path.* **a.** An inflammatory disease of the eyelids, characterized by thickening and hardening of their edges. **b.** Callosity 1890. ¶**2.** *Bot.* An intrusive growth of the wall of a cell into the cavity of a vessel in woody tissue 1876. Hence **Tylo·tic** *a. Path.* of, pertaining to, or affected with t.

Tylote (təi·loᵘt), *sb.* (*a.*) Also in L. form **tylo·tus.** 1887. [– Gr. τυλωτός knobbed, f. τυλοῦν make knobby, f. τύλος knob.] *Zool.* A sponge-spicule of the form of a cylindrical rod with a knob at each end; also *attrib.* or *adj.*

Tymp (timp). 1645. [app. abbrev. of TYMPAN.] **1.** The mouth of the hearth of a blast-furnace through which the molten metal descends; formed by an arch of masonry (*t.-arch*), or a block of stone or iron (*t.-stone, t.-plate*), or by two of these together. **2.** *Coal mining.* A horizontal piece of timber for supporting the roof; also called *bar, cap,* or *lid* 1883.

Tympan (ti·mpăn). [OE. *timpana* and ME. *timpan* (sense 1) – L. TYMPANUM; later reinforced by (O)Fr. *tympan*, †*timpan* from the same source.] **1.** A drum or similar instrument, as a timbrel or tambourine. *arch.* **b.** [Ir. *tiompan.*] An ancient Irish stringed instrument played with a bow. late ME. †**2.** = TYMPANUM 2. –1706. **3.** An appliance in a printing-press, interposed between the platen or impression-cylinder and the sheet to be printed, in order to soften and equalize the pressure; in a hand press consisting of two frames (*outer* and *inner t.*) with sheets of parchment or strong linen stretched upon them, and enclosing a packing either of blanket, rubber, etc., or sheets of paper, cloth, or other harder material, according to the nature of the work to be printed 1580. **4.** *Arch.* = TYMPANUM 3. 1704. **5.** A tense membrane or thin plate in any mechanical apparatus, e.g. in a phonograph 1883.

attrib.: **t.-sheet,** a sheet of paper, etc., laid on or fixed in the t., orig. as a guide for placing the sheets to be printed.

Tympanal (ti·mpănăl), *a.* (*sb.*) 1822. [f. TYMPANUM + -AL¹ 1.] *Anat.* and *Zool.* = next 1. **b.** *sb.* A tympanal or tympanic bone 1875.

Tympanic (timpæ·nik), *a.* (*sb.*) 1808. [f. as prec. + -IC.] **1.** *Anat.* and *Zool.* Of, pertaining to, or connected with the tympanum, or drum of the ear; of the nature of a tympanum. **2.** Pertaining to or resembling a drum; in *Path.* tympanitic 1891. **3.** *Arch.* Pertaining to a tympanum 1909.

1. T. bone, in mammals, a bone of annular or tubular form supporting the tympanic membrane and surrounding the external auditory meatus (in the adult forming part of the temporal bone); in lower vertebrates, one of several bones variously supposed to be homologous with this. **B.** as *sb.* Short for *t. bone* 1851.

Tympaniform (ti·mpăni-, timpæ·nifǫɹm], *a.* 1854. [– Fr. *tympaniforme* (Cuvier), f. L. TYMPANUM; see -FORM.] *Nat. Hist.* Having the form of a drum, or (usu.) of a drum-head; stretched like a drum-head: *spec.* applied to certain membranes in the bronchi of birds.

Tympanist (ti·mpănist). 1611. [– Fr. *tympaniste* or f. TYMPAN + -IST.] One who beats or plays upon a drum, a drummer.

‖**Tympanites** (timpănəi·tīz). late ME. [Late L. – Gr. τυμπανίτης (Galen), f. τύμπανον TYMPANUM.] *Path.* Distention of the abdomen by gas or air in the intestine, the peritoneal cavity, or the uterus.

Tympanitic (timpăni·tik), *a.* 1834. [– L. *tympaniticus*, f. *tympanites*; see prec. and -IC.] Pertaining to, characteristic of, or affected with tympanites; also, hollow-sounding.

‖**Tympanitis** (timpănəi·tis). 1797. [In sense 1 an alteration of TYMPANITES. In sense 2 f. TYMPANUM + -ITIS.] **1.** = TYMPANITES. **2.** Inflammation of the lining membrane of the tympanum 1857.

Tympano- (timpăno), bef. a vowel occas. **tympan-,** comb. form repr. Gr. τύμπανον or L. TYMPANUM; as in **Tympane·ctomy** [Gr. ἐκτομή], excision of the tympanic membrane. **Ty:mpanohy·al** *a.*, pertaining to the tympanum and the hyoid arch; epithet of a small bone or cartilage at the base of the styloid process, which in early life becomes fused with the temporal bone; *sb.* = t. bone or cartilage.

‖**Tympanum** (ti·mpănŏm). *Pl.* **tympana.** 1619. [L., drum, etc. – Gr. τύμπανον drum, f. nasalized var. of base of τύπτειν strike.] **1.** A drum or similar instrument, as a tambourine or timbrel; also, the stretched membrane of a drum, a drum-head 1675. **2.** *Anat.* The drum of the ear; the middle ear separated from the outer ear by the tympanic membrane. Also often applied to the tympanic membrane simply. 1619. **b.** *Ornith.* (*a*) Each of the two inflatable air-sacs at the sides of the neck in certain birds, as grouse. (*b*) Applied to the bony labyrinth at the base of the trachea in certain species of duck, having resonant membranes in its walls. 1873. **3.** *Arch.* **a.** The die or cubical portion of a pedestal. **b.** The vertical recessed face of a pediment, often adorned with sculpture. 1658. **4.** *Mech.* A kind of wheel (orig. drum-shaped) with curved radial partitions, used for raising water 1875.

Tympany (ti·mpăni). 1528. [– Gr. τυμπανίας (Galen), f. τύμπανον TYMPANUM.] **1.** = TYMPANITES; also sometimes used for a tumour or morbid swelling of any kind. Now *rare* or *arch.* †**b.** *transf.* or *allus.*, esp. in ref. to pregnancy –1711. **2.** *fig.* A swelling, as of pride, arrogance, self-conceit, etc., figured as a disease; a condition of being inflated or puffed up; an excess *of* something figured as a swelling; inflated style, turgidity, bombast. Now *rare* or *Obs.* 1581. **3.** = TYMPANUM 1. *Obs.* or *arch.* 1535.

1. b. A mere t...raised by a cushion DRYDEN. **2.** Puffed up with this Timpany of self conceit BURTON. Dr. Johnson..he charges..with a plethoric and tautologic t. of sentence 1828.

Tyne, obs. f. TIN, TIND, TINE.

Tynwald (ti·nwǫld, təi·n-). late ME. [– ON. *þingwall-, stem. of þingvǫllr, f. þing assembly, THING *sb.*[2] + vǫllr field, level ground.] (Also *T. Court.*) In the Isle of Man, an annual convention attended by the governor (representing the sovereign), a council acting as the upper house, and the House of Keys, at which the laws which have been enacted are proclaimed to the people.

Typal (təi·păl), *a.* 1853. [f. TYPE *sb.* + -AL[1] 1.] **1.** Of the nature of, serving as, or answering to a type, pattern, or specimen; representative; typical. **2.** Of or pertaining to printing type; typographical 1882.

Type (təip), *sb.* 1470. [– Fr. *type* or L. *typus* – Gr. τύπος blow, impression, image, figure, f. base of τύπτειν strike, beat.] **1.** That by which something is symbolized or figured; a symbol, emblem; *spec.* in *Theol.* a person, object, or event of Old Testament history, prefiguring some person or thing revealed in the new dispensation; correl. to *antitype.* †**2.** A figure or picture of something; a representation; an image or imitation (*rare*) –1774. **b.** *Numism.* The figure on either side of a coin or medal 1785. **3.** A distinguishing mark or sign; a stamp (*rare*) 1593. **4.** *Path.* The characteristic form of a fever; *esp.* the character of an intermittent fever as determined by its period. *Obs.* or merged in 5. 1601. **5.** The general form, structure, or character distinguishing a particular kind, group, or class of beings or objects; hence *transf.* a pattern or model after which something is made 1843. **b.** *Ch. Hist.* [Gr. τύπο τῆς πίστεως type of the faith.] An edict of the Emperor Constans II, promulgated A.D. 648, prohibiting further discussion of the Monothelite controversy 1727. **6.** A kind, class, or order as dist. by a particular character 1854. **7.** *transf.* A person or thing that exhibits the characteristic qualities of a class; a typical example or instance 1842. **b.** *spec.* A person or thing that exemplifies the ideal qualities or characteristics *of* a kind or order; a perfect example or specimen *of* something; a model, pattern, exemplar 1847. **8.** *techn.* **a.** *Nat. Hist.*, etc. A certain general plan of structure characterizing a group of animals, plants, etc.; hence *transf.* a group or division of animals, etc., having a common form or structure 1850. **b.** *Nat. Hist.* A species or genus which most perfectly exhibits the essential characters of its family or group, and from which the family or group is (usu.) named; an individual embodying all the distinctive characters of a species, etc. 1840. **c.** *Chem.* A simple compound taken as representing the structure of more complex compounds 1852. **d.** *Math.* A succession of symbols susceptible of + and – signs 1891. **9.** A small rectangular block, usu. of metal or wood, having on its upper end a raised letter, figure, or other character, for use in printing 1713. **b.** *sing.* Types collectively; letter. *In t.*, set up ready for printing. 1778. **c.** *transf.* A printed character or characters, or an imitation of these 1784.

1. *In* (*the*) *t.*, in symbolic representation; He offered wine not water in the t...of his bloud JER. TAYLOR. **3.** Thy Father beares the t. of the King of Naples SHAKS. Tennis and tall Stockings, Short blistred Breeches, and those types of Trauell SHAKS. **5.** The t. upon which the whole was constructed 1857. **6.** The instruction in both is of the same t. 1879. **7.** Sir Roger de Coverley is a character, as well as a t. RUSKIN. **b.** Plato is the very t. of soaring philosophy J. H. NEWMAN. **8. a.** So careful of the t. she seems, So careless of the single life TENNYSON. **9.** Musical types had.. been invented by an Italian 1880. **b.** This story goes straightway into t. DICKENS. **c.** To see small objects distinctly..such as..a small t. 1831.

attrib. and *Comb.*: **t.-bar,** (*a*) a line of t. cast in a solid bar, as by the linotype; (*b*) in a typewriter, each of the bars carrying the letters or characters; **-carriage,** in a printing-machine, a frame carrying the form; **-cutter,** one who engraves the dies or punches from which types are cast; **-cylinder,** the cylinder on which the types or plates are fastened in a rotary press; **-letter,** each of the types or letters of a typewriter; **-metal,** an alloy of lead and antimony, sometimes with tin or bismuth, of which printing types are cast; **-script,** typewritten matter or copy; also *attrib.*; **-setter,** a compositor; also, a composing-machine; so **-setting,** *sb.* and *a.*; **-theory,** *Chem.* the theory of the derivation of compounds from types by substitution; **-wheel,** a wheel with raised characters on its periphery, as in the printing telegraph and in some typewriters.

Type (təip), *v.* 1596. [f. prec.] **1.** *trans.* **a.** *Theol.* To prefigure or foreshadow as a type; to represent in prophetic similitude. **b.** = TYPIFY 1. 1836. **2.** = TYPIFY 2. (*rare*) 1627. **3.** To print (*rare*) 1736. **4.** *trans.* and *intr.* To typewrite 1888. **5.** *Med.* To determine the type of; esp. to determine the blood group to which a particular sample belongs 1927.

1. b. All nature typeth Thee and Thine 1839.

-type (təip), *suffix*, repr. Fr. *-type*, L. *-typus*, Gr. -τυπος, f. root of τύπτειν beat, strike; as in *antitype, archetype, prototype*; also, with the sense 'type, block, or plate for printing from', in *electrotype, stereotype*; and with the sense 'impression or picture', also 'process of reproduction' as in *autotype, collotype, platinotype.*

Typewrite (təi·pˌrəit), *v.* 1887. [Back-formation from next.] *trans.* To print by means of a typewriter; to type; also *intr.* to practise typewriting. So **Ty·pewri:ting** *vbl. sb.* and *ppl. a.* 1881. **Ty·pewritten** *ppl. a.*

Typewriter (təi·pˌrəi:təɹ). 1875. [f. TYPE *sb.* + WRITER.] **1.** A writing-machine having types for the letters of the alphabet, figures, and punctuation-marks, so arranged on separate rods (or on the periphery of a wheel) that as each key of the machine is depressed the corresponding character is imprinted in line on a moving sheet. †**2.** *Obs.* One who does typewriting; a TYPIST –1895.

‖**Typhlitis** (tifləi·tis). 1857. [mod.L., f. Gr. τυφλόν the cæcum or blind gut (n. of τυφλός blind) + -ITIS.] *Path.* Inflammation of the cæcum, cæcitis (often including *appendicitis*). Hence **Typhlitic** (tifli·tik) *a.*

Typhlo- (tiflo), bef. a vowel regularly **typhl-,** – Gr. τυφλο-, comb. form of τυφλός blind; occurring in a few recent pathological and surgical terms relating to the cæcum (Gr. τυφλόν; see prec.).

Typhlosole (ti·flosōul). Also **-solis.** 1859. [irreg. f. Gr. τυφλός blind + σωλήν channel, pipe.] *Zool.* A ridge or fold extending along the inner wall of the intestine and partly dividing the cavity of it, in various animals, as lampreys and certain ascidians, molluscs, and worms.

Typho- (təi·fo), – Gr. τυφο-, comb. form of τῦφος (see TYPHUS); used as comb. form of TYPHUS or TYPHOID, in recent terms of pathology, etc.; as **Typhomala·rial** *a.*, applied to a fever exhibiting both typhoid and malarial symptoms, or to typhoid fever with malarial complications, or of malarial origin. **Typhoto·xin,** a poisonous ptomaine obtained from cultures of the bacillus of typhoid fever.

Typhœan (təifī·ăn), *a.* [prop. *Typhoëan* (təifoī·ăn), f. *Typhoeus*, Gr. Τυφωεύς, name of a giant of Greek mythology; see -AN.] Belonging to or characteristic of Typhoeus. MILT.

Typhoid (təi·foid), *a.* (*sb.*) 1800. [f. TYPHUS + -OID. Cf. Fr. *typhoïde.*] *Path.* **1.** Resembling or characteristic of typhus; applied to a class of febrile diseases exhibiting symptoms similar to those of typhus, or to such symptoms themselves, esp. to a state of delirious stupor occurring in certain fevers. **2.** *T. fever*: a specific eruptive fever (formerly supposed to be a variety of typhus), characterized by intestinal inflammation and ulceration; also called *enteric fever* 1845. **b.** Of, pertaining to, characteristic of, or affected with typhoid fever 1871. **B.** *sb.* Short for *t. fever* 1861. **b.** A case of typhoid; a patient suffering from typhoid (*colloq.*) 1890. Hence **Typhoi·dal** *a.* pertaining to, characteristic of, resembling, or having the character of t. fever.

Typhomania (təifomēi·niă). 1693. [mod. L. – Gr. τυφωμανία, f. τῦφος TYPHUS + μανία MANIA; by mod. writers taken as f. TYPHUS (in the mod. sense) + MANIA.] *Path.* Delirium accompanied with stupor, occurring in typhus and other fevers.

Typhon[1] (təi·fǫn). 1592. [– L. *Typhon* – Gr. Τυφῶν, name of a giant; also, a tempestuous wind (see next), and applied to a comet or meteor.] The name of a giant or monster of ancient Greek mythology (according to Hesiod, the son of Typhoeus, and father of the Winds; later identified with Typhoeus), fabled to have been buried under Mount Etna, and represented as having a hundred heads and breathing out flames; also used as a name for the Egyptian evil divinity Set. Hence *allus.* Hence **Typho·nian** *a.* pertaining to or connected with T. or Set.

Ty·phon[2]. Now *rare* or *Obs.* 1555. [– Gr. τυφῶν; see prec. In later use partly suggested by TYPHOON.] A whirlwind, cyclone, tornado; a violent storm of wind, a hurricane.

Typhonic (təifǫ·nik), *a.* 1865. [– Gr. τυφωνικός, f. Τυφῶν; see TYPHON[1], -IC.] **1.** Having the character of a whirlwind or tornado; tempestuous. **2.** = TYPHONIAN 1874.

Typhoon (təifū·n). 1588. [In sense b – Chinese *tai fung*, dial. vars. of *ta* big, *fêng* wind. In sense a – Pg. *tufão* – Hind. (– Arab.) *ṭūfān* hurricane, tornado. Cf. TYPHON[2].] **a.** A violent storm or tempest occurring in India. **b.** A violent cyclonic storm or hurricane occurring in the China seas and adjacent regions, chiefly during the period from July to October.

Typhous (təi·fəs), *a.* 1805. [f. TYPHUS + -OUS.] *Path.* Pertaining to or having the character of typhus.

Typhus (təi·fŏs). 1643. [In sense 1 late L., in sense 2 mod.L. *typhus* (De Sauvages, 1759) – Gr. τῦφος smoke, vapour, stupor, f. τύφειν to smoke.] †**1.** Pride, haughtiness, conceit. **2.** *Path.* An acute infectious fever, characterized by great prostration and a petechial eruption, and occurring chiefly in crowded tenements, etc. Also *t. fever*. 1785.

Typic (ti·pik), *a.* 1601. [– Fr. *typique* – late L. *typicus* – Gr. τυπικός typical, f. τύπος TYPE; see -IC.] **1.** = next 1. 1610. †**2.** Of a fever: Conforming to a particular type; intermittent; periodic –1857.

Typical (ti·pikăl), *a.* 1612. [– med.L. *typicalis* (Aquinas), f. late L. *typicus*; see prec., -AL[1] 1.] **1.** Of the nature of, or serving as, a type or emblem; pertaining or relating to a type or types; symbolical, emblematic. **2.** Having the qualities of a type or specimen; serving as a representative specimen of a class or kind 1860. **b.** *Nat. Hist.* That is the type of the genus, family, etc. 1847. **3.** Of or pertaining to a type or representative specimen; distinctive, characteristic 1850. **4.** Of or pertaining to printers' type; typographical. Now *rare* or *Obs.* 1770.

1. He renewed the custome of expounding Scripture in a typicall way 1661. **2.** Horace is a t. Roman of the intellectual sort 1881. Hence **Typica·lity. Ty·pical-ly** *adv.*, **-ness.**

Typification (ti:pifikēi·ʃən). 1811. [f. next; see -FICATION.] The action of typifying; representation by a type or symbol; also, that which typifies; an exemplification.

Typify (ti·pifəi), *v.* 1634. [f. L. *typus* TYPE *sb.*; see -FY.] **1.** *trans.* To represent or express by a type or symbol; to serve as a type, figure, or emblem of; to symbolize; to prefigure. **2.** To serve as the typical specimen of (a class, family, etc.); to exhibit the essential characters of; to exemplify 1854.

1. Glorie by the wreath is typifide 1634.

Typist (təi·pist). 1843. [f. TYPE *sb.* + -IST.] **1.** One who uses type; a printer, a compositor (*rare*). **2.** One who does typewriting, esp. as a regular occupation 1885.

Typo (təipo), *sb.* (*a.*) *slang.* 1816. [Short for *typographer* or *typographic.*] A typographer, a printer; *spec.* a compositor. **b.** *attrib.* or as *adj.* = TYPOGRAPHIC 1891.

Typo- (təi·po, ti·po), bef. a vowel **typ-**, comb. form repr. Gr. τύπος TYPE *sb.*; as in **Typonym** (təi·pŏnim), *Nat. Hist.* a name based on a type or specimen; hence **Typonymal** (-ǫ·nimăl), **Typonymic** (-ŏni·mik), *adjs.*

Typograph (təi·p-, ti·pŏgrɑf). 1737. [– Fr. *typographe* (XVI) or mod.L. *typographus*; see TYPE, -GRAPH.] **1.** A typographer or typographist. **2.** A writing-machine for the blind in which pressure upon raised types causes the corresponding letters to be printed 1820.

Typographer (təip-, tipǫ·grăfəɹ). 1643. [f. Fr. *typographe* or mod.L. *typographus*; see prec., -GRAPHER.] One who is skilled in typography; a printer.

Typographic (təip-, tipŏgræ·fik), *a.* 1778. [– mod.L. *typographicus*; see TYPE, -GRAPHIC.] Of or pertaining to printing, typographical.

Typographical (təip-, tipŏgræ·fikăl), *a.* 1593. [f. as prec. + -AL[1] 1; see -ICAL.] **1.** Of or pertaining to typography or printing; connected or dealing with printing. **b.** Produced or expressed by typography or in print; printed 1803. †**2.** Emblematic; figurative. JOHNSON. Hence **Typogra·phically** *adv.*

Typo·graphist. *rare.* 1890. [f. TYPOGRAPH(Y + -IST.] One versed in the history or art of printing; a student of typography.

Typography (təip-, tipǫ·grăfi). 1641. [– Fr. *typographie* (XVI) or mod.L. *typographia*; see TYPE, -GRAPHY.] **1.** The art or practice of printing. **2.** The action or process of printing; *esp.* the setting and arrangement of types and printing from them; hence, the arrangement and appearance of printed matter 1697. **b.** *transf.* Printed matter; letterpress MILT.

Typology (təipǫ·lŏdʒi). 1845. [f. TYPO- + -LOGY.] **1.** The study of symbolic representation, *esp.* of the origin and meaning of Scripture types; also, *transf.* symbolic significance, representation, or treatment; symbolism. **2.** The study of or a discourse on printing types or printing 1882. **3.** *Archæol.* [after G.] The classification of remains and specimens according to the type they exhibit and its evolution, etc. 1886. So **Typolo·gic, -al** *adjs.*, **-ally** *adv.* **Typo·logist,** a student of t.

Tyranness (təi³·rănės). 1590. [f. L. *tyrannus* TYRANT + -ESS[1]. Cf. med.L. *tyrannissa* (XIV).] A female tyrant.

Tyrannic (ti-, təiræ·nik), *a.* 1491. [– (O)Fr. *tyrannique* – L. *tyrannicus* – Gr. τυραννικός, f. τύραννος TYRANT; see -IC.] = next.

Tyrannical (ti-, təiræ·nikăl), *a.* 1560. [f. as prec. + -AL[1] 1; see -ICAL.] **1.** Of, pertaining to, or befitting an absolute ruler or his government; arbitrary, despotic. **2. a.** Of the nature or character of a tyrant; acting or operating in an oppressive, cruel, or unjustly severe manner 1538. **b** Of, pertaining to, or befitting a tyrant; severely oppressive; despotically harsh or cruel 1579.

1. A t. dynasty 1838. **2. a.** A dark and t. superstition MORLEY. Hence **Tyra·nnical-ly** *adv.*, **-ness.**

Tyrannicide[1] (ti-, təiræ·nisəid). 1657. [– Fr. *tyrannicide* – L. *tyrannicida*, f. *tyrannus*; see -CIDE 1.] One who kills a tyrant.

Tyra·nnicide[2]. 1650. [– Fr. *tyrannicide* – L. *tyrannicidium*, f. as prec.; see -CIDE 2.] The killing of a tyrant. Hence **Tyra:nnici·dal** *a.* pertaining or relating to, disposed or inclined to, t.

Tyrannize (ti·ranəiz), *v.* 1494. [– (O)Fr. *tyranniser*, f. *tyran* TYRANT; see -IZE. Cf. late L. *tyrannizare.*] **1. a.** *intr.* To be a despot or absolute ruler; to exercise absolute rule. Const. *over.* 1590. †**b.** *trans.* To rule over or dominate with absolute power –1795. **2.** *intr.* To reign tyrannically; to rule despotically or oppressively 1494. **3.** To act tyrannically, play the tyrant; to exercise power or control oppressively or cruelly 1529. **b.** *fig.* of things 1588. **4.** *trans.* To rule or govern tyrannically; to treat tyrannically, play the tyrant to or over. Now *rare.* 1533. **b.** *fig.* of things 1588. †**5.** To render tyrannical. MILT.

1. Polycrates, who..tyrannized in Samos HOBBES. **2.** Oppressing and tyrannizing ouer her Maiesties subiects 1588. **3.** The great were not allowed to t. over the poor 1846. **b.** The influences which t. over human passions and opinions 1805. **4.** Had..rather sit still, and let his Country be tyrannized MILT. **b.** Poverty, which doth so t., crucifie, and generally depresse vs BURTON. Hence **Ty·rannizer,** one who or that which tyrannizes.

Tyrannous (ti·rănəs), *a.* 1491. [f. *tyran* TYRANT + -OUS.] **1.** Characterized by or inclined to tyranny; ruling or acting tyrannically; despotic. **2.** *transf.* Of the nature of or involving tyranny; oppressive, unjustly severe or cruel 1556.

1. The t. handes of any earthly Pharao 1577. *fig.* Yeeld vp (O Loue) thy Crowne To t. Hate SHAKS. Hence **Ty·rannous-ly** *adv.*, **-ness.**

Tyranny (ti·răni). late ME. [– (O)Fr. *tyrannie* – late L. *tyrannia*, f. L. *tyrannus* TYRANT; see -Y[3].] **1.** The government of a tyrant or absolute ruler; the position or rule of a tyrant. **b.** *gen.* Absolute sovereignty 1651. **c.** With *a* and *pl.* A state ruled by a tyrant or absolute prince; an absolute or despotic government 1605. **2.** The action or government of a tyrannical ruler; oppressive or unjustly severe government. late ME. **3.** Arbitrary or oppressive exercise of power; unjustly severe use of one's authority; harsh, severe, or unmerciful action; with *a* and *pl.*, an instance of this. late ME. **b.** Violent or lawless action. *Obs.* or *arch.* 1475.

1. Pisistratus began to affect the T. of that city 1727. **c.** In most of the cities there were erected Tyrannies HOBBES. **2.** Parliament T. began to succeed Church T. DE FOE. **3.** 'Tis t. to trample on him that prostrates himself FULLER.

Tyrant (təi³·rănt), *sb.* [ME. *tira(u)nd, tirant*, also *tyran* – OFr. *tyrant, tiran* (mod. *tyran*) – L. *tyrannus* – Gr. τύραννος. (OFr. *tyrant* is analogical after forms in -ANT.)] **1.** One who seizes upon the sovereign power in a state without legal right; an absolute ruler; a usurper. (Chiefly in ref. to ancient rulers.) †**2.** A ruler, governor, prince –1737. **3.** A king or ruler who exercises his power in an oppressive, unjust, or cruel manner; a despot ME. **4.** One who treats those under his control tyrannically ME. †**b.** By extension: Any one who acts in a cruel, violent, or wicked manner; a ruffian, desperado; a villain. Hence as a term of reproach. –1578. **c.** *fig.* Anything of which the action is likened to that of a tyrannical ruler 1508. **5.** *Ornith.* Any bird of the family *Tyrannidæ*; *esp.* any of several species of the genus *Tyrannus*, noted for attacking and driving off any other bird approaching its nesting place. Also called *t.-bird, t.-flycatcher.* 1730. **6.** *attrib.* or as *adj.* That is a tyrant, tyrannical, tyrannous; also, characteristic of a tyrant ME.

1. A tyraunt þat was kyng of sysile CHAUCER. **3.** Do not tyrants..Think men were born for slaves to kings? GAY. **4.** A plague vpon the T. that I serue SHAKS. **b.** I was a blasphemar, and a persecuter, and a tyraunt TINDALE 1 *Tim.* 1:13. **c.** Public opinion, the greatest t. of these times 1847. **6.** When t. custom had not shackled man THOMSON.

Comb.: **t.-bird**: see sense 5; **-flycatcher, -shrike,** species of *Tyrannus*, resembling, and formerly confused with, the *Muscicapidæ* and *Laniidæ*. Hence **Ty·rant** *v. intr.* to play the t., to tyrannize (also with *it*).

‖**Tyre**[1], **tyer** (təi³r). *India.* 1613. [– Tamil *tayir.*] Name in India for curdled milk and cream beginning to turn sour.

Tyre[2] (təi³ɹ). Also *U.S.* **tire.** 1796. [var. of TIRE *sb.*[2]] **1.** The iron or steel rim of a wheel, *esp.* the steel rim of the driving wheel of a locomotive. **2.** A rubber cushion around the wheel of a bicycle, motor-car, etc. 1875. Hence **Tyred** *ppl. a.* furnished with a t. or tyres: chiefly in compounds.

Tyrian (ti·riăn), *a.* and *sb.* 1513. [f. L. *Tyrius* (f. *Tyrus* Tyre) + -AN.] **A.** *adj.* Of or belonging to, native of, or made in Tyre, an ancient Phœnician city on the Mediterranean, the centre of an extensive commerce. **b.** *spec.* in ref. to the dye anciently made at Tyre from molluscs: see PURPLE B. 1. 1616. **B.** *sb.* A native or inhabitant of Tyre 1513.

b. Another finds the way to dye in Grain, And make Calabrian Wool receive the T. Stain DRYDEN.

Tyro: see TIRO.

Tyrolean (tirōᵘ·liăn) *a.* and *sb.* 1809. [f. *Tyrol* + -EAN.] **A.** *adj.* Belonging to Tyrol (often called 'the Tyrol'), a province of Austria-Hungary 1859. **B.** *sb.* A native or inhabitant of Tyrol 1809. So **Tyrolese** (-ī·z) *a.* and *sb.*

Tyrolite (ti·rŏləit). 1854. [– G. *tirolit*, f. *Tyrol*, where found; see -ITE[1] 2 b.] *Min.* Hydrous arsenate of copper, found usually in reniform masses of pale green colour.

Tyrosine (təi³·rosīn). 1857. [irreg. f. Gr. τυρός cheese + -INE[5].] *Chem.* A white crystalline substance ($C_9H_{11}NO_3$) produced by the decomposition of proteins.

‖**Tyrotoxicon** (təi³rotǫ·ksikǫn). 1886. [mod.L., f. Gr. τυρός cheese + τοξικόν poison.] *Chem.* A poisonous ptomaine (diazobenzene hydroxide, $C_6H_5N.N.OH$), produced by a microbe in stale cheese and milk; cheese-poison. Also **Tyroto·xin.**

Tyrrhene (ti·rīn, tirī·n), *a.* and *sb.* late ME. [– L. *Tyrrhenus* of or pertaining to the *Tyrrheni* or Etruscans.] = next.

Coasting the T. shore MILT.

Tyrrhenian (tirī·niăn), *a.* and *sb.* 1660. [f. L. *Tyrrhenus* (see prec.) or *Tyrrhenia* Etruria + -AN.] **A.** *adj.* Of or pertaining to the Tyrrheni or their country; Etruscan, Etrurian. **B.** *sb.* One of the Tyrrheni; an Etruscan.

A. *T. Sea*, the sea lying between the mainland of Italy and the islands of Corsica, Sardinia, and Sicily.

Tyrtæan (təɹtī·ăn), *a.* 1879. [f. proper name *Tyrtæus*, Gr. Τυρταῖος + -AN.] Pertaining to or in the style of Tyrtæus, a Greek poet of the 7th century B.C., who composed martial songs for the Spartans; martial, warlike.

Tysonite (təi·sənəit). 1880. [f. name of S. T. *Tyson* + -ITE[1] 2 b.] *Min.* A rare native fluoride of the cerium metals.

Tzar, etc.: see CZAR, TSAR.

‖**Tzigane** (tsigā·n), *sb.* and *a.* 1885. [– Fr. *tzigane* (with *tz* of G. origin) – Magyar *cigány.*] **A.** *sb.* A Hungarian gipsy 1887. **B.** *adj.* That is a Tzigane; pertaining to or consisting of Tziganes 1885.

U

U (yū), the twenty-first letter of the modern English, and the twentieth of the ancient Roman alphabet, is a differentiated form of the letter V. Latin MSS. written in capitals have V only, modified in uncial, half-uncial, and minuscule MSS. into U. In Anglo-Saxon MSS. U was regularly employed as a minuscule to denote the vowel *u*, the corresponding capital being either V or U. In ME. after continental usage, the two symbols *u* and *v* were employed without distinction in value, but with preferences (1) for *v* as initial letter and *u* elsewhere (*vnder, vain*, but *full, euer*), and (2) for *v* where it made for clearness, e.g. next to *n* or *m* (*tvne, mvse*). During the 16th century, continental printers began to distinguish *u* as the vowel symbol, and *v* as the consonantal: and by 1630 this distinction was established in English also. V remained the capital symbol for both vowel and consonant rather longer, but during the 17th century was replaced in the vowel function first by U, and later by U. From about 1700, the vowel has been denoted by U, u, and the consonant by V, v. Dictionaries and alphabetical lists continued, into the 19th century, to give the items beginning with *u* and *v* as a single series, *va-* being followed by *vb-* (= *ub-*), etc.; this practice is still continued in some book-catalogues.

The vowel sounds of *u* in OE. were two, resembling those now heard (short) in *pull* and *bush*, and (long) in *rude* and *brute*. In ME. the short sound was still represented by *u*, but the long by the new symbol *ou* adopted from French, while *u* had acquired (in addition to its old short sound in native words) the short and long sounds of French *u* (ü, ű) in words introduced from Latin and French. In mod. Eng. the ŭ of OE. and ME. has become normally (ɒ), written *u* or *o*, as in *dumb, sun, thus, some, love*, but retains its old sound universally in a few words, as *bull, bush, put*, etc., and locally in a much larger number. The OE. ū (ME. *ou*) has become the diphthong (ɑu), written *ow* or *ou*, as in *town, thou*; but the ME. ū from French and Latin has become the diphthong (iū, iūᵊ), written *u, ue, u..e*, as in *huge, due, cure*, with reduction to (ū, ūᵊ), after *s* (= ʃ, ʒ), *j*, and *r*, as in *sure, jury, brute*, and optionally after *l*, as in *lute, lure*, and more widely in American usage. (A further development of (ūᵊ) to (ōᵊ) before (r), (ɹ) is characteristic of the pronunciation of some speakers.) In combination with other vowels, *u* is employed in the groups *au* (ǭ), *eu* (iū), *ou* (with varying value as in *foul, soul, four, young, route*), *ue* and *ui* (iū, ū) as in *hue, true, nuisance, fruit*. Between *g* and a vowel, and in final *-que, u* is often silent, as in *guard, guide, plague, grotesque*: it has the value of (w) after *q* in other positions and in some words after *s* and *g* (*queen, persuade, anguish*). The pronunciation of the name of the letter has changed from (ū) to (iū) in accordance with the change in the sound which it represents in words of French or Latin origin.

I. 1. The letter or its name. **b.** = You *pron.* in IOU. **2.** With ref. to the shape of the (capital) letter, esp. *attrib.* or *Comb.*, as *U-like, U bolt, U-magnet.* **b.** Something shaped like the letter U. **3.** Used to denote serial order. **II. 1.** Abbrevs.: U = Uranium; U.C. = upcast shaft; U.K. = United Kingdom; U.P. = United Presbyterian; U.S., U.S.A. = United States (of America); U.S.S.R. = Union of Soviet Socialist Republics. **2.** *slang.* U.P., the spelling pronunciation of UP *adv.* (*adv.*[2] II. 3 c), as in *it is all U.P.*

Uberous (yū·bĕrəs), *a.* Now *rare.* 1524. [f. L. *uber* rich, fruitful + -OUS.] **1.** Of animals or the breasts: Abounding in milk 1624. †**2.** Of places: Fertile –1651. **3.** Abundant, copious 1633.

Uberty (yū·bəɹti). Now *rare.* late ME. [– OFr. *uberté* or L. *ubertas*, f. *uber*; see prec., -TY[1].] Rich growth, fertility; copiousness.

Ubication (yūbikēⁱ·ʃən). 1644. [– med.L. *ubicatio, -ōn-* whereness (XIV), f. *ubicare* situate, f. L. *ubi* where; see -ATION.] The being in or occupying a certain place; location.

Ubiety (yubəi·ėti). 1674. [– med.L. *ubietas* (XIII), f. L. *ubi* where; see -ITY.] Condition in respect of place or location; local relationship.

Ubiquarian (yūbikwēᵊ·riăn). 1737. [f. L. *ubique* everywhere; see -ARIAN.] **A.** *sb.* †**1.** *pl.* A society or club existing in the 18th cent. –1761. **2.** A person who goes everywhere (*rare*) 1767. **B.** *adj.* = UBIQUITOUS 1762.

Ubiquitarian (yubikwitēᵊ·riăn). 1640. [f. as next + -AN; see -ARIAN.] **A.** *sb.* Chiefly in *pl.*: One of those Lutherans who held that Christ's body was everywhere present at all times 1651. **B.** *adj.* **1.** Of, pertaining to, or holding this doctrine 1640. **2.** = UBIQUITOUS (*rare*) 1641. Hence **Ubiquita·rianism** = UBIQUITISM.

Ubiquitary (yubi·kwitări), *sb.* and *a.* 1585. [– mod.L. *ubiquitarius*, f. L. *ubique* everywhere; see -ARY[1].] **A.** *sb.* **1.** A person or thing that is or can be everywhere at once. Now *rare.* 1587. †**2.** = UBIQUITARIAN *sb.* –1709.

1. A Nymph..all motion, an ubiquitarie, Shee is euerywhere B. JONS.

B. *adj.* †**1.** = UBIQUITARIAN *a.* 1. –1603. **2.** = UBIQUITOUS. Now *rare.* 1609.

2. The u. Assistance of the Deity is celebrated by ..the Psalmist STEELE. A few, such as the Dandelion and the Daisy, may be said to be almost u. 1853.

Ubiquitism (yubi·kwitiz'm). 1617. [f. UBIQUITY (sense 1) + -ISM.] The doctrine of the omnipresence of Christ's body.

Ubiquitous (yubi·kwitəs), *a.* 1837. [f. UBIQUITY + -OUS.] **1.** Everywhere pervasively present, as God, an influence 1760. **b.** With joc. exaggeration, esp of persons: 'Turning up' everywhere 1752. **2.** Universally or widely distributed as a class or its members 1840.

1. Heathendom was as a beleaguered city, mastered by an u. Presence PUSEY. **b.** Here as he lay nursing himself, u. Mr. Holt reappeared THACKERAY. Hence **Ubi·quitously** *adv.*, **Ubi·quitousness.**

Ubiquity (yubi·kwĭti). 1576. [– mod.L. *ubiquitas*, f. L. *ubique* everywhere; see -ITY.] **1.** *Theol.* The omnipresence of Christ or of his body as maintained by the Ubiquitarians. **2.** The capacity of being everywhere at the same time: **a.** In general use 1597. **b.** as an attribute of God. (Variously taken as synonymous with or distinct from *omnipresence*). 1607. **c.** As expressing the Sovereign's relation to his Courts of law 1765.

1. Out of which vbiquitie of his body they gather the presence thereof with that sanctified bread and wine HOOKER. **2. a.** The attention and activity which Quentin bestowed..had in it something that gave him the appearance of u. SCOTT. **b.** By God's Omnipresence, or U., we must be understood to mean that his Power and Knowledge extend to all Places 1748. Most Christians do not believe in the omnipresence of God; they only believe in His u. 1855. **c.** The legal *u.* of the king. His majesty, in the eye of the law, is always present in all his courts. BLACKSTONE.

U-boat (yū·bōᵘt). 1916. [– G. *U-boot*, abbrev. of *unterseeboot* 'under-sea boat'.] A German submarine.

Udal (yū·dăl). 1500. [Orkney and Shetland form of ODAL.] **1.** The old native form of freehold tenure in Orkney and Shetland 1588. **b.** Land so held 1750. **2.** *attrib.* Held or holding by, or based on, this tenure 1500.

2. There are three kinds of tenure of lands in Scotland...Thirdly, the U., being a right compleat without writing. 1793. Hence **U·daller,** a tenant of land by udal right. **U·dally** *adv.*

Udder (ɒ·dəɹ). [OE. *ūder* = OFris., OS. *ūder*, MLG., MDu. *ūder* (Du. *uier, uijer*), OHG. *ūter* (G. *euter*) :– WGmc. **ūðr-*. The OE. long vowel has been shortened as in *adder, fodder.*] **1.** The pendulous baggy organ, with two or more nipples, by which the milk is secreted in some female animals OE. **b.** This part of an animal as an article of food 1474. **2.** *poet.* (in *pl.*). A dug or teat (*rare*) 1582.

1. Milk pressed from the swelling u. by the gentle hand of the beauteous milk-maid JOHNSON. **b.** Mr. Creed and I to the Leg in King Street, where he and I, and my Will had a good u. to dinner PEPYS. **2.** A Lyonesse, with vdders all drawne drie SHAKS. Hence **U·ddered** *a.*

Udometer (yudǫ·mĭtəɹ). 1825. [– Fr. *udomètre*, f. L. *udus* wet; see -METER.] A rain-gauge.

†**Uds,** var. of ODS. 1586. Common in trivial oaths in the 17th cent. –1854.

Saint. Uds Niggers, but I will...*Wood.* Uds Niggers, I confess, is a very dreadful Oath DRYDEN.

Ufer (yū·fəɹ). 1754. [– Du. *juffer* spar.] A fir pole or piece of timber from 4 to 7 in. thick and from 20 to 40 ft. long.

Ugglesome (ɒ·g'lsŏm), *a.* Now *rare.* 1561. [app. f. †*uggle* ugly + SOME[1]. Cf. UGSOME.] Fearful, horrible, gruesome.

Ugh (uʰ, ɒʰ), *int.* and *sb.* 1765. [Imitative.] **1.** A representation of the sound of a cough; the sound itself. **2.** An interjection of disgust 1837.

1. The usurer..concluded his speech with a dry 'ugh, ugh' SCOTT. **2.** It may have been a water-rat I speared, But, ugh! it sounded like a baby's shriek BROWNING.

Uglification (ɒ:glifikēⁱ·ʃən). 1820. [f. next; see -FICATION.] **1.** The action or process of uglifying. **2.** That which uglifies 1890.

Uglify (ɒ·glifəi), *v.* 1576. [f. UGLY *a.* + -FY.] *trans.* To make ugly.

The Covenanters had uglified it with pews and a gallery, and whitewash HAWTHORNE.

Ugliness (ɒ·glinės). ME. [f. UGLY + -NESS.] †**1.** Horror, dread, loathing. –late ME. **2.** The state of being ugly to look at; horrible, repulsive, unpleasing appearance ME. **b.** An ugly thing or feature 1856. **3.** Moral repulsiveness 1601.

2. The Egyptians..were..punished..with the number and vglines of them [frogs] 1608. A thing whose face, through u., frights children MIDDLETON. **3.** The Bible tells the shameful history in all its naked u. 1869.

Ugly (ɒ·gli), *a.* (*adv., sb.*) ME. [– ON. *uggligr* to be feared, f. *ugga* fear; see -LY[1]. Cf. UGSOME.] **A.** *adj.* **1.** Frightful or horrible, esp. through deformity or squalor. (Now merged in sense 3.) †**2.** Of events, times, sounds: Terrible –1725. **3.** Repulsive to the eye; unpleasant to look at; unsightly ME. **b.** *fig.* Repulsive to the imagination, unpleasant to contemplate 1440. **4.** Morally repulsive; base, degraded, vile ME. **5.** Of rank smell or taste; noisome. Now *rare.* late ME. **6.** Repugnant to refined taste; objectionable, disagreeable 1621. **7.** Troublesome, ominous, dangerous; suggestive of trouble or danger 1645. **b.** Of weather, sky, etc.: Stormy, threatening 1744. **c.** *U. customer*, a person formidable to attack or deal with 1811. **8.** Ill-tempered 1687. **9.** Comb., as *u.-faced, -looking, tempered* adjs.

1. Fayne would I die, but darksome vgly Death With-holds his darte 1594. **2.** Great numbers came down to the shore, staring at us, and making confused u. noises DE FOE. **3.** I cannot tell by what Logick we call a Toad, a Beare, or an Elephant, u. SIR T. BROWNE. You would be less zealous were the Queen old and u. 1742. The house itself was an u. residence TROLLOPE. *U. duckling*: (in allusion to the cygnet in a brood of ducks), a person of unpromising appearance or quality who ultimately proves handsome or successful. **b.** Amazement is the uggli'st shape of fear DAVENANT. **4.** Tokens that God was grievously offended with such u. deeds 1650. **5.** Stinking things have filthy and u. Vapors 1668. **6.** The one person who comes out of that strife with an u. stain upon his shield..was the Prime Minister 1888. **7.** I had an u. giddy fit last night in my chamber SWIFT. A long preface..is an u. symptom and always forebodes great sterility COWPER. The Under-Secretary for Foreign Affairs..admitted some u. facts 1890. **b.** With an u. black sky above, and an angry sea beneath KINGLAKE. **c.** You will find me, my young sir, an U. Customer! DICKENS. **8.** He turned upon her with his ugliest look DICKENS. The clever promptitude with which they manage the brutes who look at all u. 1896.

B. *adv.* Terribly; uglily; †illtemperedly. Now *rare.* late ME.

With that he looked u. upon them BUNYAN.

C. *sb.* **1.** An ugly person, animal, etc. Chiefly in *beauties and uglies.* 1755. **2.** A kind of shade projecting from a lady's hat or bonnet 1850.

2. The broad eaves project so far over that they remind you almost of a lady's 'u.' 1856. Hence **U·glily** *adv.* in an u. manner. **U·gly** *v. trans.* to uglify.

Ugrian (ū·griăn, yū·g-), *a.* and *sb.* 1841. [f. *Ugry*, the name given by early Russian writers to an Asiatic race dwelling east of the Ural mountains.] **A.** *adj.* Also **U·gric**

(see -IC) 1884. Of or belonging to a division of Ural-Altaic peoples including the Finns and Magyars. **B.** *sb.* **1.** A member of the Ugrian stock 1841. **2.** The Ugrian language 1862.

Ugsome (ʋ·gsŏm), *a.* Chiefly *north.* and *Sc.* late ME. [f. ME. *ugge*, mod. dial. *ug* + -SOME¹.] Horrible, loathsome. (The modern literary use is perhaps due to Scott.)

Such an euyl fauoured face, such an vgsome countenaunce LATIMER. Hence **U·gsomely** *adv. rare.* **U·gsomeness.**

‖**Uhlan** (ū·lăn, yū·lăn). 1753. [– Fr. *uhlan*, G. *u(h)lan* – Pol. *ulan, hulan* – Turk. *oğlan* youth, servant.] A type of cavalryman or lancer, orig. in the Polish and latterly in the German armies.

‖**Uigur** (wi·guɹ). Also **Ouigour.** 1785. [East Turk. *uighur*, f. *ui* follow + *-gur* adj. suffix.] **A.** *sb.* **1.** A Turk of the eastern branch prominent in Central Asia from the 8th to the 12th cent. 1785. **2.** The language of the Uigurs 1843. **B.** *adj.* Of or pertaining to the Uigurs 1844. So **Uigu·rean, -ian, -ic,** *adjs.* 1773.

‖**Uitlander** (oi·t-, ū·tlăndəɹ). 1892. [S. Afr. Du., f. Du. *uit* OUT + *land* LAND; see -ER¹.] = OUTLANDER b.

‖**Ukase** (yukē·s). Also **ukaz.** 1729. [– Russ. *ukáz*, f. *ukazát'* show, order, decree.] **1.** An edict of the Russian emperor as government. **2.** *transf.* Any arbitrary order 1818.

Ukrainian (yukrē·niăn). 1816. [– *Ukraine*, a southern district of Russia, – Russ. *ukráina* frontier regions, f. *u* at + *krai* edge; see -IAN.] **A.** *adj.* Of the Ukraine. **B.** *sb.* **1.** A native of the Ukraine 1823. **2.** The Ukrainian Slavonic dialect 1886.

Ukulele (yūkŭlē·li). 1900. Also **uke-.** [Hawaiian.] A four-stringed Hawaiian guitar.

-ular, *suffix*, repr. L. *-ularis* (see -ULE, -AR¹) in adjs. formed from sbs. in *-ulus, -ula, -ulum.* Of Eng. adjs. in *-ular* some, as *angular*, are adaptations of L., med.L., or mod.L. forms, while others, as *auricular*, are formed directly on L. sbs. When both the simple noun and the dim. exist as *gland* and *glandule*, the adj. in *-ular* is usu. associated with the former (*glandular* = of the glands).

Ulcer (ʋ·lsəɹ), *sb.* late ME. [– L. *ulcus, ulcer-*, rel. to Gr. ἕλκος wound, sore.] **1.** *Path.* An erosive solution of continuity in any external or internal surface of the body, forming a purulent open sore. **b.** Used in sing. as a generic term 1623. **2.** *fig.* A corroding or corrupting influence; a moral plague-spot 1592. Hence **U·lcer** *v.* (now *rare*), to ulcerate (*trans.* and *absol.*) 1590. **U·lcered** *ppl. a.* = ULCERATED *ppl. a.* 1575.

Ulcerate (ʋ·lsəreit), *v.* late ME. [– *ulcerat-*, pa. ppl. stem of L. *ulcerare*, f. *ulcus*; see prec., -ATE³.] **1.** *intr.* To form an ulcer or ulcers; to fester. **2.** *trans.* To cause ulcers in or on 1550. **3.** *fig.* To irritate or poison like an ulcer 1647. Hence **U·lcerated** *ppl. a.*, converted into, afflicted with, or characterized by an ulcer or ulcers 1547.

Ulceration (ʋlsərē·ʃən). late ME. [– L. *ulceratio, -ōn-*, f. as prec.; see -ION. Cf. (O)Fr. *ulcération.*] *Path.* **1.** The formation of ulcers; the being or becoming ulcerated; an ulcerated condition. **2.** An ulcer or group of ulcers 1580.

Ulcerative (ʋ·lsərētiv, -ătiv), *a.* 1575. [f. ULCERATE + -IVE. Cf. Fr. *ulcératif* (XV).] **1.** Causing ulceration. **2.** Of the nature of ulceration 1800. **3.** Accompanied by ulceration 1813. **4.** Caused by ulceration 1876.

Ulcerous (ʋ·lsərəs), *a.* 1577. [– L. *ulcerosus*, f. *ulcus, ulcer-*; see ULCER, -OUS.] **1.** Of the nature of an ulcer. **2.** Exhibiting ulceration 1599. **3.** Due to ulcers 1641.

-ule, *suffix*, repr. L. dim. endings *-ulus, -ula, -ulum* (e.g. *globulus, glandula, granulum*). Of current words, some correspond to L. forms, as *capsule, nodule, pustule*, others are of modern formation, as *anguillule*. Some words that appeared temporarily with this ending, as *scrupule*, have given way again to earlier forms of Fr. origin in *-le*; and others, as *formule*, to the original L. form in *-ula*.

‖**Ulema** (ūlĕmā·, ū·lĕmă, yulī·mă). 1688. [– Arab. (Turk., Pers.) *'ulamā'*, pl. of *'ālīm* learned, f. *'alama* know.] **1.** as *pl.* Those Moslems whose special training qualifies them as authorities on law and religion; *spec.* the body of Moslem doctors headed by the Sheik-ul-islam. **2.** as *sing.* A Moslem doctor or divine 1843.

-ulent, *suffix*, repr. L. adj. suffix *-ulentus*, meaning 'full of . . .', as *fraudulentus*. Many such L. adjs. have been adopted in Eng., and a few, as *flatulent*, are from mod.L. formations. *Violent, pestilent*, and a few others, show variant forms in *-olentus, -ilentus.*

‖**Ulex** (yū·leks). 1753. [mod.L. (Linnæus, 1737) – L. *ulex* (Pliny) a shrub resembling rosemary.] *Bot.* A genus of thorny papilionaceous shrubs of the family *Leguminosæ*; a plant of this genus, esp. *U. europæus*, the gorse.

Ulexine (yū·leksīn). 1887. [f. prec. + -INE⁵.] *Chem.* An alkaloid prepared from gorse seed.

Ulexite (yū·leksəit). 1867. [f. *Ulex* personal name + -ITE¹ 2 b.] *Min.* Native borate of lime and soda.

‖**Ulicon,** var. of OOLAKAN.

Uliginous (yuli·dʒinəs), *a.* 1576. [– L. *uliginosus*, f. *uligo, uligin-* moisture, or directly f. *uligin-*; see -OUS.] **1.** Of a watery or oozy nature. **2.** Of places, or soil: Waterlogged, swampy 1610. So **Uli·ginal** *a.*, *Bot.* growing in wet ground 1863. **Uli·ginose** *a.*, swampy (*rare*) 1440; also *Bot.* = ULIGINAL 1866.

Ullage (ʋ·lėdʒ), *sb.* 1444. [– AFr. *ulliage* (cf. AL. *oillagium, eol-, ull-, ocul-*) = OFr. *ouillage*, f. OFr. (also mod.) *ouiller, eullier, œiller* (cf. AL. *oillare*) :– Gallo-Rom. **oculare*, f. L. *oculus* eye, used in the sense of bung-hole; see -AGE.] **1.** The amount by which a cask or bottle falls short of being full. **b.** *On u.*, (in a cask, etc.) not completely full 1863. **2.** The amount of liquor (also *wet u.*) in a vessel that is not full 1832. **b.** *slang.* The liquor left in used wine-glasses or casks 1874. **3.** *transf.* **a.** The drainings of moist matter 1824. **b.** Waste metal cut away by the graving tool 1860. **c.** *Naut.* Off-scourings, worthless human or other material 1901. **4.** *attrib.* as *u. cask* 1743.

1. I held the bottle up to the candle to ascertain the u. MARRYAT. **b.** It is injurious to Rhenish wine to be left on u. 1863.

U·llage, *v.* 1749. [f. prec.] **1.** *trans.* To calculate the ullage in (a cask). **2. a.** To draw a little from 1881. **b.** To fill up the ullage in 1888. Hence **Ullaged** (ʋ·lėdʒd) *ppl. a.* (of a cask or bottle) short of contents 1549; (of wine) damaged by being on ullage 1907; (*transf.* of any goods) inferior, refuse 1892. **U·llager,** a gauger of ullage 1885.

Ullmannite (ʋ·lmănəit). 1839. [f. name of J. C. *Ullmann* + -ITE¹ 2 b.] *Min.* †**1.** Phosphate of manganese and iron. **2.** Sulphantimonide of nickel 1868.

Ulmate (ʋ·lmĕt). 1836. [f. ULMIC + -ATE⁴.] *Chem.* A salt of ulmic acid.

Ulmic (ʋ·lmik), *a.* 1831. [– Fr. *ulmique*, f. L. *ulmus* elm; see -IC.] *Chem.* in *U. acid*: = ULMIN.

Ulmin (ʋ·lmin). 1813. [f. L. *ulmus* elm + -IN¹; named by Thomson.] *Chem.* **1.** An exudation from the inner bark of the elm and some other trees; this as a distinct chemical principle. **2.** A dark-coloured product of the decay of wood or vegetable matter, or of the action of certain chemical agents on sugar, etc. 1843.

‖**Ulna** (ʋ·lnă). 1541. [L., related to Gr. ὠλένη and OE. *eln* ELL¹.] *Anat.* **1.** The large inner bone of the fore-arm. **2.** The corresponding bone of a quadruped's foreleg and of a bird's wing 1831. Hence **U·lnad** *adv.* towards the ulnar aspect (cf. DEXTRAD) 1803.

U·lnage, var. of ALNAGE. [– med.L. *ullnagium* (XIV), f. L. *ulna* after OFr. *aulnage* ALNAGE.] Hence **U·lnager.**

Ulnar (ʋ·lnăɹ), *a.* and *sb.* 1741. [f. ULNA + -AR¹.] *Anat.* **A.** *adj.* Of the ulna. **B.** *sb.* The ulnar nerve 1899. So **Ulno-,** comb. form, as in *ulno-carpal*.

-ulose, *suffix*, repr. L. adj. suffix *-ulosus* (see -ULE, -OSE¹) formed on sbs. in *-ulus, -ula, -ulum*. Some of the Eng. words are adaptations of L. adjs., as *calculose*: others, as *globulose*, are analogical formations. Forms in *-ulose* from the same stem as others in *-ulous* are usu. either older forms now displaced by commoner *-ulous*, or later forms differentiated for special senses.

Ulotrichous (yulǫ·trikəs), *a.* Also **oulo-.** 1857. [f. mod.L. *Ulotrichi*, f. Gr. οὖλος crisp + θρίξ, τριχ- hair; see -OUS.] *Anthrop.* Of the *Ulotrichi*, a division of mankind comprising the crisp-haired races. So **Ulo·trichan,** a u. person 1888.

-ulous, *suffix*, repr. both L. *-ulosus* (see -ULOSE), as in *fabulous, populous*, and L. *-ulus* adj., as in *garrulous, tremulous.*

Ulster (ʋ·lstəɹ). [The name of an Irish province, occurring in ME. as *Ulster, Ulvester* (= AFr. *Ulvestre*), corresp. to ON. *Ulaztir, Ulaðstir*, f. Irish *Ulaidh* men of Ulster, with an obscure suffix (cf. *Leinster, Munster*).] **1.** *pl.* Ulstermen (as troops). *rare.* 1649. **2.** The Irish king-of-arms 1552. **3.** A long loose rough overcoat, often with a waist-belt 1878.

attrib.: *U. tenant-right, U. custom*, those securing to a tenant certain rights of occupancy, disposal, or compensation, in regard to land held by him. **U·lsterman,** a native or inhabitant of Ulster. Hence (from sense 3): **U·lstered** *a.* wearing an u. **Ulstere·tte,** a small or light u. **U·lstering,** cloth for the making of ulsters.

Ult., abbrev. of ULTIMO. 1750.

I have read yours of the 30th ult. with great pleasure 1750.

Ulterior (ʋltiᵊ·riəɹ), *a.* 1646. [– L. *ulterior* further, more distant, compar. of **ulter* (cf. ULTRA and the rel. of *inferior* with *infra*); cf. Fr. *ultérieur.*] **1.** Lying beyond what is immediate or present, coming at a later stage, further, future. **b.** *spec.* Beyond what is avowed or evident; kept in the background 1735. **2.** More remote in position 1721.

1. The request was only preparatory to u. measures FROUDE. **b.** There is no reason for suspecting him of u. designs 1856. **2.** Those u. regions which are beyond the limits of our astronomy 1817. Hence **Ulterio·rity,** an u. matter. **Ulte·riorly** *adv.*, at or to a further stage.

Ultimacy (ʋ·ltimăsi). 1842. [f. next; see -ACY.] The quality or state of being ultimate.

Ultimate (ʋ·ltimĕt), *a.* (*sb.*) 1654. [– late and med.L. *ultimatus*, pa. pple. of late L. *ultimare* come to an end (Tertullian), f. L. *ultimus* last, final; see -ATE².] **A.** *adj.* **1.** Beyond which nothing is contemplated or intended. **2.** That concludes a process, course of action or series 1660. **b.** No longer alterable, definitive 1687. **c.** Precluding appeal or escape, decisive 1755. **d.** Beyond which there is no advance or progress 1794. **3.** Beyond which no advance can be made by investigation or analysis; fundamental, elemental 1659. **b.** Math. *U. ratio*, the final limiting ratio between two variable quantities which simultaneously approach definite fixed values or limits 1729. **4.** Forming a result or conclusion of a character different from the starting-point or present state; eventual 1777. **5.** Of a syllable or accent: Final; falling on the last syllable of a word 1837.

1. To be idle is the u. purpose of the busy JOHNSON. **2.** No man ever knew. . what will be the u. result. . of any given line of conduct RUSKIN. **b.** I consented to wait till then for their u. decision 1803. **c.** The u. check to population appears then to be a want of food MALTHUS. **d.** The creatures [larvae] before us were not in their u. state, but were the produce of the bee-fly 1794. **3.** There are u. truths, far above human ken 1808. The u. particles of matter TYNDALL. **4.** The quiet of the town is purchased by the ruin of the country, and the u. wretchedness of both BURKE.

B. *sb.* **1.** The final point or result; the end; the last step 1681. **2.** A final or fundamental fact or principle 1709.

1. Having now obtain'd the u. of his Desires 1728. **2.** We come down then finally to Force, as the u. of ultimates H. SPENCER.

Ultimate (ʋ·ltimeit), *v.*¹ 1834. [f. prec.; see -ATE³.] **1.** *trans.* To bring to completion 1849. **2.** *intr.* To result finally; to end (*in* something) 1834.

1. It is the soundness of the bones that ultimates itself in a peach-bloom complexion EMERSON. **2.** Unless the meditation ultimates in useful work 1868.

U·ltimate, *v.*² *rare.* 1892. [Back-formation from ULTIMATUM.] *trans.* = ULTIMATUM *v.*

Ultimately (ʋ·ltimĕtli), *adv.* 1660. [f. ULTIMATE *a.* + -LY².] **1.** In the last resort;

fundamentally. **2.** In the end; at the last 1755. **3.** Conclusively, definitively 1785.

1. All government is u. and essentially absolute JOHNSON. **2.** I doubted not that I should u. succeed MRS. SHELLEY. So **U·ltimateness,** finality.

Ultima Thule. See THULE.

Ultimation (ɒltimēⁱ·ʃən). 1791. [f. as ULTIMATE *v.*¹; see -ATION.] The action or process of bringing to an ultimate result; a final issue or development.

Ultimatum (ɒltimēⁱ·tɒ̆m), *sb. Pl.* **-ata** (-ēⁱ·tă). 1731. [subst. use of n. of *ultimatus* in the med.L. senses of 'final', 'completed' XIII (see ULTIMATE *a.*).] **1.** Terms presented by one State to another as its last word, to be complied with on pain of a diplomatic rupture or war. **b.** *transf.* A final stipulation or offer 1733. **2.** The extreme limit; an ultimate aim 1748. †**3.** *slang.* The buttocks –1825. **4.** Something unanalysable or fundamental 1858. **5.** The most distant point (to be) reached 1862.

1. b. The official shrugged his shoulders and signified that his u. had been pronounced TROLLOPE. **2.** To be married was still the u. of her wishes 1802. **4.** Certain *ultimata* of belief not to be disturbed in ordinary conversation O. W. HOLMES. **5.** Almost to the coast of the Baltic; their u. there a place called Köslin CARLYLE. Hence **Ultima·tum** *v. trans.* to present with an u.

‖**Ultimo** (ɒ·ltimo), *adv.* 1582. [L. (sc. *die* or *mense*), abl. sing. masc. of *ultimus* last.] †**1.** On the last day (of a specified month) –1682. **2.** Of last month. (Abbrev. ULT. and ULTO.) 1616.

2. Your letter of the 31st u. WASHINGTON.

Ultimoge·niture. 1882. [f. L. *ultimus* last; after PRIMOGENITURE.] Inheritance by the youngest of a family, as in borough-english.

†**Ulto.,** abbrev. of ULTIMO 2. –1847.

Ultonian (ɒltōᵘ·niăn), *a.* and *sb.* 1766. [f. med.L. *Ultonia* Ulster, f. *Ult-*, stem of OIr. *Ulaidh*; see ULSTER.] (A native or inhabitant) of Ulster.

Ultra (ɒ·ltră), *a.* (*sb.*) 1817. [Independent use of ULTRA-; orig. as an abbrev. of Fr. *ultra-royaliste*.] **A.** *adj.* **1.** Ultra-royalist. **2.** Holding extreme views 1820. **3.** Excessive 1818. **4.** Expressive of extreme views 1827. **5.** Adapted for very minute measurements, etc., as *u.-microscope* 1910.

3. A little wearied by..the u. zeal of his countrymen W. IRVING.

B. *sb.* **1.** A (French) ultra-royalist 1817. **2.** An extremist, esp. in politics or religion 1826. **3.** One who goes to the extreme of fashion 1819.

‖**Ultra** (ɒ·ltră), *prep.* 1793. [L., = beyond.] **1.** *U. vires* (vəiᵊ·rīz), beyond the powers or legal authority (*of* a person, etc.; also with ellipsis of *of*). **2.** Lying beyond (*rare*) 1883.

1. It was not *ultra vires* the directors to advance money 1884.

Ultra- (ɒ·ltră), *prefix*, repr. L. *ultra* beyond, so used in late and med.L. (see ULTRAMARINE, ULTRAMONTANE, ULTRAMUNDANE). Senses 1 and 2 below answer to these types; sense 3 apparently originated in the Fr. *ultra-révolutionnaire* and *ultra-royaliste*, and has become prolific in English and other European languages.

1. Lying on the other side of or beyond in space. In adjs., as *ultra-Gangetic, -terrestrial, -zodiacal*. **b.** *U.-red, -violet*, applied to rays lying beyond the two ends of the visible spectrum. *U.-v.* rays are used in therapeutics and photography. **2.** Exceeding or surpassing the limits of the class denoted by the simple adj. as *ultra-microscopic* too small to be microscopic, *ultra-human* beyond what is human. **b.** Exceeding in respect of number or quantity, as *ultra-centenarian* living to over a hundred. **3.** Showing the highest degree of the quality denoted by the simple adj., as *ultra-fashionable, ultra-orthodox, ultra-dolichocephalic*. **b.** Similarly in advs., as *ultra-politely*. **c.** Similarly in sbs., mostly subst. uses of, or derivatives of, adjs., as *ultra-Christian, -papist; -discipline*.

U:ltracrepidarian (-krepidēᵊ·riăn), *a.* and *sb.* 1819. [f. the L. phr. (*ne sutor*) *ultra crepidam* (let the cobbler not go) beyond his last.] **A.** *adj.* Going beyond one's province. **B.** *sb.* A person who does this, esp. an ignorant or presumptuous critic 1825. Hence **Ultracrepida·rianism, Ultracrepida·tion, -cre·pidizing.**

Ultrafidian (-fi·diăn), *a.* 1825. [f. the L. phr. *ultra fidem* beyond faith; see -IAN.] Going beyond mere faith; blindly credulous.

Ultraism (ɒ·ltră,iz'm). 1821. [f. ULTRA *a.* + -ISM.] The fact or condition of being an extremist; extreme opinions. **b.** With *pl.* Any such opinion 1824. So **U·ltraist. Ultrai·stic** *a.*

Ultramarine (ɒltrămărī·n), *a.* and *sb.* 1598. [– It. †*oltramarino* (mod. *oltre-*) in *azzurro oltramarino* 'azure from overseas'; later assim. to med.L. *ultramarinus*, f. L. *ultra* beyond + *mare* sea; see ULTRA-.] **A.** *adj.* **1.** Situated beyond the sea. Now *rare.* 1652. **2.** From beyond the sea, foreign 1656. **3.** *U. blue* (or *colour*): **a.** A pigment of various shades of blue, named with ref. to the foreign origin of lapis lazuli, from which it was orig. obtained 1686. **b.** A blue colour like that of this pigment 1781. **4.** Of a special deep-blue colour 1783.

1. He tells them that the loss of her u. dominions lessens her expences BURKE.

B. *sb.* **1.** = A. 3. 1598. **b.** With distinguishing words, as *Dutch, yellow, green, German, artificial, u.* 1728. **2.** = A. 3 b. 1695.

Ultramontane (ɒltrămǫ·nteⁱn). 1592. [– med.L. *ultramontanus* adj. and sb., f. L. *ultra* beyond + *mons, mont-* mountain; see -ANE 1.] **A.** *sb.* **1.** *Eccl. Hist.* **a.** A representative of the Roman Catholic Church north of the Alps as opposed to the ecclesiastics in Italy. Now *rare.* **b.** = ULTRAMONTANIST (named from the point of view of countries north of the Alps) 1873. **2.** An inhabitant or native of a country north of the Alps 1618. **B.** *adj.* **1. a.** Of a country north of the Alps 1618. **b.** Of the Italian party in the Roman Church; zealous for papal authority 1728. **2.** *gen.* (From) beyond the mountains 1786.

Ultramontanism (ɒltrămǫ·ntăniz'm). 1827. [– Fr. *ultramontanisme*; see prec. and -ISM.] The principles and practice of the ultramontane party in the Roman Church; the doctrine of absolute papal supremacy. So **Ultramo·ntanist,** a supporter of the absolute supremacy of the Pope 1826.

Ultramundane (ɒltrămɒ·ndeⁱn), *a.* 1656. [– L. *ultramundanus*, f. *ultra* beyond + *mundus* world; see -ANE 1.] Beyond the world; of or pertaining to things beyond the limits of the solar system.

Ultroneous (ɒltrōᵘ·niəs), *a.* 1637. [f. L. *ultroneus*, f. *ultro* of one's own accord; see -OUS.] Done, etc. of one's own accord; voluntary. **b.** *Sc. Law.* Of a witness: Not cited, but proffering testimony 1824. So **Ultro·neously** *adv.* 1627, **-ness** (*rare*) 1623.

Ululate (ɒ·liuleⁱt, yū·l-), *v.* 1623. [– *ululat-*, pa. ppl. stem of L. *ululare* howl, of imit. origin; see -ATE³.] *intr.* To howl, wail, lament loudly.

Troopes of Jackalls..all the while ululating 1638. The widow so often interrupted the service to u. 1893. So **U·lulant** *a.* howling; of, with or like howling. **Ulula·tion,** a wailing or howling 1599. **U·lulatory** *a.* ululant.

‖**Ulva** (ɒ·lvă). *Pl.* **-væ** (vī). 1706. [L., = sedge.] *Bot.* An alga, the typical genus of the *Ulvaceæ*; the laver or sea lettuce.

Ulyssean (yuli·siăn, yūlisī·ăn), *a.* 1639. [– L. *Ulysses* – Gr. Ὀδυσσεύς king of Ithaca and hero of the Odyssey; see -EAN.] Of or connected with Ulysses; *spec.* resembling him in craft or deceit, or in extensive wanderings.

Modern Greeks are U. in this respect, never telling straightforward truth, when deceit will answer the purpose 1850.

Um, 'um, var. of 'EM *pron.*, them. Now *dial.* 1606.

Um ('m), *int.* 1672. [Imitative.] = HUM *int.*

†**Um-, umb-, umbe-,** *prefixes* in many ME. verbs with the meaning 'around' 'about', as *umstand* to stand round, guard, *umbe(e)set* to beset, surround, *umbego* to go round, encircle, UMBETHINK. *Um-* is a reduced form of *umb-*. *Umb-* was – ON. *umb-*, corresponding to OE. *ymb-, ymbe-*, prefix, *ymbe* prep. *Umbe-* partly repr. OE. *ymbe-* is partly an extension of *umb-*, and partly a combination of *um-* with BE-. G. *um*, Gr. ἀμφί and L. *ambi-*, are cognate.

Umbel (ɒ·mbĕl). 1597. [– Fr. †*umbelle* (mod. *ombelle*) or L. *umbella* sunshade, dim. of *umbra* shadow; see -EL.] **1.** *Bot.* An inflorescence borne on pedicels of nearly equal length springing from a common centre. **2.** *Zool.* An umbelliform arrangement of parts 1870.

1. The white umbels of the hemlocks lining the bushy hedgerows GEO. ELIOT. Hence **U·mbelled** *a. Bot.* umbellate. **Umbe·lliform** *a.*

‖**Umbella** (ɒmbe·lă). *Pl.* **-læ** (lī). 1699. [L.; see prec.] **1.** *Bot.* An umbel. **2.** *Zool.* A more or less convex disc supporting the tentacula in Medusæ 1834.

Umbellate (ɒ·mbelĕt), *a.* 1760. [f. UMBELLA + -ATE².] **1.** *Bot.* **a.** Of flowers: Forming an umbel or umbels. **b.** Of plants: Having such flowers 1785. **2.** *Zool.* Having or forming an umbel 1870. So **U·mbellated** *ppl. a.* (in botanical senses) 1676. **U·mbellately** *adv.*

Umbellifer (ɒmbe·lifəɹ). 1718. [– Fr. †*um-, ombellifère* (XVII), f. L. *umbella* (Fr. *ombelle*) + *-fer* bearing.] *Bot.* An umbelliferous plant.

Umbelliferone (ɒmbĕli·fĕroᵘn). 1868. [f. prec. + -ONE.] *Chem.* A colourless, tasteless, crystalline substance obtained from mezereon bark, and, by distillation, from various umbellifers.

Umbelliferous (ɒmbĕli·fĕrəs), *a.* 1662. [f. as prec. + -OUS; see -FEROUS.] **1.** *Bot.* Bearing umbellate flowers; of the family *Umbelliferæ*. **2.** Produced by umbelliferous plants 1753.

Umbellule (ɒmbe·lyul). 1793. [– mod.L. *umbellula*, f. UMBELLA; see -ULE.] *Bot.* A partial or secondary umbel.

U·mber, *sb.*¹ ME. [– OFr. *umbre*, (also mod.) *ombre*, or – L. *umbra* shade; see UMBRA¹.] **1.** Shade. Now *dial.* †**b.** The shadow of the pointer on a sun-dial –1400. †**2.** *Under the u. of*, on pretence of –1518. †**3.** A visor; = UMBRERE. –1616.

1. *fig.* Vnder the vmbre and shadowe of the noble protection of our moost dradde souerayn CAXTON.

Umber (ɒ·mbəɹ), *sb.*² 1496. [– OFr. *umbre*, (also mod.) *ombre*, orig. *ombre de mer* and *de rivière* :– L. *umbra*; see UMBRA².] = GRAYLING.

U·mber, *sb.*³ 1568. [– Fr. *ombre* or It. *ombra* (also *terre d'ombre, terra di ombra* 'shadow earth'), either = L. *umbra* UMBER *sb.*¹ or from L. *Umbra*, fem. of *Umber* belonging to the ancient province of *Umbria*, Italy (cf. *Umbrica creta* 'Umbrian chalk', Pliny).] **1.** A brown earth used as a pigment, or its colour. **b.** *Burnt u.*, a special preparation of the pigment, redder in colour 1650. **2.** Any of various moths 1832. **3.** *attrib.* or *adj.* U.-coloured 1802.

1. Ile put my selfe in poore and meane attire, And with a kinde of vmber smirch my face SHAKS. **b.** To crumble burnt u. with a dry brush for foliage and foreground RUSKIN. **3.** The black woods—black, or with a faint u. shadow running through them 1866. Hence **U·mbery** *a.* umber-coloured, dark brown.

U·mber, *v.* 1610. [f. UMBER *sb.*³] *trans.* To stain or paint with umber; to colour dark brown. So **U·mbered** *ppl. a.* 1599.

Umbethi·nk, un-, *v. Obs.* exc. *dial.* ME. [See UM- and BETHINK.] †**1.** *trans.* To think about, consider –1501. **2.** *refl.* To bethink oneself ME.

2. They'll prize what I leave 'em if I could only onbethink me what they would like MRS. GASKELL.

Umbilic (ɒmbi·lik). 1607. [– Fr. *umbilic*, mod. *ombilic* (XVI), or L. UMBILICUS, f. base of UMBO; rel. to Gr. ὀμφαλός and NAVEL.] †**1.** The centre –1638. **2.** *Geom.* A point on a (curved) surface at which all the curvatures are equal 1843.

Umbilical (ɒmbi·likăl, ɒmbiləi·kăl), *a.* 1541. [– Fr. †*umbilical*, (also mod.) *ombilical*, f. †*um-, ombilic* UMBILIC + -AL¹ 1. In later use f. Eng. UMBILIC or UMBILICUS + -AL¹ 1.] **1.** *Anat., Path., Med.* Of, affecting, proceeding from, or applied to the navel. **b.** Of descent: By the female side, uterine 1888. **2.** *U. cord*: **a.** The flexible string attaching the fœtus to the placenta 1753. **b.** *Bot.* The peduncle attaching a seed to the placenta 1731. **3.** *Conch.* That has, or forms, an umbilicus 1755. **4.** *Geom.* Of or forming an umbilicus 1728. **5.** Occupying a central position 1742.

1. The bloodvessels that go to the placenta..are plainly seen issuing from the navel (being therefore called the u. vessels) GOLDSMITH. **2. a.** *fig.* He could never break the u. cord which held him to nature EMERSON. **5.** The Chapter-house is large, supported, as to its arched Roof, by one u. pillar 1742. Hence **Umbi·lically** *adv.*

Umbi·licar, *a.* 1843. [f. UMBILICUS + -AR¹.] *Geom.* Of or belonging to the umbilicus.

Umbilicate (ɒmbi·likĕt), *a.* 1698. [f. UMBILICUS + -ATE².] Navel-shaped; having a navel-like depression. So **Umbi·licated** *a.* 1698.

Umbilication (ɒmbilikē¹·ʃən). [f. next + -ATION.] *Path.* A central depression at the top of a pock or other vesicle; the condition of being so depressed.

Umbilicus (ɒmbiləi·kɒs, -bi·likɒs). *Pl.* **-ici** (-əi·səi, -isəi). 1704. [L.; see UMBILIC.] **1.** *Anat.* The navel 1799. **b.** *Bot.* The part of a seed by which it is attached to the placenta 1837. **c.** *transf.* The central point 1897. **2.** *Geom.* †**a.** A focus -1728. **b.** A point in a surface through which all its lines of curvature pass 1841. **3.** A navel-shaped depression. (Chiefly *Bot., Ent., Zool.*, etc.) 1809.

1. c. Killare.., formerly regarded as the u. of Ireland 1897. **2. b.** To determine the number of umbilici on a surface of the nth degree 1863. **3.** The u. is small or obsolete in the typical nautili 1851.

Umbles (ɒ·mb'lz). late ME. [var. of NUMBLES.] **1.** The edible inward parts of an animal, usu. of a deer. **2.** attrib. in *umble-pie* (cf. HUMBLE PIE) 1663.

1. Fine, daintie, and tender bodies, as..Umbles, Chickens, Calves feete, or any other good thing 1616. **2.** Mrs. Turner..did bring us an umble pie hot out of her oven PEPYS.

‖**Umbo** (ɒ·mbo). *Pl.* **umbones** (ɒmbōᵘ·nīz), **umbos.** 1721. [L., = shield-boss, knob. Cf. UMBILIC.] **1.** The boss in or near the centre of a shield, sometimes pointed. **2.** A round or conical projection from a surface 1753. **b.** *Conch., Ent.*, etc. Applied to protuberant parts of prominences 1822. **3.** *Path.* A central patch in the affected area in skin diseases 1822. **4.** *Anat.* The deepest point in the concavity of the tympanic membrane of the ear 1877. So **Umbonal** (ɒ·mbonăl) *a.* of, situated near, or forming an u. **U·mbonate** *a.* having an u. (chiefly *Bot.*).

‖**Umbra**¹ (ɒ·mbră). *Pl.* **-bræ** (-brī). 1599. [L.; see UMBER *sb.*¹] **1.** The shade, ghost, or spirit of one dead. **2.** An uninvited guest accompanying an invited one 1696. **3.** *Astr.* **a.** The earth's or moon's shadow in an eclipse; now *spec.* the complete shadow as dist. from the penumbra 1661. **b.** In sun-spots: The darker part (formerly called *nucleus*) as opposed to the lighter penumbra (formerly *umbra*) 1788. **4.** *Alg.* A symbol that must be paired with another to denote a quantity 1851.

1. The *umbræ* or ghosts of some three or four playes, departed a dozen yeeres since B. JONS. **2.** Most of the guests their umbra's brought 1724.

‖**U·mbra**². *rare.* 1610. [L.; see UMBER *sb.*²] **1.** The grayling. **2.** A sciænoid fish of the genus *Umbrina* 1753.

Umbrage (ɒ·mbrĕdʒ), *sb.* late ME. Also †**om-.** [- OFr. *umbrage*, (also mod.) *ombrage* :- Rom. **umbraticum* subst. use of n. of L. *umbraticus* pertaining to retirement or seclusion, f. *umbra* shadow; see -AGE.] †**1.** Shade, shadow -1763. **2.** *spec.* The shade of trees; the foliage affording it 1540. **3.** A shadowy appearance, semblance, hint, or trace (usu. *of*). Now *rare.* 1604. †**4.** A suspicion or doubt; an inkling *of* something; a ground for suspicion -1772. †**5.** Shelter, protection -1776. †**6.** A pretext; a false show -1735. †**7.** *To be* or *stand in u.*, to be in disfavour -1649. **8.** Displeasure, offence, resentment; esp: in *to give u.* (*to*), *take u.* (*at*) 1620.

1. The Sun setting that Evening without any cloudy u. 1655. [To] live..under the Badge and U. of Ignominy and Shame 1727. **2.** Where highest Woods impenetrable To Starr or Sunlight, spread thir u. broad MILT. By flowering u. shaded THOMSON. At the foot of some tree of friendly u. C. BRONTË. *fig.* The light of law was for a time obscured by the thick u. of novel facts TYNDALL. **3.** To avoid even the umbrages of suspicion 1668. Joys angelical..are all but a manifold u. of the one joy of God 1856. **4.** I say iust feare,..not out of vmbrages, light iealousnesse, apprehensions a farre off, but out of cleare foresight of imminent danger BACON. But there is not the least u. for such a conjecture to be found in the scripture 1737. **5.** Having the u. of the Editor's character to screen myself behind RICHARDSON. **6.** Truth will appear from under all the false glosses and umbrages that men may draw over it 1693. To form a Party, and maintain a Struggle for personal Power, under the Pretence and U. of Principle BOLINGBROKE. **7.** He knew Sir James stood in some u. with the King DRUMM. OF HAWTH. **8.** Fearing the captain and his lady would take u., and leave his carriage SMOLLETT. Unless my pacific disposition was displeasing, nothing else could have given u. WASHINGTON.

U·mbrage, *v.* 1647. [f. prec., or - Fr. *ombrag(i)er*, †*umbrag(i)er*, f. *ombrage*; see prec.] **1.** *trans.* To shade; also *fig.* to put in the shade. **2.** To offend, displease (*rare*) 1894.

1. A ridge or hillock heavily umbraged with the rounded foliage of evergreen oaks 1888. **2.** May I help myself to wine without umbraging you STEVENSON.

Umbrageous (ɒmbrē¹·dʒəs), *a.* 1587. [- (O)Fr. *ombrageux*, f. *ombrage* UMBRAGE; or directly f. UMBRAGE *sb.* + -OUS.] **1.** Shady; giving or abounding in shade. **b.** Of shade: Caused by thick foliage 1830. **2.** Of persons or disposition: Suspicious, jealous; apt to take offence 1601. †**3.** Obscure, dubious -1651.

1. Where the grove with leaves u. bends POPE. The u. loveliness of the surrounding country SHELLEY. **2.** The people are idle, haughty, u., fiery, quarrelsome 1874. **3.** We blesse God for the light they had, though u. and clouded 1651. Hence **Umbra·geous-ly** *adv.*, **-ness.**

Umbral (ɒ·mbrăl), *a.* 1851. [f. UMBRA¹ + AL¹ 1.] **1.** *Alg.* Based on or consisting of umbræ. **2.** *Astr.* Of the umbra of sun-spots or eclipses 1867. Hence **U·mbrally** *adv.*

Umbrated (ɒ·mbreⁱtĕd), *a.* 1486. [f. pa. ppl. stem of L. *umbrare* (f. *umbra* UMBRA¹) + -ED¹.] *Her.* Drawn merely in outline so that the field shows through.

Umbratic (ɒmbræ·tik), *a. rare.* 1677. [- L. *umbraticus*, f. *umbra* shade; see -ATIC.] **1.** = next 2. **2.** = UMBRATILE *a.* 1. 1839.

†**Umbra·tical,** *a.* 1633. [f. as prec. + -AL¹ 1; see -ICAL.] **1.** = next, A. 1. -1656. **2.** That serves as a shadow or imperfect representation of something -1683. **3.** Glozing, deceptive -1662.

Umbratile (ɒ·mbrătəil, -til), *a.* (*sb.*) 1592. [- L. *umbratilis* keeping in the shade, f. *umbra* shade; see -ILE.] **A.** *adj.* **1.** Secluded, in retirement, within doors; academic or recluse; not public or practical. **2.** Of or like a shadow or shadows 1632. **b.** Shadowy, unsubstantial, unreal. Now *rare* or *Obs.* 1647. **3.** Giving shade 1659.

1. A time of peace and security tends to foster an u. and academic science 1845. **3.** His hat was u., as of the Pilgrim Fathers BLACKMORE.

B. *sb.* One who spends his time in the shade 1888.

Many thus are umbratiles in the booths, and give themselves almost to a perpetual slumber DOUGHTY.

Umbre (ɒ·mbəɹ). Also **umber.** 1773. [- Fr. *ombre* or L. *umbra* shade, after mod.L. *umbretta* UMBRETTE.] An African bird (*Scopus umbretta*) with deep-brown plumage; the hammer-head or African crow.

Umbrella (ɒmbre·lă). 1609. [- It. *ombrella*, *ombrello* (whence Fr. *ombrelle*), dim. of *ombra* :- L. *umbra* (shadow, shade), after *umbella* UMBEL.] **1.** A large sunshade or parasol 1610. **b.** As an Oriental or African symbol of dignity 1653. **2.** A similar defence against rain, now usu. of silk, alpaca, etc., fastened on slender ribs which are attached radially to a stick and can be readily raised so as to form a circular arched canopy 1634. †**3.** *fig.* A means of shelter or protection; a screen or disguise -1734. **4.** Anything serving as protection from the sun, rain, etc. 1654. **5.** An umbrella-shaped structure 1680. **b.** *Bot.* A part of a plant resembling an umbrella 1658. **c.** *Zool.* The gelatinous disc or bell-shaped structure of a jelly-fish 1834. **d.** *Conch.* A gasteropod of the genus *Umbrella*; the part of the shell resembling an open umbrella 1841.

1. The street was in a blaze with scarlet umbrellas 1860. **2.** She always carried her stout little u. 1882.

attrib. and *Comb.*, as *u.-case, frame, -stand*; in plant-names, denoting u.-shaped, as *u.-acacia, -pine*; in names of birds, etc., as *u.-ant, -bird, -shell*, also, **u. roof,** one arched like an umbrella; **u. sail,** a kind that can be quickly set or furled; **-tree,** the *Magnolia tripetala* and other American magnolias, also various other trees of u.-like growth of leaves. Hence **Umbrellaed, -la'd** (e·lăd) *ppl. a.* **Umbre·llaless** *a.* **Umbre·lla-like** *a.*

†**U·mbrere.** late ME. [app. - AFr. **umbrere*, f. *umbre* shade, shadow; see -ER² 2. Cf. AL. (*viserium*) *umbrarium* (visor) overshadowing face (1322). Cf. UMBRIL.] The visor of a helmet -1655.

Umbre·tte. 1884. [- mod.L. *umbretta* or Fr. *ombrette* (Brisson); see UMBRE.] = UMBRE.

Umbrian (ɒ·mbriăn), *a.* and *sb.* 1601. [f. L. *Umber* or *Umbria* + -IAN, -AN; see UMBER *sb.*³] **A.** *adj.* **1.** Of ancient Umbria, its people or language. **2.** Of mediæval or modern Umbria. *U. School*, the fifteenth-century school of painting developed in Umbria. 1841. **B.** *sb.* **1.** An inhabitant of Umbria, a province of central Italy; *esp.* one of the Italic race anciently inhabiting this district 1601. **2.** The language of ancient Umbria 1858.

Umbriferous (ɒmbri·fĕrəs), *a.* 1616. [f. L. *umbrifer* (f. *umbra* shade) + -OUS; see -FEROUS.] Giving shade; umbrageous.

Umbril (ɒ·mbril). *Hist.* 1470. [Earlier *umbrel* (XV) - OFr. *ombrel* shade. Cf. UMBRERE.] A visor.

‖**Umbrina** (ɒmbrəi·nă). 1834. [mod.L. - Sp., It. *umbrina*, f. *umbra* UMBER *sb.*²] *Zool.* A fish of the genus *Umbrina*, chiefly found in warm seas.

Umbro- (ɒ·mbro), used as comb. f. L. *Umbr-*, *Umber* Umbrian.

Umbrose (ɒmbrōᵘ·s), *a. rare.* late ME. [- L. *umbrosus*, f. *umbra* shade; see -OSE¹.] Shady, giving shade; †dusky.

Umbrous (ɒ·mbrəs), *a.* 1480. [- OFr. *umbreux*, (also mod.) *ombreux*, or L. *umbrosus*; see prec., -OUS.] In the shade; shady, shadowed.

Umiak, umyak, var. ff. OOMIAK.

‖**Umlaut** (u·mlaut). 1852. [G., f. *um* about + *laut* sound.] *Philol.* A change in the sound of a vowel produced by partial assimilation to an adjacent sound (usu. that of a vowel or semi-vowel in the following syllable); = MUTATION 3. Hence **U·mlauted** *a.* modified by u.

Umph (mh), *int.* (*sb.*, *v.*) 1568. [Imitative.] = HUMPH.

Umpirage (ɒ·mpəirĕdʒ). 1490. [f. next + -AGE.] The act of umpiring; the office or power of an umpire; arbitration.

Submission of the suit to arbitration or u. shall be made a rule BLACKSTONE.

Umpire (ɒ·mpəiᵊɹ), *sb.* late ME. [Later form of late ME. †*noumpere* - OFr. *nonper*, f. *non-* NON- + *per, pair* PEER by transference of the *n-* to the indefinite article, as in *adder, apron*.] **1.** One who decides between contending parties, and whose decision is to be accepted as final; an arbitrator. **b.** *transf.* Something that serves to decide a matter 1583. **2.** *Law.* A third person appointed to decide between arbitrators who cannot agree 1464. **3.** In games a person appointed to see that rules are kept and to decide all doubtful points. (Cf. REFEREE *sb.* 3.) 1714.

1. The Lords in Parliament tooke an Oath to be indifferent umpiers betweene the Bishop and Duke 1641. **b.** The judgment, u. in the strife That grace and nature have to wage through life COWPER. **2.** If they [*sc.* the arbitrators] do not agree, it is usual to add, that another person be called in as u. BLACKSTONE. **3.** [Football], Mr. Walker officiated as referee, and Messrs. Davies and Bryan as umpires 1884. Hence **U·mpireship,** the office of u. 1565. **U·mpiress,** a female u.

U·mpire, *v.* 1592. [f. prec.] †**1.** *trans.* To appoint (a person to an office) in virtue of being 'umpire'. BACON. †**b.** To act as umpire between (persons) -1657. **2.** To settle (a matter) as umpire 1611. **b.** *transf.* Of things 1609. **3.** *spec.* To supervise (games, etc.) as umpire 1861. **4.** *intr.* To act as umpire. Also const. *between.* 1613. Hence **U·mpiring** *vbl. sb.* the action of acting as an u., esp. in games.

Umpty (ɒ·mᵖti). orig. *Army slang.* 1917. [Signallers' slang for 'dash', used in reading morse.] An indefinite (fairly large) number. Hence **Umptee·n** (also *umteen*) [see -TEEN], any (considerable) number. So **Um(p)tee·nth** *a.* **U·mptieth** *a.*

[Cf. A charming Miss of -teen summers 1887.]

Umquhile, umwhile (ɒ·mhwəil), *adv.* and *a.* In later use *Sc.* Now *Obs.* or *arch.* ME.

[repr. OE. *ymb hwīle*, with substitution of Um- for *ymb*.] **A.** *adv.* †**1.** At times, sometimes –1568. **2.** At some previous time, formerly. late ME. †**3.** At some later time, by-and-by –1513.

1. Vmquhill in plesure and prosperitie, Vmquhill in pane and greit penuritie 1535. **2.** I, Henrie Stewart, vmquhile of Scotland King 1567.

B. *adj.* Former, late. **a.** Of persons; *esp.* = now deceased. late ME. **b.** Of things (*rare*) 1548.

a. The estate which devolved on this unhappy woman by a settlement of her umwhile husband Scott. **b.** I saw my u. house existing as a bit of dingy wall 1854.

Un, 'un[1], *pers. pron.*, later dial. f. acc. Hin, hine him.

Un, 'un[2], dial. f. One *pron.* VI. 1, 2.

Un-, *prefix*[1], expressing negation, repr. OE. *un-* = OS., OHG., Goth. *un-*, ON. *ú-*, *ó-*, corresp. to OIr. *in-*, *an-*, L. *in-* (In-[3]), Gr. ἀν-, ἀ- (see A-, An-), Skr. *an-*, *a-*, Indo-Eur. **n̥*, ablaut-variant of *ne* not. The prefix has been very extensively used in English as in other Germanic langs., and is now (as compared with In-) the one which can be used with the greatest freedom in new formations.

The form of the prefix indicates that it was orig. unstressed, and normally it is still so. There is a tendency, however, to give stress to it in rare or casual formations, and esp. when the negation or contrast implied is emphasized.

The following sections enumerate the usual types of current formations. Since the actual number of compounds of *un-* is very great and their possible number indefinite, many unimportant and self-explanatory ones are omitted from the series of Main words, and others are entered in their alphabetical places, but, instead of a definition, are furnished with a reference to the section of this article under which the particular type of formation is explained; such words will usu. have appended to them the earliest (or latest, if the word is obsolete) known date of their use, or the name of the first author known to have used them.

1. *Un-* is freely prefixed to adjectives of all kinds, except where a Latin form in *in-* (*il-*, *im-*, etc.) has established itself by general preference. The two forms may, however, co-exist, and occas. a new formation with *un-* has been introduced when that with *in-* has acquired a connotation which it is sought to avoid. The form with *un-* is then purely negative, while the other may have a rather positive than a negative implication, e.g. *unmoral*, *immoral*. There is considerable restriction in the use of *un-* with short simple adjs. of native origin, the negative of these being naturally supplied by another simple word of an opposite signification; thus such forms as *unbroad*, *undeep*, *unglad*, *unfew*, *ungood*, *unstrong*, *unwhole* are now rarely found; on the other hand, derivative forms in *-able*, *-al*, *-ant*, *-ar*, *-ary*, *-ent*, *-ful*, *-ic*(*al*, *-ish*, *-ive*, *-like*, *-ly*, *-ous*, *-y*, etc., are too numerous to be recorded. (The unusual types *uncome-at-able* (1694), *unget-at-able* (1862) are later in date than the corresponding positive forms.) **2.** The prefixing of *un-* to pa. pples., common in OE. and revived in ME., was subsequently extended until it became the commonest of all uses of the prefix. **b.** Participial formations (and adjs. in *-able*) with *un-* frequently have an attached absol. prep. (usu. hyphened) as in *uncalled-for*, *unheard-of*, *unlivable-with*, *unwished-for*. Where ambiguity is not anticipated, the prep. may be dropped, as *unrepented* for *unrepented-of*. **3.** Adj. forms in *-ed*, derived from sbs., as *unbearded*, *unbodied*. The usual sense is 'not provided or furnishd with', but occas. 'not effected by', 'not treated with'. Many such compounds may be alternatively analysed as f. *un* + pa. pple. of the related vb., e.g. *uncarpeted*, *unfeathered*. **4.** The use of *un-* with pres. pples. is now frequent, and has given rise to a large number of permanent words, such as *unbecoming*, *unbending*, *unchanging*, *unfailing*, *unseeing*, *untiring*, *unwilling*. **5.** In OE. advb. formations in *-līce* were frequent. Few of them survived in ME., but additions were gradually made, and the use of *un-* with *-ly* later became common. In such formations either the suffix *-ly* is added to an existing word compounded with *un-*, or *un-* is prefixed to an already existing adv. in *-ly*. This distinction is occas. significant: e.g. *unprofessionally* formed from *unprofessional* means 'in a manner contrary to professional rules or etiquette'; formed from *professionally*, it means 'not in a professional manner or capacity'. **6.** The OE. use of *un-* with sbs. survived in ME., and many new formations of this type were then and subseq. introduced; these have been mainly words of abstract meaning, as *unchastity*, *unreality*, *unsociability*. In these the formation may not be ascertainable; e.g. *unchastity* may be f. *un-* + *chastity*, or f. *unchaste* + *-ity*. **b.** The prefixing of *un-* to nouns used attrib. is rare, and usu. joc.; e.g. *uncountry gentleman* (Byron). **7.** Verbs with prefixed *un-* have never been very numerous, and are now rare. **8.** In OE. there are few instances of *un-* with vbl. sbs. in *-ung*; none of these survive in ME., and new forms in *-ing* are rare.

Un-, *prefix*[2], expressing reversal or deprivation, repr. OE. *un-*, *on-*, = OS. *ant-*, OHG. *ant-*, *int-*, Goth. *and-*, orig. identical with And-.

1. In OE. most of the forms with *un-* have for their second part a simple vb., as *unbindan*, *undon*, and the prefix denotes a reversal of the action of the verb. Additions to this type of formation have been freely made at all subsequent periods. **2.** A small number of OE. verbs in *un-* imply removal or deprivation; the type remains rare in ME., but at a later date it became more frequent and is now common. **b.** In some vbs. *un-* implies freeing or releasing from something. This type has also become common in later use. **3.** The use of *un-* to denote the removal or extraction of a person or thing from a place or receptacle, as in *unbody*, *unearth*, *unhouse*, occurs in the 14th c., and becomes prominent at the beginning of the 17th. In some instances the sense passes into that of releasing from confinement, as in *uncage*, or of revealing to others, as in *unbosom*. **4.** From the 16th century formations in which *un-* expresses the fact or process of depriving a person or thing of a certain quality or property become frequent. **a.** When the formation has an adj. base, the adj. may be used in its simple form, with the suffix *-en*. **b.** Sbs. are similarly employed without ending. **c.** From sbs. (rarely from adjs.) there are numerous formations in *-*(*i*)*fy*, and from both sbs. and adjs. in *-ize*. Other endings, as *-ate*, are less frequent. **5.** The OE. vbs. in *un-* are almost always trans., and this is still the prevailing use. Intr. uses of some common words are found in ME., and later the usage increases to some extent, but is chiefly confined to words having some currency. **6.** Vbl. sbs., ppl. adjs., and agent-nouns from vbs. in *un-* begin to appear in the 14th c., and later become common. **7.** The redundant use of *un-* is rare, but occurs in OE. *unliesan* and ME. *unloose*, which still survives. Later instances are *unbare*, *unsolve*, *unstrip*.

Una (yū·nă). 1878. [Name of the first boat of the kind brought from America to England in 1853.] A catboat. Also *attrib.*

Unaba·shable *a.* [Un-[1] 2] 1848. **Unaba·shed** *ppl. a.* [Un-[1] 2] 1571, **-ly** *adv.* **Unaba·ted** *ppl. a.* [Un-[1] 2] 1611, **-ly** *adv.* **Unaba·ting** *ppl. a.* [Un-[1] 4] 1768, **-ly** *adv.* **Unabbre·viated** *ppl. a.* [Un-[1] 2] 1805. **Unabi·ding** *ppl. a.* [Un-[1] 4] late ME., **-ly** *adv.*

Unable (ʊnē^i·b'l), *a.* late ME. [f. Un-[1] + Able *a.*, after (O)Fr. *inhabile* or L. *inhabilis*.] **1.** Not able *to* do something specified (chiefly of persons). **b.** Const. *for* or *to* (with sbs.) 1456. **2.** Unequal to the task or need, incompetent, inefficient. Somewhat *arch.* late ME. **3.** Physically weak, feeble. Now *Sc.* 1577.

1. b. Agrippa they accounted..vnable for so great a charge 1598. **2.** No hopes of succour from such u. protectors Goldsm. **3.** As little and as vnable as a child Burton. Hence **Una·bly** *adv.* (now *rare* or *Obs.*).

Unabri·dged, *ppl. a.* 1599. [Un-[1] 2.] Not abridged; now usu. of literary works.

Una·brogated *ppl. a.* [Un-[1] 2] 1535. **Unabso·lved,** *ppl. a.* [Un-[1] 2] 1611. **Unabso·rbed** *ppl. a.* [Un-[1] 2] 1766. **Unabsu·rd** *a.* [Un-[1] 1] 1742.

Unabu·sed, *ppl. a.* 1661. [Un-[1] 2.] **1.** Not deceived or misled. **2.** Not misused or wrongly employed 1864.

2. Human greatness is, when u., a majestic sight Pusey.

Unacade·mic *a.* [Un-[1] 1] 1844. **Unacade·mical** *a.* [Un-[1] 1] 1840. **Unacce·nted** *ppl. a.* [Un-[1] 2] 1598. **Unacce·ntuated** *ppl. a.* [Un-[1] 2] 1716. **Unacce·ptable** *a.* [Un-[1] 1] 1483, **-ness.** **Unacce·ptably** *adv.* **Unacce·ptance** [Un-[1] 6] 1865. **Unacce·pted** *ppl. a.* [Un-[1] 2] 1612. **Unacce·ssory** *a.* [Un-[1] 1] 1660. **Unaccli·mated** *ppl. a.* [Un-[1] 2] 1846. **Unaccli·matized** *ppl. a.* [Un-[1] 2] 1863. **Unacco·mmodated** *ppl. a.* [Un-[1] 2] 1605. **Unacco·mmodating** *ppl. a.* [Un-[1] 4] 1790.

Unacco·mpanied, *ppl. a.* 1545. [Un-[1] 2.] **1.** Not accompanied or attended (*by* or *with*). **2.** *Mus.* With no instrumental accompaniment 1818.

Unacco·mplished, *ppl. a.* 1525. [Un-[1] 2.] **1.** Not achieved; not completed. **2.** Lacking accomplishments 1729.

1. All th' unaccomplisht works of Natures hand, Abortive, monstrous, or unkindly mixt Milt. So **Unacco·mplishment** Milt.

Unacco·rded, *a.* 1645. [Un-[1] 2.] Not agreed upon; not bestowed.

Unaccou·ntable, *a.* and *sb.* 1643. [Un-[1] 1.] **A.** *adj.* **1.** Impossible or difficult to account for; inexplicable, puzzling; of a strange or puzzling disposition. **2.** Not liable to be called to account; irresponsible 1649. **B.** *sb.* An unaccountable person, thing, or event 1748.

1. The u. and secret reasons of disaffection between man and wife Milton. With the Character of an odd u. Fellow Addison. **2.** The Acknowledgment of his Supream and U. Power 1695. Hence **Unaccountabi·lity.** **Unaccou·ntableness.** **Unaccou·ntably** *adv.*

Unaccou·nted, *ppl. a.* 1799. [Un-[1] 2, 2 b.] Not accounted *for*; of which no account is given.

Unaccre·dited *ppl. a.* [Un-[1] 2] 1828. **Unaccu·rsed, -st,** *ppl. a.* [Un-[1] 2] 1647. **Unaccu·sable** *a.* [Un-[1] 1] 1582, **-bly** *adv.* **Unaccu·sed** *ppl. a.* [Un-[1] 2] 1508.

Unaccu·stomed, *ppl. a.* 1526. [Un-[1] 2.] **1.** Not customary, unfamiliar, unusual. **2.** Not used *to* something, not wont *to* do something 1611. **b.** *attrib.* or *absol.*, without const. 1653.

1. The strange room and its u. objects Dickens. **2. b.** Phlebotomy..may prove dangerous to the u. 1653. Hence **Unaccu·stomedness.**

Unachie·vable *a.* [Un-[1] 1] 1657. **Unachi·eved** *ppl. a.* [Un-[1] 2] 1603. **Una·ching** *ppl. a.* [Un-[1] 4] Shaks. **Unacknow·ledged** *ppl. a.* [Un-[1] 2] 1583. **Unacknow·ledging** *ppl. a.* [Un-[1] 4] 1611. **Unacquai·nt** *a. Sc.* [Un-[1] 1] 1587. **Unacquai·ntance** [Un-[1] 6] 1598.

Unacquai·nted *ppl. a.* 1529. [Un-[1] 2.] †**1.** Not personally known (to one) –1607. **b.** Of things: Unfamiliar, unknown, strange –1672. **2.** Not acquainted *with* (= ignorant of) something 1563. †**b.** Const. *in*, *of*, *to* –1805. **c.** Inexperienced, ignorant 1581. **3.** Not acquainted *with* another person; not mutually acquainted, not known to each other 1633.

2. b. Being very u. in the style and form of dedications Swift. Hence **Unacquai·ntedness.**

Unacqui·red, *ppl. a.* 1653. [Un-[1] 2.] **1.** Not acquired; unattained (*rare*). **2.** Not obtained from without; innate, native 1793.

Una·ctable, *a.* 1810. [Un-[1] 1.] That cannot be acted; unsuitable for dramatic representation.

Una·cted, *ppl. a.* 1593. [Un-[1] 2. **1.** Not carried out in action; not done. **2.** *Unacted* (*up*)*on*: not affected or influenced 1794. **3.** Of a play, etc.: Not performed on the stage.

1. A thought vnacted Shaks. My sons lament.. U. crimes, and follies not their own 1706. U. desires 1789. U. upon by any extraneous influence 1825.

Una·ctive *a.* [Un-[1] 1] –1777, **-ly** *adv.* –1693, **-ness,** –1683. **Unacti·vity** [Un-[1] 6] –1740. **Una·ctuated** *ppl. a.* [Un-[1] 2] 1661. **Unadaptabi·lity** [Un-[1] 6] 1829. **Unada·ptable** *a.* [Un-[1] 1] 1882. **Unada·pted** *ppl. a.* [Un-[1] 2] 1805. **Unaddi·cted** *ppl. a.* [Un-[1] 2] 1583. **Unaddre·ssed** *ppl. a.* [Un-[1] 2] 1885.

Unade·pt, *sb.* and *a.* 1742. [Un-[1] 6, 1.] (One who is) not (an) adept.

Unadjou·rned *ppl. a.* [Un-[1] 2] 1648. **Unadju·sted** *ppl. a.* [Un-[1] 2] Johnson. **Unadmini·stered** *ppl. a.* [Un-[1] 2] 1590. **Unadmi·red** *ppl. a.* [Un-[1] 2] 1707. **Unadmi·ring** *ppl. a.* [Un-[1] 4] Carlyle, **-ly** *adv.* **Unadmi·tted** *ppl. a.* [Un-[1] 2] 1616. **Unadmo·nished** *ppl. a.* [Un-[1] 2] 1591. **Unado·pted** *ppl. a.* [Un-[1] 2] Milt. **Unado·rned** *ppl. a.* [Un-[1] 2] Milt., **-ly** *adv.*, **-ness.** **Unadu·lterate** *ppl. a.* [Un-[1] 2] 1664, **-ly** *adv.* **Unadu·lterated** *ppl. a.* [Un-[1] 2] Addison, **-ly** *adv.* **Unadva·nced** *ppl. a.* [Un-[1] 2] late ME. **Unadve·nturous** *a.* [Un-[1] 1] Milt., **-ly** *adv.*, **-ness.**

Una·dvertised, *ppl. a.* 1450. [Un-[1] 2.] †**1.** Not warned or made aware; not informed *of* –1652. **2.** Not announced or made known 1864.

Unadvi·sable, *a.* 1673. [Un-[1] 1.] **1.** That cannot or will not be advised. **2.** Inexpedient, inadvisable 1758. Hence **Unadvi·sably** *adv.*

Unadvi·sed, *ppl. a.* late ME. [Un-[1] 2.] **1.** Of acts, words etc.: Done or spoken, without due consideration; rash. **2.** Of persons, disposition, etc.: Indiscreet, thoughtless,

hasty. late ME. **b.** Not having consulted *with* another; not having been consulted *with* 1579. **3.** Lacking advice or advisers 1851.
1. An unskilful or u. treatment 1833. **2. b.** While the Parlament of England sate unadvis'd with MILT. Hence **Unadvi·sed-ly** *adv.* ME., **-ness.**

Unæsthe·tic *a.* [UN-^{1} 1] 1892. **Unafea·r(e)d** *a. arch.* [UN-^{1} 2] 1550. **Una·ffable** *a.* [UN-^{1} 1] 1603.

Unaffe·cted, *ppl. a.* 1586. [UN-^{1} 2.] **1.** Not simulated; genuine, sincere 1592. **b.** Of persons, speech, bearing, etc.: Free from affectation; simple, natural; not artificial or pretentious 1598. **c.** Sincere, honest (in some respect) 1796. **2.** Not influenced or moved; untouched 1586. **b.** Not attacked by disease or illness 1797. **3.** Not acted upon or altered *by* some agent or influence 1830.
1. A Chearfulness, the constant Companion of u. Virtue STEELE. **b.** The letters..lively, entertaining, and u. SCOTT. **c.** An u. admirer 1796. **2.** It is impossible any reader, however stoical, can remain u. 1803. Hence **Unaffe·cted-ly** *adv.*, **-ness.**

Unaffe·cting *ppl. a.* [UN-^{1} 4] 1602. **Unaffe·ctionate** *a.* [UN-^{1} 1] 1588, **-ly** *adv.* **Unaffi·liated** *ppl. a.* [UN-^{1} 2] 1849. **Unaffli·cted** *ppl. a.* [UN-^{1} 2] 1599. **Unaffri·ghted** *ppl. a.* [UN-^{1} 2] MARLOWE, **-ly** *adv.* **Unaffro·nted** *ppl. a.* [UN-^{1} 2] 1753. **Unafrai·d** *a.* [UN-^{1} 1] late ME. **Una·geing** *ppl. a.* [UN-^{1} 4] 1860. **Una·gitated** *ppl. a.* [UN-^{1} 2] 1638, **-ly** *adv.*

Unagree·able, *a.* Now *rare.* late ME. [UN-^{1} 1]. **1.** Not agreeable or pleasing; not to one's liking; disagreeable. †**2.** Unconformable *to*; incongruous *with* –1702.
1. Mr. M. was not u., though nothing seemed to go right with him JANE AUSTEN. **2.** Adventrous work, yet to thy power and mine Not u. MILTON. Hence **Unagree·ably** *adv.*

Unagree·d *ppl. a.* [UN-^{1} 2] 1525. **Unai·dable** *a.* [UN-^{1} 1] SHAKS. **Unai·ded** *ppl. a.* [UN-^{1} 2] MILT. **Unai·med** *ppl. a.* [UN-^{1} 2] 1648. **Unai·red** *ppl. a.* [UN-^{1} 2] 1616.

Unal (yū·năl), *a. rare.* 1883. [f. L. *unus* one + -AL^1 1]. Based on unity; single; that is one only.

Unala·rmed *ppl. a.* [UN-^{1} 2] 1756. **Unala·rming** *a.* [UN-^{1} 4] 1760. **Una·lienable** *a.* [UN-^{1} 1] 1611, **-bly** *adv.* **Una·lienated** *ppl. a.* [UN-^{1} 2] 1798.

Unalist (yū·nălist). *rare.* 1743. [f. L. *unus* one, after DUALIST, PLURALIST.] A holder of only one benefice.

Unali·ve *a.* [UN-^{1} 1] 1828. **Unallay·ed** *ppl. a.* [UN-^{1} 2] 1519. **Unalle·viated** *ppl. a.* [UN-^{1} 2] 1750. **Unalli·able** *a.* [UN-^{1} 1] 1740.

Unallie·d, *ppl. a.* 1663. [UN-^{1} 2.] **1.** Not allied or related (*to*). **2.** Having no ally or allies 1797.

Unallow·able *a.* [UN-^{1} 1] 1560. **Unallow·ed** *ppl. a.* [UN-^{1} 2] 1632. **Unalloy·ed** *ppl. a.* [UN-^{1} 2] 1672. **Unallu·ring** *a.* [UN-^{1} 4] 1775.

Una·lphabeted, *ppl. a.* 1799. [UN-^{1} 2; after L. *analphabetus* ANALPHABET.] Not knowing the alphabet, illiterate.

Unalterabi·lity [UN-^{1} 6] 1847. **Una·lterable** *a.* [UN-^{1} 1] 1611. **Una·lterably** *adv.* 1643. **Una·ltered,** *ppl. a.* [UN-^{1} 2] 1551. **Unama·zed** *ppl. a.* [UN-^{1} 2] 1598. **Unambi·guous** *a.* [UN-^{1} 1] CHESTERF., **-ly** *adv.* **Unambi·tion** [UN-^{1} 6] 1781.

Unambi·tious, *a.* 1621. [UN-^{1} 1.] Not ambitious or aspiring; devoid of ambition.
Those who..pass their days in u. indolence BOSWELL. The calm delights of u. piety WORDSW. Hence **Unambi·tious-ly** *adv.*, **-ness.**

Uname·nable *a.* [UN-^{1} 1] 1771. **Uname·ndable** *a.* [UN-^{1} 1] 1450. **Uname·nded** *ppl. a.* [UN-^{1} 2] WYCLIF. **Un-Ame·rican** *a.* [UN-^{1} 1] 1818. **Unamiabi·lity** [UN-^{1} 6] 1829. **Una·miable** *a.* [UN-^{1} 1] 1480, **-ness, -bly** *adv.* **Unamu·sed** *ppl. a.* [UN-^{1} 2] YOUNG. **Unamu·sing** *a.* [UN-^{1} 4] 1799, **-ly** *adv.* **Unanalo·gical** *a.* [UN-^{1} 1] 1755. **Unana·logous** *a.* [UN-^{1} 1] 1782. **Una·nalysable** *a.* [UN-^{1} 1] 1829. **Una·nalysed** *ppl. a.* [UN-^{1} 2] 1668. **Unanaly·tical** *a.* [UN-^{1} 1] MILL. **Una·nchor** *v.* [UN-^{2} 2 b] 1648. **Una·nchored** *ppl. a.* [UN-^{1} 2] 1651.

Unane·led, *ppl. a. arch.* 1602. [UN-^{1} 2.] Not having received extreme unction.
Vnhouzzled, disappointed, vnnaneld SHAKS.

Unanimate (yunæ·nimeᵗt), *v.* 1702. [f. L. *unanimus, -is* UNANIMOUS + -ATE^3.] *trans.* To cause to be unanimous.

Unanimated (vnæ·nimēᵗtėd), *a.* 1697. [UN-^{1} 2.] **1.** Not possessing life. **2.** Not lively, dull 1734. **3.** Not inspired *by* something 1856.

Unanimist (yunæ·nimist). 1921. [– Fr. *unanimiste*, f. *unanime* UNANIMOUS; see -IST.] Applied to a school of French poets.

Unanimity (yunăni·mĭti). late ME. [– (O)Fr. *unanimité* or L. *unanimitas*, f. *unanimus, -is*; see next, -ITY.] The state or quality of being unanimous; agreement in opinion or purpose.

Unanimous (yunæ·nimǝs), *a.* 1624. [f. L. *unanimus*, (late) *unanimis*, f. *unus* one + *animus* mind; see -OUS.] **1.** Of one mind, or opinion; agreed. **b.** Like-minded, of the same opinion. *arch.* 1637. **2.** Expressing or based on general agreement or consent 1675.
1. b. Let not thine u. friend..know what thou dost 1637. Hence **Una·nimously** *adv.*

Unannea·led *ppl. a.* [UN-^{1} 2] 1745. **Una·nnotated** *ppl. a.* [UN-^{1} 2] 1859. **Unannou·nced** *ppl. a.* [UN-^{1} 2] SCOTT. **Unannoy·ed** *ppl. a.* [UN-^{1} 2] 1470. **Unanoi·nted** *a.* [UN-^{1} 2] LOVELACE.

Una·nswerable, *a.* 1611. [UN-^{1} 1.] †**1.** Not corresponding or analogous (*to*) –1674. **2.** Admitting of no answer; irrefutable; insoluble 1613. **3.** Unable to answer *for*; irresponsible 1884.
2. A new u. proof BERKELEY. Embarrassing, u. questions 1894. **3.** He committed the offence.. whilst..u. for his acts 1884. Hence **Una·nswerableness, -ably** *adv.*

Una·nswered *ppl. a.* [UN-^{1} 2] late ME. **Unanta·gonized** *ppl. a.* [UN-^{1} 2] 1862. **Unanti·cipated** *ppl. a.* [UN-^{1} 2] 1779. **Una·nxious** *a.* [UN-^{1} 1] 1742, **-ly** *adv.* **Unapologe·tic** *a.* [UN-^{1} 1] 1834. **Unaposto·lic, -al** *adjs.* [UN-^{1} 1] 1675, **-ly** *adv.* **Unappa·lled** *ppl. a.* [UN-^{1} 2] 1578. †**Unappa·rel** *v. trans.* [UN-^{2} 2] 1614. **Unappa·relled** *ppl. a.* [UN-^{1} 2] BACON. **Unappa·rent** *a.* [UN-^{1} 1] 1554.

Unappea·lable, *a.* 1635. [UN-^{1} 1.] That cannot be appealed against (or *from.*).

Unappea·ling, *ppl. a.* [UN-^{1} 4] 1716. **Unappea·sable** *a.* [UN-^{1} 1] 1561, **-ness, -bly** *adv.* **Unappea·sed** *ppl. a.* [UN-^{1} 2] SHAKS. **Una·ppetizing** *ppl. a.* [UN-^{1} 4] 1884. **Unapplau·ded** *ppl. a.* [UN-^{1} 2] 1739. **Unapplie·d** *ppl. a.* [UN-^{1} 2] 1540. **Unappoi·nted** *ppl. a.* [UN-^{1} 2] 1560. **Unappre·ciated** *ppl. a.* [UN-^{1} 2] 1828. **Unappre·ciative** *a.* [UN-^{1} 1] 1857. **Unapprehe·nded,** *ppl. a.* [UN-^{1} 2] 1597. **Unapprehe·nding** *ppl. a.* [UN-^{1} 4] 1794.

Unapprehe·nsive *a.* 1624. [UN-^{1} 1.] **1.** Not apprehensive or quick to understand, unintelligent. **2.** Not afraid or anxious; not fearful *of* 1666.
1. As infants gaze at the objects which meet their eyes, in a vague u. way J. H. NEWMAN. Hence **Unapprehe·nsiveness.**

Unapproa·chable, *a.* (and *sb.*) 1581. [UN-^{1} 1.] **1.** Inaccessible. **2.** Permitting no intimacy or confidence 1848. **3.** Beyond rivalry; matchless 1831. **B.** as *sb.* One who or that which cannot be approached or equalled 1800.
1. All alone..in a place of almost u. seclusion SCOTT. **2.** Mr. Dombey is u. by anyone DICKENS. **3.** Paintings..unapproached and u. in their excellence 1856. Hence **Unapproachabi·lity. Unapproa·chableness. Unapproa·chably** *adv.*

Unappro·priate, *ppl. a.* 1767. [UN-^{1} 2.] **1.** Not appropriated or assigned. **2.** = INAPPROPIATE *a.* 1818.

Unappro·priated *ppl. a.* [UN-^{1} 2] 1756. **Unappro·ved** *ppl. a.* [UN-^{1} 2] SHAKS. **Unappro·ving** *a.* [UN-^{1} 4] 1787, **-ly** *adv.*

Una·pt, *a.* late ME. [UN-^{1} 1.] †**1.** Unfitted *to* do something –1736. **2.** Unsuited *for* some use or purpose 1513. **3.** Lacking the required qualities: †**a.** of persons –1680; **b.** of things 1588. **4.** Of language, etc.: Inappropriate, ill chosen 1553. **5.** Not readily tending or likely *to* do something 1587. **b.** Without const.: Unready, backward 1849.
1. Was neuere man ne woman yet bygete That was vnapt to suffren loues hete CHAUCER. A plot of ground u. to receive good seed 1610. **2.** Such beasts..being vncleane, and vnapt for food 1608. Princes, when..they grow u. for affairs 1648. **3. b.** The u. and violent nature of the remedies 1842. **4.** Your comparison is not u., sir GEO. ELIOT. **5.** A mind which was u. to apprehend danger SCOTT. **b.** These u. scholars MILL. Hence **Una·pt-ly** *adv.*, **-ness.**

Una·rch *v.* [UN-^{2} 1] 1598. **Una·rched** *a.* [UN-^{1} 3] 1658.

Unarchite·ctural, *a.* 1849. [UN-^{1} 1.] **1.** Not in accordance with the principles of architecture. **2.** Not skilled in architecture 1884.

Una·rguable *a.* [UN-^{1} 1] 1881. **Una·rgued** *ppl. a.* [UN-^{1} 2] B. JONS. **Unargume·ntative** *a.* [UN-^{1} 1] 1722, **-ly** *adv.*

Una·rm, *v.* ME. [UN-^{2} 2.] **1.** *trans.* To relieve (a person) of armour; to free or strip (oneself) of armour. Also *absol.* †**2.** To deprive of armour or arms; to disarm –1654.
1. Vnarme, vnarme, and doe not fight to day SHAKS. **2.** To u. his people of weapons, money, and all means, whereby thcy may resist his power RALEGH.

Una·rmed, *ppl. a.* ME. [UN-^{1} 2.] Having no armour or weapons. **b.** Of animals, plants, etc.: Not furnished with horns, teeth, prickles, thorns, etc. late ME. **c.** Of things: Not provided with anything that protects, assists, or strengthens 1693.

Una·rmoured *ppl. a.* [UN-^{1} 2] 1869. **Unarrai·gned** *ppl. a.* [UN-^{1} 2] 1595. **Unarra·nged** *ppl. a.* [UN-^{1} 2] BOSWELL. **Unarray·ed** *ppl. a.* [UN-^{1} 2] ME. **Unarre·sted** *ppl. a.* [UN-^{1} 2] late ME. **Unarri·ved** *ppl. a.* [UN-^{1} 2] 1626.

Una·rtful, *a.* 1669. [UN-^{1} 1.] **1.** Free from artifice; artless; not artificial. **2.** Lacking technical skill; inartistic 1675. Hence **Una·rtfully** *adv.*

Unarti·culated, *ppl. a.* 1700. [UN-^{1} 2.] **1.** Not articulated or distinct. **2.** Not jointed or fitted together 1861.
1. That u. language, which was before the written tongue LAMB. **2.** U. human bones 1894.

Unartifi·cial, *a.* 1591. [UN-^{1} 1.] **1.** Lacking skill; inartistic. Now *rare* or *Obs.* **2.** Natural; not artificial. Now *rare.* 1603.
1. My verse is vnartificiall, the stile rude, the phrase barbarous 1591. **2.** With an undisguised and u. goodness 1656. Hence **Unartifici·ally** *adv.*

Unarti·stic *a.* [UN-^{1} 1] 1854. **Unasce·nded** *ppl. a.* [UN-^{1} 2] SHELLEY. **Unascertai·ned** *ppl. a.* [UN-^{1} 2] 1628.

Unasha·med, *ppl. a.* 1600. [UN-^{1} 2.] Not ashamed. Hence **-ly, -ness.**

Una·sked, *ppl. a.* ME. [UN-^{1} 2.] **1.** Uninvited; without being asked. **2.** Not asked *for*; not made the subject of a request 1456.
2. He delivered his u. opinion SCOTT. An u.-for concession T. HARDY.

Una·spirated *ppl. a.* [UN-^{1} 2] 1793. **Unaspi·ring** *ppl. a.* [UN-^{1} 4] 1729, **-ness** 1681. **Unassai·lable** *a.* [UN-^{1} 1] 1596, **-ness, -ably** *adv.* **Unassai·led** *ppl. a.* [UN-^{1} 2] 1586. **Unassay·ed** *ppl. a.* [UN-^{1} 2] CHAUCER. **Unasse·rtive** *a.* [UN-^{1} 1] DICKENS. **Unassi·gned** *ppl. a.* [UN-^{1} 2] ME. **Unassi·milated** *ppl. a.* [UN-^{1} 2] 1748.

Unassi·sted, *ppl. a.* 1614. [UN-^{1} 2.] Not helped. **b.** *spec.* Of the eye or sight: Unaided, naked 1661.

Unassua·ged *ppl. a.* [UN-^{1} 2] 1654.

Unassu·ming, *ppl. a.* 1726. [UN-^{1} 4.] Free from self-assertion; unpretentious.
A very u. young woman DICKENS. The u. things that hold A silent station in this beauteous world WORDSW. Hence **Unassu·ming-ly** *adv.*, **-ness.**

Unassu·red, *ppl. a.* late ME. [UN-^{1} 2.] **1.** Not assured or safe; insecure. **2.** Not sure *of* something 1529. **3.** Not self-possessed; diffident 1627.
2. When men are by any accident u. they have slept, [dreams] seem to be reall Visions HOBBES.

Unato·nable, *a.* 1645. [UN-^{1} 1.] †**1.** Unaccordable. MILT. **2.** Irreconcilable 1683. **3.** That cannot be atoned for; inexpiable 1689.
1. Untunable or unattonable matrimony MILT.

Unatta·ched, *ppl. a.* (*sb.*) 1498. [UN-^{1} 2.] †**1.** Not taken into custody –1639. **2.** Not attached or united (*to* something) 1821. **3.** Not belonging to a particular body, institution, sphere of work, etc. **a.** Of military officers: Not attached to a particular regiment or company 1796. **b.** Of clergy: Not attached to a particular diocese or parish 1865. **c.** Of students: Not attached to any college. Also as *sb.*, an u. student. 1870. **4.** Not engaged or married 1874.

Unatta·ckable *a.* [UN-^{1} 1] 1805, **-ably** *adv.* **Unatta·cked** *ppl. a.* [UN-^{1} 2] 1663.

Unattai·nable, *a.* and *sb.* 1661. [UN-^{1} 1.] **A.** *adj.* That cannot be attained 1662. **B.** *sb.* **1.** An unattainable thing (*rare*) 1661. **2.** With *the*: That which is not attainable 1857. Hence **Unattai·nableness; -ably** *adv.*

Unattai·nted, *ppl. a.* 1592. [UN-^{1} 2.] **1.** Unstained; free from blemish. **2.** Not attainted in law 1794.
1. The u. Honour of English Knighthood MILTON.

Unatte·mpted *ppl. a* [UN-^{1} 2] 1548.

Unatte·nded, *ppl. a.* 1603. [UN-^{1} 2.] **1.** Not having attendants; unaccompanied. **b.** Of horses, vehicles, etc.: With no one in charge 1796. **2.** Not followed *by* or associated *with* some thing, circumstance, etc. 1687. **3.** Not attended *to*, disregarded 1729.

2. Night came, but u. with repose DRYDEN.

Unatte·nding *ppl. a.* [UN-[1] 4] MILT. **Unatte·sted** *ppl. a.* [UN-[1] 2] 1665. **Unatti·red** *ppl. a.* [UN-[1] 2] late ME. **Unattra·cted,** *ppl. a.* [UN-[1] 2] 1727. **Unattra·ctive** *a.* [UN-[1] 1] SHELLEY, **-ly** *adv.*, **-ness.**

‖**Unau** (yū·nǫ). 1774. [Brazilian of the island of Maranhão.] *Zool.* The S. Amer. two-toed sloth, *Cholopus didactylus.*

Unaugme·nted, *ppl. a.* 1555. [UN-[1] 2.] Not augmented or increased; *spec.* of Greek verbs.

Unauspi·cious [UN-[1] 1] –1768. **Unauthe·ntic** *a.* [UN-[1] 1] 1631. **Unauthe·nticated** *ppl. a.* [UN-[1] 2] 1787. **Unautho·ritative** *a.* [UN-[1] 1] 1644, **-ly** *adv.* **Unau·thorized** *ppl. a.* [UN-[1] 2] 1596.

Unavai·lable, *a.* 1549. [UN-[1] 1.] **1.** Of no avail; ineffectual. **2.** Not available; incapable of being used 1855.

1. U. lamentations 1850. Hence **Unavaila·bility.** **Unavai·lableness.** **Unavai·lably** *adv.*

Unavai·ling *ppl. a.* [UN-[1] 4] 1670, **-ly** *adv.* **Unave·nged** *ppl. a.* [UN-[1] 2] 1481. **Unave·rted** *ppl. a.* [UN-[1] 2] 1753.

‖**Una voce** (yū·ne[i] vō[u]·si). 1567. [L., 'with one voice'.] Unanimously.

Unavoi·dable *a.* [UN-[1] 1] 1577, **-ness, -ably** *adv.* **Unavoi·ded** *ppl. a.* [UN-[1] 2] 1565. **Unavow·ed** *ppl. a.* [UN-[1] 2] BURKE, **-ly** *adv.* **Unawa·kened** *ppl. a.* [UN-[1] 2] 1705, **-ness.**

Unaware (ɒnăwē[ə]·ɹ), *adv.* and *a.* 1592. [UN-[1] 1; see next.] **A.** *adv.* **1.** = next 1. **2.** = next 2. 1667. **3.** In phr. *at u.* = sense 1 and 2. 1598. **B.** *adj.* **1.** Not aware (*of*); not cognizant; ignorant 1704. **2.** Blind to consequences; reckless (*rare*) 1817.

A. 1. As one that u. Hath dropp'd a precious jewel SHAKS. **2.** Long have I sought for rest, and, u., Behold I find it! KEATS. **3.** A Serpent shoots his Sting at u. DRYDEN. **B. 2.** I grew desperate and u. SHELLEY. Hence **Unawa·reness.**

Unawares (ɒnăwē[ə]·ɹz), *adv.* 1535. [alt. of UNWARES (XII), var. of UNWARE (XII); see -S.] **1.** Without being aware, unconsciously, inadvertently. **b.** Without being noticed 1667. **c.** *Unawares to*, without the knowledge of, unperceived by 1548. **2.** Without warning; unexpectedly 1535. **3.** *At unawares* = sense 1, 1 b, 2.

1. I have u. run into this long account BERKELEY. **b.** Age steals upon Us u. PRIOR. **c.** U. to myself, I had moved onward RICHARDSON. **2.** The King.. came u. upon the Lady FREEMAN. Phr. *To take, catch.. u.*

Unaw·ed *ppl. a.* [UN-[1] 2] DRYDEN. **Una·zotized** *ppl. a.* [UN-[1] 2] 1828.

Unba·cked, *a.* 1592. [UN-[1] 2.] **1.** Of horses: Unmounted, untrained. **2.** Not backed or supported; not endorsed 1609. **b.** *Betting.* Having no backers 1883. **3.** Without a back or backing 1861.

Unba·g, *v.* 1611. [UN-[2] 3.] *trans.* To take or let (esp. a fox) out of a bag.

Unba·ked (ɒnbē[i]·kt), *ppl. a.* 1563. [UN-[1] 2.] **1.** Of tiles, etc.: Not baked in a kiln. **2.** Of food: Not prepared by baking 1577. †**3.** *fig.* Unfinished; immature –1635.

3. All the vnbak'd and dowy youth of a nation SHAKS.

Unba·lance *sb.* [UN-[1] 6] 1887. **Unba·lance** *v.* [UN-[2] 1] 1586.

Unba·lanced, *ppl. a.* 1650. [UN-[1] 2.] **1.** Of persons, the mind, judgement, etc.: Lacking equipoise; not balanced. **b.** Thrown out of balance; not balanced or equably poised 1732. **c.** Having no counterpoise; not offset *by* something 1818. **2.** Of an account: Not balanced 1828.

1. Interference with the old order was so far-reaching, that the minds of all were quite u. 1886. **b.** I was several times u., and on the very point of being hurled backward 1835. **c.** Valour u. by the observance of propriety 1879.

Unba·le *v.* [UN-[2] 3] 1752. **Unba·llast** *v.* [UN-[2] 2] 1684.

Unba·llasted, *ppl. a.* 1644. [UN-[1] 2.] **1.** Of vessels; Having no ballast 1657. **b.** *fig.* Not steadied by principles or solid qualities 1644. **2.** Of a railway line: Not filled in with ballast 1887.

1. b. To be tost and turmoild with their u. wits in fathomles and unquiet deeps of controversie MILTON.

Unba·ndage *v.* [UN-[2] 2] 1840. **Unba·nded** *ppl. a.* [UN-[1] 2] 1570. **Unba·nished** *ppl. a.* [UN-[1] 2] 1533. **Unba·nk** *v.* [UN-[2] 2] 1842. **Unbapti·ze** *v.* [UN-[2] 1] 1611. **Unbapti·zed** *ppl. a.* [UN-[1] 2] late ME. **Unba·r** *v.* [UN-[2] 1, 5] late ME. **Unba·rbarize** *v.* [UN-[2] 4 c] 1648.

Unba·rbed, *ppl. a.*[1] 1565. [UN-[1] 2.] Unarmed; not caparisoned.

Unba·rbed, *ppl. a.*[2] 1844. [UN-[1] 3.] Not furnished with a barb or barbs.

Unba·rded, *ppl. a.* 1598. [UN-[1] 2.] = UNBARBED *ppl. a.*[1]

Unba·re *v.* [UN-[2] 7] 1530. **Unba·rked** *ppl. a.* [UN-[1] 2] 1839.

Unba·rred, *ppl. a.* 1550. [UN-[1] 2.] **1.** Of harbours: Not obstructed with a bar 1550. **2.** Not secured or blocked with a bar or bars 1603. **3.** *Law.* Not excluded 1818. **4.** Of music: Not divided into bars 1879.

Unba·rrel *v.* [UN-[2] 3] 1611. **Unbarrica·de** *v.* [UN-[2] 2] 1623. **Unba·shful** *a.* [UN-[1] 1] 1563, **-lly** *adv.* **Unba·stardized** *ppl. a.* [UN-[1] 2] H. WALPOLE.

Unba·ted, *ppl. a.* 1596. [UN-[1] 2.] **1.** Not abated, undiminished. *arch.* †**2.** Not bated or blunted –1815.

1. With u. zeal SCOTT. **2.** You may choose A Sword vnbaited, and in a passe of practice, Requit him for your Father SHAKS.

Unbe·, *v.*[1] *rare.* late ME. [UN-[1] 7.] *intr.* To be non-existent.

Unbe·, *v.*[2] 1624. [UN-[2] 2.] *trans.* To make non-existent.

God..could as easily..unbee them as conquer them 1646.

Unbea·rable, *a.* [UN-[1] 1.] 1449. Unendurable, intolerable. Hence **-ness, -ably** *adv.*

Unbea·rded, *a.* 1560. [UN-[1] 3.] **1.** Of persons: **a.** Having no beard. **b.** Not yet bearded, youthful. **2.** Of plants: Awnless 1688.

Unbea·ten, *ppl. a.* ME. [UN-[1] 2.] **1.** Not beaten or struck. **b.** Not pounded 1607. **2.** Not beaten or trodden down; unfrequented 1617. **3.** Undefeated 1757.

2. Some new u. passage to the sky SWIFT.

Unbeau·teous *a.* [UN-[1] 1] 1660. **Unbeau·tiful** *a.* [UN-[1] 1] 1495. **Unbeau·tify** *v.* [UN-[2] 4 c] 1570.

Unbeco·me, *v.* 1628. [UN-[1] 7.] *trans.* To be unbecoming to.

Unbeco·ming, *ppl. a.* 1598. [UN-[1] 4.] Not becoming; unsuitable; improper. **a.** Without const. **b.** Governing a sb. 1658. **c.** Const. *of.* 1741.

a. A grave irony which is not u. MACAULAY. **b.** Behaviour, so u. a Christian FIELDING. **c.** What was not u. of a child would be disgraceful to a youth CHESTERF. Hence **Unbeco·ming-ly** *adv.*, **-ness.**

Unbe·d *v.* [UN-[2] 3] 1611. **Unbe·dded** *ppl. a.* [UN-[1] 2] 1842. **Unbefi·tting** *ppl. a.* [UN-[1] 4] SHAKS., **-ly** *adv.*, **-ness.** **Unbefrie·nded** *ppl. a.* [UN-[1] 2] 1628. **Unbege·t** *v.* [UN-[2] 1] 1625. **Unbe·gged** *ppl. a.* [UN-[1] 2] 1579. **Unbegi·nning** *ppl. a.* [UN-[1] 4] 1591.

Unbego·tten, *ppl. a.* 1532. [UN-[1] 2.] **1.** Not yet begotten. **2.** Not begotten, self-existent 1561. Hence **Unbego·ttenly** *adv.*, **-ness.**

Unbegu·n, *ppl. a.* OE. [UN-[1] 2.] **1.** That had no beginning; ever existent. **2.** Not yet begun 1562.

1. The myhti god, which unbegunne Stant of himself GOWER.

Unbehe·ld *ppl. a.* [UN-[1] 2] MILT. **Unbeho·ldable** *a.* [UN-[1] 1] PUSEY.

Unbeho·lden, *ppl. a.* 1674. [UN-[1] 2.] **1.** Under no obligation (*to* a person). Now *dial.* **2.** Unseen *poet.* 1820.

2. A glow-worm golden..Scattering u. Its aëreal hue SHELLEY.

Unbeknow·n, *ppl. a.* 1636. [UN-[1] 2.] **1.** *advb.* or *absol.* *Unbeknown to*, without the knowledge of. **2.** Unknown 1824.

1. *ellipt.* My love rose up so early And stole out u. HOUSMAN.

Unbeknow·nst, *adv. vulgar* and *dial.* 1854. [f. prec.] = prec. 1.

Unbelie·f. ME. [UN-[1] 6.] Absence or lack of belief; disbelief; incredulity.

Unbelie·vable *a.* [UN-[1] 1] 1548, **-ness, -ably** *adv.* **Unbelie·ve** *v.*[1] [UN-[1] 7] 1547. **Unbelie·ve** *v.*[2] [UN-[2] 2] 1605. **Unbelie·ved** *ppl. a.* [UN-[1] 2] ME.

Unbelie·ver. 1526. [UN-[1] 6.] One who does not believe; *spec.* one who does not accept a particular (esp. the Christian) religious belief; an infidel. So **Unbelie·ving** *ppl. a.* [UN-[1] 4] late ME.

Unbelo·ved *ppl. a.* [UN-[1] 2] 1597. **Unbe·lt** *v.* [UN-[2] 2, 3] 1483. **Unbe·lted** *ppl. a.* [UN-[1] 2] BYRON.

Unbe·nd, *v.* ME. [UN-[2] 1, 5.] **1.** *trans.* To relax (a bow) from tension; to unstring. †**b.** *fig.* To slacken, weaken 1605. **2.** To give relaxation or rest to (the mind, etc.) 1594. **3.** *Naut.* To unfasten, untie (a cable, line, sail) 1627. **4.** To relax the tension or severity of (the brow, face, etc.) 1718. **5.** To straighten from a bent position 1663. **6.** *intr.* To free oneself from constraint, seriousness, or ceremony; to become genial or allow oneself to relax 1746. **b.** Of the features: To relax 1818. **7.** To become straight or less bent or curved 1815.

1. b. You doe vnbend your Noble strength, to thinke So braine-sickly of things SHAKS. **2.** The Mind never unbends itself so agreeably as in the Conversation of a well chosen Friend ADDISON. **6.** In private company though he never forgot his rank, he could u. 1869.

Unbe·nding, *ppl. a.* 1688. [UN-[1] 4.] **1.** Inflexible, unyielding, obstinate. **2.** Rigid; not bending or curving; *esp.* of persons, remaining erect, not stooping 1709. Hence **Unbe·nding-ly** *adv.*, **-ness.**

Unbe·neficed *ppl. a.* [UN-[1] 2] 1623. **Unbenefi·cial** *a.* [UN-[1] 1] 1626. **Unbe·nefited** *ppl. a.* [UN-[1] 2] POPE. **Unbeni·gn** *a.* [UN-[1] 1] CROMWELL, **-ly** *adv.* **Unbe·nt** *ppl. a.* [UN-[1] 2] 1483. **Unben·umb** *v.* [UN-[2] 1] 1598. **Unbequea·thed** *ppl. a.* [UN-[1] 2] 1483. **Unbere·ft** *ppl. a.* [UN-[1] 2] 1621.

Unbesee·m, *v.* 1657. [UN-[1] 7]. **1.** *trans.* To be unseemly for or discreditable to (a person). **2.** To fail in, fall short of 1812.

2. Nor u. the promise of thy spring BYRON.

Unbesee·ming *a.* [UN-[1] 4] 1583, **-ly** *adv.*, **-ness.** **Unbesou·ght** *ppl. a.* [UN-[1] 2] MILT. †**Unbespea·k** *v.* [UN-[2] 1] –1743. **Unbespo·ken** *ppl. a.* [UN-[1] 2] 1681. **Unbestow·ed** *ppl. a.* [UN-[1] 2] 1534.

Unbethou·ght, *ppl. a.* 1558. [UN-[1] 2.] **1.** Unpremeditated, unintentional. Also as *adv.* **2.** Unthought of, unrealized 1855.

Unbetray·ed *ppl. a.* [UN-[1] 2] 1595. **Unbetro·thed** *ppl. a.* [UN-[1] 2] 1577. **Unbe·tterable** *a.* [UN-[1] 1] 1806. **Unbe·ttered** *ppl. a.* [UN-[1] 2] 1628. **Unbewai·led** *ppl. a.* [UN-[1] 2] 1586. **Unbewi·ldered** *ppl. a.* [UN-[1] 2] WORDSW. **Unbewi·tch** *v.* [UN-[2] 1] 1584. **Unbi·as** *v.* [UN-[2] 1] SWIFT.

Unbias(s)ed (ɒnbəi·ăst), *a.* 1607. [UN-[1] 2.] **1.** Of bowls, etc.: Having no bias. **2.** *fig.* Impartial, not prejudiced; not unduly influenced *by* something 1647.

2. All..which a man without authority can give,—his u. opinion BURKE. U. by mob clamour BROUGHAM. Hence **Unbi·as(s)ed-ly** *adv.*, **-ness.**

Unbi·blical *a.* [UN-[1] 1] PUSEY. **Unbi·d** *ppl. a.* (*arch.*) [UN-[1] 2] late ME. **Unbi·ddable** *a.* [UN-[1] 1] 1825.

Unbi·dden, *ppl. a.* OE. [UN-[1] 2.] Not asked or invited; not commanded or directed.

An u. Crew of graceless guests DRYDEN. Adown his cheek A tear u. stole POPE.

Unbi·nd, *v.* [OE. *unbindan*, f. UN-[2] + BIND *v.*] **1.** *trans.* To free from a band, bond or tie. **b.** *transf.* To loosen, open up or out, set free, etc. 1577. **c.** To take the bandage off (a limb or wound) 1639. **2.** To set free from bonds; to restore to personal liberty in this way OE. **3.** To untie, undo (a bond, cord, etc.) OE. **b.** *fig.* To dissolve, undo, destroy ME.

3. Then let..death u. my chain 1843. **b.** No force, no fortune, shall my vows u. DRYDEN.

Unbi·shop *v.* [UN-[2] 2, 4 b] 1598. **Unbi·shoped** *ppl. a.*[2] [UN-[2] 6] 1563.

Unbi·shoped, *ppl. a.*[1] OE. [UN-[1] 2.] **1.** Not having been confirmed. *arch.* **2.** Not consecrated as a bishop 1601.

Unbi·t, *v.* 1565. [UN-[2] 2 b.] *trans.* To free (a horse) from the bit. Also *absol.*

Unbi·tted, *ppl. a.* 1586. [UN-[1] 2.] Having no bit; unbridled, unrestrained.

fig. Our carnall Stings, or vnbitted Lusts SHAKS.

Unbla·cked *ppl. a.* [UN-[1] 2] 1836. **Unbla·ckened** *ppl. a.* [UN-[1] 2] 1864. **Unbla·m(e)able** *a.* [UN-[1] 1] 1531, **-ness, -ably** *adv.* **Unbla·med** *ppl. a.* [UN-[1] 2] late ME. **Unbla·nched** *ppl. a.* [UN-[1] 2] late ME. **Unbla·sted** *ppl. a.* [UN-[1] 2] 1589. **Unblea·ched** *a.* [UN-[1] 2] 1531.

Unble·mished, *ppl. a.* late ME. [UN-[1] 2.] **1.** Free from moral blemish or stain. **2.** Free from material blemish. Now *rare.* 1450.

1. His Spouse is chaste, vnblemisht with a spot QUARLES. All the authority which belongs to u. integrity MACAULAY. **2.** The religious houses only being spared, and left vnblemished HAKLUYT.

Unble·nched *ppl. a.* [UN-[1] 2] MILT. **Unble·nded** *ppl. a.* [UN-[1] 2] ME. **Unble·ss** *v.* [UN-[2] 1] SHAKS.

Unble·ssed, unble·st, *ppl. a.* ME. [UN-[1] 2.] **1.** Not formally blessed. **b.** Deprived of, excluded from, left without, a blessing or benediction 1590. **2.** Ill-fated, unfortunate, miserable ME. **3.** Unhallowed; evil, wicked. late ME. **4.** Not favoured or made happy *with* or *by* something 1743.

1. b. And there his corps, unbless'd, is hanging still DRYDEN. **2.** What matters, if unblest in love, How long or short my life will prove? PRIOR. **3.** Such resting found the sole Of unblest feet MILT. Hence **Unble·ssedness.**

Unbli·ghted *ppl. a.* [UN-[1] 2] COWPER. **Unbli·nd** *v.* [UN-[2] 1] 1590. **Unbli·nded** *ppl. a.* [UN-[1] 2] 1611. **Unbli·ndfold** *v.* [UN-[2] 2] late ME. **Unbli·nking** *a.* [UN-[1] 1], **-ly** *adv.* 1867. **Unbli·ssful** *a.* [UN-[1] 1] ME. †**Unbli·the** *a.* [UN-[1]] –1535. **Unblo·ck** *v.* [UN-[2] 1] 1611.

Unbloo·died, *ppl. a.* [UN-[1] 2.] Not stained with blood. SHAKS.

Unbloo·dy, *a.* 1544. [UN-[1] 1.] **1.** Not attended with (much or any) bloodshed. **2.** Not involving the shedding of blood 1548. **b.** Theol. *Unbloody sacrifice, offering, sacrament,* the Eucharist 1548. **3.** Not stained with blood 1590. **4.** Not bloodthirsty 1665.

3. *U. grave,* that of one who has not died by bloodshed. Hence **Unbloo·dily** *adv.*

Unblo·tted *ppl. a.* [UN-[1] 2] 1548.

Unblow·n, *ppl. a.*[1] 1638. [UN-[1] 1.] **1.** Not blown by the wind. Also with advs. *away, out.* **2.** Not sounded 1815.

2. The lances unlifted, the trumpet u. BYRON.

Unblow·n, *ppl. a.*[2] 1587. [UN-[1] 2.] Of flowers; Not yet open; in the bud.

fig. Ah my tender babes! My vnblowne flowers SHAKS.

Unblu·nted *ppl. a.* [UN-[1] 2] 1656. **Unblu·rred** *ppl. a.* [UN-[1] 2] 1809.

Unblu·shing, *ppl. a.* 1595. [UN-[1] 4.] **1.** Not blushing. **2.** Shameless, unabashed 1736.

2. Strenuous and u. servility MACAULAY. Hence **Unblu·shing-ly** *adv.*, **-ness.**

Unboa·stful *a.* [UN-[1] 1] 1727. **Unboa·sting** *ppl. a.* [UN-[1] 4] 1802.

Unbo·died, *a.* and *ppl. a.* 1513. [UN-[1] 3.] **1.** Separated from the body; ghostly; not invested with a body. **2.** Incorporeal; not in material form 1606. **3.** Not having a definite form 1630.

1. Lastly his vn-bodied Soule departs 1589. **2.** Art naked, abstract and u. CUDWORTH. Like an u. joy SHELLEY. **3.** I skirmish with u. air DAVENANT.

Unbo·dily *a.* (now *rare*) [UN-[1] 1] late ME. **Unbo·dy** *v.* [UN-[2] 5] 1548. **Unboi·led** *ppl. a.* [UN-[1] 2] 1611. †**Unbo·ld** *a.* [UN-[1] 1] –1825.

Unbo·lt, *v.* 1470. [UN-[2] 5 and 1.] **1.** *intr.* Of a door: To have the bolt withdrawn. **2.** *trans.* To unfasten by withdrawing a bolt or bolts 1598.

Unbo·lted, *ppl. a.*[1] 1580. [UN-[1] 2, UN-[2] 6.] **1.** Not fastened with a bolt; released by withdrawal of a bolt. **2.** Not held together with a bolt or bolts 1793.

Unbo·lted, *ppl. a.*[2] 1598. [UN-[1] 2. See BOLT *v.*[1]] Not sifted.

Unbo·ne *v.* [UN-[2] 2 b] 1570. **Unbo·ned** *ppl. a.* [UN-[1] 2] 1611.

Unbo·nnet, *v.* 1810. [UN-[2] 2, 5.] **1.** *intr.* To remove the bonnet. **b.** *esp.* To do this as a mark of respect. Also *refl.* 1821. **2.** *trans.* To remove the bonnet from 1828.

1. b. Rise, u. yourself, and be silent SCOTT.

Unbo·nneted, *ppl. a.* 1604. [UN-[1] 2.] Not wearing a bonnet; having the head uncovered; *spec.* as a mark of respect. **b.** Of the head: Not covered by a bonnet 1820.

Unboo·ked, *ppl. a.* 1586. [UN-[1] 2.] **a.** Not registered. **b.** Not pre-engaged by booking. **c.** Not book-learned.

c. The u. freshness of the Scottish peasant 1870.

Unboo·kish *a.* [UN-[1] 1] SHAKS. **Unboo·t** *v.* [UN-[2] 5] 1598. **Unbo·red** *ppl. a.* [UN-[1] 2] 1598. **Unbo·rn** *ppl. a.* [UN-[1] 2] OE. **Unbo·rrowed** *ppl. a.* [UN-[1] 2] 1638.

Unbo·som, *v.* 1588. [UN-[2] 3.] **1.** *trans.* To let out from the heart; to give vent to; to reveal, make no further secret of. **b.** *refl.* and *absol.* To disclose one's thoughts, secrets, etc. 1628. **2.** To display to the view 1610.

1. I have longed a great while to u. my sorrows DE FOE. **b.** To u. himself of his great secret THACKERAY. The last person to whom he could u. MEREDITH. **2.** Fair-handed Spring unbosoms every grace THOMSON.

†**Unbo·ttom,** *v.* 1598. [UN-[2] 2.] *trans.* To deprive of a bottom or foundation; to unsettle. Hence **Unbo·ttomed** *ppl. a.*[2]

Unbo·ttomed, *ppl. a.*[1] 1615. [UN-[1] 2.] **1.** Bottomless; unfathomable. **2.** Unfounded; not founded *on* or *in* something 1640.

2. Whether there be no Love u. on Self-love? 1675.

Unbou·ght *ppl. a.* [UN-[1] 2] OE.

Unbou·nd, *ppl. a.* OE. [UN-[1] 2.] **1.** Not bound or tied up; loose. **b.** Not under obligation; unconstrained. late ME. **2.** Not secured with a band or border of some strong material 1531. **3.** Of books: Having no binding 1541.

1. b. To constrain Thy u. spirit into bonds again COWPER.

Unbou·nded, *ppl. a.* 1598. [UN-[1] 2.] **1.** Not bounded or limited in extent or amount. **2.** Recognizing no limit; passing all bounds; uncontrolled 1608.

1. The wild u. hills we ranged SCOTT. Her..u. courage and energy 1897. **2.** U. expectations 1854. Hence **Unbou·nded-ly** *adv.*, **-ness.**

Unbow·elled *a.* [UN-[1] 3] 1592. **Unbo·x** *v.* [UN-[2] 3] 1611.

Unbra·ce, *v.* late ME. [UN-[2] 1.] **1.** *trans.* or *refl.* To free from bands or braces forming part of clothing or armour. Also *absol. arch.* **2.** *trans.* To undo, loosen (a band, grasp, etc.). *arch.* 1475. **b.** To loosen or detach by the undoing or removal of braces or bands. *arch.* 1593. **c.** To relax the tension of (a drum) 1593. †**3.** To carve (a mallard or duck) –1804. **4.** To make slack, enfeeble 1711. **b.** *absol.* To become slack, lose firmness 1693.

4. Laughter..slackens and unbraces the Mind ADDISON. So **Unbra·ced** *ppl. a.* 1510. [UN-[1] 2.]

Unbra·nched *a.* [UN-[1] 3] 1665. **Unbra·nching** *a.* [UN-[1] 4] GOLDSM. **Unbra·nded** *ppl. a.* [UN-[1] 2] MILT. **Unbrea·kable** *a.* [UN-[1] 1] 1480. **Unbrea·kfasted** *a.* [UN-[1] 3] 1646. **Unbrea·thable** *a.* [UN-[1] 1] 1846.

Unbrea·thed, *a.* 1590. [UN-[1] 2, 2 b, 3.] †**1.** Having had no training; unpractised –1644. **2. a.** Not having recovered breath 1692. **b.** Not out of breath 1901. **3.** Not breathed 1884. **b.** Not breathed *upon* 1817. **4.** Not uttered or whispered 1827.

1. A fugitive and cloister'd vertue, unexercis'd and unbreath'd MILTON.

Unbre·d, *ppl. a.* 1600. [UN-[1] 2.] †**1.** Unborn. SHAKS. **2.** Deficient in breeding; unmannerly, ill-bred 1622. **3.** Not trained *in* or *to* some occupation 1683.

Unbree·ch, *v.* 1548. [UN-[2] 2.] **1.** *trans.* To remove the breech or breeching from (a cannon). **2.** To strip of breeches 1598.

Unbree·ched, *a.* 1611. [UN-[1] 3.] Not (yet) dressed in breeches.

Unbrew·ed *ppl. a.* [UN-[1] 2] 1725. **Unbri·bable** *a.* [UN-[1] 1] 1661. **Unbri·bed** *ppl. a.* [UN-[1] 2] 1607. **Unbri·ck** *v.* [UN-[2] 2] 1598. **Unbri·cked** *ppl. a.* [UN-[1] 2] 1814. **Unbri·dged** *ppl. a.* [UN-[1] 2] WORDSW. **Unbri·dle** *v.* [UN-[2] 2 b] late ME.

Unbri·dled, *ppl. a.* late ME. [UN-[1] 2.] **1.** *fig.* Ungoverned; subject to no restraint; headstrong. **2.** Not furnished with a bridle 1553.

1. The unbridl'd impudence of this loose rayler MILT. Lands deluged by u. floods WORDSW. The u. rule of the multitude 1888. Hence **Unbri·dled-ly** *adv.*, **-ness** (*rare*).

Unbrie·fed *ppl. a.* [UN-[1] 2] 1889. **Un-Bri·tish** *a.* [UN-[1] 1] 1746. **Unbroa·ched** *ppl. a.* [UN-[1] 2] 1689.

Unbro·ken, *ppl. a.* ME. [UN-[1] 2.] **1.** Not broken or infringed; unviolated, inviolate. **2.** Not fractured; intact, whole 1495. **3.** Not humbled or subdued; not impaired 1513. **4.** Of horses, etc.: Not broken in; untrained 1538. **5.** Uninterrupted, continuous 1561. **b.** Const. *by.* 1743. **6.** Of ground: Not broken by ploughing or digging 1579. **7.** Of troops: Not thrown into disorder 1721.

1. Who first broke peace in Heav'n and Faith, till then Unbrok'n MILT. **2.** *fig.* My fortune which is u. RICHARDSON. **5.** It required an u. attention BURKE. **7.** To charge large masses of u. infantry 1898. So **Unbro·ke** *ppl. a.* **Unbro·ken-ly** *adv.*, **-ness.**

Unbro·ther *v.* [UN-[2] 4 b] 1634. **Unbro·therly** *a.* [UN-[1] 1] 1586. **Unbrou·ght** *ppl. a.* [UN-[1] 2, 2 b] TINDALE. **Unbrui·sed** *ppl. a.* [UN-[1] 2] 1440. **Unbru·shed** *ppl. a.* [UN-[1] 2] 1640.

Unbu·ckle, *v.* late ME. [UN-[2] 2 b.] **1.** *trans.* To undo the buckle of (a shoe, belt, etc.); to unfasten or set free in this way. **2.** *absol.* To undo the buckle or buckles of a belt, garment, etc. 1611. **b.** To unbend, become less stiff 1886.

1. A miser, who will not u. his purse to bestow a farthing SCOTT. **2.** U., Calladine, the day is hott DAVENANT. **b.** Even the captain..would sometimes u. a bit, and tell me of the fine countries he had visited STEVENSON.

Unbu·ckled *ppl. a.* [UN-[1] 2, UN-[2] 6] 1489. **Unbu·dded** *ppl. a.* [UN-[1] 2] KEATS. **Unbui·ld** *v.* [UN-[2] 1] SHAKS.

Unbui·lt, *ppl. a.* 1455. [UN-[1] 2, 2 b.] **1.** Not (yet) built. **b.** Not made by building 1882. **2.** Not built *on* or *upon*; not occupied with buildings 1631.

Unbu·lky *a.* [UN-[1] 1] 1678. **Unbu·ndle** *v.* [UN-[2] 1] 1606. **Unbu·ng** *v.* [UN-[2] 1] 1611.

Unbu·rden, unbu·rthen, *v.* 1538. [UN-[2] 2 b.] **1.** *trans.* To free from a burden. Chiefly *fig.*, to relieve (a person, the mind, etc.) by the removal or disclosure of something. Freq. const. *of.* **b.** *refl.* 1589. **2.** To cast off the burden of; esp. *fig.*, to disclose, reveal, confess 1593.

1. I may perhappes devise some way to be unburdened of my life 1568. We desire to unburthen the Consciences of men of needless..Ceremonies CHAS. I. **2.** In unburdening to a friend the sins and sorrows of one's life 1876. So **Unbu·rdened** *ppl. a.* [UN-[1] 2] 1548.

Unbu·ried *ppl. a.* [UN-[1] 2] OE. **Unbu·rnished** *ppl. a.* [UN-[1] 2] 1691.

Unbu·rnt, unbu·rned, *ppl. a.* ME. [UN-[1] 2.] **1.** Not consumed by fire. **2.** Not subjected to the action of fire: *esp.* of bricks, clay, lime, etc. 1626.

Unbu·rst *ppl. a.* [UN-[1] 2] 1782. **Unbu·ry** *v.* [UN-[2] 1] late ME. **Unbu·sied** *ppl. a.* (now *rare*) [UN-[1] 2] 1570. **Unbu·sinesslike** *a.* [UN-[1] 1] SCOTT. **Unbu·sy** *a.* [UN-[1] 1] 1731. **Unbu·ttered** *ppl. a.* [UN-[1] 2] 1584.

Unbu·tton, *v.* ME. [UN-[2] 1.] *trans.* To unfasten (buttons); to undo the buttons of (a garment). Also with personal obj. **b.** *absol.* To undo one's buttons; to loosen one's clothing 1605; *fig.* (*colloq.*) to be free and easy.

Thou art so fat-witted with drinking of olde Sacke, and vnbuttoning thee after Supper SHAKS. *fig.* Unbuttoning my bosom and showing him all the profitable secrets I had learnt GALT. **b.** Gluttony stuffs till it pants, and unbuttons and stuffs again 1760.

Unbu·ttoned *ppl. a.* [UN-[1] 2] 1563. **Unca·ge** *v.* [UN-[2] 3] 1620. **Unca·ged** *ppl. a.* [UN-[1] 2] POPE. **Unca·lcined** *ppl. a.* [UN-[1] 2] 1601. **Unca·lculated** *ppl. a.* [UN-[1] 2] 1828. **Unca·clulating** *a.* [UN-[1] 4] 1832, **-ly** *adv.* **Unca·lendared** *ppl. a.* [UN-[2] 6, UN-[1] 2] 1654.

Unca·lled, *ppl. a.* late ME. [UN-[1] 2, 2 b.] **1.** Not summoned; uninvited. **b.** *transf.* Of things 1586. **2.** Not called to salvation; not of the elect 1561. **3.** *Uncalled-for*, rarely *uncalled*: Not called for; not asked for or requested; unnecessary, intrusive 1610. **4.** Of capital: Not called up 1882.

1. b. Sudden tears u. spring up 1839. **2.** Either to conuert those that are vncalled, or to builde vp those which are conuerted 1619. **3.** This arbitrary, impolitic, and u.-for measure 1817.

Unca·lm *v.* [UN-[2] 4] 1655. **Unca·mbered** *ppl. a.* [UN-[1] 2] 1881. **Unca·ncelled** *ppl. a.* [UN-[1] 2] 1557. **Unca·ndid** *a.* [UN-[1] 1] 1639, **-ly** *adv.*, **-ness.** **Unca·ndour** [UN-[1] 6] 1879.

Uncanny (ʊnkæ·ni), *a.* orig. *Sc.* and *north.* 1596. [UN-[1] 1.] **1.** †Mischievous; careless; †unreliable. *dial.* **2.** Untrustworthy or inspiring uneasiness by reason of a supernatural element; uncomfortably strange or unfamiliar; mysteriously suggestive of evil or danger 1773. **3.** Dangerous, unsafe *dial.* 1785.

2. A slate quarry under the cliff—a scene of u. grandeur 1882. Hence **Unca·nnily** *adv.* **Unca·nniness.**

Uncano·nical, *a.* 1632. [UN-[1] 1.] **1.** Not in accordance with ecclesiastical canons. **b.** Unclerical; ill suited to the clergy 1747. **2.** Not included in the canon of Scripture 1835.

1. b. Begirt..with a most u. buff-belt SCOTT. Hence **Uncano·nically** *adv.*

Unca·nonize *v.* [UN-[2] 4 c] 1607. **Unca·nonized** *ppl. a.* [UN-[1] 2] 1548. **Unca·p** *v.* [UN-[2] 2] 1566. **Unca·pable** *a.* [UN-[1] 1] –1805. **Uncapa·cious** *a.* [UN-[1] 1] 1635. **Unca·pped** *ppl. a.* [UN-[1] 2] 1548. **Uncapsi·zable** *a.* [UN-[1] 1] 1883. **Unca·ptived** *ppl. a.* (*arch.*) [UN-[1] 2] 1601. **Unca·rdinal** *v.* [UN-[2] 4 b] 1642.

Unca·red-for, *a.* 1597. [UN-[1] 2 b.] Not looked after or tended; neglected.

Unca·reful, *a.* 1533. [UN-[1] 1.] **1.** Deficient in care; careless. **2.** Not taking thought *of* or *for* 1559. **3.** Free from care; untroubled 1643.

1. An vncarefull Magistrate 1604. **2.** Such [Gods] as are u. of us 1662. **3.** One of the..most u. interludes of my life HAWTHORNE. Hence **Unca·reful-ly** *adv.*, †**-ness.**

Unca·ring *ppl. a.* [UN-[1] 4] 1786. **Unca·rpeted** *a.* [UN-[1] 3] 1816. **Unca·rried** *ppl. a.* [UN-[1] 2]

1584. **Unca·rt** *v.* [UN-² 3] 1641. **Unca·rved** *a.* [UN-¹ 2] 1592.

Unca·se, *v.* 1575. [UN-² 2, 3.] **1.** *trans.* †**a.** To flay –1712. **b.** To strip, undress (a person). *arch.* 1576. **c.** *absol.* To put off a garment or garments. *arch.* 1588. **2.** To lay bare, expose, bring to light. *arch.* 1587. **3.** To take out of a case, sheath, etc. 1589.

1. a. Cambyses once uncased a corrupt judge, and made a cushion of his skin 1658. **c.** Do you not see Pompey is vncasing for the combat? SHAKS. **2.** His hypocrisie shall be uncased 1627.

Unca·shed *ppl. a.* [UN-¹ 2] 1896. **Unca·st** *ppl. a.* [UN-¹ 2] late ME. **Unca·stigated** *ppl. a.* [UN-¹ 2] 1657. **Unca·stle** *v.* [UN-² 3] 1611.

Unca·strated, *ppl. a.* 1725. [UN-¹ 2.] **1.** Not gelded. **2.** Of books, etc.: Not expurgated; unmutilated 1737.

Unca·talogued *ppl. a.* [UN-¹ 2] NEWMAN.

Unca·techized, *a.* 1619. [UN-¹ 2.] Not formally instructed or examined in religion.

Unca·tholic, *a.* and *sb.* 1601. [UN-¹ 1, 6.] **A.** *adj.* Not catholic or universal; also *spec.*, not Roman Catholic. **B.** *sb.* One who is not a Catholic 1865.

Uncau·ght *ppl. a.* [UN-¹ 2] ME. **Uncau·lked** *ppl. a.* [UN-¹ 2] 1748. **Uncau·sed** *ppl. a.* [UN-¹ 2] 1628. **Uncea·sing** *ppl. a.* [UN-¹ 4] late ME., **-ly** *adv.*, **-ness.** **Uncei·led** *ppl. a.* [UN-¹ 2] CRABBE. **Unce·lebrated** *ppl. a.* [UN-¹ 2] MILT. **Uncele·stial** *a.* [UN-¹ 1] 1661. **Unceme·nted** *ppl. a.* [UN-¹ 2] 1717. **Unce·nsored** *ppl. a.* [UN-¹ 2] 1890. **Uncenso·rious** *a.* [UN-¹ 1] 1711. **Unce·nsurable** *a.* [UN-¹ 1] 1643. **Unce·nsured** *ppl. a.* [UN-¹ 2] 1574. **Unce·ntre** *v.* [UN-² 3] 1625. **Unce·ntred** *ppl. a.* [UN-¹ 2] 1652.

U:nceremo·nious, *a.* 1598. [UN-¹ 1.] Characterized by lack of ceremony or formality; acting without ceremony. Hence **Unceremo·nious-ly** *adv.*, **-ness.**

Unce·rtain, *a.* ME. [UN-¹ 1.] **1.** Not fixed in point of time or occurrence; not determinate in amount, number, or extent. **2.** Not sure to happen; contingent ME. **b.** Liable to change or accident; mutable 1477. **3.** About which one cannot be certain or assured; not indubitable ME. **b.** Of doubtful issue or tendency. late ME. **4.** Not certainly known; doubtful, dubious ME. **b.** Ambiguous; of doubtful meaning. late ME. **c.** Unspecified; of doubtful identity 1617. **d.** Not clearly defined or outlined 1638. **5.** Not certain to remain in one state or condition; unsteady, variable, fitful; capricious 1591. **6.** Feeling no certainty; not assured *of* something. late ME. **b.** Const. *how, what, whether*, etc. 1526. **c.** Undecided; not directed to a definite end. late ME. So **Unce·rtainly** *adv.*

Unce·rtainty. late ME. [UN-¹ 6.] **1.** The quality of being uncertain in respect of duration, continuance, occurrence, etc. **b.** With *a* and *pl.* Something of which the occurrence, issue, etc. is uncertain 1619. **2.** The state of not being definitely known or perfectly clear; vagueness, doubtfulness. late ME. **b.** Something not definitely known or knowable; a doubtful point. late ME. **3.** The state or character of being uncertain in mind; hesitation, irresolution 1548.

2. Phr. (Law) *Bad* or *void for u.*

Uncerti·ficated *ppl. a.* [UN-¹ 2] DICKENS. **Unce·rtified** *ppl. a.* [UN-¹ 2] 1535. **Unchai·n** *v.* [UN-² 2] 1582. **Unchai·ned** *ppl. a.* [UN-¹ 2] 1660. **Uncha·llenged** *ppl. a.* [UN-¹ 2] 1639.

Uncha·ncy, *a.* Chiefly *Sc.* 1533. [UN-¹ 1.] **1.** Ill-omened, ill-fated, unfortunate. **b.** Inopportune, ill timed 1860. **2.** Formidable; not safe to meddle with 1786.

1. The lordis thocht that Johne was ane u. name to be ane king 1536. **2.** A stalwart u. customer, who will not be gainsaid 1833.

Uncha·ngeable *a.* [UN-¹ 1] ME., **-ness, -ably** *adv.* **Uncha·nged,** *ppl. a.* [UN-¹ 2] late ME. **Uncha·nging** *a.* [UN-¹ 4] SHAKS., **-ly** *adv.*, **-ness.** **Uncha·nnelled** (*ppl.*) *a.* [UN-¹ 2, 3] 1600. **Uncha·peroned** *ppl. a.* [UN-¹ 2] 1858.

Uncha·ractered, *ppl. a.* 1633. [UN-¹ 2.] **1.** *Phonetics.* Of a sound: Not represented by a letter or sign. **2.** Lacking moral character 1841.

Uncharacteri·stic *a.* [UN-¹ 1] 1753, **-ally** *adv.*

Uncha·rge, *v.* Now *rare.* ME. [UN-² 1.] †**1.** *trans.* To free from a burden –1430. **b.** To acquit of guilt. SHAKS. **2.** To unload (a vessel). *arch.* ME. **3.** To remove the charge from (a gun) 1687.

1. b. Euen his Mother shall vncharge the practice, And call it accident SHAKS.

Uncha·rged, *ppl. a.* 1475. [UN-¹ 2.] **1.** Not burdened (*with* something). **b.** Not formally accused 1900. **2.** Unassailed 1607. **3.** *Her.* Not furnished with a charge 1610. **4.** Not loaded with powder and shot 1719. **b.** Not charged with electricity 1815. **5.** Not subjected to a financial charge 1894.

Uncha·riot *v.* [UN-² 3] POPE. **Uncha·ritable** *a.* [UN-¹ 1] 1456, **-ness, -ably** *adv.* **Uncha·rity** [UN-¹ 6] 1548.

Uncha·rm, *v.* 1575. [UN-² 1.] **1.** *trans.* To deprive (a charm) of magical powers. **2.** To deliver from a spell or from enchantment. Also *absol.* 1621. **b.** To deprive of charm or fascination 1835.

2. That Harp, whose Charms uncharm'd the brest Of troubled Saul 1638.

Uncha·rmed *ppl. a.* [UN-¹ 2] SHAKS. **Uncha·rnel** *v.* [UN-² 3] 1805.

Uncha·rted, *ppl. a.* 1895. [UN-¹ 2.] Not marked on a chart or map.

Uncha·rtered, *ppl. a.* 1805. [UN-¹ 2.] **1.** *fig.* Not authorized as by a charter; irregular. **2.** Having no charter 1818.

1. Me this u. freedom tires WORDSW.

Uncha·ry *a.* [UN-¹ 1] SHAKS. **Uncha·ste** *a.* [UN-¹ 1] late ME., **-ly** *adv.*, **-ness.** **Uncha·stened** *ppl. a.* [UN-¹ 2] MILT. **Unchasti·sed** *ppl. a.* [UN-¹ 2] late ME. **Uncha·stity** [UN-¹ 6] late ME. **Unchea·ted** *ppl. a.* [UN-¹ 2] 1746. **Unche·cked** *ppl. a.* [UN-¹ 2] 1469. **Unchee·red** *ppl. a.* [UN-¹ 2]. WORDSW. **Unchee·rful** *a.* [UN-¹ 1] late ME., **-ly** *adv.*, **-ness.** **Unchee·ry** *a.* [UN-¹ 1] STERNE. **Unche·quered** *ppl. a.* [UN-¹ 2] 1796. **Unche·rished** *ppl. a.* [UN-¹ 2] late ME. **Unchew·ed** *ppl. a.* [UN-¹ 2] 1643. **Unchi·d** *ppl. a.* [UN-¹ 2] 1860. **Unchi·dden** *ppl. a.* [UN-¹ 2] 1472.

Unchi·ld, *v.* 1605. [UN-² 2, 4 b.] **1.** *trans.* To deprive of children, make childless. **2.** To deprive of the status of a child or of the qualities peculiar to childhood 1615. Hence **Unchi·lded** *ppl. a.*

Unchi·ldlike *a.* [UN-¹ 1] DICKENS. **Unchi·lled** *ppl. a.* [UN-¹ 2] 1794. **Unchi·pped** *ppl. a.* [UN-¹ 2] HERRICK. **Unchi·selled** *ppl. a.* [UN-¹ 2] 1772. **Unchi·valrous** *a.* [UN-¹ 1] 1846, **-ly** *adv.* **Uncho·ke** *v.* [UN-² 1] 1588. **Uncho·ked** *ppl. a.* [UN-¹ 2] 1833. **Uncho·sen** *ppl. a.* [UN-¹ 2] 1529.

Unchri·sten, *v.* 1598. [UN-² 1.] **1.** *trans.* To undo the christening of; to deprive of the baptismal name. †**2.** To deprive of the character or status of a Christian –1718.

Unchri·stened, *ppl. a.* ME. [UN-¹ 2.] **1.** Not converted to Christianity, unbaptized, pagan. **b.** Of children: Never or not yet christened 1725. **2.** Unnamed 1832.

1. The Moores..beyng infideles and vnchristened people HALL.

Unchri·stian, *a.* 1555. [UN-¹ 1, 6.] **1.** Not professing the Christian faith; devoid of Christian principles or feeling. **b.** Not Christian; of non-Christians 1816. **2.** Unbefitting a Christian; at variance with Christian principles 1581. **b.** *colloq.* Shocking to any decent person; outrageous 1630.

2. Disciples that obstinately continue in an u. life HOBBES. **b.** The unchristianest, beastliest liquor I ever tasted TRELAWNY.

†**Unchri·stian,** *v.* 1633. [UN-² 4 a.] *trans.* = UNCHRISTEN *v.* 2. –1712.

Unchristia·nity [UN-¹ 6] 1652. **Unchri·stianize** *v.* [UN-² 4 c] 1714. **Unchri·stianlike** *a.* [UN-¹ 1] 1610. **Unchri·stianly** *adv.* [UN-¹ 5] 1547. **Unchro·nicled** *ppl. a.* [UN-¹ 2] 1598.

Unchronolo·gical, *a.* 1763. [UN-¹ 1.] **1.** Not chronological; not in accordance with chronology; not chronologically arranged. **2.** Unskilled in chronology 1817. Hence **Unchronolo·gically** *adv.*

Unchu·rch, *v.* 1620. [UN-² 2, 3, 4 b.] **1.** *trans.* To deprive of church membership, excommunicate. **2.** To exclude (a church, communion, sect) from participation in the Church (or some branch of it); to divest of the character of a church; to deprive of the possession of a church 1633.

Unchu·rched, *ppl. a.* 1681. [UN-¹ 2, UN-² 6.] **1.** Excommunicated 1727. **b.** Deprived of the status of a church 1681. **2.** Having, belonging to, no church 1870. **3.** Of women: Not churched after childbirth 1727.

‖**Uncia** (ɒ·nʃ'ă). *Pl.* **-iæ** (i,ī). 1834. [L., a twelfth part (of a pound or foot). Cf. INCH, OUNCE.] A Roman copper coin, one-twelfth of the as in value.

Uncial (ɒ·nʃ'ăl), *a.* and *sb.* 1650. [– L. *uncialis*, f. UNCIA; see -AL¹. In sense 2 after late L. *unciales litteræ* (Jerome).] **A.** *adj.* **1.** Pertaining to, connected with, an inch or an ounce. **b.** Duodecimal; divided into twelve equal parts 1842. **2.** Of letters, writing: Having the large rounded forms (not joined to each other) used in early Latin and Greek manuscripts; also, more loosely, of large size, capital; hence written, cut, etc., in such characters 1712.

B. *sb.* **1.** An uncial letter; (loosely) a capital letter 1775. **b.** Uncial writing 1883. **2.** A manuscript written in uncial characters 1881. Hence **U·ncialize** *v. trans.* to convert into or write in u. characters. **U·ncially** *adv.*

Unciform (ɒ·nsifǭɹm), *a.* and *sb.* 1733. [– mod.L. *unciformis*, f. L. *uncus* hook; see -FORM.] *Anat.* **A.** *adj.* Hook-shaped; esp. *u. bone, process.* **B.** *sb.* The u. bone of the wrist 1840.

Uncinate (ɒ·nsinĕt), *a.* and *sb.* 1760. [– L. *uncinatus*, f. UNCINUS; see -ATE¹ and ².] *Anat., Bot., Zool.* **A.** *adj.* Hooked; having hooks. **B.** *sb.* An u. process 1891. So **U·ncinated** *ppl. a.* 1752.

‖**Uncinus** (ɒnsəi·nɒ̆s). *Pl.* **-ni** (-nəi). 1851. [L., f. *uncus* hook; see -INE¹.] *Zool.* A hook-shaped part or process; esp. one of the hook-like teeth of molluscs.

Unci·rcumcised, *ppl. a.* late ME. [UN-¹ 2.] **1.** Not circumcised. **b.** Not Hebrew, gentile. **2.** *fig.* Not spiritually chastened or purified. late ME. So **U:ncircumci·sion** 1526.

Unci·rcumscribed *ppl. a.* [UN-¹ 2] 1610. **Unci·rcumspect** *a.* [UN-¹ 1] 1502, **-ly** *adv.* **Uncircumspe·ction** [UN-¹ 6] 1598. **Uncircumsta·ntial** *a.* [UN-¹ 1] 1646. **Unci·ted** *ppl. a.* [UN-¹ 2] 1581.

Unci·vil, *a.* 1553. [UN-¹ 1.] **1.** Uncivilized; barbarous; unrefined. **2.** Not courteous, impolite; unmannerly 1591. **3.** Indecorous, improper 1586. **4.** Contrary to civil well-being 1597.

1. Bad and unciuill Husbandry 1632. Men cannot enjoy the rights of an u. and of a civil state together BURKE. **2.** Ruffian: let goe that rude vnciuill touch SHAKS. **3.** Her faire haire..so covered her nakedness, that no part of her body was u. to sight 1611. **4.** Our home-bred and inbred distractions and uncivill-civill warres 1642. Hence **Unci·villy** *adv.*

Uncivi·lity (now *rare*) [UN-¹ 6] 1598. **Unci·vilize** *v.* [UN-² 4 c] 1603. **Unci·vilized** *ppl. a.* [UN-¹ 2] 1607, **-ness.**

Unclad (ɒnklæ·d), arch. pa. t. and pa. pple. of UNCLOTHE, and partly of †*unclead* (cf. CLEAD *v.*) 1483.

Godiva..Unclad herself in haste TENNYSON.

Unclai·med *ppl. a.* [UN-¹ 2] SHAKS. **Uncla·mp** *v.* [UN-² 1] 1809. **Uncla·rified** *ppl. a.* [UN-¹ 2] 1591.

Uncla·sp, *v.* 1530. [UN-² 1, 5.] **1.** *trans.* To unfasten the clasp(s) of. †**b.** *fig.* To open up, display –1637. **2.** To loosen the grasp or hold of 1627. **b.** *intr.* To relax a grip or grasp 1608. **3.** *trans.* To release from a clasp or grip 1885.

1. b. In her bosome Ile unclaspe my heart SHAKS. **2. b.** I feel my feeble hands u. LONGF.

Uncla·sped *ppl. a.* [UN-¹ 2] 1609. **Uncla·ss** *v.* [UN-² 4 b] 1873. **Uncla·ssed** *ppl. a.* [UN-¹ 2] 1820. **Uncla·ssical** *a.* [UN-¹ 2] 1725, **-ally** *adv.* **Uncla·ssifiable** *a.* [UN-¹ 1] 1849. **Uncla·ssified** *ppl. a.* [UN-¹ 2] 1865.

Uncle (ɒ·ŋk'l), *sb.* ME. [– AFr. *uncle*, (O)Fr. *oncle* :– late L. *aunculus* uncle, for earlier *avunculus* maternal uncle. Superseded EME.] **1.** One's father's or mother's brother; also, an aunt's husband. **b.** *U.-in-law*, the husband of one's aunt 1561. **c.** *Welsh u.*, the first cousin of a parent 1747. **d.** *Dutch u*: in phr. *To talk to* (a person) *like a Dutch u.*, to give him advice in a kindly, heavy manner 1838. **2.** Used in addressing or designating one's uncle. late ME. **b.** *local* and *U.S.* Used as a form of address to an older or elderly man 1793. **c.** *Uncle Sam* (prob. a jocular expansion of *U.S.*) a personification of the United States of America 1813. **d.** Title of contributors to journals who write articles, etc. for young people, and of wireless broadcasters who entertain children 1880. **3.** *slang.* A pawnbroker: usu. with possessive 1756.

2. c. Uncle Sam is rather despotic as to the disposal of my time HAWTHORNE. Hence **U·ncle** *v. trans.* to address (a person) as u. SHAKS. **U·ncleship.**

Unclea·n, *a.* [OE. *unclǣne*; see UN-¹ 1.] **1.** Morally impure; unchaste; foul, obscene.

b. *U. spirit*, a devil, esp. regarded as possessing or inhabiting a person OE. **2.** Ceremonially impure; not to be used as food; not to be touched OE. **b.** Of fish: Out of season; in unwholesome condition 1861. **3.** Not physically clean; dirty, foul ME. **b.** Of the tongue: Furred 1800.

2. Meats by the Law u. MILTON. The Gentiles were no longer common or u. J. H. NEWMAN. Hence **Unclea·n-ly** *adv.*, **-ness.**

Uncleanly (ɒnkle·nli), *a.* [OE. *unclǣnlić*; see UN-¹ 1.] **1.** Morally or spiritually impure. **2.** Lacking physical cleanness; dirty. late ME.

2. Who is there so u...as to wash his feet in the water used by another? 1756.

Unclea·nsed *ppl. a.* [UN-¹ 2] OE. **Unclea·r** *a.* [UN-¹ 1] late ME., **-ly** *adv.*, **-ness.**

Unclea·red *ppl. a.* 1637. [UN-¹ 2.] **1.** Not cleared off or settled. **2.** Of land, etc.: Not cleared of trees 1772. **3.** Not freed from the imputation of guilt 1724. **4.** Not cleared *up*; not explained 1802. **5.** Of liquids: Not made clear 1837.

Uncle·nch *v.* [UN-² 1] ME. **Uncle·rical** *a.* [UN-¹ 1] 1762. **Uncle·rkly** *a.* [UN-¹ 1] 1875. **Uncle·ver** *a.* [UN-¹ 1] 1870, **-ly** *adv.*, **-ness.**

Unclew·, unclue·, *v.* 1607. [UN-² 1.] **1.** *trans.* To unwind, undo; *fig.* to ruin. **2.** To let down the clews of (a sail) 1855.

1. If I should pay you for 't as 'tis extold, It would vnclew me quite SHAKS. Dædalus himself The cheats and windings of the dome unclewed 1855.

Uncli·mbable *a.* [UN-¹ 1] 1533. **Uncli·mbed** *ppl. a.* [UN-¹ 2] 1800. **Uncli·nch** *v.* [UN-² 1] 1598. **Uncli·ng** *v.* (*rare*) [UN-² 1, 5] 1645. **Uncli·pped, -cli·pt** *ppl. a.* [UN-¹ 2] late ME.

Uncloa·k, *v.* 1598. [UN-² 2.] **1.** *trans.* To divest of a cloak. Usu. *refl.* or *absol.* **2.** *fig.* To expose, lay bare 1659. So **Uncloa·ked** *ppl. a.* 1540.

Unclo·g *v.* [UN-² 2 b] 1607. **Unclo·gged** *ppl. a.* [UN-¹ 2] 1563. **Uncloi·ster** *v.* [UN-² 3] 1611. **Uncloi·stered** *ppl. a.* [UN-¹ 2] 1627.

Unclo·se, *v.* late ME. [UN-² 1, 5.] **1.** *trans.* To cause to open. **b.** *fig.* To disclose, reveal. late ME. **2.** *intr.* To become open. late ME.

1. Unwilling I my lips u. GRAY. **b.** The briddes song I shal to the vnclose 1446. **2.** Take roses that bigynneth forto vnclose 1440. Hence **Unclo·sing** *ppl. a.* that unclose(s).

Unclo·sed *ppl. a.* [UN-¹ 2] late ME.

Unclo·the, *v.* ME. [UN-² 2.] **1.** *trans.* To undress (a person); to divest of clothing. Also *refl.* **2.** To strip of leaves or vegetation 1547. **3.** To remove a cloth or cloths from 1607.

1. *fig.* The Seleusians affirmed that He unclothed himself of His Humanity 1671. So **Unclo·thed** *ppl. a.*

Unclou·d, *v.* 1594. [UN-² 2 b.] **1.** *trans.* To free from clouds 1598. **2.** *fig.* To free from gloom or obscurity 1594. **3.** *absol.* To become clear 1874.

Unclou·ded *ppl. a.* [UN-¹ 2] 1595. **Unclo·ven** *ppl. a.* [UN-¹ 2] 1620. **Uncloy·ed** *ppl. a.* [UN-¹ 2] 1562. **Uncloy·ing** *ppl. a.* [UN-¹ 4] 1768. **Unclu·bbable** *a.* [UN-¹ 1] JOHNSON. **Unclu·tch** *v.* [UN-² 1] 1667.

Unco (ɒ·ŋkŏ), *a.*, *adv.*, and *sb.* *Sc.* and *n. dial.* late ME. [Clipped f. UNCOUTH *a.*] **A.** *adj.* **1.** Unknown, strange; unusual. **b.** Weird, uncanny 1828. **2.** Notable, great 1724.

1. Taken with an uncow disease, like unto convulsion fits 1683. It was an u. thing to bid a mother leave her ain house SCOTT. **b.** It was an u. place by night STEVENSON. **2.** She thinks an u. heep o' Mr. Ochtertyre 1869.

B. *adv.* Extremely, very 1724. **b.** *The u. guid*, rigidly moral and religious people 1786.

Whyles twalpennie-worth o' nappy Can mak the bodies u. happy BURNS.

C. *sb.* **1.** A strange thing or tale; a piece of news. Usu. *pl.* 1785. **2.** A stranger 1800.

1. Each tells the uncos that he sees or hears BURNS.

Uncoa·gulated *ppl. a.* [UN-¹ 2] 1770. **Uncoa·ted** *ppl. a.* [UN-¹ 2] 1663. **Unco·ck** *v.* [UN-² 1] 1598. **Unco·cked** *ppl. a.* [UN-¹ 2] 1721. **Unco·dified** *ppl. a.* [UN-¹ 2] 1867. **Uncoe·rced** *ppl. a.* [UN-¹ 2] 1791. **Unco·ffined** *ppl. a.* [UN-¹ 2] 1648. **Unco·gnizable** *a.* [UN-¹ 1] 1720. **Uncogno·scible** *a.* [UN-¹ 1] 1810. **Uncoi·f** *v.* (*arch.*) [UN-² 1] 1598. **Uncoi·fed** *ppl. a.* (*arch.*) [UN-¹ 2] 1611. **Uncoi·l** *v.* [UN-² 1] 1713. **Uncoi·ned** *ppl. a.* [UN-¹ 2] late ME. **Uncolla·ted** *ppl. a.* [UN-¹ 2] 1787. **Uncolle·cted** *ppl. a.* [UN-¹ 2] 1611. **Uncollo·quial** *a.* [UN-¹ 1] 1840.

Unco·loured, *ppl. a.* 1538. [UN-¹ 2.] **1.** Having no colour. **2.** Not invested with any specious or deceptive appearance or quality; not coloured *by* something 1585.

2. In naked simplicitie, in trueth vncoloured 1585.

Unco·mbated *ppl. a.* [UN-¹ 2] LOVELACE. **Unco·mbed** *ppl. a.* [UN-¹ 2] 1561. **Uncombi·ne** *v.* [UN-² 1] 1595. **Uncombi·ned** *ppl. a.* [UN-¹ 2] 1611. **Uncombi·ning** *ppl. a.* [UN-¹ 4] MILT.

Uncome-at-able (ɒnkɒmæ·tăb'l), *a.* 1694. [UN-¹ 1.] Unattainable; inaccessible.

My Honour is infallible and uncomatible CONGREVE.

Unco·mely, *a.* ME. [UN-¹ 1.] **1.** Offending against propriety or decency; unbecoming, not seemly. Now *rare.* **2.** Not pleasing to look upon; lacking beauty. late ME.

1. All such reasons are u. and unchristian to be objected 1622. **2.** Your aspect is Dusky, but not u. BYRON. Hence **Unco·meliness.**

Unco·mfortable, *a.* 1592. [UN-¹ 1.] **1.** Causing or involving discomfort or uneasiness; deficient in provision for comfort; comfortless. †**2.** Inconsolable –1667. **3.** Feeling discomfort 1796.

1. These five troublesome, u. years 1653. Most u. ruffians to meet in an unfriendly way 1873. Hence **Unco·mfortableness. Unco·mfortably** *adv.*

Unco·mforted *ppl. a.* [UN-¹ 2] 1583. **Uncomma·nded** *ppl. a.* [UN-¹ 2] late ME. **Uncomme·ndable** *a.* [UN-¹ 1] 1509, **-ably** *adv.* **Uncomme·nded** *ppl. a.* [UN-¹ 2] 1570. **Uncomme·rcial** *a.* [UN-¹ 1] 1768. **Uncommi·ssioned** *ppl. a.* [UN-¹ 2] 1659.

Uncommi·tted, *ppl. a.* late ME. [UN-¹ 2.] **1.** Not entrusted to an agent. **2.** Not committed or perpetrated 1598. **3.** Not referred to a committee 1807. **4.** Not committed to a course of action 1814.

Unco·mmon, *a.* 1548. [UN-¹ 1.] †**1.** Not held in common. UDALL. **2.** Of rare occurrence, unusual 1611. **3.** Unusual in amount, degree, or quality; remarkable, exceptional 1700. **4.** As *adv.* Very, remarkably. *colloq.* or *dial.* 1784. Hence **Unco·mmon-ly** *adv.*, **-ness.**

Uncommu·nicable *a.* [UN-¹ 1] late ME., **-ably** *adv.* **Uncommu·nicated** *ppl. a.* [UN-¹ 2] 1597. **Uncommu·nicating** *ppl. a.* [UN-¹ 4] 1650. **Uncommu·nicative** *a.* [UN-¹ 1] 1691, **-ness. Uncompa·cted** *ppl. a.* [UN-¹ 2] 1661.

Unco·mpanied, *ppl. a. arch.* 1547. [UN-¹ 2.] Unaccompanied.

Uncompa·nionable *a.* [UN-¹ 1] 1748. **Uncompa·nioned** *ppl. a.* [UN-¹ 2] 1608. **Unco·mpassed** *a.* [UN-¹ 3] 1827, *ppl. a.* [UN-¹ 2] 1577. **Uncompa·ssionate** *a.* [UN-¹ 1] SHAKS., **-ly** *adv.*, **-ness. Uncompe·lled** *ppl. a.* [UN-¹ 2] 1470. **Unco·mpensated** *ppl. a.* [UN-¹ 2] BURKE. **Uncomplai·ning** *ppl. a.* [UN-¹ 4] 1744, **-ly** *adv.*, **-ness. Unco·mplaisant** *a.* [UN-¹ 1] 1693. **Uncomple·ted** *ppl. a.* [UN-¹ 2] 1513. **Uncompli·ant** *a.* [UN-¹ 1] 1659. **Unco·mplicated** *ppl. a.* [UN-¹ 2] 1792. **Uncomplime·ntary** *a.* [UN-¹ 1] 1846. **Uncomply·ing** *ppl. a.* [UN-¹ 4] MILT.

Uncompo·sed, *ppl. a.* 1570. [UN-¹ 2.] **1.** Not composite; single. Now *rare.* **2.** Not put together in proper form 1598. **3.** Not reduced to an orderly or tranquil state; disordered, excited 1601. **b.** Unregulated, disorderly 1631. **4.** Not brought into a state of concord 1650.

2. In playne and vncomposed wordes 1610. **3. b.** The u. gestures of the drunkard 1649. **4.** No jars undecided, no differences u. 1651.

Uncompou·nded *ppl. a.* [UN-¹ 2] 1587, **-ly** *adv.*, **-ness. Uncomprehe·nded** *ppl. a.* [UN-¹ 2] 1598. **Uncomprehe·nding** *ppl. a.* [UN-¹ 4] 1838, **-ly** *adv.*

U:ncomprehe·nsive, *a.* 1606. [UN-¹ 1.] †**1.** Incomprehensible. SHAKS. †**2.** Lacking in comprehension –1667. **3.** Not comprehensive or inclusive 1862.

Unco·mpromising, *ppl. a.* 1828. [UN-¹ 4.] Not willing or seeking to compromise; unyielding, inflexible; downright; stubborn.

The most honest, fearless and u. republican of his time MACAULAY. An u. square house 1889. Hence **Unco·mpromising-ly** *adv.*, **-ness.**

Unconcea·lable *a.* [UN-¹ 1] WORDSW. **Unconcea·led** *ppl. a.* [UN-¹ 2] 1839. **Unconcei·vable** *a.* (now *rare*) [UN-¹ 1] 1611, **-ably** *adv.* **Unconcei·ved** *ppl. a.* [UN-¹ 2] late ME.

Unconcei·ving, *ppl. a.* Now *rare.* 1593. [UN-¹ 4.] Slow-witted, dull.

Unconce·rn. 1711. [UN-¹ 6.] Lack of concern, anxiety, or solicitude; indifference, equanimity.

Doing all things with a graceful U. STEELE.

Unconce·rned, *ppl. a.* 1635. [UN-¹ 2.] **1.** Devoid of concern or interest; unmoved, indifferent. **2.** Not affected by concern or anxiety; undisturbed 1660. **3.** Indifferent between two parties; impartial 1664. **4.** Not concerned or involved, having no part, *in* something 1647. Hence **Unconce·rned-ly** *adv.*, **-ness.**

Unconce·rning, *ppl. a.* Now *rare.* 1612. [UN-¹ 4.] Of no concern to one; immaterial, irrelevant. †**b.** Const. *to* or with obj. –1667.

Idly casting her eyes as upon some u. pageant LAMB. **b.** A Subject so u. my own quality 1647.

Unconce·rnment [UN-¹ 6] 1660. **Unconce·rted** *ppl. a.* [UN-¹ 2] 1594. **Unconclu·ded** *ppl. a.* [UN-¹ 2] 1564. **Unconco·cted** *ppl. a.* [UN-¹ 2] 1611. **Unconde·mned** *ppl. a.* [UN-¹ 2] 1526. **Unconde·nsed** *ppl. a.* [UN-¹ 2] 1711.

Uncondi·tional, *a.* 1666. [UN-¹ 1.] Not limited by or subject to conditions or stipulations; absolute. Hence **Uncondi·tional-ly** *adv.*, **-ness.**

Uncondi·tioned, *ppl. a.* 1631. [UN-¹ 2.] **1.** = prec. **2.** Not dependent upon, or determined by, an antecedent condition 1829. **3.** *absol.* That which is not subject to the conditions of finite existence and cognition 1829.

2. I have termed this..group of reflexes *conditioned reflexes* to distinguish them from the inborn or *u. reflexes* 1927.

Unconfe·ssed, *ppl. a.* 1500. [UN-¹ 2.] **1.** Not confessed or avowed. **b.** Of persons: Not self-avowed 1742. **2.** Not having confessed; unshriven 1607.

1. It was love mutual—u., but ardent 1863. **b.** Like princes unconfest in foreign courts YOUNG.

Unco·nfident *a.* [UN-¹ 1] 1652. **Unconfide·ntial** *a.* [UN-¹ 1] 1772. **Unconfi·nable** *a.* [UN-¹ 1] SHAKS. **Unconfi·ne** *v.* [UN-² 2 b] 1651. **Unconfi·ned** *ppl. a.* [UN-¹ 2] 1607, **-ly** *adv.*, **-ness. Unconfi·rmed** *ppl. a.* [UN-¹ 2] 1565.

†**Unconfo·rm,** *a.* 1653. [UN-¹ 1.] **1.** Not corresponding *to* –1667. **2.** Nonconformist –1676.

1. He sees, Not u. to other shining Globes, Earth MILT.

Unconfo·rmable, *a.* 1594. [UN-¹ 1.] **1.** Not conformable or correspondent *to* something. **2.** *spec.* Not conforming to the usages of the Church of England, esp. as prescribed by the Act of Uniformity of 1662. 1611. **3.** *Geol.* Not having the same direction or plane of stratification 1813. So **Unconformabi·lity. Unconfo·rmably** *adv.* **Unconfo·rmed** *ppl. a.* †nonconformist; *Geol.* = sense 3. **Unconfo·rmity,** lack of conformity (*to* something); *Geol.* the fact of being u.

Unconfou·nded *ppl. a.* [UN-¹ 2] 1577. **Unconfro·nted** *ppl. a.* [UN-¹ 2] 1656. **Unconfu·sed** *ppl. a.* [UN-¹ 2] 1609, **-ly** *adv.* **Unconfu·table** *a.* [UN-¹ 1] 1643. **Unconfu·ted** *ppl. a.* [UN-¹ 2] 1600. **Uncongea·l** *v.* [UN-² 1] 1593. **Uncongea·led** *ppl. a.* [UN-¹ 2] 1646.

Uncongе·nial, *a.* 1788. [UN-¹ 1.] **1.** Not congenial or kindred; unsympathetic 1813. **2.** Unsuited to the nature of the thing under consideration 1788. **3.** Not to one's taste; unattractive or repellent *to* 1799.

2. In England,..where..its growth is impeded by an u. climate 1788. So **Uncongenia·lity.**

Unconje·cturable *a.* [UN-¹ 1] 1806. **Unco·njugal** *a.* [UN-¹ 1] MILT.

Unconne·cted, *ppl. a.* 1736. [UN-¹ 2.] **1.** Not connected or associated *with* something. **2.** Characterized by want of connection; not in order or sequence; disconnected 1762. **3.** Not having personal connections; socially unallied 1802. Hence **Unconne·cted-ly** *adv.*, **-ness.**

Unconne·ction [UN-¹ 6] 1756.

Unco·nquerable, *a.* 1598. [UN-¹ 1.] **1.** That cannot be overcome by conquest or force of arms; *fig.* of the mind, etc. **2.** Incapable of being brought under control 1642.

1. The u. Will MILT. **2.** The u. fertility of the soil GIBBON. His u. thirst of vengeance 1828.

Unco·nquered *ppl. a.* [UN-¹ 2] 1549. **Unconscie·ntious** *a.* [UN-¹ 1] BOSWELL, **-ly** *adv.*, **-ness.**

Unco·nscionable, *a.* (*adv.*) 1565. [UN-¹ 1.] **1.** Having no conscience; unscrupulous; monstrously extortionate, harsh, etc. 1570. **b.** As an intensive 1597. **2.** Of actions, etc.: Showing no regard for conscience; irreconcilable with what is right or reasonable 1565. **b.** Excessive, immoderate, inordinate 1586. **c.** As an intensive: Egregious, arrant 1593. **3.** As *adv.* Unconscionably 1596.

1. *absol.* The u. will know no other law, but their profit, their pleasure 1623. 2. b. He had been, he said, a most u. time dying MACAULAY. Hence **Unco·nscionably** *adv.* in an u. manner; to an u. extent or degree.

Unco·nscious, *a.* 1712. [UN-[1] 1.] **1.** Unaware (*of*); not realizing the existence, occurrence, etc., of something. **2.** Not endowed with the faculty of consciousness 1712. **b.** Temporarily insensible 1860. **c.** Not present to or affecting the conscious mind; of the mind: of which the workings are not present to consciousness 1909. Also as *sb.* in *the u.* 1920. **3.** Of qualities: Of which the possessor is unaware 1800. **4.** Done, used, etc., without conscious action 1820.

1. He was u. of exercising any ascendancy KINGLAKE. The u. model, i.e. one taken unawares with a detective camera 1889. 2. Brute, u. matter 1744. b. The patient..was u. 1890. 3. [She] rode..with an u. grace 1890. 4. It is wrong to punish an u. act 1866. Hence **Unco·nscious-ly** *adv.*, **-ness.**

Unco·nsecrate *v.* [UN-[2] 1] 1598. **Unco·nsecrate** *ppl. a.* [UN-[1] 2] 1529. **Unco·nsecrated** *ppl. a.* [UN-[1] 2] 1579. **Unconseque·ntial** *a.* [UN-[1] 1] 1769. **Unconsi·dered** *ppl. a.* [UN-[1] 2] 1587. **Unconsi·dering** *ppl. a.* (now *rare*) [UN-[1] 4] 1660. **Unconso·led** *ppl. a.* [UN-[1] 2] 1814. **Unconso·lidated** *ppl. a.* [UN-[1] 2] 1802. **Unco·nsonant** *a.* [UN-[1] 1] 1535. **Unconspi·cuous** *a.* [UN-[1] 1] 1802. †**Unco·nstant** *a.* [UN-[1] 1] –1757.

U:nconstitu·tional, *a.* 1765. [UN-[1] 1.] Infringing the political constitution; contrary to the recognized principles of the state. Hence **Unconstitu·tionally** *adv.* **Unconstitutiona·lity.**

Unconstrai·ned, *ppl. a.* late ME. [UN-[1] 2.] **1.** Not acting under constraint or compulsion. **2.** Not done, made, etc., under compulsion; spontaneous 1535. **3.** Free from constraint or embarrassment; natural 1704. **4.** Not subject to restraint; unrestrained 1796. Hence **Unconstrai·nedly** *adv.*

Unconstrai·nt [UN-[1] 6] 1711. **Unconsu·lted** *ppl. a.* [UN-[1] 2] 1567. **Unconsu·mable** *a.* [UN-[1] 1] 1571. **Unconsu·med** *ppl. a.* [UN-[1] 2] 1549.

Unconsu·ming, *ppl. a.* [UN-[1] 4.] 1628. **1.** That does not waste away or suffer diminution. **2.** Of fire, etc.: That does not consume 1836.

2. God of the u. fire, On Horeb seen of old KEBLE.

Unconsu·mmate 1609, **Unco·nsummated** 1813, *ppl. adjs.* [UN-[1] 2.] **Unconta·minate** 1675, **Unconta·minated** 1611, *ppl. adjs.* [UN-[1] 2.] **Unconte·mned** *ppl. a.* [UN-[1] 2] SHAKS. **Unco·ntemplated** *ppl. a.* [UN-[1] 2] 1709. **Unconte·nted** *ppl. a.* [UN-[1] 2] 1568. **Unconte·ntious** *a.* [UN-[1] 1] 1828. **Unconte·stable** *a.* [UN-[1] 1] 1681. **Unconte·sted** *ppl. a.* [UN-[1] 2] 1678, **-ly** *adv.* **Uncontra·cted** *ppl. a.* [UN-[1] 2] 1527. **Uncontradi·cted** *ppl. a.* [UN-[1] 2] 1606.

Uncontro·llable, *a.* 1577. [UN-[1] 1.] †**1.** Irrefutable –1738. **2.** Not subject to control from a higher authority; absolute 1593. **3.** That cannot be controlled or restrained 1648.

1. Those, who think it an u. maxim, that power is always safer lodged in many hands than in one SWIFT. 2. His sentence in matters of Law and Religion is u. 1630. 3. His..fierce and uncontroulable temper RICHARDSON. Hence **Uncontro·llableness. Uncontro·llably** *adv.*

Uncontro·lled, *ppl. a.* 1513. [UN-[1] 2.] **1.** Not restrained or subjected to control; ungoverned. †**2.** Not tested by comparison with facts –1584. †**3.** Undisputed –1731. Hence **Uncontro·lledly** *adv.*

Uncontrove·rsial *a.* [UN-[1] 1] 1861. **Uncontrove·rtible** *a.* [UN-[1] 1] 1664, **-bly** *adv.*

Unconve·ntional, *a.* 1839. [UN-[1] 1.] Disregarding or not according with convention. Hence **Unconventiona·lity. Unconve·ntional-ly** *adv.*, **-ness.**

Unconve·rsable, -ible, *a.* [UN-[1] 1] 1593. **Unco·nversant** *a.* [UN-[1] 1] 1674. **Unconve·rt** *v.* [UN-[2] 1] 1825. **Unconve·rted** *ppl. a.* [UN-[1] 2] 1648. **Unconve·rtible** *a.* [UN-[1] 1] 1695. **Unconvi·cted** *ppl. a.* [UN-[1] 2] 1675.

Unconvi·nced, *ppl. a.* 1643. [UN-[1] 2.] †**1.** Not disproved or refuted MILT. **2.** Not convinced or persuaded 1675.

Unconvi·ncing *ppl. a.* [UN-[1] 4] MILT., **-ly** *adv.* **Uncoo·ked** *ppl. a.* [UN-[1] 2] 1846. **Uncoo·led** *ppl. a.* [UN-[1] 2] 1513. **Unco-o·rdinated** *ppl. a.* [UN-[1] 2] 1892. **Unco·rd** *v.* [UN-[2] 2 b] late ME. **Unco·rdial** *a.* [UN-[1] 1] 1470, **-ly** *adv.* **Unco·rk** *v.* [UN-[2] 1] POPE. **Unco·rked** *ppl. a.* [UN-[1] 2] 1791. **Uncorre·cted** *ppl. a.* [UN-[1] 2] late ME. **Uncorru·pt** *a.* [UN-[1] 1] late ME., **-ly** *adv.*, **-ness. Uncorru·pted** *ppl. a.* [UN-[1] 2] late ME., **-ly** *adv.*, **-ness. Uncorru·ptible** *a.* (now *rare*) [UN-[1] 1] late ME. **Uncorru·ption** [UN-[1] 6] late ME. **Unco·rseted** *ppl. a.* [UN-[1] 2] 1856. **Unco·stly** *a.* [UN-[1] 1] 1638. **Uncou·nselled** *ppl. a.* [UN-[1] 2] late ME.

Uncou·ntable, *a.* 1582. [UN-[1] 1.] **1.** Too numerous to be counted. **b.** Of the pulse, etc.: Too rapid to be counted 1823. **2.** Beyond estimating; immense 1858.

Uncou·nted *ppl. a.* [UN-[1] 2] 1500. **Uncou·nterfeit** *a.* [UN-[1] 1] 1542. **Uncou·nterfeited** *ppl. a.* [UN-[1] 2] 1571.

Uncou·ple, *v.* ME. [UN-[2] 2 b.] **1.** *trans.* To release (dogs) from being fastened together in couples; to set free for the chase. **b.** *absol.* late ME. **2.** *trans.* To disconnect, detach, sever 1533.

1. b. My Loue shall heare the musicke of my hounds. Vncouple in the Westerne valley. SHAKS.

Uncou·rsed, *a.* 1825. [UN-[1] 3.] Of masonry: Not laid or set in courses.

Uncou·rted *ppl. a.* [UN-[1] 2] 1595. **Uncou·rteous** *a.* [UN-[1] 1] ME., **-ly** *adv.*, **-ness. Uncou·rtly** *a.* [UN-[1] 1] 1598, **-liness.**

Uncouth (ɒnkū·þ), *a.* and *sb.* [OE. *uncūþ*, f. UN-[1] + *cūþ* COUTH *a.* See also UNCO.] **A.** *adj.* †**1.** Unknown; uncertainly known –1650. **2.** With which one is not acquainted; unfamiliar, unaccustomed. *arch.* OE. **3.** Of an unknown or unfamiliar character; unusual, strange. Now *rare.* OE. †**4.** Unseemly, shocking, repellent –1797. **5.** Of places: Unfrequented, desolate, wild 1542. **b.** Of life, surroundings, etc.: Unattractive, unpleasant, comfortless. *Obs.* or *arch.* 1611. **6.** Of strange appearance; *spec.* awkward or clumsy in shape or bearing 1513. **b.** Uncultured; of rough or uneasy manners 1732. **c.** Of language, style, etc.: Awkward; pedantic; unpolished 1694.

2. The..stranger in an u. country 1632. 3. It is no u. thing To see fresh buildings from old ruines spring B. JONSON. 4. Þis unkouþe discencioun þat is bitwixe þes popes WYCLIF. 5. b. 'Tis so u. Living i' th' country, now I'm us'd to th' city MIDDLETON. 6. c. The scholastic and u. words homogeneity, proportionateness COLERIDGE.

B. *sb.* †**1.** A stranger. –late ME. **2.** *pl.* News. Now *dial.* 1529. Hence **Uncou·th-ly** *adv.*, **-ness.**

Unco·venanted, *ppl. a.* 1648. [UN-[1] 2.] **1.** Not promised or secured by (*spec.* a Divine) covenant. **2.** Not sanctioned by, not in accordance with, a covenant 1727. **3.** Not bound by a covenant 1790. **b.** Not having subscribed the Covenant 1818.

1. I will cast me on his free u. mercy 1806. 3. b. To disclaim all allegiance to an u. Sovereign MACAULAY.

Unco·ver, *v.* ME. [UN-[2] 1, 3, 5.] **1.** *trans. fig.* To disclose, make known. **2.** To lay open by removing some covering. late ME. **b.** To strip of clothing; to expose unclothed or unveiled 1530. **3.** To bare (the head) as a mark of respect or courtesy 1530. **b.** *absol.* 1627. **4.** *Mil.* To expose, leave unprotected (troops, positions, etc.), by the moving or manœuvring of men 1796.

3. b. The House of Commons which uncovered and stood up to receive him MACAULAY.

Unco·vered, *ppl. a.* late ME. [UN-[1] 2.] **1.** Not roofed or closed in overhead. **2.** Unclothed, naked. late ME. **b.** Bare-headed 1570. **c.** Of women: Unveiled 1585. **3.** Left open or exposed; not covered *by* or *with* something 1530. **4.** Nor protected or screened 1795. **5.** Not covered by insurance 1892.

Unco·veted *ppl. a.* [UN-[1] 2] 1760. **Unco·vetous** *a.* [UN-[1] 1] 1500. **Uncow·l** *v.* [UN-[2] 2] 1611. **Uncra·cked** *ppl. a.* [UN-[1] 2] 1581. **Uncra·mped** *ppl. a.* [UN-[1] 2] 1797. **Uncra·nnied** *ppl. a.* [UN-[1] 2] –1649. **Uncrea·te** *ppl. a.* [UN-[1] 2] 1548. **Uncrea·te** *v.* [UN-[2] 1] 1633.

Uncrea·ted, *ppl. a.* 1548. [UN-[1] 2.] **1.** Not brought into existence by a special act of creation; existent without being created. **2.** Not created 1607. Hence **Uncrea·tedness.**

†**Uncre·dible** *a.* [UN-[1] 1] –1680. **Uncre·ditable** *a.* [UN-[1] 1] 1643. **Uncre·dited** *ppl. a.* [UN-[1] 2] 1586. **Uncre·sted** *ppl. a.* [UN-[1] 2] 1611. **Uncri·ppled** *ppl. a.* [UN-[1] 2] 1800.

Uncri·tical *a.* 1659. [UN-[1] 1.] **1.** Lacking in judgement or discrimination; not addicted to criticism. **2.** Not in accordance with critical canons or methods 1846.

1. An u. retailer of anecdotes 1854. *absol.* The u. who believe all they see in print 1874. 2. It is u. to judge an age by its greatest men 1874. Hence **Uncri·tically** *adv.*

Uncri·ticized *ppl. a.* [UN-[1] 2] 1846.

Uncro·pped, *ppl. a.* 1601. [UN-[1] 2.] **1.** Of flowers, etc. Not cropped, e.g. by cattle. Also *fig.* Not deflowered, virgin. **2.** Not docked or cut short 1802. **3.** Left fallow 1857.

Uncro·ss *v.* [UN-[2] 1] 1599. **Uncro·ssed** *ppl. a.* [UN-[1] 2] 1560. **Uncrow·ded** *ppl. a.* [UN-[1] 2] 1701. **Uncrow·n** *v.* [UN-[2] 2] ME. **Uncrow·ned** *ppl. a.* [UN-[1] 2] 1634. **Uncru·mple** *v.* [UN-[2] 1] 1611. **Uncru·mpled** *ppl. a.* [UN-[1] 2] 1854. **Uncru·shable** *a.* [UN-[1] 1] 1873. **Uncru·shed** *ppl. a.* [UN-[1] 2] 1626. **Uncry·stallizable** *a.* [UN-[1] 1] 1791. **Uncry·stallized** *ppl. a.* [UN-[1] 2] 1759.

Unction (ɒ·ŋkʃən). late ME. [– L. *unctio, unction-*, f. *unct-*, pa. ppl. stem of *ung(u)ere* smear; see -ION.] **1.** The action of anointing with oil as a religious rite or symbol. **b.** *Extreme unction*: see EXTREME *a.* 3. 1513. **2.** The action of anointing as a symbol of investing with an office, esp. that of kingship. late ME. **3.** *fig.* **a.** Of the Holy Ghost: chiefly in renderings and echoes of 1 John 2:20 and of the hymn *Veni, Creator Spiritus* 8. late ME. **b.** Deep spiritual feeling, or the manifestation of this in speech; a manner suggestive of religious earnestness 1692. **c.** *transf.* A manner, etc., showing appreciation or enjoyment of a subject or situation; gusto 1815. **4.** The action of anointing or rubbing with ointment or oil 1580. **5.** An unguent or ointment 1580. **b.** *fig.* A soothing influence or reflection 1602.

1. Vnctions, sacrafices, and rites Ceremoniall 1500. 2. Leo III gave Alfred the royal u. HUME. 3. Thy blessed vnction from aboue 1627. b. There is a great decay of devotional u. COLERIDGE. c. He delivered the haughty speech..with u. C. BRONTË. 5. I bought an Vnction of a Mountebanke SHAKS. b. Lay not a flattering Vnction to your soule, That..my madnesse speakes SHAKS. Hence **U·nctional** *a.* full of spiritual u.

†**U·nctious,** *a.* 1477. [var. (common c1600–1725) of UNCTUOUS, by substitution of -IOUS, prob. after UNCTION.] = UNCTUOUS *a.* 1. –1764.

Unctuosity (ɒŋktiu̯ɔ·sĭti). late ME. [– med.L. *unctuositas*, f. *unctuosus*; see next, -ITY. Cf. OFr. *unctuosité* (mod. *onct-*).] Unctuousness; oiliness, greasiness.

Unctuous (ɒ·ŋktiuəs), *a.* late ME. [– med.L. *unctuosus*, f. *unctus*, f. *unct-*; see UNCTION, -UOUS. Cf. OFr. *unctueus* (mod. *onctueux*).] **1.** Of the nature or quality of an unguent or ointment; oily, greasy. **b.** Of meat: Greasy, fat, rich. *arch.* 1495. **c.** Characterized by the presence of oil or fat 1641. **2.** Of ground or soil: Soft and adhesive, rich 1555. **3.** Of vapours, etc.: Laden with oily matter; of the nature of oil or grease 1606. **4.** Having an oily or greasy feel or appearance. Also of feel, touch, etc. 1668. **5.** Characterized by spiritual unction (now *esp.* of an assumed or superficial kind); complacently agreeable or self-satisfied 1742.

1. Gummes..and other vnctuous frutes and trees 1555. c. Their u. and epicurean paunches MILT. 4. Oak, now black with time and u. with kitchen smoke HAWTHORNE. 5. Laying an u. emphasis upon the words DICKENS. Hence **U·nctuous-ly** *adv.*, **-ness.**

Uncu·lled *ppl. a.* [UN-[1] 2] MILTON. †**Uncu·lpable** *a.* [UN-[1] 1] –1748. **Uncu·ltivable** *a.* [UN-[1] 1] 1663. **Uncu·ltivate** *ppl. a.* (*arch.*) [UN-[1] 2] 1659.

Uncu·ltivated, *ppl. a.* 1646. [UN-[1] 2.] **1.** *fig.* Not improved by education or training; uncultured. **2.** Untilled 1683. **b.** Of plants: Wild, not cultivated 1697. **3.** Not attended to or practised; not properly trained or developed 1684.

1. Such, the furniture of the u. soul! 1746. 3. Swift indeed has left..no branch of satyr u. 1751.

Uncultiva·tion [UN-[1] 6] 1796. **Uncu·lture** [UN-[1] 6] 1624.

Uncu·ltured, *ppl. a.* 1555. [UN-[1] 2.] **1.** = UNCULTIVATED 2, 2 b. **2.** *fig.* Unrefined; lacking culture 1777.

2. A rough soldier, u. as Marius and hardly less cruel 1878.

Uncu·nning *a.* (*arch.*) [UN-[1] 4] ME., **-ly** *adv.*, **-ness.** †**Uncu·rable** *a.* [UN-[1] 1] –1676. **Uncu·rb** *v.* [UN-[2] 2 b] 1580. **Uncu·rbable** [UN-[1] 1] SHAKS. **Uncu·rbed** *ppl. a.* [UN-[1] 2] 1599. **Uncu·rdled** *ppl. a.* [UN-[1] 2] 1823. **Uncu·red** *ppl. a.* [UN-[1] 2] 1548.

Uncu·rious *a.* 1570. [UN-¹ 1.] **1.** = INCURIOUS *a.* I. 2. Now *rare*, exc. as in 2. **2.** = INCURIOUS *a.* II. 2. 1684. So **Uncu·riously** *adv.* 1490.

Uncu·rl *v.* [UN-² 1, 5] SHAKS. **Uncu·rled** *ppl. a.* [UN-¹ 2] 1590. **Uncu·rling** *ppl. a.* [UN-¹ 4] 1728. **Uncu·rrent** *a.* [UN-¹ 1] SHAKS. **Uncu·rse** *v.* [UN-² 1] SHAKS. **Uncu·rsed, -st** *ppl. a.* [UN-¹ 2] 1628. **Uncurtai·led** *ppl. a.* [UN-¹ 2] 1741. **Uncu·rtain** *v.* [UN-² 2] 1628. **Uncu·rtained** *ppl. a.* [UN-¹ 1] 1804.

‖**Uncus** (ʌ·ŋkɒs). *Pl.* **unci** (ʌ·nsəi). 1826. [L., hook.] *Zool.*, etc. A hook or hook-like process.

Uncu·shioned *ppl. a.* [UN-¹ 2] 1873. **Uncu·stomary** *a.* [UN-¹ 1] 1650.

Uncu·stomed, *ppl. a.* late ME. [UN-¹ 2.] **1.** On which no custom or duty has been paid. **2.** Unaccustomed *to* something. *arch.* 1520. **3.** Not customary; unusual. *Obs.* or *arch.* 1552

Uncu·t, *ppl. a.* late ME. [UN-¹ 2.] **1.** Not cut, gashed, or wounded with a sharp-edged instrument. **2.** That has not been subjected to cutting; not mown, lopped, etc. 1548. **3.** Not fashioned or shaped by cutting 1596. **4.** Of books: **a.** Not having the leaves cut open: now styled *unopened* 1828. **b.** Having the margins not cut down 1809. **5.** Of plays, etc.: Not curtailed, without excisions 1896.

Unda·m *v.* [UN-² 1] DRYDEN. **Unda·maged** *ppl. a.* [UN-¹ 2] 1648. **Unda·mned** *ppl. a.* [UN-¹ 2] late ME. **Unda·mped** *ppl. a.* [UN-¹ 2] 1742. **Unda·ngerous** *a.* [UN-¹ 1] 1727. **Unda·ring** *ppl. a.* [UN-¹ 4] 1611. **Unda·rkened** *ppl. a.* [UN-¹ 2] 1742. **Unda·rned** *ppl. a.* [UN-¹ 2] 1797. **Unda·shed** *ppl. a.* [UN-¹ 2] 1601.

Undated (ʌ·ndeⁱtėd), *a.* Now *rare* or *Obs.* 1486. [f. med.L. *undatus*, f. L. *unda* wave; see -ED¹.] **1.** *Her.* = UNDEE *a.* **2.** *Ornith.*, *Bot.* Having wavy markings 1783.

Unda·ted, *ppl. a.* 1570. [UN-¹ 2.] **1.** Not furnished or marked with a date; of uncertain or unstated date. **2.** Having no fixed date or limit; unending 1624. **3.** Marked by no striking events 1878.

3. The dull u. life of a sleepy country town 1878.

Undau·nted, *ppl. a.* late ME. [UN-¹ 2.] †**1.** Not broken in; untamed; unbridled, unrestrained –1683. **2.** Undismayed, intrepid 1587. Hence **Undau·nted-ly** *adv.*, **-ness.**

Unda·zed *ppl. a.* [UN-¹ 2] 1757. **Unda·zzled** *ppl. a.* [UN-¹ 2] MILTON. **Unda·zzling** *ppl. a.* [UN-¹ 4] 1601. **Undea·dened** *ppl. a.* [UN-¹ 2] 1813.

Undea·dly, *a.* [OE. *undēadlić*, *undēaplić*; f. UN-¹ 1.] †**1.** Not subject to death; immortal –1612. **2.** Not causing death. CHAPMAN.

†**Undea·f** *v.* [UN-² 4 a] SHAKS. **Undea·lt** *ppl. a.* [UN-¹ 2] ME. **Undea·r** *a.* (*rare*) [UN-¹ 1] OE. **Undeba·rred** *ppl. a.* [UN-¹ 2] 1595. **Undeba·sed** *ppl. a.* [UN-¹ 2] 1753. **Undeba·ted** *ppl. a.* [UN-¹ 2] 1620. **Undecay·able** *a.* [UN-¹ 1] 1534. **Undecay·ed** *ppl. a.* [UN-² 2] 1513. **Undecay·ing** *ppl. a.* [UN-¹ 4] 1599.

Undecei·vable, *a.* 1534. [UN-¹ 1.] †**1.** Incapable of deceiving; undeceptive –1669. **2.** Incapable of being deceived 1608.

1. Sure & vndeceiuable tokens 1534. Hence **Undecei·vableness. Undecei·vably** *adv.*

Undecei·ve, *v.* 1598. [UN-² 1.] *trans.* To free (a person) from deception or mistake; to deliver from an erroneous idea. Also const. *of* (an error, etc.) Hence **Undecei·ver. Undecei·ving,** *vbl. sb.*

Undecei·ved *ppl. a.* [UN-¹ 2] late ME. **Undecei·ving** *ppl. a.* [UN-¹ 4] 1586. **Unde·cency** (now *rare* or *Obs.*) [UN-¹ 6] 1589. **Unde·cent** *a.* (now *dial.*) [UN-¹ 1] 1546, †**-ly** *adv.* –1716.

Undece·ption. 1694. [UN-² 6.] The action of undeceiving or the fact of being undeceived.

Undeci·ded, *ppl. a.* and *sb.* 1540. [UN-¹ 2.] **A.** *ppl. a.* **1.** That has not been decided; awaiting decision. **b.** Of action, opinion, etc.: Lacking in decision or definiteness 1828. **c.** *Coursing.* Resulting in no decision 1839. **2.** Irresolute, hesitating 1779. **B.** *sb. Coursing.* An indecisive course 1876. Hence **Undeci·dedly** *adv.*

Unde·cimal, *a.* 1804. [f. L. *undecim* eleven.] Characterized by the number eleven.

Undeci·pher, *v.* 1654. [UN-² 7.] *trans.* **a.** To decipher. **b.** To make undecipherable.

Undeci·pherable *a.* [UN-¹ 1] WALPOLE. **Undeci·phered** *ppl. a.* [UN-¹ 2] 1668. **Undeci·sive** *a.* [UN-¹ 1] 1661, **-ly** *adv.*, **-ness. Unde·ck** *v.* (*rare*) [UN-² 1] SHAKS.

Unde·cked, *ppl. a.* 1570. [UN-¹ 2.] **1.** Not decked or adorned. **2.** Not furnished with a deck or decks 1769.

1. Eve Undeckt, save with her self MILTON. **2.** Columbus found the New World in an u. boat EMERSON.

Undecla·red *ppl. a.* [UN-¹ 2] 1526. **Undecli·nable** *a.* [UN-¹ 1] 1530. **Undecli·ned** *ppl. a.* [UN-¹ 2] 1509. **Undecompou·nded** *ppl. a.* [UN-¹ 2] 1795. **Unde·corated** *ppl. a.* [UN-¹ 2] 1763. **Unde·dicated** *ppl. a.* [UN-¹ 2] 1661.

Undee, undé(e (ʌ·ndė), *a.* 1513. [– OFr. *undé, undée* (mod. *ondé, ondée*), f. *unde, onde* wave; see -EE¹.] *Her.* Having the form of waves; wavy.

†**Undee·ded** *a.* [UN-¹ 3] SHAKS. **Undee·med** *ppl. a.* [UN-¹ 2] ME. **Undefa·ced** *ppl. a.* [UN-¹ 2] late ME. **Undefa·med** *ppl. a.* [UN-¹ 2] 1450. **Undefea·table** *a.* [UN-¹ 1] 1640. **Undefea·ted** *ppl. a.* [UN-¹ 2] SHELLEY, **-ly** *adv.*

Undefe·nded, *ppl. a.* late ME. [UN-¹ 2.] †**1.** Not forbidden –1598. **2.** Unprotected 1564. **3.** *Law.* **a.** Not assisted by legal defence 1607. **b.** Against which no defence is raised 1898.

3. a. The accused is u. 1900. **b.** The u. petition.. for a divorce 1898.

Undefie·d *ppl. a.* [UN-¹ 2] SPENSER. **Undefi·led** *ppl. a.* [UN-¹ 2] late ME., Dan Chaucer, well of English vndefyled (SPENSER), **-ly** *adv.*, **-ness. Undefi·nable** *a.* [UN-¹ 1] LOCKE, **-ness, -ably** *adv.* **Undefi·ned** *ppl. a.* [UN-¹ 2] 1611, **-ly** *adv.*, **-ness. Undeflow·ered** *ppl. a.* [UN-¹ 2] 1533. **Undefo·rmed** *ppl. a.* [UN-¹ 2] 1672. **Undege·nerate** *a.* [UN-¹ 1] 1743. **Undegra·ded** *ppl. a.* [UN-¹ 2] 1821. **Unde·ify** *v.* [UN-² 4 c] 1637. **Undeje·cted** *ppl. a.* [UN-¹ 2] 1613. **Undelay·ed** *ppl. a.* [UN-¹ 2] late ME. **Undelay·ing** *ppl. a.* [UN-¹ 4] 1791. **Undeli·berate** *a.* [UN-¹ 1] 1550. **Undeli·ght** [UN-¹ 6] SHELLEY. **Undeli·ghted** *ppl. a.* [UN-¹ 2] MILT. **Undeli·ghtful** *a.* [UN-¹ 1] 1585, **-ly** *adv.*, **-ness. Undeli·vered** *ppl. a.* [UN-¹ 2] 1472. **Undelu·ded** *ppl. a.* [UN-¹ 2] 1746. **Unde·lved** *ppl. a.* [UN-¹ 2] 1602. **Undema·nded** *ppl. a.* [UN-¹ 2] 1513. **U:ndemocra·tic** *a.* [UN-¹ 1] 1839, **-ally** *adv.* **Undemo·lished** *ppl. a.* [UN-¹ 2] 1571. **Unde·monstrated** *ppl. a.* [UN-¹ 2] 1648.

Undemo·nstrative, *a.* 1846. [UN-¹ 1.] Not given to or characterized by outward expression (of the feelings, etc.). Hence **Undemo·nstrative-ly** *adv.*, **-ness.**

Undeni·able, *a.* 1547. [UN-¹ 1]. **1.** That cannot be denied or refuted; indisputable. **b.** Of witnesses: Irrefragable 1619. **2.** That cannot be refused; admitting or accepting no denial 1549. **3.** Not open to objection; unexceptional 1793.

1. b. The testimony of many u. Witnesses 1663. **2.** U. visitors 1839. **3.** The grapes and green figs are u. 1884. Hence **Undeni·ably** *adv.*

U:ndenomina·tional, *a.* 1871. [UN-¹ 1.] Not confined to any particular religious denomination (freq. with ref. to religious instruction in elementary schools).

Undepe·nding, *ppl. a.* Now *rare.* 1649. [UN-¹ 4.] †**1.** Not depending *from* or *on* something. MILT. **2.** Independent 1649.

Undeplo·red *ppl. a.* [UN-¹ 2] 1611. **Undepra·ved** *ppl. a.* [UN-¹ 2] 1646. **Undepre·ssed** *ppl. a.* [UN-¹ 2] 1697. **Undepri·ved** *ppl. a.* [UN-¹ 2] 1564.

Under (ʌ·ndəɹ), *sb. rare.* 1600. [f. UNDER *adv.* and UNDER- *prefix*¹.] **1.** A state of inferiority. In phr. *to be at a great u.* Now *dial.* **2.** *pl.* Under-clothes 1731.

Under (ʌ·ndəɹ), *a.* ME. [f. UNDER- *prefix*¹, detached from compounds on the analogy of OVER *a.*] **1.** Situated lower; lying beneath or at a lower level. **2.** Lying under (so as to be covered) 1547. **b.** Facing downwards 1731. **3.** Of sound: Low, subdued 1806. **4.** Subordinate; of lower rank or position 1580. **5.** Below the proper standard, amount, etc.; insufficient 1673.

1. The Morne..Gaue light to all, As well to gods, as men of th' vnder globe CHAPMAN. Now gnaw'd his u., now his upper lip TENNYSON. **2. b.** The upper and u. Surfaces of the two Leaves 1731. **3.** Those self-solacing, those under, notes Trilled by the red-breast WORDSW. **4.** For the u. characters, gather them from Homer and Virgil POPE. **5.** 'Tis best to begin rather with an u. than over Dose 1737.

Under (ʌ·ndəɹ), *prep.* [OE. *under* = OFris. *under*, OS. *undar* (Du. *onder*), OHG. *untar* (G. *unter*), ON. *undir*, Goth. *undar* :– Gmc. **under-* :– IE. **n̥dhero-*, compar. formation (cf. Skr. *ádharas* adj. lower, *adhás* below).] **I.** In senses denoting position beneath or below something, so as to have it above or overhead, or to be covered by it. **1.** With ref. to: **a.** The heavens or heavenly bodies. **b.** Particular heavenly regions, esp. as indicating terrestrial locality. late ME. **c.** The stars as having influence on persons 1583. **2.** With ref. to the surface of the earth or water OE. **3.** With words denoting natural or artificial structures or means of shelter; freq. = beneath the cover or shelter of OE. **4.** *gen.* OE. **b.** Denoting the relationship of a horse to the rider or a ship to a person on board OE. **c.** = At a point just below (a part of the body) ME. **d.** Denoting position between the arm, etc., and the body. late ME. **5.** Denoting the relationship of persons. **a.** To a head-covering OE. **b.** To something raised or carried above the head, as a standard; often as indicating military service, nationality etc. OE. **c.** *Naut.* Of ships, with ref. to the sails, etc. OE. **6.** With ref. to something which covers, clothes, envelops, or conceals OE. **b.** Denoting the relationship of land to crops grown or animals reared, on it 1569. **7.** Denoting position at the bottom or foot of something, or beside it but at a lower level OE. **8.** With verbs of motion, impulsion, etc., denoting change of place to a position below or beneath something OE.

1. a. The greatest rascal u. the canopy of heaven GOLDSM. **b.** Vnder the very pole lyeth a black and high rocke 1611. **c.** Ah lucklesse babe, borne vnder cruell starre SPENSER. **3.** *fig.* I love to shelter my self u. the Examples of Great Men 1711. **4. b.** My Lord Galway had his Horse shot u. him STEELE. **c.** I had thought t' haue yerk'd him here vnder the Ribbes SHAKS. **d.** And now he her away with him did beare Vnder his arme SPENSER. **5. a.** There may be..more pride and hypocrisy u. a close plain bonnet than u. a veil of silk 1846. **b.** A small frigate-built vessel, u. Spanish Colours DE FOE. **c.** Drove 24 hours u. bare poles 1780. **6.** Send your letters to him, u. cover, directed to Mr. Alderman Lee FRANKLIN. **b.** The marshes which were formerly u. grass 1795. **7.** The castle,..vnder which lieth a vallie very fertile 1585. **8.** Various active substances may be introduced u. the cuticle 1806.

II. In senses denoting subordination or subjection. **1.** With ref. to a person acting in a certain capacity, considered in relation to one of superior status or in authority or command OE. **b.** With ref. to derivative rights or claims 1818. **c.** Passing into the sense of 'in the time or period of' (a ruler, a dispensation, a state of affairs) OE. **2.** With abstract or other sbs. denoting authority or control, direction, care, examination, restraint, etc. OE. **b.** With words denoting a compact, obligation, etc.: Subject to, bound, or constrained (legally or morally) by 1456. **3.** With ref. to what is heavy, oppressive, or restrictive, as a burden, penalty, or disadvantage ME. **b.** With ref. to mental impressions: Possessed, swayed or affected by 1667. **c.** *ellipt.* = Under the influence of 1884.

1. The pope is the vycar generall vnder god 1531. I was commander of the ship, and had about fifty Yahoos u. me SWIFT. I made some progress in Ethics u. Professor John Bruce SCOTT. He..had fought bravely u. Monmouth MACAULAY. **b.** The acts or defaults of any person other than himself and those claiming u. him 1896. **c.** There were as many persons put to death for religious opinions u. the mild Elizabeth as u. the bloody Mary 1807. Under the reign of his present Majesty 1807. **2.** Laws u. which we were born DRYDEN. But no laurels are to be won by sitting patiently u. the knife of a surgeon COWPER. Sent u. a strong guard to the tower DICKENS. U. the editorship of Mr. Charles Burney 1885. The subject u. discussion has nothing to do with chemicals 1892. **b.** As he was also u. a promise to the church of Philippi to see them PALEY. **3.** U. Pain of never having an Husband STEELE. The glass vessels intended to retain gases u. pressure FARADAY. Wade was writing u. the dread of the halter MACAULAY. **b.** Are you u. the impression that they will be better cared for..here? 1875. **c.** Treated..u. chloroform 1892.

III. In senses implying covering or inclusion. **1.** Presented or observed in a certain form or aspect OE. **b.** With words implying a specious or deceptive appearance 1607. **c.** Beneath the form, guise, or concealment of ME. **2.** Denoting inclusion in a group, category, class, etc. OE. **b.** Denoting occurrence in a particular section of a book, etc. 1589. **3.** With words denoting protection, care, or benevolent interest OE. **4.** Denoting a state or condition (freq. one imposed by implied circumstances) ME. **5.** Denoting participation in the authoritative or confirmatory effect of a seal, signature, etc.:

Authorized, warranted, or attested by ME. **b.** Implying a statement or suggestion as to the authorship of a work 1662. **c.** = In accordance with (some regulative power or principle) 1779.

1. When the Author represents any Passion, Appetite, Virtue or Vice, u. a Visible Shape ADDISON. *U. the name of*, = by the name of; The Egyptians..had..even deified her u. the name of Isis BERKELEY. **c.** Extreme vanity sometimes hides u. the garb of ultra modesty 1854. **2.** They shall speak without Oath unless the Fact be u. Felony 1676. **b.** The day of the present voyage u. which these remarks are introduced 1823. **3.** Vnder safe conduct of the Dolphins seale 1596. **4.** U. the ballot it is as easy to vote as to pay a morning call 1884. Phr. *U. the circumstances*. **5.** A warrante vnder the kinges Maiesties owne handes 1551. **b.** Our hero..inserted his compositions, u. a fictitious signature, in his master's newspaper MAR. EDGEWORTH. **c.** U. this edict..more than fifty thousand human beings..were deliberately murdered FROUDE.

IV. In senses denoting inferiority or deficiency. **1.** Below in dignity, rank, worth OE. **2.** Less, below, in number or amount. late ME. **b.** Below (a specified age) late ME. **c.** At or for a less cost than. late ME. **d.** In less time than 1632. **e.** With less than; of less size, etc. than 1570. **f.** *ellipt.*: *and u., or u.*, placed after statements of size, price, etc. 1482. **3.** Below (a certain standard) 1615. **b.** *U. age*, below the (legal) age of majority 1590. **c.** *U.* (one's) *breath*, in a whisper 1832.

1. No person, u. a diviner, can..conduct a correspondence at such arm's length LAMB. **2.** Repeated accounts make them u. five thousand H. WALPOLE. **b.** Then was Augustus u. nineteen years old 1692. **c.** They be sold far u. the Price that they be worth 1496. **d.** Neither can any be made u. three weeks' time 1639. **e.** To sink every Spanish ship u. 100 tons 1883. **f.** As many as were two yere old and vnder TINDALE *Matt.* 2:16. **3.** So many Nets and Fish, that are u. the Statute size WALTON. **b.** Three sonnes he dying left, all vnder age SPENSER. **c.** 'Oh hang!' she added,..u. her breath 1898.

Under (ʊ·ndəɹ), *adv.* [OE. *under*; see prec.] **1.** Below, beneath. **b.** With verbs of motion OE. **c.** Lower down on a page, etc. Chiefly in comb., as *u.-mentioned*. late ME. **d.** Of the sun, etc.: Below the horizon, set 1489. **e.** Under water, submerged 1830. **f.** *Down under*, in the Antipodes 1899. **2.** In or into a position or state of subjection or submission ME. **b.** *Go u.* See GO *v.* VII. **3.** *From u.*, from below 1535. **4.** Less in amount, etc.; lower in price 1574.

1. Helped..with blessings of yᵉ depe yᵗ lyeth vnder COVERDALE *Gen.* 49:25. **b.** Let them..put no fyre vnder 1539. Pass your knife u. 1846. **d.** The sun was u. MEREDITH. **2.** Love, which doth many a wonder And many a wys man hath put u. GOWER. But I keepe vnder my body, and bring it into subiection 1 *Cor.* 9:27. The fire was got u. 1791.

Under- (ʊ·ndəɹ), *prefix*¹, repr. OE. *under-*: combining form of UNDER *adv.* and *prep.*; cf. OVER-. In OE. the prefix is common with verbs, less so with nouns, and rare with adjectives. Many of the OE. compounds are translations of Latin words in *sub-*, e.g. *underberan* = supportare, *undercuman* = subvenire. In most of its uses, *under-* may be freely employed to form new compounds, the meaning of which is usu. obvious.

I. Denoting local position. **1.** With vbs. and parts of vbs. **a.** Denoting acton (or continuance of a state) carried on under or beneath something, as in *under-build, -drain, -gird, -tie* etc. **Under-hanging,** *vbl. sb.* protrusion (of the lower jaw). **Underjawed,** *ppl. a.* underhung. **Underla·p,** *v. trans.* to extend some way beneath. **Undersi·gn,** *v. trans.* to sign one's name below (a writing). **Undertrea·d,** *v. trans.* to tread underfoot; to subdue, subjugate. **b.** Denoting the action of moving so as to be or get or place oneself under something, as *undercreep, -fall, -flow, -run*. **c.** Rarely, the sense of 'from below' is found, as in *underpeep, -peer*. **d.** A noun of action with *under-* may have the same form as the verb, as *undercut, -hang, -run, -thrust*.

2. With nouns. **a.** In names of garments worn under articles of clothing (common after the 16th century), as *under-bodice*, -PETTICOAT, *-robe*, -SKIRT, *-sleeve*, -VEST. **b.** Denoting that the thing specified is either placed below something else, or is the lower in position of two similar things. When pairs of things are contrasted *under-* becomes equivalent to *lower* (as *over-* to *upper*), and readily assumes an adjectival function. **U·nder-board,** the lower of two boards forming an organ bellows or wind-chest. **U·nderbough,** one of the lower branches of a tree. **U·nderfall,** a foot-hill slope. **U·nder-frame,** the substructure of a railway carriage, forming the frame on which the body rests. **U·nderlay:er,** a lower layer, substratum. **U·nder-lid,** the lower lid of the eye; a lid placed under another. **U·ndersoil,** subsoil. **U·nder-su:rface,** the lower surface of something. **c.** Denoting position below a surface or covering, or at a depth. **U·nder-colour,** the colour under the surface-colour (as in fur, feathers, etc.). **U·nder-down,** the down below the outer feathers of birds. **U·nder-drain,** an underground drain. **U·nder-drift,** an undercurrent. **U·nder-flow,** *sb.*, an undercurrent. **U·nderstra:tum,** an underlying layer or stratum. **U·nderswell,** a swell below the surface, an undercurrent. **d.** Denoting something which is either covered (completely or partially) by, or is subordinate to, something of the same kind, as UNDERGROWTH, UNDERWOOD. **U·nderscrub,** undergrowth, brushwood. **e.** With the sense of 'situated on the underside', as *underfeathering, -colouring*.

II. Denoting inferiority in rank or importance. **1. a.** With designations of persons, esp. of subordinate officers, officials, or servants, as *under-actor, -agent, -bailiff, -butler, -captain, -chamberlain, -clerk, -cook, -gaoler, -gardener, -god, -housemaid, -keeper, labourer, -manager, -officer, -ranger, -servant, -sexton, -shepherd, -sheriff, -steward, -teacher, -tenant, -tutor, -vassal, -warden, -workman*. **U·nderlooker, -viewer,** *Mining*, a subordinate to the manager, who superintends the miners and workings; a subordinate overseer. **b.** With other nouns, in the sense of 'subordinate, subsidiary, minor', as *under-agency, -cause, -lease, -service*. **U·nder-school,** a (or the) lower or junior school.

2. With vbs., denoting reduction to (or acceptance of) an inferior or subordinate standing, as UNDERSTUDY *v.*

III. *fig.* **1.** With vbs. **a.** In OE., various secondary meanings of *under-* are represented by such verbs as *underfōn* to receive, *understandan* to UNDERSTAND; several of these survive in ME., and a few more are added, as *undertake*. In later examples, the sense is usu. that of (secret) investigation, as *undersearch, -watch*, or of unobserved action, as †*underhear*. **b.** From the end of the 16th c. *under-* is used with vbs. in the sense of 'at a lower rate than another person', as *underbid, -buy, -quote, -sell*. **c.** occas. = 'to a point or degree below what is normal or customary', as in *undercooled*. **d.** Very rarely, subordinate action is implied, as in **Underlea·se** *v. trans.* to sub-let.

2. With nouns, denoting actions, etc., which lie or are kept beneath the surface or in the background. **U·nderlook** *sb.* a covert look or glance. **U·nderplay** *sb.* an underlying or hidden motion or action. **U·ndersense,** an underlying sense (of something). **U·nderthought,** a hidden thought, reservation, *arrière-pensée*. **b.** With words denoting sound of a subdued or subordinate character, esp. when produced or perceived at the same time as a louder or more distinct sound, as UNDERTONE. **U·ndernote,** a subdued note; an undertone or suggestion.

IV. Denoting insufficiency or defect. **a.** With verbal forms. Denoting, freq. by contrast with OVER- II. 6, that the action falls below the usual or proper standard, and thus = 'at too low a rate', 'too low', 'too little', 'insufficiently'; as in *underburn, -coloured, -dose* v., *-horsed, -masted,* †*-matched, -measure, -officered, -paid, -pay, -peopled, -play, -praise, -prize, -reckon, -roast, -staff, -staffed, -stock, -stocked, -witted*, etc. **Underbi·ll** *v. trans.* (*U.S.*), to enter (goods) at less than the actual amount or value. **Under-expo·se** *v. intr.* and *trans.*, *Photogr.* to give too little exposure to; so **Under-exposed** *ppl. a.* **Underhi·ve** *v. trans.* to place (bees) in too small a hive. **Underli·mbed** *ppl. a.* having legs too slender in proportion to the body. **Underma·tch** *v. trans.* to unite or bestow in marriage below the proper rank or condition. **Underpri·nt** *v. trans.* to print (an engraving or photograph) with insufficient depth or distinctness. **Undershoo·t** *v. trans.* and *intr.* to shoot short (of) or too low (for). **Undertru·mp** *v. trans.* and *intr.* to follow (one's partner) in trumping, but with a lower card. **b.** With nouns, in the sense of 'insufficient, deficient, defective', contrasted with OVER- II. 8; as in *underbidder*, -ESTIMATE, *-exposure, -match* sb., *-price* sb., *-production, -wit*. **c.** With adjs., as opp. to OVER- II. 7, rare except when directly suggested by the latter, as in *underhonest* (SHAKS.; in contrast to *overproud*), *under-ripe, -scrupulous*.

Under- *prefix*², originating in the coalescence of UNDER *prep.* with a following noun, the compound being then usu. employed as an adj. or adv., as UNDERFOOT, -GROUND, -HAND. In attrib. use these compounds have the stress on the prefix. **U·nder-sea,** *a.* situated or lying below the sea or the surface of the sea; intended for use below the surface of the sea. **Undersea·,** *adv.* below the sea or its surface. **U·nder-size,** *a.* below the proper or ordinary size. **U·nderturf,** *a.* of earth or soil, situated or found below the turf.

Undera·ct, *v.* 1623. [UNDER-¹ IV. a.] To perform inadequately; *spec.* to act (a theatrical part) insufficiently.

U·nder-action. 1697. [UNDER-¹ II. 1 b, IV. b.] **1.** Subordinate or subsidiary action as in the plot of a play. **2.** Insufficient or defective action 1887.

U·nder-age, *a.* and *sb.* 1594. [See UNDER *prep.* IV. 3 b, and UNDER-².] **A.** *adj.* Not of full age; immature; in one's minority.

As if I were some u. heiress T. HARDY.

†B. *sb.* The time during which a person is under age; minority –1649.

The underage and weaknesse of his succeeding sonne 1641.

U·nder-arm, *a.* 1816. [UNDER-².] **1.** *Cricket.* = UNDERHAND *a.* Also in *Lawn Tennis.* **2.** *Swimming.* Of a side-stroke: In which the arm is not lifted above the water 1905.

U·nderback. 1635. [f. UNDER-¹ I. 2 b.] *Brewing.* A vessel placed below the mash-tub to receive the raw wort from this.

Underbea·r, *v.* Now *rare.* [OE. *underberan*; see UNDER-¹ I. 1 a and BEAR *v.*] **1.** *trans.* To sustain, endure. **2.** To support, bear up. late ME.

1. Leaue those woes alone, which I alone Am bound to vnder-beare SHAKS. **2.** To help to u. with grave advice The weighty beam whereon the state depends 1595.

Underbea·rer. Now *dial.* and *U.S.* 1700. [UNDER-¹ I. 1 a.] A coffin-bearer at a funeral.

Underbi·d, *v.* 1593. [UNDER-¹ III. 1 b, IV. a.] **†1.** *trans.* To undervalue or value at a lower rate –1645. **2.** *intr.* To make too low an offer 1611. **3.** *trans.* To supplant by making a lower or better offer 1677. **4.** *Bridge.* To bid less on (a hand) than its strength warrants 1908.

†U·nderboard, *adv.* 1548. [UNDER-².] **1.** Under the table –1642. **2.** Clandestinely, underhand; not openly or honestly –1703.

1. Till they have drunk themselves underboord 1642.

U·nder-body. 1621. [UNDER-¹ I. 2 a, b.] **†1.** The lower part of a woman's dress. **b.** *U.S.* A corset-cover. **2.** The underside of an animal's body 1879. **3. a.** *Naut.* The part of a ship's hull which is below the waterline 1895. **b.** The under part of the body of a vehicle 1904.

U·nder-breath, *sb., a.,* and *adv.* 1844. [UNDER- III. 2 b.] **A.** *sb.* A whisper or low tone. **b.** Whispered rumour 1880. **B.** *adj.* Whispered 1853. **C.** *adv.* In a whisper 1865.

Underbre·d, *ppl. a.* (*sb.*) 1650. [UNDER-¹ IV. a.] **A.** *ppl. a.* **1.** Of persons or their conduct: Of inferior breeding; wanting in refinement; vulgar. **2.** Of animals: Of inferior strain, not pure bred 1890.

1. An u., fine-spoken fellow was he GOLDSM.

B. *sb.* An underbred animal (esp. a horse) 1880. So **U·nderbreeding** *vbl. sb.*

U·nderbrush. orig. *U.S.* 1813. [UNDER-¹ I. 2 c.] The shrubs or undergrowth of a forest.

A tall grove of oaks, firm under foot and clear of u. STEVENSON. Hence **U·nderbrush** *v. trans.* to clear of u. So **U·nderbush** *sb.* and *v.*

U·nder-carriage. 1794. [UNDER-¹ I. 2 b.] = UNDER-BODY 1 b. The lower framework of a vehicle which supports the superstructure.

U·nder-chap. 1607. [UNDER-¹ I. 2 b.] The lower jaw.

The stork..produces no other noise than the clacking of its under chap against the upper GOLDSM.

Undercha·rge, *v.* 1611. [UNDER-¹ IV. a.] **1.** *trans.* To charge (a person, etc.) too little; to make an inadequate charge for (a thing). Also *absol.* **2.** To charge (a gun, a receptacle) insufficiently 1794. So **U·ndercharge** *sb.*

Undercla·d, *ppl. a.* 1622. [UNDER-¹ IV. a.] Insufficiently clad.

U·nderclay. 1661. [UNDER-¹ I. 2 b.] A bed of clay beneath a seam of coal or other stratum.

U·ndercliff. 1829. [UNDER-¹ I. 2 b.] **1.** A terrace or lower cliff formed from landslips. Also *attrib.* **2.** = prec. 1883.

U·nderclothe, *v.* 1857. [Back-formation from UNDERCLOTHING.] *trans.* To provide with underclothing.

Underclo·thed, *ppl. a.* 1890. [UNDER-[1] IV. a.] Insufficiently clothed.

U·nderclothing. 1835. [UNDER-[1] I. 2 b.] Clothing worn below the upper or outer garments of ordinary indoor dress. So **U·nderclothes** 1884.

U·ndercoat. 1618. [UNDER-[1] I. 2 a, c.] **1.** A coat worn beneath another. †**2.** A petticoat –1759. **3.** The under layer of hair or down in some long-haired animals 1840.

Underconstumble, var. UNDERCUMSTUMBLE.

Undercoo·led, *ppl. a.* 1902. [UNDER-[1] III. 1 c.] Of a liquid: Brought below the normal freezing-point without crystallization.

U·nder-covert. 1805. [UNDER-[1] I. 2 b, c.] **1.** A covert of undergrowth. **2.** *Ornith.* One of the small close feathers on the underside of the wing or tail 1817.

Undercree·p, *v. Obs.* exc. *dial.* late ME. [UNDER-[1] I. 1 b, III. 1 b.] **1.** *intr.* To creep in (stealthily). **2.** *trans.* To creep under (something) 1440. **b.** *fig.* To subvert secretly; to outdo by craft or stealth 1592.

2. When we that stately wall had undercrept 1642. **b.** Now, for the price, others under-creep us, and so forestall our markets 1623.

U·ndercroft. late ME. [UNDER- I. 2 b + CROFT *sb.*[2]] A crypt; an underground vault. The monkes..buried it [*sc.* the body] immediately in the vndercraft 1601.

Undercumsta·nd, -cumstu·mble, -constu·mble, *v. dial.* and *joc. colloq.* 1824. Jocular alterations of UNDERSTAND.

U·ndercurrent, *sb.* and *a.* 1683. [UNDER-[1] I. 2 b or c.] **1.** A current flowing beneath the upper current, or below the surface. **b.** *fig.* An activity, force, tendency, etc., of a suppressed or underlying character 1817. **2.** *attrib.* or as *adj.* That runs or flows out of sight; concealed; suppressed 1855.

1. Part of this air then returns as an u. HUXLEY. **b.** A continuous under-current of feeling COLERIDGE. **2.** Blest, but for some dark u. woe TENNYSON.

U·ndercut, *sb.* 1859. [UNDER-[1] I. 2 b, 1 a, d.] **1.** The under-side of a sirloin of beef. **2.** *U.S.* A cut made in the trunk of a tree on the side towards which it is intended to fall 1883.

Undercu·t, *v.* late ME. [UNDER-[1] I. 1 a, III. 1 b.] †**1.** *trans.* To cut down. **2.** To cut (away) below or beneath 1598. **b.** *spec.* in carving 1874. **c.** *Golf.* To strike (a ball) below the centre 1891. **3.** To supplant by working for lower wages or by underselling 1884.

2. To u. the Turf 1725. Cliffs..are often undercut by streams 1881. **b.** He has undercut his Madonna's profile..too delicately for time to spare RUSKIN. **3.** We do not want the Post Office to 'undercut' private agencies at the expense of the..taxpayer 1884. Hence **U·ndercut** *ppl. a.* **U·ndercutter,** an undercutting tool. **U·ndercutting** *vbl. sb.*

U·nder-deck. 1826. [UNDER-[1] I. 2 b.] The lower deck of a vessel.

U·nder-dip, *a.* 1839. [UNDER-[1] I. 2 c.] *Mining.* Lying lower than the bottom of the engine-pit.

Underdo·, *v.* 1611. [UNDER-[1] IV. a.] **1.** *intr.* To do less than is requisite or necessary. **2.** *trans.* To do or perform insufficiently or imperfectly 1716. **b.** *spec.* To cook insufficiently 1864.

1. He must neither ouerdoe nor vnderdoe, lest he utterly undoe 1622.

U·nderdog. orig. *U.S.* 1887. [UNDER-[1] I. 2 b.] The beaten dog in a fight; hence *fig.* the worsted party; an oppressed or (socially) inferior person.

Underdone (stress var.), *ppl. a.* 1683. [UNDER-[1] IV. a.] Of meat: Insufficiently cooked; partly raw. Also *transf.*

Underdraw·, *v.* 1799. [UNDER-[1] I. 1 a, IV. a.] **1.** *trans.* To underline. **2.** To cover (the inside of a roof, the under side of a floor) with boards or with lath and plaster 1843. **3.** To depict inadequately 1865.

2. The interior of it has been..made warmer by underdrawing the roof WORDSW.

U·nderdress, *sb.* 1785. [UNDER-[1] I. 2 a.] **1.** Underclothing. **2.** A dress or gown worn beneath another, or part of a dress simulating this 1861.

Underdre·ss, *v.* 1908. [UNDER-[1] IV. a.] *intr.* To dress too plainly. So **Underdressed** (stress var.) *ppl. a.* 1784.

U·nder-earth, *sb.* 1765. [UNDER-[2].] **1.** Subsoil. **2.** The regions below the earth 1878.

U·nder-earth, *a.* 1592. [UNDER-[2].] Subterranean.

Under-e·stimate, *v.* 1812. [UNDER-[1] IV. a.] **1.** *trans.* To estimate at too low a quantity. **2.** To rate too low; undervalue 1850. So **U·nderestimate** *sb.*

1. Neither does St. Paul ignore nor u. the value.. of good works FARRAR.

Underfed (stress var.), *ppl. a.* 1835. [UNDER-[1] IV. a.] Insufficiently fed or nourished. So **Underfee·d** *v.*

†**Underfo,** *v.* Pa. t. **-feng, -fang, -fong.** Pa. pple. **-fangen, -fongen.** [OE. *underfōn*: see UNDER-[1] and FANG *v.*[1]] = next –1513.

†**Underfo·ng, -fa·ng,** *v.* ME. [UNDER-[1] III. 1 a. Cf. prec.] **1.** *trans.* To receive, accept; come to have or possess –1579. **2.** To undertake –1525. **3.** To seduce, entrap –1614.

2. To u. this labour they him prey LYDG. **3.** And some by sleight he eke doth vnderfong SPENSER.

U·nderfoot, *a.* Now *rare.* 1594. [attrib. use of next.] **1.** Lying under the foot or feet 1596. **2.** Abject, downtrodden 1594.

2. The most dejected, most u. and downetrodden Vassals of Perdition MILT.

Under foot, underfoo·t, *adv.* Also **underfeet.** ME. [UNDER *prep.*] **1.** Beneath the foot or feet; on the ground; esp. with *tread, trample.* **b.** *Naut.* See FOOT *sb.* (Phrases). **2.** *fig.* In(to) a state of subjection or inferiority ME. †**3.** Below the real or current value –1654.

1. As a dead coarse that is troden vnder fete 1539. Katerine, that Cap of yours becomes you not, Off with that bable, throw it vnder foote SHAKS. Underfoot the Violet, Crocus, and Hyacinth with rich inlay Broiderd the ground MILT. **2.** Tho was the vertu sett above And vice was put under fote GOWER. **3.** When men did let their Land underfoot, the Tenants would fight for their Landlords SELDEN.

U·nder-frame. 1855. [UNDER-[1] I. 2 b.] The substructure of a railway carriage.

U·nder-ga:rment. 1530. [UNDER-[1] I. 2 a.] An article of underclothing.

U·nder-glaze, *a.* (*sb.*) 1882. [UNDER-[2].] **1.** *U. painting,* the painting on pottery before the glaze is applied 1883. **b.** *absol.* as *sb.* 1882. **2.** Of colours: Used in, adapted for, such painting 1883.

Undergo (ʋndəɹgōᵘ·), *v.* [Late OE. *undergān*; f. UNDER-[1] I. 1 b + *gān* GO *v.*] †**1.** *trans.* To undermine; to defraud; to get the better of –1642. †**2.** To go or pass under –1627. **3.** To be subject to, to serve (*rare*) 1586. **4.** To bear, suffer, go through (pain, danger, etc.) ME. †**b.** To sustain (a burden) –1656. **5.** To submit, or be subjected, to (a law, inspection, etc.); to experience ME. **b.** To come or fall under, to experience; to have imposed on one 1599. **c.** To experience, pass through (a change) 1634. †**d.** To partake of, enjoy. SHAKS. **6.** To undertake. Now *rare.* 1601. †**b.** To discharge (an office) etc. –1726.

1. Þou hast me gyled and vndur-gone 1380. Affraid lest thou shouldest u. thy selfe in purchasing the pearle 1642. **2.** Better my shoulders underwent the earth, than thy decease CHAPMAN. **3.** So have you made our language u. you BROWNING. **4.** Much danger do I vndergo for thee SHAKS. His fine spirit was broken by the anxieties he had undergone 1832. **5.** In watir baptized he alle þo þat wolde bapteme vndir go 1425. Several clauses again underwent examination 1844. **b.** Every year thousands u. this operation LADY M. W. MONTAGU. **c.** She reviv'd And underwent a quick immortal change MILT. **6.** I haue mou'd already Some certaine of the Noblest minded Romans To vnder-goe, with me, an Enterprize SHAKS. **b.** [He is] a very young man to u. that place PEPYS.

Undergraduate (ʋndəɹgræ·diu‚ĕt), *sb.* and *a.* 1630. Also colloq. abbrev. **Undergra·d.** [UNDER-[2].] **A.** *sb.* **1.** A university student who has not yet taken a degree. **2.** *fig.* One imperfectly instructed or inexpert (*in* something) 1659.

2. Here the under graduates in iniquity commence their career with deer stealing 1795.

B. *adj.* †**1.** Of inferior importance –1659. **2.** Of undergraduate status; of or belonging to an undergraduate; characteristic of undergraduates 1685.

2. In my u. days 1889. Hence **U·ndergradue·tte,** a woman undergraduate (*slang* or *colloq.*) 1920.

U·nderground, *a.* (*sb.*) 1590. [f. next.] **A.** *adj.* **1.** Found, living, situated, acting, occurring, used, etc., below the surface of the ground 1610. **b.** *U. railway,* a railway running under the surface of the ground, esp. one beneath a city 1834. **2.** *fig.* Hidden, secret; not public, avoiding notice 1677.

1. Some Jerusalem or under-ground artichokes SOUTHEY. *fig.* The stream of London charity flows in a channel..noiseless and u. DE QUINCEY. **b.** *U.S.* (Also *u. line*) The secret system by which slaves were enabled to escape to the Free States and Canada 1852. **2.** Brougham..has been for some time in u. communication with Carlton House 1820.

B. *sb.* **1.** The region below the earth; the lower regions 1590. **b.** An underground space or passage 1594. **2.** Subsoil 1812. **b.** Ground lying at a lower level or beneath trees 1842. **3.** An underground railway 1887.

Undergrou·nd, *adv.* 1571. [UNDER-[2].] **1.** Below the surface of the ground. **2.** *fig.* In secrecy; in a hidden or obscure manner 1632.

1. Tisiphone, let loose from under Ground DRYDEN. He..wished that lady..u. rather than there THACKERAY. **2.** But in Philosophical Disputes, 'tis not allowable to work u. SHAFTESB.

U·ndergrowth. 1600. [UNDER-[1] I. 2 b, IV. b.] **1.** A growth of plants or shrubs under trees; brushwood. **b.** The shorter stems of flax and other plants 1765. **2.** A growth of (shorter and finer) hair or wool underlying the outer fur or fleece 1641. **3.** The condition of being undergrown or undersized 1891.

1. This intricate wild wilderness of trees..and u. of odorous plants SHELLEY.

U·nderhand, *a.* (*sb.*) 1592. [f. next.] **1.** Of a swimming stroke: Made with the hand below the surface of the water 1705. **b.** *Cricket.* Of bowling: With the hand under the ball and lower than the shoulder or (formerly) the elbow 1850. **c.** Of a bowler: Bowling thus 1848. **2.** Secret, surreptitious. Also *absol.* 1592. **b.** Of persons: Not straightforward 1842. **3.** Not open or obvious; unobtrusive 1600. **B.** *sb.* An underhand ball; underhand bowling 1866.

2. Several indirect and u. Practices ADDISON. **b.** I am often accused of being u. and uncandid J. H. NEWMAN. **3.** I..haue by vnder-hand meanes laboured to disswade him from it SHAKS.

Underha·nd, *adv.* OE. [UNDER-[2].] †**1.** In (or into) subjection; in (one's) possession or power; in hand, under attention or execution –1693. **2.** *Cricket.* With underhand action (see prec. 1 b) 1828. **3.** In secret; covertly, stealthily. Now *arch.* 1538.

3. He does it under hand, out of a reseru'd disposition to doe thee good without ostentation 1611. The rest being put to the sword, saue those that were vnderhand saued by the Sidonians 1615.

Underhanded (stress var.), *adv.* and *a.* 1822. [f. UNDERHAND *a.*] **A.** *adv.* = prec. 2, 3. **B.** *adj.* **1.** = UNDERHAND *a.* 2, 2 b. 1853. **2.** Short of 'hands'; undermanned 1834. Hence **Underha·nded-ly** *adv.*, **-ness.**

Underhung (stress var.), *ppl. a.* 1683. [UNDER-[1] I. 1 a.] **1.** Having the lower jaw projecting beyond the upper, or coming unusually far forward. **b.** Projecting beyond the upper jaw 1809. **2.** *Mech.* Suspended on an underlying support; *spec.* of a sliding-door moving on a rail placed below it 1855.

1. He..must lament his being very much underhung JANE AUSTEN.

Underi·vative *a.* [UN-[1] 1] 1656. **Underi·ved** *ppl. a.* [UN-[1] 2] 1630.

U·nder-jaw. 1687. [UNDER-[1] I. 2 b.] The lower jaw or mandible.

U·nder-king. OE. [UNDER-[1] II. 1 a.] A prince or ruler subordinate to a chief king.

Each having its own Ealdorman or Under-King, though united under one supreme chief FREEMAN. So **U·nder-ki:ngdom** 1581.

Underlaid (stress var.), *ppl. a.* ME. [UNDER-[1] I. 1 a.] **1.** Laid under or below. **2.** Supported or strengthened from below 1530. **b.** Supplied underneath *with* or *by* (something) 1658. **3.** *Printing.* Of type, etc.: Raised by means of an underlay 1771.

2. That man's faith is well u., that upholds it selfe by the Omnipotency of God 1618. **b.** The Floor of the Vault was all loose, and u. with several Springs 1712.

U·nderlay, *sb.* 1612. [UNDER-[1] I. 1 d.] **1. a.** A piece added to the sole of a shoe. **b.** = EKE *sb.* 2 b. 1641. **c.** A wedge or piece inserted as a prop or support, esp. so as to make one part level with another 1683. **d.**

Printing. A piece of paper or cardboard placed under type, plates, etc. to raise them to the required level 1683. **e.** Felt, etc. laid under a carpet or mattress. **2.** *Mining.* = DIP *sb.* 5. 1831.

Underlay·, *v.* [OE. *underlecgan*; see UNDER-¹ I. 1 a and LAY *v.*] **1.** *trans.* To support by placing something beneath. Const. *with.* †**b.** To sole or patch the soles of (shoes) 1530. **c.** *Printing.* To adjust (type, etc.) with an underlay (see prec. 1 d) 1683. **2.** To put (something) beneath OE. **3.** = UNDERLIE *v.* 3. 1591. **4.** intr. *Mining.* To slope, incline from the perpendicular 1728.

1. If the Board be too thin, they u. that Board upon every Joyst with a Chip 1679. **b.** *fig.* Our souls have trode awry in all mens sight, We'll u. 'em till they go upright 1622. **4.** It occurs reposing on granite, and underlaying basalt 1799.

U·nderleaf. 1707. [UNDER-¹ I. 1 b.] **1.** A variety of cider apple. **2.** The under surface of a leaf 1873.

Underle·t, *v.* 1677. [UNDER-¹ III. 1 c, d.] **1.** *trans.* To let an amount or rental less than the true value. **2.** To let to a subtenant; to sublet 1819.

1. The land indeed had been greatly underlet 1874.

U·nderlie, *sb.* 1778. [UNDER-¹ I. 1 d.] *Mining.* = UNDERLAY *sb.* 2.

Underlie·, *v.* [OE. *underlicgan*; see UNDER-¹ I. 1 a + LIE *v.*¹] †**1.** *trans.* To be ruled by, to be subject or subordinate to (a person or thing) –1594. **2.** To submit to; to undergo; to have imposed on one: **a.** a penalty, accusation, etc., OE.; **b.** *Sc.* the law 1453. **3.** To lie under; esp. *Geol.* of strata 1600. **b.** *fig.* To form a basis or foundation to; to exist beneath the surface-aspect of 1856. †**4.** *intr.* To be buried –1739. **5.** *Mining.* = UNDERLAY *v.* 4. 1778.

1. Obeye ȝe to ȝoure prouostis, or prelatis, and vndir-ligge to hem WYCLIF *Heb.* 13:17. **2.** [He] shall incur and underly the pain and punishment of death 1678. **b.** To underly the law for the said slauchter 1507. **3.** These deep-seated igneous formations must u. all the strata containing organic remains 1830. **b.** The charm which underlies the facts of rustic life SYMONDS. **4.** Here underlyes William Plowden 1739. **5.** The vein underlies west 10 degrees from the vertical 1899.

U·nderlife. 1847. [UNDER-¹ I. 2 c.] A life beneath the surface.

U·nderline, *sb.* [UNDER-¹ I. 2 b, c.] **1.** The line of the lower part of the body (of an animal). **2.** A line drawn under written or printed words. **b.** *pl.* Ruled guiding lines placed under paper that is being written on. 1888.

Underli·ne, *v.*¹ 1545. [UNDER-¹ I. 1 a.] *trans.* To furnish with an underlining; to form an underlining to.

Underli·ne, *v.*² 1531. [UNDER-¹ I. 1 a.] *trans.* To mark (words, etc.) with a line or lines drawn underneath for emphasis, as a direction to italicize, etc. **b.** *fig.* To emphasize, esp. in utterance 1880.

U·nderlinen. 1862. [UNDER-¹ I. 2 a.] Underclothing of linen (or similar) material.

U·nderling, *sb.* (*a.*) [Early ME. f. UNDER *adv.* 2 + -LING¹.] **A.** *sb.* **1.** One who is subordinate or subject to another; in later use *esp.* a lower official, an understrapper. **b.** A weakly plant, animal, or child. Now *dial.* 1688. **2.** *predic.*, passing into adj. Subject, subordinate (*to*). late ME. **b.** So in attrib. use 1615.

1. My lord..I am ȝoure knyght and ȝoure vndirlyng 1400. He undoubtedly felt..an impatience of fools and underlings EMERSON. **2.** Lilis..would not be vnderling, and Adam would not endure her his equall PURCHAS. **b.** The u. Pedlars amongst the Presbyterians may write what they please 1693.

B. *adj.* **1.** Undersized, small, weak 1722. **2.** Low-growing 1830. **3.** Unimportant 1804.

2. A most troublesome u. weed 1830. **3.** While they can employ me more to their own advantage in little u. works SOUTHEY.

U·nderlining, *sb.* 1580. [UNDER-¹ I. 2 c.] The inner lining of a garment, etc.; a lining under the brim.

Underli·ning, *vbl. sb.* 1864. [f. UNDERLINE *v.*²] The action of the vb. UNDERLINE; a line or lines drawn beneath words, etc.

U·nderlip. 1669. [UNDER-¹ I. 2 b. Cf. G. *unterlippe.*] The lower lip of a person, animal, or insect.

U·nderlying, *ppl. a.* 1611. [f. UNDERLIE *v.*] Lying under or beneath.

The stones That name the under-lying dead TENNYSON. The identity of phraseology does but serve to bring into prominence the u. differences 1882.

Undermanned (stress var.), *ppl. a.* 1867. [UNDER-¹ IV. a.] Not furnished with a sufficient number of men; short-handed.

U·ndermaster. late ME. [UNDER-¹ II. 1 a.] A subordinate instructor; esp. an assistant teacher in a school.

Under-mentioned (stress var.), *ppl. a.* 1640. [UNDER *adv.* 2 b.] Named or noted below or in a place beneath.

Undermi·ne, *v.* Also †**undermind**(e. ME. [f. UNDER-¹ I. 1 a + MINE *v.*, prob. after MDu. *ondermineren* (cf. Du. *ondermijnen*).] **1.** *trans.* To excavate beneath, to make a passage or mine under (a wall, etc.), esp. as a military operation; to sap. **b.** *absol.* To make mines. late ME. **c.** *fig.* late ME. **2. a.** Of water: To work under and wash away (ground, etc.). late ME. **b.** Of animals: To burrow under or in; to make insecure through burrowing; to make (a passage) by burrowing 1526. **c.** *Path.* To erode below the surface 1879. **3.** *fig.* To work secretly against (a person); to overthrow or supplant by underhand means. late ME. **4.** To win over, pervert, by subtle means 1457. **5.** To weaken, injure, destroy or ruin, insidiously 1569. **b.** To sap (the health or constitution) by degrees 1812.

1. The wal of Babilon..with vndermyning shal be vndermyned WYCLIF *Jer.* 51:58. **c.** As yet, the house is not fallen; but it is completely undermined BURKE. **2. a.** A strong heady streame, undermining great hygh bankes 1562. **b.** There was a Towne in Spayne vndermined with Connyes LYLY. **3.** He maye well be called Iacob, for he hath vndermined me now two tymes COVERDALE *Gen.* 27:36. He..with slie shiftes and wiles did vnderminde All noble Knights SPENSER. **4.** She undermin'd my Soul With Tears DRYDEN. **5.** Goe not aboute to vndermine my life SIR T. MORE. A dangerous sort of men that would u. received principles BERKELEY. **b.** But years advancing undermined his health CRABBE. Hence **Undermi·ning** *vbl. sb.* and *ppl. a.* **Undermi·ningly** *adv.*

U·ndermost, *a.* 1555. [UNDER *adv.* + -MOST.] **1.** *adj.* Holding the lowest place or position. **2.** *predic.* In the lowest or lower place or position 1617.

1. The fall is greater from the first to the second, then from the second to the vndermost SIDNEY. **2.** The assailant..flung himself above the struggling Saracen, and..kept him u. SCOTT.

Undern (ʊ·ndəɹn). *Obs.* exc. *arch.* and *dial.* [OE. *undern* = OFris. *undern, -en,* OS. *undorn, -ern,* OHG. *untorn, -arn* (Du. dial. *onder,* G. dial. *untern, undern, unnern*), ON. *undorn, -arn,* Goth. in *undaurni*|*mats* ἄριστον; Gmc. formation meaning 'morning' or 'midday', prob. f. UNDER in the sense of 'between'.] †**1.** The third hour of the day; about 9 a.m.; in eccl. use = tierce –1500. †**2.** The sixth hour; midday –1493. **3.** The afternoon or evening. Now *dial.* 1470. **4.** *dial.* A light or intermediate meal esp. one taken in the afternoon 1691. †**5.** *attrib.* in *u. tide, time.*

1. Whanne it is the thridde our of the day, or vndirne WYCLIF *Acts* 2:15. **2.** Sothli the our was, as the sixte, or vndurn WYCLIF *John* 4:6. **3.** *The Aunder,* or as they pronounce it in Cheshire, Oneder; the afternoon RAY. **4.** *Oanders,* the afternoon meal, often sent out in harvest time to the labourers in the fields 1887.

Undernamed (stress var.), *ppl. a.* 1599. [UNDER *adv.* 2 b.] Named or specified below.

Underneа·th, *prep., adv.,* and *sb.* [OE. *underneoþan,* f. UNDER *prep.* and *adv.* + *neoþan* beneath.] **A.** *prep.* **1.** Beneath or below (in local position). **b.** *fig.* Under the form, cover, protection, authority, etc., of. late ME. **2.** Under the power or control of. Now *arch.* late ME.

1. Vndernethe that castel they sawe a knyghte standynge MALORY. **b.** The truths which lay u. its false worship 1845. **2.** A man u. many Passions, but above fear 1651.

B. *adv.* **1.** Down below; at a lower level OE. **b.** Below or beneath other clothing. late ME. **c.** Lower down on a sheet of paper, etc. late ME. **2.** On the under side 1776.

1. Lyke as they yᵗ wrestleth be somtyme aboue, & somtyme vnderneath 1526. *fig.* If such a Union as this be not accepted on the Army's part, be confident there is a single Person u. MILT. **b.** He wore a suit of black armour..and u. a shirt of close mail 1856. **2.** The leaves..not shining or hoary u. 1812.

C. *sb.* The under part or side 1676.

U·nderpart. 1662. [UNDER-¹ I. 2 b, II. 1 b.] **1.** A lower part or portion. **b.** *pl.* The underside of the body (of a bird or animal) 1783. **2.** A minor role, esp. in a play; a subordinate actor 1679. **3.** A subdivision 1711.

2. Making..even Jocasta but an u. to him DRYDEN. **3.** Uniform Division into Parts and Under-Parts 1711.

U·nder-pe·tticoat: see UNDER-¹ I. 2 a.

Underpi·n, *v.* 1522. [UNDER-¹ I. 1 a.] **1.** *trans.* To support, strengthen (a building, etc.) from beneath, *spec.* by laying a solid underground foundation or substituting stronger or more solid for weaker materials 1533. **b.** *fig.* To support, corroborate 1522. **2.** To form a base or support to 1878.

1. We underpinned that West End of it, where we found that there was nothing supporting the upper Work, but the Bond of the Stones 1776. **b.** Was it unlawfull..to u. Episcopacy with some Texts of Scripture? 1646. Hence **Underpi·nning** *vbl. sb.* the action of the vb.; the materials or structure used for this; *fig.* a prop.

U·nderplay, *sb.* 1845. [UNDER-¹ II. 1 b, UNDER *adj.*] **1.** An underlaying action or motion. **2.** *Cards.* The leading of a low card when a higher card is in the hand 1850.

U·nderplay, *v.* 1733. [UNDER *adv.*] **1.** *refl.* To play below one's ability. **2.** *intr.* To play a low card when holding a high one 1850.

U·nderplot. 1668. [UNDER-¹ II. 1 b, III. 2.] **1.** A (dramatic or literary) plot subordinate to the main plot. **2.** An underhand scheme or trick 1668.

1. I have laid my under-plot in low life SHERIDAN. **2.** They still suspect an Under-Plot in every female Action ADDISON.

U·nderprop, *sb.* 1579. [UNDER-¹ I. 2 b.] A prop or support placed under a thing.

Underpro·p, *v.* 1513. [UNDER-¹ I. 1 a.] **1.** *trans.* To support with or as with a prop or props 1532. **2.** *fig.* To support; to maintain 1513. **3.** To form a prop or support to (something) 1590.

1. This doctrine is a..Pillar, to under prop the Chamber in Hell, which they call Purgatory 1645. **2.** He thought fit to u. it with his earthly God, the Leviathan WARBURTON. **3.** Six columns..underpropt a rich Throne of the massive ore TENNYSON.

Underra·te, *v.* 1623. [UNDER-¹ IV. a.] †**1.** *trans.* To depreciate –1649. **2.** To assess (for taxation) too low 1641. **3.** To rate or estimate at too low a value or worth 1650. **4.** To underestimate in amount or extent 1691.

Underru·n, *v.* 1547. [UNDER-¹ I. 1 a, b.] **1.** *trans.* To run, flow, or pass beneath 1594. **2.** *Naut.* To overhaul or examine (a cable, etc.) on the under side, *spec.* by drawing a boat along under it 1547. **b.** To pull in (a net or trawl) in order to clear it of the catch and reset it 1883. **3.** In pa. pple.: see quot. 1855.

1. The granite is under-run by schistose earth 1799. The principle..underran all these modifications 1882. **2.** The harbour..is..very rocky, the bottom so much so as to make it necessary to under-run every cable 1798. **b.** Underrunning a trawl means pulling it in on one side of the dory, picking off the fish, rebaiting the hooks, and passing them back to the sea again KIPLING. **3.** Cut away all hoof that is separated from the sensitive parts, or..'under-run' 1855.

U·nder-ru·nner. 1882. [UNDER-¹ I. 1 b.] *Printing.* A side-note continued across the foot of the page.

Undersco·re, *v.* 1771. [UNDER-¹ I. 1 d.] *trans.* To underline.

†**Underscri·ber.** 1681. [UNDER-¹ I. 1 b.] A subscriber to a document –1785.

U·nder-se·cretary. 1687. [UNDER-¹ II. 1 a.] An assistant secretary; esp. as the title of the official immediately subordinate to or ranking next in a department below a Secretary of State. Hence **U·nder-se·cretaryship.**

Underse·ll, *v.* 1622. [UNDER-¹ III. 1 b, IV. a.] **1.** *trans.* To sell at a lower price than (another person). **b.** *transf.* (Said of the thing sold) 1757. **2.** To sell at too low a price 1647.

2. The farmer for haste is forced to under-sell his corn 1662.

U·nderset, *sb.* 1747. [UNDER-¹ I. 2 b.] **1.** *Mining.* A lower vein of ore. **2.** An undercurrent running counter to the surface motion of water 1815.

Underse·t, *v.* ME. [UNDER-¹ I. 1 a.] **1.** *trans.* To support or strengthen by something placed beneath; to prop up. **b.** To serve as a support to (*rare*) ME. **2.** *fig.* To support, sustain, or strengthen. late ME. **3.** To set or place under something ME. **4.** To sublet 1804.

1. He shall prepare props.. to vnder set his vines 1600. The Custom House, London, was underset some years ago, a new foundation having been made to it without the superstructure being disturbed 1842. **2.** Yf oure soules be truely vnderset wyth sure hope TINDALE. **3.** Iulian the Apostata did vnderset his shoulder, to shore vp the seruice of the false Gods 1587. **4.** These middle-men will u. the land, and live in idleness MAR. EDGEWORTH. Hence **Underse·tter,** a supporter, a prop. **Underse·tting** *vbl. sb.*

U·nderse:ttle. *Obs.* exc. *Hist.* ME. [f. UNDER-¹ II. 1 a + *-set(t)le* = OE. *-setla*, f. *set-*, root of SIT *v.*] One who occupies a house (or part of one) held by another; a subtenant.

U·ndershirt. 1648. [UNDER-¹ I. 2 a.] A garment worn under a shirt; a vest.

Undersho·re, *v.* late ME. [UNDER-¹ I. 1 a.] **1.** *trans.* To prop up; to strengthen with shores. **2.** *fig.* To support, strengthen 1500.

1. To vnder-shore the ruinous walls 1608. **2.** Yf ye wyll vnder-shore Hys croked old age 1500.

U·ndershot, (*ppl.*) *a.* (and *sb.*) 1510. [UNDER-¹ I. 1 a.] **1.** Of a mill-wheel: Driven by water passing under the wheel; so of a mill. **2.** = UNDERHUNG *ppl. a.* 1. 1881. **B.** *sb.* An undershot wheel or mill 1705.

U·ndershrub. 1598. [UNDER-¹ I. 2 d.] A low-growing shrub; *spec.* in *Bot.*, a plant with a shrubby base.

U·nderside. 1680. [UNDER-¹ I. 2 b.] The under or lower side or surface.

Undersigned, *ppl. a.* 1643. [Cf. SUBSIGN *v.*] Whose signature is below.

Under-sized (stress var.), *ppl. a.* 1706. [UNDER-¹ IV. a.] Below the proper or ordinary size.

U·nder-skirt. 1861. [UNDER-¹ I. 2 a.] **1.** A skirt worn under another, a petticoat. **2.** A foundation for the drapery of the skirt 1883.

U·ndersong. 1579. [UNDER-¹ III. 2 b.] **1.** A subordinate song or strain, esp. one serving as an accompaniment or burden to another. Freq. *transf.* of natural sounds. **2.** *fig.* An underlying meaning; an undertone 1631.

1. Who the Roundelay shoold singe And who againe the vndersong should beare DRAYTON. **2.** If there is any fault in the Preface, it is not affectation, but an u. of disrespect to the public KEATS.

Understand (ʌndəɹstæ·nd), *v.* [OE. *understandan* = OFris. *understonda*, OIcel. (as a foreign word) *undirstanda*; cf. MLG. *understān* understand, step under, MDu. *onderstaen* (Du. *-staan*), MHG. *understān, -stēn* (G. *unterstehen*), and with another prefix, OE. *forstandan*, OS. *farstandan*, OHG. *firstantan*, MHG. *verstān, -stēn* (G. *verstehen*), MDu. *verstaen* (Du. *-staan*).] **1.** *trans.* To comprehend; to apprehend the meaning or import of. **b.** To be expert with or at by practice 1533. **c.** To apprehend clearly the character or nature of (a person) 1587. **†d.** *refl.* To know one's place –1745. **2.** To be able to interpret (a language, words, signs) OE. **b.** *To u. each other*, to be agreed or in collusion 1663. **3.** To comprehend as a fact; to realize. Chiefly with clause as obj. OE. **4.** To accept as true or existent; to regard as settled or implied without specific mention OE. **b.** To have knowledge of, to know or learn, by information received ME. **c.** To take or accept as a fact, without positive knowledge or certainty; to believe 1751. **5.** To interpret or view in a certain way OE. **b.** To regard as denoted *by* (the expression used) ME. **c.** To regard (an expression, etc.) as used *of* or applied to 1549. **6.** To supply mentally (something not expressly stated). Chiefly *Gram.* 1530. **b.** In pa. pple.: Implied, though not expressed 1580. **7.** To stand under. late ME. **8.** *intr.* To have comprehension or understanding (in general or in a particular manner) OE. **b.** Const. *about*, etc. OE. **9.** In parenthetic use (chiefly *I u.*): To believe or assume, on account of information received or by inference ME.

1. The multytude of dyuerse ceremonyes..not being vnderstanded nor perceyued of the comen sorte 1523. Now clear I u. What oft my steddiest thoughts have searcht in vain MILT. One half of the world cannot u. the pleasures of the other JANE AUSTEN. **b.** He..understood a small Sword excellently well 1727. **c.** It is my misfortune to be little understood 1846. **d.** You doe not vnderstand your selfe so cleerely, As it behoues my Daughter, and your Honour SHAKS. **2.** Now herkeneth, euery maner man That englissh understonde kan CHAUCER. **b.** 'You trust me', replied Leather..with a look as much as to say, 'we u. each other' SURTEES. **3.** Howbeit they vnderstode not, that he spake of the father COVERDALE *John* 8:27. This Œdipus, you must u...was son to a King of Thebes ADDISON. **4.** Warr then, Warr Open or understood must be resolv'd MILT. **b.** When the colonell's wife understood her husband's bad accommodation 1664. **c.** The General, I u. by his last letter, is in town COWPER. **5.** I shewed hym that it was not necessary, that the words shulde so be vnderstonde as they sownde 1533. **b.** We do not u. by this advancement, in general, the mere making of money RUSKIN. **c.** Which is true, if understood only of the Rivers of Italy ADDISON. **6.** The Ancient Romans said *Saturam* understanding *Lancem* 1704. An exception in favour of the Nabob was, from standing usage, so much understood, that to express it had appeared altogether useless JAMES MILL. **7.** Thy rude hand Would lift a shield, thou canst not vnder stand HEYWOOD. **8.** They know not nor will u., In darkness they walk on MILT. **b.** You quite u. about that little matter of business being safe in my hands? 1860. **9.** Hire fader was a man of grete powre, And kyng of aufrike as I vnderstonde 1440. Hence **Understa·ndable** *a.*, **-ably** *adv.* **Understa·nder** (now *rare*).

Understanding (ʌndəɹstæ·ndiŋ), *vbl. sb.* OE. [f. prec. + -ING¹.] **1.** Ability to understand; intelligence, judgement. **b.** *Of u.*, intelligent, capable of judging with knowledge. late ME. **c.** With *the*: The faculty of comprehending and reasoning; the intellect. late ME. **2.** The degree or quality of the intellectual faculty in a particular person or set of persons. late ME. **†3.** Meaning, signification –1728. **4.** *A good u.*, amicable or friendly relations 1649. **b.** An agreement of an informal but more or less explicit nature 1812. **5.** *slang. pl.* **a.** Boots, shoes 1822. **b.** Legs, feet 1828.

1. Vnderstanding is a power of the Soule, by which we perceiue, know, remember, and Iudge 1621. **c.** The U., like the Eye..takes no notice of it self LOCKE. **2.** It gave him..a very mean opinion of our understandings SWIFT. **3.** Single words haue their sence and vnderstanding altered 1589. **4.** To cultivate a good u. between the two countries 1762. **b.** With this u. we parted for the night TYNDALL.

Understa·nding, *ppl. a.* ME. [f. as prec. + -ING².] Having knowledge and judgement; discerning, intelligent, sagacious.

Geue therfore vnto thy seruaunt an vnderstandyng hert BIBLE (Great) 1 *Kings* 3:9. An elephant (an vnderstanding beast) SIR T. HERBERT. Aristotle..was an u. fellow OTWAY. Hence **Understa·ndingly** *adv.*

Understa·te, *v.* 1824. [UNDER- IV. a.] *trans.* To fall below the truth in stating; to put too low. Also *absol.* So **Understa·tement** 1799.

U·nder-stew:ard. 1472. [UNDER-¹ II.] Hence **U:nder-stew·ardship.**

Understoo·d, *ppl. a.* 1605. [f. UNDERSTAND *v.*] **1.** Comprehended; known; appreciated, realized. **2.** Agreed upon; assumed as known or fixed 1607. **3.** *Gram.* Implied but not expressed 1848.

2. It was an u. thing that no one was to be ill or tired MRS. GASKELL.

U·nderstra:pper. 1704. [f. UNDER-¹ II. 1 a + STRAP *v.*] A subordinate; an underling. So **U·nderstra:pping** *a.* of a subordinate or inferior character or standing.

Understu·dy, *v.* 1874. [UNDER-¹ II. 2.] **1.** *trans.* To study (a theatrical part) in readiness to take the place of a principal actor or actress if necessary. **2.** To act as understudy to (an actor or actress) 1884. Hence **U·nderstu:dy** *sb.* one who understudies a part 1882.

Undertake (ʌndəɹtēⁱ·k), *v.* ME. [f. UNDER-¹ III. 1 a + TAKE *v.*, superseding OE. *underfōn*, ME. *underfo, -fong* (see FANG *v.*¹), and *underniman* (see NIM), ME. *undernime*, which survived till XV.] **†1.** *trans.* To overtake, seize –1470. **†b.** To rebuke –1691. **†2.** To receive, accept –1623. **†b.** To hear –1596. **†c.** To understand –1510. **3.** To take upon oneself; to take in hand; freq. = to enter upon, begin ME. **b.** Const. *to* with inf. (Sometimes implying a solemn pledge or promise.) ME. **c.** To give a formal promise or pledge *that*; to venture to assert. late ME. **d.** *I* (*dare*) *u.*, added to a statement. late ME. **4.** To take in charge, accept the charge of ME. **b.** To engage in combat with 1470. **c.** To take in hand to deal with (a person) 1601. **†5.** To pretend to, assume –1608. **†6.** *intr.* To enter upon, commit oneself to, an enterprise –1639. **7.** To give a pledge or promise 1475. **8.** To become surety or make oneself answerable *for* 1548.

1. So sire Tristram endured there grete payne, for sekenesse had vndertake hym MALORY. **2. b.** Whose voice so soone as he did vndertake, Eftsoones he stood as still as any stake SPENSER. **3.** He which þat no þyng vnder-taketh No þyng ne acheueth CHAUCER. [They] are readie to u. more than they are able to undergo 1654. **b.** I alone first undertook To wing the desolate Abyss MILT. **c.** He undertook to me, that the King should ask me no question BURNET. **d.** Wel coude he peynte, I vndirtake, That sich ymage coude make CHAUCER. You have gallants among you, I dare u., that have made the Virginia voyage SCOTT. **4.** The Holy Ghost undertakes every man amongst us and would make every man fit for Gods service DONNE. **b.** Sir, he shall yeeld you all the honor of a competent aduersarie, if you please to vnder-take him B. JONSON. **5.** You are like to Sir Vincentio. His name and credite shal you vndertake. SHAKS. **6.** Hardy he was and wys to vndertake CHAUCER. **7.** I, as I undertook,..Have found him MILT. **8.** She..undertook for her brother John's good behaviour ARBUTHNOT. Hence **Underta·kable** *a.* **Underta·ken** *ppl. a.*

Undertaker (ʌ·ndəɹtēⁱkəɹ). late ME. [f. prec. + -ER¹.] **†1.** A helper or protector –1645. **†b.** A surety –1706. **†c.** A baptismal sponsor –1697. **2.** One who undertakes a task or enterprise. late ME. **3.** *Hist.* **a.** One who undertook to hold crown lands in Ireland in the 16th and 17th centuries 1586. **b.** One of those who in the reigns of the first three Stuart kings of England undertook to influence the action of Parliament, esp. with regard to the voting of supplies 1620. **c.** One of those Lowland Scots who attempted to colonize the Island of Lewis in the late 16th c. 1819. **4.** A contractor. Now *rare.* 1602. **b.** One who makes a business of carrying out the arrangements for funerals 1698. **5.** One who embarks on or takes part in some business enterprise. Now *rare.* 1615. **†b.** One who undertakes the preparation of a literary work –1800. **†c.** A publisher –1823 **†d.** A dramatic producer or impresario –1740.

1. Columbus..repaires to some Christian Princes for his vndertakers SIR T. HERBERT. **c.** A venerable old Deacon who had been the U. for him at his Baptism 1673. **2.** The Devil..Who was the first bold U. of bearing Arms against his Maker 1680. **3. a.** These lands in the counties of Cork and Kerry..were parcelled out among English undertakers at low rents HALLAM. **4.** An Agreement is concluded with Undertakers for furnishing the Magazines..with Forage 1710. **b.** His appearance has a stronger effect on my spirits than an undertaker's shop GOLDSM. **5.** The mine..yielded vast profit to the undertakers 1752. **b.** The u. himself will publish his proposals with all convenient speed SWIFT. **d.** No Company could flourish while the chief Actors and Undertakers were at variance CIBBER.

Underta·king, *vbl. sb.* late ME. [f. as prec. + -ING¹.] **†1.** Energy, enterprise (*rare*). **2.** Something undertaken or attempted; an enterprise. late ME. **b.** The action of taking in hand 1600. **c.** *spec.* The business of a funeral undertaker 1850. **3.** A pledge, promise; a guarantee. late ME.

2. The consequences, which would naturally attend such a rash u. CLARENDON. **b.** That which is required of each one towardes the vndertaking of this aduenture HAKLUYT. **3.** Three hundred pounds a year, which he proposed to pay to her on an u. that she would never trouble him THACKERAY.

U·nderthings, *sb. pl.* 1864. [UNDER-¹ I. 2 b.] Underclothing.

Under-time, var. UNDERN-*time.*

U·ndertone, *sb.* 1806. [UNDER-¹ I. 2 c, III. 2, 2 b.] **1.** A low or subdued tone: **a.** of utterance. **b.** of sound 1833. **2.** *fig.* An underlying tone or undercurrent (*of* feeling, etc.) 1861. **b.** A subdued or underlying tone of colour 1891. **c.** The general basis of Exchange or market dealings in any stock or commodity 1897.

2. Throughout all these high reasonings..there runs an u. of controversy 1879. **c.** Maize has had a weak u. during the entire session 1902. Hence **U·ndertone** *v. trans.* to accompany as an u. **U·ndertoned** *ppl. a.*[1] expressed in an u.

U:nderto·ned, *ppl. a.*[2] 1849. [UNDER-[1] IV. a.] Defective in tone.

U·ndertow. 1817. [UNDER-[1] I. 2 c.] A current below the surface of water, moving in a contrary direction to that of the surface current.

U·nder-trea:surer. 1447. [UNDER-[1] II. 1 a.] A deputy treasurer; *spec.* the officer immediately subordinate to the Lord High Treasurer of England.

U:nderva·lue, *v.* 1596. [UNDER-[1] IV. b.] †**1.** *trans.* To rate as inferior in value *to* –1612. **2.** To rate at too low a monetary value 1599. **b.** To reduce or diminish in value 1622. **3.** To estimate too low; to value or appreciate insufficiently; to depreciate 1611.

1. Or shall I thinke in Siluer she's immur'd Being ten times vndervalued to tride gold SHAKS. **2. b.** The currency has been undervalued by the fraudulent issue 1866. **3.** He who undervalues himself is justly undervalued by others HAZLITT. Hence **U:ndervalua·tion. U·nderva:lue** *sb.* **U:nderva·luer.**

U·ndervest. 1813. [UNDER-[1] I. 2 a.] A vest worn underneath a shirt.

U·nderwa:ter, *sb.* 1637. [UNDER-[1] I. 1 a, 2 a, b.] **1.** Water below the surface of the ground. **2.** Water entering a vessel from beneath 1645.

U·nderwa:ter, *a.* 1627. [attrib. use of phr. *under water.*] **1.** Placed, situated, carried on, etc., under water. **2.** *spec.* In ships: Situated below the water-line 1882.

U·nderwear. 1880. [UNDER-[1] I. 2 a.] Underclothing.

U·nderweight. 1596. [UNDER-[1] IV. b.] Insufficient weight; deficiency in weight.

U·nderwing. 1535. [UNDER-[1] I. 2 b, UNDER-[2].] **1.** A wing placed under, or partly covered by, another. **2.** Used *attrib.*, with adjs. of colour, in collectors' names of moths 1749. **b.** *ellipt.* an u. moth 1819.

2. The great yellow-u. moth 1749. **b.** The common yellow under-wings DARWIN.

U·nderwood. ME. [UNDER-[1] I. 2 d.] **1.** Small trees or shrubs growing beneath timber trees; brushwood. **2.** With *a* and *pl.* A quantity or stretch, a special kind, of this 1541.

1. Thinke when an oake fals, vnderwood shrinkes downe, And yet may liue, though brusd 1596. *fig.* But these are the Under-Wood of Satire, rather than the Timber-Trees DRYDEN. **2.** Our little habitation was..sheltered with a beautiful u. behind GOLDSM.

U·nderwork, *sb.* 1624. [UNDER-[1] I. 2 c, III. 2, IV. b.] **1.** A structure placed under or supporting something. **2.** Subordinate or inferior work 1645. **b.** Underhand or secret work 1814.

Underwo·rk, *v.* 1595. [UNDER-[1] III. 1 a, b, IV. a.] †**1.** *trans.* To work secretly against –1659. **2.** To impose too little work on 1882. **b.** *intr.* To do too little work 1902. **3.** *trans.* To work for less wages than (another) 1695.

U·nderworld. 1608. [UNDER-[1] I. 2 b, 1 c.] **1.** The sublunary or terrestrial world 1609. **2.** The abode of the dead; the nether world 1608. **b.** Any subterranean region 1885. **3.** The Antipodes; also, the part of the earth beyond the horizon 1847. **4.** A sphere or region lying below the ordinary one. Also *fig.*, the lowest stratum of society. 1859.

2. The western Hades, the u. of night and death 1871. **b.** The u. in the Potteries is honeycombed with coal mines 1885. **3.** The first beam glittering on a sail, That brings our friends up from the u. TENNYSON.

U·nderwrite, *v.* late ME. [f. UNDER-[1] I. 1 a, after L. *subscribere.*] **1.** *trans.* To write (words, etc.) below something, esp. after other written matter. †**b.** To sign (one's name) to a document –1793. †**2.** To subscribe (a document) with one's name –1748. **b.** To subscribe (a policy of insurance) thereby accepting the risk of insurance 1622. **c.** *absol.* To carry on the business of insurance 1784. **3.** To subscribe to (a decision, statement, etc.); to agree to or confirm by signature 1606. †**4.** To guarantee to contribute (a certain sum of money, etc.) –1705. **b.** To agree to take up, in a new company or new issue (a certain number of shares if not applied for by the public) 1889.

1. Each Subscriber should u. his Reason for the Place he allots his Candidate 1709. **b.** The Acceptant, when he accepts, must u. his Name 1682. **2.** No importunity could prevail with him to u. this will 1655. **b.** Whosoever..hath underwritten any Policy of Insurance on the Ship Samuel 1703. **3.** I could, with a safe conscience, u. all that he there relates 1853. **4.** The Subscription-Money did not come in with the same readiness, with which it had been underwritten 1705. **b.** A promoter of a company who had agreed to u. 10,000 shares 1889. Hence **U·nderwriting** *vbl. sb.* the action of the vb.; the action or practice of (marine) insurance.

U·nderwri:ter. 1622. [f. prec.] **1.** One who underwrites an insurance policy; *spec.* one who carries on an insurance business, esp. of shipping. **2.** One who underwrites company shares 1889.

Underwri·tten, *ppl. a.* late ME. [UNDER-[1] I. 1 a.] **1.** Written (out), expressed in writing, below; following upon what is already written; specified or set down in writing below, etc. **2.** Of persons: Whose names are written or signed below, etc. late ME.

Undescri·bable *a.* [UN-[1] 1] 1728.

Undescri·bed, *ppl. a.* 1575. [UN-[1] 2.] Not described. **b.** *Nat. Hist.* = NONDESCRIPT *a.* 1. 1680.

Undescrie·d *ppl. a.* [UN-[1] 2] 1595. **Undescri·ptive** *a.* [UN-[1] 1] 1744. **Undese·rve** *v.* [UN-[1] 7] 1621.

Undese·rved, *ppl. a.* late ME. [UN-[1] 2.] †**1.** Without having deserved it; undeserving –1593. **2.** Not deserved better or worse than has been deserved. late ME. Hence **Undese·rved-ly** *adv.*, **-ness.**

Undese·rver. Now *rare.* 1597. [UN-[1] 6.] One who is not deserving (*of* something); an unworthy person.

Undese·rving, *vbl. sb.* 1598. [UN-[1] 8.] Want of desert or merit.

Undese·rving, *ppl. a.* 1549. [UN-[1] 4.] **1.** Lacking desert or merit, not deserving (something good). **b.** With direct object 1603. **2.** Not deserving (bad fortune, etc.); guiltless, innocent 1586. †**3.** Undeserved, unmerited. SHAKS.

1. The vndeseruing rich man COVERDALE. Though u. of our Love 1748. **b.** Creatures u. respect 1860. **2.** To destroy this sonne..u. destruction SIDNEY. If your hard decrees.. Have doomed to death his u. head DRYDEN. Hence **Undese·rvingly** *adv.*

Undesi·gned, *ppl. a.* 1654. [UN-[1] 2.] Not resulting from design; unintentional. Hence **Undesi·gned-ly** *adv.*, **-ness.**

Undesi·gning, *ppl. a.* 1673. [UN-[1] 4.] **1.** Not designing or planning (*rare*). **2.** Having no ulterior or selfish designs; free from designing or underhand motives 1697.

Undesi·rable, *a.* and *sb.* 1667. [UN-[1] 1.] **A.** *adj.* Not to be desired; objectionable. **B.** *sb.* An undesirable person or thing 1883. Hence **Undesirabi·lity. Undesi·rableness, -ably** *adv.*

Undesi·red, *ppl. a.* 1470. [UN-[1] 2.] **1.** Not asked or requested; uninvited. Now *rare.* **2.** Not wished for; unwelcome 1599.

Undesi·ring *ppl. a.* [UN-[1] 4] DRYDEN. **Undesi·rous** *a.* [UN-[1] 1] 1654. **Undespai·ring** *ppl. a.* [UN-[1] 4] 1730. **Undestroy·ed** *ppl. a.* [UN-[1] 2] 1450. **Undete·cted** *ppl. a.* [UN-[1] 2] 1593. **Undete·riorated** *ppl. a.* [UN-[1] 2] 1856. **Undete·rminable** *a.* [UN-[1] 1] 1581. **Undete·rminate** *a.* (now *rare*) [UN-[1] 1] 1603, **-ly** *adv.*, **-ness.**

Undete·rmined, *ppl. a.* 1442. [UN-[1] 2.] **1.** Not authoritatively decided or settled. **b.** Not yet decided; still subject to alteration or uncertainty 1668. **2.** Not certainly known or identified 1588. **3.** Of indefinite meaning or application 1611. **4.** Not restrained within limits 1627. **5.** Not determined or fixed in respect of character, action, etc. 1676. **6.** Undecided, irresolute 1718.

1. The question..was..left u. in the case of Reg. *v.* Robson 1885. **b.** The combat was yet within the u. doom of Providence SCOTT. **2.** Though the date be u. 1697. **3.** Such u. expressions as wide, narrow, deep BERKELEY. **4.** Too absolute and vndetermined a power 1627.

Undete·rred *ppl. a.* [UN-[1] 2] 1607. **Undeve·loped** *ppl. a.* [UN-[1] 2] 1736. **Undeviating** *ppl. a.* [UN-[1] 4] 1732, **-ly** *adv.*

Unde·vil, *v. arch.* 1632. [UN-[2] 2 b, 4.] **1.** *trans.* To free from demoniacal possession. **2.** To deprive of the qualities of a devil 1726.

Undevi·sed *ppl. a.* [UN-[1] 2] 1766. **Undevou·red** *ppl. a.* [UN-[1] 2] 1661. **Undevou·t** *a.* [UN-[1] 1] late ME., **-ly** *adv.* **Unde·xt(e)rous** *a.* [UN-[1] 1] 1688, **-ly** *adv.* **Undiagno·sed** *ppl. a.* [UN-[1] 2] 1864. **Undicta·ted** *ppl. a.* [UN-[1] 2] 1797.

Undies (*ʊ*·ndiz) *sb. pl. colloq.* 1918. [Intended as a euphemistic abbrev. of *under-clothes, -garments,* prob. after *frillies* (1900).] Women's or children's undergarments.

Women's under-wear or 'undies' as they are coyly called 1918.

U:ndifferentiated *ppl. a.* [UN-[1] 2] 1862. **Undi·g** *v.* [UN-[2] 3] 1641.

Undige·sted, *ppl. a.* 1528. [UN-[1] 2.] **1.** Not brought to a mature or proper condition by natural physical change. *arch.* **2.** Not digested in the stomach 1597. **3.** Not reduced to order or harmony; not arranged or classified; chaotic; confused 1598. **b.** Of discourse, ideas, etc. 1655.

1. When we behold the sunne through thicke clouds and u. vapors 1586. **2.** *fig.* His reading, too, though u., was of immense extent MACAULAY. **3. b.** A volume of u. observations 1742.

Undi·ght, *ppl. a. arch.* or *dial.* 1555. [UN-[1] 2.] Not decked, adorned, or put in order.

Undi·gnified, *ppl. a.* 1689. [UN-[1] 2.] †**1.** Of clergy: Not ranking as a dignitary –1833. **2.** Not dignified *by* or *with* something; undistinguished 1716. **3.** Lacking in dignity of manner, etc. 1782.

1. A great number of the u. clergy 1776. **2.** No prosperous event passed u. by poetry JOHNSON. **3.** Genuine emotion..is never u. 1836. Hence **Undi·gnifiedly** *adv.*

Undi·gnify *v.* [UN-[2] 4 c] 1702. **Undi·ligent** *a.* [UN-[1] 1] 1547, **-ly** *adv.* **Undilu·ted** *ppl. a.* [UN-[1] 2] 1756. **Undimi·nishable** *a.* [UN-[1] 1] 1653. **Undimi·nished** *ppl. a.* [UN-[1] 2] 1587. **Undi·mmed** *ppl. a.* [UN-[1] 2] 1723.

Undine (*ʊ*·ndīn). Also **ondine.** 1657. [– mod.L. *undina,* also *undena* (Paracelsus), f. L. *unda* wave; see -INE[1]; whence also Fr. *ondine,* G. *undine.*] A female water-sprite; a nymph.

Spirits of nature, embodiments..of the four elements, sylphs, salamanders, gnomes, and ondines 1865.

Undi·ned *ppl. a.* [UN-[1] 2] 1500. **Undi·nted** *ppl. a.* [UN-[1] 2] SHAKS. **Undiploma·tic** *a.* [UN-[1] 1] 1831.

Undi·pped, *ppl. a.* 1648. [UN-[1] 2.] Not dipped. **b.** *spec.* Unbaptized 1693.

Undire·cted *ppl. a.* [UN-[1] 2] SPENSER. **Undisba·nded** *ppl. a.* [UN-[1] 2] 1641. **Undisce·rned** *ppl. a.* [UN-[1] 2] 1529. **Undisce·rnible** *a.* [UN-[1] 1] 1624, **-ness, -ably** *adv.* **Undisce·rning** *sb.* [UN-[1] 8] STEELE. **Undisce·rning** *ppl. a.* [UN-[1] 4] 1589, **-ly** *adv.*

Undischa·rged, *ppl. a.* 1585. [UN-[1] 2.] **1.** Not paid; not cleared off or settled. **2.** Not freed from obligations or engagements; not discharged in bankruptcy 1603. **3.** Not accomplished or carried out 1705. **4.** Not fired off 1798. **5.** Of cargo: Not unloaded 1864.

2. I know myself an u. debtor COLERIDGE.

Undi·sciplinable *a.* [UN-[1] 1] 1652. **Undi·scipline** [UN-[1] 6] 1827.

Undi·sciplined, *ppl. a.* late ME. [UN-[1] 2.] **1.** Not subjected to discipline; untrained. **2.** Not properly subjected or submissive to military discipline 1718.

Undisclo·sed *ppl. a.* [UN-[1] 2] 1571. **Undisco·loured** *ppl. a.* [UN-[1] 2] 1666. **Undisco·mfited** *ppl. a.* [UN-[1] 2] CHAUCER. **Undisconti·nued** *ppl. a.* [UN-[1] 2] 1629. **Undiscou·rageable** *a.* [UN-[1] 2] 1571. **Undiscou·raged** *ppl. a.* [UN-[1] 1] 1628. **Undisco·verable** *a.* [UN-[1] 1] 1642, **-ably** *adv.* **Undisco·vered** *ppl. a.* [UN-[1] 2] 1542. †**Undiscree·t** *a.* [UN-[1] 1] –1704, †**-ly** *adv.* **Undiscri·minating** *ppl. a.* [UN-[1] 4] COWPER, **-ly** *adv.*, **-ness.** **Undiscu·ssed** *ppl. a.* [UN-[1] 2] ME. **Undisea·sed** *ppl. a.* [UN-[1] 2] 1450. **Undisfi·gured** *ppl. a.* [UN-[1] 2] 1720. **Undisgra·ced** *ppl.a* [UN-[1] 2] 1748. **Undisgui·sable** *a.* [UN-[1] 1] 1673. **Undisgui·se** *sb.* [UN-[1] 6] 1804. **Undisgui·se** *v.* [UN-[2] 2] 1638. **Undisgui·sed** *ppl. a.* [UN-[1] 2] 1500, **-ly** *adv.*, **-ness.** **Undisho·noured** *ppl. a.* [UN-[1] 2] SHAKS. **Undismay·ed** *ppl. a.* [UN-[1] 2] 1615. **Undismi·ssed** *ppl. a.* [UN-[1] 2] COWPER. **Undispa·tched** *ppl. a.* [UN-[1] 2] 1589. **Undispe·lled** *ppl. a.* [UN-[1] 2] 1860.

Undispe·nsed, *ppl. a.* ME. [UN-[1] 2.] Not absolved or released by dispensation.

Undispo·sed, *ppl. a.* late ME. [UN-[1] 2 b.] †**1.** Unfitted –1449. †**2.** Disordered; out of condition –1645. †3. Ill-disposed, unfriendly –1621. **4.** Not disposed of; not put to any purpose 1483. **b.** With *of* (now usual) 1626. **5.** Without inclination, indisposed (*to* or *to do* something) 1590.

3. Some curse Fate, Others..rate Their vndisposed Starres 1621. **4.** The Fens and other Waste and u. Places 1653. The house took care..to prevent the recurrence of an u. surplus HALLAM. **5.** The greater part is carelesse and vndisposed to ioine with them HOOKER.

Undisproved *ppl. a.* [UN-^{1} 2] 1579. **Undi·sputable** *a.* (now *rare*) [UN-^{1} 1] 1598. **Undispu·ted** *ppl. a.* [UN-^{1} 2] 1570, **-ly** *adv.* **Undisse·mbled** *ppl. a.* [UN-^{1} 2] 1651. **Undisse·mbling** *ppl. a.* [UN-^{1} 4] 1613, **-ly** *adv.* **Undi·ssipated** *ppl. a.* [UN-^{1} 2] 1661. **Undisso·lvable** *a.* [UN-^{1} 1] 1611. **Undisso·lved** *ppl. a.* [UN-^{1} 2] 1535. **Undiste·mpered** *ppl. a.* [UN-^{1} 2] 1589. **Undisti·lled** *ppl. a.* [UN-^{1} 2] 1600.

Undisti·nguishable, *a.* 1590. [UN-^{1} 1.] **1.** Incapable of being made out or discerned; imperceptible. **2.** Not to be known apart, too much alike to be distinguished; of which the different elements cannot be distinguished 1679. Hence **Undisti·nguishably** *adv.*

Undisti·nguished, *ppl. a.* 1598. [UN-^{1} 2.] **1.** Not separated or kept distinct. **b.** In which no distinction is or can be made 1608. **c.** Not distinguished *from* or *by* something 1612. **2.** Indistinctly articulated. Now *rare*. 1595. **b.** Not clearly seen; unrecognized 1814. **3.** Not marked by any distinction; not noted or elevated above others 1600.

1. U. clouds, and rocks WORDSW. **c.** Though undistinguish'd from the crowd By wealth or dignity COWPER. **2. b.** Finding herself u. in the dusk JANE AUSTEN.

Undisti·nguishing *ppl. a.* [UN-^{1} 4] 1599, **-ly** *adv.* **Undisto·rted** *ppl. a.* [UN-^{1} 2] 1647. **Undistra·cted** *ppl. a.* [UN-^{1} 2] 1648, **-ly** *adv.*, **-ness. Undistre·ssed** *ppl. a.* [UN-^{1} 2] 1582.

Undistri·buted, *ppl. a.* 1483. [UN-^{1} 2.] Not distributed. **b.** *spec.* in *Logic*. Of a term: Not given its fullest extension, not made universal 1827.

b. It would have an u. middle WHATELEY.

Undistu·rbed *ppl. a.* [UN-^{1} 2] 1610, **-ly** *adv.*, **-ness. Undive·rted** *ppl. a.* [UN-^{1} 2] 1665. **Undive·rting** *ppl. a.* [UN-^{1} 4] 1697. **Undivi·dable** *a.* (now *rare*) [UN-^{1} 1] 1548. **Undivi·ded** *ppl. a.* [UN-^{1} 2] late ME., **-ly** *adv.*, **-ness. Undivi·ne** *a.* [UN-^{1} 2] 1685, **-ly** *adv.* **Undivi·ned** *ppl. a.* [UN-^{1} 2] 1852. **Undivu·lged** *ppl. a.* [UN-^{1} 2] SHAKS.

Undo (ʋndū·), *v.* [OE. *undōn* = OFris. *un(d)dua*, MDu. *ontdoen*, OHG. *intuon*; see UN-^{2}, DO.] **1.** *trans.* To unfasten and open (a door, a receptacle, etc.). **2.** To unfasten by untying or by releasing from a fixed position OE. **b.** To unfasten the clothing of (a person) 1633. †**3.** To cut open; to open with a knife –1688. **4.** *intr.* To come open or undone. Now only *colloq.* ME. **5.** *trans.* To annul, cancel, rescind; to reduce to the condition of not having been done, decided, etc. Also *absol.* OE. **b.** To reverse the doing or making of (some material thing or effect) so as to restore the original form or condition. late ME. **6.** To destroy, put an end to; to take away, remove. Now *rare*. OE. **b.** To ruin, cause the downfall of. late ME. **c.** To ruin by seducing. *arch.* 1612. **7.** To explain, interpret, expound. Now *rare*. ME.

1. The wyndow she vndoth CHAUCER. Then made he men to vndo þe tombe 1450. **2.** Oure lady..vndyd his bondes 1450. **3.** George undid the Dragon just as you'd u. an oyster 1688. **5.** Warwicke as our Selfe, Shall do, and vndo as him pleaseth best SHAKS. **6.** Nor tell him that which will u. his Quiet 1703. **b.** Our Folly has undon us 1612. **c.** Losing Her I am undone, Yet would not gain Her to u. Her PRIOR. **7.** Such as can u. a Text..with as much ease as a bow-knot 1654. Hence **Undo·er.**

Undo·cked *ppl. a.* [UN-^{1} 2] 1677. **Undo·ctor** *v.* [UN-^{2} 4 b] 1833. **Undo·cumented** *ppl. a.* [UN-^{1} 2] 1883. **Undogma·tic** *a.* [UN-^{1} 1] PUSEY.

Undo·ing, *vbl. sb.* ME. [f. UNDO *v.*] †**1.** Interpretation –1440. **2.** The action of unfastening, opening, loosening, etc. late ME. **3.** The action of destroying or ruining; the fact of being so dealt with; also, an instance of this. late ME. **b.** With possessive. Chiefly in passive sense. late ME. **4.** A cause of ruin or destruction. late ME. **5.** The action of reversing, annulling, etc. 1540.

3. b. He was not the first that has..brought about his own u. THACKERAY. Phr. *To* (one's) *u.*; All his creditors came upon him to his utter undoinge 1621. **4.** The Chocolate-houses are his U. GAY. **5.** Our Trade of doing, and u., will be endlesse 1650.

Undo·ne, *ppl. a.*^{1} ME. [UN-^{1} 2.] Not done; unaccomplished, uneffected.

Nought done the Hero deem'd, while ought u. remain'd PRIOR.

Undo·ne, *ppl. a.*^{2} ME. [pa. pple. of UNDO *v.*] **1.** Brought to decay or ruin; destroyed. **2.** Unfastened, untied, etc. 1565.

1. Keepe hop from sunne, and hop is vndunne 1573. Whichever way I turn, I am u. DICKENS.

Undou·ble, *v.* 1611. [UN-^{2} 4.] **1.** *trans.* and *intr.* To unfold. **2.** *Chess.* (*trans.*) To move (pawns) so that one no longer stands directly in front of the other 1868.

Undou·bted, *ppl. a.* 1460. [UN-^{1} 2.] **1.** Not held doubtful in respect of fact. **2.** Of persons: Not called in question in respect of status or character 1460. **3.** Not impaired by doubt; absolute, complete. Now *rare* or *Obs.* 1489. **4.** About the nature, truth, authenticity, etc., of which there is no doubt 1513.

Undou·btedly, *adv.* 1500. [UN-^{1} 5.] **1.** Admittedly, certainly; beyond or without any doubt. †**2.** With verbs of statement: Positively, in no doubtful terms –1653.

Undou·btful *v.* [UN-^{1} 1] 1450. **Undoubting** *ppl. a.* [UN-^{1} 4] late ME., **-ly** *adv.*, **-ness. Undow·ered** *ppl. a.* [UN-^{1} 2] 1803. **Undrai·nable** *a.* [UN-^{1} 1] 1611. **Undrai·ned** *ppl. a.* [UN-^{1} 2] TUSSER.

Undrama·tic, *a.* 1754. [UN-^{1} 1.] **1.** Lacking the essential qualities of drama, unsuited for the theatre. **2.** Not gifted with or exhibiting dramatic power 1769. **b.** Unappreciative of drama 1836. **3.** Not in the form of drama 1840. Hence **Undrama·tically** *adv.*

Undra·ped *ppl. a.* [UN-^{1} 2] 1814. **Undra·peried** *ppl. a.* [UN-^{1} 2] 1802.

Undraw·, *v.* 1677. [UN-^{2} 1.] **1.** *trans.* To draw back (esp. a curtain); to unfasten by pulling. **2.** *intr.* Of bolts: To move back 1794.

Undraw·n *ppl. a.* [UN-^{1} 2] 1527. **Undrea·ded** *ppl. a.* [UN-^{1} 2] 1535. **Undrea·med, -drea·mt** *ppl. a.* [UN-^{1} 2] SHAKS.

U·ndress, undre·ss, *sb.* 1683. [UN-^{1} 6.] **1.** Partial or incomplete dress; dress of a kind not ordinarily worn in public; dishabille. Also (esp. of men), informal or ordinary as opposed to ceremonial or special dress. **b.** In the services, uniform authorized to be worn on ordinary occasions, as dist. from *full* or *service dress* 1748. **2.** *attrib.* Worn when in undress; constituting an undress 1829.

1. *fig.* This famine..'Tis death in an u. of skin and bone DRYDEN. **b.** A young officer, in a cavalry u. 1849. **2.** *fig.* The simple, idiomatic, u., conversational tone of Lessing's blank verse 1806.

Undre·ss, *v.* 1596. [UN-^{2} 2.] **1.** *refl.* To divest (oneself) of clothes. **b.** *intr.* To take off one's clothes 1625. **2.** *trans.* To divest or strip (a person) of clothes 1615. **b.** To strip *of* something 1641. †**3.** To undo (the hair) –1652.

2. *fig.* Till I slumber, and death shall undresse me 1633. **b.** The protestant religion..must undresse them of all their guilded vanities MILT. Hence **Undre·ssing** *vbl. sb.*

Undre·ssed, *ppl. a.* 1445. [UN-^{1} 2.] **1. a.** Of the hair, etc.: Not trimmed or put in order. **b.** Of textiles, leather, stone, wood, etc.: With the surface not artificially smoothed or prepared 1535. **c.** Not treated with surgical dressings 1597. **d.** Not pruned or clipped 1611. **e.** Not cooked or prepared for the table 1647. **f.** Of a shop-window: Not attractively set out 1883. **2.** Not clothed; naked (or nearly so) 1613. **b.** In undress; not fully dressed; informally dressed 1605.

1. b. Strict Lawes are made..that the web vndressed be viewed by three skillfull men 1617. Enveloped in an u. seal-skin 1853. **d.** Thou shalt not..gather the grapes of thy Vine vndressed *Lev.* 25:5. **e.** The flesh of an u. lobster 1806.

Undrie·d *ppl. a.* [UN-^{1} 2] 1440. **Undri·nkable** *a.* [UN-^{1} 1] 1611. **Undri·ven** *ppl. a.* [UN-^{1} 2] 1615. **Undroo·ping** *ppl. a.* [UN-^{1} 4] 1736. **Undrow·ned** *ppl. a.* [UN-^{1} 2] 1573. **Undru·gged** *ppl. a.* [UN-^{1} 2] 1868. **Undru·nk** *ppl. a.* [UN-^{1} 2] 1637. **Undu·bbed** *ppl. a.* [UN-^{1} 2] 1602. **Undu·bitable** *a.* (now *rare*) [UN-^{1} 1] 1643, **-ably** *adv.*

Undue·, *a.* late ME. [UN-^{1} 1, after (O)Fr. *indu*.] **1.** Not owing. **2.** Not appropriate or suitable; improper; unseasonable. late ME. **3.** Unjustifiable, illegal. late ME. **4.** Going beyond what is appropriate, warranted, or natural; excessive 1684.

2. At an vndue houre of a leuen a clocke in the night 1541. The u. awarding of honours 1875. **3.** Such miscreants..had by u. ways devoured the patrimony of the Church 1660. The Laws relating to Bribery, Treating, and u. Influence at Elections 1854. **4.** Instances of u. Warmth and Zeal 1739.

Undu·g *ppl. a.* [UN-^{1} 2] 1657. **Undu·ke** *v.* [UN-^{2} 4 b] 1611.

Undulant (ʋ·ndiŭlănt), *a.* 1830. [f. UNDULATE *v.*, perh. after Fr. *ondulant* (XVIII); see -ANT.] Undulating. *U. fever* = MALTA *fever*.

Undulate (ʋ·ndiŭlĕt), *a.* 1658. [In XVII prob. – L. *undulatus* waved (Varro), f. late L. *undula* (Boethius), f. *unda* wave; see -ULE, -ATE^2. Cf. next.] = UNDULATED *ppl. a.*; *spec.* in *Bot.* and *Zool.*

Undulate (ʋ·ndiŭlēˡt), *v.* 1664. [– *undulat-*, pa. ppl. stem of late and med.L. **undulare* (cf. cl. L. *undare*, late L. *undula* Boethius); see -ATE^3.] **1.** *intr.* To move in, or like, waves. **b.** *transf.* Of sound, etc. 1760. **2.** *trans.* To cause to move, esp. to rise and fall, like waves 1669. **b.** To impart a wavy appearance to 1730. **3.** *intr.* To present a wavy surface, outline, or appearance 1833.

2. The first dancing of all Ghawâzi is..undulating the body 1873. **3.** The vast plain undulates in hills and valleys 1833. Hence **U·ndulator** in *Wireless Telegr.*

Undulated (ʋ·ndiŭlēˡtėd), *ppl. a.* 1623. [f. prec. + -ED^1.] **1.** Having a wavy surface or outline. **2.** Having wavy markings 1664. **b.** *spec.* In the names of birds or fishes 1785.

U·ndulating, *ppl. a.* 1700. [f. as prec. + -ING^2.] That undulates. **b.** *fig.* Exhibiting variations comparable to the rising and falling of waves 1815.

b. The u. and tumultuous multitude BENTHAM. Hence **U·ndulatingly** *adv.*

Undulation (ʋndiŭlē·ʃən). 1646. [In XVII – mod.L. *undulatio* f. **undulare*; see UNDULATE *v.*, -ATION. Later directly f. the Eng. vb.] **1.** The action of moving in a wave-like manner; a gentle rising and falling in the manner of waves. **b.** A wave-like motion of the air, ether, etc., as in the propagation of light 1658. **c.** *transf.* Of sound 1668. **2.** A wave-like curve or a series of these; a surface defined by such curves; an undulating rise and fall of level 1670. **b.** An instance of this; also, a single rise and fall of this nature 1823.

1. Porpoises progress by..undulations in a vertical plane 1854. Hence **Undula·tionist,** one who holds the undulatory theory of light.

Undulatory (ʋ·ndiŭlătəri), *a.* 1728. [f. UNDULATE *v.* + -ORY^2; cf. Fr. *ondulatoire* (XVIII), perh. partly the source.] **1.** Of the nature of undulation; exhibiting or consisting of wave-movement. **b.** *U. theory, hypothesis*, the theory that light consists in an undulatory movement of an elastic medium pervading space 1802. **2.** Forming a series of wave-like curves; of ground, etc., having undulations 1796.

Undulous (ʋ·ndiŭləs), *a.* 1728. [f. UNDULATE *v.*, -ATION + -OUS, after *populate, population, populous.* Cf. Fr. *onduleux* (XVIII).] Of an undulating nature.

Unduly (ʋndiū·li), *adv.* late ME. [UN-^{1} 5.] **1.** Without due cause or justification; unrightfully, undeservedly. **2.** To excess; beyond the due degree 1779.

1. Malvern hills, for mountains counted Not u. E. B. BROWNING. **2.** William had never been u. harsh FREEMAN.

Undu·rable *a.* [UN-^{1} 1] COVERDALE. **Undu·sted** *ppl. a.* [UN-^{1} 2] 1648. **Undu·teous** *a.* [UN-^{1} 1] SHAKS. **Undu·tiful** *a.* [UN-^{1} 1] 1582, **-ly** *adv.*, **-ness.**

U·ndy, *a.* 1592. [Anglicized f. UNDEE *a.*; see -Y^5.] *Her.* Wavy.

Undy·ing, *ppl. a.* ME. [UN-^{1} 4.] That does not die; immortal.

Driven down To chains of Darkness, and th' u. Worm MILTON. The u. interest..felt by kindly women in a question of love or marriage 1885. Hence **Undy·ing-ly** *adv.*, **-ness.**

Unea·red, *ppl. a. arch.* OE. [UN-^{1} 2.] Untilled.

Unea·rned, *ppl. a.* ME. [UN-^{1} 2.] **1.** Not earned by merit or desert; undeserved (as reward or punishment). **2.** Not earned by work or service 1667. **b.** *U·nearned increment*, increase in the value of land or property not due to action or expenditure on the part of the owner 1873.

Unea·rth, *v.* 1450. [UN-^{2} 3.] **1.** *trans.* To exhume, dig out; to expose by removing earth. **b.** To force out of a hole or burrow

1622. **2.** *fig.* To bring to light; to disclose, reveal, discover 1820. Hence **Unea·rthed** *ppl. a.*[1]

Unea·rthed, *ppl. a.*[2] 1513. [UN-[1] 2.] †**1.** Unburied. **2.** *Electr.* Not furnished with an earth 1905.

Unea·rthly, *a.* 1611. [UN-[1] 1.] **1.** Rising above what is characteristic of earth; sublime; heavenly. **2.** Not belonging to this earth; supernatural, ghostly, weird 1802. **b.** colloq. *U. hour, time,* an absurdly early or inconvenient time 1865. Hence **Unea·rthliness.**

Unea·se [UN-[1] 6] ME. **Unea·seful** *a.* (now *rare*) [UN-[1] 1] 1515.

Unea·sily, *adv.* ME. [UN-[1] 5.] †**1.** With difficulty –1725. **2.** Restlessly, with discomfort or embarrassment. late ME.

Unea·siness. late ME. [UN-[1] 6.] †**1.** The quality of being troublesome –1712. †**2.** Difficult nature or character –1691. †**b.** Reluctance –1737. **3.** Discomfort, anxiety or trouble as affecting one's circumstances or welfare; an instance of this 1599. **b.** Bodily discomfort (falling short of actual or definite pain) 1665. **c.** Mental discomfort; anxiety, apprehension 1682.

Unea·sy, *a.* ME. [UN-[1] 1.] **1.** Causing physical discomfort; preventing ease. †**b.** Disquieting to the mind –1798. **c.** Characterized by absence of ease or comfort; suggesting or manifesting discomfort of body or mind 1513. †**2.** Of persons: Disagreeable, unfriendly, dissatisfied –1737. **b.** Rigid, uncompromising 1819. **3.** Not easy or simple; difficult, hard, troublesome. Now *rare.* late ME. **4.** Disturbed in mind; anxious, apprehensive 1680. **b.** Restless, unsettled, fidgety 1855. **c.** Suffering physical discomfort 1725. **5.** quasi-*adv.* Uneasily 1596.

1. Golden fetters are as uneasie as those of Iron 1660. **2. b.** Ladies even of the most u. virtue BYRON. **3.** 'The road will be u. to find,' answered Gurth SCOTT. **5.** Vneasie lyes the Head, that weares a Crowne SHAKS.

Unea·table *a.* [UN-[1] 1] 1611. **Unea·ten** *ppl. a.* [UN-[1] 2] ME.

Uneath (vnī·þ), *adv. arch.* [OE. *unēaþe,* f. *un-* UN-[1] 5 + *ēaþe* EATH *adv.*] Not easily; (only) with difficulty; scarcely, hardly. So **Unea·th** *a.* difficult, hard, troublesome.

Uncli·psed *ppl. a.* [UN-[1] 2] 1649.

U:necono·mic, *a.* 1909. [UN-[1] 1.] Not based on or out of relation to economics. **b.** *U. rent,* one too low to repay builder or owner.

Unecono·mical *adj.* [UN-[1] 1] BENTHAM, **-ly** *adv.* **Une·dge** *v.* [UN-[2] 2] 1614. **Une·dified** *ppl. a.* [UN-[1] 2] 1618. **Une·difying** *ppl. a.* [UN-[1] 4] 1641. **Une·dited** *ppl. a.* [UN-[1] 2] 1829. **Une·ducated** *ppl. a.* [UN-[1] 2] SHAKS., **-ness.** †**Une·ffable** *a.* [UN-[1] 1] –1689. **Unela·borate** *a.* [UN-[1] 1] 1663. **Unela·stic** *a.* [UN-[1] 1] 1728. **Unela·ted** *ppl. a.* [UN-[1] 2] 1710. **Une·lbowed** *ppl. a.* [UN-[1] 2] POPE. **Unele·cted** *ppl. a.* [UN-[1] 2] 1581. **Unele·ctrified** *ppl. a.* [UN-[1] 2] 1747. **Une·levated** *ppl. a.* [UN-[1] 2] 1627. **Une·loquent** *a.* [UN-[1] 1] 1565, **-ly** *adv.*

Unemba·rrassed, *ppl. a.* 1708. [UN-[1] 2.] **1.** Not encumbered, hampered, or impeded. **2.** Unconstrained; free from self-consciousness or awkwardness 1746.

Unemba·ttled, *ppl. a.* 1615. [UN-[1] 2; see EMBATTLED *ppl. a.*[2]] Without battlements.

Unembe·llished *ppl. a.* [UN-[1] 2] 1630. **Unembi·ttered** *ppl. a.* [UN-[1] 2] 1711. **Unembo·died** *ppl. a.* [UN-[1] 2] 1662. **Unemo·tional** *a.* [UN-[1] 1] 1876, **-ly** *adv.* **Unempha·tic** *a.* [UN-[1] 1] 1800, **-ally** *adv.*

Unemploy·able, *a.* and *sb.* 1887. [UN-[1] 1.] (One) unfit to be employed as a paid worker.

Unemploy·ed, *ppl. a.* and *sb.* 1600. [UN-[1] 2.] **1.** Not used; not occupied; not in use. **2.** Of persons: Having no occupation; disengaged, at leisure; *spec.* temporarily out of work 1667. **b.** *absol.* or as *sb.* (chiefly pl. with *the,* occas. sing. with *an*) 1882. **c.** Pertaining to or connected with unemployed persons 1844.

2. Other Creatures all day long Rove idle unimploid MILT. The destinies of the u. workmen RUSKIN.

Unemploy·ment. 1888. [UN-[1] 6.] The state or fact of being unemployed; the prevalence or extent of this state.

Une·mptied *ppl. a.* [UN-[1] 2] 1624. **Unena·cted** *ppl. a.* [UN-[1] 2] 1802. **Unencha·nted** *ppl. a.* [UN-[1] 2] MILT. **Unenclo·sed** *ppl. a.* [UN-[1] 2] 1676. **Unencu·mbered** *ppl. a.* [UN-[1] 2] 1722. **Unenda·ngered** *ppl. a.* [UN-[1] 2] 1658.

Une·nded, *ppl. a.* Now *rare.* ME. [UN-[1] 2.] **1.** Endless, infinite. **2.** Unfinished. late ME.

1. For thi myche malice, and thi wickidnessis vnendid WYCLIF *Job.* 22:5.

Une·nding *ppl. a.* [UN-[1] 4] 1661, **-ly** *adv.*, **-ness.** **Unendow·ed** *ppl. a.* [UN-[1] 2] 1647. **Unendue·d** *ppl. a.* [UN-[1] 2] 1647. **Unendu·rable** *a.* [UN-[1] 1] 1630, **-ly** *adv.* **U:nenerge·tic** *a.* [UN-[1] 1] 1805. **Unenfo·rced** *ppl. a.* [UN-[1] 2] 1607. **Unenfra·nchised** *ppl. a.* [UN-[1] 2] 1832.

Unenga·ged, *ppl. a.* 1656. [UN-[1] 2.] **1.** Not bound or committed. **2.** *spec.* Not betrothed 1702. **3.** Not hired 1654. **4.** Not occupied or busied (*in* something) 1712. **b.** Not occupied or involved in fighting 1806. **5.** Not allocated or assigned 1732.

4. If your Thoughts are u., I shall explain myself further POPE.

Un-E·nglish, *a.* 1633. [UN-[1] 1.] **1.** Not English in character; lacking the qualities regarded as typically English. **2.** Not English by occupation or possession 1738.

Une·nglished, *ppl. a. arch.* 1546. [UN-[1] 2.] Not translated into English.

Unenjoy·able *a.* [UN-[1] 1] 1797. **Unenjoy·ed** *ppl. a.* [UN-[1] 2] MILT. **Unenjoy·ing** *ppl. a.* [UN-[1] 4] 1697, **-ly** *adv.*

Unenli·ghtened, *ppl. a.* 1656. [UN-[1] 2.] **1.** Not illuminated or lit up. Now *rare.* 1662. **2.** Not mentally illuminated; uninstructed 1656. **b.** Uninformed *on* some matter 1829. **3.** Marked by lack of enlightenment 1792.

Unenli·vened *ppl. a.* [UN-[1] 2] 1692. **Unenqui·ring** *ppl. a.* [UN-[1] 4] 1813, **-ly** *adv.* **Unenri·ched** *ppl. a.* [UN-[1] 2] 1723. **Unentai·led** *ppl. a.* [UN-[1] 2] 1713. **Unenta·ngled** *ppl. a.* [UN-[1] 2] 1586.

Une·ntered, *ppl. a.* 1482. [UN-[1] 2.] **1.** Not recorded by an entry in a book. †**2.** Not initiated –1642. **b.** Of hounds: Not yet put into a pack 1896. **3.** Of places: Not entered 1775.

Une·nterprising *ppl. a.* [UN-[1] 4] 1777. **Unentertai·ned** *ppl. a.* [UN-[1] 2] 1628. **Unentertai·ning** *ppl. a.* [UN-[1] 4] 1697, **-ly** *adv.*, **-ness.** **Unenthra·lled** *ppl. a.* [UN-[1] 2] MILT. **Unenthusia·stic** *a.* [UN-[1] 1] 1805. **Unenti·tled** *ppl. a.* [UN-[1] 2] 1768. **Une·nviable** *a.* [UN-[1] 1] MILT., **-ably** *adv.*

Une·nvied, *ppl. a.* late ME. [UN-[1] 2.] †**1.** Unmixed with envy. late ME. only. **2.** Not regarded with envy 1615. **3.** Not enviously desired or grudged 1645.

Une·nvious *a.* [UN-[1] 1] 1656, **-ly** *adv.*

Unepi·scopal, *a.* 1659. [UN-[1] 1.] **1.** Not controlled by bishops; not episcopalian in character or government. **2.** Not pertaining to or befitting a bishop 1661.

2. The Bishop lost his temper, and used very u. language 1897. Hence **Unepi·scopally** *adv.*

Une·qual, *a., sb., adv.* 1535. [UN-[1] 1, 6.] **A.** *adj.* **1.** Not equal in amount, size, quality, etc.: **a.** Of two or more things or persons in comparison with each other 1565. **b.** With abstract sbs. in the singular 1593. **c.** Of single persons or things 1677. **2.** Not divisible into two equal numbers, odd 1697. **3.** †**a.** Of things: Inadequate –1736. **b.** Not equal or adequate *to* some task, etc. 1694. **4.** Variable or uneven in quality 1565. †**5.** Inequitable, unjust, unfair –1761. **6.** In which the two parties are not on equal terms, or have not equal advantage 1552. **b.** *esp.* Of combats or contests 1654.

1. a. If your horses be unequall for height 1653. **b.** Halting on crutches of u. size COWPER. **c.** A match with one so u. in birth SCOTT. **2.** Thrice bind about his thrice devoted Head,..U. numbers please the Gods DRYDEN. **3. b.** Four..were ..rejected as u. to the burden GIBBON. **4.** A fine, but u. poem SCOTT. An u. distribution of heat 1836. **5.** To punnish me for what you make me do Seemes much vnequall SHAKS. **6.** So u. a bargain 1748. **b.** In such u. strife DRYDEN.

B. *sb. pl.* **1.** Persons who are not on an equality with each other in rank or social standing 1565. **2.** Things unequal to each other 1611.

1. Among unequals what societie Can sort, what harmonie or true delight? MILTON.

C. *adv.*, or quasi-*adv.* Unequally 1602. So **Une·qual-ly** *adv.*, **-ness.**

Une·qualled *ppl. a.* [UN-[1] 2] 1622. **Une·quitable** *a.* [UN-[1] 1] 1647, **-ably** *adv.*

Unequi·vocal, *a.* 1784. [UN-[1] 1.] Of unmistakable meaning, free from ambiguity. Hence **Unequi·voca-ly** *adv.*, **-ness.**

Unera·dicable *a.* [UN-[1] 1] BYRON. **Une·rrancy** [UN-[1] 6] 1646.

Unerring (vnǝ̄·riŋ), *ppl. a.* 1621. [UN-[1] 4.] **1.** Making no error; not going or leading astray 1660. **2.** Not diverging from a standard or aim; exact 1665. **3.** Of missiles, aim, etc.: Not going astray from the intended mark; sure 1621.

1. The U. Authority of the Catholic Church in matters of Faith 1732. **3.** How deadly thine u. bow! SCOTT. Hence **Une·rring-ly** *adv.*, **-ness.**

Unesca·pable *a.* [UN-[1] 1] DONNE. **Uneschew·able** *a.* [UN-[1] 1] CHAUCER. **Unesco·rted** *ppl. a.* [UN-[1] 2] 1774. **Unespie·d** *ppl. a.* [UN-[1] 2] CHAUCER. **Unessay·ed** *ppl. a.* [UN-[1] 2] 1642.

Une·ssence, *v.* 1642. [UN-[2] 2.] *trans.* To deprive of essence or essential properties.

Unesse·ntial, *a.* and *sb.* 1656. [UN-[1] 1.] **1.** Having no essence or substance; immaterial 1667. **2.** Not affecting or pertaining to the essence of a matter; unimportant 1656.

1. The void profound of u. Night MILT. **2.** Those, who differed from him in the u. Parts of Christianity ADDISON.

B. *sb.* An unessential thing or feature 1828. **b.** That which is not essential 1840.

b. Who is to determine..the limit of the U.? 1841.

Unesta·blish *v.* [UN-[2] 1] MILT. **Unesta·blished** *ppl. a.* [UN-[1] 2] 1646. **Unestee·med** *ppl. a.* [UN-[1] 2] 1550. **Unestra·nged** *ppl. a.* [UN-[1] 2] 1851. **Une·thical** *a.* [UN-[1] 1] 1871. **Uneva·dable** *a.* [UN-[1] 1] 1839. **U:nevange·lical** *a.* [UN-[1] 1] 1648.

Une·ven, *a.* [OE. *unefen,* f. UN-[1] 1 + *efen* EVEN *a.*] **1.** Not corresponding or matching; unequal. Now *rare.* **b.** Of numbers: Odd. Of things: Making up, or marked by, an odd number 1577. †**2.** Unequitable; unjust –1641. **3.** Diverging from a straight or exactly parallel position. late ME. **4.** Not smooth or level; irregular, broken, rugged ME. **b.** *transf.* and *fig.* (of immaterial things, sounds, etc.) 1596.

1. So forth they traueld an vneuen payre SPENSER. **3.** The windows were u. 1862. **4.** Which causeth cloth to cockle and be u. HAKLUYT. **b.** Such is the u. State of human Life DE FOE. Hence **Une·ven-ly** *adv.*, **-ness.**

Uneve·ntful *a.* [UN-[1] 1] 1800, **-ly** *adv.*, **-ness.** **Une·videnced** *ppl. a.* [UN-[1] 2] 1842. **Une·vident** *a.* [UN-[1] 1] late ME. **Unexa·ct** *a.* [UN-[1] 1] 1758. **Unexa·ggerated** *ppl. a.* [UN-[1] 2] 1770. **Unexa·lted** *ppl. a.* [UN-[1] 2] 1611. **Unexa·mined** *ppl. a.* [UN-[1] 2] 1495. **Unexa·mining** *ppl. a.* [UN-[1] 4] 1682.

Unexa·mpled, *ppl. a.* 1610. [UN-[1] 2.] Having no preceding or similar example; unprecedented, unparalleled.

Unexce·lled *ppl. a.* [UN-[1] 2] 1800. **Unexce·pted** *ppl. a.* [UN-[1] 2] 1614.

Unexce·ptionable, *a.* 1664. [UN-[1] 1.] **1.** To whom or which no exception can be taken; perfectly satisfactory or adequate. **2.** Admitting of no exception (*rare*) 1871. Hence **Unexceptionabi·lity. Unexce·ptionableness. Unexce·ptionably** *adv.*

Unexce·ptional, *a.* 1775. [UN-[1] 1.] **1.** = prec. 1. **2.** Admitting of or subject to no exception 1844.

2. The orders received..were imperative, and u. 1844.

Unexcha·nged *ppl. a.* [UN-[1] 2] 1618. **Unexci·sed** *ppl. a.* [UN-[1] 2, 3] 1871. **Unexci·table** *a.* [UN-[1] 1] 1839. **Unexci·ted** *ppl. a.* [UN-[1] 2] 1735. **Unexci·ting** *ppl. a.* [UN-[1] 4] 1833. †**Unexcu·sable** *a.* [UN-[1] 1] –1685. **Une·xecuted** *ppl. a.* [UN-[1] 2] 1585. **Unexe·mplary** *a.* [UN-[1] 1] 1649. **Unexe·mplified** *ppl. a.* [UN-[1] 2] 1634. **Unexe·mpt, unexe·mpted** *ppl. adjs.* [UN-[1] 2] MILT. **Une·xercised** *ppl. a.* [UN-[1] 2] late ME. **Unexe·rted** *ppl. a.* [UN-[1] 2] 1675. **Unexhau·sted** *ppl. a.* [UN-[1] 2] 1602. **Unexhau·stible** *a.* (now *rare*) [UN-[1] 1] 1656. **Unexi·stence** [UN-[1] 6] 1593. **Unexi·stent** *a.* [UN-[1] 1] 1682. **Unexi·sting** *ppl. a.* [UN-[1] 4] 1785. **Une·xorcised** *ppl. a.* [UN-[1] 2] 1750. **Unexpa·nded** *ppl. a.* [UN-[1] 2] 1664. **Unexpa·nsive** *a.* [UN-[1] 1] 1846. **Unexpe·ctable** *a.* [UN-[1] 1] 1598. **Unexpe·ctant** *a.* [UN-[1] 1] 1811. **Unexpe·cted** *ppl. a.* [UN-[1] 2] 1586, **-ly** *adv.*, **-ness.** **Unexpe·nded** *ppl. a.* [UN-[1] 2] 1571. **Unexpe·nsive** *a.* [UN-[1] 1] MILT., **-ly** *adv.*, **-ness.**

Unexpe·rienced, *ppl. a.* 1569. [UN-[1] 2.] **1.** Not furnished with or taught by experience; not skilled or trained in this way. **2.** Not known or felt by experience 1698.

Unexpe·rimented, *ppl. a.* 1594. [UN-[1] 2.] †**1.** Inexperienced –1635. **2.** Not tried, known, or ascertained by experiment 1594.

†**Unexpe·rt** *a.* [UN-[1] 1] –1778. **Une·xpiated** *ppl. a.* [UN-[1] 2] 1681. **Unexpi·red** *ppl. a.* [UN-[1] 2]

1570. **Unexplai·nable** *a.* [UN-¹ 1] 1711. **Unexplai·ned** *ppl. a.* [UN-¹ 2] 1721. **Unexpla·natory** *a.* [UN-¹ 1] BENTHAM. **Une·xplicated** *ppl. a.* [UN-¹ 2] 1666. **Unexpli·cit** *a.* [UN-¹ 1] 1838, **-ly** *adv.* **Unexplo·red** *ppl. a.* [UN-¹ 2] 1697. **Unexpo·sed** *ppl. a.* [UN-¹ 2] 1691. **Unexpre·ssed** *ppl. a.* [UN-¹ 2] 1561. **Unexpre·ssible** *a.* [UN-¹ 1] 1621.

Unexpre·ssive, *a.* 1600. [UN-¹ 1.] †**1.** Inexpressible, beyond description –1637. **2.** Not expressive; that fails to convey a meaning or feeling 1755.

1. The faire, the chaste, and vnexpressiue shee SHAKS. Hence **Unexpre·ssive-ly** *adv.*, **-ness.**

Unexpu·gnable *a.* (now *rare*) [UN-¹ 1] WYCLIF. **Unexpu·nged** *ppl. a.* [UN-¹ 2] 1826. **Une·xpurgated** *ppl. a.* [UN-¹ 2] 1882.

Unexte·nded, *ppl. a.* 1648. [UN-¹ 2.] **1.** Not held out, opened, or spread. **b.** Of an athlete, horse, etc.: Without being obliged to exert himself to the full. **2.** *spec.* Having no extension (EXTENSION 4) 1674.

2. Aristotle..did suppose Incorporeal Substance to be u. CUDWORTH. Hence (in sense 2) **Unexte·nded-ly** *adv.*, **-ness.**

Unexte·nuated *ppl. a.* [UN-¹ 2] JOHNSON. **Unexti·nct** *a.* [UN-¹ 1] 1622. **Unexti·nguishable** *a.* [UN-¹ 1] 1642, **-ness, -ably** *adv.* **Unexti·nguished** *ppl. a.* [UN-¹ 2] DRYDEN. **Une·xtirpated** *ppl. a.* [UN-¹ 2] 1663. **Unexto·rted** *ppl. a.* [UN-¹ 2] SWIFT.

Uneyed (ʌnəi·d), *ppl. a.* 1616. [UN-¹ 2.] Not looked at, unseen.

Unfa·ce, *v.* 1611. [UN-² 2.] *trans.* To strip of a facing or disguise, to expose the face of.

Unfa·dable *a.* [UN-¹ 1] 1626. **Unfa·ded** *ppl. a.* [UN-¹ 2] 1550. **Unfa·ding** *ppl. a.* [UN-¹ 4] 1652, **-ly** *adv.*, **-ness.**

Unfai·ling, *ppl. a.* late ME. [UN-¹ 4.] **1.** Not failing or giving way. **2.** Unceasing, continual. late ME. **3.** Infallible, certain. late ME.

2. A country..watered by u. rivers 1876. **3.** The undoubted truth of gods u. word 1553. Hence **Unfai·ling-ly** *adv.*, **-ness.**

Unfai·n, *a. arch.* and *dial.* [OE. *unfæġen*, f. UN-¹ 1 + *fæġen* FAIN *a.*] Not glad; ill-pleased; reluctant.

Unfai·r, *a.* [OE. *unfæġer*, f. UN-¹ 1 + *fæġer* FAIR *a.*] †**1.** Not fair or beautiful; uncomely; ugly –1648. **2.** Not fair or equitable; unjust 1713. **b.** *spec.* Not paying the usual rate of wages. Of wages, etc.: Below the normal rate. 1886. **3.** Of the wind: Unfavourable. 1801. **4.** *Ship-building.* Not fitting or corresponding exactly 1869. Hence **Unfai·r-ly** *adv.*, **-ness.**

Unfai·thful, *a.* late ME. [UN-¹ 1.] **1.** Not holding the true faith; infidel. **2.** Not keeping good faith; acting falsely or treacherously. late ME. **b.** *transf.* Of things: Disappointing expectation, deceptive, unreliable 1586. **c.** Misrepresenting the original; incorrect, inexact 1697. **d.** *spec.* Not faithful in wedlock 1828. **3.** Of conduct: Characterized by want of good faith; not honest or upright 1565.

1. Vnfeithful men schulen be conuertid to thee WYCLIF *Ps.* 50:15. **2.** The combined offence of two u. servants WELLESLEY. **b.** Sea-sand..is..u. in supporting great Weights 1726. **c.** He..is much blamed for his unfaithfull quotations 1697. Hence **Unfai·thful-ly** *adv.*, **-ness.**

Unfa·llen *ppl. a.* [UN-¹ 2] 1653. **Unfa·ltering** *ppl. a.* [UN-¹ 4] 1727, **-ly** *adv.* **Unfa·med** *ppl. a.* [UN-¹ 2] SHAKS. **Unfami·liar** [UN-¹ 1] 1594. **Unfamilia·rity** [UN-¹ 6] 1755. **Unfami·liarized** *ppl. a.* [UN-¹ 2] 1775. **Unfana·tical** *a.* [UN-¹ 1] 1826. **Unfa·ncied** *ppl. a.* [UN-¹ 2] 1655. **Unfanta·stic** *a.* [UN-¹ 1] 1794.

Unfa·shion, *v.* 1569. [UN-² 2.] *trans.* To undo the fashion or make of.

Unfa·shionable, *a.* and *sb.* 1563. [UN-¹ 1.] **A.** *adj.* †**1.** That cannot be fashioned or shaped –1607. †**2.** Badly shaped or formed –1663. **3.** Of clothes, behaviour, opinions, etc.: Not in accordance with the prevailing fashion 1644. **4.** Not belonging to fashionable society; not conforming to current fashions 1660.

1. The invisible and u. God 1563. **2.** He was..of body somewhat grosse and vnfashionable 1611. **3.** It is there u. not to be a man of business 1776. **B.** *sb.* An u. person 1822. Hence **Unfa·shionableness. Unfa·shionably** *adv.*

Unfa·shioned, *ppl. a.* 1538. [UN-¹ 2.] **1.** Not wrought into form or shape. †**2.** Not refined; lacking culture or elegance –1821.

2. A plump goodnatured u. girl 1821.

Unfa·sten, *v.* ME. [UN-² 1, 5.] **1.** *trans.* **a.** To unfix; to make loose or slack. Also *absol.* **b.** To detach; to undo or release 1440. **2.** *intr.* To become detached or loose; to open ME.

Unfa·stened *ppl. a.* [UN-¹ 2] 1587. **Unfasti·dious** *a.* [UN-¹ 1] 1815.

Unfa·thered, *a.*¹ 1597. [UN-¹ 3.] **1.** Having no (known or acknowledged) father; illegitimate. **2.** Of obscure origin; unauthenticated 1830.

Unfa·thered, *a.*² 1586. [UN-² 2, 6.] Deprived of a father.

Unfa·thomable, *a.* 1617. [UN-¹ 1.] **1.** *fig.* Of feelings, qualities, conditions, etc.: Incapable of being fully ascertained, explored, exhausted, etc. **2.** Incapable of being fathomed or measured; immeasurable, vast 1640. **b.** *fig.* Of the eyes 1817.

1. The Goodness is u. 1663. **2.** O the u. Abysse of Eternity! 1672. Stretching into u. distance 1879. **b.** Her u. eyes THACKERAY. Hence **Unfa·thomableness. Unfa·thomably** *adv.*

Unfa·thomed *ppl. a.* [UN-¹ 2] 1623. **Unfati·guable** *a.* [UN-¹ 1] 1799. **Unfati·gued** *ppl. a.* [UN-¹ 2] 1705. **Unfati·guing** *ppl. a.* [UN-¹ 4] 1808. **Unfau·lty** *a.* [UN-¹ 1] 1548.

Unfa·vourable, *a.* 1548. [UN-¹ 1.] **1.** Not favourable in various senses. **2.** Ill-favoured; unprepossessing. Now *rare.* 1776.

1. An u. wind detained them GIBBON. Viewed with an u. eye 1835. The prognosis was u. 1890. **2.** With u., long, and saturnine countenances 1776. Hence **Unfa·vourableness. Unfa·vourably** *adv.*

Unfa·voured *ppl. a.* [UN-¹ 2] 1774. **Unfa·vouring** *ppl. a.* [UN-¹ 4] 1835. **Unfea·red** *ppl. a.* [UN-¹ 2] late ME. **Unfea·rful** *a.* [UN-¹ 1] 1544, **-ly** *adv.* **Unfea·ring** *ppl. a.* [UN-¹ 4] 1796, **-ly** *adv.* **Unfea·sible** *a.* [UN-¹ 1] 1527. **Unfea·ther** *v.* [UN-² 2] 1483.

Unfea·thered, *a.* 1570. [UN-¹ 3.] **1.** Of birds, etc.: Not provided or covered with feathers. **2.** Not of the feathered kind: applied spec. (after L. *implumis*) to man 1600. **3.** Of arrows: Not fitted with feathers 1611.

2. The *animal implume bipes*, the two-leg'd u. Philosopher 1754. **3.** U. arrows of reed LYTTON.

Unfea·tured *a.* [UN-¹ 3] DRYDEN. **Unfe·cundated** *ppl. a.* [UN-¹ 2] 1857. **Unfe·d** *ppl. a.* [UN-¹ 2] ME. **Unfee·d** *ppl. a.* [UN-¹ 2] SHAKS.

Unfee·ling, *ppl. a.* OE. [UN-¹ 4.] **1.** Devoid of sensation; insensible; *fig.* not sensitive to impressions, etc. **2.** Without kindly or tender feeling; callous, unsympathetic 1596.

1. So one..Woo'd an u. statue for his wife COWPER. **2.** Can it be? That men should liue with such vnfeeling soules? B. JONSON. Hence **Unfee·ling-ly** *adv.*, **-ness.**

Unfei·gned, *ppl. a.* late ME. [UN-¹ 2.] **1.** Not feigned or pretended; genuine, true, real. **2.** Of persons, the heart, etc.: Honest or sincere in feeling or action. late ME.

2. They parceyued well howe he spake them with all his herte vnfayned 1525. Your unfeined, trusty, and assured friend 1573. Hence **Unfei·gnedly** *adv.*

Unfei·gning *ppl. a.* [UN-¹ 4] late ME., **-ly** *adv.* **Unfe·lled** *ppl. a.* [UN-¹ 2] 1543. **Unfe·llowed** *a.* [UN-¹ 3] 1597. **Unfe·lt** *ppl. a.* [UN-¹ 2] 1586. **Unfe·minine** *a.* [UN-¹ 1] 1757, **-ness.**

Unfe·nced, *ppl. a.* 1548. [UN-¹ 2.] **1.** Undefended, unprotected. *arch.* **2.** Unenclosed; without fences 1608. **b.** Not provided with a guard or the like 1683.

Unferme·nted *ppl. a.* [UN-¹ 2] 1663. **Unfe·rtile** *a.* [UN-¹ 1] 1596. **Unfe·rtilized** *ppl. a.* [UN-¹ 2] 1893. **Unfe·tter** *v.* [UN-² 2 b] late ME.

Unfe·ttered, *ppl. a.* 1601. [UN-¹ 3.] Not in fetters. Chiefly in fig. use: Unrestrained, unrestricted. Const. *by.*

A new estate u. by conditions 1800. Accustomed ..to the u. exercise of their faculties PRESCOTT.

Unfi·gured, *ppl. a.* 1577. [UN-¹ 2, 3.] **1.** Not expressed in or employing figurative speech. **2.** Not marked with a numerical figure or figures 1596. **3.** *Zool.* etc. Not (yet) depicted by a figure 1822. **4.** *Logic.* Of a syllogism: Not belonging to one of the usual figures 1838.

1. The u. language of highly cultivated nations 1827.

Unfi·led, *ppl. a.*¹ 1590. [UN-¹ 2 + FILE *v.*¹] **1.** Not smoothed with the file. **b.** *fig.* Rude, unpolished 1633. **2.** Of coin: Not reduced by filing 1774.

1. He was all armd in rugged steele vnfilde SPENSER. **2.** Unfil'd, unsweated, all of sterling weight 1774.

Unfi·led, *ppl. a.*² 1571. [UN-¹ 2 + FILE *v.*³] Not arranged in or as in a file; not placed on a file.

Unfi·lial *a.* [UN-¹ 1] SHAKS. **Unfi·llable** *a.* (now *rare*) [UN-¹ 1] ME. **Unfi·lled** *ppl. a.* [UN-¹ 2] late ME. **Unfi·ne** *a.* (now *rare*) [UN-¹ 1] late ME.

Unfi·ngered, (*ppl.*) *a.* 1603. [UN-¹ 2, 3.] **1.** Not provided with fingers. **2.** Not touched with the fingers 1811.

Unfi·red, *ppl. a.* 1590. [UN-¹ 2.] **1.** Not set on fire. **2.** Not subjected or exposed to fire 1791. **3.** Of firearms: Not discharged by firing 1892.

1. Not leave One house u. MASSINGER. *fig.* The human Brute, who view'd her Charms unfir'd 1729. **2.** These un-fired bricks lasted perfectly well 1888.

Unfi·rm, *a.* Now *rare.* 1592. [UN-¹ 1.] **1.** Lacking solidity or rigidity. †**2.** Weak, feeble, infirm –1660. †**3.** Unsteady, flighty. SHAKS. **4.** Unstable, unsteady; liable to slip or fall 1697.

1. What is the reason that most Veal is so u. and like a Jelly? 1683. **3.** Our fancies are more giddie and vnfirme..Then womens are SHAKS. So **Unfi·rmly** *adv.*

Unfit, *a.* 1545. [UN-¹ 1.] **1.** Not fit or suitable, not fitted or suited (*for* some purpose, action, or end, *to* do something, or *to be* done something to). **b.** Unsuitable, ill fitted for the purpose, etc. 1551. **2.** Not physically fit 1665. *sb.* an u. person. So **Unfi·t-ly** *adv.*, **-ness.**

Unfi·t, *v.* 1611. [UN-² 4.] *trans.* To render unfit; to disqualify.

Unfi·tted, *ppl. a.* 1592. [UN-¹ 2.] **1.** Not adapted or suited; unfit. **2.** Not fitted up or out; not properly furnished 1708. **3.** Not adjusted by fitting 1895.

Unfi·tting, *ppl. a.* 1590. [UN-¹ 4.] Not fitting or suitable; unbecoming, improper.

Qualities mis-seeming his place, and u. his calling FLORIO. A thing which..is altogether u. to be named 1656. This is an u., it is a dangerous, state of things BURKE. So **Unfi·tting-ly** *adv.*, **-ness.**

Unfi·x, *v.* 1597. [UN-² 1, 5.] **1.** *trans.* To unfasten, loosen. **b.** *spec.* in military use 1802. **2.** *fig.* To unsettle; to render uncertain or doubtful 1650. **3.** *intr.* To become unfixed 1844.

1. b. U. Bayonet, on which the soldier disengages the bayonet from his piece, and returns it to the scabbard 1802. **2.** The shock..had..unfixed all his opinions MACAULAY. **3.** But the ruthless talons refuse to u. HOOD.

Unfi·xed, *ppl. a.* 1598. [UN-¹ 2.] **1.** Not fixed in a definite place or position; loose, free. **b.** Of bayonets: Not attached to the rifles 1844. **2.** *fig.* Unsettled, uncertain, undetermined; fluctuating, variable 1654. **b.** Unstable; lacking permanency 1669.

1. In a rusty u. grate DICKENS. **2.** He is totally u. in his principles, and wants to puzzle other people JOHNSON.

Unfla·gging *ppl. a.* [UN-¹ 4] 1715, **-ly** *adv.* **Unfla·nked** *ppl. a.* [UN-¹ 2] 1553. **Unfla·ttered** *ppl. a.* [UN-¹ 2] 1634. **Unfla·ttering** *ppl. a.* [UN-¹ 4] 1581. **Unflaw·ed** *ppl. a.* [UN-¹ 2] 1665. **Unfle·cked** *ppl. a.* [UN-¹ 2] 1865.

Unfle·dged, *ppl. a.* 1602. [UN-¹ 2.] **1.** Not yet fledged; callow, unfeathered 1611. **b.** Of an arrow: Unfeathered 1752. **2.** Of persons: Immature, inexperienced 1602. **3.** Of things: Not fully developed; still in a crude or imperfect state 1615. **4.** Pertaining to or characteristic of youth and inexperience 1611.

1. The two-legged and u. species called mankind SCOTT. **3.** Newly hatched u. opinions 1790. **4.** In those vnfledg'd dayes, was my Wife a Girle SHAKS.

Unfle·sh, *v.* 1598. [UN-² 2.] *trans.* To strip of flesh. So **Unfle·shed** *ppl. a.*²

Unfle·shed, *ppl. a.*¹ 1542. [UN-¹ 2.] Not yet stimulated by tasting flesh; *fig.* untried, inexperienced, new.

Unfle·shly *a.* [UN-¹ 1] 1855. **Unfli·nching** *ppl. a.* [UN-¹ 4] 1728, **-ly** *adv.* **Unflu·ctuating** *ppl. a.* [UN-¹ 4] 1723. **Unfoi·led** *ppl. a.*¹ [UN-¹ 2] 1579.

Unfoi·led, *ppl. a.*² 1640. [UN-¹ 2.] Not coated or backed with foil.

Unfo·ld, *v.*¹ [OE. *unfealdan*, f. UN-² + *fealdan* FOLD *v.*¹] **1.** *trans.* To open or unwrap the folds of; to spread open; to expand; to straighten out. **b.** To open (the lips or eyes, a gate, etc.) ME. **2.** To disclose or reveal by statement or exposition; to explain OE. **3.** To disclose to view; to display. late ME. **4.** To unwrap; to release or extract from wrappings 1553. **5.** *intr.* To come open; to spread out or expand; to become patent or plain ME.

1. U. thy forehead gather'd into frowns 1633. U. your arms from about my patient SCOTT. *refl.* Would some new rosebud now u. itself? 1891. **b.** He would not once vnfold his lips SHELTON. Hell shall unfould..her widest Gates MILT. **2.** I will vnto you all vnfold Our royall mind 1595. **3.** The lightning..That..vnfolds both heauen and earth SHAKS. The hollow vales their smiling pride u. 1713. **5.** And now Olympus' shining gates u. POPE. The queen's scheme began gradually to u. 1759. So **Unfo·lded** *ppl. a.*^{1} **Unfo·lder.**

Unfo·ld, *v.*^{2} 1530. [Un-^{2} 2 b.] *trans.* To release (sheep) from a fold or folds. So **Unfo·lded** *ppl. a.*^{2}

Unfo·llowed *ppl. a.* [Un-^{1} 2] 1508. **Unfoo·l** *v.* [Un-^{2} 4 b] SHAKS. **Unfoo·ted** *ppl. a.* [Un-^{1} 2] 1808. **Unforbi·d** 1667, **unforbi·dden** 1535, *ppl. adjs.* [Un-^{1} 2], **-ly** *adv.*, **-ness.**

Unfo·rced, *ppl. a.* 1598. [Un-^{1} 2.] **1.** Not acting or done under compulsion, voluntary. **b.** Of plants: Not forced 1868. **2.** Not strained, arrived at or effected without abnormal effort, spontaneous, natural 1604.

2. A natural and unforc'd order of words 1665. Here we have a fair u. example of coincidence PALEY. Hence **Unfo·rcedly** *adv.*

Unfo·rdable *a.* [Un-^{1} 1] 1611. **Unforeknow·n** *ppl. a.* [Un-^{1} 2] MILT. **Unforesee·able** *a.* [Un-^{1} 1] 1672, **-ably** *adv.*, **-ness. Unforesee·ing** *ppl. a.* [Un-^{1} 4] 1602, **-ly** *adv.* **Unforesee·n** *ppl. a.* [Un-^{1} 2] 1651. **Unfo·rested** *ppl. a.*^{1} [Un-^{1} 2] 1885. **Unfo·rested** *ppl. a.*^{2} [Un-^{2} 4 b, 6] 1502. **Unforewa·rned** *ppl. a.* [Un-^{1} 2] 1651. **Unfo·rfeit** *a.* [Un-^{1} 1] 1631. **Unfo·rfeited** *ppl. a.* [Un-^{1} 2] SHAKS. **Unfo·rged** *ppl. a.* [Un-^{1} 2] late ME. **Unforge·ttable** *a.* [Un-^{1} 1] 1806. **Unforge·tting** *ppl. a.* [Un-^{1} 4] 1777. **Unforgi·v(e)able** *a.* [Un-^{1} 1] 1548, **-ably** *adv.* **Unforgi·ven** *ppl. a.* [Un-^{1} 2] 1565. **Unforgi·veness** [Un-^{1} 6] 1611. **Unforgi·ving** *ppl. a.* [Un-^{1} 4] 1713, **-ness. Unforgo·t** (*arch.*) 1653, **Unforgo·tten** 1813, *ppl. adjs.* [Un-^{1} 2]. **Unfo·rm** *v.* [Un-^{2} 2] 1621. **Unfo·rmal** *a.* (now *rare*) [Un-^{1} 1] 1449.

Unfo·rmed, *ppl. a.* ME. [Un-^{1} 2.] **1.** Not formed or fashioned into a regular shape; formless. **b.** *transf.* Of immaterial things: Not brought to a definite or properly developed state; crude 1689. **c.** Of persons (or the mind): Not developed by education; unpolished 1711. **2.** Not formed or made; uncreated ME.

1. The u. matter of the World, was a God, by the name of Chaos HOBBES. **b.** Every science is in an u. state until its first principles are ascertained 1774. **3.** Vnfourmed is þe fader, vnfourmed is þe sone, vnfourmed is þe holi gost 1325. The New Ministry yet u. 1757.

Unfo·rmidable *a.* [Un-^{1} 1] 1667. **Unfo·rmulated** *ppl. a.* [Un-^{1} 2] 1866. **Unforsa·ken** *ppl. a.* [Un-^{1} 2] 1648. **Unfo·rtified** *ppl. a.* [Un-^{1} 2] 1525.

Unfo·rtunate, *a.* and *sb.* 1530. [Un-^{1} 2.] **A.** *adj.* **1.** Not favoured by fortune; meeting with bad fortune; unlucky. **b.** euphemistically, *U. woman, female*, a prostitute 1796. **2.** Marked by or associated with misfortune or mishap; disastrous, inauspicious. Also, untoward, regrettable, unlucky 1548.

1. U. in most of his counsels 1652. She shall..fall a Sniveling and call herself the most u. of Women 1680. *absol.* Every gate is shut against the u. GIBBON. **2.** Sith that vnfortunate day 1548. My rash but more u. misdeed MILT. The word 'massage' seems rather an u. one to apply to the procedure 1890.

B. *sb.* **1.** An unfortunate person 1683. **2.** A prostitute 1844.

2. One more U...Gone to her death! HOOD.

Unfo·rtunately, *adv.* 1548. [Un-^{1} 5.] **1.** In an unfortunate way, to a regrettable extent, not successfully, without good results, unaptly. Now *rare.* **2.** Used as a comment on the statement: = Sad to say; what is regrettable; a fact that has bad results. (The current use.) 1706. So **Unfo·rtunateness** 1561.

Unfo·rtune (*arch.*) [Un-^{1} 6] 1470. **Unfo·stered** *ppl. a.* [Un-^{1} 2] 1744. **Unfou·ght** 1523, **unfou·ghten** 1475 (*arch.*) *ppl. adjs.* [Un-^{1} 2]. **Unfou·nd** *ppl. a.* [Un-^{1} 2] 1584.

Unfou·nded, *ppl. a.* 1648. [Un-^{1} 2.] Groundless, not based on facts; chiefly *fig.*, unwarranted. Hence **Unfou·ndedly** *adv.*

Unfra·me *v.* [Un-^{2} 1] ME. **Unfra·med** *ppl. a.* [Un-^{1} 2] 1548. **Unfra·nchised** *ppl. a.* [Un-^{1} 2] 1648. **Unfra·nked** *ppl. a.* [Un-^{1} 2] 1765. **Unfra·ternal** *a.* [Un-^{1} 1] 1865.

Unfree·, *a.* late ME. [Un-^{1} 1.] **1.** Characterized by want of freedom; not possessed of personal liberty. **2.** Not holding the freedom of a corporation. *Obs.* or *arch.* 1442. **3.** Not free of duty, tax, or impost 1678. Hence **Unfree·man** (now *arch.*), one who is not a freeman of a corporation.

Unfree·d *ppl. a.* [Un-^{1} 2] 1565. **Unfree·dom** [Un-^{1} 6] late ME. **Unfre·eze** *v.* [Un-^{2} 1, 5] 1584. **Un-Fre·nch** *a.* [Un-^{1} 1] 1830. **Unfre·quency** (now *rare*) [Un-^{1} 6] 1611. **Unfre·quent** *a.* [Un-^{1} 1] 1611, **-ly** *adv.* **Unfreque·nted** *ppl. a.* [Un-^{1} 2] SHAKS., **-ness. Unfre·tted** *ppl. a.* [Un-^{1} 2] 1577.

Unfrie·nd. ME. [Un-^{1} 6.] **1.** One who is not a friend (*to* or *of* a person, cause, etc.). In early use chiefly *Sc.*, app. revived in the 19th c. by Scott. **2.** One who is not a member of the Society of Friends 1828.

1. He is a very unquiet neighbour to his unfriends SCOTT. Mr. Courtney, certainly no u. of the Parnellites 1888. **2.** *attrib.* Adding the names of u. ladies to their committee 1846.

Unfrie·nded, *a.* 1513. [Un-^{1} 2.] Not provided with friends; friendless.

Unfrie·ndly, *a.* late ME. [Un-^{1} 1.] **1.** Indicating or caused by dislike or hostility. **2.** Not having the qualities or disposition of a friend; *esp.* unfavourably disposed, inimical, hostile 1483. **3.** Not propitious or favourable (*to* or *for*) 1513.

1. This would be looked upon by other countries as an 'u. act' 1898. **3.** A coarse, u., stiff soil 1805. Hence **Unfrie·ndliness.**

Unfrie·ndly *adv.* (now *rare*) [Un-^{1} 5] OE. **Unfrie·ndship** (*arch.*) [Un-^{1} 6] ME. **Unfri·ghted** *ppl. a.* [Un-^{1} 2] 1611. **Unfri·ghtened** *ppl. a.* [Un-^{1} 2] 1675.

Unfro·ck, *v.* 1644. [Un-^{2} 2.] *trans.* To strip (an ecclesiastic) of his frock as a sign of degradation; hence, to deprive of the right of exercising the priestly function or office.

It is not the unfrocking of a Priest..that will make us a happy Nation MILTON. Who..had unfrocked himself to become a statesman L. HUNT. Hence **Unfro·cked** *ppl. a.*

Unfro·zen *ppl. a.* [Un-^{1} 2] 1596. **Unfru·ctuous** *a.* (now *rare*) [Un-^{1} 1] late ME. **Unfru·gal** *a.* [Un-^{1} 1] 1629.

Unfrui·tful, *a.* late ME. [Un-^{1} 1.] **1.** Not producing offspring; barren. **2.** Not productive of good results; unprofitable, fruitless. late ME. **3.** Of trees: Not bearing fruit 1531. **4.** Of ground, climate, etc.: Not yielding fruit or crops; unproductive 1545.

1. Unhappy and u. marriage BERKELEY. **2.** A time of idle and u. laughter SCOTT. Hence **Unfrui·tful-ly** *adv.*, **-ness.**

Unfru·strable *a.* (*rare*) [Un-^{1} 1] 1714, **-ably** *adv.* **Unfu·elled** (*ppl.*) *a.* [Un-^{1} 2] 1687. **Unfulfi·lled** *ppl. a.* [Un-^{1} 2] late ME. **Unfu·nded** *ppl. a.* [Un-^{1} 2] 1776.

Unfu·rl, *v.* 1641. [Un-^{2} 1.] **1.** *trans.* To spread (a sail or flag) to the wind. **b.** *transf.* To open (a fan, umbrella, etc.) 1678. **2.** *intr.* To open to the wind 1813.

1. b. The next Motion is that of unfurling the Fan ADDISON. **2.** As to the breeze a flag unfurls 1854.

Unfu·rnish, *v.* 1580. [Un-^{2} 2.] **1.** *trans.* To remove the garrison or other means of defence of (a town, etc.). Now *rare.* **2.** To strip of fittings or furniture; to dismantle 1598. †**3.** To deprive *of* something –1664.

1. English troops should, without unfurnishing Lisbon, co-operate for the relief of Oporto 1829. **3.** That, which may Vnfurnish me of Reason SHAKS.

Unfu·rnished, *ppl. a.* 1541. [Un-^{1} 2.] **1.** Not furnished; unprovided (*with* or †*of* something), unequipped, unprepared. **2.** Of houses or apartments: Not provided with furniture; *spec.* not furnished by the landlord or person letting; requiring to be furnished by the tenant 1581.

1. We shall be much vnfurnisht for this time SHAKS. The sayd place is..unfurnyshed with a convenient Schole howse 1611. To fill the void of an unfurnish'd brain COWPER. The treasury was u. 1860. **2.** A Fair House to be Lett Furnished or U. 1680.

Unfu·rred (*ppl.*) *a.* [Un-^{1} 2] 1450. **Unfu·rrowed** *ppl. a.* [Un-^{1} 2] 1566. **Ungai·n** *a.* (now chiefly *dial.*) [Un-^{1} 1] late ME. **Ungai·ned** *ppl. a.* [Un-^{1} 2] SHAKS. **Ungai·nful** *a.* [Un-^{1} 1] 1599.

Ungai·nly, *a.* 1611. [Un-^{1} 1.] Awkward, clumsy, ungraceful.

The tall u. figure..of Ebenezer SCOTT. So **Ungai·nly** *adv.* in an u. manner.

Ungainsai·d *ppl. a.* [Un-^{1} 1] 1587. **Ungainsay·able** *a.* [Un-^{1} 1] 1618, **-ably** *adv.* **Unga·llant** *a.* [Un-^{1} 1] 1710, **-ly** *adv.* **Unga·lled** *ppl. a.* [Un-^{1} 2] SHAKS. **Unga·rbled** *ppl. a.* [Un-^{1} 2] late ME. **Unga·rmented** *ppl. a.* [Un-^{1} 2] 1798. **Unga·rnered** *ppl. a.* [Un-^{1} 2] 1850. **Unga·rnish** *v.* [Un-^{2} 2] 1530. **Unga·rnished** *ppl. a.* [Un-^{1} 2] late ME. **Unga·rrisoned** *ppl. a.* [Un-^{1} 2] 1660. **Unga·rter** *v.* [Un-^{2} 2 b] 1594. **Unga·rtered** *ppl. a.* [Un-^{1} 2] SHAKS. **Unga·thered** *ppl. a.* [Un-^{1} 2] 1461. **Ungau·ged** *ppl. a.* [Un-^{1} 2] 1745. **Ungau·ntleted** (*ppl.*) *a.* [Un-^{1} 2] 1800.

Ungea·r, *v.* 1611. [Un-^{2} 1, 2 b.] **1.** *trans.* To unharness. Now *dial.* **2.** To disconnect the gearing of 1828.

Ungea·red, *a.* [Un-^{1} 3.] †**1.** Without fittings or accessories –1588. **2.** Not provided with gears or gearing (cf. GEARING 3).

Unge·lded, unge·lt *ppl. a.* [Un-^{1} 2] late ME. **Unge·nerated** *ppl. a.* [Un-^{1} 2] 1614. **Ungenero·sity** [Un-^{1} 6] 1757.

Unge·nerous, *a.* 1641. [Un-^{1} 1.] Not generous or large-minded; illiberal, ignoble, mean. Hence **Unge·nerous-ly** *adv.*, **-ness.**

Unge·nial *a.* [Un-^{1} 1] 1726, **-ly** *adv.* **Ungentee·l** *a.* [Un-^{1} 1] 1633, **-ly** *adv.*, **-ness. Ungenti·lity** [Un-^{1} 6] 1822.

Unge·ntle, *a.* late ME. [Un-^{1} 1.] †**1.** Not of gentle birth –1688. **2.** Lacking the qualities associated with gentle birth or breeding; unchivalrous; discourteous, unmannerly. Now *arch.* late ME. **b.** Not appropriate to or befitting one of gentle birth or breeding 1565. **3.** Not gentle in action; rough, harsh, unkind; rigorous, hard, severe 1509.

1. He is ashamed of hys vngentil lynage CHAUCER. **2.** Sith the vngentle king Of Fraunce refuseth to giue aide..To this distressed Queene MARLOWE. **b.** Where so loose life, and so vngentle trade Was vsd of Knights and Ladies seeming gent SPENSER. **3.** To crush our old limbes in vngentle Steele SHAKS. His temper, naturally u., had been exasperated by his domestic vexations MACAULAY.

Unge·ntleman *v.* (now *rare*) [Un-^{2} 4 b] 1671. **Unge·ntlemanlike** *a.* and *adv.* [Un-^{1} 1] 1592. **Unge·ntlemanly** *a.* and *adv.* [Un-^{1} 1, 5] 1562. **Unge·ntleness** [Un-^{1} 6] late ME. **Unge·ntly** *adv.* [Un-^{1} 5] 1440. **Unge·nuine** *a.* (*rare*) [Un-^{1} 1] 1665, **-ness. U:ngeome·trical** *a.* [Un-^{1} 1] 1570. **Unge·t** *v.* [Un-^{2} 1] 1775.

Unget-a·t-able, *a.* 1862. [Un-^{1} 1.] Difficult to get at; inaccessible.

Ungho·stly, *a.* 1526. [Un-^{1} 1.] **1.** Not spiritual, secular. **2.** Not of or like a ghost 1888.

1. Martin Luther the first preacher of this vnghostely ghospell 1565.

Ungi·fted (*ppl.*) *a.* [Un-^{1} 2, 3] 1631. **Ungi·ld** *v.* [Un-^{2} 2] 1611. **Ungi·lded** 1674, **ungi·lt** 1444 *ppl. adjs.* [Un-^{1} 2]. **Ungi·rd** *v.* [Un-^{2} 2, 2 b] OE. **Ungi·rded** *ppl. a.* [Un-^{1} 2] late ME. **Ungi·rdled** *ppl. a.* [Un-^{1} 2] 1611.

Ungi·rt, *ppl. a.* ME. [Un-^{1} 2.] **1.** Not girded or wearing a girdle; with the girdle or belt removed or slackened. **2.** *fig.* Not braced up for action; not drawn together; left loose or incompact 1579.

1. The idle and sluggish person..goeth loose and vngirt 1586. **2.** What in most English wryters vseth to be loose, and as it were vngyrt, in this Authour is..strongly trussed vp together SPENSER.

Ungi·rth *v.* [Un-^{2} 2 b] 1580. **Ungi·rthed** (*ppl.*) *a.* [Un-^{1} 2] 1628. **Ungi·ven** *ppl. a.* [Un-^{1} 2] ME. **Ungi·ving** *ppl. a.* [Un-^{1} 4] 1682. **Ungla·d** *a.* [Un-^{1} 1] OE., **-ly** *adv.*, **-ness. Ungla·ddened** *ppl. a.* [Un-^{1} 2] 1851.

Ungla·zed, *ppl. a.* 1599. [Un-^{1} 2.] **1.** Not glazed or having a smooth shining surface. **2.** Not filled in with glass; without glass windows 1608.

Unglea·ned *ppl. a.* [Un-^{1} 2] 1858. **Unglo·rified** *ppl. a.* [Un-^{1} 2] late ME. **Unglo·rify** *v.* [Un-^{2} 4 c] 1740. **Unglo·rious** *a.* (now *rare*) [Un-^{1} 1] late ME. **Unglo·ssed** *ppl. a.* [Un-^{1} 2] 1802. **Unglo·ssy** *a.* [Un-^{1} 1] 1822. **Unglo·ve** *v.* [Un-^{2} 2] late ME. **Unglo·ved** (*ppl.*) *a.* [Un-^{1} 2] 1626.

Unglue·, *v.* 1548. [Un-^{2} 1, 4.] **1.** *trans.* To sever or detach (a glued article, joint, or part). **b.** *transf.* To part the lids of, open (the eyes) 1606. **c.** *fig.* To bring (a union, etc.) to an end, dissolve 1619. **2.** *intr.* To lose cohesion, come apart 1693.

1. c. Enough to unglew all naturall and civill relations 1649.

Unglu·tted *ppl. a.* [Un-^{1} 2] 1813. **Ungo·d** *v.* [Un-^{2} 4 b] 1627. **Ungo·ddess** *v.* [Un-^{2} 4 b] 1760. **Ungo·dlike** *a.* [Un-^{1} 1] 1652.

Ungo·dly, *a.* 1526. [Un-^{1} 1.] **1.** Of persons: Not fearing or reverencing God; irreligious, impious, wicked. **2.** Of actions, etc.: Not in accordance with the law or will of God; wicked 1526. **3.** *colloq.* Outrageous, dreadful 1887.

1. They sayde it was vngodly to feyght..not beinge prouoked 1555. But no Success th' U. find

WESLEY. **3.** The wind['s] u. and unintermittent uproar STEVENSON. So **Ungo·dly** *adv.* (*arch.*) in an u. manner.

Ungo·rged *ppl. a.* [UN-¹ 2] 1623. **Ungo·spel-like** *a.* [UN-¹ 1] 1574. **Ungo·t** *ppl. a.* [UN-¹ 2] late ME. **Ungo·tten** *ppl. a.* [UN-¹ 2] late ME.

Ungo·vernable, *a.* 1673. [UN-¹ 1.] That cannot be governed; uncontrollable.

The u. spirit of a Barbarian host GIBBON. The abbess..will have an u. penitent under her charge SCOTT. He fell into a most u. passion 1843. Hence **Ungo·vernableness. Ungo·vernably** *adv.*

Ungo·verned *ppl. a.* [UN-¹ 2] SHAKS. **Ungow·ned** *ppl. a.* [UN-¹ 2] 1611. **Ungra·ce** (now *rare*) [UN-¹ 6] late ME. **Ungra·ced** *ppl. a.* [UN-¹ 2] 1595. **Ungra·ceful** *a.* [UN-¹ 1] MILT., **-ly** *adv.*, **-ness.**

Ungra·cious, *a.* ME. [UN-¹ 1.] †**1.** Of persons: Devoid of spiritual grace; graceless, wicked -1820. †**2.** Unfortunate, unlucky, unfavourable -1634. †**3.** Rude, unmannerly -1606. †**4.** Not in favour; disliked -1761. **b.** Unpleasant and unappreciated 1807. **5.** Ungraceful, unattractive 1647. **6.** Not gracious; lacking in courtesy or responsiveness; offending the sensibilities of others 1745.

1. Emong yᵉ holy apostles vngratious Iudas 1579. **2.** The .xv. day ys noght spedeful to begynne ony werke vp-on, for yt ys ongracyus 1445. **4.** Prince Rupert, at that time, was generally very u. in England CLARENDON. **b.** The u. duties inseparable from his office 1844. **5.** Show no parts which are u. to the Sight, as all foreshortnings usually are DRYDEN. **6.** The meek and affable duchess turned out an u. and haughty queen MACAULAY. Refusal on my part would be too u. DICKENS. Hence **Ungra·cious-ly** *adv.*, **-ness.**

Ungra·ded *ppl. a.* [UN-¹ 2] 1879.

Ungra·duated, *ppl. a.* 1783. [UN-¹ 2.] **1.** That has not graduated at a university. **2.** Without gradations; abrupt, not gradual 1841.

Ungra·fted *ppl. a.* [UN-¹ 2] 1657.

Ungramma·tical, *a.* 1654. [UN-¹ 1.] **1.** Not grammatical; breaking or offending against the rules of grammar. **2.** At variance with correct rule or method 1851.

2. Some really u. and false picture RUSKIN. Hence **Ungramma·tical-ly** *adv.*, **-ness.**

Ungra·nted *ppl. a.* [UN-¹ 2] 1570. **Ungra·spable** [UN-¹ 1] 1741.

Ungra·teful, *a.* 1553. [UN-¹ 1.] **1.** Not feeling or displaying gratitude. **b.** Of soil, etc.: Not responding to cultivation 1681. **2.** Unpleasant, distasteful, unwelcome 1596.

1. b. The land is u. and barren BORROW. **2.** Good wine which..is rendred..acid and u. to our palate 1663. Some sounds..are very harsh and u. 1690. The u. rumour reached his ears GIBBON. Then are these songs I sing of thee Not all u. to thine ear TENNYSON. Hence **Ungra·teful-ly** *adv.*, **-ness.**

Ungra·tified *ppl. a.* [UN-¹ 2] 1613. †**Ungra·titude** [UN-¹ 6] 1548. **Ungra·ve** *v.* [UN-² 3] 1664. **Ungra·vely** *adv.* (now *rare*) [UN-¹ 5] SHAKS. **Ungra·ven** *ppl. a.* [UN-¹ 2] late ME. **Ungrea·sed** *ppl. a.* [UN-¹ 2] 1440. **Un-Gree·k** *a.* [UN-¹ 1] 1846. **Ungree·ted** *ppl. a.* [UN-¹ 2] 1611. **Ungrou·nd** *ppl. a.* [UN-¹ 2] late ME.

Ungrou·nded, *ppl. a.* late ME. [UN-¹ 2.] **1.** Not based or established *in* something. **2.** Having no sound basis; unfounded, groundless. late ME. **3.** Not properly instructed or informed (*in* a subject) 1449.

1. Euyle lawis vngroundid in holy writt & reson WYCLIF. **2.** My former Letter, by which that conjecture will appear to be u. NEWTON. Hence **Ungrou·nded-ly** *adv.*, **-ness.**

Ungrow·n *ppl. a.* [UN-¹ 2] SHAKS. **Ungru·dged** *ppl. a.* [UN-¹ 2] 1631. **Ungru·dging** *ppl. a.* [UN-¹ 4] 1768, **-ly** *adv.*, **-ness.**

Ungual (*ʊ·ŋgwăl*), *a.* and *sb.* 1834. [f. L. *unguis* nail + -AL¹ 1.] **A.** *adj.* **1.** *Anat.* Pertaining to, connected with, a nail or claw; esp. *u. phalanx*, the terminal bone of a digit. **2.** *Path.* Affecting the nail 1872. **B.** *sb.* An ungual phalanx, claw, or bone.

Ungua·rd, *v.* 1745. [UN-² 2.] To deprive of a guard or defence; to lay open to attack. **b.** *Whist*, etc. To expose (a high card) to the risk of loss by discarding a lower and protecting card 1862.

Some well-chosen presents..so..unguarded the girl's heart FIELDING.

Ungua·rded, *ppl. a.* 1593. [UN-¹ 2.] **1.** Not furnished with, or protected by a guard; left open to attack, spoliation, etc. **b.** *Chess, cards*, etc. Not protected by other pieces or cards 1808. **2.** Not on one's guard; incautious 1640. **b.** Of times: Characterized by the absence of guard or caution 1680. **c.** Of actions, etc.: Incautious, imprudent; careless 1714. **3.** Having no screen, shield, fence, case, etc. 1771.

1. The u. passes of the Apennine GIBBON. **2.** Sir Robert was frequently very u. in his expressions 1763. **b.** I'll..Wait on and watch her loose u. hours OTWAY. **3.** Dust or gas..ignited by an u. lamp 1900. Hence **Ungua·rded-ly** *adv.*, **-ness.**

Unguent (*ʊ·ŋgwĕnt*), *sb.* 1440. [- L. *unguentum*, f. *unguere* anoint.] An ointment or salve. Hence **U·nguent** *v.* (*rare*) *trans.* to anoint.

‖**Unguentarium** (*ʊŋgwentēᵊ·riŏm*). 1859. [subst. use of n. (sc. *vas* vessel) of L. *unguentarius*; see next, -ARIUM.] *Archæol.* A vessel for holding ointment.

Unguentary (*ʊ·ŋgwĕntări*), *sb.* and *a.* Now *rare*. late ME. [- L. *unguentarius* (adj. and sb.), f. *unguentum* UNGUENT; see -ARY¹.] **A.** *sb.* **1.** A maker of or dealer in (perfumed) ointment; a perfumer. **2.** = prec. 1911. **B.** *adj.* Adapted for use in, suitable for or connected with ointments 1657.

Ungue·rdoned *ppl. a.* [UN-¹ 2] late ME. **Ungue·ssable** *a.* [UN-¹ 1] 1832. **Ungue·ssed** *ppl. a.* [UN-¹ 2] late ME.

Unguiculate (*ʊŋgwi·kiŭlĕt*), *a.* and *sb.* 1802. [- mod.L. *unguiculatus* (Ray, 1693), f. *unguiculus*, dim. of UNGUIS; see -CULE, -ATE².] **A.** *adj.* **1.** *Bot.* Of petals: Having an unguis. **2.** *Zool.* Ending in or of the form of a nail or claw 1826. **3.** *Zool.* Of quadrupeds: Having nails or claws; belonging to the order *Unguiculata* 1839. **B.** *sb.* An u. quadruped 1840. So **Ungui·culated** *a.* 1752.

Ungui·ded, *ppl. a.* 1585. [UN-¹ 2.] Not guided in a particular path or direction; left to take one's own course or way. **b.** *fig.* Of action, etc.: Undirected, uncontrolled 1597.

U·nguiform, *a.* 1726. [f. L. *unguis* nail + -FORM.] Having the form of a nail or claw.

Unguilloti·ned *ppl. a.* [UN-¹ 2] 1837. **Ungui·lty** *a.* [UN-¹ 1] OE.

‖**Unguis** (*ʊ·ŋgwis*). *Pl.* **ungues** (-*īz*). 1728. [L., 'nail, claw'.] **1.** *Bot.* The narrow part of a petal, by which it is attached to the receptacle. **2.** *Zool.*, etc. A nail or claw 1790.

‖**Ungula** (*ʊ·ŋgiŭlă*). 1710. [L., claw, hoof, f. *unguis* nail; see -ULE.] *Geom.* An obliquely truncated cone or cylinder.

‖**Ungulata** (*ʊŋgiŭlēⁱ·tă*), *sb. pl.* 1839. [L., n. pl. *ungulatus*; see next.] The order or division of ungulate animals.

Ungulate (*ʊ·ŋgiŭlĕt*), *a.* and *sb.* 1802. [- late L. *ungulatus*, f. UNGULA; see -ATE.] **A.** *adj.* **1.** Hoof-shaped. **2.** Of quadrupeds: Having hoofs 1839. **B.** *sb.* An u. animal 1842.

Unguled (*ʊ·ŋgiŭld*), *a.* 1572. [f. L. UNGULA + -ED².] *Her.* Of animals: With hoofs or claws of a different tincture from the body.

An ox gu., armed and u. or 1864.

Ungulite (*ʊ·ŋgiŭləit*). 1850. [f. L. *ungula* hoof + -ITE¹ 2 a.] *Palæont.* A Palæozoic brachiopod, the obolus.

Ungu·m *v.* [UN-² 2 b] 1598. **Ungu·mmed** *ppl. a.* [UN-¹ 2] 1799. **Ungy·ve** *v.* [UN-² 2 b] 1531. **Ungy·ved** *ppl. a.* [UN-¹ 2] 1607. **Unha·bitable** *a.* (now *rare*) [UN-¹ 1] late ME. **Unhabi·tuated** *ppl. a.* [UN-¹ 2] 1796. **Unha·cked** *ppl. a.* [UN-¹ 2] SHAKS. **Unha·ckneyed** *ppl. a.* [UN-¹ 2] 1759. **Unhai·led** *ppl. a.* [UN-¹ 2] 1715.

Unhai·r, *v.* late ME. [UN-² 2.] **1.** *trans.* To deprive (the head, etc.) of hair. **b.** *Tanning.* To remove the hair from (a skin) 1845. **2.** *intr.* To lose the hair; to become free of hair 1843.

Unhallow *v.* [UN-² 2] COVERDALE.

Unha·llowed, *ppl. a.* [OE. *unhālgod*, f. UN-¹ 2 + pa. pple. of HALLOW *v.*] **1.** Not formally hallowed or consecrated; left secular or profane. **2.** Not having a hallowed or sacred character; unholy, impious, wicked 1588.

1. Men vnhallowed and vnconsecrated 1587. **2.** In this unhallow'd air MILTON. In impious feasting, and unhallow'd joy POPE.

Unha·lter *v.* [UN-² 2 b] 1584. **Unha·lting** *ppl. a.* [UN-¹ 4] 1832. **Unha·mpered** *ppl. a.* [UN-¹ 2] 1699.

Unha·nd, *v.* 1602. [UN-² 2 b.] *trans.* To take the hand off; to release from one's grasp; to let go. Chiefly *arch.* in the phrase *unhand me.*

Unha·ndcuffed *ppl. a.* [UN-¹ 2] 1861. **Unha·ndily** *adv.* [UN-¹ 5] 1706. **Unha·ndiness** [UN-¹ 6] 1706. **Unha·ndled** *ppl. a.* [UN-¹ 2] 1558.

Unha·ndsome, *a.* 1530. [UN-¹ 1.] **1.** Not handsome in appearance; plain, uncomely. †**2.** Unhandy, inconvenient -1690. †**3.** Inexpert, unskilful. SHAKS. **4.** Unfitting, unbecoming, unseemly; discourteous, mean 1645. **b.** Not generous or liberal 1800.

1. Socrates was the most nasty and unhandsom of all men living 1653. Being generally well-shaped, and not u. 1787. A large u. house 1895. **2.** The night (perdy) is unhansome to woorke in UDALL. **4.** The u. attributes you so often give me HOBBES. Let mee conjure you not to doe a thing soe unhandsom 1658. Hence **Unha·ndsome-ly** *adv.*, **-ness.**

Unha·ndy, *a.* 1664. [UN-¹ 1.] **1.** Not easy to handle or manage; awkward, clumsy. **2.** Not skilful in using the hands, lacking in dexterity 1669. Hence **Unha·ndily** *adv.* KIPLING.

Unha·ng, *v.* late ME. [UN-² 1.] **1.** *trans.* To take down from a hanging position. **b.** *Naut.* To unship (a rudder) 1600. **2.** To undo the hanging of (a person) 1829.

Unha·nged, *ppl. a.* 1440. [UN-¹ 2.] Not (yet) executed by hanging.

There liues not three good men vnhang'd in England SHAKS. The greatest rascal u. THACKERAY.

Unha·ppily, *adv.* late ME. [UN-¹ 5.] **1.** By mischance; unfortunately, unluckily; regrettably. **b.** Used parenthetically or in loose construction 1586. **2.** In an unsatisfactory way; disastrously; unsuccessfully. late ME. **3.** Without happiness 1687. †**4.** Unpleasantly near the truth -1602. †**b.** Unfavourably. SHAKS.

1. Worc'ster (who had escap'd vnhappily His death in battel) on a Scaffold dies DANIEL. That War in which the King was so unhappyly engaged against Spain CLARENDON. **b.** U. the splendid qualities of John Churchill were mingled with alloy of the most sordid kind MACAULAY. **2.** I promise you, the effects he writes of, succeede vnhappily SHAKS. The giddy girl who married u. 1770. Persons who manage so u. what they mean for civilities SCOTT. **3.** Where little Rawdon passed the first months of his life, not u. THACKERAY. **4.** *Ham.* IV. v. 13.

Unha·ppiness. 1470. [UN-¹ 6.] **1.** Misfortune, mishap, ill luck. *Obs.* or *arch.* **2.** The condition of being unhappy in mind 1722.

1. I haue not that vnhappinesse, to be A Rich Mans Sonne 1621.

Unha·ppy, *a.* ME. [UN-¹ 1.] **1.** Causing misfortune or trouble (to oneself or others); objectionable or miserable on this account. **2.** Illfated, unlucky; miserable in lot or circumstances. Also, in later use, wretched in mind, ill content. late ME. **b.** Unsuccessful; apt to make mistakes 1651. **c.** Of places: Subject to, suffering from, misfortunes or evils 1591. **3.** Associated with, bringing about or causing, misfortune or mishap; disastrous. late ME. **b.** Inauspicious 1533. **c.** Infelicitous 1719. **4.** Of conditions: Marked by misfortune or mishap; miserable, wretched. late ME.

1. These u. Highland clans are again breaking into general commotion SCOTT. **2.** The seamen might conjecture some u. mortal to be shut up in the box SWIFT. **b.** He is as u. a person in Philology, as any that have pretended so much acquaintance with it 1662. **c.** The bands which.. wasted these u. districts MACAULAY. **3.** He had an u. propensity to drinking LOCKHART. **b.** Wretches borne vnder vnhappie starre SPENSER. **4.** You oft declaim on man's u. fate 1712. Their u. social position 1838. So †**Unha·ppy** *v. trans.* to make u. or unfortunate -1653.

Unha·rbour, *v.* 1576. [UN-² 3.] *trans.* To dislodge (a deer) from covert.

Unha·rdened *ppl. a.* [UN-¹ 2] SHAKS. **Unha·rdy** *a.* [UN-¹ 1] late ME. **Unha·rmed** *ppl. a.* [UN-¹ 2] ME. **Unha·rmful** *a.* [UN-¹ 1] 1538, **-ly** *adv.* **Unha·rming** *ppl. a.* [UN-¹ 4] 1795. **Unharmo·nious** *a.* [UN-¹ 1] 1634, **-ly** *adv.*

Unha·rness, *v.* late ME. [UN-² 2, 2 b.] **1.** *trans.* To divest of armour. **2.** To take off the harness from; to unyoke 1611.

2. *fig.* When two unfortunately met are by the Canon forc't to draw in that yoke..till death unharnesse 'em MILT. Hence **Unha·rnessed** *ppl. a.*²

Unha·rnessed, *ppl. a.*¹ 1513. [UN-¹ 2.] **1.** Not in armour. **2.** Not harnessed 1608. **b.** Not adapted for industrial use 1903.

2. b. U. rapids wasting fifty thousand head an hour KIPLING.

Unha·rvested *ppl. a.* [UN-¹ 1] 1867. **Unha·sp** *v.* [UN-² 2 b] late ME. **Unha·sting** *ppl. a.* [UN-¹ 4] 1839. **Unha·sty** *a.* [UN-¹ 1] SPENSER.

Unha·t *v.* [UN-[2] 2, 5] 1611. **Unha·tched** *ppl. a.*[1] [UN-[1] 2] 1601.

†**Unha·tched,** *ppl. a.*[2] 1601. [UN-[1] 2.] Unhacked; unstained –1619.

He is a knight dubb'd with vnhatch'd Rapier SHAKS.

Unha·tted *a.* [UN-[1] 3] 1832. **Unhau·nted** *ppl. a.* [UN-[1] 2] 1533. **Unha·zarded** *ppl. a.* [UN-[1] 2] 1588. **Unha·zardous** *a.* [UN-[1] 1] 1682.

Unhea·d, *v.* late ME. [UN-[2] 2.] **1.** *trans.* To behead. Now *rare.* **2.** To deprive or divest of a top, or end 1611.

Unhea·ded *a.* [UN-[1] 3] 1586. **Unhea·lable** *a.* [UN-[1] 1] late ME. **Unhea·led** *ppl. a.* [UN-[1] 2] ME. **Unhea·lth** [UN-[1] 6] OE. **Unhea·lthful** *a.* [UN-[1] 1] 1580, **-ness.**

Unhealthy (ʊnhe·lþi), *a.* 1595. [UN-[1] 1.] **1.** Not possessed of good health; weak, sickly 1611. **b.** *Path.* Not in a sound or healthy condition; diseased 1813. **2.** Prejudicial to health; insalubrious; unwholesome; in recent use, trivially (*War slang*), unsafe. 1595. **3.** *fig.* Deleterious to morals or character 1821.

1. b. When a wound becomes u., as surgeons term it 1877. **2.** The most u. season of the year 1806. **3.** I do feel the differences of mankind . . to an u. excess LAMB. Hence **Unhea·lthily** *adv.*, **-ness.**

Unhea·rd, *ppl. a.* ME. [UN-[1] 2.] **1.** Not apprehended by the sense of hearing; not heard. **b.** Not having been allowed a hearing 1595. **2.** Not before heard of; unknown, new, strange. (Now always with *of.*) late ME.

1. He drew not nigh u. MILT. **b.** I will not condemn you u. 1655. **2.** The vngracious and vnherde wickednesse of Iason COVERDALE 2 *Macc.* 4:13. Inflicting vnheard-of tortures 1615.

Unhea·rt, *v.* 1593. [UN-[2] 2.] To deprive of heart; to dishearten.

Yet to bite his lip, And humme at good Cominius, much vnhearts mee SHAKS.

Unhea·rty *a.* (now *rare*) [UN-[1] 1] 1440. **Unhea·ted** *ppl. a.* [UN-[1] 2] 1691. **Unhea·ven** *v.* [UN-[2] 3] 1609. **Unhea·venly** *a.* [UN-[1] 1] 1752. **Unhe·dged** *ppl. a.* [UN-[1] 2] 1648. **Unhee·d** *v.* [UN-[1] 7] 1847. **Unhee·ded** *ppl. a.* [UN-[1] 2] 1611, **-ly** *adv.* **Unhee·dful** *a.* [UN-[1] 1] 1570, **-ly** *adv.*, **-ness.**

Unhee·ding, *ppl. a.* 1737. [UN-[1] 4.] **1.** Heedless, inattentive. **2.** Const. *of*, or with direct obj. 1795.

2. I ramble . . u. of the storm 1795. Then, u. his proffered aid, Erma descends 1892. Hence **Unhee·dingly** *adv.*

Unhe·le, *v. Obs.* exc. *dial.* [OE. *unhelan*, f. UN-[2] + HELE *v.*] To uncover; to strip of covering; *fig.* to discover, reveal.

Unhe·lm *v.* [UN-[2] 2, 5] late ME. **Unhe·lmed** (*ppl.*) *a.* [UN-[1] 2] 1795. **Unhe·lmeted** (*ppl.*) *a.* [UN-[1] 2] 1823. **Unhe·lpable** *a.* [UN-[1] 1] 1886. **Unhe·lped** *ppl. a.* [UN-[1] 2] late ME. **Unhe·lpful** *a.* [UN-[1] 1] SHAKS., **-ness.** **Unhe·lping** *ppl. a.* [UN-[1] 4] 1604. **Unhe·mmed** *ppl. a.* [UN-[1] 2] 1561. **Unhe·ralded** *ppl. a.* [UN-[1] 2] 1845. **Unhero·ic** *a.* [UN-[1] 1] 1732, **-ally** *adv.* **Unhe·sitating** *ppl. a.* [UN-[1] 4] 1753, **-ly** *adv.*, **-ness.** **Unhew·ed** *ppl. a.* [UN-[1] 2] late ME.

Unhew·n, *ppl. a.* late ME. [UN-[1] 2.] **1.** Not hacked or cut with weapons. **2.** Not hewn or cut into shape; not shaped by hewing. late ME. **b.** *fig.* Rugged, unpolished, rough 1659.

2. b. The difference between a rough, u. soldier, and a polish'd Gentleman 1703.

Unhi·d *ppl. a.* [UN-[1] 2] ME. **Unhi·dden** *ppl. a.* [UN-[1] 2] SHAKS. **Unhi·de** *v.* [UN-[2] 1] ME. **Unhi·ndered** *ppl. a.* [UN-[1] 2] 1615.

Unhi·nge, *v.* 1612. [UN-[2] 1.] **1.** *trans.* To take (a door, etc.) off the hinges; to remove the hinges from; to open in this way 1616. **2.** To unbalance, unsettle, upset, disorder (the mind, a person, his opinions, convictions, etc.) 1612. **3.** To deprive of stability or fixity; to throw into confusion or disorder 1664. **b.** *esp.* To unsettle (an established order of things) 1679. **4.** To detach or dislodge *from* something 1655.

1. Our hogges having found a way to unhindge their barne doores 1634. **2.** The nerves of Mahomet were completely unhinged 1867. **b.** One Blow from unforeseen Providence unhing'd me at once DE FOE. **3.** The supplies are coming in very irregularly and u. the trade 1886. **4.** Minds that have been unhinged from their old faith and love GEO. ELIOT. Hence **Unhi·nged** *ppl. a.* **Unhi·ngement,** the act of unhinging; the fact of being unhinged.

Unhi·red *ppl. a.* [UN-[1] 2] 1617. **Unhisto·ric** *a.* [UN-[1] 1] 1862.

Unhisto·rical, *a.* 1611. [UN-[1] 1.] **1.** Not in accordance with history. **2.** Not recorded in true history; not having actually occurred 1848. Hence **Unhisto·rically** *adv.*

Unhi·tch, *v.* 1706. [UN-[2] 2 b.] **1.** *trans.* To detach (a horse, etc.) from a vehicle, etc. or from something to which its head is tied. **2.** To detach or unfasten (a thing) 1876.

Unhi·ve *v.* [UN-[2] 3] 1729. **Unhoa·rd** *v.* [UN-[2] 3] MILT. **Unho·lpen** *ppl. a.* (*arch.*) [UN-[1] 2] late ME.

Unho·ly, *a.* and *sb.* [OE. *unhāliġ*, f. UN-[1] + *hāliġ* HOLY *a.*] **1.** Not holy, impious, profane, wicked. **2.** *colloq.* Awful, dreadful 1865. **B.** *sb.* An u. person or thing (*rare*) 1831. Hence **Unho·lily** *adv.* **Unho·liness.**

Unho·mely *a.* [UN-[1] 1] 1871. **Unhomoge·neous** *a.* [UN-[1] 1] 1828.

Unho·nest, *a.* Now *arch.* or *dial.* ME. [UN-[1] 1.] **1.** Physically or morally objectionable, offensive, or unpleasant; indecent, filthy, vile. **b.** Unseemly, unbecoming, improper. late ME. **2.** Morally unfitting or unbecoming; unseemly, immodest, lewd; dishonourable, discreditable. late ME. **3.** Of persons: Not honourable, respectable, or of good repute; bad or immoral in character or conduct. late ME. **4.** Dishonest 1545.

1. Whatsoever thyng wer not of it self u., he affermed not to bee unhoneste in open presence UDALL. **2.** Taking delight in hearing u. things 1645. **3.** This untrew, u. and perjured persone HALL. **4.** How vnhonest is that labourer, who will not worke for his wages? 1603. So **Unho·nestly** *adv.* (*obs.* or *dial.*). **Unho·nesty** (*obs.* or *dial.*).

†**Unho·nourable** *a.* [UN-[1] 1] –1635. **Unho·noured** *ppl. a.* [UN-[1] 2] 1513. **Unhoo·d** *v.* [UN-[2] 2] 1575. **Unhoo·ded** *ppl. a.* [UN-[1] 2] 1575.

Unhoo·k, *v.* 1611. [UN-[2] 2 b.] **1.** *trans.* To detach from a hook; to unfasten or open in this way. **2.** To unfasten the hooks of (a dress). Also with personal obj. 1840. **3.** To disengage (one's arm) from another's 1865.

Unho·ped, *ppl. a.* late ME. [UN-[1] 2.] †**1.** Unforeseen –1697. **2.** Not hoped for. Now *rare*. late ME. †**b.** *advb.* By unexpected good fortune, beyond hopes –1830. **3.** Not hoped [†or looked) *for* 1598.

1. Amazed at this u. danger 1575. **2.** Such, as fill my heart with vnhop'd ioyes SHAKS. **b.** Though Jove hath given me to behold, Unhop'd, the land again COWPER. **3.** These u.-for circumstances 1857.

Unho·peful *a.* [UN-[1] 1] 1450, **-ly** *adv.*, **-ness.** **Unho·ping** *ppl. a.* [UN-[1] 4] 1628. **Unho·rned** *ppl. a.* [UN-[1] 2] 1570.

Unho·rse, *v.* late ME. [UN-[2] 1.] **1.** *trans.* To throw or drag (a rider) from his horse, esp. in battle. **b.** *fig.* To discomfit, overthrow. Now *rare*. 1577. **c.** *pass.* To be thrown from a horse 1583. **2.** To unharness the horses from (a carriage, gun, etc.) 1654.

1. b. Thou hast unhorsed me with that very word SCOTT.

Unho·spitable *a.* (now *rare*) [UN-[1] 1] SHAKS. **Unhou·se** *v.* [UN-[2] 3] late ME. **Unhou·sed** *ppl. a.* [UN-[1] 2] 1582.

Unhouseled (ʊnhau·z'ld), *ppl. a.* Now only after Shaks. [UN-[1] 2] Not having received Holy Communion.

Vnhouzzled, disappointed, vnnaneld *Ham.* I. v. 77.

Unhu·man, *a.* 1549. [UN-[1] 1.] **1.** Inhuman, inhumane, unmerciful, cruel. Now *rare.* **2.** Transcending the human; super-human 1782. **3.** Not pertaining to mankind 1885.

1. He was sent away pennyless . . from the house of his u. father FIELDING. **2.** Exalted to u. happiness 1782. **3.** 'How is this?', he cried, in a sharp u., voice 1885.

Unhu·manize *v.* [UN-[2] 4 c] 1752. **Unhu·mble** *a.* [UN-[1] 1] 1611. **Unhu·mbled** *ppl. a.* [UN-[1] 2] 1604. **Unhu·morous** *a.* [UN-[1] 1] 1881.

Unhu·ng, *ppl. a.* 1648. [UN-[1] 2.] **1.** Not furnished with hangings. Now *rare.* **2.** Not (yet) hanged 1840. **b.** Not hung up (for exhibition) 1880.

2. One of the greatest scoundrels u. DICKENS.

Unhu·nted, *ppl. a.* 1572. [UN-[1] 2.] **1.** Of districts, etc.: Not hunted in. **2.** Not hunted or chased 1648.

Unhu·rried *ppl. a.* [UN-[1] 2] 1768, **-ly** *adv.* **Unhu·rrying** *ppl. a.* [UN-[1] 4] 1768. **Unhu·rt** *ppl. a.* [UN-[1] 2] ME. **Unhu·rtful** *a.* [UN-[1] 1] 1549, **-ly** *adv.*, **-ness.** **Unhu·rting** *ppl. a.* [UN-[1] 4] 1613.

Unhu·sbanded, *ppl. a.* 1538. [UN-[1] 2.] **1.** Not improved by husbandry; untilled, uncultivated. **2.** Having no husband 1797.

Unhu·sk, *v.* 1596. [UN-[2] 3.] **1.** *trans.* To divest of husk or shell 1598. **2.** *fig.* To strip of a covering or disguise; to expose 1596. Hence **Unhu·sked** *ppl. a.*[2]

Unhu·sked, *ppl. a.*[1] 1769. [UN-[1] 2.] Not stripped of the husk.

Unhygie·nic *a.* [UN-[1] 1] 1883, **-ally** *adv.* **Unhy·mned** *ppl. a.* [UN-[1] 2] 1851. **Unhypo·thecated** *ppl. a.* [UN-[1] 2] 1802. **Unhyste·rical** *a.* [UN-[1] 1] 1886.

Uni- (yū·ni), repr. L. *uni-*, comb. form of *unus* one, forming the first element in many words with the sense 'having, composed or consisting of, or characterized by one (thing specified by the second element)'. The older examples are directly adopted from French or Latin, as UNANIMOUS, UNIVERSAL. In the 15th and 16th centuries additional words were formed of L. elements and on L. analogy; in the 17th and 18th the prefix gained currency and appeared in some abnormal functions, as *unifold, unisoil*; and in the 19th it came into frequent use in forming scientific and technical terms, esp. in *Bot.* and *Zool.* The second element of these compounds is usually of L. origin, but the prefix has been combined with English forms or words, and has been used occas. in place of the Gr. equivalent MONO-. (In scientific works the figure 1 is often substituted for *uni-*, as in 1-*bracteate.*)

1. Forming adjs. with the general sense 'having, provided with, composed or consisting of, characterized by one (thing specified or connoted by the second element)'. Many of these compounds are self-explanatory. **U:niarti·culate** *Ent., Zool.,* having a single joint. **U:niauri·culate(d** *Zool.,* having a single auricle or auriculate process. **Unia·xial** *Optics* and *Cryst.,* having one optical axis; *Bot.* and *Zool.* = MONAXIAL *a.* **Unica·meral,** having, consisting of, or characterized by one legislative chamber. **Unico·lor, Unico·lorous, Unico·loured** *Nat. Hist.,* of a single uniform colour. **Unico·rneal** *Zool.,* of an ocellus: having a single cornea. **Unicu·spidate,** ending in one cusp or point. **U:nidime·nsional,** of one dimension. **U:nidire·ctional** *Electr.,* (of currents) moving in one direction. **Uni filar** (-fəi·lăɹ), of a magnetometer, etc., having or suspended by a single thread or fibre. **Uniflo·rous** *Bot.,* having or bearing only one flower. **Unifo·liate, -fo·liolate** *Bot.,* of leaves, etc.: consisting of one leaflet; of plants: having such leaves. **Unila·biate** *Bot., Ent.,* having one lip. **Unili·near** *Math.,* involving one line only. **Unili·ngual,** pertaining to one language only; knowing or employing only one language. **Unili·teral,** involving the use of, or consisting of, only one letter. **Unilo·bular** *Path.,* of cirrhosis: characterized by hypertrophy of single lobules; hypertrophic. **Unilo·cular,** having, consisting of, characterized by, only one loculus; one-celled. **Unino·dal,** having one node or nodal point. **Uninu·clear,** having, or characterized by, one nucleus. **Unio·cular,** of, pertaining to, or affecting one eye; *fig.* characterized by the use of one eye only. **Unio·vular, -o·vulate,** produced by or containing one ovule. **Unipa·rient** = UNIPAROUS 1. **Unipa·rtite** *Math.,* consisting of or involving a single part. **U·niped,** having only one foot (or leg). **Unipe·rsonal,** consisting of a single person or individual; having or existing as one person; hence **U:nipersona·lity.** **Unise·rial, -se·riate** *Bot., Zool.,* etc., arranged in or consisting of one series or row; characterized by such a form or arrangement. **U:nitenta·cular.** **U:niungui·culate,** having one unguis or claw.

2. Forming sbs. **U·nicell** *Bot.,* a unicellular plant. **U·nicode,** a telegraphic code in which one word or set of letters represents a sentence or phrase; a telegram or message in this. **U·nicycle** *U.S.,* a vehicle having only one wheel; esp. a monocycle used by acrobats or for gymnastic displays. **U·niped,** a creature having only one foot (or leg). **U·nireme** [L. *remus* oar], an ancient vessel or galley having one bank of oars. **Unitri·nity,** unity in trinity.

Uniat, Uniate (yū·niæt, -ēt). 1833. [– Russ. *úniyat*, f. *úniya* – L. *unio* UNION.] A Russian, Polish, or other member of that part of the Greek Church which, while retaining its own liturgy, acknowledges the Pope's supremacy. **b.** *attrib.* or as *adj.* Of, adhering or pertaining to, or denominating the United Greek Churches 1855.

b. The much persecuted Uniate or Greek Catholic creed 1905.

Unica·psular, *a.* 1720. [f. UNI- + CAPSULE + -AR[1].] *Bot.* Of a pericarp: Having a single capsule. Of a plant: Having such a pericarp.

Unicellular (yūni,se·liŭlăɹ), *a.* 1858. [f. UNI- + CELLULE + -AR[1].] *Biol.* **1.** Composed or consisting of a single cell; applied esp. to organisms belonging to the primary divisions of the animal and vegetable kingdoms. Also as *sb.* **2.** Characterized by the formation or presence of a single cell or cells 1863. Hence **Unicellula·rity.**

Unicist (yū·nisist). 1807. [f. L. *unicus* one + -IST.] **1.** A believer in the unicity of the Godhead. **2.** *Med.* A believer in unicity 1890.

Unicity (yūni·siti). 1691. [XVII poss. – med.L. *unicitas* (Blaise), var. of *unitas* (of the Trinity); otherwise f. L. *unicus* one, unique; see -ITY. Cf. Fr. *unicité.*] **1.** The fact of being or consisting of one; oneness. **b.** *Med.* The theory that syphilis is caused by one kind only of venereal virus 1861. **2.** The fact or quality of being unique 1859.

Unicorn (yū·nikǭɹn). ME. [– (O)Fr. *unicorne* – L. *unicornis* one-horned, (Vulg.) unicorn, f. *unus* one + *cornu* horn, rendering Gr. μονόκερως.] **1.** A legendary animal usu. regarded as having a horse's body and a single long straight horn projecting from its forehead. (The horn of this animal was reputed to possess medicinal or magical properties, esp. as an antidote to or preventive of poison.) **b.** Used in ME. and later versions of the OT. to render the Vulgate *unicornis* or *rhinoceros* (Greek μονόκερως), as tr. Heb. *rᵉ'em*, where the R. V. has *wild-ox*. ME. **2.** A representation of this animal, esp. in *Her.* as a charge or (usu.) as a supporter of the Royal Arms. late ME. **3.** *Sc.* One of the pursuivants of the Lyon King of Arms 1445. **4.** *Hist.* A Scottish gold coin (= 18 shillings Scots) current in the 15th and 16th centuries 1487. **5.** *Astr.* A southern constellation 1771. **6.** A carriage, etc., drawn by three horses, two abreast and one in front; now usu., a team of horses so arranged 1785. †**7.** The one-horned rhinoceros –1700. **8.** The narwhal or sea-unicorn 1694. **b.** A unicorn-shell 1711.

Comb., chiefly in names of animals or plants characterized by a projecting horn-like process or spine suggesting the unicorn's horn: **u.-bird,** the horned screamer, *Palamedea cornuta*; **-fish, narwhal** = sense 8; **-plant,** any of various N. Amer. plants, esp. *Martynia proboscidea*, the capsule of which terminates in two horn-like spines; **-shell,** a marine gasteropod having a horn-like lip projecting from the shell, now esp. one belonging to the genus *Monoceros*. **b.** Comb. with *unicorn's*: **unicorn's horn,** a horn of the rhinoceros, narwhal, or other animal reputed to be obtained from a u., freq. mounted or made into a cup, and employed as a preventive of or charm against poison; †the material of this powdered and used medicinally, esp. as an antidote against poison. Hence **Unico·rnic** *a.* (*rare*) resembling, having the form of, a u.

‖**Unicum** (yū·nikǒm). *Pl.* **unica** (yū·nikă). 1885. [L., n. sing. of *unicus* UNIQUE *a.*] A unique specimen.

Unicursal (yūnikǒ·ɹsăl), *a.* and *sb.* 1866. [f. UNI- + L. *cursus* course + -AL[1] 1.] *Math.* **A.** *adj.* Having, traversing, or being on one course or path. **B.** *sb.* A unicursal curve.

Unidea'd (ɒn,əidī·ăd), *a.* 1752. [UN-[1] 2.] Not furnished with an idea.

Unideal (ɒn,əidī·ăl), *a.* 1751. [UN-[1] 1.] †**1.** Conveying or expressing no idea –1792. †**2.** Destitute of ideas –1801. **3.** Not following an ideal 1760. **4.** Not inspired by or exhibiting idealism 1846.

Unide·ntified *ppl. a.* [UN-[1] 2] 1860. **U:nidioma·tic** *a.* [UN-[1] 1] 1822. **Unido·latrous** *a.* [UN-[1] 1] 1841.

Unific (yuni·fik), *a.* 1788. [f. UNIFY, after *deify/deific, pacify/pacific*; see -FIC. Cf. med.L. *unificus* unifying (IX).] That unifies; producing unity.

Unification (yū:nifikē[1]·ʃən). 1851. [f. UNIFY (see -FICATION), perh. after Fr. *unification.*] The action or process of unifying; reduction to unity or to a uniform system; the result of this.

Uniform (yū·nifǭɹm), *sb.* 1748. [After Fr. *uniforme*, subst. use of the adj.] **1.** A distinctive dress of uniform materials, colour, and cut, worn by all the members of a particular military, naval, or other force to which it is recognized as properly belonging and peculiar. **b.** A distinctive uniform dress worn by the members of any civilian body or association of persons 1837. **c.** A single suit of such dress 1783. **2.** *attrib.* **a.** Belonging to or forming part of a uniform, as *u. coat* 1807. **b.** Wearing uniform, uniformed, as *u. policeman* 1895.

1. None shall fight who do not wear the u. of one of the armies engaged 1879. **b.** The proposed u., sir, of the Pickwick Club DICKENS. Hence **U·niformed** *a.* dressed in or wearing u.

Uniform (yū·nifǭɹm), *a.* 1540. [– (O)Fr. *uniforme* or L. *uniformis*, f. *unus* UNI- + *forma* FORM.] **1.** Having, maintaining, or occurring in the same form always; the same or alike under all conditions; unvarying. **b.** Of persons, etc. Hence, constant in respect of conduct or opinion; consistent. 1551. **c.** Of clothing, etc.: Of the same pattern, colour, and material amongst a number or body of persons 1746. **2.** Having or presenting the same appearance or aspect; hence, having a plain, unbroken, or undiversified surface or exterior 1550. **3.** Of motion, dimensions, etc.: Free from fluctuation or variation in respect of quantity or amount 1559. **4.** Of the same form, character, or kind as another or others; conforming to one standard, rule, or pattern; alike, similar 1548.

1. That all our Subjects could be brought to agree in a uniforme Worship of God 1662. **b.** A man so u. as to have nothing of Inequality..in his Actions DRYDEN. **c.** The practice of clothing soldiers, by regiments, in one u. dress 1890. **2.** The street..is one of the longest, straightest, and most u. in Europe 1756. His jerkin, hose, and cloak, were of a dark u. colour SCOTT. This piece of glass..being perfectly u. in its internal structure FARADAY. **3.** Velocity..may be u., *i.e.* the same at every instant 1879. **4.** How far churches are bound to be u. in their ceremonies HOOKER. When two figures are composed of similar parts, they are said to be u. 1762. The copies sold..were found to be exactly u. 1867. Hence **U·niform-ly** *adv.* 1549, **-ness.**

U·niform, *v.* 1681. [f. UNIFORM *sb.* and *a.*] **1.** *trans.* To make uniform. **2.** To put into uniform 1894.

1. The..travesties which words underwent before they were uniformed by Johnson and Walker 1870.

Unifo·rmal, *a.* Now *rare.* 1573. [f. UNIFORM *a.* + -AL[1] 1.] Uniform.

U·niformist. 1885. [f. UNIFORM *a.* + -IST.] One who believes in or advocates uniformity, esp. in respect of religious doctrine or observance.

Uniformitarian (yū:nifǭɹmitē[ə]·riăn), *sb.* and *a.* 1840. [f. next + -ARIAN.] **A.** *sb.* **1.** *Geol.* One who attributes geological processes and phenomena to forces operating continuously and uniformly. (Opp. to CATASTROPHIST.) **2.** = prec. (*rare*) 1890. **B.** *adj.* **1.** *Geol.* Of, characteristic of, or held by uniformitarians 1840. **b.** In accordance with the theory of the uniformitarians 1869. **c.** Of persons: That is a uniformitarian 1864. **2.** Of or pertaining to, advocating or practising, uniformity in something 1897. Hence **U:niformita·rianism.**

Uniformity (yūnifǭ·ɹmĭti). late ME. [– (O)Fr. *uniformité* or late L. *uniformitas*, f. L. *uniformis*; see UNIFORM *a.*, -ITY.] The quality or condition of being uniform, in various senses. **b.** Conformity to (or compliance with) one standard of opinion, practice, or procedure, esp. in religious observance 1549. **c.** *spec.* in *Geol.* Cf. UNIFORMITARIAN. 1837. **d.** With *a* and *pl.* A particular instance of this condition; a uniform feature, law, etc. 1665.

The u. of life must be sometimes diversified JOHNSON. Variety is more pleasing than u. HOGARTH. **b.** Three..Reverend Divines, who..can give a good Account of his Vertue, U., and Learning 1708. *Act of U.*, in *Eng. Hist.*, any of three Acts (1549, 1559, 1662) regulating public worship, which prescribed the use and acceptance of the Books of Common Prayer published in those years. **c.** It is very conceivable that catastrophes may be part and parcel of u. HUXLEY.

Unify (yū·nifəi), *v.* 1502. [– (O)Fr. *unifier* or late L. *unificare*; see UNI-, -FY.] *trans.* To make, form into, or cause to become one; to unite, consolidate. Hence **U·nifying** *ppl. a.*

Unige·niture. 1659. [– late (eccl.) L. *unigenitus* only-begotten, or f. UNI- + GENITURE.] **1.** *Theol.* The fact of being the only-begotten Son. **2.** The fact of being an only child; the practice of having only one child 1887.

Unila·teral, *a.* 1802. [f. UNI- + LATERAL. Cf. Fr. *unilatéral.*] **1. a.** *Bot.* Of a raceme or panicle; Having the flowers on one side of the peduncle. Also, of a cyme: Having a branch or axis on one side only. **b.** *Bot., Zool.* Arranged or produced on one side of an axis or surface; directed towards one side 1870. **2.** Of or pertaining to, occurring on or affecting, one side of an organ or part 1843. **b.** *Path.* Affecting or developed on one side of the body only 1876. **c.** *Phonetics.* Produced with the glottis open on one side only 1867. **3.** Of one party or side only, not reciprocal 1802. **b.** *Law.* Binding or imposed on one party only; without reciprocal obligation 1802. **4.** One-sided, partial, incomplete 1830.

4. This is a u. view of the social contract, and omits the element of reciprocity MORLEY. Hence **Unilatera·lity. Unila·terally** *adv.*

Unillu·minated, *ppl. a.* 1579. [UN-[1] 2.] **1.** Not spiritually or mentally enlightened. **2.** Not lighted up 1824.

Unillu·minating *ppl. a.* [UN-[1] 4] 1882. **Unillu·mined** *ppl. a.* [UN-[1] 2] 1826. **Uni·llustrated** *ppl. a.* [UN-[1] 2] 1828. **Uni·maged** *ppl. a.* [UN-[1] 2] 1648. **Unima·ginable** *a.* [UN-[1] 1] 1611, **-ness, -ably** *adv.* **Unima·ginative** *a.* [UN-[1] 1] WORDSW., **-ly** *adv.*, **-ness. Unima·gined** *ppl. a.* [UN-[1] 2] 1548. **Uni·mitated** *ppl. a.* [UN-[1] 2] 1610. **Unimme·rsed** *ppl. a.* [UN-[1] 2] 1835. **Unimmo·rtal** *a.* [UN-[1] 1] MILT. **Unimpai·rable** *a.* [UN-[1] 1] 1627. **Unimpai·red** *ppl. a.* [UN-[1] 2] 1583. **Unimpa·rted** *ppl. a.* [UN-[1] 2] 1655. **Unimpa·ssioned** *ppl. a.* [UN-[1] 2] 1744.

Unimpea·chable, *a.* 1784. [UN-[1] 1.] That cannot be called in question, doubted, or discredited, of evidence, witnesses, good qualities, etc. Hence **Unimpeachabi·lity. Unimpea·chableness. Unimpea·chably.** *adv.*

Unimpea·ched, *ppl. a.* late ME. [UN-[1] 2.] †**1.** Not impeded. –late ME. **2.** Not assailed, accused, or called in question 1583.

Unimpe·ded *ppl. a.* [UN-[1] 2] 1760. **Unimplo·red** *ppl. a.* [UN-[1] 2] MILT. **Unimpo·rtance** [UN-[1] 6] JOHNSON. **Unimpo·rtant** *a.* [UN-[1] 1] 1727. **Unimpo·sing** *ppl. a.* [UN-[1] 4] 1736. **Unimpre·gnated** *ppl. a.* [UN-[1] 2] 1744.

Unimpre·ssed, *ppl. a.* 1743. [UN-[1] 2.] †**1.** Not under restraint. YOUNG. **2.** Not affected by feelings of respect or awe 1861. **3.** Not bearing an impression 1868.

Unimpre·ssible *a.* [UN-[1] 1] 1828. **Unimpre·ssionable** *a.* [UN-[1] 1] 1847. **Unimpre·ssive** *a.* [UN-[1] 1] 1796, **-ly** *adv.*, **-ness. Unimpri·soned** *ppl. a.* [UN-[1] 2] 1659.

Unimpro·vable, *a.* 1660. [UN-[1] 1.] **1.** That cannot be cured of faults, etc.; hopelessly bad, not to be made better. **2.** Perfect, having no fault or deficiency 1822.

1. A people the most unprincipled and unimproveable of all GROTE. **2.** You show an absolute and u. acquaintance with..mankind SCOTT.

Unimpro·ved, *ppl. a.* 1665. [UN-[1] 2.] **1.** Not made better; not raised in quality. **2.** Not turned to use; not taken advantage of 1781.

2. They preferred leaving their victory u., to the hazard of a general battle 1850.

Unimpro·ving *ppl. a.* [UN-[1] 4] 1747. **Unimpu·gnable** *a.* [UN-[1] 1] 1832. **Unimpu·gned** *ppl. a.* [UN-[1] 2] 1838. **Unimpu·lsive** *a.* [UN-[1] 1] 1856, **-ness. Uninca·rnate** *a.* [UN-[1] 1] 1687. **Unince·nsed** *ppl. a.* [UN-[1] 2] 1594. **Uninclu·ded** *ppl. a.* [UN-[1] 2] 1775. **Uninco·rporate** *a.* [UN-[1] 1] 1821. **Uninco·rporated** *ppl. a.* [UN-[1] 2] 1715. **Unincrea·sable** *a.* [UN-[1] 1] 1648. **Unincrea·sed** *ppl. a.* [UN-[1] 2] 1824. **Uninde·bted** *ppl. a.* [UN-[1] 2] DRYDEN, **-ness. Uninde·nted** *ppl. a.* [UN-[1] 2] 1750. **Uni·ndexed** *ppl. a.* [UN-[1] 2] 1832.

Unindi·fferent, *a.* 1565. [UN-[1] 1.] **1.** Not impartial; prejudiced. Now *arch.* **2.** Not unconcerned; interested 1813. So **Unindi·fference. Unindi·fferency** (now *arch.*). **Unindi·fferently** *adv.*

Unindu·strious *a.* [UN-[1] 1] 1599. **Uninfe·cted** *ppl. a.* [UN-[1] 2] 1628. **Uninfe·ctious** *a.* [UN-[1] 1] 1744. **Uninfe·sted** *ppl. a.* [UN-[1] 2] MILT.

Uninfla·med, *ppl. a.* 1626. [UN-[1] 2.] †**1.** Not set on fire –1794. **2.** *fig.* Not fired with passion, enthusiasm, etc. 1714. **3.** *Path.* Free from inflammation 1793.

1. Rise odours sweet from incense uninflam'd? YOUNG.

Uninfla·mmable *a.* [UN-[1] 1] 1666. **Uninfla·ted** *ppl. a.* [UN-[1] 2] 1861. **Uninfle·cted** *ppl. a.* [UN-[1] 2] 1713. **Uni·nfluenced** *ppl. a.* [UN-[1] 2] 1734. **Uninflue·ntial** *a.* [UN-[1] 1] 1661.

Uninfo·rmed, *ppl. a.* 1597. [UN-[1] 2.] **1.** Not informed, instructed, or enlightened on some matter or in some respect. **2.** Uneducated, uninstructed, ignorant 1647. **b.** Marked by lack of enlightenment, information, or knowledge 1796. **3.** Not showing animation; lifeless, mechanical 1709.

3. Without this irradiating Power..her most perfect Features are Uninform'd and Dead STEELE.

Uninfo·rming *ppl. a.* [UN-^{1} 4] 1709. **Unin-fri·nged** *ppl. a.* [UN-^{1} 2] 1610. **Uninge·nious** *a.* [UN-^{1} 1] 1638. †**Uninge·nuous** *a.* [UN-^{1} 1] –1670, †**-ly** *adv.* **Uninha·bitable** *a.* [UN-^{1} 1] 1448, **-ness.** **Uninha·bited** *ppl. a.* [UN-^{1} 2] 1571. **Unini·tiate** *ppl. a.* [UN-^{1} 2] 1801. **Un-ini·tiated** *ppl. a.* [UN-^{1} 2] 1678. **U:ninitia·tion** [UN-^{1} 6] 1834. **Uni·njured** *ppl. a.* [UN-^{1} 2] 1578. **Uninju·rious** *a.* [UN-^{1} 1] 1809, **-ly** *adv.*

Unino·minal (yūni-), *a.* 1881. [– Fr. *uninominal* (1878); see UNI-, NOMINAL *a.*] **1.** Based on the principle of one member being separately elected by each constituency. **2.** Having or involving one name, *spec.* in *Nat. Hist.* 1885.

Uninqui·ring *ppl. a.* [UN-^{1} 4] 1804. **Uninqui·sitive** *a.* [UN-^{1} 1] 1609. **Uninscri·bed** *ppl. a.* [UN-^{1} 2] 1704. **Uninspe·cted** *ppl. a.* [UN-^{1} 2] 1858. **Uninspi·red** *ppl. a.* [UN-^{1} 2] LOCKE. **Uninspi·ring** *ppl. a.* [UN-^{1} 4] 1815.

Uninstru·cted, *ppl. a.* 1598. [UN-^{1} 2.] **1.** Not instructed or informed; unenlightened, ignorant. **2.** Not furnished with instructions 1892. Hence **Uninstru·ctedness.**

Uninstru·ctive *a.* [UN-^{1} 1] 1666, **-ly** *adv.* **Uni·nsulate** *v.* [UN-^{2} 1] 1844. **Uni·nsulated** *ppl. a.* [UN-^{1} 2] 1794. **Uninsu·rable** *a.* [UN-^{1} 1] 1864. **Uninsu·red** *ppl. a.* [UN-^{1} 2] 1799. **U:n-intelle·ctual** *a.* [UN-^{1} 1] 1676.

Uninte·lligent, *a.* 1609. [UN-^{1} 1.] **1.** Without knowledge or understanding *of* something. Now *rare.* **2.** Devoid of intelligence 1664. **3.** Deficient in intelligence; dull, stupid 1676. †**4.** Unintelligible –1756.

1. China,..too u. of us and too unintelligible to us CARLYLE. **2.** Time,..the most spiritual of the u. creatures of God PUSEY. So (in sense 3) **Uninte·lligence.** **Uninte·lligently** *adv.*

U:nintelligibi·lity [UN-^{1} 6] 1665. **Unin-te·lligible** *a.* [UN-^{1} 1] 1616, **-ness, -bly** *adv.* **Uninte·nded** *ppl. a.* [UN-^{1} 2] MILT., **-ly** *adv.* **Uninte·ntional** *a.* [UN-^{1} 1] 1782, **-ly** *adv.*

Uni·nterested, *ppl. a.* 1646. [UN-^{1} 2.] †**1.** Impartial; disinterested –1767. **2.** Taking no interest; indifferent 1771. Hence **Uni·nterested-ly** *adv.*, **-ness.**

Uni·nteresting *ppl. a.* [UN-^{1} 4] BURKE, **-ly** *adv.*, **-ness.** **U:nintermi·tted** *ppl. a.* [UN-^{1} 2] 1611, **-ly** *adv.* **Unintermi·ttent** *a.* [UN-^{1} 1] 1850, **-ly** *adv.* **Unintermi·tting** *ppl. a.* [UN-^{1} 4] 1661, **-ly** *adv.*, **-ness.** **Unintermi·xed** *ppl. a.* (now *rare*) [UN-^{1} 2] 1595. **Uninte·rpretable** *a.* [UN-^{1} 1] 1625. **Uninte·rpreted** *ppl. a.* [UN-^{1} 2] 1662. **Uninte·rred** *ppl. a.* [UN-^{1} 2] 1648.

U:ninterru·pted, *ppl. a.* 1602. [UN-^{1} 2.] **1.** Not interrupted or broken in respect of continuity or sequence; unintermittent, continuous. **b.** Continuous in surface; having no intervals between the parts 1791. **2.** Not disturbed or broken into; not interrupted *by* something 1657.

1. b. The cascade..falls..in one u. sheet 1791. Hence **U:ninterru·pted-ly** *adv.*, **-ness.**

U:ninterru·ption [UN-^{1} 6] 1647. **Uninti·midated** *ppl. a.* [UN-^{1} 2] 1764. **Uninto·xicating** *ppl. a.* [UN-^{1} 4] 1773. **U:nintrodu·ced** *ppl. a.* [UN-^{1} 2] 1743. **Uninu·red** *ppl. a.* [UN-^{1} 2] 1708. **Uninva·ded** *ppl. a.* [UN-^{1} 2] 1647. **Uninve·nted** *ppl. a.* [UN-^{1} 2] 1611. **Uninve·ntive** *a.* [UN-^{1} 1] 1776, **-ness.** **Uninve·sted** *ppl. a.* [UN-^{1} 2] 1802. **Uninve·stigable** *a.* [UN-^{1} 1] 1677. **Uninve·stigated** *ppl. a.* [UN-^{1} 2] 1816. **Uninvi·te** *v.* [UN-^{2} 1 or UN-^{1} 7] 1665. **Uninvi·ted** *ppl. a.* [UN-^{1} 2] 1631. **Uninvi·ting** *ppl. a.* [UN-^{1} 4] 1686. **Uninvo·ked** *ppl. a.* [UN-^{1} 2] 1718. **Uninvo·lved** *ppl. a.* [UN-^{1} 2] 1793.

‖**Unio** (yū·nio). *Pl.* **unios** (-ōᵘz), ‖**uniones** (-ōᵘ·nīz). 1824. [L., 'a single large pearl'.] *Zool.* A genus of freshwater bivalves typical of the family *Unionidæ*; a mussel of this or a related genus, esp. one yielding pearls. Hence **U·nioid** *a.* resembling or shaped like (that of) a u.

Union^1 (yū·niən, yū·nyən). late ME. [– (O)Fr. *union* or eccl.L. *unio, uniōn-* the number one, unity, f. L. *unus* ONE; see -ION.] **1.** The action of uniting one thing to another or others, or two or more things together, so as to form one whole or complete body; the state or condition of being so joined or united; combination, conjunction. **b.** Of persons or countries with ref. to joint action or policy 1608. **c.** *spec.* in *Surg.* The growing together in the process of healing of parts separated by fracture, cutting, etc. 1631. **d.** With *a* and *pl.* An instance or occasion of this 1570. **e.** Sexual conjunction (*rare*) 1728. **2.** The uniting together of the different sections, parties, or individuals of a nation or other body so as to produce general agreement or concord; the condition resulting from this 1460. **b.** Harmony of colour or design between the parts of a picture 1704. **3. a.** *Scots Law.* The uniting into one tenantry of non-contiguous lands or tenements 1503. **b.** *Eccl.* The uniting of two or more churches or benefices into one 1529. **4.** The action of uniting, or fact of being united, into one political body; esp. formation or incorporation into a single state, kingdom, or political entity, usu. with one central legislature 1547. **b.** *Eng. Hist.* (with *the* and capital): The uniting of the English and Scottish crowns in 1603, or parliaments in 1707; or of the parliaments of Great Britain and Ireland, dating from 1 Jan. 1801. 1603. **5.** The joining of two persons in matrimony; an instance of this, a marriage 1595. **6.** That which is united or combined into one; a whole formed by conjunction of parts; a combination or compound 1660. **b.** An association or league of persons or states formed for some common purpose or action. Now esp. = TRADE-UNION. 1660. **c.** *spec.* A legislative confederacy of states or provinces; a confederation or federation; esp. the United States of America. (In American use occas. restricted to the northern or federal States.) 1775. **d.** A number of parishes combined under one Board of Guardians for poor-law administration; an area or sub-district so formed and administered 1834. **e.** A textile fabric composed of two or more different materials woven together, esp. of cotton with linen, wool, or jute 1844. **7.** That which unites or connects one thing to another; *techn.*, a coupling for pipes or tubes 1850. **8.** *Brewing.* One of a series of casks or vats used in the union system of cleansing beer 1876. **9.** *ellipt.* with *the* **a.** = *U.-flag*, UNION JACK 1769. (*b*) *spec.* The union flag inserted in the upper inner canton of the ensign; freq. in phr. *u. down* or *downwards*, i.e. with the flag inverted as a sign of distress 1804. **b.** = *U. House* 1843. **c.** = *U. Society*; also, the buildings of such a society 1835. **10.** *attrib.* and *Comb.*, passing into adj. **a.** With the sense 'of or belonging to, promoting or advocating, etc. (a particular) legislative union' 1707. **b.** *gen.* 1723. **c.** In sense 6 e, as *u. cloth, goods*, etc. 1862.

1. The U. of the human Nature with the Divine 1728. Persecution, said Mr. Fox, is a bond of u. 1789. By the u. and investigation of several data 1800. **d.** A colony having an u. of interest 1817. **2.** There shalbe perfite vnion amonges them without striffe CROMWELL. **b.** A figure..though deviating from beauty, may still have a certain u. of the various parts SIR J. REYNOLDS. **5.** Her grandfather had been..very much averse to our u. THACKERAY. **6. b.** The increase of wages is not confined to those trades which have unions 1878. **c.** The South will come back to the U. 1865. **9. a.** A barge with the U. hoisted at the stern 1865. **b.** I wonder..if I am doomed to die in the Union HARDY. **c.** There existed at Cambridge a certain debating club, called the 'Union' THACKERAY.

Special combs.: **U. flag,** the national flag of Great Britain, and (from 1801) of the United Kingdom, formed by combining the crosses of St. George, St. Andrew, and St. Patrick, retaining the blue ground of the banner of St. Andrew; **U. House,** the workhouse of a Poor Law u.; **-joint,** see sense 7; **u. nut,** (*a*) a nut used with a screw to unite one part to another; (*b*) the Australian timber tree *Bosistoa sapindiformis* or its wood; **-room** *Brewing*, the room containing the unions or cleansing vats; **-rustic,** a British moth, *Apamea connexa*; **U. Society,** at universities: a general club and debating society usu. open to all members or all undergraduates of the university; **u. suit** *U.S.*, men's or boys' combinations; **u. system** *Brewing*, a method of beer-cleansing. Hence **Unionic** (yūniǫ·nik) *a.* of, pertaining to, characteristic of, a union or Union Society.

U·nion^2. *arch.* ME. [– L. *unio, uniōn-* (Pliny); see prec., and cf. ONION.] A pearl of large size, good quality, and great value.

Unionid (yū·nionid). 1861. [– mod.L. *Unionidæ*, f. L. *unio* UNIO; see -ID^3.] *Zool.* A member of the *Unionidæ*, a family of bivalve molluscs typified by the genus *Unio.*

Unionism (yū·niəniz'm). 1845. [f. UNION^1 + -ISM.] The principle or policy of combining; combination in union as a system of social organization. **b.** = TRADE(S)-UNIONISM 1869. **c.** *U.S.* Advocacy of or belief in legislative union between States 1864. **d.** Loyalty to or advocacy of the principles, views, or programme of the Unionist Party; the political tenets of a Unionist 1886.

Unionist (yū·niənist), *sb.* and *a.* 1799. [f. as prec. + -IST.] **A.** *sb.* **1.** A believer in unionism as a political principle or system of organization; esp. one who advocates or supports the formation of some particular legislative union (usu. with initial capital). **b.** *U.S.* A supporter of the Federal Union of the U.S.A.; esp. an opponent of Secession in the Civil War of 1861–5. 1830. **c.** *British Politics.* A member of the political party which advocated or supported maintenance of the parliamentary union between Great Britain and Ireland, formed by coalition between Conservatives and Liberal Unionists in 1886, and later known indifferently as 'Unionist' or 'Conservative' 1886. **2.** = TRADE-UNIONIST 1834. **3.** One who advocates or endeavours to promote the union of churches 1852.

2. The charges of conspiracy and violence brought against unionists 1879.

B. *attrib.* or as *adj.* **1.** Pertaining to or supporting a legislative union, esp. that between Great Britain and Ireland 1816. **b.** Of or belonging to the Unionist party 1886. **2.** Of or belonging to trade-unionism or trade-unionists 1879. Hence **Unioni·stic** *a.*

U·nionize, *v.* 1841. [f. UNION^1 + -IZE.] *trans.* To form into a union; to bring (work) under trade-union rules; to attract or form (workers) into trade-unions.

Union Jack. 1674. [JACK *sb.*^{3}] Orig. and prop., a small British union flag flown as the jack of a ship; later extended to any size or adaptation of the union flag, whether used as a jack or not, and regarded as the national ensign. **b.** A figure or representation of this 1848.

Union pipes, *sb. pl.* 1851. [perh. – Ir. *piob uilleann*, f. *piob* pipe + *uilleann* gen. sing. of *uille* elbow.] Irish bagpipes, in which the bag is inflated by bellows worked by the elbow.

Uniparous (yuni·părəs), *a.* 1646. [f. mod.L. *uniparus*; see UNI- and -PAROUS.] **1.** Bearing one at a birth; characterized by this kind of parturition. **2.** *Bot.* Of a cyme: Having only one axis or branch; developing a single axis at each branching 1839.

Unipla·nar, *a.* 1866. [f. UNI- + PLANE *sb.* + -AR^1.] **1.** *Geom.* Having or characterized by coincident planes. *U. node* (or *point*), a form of node or conical point in which the tangent cone has become a pair of coincident planes. **2.** *Mech.* Of motion: Confined to one plane; of or pertaining to such motion 1882.

Unipo·lar, *a.* 1812. [f. UNI- + POLE *sb.*^{2} + -AR^1.] **1.** *Electr.* Produced by, proceeding from, one magnetic pole; exhibiting one kind of polarity. **b.** Of apparatus: Having, or operating by means of, one magnetic pole 1876. **2.** *Biol.* Of nerve cells: Having one pole or fibrous prolongation; connected to the nerve-fibre by a single fibrous process 1859. Hence **Unipola·rity.**

Unique (yunī·k), *a.* and *sb.* 1602. [– Fr. *unique*, †*unic* masc. – L. *unicus* one and only, alone of its kind, f. *unus* ONE; see -IC.] **A.** *adj.* **1.** Of which there is only one; one and only; single, sole, solitary. **2.** Having no like or equal; superior to or different from all others; unparalleled, unrivalled 1618.

1. He hath lost..his unic Son 1645. A man..who made Latin scholarship his u. intellectual purpose 1873. **2.** This is a soueraigne and vnicke remedie 1618. Such a u. mortal..no man can describe 1871.

B. *sb.* **1.** A thing of which there is only one example, copy, or specimen; esp. such a coin or medal 1714. **2.** A thing, fact, person, etc., that is without equal or parallel in its kind 1758.

1. A coin, which I have reason to think is a Unic 1774. **2.** He is..quite an u. in this country COWPER. Of Lamb's writings..some were so memorably beautiful as to be uniques in their class DE QUINCEY. Hence **Uni·que-ly** *adv.*, **-ness.** **Uni·quity,** uniqueness.

Un-i·rish *a.* [UN-¹ 1] 1842. **Uni·roned** *ppl. a.* [UN-¹ 2] late ME. **Uni·rritating** *ppl. a.* [UN-¹ 4] 1797.

Unisexual (yūnise·ksiuăl), *a.* 1802. [f. UNI- + SEXUAL.] **1.** Of one sex; having the reproductive organs of one or other sex developed or present in individuals: **a.** *Bot.* Of flowers: With either stamens or pistils absent or suppressed. Of plants: Having such flowers. 1802. **b.** Of animals or their organs 1830. **2.** Pertaining or restricted to one sex 1885. Hence **U:nisexua·lity,** the condition of being u. **U:nise·xually** *adv.*

Unison (yū·nisən, -zən), *sb.* and *a.* 1574. [– OFr. *unison* (mod. *unisson*) or late L. *unisonus* of the same sound, f. L. *unus* one + *sonus* SOUND *sb.*²] **A.** *sb.* **1.** *Mus.* and *Acoustics.* A note of the same pitch as another; also loosely, a note from which intervals are reckoned. Now *rare.* **b.** Identity of pitch; the relation of two notes of the same pitch reckoned as one of the musical 'intervals' 1575. **c.** In phr. *in u.*: with identity of note and pitch 1616. **d.** A passage in which different voices or instruments execute a melody that is the same for all parts (or, loosely, different only by an interval of an octave or octaves) 1724. **e.** *ellipt.* for *u. string* 1820. **2.** A union or combination of concordant sounds; a united and unanimous utterance 1806. **3.** *fig.* A thing perfectly agreeing or consonant with another. Now *rare* or *Obs.* 1650. **b.** Perfect agreement, concord, or harmony; harmonious combinations 1654. **c.** *In unison* (*with*), in agreement or harmony, consonant, harmonious 1780.

1. Unisons, 'tis plain, cannot possibly have any Variety 1728. **c.** The nymphs joined in u., and their swains an octave below them STERNE. **d.** In Unisons, or passages where all instruments play the same melody, though in different Octaves 1799. **3. b.** Friendship the Vnison of well tun'd Hearts 1674. **c.** It was all in u.; words, conduct,.. told the same story JANE AUSTEN.

attrib.: **u. stop,** in an organ, a stop of the same pitch as the diapasons; **u. string,** in a pianoforte or other instrument, a string tuned to the same pitch as (or loosely an octave higher than) another; **u. tune,** one to be sung in u.; **-tuning,** the tuning of strings (of a pianoforte, etc.) in u.

B. *adj.* †**1.** Sounding together; *fig.* in complete agreement, unanimous –1762. **2.** Identical in pitch; singing or sounding in unison. Now *rare* or *Obs.* 1614. So **Uni·sonal** *a. Mus.* = next 1; **-ly** *adv.* **Uni·sonance** (*rare*), agreement or identity of sounds. **Uni·sonant** *a.* of the same pitch or sound.

Unisonous (yuni·sŏnəs), *a.* 1781. [f. late L. *unisonus* UNISON + -OUS.] **1.** *Mus.* Of the same pitch for the different voices or instruments; in unison or octaves, not in parts. **2.** Agreeing, concordant 1812.

Unit (yū·nit), *sb.* (and *a.*). 1570. [f. L. *unus* one; introduced by John Dee (1570), prob. after *digit*, repl. earlier UNITY.] **1.** *Math.* A single magnitude or number regarded as an undivided whole and as the ultimate base of all number; *spec.* in *Arith.*, the least whole number; the numeral 'one', represented by the figure 1. **b.** Any determinate quantity, dimension, etc., adopted as a standard of measurement 1738. **c.** A substance adopted as a standard for estimating specific gravity 1829. **2.** One of the separate parts or members of which a complex whole or aggregate is composed or into it may be analysed 1642. **b.** The lowest constituent part of a collective body or whole having a distinctive existence; such a division or group of individuals considered as a basis of formation or administration 1847. **3.** *attrib.*, passing into *adj.* Of, pertaining or equivalent to (that of) a unit; produced or caused by a u.; consisting of, containing, or forming a unit or units 1839. **4.** As *adj.* Having the distinct or individual existence of a unit 1870.

1. Note the worde, Vnit, to expresse the Greke Monas, and not Vnitie: as we haue all, commonly, till now, vsed JOHN DEE. If, as some affirm, the unite be no number, but only the source of all others 1726. **b.** The necessity..of the adoption of a money U. 1825. The ohm is a u. of resistance, in the same manner that an inch is a u. of length 1870. **c.** As water is taken as the u. for solids and liquids, so is atmospheric air for gases 1829. **2.** The u. of that life..was for ever withdrawn from the sum of human existence SCOTT. **b.** The village is a fraction, but the city is an u. 1847. A company is the u. of a regiment 1876. **3.** The u. current flowing through a conductor u. of length will exert the u. force on the u. pole at the u. distance 1867. The consumption of wheat per head of the population (u. consumption) was over 6 bushels per annum 1898. **4.** All things in the exterior world are u. and individual J. H. NEWMAN.

Unitable (yūnəi·tăb'l), *a.* [f. UNITE *v.* + -ABLE.] That can be united; capable of union.

Unital (yū·nităl), *a.* 1860. [f. UNIT or UNITY + -AL¹ 1.] That unites; causing or producing unity or union; of the nature of a unit.

Unitarian (yūnitēᵊ·riăn), *sb.* and *a.* 1687. [f. mod.L. *unitarius* (XVII), f. L. *unitas* unity; see -ARIAN.] **A.** *sb.* **1.** *Theol.* One who affirms the unipersonality of the Godhead, esp. as opp. to an orthodox Trinitarian; *spec.* a member of a Christian religious body or sect holding this doctrine. (Usu. with initial capital.) **b.** Any monotheist, esp. a Moslem 1708. **2.** An advocate of a theory or system based on unity, e.g. of MONISM in philosophy, of centralization, federation, or national unity in politics, etc. 1836.

1. b. His preachers..called aloud on the unitarians, manfully to stand up against the Christian idolaters GIBBON.

B. *adj.* **1.** *Theol.* Of or pertaining to, connected with, the Unitarians or their doctrines; of the nature of, characteristic of, Unitarianism 1687. **b.** Accepting the doctrines, or belonging to a religious body or sect, of Unitarians 1691. **2.** Of or pertaining to, based or founded on, characterized by, unity, in various senses 1836.

1. The U. [conception], which conceives of Christ as an exalted human teacher merely 1889. **2.** These two theories, the one dualistic, the other u. 1875. The King of U. Italy 1865. Hence **Unita·rianism,** belief in or affirmation of the unity of God, esp. the tenets, principles, or views of the Unitarians.

Unitary (yū·nitări), *a.* 1842. [f. UNIT or UNITY + -ARY¹.] **1.** Of or pertaining to, characterized by, or based upon unity 1847. **2.** *Philos.* Of or pertaining to, involving, unity of being or existence 1842. **3.** Of the nature of a unit; individual, uncompounded 1861. **b.** Serving as a unit of measurement or calculation 1889. **4.** Of or pertaining to a unit or units. **a.** *Chem.* Applied to a theory or system in which the molecules of all bodies are regarded as units 1865. **b.** Of an alphabet, etc.: In which a single symbol represents each sound 1874. **c.** *Arith.* Applied to a modification of the 'rule of three', by which the value, extent, etc., of one unit being first determined, that of any number is found by multiplication 1877. **5.** Forming a unit *with* something 1868.

1. The national and u. tendencies of the people LOWELL. **2.** Man loves the Universal, the Unchangeable, the U. 1842. **3.** Each man is at once profoundly u. and almost infinitely composite 1901. Hence **U·nitarist,** an advocate of a u. system of government; *spec.* a supporter of the unity of Italy.

Unite (yū·nəit, yunəi·t), *sb.* 1604. [f. †*unite* united – L. *unitus*; see next.] *Numism.* An English gold coin first issued by James I in 1604 (named with ref. to the Union of the Crowns).

Unite (yunəi·t), *v.* late ME. [– *unit-*, pa. ppl. stem of L. *unire* join together, f. *unus* one.] **1.** *trans.* To combine or join (a thing or things) *to* or *with* another or others, to bring or put (separate or divided things) together, so as to make a connected or contiguous whole; to form into, make or cause to be, one. **b.** To combine or amalgamate into one body 1591. **c.** To join (hands), esp. in the marriage ceremony 1602. **2.** To bring to agreement; to combine (persons, etc.) in action or interest, or for some purpose 1547. **b.** To join (persons) in marriage 1728. **3.** To have, possess, or exhibit (functions, qualities, etc.) in combination 1796. **4.** *intr.* To enter into association or union; to combine forces, act in concert *with* others (*in* some action or *to* do something) 1613. **b.** To become one in feeling or sentiment 1766. **5.** To form one material whole; to combine physically; to coalesce 1667. **b.** *spec.* in *Chem.* To combine by chemical affinity or attraction 1800. **c.** Of troops, etc.: To form one combined or conjoint body 1700. **d.** Of immaterial things or in non-physical connection 1795.

1. Like a broken Limbe vnited SHAKS. Where the publique and private interest are most closely united HOBBES. **b.** Not believing that the enemy could be so soon united CLARENDON. **c.** Their hands were united by the Protestant preacher SCOTT. **2.** If Sympathy of Loue vnite our thoughts SHAKS. **3.** D'Aubigné's style, which unites the severe and the ludicrous 1798. **4.** Is it best for the States to u. or not to u.? WASHINGTON. **5. d.** The whole body of the coheirs..must u. to constitute the heir 1795. Hence **Uni·ting** *vbl. sb.* and *ppl. a.*

United (yunəi·tĕd), *ppl. a.* 1552. [f. prec. + -ED¹.] **1.** Joined together; combined, made one. **2.** Conjoint, in combination; not of single origin or constituents; resulting from a union (freq. in titles of amalgamated churches and societies) 1586.

Special Collocations: *U. Brethren,* the Moravians; *U. Colonies,* †(*a*) the four colonies of the New England Confederation of 1643; (*b*) the thirteen colonies forming the original Republic of N. America; *U. Greek,* a Uniat; *U. Irishmen,* a political association orig. formed to promote union between Protestants and Catholics, which became a separatist secret society and was concerned in the rebellion of 1798; so *U. Irishman*; **U. Kingdom** (abbrev. *U.K.*), the kingdom of Great Britain or (from 1801 to 1922) of Great Britain and Ireland; **U. Provinces,** (*a*) the seven northern provinces of the Netherlands, allied from 1579, and later developed into the kingdom of Holland; (*b*) in full *U. Provinces of Agra and Oudh,* a district in north British India, consisting of the provinces of Agra and Oudh united under a governor. Hence **Uni·ted-ly** *adv.,* **-ness.**

United States. 1617. **1.** The proper name or title of a confederation, federation, or union of states. **a.** = United Provinces of the Netherlands (now *rare* or *Hist.*). **b.** The Republic of N. America. Abbrev. *U.S.* or *U.S.A.* 1781. **c.** In other applications 1864. **2.** The form of English spoken in the U.S. or regarded as distinctly American 1891.

Uni·ter. 1587. [f. UNITE *v.* + -ER¹.] A person or agency that brings about union.

Uniters of states and cities BACON. Money..the great u. of a most divided people SWIFT.

Unition (yuni·ʃən). Now *rare.* 1511. [– late and med.L. *unitio, -ōn-,* f. *unit-*; see UNITE, -ION.] The action of uniting; the fact or condition of being united; union, junction.

The vnition of two [livings] in one man 1587. The Union or rather U. of a particular Soul and particular Body 1733.

Unitive (yū·nitiv), *a.* 1526. [– late and med.L. *unitivus*, f. as prec.; see -IVE. Cf. Fr. *unitif, -ive* (XV).] **1.** Uniting; causing or involving union; *spec.* in *Anat.* of fibres. **2.** Bringing about spiritual union with God 1659. **b.** *spec.* in *unitive life, way,* etc., applied to the third and final stage of spiritual advancement 1649.

1. The u. power of the Intellect 1647. **2.** This u. power of the Eucharist 1879. **b.** The purgative, illuminative, and u. stages of devotion 1830. Hence **U·nitive-ly** *adv.,* **-ness.**

Unity (yū·nĭti). ME. [– (O)Fr. *unité* – L. *unitas, -tat-,* f. *unus* one; see -ITY.] **1.** The fact, quality, or condition of being one in number; oneness, singleness. **b.** *Math.* The condition of the unit or number one; the numeral one regarded abstractly as the basis of number 1570. **c.** A quantity, magnitude, or substance, adopted as the unit of comparison or measurement 1728. **2.** †**a.** = UNIT 1. –1837. **b.** One separate or single thing, quality, etc.; something complete in itself or regarded as such 1587. **3.** The quality or condition of being one in feeling, action, purpose, etc.; harmonious combination of parties or persons ME. **b.** *At unity,* in concord or harmony; at one. late ME. **c.** Agreement or concord between things. late ME. **4.** The fact of forming or being united into one whole; union (of persons or things, or one *with* another or others). late ME. **b.** A body formed by union, esp. *the Unity of the* (Moravian) *Brethren* 1780. **5.** The quality or fact of being one body or whole, esp. as made up of two or more parts; an undivided whole, as dist. from its parts. late ME. **6.** Singleness of design or effect in a work of art; consonance of parts with each other and the whole 1712. **b.** *The unities*, the three principles of the canon of dramatic composition laid down by Aristotle and observed in the classical French drama, according to which a play should consist of one main action, represented as occurring at one time (i.e. one day) and in one place 1668. **7.** Continuity, homogeneity; unvaried nature; singleness of aim, purpose, or action 1802. **8.** Law. *U. of possession*, the joint possession of two rights by separate titles 1607.

1. Our God is one, or rather very oneness, and meere unitie HOOKER. **b.** The quotient is u. when the Dividend and the Divisor are equal 1869. **2. b.** The life and strength of a multitude consisteth in vnities 1600. **3.** The vnity and married calme of States SHAKS. Laud..contemplated establishing u. by uniformity 1830. **b.** Ierusalem is buylded as a cite, that is at vnitie in it self COVERDALE *Ps.* 121. **c.** There is such vnitie in the proofes SHAKS. **4.** Our Lord claimed for himself a mysterious u. with the Father 1871. **5.** Every grain Is sentient both in u. and part SHELLEY. **6.** Aristotle..allows, that Homer has nothing to boast of as to the U. of his Fable ADDISON. **7.** The possession of this child would give u. to her life GEO. ELIOT.

Univalent (yuni·vǎlěnt), *a.* 1869. [f. UNI- + *valent*, deduced from VALENCY 2.] *Chem.* Having a valency of one, having the combining power of one atom of hydrogen. So **Uni·valence. Uni·valency.**

Univalve (yū·nivælv), *a.* and *sb.* 1661. [f. UNI- + VALVE *sb.*[1]] *Nat. Hist.* **A.** *adj.* **a.** *Conch.* Of shells: Composed of a single valve or piece. Of molluscs: Having such a shell. **b.** *Ent.* Having one valve 1826. **B.** *sb. Conch.* A u. mollusc or shell 1668. Hence **U·nivalved, Univa·lvular** *adjs. Bot.* having or consisting of one valve.

Universal (yūnivǝ·ɹsǎl), *a.* and *sb.* late ME. [– Fr. *universal* (mod. *-el*) or L. *universalis*, f. *universus*; see UNIVERSE, -AL[1] 1.] **A.** *adj.* **1.** Extending over, comprehending, affecting, or including the whole of something specified or implied. **b.** Proceeding from the whole body or number without exception; unanimous 1586. **c.** Qualifying agent-nouns, personal designations, or titles; freq. in *u. bishop*, a title assumed by or given to some popes. late ME. **d.** *Law.* Of or in respect of the whole estate or property 1669. **2.** Of or throughout the universe, the world, or all nature; existing or occurring everywhere or in all things. late ME. **b.** Of language, etc.: Adopted, (intended to be) used, understood, etc., everywhere or by all nations; freq. = Latin 1652. **3.** Of the Church: Including all Christians; catholic 1483. **4.** Constituting or forming, existing or regarded as, a complete whole; entire, whole. (In 16th c., freq. of the world, earth, etc.) 1470. **5.** Of persons, etc.: Having a wide range of knowledge or interest; widely accomplished; not specialized; versatile 1520. **c.** Embracing or covering all (or a great variety of) subjects, branches of knowledge, etc. 1638. **6.** *Logic.* Applicable to, relating to, involving, the whole of a class or genus, or all the individuals or species composing it; *spec.* of a proposition: Predicable of each of the things denoted by the subject 1551. **b.** Of a law or rule: Valid in all cases 1583. **7.** Of implements, machines or their parts, etc.: Adjustable to all requirements; adapted to various purposes, sizes, etc. Freq. *u. joint*, one allowing free movement in any direction of the parts joined. 1676. **8.** *absol.* The whole of, all of (something expressed or implied); *spec.* in *Logic* and *Philos.*, the whole class or genus, as dist. from the individuals comprising it. late ME.

1. Grammar u.; that grammar which..only respects those principles that are essential to them all 1751. The battle was general, the overthrow universal DISRAELI. **2.** Her inchanting son Whom U. nature did lament MILT. **3.** The Catholick Church, that is, God's whole or universall Assembly 1645. **4.** 'Twas for nothing in the u. world but for killing a rich Patient 1649. Thine this u. Frame MILT. **5.** Shakespeare had an u. mind DRYDEN. He sets up for an u. man, because he has a small tincture of every science SMOLLETT. **7.** An u. chuck for holding any kind of work which is to be turned 1825.

Collocations: **u. arithmetic,** algebra; **u. suffrage,** a suffrage extending to the whole of a community, esp. one in which all persons over a fixed age, except lunatics, aliens, and criminals, have the right to vote for representatives to a legislative assembly.

B. *sb.* **1.** *Logic* and *Philos.* What is predicated of all the individuals or species of a class or genus; an abstract or general concept regarded as having an absolute, mental, or nominal existence; a universal proposition; a general term or notion 1553. **2.** That which is universal; esp. one who or that which is universally potent, current, etc. Now *rare.* 1556.

1. An abstract u., which is properly nothing, a conception of our own making BENTLEY. The long controversies between the Realists and Nominalists concerning the nature of universals 1837.

Universalism (yūnivǝ·ɹsǎliz'm). 1805. [f. prec. + -ISM. Cf. Fr. *universalisme.*] **1.** *Theol.* The doctrine of universal salvation or redemption. **2.** The pursuit of universal knowledge or skill; extreme versatility 1827. **3.** The fact or condition of being universal in scope or character; universality 1840. So **Unive·rsalist** *sb.* esp. *Theol.* one who believes or maintains the doctrine that redemption or election is extended to the whole of mankind; *spec.* in *U.S.* a member of a sect holding this doctrine; *adj.* universalistic. **U:niversali·stic** *a. Theol.* of or pertaining to Universalism; universal in scope or character.

Universality (yū:nivǝɹsæ·lĭti). late ME. [– (O)Fr. *universalité* or late L. *universalitas* (Boethius), f. L. *universalis*; see UNIVERSAL, -ITY.] **1.** The fact, quality, or condition of being universal, in various senses. **2.** The collective whole *of* something regarded collectively, as the world, a people, a nation. Now *arch.* 1561. †**b.** The whole people or state –1675. †**3.** A general statement, a generality –1647.

1. The antiquitie, and vniuersalitie, of the Catholicke Religion 1559. The u. of this mathematical rule BERKELEY. **2. b.** The Common happiness of the vniuersalitie RALEGH.

Universalize (yūnivǝ·ɹsǎlǝiz), *v.* 1642. [f. UNIVERSAL *a.* + -IZE.] **1.** *trans.* To make or render universal; to give a universal character to; to convert from particular or individual to general. **2.** To bring into universal use, acceptance, or currency 1809.

Universally (yūnivǝ·ɹsǎli), *adv.* late ME. [f. as prec. + -LY[2].] **1.** In every instance; without any exception; in every part or place; by, among, to, etc., all the persons concerned. **2.** *Logic* and *Metaph.* In relation to all the members of a class or genus 1551.

1. Rye is generally (nay u., I think) allowed to be a better bearer than wheat 1765. **2.** The term 'necessary to life' is affirmed of food, but not u.; for it is not said of every kind of food WHATELY.

Universe (yū·nivǝɹs). 1589. [– (O)Fr. *univers* or L. *universum* the whole world, subst. use of n. of *universus* all taken together, lit. 'turned into one', f. *unus* UNI- + *versus*, pa. pple. of *vertere* turn.] **1.** The whole of created or existing things regarded collectively; all things, including the earth, the heavens, and all that is in them, considered as constituting a systematic whole. **b.** With *a* and *pl.* 1667. **2.** The world or earth, esp. as the abode of man or as the scene of human activities 1630. **b.** *transf.* The inhabitants of the earth; mankind in general 1742.

1. *transf.* The four Faculties are supposed to make the World or U. of Study 1728. Into the heights of Love's rare U. SHELLEY. **b.** A U. of death, which God by curse Created evil MILTON. To Newton and to Newton's Dog Diamond, what a different pair of Universes! CARLYLE. **2.** [Wesley] took the u. for his parish 1791. **b.** Our good Edmund,..Who, born for the u.,..to party gave up what was meant for mankind GOLDSM.

Universitarian (yū:nivǝɹsitēᵊ·riǎn), *a.* 1834. [f. UNIVERSITY + -ARIAN.] Of or pertaining to, characteristic of, obtaining in, a university.

‖**Universitas** (yūnivǝ·ɹsitæs). 1765. [L.; see next.] *Sc. Law.* The whole (of an estate or inheritance).

University (yūnivǝ·ɹsĭti). ME. [– (O)Fr. *université* – L. *universitas* the whole, the whole number (of), the universe, (in later juridical lang.) society, guild, corporation (whence the med. academic use *universitas magistrorum et scholarium*), f. *universus*; see UNIVERSE, -ITY.] **1.** The whole body of teachers and students pursuing, at a particular place, the higher branches of learning; such persons associated together as a society or corporate body, having the power of conferring degrees and other privileges, and forming an institution for the promotion of education in the higher branches of learning; the colleges, buildings, etc., belonging to such a body. †**2.** The whole number or aggregate *of* creatures, persons, things, etc. –1677. †**b.** The universe –1642. **3.** Law. *University of rights and duties*, the complex aggregate of these attached to a succession, etc. 1832. †**4.** A class of persons regarded collectively; a corporate body –1678. **5.** *attrib.* passing into *adj.* Of or belonging to, characteristic of, a u.; that is or has been a member of a u.; attached to or connected with a u.; etc. late ME.

1. They labour to put out the eyes of this land (the Vniuersityes I meane) 1579. The u. of the chancellor, masters, and scholars, is one corporation 1868. *transf.* I think you were broght vp in the vniuersitie of bridewell; you haue your rhetorick so ready at your toongs end 1595. **2.** In al the hool vnyuersite of thingis and of beingis 1449. **b.** Man is a little world and beares the face And picture of the Vniuersitie 1598. **4.** Although kings doe die, the people in the mean time (as niether any other Vniversitie) never dyeth 1643.

attrib., as *u. chair, chest* (CHEST *sb.*[1] 1), *course, extension* (EXTENSION 7), *lecturer, man, sermon.*

Univocal (yuni·vǒkǎl), *a.* and *sb.* 1615. [– late L. *univocus* having one meaning (f. L. *unus* UNI- + *vox, voc-* VOICE) + -AL[1] 1.] **A.** *adj.* **1.** Having only one meaning or signification; not equivocal; unambiguous 1656. †**2.** Uniform, homogeneous –1727. †**3.** Of or belonging to, characteristic of, things of the same name or species; esp. in *u. generation*, normal generation between members of the same species –1822. †**4.** Uttered with or as with one voice; unanimous –1734. **B.** *sb.* A univocal term 1728. Hence **Uni·vocally** *adv.* 1593.

Univo·ltine, *sb.* and *a.* 1874. [– Fr. *univoltin, -tain*, f. *uni-* UNI- + It. *volta* turn.] **A.** *sb.* One of a breed of silkworms producing one brood a year. **B.** *adj.* Having only one brood each year 1883.

Unja·ded *ppl. a.* [UN-[1] 2] 1779. **Unjaundiced** *ppl. a.* [UN-[1] 2] 1792. **Unjea·lous** *a.* [UN-[1] 1] 1673. **Unjoi·n** *v.* (now *rare*) [UN-[2] 1] ME.

Unjoi·nt, *v.* late ME. [UN-[2] 1.] **1.** *trans.* To take apart at the joints; to disjoint, dislocate. **2.** *fig.* To disunite, sever 1561.

Unjoi·nted, *a.* 1588. [UN-[1] 3.] **1.** *fig.* Incoherent, disjointed. *arch.* **2.** Without joints 1681.

1. This bald, vnioynted Chat of his SHAKS.

Unjoy·ful *a.* [UN-[1] 1] ME., **-ly** *adv.* **Unjoy·ous** *a.* [UN-[1] 1] MILT. **Unju·dged** *ppl. a.* [UN-[1] 2] 1647. **Unjudi·cial** [UN-[1] 1] 1599, **-ly** *adv.* **Unjudi·cious** *a.* (now *rare* or *Obs.*) [UN-[1] 1] 1614. **Unju·mpable** *a.* [UN-[1] 1] 1886.

Unju·st, *a.* late ME. [UN-[1] 1.] **1. a.** Not acting justly or fairly; not observing the principles of justice or fair dealing. **b.** Not in accordance with justice or fairness. late ME. **2.** Not upright or free from wrong-doing; faithless, dishonest. Now *rare.* 1500.

1. a. To compare the universal with the limited is to be u. to both 1876. **b.** Vsurie and vniust gaine *Prov.* 28:8. **2.** The lorde commended the uniust stewarde TINDALE *Luke* 16:8. Hence **Unju·st-ly** *adv.*, **-ness.**

Unju·stifiable *a.* [UN-[1] 1] 1641, **-ness, -ably** *adv.*

Unju·stified, *ppl. a.* ME. [UN-[1] 2.] †**1.** Not brought to justice, not executed –1596. **2.** Not justified, e.g. by faith 1651. **3.** Lacking justification, done without due cause, improper, unwarranted. (The current use.) 1685.

Unked, unkid (v·ŋkėd), *a.* Now *dial.* [ME. *unkid(d*, f. UN-[1] + pa. pple. of KITHE *v.*] **1.** Unknown, strange. **2.** Awkward or troublesome from unfamiliarity or novelty 1634. **3.** Unfamiliarly lone or dreary; solitary, forlorn; lonely 1706. **4.** Uncanny, eerie, weird 1800.

3. Weston is sadly u. without you COWPER. **4.** They would not pass at night, Lest they should hear an u. strain Or see an u. sight CHRISTINA ROSSETTI.

Unkee·led *ppl. a.* [UN-[1] 2] 1807.

Unke·mbed, *ppl. a.* Now *rare.* late ME. [Un-1 2.] = next.

Unke·mpt, *ppl. a.* 1579. [Un-1 2.] **1.** Of hair, etc.: Uncombed 1742. **b.** With uncombed hair, dishevelled 1748. **c.** Untidy; of neglected appearance; untrimmed; rough 1861. †**2.** Of language: Inelegant, unpolished; rude –1606.

1. c. Filthy habits and u. attire 1879. **2.** To well I wote..howe my rymes bene rugged and vnkempt SPENSER.

Unke·nnel, *v.* 1576. [Un-2 3.] **1.** *trans.* To dislodge (a fox) from its hole. Also *absol.* **b.** *intr.* To come out of a hole or lair 1760. **2.** *fig.* (*trans.*) To dislodge, fetch out; to bring to light 1612. **3.** To let (hounds) out of a kennel 1607.

Unke·pt *ppl. a.* [Un-1 2] ME. **Unkey·** *v.* [Un-2 2] 1751. **Unki·llable** *a.* [Un-1 1] 1878. **Unki·lled** *ppl. a.* [Un-1 2] 1535.

Unkind (ɒnkəi·nd), *a.* ME. [Un-1 1.] †**1.** Strange, foreign –late ME. **2.** Of weather, etc.: Not mild or pleasant; ungenial. Now *dial.* or *arch.* ME. †**b.** Physically unnatural; contrary to the usual course of nature –1603. **c.** Naturally bad or hurtful; unsuitable; injurious. Now *dial.* late ME. †**3.** Lacking in natural gratitude, filial affection or respect, or natural goodness –1649. †**4.** Contrary to nature; *esp.* unnaturally bad or wicked –1656. **5.** Lacking in kindness or kindly feeling; acting harshly or ungently. late ME. **b.** Of actions, etc.: Characterized by want of kindness. late ME.

2. The climate is u. and the ground penurious JOHNSON. **b.** They doe quench and allay thirst, and coole u. heat HOLLAND. **c.** The East-wind being cold..is verie vnkind for Bees 1609. **3.** The Redeemer of unkinde mankinde 1649. **4.** Such vnlawfull lust, such vnkinde desires GREENE. Making thyself unkinde and monstrous in murthering of thy mother 1635. **5.** To the Noble minde, Rich gifts wax poore, when giuers proue vnkinde SHAKS. **b.** This was the most vnkindest cut of all SHAKS. Hence **Unki·nd-ly** *adv.*; phr. *to take u.*, to resent; **-ness**; *an u.*, an unkind act.

Unki·ndled *ppl. a.* [Un-1 2] 1513. **Unki·ndliness** [Un-1 6] 1470.

Unki·ndly, *a.* ME. [f. Un-1 1 + KINDLY *a.* Cf. OE. *ungecyndelić.*] †**1.** Unnaturally wicked or vile –1614. †**b.** Unrestrained by natural bonds of kindred, etc. –1647. †**2.** Unnatural in respect of physical qualities or actions –1639. **b.** Of weather, soil, etc.: Unnaturally bleak or cold; unfruitful; unfavourable. late ME. **c.** Of plants, animals, etc.: Ill-conditioned, not well developed. Now *dial.* or *arch.* late ME. †**d.** Prejudicial to health; not developing in a natural healthy manner –1827. **3.** Devoid of kindness; unkind 1805.

Unki·ng, *v.* 1578. [Un-2 4 b.] **1.** To deprive of the position of king; to depose from sovereignty. **b.** *refl.* To abdicate 1647. **2.** To deprive (a country) of a king 1647.

1. These men do design To un-king the Queen 1711. **2.** A wife's dishonour unking'd Rome for ever BYRON. Hence **Unki·nged** *ppl. a.* God saue King Henry, vn-King'd Richard sayes SHAKS.

Unki·ngly *a.* [Un-1 1] 1600; *adv.* [Un-1 5] late ME. **Unki·ss** *v.* [Un-2 1] 1562.

Unki·ssed, *ppl. a.* late ME. [Un-1 2.] Not kissed. †**b.** *Uncouth* (*unknown, unkent*), *u.*, the kiss of greeting is not given to strangers; *transf.* the unknown is neglected 1697.

Unkni·ght *v.* [Un-2 4 b] 1623. **Unkni·ghted** *ppl. a.* [Un-1 2] 1631. **Unkni·ghtly** *a.* [Un-1 1] late ME.; *adv.* [Un-1 5] 1586.

Unkni·t, *v.* [OE. *uncnyttan*, f. Un-2 2 b.] **1.** *trans.* To undo (a knot or something tied). Now *arch.* **b.** *fig.* To loosen, dissolve (a bond, union). *poet.* and *arch.* ME. **c.** To relax (a knitted brow) 1596. **d.** To disjoint, disunite; to unclasp (*rare*) 1580. **2.** *fig.* To disperse, dissolve, undo, destroy; to relax or weaken. Also *absol.* late ME. **b.** To sever, divorce. late ME. **3.** *intr.* To become unknit, in various senses 1574.

1. c. Fie, fie, vnknit that threatning vnkinde brow SHAKS. **2.** Logike is bound..to knit true arguments and u. false 1551. **3.** The ligaments, hindring the parts from unknitting 1677.

Unkni·t *ppl. a.* [Un-1 2] 1607. **Unkno·t** *v.* [Un-2 1] 1598. **Unkno·tted** *ppl. a.* [Un-1 2] 1642. **Unknow·** *v.*1 (now *rare*) [Un-1 7] late ME. **Unknow·** *v.*2 [Un-2 1] 1586. **Unknow·able** *a.* [Un-1 1] late ME.

Unknow·ing, *ppl. a.* ME. [Un-1 4.] **1.** Not knowing; ignorant, uninformed. **2.** Without knowledge *of* something ME. **b.** Const. direct obj., or obj. clause. late ME. **c.** Const. with inf. 1666. **3.** Unknown *to* (a person). Now *dial.* late ME. **4.** As quasi-*adv.* Unknowingly. late ME.

1. Symple and unknouuing men 1386. Winds that pilfer from u. flowers Their balmy breaths 1845. **2.** The residue wer vnknowying of this thyng UDALL. **b.** Mankind wanders, u. his way GOLDSM. U. where my course is bound SCOTT. **c.** U. whitherward to bend his way SOUTHEY. **3.** He..sodenly departed (vnknowing to the Ladies) 1577. Hence **Unknow·ing-ly** *adv.*, **-ness.**

Unknow·n, *ppl. a.* and *sb.* ME. [Un-1 2.] **A.** *adj.* **1.** Not known; unfamiliar, strange. **2.** In absolute const.: Without its being known (*to* one); without the knowledge *of* (some one). late ME.

1. Vnto the vnknowen God TINDALE *Acts* 17:23. To..walke through unknowen places without a guide 1586. Death is the knownest and vnknownest thing in the world 1622. The fishes of the u. deep COWPER. Some u.-of isle 1839. *U. warrior*: see WARRIOR 1. Phr. *U. quantity*, in algebra, a quantity of which the value is not determined; also freq. *fig.* Provb. phr. *U., unkissed* (see UNKISSED b); Unknowen vnkist, and beyng knowen I weene, Thou art neuer kist, where thou mayst be seene HEYWOOD. **2.** Being done vnknowne, I should haue found it afterwards well done SHAKS. The Patient, u. to me, pursued his intention 1672.

B. *sb.* **1.** An unknown person 1597. **2.** That which is unknown 1656. **3.** *Math.* An unknown quantity 1817.

1. The faire Unknowne 1652. **2.** The dark u. of legal perplexities 1846.

Unla·belled *ppl. a.* [Un-1 2] 1844. **Unlabo·rious** *a.* [Un-1 1] MILT. **Unla·boured** *ppl. a.* [Un-1 2] 1473. **Unla·bouring** *ppl. a.* [Un-1 4] 1619.

Unla·ce, *v.* ME. [Un-2 1.] **1.** *trans.* To undo the lace or laces of (armour, clothing, etc.); to unfasten or loosen thus. **2.** To free or relieve (a person, the body, etc.) by undoing a lace or laces. Also *absol.* ME. †**3.** To carve (*spec.* a rabbit); to cut off in carving –1771.

1. He vnlaced his helme and gate hym wynde MALORY. Hence **Unla·ced** *ppl. a.*

Unla·de, *v.* late ME. [Un-2 2.] **1.** *trans.* To take a load off (a horse, cart, etc.). **b.** To take the cargo out of (a ship) 1489. **c.** To unburden, relieve (*of* a load, care, sin, etc.) 1581. **2.** To discharge (a cargo, etc.) from a ship. late ME. **b.** To lay down (a load, care, etc.); to unpack (goods); to bring forth (news, ideas) 1591. **3.** *absol.* To discharge a cargo or cargoes, a burden, etc. 1547.

2. b. He..unlades his stock of ideas in perfect order LAMB. **3.** What adventure is this you are so full of? come, u., u. 1717. Hence **Unla·ding** *vbl. sb.*

Unla·den *ppl. a.* [Un-1 2] 1802. **Unla·dylike** *a.* [Un-1 1] MISS MITFORD. **Unlai·d** *ppl. a.* [Un-1 2] 1468. **Unlame·nted** *ppl. a.* [Un-1 2] 1595. **Unla·nded** *a.* [Un-1 3] 1488.

Unla·nguaged, *a.* 1654. [Un-1 3.] **1.** Not gifted with speech. **2.** Not put into words 1846.

Unla·p, *v.* Now *rare.* late ME. [Un-2 2.] *trans.* To unwrap.

Unla·sh *v.* [Un-2 2 b] 1748. **Unla·tch** *v.* [Un-2 1] 1642. **Unla·tched** *ppl. a.* [Un-1 2] 1888. **Unlau·dable** *a.* [Un-1 1] 1550.

U·nlaw, *sb.* [OE. *unlagu* = ON. *úlǫg*; see Un-1 12, LAW.] Illegal action; illegality. (Revived by recent writers.)

Unlaw·, *v.* 1491. [f. prec. or Un-2.] †**1.** *trans.* To fine. *Sc.* –1732. **2.** To annul (a law). *rare.* 1644.

Unlaw·ful, *a.* ME. [Un-1 1.] **1.** Prohibited by law; illegal. **b.** spec. *U. assembly*: the meeting of large numbers of people together with such circumstances of behaviour as to raise the fears of their fellow-subjects and to endanger the public peace 1485. **c.** Of offspring: Illegitimate 1606. **2.** Offending against morals or religion 1475. **3.** Of persons: Not obeying the law; acting illegally; with no right to the specified status. late ME. **4.** Against rules; irregular 1792.

3. To execute worthy punishment on me as an u. wife ANNE BOLEYN. The u. opener of a letter DICKENS. **4.** It is u. to divide the anapæst between two words 1836. Hence **Unlaw·ful-ly** *adv.*, **-ness.**

Unlay·, *v.* 1726. [Un-2 1.] *trans.* To untwist (a rope) into separate strands.

Unlead (ɒnle·d), *v.* 1591. [Un-2 2.] To strip (a roof or building) of lead. So **Unlea·ded** *ppl. a.* not weighted with lead; *Typog.* not spaced with leads.

Unlea·rn, *v.* 1450. [Un-2 1.] **1.** *trans.* To discard from knowledge or memory; to give up knowledge of (something). **b.** *absol.* or const. with inf. 1530. **2.** To unteach 1664.

1. The most necessary learning for mans life, is to u. that which is nought and vain 1686. **2.** Legal learning..can never have unlearnt a man the difference between three and one and a half BENTHAM.

Unlearned (ɒnlɔ̄·ɹnéd), *ppl. a.* late ME. [Un-1 2.] **1.** Having no learning; untaught; ignorant. **2.** Not skilled or versed *in* something 1565. **3.** Characterized by want of learning; pertaining to the unlearned class 1526. **4.** (ɒnlɔ̄·ɹnd) Not acquired by learning 1534. **5.** *absol.* Those who have no learning 1500.

3. The u. and vulgar passion of admiration BURKE. Hence **Unlea·rned-ly** *adv.*, **-ness.**

Unlea·rnt *ppl. a.* [Un-1 2] 1879. **Unlea·sed** *ppl. a.* [Un-1 2] 1716. **Unlea·sh** *v.* [Un-2 2 b] 1671. **Unlea·shed** *ppl. a.* [Un-1 2] 1821. **Unlea·vened** *ppl. a.* [Un-1 2] TINDALE. **Unle·d** *ppl. a.* [Un-1 2] 1569. **Unle·galized** *ppl. a.* [Un-1 2] 1830. **Unlei·sured** *a.* [Un-1 3] SIDNEY. **Unle·nt** *ppl. a.* [Un-1 2] 1887.

Unless (ɒ̆nle·s), *prep. phr.*, *prep.*, *conj.* and *sb.* [Late ME. (Maundev.) phr. *o(n lesse*, also *in lesse* (followed by *than*), modelled on (O)Fr. *à moins que*; when the phr. had coalesced into one word (*onless*), lack of stress on the first syll. together with the negative implication of the word led to assim. to Un-1.] **A.** *prep. phr.* †**1.** On a less or lower condition, footing, etc., *than* (what is specified) –1500. **2.** Except, if..not. †**a.** With *than, that* –1596. **b.** With omission of conjunction before the subordinate clause, thus passing into *conj.* 1509. **c.** With ellipsis of verb, etc. in the clause 1548. **B.** *prep.* Except, but 1531. †**C.** *conj.* Lest –1592. **D.** *sb.* An instance or utterance of the word; a reservation 1861.

2. a. Onlesse that our kyng haue more chyualry, ..he shal be ouercome MALORY. **b.** For one is to much, onles it be well spent 1563. **c.** But I dare not shew them, u. to you 1789. **B.** All forbeare this place, vnlesse the Princess HEYWOOD. **D.** Let us have no unlesses, sir DICKENS.

Unle·ssoned *ppl. a.* [Un-1 2] 1550. **Unle·t** *ppl. a.* [Un-1 2] 1453.

Unle·ttered, *a.* ME. [Un-1 3.] **1.** Not instructed in letters; not possessed of book-learning. **b.** Pertaining to or characterized by ignorance of letters 1588. **2.** Not marked with or expressed in letters 1633.

1. Plain u. Men WESLEY. **b.** Learned men in an u. age HAZLITT. **2.** This u. tomb 1782.

Unle·vel *a.* [Un-1 1] 1571. **Unle·vel** *v.* [Un-2 4 b] 1586. **Unle·velled** *ppl. a.* [Un-1 2] 1622. **Unle·vied** *ppl. a.* [Un-1 2] 1450. **Unli·able** *a.* [Un-1 1] 1624.

Unli·censed, *ppl. a.* 1608. [Un-1 2.] **1.** Not authorized by a formal licence to carry on some occupation, etc. 1634. **b.** Not furnished with authority, sanction, or formal permission to do something 1608. **2.** Of books, etc.: Published without licence 1643. **b.** Not authorized or sanctioned 1649. **3.** Free from requiring a licence 1644.

1. b. The Papists restraint of the Laity u., from reading it translated in a known Tongue 1685. **3.** For the Liberty of Vnlicenc'd Printing MILT.

Unli·cked, *ppl. a.* 1593. [Un-1 2.] **1.** Not licked into shape (see LICK *v.* 4). Chiefly *fig.*, esp. with *cub* (or *whelp*). **b.** *fig.* Not reduced to form or order; unpolished, rude or crude 1661. **2.** Not licked 1861.

1. b. Clumsy verse, unlickt DRYDEN.

Unli·d *v.* [Un-2 2] ME. **Unli·dded** *ppl. a.* [Un-1 2] 1819. **Unli·felike** *a.* [Un-1 1] 1818. **Unli·ghted** *ppl. a.* [Un-1 2] 1699. **Unli·ghtened** *ppl. a.* [Un-1 2] 1587. **Unli·ghtsome** *a.* (now *rare*) [Un-1 1] 1592.

Unlike (ɒnləi·k), *a.* and *sb.* [The early distribution of the word suggests orig. accommodation of ON. *úlíkr, úglíkr* = OE. *unġelić* (ME. *unliche*); see Un-1 1, LIKE *a.*] **A.** *adj.* **1.** Not like or resembling, different from (some other person or thing). **b.** Const. *to* ME. **2.** Not like each other; dissimilar ME. **3.** Dissimilar to the thing or person in question. late ME. **4.** Not uniform or even; unequal. late ME. **5.** Unlikely, improbable. Now *dial.* or *arch.* late ME.

1. He was unlich alle othre there GOWER. **b.** Vnlyk is my word to my dede 1400. **2.** How much u. they look CRABBE. **3.** Nor a muche vnlyke aunswere dyd Wylliam..gyue vnto me UDALL. **4.** Whan an vnlike pare of oxen must drawe together COVERDALE *Ecclus.* 26:7. **5.** It is not vnlike but that the saide Duke hathe ben deceyued CROMWELL. He thought the Match very u. to be effected 1626.

B. *sb.* **1.** *pl.* Dissimilar things or persons 1612. **2.** A person unlike another or others ME.

1. In a comparison of unlikes 1612. **2.** The just does not desire more than his like but more than his u. JOWETT.

Unli·ke, *adv.* ME. [UN-1 5.] †**1.** Unevenly, unequally. –late ME. **2.** †**a.** Differently, diversely –1595. **b.** In a manner different from (that of a specified person) 1593. †**3.** Improbably –1596.

2. b. The Master had treated me u. a gentleman SCOTT.

Unli·k(e)able *a.* [UN-1 1] 1841. **Unli·ked** *ppl. a.* (now *rare*) [UN-1 2] 1561. **Unli·kelihood** [UN-1 6] 1483.

Unli·kely, *a.* late ME. [UN-1 1.] **1.** Not likely to occur or come to pass. **b.** Not likely to be true or correct 1592. **c.** Not likely, in various senses 1535. **2.** With complement: **a.** With *to* and inf. late ME. **b.** With *that* and clause. late ME. **3.** Unseemly, unbecoming; of unattractive appearance. Now *dial.* 1456.

1. b. They tell, for news, such u. stories! DRYDEN. **c.** An U. way of gaining Proselytes 1694. A succession [of swifts] still haunts the same u. roofs G. WHITE. A poor lad was come, at that u. time, to fetch Mr. Rivers C. BRONTË. **3.** The most u. person..that in any countrye might be found 1590. Hence **Unli·keliness.** late ME.

Unli·kely, *adv.* 1449. [UN-1 5.] Improbably. (Usu. with negative.)

The..epistle..ascryued vnlikeli to Constantyn 1449. [He] may fall not u...into an uncouth opinion MILT.

Unli·keness. ME. [UN-1 6.] †**1.** Strangeness. –late ME. **2.** The quality of being unlike; dissimilarity. late ME. **3.** With *a* and *pl.* An instance of this 1662. **2.** A bad or poor likeness 1729.

Unli·king [UN-1 4, 8] late ME. **Unli·mber** *v.* [UN-2 3] 1802. **Unli·med** *ppl. a.* [UN-1 2] 1622.

Unli·mited, *ppl. a.* 1445. [UN-1 2.] **1.** Of rule, power, etc.: Free from restriction or control. **2.** Not limited or restricted in amount, extent, degree, or number 1586.

1. It must be an u. Monarchy SIDNEY. **2.** Four Wives the Law tolerates, Concubines are u. 1665. My confidence in his talents..is u. 1846. Hence **Unli·mited-ly** *adv.*, **-ness.**

Unli·neal *a.* [UN-1 1] 1593. **Unli·ned** *ppl. a.*1 (see LINE *v.*1) [UN-1 2] 1521. **Unli·ned** *ppl. a.*2 (see LINE *v.*2) [UN-1 2] 1865.

Unli·nk, *v.* 1600. [UN-2 2 b.] **1.** *trans.* To undo the links of; to sever, unfasten (a chain, bond, connection). **b.** To release or separate thus 1655. **2.** *intr.* To lose connection; to part; to become relaxed 1641.

Unli·nked *ppl. a.* [UN-1 2] 1813. **Unli·quid** *a.* [UN-1 1] 1547. **Unli·quidated** *ppl. a.* [UN-1 2] 1765. **Unli·quored** *ppl. a.* [UN-1 2] MILT. **Unli·stened** *ppl. a.* [UN-1 2] 1787. **Unli·stening** *ppl. a.* [UN-1 4] 1736. **Unli·t** *ppl. a.* [UN-1 2] 1852. **Unli·terary** *a.* [UN-1 1] LAMB.

Unli·ve, *v.* 1593. [UN-2 1, 2.] †**1.** *trans.* To deprive of life –1702. **2.** To reverse, undo, or annul (past life or experience) 1614.

1. Where shall I live now Lucrece is unlived? SHAKS. **2.** We must u. our former lives 1661.

Unli·v(e)able, *a.* 1869. [UN-1 1.] **1.** Of life: Not to be lived, not worth living. **2.** *U.(-in)*, uninhabitable 1898.

Unli·vely *a.* [UN-1 1] 1563, **-liness.**

Unli·ver, *v.* Now *rare* or *Obs.* 1637. [UN-2 7.] *trans.* To discharge (a ship or cargo). Also *absol.*

Unli·very. 1805. [f. prec.] *Law.* Discharge of a ship or cargo.

Unli·ving *ppl. a.* [UN-1 4] 1561.

Unloa·d, *v.* 1523. [UN-2 1.] **1.** *trans.* To take off (something carried or conveyed); to discharge (a cargo). Also *absol.* **b.** *absol.* Of vessels: To discharge cargo 1799. **2.** *fig.* To give vent to (feelings); to communicate *to* another 1593. **3.** *trans.* (and *refl.*) To free, relieve, or divest of a load, burden, or weight 1591. **b.** *Med.* To relieve by evacuation 1653. **c.** To relieve (the heart, etc.) by utterance 1720. **d.** To rid *of* something burdensome 1721. **4.** To discharge the cargo from (a vessel) 1599. **5.** To withdraw the charge from (a fire-arm, etc.) 1709. **6.** *Stock Exch.* To get rid of, sell out (stock, etc.). Also *absol.* 1876. Hence **Unloa·ded** *ppl. a.*2 **Unloa·ding** *vbl. sb.* 1522.

Unlo·aded *ppl. a.*1 [UN-1 2] 1648. **Unlo·calized** *ppl. a.* [UN-1 2] LAMB. **Unloca·ted** *ppl. a.* [UN-1 2] 1776.

Unlo·ck, *v.* late ME. [UN-2 1.] **1.** *trans.* To undo the lock of (a door, etc.) by turning the key. **2.** To set free by undoing a lock; chiefly *fig.* late ME. **b.** To give or obtain access to; to bring to light 1593. **3.** *fig.* To cause to open or unclose 1531. **b.** To explain, provide a key to (something obscure) 1636. **4.** To open, or cause to open, by physical action 1586. **b.** To undo or unfasten by some mechanical operation, or by force 1606. **c.** To free from being fixed or immovable 1735. **5.** *intr.* To become unlocked 1470.

1. This can u. the gates of Joy GRAY. **2.** When the kind early Dew Unlocks th' embosom'd Odors 1708. Capital..is so very hard to u. 1884. **b.** These hoards of truth you can u. at will WORDSW. **3.** I know you have a key to u. hearts GEO. ELIOT. **b.** With a Key Præfixed to vnlock the whole Story 1636. **4.** [Clay-lands] hardning with the Sun and Wind, till they are unlocked by industry 1707. U. your jaws, sirrah SHERIDAN. **b.** Those stops, which..lock and u. the Clock in striking 1704. **c.** At first he could u. the knee easily 1902. Hence **Unlo·cked** *ppl. a.*1

Unlo·cked *ppl. a.*2 [UN-1 2] 1603. **Unlocomo·tive** *a.* [UN-1 1] SCOTT. **Unlo·dge** *v.* (now *rare*) [UN-2 3, 7] 1560. **Unlo·gic** [UN-1 6] CARLYLE. **Unlo·gical** *a.* (now *rare*) [UN-1 1] 1661.

Unloo·ked, *ppl. a.* ME. [UN-1 2.] †**1.** Not looked to, neglected. ME. only. **b.** Not looked *at*, *on*, *to*, etc.; unexamined, unheeded, unregarded 1563. **2.** Not looked *for*; unexpected, unanticipated 1535. †**b.** Unlooked for –1618.

2. b. But by some vnlook'd accident cut off SHAKS.

Unloo·sable *a.* [UN-1 1] late ME. **Unloo·se** *v.* [UN-2 7] late ME. **Unloo·sed** *ppl. a.* [UN-1 2] late ME. **Unloo·sen** *v.* [UN-2 7] 1450. **Unlo·pped** *ppl. a.* [UN-1 2] 1573. **Unlo·rd** *v.* [UN-2 4 b] 1572. **Unlo·rded** *ppl. a.* [UN-1 2] MILT. **Unlo·rdly** *a.* [UN-1 1] 1575. **Unlo·sable** *a.* [UN-1 1] 1647. **Unlo·st** *ppl. a.* [UN-1 2] 1513. **Unlo·v(e)able** *a.* [UN-1 1] 1570. **Unlo·ve** *v.* [UN-2 1] CHAUCER. **Unlo·ved** *ppl. a.* [UN-1 2] late ME.

Unlo·vely, *a.* late ME. [UN-1 1.] **1.** Not evoking feelings of love or affection; unattractive, repellent. **2.** Lacking beauty, ugly. late ME.

1. This very u. quarrel 1889. **2.** A ful old man.. that onlovely was of face 1450. Hence **Unlo·veliness.**

Unlo·verlike *a.* [UN-1 1] JANE AUSTEN. **Unlo·ving** *ppl. a.* [UN-1 4] 1529, **-ly** *adv.*, **-ness.** **Unlu·ck** [UN-1 6] 1838.

Unlu·ckily, *adv.* 1530. [UN-1 5.] Unfortunately, unhappily (usu. parenthetic or in loose construction). **b.** With verbs of happening, succeeding, etc. With ill success or results, not well 1550.

Blind Fortune..made them u. to be killed SIDNEY. U. all our money had been laid out..in provisions GOLDSM. **b.** It has turned out u. SHELLEY.

Unlu·cky, *a.* 1530. [UN-1 1.] **1.** Having an unfortunate character or issue; marked by misfortune or failure. **2.** Boding or involving misfortune; ill-omened 1547. **3.** Having ill-luck; meeting with misfortune or mishap 1552. **4.** Bringing ill-luck; mischievous, malicious. Now *dial.* 1586. **5.** Of an unfortunate or regrettable nature; not entitled to commendation 1628.

Brought hither in a most vnluckie houre SHAKS. The year..had certainly been u. MACAULAY. **2.** The Scottes..thought John an unluckie name for a King 1568. **3.** Some Ships.. are so vnlucky, that they neuer make a good voyage 1627. **5.** If some u. Barber notch my Hair 1746. Hence **Unlu·ckiness.**

Unlu·crative *a.* [UN-1 1] 1771. **Unlu·minous** *a.* [UN-1 1] 1773. **Unlu·strous** *a.* [UN-1 1] 1709. **Unlu·sty** *a.* (now only *dial.*) [UN-1 1] ME. **Unluxu·rious** *a.* [UN-1 1] 1700. **Unmaca·damized** *ppl. a.* [UN-1 2] 1840. **Unma·ddened** *ppl. a.* [UN-1 2] COLERIDGE.

Unma·de, *ppl. a.* ME. [UN-1 2.] **1.** Not (yet) made, in senses of the vb. **b.** *spec.* Not trained 1856. **c.** With advs. Not made *out*, *up*, etc. 1600. **2.** Existing without having been made; uncreated but existent ME.

1. Lawes..are farre better vnmade, then vnkept 1623. **b.** U. hunters and carriage-horses 1856. **c.** He wears his little Learning, unmade-up, puts it on, before it was half finished 1680. **2.** U., Self-existent, independent Deities 1682.

Unmagna·nimous *a.* [UN-1 1] 1856. **Unmagne·tic** *a.* [UN-1 1] 1805. **Unma·gnetized** *ppl. a.* [UN-1 2] 1834. **Unmai·den** *v.* [UN-2 4 b] 1579. **Unmai·denly** *a.* [UN-1 1] 1634, **-liness.** **Unmai·lable** *a.* (*U.S.*) [UN-1 1] 1875. **Unmai·med** *ppl. a.* [UN-1 2] MALORY. **Unmaintai·nable** *a.* [UN-1 1] 1625.

Unma·ke, *v.* late ME. [UN-2 1.] **1.** To reverse or undo the making of; to reduce again to an unmade condition. Also *absol.* **2.** To deprive of a particular rank or station; to depose 1554. **b.** To deprive of a certain character or quality; to change the nature of 1616. **3.** *fig.* To undo; to ruin; to bring to nothing 1605.

1. Prelaty..must be forc't to dissolve and u. her own pyramidal figure MILTON. When a statute.. has been unmade by the authority that made it BENTHAM. **2.** They made and unmade Popes at their pleasure 1670. **b.** You are so pure—That.. Heaven would u. it sin! DRYDEN. **3.** The machine unmakes the man EMERSON. Hence **Unma·ker.**

Unmali·cious *a.* [UN-1 1] 1649. **Unma·lleable** *a.* [UN-1 1] 1609, **Unmalleabi·lity.** **Unma·lted** *ppl. a.* [UN-1 2] 1651.

Unma·n, *sb. rare.* late ME. [UN-1 6.] †**1.** A being below the status of man –1641. **2.** A monster 1879.

Unma·n, *v.* 1598. [UN-2 4 b.] **1.** *trans.* To deprive of the attributes of a man; to remove from the category of men. **2.** To reduce below the level of man; to degrade, brutalize 1637. **3.** To deprive of manly courage or fortitude; to make weak or womanish 1600. **b.** *trans.* and *intr.* To bring or come back to childhood (*rare*) 1672. **4.** To emasculate, castrate 1684. **5.** To remove the men from (a vessel or fleet) 1687.

2. Habits of Vice u. Men's minds 1701. **3.** The sight of her unmans me ADDISON. **5.** He could not venture to u. his Fleet NELSON.

Unma·nacle *v.* [UN-2 2 b] 1582. **Unma·nacled** *ppl. a.* [UN-1 2] 1726.

Unma·nageable, *a.* 1632. [UN-1 1.] **1.** Not amenable to control; unruly, headstrong. **2.** Incapable of being properly or conveniently handled or manipulated 1658.

1. That tough, lofty, u. Monarch [Henry VIII] 1728. Each fresh gambade of his u. horse SCOTT. **2.** An index of an u. length 1779. Hence **Unma·nageableness.** **Unma·nageably** *adv.*

Unma·naged, *ppl. a. arch.* 1603. [UN-1 2.] Not well trained or disciplined; not controlled. **b.** Of language: Unrestrained, immoderate 1771.

b. Accusations, so heavy in the matter and u. in the epithets BURKE.

Unma·nfully *adv.* [UN-1 5] late ME. **Unma·ngled** *ppl. a.* [UN-1 2] 1557. **Unma·nifest** *a.* [UN-1 1] 1535. **Unma·nifested** *ppl. a.* [UN-1 2] 1683. **Unma·nlike** *a.* and *adv.* [UN-1 1, 5] 1579.

Unma·nly, *a.* 1475. [UN-1 1.] **1.** Dishonourable or degrading to a man. **2.** Womanish; effeminate; cowardly; poor-spirited 1547. So **Unma·nliness.** **Unma·nly** *adv.* late ME.

Unma·nned, *ppl. a.* 1544. [UN-1 2.] **1.** Not furnished with men. **2.** Unsupported; unassisted 1620. **b.** Without inhabitants 1680. **3.** Not trained or broken in; *spec.* of a hawk. Now *rare.* 1592.

3. Like a wild Kestrell or vnmand Hawke 1623.

Unma·nnered, *ppl. a.* 1594. [UN-1 2.] **1.** Not possessed of good manners; unmannerly, rude. **2.** Of conduct: Characterized by want of manners 1760. †**3.** Free from mannerisms. LAMB.

1. Vnmanner'd Dogge, Stand'st thou when I commaund SHAKS.

Unma·nnerly, *a.* late ME. [UN-1 1.] **1.** Of persons: Ill-bred; lacking manners; behaving rudely or discourteously. **2.** Of actions, etc.: Showing want of manners. late ME. So **Unma·nnerliness.** **Unma·nnerly** *adv.* in an u. fashion ME.

Unma·ntle, *v.* 1598. [UN-2 2, 5.] **1.** *trans.* To take off a mantle or a covering from. **b.** *intr.* To take off one's mantle 1822. **2.** *trans.* To dismantle (a room, etc.) *rare.* 1828.

2. The Tapestried Chamber to be unmantled SCOT.

Unma·ntled *ppl. a.* [UN-1 2] 1800. **Unmanufa·ctured** *ppl. a.* [UN-1 2] 1796.

Unmanu·red, *ppl. a.* 1570. [UN-1 2.] †**1.** Not tilled –1721. †**b.** *fig.* Of the mind, etc.: Untrained, uncultivated –1700. **2.** Without manure 1828.

1. All rough and u. places 1578. b. It argueth an u. wit 1594.

Unma·pped *ppl. a.* [UN-[1] 2] 1805.

Unma·rked, *ppl. a.* late ME. [UN-[1] 2.] **1.** Having received no mark or impress. **b.** Not marked off or out, not distinguished or characterized (*by* something) 1815. **2.** Unobserved, unnoticed 1533.

1. *Maverick*, used in Texas to designate an u. yearling 1872. b. Virgil's characters are mostly cold, u., and not attaching 1815. 2. The hours.. have stol'n unmark'd away AKENSIDE.

Unma·rketable *a.* [UN-[1] 1] 1654. **Unma·rred** *ppl. a.* [UN-[1] 2] ME. **Unma·rriageable** *a.* [UN-[1] 1] 1775.

Unma·rried, *ppl. a.* ME. [UN-[1] 2.] **1.** Not married. **2.** Lived without marriage 1648.

Unma·rry, *v.* 1530. [UN-[2] 1, 5.] **1.** *trans.* To dissolve the marriage of; to divorce. **b.** To put away (a wife) 1645. **2.** *intr.* To free oneself from marriage 1635.

1. I did marry you;..I would there were a parson to u. us! 1637. b. Though he did not live with her, he could not u. her 1797. 2. We are unmarrying among the great; the Duke of Grafton's divorce was finished this morning 1769.

Unma·rtyred *ppl. a.* [UN-[1] 2] 1580. **Unma·sculine** *a.* [UN-[1] 1] MILT.

Unma·sk, *v.* 1586. [UN-[2] 2, 5.] **1.** *trans.* To remove a mask or covering from (the face, a masked person, etc.). **2.** *fig.* To strip of disguise; to disclose the real nature of; to bring into the light 1593. **3.** *absol.* To take off one's mask 1603. **b.** *fig.* To reveal one's true character 1622. **4.** *Mil.* To reveal the presence (of a gun or battery) by opening fire 1747. **b.** To make patent; to show plainly 1816.

1. If she vnmaske her beauty to the Moone SHAKS. 2. The true God hath vnmasked the errors of those times 1611. 4. The Chinese, unmasking a mountain gun, fired on the Bayard 1884. b. With a view of making the Afghan commandant..u. his force 1879. Hence **Unma·sked** *ppl. a.* **Unma·sking** *vbl. sb.*

Unma·stered *ppl. a.* [UN-[1] 2] 1561. **Unma·sticated** *ppl. a.* [UN-[1] 2] 1815. **Unma·tchable** *a.* [UN-[1] 1] 1544, **-ably** *adv.*

Unma·tched, *ppl. a.* 1581. [UN-[1] 2.] **1.** Having no equal; matchless; unrivalled. **2.** Not provided with something equal or alike 1645.

2. Old-fashioned u. chairs 1824.

Unma·ted *ppl. a.* [UN-[1] 2] 1614. **Unmate·rial** *a.* [UN-[1] 1] late ME. **Unmate·rnal** *a.* [UN-[1] 1] 1821. **Unmathema·tical** *a.* [UN-[1] 1] 1720, **-ly** *adv.*

Unmea·ning, *ppl. a.* 1704. [UN-[1] 4.] **1.** Of features, etc.: Expressionless, vacant. **b.** Of persons: Having no serious aim or purpose 1746. **2.** Having no meaning or significance; meaningless 1709. Hence **Unmea·ningly** *adv.*

Unmea·nt *ppl. a.* [UN-[1] 2] 1634. **Unmea·surable** *a.* [UN-[1] 1] late ME. **Unmea·surably** *adv.* (now *rare*) [UN-[1] 5] late ME.

Unmea·sured, *ppl. a.* late ME. [UN-[1] 2.] **1.** Not limited or known by measurement; immense in size, extent, or amount. **2.** Not composed of measured syllables 1715. **3.** Immoderate, unrestrained 1820.

1. Gods vnmesured bountee 1450. Along th' unmeasur'd shore CHAPMAN. Of an u. fluid, we can only reason by conjecture 1794. 2. A kind of u. Poetry 1728. 3. The u. eulogies he bestows upon him 1839.

Unmecha·nical *a.* [UN-[1] 1] 1674, **-ly** *adv.* **Unme·chanize** *v.* [UN-[2] 4 c] 1687. **Unme·ddled** *ppl. a.* [UN-[1] 2] late ME. **Unme·ddling** *ppl. a.* [UN-[1] 4] 1765. **Unme·ditated** *ppl. a.* [UN-[1] 2] 1624. **Unme·ditative** *a.* [UN-[1] 1] 1842. **Unmee·k** *a.* (*arch.*) [UN-[1] 1] ME.

Unmee·t, *a.* [OE. *unmǣte*, f. UN-[1] 1 + MEET *a.*] †**1.** Immoderate or excessive in amount or size –1475. †**2.** Unequal; unevenly matched –1760. **3.** Unbecoming, improper 1529. **4.** Unfit or unsuited for some end or purpose 1513.

2. Litle Iulus..With wnmeit paiss his fader fast followand 1513. 3. While they contending were with words u. HOBBES. Christ thought..a ship no u. place to preach in 1703. 4. The lot fell oft vpon the vnmeetest 1598. The Pastor is the unmeetest person to meddle in it BAXTER. Mr. Blair was now infirm and u. for travel 1676. Hence **Unmee·t-ly** *adv.*, **-ness.**

Unme·llowed *ppl. a.* [UN-[1] 2] 1573. **Unmelo·dious** *a.* [UN-[1] 1] 1665, **-ly** *adv.* **Unme·lted** *ppl. a.* [UN-[1] 2] 1549. **Unme·lting** *ppl. a.* [UN-[1] 4] 1743. **Unme·morable** *a.* [UN-[1] 1] 1598. **Unme·naced** *ppl. a.* [UN-[1] 2] 1821. **Unme·ndable** *a.* [UN-[1] 1] 1584. **Unme·nded** *ppl. a.* [UN-[1] 2] 1880.

Unme·ntionable, *a.* and *sb.* 1830. [UN-[1] 1.] **A.** *adj.* Not fit to be mentioned; too scandalous, disgusting, etc., for mention 1837. **B.** *sb. pl.* Trousers 1830.

Hence **Unme·ntionably** *adv.*

With an unmentionably vulgar oath W. COLLINS.

Unme·ntioned *ppl. a.* [UN-[1] 2] 1545. **Unme·rcenary** *a.* [UN-[1] 1] 1643. **Unme·rchantable** *a.* [UN-[1] 1] 1602. **Unme·rciful** *a.* [UN-[1] 1] 1481, **-ly** *adv.*, **-ness.**

Unme·ritable, *a.* Now *rare.* 1594. [UN-[1] 1.] Of no merit.

This is a slight vnmeritable man SHAKS.

Unme·rited *ppl. a.* [UN-[1] 2] 1648, **-ly** *adv.*, **-ness. Unme·riting** *ppl. a.* [UN-[1] 4] 1594. **Unmerito·rious** *a.* [UN-[1] 1] 1855, **-ly** *adv.* **Unme·rry** *a.* (now *rare*) [UN-[1] 1] OE. **Unme·sh** *v.* [UN-[2] 2 b] 1822. **Unme·t** *ppl. a.* [UN-[1] 2] 1603. **Unme·talled** *ppl. a.* [UN-[1] 2] 1843. **Unmeta·llic** *a.* [UN-[1] 1] 1757. **Unmetamo·rphosed** *ppl. a.* [UN-[1] 2] 1600. **Unmetaphy·sical** *a.* [UN-[1] 1] 1691. **Unmetho·dical** *a.* [UN-[1] 1] 1601, **-ly** *adv.* **Unme·thodized** *ppl. a.* [UN-[1] 2] 1677. **Unme·trical** *a.* [UN-[1] 1] 1791. **Unmew·** *v.* (*rare*) [UN-[2] 3] KEATS. **Unmi·ghty** *a.* (*arch.*) [UN-[1] 1] OE.

Unmi·litary, *a.* 1777. [UN-[1] 1.] **1.** Not in accordance with military practice or standards. **2.** That is not a soldier, not belonging to the army. **b.** Of nations, etc.: Averse, or not prone, to soldiering. 1802.

1. Defence—the very word is u. 1806.

Unmi·lked *ppl. a.* [UN-[1] 2] 1648. **Unmi·lled** *ppl. a.* [UN-[1] 2] 1555. **Unmi·nded** *ppl. a.* [UN-[1] 2] 1513.

Unmi·ndful, *a.* late ME. [UN-[1] 1.] Not bearing something in mind; forgetful or oblivious *of* something; careless, heedless.

Dull vnmindfull Villaine, Why stay'st thou here? SHAKS. Careless of Night, u. to return DRYDEN. Every person was willing to save himself, u. of others GOLDSM.

Unmi·ngled *ppl. a.* [UN-[1] 2] 1548. **Unmi·nished** *ppl. a.* (*arch.*) [UN-[1] 2] 1533. **Unministe·rial** *a.* [UN-[1] 1] 1727. **Unmi·nted** *ppl. a.* [UN-[1] 2] 1611. **Unmira·culous** *a.* [UN-[1] 1] 1746. **Unmi·rthful** *a.* [UN-[1] 1] 1815, **-ly** *adv.* **Unmisgi·ving** *ppl. a.* [UN-[1] 4] 1693, **-ly** *adv.* **Unmi·ssed** *ppl. a.* [UN-[1] 2] late ME. **Unmista·kable** *a.* [UN-[1] 1] 1666, **-ness, -ably** *adv.* **Unmistru·sting** *ppl. a.* [UN-[1] 4] 1598. **Unmi·tigable** *a.* [UN-[1] 1] SHAKS., **-ably** *adv.*

Unmi·tigated, *ppl. a.* 1599. [UN-[1] 2.] **1.** Not softened in respect of severity or intensity. **2.** Not modified or toned down; absolute 1840.

1. The u. glare of day JANE AUSTEN. 2. An u. fib C. BRONTË. An u. humbug 1860. Hence **Unmi·tigatedly** *adv.*

Unmi·tred *ppl. a.* [UN-[1] 2] 1688. **Unmi·x** *v.* [UN-[2] 1] 1558. **Unmi·xed** *ppl. a.* [UN-[1] 2] 1526, **-ly** *adv.*, **-ness. Unmo·cked** *ppl. a.* [UN-[1] 2] 1648. **Unmo·dern** *a.* [UN-[1] 1] 1757. **Unmo·dernized** *ppl. a.* [UN-[1] 2] JANE AUSTEN. **Unmo·difiable** *a.* [UN-[1] 1] 1825. **Unmo·dified** *ppl. a.* [UN-[1] 2] BURKE. **Unmo·dish** *a.* (*arch.*) [UN-[1] 1] 1665. **Unmo·dulated** *ppl. a.* [UN-[1] 2] JANE AUSTEN. **Unmoi·st** *a.* [UN-[1] 1] 1611. **Unmoi·stened** *ppl. a.* [UN-[1] 2] 1625. **Unmole·sted** *ppl. a.* [UN-[1] 2] 1531, **-ly** *adv.* **Unmo·lten** *ppl. a.* [UN-[1] 2] 1525. **Unmo·narch** *v.* [UN-[2] 4 b] 1667. **Unmo·neyed** *ppl. a.* [UN-[1] 2] 1677.

Unmoo·r, *v.* 1497. [UN-[2] 2 b.] *Naut.* **1.** *trans.* To free from moorings; *spec.* to reduce the moorings of (a ship) till she rides by a single anchor. **2.** *intr.* To cast off moorings 1611.

1. They lye Unmored, and ride single, and intend to Sail 1681. 2. The next Morning we unmoor'd.. and at Six weigh'd 1745.

Unmo·ral, *a.* 1841. [UN-[1] 1.] Non-moral; not influenced by, or connected with, moral considerations.

The Lower animism is not immoral, it is u. TYLOR. So **Unmora·lity.**

Unmo·ralized *ppl. a.* [UN-[1] 2] 1668. **Unmo·rtared** *ppl. a.* [UN-[1] 2] 1656. **Unmo·rtgaged** *ppl. a.* [UN-[1] 2] 1638. **Unmo·rtified** *ppl. a.* [UN-[1] 2] 1450. **Unmo·thered** *ppl. a.* [UN-[1] 2] 1607. **Unmo·therly** *a.* [UN-[1] 1] 1593. **Unmo·tived** *ppl. a.* [UN-[1] 2] COLERIDGE.

Unmou·ld, *v.* 1611. [UN-[2] 1, 3, 5.] **1.** *trans.* To destroy the mould or form of. **b.** To take out of a mould 1900. **2.** *intr.* or *absol.* To lose form or shape 1834.

1. His baneful cup..unmoulding reasons mintage Character'd in the face MILT.

Unmou·lded *ppl. a.* [UN-[1] 2] 1620.

Unmou·nt, *v.* 1680. [UN-[2] 1, 6.] **1.** *trans.* To remove from a mount; to unfix and take down. **2.** To dismount. Also *intr.* (*rare.*) 1787.

2. The German Emperor has had to u. his high horse 1892.

Unmou·nted, *ppl. a.* 1592. [UN-[1] 2.] **1.** Not provided with or riding on a horse or horses. **2.** Of cannon: Not on carriages 1627. **3.** Of specimens, pictures, etc.: Not mounted; not provided with a mount or mounts 1888.

Unmou·rned *ppl. a.* [UN-[1] 2] 1650. **Unmo·vable** *a.* (now *rare*) [UN-[1] 1] late ME., **-ness, -ably** *adv.*

Unmo·ved, *ppl. a.* late ME. [UN-[1] 2.] **1.** Unaffected by emotion or excitement; collected, undisturbed; calm, steadfast. **2.** Not moved in position; remaining fixed or steady 1440.

1. He found the Duke u. by all the considerations and arguments..he had offered CLARENDON. My soul is still the same, U. with fear DRYDEN. Hence **Unmo·vedly** *adv.*

Unmo·ving *ppl. a.* [UN-[1] 4] late ME., **-ly** *adv.* **Unmow·n** *ppl. a.* [UN-[1] 2] 1549. **Unmu·ffle** *v.* [UN-[2] 2] 1611. **Unmu·rdered** *ppl. a.* [UN-[1] 2] 1586. **Unmu·rmuring** *ppl. a.* [UN-[1] 4] 1784, **-ly** *adv.*

Unmu·sical, *a.* 1607. [UN-[1] 1.] **1.** Of sounds: Not musical; unmelodious, harsh. **2.** Of persons: Not appreciative of or not expert in music 1634. **3.** Not based on musical principles 1786.

1. A name vnmusicall to the Volcians eares SHAKS. His voice was singularly u. 1880. 2. The u. admired her singing 1896. Hence **Unmu·sically** *adv.*

Unmu·tilated *ppl. a.* [UN-[1] 2] 1790. **Unmu·zzle** *v.* [UN-[2] 2 b] 1600. **Unmu·zzled** *ppl. a.* [UN-[1] 2] SHAKS. **Unmyste·rious** *a.* [UN-[1] 1] 1746.

Unnai·l, *v.* 1470. [UN-[2] 1.] **1.** *trans.* To extract the nails or rivets from; to undo or unfasten thus. **2.** To detach by the removal of nails 1598.

1. They made all y[e] bridge to be vnnayled, redy to be broken downe LD. BERNERS. Caus'd the Coffin to be unnail'd again 1704. 2. Whiles Joseph of Arimathea and Nicodemus un-nail our Lord EVELYN.

Unna·m(e)able, *a.* 1610. [UN-[1] 1.] That cannot be named.

God is celestiall, ineffable, and un-name-able 1610. Her lustrous eyes wide distended with unnamable horror 1874.

Unna·med, *ppl. a.* 1509. [UN-[1] 2.] **1.** Not mentioned or specified by name. **2.** Having no name 1611. **b.** *U. bone*, the INNOMINATE bone 1845.

1. Throwing the burden..on some u. third person MEREDITH. 2. Flowers of u. colours bright MORRIS.

Unna·tional *a.* [UN-[1] 1] 1753. **Unna·tive** *a.* [UN-[1] 1] 1712.

Unna·tural, *a.* late ME. [UN-[1] 1.] **1.** Not in accordance with the physical nature of persons or animals. **2.** Not in accordance with the usual course of nature 1513. **b.** Monstrous, abnormal 1516. **c.** Devoid of natural qualities or characteristics; artificial 1746. **3.** Outraging natural feeling or moral standards, monstrously cruel or wicked 1529. **4.** At variance with what is natural, usual, or expected; unusual, strange 1586.

1. The tones of their voice sounded..hollow, hoarse and u. 1846. 2. c. Timid, stiff, u., and ill at ease LYTTON. 3. As vnnatural as children that seek the ruin of their parents 1685. In yon fatal apartment incest and u. murder were committed SCOTT. 4. It is u. for any one in a gust of passion to speak long together DRYDEN. Hence **Unna·tural-ly** *adv.*, **-ness.**

Unna·turalism [UN-[1] 6] 1754. **Unnatura·lity** (*rare*) [UN-[1] 6] 1548.

Unna·turalize, *v.* 1613. [UN-[2] 4 c.] **1.** *trans.* To change the nature of; to deprive of natural character; to make unnatural. **2.** To deprive of the status or privileges of a native-born subject 1698. **3.** To make unnatural or artificial 1741.

1. It may..u. the incidents RICHARDSON.

Unna·turalized *ppl. a.* [UN-[1] 2] 1611. **Unna·ture** *sb.* (*rare*) [UN-[1] 6] 1843. **Unna·ture** *v.* [UN-[2] 4 b] 1586. **Unnau·tical** *a.* [UN-[1] 1] 1852. **Unna·vigable** *a.* [UN-[1] 1] 1579. **Unna·vigated** *ppl. a.* [UN-[1] 2] 1777. **Unnea·t** *a.* [UN-[1] 1] 1648.

Unne·cessary, *a.* and *sb.* 1548. [UN-[1] 1, 6.] **A.** *adj.* **1.** Not necessary or requisite; needless. **b.** With *it* (etc.) as subj., and usu. const. *to* with inf. 1597. †**2.** Not requiring much. SHAKS.

1. From a nice, u. scruple SWIFT. Addicted to u. haste 1898. b. It is u. to pursue the argument any farther '*Junius*' *Lett.*

B. *sb. pl.* Unnecessary things 1559.

The unnecessaries of life 1881. Hence **Unne·cessarily** *adv.* **Unne·cessariness.**

Unnece·ssitated *ppl. a.* [Un-1 2] 1635. **Unnee·ded** *ppl. a.* [Un-1 2] 1844. **Unnee·dful** *a.* [Un-1 1] late ME., **-ly** *adv.* **Unnei·ghboured** *ppl. a.* [Un-1 2] 1657. **Unnei·ghbourly** *a.* and *adv.* [Un-1 1, 5] 1583.

Unne·rve, *v.* 1621. [Un-2 1.] **1.** *trans.* To destroy the strength of; to enfeeble, weaken. **2.** To deprive (the mind, etc., or a person) of courage or energy; to render incapable of acting with ordinary firmness or energy 1704.

1. Pale sudden feare vn-nerves his quaking thighs 1621. The Precepts..weaken and un-nerve his Verse Addison. **2.** The fear..completely unnerved the Romans 1878. Hence **Unne·rved, Unne·rving** *ppl. adjs.*

Unne·st *v.* (chiefly *fig.*) [Un-2 3] late ME. †**Unne·stle** *v.* [Un-2 1] –1694. **Unne·tted** *ppl. a.* [Un-1 2] 1833. **Unneu·tralized** *ppl. a.* [Un-1 2] 1758. **Unni·mble** *a.* (now *rare*) [Un-1 1] 566.

Unno·ble, *a.* late ME. [Un-1 1.] **1.** Not of noble birth or high rank. **2.** Without magnanimity or generosity; mean, base, ignoble *arch.* 1566.

1. The noble men bare a garment vnlyke to them that were vnnoble Caxton. It is an almost universal weakness of the u. in England to parade an acquaintance with the noble 1832.

Unno·table *a.* [Un-1 1] 1528. **Unno·tched** *ppl. a.* [Un-1 2] 1811.

Unno·ted, *ppl. a.* 1563. [Un-1 2.] **1.** Not noticed or observed; unmarked. **2.** Not specially noticed or observed; obscure, undistinguished 1592.

Unno·ticeable *a.* [Un-1 1] 1775, **-ness, -ably** *adv.* **Unno·ticed** *ppl. a.* [Un-1 2] 1720. **Unno·ticing** *ppl. a.* [Un-1 4] 1782. **Unno·tified** *ppl. a.* [Un-1 2] 1802. **Unnou·rishing** *ppl. a.* [Un-1 4] 1605. **Unnu·mberable** *a.* (now *rare*) [Un-1 1] ME.

Unnu·mbered, *ppl. a.* late ME. [Un-1 2.] **1.** Not numbered or reckoned up; countless. **2.** Not marked with or identified by a number or numbers 1533.

1. The Skies are painted with vnnumbred sparkes Shaks. **2.** I have receaved yours (unnumbred) of the 8th of Dec. 1654.

Unnu·rsed *ppl. a.* [Un-1 2] 1875. **Unnu·rtured** *ppl. a.* [Un-1 2] 1548. **Unobe·dient** *a.* [Un-1 1] Wyclif. **Unobey·ed** *ppl. a.* [Un-1 2] 1595. **Unobje·cted** (*to*) *ppl. a.* [Un-1 2] Atterbury. **Unobje·ctionable** *a.* [Un-1 1] 1793, **-ness, -ably** *adv.* **Unobli·ged** *ppl. a.* [Un-1 2] 1648. **Unobli·terated** *ppl. a.* [Un-1 2] 1644.

Unobno·xious, *a.* 1609. [Un-1 1.] **1.** Not exposed or liable *to* something. **2.** Not objectionable or offensive 1678.

1. Unwearied, u. to be pain'd By wound Milt. The soul is..u. to error 1862.

Unobscu·red *ppl. a.* [Un-1 2] 1646. **Unobse·rvable** *a.* [Un-1 1] Hobbes. **Unobse·rvance** [Un-1 6] 1654. **Unobse·rvant** *a.* [Un-1 1] 1661, **-ly** *adv.* **Unobse·rved** *ppl. a.* [Un-1 2] 1612, **-ly** *adv.* **Unobse·rving** *ppl. a.* [Un-1 4] 1690. **Unobstru·cted** *ppl. a.* [Un-1 2] 1659, **-ly** *adv.* **Unobtai·nable** *a.* [Un-1 1] 1860. **Unobtai·ned** *ppl. a.* [Un-1 2] 1594. **Unobtru·sive** *a.* [Un-1 1] 1743, **-ly** *adv.*, **-ness. Uno·bvious** *a.* [Un-1 1] 1643.

Uno·ccupied, *ppl. a.* late ME. [Un-1 2.] **1.** Not occupied or engaged in some work or pursuit; at leisure. **2.** Not put to use; left idle. (In later use only of time) 1448. **3.** Without occupants or users; uninhabited, untilled, unfrequented. late ME. **b.** Not taken up or appropriated 1701.

1. She led a blameless, u., and apparently purposeless life 1898. **2.** They..loste theyr puissa nce and brightnesse, lyke yron vnoccupied 1561. **3.** The hye wayes were vnoccupied Bible (1560) *Judges* 5:6. Not an inch of ground lies waste and u. 1807. **b.** Leaving the ear u. for any measure which may follow 1832.

Unoffe·nded *ppl. a.* [Un-1 2] 1481, **-ly** *adv.* **Unoffe·nding** *ppl. a.* [Un-1 4] 1569. **Uno·ffered** *ppl. a.* [Un-1 2] 1526. **Uno·fficered** *ppl. a.* [Un-1 2] 1655. **Uno·fficerlike** *a.* [Un-1 1] 1803.

Unoffi·cial, *a.* 1798. [Un-1 1.] **1.** Not having an official character or stamp. **2.** Of persons: Not holding an official position; not acting in an official capacity 1829. Hence **Unoffi·cially** *adv.*

Unoffi·cious *a.* [Un-1 1] 1611. **Uno·ften** *adv.* [Un-1 5] 1741. **Unoi·led** *ppl. a.* [Un-1 2] 1728. **Uno·pened** *ppl. a.* [Un-1 2] 1600. (Cf. Uncut *ppl. a.* 4 a.) **Unoppo·sed** *ppl. a.* [Un-1 2] 1659. **Unoppre·ssed** *ppl. a.* [Un-1 2] 1572. **Unoppre·ssive** *a.* [Un-1 1] 1648, **-ly** *adv.*

Unordai·ned, *ppl. a.* ME. [Un-1 2.] †**1.** Not controlled. ME. only. **2.** Not ecclesiastically ordained 1653. **3.** Not appointed or decreed 1815.

Uno·rder *v.* [Un-2 1] 1440.

Uno·rdered, *ppl. a.* late ME. [Un-1 2.] †**1.** Not belonging to a religious order; not in ecclesiastical orders –1607. **2.** Not put in order 1477. †**3.** Disorderly, uncontrolled –1611. **4.** Not ordered or bespoken 1981.

1. Wedded or sengle, ordered or unordred,.. clerk or seculeer Chaucer. **2.** Those various and u. ideas 1877. **3.** The vnordred appetites of the body 1611.

Uno·rderly *a.* (now *rare*) [Un-1 1] 1483; *adv.* [Un-1 5] 1470. **Uno·rdinary** *a.* [Un-1 1] 1547.

Uno·rganized, *ppl. a.* 1690. [Un-1 2.] **1.** Inorganic, not possessed of organs or life. **2.** Not formed into an orderly whole 1836.

1. To me it seems that stones are vegetables u. Berkeley. **2.** The u. valour of the English nation 1836.

Unori·ginal, *a.* 1667. [Un-1 1.] †**1.** Without origin; uncreated. Milt. **2.** Not original; derivative; borrowed or plagiarized 1774.

1. U. Night and Chaos wilde Milt. **2.** The 'Song of Roland' is comparatively late and u. 1897. Hence **Unorigina·lity.**

Unori·ginate, *a.* and *sb.* 1719. [Un-1 2.] **A.** *adj.* Self-existent; without origin; not created.

One spirit,..self-existent, u., the first cause of the universe 1755.

B. *sb.* An u. being 1724. Hence **Unori·ginate-ly** *adv.*, **-ness.**

Unori·ginated *ppl. a.* [Un-1 2] 1696. **Unorname·ntal** *a.* [Un-1 1] 1747. **Unorname·nted** *ppl. a.* [Un-1 2] 1697. **Uno·rthodox** *a.* [Un-1 1] 1657. **Uno·rthodoxy** [Un-1 6] 1704. **Uno·ssified** *ppl. a.* [Un-1 2] 1726. **Unostenta·tious** *a.* [Un-1 1] 1747, **-ly** *adv.* **Unoverco·me** *ppl. a.* [Un-1 2] late ME. **Unoverthrow·n** *ppl. a.* [Un-1 2] 1535.

Unow·ned, *ppl. a.* 1611. [Un-1 2.] **1.** Not possessed as property; having no owner. **2.** Unacknowledged; unadmitted 1715.

Uno·xidized *ppl. a.* [Un-1 2] 1827. **Unoxy·genated** *ppl. a.* [Un-1 2] 1790. **Unpaci·fic** *a.* [Un-1 1] 1774. **Unpa·cified** *ppl. a.* [Un-1 2] 1570.

Unpa·ck, *v.* 1472. [Un-2 1, 3.] **1.** *trans.* To undo or open (a bale, luggage, etc.) and remove or release the contents. **2.** To take (something) out of a pack or packing 1598. **b.** *refl.* or *pass.* To get one's furniture, luggage, etc., unpacked 1791. **c.** *absol.* To undo things from a packed state 1837. **3.** To unload (a pack-horse, cart, etc.) 1570.

1. *fig.* That I..Must..vnpacke my heart with words Shaks. **2.** *transf.* A red-haired man..had unpacked himself from a cab Dickens. **3.** His first care was to u. his horses W. Irving.

Unpa·cked *ppl. a.* [Un-1 2] 1495. **Unpa·dlocked** *ppl. a.* [Un-1 2] 1681. **Unpa·ged** *ppl. a.* [Un-1 2] 1874.

Unpai·d, *ppl. a.* late ME. [Un-1 2.] **1.** To whom payment has not been made; not receiving payment. **2.** Not met or cleared off by payment, undischarged; not handed over or given in payment. late ME. **b.** Not rendered or discharged 1611. **3.** Not paid *for*. Also without prep. 1465.

1. Whilst thy unpay'd Musicians, Crickets sing Lovelace. Phr. *The* (*Great*) *U.*, the class of u. magistrates or judges. **2.** She remembers she has u. bills 1887. *fig.* Coming to receive from us Knee-tribute yet u. Milt. **b.** What can atone.. Thy fate unpity'd, and thy rites u.? Pope. **3.** Rustling in vnpayd-for Silke Shaks. Letters posted u. are charged double postage 1886.

Unpai·ned *ppl. a.* [Un-1 2] Wyclif. **Unpai·nful** *a.* [Un-1 1] 1570, **-ly** *adv.* **Unpai·nt** *v.* [Un-2 2] 1611. **Unpai·ntable** *a.* [Un-1 1] 1849. **Unpai·nted** *ppl. a.* [Un-1 2] 1555. **Unpai·red** *ppl. a.* [Un-1 2] 1648.

Unpa·latable, *a.* 1682. [Un-1 1.] **1.** Not agreeable to the palate. **2.** Unpleasant, distasteful, disagreeable 1711.

Unpa·lled *ppl. a.* [Un-1 2] 1770. **Unpa·lliated** *ppl. a.* [Un-1 2] 1798. **Unpa·lpable** *a.* (now *rare*) [Un-1 1] 1538. **Unpa·mpered** *ppl. a.* [Un-1 2] 1794. **Unpa·nelled** *ppl. a.* [Un-1 2] 1883. **Unpa·per** *v.* [Un-2 2] 1714. **Unpa·pered** *ppl. a.* [Un-1 2] 1851.

Unpa·radise, *v.* 1592. [Un-2 1, 4 b.] **1.** *trans.* To expel from Paradise. **2.** To deprive of the character of Paradise 1647.

Unpa·ragoned *ppl. a.* [Un-1 2] 1611. **Unpa·rallel** *a.* [Un-1 1] 1652. **Unpa·rallelable** *a.* [Un-1 1] 1640.

Unpa·ralleled, *ppl. a.* 1594. [Un-1 2.] That has no parallel or equal, unmatched. Hence **Unpa·ralleled-ly** *adv.*, **-ness.**

Unpa·ralyzed *ppl. a.* [Un-1 2] 1846. **Unpa·rcelled** *ppl. a.* [Un-1 2] 1840. **Unpa·rdonable** *a.* [Un-1 1] 1525, **-ness, -ably** *adv.* **Unpa·rdoned** *ppl. a.* [Un-1 2] 1565. **Unpa·rdoning** *ppl. a.* [Un-1 4] Milt. **Unpa·red** *ppl. a.* [Un-1 2] ME. **Unpa·rented** *ppl. a.* [Un-1 2, Un-2 6] 1650.

U:nparliame·ntary, *a.* 1626. [Un-1 1.] Not suitable or belonging to Parliament; unsanctioned by Parliament; transgressing parliamentary rules; applied esp. to discourteous language in debate.

I am come here to shew you your..u. proceedings in this Parliament Jas. I. All U. raising of Mony upon the Subjects Hobbes. A member had used u. language 1810. Hence **U:nparliame·ntarily** *adv.*

Unpa·rriable *a.* [Un-1 1] Scott. **Unpa·rted** *ppl. a.* [Un-1 2] 1561. **Unpa·rtial** *a.* (now *rare*) [Un-1 1] 1579. **Unparti·cipated** *ppl. a.* [Un-1 2] 1678. **Unparti·cipating** *ppl. a.* [Un-1 4] 1795. **Unparti·cularized** *ppl. a.* [Un-1 2] 1823. **Unpa·ssable** *a.* [Un-1 1] 1553. **Unpa·ssed** *ppl. a.* [Un-1 2] 1541. **Unpa·ssionate** *a.* [Un-1 1] 1593, **-ly** *adv.*, **-ness. Unpa·ssioned** *ppl. a.* [Un-1 2] 1618. **Unpa·storal** *a.* [Un-1 1] 1782. **Unpa·stured** *ppl. a.* [Un-1 2] 1548. **Unpa·tented** *ppl. a.* [Un-1 2] 1719. **Unpa·thed** *ppl. a.* [Un-1 2] Shaks. **Unpathe·tic** *a.* [Un-1 1] 1782. **Unpatrio·tic** *a.* [Un-1 1] 1828, **-ally** *adv.* 1783. **Unpa·tronized** *ppl. a.* [Un-1 2] 1620.

Unpa·tterned, *ppl. a.* 1621. [Un-1 2.] **1.** Unexampled, unequalled. *arch.* **2.** Not decorated with a pattern 1884.

Unpau·sing *ppl. a.* [Un-1 4] 1837. **Unpa·ve** *v.* [Un-2 2] 1598. **Unpa·ved** *ppl. a.* [Un-1 2] 1533. **Unpavi·lioned** *a.* [Un-1 3] Shelley. **Unpa·wned** *ppl. a.* [Un-1 2] 1638. **Unpay·able** *a.* [Un-1 1] 1463. **Unpay·ing** *ppl. a.* [Un-1 4] 1682. **Unpea·ce** (*arch.*) [Un-1 6] ME. **Unpea·ceable** *a.* (now *rare*) [Un-1 1] 1520, **-ness** 1475, **-ably** *adv.* **Unpea·ceful** *a.* [Un-1 1] 1611. **Unpeda·ntic** *a.* [Un-1 1] 1796. **Unpe·destal** *v.* [Un-2 3] 1821. **Unpe·digreed** *ppl. a.* [Un-1 2] 1827. **Unpee·led** *ppl. a.* [Un-1 2] 1599. **Unpee·red** *ppl. a.* (*arch.*) [Un-1 2] 1602. **Unpe·g** *v.* [Un-2 2 b] Shaks. **Unpe·n** *v.* [Un-2 3] 1592. **Unpe·netrated** *ppl. a.* [Un-1 2] 1781. **Unpe·nitent** *a.* (now *rare*) [Un-1 1] 1546. **Unpe·nsioned** *ppl. a.* [Un-1 2] Pope. **Unpe·nt** *ppl. a.* [Un-1 2] Shelley. **Unpeo·ple** *v.* [Un-2 2] 1533. **Unpeo·pled** *ppl. a.* [Un-1 2] 1586. **Unpercei·vable** *a.* [Un-1 1] late ME., **-ably** *adv.* **Unpercei·ved** *ppl. a.* [Un-1 2] ME., **-ly** *adv.* **Unpercei·ving** *ppl. a.* [Un-1 4] 1723. **Unperce·ptive** *a.* [Un-1 1] 1668.

Unpe·rch, *v.* 1579. [Un-2 3.] *trans.* To dislodge from a perch.

Either rowse the Deer, or vnpearch the Phesant Lyly. If he but offers to tune his note contrary to the true Dialect of State he is straight unperched 1659.

†**Unpe·rfect** *a.* [Un-1 1] –1858. **Unpe·rfected** *ppl. a.* [Un-1 2] 1513. **Unpe·rforated** *ppl. a.* [Un-1 2] 1676. **Unperfo·rmed** *ppl. a.* [Un-1 2] 1442. **Unperfo·rming** *ppl. a.* [Un-1 4] 1670. **Unperfumed** *ppl. a.* [Un-1 2] 1706. **Unpe·rilous** *a.* [Un-1 1] 1621. **Unpe·rishable** *a.* (now *rare*) [Un-1 1] 1548. **Unpe·rished** *ppl. a.* [Un-1 2] late ME. **Unpe·rishing** *ppl. a.* [Un-1 4] 1561. **Unpe·rmanent** *a.* [Un-1 1] 1630. **Unpermi·tted** *ppl. a.* [Un-1 2] 1598. **Unperple·x** *v.* [Un-2 1] 1631.

Unperple·xed, *ppl. a.* 1558. [Un-1 2.] **1.** Not puzzled or made uncertain. **2.** Not involved or intricate 1653.

2. That good, plain, unperplext Catechism, that is printed with the old service book Walton.

Unpe·rsecuted *ppl. a.* [Un-1 2] Milt. **Unpersua·dable** *a.* [Un-1 1] 1586, **-ness. Unpersua·ded** *ppl. a.* [Un-1 2] 1534. **Unpersua·sive** *a.* [Un-1 1] Richardson, **-ly** *adv.* **Unpertu·rbed** *ppl. a.* [Un-1 2] late ME., **-ness. Unperve·rted** *ppl. a.* [Un-1 2] 1653. **Unpe·stered** *ppl. a.* [Un-1 2] 1588. **U:nphiloso·phical** *a.* [Un-1 1] Milt., **-ly** *adv.* **Unphone·tic** *a.* [Un-1 1] 1857. **Unphra·sed** *ppl. a.* [Un-1 2] 1663. **Unphy·sical** *a.* [Un-1 1] 1593. **Unphy·sicked** *ppl. a.* [Un-1 2] 1596.

Unpi·ck, *v.* late ME. [Un-2 7.] †**1.** *trans.* To pick (a lock); to open (a door, etc.) in this way –1661. **2.** To take out (stitches); to undo the sewing of (a seam, garment, etc.) 1809.

Unpi·ckable *a.* [Un-1 1] 1612. **Unpi·cked** *ppl. a.* [Un-1 2] 1587. **Unpi·cketed** *ppl. a.* [Un-1 2] 1860. **U:npicture·sque** *a.* [Un-1 1] 1791, **-ly** *adv.*, **-ness. Unpie·rceable** *a.* [Un-1 1] 1600. **Unpie·rced** *ppl. a.* [Un-1 2] 1593.

Unpi·le, *v.* 1611. [Un-2 1, 3.] *trans.* To remove from a pile. **b.** Mil. *U. arms*, a command to detach rifles from stacks in which they are interlocked 1847.

Unpi·llowed *ppl. a.* [Un-1 2] Milt. **Unpi·loted** *ppl. a.* [Un-1 2] Coleridge.

Unpi·n, *v.* ME. [Un-2 1, 2.] **1.** *trans.* To withdraw the pin or bolt of (a door). **2.** To remove pins or pegs from; to unfasten or detach in this way 1611. **3.** To undo the dress of (a person) by removing pins 1604. **4.** To remove a pin or pins from (a garment, etc.); to detach by removing a pin or pins 1605.

1. Þe porter vnpynned þe ȝate LANGL. 2. When the upper part of the frame..is unpinned and removed 1825. 3. Mrs. Etoff, who had the honour to pin and u. the Lady Bellaston FIELDING. 4. She..began to u. her hood STEELE.

Unpi·nioned *ppl. a.* [UN-1 2] 1593. **Unpi·teous** *a.* [UN-1 1] late ME., **-ly** *adv.* **Unpi·tiable** *a.* [UN-1 1] 1646. **Unpi·tied** *ppl. a.* [UN-1 2] SIDNEY. **Unpi·tiful** *a.* [UN-1 1] 1449, **-ly** *adv.* **Unpi·tying** *ppl. a.* [UN-1 4] DRAYTON, **-ly** *adv.* **Unpla·ce** *v.* (now *rare*) [UN-2 3] 1554.

Unpla·ced, *ppl. a.* 1512. [UN-1 2.] **1.** Not assigned to, or set in, a definite place. **b.** *Racing.* Not among the placed competitors 1881. **2.** Not appointed to a place or office 1558.

Unpla·gued *ppl. a.* [UN-1 2] 1550. **Unplai·t** *v.* [UN-2 1] CHAUCER. **Unplai·ted** *ppl. a.* [UN-1 2] 1659. **Unpla·ned** *ppl. a.* [UN-1 2] 1810. **Unpla·nted** *ppl. a.* [UN-1 2] late ME. **Unpla·stered** *ppl. a.* [UN-1 2] 1648. **Unplau·sible** *a.* [UN-1 1] 1575, **-bly** *adv.* **Unplay·able** *a.* [UN-1 1] 1833. **Unplay·ed** *ppl. a.* [UN-1 2] 1850. **Unplea·dable** *a.* [UN-1 1] 1716.

Unplea·sant, *a.* 1535. [UN-1 1.] **1.** Not pleasant, disagreeable: **a.** To the senses 1538. **b.** To the mind or feelings 1535. **2.** Unentertaining, unfacetious 1712. **3.** Unamiable 1654.

1. Flies prefer u. smells 1879. **b.** Tho' your Majesty permitts me to wryte even on ane u. subject 1721. A commission which would require them to deliver many u. truths 1839. Hence **Unplea·santly** *adv.*

Unplea·santness. 1548. [UN-1 6.] The quality of being unpleasant. **b.** Ill-feeling or unpleasant relations between persons; an instance of this 1830. So **Unplea·santry** 1830.

Unplea·sed *ppl. a.* (now *rare*) [UN-1 2] 1450. **Unplea·sing** *ppl. a.* [UN-1 4] 1480, **-ly** *adv.*, **-ness.** **Unplea·surable** *a.* [UN-1 1] 1768, **-ably** *adv.* **Unplea·ted** *ppl. a.* [UN-1 2] 1612. **Unple·dged** *ppl. a.* [UN-1 2] 1605. **Unpli·able** *a.* [UN-1 1] late ME., **-ness.** **Unpli·ancy** [UN-1 6] 1737. **Unpli·ant** *a.* [UN-1 1] 1624. **Unplou·ghed** *ppl. a.* [UN-1 2] 1580. **Unplu·cked** *ppl. a.* [UN-1 2] 1568. **Unplu·mbed** *ppl. a.* [UN-1 2] 1623. **Unplu·me** *v.* [UN-2 3] 1587. **Unplu·med** *ppl. a.* [UN-1 2] 1601. **Unplu·ndered** *ppl. a.* [UN-1 2] 1655. **Unpo·cket** *v.* [UN-2 3] 1611. **Unpoe·tic** 1619, **-al** 1746, *adjs.* [UN-1 1], **-ly** *adv.*

Unpoi·nted, *ppl. a.* 1574. [UN-1 2.] †**1.** Of garments: Not tagged for tying. **2.** Unpunctuated 1593. **b.** Without vowel points or diacritical marks 1640. **3.** Without point; dull or irrelevant 1632. **b.** Without a point, not sharpened at the end 1887. **4.** Not pointed *at* 1555.

Unpoi·sed *ppl. a.* [UN-1 2] 1600. **Unpoi·son** *v.* [UN-2 4 b] 1598. **Unpoi·soned** *ppl. a.* [UN-1 2] 1821. **Unpo·larized** *ppl. a.* [UN-1 2] 1827. **Unpoli·ced** *ppl. a.* [UN-1 2] 1797. **Unpo·licied** *ppl. a.* [UN-1 2] –1738. **Unpo·lishable** *a.* [UN-1 1] 1687. **Unpo·lished** *ppl. a.* [UN-1 2] late ME.

Unpoli·te, *a.* 1646. [UN-1 1.] †**1.** Without refinement, unpolished –1727. †**b.** Unfashionable, inelegant –1753. **2.** Lacking in politeness; impolite 1709. Hence **Unpoli·tely** *adv.*, **-ness.**

Unpo·litic *a.* (now *rare*) [UN-1 1] 1548. **Unpoli·tical** *a.* [UN-1 1] 1643. **Unpo·llarded** *ppl. a.* [UN-1 2] 1830. **Unpo·lled** *ppl. a.* [UN-1 2] 1647. **Unpollu·ted** *ppl. a.* [UN-1 2] SHAKS. **Unpo·pe** *v.* [UN-2 4 b] 1563. **Unpo·pular** *a.* [UN-1 1] 1647. **Un:popula·rity** [UN-1 6] 1735. **Unpo·pulated** *ppl. a.* [UN-1 2] 1885. **Unpo·pulous** *a.* [UN-1 1] SCOTT. **Unpo·rtable** *a.* [UN-1 1] –1782. **Unpo·rtioned** *ppl. a.* [UN-1 2] 1744.

Unposse·ssed, *ppl. a.* 1586. [UN-1 2.] **1.** Not possessed or owned; unoccupied 1594. †**2.** Unprejudiced –1685. **3.** Not having possession *of* something 1795.

1. A grace by thee unsought and unpossest WORDSW. 2. To any thinking and u. Man 1685.

Unpo·ssible *a.* (now *dial.*) [UN-1 1] late ME. **Unpo·sted** *ppl. a.* [UN-1 2] 1860. **Unpow·dered** *ppl. a.* [UN-1 2] 1440. **Unpow·erful** *a.* (*rare*) [UN-1 1] 1611. **Unpra·cticable** *a.* [UN-1 1] 1647, **-ness.** **Unpra·ctical** *a.* [UN-1 1] 1637, **-ly** *adv.*, **-ness.**

Unpra·ctised, *ppl. a.* 1540. [UN-1 2.] **1.** Not familiarized or skilled by practice; inexpert 1551. **2.** Not practised; unemployed 1540.

1. The most destructive arms in..u. hands 1748. 2. The old prouerbe..is not lefte vnpractised 1540.

Unprai·sed *ppl. a.* [UN-1 2] late ME. **Unpray·** *v.* [UN-2 1] 1611. **Unpray·ed** *ppl. a.* [UN-1 2] late ME. **Unprea·ch** *v.* [UN-2 1] 1692. **Unprea·ching** *ppl. a.* [UN-1 4] 1549. **Unpreca·rious** *a.* [UN-1 1] 1712.

Unpre·cedented, *ppl. a.* 1623. [UN-1 2.] For which no precedent can be cited; of an unexampled kind, degree, etc. Hence **Unpre·cedented-ly** *adv.*, **-ness.**

Unpreci·se *a.* [UN-1 1] 1782, **-ly** *adv.* **Unpredi·ctable** *a.* [UN-1 1] 1857. **Unpre·faced** *ppl. a.* [UN-1 2] 1801. **Unprefe·rred** *ppl. a.* [UN-1 2] 1483. **Unpre·gnant** *a.* [UN-1 1] SHAKS.

Unpre·judiced, *ppl. a.* 1613. [UN-1 2.] †**1.** Not affected prejudicially. **2.** Free from prejudice 1637. Hence **Unpre·judiced-ly** *adv.*, **-ness.**

Unprela·tical *a.* [UN-1 1] 1647. **Unpreme·ditate** *ppl. a.* (*arch.*) [UN-1 2] 1551. **Unpreme·ditated** *ppl. a.* [UN-1 2] 1591, **-ly** *adv.*, **-ness.** **Unpreo·ccupied** *ppl. a.* [UN-1 2] 1827.

Unprepa·re, *v. rare.* 1598. [UN-2 1, or UN-1 7.] **1.** *trans.* To undo the preparation of. **2.** To make unprepared; to unfit 1645.

Unprepa·red, *ppl. a.* 1549. [UN-1 2.] **1.** Of persons: Not in a state of preparation; not ready (for defence, reply, etc.). **b.** Const. *for*, or *to* with inf. 1549. **c.** *spec.* Not prepared for death 1594. **2.** Left, introduced, taken, etc., without special preparation 1595.

2. Events..appear to us very often original, u., single, and un-relative 1751. So **Unprepa·red-ly** *adv.*, **-ness.**

U:nprepose·ssed *ppl. a.* [UN-1 2] 1648. **U:nprepose·ssing** *ppl. a.* [UN-1 4] 1816. **Unpre·scient** *a.* [UN-1 1] 1866. **Unprescri·bed** *ppl. a.* [UN-1 2] 1642. **Unprese·ntable** *a.* [UN-1 1] 1828, **-ness.** **U:npresentabi·lity** [UN-1 6] 1882. **Unprese·nted** *ppl. a.* [UN-1 2] 1523. **Unprese·rved** *ppl. a.* [UN-1 2] 1648. **Unpre·ssed** *ppl. a.* [UN-1 2] 1552. **Unpresu·ming** *ppl. a.* [UN-1 4] 1770, **-ness.** **Unpresu·mptuous** *a.* [UN-1 1] 1704, **-ly** *adv.* **Unprete·nding** *ppl. a.* [UN-1 4] 1697, **-ly** *adv.*, **-ness.** **Unprete·ntious** *a.* [UN-1 1] 1859, **-ly** *adv.*, **-ness.** **Unpre·tty** *a.* [UN-1 1] MME. D'ARBLAY. **Unprevai·ling** *ppl. a.* [UN-1 4] SHAKS. **Unpreve·ntable** *a.* [UN-1 1] 1616, **-ness, -ably** *adv.* **Unpreve·nted** *ppl. a.* [UN-1 2] 1585. **Unpri·ced** *ppl. a.* [UN-1 2] 1857. **Unpri·cked** *ppl. a.* [UN-1 2] 1588. **Unprie·st** *v.* [UN-2 4 b] 1550. **Unprie·stly** *a.* [UN-1 1] 1537. **Unpri·mitive** *a.* [UN-1 1] 1708. **Unpri·ncely** *a.* [UN-1 1] 1536.

Unpri·ncipled, *ppl. a.* 1634. [UN-1 2.] †**1.** Not instructed or grounded *in* MILT. **2.** Not possessed of fixed, sound, or honourable principles of conduct 1644. **3.** Based upon, or exhibiting want of principle 1782.

1. I do not think my sister so..unprincipl'd in vertues book MILT. 2. A couple of u. rascals 1878. 3. Many who are esteemed good sort of persons, but whose goodness is u. 1782.

Unpri·ntable *a.* [UN-1 1] 1871. **Unpri·nted** *ppl. a.* [UN-1 2] MORE. **Unpri·son** *v.* [UN-2 3] late ME. **Unpri·vileged** *ppl. a.* [UN-1 2] 1590.

†**Unpri·zable,** *a.* 1601. [UN-1 1.] **1.** Not to be prized; of little worth. SHAKS. **2.** Beyond all price; inestimable –1634.

1. A bawbling Vessell..For shallow draught and bulke vnprizable SHAKS.

Unpri·zed *ppl. a.* [UN-1 2] 1445. **Unpro·bed** *ppl. a.* [UN-1 2] 1827. **Unproclai·med** *ppl. a.* [UN-1 2] 1648. **Unprocu·rable** *a.* [UN-1 1] 1607. **Unprodu·ced** *ppl. a.* [UN-1 2] 1674. **Unprodu·ctive** *a.* [UN-1 1] BURKE, **-ly** *adv.*, **-ness.** **Unprofa·ned** *ppl. a.* [UN-1 2] 1650. **Unprofe·ssed** *ppl. a.* [UN-1 2] late ME.

Unprofe·ssional, *a.* and *sb.* 1806. [UN-1 1, 6.] **A.** *adj.* Not professional. **b.** Contravening the rules or etiquette of the profession concerned 1899. **B.** *sb.* One who belongs to no profession or is outside the one in question 1863. Hence **Unprofe·ssionally** *adv.*

Unpro·fit (now *rare*) [UN-1 6] late ME. **Unpro·fitable** *a.* [UN-1 1] ME., **-ness, -ably** *adv.* **Unpro·fited** *ppl. a.* [UN-1 2] SHAKS. **Unpro·fiting** *ppl. a.* [UN-1 4] 1616. **Unprogre·ssive** *a.* [UN-1 1] 1851, **-ly** *adv.*, **-ness.** **Unprohi·bited** *ppl. a.* [UN-1 2] MILT. **Unproje·cted** *ppl. a.* [UN-1 2] CROMWELL. **Unproli·fic** *a.* [UN-1 1] 1676. **Unpro·mise** *v.* (now *rare*) [UN-2 1] 1598.

Unpro·mising, *ppl. a.* 1632. [UN-1 4.] **1.** Not giving promise of excellence or success 1663. †**2.** Unprepossessing –1669. Hence **Unpro·misingly** *adv.*

Unpro·mpted *ppl. a.* [UN-1 2] 1659. **Unpro·mulgated** *ppl. a.* [UN-1 2] 1802. **Unpronou·nceable** *a.* [UN-1 1] SCOTT. **Unpronou·nced** *ppl. a.* [UN-1 2] 1611. **Unpro·per** *a.* (now *dial.*) [UN-1 1] late ME., †**-ly** *adv.* **Unpro·pertied** *ppl. a.* [UN-1 2] 1793. **Unprophe·tic** *a.* [UN-1 1] 1725. **Unpropi·tious** *a.* [UN-1 1] 1699. **Unpropo·rtionable** *a.* [UN-1 1] –1766. **Unpropo·rtionate** *a.* (now *rare*) [UN-1 1] 1581, **-ly** *adv.* **Unpropo·rtioned** *ppl. a.* [UN-1 2] 1586. **Unpro·pped** *ppl. a.* [UN-1 2] 1616. **Unpro·secuted** *ppl. a.* [UN-1 2] 1655. **Unprospe·rity** [UN-1 6] 1628. **Unpro·sperous** *a.* [UN-1 1] 1578, **-ly** *adv.*, **-ness.** **Unpro·stituted** *ppl. a.* [UN-1 2] 1721. **Unprote·cted** *ppl. a.* [UN-1 2] 1593, **-ly** *adv.*, **-ness.** **Unpro·testant** *a.* [UN-1 1] 1841. **Unpro·testantize** *v.* [UN-2 4 c] 1833. **Unprou·d** *a.* [UN-1 1] 1570. **Unpro·vable** *a.* [UN-1 1] late ME.

Unpro·ved, *ppl. a.* 1440. [UN-1 2.] **1.** Not tested, untried. Now *rare.* **2.** Not demonstrated to be true or genuine 1532.

1. For to find a fresh vnproued knight SPENSER.

Unprovi·ded, *ppl. a.* 1514. [UN-1 2.] **1.** Not furnished, supplied, or equipped (*with* something) 1523. **b.** Not provided for 1640. **2.** Not in a state of preparation or readiness; unprepared 1525. **3.** Against which provision has not been made; unforeseen 1514. **4.** Not provided *for* 1575. **5.** Not furnished, supplied, or made ready 1621.

1. Courts are seldom u. of persons under this character SWIFT. Since you will go, you must not go u. 1760. Assailants..u. with regular means of attack KINGLAKE. 2. If they dye vnprouided SHAKS. 3. Sodayne tempeste, and unprovyded colde 1514. The u. expenditure of the year 1841. 4. The necessary Subsistence of the household was u. for CLARENDON. Hence **Unprovi·ded-ly** *adv.*, **-ness.**

Unprovo·cative *a.* [UN-1 1] 1821. †**Unprovo·ke** *v.* [UN-2 1] SHAKS. **Unprovo·ked** *ppl. a.* [UN-1 2] 1585, **-ly** *adv.*, **-ness.** **Unprovo·king** *ppl. a.* [UN-1 4] 1710. **Unprude·ntial** *a.* [UN-1 1] 1650. **Unpru·ned** *ppl. a.* [UN-1 2] 1588. **Unpu·blishable** *a.* [UN-1 1] 1815, **-ably** *adv.* **Unpu·blished** *ppl. a.* [UN-1 2] SHAKS. **Unpu·lled** [*ppl. a.* UN-1 2] 1440. **Unpu·nctual** *a.* [UN-1 1] 1740, **-ly** *adv.* **Unpunctua·lity** [UN-1 6] 1828. **Unpu·nctuated** *ppl. a.* [UN-1 2] 1866. **Unpu·nishable** *a.* [UN-1 1] 1531. **Unpu·nished** *ppl. a.* [UN-1 2] ME. **Unpu·rchas(e)able** *a.* [UN-1 1] 1611. **Unpu·rchased** *ppl. a.* [UN-1 2] 1545. **Unpu·rged** *ppl. a.* [UN-1 2] 1530. **Unpu·rified** *ppl. a.* [UN-1 2] 1574. **Unpu·rposed** *ppl. a.* [UN-1 2] 1570.

Unpu·rse, *v.* late ME. [UN-2 3, 2, 1.] **1.** *trans.* To take (money) out of a purse; to disburse. **2.** To steal the purse of 1827. **3.** To relax from a pursed state. Also *intr.* 1871.

3. Now I permit your plump lips to u. BROWNING.

Unpursu·ed *ppl. a.* [UN-1 2] 1469. **Unpu·t** *ppl. a.* [UN-1 2] 1470. **Unpu·trefied** *ppl. a.* [UN-1 2] 1579. **Unquai·ling** *ppl. a.* [UN-1 4] 1836, **-ly** *adv.* **Unqua·kerish** *a.* [UN-1 1] LAMB. **Unqua·lifiable** *a.* [UN-1 1] 1734.

Unqua·lified, *ppl. a.* 1556. [UN-1 2.] **1.** Not qualified or fitted; not having the necessary qualifications. **2.** Not endowed with specific qualities 1678. **3.** Not modified, limited, or restricted 1796. Hence **Unqua·lified-ly** *adv.*, **-ness.**

Unqual·lify *v.* [UN-2 1] 1655. **Unqua·litied** *ppl. a.* (*rare*) [UN-1 2] SHAKS. **Unqua·rried** *ppl. a.* [UN-1 2] 1788. **Unquee·n** *v.* [UN-2 2, 4 b] 1579. **Unquee·nly** *a.* [UN-1 1] 1865. **Unque·lled** *ppl. a.* [UN-1 2] late ME. **Unque·nchable** *a.* [UN-1 1] late ME., **-ably** *adv.* **Unque·nched** *ppl. a.* [UN-1 2] ME.

Unque·stionable, *a.* 1600. [UN-1 1.] **1.** Having an assured character or position; unexceptionable 1603. **2.** Incapable of being doubted or disputed; indubitable, certain 1631. **3.** Not submitting to question (*rare*) 1600.

2. Authentic facts, and u. evidence 1782. 3. An vnquestionable spirit SHAKS. Hence **Unque·stionably** *adv.*

Unque·stioned *ppl. a.* [UN-1 2] 1601. **Unque·stioning** *ppl. a.* [UN-1 4] 1828, **-ly** *adv.* **Unqui·ckened** *ppl. a.* [UN-1 2] 1610.

Unqui·et, *sb.* 1551. [UN-1 6.] Absence or want of quiet; disquiet, disturbance.

Unqui·et, *a.* 1523. [UN-1 1.] **1.** Marked by unrest, disturbance, or disorder. **2.** Of persons, emotions, etc.: Restless, active, turbulent 1526. **3.** Perturbed, anxious, not at ease 1535. Hence **Unqui·et-ly** *adv.*, **-ness.**

Unqui·et, *v. arch.* late ME. [UN-2 1.] *trans.* To disturb the quiet of; to disquiet.

Unqui·vering *ppl. a.* [UN-1 4] 1811. **Unquo·table** *a.* [UN-1 1] 1843. **Unquo·ted** *ppl. a.* [UN-1 2] 1825. **Unrai·sed** *ppl. a.* [UN-1 2] 1523. **Unra·ked** *ppl. a.* [UN-1 2] SHAKS. **Unra·nsacked** *ppl. a.* [UN-1 2] 1529. **Unra·nsomed** *ppl. a.* [UN-1 2] 1554. **Unra·table** *a.* [UN-1 1] 1629. **Unra·ted** *ppl. a.* [UN-1 2] 1648. **Unra·tified** *ppl. a.* [UN-1 2] 1611. **Unra·vaged** *ppl. a.* [UN-1 2] BURKE.

Unra·vel, *v.* 1603. [UN-2 1.] **1.** *trans.* To undo from a ravelled, tangled or woven state; to disentangle; to untwist (rope). †**2.** *fig.* To reverse, undo, annul –1766. **3.** To free from intricacy or obscurity; to reveal or disclose 1660. **4.** *intr.* To come undone; to become unknit or disentangled 1650.

4. As the burning threads Of woven cloud u. in pale air SHELLEY. Hence **Unra·veller. Unra·velling** *vbl. sb.* **Unra·velment.**

Unra·vished *ppl. a.* [UN-[1] 2] 1622. **Unra·zored** *ppl. a.* [UN-[1] 2] MILT. **Unrea·chable** *a.* [UN-[1] 1] 1593, **-ably** *adv.* **Unrea·ched** *ppl. a.* [UN-[1] 2] 1611.

Unrea·d, *ppl. a.* 1456. [UN-[1] 2.] **1.** Not read; unperused. **2.** Not instructed by reading 1606. **b.** Const. *in* 1602.

2. The clown u., and half-read gentleman DRYDEN. **b.** Algernon was u. in the hearts of women MEREDITH.

Unrea·dable, *a.* 1802. [UN-[1] 1.] **1.** Too dull or distasteful to read. **2.** Illegible 1830. Hence **Unreadabi·lity, Unrea·dableness.**

Unrea·dy, *a.*[1] ME. [UN-[1] 1.] **1.** Not in a state of readiness or preparation. **2.** Not prepared or made ready. late ME. **3.** Undressed; in deshabille. *Obs.* or *dial.* 1591. **4.** Given to hesitation; irresolute; slow 1594.

1. For the most part our witts be best When wee be takyne most vnrediest 1560. I express'd my self u. to vote for it 1707. Hence **Unrea·dily** *adv.* **Unrea·diness.**

Unrea·dy, *a.*[2] 1580. [Later form of late ME. *unredy*, f. UN-[1] 1.] = REDELESS *a.* (only as an epithet of Ethelred II, d. 1016).

Unreal (ʊnrī·ăl), *a.* 1605. [UN-[1] 1.] Not real. **b.** *Gram.* Applied to suppositions implying non-fulfilment.

Hence horrible shadow, Vnreall mock'ry hence SHAKS.

Unreali·stic *a.* [UN-[1] 1] 1865. **Unrea·lity** [UN-[1] 6] 1751. **Unre·alizable** *a.* [UN-[1] 1] 1840. **Unre·alize** *v.* [UN-[2] 1] 1804. **Unre·alized** *ppl. a.* [UN-[1] 2] 1803. **Unrea·ped** *ppl. a.* [UN-[1] 2] 1577.

Unrea·son. ME. [UN-[1] 6.] †**1.** Injustice, impropriety –1609. **2.** *Abbot of U.*: see ABBOT. *Hist.* 1496. **3.** Absence of reason; indisposition or inability to act or think rationally or reasonably 1827.

Unrea·sonable, *a.* ME. [UN-[1] 1.] **1.** Not having the faculty of reason; irrational. **2.** Not acting in accordance with reason or good sense; claiming or expecting more than is reasonable. late ME. **3.** Not based on reason or good sense ME. **4.** Going beyond what is reasonable or equitable; excessive. late ME. Hence **Unrea·sonableness. Unrea·sonably** *adv.*

Unrea·soned *ppl. a.* [UN-[1] 2] 1582. **Unrea·soning** *ppl. a.* [UN-[1] 4] 1751, **-ly** *adv.* **Unrebe·llious** *a.* [UN-[1] 1] 1570. **Unrebu·ked** *ppl. a.* [UN-[1] 2] 1445. **Unreca·lled** *ppl. a.* [UN-[1] 2] 1601. **Unrecei·pted** *ppl. a.* [UN-[1] 2] 1881. **Unrecei·vable** *a.* [UN-[1] 1] 1611. **Unrecei·ved** *ppl. a.* [UN-[1] 2] 1540. **Unrece·ptive** *a.* [UN-[1] 1] 1778. **Unre·ckoned** *ppl. a.* [UN-[1] 2] ME. **Unreclai·mable** *a.* [UN-[1] 1] 1577, **-ably** *adv.* **Unreclai·med** *ppl. a.* [UN-[1] 2] 1470. **Unrecogni·tion** [UN-[1] 6] 1869. **Unre·cognizable** *a.* [UN-[1] 1] 1817, **-ably** *adv.* **Unre·cognized** *ppl. a.* [UN-[1] 2] 1813. **Unre·cognizing** *ppl. a.* [UN-[1] 4] 1814, **-ly** *adv.* **Unrecolle·cted** *ppl. a.* [UN-[1] 2] 1733. **U:nrecomme·nded** *ppl. a.* [UN-[1] 2] 1550. **Unre·compensed** *ppl. a.* [UN-[1] 2] 1469. **Unre·concilable** *a.* [UN-[1] 1] 1577. **Unre·conciled** *ppl. a.* [UN-[1] 2] 1450. **Unreconstru·cted** *ppl. a.* [UN-[1] 2] 1869. **Unreco·rded** *ppl. a.* [UN-[1] 2] 1585.

Unreco·verable, *a.* late ME. [UN-[1] 1.] †**1.** That cannot be recovered; completely lost –1650. **2.** That cannot be recovered from; past remedy 1561.

Unreco·vered *ppl. a.* [UN-[1] 2] 1611. **Unrecrui·ted** *ppl. a.* [UN-[1] 2] 1649. **Unre·ctified** *ppl. a.* [UN-[1] 2] 1638. **Unredee·mable** *a.* [UN-[1] 1] 1584.

Unredee·med, *ppl. a.* 1548. [UN-[1] 2.] **1.** Not spiritually redeemed; unregenerate. **2.** Not recovered, ransomed, or released, by purchase or otherwise 1554. **b.** *spec.* Not recovered from pawn 1859. **3.** Having no redeeming qualities; unmitigated 1805. **4.** Of promises, etc.: Not performed or realized 1812.

Unredre·ssed *ppl. a.* [UN-[1] 2] 1563. **Unredu·ced** *ppl. a.* [UN-[1] 2] 1572. **Unredu·cible** *a.* [UN-[1] 1] MILT. **Unree·l** *v.* [UN-[2] 1] 1567. **Unree·lable** *a.* [UN-[1] 1] 1611. **Unree·ve** *v.* [UN-[2] 1] 1600.

Unrefi·ned, *ppl. a.* 1595. [UN-[1] 2.] **1.** Not refined in manners, feelings, or speech. **2.** Not freed from impurities; crude 1610.

Unrefle·cted *ppl. a.* [UN-[1] 2] 1670. **Unrefle·cting** *ppl. a.* [UN-[1] 4] 1665. **Unrefle·ctive** *a.* [UN-[1] 1] 1854, **-ly** *adv.* **Unrefo·rmable** *a.* [UN-[1] 1] 1583.

Unrefo·rmed, *ppl. a.* 1528. [UN-[1] 2.] **1.** Of faults, etc.: Not amended or made good. *arch.* **2.** Of persons, institutions, etc.: Not reformed or improved 1583. **3.** Of churches: Not affected by the Reformation 1788.

Unrefra·cted *ppl. a.* [UN-[1] 2] 1676. **Unrefre·shed** *ppl. a.* [UN-[1] 2] 1736. **Unrefu·ted** *ppl. a.* [UN-[1] 2] 1589. **Unre·gal** *a.* [UN-[1] 1] 1611. **Unrega·rded** *ppl. a.* [UN-[1] 2] 1561, **-ly** *adv.* **Unrega·rdful** *a.* [UN-[1] 1] 1598. **Unrega·rding** *ppl. a.* [UN-[1] 4] 1585.

Unrege·nerate, *a.* 1612. [UN-[1] 1.] Not regenerate; often used vaguely = wicked, bad. Also *sb.* So **Unrege·neracy** 1622. **Unrege·nerated** *ppl. a.* 1579. **U:nregenera·tion** 1625.

Unre·gistered *ppl. a.* [UN-[1] 2] 1604. **Unregre·tted** *ppl. a.* [UN-[1] 2] 1676. **Unre·gulated** *ppl. a.* [UN-[1] 2] 1721. **Unrehea·rsed** *ppl. a.* [UN-[1] 2] 1472. **Unrei·n** *v.* [UN-[2] 2 b] 1603. **Unrei·ned** *ppl. a.* [UN-[1] 2] 1609. **Unrejoi·cing** *ppl. a.* [UN-[1] 4] 1726.

Unrela·ted, *ppl. a.* 1661. [UN-[1] 2.] **1.** Not connected by blood; not akin. **2.** Not standing in relationship or connection 1668. **3.** Not recounted or told 1764.

2. Detached and u. offences BURKE.

Unre·lative *a.* [UN-[1] 1] 1751. **Unrela·xed** *ppl. a.* [UN-[1] 2] 1508. **Unrela·xing** *ppl. a.* [UN-[1] 4] 1781. **Unrelea·sed** *ppl. a.* [UN-[1] 2] late ME. **Unrele·nting** *ppl. a.* [UN-[1] 4] SHAKS., **-ly** *adv.*, **-ness.**

Unreli·able, *a.* 1840. [UN-[1] 1.] That cannot be relied upon.

Alcibiades..was too unsteady, and (according to Mr. Coleridge's coinage) 'u.' DE QUINCEY. Hence **Unreliabi·lity. Unreli·ableness.**

Unrelie·vable *a.* [UN-[1] 1] 1586.

Unrelie·ved, *ppl. a.* 1533. [UN-[1] 2.] **1.** Not freed from an obligation; not provided with relief; not aided or assisted. **2.** Lacking the relief of diversity or contrast; monotonous, not varied (*by* something) 1764. Hence **Unrelie·vedly** *adv.*

Unreli·gious, *a.* late ME. [UN-[1] 1.] **1.** Irreligious. Now *rare.* **2.** Not connected with or related to religion 1855.

2. The popular poetry..became profane, u., at length in some parts irreligious MILMAN. Hence **Unreli·gious-ly** *adv.*, **-ness.**

Unreli·nquished *ppl. a.* [UN-[1] 2] COWPER. **Unrelu·ctant** *a.* [UN-[1] 1] 1737, **-ly** *adv.* **Unrema·rkable** *a.* [UN-[1] 1] 1611. **Unrema·rked** *ppl. a.* [UN-[1] 2] 1793. **Unre·medied** *ppl. a.* [UN-[1] 2] 1563. **Unreme·mberable** *a.* [UN-[1] 1] 1803. **Unreme·mbered** *ppl. a.* [UN-[1] 2] late ME. **Unreme·mbering** *ppl. a.* [UN-[1] 4] 1540.

Unremi·tted, *ppl. a.* 1646. [UN-[1] 2.] **1.** Of debt, penalty, etc.: Not cancelled or forgiven. **2.** Of effort, etc.: Constant, sustained 1722. **b.** Of persons: Persistent in effort 1796. Hence **Unremi·ttedly** *adv.*

Unremi·tting, *ppl. a.* 1728. [UN-[1] 4.] Never relaxing or slackening; continuing with the same force; incessant. Hence **Unremi·ttingly** *adv.*, **-ness.**

Unremo·rseful *a.* [UN-[1] 1] 1611, **-ly** *adv.* **Unremo·vable** *a.* (now *rare*) [UN-[1] 1] 1500. **Unremo·ved** *ppl. a.* [UN-[1] 2] 1450. **Unremu·nerative** *a.* [UN-[1] 1] 1854, **-ly** *adv.*, **-ness.** **Unre·ndered** *ppl. a.* [UN-[1] 2] 1851. **Unrenew·ed** *ppl. a.* [UN-[1] 2] 1579. **Unrenow·ned** *ppl. a.* [UN-[1] 2] 1570. **Unre·nt** *ppl. a.* [UN-[1] 2] SPENSER. **Unrepai·d** *ppl. a.* [UN-[1] 2] 1655. **Unrepai·r** [UN-[1] 6] 1873. **Unrepai·red** *ppl. a.* [UN-[1] 2] 1523. **Unrepa·ssable** *a.* [UN-[1] 1] 1600. **Unrepea·lable** *a.* [UN-[1] 1] 1601. **Unrepea·led** *ppl. a.* [UN-[1] 2] 1479.

Unrepea·table, *a.* 1843. [UN-[1] 1.] **1.** Too coarse or indecent to be repeated. **2.** That cannot be done or made again 1880.

Unrepea·ted *ppl. a.* [UN-[1] 2] 1586. **Unrepe·lled** *ppl. a.* [UN-[1] 2] 1795. **Unrepe·ntance** [UN-[1] 6] late ME. **Unrepe·ntant** *a.* [UN-[1] 1] late ME., **-ly** *adv.* **Unrepe·nted** *ppl. a.* [UN-[1] 2] 1597. **Unrepe·nting** *ppl. a.* [UN-[1] 4] 1586, **-ly** *adv.*, **-ness. Unrepi·ning** *ppl. a.* [UN-[1] 4] 1637, **-ly** *adv.* **Unrepla·ceable** *a.* [UN-[1] 1] 1801. **Unreple·nished** *ppl. a.* [UN-[1] 2] 1562. **Unreply·ing** *ppl. a.* [UN-[1] 4] 1791. **Unrepo·rtable** *a.* [UN-[1] 1] 1611. **Unrepo·rted** *ppl. a.* [UN-[1] 2] 1622. **U:nreprese·ntative** *a.* [UN-[1] 1] 1832. **U:nrepprese·nted** *ppl. a.* [UN-[1] 2] 1681. **Unrepre·ssed** *ppl. a.* [UN-[1] 2] 1583. **Unreprie·vable** [UN-[1] 1] 1593, **-ably** *adv.* **Unreprie·ved** *ppl. a.* [UN-[1] 2] MILT. **Unrepri·nted** *ppl. a.* [UN-[1] 2] 1872. **Unreproa·ched** *ppl. a.* [UN-[1] 2] 1648. **Unreproa·chful** *a.* [UN-[1] 1] 1720, **-ly** *adv.* **Unreproa·ching** *ppl. a.* [UN-[1] 4] 1742. **U:nreprodu·cible** *a.* [UN-[1] 1] 1880. **Unrepro·vable** *a.* (now *rare*) [UN-[1] 1] late ME. **Unrepro·ved** *ppl. a.* [UN-[1] 2] late ME. **Unrepu·gnant** *a.* [UN-[1] 1] 1594. **Unreque·sted** *ppl. a.* [UN-[1] 2] 1576. **Unrequi·red** *ppl. a.* [UN-[1] 2] late ME. **Unrequi·table** *a.* [UN-[1] 1] 1584.

Unrequi·ted, *ppl. a.* 1542. [UN-[1] 2.] Not requited or reciprocated. Hence **Unrequi·ted-ly** *adv.*, **-ness.**

Unrese·mbling *ppl. a.* [UN-[1] 4] 1598. **Unrese·nted** *ppl. a.* [UN-[1] 2] 1705. **Unrese·ntful** *a.* [UN-[1] 1] 1773, **-ly** *adv.*, **-ness. Unrese·nting** *ppl. a.* [UN-[1] 4] 1716.

Unrese·rve. 1751. [UN-[1] 6.] Absence of reserve; frankness.

Unrese·rved, *ppl. a.* 1539. [UN-[1] 2.] **1.** Unrestricted, unlimited, absolute. **b.** Of seats, etc.: Not reserved for a particular person or persons. **2.** Frank, outspoken 1713. Hence **Unrese·rved-ly** *adv.*, **-ness.**

Unresi·sted *ppl. a.* [UN-[1] 2] 1526. **Unresi·stible** *a.* (now *rare*) [UN-[1] 1] 1608. **Unresi·sting** *ppl. a.* [UN-[1] 4] 1625, **-ly** *adv.*, **-ness. Unreso·lvable** *a.* [UN-[1] 1] 1611.

Unreso·lved, *ppl. a.* 1577. [UN-[1] 2.] **1.** Of questions, etc.: Undetermined, undecided, unsolved. **2.** Uncertain or undetermined how to act; irresolute 1594. **b.** Uncertain in opinion; undecided 1597. **3.** Not broken up or dissolved 1801.

Unrespe·ctable *a.* [UN-[1] 1] 1765. **Unrespe·cted** *ppl. a.* [UN-[1] 2] 1586.

Unrespe·ctive, *a.* Now *rare.* 1594. [UN-[1] 1.] †**1.** Inattentive, heedless –1633. **2.** Indifferent; undiscriminating 1606.

Unre·spirable *a.* [UN-[1] 1] 1807. **Unrespited** *ppl. a.* [UN-[1] 2] 1593. **Unrespo·nsible** *a.* [UN-[1] 1] 1634. **Unrespo·nsive** *a.* [UN-[1] 1] 1668, **-ly** *adv.*, **-ness.**

Unre·st. ME. [UN-[1] 6.] Absence of rest; disturbance, turmoil, trouble.

Unre·stful, *a.* late ME. [UN-[1] 1.] **1.** Restless, stirring, unquiet. **2.** Marked by absence of rest or quiet. late ME.

2. The bedde of a persone beeyng in greate debte is an unrestefull thyng 1542. So **Unre·stfulness.**

Unre·sting *ppl. a.* [UN-[1] 4] 1582. **Unresto·red** *ppl. a.* [UN-[1] 2] 1445. **Unrestrai·nable** *a.* [UN-[1] 1] late ME.

Unrestrai·ned, *ppl. a.* 1586. [UN-[1] 2.] **1.** Not kept in check or under control; allowed free course or vent 1600. **b.** Not restricted or limited 1622. **2.** Not subject (or subjected) to restraint in respect of action or conduct 1586. **b.** *appositive.* Without restraint; unrestrainedly 1596. **3.** Not constrained; easy, natural 1856. Hence **Unrestrai·nedly** *adv.*

Unrestri·cted *ppl. a.* [UN-[1] 2] 1766, **-ly** *adv.*, **-ness. Unreta·rded** *ppl. a.* [UN-[1] 2] 1615. **Unrete·ntive** *a.* [UN-[1] 1] 1748. **Unretra·cted** *ppl. a.* [UN-[1] 2] 1646. **Unretu·rnable** *a.* [UN-[1] 1] 1513.

Unretu·rned, *ppl. a.* 1589. [UN-[1] 2.] **1.** Not having returned or come back. **2.** Not reciprocated, unrequited 1643.

Unretu·rning *ppl. a.* [UN-[1] 4] 1628, **-ly** *adv.* **Unrevea·led** *ppl. a.* [UN-[1] 2] 1529. **Unrevea·ling** *ppl. a.* [UN-[1] 4] 1628. **Unreve·nged** *ppl. a.* [UN-[1] 2] 1533. **Unre·verenced** *ppl. a.* [UN-[1] 2] 1470.

Unre·verend, *a.* 1562. [UN-[1] 1.] †**1.** Irreverent –1820. **2.** Unworthy of reverence 1828.

1. They rather hold such curiosities to be impertinent—u. LAMB.

Unre·verent *a.* (now *rare*) [UN-[1] 1] late ME. **Unreve·rsed** *ppl. a.* [UN-[1] 2] SHAKS. **Unreview·ed** *ppl. a.* [UN-[1] 2] 1819. **Unrevi·sed** *ppl. a.* [UN-[1] 2] 1845. **Unrevi·ved** *ppl. a.* [UN-[1] 2] 1631. **Unrevo·ked** *ppl. a.* [UN-[1] 2] 1479. **Unrewa·rded** *ppl. a.* [UN-[1] 2] late ME. **Unrewa·rding** *ppl. a.* [UN-[1] 4] 1653. **Unrheto·rical** *a.* [UN-[1] 1] 1822. **Unrhy·med** *ppl. a.* [UN-[1] 2] 1828. **Unrhy·thmical** *a.* [UN-[1] 1] 1777, **-ly** *adv.* **Unri·bbed** *ppl. a.* [UN-[1] 2] 1834. **Unri·dden** *ppl. a.* [UN-[1] 2] 1574.

Unri·ddle, *v.* 1586. [UN-[2] 1.] *trans.* To solve, explain (a mystery, etc.). Hence **Unri·ddler.**

Unrid(e)able *a.* [UN-[1] 1] 1881. **Unri·fled** *ppl. a.* [UN-[1] 2] 1603. **Unri·g** *v.* [UN-[2] 2] 1579. **Unri·gged** *ppl. a.* [UN-[1] 2] 1593. ‡**Unri·ght** *sb.* [UN-[1] 6] –1610. **Unri·ght** *a.* (*arch.*) [UN-[1] 1] OE., **-ly** *adv.* **Unri·ghted** *ppl. a.* [UN-[1] 2] 1883.

Unri·ghteous, *a.* [OE. *unrihtwīs*, f. UN-[1] 1 + RIGHTEOUS.] Not righteous; unjust, wicked. Hence **Unri·ghteous-ly** *adv.*, **-ness.**

Unri·ghtful *a.* (now *rare*) [UN-[1] 1] ME., **-ly** *adv.*, **-ness. Unri·nged** *ppl. a.* [UN-[1] 2] 1510. **Unri·nsed** *ppl. a.* [UN-[1] 2] 1661.

Unri·p, *v.* 1513. [UN-[2] 7.] **1.** *trans.* To strip (a house or roof) of tiles, etc. Now *dial.* **2.** To lay open, slit up, or detach, by ripping 1534.

Unri·pe, *a.* [OE. *unripe*, f. Un-[1] 1 + *ripe* Ripe *a.*] †**1.** Of death: Premature –1633. **2.** Immature; not arrived at full development ME. **b.** Of fruit, etc.: Not matured by growth ME. Hence **Unri·pe-ly** *adv.*, **-ness.**

Unri·pened *ppl. a.* [Un-[1] 2] 1588. **Un-ri·ppled** *ppl. a.* [Un-[1] 2] 1816. **Unri·sen** *ppl. a.* [Un-[1] 2] 1806. **Unri·valled** *ppl. a.* [Un-[1] 2] Shaks. **Unri·ven** *ppl. a.* [Un-[1] 2] late ME.

Unri·vet, *v.* 1591. [Un-[2] 1.] **1.** *trans.* To unfasten or detach by the removal of rivets. **2.** *fig.* To undo, loosen, detach, relax, etc. 1620.

2. Before I had..unriveted my gaze 1853.

Unroa·sted *ppl. a.* [Un-[1] 2] late ME. **Unro·bbed** *ppl. a.* [Un-[1] 2] late ME. **Unro·be** *v.* [Un-[2] 2] 1598. **Unro·bed** *ppl. a.* [Un-[1] 2] 1861.

Unro·ll, *v.* late ME. [Un-[2] 1, 2, 5.] **1.** *trans.* To open out from a rolled-up state; to uncoil. **b.** To extend, spread out 1813. **c.** *fig.* To develop or expand fully 1854. **2.** *intr.* To become unrolled 1588. †**3.** *trans.* To remove from a roll or list. Shaks.

1. Time has unrowl'd her Glories to the last, And now clos'd up the Volume Dryden. The operation of unrolling the ancient papyri 1828. **2.** Euen as an Adder when she doth vnrowle Shaks.

Unro·lled *ppl. a.* [Un-[1] 2] 1573. **Un-Ro·man** *a.* [Un-[1] 1] 1682. **Unro·manized** *ppl. a.* [Un-[1] 2] 1771. **Unroma·ntic** *a.* [Un-[1] 1] 1731, **-ally** *adv.* **Unroo·f** *v.* [Un-[2] 2] 1598. **Unroo·fed** *ppl. a.* [Un-[1] 2] 1550. **Unroo·st** *v.* (now *rare*) [Un-[2] 3, 5] 1598.

Unroo·t, *v.* 1449. [Un-[2] 2 b, 5.] **1.** *trans.* To tear up by the roots, overthrow from a fixed base, displace by force 1570. **b.** *fig.* To eradicate, get rid of 1449. **2.** *intr.* To lose root-hold; to become detached (*rare*) 1616.

1. Whole plains unrooted from the main lands, by floods and tempests Goldsm. **b.** Vices be so euill to be vnrooted where they once take place 1574.

Unroo·ted *out, ppl. a.* [Un-[1] 2, Root *v.*[1] II. 2] 1550. **Unro·pe** *v.* [Un-[2] 2 b] 1883. **Unro·ped** *ppl. a.* [Un-[1] 2] 1881. **Unro·tted** *ppl. a.* [Un-[1] 2] 1440. **Unro·tten** *a.* [Un-[1] 1] 1574. †**Unrou·gh** *a.* [Un-[1] 1] –1605. **Unrou·nd** *a.* [Un-[1] 1] 1588.

Unrou·nd, *v.* 1611. [Un-[2] 4 a.] **1.** *trans.* To break or distort the roundness of 1611. **2.** *Phonetics.* To delabialize (a vowel) 1874.

Unrou·nded *ppl. a.* [Un-[1] 2] 1519. **Unrou·sed** *ppl. a.* [Un-[1] 2] 1802. **Unroy·al** *a.* [Un-[1] 1] 1586, **-ly** *adv.* **Unru·bbed** *ppl. a.* [Un-[1] 2] late ME. **Unru·ffle** *v.* [Un-[2] 1, 5] 1697.

Unru·ffled, *ppl. a.* 1659. [Un-[1] 2.] **1.** Not affected by any violent feeling; not agitated or disturbed; calm, unmoved. **2.** Not physically ruffled or made rough 1713. **3.** Not furnished with ruffles 1825. Hence **Unru·ffledness.**

Unru·ined *ppl. a.* [Un-[1] 2] 1610. **Unru·lable** *a.* [Un-[1] 1] 1680. **Unru·le** [Un-[1] 6] late ME. **Unru·led** *ppl. a.* [Un-[1] 2] late ME.

Unruly, *a.* late ME. [Un-[1] 1.] **1.** Not amenable to rule or discipline; ungovernable; disorderly, turbulent. **b.** Characterized by disorder or disquiet. late ME. **2.** Stormy, tempestuous, impetuous 1593.

1. Ouer kind fathers make vnruly daughters 1592. **b.** These vnrulye reuels 1582. **2.** U. blasts wait on the tender spring Shaks. Hence **Unru·liness.**

Unru·mple *v.* [Un-[2] 1] 1694. **Unru·mpled** *ppl. a.* [Un-[1] 2] 1641. **Unru·ng** *ppl. a.* [Un-[1] 2] late ME. **Unru·ptured** *ppl. a.* [Un-[1] 2] 1862. **Unru·sted** *ppl. a.* [Un-[1] 2] 1653. **Unru·th** (*arch.*) [Un-[1] 6] 1440. **U:nsacerdo·tal** *a.* [Un-[1] 1] 1847. **Unsa·cked** *ppl. a.* [Un-[1] 2] 1590. **Unsa·cred** *a.* [Un-[1] 1] 1608.

Unsa·ddle, *v.* late ME. [Un-[2] 2, 3.] **1.** *trans.* To remove the saddle from (a horse, etc.). Also *absol.* **2.** To dislodge from the saddle 1470.

Unsa·ddled *ppl. a.* [Un-[1] 2] 1623.

Unsa·fe, *a.* 1597. [Un-[1] 1.] **1.** Not enjoying safety; exposed to danger or risk 1605. **2.** Involving, or not free from, danger or risk 1597. **b.** Of places, etc.: Presenting or beset with dangers 1621. **3.** Unreliable; not to be trusted to 1601. So **Unsa·fe-ly** *adv.*, **-ness. Unsa·fety.**

Unsai·d *ppl. a.* [Un-[1] 1.] OE. **Unsai·led** *ppl. a.* [Un-[1] 2] 1572. **Unsai·lorlike** *a.* [Un-[1] 1] 1841. **Unsai·nt** *v.* [Un-[2] 4 b] 1572. **Unsai·nted** *ppl. a.* [Un-[1] 2] 1642. **Unsai·ntly** *a.* [Un-[1] 1] 1659. **Unsa·laried** *ppl. a.* [Un-[1] 2] Disraeli. **Unsa·leable** *a.* [Un-[1] 1] 1565; hence **Unsaleabi·lity. Unsa·lted** *ppl. a.* [Un-[1] 2] 1440. **Unsa·lutary** *a.* [Un-[1] 1] 1770. **Unsalu·ted** *ppl. a.* [Un-[1] 2] 1542. **Unsa·lvable** *a.* [Un-[1] 1] 1624. **Unsa·mpled** *ppl. a.* [Un-[1] 2] 1890. **Unsa·nctified** *ppl. a.* [Un-[1] 2] 1570. **Unsa·nctify** *v.* [Un-[2] 4 c] 1594. **Unsa·nctioned** *ppl. a.* [Un-[1] 2] 1784. **Unsa·ndalled** *ppl. a.* [Un-[1] 2] 1772. **Unsa·nguine** *a.* [Un-[1] 1] 1728. **Unsa·nitary** *a.* [Un-[1] 1] 1871. **Unsa·ted** *ppl. a.* [Un-[1] 2] 1693. **Unsa·tiable** *a.* (now *rare*) [Un-[1] 1] late ME. **Unsa·tiated** *ppl. a.* [Un-[1] 2] 1701. **U:nsatisfa·ction** [Un-[1] 6] 1643.

U:nsatisfa·ctory, *a.* 1637. [Un-[1] 1.] That fails to meet requirements or fulfil hopes; giving ground for complaint, criticism, or suspicion. Hence **Unsatisfa·ctorily** *adv.*, **-ness.**

Unsa·tisfiable *a.* [Un-[1] 1] 1539.

Unsa·tisfied, *ppl. a.* late ME. [Un-[1] 2.] **1.** Not satisfied in respect of something desired; not having obtained all that, or as much as, is wished for. **2.** Not satisfied in respect of information or knowledge; doubtful, dubious 1575. **3.** Not satisfied with some circumstance, result, etc.; displeased. Now *rare.* 1648. **4.** Of requirements, debts, doubts, etc.: Not settled 1588.

3. Mr. Freeman is..u. with the review 1883. Hence **Unsa·tisfiedness.**

Unsa·tisfying *ppl. a.* [Un-[1] 4] 1656. **Unsa·turated** *ppl. a.* [Un-[1] 2] 1758. **Unsa·ved** *ppl. a.* [Un-[1] 2] 1648.

Unsa·voury, *a.* ME. [Un-[1] 1.] †**1.** Flavourless; insipid; tasteless –1634. **2.** Disagreeable to the taste. late ME. **b.** Distasteful or offensive to the sense of smell, or to refined feelings 1539. **3.** Unpleasant, disagreeable, distasteful. late ME. **4.** Morally offensive; having an unpleasant or disagreeable character or association. late ME.

2. b. U. stench of oil Pope. **3.** All that tended to safety was vnsauory 1591. **4.** Grim anecdotes and u. details 1882. Hence **Unsa·vourily** *adv.* **Unsa·vouriness.**

Unsaw·n *ppl. a.* [Un-[1] 2] 1572. **Un-Sa·xon** *a.* [Un-[1] 1] 1848.

Unsay·, *v.* 1460. [Un-[2] 1, 5.] †**1.** *trans.* To deny. **2.** To retract, revoke (something said or written). Also *intr.* 1483.

Unsca·bbard *v.* [Un-[2] 3] 1611. **Unsca·bbarded** *ppl. a.* [Un-[1] 1] 1562. **Unsca·lable** *a.* [Un-[1] 1] 1579. **Unsca·le** *v.* [Un-[2] 2, 2 b] 1510. **Unsca·led** *ppl. a.* [Un-[1] 2] 1812. **Unsca·lped** *ppl. a.* [Un-[1] 2] 1814. **Unsca·nned** *ppl. a* [Un-[1] 2] 1577. **Unsca·red** *ppl. a.* [Un-[1] 2] 1742. **Unsca·rred** *ppl. a.* [Un-[1] 2] Shaks.

Unsca·thed, *ppl. a.* orig. *Sc.* and *rare.* late ME. [Un-[1] 2.] Uninjured.

Unsce·nted *ppl. a.* [Un-[1] 2] Cowper. **Unsce·ptred** *ppl. a.* [Un-[1] 2] 1752. **Unscho·larlike** *a.* [Un-[1] 1] 1616. **Unscho·larly** *a.* [Un-[1] 1] 1784. **Unschola·stic** *a.* [Un-[1] 1] 1690. **Unschoo·l** *v.* [Un-[2] 1] 1820.

Unschoo·led, *ppl. a.* and *a.* 1589. [Un-[1] 2, 3.] **1.** Uneducated, untaught 1594. **b.** *spec.* Not educated at school 1841. **2.** Untrained, undisciplined 1589. **b.** Not affected or made artificial by education; natural, spontaneous 1815.

Unsci·ence. late ME. [Un-[1] 6.] **1.** Lack of knowledge, ignorance. **2.** False conceptions or methods in scientific inquiry 1878.

1. It nys nat oonly vnscience, but it is deceiuable oppinioun Chaucer. **2.** Un-science, not Science, Adverse to Faith Pusey.

U:nscienti·fic, *a.* 1775. [Un-[1] 1.] Not versed in or concerned with science; now usu., not in accordance with or adopting scientific methods. So **Unscienti·fically** *adv.*

Unsci·ssored *ppl. a.* [Un-[1] 2] Shaks. **Unsco·rched** *ppl. a.* [Un-[1] 2] Shaks. **Unsco·red** *ppl. a.* [Un-[1] 2] 1596. **Unsco·rned** *ppl. a.* [Un-[1] 2] late ME. **Un-Sco·ttish** *a.* [Un-[1] 1] 1825. **Unscou·red** *ppl. a.* [Un-[1] 2] 1460. **Unscou·rged** *ppl. a.* [Un-[1] 2] late ME. **Unscra·ped** *ppl. a.* [Un-[1] 2] 1725. **Unscra·tched** *ppl. a.* [Un-[1] 2] Shaks. **Unscree·n** *v.* (now *rare*) [Un-[2] 3] 1628. **Unscree·ned** (*ppl.*) *a.* [Un-[1] 2, 3] 1648.

Unscrew·, *v.* 1605. [Un-[2] 1, 5.] **1.** *trans.* To slacken or detach by turning a screw; to remove or loosen (a screw) by turning. Also *fig.* **2.** *intr.* To be unscrewed or admit of being unscrewed 1822.

2. Courtiers will..u. their features 1761.

Unscri·ptural, *a.* 1653. [Un-[1] 1.] Not authorized by or based on Holy Scripture. So **Unscriptura·lity. Unscri·ptural-ly** *adv.*, **-ness.**

Unscru·bbed *ppl. a.* [Un-[1] 2] 1900. **Unscru·pulous** *a.* [Un-[1] 1] 1803, **-ly** *adv.*, **-ness Unscru·tinized** *ppl. a.* [Un-[1] 2] 1728. **Unscu·lptured** *ppl. a.* [Un-[1] 2] Shelley.

Unsea·l, *v.* late ME. [Un-[2] 1, 2.] **1.** *trans.* To remove the seal from; to break the seal of (a letter, etc.). **2.** To free from constraint; to allow free action to 1589. **b.** To free from the condition (or necessity) of remaining closed 1586. **3.** To disclose, reveal 1640.

Unsea·led, *ppl. a.* late ME. [Un-[1] 2.] **1.** Not stamped or marked with a seal. **2.** Not closed with a seal; not having a seal imposed or attached. late ME. **3.** *fig.* Not formally ratified 1601.

1. [They]..sell beere and wyne by vnlawful and vnsealled measures 1550. **2.** A promissory note u. Berkeley. **3.** Prophecies..unseal'd by any divine Sign 1665.

Unsea·m, *v.* 1592. [Un-[2] 2.] **1.** *trans.* To undo the seams of; to rip. **2.** *fig.* To rip up, tear open 1605.

2. Till he vnseam'd him from the Naue to th' Chops Shaks.

Unsea·manlike *a.* [Un-[1] 1] 1726. **Unsea·med** *ppl. a.* [Un-[1] 2] 1592.

Unsea·rchable, *a.* late ME. [Un-[1] 1.] That cannot be searched into; inscrutable. Hence **Unsea·rchableness. Unsea·rchably** *adv.*

Unsea·rched *ppl. a.* [Un-[1] 2] 1526. **Unsea·red** *ppl. a.* [Un-[1] 2] 1599. **Unsea·son** *v.* [Un-[2] 2] 1590.

Unsea·sonable, *a.* 1448. [Un-[1] 1.] **1.** Not suited to or not in accordance with the time or occasion; untimely, inopportune. **b.** Of time: Not suitable; ill chosen, inconvenient; unusual 1595. **2.** Of fish, etc.: Not in season 1450. **3.** Of weather: Not appropriate to the season of the year; *esp.* stormy, tempestuous. Also of days, seasons, etc. 1513.

1. To chuse tyme is to save tyme, and an vnseasonable mocion is but beating the ayre Bacon. The omission..was u. and injudicious 1844. **b.** If he endeavoured at so u. an hour, to force an entrance Lytton. Hence **Unsea·sonableness. Unsea·sonably** *adv.*

Unsea·soned, *ppl. a.* 1582. [Un-[1] 2.] **1.** Not made palatable by seasoning. **2.** Not matured by growth or time 1601. **b.** Not habituated by time or experience 1601.

Unsea·t, *v.* 1596. [Un-[2] 3.] **1.** *trans.* To dislodge from a seat, *esp.* on horseback. **2.** To dislodge from some place or position; to deprive of rank or office 1611. **b.** *spec.* To deprive of a seat in Parliament or other representative body 1834.

Unsea·worthiness [Un-[1] 6] 1824. **Unsea·worthy** *a.* [Un-[1] 1] 1820. **Unse·conded** *ppl. a.* [Un-[1] 2] Shaks. **Unse·cret** *a.* (now *rare*) [Un-[1] 1] 1586. **Unsecta·rian** *a.* and *sb.* [Un-[1] 1, 6] 1847. **Unse·cular** *a.* [Un-[1] 1] 1846. **Unsecu·red** *ppl. a.* [Un-[1] 2] 1780. **Unsedu·ced** *ppl. a.* [Un-[1] 2] 1565. **Unsee·able** *a.* [Un-[1] 1] late ME.

Unsee·ing, *ppl. a.* ME. [Un-[1] 4.] †**1.** Invisible. ME. only. **2.** Not seeing; lacking sight 1591. **b.** Without seeing (something) 1632.

2. I should haue scratch'd out your vnseeing eyes Shaks. He looked at his friend's face with blank u. eyes 1873. **b.** I sat..u. all Around me Southey.

Unsee·mly, *a.* ME. [Un-[1] 1.] **1.** Unbecoming, indecorous; indecent. **2.** Uncomely, unhandsome. Now *rare.* ME. Hence **Unsee·mliness.**

Unsee·mly, *adv.* late ME. [Un-[1] 5.] In an unseemly or unbecoming manner.

English women..rode very unseemely astride, like as men doe 1610.

Unsee·n, *ppl. a.* and *sb.* ME. [Un-[1] 2, 6.] **A.** *adj.* **1.** Not seen; not apprehended by sight; invisible. **b.** Const. *of* (= by) 1586. **2.** Not seen previously or hitherto; *esp.* †unfamiliar, strange ME. **b.** Of passages for translation: Not previously read 1879. **B.** *sb.* An unprepared passage for translation 1882.

Unse·gmented *ppl. a.* [Un-[1] 2] 1848. **Unsei·zable** *a.* [Un-[1] 1] 1862. **Unsei·zed** *ppl. a.* [Un-[1] 2] late ME.

Unse·ldom, *adv.* 1658. [Un-[1] 5.] *Not u.* (misused for) not rarely, not infrequently.

Unsele·ct *a.* [Un-[1] 1] 1826. **Unse·lf** *v.* [Un-[2] 4 b, 6] 1654. **Unselfco·nscious** *a.* [Un-[1] 1] 1866, **-ly** *adv.*, **-ness. Unse·lfish** *a.* [Un-[1] 1] 1698, **-ly** *adv.*, **-ness. Unsensa·tional** *a.* [Un-[1] 1] 1865, **-ly** *adv.* **Unse·nse** *v.* (now *rare*) [Un-[2] 4 b] 1611. **Unse·nsed** *ppl. a.* [Un-[1] 2] 1667. **Unse·nsible** *a.* (*Obs.* exc. *dial.*) [Un-[1] 1] late ME. **Unse·nsitive** *a.* [Un-[1] 1] 1610. **Unse·nsualize** *v.* [Un-[2] 4 c] 1792. **Unse·nt** *ppl. a.* [Un-[1] 2] 1501. **Unse·ntenced** *ppl. a.* [Un-[1] 2] 1526, **Unse·ntient** *ppl. a.* [Un-[1] 1] 1768. **U:nsentime·ntal** *a.* [Un-[1] 1] 1810, **-a·lity, -ly** *adv.* **Unse·parated** *ppl. a.* [Un-[1] 2] 1545. **Unse·pulchred** *ppl. a.*

[Un-[1] 2] 1611. **Unse·rious** *a.* [Un-[1] 1] 1655. **Unse·rved** *ppl. a.* [Un-[1] 2] ME. **Unse·rviceable** *a.* [Un-[1] 1] 1535, **-ness, -ably** *adv.* **Unse·rvile** *a.* [Un-[1] 1] 1701. **Unse·t** *v.* [Un-[2] 1, 5] 1602. **Unse·t** *ppl. a.* [Un-[1] 2] late ME. **Unse·tting** *ppl. a.* [Un-[1] 4] 1567.

Unse·ttle, *v.* 1598. [Un-[2] 1, 5.] **1.** *trans.* To undo from a fixed position; to displace, unfix (*rare*). **2.** To force out of a settled condition; to make insecure or unquiet; to disturb 1644. **3.** *intr.* To become unsettled 1605. Hence **Unse·ttling** *ppl. a.*

Unse·ttled, *ppl. a.* 1591. [Un-[1] 2.] **1.** Not peaceful or orderly; not (yet) quietly or firmly established. **b.** Of weather, etc. Changeable, variable 1707. **c.** That has not yet settled down 1691. **2.** Not settled in a particular place or position 1594. **3.** Not settled, tranquil, calm, or staid in character; restless, turbulent 1594. **4.** Undecided, undetermined 1593. **5.** Unbalanced, disturbed 1611. **b.** Of persons: Mentally affected 1611. **6.** Not assigned by will 1671. **b.** Undischarged, unpaid 1811. **c.** Not freed from doubt or uncertainty; undecided 1844. **7.** Not occupied by settlers 1724. Hence **Unse·ttledness.**

Unse·ttlement. 1648. [f. Unsettle *v.* or Un-[1] 6.] **1.** The act or process of unsettling. **2.** Unsettled state or condition 1650.

Unse·vered *ppl. a.* [Un-[1] 2] 1453. **Unsew·** *v.* [Un-[2] 1] late ME. **Unsew·ed** *ppl. a.* [Un-[1] 2] ME. **Unsew·n** *ppl. a.* [Un-[1] 2] 1648.

Unse·x, *v.* 1605. [Un-[2] 4 b.] *trans.* To deprive or divest of sex, or of the typical qualities of one or other (*esp.* the female) sex. Hence **Unse·xed** *ppl. a.*

Unse·xual *a.* [Un-[1] 1] 1819, **-ly** *adv.* **Unsha·ckle** *v.* [Un-[2] 2 b] 1611. **Unsha·ckled** *ppl. a.* [Un-[1] 2] 1776. **Unsha·ded** *ppl. a.* [Un-[1] 2] 1668. **Unsha·dow** *v.* [Un-[2] 2 b] 1550. **Unsha·dowed** *ppl. a.* [Un-[1] 2] 1593. **Unsha·keable** *a.* [Un-[1] 1] 1611, **-ably** *adv.* **Unsha·ken** *ppl. a.* [Un-[1] 2] 1460. **Unsha·med** *ppl. a.* [Un-[1] 2] late ME. **Unsha·pe** *v.* [Un-[2] 1, 2] late ME. **Unsha·ped** *ppl. a.* [Un-[1] 2] 1572. **Unsha·peliness** [Un-[1] 6] 1741. **Unsha·pely** *a.* [Un-[1] 1] ME. **Unsha·pen** *ppl. a.* [Un-[1] 2] ME. **Unsha·red** *ppl. a.* [Un-[1] 2] 1616. **Unsha·ttered** *ppl. a.* [Un-[1] 2] 1634. **Unsha·ved** *ppl. a.* [Un-[1] 2] 1648. **Unsha·ven** *ppl. a.* [Un-[1] 2] late ME. **Unshaw·l** *v.* [Un-[2] 2, 5] 1817.

Unshea·the, *v.* late ME. [Un-[2] 2, 3.] †**1.** *trans.* To dislodge –1593. **2.** To draw (a weapon) from the sheath or scabbard 1542. **3.** To strip off a sheath or covering 1638.

1. Til I my soule out of my breste vnshepe Chaucer. **2.** *To u. the sword*, to begin hostilities. Hence **Unshea·thed** *ppl. a.*

Unshe·d *ppl. a.* [Un-[1] 2] 1450. **Unshe·ll** *v.* [Un-[2] 3] 1599. **Unshe·lled** *ppl. a.* [Un-[1] 2] 1594. **Unshe·ltered** *ppl. a.* [Un-[1] 2] 1599. **Unshe·ltering** *ppl. a.* [Un-[1] 4] 1614. **Unshe·nt** *ppl. a.* (*arch.*) [Un-[1] 2] ME. **Unshe·pherded** *ppl. a.* [Un-[1] 2] 1850. **Unshie·lded** *ppl. a.* [Un-[1] 2] Dryden. **Unshi·fted** *ppl. a.* [Un-[1] 2] 1643. **Unshi·fting** *ppl. a.* [Un-[1] 4] Wordsw.

Unshi·p, *v.* 1450. [Un-[2] 3, 2, 5.] **1.** *trans.* To take out of, remove, or discharge from a ship; to disembark. **2.** *Naut.* To detach or remove (esp. a mast, rudder, or oar) from a fixed place or position 1598. **b.** *gen.* 1793. **3.** *intr.* **a.** To admit of being detached or removed 1834. **b.** To become detached 1867. Hence **Unshi·pment.**

Unshi·pped *a.* [Un-[1] 3] 1720. **Unsho·cked** *ppl. a.* [Un-[1] 2] 1712.

Unsho·d, *ppl. a.* OE. [Un-[1] 2.] **1.** Without shoes, barefooted. **2.** Of horses: Having cast a shoe or shoes; not furnished with shoes 1523. **3.** Not protected with an iron rim, toe-piece, etc. 1497.

Unshoe *v.* [Un-[2] 2] 1481. **Unsho·rn** *ppl. a.* [Un-[1] 2] 1449. **Unsho·rtened** *ppl. a.* [Un-[1] 2] 1744. **Unsho·t** *ppl. a.* [Un-[1] 2] 1544. **Unshou·lder** *v.* [Un-[2] 2] 1598. **Unshow·ered** *ppl. a.* [Un-[1] 2] Milt. **Unshow·n** *ppl. a.* [Un-[1] 2] Shaks. **Unshri·ne** *v.* [Un-[2] 3] 1599. **Unshri·nkable** *a.* [Un-[1] 1] 1885. **Unshri·nking** *ppl. a.* [Un-[1] 4] Shaks., **-ly** *adv.* **Unshri·ven** *ppl. a.* [Un-[1] 2] ME. **Unshrou·d** *v.* [Un-[2] 1, 3] 1594. **Unshrou·ded** *ppl. a.* [Un-[1] 2] late ME. **Unshru·nken** *ppl. a.* [Un-[1] 2] 1862. **Unshu·ffled** *ppl. a.* [Un-[1] 2] 1775. **Unshu·nnable** *a.* [Un-[1] 1] Shaks. **Unshu·t** *v.* (now *rare*) [Un-[2] 1, 5] ME. **Unshu·t** *ppl. a.* [Un-[1] 2] late ME. **Unshu·ttered** *ppl. a.* [Un-[1] 2] 1845.

Unsi·fted, *ppl. a.* 1589. [Un-[1] 2.] **1.** Not passed through a sieve; unstrained. **2.** *fig.* Not classified, scrutinized, or tested 1620. †**3.** Untried, inexperienced. Shaks.

Unsi·ghing *ppl. a.* [Un-[1] 4] 1743.

Unsi·ght, *v.* 1615. [Un-[2] 2 b.] **1.** *trans.* To blind (*rare*). **2.** In *pa. pple.* Cut off from seeing an object 1825.

Unsi·ghted *ppl. a.* [Un-[1] 2] 1584.

Unsi·ghtly, *a.* late ME. [Un-[1] 2.] Unpleasing to look at; ugly. **b.** Applied to immaterial things 1605. Hence **Unsi·ghtliness.**

Unsi·gnalled *ppl. a.* [Un-[1] 2] 1868. **Unsi·gned** *ppl. a.* [Un-[1] 2] 1598. **Unsi·gnifying** *ppl. a.* [Un-[1] 4] 1665. **Unsi·lenceable** *a.* [Un-[1] 1] 1678. **Unsi·lenced** *ppl. a.* [Un-[1] 2] 1615. **Unsi·lvered** *ppl. a.* [Un-[1] 2] 1772. **Unsi·milar** *a.* [Un-[1] 1] 1768. **Unsi·mple** *a.* [Un-[1] 1] 1541.

Unsi·n, *v.* 1628. [Un-[2] 2 b, 4 b.] **1.** *trans.* To annul (a sin) by subsequent action. **2.** To maintain or prove to be no sin 1682.

Unsince·re *a.* [Un-[1] 1] 1577. **Unsi·new** *v.* [Un-[2] 2, 4 b] 1598. **Unsi·newed** *ppl. a.* [Un-[1] 2] 1541. **Unsi·newy** *a.* [Un-[1] 1] 1622. **Unsi·nful** *a.* [Un-[1] 1] 1598, **-ly** *adv.*, **-ness.** **Unsi·nged** *ppl. a.* [Un-[1] 2] 1599. **Unsi·nkable** *a.* [Un-[1] 1] 1655, **-ness, -bi·lity.** **Unsi·nking** *ppl. a.* [Un-[1] 4] 1705. **Unsi·nning** *ppl. a.* [Un-[1] 4] late ME. **Unsi·ster** *v.* [Un-[2] 4 b] 1875. **Unsi·sterly** *a.* [Un-[1] 1] 1747.

Unsi·zeable, *a.* 1653. [Un-[1] 1.] †**1.** Unequal in size –1716. †**2.** Too large, unwieldy –1759. **3.** Of fish: Not grown to a proper size; immature 1746.

Unsi·zed, *ppl. a.*[1] 1700. [Un-[1] 2 + Size *v.*[1]] Not made to size, not sorted into sizes.

Unsi·zed, *ppl. a.*[2] 1794. [Un-[1] 2 + Size *v.*[2]] Not stiffened or coated with size.

Unski·lful, *a.* late ME. [Un-[1] 1.] †**1.** Ill-advised, unwise; ignorant *of* something –1667. **2.** Lacking in skill; inexpert 1565. **b.** Displaying lack of skill; clumsy 1586. Hence **Unski·lful-ly** *adv.*, **-ness.**

Unski·ll (*arch.*) [Un-[1] 6; cf. ON. *úskil*] ME.

Unski·lled, *ppl. a.* 1581. [Un-[1] 2.] **1.** Not skilled or expert *in* something; ignorant *of*; not qualified *to* do something. **b.** Inexpert, inexperienced 1693. **c.** *spec.* Not skilled in some handicraft; without technical training 1851. **2.** Not involving or requiring skill; displaying lack of skill 1833.

Unski·mmed *ppl. a.* [Un-[1] 2] 1634. **Unski·n** *v.* (now *rare*) [Un-[2] 2] 1598. **Unski·nned** *ppl. a.* [Un-[1] 2] 1882. **Unsla·cked** *ppl. a.* [Un-[1] 2] 1593. **Unsla·ckened** *ppl. a.* [Un-[1] 2] 1770. **Unsla·ckening** *ppl. a.* [Un-[1] 4] 1768. **Unslai·n** *ppl. a.* [Un-[1] 2] ME. **Unsla·ked** *ppl. a.* [Un-[1] 2] 1598. **Unsla·te** *v.* [Un-[2] 2] 1598. **Unslau·ghtered** *ppl. a.* [Un-[1] 2] 1719. **Unsla·ve** *v.* [Un-[2] 2 b] 1618. **Unslee·ping** *ppl. a.* [Un-[1] 4] Milt., **-ly** *adv.*

Unsle·pt, *ppl. a.* 1500. [Un-[1] 2.] **1.** Not having slept. **2.** Of a bed, etc.: Not slept *in* 1864. **3.** Of a carouse, etc.: Not slept *off* 1821.

1. Pale, as man longe u. 1500. I hurry on board, unsupped and u. Froude.

Unsli·ng *v.* [Un-[2] 1, 2 b] 1630. **Unsli·p** *v.* [Un-[2] 1, 2 b] 1611. **Unsli·pping** *ppl. a.* [Un-[1] 4] Shaks.

Unslui·ce, *v.* 1611. [Un-[2] 2 b, 5.] **1.** To let out as from a sluice; to allow to flow. **2.** To furnish with an outlet 1652.

Unslu·mbering *ppl. a.* [Un-[1] 4] 1718. **Unsma·rt** *a.* [Un-[1] 1] 1480. **Unsme·lted** *ppl. a.* [Un-[1] 2] 1824. **Unsmi·led** *ppl. a.* [Un-[1] 2] 1841. **Unsmi·ling** *ppl. a.* [Un-[1] 4] 1826, **-ly** *adv.*, **-ness.** **Unsmi·rched** *ppl. a.* [Un-[1] 2] Shaks. **Unsmi·tten** *ppl. a.* [Un-[1] 2] late ME. **Unsmo·ked** *ppl. a.* [Un-[1] 2] 1648. **Unsmoo·th** *a.* [Un-[1] 1] 1597. **Unsmoo·th** *v.* [Un-[2] 4 b] 1621. **Unsmoo·thed** *ppl. a.* [Un-[1] 2] 1614. **Unsmo·therable** *a.* [Un-[1] 1] Donne. **Unsna·p** *v.* [Un-[2] 1, 5] 1862.

Unsna·rl, *v.* 1555. [Un-[2] 1.] *trans.* To disentangle.

Unsnu·bbable *a.* [Un-[1] 1] 1847. **Unsnu·ffed** *ppl. a.* [Un-[1] 2] 1825.

Unso·ber, *a.* late ME. [Un-[1] 1.] †**1.** Uncontrolled, immoderate –1680. **2.** Unregulated in conduct; not staid or grave 1542. **3.** Affected by or addicted to drinking 1611.

1. The sea was vnsober 1400. Hence **Unso·berly** *adv.*, **-ness.**

Unso·ciable, *a.* 1600. [Un-[1] 1.] **1.** Not sociable or companionable; not readily or pleasantly associating with others. **2.** Ill matched; incongruous, incompatible 1611. **3.** Interfering with social intercourse 1638.

2. This..text..seemeth vnsociable to our begunne Subiect 1611. **3.** Sunder'd by savage seas u. From kin and country 1861. So **U:nsociabi·lity. Unso·ciableness. Unso·ciably** *adv.*

Unso·cial, *a.* 1731. [Un-[1] 1.] Not living or lived in communities, isolated or secluded or independent; ill adapted to or not fond of social life. Hence **Unsocia·lity.**

Unso·cket *v.* [Un-[2] 3] 1711. **Unso·dden** *ppl. a.* [Un-[1] 2] OE. **Unso·ftened** *ppl. a.* [Un-[1] 2] 1645. **Unsoi·led** *ppl. a.* [Un-[1] 2] Marlowe. **Unso·ld** *ppl. a.* [Un-[1] 2] late ME. **Unso·lder** *v.* [Un-[2] 1] 1538. **Unso·ldered** *ppl. a.* [Un-[1] 2] 1641. **Unso·ldier** *v.* [Un-[2] 2, 4 b] 1611. **Unso·ldierlike** *a.* [Un-[1] 1] 1590. **Unso·ldierly** *a.* [Un-[1] 2] 1598. **Unso·lemn** *a.* [Un-[1] 1] late ME. **Unsoli·cited** *ppl. a.* [Un-[1] 2] Shaks. **Unsoli·citous** *a.* [Un-[1] 1] 1668. **Unso·lid** *a.* [Un-[1] 1] 1593, **-ly** *adv.*, **-ness.** **Unso·lvable** *a.* [Un-[1] 1] 1821. **Unso·lved** *ppl. a* [Un-[1] 2] 1665. **Unso·n** *v.* [Un-[2] 4 b] 1652. **Unso·nlike** *a.* [Un-[1] 1] 1657. **Unsoo·thed** *ppl. a.* [Un-[1] 2] 1648. **Unsophi·stical** *a.* [Un-[1] 1] Landor, **-ly** *adv.* **Unsophi·sticate** *ppl. a.* (now *rare*) [Un-[1] 2] 1607.

Unsophi·sticated, *ppl. a.* 1630. [Un-[1] 2.] **1.** Unadulterated, unmixed. **2.** Not tampered with, altered, or falsified; uncorrupted, genuine 1664. **3.** Not sophisticated in habits, manners, or mind; natural, ingenuous 1665.

1. Vnsophisticated drinke, That neuer makes men stagger 1630. **2.** The correspondence in its genuine u. state 1843. **3.** What an u. little country creature you are! Thackeray.

U:nsophistica·tion [Un-[1] 6] 1825. **Unso·rted** *ppl. a.* [Un-[1] 2] 1533.

Unsou·ght, *ppl. a.* ME. [Un-[1] 2.] **1.** Not searched out or sought for. **b.** Not obtained by search or effort ME. **2.** Unasked; without being requested 1500. **3.** Unexamined, unexplored. late ME. **4.** Not resorted to; untried 1582.

Unsou·l, *v.* 1634. [Un-[2] 2, b.4] **1.** *trans.* To dispirit. Now *rare*. **2.** To deprive of soul; to make soulless 1652.

1. Your sad appearance..Would half u. your army Chapman.

Unsou·led *ppl. a.* [Un-[1] 2] Spencer.

Unsou·nd, *a.* ME. [Un-[1] 1.] **1.** Of persons, etc.: Not physically sound; unhealthy, diseased. **b.** *transf.* Of wounds, ailments, etc. late ME. **c.** Of substances, plants, etc.: Not in sound or good condition 1617. **2.** Morally corrupt; wicked, evil. late ME. **3.** Not mentally sound or normal; not sane 1547. **4.** Not soundly based in fact or reasoning 1595. **b.** Holding such opinions, etc. 1597. **5.** Lacking in solidity or firmness 1590. **6.** Of sleep: Broken or disturbed 1584.

2. Lewd my hauiour was, vnsound my carriage 1601. **4. b.** St. John, I have even heard, was u. about Old Testament dates 1891. Hence **Unsou·nd-ly** *adv.*, **-ness.**

Unsou·ndable *a.* [Un-[1] 1] 1627. **Unsou·nded** *ppl. a.*[1] [Un-[1] 2 + Sound *v.*[1]] 1530. **Unsou·nded** *ppl. a.*[2] [Un-[1] 2 + Sound *v.*[2]] Shaks. **Unsou·red** *ppl. a.* [Un-[1] 2] Bacon. **Unsow·n** *ppl. a.* [Un-[1] 2] late ME. **Unspa·red** *ppl. a.* [Un-[1] 2] ME.

Unspa·ring, *ppl. a.* 1586. [Un-[1] 4.] **1.** Showing no forbearance or mercy; sparing no effort; zealous. **2.** Not niggardly; liberal, lavish 1667. Hence **Unspa·ringly** *adv.*

Unspaw·ned *ppl. a.* [Un-[1] 2] 1814. **Unspea·k** *v.* [Un-[2] 1] Shaks.

Unspea·kable, *a.* late ME. [Un-[1] 1.] **1.** Incapable of being expressed in words; inexpressible, ineffable. **b.** *spec.* Indescribably or inexpressibly bad or objectionable 1831. **2.** *U.S.* Unwilling or unable to speak 1888.

1. It is chaunged by an vnspeakeable woorking, although it seme bread to vs 1534. I had the u. mortification to see my favours sometimes not inserted 1754. **b.** The u. Turk should be immediately struck out of the question Carlyle. Hence **Unspea·kableness. Unspea·kably** *adv.*

Unspea·king *ppl. a.* [Un-[1] 4] late ME. **Unspe·cialized** *ppl. a.* [Un-[1] 2] 1874. **Unspeci·fic** *a.* [Un-[1] 1] 1807. **Unspe·cified** *ppl. a.* [Un-[1] 2] 1624. **Unspe·ctacled** *ppl. a.* [Un-[1] 2] 1791. **Unspe·culative** *a.* [Un-[1] 1] 1659.

Unspe·d, *ppl. a. arch.* ME. [Un-[1] 2.] Not having succeeded or attained one's or its object; without success.

So was he come ayein u. Gower.

Unspe·ll, *v.* 1611. [Un-[2] 1.] **1.** *trans.* To undo (a spell). **2.** To free from a spell 1635. **3.** *Typog.* In distributing type, to detach letter from letter in (a word) 1846.

Unspe·llable *a.* [Un-[1] 1] 1852.

Unspe·nt, *ppl. a.* 1466. [Un-[1] 2.] **1.** Not expended or used. Of money, food, cartridges, etc. **2.** Not at an end or worn out, with force or strength remaining, unexhausted 1611.

Unsphe·re, *v.* 1611. [UN-2 3.] *trans.* To remove (a heavenly body, *fig.* a spirit) from its place in the sky.

Though you would seek t' vnsphere the Stars with Oaths SHAKS. Unsphear The spirit of Plato MILTON. Hence **Unsphe·red** *ppl. a.* 1598.

Unspi·ced *ppl. a.* [UN-1 2] 1655. **Unspie·d** *ppl. a.* [UN-1 2] late ME. **Unspi·ke** *v.* [UN-2 1, 2 b] 1680. **Unspi·lled, -spi·lt** *ppl. a.* [UN-1 2] 1573. **Unspi·n** *v.* [UN-2 1] 1585. **Unspi·ritual** *a.* [UN-1 1] MILT., **-ly** *adv.*, **-ness. Unspi·ritualize** *v.* [UN-2 4 c] 1716. **Unspli·t** *ppl. a.* [UN-1 2] 1656.

Unspoi·led, *ppl. a.* 1500. [UN-1 2.] **1.** Not despoiled or plundered. **2.** Not spoiled or deteriorated 1732. So **Unspoi·lt** *ppl. a.* 1796, in sense 2.

Unspo·ken, *ppl. a.* late ME. [UN-1 2.] **1.** Not spoken *of*. **2.** Not uttered; not expressed in speech 1449. **3.** Not spoken *to* 1616.

Unsponta·neous *a.* [UN-1 1] 1791. **Unspo·rting** *ppl. a.* [UN-1 4] 1859. **Unspo·rtsmanlike** *a.* [UN-1 1] 1754.

Unspo·tted, *ppl. a.* late ME. [UN-1 2.] **1.** Free from any spot or stain. **b.** *Nat. Hist.* Not marked with spots 1804. **2.** Not morally stained; unblemished, pure. late ME.

Unsprea·d *ppl. a.* [UN-1 2] 1589. **Unspu·n** *ppl. a.* [UN-1 2] 1545. **Unspu·rred** (*ppl.*) *a.* [UN-1 2, 3] 1635. **Unsqua·ndered** *ppl. a.* [UN-1 2] 1799. **Unsqua·red** *ppl. a.* [UN-1 2] 1549. **Unsquee·zed** *ppl. a.* [UN-1 2] 1683.

Unsta·ble, *a.* ME. [UN-1 1.] **1.** Apt to move or be moved about; not stationary. **b.** Not steady in position; readily swaying or shaking; liable to swing or fall. late ME. **c.** Of movement: Unsteady; irregular 1549. **d.** *Mech.* Of equilibrium 1839. **2.** Not stable in purpose; vacillating, unreliable, changeable ME. **3.** Not fixed in character or condition; apt to change or alter; variable ME. **b.** *Chem.* Of compounds: Readily broken up 1849.

1. b. Thilke u. whel, Which evere torneth GOWER. **d.** The body will be in a state of u. equilibrium 1839. **3.** All oligarchies and democracies are u. 1863. So **Unstabi·lity** 1470. Hence **Unsta·bleness. Unsta·bly** *adv.*

Unstai·d *a.* (*arch.*) [UN-1 1] 1550, **-ly** *adv.*, **-ness. Unstai·nable** *a.* [UN-1 1] 1584. **Unstai·ned** *ppl. a.* [UN-1 2] 1555. **Unsta·mped** *ppl. a.* [UN-1 2] 1594. **Unsta·nchable** *a.* [UN-1 1] late ME.

Unsta·nched, *ppl. a.* late ME. [UN-1 2.] **1.** Not satisfied; unsated. *arch.* **b.** Of wounds: Still bleeding 1826. **2.** Not made staunch or water-tight. *arch.* 1607.

Unsta·rched *ppl. a.* [UN-1 2] 1827. **Unsta·rred** *ppl. a.* [UN-1 2] 1849. **Unsta·rtled** *ppl. a.* [UN-1 2] 1659. **Unsta·te** *v.* [UN-2 4 b] 1586. **Unsta·ted** *ppl. a.* [UN-1 2] 1864. **Unsta·tesmanlike** *a.* [UN-1 1] 1796. **Unsta·tutable** *a.* [UN-1 1] 1634, **-ably** *adv.* **Unstay·ed** *ppl. a.*[1] [UN-1 2 + STAY *v.*[1]] 1600. **Unstay·ed** *ppl. a.*[2] [UN-1 2 + STAY *v.*[2]] 1594. **Unstay·ed** *ppl. a.*[3] [UN-1 2 + STAY *sb.*[2]] 1820. **Unstay·ing** *ppl. a.* [UN-1 4] 1616. **Unstea·dfast** *a.* [UN-1 1] ME., **-ly** *adv.*, **-ness.**

Unstea·dy, *a.* 1598. [UN-1 1.] **1.** Not steady in position; not firm or secure. **2.** Not steady or constant in conduct or purpose; fluctuating, fickle, wavering 1598. **3.** Marked or characterized by absence of steadiness or regularity; not regular, even, or uniform 1690. Hence **Unstea·dily** *adv.* **Unstea·diness.**

Unstea·dy *v.* [UN-2 4 a] 1532. **Unstee·ped** *ppl. a.* [UN-1 2] 1626. **Unste·p** *v.* [UN-2 3, 5] 1853. **Unsti·ffen** *v.* [UN-2 4] 1611. **Unsti·ffened** *a.* [UN-1 2] 1648. **Unsti·fled** *ppl. a.* [UN-1 2] 1742. **Unsti·lled** *ppl. a.* [UN-1 2] 1648. **Unsti·mulated** *ppl. a.* [UN-1 2] 1800. **Unsti·mulating** *ppl. a.* [UN-1 4] 1844. **Unsti·nted** *ppl. a.* [UN-1 2] 1480, **-ly** *adv.* **Unsti·nting** *ppl. a.* [UN-1 4] 1845, **-ly** *adv.* **Unsti·rred** *ppl. a.* [UN-1 2] ME. **Unsti·rring** *ppl. a.* [UN-1 4] 1684. **Unsti·tch** *v.* [UN-2 1] 1538. **Unsti·tched** *ppl. a.* [UN-1 2] 1599.

Unsto·ck, *v.* 1547. [UN-2 2, 3.] **1.** *trans.* **a.** To remove (a ship) from the stocks. **b.** To dismount (a gun) 1598. **c.** To remove the stock from (a gun, etc.) 1706. **2.** To deplete of cattle, inhabitants, plants, etc. 1647.

2. The conflict of the Roses did not u...England 1865. So **Unsto·cked** *ppl. a.* [UN-1 2] late ME.

Unsto·ckinged *ppl. a.* [UN-1 2] 1812. **Untoo·ping** *ppl.a.* [UN-1 4] SHAKS.

Unsto·p, *v.* late ME. [UN-2 1.] **1.** *trans.* To free from being stopped up or closed. **2.** To pull out (an organ-stop) 1855. **3.** *Naut.* To let (the cable or engine) run again after stopping. Also *absol.* 1840.

1. The eares of the deafe shalbe vnstopped *Isaiah* 35:5.

Unsto·ppable *a.* [UN-1 1] 1836.

Unsto·pped, *ppl. a.* late ME. [UN-1 2.] **1.** Not closed, stuffed up, corked, or bunged. **b.** Of a tooth or dental cavity: Not filled with stopping 1825. **c.** Of a hunting country: With the earths not stopped 1887. **2.** Not checked, unhindered 1621. **3.** *Phonetics.* Of a consonant: Open (cf. STOPPED) 1874. **4.** Of blank verse: Not end-stopped (see END *sb.*) 1874.

Unsto·pper *v.* [UN-2 1, 2] 1839. **Unsto·re** *v.* [UN-2 2, 3] 1618. **Unsto·red** *ppl. a.* [UN-1 2] 1603.

Unstow·, *v.* 1726. [UN-2 1.] *Naut.* To take out of stowage; to clear (a hold, etc.) of the articles stowed in it.

Unstrai·ned, *ppl. a.* late ME. [UN-1 2.] **1.** Not drawn tight; not subjected to a strain. **2.** Not forced or produced by effort 1580. **3.** Not passed through a strainer 1828.

Unstra·p *v.* [UN-2 2 b] 1828. **Unstra·tified** *ppl. a.* [UN-1 2] 1802. **Unstrea·ked** *ppl. a.* [UN-1 2] 1861. **Unstre·ngthened** *ppl. a.* [UN-1 2] 1597. **Unstre·ssed** *ppl. a.* [UN-1 2] 1883. **Unstre·tch** *v.* [UN-2 1, 5] 1611. **Unstri·cken** *ppl. a.* [UN-1 2] 1548.

Unstri·ng, *v.* 1611. [UN-2 2, 2 b.] **1.** *trans.* To relax or remove the string(s) of (a bow, lyre, etc.). **b.** To undo the strings of (a purse). Also *absol.* Now *rare.* 1681. **2.** To detach from a string 1697. **3.** To render lax or weak; to disorder (the nerves, etc.) 1700.

Unstri·nged *ppl. a.* [UN-1 2] SHAKS. **Unstri·p** *v.* (now *dial.* and *rare*) [UN-2 7] 1596. **Unstri·ped** *ppl. a.* [UN-1 2] 1841. **Unstri·pped** *ppl. a.* [UN-1 2] 1676. **Unstru·ck** *ppl. a.* [UN-1 2] 1615.

Unstru·ng, *ppl. a.* 1598. [f. UNSTRING *v.*, or UN-1 2.] **1.** Having the string(s) removed or relaxed. **2.** Weakened, relaxed; unnerved 1692.

Unstu·died, *ppl. a.* late ME. [UN-1 2.] **1.** Not meditated on; neglected as a subject of study or thought. **2.** Not having studied; unversed (*in* something) 1642. **3.** Not elaborated by study or care; not laboured or artificial 1657.

1. Þus..is goddis lawe vnstudied WYCLIF. **2.** I..was not u. in those authors which are most commended MILT. **3.** Express'd in ready and u. Words DRYDEN.

Unstu·dious *a.* [UN-1 1] 1663. **Unstu·ffed** *ppl. a.* [UN-1 2] 1480. **Unstu·ng** *ppl. a.* [UN-1 2] 1615. **Unsty·lish** *a.* [UN-1 1] 1863. **Unsubdu·able** *a.* [UN-1 1] 1611. **Unsubdue·d** *ppl. a.* [UN-1 2] 1590, **-ness. Unsu·bject** *a.* [UN-1 1] late ME. **Unsubje·cted** *ppl. a.* [UN-1 2] late ME. **Unsubli·med** *ppl. a.* [UN-1 2] 1694. **Unsubme·rged** *ppl. a.* [UN-1 2] 1883. **Unsubmi·ssive** *a.* [UN-1 1] 1653, **-ness. Unsubmi·tting** *ppl. a.* [UN-1 4] 1730. **Unsubo·rned** *ppl. a.* [UN-1 2] 1656. **Unsubscri·bed** *ppl. a.* [UN-1 2] 1571. **Unsubscri·bing** *ppl. a.* [UN-1 4] 1790. **Unsu·bsidized** *ppl. a.* [UN-1 2] 1756.

Unsubsta·ntial, *a.* 1455. [UN-1 1.] **1.** Having no real basis or foundation in fact. **2.** Having no bodily or material substance 1592. **b.** Lacking in substance or solidity 1617.

1. These deep but u. meditations GIBBON. **2.** Hill and plain, apparently u. as a mountain mist 1871. **b.** A nutriment that is watry and u. 1773. Hence **U:nsubstantia·lity. Unsubsta·ntially** *adv.*

U:nsubsta·ntiate *v.* [UN-2 4] 1799. **U:nsubsta·ntiated** *ppl. a.* [UN-1 2] 1837. **Unsubve·rted** *ppl. a.* [UN-1 2] WORDSW. **Unsucce·ss** [UN-1 6] SIDNEY. **Unsucce·ssful** *a.* [UN-1 1] 1617, **-ly** *adv.*, **-ness. Unsucce·ssive** *a.* (now *rare*) [UN-1 1] 1617. **Unsu·ccoured** *ppl. a.* [UN-1 1] late ME. **Unsu·cked** *ppl. a.* [UN-1 2] 1652. **Unsue·d** *ppl. a.* [UN-1 2] 1594. **Unsu·fferable** *a.* (now *rare*) [UN-1 2] ME., **-ably** *adv.* **Unsuffi·ced** *ppl. a.* [UN-1 1] 1586. †**Unsuffi·cient** *a.* [UN-1 1] –1656. **Unsu·gared** *ppl. a.* [UN-1 2] 1592. **Unsugge·stive** *a.* [UN-1 1] LAMB.

Unsui·t, *v.* 1635. [UN-1 7.] **1.** *trans.* To be at variance with (*rare*). **2.** To render unsuitable 1869.

Unsui·table, *a.* 1586. [UN-1 1.] Not suitable, unfitting. Const. *to*, *for*. Hence **Unsuitabi·lity. Unsui·tably** *adv.* **Unsui·tableness.**

Unsui·ted, *ppl. a.* 1598. [UN-1 2.] **1.** Lacking the qualities required. Const. *to*, *for*. **2.** Not accommodated or supplied with what is desired 1796.

2. So that no constitution-fancier may go u. from his shop BURKE.

Unsui·ting *ppl. a.* [UN-1 4] 1596. **Unsu·llied** *ppl. a.* [UN-1 2] SHAKS., **-ness. Unsu·mmed** *ppl. a.* [UN-1 2] late ME. **Unsu·mmerlike** *a.* [UN-1 1] 1869. **Unsu·mmoned** *ppl. a.* [UN-1 2] 1474.

Unsu·ng, *ppl. a.* late ME. [UN-1 2.] **1.** Not sung. **2.** Not celebrated in or by song 1667.

Unsu·nk *ppl. a.* [UN-1 2] ME.

Unsu·nned, *ppl. a.* 1607. [UN-1 2.] **1.** Not penetrated or reached by sunlight; not exposed or accessible to the sun. **b.** *fig.* Not made patent or public 1809. **2.** Not touched or affected by the light or heat of the sun 1611. **b.** Not coloured or tanned by the sun 1821. **3.** Not lighted up by the sun 1840.

1. The unsun'd heaps Of Misers treasure MILT. **b.** The u. historical treasures in the possession of the London Corporation 1862. **2.** As Chaste, as vn-Sunn'd Snow SHAKS.

Unsupe·rfluous *a.* [UN-1 1] 1571. **Unsu·pervised** *ppl. a.* [UN-1 2] 1899. **Unsu·pped** *ppl. a.* [UN-1 2] late ME. **Unsupplie·d** *ppl. a.* [UN-1 2] 1599. **Unsuppo·rtable** *a.* [UN-1 1] 1586.

Unsuppo·rted, *ppl. a.* late ME. [UN-1 2.] **1.** Not supported by aid or assent; not backed up or corroborated. **b.** Const. *by*. 1694. **2.** Not physically supported or sustained 1635.

Unsuppo·sable *a.* [UN-1 1] 1650. **Unsuppre·ssed** *ppl. a.* [UN-1 2] 1621.

Unsure (ʊnʃūə·ɹ), *a.* late ME. [UN-1 1.] **1.** Not safe against attack or mishap; liable to danger or risk; exposed to peril; insecure. Now *rare.* **b.** Not affording or conducive to safety; unsafe, liable to yield or give way. late ME. **2.** Marked by uncertainty or unsteadfastness; dependent on chance or accident; precarious, uncertain. late ME. **3.** Of persons, etc.: Unreliable, untrustworthy. Now *rare.* 1445. **4.** Open to doubt; not fixed, sure, or certain; doubtful 1445. **5.** Lacking certainty, assurance, or confidence; in doubt; not sure *of* something; not knowing *whether*, *when*, etc. late ME. **6.** Irresolute, faltering, vacillating 1633. Hence **Unsu·re-ly** *adv.* (*rare*), **-ness.**

Unsurmou·ntable *a.* [UN-1 1] 1611. **Unsurpa·ssable** *a.* [UN-1 1] 1611, **-ably** *adv.* **Unsurpa·ssed** *ppl. a.* [UN-1 2] 1818. **Unsurpri·sed** *ppl. a.* [UN-1 2] 1591. **Unsurre·ndered** *ppl. a.* [UN-1 2] 1800. **Unsurrou·nded** *ppl. a.* [UN-1 2] 1813. **Unsurvey·able** *a.* [UN-1 1] 1833. **Unsurvey·ed** *ppl. a.* [UN-1 2] 1546. **U:nsusceptibi·lity** [UN-1 6] 1805. **Unsusce·ptible** *a.* [UN-1 1] 1692.

Unsuspe·cted, *ppl. a.* 1530. [UN-1 2.] **1.** Not incurring suspicion; escaping suspicion or detection. **2.** Not suspected to exist, or to bear a certain character 1620.

1. The courage of our common seamen is hitherto generally u. 1747. I had..stolen unnotic'd on them, And u...heard the whole COLERIDGE. **2.** A close, secret and u. Christian FULLER. Hence **Unsuspe·ctedly** *adv.*

Unsuspe·cting *ppl. a.* [UN-1 4] 1595, **-ly** *adv.* **-ness. Unsuspe·nded** *ppl. a.* [UN-1 2] 1701. **Unsuspi·cion** [UN-1 6] 1792. **Unsuspi·cious** *a.* [UN-1 1] 1589, **-ly** *adv.*, **-ness. Unsustai·nable** *a.* [UN-1 1] 1677. **Unsustai·ned** *ppl. a.* [UN-1 2] 1630. **Unsustai·ning** *ppl. a.* [UN-1 2] 1818. **Unswa·ddle** *v.* [UN-2 2] 1580. **Unswa·llowed** *ppl. a.* [UN-1 2] late ME. **Unswa·the** *v.* [UN-2 2] late ME. **Unsway·ed** *ppl. a.* [UN-1 2] SHAKS. **Unswea·r** *v.* [UN-2 1, 5] SHAKS. **Unsweet** *a.* [UN-1 1] OE., **-ly** *adv.* **Unswee·tened** *ppl. a.* [UN-1 2] 1817. **Unswe·ll** *v.* (now *rare*) [UN-2 1] late ME. **Unswe·pt** *ppl. a.* [UN-1 2] 1597. **Unswe·rving** *ppl. a.* [UN-1 4] 1694, **-ly** *adv.* **Unswo·llen** *ppl. a.* [UN-1 2] 1648.

Unswo·rn, *ppl. a.* 1529. [UN-1 2.] **1.** Not put on oath; not bound by or having taken an oath. **2.** Not confirmed by, or sworn as, an oath 1623.

Unsy·llabled *ppl. a.* [UN-1 2] 1594. **Unsymme·trical** *a.* [UN-1 1] 1755, **-ly** *adv.* **Unsympathe·tic** *a.* [UN-1 1] 1823, **-ally** *adv.* **Unsy·mpathizing** *ppl. a.* [UN-1 4] 1735, **-ly** *adv.* **U:nsystema·tic** 1770, **-al** 1780, *adjs.* [UN-1 1], **-ly** *adv.* **Unsy·stematized** *ppl. a.* [UN-1 2] 1849. **Unta·ck** *v.* [UN-2 1] 1641.

Unta·ckle, *v.* 1552. [UN-2 2, 2 b.] **1.** To strip (a vessel) of tackle. **2.** To unharness (a horse) 1573. **3.** To free from tackling or fastenings 1905.

Unta·ctful *a.* [UN-1 1] 1860. **Untai·led** *ppl. a.* [UN-1 2] 1611. **Untai·nted** *ppl. a.* [UN-1 2] 1590. **Unta·ken** *ppl. a.* [UN-1 2] ME. **Unta·king** *ppl. a.* [UN-1 4] 1587. **Unta·lented** *ppl. a.* [UN-1 2] 1753. **Unta·lked** *ppl. a.* [UN-1 2] SHAKS. **Unta·me** *a.* [UN-1 1] late ME., **-ness. Unta·m(e)able** *a.* [UN-1 1] 1567, **-ness, -ably** *adv.* **Unta·med** *ppl. a.* [UN-1 2] ME., **-ly** *adv.*, **-ness.**

Unta·mpered *ppl. a.* [UN-1 2] 1682. **Unta·ngle** *v.* [UN-2 1, 5] 1550. **Unta·nned** *ppl. a.* [UN-1 2] 1535. **Unta·pped** *ppl. a.* [UN-1 2] 1779. **Unta·rnished** *ppl. a.* [UN-1 2] 1732. **Unta·rred** *ppl. a.* [UN-1 2] 1579. **Unta·sted** *ppl. a.* [UN-1 2] 1538.

Untau·ght, *ppl. a.* ME. [UN-1 2.] **1.** Having had no teaching; uninstructed, untrained, ignorant. **b.** Const. with inf., *in*, or obj. complement 1581. **c.** Of animals, etc. 1697. **2.** Not imparted or acquired by teaching; hence, natural, spontaneous 1445.

1. Better it is to be wnborne than wntawght 1530. **b.** U. The knowledge of the world COWPER. **2.** I have..a pretty u. Step in Dancing STEELE.

Unta·x *v.* [UN-2 2 b] 1831. **Unta·xable** *a.* [UN-1 1] 1610. **Unta·xed** *ppl. a.* [UN-1 2] 1460. **Untea·ch** *v.* [UN-2 1] 1531. **Untea·chable** *a.* [UN-1 1] 1475. **Untea·m** *v.* (now *rare*) [UN-2 2 b] 1548. **Untea·rable** *a.* [UN-1 1] 1648. **Unte·chnical** *a.* [UN-1 1] 1845, **-ly** *adv.* **Unte·llable** *a.* [UN-1 1] late ME.; **-ably** *adv.* not recorded in 17th and 18th cc.; freq. from 1880.

Unte·mpered, *ppl. a.* late ME. [UN-1 2.] **1.** Unregulated, uncontrolled; not held in check. **b.** Not modified or qualified (*by* something) 1768. **2.** Of lime or mortar: Not properly mixed and prepared 1440. **3.** Of steel, etc.: Not tempered or hardened 1820.

Unte·mpted *ppl. a.* [UN-1 2] 1607. **Unte·mpting** *ppl. a.* [UN-1 4] 1824. **Untenabi·lity** [UN-1 6] 1644. **Unte·nable** *a.* [UN-1 1] 1647, **-ness.** **Unte·nant** *v.* [UN-2 2, 3] 1614. **Unte·nantable** *a.* [UN-1 1] 1661. **Unte·nanted** *ppl. a.* [UN-1 2] 1673. **Unte·nded** *ppl. a.* [UN-1 2] 1598. **Unte·nder** *a.* [UN-1 1] SHAKS., **-ly** *adv.*, **-ness.** **Unte·ndered** *ppl. a.* [UN-1 2] 1607. **Unte·nted** *ppl. a.* (*arch.*) [UN-1 2 + TENT *v.*2] SHAKS. **Unte·rrified** *ppl. a.* [UN-1 2] 1609. **Unte·rrifying** *ppl. a.* [UN-1 4] 1691. **Unte·sted** *ppl. a.* [UN-1 2] 1570. **Unte·ther** *v.* [UN-2 2b] 1888. **Untha·nked** *ppl. a.* [UN-1 2] 1562.

Untha·nkful, *a.* late ME. [UN-1 1.] **1.** Not earning thanks or gratitude; thankless, unappreciated; unwelcome. **2.** Giving no thanks, ungrateful (*to* a person, *for* a thing) 1499. **3.** Characterized by ingratitude 1614.

1. One of the most u. offices in the world GOLDSM. Hence **Untha·nkful-ly** *adv.*, **-ness.**

Untha·tched *ppl. a.* [UN-1 2] 1570. **Unthaw·** *v.* (now *dial.*) [UN-2 5, 7] 1598. **Unthaw·ed** *ppl. a.* [UN-1 2] 1611. **Unthea·trical** *a.* [UN-1 1] 1745. **U:ntheolo·gical** *a.* [UN-1 1] MILT. **Unthi·ckened** *ppl. a.* [UN-1 2] 1870. **Unthi·nk** *v.* [UN-2 1] 1600.

Unthi·nkable, *a.* late ME. [UN-1 1.] **1.** Beyond the scope of thought; too great, numerous, etc. to be conceived. **2.** Incapable of being framed or grasped by thought 1445. Hence **Unthi·nkably** *adv.*

Unthi·nking, *ppl. a.* 1676. [UN-1 4.] **1.** Not exercising the faculty of thought; thoughtless; unreflecting; undiscriminating. **2.** Characterized by absence of thought 1688. **3.** Not possessing the faculty of thought 1688. Hence **Unthi·nking-ly** *adv.*, **-ness.**

Unthi·nned *ppl. a.* [UN-1 2] 1648. **Unthou·ght** *ppl. a.* [UN-1 2] 1538. **Unthou·ghtful** *ppl. a.* [UN-1 1] 1456, **-ly** *adv.*, **-ness.** **Unthra·ll** *v.* [UN-2 2 b] 1586. **Unthra·shed, -thre·shed** *ppl. a.* [UN-1 2] 1561. **Unthrea·d** *v.* [UN-2 1] SHAKS. **Unthrea·tened** *ppl. a.* [UN-1 2] 1647.

Unthrift (stress var.). late ME. [UN-1 6.] †**1.** A fault or folly. **2.** Want of thrift or economy; wastefulness; †loose living. late ME. **3.** An unthrifty, shiftless, or dissolute person; a spendthrift, prodigal. Now *rare.* ME. **4.** *attrib.* or as *adj.* Prodigal, spendthrift 1562.

2. Ful of ydelnes and al maner vnthrifte 1400. **3.** If he played the u. with this golden occasion 1639. **4.** The u. Sunne shot vitall gold A thousand peeces VAUGHAN.

Unthri·fty, *a.* late ME. [UN-1 1.] **1.** Not profitable or serviceable; leading to no good; tending to waste or harm. **2.** Not vigorous or thriving; weakly, unpromising. Now *rare.* 1440. **b.** Characterized by absence of well-being; unprosperous. late ME. †**3.** Unchaste, wanton, profligate –1571. **4.** Not thrifty; improvident; wasteful, extravagant, prodigal 1532. **b.** Prodigal or lavish *of* something 1620.

2. The Cow was very u., for which they gave her Cow Physick 1709. **3.** Suche u. Carnall and abhomynable lyvyng 1535. **4.** The wormes shall have his carkass, and u. heires his estate 1662. Hence **Unthri·ftily** *adv.* **Unthri·ftiness.**

Unthri·ving *ppl. a.* [UN-1 4] ME., **-ly** *adv.* **-ness.** **Unthro·ne** *v.* [UN-2 2] 1611. **Unthrow·n** *ppl. a.* [UN-1 2] 1547. **Unthu·mbed** *ppl. a.* [UN-1 2] 1797. **Unthwa·rted** *ppl. a.* [UN-1 2] WORDSW.

Unti·dy, *a.* ME. [UN-1 1.] †**1.** Unseasonable; unsuitable, unseemly –1661. **2.** Not neat or orderly; not kept in good order ME. Hence **Unti·dily** *adv.* **Unti·diness.**

Unti·dy *v.* [UN-2 1] 1891.

Untie (ɒntəi·), *v.* [OE. *untīgan*, f. UN-2 1, 5 + TIE *v.*] **1.** *trans.* To release, set free, detach, by undoing a cord or similar fastening. **b.** To free from a confining or encircling cord, bond, etc. 1450. **c.** *fig.* ME. **2.** To undo (a cord, knot, etc.) 1590. **b.** *fig.* To solve (a difficulty); esp. with *knot* in fig. sense 1586. **c.** *fig.* To dissolve (a bond, esp. of union) 1634. **3.** *intr.* To become untied 1590. Hence **Untie·d** *ppl. a.*1

Untie·d, *ppl. a.*2 [UN-1 2.] Not tied.

For tunges vntayde be rennyng astray SKELTON. Unty'd to a man RAMSAY. An u. beerhouse 1888.

Until (ɒnti·l), *prep.* and *conj.* ME. [First in northern and eastern texts f. ON. **und*, retained in *unz, undz*, for **und es* 'till that', and corresp. to OE., OFris., OS. *und* (combined with **te* in OS. *unti, unt*, OHG. *unzi, unz*, Goth. *unte*) + TILL *prep.*, the meaning being thus duplicated.] **A.** *prep.* **1.** To, unto (a person or place). Now *Sc.* and *north.* **b.** Up to (a point or limit); so as to reach. Now *Sc.* and *north.* ME. **2.** Onward till (a time specified or indicated); up to the time of (an action, occurrence, etc.) ME. **b.** With (usu. after) a negative 1543. **c.** Followed by an adv. (or advb. phr.) of time ME. **3.** Before (a specified time) 1887.

1. Then came vntyll hym the tempter TINDALE *Matt.* 4:3. He..hastned them vntill SPENSER. **2.** To hang them up u. the end of February 1721. **b.** Things growing are not ripe vntill their season SHAKS. **c.** U. four years ago 1873.

B. *conj.* Up to the time that; till the point when.

Now get you in, vntill I call for you 1602. A silly wench who has heard stories of apparitions u. she believes them H. WALPOLE. U. that the day began to daw 1802. After this, u. feathered, they should be fed on rich food 1855. *To think (it) long u.*: see LONG *a.* II. 4, THINK *v.*2 III. 2.

Unti·le *v.* [UN-2 2] late ME. **Unti·led** *ppl. a.* [UN-1 2] late ME. **Unti·llable** *a.* [UN-1 1] 1714. **Unti·lled** *ppl. a.* [UN-1 2] ME. **Unti·mbered** *ppl. a.* [UN-1 2] 1606.

Unti·mely, *a.* 1535. [UN-1 1.] **1.** Coming before the proper or natural time; premature, immature. **2.** Unseasonable (in respect of time of year) 1576. **3.** Ill-timed, inopportune, unseasonable 1581.

1. Euen as a figge tree casteth her vntimely figges BIBLE (Bishops') *Rev.* 6:13. Abortion or u. birth 1634. **2.** By u. rains or untimelier heat LONGF. **3.** All this u. activity FREEMAN.

Unti·mely, *adv.* ME. [UN-1 5.] **1.** Unseasonably, inopportunely. **2.** Prematurely 1586.

Untimeous (ɒntəi·məs), *a.* Chiefly *Sc.* 1500. [Alteration of earlier *untimes*, advb. gen. of †*untime* wrong time, by assimilation to adjs. in -(E)OUS.] = UNTIMELY *a.* Hence **Unti·meously** *adv.*

Unti·nctured *ppl. a.* [UN-1 2] 1760. **Unti·nged** *ppl. a.* [UN-1 2] 1664. **Unti·nned** *ppl. a.* [UN-1 2] 1825. **Unti·rable** *a.* [UN-1 1] 1607. **Unti·red** *ppl. a.* [UN-1 2] SHAKS. **Unti·ring** *ppl. a.* [UN-1 4] 1822, **-ly** *adv.* **Unti·thed** *ppl. a.* [UN-1 2] 1621. **Unti·tled** *ppl. a.* [UN-1 2] SHAKS.

Unto (ɒ·ntu, *formerly* also ɒntū·), *prep.* and *conj.* Now chiefly *arch.* and *literary.* ME. [Modelled on UNTIL *prep.* by substitution of TO *prep.* for the northern equivalent *til* TILL *prep.*] **A.** *prep.* **I.** Indicating spatial or local relationship. **1.** = TO *prep.* I. 1, 2, 3, 5. **2.** Expressing relative location (esp. with *nigh* or *near*) 1526.

1. Wilt thou flout me thus vnto my face? SHAKS. I will vnto Venice SHAKS. The Root smelled vnto is good for the same purpose 1670. She..lean'd her head u. the kindly tree 1768. I bow'd fu' low u. this maid BURNS. My throat is cut u. the bone WORDSW.

II. Indicating a temporal relationship. **1.** = TO *prep.* II. 1. ME. †**2.** After a negative: = UNTIL *prep.* 2 b. –1559.

1. The wulf..hyd hym self nyghe them vnto the nyght CAXTON.

III. Expressing the relation of aim, design, destination, result, consequent status or condition. = TO *prep.* III. ME.

Many bold knyghtes wente vnto mete MALORY. For hokes and hengles u. the skolehouse dore 1487. Hee hath turnd a heauen vnto a hell! SHAKS. To destroy and bring us u. nought DRAYTON. They..provoke Him u. ire DRAYTON. Such personal estate as he..shall become..intitled u. 1738.

IV. Followed by an expression denoting or indicating a limit in extent, number, amount, or degree. = TO *prep.* IV. 1 b. *arch.* ME. **b.** Down to (an ultimate grade, point, or number). *arch.* ME.

What may the Kings whole Battaile reach vnto? *Vernon.* To thirty thousand. SHAKS. **b.** The whole world perished u. eight persons before the floud Sir T. BROWNE.

V. Expressing addition or accumulation, attachment, appurtenance, or possession. = TO *prep.* V. ME.

A ful noble Knyghte nyghe kynne vnto sire Launcelot MALORY. There maye nothinge be taken from them, nothinge maye be put vnto them COVERDALE *Ecclus.* 18:6. Until the Earth seems join'd u. the Sky DRYDEN. So may'st thou be..a Father u. thy contemporaries SIR T. BROWNE.

VI. Expressing comparison or correspondence, relation to a standard, etc. = TO *prep.* VI. ME.

Like vnto the turtill 1460. Likewise reckon yee also your selues to be dead indeed vnto sinne *Rom.* 6:11. All thy passions, match'd with mine, Are as moonlight u. sunlight TENNYSON. U. all seeming, life went merrily WM. MORRIS.

VII. Expressing relations in which the idea of course or direction tends to blend with the dative use. = TO *prep.* VII. ME.

He fell vnto his prayers 1440. Then gather strength, and march vnto him straight SHAKS. Now vnto thy bones good night SHAKS. These words of the Prophet vnto Heli 1610. To say Amen, u. Isaiahs Description of our Lord 1710.

VIII. Supplying the place of, assuming or taking over the functions of, the dative. = TO *prep.* VIII. ME.

I am now in great haste, as may appeare vnto you SHAKS. This could not but be a great grief u. him BUNYAN. An excellent Lore, That u. your Wives you may teach 1714. The Lord be good u. me! 1796. One..Known u. few WORDSW.

†**B.** *Conj.* = UNTIL *conj.* –1573.

Untoi·led, *ppl. a.* 1578. [UN-1 2.] †**1.** Not tilled –1683. **2.** Not subjected to or overcome by toil 1598. **3.** Not toiled *for* 1651.

Unto·ld, *ppl. a.* [OE. *untēald*: UN-1 2.] †**1.** Not counted up or counted out –1607. **2.** Uncounted or unreckoned because of amount or numbers; indefinitely many or numerous, numberless, countless. late ME. **b.** Unmeasured, unlimited 1781. **3.** Not related or recounted. late ME. †**4.** Not informed. SPENSER.

2. All the u. riches of his treasury 1853. *U. gold* (colloq.): any amount of money. **b.** It had..cost ..u. suffering 1875.

Unto·mb *v.* [UN-2 3] 1594. **Unto·mbed** *ppl. a.* [UN-1 2] 1560.

Unto·ngue, *v.* Now *rare.* 1598. [UN-2 2.] *trans.* To make speechless; to deprive of (the use of) the tongue. So **Unto·ngued** *ppl. a.*

Untoo·thsome *a.* [UN-1 1] 1548. **Untor·me·nted** *ppl. a.* [UN-1 2] late ME. **Unto·rn** *ppl. a.* [UN-1 2] 1547.

Untou·chable, *a.* 1567. [UN-1 1.] †**1.** Intangible. **b.** Beyond the reach of touch 1622. **c.** *fig.* Unapproachable, unrivalled 1867. **2.** Exempt from touch; that one may not touch; sacred 1607. **b.** *spec.* That cannot legally be interfered with or made use of 1734. **3.** Too bad or unpleasant to touch 1873. *sb.* A Hindu whose touch pollutes 1921.

Untou·ched, *ppl. a.* late ME. [UN-1 2.] **1.** Not handled; not having suffered contact. **b.** Of places: Not reached or visited 1628. **2.** Not affected physically; unhurt, intact. late ME. †**b.** Sexually intact; unviolated –1683. **c.** Not used or drawn upon; *esp.* untasted 1538. **3.** Not worked upon or at; left or remaining in the previous state 1726. **4.** Not subjected to discussion, amendment, or criticism; unedited; ignored in argument, etc.; unmentioned. late ME. **5.** Not affected, modified, or influenced, esp. injuriously 1586. **b.** Not emotionally affected; unmoved, calm, undisturbed 1616. **6.** Unequalled; unexampled, unparalleled 1736.

Untou·ching *ppl. a.* [UN-1 4] 1602.

Untoward (ɒntōᵘ·wăɹd, ɒntŭwǭ·ɹd), *a.* 1526. [UN-1 1.] †**1.** Averse *to*, not ready or disposed *for* something; disinclined –1665. **2.** Intractable, unruly, perverse 1526. **b.** Of things: Hard to manage; stubborn, stiff 1566. †**c.** Ungainly; awkward –1791. **3.** Unlucky; unfavourable; turning out badly 1570. **4.** Unseemly, improper; foolish 1628.

2. The very u. Spanish Mules 1656. **b.** What a rascally vntoward thing this poetrie is B. JONSON.

c. Knees that..grow u. and unshaped 1658. **3.** When the times are u. 1868. She could hardly have made a more u. choice J. AUSTEN. **4.** When I with these u. thoughts had striven WORDSW. Hence **Unto·ward-ly** *adv.*, **-ness.**

Unto·wardly, *a.* Now *rare.* 1483. [UN-1 1.] †**1.** Unbecoming, improper. **b.** Froward, perverse 1561. **2.** Awkward, ungainly 1611. **3.** Adverse, unfavourable 1756. Hence **Unto·wardliness.**

Untra·ceable *a.* [UN-1 1] 1661, **-ness, -ably** *adv.* **Untra·ced** *ppl. a.* [UN-1 2] 1641. **Untra·cked** (*ppl.*) *a.* [UN-1 2, 3] 1603. **Untra·ctable** *a.* (now *rare*) [UN-1 1] 1538, **-ness. Untrai·ned** *ppl. a.* [UN-1 2] 1548, **-ness. Untra·mmelled** *ppl. a.* [UN-1 2] 1795. **Untra·mpled** *ppl. a.* [UN-1 2] 1648. **Untra·nquil** *a.* [UN-1 1] KEATS. **Untra·nsferable** *a.* [UN-1 1] 1649. **Untransfo·rmable** *a.* [UN-1 1] 1570. **Untransfo·rmed** *ppl. a.* [UN-1 2] 1890. **Untransla·table** *a.* [UN-1 1] 1655, **-ness, -ably** *adv.* **Untransla·ted** *ppl. a.* [UN-1 2] 1530. **Untranspa·rent** *a.* [UN-1 1] 1591. **Untranspo·sed** *ppl. a.* [UN-1 2] JOHNSON. **Untra·pped** *a.* [UN-1 3] 1860.

Untra·velled, *ppl. a.* 1585. [UN-1 2.] **1.** That has not travelled. **2.** Not travelled over or through, unvisited 1646.

Untrea·d *v.* [UN-2 1] SHAKS. **Untrea·sure** *v.* [UN-2 2, 3] SHAKS. **Untrea·table** *a.* [UN-1 2] late ME. **Untrea·ted** *ppl. a.* [UN-1 2] 1456. **Untre·mbling** *ppl. a.* [UN-1 4] 1570, **-ly** *adv.* **Untre·nched** *ppl. a.* [UN-1 2] 1807.

Untre·ssed, *ppl. a.* late ME. [UN-1 2.] Not arranged in tresses; loose, dishevelled.

Untrie·d, *ppl. a.* 1526. [UN-1 2.] **1.** Not tried, proved, or tested. **2.** Not tried by a judge 1618.

2. Condemn'd u. COWPER. U. offenders DICKENS.

Untri·lled *ppl. a.* [UN-1 2] 1869. **Untri·m** *v.* [UN-2 1] SHAKS. **Untri·mmed** *ppl. a.* [UN-1 2] 1532. **Untro·d** 1593, **untro·dden** ME., *ppl. adjs.* [UN-1 2]. **Untrou·bled** *ppl. a.* [UN-1 2] 1484.

Untrue·, *a.* and *adv.* [OE. *untrēowe*, *untrew(e*, etc., f. UN-1 1, 5.] **A.** *adj.* **1.** Of persons: Unfaithful, faithless. **2.** Contrary to fact; false. late ME. **3.** Dishonest; unfair, unjust; wrong. Now *rare.* late ME. **4.** Not straight; inexact; not agreeing with a standard ME.

3. Be cause it was of u. makyng, and untru stuff, no man sette therby 1444. **4.** Untrewe Beames and Scales 1503. Whose hand is feeble, or his aim u. COWPER.

†**B.** *adv.* Untruly –1622.

Some fooles would say I flatter'd, spake untrue 1622. Hence **Untru·ly** *adv.*

Untru·ss, *v.* late ME. [UN-2 2 b.] **1.** *trans.* To free from a pack or burden (*rare*). **2.** To undo (a pack, etc.); to remove or free from some fastening. late ME. **3.** *Hist.* To untie (a 'point' or tag of a garment) 1577. **b.** *absol.* To undo one's dress or breeches 1592. **c.** To undo or unfasten the garments of 1625. †**4.** To take apart, dissect, disclose –1651.

Untru·ssed *ppl. a.* [UN-1 2] ME. **Untru·st** (now *rare*) [UN-1 6] ME. **Untru·sted** *ppl. a.* [UN-1 2] 1552. **Untru·stworthiness** [UN-1 6] 1808. **Untru·stworthy** *a.* [UN-1 1] 1846. **Untru·sty** *a.* [UN-1 1] late ME.

Untru·th. [OE. *untrēowþ*, *untrīewþ*, f. UN-1 6.] **1.** Unfaithfulness; disloyalty. *arch.* **2.** Falsehood, falsity. late ME. **b.** A false or incorrect statement; a lie 1449.

Untru·thful *a.* [UN-1 1] 1847, **-ly** *adv.*, **-ness. Untu·ck** *v.* [UN-2 1] 1611. **Untu·mbled** *ppl. a.* [UN-1 2] 1675. **Untumu·ltuous** *a.* [UN-1 1] 1741. **Untu·nable** *a.* [UN-1 1] 1545, **-ness, -ably** *adv.* **Untu·ne** *v.* [UN-2 2] 1598. **Untu·ned** *ppl. a.* [UN-1 2] SHAKS. **Untu·neful** *a.* [UN-1 1] 1709, **-ly** *adv.*, **-ness. Untu·rned** *ppl. a.* [UN-1 2] 1550. **Untu·rning** *ppl. a.* [UN-1 4] 1591.

Untu·tored, *ppl. a.* 1593. [UN-1 2.] **1.** Untaught; simple, unsophisticated; †boorish. **2.** Not resulting from instruction; native, instinctive 1593. **3.** Not subject to a tutor or tutors 1641.

1. The u. parts of the earth 1760. The u. many BENTHAM. **2.** The u. wisdom of Romulus GIBBON. **3.** A free and untutor'd Monarch MILT.

Untwi·ne, *v.* late ME. [UN-2 1.] **1.** *trans.* To undo by untwisting or disentangling. **b.** *fig.* To dissolve, undo, destroy. late ME. **2.** To detach, release, etc. by untwisting 1568. **3.** *intr.* To become untwisted 1592.

Untwi·st *v.* [UN-2 1, 5] 1538. **Untwi·sted** *ppl. a.* [UN-1 2] 1575. **Unty·pical** *a.* [UN-1 1] 1848. **U:nundersta·ndable** *a.* [UN-1 1] 1631. **U:nundersta·nding** *ppl. a.* [UN-1 4] 1611. **U:nunderstoo·d** *ppl. a.* [UN-1 2] 1639. **Unu·niform** *a.* [UN-1 1] 1659, **-ly** *adv.* **Ununi·ted** *ppl. a.* [UN-1 2] 1587. **Unupbrai·ded** *ppl. a.* [UN-1 2] 1682. **Unupbrai·ding** *ppl. a.* [UN-1 4] 1780. **Unu·rged** *ppl. a.* [UN-1 2] SHAKS. **Unu·sable** *a.* [UN-1 1] 1825.

Unused (ʊnyū·zd), *ppl. a.* ME. [UN-1 2.] **1.** Unaccustomed (esp. *to* something, or with inf.). **2.** Not made use of. late ME. **3.** Not in use; unusual. *arch.* 1513.

1. Albeit vn-vsed to the melting moode SHAKS. **3.** Inuentyng..vnused termes 1568.

Unu·seful *a.* [UN-1 1] 1598, **-ly** *adv.*, **-ness.**

Unu·sual, *a.* 1582. [UN-1 1.] Not often occurring or observed, different from what is usual; out of the common, remarkable, exceptional. Hence **U:nusua·lity. Unu·sual-ly** *adv.*, **-ness.**

Unu·tterable, *a.* and *sb.* 1586. [UN-1 1.] **1.** Transcending utterance; inexpressible. **b.** In the phr. *u. things* 1711. **2.** That may not be uttered or spoken 1656. **b.** Unpronounceable 1852.

1. He is, Sir, the most u. coward FLETCHER. Those u. Beatitudes 1746. U. scorn 1880. **2.** Witness th' u. Name COWLEY.

B. *sb.* **1.** An u. thing 1788. **2.** *pl.* Trousers 1843. Hence **Unu·tterably** *adv.*

Unu·ttered *ppl. a.* [UN-1 2] 1463. **Unva·ccinated** *ppl. a.* [UN-1 2] 1871. **Unva·luable** *a.* (now *rare*) [UN-1 1] 1569. **Unva·lued** *ppl. a.* [UN-1 2] 1586. **Unva·nquishable** *a.* [UN-1 1] late ME. **Unva·nquished** *ppl. a.* [UN-1 2] late ME. **Unva·riable** *a.* (now *rare*) [UN-1 1] late ME. **Unva·ried** *ppl. a.* [UN-1 2] 1570.

Unva·rnished, *ppl. a.* 1604. [UN-1 2.] **1.** *fig.* Of statements, etc.: Plain, straightforward; not adorned or specious. **b.** Of persons, etc.: Direct; unsophisticated 1827. **2.** Not varnished 1758.

1. A round vn-varnish'd Tale SHAKS.

Unva·rying *ppl. a.* [UN-1 4] 1690, **-ly** *adv.*, **-ness.**

Unvei·l, *v.* 1599. [UN-2 2, 2 b.] **1.** *trans.* To free (the eyes, etc.) from a veil. **2.** To make (objects) visible by removing a veil or covering. Also *absol.* 1657. **b.** *spec.* To remove the covering from (a statue, etc.) so as to display it for the first time to the public 1865. **3.** *fig.* To disclose, reveal 1606. **b.** To display to the sight; to make visible 1656. **4.** *intr.* To emerge from a veil; to become visible 1655. Hence **Unvei·ling** *vbl. sb.*

Unvei·led *ppl. a.* [UN-1 2] 1606. **Unve·ndible** *a.* [UN-1 1] 1642. **Unve·nerable** *a.* [UN-1 1] SHAKS.

Unve·ntilated, *ppl. a.* 1712. [UN-1 2.] **1.** Not provided with means of ventilation. **2.** Not ventilated or discussed 1872.

Unve·ntured *ppl. a.* [UN-1 2] 1605. **Unvera·cious** *a.* [UN-1 1] 1845, **-ly** *adv.* **Unve·rified** *ppl. a.* [UN-1 2] 1816. **Unve·rsed** *ppl. a.* [UN-1 2] 1675. **Unve·st** *v.* [UN-2 2] 1609. **Unve·xed** *ppl. a.* [UN-1 2] 1456. **Unvi·ctualled** *ppl. a.* [UN-1 2] 1484. **Unview·ed** *ppl. a.* [UN-1 2] 1570. **Unvi·olated** *ppl. a.* [UN-1 2] 1555. **Unvi·rtuous** *a.* [UN-1 1] late ME., **-ly** *adv.*, **-ness. Unvi·sited** *ppl. a.* [UN-1 2] 1549. **Unvi·tal** *a.* [UN-1 1] 1661. **Unvi·tiated** *ppl. a.* [UN-1 2] 1632. **Unvi·trifiable** *a.* [UN-1 1] 1758. **Unvi·trified** *ppl. a.* [UN-1 2] 1779. **Unvo·cal** *a.* [UN-1 1] 1773.

Unvoi·ce, *v.* 1637. [UN-2 2.] *trans.* To deprive of voice; *spec.* in *Phonetics*, to utter with 'breath' instead of 'voice'.

Unvoi·ced, *ppl. a.* 1859. [UN-1 2.] **1.** Of opinions, etc.: Not expressed. **2.** Of organ-pipes: Not having had the tone regulated 1881. **3.** *Phonetics.* Uttered without vibration of the vocal chords 1879.

Unvo·luntary *a.* (now *rare*) [UN-1 1] 1570. **Unvo·te** *v.* [UN-2 1, 5] 1647. **Unvou·ched** *ppl. a.* [UN-1 2] 1775. **Unvow·ed** *ppl. a.* [UN-1 2] 1570. **Unvoy·ageable** *a.* [UN-1 1] MILT. **Unvu·lgar** *a.* [UN-1 1] 1598. **Unwa·kened** *ppl. a.* [UN-1 2] 1621. **Unwa·lled** *ppl. a.* [UN-1 2] 1440. **Unwa·ndered** *ppl. a.* [UN-1 2] 1654. **Unwa·ndering** *ppl. a.* [UN-1 4] 1568. **Unwa·nted** *ppl. a.* [UN-1 2] 1697. **Unwa·rded** *ppl. a.* [UN-1 2] late ME. †**Unwa·re** *a.*, *sb.*, and *adv.* [UN-1 1, 5, 6] –1875. **Unwa·reness** (*arch.*) [UN-1 6] late ME.

Unwa·res, *adv. arch.* [Late OE. *unwæres*, f. *unwær* UNWARE + *-es* -S suffix; see UN-1 1, and cf. UNAWARES.] Unexpectedly, suddenly; unwittingly.

Unwa·rily *adv.* [UN-1 5] 1568. **Unwa·riness** [UN-1 6] 1544. **Unwa·rlike** *a.* [UN-1 1] 1590. **Unwa·rmed** *ppl. a.* [UN-1 2] 1625. **Unwa·rming** *ppl. a.* [UN-1 4] 1736. **Unwa·rned** *ppl. a.* [UN-1 2] OE. **Unwa·rp** *v.* [UN-2 1] 1659. **Unwa·rped** *ppl. a.* [UN-1 2] 1744. **Unwa·rrantable** *a.* [UN-1 1] 1612, **-ness, -ably** *adv.*

Unwa·rranted, *ppl. a.* 1577. [UN-1 2.] Not warranted or guaranteed, in various senses.

Ignorant and u. Physitians 1633. The Assembly cannot Represent any man in things u. by their Letters HOBBES. I should be utterly u. in supposing that..they were insane LYTTON.

Unwa·ry *a.* [UN-1 1] 1579.

Unwa·shed, *ppl. a.* late ME. [UN-1 2.] **1.** Not washed. **2.** *spec.* Of persons: Not having washed; not usually washed or in a clean state 1595. **b.** *absol.*, freq. in *The (Great) U.*, the lower orders 1833. **3.** Not washed *off* or *out* 1628.

2. Another leane, vnwash'd Artificer SHAKS. **b.** Whenever I speak of..the working classes, it is in the 'great-u.' sense 1868. So **Unwa·shen** *ppl. a.* (*arch.*) OE.

Unwa·sted *ppl. a.* [UN-1 2] ME. **Unwa·sting** *ppl. a.* [UN-1 4] late ME. **Unwa·tched** *ppl. a.* [UN-1 2] late ME. **Unwa·tchful** *a.* [UN-1 1] 1611, **-ly** *adv.*, **-ness. Unwa·ter** *v.* [UN-2 2] 1642.

Unwa·tered, *ppl. a.* 1440. [UN-1 2.] **1.** Not treated or supplied with water. **b.** Of silk fabrics, etc.: Plain, not watered 1535. **2.** Not diluted with water 1562. **b.** Of capital: Not increased merely in nominal amount by share-issuing 1893. **3.** Waterless, dry 1600.

Unwa·tery *a.* [UN-1 1] OE. **Unwa·vering** *ppl. a.* [UN-1 4] 1570, **-ly** *adv.* **Unwa·xed** *ppl. a.* [UN-1 2] late ME. **Unwea·kened** *ppl. a.* [UN-1 2] 1648. **Unwea·lthy** *a.* [UN-1 1] late ME. **Unwea·ned** *ppl. a.* [UN-1 2] 1581. **Unwea·poned** *ppl. a.* [UN-1 2] ME. **Unwea·riable** *a.* [UN-1 1] 1561, **-ness, -ably** *adv.* **Unwea·ried** *ppl. a.* [UN-1 2] ME., **-ly** *adv.*, **-ness. Unwea·ry** *a.*, [UN-1 1] OE. **Unwea·rying** *ppl. a.* [UN-1 4] 1600, **-ly** *adv.* **Unwea·thered,** *ppl. a.* [UN-1 2] 1843. **Unwea·ve** *v.* [UN-2 1, 5] 1542. **Unwe·bbed** *ppl. a.* [UN-1 2] 1768. **Unwe·d** 1513, **Unwe·dded** ME. *ppl. adjs.* [UN-1 2].

Unwe·dgeable, *a.* 1603. [UN-1 1.] Incapable of being split by wedges; uncleavable.

The vn-wedgable and gnarled Oke SHAKS.

Unwee·ded *ppl. a.* [UN-1 2] 1602. **Unwee·ting** *ppl. a.* (*arch.*) [f. UN-1 4 + WEET *v.*1] ME, **-ly** *adv.* **Unwei·ghed** *ppl. a.* [UN-1 2] 1481. **Unwei·ghted** *ppl. a.* [UN-1 2] 1883. **Unwe·lcome** *a.* [UN-1 2] ME., **-ly** *adv.*, **-ness. Unwe·lcomed** *ppl. a.* [UN-1 2] 1548.

Unwe·ll, *a.* 1450. [UN-1 1.] Not in good health; slightly or temporarily ill; indisposed. (In early use chiefly *dial.* or *U.S.*) Hence **Unwe·llness** (*rare*).

Unwe·mmed, *ppl. a. arch.* or *dial.* [OE., f. UN-1 2.] Spotless, pure, immaculate; unblemished.

Unwe·pt, *ppl. a.* 1594. [UN-1 2.] Not wept or mourned for; unlamented.

Unwept, unhonour'd, and unsung SCOTT.

Unwe·t *a.* [UN-1 1] late ME. **Unwe·tted** *ppl. a.* [UN-1 2] 1664. **Unwhi·pped, -whi·pt** *ppl. a.* [UN-1 2] SHAKS. **Unwhi·skered** *ppl. a.* [UN-1 2] 1812. **Unwhi·spered** *ppl. a.* [UN-1 2] 1821. **Unwhi·tewashed** *ppl. a.* [UN-1 2] 1846.

Unwho·lesome, *a.* ME. [UN-1 1.] **1.** Not beneficial, salutary, or conducive to morals, etc.; detrimental or prejudicial to health of mind. **b.** Hurtful, noxious. late ME. **2.** Unfavourable or injurious to bodily health ME. **3.** Of persons: Morally or physically unsound; tainted or corrupted. late ME.

1. b. Perhaps farther stay were u. for my safety SCOTT. **3.** The people muddied, Thicke and vnwholsome in their thoughts and whispers SHAKS. Hence **Unwho·lesome-ly** *adv.*, **-ness.**

Unwieldy (ʊnwī·ldi), *a.* late ME. [UN-1 1.] †**1.** Of persons, etc.: Lacking strength; weak, feeble –1685. **2.** Moving ungracefully or with difficulty; not active; awkward, clumsy 1530. **b.** Of clumsy make or size; ponderously big 1582. **c.** Of action, etc.: Ungraceful, awkward 1635. **3.** Difficult to wield or manage owing to size, weight or shape 1547. **b.** *transf.* and *fig.* 1538. **4.** Restive, indocile; rejecting control. Now *rare.* 1513.

1. So vnweeldy was this sory palled goost CHAUCER. **2. b.** Elephants and whales please us with their u. greatness HOGARTH. Two cases of u. corpulence 1793. **3. b.** The u. haughtiness of a great ruling nation BURKE. **4.** The Flemings grew vnweildie to his commandements 1611. Hence **Unwie·ldily** *adv.* **Unwie·ldiness.**

Unwi·lful *a.* [UN-1 1] late ME. **Unwi·ll** *v.* [UN-2 1] 1650. **Unwi·lled** *ppl. a.* [UN-1 2] 1540.

Unwi·lling, *ppl. a.* [OE. *unwillende*, f. UN-1 4 + WILLING *ppl. a.*] †**1.** Not intending the act in question –ME. **2.** Not willing or ready; reluctant, disinclined, loath OE. **b.** *transf.* of things 1592. †**3.** Involuntary, not intended –1687. **4.** Done, expressed, etc., reluctantly or unwillingly 1613.

2. I own I were u. he should learn what nowise concerns him SCOTT. **b.** Why shou'd you pluck the green distasteful Fruit From the u. Bough DRYDEN. **4.** That sagacity..which had..extorted the u. admiration of his enemies MACAULAY. Hence **Unwi·lling-ly** *adv.*, **-ness.**

Unwi·nd, *v.* ME. [Un-^{2} 1.] **1.** *trans.* To wind off (a wrapping, bandage, etc.); to undo the windings of (thread, tape, or the like). **b.** To cause to uncoil; to free from a coiled state 1634. **2.** To roll, twist, or turn back the wrapping, bandaging or covering of (a body, etc.); to untwine thread from (a reel); to free (a person) *from* bonds 1596. **3.** *intr.* To become unwound or uncoiled 1656. **4.** *trans.* To trace or retrace to an issue, outlet, or end 1716.

1. *fig.* As you vnwinde her loue from him SHAKS. **2.** †*fig.* You could u. yourself from all these dangers DRYDEN. **3.** As the spring unwinds and acts with less power 1834. **4.** Till Ariadne's clue unwinds the way GAY. Hence **Unwi·nding** *vbl. sb.*

Unwi·nged *ppl. a.* [Un-^{1} 2] 1601. **Unwi·nking** *ppl. a.* [Un-^{1} 4] 1782, **-ly** *adv.* **Unwi·nning** *ppl. a.* (*rare*) [Un-^{1} 4] 1655. **Unwi·nnowed** *ppl. a.* [Un-^{1} 2] 1552. **Unwi·ped** *ppl. a.* [Un-^{1} 2] 1605. **Unwi·sdom** [Un-^{1} 6] OE.

Unwi·se, *a.* [OE. *unwis*, f. Un-^{1} 1.] **1.** Lacking or deficient in (practical) wisdom, discretion, or prudence; foolish. Often *absol.* **2.** Not marked or prompted by (practical) wisdom; injudicious. late ME. Hence **Unwi·se-ly** *adv.*, **-ness.**

Unwi·sh, *v.* 1594. [Un-^{2} 1.] **1.** *trans.* To revoke (a wish). **2.** To wish non-existent, desire the annihilation or absence of 1599. **b.** To wish or desire (a circumstance or thing) not to be 1628.

2. Now thou hast vnwisht fiue thousand men SHAKS. **b.** How many shall u. themselves Christians 1615.

Unwi·shed *ppl. a.* [Un-^{1} 2] 1583. **Unwi·shful** *a.* [Un-^{1} 1] 1876. **Unwi·st** *ppl. a.* (*Obs.* or *arch.*) [Un-^{1} 2] late ME. †**Unwi·t** *v.* [Un-^{2} 2] SHAKS. **Unwi·tch** *v.* (*arch.*) [Un-^{2} 1] 1580. **Unwithdraw·ing** *ppl. a.* [Un-^{1} 4] MILT. **Unwithdraw·n** *ppl. a.* [Un-^{1} 2] 1829. **Unwi·thered** *ppl. a.* [Un-^{1} 2] 1599. **Unwi·thering** *ppl. a.* [Un-^{1} 4] 1743. **Unwithstoo·d** *ppl. a.* [Un-^{1} 2] 1595. **Unwi·tnessed** *ppl. a.* [Un-^{1} 2] late ME.

Unwi·tting, *ppl. a.* [OE. *unwitende*, f. Un-^{1} 4. Rare after *c*1600, until revived *c*1800. Cf. UNWEETING.] **1.** Unconscious; not aware; without knowing; unheeding. Occas. quasi-*adv.* **b.** Const. *of*, or with direct obj. or obj. clause. late ME. †**2.** In absolute constructions –1622. †**3.** Without the knowledge *of* (or with poss. adj.), unbeknown *to* –1633. **4.** Done unwittingly; unintentional 1818.

1. Of which he had been the u. cause 1833. **b.** U. the frightful truth that lay in the words 1869. **2.** Unwittand his ost, he passis fra his company 1456. **3.** My wif delyvered all, myn unwetyng 1454. The two Earles..vnwitting to the rest, presently withdrew themselues 1630. Hence **Unwi·tting-ly** *adv.*, **-ness.**

Unwi·tty, *a.* [OE. *unwittiġ*, f. Un-^{1} 1.] **1.** Lacking in wit, intelligence, or knowledge; foolish; of weak understanding. Now *rare*. **2.** Lacking verbal wit; not witty 1637.

1. These u. wandering wits of mine TENNYSON. **2.** It was an old, but not u. application 1637. Hence **Unwi·ttily** *adv.*

Unwi·ve *v.* [Un-^{2} 1] 1611. **Unwi·ved** *ppl. a.* [Un-^{1} 2] 1570. **Unwo·man** *v.* [Un-^{2} 4 b] 1611. **Unwo·manly** *a.* [Un-^{1} 1] 1529, *adv.* [Un-^{1} 5] late ME. **Unwo·n** *ppl. a.* [Un-^{1} 2] 1593. **Unwo·nt** *a.* (now *rare* or *Obs.*) [Un-^{1} 1] late ME.

Unwo·nted, *ppl. a.* 1553. [Un-^{1} 2.] **1.** Not wonted, usual, or habitual; infrequent. **2.** Not accustomed (*to* something or *to* do something) 1586.

1. New rules and u. tasks C. BRONTË. **2.** Her feete, u. to feele the naked ground SIDNEY. These chambers..That with their splendour load my u. eyes 1822. Hence **Unwo·nted-ly** *adv.*, **-ness.**

Unwoo·ded *ppl. a.* [Un-^{1} 2] 1628. **Unwoo·ed** *ppl. a.* [Un-^{1} 2] 1570. **Unwo·rdable** *a.* [Un-^{1} 1] 1660. **Unwo·rded** *ppl. a.* [Un-^{1} 2] 1860.

Unwo·rkable, *a.* 1839. [Un-^{1} 1.] **1.** Of systems, machines, etc.: That cannot be made to work or function. **b.** Too much, many, large, etc., to be rightly controlled or managed 1862. **2.** Of materials: Too hard, soft, brittle, etc., for shaping or using 1854. Hence **Unworkabi·lity. Unwo·rkableness.**

Unwo·rked, *ppl. a.* 1730. [Un-^{1} 2.] **1.** Of flint, etc.: Not artificially shaped. **2.** Not worked in or operated upon 1817. **3.** Of persons, beasts, tools, etc.: Not set to work or used.

Unwo·rking *ppl. a.* [Un-^{1} 4] 1696. **Unwo·rkmanlike** *a.* [Un-^{1} 1] 1647. **Unwo·rld** *v.* [Un-^{2} 4 b] 1647.

Unwo·rldly, *a.* 1707. [Un-^{1} 1.] **1.** Of a type transcending or exceeding what is usually found or experienced in the world. **2.** Free from worldliness; spiritually minded 1825. **3.** Not belonging to this world; celestial 1765. Hence **Unwo·rldliness.**

Unwo·rn, *ppl. a.* 1586. [Un-^{1} 2.] **1.** Not impaired, decayed, or wasted by use, weather, etc. **2.** Not deteriorated or weakened; unimpaired, fresh 1757. **3.** Never yet worn 1798.

Unwo·rried *ppl. a.* [Un-^{1} 2] KEATS. **Unwo·rshipful** *a.* [Un-^{1} 1] late ME. **Unwo·rshipped** *ppl. a.* [Un-^{1} 2] late ME. **Unwo·rshipping** *ppl. a.* [Un-^{1} 4] 1828. **Unwo·rth** *sb.* [Un-^{1} 6] ME.

Unwo·rth, *a.* 1587. [Un-^{1} 1.] Not worthy of. Chiefly in phr. *not u.* (one's) *while.*

Unworthy (ɒnwɔ̄·ɹði), *a.* ME. [Un-^{1} 1.] **1.** Of little or no value; worthless. **b.** Discreditable; hurtful or injurious to reputation 1693. **2.** Of persons: Not worthy; undeserving; despicable ME. **b.** Used as a conventional or devotional expression of humility 1532. **3.** Not worthy *to* (with infin.) or *of* something ME. **4.** Of treatment, fortune, etc.: Not deserved or justified; unmerited. late ME. **5.** Unbecoming or inadequate to the character or dignity *of* a person, etc.; undeserving *of* notice, etc.; inferior to or below what is merited or deserved 1533. **6.** With ellipse of *of.* Not worthy of, not deserving (something). late ME. **b.** Not befitting or suiting, derogatory to (a person, one's repute, etc.) 1646. **7.** As *adv.* Unworthily. Now *rare.* 1661. **8.** As *sb.* An unworthy person 1616.

1. A litill toune and vnworthy 1375. **b.** Narrow schemings and u. cares SHELLEY. **2.** An u. blackguard of that name 1835. **4.** With tender ruth for her vnworthy griefe SPENSER. **5.** I will take care to suppress things u. of him POPE. **6.** How much he is vnworthy so good a lady SHAKS. **b.** Boyish folly, u. his experience and maturity 1885. **7.** I hope I shall not behave u. of the good Instructions RICHARDSON. Hence **Unwo·rthily** *adv.* **Unwo·rthiness.**

Unwou·nd *ppl. a.* [Un-^{1} 2] 1648. **Unwou·ndable** *a.* [Un-^{1} 1] 1611. **Unwou·nded** *ppl. a.* [Un-^{1} 2] OE. **Unwo·ven** *ppl. a.* [Un-^{1} 2] late ME. **Unwra·p** *v.* [Un-^{2} 1, 2, 5] late ME. **Unwrea·ked** *ppl. a.* [Un-^{1} 2] 1590. **Unwrea·the** *v.* [Un-^{2} 1] 1591. **Unwre·cked** *ppl. a.* [Un-^{1} 2] 1748. **Unwre·nched** *ppl. a.* [Un-^{1} 2] 1784. **Unwre·sted** *ppl. a.* [Un-^{1} 2] 1653. **Unwri·nkle** *v.* [Un-^{2} 1] 1611. **Unwri·nkled** *ppl. a.* [Un-^{1} 2] 1576. **Unwri·te** *v.* [Un-^{2} 1] 1586. **Unwri·teable** *a.* [Un-^{1} 1] 1780.

Unwri·tten, *ppl. a.* late ME. [Un-^{1} 2.] **1.** Not put in writing; unrecorded. **b.** Of laws, etc.: Not formulated in written codes or documents; oral 1456. **c.** Not written *of* 1651. **2.** Not written upon or *on* 1542.

1. b. The u., or common law; and..the written, or statute law BLACKSTONE. *U. law* (colloq.), the assumption that murder committed in the defence of personal honour (e.g. to avenge seduction) is justifiable.

Unwro·nged *ppl. a.* [Un-^{1} 2] 1598.

Unwrou·ght, *ppl. a.* late ME. [Un-^{1} 2.] **1.** Not brought to completion, left unfinished 1375. **2.** Of materials, etc.: In the crude state, not fashioned or worked on. late ME. **3.** Of mines: Not worked 1669.

Unwru·ng *ppl. a.* [Un-^{1} 2] SHAKS.

Let the gauled Iade winch, our withers are vnwrong *Ham.* III. ii. 253 (Q 2).

Unyie·lding, *ppl. a.* 1592. [Un-^{1} 4.] **1.** Of substances: Not yielding to force or pressure 1658. **2.** Of persons, temper, etc.: Steadfast, obstinate 1592. Hence **Unyie·lding-ly** *adv.*, **-ness.**

Unyo·ke, *v.* [OE. *unġeocian*; Un-^{2} 2 b.] **1.** *trans.* To release (a beast) from the yoke. **b.** To disconnect (the plough) from a draught-animal. SCOTT. **2.** To free from oppression or subjection. late ME. **3.** To disjoin, unlink 1595. **4.** *absol.* To remove the yoke from an animal 1573. **b.** *fig.* To cease from labour, etc. 1594.

Unyo·ked *ppl. a.* [Un-^{1} 2] 1573. **Unzo·ned** *ppl. a.* [Un-^{1} 2] 1718.

-uous (-juəs), a compound suffix repr. L. *-uosus*, OFr. or AFr. *-uous*, *-uos* (Fr. *-ueux*) occurring in adoptions from Latin or French, as *impetuous, tempestuous*, and by analogy, with the sense 'of the nature of, consisting of', in a few English formations on Latin stems, as *ambiguous, strenuous.*

Up (ɒp), *sb.* 1536. [f. UP *adv.*^{1,2} or *a.*] **1.** A person or thing that is up (*rare*). **2.** Usu. *pl.* and assoc. with *downs* (see UP AND DOWN D): **a.** A rise in the ground 1637. **b.** A rise in life; a spell of prosperity 1844. **c.** A rise in price or value 1897. **3.** An 'up' train 1884.

Up (ɒp), *a.* ME. [f. UP *adv.*^{1,2}.] **1.** Of regions or their inhabitants: High, upland (*rare*). **2.** Of trains, coaches, etc.: Going or running up (see UP *adv.*^{1} 6) 1784. **b.** Belonging to, connected with, such trains, etc. 1840. **3.** Of sparkling wines, beer, soda-water, etc.: Effervescing; effervescent. Usu. predic. 1815. **b.** *fig.* Animated, vivacious 1815. **4.** Ascending; upward 1869.

2. b. The booking-office..is on the up platform 1885. **4.** Horizontal, or with slight up gradient 1901.

Up, *v.* 1560. [f. UP *adv.*^{1}] **1.** *trans.* To drive up (swans) for marking. **2.** To lift up (a weapon), esp. to or upon the shoulder 1885. **3.** *Naut.* To put (the helm) or haul (a trawl, etc.) up 1890. **4.** *intr.* To stand up; to get up; to rise from bed. **b.** colloq. *To up and* (do something), to do it abruptly or boldly 1831. **5.** *To up and down*, to rise and fall by turns 1737. **6.** *To up with*, to raise (the arm, a weapon, etc.) 1760.

2. Good..upped gun, and let drive at..a young cow 1885. **4. b.** All of a sudden the doctor ups and turns on them MARK TWAIN. **6.** He ups with the spade in a minute 1887.

Up (ɒp), *adv.*^{1} [OE. *up, upp* = OFris. *up, op*, OS. *up* (Du. *op*), ON. *upp*; rel. to OHG. *ūf* (G. *auf*).] **I. 1.** To or towards a point or place higher than another and lying directly (or almost directly) above it. **b.** Towards or above the level of the shoulders or head OE. **c.** So as to raise into a more erect (or level) as well as elevated position OE. **d.** So as to raise a thing from the place in which it is lying, placed, or fixed OE. **e.** So as to invert the relative position of things or surfaces; so as to have a particular surface facing upwards ME. **2.** Towards a point above the ground; into the air OE. **b.** To some height above the ground or other surface; *spec.* to a seat on horseback OE. **c.** So as to be suspended aloft or on high OE. **3.** Of stars, etc.: From below the horizon to the line of vision OE. **b.** From below to the surface of water, the ground, etc. OE. **c.** Out from the ground; from the stomach into, or out at, the mouth; out of the sea on to the shore, etc. OE. **4.** So as to extend or rise to a higher point or level, esp. above the surface of the ground OE. **b.** So as to form a heap or pile, or become more prominent ME. **5.** So as to raise or rise to an upright or nearly upright position OE. **b.** Upon one's feet from a recumbent or reclining posture; *spec.* out of bed OE. **c.** So as to rise from a sitting, stooping, or kneeling posture and assume an erect attitude OE. **6.** So as to mount or rise by gradual ascent, in contact with a surface, to a higher level; sometimes *spec.* = upstairs OE. **b.** To a point on a river, channel, etc., further from the sea OE. **c.** To or in any place regarded as important, e.g. London, a university, a capital city, etc. 1475. **d.** *Naut.* To windward 1591. **7.** So as to direct the sight to a higher point or level OE. **b.** So as to cause sound to ascend, increase, or swell OE.

1. After he has pulled up his stockings 1766. **b.** Eliza's hands went up in horror 1887. **e.** In trumps, if king or queen is turned up 1863. **2.** Doubting least S. Richard would haue blowne them vp and himselfe RALEGH. The gentle larke..mounts vp on hie SHAKS. **3.** Never sleep the Sun up 1655. **b.** To se the water ryse up..out of a spring 1530. The taking up oysters from great depths 1748. **4.** Lighthouses..put up to prevent shipwrecks 1873. **5.** Drew himself up in offended dignity 1850. I..did not get up till the lamps were being lighted 1865. **6.** The moving Moon went up the sky COLERIDGE. **c.** Resolved to go up to London 1820.

II. *transf.* and *fig.* **1.** From a lower to a higher status in respect of rank, affluence, credit, repute, etc. OE. **2. a.** To a higher spiritual or moral level or object OE. **b.** To a state of greater cheerfulness, resolution, etc. ME. **c.** Into a state of activity, commotion, or excitement ME. **d.** To or at a higher pitch, speed, rate, amount, number, price, etc. 1538. **3.** To or towards maturity or proficiency OE. **4.** Into existence, prominence, etc.; so as to appear or prevail OE. **b.** So as to be heard ME. **5.** To the notice of a person or body of persons (*spec.* of one in authority) ME. **b.** Before a judge, magistrate, etc. 1440. **c.** So as to divulge, reveal, etc. 1593. **d.** As a charge or accusation 1604. **6.** Into the hands or possession of another ME. **b.** So as to relinquish or forsake ME. **7.** Into a receptacle or place of storage ME. **8.** Into one's possession, charge, custody, etc. late ME. **9.** Into the position or state of being open ME. **10.** Into an open or loose condition of surface. late ME. **b.** So as to separate or divide, esp. into many fragments or parts. late ME. **11.** To or towards a state of completion or finality ME. **12.** By way of summation or enumeration. late ME. **b.** To a final or total sum or amount ME. **13.** Into a close or compact form; so as to be confined or secured. late ME. **b.** Into a closed or enclosed state 1489. **c.** So as to cover or envelop. late ME. **14.** Into a state of union, conjunction or combination 1450. **b.** So as to supply deficiencies, defects, etc. 1568. **15.** To or towards a person or place; so as to approach or arrive. late ME. **b.** To or towards a particular point or state 1513. **c.** To or into later life 1535. **d.** So as to find, overtake, or keep on the track of 1622. **16.** To a stop or halt 1623.

1. Getting up in the world 1832. A preacher-up of Nature 1871. **2. b.** I..could not pluck up courage 1894. **c.** Work the crowds up 1901. **d.** Carry had better hurry up 1900. **3.** Brought up to no profession 1894. **4.** Smyth..had not turned up 1902. **b.** The bell..strikes up 1853. **5.** The writ went up to the Lords 1844. **c.** If his two companions..would not own up 1884. **7.** The heat of the sun is stored up in coal 1879. **10.** Taking up all the streets in South London 1895. **b.** Engaged in tearing up old newspapers 1837. **11.** Cloves.. boil'd Up with the coffee BYRON. I polished up the handle of the big front door W. S. GILBERT. The spendthrift had..sold up the remainder 1894. **12.** All my years when added up are many JOWETT. **13.** Visitors huddled up in corners LAMB. **c.** If the wound is covered closely up 1837. **14.** That he could draw up..a hole in his breeches STERNE. **15.** The Spring comes slowly up this way COLERIDGE. **b.** To even up my account with his people 1901. **c.** From his youth up 1890. **16.** A man..pulled up his coach 1623.

III. *ellipt.* **1.** *imper.* or with auxiliary vb. ME. **2.** Followed by a sb. in obj. relationship to an unexpressed verbal notion. Orig. in imper., later in other uses, thus passing into UP *v.* 2, 3. late ME.

1. 'Up Guards, and at them', cried the Duke of Wellington SCOTT. **2.** We'll up anchor 1832. *Up Jenkins* = TIP-IT.

With preps., etc. **Up against —.** *To knock* or *run up against*, to fall in with. **Up till —.** = *up to.* **Up to —. a.** As high or as far as. **b.** Up towards. **c.** So as to arrive at. (*b*) Until. **d.** Confronting (a person) as a task. **e.** So as to reach or attain (a specified point or stage). (*b*) As many or much as (a specified number or amount). **Up with —. a.** So as to overtake. **b.** *To put up with*: see PUT *v.*[1] **c.** *ellipt.* (*a*) Denoting the raising of a weapon, the hand, etc., esp. so as to strike. (*b*) Denoting erecting, pulling up, etc. (*c*) To drink off, consume. (*d*) To 'come out' with (something). (*e*) Denoting support or advocacy of a person or thing. **Up and —,** *ellipt.*, denoting the act of rising or starting up, accompanied by subsequent action.

Up (ʊp), *adv.*[2] [OE. *uppe* = OFris., OS. *uppa*, ON. *uppi.*] **I. 1.** At some distance above the ground or earth; aloft. **b.** Of the heavenly bodies: Risen above the horizon OE. **2.** On high or (more) elevated ground; more inland OE. **3.** In an elevated position OE. **b.** Of an adjustable device or part: Raised 1599. **c.** *colloq.* On horseback, riding 1812. **4.** High, in respect of the river-bank or shore. late ME. **b.** On or above the surface of the ground or water 1835. **5. a.** In a standing posture; standing (and delivering a speech) ME. **b.** In an upright position 1669. **c.** Erected, built 1613. **6. a.** Out of bed; risen. late ME. **b.** Not (yet) gone to bed 1535. **c.** Of game: Roused, started 1611. **7.** Further away from the mouth of a river, etc. 1600. **b.** Towards a place or position; advanced in place 1613. **c.** At or in a place of importance (*spec.* London) 1845. **d.** *colloq.* At or in school or college 1847. **8.** Facing upward 1683. **9.** With the surface broken or removed 1886.

1. b. Tho' the Moon was up DE FOE. **2.** The City..is 20 mile up in the Country 1697. **3. b.** His coat-collar was up MEREDITH. **c.** To pace the paddock when Archer 's up 1886. **4.** The tide was up DE FOE. **6. b.** They were up all last night DICKENS. **7. b.** If the ball is a half-volley or well up 1903. **9.** Streets that are up 1886.

II. *fig.* **1.** In a state of disorder, revolt, or insurrection. late ME. **b.** *Up in arms*, risen, levied, or marshalled as an armed host. Also *fig.* 1590. **c.** Actively stirring or moving about 1460. **d.** In a state of agitation, exaltation, confidence, etc. 1470. **2.** In a state of prevalency, performance, or progress (now chiefly with KEEP *v.*) ME. **b.** Much or widely spoken of. Now *rare.* 1618. **c.** *colloq.* Occurring (as an unusual or undesirable event); going on 1849. **d.** Amiss *with* a person, etc. 1887. **3.** Completed; expired; over; (at) the number or limit agreed on as the game; of an assembly: risen, adjourned, over. late ME. **b.** Come to a fruitless or undesired end 1787. **c.** *All up*, completely finished (*with*). Also, *all U.P.* (yū pī). 1825. **4.** Higher in respect of position, rank, fortune, etc. 1509. **b.** Increased in strength, power, etc.; ready for action 1547. **c.** Advanced or high in number, value, or price 1546. **d.** (So many points, etc.) in advance of a competitor 1894. **e.** At a high or lofty pitch 1902. **5.** Before a magistrate, etc. in court. **b.** Offered or exposed for sale 1921.

1. The eastern counties were up MACAULAY. **c.** Let us, then, be up and doing LONGF. **d.** When his temper is up 1891. **3.** As his leave was nearly up 1889. **4. b.** A Government steamer.., with steam up 1848.

With preps. **Up against —,** faced or confronted by (difficulties, etc.). *colloq.* (orig. *U.S.*). **Up in —,** expert or versed, etc., in a subject, etc. *colloq.* **Up to —. a.** Able to perform or undertake; fit or qualified for. (*b*) Prepared for; a match for. (*c*) Expert or versed in. (*d*) Ready for. **b.** Equal in quality or quantity to; on a level with. (*b*) *Not up to much*, of no great ability, importance, or worth. **c.** Engaged in or bent on (an activity, esp. of a reprehensible nature); doing or planning. **d.** *colloq.* Obligatory or incumbent upon. **Up with —.** On a level with (a person, place, etc.).

Up (ʊp), *prep.* 1509. [By ellipsis of prepositions, such as *against*, *along*, etc., a new prep. was developed to form collocations like *upstairs.*] **1.** Upwards on or along (an ascent). **2.** Towards the source or head of (a river, lake, etc.) 1513. **b.** *Up* (*the*) *wind*, towards the quarter it blows from 1611. **3.** Into or towards the interior of (a country); towards the upper end of (a room) 1596. **4.** Along towards the other end of (a street, town, passage, line, etc.) 1669. **5.** Of situation: In or at the higher, interior, or more remote part of (a stream, country, state, area) 1667. **6.** At the top of; at some distance above the bottom of 1645.

1. Phr. *Up hill and down dale*, over hill and valley (in pursuit or flight); *transf.* and *fig.*, headlong; thoroughly (as 'to curse up hill and down dale'). **2.** There was a nice up Channel breeze 1898. **3.** They passing in Went vp the hall SPENSER. William's army began to march up the country MACAULAY. **5.** All those five tenements up the yard 1799. *Up stage*: on a part of the stage distant from the footlights or the spectators; *fig.* (orig. *U.S.*) keeping oneself at a distance, distant (in behaviour). *Up-State* (U.S.), freq. with ref. to the State of New York. **6.** A small chamber up four pair of stairs 1714.

Up-, *prefix*, repr. OE. *up-*, *upp-*, corresp. to OFris. *op-*, *up-*, (M)Du. *op-*, OS., (M)LG. *up-*, OHG. *ūf-* (G. *auf-*), ON. *upp-*. The prefix is identical with UP *adv.*[1]

I. In comb. with sbs. **1.** In OE. *up-* occurs freely with sbs., in the sense of 'occupying a higher position', 'upper', as in *upflōr*. In ME. this type practically disappears, and in later use is represented chiefly by UPLAND *sb.* and UPSIDE. **b.** In the sense of 'in a supported state', in OE. *upheald*, etc., ME. *uptie* (naut.), and the modern *upkeep*.

2. In the sense of 'upwards' OE. had compounds with nouns, mainly derived from intr. vbs., as *up-cyme*, *-spring*, etc. Many of these disappeared in ME., but new formations were added, and since 1800 the type has become common. Examples are *upbreak*, *-burst*, *-curve*, *-glance*, *-growth*, *-leap*, *-look*, *-shoot*, *-sweep*, *-turn*. **b.** More rarely *up-* is employed in the sense of 'upwards' with other nouns than those of action, as OE. *upweġ*, and the recent *up-grade*, *-road*, etc.

II. *Up-* is rarely employed in comb. with adjs.: **U·phand** *a.* operated, or performed by raising the hand or hands. †**U·pspring** *a.* upstart, newly arisen or come in.

III. 1. With vbs., participles, agent-nouns, etc. In OE., *up* was placed immediately before a vbl. form only in a limited number of instances, as *upgān*, *-hebban*, etc.; it is difficult to determine in how many of these the adv. had become a real prefix. In ME. the use of the prefix is thoroughly established and new formations have been constantly added during the following centuries. A considerable proportion, however, occur only in poetry, and are simple substitutions for the vb. followed by the adv., although they are regarded as real compounds and written as one word. Examples are: **uparise, -bear, -blaze, -blow, -boil, -break, -buoy, -call, -drag, -draw, -fill, -grow, -jet, -keep, -look, -move, -roll, -rouse, -shoot, -snatch, -stir, -tear, -thrust, -wind, -wrap.**

2. The use of *up* with pa. pples. gave rise to compounds of which several had already so far established themselves in OE. that derivatives in *-nes* and *-lice* were formed from them. The type is still usual, but at all periods these forms have been mainly employed in verse. When they are used *attrib.*, the stress is normally on the prefix. Examples are: **up-blown, -choked, -flung, -looped, -ploughed, -poised, -propped, -ripped, -rolled, -swept, -wrapped.**

3. The use of *up* before pres. pples. is somewhat rare in OE.; ME. furnishes a few instances, but this type of formation becomes common only after 1500. Examples are: **uparising, -blazing, -brimming, -gliding, -keeping, -rousing, -staring, -steaming, -swarming, -wreathing.** **b.** In the earlier periods these forms in *-ing* were not used *attrib.*; examples of this use begin to appear in the 16th c., but are not common before the 19th. As adjs., such compounds normally have the main stress on the prefix, but in verse the stress is freq. on the stem. Examples are: **upbearing, -creeping, -cropping, -flashing, -gushing, -lying, -pouring, -sticking, -stretching, -striving, -struggling.**

4. In OE. the comb. of *up-* with a vbl. sb. is limited to one instance, *uphebbing*; in ME. the type is also rare, but it becomes common in the 16th c. and again in the 19th. Examples are †**uparising, -bubbling,** †**-crying, -gushing, -piling, -putting, -sealing, -surging, -swelling, -working.**

5. The use of *up-* with agent-nouns first appears in the 14th c., in *upstyer*, *uptaker*, etc. Similar forms appear in the 16th c. (but chiefly Sc.), as *up-creeper*, *-lifter*, *-looker*, and a few in the 17th as *upbringer*, *-riser*. Later formations are mainly from the 19th c., as *upbuilder*, *-climber*, *-stander*.

U·p-a-daisy, *int.* Now *dial.* or *colloq.* 1711. [f. UP *adv.*[1]; also *upsidaisy.*] An exclam. addressed to a child that has fallen, or when raising it in the arms.

Up-a·nchor, *v.* 1897. [UP *adv.*[1], UP *v.* 3.] *intr.* To weigh anchor.

Up and coming, *a. U.S.* 1889. [UP *adv.*[2]] Active, alert, wide-awake.

Up and down, *adv.*, *prep.*, *a.*, and *sb.* ME. [f. UP *adv.*[1] and *adv.*[2] + DOWN *adv.*] **A.** *adv.* **1.** Alternately on or to a higher and a lower level or plane. **2.** To and fro; backward and forward ME. **3.** At various points; here and there ME. **b.** Here and there in a book or author; passim 1668. **4.** *Naut.* In or into a vertical position; vertically 1669. **5.** In every respect; entirely. Now *dial.* 1542. **6.** *U.S. colloq.* Bluntly; in plain words 1869.

3. He..liu'd obscurely vp and downe in boothes, and taphouses B. JONSON. **4.** When the cable is in that condition, the boatswain calls, 'Up and down, sir' 1867. **5.** This is the Pharisee up and down, 'I am not as other men are' MILT.

B. *prep.* **1.** To and fro, backward and forward, in, along or upon. late ME. **b.** Here and there in or upon 1597. **2.** Alternately on or to higher and lower parts of (hills, etc.) 1665.

1. b. As is evident up and down the Scripture 1675.

C. *adj.* (now usu. hyphened). **1.** Acting, directed, etc., alternately or indifferently upward and downward 1616. **2.** Vertical, not horizontal or sloping 1710. **b.** *U.S.* Downright; straightforward 1836. **3.** Having an uneven or irregular surface; consisting of ups and downs 1775. **4.** Moving from place to place; migratory, oscillating 1824.

2. Clothes hanging in folds upon her up-and-down figure 1897.

D. *sb.* **1.** *pl.* **Ups and downs. a.** Irregularities of surface 1682. **b.** Undulatory motions, tracings, etc. 1860. **c.** Vicissitudes 1659. **2.** *sing.* (usu. hyphened). **a.** Alternate rise and fall, esp. *fig.* in respect of fortune, position, etc. 1775. **b.** An undulating surface or marking 1856.

Upanishad (ʊpæ·niʃæd). 1805. [– Skr. *upa-nishád*, f. *upa* near to + *ni-shad* sit or lie down.] In Sanskrit literature, one or other of various speculative metaphysical treatises forming a division of the Vedic literature.

‖**Upas** (yū·pǎs). 1783. [– Malay *ūpas* poison, in the comb. *pōhun ūpas* poison-tree.] **1.** In full *upas-tree*, a fabulous Javanese tree so poisonous as to destroy all life for many miles round. **b.** *fig.* A baleful power or influence 1801. **2.** The Javanese tree *Antiaris toxicaria*, yielding a poisonous juice 1814. **3.** The poison obtained from the upas-tree 1783.

U·pbeat. 1869. [UP- I. 2.] **1.** *Mus.* An unaccented beat in a bar, during which the hand is raised in beating time. **2.** *Pros.* **a.** An anacrusis. **b.** An arsis or stressed syllable. 1883.

Upbraid (ʊpbrēⁱ·d), *v.* [Late OE. *upbrēdan*, perh. after ON. **uppbregða*, f. *upp-* UP- + *bregða* = OE. *breġdan* BRAID *v.*¹] †**1.** *trans.* To adduce or allege (a matter) as a ground for censure or reproach –1718. **b.** To censure, find fault with, carp at ME. **2.** To reprove, reproach (a person, etc.) ME. **b.** Const. *with* or †*of* (the cause of censure) ME.

1. It shall bee vpbraided vs that wee haue turned our heartes backe 1583. **b.** How much doth thy kindnesse upbraide my wickednesse? SIDNEY. **2. b.** Lest he of eny vntrouthe her vpbreyde CHAUCER. Hence **Upbrai·der. Upbrai·ding** *vbl. sb.* the action of the vb.; a reproach or reproof. **Upbrai·ding** *ppl. a.*

U·pbringing, *vbl. sb.* 1520. [f. †*upbring* to rear + -ING¹.] The action of bringing up; the fact of being brought up, or the manner of this; early rearing and training.

U·pcast, *sb.* 1611. [UP- I. 2.] **1.** A chance or accident. Now *rare.* **2.** *Mining* and *Geol.* An upward dislocation or shifting of a seam or stratum; a fault caused by this 1793. **3.** *Upcast shaft* (or *pit*), the pit-shaft by which the ventilating air is returned to the surface 1816. **4.** Material thrown up in digging 1883.

1. *Cymb.* II. 1. 2.

Upca·st, *v.* late ME. [UP- III. 1.] *trans.* To cast or fling up. Hence **Upca·sting** *vbl. sb.*

U·pcast, *ppl. a.* late ME. [UP- III. 2.] **1.** Of the eye or look; Turned or directed upwards. **2.** Mining. *Upcast dyke* = UPCAST *sb.* 2. 1810. **3.** Thrown upwards 1823.

U·p-country, up-cou·ntry, *sb., a.,* and *adv.* 1835. [UP *a.* and *prep.*] **A.** *sb.* The inland or more remote part of a country 1837. **B.** *adj.* Of or situated in the inland part of a country 1835. **C.** *adv.* In or to the inland part of a country 1864.

Up-e·nd, *v.* orig. *dial.* 1823. [UP *adv.*¹] **1.** *trans.* To set (something) on its end; to turn end upwards. **2.** *intr.* To rise up on end 1897.

U·p-grade, *sb.* and *adv.* orig. *U.S.* 1888. [UP- I. 2 b.] **A.** *sb.* An upward slope or incline. **b.** *On the up-grade*: ascending, rising; *fig.* improving, making progress 1892. **B.** *adv.* Uphill 1899. Hence **Upgra·de** *v. trans.* to raise to a higher grade of wages, etc.

Upheaval (ʊphī·vǎl). 1838. [f. next + -AL¹ 2.] **1.** *Geol.* The action of raising, or fact of being raised, above the original level, esp. by volcanic action. **b.** An instance of this; an upward displacement of some part of the earth's crust 1849. **c.** *gen.* 1890. **2.** A great and sudden convulsion or alteration of society 1850. Hence **Uphea·valist,** one who attributes geological changes to upheaval.

Uphea·ve, *v.* ME. [UP- III. 1.] **1.** *trans.* To heave or lift up; to raise. **b.** *esp.* To toss or throw up with violence; *spec.* in *Geol.* 1708. **2.** *intr.* To rise up 1649.

1. The fader Eneas. .His handis bayth vphevis towartis hevin 1513. **2.** The surface of the bay. . upheaved with a slow, majestic movement 1850. Hence **Uphea·ved** *ppl. a.* **Uphea·vement. Uphea·ver. Uphea·ving** *vbl. sb.* and *ppl. a.*

U·phill, u·p-hill, *sb.* and *a.* 1548. [f. UP *prep.*] **A.** *sb.* An ascent; a high or steep rise. **B.** *adj.* **1.** Situated on high ground 1613. **2.** Ascending; sloping upwards, esp. steeply 1622. **b.** Of a task, struggle, etc.: Difficult; involving prolonged effort; arduous 1622.

Uphi·ll, *adv.* 1607. [UP *prep.*] Towards higher ground; upwards on a (steep) slope. Hence **Uphi·llward** *adv.* and *a.*

Upho·ld, *v.* ME. [UP- III. 1.] **1.** *trans.* To support or sustain physically; to keep from falling or sinking. **2.** To support the cause or contribute to the preservation or prosperity of ME. **b.** To maintain at the same level or standard 1523. **c.** To sustain spiritually 1820. **3.** To maintain in good condition or in a proper state of repair 1511. **4.** To maintain or confirm the validity or truth of; to sustain against objection or criticism 1485. **5.** To raise or lift up; to direct upwards. late ME.

1. Whose feeble thighes, vnhable to vphold His pined corse, him scarse. .could beare SPENSER. **4.** The decision of the registrar was upheld 1893.

Upho·lder. ME. [f. prec. + -ER¹.] **1.** (also †*uphol(d)ster*). †**a.** A dealer in or maker of small wares, furniture, etc. –1812. **b.** An upholsterer. Now *rare.* 1688. **c.** An undertaker. Now *Hist.* 1709. **2.** One who upholds a person, cause, doctrine, etc.; a supporter *of.* late ME. **b.** A support or prop. late ME.

1. c. Th' U., rueful Harbinger of Death, Waits with Impatience for the dying Breath GAY.

Upho·lster, *v.* orig. *U.S.* 1861. [Back-formation from UPHOLSTERER or UPHOLSTERY.] **1.** *trans.* To cover with or as with upholstery 1864. **2.** *intr.* To do upholstery work 1861.

Upho·lstered, *ppl. a.* 1837. [f. as prec. + -ED¹.] Furnished or fitted with upholstery.

Upholsterer (ʊphōᵘ·lstərəɹ). 1613. [Extended form with -ER¹ 3 of †*upholster sb.* (XV), f. UPHOLD + -STER.] A maker, finisher, or repairer of articles of furniture and other house-furnishings in which woven or similar fabrics, or materials used for stuffing these, are employed. **b.** *transf.* Applied to certain bees and birds 1830.

Upho·lstery. 1649. [f. as prec.; see -ERY 2.] Upholsterer's work, materials, or products; the collective use of these in a room or house.

U·pkeep. 1884. [UP- I. 1 b.] Maintenance in good condition or repair; the cost of this.

Upland (ʊ·plænd), *sb.* and *a.* 1566. [f. UP *a.* 1 + LAND *sb.*] **A.** *sb.* **1.** The part of a country lying away from the sea. *arch.* 1579. **2.** High ground; a piece of high, hilly, or mountainous country. Usu. in *pl.* 1566. **3.** (A stretch of) raised land not liable to flooding. Chiefly *local* and *U.S.* 1572. **4.** *ellipt.* in *pl.* Upland cotton 1858.

1. He determined to draw these pirats from the sea into the vpland NORTH. **2.** These to the u., to the valley those COWPER. At the foot of this hill, one stage or step from the uplands, lies the village 1787.

B. *attrib.* or as *adj.* **1.** Lying away from the sea; inland, remote 1575. **b.** Living inland 1716. **2.** Lying higher than the surrounding country 1610. **b.** Living, growing, or found on high ground 1622. **c.** Of water: Flowing from higher ground 1653.

1. The vpland townes are fairer and richer, then those that stand nearer the sea 1601. **2.** *U. cotton*, a class of short-stapled cotton. Hence **U·plander,** an inhabitant or native of the uplands.

U·plift, *sb.* 1845. [UP- I. 2.] **1.** The fact of being raised or elevated. **b.** *spec.* A rise in level, esp. of part of the earth's surface 1853. **2.** *fig.* An elevating effect, result, or influence in the sphere of morality, emotion, physical condition, etc.; often *gen.* without article. Also *attrib.* orig. *U.S.* 1873.

Upli·ft, *v.* ME. [UP- III. 1.] **1.** *trans.* To lift up to a higher level or more erect position; to raise. **b.** To raise to higher rank, repute, wealth, etc. Now *rare.* ME. **c.** To elevate morally 1883. **2.** *Sc.* To levy (rents, etc.); to draw (wages) 1508. **3.** To raise (the voice); to utter (hymns, cries, praise, etc.) 1816. Hence **Upli·ft** (*poet.*), **Upli·fted** *pa. pples.* and *ppl. adjs.* **Upli·fter. Upli·fting** *vbl. sb.*

U·plong. 1819. [f. UP *adv.*² + *long* ALONG.] A strengthening bar along the sail of a windmill.

Upmost (ʊ·pmǒst), *a.* 1560. [f. UP *adv.*² + -MOST.] = UPPERMOST *a.*

Upon (ǒpǫ·n), *prep.* ME. [First in eastern and northern texts; f. UP *adv.*¹ and *adv.*² + ON *prep.*, after ON. *upp á* (OSw. *up a*, *uppa*, Sw. *på*, Norw., Da. *paa*); distinct from OE. *uppan*, ME. *uppon*, *uppe(n*, *up* prep. on, upon.] = ON *prep.*, in all senses. (The use of one form or the other is usu. a matter of individual choice (on grounds of rhythm, emphasis, etc.) or of simple accident, although in certain contexts and phrases there may be a general tendency to prefer the one to the other.) **I.** Of position: = ON *prep.* I–V. **1.** Above and in contact with or supported by. **b.** Denoting that on which the hand is placed in taking the oath, or the basis of an oath ME. **c.** With *sit*, *serve*, etc.: On the panel of (a jury, inquest) 1516. **d.** In phrases now used *fig.* See esp. CARPET *sb.* 1, HAND *sb.* V. d, LEVEL *sb.* 1, 2. **2.** In contact with (any surface) ME. **b.** Of immaterial actions or *fig.* late ME. **c.** Conformably to (an axis, pivot, base) 1570. **3.** Close to, beside, near ME. **4.** Expressing position with ref. to a place or thing: = ON I. 4. ME. **b.** With vbs., as *border*, *touch*, *verge* ME. **c.** At close quarters with, about to attack 1568. **d.** Indicating the side or part espoused or supported by the agent. late ME. **5.** In the course of (a day, night time) ME. **b.** With vbl. sbs., etc.: On the point of. late ME. **c.** On the occasion of, because of 1440. **d.** Immediately after; following upon. late ME. **6.** About, engaged in, intent on ME. **b.** Of state, condition, action: = ON IV. 3. ME. **c.** Indicating a sphere of activity or existence 1487. **7.** On the basis of, on the model of, by reason of, in reliance on, according to, on the strength of, by means of ME.

1. When they sawe him walkinge apon the see TINDALE *Mark* 6:48. Gallantry strutting u. his Tiptoes STEELE. The castle u. yonder hill 1732. Mrs. Honour is u. the stairs FIELDING. U. her palfrey she is set SOUTHEY. **2.** A greate clothe of redd silke. .with lions of golde u. it 1552. Vpon the next Tree shall thou hang SHAKS. Those clothes would not look so well u. Oswald MARRYAT. **b.** Every one's eyes were u. me RICHARDSON. **c.** The Circle. .is described u. the Centre A 1679. **3.** Countries lying u. the Ocean 1662. **4.** My Lord Ambassador beinge plac'd. .u. his left hand 1644. **c.** The roundheads are u. us 1721. **d.** Famine. .shall wage war u. our side! SHELLEY. **5.** U. a Sabbath-day it fell KEATS. Phr. *Once u. a time*: see ONCE *adv.* **b.** The truce. .was just u. expiring GOLDSM. **c.** If one kill another u. a suddaine quarrell BACON. They. .were cast into Hell u. their Disobedience ADDISON. **d.** [They] conquered. .townes and castels one vpon the other LD. BERNERS. **6.** When Mankind. .were u. Building a City together LOCKE. **b.** A Granadeer . .absent u. Furlow 1706. **c.** The Reception these Gentleman met with u. Change STEELE. **7.** Al min hope is uppon þe 1250. Let vs borowe money of the kinge vpon vsury COVERDALE. Aspshawe is a very poore man, and liveth apon his neibours 1564. Vpon my Blessing I command thee goe SHAKS. My life vpon her faith SHAKS. He has solved. .Phænomena of Nature u. sound Principles 1697. He order'd every man u. the pain of death to bring in all the money he had 1699. A young Horse may look pretty sleek u. Hay only 1737. Mr. Belford gives the substance of it u. his memory RICHARDSON. The new constitution. . is formed very much u. that of France 1863. A commission of over 60 per cent. u. the sums received 1892.

II. Of motion or direction towards something = ON *prep.* VI–VIII. **1.** Upward so as to place or be on a surface, etc. ME. **b.** To or towards a position on (a surface, etc.) ME. **c.** After vbs., etc., of seizing, striking, etc.: = ON VI. 1. ME. **d.** In pursuance of (a voyage, course, etc.) late ME. **2.** Into contact or collision with, against ME. **3.** In the direction of (esp. after vbs. of looking, etc.) ME. **4.** Into or on (some action, occupation, course, etc.) ME. **5.** Indicating the person or thing that action or feeling is directed towards or against, or that is influenced by it: with vbs., as *attend*, *bestow*, adjs., as *keen*, sbs., as *attempt*, *entrance*. ME. **6.** With regard or in reference to, as to, about. late ME.

1. He lep up on a stede HAVELOK. **b.** [They] fell vpon the kne, & worshipped him COVERDALE.

Her head sunk down u. her breast MARSTON. A light broke in u. my brain BYRON. **c.** Sir Tristram gaf him suche a buffet vpon the helme MALORY. The paynes of hell gat holde vpon me COVERDALE *Ps.* 114:3. Sentu. a long Voyage ADDISON. **2.** *ellipt.* Aduance your standards, & vpon them Lords SHAKS. **d.** He cast his eye vpon Emelya CHAUCER. Our Fleet..bore down u. them 1716. **4.** It put the Church u. the alert 1813. **5.** The peple roos vp-on hym CHAUCER. Reuenge my death vpon his traiterous head 1595. Able to play vpon an oaten pipe 1621. They were sufficiently railed u. in the streets LAUD. He..had made their places be conferred u. men void of counsel 1656. Encroachments u. his Dominions 1678. The French have..refin'd too much u. Horace's Rule ADDISON. He shows me a bill u. me, drawn by my wife DE FOE. The constitution..is sacredly obligatory u. all 1796. O'Connell is bent u...disruption 1843. Softly turning the key u. him DICKENS.

†**Upo·n,** *adv.* ME. [ellipt. use of prec.] **1.** Upon it; upon its surface; upon one's person –1611. **2.** Thereupon, thereafter –1606.

1. His gloues, his gyrdell, the kynge had vpon 1513. A clothe..wroughte with goulde vpon 1567. **2.** Indeed my Lord, it followed hard vpon SHAKS.

U·pper, *sb.* 1845. [f. next.] **1.** The upper part of a boot or shoe; that part above the sole and welt. Usu. *pl.* **b.** *U.S.* An ankle gaiter, spat 1891. **c.** *On* one's *uppers*, in want. *colloq.* (orig. *U.S.*) 1891. **2.** An upper jaw, dental plate, or tooth 1878.

Upper (ʌ·pəɹ), *a.* ME. [f. UP *a.* + -ER[3]; cf. MDu. *upper* (Du. *opper*), LG. *upper.*] Comparative of UP *a.* **I. 1.** Consisting of or occupying higher (and usu. more inland) ground ME. **2.** Situated higher than or above another or others. Freq. in proper names of villages, etc. 1467. **b.** Of rooms, etc.: Occupying or forming (part of) the higher or highest portion of a building 1522. **3.** With partitive terms, esp. *end, part, side* 1484. **4.** That forms the higher of a pair of corresponding things or sets 1460. **5. a.** Of garments, etc.: Outer, exterior 1526. **b.** Furthest removed from the door or entrance; innermost. Usu. with *end.* 1590. **6.** That is on or above the earth's surface, not subterranean or infernal 1667. **7.** Of strata: Lying nearer the surface or formed later 1696. **8.** Occurring in a higher or the highest position; directed upwards 1607.

1. The Lower and U. Cossacks 1790. **2.** Clouds.. driven along by u. currents of air 1873. **b.** *fig.* 'Ill-furnished in the u. story'; a head without brains 1870. **4.** *U. case* (Printing): see CASE *sb.*[2] 6. *U. bench*, during the exile of Chas. II, the KING'S BENCH (*Hist.*). **6.** Longing the common Light again to share, and draw the vital breath of u. Air DRYDEN. **8.** During the u. stroke [of the piston] 1815. *U. cut* (Pugilism) a blow delivered upwards 'when an opponent leads off or rushes in with his head down'.

II. *transf.* **1.** Of higher (or the highest) rank, station, authority, wealth, or dignity 1477. **2.** Of studies or students: More advanced 1629. **3.** Of notes, voices, etc.: Of higher pitch 1843.

1. By the Extortion of U. Servants STEELE. Finishing schools for the u. classes EMERSON. **3.** The u. or female voice part of the scale 1843.

Special collocations. **Upper crust: a.** The top crust of a loaf. †**b.** The surface of the earth. **c.** *slang.* The human head. **d.** *colloq.* The aristocracy. **Upper deck,** the highest continuous deck of a ship. **Upper hand. a.** The mastery or control (*of, over*); predominance, rule, dominion. Usu. after vbs., as *get, have, gain.* †**b.** The place of honour; precedence. **Upper house.** The House of Lords; the higher of the two chambers of any deliberative assembly. **Upper leather. a.** (Leather forming) the upper of a boot or shoe. **b.** Leather prepared or suitable for this. **Upper lip. a.** The superior lip of a person, animal, or insect. *To keep a stiff upper lip*, to show no sign of weakening, yielding, or suffering. **b.** The higher of two edges of an organ-pipe mouth. **c.** *Bot.* The superior division of a bilabiate corolla or calyx. **Upper ten,** the upper classes; the aristocracy. *colloq.* Orig. (U.S.) *u. ten thousand.* **Upper works. a.** The part of a ship above the waterline when it is ready or laden for a voyage. **b.** *slang.* The head, brains, wits.

U·pperest, *a.* Now *rare* or *Obs.* ME. [f. prec. + -EST.] Uppermost.

On what might be called the u. Thames W. MORRIS.

Uppermost (ʌ·pəɹmōst), *adv.* and *a.* 1481. [f. as prec. + -MOST.] **A.** *adv.* **1.** In or to the highest or upmost position or place. **b.** In the first place in respect of precedence, rank, importance, etc. 1526. **2.** Foremost in or into the mind, thoughts, conversation, etc. 1693.

1. Shee was turned topse-turvie, her Kele vppermost 1622. **2.** Perpetual Chat on whatever comes u. 1693.

B. *adj.* **1.** Occupying the highest position or place; loftiest; furthest up (on a river, etc.) 1500. **b.** Outermost, most external 1548. **2.** Highest in rank, importance, precedence, etc. 1680. **b.** Having the chief power, control, or authority; predominant 1691.

1. Ye love the vppermost seates in the sinagoges TINDALE *Luke* 11:43. The vppermost village neere the mountaines 1623. **b.** The Adder.. casteth off yearely his u. skin 1567.

U·pping, *vbl. sb.* 1560. [f. UP *v.* + -ING[1].] **1.** = SWAN-UPPING. **2.** The action of getting up; only *attrib.* in *u.-block, -stock, -stone,* a mounting-stone 1796.

Uppish (ʌ·piʃ), *a.* 1678. [f. UP *adv.*[2] + -ISH[1].] †**1.** Flush of money –1700. **2.** †**a.** Elated –1802. †**b.** Excited with drink –1728. **c.** Irritable, testy. Now *dial.* or *Obs.* 1778. **2.** Characterized by presumption or affectation of superiority 1734. **3.** Slightly elevated or directed upwards 1862. Hence **U·ppishness.**

Uprai·se, *v.* ME. [UP- III. 1.] †**1.** *trans.* To raise from the dead –1533. †**2.** To laud, extol –1595. **3.** To raise to a higher level; to lift up (esp. the head, hands, etc.) ME. **b.** To raise from a prostrate, low, or dejected state; to assist, encourage, or cheer ME. **4.** To erect, build. Now *rare.* ME. Hence **U·praised** *ppl. a.* **Uprai·sing** *vbl. sb.* and *ppl. a.*

Uprea·r, *v.* ME. [UP- III. 1.] **1.** *trans.* To raise up, elevate, erect, etc. **b.** To raise in dignity; to exalt. late ME. **2.** To bring up; to tend. late ME. **3.** To excite, stir up. *arch.* 1486. **4.** *intr.* To rise up 1828.

1. So in the field..Uprears some antient Oak his rev'rend head 1718. **b.** Now I shal ben enhauncid, now I shal ben vp rered WYCLIF *Isaiah* 33:10. **4.** Steeds Were seen uprearing 1828. Hence **U·preared** *ppl. a.* **Uprea·ring** *vbl. sb.*

Upright (ʌ·prəit, †ʌprəi·t), *a.* and *sb.* [OE. *upriht*, corresp. to OFris. *upriuht*, (M)Du. *oprecht*, OHG. *ūfreht* (G. *aufrecht*), ON. *upréttr*; see UP *adv.*[1], -RIGHT.] **A.** *adj.* **1.** *predic.* Erect on the feet or end; in or into a vertical position; perpendicular to the ground or other surface. †**2.** *predic.* Lying or so as to lie at full length on the back; supine. Usu. with *lie* vb. –1627. **3.** Having the chief axis or distinctive part perpendicular to a surface; pointed or directed upwards; not inclined or leaning over. late ME. **b.** Marked by perpendicular position or attitude; erect OE. **4.** Of persons: Erect in carriage. late ME. **5. a.** Of a hill, etc.: Very steep 1596. **b.** Of a rectangular superficies; Having the height greater than the breadth 1888. †**6.** Of a shoe: That may fit either foot –1642. **7.** *fig.* Of persons, principles, conduct: Of unfailing integrity or rectitude; morally just, honest, or honourable 1530.

1. My stiffned haire stands vpright 1607. Supported by pillows, she sat almost u. MISS BURNEY. *fig.* While the honour of the Britons stood vpright 1570. **2.** Sleeping u. upon the back be not healthfull 1620. **3.** It cost me a Month to shape it ..to something like the Bottom of a Boat, that it might swim u. DE FOE. *U. pianoforte*: see PIANOFORTE. *U. Grand Piano*..applied..to the better kinds of the cottage piano 1896.

B. *sb.* †**1.** A vertical front, face, or plane –1726. †**b.** = ELEVATION II. 3. –1842. **2.** An upright or vertical position; the perpendicular 1683. **3.** Something set or standing upright; a perpendicular stone, post, part, etc. 1742. **b.** *spec.* One of the vertical members of a framing, etc. 1700. **c.** An upright pianoforte 1860. **d.** A kind of fly-hook 1878. **4.** *slang.* A drink of beer and gin mixed 1796.

1. b. There are not many uprights, but several ground plans of some of the palaces H. WALPOLE. **2.** The mullion was much out of u. 1905. **3.** A beam laid cross-wise upon two uprights 1845.

U·pright, *adv.* 1509. [f. prec.] †**1.** = UPRIGHTLY 1. –1624. **2.** Vertically upwards 1590.

2. Wownded on his hed by his own wanton throwing of a brik-bat u., and not well avoyding the fall of it 1591.

U·pright, *v.* ME. [f. as prec.] *trans.* To raise to an upright or vertical position; to erect.

Upri·ghteousness. 1549. [f. UPRIGHT *a.*, after RIGHTEOUSNESS.] †**1.** = Uprightness –1623. **2.** Show of virtue, sanctimony (*rare*) 1904.

U·prightly, *adv.* 1549. [f. as prec. + -LY[2].] **1.** In a just or upright manner; with strict observance of justice, honesty, or rectitude. †**b.** Candidly –1630. **2.** In an upright position. Now *rare.* 1601.

2. I have..seen him..walk..as u. as you can walk 1826.

U·prightness. 1541. [f. as prec. + -NESS.] **1.** The state or condition of being upright; moral integrity or rectitude. **b.** Const. *of* (heart, conduct, etc.) 1560. **2.** The state or character of being vertical, erect, or upright; erectness 1645.

2. Mrs. Croft..had a squareness, u., and vigour of form JANE AUSTEN.

Upri·sal. 1871. [f. UPRISE *v.* + -AL[1] 2.] Uprising.

Uprise (ʌprəi·z, ʌ·prəiz), *sb.* ME. [UP- I. 2.] †**1.** Resurrection. ME. only. **2.** Rising (of the sun, etc.); dawn (of day) 1588. **b.** The act of rising to a higher level; ascent 1690. **c.** The beginning of an ascent; an ascending shaft in a mine 1875. **3.** Ascent to power or dignity; rise to wealth or importance 1810. **b.** The act of coming into existence or notice 1817.

Uprise (ʌprəi·z), *v.* ME. [UP- III. 1.] **1.** *intr.* To rise to one's feet; to stand up. **b.** To rise from bed ME. **2.** Of the sun: To rise ME. **3.** To rise from the dead ME. **b.** To come from the underworld 1550. **4.** To rise or ascend to a higher level; to rise into view ME. **b.** To become erect 1796. **5.** To ascend as a sound 1503. **6.** To come into existence 1471. Hence **Upri·sen, Upri·sing,** *ppl. adjs.*

Upri·sing, *vbl. sb.* ME. [UP- III. 4.] **1.** The action of rising from death; resurrection. Now *rare.* **2.** The action of rising from bed; or from a sitting, kneeling, or recumbent posture ME. **3.** The action of rising after a fall ME. **4.** The rising of the sun ME. **5.** Advancement in a place or power; increase of prosperity. Now *rare.* late ME. **6.** An insurrection; a popular rising 1587. **7.** The process or fact of coming into existence or notice 1587.

2. Thou knowest my downe syttinge & my vprisynge COVERDALE *Ps.* 138:2. **6.** The great communistic u. under Wat Tyler 1861. **7.** The u. of a new aristocracy of wealth and intellect 1851.

U·p-ri:ver, *a.* 1877. [UP *prep.* 2.] Belonging to, situated, etc. farther up, or near the source of, a river. **b.** Leading or directed towards the source of a river 1890.

Uproar (ʌ·prōᵊɹ), *sb.* 1526. [– Du. *oproer*, in MDu. *uproer*, MLG. *uprōr*, f. *op-* UP + *roer* confusion; see ROAR *sb.*[2] In sense 2 assoc. with ROAR *sb.*[1]] **1.** An insurrection or popular rising; a serious tumult or outbreak of disorder among the people or a body of persons. Now *rare.* **2.** Loud outcry; noise of shouting or tumult 1544. **b.** With article and in pl. 1572. **3.** *In (an) u.*, in a state of tumult, commotion, or excitement 1548.

1. Athalia rente hir clothes, & sayde vproure, vproure COVERDALE 2 *Kings* 11:14.

Uproa·r, *v. rare.* 1605. [f. prec.] **1.** *trans.* To throw into confusion. **2.** *intr.* To make an uproar 1831.

1. I should..Vprore the uniuersall peace SHAKS.

Uproarious (ʌprōᵊ·riəs), *a.* 1819. [f. UPROAR *sb.* + -IOUS.] **1.** Making, or given to making, an uproar. **2.** Characterized by uproar 1849. Hence **Uproa·rious-ly** *adv.*, **-ness.**

Uproo·t, *v.*[1] 1620. [UP- III. 1 + ROOT *v.*[1]] *trans.* To tear up by the roots; to remove from a fixed position 1695. **b.** *fig.* To destroy as by tearing up; to exterminate, eradicate 1620. So **Uproo·ted** *ppl. a.* 1593.

Uproo·t, *v.*[2] 1726. [UP- III. 1 + ROOT *v.*[2]] *trans.* To grub up.

U·prush, *sb.* 1873. [UP- I. 2.] An upward rush or flow.

Upru·sh, *v.* 1818. [UP- III. 1.] *intr.* To rush up.

U·psaddle, *v. S. Afr.* 1863. [– Du. *opzadelen*, f. *op-* UP- + *zadelen* SADDLE *v.*] *intr.* To saddle a horse.

Upset (ʌ·pset), *sb.* late ME. [UP- I. 2.] †**1.** A revolt. late ME. only. †**2.** *north.* and *Sc.* (The fee paid upon) setting up in business as a master or becoming a freeman in a trade

–1687. **3.** The overturning of a vehicle or boat; the fact of being overturned 1804. **b.** An overturning or overthrow *of* ideas, plans, etc. 1822. **c.** A physical or (more commonly) mental disturbance or derangement 1866. **d.** A quarrel; a misunderstanding 1887.

3. b. What a strange u. of old principles and old measures! SOUTHEY.

Upset (ʊpse·t), *v.* 1440. [UP- III. 1.] **1.** *trans.* †**a.** To set up, establish –1608. **b.** *techn.* To force back the end of (a metal bar, etc.) by hammering or beating, esp. when heated 1677. **2.** *intr.* To be overturned or capsized (said of a vehicle, boat, etc., or of persons in it) 1799. **3.** *trans.* To overturn; to capsize; to knock over 1803. **b.** To involve (persons) in the accidental overturning of a vehicle or boat. Chiefly *pass.* 1807. **c.** *fig.* To overthrow, undo, put out of joint 1818. **4.** To throw into mental disorder or discomposure; to trouble, distress: freq. *pass.* 1805. **b.** To disorder physically 1845.

3. Phr. *To u.* a person's or the *applecart*, fig. to overthrow his projects. **4.** I never was so shocked or so completely upset 1805. **b.** A young person.. easily upset by any imprudence in diet 1845. Hence **Upse·tter. Upse·tting** *vbl. sb.* and *ppl. a.*

U·pset, *pa. pple.* and *ppl. a.* ME. [UP- III. 2.] **1.** Set up, erected, raised up, etc. Now *rare.* **2.** Of price: Stated as the lowest sum for which property exposed to auction will be sold; named as the sum from which bidding may start. Orig. *Sc.* and *U.S.* 1814. **3.** Overturned, capsized 1842.

U·pshot. 1531. [UP- I. 2.] †**1.** A final shot in a match at archery; chiefly *fig.* a closing or parting shot –1618. †**2.** A mark aimed at –1754. †**3.** An end, conclusion, or termination; the climax or completion *of* something –1662. **b.** The extreme limit (*rare*) 1699. **4.** The result, issue, or conclusion (*of* some course of action, etc.) 1604.

1. As it were for an vp-shot to all the fooles thunderbolts they had let flie 1614. **2.** The U. of all Religion is to please God 1754. **3.** Through fear of death the u. of evils 1617. **b.** That threescore years and ten make the u. of man's pleasurable existence DE QUINCEY. **4.** The u. of all was, our Lord vanquished the devil 1680. Phr. *In the upshot,* in the end, at last.

Upsidaisy, var. UP-A-DAISY.

U·pside. 1611. [UP- I. 1.] **1.** The upper side or part (*of* a thing). **2.** The side of a railway or station on or into which the 'up' trains run 1880.

U·pside dow·n, *adv.* (*a.*) ME. [orig. *up so down,* the *so* perh. meaning 'as if'.] **A.** *adv.* **1.** So that the upper part or surface becomes the under or lower. Freq. in phr. *to turn u.* **2.** *fig.* In or into a state of overthrow, reversal, or disorder ME. **B.** *adj.* (Written with hyphen or as one word.) Inverted 1866.

A. 1. The cradel and the child thai found Up so doun upon the ground ME. Transuersed or turned vp set downe 1520. **2.** As for the waye of yᵉ vngodly, he turneth it vpsyde downe COVERDALE *Ps.* 145[6]:9.

U·pside dow·nward(s, *advs.* 1611. [f. prec. + -WARD, -WARDS.] = prec. A.

U·psides, *adv.* 1746. [f. UPSIDE + -S.] **1.** *U. with,* even, equal, or quits with (a person). *dial.* (orig. *Sc.*) or *colloq.* **2.** *colloq.* On a level *with,* alongside *of* 1883.

Upsilon (yupsəi·lǫn). 1642. [– Gr. ὖ ψιλόν 'slender u', the adj. having reference to its later sound (ü).] The Greek letter Υ, υ, representing the vowel *u.* Also *attrib.* = having the form of this letter. (Cf. HYPSILOID.)

Upspri·ng, *v.* OE. [UP- III. 1.] **1.** *intr.* Of plants, etc.: To spring up, to grow. **b.** *fig.* To come into being. late ME. **2.** To ascend; to spring or leap upwards; to start to one's feet. late ME.

1. b. The hour When Paradise upsprung BYRON. **2.** Upsprang she then, and kiss'd them R. BRIDGES. Hence **Upspri·nging** *ppl. a.*

U·pstair, *adv.* and *a.* 1627. [UP *prep.* 1, 6.] = next A. 1, B.

Upstairs, *adv., sb.,* and *a.* 1596. [See UP *prep.* 1, 6.] **A.** *adv.* (ʊpstēᵊ·ɹz, exc. when contrasted with *dow·nstairs*). **1.** So as to ascend a flight of stairs; to the floor at the top of a staircase. **2.** At the top of, on a floor or in a room reached by, a flight of stairs; in an upper storey 1781. **b.** quasi-*sb.* 1842. **c.** as *sb.* An upper storey or floor. Also *transf.*, a person or persons living on an upper floor 1884.

1. *Phr. To kick u.*; see KICK *v.* 5. **2. b.** The ogre's voice from u. LOVER.

B. *adj.* (ʊ·pstēᵊɹz). Situated on an upper storey or at the top of a flight of steps 1782. **b.** Belonging to, connected with, the upper rooms or parts of a house 1839.

U·pstanding, *ppl. a.* OE. [UP- III. 3.] **1.** Standing up; erect. **2.** Of animals (esp. horses) or persons: Having an erect carriage; well set up 1835. **b.** *fig.* Of independent, open, or honest bearing; straightforward, downright 1863. **3.** *U. wage,* a regular or fixed wage (as opp. to one dependent on circumstances) 1888.

1. A coronal of high u. plumes SOUTHEY.

Upstart (ʊ·pstaɹt), *sb.* and *a.* 1555. [UP- I. 2, II.] **A.** *sb.* **1.** One who has newly or suddenly risen in position, rank, or importance; a parvenu. **2.** The meadow-saffron, *Colchicum autumnale* 1852.

1. Mary gyp goodman vpstart, who made your father a gentleman? 1592.

B. *adj.* **1.** Of things: Lately come into existence or notice; new-fangled 1565. **b.** Characteristic of upstarts 1593. **2.** Of persons, families, etc.; Lately or suddenly risen to prominence or dignity 1566.

1. This up-start fansie is far from God's ordinance 1593. **b.** He dreaded their u. ambition GIBBON.

Up-stream, *adv.* and *a.* 1681. [UP *prep.* 2, 5.] **A.** *adv.* (even stress, and freq. as two words). In a direction contrary to the flow of a stream; towards the source of a stream. **B.** *adj.* (ʊ·pˌstrīm). **1.** Situated higher up a stream 1838. **2.** Directed or taking place upstream 1826.

U·p-stroke. 1828. [UP- I. 2.] **1.** A stroke delivered upwards. **2.** The upward stroke of a pen, etc. 1848.

†**U·psy.** 1590. [– Du. *op zijn* (ǫp sei) lit. 'on his (her or its)', used in such expressions as *op zijn Vriesch* 'in the Frisian fashion'.] *U. Friese, u. Dutch,* deeply, heavily, to excess 1592. *U. Friese,* a mode of drinking or carousing 1590. *U. Dutch,* suggestive of having drunk too deeply, heavy 1610.

Drinke Duch like gallants, lets drinke vpsey freeze 1601. Sit downe Lads, And drink me upsey-Dutch FLETCHER.

U·ptake. 1816. [UP- I. 2.] **1.** The action of, or capacity for, understanding; comprehension. Usu. *quick* (etc.) *in the u.*; orig. (and still chiefly) *Sc.* **2.** = TAKE-UP 4. 1839. **3.** A ventilating shaft by which foul air ascends 1889.

Upthrow (ʊ·pþrōᵘ). 1807. [UP- I. 2.] **1.** *Geol.* and *Mining.* An upward dislocation of a stratum or seam. **2.** *Geol.* An upheaval of part of the earth's crust or surface 1833. **3.** The action of throwing up 1898.

1. *attrib.* A true fault with an u. and downthrow side 1882.

U·pthrust. 1846. [UP- I. 2.] The action of thrusting or the fact of being thrust upwards, esp. by volcanic action.

Up to date, *adv. phr.* and *a.* 1868. [UP *adv.*¹] **A.** *adv. phr.* (u·p to da·te). **1.** Until the present time, the time in question, or the time of writing. **2.** Not behind the times; with the latest information, appliances, etc. 1889.

2. The improvements..render this camera quite 'up to date' 1892.

B. *adj.* (predic. u:p-to-da·te; attrib. u·p-to-date). **1.** Extending to the present time; presenting or inclusive of the latest facts, details, etc.; employing or involving the latest methods or devices 1888. **2.** Of persons: Having or employing the latest information, facts, or methods; keeping abreast of the times; having tastes, manners, etc., regarded as prevailing at or characteristic of the present time 1891. Hence **Up-to-da·teness.**

1. General up-to-date smartness 1894.

Up town, up-tow·n, *adv.,* **u·p-town,** *a.* 1838. [UP *prep.*] **A.** *adv.* In, to, or into the higher or upper part of a town, or (*U.S.*) the residential portion of a town or city 1855. **B.** *adj.* Situated or dwelling up-town 1838.

A. I had heard of Miss Havisham up town DICKENS.

Uptu·rn, *v.* ME. [UP- III. 1.] †**1.** *trans.* To overthrow, subvert –late ME. **2.** To turn, throw, or tear up; to cast or turn over 1567. **3.** To turn (the eyes, face, etc.) upwards 1667. **4.** *intr.* To turn or move up or towards 1805.

2. Boreas and Cæcias..rend the Woods and Seas u. MILTON. Hence **Uptu·rning** *vbl. sb.*

U·pturned, *ppl. a.* 1592. [UP- III. 2.] **1.** Turned or directed upwards. **2.** Turned upside-down; overturned; turned up by digging, etc. 1816. **3.** Turned upwards at the point or end; curved 1843.

Upward (ʊ·pwǫ̈ɹd) *adv., prep., a.,* and *sb.* [OE. *upweard,* f. *up* UP *adv.*¹ + *weard* -WARD.] **A.** *adv.* **I. 1.** To or towards a higher position or plane: **a.** In ref. to movement or extension through space. **b.** In ref. to aspect, attitude, or direction OE. **c.** *fig.* In respect of thought, life, merit, rank, etc. ME. **d.** Higher in respect of price or value 1874. **2.** Up along the course of a stream, etc.; further into the interior of a country; to or towards a centre, metropolis, source, etc. ME. **b.** Towards the body or head 1600. **3.** In, occupying, or so as to occupy a higher or the highest position or place ME. **b.** In respect of the upper part or parts. late ME. **4.** With (vertical) extension *from* a point or part (esp. of the body) to another expressed or implied. late ME.

1. a. Herons,..mounting u...soar above the Sight DRYDEN. *fig.* U. steals the life of man, As the sunshine from the wall LONGF. **b.** If yee looke u., yee see there infinite bodies SIDNEY. **c.** *Macb.* IV. ii. 24. **2.** Trace the Muses u. to their spring POPE. **3.** Lying with the face u. JOHNSON. **b.** U. Man And downward Fish MILT. **4.** A Spaniard from the hip vpward SHAKS.

II. 1. Backward in order of time; continuously into the past OE. **2. a.** To or into later life 1530. **b.** *And* (*or*) *u.* = UPWARDS *adv.* 2. 1555. **3.** *U. of,* more than; also, rather less than 1613.

1. Consider now from this day, and vpward *Haggai* 2:18. **2. a.** I am, and ever have been from my Youth u., one of the greatest Liars STEELE. **b.** To the number of two thousand people and vpward 1608. **3.** I haue beene your Wife, in this Obedience, Vpward of twenty yeares SHAKS.

†**B.** *prep.* Up; along the line of ascent of –1818. **C.** *adj.* †**1.** Facing upwards; supine –1646. **2.** Directed, taking place, or inclined upwards; ascending 1607. **b.** Having a course which indicates advance, progress, or increase 1596. **3.** Situated above; higher; lofty 1622. **4.** Directed, moving, taking place, etc. upstream 1731. †**D.** *sb.* The top part. SHAKS.

2. b. The u. movement which raised the lower labouring classes 1914. **3.** With strong wings Scaling the u. sky SHELLEY. **4.** The..chief Boatman of any u. boat 1731. Hence **U·pward-ly** *adv.,* **-ness.**

Upwards (ʊ·pwǫ̈ɹdz), *adv.* and *prep.* [OE. *up(p)weardes,* f. *upweard* UPWARD + *-es* of advb. gen.; see -WARDS.] **A.** *adv.* **1.** = UPWARD *adv.* I. **b.** *U. of,* to or at a higher level than; above 1853. **2.** To a higher aggregate, figure, or the like. Usu. *and u., or u.* 1523. **c.** To later life 1805. **3.** Backwards in time; into the past 1654. **4.** *U. of,* rather more than; rather less than 1721. †**B.** *prep.* = UPWARD *prep.* –1601.

1. Prisoners..of the degree of a Baron, or uppwardes 1557. A Fire that naturally mounts u. ADDISON. Looking u. we saw a series of coloured rings TYNDALL. We followed this stream u. 1869. **2.** Hotel accommodation..for two and a half or three guineas a week, u. 1910. **4.** U. of three thousand years ago 1893.

Up-wind (ʊ:pwi·nd), *adv.* 1838. [UP *prep.* 4.] Contrary to the course of or against the wind.

Ur (ɔɹ). 1846. [var. of ER.] An inarticulate sound, uttered instead of a word that the speaker is unable to remember or bring out.

‖**Ur-** (ūᵊr), *prefix,* repr. G. *ur-* 'primitive, original, earliest', and occurring in a few terms.

The *Ur-Hamlet* may have contained a number of these borrowings 1901. **Ursprache** (ū·rʃprāχə) *Philol.*, hypothetically primitive language reconstructed from a group of historically cognate languages.

‖**Urachus** (yū̆ᵊ·răkǒs). 1578. [mod.L. – Gr. οὐραχός urinary canal of a fœtus.] *Anat.* A fibrous cord binding the apex of the bladder to the anterior abdominal wall and the peritoneal folds. Hence **U·rachal** *a.*

‖**Uræmia** (yuri·miă). 1857. [mod.L., f. Gr. οὖρον urine + αἷμα blood.] *Path.* A morbid condition resulting from the presence in the blood of urinary constituents normally eliminated by the kidneys. So **Uræ·mic** *a.* of, marked by, or affected by uræmia 1855.

‖**Uræus** (yurī·ŏs). *Pl.* **uræi** (-əi). 1832. [mod. latinization of Gr. οὐραῖος (perh. influenced by Gr. οὐραῖος, f. οὐρά tail) repr. the Egyptian word for 'cobra'.] *Egypt. Antiq.* A representation of the sacred asp, or of its head and neck, employed as an emblem of supreme power, occas. *spec.* as worn on the head-dress of ancient Egyptian divinities and sovereigns.

Ural[1] (yūᵊ·răl, yurā·l). 1785. The name of a mountain-chain (more freq. *Urals, U. mountains*) forming the north-eastern boundary of Europe with Asia, used attrib. in specific appellations of animals, etc., as *U. duck, lizard.* **b.** *U.-Altaic*, pertaining or belonging to the region including the Ural and Altaic mountains, its people, or their speech. Also *absol.*, the family of agglutinative languages spoken in eastern Europe and northern Asia; Turanian; Finno-Tartar 1855.

Ural[2] (yūᵊ·răl). 1891. [irreg. f. URETHANE; see -AL[2].] *Med.* A preparation of chloral hydrate and urethane, used as a hypnotic.

‖**Urali** (urā·li). 1862. [var. of OORALI.] The urari-plant, *Strychnos toxifera*, or the poison obtained from this.

Uralian (yurē¹·liăn), *a.* 1801. [f. URAL[1] + -IAN. Cf. Fr. *ouralien.*] Of or pertaining to, dwelling in or near, the Ural mountains; also, Ural-Altaic. So **Uralic** (yuræ·lik), *a.*

Uralite (yūᵊ·rāləit). 1835. [- G. *uralit*, f. URAL[1] + -ITE[1] 2 b.] *Min.* Pyroxene altered to amphibole. Hence **Urali·tic** *a.*

Uralium (yurē¹·liŏm). 1889. [See URAL[2] and -IUM.] *Med.* = URAL[2].

Uralo- (yurē¹·lo), comb. form of URAL[1], as in *Uralo-Altaic, -Caspian, -Finnic.*

Uramil (yuræ·mil). 1839. [- G. *uramil*, f. mod.L. *ur(ea* + *am(monia* + *-il* -YL.] *Chem.* Murexan. Hence **Urami·lic** *a.* 1839.

Uran- (yūᵊ·răn), comb. form of URANITE, URANIUM, as in *uran-mica, -ochre.*

Uranate (yūᵊ·rănĕt). 1842. [f. URANIC *a.*[1] + -ATE[4].] *Chem.* A salt produced by the action of uranic acid upon a base.

Urania (yurē¹·niă). 1614. [L. (the muse of astronomy) – Gr. Οὐρανία fem. of οὐράνιος heavenly, f. οὐρανός heaven.] **1.** As the title of a book or poem dealing with celestial or astronomical themes, etc. **2.** *Astr.* One of the planetoids or asteroids 1865.

Uranian (yurē¹·niăn), *a.*[1] 1600. [f. prec. + -AN.] **1.** Pertaining to or befitting heaven; heavenly, celestial. **b.** As a distinctive epithet of Venus (or Aphrodite): Heavenly, spiritual 1768. **2.** Pertaining, belonging, or dedicated to (the muse) Urania 1656. **b.** Astronomical 1761.

1. He sees the earthly image of U. Love SHELLEY.

Uranian (yurē¹·niăn), *a.*[2] and *sb.* 1844. [f. URANUS + -IAN.] **A.** *adj.* Of or pertaining to the planet Uranus. **B.** *sb.* An inhabitant of Uranus 1870.

Uranic (yuræ·nik), *a.*[1] 1837. [f. URANIUM + -IC.] Formed from or related to the higher oxide of uranium.

Ura·nic, *a.*[2] 1901. [f. Gr. οὐρανός palate + -IC.] *Anthropol.* Pertaining or relating to the palate. Freq. in *u. index.*

Uraninite (yuræ·ninəit). 1879. [f. URANIUM + -IN[1]; see -ITE[1] 2 b.] *Min.* Pitchblende.

Uranism (yūᵊ·răniz'm). 1899. [- G. *uranismus*, f. Gr. οὐράνιος heavenly, taken to mean 'spiritual'; see -ISM.] Homosexuality.

Uranite (yūᵊ·rănəit). 1794. [- G. *uranit* (Klaproth, 1789), or Fr. *uranite*, f. URANIUM + -ITE[1] 2 b (sense 2).] †**1.** *Chem.* = next 1. –1821. **2.** *Min.* An ore or mineral composed largely of uranium, and occurring in two varieties, autunite and torbernite 1802. Hence **Urani·tic** *a.* of, pertaining to, or containing u. or uranium.

Uranium (yurē¹·niŏm). 1797. [mod.L. (Klaproth, 1789), f. URANUS + -IUM; cf. TELLURIUM.] **1.** A rare, heavy, greyish metallic element, found esp. in pitchblende and uranite. **2.** *ellipt.* A solution of a salt or nitrate of uranium 1878.

Urano-[1] (yūᵊ·răno, yūᵊrănǫ·), comb. form of Gr. οὐρανός sky, heaven(s, roof of the mouth.

Urano·graphy, the science of describing or delineating, a delineation or description of, the sidereal heavens; hence **Urano·grapher. Uranogra·phic, -al** *adjs.* **Urano·logy,** (a treatise or discourse on) astronomy; hence **Uranolo·gical** *a.* **Urano·metry,** (a treatise on) the measurement of the magnitudes and relative distances of heavenly bodies, esp. the fixed stars; hence **Uranome·trical** *a.* **U·ranopla·sty** *Surg.*, plastic surgery of the hard palate; hence **U·ranopla·stic** *a.* **Urano·scopus,** *Ichth.* = STAR-GAZER 2.

Urano·so-, comb. form of next occurring in a few chemical terms, as *uranoso-ammonic, -potassic, -uranic.*

Uranous (yūᵊ·rănəs), *a.* 1842. [f. URANIUM + -OUS c.] *Chem.* **1.** Formed from or related to the lower oxide of uranium. **2.** Of, pertaining to or typical of uranium 1878.

Uranus (yūᵊ·rănŏs, pop. yuᵊrē¹·nŏs). [L. *Uranus* – Gr. Οὐρανός husband of Gæa (Earth) and father of Cronos (Saturn).] *Astr.* The most remote but two of the planets, situated between Saturn and Neptune, and discovered in 1781 by Sir Wm. Herschel.

Uranyl (yūᵊ·rănil). 1850. [f. URANIUM + -YL.] *Chem.* A radical (UO_2) held to exist in many compounds of uranium. Hence **Urany·lic** *a.*

‖**Urari** (urā·ri). 1838. [See CURARE, and cf. URALI, OORALI, WOORALI.] = CURARE.

Urate (yūᵊ·rĕt). 1800. [– Fr. *urate*; see URIC, -ATE[4].] *Chem.* A salt produced by the action of uric acid on a base. Hence **Ura·tic** *a.* of or pertaining to, containing or consisting of, a u. or urates.

Urban (ŏ·ɹbăn), *a.* and *sb.* 1619. [– L. *urbanus*, f. *urbs, urb-* city; see -AN and cf. next. Rare before XIX.] **A.** *adj.* **1.** Pertaining to or characteristic of, situated or occurring in, a city or town. **b.** Constituting, forming, or including a city, town, or burgh 1841. **2.** Exercising authority, control, etc., in or over a city or town 1651. **b.** Residing, dwelling, or having property in a city or town 1837.

1. The strength of u. Toryism GLADSTONE. **2.** All Magistrats are either U. or Forren, viz. of Town or Countrey 1651. **b.** The vehemence of u. democracy 1849.

B. *sb.* A town-dweller (*rare*) 1891.

Urbane (ɒɹbē¹·n), *a.* 1533. [– (O)Fr. *urbain, -aine* or L. *urbanus*; see prec., -ANE. For the difference of form, stress, and meaning between *urban* and *urbane*, cf. *human, humane.*] **1.** Of or pertaining to, characteristic of or peculiar to, a town or city. Now *Obs.* or *arch.* **2.** Having the manners, refinement, or polish regarded as characteristic of a town; courteous, at ease in society; also, blandly polite, suave 1623. **b.** Characterized by urbanity, courtesy, or politeness 1679.

1. Raising. . savage life To rustic, and the rustic to u. WORDSW. Béranger, an u. or city poet LOWELL. **2.** I feel never quite sure of your u. and smiling coteries STEVENSON. **b.** His manners were gentle, affable, and u. W. IRVING. Hence **Urba·nely** *adv.*

U·rbanist. 1523. [f. the Papal name *Urban* + IST; in XVI perh. – med.L. *urbanista* (1385). Cf. Fr. *Urbaniste* in sense 2.] **1.** An adherent of Pope Urban VI against Clement VII (*rare*). **2.** A nun of a branch of the Poor Clares, following the rule as mitigated in 1264 by Pope Urban IV. 1687.

Urbanity (ɒɹbæ·nĭti). 1535. [– (O)Fr. *urbanité* or L. *urbanitas*, f. *urbanus* URBAN; see -ITY.] **1.** The character or quality of being urbane; refined or bland politeness or civility. **b.** *pl.* Civilities, courtesies 1646. †**2.** Cheerful, witty, or pleasant talk; polished wit or humour –1693. **3.** The state, condition, or character of a town or city; life in a city 1549.

1. His U., that is, his Good Manners DRYDEN. **b.** The passages of societie and daily urbanities of our times SIR T. BROWNE. **2.** Moral Doctrine,. . and U., or well-manner'd Wit,. . constitute the Roman Satire DRYDEN.

Urbanize (ŏ·ɹbănəiz), *v.* 1642. [In sense 1 f. URBAN *a.* or URBANE + -IZE; in sense 2 – Fr. *urbaniser.*] **1.** To make urbane, or more refined or polished. Now *rare.* **2.** To make of an urban character; to convert into a city 1884.

In order to. . u. their savage Disposition 1785. Hence **Urbaniza·tion.**

Urceolate (ŏ·ɹsiŏlĕt), *a.* 1760. [f. URCEOLUS + -ATE[2].] **1.** Pitcher-shaped; esp. in *Bot., Anat.*, etc. **2.** Furnished with or contained in an urceolus 1891. So **U·rceolated** *a. Zool.* = sense 1. 1752.

‖**Urceolus** (ɒɹsī·ŏlŏs). 1832. [L., dim. of *urceus* pitcher.] A pitcher-shaped sheath or tube, esp. as a protective part in plants or animals.

Urchin (ŏ·ɹtʃin). [ME. *urcheon, hirchon* – ONFr. *herichon, *urchon*, vars. of OFr. *heriçon* (mod. *hérisson*, dial. *hérichon, hurchon*) :– Rom. **hericio, -ōn-*, f. L. *hericius*, late form of *ericius* HEDGEHOG.] **1.** = HEDGEHOG 1. †**b.** A goblin or elf –1614. **2.** A sea-urchin; = ECHINUS 1. 1601. **3.** One who is deformed in body; a hunchback. Now *dial.* 1528. **4.** A pert, mischievous, or roguish youngster; a brat 1530. **b.** *poet.* Applied to Cupid 1709. **5.** A little fellow; a boy or youngster 1556. **6.** *techn.* One of a pair of rapidly rotating small card cylinders of a carding-machine 1835.

1. b. An old wiues tale of diuells and vrchins 1594. **2.** The Vrchins of the sea called Echini 1601. **3.** An vrchine: by which name also we call a man that holdeth his Necke in his bosome 1607. **4. b.** The subtile line Wherewith the u. angled for my Heart SOUTHEY. **5.** The gutter urchins 1839.

Urdee (ŏ·ɹdi), *a.* Also **urdé, urdy.** 1562. [Origin obsc.; perh. due to a misreading of Fr. *vidée* in the phr. *croix aiguisée et vidée.*] *Her.* **1.** Of a cross: Having the extremities pointed. **2.** Of a bend, etc.: Having the margin broken into parallel pointed projections. Also of a line broken thus. 1688.

Urdu (ūᵊ·ɹdū), *sb.* and *a.* 1796. [– Hind. *urdū*, of Pers. origin, for *zabān i urdū* language of the camp; Pers. *urdū* camp – Turk. *ordu* (see HORDE).] **A.** *sb.* = HINDUSTANI *sb.* 2. **B.** *adj.* Of or pertaining to, printed, written, or composed in the Hindustani language 1845.

†**Ure**[1]. late ME. [– AFr. **eure* = OFr. *evre, euvre, uevre* (mod. *œuvre*) :– L. *opera*, pl. of *opus* work, used as fem. sing. (see OPERA). Cf. INURE, MANURE.] **1.** *In ure*, in or into use, practice, or operation –1711. **2.** *Out of ure*, disused, obsolete –1600. **3.** Custom, habit –1600.

†**Ure**[2]. *Orkney* and *Shetland.* 1534. [– ONorw. *øyrir* (Norw. *øyre, øre*) = (M)Sw. *öre*, (M)Da. *øre*, Icel. *eyrir* – L. *aureus* gold solidus. Cf. ORA[1].] *Urisland* [ON. *øyrisland*], *u. of land*, land yielding rent of one-eighth of a mark; also *ellipt.*

-ure (iŭɹ), *suffix*, repr. Fr. *-ure*, L. *-ura*, in words of Fr. or L. origin. The meaning, in L. action or process, hence the result of this, office, rank, dignity, after further development in Fr. and Eng. is now extended to action or process, the results or product of this (e.g. *enclosure, figure, scripture*), state, rank, office or function (e.g. *judicature, prefecture*), a collective body (e.g. *legislature*), and that by which the action is effected (*ligature*). Many words are early adoptions from Fr. (as *figure, censure, tonsure*), a few direct adaptations from L. (*aperture*), some formed by addition of *-ure* to Eng. stems of L. origin (e.g. *composure, unigeniture*). The suffix was further used with stems of Romance origin and with native or other stems, as in *wafture.*

‖**Urea** (yūᵊ·rĭă). 1806. [mod.L. – Fr. *urée*, f. Gr. οὖρον URINE or οὐρεῖν urinate.] *Chem.* A soluble crystalline compound, forming an organic constituent of the urine in mammalia, birds, and some reptiles, and also found in blood, milk, etc.; carbamide, $CO(NH_2)_2$. Hence **U·real** *a.*

Uredine (yurī·dəin), *sb.* and *a.* 1889. [f. the pl. UREDINES.] *Bot.* **A.** *sb.* A fungus of the family *Uredineæ* of minute ascomycetal fungi (including mildew, rust, smut, etc.), parasitic on plants. **B.** *adj.* Pertaining or belonging to the Uredines 1889.

‖**Uredines** (yurī·dinīz). 1753. [L., pl. of UREDO. Cf. Fr. *urédinées.*] *Bot.* Species of fungi parasitic upon and injurious to plants, etc.

Uredinous (yurī·dinəs), *a.* 1865. [f. L. *uredin-* (see next) + -OUS.] **1.** *Bot.* Of the nature of a uredine; belonging to the *Uredines*. **2.** *Path.* Affected with or of the nature of nettlerash 1891.

‖**Uredo** (yuᵊrī·do). 1706. [L. (pl. *uredines*) blight, blast, itch, f. *urere* to burn. *Bot.* **1.** A form of blight, = BRAND *sb.* 6 (*rare*). **2.** The intermediate stage of the *Uredineæ* or rust fungi, parasitic on grain and other plants; formerly regarded as a separate genus. Usu. with capital. 1836. **b.** A species or plant of this 1836. **3.** *attrib.*: **u.-fruit,** a group of uredospores; **u. stage,** the summer stage of certain rust fungi.

Ure·dospore. 1875. [f. prec. + SPORE.] *Bot.* One of the peculiar summer spores developed during the uredo stage in rust fungi.

Ureide (yūᵊ·rīəid). 1857. [f. UREA + -IDE, -ID⁴.] *Chem.* A derivative of urea containing acid radicles.

Ureo- (yūᵊ·rīo), comb. form of UREA, as in *ureo-carbonate, ureometer.*

Ure-ox (yūᵊ·rǫks). 1607. [– G. *urochs*, var. of *auerochs*; see URUS, UROCHS.] = AUROCHS.

-uret (iŭret), *Chem.*, a suffix, – mod.L. *-uretum -oretum*, now replaced by -IDE, forming names of simple compounds of an element with another element or a radical.

Ureter (yurī·təɹ). 1578. [– Fr. *uretère* or mod.L. *ureter* – Gr. οὐρητήρ, f. οὐρεῖν make water, f. οὖρον URINE.] *Anat.* Either of the fibro-muscular tubes or vessels conveying urine from the kidneys to the bladder; a urinary duct. Usu. in pl. Hence **Ure·teral, Ureteric** (yūᵊrite·rik) *adjs.* pertaining to, affecting, or connected with a u. or the ureters.

Ureteritis (yurītĕrəi·tis). 1823. [f. URETER + -ITIS.] *Path.* Inflammation of a ureter.

Uretero- (yurī·tĕro), comb. form of URETER, occurring in various surgical and medical terms, as in **uretero·tomy, -ge·nital, -ve·sical** *adjs.*, etc.

Urethane (yure·þēⁱn). 1838. [– Fr. *uréthane*; see UREA and ETHANE.] *Chem.* Ethyl carbamate, valued as an anæsthetic.

Urethra (yurī·þră). 1634. [– late L. *urethra* – Gr. οὐρήθρα, f. οὐρεῖν make water.] *Anat.* The membranous tube through which the urine is discharged from the bladder. Hence **Ure·thral** *a.* of or pertaining to, connected with, or affecting the u.; adapted for, used in, operating on the u.

Urethritis (yūᵊrīþrəi·tis). 1823. [f. prec. + -ITIS.] *Path.* Inflammation of the urethra.

Urethro- (yurī·þro), comb. form of URETHRA, as in **urethrocele, -meter, -rrhaphy, -scope, -tomy; -plastic, -sexual** *adjs.*

Urethylane (yure·þilēⁱn). 1844. [f. UREA; see ETHYL and -ANE 2.] *Chem.* Methyl-urethane; methyl carbamate.

Urge (ŏɹdʒ), *sb.* 1618. [f. next.] **1.** The action of urging or fact of being urged or prompted (*rare*). **2.** An impelling motive, force, pressure, etc.; an inner striving or yearning towards development or action 1884.

1. That we may pray without all u. 1618. 2. There is an inward u. that forces it upwards 1914.

Urge (ŏɹdʒ), *v.* 1560. [– L. *urgēre* press, drive, compel.] **1.** *trans.* To bring forward, present or press upon the attention (a fact, reason, etc.) in an urgent manner; to plead as an excuse or argument; to allege or state, esp. in justification, extenuation, or defence. **2.** To advocate (a course of action, etc.); to claim or demand pressingly 1592. **3.** To entreat or plead with pertinaciously; to importune, ply with arguments or strong persuasion. Also, with impersonal subject: To incite or impel strongly. 1565. **4.** To serve or act as a constraining influence on (a person's feelings, etc.). **5.** To press forward, prosecute vigorously (a proceeding, enterprise, etc.) 1565. **6.** To drive or force in some direction. Also with preps. or advs., as *against, through.* 1594. **b.** To accelerate the pace of; to speed up. Usu. with advs. or preps. 1721. **c.** To pursue (one's flight, way, the chase); to hasten (one's pace, etc.) 1697. **7.** To stimulate to expression or action; to provoke; to increase or intensify 1594. **8.** To ply vigorously 1697. **9.** *intr.* To adduce or bring forward arguments, allegations, etc.; to press by inquiry 1592. **b.** To press solicitously, make a strong claim *for* something 1607. **10.** To press, push, or hasten on 1605. **11.** To act as an impelling or prompting motive, stimulus, or force; to exercise pressure or constraint 1645.

1. I am at a loss what more to u. BERKELEY. 'Don't break out, Lammle,' urged Fledgeby DICKENS. 2. He hath ever urged peace with the malignants SCOTT. 3. The barbarian..moves when he is urged by appetite J. H. NEWMAN. 5. While Turnus urges thus his Enterprise DRYDEN. 6. From Stage to Stage the licens'd Earl may run, ..the Senator at Cricket u. the Ball POPE. Evening must usher night, night u. the morrow SHELLEY. b. Vesper! u. thy lazy car! SHELLEY. 7. Then u. the fire gradually 1800. 9. He again urged for her hand, and for a private marriage RICHARDSON. 11. The combat urges, and my soul's on fire POPE. Hence **U·rger. U·rging** *vbl. sb.* and *ppl. a.*, **-ly** *adv.*

Urgence (ŏ·ɹdʒĕns). 1592. [– Fr. *urgence* (XVI), or f. URGENT; see -ENCE.] **1.** = next 1, 2. **2.** Expedition, haste 1612. **3.** = next 4. 1874.

1. At the united u. of France and England.. [he] resigned 1893. 2. Late despatches sent With u. GEO. ELIOT.

Urgency (ŏ·ɹdʒĕnsi). 1540. [f. next; see -ENCY.] **1.** The state, condition, or fact of being urgent; pressing importance. **b.** *spec.* The status of parliamentary business that has been voted urgent 1883. **2.** Pressure by importunity or entreaty; urgent solicitation 1611. **3.** Stress *of* wind, weather, etc. 1660. **4.** Impelling or prompting force or quality 1816. **5.** An urgent need or situation 1647. **6.** A driving or constraining impulse or motive 1664. **7.** *pl.* Earnest representations or entreaties 1823.

2. By your great and frequent u., you prevailed on me SWIFT. 4. From no apparent impulse but the u. of conscience SCOTT. 5. Collections through the Kingdom being too slow for such an u. 1647. 6. Quick urgencies of Devotion 1664.

Urgent (ŏ·ɹdʒĕnt), *a.* 1496. [– (O)Fr. *urgent* – L. *urgens, urgent-*, pr. pple. of *urgēre* URGE *v.*; see -ENT.] **1.** Pressing; demanding prompt action; marked or characterized by urgency. **b.** Of messages, commands, etc., by which a matter is strongly pressed upon a person's attention 1611. **2.** Of persons: Importunate, insistent 1548. **b.** Eagerly desirous *to* do something 1753. **3.** Pressing forward, hurrying on. Now *poet.* 1546. †**4.** Oppressive; severe; heavy –1699. †**5.** Of time: Pressing; passing quickly –1791.

1. U. appetites of the flesche 1559. 2. Most vrgent suiters for my loue MARLOWE. His family have been very u. for him to make an expedition to Margate W. IRVING. 3. A shapen prow Borne by the mastery of its u. wings R. BRIDGES. 4. The heat is very vrgent HAKLUYT. 5. *Wint. T.* I. ii. 465. Hence **U·rgently** *adv.*

-uria (yūᵊ·riă), a second element, latinized from Gr. -ουρία, employed in pathological terms denoting morbid conditions of the urine, as *albuminuria, glycosuria, hæmaturia, pyuria.*

Uric (yūᵊ·rik), *a.* 1797. [– Fr. *urique*, f. *urine* URINE; see -IC.] *Chem.* **1.** *U. oxide*: earlier name of XANTHINE. **2.** *U. acid*, a crystallizable acid, $C_5H_4N_4O_3$, found in the urine of man and certain of the lower animals 1800.

Comb.: **u.-acidæmia** = URICÆMIA; **u. acidity,** the condition of containing an excess of u. acid.

Uricæmia (yūᵊrisī·miă). 1867. [mod.L., f. *uricus* URIC *a.* + Greek αἷμα blood + -IA¹.] *Path.* = LITHÆMIA. Hence **Uricæ·mic** *a.*

Uriconian (yūᵊrikōᵘ·niăn), *a.* 1886. [f. *Uriconium*, name of a Roman town at Wroxeter + -AN.] *Geol.* Consisting of or pertaining to a series of volcanic rocks such as constitute the Wrekin in Shropshire.

-urient (yūᵊ·riĕnt), *suffix*, – L. *-urient-*, pres. ppl. stem of desiderative vbs., occurring in a few direct adoptions from L., as *parturient*, and hence occas. added to L. stems to form adjs. with the meaning 'desiring, characterized by a desire (to do something)', as *nupturient.*

‖**Urim** (yūᵊ·rim). 1537. [– Heb. *'ûrîm* pl., referred to *'ôr* light, pl. *'ôrîm*, and by some taken as = lights, φωτισμοί 'illuminations'.] Certain objects, the nature of which is not known, worn in or upon the breastplate of the Jewish high-priest, by means of which the will of Jehovah was held to be declared. (Chiefly in *Urim and Thummim*, rendered in the LXX δήλωσις καὶ ἀλήθεια, in the Vulgate *doctrina et veritas*, whence Wyclif *doctryne and trewthe*, and in Coverdale *light and perfectnesse*, following Luther's *licht und recht*; in later English versions the words are left untranslated.)

The Counsel would be as the Oracle U. and Thummim, those oraculous gems On Aaron's breast MILT.

Urinal (yūᵊ·rinăl), *sb.* ME. [– (O)Fr. *urinal* – late L. *urinal*, subst. use of n. of late L. *urinalis* urinary, f. *urina* URINE; see -AL¹ 1.] †**1.** A glass vessel for the medical examination or inspection of urine –1858. †**2.** *Alchemy.* A phial for solutions, etc. –1738. **3.** A chamber-pot 1475. **b.** *Med.* A bottle for passing urine in bed. **4.** A vessel with conductor worn on the person for incontinence of urine 1855. **5.** A place of accommodation for passing urine 1851.

U·rinal, *a.* Now *rare* or *Obs.* 1541. [– Fr. *urinal* (XVI) – late L. *urinalis*; see prec.] = URINARY *a.*

Urinary (yūᵊ·rinări), *a.* 1578. [– med.L. **urinarius*, f. L. *urina* URINE; see -ARY¹.] Affording passage to urine; effecting or assisting in the secretion and discharge of urine. **2.** Of the nature of urine; excreted as urine 1646. **3. a.** Adapted for using on the urinary passage 1688. **b.** Adapted for receiving urine 1822. **4. a.** Lodged or formed in the urinary organs or bladder; excreted in the urine 1793. **b.** Of, pertaining to, affecting, or occurring in the urinary system or organs 1822.

Urinate (yūᵊ·rineⁱt), *v.* 1599. [– *urinat-*, pa. ppl. stem of med.L. *urinare* (in cl. L. dive), f. L. *urina* URINE; see -ATE³.] **1.** *intr.* To discharge urine; to make water. **2.** *trans.* To wet with urine 1768. **b.** To pass as or after the manner of urine 1915. So **Urina·tion,** the action of passing water, micturition 1599.

†**U·rinator.** 1648. [– L. *urinator* diver, f. *urinari, -are* dive.] A diver –1691.

Urine (yūᵊ·rin), *sb.* ME. [– (O)Fr. *urine* – L. *urina.*] The fluid secreted from the blood by the kidneys in man and the higher animals, stored in the bladder, and voided at intervals through the urethra. (Freq. in *Path.* with qualifying terms, denoting morbid condition.) **b.** With *an* and *pl.* 1483.

A physycyen, truely, can lyttel descerne Ony maner sekenes wythout syght of uryne 1509. Hence **U·rine** *v.* (now *rare* or *Obs.*) = URINATE.

Urini·ferous, *a.* 1744. [– mod.L. *urinifer*us; see URINE, -FEROUS.] *Anat.* Conveying urine. Usu. with *tube*, also with *duct, tubule.*

Urino- (yūᵊ·rino, -ǫ·), comb. form of L. *urina* URINE.

U:rinoge·nital *a.*, = UROGENITAL *a.*, affecting or occurring in the urogenital organs. **Urino·logy,** = UROLOGY; hence **Urino·logist. U·rinomancy,** diagnosis of diseases by examination of the urine. **Urino·meter,** an instrument for determining the specific gravity of urine. **U:rinosco·pic** *a.*, of or pertaining to the inspection of urine as a means of diagnosing diseases; hence **Urino·scopist, -scopy.**

Urinous (yūᵊ·rinəs), *a.* 1644. [f. URINE + -OUS.] **1.** Having or partaking of the essential properties of urine. **b.** Characteristic or suggestive of that of urine 1670. **2.** Of the nature of urine 1669. **3.** Marked by the presence or prevalence of urine 1788.

Urn (ŏɹn), *sb.* late ME. [– L. *urna* (:- **urcna*), rel. to *urceus* pitcher.] **1.** An earthenware or metal vessel of a rounded or ovaloid form and with a circular base, used by the ancient Greeks and Romans and others to preserve the ashes of the dead. **2.** A receptacle for holding voting-tablets, lots, or balls, in casting lots, voting, etc. Chiefly *Rom. Antiq.* 1513. **b.** A ballot-box 1888. **3.** A hollow vessel, usu. of earthenware, of an oviform or rounded shape, and having a circular base, used for various purposes 1639. **b.** A sculptured ornament representing or shaped like an urn 1653. **4.** An oviform pitcher or vessel for water, wine, etc. 1613. **b.** The source of a stream, etc.; a spring or fountain 1728. **c.** A tear-bottle (freq. with *lachrymal*) 1753. **d.** *Astr.* The constellation of Aquarius 1633. **5.** Short for *tea-urn* 1781.

6. a. *Bot.* The spore-case or capsule of urn-mosses 1840. **b.** *Biol.* An urn-shaped process or part 1877.

1. Alasse, how small an Vrne containes a King! DEKKER. **3.** *fig.* The haughty day Fills his blue u. with fire EMERSON. **b.** Her statue..set uppon an Urne or Pedestall 1653. **4. b.** Ten thousand rivers poured..From urns that never fail COWPER.

Comb.: **u.-moss** (see sense 6 a). Hence **Urn** *v. trans.* to deposit (ashes, bones) in a cinerary u.; to enclose in or as in an u. †**U·rnal** *a.* of the nature of a cinerary u.; effected in a sepulchral u.

Urning (ǖ·ɹniŋ). 1890. [– G. *urning*, f. (Venus) *Urania* (Ulrichs); cf. URANISM.] A homosexual person.

Uro-¹ (yūᵊ·ro), comb. form of Greek οὖρον urine, in terms of physiological chemistry, etc., denoting esp. (*a*) pigments present in or derived from urine, as *urocy·anin*; (*b*) morbid conditions of the urine or urinary organs, as *urocysti·tis*; (*c*) instruments for examining urine, as *urogravi·meter*; also in adjs., as *urose·xual*.

Urobe·nzoate, = HIPPURATE. **Urobenzo·ic** *a.*, in *u. acid*, hippuric acid. **Urobilin** (-bəi·lin), a brownish resinous pigment found in the urine; hence **U:robilinu·ria**, a morbid condition characterized by excess of urobilin. **U·rochrome**, a yellow amorphous pigment found in the urine. **Uroe·rythrin**, a reddish pigment found in the urine of persons suffering from fevers, esp. rheumatic fever. **Uroglaucin** (glǭ·sin), a blue pigment found in the urine in certain diseases, as scarlet fever. **Urohæ·matin**, a variety of hæmatin forming the colouring matter of the urine. **Uroto·xic**, *a.* of or pertaining to the toxicity or toxic materials of the urine. **U·rotoxy, -toxi·city**, the toxic quality of the urine; a unit of urine in respect of its toxicity. **Uroxa·nic** *a.*, of an acid, obtained by oxidation of uric acid in alkaline solution. **Uroxanthin** (-zæ·nþin), = INDICAN.

Uro-² (yūᵊ·ro), comb. form of Greek οὐρά tail, occurring in terms of comparative anatomy, etc., designating or relating to a posterior, caudal, or tail-like part, region, segment, or process.

U·rochord, the notochord of ascidians and tunicates, regarded as corresponding to the primordial spinal column in vertebrates; one of the *Urochorda*, a branch of *Chordata* comprising ascidians and tunicates. **U·rodele** [Gr. δῆλος evident] *sb.* a member of the order *Urodela* of amphibians, in which the larval tail persists in adult life; *adj.* belonging to this order; so **Urode·lan. Urohy·al** *a.* forming or relating to a median posterior process or part of the hyoid arch in fishes or birds; *sb.* the bone forming this. **U·rostyle,** *Biol.*, the posterior unsegmented portion of the vertebral column in certain fishes and amphibians.

‖**Urochs** (ū̆ᵊ·r-, yūᵊ·rǫks). 1839. [G. *urochs*; see URE-OX.] = AUROCHS.

Uroge·nital, *a.* 1848. [f. URO-¹ + GENITAL *a.*] Pertaining to or belonging to the urinary and genital organs or products.

Urology (yuᵊrǫ·lŏdʒi). 1753. [f. URO-¹ + -LOGY.] †**a.** A treatise or discourse on urines. **b.** The scientific study of urine. Hence **Urolo·gical** *a.* **Uro·logist.**

Uroo (yūᵊ·ru). *Austral.* 1866. [Native name.] A species of kangaroo.

Uropoietic (yūᵊropoiˌe·tik), *a.* 1783. [f. URO-¹ + Gr. ποιητικός active, effective, f. ποιεῖν do, make; see -IC.] Of, pertaining to, concerned with the secretion of urine; secreting or excreting urine.

‖**Uropygium** (-pi·dʒiŏm). 1813. [med.L. *uropygium* – Gr. οὐροπύγιον.] *Ornith.* The rump in birds. So **Uropy·gial** *a.* situated on or belonging to the u.; *sb.* a rump-feather.

Uroscopy (yurǫ·skŏpi). 1646. [f. URO- + -SCOPY.] The scientific examination of urine, esp. as a means of diagnosing diseases. Hence **Urosco·pic** *a.* **Uro·scopist.**

Urrhodin (yūᵊrŏdin). 1846. [– G. *urorhodin* (Heller), f. *uro-* URO-¹ + Gr. ῥόδον the rose + -IN¹.] *Chem.* A red pigment found in the urine in certain morbid conditions. Hence **Urrhodi·nic** *a.*

‖**Ursa** (ǖ·ɹsă). OE. [L., bear (esp. she-bear), the Great Bear.] *Astr.* **1.** = sense 2. **2.** *Ursa Major*: The northern constellation also called the Great Bear, the Plough, and Charles's Wain. late ME. **b.** *joc.* A bearish person 1773. **3.** *Ursa Minor*: the northern constellation called the Little Bear 1597.

U·rsal, *a.* 1837. [f. L. *ursus* bear + -AL¹ 1.] Bear-like; *fig.*, bearish.

Ursine (ǖ·ɹsəin), *a.* 1550. [– L. *ursinus*, f. *ursus* bear; see -INE¹.] **1.** Of or pertaining to, characteristic of, or due to a bear or bears. **2.** Of the nature of, resembling, or having the essential characteristics of a bear; consisting of bears 1833. **b.** In specific names of beasts 1778. **3.** Suggesting that or those of a bear; bear-like 1837.

1. Full corpolent he was with breist ursyne, . and sperit leonine 1550. The u. fate of prophet-mockers 1841. **3.** Noted for u. manners SOUTHEY.

Urson (ǖ·ɹsən). 1774. [– Fr. *ourson* (XVI), dim. of *ours* bear.] *Zool.* The Canada porcupine, *Erethizon dorsatus*.

Ursone (ǖ·ɹsoᵘn). 1866. [f. L. (*uva*) *ursi* (see UVA) + -ONE.] *Chem.* A crystalline principle obtained esp. from the leaves of the bearberry.

Ursuline (ǖ·ɹsiuləin, -in, -īn), *sb.* and *a.* 1693. [f. name of St. *Ursula* + -INE¹.] **A.** *sb. pl.* An order of nuns established in 1572 with the rule of St. Augustine, for the teaching of girls, nursing of the sick, and the sanctification of the lives of its members. **B.** *adj.* Pertaining or belonging to the Ursulines 1739.

‖**Urtica** (ǖ·ɹtikă, ɒɹtəi·kă). 1706. [L. *urtica* nettle, f. *urere* burn.] A genus of apetalous plants, typical of the family *Urticaceæ*, including the true nettles; also, a plant of this, a stinging-nettle. So **Urtica·ceous** *a.* belonging to, consisting of, the *Urticaceæ*; resembling a nettle.

Urtical (ǖ·ɹtikăl, ɒɹtəi·kăl), *a.* and *sb.* 1846. [f. L. *urtica* nettle + -AL¹ 1.] *Bot.* **A.** *adj.* Pertaining to or belonging to the stinging-nettles. **B.** *sb.* An exogenous plant of the genus *Urtica* 1846.

‖**Urticaria** (ǖɹtikēᵊ·riă). 1771. [mod.L., f. L. URTICA.] *Path.* = NETTLE-RASH. Hence **Urtica·rial, Urtica·rious** *adjs.* of or pertaining to, appearing in, characteristic of, or resembling u.

Urticate (ǖ·ɹtikeⁱt), *v.* 1843. [– *urticat-*, pa. ppl. stem of med.L. *urticare* sting, f. *urtica* nettle; see -ATE³.] **1.** *intr.* To have the property of stinging like a nettle; to affect with a tingling pain or stinging sensation. **2.** *trans.* To flog with stinging-nettles 1861. **b.** To affect with a stinging pain; to produce urtication in or on 1862. **3.** To nettle, irritate 1873.

Urtication (ɒɹtikēⁱ·ʃən). 1655. [– med.L. *urticatio, -ōn-*, f. as prec.; see -ION.] **1.** The action or function of stinging like or as a nettle. **b.** A sensation suggestive of stinging 1859. **2.** The flogging or pricking of a benumbed part or paralytic limb with nettles as a means of restoring sensation, etc. 1837.

‖**Urubu** (ūrubū·). 1672. [– Brazilian (Tupi) *urubú*.] The black vulture, *Cathartes fœtens* or *atrata*, of the southern U.S. and South America.

‖**Urucu** (ūrukū·). 1613. [– Brazilian (Tupi) *urucú* anatta.] = ROUCOU 1, †2.

‖**Urucuri** (ūrukū·ri). 1863. [– Brazilian (Tupi) *urucuri* palm.] The Brazilian palm-tree, *Attalea excelsa*.

‖**Urus** (yūᵊ·rŏs). *Pl.* **uri** (yūᵊ·rəi), **uruses.** 1601. [– L. *urus* (Gr. οὖρος) – Gmc. *ūrus (OE., OHG. *ūr*, ON. *úrr*). See URE-OX.] *Zool.* **1.** = AUROCHS. **2.** Applied to species of fossil or prehistoric oxen 1823.

Us (ɒs), *pers.* and *refl. pron.* [OE. *ūs* = OFris., OS. *ūs*, (M)Du. *ons*, (O)HG. *uns*, ON. *oss*, Goth. *uns* :– Gmc. **uns* :– IE. **n̥s*, reduced grade of **nes* (Skr. *nas*).] The objective case of the pron. WE, repr. the OE. acc. and dat. **I.** With ref. to two or more persons. **1. a.** As direct obj. of a verb. **b.** As indirect obj., = To us OE. **c.** As obj. of a prep. (or other governing word or phrase) OE. **d.** With participles in absolute construction 1549. **e.** In ethic dative. *arch.* 1685. **2.** *refl.* Ourselves. Now only *arch.* or *dial.*, after some verbs of motion or posture. OE. **3.** With defining term. late ME. **4.** As nom., in place of WE. Now *dial.* or *vulg.* 1607. **b.** With sb. or adj. numeral in apposition 1489. **c.** In continuative or exclamatory clauses after *and* 1848. **d.** *predic.* after the vb. *to be*. *dial.* and *colloq.* 1883. **5.** *Naut.* = Our ship 1622.

1. a. To the soper sette he vs anon, And serued vs with vitaille CHAUCER. **b.** We myȝte be lordes aloft and lyue as vs luste LANGL. It mighte cost vs oure neckes COVERDALE 1 *Chron.* 13:19. Give us clothes, father! SHELLEY. **c.** Spanish men of warre..came vp with vs and fired at vs 1659. **d.** Vntill he ascended vp (all vs beholdyng hym) to heauen 1549. **e.** They wounded us only one Man 1711. **2.** For we may not hide us from þin iȝe 1430. Let's make vs Med'cines of our great Reuenge SHAKS. Let vs hye vs to Wakefield 1599. We sat us dahn on a wall top 1892. **3.** Bacon-fed Knaues, they hate vs youth SHAKS. Concerning the loyalty of us Catholics 1641. **4.** Come my Lords, shall vs march? 1607. **b.** A thing us men ought.. to bless God for 1814. **c.** And him so rich..And us so poor! DICKENS. **d.** It's us must break the treaty when the times come STEVENSON. **5.** We had taken the Vice-admirall, the first time shee bourded with vs 1622.

II. With ref. to a single person. **1.** Used by a sovereign or other potentate or magnate ME. **b.** In editorial or authorial use 1835. **2.** *dial.* and *colloq.* Me; to me 1828.

1. Tell Our Army from Vs Q. ELIZ. His Holiness was pleased to raise us..to the rank of Cardinal Priest of the Holy Roman Church CDL. WISEMAN. **b.** The one public man who is supposed never to read Us 1895.

Usable (yū·zăb'l), *a.* Also **useable.** late ME. [– (O)Fr. *usable* f. USER; see USE *v.*, -ABLE.] That may or can be used.

The candelstik, lanterns, and the vsable thingis of it WYCLIF *Exod.* 39:36. Hence **Usabi·lity. U·s(e)ableness.**

Usage (yū·zėdʒ). ME. [– (O)Fr. *usage*, f. *us* USE *sb.* + *-age* -AGE.] **1.** Habitual use, established practice, customary mode of action, on the part of a number of persons. **2.** With *a* and *pl.* An established or recognized mode of procedure, action, or conduct; a custom; *spec.* one which has force in law ME. **b.** *The Usages*, the eucharistic ceremonies of mixing water with the wine, prayer for the dead, prayer for the descent of the Holy Spirit on the elements, and the prayer of oblation 1718. **c.** *local.* A right-of-way 1829. **3.** The rules and customs *of* a particular body, class, craft, or pursuit ME. †**4.** Manner of (ordinarily) bearing or comporting oneself; usual conduct or behaviour; a practice or habit –1655. **5.** The action of using something; the fact of being used; employment, use. late ME. **6.** Action, behaviour, or conduct towards a person, etc.; manner of using or being used; treatment 1563. **7.** Established or customary use of words, language, expressions, etc. 1697.

1. Laws..corrected, altered, and amended by acts of parliament and common u. BLACKSTONE. **2.** Dyvers Privileges, Liberties and free Usages 1473. All I have here related was a receiv'd u. 1734. **c.** Crooked U. is a narrow lane..[in] Chelsea 1884. **3.** Of woodecraft wel koude he al the vsage CHAUCER. Married..according to the u. of the church of England 1827. **5.** Þe vsage and exercitacioun of pacience CHAUCER. Thou haste the vsage of reason CAXTON. **6.** Another..surrendred of her own accord, in hopes of better u. 1687. To inquire into the u. of children legally bound out 1799. Without fear of their being injured by the roughest u. 1892. Hence **U·sager,** a member of that section of nonjurors which observed 'the Usages'.

Usance (yū·zăns). late ME. [– OFr. *usance* :– Rom. **usantia*, f. **usare*; see USE *v.*, -ANCE. In med.L. *usantia, -cia*.] **1.** = prec. 1, 1 b. Now *arch.* or *poet.* **2.** = prec. 5. *arch.* 1460. **3.** †**a.** The practice or fact of lending or borrowing of money at interest (*rare*) –1611. **b.** Interest on money lent. (In 19th c. as a literary revival.) 1584. **4.** The period allowed by commercial usage or law for the payment of a bill of exchange, esp. as drawn in a foreign or distant land 1617. **b.** In the phr. *at u.*, *at..usance(s)* 1487.

1. Edicts, which have lost their validity by contrary u. 1656. I have in this way heard something of the prospects and usances of teachers 1860. Things to which we have grown so accustomed.., that u. has begotten familiarity 1862. **3. a.** You have rated me About my monies and my vsances SHAKS. **b.** The old Catholic doctrine that no u. whatever could be unsinfully received for the use of money 1862. **4.** Touching the exchange from London to Venice farther distant, by the word vsance three moneths are signified, and by double vsance six moneths 1617. **b.** No bills are now drawn in London at u. 1878.

Use (yūs), *sb.* [ME. *us* – (O)Fr. *us* :– L. *usus* use, usage, f. *us-*, pa. ppl. stem of *uti* use.] **I.** Act of using or fact of being used. **1.** The act of using a thing for any (esp. a profitable) purpose; the fact, state, or condition of being so used; utilization or employment for or with some aim or purpose; application or conversion to some (esp. good or useful) end. **b.** In *Law*, coupled with *occupation* (or *occupancy*) 1738. **c.** Freq. *to make* or *take* (*free, full*, etc.) *use of* 1591. **2.** In special senses: **a.** The act of using or fact of being used as food, etc.; consumption 1586. **b.** Employment or maintenance for sexual purposes 1565. **3.** *Law*. The act or fact of using, holding, or possessing land or other property so as to derive revenue, profit, or other benefit from it 1535. **b.** A trust or confidence reposed in a person for the holding of property, etc., of which another receives or is entitled to the profits or benefits 1535. **4.** The fact of using money borrowed or lent at a premium 1603. **b.** Such premium; interest, usury. Now *dial.* or *arch.* 1598. **5.** Employment or usage resulting in or such as to cause impairment, wear, etc. 1440.

1. To lend me the vse of one of your maskes 1558. The..confusion that is so hard to be avoided in the U. of Words LOCKE. **c.** Perhaps she had only made u. of him as a convenient aid to her intentions HARDY. Phrases. *In u.*; a low word not in u. JOHNSON. *To u.*; Every moment may be put to some u. CHESTERF. *Out of u.*; The name..had in some way gone out of u. 1892. *Of u.*; Words.. of very frequent u. in the New Testament 1648. **2. a.** A moderate u. of generous liquors 1772. **b.** His step-mother desired the u. of his body 1647. **3.** The property or possession of the soil being vested in one man, and the u., or profit thereof, in another BLACKSTONE. **b.** The Statute of Uses (A.D. 1535) was passed in order to prevent the severance of legal from beneficial ownership 1882. **4.** When money is lent on a contract to receive.. an increase by way of compensation for the u. BLACKSTONE. **b.** Human life Is but a loan to be repaid with u. COWPER. Phr. *At, to, †u.* (now *dial.*); You are my own son; — you have put my money out to u. already 1785. *†U. upon u.*, compound interest. **5.** Everything told of long u. and quiet slow decay DICKENS.

II. Habit of using. **1.** The habitual, usual, or common practice; continual, repeated, or accustomed employment or exercise; habit, custom ME. **2.** A custom, habit, or practice ME. **3.** Without article: Accustomed practice or procedure; usage, wont, habit. Often *use and wont*. **4.** Opportunity, occasion, habit or practice of using. Chiefly *to have the u. of*. ME. **b.** The power of using some faculty, etc.; ability to use or employ 1483. **5.** Long practice in something; practised condition, skill. late ME. **6.** *Eccl.* The distinctive ritual and ceremonial of a particular church, diocese, community, etc. late ME. **b.** Religious rite or ceremony observed in particular services of the church; a customary form of religious observance or service. late ME. **7.** The usage or fashion obtaining or prevailing in a country or community. late ME.

1. His vse was to ride with a thousande horses 1568. It is the vse of Cowards to doe that which thou dost 1612. According to the U. of those Days 1720. **2.** Englande hath an euyll vse in syttynge longe at dyner 1542. She knows not yet the uses of the world SHELLEY. **3.** Long U. obtaineth the authority of a Law HOBBES. **4.** The Pict..hath generally no vse of apparell HOLINSHED. **b.** Till a Person is come to the U. of Reason 1753. 'Little darling' has lost the u. of an arm 1860. **5.** When men can by muche vse, leape, wrastle, or cast the barre, better then any other 1551. I frequented all the fencing-schools to keep my hand in vse GOLDSM. **6.** Some folowyng Salsbury vse, some Herford vse, some the vse of Bangor 1548. **b.** Some very remarkable 'uses'.., such as mixing water with the wine 1877. **7.** The vse of that cuntre differethe from the rite of Englonde in clothenge 1432.

III. Manner of using. Manner or a manner or method of employing, applying, turning to account, etc.; an instance of this ME.

Perverts best things To worst abuse, or to thir meanest u. MILT. As its u. is very easie, so its convenience is very great 1703. Some of these uses of the word are confusing JOWETT.

IV. Purpose served. **1.** A purpose, object, or end, esp. of a useful or advantageous nature ME. **†b.** A practical application of doctrine in a sermon or homily –1816. **2.** The fact or quality of serving the needs or ends *of* a person or persons ME. **3.** *Law*. The advantage *of* a specified person or persons in respect of profit or benefit from lands, etc. late ME. **4.** Office; function; service 1509. **5.** The character, property, or quality which makes a thing useful or suitable for some purpose; utility; advantage, benefit 1598. **b.** In the phr. *of* or *to* (*no, little*, etc.) *use*. late ME. **c.** With ellipsis of prep. 1820. **6.** Need or occasion for using; necessity, demand 1604. **b.** *To have no use for*: to find superfluous, regard as a nuisance; to dislike, *colloq.*, orig. *U.S.* 1887.

1. The prestes..take the golde.., and put it to their owne vses COVERDALE *Baruch* 6:10. I had the tallow..for greasing my boat, and other uses SWIFT. **b.** I proceed now to the Uses which may be drawn from the Truths delivered 1679. **2.** Coffee..for the u. of the Grand Seignior MILT. **3.** A rente charge paiable to the vs and profit of his chanterie 1393. **4.** The u. of the sand in these processes is to prevent the amber..from passing over into the receiver 1811. **5.** Their u. is not answerable to the great Stress which seems to be laid on them LOCKE. What is the u. of making up my mind? 1880. **b.** Birds..that are of Assistance and U. to Man ADDISON. I had good reason to hope that I was being of u. 1859. **c.** Alas! it is no u. to say, 'I'm poor!' SHELLEY. **6.** Giue it me..I haue vse for it SHAKS.

Use (yūz), *v.* ME. [– (O)Fr. *user* †employ (now *user de*), consume, wear out :– Rom. **usare*, f. L. *us-* (see prec.). In med.L. *usare*.] **I. †1.** *trans.* To observe (a rite, custom, etc.); to keep as a custom; *pass.*, of a practice: to be customary –1889. **†2.** To comply with, put in practice (a law, etc.) –1609. **3.** To prosecute or pursue (a course of action). Now *rare*. ME. **†4.** To follow (a trade, etc.); to perform the functions of (an office) –1773. **†b.** To follow or pursue (a manner or course of life) –1821. **c.** To spend (a period of time) in a certain way. (Now only with implication of sense II. 1.) 1477. **†d.** To frequent (a person's company) –1599. **†5.** To engage in or practise (a game, etc.) –1801. **6.** To put into practice or operation; to carry into action or effect. late ME.

1. It shall be lawful, as it hath been used heretofore, to make Probates of wills..in the Colony 1650. **2.** Al Barons sall receaue, and vse the lawes, as they are vsed in the Kings court 1609. **3.** The chiefest Market place, where all the buying and selling was used 1648. **4.** Then let them vse the office of a Deacon 1 *Tim.* 3:10. **b.** The wicked life that I did vse 1578. **c.** *Timon* III. i. 39. **5.** A corpulent Man, who lived freely and used no Exercise 1764. **6.** 'Twas a good world when such simplicitie was vsed 1589.

II. 1. To make use of (some immaterial thing) as a means or instrument; to employ for a purpose ME. **b.** To employ (a standard, type, etc.) ME. **2.** To employ (an article, etc.), esp. for a profitable end; to turn to account ME. **b.** To wear as an article of apparel. late ME. **3.** To work, manipulate (a member, tool, etc.) ME. **4.** To employ (a person, animal, etc.) in some function or capacity, esp. for an advantageous end. late ME. **b.** To have sexual intercourse with. Now *dial.* late ME. **5.** To take or partake of as food, drink, etc. Now *rare*. late ME. **6.** To expend, consume, or exhaust by use 1440. **7.** *To use up*: **a.** To come to the end of (a stock, etc.) 1785. **b.** To exhaust the vigour of, tire out (a person) *colloq.* 1850. **8.** To speak or write (a language) ME. **b.** To avail oneself of, express oneself by or in (a style, a word, etc.) ME. **9.** To frequent, haunt (a place). Now *rare*. late ME. **b.** *To use the sea(s)*, to be a sailor. *arch.* 1634. **10.** To treat or deal with (a person or thing), behave to (a person) in a specified way 1483. **†b.** *refl.* To conduct or comport oneself –1860.

1. Freedom is either a blessing or a curse as men u. it BERKELEY. The arguments used..to detain her brother 1798. **2. b.** Buskins of shels all siluered vsed she MARLOWE. **3.** Good Launcelot Iobbo, vse your legs,..run awaie SHAKS. I am against the prophets..that vse their tongues *Jer.* 23:31. He..used a *perspicillum* or simple lens 1880. **4.** Were not his purpose To u. him further yet in some great service MILT. **5.** And vse these thynges, Cowe mylke, Almon mylke, yolkes of rere egges 1542. **6.** A Cook that used six Pounds of butter to fry twelve Eggs MRS. GLASSE. **7.** The genuine Roman race must have been almost used up in the desperate warfare 1875. **b.** We have used up no fewer than six Irish Secretaries 1887. **8.** [He] should be able to u. Latin, not merely to understand it 1888. **b.** A man y[t] vseth moch swearing BIBLE (Great) *Ecclus.* 23:11. **9.** Like a wilde Asse, that vseth the wildernesse COVERDALE *Jer.* 2:23. He useth the Queen's-head Ale-house 1708. **b.** These many years.. have I used the seas 1681. **10.** My Collonel useth me with very greate courtesy 1639. **b.** He used himself more like a Fellow to your Highness, than like a Subject 1648.

III. 1. To make (a person, etc.) familiar or accustomed by habit or practice; to habituate, accustom; to inure. Const. †*in*, †*with*, *to*. Now chiefly in pa. pple. ME. **2.** *intr.* To do a thing customarily; to be wont to do. (Now only literary and chiefly in clauses introduced by *as*.) late ME. **3.** To be accustomed or wont *to* do something. Now only in pa. t. *used to* (yūst tu, yū·stŭ). ME. **4.** To frequent a place; to go often *to* a person or place. Now *dial.* and *U.S.* 1470.

1. This man had accesse unto the queene..to u. hir with..courtlie pastimes HOLINSHED. You shall do well also to u. your Horse to Swimming 1643. As soon as it perceives any thing it is not us't to 1682. I'm not used to be used in this manner! MME. D'ARBLAY. He wanted to u. her by degrees to live without meat SCOTT. **2.** We should, as learned Poets u., Invoke the Assistance of some Muse 1663. **3.** Your silke-worme useth to fast every third day WEBSTER. Jewels do not u. to lie upon the surface of the earth 1662. **4.** Sertaine lewde fellowes..doe frequente and u. about Layton heath 1599. Ye valleys low where the milde whispers u., Of shades and wanton winds MILT. Hence **U·ser**[1], one who uses or employs a thing.

Used (yūzd), *ppl. a.* late ME. [f. prec. + -ED[1].] **†1.** Usual, wonted –1655. **b.** That is or has been made use of 1594. **2. Used up. a.** Thoroughly exhausted by physical exertion; tired out, 'done up'; exhausted by use, rendered unserviceable. *slang* or *colloq.* 1840. **b.** *U.S.* Fully discussed 1839. **c.** Worn out, debilitated, rendered useless, as with hard work, dissipation, age, etc. 1848.

Useful (yū·sfŭl), *a.* 1483. [f. USE *sb.* + -FUL.] Having the qualities to bring about good or advantage; helpful in effecting a purpose; suitable for use; serviceable. Hence **U·seful-ly** *adv.*, **-ness.**

Useless (yū·slės), *a.* 1593. [f. as prec. + -LESS.] That is of no use; unserviceable, ineffectual, unavailing. **b.** Of persons: Incompetent, inefficient; performing no service 1670. Hence **U·seless-ly** *adv.*, **-ness.**

U·se-mo:ney. Now *dial.* 1616. [f. USE *sb.* I. 4 b.] = INTEREST *sb.* II. 2.

User[2] (yū·zəɹ). 1835. [Evolved from ABUSER[2], NON-USER.] *Law*. Continued use, exercise, or enjoyment of a right; presumptive right arising from use.

‖**Ushabti** (uʃa·bti). 1912. [Egyptian.] Statuettes of servants deposited in the tomb of a mummy.

Usher (ɒ·ʃəɹ), *sb.* late ME. [– AFr. *usser* = OFr. *ussier, uissier* (mod. *huissier*); see HUISHER. For *-sh-* from OFr. *-ss-* cf. CUSHION, -ISH[2], PUSH.] **1.** An official or servant who has charge of the door and admits people to a hall, chamber, etc.; in later use, esp. an officer in a law-court or an attendant who conducts people to seats in a church or place of assembly. **2.** An officer at court, in a great household, etc., who walks before a person of high rank; also, a chamberlain 1518. **†b.** A male attendant on a lady –1809. **3.** One who precedes or arrives before another, esp. a higher dignitary or personage; a precursor 1548. **b.** *transf.* That which precedes or gives intimation of the approach or advent of a person or thing 1586. **c.** *Ent.* A species of moth 1819. **4.** A schoolmaster's assistant; an under-master. Now only as a traditional title, or as a depreciatory synonym for (*assistant-*)*master*. 1512.

1. *fig.* Arminianisme is but a Bridge, an Vsher vnto grosse Popery PRYNNE. **2.** The Duke of Northfolke..claymethe to be highe vssher the daye of the coronacion 1553. *U. of the Black Rod*: see BLACK ROD; The U. of the Black Rod commanded their Attendance in the House of Lords 1718. *U. of the Green Rod*, an officer of the Order of the Thistle. *transf.* The wife of Anttony Should haue an Army for an Vsher SHAKS. **3.** By his ussher and messenger John UDALL. **b.** Fasts haue beene set as Vshers of festiuall dayes HOOKER. **4.** Country Vshers..are vnder the Headmaister, equall with the chiefe Schollers, and aboue the lesser boyes 1632. Hence **U·sheress, -ette,** a female usher. **U·sherless** *a.* lacking an u., herald, or harbinger. **U·shership,** the functions or office of an u.

Usher (ʊ·ʃəɹ), *v.* 1594. [f. prec.] **1.** *trans.* To act as usher to; to conduct, attend, or introduce with ceremony *from, to,* or esp. *into* (a place), etc.; to announce or bring *in,* show *in* or *out.* **2.** To precede or escort (a dignitary) ceremonially as an usher 1612. **b.** To precede; to lead up to 1607. **3.** To introduce or preface (an utterance, etc.) 1635. **4.** To introduce or bring *into* the world 1679.

1. *fig.* The blushing dawn out of the chearfull east Is ushering forth the day DRAYTON. **2. b.** Pitchy tempests threat, Usher'd with horrid gusts of wind CHAPMAN. **3.** Oh name for ever sad!..still ushered with a tear POPE.

To usher in: (see also 1). **a.** To bring in (a banquet, etc.) in state. **b.** To inaugurate (a period). **c.** To precede, come before. **d.** To mark the introduction, beginning, or occurrence of. **e.** To preface. Hence **U·sherer, U·shering** *vbl. sb.* and *ppl. a.*

‖**Usine** (yuzī·n, Fr. üzin). 1858. [Fr.] A factory, *esp.* a West Indian sugar factory.

‖**Usnea** (ʊ·snĭă). 1597. [med.L. – Arab. and Pers. *'ušna* moss.] A genus of gymnocarpous lichens, typical of the family *Usneidæ.*

Usnic (ʊ·snik), *a.* 1847. [f. prec. + -IC 1 b.] *Chem. U. acid,* an acid found in lichens.

Usnin (ʊ·snin). 1861. [f. as prec. + -IN¹.] *Chem.* Usnic acid.

Usquebaugh (ʊ·skwĭbǭ). 1581. [– Irish and Sc. Gaelic *uisge beatha* 'water of life', f. *uisge* water, and *beatha* life.] = WHISKY *sb.*¹

‖**Ustilago** (ʊstilē¹·go). *Pl.* **-agines** (-ē¹·dʒinīz). 1578. [mod. use of late L. *ustilago,* f. *ust-,* pa. ppl. stem of L. *urere* burn.] *Bot.* Smut on grain; *spec.* a genus of parasitic fungi, typical of the family *Ustilagineæ* (brand fungi). So **Ustilagi·neous** *a.* of or pertaining to the *Ustilagineæ.* **Ustila·ginous** *a.,* resembling, or belonging or allied to *U.*

†**U·stion.** 1567. [– (O)Fr. *ustion* – L. *ustio, ustiōn-,* f. as prec.; see -ION.] **1.** The action of burning or fact of being burnt –1802. **2.** Cauterization –1737.

Ustulation (ʊstiŭlē¹·ʃən). 1658. [– late and med.L. *ustulatio, -ōn-,* f. *ustulat-,* pa. ppl. stem of L. *ustulare* burn, f. as prec.; see -ION.] The action of burning or fact of being burnt; *spec.* in later use, roasting.

Usual (yū·ʒ¹uăl, yū·ziuăl), *a.* late ME. [– OFr. *usual,* (also mod.) *usuel,* or late L. *usualis,* f. L. *usus* USE *sb.*; see -AL¹ 1.] **1.** That is in ordinary use or observance; commonly observed or practised; current, prevalent. **2.** Ordinarily used; in common use; ordinary, customary 1444. **b.** Of persons: Commonly employed or serving in a particular capacity 1590. **3.** That ordinarily happens, occurs, or is to be found; common, wonted 1577. **b.** Customary on the part of a person or persons *to* do something 1605. **c.** Common or habitual *to* a person or thing 1655. **d.** *As* (or *than*) *u.,* as (or than) is or was customary or habitual. Also, in facetious use, *as per u.* 1716. **4.** *absol. The* (*his,* etc.) *usual,* what is usual, customary, or frequent (esp. with a person or persons) 1876.

1. Fortie markis wsuall money of Scotland 1575. He never goes thither at the u. hours 1687. **2.** The u. expressions of friendship 1836. Beer in the u. stately German flagons with pewter covers 1883. **b.** Where is our vsuall manager of mirth? SHAKS. **3. b.** It was u. for him to show the Delicacy of his Taste by [etc.] ADDISON. **d.** Our Conversation opened, as u., upon the Weather ADDISON. The huddled buildings looked lower than u. DICKENS. **4.** To-day the drivers outdid their u. 1892. Hence **U·sualness.**

Usually (yū·ʒ¹uăli, yū·ziuăli), *adv.* 1477. [f. prec. + -LY².] **1.** In a usual or wonted manner; according to customary, established, or frequent usage; as a rule. †**2.** In a regular manner –1605.

1. Phr. †*As u.*; The company behaved as u. on these Occasions FIELDING. *Than u.* (now only when followed by an adj.); The mind of man has been more than u. active in thinking about man JOWETT.

Usuca·pient. 1875. [– L. *usucapiens, -ent-,* pr. pple. of *usucapere*; see next, -ENT.] *Roman Law.* An owner or claimant by usucapion.

Usucapion (yūziukē¹·piǫn). 1606. [– Fr. *usucapion* or L. *usucapio, -ōn-,* f. *usucapere* acquire ownership by prescription, f. *usu,* abl. of *usus* USE *sb.* + *capere* take, seize; see -ION.] *Roman* and *Civil Law.* The acquisition of ownership by long use or enjoyment.

Usucapt (yū·ziukæpt), *v.* 1880. [– *usucapt-,* pa. ppl. stem of L. *usucapere*; see prec.] *Roman Law. trans.* To acquire ownership of or title to (a property, etc.) by usucapion. So **Usuca·ption** = USUCAPION 1656.

Usufruct (yū·ziufrʊkt). 1630. [– med.L. *usufructus,* for L. *ususfructus,* more fully *usus et fructus, usus fructusque* use and enjoyment; see USE *sb.,* FRUIT.] **1.** *Law.* The right of temporary possession, use, or enjoyment of the advantages of property belonging to another, so far as may be had without causing damage or prejudice to it. **2.** Use, enjoyment, or profitable possession (*of* something) 1811.

2. In the rich man's houses and pictures..I have a temporary u. at least LAMB.

Usufructuary (yūziufrʊ·ktiuări), *sb.* 1618. [– late L. *usufructuarius,* f. *usufructus* USUFRUCT; see -ARY¹.] **1.** *Law.* One who enjoys the usufruct of a property, etc. **2.** *gen.* One who has the use or enjoyment *of* something 1621.

1. The Parsons of Parishes are not in Law accounted Proprietors, but only Usufructuaries 1726. **2.** The present usufructuaries of the blessings of civilization 1886.

Usufru·ctuary, *a.* 1710. [– late L. *usufructuarius*; see prec.] Pertaining or relating to, or of the nature of usufruct.

†**U·sufruit.** 1478. [– (O)Fr. *usufruit* – med.L. *usufructus* USUFRUCT.] = USUFRUCT –1728.

†**Usure.** ME. [– (O)Fr. *usure* – L. *usura,* f. *usus* USE *sb.* See -URE, USURY.] = USURY.

Usurer (yū·ʒŭrəɹ, yū·ziŭrəɹ). ME. [– AFr. *usurer,* OFr. *usureor,* (also mod.) *usurier,* f. *usure*; see prec. -ER² 2. Cf. med.L. *usurarius.*] One who practises usury; a money-lender, esp. one who charges an excessive rate of interest.

No Christian is an vsurer 1551. The u., who derived from the interest of money a silent and ignominious profit GIBBON. I know myself to be an u. as long as I take interest on any money RUSKIN.

Usurious (yuʒū³·riəs, yuziū³·riəs), *a.* 1610. [f. USURY + -OUS.] **1.** Characterized by, of the nature of, or involving usury or excessive interest. **b.** Of interest, etc.: Charged by way of usury; exorbitant, excessive 1611. **2.** Practising usury; exacting excessive interest on loaned money 1631. **b.** Characteristic of a usurer 1727. Hence **Usu·riously** *adv.*

Usurp (yuzɒ̄·ɹp), *v.* ME. [– (O)Fr. *usurper* – L. *usurpare* seize for use.] **1.** *trans.* To appropriate wrongfully to oneself (a right, prerogative, etc.); *esp.* to assume or arrogate to oneself (political power, rule, authority, etc.) by force; to claim unjustly. **2.** To take possession or assume rule of (territory, etc.) wrongfully or illegally. late ME. **b.** *transf.* To take the place of or encroach upon physically 1635. **c.** Of feelings: To gain control of or fill (the heart, etc.) 1749. **d.** *To usurp the place of,* to oust, be substituted for 1573. †**3.** To appropriate by ruse or violence; to steal –1643. **4.** To make use of, employ (something not properly belonging to one or one's estate). late ME. **b.** To pretend to, assume as one's own (a name or style) 1549. **c.** To take into use, borrow (a word, etc.) from another language, source, etc. Now *rare.* 1531. **6.** To oust, supplant (*rare*) ME. **7.** *intr.* To play the usurper. Now *rare.* late ME. **8.** *To usurp on* or *upon*: **a.** To practise usurpation upon (a person) 1470. **b.** To encroach upon or infringe (a right, sphere, etc.) 1493. **c.** To intrude upon and seize (territory, etc.) without right or just cause 1630.

2. Whereat a sudden pale..Usurps her cheek SHAKS. Blasphemous and ignorant mechanics usurping the pulpets every where EVELYN. **b.** The white-mouth'd Water now usurpes the Shore QUARLES. **c.** Distemper'd passion..Usurped my troubled bosom SMOLLETT. **3.** *Ham.* I. i. 46. **4.** Some inferior dauber has usurped the pencil of Apelles SCOTT. **b.** Love to heaven is fled,. Since sweating Lust on earth usurp'd his name SHAKS. **c.** Stadium..is vsurped, for a place where men exercise their horse 1559. **6.** The erle..wyllynge to usurpe her of her duchy 1512. **8. a.** When any of the three estates have usurped upon the others 1760. The Saxon and the Norman kings gradually usurped upon the freedom of the Church MANNING. Hence **Usu·rping** *vbl. sb.* and *ppl. a.*

Usurpation (yūzɒɹpē¹·ʃən). late ME. [– (O)Fr. *usurpation* or L. *usurpatio, -ōn-,* f. *usurpare*; see prec., -ATION.] **1.** Unwarranted assumption of or pretension to something. **2.** Unlawful seizure or occupation of other's property; encroachment on or intrusion into the office, right, etc., of another. late ME. **b.** *esp.* The unlawful or forcible seizure or occupation of a throne, sovereign power, etc. 1470. **c.** With *a* and *pl.* An act of usurping or encroachment 1638. **3.** *Eccl. Law.* The action on the part of a stranger of dispossessing a lawful patron of the right of presenting to a benefice 1596. †**4.** Usurpatory rule or power (*rare*) –1761. **b.** *The u.,* the period of the Commonwealth 1682. **5.** The action of taking a thing into use; usage, employment. Now *rare.* 1583.

1. As he usurped divine honours, so he made a figure suitable to his u. DE FOE. **2.** Whatsoeuer the Popes of Rome gained upon us..was meer tyranny and u. 1654. **b.** Nameinge hymself, by usurpacion, King Richard the III[d] 1485. **c.** Usurpations of unconstitutional powers by the House of Commons 1863. **5.** Which worde [*sc.* priests] is taken vp by common vsurpation, to signifie sacrificers 1583.

Usurpative (yuzɒ̄·ɹpătiv), *a.* 1797. [– late L. *usurpativus,* f. L. *usurpare*; see -IVE.] Of the nature of, marked by, or characterized by usurpation.

Usurpatory (yuzɒ̄·ɹpətəri), *a.* 1847. [f. USURPATION + -ORY², after similar pairs.] Marked or characterized by usurpation; usurping.

Usurpature (yū·zɒɹpē¹·tiūɹ). *poet.* 1845. [f. as prec. + -URE.] Usurpation.

Usurper (yuzɒ̄·ɹpəɹ). late ME. [– OFr. *usurpeur,* or f. USURP *v.* + -ER¹.] One who usurps a crown or throne, or supreme power or authority. **b.** One who illegally or unjustly seizes or intrudes into any office, property, rights, etc. late ME.

Usury (yū·ʒŭri, yū·ziŭri). ME. [– AFr. *usurie (= (O)Fr. *usure*) or med.L. *usuria,* f. L. *usura,* f. *usus* USE *sb.*; see -Y³.] **1.** The fact or practice of lending money at interest; esp. in later use, the practice of charging excessive or illegal rates of interest for money on loan. **2.** Premium or interest on money (or goods) lent. Also *fig.* Now *arch.* 1440.

1. To whom þat vsery ys lefe, Gostely he ys a þefe 1303. The crime of u., before the Reformation, consisted in the taking of *any* interest for the use of money; and now in taking an higher rate of interest than is authorised by law 1754. I know of but two definitions that can possibly be given of u.: one is, the taking of a greater interest than the law allows of...The other is the taking of a greater interest than it is usual for men to give and take BENTHAM. The statutes against u...are repealed, so that you may take for your money whatever amount of interest you can get LD. ST. LEONARDS. **2.** þer was ane vsurar þat wolde neuer restore his vsurie agayn 1440. I repay you with u. yor kinde Wishes PEPYS.

Usward (ʊ·swəɹd), *adv.* Now *arch.* late ME. [f. US; see -WARD.] orig. (and chiefly) *to u.,* towards us. Also *from u.*

Ut (ut, ʊt). ME. [– (O)Fr. *ut*; the lowest of the series *ut, re, mi, fa, sol, la, si,* being the initial syllables of half-lines of the sapphic stanza of the office hymn for the Nativity of St. John Baptist, *Ut* queant laxis *re*sonare fibris *Mi*ra gestorum *fa*muli tuorum, *Sol*ve polluti *la*bii reatum, *S*ancte *I*ohannes. Cf. GAMUT.] *Mus.* The first note in Guido's hexachords, and in the modern octave, now commonly Do *sb.*²; the note C in the natural scale of C major.

Utas (yū·tæs). *Hist.* late ME. [Reduced form of *utaves* – OFr. *outaves* :– L. *octavas* (*dies*), acc. pl. of *octava* (*dies*) eighth day. See OCTAVE.] = OCTAVE 1 a, b.

The Octave or U. of each Feast 1833.

Utensil (yute·nsĭl). late ME. [– OFr. *utensile* (mod. *ustensile*) – med.L. *utensile,* subst. use of n. of L. *utensilis* fit for use, useful (n. pl. *utensilia* implements), f. *uti* use.] †**1.** *collect. sing.* Domestic vessels, appliances, and furniture. Chiefly *Sc.* –1535. **2.** Any article useful or necessary in a household; a domestic implement, vessel, or article of furniture; now *esp.* an instrument or vessel in common use in a kitchen, dairy, etc. 1484.

b. Any vessel (†or other article) serving a useful end or purpose 1502. c. *esp.* A tool or implement used by artisans, farmers, etc. 1604. 3. One who is made use of (*rare*) 1678. 4. A sacred vessel, etc., belonging to, and esp. used in the services of a place of worship 1650. 5. (*Chamber*) *utensil*, a chamber-pot 1699.

1. Y be-qweythe to lucye my wyfe..alle þe vtensyl of myn hows 1411. 2. He ha's braue Vtensils..Which when he ha's a house, hee'l decke withall SHAKS. No expences are calculated for the dairy, such as wood, utensils, &c. 1767. b. Waggons fraught with Utensils of war MILT. *transf.* A large Library, and other literary utensils 1657. 3. A Sot, a Beetle, a Droan of a Husband, a mere U. OTWAY.

Uterine (yū·tĕrəin, -rin), *a.* late ME. [– late L. *uterinus* (in sense 1), f. *uterus* + *-inus* -INE[1]. Cf. (O)Fr. *utérin, -ine*. In other senses f. UTERUS + -INE[1].] 1. Born of one womb; having the same mother, but not the same father. b. Related through the mother (*rare*) 1632. 2. *Surg.* Adapted for using or operating on or in the womb 1615. 3. Of, pertaining or belonging to, situated in, or connected with the womb 1646. b. Affecting, occurring, or taking place in the uterus 1661. 4. Of vellum: Made from the skin of a fœtal or abortive calf or lamb 1870.

1. Brothers or sisters of the deceased by the mother only, who are called *u.* ERSKINE. b. The property..devolves to his brothers or u. uncles 1816.

Utero- (yū·tĕro), comb. form of UTERUS in medical and surgical terms, esp. with the sense 'of or for the womb and another part'.

Utero-abdo·minal, *a.* relating to or suitable for the womb and the abdomen. **Utero-gesta·tion,** the development of the embryo in the womb from conception till birth. **Utero-inte·stinal,** *a.* of the womb and intestines. **Utero·ova·rian,** *a.* of or pertaining to the uterus and ovary. **U·terotome,** an instrument for incising the womb. **Utero·tomy,** surgical incision of the uterus. **Uterovaginal** (stress var.) *a.* pertaining to or connected with the uterus and the vagina.

‖**Uterus** (yū·tĕrŏs). *Pl.* **uteri** (əi). 1615. [L.] 1. In the primates; The organ in which the young are conceived, developed, and protected till birth; the female organ of gestation; the womb. b. In other animals: The matrix; the ovary 1753. 2. *Bot.* a. = PERICARP 1676. b. In fungi: The envelope of the sporophore 1829.

Utile (yū·təil), *a.* Now *rare*. 1484. [–(O)Fr. *utile* – L. *utilis*, f. *uti* use; see -ILE.] Useful, profitable, advantageous.

Utilitarian (yutilitē·riăn), *sb.* and *a.* 1781, [f. UTILITY + -ARIAN.] A. *sb.* An adherent of utilitarianism; one who considers utility the standard of whatever is good for man; *loosely*, a person devoted to mere utility or material interests.

I thought they had more sense than to secede from Christianity to become Utilitarians 1821.

B. *adj.* 1. Of philosophy, principles, etc.: Based upon utility; *spec.* that regards the greatest good or happiness of the greatest number as the chief consideration or rule of morality 1802. b. Of, pertaining, or relating to utility or mere material interests 1830. c. More useful than beautiful, made, etc., primarily for utility 1847. 2. Of persons: Believing in or supporting utilitarianism; also, preferring mere utility to beauty or amenity 1802. 3. Of times: Marked or characterized by prevalence of utilitarian doctrine, principles, or views 1828.

1. The u. doctrine is, that happiness is..the only thing desirable, as an end MILL. b. Turning from the picturesque or romantic, to the u. view of this tree 1859. c. All exceedingly u., well kept, stiff, and disagreeable 1847. 3. In these hard, unbelieving u. days CARLYLE.

Utilitarianism (yutilitē·riăniz'm). 1827. [f. prec. + -ISM.] Utilitarian doctrine, principles, theories, or practices; *spec.* in *Philos.*, the doctrine that the greatest happiness of the greatest number should be the guiding principle of conduct.

A life..of sordid godless U. 1827. U., therefore, could only attain its end by the general cultivation of nobleness of character MILL.

Utility (yuti·lĭti). late ME. [– (O)Fr. *utilité* – L. *utilitas, -at-*, f. *utilis* useful; see UTILE, -ITY.] 1. The fact, quality, or character of being useful; fitness for a purpose; usefulness, serviceableness. b. In the phr. *Of* (*great, no,* etc.) *utility* 1440. c. *Philos.* The ability or capacity of a person, action, or thing to satisfy the needs or gratify the desires of the majority, or of the human race as a whole 1751. †2. Personal convenience or profit –1752. 3. A useful thing or feature; a use. Chiefly in pl. 1483. b. *Pol. Econ.* An object that can satisfy a human need 1848. 4. Short for *u. actor*, etc. (see 5) 1885. 5. *attrib.* passing into *adj.* a. **U. actor,** an actor of the smallest speaking-parts in a play; **u. man,** a u. actor, also (U.S.) an all-round substitute at base-ball. b. Of a dog, fowl, etc.: That is bred or kept for some useful object as dist. from purposes of display, show, etc. 1877.

1. The u. of Prayer for the Dead HOBBES. The circular court is a picturesque thought, but without meaning or u. H. WALPOLE. c. The creed which accepts as the foundation of morals, U., or the Greatest Happiness Principle MILL. 2. This is ayenst your prosperite and utilite CAXTON. 3. Of several of his creatures, whereof men.. make some uses, they shall hereafter discover other utilities BOYLE. Heinzman wanted the improvements..sold as a public u. to the highest bidder S. E. WHITE. Also *pl.* = *public utilities* (PUBLIC *a.* I. 2). b. A good or u. is anything which can satisfy a human want 1904. 4. She was playing u., that is to say, going on for anything 1889.

Utilize (yū·tiləiz), *v.* 1807. [– Fr. *utiliser* (1792) – It. *utilizzare*, f. *utile*; see UTILE, -IZE.] *trans.* To make useful, turn to account. So **U·tilizable** *a.* **U:tiliza·tion. U·tilizer.**

Utmost (ɒ·tmoᵘst, -məst), *a.* and *sb.* [OE. *ūtmest*, var. of *ūtemest*, f. *ūt, ūte* + *-mest*; see OUT *adv.*, -MOST.] I. 1. Situated, dwelling, etc., farthest from the centre; most external or remote; outermost, uttermost. b. Reaching furthest; of greatest length, extent, etc. 1709. 2. Of the greatest or highest degree; of the largest amount, etc.; extreme ME. 3. Latest in oruer or time; last, final. Now *rare*. 1460.

1. The u. extremities of the north of Britain 1729. b. All..that I could reach with my u. sight and keenest listening was still KINGLAKE. 3. In these sad words she spent her vtmost breath SPENSER.

II. *absol.* and as *sb.* 1. That which is most outward, distant, or remote; the farthest part *of* something. *arch.* OE. 2. That which is greatest or of the highest degree; the utmost point, extreme limit or degree (*of* something) 1472. b. With possessive adjs.: The highest, greatest, or best of one's ability, powers, etc. Often with *do*. 1611. 3. The end, finish, or issue *of* something. Now *rare*. 1603. 4. *To the u.*, to the extreme (*of* one's power, etc.) 1450. 5. *At the u.* (†*at u.*), at the most; taking the highest possible estimate 1618.

1. A City..on the u. of the ridge of a hill 1615. 2. Thinking the vtmost of their force to trie SPENSER. b. To rally up all one's little U. into one Discourse 1660. 3. *Meas. for M.* II. i. 36. 4. The wrath off God is come on them, even to the vtmost TINDALE I *Thess.* 2:16. 5. The Modern Age of Men at the u. is not 80. 1722.

Utopia (yutōᵘ·piă). 1551. [– mod.L. *Utopia* 'no-place', f. Gr. οὐ not + τόπος place; see -IA[1].] 1. An imaginary island, depicted by Sir Thomas More as enjoying a perfect social, legal, and political system. b. *transf.* Any imaginary or indefinitely-remote region, country, or locality 1610. 2. A place, state, or condition ideally perfect in respect of politics, laws, customs, and conditions 1613. b. An impossibly ideal scheme, esp. for social improvement 1734.

1. b. Ignorant where this River rises,..whether in Asia, in Africa, or in U. 1684. 2. b. Averse to all enthusiasm, mysticism, utopias, and superstition LECKY.

Utopian (yutōᵘ·piăn), *a.* and *sb.* 1551. [– mod.L. *Utopianus* (More, 1516); see prec., -AN.] A. *adj.* 1. Of or belonging to the imaginary island of Utopia or its people. †b. Nowhere existing –1689. 2. Impracticably ideal; of impossible and visionary perfection, esp. in respect of politics, social organization, etc. 1613. 3. Indulging in impracticably ideal projects for social welfare, etc.; believing in or aiming at the perfecting of polity or social conditions 1597.

1. b. In certain intermundane spaces and U. regions without the world 1678. 2. When he was laying out so magnificent, charitable, and philosophic an U. villa H. WALPOLE. An U. sketch of a perfect government 1798. 3. You are. a Theoretical Common-wealthsman, an U. Dreamer COWLEY.

B. *sb.* 1. A native or inhabitant of Utopia; a dweller in some Utopia 1551. 2. One who conceives or proposes schemes for the perfecting of social and political conditions; an advocate of visionary reform 1873.

2. Utopians who are equally ignorant of capital, labour, or hard work 1887. Hence **Uto·pianism. Uto·pianize** *v. trans.* to render U. **U·topism** = UTOPIANISM. **U·topist** = sense B. 2.

Utraquist (yū·trăkwist), *sb.* and *a.* 1836. [– mod.L. *Utraquista*, f. L. *utraque* each, both, in the phr. *sub utraque specie* under each kind; see -IST.] A. *sb. Hist.* = CALIXTIN 1. B. *adj. Hist.* Belonging to the Utraquists; insisting on Communion in both kinds 1894. So **U·traquism,** the doctrine of the Utraquists.

Utrecht (yū·trekt, ū·trext). 1848. The name of a Dutch town and province, used attrib. in *U. velvet*, a strong thick kind of plush used in upholstery.

Utricle[1] (yū·trik'l). 1731. [– Fr. *utricule*, or L. UTRICULUS[1].] 1. *Bot.* A small sac or bladder-shaped body; a bottle-shaped part. 2. *Anat.* and *Biol.* A small cell, sac, or bladder-like process 1822. b. The larger of two sacs in the membranous labyrinth of the ear 1837. 3. *gen.* A small bladder-like body; a globule 1858. So **Utri·cular** *a.*[1] of the nature of or resembling a u.; composed of utricles or small bladders.

U·tricle[2]. 1861. [– Fr. *utricule*, or L. UTRICULUS[2].] *Anat.* A small cul-de-sac in the prostatic portion of the urethra in man; the prostatic vesicle.

Utricular (yutri·kiŭlăɹ), *a.*[2] 1827. [f. L. UTRICULUS[2] + -AR[1].] Of or pertaining to the uterus or abdomen; uterine.

‖**Utricularia** (yutrikiŭlēᵊ·riă). *Pl.* **-iæ** (i,ī·). 1753. [mod.L., f. UTRICULUS[1]. See -ARY[1] 3.] *Bot.* A genus of scrophulariaceous plants, bearing small bladders at the margins of the leaves; bladderwort, hooded (water) milfoil; a species or plant of this.

‖**Utriculus**[1] (yutri·kiŭlŏs). 1753. [L., dim. of *uter* leathern bottle or bag; see -CULUS.] 1. *Bot.* = UTRICLE[1] 1. 2. *Anat.* = UTRICLE[1] 2 b. 1847.

‖**Utri·culus.**[2] 1848. [L., dim. of *uterus* UTERUS; see -CULUS.] *Anat.* = UTRICLE[2].

Utriform (yū·trifǫɹm), *a. rare*. 1860. [– mod.L. *utriformis* (Mayne), f. L. *utris, uter* bag, bottle, etc.; see -FORM.] Shaped like a leathern bottle.

‖**Utrum** (yū·trŏm). *Obs.* or *Hist.* ME. [AFr., AL. *utrum* (XII) = L. *utrum*, n. sing. of *uter* which, whether.] A writ authorizing the holding of an assize to decide the status of a property. Usu. *assize of utrum*.

Utter (ɒ·təɹ), *sb.* 1853. [See quot.] *Mech. pl.* Irregular marks made on a surface by the vibration or too great pressure of a tool.

Fine lines or striæ, also called 'utters',..from the sound emitted by the work when in vibration against the tool 1879.

Utter (ɒ·təɹ), *a.* [OE. *ūter(r)a. ūttra*, compar. formation (see -ER[3]) on *ūt* OUT *adv.*, corresp. to OFris. *utt(e)ra, ūtera*, MDu. *ūtere* (Du. *uiter-*), OHG. *ūȥaro* (G. *äusser*); for shortening of *ū* cf. *udder*.] 1. That is farther out than another; forming the exterior part or outlying portion; exterior, outward, external; also, indefinitely remote. Now only *poet.* exc. in *u. bar, barrister* (taken after 1600 to mean a junior counsel pleading outside the bar in lawcourts, as distinguished from a K.C. within it: see BAR *sb.*[1] III. 3, BARRISTER). b. With partitive words, as *end, part, side*. Now *rare*. ME. †2. = OUTER *a.* 2. –1450. †3. OUTWARD *a.* 4. –1593.

I. The kyngis cote, vndir his vttir garnement 1435. Cast that vnprophetable servaunt into vtter dercknes TINDALE *Matt.* 25:30. 3. Lyke the Geometritians, they square about poynts and lynes and the vtter shew of things NASHE.

II. 1. Going to the utmost point; extreme, absolute, complete, total. Freq. of destruction, ruin, etc. late ME. b. Of answers, decisions, etc.: Unqualified, decisive, definite 1456. **c.** Of darkness, etc.; Complete, absolute 1596. **2.** Of persons: That is such to an absolute degree; out-and-out, complete, 'perfect'. late ME. **b.** In affected use: Indescribably beautiful, intense, or æsthetic 1881.

1. The vtter losse of all the Realme SHAKS. Two Things which were his u. Aversion PRIOR. **b.** This is my vtter minde and will, That [etc.] 1560. The u. refusal of the..regiments to march farther CLARENDON. **c.** They blew out their lights.., and left the knight in u. darkness SCOTT. **2.** The Kinges u. enemye 1555. Ye be u. strangers to me BUNYAN. **b.** Are they not quite too all-but?.. They are indeed jolly u. W. S. GILBERT. Hence **U·tterness** (*rare*).

Utter (*ɒ·təɹ*), *v.* late ME. [– MDu. *ūteren* (Du. *uiteren*) drive away, speak, show, make known = OFris. *ūtia, ūtria*, MLG. *ūtern* turn out, sell, speak, demonstrate, with assim. to UTTER *a.*; prob. introduced partly as a term of commerce.] **I.** †**1.** *trans.* To put (goods, wares, etc.) forth or upon the market; to vend, sell –1863. **2.** To give currency to (money, coin, etc.); esp. to pass or circulate (forged coin, notes, etc.), as legal tender. Also *absol.* 1483. **3.** To put or thrust forth, shoot or urge out; to discharge, emit, eject. Now *dial.* 1536.

1. Booksellers were..prohibited from uttering Tindale's translation of the Bible 1863. **2.** To u. or cause to be uttered false mony knowing it to be false 1602. *absol.* The punishment of forging, uttering, and the like 1863.

II. 1. To give vent to (joy, etc.) in sound; to burst out with (a cry, etc.); to give out in an audible voice. late ME. **b.** With advs., esp. *forth* 1594. **2.** To give utterance to (words, speech, etc.). late ME. **b.** To give expression to, put in words, describe (thoughts, a subject, theme, etc.); to speak of or about 1449. **c.** With clause as obj. 1449. †**3.** To disclose or reveal (something unknown, secret, or hidden); to declare, divulge –1677. **4.** *refl.* To express oneself in words 1600. **5.** *intr.* To exercise the faculty of speech; to speak. late ME. **b.** Of words, etc.: To be spoken; to undergo utterance. *rare.* 1857.

1. A shout..sweet As from blest voices, uttering joy MILT. **2.** While he was uttering the words of Consecration HOBBES. **b.** His heart will worke iniquitie,..to vtter errour against the Lord *Isaiah* 32:6. This dire change, Hateful to u. MILT. **c.** Then didst thou vtter, I am yours for euer SHAKS. **3.** With what gravity..his Tongue and Pen uttered Heavenly Mysteries WALTON. **4.** *transf.* An excellent Musician..cannot u. himself upon a defective instrument 1648. **5.** My trembling was so great..that I could not u. 1774. **b.** Wishes that cannot be understood, and words that will not u. 1857.

Utterable (*ɒ·tərăb'l*), *a.* 1581. [f. prec. + -ABLE.] †**1.** That may be disposed of by sale –1611. **2.** That can be said; expressible in words 1648. Hence **Utterabi·lity.**

Utterance[1] (*ɒ·tərăns*). late ME. [f. as prec. + -ANCE.] †**1.** The disposal of goods, etc. by sale or barter –1632. **2.** The action of uttering with the voice; vocal expression; speaking, speech. *To give utterance to*, to express in words. 1456. **b.** *transf.* Musical or visible expression 1602. **3.** The faculty or power of speech; manner of speaking 1474. **4.** That which is uttered; a spoken (or written) statement or expression; an articulated sound 1454.

2. Oftetymes they selle as welle theyr scilence as theyr vtterance CAXTON. **3.** Because God has not bestow'd on them the gift of u. DRYDEN. The King's difficult u. rendered his addresses..painful to himself and the Parliament 1828. **4.** To hear a whole series and river of the most memorable utterances CARLYLE.

U·tterance[2]. Now *literary* or *arch.* late ME. [– (with assim. to UTTER *a.*) (O)Fr. *outrance*, †*oultrance* OUTRANCE.] *To the u.*, to the last extremity; to the bitter end. Freq. with *fight*, etc.

Come Fate into the Lyst, And champion me to th' vtterance SHAKS. I will fight him to the u. upon this quarrel SOUTHEY.

Utterer (*ɒ·tərəɹ*). 1509. [f. UTTER *v.* + -ER[1].] †**1.** A seller, vendor –1653. **b.** One who utters counterfeit coin, etc. 1731. **2.** One who utters, speaks, or expresses in language 1509. †**b.** A revealer –1590.

b. The coiners manufacture, and the utterers buy and distribute 1887. **2.** Falsehood..brings dishonour on its u. 1785. **b.** The vtterer of which conspiracie was one White HOLINSHED.

U·tterest, *a.* Now *rare.* ME. [f. UTTER *a.* + -EST.] †**1.** Most remote, furthest –1491. **2.** = UTMOST *a.* I. 2. late ME. †**3.** Last, final –1470. **4.** *absol.* or as *sb.* †**a.** = UTMOST II. 2, 2 b. –1577. **b.** *To the u.* = To the utmost. late ME.

2. The u. fool..in all the universe 1873.

Utterless (*ɒ·təɹlės*), *a.* 1643. [f. UTTER *v.* + -LESS.] Incapable of being uttered; unutterable. **b.** Inexpressible 1832.

Utterly (*ɒ·təɹli*), *adv.* ME. [f. UTTER *a.* + -LY[2].] †**1.** Sincerely, outspokenly –1559. **2.** In a complete or utter manner; altogether, entirely; fully, out-and-out. late ME. **b.** Freq. with verbs of perishing, refusal, etc. late ME. **c.** Qualifying adjs. (esp. with words implying negation, defect or opposition). late ME.

Uttermost (*ɒ·təɹmoᵘst, -məst*), *a.* ME. [f. as prec. + -MOST.] **1.** Farthest out or off; remotest. **b.** Greatest in extent; longest (*rare*) 1586. **2.** Extreme ME. †**3.** Last in time; final –1600. **b.** Last of a series, store, etc.; usu. in *u. farthing* 1553. **4.** *absol.* = UTMOST II. ME.

1. From the u. parts of the Earth HOBBES. **b.** The vttermost time presupposed in it, should be.. but one day SIDNEY. **2.** As they will answere.. for the same att their u. perilles 1544. A voice of u. joy WORDSW. **3.** To the vttermost dayes of my lyf MALORY. **b.** Thou shalt by no meanes come out thence, till thou hast payd the vttermost farthing *Matt.* 5:26. **4.** Ile..seeke to effect it to my vttermost SHAKS. To withstand the stranger to the u. FREEMAN.

‖**Utu** (*ū·tū*). *New Zealand.* 1840. [– Maori, = requital.] Satisfaction, price paid for injuries received.

Uva (*yū·vă*). 1670. *Pl.* **uvæ** (*yū·vī*). [– L. *uva* grape, uvula, etc.] **1.** *Bot.* A grape or raisin; a grape-like fruit. **2.** *U. ursi*, the bearberry, *Arctostaphylos uva-ursi*, a trailing plant furnishing an astringent tonic 1753. **b.** *Med.* (An infusion of) bearberry leaves 1805.

Uvarovite (*uvæ·rŏvəit*). 1837. [Named after Count S. S. *Uvarov*; see -ITE[1] 2 b.] *Min.* An emerald-green variety of garnet.

‖**Uvea** (*yū·viă*). 1525. [med.L., f. L. *uva* UVA.] *Anat.* †**1.** The posterior coloured surface or choroid coat of the eye –1797. **2.** A layer of pigmented cells forming the posterior covering of the iris; the choroid, iris, and ciliary body, forming the vascular tunic of the eye 1745. Hence **U·veal·** *a.* **Uveitis** (*yūvĭəi·tis*), inflammation of the u.

Uvula (*yū·viŭlă*). late ME. [– late L. *uvula*, dim. of L. *uva*; see UVA, -ULE.] *Anat.* The conical fleshy prolongation hanging from the middle of the pendent margin of the soft palate in man and some other primates. **b.** A small eminence forming the apex of the trigone, and projecting into the urethral orifice 1835. **c.** A lobe or triangular elevation between the two tonsils of the cerebellum 1848. Hence **U·vulatome, U·vulotome,** an instrument for cutting or removing the u. **Uvula·tomy, -o·tomy.**

Uvular (*yū·viŭlăɹ*), *a.* (*sb.*). 1843. [f. UVULA + -AR[1].] **1.** Pertaining or belonging to the uvula. **2.** *Phonetics.* Produced by vibration of the uvula 1873. **b.** as *sb.* A uvular consonant 1884.

2. The u. trill in French Paris 1873. Hence **U·vularly** *adv.* with a thick utterance, as when the uvula is unduly long.

‖**Uvularia** (*yūviulēᵊ·riă*). 1829. [mod.L., f. late L. UVULA. See -ARY[1] 3.] *Bot.* One or other species of *Uvularia*, a liliaceous genus typical of the family *Uvulareæ* of melanthaceous plants.

Uvulitis (*yūviŭləi·tis*). 1848. [f. UVULA + -ITIS.] *Path.* Inflammation of the uvula.

Uxorial (*ɒksōᵊ·riăl*), *a.* 1800. [f. L. *uxor* wife; see -IAL. In sense 2 var. of UXORIOUS.] **1.** Of or pertaining to a wife or wives. **2.** = UXORIOUS *a.* 2. 1853.

1. The rather generous u. laws of Islam 1896.

Uxoricide[1] (*ɒksōᵊ·risəid*). 1860. [f. L. *uxor* wife; see -CIDE 1.] One who murders his wife.

Uxo·ricide[2]. 1854. [f. L. *uxor* wife; see -CIDE 2.] The murder of one's wife.

Uxorious (*ɒksōᵊ·riəs*), *a.* 1598. [f. L. *uxoriosus* (f. *uxor* wife) + -OUS.] **1.** Dotingly or submissively fond of a wife; devotedly attached to a wife. **2.** Of actions, etc.: Marked or characterized by excessive affection for one's wife 1623.

1. Effeminate and U. Magistrates, govern'd and overswaid at home under a Feminine usurpation MILT. Hence **Uxo·rious-ly** *adv.*, **-ness.**

V

V (*vī*), the 22nd letter of the modern English and the 20th of the ancient Roman alphabet, was in the latter an adoption of the early Greek vowel-symbol V, now also represented by U and Y, but in Latin was employed also with the value of the Greek digamma, viz. (w), to which it corresponds phonologically. Under the Empire, the semi-vocalic sound gradually changed to a bilabial consonant, and finally became the labio-dental voiced open consonant (spirant) now denoted by this letter in English and various other languages.

The use of *v* in English first became established with the influx of French words into literature, and it is subsequently used freely in native words as well as in those of Latin or other origin. It had a double function, like U (q.v.), until in the 17th century *u* and *v* were finally distinguished as vowel and consonant symbols; even in the 19th century words beginning with either letter continued to form one series in some dictionaries, and this arrangement survives still in some catalogues.

Elision of *v* when not initial has taken place extensively in dialects. In standard English this is represented by such words as *hawk, head, lark, lord*, and is specially indicated in a few archaic or poetic forms, as *e'en* even, *e'er* ever, *ne'er* never, *o'er* over.

I. 1. The letter or its name. **2.** Used with ref. to the shape of the letter; an object having this shape; a V-shaped, acute-angled formation; also *attrib.*, freq. in the sense 'shaped like the letter V'; *v.neck*, a neck (as of a dress) cut in front in the shape of a letter V. **3.** Used to denote serial order, as V Battery, MS. V, or as a symbol of some thing or person.

II. The Roman numeral symbol for: Five (†or fifth). **b.** *V, V-spot, V-note*, a five-dollar note. *U.S.*

III. *Abbreviations.* **a.** Of various Latin words or phrases: v. = *verso* the back of the leaf, *versus* against, *vide* see; v.g. = *verbi gratia.* **b.** Of English words and phrases: V. = various proper names as Victoria, Vincent, etc.; the chemical symbol of Vanadium; v. = verb, verse, vision (in *Med.*), volt, etc.; very (as v.g. very good, v.h.c. very highly commended, etc.); V.A. = Vicar-Apostolic; V.C. = Victoria Cross; v.d. = various dates; V.M. = Virgin Mary; V.P. = Vice-President; v.r. = variant or various reading; V.S. = veterinary surgeon. **c.** In music an abbrev. of various Italian words, as *verte* turn, *violino* violin, *voce* voice, *volta* time.

Vac (*væk*). 1709. Abbreviation (chiefly in University colloq. use) of VACATION *sb.*

Vacancy (*vē̆ᵢ·kănsi*). 1580. [f. next (see -ANCY) or – late and med.L. *vacantia*, f. *vacant-*; see next.] **I. 1.** = VACATION 2. Also in pl. Now *arch.* †**2.** Temporary freedom from business or some usual occupation –1775. †**b.** Unoccupied time; leisure –1656. †**c.** An interval of leisure –1748. **3.** The state or condition of being unoccupied; absence of occupation; idleness; inactivity. Now *rare.* 1615. †**b.** Freedom from mental preoccupation –1856.

3. Nor does the v. of a Bath life suit complaints 1782. **b.** The fishers..whistle o'er their lazy task In happy v. 1856.

II. †**1.** An unoccupied period or interval; a time of absence *of* some activity –1663. **2.** The fact or condition of an office or post being, becoming, or falling vacant; an occasion or occurrence of this 1607. **3.** A vacant or unoccupied office, post, or dignity 1693.

1. *Twel. N.* v. i. 90. **2.** The V. of a Bishoprick 1726. The v. among the Chancery taxing masters 1896. **3.** How could there be an election without a v.? MACAULAY.

III. 1. Empty or void space 1602. **2.** A vacant, unfilled, or unoccupied space; an open space between objects or things, or in a row or series; a breach, gap, or opening 1652. **b.** *transf.* A blank, gap, or deficiency 1759. **3.**

The state or condition of being vacant, empty, or unoccupied; emptiness 1788. **b.** Lack of intelligence; inanity; vacuity 1841.

1. You bend your eye on vacancie, And with the incorporall ayre do hold discourse SHAKS. **3.** He contemplated with horror the v. and solitude of the city GIBBON.

Vacant (vē¹·kănt), *a.* ME. [In early use – (O)Fr. *vacant*; in XVI taken in afresh – L. *vacans, vacant-*, pr. pple. of *vacare* be empty or unoccupied; see -ANT.] **1.** Of a benefice, office, position, etc.: Not filled, held, or occupied. **2.** Devoid of all material contents or accessories; empty, void. late ME. **b.** Devoid of an occupant; not taken up by any one 1599. **c.** Of land, houses, etc.: Uninhabited, unoccupied, untenanted. Also of a room: Not in use, disengaged. 1518. Also *transf.* in *v. possession.* **d.** Marked by the absence of life, activity, or sound 1791. **3.** With *of*: Devoid or destitute of, entirely lacking or free from something. late ME. **4.** Of time: Free from or unoccupied with affairs, business or customary work; leisure 1531. †**b.** Of persons: At leisure; also, having nothing or little to do –1782. **c.** Characterized by or arising or proceeding from absence of occupation, leisure, or idleness; undisturbed by business or work. Now *rare.* 1615. **5.** Of the mind or brain: Devoid of or unoccupied with thought or reflection. Chiefly *poet.* 1579. **6.** Characterized by, proceeding from, or exhibiting absence of intelligence or thought; inane 1712.

2. Instant to his aid The Goddess hasted, to his v. hand His whip restored COWPER. **b.** To see the v. chair, And think 'How good! how kind! and he is gone' TENNYSON. **d.** The stillness of the v. night COWPER. **3.** A company of select friends, v. of business, and full of chearfulness 1663. **4.** The Memory relieves the Mind in her v. Moments ADDISON. **c.** An idle and v. life 1866. **5.** The loud laugh that spoke the v. mind GOLDSM. **6.** Yet folly ever has a v. stare COWPER. Hence **Va·cant-ly** *adv.*

Vacate (văkē¹·t, *U.S.* vē¹·ke¹t), *v.* 1643. [– *vacat-*, pa. ppl. stem of L. *vacare* be empty or unoccupied; see -ATE³.] **1.** *trans.* To make void in law; to annul or cancel. **b.** *transf.* To deprive of force, efficacy, or value; to render inoperative. Now *Obs.* or *rare.* 1655. **2.** To make or render (a post or position) vacant; to deprive of an occupant or holder 1697. **b.** To leave (an office, position, etc.) vacant by death, resignation, or retirement; to give up, relinquish, or resign the holding or possession of. Also *absol.* 1812. **3.** To leave or withdraw from (a place, seat, etc.); to quit or give up 1791.

1. Such omission..will not v. the contract 1817. **2.** As a Garter was vacated by the death of Lord Strafford 1697. **3.** I have determined..to remove him to the berth Riley has vacated 1856.

Vacation (văkē¹·ʃən, *U.S.* ve¹kē¹·ʃən). late ME. [– (O)Fr. *vacation* or L. *vacatio, -ōn-*, f. as prec.; see -ION.] **I. 1.** Freedom, release, or rest *from* some occupation, business, or activity. **b.** Without const. Freedom or respite from work, etc.; time of rest or leisure. late ME. **2.** A period during which there is a formal suspension of activity; one or other part of the year during which the normal functions of law-courts, universities, or schools are suspended; holidays 1456. **b.** A holiday (chiefly *U.S.*) 1878. **3.** †**a.** A state or period characterized by the intermission or absence *of* something –1711. **b.** A state or period of inactivity 1644. **4.** A time of freedom or respite 1614.

1. What vacacion had they from the warres? 1531. **2.** In the Easter V. we went for a short walking tour in Norfolk 1904. *attrib.* At a V. Exercise in the Colledge MILT. **3. a.** Sleep's a V. of our Pow'rs 1711. **4.** Let..a V. from Labour be given him 1748.

†**II.** The fact of an office or post becoming or being vacant; the time during which the vacancy lasts –1709.

III. The action of vacating, of leaving (or being left) vacant or unoccupied 1876.

Hence **Vaca·tion** *v. intr.* (U.S.), to take a v. or holiday; to pass one's v. 1896.

Vaccary (væ·kări). Now *Hist.* 1471. [– med.L. *vaccaria*, f. L. *vacca* cow; see -ARY¹.] A place where cows are kept or pastured; a dairy-farm.

Vaccinal (væ·ksinăl, væksəi·năl), *a.* 1888. [f. VACCINE + -AL¹ 1; cf. Fr. *vaccinal*, perh. partly the source.] Of, pertaining to, or connected with vaccine or vaccination.

Vaccinate (væ·ksine¹t), *v.* 1803. [f. VACCINE *sb.* + -ATE³. Cf. Fr. *vacciner* (*a*1803).] **1.** *trans.* To inoculate with the virus of cow-pox as a protection against small-pox. **b.** *transf.* To inoculate with a virus 1904. **2.** *intr.* To perform or practise vaccination 1837.

Vaccination (væksinē¹·ʃən). 1800. [f. VACCINATE + -ION; see -ATION. Cf. Fr. *vaccination* (*a*1803).] The action or practice of inoculating with vaccine matter as a preventative of small-pox. **b.** Inoculation with a virus 1891.

attrib. as *v. act, law, scar.* Hence **Vaccina·-tionist.**

Vaccinator (væ·ksinē¹təɹ). 1808. [f. as prec. + -OR 2. Cf. Fr. *vaccinateur.*] **1.** One who performs, practises, or advocates vaccination. **2.** An instrument used in performing vaccination 1875.

Vaccine (væ·ksīn, -in), *sb.* 1846. [subst. use of next. Cf. Fr. *vaccin* (1812) vaccine matter, *vaccine* (1800) cowpox, vaccination.] Vaccine matter used in vaccination. **b.** A preparation of some virus used for the purpose of inoculation 1894.

Vaccine (væ·ksīn, -in), *a.* 1799. [– L. *vaccinus*, as used in mod.L. *variolæ vaccinæ* cowpox (E. Jenner, 1798), *virus vaccinus* virus of cowpox used in vaccination; f. *vacca* cow; see -INE¹.] **1.** *V. disease, pock* = COW-POX. **b.** Appearing in or characteristic of the disease of cow-pox 1800. **2.** *V. lymph, matter, virus*, the characteristic virus of cow-pox (obtained directly or from human subjects) which is employed in vaccination 1799. **3.** *V. inoculation* = VACCINATION 1799. **b.** Connected with vaccination 1812. **4.** Derived from, pertaining or relating to, cows 1804.

4. We have milk..butter..cheese. All this is v. matter. 1804.

‖**Vaccinia** (væksi·niă). 1803. [mod.L., f. L. *vaccinus* VACCINE *a.*; see -IA¹.] *Path.* Cow-pox.

Vaccinist (væ·ksinist). 1847. (Cf. *anti-vaccinist* 1822.) [f. VACCINE *sb.* or *a.* + -IST.] A vaccinator; a supporter or advocate of vaccination.

‖**Vaccinium** (væksi·niŏm). 1706. [L. *vaccinium* blueberry.] *Bot.* **a.** A large genus of plants, chiefly belonging to the northern hemisphere, many species of which bear edible berries. **b.** One or other species of this genus; *spec.* a bilberry.

Vacillant (væ·silănt), *a.* 1521. [– L. *vacillans, -ant-*, pr. pple. of *vacillare*; see next, -ANT. Cf. (O)Fr. *vacillant.*] **1.** Uncertain, hesitating, wavering. **2.** *Ent.* Unsteady; swaying readily 1860. Hence **Va·cillancy** (now *rare*), vacillation.

Vacillate (væ·sile¹t), *v.* 1597. [– *vacillat-*, pa. ppl. stem of L. *vacillare* sway, totter, after (O)Fr. *vaciller*; see -ATE³.] **1.** *intr.* To swing or sway unsteadily; to be in unstable equilibrium; to stagger. **b.** To hover doubtfully 1841. **2.** To alternate or waver between different opinions or courses of action 1623.

1. When a spheroid..turns upon an axis which is not permanent..it is always liable to shift and v. from one axis to another 1802. **2.** He may..tremble, but he must not v. RUSKIN.

Va·cillating, *ppl. a.* 1814. [f. prec. + -ING².] **1.** Of persons: Given to vacillation. **2.** Of conduct, etc.: Marked by vacillation 1828. **3.** Of things: **a.** Varying, changeful. **b.** Unsteady, swaying. 1822.

2. The v. expression of a mind unable to concentrate itself strongly 1863. Hence **Va·cillat-ingly** *adv.*

Vacillation (væsilē¹·ʃən). late ME. [– L. *vacillatio, -ōn-*, f. *vacillat-*; see VACILLATE, -ION. Cf. Fr. *vacillation.*] **1.** The action or quality of alternating or wavering in respect of opinion or conduct; hesitation, uncertainty; an instance of this. **2.** The action or an act of swaying or swinging unsteadily to and fro 1632.

1. Christopher Smart, with whose unhappy v. of mind he..sympathised BOSWELL. The agents.. were shocked at the vacillations of their own Cabinets 1828.

Vacillatory (væ·silătŏri), *a.* 1734. [f. VACILLATE + -ORY².] **1.** Marked by vacillation. **2.** Of persons: Tending to vacillate 1854.

†**Va·cuate,** *v.* 1572. [– *vacuat-*, pa. ppl. stem of L. *vacuare*, f. *vaccus* empty; see -ATE³.] *trans.* = EVACUATE *v.* 1, 4, 5. –1765.

†**Vacua·tion.** 1590. [– late and med.L. *vacuatio, -ōn-*, f. as prec.; see -ION.] = EVACUATION 1 a, b. –1721.

Vacuity (vækiū·iti). 1541. [– (O)Fr. *vacuité* or L. *vacuitas*, f. *vacuus* empty; see -ITY.] **I. 1.** Absolute emptiness of space; complete absence of matter 1546. **2.** Emptiness consisting in the absence of solid or liquid matter 1579. **b.** Complete emptiness in respect of things or persons 1660. **c.** The fact of being unfilled or unoccupied 1664. **3.** *fig.* The quality or fact of being empty, in various fig. senses; esp. emptiness as a condition or state having a kind of real existence 1603. **4.** Complete absence of ideas; vacancy of mind or thought 1594. **5.** Complete absence or lack *of* something, or †freedom or exemption *from* something 1601. **6.** Lack of occupation; idleness 1817.

1. There is no voidnesse or v. in nature HOLLAND. **2. b.** Sunbeams..lost themselves in the v. of the vaults SCOTT. **3.** The emptiness, v., and no worth of man FLORIO. Thou all-sufficient art, and I Am nothing but v. 1711. **4.** The mental v. of the savage 1885.

II. 1. A hollow or enclosed space empty of matter; *esp.* a small internal cavity or interstice of this kind in a solid body 1541. **b.** A cosmic space empty of matter 1643. **2.** An empty space left or contrived in something 1624. **b.** An open space, gap, or interval left between or among things (*rare*) 1658. **c.** An empty space due to the disappearance or absence of some special thing 1822. **3.** *fig.* An emptiness, an empty space, a blank 1631. **4.** An empty or inane thing 1648.

1. b. That seat soon failing, [he] meets A vast vacuitie MILT. **2. b.** The Scots and Picts.. rushed with redoubled violence into this v. BURKE. **3.** A filling of all former vacuities, a supplying of all emptinesses in our souls DONNE.

Vacuole (væ·kiu₁ōᵘl). 1853. [– Fr. *vacuole* (Dujardin), dim. f. L. *vacuus* empty.] **1.** A small cavity or vesicle in organic tissue or protoplasm, freq. containing some fluid. **2.** An empty or open space (in a comet) 1881. So **Va·cuolar** *a.* of, pertaining to or of the nature of a v. or vacuoles 1852. **Va·cuolated** *ppl. a.* rendered vacuolar; modified or altered by vacuolation. **Vacuola·tion,** the formation of vacuoles, change to a vacuolar state.

Vacuous (væ·kiu₁əs), *a.* 1655. [f. L. *vacuus* empty + -OUS.] **1.** Empty of matter; not occupied or filled with anything solid or tangible. **b.** Empty of air or gas; in which a vacuum has been produced 1669. **2.** Empty of ideas; unintelligent; expressionless 1848. **3.** Devoid of content or substance 1870. **4.** Unoccupied, idle, indolent 1872.

1. The water..is not able to fill it, hence a v. space must be formed in the cell TYNDALL. **2.** A v., solemn..Snob THACKERAY. **4.** Many rich people..lead such mean and v. lives 1897. **Va·cuous-ly** *adv.*, **-ness.**

Vacuum (væ·kiu₁ŏm). *Pl.* **vacua, vacuums.** 1550. [L. *vacuum*, mod. subst. use of n. sing. of *vacuus* empty, repr. Aristotle's *τὸ κενόν* 'the empty', defined as *τόπος ἐστερημένος σώματος* 'place bereft of body'.] **1.** Emptiness of space; space unoccupied by matter. Now *rare* or *Obs.* **2.** A space entirely empty of matter 1607. **b.** A space empty of air, esp. one from which the air has been artificially withdrawn 1652. **3.** An empty space; a portion of space (left) unoccupied or unfilled with the usual or natural contents 1589.

2. There are objections against a *plenum*, and objections against a *vacuum*; yet one of them must..be true JOHNSON. **b.** Count Rumford proved the passage of heat through a Torricellian v., that is, the space left at the top of a barometer by the mercury falling 1829. **3.** *fig.* They filled up the v. of the unrecorded past GROTE.

attrib. and *Comb.*: **v.-brake,** a form of steam-operated brake used on railways; **-cleaner,** an apparatus for removing dust, etc., by suction; **-flask,** a flask with two walls separated by a vacuum, the existence of which keeps the contents of the inner receptacle at their original temperature for a considerable period; **-gauge,** a contrivance for testing the pressure consequent on the production of a v.; **-pan,** a large closed metallic retort, so connected with an exhausting apparatus that a partial v. is formed within; used in sugar manufacture for boiling down syrup; **-pump,** a pump for producing a v.; **-tube,** a tube from which the gas has been exhausted, or in which the gas pressure is less than normal, as the bulb of an electric incandescent light or a wireless valve; **-valve,** a safety-valve opening inwards (cf. SAFETY-VALVE 1).

†**Vade,** var. of FADE *v.* –1678.

Seize the short Ioyes then, ere they v. MARVELL.

Vade-mecum (vē¹·dĭ mī·kŏm). Also **vade mecum.** 1629. [– Fr. (XVI) – mod.L. *vade-mecum,* subst. use of L. *vade mecum* go with me.] **1.** A book or manual suitable for carrying about with one for ready reference. **2.** A thing commonly carried about by a person as being of some service to him 1632.

Vagabond (væ·găbǫnd), *a.* and *sb.* late ME. [– (O)Fr. *vagabond* or L. *vagabundus,* f. *vagari* wander.] **A.** *adj.* **1.** Of persons, etc.: Roaming or wandering from place to place without settled habitation or home; nomadic. **2.** Leading an unsettled, irregular, or disreputable life; good-for-nothing, rascally, worthless 1630. **3.** Of or pertaining to, characteristic or distinctive of a homeless wanderer 1585. **4.** *fig.* Roving, straying; not subject to control or restraint 1635.

1. A v. and useless tribe there eat Their miserable meal COWPER. *fig.* To Heav'n thir prayers Flew up, nor missed the way, by envious windes Blow'n v. or frustrate MILT. **2.** A most v. crew! 1777. **3.** Voyages by Sea and Land, and a v. life 1653. **4.** My heart is a vain heart, a v. and unstable heart QUARLES.

B. *sb.* **1.** One who has no fixed abode or home, and who wanders about from place to place; *spec.* an itinerant beggar, idle loafer, or tramp; a vagrant 1485. **2.** A disreputable or worthless person; an idle good-for-nothing fellow; a rascal or rogue 1686.

1. A Bill..for the more effectual punishing Rogues and Vagabonds 1736. **2.** The dishonest, scheming vagabonds! 1890. Hence **Va·gabond** *v. intr.* to wander (*about*) as or like a v. **Va·gabondism** = next. **Va·gabondry** = next 1.

Vagabondage (væ·găbǫndėdʒ). 1813. [f. prec. + -AGE, or – Fr. *vagabondage* (1798).] **1.** The state, condition, or character of a vagabond; idle or unconventional wandering or travelling; vagabondism. **2.** Vagabonds collectively 1855.

Vagabondize (væ·găbǫndəiz), *v.* 1611. [f. as prec. + -IZE.] *intr.* To live, wander, or go about as, or in the manner of, a vagabond; to play the vagabond. Also with *it.*

Vagal (vē¹·găl), *a.* 1854. [f. VAGUS + -AL¹ 1.] *Anat.* and *Path.* **a.** *V. nerve,* the vagus or pneumogastric nerve. **b.** Of, pertaining to, or affecting this.

Vagarious (văgēᵊ·riəs), *a.* 1827. [f. next + -OUS; see -IOUS.] **1.** Marked or characterized by, full of, or subject to vagaries; erratic. **2.** Wandering, roving 1882.

Vagary (văgēᵊ·ri, vē¹·gəri). 1577. [– L. *vagari* wander.] †**1.** A wandering or devious journey or tour; an excursion, ramble, stroll –1826. †**2.** A wandering in speech or writing; a digression or divagation –1762. **3.** A departure or straying from the ordered, regular, or usual course of conduct, decorum, or propriety; a frolic or prank, esp. one of a freakish nature. Now *rare* or *Obs.* 1588. **4.** A capricious, fantastic, or eccentric action or piece of conduct 1629. **b.** A caprice or trick *of* fortune, fancy, the brain, a malady, etc. 1717. **5.** A fantastic, eccentric, or extravagant idea or notion 1753.

3. Strait they chang'd thir minds, Flew off, and into strange vagaries fell, As they would dance MILT. **4.** The Vagaries of a Child STEELE. **b.** To follow the vagaries of fashion 1871. **5.** The vagaries of Apocalyptic interpretation 1882.

Vagina (vădʒəi·nă). *Pl.* **-æ** (ī), **-as.** 1682. [– L. *vagina* sheath, scabbard.] **1.** *Anat.* and *Med.* The membranous canal leading from the vulva to the uterus in women and female mammals. **b.** A genital passage in other animals 1826. **2.** A sheath-like covering, organ, or part; a theca 1713. **b.** *Bot.* = SHEATH *sb.* 2 b. 1720.

Vaginal (vădʒəi·năl, væ·dʒinăl), *a.* and *sb.* 1726. [f. prec. + -AL¹ 1.] **A.** *adj.* **1.** *Anat.* and *Med.* Of the nature of or having the form or function of a sheath; serving as a sheath. **2.** Of, pertaining to, or affecting the vagina 1825. **b.** Of instruments: Used in dealing with or operating on the vagina 1825. **B.** *sb.* A vaginal artery or muscle 1872.

Va·ginant, *a.* 1760. [f. VAGINA (sense 2) + -ANT.] *Bot.* Constituting an investing sheath.

Va·ginate, *a. rare.* 1849. [f. VAGINA (sense 2) + -ATE².] Enclosed in a sheath or vagina; invaginate. So †**Vaginated** *ppl. a.*

Vaginitis (vædʒinəi·tis). 1846. [f. L. *vagina* + -ITIS.] *Path.* Inflammation of the vagina.

Vagino- (vădʒəi·no), used as a comb. form of L. *vagina,* as in **vagi·noscope,** an instrument for examining the vagina.

‖**Vaginula** (vădʒəi·niŭlă). *Pl.* **-æ** (-ī). 1843. [mod.L., dim. of VAGINA (sense 2); see -ULE.] *Zool.* and *Bot.* A little sheath or vagina; *esp.* in *Bot.* the capsule or theca enclosing the base of the seta in certain mosses. So **Vagi·nule.**

Vagrancy (vē¹·grănsi). 1642. [f. VAGRANT *a.*; see -ANCY.] **1.** The action or fact of wandering or digressing in mind, opinion, thought, etc.; an instance of this. **2.** The state, condition, or action of roaming abroad or wandering about from place to place 1677. **b.** *spec.* Idle wandering with no settled habitation, occupation, or obvious means of support; conduct or practices characteristic of vagrants 1706.

2. b. He ought to be taken up for v. as having no visible means of support 1876.

Vagrant (vē¹·grănt), *sb.* and *a.* 1444. [– AFr. *vagarant, -aunt(e,* perh. alt. of AFr. *wakerant, wacrant, walcrant* by assoc. with (O)Fr. *vaguer,* L. *vagari* wander; see -ANT.] **A.** *sb.* **1.** One of a class of persons who, having no settled home or regular work, wander from place to place, and maintain themselves by begging or in some disreputable or dishonest way; an itinerant beggar, idle loafer, or tramp. **2.** One who leads a wandering life; a rover 1590.

1. Vagrants who on falsehood live, Skill'd in smooth tales, and artful to deceive POPE. **2.** The Israelites, poor vagrants who had not a foot of ground of their own 1770.

B. *adj.* **1.** Wandering about without proper means of livelihood; of or belonging to the class of vagrants or itinerant beggars 1461. **2.** *fig.* Wandering, roving; unsettled, wayward 1522. **3.** Leading a wandering or nomadic life; ranging or roaming from place to place; straying, straggling 1546. **4.** Of or belonging to a vagrant or wanderer; characterized by, peculiar to, or devoted to vagrancy or wandering 1583. **5.** Of things: Not fixed or stationary; moving hither and thither; *spec.* in *Path.* of certain blood-cells 1586.

1. His house was known to all the v. train GOLDSM. **2.** The offspring of a v. and ignoble love MACAULAY. **3.** The v. soldiers were recalled to their standard GIBBON. The soft murmur of the v. Bee WORDSW. **4.** That Beauteous Emma v. Courses took; Her Father's House and civil Life forsook PRIOR. **5.** Those v. worlds, the comets 1794. Hence **Va·grantly** *adv.*

Vagrom (vē¹·grəm), *a.* 1599. [Illiterate alteration of VAGRANT *a.* In mod. use only after SHAKS.] Vagrant, vagabond, wandering.

You shall comprehend all v. men SHAKS.

Vague (vē¹g), *a.* (*adv., sb.*) 1548. [– Fr. *vague* or L. *vagus* wandering, inconstant, uncertain.] **1.** Of statements, ideas, etc.: Couched in general or indefinite terms; not precisely expressed; lacking in definiteness or precision; indefinite. **2.** Lacking physical definiteness of form or outline; indistinctly seen or perceived; obscure, shadowy 1822. **3.** Of persons, the mind, etc.: Unable to think with clearness or precision; indefinite or inexact in thought or statement 1806. **4.** Of the Egyptian month or year: Beginning at varying seasons; moveable, shifting 1656. **5.** As *adv.* Vaguely; indistinctly 1864. **6.** *absol.* as *sb.,* esp. *the v.,* the vague aspect or consideration of things 1851. **b.** The vague or undefined expanse *of* something 1870.

1. Their answers, v., And all at random COWPER. An indiscriminate use of v. terms 1813. A v. analogy 1881. Man's sense of v. wonder in the presence of powers whose force he cannot measure 1885. **2.** Countries where every feature of the scenery is v. 1879. **6.** *In the v.,* in a v. or indefinite state or condition; in general. Hence **Va·gue-ly** *adv.,* **-ness.**

Vague (vē¹g), *v.* Chiefly *Sc.* Now *rare* or *Obs.* late ME. [– L. *vagari* wander. Cf. (O)Fr. *vaguer* (XIV).] *intr.* To wander; to range, roam; to ramble idly or as a vagrant.

These robbers that v. about our country HOLLAND.

Vagus (vē¹·gŏs). *Pl.* **vagi** (vē¹·dʒəi). 1840. [– L. *vagus* wandering, straying.] *Anat.* and *Path.* The pneumogastric nerve.

Vail (vē¹l), *sb.*¹ Now *arch.* or *dial.* late ME. [f. VAIL *v.*¹ Cf. AVAIL *sb.*] †**1.** Advantage, profit –1550. **2.** Usu. *pl.* Now *arch.* or *Obs.* A casual or occasional profit or emolument in addition to salary or other regular payment, esp. one accruing or attached to an office or position; a fee or offering of this nature. 1450. **b.** A dole or gratuity given to one in an inferior position 1622. **3.** A gratuity given to a servant or attendant; a tip; *spec.* one of those given by a visitor on his departure to the servants of the house in which he has been a guest. *arch.* 1605. **4.** *pl.* = PERQUISITE 3 b. Now *rare.* 1592.

3. Why should he, like a Servant, seek Vails over and above his Wages? MILT.

†**Vail,** *sb.*² 1606. [f. VAIL *v.*²] The going down or setting *of* the sun. SHAKS.

†**Vail,** *v.*¹ ME. [– *vail-,* tonic stem of (O)Fr. *valoir* be of value – L. *valēre* be strong, powerful, of value. Cf. AVAIL *v.*] **1.** *intr.* To be of use or service; to avail or profit –1601. **2.** *trans.* To be of use, advantage, or benefit to; to aid, assist, or help –1813.

Vail (vē¹l), *v.*² *arch.* or *Obs.* ME. [Aphetic f. *avail* AVALE *v.*] **I.** *trans.* **1.** To lower (a weapon, banner, etc.); to cause or allow to descend or sink. **b.** *spec.* To lower in sign of submission or respect 1599. **c.** To lower or cast down (the eyes); to bend, bow down (the head, etc.); to hang (the tail) 1586. **2.** To doff or take off (a bonnet, hat, crown, etc.), esp. out of respect or as a sign of submission; also *fig.* with *bonnet,* to manifest submission; to yield, give way; to show respect *to* 1460. †**3.** *Naut.* To lower, to let or haul down (a sail) –1635. †**4.** *fig.* To abase, humble, or lower (one's courage, the heart, etc.); to submit, subject, or yield (one thing) *to* (another) –1827.

1. c. Voice of the wise of old! Go..teach proud Science where to v. her brow KEBLE. **2.** The bonnets, which hitherto each Chief had worn..were now at once vailed in honour of the royal warrant SCOTT. **4.** Now vaile your pride you captiue Christians 1592.

II. *intr.* †**1.** To fall (*down*); to descend –1624. **2.** Of a bonnet or banner: To be doffed or lowered in token of respect or submission 1550.

1. His jollity is down, valed to the ground 1624.

III. *absol.* †**1.** *Naut.* To lower the sail –1650. **2.** To doff or take off the cap or hat (*to* a person, etc.) 1599. **3.** *fig.* To submit, yield, give place *to* (or *unto*); to acknowledge the superiority or supremacy of 1610. †**b.** To do homage *to.* SHAKS.

3. The Ministry v. to every measure to humour the people 1779.

†**Vai·lable,** *a.* ME. [f. VAIL *v.*¹ + -ABLE. Cf. AVAILABLE.] **1.** Of avail, advantage, or benefit; beneficial; profitable, efficacious –1577. **2.** Legally valid or effective –1652.

Vain (vē¹n), *a.* and *sb.* ME. [– (O)Fr. *vain, vaine* :– L. *vanus, -a* empty, without substance.] **A.** *adj.* **1.** Devoid of real value, worth, or significance; idle, unprofitable, useless; of no effect, force, or power; fruitless, unavailing. †**2.** Empty, vacant, void. Also const. *of.* –1544. **3.** Of persons: Devoid of sense or wisdom; foolish, thoughtless; of an idle or futile disposition. Now *rare* or *Obs.* late ME. **4.** Given to indulging in personal vanity; having an excessively high opinion of one's own appearance, attainments, qualities, possessions, etc.; delighting in or desirous of attracting the admiration of others; conceited. Const. *of.* 1692.

1. For the loue of a vayn thynge men ought not to leue that whiche is certeyn CAXTON. In v. regrets for the past, in vainer resolves for the future 1853. **3.** He is veyne that puttiþ his hope in men or in creatures 1450. **4.** A good, honest, plain girl, and not v. of her face FIELDING.

In vain, to no effect or purpose; ineffectually, uselessly, vainly. *To take..in v.* (with *name* as object): To use or utter (the name of God) lightly, needlessly, or profanely; *transf.* to mention or speak of casually or lightly. [After L. *in vanum*, Fr. *en vain.*]

†**B.** as *sb.* Vanity; a vain thing –1742. Hence **Vai·n-ly** *adv.*, **-ness.**

Vainglorious (vēinglōəriəs), *a.* 1480. [After OFr. *vaneglorieus*, med.L. *vanagloriosus* (*vaniglorius*).] **1.** Filled with, given to, or indulging in, vainglory; inordinately boastful or proud of one's own abilities, actions, or qualities; excessively and ostentatiously vain. **2.** Characterized by, indicative of, or proceeding from vainglory 1533.

1. Where is the fame Which the v. mighty of the earth Seek to eternize? SHELLEY. **2.** Wandring.. in a vayne glorious oppinion of their owne wit GASCOIGNE. Hence **Vainglo·rious-ly** *adv.*, **-ness.**

Vainglory (vēinglōəri), *sb.* ME. [After (O)Fr. *vaine gloire*, L. *vana gloria.*] **1.** Glory that is vain, empty, or worthless; inordinate or unwarranted pride in one's accomplishments or qualities; disposition or tendency to exalt oneself unduly; idle boasting or vaunting. **2.** A vainglorious thing, action, etc. (*rare*) 1450.

1. For he that doth a thing secretly..how seketh he vaynglory? 1535. **2.** What needs these Feasts, pompes, and Vaine-glories? SHAKS. Hence **Vainglo·ry** *v. intr.* to indulge in v.

Vair (vēəɹ), *sb.* ME. [– (O)Fr. *vair* :– L. *varius* particoloured.] **1.** A fur obtained from a variety of squirrel with grey back and white belly, much used in the 13th and 14th centuries as a trimming or lining for garments. Now *arch.* **2.** A weasel or stoat. Now *dial.* late ME. **3.** *Her.* One of the heraldic furs, represented by bell- or cup-shaped spaces of two (or more) tinctures, usu. azure and argent, disposed alternately (in imitation of small skins arranged in a similar manner) 1562.

Vairy (vēəri), *a.* 1486. [– OFr. *vairy*, f. *vair*; see prec., -Y[5].] *Her.* Of a coat, charge, etc.: Varied or variegated with two or more colours; having divisions and tinctures like those of vair.

‖**Vaisya** (vai·syă). 1794. [Skr. *vaiśya* peasant, labourer.] The third of the four great Hindu castes, comprising the merchants and agriculturists; a member of this caste.

Vaivode (vēi·vōud). Now *Hist.* 1560. [ult. – early Magyar *vajvoda* (now *vajda*), repr. the common Slavonic *voj(e)voda* VOIVODE. The immed. source is partly mod.L. *vayvoda* or Fr. *vayvode*. See also WAYWODE.] A local ruler or official in various parts of south-eastern Europe (in older use esp. in Transylvania).

‖**Vakeel, vakil** (văkī·l). *India.* 1622. [Urdu *vakīl*, *wakīl*.] **1.** An agent or representative; *esp.* a minister, envoy, or ambassador. **2.** A native attorney or barrister; a pleader in the Hindu law-courts 1858.

Valance (væ·lăns), *sb.* 1450. [perh. – AFr. **valance*, f. *valer*, aphetic f. (O)Fr. *avaler*; see AVALE *v.* (VAIL *v.*[2]), -ANCE. But the occurrence of pl. forms such as *valandes* (XVI), *-ents* (XVII) may indicate deriv. from the pl. of the pr. pple. used subst. (cf. ACCIDENCE).] **1.** A piece of drapery attached lengthways to a canopy, altar-cloth, or the like, so as to hang in a vertical position 1463. **2.** *spec.* **a.** A border of drapery hanging round the canopy of a bed; in later use, a short curtain around the frame of a bedstead, etc. serving to screen the space underneath 1450. **b.** A short window-curtain (*rare*) 1726. **3.** A pendant border or edging of velvet, leather, or other material 1700. **b.** A flap attached to a head-dress, esp. as a protection against the sun 1791.

1. A tent, striped with white and gold..and the v., of the same colours H. WALPOLE. **2. a.** An iron bedstead (no vallance, of course), and hair mattress F. NIGHTINGALE. **3. b.** Like the cap with a v. named from the East Indian hero 'Havelock' 1875. So **Va·lance** *v.* (*rare*) *trans.* to drape or fringe with, or as with, a v.

Valanced (væ·lănst), *ppl. a.* 1548. [f. VALANCE *sb.* or *v.* + -ED.] Provided or furnished *with* a valance or draped edging of a specified material. **b.** *transf.* Also *ellipt.*, fringed with hair 1602.

An old set-stich'd chair, v. and fringed around with..worsted bobs STERNE. **b.** *Haml.* II. ii. 403.

Vale (vēil), *sb.*[1] ME. [– (O)Fr. *val* :– L. *valles*, *vallis*; cf. VALLEY.] A tract of land lying between two ranges of hills, or stretches of high ground, and usu. traversed by a river or stream; a dale or valley. In later use chiefly *poet.* Freq. const. *of* (the distinctive name of the v.). **b.** The world regarded as a place *of* trouble, sorrow, etc., or as the scene of life. late ME.

And thou Moon [stand] in the v. of Aialon, Till Israel overcome MILT. A slumber seems to steal O'er v. and mountain WORDSW. **b.** What could you find in the vail of tears? RALEGH. Phr. *The v. of years*, the declining years of a person's life, old age; I am declin'd Into the v. of yeares SHAKS.

‖**Vale** (vēi·li), *int.* and *sb.*[2] 1550. [L. *vale*, imper. of *valēre* be strong or well.] **A.** *int.* Farewell; goodbye; adieu. **B.** *sb.* A farewell greeting, letter, etc.; a goodbye, farewell, or leave-taking 1580.

I am going to say my *vales* to you for some weeks SCOTT.

Valediction (vælĭdi·kʃən). 1614. [f. L. *vale* (prec.) or *valedicere* (to say '*vale*'), after BENEDICTION (L. *benedictio*).] **1.** The action of bidding or saying farewell (*to* a person, etc.); an instance of this; a farewell or leave-taking. **2.** An utterance, discourse, etc. made on (or by way of) leave-taking or bidding farewell 1619.

2. Their last v., thrice uttered by the attendants, was..very solemn SIR T. BROWNE.

Valedictory (vælĭdi·ktŏri), *a.* and *sb.* 1651. [f. VALEDICTION + -ORY.] **A.** *adj.* **1.** Uttered or bestowed in bidding or on taking farewell; of the nature of a valediction. **2.** Manifested, performed, or done by way of valediction 1806.

1. The Bishop who delivered the v. address SOUTHEY. **2.** Lord Ripon's v. tour..in the Punjab 1884.

B. *sb.* **1.** *U.S.* A valedictory oration 1847. **2.** A statement or speech made by way of valediction on leaving a position, person, etc. 1892.

2. In his V. on retiring from the Editorship 1892. Hence **Valedicto·rian** (*U.S.*), in colleges, academies, etc., the student appointed on grounds of merit to deliver the v. oration on Commencement Day.

Valence (vēi·lĕns). 1884. [var. of VALENCY; see -ENCE.] *Chem.* = VALENCY 2.

Valencia (văle·nʃiă). Also **Valentia.** 1796. [See def.] **1.** *attrib.* Of, pertaining to, cultivated in, or obtained from Valentia, a province and town of eastern Spain. **2.** A mixed fabric for waistcoats, etc., having a wool weft with a warp of silk, silk and cotton, or linen, and usu. striped 1850. **3.** *ellipt.* in *pl.* Valencia almonds or raisins 1867. **b.** A variety of orange. So **Vale·ncian** *a.* 1753.

Valenciennes (valaṅsyeṅ, vælənsī·nz). 1717. [See def.] **1.** The name of a town in northern France, celebrated for the manufacture of lace, used *attrib.* in *V. lace.* **2.** *ellipt.* A variety of lace orig. manufactured at Valenciennes; a ruffle or the like made of this 1764.

Valency (vēi·lĕnsi). 1869. [– L. *valentia* power, competence, f. *valēre* be powerful; see -ENCY.] **1.** *Physics.* Energy, active force. **2.** *Chem.* The power or capacity of certain elements to combine with or displace a greater or less number of hydrogen (or other) atoms; atomicity 1876. **b.** A unit of this capacity. Usu. in pl. 1891.

Valentine (væ·lĕntəin). late ME. [– (O)Fr. *Valentin* – L. *Valentinus* name of two Italian saints whose festival falls on 14 February.] **1.** (*St.*) *Valentine's day*, the 14th of February. (Freq. mentioned with ref. to the choosing of sweethearts or the mating of birds.) **2.** A person of the opposite sex chosen, drawn by lot, or otherwise determined, on St. Valentine's day, as a sweetheart, lover, or special friend for the ensuing year 1450. **3.** A folded paper inscribed with the name of a person to be drawn as a valentine 1553. **b.** A written or printed letter or missive, a card with verses or other words, esp. of an amorous or sentimental nature, sent on St. Valentine's day to a person of the opposite sex; in later use also, a printed sheet consisting of a more or less grotesque picture with humorous or satirical rhymes (more exactly called a *mock v.*) 1824.

1. *ellipt.* Saint V. is past, Begin these wood birds but to couple now? SHAKS.

Valentinian (vælĕnti·niăn), *sb.* and *a.* 1449. [See def.] **A.** *sb.* A follower of the Egyptian theologian Valentinus (*c*150 A.D.), founder of a Gnostic sect. **B.** *adj.* Adhering or belonging to the Gnostic sect instituted by the heresiarch Valentinus; taught or disseminated by Valentinus or his followers 1579. Hence **Valenti·nianism.**

Valerate (væ·lĕrĕt). 1852. [f. VALERIC *a.* + -ATE[4].] *Chem.* = VALERIANATE.

Valerian (vălīə·riăn). late ME. [– (O)Fr. *valériane* – med.L. *valeriana* (sc. *herba* plant), app. fem. sing. of L. adj. *Valerianus*, f. the pers. name *Valerius*; see -IAN.] **1.** Any of the various species of herbaceous plants belonging to the genus *Valeriana*, many of which have been used medicinally as stimulants or antispasmodics. **2.** With distinctive terms, denoting varieties of true v., or plants of other genera 1548. **3.** The drug derived from the rootstocks of the wild valerian or other species 1794.

2. *Red, spur-v.* = *Centranthus ruber. Greek v.*, Jacob's ladder, *Polemonium cæruleum.*

Valerianate (vălīə·riănĕt). 1845. [f. next + -ATE[4].] *Chem.* A salt produced by the action of valeric acid on a base.

Valerianic (vălīəriæ·nik), *a.* 1838. [f. VALERIAN + -IC.] *Chem.* Derived or obtained from valerian. So **Valeric** (vălīə·rik) *a.* esp. in *valeric acid*, a fatty acid of the formula $C_5H_{10}O_2$. **Valerin** (væ·lĕrin), a glyceride produced by heating valeric acid with glycerin.

Valero- (væ·lĕro-), before a vowel **valer-**, comb. form of VALERIAN or VALERIC *a.*; e.g. *valerolactic*, in *valerolactic acid*, ethyl-lactic acid; *valero-nitrile*, cyanide of tetryl.

Valerone (væ·lĕrōun). 1839. [f. VALERIAN + -ONE.] *Chem.* A transparent, colourless, mobile liquid, a ketone of valeric acid.

Va·leryl. 1852. [f. as prec. + -YL.] *Chem.* The hypothetical radical, C_5H_9O, of valeric acid.

Valet (væ·lĕt, væ·lei), *sb.* 1567. [– (O)Fr. *valet*, also †*vaslet*, †*varlet* (see VARLET) :– Rom. **vassellittus*, dim. of **vassus* (see VASSAL).] A man-servant performing duties chiefly relating to the person of his master; a gentleman's personal attendant. Hence **Va·let** *v. trans.* to wait upon, to attend or serve, as a v. **Va·letry,** valets collectively; the office of a v.

‖**Valetaille** (valtaiy). 1858. [Fr., f. *valet* VALET *sb.*] A number or retinue of valets.

‖**Valet-de-chambre** (vale d ʃāṅbr). 1646. [Fr., lit. 'chamber-valet'.] = VALET *sb.*

No man is a hero to his valet de chambre 1764.

‖**Valet-de-place** (vale də plas). 1750. [Fr., lit. 'place-servant'.] A man who acts as a guide to strangers or tourists; a cicerone.

†‖**Valetudinaire,** *a.* and *sb.* *rare.* 1682. [Fr.; cf. next.] = next –1715.

Valetudinarian (væ:lĭtiūdinēə·riăn), *sb.* and *a.* 1703. [f. next + -IAN; see -ARIAN.] **A.** *sb.* A person in weak health, esp. one who is constantly concerned with his own ailments; an invalid.

Every one knows how hard..it is to cure a v. 1787.

B. *adj.* = next A. 1713.

The v., feeble Part of Mankind 1713. Hence **Valetudina·rianism,** the condition of a v.; *esp.* tendency to be much concerned about one's own health.

Valetudinary (vælĭtiū·dinări), *a.* and *sb.* 1581. [– L. *valetudinarius* in ill health, f. *valetudo, -din-* state of health, f. *valēre* be strong or well; see -ARY[1].] **A.** *adj.* **1.** Not in robust or vigorous health; more or less weakly, infirm, or delicate; invalid. (In later use freq. implying anxious attention to the state of one's own health.) **2.** Of conditions, etc.: Characterized by weak or feeble health 1620.

1. I carry an infirm and V. body DONNE. Though v., he lived to be nearly ninety SCOTT.

B. *sb.* = prec. A. 1785.

‖**Valgus** (væ·lgŏs). 1800. [L., bandy-legged.] *Path.* A variety of club-foot in which the foot is turned outwards (or †inwards).

Valhalla (vælhæ·lă). 1768. [– mod.L. *Valhalla* – ON. *Valhall-*, *-hǫll*, f. *valr* those slain in battle (= OE. *wæl*, OS., OHG. *wal*) + *hǫll* HALL. See VALKYRIE.] In Scandinavian mythology, the hall assigned to those who have died in battle, in which they feast with Odin. **b.** *transf.* and *fig.* A place or sphere assigned to persons, etc., worthy of special honour 1845.

V., the·hall of Odin, or paradise of the Brave GRAY. **b.** That St. Paul's might fitly become a V. for English worthies 1868.

‖**Vali** (vālī·). 1753. [– Turk. *vali* – Arab. *wālī* WALI; cf. VILAYET.] A civil governor of a Turkish province or vilayet.

Valiance (væ·liăns). 1456. [– AFr. *valiance*, (O)Fr. *vaillance*, f. *valiant*, *vaillant*; see next, -ANCE.] **1.** Bravery, valour. **2.** A valiant act or deed; a feat of valour or bravery. Now *arch.* 1470.

1. In spite of our v., The victory lay with Malbrook THACKERAY. So **Va·liancy.**

Valiant (væ·liănt), *a.* (and *sb.*) ME. [– AFr. *valiaunt*, OFr. *vailant*, (also mod.) *vaillant* :– Rom. **valient-*, for *valens*, *valent-*, pr. pple. of L. *valēre* be strong; see VAIL *v.*[1], -ANT.] **A.** *adj.* **†1.** Of persons: Stalwart *of* body, bone, hands –1548. **2.** Having or possessing courage; *esp.* acting with boldness or bravery on the field of battle; brave, stout-hearted ME. **b.** *absol.* with *the* 1560. **3.** Characterized by, performed with, or exhibiting valour or courage; of a valorous character or nature ME. **4.** As *sb.* One who is valiant; a brave or courageous person 1609.

1. Sir Moreau of Fyennes..was a right valyant man of his handes 1523. **2.** In all these castles.. William placed trusty and v. captains FREEMAN. **b.** O harmless Death! whom still the v. brave DAVENANT. **3.** The v. deeds of the great reign of Elizabeth 1907. Hence **Va·liant-ly** *adv.*, **-ness.**

Valid (væ·lid), *a.* 1571. [– Fr. *valide* or L. *validus* strong, f. *valēre* be strong; see -ID[1].] **1.** Good or adequate in law; legally binding or efficacious. **b.** *Eccl.* Technically perfect or efficacious 1674. **2.** Of arguments, assertions, etc.: Well founded and applicable; sound and to the point; against which no objection can fairly be brought 1648. **b.** *gen.* Effective, effectual; sound 1651. **3.** Of things: Strong, powerful. Now *arch.* 1656. **4.** Of persons: Sound or robust in body; possessed of health and strength. Also said of health. 1652.

1. The nature of Justice, consisteth in keeping of v. Covenants HOBBES. Those, who held rent-free lands by titles that might be declared v. 1844. **2.** For when One's Proofs are aptly chosen; Four are as v. as four Dozen PRIOR. **b.** The only v. method of investigating the relation between thought and speech 1860. **4.** The Boers have evidently put every v. male into the field 1899. Hence **Va·lid-ly** *adv.*, **-ness.**

Validate (væ·lideɪt), *v.* 1648. [– *validat-*, pa. ppl. stem of med.L. *validare* render (legally) valid (earlier 'strengthen'), f. L. *validus*; see VALID, -ATE[3]. Cf. Fr. *valider* (XVI).] **1.** *trans.* To render or declare legally valid; to confirm the validity of (an act, contract, deed, etc.); to legalize. **b.** *spec.* [Now after Fr. *valider.*] To declare (an election) valid; to declare (a person) duly and properly elected 1658. **2.** To make valid or of good authority; to confirm, corroborate, substantiate, support 1775.

1. **b.** The Chamber has validated the election for Passy of M. Cailla 1883. **2.** You must v. my report, for I learnt it of you 1803. Hence **Valida·tion,** the action of validating.

Validity (văli·dĭti). 1550. [– Fr. *validité* or late L. *validitas*, f. *validus* VALID; see -ITY.] **1.** The quality of being valid in law; legal authority, force, or strength. **2.** The quality of being well-founded and applicable to the case or circumstances; soundness and strength (of argument, proof, authority, etc.) 1581. **†3.** The quality or state of being (physically) strong or sound –1750. **4.** Value or worth; efficacy 1593.

1. Much as they hated him, they could not question the v. of his commission MACAULAY. **2.** A mere coniecture, and of no valydytye 1599. I do not..understand the v. of this objection 1804. **4.** The v. of regular troops 1788.

Valise (vălī·s, vălī·z). 1633. [– Fr. *valise* – It. *valigia*; in med.L. *valesia*, *-ium*, *-isia*; of unkn. origin.] A travelling case or portmanteau, now usu. made of leather and of a size suitable for carrying by hand, formerly also for strapping to the saddle of a horse. Now chiefly *U.S.* **b.** *Mil.* A cylindrical cloth or leather case for carrying the kit or outfit of a soldier, esp. of a cavalryman or artilleryman 1833.

Valkyrie (væ·lkiri, vælki·ri, -kīə·ri, -kəiə·ri). 1768. [– ON. *Valkyrja* 'chooser of the slain', f. *valr* those slain in battle (see VALHALLA) + **kur-* :– **kuz-*, reduced grade of **keuz-* CHOOSE.] In Scandinavian mythology, any of the twelve war-maidens who hovered over battlefields and conducted the fallen warriors (of their choice) to Valhalla. Hence **Valky·rian** *a.* of or concerning the valkyries.

Vallar (væ·lăɹ), *a.* 1542. [– L. *vallaris*, f. *vallum* or *vallus* rampart.] *Rom. Antiq.* Of a crown or garland: Bestowed as a distinction on the first soldier to mount the enemy's rampart. So **Va·llary** *a.*

‖**Vallecula** (væle·kiŭlă). *Pl.* **-æ** (*-i*). 1856. [Late L., var. of L. *vallicula*, dim. of *valles*, *vallis* VALLEY *sb.*] **1.** *Anat.* A furrow, fissure, or fossa; *spec.* = next 4. 1859. **2.** *Bot.* A groove or channel; a sulcus or stria 1856. Hence **Valle·cular** *a.*

Valley (væ·li). ME. [– AFr. *valey*, OFr. *valée* (mod. *vallée*) :– Rom. **vallata*, f. L. *vallis*, *valles*; see VALE *sb.*[1], -Y[5].] **1.** A long depression or hollow lying between hills or stretches of high ground and usu. having a river or stream flowing along its bottom. (Usu. dist. from a *vale* as having less width and a steeper slope on either side.) Freq. in *fig.* uses. **b.** The extensive stretch of flattish country drained or watered by one or other of the larger river-systems of the world 1790. **2.** *transf.* A depression or hollow suggestive of a valley; *esp.* a trough between sea-waves 1611. **3.** *techn.* The depressed angle formed by the meeting (at the bottom) of two sloping sides of a composite roof, or by the slope of a roof and a wall; a gutter 1690. **4.** *Anat.* A depression between the hemispheres of the cerebellum 1842.

1. Euery v. shalbe fylled, and euery mountayne & hyll shalbe brought lowe COVERDALE *Luke* 3:5. The pleasant Vally of Hinnom MILT. *Valleys of elevation*, those which seem to have originated in a fracture of the strata, and a movement of the fractured part upwards 1839. fig. *V. of the shadow* (*of death*): see SHADOW *sb.* I. 1. *V. of tears*: the world regarded as a place of trouble, sorrow, misery, or weeping.

‖**Vallum** (væ·lŏm). 1610. [L., collect. f. *vallus* stake, palisade.] **1.** A wall or rampart of earth, sods, or stone, erected as a permanent means of defence; *esp.* one of those constructed by the Romans in northern England and central Scotland. **2.** In Roman castrametation, a palisaded bank or mound, formed of the earth cast up from the ditch or fosse around a camp or station 1806.

Valonia (vălōᵘ·niă). 1722. [– It. *vallonia* – mod. Gr. βαλάνια, βελάνια, pl. of βαλάνι, βελάνι (Gr. βάλανος) acorn.] **1.** The large acorn-cups and acorns of *Quercus ægilops* (and the related *Q. vallonea*), a species of oak of the north-eastern Mediterranean region, valued for the abundant tannin they contain. **2.** *V. Oak*, the Levantine species *Q. ægilops*. Also *ellipt.*

Valor (væ·lǫɹ). 1467. [var. of VALOUR; see -OR 1.] **†1.** = VALUE *sb.* I. 2. –1676. **2.** Power, import, significance 1676. **3.** Courage, bravery. Now chiefly *U.S.* 1586.

1. An horse..to such a v. 1577. **2.** If I may make an English word to express the v. of the Greek word 1808. **3.** The v. of the French 1586.

Valorization (væ:lǫrəizēɪ·ʃən). 1907. [– Fr. *valorisation*; cf. REVALORIZATION.] Fixing the price or value of a commodity, etc., esp. by a centrally organized scheme. So **Va·lorize** *v. trans.*

Valorous (væ·lərəs), *a.* 1477. [– OFr. *valerous* (mod. *valeureux*) or med.L. *valorosus* valiant, valuable, f. L. *valor*; see next, -OUS.] **1.** Of persons: Endowed with valour; valiant, courageous; brave, bold. **2.** Of actions, etc.: Characterized by valour courage, or bravery 1490. Hence **Va·lorous-ly** *adv.*

Valour (væ'ləɹ). Also (now *U.S.*) **valor.** ME. [– OFr. *valour* (mod. *valeur* value) :– late L. *valor*, *valōr-*, f. *valēre* be strong, etc.; see -OUR, -OR.] **1. †a.** Worth or importance due to personal qualities or to rank –1586. **b.** The quality of mind which enables a person to face danger with boldness or firmness; courage or bravery, esp. as shown in warfare or conflict; valiancy, prowess 1581. **c.** Used as a personal name or as a quasi-title; also, a person of courage 1606. **†2.** = VALUE *sb.* II. 2. –1642.

1. **a.** A damisel of gret v. 1330. **b.** Our fortunate and oft prooued v. in warres abroad JAS. I. **2.** A launce he tok of gret v. 1330.

Valsalvan (vælsæ·lvăn), *a.* 1878. [f. the name of the Italian anatomist A. M. *Valsalva* (1666–1723); see -AN.] *Med.* Associated with Valsalva's researches on the organs of hearing; introduced or used by Valsalva.

Valse (vǫls), *sb.* 1796. [– Fr. *valse* – G. *walzer* WALTZ.] A round dance in triple time, a waltz; the music for this. So **Valse** *v. intr.* to waltz.

Valuable (væ·liu,ăb'l), *a.* and *sb.* 1589. [f. VALUE *v.* + -ABLE.] **A.** *adj.* **1.** Of material or monetary value; having value for use or for exchange. **2.** Having value or worth, of great use or service, *to* a person or *for* a purpose 1647. **b.** Possessed of qualities which confer value or bring into high estimation 1638. **†c.** Of persons: Estimable –1730. **†3.** That can be valued (*rare*) –1690.

1. Jewels, or other v. effects 1776. Phr. *V. consideration*: see CONSIDERATION 6; Natural affection was formerly called *good consideration*, as contrasted with *v. consideration*, or that which is deemed to have value in a pecuniary sense O.E.D. **2.** Quinine is v. for curing fevers 1878. **b.** Yᵉ ancient Classicks, and other v. authors H. WALPOLE. **c.** Mr. Pepys, who was a very v. person..is dead 1703.

B. *sb.* An article of worth or value. Usu. in pl., valuable goods or possessions 1775.

I..sent all my valuables to the hammer LYTTON.

Valuation (væliu,ēɪ·ʃən). 1529. [f. VALUE *v.* + -ATION. Cf. OFr. *valuacion*, *-tion.*] **1.** The action of valuing; the process of assessing the value of a thing. **b.** Estimated value 1631. **†2.** Value or worth; *spec.* Current value (of money) –1776. **3.** Appreciation or estimation of anything in respect of excellence or merit 1548.

1. A new v. of all private property had been made THIRLWALL. **b.** Mr. Hardwicke..had also taken the furniture at a v. 1888. **3.** The outside public appear disposed to take Mr. Chaplin at his own v. 1884.

Valuator (væ·liu,ēɪtəɹ). 1731. [f. VALUATION + -OR 2; see -ATOR.] One who estimates the value of things; *esp.* one appointed or licensed to do so; an appraiser.

Value (væ·liu), *sb.* ME. [– OFr. *value*, fem. pa. ppl. formation from *valoir* be worth :– L. *valēre* be strong, be worth.] **I. 1.** That amount of some commodity, medium of exchange, etc., which is considered to be an equivalent for something else; a fair or adequate equivalent or return. **2.** The material or monetary worth of a thing; the amount at which it may be estimated in terms of some medium of exchange or other standard of a like nature ME. **3.** The equivalent (in material worth) *of* a specified sum or amount. late ME. **b.** The extent or amount *of* a specified standard or measure of length, quantity, etc. Now *dial.* 1600. **4.** *Ethics.* That which is worthy of esteem for its own sake; that which has intrinsic worth.

1. We hardly could be said to have had v. for our money 1806. **2.** The v. of the stock I hold has doubled 1885. Phr. *Of v.*, valuable. *Of..v.*, possessed of (a specified) material or monetary worth; Gold and Siluer is of no v. amongst them 1634. *Under v.*, below the proper v. **3.** Bronze coinage..to the v. of £57,563. 1887.

II. †1. Worth or worthiness (of persons) in respect of rank or personal qualities –1639. **†b.** Valour –1614. **2.** The relative status of a thing, or the estimate in which it is held, according to its real or supposed worth, usefulness, or importance. late ME. **†b.** Estimate *of* or liking *for* a person or thing –1794. **3. a.** *Math.* The number or quantity represented by a figure or symbol 1542. **b.**

Mus. The relative length or duration of a tone signified by a note 1662. **c.** Of cards, chessmen, or the like: Relative rank or importance according to the conventions of the game; the amount at which each (or each set) is reckoned in counting the score 1670. **d.** *Painting.* Due or proper effect or importance; relative tone of colour in each distinct section of a picture; a patch characterized by a particular tone 1778.

1. b. Alceste by his v. brought My father..to such distress 1591. **2.** [Let men] rate themselves at the highest V. they can; yet their true V. is no more than it is esteemed by others HOBBES. **b.** I must esteem one for whom..Mr. Allworthy hath so much v. FIELDING. Phr. *To set a..v. on* or *upon*, to estimate at a specified rate; Wolsey set much v. upon the study of Greek 1868. **3. d.** A certain quantity of cold colours is necessary to give a value and lustre to the warm colours SIR J. REYNOLDS.

Value (væ·liu), *v.* 1482. [f. the sb.] **I. 1.** *trans.* To estimate or appraise as being worth a specified sum or amount. **2.** To estimate the value of (goods, property, etc.); to appraise in respect of value 1509. **3.** To estimate or regard as having a certain value or worth 1589.

1. I valued it at Ten Pounds 1686. **3.** The Queene is valued thirtie thousand strong SHAKS. He.. does not v. his life at a boot-lace 1892.

II. 1. To consider of worth or importance; to rate high; to esteem; to set store by 1549. †**2.** With neg.: To take account of; to heed or be concerned about; to care –1765. **3.** *refl.* **a.** To pride or plume (oneself) *on* or *upon* a thing 1667. **b.** To think highly of (oneself) *for* something 1687.

1. He valued money, as a man values it who has been poor 1880. **2.** People infected..valued not who they injur'd DE FOE. **3. b.** Every one is in danger of valuing himself for what he does J. H. NEWMAN.

†**III.** To equal in value; *esp.* to have the value of (so much money); to be worth (nothing, more, etc.) –1799.

Valued (væ·liŭd), *ppl. a.* 1605. [f. prec. + -ED[1].] †**1.** In which value is indicated. SHAKS. **2.** Estimated, appraised 1607. **3.** Highly esteemed 1665.

1. The v. file Distinguishes the swift, the slow, the subtle SHAKS. **3.** The Epicureans..were the only valued Sects of Philosophers 1665.

Valueless (væ·liulės), *a.* 1595. [f. VALUE *sb.* + -LESS.] Having no value. Hence **Va·luelessness.**

Valuer (væ·liu,əɹ). 1611. [f. VALUE *v.* + -ER[1].] **a.** One who estimates values; a valuator. **b.** One who values something; an appreciator.

†**Valure.** late ME. [alt. f. OFr. *valur* VALOUR, after forms in -URE.] = VALOUR, VALUE *sbs.* –1641.

‖**Valuta** (vălū·tă). 1924. [It. 'value'.] A standard money.

Valvate (væ·lvėt), *a.* 1829. [– L. *valvatus* having folding doors, f. *valva* VALVE, or f. VALVE *sb.* I. 3 + ATE[2].] **1.** Of sepals or petals: Applied to each other by the margins only 1830. **b.** Of a calyx: Composed of sepals so united 1858. **2.** Of æstivation or vernation: Characterized by this arrangement of parts 1829.

Valve (vælv), *sb.* late ME. [– L. *valva* leaf of a door (usu. pl. *valvæ* a folding door).] **I. 1.** One or other of the halves or leaves of a double or folding door. **b.** A door controlling the flow of water in a sluice 1790. **2.** *Conch.* One of the halves of a hinged shell; a single shell of similar form; a single part of a compound shell 1661. **3.** *Bot.* **a.** One of the halves or sections of a dehiscent pod, pericarp, or capsule 1760. **b.** A lid-like portion of some anthers 1812.

1. Throwing open the valves, we entered the chapel BECKFORD.

II. 1. *Anat.* A membranous fold in an organ or passage of the body (esp. in the heart, arteries, and veins), which automatically closes after the manner of a trap-door to prevent the reflux of blood or other fluid 1615. †**2.** A supposed check (similar to above) to the reflux of sap in plants –1807. **3.** *Mech.* A device of the nature of a flap, lid, plug, etc., applied to a pipe or aperture to control the passage of air, steam, water, or the like, acting automatically by yielding to pressure in one direction only 1659. **b.** *Electr.* An arrangement of filaments, etc., in a vacuum bulb, designed to regulate or modify a current; a vacuum tube. Also, *thermionic, wireless v.* 1905.

Comb.: **v.-shell,** a gasteropod of the genus *Valvata*; **v. set,** a wireless receiving apparatus with thermionic valves. Hence **Va·lval** *a.* (*Bot.*) in *valval view*, that aspect of a diatom in which one of the valves is turned to the observer; a side-view. **Va·lvar** *a.* (*rare*) of the nature of or pertaining to a v. **Valve** *v.* (*rare*) *trans.* to furnish with a v. or valves; to govern, check, or hold *back* by a v. or similar device; *intr.* to make use of a v. or valves, *spec.* in ballooning, to open a v. in order to descend. **Valved** (vælvd) *a.* provided with a v. or valves. **Va·lveless** *a.*

‖**Valvula** (væ·lviŭlă). *Pl.* **-æ** (-ī). 1615. [mod.L. dim. of L. *valva*; see -ULE.] *Anat.* A valve or valvule.

Valvular (væ·lviŭlăɹ), *a.* 1797. [f. prec. + -AR[1].] **1.** Having the form or function of a valve; composed or consisting of valves. Chiefly *Anat.* and *Bot.* **2.** Furnished with a valve or valves 1808. **3.** Of or pertaining to a valve or valves 1866.

1. The calyx is v. LINDLEY. **3.** V. disease of the heart 1881.

Valvule (væ·lviŭl). 1755. [Anglicized f. VALVULA or – Fr. *valvule.*] A small valve. **b.** *Bot.* = PALEA.

‖**Valvulitis** (vælviuləi·tis). 1891. [f. VALVULA + -ITIS.] *Path.* Inflammation of the valves of the heart.

Valylene (væ·lilīn). 1868. [f. VALERIAN *sb.* + -YL + -ENE.] *Chem.* A hydrocarbon, C_5H_6, found among the products of the action of alcoholic potash on valerylene.

Vambrace (væ·mbrēⁱs). Now *Hist.* [ME. *vaun(t)bras* – AFr. *vauntbras*, aphetic f. OFr. *avantbras*, f. *avant* before + *bras* arm. See VANTBRACE.] Defensive armour for the (fore-)arm. Hence **Va·mbraced** *a.* (*Her.*) of an arm: defended or covered by a v.

Vamose (vămōᵘ·s), **vamoose** (vămū·s), *v.* orig. *U.S. colloq.* 1848. [– Sp. *vamos* let us go.] **1.** *intr.* To depart, make off, decamp, disappear. **2.** *trans.* To decamp or disappear from; to quit hurriedly 1852.

2. On the old Californian principle of 'making a "pile" and vamosing the ranche' 1852.

Vamp (væmp), *sb.*[1] ME. [– AFr. **vaumpé*, aphetic f. OFr. *avantpié* (mod. *avantpied*), f. *avant* before + *pie(d* foot.] **1.** That part of hose or stockings which covers the foot and ankle; also, a short stocking, a sock. Now *dial.* **2.** The part of a boot or shoe covering the front of the foot; *U.S.*, that part between the sole and the top in front of the ankle-seams 1654.

Vamp (væmp), *sb.*[2] 1884. [f. VAMP *v.*[1]] Anything vamped, patched up, or refurbished; a patchwork; a book of this nature.

Vamp (væmp), *sb.*[3] 1918. *colloq.* [abbrev. of VAMPIRE *sb.*] A woman who sets out to charm or captivate men (freq. from disreputable or dishonest motives) by an unscrupulous use of sexual attractiveness. Hence **Vamp** *v.*[2] *trans.* **Va·mpish** *a.* **Va·mpishness.**

Vamp (væmp), *v.*[1] 1599. [f. VAMP *sb.*[1]] **I. 1.** *trans.* To provide or furnish with a (new) vamp; to mend or repair with or as with patches; to furbish up, renovate, or restore. Also with *up.* **2.** *transf.* To make or produce by or as by patching; to serve up (something old) as new by addition or alteration. Also with *up.* 1644. **3.** *Mus.* To improvise or extemporize (an accompaniment, tune, etc.) Also *intr.* 1789.

1. *fig.* The expedient of vamping up an old Sermon 1825. **2.** The veriest drudge that vamps books together for his daily bread 1880.

II. *intr.* To make one's way on foot; to tramp or trudge. Now *dial.* 1654. Hence **Va·mper,** one who vamps.

Vampire (væ·mpəiᵊɹ). 1734. [– Fr. *vampire* or G. *vampir* – Magyar *vampir* – identical form in Slav. langs.; the ult. origin may be Turk. *uber* witch.] **1.** A preternatural being of a malignant nature (in the orig. and usual form of the belief, a reanimated corpse), supposed to seek nourishment, or do harm, by sucking the blood of sleeping persons; a man or woman endowed with similar habits. **2.** *transf.* A person of a malignant and loathsome character, esp. one who preys ruthlessly on others; a vile and cruel exactor or extortioner 1741. **3.** *Zool.* One or other of various bats, chiefly S. Amer., known or popularly believed to be blood-suckers 1774. **4.** A double-leaved trap-door, closing by means of springs, used in theatres to effect a sudden disappearance from the stage 1881.

1. Walter Mapes..gives some curious stories of English vampires in the twelfth century 1846.

attrib. and *Comb.*: **v.-bat,** = sense 3; **v. trap,** = sense 4. Hence **Vampirism** (væ·mpəiriz'm), the collective facts or ideas connected with the supposed existence and habits of vampires.

Vamplate (væ·mplēⁱt). Now *Hist.* ME. [– AFr. *vauntplate*, f. *vaunt-* VANT- + *plate* PLATE *sb.*] A plate fixed on a spear or lance to serve as a guard for the hand, esp. in tilting.

Van (væn), *sb.*[1] 1450. [Southern and western var. of FAN *sb.* prob. reinforced by (O)Fr. *van* or L. *vannus*. For initial *v* repl. *f* cf. VANE, VAT, VENEER, VIXEN.] **1.** A winnowing basket or shovel. **b.** A shovel used for lifting charcoal or testing ore 1664. **c.** A process of testing ore on a shovel; the amount of metal obtained by this test 1778. **2.** = FAN *sb.*[1] 4. Chiefly *poet.* 1667. **3.** A sail of a windmill 1837.

2. Strait a fiery Globe Of Angels on full sail of wing flew nigh, Who on their plumy Vans receiv'd him soft MILT. **3.** With his arms flying.. like the vans of a windmill 1860.

Van (væn), *sb.*[2] 1610. [Shortening of VANGUARD.] **1.** The foremost division or detachment of a military or naval force when advancing or set in order for doing so 1633. **2.** The foremost portion of, or the foremost position in, a company or train of persons moving or prepared to move forwards or onwards 1610.

1. Standards, and Gonfalons twixt V. and Reare Streame in the Aire MILT. **2.** *fig.* Moses led the v. of these testimonies 1772. Our position in the v. of industrial nations 1879.

Van (væn), *sb.*[3] 1829. [Shortened f. CARAVAN.] **1.** A covered vehicle chiefly employed for the conveyance of goods, usu. resembling a large wooden box with arched roof and opening from behind, but varying in size and form. **2.** A closed carriage or truck used on railways for conveying passengers' luggage and the guard of the train, or in goods trains for smaller articles 1868. Hence **Van** *v.*[2] *trans.* to send in a v.

Van, *sb.*[4] Abbrev. of VANTAGE *sb.* 5.

Van (væn), *v.*[1] ME. [var. of FAN *v.*[1]; see VAN *sb.*[1]] †**1.** *trans.* To winnow with a fan –1706. **2.** To separate and test (ore) by washing on a van or shovel 1839.

Vanadate (væ·nădēt). 1835. [f. VANADIUM + -ATE[4].] *Chem.* A salt produced by the combination of vanadic acid with a base. So **Vanadiate** (vănēⁱ·diėt).

Vanadic (vănæ·dik, vănēⁱ·dik), *a.* 1835. [f. VANADIUM + -IC.] *Chem.* Of, pertaining to, or derived from vanadium; *spec.* containing vanadium in its higher valency, as opp. to VANADIOUS *a.* Chiefly in *v. acid.*

Vanadinite (vănæ·dinəit). 1855. [f. VANADIUM + -IN[1] + -ITE[1] 2 b.] *Min.* A mineral consisting of vanadate of lead and chloride of lead, occurring in brilliant crystals of various colours.

Vanadious (vănēⁱ·diəs), *a.* 1868. [f. VANADIUM + -OUS.] *Chem.* Containing vanadium in its lower valency, as opp. to VANADIC *a.*; esp. in *v. acid.* So **Va·nadite,** a salt of v. acid.

Vanadium (vănēⁱ·diŏm). 1835. [– mod.L. *vanadium* (Sefström, 1830), f. ON. *Vanadís* name of the Scand. goddess Freyja; see -IUM.] *Chem.* A rare chemical element (symbol V), occurring in certain iron, lead, and uranium ores, some of the compounds of which are used in the production of aniline blacks and other dyeing materials.

Vanbrace, -bras, vars. VAM-, VANTBRACE.

Van-courier (væ·nkūᵊ:riəɹ). 1581. [Variant of *vant-*, VAUNT-COURIER.] A vaunt-courier or forerunner.

Vanda (væ·ndă). 1801. [mod.L. – Skr. and Hindi *vandā.*] *Bot.* A genus of epiphytal orchids of tropical Asia, having large showy flowers; a plant of this genus.

Vandal (væ·ndăl), *sb.* and *a.* 1555. [– L. *Vandalus*, pl. *Vandali* (Pliny), *-alii*, *-ilii* (Tacitus), *-uli* – Gmc. **Wandal-*, *-il-*, *-ul-* (repr. by OE. *Wendlas* pl., OHG. *Wentil-* in pers. names, G. *Wandale*, ON. *Vendill*).] **A.** *sb.* **1.** A member of a Germanic tribe, which in the 4th and 5th centuries invaded Western Europe, and established settlements, esp. in Gaul and Spain, finally in 428–9 migrating to Northern Africa. Chiefly in pl. **2.** *transf.* One who acts like a Vandal or barbarian; a wilful or ignorant destroyer of anything beautiful, venerable, or worthy of preservation 1663.

1. Till Goths, and Vandals, a rude Northern race, Did all the matchless Monuments deface DRYDEN. **2.** The Vandals of our isle..Have burnt to dust a nobler pile Than ever Roman saw! COWPER.

B. *adj.* **1.** Of or pertaining to the Vandals (or a Vandal) 1613. **2.** Acting like a Vandal; recklessly or ruthlessly destructive; barbarous, rude, uncultured 1700. **3.** Characterized by vandalism or lack of culture 1752. So **Vanda·lic** *a.* characteristic of the Vandals; barbarously or ignorantly destructive; of, pertaining to, or consisting of the Vandals. **Vandali·stic** *a.* characterized by or given to vandalism. **Va·ndalize** *v. trans.* to render V. in respect of culture; to treat in a vandalistic manner.

Vandalism (væ·ndăliz'm). 1787. [– Fr. *vandalisme* (Henri Grégoire, *c*1793); see prec., -ISM.] The conduct or spirit characteristic of the Vandals in respect of culture; ruthless destruction or spoiling of anything beautiful or venerable; in weakened sense, barbarous, ignorant, or inartistic treatment.

Vandyke (vændəi·k, væ·ndəik), *sb.* 1751. [f. name of Sir Anthony *Vandyke* (anglicized spelling of *Van Dyck*), Flemish painter (1599–1641).] **1.** A painting or portrait by Vandyke. **2.** A broad lace or linen collar or neckerchief with a deeply cut edge, imitating a type of collar freq. depicted in portraits by Vandyke and fashionable in the 18th c. 1755. **3.** usu. *pl.* One of a number of deep-cut points on the border or fringe of an article of apparel 1827. **4.** *transf.* A notched, deeply indented, or zigzag border, edging, or formation 1846. **5.** *attrib.* or as *adj.* designating things associated in some way with Vandyke or his paintings, as *V. beard*, a small pointed beard, *V. brown*, *collar* 1757.

1. The whole-length Vandykes went for a song! H. WALPOLE. **5.** *V. Brown*,..a species of peat or bog-earth, of a fine deep semi-transparent brown colour 1850.

Vandyke (vændəi·k, væ·ndəik), *v.* 1800. [f. as prec.] **1.** *trans.* To furnish or provide (a dress material) with vandykes or deep-cut points, after the manner represented in Vandyke's paintings; to cut or shape with deep angular indentations. Chiefly in pa. pple. **b.** Said of the thing forming the indentations 1854. **†2.** *intr.* To go or proceed in an irregular zigzag manner; to take a zigzag course –1845.

1. b. Tongues of sea-sand..vandyking its borders 1854.

Vane (vēⁱn). late ME. [Southern and western var. of FANE *sb.*¹ Cf. VAN *sb.*¹] **1.** A plate of metal, usu. of an ornamental form, fixed at an elevation upon a vertical spindle, so as to turn readily with the wind and show the direction from which it is blowing; a weather-cock. **b.** *fig.* An unstable or constantly changing person or thing 1588. **c.** *Naut.* A piece of bunting fixed to a wooden frame, which turns on a spindle at the masthead to show the direction of the wind 1706. **2. a.** A sail of a windmill 1581. **b.** A blade, wing, or similar projection attached to an axis, wheel, etc., so as to be acted upon by a current of air or liquid or to produce a current by rotation 1815. **c.** A revolving fan or wheel 1810. **3.** A sight of a levelling-staff, forestaff, quadrant, or other surveying instrument 1594. **4.** The web of a feather 1713.

1. b. What plume of feathers is hee that indited this Letter? What veine? What Wether-cocke? SHAKS.

‖**Vanessa** (văne·să). 1863. [mod.L. (Fabricius).] *Ent.* A genus of butterflies (including the *red admiral* and *peacock*); a butterfly of this genus.

Va·n-foss(e. 1728. [– Fr. *avant-fossé*, after *vanguard*, etc., and FOSSE.] *Mil.* A ditch usu. full of water at the outer foot of the glacis.

Vang (væŋ). 1769. [Later var. of FANG *sb.* III. 1 a.] *Naut.* One or other of the two ropes used for steadying the gaff of a fore-and-aft sail.

Vanguard (væ·ngāɹd). 1487. [Earlier *vandgard*, var. of †*vantgard*, aphetic f. †*avantgard* (XV) – (O)Fr. *avant-garde*, †*avangarde*, f. *avant* before + *garde* GUARD.] **1.** *Mil.* The foremost division of an army; the forefront or van. **2.** *ellipt.* The name of a variety of peach 1786.

Vanilla (văni·lă). 1662. [– Sp. *vainilla*, dim. of *vaina* sheath – L. *vagina* VAGINA. In early use in various (esp. perverted) forms, finally assim. to Fr. *vanille*.] **1.** A pod produced by one or other species of the genus *Vanilla* (see sense 2), esp. *V. planifolia*. Chiefly in pl. **2.** The climbing orchid *V. planifolia*, or other species related to this; the tropical (Amer.) genus to which these belong 1698. **b.** With pl. One or other species of this genus 1827. **3.** The aromatic substance composed of or obtained from the slender pod-like capsule of *V. planifolia* or related species, much used as a flavouring or perfume 1728. **b.** A kind or variety of this 1753.

attrib. and *Comb.*, as *v. bean*, *essence*, *ice*; **v. grass**, Seneca grass, *Hierochloa borealis*; **v. plant** (*a*) = sense 2; (*b*) an Amer. species of *Liatris*.

Vanille (văni·l). 1845. [– Fr. *vanille* – Sp. *vainilla*; see prec.] **1.** = prec. 3. **2.** *V. ice*, ice cream flavoured with vanilla essence 1846.

Vanillic (văni·lik), *a.* 1868. [f. VANILLA + -IC 1 b.] *Chem.* In *v. acid*, vanillin, or an oxidized form of this.

Vanillin (văni·lin). 1868. [f. as prec. + -IN¹.] *Chem.* The neutral odoriferous principle of vanilla, $C_8H_8O_3$.

Vanish (væ·niʃ), *v.* ME. [Aphetic – *e(s)vaniss-*, lengthened stem (see -ISH²) of OFr. *e(s)vanir* EVANISH.] **1.** *intr.* To disappear from sight or become invisible, esp. in a rapid and mysterious manner. **2.** To disappear by decaying, coming to an end, or ceasing to exist ME. **b.** *Math.* Of numbers or quantities: To become zero 1715. **3.** *trans.* To cause to disappear; to remove from sight 1440.

1. Therwith merlyn vanysshed awey sodenly MALORY. **2.** The heauens shal v. awaye like smoke COVERDALE *Isa.* 51:6. The cold began to v. and the north-east wind change 1695. If the cock be heard to crow The charm will v. into air HOGG. **3.** Then he vanishes a birdcage and its occupant 1886. Hence **Va·nish** *sb.* †disappearance, *spec.* a gradual cessation of sound; a glide. **Va·nisher. Va·nishment.**

Vanishing (væ·niʃiŋ), *vbl. sb.* late ME. [f. prec. + -ING¹.] The action or fact of disappearing.

V. point, in perspective, the point in which receding parallel lines, if continued, appear to meet. Similarly *v. line*, *plane*.

Vanishing (væ·niʃiŋ), *ppl. a.* late ME. [f. as prec. + -ING².] **1.** Disappearing from sight or from existence. **2.** *Math.* Becoming zero 1823.

1. *V. cream*, invisible face cream. **2.** Much discussion has arisen as to whether v. fractions have values or not 1838. Hence **Va·nishingly** *adv.*

Vanity (væ·nĭti). ME. [– (O)Fr. *vanité* :– L. *vanitas*, *-tat-*, f. *vanus* VAIN *a.*; see -ITY.] **1.** That which is vain, futile, or worthless; that which is of no value or profit. **b.** Vain and unprofitable conduct or employment of time ME. **2.** The quality of being vain or worthless; the futility or worthlessness *of* something ME. **†b.** The quality of being foolish or of holding erroneous opinions –1660. **3.** The quality of being personally vain; high opinion of oneself; self-conceit and desire for admiration; an instance of this ME. **b.** A thing of which one is vain 1837. **4.** A vain, idle, or worthless thing; a thing or action of no value ME. **†b.** An idle tale or matter –1660.

1. All is but vanite (sayeth the preacher) all is but playne Vanite COVERDALE *Eccl.* 12:8. **b.** In V. ye waste your Days 1751. **2.** He hath pleasure in the vanyte of wickednes COVERDALE *Ecclus.* 17:31. **3.** The intention of this discourse was not fond ambition or the v. to get a Name MILT. His v. was so mingled with good nature that it became graceful LYTTON. **4.** I had forsaken the vanytees of the world MALORY.

attrib. and *Comb.*: **v.-bag, -box, -case**, a small hand-bag, etc., fitted with a mirror and powder-puff; **V. Fair** (after Bunyan *Pilgrim's Progress*), a place where all is frivolity and empty show; the world or a section of it as a scene of idle amusement and unsubstantial display.

Vanner (væ·nəɹ). 1552. [f. VAN *sb.*¹ and *v.*¹ + -ER¹.] **1.** One who winnows with a fan (*rare*). **2.** *Mining.* One who tests the quality of ore by washing it on a shovel 1671. **b.** An apparatus for separating minerals from the gangue 1882.

Va·nning, *vbl. sb.* 1552. [f. VAN *v.*¹ + -ING¹.] **†1.** The action of winnowing with a fan –1626. **2.** The action or process of separating ore on a shovel 1671.

Vanquish (væ·ŋkwiʃ), *v.* [Early forms *vencus*, *venquis*, *venquisshe*, the *ven-* forms being superseded by *van-* in XVI, by assoc. with late OFr. *vain-*, and the ending assim. to -ISH² in XV; f. pa. pple. *vencus* and pa. t. *venquis* of OFr. *veintre*, *vaintre* (mod. *vaincre*) :– L. *vincere* conquer.] **1.** *trans.* To overcome or defeat (an opponent or enemy) in conflict or battle; to reduce to subjection or submission by superior force. **b.** *fig.* To overcome by spiritual power. late ME. **2.** To overcome (a person) by other than physical means. Also const. *of* (= in respect of). late ME. **3.** With impers. object: To overcome, subdue, suppress or put an end to (a feeling, state of things, etc.). late ME. **†4.** To win or gain (a battle or other contest) –1548. **5.** *absol.* To be victorious; to have the victory. late ME.

1. David vanquished the Ammonites NEWTON. **b.** The Son of God Now entring his great duel,.. to v. by wisdom hellish wiles MILT. **2.** I my self, Who vanquisht with a peal of words..Gave up my fort of silence to a Woman MILT. **3.** Till it thus v. shame and fear SHELLEY. Hence **Va·nquishable** *a.* capable of being vanquished. **Va·nquisher**, a conqueror, subduer. **Va·nquishment**, the act of vanquishing.

Vansire (væ·nsiᵊɹ). 1774. [– Fr., formed by Buffon from the Malagasy name.] *Zool.* The marsh-ichneumon (*Herpestes galera*) of S. Africa.

Vant-, *prefix*, repr. AFr. *vant-*, aphetic f. *avant-* AVANT-; see VANT-BRACE, etc. In a number of compounds the *t* was elided, as in VANBRACE, -COURIER. Before labials the *n* by assimilation became *m*, as in VAMBRACE, VAMPLATE; and a further reduction appears in *vamure* VAUMURE and VAWARD.

Vantage (vɑ·ntėdʒ), *sb.* ME. [– AFr. *vantage*, aphetic f. OFr. *avantage* ADVANTAGE.] **1.** Advantage, benefit, profit, gain. Now *arch.* **†2.** An additional amount or sum –1706. **3.** Advantage or superiority in a contest; position or opportunity likely to give superiority; vantage-ground 1523. **†4.** With *a* and *pl.* An advantage; a position or state of superiority. Freq. with *at* or *for*. –1642. **5.** *Lawn Tennis.* = ADVANTAGE *sb.* 2. 1884.

1. Then at my commynge shulde I have receaved my money with vauntage TINDALE *Matt.* 25:27. **2.** *For* or *to the v.*, in addition. **3.** To each knight their care assigned Like v. of the sun and wind SCOTT. Phr. *Coign* (see COIGN 1), *place*, *point*, (etc.) *of v. To catch*, *have*, *hold*, *take* (one) *at v.*

Vantage (vɑ·ntėdʒ), *v.* Now *arch.* 1460. [f. prec.] *trans.* To profit or benefit (one). Hence **†Va·ntageable** *a.* profitable –1610.

Va·ntage-ground. 1612. [VANTAGE *sb.*] A position which places one at an advantage for defence or attack.

Va·ntbrace. Now *arch.* or *Hist.* late ME. [– AFr. *vauntbras*; see VANT-, VAMBRACE.] = VAMBRACE.

†Va·ntguard. 1450. [Aphetic f. AVANT-GUARD. See VANGUARD.] = VANGUARD 1, 1 b. –1754.

Va·nward, *a.* 1820. [f. VAN *sb.*² + -WARD.] Situated in the van or front. So **Va·nward** *adv.* towards or in the front; forward.

Vapid (væ·pid), *a.* 1656. [– L. *vapidus* savourless, insipid; see -ID¹.] **1.** Devoid of briskness; flat, insipid. **b.** *Med.* Of blood:

Devoid of strength or vigour; weak, inert 1684. **2.** *fig.* Devoid of animation, zest, or interest; dull, flat, lifeless, insipid 1758. †**3.** Of a damp or steamy character; dank; vaporous –1690.

1. He..made his own cold tea, and drank it weak and v. MME. D'ARBLAY. It gives to the beer a v. disagreeable flavour 1826. **2.** Conversation would become dull and v. JOHNSON. One continued round of v. amusements 1825. A smile is..in general v. DISRAELI. Hence **Vapi·dity,** the quality or fact of being v.; a v. remark, idea, feature, etc. **Va·pid-ly** *adv.*, **-ness.**

Vaporable (vē^i·pŏrăb'l), *a.* late ME. [– med.L. *vaporabilis*, f. L. *vaporare* emit steam or vapour; see VAPOUR, -ABLE.] Capable of being converted into vapour. Hence **Va:porabi·lity,** capability of being vaporized.

Vaporific (vē^ipŏri·fik), *a.* 1781. [f. VAPOUR + -FIC.] **1.** Associated, connected with, producing, or causing vaporization. **2.** Vaporous 1797.

1. A great quantity of v.,..or, as it is called, latent heat 1799.

Vapori·meter (vē^ipŏr-). 1878. [f. VAPOUR + -METER.] An instrument for measuring the amount of vapour.

Vaporize (vē^i·pŏrəiz), *v.* 1634. [f. VAPOUR + -IZE.] †**1.** *trans.* To smoke (tobacco). SIR T. HERBERT. **2.** To convert into vapour 1803. **3.** *intr.* To become vaporous 1828. **4.** *trans.* To spray with fine particles of liquid 1900.

1. Forty load of Tobacco vaporized 1634. **3.** *fig.* Money seems somehow to have vaporised away, and none knows anything about it 1892. Hence **Va·porizable** *a.* vaporable. **Vaporiza·tion,** the action or process of converting or of being converted into vapour. **Va·porizer,** a device or apparatus by which conversion into vapour is accomplished.

†**Vaporo·se,** *a. rare.* late ME. [– L. *vaporosus* f. *vapor*; see VAPOUR, -OSE¹.] Vaporous; easily vaporizing –1731. So **Vaporo·sity** (*rare*), vaporous quality or qualities.

Vaporous (vē^i·pŏrəs), *a.* 1527. [f. late L. *vaporus* + -OUS, or – L. *vaporosus* (see prec.). Cf. Fr. *vaporeux*. In later use also f. VAPOUR.] †**1.** Of a bath: Consisting or composed of vapour –1706. **2.** Emitting or exhaling vapour; †*spec.* of food in the stomach 1544. **3.** Filled with vapour, thick or dim with mist; foggy, misty 1593. **b.** Covered or obscured with vapour 1687. **4.** Having the form, nature, or consistency of vapour 1604. **b.** *fig.* Of ideas, feelings, etc.: Fanciful, idle, unsubstantial, vain 1605. **c.** Of fabrics or garments: Gauzy, filmy 1863. **5.** Of persons or minds: Inclined to be fanciful, vague, or frothy, in ideas or discourse 1605. **6.** Of state or condition: Characteristic of vapour 1661.

2. Such things as bee most v. do most dispose us to sleepe 1584. **3.** The waveless plain of Lombardy, Bounded by the v. air SHELLEY. **b.** The lower cloud field—itself an empire of v. hills TYNDALL. **4. b.** Such v. conjecture passed away as quickly as it came GEO. ELIOT. **6.** We have matter in the v. or gaseous form TYNDALL. Hence **Va·porous-ly** *adv.*, **-ness.**

Vapour (vē^i·pəɹ), *sb.* Also (now *U.S.*) **vapor.** late ME. [– (O)Fr. *vapeur*, †*vapour* or L. *vapor*, *vapōr-* steam, heat; see -OUR.] **1.** Without article: Matter in the form of a steamy or imperceptible exhalation; *esp.* the form into which liquids are naturally converted by the action of a sufficient degree of heat. **2.** An exhalation of the nature of steam, or an emanation consisting of imperceptible particles, usu. due to the effect of heat upon moisture. late ME. **b.** An exhalation rising by natural causes from the ground or from some damp place; freq., a mist or fog. late ME. **c.** *fig.* Used esp. to denote something unsubstantial or worthless. late ME. **3.** *pl.* In older medical use: Exhalations supposed to be developed within the organs of the body (esp. the stomach) and to have an injurious effect upon the health. late ME. **b.** A morbid condition supposed to be caused by the presence of such exhalations; depression of spirits, hypochondria, hysteria, or other nervous disorder. Now *arch.* 1662. **c.** So *The vapours* 1711. †**4.** A fancy or fantastic idea; a foolish brag or boast –1738.

1. V. is a moist kinde of fume extracted chiefly out of the water 1610. **2.** The vapoure of the fyre brenneth his flesh. COVERDALE *Ecclus.* 38:28. Vapours of ammonia will be evolved if nitrogen be present 1857. **b.** The vapours which are raised by the Sun under the Torrid Zone 1698. **c.** Forsothe what is ȝoure lijf? A v., to a litel semynge. WYCLIF *Jas.* 4:15. **3.** Vapours from an empty Stomach DE FOE. **b.** Sometimes, thro' pride, the sexes change their airs; My lord has vapours, and my lady swears YOUNG. **4.** These are mere vapours, indeed—Nothing but vapours STEELE.

attrib. and *Comb.*: **v.-burner,** a device for burning previously vaporized liquid hydrocarbons; **-density,** the density of a substance in a state of v. Hence **Va·poured** *ppl. a.* affected with the vapours, suffering from nervous depression.

Vapour (vē^i·pəɹ), *v.* Also (now *U.S.*) **vapor.** late ME. [f. prec. Sense 1 may reflect L. *vaporare* emit vapour or steam.] **1.** *intr.* To rise, ascend, be emitted or diffused in the form of vapour. Also with *out*, *up*. **b.** To pass *away* in the form of vapour 1555. **c.** To pass *into* a state of vapour or moisture (*rare*) 1567. **2.** *trans.* **a.** To cause to rise *up* or ascend in the form of vapour. late ME. **b.** To cause to pass *away* in the form of vapour 1460. **c.** With *out* or *forth*: To evaporate 1530. **d.** To convert into vapour. Chiefly with *to*. 1591. **3.** *intr.* To use language as light or unsubstantial as vapour; to talk fantastically, grandiloquently, or boastingly; to brag or bluster 1628. **b.** *trans.* To declare or assert in a boasting or grandiloquent manner 1658. **4.** *intr.* To act in a fantastic or ostentatious manner; to show off; to swagger 1652. **5.** *trans.* †To give (one) the vapours; to depress or bore –1804.

1. b. *fig.* Their whole life hath vapoured away in hopes 1638. **2. b.** Then upon a gentle heat v. away all the Spirit of Wine BACON. **3.** Poets indeed use to vapor much after this manner MILT. Strutting and vapouring about his own pretensions HAZLITT. **4.** The robbers vapouring about in the court below BORROW. Hence **Va·pouring** *ppl. a.*, **-ly** *adv.*

Va·pour-bath. Also **vapour bath.** 1719. **1.** A bath consisting of vapour. Also, an apartment in which such a bath is used. **2.** *Chem.* A vessel or receptacle in which hot vapour is generated in order to heat or melt a substance 1728.

1. *transf.* One day in August, when all Chowringhee is a vast v. TREVELYAN.

Vapourer (vē^i·pərəɹ). 1653. [f. VAPOUR *v.* + -ER¹.] **1.** One who vapours; a bragging, grandiloquent, or fantastical talker. **2.** *V. moth*, a British moth of the genus *Orgyia*, esp. *O. antiqua*, the male of which flies with a rapid quivering motion 1782.

Vapourish (vē^i·pəriʃ), *a.* Also (*U.S.*) **vaporish.** 1647. [f. VAPOUR *sb.* + -ISH¹.] **1.** Of the nature of vapour; dim through the presence of vapour; vapoury. **2.** Apt to be troubled with the vapours; inclined to depression or low spirits 1716. **b.** Of the nature of, connected with, or arising from nervous depression 1733.

2. For, as most other old Maids, she is exceedingly v. and fanciful 1716. Hence **Va·pourishness.**

Vapoury (vē^i·pəri), *a.* Also (*U.S.*) **vapory.** 1598. [f. VAPOUR *sb.* + -Y¹.] **1.** Of the nature or consistency of vapour; composed of or caused by vapour. **b.** *fig.* Unsubstantial, indefinite, vague 1818. **2.** Rendered dim or obscure by the presence of vapour 1818.

1. The Jungfrau..had wrapped her v. veil around her TYNDALL.

‖**Va·ppa.** Now *rare* or *Obs.* 1629. [L.] Flat or sour wine.

Vapulate (væ·piŭlē^it), *v. rare.* 1603. [– *vapulat-*, pa. ppl. stem of L. *vapulare* be beaten; see -ATE³.] **1.** *trans.* To beat or strike. **b.** *absol.* To administer a flogging 1818. **2.** *intr.* To suffer flogging 1783.

Vapulation (væpiulē^i·ʃən). *rare.* 1656. [f. prec. + -ION. Cf. med.L. *vapulatio* flogging (XI).] A beating or flogging.

‖**Vaquero** (văkē^ə·ro). 1837. [Sp., f. *vaca* cow.] In Spanish America: A cowboy or cowherd; a herdsman or cattle-driver.

‖**Vara** (vā·ră). 1674. [Sp. and Pg., 'rod, yard-stick' :– L., 'forked pole, trestle', f. *varus* bent.] A linear measure used in Spain, Portugal, and S. America, usu. about 33 inches long; a Spanish yard.

Varan (væ·răn). 1843. [– mod.L. *Varanus*, f. Arab. *waran*, var. of *waral* monitor lizard.] *Zool.* A lizard belonging to the genus *Varanus* or family *Varanidæ*; a monitor or varanian.

Varangian (văræ·ndʒiăn), *sb.* and *a.* 1788. [f. med.L. *Varangus* – med. Gr. βάραγγος – (through Slav. langs.) ON. *Væringi* (pl. *Væringjar*), prob. f. *vár* (pl. *várar*) plighted faith; see -IAN.] **A.** *sb.* One of the Scandinavian rovers who in the 9th and 10th centuries overran parts of Russia and reached Constantinople; a Northman (latterly also an Anglo-Saxon) forming one of the bodyguard of the later Byzantine Emperors. **B.** *adj.* Of or pertaining to the Varangians, e.g. *V. Guard*; composed of Varangians 1788.

Varanian (vărē^i·niăn), *sb.* and *a.* 1840. [f. mod.L. *Varanus* VARAN + -IAN.] **A.** *sb.* A lizard belonging to the family *Varanidæ* of scaled saurians; a monitor or varan 1841. **B.** *adj.* Belonging to or characteristic of the varans or monitors 1840.

†**Va·rdingale.** 1552. [Early forms *vard-*, *verd-*, *fardingale*; see FARTHINGALE.] = FARTHINGALE –1753.

†**Vare.** 1545. [– Sp. *vara* or its source L. VARA.] **1.** = VARA –1604. **2.** A rod, staff, or wand, esp. as a symbol of judicial office or authority –1681.

2. His Hand a V. of Justice did uphold DRYDEN.

‖**Varec** (væ·rek). Also **varech.** 1676. [– Fr. *varec(h*, OFr. *warec*, *vrec* – ON. **wrek* WRECK.] **1.** Seaweed. **2.** An impure carbonate of soda obtained from sea-weed 1844.

†‖**Varella** (văre·lă). 1588. [Pg. and It., of doubtful origin.] A pagoda –1662.

‖**Vari** (vā·ri). 1774. [f. *vari(kandana* or *vari(anda*, the Malagasy name.] The ruffed lemur, *Lemur varius*.

Variability (vē^əriăbi·lĭti). 1771. [f. next + -ITY. Cf. Fr. *variabilité*.] **1.** The fact or quality of being variable in some respect; tendency towards or capacity for variation or change. **2.** *spec.* **a.** The fact of, or capacity for, varying in amount, magnitude, or value 1816. **b.** *Biol.* Capability in plants or animals of variation or deviation from a type 1832.

Variable (vē^ə·riăb'l), *a.* and *sb.* late ME. [– (O)Fr. *variable* – L. *variabilis*, f. *variare*; see VARY *v.*, -ABLE.] **A.** *adj.* **1.** Liable or apt to vary or change; (readily) susceptible of variation; mutable, changeable, fluctuating, uncertain. **2.** Of persons: Apt to change from one opinion or course of action to another; inconstant, fickle, unreliable. late ME. **3. a.** Of the weather, seasons, etc.: Liable to vary in temperature or character; changeable 1480. **b.** Of wind or currents: Shifting 1665. **c.** Of a star: That varies periodically in respect of brightness or magnitude 1788. **d.** *Biol.* Liable to deviate from a type; admitting of such deviation 1859. †**4.** Differing, diverse, various –1613. **5.** Susceptible or admitting of increase or diminution in respect of size, number, amount, or degree 1607. **b.** Of quantity, number, etc.: Liable to vary 1710. **6.** That may be varied, changed, or modified; alterable 1597. **7.** *Nat. Hist.* Of various colours, or varying in colour according to the season, etc. 1776.

1. A doubtfull and v. fight 1610. Subjects of v. fancy RUSKIN. **2.** My word nor I shall not be v., But alwaies..firme and stable WYATT. **3. a.** The weather..was very v., but upon the whole mild 1808. **b.** We had the wind v. DE FOE. **d.** Beings low in the scale of nature are more v. than those which are higher DARWIN. **5.** The pressure of the atmosphere is v. 1815.

B. *sb.* **1.** *Math.* and *Phys.* A quantity or force which, throughout a mathematical calculation or investigation, is assumed to vary or be capable of varying in value 1816. **2. a.** A variable or shifting wind; *spec.* in *pl.*, parts of the sea where a steady wind is not expected 1846. **b.** A variable star 1868. **3.** Something which is liable to vary or change; a changeable factor, feature, or element 1846.

2. a. The Variables, which are found South of the border of the South-east Trades 1857. Hence **Va·riableness. Va·riably** *adv.*

Variance (vē^ə·riăns). ME. [– OFr. *variance* – L. *variantia*, f. *variare* VARY *v.*; see

-ANCE.] I. 1. The fact or state of undergoing change or alteration; tendency to vary or become different; variation. †b. Inconstancy in persons; variableness, changeableness –1520. 2. The fact or quality of varying or differing; difference, divergency, discrepancy. late ME. 3. a. *Law*. A difference or discrepancy between two statements or documents. late ME. b. *gen.* A difference or discrepancy; a divergent feature 1497.

1. Uncarefull of Fortunes varyaunce 1559. 2. It is evident that v. of opinion proves error somewhere 1839. 3. b. Variances in the spelling of proper names 1860.

II. 1. The state or fact of disagreeing or falling out; discord, dissension, contention, debate. late ME. 2. A disagreement, quarrel, or falling out; a dispute. late ME.

1. She makes V. betwixt Rulers and Subjects, betwixt Parents and Children BUNYAN.

Phr. **At v. a.** Of persons: In a state of discord, dissension, or enmity. b. Of things: In a state of disagreement or difference; conflicting, differing. Usu. const. *with*.

Variant (vēᵊ·riănt), *a.* and *sb.* late ME. [– (O)Fr. *variant*, pr. pple. of *varier* VARY *v.*; see -ANT.] A. *adj.* 1. Of persons: Changeful in disposition or purpose; inconstant, fickle. Now *rare*. 2. Of things: Exhibiting variation or change; tending to vary or alter; not remaining uniform. late ME. 3. Exhibiting difference or variety; diversified; diverse. late ME. 4. Differing or discrepant *from* something. late ME. b. *Biol.* Varying from type 1881.

1. Calm and resolute, if occasionally v. of mood 1890. 3. They who would trauerse earths v. face 1632.

B. *sb.* 1. A form or modification differing in some respect from other forms of the same thing 1848. b. A various reading 1861. 2. A variation of the original work, story, song, etc. 1872. 3. *Nat. Hist.* A variant form or type 1895.

†**Va·riate,** *v.* 1566. [– *variat-*, pa. ppl. stem of L. *variare*; see VARY *v.*, -ATE³.] *trans.* and *intr.* To alter, vary, change –1770.

Variation (vēᵊriēⁱ·ʃən). late ME. [– (O)Fr. *variation* or L. *variatio, -ōn-*, f. as prec.; see -ION.] †I. Difference, divergence, or discrepancy between two or more things or persons –1637. II. 1. The fact of varying in condition, character, degree, or other quality; the fact of undergoing modification or alteration, esp. within certain limits 1502. b. The action of making some change or alteration 1704. 2. *V. of the compass* or *needle*, = DECLINATION 8 b. Also *ellipt.* 1556. 3. The fact, on the part of the mercury, of standing higher or lower in the tube of a barometer or thermometer; the extent or range of this 1719. 4. *Astr.* = LIBRATION 2. 1704. 5. *Math.* †a. = PERMUTATION 3. –1728. b. Change in a function or functions of an equation due to an indefinitely small increase or decrease in the value of the constants 1743. 6. *Biol.* Deviation or divergence in the structure, character, or function of an organism from those typical of or usual in the species or group 1859.

1. According to the varying gravity of the atmosphere; which v. has.. a very considerable influence on the weather-glass BOYLE. b. Powers.. to control the v. of investments 1885.

III. 1. An instance of varying or changing; an alteration or change in something, esp. within certain limits; a difference due to the introduction or intrusion of some change 1611. b. *Biol.* A slight departure or divergence from a type 1835. c. A variety, variant 1863. 2. A deviation or departure *from* something 1647. 3. Math. *Calculus of variations*, a form of calculus applicable to expressions or functions in which the law relating the quantities is liable to variation 1810. 4. *Mus.* A modification with regard to the tune, time, and harmony of a theme, by which on repetition it appears in a new but still recognizable form; *esp.* in *pl.*, embellishments in an air for giving variety on repetition after playing it in its simple form 1801.

1. Variations of the Compass DE FOE. c. The Matadore Game..is a v. of All Fives 1868. 4. She ran a set of variations on 'Kenmure's on and awa'' SCOTT. Hence **Varia·tional** *a.* characterized by, dealing with, or concerning v.

‖**Varicella** (værise·lă). 1771. [mod.L. (Vogel, 1764), irreg. dim. of VARIOLA.] *Path.* Chickenpox. Hence **Varice·llous** *a.* of, relating to, affected with, or of the nature of v.

Varicocele (væ·rikosīːl). 1736. [f. *varic-*, comb. form of VARIX + Gr. κήλη tumour; see -O-.] *Path.* Varicose condition or dilatation of the spermatic veins.

Vari-coloured, varicoloured (vēᵊ·ri-kɒːləɹd), *a.* 1665. [f. L. *varius* VARIOUS *a.* + COLOURED *ppl. a.*] Of various or different colours; variegated in colour. b. *fig.* Different, diverse, diversified 1855.

Varicose (væ·rikoᵘs), *a.* 1730. [– L. *varicosus*, f. *varix, varic-* dilated vein; see -OSE¹.] 1. *Path.* or *Med.* Affected with, characterized by, or of the nature of a varix or varices. b. Of veins: Unnaturally swollen or dilated 1797. 2. *Ent.* and *Bot.* Unusually enlarged or swollen; resembling a varix 1826. 3. Of appliances: Designed or used for the treatment of varicose veins 1858.

1. b. *fig.* Milton has..not a sinew sharp or rigid, not a vein v. or inflated LANDOR. So †**Va·ricous** *a.* –1786.

Varicosity (værikǫ·sĭti). 1842. [f. prec. + -ITY.] 1. A varicose swelling or distension. 2. The state or condition of being varicose or abnormally swollen; an instance or case of this 1876. 3. The state of having varicose veins 1879.

1. Irregular dilatations or varicosities of the absorbent vessels 1842.

Varied (vēᵊ·rid), *ppl. a.* 1588. [f. VARY *v.* + -ED¹.] 1. Differing from one another; of different or various sorts or kinds. 2. Marked by variation or variety; presenting different forms or qualities on this account 1732. 3. Vari-coloured; *esp.* in the names of birds or beasts 1715.

1. So v., extensive and pervading are human distresses 1851. 2. Observe..What vary'd Being peoples ev'ry star POPE. The v. actor flies from part to part CHURCHILL. Hence **Va·ried-ly** *adv.*, **-ness** (*rare*).

Variegate (vēᵊ·rigeⁱt), *v.* 1653. [– *variegat-*, pa. ppl. stem of L. *variegare* make varied, f. *varius* VARIOUS; see -ATE³.] 1. *trans.* To diversify; to invest with variety; to enliven with differences or changes. b. *esp.* To mark or cover with patches of different colours or objects 1728. 2. To vary by change or alteration (*rare*) 1674.

1. b. The Shells are filled with a white Spar, which variegates and adds to the Beauty of the Stone 1728.

Variegated (vēᵊ·rigēⁱtėd), *ppl. a.* 1661. [f. prec. + -ED¹.] 1. Marked with patches or spots of different colours; varied in colour; many-coloured, vari-coloured; *spec.* in *Bot.* (see next 1). 2. Marked or characterized by variety; of a varied character, form, or nature; diverse 1662. 3. Varied or diversified *with* something 1678.

1. A v. flowing robe of silk GIBBON. 3. Corolla blue v. with white inside 1870.

Variegation (vēᵊrigēⁱ·ʃən). 1646. [f. VARIEGATE + -ION. Cf. mod.L. *variegatio* (1620).] 1. The quality or condition of being variegated or varied in colour; diversity of colour or the production of this; *spec.* in *Bot.*, the presence of two or more colours in the leaves, petals, or other parts of plants; also, defective or special development leading to such colouring. b. With *a* and *pl.* Also, a variegated marking. 1664. 2. The action or process of diversifying; an instance or occasion of this 1668.

Varietal (vărəi·ėtăl), *a.* 1866. [f. next + -AL¹ 1.] *Zool.* and *Bot.* Of, pertaining to, or connected with, indicating, etc., a distinct variety of animal or plant. Opp. to *specific* or *generic*. Hence **Vari·etally** *adv.*

Variety (vărəi·ėti). 1533. [– (O)Fr. *variété* or L. *varietas*, f. *varius* VARIOUS; see -ITY.] †1. a. Variation or change of fortune –1617. b. Tendency to change; fickleness –1579. 2. Difference or discrepancy between things or in the same thing at different times 1552. 3. The fact, quality, or condition of being varied; absence of monotony, sameness, or uniformity 1548. b. *pl.* A series or succession of different forms, conditions, etc.; variations 1604. 4. Used as a collective to denote a number *of* things, qualities, etc., different or distinct in character 1553. 5. A different form *of* some thing, quality, or condition; a kind or sort 1617. b. *Zool.* and *Biol.* A plant or animal differing from those of the species to which it belongs in some minor but permanent or transmissible particular; a group of such individuals constituting a sub-species or other subdivision of a species; also, a plant or animal which varies in some trivial respect from its immediate parent or type 1629. c. So in the classification of inorganic substances or of diseases 1753. 6. *attrib.* a. *V. shop* or *store* (*U.S.*), one in which small goods of various kinds are sold; a general store 1824. b. Used to designate music-hall or theatrical entertainments of a mixed character (songs, dances, impersonations, etc.). Also applied to things or persons connected with such entertainments. c. *ellipt.*, v. performances or entertainments. 1886. d. attrib., *v. theatre*.

2. Many, according to the varietie of their opinions, attribute this to diverse causes 1604. 3. Age cannot wither her, nor custome stale Her infinite v. SHAKS. V. is the mother of enjoyment DISRAELI. b. He had passed through all varieties of fortune, and had seen both sides of human nature MACAULAY. 4. Like Proteus, he transforms himself into a v. of shapes 1875. A v. of hooks were used for different kinds of fish 1887. 5. Even the varieties of good character are almost infinite 1860.

Variform (vēᵊ·rifǭɹm), *a.* 1662. [f. L. *varius* + -FORM.] Of various forms; varied or different in form; diversiform.

†**Va·rify,** *v.* 1606. [f. L. *varius* + -FY.] *trans.* To make varied; to vary; to variegate –1741.

‖**Variola** (vărəi·ŏlă). 1771. [– late and med.L. *variola* pustule, pock, f. L. *varius* VARIOUS.] *Path.* The small-pox. So **Vari·olar** *a.* of, pertaining to, or resembling (that of) v. **Vario·lic** *a.* (*rare*) of v.

Variolate (vēᵊ·riŏleⁱt), *v.* 1792. [f. prec. + -ATE³.] *Med. trans.* To infect with variola; to inoculate with the virus of variola or small-pox. Hence **Va:riola·tion,** inoculation with the virus of small-pox.

Variolite (vēᵊ·riŏləit). 1796. [f. VARIOLA + -ITE¹ 2 b.] *Geol.* A kind of rock embedded with spherulites which give it the appearance of being pock-marked; esp. the diabase (diorite) of Brongniart. Hence **Va:rioli·tic** *a.* of the nature of or containing v.: spherulitic.

Varioloid (vēᵊ·riŏloid), *a.* and *sb.* 1821. [f. VARIOLA + -OID.] *Path.* A. *adj.* Resembling variola or small-pox; like that of variola. B. *sb.* A modified form of variola, esp. a mild variety occurring after vaccination or in those who have previously had small-pox 1828.

Variolous (vărəi·ŏləs), *a.* 1668. [f. VARIOLA + -OUS.] 1. Of the nature of or resembling (that of) variola or small-pox; of, pertaining to, appearing in, or characteristic of variola 1676. 2. Of persons: Affected with or suffering from small-pox 1668.

1. *V. matter* (*fluid* or *virus*), the virus of small-pox, esp. as used for inoculation.

Variometer (vēᵊriǫ·mėtəɹ). 1889. [f. *vario-*, taken as comb. form of L. *varius* VARIOUS + -METER.] An instrument used to show or determine variations in barometric pressure, magnetic force, etc.; in wireless telephony and telegraphy, a tuning coil the inductance of which is varied by altering the relative position of its two parts.

‖**Variorum** (vēᵊriōᵊ·rŏm). 1728. [L., gen. pl. masc. of *varius* VARIOUS *a.*, in the phr. *editio cum notis variorum* (see def.).] An edition, esp. of the complete works of a classical author, containing the notes of various commentators or editors. Also *v. edition*.

V. Shakespeare; The book-sellers have chosen to call the 1803 and 1813 editions of Johnson and Steevens the *First* and *Second V. Shakespeares*, and the 1821 edition of Malone, although of different origin, the *Third V.* E. K. CHAMBERS.

Various (vēᵊ·riəs), *a.* 1552. [f. L. *varius* changing, diverse: see -IOUS.] †I. 1. Of things: Undergoing, exhibiting, or subject to variation or change; variable, changeful –1775. 2. Of persons: Unstable; fickle –1820.

1. As the condition of the Court is ever v. and unconstant 1647. 2. The v. character of that

emperor, capable, by turns, of the meanest and the most generous sentiments GIBBON.

II. †**1.** Of persons: Versatile in knowledge or acquirements; exhibiting variety in work or writings –1681. **2. a.** Varied in colour; vari-coloured. Chiefly *poet.* 1618. **b.** Exhibiting variety in appearance 1656. **3.** Characterized by variation or variety of attributes or properties; varied in nature or character 1633. †**b.** Calculated to cause difference. MILT. **4.** Marked by variety of incident or action 1634. **5. a.** Exhibiting variety of subject or topic 1677. **b.** Exhibiting variety in the different persons or things forming a collective whole 1769.

1. A delectable Author, very v. SIR T. BROWNE. **2.** Birds of v. plumage LONGF. **b.** A prospect wide And v. MILT. **3.** After conviction their behaviour was very v. 1780. **5. a.** One whose conversation was so v., easy, and delightful THACKERAY. **b.** A v. host they came SCOTT.

III. 1. With pl. sb. Different from one another; of different kinds or sorts 1634. **b.** With a sing. sb., and freq. preceded by *each* or *every* 1721. **2.** In weakened sense, as an enumerative term: Different, divers, several, many, more than one 1696.

1. The woodland scene, Diversified with trees of ev'ry growth, Alike, yet v. COWPER. **b.** In every v. Change of Life the same 1746. Phr. *V. reading(s*; It may rest upon a v. reading in the Hebrew 1910. Hence **Va·rious-ly** *adv.*, **-ness.**

‖**Varix** (vēᵊ·riks). *Pl.* **varices** (vēᵊ·risīz). late ME. [L. *varix, varic-*.] **1.** *Path.* An abnormal dilatation or enlargement of a vein or artery, usu. accompanied by a tortuous development; a varicose vein. **b.** The diseased condition characterized by this, as a specific malady 1813. **2.** *Conch.* A longitudinal elevation or swelling on the surface of a shell 1822.

Varlet (vā·ɹlėt). 1456. [– OFr. *varlet*, var. of *vaslet, vadlet* VALET. Cf. AL. *vadlettus, vaslettus* (XII/XIII).] **1.** A man or lad acting as an attendant or servant; a menial, a groom. Now *arch.* **b.** *spec.* An attendant on a knight or other person of military importance. Now *Hist.* 1470. **2.** A person of a low, mean, or knavish disposition; a knave, rogue, rascal. (In later use, freq. without serious implication of bad qualities.) 1550. †**3.** The knave in cards. [So Fr. *valet.*] –1625.

2. A little contemptible v., without the least title to birth, person, wit SWIFT.

Varletry (vā·ɹlėtri). 1606. [f. prec. + -RY.] Varlets collectively; a crowd of menials.

Shall they hoyst me vp, And shew me to the showting Varlotarie Of censuring Rome? SHAKS.

Varment, varmint (vā·ɹmėnt), *sb. dial.* and *U.S.* 1539. [var. of *varmin* VERMIN, with parasitic *t* as in *peasant, tyrant.*] **1. a.** *collect.* Vermin. **b.** An animal of a noxious or objectionable kind 1689. **c.** In hunting parlance, the fox. **2.** An objectionable or troublesome person or persons; a mischievous boy or child 1773.

1. b. The granger came out with his rifle and shot the varmint [*viz.* a panther] 1889.

Varnish (vā·ɹniʃ), *sb.*[1] [ME. *vernisch* – (O)Fr. *vernis* :– med.L. *veronix, -ic-* (VIII) fragrant resin, sandarac, or – med. Gr. *βερενίκη*, prob. appellative use of the town-name (Berenice, in Cyrenaica).] **1.** Resinous matter dissolved in some liquid and used for spreading over a surface in order to give this a hard, shining, transparent coat, by which it is made more durable or ornamental. **b.** With *a* and *pl.* A special preparation of this nature 1667. **c.** A solution of this kind spread on a surface; the coating or surface so formed 1643. **2.** *fig.* A specious gloss or outward show; a pretence 1565. **3.** A means of embellishment or adornment; a beautifying or improving quality or feature 1591. **4.** An external appearance or display of some quality without underlying reality. (Cf. VENEER *sb.*) 1662.

2. For the better v., the Duke would not be his own Judge 1647. **3.** A cloudy and rainy day takes the v. off the scenery HAWTHORNE. **4.** The youth comes up with a v. of accomplishment beyond his real powers 1868.

attrib. and *Comb.*: **v. sumach**, the Japanese tree *Rhus vernicifera* from which lacquer is obtained; **-tree**, one or other of various trees yielding a resinous substance used as a v.

Va·rnish, *sb.*[2] 1601. [f. the vb.] An act of varnishing; an application of varnish.

Varnish (vā·ɹniʃ), *v.* late ME. [– OFr. *verniss(i)er, -ic(i)er* (mod. *vernir* is a new formation on the sb.), f. *vernis* VARNISH *sb.*[1]; see -ISH[2].] **1.** *trans.* To paint *over* or coat with varnish; to overlay with a thin coating composed of varnish. **b.** *transf.* To invest with a bright or glossy appearance; to smear or stain with some substance similar to varnish. late ME. **2.** To embellish or adorn; to improve, trick out, furbish *up.* late ME. **3.** To cover or overlay with a specious or deceptive appearance; to gloss over, disguise 1571.

1. These pictures, I am persuaded, were afterwards constantly varnished 1821. **b.** The Leaves fresh varnisht lively green SYLVESTER. **2.** To dress up and v. the Story of Pausanias BENTLEY. **3.** Cato's voice was ne'er employed To clear the guilty, and to vernish crimes ADDISON. To v. over these distinctions 1871. Hence **Va·rnisher,** one who varnishes; *spec.* one who makes a business or trade of varnishing.

Varnishing (vā·ɹniʃiŋ), *vbl. sb.* 1505. [f. prec. + ING[1].] The action of applying varnish or of coating anything with varnish. *attrib.* In the year 1809..the 'v. days' were appointed, whereby the members of the Academy were granted the privilege of retouching and varnishing their pictures after they were hung, and prior to the opening of the exhibition 1862.

Varronian (værōᵘ·niăn), *a.* 1693. [– L. *Varronianus*, f. *Varro, Varron-*; see def., -IAN.] Of or pertaining to the Roman author M. Terentius Varro (116–27 B.C.); admitted as genuine by Varro.

Varsal (vā·ɹsăl), *a.* Now *dial.* 1696. [Illiterate abbrev. of UNIVERSAL *a.* Cf. VERSAL.] **1.** Universal, whole. Only in the phr. *in the v. world.* **2.** Single, individual (*rare*) 1765.

Varsity (vā·ɹsĭti). Also **'varsity.** 1846. Clipped form of UNIVERSITY. Cf. prec.

Vartabed (vā·ɹtăbed). Also **-bied, -bet.** 1718. [Armenian.] An ecclesiastic in the Armenian church whose function it is to teach and preach.

‖**Varus**[1] (vēᵊ·rŏs). 1800. [L., 'knock-kneed'.] *Path.* A physical deformity in which the foot is turned inwards.

‖**Varus**[2] (vēᵊ·rŏs). 1822. [L., 'pimple'.] *Path.* **a.** Stone-pock. **b.** A papule (of small-pox).

Varvel (vā·ɹvĕl). 1537. [Earlier †*vervel* – (O)Fr. *vervelle*, †*varvelle*, syncopated form of *vertevelle* :– Rom. **vertibella*, beside **vertibellum*, dim of late L. *vertibulum* joint, f. *vertere* turn. Cf. dial. *vardle* XVI, *vartiwell* XVIII eye of a hinge, hinge.] A metal ring attached to the end of a hawk's jess and serving to connect this with the leash.

Va·ry, *sb. rare.* 1600. [f. next.] A variation; †a hesitation or vacillation.

Vary (vēᵊ·ri), *v.* ME. [– (O)Fr. *varier* or L. *variare*, f. *varius* VARIOUS.] **I.** *intr.* **1.** Of things: To undergo change or alteration; to pass from one condition, state, etc., to another. late ME. **2.** To differ, to exhibit or present divergence, *from* something else. late ME. **3.** Of persons: To differ, diverge, or depart, in respect of practice or observance (*from* some standard). late ME. †**4.** To differ in respect of statement; to give a different or divergent account –1607. **b.** Const. *from* (another or each other). In later use, to depart *from* an author by some change of statement. 1513. †**5.** To differ in opinion, to disagree (*about, for, in,* or *of* something); to dissent *from* another –1657. †**b.** To fall at variance –1577. **6.** To change or alter in respect of conduct, direction, etc. 1481. **7.** To be inconsistent in one's statements; to introduce a difference or discrepancy 1557.

1. When the organisation has once begun to v., it generally continues to v. for many generations DARWIN. **2.** This edition varies very little from its predecessor 1891. **3.** I v. from his wordes, as all Translators must doe 1621. **4. b.** I have in.. other places varied somewhat from him 1653. **7.** For drawing wittnesses to varie from their former depositions 1637.

II. *trans.* **1.** To cause to change or alter; to introduce changes or alterations into (something); in later use freq., to adapt to certain circumstances or requirements by appropriate modifications ME. **b.** To dispose, obtain, occupy in a manner characterized by variety or variation 1697. †**2.** To express in different words –1682.

1. The court, after such notice,..may v. such order in such manner..as it may think fit 1891. **b.** To v. a whole week with joy, anxiety, and conjecture JOHNSON. **2.** Let your ceasless change Varie to our great Maker still new praise MILT. Hence **Va·rier** †(*a*) = PREVARICATOR 4; (*b*) one who varies or dissents *from* something. **Va·rying** *vbl. sb.*

Varying (vēᵊ·ri,iŋ), *ppl. a.* ME. [f. prec. + -ING[2].] That varies.

V. hare, a species of hare, inhabiting northern or elevated regions, the fur of which turns white in winter; the Alpine, blue, or mountain hare. Hence **Va·ryingly** *adv.*

‖**Vas** (væs). *Pl.* **vasa** (vē¹·să). 1651. [L., vessel.] **a.** *Anat.* A hollow organ serving for the conveyance of a liquid in the body: often *ellipt.* for *vas deferens*, etc. **b.** *Bot.* (See quot.) 1843.

b. *Vasa*, the tubes which occur in the interior of plants, and serve for the conveyance of sap or air 1866. Hence **Va·sal** *a.*

Vascular (væ·skiŭlăɹ), *a.* 1672. [– mod.L. *vascularis*, f. L. *vasculum*, dim. of *vas* VAS; see -AR[1].] **1.** *Bot.* Of fibres, tissue, etc.: Having the form of tubular vessels; consisting of continuous tubes of simple membrane. **b.** Of structure: Characterized by the prevalence of tubular vessels 1728. **c.** Of plants: Having a vascular structure 1830. **2.** *Anat.* or *Phys.* Having the character or properties of a conveying vessel or vessels 1728. **b.** Affecting the vascular system or tissue 1869.

1. The v. fibres of the bark 1791. *V. system*, the aggregate of tubular vessels in a plant. **2.** All the Flesh in an animal Body is found to be V. 1728. *V. system*; The v. system comprises the heart, arteries, veins, and capillaries; the lymphatic glands and vessels, together with certain ductless glands; and the blood with its tributary fluids 1876. Hence **Vascula·rity,** v. form or condition. **Va:sculariza·tion,** conversion to a v. condition. **Va·scularize** *v. trans.* to render v. **Va·scularly** *adv.*

Vasculose (væ·skiŭlōᵘs). 1883. [f. VASCULAR + -OSE[2].] The principal constituent of the vascular tissue in plants.

‖**Vasculum** (væ·skiŭlŏm). 1832. [L., dim. of *vas* vessel; see -CULE.] **1.** *Bot.* = ASCIDIUM 2. **2.** A special case used by botanists for carrying newly-collected specimens 1844.

Vase (vāz, *occas.* vǭz; earlier and still *U.S.* vē¹s, vē¹z). 1563. [– Fr. *vase* – L. *vas* vessel.] **1.** *Arch.* †**a.** = BELL *sb.*[1] 4. –1753. **b.** An ornament having the form of a vase (sense 2) 1706. **2.** A vessel, usu. of an ornamental character, commonly of circular section, tall in proportion to its diameter, and made either of earthenware, metal, glass, etc., but varying greatly in form and use 1629. **b.** A calyx or other growth resembling a vase 1728.

2. No chargers then were wrought in burnish'd gold, Nor silver vases took the forming mold POPE.

Vaseline (væ·sĕlīn, -in, væ·z-), *sb.* 1874. [irreg. f. G. *wasser* water + Gr. *ἔλαιον* oil + -INE[5].] Proprietary name (introduced by R. A. Chesebrough, 1872) of a soft greasy substance used as an ointment or lubricant, obtained by evaporating petroleum and passing the residuum through animal charcoal. Hence **Va·seline** *v. trans.* to lubricate, rub, or anoint with v.

Vasiform (vē¹·zifǭɹm, vē¹·s-), *a.* 1835. [f. L. *vas* vessel + -FORM.] **1.** Having the form of a duct or similar conveying vessel; tubular. **2.** Shaped like a vase 1846.

1. *V. tissue*, ducts, that is tubes having the appearance of spiral vessels and bothrenchyma 1866.

Vaso- (vē¹·so), comb. form, on Gr. types, of L. *vas* VAS, employed in terms of *Phys.* and *Path.* relating to the vascular system or parts of this, as **vaso-cellular** *a.*, **-constrictor, -dentine, -dilator, -ganglion, -inhibitory** *a.*, **-motive** *a.*

Va·so-mo:tor, *a.* and *sb.* 1865. [f. prec.] *Phys.* **A.** *adj.* **1.** Acting upon the walls of the blood-vessels, so as to produce constriction or dilatation of these and thus regulate or affect the flow of the blood. Chiefly with *nerve* and *centre.* **2.** Affecting the vaso-motor nerves or centres 1879. **B.** *sb.* A vaso-motor nerve 1887.

Vassal (væ·săl), *sb.* and *a.* ME. [– (O)Fr. *vassal* :– med.L. *vassallus* man-servant, retainer, of Celtic origin; the simplex *vassus* (see VAVASOUR) corresp. to OGaulish *-vassus* in pers. names, e.g. *Dagovassus*, OBret. *uuas* (Bret. *goaz*), W. *gwas*, Ir. *foss* servant.] **A.** *sb.* **1.** In the feudal system, one holding lands from a superior on conditions of homage and allegiance; a feudatory; a tenant-in-fee. Now *Hist.* **2.** *transf.* One who holds, in relation to another, a position similar or comparable to that of a feudal vassal 1563. **b.** *esp.* A humble servant or subordinate; one devoted to the service of another 1500. **c.** One who is completely subject to some influence. Const. *of* or *to*. 1614. **3.** A base or abject person; a slave 1589. **4.** *attrib.* or *adj.* **a.** Subject, subordinate. Chiefly *fig.* 1593. **b.** Of, pertaining to, or characteristic of a v. 1588.

2. b. Damoyselle, . . as to my part, your vassall & seruaunt shal I euer be 1500. *transf.* Thy thoughts, low vassals to thy state SHAKS. **c.** The feeble vassals of wine and anger and lust TENNYSON. **3.** *Lear* I. i. 163. **4. a.** Thy proud hearts slaue and vassall wretch to be SHAKS. Hence **Va·ssalize** *v. trans.* = next. **Va·ssalry** = VASSALAGE 3, 4. **Va·ssalship.**

Vassal (væ·săl), *v.* Now *rare.* 1606. [f. prec.] **1.** *trans.* To make subject or subordinate *to* some thing or person 1613. **2.** To reduce to the position of a vassal; to subdue or subjugate 1606.

Vassalage (væ·sălėdʒ). ME. [– OFr. *vassalage* (mod. *vasselage*), f. *vassal* VASSAL *sb.*; see -AGE.] **1.** Action befitting a good vassal or a man of courage and spirit; prowess. *Obs.* exc. *arch.* **2.** The state or condition of a vassal; subordination, homage, or allegiance characteristic of or resembling that of a vassal 1594. **3.** Subjection, subordination, servitude; service 1595. **4.** A body or assemblage of vassals 1807.

2. Like v. at vnawares encountring The eye of Maiestie SHAKS. Phr. *To hold* (lands) *in v.* **3.** Princes. ., Born to the pompous v. of state 1767.

Vast (vɑst), *sb.* 1604. [f. the adj.] **1.** A vast or immense space. Chiefly *poet.* **2.** *dial.* A very great number or amount 1793.

1. Thou god of this great v., rebuke these surges SHAKS. The v. of Heav'n MILT. **2.** I took a v. of trouble (as the country folks say) about it HUXLEY.

Vast (vɑst), *a.* and *adv.* 1575. [– L. *vastus* void, immense.] **A.** *adj.* **1.** Of very great or large dimensions or size; huge, enormous. **2.** Of great or immense extent or area; extensive, far-stretching 1590. **3.** Of the mind, etc.: Unusually large or comprehensive in grasp or aims 1610. **4.** Very great in respect of amount, quantity, or number 1637. **5.** As a mere intensive 1695.

1. A v. ruff, a vaster fardingale H. WALPOLE. **2.** One sees more diuels then vaste hell can hold SHAKS. His v. breadth of shoulder 1865. Science is grown too v. for any one head KINGSLEY. **4.** V. herds of cattle 1838. His reading was v. 1856. I saw a v. number 1884. **5.** Their wise heads go. . nodding with v. solemnity 1861.

B. *adv.* Vastly. Now *dial.* 1687. Hence **Va·st-ly** *adv.* immensely; in weakened sense as a mere intensive, exceedingly, very (freq. in fashionable use in the 18th cent.); **-ness.**

Vastation (væstēi·ʃən). 1545. [– L. *vastatio*, *-ōn-*, f. pa. ppl. stem of *vastare* lay waste, f. *vastus*; see prec., -ION.] †**1.** The action of laying waste, devastating, or destroying –1663. †**2.** The fact or condition of being devastated or laid waste –1653. **3.** The action of purifying by the destruction of evil qualities or elements 1847.

Vastitude (vɑ·stitiūd). 1623. [– L. *vastitudo*, f. *vastus* VAST *a.*; see -TUDE.] **1.** The quality of being vast; immensity. **2.** A vast extent or space 1841.

Vastity (vɑ·stiti). Now *rare.* 1545. [– L. *vastitas*, f. as prec.; see -ITY.] †**1.** The fact or quality of being desolate, waste, void, or empty –1651. **2.** The quality of being vast or immense 1603.

2. Th' unbounded Sea and Vastitie of shore HEYWOOD.

Vasty (vɑ·sti), *a.* 1596. [f. VAST *a.* + -Y[1].] Vast, immense. (In mod. use after Shaks.)

I can call Spirits from the vastie Deepe SHAKS. Hence **Va·stily** *adv.*

Vat (væt), *sb.* ME. [Southern and western var. of FAT *sb.*[1]] **1.** A cask, tun, or other vessel used for holding or storing water, beer, or other liquid; usu. one of some size in which a liquor, esp. beer or cider, undergoes fermentation or is prepared. **b.** A vessel, cauldron, or cistern containing the liquid used in dyeing or some other process 1548. **2.** *spec.* **a.** = CHEESE-*vat* 1669. **b.** = TAN-*vat* 1777. **c.** *Mining.* A wooden tub used in washing ore, etc. 1802. **d.** *Salt-making.* A salt-pit 1860. **3.** = FAT *sb.*[1] 3. 1766. †**b.** Formerly used as a measure of capacity for coal –1821. **4.** *Dyeing.* The liquid solution in which the material to be dyed is immersed; the dyeing liquor 1755. Hence **Vat** *v. trans.* to place or store in a v.; to immerse in a dyeing solution or v.

‖**Vates** (vēi·tīz). 1625. [L.] **1.** A poet or bard, esp. one who is divinely inspired; a prophet-poet. **2.** *pl.* One of the classes of the old Gaulish druids 1728. Hence **Va·tic,** †**-ical** *adjs.* of, pertaining to, or characteristic of a prophet or seer; prophetic, inspired 1594.

Vatican (væ·tikăn). 1555. [– Fr. *Vatican* or L. *Vaticanus* (sc. *collis* hill, *mons* mountain); see -AN.] **1.** (With initial capital, and now always with *the*.) The palace of the Pope built upon the Vatican Hill in Rome. Also, in recent use, the papal authorities or the system which they represent; the papacy. **b.** Used with ref. to the artistic or literary treasures of the Vatican 1600. **2.** *attrib.* or as *adj.* Of or pertaining to the Vatican or its library 1638.

1. b. I. . would not part with his Book for half a V. 1694. **2.** *V. Council*, the council of 1869–70 which proclaimed the infallibility of the Pope.

Vaticanism (væ·tikăniz'm). 1875. [f. prec. + -ISM.] The policy or principles of the Vatican, esp. in respect of papal infallibility and particularly with ref. to the Vatican Council of 1869–70.

Vaticanist (væ·tikănist), *sb.* and *a.* 1846. [f. as prec. + -IST.] **A.** *sb.* An adherent or supporter of the Vatican or of Vaticanism. **B.** *adj.* Of or pertaining to Vaticanism or its adherents 1892.

Vaticide (væ·tisəid). 1728. [f. L. *vates* + -CIDE 1.] One who kills a prophet.

Vaticinal (văti·sinăl), *a.* 1586. [f. L. *vaticinus* prophetic (see next) + -AL[1] 1.] Of the nature of or characterized by vaticination; prophetic, vatic.

Vaticinate (văti·sineit), *v.* 1623. [– *vaticinat-*, pa. ppl. stem of L. *vaticinari* prophecy, f. *vates* prophet; see -ATE[3].] **1.** *intr.* To speak as a prophet or seer; to utter vaticinations; to foretell events. **2.** *trans.* To foretell, predict, prognosticate, or prophesy (a future event) 1652.

Vaticination (vătisinēi·ʃən). 1603. [– L. *vaticinatio*, *-ōn-*, f. as prec.; see -ION.] **1.** A prediction of an oracular or inspired nature; a prophecy, a prophetic utterance or forecast. **2.** The action or fact of vaticinating; also, the power or gift of this 1623.

2. The ambiguous v. of the heathen oracles 1874.

Vaticinator (væti·sineitǫɹ). Now *rare* or *Obs.* 1652. [– L. *vaticinator*, f. as prec.; see -OR 2.] One who writes or utters vaticinations; a prognosticator or prophet.

Vatted (væ·tėd), *ppl. a.* 1843. [f. VAT *v.* + -ED[1].] Placed or stored in a vat; said esp. of wine. Also *fig.*, mellow.

‖**Vaudeville** (vōu·dəvil, Fr. vodvil). 1739. [Fr., earlier *vau* (pl. *vaux*) *de ville*, *vau de vire*, and in full *chanson du Vau de Vire* a song of the valley of Vire (in Calvados, Normandy).] **1.** A light popular song, commonly of a satirical or topical nature; *spec.* a song of this nature sung on the stage. Now *rare* or *Obs.* **2.** A play or stage performance of a light and amusing character interspersed with songs. Also, without article, this species of play or comedy. 1833. **3.** orig. *U.S.* = VARIETY 6 c, d. 1891.

2. Country people always go to see tragedies. None of your flimsy vaudevilles for them! 1862. So **Vaudevi·llian** *a.* and *sb.* **Vau·devillist.**

‖**Vaudois** (vodwa), *sb.* and *a.* 1560. [Fr., repr. med.L. *Valdensis*; see WALDENSES.] **A.** *sb. pl.* Waldensians. **B.** *adj.* Waldensian.

‖**Vaudoux** (vodu). 1864. [Fr.] = VOODOO *sb.*

Vault (vǫlt), *sb.*[1] [ME. *voute*, *vaute* – OFr. *voute*, *vaute* (mod. *voûte*) :– Rom. **volta*, **volvita*, pa. pple. fem. (for *voluta*) of L. *volvere* turn. The sp. with *l* appeared XV (after OFr. usage), and permanently influenced the pronunc. as in FAULT.] **1.** A structure of stones or bricks so combined as to support each other over a space and serve as a roof or covering to this; an arched roof or ceiling. **b.** *transf.* An arching roof or covering resembling a structure of this kind 1470. **c.** The apparent concave surface formed by the sky. Chiefly *poet.* 1586. **d.** *Anat.* One or other of certain concave structures or surfaces normally facing downwards 1594. **e.** The inner portion of a steel furnace 1825. **2.** An enclosed space covered with an arched roof; *esp.* a lower or underground apartment or portion of a building constructed in this form. late ME. **b.** A place of this kind used as a cellar or storeroom for provisions or liquors 1500. **3.** †**a.** An arched space under the floor of a church, used for ecclesiastical purposes; a crypt –1511. **b.** A burial chamber (orig. with arched roof), usu. altogether or partly under ground 1548. †**4.** A covered conduit for carrying away water or filth; a drain or sewer –1700. **5.** A natural cavern, cave, or overarched space; †a deep hole or pit 1535.

1. The long-drawn isle and fretted v. GRAY. **b.** They frequently passed under vaults, formed by fragments of the rock 1773. **c.** When evening turns the blue v. grey COWPER. **d.** The cranial v. 1849. **2.** A paper currency is employed, when there is no bullion in the vaults EMERSON. **3. b.** In as few years their successors will go to the family v. of 'all the Capulets' BURKE. **5.** The v. at the end of the glacier TYNDALL.

Vault (vǫlt), *sb.*[2] 1576. [f. VAULT *v.*[2]] An act of vaulting; a leap or spring.

Vault (vǫlt), *v.*[1] late ME. [– OFr. *vouter* (mod. *voûter*), f. *voute* VAULT *sb.*[1]] **1.** *trans.* To construct with or cover in with a vault or arched roof. Also with *over*. **b.** Of things: To form a vault over (something); to cover like a vault; to overarch 1667. **2.** To bend, arch, or raise (something) after the manner of a vault 1552. **3.** *intr.* To curve in the form of a vault 1805.

1. The various attempts made to v. the naves 1894. **b.** Have I not seen whole armies vaulted o'er With flying jav'lins? 1719. **2.** Hateful is the dark-blue sky, Vaulted o'er the dark-blue sea TENNYSON. **3.** Her mighty orbit vaults like the fresh rainbow into the deep EMERSON.

Vault (vǫlt), *v.*[2] 1568. [– OFr. *volter*, *voulter* turn (a horse), gambol, leap :– Rom. **voltare*, **volutare* or **volvitare*, frequent. of L. *volvere* roll. Assim. to VAULT *v.*[1]] **1.** *intr.* To spring or leap; *spec.* to leap with the assistance of the hand resting on the thing to be surmounted, or with the aid of a pole. **2.** *trans.* To get over, surmount in this way 1884.

1. Vaulting from the ground, His saddle every horseman found SCOTT. *fig.* He was ordained priest a day or two only before he vaulted into the Archbishopric of Canterbury 1882. **2.** The foot-passengers have to v. the gate 1884. Hence **Vau·lter,** one who vaults or leaps.

Vaultage (vǫ·ltėdʒ). 1599. [f. VAULT *sb.*[1] + -AGE.] A vaulted place or area; a series of vaults.

Vaulted (vǫ·ltėd), *ppl. a.* 1553. [f. VAULT *sb.*[1] or *v.*[1] + -ED.] **1.** Having the form of a vault; arched or rounded. **2.** Constructed or furnished with an arched roof; covered in or roofed by a vault 1601.

Vaulting (vǫ·ltiŋ), *vbl. sb.*[1] and *sb.* 1512. [f. VAULT *sb.*[1] and *v.*[1] + -ING[1].] **1.** The construction of a vault or vaults; the operation of covering or roofing with a vault. **2.** The work or structure forming a vault 1513. **b.** With *a* and *pl.* A species, example, or piece of such work 1750.

Vaulting (vǫ·ltiŋ), *vbl. sb.*[2] 1531. [f. VAULT *v.*[2] + -ING[1].] The action of leaping with a vault, esp. as a gymnastic exercise.

V. horse: †**a.** a horse mounted by vaulting, esp. one used for the exercise of leaping into the saddle without the help of a stirrup; **b.** in gymnastics, a wooden figure of a horse employed for exercise in vaulting.

Vaulty (vǫ·lti), *a.* 1545. [f. VAULT *sb.*[1] + -Y[1].] Resembling a vault; having the arching form of a vault.

Sound..which resounds in v. and hollow places 1651.

†**Vaumure.** 1475. [Reduced f. AFr. *vauntmur; see VAUNTMURE.] An advanced wall or earthwork thrown out in front of the main fortifications; the outer wall or series of walls of a fortification or fortress –1656.

Vaunt (vǫnt, *U.S.* vānt), *sb.*[1] Now *rhet.* or *arch.* late ME. [Aphetic f. AVAUNT *sb.*[1]] **1.** Boasting, bragging; arrogant assertion or bearing. **2.** A boasting assertion, speech, or statement; a boast or brag 1597. **3.** A cause or subject of boasting (*rare*) 1791.

1. With all the v. and insolent port of a conqueror 1838. Phr. *To make (one's* or *a) v.*, to boast or brag (now *rare*). **2.** The spirits beneath, whom I seduc'd With other promises and other vaunts Then to submit, boasting I could subdue Th' Omnipotent MILT. Hence **Vau·ntful** (*arch.*) *a.* boastful; *adv.* (*rare*) boastfully.

†**Vaunt,** *sb.*[2] 1589. [Independent use of VANT-, VAUNT- *prefix.*] A front part or portion, *esp.* the van of an army –1624.

Vaunt (vǫnt, *U.S.* vānt), *v.* Now *rhet.* or *arch.* late ME. [– AFr. *vaunter*, (O)Fr. *vanter* :– late L. *vanitare*, later *vantare*, f. L. *vanus* VAIN; partly aphetic f. earlier AVAUNT *v.*[1]] **1.** *intr.* To boast or brag; to use bragging or vainglorious language. Now *rare* or *Obs.* **2.** *trans.* To boast of (something); to commend or praise in a vainglorious manner 1592.

1. He talk'd little, never vaunted, observ'd much, was very secret TEMPLE. Attila vaunted that the grass never grew again after his horse's hoof 1853. **2.** This country, which does not always err in vaunting its own productions H. WALPOLE. So **Vau·nter** (now *arch.*) a boaster, braggart. **Vau·ntery** (now *Obs.* or *arch.*) vaunting, boasting; †a vaunt. **Vau·ntingly** *adv.*

Vaunt-, *prefix*, an AFr. variant of VANT-.

Vaunt-courier (vǫ·nt-, vā·nt‚kūᵊ:riəɹ). Also †**vantcourier.** 1560. [Aphetic f. AVANT-COURIER – Fr. *avant-courrier.* Cf. VAN-COURIER.] †**1.** A soldier or horseman sent out in advance of the main body. Usu. in pl. –1677. **2.** *transf.* One who goes or is sent out in advance in order to prepare the way or to announce the approach of another; a forerunner. Freq. of things. 1561.

†**Vauntmure.** 1562. [Aphetic f. AVANTMURE; see VANT-, VAUNT-.] = VAUMURE –1605.

Vauquelinite (vōᵘ·klinəit). 1823. [f. the name of the French chemist L. N. *Vauquelin* (1768–1829) + -ITE[1] 2 b.] *Min.* Chromate of lead and copper, found in amorphous masses or crystalline crusts of a green or brownish colour.

‖**Vaurien** (vorуæ̃n). Also **vaut-rien, vaut rien.** 1825. [Fr., f. *vaut*, 3rd sing. pres. ind. of *valoir* be worth + *rien* nothing.] A worthless good-for-nothing fellow; a scamp.

Vavasour (væ·văsūᵊɹ). Now *arch.* and *Hist.* ME. [– OFr. *vavas(s)our* (mod. *vavasseur*) – med.L. *vavassor*, supposed, but without conclusive evidence, to derive from med.L. *vassus vassorum* 'VASSAL of vassals'.] A feudal tenant ranking immediately below a baron.

Was nowher such a worthi vauaser CHAUCER. So **Va·vasory,** an estate held by a v.

Va·ward. *Obs.* exc. *arch.* late ME. [Reduced form of †*vaumward*, †*vamward* vanguard. See VANT- *prefix.*] *Mil.* = VANGUARD 1. **b.** *fig.* The forefront; the early part 1597.

b. We that are in the v. of our youth SHAKS.

've, reduced form of HAVE *v.* appended to pronouns in rapid or unstudied speech; e.g. *they've* = they have.

Veal (vīl), *sb.* late ME. [– AFr. *vel*, *veel* = OFr. nom. *veiaus*, obl. *veel* (mod. *veau*) :– L. *vitellus* dim. of *vitulus* calf.] **1.** The flesh of a calf as an article of food. **2.** A calf, esp. as killed for food or intended for this purpose. Now *rare.* late ME. Hence **Veal** *v. trans.* (*U.S.*) to rear (calves) for use as v. **Vea·ly** *a.* resembling v.; *fig.* imperfectly developed; immature.

‖**Vectis** (ve·ktis). 1648. [L., 'lever, crowbar'.] †**1.** A lever –1674. **2.** *Surg.* **a.** An obstetrical instrument used as a lever to free the head of the child 1790. **b.** An instrument employed in operations on the eye 1882.

Vectita·tion. *rare.* 1656. [f. L. *vectitare*, frequent. of *vectare* carry, convey. Cf. L. *vectatio.*] The action of carrying or conveying; the fact of being carried or conveyed.

Vector (ve·ktǫɹ). 1704. [– L. *vector* carrier, traveller, rider, f. *vect-*, pa. ppl. stem of *vehere* carry; see -OR 2.] †**1.** *Astr.* An imaginary straight line joining a planet moving round a centre, or the focus of an ellipse, to that centre or focus. Also *v. radius* = *radius v.* (RADIUS 3 d) –1796. **2.** *Math.* A quantity having direction as well as magnitude, denoted by a line drawn from its original to its final position 1865. **3.** A carrier of disease 1926. Hence **Vecto·rial** *a.* of, pertaining to, or connected with a v. or radius vector.

‖**Veda** (vē[1]·dă). 1734. [– Skr. *vēda* knowledge, sacred knowledge, sacred book, f. **wid-* know (see WIT *sb.*).] One or other of the four ancient sacred books of the Hindus (called the *Rig-*, *Yajur-*, *Sāma-*, and *Atharva-vēda*); the body of sacred literature contained in these books. Hence **Veda·ic** *a.* = VEDIC *a.*; **Ve·daism** = VEDISM.

‖**Vedanta** (vĕdā·ntă, -æ·ntă). 1823. [Skr. *vēdānta*, f. *vēda* VEDA + *anta* end.] One of the leading systems of Hindu philosophy.

The V. system shows us..how pantheism must logically result in scepticism 1849. Hence **Veda·ntic** *a.* **Veda·ntism, Veda·ntist.**

Vedda (ve·dă). Also **Wedda.** 1681. [Sinhalese *veddā* archer, hunter.] A member of a primitive race inhabiting the forest districts of Ceylon.

‖**Vedette** (vĭde·t). 1690. [– Fr. *vedette* scout, sentinel – It. *vedetta*, alt. (after *vedere* see) of south It. *veletta*, f. Sp. *vela* watch, f. *velar* watch :– L. *vigilare.*] *Mil.* A mounted sentry placed in advance of the outposts of an army to observe the movements of the enemy.

V. boat, a small vessel used for scouting purposes in naval warfare.

Vedic (vē[1]·dik), *a.* and *sb.* 1859. [– Fr. *védique* or G. *vedisch*; see VEDA, -IC.] **A.** *adj.* Of, pertaining to, contained, mentioned in, or contemporary with the Vedas. **B.** *sb.* The language of the Vedas, an early form of Sanskrit.

Vedism (vē[1]·diz'm). 1882. [f. VEDA + -ISM.] The system of religious beliefs and practices contained in the Vedas.

‖**Vedro** (vedrō·). 1753. [Russ., 'pail'.] A Russian liquid measure equal to 2·7 imperial gallons.

Veer (vīᵊɹ), *sb.* 1611. [f. VEER *v.*[2]] An act or instance of veering; a change of direction.

Veer (vīᵊɹ), *v.*[1] 1460. [– (M)Du. *vieren* let out, slacken = OHG. *fiaren*, *fieren* give direction to.] †**1.** *trans.* To allow (a sheet or other sail-line) to run out to some extent; to let *out* by releasing –1694. **b.** To let *out* (any line or rope); to allow to run *out* gradually to a desired length 1574. **2.** To allow (a boat, buoy, etc.) to drift further off by letting out a line attached to it 1539. **3.** To let out or pay out (a cable) 1604.

1. b. They rowed it towards the rock, veering out a rope, which they had fastened to the large boat 1793. **2.** They veered out a buoy with a line, which we got hold of MARRYAT. **3.** After veering cable we went to quarters 1870. *To v. and haul*, is to haul and slack alternately on a rope, as in warping, until the vessel or boat gets headway R. H. DANA.

Veer (vīᵊɹ), *v.*[2] 1582. [– (O)Fr. *virer* :– Rom. **virare*, perh. alt. of L. *gyrare* GYRATE, by assoc. with a verb beginning with *v*, e.g. *vertere* turn or *vibrare* shake.] **1.** *intr.* Of the wind: To change gradually; to pass by degrees from one point to another, *spec.* in the direction of the sun's course. orig. *Naut.* **2.** *Naut.* Of a ship: To change course; *spec.* to turn round with the head away from the wind in order to sail on another tack 1620 **3.** To turn round or about; to change from one direction or course to another 1633. **4.** *fig.* To change or alter; to pass from one state, position, tendency, etc. to another; to be variable or changeable 1669. **5.** *absol.* To alter the course of a ship, *spec.* by causing it to swing round with the stern to windward so as to sail on another tack. Also of a ship: To admit of veering. 1625. **6.** *trans.* To turn from one course or direction to another 1647.

1. The next night the wind veered to the eastward 1899. **2.** A-head of all the Master Pilot steers, And, as he leads, the following navy veers DRYDEN. **3.** Grief a fixed star, and joy a vane that veers SWINBURNE. The amazed horse veered quickly to one side 1879. **4.** Seldom has the fortune of war veered round so rapidly 1878. He is a man to v. about like a weathercock 1884. **5.** My lads, lie to, then v. and sail against the wind 1884.

Veery (vīᵊ·ri). *U.S.* 1845. [perh. imitative.] A N. Amer. thrush (*Turdus fuscescens*), also called *tawny* and *Wilson's thrush.*

‖**Vega**[1] (vē[1]·gă). 1645. [– Sp. (Cat.) *vega* = Pg. *veiga.*] In Spain and Spanish America, an extensive, fertile, and grass-covered plain or tract of land.

Vega[2] (vī·gă). 1638. [– Sp. (med.L.) *vega* – Arab. (*al-nasr*) *al-wāḳiᶜ* 'the falling vulture', constellation Lyra.] The brightest star in the constellation Lyra; α Lyræ.

Vegetability (ve:dʒĭtăbi·lĭti). late ME. [– med.L. *vegetabilitas*, f. late L. *vegetabilis*; see next, -ITY.] †**1.** A vegetable organism. late ME. only. **2.** Vegetable character, quality, or nature 1646.

Vegetable (ve·dʒĭtăb'l), *sb.* 1582. [f. the adj.] **1.** A living organism belonging to the vegetable kingdom or the lower of the two series of organic beings; a growth devoid of animal life; = PLANT *sb.* I. 2. †**b.** *pl.* in collective sense: Vegetation –1821. **2.** A plant cultivated for food; *esp.* an edible herb or root used for human consumption and commonly eaten, either cooked or raw, with meat or other articles of food 1767.

2. At a stinted repast of milk and vegetables 1796.

attrib., as *v. dish, garden, soup.*

Vegetable (ve·dʒĭtăb'l), *a.* late ME. [– (O)Fr. *végétable* or late L. *vegetabilis* animating, vivifying, f. *vegetare*; see VEGETATE *v.*, -ABLE.] †**1.** Having the vegetating property of plants; living and growing as a plant or organism endowed with the lowest form of life –1678. **2.** Of or pertaining to, composed or consisting of, or derived or obtained from plants or their parts; of the nature of or resembling a vegetable. Freq. as contrasted with animal or mineral products. 1582. **3.** *V. creation, kingdom, world*, etc., that division of organic nature to which plants belong 1668. **4.** Of, composed or consisting of, or made from esculent vegetables 1746. **5.** Resembling that of a vegetable; *esp.* uneventful, monotonous, dull 1854.

1. Comparysownyd..To a sowle þatw ere v., þe whiche, with-oute sensibilite, Mynystreth lyf in herbe, flour, and tre LYDG. **2.** The superiority of coal to v. tar 1800. The subject of v. development 1842. **5.** The pauper peasantry, weary of a merely v. life, were glad of any pretext for excitement 1854.

Special collocations: **V. acid,** an organic acid derived from a plant. **V. alkali,** carbonate of potash. **V. butter,** the name given to the concrete oil of certain vegetables, because of its resemblance to the butter obtained from the milk of animals, and because it is employed for similar purposes. *V. casein* = LEGUMIN. *V. ivory* (see IVORY 2); also *attrib.* **V. leather,** the plant *Euphorbia punicea*; also, imitation leather made from cotton waste. **V. marrow:** see MARROW[1] 3. **V. mould,** mould having a large proportion of decayed v. matter in it. **V. parchment:** see PARCHMENT 1. **V. silk,** a cotton-like material obtained from the seed-pods of *Chorisia speciosa.* **V. tallow,** a fatty substance obtained from *Stillingia sebifera*, and other plants. **V. wax,** a wax or wax-like substance obtained from plants or v. growths.

Vegetal (ve·dʒĭtăl), *a.* and *sb.* late ME. [– med.L. *vegetalis*, f. *vegetare*; see VEGETATE, -AL[1] 1.] **A.** *adj.* **1.** Characterized by, exhibiting, or producing the phenomena of physical life and growth. Now usu. in contrast with *animal.* **b.** In expressed or implied contrast with *sensible* (or *sensitive*) and *rational.* *Obs.* exc. *Hist.* 1621. **2.** Of or pertaining to, derived or obtained from, plants or vegetables 1596. **3.** = prec. 3. 1664.

1. Phenomena of animal and v. life SPENCER. **b.** All creatures, v., sensible, and rational BURTON. **2.** Manna, Cassia, and v. Salt 1758.

B. *sb.* = VEGETABLE *sb.* 1. 1599.

Vegetant (ve·dʒĭtănt), *a.* and *sb.* 1576. [– L. *vegetans*, *-ant-*, pr. pple. of *vegetare*; see

VEGETATE *v.*, -ANT.] **A.** *adj.* †**1.** Animating, vivifying, invigorating (*rare*) –1615. **2.** Vegetating; vegetable, vegetal. Now *rare.* 1610. †**B.** *sb.* = VEGETABLE *sb.* 1. –1610.

Vegetarian (vedʒĭtēᵊ·riăn), *sb.* and *a.* 1842. [irreg. f. VEGETABLE + -ARIAN.] **A.** *sb.* **1.** One who lives wholly or principally upon vegetable foods; *esp.* one who abstains from animal food obtained by the direct destruction of life. **2.** A member of a fanatical Chinese sect 1895. **B.** *adj.* **1.** Of or pertaining to vegetarians or vegetarianism; practising or advocating vegetarianism 1849. **2.** Of animals: Living on vegetables 1856. **3.** Consisting of vegetables or plants 1868.

Vegetarianism (vedʒĭtēᵊ·riăniz'm). 1853. [f. prec. + -ISM.] The principles or practice of vegetarians; abstention from eating meat, fish, or other animal products.

Is it contrary to the rules of V. to eat eggs? TYNDALL.

Vegetate (ve·dʒĭteᶦt), *v.* 1605. [– *vegetat-*, pa. ppl. stem of L. *vegetare* animate, enliven, f. *vegetus* active, f. *vegēre* be active; see -ATE³.] **1.** *intr.* Of plants, seeds, etc.: To exercise or exhibit vegetative faculties or functions; to grow or develop, or begin to do so. **b.** *transf.* To increase as if by, or present the appearance of, vegetable growth 1744. **2.** *fig.* Of persons, etc.: To live a merely physical life; to lead a dull, monotonous existence, devoid of intellectual activity or social intercourse; to live in dull retirement or seclusion 1740. †**3.** *trans.* To cause to grow; to animate, quicken –1678.

1. A young oak, just vegetating from the acorn 1791. **b.** Naturalists have observed that ore in swamps and pondy ground vegetates and increases 1796. **2.** In short, we rather vegetated than lived 1777. The vast empire of China..has vegetated through a succession of drowsy ages W. IRVING.

Vegetation (vedʒĭtēᶦ·ʃən). 1564. [– L. *vegetatio, -ōn-*, in med.L. sense 'power of growth', etc., f. as prec.; see -ION.] **I. 1.** The action of vegetating or growing; the faculty, process, or phenomena of growth and development as possessed by certain organic substances; vegetal activity or property. †**2.** *transf.* The production of a plant-like formation –1842. **3.** *fig.* Existence similar or comparable to that of a vegetable; dull, empty, or stagnant life spent in retirement or seclusion 1797.

2. The Influence of the Air and Light upon the V. of Salts 1823. **3.** Hedouville..went to spend a life of mere v. in Spain 1854.

II. 1. †**a.** A vegetable form or growth; a plant –1707. **b.** A plant-like growth or formation due to chemical action 1790. **c.** *Path.* A morbid fungoid growth or excrescence occurring on some part of the body 1835. **2.** Plants collectively; plants or vegetal growths as a product of the soil 1727.

2. When an American forest is cut down, a very different v. springs up DARWIN.

Vegetative (ve·dʒĭteᶦtiv), *a.* and *sb.* late ME. [– (O)Fr. *végétatif, -ive* or med.L. *vegetativus*, f. as prec.; see -IVE.] **A.** *adj.* **1.** Having the function of vegetation; endowed with the power or faculty of growth. **b.** *spec.* in *Phys.* and *Bot.* Concerned with growth and development, as opp. to *reproductive* 1857. **2.** Of or pertaining to, concerned or connected with, or characterized by vegetation or growth. late ME. **3.** Causing or promoting vegetation; productive, fertile 1594. **4.** = VEGETABLE *a.* 3. 1677. **5.** *Path.* Characterized by the exercise or activity of the physical functions only 1893.

3. Fullers-earth is..very full of that v. Salt that helps the growth of Plants 1707. **5.** Idiots of v. grade 1899.

†**B.** *sb.* An organic body capable of growth and development but devoid of sensation and thought; a vegetable or plant –1764. Hence **Ve·getative-ly** *adv.*, **-ness.**

Vegete (vīdʒī·t), *a.* Now *rare.* 1639. [– L. *vegetus*; see VEGETATE *v.*] **1.** Healthy and active, flourishing in respect of health and vigour. **2.** Of plants or their parts: Healthy, vigorous; growing strongly or promoting active growth 1651.

1. Even her body was made aëry and v. JER. TAYLOR. **2.** The lower leaf dies..as the upper leaf becomes v. 1800.

Vegetive (ve·dʒĭtiv), *a.* and *sb.* 1526. [Reduced f. VEGETATIVE *a.*, after L. *vegetare* or *vegetus.*] **A.** *adj.* **1.** = VEGETATIVE *a.* 2. **2.** Endowed with the faculty of vegetation or growth 1615. †**B.** *sb.* = VEGETABLE *sb.* 2. –1819.

Vegeto- (ve·dʒĭto), taken as comb. form of the L. stem *veget-*, (see -O-) used in the sense of 'vegetable and..' or 'having a vegetable origin', as *v.-animal, -mineral.*

†**Vegetous,** *a.* 1609. [f. L. *vegetus* VEGETE + -OUS.] = VEGETE *a.* –1696.

Vehemence (vī·ĭmĕns, vī·hĭmĕns). 1529. [– Fr. *véhémence* – L. *vehementia*; see next, -ENCE.] **1.** Intensity or strength *of* smell or colour (*rare*) 1535. **2.** Impetuosity, great force or violence, of physical action or agents 1542. **3.** Great or excessive ardour, eagerness, or fervour of personal feeling or action; passionate force or violence 1529.

3. With an almost savage v. of gesticulation 1839.

Vehemency (vī·ĭmĕnsi, vī·h-). Now *rare.* 1538. [– L. *vehementia*, f. *vehemens, -ent-*; see next, -Y³, -ENCY.] **1.** = prec. 3. **2.** Intensity or severity 1543. **3.** = prec. 2. 1555.

1. You'll learn henceforth to chide with far less v. 1830. **2.** The vehemencie of the fire forceth.. vp an aboundance of vapours 1604.

Vehement (vī·ĭmĕnt, vī·h-), *a.* 1485. [– (O)Fr. *véhément* or L. *vehemens, -ent-* impetuous, violent, perh. for **vemens* 'deprived of mind' (cf. *vecors* cowardly), alt. by assoc. with *vehere* carry.] **I. 1.** Intense, severe; rising to a high degree or pitch. **2.** Of natural forces: Operating with great strength or violence; *esp.* of wind, blowing very strongly or violently 1531. **3.** Of actions: Characterized by great physical exertion; performed with unusual force or violence 1531. †**4.** Of remedies, etc.: Having a powerful effect upon the system –1656.

1. V. dolour and payne 1563. Salt of Tartar requires a v. fire to flux it BOYLE. **2.** The Rain was so v. 1701. **3.** *transf.* These v. exertions of intellect cannot be frequent JOHNSON.

II. 1. a. Of suspicion or likelihood: Very strong. Now *arch.* 1516. †**b.** Of proof, etc.: Strong, cogent; capable of producing conviction –1731. **2.** Of thoughts, feelings, etc.: Extremely strong or deep; eager, passionate; violent, intense 1526. **3.** Of language: Very forcibly or passionately uttered or expressed; resulting from strong feeling or excitement 1533. **4.** Of persons, their character, etc.: Acting or tending to act in a manner displaying passion or excitement 1560. **5.** Of debate, strife, etc.: Characterized by great heat or bitterness 1620.

2. The Queen's v. partisanship 1907. **3.** The most v. protestations of gratitude and fidelity 1848. **4.** For the woman..Ever prefers the audacious, the wilful, the v. hero 1848. **5.** Powerful and v. opposition 1844. Hence **Ve·hement-ly** *adv.*, **-ness.**

Vehicle (vī·ĭk'l; chiefly *U.S.* vī·hik'l), *sb.* 1612. [– Fr. *véhicule* (Paré) or L. *vehiculum*, f. *vehere* carry.] **I. 1.** A substance, *esp.* a liquid, serving as a means for the readier application or use of another substance mixed with or dissolved in it: **a.** *Med.* A medium in which strong or unpalatable drugs or medicines are administered. **b.** *Painting.* A fluid (as water, oil, etc.) with which pigments are mixed for use 1787. **2.** That which serves as a means of transmission, or as a material embodiment or manifestation of something 1650. **3.** A means or medium by which ideas or impressions are communicated or made known; a medium of expression or utterance 1652. **4.** The form, the material or other shape, in which something spiritual is embodied or manifested 1652.

2. If the water be in reality the v. of this disease 1779. The..use of paper as the v. of writing instead of parchment 1837. **3.** Music is not made the v. of poetry, but poetry of music HAZLITT. **4.** When our souls are divested of their grosser vehicles 1670.

II. 1. A material means, channel, or instrument by which a substance or some property of matter (as sound or heat) is conveyed or transmitted from one point to another 1615. **2.** A means of conveyance provided with wheels or runners and used for the carriage of persons or goods; a carriage, cart, wagon, sledge, etc. 1656. **3.** A receptacle in which anything is placed in order to be moved 1678.

1. Air is the usual v. of Sound 1803. **2.** The rumbling and jolting v. stopped at the door of a tavern 1829. Hence **Ve·hicle** *v. trans.* to place or convey in a v.

Vehicular (vĭhi·kiŭlăɹ), *a.* 1616. [– late L. *vehicularis*, f. *vehiculum* VEHICLE *sb.*; see -AR¹.] **a.** Of, pertaining to, associated or connected with a (wheeled) vehicle. **b.** Made, performed, or carried on by means of a vehicle or vehicles 1742. **c.** Of the nature of or serving as a vehicle 1807.

b. V. traffic was almost entirely suspended 1879.

Vehiculate (vĭhi·kiŭleᶦt), *v. rare.* 1660. [f. L. *vehiculum* (current in Eng. contexts XVII–XVIII) + -ATE³.] **a.** *trans.* To carry or convey in or as in a vehicle. **b.** *intr.* To travel, ride, or drive, in a vehicle. So **Vehicula·tion,** conveyance by means of a vehicle or vehicles; vehicular activity or traffic. **Vehi·culatory** *a.* of the nature of, pertaining or relating to, vehicles.

‖**Vehiculum** (vĭhi·kiŭlŏm). Now *rare* or *Obs. Pl.* **vehicula.** 1624. [L.] = VEHICLE *sb.* I. 1, 2, 4, II. 2.

‖**Vehme** (vēᶦ·mə, ‖fē·mə). *Hist.* Also **Fehm.** 1829. [– early mod.G. *Vehme*, now *Fehme, Feme*, MHG. *veme, veime* judgement, punishment.] = next. Hence **Veh·mic** *a.* pertaining to or connected with the Vehmgericht.

‖**Vehmgericht** (vēᶦ·m-, ‖fē·mgərixᵗt). *Hist.* 1829. [– G. *vehmgericht* (now *fe(h)mgericht*), f. *vehm* (of unkn. origin) + *gericht* court, tribunal, rel. to *recht* RIGHT.] A form of secret tribunal which exercised great power in Westphalia from the end of the 12th to the middle of the 16th century.

Veil (vēᶦl), *sb.* ME. [– AFr. *veile* and *veil* = OFr. *voile* and *voil* (mod. *voile* masc. veil, fem. sail) :– L. *vela* pl. sails and *velum* sing. sail, curtain, veil.] **1.** A piece of woollen material forming the outer part of the distinctive head-dress of a nun, and worn so as to drape the head and shoulders. **2.** An article of attire worn, esp. by women, over the head or face, either as a part of the ordinary head-dress, or in order to conceal or protect the face; freq. a piece of net or thin gauzy material tied to the hat and covering the face in order to protect it from the sun or wind ME. **3.** A piece of cloth or other material serving as a curtain or hanging: **a.** *Jewish Antiq.* The piece of precious cloth separating the sanctuary from the body of the Temple or the Tabernacle ME. **b.** *Eccl.* The curtain hung between the altar and the choir, esp. during Lent. Now *Hist.* late ME. **4.** A piece of silk or other material used as a covering, *spec.* (*Eccl.*) to drape a crucifix, image, picture, etc., esp. during Lent, or to cover the chalice, etc. late ME. **5.** *fig.* Something which conceals, covers, or hides; a disguising or obscuring medium or influence; a cloak or mask. late ME. **6.** In various specific uses: A veil-like membrane; a membranous appendage or part serving as a cover or screen; a velum 1760.

1. Phr. *To take the v.*, to become a nun; to enter a convent or nunnery. *The v.*, the life of a nun. **2.** Over her face a v., so transparent as not to conceal 1774. A bridal v. of old Brussels lace (*mod.*). **3. a.** Phr. *Behind, beyond,* or *within the v.*: used fig. or allus., chiefly after Heb. 6:19; now commonly with ref. to the next world. **5.** The v. of anonymity 1882. Phr. *To draw, throw,* or *cast a v. over*: to hide or conceal, to refrain from discussing, to hush up or keep from public knowledge. Hence **Vei·lless** *a.* having no v.; unshaded, unclouded.

Veil (vēᶦl), *v.* late ME. [f. prec.] **1.** *trans.* To cover (a person, etc.) with or as with a veil; to conceal or hide (the face, etc.) by means of a veil or other material; to enveil. **b.** *refl.* To hide, cover, or wreathe (oneself) *in* something 1799. **2.** To bestow the veil of a nun upon (a woman); to admit into the religious life as a nun. late ME. **3.** To cover, enshroud, or screen as or in the manner of a veil; to serve as a veil to (something) 1513. **4.** *fig.* To conceal (some immaterial thing, condition, quality, etc.) from apprehension, knowledge, or perception; to hide the real nature or meaning of (something): freq. with implication of bad motives. 1538. **5.** To render less distinct or apparent; to reduce, soften, tone down 1843.

1. She bow'd as if to v. a noble tear TENNYSON. Psyche, all in lily-whiteness veil'd BRIDGES. **3.** Ornament is but..The beautious scarfe Vailing an Indian beautie SHAKS. Yonder blazing Cloud that veils the Hill MILT. **4.** Pythagoras learned to v. his precepts 1770.

Veiled (vēⁱld), *ppl. a.* 1593. [f. VEIL *v.* or *sb.* + -ED.] **1.** Covered with or wearing a veil; shrouded in a veil. **b.** *Bot.* Having a velum; velate 1793. **2.** Concealed, covered, hidden, as if by a veil; obscure, unrevealed 1612. **b.** *fig.* Covert, disguised; not openly declared, expressed, or stated 1875. **3.** Of sound, the voice, etc.: Indistinct, muffled, obscure 1834.

1. What v. form sits on that ebon throne? SHELLEY. **2.** The more vailed and pregnant parts of Scripture 1612. **b.** The scarcely v. sneer which marked his tone of voice 1891.

Veiling (vēⁱ·liŋ), *vbl. sb.* late ME. [f. as prec. + -ING¹.] **1.** The action of VEIL *v.* 1586. **2.** Something serving as a veil, curtain, or screen. late ME. **b.** Material of which veils are made. Also *pl.* 1882.

2. *Nun's v.*: see NUN *sb.*

Vein (vēⁱn), *sb.* ME. [– (O)Fr. *veine* :– L. *vena*.] **I. 1.** One or other of the tubular vessels in which the blood is conveyed through the animal body; in later use *spec.* one of those by which the blood is carried back to the heart from the extremities (opp. to *artery*). **2.** *Bot.* A slender bundle of fibro-vascular tissue forming an extension of the petiole in the parenchyma of a leaf 1513. **b.** *Ent.* A nervure of an insect's wing 1817. **3.** A marking or an appearance suggestive of a vein; *esp.* an irregular stripe or streak of a different colour in marble or other stone 1642. **b.** A streak or seam of a different material or texture from the main substance 1663.

1. *fig.* In equity and reason the benefitt of trade should be equally disposed into all the vaines of the Commonwealth 1651. **3.** The blue veins of the glacier are beautifully shown TYNDALL. **b.** The spectrum formed by a fine prism of flint glass, free of veins 1831.

II. 1. A small natural channel or perforation within the earth through which water trickles or flows; a flow of water through such a channel ME. **2.** *Min.* A deposit of metallic or earthy material having an extended or ramifying course under ground; a seam or lode; *spec.* a continuous crack or fissure filled with matter (esp. metallic ore) different from the containing rock. late ME. **3.** †**a.** A strip of ground or soil, *esp.* one having a particular character or quality –1693. **b.** A channel or lane of water 1606. **c.** A current of wind; the track in which this moves 1792. **III.** *fig.* **1.** A strain or intermixture *of* some quality traceable in personal character or conduct, in a discourse or writing, etc. 1565. **b.** A line or course *of* thought, etc.; a source *of* information 1704. **2.** A natural tendency towards or a special aptitude or capacity for the production of literary or artistic work; a particular strain of talent or genius 1577. **3.** A special or characteristic style of language or expression in writing or speech 1548. †**4.** A habit or practice –1725. †**b.** An inclination or desire towards something specified –1673. **5.** Personal character or disposition; also, a particular element or trait in this 1565. **b.** A humour or mood 1577.

1. A v. of Superstition ran through all his Actions 1701. **b.** Delay opens new veins of thought JOHNSON. **2.** If I had Virgilles vayne to indite, or Homers quill 1577. **3.** An inscription, somewhat in the v. of Ancient Pistol SCOTT. **5.** When the peacock v. rises, I strut a Gentleman Commoner LAMB. **b.** Phr. *In the v.*, in a fit or suitable mood for something; Nobody can be more amusing when she is in the v. 1905. Hence **Vei·nless** *a.* having no veins: chiefly *Bot.* of leaves. **Vei·nlet**, a small or minor v.; *spec.* in *Bot.* a branch or subdivision of a v.

Vein (vēⁱn), *v.* 1686. [f. prec.] **1.** *trans.* To ornament with coloured, incised, or impressed lines or streaks suggestive of veins. Also with *in*. **2.** Of things: To extend over or through (something) after the manner of veins. Chiefly *poet.* 1807.

2. All the gold That veins the world TENNYSON.

Veined (vēⁱnd), *ppl. a.* 1529. [f. VEIN *sb.* + -ED².] **1.** Furnished or marked with veins (in various senses). **2.** Intersected or marked *with* something (esp. a colour) suggestive of veins 1612.

1. The v. structure of the ice TYNDALL. The million leaves, v. and edge-cut, on bush and tree 1883.

Veining (vēⁱ·niŋ), *vbl. sb.* 1686. [f. VEIN *sb.* or *v.* + -ING.] **1.** The action or process of ornamenting with vein-like markings. **2.** The arrangement of veins or vein-like markings on or in something; a veined appearance or structure; venation 1826.

Veinous (vēⁱ·nəs), *a.* 1634. [f. as prec. + -OUS.] **1.** *Physiol.* **a.** Full of or traversed by veins. **b.** Occupying the veins 1801. **2.** Having large or prominent veins (also *transf.*); formed by out-standing veins 1848.

2. She clasped her v. and knotted hands together DICKENS.

Vei·n(-)stone. 1709. [f. VEIN *sb.*] **1.** Stone or earthy matter composing a vein and containing metallic ore; gangue, matrix. **b.** With pl.: A portion or variety of this 1728. **2.** = PHLEBOLITE, -LITH 1835.

Veiny (vēⁱ·ni), *a.* 1594. [f. VEIN *sb.* + -Y¹.] Full of veins; traversed by veins; marked by veins of colour.

Six blocks of very superior veiny marble 1800.

‖**Velamen** (vĭlēⁱ·mĕn). *Pl.* **-amina.** 1882. [L., f. *velare* to cover.] *Bot.* The outer envelope or covering of the aerial roots of some arums and orchids.

Velar (vī·lăɹ), *a.* and *sb.* 1726. [– L. *velaris* (whence Fr. *vélaire*, etc.), f. *velum* curtain; see VELUM, -AR¹.] **A.** *adj.* **1.** *Arch. V. cupola*: a cupola or dome, terminated by four or more walls. **2.** *Phonetics.* Of sounds: Produced by contact with the soft palate 1876. **3.** *Zool.* Of or pertaining to a velum 1878. **B.** *sb.* A velar guttural 1886.

‖**Velarium** (vĭlēᵊ·riŏm). *Pl.* **-ia.** 1834. [L. *velarium*, f. *velum*; see VELUM, -ARIUM.] **1.** *Rom. Antiq.* A large awning used to cover a theatre or amphitheatre as a protection against sun or rain. **2.** *Zool.* A thin marginal rim on the bell of certain hydrozoans 1888.

Velate (vī·lĕt), *a.* 1857. [f. VELUM + -ATE².] **a.** *Bot.* Furnished with a veil; veiled. **b.** *Zool.* Having a velum. So **Ve·lated** *a.* 1835.

Veld, veldt (velt, felt). Also **velt.** 1801. [S.Afr. Du. *veld*, earlier *veldt* FIELD.] In South Africa, the unenclosed country, or open pasture-land.

Comb.: **v.-cornet,** = *field-cornet*; **v. pig,** the Ethiopian wart-hog (*Phacocœrus ethiopicus*); **v. rat,** the striped rat of S. Africa.

Veld-, veldt-shoe (ve·lt,ʃū, felt-). *S. Afr.* Also **velschoen** (*pl.*); **veldtschoon.** 1822. [– S. Afr. Du. *veldschoen* (Afrikaans *velskoen*), ult. by assim. to VELD of earlier *velschoen*, f. *fel* skin, FELL *sb.*¹ + *schoen* SHOE *sb.*] A light shoe made of untanned hide.

‖**Velella** (véle·lă). 1834. [mod.L. (Gmelin and Lamarck), f. L. *velum* sail.] *Zool.* A genus of siphonophorous oceanic hydrozoans; a member of this genus.

Veliferous (vĭli·fĕrəs), *a.* 1656. [– L. *velifer*, f. *velum* sail; see VELUM, -FEROUS.] †**1.** Carrying sails –1697. **2.** *Zool.* Bearing a velum; membranous 1871.

Veliger (vī·lidʒəɹ). 1877. [mod.L., f. VELUM (sense 2) + L. *-ger* bearing.] *Zool.* A molluscan larva furnished with a velum or ciliated swimming-membrane.

Veligerous (vĭli·dʒĕrəs), *a.* 1877. [f. as prec.: see -GEROUS.] *Zool.* Of certain larval forms: Bearing or furnished with a velum.

Velitation (velitēⁱ·ʃən). Now *rare.* 1607. [– L. *velitatio*, *-ōn-*, f. *velitari* skirmish, f. *veles*; see next, -ATION.] **1.** A slight engagement; a skirmish 1616. **2.** *fig.* A wordy skirmish or encounter 1607.

2. All the velitations were peaceably furled up in this result 1702.

Velites (vī·litīz), *sb. pl.* 1600. [L. *velites*, pl. of *veles*, *velit-*.] Light-armed soldiers employed as skirmishers in the Roman armies. So †**Ve·litary** *a.* of or pertaining to light-armed troops.

Velleity (velī·iti). 1618. [– med.L. *velleitas* (whence also Fr. *velléité*, etc.), f. L. *velle* wish, will; see -ITY.] **1.** The fact or quality of merely willing, wishing, or desiring, without any effort or advance towards action or realization. **2.** With *a* and *pl.* A mere wish, desire, or inclination 1624.

Vellicate (ve·likeⁱt), *v.* Now *rare* or *Obs.* 1604. [– *vellicat-*, pa. ppl. stem of L. *vellicare*, frequent. of *vellere* pluck; see -ATE³.] **1.** *trans.* Of things: To act upon or affect so as to irritate; *esp.* to pluck, nip, pinch, or tear by means of small or sharp points. **b.** Of persons: To tickle or titillate 1755. †**2.** *fig.* To carp at –1686. **3.** *intr.* To twitch; to contract or move convulsively (*rare*) 1670.

1. A hairy, bristly substance, which..will, by pricking and vellicating the coats of stomach and bowels, many times occasion sickness 1783.

Vellication (velikēⁱ·ʃən). Now *rare* or *Obs.* 1623. [– L. *vellicatio*, *-ōn-*, f. as prec.; see -ION.] **1.** The action or process of pulling or twitching; irritation or stimulation by means of small or sharp points; titillation or tickling. **2.** An instance or occasion of this; also, a twitching or convulsive movement, esp. of a muscle or other part of the body 1665.

‖**Vellon** (velyō·n). 1676. [Sp. *vellon*. Cf. BILLON.] Copper, as used in Spanish coinage: esp. in *real (of) v.*

Vellum (ve·lŏm). late ME. [Earlier *velim* (XV) – (O)Fr. *vélin*, f. OFr. *veel* VEAL + *-in* -INE¹; for the change of *n* to *m* cf. *pilgrim*, *venom*.] **1.** A fine kind of parchment prepared from the skins of calves (lambs or kids) and used especially for writing, painting, or binding; also, any superior quality of parchment or an imitation of this 1440. **2.** A piece or sheet of this material; a manuscript or testimonial written on vellum. late ME.

attrib. and *Comb.*: **v. cloth,** tracing-cloth; **v. paper,** a paper made to imitate v. Hence **Ve·llumy** *a.* relating to or resembling v.

Velocimeter (velŏsi·mĭtəɹ). 1842. [f. L. *velox*, *veloc-* swift + -METER.] An instrument or apparatus (variously constructed) for measuring the velocity of engines, vessels, projectiles, etc.

Velocipede (vĭlǫ·sipīd). 1819. [– Fr. *vélocipède*, f. L. *veloc-* (see next) + *pes*, *ped-* foot.] **1.** = HOBBY *sb.*¹ 4. *Obs.* exc. *Hist.* **2.** A travelling-machine having wheels turned by the pressure of the foot upon pedals; *esp.* an early form of the bicycle or tricycle; a 'bone-shaker'. Now *rare.* 1849. Hence **Velo·cipedist** [– Fr. *vélocipédiste*], one who rides a v.

Velocity (vĭlǫ·sĭti). 1550. [– (O)Fr. *vélocité* or L. *velocitas*, f. *velox*, *veloc-* swift, rapid; see -ITY.] **1.** Rapidity or celerity of motion; swiftness, speed. Also, relative rapidity or rate of motion. **2.** Rapidity (absolute or relative) of operation or action; quickness 1674.

1. His Blood flows with its due V. 1704. A v. of upwards of three knots per hour 1880. **2.** Colonel Braithwaite was instructed to anticipate resistance by v. of completion JAS. MILL.

‖**Velours** (vəlūᵊ·ɹ). Also **velour.** 1706. [Fr. *velours* velvet. See VELURE.] **1.** A hatter's velvet pad for smoothing and polishing a hat. **2. a.** A kind of velvet or plush for furniture, carpets, etc. manufactured in Prussia 1858. **b.** A woollen dress-stuff with a velvet pile; also, a material for making hats, usu. with a short soft pile like velvet 1884.

‖**Velum** (vī·lŏm). *Pl.* **vela** (vī·lă). 1771. [mod. use of L. *velum* sail, etc.] **1.** *Anat.* **a.** The soft palate; the membranous septum extending backwards from the hard palate. **b.** One or other of two membranes extending from the vermiform process of the brain 1840. **c.** A triangular fold of the pia mater lying between the third ventricle and the fornix of the brain 1845. **d.** A small triangular space in the inferior region of the bladder 1835. **2.** *Zool.* A membrane or membranous integument, esp. one occurring in molluscs, medusæ, or lower forms of animal life 1826. **3.** *Bot.* A membranous structure or covering in certain fungi 1832.

Velure (vĭlⁱūᵊ·ɹ). 1587. [– OFr. *velour*, *velous* (mod. *velours*); see VELOURS.] †**1.** Velvet –1748. **2.** = VELOURS 1. 1880. **3.** A fabric of linen, silk, or jute resembling velvet.

Velu·tinous, *a.* 1826. [perh. f. It. *vellutino*

(= Fr. *velouteux*) in the same sense, f. *velluto* velvet; but the relations are undetermined.] *Ent.* and *Bot.* Having a surface resembling velvet; velvety.

Ve·lveret. Now *rare.* 1769. [irreg. f. next.] A variety of fustian with a velvet surface.

Velvet (ve·lvėt). [ME. orig. three syll. (cf. the vars. *velowet, velewet*) – OFr. *veluotte*, f. *velu* velvety – med.L. *villutus*, f. L. *villus* down; *veluet* passed through the stage *velwet* (XV–XVI) on its way to *velvet.*] **I. 1.** A textile fabric of silk having a short, dense, and smooth piled surface; a kind or variety of this. **b.** A piece of this material (*rare*). late ME. **2.** *transf.* The soft downy skin which covers a deer's horn while in the growing stage. late ME. **3.** A surface, substance, etc. comparable to velvet in respect of softness or general appearance 1597. **4.** Profit, gain, winnings 1901.

1. Phr. *On v.*, in a position of ease or advantage; in an advantageous or prosperous condition. *colloq.*

II. *attrib.* **a.** In the sense 'made of v.', as *v. bag, gown*, or 'covered with v.', as *v. cushion* ME. **b.** In the sense 'smooth or soft like v., velvety', as *v. down, hand, leaf.* Also with names of colours, esp. *v. black.* 1588.

Comb.: **v.-brush**, a velvet-covered brush used to remove dust, etc. from garments made of v.; **-cloth**, a plain cloth with a gloss, used in eccl. embroidery, and as a material for womens' jackets; **-cork**, the best kind of cork bark, which is of a reddish colour; **-pile** (a carpet or cloth) having a pile like that of v.

b. In names of plants or animals, as **v.-bean**, an annual climbing plant (*Mucuna utilis*) bearing velvety pods; **v. crab**, a species of swimming crab (*Portunus puber*); **-dock**, common mullein; **-duck**, a species of scoter (*Œdemia fusca*); **-grass**, *Holcus lanatus*; **†v. runner**, the water-rail; **v. scoter** = *velvet-duck*; **v. wheat**, a variety of white wheat with downy ears. Hence **Ve·lveted** *a.*, covered with or dressed in v. **Ve·lveting**, velvet as a commercial fabric, esp. *pl.* v. goods.

Velveteen (velvėtī·n, *attrib.* ve·lvėtīn). 1776. [f. VELVET *sb.*] **1.** A fabric having the appearance and surface of velvet, but made from cotton in place of silk. **b.** *attrib.* Made of this material 1824. **2.** *pl.* **a.** Trousers or knickerbockers made of v. 1863. **b.** *transf.* A gamekeeper (as usu. wearing velveteen clothes) 1857.

†Velvet head. 1576. [f. VELVET 2.] The head of a deer while the horns are still covered with velvet –1674.

Velvet-leaf. 1707. [f. VELVET II. *b.*] **1.** The tropical shrub *Cissampelos pareira*, the root and bark of which are employed medicinally. **2.** The tree-mallow, *Lavatera arborea*, or a leaf of this 1728.

Velvety (ve·lvėti), *a.* 1752. [f. VELVET + -Y[1].] **1.** Having the smooth and soft appearance or feel of velvet. **b.** Applied to colours 1819. **2.** Characteristic of velvet; similar to that of velvet 1846. **3.** *fig.* Unusually or attractively smooth, soft, or gentle 1861.

1. b. The v. brown of a stag's throat 1883. **3.** The other's v. manner made him chafe and fret 1861.

‖**Vena** (vī·nă). *Pl.* **venæ** (vī·ni). late ME. [L.] A vein. (Used only in conjunction with Latin adjs. or genitives.)

The abdominal branches of the v. portæ 1822. The aortic and v. cava pressures 1899.

Venal (vī·năl), *a.*[1] 1652. [– L. *venalis*, f. *venum* that which is sold or for sale; see -AL[1] 1.] **1.** Of things: **a.** Exposed or offered for sale, that may be bought, as an ordinary article of merchandise. Also, associated or connected with ordinary sale or purchase. Now *arch.* 1662. **b.** Of offices, privileges, etc.: Capable of being acquired by purchase, instead of being conferred on grounds of merit or regarded as above bargaining for 1675. **c.** Of support, favour, etc.: That may be obtained for a price 1652. **2.** Of persons: Capable of being bought over; of an unprincipled and hireling character 1670. **3.** Subject to mercenary or corrupt influences 1718.

1. a. The figs..might be v. at the nearest stall 1888. **b.** The V. Indulgences and pardons of the Church of Rome 1839. **c.** You may command a v. vote '*Junius' Lett.* **2.** Rome was as v. under the popes as Jugurtha found her under the Republic FROUDE. **3.** Corruption on her v. throne THOMSON.

Venal (vī·năl), *a.*[2] Now *rare* or *Obs.* 1615. [f. L. *vena* VEIN *sb.* + -AL[1].] **1.** Of blood: Contained in the veins. **2.** Of, connected with, forming, or of the nature of a vein or veins 1661.

Venality (vĭnæ·lĭti). 1611. [– Fr. *vénalité*, or late L. *venalitas* f. L. *venalis* VENAL *a.*[1]; see -ITY.] **1.** The quality or fact of being for sale (*rare*). **2.** The quality of being venal; readiness to give support or favour in return for profit or reward; prostitution of talents or principles for mercenary considerations 1683.

Venatic (vĭnæ·tik), *a.* 1656. [– L. *venaticus*, f. *venat-*, pa. ppl. stem of *venari* hunt; see -ATIC.] Of, pertaining to, employed in, or devoted to hunting.

I adore, with a sort of v. worship, both a fox and a hound 1889. So **Vena·tical** *a.*, **-ally** *adv.*

Vena·tion[1]. Now *rare* or *Obs.* late ME. [– L. *venatio, -ōn-*, f. as prec.; see -ION.] The action or occupation of hunting wild animals.

Venation[2] (vinēi·ʃən). 1830. [f. L. *vena* vein + -ATION.] *Bot.* and *Ent.* The arrangement or structure of the veins in the leaves of plants or the wings of insects.

Venatorial (venătōə·riăl), *a.* 1830. [f. L. *venatorius* + -AL[1] 1.] **1.** Connected with hunting. **2.** Given to hunting; addicted to the chase 1881. So **Ve·natory** *a.*

Vend, *sb.* 1618. [f. next.] **1.** Sale; opportunity of selling. **2.** *spec.* Sale of coals from a colliery; the total amount sold during a certain period 1708.

Vend (vend), *v.* 1622. [– (O)Fr. *vendre* or L. *vendere* sell, f. *venum* (see VENAL *a.*[1]) + *-dere*, var. of *dare* give.] **1.** *intr.* To be disposed of by sale; to find a market or purchaser. **2.** *trans.* To sell; to dispose of by sale; to trade in as a seller 1651. **3.** *fig.* To give utterance to, to put forward, advance (an opinion, etc.) 1657.

1. No Books v. so nimbly, as those that are sold (by Stealth as it were) and want Imprimaturs 1689. **2.** The right to v. books and newspapers 1879. **3.** He is not free to v. in his pulpit the extravagances of an eccentric individualism 1907. Hence **Ve·ndable** *a.* (now *rare*) = VENDIBLE *a.* late ME.

Vendace (ve·ndės). 1769. [– OFr. *vendese, -oise* (mod. *vandoise*) – Gaulish **vindesia*, f. **vindos* white (cf. OIr. *find*, W. *gwynn* white).] **a.** A species of small freshwater fish (*Coregonus vandesius*) belonging to the same genus as the pollan, found in the lake of Lochmaben in Scotland. **b.** A closely-allied species (*C. gracilior*) found in Derwentwater.

Vendean (vendī·ăn), *sb.* and *a.* 1796. [– Fr. *vendéen*, f. *Vendée*, a maritime department in western France; see -AN.] **A.** *sb.* An inhabitant of La Vendée, esp. one who took part in the insurrection of 1793 against the Republic. **B.** *adj.* Of or pertaining to La Vendée, esp. in connection with that insurrection 1796.

Vendee (vendī·). 1547. [f. VEND *v.* + -EE[1].] The person to whom a thing is sold; the purchaser.

Vender (ve·ndəɹ). 1596. [f. VEND *v.* + -ER[1].] One who sells; a seller: occas., a street-seller.

‖**Vendetta** (vende·tă). 1855. [It. :– L. *vindicta* vengeance.] **1.** A family blood-feud, usu. of a hereditary character, as customary among the Corsicans. **2.** A similar blood-feud in other communities 1861.

Vendible (ve·ndĭb'l), *a.* and *sb.* late ME. [– L. *vendibilis*, f. *vendere* sell; see -BLE.] **A.** *adj.* **1.** Capable of being vended or sold; that may be disposed of by sale; saleable, marketable. **b.** = VENAL *a.*[1] 1 b, c. 1579. **†c.** Of persons: = VENAL *a.*[1] 2. –1668. **†2.** Offered for sale; that may be bought –1756. **†3.** *fig.* Current, accepted, acceptable –1678.

1. They cannot therefore bee v. because they are not valuable 1633. **2.** Houses, like our Tauernes. Where is v. Wine. 1634.

B. *sb.* A thing admitting of being sold or offered for sale 1681. Hence **Ve·ndibleness. Ve·ndibly** *adv.*

†Ve·nditate, *v.* 1600. [– *venditat-*, pa. ppl. stem of L. *venditare*, frequent. of *vendere* sell; see -ATE[3].] *refl.* and *trans.* To set out as if for sale; to exhibit ostentatiously –1678. So **†Vendita·tion**, the action of putting forward or displaying in a favourable or ostentatious manner –1854.

Vendition (vendi·ʃən). 1542. [– L. *venditio*, f. pa. ppl. stem of *vendere* sell; see -ITION.] The action of selling; disposal or transfer by sale.

Vendor (ve·ndǭɹ). 1594. [– AFr. *vendor, -dour* (mod. Fr. *vendeur*); see VEND, -OR 2.] orig. *Law.* One who disposes of a thing by sale; a seller.

Vendue (vendiū·). *U.S.* and *W. Indies.* 1686. [– Du. *vendu*, †*vendue* – (O)Fr. (now dial.) *vendue* sale, f. *vendre* VEND.] A public sale; an auction: freq. in phr. *at v., by v.*

Veneer (və-, vĭnīə·ɹ), *sb.* 1702. [– G. *furni(e)r, fourni(e)r*; see next and VENEERING.] **1.** One of the thin slices or slips of fine or fancy wood, or other suitable material, used in veneering. **2.** Material prepared for use in veneering, or applied to a surface by this or some similar process 1750. **3.** *fig.* A merely outward show or appearance *of* some good quality 1868. **4.** One or other of many species of moths of the genus *Crambus* or family *Crambidæ*; a grass-moth 1819.

3. Heartfelt courtesy..was replaced by a superficial v. of forced politeness 1882.

Veneer (və-, vĭnīə·ɹ), *v.* 1728. [Later form of FINEER *v.*[1] – G. *furni(e)ren* – (O)Fr. *fournir* FURNISH *v.*] **1.** *trans.* To apply or fix as veneering. **2.** To cover or face with veneer 1742. **b.** *fig.* To invest with a merely external or specious appearance of some commendable or attractive quality. Usu. const. *with.* 1847.

2. b. And one the Master, as a rogue in grain Veneer'd with sanctimonious theory TENNYSON.

Venee·ring, *vbl. sb.* 1706. [Later f. *faneering, fineering* – G. *furni(e)rung, fourni(e)rung*; see prec.] **1.** The process of applying thin flat plates or slips of fine wood (or other suitable material) to cabinet-work or similar articles; also, the result obtained by this process. Often *fig.* **2.** Wood or other material in the form of veneer; a facing of this 1789.

†Vene·fic, *a.* 1646. [– L. *veneficus*, f. *venenum* poison; see -FIC.] Practising, or dealing in, poisoning; acting by poison; having poisonous effects –1702. So **†Vene·fical** *a.* venefic; practising or associated with malignant sorcery or witchcraft 1584–1716.

†Ve·nefice. late ME. [– L. *veneficium*, f. *veneficus*; see prec.] The practice of employing poison or magical potions; the exercise of sorcery by such means –1652. Hence **†Venefi·cial, Venefi·cious** (now *rare*) *adjs.* = VENEFICAL *a.*

Venenose (ve·nĕnōᵘs), *a.* Now *rare.* 1673. [– late L. *venenosus*, f. *venenum* poison; see -OSE[1].] Poisonous, venomous. So **Vene·nous** *a.* (now *rare*). late ME. **†Veneno·sity**, poisonous quality or property 1539.

Venerable (ve·nĕrăb'l), *a.* and *sb.* late ME. [– (O)Fr. *vénérable* or L. *venerabilis*, f. *venerari* VENERATE; see -ABLE.] **1.** Of persons: Worthy of being venerated, revered, or highly respected and esteemed, on account of character or position. **a.** As an epithet of ecclesiastics (or ecclesiastical bodies), now *spec.* of archdeacons or, in the R.C. Church, of those who have attained the first degree of canonization. (Abbreviated *Ven.*) late ME. **b.** *gen.* (*rare*) 1641. **2.** Commanding veneration or respect in virtue of years and high personal qualities 1480. **b.** Applied to personal features or attributes of these 1726. **3.** Of things: **a.** Worthy of religious reverence 1504. **b.** Worthy of veneration or deep respect on account of noble qualities or associations 1601. **c.** Impressive, august 1615. **4.** Worthy of veneration or respect on account of age or antiquity 1610. **b.** Ancient, antique, old 1792. **†5.** Reverent, reverential –1710.

1. The Archbishop of Arles, v. for his years and his virtues 1849. **a.** Peter the V., of Cluny 1834. **2.** A white beard which made him look v. 1862. **3. b.** Holy Writers, and such whose names are v. unto all posterity SIR T. BROWNE. **4.** His looks adorn'd the v. place GOLDSM. **b.** Those muskets cased with v. rust 1792. Hence **Venerabi·lity. Ve·nerableness. Ve·nerably** *adv.*

Venerate (ve·nĕreⁱt), *v.* 1623. [– *venerat-*, pa. ppl. stem of L. *venerari* (*-are*) reverence, adore; see -ATE³.] **1.** *trans.* To regard with feelings of respect and reverence; to look upon as something exalted, hallowed, or sacred; to reverence or revere. **2.** To pay honour to (something) by an act of reverence 1844.

1. Who v. themselves, the world despise YOUNG. The ruined chapels are still venerated 1851. **2.** Thrice he venerated the sacred remains 1844. So **Ve·nerator,** one who venerates; a reverencer of something.

Veneration (venĕrēⁱ·ʃən). late ME. [– (O)Fr. *vénération* or L. *veneratio, -ōn-*, f. as prec.; see -ION.] **1.** A feeling of deep respect and reverence directed towards some person or thing. **2.** The action or fact of showing respect and reverence; the action or practice of venerating 1526. **3.** The fact or condition of being venerated 1625.

1. She expressed a great v. for the liturgy of the Church of England 1759. Phr. *To have* or *hold in v.* **2.** The v. paid to Mary in the early Church 1852. **3.** Princes are like to Heauenly Bodies.. which haue much V., but no Rest BACON.

Venereal (vĭnīᵊ·riăl), *a.* and *sb.* late ME. [f. L. *venereus* (f. *venus, vener-* love) + -AL¹ 1.] **1.** Of or pertaining to, associated or connected with sexual desire or intercourse. **2.** Resulting from or communicated by sexual intercourse with an infected person; symptomatic of or associated with a disease so caused 1658. **b.** Of persons: Infected with or suffering from venereal disease 1683. **c.** *ellipt.* as *sb.* Venereal disease 1843. †**3.** Of persons: Under the influence of Venus; addicted to venery or lust –1728.

7. Such is hunger and thirst, and the venereall affect, vsually called lust 1610. **2.** A lusty robust Souldier dangerously infected with the V. Disease 1667.

†**Vene·rean,** *a.* (and *sb.*) 1550. [f. as prec. + -AN.] **1.** Connected or associated with, relating or pertaining to Venus or her service –1685. **2.** Of or pertaining to sexual desire or intercourse –1700. **3.** Addicted to venereal pleasures. Also as *sb.*, a person of this character. –1631.

†**Vene·reous,** *a.* 1509. [f. as prec. + -OUS.] **1.** Addicted to or desirous of sexual enjoyment; libidinous, lustful –1713. **2.** = VENEREAL *a.* 1. –1795. **3.** Exciting or stimulating sexual desire –1694.

Ve·nerer. *arch.* 1845. [f. VENERY¹ + -ER¹.] A huntsman.

†**Ve·nerous,** *a.* 1562. [f. L. *venus, vener-* love + -OUS.] **1.** = VENEREAL *a.* 1. –1651. **2.** = VENEREOUS *a.* 3. –1651.

Venery¹ (ve·nĕri). Now *arch.* ME. [– (O)Fr. *vénerie*, f. *vener* :– Rom. **venare*, for L. *venari* hunt; see -ERY.] **1.** The practice or sport of hunting beasts of game; the chase. †**2.** Wild animals hunted as game –1630.

1. Phr. *Beasts, game, hounds of v.*

Venery² (ve·nĕri). 1497. [– med.L. *veneria*, f. L. *venus, vener-* love; see -Y³.] **1.** The practice or pursuit of sexual pleasure; indulgence of sexual desire *arch.* †**2.** *fig.* A source of great enjoyment –1625.

Venesection (venĭse·kʃən). 1661. [– med. L. *venæ sectio* 'cutting of a vein'; see VEIN, SECTION.] *Med.* **1.** The operation of cutting or opening a vein; phlebotomy; the practice of this as a medical remedy. **2.** An instance of this 1834. Hence **Ve·nesect** *v. intr.* to practise v.

Venetian (vĭnī·ʃăn, və-), *sb.* and *a.* [Late ME. *Venicien* – OFr. *Venicien* (mod. *Vénitien*); later assim. to med.L. *Venetianus*, f. L. *Venetia* (It. *Venezia*).] **A.** *sb.* **1.** A native or inhabitant of Venice. †**2.** *pl.* Hose or breeches of a particular fashion originally introduced from Venice –1612. †**3.** A sequin of Venice, as current in India, etc. –1835. **4.** A closely-woven cloth having a fine twilled surface, used as a suiting or dress material 1710. **5.** *ellipt.* A Venetian blind 1816. **B.** *adj.* **1.** Of or pertaining to Venice 1554. **2.** In special collocations, denoting things characteristic of Venice, esp. articles produced there, or others made in imitation of these 1548.

1. *V. School*: (*a*) a school of painting, distinguished by its mastery of colouring, which originated in the 15th c. and reached its climax in the 16th; (*b*) a school of Italian architecture originating in the early part of the 16th c. **2.** **V. blind,** a window blind composed of narrow horizontal slats so fixed on strong tapes as to admit of ready adjustment for the exclusion or admission of light and air. **V. carpet,** a common make of carpet, usu. striped, in which the warp alone is shown. **V. chalk,** a white compact talc or steatite, used for marking on cloth. **V. door,** a door having side lights on each side for lighting an entrance hall. **V. glass,** Venice glass. †**V. hose,** = sense A. 2. **V. mast,** a tall pole ornamented with spiral bands of colour, used in the decoration of streets or open spaces on special occasions. **V. pearl,** a solid artificial pearl. **V. point,** a variety of point-lace. **V. sumach,** the southern European shrub *Rhus cotinus.* **V. window,** a window in three separate apertures, the two side ones being narrow, and separated from the centre by timber only.

Venge (vendʒ), *v.* Now *arch.* ME. [– OFr. *vengier*, (also mod.) *venger* :– L. *vindicare* VINDICATE.] = AVENGE *v.* So **Ve·nger,** an avenger (now *poet.* or *rhet.*) †**Ve·ngeress.**

Vengeable, *a. Obs.* or *dial.* late ME. [– AFr. *vengable*, f. *venger*; see prec., -ABLE.] **1.** Inclined or ready to take vengeance or inflict retaliative injury. **2.** Characterized by or arising from vengeance or revenge; cruel, dreadful. late ME. **3.** As an intensive: Very great, severe, intense, etc. 1532. Hence **Ve·ngeably** *adv.* late ME.

Vengeance (ve·ndʒăns,) *sb.* (and *adv.*) ME. [– (O)Fr. *vengeance*, f. *venger*; see VENGE, -ANCE.] **1.** The act of avenging oneself or another; retributive infliction of injury or punishment. **2.** With *a* and *pl.* An act or instance of retributive or vindictive punishment ME. **b.** In imprecations, usu. with *on. Obs.* or *arch.* 1500. †**3.** Used to strengthen interrogations –1828. †**b.** As *adv.* Extremely, intensely –1711.

1. Thou God to whom vengeaunce belongeth, shewe thy self COVERDALE *Ps.* 93:1. Where was thine arm, O V.! CAMPBELL. Phr. *To take v.* **2.** Taking..a cruel v. on these deluded wretches BURKE. **b.** A veng'ance on 't, there 'tis SHAKS.

Phr. *With a v.*: †**a.** With a curse or malediction. **b.** As an intensive: With great force or violence; in an extreme degree; to an unusual extent.

Vengeful (ve·ndʒfŭl), *a.* 1586. [f. VENGE + -FUL, after *revengeful*; cf. *avengeful* (XVI).] **1.** Harbouring revenge; seeking vengeance; vindictive 1599. **b.** Inflicting vengeance; serving as an instrument of vengeance. Said of a weapon, the hand or arm, etc. 1586. **2.** Of actions or feelings: Characterized or prompted by revengeful motives; arising from a desire for vengeance 1635.

1. Ulysses is..subtle, v., cunning 1873. **b.** So could he bid the v. fire fall from heaven 1869. **2.** Pond'ring v. Wars PRIOR. Hence **Ve·ngeful-ly** *adv.*, **-ness.**

Venial (vī·niăl), *a.* and *sb.* ME. [– OFr. *venial* (mod. *véniel*) – late L. *venialis*, f. *venia* forgiveness.] **A.** *adj.* **1.** Worthy or admitting of pardon, forgiveness, or remission; not grave or heinous; pardonable, light: **a.** Of sin; *spec.* in *Theol.* as opp. to *deadly* or *mortal.* **b.** Of crimes, offences, etc. 1604. **2.** Of an error or fault: That may be excused or overlooked; light, unimportant, trivial 1581. †**3.** Permissible; blameless (*rare*) –1725.

1. a. In þis wise skippith v. in to dedly synne CHAUCER. **b.** If they do nothing, 'tis a Veniall slip SHAKS. **2.** If a boy has committed some.. quite v. fault 1876. **3.** Where God..With Man.. us'd To sit indulgent,..permitting him the while V. discourse unblam'd MILT.

†**B.** *sb.* A venial sin or offence; a light fault or error –1671. Hence **Venia·lity,** the property or quality of being v.; a matter of favour or grace. **Ve·nially** *adv.*

Venice (ve·nis). 1506. [– Fr. *Venise* :– L. *Venetia*; see def.] The name of a city (the capital of the province of the same name) in the north-east of Italy, used attrib. to designate various articles made there or having some connection with the locality.

V. crown, (*Her.*) the crown, or cap of state, worn by the Doge of V. **V. glass** (*a*) a very fine and delicate kind of glass, orig. manufactured at Murano, near V.; (*b*) an article made of this, esp. a drinking vessel or vial; (*c*) a Venetian mirror. **V. talc,** steatite or soap-stone. **V. treacle** (now *arch.*), in old pharmacy, an electuary composed of many ingredients and supposed to possess universal alexipharmic and preservative properties.

‖**Venire** (vĭnəiᵊ·ri). 1665. [ellipt. for next.] *Law.* = next 1.

V. de novo = next 1 b. *V. man* (*U.S.*) one summoned to serve on a jury under a writ of *V. facias*, a juryman.

‖**Venire facias** (vĭnəiᵊ·ri fēⁱ·ʃiæs). 1444. [L., lit. 'make or cause to come'.] *Law.* **1.** A former judicial writ directed to a sheriff requiring him to summon a jury to try a cause or causes at issue between parties. *Obs.* or *Hist.* **b.** *Venire facias de novo*, an order for a new trial of a cause, upon the same record, owing to some defect or irregularity in the first trial 1797. †**2.** A writ issued against a person indicted of a misdemeanour, summoning him to appear before the court –1769.

Venison (ve·nz'n, ve·niz'n). [ME. *veneso(u)n, venisoun* – OFr. *veneso(u)n, -ison* (mod. *venaison*) :– L. *venatio, -ōn-*; see VENATION¹, -ISON.] **1.** The flesh of an animal killed in the chase or by hunting and used as food; formerly applied to the flesh of the deer, boar, hare, or other game animal, now almost entirely restricted to the flesh of various species of deer. **2.** Any beast of chase or other wild animal, esp. of the deer kind, killed by hunting. Now *arch.* ME. **b.** *collect.* Now *arch.* ME.

‖**Venite** (vĭnəi·ti). ME. [L.; 2nd pers. pl. imp. of *venire* come.] The ninety-fifth psalm (beginning *Venite, exultemus Domino* 'O come, let us sing unto the Lord') used as a canticle at Matins or Morning Prayer; the invitatory psalm; also, a musical setting of this.

Venom (ve·nəm), *sb.* and *a.* [ME. *venim* – OFr. *venim*, (also mod.) *venin* :– Rom. **venimen*, alt. (after L. words in *-īmen*) of *venenum* potion, drug, poison; for the change of *n* to *m* cf. *pilgrim, vellum.*] **A.** *sb.* **1.** The poisonous fluid normally secreted by certain snakes and other animals and used by them in attacking living creatures. **2.** Poison, esp. as administered to or drunk by a person; any poisonous or noxious substance, preparation, or property; a morbid secretion or virus. Now *rare.* ME. **3.** *fig.* Something comparable to or having the effects of poison; any baneful, malign, or noxious influence or quality; bitter or virulent feeling, language, etc. ME. **4.** With *a* and *pl.* A poison; a particular kind of poison or virus. late ME.

1. What the..hurtfull Worm with canker'd v. bites MILT. **2.** Anoynted let me be with deadly Venome SHAKS. **3.** The veneme of this Book wrought upon the hearts of men CLARENDON. So **Ve·nom** *v.* (*Obs.* or *arch.*) *trans.* = ENVENOM *v.*

Venomous (ve·nəməs), *a.* ME. [– (O)Fr. *venimeux*, f. OFr. *venim*, after late L. *venenosus*, f. *venenum*; see prec., -OUS.] †**1.** *fig.* Morally or spiritually hurtful; pernicious –1610. **2.** Containing, consisting or full of, infected with venom; destructive of, harmful or injurious to life on this account ME. †**b.** Of a wound, etc.: Envenomed –1774. †**c.** Harmful or injurious *to* something –1691. **3.** Of animals, *esp.* snakes, or their parts: Secreting venom; having the power or property of communicating venom by means of bites or stings; inflicting or capable of inflicting poisonous wounds in this way ME. **4.** *fig.* Having the virulence of venom; rancorous, spiteful, malignant; embittered, envenomed ME. †**5.** Treated with venom or poison –1631. **6.** Of, pertaining to, or of the nature of venom. late ME.

1. That venemous Pelagian Heresie 1610. **2.** Of the venemous apples wherwith the Canibales inuenime theyr arrowes 1555. **c.** *Cor.* IV. i. 23. **3.** The poisonous Snakes are divided into two groups—the Viperiform Snakes and the V. Colubrines 1880. **4.** The Venemous Mallice of my swelling heart SHAKS. The doctor seemed to me a v. little creature 1911. **6.** The glands that serve to fabricate this v. fluid GOLDSM. Hence **Ve·nomous-ly** *adv.*, **-ness.**

Venose (vī·nōᵘs), *a.* 1661. [– L. *venosus*, f. *vena* VEIN *sb.*; see -OSE¹.] Venous; *spec.* in *Bot.* and *Ent.* Hence **Veno·sity** *Path.*, the state of being venous; *spec.* of the blood.

Venous (vī·nəs), *a.* 1626. [– L. *venosus*, or f. L. *vena* + -OUS.] **1.** Filled with, full of, or having veins; veined; veiny. **2.** *Anat.* and *Phys.* Of, pertaining to, or of the nature of a blood-vein or veins; having the form or function of a vein 1681. **b.** Of blood: Contained in the veins; characterized by a dusky or blackish red colour due to loss of oxygen. (Opp. to *arterial.*) 1728. **c.** Consisting or composed of veins 1826. **3.** Of, pertaining to, or characteristic of vein-blood 1845.

1. If the veins diverge from the midrib towards the margin, ramifying as they proceed, such a leaf has been called a v. or reticulated leaf 1832. **2. c.** *V. system*, the aggregate of veins by which the blood is conveyed from the various parts of the body to the heart. Hence **Ve·nous-ly** *adv.*, **-ness.**

Vent (vent), *sb.*[1] late ME. [var. of FENT *sb.*; for the *v*, see VAN *sb.*[1]] An opening or slit in a garment; now *spec.* the slit in the back of a coat.

Vent (vent), *sb.*[2] 1508. [Partly – Fr. *vent* wind; partly after Fr. *évent*, f. *éventer* EVENT *v.*[2]] **I. 1.** The action of emitting or discharging; emission or discharge *of* something; utterance *of* words (*rare*). **2.** The action, usu. on the part of something confined or pent up in a comparatively small space, of escaping or passing out; means, power, or opportunity to do this; issue, outlet 1558. **b.** The windage of a firearm or gun 1644. **3.** *fig.* Means of outlet afforded to or obtained by a feeling, faculty, activity, etc.; expression or utterance, or the relief afforded by these 1603. **4.** With *a*: An opportunity or occasion of escaping or issuing from a receptacle; a discharge or evacuation 1644. **5.** Something which serves as an outlet for an emotion, energy, etc. 1667.

1. Phr. †*To make v. of*, to speak or talk of; Thou didst make tollerable v. of thy trauell SHAKS. **2.** Phr. *To find, get, have, make, want v.*; The smoke found ample v. through the holes TYNDALL. *To give v.*, (*a*) to cause or allow to issue or flow out; (*b*) *fig.* to give outlet, expression, or utterance (to an emotion, faculty, etc.); to relieve in this way. †*To take v.*, (*a*) of news, etc., to become known, to be divulged or let out; (*b*) of a mine or powder, to explode imperfectly; to lose explosive power. **3.** Passion found v. in words 1880. **4.** *fig.* For, though in whispers speaking, the full heart Will find a v. WORDSW. **5.** Laughter is a v. of any sudden joy 1713.

II. 1. †**a.** An opening by which blood issues from the body –1606. **b.** The anus, anal or excretory opening of (†persons or) animals, esp. of certain non-mammalians, as birds, fishes, and reptiles 1587. **2.** An aperture or opening occurring or made in something and serving as an outlet for air, liquid, or other matter; a passage or hole by which matter is carried off or discharged from the interior of something; a vent-hole 1570. **b.** *spec.* The funnel or pipe of a volcano 1604. **3.** An opening, aperture, or hole; occas., one by which air, etc. enters or is admitted 1593. **b.** The hole or channel in the breech of a cannon or firearm through which fire is communicated to the charge; the touch-hole; the adjustable part of a gun containing this, a vent-piece 1667. **4.** Any outlet or place of issue; a passage, exit, or way out. Chiefly *fig.* 1602.

1. a. *Ant. & Cl.* v. ii. 353. **2. b.** A 'solfatara' or v. emitting only gaseous discharges 1882. **3.** Through little vents and crannies of the place The wind wars with his torch to make him stay SHAKS. **4.** Winds for ages pent In earth's dark womb have found at last a v. COWPER.

III. Of an otter: The action of coming to the surface of the water in order to breathe; an instance or occasion of this 1653.

attrib. and *Comb.*, as *v.-cock*, *-pipe*; **v. feather,** one of the feathers covering or surrounding a bird's v.; **v.-piece** *Gunnery*, (*a*) a plug of steel or wrought iron containing the v.; (*b*) the block which closes the rear of the bore in a breech-loader.

Vent, *sb.*[3] *Obs.* exc. *arch.* 1545. [– (O)Fr. *vente* :– Rom. **vendita*, fem. pa. ppl. formation on L. *vendere* VEND.] **1.** The fact of commodities being disposed of by sale or of finding purchasers. **2.** The fact, on the part of persons, of disposing of goods by sale; opportunity for selling; market or outlet for commodities 1548. †**3.** An inn or tavern; a baiting or posting house –1625.

1. Like fish that could not find v. in London H. WALPOLE. **2.** If husbandmen..have a ready v. for their commodities HUME.

Vent (vent), *v.*[1] late ME. [prob. aphetic f. †*avent* (XIV) – OFr. *aventer*, var. of *esventer* (mod. *éventer*) create wind, expose to the air, divulge, scent :– Rom. **exventare*, f. L. *ex* Ex-[1] + *ventus* wind.] **I.** *trans.* †**1.** To provide (a liquor cask, etc.) with a vent or outlet for gas or vapour –1703. **b.** *fig.* To relieve or unburden (one's heart or soul) in respect of feelings or emotions. Also *refl.* 1626. †**2.** To discharge, eject, cast or pour out (liquid, smoke, etc.); to carry off or away; to drain in this way. Also with advs. –1793. †**b.** Of persons, animals or their organs: To cast out, expel, or discharge, esp. by natural evacuation –1846. **3.** *fig.* To give vent to (an emotion, feeling, a sigh, groan); to give free course or expression to; to make manifest or known 1596. **b.** To let loose, pour out, wreak (one's anger, spleen, etc.) *on* or *upon* a person or thing 1697. **4.** *fig.* To give out or forth, publish or spread abroad, by or as by utterance; to utter (a word, expression, etc.). Now *rare* or *arch.* 1602. **5.** *refl.* Of a thing: To discharge itself; to find issue or exit; *esp.* of an emotion, faculty, quality, etc.: to express or show itself *in* something 1650. **6.** To supply (a gun) with a vent or vent-piece 1828.

1. b. To v. an Heart overflowing with Sense of Success STEELE. **3.** I..v. a heaving sigh MARSTON. I must v. my griefes, or heart will burst MARSTON. **b.** To v. their spleen on the first idle coxcomb they can find 1816. **5.** The Presidency v. the most bitter complaints 1817. **6.** The coffee houses were the chief organs through which the public opinion of the metropolis vented itself MACAULAY.

II. *intr.* **1.** Of an exhalation, liquid, smoke, etc.: To find or make an outlet or way of escape from a confined space; to come, flow, pass, or pour *out* or *away* by a vent or opening. Now *rare.* 1540. †**2.** Of a bottle, confined space, etc.: To have or obtain an outlet by which the contained matter can escape –1655.

1. New wine..by venting bursteth the bottle 1604.

III. †**1.** *intr.* Of an animal: To snuff up the air, esp. in order to pick up the scent of something –1660. †**2.** = SCENT *v.* 1. –1735. **3.** Of an otter, or beaver: To rise to the surface in order to breathe 1590.

2. The Fox,..if he vents any thing which causes fear, returns to ground again 1660. Hence **Ve·nter**[2], one who gives vent to a statement, doctrine, etc., esp. of an erroneous, malicious, or objectionable nature.

Vent, *v.*[2] Now *dial.* 1478. [– Fr. *vente* VENT *sb.*[3]] **1.** *trans.* To sell or vend (commodities or goods); to dispose of by sale. †**2.** *intr.* Of goods: To have or find sale; to sell, go off (well or ill) –1670.

‖**Venta** (ve·ntă). 1610. [Sp.] A Spanish hostelry or wayside inn.

Ventage (ve·ntėdʒ). 1602. [f. VENT *sb.*[2] + -AGE.] **1.** One of the series of apertures or holes in the length of a wind instrument for controlling the notes; a finger-hole. (In mod. use, perh. after Shakespeare.) **2.** An air-hole or vent-hole 1623.

Ventail (ve·ntēⁱl). Now *Hist.* ME. [– OFr. *ventail* or *ventaille*, f. *vent* wind; see -AL[1] 2.] †**1.** A piece of armour protecting the neck, upon which the helmet fitted; a neck-piece –1450. **2.** The lower movable part of the front of a helmet, as distinct from the vizor; latterly, the whole movable part including the vizor. late ME.

2. Through whose bright ventayle..His manly face..lookt foorth SPENSER.

Venter[1] (ve·ntəɹ). 1544. [In I – law-Fr. *venter*, for (O)Fr. *ventre* :– L. *venter* belly; in II immed. – L.] **I. 1.** One or other of two or more wives who are sources of offspring to the same person; orig. (and in later use (chiefly) *Law.* **2.** The womb as the source of one's birth or origin; hence *transf.*, a mother in relation to her children 1579.

1. To his Sons by another V...he gave Money-portions 1665. **2.** My Sister, by one V. 1630.

II. †**1.** In man, quadrupeds, etc.: One or other of the three chief cavities containing viscera, consisting of the abdomen, thorax, and head. Usu. in pl. or qualified –1771. **2.** †**a.** One of the four stomachs in ruminants –1706. **b.** *Anat.* The abdomen, the belly 1706. **c.** That part in lower forms of animal life corresponding in function or position to the belly of mammals 1790. **3.** *Anat.* †**a.** The belly or body of a muscle, into which are inserted arteries and nerves –1728. **b.** The belly or hollowed surface of a bone 1851.

Ve·nt-hole. Also **venthole, vent hole.** 1577. [f. VENT *sb.*[2] + HOLE *sb.*] **1.** A hole or opening for the admission or passage of air, light, etc. **2.** A hole or opening in a furnace, etc., for the escape of smoke and gases or the admission of fresh air 1612. **b.** Any hole by which an enclosed space communicates with the outside air 1750. **3.** *spec.* An air-hole in a cask; a vent 1669.

Ventiduct (ve·ntidɒkt). 1615. [f. L. *ventus* wind + *ductus* DUCT.] A pipe or passage serving to bring cool or fresh air into an apartment or place, esp. in Italy and other warm climates. **b.** A conduit for the passage of wind, air, or steam 1685.

Ventil (ve·ntil). 1876. [– G. *ventil* – It. *ventile* – med.L. *ventile* sluice.] *Mus.* One or other of the valves or shutters which control the wind-supply of the various groups of stops in an organ.

Ventilate (ve·ntilēⁱt), *v.* 1527. [– *ventilat-*, pa. ppl. stem of L. *ventilare* brandish, fan, winnow, agitate, in late L., discuss, air a subject, f. *ventus* wind; see -ATE[3].] **I. 1.** To fan or winnow (corn, etc.) 1609. †**2.** To increase (a fire or flame) by blowing or fanning –1742. †**3.** To put or set (air) in motion; to move or agitate; to renew or freshen in this way –1775. **4. a.** To expose (blood) to the chemical action of the air; to aerate, oxygenate 1668. **b.** To expose (substances, etc.) to fresh air so as to keep in or restore to good condition 1755. **5.** Of air: To blow upon, to pass over or circulate through, so as to purify or freshen 1695. **6.** To supply (a room, building, mine, etc.) with fresh air in place of that which is vitiated, exhausted, or stagnant; to produce a free current of air in (some enclosed space) so as to maintain a fresh supply 1758.

4. a. Lungs v. the blood 1891. **b.** The wheat should be kept cool, well ventilated, and frequently moved 1855. **5.** Sweeping breezes v. each street 1810. **6.** How to v. and purify his cottages 1888.

II. 1. *trans.* To examine or investigate (a question, topic, etc.) freely or thoroughly by discussion or debate; to bring to public notice or consideration in this way 1527. **2.** To publish *abroad*; to make public (*rare*) 1530. **3.** To utter; to make known to others 1637. †**4.** To carry on or take part in (a controversy) –1678.

1. Politicians do not 'discuss' subjects in the year of grace 1857: they 'v.' them 1857. **3.** The habit.. of using novels to v. opinions 1855. Hence **Ve·ntilative** *a.* of, pertaining to, or promoting ventilation.

Ventilation (ventilēⁱ·ʃən). 1456. [– (O)Fr. *ventilation* or L. *ventilatio*, *-ōn-* (exposure to the air, Pliny; in AL. discussion), f. as prec.; see -ION.] **I.** †**1.** A stir or motion of the air; a current of air; a breeze –1752. **2.** Movement or free course of the air 1605. **3.** Oxygenation of the blood, *spec.* in the act of respiration 1615. **4.** The admission of a proper supply of fresh air, esp. to a room, building, mine, or other place where the air readily becomes stagnant and vitiated; the means or method by which this is accomplished 1664.

2. Upon such consideration of winds and v. the Ægyptian granaries were made open SIR T. BROWNE. **3.** The lungs,..in which the air undergoes the important process of v. 1822. **4.** Before v., the foul air..became infectious 1753.

II. 1. The action of fanning or blowing; †the winnowing of corn in this way 1519. **2.** *fig.* Free or open discussion or debate upon a doctrine, question, or subject of public interest; the action or fact of bringing to public notice in this way 1614.

2. Careful v. of questions 1850.

Ventilator (ve·ntilēⁱtəɹ). 1743. [f. VENTILATE + -OR 2.] **1.** A mechanical contrivance or apparatus by which the vitiated or heated air is drawn or removed from a building, ship, mine, etc., and a fresh supply introduced; also freq., a simple opening or open shaft, so placed or contrived as to facilitate renewal of the air. **b.** The former Ladies' Gallery in the House of Commons 1832. **2.** One charged with ventilating a building, etc. 1750.

†**Ventose,** *sb.* 1500. [– OFr. *ventose,* (also mod.) *ventouse* – late L. *ventosa* (cf. *ventosa cucurbita* Juvenal), fem. of *ventosus*; see next.] *Surg.* A species of cupping-glass –1704.

Ventose (ve·ntōᵘs), *a. rare.* 1721. [– L. *ventosus*, f. *ventus* wind; see -OSE¹.] Windy, flatulent.

Ventosity (ventǫ·sĭti). Now *rare* or *Obs.* late ME. [– (O)Fr. *ventosité* or late L. *ventositas* flatulence, f. *ventosus*; see VENTOSE *a.*, -ITY.] **1.** *Path.* The state of having the stomach or other part of the alimentary canal charged with wind; flatulency. **b.** *pl.* Gases generated in the stomach or bowels; attacks of flatulence. late ME. **†2.** A blast or puff of wind, esp. one coming from the stomach –1725. **†3.** The state of being windy; windiness –1661. **4.** *fig.* Pompous conceit, vanity, or bombast 1550. **†b.** An instance of this; an idle conceit –1681.

4. Vaine glory..is windy and full of v., consisting of popular applause 1631.

Ve·nt-peg. 1707. [f. VENT *sb.*²] A small peg for inserting in the vent-hole of a cask; a spile.

Ventrad (ve·ntræ̆d), *adv.* 1847. [f. L. *venter, ventr-* abdomen + -AD II.] *Anat.* and *Zool.* Toward the ventral surface of the body.

Ventral (ve·ntrăl), *a.* and *sb.* 1739. [f. VENTER¹ II + -AL¹ 1. Cf. Fr. *ventral.*] **A.** *adj.* **1.** Occurring or taking place in the region of the abdomen; abdominal. **2.** *Anat.* and *Zool.* Of, pertaining to, or situated in or on the abdomen; abdominal 1752. **3.** *Bot.* Of or belonging to the anterior or lower surface 1832. **4.** *V. segment*, in Acoustics: the part of a vibrating string, air column, etc. between two nodes 1830.

1. V. rupture is a protrusion of some of the bowels through the interstices of the abdominal muscles 1797. To..shake luxuriously with a silent r. laughter GEO. ELIOT. **2.** The v. fins, serve to raise and depress the fish 1802. The v. (or front) aspect of the body HUXLEY.

B. *sb.* **1.** A ventral fin; one of the fins corresponding to the hind legs of quadrupeds 1834. **2.** *Ent.* One or other of the segments of the abdomen, esp. in *Coleoptera* 1891. Hence **Ve·ntrally** *adv.* in a v. direction; with respect to the venter or abdomen.

Ventri- (ve·ntri), comb. form of L. *venter* VENTER¹, as in **Ventrico·rnu** *Anat.*, the ventral extension of gray matter in the substance of the spinal cord; hence **Ventrico·rnual** *a.*; **Ventrime·son** *Anat.*, the median line on the ventral surface of the body; hence **Ventrime·sal** *adj.*

Ventricle (ve·ntrik'l). late ME. [– L. *ventriculus*, dim. of *venter* VENTER¹; see -CULE.] *Anat.* and *Zool.* **1.** One or other of the two cavities in the heart by means of which the blood is circulated through the body; also, the cavity of the heart in certain animals which fulfils this function. **2.** One or other of a series of cavities in the brain (normally numbering four in the adult human being) formed by enlargements of the neural canal. late ME. **†3.** The stomach in man or quadrupeds –1806. **b.** The digestive sac or organs in birds, fishes, insects, and certain reptiles 1575. **4.** Any small hollow or cavity in an animal body, serving as a place of organic function; in later use, the recess or space between the true and false vocal cords on each side of the larynx 1641.

2. *Pineal v.*: see PINEAL *a.* b. **3.** Whether I will or not,..my Heart beats,..my V. digests what is in it 1676. So **Ve·ntricule.**

Ventricose (ve·ntrikōᵘs), *a.* 1756. [app. irreg. f. VENTRICLE + -OSE¹. The AL. *ventricosus* pot-bellied is not continuous with this word.] **1.** Swelling out in the middle or on one side, after the manner of an animal's belly; bellied, protuberant, strongly convex. **2.** Of persons: Big-bellied 1843.

1. The flowers are white and v. 1841. So **Ve·ntricoseness, Ventrico·sity. Ve·ntricous** *a.* (1702).

Ventricular (ventri·kiŭlăɹ), *a.* 1822. [f. VENTRICULUS + -AR¹.] **1.** Of or pertaining to the stomach; abdominal, gastral, ventral. **2.** Of, pertaining to, forming part of, or affecting a ventricle 1838. **3.** Of the nature of a ventricle 1841.

Ventriculite (ventri·kiŭləit). 1822. [– mod.L. *Ventriculites*, f. L. *ventriculus* ventricle; see -ITE¹ 2 a.] A fossil sponge belonging to the genus *Ventriculites* or the family *Ventriculitidæ.*

‖**Ventriculus** (ventri·kiŭlŏs). 1710. [L., dim. of *venter* VENTER¹.] **1.** *Anat.* and *Zool.* = VENTRICLE 2. **b.** The gizzard in birds and insects 1891. **2.** = VENTRICLE 1. 1771. **3.** The body-cavity of a sponge 1877.

Ventriloquial (ventrilōᵘ·kwiăl), *a.* 1836. [f. VENTRILOQUY + -AL¹ 1.] **1.** Of sounds: Such as are produced by ventriloquism. **2.** Of, belonging to, or consisting of ventriloquism 1838.

Ventriloquism (ventri·lŏkwiz'm). 1797. [f. VENTRILOQUY + -ISM.] **1.** The art or practice of speaking or producing sounds in such a manner that the voice appears to proceed from some person or object other than the speaker, and usu. at some distance from him. **b.** An instance of this; a ventriloquial sound 1839. **2.** The fact or practice of speaking or appearing to speak from the abdomen 1818.

Ventriloquist (ventri·lŏkwist). 1656. [f. as prec. + -IST.] One who practises or is expert in ventriloquism. Also applied to birds and beasts. Hence **Ventriloqui·stic** *a.* using or practising ventriloquism; ventriloquial.

Ventriloquize (ventri·lŏkwəiz), *v.* 1832. [f. as prec. + -IZE.] **1.** *intr.* To use or practise ventriloquism; to cast the voice. **2.** *trans.* To utter as a ventriloquist 1865.

Ventriloquous (ventri·lŏkwəs), *a.* 1713. [f. L. *ventriloquus* (used 1644–1762 in Engl.) ventriloquist, f. *venter* VENTER¹ + *loqui* to speak, after Gr. ἐγγαστρίμυθος + -OUS.] **1.** Using or practising ventriloquism. **2.** Produced by or as by ventriloquy; ventriloquial 1768.

Ventriloquy (ventri·lŏkwi). 1584. [– mod. L. *ventriloquium*, f. L. *ventriloquus* ventriloquist; see prec.] = VENTRILOQUISM.

Ventripotent (ventri·pǫtĕnt), *a.* Now *rare.* 1611. [– Fr. *ventripotent* (Rabelais), in XIX prob. allusive. Cf. med.L. *ventripotens* (XII), whence the Rabelaisian word.] **a.** Big-bellied. **b.** Gluttonous 1823.

Ventro- (ve·ntro), comb. form, on Gr. models, of VENTER¹, as in **v.-i·nguinal** *a.*, of or pertaining to the abdominal cavity and the inguinal canal; **-la·teral** *a.*, of or belonging to the ventral and lateral sides of the body.

Venture (ve·ntiŭɹ, -tʃəɹ), *sb.* 1450. [Aphetic f. *aventure* ADVENTURE, partly through apprehending *a-* as the indef. article (esp. in phr. *at aventure*).] **†1.** Fortune, luck; chance. **b.** *At a v.*, at random, by chance, without due consideration or thought 1509. **†2.** Danger, jeopardy, hazard, or peril; the chance or risk of incurring harm or loss –1823. **3.** A course or proceeding the outcome of which is uncertain, but which is attended by the risk of danger or loss 1566. **4.** A commercial enterprise in which there is considerable risk of loss as well as chance of gain 1584. **b.** That which is ventured in a commercial enterprise or speculation 1597. **5.** The (or an) act of venturing upon something; also, the means or result of so venturing 1842.

1. b. A certain man drew a bow at a v. 1 *Kings* 22:34. **3.** I'll be your scholar, I cannot lose much by the v. sure FLETCHER. **4.** Hath all his ventures faild, what not one hit? SHAKS. **b.** He lost his v., sheep and gold 1764. **5.** On her great v., Man, Earth gazes MEREDITH.

Venture (ve·ntiŭɹ, -tʃəɹ), *v.* late ME. [Aphetic f. *aventure* ADVENTURE *v.*] **I. 1.** *trans.* To risk the loss of (something); to hazard, risk, or stake. **2.** *refl.* To risk (oneself); to dare to go. Now *arch.* 1572. **3.** To take the risk of sending or causing to go where loss or detriment is possible. Now *rare.* 1599.

1. To v. a greater Good for a less LOCKE. Provb. *Nought* (or *nothing*) *v., nought* (or *nothing*) *have.* **3.** The streame..he found so exceeding swift, that it was like to be dangerous to v. our horses ouer 1617.

II. 1. To run or take the risk of (something dangerous or harmful); to brave the dangers of (ice, water, etc.). Now *rare.* 1548. **b.** To risk trusting or confiding in (a person) 1777. **2.** To dare or have the courage to attempt or undertake (some action); to risk the issue or result of; to venture upon 1595. **b.** To dare to give, put forth, or express (an opinion, statement, etc.); to make or utter tentatively or with some degree of presumption 1638.

1. That they had rather venter hanging than starving 1675. **2.** I am afraide, and yet Ile v. it SHAKS. **b.** I..ventured a sly joke at the good effects of matrimony LYTTON.

III. 1. *intr.* To risk oneself; to brave the risks or chances of a journey, voyage, etc.; to dare to go or proceed 1534. **2.** To run or take risks; to incur the chance of danger, peril, loss, disapproval, etc. 1560. **3.** With inf.: To dare, presume, go so far as, be so bold as (*to* do something) 1559.

1. Your marchantes..venteryng to Iseland for Fysshe 1534. **2.** You have deeply ventured; But all must do so who would greatly win BYRON. **3.** I humbly v. to say, all these things may be done 1687.

Phr. **To v. on** or **upon:** †**a.** To dare to advance upon, approach, or attack (a person or animal). **b.** To accept or take the risk of (an action, etc.), to dare to do, make, or take (something), realizing that a risk is being run. *To v. at*, to make a venture or attempt at; to guess at. Hence **Ve·nturer,** one who ventures, an adventurer; one who undertakes or shares in a commercial or trading venture, esp. by sending goods or ships beyond seas, a merchant-venturer.

Ve·nturesome, *a.* 1661. [f. VENTURE *sb.* or *v.* + -SOME¹.] **1.** Of persons: = next 1. 1677. **2.** Hazardous, risky 1661.

1. He was most v. in his schemes for action 1863. Hence **Ve·nturesome-ly** *adv.*, **-ness.**

Venturous (ve·ntiŭrəs, ve·ntʃərəs), *a.* 1565. [Aphetic f. ADVENTUROUS *a.*, after VENTURE *sb.* and *v.*] **1.** Of persons, etc.: Disposed to venture upon or undertake something of a dangerous or risky nature; bold, daring, or enterprising in action or opinion; adventurous. **2.** Of the nature of a venture; hazardous, risky 1570. **3.** Arising from or indicative of a readiness to encounter hazard or risk; bold, daring 1584. **b.** Of opinions, etc.: Daringly bold or original; going further than the evidence or facts appear to warrant 1608.

1. Those who at the Spear are bold And ven-t'rous MILT. He..drives his v. plough-share to the steep GOLDSM. **2.** Bloody Wreaths in vent'rous Battels won PRIOR. **3.** There was something of romance in Jeanie's v. resolution SCOTT. Hence **Ve·nturous-ly** *adv.*, **-ness.**

Venue (ve·niu). ME. [– (O)Fr. *venue*, subst. use of pa. pple. fem. of *venir* :– L. *venire* come.] **†I. 1.** An assault or attack. ME. only. **2.** A thrust or hit in fencing; a stroke or wound with a weapon –1662. **3.** A bout or turn of fencing –1659.

II. *Law.* The county, district, or locality where an action is laid; the place where a jury is summoned to come for the trial of a case 1531. **b.** The scene of a real or supposed action or event; also *fig.*, a position taken up by a disputant 1843. **c.** An appointed place of meeting, esp. for a match or competition 1857.

Thus we say, Twelve of the Assize ought to be of the same Venew where the Demand is made 1728. The Attorney-General may lay the venue where he pleases 1838. Phr. *To change the v.*, (*a*) *change of v.* **b.** Here Mr. Froude changes the v. and joins issue on the old battle ground SPENCER.

Venule (ve·niul). 1850. [– L. *venula*, dim. of *vena* VEIN *sb.*] A small or minor vein.

Venus (vī·nŏs). *Pl.* **Venuses,** †**Veneres.** OE. [– L. *Venus* (gen. *Veneris*).] **I. 1.** *Myth.* The ancient Roman goddess of beauty and love (esp. sensual love), or the corresponding Greek goddess Aphrodite. **b.** A representation, esp. a statue or image, of Venus 1568. **c.** A local or other distinct conception of the goddess; also *transf.* a goddess in other mythologies corresponding to Venus 1770. **d.** A beautiful or attractive woman 1579. **†2.** The desire for sexual intercourse; indulgence of sexual desire; lust, venery –1746. **†3.** A quality or characteristic that excites love; a charm, grace, or attractive feature –1711.

1. c. Under the special protection of Hathor, the Egyptian V. 1877. **d.** The dreams..of the sable Venuses which they were to find on the banks of the Congo 1816. **3.** All the Graces, Veneres, pleasures, elegances attend him BURTON.

II. 1. *Astr.* The second planet in order of distance from the sun, revolving in an orbit between those of Mercury and the earth; the morning or evening star ME. †**2.** *Alch.* Copper. So in *crystals, saffron, salt, vinegar, vitriol of V.* –1807. †**3.** *Her.* A name for the tincture green or vert when the names of planets are used in blazoning –1704. **4.** The highest cast or throw in playing with huckle-bones 1611. **5.** *Zool.* A genus of bivalve molluscs typically representing the family *Veneridæ*; a member of this genus or family; a venerid 1770.

Comb. (of the possessive, with or without *'s*): **Venus's hair-stone, pencil,** names applied to rock crystals enclosing slender hair-like or needle-like crystals of hornblende, asbestos, oxide of iron, oxide of manganese, etc.

b. *Bot.* **Venus's basin, bath,** the wild teasel, *Dipsacus sylvestris*; **Venus's comb,** the shepherd's needle, *Scandix pecten-veneris*; **Venus's flytrap,** the N. Amer. marsh-plant *Dionæa muscipula*; **Venus' hair,** the maiden-hair, *Adiantum capillus-veneris*; **Venus('s) looking-glass,** one or other of certain plants belonging to the genus *Specularia*, esp. *S.* (or *Campanula*) *speculum*; **Venus's navelwort,** (*a*) the penny-wort, *Cotyledon umbilicus*; (*b*) one or other species of annual plants belonging to the genus *Omphalodes*, esp. *O. linifolia*; **Venus's slipper,** the lady's slipper, *Cypripedium calceolus*.

c. *Zool.* **Venus's comb,** the shell of *Murex tribulus*, which has many long thin spines; **Venus's fan,** a sea-fan, esp. *Rhipodogorgia* (*Gorgonia*) *flabellum*; **Venus's flower-basket, purse,** a glass-sponge of the genus *Euplectella*, esp. *E. aspergillum*; **Venus-shell,** a bivalve mollusc belonging to the family *Veneridæ* or related species; a venus, murex, or cowry; **Venus's slipper,** any shell of the genus *Carinaria*.

Ve·ny. *Obs.* exc. *dial.* 1578. [Phonetic var. of VENUE.] **1.** = VENUE 2. Also *fig.*, *esp.* a sharp retort, a pungent remark. **2.** = VENUE 3. 1594.

†**Ver.** late ME. [– L. *ver* or OFr. *ver*.] The season of spring; springtime –1630.

Veracious (vĕrēⁱ·ʃəs), *a.* 1677. [f. L. *verax, verac-*, f. *verus* true; see -ACIOUS.] **1.** Habitually speaking or disposed to speak the truth; observant of the truth; truthful. **2.** Characterized by veracity; conforming to truth; true, accurate 1777. **3.** That estimates or judges truly or correctly 1851.

1. The testimony of the two v. and competent witnesses DICKENS. **2.** The v. narrative of Balaam and his ass 1868. **3.** The young ardent soul that enters on this world..with v. insight,..will find this world a very mad one CARLYLE. Hence **Vera·cious-ly** *adv.*, **-ness.**

Veracity (vĕræ·sĭti). 1623. [Earliest in Cockeram, app. f. VERACIOUS after *capacious/capacity*, etc. Fr. *véracité* may be of independent origin (cf. OFr. *verace* true), and poss. partly the source of the Eng., but the relation cannot be determined.] **1.** The quality or character in persons of speaking or stating the truth; habitual observance of the truth; truthfulness, veraciousness. **2.** Agreement of statement or report with the actual fact or facts; accordance with truth; correctness, accuracy 1736. **3.** Correspondence with external facts; exactness in the indication of these 1666. **4.** That which is true; a truthful statement; a truth 1852.

1. Phr. *Of v.*, trustworthy, veracious, truthful; Authors..of the greatest authority and v. 1671. **2.** Narratives where historical v. has no place JOHNSON. **3.** He was under the painful necessity of omitting the v. of his optics DICKENS.

Veranda, verandah (vĕræ·ndă). 1711. [– Hindi *varandā* (cf. Bengali *bārāndā*) – Pg. *varanda*, †Sp. *baranda* railing, balustrade, balcony, of unkn. origin.] An open portico or roofed gallery extending along the front (and occas. other sides) of a dwelling or other building, erected chiefly as a protection or shelter from the sun or rain.

After dinner we will sit in the verandah 1879. Hence **Vera·nda(h)ed** *a.* furnished with a v. or verandahs.

Veratr-, comb. form or stem of VERATRUM, occurring in chemical terms, as **veratrate,** a salt of veratric acid; **veratric** *a.*, derived from or contained in species of *Veratrum*; **veratrol,** a colourless aromatic oil obtained by distilling veratric acid with excess of baryta.

Veratria (vĕrēⁱ·triă). 1821. [f. VERATRUM + -IA¹.] *Chem.* = next.

Veratrine (ve·rătrīn). 1822. [– Fr. *vératrine*, f. next; see -INE⁵.] *Chem.* A poisonous vegetable alkaloid or mixture of alkaloids, obtained esp. from various species of *Veratrum*, and used medicinally as an ointment for the relief of neuralgia, rheumatism, etc.; veratria.

‖**Veratrum** (vĕrēⁱ·trŏm). 1577. [L., hellebore.] *Bot.* A perennial genus typical of the family *Veratreæ* of liliaceous plants; a plant belonging to this genus, esp. the white hellebore (*V. album*); also, the rhizome of this.

Comb.: **v.-resin,** a brownish resin extracted from the seeds of sabadilla (*V. sabadilla*).

Verb (vɔ̄ɹb). late ME. [– (O)Fr. *verbe* or L. *verbum* word, verb.] *Gram.* That part of speech which is used to express action or being.

Active, auxiliary, deponent, desiderative, frequentative, inchoative, intransitive, transitive, etc. *verb*: see the adjs. *Principal v.*, the chief verb in a sentence; †*fig.* the chief or most important thing; The violin was scarce knowne tho' now the principall v. 1728.

Verbal (vɔ̄·ɹbăl), *a.* and *sb.* 1484. [– (O)Fr. *verbal* or late L. *verbalis*, f. *verbum*; see prec. -AL¹ 1.] **A.** *adj.* **1.** Of persons: **a.** Dealing in or with words, esp. with mere words. †**b.** Using many words; talkative, verbose –1647. **c.** Interested in or attending to the mere words of a literary composition 1709. **2.** Consisting or composed of words; also, pertaining to or manifested in, words 1530. **b.** Of the nature of or denoting a word 1605. **3.** Concerned with, affecting, or involving words only, without touching things or realities 1605. **b.** Finding expression in words only, without being manifested in action 1622. **c.** Consisting merely in words or speech 1618. **4.** Expressed or conveyed by speech instead of writing; stated or delivered by word of mouth; oral 1591. **5.** = VERBATIM *a.* 1. 1612. **b.** In respect of each single word 1790. **6.** Of, pertaining to, or derived from a verb 1530.

1. b. *Cymb.* II. iii. 111. **c.** The labours of v. critics 1782. **2.** A series of v. quibbles and jingles 1791. Phrases. *V. inspiration*: see INSPIRATION II. 1 a. *V. note*, in diplomacy, an unsigned note or memorandum sent as a mere reminder of some matter not of immediate importance. **3.** The opposition between these two modes of speaking is rather v. than real JOWETT. **4.** He did it by v. order from Sir W. Coventry PEPYS. **5.** You will perceive that it is almost a v. Copy 1786. **b.** The sacred writers never aim at v. accuracy in their quotations FARRAR. **6.** *Verbals* or *V. Nouns*, those Nouns that are derived from Verbs 1706.

B. *sb.* A noun or other part of speech derived from a verb 1530.

Verbalism (vɔ̄·ɹbăliz'm). 1787. [f. prec. + -ISM.] **1.** A verbal expression; a word or vocable. **2.** Predominance of what is merely verbal over reality or real significance 1871.

Verbalist (vɔ̄·ɹbălist). 1609. [f. as prec. + -IST.] **1.** One who deals in or directs his attention to words only, apart from reality or meaning. **2.** One who is skilled in the use or knowledge of words 1794.

Verbality (vəɹbæ·lĭti). 1645. [f. as prec. + -ITY.] The quality of being (merely) verbal; that which consists of mere words or verbiage. **b.** *pl.* Verbal expressions or phrases 1840.

Verbalize (vɔ̄·ɹbăləiz), *v.* 1609. [– Fr. *verbaliser*, or f. VERBAL *a.* + -IZE.] **1.** *intr.* To use many words; to be verbose. **2.** *trans.* To make into a verb 1659. **3.** To express in words 1875. Hence **Ve:rbaliza·tion,** the action of verbalizing or the fact of being verbalized.

Verbally (vɔ̄·ɹbăli), *adv.* 1588. [f. VERBAL *a.* + -LY².] **1.** Word for word; in respect of each word. **2.** In or with (mere) words, without accompanying action or reality 1610. **b.** So far as words (only) are concerned 1855. **3.** In actual words; by means of words or speech 1646. **b.** In speech, as contrasted with writing 1637.

2. This passion of Christ, the reprobate preach verballie only 1610.

Verbarian (vəɹbēᵊ·riăn), *a.* and *sb.* 1830. [f. L. *verbum* word, after forms in -ARIAN.] **A.** *adj.* Having to do with words. **B.** *sb.* An inventor or coiner of words 1873.

In *The Doctor*, Southey gives himself free scope as a v. 1873.

‖**Verbascum** (vəɹbæ·skŏm). 1562. [L. (Pliny).] = MULLEIN 1; one or other species of this.

Verbatim (vəɹbēⁱ·tim), *adv.*, *a.*, and *sb.* 1481. [– med.L. *verbatim*, f. L. *verbum* word. Cf. LITERATIM.] **A.** *adv.* **1.** Word for word; in the exact words. †**2.** In so many words; exactly, precisely –1638.

1. A translation v. from the french 1815. Phr. *V. et literatim*; It was, *v. et literatim*, a copy of the log-book of the brig 1828.

B. *adj.* **1.** Corresponding with or following an original word for word 1737. **2.** *transf.* Able to take down a speech word for word (in shorthand) 1882.

1. A machine for *v.* reporting 1880. **2.** The fastest 'v.' hands seemed to be embarrassed 1897.

C. *sb.* A verbatim report 1898.

Verbena (vəɹbī·nă). 1562. [In sense 1 – L. (usu. in pl. *verbenæ*), in sense 2 med. and mod.L. (= L. *verbenaca*).] **1.** *Rom. Antiq.* In *pl.*, the leaves or twigs of certain plants or shrubs (as olive, myrtle, laurel, etc.) having a sacred character and employed in religious ceremonies 1600. **2.** The plant VERVAIN; also, one or other plant of the genus *Verbena* or the order *Verbenaceæ* 1562. **3.** A perfume obtained from the leaves of vervain 1858.

2. The *Aloysia citriodora* is the Lemon-scented V. of the gardens 1866. Hence **Verbena·ceous** *a.* *Bot.* of or pertaining to the *Verbenaceæ*, an extensive family of monopetalous (chiefly tropical) plants.

Verberate (vɔ̄·ɹberēⁱt), *v.* 1587. [– *verberat-*, pa. ppl. stem of L. *verberare* beat, flay, f. *verber* lash, scourge; see -ATE³.] **1.** *trans.* **a.** To strike so as to produce a sound (*rare*). **b.** To beat or strike so as to cause pain, esp. by way of punishment 1625. **2.** *intr.* To vibrate or quiver 1755.

1. The sounde..Reboundes againe, and verberates the skies 1587.

Verberation (vɔ̄ɹbĕrēⁱ·ʃən). 1610. [– L. *verberatio, -ōn-*, f. as prec.; see -ION. Cf. (O)Fr. *verbération*.] **1.** The action of beating or striking, or the fact of being struck, so as to produce sound; percussion. **2.** The action of beating or striking so as to cause pain or hurt; also, a blow or stroke 1730.

Verbiage (vɔ̄·ɹbiėdʒ). 1721. [– Fr. *verbiage*, f. †*verbeier* chatter, f. *verbe* word + *-eier*; see -AGE.] **1.** Abundance of words without necessity or without much meaning; excessive wordiness. **2.** Diction, wording, verbal expression 1804.

1. The Homeric phrase is thus often muffled and deadened by Pope's v. 1880. **2.** All that is nothing; the previous v. [of the treaty] is thought sufficient to bind us WELLINGTON.

Verbify (vɔ̄·ɹbifəi), *v.* 1813. [f. VERB + -FY.] *trans.* To convert (a noun, etc.) into a verb. Also *absol.*

Verbigerate (vəɹbi·dʒĕrēⁱt), *v.* 1892. [– *verbigerat-*, pa. ppl. stem of L. *verbigerare* chat, f. *verbum* word + *gerere* carry on; see -ATE³.] *Path. intr.* To go on repeating the same word or phrase in a meaningless fashion, as a symptom of mental disease. So **Verbigera·tion** 1891.

Verbose (vəɹbōᵘ·s), *a.* 1672. [– L. *verbosus*, f. *verbum* word; see -OSE¹.] **1.** Expressed in an unnecessary number of words; prolix, wordy. **2.** Using an excessive number of words; long-winded 1692.

1. Any v. circumlocutory appeal 1826. Countless papers, expressed in..v. and tedious tenor 1870. **2.** The conveyances of a v. attorney ADAM SMITH. Hence **Verbo·se-ly** *adv.*, **-ness.**

Verbosity (vəɹbǫ·sĭti). 1542. [– L. *verbositas*, f. *verbosus*; see prec., -ITY. Cf. Fr. *verbosité*.] The state or quality of being verbose; superfluity of words; wordiness, prolixity. **b.** With pl. An instance of this 1665.

He draweth out the thred of his verbositie, finer then the staple of his argument SHAKS.

‖**Verbum sap.** 1818. Also **verb. sap. (sat).** [Shortening of L. *verbum sapienti sat est* 'a word is sufficient to a wise man'.] A phrase used in place of making a full statement or explanation, implying that an intelligent person may easily infer what is left unsaid, or understand the reasons for reticence.

‖**Verbum sat.** Also **sat verbum.** 1649. [See prec.] A phrase used to conclude a statement, implying that further comment is unnecessary or unadvisable.

Verdancy (vɔ̄·ɹdănsi). 1631. [f. VERDANT; see -ANCY.] **1.** The quality, condition, or character of being verdant; greenness. **2.** *fig.* Innocence, inexperience; rawness, simplicity 1849.

Verdant (vǝ̄·ɹdǎnt), *a.* 1581. [Of obscure origin; perh. – OFr. *verdeant*, pr. pple. of *verdoier* (mod. *-oyer*) = It. *verdeggiare* (*-iante*) :– L. **viridiare*, f. *viridis* green; with reduction to two syll. after pr. pples. in -ANT and assoc. with VERDURE.] **1.** Of a green hue or colour; green. **2.** Green with vegetation; characterized by abundance of verdure 1590. **3.** *fig.* Of persons: Green, inexperienced, gullible 1824.

1. When eve embrowns the v. grove 1764. **2.** As I tread The walk, still v., under oaks and elms COWPER. **3.** With the..object of warning 'v.' purchasers 1854. Hence **Ve·rdantly** *adv.*

‖**Verd-antique, verd antique** (vǝ̄:ɹd æntī·k). 1745. [– Fr. †*verd antique* (now *vert a.*); see VERT *sb.*[1], ANTIQUE.] **1.** An ornamental variety of marble, consisting chiefly of serpentine mixed with calcite and dolomite. **b.** *Oriental v.*, green porphyry 1852. **2.** A green incrustation on brass or copper; verdigris 1835.

‖**Verde antico.** 1753. [It.] = prec. 1.

Verderer (vǝ̄·ɹdǝrǝɹ). Also **-or.** 1541. [– AFr. *verderer*, extended form (see -ER[1] 3) of *verder* = (O)Fr. *verdier* :– Gallo-Rom. **viridarius* (also AL. XIII), f. L. *viridis* green; see VERT *sb.*[1], -ER[2] 2.] 'A judicial officer of the King's forest..sworn to maintain and keep the assises of the forest, and also to view, receive, and enroll the attachments and presentments of all manner of trespasses of the forest, of vert and venison' (Manwood).

Verdict (vǝ̄·ɹdikt). [ME. *verdit* – AFr. *verdit* = OFr. *veir-*, *voirdit*, f. *veir*, *voir* :– L. *verum* true + *dit* :– L. *dictum* saying, speech, subst. use of n. pa. pple. of *dicere* say; see VERY *adj.*] **1.** *Law.* The decision of a jury in a civil or criminal cause upon an issue which has been submitted to their judgement. **2.** *transf.* and *fig.* A judgement given by some body or authority acting as or likened to a jury. late ME. **3.** *transf.* A finding, conclusion, or judgement upon some matter or subject. late ME.

1. The Agreement of Twelve Men is a V. in Law 1726. **2.** They are here presently to abide the verdite of battaile 1611. **3.** No controversy is supposed to be closed till the *Times* has given its v. 1882.

Verdigris (vǝ̄·ɹdigris, -grīs). [ME. *verdegres*, *vertegres* – OFr. *verte-gres*, earlier *vert de Grece* (mod. *vert-de-gris*) 'green of Greece' (see VERT *sb.*[1]), latinized *viride grecum*.] A green or greenish blue substance obtained artificially by the action of dilute acetic acid on thin plates of copper (or as a green deposit naturally forming on copper or brass), and much used as a pigment, in dyeing, the arts, and medicine; basic acetate of copper.

attrib.: **v. green,** a green of a bright, bluish hue; æruginous green. Hence **Ve·rdigrised** *ppl. a.* coated or tainted with v.

Verditer (vǝ̄·ɹditǝɹ). 1505. [– OFr. *verd de terre* (mod. *vert de terre*) 'green of earth'; cf. prec., VERT *sb.*[1]] **1.** A pigment of a green, bluish green, or (more freq.) light blue colour, usu. prepared by adding chalk or whiting to a solution of nitrate of copper, and much used in making crayons and as a water-colour. **2.** The blue or green colour characteristic of verditer 1819.

†**Verdour.** 1447. [– OFr. *verdour*, f. *verd* green; see VERT *sb.*[1], -OUR.] = VERDURE, in various senses –1646.

Verdoy, *a.* 1562. [– Fr. *verdoyé*, pa. pple. of *verdoyer*, f. OFr. *verd* green; see VERT *sb.*[1]] *Her.* Of a bordure: Charged with leaves, flowers, fruits, etc.

Verdure (vǝ̄·ɹdiŭɹ, -dʒǝɹ). late ME. [– (O)Fr. *verdure*, f. OFr. *verd* green; see VERT *sb.*[1], -URE.] **I. 1.** The fresh green colour of vegetation; greenness, viridity. **2.** Green vegetation; plants or trees, or parts of these, in a green and flourishing state. late ME. **b.** *esp.* Green grass or herbage 1447. †**c.** *pl.* Green plants or herbs –1722.

1. The perennial v. of cypress and pine 1910. **2. b.** [Thoughts] and the pleasant v. of the fields Made me forget the way COWLEY.

II. †**1.** Freshness or agreeable briskness of taste in fruits or liquors; also simply, taste, savour –1630. †**2.** Smell; odour –1716. **3.** *fig.* Fresh or flourishing condition 1586.

3. Those years make the prime and v. of our lives 1829. Hence **Ve·rdured** *ppl. a.* clad with v. or vegetation, covered with grass. **Ve·rdureless** *a.* destitute of v.; bare, bleak.

Verdurous (vǝ̄·ɹdiŭrǝs, -dʒǝrǝs), *a.* 1604. [f. VERDURE + -OUS.] **1.** Of vegetation: Rich or abounding in verdure; flourishing thick and green. **b.** Of places, etc.: Displaying a rich (green) vegetation 1717. **2.** Consisting or composed of verdure 1667. **3.** Of, pertaining to, or characteristic of verdure 1820.

1. Where the lowing Herd Chews verd'rous Pasture 1708. **b.** That v. hill with many a resting-place COLERIDGE. **3.** Through v. glooms and winding mossy ways KEATS. Hence **Ve·rdurousness.**

Verecund (ve·rīkʊnd), *a.* 1550. [– L. *verecundus*, f. *verēri* to reverence, fear.] Modest, bashful; shy, coy.

Veretilliform (verīti·lifǭɹm), *a.* 1838. [f. mod.L. *Veretillum* + -FORM.] *Zool.* Having the form of a member of *Veretillum*, the typical genus of *Veretillidæ*, a family of pennatuloid polyps.

Verey (*lights*), variant of VERY.

Vergaloo (vǝ̄ɹgălū·). *U.S.* Also **virgalieu.** 1828. [var. of VIRGOULEUSE, prob. taken as a pl.] The white doyenné or Warwickshire bergamot.

Verge (vǝ̄ɹdʒ), *sb.* late ME. [– (O)Fr. *verge* :– L. *virga* rod.] **I. 1.** †**a.** The penis. late ME. only. **b.** *Zool.* [after mod.Fr. use.] The male organ of a mollusc, crustacean, or other invertebrate 1774. **2. a.** A rod or wand carried as an emblem of authority or symbol of office; a staff of office; a warder, †sceptre, mace 1494. †**b.** A rod or wand put in a person's hand when taking the oath of fealty to the lord on being admitted as a tenant, and delivered back on the giving up of the tenancy. Also in phr. *tenant by the v.* –1651. **3.** *Watchmaking.* The spindle or arbor of the balance in the old vertical escapement 1696. **b.** *ellipt.* A verge watch 1871. **4.** *U.S.* That part of a linotype machine which carries the pawls by which the matrices are released 1909.

†**II.** *V. of land* [tr. OFr. *verge de terre*, med.L. *virga terræ*] = VIRGATE (*rare*) –1672.

III. 1. *Within the v.* [AFr. *dedeinz la verge*], within an area subject to the jurisdiction of the Lord High Steward, defined as extending to a distance of twelve miles round the King's court. In the 18th c. commonly denoting the precincts of Whitehall as a place of sanctuary. *Obs.* exc. *Hist.* 1509. **b.** Hence *The v.* (*of the court*), etc., employed to designate this area or jurisdiction 1529. **2.** The bounds, limits, or precincts *of* a particular place 1641. †**3.** In phrases. **a.** The range, sphere, or scope *of* something –1734. **b.** The pale or limit *of* a class or community –1768. **c.** The power, control, or jurisdiction of a person or persons –1704.

2. She should be beheaded within the v. of the Tower HUME. **3. a.** They do not fall within the V. of my Undertaking in the present 1734.

IV. 1. The edge, rim, border, or margin *of* some object of limited size or extent. Now *rare.* †**b.** With *a* and *pl.*, etc.: A brim or rim; a circle of metal, etc. –1710. **c.** *Arch.* The edge of the tiling projecting beyond the gable of a roof 1833. **2.** The extreme edge, margin, or bound *of* a surface of an extensive nature, but regarded as having definite limits 1593. **b.** *fig.* The end *of* life 1750. **c.** The utmost limit to which a thing or matter extends; the distinctive line of separation between one subject and another 1796. **3. a.** The extreme edge of a cliff or abrupt descent 1605. **b.** The margin *of* a river or the sea 1606. **c.** *poet.* The horizon 1822. **4.** With *a* and *pl.* A limit or bound; a limiting or bounding belt or strip. Somewhat *rare.* 1660. **b.** *spec.* A narrow grass edging separating a flower border, etc. from a walk 1728. **5.** The brink or border *of* something towards which there is progress or tendency (from without); the point at which something begins. Usu. in phrases *on* or *to the v. of.* 1602. **6.** The space within a boundary; room, scope 1690.

2. The furthest V. That euer was suruey'd by English eye SHAKS. **c.** Having lived up to the very v. of his yearly income MME. D'ARBLAY. **3.** *fig.* You see him often tottering on the v. of laughter GRAY. **c.** The v. where brighter morns were wont to break BYRON. **5.** He seems to have been driven to the very v. of despair 1842. Phr. *On the v. of* (with vbl. sbs.), on the very point of (doing something); Twice she was on the v. of telling all 1887. **6.** Give ample room, and v. enough The characters of hell to trace GRAY.

Verge (vǝ̄ɹdʒ), *v.*[1] 1605. [f. prec.] †**1.** *trans.* To provide *with* a specified kind of verge or border; to edge. Chiefly in pass. –1708. **2.** *intr.* **a.** To be contiguous or adjacent to; to lie on the verge of. Const. *on* or *upon*, *along.* 1787. **b.** To border *on* or *upon* some state, condition, etc. 1825.

2. b. Your generosity must have verged on extravagance C. BRONTË.

Verge (vǝ̄ɹdʒ), *v.*[2] 1610. [– L. *vergere* bend, incline.] **1.** *intr.* Of the sun: To descend towards the horizon; to sink, or begin to do so. **2.** To move in a certain direction (esp. downwards); also, to extend or stretch 1661. **b.** To diverge or deflect 1692. **3.** To incline or tend, to approach or draw near, *towards* or *to* some state or condition 1664. **b.** To pass or undergo gradual transition *into* something else 1756. **4.** To have a particular direction; to lie or extend towards a specified point 1726.

3. A man of light wit, verging towards fourscore CARLYLE. **b.** Fast verging into a state of monomania 1854. **4.** Whose rays..V. to one point and blend for ever there SHELLEY.

Ve·rge-board. 1833. [f. VERGE *sb.* IV. 1 c.] *Arch.* = BARGE-BOARD.

Vergency (vǝ̄·ɹdʒĕnsi). 1649. [f. VERGE *v.*[2] + -ENCY.] †**1.** The act or fact of verging or inclining towards some condition, etc.; tendency, leaning; an instance of this –1702. **2.** The fact or condition of being inclined toward some object or in some direction 1668. **b.** *Optics.* The reciprocal of the focal distance, being the measure of the degree of divergence or convergence of a pencil of rays 1832.

†**Ve·rger**[1]. ME. [– (O)Fr. *verger* :– L. *virdiarium*, for *viridiarium*, *viridarium*, f. *viridis* green; see -ER[2] 2.] A garden or orchard; a pleasure-garden –1501.

Verger[2] (vǝ̄·ɹdʒǝɹ). 1472. [– AFr. **verger* (AL. *virgarius* verger (XIII); cf. late L. 'lictor'), f. *verge*; see VERGE *sb.*, -ER[2] 2.] An official who carries a rod or similar symbol of office before the dignitaries of a cathedral, church, or university. **b.** One whose duty it is to take care of the interior of a church, and to act as attendant 1707. See also VIRGER.

Vergobret (vǝ̄·ɹgǒbret). 1563. [– L. *vergobretus* (Cæsar), of Gaulish origin.] The chief magistrate among the ancient Ædui of Gaul.

Veridical (vĭri·dikăl), *a.* 1653. [f. L. *veridicus*, f. *verum* truth + *dic-*, stem of *dicere* to speak; see -AL[1].] **1.** Speaking, telling, or relating the truth; veracious. **2.** *spec.* in *Psychol.* Of hallucinations, phantasms, etc.: Coincident with, corresponding to, or representing real events or persons 1884.

Verifiable (ve·rifǝi,ăb'l), *a.* 1593. [f. VERIFY *v.* + -ABLE.] That can be verified or proved to be true, authentic, accurate, or real; capable of verification. Hence **Ve:rifiabi·lity. Ve·rifiableness. Ve·rifiably** *adv.*

Verification (ve:rifikē[i]·ʃǝn). 1523. [– (O)Fr. *vérification* or med.L. *verificatio*, *-ōn-*, f. *verificat-*, pa. ppl. stem of *verificare*; see VERIFY, -FICATION.] **1.** The action of demonstrating or proving to be true or legitimate by means of evidence or testimony; formal assertion of truth. Now *rare.* **2.** Demonstration of truth or correctness by facts or circumstances 1541. **3.** The action of establishing or testing the truth or correctness of a fact, theory, statement, etc., by means of special investigation or comparison of data 1603. **b.** The action of verifying or testing the correctness of an instrument, or the quality of goods 1832. **4.** [After Fr.] Ratification 1845.

4. By the old constitution of France, these letters patent required the v. of the Parliament M. ARNOLD.

Verificatory (ve·rifikē[i]:tǝri), *a.* 1834. [f. VERIFICATION + -ORY[2].] That verifies; of the nature of or serving as a verification.

Verify (ve·rifəi), *v.* ME. [– (O)Fr. *vérifier* – med.L. *verificare*, f. L. *verus* true; see VERY, -FY.] **1.** *trans. Law.* To prove by good evidence or valid testimony; to testify or affirm formally or upon oath. **b.** *gen.* To testify to, to assert as true or certain. Now *rare.* 1525. †**c.** To support by testimony. SHAKS. **2.** To show to be true by demonstration or evidence; to substantiate. Now *rare* of persons. late ME. **3.** *pass.* To be proved true or correct by the result or event, or by some confirming fact or circumstance; to be fulfilled or accomplished in this way. late ME. **b.** Used actively of the circumstances, person, etc., serving as proof or confirmation. late ME. **4.** To ascertain or test the accuracy or correctness of (something), esp. by examination or by comparison with known data or some standard; to check or correct in this way 1527. **b.** To establish by investigation 1801.

1. The said charge to be verified by the oath of the said Frazer BURKE. **2.** 'Prosperitee is blynd': ..And verifie I can wel it is so HOCCLEVE. The strongest evidence by which the fact of a death was ever verified MACAULAY. **3.** If he doth, I fear it will be verified in him, that a 'fool and his money is soon parted' 1629. **4.** Hours..spent in casting up and verifying accounts 1802. Hence **Ve·rifier,** one who or that which verifies.

Verily (ve·rili), *adv.* Now *arch.* or *rhet.* ME. [f. VERY *a.* + -LY², after OFr. *ver-rai(e)ment* (mod. *vraiment*), and AFr. *veirement* = OFr. *voirement.*] In truth; as a matter of truth or fact; in deed, fact, or reality; really, truly. **b.** Placed in front of a sentence or statement as an emphatic asseveration of its truth or accuracy; freq. connoting the truth of a preceding statement ME. **c.** Used to emphasize a negative or affirmative particle 1489.

He..v. believes him an honest man '*Junius' Lett.* **b.** V., Mr. Spectator, we are much offended at the Act for Importing French Wines 1711. **c.** Yes, v.,..so you must 1865.

Verisimilar (verisi·milăɹ), *a.* 1681. [f. L. *verisimilis, veri similis* 'like the truth', i.e. gen. sing. of *verus* true, *similis* like; see -AR¹, SIMILAR.] Having the appearance of truth or reality; appearing true or real; probable.

Are these dramas of his not v. only but true? CARLYLE.

Verisimilitude (ve:risimi·litiūd). 1603. [– L. *verisimilitudo, veri similitudo,* f. *verisimilis*; see prec., -TUDE.] **1.** The fact or quality of being verisimilar; the appearance of being true or real, probability. **2.** A statement, etc., which has the mere appearance or show of being true or in accordance with fact 1783.

1. Truth has no greater Enemy than v. and likelihood 1654. **2.** I felt..that there was more truth in the verisimilitudes of fiction than in the assumptions of history L. HUNT. So †**Verisimi·lity** –1706.

Verist (vīᵊ·rist). 1884. [f. L. *verum* or It. *vero* true + -IST.] One who believes in or practises the rigid representation of the truth or reality in literature or art. So **Ve·rism,** the style practised or advocated by the verists. **Veri·stic** *a.*

Veritable (ve·rităb'l), *a.* 1474. [– (O)Fr. *véritable*, f. *vérité*; see next, -ABLE.] †**1.** Of a statement, etc.: That is in accordance with the truth; true –1649. †**b.** Of persons: Veracious –1594. **2.** Genuine, real, true; correctly or properly so called 1483. **3.** In extended use, denoting possession of all the distinctive qualities of the person or thing specified 1862.

1. *Oth.* III. iv. 76. **2.** A v. personage was Whittington 1852. A moral relish for v. proofs of honesty 1872. **3.** They had a succession of governors who were v. brigands 1869. Hence **Ve·ritably** *adv.*

Verity (ve·rĭti). [ME. *verite* – (O)Fr. *vérité*, repl. OFr. *verté* :– L. *veritas, -tat-*, f. *verus* true; see -ITY.] **1.** Without article. Truth; conformity to fact or reality. **2.** With article or pronoun. The truth; the true or real facts or circumstances. late ME. **b.** Said of God or Christ. Usu. with defining adj. preceding. 1535. †**c.** The exact wording and meaning of the original Hebrew or Greek text of the Bible –1771. **d.** The actuality or reality *of* something 1633. **3.** With *a* and *pl.* A true statement, doctrine, or opinion; an established fact, a reality; a truth 1533. †**4.** Truthfulness, veracity, sincerity –1848.

1. Betweene veritie & falsitie there is no meane 1579. **2.** Telle me what ye be, and of youre felowes telle me the verite 1450. The v. of his Miracles HOBBES. **b.** God being the Prime V. 1645. **3.** The quarrel and the reconciliation are unquestionable verities FREEMAN. Phr. *Of a v.*, truly, assuredly. **4.** Thou hast sworen to Dauid in thy verite 1565.

Verjuice (vɔ̄·ɹdʒūs), *sb.* ME. [– OFr. *vertjus*, (also mod.) *verjus*, i.e. *vert jus* 'green juice'; see VERT *sb.*¹, JUICE.] The acid juice of green or unripe grapes, crab-apples, or other sour fruit, expressed and formed into a liquor; formerly much used in cooking, etc.

fig. Miss Budd, although she said nothing, looked vinegar and v. 1833. Hence **Ve·rjuice** *v. trans.* to make sour.

Vermeil, vermil (vɔ̄·ɹmil), *a.* and *sb.* late ME. [– (O)Fr. *vermeil* :– L. *vermiculus*, dim. of *vermis* worm. See VERMILION.] **A.** *adj.* Of a bright scarlet or red colour; vermilion. Chiefly *poet.* **b.** With names of colours; esp. *v. red* 1590.

Take not colde water in stede of vermayll wine 1509. **b.** In her cheekes the vermeill red did shew SPENSER.

B. *sb.* **1.** Vermilion hue or colour 1590. †**b.** *transf.* Blood (*rare*) –1812. **2.** An orange-red garnet 1796. **3.** Silver gilt; gilt bronze 1858. Hence **Vermeil, vermil** *v. trans.* to colour or suffuse, to stain *over*, with or as with vermilion.

‖**Vermes** (vɔ̄·ɹmīz). 1693. [L., pl. of *vermis* worm.] **1.** *Path.* A disease caused by the presence of parasitic worms. **2.** *Zool.* One or other of the primary divisions, sub-kingdoms, or groups of the animal kingdom proposed or adopted at various times, comprising worms and allied forms 1771.

Vermetid (vɔ̄·ɹmĕtid). 1860. [– mod.L. *Vermetidæ*, f. L. VERMES; see -ID³.] *Zool.* An individual of the family *Vermetidæ* of holostomatous gasteropods.

Vermi- (vɔ̄·ɹmi), comb. form of L. *vermis*, as in VERMICIDE, VERMIFORM, VERMIFUGE, *adjs.*; also in other terms, as **Vermi·ferous,** *a.* producing worms; **-i·gerous** *a.* infested with worms.

Vermian (vɔ̄·ɹmiăn), *a.* 1878. [f. VERMES + -IAN.] **1.** Of or pertaining to *Vermes*; characteristic of worms; worm-like. **2.** *Anat.* Pertaining or belonging to the vermis of the cerebellum.

Vermicelli (vəɹmise·li, vəɹmitʃe·li). 1669. [– It. *vermicelli*, pl. of *vermicello*, dim. of *verme* :– L. *vermis* worm.] **1.** A wheaten paste, of Italian origin, now usu. made of flour, cheese, yolks of eggs, sugar and saffron, prepared in the form of long, slender, hard threads, and used as an article of diet. **2.** *ellipt.* Vermicelli soup 1771.

Vermicide (vɔ̄·ɹmisəid). 1849. [f. VERMI- + -CIDE 1.] *Med.* A medicine for killing intestinal worms; an anthelmintic.

Vermicle (vɔ̄·ɹmik'l). late ME. [– L. *vermiculus*; see VERMICULE.] †**1.** = VERMILION *sb.* 3. WYCLIF. **2.** *Biol.* A vermicule 1657.

Vermicular (vəɹmi·kiŭlăɹ), *a.* 1672. [– med.L. *vermicularis*, f. L. *vermiculus* VERMICULE; see -AR¹.] **1.** = PERISTALTIC *a.* **2.** Having the sinuous shape or form characteristic of a worm; consisting of or characterized by tortuous outlines or markings; sinuous, wavy 1712. **3.** Of, pertaining to, or characteristic of a worm or worms; resembling or like a worm 1713. **b.** Accomplished or made by worms; performed by means of worms 1715. **4.** Of the nature of a worm; consisting of worms 1784. **5.** *Path.* Of diseases: Due to or caused by intestinal worms 1794.

1. The v. motion of the intestine 1881. **2.** A generation more refin'd..made three legs four, Gave them a twisted form v. COWPER. **4.** *V. ascaris*, the thread-worm, *Oxyurus* (*Ascaris*) *vermicularis*. Hence **Vermi·cularly** *adv.*

Vermiculate (vəɹmi·kiŭlĕt), *a.* 1605. [– L. *vermiculatus*, pa. pple. of *vermiculari*, f. *vermiculus*; see VERMICULE, -ATE².] Vermiculated, vermicular, sinuous.

Subtile, idle, vnholesome, and (as I may tearme them) v. questions BACON.

Vermiculated (vəɹmi·kiulēⁱtĕd), *ppl. a.* 1623. [See prec. and -ED¹.] **1.** Worm-eaten; covered or ornamented with vermicular markings. **b.** *Arch.* Of stone-work or other surfaces so carved or moulded as to present the appearance of worm-tracks 1788. **2.** Of mosaic work (after L. (*opus*) *vermiculatum*): Wrought, ornamented, or inlaid in a pattern resembling the sinuous movements or tracks of worms 1656. **3.** Ornamented *with* sinuous or wavy lines or markings of a specified colour 1872.

Vermiculation (vəɹmikiŭlēⁱ·ʃən). 1611. [– L. *vermiculatio, -ōn-*, f. as VERMICULATE *a.*; see -ION.] **1.** The fact or condition of being infested with or eaten by worms; conversion into small worms. †**2.** *Path.* Peristalsis –1710. **3.** With *pl.* A tortuous boring or marking made by or resembling the track of a worm 1670. **b.** Without article. Vermicular marking or ornamentation 1866.

3. The face of the boards is shown to be eaten into innumerable vermiculations T. HARDY.

Vermicule (vɔ̄·ɹmikiūl). 1713. [– L. *vermiculus*, dim. of *vermis* worm; see -CULE.] *Biol.* A small worm or worm-like creature; a maggot or grub.

Vermiculite (vəɹmi·kiŭləit). 1824. [f. L. *vermiculari* (see VERMICULATE) + -ITE¹ 2 b.] *Min.* Any of a number of hydrous silicates; chiefly resulting from alterations of mica, and occurring in small foliated scales.

Vermiculous (vəɹmi·kiŭləs), *a.* 1690. [– late L. *verminculosus*, f. *vermiculus* VERMICULE; see -OUS.] †**1.** Full of worms (*rare*). **2.** Of or pertaining to worms 1813. **3.** Having a wormy appearance 1818. So **Vermiculo·se** *a.* (*rare*) infested with worms, worm-like.

Vermiform (vɔ̄·ɹmifǭɹm), *a.* 1730. [f. L. *vermis* worm + -FORM. Cf. Fr. *vermiforme.*] **1.** Having the form of a worm; long, thin, and more or less cylindrical. **2.** Of, pertaining to, or characteristic of a worm; like or resembling that of a worm; vermicular 1822.

1. *V. appendix* (or *appendage*), a small worm-like process or diverticulum extending from the cæcum in man and a few other mammals. *V. process*, the median lobe of the cerebellum, the upper and lower laminæ of which are distinguished as the *superior* and *inferior v. processes.*

Vermifuge (vɔ̄·ɹmifiūdʒ), *a.* and *sb.* 1697. [f. L. *vermis* worm + -FUGE. Cf. Fr. *vermifuge* adj. and sb.] **A.** *adj.* Causing or promoting the expulsion of worms or other animal parasites from the intestines; anthelmintic. **B.** *sb.* An anthelmintic 1718. So **Vermi·fugal** *a.*

Vermilion (vəɹmi·lyən), *sb.* and *a.* [ME. *vermelyon* – OFr. *vermeillon*, f. *vermeil* VERMEIL *a.*] **A.** *sb.* **1.** Cinnabar or red crystalline mercuric sulphide, esp. in later use that obtained artificially, much valued on account of its brilliant scarlet colour, and used as a pigment or in the manufacture of red sealing-wax; also, any red earth resembling this and similarly used as a pigment. **2.** The colour of this pigment; a bright red or scarlet. late ME. †**3.** Scarlet wool or fabric –1641.

2. Streight the Vermillion vanish'd from her Face 1708.

B. *adj.* Having the colour of vermilion; of a bright red or scarlet colour 1589. Hence **Vermi·lion** *v. trans.* to colour or paint with, or as with v.; to give the colour of v. to (the face, etc.).

Vermin (vɔ̄·ɹmin), *sb.* ME. [– OFr. *vermin*, (also mod.) *vermine* :– Rom. **verminum, -ina*, collective deriv. f. L. *vermis* worm.] **1.** *collect.* Animals of a noxious or objectionable kind: **a.** Orig. applied to reptiles, stealthy or slinking animals, and various wild beasts; now, exc. in *U.S.* and *Austral.*, almost entirely restricted to those animals or birds which prey upon preserved game. **b.** Applied to creeping or wingless insects (and other minute animals) of a loathsome or offensive appearance or character, esp. those which infest or are parasitic on living beings and plants ME. †**2.** With *a, that, this,* etc. **a.** A kind or class of obnoxious animals –1774. **b.** A single animal or insect of this kind –1809. **3.** *fig.* Applied to persons of a noxious, vile, objectionable, or offensive character or type 1562.

1. A hole..filled with Snakes, Lizards, and other poisonous Virmin 1684. That the stock of partridges, grouse, and hares on any large estate depends chiefly on the destruction of v. DARWIN. **b.** Vermyn, as flees, lyse, wormes, etc. 1552. **2. a.** This Crocodile is..a dangerous vermine used to both elements HOLLAND. **3.** Knaves, cheats, hypocrites; the v. of this earth 1690.

Verminate (vǝ·ɹminēit), *v. rare.* 1693. [– *verminat-*, pa. ppl. stem of L. *verminare* have worms, f. *vermis* worm; see -ATE[3].] *intr.* To breed parasitic vermin.

Vermination (vǝɹminēi·ʃǝn). 1628. [– L. *verminatio, -ōn-*, f. as prec.; see -ION.] †**1.** The fact or condition of being gnawed by worms; vermiculation. DONNE. †**2.** The breeding, growth, or production of vermin, esp. parasitic vermin –1713. **3.** The fact of being infested with parasitic vermin; esp. *Med.*, the morbid condition due to this 1818.

Verminous (vǝ·ɹminǝs), *a.* 1616. [– OFr. *verminous*, (also mod.) *vermineux*, or L. *verminosus*, f. *vermis* worm; see -OSE[1].] **1.** Of the nature of or consisting of vermin; like vermin in character; noxious, objectionable, offensive. **2.** Infested with vermin, esp. parasitic vermin; foul or offensive on this account 1632. **3.** Of diseases or morbid conditions, etc.: Due to or characterized by the presence of parasitic vermin or intestinal worms 1666. **b.** Of persons: Subject to vermin or intestinal worms 1860.

2. A v., over-crowded vagrant ward 1865. **3.** Instances of v. abscess 1897. Hence **Ve·rminously** *adv.*, **-ness.**

Vermi·parous, *a. rare.* 1646. [f. VERMI- + -PAROUS.] **1.** Producing young, or produced as young, in the form of small worms or maggots. **2.** Producing verminous parasites 1860.

‖**Vermis** (vǝ·ɹmis). 1890. [L., worm.] *Anat.* The vermiform process of the cerebellum.

Vermivorous (vǝɹmi·vǒrǝs), *a.* 1704. [f. VERMI- + -VOROUS.] Feeding on worms, grubs, or insect vermin; said esp. of certain birds.

Vermouth (vēǝ·ɹmūt, vǝ·ɹmūþ). Also **vermuth.** 1806. [– Fr. *vermout* – G. *wermut* (see WORMWOOD), with assim. to the early G. sp. *wermuth.*] White wine flavoured with wormwood or other aromatic herbs and taken to stimulate the appetite. **b.** A glass of vermouth 1899.

Vernacular (vǝɹnæ·kiŭlăɹ), *a.* and *sb.* 1601. [f. L. *vernaculus* domestic, native, indigenous, f. *verna* home-born slave; see -AR[1].] **A.** *adj.* **1.** That uses the native or indigenous language of a country or district. **2.** Of a language or dialect: That is naturally spoken by the people of a particular country or district; native, indigenous 1645. **3.** Of literary works, etc.: Written, spoken in, or translated into the native language of a particular country or people 1661. **4.** Of words, etc.: Of or pertaining to the native language 1716. **5.** Connected or concerned with the native language 1845. **6.** Of arts, etc.: Native or peculiar to a particular country or locality 1857.

1. The Learned v. Editor of Hippocrates's Works in French 1716. **2.** The congregation here being chiefly peasants, and artisans, a sermon was delivered in the v. dialect 1832. He began to translate the Bible into clear v. German FROUDE. **3.** A history of our v. literature D'ISRAELI. **4.** A word entirely English and v. POPE. **6.** The v. cottage-building of the day 1857.

B. *sb.* **1.** The native speech or language of a particular country or district 1706. **2.** With *a* and *pl.* A native or indigenous language 1715. **3.** *transf.* The phraseology or idiom *of* a particular profession, trade, etc. 1876.

1. No one of them was qualified..to preach in the v. 1889. **3.** To use the v. of engineers 1876. Hence **Verna·cularism**, a v. word, idiom, or mode of expression. **Vernacula·rity**, the fact of belonging or adhering to the v. or native language. **Verna·cularly** *adv.*

Vernacularize (vǝɹnæ·kiŭlărǝiz), *v.* 1821. [f. prec. + -IZE.] *trans.* To render or translate into the native speech of a people; to make vernacular. Hence **Verna:culariza·tion.**

†**Verna·culous**, *a.* 1605. [f. L. *vernaculus*; see VERNACULAR, -OUS.] **1.** Low-bred, scurrilous. B. JONS. **2.** Indigenous, native –1657. **3.** = VERNACULAR *a.* 1, 2. –1682.

†**Ve·rnage.** late ME. [– OFr. *vernage*, *vernace* – It. *vernaccia* 'kind of strong wine'. Cf. med.L. *vernagium, vernacium.*] A kind of white Italian wine –1500.

Vernal (vǝ·ɹnăl), *a.* (and *sb.*) 1534. [– L. *vernalis*, f. *vernus* of the spring, f. *ver* spring; see -AL[1] 1. Cf. (O)Fr. *vernal.*] **1.** Coming, appearing, happening, etc., in spring. **2.** Pertaining or belonging to the spring-time; spring-like 1611. **b.** *fig.* Suggestive of spring; having the mildness or freshness of spring; early, youthful 1790. **3.** Of flowers, plants, etc.: Appearing or blooming in spring-time 1695. **b.** *V. grass*, one of the grasses commonly cultivated for hay 1762. **4.** *ellipt.* or as *sb.* = *V. grass* 1771.

1. V. Birds, such as the Cuckow 1709. Sweet is the breath of v. shower GRAY. *V. equinox* (or †*equinoctial*): see EQUINOX 1, 2. **2.** The freshest v. airs 1847. *V. season*, the season of spring. **b.** Late in beauty's v. bloom SOUTHEY. **3.** As thick as bees o'er v. blossoms fly POPE. **b.** The sweet scented v. grass (anthoxanthum odoratum) 1799. Hence **Ve·rnally** *adv.* (*rare*).

Vernant, *a.* Now *rare* or *Obs.* 1440. [– OFr. *vernant* – L. *vernans, -ant-*, pr. pple. of *vernare* flourish, be verdant, f. *vernus*, f. *ver* spring; see -ANT.] Flourishing or growing in or as in spring.

Vernation (vǝɹnēi·ʃǝn). 1793. [– mod.L. *vernatio* (Linnæus), f. *vernare* bloom, f. *vernus* of the spring; see VERNAL, -ATION.] *Bot.* The arrangement or formation of the leaves of plants or fronds of ferns in the bud; the manner in which the rudimentary or unexpanded leaves are disposed; prefoliation.

Verneuk (vǝrnū·k), *v.* 1871. [– S. Afr. Du. *verneuken.*] *S. Afr. slang.* To humbug.

Vernicle (vǝ·ɹnik'l). late ME. [– OFr. *vernicle*, alt. of *vernique*, (also mod.) *véronique* – med.L. *veronica*, which has been supposed to be a perversion of **vēra īcōn* 'true image', and was subsequently taken as the name of the woman herself. For the parasitic *l* cf. *barnacle, chronicle.*] **1.** The picture of the face of Christ said to have been impressed upon the handkerchief of St. Veronica; any similar picture of Christ's face; an ornament or token bearing this as worn by pilgrims. **2.** The cloth or kerchief, alleged to have belonged to St. Veronica, with which, according to legend, she wiped the face of Christ on the way to Calvary, and upon which his features were miraculously impressed. late ME.

1. A vernycle hadde he sowed vp on his cappe CHAUCER.

Vernier (vǝ·ɹniǝɹ). 1766. [Named after the inventor, Paul *Vernier* (1580–1637).] A device consisting of a short movable scale, by which more minute measurements may be readily obtained from the divisions of the graduated scale of astronomical, surveying, or other mathematical instruments to which it is attached.

attrib., as *v. circle, scale*; also in the names of instruments or tools having a v. scale or attachment, as *v. caliper, compass.*

Veronal (ve·rǒnăl). 1903. [– G. *veronal* (Emil Fischer), f. *Verona*, name of an It. town; see -AL[2].] *Chem.* Diethyl-malonylurea, a white crystalline substance used as a hypnotic.

Veronese (verǒnī·z, ve·rǒnīz), *a.* and *sb.* 1757. [– It. *Veronese*, f. *Verona*; see prec., -ESE.] **A.** *adj.* Of, belonging to, made in, or obtained from Verona in the north of Italy. **B.** *sb.* The natives or inhabitants of Verona. Also as *sing.* 1757.

‖**Veronica**[1] (vĕ-, vėrǫ·nikă). 1527. [Obscure use in med.L. of the name *Veronica* (see VERNICLE).] **1.** *Bot.* A large genus of scrophulariaceous plants (herbs or shrubs) having leafy stems and blue (rarely white or pink) flowers borne in racemes or spikes. **2.** With *a* and *pl.* A plant or species of the genus Veronica 1855.

Vero·nica[2]. 1700. = VERNICLE, q.v.

‖**Verruca** (verū·kă). *Pl.* **verrucæ** (verū·si). 1565. [L., wart, excrescence on precious stones.] **a.** A wart. **B.** *Bot., Conch., Ent.* A wart-like formation, growth, or prominence. So **Ve·rrucated** *a. Conch.* having or covered with verrucæ or warty growths.

Verruci- (si), combining form of L. *verruca* VERRUCA, as in **Verruci·ferous** *a.*, of a zoophyte, bearing verrucæ. **Verru·ciform** *a.*, wart-shaped.

Verrucose (ve·rukōus), *a.* 1686. [– L. *verrucosus*, f. *verruca*; see prec., -OSE[1].] **1.** Covered, furnished with, or full of verrucæ or wart-like excrescences or growths. Now *Nat. Hist.* and *Path.* **2.** *Bot.* Studded with warty swellings or protuberances; tubercular 1802.

Verrucous (verū·kǝs), *a.* 1656. [f. as prec.; see -OUS.] **1.** = prec. (*rare*). **2.** *Path.* Of the nature of a wart or warts; characterized by the formation of warts 1728.

Verruculose (verū·kiŭlōus), *a.* 1846. [f. VERRUCA, after *globulose*, etc.; see -ULOSE.] Covered with small verrucæ or warts.

‖**Verruga** (verū·gă). 1897. [Sp., wart :– L. *verruca* VERRUCA.] *Path.* A febrile disease endemic in Peru and characterized by warty eruptions or tumours on the skin; Peruvian wart.

†**Ve·rry**, *a.* (and *sb.*) 1550. [var. of *varry* VAIRY *a.*] *Her.* = VAIRY *a.* 1. –1780.

†**Versabi·lity.** 1673. [f. L. *versabilis* changeable, f. *versare* VERSE *v.*[2]; see -ITY. Cf. late L. *versibilitas.*] **a.** = VERSATILITY. **b.** Aptness or readiness to be changed or turned (round). –1762.

Versal (vǝ·ɹsăl), *a. Obs.* or *dial.* 1592. [Illiterate or colloq. abbrev. of UNIVERSAL *a.* Cf. VARSAL *a.*] **1.** Universal; whole. Usu. coupled with *world.* **2.** Single; individual 1709.

Versant (vǝ·ɹsănt), *sb.* 1851. [– Fr. *versant*, f. *verser*; see VERSE *v.*[2], -ANT.] **1.** The slope, side, or descent of a mountain or mountain-chain; the area or region covered by this. **2.** Tendency to slope or descend; declination 1859.

Versant (vǝ·ɹsănt), *a.* 1645. [– L. *versans*, *-ant-*, pr. pple. of *versare, -ari*; see VERSE *v.*[2]] **1.** Concerned *about*, occupied or engaged *in* or *with*, something. **2.** Of persons: **a.** = VERSED *ppl. a.*[1] Now *rare.* 1766. **b.** Conversant or intimately acquainted *with* a subject or person 1787.

2. b. A man not v. with courts of justice SYD. SMITH.

Versatile (vǝ·ɹsătǝil, vǝ·ɹsătil), *a.* 1605. [– Fr. *versatile* or L. *versatilis*, f. *versat-*, pa. ppl. stem of *versare*; see VERSE *v.*[2], -ATILE.] **I. 1.** Marked by changeability or inconstancy; subject to change or fluctuation; variable, changeable. **b.** Of persons: Fickle, inconstant (*rare*) 1682. **2.** Characterized by readiness or facility in turning from one subject, pursuit, etc., to another; marked by many-sidedness or variety of talent 1656. **3.** Of persons: Turning easily or readily from one subject or occupation to another; showing facility in varied subjects; many-sided 1762.

1. The v. tenderness which marks the irregular and capricious feelings of the populace BURKE. **2.** Chaucer's genius was vast, v. and original 1828. **3.** He was an able man of business, v., politic 1874.

II. Capable of being turned round on, or as on, a pivot or hinge; that may be turned different ways 1658. **b.** *Bot.* Of an anther: Swinging or turning about freely on the filament to which it is attached 1760.

The Head..is sometimes v. 1826. Hence **Ve·rsatile-ly** *adv.*, **-ness.**

Versatility (vǝɹsăti·lĭti). 1755. [– Fr. *versatilité*, or from prec. + -ITY.] The condition or quality of being versatile, in various senses.

Verse (vǝɹs), *sb.* [OE. *fers*, corresp. to OFris. *fers*, MLG., OHG. (Du., G.), ON. *vers* – L. *versus* turn of the plough, furrow, line, row, line of writing, verse, f. *vers-*, pa. ppl. stem of *vertere* turn; reinforced or repl. in ME. by adoption of (O)Fr. *vers* from the same L. source.] **1.** A succession of words arranged according to rules of prosody and forming a complete metrical line; one of the lines of a poem or piece of versification. **2.** *Liturg.* = VERSICLE 1. Now *rare.* OE. **3.** One of the sections of a psalm or canticle corresponding to the compound unit (usu. a couplet) of Hebrew poetry. (Now merged in next.) ME. **b.** One of the sections into which a chapter of the Bible is divided 1560.

4. A stanza ME. **5.** Without article: Metrical composition, form, or structure; language or literary work written or spoken in metre; poetry, esp. with ref. to metrical form. Opp. to *prose*. ME. **6.** The metrical or poetical compositions of a particular author, etc.; a certain amount of metrical work or poetry considered as a whole 1586.

1. Some mens behauiour is like a v. wherein euery sillable is measured BACON. **3. b.** The first edition of the New Testament divided into our present verses was printed by Robert Stephens at Geneva in 1551. **4.** I remember the two last lines of a v. in some of the old songs of 'Logan Water' BURNS. **5.** In antient time, before letters were in common use, the Lawes were many times put into v. HOBBES. Phr. *In v.*, in metrical form. *Adonic, Alexandrine, blank, elegiac, heroic(al, hexameter, Leonine, Saturnian v.*: see these words. **6.** Thus your V. Flow'd with her Beautie once SHAKS. Hence **Ve·rselet,** a small poem. **Ve·rsema:ker,** one who makes or writes verses; a versifier. **Ve·rseman,** a man who writes v.; a poet, esp. (in recent use) a minor poet or versifier. **Ve·rsemonger,** a versifier, esp. one who writes poor or indifferent v.

Verse (vɔ̄ɹs), *v.*[1] OE. [f. prec.] **1.** *intr.* To compose or make verses; to versify. Also with *it*. **2.** *trans.* To tell in verse; to turn into verse 1446.

2. Versing loue To amorous Phillida SHAKS. Hence **Versed** (vɔ̄ɹst) *ppl. a.*[2] composed in verse, turned into verse. **Ve·rser,** a writer of verse, a verseman.

Verse (vɔ̄ɹs), *v.*[2] 1556. [– (O)Fr. *verser* or L. *versare*, frequent. of *vertere* turn. In sense 2 app. a back-formation from VERSED *ppl. a.*[1]] †**1.** To turn over (a book) in study or investigation –1656. **2.** To instruct, to make (a person) conversant or experienced *in* something. Now *refl.* 1673.

Versed (vɔ̄ɹst), *a.* 1596. [tr. mod.L. *sinus versus*, i.e. L. *sinus* SINE, *versus* turned, pa. pple. of *vertere* turn.] *V. sine.* **a.** *Trig.* orig. The segment of the diameter intercepted between the foot of the sine and the extremity of the arc; in mod. use, the ratio of this line to the radius, or (equivalently, as a function of an angle) the quantity obtained by subtracting the cosine from unity. **b.** *Bridge-building.* The rise of an arch 1838.

Versed (vɔ̄ɹst), *ppl. a.*[1] 1610. [– Fr. *versé* or its source L. *versatus*, pa. pple. of *versari* stay, be situated, be occupied or engaged, pass. of *versare*; see VERSE *v.*[2], -ED[1].] Of persons: Experienced, practised, or skilled *in* a subject, matter, art, etc.; conversant with or having an intimate knowledge of something.

Versed, *ppl. a.*[2]: see VERSE *v.*[1]

Verset (vɔ̄·ɹsėt). ME. [– (O)Fr. *verset*, f. *vers* VERSE *sb.*; see -ET.] **1.** = VERSICLE 1. Now *Hist.* **2.** A little or short verse, esp. one of the Bible or a similar book; a short piece of verse 1625.

Versicle (vɔ̄·ɹsik'l). late ME. [– (O)Fr. *versicule* or L. *versiculus*, dim. of *versus* VERSE *sb.*; see -CULE.] **1.** *Liturg.* One of a series of short sentences, said or sung antiphonally in divine service; *spec.* one said by the officiant and followed by the RESPONSE of the congregation or people; often *collect. pl.*, a set of these with their accompanying responses. **2.** A little verse. †**a.** A short clause or sentence –1721. **b.** †A verse of the Psalms or the Bible; now *spec.* one of the subdivisions of a Hebrew verse 1624. **c.** A short or single metrical line; a little verse 1573.

2. b. That v. of Psal. 119, 'Righteous art thou, O Lord, and right are thy Judgements' 1641. So **Versi·cular** *a.* of, pertaining to, characterized by, or consisting of versicles or verses, esp. Biblical verses.

Versicoloured (vɔ̄·ɹsikʌlɔɹd), *a.* 1721. [f. L. *versicolor*, f. *versus*, pa. pple. of *vertere* turn + *color* COLOUR; see -ED[2].] Changing or varying in colour; iridescent; also, variegated.

A rocket..drops its v. shower 1873.

Versification (vɔ̄ɹsifikē[i]·ʃən). 1603. [– L. *versificatio*, *-ōn-*, f. *versificat-*, pa. ppl. stem of *versificare*; see VERSIFY, -FICATION.] **1.** The action of composing verse; the art or practice of versifying. **2.** The form or style in which the words in a poetical composition are arranged; the structure of poetry or verse; measure, metre 1693. **3.** A metrical version *of* something 1821.

Versificator (vɔ̄·ɹsifikē[i]:təɹ). 1611. [– L. *versificator*, f. as prec.; see -OR 2.] One who writes verse; a poet, versifier.

Statius, the best V. next to Virgil DRYDEN.

Versifier (vɔ̄·ɹsifəi,əɹ). ME. [– AFr. *versifiur*, OFr. *-fiour*, *-fieur*, f. *versifier*; see VERSIFY, -ER[2] 3.] **1.** One who versifies or composes verses; a verse-maker; a poet. **2.** A mere or poor writer of verse(s); a rhymester, poetaster 1531.

1. He was a good classic and an excellent v. 1828. **2.** She thought Byron an ephemeral v. 1880.

Versify (vɔ̄·ɹsifəi), *v.* late ME. [– (O)Fr. *versifier* – L. *versificare* (Lucilius); see VERSE *sb.*, -FY.] **1.** *intr.* To make or compose verses; to write poetry. **2.** *trans.* To narrate or recount in verse; to treat as the subject of verse. late ME. **3.** To turn or convert (a literary piece) into verse; to translate or rewrite in verse-form 1735.

1. Never straining hard to v. BYRON. **2.** I v. the truth, not poetize DANIEL. **3.** Bolingbroke really wrote the 'Essay on Man', which Pope versified D'ISRAELI. Hence **Ve·rsifying** *vbl. sb.*

Version (vɔ̄·ɹʃən), *sb.* 1582. [– (O)Fr. *version* – med.L. *versio*, *-ōn-*, f. *vers-*, pa. ppl. stem of L. *vertere* turn; see -ION.] **1.** A rendering of some text or work, or of a single word, passage, etc., from one language into another; a translation; also (*rarely*), the action or process of translating. **2.** The particular form of a statement, account, report, etc., given by one person or party; an account resting upon limited authority or embodying a particular point of view 1788. **b.** A particular form or variant of something 1835. †**3.** A turning about; a change of direction –1706. **b.** *Obstet.* The operation of manually turning the child so as to facilitate delivery 1853. †**4.** Conversion, transformation –1666.

1. The English v. of the Bible 1874. **2.** The v. generally received of what he actually did say FROUDE. **b.** This painting is a larger v. of one at Windsor Castle 1908. **4.** The V. of Aire into Water BACON. Hence **Ve·rsion** *v. trans.* to translate. **Ve·rsionist,** a translator.

‖**Vers libre** (vēr lībr). 1909. [Fr., 'free verse'.] Versification in which the ordinary rules of prosody are or may be disregarded; verse consisting of an irregular alternation of long and short lines, freq. unrhymed. Hence **Vers-li·brist,** a writer of such verse.

‖**Verso** (vɔ̄·ɹso). 1839. [– L. *verso* (sc. *folio*) '(the leaf) being turned', abl. sing. n. of pa. pple. of *vertere* turn.] **1.** The back of a leaf in a manuscript or printed book; the side presented to the eye when the leaf has been turned over in a forward direction. Abbreviated *v.*, *v°*. **2.** The reverse of a coin, medal, or the like 1891.

1. The left-hand page of a book is the verso of that leaf, and faces the RECTO of the next O.E.D.

Versor (vɔ̄·ɹsǫɹ). 1640. [In sense 2 mod.L. f. *vers-*, pa. ppl. stem of L. *vertere* turn + -OR 2. In sense 1 app. for mod.L. *versorium* (Bacon).] †**1.** The needle of a compass. **2.** *Math.* In quaternions, an operator which changes the direction of a vector without altering its length 1865.

Verst (vɔ̄ɹst). 1555. [– Russ. *verstá*, partly through G. *werst* and Fr. *verste*.] A Russian measure of length equal to 3500 English feet or about two-thirds of an English mile.

‖**Versus** (vɔ̄·ɹsɒs), *prep.* 1447. [– med.L. (XII) use of L. *versus* towards, in the sense of *adversus* against.] Against; employed in *Law* to denote an action by one party against another. Freq. abbrev. *v.* (also *vs.*).

The jugement by twene..John Husset *versus* John Notte 1447. *transf.* Free will *versus* necessity H. SPENCER.

Versute (vəɹsiū·t, vɔ̄·ɹsiut), *a.* Now *rare.* 1616. [– L. *versutus*, f. *vers-*, pa. ppl. stem of *vertere* turn.] Cunning, crafty, wily.

Vert (vɔ̄ɹt), *sb.*[1] (and *a.*). late ME. [– (O)Fr. *vert* :– L. *viridis*, *virid-* green, rel. to *virēre* be green; see -ID[1].] **1.** Green vegetation growing in a wood or forest and capable of serving as cover for deer. **2.** *ellipt.* The right to cut green trees or shrubs in a forest. Now *arch.* 1639. †**3.** A green colour or pigment –1582. **4.** *spec.* in *Her.* The tincture green. Also as *adj.* 1507.

1. The oversight of verte and venyson, in all the Parkes 1455.

Vert (vɔ̄ɹt), *sb.*[2] Also **'vert.** 1864. [Short for CONVERT *sb.*, PERVERT *sb.*] A convert or pervert from one religion to another, esp. to the Roman Catholic faith.

Vert, *v.*[1] 1590. [– L. *vertere* turn.] *trans.* To turn in a particular direction; to turn or twist out of the normal position. Now *spec.* in *Path.* or *Anat.*

Vert, *v.*[2] Also **'vert.** 1888. [f. VERT *sb.*[2]] *intr.* To become a convert or pervert from one religion to another, esp. to Roman Catholicism.

Vertebra (vɔ̄·ɹtĭbră). *Pl.* **-æ** (-ī). 1615. [– L. *vertebra*, f. *vertere* turn.] **1.** *Anat.* and *Zool.* One or other of the joints composing the spinal column in man or other vetebrate animals; any segment of the backbone. **2.** *pl.* (with *the*). The vertebral column; the spine or backbone 1627. **3.** *Zool.* One or other of the axial ossicles of the arms of starfishes 1704.

Vertebral (vɔ̄·ɹtĭbrăl), *a.* and *sb.* 1681. [– mod.L. *vertebralis*, f. *vertebra*; see prec., -AL[1] 1.] **A.** *adj.* **1.** Of, pertaining to, or situated on or near the vertebræ; spinal. **2.** Composed of vertebræ; spinal. Freq. in *v. column.* 1822. **3.** Of the nature of a vertebra 1847. **4.** = VERTEBRATE *a.* 1. 1816. **B.** *sb.* A vertebral artery or vein 1718. Hence **Ve·rtebrally** *adv.*

Vertebrarterial (vɔ̄:ɹtĭbraɹtī[ə]·riăl), *a.* 1884. [f. VERTEBRA + ARTERIAL *a.*] *Anat.* and *Zool.* Of or belonging to a vertebra and an artery; vertebro-arterial.

‖**Vertebrata** (vɔ̄ɹtĭbrē[i]·tă). 1826. [mod.L. (Cuvier) – L. *vertebrata* (sc. *animalia*), n. pl. of *vertebratus*; see next.] **1.** With *the.* A division of the animal kingdom including all animals which have a backbone or its equivalent. **2.** A group or class of these; a number of vertebrate animals 1851.

Vertebrate (vɔ̄·ɹtĭbrĕt), *a.* and *sb.* 1826. [– L. *vertebratus* (Pliny) jointed, articulated, f. *vertebra* VERTEBRA; see -ATE[2].] **A.** *adj.* **1.** *Zool.* Of or belonging to the Vertebrata; characterized by having a backbone or spinal column. **2.** Of, pertaining to, characteristic of, or found in a vertebrated animal or animals 1848. **3.** *fig.* Of writings, etc.: Connectedly put together; characterized by strength or consistency 1882. **B.** *sb.* A member of the Vertebrata 1826. Similarly **Ve·rtebrated** *ppl. a.* 1828. (*a*) = sense A. 1; (*b*) consisting of vertebræ; (*c*) *transf.* constructed in a manner suggestive of vertebræ.

Vertebration (vɔ̄ɹtĭbrē[i]·ʃən). 1884. [f. VERTEBRA + -ATION.] Vertebral formation; division into segments like those of the spinal column; *fig.* 'backbone', strength or firmness.

†**Ve·rtebre.** 1578. [– Fr. *vertèbre* (XVI) – L. *vertebra* VERTEBRA.] = VERTEBRA 1 –1843.

Vertebro- (vɔ̄·ɹtĭbro), used as comb. form (see -o-), of VERTEBRA, as in *v.-arterial*, *-costal*, *-iliac.*

Vertex (vɔ̄·ɹteks). *Pl.* **vertices** (vɔ̄·ɹtisīz); also **vertexes.** 1570. [– L. *vertex*, *vertic-* whirl, vortex, crown of the head, highest point, f. *vertere* turn.] **1.** *Geom.* The point opposite to the base of a (plane or solid) figure; the point in a curve or surface at which the axis meets it; an angular point, as of a triangle or polygon. **b.** *Optics.* The point at which the axis cuts the surface of a lens 1704. **2.** The point in the heavens vertically overhead, or directly above a given place; the zenith 1646. **3.** *Anat.* and *Zool.* The crown or top of the head; *esp.* in man, the part lying between the occiput and the sinciput 1638. **4.** The top, summit, or highest point of something, esp. a hill or structure; the crown of an arch. Also, †a high piece of land, an eminence. 1641.

†**Ve·rtible,** *a.* 1447. [– OFr. *vertible* or late and med.L. *vertibilis*, f. *vertere* turn; see -IBLE.] Capable of turning or being turned; inconstant, mutable –1667. So †**Vertibi·lity** –1675.

Vertical (vɔ̄·ɹtikăl), *a.* and *sb.* 1559. [– Fr. *vertical* or late L. *verticalis*, f. L. *vertex*, *vertic-*; see VERTEX, -AL[1].] **A.** *adj.* **1.** Of, pertaining to, placed or situated at, or passing through the vertex or zenith; occupying a position in the heavens directly overhead or above a given place or point; †*fig.* pertaining to or denoting the period or position of greatest eminence or perfection. **2.** *V. angle*: **a.** Either of the two angles lying on opposite sides of two intersecting lines or planes; an opposite angle. †**b.** The angle opposite the base of a triangle or polygon. 1571. **c.** *Astr.* An angle measured on a vertical circle. **3.** Placed or extending at right angles to the plane of the horizon; perpendicular, upright 1704. **b.** Of mechanical appliances or structures. Also in techn. use applied to machines which operate vertically. 1825. **4.** Having a position at right angles to the plane of the axis, body, or supporting surface; pointing or situated directly upwards or downwards 1776. **5.** *Zool.*, *Anat.*, etc. Of, pertaining to, situated on, or affecting the vertex of the head 1826.

1. At each equinox the sun appears v. over the equator 1880. †*V. point*, = VERTEX 2. *V. circle*, an azimuth-circle (see AZIMUTH 1). **3.** The adaptation of the Virginian Creeper to climbing up v. walls 1882. **b.** *V. Boring-machine*, a drill.. having a v. spindle 1875. *V. engine*, an upright engine, as distinct from a 'horizontal one 1888. Special collocations: **v. anthers,** anthers attached to the top of the filaments and pointing in the same direction as the filaments; **v. escapement,** *Watch-making*, an old type of escapement in which the balance staff was at right angles to the axis of the escape wheel; **v. fire** (*Naval* and *Mil.*), fire at such a high angle that it will fall nearly vertically on the target; **v. index,** the ratio of the height of the cranium to its length; **v. limb,** a graduated arc attached to a theodolite or other instrument for measuring v. angles; **v. line,** a line at right angles to the plane of the horizon, or to any other line or plane taken as a base.

B. *sb.* [The adj. used ellipt.] †**1.** The vertex or zenith –1655. **2.** A vertical circle, line, or plane 1669. **3.** A vertical dial 1669.

2. *Prime v.*: see PRIME *a.* Phr. *The v.*, the perpendicular. Hence **Ve·rtical-ly** *adv.*, **-ness.**

Verticality (vɔ̄ɹtikæ·lĭti). 1570. [f. prec. + -ITY. Cf. Fr. *verticalité.*] **1.** The condition of the sun or other celestial body when it is vertical or at the vertex or zenith. **2.** Vertical position; perpendicularity 1799.

1. For unto them the Sunne is verticall twice a year, making two distinct Summers in the different points of v. SIR T. BROWNE.

Verticil (vɔ̄·ɹtisil). 1793. [– L. VERTICILLUS.] *Bot.* A number or set of organs or parts arranged, disposed, or produced in a circle round an axis; a whorl.

Verticillaster (vɔ̄ːɹtisilæ·stəɹ). 1832. [mod. L., f. L. VERTICILLUS + -ASTER.] *Bot.* A form of inflorescence occurring in certain labiate plants; a false whorl.

Verticillate (vɔ̄ɹtisi·lĕt, vəɹti·silĕt), *a.* Also †**verticellate.** 1668. [f. VERTICILLUS + -ATE[2].] *Bot.* and *Zool.* Arranged in whorls; disposed in or forming verticils or whorls; having leaves, flowers, hair, etc. so disposed or arranged. So **Verti·cillated** *a.* (now *rare.*) **Verticilla·tion,** the formation of verticils; a verticil.

‖**Verticillus** (vɔ̄ɹtisi·lɒ̆s). *Pl.* **-li** (-ləi). 1760. [L., whorl (sc. of a spindle), dim. of *vertex* VERTEX.] *Bot.* A verticil or whorl.

Verticity (vəɹti·sĭti). Now *rare.* 1625. [– mod.L. *verticitas*, f. *vertex*, *vertic-* VERTEX; see -ITY.] **1.** The faculty of turning, or tendency to turn, towards a vertex or pole, esp. as exhibited in the loadstone or magnetic needle. Now *rare* or *Obs.* †**2.** The power of turning or revolving; rotation, revolution –1819.

1. The little magnet or needle turned itself briskly,..shewing great v. 1837.

Vertiginate (vəɹti·dʒineᶦt), *v. rare.* 1767. [f. L. *vertigo*, *-gin-* VERTIGO; see -ATE[3].] *intr.* To turn round, spin, or rush dizzily.

Vertiginous (vəɹti·dʒinəs), *a.* 1608. [– L. *vertiginosus* one suffering from giddiness, f. *vertigo*, *-gin-*; see next, -OUS.] **1.** Of persons, the head, etc.: Affected with vertigo or giddiness; giddy, dizzy 1621. **b.** *fig.* Inconstant; marked by instability or rapid change 1609. **2.** Of the nature of or characterized by vertigo 1608. **3.** Liable to cause vertigo; inducing giddiness 1649. **4.** Of motion: Having the character of rotation or revolution; rotatory 1663.

7. They grew v. and fell from the battlements of heaven JER. TAYLOR. **2.** V. attacks became troublesome at times 1901. **3.** Crowded rooms and the v. influence of the dance 1899. **4.** We see, with whirl v., the Sun From west to east around his axis run 1766. Hence **Verti·ginous-ly** *adv.*, **-ness.**

‖**Vertigo** (vɔ̄·ɹtigo, vəɹtəi·go, vəɹtī·go). 1528. [L. *vertigo*, *vertigin-* whirling about, giddiness, f. *vertere* turn.] **1.** *Path.* A disordered condition in which the person affected has a sensation of whirling, either of external objects or of himself, and tends to lose equilibrium and consciousness; swimming in the head; giddiness, dizziness. **2.** *fig.* A disordered state of mind, or of things, comparable to giddiness 1634.

‖**Verumontanum** (vīᵊːruˌmǫntēᶦ·nɒ̆m). 1728. [mod.L. *veru* spit + *montanum*, n. of *montanus* hilly.] *Anat.* A small prominence at the point where the seminal ducts enter the prostatic part of the urethra.

Vervain (vɔ̄·ɹvēᶦn). late ME. [– (O)Fr. *verveine* – L. *verbena* VERBENA.] **1.** The common European herbaceous plant *Verbena officinalis*, formerly much valued for its reputed medicinal properties. Also rarely, some other species of the genus *Verbena*, or the genus itself. **b.** With distinguishing terms, denoting varieties of this or other species of *Verbena*. Also applied to other plants resembling or allied to the vervains. 1578. **c.** With *a* and *pl.* A single species or plant of the genus *Verbena* 1597. **2.** Incorrectly used to render L. *verbena*; see VERBENA 1. 1548.

attrib.: **v. humming bird,** the small Jamaican species, *Mellisuga minima*; **v. mallow,** a species of mallow, *Malva alcea.*

Verve (vɔ̄ːɹv). 1697. [– (O)Fr. *verve* †form of expression, †empty chatter, †whim, vigour – L. *verba*, pl. of *verbum* word.] **1.** Special bent, vein, or talent in writing. Now *rare* or *Obs.* **2.** Intellectual vigour or energy, esp. as manifested in literary productions; great vivacity of ideas and expression 1803. **3.** *gen.* Energy, vigour, spirit 1863.

2. That thorough enjoyment of the labour, which is necessary to give life and v. to any creation, whether of the poet or the orator 1879.

Vervet (vɔ̄·ɹvĕt). 1884. [– Fr. *vervet* (Cuvier), of obscure origin.] *Zool.* A species of monkey (*Cercopithecus pygerythrus* or *C. lalandii*) native to various parts of Africa.

Very (ve·ri). Also **verey.** The name of the inventor, Samuel W. *Very*, used attrib. in *V. lights*, lights used in night-signalling or for illuminating the enemy's position; so *V. flare*; *V. pistol*, the pistol from which these lights or flares are fired 1915.

Very (ve·ri), *a.* and *adv.* [ME. *verray* – OFr. *ver(r)ai* (mod. *vrai*) :– Gallo-Rom. **veraius*, obscurely f. L. *verus* true. The termination was assim. to -Y[1].] **A.** *adj.* **I.** †**1.** Really or truly entitled to the name or designation; = TRUE *a.* 5. **2.** With limitation (usu. expressed by *the* or a possessive) to particular instances: The true or real; that is truly or properly entitled to the name. Now *arch.* late ME. **3.** In emphatic use, denoting that the person or thing may be so named in the fullest sense of the term, or possesses all the essential qualities of the thing specified. late ME. **4.** †**a.** Truthful, true; sure, reliable –1505. **b.** Of truth: Exact, simple, real, actual. late ME. †**5.** Exact or precise, as opp. to *approximate* –1657. †**6.** Of a friend, servant, etc.: True, faithful, sincere, staunch –1676. †**7.** Of persons: Rightful, lawful, legitimate –1606.

1. Very God of very God *Bk. Com. Pr.*, *Nicene Creed* 1549. God is a v. spirit 1615. The Law of Nature [is] v. justice HOBBES. **2.** What would you say to me now, and I were your verie, verie Rosalind? SHAKS. The reall, and v. object HOBBES. **3.** They shall become a v. desolacion and curse COVERDALE 2 *Kings* 22:19. A Region, which is the v. Reverse of Paradise ADDISON. A thing..so v. a nothing in itself 1747. A verier knave ne'er stepped the earth 1856. The veriest schoolboy 1859. **4. a.** Phr. *In* (or †*of*) *v. deed*; see DEED. **b.** To speak the v. truth 1668. **6.** A Gentleman a verie friend of mine 1608.

II. 1. Used as an intensive, either to denote the inclusion of something regarded as extreme or exceptional, or to emphasize the exceptional prominence of some ordinary thing or feature. late ME. **b.** Emphasizing sbs. which denote extremity of degree or extent. late ME. **2.** Neither more nor less than (that expressed by the sb. qualified); sheer. late ME. **b.** = MERE *a.* 5. 1546. **3.** Used (after *the, this, that*, etc.) to denote or emphasize complete or exact identity 1582. **b.** Of words: Exactly corresponding to those of an original or previous statement 1598.

1. The v. heauens declare his rightuousnes COVERDALE *Ps.* 96:6. The room was crammed to the v. door 1832. His v. defects were a main cause of his popularity 1880. **b.** A bankrupt from the v. outset 1851. **c.** Coupled with *own*; I had to have it for my v. own. 1884. **2.** The sailors mutinied from v. hunger MACAULAY. **b.** The Governor-General treated the v. request as a high offence 1817. **3.** She died just this v. Day Seven Years SWIFT. Phr. *The v. thing*, the thing exactly suitable or requisite. **b.** Those were my v. words! 1865.

B. *adv.* †**1.** Truly, really, genuinely; in or with truth or reality; truthfully –1593. **2.** In a high degree or measure; to a great extent; exceedingly, extremely 1448. **b.** Qualifying pa. pples. used predic. or attrib.: = Very much 1641. **c.** With a neg., freq. denoting: Only moderately or slightly 1710. **d.** Repeated in order to convey greater emphasis 1649. **3.** In purely intensive use 1500.

2. My father..ys a verye old man 1588. V. near as long as the Iliad it self ADDISON. **b.** A v. overrated man 1804. **c.** Then it went off, leaving me sickish, but not v. SWIFT. **d.** It was indeed v., v., v. dreadful DE FOE. **3.** The City was now reduc'd to the v. last Extremity 1684. The v. same day the year before 1662.

‖**Vesania** (vĭsēᶦ·niă). 1693. [L., f. *vesanus* mad, f. *ve-* not + *sanus* sane.] *Path.* Mental derangement.

‖**Vesica** (vĭsəi·kă). 1683. [L., bladder, blister.] **1.** *Anat.* A bladder 1693. †**2.** A copper vessel used in distilling –1728. **3.** In full, *V. piscis* (also *piscium*): a pointed oval figure, the sides of which are properly parts of two equal circles passing through each other at their centres, freq. employed as an architectural feature and by early artists as an aureole enclosing figures of Christ, the Virgin, etc. 1809.

3. Vesica piscium cannot, therefore, signify a fish's bladder, but a bladder which when filled with wind, would be in the form of a fish 1813. Hence **Ve·sical** *a.* of, pertaining to, or formed in the urinary bladder; having the form of a v.

Vesicant (ve·sikănt), *sb.* and *a.* 1661. [f. VESICATE *v.* + -ANT. Cf. Fr. *vésicant.*] *Med.* **A.** *sb.* A vesicatory. **b.** A blister gas 1938. **B.** *adj.* Causing blisters; vesicatory 1826.

Vesicate (ve·sikeᶦt), *v.* 1657. [– *vesicat-*, pa. ppl. stem of late and med.L. *vesicare*, *-ari* (intr.) form pustules, f. VESICA; see -ATE[3].] Chiefly *Med.* **1.** *trans.* To cause to rise in a blister or blisters; to raise blisters on (the skin, etc.). **b.** In *pa. pple.* Covered with or converted into blisters 1676. **2.** *absol.* To produce blisters 1809. **3.** *intr.* To become blistered 1899.

Vesication (vesikēᶦ·ʃən). 1543. [– med.L. *vesicatio*, *-ōn-* formation of pustules, f. as prec.; see -ION. Cf. Fr. *vésication* (XVI).] *Med.* **1.** The result of blistering or of rising in blisters; a blister or a group of these. **2.** The formation or development of blisters; the action or fact of blistering 1753.

Vesicatory (ve·sikeᶦtəri, vesi·kătəri), *sb.* and *a.* 1604. [prob. f. VESICATION; see -ORY.] *Med.* **A.** *sb.* An ointment, plaster, or other application for raising blisters on the skin. **B.** *adj.* Of the nature of a vesicatory; capable of or characterized by raising blisters 1612.

Vesicle (ve·sik'l). 1578. [– Fr. *vésicule* or L. *vesicula*, dim. of VESICA; see -ULE.] **1. a.** *Anat.*, *Bot.*, *Zool.* A small bladder-like vessel; a cavity or cell with a membranous integument; a small sac or cyst. (Freq. with defining terms, as *blood-*, *seminal*, *umbilical vesicles.*) **b.** *Physics.* A minute bubble or spherule of liquid or vapour, esp. one of those composing a cloud or fog 1731. **c.** *Geol.* A small spherical or oval cavity produced by the presence of bubbles of gas or vapour in volcanic rocks 1811. **2.** *Path.* A small, usually round, elevation of the cuticle containing fluid matter 1799.

Vesico- (ve·siko), used as comb. form (see -o-) of VESICA, occurring in terms referring to the bladder in connection with some other part of the body denoted by the second element, as *v.-cervical*, *-prostatic*, *-rectal*.

‖**Vesicula** (vĭsi·kiŭlă). *Pl.* **-æ** (-ī). 1715. [L., dim. of VESICA; see -ULE.] = VESICLE 1 (usu. in pl.), 2.

Vesicular (vĭsi·kiŭlăɹ), *a.* 1715. [f. VESICULA + -AR¹.] **1.** Having the form or structure of a vesicle; bladder-like 1720. **2.** Characterized by the presence of vesicles; composed of parts having the form of vesicles 1715. **3.** *Path.* **a.** Characterized by the formation or presence of vesicles on the skin 1818. **b.** Affecting or connected with the vesicles or air-cells of the lungs 1829.

1. It was formerly advanced that these minute drops of rain or fog were v.—that is, hollow spheres! 1860. **2.** V. Lava 1811. **3. a.** V. Fever 1818. **b.** It is commonly called the 'v. murmur', having been so named when the idea that it arose in the air cells of the lung was accepted without question 1883.

Vesiculated (vĭsi·kiŭlēⁱtėd), *a.* 1703. [f. VESICULA + -ATE² + -ED¹.] **1.** Having or full of small cavities or air-cells. **2.** Of the nature of a vesicle or vesicula 1898. **3.** *Path.* Covered with vesicles 1858

Vesiculation (vĭsikiŭlēⁱ·ʃən). 1876. [f. VESICULA + -ATION.] *Path.* The formation of vesicles, esp. on the skin; a vesicular condition or pustule.

‖**Vesiculitis** (vĭsikiŭləi·tis). 1861. [f. VESICULA + -ITIS.] *Path.* Inflammation of a vesicle, esp. of the seminal vesicles.

Vesiculose (vĭsi·kiŭlōᵘs), *a.* 1817. [f. VESICULA + -OSE¹ or f. VESICA + -ULOSE.] Full of vesicles; vesicular. So †**Vesi·culous** *a.* –1712.

Vesper (ve·spəɹ). late ME. [Partly – L. *vesper* evening star, evening = Gr. ἕσπερος; partly – OFr. *vespres* (mod. *vêpres*) – eccl. L. *vesperas*, acc. pl. of L. *vespera* evening, eventide (= Gr. ἑσπέρα), modelled on *matutinas* MATINS.] **I.** In the sing. form. **1.** *poet.* (or *rhet.*). With capital. The evening star; Hesper, Hesperus. †**2.** Evening, eventide; an evening –1849. **3.** Vespers, evensong 1636. **4.** *ellipt.* The vesper-bell 1808.

4. But, hark! the v. calls to pray'r MOORE.

II. In collect. pl. **Vespers.** †**1. a.** In University use; The public disputations and accompanying ceremonies immediately preceding the inception or commencement of a Bachelor of Arts; esp. in later use at Oxford, the day on which these were held, the eve *of* the Act –1715. †**b.** The eve *of* a festival or *of* the Passion –1697. **2.** *Eccl.* The sixth of the canonical hours of the breviary, said or sung (orig.) towards evening; evensong; also, the time of this office 1611. **b.** *poet.* Evening prayers or devotions 1814. **3.** *transf.* The evening song of a bird. Chiefly *poet.* 1678.

2. *Sicilian vespers*: see SICILIAN *a.*

Vesperal (ve·spĕrăl), *a.* and *sb.* 1623. [– Fr. *vespéral* adj. and sb., f. L. *vespera* (see prec.) + *-al* -AL¹ 1 (in the sb. = med.L. *-ale* as in *missale* MISSAL).] **A.** *adj.* Pertaining to the evening or to vespers (*rare*). **B.** *sb. Eccl.* An office-book containing the psalms, canticles, antiphons, etc., used at vespers; an antiphonary containing the vesperchants 1869.

‖**Vespertilio** (vespəɹti·lio). 1665. [L. *vespertilio* bat, f. *vesper* VESPER.] A bat (*rare*); in mod. *Zool.*, one of the many genera of *Cheiroptera*.

Vesperti·lionid, *a.* 1875. [– mod.L. *Vespertilionidæ*; see prec., -ID³.] *Zool.* Of or belonging to the *Vespertilionidæ*, a large family of insectivorous bats including the common British species.

Vespertine (ve·spəɹtəin, -in), *a.* 1502. [– L. *vespertinus*, f. *vesper* VESPER; see -INE¹.] **1.** Of or pertaining to the evening; coming, occurring, or taking place in the evening. **b.** Of animals, birds, etc.: Appearing or especially active in the evening 1607. **2.** *Astr.* and *Astrol.* Of a star, planet, etc.: Setting at or just after sunset 1601. **3.** *Geol.* Used to designate the lowest carboniferous formation of the Pennsylvanian coal-measures 1858. So **Vesperti·nal** *a.*

Vespiary (ve·spiări). 1817. [irreg. f. L. *vespa* wasp, after *apiary*.] A wasps' nest.

Vespine (ve·spəin), *a.* 1843. [f. L. *vespa* wasp + -INE¹.] Of or pertaining to a wasp or wasps; consisting of wasps.

Vessel (ve·sĕl), *sb.* ME. [– (i) AFr. *vessel* = OFr. *vaissel* (mod. *vaisseau* vessel, vase, ship) :– late L. *vascellum* small vase, dim. of *vas* vessel (see VASE); (ii) AFr. *vessele* = (O)Fr. *vaisselle* pots and pans, plate :– Rom. **vascella*, pl. of L. *vascellum* used as coll. sing. fem.] †**1.** In collect. sing.: = PLATE *sb.* II. 3. –1664. **2.** A receptacle for a liquid or other substance, often one of circular section and made of some durable material; *esp.* a utensil of this nature in domestic use, employed in connection with the preparation or serving of food or drink, and usu. of a size suitable for carrying by hand ME. **3.** *fig.* (chiefly in or after Biblical use). **a.** Said of a person regarded as having the containing capacity or function of a vessel. Now *arch.* ME. †**b.** Said of the body, esp. as the receptacle of the soul –1704. **4.** A craft or ship of any kind, now usu. one larger than a rowing-boat and often restricted to seagoing craft or those plying upon the larger rivers or lakes ME. **5.** *Anat.* and *Zool.* One of the membranous canals, ducts, or tubes in which the fluids of the body are contained and by means of which they are circulated; freq., a blood-vessel. late ME. **b.** *Bot.* One of the cellular or tubular structures composing the vascular system of plants and having the function of containing or carrying sap or other secretion; a duct 1671. **6.** *Bot.* = PERICARP (*rare*) 1691.

1. All his Vessell was of golde and siluer, pottis, basons, ewers, dysshes, flagons, barels, cuppes, and all other thyngis LD. BERNERS. **2.** To my great Misfortune, I had no V. to boil or stew any Thing DE FOE. *fig.* When creeping Murmure.. Fills the wide Vessell of the Vniuerse SHAKS. *Prov.* But the saying is true, The empty v. makes the greatest sound SHAKS. **3. a.** We know there are vessels of wrath 1597. Phr. *The weaker v.*: see WEAK *a.* **3. b.** WYCLIF 1 *Thess.* 4:4. **4.** *fig.* In 1832 the v. of Reform was still labouring heavily 1876. Hence †**Ve·ssel** *v. trans.* to put or enclose (a liquid, etc.) in a v. **Ve·sselful,** as much or as many as a v. will hold.

Vest (vest), *sb.* 1613. [– Fr. *veste* – It. *veste* garment :– L. *vestis* clothing, attire, garment.] **1.** A loose outer garment worn by men in Eastern countries or in ancient times; a robe or gown. **b.** A similar garment worn by women. Chiefly *poet.* 1700. **c.** A garment, in various fig. uses 1655. **2.** An ecclesiastical vestment (*rare*) 1663. **3. a.** A sleeveless garment of some length worn by men beneath the coat. (Introduced by Charles II.) Now *Hist.* **b.** A waistcoat. (Now in tradesman's use and *U.S.*) 1666. **c.** A knitted or woven under-garment for the upper part of the body, worn next to the skin 1851. **d.** A piece of lace, net, silk, or other soft material worn so as to be completely or partly visible at the front of the bodice of a low-necked garment 1887.

1. The Persians make their long vests of such cloths DE FOE. **b.** Attended by her Maiden Train, Who bore the Vests that Holy Rites require DRYDEN. **c.** Ev'ning in her sober v. COWPER.

Vest (vest), *v.* late ME. [In both I. and II. first in pa. pple. *vested* – OFr. *vestu*, pa. pple. of *vestir* (mod. *vêtir*) clothe, †invest :– L. *vestire* clothe, spec. with the Imperial purple, in med.L. put in possession, as by investing a person with the insignia of an office, f. *vestis* VEST *sb.*] **I. 1.** *trans.* = INVEST *v.* I, 5, 6. Chiefly in pass., and usu. const. *in.* **b.** To invest (a person) *with* some quality, esp. power, authority, etc. Chiefly in pass. 1674. **2.** *intr.* To become vested *in* a person; to descend or devolve *upon* a person as possessor 1592.

1. No Legiance is due to him, before the Crown is vested upon him 1651. There is a particular jurisdiction vested in the officers 1756. Miltiades thus vested in the supreme command GOLDSM. **b.** They may be reasonably supposed to be vested with the same powers 1727. **2.** The property vests in the official receiver *qua* trustee 1885.

II. 1. *trans.* In pa. pple.: Dressed, clothed, robed (*in* some garment) 1513. **2.** Of a garment: To clothe or cover (a person) 1582. **3.** To dress (a person) in a robe or garment, esp. as a formal act or ceremony 1648. **b.** *Eccl.* To drape or cover (an altar) 1867. **4.** *refl.* To apparel or robe oneself, esp. in ecclesiastical vestments. Also *absol.* 1668.

1. My late espoused Saint..Came vested all in white, pure as her mind MILT. **4.** Just before the Bishop vested himself to say Mass 1771.

III. *trans.* = INVEST *v.* II. 1719.

Vesting this Hundred Pounds in English Goods DE FOE.

‖**Vesta** (ve·stă). late ME. [L., corresp. to Gr. Ἑστία, identical with ἑστία hearth, house, household.] **1.** *Myth.* A Roman female divinity, the daughter of Saturn and goddess of the hearth and household. **2.** *Astr.* One of the minor planets, revolving in an orbit between Mars and Jupiter 1807. **3.** orig. *v. match*: A kind of short match, orig. of wax 1839.

Vestal (ve·stăl), *a.* and *sb.* late ME. [– L. *vestalis*, f. VESTA; see -AL¹ 1.] **A.** *adj.* **1.** *V. virgin*, one of the priestesses (orig. four, subseq. six in number) who had charge of the sacred fire in the temple of Vesta at Rome. **2.** Of fire, etc.: Of or pertaining to Vesta 1599. **3.** Resembling a priestess of Vesta in respect of chastity; chaste, pure, virgin 1595. **4.** Pertaining to or characteristic of a vestal virgin or virgins; marked by chastity or purity 1592.

2. She sprinkl'd thrice, with Wine, the V. Fire DRYDEN. **3.** *transf.* V. primroses KEATS. **4.** A Song fit for a v. Ear 1729.

B. *sb.* **1.** A vestal virgin 1579. **2.** A virgin; a chaste woman; a nun 1590.

2. She was the most hospitable and jovial of old vestals, and had been a beauty in her day THACKERAY.

Vested (ve·stėd), *ppl. a.* 1671. [f. VEST *v.* + -ED¹.] **1.** Clothed, robed, dressed, *spec.* in ecclesiastical vestments. **2.** Established, secured, or settled in the hands of, or definitely assigned to a certain possessor; *esp.* with *right* or *interest* 1766.

1. The V. Priest before the Altar stands WORDSW. **2.** V. remainders..are where the estate is invariably fixed, to remain to a determinate person, after the particular estate is spent BLACKSTONE.

Vestiarian (vesti,ēᵊ·riăn), *a.* 1850. [f. VESTIARY + -IAN.] Of, relating to, or concerned with ecclesiastical vestments.

Vestiary (ve·sti,ări), *sb.* ME. [– OFr. *vestiarie*, (also mod.) *vestiaire* – L. *vestiarium* clothes-chest, wardrobe (in med.L. = vestry XI), subst. use of n. sing of *vestiarius* adj., f. *vestis* clothing, vesture.] The vestry of a church. Now *rare* or *Obs.* **b.** A room or building, esp. in a monastery or other large establishment, in which clothes were kept. *Hist.* 1450.

Vestiary (ve·sti,ări), *a.* 1622. [– L. *vestiarius*; see prec. and -ARY¹.] Of, pertaining to, or relating to clothes or dress.

Vestibular (vesti·biŭlăɹ), *a.* 1836. [f. next + -AR¹.] Of, pertaining to, of the nature of, resembling, or serving as a vestibule.

The v. termination of the auditory nerve 1899.

Vestibule (ve·stibiŭl). 1623. [– Fr. *vestibule* (perh. – It. *vestibulo*) or L. *vestibulum* entrance-court, fore-court, entrance.] **1.** The enclosed or partially enclosed space in front of the main entrance of an ancient Roman or Greek house or building; an entrance-court or fore-court. **b.** A chamber or hall immediately between the entrance-door and the interior of a building or house (usu. one of some size), to which it gives admittance; an ante-chamber, entrance-hall, or lobby 1730. **c.** An enclosed and covered-in portion at either end of a railway carriage, serving as a means of passage from one carriage to another. Also *attrib.* in *v. train*. orig. *U.S.* 1889. **2.** *Anat.* and *Zool.* One or other of various cavities or hollows regarded as forming an approach or entrance to another, usu. a larger or more important part 1728.

2. *V. of the ear*, the osseous cavity which forms the central portion of the labyrinth of the ear and is situated between the tympanum and the internal auditory canal immediately behind the cochlea.

‖**Vestibulum** (vesti·biŭlǒm). 1662. [L.; see prec.] **a.** = prec. 1, 2. **b.** *Zool.* The cavity or chamber in certain infusorians into which the œsophagus and anus open 1859.

Vestige (ve·stidʒ). 1602. [– Fr. *vestige* – L. *vestigium* sole of the foot, footprint, trace.] **I. 1.** A mark, trace, or visible sign *of* something which no longer exists or is present; a piece of material evidence of this nature; something which remains after the destruction or disappearance of the main portion. **b.** A surviving memorial or trace *of* some condition, quality, practice, etc., serving as an indication of its former existence. Usu. in pl. 1700. **c.** A very small or slight trace, indication, or amount (*of* something) 1756. **2.** *Biol.* A surviving trace *of* some part formerly existing in the species; a vestigial organ or structure 1859.

1. Descending the Mons Cælius we come against the vestiges of the Palazzo Maggiore EVELYN. **b.** The vestiges of a patriarchal state still surviving 1875. **c.** Not a v. of green pasturage was to be descried 1834. **2.** Rudimentary organs,..as..the v. of an ear in earless breeds DARWIN.

II. A mark or trace left on the ground by the foot; a footprint; a track (*rare*) 1656.

Vestigial (vesti·dʒiăl), *a.* 1884. [f. VESTIGE + -IAL.] Of the nature of a vestige; remaining or surviving in a degenerate, atrophied, or imperfect condition or form.

‖**Vestigium** (vesti·dʒiǒm). *Pl.* **-ia.** Now *rare* or *Obs.* 1637. [L. See VESTIGE.] A vestige or trace; a mark or indication left by something destroyed, lost, or no longer present.

†**Ve·stiment.** ME. [– OFr. *vestiment* or L. *vestimentum* clothes, f. *vestire* clothe; see VEST *v.*, -MENT.] A vestment, esp. one worn by an ecclesiastic –1850. Hence **Vestime·ntal** (*rare*), **Vestime·ntary** *adjs.* of or pertaining to clothes or dress; vestiary.

Ve·sting. 1828. [f. VEST *sb.* 3 b + -ING¹.] Cloth or other material for making vests or waistcoats. Usu. in pl.

Vestiture (ve·stitiŭɹ, -tʃəɹ). late ME. [– med.L. *vestitura*, f. L. *vestire* VEST *v.*; see -URE.] **1.** = INVESTITURE 2, 3. (*rare*). **2.** *concr.* Clothes, clothing, vesture 1842.

Vestment (ve·stmĕnt). [ME. *vestiment*, *vestement* (3 syll.) – OFr. *vestiment*, *vestement* (mod. *vêtement*) – L. *vestimentum*; see VESTIMENT.] **1.** A garment or article of clothing, esp. one of the nature of a robe or gown. Also *collect.*, clothing, dress, vesture. **2.** A garment worn by a priest or ecclesiastic on the occasion of some service or ceremony; a priestly robe ME. **b.** An article of attire worn by the clergy, or by certain of their assistants, during divine service or on some special occasion; *spec.* a chasuble ME. **c.** *transf.* and *fig.* Something which covers as a garment; a covering 1483.

2. The Surplice, a v. of the Pagan Priests, introduced into churches 1796. **3.** Green,..which colour nature hath chosen for the v. of the earth HOGARTH.

Vestry (ve·stri). late ME. [– AFr. *vest(e)rie, alt. of (O)Fr. *vestiaire*, †*vestiarie* (see VESTIARY), by assoc. with *-erie*, -ERY.] **1.** A room or part of a church in which the vestments, vessels, records, etc. are kept, and in which the clergy and choir robe for divine service; a room used for similar purposes in connection with any church, chapel, or other place of worship. **b.** A place or room where clothes (†or valuables) are kept 1574. **2.** In English parishes: An assembly or meeting of the parishioners or a certain number of these, held usu. in the vestry of the parish church, for the dispatch of parochial business 1589. **b.** The body of parishioners meeting in this way and constituting a parochial board or council of management 1672.

1. b. Then said the Interpreter.., Go into the V. and fetch out Garments for these People BUNYAN. **2.** I did speechify once at a v. 1762. **b.** The Lower House..had degenerated into something noisier than a v. 1882.

Comb.: **v.-book,** (*a*) a book in which the proceedings of the parish v. are recorded; (*b*) a book kept in a v. in which the births, marriages, and deaths of the parishioners are registered; **-clerk,** the clerk of a parochial v.; **-room,** the v. of a church; the room in which the parochial v. assembles. Hence **Ve·stryman,** a member of a parochial v.

Vestuary (ve·stiu‚ări). Now *arch.* 1490. [– OFr. *vestuaire* – med.L. *vestuarium*, alt. (after *vestura*) f. *vestiarium* VESTIARY, VESTRY.] A vestiary or vestry; a wardrobe.

Vesture (ve·stiŭɹ, -tʃəɹ), *sb.* late ME. [– OFr. *vesture* (mod. *vêture*) – med.L. *vestura*, for late L. *vestitura*, f. L. *vestire* clothe; see -URE.] **1.** That with which a person is clothed or dressed; clothes, clothing. **2.** *Law.* All that grows upon or covers the land, with the exception of trees; one or other of the products of land, such as grass or corn 1455.

1. Pharaoh..arayed him in vestures of fine linnen *Gen.* 41:42. *collect.* They haue..cast lottes vpon my v. COVERDALE *Ps.* 21:18. *fig.* To clothe ourselves with the comely v. of innocency 1575. **2.** In English Law it has been held that one person may have a freehold in the soil and another in the v. 1869. Hence **Ve·stured** *ppl. a.* clothed or dressed in v.; wearing v.

Vesuvian (vĭsiū·viăn), *a.* and *sb.* 1673. [f. *Vesuvius*, the active volcano on the Bay of Naples in Italy; see -AN.] **A.** *adj.* Of or pertaining to Vesuvius; *esp.* like or resembling Vesuvius, or that of Vesuvius, in volcanic violence or power. **B.** *sb.* **1.** *Min.* A silicate or aluminium, lime, and iron or other base, occurring massive but more freq. in square crystals of various colours, and found orig. in the ancient Vesuvian lavas; idocrase 1796. **2.** A kind of match or fusee, used esp. for lighting cigars or pipes in the open air 1853. Hence **Vesu·vianite** = B 1.

Vesuvin (vĭsiū·vin). 1885. [– G. *vesuvin*, f. *Vesuvius*, from its explosive property; see -IN¹.] *Chem.* Phenyl-brown, used esp. as a staining matter for histological preparations.

Vet, *sb.* 1862. [colloq. contr. of VETERINARIAN or VETERINARY.] A veterinary surgeon. Hence **Vet** *v. trans.* to submit (an animal) to veterinary examination or treatment 1891; *transf.* to examine or treat (a person) medically; *fig.* (*colloq.*) to examine, scrutinize, test 1904.

Vet. U.S. abbrev. of VETERAN.

Vetch (vetʃ). late ME. [– AFr., ONFr. *veche* = OFr. *vece* (mod. *vesce*) :– L. *vicia*).] **1.** The bean-like fruit of various species of the leguminous plant *Vicia*. **2.** *pl.* Plants belonging to the genus *Vicia*, esp. to the species *V. sativa*, the common tare. late ME. **3.** In generic use as a plant-name (or, in early use, as that of a grain); also occas., with *a* and *pl.*, one or other species of the genus *Vicia*. late ME. **4.** Applied, with distinguishing terms, to plants of various genera more or less resembling vetches 1562. Hence **Ve·tchy** *a.* composed of or abounding in vetches.

Vetchling (ve·tʃliŋ). 1578. [f. prec. + -LING¹.] *Bot.* A plant or species of the genus *Lathyrus*; the genus itself.

Veteran (ve·tĕrăn), *sb.* and *a.* 1509. [– Fr. *vétéran* or L. *veteranus*, f. *vetus*, *veter-* old; see -AN.] **A.** *sb.* **1.** One who has had long experience in military service; an old soldier. **2.** One who has seen long service in any office or position, an experienced or aged person 1597. **3.** An ex-service man (*U.S.*) 1906.

B. *adj.* **1.** Of soldiers: Long practised or exercised in war 1611. **2.** Of persons in general: Grown old in service; experienced by long usage or practice 1728. **3.** Of things: Old; long-continued (*rare*) 1653.

1. The loss of a v. army GIBBON. **2.** The self-possession of a v. courtier MACAULAY. Hence **Ve·teranize** *v.* (*U.S.*) *trans.* to render a v.; *intr.* to re-enlist as a soldier.

Veterinarian (ve:tĕrinē³·riăn), *sb.* and *a.* 1646. [f. L. *veterinarius* (see next) + -AN.] **A.** *sb.* One who is skilled in or professionally occupied with the medical and surgical treatment of cattle and domestic animals; a veterinary surgeon. **B.** *adj.* = next A. 1656.

Veterinary (ve·tĕrinări), *a.* and *sb.* 1790. [– L. *veterinarius*, f. *veterinus* pertaining to cattle (*veterinæ* fem. pl., *veterina* n. pl. cattle), perh. f. *vetus*, *veter-* old, as if the orig. ref. was to animals past work; see -INE¹, -ARY¹.] **A.** *adj.* Of, pertaining to, connected or concerned with the medical or surgical treatment of cattle or domestic animals.

V. surgeon = prec. A.

B. *sb.* = prec. A. 1861.

Vetiver (ve·tivəɹ). Also **-vert.** 1858. [– Fr. *vétiver*, *vétyver* – Tamil *veṭṭivēru* (f. *vēr* root).] = CUSCUS².

Veto (vī·to), *sb.* 1629. [– L. *veto* I forbid, the word by which the Roman tribunes of the people opposed measures of the Senate or actions of the magistrates.] **1.** A prohibition having for its object or result the prevention of a proposed or intended act; the power of thus preventing or checking action by prohibition. **2.** *spec.* The act on the part of a competent person or body of preventing or checking legislative or other political action by the exercise of a prohibitory power; the right or power to interpose prohibition against the passing or putting in force of an enactment or measure 1792.

1. Phr. *To put* (also *place, set*) *a v. on* or *upon* (something); The Rector had beforehand put a v. on any Dissenting chairman GEO. ELIOT. **2.** The President's v. kills off some vicious measures 1888. Hence **Ve·toist,** one who exercises the right, or supports the use, of the v.

Veto (vī·to), *v.* 1706. [f. prec.] **1.** *trans.* To put a veto on, refuse consent to; to stop or block by this means. **2.** To refuse to admit or accept (a person) 1885.

1. Washington vetoed..two bills only 1888.

‖**Vettura** (vetū·ra). 1792. [It. :– L. *vectura* transportation, f. *vect-*, pa. ppl. stem of *vehere* convey. Cf. VOITURE.] A four-wheeled carriage used in Italy.

‖**Vetturino** (veturī·no). *Pl.* **-ini.** 1617. [It., f. *vettura*; see prec.] **1.** In Italy: One who lets out carriages or horses on hire; also, a driver of a vettura. **2.** = prec. 1789.

Vex (veks), *v.* late ME. [– (O)Fr. *vexer* – L. *vexare* shake, agitate, disturb.] **I. 1.** *trans.* To trouble, afflict, or harass (a person, etc.) by aggression, encroachment, or other interference with peace and quiet. **2.** Of diseases, etc.: To afflict or distress physically. Now *poet.* 1489. **3.** To afflict with mental agitation or trouble; to make anxious or depressed; to distress deeply or seriously. late ME. **4.** To affect with a feeling of dissatisfaction, annoyance, or irritation; to cause (a person) to fret, grieve, or feel unhappy 1450. **b.** To irritate or tease (an animal) 1700. †**5.** *intr.* To be distressed in mind; to feel unhappy or dissatisfied; to fret or grieve. Also const. *at.* –1804.

1. When intestine divisions v. a state 1845. **2.** Sore vexed with the gout 1548. **3.** V. not his ghost, O let him passe SHAKS. Why will you v. yourself about your father? 1873. **4.** Your letter very much vexed me 1714.

II. 1. *trans.* To disturb by causing physical movement, commotion, or alteration; to agitate, toss about, work, etc. 1627. **b.** *fig.* To press, strain, or urge 1678. **2.** To subject (a matter) to prolonged or severe examination or discussion 1614.

1. Some English wool, vex'd in a Belgian Loom, And into Cloth of spungy softness made DRYDEN. **2.** And not vexing a question..let us own that he was..a gentleman 1869. Hence **Ve·xer,** one who or that which vexes or annoys.

Vexation (veksē¹·ʃən). late ME. [– (O)Fr. *vexation* – L. *vexatio*, *-ōn-*, f. *vexat-*, pa. ppl. stem of *vexare*; see prec., -ION.] **1.** The action of troubling or harassing by aggression or interference (occas. *spec.* by unjustifiable claims or legal action); the fact of being troubled or harassed in this way. †**2.** The action of troubling, disturbing, or irritating by physical means; the fact or state of being so troubled or distressed –1704. **3.** The state or fact of being mentally troubled or distressed, in later use esp. by something causing annoyance, irritation, dissatisfaction, or disappointment 1465. **4.** A source or cause of mental trouble or distress; a grief or affliction. Chiefly with *a.* 1594.

1. I still had hopes, my long vexations past, Here to return GOLDSM. **2.** The fierce v. of a dreame SHAKS. **3.** The King..heard of this new trouble with much v. SCOTT. Phr. *V. of mind, spirit.* **4.** Your Children were v. to your youth, But mine shall be a comfort to your Age SHAKS.

Vexatious (veksē¹·ʃəs), *a.* 1534. [f. prec.; see -IOUS.] **1.** Causing or tending to cause vexation. **b.** *spec.* Of legal actions: Instituted without sufficient grounds for the purpose of causing trouble or annoyance to the defendant 1677. †2. Full of trouble or uneasiness –1671.

1. The Towsmen..are..turbulent and v. to the Regiment 1715. b. Their courts were unceasingly occupied with v. suits FROUDE. 2. Riches and honours which bring not a pleasant, but rather a careful and v. life 1671. Hence **Vexa·tious-ly** *adv.*, **-ness.**

Vexed (vekst), *ppl. a.* 1440. [f. VEX *v.* + -ED[1].] **1.** Troubled, harassed. **2.** Distressed, grieved; annoyed, irritated 1602. **3.** Subjected to physical force or strain; tossed about, agitated 1610. **4.** *V. question*, a much debated or contested question 1657. Hence **Ve·xed-ly** *adv.*

Vexillary (ve·ksilări). 1591. [– L. *vexillarius* standard-bearer, f. *vexillum*; see VEXILLUM, -ARY[1].] **a.** One of the oldest class of veterans in the Roman army, who served under a special standard. **b.** A Roman standard-bearer.

Vexillation (veksilēⁱ·ʃən). 1656. [– L. *vexillatio, -ōn-*, f. *vexillum*; see next, -ATION.] A company of veteran soldiers (see prec. a) or of soldiers grouped under one standard.

‖**Vexillum** (veksi·lɒ̆m). 1726. [L. (in sense 1) f. the stem of *vehere* carry.] **1. a.** A flag or banner carried by Roman troops; a body of men grouped under one banner. **b.** *Eccl.* A piece of linen or silk attached to the upper part of a crozier 1877. **2.** *Bot.* The large external petal of a papilionaceous flower 1727. **3.** *Ornith.* The vane or web of a feather 1867.

‖**Via** (vəi·ă), *sb.* 1615. [L., a road, way.] **1.** *V. Lactea*, the Milky Way. **2.** A way or road; a highway 1787. **3.** *V. media*, a middle way; an intermediate course 1845.

‖**Via** (vəi·ă), *int. Obs.* exc. *arch.* 1596. [It. (special use of *via* way; see prec.).] **1.** As an exclam. = Onward, come on, come along. **2.** As an exhortation or command to depart = Away, be off, begone 1596. **b.** Used to check argument or reply, or to dismiss a subject 1598.

1. Then *v.* for the spatious bounds of Fraunce 1596. 2. b. *Merry W.* II. ii. 159.

‖**Via** (vəi·ă), *prep.* Also **viâ.** 1779. [L., abl. sing. of VIA *sb.*] By way of; by the route which passes through or over (a specified place).

To proceed through Spain and *viâ* Paris, home 1882.

Viability (vəiăbi·lĭti). 1843. [– Fr. *viabilité* (1812), or f. VIABLE *a.*; see -ITY.] The quality or state of being viable; capacity for living; ability to live under certain conditions.

Viable (vəi·ăb'l), *a.* 1828. [– Fr. *viable* (XVI), f. *vie* life; see -ABLE.] Capable of living; able to maintain a separate existence.

Such..deformity of the female pelvis..as will absolutely preclude the birth of a v. child 1881.

Viaduct (vəi·ădɒkt). 1816. [f. L. *via* way, after AQUEDUCT.] An elevated structure, consisting of a series of arches or spans, by means of which a railway or road is carried over a valley, road, river, etc.

Viage, obs. f. VOYAGE.

Vial (vəi·ăl), *sb.* [ME. *viole*, alt. of *fiole* PHIAL. For the *v* cf. VENT *sb.*[1], VAN *sb.*[1]] A vessel of a small or moderate size used for holding liquids; *spec.*, in later use a small glass bottle, a phial.

Put a spoonful of this Water in a V. WESLEY. *fig.* (after Rev. 16:1) The vials of God's wrath poured out KINGSLEY. Hence **Vi·al** *v. trans.*, to put into a v.

Viand (vəi·ănd). late ME. [– (O)Fr. *viande* †food, (now) meat :– Rom. **vi(v)anda* fem. sb. alt. of L. *vivenda*, n. pl. gerundive of *vivere* live.] **1.** *pl.* Articles of food; provisions, victuals. **2.** *sing.* **a.** *collect.* Food, sustenance 1450. **b.** With *a* and *pl.* An article or kind of food 1527.

1. Flesche and dyverse vyaundes MAUNDEV. 2. All things necessary both for viande and apparell 1643.

†**Vi·ander**[1]. ME. [– AFr. *via(u)ndour, viandere*, OFr. *viandier, -iere*, f. *viande* VIAND; see -ER[2] 2.] **1.** One who provides viands or good cheer for his household or guests; a (liberal) host or entertainer –1577. **2.** One who provides himself with good cheer; one who is fond of good living –1780. **3.** A supplier or seller of provisions –1622.

†**Vi·ander**[2]. 1548. [– OFr. *viandier*, f. as prec.] Viands, victuals, food –1625. So †**Vi·andry.**

Viatical (vəiæ·tikăl), *a.* and *sb. rare.* 1855. [f. L. *viaticus* pertaining to a road or journey, f. *via* way; see -ATIC, -AL[1] 1.] **A.** *adj.* Of or pertaining to a way or road; relating to a journey. **B.** *sb. pl.* Articles for use on a journey.

‖**Viaticum** (vəiæ·tikɒ̆m, vi-). *Pl.* **viatica.** 1562. [L. *viaticum* travelling money, provisions for a journey, subst. use of n. of *viaticus*.] **1.** *Eccl.* The Eucharist when administered to or received by one who is dying or in danger of death. **2.** A supply of money or other necessaries for a journey; a sum given or taken to cover travelling expenses 1582. **b.** Provisions taken for use on a journey 1663.

Viator (vəiēⁱ·tǫɹ). 1504. [– L. *viator*, f. *via* way.] A traveller, wayfarer.

‖**Vibex** (vəi·beks). *Pl.* **vibices** (vəi-, vibəi·sīz). 1771. [L., weal.] *Path.* A long and narrow mark or patch in the skin caused by the subcutaneous extravasation of blood, occurring esp. in some fevers. Usu. in pl.

‖**Vibraculum** (vəibræ·kiŭlɒ̆m). *Pl.* **-cula.** 1854. [mod.L., f. L. *vibrare* shake.] *Zool.* One of the long whip-like movable processes or organs possessed by certain polyzoans; now regarded as a modified zooid. Hence **Vibra·cular** *a.* of, pertaining to, or furnished with vibracula.

Vibrant (vəi·brănt), *a.* 1616. [– L. *vibrans, -ant-*, pr. pple. of *vibrare* VIBRATE; see -ANT.] **1.** Moving or quivering rapidly; vibrating. **2.** Of sound, the voice: Characterized by or exhibiting vibration; resonant 1848. Hence **Vi·brancy**, the condition or quality of being v.

Vibrate (vəibrēⁱ·t, vəi·breⁱt), *v.* 1647. [– *vibrat-*, pa. ppl. stem of L. *vibrare* move rapidly to and fro, brandish, shake, etc.; see -ATE[3].] **I. 1.** *intr.* Of a pendulum, etc.: To swing to and fro; to oscillate 1667. **2. a.** Of sounds: To strike *on* or sound *in* the ear, etc., with an effect like that of a vibrating chord; to resound; to continue to be heard. Chiefly *poet.* 1735. **b.** To circulate *about*, move or pass *through*, pierce or penetrate *to*, by or as by vibration 1756. **3.** To move or swing backwards and forwards, or upwards and downwards, with some degree of rapidity; to quiver, shake, tremble 1756. **b.** *spec.* in *Physics* (see VIBRATION 2) 1774. **4.** *fig.* To move or oscillate *between* two extreme conditions, opinions, etc.; to fluctuate or vary *from* one extreme *to* another. Also without const. To vacillate in opinion. 1782.

1. Long pendulums v. more slowly than short ones 1827. 2. a. Music, when soft voices die, Vibrates in the memory SHELLEY. b. Those powers that..Catch every nerve, and v. through the frame GOLDSM. 3. Palm trees vibrating in the breeze 1816. b. When a hammer strikes a bell, the latter vibrates TYNDALL. 4. The life of a man of fashion vibrated between frivolity and excess 1874.

II. 1. *trans.* To throw with vibratory motion; to launch or hurl (a thunderbolt, sentence, etc.). Now *Obs.* or *arch.* 1641. **b.** To emit, give forth (light, sound, etc.) by or as by vibration or vibratory motion 1643. **2.** Of a pendulum, etc.: To measure (seconds) by vibration; also, to swing (so many times) 1667. **3.** To give a vibratory motion to (something); to set in vibration 1700.

1. b. Star to star vibrates light TENNYSON. 2. A pendulum which vibrates seconds in very small arcs 1803. 3. Virginian rattlesnakes..swiftly vibrating and shaking their tailes EVELYN.

Vibratile (vəi·brătəil, -il), *a.* 1826. [var., by substitution of suffix, of VIBRATORY *a.*, after *pulsatile*, etc.; see -ATILE.] **1.** Of the nature of vibration; vibratory. **2.** Of cilia, etc.: Endowed with the power of vibration; having a rapid and constant oscillatory movement 1835.

1. The v., lashing action of the spermatozoon 1881.

Vibration (vəibrēⁱ·ʃən). 1655. [– L. *vibratio, -ōn-*, f. *vibrat-*; see VIBRATE *v.*, -ION.] **1.** The action on the part of a pendulum, etc. of moving or swinging to and fro; oscillation 1668. **b.** A single instance of this 1667. **2.** *Physics.* The rapid alternating or reciprocating motion to and fro or up and down, produced in the particles of an elastic body by the disturbance of equilibrium; the motion in the particles of a sonorous body by which sound is produced 1656. **b.** A single movement of this kind 1666. **c.** *spec.* A supposed movement of this kind in the nerves, regarded as the means by which external impressions are conveyed to the mind. *Obs.* exc. *Hist.* 1728. **3.** In wider sense: Movement to and fro or up and down, esp. when quick and more or less continuous; a quivering, swaying, or tremulous motion of any kind; an instance of this 1655. **4.** The action or fact of vacillating in respect of conduct or opinion; an instance of this 1785.

2. The v. of the Air and its Undulation PRIOR. b. The deep vibrations of his witching song THOMSON. 3. The vibration and smells of the modern steamer 1901. 4. In Virginia there had been a great v. of opinion 1882. Hence **Vibra·tional** *a.* of or pertaining to v.; vibratory.

Vibratiuncle (vəibrēⁱ·ʃiɒŋk'l). 1718. [f. VIBRATION + dim. element *-uncle* as in *peduncle*.] A minute or slight vibration.

Vibrative (vəi·brătiv), *a.* Now *rare.* 1667. [f. VIBRATE *v.* + -IVE; see -ATIVE.] Vibrating, vibratory.

‖**Vibrato** (vibrā·to), *adv.* and *sb.* 1861. [It., pa. pple. of *vibrare* VIBRATE.] *Mus.* **A.** *adv.* With much vibration of tone. **B.** *sb.* A tremulous quality of tone 1876.

Vibrator (vəibrēⁱ·tǫɹ, vəi·breⁱtəɹ). 1862. [f. VIBRATE *v.* + -OR 2.] That which vibrates or causes vibration. **a.** One of the vibrating reeds of an organ, harmonium, etc. **b.** One or other of various appliances, instruments, or parts which have or cause a vibratory motion or action 1888.

Vibratory (vəi·brătəri), *a.* 1728. [f. VIBRATE *v.* + -ORY[2].] **1.** Of the nature of vibration; characterized by or consisting of vibration. **2.** Causing or producing vibration 1756. **3.** Of or pertaining to vibration 1831. **4.** Capable of vibrating; readily admitting of vibration 1839. **b.** Of the voice: Vibrant 1890.

1. The v. Motion of the Nerves 1728. 2. Human throats Have v. powers 1812. 3. The v. theory of light 1889. 4. The v. rays of the spectrum 1862. b. A voice v. with excitement 1891.

‖**Vibrio** (vəi·brio, vi·brio). *Pl.* **vibriones** (-ōᵘ·nīz), **vibrios.** 1835. [mod.L., f. L. *vibrare* VIBRATE after Fr. *vibrion*.] †**1.** A genus of minute nematode worms; an anguillule –1839. **2.** A group or genus of bacteroid or schizomycetous organisms characterized by vibratory motion; a member of this genus; *spec.* in *Bacteriol.*, a form of bacterium having vibratile cilia and closely resembling spirilla 1870.

†**Vi·brion.** 1853. [– Fr. *vibrion*; see prec.] **1.** A vibratile filament or appendage. **2.** *Bacteriol.* A vibrio 1882.

‖**Vibrissæ** (vəibri·sī), *sb. pl.* 1693. [L. (Festus) f. *vibrare* VIBRATE.] **1.** *Anat.* The hairs which grow in the nostrils. **2.** *Zool.* Stiff or bristly hairs, esp. those growing about the mouth or other parts of the face in certain animals 1839. **b.** *Ornith.* The coarse hairs or bristles growing about the rictus of certain birds, esp. of insectivorous species 1874.

Vibro- (vəi·bro), irreg. comb. form of L. *vibrare* vibrate, as in **vibro-massage; vi·broscope**, an instrument used for counting the vibrations of a tuning-fork.

‖**Viburnum** (vəibɒ̄·ɹnɒ̆m). 1731. [L., the wayfaring-tree.] An extensive genus of shrubs, natives of Europe, Asia, and N. America, to which the guelder-rose and laurustinus belong; a species or plant of this genus.

Vicar (vi·kăɹ). ME. [In XIV *vikere*, etc., *vicar* – AFr. *vikere, vicare*, (O)Fr. *vicaire* (now) assistant curate, deputy – L. *vicarius* substitute, deputy, f. **vicis* change, alteration, time, turn; see VICE *prep.*, -AR[2].] One who takes the place of or acts instead of another; a substitute, representative, or proxy. Chiefly *Eccl.* **1.** Applied to persons, etc., as earthly representatives of God or Christ. **b.** *spec.* (*V. of Christ*, etc.) Applied to the Pope; also to St. Peter in a similar sense ME. **2.** In early use, a person acting as priest in a parish in place of the parson or rector, or as the representative of a religious community to whom the tithes had been appropriated; hence, in later and mod. use, the incumbent of a parish of which the tithes are impropriated or appropriated, in contrast to a RECTOR ME. **3.** One of the minor clergy or laymen (also called *lay vicar*) in a cathedral whose duty it is to sing p.rts of the services. Cf. VICAR-CHORAL. late ME. **4.** One who takes the place of, or acts as the representative of, another (esp. the Pope or other high dignitary) in the performance of ecclesiastical functions; *spec.* in the R. C. Ch., a bishop's deputy. late ME. **5.** In general use: One acting or appointed to act in place of another, esp. in administrative functions; a vicegerent. late ME.

1. b. Proclaiming that to the Pope, as God's v,. all mankind are subject, and all rulers responsible BRYCE. **2.** *V. of Bray*, one who readily changes his principles to suit the times or circumstances (chiefly in allusion to the song of that name). **4.** *V. apostolic*; Where the succession of the Catholic hierarchy has been interrupted, as in England,.. the bishops who superintend the Catholic church and represent the papal authority, are known by the name of vicars apostolic 1836. *V. forane*, in the R. C. Ch., a dignitary or parish priest, appointed by a bishop to exercise a limited jurisdiction in a particular town or district of his diocese 1888.

Vicarage (vi·kărėdʒ). late ME. [In XV *viker-*, *vicarage*, app. f. VICAR + -AGE. Not recorded before 1425, but prob. much older; cf. AL. *vicaragium* 1250. See VICARY[2].] **1.** The benefice or living of a vicar. **2.** The house or residence of a vicar; also, its occupants 1530. †**3.** The position, office, or duties of a vicar or representative (*rare*) –1734.

Vicar(-)choral. 1530. [tr. AL. *vicarius choralis* (XV); see VICAR 3.] = VICAR 3.

Vicaress (vi·kărės). 1613. [f. VICAR + -ESS[1].] **1.** The sister ranking immediately below the abbess or mother superior in a nunnery or convent. **2.** The wife of the vicar of a parish 1770.

Vicar(-)general. late ME. [VICAR 4, after med.L. *vicarius generalis*.] †**1.** The title assumed by or bestowed upon the Pope as head of the Church under Christ –1651. **2.** An ecclesiastical officer, usu. a cleric, appointed by a bishop as his representative in matters of jurisdiction or administration; also, in post-Reformation use in the Church of England, *spec.* a permanent lay official serving as a deputy or assistant to a bishop, or to the Archbishop of Canterbury or York, in certain ecclesiastical causes 1450. **3.** *Hist.* The title given to Thomas Cromwell in 1535 as representative of the King in ecclesiastical affairs 1679.

Vicarial (vəi-, vikēᵊ·riăl), *a.* 1617. [f. VICAR + -IAL, after *ministerial*. Cf. Fr. *vicarial*.] **1.** Delegated, deputed; vicarious. **2.** Of or belonging to a vicar or vicars 1744.

1. V. and deputed power 1803. **2.** A v. tithe 1765.

Vicarian (vəi-, vikēᵊ·riăn), *sb.* and *a.* 1598. [orig. – late L. *vicarianus*, of a *vicarius* deputy; see VICAR, -IAN.] **A.** *sb.* †**1.** A substitute or deputy. MARSTON. **2.** One who accepts the view of religious vicariousness 1851. **B.** *adj.* Of, pertaining to, or governed by a deputy ruler 1643.

Vicariate (vəi-, vikēᵊ·riĕt). 1610. [– med.L. *vicariatus*, f. L. *vicarius*; see VICAR, -ATE[1].] **1.** The office or authority of a vicar in a religious or ecclesiastical sense. **2.** A political office held by a person as deputy for another; deputed exercise of authority by a person or governing body 1619. **3. a.** A district under the rule of a deputy governor 1755. **b.** *R. C. Ch.* A district under the charge of a vicar apostolic; the see of a vicar apostolic 1818.

2. The vicariat of that part of Germany which is governed by the Saxon laws, devolved to the elector of Saxony ROBERTSON.

Vicarious (vəi-, vikēᵊ·riəs), *a.* 1637. [f. L. *icarius*, f. **vicis* change, stead; see -ARIOUS.] **1.** That takes or supplies the place of another thing or person; substituted instead of the proper thing or person. **2.** Of punishment, etc.: Endured or suffered by one person in place of another; accomplished or attained by the substitution of some other person, etc., for the actual offender. Freq. in *Theol.* with ref. to the suffering and death of Christ. 1692. **3.** Of power, authority, etc.: Exercised by one person or body of persons as the representative or deputy of another 1706. **4.** Performed or achieved by means of another, or by one person, etc., on behalf of another 1806. **b.** Of qualities, etc.: Possessed by one person but reckoned to the credit of another 1812. **c.** Of methods, principles, etc.: Based upon the substitution of one person for another 1857. **5.** *Physiol.* Denoting the performance by or through one organ of functions normally discharged by another; substitutive 1780.

1. The University and Colleges are thus neither identical, nor v. of each other 1831. **2.** V. Punishments may be..absolutely necessary 1736. **3.** Exercising a kind of v. jurisdiction JOHNSON. Hence **Vica·rious-ly** *adv.*, **-ness.**

Vi·carship. 1534. [f. VICAR + -SHIP.] The office or position of a vicar.

†**Vi·cary**[1]. ME. [– L. *vicarius* VICAR.] = VICAR –1648.

†**Vi·cary**[2]. 1420. [– OFr. *vicarie* or med.L. *vicaria* (XII), f. *vicarius* VICAR; see -Y[3].] The office or position of a vicar; a benefice held by a vicar –1712.

Vice (vəis), *sb.*[1] ME. [– (O)Fr. *vice* – L. *vitium* physical or other defect, fault, vice.] **1.** Depravity or corruption of morals; evil, immoral, or wicked habits or conduct; indulgence in degrading pleasures or practices. **2.** A habit or practice of an immoral, degrading, or wicked nature ME. **b.** In horses: A bad habit or trick 1726. **3.** A character in a morality play representing one or other vice; hence, a stage jester or buffoon. Now *Hist.* (with cap.) 1551. **4.** Moral fault or defect (without implication of serious wrong-doing); a flaw in character or conduct ME. **5.** A fault, blemish, or imperfection. late ME. **6.** Viciousness, harmfulness 1837.

1. Fy upon slouth, the nourysher of vyce 1509. **2.** The Gods are iust, and of our pleasant vices Make instruments to plague vs SHAKS. **b.** Of all the vices incidental to the horse, shying is one of the worst 1847. **3.** A favourite piece of horse-play in the old miracles and morals, when the V. belabours the Devil 1886. **4.** Contempt, prior to examination, is an intellectual v. PALEY. **5.** I perceive I doe anticipate the vices of age SIR T. BROWNE.

Vice (vəis), *sb.*[2] Also (now *U.S.*) **vise.** ME. [– (O)Fr. *vis* :– L. *vitis* vine, vine stem, prop. tendril, plant with tendrils.] **1.** A winding or spiral staircase. *Obs.* exc. *arch.* †**2.** A mechanical contrivance or device by which some piece of apparatus, etc., is worked –1650. †**3.** A screw –1611. †**4.** A tap or a vessel; a screw-stopper –1653. **5.** A tool composed of two jaws, opening and closing by means of a screw, which firmly grip and hold a piece of work in position while it is being operated upon; used esp. by workers in metal and carpenters 1500. **6.** A tool used for drawing lead into grooved rods for lattice windows 1706.

5. To secure him with a grasp like that of his own iron v., was, for the powerful Smith, the work of a single moment SCOTT.

Vice (vəis), *sb.*[3] 1597. [absol. use of VICE-*prefix*.] One who acts in the place of another; a substitute or deputy.

Vice (vəis), *v.* 1602. [f. VICE *sb.*[2]] *trans.* To force, strain, or press hard as by the use of a vice; to fix, jam, or squeeze tightly.

‖**Vice** (vəi·si), *prep.* 1770. [L., abl. of **vix* change, place, stead.] In place of; in succession to.

Vice- (vəis), *prefix*, repr. L. *vice* in place of; see prec. The older examples in English, having been taken immediately from French, also present the prefix in the reduced forms *vis-* (*vys-*, *viz-*) and *vi-* (*vy-*), subsequently replaced by *vice-*, except in VISCOUNT.

a. With personal designations, especially titles of office, indicating that the person so called acts temporarily or regularly in place of, in the absence of, or as assistant to another who properly holds the office or bears the title or name, as *v.-abbot*, *-agent*, *-architect*, *-captain*, etc. A group of these words appears in English in the 16th and early 17th cc. which includes *vice-god*, *-governor*, *-king*, *-rector*; **vice-chamberlain,** *spec.* an officer of the Royal Household under the Lord Chamberlain; **-legate,** one who acts as the representative or deputy of a (Papal) legate; **-queen,** (*a*) a woman ruling as the representative of a queen; (*b*) the wife of a viceroy; **-treasurer,** *spec.* formerly in the government of Ireland; **-warden,** *esp.* a deputy warden of the Stannaries or the Borders. **b.** With nouns or adjs. derived from personal designations, as *v.-apostolical* *-deity*, *-duchy*, etc., or associated in some way with the holding of office, as *v.-chair*, *-government*, *-throne*.

Vice-a·dmiral. 1520. [– AFr. *visadmirail*, OFr. *visamiral*, or AL. *viceadmirallus* (XIV); see VICE-, ADMIRAL.] **1.** A naval officer ranking next to an admiral. **b.** A civil officer appointed by the lords-commissioners of the Admiralty for the execution of jurisdiction 1618. †**2.** A vessel commanded by a vice-admiral –1693.

Vice-a·dmiralty. 1602. [f. prec. + -TY[1].] The office or jurisdiction of a vice-admiral (in sense 1 b); an area under the jurisdiction of a vice-admiral.

V. courts, branches of the High Court of Admiralty, instituted for carrying on the like duties in several of our colonies, prize-courts, &c. 1867.

Vice-cha·ncellor. late ME. [– OFr. *vi(s)chancelier* (mod. *vice-*), or med.L. *vicecancellarius* (XII); see VICE-, CHANCELLOR.] **1.** The deputy or substitute of an ecclesiastical chancellor; *spec.* the cardinal at the head of the Papal Chancery. **2.** The acting representative of the Chancellor of a university, usu. the head of a college, appointed to the office for a limited time, or the principal of the university 1530. **3.** A deputy or subordinate of one or other state official bearing the title of Chancellor 1587. **b.** *spec.* One of the higher judges in the former Court of Chancery 1813. Hence **Vice-cha·ncellorship,** the office or dignity of a v.; the period during which this is held.

Vice-co·nsul. 1559. [VICE-.] †**1.** A Roman proconsul –1601. **2.** The assistant or deputy of a consul 1601.

Vice-cou·nty. 1859. [f. VICE- + COUNTY[1] 2.] A division of a large county treated as a county-area with regard to the distribution of species of plants, etc.

Vicegerency (vəisˌdʒīᵊ·rĕnsi, -dʒe·rĕnsi). 1596. [See next and -ENCY.] The office, dignity, or rule of a vicegerent; the fact of ruling or administering as representative of another. **b.** A district or province ruled by a vicegerent 1865. So **Vicege·rence** (now *rare*) 1527.

Vicegerent (vəisˌdʒīᵊ·rĕnt, -dʒe·rĕnt), *sb.* and *a.* 1536. [– med.L. *vicegerens*, *-gerent-* deputy (1274); see VICE-, GERENT.] **A.** *sb.* **1.** A person appointed by a king or other ruler to act in his place or exercise certain of his administrative functions. **b.** *gen.* One who takes the place of another in the discharge of some office or duties 1549. **c.** A ruler or commander *of* a country, etc., in virtue of deputed power 1577. **2.** Applied to rulers and magistrates as representatives of the Deity. Also to priests, and *spec.* to the Pope, as representatives of God or Christ. 1547. **b.** Similarly applied to man in general, and to persons as representing some other supernatural or spiritual power 1588.

1. He was trusted by the sultan as the faithful vicegerent of his power GIBBON. **c.** Aspasius the v. of Rome 1610. **2.** Princes, being by God put in authority, are His vice-gerents, and should therefore require obedience 1547. The Pope, Christ's Vicar and V. 1593.

B. *adj.* (or *attrib.*). **1.** Taking the place or performing the functions of another 1577. **2.** Characterized by deputed or vicarious power 1667.

2. Under his great Vice-gerent Reign abide,.. For ever happie MILT.

Vice-pre·sident. 1574. [f. VICE- + PRESIDENT; cf. AL. *vicepresidens* (1535).] One who acts as the representative or deputy of a president; an official ranking immediately below a president. **Vice-pre·sidentship, -pre·sidency.**

Vice-re·gal, *a.* 1839. [f. VICE- + REGAL, after VICEROY, -AL.] Of, pertaining to, or associated with a viceroy.

Vice-re·gent. 1556. [f. VICE- + REGENT; in XVI perh. erron. for contemp. *vice-gerent*, AL. *vicegerens* (XIII).] One who acts in place of a regent. Hence **-re·gency.**

‖**Vicereine** (vəisrēn). 1823. [– Fr. *vicereine*, f. *vice-* VICE- + *reine* queen.] The wife of a viceroy; also (less usu.), a woman ruling as the representative of a queen.

Viceroy (vəi·sroi). 1524. [– Fr. *viceroy*, †*visroy* (mod. *viceroi*), f. *vice-* VICE- + *roy*, *roi* king.] **1.** One who acts as the governor of a country, province, etc., in the name and by the authority of the supreme ruler; a vice-king. **2.** *transf.* One having authority or rank comparable to that of a viceroy 1590. **3.** *Ent.* An Amer. species of butterfly, *Basilarchia archippus*, distinguished by handsome red and black colouring 1881. Hence **Vi·ceroyal** *a.* of or pertaining to a v. **Vi·ceroyship,** viceroyalty.

Viceroyalty (stress variable). 1703. [– Fr. *vice-royauté*; see VICE- and ROYALTY.] **1.** The office, rank, or authority of a viceroy. **b.** In quasi-concr. use: A viceroy or viceregal household 1842. **2.** A province or dependency commonly administered by a viceroy 1715. **3.** The period during which a particular viceroy holds office 1849.

Vice versa (vəi·si vō·ɹsă), *adv. phr.* 1601. [– L. *vice versa* 'the position being reversed'; *vice*, abl. of **vix* (see VICE *prep.*), and abl. sing. fem. of *versus*, pa. pple. of *vertere*; see VERSE *v.*[2]] With a reversal or transposition of the main items in the statement just made; contrariwise, conversely.

Nor can we ask his favour upon occasion, and so *vice versa* he can make no use of us 1710.

‖**Vichy** (vi·ʃi). 1858. [See def.] The name of a town in the department of Allier in Central France, used *attrib.* and *ellipt.* to designate a mineral water obtained from springs there.

Vicinage (vi·sinėdʒ). ME. [– OFr. *vis(e)nage*, also *visné*, AL. *visnetum* XII (mod. *voisinage*) – Gallo-Rom. **vēcīnatus*, f. *vēcinus*, for L. *vicinus* neighbour.] **1.** A number of places lying near to each other taken collectively; an area extending to a limited distance round a particular spot; a neighbourhood. **b.** *transf.* The people living in a certain district or neighbourhood 1647. **2.** The fact of being or living close to one another or others; nearness, proximity 1598.

1. The Metropolis and its V. BURKE. The French ladies in my v. H. WALPOLE. **2.** Common because of v., or neighbourhood, is where the inhabitants of two townships, which lie contiguous to each other, have usually intercommoned with each other BLACKSTONE.

Vicinal (vi·sinăl, visəi·năl), *a.* 1677. [– Fr. *vicinal* (XVI) or L. *vicinalis*, f. *vicinus* neighbour; see -AL[1] 1.] **1.** *V. way* or *road*, a local common way as dist. from a highway; a by-road or cross-road. **2.** Neighbouring, adjacent, near 1739. **b.** *Math.* and *Min.* Nearly coincident with a given surface or plane 1895. **c.** *Organ. Chem.* Of substituted groups or atoms: Lying in consecutive order; adjacent to each other 1898.

Vicinity (visi·nĭti). 1560. [– L. *vicinitas*, f. *vicinus*; see prec. and -ITY.] **1.** The state, character, or quality of being near in space; propinquity. †**2.** Nearness in degree or quality; close relationship or connection; resemblance, likeness –1676. **3.** = VICINAGE 1. 1781.

1. The Abundance and v. of country seats SWIFT. This v. to the great capital 1858. **3.** We were glad..to escape the v. of that ugly crevasse TYNDALL.

Phr. *In the v.* (*of*), in the neighbourhood (of), near or close (to).

Vicious (vi·ʃəs), *a.* ME. [– OFr. *vicious* (mod. *vicieux*) – L. *vitiosus*, f. *vitium* VICE *sb.*[1]; see -IOUS.] **I. 1.** Of habits, practices, etc.: Of the nature of vice; contrary to moral principles; depraved, immoral, bad. **2.** Of persons: Addicted to vice or immorality; of depraved habits; profligate, wicked. late ME. **3.** Falling short of or varying from what is morally or practically commendable; reprehensible, blameworthy, mischievous. late ME. **4.** Of animals (*esp.* horses): Inclined to be savage or dangerous, or to show bad temper; not submitting to be thoroughly tamed or broken in 1711. **b.** Full of malice or spite; malignantly bitter or severe 1825.

1. Richard Iohnson caused the English, by his v. liuing, to bee worse accounted of then the Russes 1613. **2.** V. as the stage was, it only reflected the general vice of the time 1874. **3.** It had beene v. To haue mistrusted her SHAKS. **4.** A v. animal, having injured any person, was forfeited 1818. **b.** Three nasty v. letters 1908.

II. 1. *Law.* Marred or rendered void by some inherent fault or defect; not satisfying legal requirements or conditions; unlawful, illegal. late ME. **2.** Impaired or spoiled by some fault, flaw, blemish, or defect; faulty, defective, imperfect, bad; corrupt, impure, debased 1589. †**3.** Foul, impure, noxious, morbid –1831. †**4.** Of a part or function of the body: Morbid, diseased; irregular –1733.

2. If from true premisses follows what is false, it is a sign that the form of the syllogism is vitious 1697. The foundations of the bridge were originally v. 1846.

Phr. *V. circle.* **a.** *Logic.* See CIRCLE *sb.* Also *gen.* **b.** *Path.* A morbid process consisting in the reciprocal continuation and aggravation of one disorder by another. The practice proceeds, in a v. circle of habit 1839. The authority of the law is demanded, and he cites the disputed passage. A more..v. circle was never devised 1876. Hence **Vi·cious-ly** *adv.*, **-ness.**

Vicissitude (vəi-, visi·sitiūd). 1570. [– (O)Fr. *vicissitude* or L. *vicissitudo*, f. *vicissim* by turns, f. *vic-* turn; see VICE *prep.*, -TUDE.] **1.** The fact of change or mutation taking place in a particular thing or within a certain sphere; the uncertain changing or mutability *of* something. **2.** Without article: Change, mutation, mutability; successive substitution of one thing or condition for another taking place from natural causes 1596. **3.** A change or alteration in condition or fortune; an instance of mutability in human affairs 1616. **4.** Alternation, mutual or reciprocal succession, of things or conditions 1624. **5.** An instance of alternation or succession 1648.

1. The notice, that our Senses take of the constant V. of Things LOCKE. **2.** This is a world of conflict, and of v. amid the conflict 1833. **3.** The vicissitudes of War 1665. **4.** The succession of light and darkness,..the v. of the seasons 1835. **5.** The vicissitudes of tides are scarcely felt in those seas GIBBON. Hence †**Vicissitu·dinary** *a.* marked by alternation –1650. **Vicissitu·dinous** *a.* marked by vicissitudes.

†**Vico·ntiel,** *sb.* and *a.* 1548. [– AFr *vicontiel* (= OFr. *vi(s)contal*, AL. *vicecomitalis* XIV); see VISCOUNT, -IAL.] **A.** *sb. pl.* Certain sums regularly payable to the Crown by a sheriff and charged against him in the Exchequer accounts –1738. **B.** *adj.* **1.** Of or pertaining to a sheriff –1798. **2.** Of a writ: That is to be executed by the sheriff –1768.

Victim (vi·ktim). 1497. [– L. *victima.*] **1.** A living creature killed and offered as a sacrifice to some deity or supernatural power. **2.** A person who is put to death or subjected to torture by another; one who suffers severely in body or property through cruel or oppressive treatment 1660. **b.** One who is reduced or destined to suffer under some oppressive or destructive agency 1718. **c.** One who perishes or suffers in health, etc. from some enterprise or pursuit voluntarily undertaken 1726. **d.** In weaker sense: One who suffers some injury, hardship, or loss, is badly treated or taken advantage of, or the like 1781.

1. Select four Brawny Bulls for Sacrifice,..From the slain Victims pour the streaming Blood DRYDEN. **2.** If he had not died the v. of a tyrant 1839. **b.** The houses..continued to collapse and make fresh victims 1890. **d.** He went off.., and left his respected v. to settle the bill DICKENS.

Phr. *To fall a v. to* (some thing or person).

Victimize (vi·ktiməiz), *v.* 1830. [f. prec. + -IZE.] **1.** *trans.* To make a victim of; to cause to suffer discomfort, inconvenience, etc.; to cheat, swindle, or defraud. **2.** To put to death as, or in the manner of, a sacrificial victim; to slaughter 1853. **b.** To spoil or destroy (plants) completely 1849. Hence **Victimiza·tion. Vi·ctimizer.**

Victor (vi·ktəɹ), *sb.* ME. [– AFr. *victo(u)r* or L. *victor*, *-ōr-*, f. *vict-*, pa. ppl. stem of *vincere* conquer; see -OR 2.] One who overcomes or vanquishes an adversary; the leader of an army which wins a battle or war. Sometimes *collect. sing.* with *the*, the winning army or nation. **b.** *transf.* and *fig.* One who overcomes in any contest or struggle. late ME.

1. The Huns..soon withdrew from the presence of an insulting v. GIBBON. **b.** There, V. of his health, of fortune, friends, And fame, this lord of useless thousands ends POPE. Hence †**Vi·ctor** *v. trans.* to overcome, vanquish –1683.

‖**Victoria**[1] (viktō°·riă). 1638. [L. (or Sp., Pg.) *victoria* VICTORY.] A word employed as a shout of triumph.

Victoria[2] (viktō°·riă). 1846. [Name of Queen *Victoria* of England (1837–1901) used attrib. or ellipt.] **1.** A light, low, four-wheeled carriage having a collapsible hood, with seats (usu.) for two persons and an elevated seat in front for the driver 1870. **2.** *Bot.* A gigantic species of water-lily, *Victoria regia*, indigenous to South America 1846. **3.** *Astr.* One of the minor planets, discovered in 1850 by Hind. **4.** A variety of domestic pigeon 1879. **5.** A variety of plum characterized by its luscious flavour and rich red colour 1860. **6.** attrib. *V. Cross* (abbrev. V.C.), the highest British military and naval decoration, bestowed for conspicuous bravery in battle. 1856. *V. Day*, the anniversary of the birthday of Queen Victoria, May 24 (now usu. called *Empire Day*).

Victo·rian, *a.*[1] 1728. [f. the name of *Victorius*, an ecclesiastic of the 5th c.] *V. cycle*, *period* (see quot. and DIONYSIAN *a.*).

V. period, an Interval of 532 Julian Years, which elaps'd, the new and full Moons return on the same Day of the Julian Year 1728.

Victorian (viktō°·riăn), *a.*[2] and *sb.* 1875. [f. VICTORIA[2] + -AN.] **A.** *adj.* Of, belonging to, designating, or typical of the reign of Queen Victoria (1837–1901). **B.** *sb.* A person who lived in or has the characteristics typical of the reign of Queen Victoria 1876. Hence **Victo·rianism.**

Victo·rian, *a.*[3] 1857. [See def.] Of, belonging, or native to the colony of Victoria in Australia (named in 1851 after Queen Victoria).

Victorine (vi·ktŏrīn). 1849. [f. VICTORIA[2] + -INE[4].] A kind of fur tippet formerly worn by ladies, fastening in front of the neck and having two loose ends hanging down.

Victorious (viktō°·riəs), *a.* late ME. [– AFr. *victorious* = (O)Fr. *victorieux* – L. *victoriosus*, f. *victoria*; see next, -OUS.] **1.** Having gained victory or obtained supremacy as victor; successful in any contest or struggle. **2.** Of, belonging to, or characterized by victory; producing victory; emblematic of victory 1490.

1. Giacomo da Pesaro,..v. over the Turks in war, and over himself in peace 1757. *transf.* Now the distemper, spite of draught or pill, V. seem'd COWPER. **2.** Those just Spirits that wear v. Palms MILT. Hence **Victo·rious-ly** *adv.*, **-ness.**

Victory (vi·ktŏri). ME. [– AFr. *victorie* = (O)Fr. *victoire* – L. *victoria*, f. *victor*; see VICTOR, -Y[3].] **1.** The position or state of having overcome an enemy or adversary in combat, battle, or war; supremacy or superiority achieved as the result of armed conflict. **b.** Used interjectionally as an expression of triumph or encouragement 1591. **2.** An instance or occasion of overcoming an adversary in battle, etc. ME. **3.** Supremacy, superiority, triumph, or ultimate success in any contest, struggle, or enterprise ME. **4.** The Roman goddess representing or typifying victory; a figure or statue of this 1569.

1. V. is the fruit of moral as well as military virtue GIBBON. *personified.* Fortune, and V. sit on thy Helme SHAKS. Phr. *To have* (*get, win*) *the v.* **b.** Saint George, and V.; fight Souldiers, fight SHAKS. **2.** Phr. *Cadmean, Pyrrhic v.*: see these words. *Moral v.*: see MORAL *a.* 7 b. **3.** Such is euer-more the finall victorie of all truth HOOKER. **4.** Crowned with a winged figure of Victory GIBBON.

Victress (vi·ktrės). 1601. [f. VICTOR + -ESS[1], after L. *victrix.*] A female victor or vanquisher.

‖**Victrix** (vi·ktriks). 1651. [L., fem. of VICTOR.] = prec. So †**Vi·ctrice** –1633.

Victual (vi·t'l), *sb.* [ME. *vitaile(s* – OFr. *vitaille*, later (and mod.) *victuaille* :– late L. *victualia*, n. pl. of *victualis*, f. L. *victus* livelihood, f. base of *vivere* live; see -AL[1] 1. The spelling has been assimilated to the L. original, while the pronunc. still repr. the older forms *vittel, vittle*.] **1.** *collect.* Whatever is normally required or may naturally be used for consumption in order to support life; food or provisions of any kind. †**b.** Produce of the ground capable of being used as food –1799. **2.** *pl.* Articles of food; supplies or various kinds of provisions; in later use *esp.* articles of ordinary diet prepared for use ME.

1. Twise a day giue him fresh vittle and drinke 1573. A fair-hair'd youth, that in his hand Bare v. for the mowers TENNYSON. **2.** The Wages of a..Labourer..is 4s. per week without Victuals 1687. Hence **Vi·ctualage** (*rare*) victuals.

Victual (vi·t'l), *v.* ME. [– OFr. *vitaillier, vi(c)tuaillier*, f. *vitaille*; see prec.] **1.** *trans.* To supply or furnish (a ship, castle, garrison, body of troops, etc.) with victuals, esp. with a store to last for some time. **2.** *intr.* **a.** To partake of victuals; to eat. Also of animals, to feed or pasture. 1577. **b.** To lay in or obtain a supply of victuals 1615.

1. This squadron..was victualed for twelve months 1777. **2. b.** Which was a voyage of such a length, that no ship could v. for DE FOE. Hence **Vi·ctualled** *ppl. a.*

Victualler (vi·t'ləɹ). late ME. [– OFr. *vitaill(i)er, -our*, f. *vitaille* VICTUAL *sb.*; see -ER[2] 2.] **1.** A purveyor of victuals or provisions; *spec.* the keeper of an eating-house, inn, or tavern; a licensed victualler. **2.** *spec.* **a.** One who supplies or undertakes to supply an army or armed force with necessary provisions; †*pl.* those engaged in bringing up victuals to an armed force. late ME. **b.** One who furnishes a ship or navy with provisions. late ME. **3.** A ship employed to carry provisions for a fleet or squadron (or for troops overseas); a victualling ship 1572.

1. *Licensed v.*, one who has a licence to sell food or drink, but esp. the latter, to be consumed on the premises; a publican.

Victualling (vi·t'liŋ), *vbl. sb.* 1462. [f. VICTUAL *v.* + -ING[1].] **1.** The action of providing or storing a ship, town, army, etc. (now esp. the Navy) with victuals. **b.** The business of supplying food and drink for payment; supply of food for this purpose 1534. **2.** A supply of food for personal use 1532.

attrib.: **v.-house,** an eating-house, inn, or tavern; **-office,** an office concerned with the v. of ships, esp. of ships of the Royal Navy; *Boxing slang*, the stomach.

‖**Vicuña** (vikū·nʸă), **vicuna** (vikiū·nă). 1622. [Sp. *vicuña* (Pg. *vicunha*) – Quechua.] **1.** A S. Amer. animal (*Auchenia vicunna*), closely related to the llama and alpaca, inhabiting the higher portions of the northern Andes and yielding a fine silky wool used for textile fabrics. **2.** *ellipt.* Vicuña cloth; also, a garment made of this 1851.

Comb.: **v.-cloth,** cloth made of **v. wool,** (*a*) wool or fur of the v.; (*b*) a mixture of fine wool and cotton.

‖**Vidame** (vī·dam). 1523. [– Fr. *vidame*, OFr. *visdame* :– late and med.L. *vicedominus* (VIII), f. *vice-* VICE- + *dominus* lord.] Formerly in France, one who held lands from a bishop as his representative and defender in temporal matters.

‖**Vide** (vəi·di), *v. imp.* 1565. [L., imp. sing. of *vidēre* see.] 'See, refer to, consult'; a direction to the reader to refer elsewhere for fuller or further information.

‖**Videlicet** (vəi-, vide·liset, vəidī·liset, vi-), *adv.* and *sb.* 1464. [L., f. *vide-*, stem of *vidēre* + *licet* it is permissible.] **A.** *adv.* That is to say; namely; to wit; used to introduce an amplification or more precise explanation of a previous statement or word. Abbrev. *viz.*

One of Rob's original profession, *v.* a drover SCOTT.

B. *sb.* The word itself as used to introduce an explanation or amplification, esp. in legal documents 1658.

Vidian (vi·diăn), *a.* 1831. [f. Vidus *Vidius*, latinized form of Guido Guidi, an Italian anatomist (died 1569); see -AN.] *Anat.* The special designation of certain anatomical features of the head, as *V. artery, canal, nerve.*

‖**Vidimus** (vəi·dimŏs). late ME. [L., = 'we have seen'.] **1.** A copy of a document bearing an attestation that it is authentic or accurate. **b.** An examination or inspection, as of accounts 1850. †**2.** *Arch.* A design for a painted or stained-glass window –1762.

‖**Vidonia** (vidōᵘ·niă). 1723. [Of unkn. origin.] A dry white wine made in the Canary Islands.

Viduage (vi·diuˌėdʒ). 1832. [f. L. *vidua* widow; see -AGE.] The condition of widowhood, viduity; widows collectively.

Vidual (vi·diuˌăl), *a.* 1550. [– late L. *vidualis*, f. *vidua* widow; see -AL[1] 1.] Of or belonging to, befitting, a widow or widowhood; widowed.

Viduity (vidiū·ĭti). late ME. [– (O)Fr. *viduité* or L. *viduitas, -tat-*, f. *vidua* widow; see -ITY.] The state of being or remaining a widow; the time during which a woman is a widow; widowhood.

†**Vie,** *sb.* 1533. [Aphetic – Fr. *envi* increase of stake (in OFr., challenge, provocation), f. *envier* increase the stake; see ENVY *v.*[2]] **1.** In card-playing: A challenge, venture, or bid; a sum staked on one's cards –1680. **2.** A challenge to contest or rivalry; a display of rivalry or emulation; a contest or competition –1674. **3.** A challenge as to the accuracy of something; an objection or difficulty (*rare*) –1640.

2. They..beganne a v., who should be first in shewing their alteration 1611.

Vie (vəi), *v.* 1565. [prob. aphetic f. ME. *avie, envie*; see ENVY *v.*[2]] †**1.** *intr.* In card-playing: To make a 'vie'; to hazard a sum on the strength of one's hand –1640. †**2.** *trans.* To hazard (a certain sum, etc.) on a hand of cards –1659. †**3.** To back (cards) for a certain sum; to declare oneself able to win (a game, etc.) –1655. **4.** To display, advance, practise, etc., in competition or rivalry *with* another person or thing; to contend or strive *with* in respect of (something). *Obs.* or *arch.* 1570. **5.** To match (one thing) *with* another by way of return, rivalry, or comparison. Now *arch.* 1583. †**6.** To increase in number by addition or repetition –1633. **7.** *intr.* To enter into or carry on rivalry; to be rivals or competitors; to compete for superiority in some respect 1615.

1. They v. and reuie till some ten shillings bee on the stake 1591. **4.** One eye vied drops with the other 1660. **5.** I will take your advice, and v. my state with others 1685. **6.** *Tam. Shr.* II. i. 311. **7.** Fruits that v. In glowing colours with the Tyrian dye POPE. They all vied in paying me every attention 1806.

‖**Vielle** (vie·l). 1768. [– Fr. *vielle*, OFr. *viele*; see VIOL[1].] A musical instrument with four strings played by means of a small wheel; a hurdy-gurdy.

Vienna (viˌe·nă), name of the capital of Austria used in various collocations, as **V. caustic,** = *V. paste*; **V. paste,** a paste made up of equal parts of caustic potash and quicklime. **b.** The distinctive name of a grade of wheatflour, and of certain forms of plain or fancy bread.

Viennese (viĕˌnī·z), *sb.* and *a.* 1839. [f. prec. + -ESE.] **A.** *sb.* **a.** A native or inhabitant of Vienna; also *collect.* **b.** The variety of German spoken in Vienna. **B.** *adj.* Of or belonging to Vienna; originating in Vienna 1839.

View (viū), *sb.* late ME. [– AFr. *vewe, vieue*, OFr. *vëue* (mod. *vue*), pa. ppl. sb. from *vëoir* (mod. *voir*) see :– L. *vidēre* see.] **I. 1. a.** A formal inspection or survey of lands, tenements, or ground for some special purpose. Now *rare* or *Obs.* †**b.** A formal examination or inspection of something, made by a properly appointed or qualified person; the charge or office of inspecting something –1827. †**c.** A review (of troops, etc.) –1721. **2.** *gen.* An examination, inspection, or survey 1568. **3.** The exercise of the faculty of sight; the faculty or power of vision; the possibility or opportunity of seeing something 1573. **b.** Range of sight or vision 1591. **4.** An act of looking or beholding; a sight, look, or glance 1581. **5.** The sight or vision *of* something 1588. **b.** = VIEW-HALLOO 1825. †**6.** Visual appearance or aspect –1812. **7.** †**a.** *Hunting.* The footprints of a buck or fallow-deer –1679. **b.** A sight or prospect of some landscape or extended scene; an extent or area covered by the eye from one point 1606. **c.** A drawing, painting, print, etc. representing a landscape or other prospect 1700.

1. b. *V. of frank-pledge*: see FRANK-PLEDGE. **2.** Surveying Nature with too nice a v. DRYDEN. **3.** Tom was already lost to v. 1852. **b.** Somewhere, out of human v., Whate'er thy hands are set to do Is wrought TENNYSON. **4.** The first v. would displease many 1581. **5.** Pisa's Mount, that intercepts the v. Of Lucca GRAY. **b.** From a find to a check, from a check to a v., From a v. to a death in the morning *c*1825. **6.** A happy rural seat of various v. MILT. **7. b.** From the flat roof of the church we had a delightful v. of the village 1808. **c.** A photographist preparing to take a v. of the castle 1854.

II. 1. Mental contemplation or vision; observation, notice 1440. **b.** A single act of contemplation or attention to a subject 1570. **2.** A particular manner or way of considering or regarding a matter or question; a conception, opinion, or theory formed by reflection or study 1573. **b.** An aspect or light in which something is regarded or considered 1713. **c.** *pl.* Opinions, ideas, or theories of an individual or speculative character held or advanced with regard to some subject 1769. **3.** A survey; a general or summary account 1604. **4.** An aim or intention; a design or plan; an object or purpose 1634. **5.** A prospect, anticipation, expectation, or outlook 1719.

1. But I hate to have my secrets laid open to everybodie's v. 1642. *Point of v.*: see POINT *sb.*[1] **2.** Let us take the most impartial V. we can 1679. **c.** Nor did his political views and maxims seem less strange 1769. **3.** It may not be amiss to give the reader the whole argument here in one v. 1729. **4.** I have told you my views for Jemima 1831. **5.** I entertain no v. of any emolument whatever from the present publication 1827.

Phrases. †*At, to the v.* (in hawking or hunting): By sight. **In** (..) **v.: a.** *In* (*the*) *v. of*, in the sight of, so as to be seen by; also, within sight of, near enough to see. **b.** *In v.*, in sight; also (*b*) in contemplation or notice, under attention; (*c*) as an end or object aimed at. **c.** *In v. of*, (*a*) in prospect or anticipation of, with a view to; (*b*) in consideration or regard of, on account of. **On** (..) **v.: a.** *On* or *upon* (*the*) *v. of*, on ocular inspection or perception of, *spec.* by way of inquest. **b.** *On v.*, on exhibition, open to general or public inspection. **With** (..) **v.: a.** *With the* (or *a*) *v. of*, with the object or design of (doing something). **b.** *With a v. to*, (*a*) with the aim or object of attaining, effecting, or accomplishing something; (*b*) with regard to; (*c*) in view of. **c.** *With this* (or *that*) *v.*, with this intention or aim, for this purpose. *To take a v. of*, to take a look at, to make an examination or survey of. *To take the long v.*, to provide for the future.

Comb.: **v.-finder,** an attachment to a camera by which it is more readily adjusted to photograph a particular view.

View (viū), *v.* 1523. [f. prec.] **1.** *trans.* To inspect or examine in a formal or official manner; to survey carefully or professionally; †to review (troops). †**b.** *spec.* To inspect or examine (records, accounts, etc.) by way of check or control –1647. †**c.** To survey or explore (a country, coast, etc.) –1796. **2.** To look at (something) more or less attentively; to scrutinize; to observe closely 1548. **b.** To see or behold; to catch sight of 1586. **c.** *Hunting.* With *away*: To see (a fox) break cover; to give notice of (the fox as doing so) by hallooing 1853. **3.** To survey mentally; to consider 1591. **b.** To regard or consider in a certain light 1765.

1. The Surgeon,..having viewed the wound,.. ordered his Patient instantly to bed FIELDING. **2.** Looke where she comes: Æneas, viewe her well 1593. **b.** The fox was viewed several times by the horsemen 1810. **3.** Bede viewed the world only from the retirement of his cell 1845. **b.** A third manner of viewing mixed governments 1832.

Viewer (viū·əɹ). late ME. [f. VIEW *v.* + -ER[1].] **1.** One who views. **2.** A person appointed to examine or inspect something, either on a special occasion or permanently; in later use *esp.* an inspector or examiner of goods supplied by contract; †*spec.* in *Law*, one appointed by a court to inspect a place, property, etc., and report upon it. late ME.

View-halloo (viūˌhălū·) 1761. [f. VIEW *sb* + HALLOO.] The shout given by a huntsman on seeing a fox break cover.

Viewless (viū·lės), *a.* 1603. [f. VIEW *sb.* or *v.* + LESS.] **1.** That cannot be perceived by the eye; incapable of being seen; invisible. Orig. and chiefly *poet.* **2.** Devoid of a view or prospect 1840. **3.** Having no views or opinions 1885.

1. To be imprison'd in the viewlesse windes SHAKS. Hence **View·lessly** *adv.* invisibly.

View·-point, view·point. 1856. [f. VIEW *sb.*] A point of view.

Viewy (viū·i), *a.* 1848. [f. VIEW *sb.* + -Y¹.] Given to adopting speculative views on particular subjects; inclined to be unpractical or visionary. **2.** *slang.* Attractive in appearance; showy 1851.

1. I doubt whether the public care much about v. books 1883. **2.** Odds and ends of the ham, such as isn't quite v. enough for the public 1851. Hence **Vie·winess.**

Vigesimal (vəi-, vidʒe·simăl), *a.* 1656. [f. L. *vigesimus*, var. of *vicesimus*, f. *viceni* distrib. of *viginti* twenty; see -AL¹ 1.] Of or pertaining to twenty; based on the number twenty.

Vige·simo-qua·rto. 1864. = TWENTY-FOURMO.

‖**Vigia** (vi·dʒiă). 1867. [– Pg. *vigia* look-out, f. *vigiar* :– L. *vigilare* watch (see next).] A warning on a sea chart to denote some hidden danger.

Vigil (vi·dʒil). ME. [– (O)Fr. *vigile* – L. *vigilia* watch, watchfulness, f. *vigil* awake, alert, rel. to *vigēre* be vigorous or lively.] **1.** *Eccl.* The eve of a festival or holy day, esp. as an occasion of religious observance. **b.** A devotional watching, *esp.* the watch kept on the eve of a festival or holy day; formerly, a nocturnal service or devotion. Chiefly in pl. late ME. **c.** *pl.* Prayers said or sung at a nocturnal service, *spec.* for the dead. *arch.* 1483. †**2.** One or other of the four watches into which the Romans divided the night –1656. **3.** An occasion or period of keeping awake for some special reason or purpose 1711. **b.** Without article: Watching, watch 1816. **4.** A state or period of wakefulness or inability to sleep. Somewhat *rare. poet.* 1747.

1. He that shall see this day, and liue old age, Will yeerely on the V. feast his neighbours, And say, to morrow is Saint Crispian SHAKS. **b.** The solemnity of the Easter v. 1896. Phr. *To keep (a) v.* or *vigils.* **3.** His delicate frame worn out by the labours and vigils of many months MACAULAY. **b.** Hermas and the twelve virgins keep v. by the tower 1892.

Vigilance (vi·dʒilăns). 1570. [– Fr. *vigilance* or L. *vigilantia*, f. as next; see -ANCE.] **1.** The quality or character of being vigilant; alertness or closeness of observation. †**b.** A guard or watch. MILT. **2.** The state of being awake; *spec.* in *Path.*, abnormal wakefulness, inability to sleep, insomnia 1748.

1. What constant v. it requires to preserve the public health in a large city 1875. **b.** In at this Gate none pass The v. here plac't MILT.

attrib.: **v. committee** *U.S.*, a self-appointed committee for the maintenance of justice and order in an imperfectly organized community; hence *v. man, work.*

†**Vi·gilancy.** 1537. [– L. *vigilantia*, f. as next: see -ANCY.] = prec. –1767.

Vigilant (vi·dʒilănt), *a.* 1480. [– L. *vigilans, -ant-*, pr. pple. of *vigilare* keep awake, f. *vigil*; see VIGIL, -ANT.] **1.** Wakeful and watchful; keeping steadily on the alert. **2.** Of attention, etc.: Characterized by vigilance 1531.

1. Be sober, be v. 1 *Pet.* 5:8. Disperse then to your posts: be firm and v. BYRON. **2.** They kept a v. eye..upon every height where a scout might be posted 1836. Hence **Vi·gilant-ly** *adv.*, †**-ness.**

Vigilante (vidʒilā·nte). 1865. [– Sp. *vigilante* = VIGILANT.] *U.S.* A member of a vigilance committee.

‖**Vigneron** (vinʸəroṅ). 1456. [(O)Fr. *vigneron*, f. *vigne* VINE, with intercalated r.] One who cultivates grape-vines; a wine-grower.

Vignette (vinye·t, vine·t), *sb.* 1751. [– (O)Fr. *vignette*, dim. of *vigne* VINE; see -ETTE, and cf. VINET.] **1.** An ornamental or decorative design, usu. of relatively small size, on a blank space in a book or among printed matter, esp. at the beginning or end of a chapter or other division; *spec.* any embellishment, illustration, or picture unenclosed in a border, or having the edges shading off into the surrounding paper; the head-piece or tail-piece of a book or article. **b.** An ornamental design, drawing, or picture in a manuscript or written document 1830. **2.** A photographic portrait, showing only the head or the head and shoulders, with the edges of the print shading off into the background 1862.

Vignette (vinye·t, vine·t), *v.* 1853. [f. prec.] *trans.* To make a vignette of; *spec.* in *Photogr.*, to produce (a picture or portrait) in the style of a vignette by softening away or shading off the edges, leaving only the central portion.

‖**Vigogne** (vigonʸ). 1660. [Fr. *vigogne* – Sp. *vicuña.*] **1.** = VICUÑA 1. **2.** Vicuña-cloth 1876. **3.** *V. yarn*, a mixture of vicuña wool, or other fine wool, and cotton 1885.

Vigonia (vigōᵘ·niă). 1763. [Latinized form of prec.] = prec. 1, 2.

Vigorous (vi·gŏrəs), *a.* ME. [– OFr. *vigorous* (mod. *vigoureux*) – med.L. *vigorosus*, f. L. *vigor*; see next, -OUS.] **1.** Of persons or animals: Strong and active in body; robust in health or constitution. So of the body or its parts, health, etc. **b.** Of plants, etc.: Growing strongly and freely 1706. **c.** Marked by, requiring or involving physical strength or activity 1697. **2.** Full of or characterized by vigour or active force; powerful, strong 1548. **b.** Of language, etc.: Energetic, forcible, powerful 1821. **3.** Of actions, measures, etc.: Characterized by, attended, carried out, or enforced with vigour or energy 1599. **b.** Of persons, etc.: Acting, or prepared to act, with vigour 1638.

1. Men are Conservatives when they are least v., or when they are most luxurious EMERSON. The ..v. pulse, and undimmed eye 1870. **b.** Some Trees are weak, others strong and v. 1706. **c.** The keenness of youth's v. day 1836. **2.** *Elaterium* is a v. Purge 1728. The air was dark and heavy, for want of that v. heat which clears..it 1770. Where the opportunities of v. intellectual exercise were frequent MACAULAY. **b.** A copious fount of v. English 1864. **3.** A v. defence 1777. **b.** An able, v., and well-informed statesman BURKE. Hence **Vi·gorous-ly** *adv.*, **-ness.**

Vigour (vi·gəɹ). Also (*U.S.*) **vigor.** late ME. [– OFr. *vigour* (mod. *vigueur*) – L. *vigor*, *vigōr-* liveliness, activity, f. *vigēre* be lively, flourish; see -OR 1, -OUR.] **1.** Active physical strength as an attribute or quality of living things; active force or power; activity or energy of body or constitution. **2.** Mental or moral strength, force, or energy; activity, animation, or liveliness of the mind or the faculties 1587. **3.** Active force or strength as an attribute of things, natural agencies, conditions, or qualities; intensity of effect or operation 1445. †**4.** Legal or binding force; validity. *In v.*, in force or operation. –1678. **5.** Strong or energetic action esp. in administration or government; the power, exercise, or use of this, esp. as possessed by or as an attribute of a ruler or governor. (Freq. implying some degree of severity or rigour.) 1618. **6.** The condition or state of greatest strength or activity, esp. in the life of a man; *spec.* in *Med.*, the height or acme of a disease 1563.

1. The sinnowy v. of the trauailer SHAKS. In order to..maintain a sufficient degree of v. in the vines 1842. **2.** The mind retains its utmost v. to forty-nine 1823. **3.** My bones beares witnesse, That since haue felt the vigor of his rage SHAKS. The whole picture is wanting in v. and contrast 1873. **4.** The Five Mile Act and the Conventicle Act were in full v. MACAULAY. **5.** The Star Chamber.. was invested with a v. beyond the laws 1830. **6.** He was then in the V. of his years 1697.

Viking (vəi·kiŋ, vī·kiŋ). Also **vikingr, wi(c)king.** 1807. [– ON. (Icel.) *víkingr* (X), commonly held to be f. *vík* creek, inlet + *-ingr* -ING³, as if 'frequenter of inlets of the sea'; but the existence of the word in Anglo-Frisian (OE. VIII) suggests that it originated in that linguistic area, in which case it was prob. f. OE. *wīc*, OFris. *wīk* (see WICK²), in the sense of 'camp', the formation of temporary encampments being a prominent feature of viking raids.] *Hist.* One of those Scandinavian adventurers who practised piracy at sea, and committed depredations on land, in northern and western Europe from the 8th to the 11th c.; occas. *gen.*, a warlike pirate or sea-rover.

A fleet of vikings from Norway ravaged the western coasts 1848.

‖**Vilayet** (vilā·yet). 1869. [Turk. *vilâyet* – Arab. *wilāya* district, dominion. Cf. VALI.] A province of the Turkish empire ruled by a vali or governor-general.

Vild (vəild), *a. Obs.* exc. *arch.* or *dial.* 1560. [Variant of VILE *a.*, with excrescent *d.*] = VILE *a.* Hence **Vi·ldly** *adv.*

Vile (vəil), *a.* and *adv.* ME. [– (O)Fr. *vil* masc., *vile* fem. :– L. *vilis* of low value or price, cheap, common, mean, base.] **A.** *adj.* **1.** Of actions, conduct, character, etc.: Despicable on moral grounds: characterized by baseness or depravity. **b.** Of epithets, etc.: Implying (moral) baseness or depravity 1560. **2.** Of persons: Of a base or despicable character; morally depraved or degraded ME. **3.** Physically repulsive, esp. through filth or corruption; horrid, disgusting ME. **b.** Of clothes, etc.: Mean, wretched 1526. **4.** Of conditions, situations, treatment, etc.: Base or degrading in character or effect; ignominious ME. **5.** Of little worth or account; mean or paltry in respect of value; held in no esteem. Also *absol.* ME. †**b.** Cheap, low (in price) –1601. **6.** Of poor or bad quality; wretchedly bad or inferior ME. **b.** Used as an intensive emphasizing some bad quality or condition; also *colloq. trivially* (cf. *foul*). late ME.

1. Let their v. thoughts the thinckers ruine be SIDNEY. **b.** The vilest epithet in the English language 1868. **2.** A victim to the snare, That v. attorneys for the weak prepare CRABBE. **3.** My v. body I bequeath to the dust 1637. **b.** A poore man in vyle raiment TINDALE *Jas.* 2:2. **4.** He had been a slave, in the vilest of all positions 1879. Phr. *Durance v.*: see DURANCE 5. **5.** The vilest and commonest stones 1677. A clamorous v. plebeian POPE. **6.** A V. compound..called Olla podrida 1841.

B. *adv.* = VILELY *adv.* Now only in combs. ME. Hence **Vi·le-ly** *adv.*, **-ness.**

†**Viliaco.** 1593. [– It. *vigliaco*, f. L. *vilis* VILE *a.*] A vile or contemptible person –1651.

Vilification (vi:lifikēⁱ·ʃən). 1653. [– Fr. †*vilification* (XV) or med.L. *vilificatio, -ōn-*, f. L. *vilis*; see VILE, -FICATION.] The action of vilifying by means of abusive language; reviling; an instance of this.

Vilify (vi·lifəi), *v.* 1450. [– late L. *vilificare* (Jerome), f. L. *vilis*; see VILE, -FY.] **1.** *trans.* To lower or lessen in worth or value; to reduce to a lower standing or level. Also *refl.* Now *rare* or *Obs.* †**b.** To make morally vile; to degrade; also, to defile or dirty –1781. †**c.** To bring disgrace or dishonour upon –1749. **2.** †To depreciate or disparage in discourse; to defame or traduce; to speak evil of 1586. †**3.** To regard as worthless or of little value; to contemn or despise –1671.

1. b. Thir Makers Image..then Forsook them, when themselves they villifi'd To serve ungovern'd appetite MILT. **2.** Mother-in-Lawes, Poets much Vilifie 1659. Hence **Vi·lifier,** a defamer or abuser.

Vilipend (vi·lipend), *v.* 1470 [– (O)Fr. *vilipender* or L. *vilipendere*, f. *vilis* VILE + *pendere* consider.] **1.** *trans.* To rate or regard as being of little value or consequence; to contemn or despise; to treat slightingly. **2.** To abuse or vilify 1529.

2. Even Dryden, who speaks with proper respect of Corneille, vilipends Racine 1806. Hence †**Vilipe·ndency,** the expression of disparagement or contempt (*rare*)

Vility (vəi·liti). *Obs.* exc. *arch.* late ME. [– L. *vilitas*, f. *vilis* VILE; see -ITY.] **1.** Vileness of character or conduct; moral baseness. †**2.** Meanness or lowliness of condition –1696. †**b.** Cheapness –1674.

Vill (vil). 1596. [– AFr. *vill* = OFr. *vile*, *ville* farm, country house, etc. (mod. *ville* town) – L. *villa*; see next.] **1.** *Law* and *Hist.* A territorial unit or division under the feudal system, consisting of a number of houses or buildings with their adjacent lands, more or less contiguous and having a common organization; corresponding to the Anglo-Saxon tithing and to the modern township or civil parish. **2.** *poet.* A village 1700.

1. Any Parish, Township, Vill, or Extraparochial Place 1721. **2.** Parochial Priests were fix'd in ev'ry Vill 1700.

Villa (vi·lă). 1611. [Partly – L. *villa* country house, farm; partly – It. *villa* from the same source.] *orig.* A country mansion or residence, together with a farm, farm-buildings, or other houses attached, built or occupied by a person of some position and wealth; a country seat or estate; later, a residence in the country or in the neighbourhood of a town, usu. standing in its own grounds. **b.** Hence, any residence of a superior type, in the suburbs of a town or in a residential district, such as is occupied by a person of the middle-class; also, any small better-class dwelling house, usu. one which is detached or semi-detached 1755. Hence **Vi·lladom**, the world of villas; suburban villas or their residents collectively.

Village (vi·lėdʒ), *sb.* late ME. [– (O)Fr. *village*, collective deriv. of L. *villa*; see prec., -AGE.] **1.** A collection of dwelling-houses and other buildings, larger than a hamlet and smaller than a town, or having a simpler organization and administration than the latter. Sometimes applied joc. to a large town or city. **b.** *U.S.* A minor municipality with limited corporate powers 1888. **2.** The inhabitants or residents of a village; the villagers 1529. **3.** *transf.* A small group or cluster of the burrows of prairie-dogs 1808.

1. A wall'd Towne is more worthier then a v. SHAKS. Birmingham is called 'the hardware village' 1874. Hence **Vi·llage** *v. intr.* to settle down to a villeggiatura. **Vi·llager,** one who lives in a v.; now usu., a working-class inhabitant of a v. **Vi·llagery,** villages collectively.

Villain (vi·lən), *sb.* [ME. *vilein, vilain* – OFr. *vilein, vilain* (mod. *vilain*; also adj. ugly, vile, low) :– Rom **villanus* (med.L. *villanus* villein in Domesday Book), f. L. VILLA.] **1.** *orig.* A low-born, base-minded rustic; a man of ignoble ideas or instincts; in later use, an unprincipled or depraved scoundrel; a man naturally disposed to base or criminal actions, or deeply involved in the commission of disgraceful crimes. **b.** Used playfully. Also applied to a woman 1590. **c.** (Usu. with *the*.) That character in a play, novel, etc., whose evil motives or actions form an important element in the plot 1822. **2.** A person or animal of a troublesome character in some respect. Const. *to* with inf. 1895.

1. Now knocke when I bid you: sirrah villaine SHAKS. There were two desperate Villains among them DE FOE. **b.** Ile fetch her; it is the prettiest villaine SHAKS. I shall telegraph to the young v. 1908. **c.** Arnulf, as usual, appears as the v. of the piece 1867. Hence **Vi·llainess,** a female v.

Villain (vi·lən), *a.* Now *rare.* ME. [– OFr. *vilein, vilain*; see prec.] †**1.** Boorish, clownish. –late ME. **2.** Base in character or disposition; given to committing vile or criminal acts ME. **3.** Partaking of the nature of villainy ME. **4.** Low or mean in respect of birth or position 1483.

2. Where gloomily retired The v. spider lives, cunning and fierce THOMSON. **3.** Narrowness or spite, Or v. fancy fleeting by TENNYSON.

Villain: see VILLEIN.

Villainize (vi·lănəiz), *v.* 1623. [f. VILLAIN *sb.* + -IZE.] **1.** *trans.* To render villainous; to debase or degrade. **2.** To treat or revile as a villain 1857.

Villainous (vi·lənəs), *a.* late ME. [f. VILLAIN *sb.* + -OUS, in XVI repl. VILLAIN *a.* and *villains* adj. (XIV–XVI). In earliest use 'churlish, ill-bred' (XIV) – Fr. *vileneus.*] **1.** Of persons: Having the character or disposition of a villain: infamously depraved or wicked; vilely criminal 1550. **2.** Of actions: Of the nature of villainy; marked by depravity or vileness of conduct. late ME. **b.** Of looks, etc.: Indicative of villainy 1828. **3.** Of words, etc.: Pertaining to or characteristic of a villain 1470. †**4.** Shameful, atrocious, horrible –1616. **5.** Extremely bad or objectionable; atrocious, detestable 1596. **6.** Low or base in respect of social position; servile –1766.

1. There is nothing but Roguery to be found in Villanous man SHAKS. **2.** A Vilanous and shamefull act 1573. **b.** A most sinister and v. squint DICKENS. **3.** A v., low oath STEVENSON. **4.** Phr. †*V. judgement*, a sentence of extreme severity passed on one found guilty of conspiracy or other grave offence. **5.** Thou art ugly and old, And a v. Scold ADDISON. The weather was v. 1884. Hence **Vi·llainous-ly** *adv.*, **-ness.**

Villainy (vi·lăni). ME. [– (O)Fr. *vilenie* (med.L. *vilania, -enia*); see VILLAIN *sb.*, -Y[3]. Until XIX *villany* was the more prevalent spelling.] **1.** Action or conduct befitting, characteristic or typical of, a villain; evil or wrongdoing of a foul, infamous, or shameful nature; extreme wickedness on the part of a person in dealing with others. **b.** With *a* and *pl.*: An instance or case of this. late ME. †**2.** Ill-usage, indignity, insult –1590. †**3.** Disgrace, dishonour; ignominy; discredit –1594. †**4.** Lack of courtesy or politeness; incivility, rudeness; boorishness –1694. †**5.** The condition or state of a villein; bondage, servitude; hence, moral degradation –1543.

1. Age's firm, cold, subtle v. SHELLEY. **b.** Robberies and all manner of Villanies 1691. **2.** To see villanie offered him, and to holde his peace 1590. Phrases. †*To say* or *speak* (*a, no*, etc.) *v.*, to speak (no) evil, to use (refrain from) low, obscene, or opprobrious language. †*To speak v. of*, to defame (a person). So †*words of v.*

Villakin (vi·lăkin). 1730. [f. VILLA + -KIN.] A little villa; a villa-residence. Chiefly *familiar* or *joc.*

I am every day building villakins and have given over that of castles GAY.

Villan (vi·lăn). *Hist.* 1552. [– med.L. *villanus* villager, f. L. *villa* VILLA.] A villein; an occupier of land in the feudal vill.

‖**Villanella** (vilăne·lă). *Pl.* **-elle.** 1597. [It., fem. of *villanello* rural, rustic, f. *villano*; see VILLAIN *sb.* and *a.*] An unaccompanied part-song, of light rustic character.

‖**Villanelle** (vilăne·l). 1586. [– Fr. *vilanelle* – It. *villanella*; see prec.] †**1.** = prec. –1685. **2.** A poem of fixed form, usu. of a pastoral or lyric nature, consisting normally of five three-lined stanzas and a final quatrain, with only two rhymes throughout 1877.

2. A dainty thing's the V. Sly, musical, a jewel in rhyme HENLEY.

Villarsite (vilā·ɹzəit). 1846. [– Fr. *villarsite*, f. name of D. *Villars* (1745–1814), a French botanist; see -ITE[1] 2 b.] *Min.* A hydrous silicate of magnesium occurring massive or in rounded grains at Traversella, Piedmont.

Villatic (vilæ·tik), *a.* 1671. [– L. *villaticus*, f. *villa* VILLA; see -ATIC.] Of or pertaining to a villa or villas or to the inhabitants; *esp.* rural, rustic.

The perched roosts, And nests in order rang'd Of tame v. Fowl MILT.

‖**Villeggiatura** (viledʒiătū·ră). 1742. [It., f. *villeggiare* live at a villa or in the country, f. *villa* VILLA.] Residence at a country villa or in the country; a holiday spent in this way.

Lord Byron is in *v.*, near Leghorn SHELLEY.

Villein (vi·lĕn). Now *Hist.* Also **villain.** ME. [var. sp. of VILLAIN *sb.*] One of the class of serfs in the feudal system; *spec.* a peasant occupier or cultivator entirely subject to a lord (*v. in gross* GROSS *sb.*[3] 2 e.) or attached to a manor (*v. regardant* REGARDANT *a.* 1.); a tenant in villeinage; also applied to a person regarded as holding a similar position in other communities; a bondsman. †Hence formerly in general use, a peasant, country labourer, or low-born rustic.

The villain was not a slave, but a freeman minus the very important rights of his lord 1876.

attrib.: **v. service,** service which a villein was bound to render to his lord as a condition of holding his land: **-socage,** socage or tenure by v. service.

Villeinage (vi·lĕnėdʒ). ME. [– AFr., OFr. *vilenage*, med.L. *villenagium*; see prec., -AGE.] **1.** The tenure by which a feudal villein held or occupied his land; tenure of lands by bond-service rendered to the lord or superior. Also called *tenure in v.* **2.** The state or condition of a feudal villein; complete subjection, bondage, serfdom, servitude 1531.

1. Copy-holders is but a new Name, for anciently they were called Tenants in villenage 1672. **2.** Reduced to the terms of the Peasants of France, of v. and slavery MILT. *fig.* As if sin were condemn'd in a perpetual v.. never to be manumitted MILT.

Villiform (vi·lifǭɹm), *a.* 1849. [f. VILLUS + -FORM.] *Zool.* Of the teeth of certain fishes: Having the form of villi; so numerous, slender, and closely set as to resemble the pile of velvet.

Villose (vi·lōᵘs), *a.* 1727. [f. L. *villosus* hairy, rough, f. *villus* VILLUS; see -OSE[1].] *Bot.* and *Ent.* = VILLOUS *a.*

Villosity (vilǫ·sĭti). 1777. [f. prec. + -ITY; see -OSITY.] **1.** *Bot., Zool.*, etc. The condition or fact of being villose or villous. **2. a.** A villous formation or surface. **b.** A villus. 1828.

Villous (vi·ləs), *a.* late ME. [– L. *villosus*; see VILLOSE, -OUS.] **1.** *Anat.* Covered with numerous thick-set slender projections resembling short hairs. **2.** Of the nature of villi 1664. **3.** *Bot.* Of parts of plants: Thickly covered with long soft hairs 1766. Hence **Vi·llously** *adv.*

‖**Villus** (vi·lŏs). *Pl.* **villi** (vi·ləi). 1704. [L., tuft of hair, shaggy hair.] **1.** *Bot.* A long, slender, soft hair. **2.** *Anat.* A slender hair-like process or minute projection forming one of a number closely set upon a surface 1728.

Vim (vim). orig. *U.S.* 1850. [usu. supposed to be – L. *vim*, acc. of *vis* strength, energy; but it is poss. a symbolic formation.] Force or vigour, energy, 'go'.

Vimineous (vimi·nĭəs), *a.* Now *rare.* 1657. [f. L. *vimineus*, f. *vimen, vimin-* osier; see -EOUS.] **1.** Made of pliable twigs or wickerwork. **2.** *Bot.* Producing long, flexible shoots or twigs 1664.

‖**Vina** (vī·nă). 1796. [Skr. and Hindi *viṇā.*] An Indian musical instrument consisting of a fretted fingerboard, to which seven strings fitted with pegs are attached, with a gourd at each end; an Indian lyre.

Vinaceous (vəinēⁱ·ʃəs), *a.* 1688. [f. L. *vinaceus*, f. *vinum* wine; see -ACEOUS.] Of the reddish colour of wine; wine-coloured. Also *ellipt.* or as *sb.*

‖**Vinaigrette** (vinēⁱgre·t). 1698. [Fr. f. *vinaigre* VINEGAR *sb.*; see -ETTE.] **1.** A small two-wheeled carriage drawn or pushed by hand, formerly in use in France. Now *Hist.* **2.** A small ornamental bottle or box usu. containing a sponge charged with some aromatic or pungent salts; a smelling-bottle 1811.

Vinal (vəi·năl), *a.* Now *rare.* 1658. [f. L. *vinum* + -AL[1] 1.] Produced by or originating in wine.

Vincentian (vinse·nʃăn), *sb.* and *a.*[1] 1854. [f. *Vincent* (see def.) + -IAN.] **A.** *sb.* A member of the Congregation of the Priests of the Mission founded by St. Vincent de Paul (1576–1660). **B.** *adj.* Of or pertaining to this.

Vincentian (vinse·nʃăn), *a.*[2] 1875. [f. *Vincent* (see def.) + -IAN.] Originating or associated with St. Vincent of Lerins (died *c* 450 A.D.).

The meaning of 'Semper' in the Vincentian Canon [viz. *quod ubique, quod semper, quod ab omnibus creditum est*] LIDDON.

Vincible (vi·nsĭb'l), *a.* 1548. [– L. *vincibilis*, f. *vincere* overcome; see -IBLE. Cf. Fr. †*vincible.*] **1.** Of persons: That may be overcome or vanquished; susceptible of defeat or overthrow. **2.** Of material or immaterial things, obstacles, arguments, etc.: That may be overcome; conquerable, surmountable 1568.

1. He not easily v. in spirit. .drew his sword 1630. **2.** Nought is so hard but v. by paines FULLER. *V. ignorance*, an ignorance the means of overcoming which are possessed by the ignorant person himself. Hence **Vincibi·lity, Vi·ncibleness. Vi·ncibly** *adv.*

‖**Vinculum** (vi·ŋkiŭlŏm). *Pl.* **vincula.** 1678. [L., f. *vincire* bind; see -ULE.] **1.** A bond of union; a tie. Usu. *fig.* **2.** *Math.* A straight line drawn over two or more terms, denoting that these are to be considered as subject to the same operations of multiplication, division, etc., by another term 1710. **3.** *Anat.* A ligament or frenum 1859.

Vindemiate (vindĭ·mieⁱt), *v.* 1664. [– *vindemiat-*, pa. ppl. stem of L. *vindemiare*, f. *vindemia* vintage; see -ATE[3].] *intr.* To gather ripe fruit, esp. grapes (*rare*). So **Vindemia·tion,** the gathering of grapes or other fruit 1609.

‖**Vindemiatrix** (vindĭmiēⁱ·triks). 1704. [med. or mod.L. fem. of *vindemiator* vintager, star in Virgo, f. L. *vindemiare*; see prec., -TRIX.] A bright fixed star in the constellation Virgo.

Vindicable (vi·ndikăb'l), *a.* 1647. [f. VINDICATE + -ABLE.] Capable of being vindicated, justified, or maintained

Vindicate (vi·ndikeⁱt), *v.* 1623. [– *vindicat-*, pa. ppl. stem of L. *vindicare* claim, set free, punish, avenge, f. *vindex, vindic-* claimant, avenger; see -ATE[3].] †1. *trans.* To avenge or revenge (a person, cause, wrong, etc.) –1713. †b. To punish –1770. †2. To make or set free; to deliver or rescue. Usu. const. *from.* –1761. 3. To clear from censure, criticism, suspicion, or doubt, by means of demonstration; to justify or uphold by evidence or argument 1635. b. To provide justification for (something); to justify by facts or results 1702. 4. To assert, maintain, or make good by one's action, esp. in one's own interest; to defend against encroachment or interference 1650. 5. To claim as properly belonging *to* oneself or another; to assert or establish possession of (something) *for* oneself or another 1680. b. Without const.: To claim for oneself or as one's rightful property; *spec.* in *Law* 1725.

1. But Cupid, full of mischief, longs To v. his mother's wrongs SWIFT. b. Because our grievances are..not..those which we bore from the Tudors, or vindicated on the Stuarts BURKE. 3. The design of this treatise is not to v. the character of God 1736. I must v. Sterne from a charge of plagiarism 1798. b. What have I ever shewn to v. this presumption of yours? FARQUHAR. 4. Arise and v. Thy Glory, free thy people from thir yoke MILT. 5. Though Christ's Appeal to the 110th vindicates that Psalm to David 1737. b. Is thine alone the seed that strews the plain? The birds of heav'n shall v. their grain. POPE.

Vindication (vindikēⁱ·ʃən). 1484. [– OFr. (now dial.) *vindication* vengeance or L. *vindicatio, -ōn-,* f. as prec.; see -ION.] †1. The action of avenging or revenging –1690. 2. The action of vindicating against censure, calumny, etc.; justification by proof or explanation 1647. b. A justifying fact or circumstance 1846. 3. The action of asserting or maintaining 1871.

2. Leave the v. of your character to your children 1825. Phr. *In v. of.* 3. The bulk of the members supported Eliot in his last v. of English liberty 1874.

Vindicative (vi·ndikeⁱtiv, vindi·kătiv), *a.* 1521. [– (O)Fr. *vindicatif, -ive* or med.L. *vindicativus,* f. as prec.; see -IVE.] †1. = VINDICTIVE *a.* 1. –1734. 2. = VINDICTIVE *a.* 2. Now *rare.* 1610. 3. Serving to vindicate by defence or assertion 1660.

1. They discerned not between a zealous and a v. spirit DONNE. 2. They will find it ill striving against the Stream and Current of V. Justice 1679. Hence **Vindi·cativeness,** vindictiveness.

Vindicator (vi·ndikēⁱtəɹ). 1566. [– late (eccl.) L. *vindicator,* f. as prec.; see -OR 2.] One who vindicates. Hence **Vi·ndicatress.**

Vindicatory (vi·ndikāⁱtəri), *a.* 1647. [f. VINDICATE *v.* + -ORY[2].] 1. Serving to vindicate; justificatory, defensive. 2. Avenging; punitive; retributive 1655.

2. The afflictions of Job were no v. punishments to take vengeance of his sins 1655. Hence **Vi·ndicatorily** *adv.* in a v. manner.

Vindictive (vindi·ktiv), *a.* 1616. [f. L. *vindicta* vengeance, revenge + -IVE.] 1. Of persons: Given to revenge; having a revengeful disposition. b. Of actions, qualities, etc.: Characterized by a desire for, or the exercise of, revenge 1627. 2. Involving retribution or punishment; punitive, retributive; avenging. Now *rare.* 1623. b. Of deities: Inflicting punishment for wrongdoing 1703.

1. He is as v. as a demon 1875. b. When..you engage To meet high Heaven's v. Rage 1743. 2. The..debts we owe to thy v. justice 1711. *V. damages,* damages awarded not only as compensation to the plaintiff but also as a punishment to the defendant. b. V. Jove prepares his Thunder 1703. Hence **Vindi·ctive-ly** *adv.*, **-ness.**

Vine (vəin), *sb.* ME. [– OFr. *vine,* (also mod.) *vigne* :– L. *vinea* vineyard, vine, subst. use of fem. of *vineus* pertaining to wine, f. *vinum* WINE.] I. 1. The trailing or climbing plant, *Vitis vinifera,* bearing the grapes from which ordinary wine is made (= GRAPE-VINE); also gen., any plant of the genus *Vitis.* b. A single plant or tree of this species or genus ME. c. A representation of a vine in metal, embroidery, etc. late ME.; also, an ornamental figure cut by a skater. 2. *fig.* a. Applied to Christ, in renderings or echoes of John 15:1 and 5. ME. b. In allusion to Ps. 128:3. 1787. 3. Applied, with distinguishing epithets, to some species of *Vitis* distinct from the ordinary grape-vine, and to many plants of other genera which in some feature resemble this. late ME. 4. The stem of any trailing or climbing plant. Also *collect.* without article. 1563. b. *U.S.* A trailing or climbing plant 1842.

1. Then sayde the trees vnto the vyne: Come thou and be oure kinge COVERDALE *Judg.* 9:12. b. Raisins from the Grapes of Psythian Vines DRYDEN. 2. a. That true V. whereof wee both spiritually and corporally are branches HOOKER. b. A wife, who bids fair to be a fruitful v. 1787. 3. *Wild v.,* the fox-grape, *Vitis labrusca* (now *rare* or *Obs.*); also, one or other of several climbing or trailing plants, esp. bryony and traveller's joy.

II. †1. A vineyard –1560. 2. A grape. *Obs.* or *poet.* late ME. 3. *Rom. Antiq.* = VINEA (*rare*) 1563.

attrib. and *Comb.*, as *v.-branch, -grounds, -leaf, -prop, -stock.* **v. bower,** a species of clematis (*Clematis viticella*); **-disease,** one or other disease attacking vines, esp. v.-mildew and the v.-pest (*Phylloxera*); **-fretter** (now *rare* or *Obs.*), **-grub,** a grub or insect (esp. a species of aphis) feeding upon vines; **-leek,** round-headed garlic (*Allium ampeloprasum*); **-louse,** the phylloxera; **-mildew** a disease of vines caused by the fungus *Oidium tuckeri*; the fungus or mould itself; **-moth,** a species of pyralis infesting vines; **-pest,** the phylloxera; **-rod,** a rod of v.-wood, *spec.* as the staff of a Roman centurion; **-sawfly,** a species of sawfly, the larvæ of which feed on the v.; **-scrub,** in Australia, scrub abounding in various species of *Vitis*; **-snail** [Fr. *escargot des vignes*], the Roman snail; **-weevil,** a small weevil destructive to vines. Hence **Vine** *v. trans.* to graft (*in* or *into* a vine); *intr.* to develop tendrils like a vine.

‖**Vinea** (vi·niă). 1601. [L.; see VINE *sb.*] A kind of protective shed or penthouse anciently used in siege operations.

Vineal (vi·niăl), *a. rare.* 1659. [– L. *vinealis,* f. *vinea* VINE *sb.*; see -AL[1] 1.] Of or pertaining to vines or wine; living on vines; consisting of wine.

Vi·ne-dresser. 1560. [VINE *sb.*] One occupied in the pruning, training, and cultivation of vines.

Vinegar (vi·nĕgăɹ), *sb.* [ME. *vinegre* – OFr. *vyn egre* (mod. *vinaigre*), repr. Rom. **vinum acrum* (for L. *acre*) 'sour wine'.] 1. A liquid (consisting of acetic acid in a dilute form) produced by the acetous fermentation of wine and some other alcoholic liquors or special compounds, and employed in the preparation of food (or as a relish to this), and in the arts, etc. b. With *a* and *pl.* A particular kind or special preparation of vinegar 1839. 2. *fig.* Speech, temper, etc. of a sour or acid character 1601.

1. *allus.* Our desire is..not to pour Vinegar but Oyl into the Wounds 1656. 2. Heere's the Challenge..: I warrant there's v. and pepper in't SHAKS.

attrib. and *Comb.*, as *v. bottle, -cruet*; (= sour) *v.-faced* adj. **V. Bible,** an edition printed by Baskett in 1717, so called from an error in the running title at St. Luke, chap. 20, where it reads 'the parable of the v.', instead of 'the parable of the vineyard'; **v.-eel,** a minute nematoid worm (*Anguillula aceti*) breeding in v.; **v. mother** = *vinegar-plant* (b); **-plant,** (*a*) the Virginian sumach, *Rhus typhina*; (*b*) a mould which grows on the surface of liquids undergoing acetous fermentation; **-tree,** = *v.-plant* (*a*); **-yard,** a yard or open space in which v. casks are arranged. Hence **Vi·negar** *v. trans.* to treat with v. in some way; to add or apply v. to; to restore by means of v. **Vi·negary** *a.* resembling v.; sour like v.

Vinery (vəi·nəri). late ME. [In sense 1 – OFr. *vignerie* (med.L. *vinarium*); in sense 2 f. VINE + -ERY.] †1. A vineyard –1513. 2. A glass house or hot-house constructed for the cultivation of the grape-vine 1789. 3. Vines collectively 1883.

†**Vinet.** late ME. [– (O)Fr. *vignette*; see VIGNETTE, which was readopted XVIII.] 1. A running or trailing ornament or design in imitation of the branches, leaves, or tendrils of the vine, employed in architecture or decorative work –1601. 2. = VIGNETTE *sb.* 1, 1 b. –1637. 3. An ornamental title-page or the like containing various symbolical designs or figures –1625.

Vineyard (vi·nyăɹd). ME. [f. VINE *sb.* + YARD *sb.*[1]; superseding ME. *winyard,* OE. *wingeard* = OS. *wingardo,* OHG. *wingart,* ON. *vingarðr,* Goth. *weinagards.*] A piece of ground in which grape-vines are cultivated; a plantation of vines. b. *fig.* A sphere of action or labour, esp. of an elevated or spiritual character. (See Matt. 20:1 and 21:28, 40.) late ME.

b. The v. of methodism lies before you SMOLLETT. Hence **Vi·neyardist,** one who engages in vine-growing.

‖**Vingt-et-un** (vænt e öñ), **vingt-un** (vænt-öñ). 1781. [Fr., 'twenty-one'.] A round game of cards in which the object is to make the number of twenty-one or as near this as possible without exceeding it, by counting the pips on the cards, court-cards counting as ten, the ace one or eleven as the holder chooses.

Vinic (vəi·nik), *a.* 1835. [f. L. *vinum* wine + -IC.] *Chem.* Obtained or derived from wine or alcohol.

Viniculture (vəi·ni-). 1871. [f. L. *vinum* wine + CULTURE.] The cultivation of grapes for the production of wine. Hence **Vinicu·ltural** *a.*

Vinification (vəi:nifikēⁱ·ʃən). 1880. [f. as prec.; see -FICATION.] The conversion of grape juice or the like into an alcoholic liquid by fermentation.

Vino- (vəi·no), used as comb. f. L. *vinum* wine, as in *vino-acetous, -sulphureous,* adjs.; see -O-.

Violent (vəi·nŏlĕnt), *a.* late ME. [– L. *vinolentus,* f. *vinum* wine.] Addicted to drinking wine; tending to drunkenness. So **Vi·nolence, Vi·nolency,** drunkenness. *rare.*

Vinose (vəi·nōᵘs), *a.* 1727. [– L. *vinosus* full or fond of wine; see -OSE[1].] = VINOUS *a.*

Vinosity (vəinǫ·sĭti). 1624. [f. VINOUS + -ITY.] The quality or state of being vinous.

Vinous (vəi·nəs), *a.* 1664. [f. L. *vinum* + -OUS. Cf. Fr. *vineux.*] 1. Of the nature of wine; having the qualities of wine; tasting or smelling like wine; made of or prepared with wine. 2. Pertaining to or characteristic of wine 1708. 3. Caused by or resulting from indulgence in wine 1776. b. Affected by the use of wine 1847. 4. Addicted to wine 1816. 5. With names of colours: Like that of (red) wine; having a wine-coloured tinge 1834.

1. So will the Liquor be V. in Smell 1694. 2. A v. and delicious Taste 1719. 3. I was seized with a v. inspiration 1874. b. Winking..with a pair of v. eyes THACKERAY. 5. Cup..rough, vinous-brown 1887. Hence **Vi·nous-ly** *adv.*, **-ness.**

Vint, *sb.* 1898. Also **wint.** [Russ.] A Russian card-game resembling auction bridge.

Vint (vint), *v.* 1857. [Back-formation from VINTNER or VINTAGE.] *trans.* To make (wine or strong liquor).

The best wine that ever was vinted TROLLOPE.

Vintage (vi·ntĕdʒ), *sb.* 1450. [alt., by assoc. with VINTER, VINTNER, and assim. of the ending to -AGE, of late ME. *vyndage, vendage* – (O)Fr. *vendange* :– L. *vindemia,* f. *vinum* WINE + *demere* take away.] 1. The produce or yield of the vine, either as grapes or wine; the crop or yield of a vineyard or district in a single season. Now *rare* or *Obs.* b. *poet.* Wine, esp. of good or rare quality 1604. c. Used with ref. to the age or year of a particular wine, usu. connoting one of good or outstanding quality; now *spec.* a wine made from the grape-crop of a certain district in a good year and kept separate on account of its quality 1746. 2. The gathering of the ripe grapes in order to make them into wine, including the preliminary processes of wine-making, as pressing and placing the juice in the fermenting vats, etc.; the grape-harvest 1540. b. The season or time when this is done. Also with *a* and *pl.* 1616.

1. The gen'rous V. of the Chian Vine DRYDEN. b. O! for a draught of v., that hath been Cool'd a long age in the deep-delved earth KEATS. c. Taste my wine; 'Tis of an ancient v. BYRON. *attrib.* The market for v. wines 1895. 2. The grape-gatherer in time of Vintage HOLLAND.

Vintage, *v.* 1618. [f. prec.] *trans.* †a. To strip (vines or a vineyard) of grapes at the vintage –1694. b. To gather (grapes) in order to make wine; to make (wine) from gathered grapes 1888. Hence **Vi·ntaging** *vbl. sb.* the action or process of gathering the grapes at the v.

Vintager (vi·ntădʒəɹ). 1588. [f. VINTAGE *sb.* + -ER[1].] 1. One who gathers grapes in the vintage 1589. 2. A bright star in the constellation Virgo 1588.

‖**Vintem** (vinte·m). 1584. [Pg. *vintem,* f. *vinte* twenty.] A small silver (or copper) coin of the value of 20 reis.

†**Vi·nter.** ME. [See VINTNER.] A vintner –1486.

Vintner (vi·ntnəɹ). late ME. [– AL. *vintenarius* (XIV), var. of *vinetarius* (XII) – AFr. *viniter, vineter* (whence VINTER, which VINTNER superseded), OFr. *vinetier* – med.L. *vinetarius, vinatarius*, f. L. *vinetum* vineyard, f. *vinum* wine; see -ER² 2.] One who deals in or sells wine; a wine-merchant; †an innkeeper selling wine.

Vintry (vi·ntri). Now *arch.* or *Hist.* ME. [f. VINTER + -Y³; see -RY. Cf. AL. *vin(i)tria* XV.] A place where wine is sold or stored; a wine-shop; a wine-vault, or a number of these. **b.** With *the* (and usu. with initial cap.): A large wine-store formerly existing in the City of London; also, the immediate neighbourhood of this as a part of the city 1456.

Viny (vəi·ni), *a.* 1570. [f. VINE *sb.* + -Y¹.] **1.** Of, pertaining to or of the nature of vines; composed or consisting of vines. **2.** Abounding in, full of, or covered with vines; bearing vines 1612.

Vinyl (vəi·nil). 1863. [f. L. *vinum* + -YL.] *Chem.* The compound univalent radical CH_2CH, isomeric with ethenyl, and characteristic of many derivatives of ethylene (which is the hydride of vinyl).

Viol¹ (vəi·əl). 1483. [Earlier forms *vyell* (Caxton), *viall* – OFr. *viel(l)e* (mod. *vielle* viol, hurdy-gurdy), alt. of *viole* – Pr. *viola, viula*, prob. rel. to FIDDLE *sb.*; the present form (– Fr. *viole*) dates from XVI.] **1.** A musical instrument having five, six, or seven strings and played by means of a bow. Now *Hist.* or *arch.* **2.** With distinguishing terms, denoting esp. the form or tone of the instrument. See also BASS-VIOL, VIOL DA GAMBA, etc. 1611. **b.** *Viol d'amore* or *viol(e d'amour*, a viol with five or six metal strings 1700.

1. For I wil not heare the melodie of thy violes BIBLE (Genev.) *Amos* 5:23.

†**Vi·ol**². Also **voyol, voyal.** 1627. [Of unkn. origin.] *Naut.* A large rope formerly used in weighing an anchor. Also *attrib.*, esp. in *v.-block.* –1869.

Viola¹ (vəi·ŏlă). late ME. [– L. *viola* violet.] †**1.** The violet (*rare*) –1480. **2.** A large genus of herbaceous plants of the order *Violaceæ*, including violets and pansies; a plant or species of this genus 1731. **b.** A hybrid garden-plant of this genus, distinguished from the pansy by a more delicate and uniform colouring of the flowers 1871. **3.** *attrib.* In chemical terms denoting substances derived from the violet or pansy 1868.

‖**Viola**² (vəi,ōᵘ·lă, vi,ōᵘ·lă). 1797. [– Sp., It. *viola*, prob. – Pr. *viola*, whence Fr. *viole*; see VIOL¹.] **1.** A four-stringed musical instrument slightly larger than a violin; the alto or tenor violin. **b.** One who plays the viola 1894. **2.** *V. da* (also *di*) *gamba*, = VIOL DA GAMBA 1724. **3.** *V. d'amore* (or †*d'amour*) = viol d'amore (see VIOL¹ 2 b) 1724.

Violable (vəi·ŏlăb'l), *a.* 1552. [– L. *violabilis*, f. *violare* VIOLATE *v.*; see -ABLE. Cf. (O)Fr. *violable*, perh. partly the source.] Capable of being violated. Hence **Vi·olableness.**

Violaceous (vəiŏlēⁱ·ʃəs), *a.* 1657. [f. L. *violaceus* violet-coloured, f. *viola* VIOLA¹; see -ACEOUS.] **1.** Of a violet colour; purplish blue. **2.** *Bot.* Belonging to or resembling the family *Violaceæ* 1889.

Violan (vəi·ŏlăn). 1850. [f. L. *viola* VIOLA¹ (A. Breithaupt, 1838).] *Min.* A silicate of aluminium, calcium, magnesium, and sodium.

Violate (vəi·ŏleⁱt), *v.* late ME. [– *violat-*, pa. ppl. stem of L. *violare* treat with violence, etc.: see -ATE³.] **1.** *trans.* To break, infringe, or transgress unjustifiably; to fail to keep or observe duly. **2.** To ravish or outrage (a woman) 1440. **3.** To do violence to; to treat irreverently; to desecrate, dishonour, profane, or defile 1490. **b.** To destroy (a person's chastity) by force 1592. **c.** To interfere with by appropriation 1823. †**4.** To vitiate, corrupt, or spoil, esp. in respect of physical qualities –1656. †**b.** To damage or injure by violence –1675. **5.** To break in upon; to interrupt or disturb; to interfere with rudely or roughly 1667. **6.** To treat without proper respect or regard; to do violence or injury to (feelings, etc.) in this way 1692.

1. If any man be affraid to violat the oth of obedience, which they haue made to suche monstres KNOX. Her priests haue violated my law *Ezek.* 22:26. He that would not v. truth, must avoid all injustice 1722. **5.** Legislation passes its limits when it violates the purse JOHNSON. So **Vi·olate** *pa. pple.* and *ppl. a.* (now *poet*). **Vi·olater** (now *rare*) = VIOLATOR. **Vi·olative** *a.* (chiefly *U.S.*) involving or causing violation (*of* something).

Violation (vəiŏlēⁱ·ʃən). late ME. [– (O)Fr. *violation* or L. *violatio, -ōn-*, f. as prec.; see -ION.] The action of violating. **1.** Infringement, flagrant disregard, or non-observance *of* some principle or standard of conduct or procedure, as an oath, promise, law, etc.; an instance of this. †**2.** The action of treating or handling violently and injuriously –1699. **3. a.** Defilement *of* chastity, etc.; in later use esp. by means of violence 1497. **b.** Ravishment, outrage, rape 1599. **4.** Desecration or profanation of something sacred 1546.

1. V. of the principles of the constitution GIBBON. A flagrant v. of treaty 1863. **4.** The v. of a sacred place by murder 1856.

Violator (vəi·ŏleⁱtǫɹ, -əɹ). late ME. [– L. *violator*, f. as prec.; see -OR 2.] One who violates; a ravisher or outrager of women; a desecrator or profaner; an infringer, breaker, or transgressor (of a law, compact, etc.).

‖**Viol da gamba** (vi·ŏl da ga·mbă). 1597. [– It. *viola da gamba* 'leg-viol'.] **1.** A viol held between the legs of the player while being played; in later use restricted to the bass viol corresponding to the modern violoncello. **2.** An organ-stop having a tone resembling that of the viol da gamba 1852.

Violence (vəi·ŏlĕns), *sb.* ME. [– (O)Fr. *violence* – L. *violentia*, f. *violens, -ent-*, beside *violentus* VIOLENT *a.*; see -ENCE.] **1.** The exercise of physical force so as to inflict injury on or damage to persons or property; action or conduct characterized by this. **b.** In weakened sense: Improper treatment or use of a word; wresting or perversion of meaning or application; unauthorized alteration of wording 1596. **c.** Undue constraint applied to some natural process, habit, etc. 1715. **2.** With *a* and *pl.* An instance or case of violent, injurious, or severe treatment. late ME. **3.** Force or strength of physical action or natural agents; forcible, powerful, or violent action or motion (in early use freq. connoting destructive force or capacity). late ME. **4.** Great force, severity, or vehemence; intensity *of* some condition or influence. late ME. **5.** Vehemence of personal feeling or action; great, excessive, or extreme ardour or fervour; also, violent or passionate conduct or language; passion, fury. late ME.

1. Promises proceeding from fear of death, or v., are no Covenants HOBBES. The v. of war admits of no distinction JOHNSON. Phr. *To do v. to, unto* (or with indirect object), to inflict harm or injury upon; to outrage or violate. **b.** The v. of the proposed interpretation is..conspicuous 1875. **2.** The violences inseparable from the best-ordered ancient society 1864. **3.** He knocked a fourth time, and with v. 1841. **4.** All the v. of her disorder was passed 1794. **5.** The v. of party spirit 1818. Hence †**Vi·olence** *v. trans.* to do v. to, to violate; to compel or constrain.

†**Vi·olency.** 1545. [– L. *violentia*; see prec., -ENCY.] Violence –1660.

Violent (vəi·ŏlĕnt), *a.* ME. [–(O)Fr. *violent* – L. *violentus*, or *violens, violent-*.] **I. 1.** Of things: Having some quality or qualities in such a degree as to produce a very marked or powerful effect (esp. in the way of injury or discomfort); intense, vehement, very strong or severe. **b.** Of colour: Intensely or extremely bright or strong; vivid. Also *fig.* of outline. 1768. **2.** Of natural forces: Possessed of or operating with great force or strength; moving, flowing, blowing, etc. strongly and impetuously. late ME. **b.** Of noise: Extremely loud 1602. **3.** Of persons: Acting with or using physical force or violence, esp. in order to injure, control, or intimidate others; committing harm or destruction in this way; †acting illegally, taking illegal possession. late ME. **b.** Of the hand. Chiefly in phr. *to lay v. hands on* or *upon.* late ME. **4.** Of actions: **a.** Characterized by the doing of harm or injury; accompanied by the exercise of violence. late ME. **b.** Characterized by the exertion of great physical force or strength; done or performed with intense or unusual force, and with some degree of rapidity; not gentle or moderate. late ME. **5.** †**a.** Due or subject to constraint or force; forced –1667. **b.** Of death: Caused by or due to physical violence; not natural 1588. **6.** Of persons, their temper, etc.: Displaying passion, excessive ardour, or lack of moderation in action or conduct 1647. **7.** Of language or writings: Resulting from, indicating, or expressive of strong feeling 1749.

1. So v. and fervent was þe hete LYDG. Parker was a man of v. passions 1808. **b.** Her hair, which was a very v. red 1873. **2.** For v. fires soone burne out themselues SHAKS. **3.** A man so v. and unprincipled as Goodenough MACAULAY. **4. a.** [To use] v. thefts, And rob in the behalfe of charitie SHAKS. **b.** Feverish with v. exercise 1798. **5. b.** I pray thee doe on them some v. death SHAKS. **6.** Some of the violenter sort of the other partie 1654. **7.** He wrote v. letters, protesting his innocence 1826.

II. In intensive use: Very or extremely great, strong, or severe 1516.

V. presumption is many times equal to full proof BLACKSTONE. I cannot make use of so v. a metaphor 1807. The intemperate life has v. delights, and still more v. desires 1875. Hence **Vi·olent-ly** *adv.*, †**-ness.**

†**Vi·olent,** *v.* 1598. [– (O)Fr. *violenter* or med.L. *violentare* compel by force; see prec.] **1.** *trans.* To constrain or force by violence; to compel or coerce (a person) –1730. **2.** To perpetrate or attempt with violence –1661.

Violer (vəi·ŏləɹ). Chiefly *Sc.*, now *arch.* 1551. [– OFr. *violeur*, f. *violer* play, sing to, the *viole*; see VIOL¹, -ER² 3.] A player of the viol.

Violet (vəi·ŏlĕt), *sb.* ME. [– (O)Fr. *violette*, †*-ete* in all Eng. senses, and (O)Fr. *violet* in 3 and 4; dims. of *viole* – L. *viola* VIOLA¹; see -ET.] **1.** A plant or flower of the genus *Viola*, esp. *V. odorata*, the sweet-smelling violet, growing wild, and cultivated in gardens; the flowers are usu. purplish blue, mauve, or white. **b.** *collect.* and *pl.* The plant, or more usu. the flowers, pulled or plucked for use in medicine or in making confections. late ME. **2.** With specific epithets: **a.** Denoting species of *Viola*, or varieties of the common violet 1578. **b.** Applied to plants of other genera, as *bulbous, dog's-tooth, false v.* 1578. **3.** Cloth, dress, or vestments of a violet colour. late ME. **4.** A purplish blue colour resembling that of the violet; a pigment or dye of this colour. late ME.

1. Underfoot the V., Crocus, and Hyacinth with rich inlay Broiderd the ground MILT. *fig. Rich. II*, V. ii. 46. **2. a.** *Viola canina syluestris.* Dogs Violets or wilde Violets. 1597. **3.** Where be my gounes of scarlet,..Grenes also, and þe fayre v.? HOCCLEVE.

Comb.: **v.-blind,** *a.* colour-blind as regards the violet rays of the spectrum; **-powder,** a violet-scented variety of toilet-powder; **-wood,** (*a*) kingwood; (*b*) the wood of the Australian *Acacia pendula*; (*c*) the wood of *Andira violacea*, a tree of Guiana.

Violet (vəi·ŏlĕt), *a.* late ME. [– (O)Fr. *violet* adj., attrib. use of the sb.; see prec.] **1.** Having the colour of violets; of a blue or bluish-purple colour. **2. a.** In names of varieties of fruits or plants, as *v. clover, maize, plum* 1706. **b.** In names of birds, insects, etc., as *v. bee, cormorant, crab, heron, swallow*; **v.-ear,** one or other species of the genus *Petasophora* of humming-birds; **v.-fly,** an artificial fly used in angling; **v.-tip,** an American butterfly (*Polygonia interrogationis*) 1676.

V. ray, the shortest ray of the visible spectrum, producing v. colour; also = *ultra-violet ray* 1903.

Violet (vəi·ŏlĕt), *v.* 1623. [f. VIOLET *sb.* or *a.*] **1.** *trans.* To tinge with a violet hue. **2.** *intr.* To gather violets 1813.

Vi·olet-co:loured, *a.* 1552. [VIOLET *sb.* or *a.*] Of bluish-purple colour.

Violin (vəi,ŏli·n). 1579. [– It. *violino*, f. *viola* VIOLA².] **1.** A musical instrument having four strings tuned in fifths and played with a bow; a fiddle. **2.** One who plays on the violin; a violinist 1667.

1. Phr. *To play first v.*, freq. fig., to take the leading part.

Violine¹ (vəi·ŏləin). 1831. [– Fr. *violine*, f. *viole* VIOLA¹ + -INE⁵.] *Chem.* A bitter emetic principle found in the common violet.

Violine² (vəi·ŏləin). 1859. [f. L. *viola* VIOLA¹ + -INE⁵.] *Chem.* A violet-blue colouring matter or colour.

Violinist (vəiₗŏli·nist). 1670. [f. VIOLIN + -IST.] A player of or performer on the violin.

Violist (vəi·ŏlist). 1670. [f. VIOL *sb.*[1] + -IST.] A player on the viol.

Violon (vəi·ŏlǫn). 1552. [– Fr. *violon* (XVI) violin or (in sense 2). It. *violone* bass-viol; see -OON.] †**1.** A violin. Also, a violinist. –1606. **2.** A variety of organ-stop 1852.

‖**Violoncello** (vəiŏlǫntʃe·lo, vīₗŏ-). 1724. [It., dim. of *violone*; see VIOLON.] **1.** A large four-stringed instrument of the violin class; a bass violin. Abbreviated 'CELLO. **2.** An organ-stop having a tone similar to that of a violoncello 1876. Hence **Violonce·llist.**

‖**Violone** (vīₗŏlō·ne). 1724. [It., f. *viola* VIOLA[2].] The double-bass viol.

Violuric (vəiₗŏliū°·rik), *a.* 1866. [f. VIOL(ET + URIC *a.*] *Chem.* In *v. acid*, an acid produced by the action of nitric on hydurilic acid. Hence **Violu·rate,** a salt of v. acid.

Viper (vəi·pəɹ). 1526. [– (O)Fr. *vipère* or L. *vipera* serpent :– **vivipera*, f. *vivus* alive + *parere* bring forth.] **1.** The small ovo-viviparous snake *Pelias berus* (formerly *Coluber berus* or *Vipera communis*), abundant in Europe and the only venomous snake found in Great Britain; the adder; in general use, any venomous, dangerous, or repulsive snake or serpent. **b.** *Zool.* Applied with distinguishing terms to other species of the genus *Vipera*, the sub-order *Viperina*, or snakes resembling the common viper 1736. **c.** *Zool.* One or other of the snakes belonging to the genus *Vipera*, of which the common viper is the type, or to the family *Viperidæ* 1802. **2.** *fig.* A venomous, malignant, or spiteful person; a villain or scoundrel 1591. **3.** †**a.** In allusion to the supposition that the female viper was killed by her young eating their way out at birth –1608. **b.** In allusion to the fable of the viper reared or revived in a person's bosom 1596.

3. a. *Per.* I. i. 64. **b.** He is the brother of that wicked v. which I have so long nourished in my bosom FIELDING.

Comb.: **v.-fish,** a deep-sea fish of the family *Chauliodontidæ*, esp. *Chauliodus sloani*; **-grass,** = *viper's grass*. **b.** Special collocations with *viper's*, forming names of plants, as **viper's bugloss,** the plant *Echium vulgare* or a variety of this; **viper's grass,** a plant of the genus *Scorzonera*, esp. *S. hispanica*. Hence **Vi·perish** *a.* viper-like; *fig.* venomous, viperish.

Viperine (vəi·pĕrəin, -in), *a.* and *sb.* 1550. [– L. *viperinus*, f. *vipera* VIPER; see -INE[1].] **A.** *adj.* **1.** Resembling a viper or that of a viper; having the nature or character of a viper; venomous, viperous; viper-like. **2.** Of or pertaining to a viper; obtained from or natural to vipers 1608. **3.** *Zool.* Of snakes: Resembling or related to the common viper; now *spec.* belonging to the sub-order *Viperina* (*Solenoglypha*) 1802. **B.** *sb.* *Zool.* A snake belonging to the *Viperina* 1887.

Viperous (vəi·pĕrəs), *a.* 1535. [f. VIPER + -OUS.] **1.** Of or pertaining to a viper or vipers. **2.** Composed or consisting of vipers 1538. **3.** Of actions, qualities, etc.: Worthy of or befitting a viper; malignant, treacherous, venomous. Now *rare* or *arch.* 1542. **4.** Of the nature of a viper; having the attributes or evil qualities of a viper. Now *rare.* 1591.

1. Censure spreads the v. hiss around 1765. **2.** Phr. *V. brood* or *generation*. **3.** The v. malice of this Monkish broode 1631. **4.** *fig.* The stings of v. remorse WORDSW. Hence **Vi·perously** *adv.* **Vi·perousness** (*rare*).

Viraginian (virădʒi·niăn), *a.* and *sb.* 1642. [f. L. *virago, -gin-* VIRAGO + -IAN.] **A.** *adj.* = next. **B.** *sb.* The language of a virago 1899.

Viraginous (viræ·dʒinəs), *a.* 1666. [f. as prec. + -OUS.] Of the nature of or having the characteristics of a virago.

Virago (virē[i]·go, virā·go). OE. [– L. *virago* a man-like or heroic woman, etc., obscurely f. *vir* man.] †**1.** Woman. (Only as the name given by Adam to Eve, after the Vulgate rendering of Gen. 2:23.) –1576. **2.** A man-like, vigorous, and heroic woman; a female warrior; an amazon. Now *rare.* late ME. †**b.** Applied to a man (*rare*) –1601. **3.** A bold, impudent (or †wicked) woman; a termagant, a scold. late ME.

1. And Adam seide. . This schal be clepid v., for she is takun of man WYCLIF *Gen.* 2:23. **2.** To arms! to arms! the fierce v. cries, And swift as lightening to the combate flies POPE. **b.** *Twel. N.* III. iv. 300. **3.** God sets this black brand upon this v. Jezabel 1680.

Virelay (vi·rĕlē[i]). Now *Hist.* or *arch.* late ME. [– (O)Fr. *virelai*, alt. of †*vireli* (perh. orig. a refrain) after *lai* LAY *sb.*[2]] A song or short lyric piece, of a type originating in France, usu. consisting of short lines arranged in stanzas with only two rhymes, the end rhyme of one stanza being the chief one of the next.

He made. . manye an ympne for your halydayis That hightyn baladis, roundelys, & vyrelayes CHAUCER.

Virent (vəi°·rĕnt), *a.* 1595. [– L. *virens, -ent-*, pr. pple. of *virēre* be green; see -ENT.] †**1.** Verdant; fresh, not faded –1646. **2.** Green in colour 1830.

Vireo (vi·riₗo). 1834. [– L. *vireo*, perhaps the greenfinch.] *Ornith.* Any small Amer. bird belong to the genus *Vireo* or the family *Vireonidæ*; a greenlet, a fly-catcher.

Virescent (vire·sĕnt), *a.* 1826. [– L. *virescens, -ent-*, pr. pple. of *virescere* become green, f. *virēre* be green; see -ESCENT.] Greenish; turning or becoming green. Hence **Vire·scence,** (*a*) *Bot.* regular or abnormal development of a green colour in leaves or flowers; (*b*) greenness.

Virgate (vɔ̄·ɹgĕt), *sb.* *Hist.* 1655. [– med.L. *virgata* (Domesday Book), f. L. *virga* rod; a rendering of OE. *ġierdland* (YARD *sb.*[1], LAND); see -ATE[1].] **1.** An early English land-measure, varying greatly in extent, but in many cases averaging thirty acres. **2.** As a linear measure: A rod or pole 1772.

Virgate (vɔ̄·ɹgĕt), *a.* 1821. [– L. *virgatus*, f. *virga* rod; see -ATE[2].] *Bot.* and *Zool.* Rod-like; long, slender, and straight. So **Vi·rgated** *a.* (*rare*) 1752.

†**Virge.** 1540. [var. of VERGE *sb.*, after L. *virga.*] **1.** = VERGE *sb.* III. 1. –1671. **2.** A rod or wand; *esp.* a rod of office –1727.

Vi·rger. 1671. [var. of VERGER[2], after prec. or med.L. *virgarius.*] An official rod-bearer; a verger.

This spelling is still retained in various cathedrals, e.g. St. Paul's and Winchester.

Virgilian (vəɹdʒi·liăn), *a.* and *sb.* 1513. [– L. *Vergilianus* (f. Publius *Vergilius* Maro); see -IAN. The sp. with *-ir-* is found in Eng. use as early as the OE. translation of Boethius; cf. Fr., Sp., Pg., It. usage (all with *-ir-*).] **A.** *adj.* **1.** Of, pertaining to, or characteristic of the poet Virgil; agreeing with or suggestive of the style of Virgil. **2.** Of agriculture: Practised according to the methods described in the *Georgics* of Virgil. Also of persons following these methods. 1724. **B.** *sb.* One who is specially devoted to or skilled in the study of Virgil's works 1577.

Virgin (vɔ̄·ɹdʒin), *sb.* and *a.* ME. [– AFr., OFr. *virgine, -ene* (mod. *vierge*) – L. *virgo, virgin-.*] **I. 1.** *Eccl.* An unmarried or chaste maiden or woman, distinguished for piety or steadfastness in religion, and regarded as having a special place among the members of the Christian church on account of these merits. **2.** A woman (esp. a young woman) who is or remains in a state of inviolate chastity; an absolutely pure maiden or maid. Also *transf.* of things. ME. **b.** *Ent.* A female insect producing fertile eggs by parthenogenesis 1883. **3.** A young woman or maiden of an age and character affording presumption of chastity ME. **4.** *The* (*Blessed*) *V. Mary* (abbrev. B.V.M.), or *the* (*blessed, holy*) *V.*, the mother of Jesus Christ. Also (now *rare*) an image or picture representing her, a madonna ME. **b.** *attrib.* or in possessive, in pop. names of plants 1703. **5.** A youth or man who has remained in a state of chastity ME. **6.** *Astr.* = VIRGO 1480. **7.** *Ent.* Applied to species of moths and butterflies 1832.

1. St. Ursula and her eleven thousand virgins 1862. **2.** [Thou] toldst her doubting how these things could be To her a V., that on her should come The Holy Ghost MILT. *transf.* In Africa, the highest mountain is still a v. 1897. **3.** She seemed a v. of the Spartan blood DRYDEN. **4.** God, that of the vyrgyn was borne in bedeleym CAXTON. **5.** He was reputed a Pure V. 1700.

II. *attrib.* passing into *adj.* **1.** Of persons (usu. of the female sex): Being a virgin or virgins; remaining in a state of chastity 1560. **b.** *The V. Mother*, the Virgin Mary 1711. **c.** *V. widow*, a widow who has been deprived of her husband before the consummation of the marriage 1644. **d.** Of a fortress, city, etc.: That has never been taken or subdued 1780. **e.** *V. generation, procreation*, or (*re*)*production*, parthenogenesis 1849. **2.** Composed or consisting of virgins 1586. **3.** Of or pertaining to a virgin; appropriate to or characteristic of virgins 1586. **4.** Comparable to a virgin in respect of purity or freedom from stain; unsullied; not yet touched, handled, or employed for any purpose. late ME. **5.** Employed for the first time; coming at the beginning or outset 1627.

1. Pardon, goddesse of the night, Those that slew thy v. knight SHAKS. *The V. Queen*, Queen Elizabeth I of England. **d.** Kerak, whose proud boast is that it yet remains a v. city 1873. **2.** In this tryumphant song, A v. army did their voices try 1586. **3.** Yet ne'er again. . the v. snood did Alice wear SCOTT. Humble v. simplicity 1848. **4.** The v. Lillie, and the Primrose trew SPENSER. Salmon. . hatched in perfectly v. waters 1867. **5.** His v. sword Ægysthus' veins imbru'd POPE. The v. energy of the session 1891.

Collocations: **v. earth, soil,** soil which has not been brought into cultivation, freq. *fig.*; **v. forest,** a forest of natural growth untouched by man. *Comb.*: **v.-bower,** = VIRGIN'S BOWER; **-stock,** the Virginian stock; **-tree,** Oriental sassafras. Hence **Vi·rginhood,** virginity.

Virginal (vɔ̄·ɹdʒinăl), *sb.* 1530. [f. as next; perh. so called because it was intended for young ladies, Parthenia (i.e. maidens' songs) being the title of the first music published for it in England.] A keyed musical instrument (common in England in the 16th and 17th centuries), resembling a spinet, but set in a box or case without legs. **a.** in plural form, applied to a single instrument. Also a *pair of virginals*. **b.** as sing., with *pl.* denoting more than one instrument 1566.

Virginal (vɔ̄·ɹdʒinăl), *a.* late ME. [– (O)Fr. *virginal* or L. *virginalis*, f. *virgo, virgin-*; see prec., -AL[1] 1.] **1.** Of or pertaining to a virgin or to virginity. **2.** Of qualities, actions, etc.: Proper to or characteristic of a virgin. late ME. **3.** Of persons: Continuing in a state of virginity 1483. **4.** *transf.* Fresh, pure, unsullied, untouched 1659.

1. In the vyrgynall wombe of blessed marye 1513. Phr. *V. generation*, parthenogenesis. **2.** A. . v. and spotless innocence 1850. **3.** The vyrgynal companye of thynnocentes CAXTON. **4.** Mountain flowers More v. and sweet than ours M. ARNOLD. Hence **Vi·rginally** *adv.*

Virginia (vəɹdʒi·niă). 1609. [f. L. *virgo, virgin-* VIRGIN *sb.* + -IA[1].] **1.** The name of that part of North America in which the first English settlement was made in 1607, subsequently one of the original thirteen States of the North American Union, used attrib. in *V. company, tobacco, trade*, etc. **2.** *ellipt.* A variety of tobacco grown and manufactured in Virginia 1618. **3.** *Astr.* One of the minor planets 1868.

1. V. creeper, *Ampelopsis hederacea* and *quinquefolia*, common climbing plants of the family *Vitaceæ*; **V. fence,** a rail fence made in a zig-zag manner; **V. nightingale,** the cardinal grosbeak; **V. reel,** a country-dance; **V. stock** = *Virginian stock* (STOCK *sb.*[1] V. 4 b).

Virginian (vəɹdʒi·niăn), *sb.* and *a.* 1588. [f. prec. + -AN.] **A.** *sb.* One of the aboriginal natives or inhabitants of Virginia. **b.** A white settler in Virginia; a native or inhabitant of the modern State of Virginia 1797. **B.** *adj.* Belonging or relating to the State of Virginia; connected with or interested in Virginia 1609.

V. creeper, = VIRGINIA *creeper*.

Virginity (vəɹdʒi·nĭti). ME. [– (O)Fr. *virginité* – L. *virginitas, -tat-*, f. *virgo, virgin-* VIRGIN *sb.*; see -ITY.] **1.** The condition of being or remaining in a state of chastity; abstinence from or avoidance of all sexual relations; bodily chastity; the mode of life characterized by this, esp. as adopted from religious motives. **2.** The state or condition of a virgin or chaste woman; chastity; maidenhood. Also, a condition affording presumption of chastity; spinsterhood. ME. **3.** *fig.* The state of being virgin, fresh, or new 1610.

2. Some pleaded their unspotted V.; others their numerous issue ADDISON.

Virgin's bower. 1597. [VIRGIN *sb.*] The British climbing shrub *Clematis vitalba*, traveller's joy. **b.** Applied to other species of *Clematis*, esp. to the Amer. species *C. virginiana*, or employed as a book-name for the whole genus 1668.

†Virgin's milk. 1600. [tr. med.L. *lac virginis*.] A chemical preparation having a milky appearance; a cosmetic preparation or wash for cleansing or purifying the face or skin –1835.

Virgin wax. Also **virgin-wax; †virgin's wax.** ME. [tr. med.L. *cera virginea*. So Fr. *cire vierge*.] *orig.* Fresh, new, or unused bees-wax; in later and more general use, a purified or fine quality of wax, esp. as used in the making of candles; white wax.

‖**Virgo** (vǝ̄·ɹgo). OE. [L.; see VIRGIN *sb.*] **a.** The zodiacal constellation lying between Leo and Libra; the Virgin. **b.** The sixth sign of the zodiac, which the sun enters about Aug. 20–23.

‖**Virgouleuse** (virgulǭz). 1698. [Fr., f. *Virgoulée*, the pop. pronunc. of *Villegoureix*, name of a village in Limousin. Cf. VERGALOO.] In full *V. pear*: A juicy variety of winter pear.

Virgule (vǝ̄·ɹgiŭl). 1837. [– Fr. *virgule* comma – L. *virgula*, dim. of *virga* rod; see -ULE.] A thin sloping or upright line (/, |) occurring in mediæval MSS. as a mark for the cæsura or as a punctuation-mark (freq. with the same value as the modern comma).

Virial (vi·riăl). 1870. [– G. *virial* (Clausius), f. *vir-*, pl. stem of *vis* force, strength.] *Physics.* In Clausius' kinetic theorem of gases, half the product of the stress due to the attraction or repulsion between a pair of particles multiplied by the distance between them; also, half the sum of such products for all pairs in a system.

Virid (vi·rid), *a. poet.* and *rhet.* 1600. [– L. *viridis*, f. *virēre* be green; see -ID[1].] Green, verdant.

‖**Viridarium** (viridēᵊ·riǝm). 1700. [L., pleasure-garden, f. *viridis* VIRID *a.*; see -ARIUM.] *Rom. Antiq.* A pleasure-garden or green court of an ancient Roman villa or palace.

Viride·scent, *a. rare.* 1847. [– late L. *viridescens, -ent-*, pr. pple. of *viridescere* become green, f. L. *viridis*; see VIRID, -ESCENT.] Somewhat green or virid. So **Viride·scence** (*rare*), the quality of being v. 1841.

Viridian (viri·diăn), *sb.* and *a.* 1882. [f. L. *viridis* VIRID *a.*] **A.** *sb.* Veronese green. **B.** *adj.* Of or pertaining to this colour.

Viridine (vi·ridīn). 1837. [f. as prec. + -INE[5]. Cf. Fr. *viridine*.] **1.** *Bot.* = CHLOROPHYLL, CHROMULE. **2.** *Dyeing.* A green aniline dye 1875. **3.** *Chem.* = JERVINE 1877.

Viridite (vi·ridǝit). 1879. [f. as prec. + -ITE[1] 2 b.] *Min.* A mineral compound occurring in certain rocks in the form of minute greenish particles.

Viridity (viri·dĭti). Now *rare.* late ME. [– (O)Fr. *viridité* or L. *viriditas, -tat-*, f. *viridis* VIRID; see -ITY.] **1.** The quality or state of being virid or green; greenness, verdancy. **2.** *fig.* = VERDANCY 2. 1825.

Virile (vi·rǝil, vǝiᵊ·rǝil), *a.* 1490. [– (O)Fr. *viril* or L. *virilis*, f. *vir* man; see -ILE.] **1.** Of, belonging to, or characteristic of a man; manly, masculine; marked by strength or force. **b.** Of dress: Denoting the attainment of man's estate; distinctively belonging to men in contrast to youths (or women) 1603. **2.** Of persons: Full of masculine energy or strength; not weak or effeminate; also *spec.* (cf. next 2) 1512.

1. The V. Age..*viz.* from thirty to forty-five Years 1728. *V. member* [L. *membrum virile*], the male organ of generation. **b.** The assumption of the v. jacket and pantaloons THACKERAY.

Virility (viri·lĭti). 1586. [– (O)Fr. *virilité* or L. *virilitas, -tat-*, f. *virilis*; see prec., -ITY.] **1.** The period of life during which a person of the male sex is in full vigour; fully developed manhood or masculine force. **b.** Masculine vigour; masculinity of sex 1890. **2.** Capacity for sexual intercourse 1721. **3.** Manly strength and vigour of action or thought; energy or force of a virile character 1597.

1. b. Literary men of more sensitiveness than v. 1898.

Virose (vǝiᵊ·rōᵘs), *a.* Now *rare.* 1680. [– L. *virosus*, f. VIRUS; see -OSE[1].] Poisonous; suggestive of poisonous qualities; rank and unwholesome. So **Vi·rous** *a.* (*rare*).

‖**Virtu, vertu** (vǝ̄ɹtū·, vǝ̄·ɹtū). Also **vertù, virtù.** 1722. [– It. *virtù* (see VIRTUE); the form *vertu* follows French sp. without justification.] **1.** A love of or taste for works of art or curios; a knowledge of or interest in the fine arts; the fine arts as a subject of study or interest. **2.** *collect.* Objects of art; curios 1746.

1. Phr. *Man* (or *gentleman*) *of v.*, a virtuoso. *Article, object, piece*, etc., *of v.*, an article such as virtuosos are interested in; a curio, antique, etc. **3.** My books, my *v.*, and my other follies and amusements H. WALPOLE.

Virtual (vǝ̄·ɹtiuăl), *a.* late ME. [– med.L. *virtualis*, f. L. *virtus* virtue, after L. *virtuosus*.] **1.** Possessed of certain physical virtues or capacities; effective in respect of inherent natural qualities or powers; capable of exerting influence by means of such qualities. Now *rare.* **b.** Of herbs: Possessing specific virtues (*rare*) 1660. **†2.** Capable of producing a certain effect or result; effective, potent, powerful –1683. **3.** That is so in essence or effect although not formally or actually; admitting of being called by the name so far as the effect or result is concerned 1654. **b.** *Optics.* Applied to the apparent focus or image resulting from the effect of reflection or refraction upon rays of light 1704. **c.** *Dynamics.* Of velocity or momentum (see quot.); (usu. =) possible and infinitesimal 1818.

1. See if the Virtuall Heat of the Wine, or Strong Waters will not mature it BACON. **3.** One part of it could not be yielded..without a v. surrender of all the rest BURKE. The simplest conscious action involves actual or v. thought 1883. **b.** The image of an object under water is *v.* 1859. **c.** If the point of application of a force be displaced through a small space, the resolved part of the displacement in the direction of the force has been called its V. Velocity. ..The product of the force, into the v. velocity of its point of application, has been called the V. Moment of the force THOMSON & TAIT. So *v. displacement, eccentric, work.*

Virtuality (vǝ̄ɹtiuæ·lĭti). 1483. [– med.L. *virtualitas*, f. *virtualis*; see prec., -ITY.] **†1.** The possession of force or power. CAXTON. **2.** Essential nature or being, apart from external form or embodiment 1646. **3.** A virtual (as opp. to an actual) thing, capacity, etc.; a potentiality 1836.

2. In one graine of corne..there lyeth dormant the v. of many other, and from thence sometimes proceed an hundred eares SIR T. BROWNE.

Virtually (vǝ̄·ɹtiuăli), *adv.* late ME. [f. VIRTUAL *a.* + -LY[2].] **1.** As far as essential qualities or facts are concerned. **b.** In effect; practically; to all intents; as good as 1600. **2.** Virtuously, morally (*rare*) 1539.

Virtue (vǝ̄·ɹtiu). ME. [– (O)Fr. *vertu* (= OIt. *vertù*; see VIRTU) :– L. *virtus, virtut-* valour, worth, merit, moral perfection, f. *vir* man.] **I.** As a quality of persons. **1.** The power or operative influence inherent in a supernatural or divine being. Now *arch.* or *Obs.* **b.** An embodiment of such power; esp. *pl.*, one of the orders of the celestial hierarchy ME. **†c.** An act of superhuman or divine power; a 'mighty work'; a miracle –1526. **2.** Conformity of life and conduct with the principles of morality; voluntary observance of the recognized moral laws or standards of right conduct ME. **b.** *spec.* Chastity, sexual purity, esp. in women. *Of easy v.*: see EASY *a.* 11. 1599. **3.** With *a* and *pl.* A particular moral excellence; a special manifestation of the influence of moral principles in life or conduct ME. **4.** Superiority or excellence; unusual ability, merit, or distinction. late ME. **b.** An accomplishment. Now *rare* or *Obs.* 1550. **†5.** Physical strength, force, or energy –1500. **6.** The possession or display of manly qualities; manly excellence, manliness, valour ME.

1. In his owne vertue he rose agayne *N.T.* (Geneva) Epist. *iiii. **b.** Dominations first; next them, Virtues; and powers the third CARY. **2.** Lessons of honour, courage,..humanity, and in one word, v. in its true signification CHATHAM. **3.** Neither faith, hope, nor charity enters into the virtues of a savage 1865. *Cardinal virtues*: see CARDINAL *a.* 1. *Theological virtues*: see THEOLOGICAL *a.* 1. **4.** That unsparing impartiality which is his most distinguishing v. MACAULAY.

Phr. *To make (a) v. of necessity* [after Fr. *faire de nécessité vertu*, L. *facere de necessitate virtutem* (Jerome)], to do as if performing a meritorious action what one in reality cannot help doing; to submit to circumstances with a good grace. *To make a v. of*, to make a merit of, to gain credit by.

II. As a quality of things. **1.** In the prep. phrases *in* or *by* (also *†through* or *with*) *v. of*, by the power or efficacy of; hence, in later use, by the authority of, in reliance upon, in consequence of, because of ME. **2. †a.** Of precious stones: Occult efficacy or power: in later use, great worth or value –1509. **b.** Of plants, waters, etc.: Efficacy arising from physical qualities; strengthening, sustaining, or healing properties ME. **c.** Efficacy of a moral nature; influence working for good upon human life or conduct ME. **d.** Worth or efficacy of any kind. late ME. **3.** With *a* and *pl.* A particular power, efficacy, or good quality inherent in or pertaining to something. late ME.

1. The planets..rise and set by v. of the Earth's rotation 1868. He remained a senator in v. of his quæstorship FROUDE. **2. b.** All Simples that haue Vertue Vnder the Moone SHAKS. **d.** There is v. in a bushel of coals properly consumed, to raise seventy millions of pounds weight a foot high 1830. **3.** I declare also the vertues of euery herbe 1551. If the Loadstone be of such a vertue, let it show it by attracting the Iron to it 1628. Hence **Vi·rtued** *a.* (*rare*) endued with v. or efficacy.

Vi·rtueless, *a.* late ME. [f. VIRTUE *sb.* + -LESS.] **1.** Destitute of efficacy or excellence; ineffective, worthless. **2.** Destitute of moral goodness; immoral, vicious. late ME.

1. Wo worth þe faire gemme vertules CHAUCER.

‖**Virtuosa** (vǝɹtiu,ōᵘ·să). Now *rare.* 1668. [It., fem. of VIRTUOSO.] A female virtuoso.

Virtuosity (vǝ̄ɹtiu,ǫ·sĭti). 1673. [f. next + -ITY.] **1.** The pursuits, interests, or temperament characteristic of a virtuoso; interest or taste in the fine arts, esp. of a dilettante or trifling nature. **b.** *spec.* Excessive attention to technique or to the production of special effects in vocal or instrumental music (also *transf.* in art or literature) 1865. **2.** Virtuosi collectively 1831.

1. Charles-Augustus had imbibed..a taste for merit, a v. in human excellence, to employ his preceptor's phrase 1823.

‖**Virtuoso** (vǝ̄ɹtiu,ōᵘ·so). *Pl.* **virtuosi, virtuosos.** 1651. [– It. *virtuoso* learned, skilful – late L. *virtuosus*; see next.] **†1.** One who has a general interest in arts and sciences, or who pursues special investigations in one or more of these; a learned person; a scientist, savant, or scholar –1778. **2.** One who has a special interest in, or taste for, the fine arts; a student or collector of antiquities, natural curiosities or rarities, etc.; a connoisseur; freq., one who carries on such pursuits in a dilettante or trifling manner 1662. **3.** One who has special knowledge or skill in music; *spec.*, in mod. use, one who devotes special attention to technique in playing or singing 1743.

1. Another excellent V. of the same Assembly, Mr. John Evelyn, hath very considerably advanced the History of Fruit and Forest-Trees 1676. **3.** All these *virtuosi*..were either *contraltos* of the softest note, or *sopranos* of the highest squeakery 1834. Hence **Virtuo·soship.**

Virtuous (vǝ̄·ɹtiu,ǝs), *a.* ME. [– OFr. *vertuous*, (also mod.) *vertueux* – late L. *virtuosus*, f. L. *virtus* VIRTUE; see -OUS.] **I.** Of persons, personal qualities or actions, etc. **†1.** Distinguished by manly qualities; valiant, valorous –1611. **†b.** Of an act: Evincing a manly spirit; brave, heroic, courageous (*rare*) –1653. **2.** Possessing or showing virtue in life and conduct; acting with moral rectitude or in conformity with moral laws; good, just, righteous ME. **b.** Of women. Freq. = CHASTE *a.* late ME. **†c.** Used as a title of courtesy in addressing or referring to persons, esp. ladies of rank or eminence –1700. **d.** *absol.* (as *pl.*), chiefly with *the.* late ME. **3.** Of acts, life, manners, etc.: Characterized by or of the nature of virtue; morally good or justifiable. late ME.

1. But young Deiphobus, Old Priam's son, amongst them all was chiefly v. CHAPMAN. **2.** A man may be counted a vertuous man, though hee haue made many slips in his life 1611. **b.** A vertuous woman is a crowne to her husband *Prov.* 12:4. **c.** I saw the tragedy of 'Horace' (written by the v. Mrs. Phillips) EVELYN. **d.** The esteem of the noble and v. 1846. **3.** Can any act be truly v., if done in pride? 1836.

II. Of things, their operations, etc. **1.** Producing or capable of producing (great) effect; powerful, potent, strong ME. **2.** Endowed with or possessed of inherent or natural virtue or power (often of a magical, occult, or supernatural kind); potent in effect, influence, or operation on this account; *spec.* having potent medicinal qualities; efficacious in healing. late ME.

1. With one vertuous touch Th' Arch-chimick Sun, so farr from us remote..Produces..so many precious things MILT. **2.** Canace.., That own'd the vertuous Ring and Glass MILT. These our mountaines are full of vertuous herbes 1632. Hence **Vi·rtuous-ly** *adv.*, **-ness.**

Virulence (vi·rʼŭlĕns). 1663. [f. VIRULENT; see -ENCE. Cf. Fr. *virulence* (XVI), perh. partly the source.] **1.** Extreme acrimony of temper or speech; violent malignity or rancour. **2.** The property or quality of being physically virulent or full of virus; malignity or violence (of disease) 1748.

1. Our v. is thrown On others' fame, thro' fondness for our own YOUNG. **2.** The v. of distemper 1815. So **Vi·rulency** 1617.

Virulent (vi·rʼŭlĕnt), *a.* late ME. [– L. *virulentus* poisonous, f. *virus*; see next, -ULENT.] **1.** *Med.* †**a.** Of wounds or ulcers: Characterized by the presence of corrupt or poisonous matter –1728. **b.** Of diseases, etc.: Extremely malignant or violent 1563. **2.** Of serpents, material substances, plants, etc.: Possessing venomous or strongly poisonous qualities; extremely noxious 1577. **3.** *fig.* Violently bitter, spiteful, or malignant; full or acrimony or enmity 1607.

1. b. Scurvy in its most v. form 1866. **2.** Herbs or mineralls, with V., and Deleterious Qualities 1671. **3.** The v. Pen of that Rascal the Examiner STEELE. His enemies here are as v. as ever 1792. She was hated by Whig beauties with v. wrath 1867. Hence **Vi·rulent-ly** *adv.*, **-ness** (*rare*).

‖**Virus** (vəiᵊ·rŏs). 1599. [L. *virus* slimy liquid, poison, offensive odour or taste.] **1.** Venom, such as is emitted by a poisonous animal. **2.** *Path.* A morbid principle or poisonous substance produced in the body as the result of some disease, esp. one capable of being introduced into other persons or animals by inoculation or otherwise and of developing the same disease in them 1728. **3.** *fig.* A moral or intellectual poison or poisonous influence 1778.

1. Cleopatra..pouring the V. of an Asp into a Wound..in her Arm 1702. **2.** The pustules..contain a perfect Small-pox v. 1800. **3.** Venice is a stink-pot, charged with the very v. of hell! 1778.

‖**Vis** (vis). *Pl.* **vires** (vəiᵊ·rīz). 1601. [L.] Strength, force, energy, vigour.

V. a fronte, a force operating from in front (as in attraction or suction); **v. a tergo,** a force operating from behind, a propulsive force; **v. inertiæ,** the resistance naturally offered by matter to any force tending to alter its state in respect of rest or motion; also *transf.* tendency on the part of persons, etc., to remain inactive or unprogressive; **v. major,** such a degree of superior force that no effective resistance can be made to it; **v. vitæ,** vital force; **v. viva,** the operative force of a moving or acting body, reckoned as equal to the mass of the body multiplied by the square of its velocity.

‖**Visa** (vī·ză), *sb.* 1831. [– Fr. *visa* – mod. use of L. *visa* 'things seen', n. pl. of pa. pple. of *vidēre* see. Superseding VISÉ.] = VISÉ *sb.* Hence **Vi·sa** *v. trans.* to visé.

Visage (vi·zėdʒ), *sb.* ME. [– (O)Fr. *visage*, f. OFr. *vis* (cf. next) :– L. *visus* sight, appearance, in Rom. face, f. pa. pple. of *vidēre* see; see -AGE.] **1.** The face, the front part of the head, of a person (rarely of an animal). **2.** The face with reference to the form or proportions of the features ME. **3.** The face or features as expressive of feeling or temperament; the countenance ME. **4.** *transf.* The face or visible side of the sun or moon. late ME. **5.** An appearance or aspect. late ME. †**6.** An assumed appearance; an outward show; a pretence or semblance –1684.

1. There are no wrinkles in his v. 1797. **2.** I neuer sawe..soo fayre a creture in yᵉ v. 1533. **3.** A plodding invalid..with..dreary v. 1860. **4.** And thou fair Moon..Stoop thy pale v. through an amber cloud, And disinherit Chaos MILT. Hence †**Vi·sage** *v. trans.* to confront; to regard, observe –1531. **Vi·saged** *a.* having a v. of a specified kind.

‖**Vis-à-vis** (vīz-, vizăvī·), *sb.*, *prep.*, and *adv.* 1753. [(O)Fr. 'face to face'; OFr. *vis* face (see prec.), *à* to, *vis*.] **A.** *sb.* **1.** A light carriage for two persons sitting face-to-face. *Obs.* exc. *Hist.* **2.** One or other of two persons or things facing or situated opposite to each other 1757. **3.** A meeting face to face; an encounter 1867.

2. Partners were scrambling for v. and places 1877.

B. *prep.* Over against, in comparison with, in relation to; also *lit.*, face to face with 1755.

He is responsible v. the Government for their efficiency 1907.

C. *adv.* Opposite, so as to face (another or each other) 1807. Hence **Vis-à-vis** *v. trans.*

Viscacha (viska·tʃă). Also **vizcacha.** 1604. [– Sp. *viscacha* (also *biscacha*) – Quechua (*h*)*uiscacha*.] One or other of two large burrowing rodents of S. America, related to the chinchilla. **a.** The *Lagidium cuvierii*, inhabiting the upper Andes from Chile to Ecuador; the Alpine viscacha. **b.** The *Lagostomus trichodactylus* of the southern Argentine pampas 1836.

‖**Viscera** (vi·sĕră), *sb. pl.* 1651. [L., internal organs, pl. of *viscus* VISCUS.] **1.** *Anat.* The soft contents of the principal cavities of the body; *esp.* the internal organs of the trunk; the entrails or bowels together with the heart, liver, lungs, etc. **2.** *transf.* The interior; the inner parts 1709.

Visceral (vi·sĕrăl), *a.* 1575. [Sense 1 – OFr. *visceral* or med.L. *visceralis* in same sense; senses 2–5 f. VISCERA + -AL¹ 1.] †**1.** Affecting the viscera or bowels regarded as the seat of emotion; pertaining to or touching deeply inward feelings –1640. **2.** *Phys.* Of disorders or diseases: Affecting the viscera or internal organs 1794. **3.** *Anat.* Of, pertaining to, consisting of, or situated in or among the viscera 1826. **4.** Pertaining to the viscera of animals used as a means of divination 1833. **5.** *Anat.* **a.** *V. layer*, a portion of the arachnoid membrane 1840. **b.** *V. arch*, one of a set of parallel ridges in the region of the mouth in the embryonic skull. *V. cleft*, one of the intervals between the visceral arches. 1870.

3. *V. cavity*, that part of an animal body in which the viscera are contained.

Vi·scerate, *v. rare.* 1727. [f. VISCERA + -ATE³, after *eviscerate*.] *trans.* To eviscerate, disembowel.

Viscero- (vi·sĕro), used as comb. form (see -O-) of L. *viscera* VISCERA, as in *v.-branchial*, *-pericardial*.

Viscid (vi·sid), *a.* 1635. [– late L. *viscidus*, f. L. *viscum* birdlime; see -ID¹.] **1.** Of fluid or soft substances: Having a glutinous or gluey character; sticky, adhesive, ropy. **2.** Of surfaces: Covered with a glutinous or sticky secretion. Chiefly *Bot.* of leaves. 1760.

Viscidity (visi·dĭti). 1611. [f. prec. + -ITY.] **1.** The quality of being viscid; glutinousness, stickiness, ropiness. **2.** Viscid matter or substance 1720.

Viscin (vi·sin). 1838. [– Fr. *viscin* (Macaire), f. *viscum* birdlime; see -IN¹.] *Chem.* A substance which forms the main constituent of birdlime, chiefly obtained from the berries and other parts of the mistletoe.

Viscose (vi·skōᵘs). 1896. [– late L. *viscosus*; see VISCOUS, -OSE¹.] Cellulose reduced to a viscous solution, largely used in the manufacture of artificial silk. Also *attrib.*, as *v. silk.*

Viscosimeter (viskosi·mĭtəɹ). 1868. [f. L. *viscosus* VISCOUS; see -METER.] An instrument for measuring the viscosity of liquids.

Viscosity (viskǫ·sĭti). late ME. [– (O)Fr. *viscosité* or med.L. *viscositas*, f. late L. *viscosus*; see VISCOUS, -ITY.] **1.** The quality or fact of being viscous; viscidity. **2.** A viscous substance; a collection of viscous matter 1545.

1. *Magnetic v.*, tendency on the part of a magnetic medium to retard the magnetizing force.

Viscount (vəi·kaunt). late ME. [– AFr. *viscounte* (OFr. *vi*(*s*)*conte*, mod. *vicomte*) – med.L. *vicecomes*, *-comit-*; see VICE-, COUNT *sb.*²] **1.** *Hist.* One acting as the deputy or representative of a count or earl in the administration of a district; in Eng. use *spec.* a sheriff or high sheriff. **2.** A member of the fourth order of the British peerage, ranking between an earl and a baron. Abbreviated *Visc.*, *Visct.* 1450. Hence **Vi·scountcy,** the title, dignity, or rank of a viscount. **Vi·scountship,** the dignity of a v.; a viscountcy.

Viscountess (vəi·kauntės). 1475. [f. prec. + -ESS¹.] The wife of a viscount; a peeress of the fourth order of nobility.

Viscounty (vəi·kaunti). 1611. [f. VISCOUNT + -Y³.] **1.** *Hist.* The office or jurisdiction of or the territory under the authority of a viscount 1611. **2.** = VISCOUNTCY 1859.

Viscous (vi·skəs), *a.* late ME. [– AFr. *viscous* (Gower) or late L. *viscosus*, f. *viscum* birdlime; see -OUS.] **1.** Of substances: Having a glutinous or gluey character. **b.** *Physics.* Imperfectly fluid; adhesively soft 1830. **2.** *fig.* Adhesive, sticky 1605. **3.** *Bot.* Of leaves: = VISCID *a.* 2. 1712. Hence **Vi·scous-ly** *adv.*, **-ness** (now *rare*). So †**Vi·scuous** *a.*

‖**Viscus** (vi·skŏs). 1728. [L., usu. in pl. *viscera* VISCERA.] *Anat.* One or other of the soft internal organs of the body.

Vise, var. (now usu. *U.S.*) of VICE *sb.*²

‖**Visé** (vī·zeⁱ), *sb.* 1858. [Fr. *visé*, pa. pple. of *viser* look attentively at, scrutinize :– Rom. **visare*, f. L. *vis-*, pa. ppl. stem of *vidēre* see.] An entry or note on a passport, certificate, or other official document signifying that it has been examined and found correct; a formal official signature or entry of this nature. Hence ‖**Visé** *v. trans.* to put a v. on (a passport or other document); to endorse or sign as correct and in due order.

Vishnu (vi·ʃnu). 1638. [Skr. *Vishṇu*, prob. from the root *vish*, and meaning 'all-pervader' or 'worker'.] One of the principal Hindu deities, holding the second place in the great triad, but by his worshippers identified with the supreme deity and regarded as the preserver of the world. Hence **Vi·shnuism,** the worship of V. **Vi·shnuite,** a worshipper of V.

Visibility (vizĭbi·lĭti). 1581. [– Fr. *visibilité* or late L. *visibilitas* (Tertullian), f. L. *visibilis*; see next, -ITY.] **1.** The condition, state, or fact of being visible; capacity of being seen (in general, or under special conditions). **b.** *spec.* The possibility of (a vessel, etc.) being seen under the conditions of distance, light, atmosphere, etc., existing at a particular time; hence conversely, the possibility of seeing, or the range of vision, under such conditions 1914. **2.** With *a* and *pl.* A visible thing or object 1628. †**3.** Sight, vision (*rare*) –1733.

1. b. The v. early on 1st June (three to four miles) was less than on 31st May SIR J. JELLICOE.

Visible (vi·zĭb'l), *a.* and *sb.* ME. [– (O)Fr. *visible* or L. *visibilis*, f. *vis-*, pa. ppl. stem of *vidēre* see; see -IBLE.] **A.** *adj.* **1.** Capable of being seen; perceptible by the sense of sight. **2.** That may be mentally perceived or observed; clearly or readily evident; manifest, obvious 1613. **3.** That can be seen under certain conditions, at a certain time, or by a particular person; in sight; open or exposed to sight or view 1667. **b.** *Comm.* Of stocks or supply: Actually in hand or to be seen 1882. **4.** Of persons: Capable of being seen or visited; accessible to others; now *esp.*, 'at home' to visitors 1722. **5.** *V. direction*, in *Optics*, the apparent direction in which an object is seen 1829.

1. He was neuer visyble to the mortall eye COVERDALE. It pleased God to unite Christians in communities or visible churches BUTLER. The conversion of v. energy into heat 1878. *V. speech*, a system of phonetic notation devised by A. M. Bell, consisting of characters or symbols intended to represent the actual position of the vocal organs in the production of speech-sounds. **2.** Pneumonia..may..arise without any v. cause 1908. **3.** On this Mount he appeerd, under this Tree Stood v. MILT. *V. horizon*: see HORIZON *sb.* 1. **b.** Statistics relating to the v. supply of grain 1882.

B. *sb.* **1.** A visible thing or entity. Chiefly in pl. 1614. **2.** *The v.*, that which is visible, esp. the visible world 1742. Hence **Vi·sibleness. Vi·sibly** *adv.*

Visigoth (vi·zigǫþ). 1647. [– late L. *Visigothus* (usu. in pl. *-gothi*; so Gr. Οὐισίγοτθοι), the first element of which may mean 'west', as opp. to OSTROGOTH 'East Goth'.] **1.** A member of that branch of the Gothic race which entered Roman territory towards the end of the fourth century and subsequently established a kingdom in Spain, overthrown by the Moors in 711–12; a West-Goth. Chiefly in *pl.* **2.** *transf.* An uncivilized or barbarous person 1749. Hence **Visigo·thic** *a.*

Visile (vi·zəil), *a.* and *sb.* 1909. [f. L. *vis-*, pa. ppl. stem of *vidēre* see + -ILE.] (One who is) characterized by strong visual perception.

Vision (vi·ʒən), *sb.* ME. [– (O)Fr. *vision* – L. *visio, visiōn-* sight, thing seen, f. as prec.; see -ION.] **1.** Something which is apparently seen otherwise than by ordinary sight; *esp.* an appearance of a prophetic or mystical character, or having the nature of a revelation, supernaturally presented to the mind in sleep or in an abnormal state. **b.** A mental concept of a distinct or vivid kind; a highly imaginative scheme or anticipation 1592. **c.** A person seen in a dream or trance 1611. **d.** *transf.* A person, scene, etc. of unusual beauty 1823. **2.** The action or fact of seeing or contemplating something not actually present to the eye; mystical or supernatural insight or foresight. late ME. **3.** The action of seeing with the bodily eye, the exercise of the ordinary faculty of sight, or the faculty itself 1491. **b.** An instance of seeing; a look 1855. **4.** A thing actually seen; an object of sight. SHAKS.

1. Visions of glory, spare my aching sight GRAY. The art renown'd, V. and omen to expound SCOTT. **b.** The visions of romantic youth CAMPBELL. **c.** The v. bright, As with a smile more brightn'd, thus repli'd MILT. **2.** Ministers..neither have v. to foretell, nor power to confer, blessing 1657. **3.** Even the v. of natural objects presents to us insurmountable difficulties 1832.

Vision (vi·ʒən), *v.* 1594. [f. prec.] **1.** *trans.* To show as in a vision; to display to the eye or mind. **2.** To see as in a vision; to bring before the eye of the mind 1795.

2. We in the morning eyed the pleasant fields Vision'd before SOUTHEY.

Visional (vi·ʒənăl), *a.* 1588. [f. VISION *sb.* + -AL¹ 1.] **1.** Connected with, relating to, based upon, a vision or visions. **2.** Of the nature of a vision; seen or occurring in a vision; visionary, unreal 1647. Hence **Vi·sionally** *adv.* as or in a vision.

Visionary (vi·ʒənări), *a.* and *sb.* 1648. [f. VISION *sb.* + -ARY.] **A.** *adj.* **1.** Able or accustomed to see visions; capable of receiving impressions by means of visions 1651. **b.** Given to fanciful and unpractical views; speculative, dreamy 1727. **2.** Of the nature of a vision; presented or apprehended in a vision 1648. **b.** Seen only in a vision; unreal, spectral 1697. **c.** Connected with or pertaining to visions 1727. **3.** Existing in imagination only; not actual or real 1725. **b.** Of schemes, plans, etc.: Incapable of being carried out or realized; fantastic, unpractical 1727. **c.** Characterized by fantasy or imagination without corresponding reality 1777.

1. What spells entrance my v. mind 1792. **b.** Knox was no v. enthusiast 1902. **2.** The v. emblem seen By him of Babylon COWPER. **b.** The v. fabric melted into air GIBBON. **c.** The v. hour, When musing midnight reigns THOMSON. **3.** Vanish'd are all the v. joys POPE. **b.** Vain, idle, v. thoughts SWIFT. **c.** To withdraw from active life into a v. world 1840.

B. *sb.* **1.** One who has visions; one to whom unknown or future things are revealed in visions 1706. **2.** One who indulges in fantastic ideas or schemes; an unpractical enthusiast 1702.

1. Of such honourable repute was the name Seer, or v., in those times 1778. Hence **Vi·sionarily** *adv.* **Vi·sionariness.**

Visioned (vi·ʒənd), *ppl. a.* 1510. [f. VISION *sb.* or *v.* + -ED.] **1.** Seen in a vision. **2.** Associated with or arising from a vision or visions 1817. **3.** Having the power of seeing visions 1813. **4.** Full of visions 1815.

3. The v. poet in his dreams SHELLEY.

Visionist (vi·ʒənist). 1665. [f. VISION *sb.* + -IST.] One who has or professes to have visions; a professed visionary.

Visionless (vi·ʒənlės), *a.* 1820. [f. VISION *sb.* + -LESS.] **1.** Destitute of vision; sightless, blind. **2.** Devoid of higher insight or inspiration 1856.

Visit (vi·zit), *sb.* 1621. [– Fr. *visite*, f. *visiter*; or immed. f. the vb.] **1.** An act of visiting a person; a friendly or formal call upon a person or a shorter or longer stay with him, as a feature of social intercourse. **b.** An excursion *to* a place for the purpose of sight-seeing; a short or temporary stay at a place. Also *transf.* of animals or birds. 1800. **c.** An occasion of going *to* a doctor, dentist, etc., for examination or treatment 1884. **2.** **a.** A call made by a minister of religion as part of his pastoral duties 1724. **b.** A professional call made by a doctor on a patient 1719. **3.** An instance (or the action) of going to a place, house, etc., for the purpose of inspection or examination 1787.

1. Phr. *To make, pay a v., to return a v.* **b.** A v. to Lyme 1839. **3.** The right of v. and search. A belligerent has the right..to visit and search every merchant ship at sea in time of war. 1897.

Visit (vi·zit), *v.* ME. [The earlier uses (I. 1–6, II. 1) are based on those of L. *visitare* in the Vulgate. – (O)Fr. *visiter* – L. *visitare* go to see, frequent. of *visare* view, see to, visit, f. *vis-*, pa. ppl. stem of *vidēre* see.] **I. 1.** *trans.* Of the Deity: To come to (a person) in order to comfort or benefit him. †**2.** To come to (a person) in order to observe or examine his conduct or disposition; to make trial of; to subject to test or scrutiny –1667. **3.** To inflict hurt, harm, or punishment upon; to deal severely or hardly with (persons or things); †to cut off, cause to die. late ME. **b.** To afflict or distress *with* sickness, poverty, or the like. late ME. **4.** Of sickness, etc.: To come upon, assail, afflict ME. **5.** To punish or requite (wrongdoing) ME. **b.** To avenge, or inflict punishment for (wrongdoing) *on* or *upon* a person. late ME. **6.** *absol.* To take vengeance or inflict punishment. late ME.

1. For He..Shall v. earth in Mercy COWPER. **3.** Therfore will I vyset you in all youre wickednesses COVERDALE *Amos* 3:2. **b.** It pleased God to visite me with a quartan 1624. **5.** Mild offences were visited with the loss of eyes or ears 1879. **b.** The Lorde..vysiteth the myszdede of the fathers vpon the children COVERDALE *Numb.* 14:18.

II. 1. To go to see (a person in sickness or distress) in order to comfort or assist him, out of charity or devotion or in the fulfilment of pastoral duty ME. **2.** To go to see (a person) in a friendly or sociable manner; also, to stay with for a short time as a guest ME. **b.** Of a medical man: To attend (a patient) professionally 1585. **c.** *transf.* To go to (a person, etc.) with hostile intentions 1533. **d.** *absol.* To make a call or calls; to pay calls; to maintain friendly or social intercourse by this means; also, to spend a short time with one as a guest; to pay visits of this kind; *spec.* to make pastoral visits 1626. **3.** To go to look at (†or explore); to inspect or examine; to look into or see to (something); in later use *esp.* to examine (vessels, goods, baggage, etc.) officially ME. **b.** *spec.* To go to (an institution) for the purpose of seeing that everything is in due order; to exercise a periodical surveillance or supervision over, or make a special investigation into (management or conduct) ME. **4.** To go to (a temple, shrine, etc.) for the purpose of worship or as a religious duty ME. **b.** To go to (a place) for the purpose of sight-seeing or on some special errand. late ME. **c.** Of birds, etc.: To resort to or frequent (land or sea, a country, etc.) for a limited period or at certain seasons 1774.

1. Ye must v. the Sick and these who are in Distress 1687. Sent for..to v. a sick parishioner 1808. **2.** He comes here visiting his relation DICKENS. **c.** *Cor.* IV. v. 148. **d.** A spinster..who spends her life visiting from place to place 1894. Go se and vysyte our wethers in the cote 1514. **b.** A faculty empowering Wolsey to v. those English monasteries 1868. **4.** He had visited the Holy Land SCOTT. *transf.* Dear, as the light that visits these sad eyes GRAY. Hence **Vi·sitable** *a.* liable to visitation; capable of being visited; such as admits of receiving visitors.

Visitant (vi·zitănt), *sb.* and *a.* 1599. [– Fr. *visitant*, pr. pple. of *visiter*, or – L. *visitans, -ant-*, pr. pple. of *visitare*; see prec., -ANT.] **A.** *sb.* **1.** One who pays a visit; a visitor. **b.** Applied to supernatural beings or agencies, etc., esp. as revealing themselves to mortals 1667. **2.** One who visits some place or object of interest 1677. **b.** A stranger who spends a short time in a place; a temporary resident 1751. **3.** A thing which comes to one in a casual or temporary manner 1742. **4.** A migratory bird, etc., as temporarily frequenting a particular locality 1770.

1. b. Adam..to Eve, While the great V. approachd, thus spake MILT. **4.** The Hooded Crow.. being..in some localities a winter visitant only, in others a resident 1894.

B. *adj.* Paying a visit or visits; having the position or character of a visitor 1653.

Visitation (vizitēⁱ·ʃən). ME. [– (O)Fr. *visitation* or late L. *visitatio, -ōn-* (Tertullian, Vulgate), f. L. *visitare* VISIT *v.*; see -ATION. Now rare in I. 2, 3, 4.] **I. 1.** The action, on the part of one in authority, or of a duly qualified or authorized person, of going to a particular place in order to make an inspection and satisfy himself that everything is in order; an instance of such inspection or supervision. **b.** *esp.* A visit by an ecclesiastical person (or body) to examine into the state of a diocese, parish, religious institution, etc.; *spec.* in English use, such a visit paid by a bishop or archdeacon; a meeting of persons concerned in such a visit ME. **c.** A periodic visit made to a district by heralds to examine and enrol arms and pedigrees. Now *Hist.* 1572. **d.** Examination of goods by a customs officer or similar official; the action on the part of a belligerent vessel of ascertaining, by entry or close examination, the character of a merchant ship belonging to a neutral state 1755. **2.** The action of going to a place, either for some special purpose or merely in order to see it; an instance of this. late ME. **3.** The action or practice of visiting sick or distressed persons as a work of charity or pastoral duty. late ME. **4.** The action of making a friendly or formal call or calls; social intercourse of this nature; visiting 1586. **b.** An instance of this; a visit 1581.

1. d. The law of nations gives to every belligerent cruiser the right of v. and search of all merchant ships 1867. **3.** The Church of England..retains private confession in the rubric for v. of the sick 1862. *The V.* (*of our Lady, of the Blessed Virgin Mary*), the visit paid by the Virgin Mary to Elizabeth, recorded in Luke 1:39 ff. and commemorated by the Church on July 2; hence *ellipt.*, the day on which this is commemorated, the feast so observed; also, a picture representing the event. *The* (*order of the*) *V.*, the Order founded in 1610 by Mme. de Chantal (St. Frances) under the direction of St. Francis of Sales.

II. 1. The action, on the part of God or some supernatural power, of coming to, or exercising power over, a person or people for some end ME. **2.** A heavy affliction, blow, or trial, regarded as an instance of divine dispensation; retributive punishment operating by this means 1450. **3.** The fact of some violent or destructive agency or force coming or falling upon a people, country, etc. 1535. **4.** The fact of some immaterial power or influence acting or operating on the mind 1791.

1. Mercies are visitations; when God comes in kindness and love to do us good, he visiteth us 1643. A verdict of 'died by the v. of God' was recorded 1820. **2.** War is here regarded..as a punitive v., as a form of retribution for our sins 1885. **3.** The period..was marked by the visitations of pestilence, as well as those of war 1838. **4.** Or was he moved by some v. of compunction? 1873.

Visitatorial (vizitătōə·riăl), *a.* 1688. [f. *visitator* (XVI – late and med.L.) + -IAL, or f. *visitatory* (XVII – med.L. *visitatorius*) + -AL¹ 1; see -ORIAL.] **1.** Pertaining to, connected with, involving or implying, official visitation. **2.** Having the power of visitation; exercising authority of this kind 1880.

1. Deriving the v. power from the property of the donor 1834. **2.** Leave of absence granted by v. boards 1881.

Visite (vizi·t). 1852. [– Fr. *visite*, VISIT *sb.*] A light cape or short sleeveless cloak worn by women in the 19th c.

Visiter (vi·zitəɹ). Now *rare*. late ME. [f. VISIT *v.* + -ER¹.] = VISITOR.

Visiting (vi·zitiŋ), *vbl. sb.* ME. [f. VISIT *v.* + -ING¹.] The action of coming or going to a person or place for some special purpose. *attrib.*: **v.-book,** a book containing the names of persons to be visited; **-card,** a small card bearing a person's name (and address), to be presented or left on paying a visit; **-list,** a list of persons to be visited.

Visiting (vi·zitiŋ), *ppl. a.* 1606. [f. VISIT *v.* + -ING².] **1.** That visits; that pays visits or is engaged in visiting. **2.** That visits officially for the purpose of inspection or examination 1713.

1. *V. ant*, the driver ant.

Visitor (vi·zitəɹ). late ME. [– AFr. *visitour*, (O)Fr. *visiteur*, f. *visiter* VISIT *v.*; see -ER[2] 3.] **1.** One who visits officially for the purpose of inspection or supervision, in order to prevent or remove abuses or irregularities. **2.** One who visits from charitable motives or with a view of doing good. late ME. **3.** One who pays a visit to another person or to a household; one who is staying for a time with friends 1607. **4.** One who visits a place, country, etc., esp. as a sightseer or tourist 1728. **b.** An animal or bird which occasionally or at regular seasons frequents a certain locality or area 1859.

1. In certain Colleges..fundamental statutes can only be changed by visitors 1832. **2.** Vertuous visitour to folkys in prisoun LYDG. **3.** You see this confluence, this great flood of visitors SHAKS. **4.** Visitors to the Montauvert 1860. **b.** The Glead or Kite..is a very rare v. 1870.

Visitress (vi·zitrės). 1827. [f. VISITOR; see -ESS[1].] **1.** A female visitor. **2.** *spec.* A woman who undertakes regular visiting of the poorer households of a district in order to help or advise 1861.

†**Vi·sive,** *a.* 1543. [– Fr. †*visif*, *-ive* (XV) or late and med.L. *visivus*, f. L. *visus* seeing, sight; see -IVE.] Of or pertaining to sight or the power of seeing; visual. **1.** *V. faculty, power, virtue*, etc.: the faculty of sight; the power of vision –1838. **2.** Forming the object of vision; capable of being seen –1647. **b.** *Optics.* Falling upon or appearing to the eye –1690.

Visne (vī·ni). 1449. [– AFr., OFr. *visné* :– Rom. **vicinatus*, f. L. *vicinus* neighbour; see VICINITY, -ATE[1].] *Law* or *Hist.* **1.** A neighbourhood or vicinage, esp. as the area from which a jury is summoned. **2.** A jury summoned from the neighbourhood in which the cause of action lies 1633.

Visnomy (vi·znŏmi). Now *arch.* or *dial.* 1509. [var. of ME. *fisnomye* PHYSIOGNOMY.] = PHYSIOGNOMY 3.

Vison (vəi·sən). 1781. [– Fr. *vison* (Buffon), of unkn. origin.] The American mink.

Visor, vizor (vəi·zəɹ), *sb.* [ME. *viser* – AFr. *viser* = (O)Fr. *visière*, f. OFr. *vis* face; see VISAGE, -OR 2. Cf. VIZARD *sb.*] **1.** The front part of a helmet, covering the face but provided with holes or openings to admit of seeing and breathing, and capable of being raised and lowered; sometimes *spec.* the upper portion of this. **b.** *U.S.* The peak of a cap 1864. **2.** A mask to conceal the face; a vizard ME. **3.** *fig.* An outward appearance or show under which something different is hid; a mask or disguise 1532. †**4.** A face or countenance; an outward aspect or appearance –1693.

2. They were disguised in cloaks and visors 1797. **3.** He concealed his dislike (their enmity being covered yet under a fair visour) 1653.

Comb.: **v.-mask,** (*a*) a form of disguising mask, a domino (*Hist*); †(*b*) a prostitute. Hence **Vi·sor, vi·zor** *v.* (*rare*) *refl.* to disguise (oneself) with a v.; *trans.* to cover *up* with a v.

Visored, vizored (vəi·zəɹd), *ppl. a.* late ME. [f. prec. + -ED[1].] **1.** Of persons: Having the face covered or hid with a visor or mask. **2.** Of helmets: Furnished with a visor 1834.

1. Visor'd falshood, and base forgery MILT.

‖**Viss** (vis). 1626. [– Tamil *vīsai.*] A weight used in Southern India and Burma equal to about 3⅛ lbs.

Vista (vi·stă). Also †**visto.** 1657. [– It. *vista* view.] **1.** A view or prospect, esp. one seen through an avenue of trees or other long and narrow opening. **2.** A long narrow opening in a wood, etc., through which a view may be obtained, or which in itself affords a pleasant prospect; an avenue or glade 1671. **b.** An open corridor or long passage in or through a large building; an interior portion of a building affording a continuous view 1708. **3.** *fig.* A mental view or vision of a far-reaching nature 1673. **4.** *In v.*, in continuous view 1758.

1. A Visto by Canalleto 1742. A piny dell gave some v. of the broad sea we were leaving 1873. **2.** He employed hands to cut a v. through a coppice RICHARDSON **b.** The central aisle..forming in itself the grandest architectural v. in Europe 1806. **4.** A long v. of years stretching out before them 1888.

Vistaed (vi·stăd), *a.* 1835. [f. prec. + -ED[2].] **1.** Placed or arranged so as to make a vista or avenue. **2.** Provided with vistas 1862. **3.** *fig.* Seen as it were in prospect by the imagination 1849.

3. The vista'd joys of Heaven's eternal year 1851.

Visual (vi·ʒiuăl, vi·ziu,ăl), *a.* and *sb.* late ME. [– late L. *visualis*, f. L. *visus* sight; see -AL[1] 1.] **A.** *adj.* **1.** Of beams: Coming, proceeding, or directed from the eye or sight. *Obs.* or *arch.* **2.** Of power or faculty: Pertaining or relating to, concerned or connected with, sight or vision 1603. **3.** Of organs: Endowed with the power of sight; having the function of producing vision 1626. **4. a.** Of knowledge: Attained or obtained by sight or vision 1651. **b.** Carried out or performed by means of vision 1849. **c.** Of impressions, etc.: Received through the sense of sight; based upon something seen 1833. **5.** Of or pertaining to vision in relation to the object of sight; optical; as in *v. angle, axis, focus, point* 1710. **6.** Perceptible, visible 1756. **7.** Of the nature of a mental vision 1845.

1. For inward light alas Puts forth no v. beam MILT. *V. line*, the direct line from the eye to the object or point of vision; the line of sight. *V. ray*, a ray proceeding from the eye to the object seen, or in later use from the object to the eye. **2.** The Spirits of the Mind Are busy..Upon the rights of v. sense Usurping WORDSW. **3.** The virtue of the V. nerve SWIFT. **4. b.** The v. test however is independent 1882. **c.** All parts of the retina are not equally sensitive to v. impressions 1879.

B. *sb.* **1.** A visual ray 1726. **2.** One whose memory, imagination, etc., is wholly or largely visual 1886. **Visua·lity,** mental visibility; a mental picture or vision. CARLYLE. **Vi·sually** *adv.*

Visualize (vi·ʒiuăləiz, vi·ziu-), *v.* 1817. [f. prec. + -IZE.] **1.** *trans.* To form a mental vision, image, or picture of. **2.** *absol.* To construct a visual image in the mind 1871.

Vi:sualiza·tion, the action, fact, or power of visualizing; a picture formed by visualizing. **Vi·sualizer.**

Vita glass (vəi·tă glɑs). 1925. [f. L. *vita* life.] Trade name of a variety of glass which permits the passage of a large part of the ultra-violet rays of sunlight.

Vital (vəi·tăl), *a.* and *sb.* late ME. [– (O)Fr. *vital* – L. *vitalis*, f. *vita* life; see -AL[1] 1.] **A.** *adj.* **I. 1.** Consisting in, constituted by, that immaterial force or principle which is present in living beings or organisms and by which they are animated and their functions maintained. Now chiefly *Phys.* or *Biol.* **2.** Maintaining, supporting, or sustaining life 1450. **3.** Of parts, organs, etc.: Essential or necessary to life 1482. **b.** *transf.* 1647. **4.** Of, pertaining or relating to, accompanying, or characteristic of life 1565. **b.** Of statistics: Concerned with or relating to the facts of life, e.g. birth, marriage, death, etc. 1837. **5.** Invigorating, vitalizing; life-giving. Chiefly *poet.* 1590. **6.** Affecting life; fatal to or destructive of life 1612. **7.** *fig.* That is essential to the existence of something; absolutely indispensable, necessary, or requisite. Also, in wider sense, of supreme importance. 1619. **b.** Paramount, supreme, very great 1810.

1. This internal energy, which is peculiar to living protoplasm, is frequently spoken of as v. force BENTLEY. Phr. *V. spark* (†or *flame*); The v. spark was extinct 1826. **2.** The Spirit of God..v. vertue infus'd, and v. warmth throughout the fluid Mass MILT. Dream not that the amorous Deep Will yet restore him to the v. air SHELLEY. Phr. *V. fluid*, in *Bot.* = LATEX 2. †*V. air*, in *Old Chem.* = OXYGEN 1. **3.** The V. Parts are the Heart, Brain, Lungs and Liver 1696. **b.** Such v. parts as the machinery, magazines, and steering gear 1889. **4.** When I haue pluck'd thy Rose, I cannot giue it vitall growth againe SHAKS. A gradual decay of the v. powers from old age 1826. *V. affinity*: see AFFINITY 9. *V. capacity*, in *Phys.*, the breathing or respiratory capacity of the lungs. **5.** Vitall and comfortable heate..from the bodie of the sunne 1608. **6.** Those that hold the v. shears MILT. **7.** Our own v. interests 1809. A cause which was so v. to both nations 1860. This question—quite v. to all social happiness RUSKIN. **b.** This inquiry..is..of v. moment 1850.

II. 1. Endowed with or possessed of life; animate, living. Now *poet.* or *rhet.* 1513. **b.** Of places: Full of life or activity 1742. †**2.** As an epithet of *life* –1645. †**3.** = VIABLE *a.*[1] –1646.

1. That bright shape of v. stone which drew the heart out of Pygmalion SHELLEY.

B. *sb.* A vital part or organ (*rare*) 1710. Hence **Vi·tally** *adv.*

Vitalism (vəi·tăliz'm). 1822. [– Fr. *vitalisme*, or f. prec. + -ISM.] *Biol.* The doctrine that the origin and phenomena of life are due to or produced by a vital principle, as dist. from a purely chemical or physical force.

Vitalist (vəi·tălist). 1860. [f. prec. + -IST.] An advocate of or believer in vitalism. Also as *adj.* = next.

Vitalistic (vəităli·stik), *a.* 1865. [f. prec. + -IC.] **1.** Of, pertaining to, involving, or denoting vitalism, or a hypothetical vital principle. **2.** Pertaining to or denoting the germ-theory, esp. in its relation to fermentation 1891.

Vitality (vəitæ·lĭti). 1592. [– L. *vitalitas*, *-tat-*, f. *vitalis* VITAL; see -ITY.] **1.** Vital force, power, or principle as possessed or manifested by living things; the principle of life; animation. **b.** Of plants or vegetative organisms. Also *spec.* of seeds: Germinating power. 1829. **2.** *fig.* Power of enduring or continuing 1844. **3.** *fig.* Active force or power; mental or physical vigour 1858. **4.** With *a* and pl. Something possessed of vital force 1851.

2. The v. of Pope's writings 1874. **3.** Such was the intense v. of the Béarnese prince 1860.

Vitalize (vəi·tăləiz), *v.* Also **-ise.** 1678. [f. VITAL *a.* + -IZE.] **1.** *trans.* To give life or animation to (the body, etc.); to endow with vital force or principle. **2.** *fig.* To make living or active; to infuse vitality or vigour into (something); to animate 1805. **b.** To put life into (a literary or artistic conception) 1884.

2. b. He is not an artist. He cannot v. his material. 1907. Hence **Vitaliza·tion,** the action or process of vitalizing, or the state of being vitalized; an instance of this.

Vitals (vəi·tălz), *sb. pl.* 1610. [– L. *vitalia*, n. pl. of *vitalis* VITAL, used subst.] **1.** Those parts or organs of the body, esp. the human body, essential to life, or upon which life depends; usu. applied vaguely, but occas. *spec.* the brain, heart, lungs, and liver. **2.** *transf.* Essential parts or features 1657. **b.** The vital parts of a ship 1884.

1. The weapon has missed your v. 1760. *fig.* Such immense sums, drawn from the v. of all France BURKE. **2.** The very vitals of religion 1702.

Vitamin (vi·tămin, vəi·tă-, -in). 1912. Also **-ine.** [Eng. orig. *vitamine* (1912, Casimir Funk) – G. *vitamin*, f. L. *vita* life + G. *amin* AMINE. So named because it was first believed that an amino-acid was present, the sp. being later modified in order to avoid the suggestion.] Any of the accessory food-factors (distinguished as *v. A, B*, etc.) occurring naturally in minute quantities in many foodstuffs and regarded as essential to normal growth. Hence **Vitami·nic, Vita·minous** *adjs.* **Vi·taminize** *v. trans.*

Vitascope (vəi·tăskōᵘp). *U.S.* 1896. [f. L. *vita* life + -SCOPE.] A variety of cinematograph.

‖**Vitellarium** (vitelēᵊ·riŏm). *Pl.* **-aria.** 1865. [mod.L. f. VITELLUS + -ARIUM.] *Anat.* An accessory gland in the female productive organs of some worms, by which the vitellus for the eggs is secreted; a yolk-gland. Hence **Vitella·rian** *a.*

Vitellary (vi·telări, vite·lări, vəi-), *sb.* and *a.* 1650. [f. L. VITELLUS + -ARY; cf. prec.] †**A.** *sb.* The place or part where the yolk of an egg is formed –1687. **B.** *adj.* Vitelline 1846.

Vitelli-, comb. f. L. *vitellus* VITELLUS, as in **vitelli·genous** *a.* producing the vitellus.

Vitellin (vite·lin, vəi-). 1857. [f. VITELLUS + -IN[1].] *Chem.* **1.** The albuminoidal substance in the yolk of an egg, a mixture of albumin and casein. **2.** A related substance found in the seeds of plants 1882.

Vitelline (vite·ləin, -in, vəi-), *a.* and *sb.* late ME. [– med.L. *vitellinus*, f. VITELLUS; see -INE[1]. Cf. (in sense 1) (O)Fr. *vitellin.*] **A.** *adj.* **1.** Coloured like the yolk of an egg; deep-yellow with a tinge of red. **2.** *Biol.* Of or belonging to the vitellus or yolk of an egg 1835. **b.** *V. membrane, sac*, the transparent membrane which surrounds the yolk of an egg; the yolk-sac; the investing membrane of the embryo 1845. **B.** *sb.* The yolk, the vitellary substance 1891.

Vite·llo-, comb. f. VITELLUS, as in **vitello·genous** *a.*, producing the vitellus or yolk.

||**Vitellus** (vite·lŏs, vəi-). 1728. [L., yolk of an egg.] **1.** *Embryol.* The yolk of an egg; the germinative contents of an ovum-cell. **2.** *Bot.* A fleshy sac situated between the albumen and the embryo in a seed 1807.

Viti-, comb. form of L. *vitis* vine, as in **viti·ferous** *a.* [L. *vitifer*].

Vitiate (vi·ʃiĕt), *ppl. a.* Now *rare.* late ME. [L. *vitiatus*, pa. pple. of *vitiare*; see next, -ATE².] Vitiated.

Vitiate (vi·ʃieᶦt), *v.* 1534. [– *vitiat-*, pa. ppl. stem of L. *vitiare*, f. *vitium* VICE *sb.*¹; see -ATE³.] **1.** *trans.* To render incomplete, imperfect, or faulty; to impair or spoil. **b.** To corrupt (*a*) literary works or (*b*) language by carelessness, arbitrary changes, or the introduction of foreign elements 1659. **2.** To render corrupt in morals; to lower the moral standard of (persons) 1534. **b.** Similarly with impersonal objects 1584. **c.** To pervert (the eye, taste, etc.), so as to lead to false judgements or preferences 1806. †**3.** To deflower or violate (a woman) –1791. **4.** To corrupt in respect of substance; to make bad, impure, or defective 1572. **5.** To render of no effect; to invalidate either completely or in part; *spec.* to destroy or impair the legal force of (a deed, etc.) 1621. **b.** To render (an argument, etc.) unsatisfactory 1748. †**6.** To adulterate –1728.

1. A continual Anxiety for Life vitiates all the Relishes of it ADDISON. **b.** Many barbarous terms and phrases, by which other dictionaries may v. the style, are rejected from this JOHNSON. **2.** The suppression of those habits with which I was vitiated JOHNSON. **b.** One sin of youth vitiates a protracted life 1847. **4.** A malady that has permanently vitiated the sight 1863. The impurity of the air vitiated by respiration 1869. **5.** If an undefined portion of a bequest is to be applied to a purpose void by the statute, it vitiates the whole 1827. Hence **Vi·tiated** *ppl. a.*

Vitiation (viʃiēᶦ·ʃən). 1635. [– L. *vitiatio*, *-ōn-*, f. as prec.; see -ION. Later, f. VITIATE *v.*] The action of vitiating, the fact or state of being vitiated.

Viticulture (vi·tikɒltiŭɹ, vəi·ti-, -tʃəɹ). 1872. [f. VITI- + CULTURE.] The cultivation of the vine; vine-growing. Hence **Viticu·ltural** *a.* of or pertaining to v. 1865. **Viticu·lturer, Viticu·lturist**, a vine-grower.

||**Vitiligo** (vitiləi·go). 1657. [L. *vitiligo* tetter.] *Path.* A skin disease characterized by the presence of smooth white shining tubercles on the face, neck, and other parts of the body; a species of leprosy. Hence **Vitili·ginous** *a.* of, connected with, or of the nature of v.

Vitiosity (viʃiǫ·sĭti). 1538. [– L. *vitiositas*, f. *vitiosus* VICIOUS; see -ITY.] †**1.** A defect or fault; an imperfection –1665. **2.** The state or character of being morally vicious 1603. †**b.** An instance of this; a vice –1657. †**3.** The quality of being physically impaired or defective –1651. **4.** *Sc. Law.* The quality of being legally faulty or improper 1765.

2. My untamed affections and confirmed v. makes mee dayly doe worse SIR T. BROWNE.

||**Vitrage** (vi·trāʒ). 1886. [Fr. *vitrage* glass windows, f. *vitre* glass.] *V. net* (also *cloth*), a lace-net or thin fabric suitable for window-curtains.

Vitreous (vi·triəs), *a.* 1646. [f. L. *vitreus*, f. *vitrum* glass; see -EOUS.] **1.** Of, belonging to, or consisting or composed of glass; of the nature of or resembling glass; glassy. **b.** *Geol.* and *Min.* Resembling glass in brittleness, hardness, lustre, and mode of cleavage 1774. **c.** *Chem.* Resembling glass in composition 1800. **2.** *V. humour* (or *body*), the transparent gelatinous substance occupying the posterior and larger part of the eyeball 1663. **b.** *ellipt.* as *sb.* = a. 1869. **3.** *V. electricity*, positive electricity obtained from glass by friction 1759. **4.** Resembling that of glass; characteristic of glass 1811. **b.** Having the colour or appearance of glass 1874.

1. The final stiffening of a v. mass into solid stone 1882. **b.** V. lava 1811. Hence **Vi·treousness.**

Vitreously (vi·triəsli), *adv.* 1794. [f. prec. + -LY².] In a vitreous manner: **a.** With positive electricity. **b.** Like glass 1904.

Vitrescence (vitre·sĕns). 1796. [f. next; see -ENCE.] The state of becoming vitreous or glassy; vitrified or vitreous condition. So **Vitre·scency** (*rare*) 1756.

Vitrescent (vitre·sĕnt), *a.* 1756. [f. L. *vitrum* glass + -ESCENT.] Tending to become glass; susceptible of being turned into glass; glassy.

Vitrescible (vitre·sib'l), *a.* 1754. [– Fr. *vitrescible*, f. *vitre* glass, after formal parallels.] That can be vitrified; vitrifiable. Hence **Vitrescibi·lity.**

Vitrifaction (vitrifæ·kʃən). 1728. [var. of earlier VITRIFICATION; see -FACTION.] = VITRIFICATION.

Vitrifiable (vi·trifəiăb'l), *a.* 1646. [f. VITRIFY *v.* + -ABLE.] Capable of being vitrified; admitting of conversion by heat into a glassy substance.

Vitrification (vi:trifikēᶦ·ʃən). 1612. [– med.L. *vitrificatio*, f. **vitrificare*; see VITRIFY, -FICATION. Cf. Fr. *vitrification* (XVI).] **1.** The action or process of vitrifying; conversion into a glassy substance by fusion due to heat; the fact of being so converted. **b.** With *a* and *pl.*: An instance of such conversion 1626. **3.** The result or product of vitrifying; a vitrified substance or body 1651.

3. He had but to cover this material with a v. of transparent glaze 1860.

Vitrified (vi·trifəid), *ppl. a.* 1646. [f. VITRIFY + -ED¹.] Converted into glass or a glassy substance by exposure to heat; rendered glassy; glazed. †**b.** *fig.* Icy, frozen. CRABBE.

V. fort, a hill-fort of a type occurring in Scotland and some parts of the Continent, the stones of which have been converted into a vitreous substance by the action of fire.

Vitriform (vi·trifǫɹm), *a.* 1796. [f. L. *vitrum* glass + -FORM.] Having the form or appearance of glass.

Vitrify (vi·trifəi), *v.* 1594. [– Fr. *vitrifier* or med.L. **vitrificare* (cf. *vitrificatio* 1652) f. L. *vitrum* glass; see -FY.] **1.** *trans.* To convert into glass or a glass-like substance; to render vitreous by fusion due to heat. **2.** *intr.* To become vitreous; to turn into glass or a glass-like substance 1626.

||**Vitrine** (vi·trĭn). 1886. [– Fr., f. *vitre* glass.] A glass show-case for specimens or for objects of art.

Vitriol (vi·triǫ̆l). late ME. [– (O)Fr. *vitriol* or med.L. *vitriolum* (XIII), f. L. *vitrum* glass.] **1.** One or other of various native or artificial sulphates of metals used in the arts or medicinally, esp. sulphate of iron. **b.** *Oil of v.*, concentrated sulphuric acid 1580. Also short for this. **2.** *fig.* (In allusion to the corrosive properties of v.) Virulence or acrimony of feeling or utterance 1769.

1. *Blue, green, red, white v.*, sulphate of copper, iron, cobalt, and zinc respectively. *Oil of v.*, concentrated sulphuric acid. *Spirit(s of v.*, a distilled essence of v.

†**Vi·triolate**, *a.* 1646. [– med.L. **vitriolatus*, f. *vitriolum*; see prec., -ATE².] **1.** Of, belonging to, or resembling that of vitriol –1672. **2.** Treated with vitriol –1782. **3.** Affected by or impregnated with vitriol –1751.

Vi·triolated, *ppl. a.* 1626. [f. as prec. + -ED¹.] **1.** Impregnated with vitriol. **b.** Of minerals, etc., affected by native sulphates 1794. **2.** Treated with vitriol, as *v. tartar*, sulphate of potassium 1694.

Vitriolic (vitriǫ·lik), *a.* and *sb.* 1670. [f. VITRIOL + -IC. Cf. Fr. *vitriolique* (XVI).] **A.** *adj.* **1.** Of or belonging to vitriol; having the nature or qualities of vitriol; impregnated with vitriol. **2.** *fig.* Of language, persons, etc.: Extremely caustic or scathing; bitterly malignant 1841.

1. *V. acid*, oil of vitriol. **2.** A..Parliamentary critic of the acrid and v. style 1879.

Vitriolize (vi·triŏləiz), *v.* 1694. [f. VITRIOL + -IZE.] **1. a.** *trans.* To convert into vitriol; to vitriolate. Also *absol.* **b.** *intr.* To become vitriolated or vitriolic 1757. **2.** *trans.* To injure with vitriol; to throw vitriol at (a person) with intent to injure 1886. Hence **Vitrioliza·tion**, the process of converting, or of being converted, into a vitriol. **Vi·triolizer**, one who throws vitriol with intent to injure.

Vitrite (vi·trəit). 1866. [f. L. *vitrum* glass + -ITE¹ 2 b.] *Min.* 'The matrix of Bohemian pyrope, related to pitchstone'.

Vi·tro-, comb. form (see -O-) of L. *vitrum* glass, as in **v.-de·ntine**, the hard external layer of dentine in a tooth.

Vi·trous, *a. rare.* 1657. [f. L. *vitrum* glass; see -OUS. Cf. (O)Fr. *vitreux*.] Vitreous.

Vitruvian (vitrū·viăn), *a.* 1762. [f. the name of M. *Vitruvius* Pollio, a Roman architect and writer (*c* 10 B.C.); see -AN.] Of, relating to, or in the style of Vitruvius. **b.** *V. scroll*, a convoluted scroll-pattern employed as an architectural ornament 1837.

†**Vi·try.** late ME. [– Fr. *Vitré*, name of a town in Brittany.] In full *V. canvas*, a kind of light durable canvas –1867.

||**Vitta** (vi·tă). *Pl.* **-æ** (-ī). 1819. [L. *vitta* band, fillet, chaplet.] **1.** *Zool.* A band or stripe of colour. **2.** *Bot.* One of the oil-tubes occurring in the pericarp of the fruit of most umbelliferous plants. Usu. in pl. 1830.

Vittate (vi·tet), *a.* 1826. [f. prec. + -ATE².] **1.** *Zool.*, *Bot.*, etc. Marked or striped with vittæ. **2.** *Bot.* Having a vitta or vittæ 1870. So **Vi·ttated** *a.* (*rare*) = sense 1. 1790.

Vituline (vi·tiŭləin), *a. rare.* 1656. [– L. *vitulinus*, f. *vitulus* calf; see -INE¹.] Of or belonging to a calf or calves; resembling that of a calf.

Vitu·perable, *a.* Now *rare* or *Obs.* 1450. [– L. *vituperabilis*, f. *vituperare*; see next, -ABLE. Cf. OFr. *vituperable*.] That deserves vituperation; censurable; reprehensible; disgraceful.

Vituperate (vəitiū·pĕreᶦt, vi-), *v.* 1542. [– *vituperat-*, pa. ppl. stem of L. *vituperare*, f. *vitu-*, for *viti-*, stem of *vitium* VICE *sb.*¹; see -ATE³.] *trans.* To blame, speak ill of, find fault with, in strong or violent language; to assail with abuse; to rate or revile. Also *absol.* or *intr.*

Vituperation (vəitiūpĕrēᶦ·ʃən, vi-). 1481. [– OFr. *vituperation* or L. *vituperatio*, *-ōn-* blaming, censuring, etc., f. as prec.; see -ION.] The action, fact, or process of vituperating; blame, censure, reproof, or (esp. in later use) the expression of this, in abusive or violent language; abuse, railing, rating. Also, vituperative or abusive language.

Few nations can surpass the Spaniards in the language of v. 1845.

Vituperative (vəitiū·pĕrĕtiv, vi-), *a.* 1727. [– late L. *vituperativus* (Priscian), f. as prec.; see -IVE.] **1.** Of words, language, etc.: Containing, conveying, or expressing strong depreciation; violently abusive or fault-finding; contumelious. Also, of or pertaining to vituperation. **2.** Characterized by vituperation or abuse 1754. **3.** Of persons: Given to vituperation 1819.

1. In utter despair at this v. epithet SCOTT. **3.** A Whig is a v. animal 1819. Hence **Vitu·peratively** *adv.*

Vituperator (vəitiū·pĕreᶦtəɹ, vi-). 1837. [f. VITUPERATE + -OR 2.] One who vituperates; an abuser.

Vitu·peratory, *a.* Now *rare* or *Obs.* 1586. [f. VITUPERATE + -ORY².] Expressive of blame or censure; vituperative, violently abusive.

||**Viva** (vī·vă), *sb.*¹ 1700. [It., 3rd pers. sing. pres. subj. of *vivere* (:– L. *vivere*) live.] A cry of *viva!* ('long live') as a salute or greeting; a shout of applause; a cheer or hurrah.

Viva (vəi·vă), *sb.*² *Univ. colloq.* 1891. [abbrev. of VIVA VOCE.] = VIVA VOCE *sb.* Hence **Vi·va** *v. trans.* to subject to a viva voce examination; *intr.* to examine viva voce.

||**Vivace** (vivā·tʃe), *adv.* (and *sb.*) 1683. [It., 'brisk, lively' :– L. *vivax*, *vivac-*; see next.] *Mus.* A direction indicating brisk or lively performance.

Vivacious (vəivēᶦ·ʃəs, vi-), *a.* 1645. [f. L. *vivax*, *vivac-* conscious or tenacious of life, lively, vigorous, f. *vivus* alive, *vivere* live; see -ACIOUS.] **1.** Full of, characterized by, or exhibiting vivacity or liveliness; animated, brisk, lively, sprightly. **2.** Continuing to live; remaining alive for a long time; long-lived. Now *rare* or *Obs.* 1655. **b.** Of plants; †*spec.* perennial 1676. **3.** Possessing or exhibiting tenacity of life; difficult to kill or destroy (*rare*) 1660.

1. V. nonsense 1788. V. pupils should from time to time be accustomed to an exact enumeration of particulars 1798. **2.** Hitherto the English Bishops had been v. almost to wonder FULLER. Hence **Viva·cious-ly** *adv.*, **-ness.**

Vivacity (vəivæ·sĭti, vi-). late ME. [– (O)Fr. *vivacité* – L. *vivacitas, -tat-* natural vigour, f. as prec.; see -ITY.] **1.** Intellectual or mental animation, acuteness, or vigour; quickness or liveliness of conception or perception. †**2.** Vital force or power; vitality –1747. **b.** *transf.* and *fig.* Active force, power, vigour 1649. **3.** Longevity. Now *rare.* 1616. †**b.** Tenacity of life –1664. **4.** Vigorous or energetic action; activity, energy, vigour; spirit. Now *rare.* 1652. **5.** The quality, condition, or fact of being vivacious; animation or liveliness of demeanour or disposition; briskness, sprightliness 1647. **b.** A vivacious or lively act, expression, scene, etc. Usu. in *pl.* 1692. **6.** Brightness, brilliancy (of light or colour) 1734.

1. He hath this viuacite or quycknes of wytte. 1526. His conceptions were..full of fire and v. 1704. **2. b.** The v. of an excellent example JER. TAYLOR. **3.** The v. of some of these Pensioners is little lesse than a Miracle, they survived so long FULLER. **5.** As V. is the Gift of Women, Gravity is that of Men ADDISON.

‖**Vivandier** (vivandye). 1591. [Fr., = sutler.] In the French or other continental armies: A person who supplies victuals to troops in the field; a sutler. So **Vivandière** *fem.*

Vivarium (vəivēə·riŏm, vi-). *Pl.* **vivaria,** also **-iums.** 1600. [– L. *vivarium* warren, fishpond, subst. use of *vivarius*, f. *vivus* alive living, f. *vivere* live; see -ARIUM.] **1.** A place where living animals, esp. fish, are maintained or preserved for food; a fish-pond or fish-pool. **2.** A place specially adapted or prepared for the keeping of living animals under their normal conditions, either as objects of interest or for the purpose of scientific study; freq. in later use, an aquarium 1684. **b.** A glass bowl, case, etc., in which fish or other aquatic animals are kept, esp. for study 1855.

Vivary (vəi·vări). 1601. [– L. *vivarium* VIVARIUM; see -ARY[1].] **1.** = prec. 2. Now *rare* or *Obs.* **2.** = prec. 1. 1628.

1. That cage and vivarie Of fowles, and beasts DONNE. **2.** In stagnant vivaries they lie Forgetful of their ancient haunts 1858.

Vivat (vəi·væt), *int.* and *sb.* 1663. [– L., 3rd pers. sing. pres. subj. of *vivere* live. So Fr. *vivat.*] **A.** *int.* A word of acclamation wishing a person (long) life and prosperity, or expressing applause or approval. **B.** *sb.* An utterance of this word by way of acclamation or applause 1821.

‖**Viva voce** (vəi·vă vōᵘ·si), *adv. phr.*, *a.* and *sb.* 1581. [med.L., lit. 'by or with the living voice'.] **A.** *adv.* By word of mouth; in speech; orally.

The Apostles taught *viua voce*, by liuely voyce 1581.

B. *adj.* Conveyed or expressed in speech instead of writing; spoken; oral 1718. **b.** Of an examination, etc.: Conducted by speech 1815. **C.** *sb.* A viva voce examination; freq. abbrev. VIVA *sb.*[2] 1842. Hence **Viva-voce** *v. trans.* to examine orally.

Vi·vda. *Orkn.* and *Shetl. dial.* Also **vifda.** 1688. [perh. – ON. *vǫðva* muscular flesh.] Meat smoked, or dried in the air, without being salted.

Vive, *a.* Now only *Sc.* or *arch.* 1477. [– (O)Fr. *vive*, fem. of *vif* :– L. *viva, vivus* living, alive, or directly from the L. word.] **1.** Lively, forcible, or brisk (*rare*). **2.** Of images, pictures, etc.: Life-like 1585. **3.** Of colours: Bright, vivid 1591. Hence **Vi·vely** *adv.* (now *Sc.* or *Obs.*).

Vivency (vəi·vĕnsi). *rare.* 1646. [f. L. *vivere* live + -ENCY.] Manifestation of the principle of life; vitality.

‖**Viverra** (vive·ră, vəi-). 1706. [L., ferret.] *Zool.* †**a.** The ferret. **b.** The civet-cat (*V. civetta*), or other species of the type-genus of the civet family (*Viverridæ*).

Viverrine (vive·rəin, vəi-), *a.* and *sb.* 1800. [– mod.L. *viverrinus*, f. VIVERRA; see -INE[1].] **A.** *adj.* Resembling or related to the civet, or the civet family; *spec.* belonging to the sub-family *Viverrinæ.* **B.** *sb.* An individual of the sub-family *Viverrinæ* 1880.

Vivers (vəi·vəɹz), *sb. pl.* orig. and chiefly *Sc.* 1536. [– (O)Fr. *vivres*, subst. use of *vivre* live.] Food, provisions, victuals, eatables.

Vives (vəivz), *sb. pl.* 1523. [Aphetic f. AVIVES.] Hard swellings of the submaxillary glands of a horse.

Vivi- (vi·vi), comb. form of L. *vivus* alive, living, as in **vivise·pulture,** burying alive.

Vivianite (vi·viănəit). 1823. [f. name of J. G. *Vivian* the discoverer; see -ITE[1] 2 b.] *Min.* A phosphate of iron usu. occurring in crystals of blue and green colour.

Vivid (vi·vid), *a.* 1638. [– L. *vividus*, f. *vivere* be living, *vivus* alive, lively; see -ID[1].] **1.** Full of life; vigorous, active, or energetic on this account; lively or brisk. **2.** Of actions or operations: Proceeding or taking place with great vigour or activity 1702. **b.** Of utterances: Strongly or warmly expressed 1806. **c.** Of intellectual faculties: Capable of ready and clear creation of ideas or concepts 1814. **d.** Of description, etc.: Presenting subjects or ideas in a clear and striking manner 1837. **3.** Of colour, light, etc.: Brilliant, fresh, lively, bright 1665. **b.** Of things in respect of colour or brightness 1686. **4.** Clearly or distinctly perceived or perceptible 1690. **b.** Intensely or strongly felt 1704. **5.** Quasi-*adv.* Vividly, brightly 1819.

1. They have a sprightly v. countenance 1769. This v. and volatile instrument [*sc.* the violin] 1818. Her face expressed v. interest 1860. **2.** The combustion that ensues is exceedingly v. and beautiful 1815. **c.** Edward's power of imagination ..was v. SCOTT. **d.** A most v. history of the time FREEMAN. **3.** A deep v. blue 1815. **b.** Like a v. circular rainbow quite round the sun TYNDALL. **4.** A..v. impression of the growth of Russian influence 1869. Hence **Vi·vid-ly** *adv.*, **-ness.**

Vividity (vivi·dĭti). 1616. [f. prec. + -ITY.] †**1.** Living force, vitality. **2.** The quality or state of being vivid; vividness 1772.

Vivific (vivi·fik), *a.* 1551. [– L. *vivificus*, f. *vivus* living; see -FIC.] Life-giving, enlivening, vivifying. So †**Vivi·fical** *a.*

Vivificate (vivi·fikeᶦt), *v.* late ME. [– *vivificat-*, pa. ppl. stem of late (eccl.) L. *vivificare* make alive, etc., f. *vivus* alive; see -ATE[3].] *trans.* = VIVIFY *v.* 1.

Vivification (vi:vifikēᶦ·ʃən). 1548. [– late (eccl.) L. *vivificatio, -ōn-*, f. as prec.; see -ION.] **1.** The process or fact of being vivified in a spiritual sense. **2.** The action or fact of enduing with life; the fact of being vivified physically 1626. †**3.** Restoration of a metal to its original state –1728. **4.** The action or fact of investing with an air of vitality or reality 1858.

4. An industrious scholar..but we do not know that he has the gift of v. 1890.

Vivify (vi·vifəi), *v.* 1545. [– (O)Fr. *vivifier* – late L. *vivificare* VIVIFICATE; see -FY.] **1.** *trans.* To give life to; to endue with life; to animate; to quicken. **2.** To make brighter, more brilliant, or more striking 1791. **3.** *absol.* To impart life or animation 1626. **4.** *intr.* To acquire life; to become alive 1737.

1. An indraught—slight no doubt, but..sufficient to contaminate or vivify the infusion TYNDALL. *fig.* That Promethean fire, which.. vivifies the marble SIR J. REYNOLDS. **3.** It [a fire] talks to us;..it is vivified at our touch; it vivifies in return L. HUNT. Hence **Vi·vifier,** one who or that which gives life.

Viviparity (vivipæ·rĭti). 1864. [f. next + -ITY; cf. contemp. *oviparous, oviparity.*] *Zool.* and *Bot.* The condition or character of being viviparous.

Viviparous (vivi·părəs, vəi-), *a.* 1646. [f. L. *viviparus* + -OUS; see VIVI-, -PAROUS.] **1.** Involving the production of young in a living state. **2.** Of animals: Bringing forth young in a live state. (Usu. in contrast with *oviparous.*) 1651. **3.** *Bot.* Reproducing from seeds or bulbs which germinate while still attached to the parent plant 1777. **b.** Characterized by this mode of reproduction 1802. Hence **Vivi·parous-ly** *adv.*, **-ness.**

Vivisect (vi·visekt), *v.* 1864. [Back-formation from next.] **1.** *trans.* To dissect (an animal) while living; to perform vivisection upon. **2.** *intr.* To practise vivisection 1883.

Vivisection (vivise·kʃən). 1707. [f. VIVI- + SECTION, after *dissection.*] The action of cutting or dissecting some part of a living organism; *spec.* the action or practice of performing surgical experiment upon living animals as a method of physiological or pathological study. **b.** An operation of this nature 1859.

Vivisectional (vivise·kʃənăl), *a.* 1866. [f. prec. + -AL[1] 1.] **1.** Of, belonging to, or of the nature of vivisection. **2.** Performing vivisection 1882.

Vivisectionist (vivise·kʃənist). 1879. [f. as prec. + -IST.] One who practises or defends vivisection.

Vivisector (vi·visektəɹ). 1863. [f. VIVISECT + -OR 2.] One who vivisects or practices vivisection.

†‖**Vivres** (vī·vəɹz). 1650. [Fr.; see VIVERS.] Victuals, provisions –1852.

Vixen (vi·ks'n), *sb.* and *a.* [In XV *fixen(e of the foxe*; not recorded in OE., which had *fyxe* and adj. *fyxen*, but there is a parallel sb. in late OHG. *fuhsin*, MHG. *vühsinne* (G. *füchsin*); see FOX, -EN[2]. For initial *v*, not recorded before late XVI, cf. VAN *sb.*[1], VANE; the *f*-form continued till early XVIII.] **1.** The female of the fox; a she-fox. **2.** An ill-tempered quarrelsome woman; a shrew, a termagant 1575. †**b.** Applied to a child or a man (*rare*) –1738. **3.** *attrib.* **a.** Appositive with *fox*, = sense 1. late ME. **b.** = VIXENISH *a.* 1660.

2. She's a pestilent v. when she's angry, and as proud as Lucifer 1644. **3. b.** What a Vixon trick is this? CONGREVE. The old v. queen 1842.

Vixenish (vi·ks'niʃ), *a.* 1828. [f. prec. + -ISH[1].] **1.** Resembling a vixen in temper; cross, ill-tempered, snappish. **2.** Characteristic of or appropriate to a vixen 1838. Hence **Vixenish-ly** *adv.*, **-ness.**

Vixenly (vi·ks'nli), *a.* and *adv.* 1677. [f. as prec. + -LY.] **A.** *adj.* Like a vixen in disposition. **B.** *adv.* Crossly, ill-naturedly.

‖**Viz.,** *adv.* and *sb.* 1540. [abbrev. of VIDELICET; the abbrev. repr. the ordinary med.L. symbol of contraction for *-et.*] **A.** *adv.* = VIDELICET *adv.* **B.** *sb.* = VIDELICET *sb.* Also, a special clause in a deed introduced by *viz.* 1750.

†**Vizament,** alteration of ADVISEMENT or *visement* (1414–1568). SHAKS.

Vizard (vi·zăɹd), *sb.* Now *arch.* 1558. [Altered form of *vysar, viser, vizar* VISOR, by confusion of ending; see -ARD; for a similar substitution cf. MAZARD *sb.*[1]] **1.** = VISOR *sb.* 2, 3. †**2.** In depreciatory use: A face suggestive of a mask –1625. †**3.** A person wearing a visor or mask; *spec.* a woman of loose character wearing a mask in public, a prostitute –1719.

1. Men are glad to pull of their Vizards, and resume themselves again SIR T. BROWNE. Hypocrisy and Superstition wear the V. of Piety WATTS.

Vi·zard, *v.* Now *rare.* 1609. [f. prec.] †**1.** *trans.* To conceal or disguise (something) under a false outward show or appearance; to represent falsely or speciously –1660. **2.** To cover or disguise (the face, etc.) with or as with a vizard; to mask 1609. Hence **Vi·zarded** *ppl. a.* disguised with or wearing a vizard; *fig.* assumed, pretended 1593.

Vizard-mask. *arch.* 1667. [f. as prec.] **1.** A mask worn to conceal the face; a domino. **2.** A woman who wears such a mask; a prostitute 1670.

Vizier (viziᵊ·ɹ, vi·zyəɹ, vi·ziəɹ). 1562. [Early forms *vezir, vizir* – Fr. *visir, vizir* or Sp. *visir* – Turk. *vezir* – Arab. *wazīr* senior minister of a caliph.] **1.** In the Turkish empire, Persia, or other Moslem country: A high state official or minister, freq. one invested with vice-regal authority; a governor or viceroy of a province; now esp. the chief minister of a sovereign. **2.** *Grand v.*, the chief minister or administrator of a Moslem ruler, esp. of the Sultan of Turkey 1597.

1. All Pashas, before whom are carried the three horse-tails, have the title of Visier 1819.

Vizierate (viziᵊ·rĕt). 1687. [– Arab. *wizāra* office of *wazīr*, with assim. to prec. and -ATE[1].] **1.** The dignity, position, or authority of a vizier or grand vizier; also, the period of office of a vizier. **2.** A province or district governed by a Turkish vizier 1876.

Vizierial (viziᵊ·riăl), *a.* 1849. [f. VIZIER + -IAL.] **1.** Of a letter or rescript: Issued by or under the authority of a vizier or grand vizier. **2.** Of or pertaining to a vizier 1876.

Viziership (viziᵊ·ɹʃip). 1655. [f. VIZIER + -SHIP.] The office or function of a vizier; rule or government as a grand vizier.

Vlach (vlæk). 1841. [– Bulg., Serb. *Vlach* = OSl. *Vlachŭ* Rumanian, Italian, Czech *Vlach* Italian, Russ. *Volókh*, etc. – Gmc. (OHG.) *Walh* (cf. OE. *wealh*) foreigner. Cf. WALACHIAN.] A member of the Latin-speaking race occupying parts of south-eastern Europe; a Walachian or Roumanian. Hence **Vlachian** (vlē^{i}·kiăn) *a.*

‖**Vlei** (vləi). 1849. [Du. dial., reduced f. Du. *vallei* valley.] **1.** In South Africa: A shallow pool of water; a piece of low-lying ground covered with water during the rainy season. **2.** *local U.S.* A swamp 1880.

Vocable (vō^{u}·kăb'l), *sb.* 1530. [– Fr. *vocable* or L. *vocabulum*, f. *vocare* call; see -BLE.] **1.** A word or term (app. reintroduced in the 18th c.) †**2.** A name or designation (*rare*) –1623.

Vo·cable, *a.* [f. L. *vocare* + -ABLE.] Capable of utterance. MEREDITH. Hence **Vo·cably** *adv.*

Vocabular (vŏkæ·biŭlăɹ), *a.* 1608. [f. L. *vocabulum* VOCABLE *sb.* + -AR[1].] Of, pertaining to, or concerning words.

Vocabulary (vŏkæ·biŭlări). 1532. [– med.L. *vocabularius*, *-um*, f. L. *vocabulum* VOCABLE *sb.*; see -ARY[1].] **1.** A collection or list of words with brief explanations of their meanings; now *esp.* one given in an elementary grammar or reading-book of a foreign language. **2.** The range of language of a particular person, class, profession, or the like 1753. **3.** The sum or aggregate of words composing a language 1782.

1. This is the proper signification of the word,.. Greeke vocabularies thus expound it SIR T. BROWNE. 2. An Innocent, in Shakesperian v., signifies an Idiot 1851. The rank v. of malice and hate 1872.

Vocal (vō^{u}·kăl), *a.* and *sb.* late ME. [– L. *vocalis*, f. *vox*, *voc-* voice; see -AL[1] 1.] **A.** *adj.* **I. 1.** Uttered or communicated by the voice; spoken, oral. **b.** Of sound: Produced by the voice; *spec.* of the nature of words or speech 1623. **2.** Of music: Performed by or composed for the voice. (Opp. to *instrumental.*) 1586. **b.** Connected with singing 1799. **3. a.** Having the character of a vowel; vocalic 1589. †**b.** Actually sounded. JOHNSON. **c.** *Phonetics.* Uttered with voice (as dist. from *breath*); voiced, sonant 1668.

1. They were not vocall but mentall Prayers 1641. The human pair..joyned thir v. Worship to the Quire Of Creatures wanting voice MILT. **b.** V. sound is the Matter of speech 1864.

II. 1. Endowed with a voice, possessed of utterance; exercising the power of speech or of uttering sounds 1601. **2.** *fig.* Conveying impressions or ideas as if by speech; expressive, eloquent 1608. **3.** Operative or concerned in the production of voice. Freq. in *v. chords*, *organs*, etc. 1644. **4.** Of or belonging to the voice (†or sound) 1644. **b.** Of the nature of voice or sound 1826. **5.** Full of voice or sound; sounding, resounding 1667. **6.** Readily or freely expressing oneself in speech; giving vent to one's views or opinions 1871.

1. These insects are generally v. in the midst of summer GOLDSM. *transf.* The v. statue of the supposed Memnon is of Amunoph III. 1837. 4. His vocall impediment 1654. 5. Hill, or Valley, Fountain, or fresh shade Made v. by my song MILT. 6. The most v. class in the whole community 1887.

B. *sb.* †**1.** A vowel –1586. **2.** A member of a Roman Catholic body who has a right to vote in certain elections 1660.

Vocalic (vokæ·lik), *a.* 1814. [f. VOCAL *a.* + -IC.] **1.** Rich in vowels; composed mainly or entirely of vowels. **b.** Characterized by a vowel or vowels 1874. **2.** Consisting of a vowel or vowels; of the nature of a vowel 1852. **3.** Of, pertaining to, affecting, or concerning a vowel or vowels 1861.

1. The Gaelic language being uncommonly v. SCOTT. **b.** The varying v. forms of the Imperfect 1874. 2. The series of v. and consonantal sounds 1852.

Vocalion (vokē^{i}·liən). 1882. [f. VOCAL *a.*, after *accordion*, *orchestrion*.] A musical instrument of the nature of a harmonium with broad reeds, producing sounds somewhat resembling the human voice.

Vocalism (vō^{u}·kăliz'm). 1864. [f. VOCAL *a.* + -ISM.] **1.** The exercise of the voice or vocal organs in speech. **b.** The art of exercising the voice in singing 1884. **2.** A vocal sound or articulation 1873. **b.** A system of vowels; the use of vowels, vocalic conditions 1873.

Vocalist (vō^{u}·kălist). 1613. [f. as prec. + -IST.] †**1.** A speaker. **2.** A vocal musician; a singer 1834.

Vocality (vokæ·lĭti). 1597. [– med.L. *vocalitas* utterance (c1430); see VOCAL *a.*, -ITY.] **1.** The quality of having voice or utterance; the possession or exercise of vocal powers. **2.** The quality or fact of being uttered or utterable; vocal quality or nature 1623. **b.** *pl.* Vocal properties or sounds, *spec.* as displayed in singing 1667. **3.** *Phonetics.* The quality of being (*a*) voiced or (*b*) vocalic 1669.

Vocalization (vō^{u}:kăləizē^{i}·ʃən). 1842. [f. next + -ATION.] **1.** The action of vocalizing or the fact of being vocalized; utterance with the voice. **b.** Mode of pronunciation, esp. of vowel sounds 1855. **2.** *Mus.* The action or art of producing musical sounds with the voice; exercise of the voice in singing 1852. **b.** *spec.* The action of singing upon a vowel to one or more notes 1889. **3.** The insertion of vowel-signs in forms of writing consisting mainly or entirely of consonants 1845. **4.** *Phonetics.* Conversion into a voiced sound 1874.

3. The question of v...is one of the highest importance in Biblical criticism 1848.

Vocalize (vō^{u}·kăləiz), *v.* 1669. [f. VOCAL *a.* + -IZE.] **1.** *trans.* To form into voice; to utter or articulate. **b.** To sing 1798. **2.** *Phonetics.* **a.** To convert into a vowel 1844. **b.** To utter with voice (as dist. from *breath*); to render sonant 1836. **3.** To endow with voice; to render vocal or articulate 1858. **4.** To furnish with vowels or vowel-signs 1845. **5.** *intr.* To perform vocal music; to sing 1830. **b.** *spec.* To sing upon a vowel to one or more notes 1873.

1. A faithful copy of the native pronunciation which readers in all countries will v. alike 1867. Hence **Vo·calizer.**

Vocally (vō^{u}·kăli), *adv.* 1483. [f. VOCAL *a.* + -LY[2].] **1.** In a vocal manner; in spoken words. **2.** By means of singing; in vocal music 1716. **3.** In respect of vowels 1873.

1. I 'never told my love' v. EMILY BRONTË.

Vocation (vŏkē^{i}·ʃən). late ME. [– (O)Fr. *vocation* or L. *vocatio*, *-ōn-*, f. *vocat-*, pa. ppl. stem of *vocare* call; see -ION.] **1.** The action of God in calling a person to exercise some special (esp. spiritual) function, or to fill a certain position; divine influence or guidance towards a definite (esp. religious) career; the fact of being so called or directed towards a special work in life; natural tendency to or fitness for such work. **b.** The action of God (or Christ) in calling persons or mankind to a state of salvation or union with Himself; the fact or condition of being so called 1502. **2.** The particular function or station to which a person is called by God 1487. **b.** One's ordinary occupation, business, or profession 1553. †**c.** *collect.* Those who follow a particular business or profession –1651. **3.** The action on the part of an ecclesiastical body of calling a person to the ministry or to a particular office or charge in the Church 1578.

1. None are to enter the Ecclesiastick or Monastick State, without a particular Vocation 1728. 2. Heaven is his v., and therefore he counts earthly employments avocations FULLER. **c.** Euerie function and seuerall v. striueth with other 1587. 3. A v. to pastoral duty in the manufacturing districts 1860. Hence **Voca·tional** *a.*, **-ly** *adv.*

Vocative (vǫ·kătiv), *a.* and *sb.* 1440. [– (O)Fr. *vocatif* or L. *vocativus*, f. as prec.; see -IVE.] **A.** *adj.* **1.** *V. case*: That case of nouns, adjectives, or pronouns, which in inflected languages is used to express address or invocation. **2.** Characteristic of or pertaining to calling or addressing 1644. **B.** *sb.* **1.** The vocative case 1522. †**2.** An invocation or appeal. RICHARDSON.

Vociferance (vosi·fĕrăns). 1838. [f. next; see -ANCE.] **a.** Clamour or noise of shouting. **b.** Vociferant quality.

Vociferant (vosi·fĕrănt), *a.* 1609. [– L. *vociferans*, *-ant-*, pr. pple. of *vociferari*; see next, -ANT.] Clamouring, bawling, vociferating.

Vociferate (vosi·fĕrē^{i}t), *v.* 1623. [– *vociferat-*, pa. ppl. stem of L. *vociferari*, f. *vox*, *voc-* voice + *fer-*, stem of *ferre* carry; see -ATE[3].] **1.** *intr.* To cry out loudly; to bawl, shout. **2.** *trans.* To utter in a loud voice; to shout out clamorously; to declaim or assert with loud vehemence 1748.

1. So they vociferating to the Greeks, Stirr'd them to battle COWPER. 2. He entered, vociferating oaths dreadful to hear EMILY BRONTË. Hence **Voci·ferator,** one who or that which vociferates.

Vociferation (vosifĕrē^{i}·ʃən). late ME. [– OFr. *vociferation* (mod. *-tions* pl.) or L. *vociferatio*, *-ōn-*, f. as prec.; see -ION.] The action or an act of vociferating, shouting, or speaking loud.

Vociferous (vosi·fĕrəs), *a.* 1611. [f. L. *vociferari* VOCIFERATE + -OUS.] **1.** Uttering loud cries or shouts; clamorous, bawling, noisy. **2.** Of the nature of vociferation; uttered with or accompanied by clamour; characterized by loud declamation 1631.

1. The whole audience..became v. 1875. 2. V. ill-nature CIBBER. Hence **Voci·ferous-ly** *adv.*, **-ness.**

Vocular (vǫ·kiŭlăɹ), *a.* *rare.* 1813. [f. L. *vocula* VOCULE + -AR[1].] **1.** Vowel, vocalic. **2.** Vocal. DICKENS.

Vocule (vǫ·kiŭl). 1833. [– L. *vocula* soft note or tone, dim. of *vox*, *voc-* voice; see -ULE.] The faint final sound produced in pronouncing certain consonants.

‖**Vodka** (vǫ·dkă). Also **vodki, -ky, votky.** 1802. [Russ., pronounced (vo·tka), f. *vodá* water.] An ardent spirit peculiar to Russia, chiefly distilled from rye.

Voe (vō^{u}). *Orkn.* and *Shetl. dial.* 1688. [Norw. *vaag*, ON., Icel. *vágr* = OE. *wǣġ* wave.] A bay, creek, or inlet.

‖**Vogt** (vōɣt, fōɣt). 1694. [G. *vogt* – med.L. use of L. *vocatus*, pa. ppl. of *vocare* call.] A steward, bailiff, or similar official.

Vogue (vō^{u}g). 1571. [– Fr. *vogue* – It. *voga* rowing, fashion, f. *vogare* row, be going well.] †**1.** *The v.*, the principal or foremost place in popular repute or estimation; the greatest currency or prevalence –1788. **2.** Without article: Popularity; general acceptance or currency; success in popular esteem 1604. **3.** With *a*, *the*, etc.: A prominent place in popular favour or fashion; a course or period of success or distinction in this connection 1645. †**4.** General course or tendency; general character or condition –1729. †**5.** The current opinion or belief; the general report or rumour –1730. **6.** The prevailing fashion or tendency 1648.

1. A theory of electricity, which then had the general v. FRANKLIN. 2. Mr.—..seems to have a good deal of v. as a sculptor HAWTHORNE. Phr. *In* (or *out of*) *v.*, *in full v.*, etc. 3. Authority..may give a temporary v. to a bad poet 1752. 4. They go with the v. and stream of times 1660. 6. An age when burlesque is the v. 1860.

Voice (vois), *sb.* ME. [– AFr. *voiz*, *voice*, OFr. *vois*, *voiz*, (also mod.) *voix* :– L. *vox*, *voc-* voice, sound.] **I. 1.** Sound, or the whole body of sounds, made or produced by the vocal organs of man or animals in their natural action; esp. sound formed in or emitted from the human larynx in speaking, singing, or other utterance; vocal sound as the vehicle of human utterance or expression. Also occas., the faculty or power of producing this; or concretely, the organs by which it is produced. **b.** Utterance or expression (of feeling, etc.) 1855. **c.** *Phonology.* Sound uttered with vibration or resonance of the vocal chords, as dist. from BREATH 10. 1842. **2.** The right of speaking or voting in a legislative assembly, etc.; part or share in the control, government, or deciding of something. late ME. **3.** The expressed opinion, judgement, will, or wish *of* the people, a number of persons, a corporate body, etc.; occas. as indicated by the exercise of the suffrage. late ME. †**4.** That which is generally or commonly said; common talk; rumour or report –1652. †**b.** A report or rumour –1652. **5.** *Gram.* The form of a verb by which the relation of the subject to the action implied is indicated; one or other of the modes of inflecting or varying a verb according to the distinctions of *active*, *passive*, or *middle*. late ME.

1. A..iustice, which speaketh in action though not in voyce 1608. They that haue the voyce of Lyons and the act of Hares: are they not Monsters? SHAKS. Phr. *In* (..) *v.*, (of persons) having the v., or vocal organs in fit condition for speaking or singing; so *out of v.* **b.** Phr. *To give v. to, to find v. in.* **2.** If we had more v. in the management of affairs 1873. **3.** The whole v. of the commons was to yelde, yeld, rather than starue HALL. The common voyce do cry it shall be so SHAKS.

II. 1. In limited sense: The sounds naturally made by a single person or animal in speech or other form of vocal utterance; these sounds regarded as characteristic of the person and as distinguishing him from another or others; also freq., the individual organic means or capacity of producing such sounds ME. **b.** Used in ref. to the expression of opinion or protest, or the issuing of a command 1667. **2. a.** The sound *of* prayer, etc. ME. **b.** *transf.* A sound or sounds produced or emitted by something inanimate, as a stream, thunder, the wind, etc., or musical instruments ME. †**3.** An articulate sound; a vocable, term, or word –1697. **4.** An expression of opinion, choice, or preference uttered or given by a person; a single vote. late ME. †**b.** Support or approval in a suit or petition. SHAKS. **c.** A right or power to take part in the control or management of something. Chiefly in the phr. *to have a v. in.* 1835. **5.** *Mus.* The vocal capacity of one person in respect of its employment for musical purposes, esp. in combination with others; a person considered as the possessor of a voice so employed; a singer. Chiefly in pl. 1607. **b.** A vocal part in music 1666. **6.** The agency or means by which something specified is expressed, represented, or revealed 1600.

1. Return Alpheus, the dread v. is past, That shrunk thy streams MILT. A talent for music and a good v. H. WALPOLE. Within such distance as a v. may reach COWPER. Phr. *The v. of God*, freq. = 'the expressed will or desire of God, etc.; the divine command, ordinance, or word'. *To lose the v.*, to be (temporarily) deprived of the power of using the voice for singing or speaking. **b.** A convention..ratified the constitution without a dissenting v. 1796. Phr. *With one v.*, unanimously. †*In my v.*, in my name SHAKS. **2. a.** Thou heardest the v. of my supplications when I cryed vnto thee *Ps.* 31:22. **b.** Fro the voises of manye watris WYCLIF *Ps.* 92[3]:3. Two Voices are there; one is of the sea, One of the mountains; each a mighty V. WORDSW. *fig.* The v. of tradition 1839. **4. b.** *Merry W.* I. iv. 167. **c.** A v. in the management of the workhouse 1888. **5.** [He] hath sent for voices and painters and other persons from Italy PEPYS. **6.** Poetry is the v. of imagination 1854. Lord Cranborne, the present v. of the Foreign Office in the House of Commons 1903.

Comb., as *v.-production, -trainer, -training*; **v.-box,** the larynx; **-figure,** a figure or graphic representation of a vocal sound; **-part,** *Mus.* a part or melody written for the v., a vocal part; **-pipe, -tube,** a tube or pipe for conveying the v., a speaking-tube, esp. as used on ships.

Voice (vois), *v.* 1453. [f. prec.] **I.** *trans.* †**1.** *pass.*: To be commonly said or stated; to be spoken of generally or publicly; to be reported, rumoured, or bruited *abroad* –1822. †**2.** To speak of, state, report, proclaim, etc. –1672. †**3.** To speak much or highly of; to cry *up* (a person or thing). Usu. *pass.* –1673. †**4.** To elect (a person) by voice or vote; to nominate or appoint to an office –1670. **5.** To speak or utter (a word, etc.) 1638. **6.** To give voice, utterance, or expression to (an emotion, opinion, etc.); to proclaim openly or publicly 1607. **b.** To act as the mouthpiece or spokesman of, to express the opinions of (a body of persons) 1893. **7.** *poet.* or *rhet.* To endow with voice, or the faculty of speech or song 1711. **b.** *Organ-building.* To give the correct quality of tone to (an organ or organ-pipe) 1708. **8.** *Phonology.* To utter (a sound) with vibration of the vocal chords 1877.

1. Your father was voiced generally as..one of the bravest men of Scotland SCOTT. **5.** Words.. voyced like the Irish 1638. **6.** Rather assume thie right in silence..then voyce it with claimes and Challenges BACON. **b.** To v. the Opposition 1893. **7.** The God of Harmony voic'd all their Throats KEN.

†**II.** *intr.* **1.** To use the voice; to cry out, exclaim. Also *to v. it.* –1682. **2.** To vote –1642. Hence **Voi·cer,** esp. in sense I. 7 b.

Voiced (voist), *ppl. a.* 1600. [f. VOICE *sb.* and *v.* + -ED.] **1.** Endowed with or possessing a voice. **b.** Having a voice of a specified kind, quality, or tone 1637. †**2.** Much spoken of; famed –1661. **3.** *Phonetics.* Uttered with voice (or vibration of the vocal chords) as opp. to *breath*; sonant. Said esp. of certain consonants, in opposition to VOICELESS *a.* 5. 1867.

Voiceful (voi·sfŭl), *a.* Chiefly *rhet.* or *poet.* 1611. [f. VOICE *sb.* + -FUL.] **1.** Endowed with or as with a voice; having voice or power of utterance; vocal. **b.** Vocal *with* or expressive *of* something 1856. **2.** Of or pertaining to the voice; uttered by the voice or voices 1821.

1. That blind Bard, who..Beheld the Iliad and the Odyssee Rise to the swelling of the v. sea COLERIDGE. **b.** The mountains were thus v. with perpetual rebuke RUSKIN. Hence **Voi·cefulness.**

Voi·celess, *a.* 1535. [f. VOICE + -LESS.] **1.** Having no voice; uttering no words or speech; dumb, mute. †**b.** Having no voice in the management of affairs –1634. **c.** Silent, mute 1863. **2.** Characterized by the absence of sound; silent, still 1815. **3.** Unspoken, unuttered 1816. **4.** Characterized by or causing loss of speech or vocal utterance; speechless 1818. **5.** *Phonetics.* Produced or uttered without voice or vocalic tone; surd. Said esp. of certain consonants in opposition to VOICED *ppl. a.* 3. 1867.

1. Mute As creatures v. thro' the fault of birth TENNYSON. **c.** The v., helpless masses of the population 1884. **2.** A silent and v. desert 1868. **3.** The spirit's v. prayer LONGF. **4.** The Niobe of nations! there she stands, Childless and crownless, in her v. woe BYRON. Hence **Voi·celess-ly** *adv.*, **-ness.**

Void (void), *a.* and *sb.* ME. [– OFr. *voide*, dial. var. of *vuide* (mod. *vide*) fem., superseding *vuit* masc. :– Rom. **vocitus*, pa. ppl. formation on **voc-*, repr. also in L. *vocivus*, with parallel *vac-* of *vacare* (see VACANT).] **A.** *adj.* **I. 1.** Of a see, benefice, etc.: Unoccupied, vacant. Also of secular offices. **2.** Of a seat, saddle, etc.: Having no occupant; empty ME. **b.** Of a house or room: Unoccupied; untenanted. Now chiefly *dial.* 1479. **3.** Of places: Not occupied or frequented by living creatures; deserted, empty ME. **b.** Not occupied by buildings or other useful structures; vacant 1442. **4.** Not occupied by visible contents; empty, unfilled. late ME. †**b.** Of paper: Blank –1748. **5.** †**a.** Of persons, etc.: Worthless –1728. **b.** Ineffective, useless, leading to no result. late ME. **6.** Having no legal force; legally null, invalid, or ineffectual. late ME. **b.** *gen.* Null, invalid 1526. **7.** Of time: Unemployed, idle, leisure. Now *rare.* 1450. †**b.** Vacant in respect of office –1614.

1. Winchester lay v. six, and Sherburn seven years FULLER. **2.** I..sate down on the first v. Seat 1713. **3.** As for Ierusalem, it laye voyde, and was as it had bene a wyldernesse COVERDALE 1 *Macc.* 3:45. **4.** The Spaces between..left v. to admit the Light 1697. **6. a.** They that do persecute, be voyde, and without all truth FOXE. **b.** The end ought to be, from both philosophies to separate..whatsoever is empty and v., and to preserve..whatsoever is solid and fruitful BACON. **6.** The Force us'd on me made that Contract v. DRYDEN. *Null and v.*: see NULL *a.* 1. **b.** This makes v. that common conceit and tradition of the Fish called *Faber marinus* SIR T. BROWNE.

II. Const. *of* (occas. †*from*). **1.** Devoid of, free from, or not tainted with (some bad quality, fault, or defect); not affected or impaired by (something unpleasant or hurtful). late ME. **2.** Destitute of (some virtue or good quality); lacking or wanting (something desirable or natural). late ME.

1. The lambish peple, voyd of alle vyce CHAUCER. V. of Care and Strife, To lead a soft, secure, inglorious Life DRYDEN. **2.** Bad Fruit of Knowledge,..Which leaves us naked thus, of Honour v. MILT. It would not at first view be altogether v. of probability BERKELEY.

B. *sb.* **1.** A state or condition devoid *of* something; a lack or want (*rare*) 1786. **2.** Emptiness, vacancy, vacuity, vacuum 1618. **3. a.** *Arch.* A space left in a wall for a window or door; the opening of an arch; any unfilled space in a building or structure 1616. **b.** An empty or vacant space, an unoccupied place or opening; a vacancy caused by the removal of something 1697. **c.** *spec.* An absolutely empty space; a vacuum 1727. **d.** One of the small unoccupied spaces in a heap or mass which is not perfectly solid 1837. **4.** *spec.* With *the*: The empty expanse of space 1667. **b.** Const. *of* (heaven, etc.) 1667. **5.** *fig.* **a.** An unsatisfied feeling or desire 1779. **b.** A blank in a record 1866. **6.** A period during which a house or farm is unoccupied or unlet 1885.

1. Men in whom pride..supplies the v. of sense WESLEY. **3. b.** Phr. *To fill the v.* **4.** He sung.. How Seas, and Earth, and Air, and active Flame, Fell through the mighty V. DRYDEN. **b.** To tempt with impious wings the v. of air 1743. *fig.* The dark v. of infidelity 1829. **5. a.** They have left an aching v., The world can never fill COWPER. Hence **Voi·dness,** the state or condition of being v.; a v. or vacant space.

Void (void), *v.* ME. [Partly – OFr. *voider*, *vuider* (mod. *vider*) :– Rom. **vocitare*, f. **vocit-* (see prec.); partly aphetic f. AVOID *v.*] **I. 1.** *trans.* To clear (a room, house, place) *of* (or †*from*) occupants; to empty or clear (a place, receptacle, etc.) *of* something. Now *arch.* **b.** To rid *of* (or †*from*) some quality or condition ME. †**2.** Without const. To clear (a table) of dishes, etc.; to clear or empty (some thing or place) of its contents or occupants –1658. †**b.** To render (a benefice) vacant –1703. **3.** To deprive (something) of legal validity; to annul or cancel ME. **b.** To deprive of efficacy, force, or value; to set aside or nullify. Now *rare.* ME. †**c.** To confute or refute –1699.

1. Whan that the house voyded was of alle CHAUCER. **b.** Having voided thy mind of what is earthly and carnal 1668. **3.** Unless you intend to ..v. Bargains lawfully made LOCKE. **b.** We defeat our own hope and v. our own prayer 1874.

II. †**1.** To send or put (a person) away; to dismiss or expel –1644. †**2.** To go away, depart, or withdraw from (a place); to move out of (the way) –1732. **3.** To remove (something) so as to leave a vacant space; to take, put, or clear away; occas., to remove by emptying or taking out. Now *rare.* late ME. †**b.** With immaterial obj. –1656. **4.** Of persons, animals, or their organs: To discharge (some matter) from the body through a natural vent or orifice, esp. through the excretory organs; also, †to spit or pour forth (venom). late ME. **b.** *absol.* To evacuate; to vomit. late ME. †**5.** To carry off or drain *away* (water, etc.); to discharge or let out –1707.

2. To voyde the realme of Fraunce 1523. The whole shoal of virtuosoes..voided the room 1732. **4.** My brother..fell, and voided much blood at the nose 1617. *fig.* That's base wit, That voyds but filth and stench VAUGHAN.

†**III. 1.** To leave alone, avoid; to abstain or refrain from; to have nothing to do with –1681. **2.** To escape from or evade (something injurious or troublesome) –1677. **3.** To prevent; to keep or ward *off* –1722.

1. For if I had fear'd death, Of all the Men i th' world I would haue voided thee SHAKS.

IV. 1. *intr.* To go away, withdraw; to retire or retreat; to give place; to vanish. Now *Obs.* or *arch.* ME. †**2.** Of a benefice, etc.: To become, fall, or remain vacant –1531. †**3.** Of matter, etc.: To come, flow, or pass out, esp. in or by evacuation or excretion; to issue –1774. Hence **Voi·ding** *vbl. sb.* the action of the vb.; also *concr.* that which is voided or evacuated.

Voidable (voi·dăb'l), *a.* 1485. [f. prec. + -ABLE.] **1.** Capable of being annulled or made legally void; *spec.* (as dist. from *void*) that may be either voided or confirmed. **2.** Capable of being voided or evacuated (*rare*) 1663.

1. These civil disabilities make the contract void *ab initio*, and not merely v. BLACKSTONE. Hence **Voidabi·lity. Voi·dableness.**

Voidance (voi·dăns). late ME. [– OFr. *voidance*, *vuidance* (see VOID *a.*), f. *voider*, *vuider*; see VOID *v.*, -ANCE.] The action of voiding or making void. **1.** The action or process of emptying out the contents of something. Now *rare.* †**2.** The action or fact of removing, clearing away, or getting rid of something; removal –1677. **3.** *Eccl.* The fact of a benefice, etc., becoming or being void. late ME. **4.** Annulment 1488. †**5.** A verbal evasion; an evasive answer or argument. BACON.

Voi·ded, *ppl. a.* late ME. [f. VOID *v.* + -ED[1].] †**1.** Made void or empty; emptied or cleared of contents –1563. **2.** Having a part or portion cut out so as to leave a void or vacant space. †**a.** Of shoes or a garment

–1623. **b.** *Her.* of a charge or ordinary 1572. **3.** Evacuated (*rare*) 1784.

2. b. *V.* is a term applied to any ordinary,.. when it is pierced through, so that the field appears, and nothing remains of the charge but its edge 1780.

Voidee (voi·dī). Now only *Hist.* late ME. [– AFr. *voidé(e, pa. pple. of *voider* VOID *v.*, with ref. app. to the withdrawing from a hall or chamber of those who were not to sleep there; see -EE¹.] A collation consisting of wine with spices, comfits, or the like, partaken of before retiring to rest or before the departure of guests; a repast of this nature following upon a feast or fuller meal; a parting dish.

Voider (voi·dəɹ). late ME. [f. VOID *v.* + -ER¹.] †**1.** That which keeps off or away; a screen or defence –1550. **2.** A receptacle into which something is voided or emptied: **a.** A tray, basket, etc. in which dirty dishes, fragments of broken food, etc. are placed in clearing the table or during a meal. *Obs.* exc. *dial.* 1466. †**b.** A tray, basket, or large plate for holding, carrying, or handing round sweetmeats. Also *transf.* a quantity or amount carried in this –1706. **c.** A clothes-basket; a wicker basket of any kind. *dial.* 1707. **3.** *Her.* As the name of an ordinary (see quot.) 1562. **4.** One who or that which voids, clears away, or empties (*rare*) 1589.

2. a. I sent my old silver voyder..to be exchandged for a new 1620. **3.** *V.*, is an ordinary much resembling the flanch, but is not quite so circular towards the centre of the field 1780.

‖**Voile** (voil, vwal). 1889. [Fr., VEIL *sb.*] A thin semi-transparent cotton or woollen material used for blouses and dresses.

‖**Voir dire** (vwār dīr). 1676. [OFr. *voir* true, the truth + *dire* say.] *Law.* (See quot.)

If however the court has, upon inspection, any doubt of the age of the party,..it may..examine the infant himself upon an oath of *voir dire, veritatem dicere*, that is, to make true answer to such questions as the court shall demand of him BLACKSTONE.

‖**Voiture** (vwatǖr). 1698. [Fr. *voiture.* Cf. VETTURA.] A carriage or conveyance; a vehicle.

‖**Voiturier** (vwatürye). 1763. [Fr., f. prec.; see -IER.] The driver of a carriage or coach.

‖**Voiturin** (vwatüræn). 1768. [Fr., f. *voiture*, after It. *vetturino.*] **1.** = prec. **2.** A carriage for hire, a voiture 1768.

Voivode (voi·vōᵘd). 1570. [– earlier Magyar *vajvoda* (now *vajda*) and Bulg., Serb. *vojvoda*, Czech *vojevoda.* See VAIVODE, WAYWODE.] = VAIVODE.

Vol (vǫl). 1722. [– Fr. *vol* flight, f. *voler* :– L. *volare* fly.] *Her.* Two wings displayed and joined at the base.

Vol., abbrev. of VOLUME.

Volage (volā·ʒ), *a.* late ME. [– (O)Fr. *volage*, semi-pop. – L. *volaticus* winged, flighty, f. *volare* fly; see -AGE, -ATIC.] Giddy, foolish, fickle, inconstant.

Not yit twelve yeer of age, With herte wylde, and thought v. CHAUCER.

Volant (vōᵘ·lănt), *a.* and *sb.* 1548. [– Fr. *volant*, pr. pple. of *voler*; see prec., -ANT.] **A.** *adj.* †**1. a.** Riding at full gallop (*rare*). **b.** *Mil.* So constituted as to be capable of rapid movement or action –1647. **2.** *Her.* Of birds, etc.: Represented as flying; having the wings expanded as if in flight 1572. **3.** Flying; capable of flight 1665. **4.** Of things: Passing rapidly through the air or space, as if by flight; floating lightly in the air 1603. **b.** Moving rapidly or lightly; active, nimble. Also *fig.* of discourse. 1650. **5.** Characterized by or the nature of flight 1818.

1. b. Sir Henrie Powers squadron v. (or flying Regiment) 1617. **3.** A kind of v. beetle MRS. PIOZZI. **4.** The v. shadows that cross our British hills MRS. PIOZZI. **b.** Bards with v. touch Traverse loquacious strings 1708.

B. *sb.* †**1.** *To act* or *keep* (*upon*) *the v.*, to hover between two parties, sides, or opinions –1734. **2.** A flounce or frill 1882.

‖**Volante** (vola·nte). 1791. [Sp., pr. pple. of *volar*; cf. prec.] A two-wheeled covered carriage drawn by a horse ridden by a postilion (freq. with another horse attached at the side), used in Spanish countries.

Volapük, -puk (vǫ·läpük, -puk). 1885. [f. *vol* world (alt. of Eng. *world*) + *a*, connecting vowel + *pük* speech (alt. of Eng. *speak*).] An artificial language, invented in 1879 by a German priest, Johann M. Schleyer, as a means of international communication.

Volar (vōᵘ·lăɹ), *a.* 1814. [f. L. *vola* hollow of hand or foot + -AR¹.] *Anat.* Of or belonging to the palm of the hand or the sole of the foot; palmar.

Volary (vōᵘ·lări). Now *rare.* 1630. [– Fr. *volière*, f. *voler* fly; see -ARY¹.] **1.** A large bird-cage; an aviary. **2.** *collect.* The birds kept in an aviary 1693.

Volatic (vŏlæ·tik), *sb.* and *a.* Now *rare* or *Obs.* 1643. [– L. *volaticus* winged, inconstant, f. as next; see -ATIC.] **A.** *sb.* A winged creature. **B.** *adj.* That flies or flits about; *spec.* in *Path.* of a variety of itch 1684.

Volatile (vǫ·lătəil, -il), *sb.* and *a.* ME. [– (O)Fr. *volatil* or L. *volatilis*, f. *volat-*, pa. ppl. stem of *volare* fly; see -ATILE.] **A.** *sb.* †**1.** *collect.* Birds, *esp.* wild-fowl –1660. **2.** A winged creature; a bird, butterfly, or the like; a fowl. Usu. in pl. ME. **3.** A volatile matter or substance 1686. **B.** *adj.* **1.** Flying, capable of flying, volant 1626. **b.** Moving or flitting from one place to another, esp. with some degree of rapidity 1654. **2.** Of substances: Liable to or susceptible of evaporation and diffusion at ordinary temperatures 1605. **3.** Changeable, fickle; marked or characterized by levity or flightiness 1647. **4.** Evanescent, transient; readily vanishing; difficult to seize, retain, or fix permanently 1665.

1. Conveyed by some v. insect 1865. **2.** Sulphur is fixt and not v. 1671. *V. salt* or *salts*, sal volatile. *V. alkali*, ammonia. *V. oil*: see ESSENTIAL 5. **3.** The fickle, inconstant, v. temper of the people 1861. **4.** The incidents which give excellence to biography are of a v. and evanescent kind BOSWELL. Hence **Vo·latileness, Volati·lity**, the quality, state, or condition of being v.

Volatilize (vǫ·lătiləiz, volæ·tiləiz), *v.* 1657. [f. VOLATILE *a.* + -IZE. Cf. Fr. *volatiliser* (XVII).] **1.** *trans.* To render volatile; to cause to evaporate or disperse in vapour. **b.** *fig.* To render light, airy, unsubstantial, etc. 1664. **2.** *intr.* To become volatile; to evaporate 1728.

1. Hence we see how necessary heat is, to v. the rancid oil 1755. Hence **Vo·latili:zable** *a.* capable of being volatilized. **Vo:latiliza·tion**, the action or process of making volatile; volatilized state.

†**Vo·latize**, *v.* 1650. [Syncopated form of prec.] = prec. –1826.

‖**Vol-au-vent** (volovaṅ). 1828. [Fr., lit. 'flight in the wind'.] A kind of raised pie, formed of a light puff paste filled with meat, fish, or the like.

Volborthite (vǫ·lbǫɹþəit). 1844. [Named after its discoverer, A. von *Volborth*, a Russian scientist (1837); see -ITE¹ 2 b.] *Min.* Hydrous vanadate of copper, barium, and calcium, found in small yellowish-green crystals.

Volcan (vǫ·lkăn). Now *rare.* 1577. [– Fr. and Sp. *volcan* – It. *volcano* – L. *Volcanus, Vulcanus* VULCAN.] = VOLCANO 1.

Volca·nian, *a. rare.* 1820. [f. VOLCANO + -IAN.] = next.

Volcanic (vǫlkæ·nik), *a.* 1774. [– Fr. *volcanique*, f. *volcan* VOLCAN.] **1.** Discharged from or produced or ejected by a volcano or volcanoes. **2.** Due to or caused by a volcano or volcanoes 1776. **b.** Of or pertaining to a volcano or volcanoes 1797. **3.** Characterized by the presence of volcanoes; composed of volcanoes; consisting of materials produced by igneous action 1789. **b.** Of the nature of a volcano 1833. **4.** *fig.* Resembling or characteristic of a volcano, or the attributes of this; violently explosive, latently capable of sudden and violent activity 1854.

1. V. cinders 1774. *V. tufa, tuff*: see TUFA. *V. glass*, obsidian. **2.** V. shocks 1817. **3.** Hot springs are common to the v. districts of different parts of the world 1832. **4.** His v. soul was tossed with an inward ocean of fire 1870. Hence **Volca·nically** *adv.* like or in respect of a volcano or volcanoes.

Volcanicity (vǫlkăni·sĭti). 1836. [– Fr. *volcanicité* or f. prec. + -ITY.] Volcanic action, activity, or phenomena.

Volcanism (vǫ·lkăniz'm). 1869. [– Fr. *volcanisme*; cf. prec. and VULCANISM.] The state, condition, or character of being volcanic; volcanic action or phenomena.

Volcanist (vǫ·lkănist). 1796. [– Fr. *volcaniste* or f. VOLCANO + -IST; cf. VULCANIST.] **1.** One who asserts the igneous origin of certain geological formations; a Plutonist or Vulcanist. **2.** One who studies or is versed in volcanoes 1828.

Vo·lcanized, *ppl. a. rare.* 1792. [– Fr. *volcanisé*, f. *volcan* VOLCAN; see -IZE.] Affected or altered by volcanic action or heat. Hence **Vo·lcanize** *v. trans.*

Volcano (vǫlkēⁱ·no). *Pl.* **volcanoes** (†**-os, -o's**). 1613. [– It. *volcano*, †*vulcano* – L. *Volcanus, Vulcanus* VULCAN.] **1.** *Physiog.* A more or less conical hill or mountain, composed wholly or chiefly of discharged matter, communicating with the interior of the globe by a funnel or crater, from which in periods of activity steam, gas, ashes, rocks, and freq. streams of molten materials are ejected. **2.** *fig.* A violent feeling or passion, esp. one in a suppressed state 1697. **b.** A state of things liable to burst out violently at some time 1853.

2. Nursing this v. of wrath in his breast 1872. **b.** The social v. which some think exists below modern society 1890.

Vole (vōᵘl), *sb.*¹ 1679. [– Fr. *vole* (XVII), f. *voler* :– L. *volare* fly.] The winning of all the tricks in certain card-games, as écarté, quadrille, or ombre. Phr. *to win the v.* **b.** *To go the v.*, to run every risk in the hope of great gain; to try all shifts. Hence **Vole** *v. intr.* to win the v. POPE.

Vole (vōᵘl), *sb.*² 1805. [orig. *vole-mouse* – Norw. *vollmus, f. *voll* field + *mus* mouse.] One or other of various rat- or mouse-like quadrupeds; esp. the short-tailed field-mouse, *Microtus* (formerly *Arvicola*) *agrestis*; the water-rat, *M. amphibius*; and the red or bank vole, *Evotomys glareolus.*

Volent (vōᵘ·lĕnt), *a. rare.* 1654. [– L. *volens, volent-*, pr. pple. of *velle* will, wish, desire; see -ENT.] Exercising or capable of exercising will or choice in respect of one's conduct or course of action.

‖**Volet** (vole). 1847. [– (O)Fr. *volet* (mod. 'shutter', etc.), f. *voler* :– L. *volare* fly.] One of the wings or side compartments of a triptych.

Volitant (vǫ·litănt), *a.* 1847. [– L. *volitans, -ant-*, pr. pple. of *volitare*, frequent. of *volare* fly; see -ANT.] Flitting, flying, or constantly moving about.

Volitate (vǫ·liteⁱt), *v.* 1866. [– *volitat-*, pa. ppl. stem of L. *volitare*; see prec., -ATE³.] To fly with a fluttering motion.

Volitation (vǫlitēⁱ·ʃən). 1646. [– late and med.L. *volitatio, -ōn-*, f. as prec.; see -ION.] Flying, flight.

Volition (vŏli·ʃən). 1615. [– Fr. *volition* or med.L. *volitio, -ōn-*, f. *volo* I wish, will; see -ITION.] **1.** With *a* and *pl.* An act of willing or resolving; a decision or choice made after due consideration or deliberation. **2.** The action of consciously willing or resolving; exercise of the will 1660. **b.** The power or faculty of willing 1738. **c.** Will-power 1844.

1. A determination to suspend a v. is, in fact, another v. 1777. **2. b.** The individuality of a mind ..or its v., that is, its power of originating motion PALEY. **c.** Montacute..acted upon a stronger v. than his own DISRAELI. Hence **Voli·tional** *a.* of or belonging to v.; endowed with or exercising the faculty of v.; leading or impelling to action; arising from the exercise of v.

Volitive (vǫ·litiv), *a.* and *sb.* 1660. [– med.L. *volitivus* (XIII), f. as prec.; see -IVE.] **A.** *adj.* **1.** Of or pertaining to the will; volitional. **2.** Arising from the will 1675. **3.** *Gram.* Expressive of a wish or desire; desiderative 1864.

1. The V. or chusing faculty JER. TAYLOR.

B. *sb.* A desiderative verb, mood, etc. 1813.

Volitorial (vǫlitōᵊ·riăl), *a.* 1872. [f. mod.L. *Volitores* birds capable of flight + -IAL.] Of or pertaining to flight; having the power of flight.

‖**Volksraad** (vǫ·lksrāt). 1852. [f. Du. *volk* FOLK + *raad* senate, council. Cf. REDE *sb.*] The chief legislative assembly in either of the former South African republics of the Transvaal or the Orange Free State.

Volley (vǫ·li), *sb.* 1573. [– (O)Fr. *volée* :– Rom. *volata flight, subst. use of pa. pple. fem. of L. *volare* fly; see -Y⁵.] **1.** A simultaneous discharge of a number of fire-arms or artillery; a salvo. **2.** A shower or simultaneous flight of many missile weapons, as arrows, stones, etc. 1598. **b.** *poet.* A storm or shower of hail, rain, etc. 1737. **3.** An uttering or outpouring *of* numerous words, oaths, shouts, etc., in smart or rapid succession. Also without const. 1590. **4.** *Tennis.* The flight of a ball in play before it has touched the ground 1596. **b.** *Tennis, Lawn-tennis, Cricket*, etc. A return stroke or hit at a ball before it has touched the ground; the action of so returning the ball 1862.

1. A v. of small shot SCOTT. After firing a v., the troops charged 1844. *fig.* Large black eyes that flash on you a v. Of rays BYRON. **2.** *P. L.* VI. 213. **3.** Volleys of laughter 1786. **4. c.** *attrib.* **v.-ball** (*U.S.*) a game played by volleying a large inflated ball with the hands over a high net.

Volley (vǫ·li), *v.* 1591. [f. prec.] **1.** *trans.* **a.** To utter (words, etc.) rapidly or impetuously. Usu. with advs. as *forth, off, out.* **b.** To discharge (arrows, shot, etc.) in a volley 1839. **c.** *Tennis*, etc. To return (a ball) in play before it touches the ground; to reply to (a service) in this way 1875. **2.** *absol.* **a.** To fire a volley or volleys 1606. **b.** *Tennis*, etc. To hit or return the ball before it bounces; to make a volley-stroke 1819. **3.** *intr.* **a.** To emit or produce sounds simultaneously or continuously, in a manner suggestive of firearms or artillery 1810. **b.** To rush, roll, or stream with simultaneous motion 1853. **c.** To issue or be discharged in or after the manner of a volley 1887. Hence **Vo·lleyer** *Tennis*, etc. one who volleys.

Volleyed (vǫ·lid), *ppl. a.* 1616. [f. prec. + -ED[1].] **1.** Shouted or uttered in the manner of a volley. **2.** Of thunder or lightning: Discharged with the continuous effect of a volley 1667. **3.** Of missiles, etc.: Discharged or cast in or as in a volley 1759.

2. When in Battel to thy aide The blasting volied Thunder made all speed MILT. **3.** Our vollied darts 1759.

Volplane (vǫ·pleⁱn), *sb.* 1910. [For Fr. *vol plané*, i.e. *vol* flight (f. *voler* fly), *plané* pa. pple. of *planer* (see PLANE *v.*[2]).] A dive, descent, or downward flight at a steep angle on the part of an aeroplane under control, and with the engine stopped or shut off. Hence **Vo·lplane** *v. intr.* to make a v.

Volscian (vǫ·lʃⁱăn), *sb.* and *a.* 1513. [f. L. *Volsci*, pl. of *Volscus*; see -IAN.] **A.** *sb.* **1.** *Hist.* One of an ancient warlike people formerly inhabiting the east of Latium, subdued by the Romans in the 4th century B.C. **2.** The Italic language spoken by the Volscians 1897. **B.** *adj.* Of, pertaining to, or belonging to the Volscians; that is a Volscian 1601.

Volt (vōᵘlt, vǫlt), *sb.* 1873. [f. the name of *Volta*; see VOLTAIC *a.*] The practical unit of electromotive force; the difference of potential capable of sending a current of one ampère through a conductor whose resistance is one ohm. Also *attrib.* (with numeral preceding).

Volt (vǫlt, vōᵘlt), *v.* 1692. [– Fr. *volter*, f. *volte* VOLTE.] *Fencing.* To make a volte.

‖**Volta** (vǫ·ltă). 1642. [It.; see VOLTE.] = LAVOLTA.

Volta- (vǫ·ltă), comb. form of VOLTAIC used in a few technical terms, as *v.-electric, -electrometer.*

Voltage (vōᵘ·ltėdʒ, vǫ·ltėdʒ). 1890. [f. VOLT *sb.* + -AGE.] Electromotive force reckoned or expressed in volts.

Voltaic (vǫltē·ik), *a.* 1812. [f. name of Alessandro *Volta*, Italian physician and scientist (1745–1827) + -IC.] **1.** Of apparatus: Used in producing electricity by chemical action after the method discovered by Volta; esp. *v. battery, v. pile.* **2.** Of electricity: Generated by chemical action 1816. **b.** Of a current: Consisting of voltaic electricity 1834. **3.** Of, pertaining to, connected with, or caused by electricity due to chemical action 1820. **b.** *V. brass*, brass deposited by the action of electricity 1860.

2. The application of v. electricity to the welding and fusion of metals 1890. Hence **Volta·ically** *adv.* by means of or in respect of v. electricity; after the manner of a v. battery.

Voltairean, Voltairian (vǫltēᵊ·riăn), *sb.* and *a.* 1871. [f. the later name, *de Voltaire*, of the French author François Marie Arouet (1694–1778); see -EAN, -IAN.] **A.** *sb.* A follower or adherent of Voltaire; one whose views on social and religious questions are characterized by a critical and mocking scepticism. **B.** *adj.* Of, belonging to, or resembling Voltaire; holding opinions like those of Voltaire, or expressing them in his style 1876. So **Voltai·rianism** 1848, **Voltai·rism** 1776, the body of opinions or views expressed by Voltaire; the mocking and sceptical attitude characteristic of these.

Voltaism (vǫ·ltă,iz'm). 1811. [f. *Volta* (see VOLTAIC *a.*) + -ISM.] The production of an electric current by the chemical action of a liquid on metals; galvanism as produced by Volta's methods.

Voltameter (vǫltæ·mĭtəɹ). 1836. [f. VOLTA- + -METER.] An instrument used for the quantitative measurement of electricity by means of the results of electrolysis.

Volte, volt (vǫlt, vōᵘlt). 1586. [– Fr. *volte* – It. *volta*, subst. use of fem. pa. pple. of *volgere* turn :– L. *volvĕre* roll.] †**1.** = LAVOLTA –1610. **2.** *Fencing.* A sudden dexterous movement to avoid a thrust 1688. **3.** In the manège, a circular movement executed by a horse 1727.

‖**Volte-face** (volt(ə)fas). 1819. [– Fr. *volte-face* – It. *voltafaccia* 'turn-face', f. *voltare* :– Rom. **volvitare*, frequent. of L. *volvere* roll.] The act of turning so as to face in the opposite direction; *fig.* a complete change of attitude or opinion.

‖**Voltigeur** (voltiʒőr). 1805. [Fr., f. *voltiger* hover, flutter, vault, etc.] Formerly in the French Army, a member of a special skirmishing company attached to each regiment of infantry.

Voltmeter (vōᵘ·ltmīːtəɹ, vǫ·lt-). 1882. [f. VOLT *sb.* + METER.] An instrument for measuring the pressure of electricity in volts.

‖**Vo·lto.** 1700. [It. *volto* = *volta* vault (the same word as VOLTA).] = VAULT *sb.*[1] 1.

Voltzite (vǫ·ltsəit). 1835. [f. name of P. L. *Voltz*, French inspector of mines + -ITE[1] 2 b.] *Min.* A native oxysulphide of zinc.

Volubility (vǫliŭbi·lĭti). 1579. [– Fr. *volubilité*, or – L. *volubilitas*, f. *volubilis*; see next and -ITY.] †**1.** Versatility (*rare*) –1605. **2.** The capacity of rolling, revolving, or turning round; aptness to rotate about an axis or centre 1594. †**3.** Changeableness, mutability –1699. **4.** Ready flow *of* speech, etc. 1589. **b.** Smooth, easy, or copious flow of verse 1589. **5.** The character or state of being voluble in speech; fluency, garrulousness 1596. **6.** Extreme readiness *of* the tongue, voice, etc. in speech or discourse 1612.

Voluble (vǫ·liŭb'l), *a.* 1575. [– Fr. *voluble* or L. *volubilis*, f. *volu-*; see VOLUME, -BLE.] **I. 1.** Liable to change; inconstant, variable, mutable. Now *rare.* **2.** Capable of ready rotation on a centre or axis; apt to revolve in this manner. Now *rare.* 1589. **3.** Moving rapidly and easily, esp. with a gliding or undulating movement 1589. **4.** *Bot.* Twining, twisting 1753.

1. Nothing abides at a stay; all things are unstable, and v. 1647. **4.** Plants with v. stems 1789.

II. 1. Characterized by fluency or glibness of utterance; fluent 1588. **2.** Of discourse, words, etc.: Characterized by great fluency or readiness of utterance 1588.

1. A most acute Iuuenall, v. and free of grace SHAKS. Her tongue, so v. and kind, It always runs before her mind PRIOR. **2.** A discours, v. anough, and full of sentence MILT. Hence **Vo·lubleness. Vo·lubly** *adv.*

Volume (vǫ·liŭm), *sb.* [Late ME. *volym, volum(e* – OFr. *volum*, (also mod.) *volume* – L. *volumen* roll of writing, book, etc., f. *volu-* var. of base **wolw-* of *volvere* roll.] **I. 1.** *Hist.* A roll of parchment, papyrus, etc. containing written matter; a literary work or part of one, recorded or preserved in this form, which was customary in ancient times. **2.** A collection of written or printed sheets bound together so as to form a book; a tome. late ME. **3.** *fig.* Something comparable to a book; *esp.* something which may be studied after the manner of a book 1592. **4.** A separately bound portion or division of a work; one of a number of books forming a related set or series 1523.

1. In history a great v. is unrolled for our instruction BURKE. **2.** Lo, here a little v., but great book! CRASHAW. *The sacred v.*, the Bible. *The Christian v.*, the New Testament. **3.** This night you shall..Read ore the v. of young Paris face, And find delight, writ there with Beauties pen SHAKS. Phr. *To speak* (also *tell, express*) *volumes*, to be highly expressive or significant. **4.** Thus endeth the first v. of sir Johan Froissart LD. BERNERS.

II. †**1.** Size, bulk, or dimensions (of a book) –1683. **2.** A particular bulk, mass, or quantity as an attribute of a thing 1621. **b.** *concr.* A quantity or mass (esp. a large one) regarded as matter occupying space 1647. **c.** *Chem.* A determinate quantity or amount, in terms of bulk, of any substance 1812. **3.** The bulk, size, or dimensions *of* a thing. Also *concr.*, the mass or solid body *of* something 1792. **b.** *gen.* The amount or quantity *of* something 1882. **c.** *spec.* The cubic contents of any enclosed space or solid, e.g. as determined by the length × breadth × height 1841. **4.** Without article: Bulk, mass, dimensions 1794. **5.** *Mus.* Quantity, strength or power, combined mass, of sound 1801.

2. Certain gases, which, in assuming a larger v., have caused the explosion 1862. **b.** The v. of mercury in the stem of a thermometer 1871. **c.** Instead of a given v. or measure, a given weight of air is examined HUXLEY. **3.** The v. of the Sun is 1,200,000 times greater than that of the Earth 1868. **b.** The v. of business 1892. **4.** The brook is ..of..moderate v. 1868. **5.** *V.*, a term applied to the power and quality of the tone of a voice or instrument 1876.

III. *poet.* A coil, fold, wreath, convolution, esp. of a serpent 1648. **b.** A winding of a stream 1716.

So glides some trodden Serpent on the Grass, And long behind his wounded V. trails DRYDEN. The ivy and the wild-vine interknit The volumes of their many-twining stems SHELLEY. Hence †**Vo·lumist**, one who writes a v. MILT.

Volume (vǫ·liŭm), *v.* 1815. [f. prec.] **1. a.** *trans.* To send up, pour out, in volumes. **b.** *intr.* To rise or roll in a volume or cloud 1824. **2.** *trans.* To collect or bind in a volume 1853.

1. a. More and more the nightingales volumed their notes MEREDITH.

Volumed (vǫ·liŭmd), *a.* 1596. [f. VOLUME *sb.* and *v.* + -ED.] **1.** Made into a volume or volumes of a specified size, number, etc. **b.** Filling a volume or volumes 1746. **2.** Formed into a rolling, rounded, or dense mass 1803.

1. Margents of great volum'd bookes 1609. **2.** Gasping with the v. smoke BYRON.

Volumetric (vǫliume·trik), *a.* 1862. [f. VOLUME *sb.* + METRIC *a.*[2]] Of, pertaining to, or noting measurement by volume. So **Volume·trical** *a.* 1853; **-ly** *adv.*

Voluminosity (vŏliŭminǫ·sĭti). 1782. [f. next + -OSITY.] **1.** The state of being voluminous in respect of literary production. **2.** The fact of turning or winding; an instance of this 1841.

Voluminous (vŏliū·minəs), *a.* 1611. [Sense 1 – late L. *voluminosus* with many coils, sinuous; other senses based on those of VOLUME *sb.*] **1.** Full of turnings or windings; containing or consisting of many coils or convolutions. **2.** Writing so much as to fill volumes; writing or discoursing at great length 1611. **3.** Forming a large volume; extending to or consisting of many volumes; extensive or copious in treatment 1612. **4.** Of matter of discourse: Extremely full or copious; forming a large mass or collection 1647. **b.** *gen.* Extensive, vast 1652. **5.** Of great volume or size; massive, bulky, large, swelling 1635.

1. Many a scaly fould V. and vast, a Serpent arm'd With mortal sting MILT. **2.** The very learned and v. Grotius 1782. **3.** Fames v. booke DEKKER. **4.** V. roundabout descriptions HAZLITT. **5.** That young lady with the v. light brown hair 1872. Hence **Volu·minous-ly** *adv.*, **-ness.**

Voluntariate (vǫlǫntēᵊ·riĕt). 1881. [– Fr. *volontariat* (1866), f. *volontaire* VOLUNTARY *a.*; see -ATE[1].] Voluntary service, *spec.* of a military character.

Voluntarily (vǫ·lŏntărili), *adv.* late ME. [f. VOLUNTARY *a.* + -LY[2].] In a voluntary manner; of one's own free will or accord; naturally, spontaneously.

Vo·luntariness. 1612. [f. as prec. + -NESS.] The state or condition of being voluntary; absolute freedom or liberty in respect of choice, determination, or action; spontaneity; also, an instance of this.

Voluntarism (vǫ·lŏntăriz'm). 1838. [irreg. f. VOLUNTARY *a.* + -ISM.] **1.** = VOLUNTARYISM 1. **2.** *Philos.* One or other theory or doctrine which regards will as the fundamental principle or dominant factor in the individual or the universe 1896.

Voluntarist (vǫ·lŏntărist). 1841. [f. as prec. + -IST.] An advocate or adherent of the voluntary principle or method in the Church or in philosophy. Also, in more recent use, an advocate of voluntary military service, as opp. to conscription.

Voluntary (vǫ·lŏntări), *a.*, *adv.*, and *sb.* late ME. [– (partly after (O)Fr. *volontaire*, †*voluntaire*) L. *voluntas* will; see -ARY[1].] **A.** *adj.* **I. 1. a.** Of feelings, etc.: Arising or developing in the mind without external constraint; purely spontaneous. **b.** Of actions: Performed or done of one's own free will, impulse, or choice; not constrained, prompted, or suggested by another 1449. **c.** Of oaths, etc.: Proceeding from the free, unprompted, or unconstrained will of a person; *spec.* in *Law* 1595. **d.** *Law.* Of documents, proceedings, etc. 1625. **2.** *Physiol.* Of bodily actions: Subject to the will. late ME. **3.** Of conditions, etc.: Freely chosen or undertaken. late ME. **b.** Brought about by one's own choice or deliberate action; self-inflicted, self-induced 1548. **c.** Entered into of free choice 1612. **4.** Done of deliberate intent or purpose; designed, intentional 1495. **b.** *Law.* Of escapes: Deliberately permitted or connived at 1660. **5.** Of gifts, etc.: Freely or spontaneously bestowed, rendered, or made; contributed voluntarily 1580.

1. Albeit we sweare A v. zeale, and an vn-urg'd Faith SHAKS. **b.** Thy v. wandring, and vnconstrayned exyle 1632. **d.** V. conveyances of estates in land, that is, conveyances without any consideration, such as money or marriage 1875. **2.** Imagination is the first internal beginning of all V. Motion HOBBES. **3.** They discover what nothing but v. blindness before had concealed JOHNSON. **b.** Voluntarie death ought not to be attempted of any wise man 1576. **c.** *V. association*, . . a society which is unincorporated, but is not a partnership, in that the members are not agents for one another 1889. **4.** Waste is either v., which is a crime of commission, as by pulling down a house; or it is permissive BLACKSTONE. **5.** Nor is it every contribution, called v., which is according to the free will of the giver BURKE.

II. †**1.** Of the will: Free, unforced, unconstrained –1563. **2.** Of persons: That is such of one's own accord or free choice; acting voluntarily, willingly, or spontaneously in a specified capacity; also, endowed with the faculty of willing 1594. †**b.** Serving as a volunteer soldier; that is a volunteer; also, composed of volunteers –1647. **c.** *poet.* Of a sword: Offered freely or willingly in aid of some cause 1761. †**3.** Willing, ready (*to* do something) –1768. **4.** Of institutions: Maintained or supported solely or largely by freewill offerings or contributions, and free from State interference or control 1745. **b.** Of, pertaining to, concerned, or connected with voluntaryism 1834. **c.** Of persons: Advocating or supporting the voluntary principle as opp. to State establishment and control 1835. **5.** Of muscles, etc.: Acting in response to the volition; directing or controlling voluntary movements 1788.

2. V. exiles GIBBON. **c.** At Aix his v. sword he drew GRAY. **4.** Private or V. Schools 1837. **b.** The v. system. . is almost universal in Australia 1891.

†**III.** Growing wild or naturally; of spontaneous growth –1718.

The wilde or v. Strawberries 1620.

†**B.** *adv.* = VOLUNTARILY *adv.* –1769.

C. *sb.* **I.** †**1.** Free will or choice –1633. **2.** †**a.** Music added at the will of the performer to a piece played or sung –1597. **b.** A musical piece or movement performed spontaneously or of one's free choice, esp. by way of prelude to a more elaborate piece, song, etc. 1598. **c.** *esp.* A piece or solo played upon the organ before, during, or after any office of the Church; also, the music for this 1712. **3.** An extempore, optional, or voluntary piece of writing or composition 1690. **4.** The parting of a rider from his horse without adequate cause. Phr. *to cut a v.* = VOLUNTEER *v.* 2 b. 1863. **5.** A voluntary examination 1894.

2. b. *fig.* He. . ran off in a wild v. of fanciful mirth SCOTT.

II. †**1.** = VOLUNTEER *sb.* 1. –1670. **2.** = VOLUNTEER *sb.* 2. 1609. **3.** One who holds or advocates that the Church (or educational institutions) should be maintained by voluntary contributions instead of by the State 1834.

Voluntaryism (vǫ·lŏntări,izm). 1835. [f. prec. + -ISM.] **1.** The principle or tenet that the Church and educational institutions should be supported by voluntary contributions instead of by the State. **2.** A system which rests upon voluntary action or principles 1883.

Voluntaryist (vǫ·lŏntări,ist). 1842. [f. as prec. + -IST.] = VOLUNTARY C: II. 3. Also, in recent use, an advocate of voluntary military service.

Voluntative (vǫ·lŏntĕtiv), *a.* and *sb.* 1870. [f. L. *voluntas*, *voluntat-* + -IVE (see -ATIVE), after similar terms, as *cohortative*, *desiderative*, *prohibitive*, etc.] **A.** *adj.* **a.** *Hebrew Gram.* Of a verbal form: Expressive of a desire; desiderative. **b.** Having the ability to act or accomplish at will; voluntary. **B.** *sb.* *Hebrew Gram.* A verbal form expressive of a desire to do the action denoted by the verb; a desiderative 1870.

Volunteer (vǫlŏntī°·ɹ), *sb.* and *a.* Also †**-ier.** 1600. [– Fr. *volontaire* – L. *voluntarius* (pl., sc. *milites* soldiers); the suffix was assim. to -IER and (later) -EER[1].] **A.** *sb.* **1.** *Mil.* One who voluntarily offers or enrols himself for military service, in contrast to those who are under obligation to do so, or who form part of a regular army or military force. **b.** *spec.* A member of an organized military company or force, formed by voluntary enrolment and distinct from the regular army. In later use, a civilian forming part of the 'auxiliary forces' of a country as a member of such a body. 1642. †**c.** One voluntarily serving in the Navy –1720. **2.** One who of his own free will takes part in any enterprise 1638. **3.** *Law.* One to whom a voluntary conveyance is made; one who benefits by a deed made without valuable consideration 1744. **B.** *attrib.* or as *adj.* **1. a.** Of troops, etc.: Consisting or composed of persons undertaking military service as volunteers 1662. **b.** Of persons: Serving as a volunteer in the army (†or the navy) 1649. **c.** Of or pertaining to a volunteer or volunteers 1724. **2.** Voluntarily undertaking or performing any action or service 1661. **b.** Of vegetation: Growing spontaneously 1794. **3.** Of services, actions, etc.: Rendered or performed voluntarily 1724.

1. a. Officers of. . V. Corps 1811. **c.** Trailing a v. pike in the Artillery ground SHERIDAN. **2. b.** V. or self-sown oats 1882. **3.** I am not very fond of any v. modes of raising money for public service BURKE.

Voluntee·r, *v.* 1755. [Back-formation from next.] **1.** *intr.* To undertake military service voluntarily, esp. on a special occasion. Freq. const. *for*. **2.** To offer of one's own accord *to* do something 1840. **b.** To be thrown from a horse without adequate cause 1890. **3.** *trans.* To offer (one's services) for some special purpose or enterprise 1800. **4.** To offer to undertake or perform (something) 1818. **5.** To communicate (information, etc.) on one's own initiative 1839. **6.** To offer to give or supply 1873.

1. John Sheffield. . volunteered to serve at sea against the Dutch MACAULAY. **2.** My guide volunteered to cut the steps for me TYNDALL. **5.** He volunteered no information about himself GEO. ELIOT.

Voluntee·ring, *vbl. sb.* 1691. [f. VOLUNTEER *sb.* + -ING[1].] The action of serving or offering one's services as a volunteer.

†**Volunty.** [ME. *volunte* – (O)Fr. *volonté* – L. *voluntas*, *-tat-* will, f. *vol-* (*volo* I will); see -TY[1].] Will, desire, pleasure; that which one wishes or desires –1652.

Voluptuary (vŏlɒ·ptiu,ări), *sb.* and *a.* 1605. [– L. *voluptuarius*, later form of *voluptarius*, f. *voluptas* pleasure; see -ARY.] **A.** *sb.* One who is addicted to sensuous pleasures; one given up to indulgence in luxury or the gratification of the senses; a sybarite 1610.

A good-humoured, but hard-hearted, v. SCOTT.

B. *adj.* Of, pertaining to, or characterized by sensuous or luxurious pleasures 1605.

Voluptuo·sity. Now *rare* or *Obs.* late ME. [– OFr. *voluptuosité* or med.L. *voluptuositas*, f. L. *voluptuosus*; see next, -OSITY.] The quality or state of being voluptuous; voluptuousness.

Voluptuous (vŏlɒ·ptiu,əs), *a.* late ME. [– (O)Fr. *voluptueux*, *-euse* or L. *voluptuosus*, f. *voluptas* pleasure; see -UOUS.] **1.** Of, pertaining to, derived from, resting in or characterized by gratification of the senses, esp. in a refined or luxurious manner; marked by indulgence in sensual pleasures; luxuriously sensuous. **2.** Addicted to sensual pleasures or the gratification of the senses; inclined to ease and luxury; fond of elegant or sumptuous living 1440. **3.** Imparting a sense of delicious pleasure; suggestive of sensuous pleasures, esp. of a refined or luxurious kind 1816. **b.** Suggestive of sensuous pleasures by fullness and beauty of form 1839.

1. V. liuing, one of the thornes that choke the worde 1582. V. Feasts 1638. The luxuriant charms of v. Italy 1832. **2.** The poore are not so v.: they content themselves with drie ryce, herbs, roots SIR T. HERBERT. **3.** And when Music arose with its v. swell, Soft eyes look'd love to eyes which spake again BYRON. **b.** The v. image of a Corinthian courtezan JOWETT. Hence **Volu·ptuous-ly** *adv.*, **-ness.**

†‖**Voluta** (vŏliū·tă). 1563. [L.; see VOLUTE.] *Arch.* = VOLUTE *sb.* 1. –1753.

Volutation (vǫliutē[i]·ʃən). Now *rare* or *Obs.* 1610. [– L. *volutatio*, *-ōn-*, f. *volutat-*, pa. ppl. stem of *volutare*, frequent. of *volvere* roll; see -ION. Cf. OFr. *volutation*.] The action of rolling or causing to roll; revolution combined with progression. **b.** Wallowing 1655.

Volute (vŏliū·t), *sb.* 1696. [– Fr. *volute* or L. *voluta*, subst. use of pa. pple. fem. of *volvere* roll, wrap.] **1.** *Arch.* A spiral scroll forming the chief ornament of the Ionic capital and employed also in those of the Corinthian and Composite orders. **2.** A spiral conformation; a convolution, twist, or turn; a thing or part having a spiral form 1756. **3.** The spiral shell of a gasteropod of the genus *Voluta*; also, the animal itself 1753.

Volute (vŏliū·t), *a.* 1845. [– L. *volutus*, or attrib. use of prec.] Having the form of a volute; forming a spiral curve or curves.

Volu·ted, *a.* 1801. [f. VOLUTE *sb.* + -ED[2].] **1.** Spirally twisted or grooved. **2.** *Arch.* Furnished with a volute or spiral scroll 1810.

Volution (vŏliū·ʃən). 1610. [f. *volut-*, pa. ppl. stem of L. *volvere* turn (see -ION), after *revolution*, etc. Cf. late L. *volutio* rolling, twisting.] **1.** A rolling or revolving movement. **2.** A spiral turn or twist; a coil or convolution 1752. **3.** A whorl of a spiral shell 1884.

‖**Volva** (vǫ·lvă). 1753. [L., f. *volvere* roll, wrap.] *Bot.* The membranous covering which completely encloses many fungi in the early stage of growth.

Volvelle (vǫ·lvel). *Obs.* exc. *Hist.* late ME. [– med.L. *volvella* or *volvellum*, app. f. L. *volvere* turn.] An old device consisting of one or more movable circles surrounded by other graduated or figured circles, serving to ascertain the rising and setting of the sun and moon, the state of the tides, etc.

‖**Volvox** (vǫ·lvǫks). 1798. [mod.L., f. L. *volvere* turn.] *Bot.* A genus of freshwater organisms having a spherical form and provided with cilia which enable them to roll over in the water; an individual of this genus.

‖**Volvulus** (vǫ·lviŭlŏs). 1679. [mod.L., f. L. *volvere* turn, twist.] *Path.* A form of intestinal obstruction caused by a twisting or knotting of the bowel. †Also in pl. *volvuli*. **b.** With *a*: An instance of this 1758.

Vomer (vō[u]·məɹ). 1704. [– L. *vomer* ploughshare.] **1.** *Anat.* A small thin bone forming the posterior part of the partition between the nostrils in man and most vertebrate animals. **2.** *Ichth.* A bone forming the front part of the roof of the mouth, and often bearing teeth 1828. **3.** *Ornith.* The pygostyle 1872. Hence **Vo·merine** *a.* of or belonging to the v.; composing the v.; of teeth, situated on the v.

‖**Vomica** (vǫ·mikă). *Pl.* **vomicæ** (-isī),

vomicas. 1572. [L. 'boil, ulcer', f. *vomere* eject, vomit.] **1.** †**a.** A vent or opening. **b.** A place at which water issues 1838. **2.** *Path.* An ulcerous cavity or abscess in the substance of the lungs or (more rarely) some other internal organ 1693.

Vomit (vǫ·mit), *sb.* late ME. [– OFr. *vomite* or L. *vomitus*, f. *vomere* vomit (whence Fr. *vomir*); see next.] **1.** The act of ejecting the contents of the stomach through the mouth. **2.** Matter ejected from the stomach by vomiting. late ME. **3.** An emetic. late ME.

1. Nvx vomica..causeth a strong vomite 1579. **2.** *Black v.*, a blackish matter, resembling coffee grounds and due to hæmorrhage, vomited in severer cases of yellow fever; also, the disease of yellow fever itself. *fig.* (with allusion to *Prov.* 26:11); Now that ye have started back from the purity of Scripture..to the old v. of your traditions MILT. **3.** I have taken a v. to-day, and hope I shall be better SWIFT.

Vomit (vǫ·mit), *v.* late ME. [– *vomit-*, pa. ppl. stem of L. *vomere* or – L. frequent. *vomitare.*] **1.** *intr.* To bring up and eject the contents of the stomach by the mouth. **2.** *trans.* To bring up and discharge (swallowed food or drink) through the mouth; to cast out (a matter or substance) in this way 1541. **3.** *fig.* To eject, reject, cast *out* or *up*, esp. with abhorrence or loathing 1562. **b.** To give vent to or utter (abusive or objectionable language) 1592. **4.** *transf.* To discharge, to give, send, or throw out copiously or with force; to send *out* or pour *forth* in a manner suggestive of vomiting 1552. **5.** (All now *rare* or *Obs.*) *absol.* Of emetics: To cause vomiting 1651. **b.** *trans.* To cause (a person) to vomit 1662. **c.** Said of a person administering the emetic; or *pass.* of the patient 1684. **6.** *intr.* To issue with force or violence; to rush *out*, to spout *up* 1632.

2. The fish..vomited out Jonas upon the dry land BIBLE (Douay) *Jonah* 2:11. **3. b.** All these abominable names Thou vomits forth so fluently COTTON. **4.** He and his curst crew..like the sons of Vulcan, v. smoke MILT. An incredible quantity of nonsense is vomited from the press 1834. Hence **Vo·miting** *vbl. sb.* the act of ejecting the contents of the stomach through the mouth; an instance of this; †*concr.* matter which is vomited.

Vomition (vomi·ʃən). 1656. [– Fr. †*vomition* or L. *vomitio, -ōn-*, f. as prec.; see -ION.] The action of vomiting.

†**Vo·mitive,** *a.* and *sb.* 1580. [– (O)Fr. *vomitif, -ive* or med.L. *vomitivus* (XIII), f. as prec.; see -IVE.] **A.** *adj.* **1.** Of medicines: Causing vomiting; vomitory; emetic –1754. **2.** Of or pertaining to vomiting –1691. **B.** *sb.* = VOMITORY *sb.* 1. –1756.

‖**Vomito** (vǫ·mito). 1833. [Sp. (and Pg.) *vómito* – L. *vomitus* VOMIT *sb.*] The yellow fever in its virulent form, when it is usu. accompanied by black vomit.

Vomitorium (vǫmitōᵊ·riŏm). *Pl.* **-ia.** 1754. [f. late L. (pl.) *vomitoria* (Macrobius), subst. use of n. pl. of *vomitorius*; see next, -ORIUM.] A passage or opening in an ancient amphitheatre or theatre, leading to or from the seats. Usu. *pl.*

Vomitory (vǫ·mitŏri), *sb.* 1601. [Sense 1, subst. use of next; sense 2, anglicization of prec.; see -ORY¹. Cf. Fr. *vomitoire* in same senses.] †**1.** An emetic –1753. **2.** An opening door, or passage in a theatre, playhouse, or the like, affording ingress or egress to the spectators; orig. (and usu.) = prec. 1730. **3.** A funnel, vent, or other opening through which matter is emitted or discharged 1822.

2. Sixty-four *vomitories*..poured forth the immense multitude GIBBON.

Vomitory (vǫ·mitŏri), *a.* 1620. [– L. *vomitorius* (Pliny), f. *vomit-*; see VOMIT *v.*, -ORY².] **1.** Of or pertaining to vomiting. **2.** Efficacious in promoting vomiting; causing vomiting; emetic 1634.

Vomiturition (-iuri·ʃen). 1842. [f. *vomit-* (see prec.) after *micturition*, perh. after Fr. *vomituration.*] Ineffectual attempts to vomit.

Voodoo (vū·dū), *sb.* 1880. [Dahomey *vodu.* Cf. VAUDOUX, HOODOO.] **1.** A body of superstitious beliefs and practices, including sorcery, serpent-worship, and sacrificial rites, current among Negroes and persons of Negro blood in the West Indies and southern United States, and ultimately of African origin. **2.** One who practises voodoo; a negro sorcerer or witch 1880. **3.** *attrib.* as *v. dance, doctor, priest* 1885. Hence **Voo·doo** *v. trans.* to bewitch by means of v. arts. **Voo·dooism,** the system of beliefs and practices constituting v.; the belief in or practice of v. as a superstition or form of sorcery.

‖**Voorlooper** (vōrlō·pəɹ). *S. Afr.* 1852. [Du., f. *voor-* before + *loopen* run.] A native boy who walks with the foremost pair of a team of oxen in order to guide them.

‖**Voortrekker** (vōrtre·kəɹ). *S. Afr.* 1878. [Du., f. *voor-* before + *trekken* TREK *v.*] One of the original Dutch emigrants into the Transvaal; a Boer pioneer.

Voracious (vŏrēⁱ·ʃəs), *a.* 1635. [f. L. *vorax, vorac-*, f. *vorare* devour; see -IOUS.] **1.** Of animals (rarely of persons, or of the throat): Eating with greediness; devouring food in large quantities; gluttonous, ravenous. Also const. *of.* 1693. **b.** *fig.* Of persons: Excessively greedy or eager in some desire or pursuit. Also const. *of.* 1746. **c.** *transf.* Of things 1767. **2.** Characterized by voracity or greediness 1635. **b.** *fig.* Of desires, interests, etc.: Insatiable 1712.

1. The v. and highly organized tribe of sharks 1855. **b.** A v. reader 1883. **2.** He had such a v. appetite that he would take with indifference either medicine or food 1800. **b.** His appetite for argument was..v. 1854. Hence **Vora·cious-ly** *adv.*, **-ness.**

Voracity (vŏræ·sĭti). 1526. [– (O)Fr. *voracité* or L. *voracitas*, f. as prec.; see -ACITY.] The quality or character of being voracious; greediness in eating.

†**Vora·ginous,** *a.* 1624. [– L. *voraginosus*, f. *vorago, voragin-*; see next, -OUS.] **1.** Of or belonging to an abyss or whirlpool; resembling a chasm or gulf –1747. **2.** Devouring, voracious –1691.

‖**Vorago** (vŏrēⁱ·go). Now *rare.* 1654. [– L. *vorago* abyss, etc., f. *vorare* devour.] An abyss, gulf, or chasm.

Vorant (vōᵊ·rănt), *a.* 1618. [– L. *vorans, -ant-*, pr. pple. of *vorare* devour; see -ANT.] †**1.** Devouring (*rare*) –1639. **2.** *Her.* Of animals: Devouring or swallowing something 1766.

-vorous, *suffix*, forming adjs., after L. *-vorus* devouring, eating, in *carnivorus, omnivorus.* Examples are *carnivorous, herbivorous, omnivorous.*

Vortex (vǭ·ɹteks). *Pl.* **vortices** (-isīz). 1652. [– L. *vortex* eddy, whirlpool, whirlwind, var. of *vertex* VERTEX.] **1. a.** In older theories of the universe (esp. that of Descartes), a supposed rotatory movement of cosmic matter round a centre or axis, regarded as accounting for the origin or phenomena of the terrestrial and other systems; a body of such matter rapidly carried round in a continuous whirl 1653. **b.** In mod. scientific use: A rapid movement of particles of matter round an axis; a whirl of atoms, fluid, or vapour 1847. **2.** An eddying or whirling mass of fire or flame 1652. **3.** A whirl or swirling mass of water; a strong eddy or whirlpool 1704. **4.** A violent eddy or whirl of the air; a whirlwind or cyclone, or the central portion of this 1700. **5.** *fig.* A state or condition of human affairs or interests comparable to a whirl or eddy by reason of rush or excitement, rapid change, or absorbing effect 1761. **b.** A constant round *of* excitement or pleasure 1792. **c.** A situation into which persons or things are steadily drawn, or from which they cannot escape 1779.

5. To be drawn into the v. of New York politics W. IRVING. **b.** She..lived in a v. of gaiety 1877. **c.** Whirled round again in the v. of dissipation and gaming 1779.

attrib. **v. turbine** or **wheel,** a turbine in which the water enters tangentially at the circumference and is discharged at the centre.

Vortical (vǭ·ɹtikăl), *a.* 1653. [f. L. *vortex, vortic-* (see prec.) + -AL¹ 1.] **1.** Of motion: Like that of a vortex; rotating, eddying, whirling. **2.** Moving in a vortex; whirling round 1728. Hence **Vo·rtically** *adv.*

‖**Vorticella** (vǭɹtise·lă). 1787. [mod.L. dim. of *vortex*; see prec., -EL².] *Zool.* The typical genus of *Vorticellidæ*, a family of sedentary infusorians; an individual belonging to this genus; a bell-animalcule. So **Vortice·llid,** an individual belonging to the *Vorticellidæ.*

Vorticist (vǭ·ɹtisist). 1866. [f. *vortici-*, comb. f. of VORTEX + -IST.] **1.** An advocate of the theory of vortices (VORTEX 1). **2.** *Painting,* etc. One of a school of artists who emphasize the expression of movement and activity and are characterized by a dynamic quality; also *attrib.* 1915. So **Vo·rticism.**

Vorticose (vǭ·ɹtikōᵘs), *a.* 1783. [– L. *vorticosus*, f. *vortex, vortic-*; see VERTEX, -OSE¹.] **1.** Of motion: = VORTICAL *a.* 1. **2.** Resembling a vortex 1870.

Vorticular (vǭɹti·kiŭlăɹ), *a.* 1838. [f. as prec. + -ULAR.] Of motion: Vortical, vorticose.

Vortiginous (vǭɹti·dʒinəs), *a.* 1671. [f. L. *vortigo, vortigin-*, var. of *vertigo*; see VERTIGINOUS.] **1.** Of motion: Vortical, vorticular. **2.** Moving in a vortex or vortices; rushing in whirls or eddies 1791.

Votal (vōᵘ·tăl), *a.* 1610. [f. L. *votum* vow, wish + -AL¹ 1.] †**1.** Existing in will or wish, though not carried out in fact –1624. **2.** Of the nature of a vow or solemn engagement 1632. †**3.** Bound by vows; devoted to a religious life; appropriate to one under vows –1656. **4.** Of offerings: Votive 1846.

2. Strong objections to take any further v. obligations 1855.

Votaress (vōᵘ·tărės). 1589. [f. VOTARY + -ESS¹.] A female votary; *esp.* a woman devoted to a religious life or to a special saint.

Votarist (vōᵘ·tărist). 1603. [f. VOTARY + -IST; cf. *plagiary, plagiarist*, etc.] One bound by a vow; a devotee, votary.

Votary (vōᵘ·tări), *sb.* 1546. [f. *vot-* pa. ppl. stem of L. *vovēre* vow + -ARY¹.] **I. 1.** One who is bound by vows to a religious life; a monk or nun. **b.** One who has made or is bound by a special vow 1588. **2.** One who is devoted to a particular religion, or to some form of worship or religious observance 1704. **b.** A devout worshipper 1823. **3.** A devoted or zealous worshipper of God, Christ, a saint, etc. 1690.

1. b. The votarie that will not cut his haire, Vntill the expiration of his vow 1596. **3.** Hear, Goddess, hear thy V. PRIOR.

II. 1. One who is devoted or passionately addicted to some particular pursuit, occupation, study, aim, etc. 1591. **2.** A devoted adherent or admirer of some person, institution, etc. 1647.

1. We know..You are already loues firme v. SHAKS.

†**Votary,** *a.* 1564. [f. as prec. + -ARY².] **1.** Consecrated by a vow; subject to vows –1656. **2.** Of the nature of a vow –1612.

Votation (votēⁱ·ʃən). 1816. [f. VOTE *v.* + -ATION.] The action of voting in an election or at a meeting.

Vote (vōᵘt), *sb.* 1460. [– L. *votum* vow, wish, subst. use of n. pa. pple. of *vovēre* vow, desire. Fr. *vote* (XVIII) is – Eng.] †**I. 1.** A vow –1715. **2.** A prayer –1664. **3.** An ardent wish or desire –1667. **II. 1.** An indication, by some approved method, of one's opinion or choice on a matter under discussion; an intimation that one approves or disapproves, accepts or rejects, a proposal, motion, candidate for office, or the like 1460. **b.** A means of signifying choice, approval, etc.; a voting tablet or ticket 1817. **2.** The collective opinion or assent of an assembly or body of persons 1582. **b.** In phr. *To put to the v.*, to submit to the decision of a meeting. Similarly (of a question), *to go to the v.* 1599. **c.** The collective support of a special number or class of persons in a deliberative decision, election, etc. 1851. **3.** The right or privilege of exercising the suffrage; esp. in phr. *to have a v.* 1585. †**b.** A person regarded merely as an embodiment of the right to vote; also, a person possessing the right to vote; a voter –1806. **c.** The aggregate of voters, esp. of a certain class 1888. **4.** A resolution or decision passed by, or carried in, an assembly as the result of voting; an expression of opinion formerly adopted by a meeting of any kind 1641. †**5.** A declaration or statement of opinion –1680.

1. *Casting v.*: see CASTING *ppl. a.* 2. **b.** *To give (record) a v.* The citizens of each tribe cast their votes of condemnation or acquittal into one urn 1838. **2.** Phr. *To take a v.*, to ascertain the opinion of a meeting by formal reference. **3.** The common people ceased to have votes 1782. **b.** To enter the votes' houses up and down WOLCOT. **4.** A v. of thanks DICKENS. Marlborough was..condemned as guilty by a v. of the House of Commons 1874. A v. of censure 1881.

Comb.: **V. Office,** the office from which Parliamentary bills and papers are issued to members of the House of Commons.

Vote (vǭᵘt), *v.* 1533. [f. *vot-*, pa. ppl. stem of L. *vovēre* (see prec.). Fr. *voter* (XVIII) is – Eng.] **1.** *refl.* and *trans.* To assign by a vow; to devote religiously. Now *rare.* **2.** *intr.* To give a vote; to express a choice or preference by ballot or other approved means 1552. **3.** *trans.* Of assemblies, etc.: To choose, elect, enact, or establish by vote; to ratify or determine by formal expression of will 1568. **4.** *To v. down*, to defeat, put down, or suppress by a vote 1642. **5.** To grant, allow, or confer by vote 1710. **6.** To declare by common assent; hence *gen.* to characterize by an expression of opinion; to pronounce 1663. **b.** *colloq.* To propose, suggest 1814.

2. The right to v. makes a safety-valve of every voter 1887. **3.** They v. a message to their absent chief DRYDEN. **6.** He..spoke no more during the whole debate, which I am sure he was ready to v. a bore MME. D'ARBLAY. **7.** *U.S.* To influence or control in voting; also, to present for voting, to record the votes of (electors) 1859.

Voter (vǭᵘ·tə.ı). 1578. [f. prec. + -ER¹.] One who has a right to vote; *esp.* an elector. **b.** One who gives a vote (*rare*) 1701.

Voting (vǭᵘ·tiŋ), *vbl. sb.* 1575. [f. VOTE *v.* + -ING¹.] The action of giving a vote.

attrib.: **v.-paper,** a paper on which a vote is recorded; a ballot-paper.

†**Vo·tist.** *rare.* 1613. [f. VOTE *sb.* or *v.* + -IST.] One who makes a vow; a votary –1711.

Votive (vǭᵘ·tiv), *a.* 1611. [– L. *votivus*, f. *votum* VOTE *sb.*; see -IVE.] **1.** Dedicated, consecrated, offered, erected, etc. in consequence of or in fulfilment of a vow. **b.** Observed, practised, undertaken, etc. in consequence of a vow 1628. **2.** Consisting in or expressive of a vow, desire, or wish 1597. **3.** *V. mass*, a special or extraordinary mass said at the personal desire of the priest 1738.

1. The jewels given as v. offerings 1789. V. pictures 1841. **b.** Votiue Abstinence 1628. **2.** Fanes..that echoed to the v. strains WORDSW. **3.** Masses..called v. masses, because said according to the votum, i.e. the intention or desire of the celebrant 1881. Hence **Vo·tively** *adv.*

Votress (vǭᵘ·trės). 1590. [var. of VOTARESS, after forms like *enchantress*, etc.] A female votary.

The imperiall Votresse passed on, In maiden meditation, fancy-free SHAKS.

Vouch, *sb.* 1603. [f. next.] †**1.** = VOUCHER *sb.*¹ 1. –1621. **2.** An assertion, allegation, or declaration; a formal statement or attestation of truth or fact. Now chiefly *colloq.* 1603.

2. *Oth.* II. i. 147.

Vouch (vautʃ), *v.* ME. [– OFr. *vocher, voucher* summon, invoke, claim, obscurely repr. L. *vocare* call.] **1.** *trans.* Law. *To v. to warrant* or *to* (also †*for*) *warranty*, to cite, call, or summon (a person) into court to give warranty of title. Also *ellipt.* (with omission of *to warrant*). **b.** With *over.* Of a vouchee: To cite (another person) into court in his stead. Also *absol.* 1511. **2.** To take or call (a person) to witness. late ME. **b.** To cite or appeal to (authority, example, doctrine, authors, works, etc.) in support of one's views or statements or as justification for a course of action 1531. **3.** To allege, assert, affirm, or declare. Also const. *upon* or *against* (a person). Now *rare* or *Obs.* late ME. **4.** To assert or affirm to be true or according to fact; to attest or certify. Also const. *against* (a person). 1591. **5.** To support or uphold by satisfactory evidence; to back with proofs of a practical or substantial character 1579. **b.** To attest or substantiate by written evidence 1745. **6.** To become sponsor for (a person or thing). *rare.* 1590. **b.** To affirm or guarantee (the truth of a statement) 1607. **7.** *intr.* with *for.* **a.** To speak or bear witness on behalf of (a person); to be surety or sponsor for 1687. **b.** Of things: To supply evidence or assurance of (some fact) 1755. **c.** To give personal assurance of the truth or accuracy of (a statement or fact) 1777. †**8.** To guarantee the title to or legal possession of (something). *rare.* –1661. †**9.** = VOUCHSAFE *v.*, in various senses –1848.

1. If the Heir at Common Law be vouched for Warranty 1741. **b.** He vouches the tenant in tail, who vouches over the common vouchee BLACKSTONE. **2. b.** A solicitor cannot v. his privilege in such a case as this 1885. **3.** What can you v. against him, Signor Lucio? SHAKS. **4.** The saying of Pliny..that there is no lie so impudent which is not vouched by authority 1750. Peter vouches that he had seen our Saviour 1806. **5.** He afterwards honourably vouched his words by his deeds 1828. **b.** All expenses so claimed must be strictly vouched 1886. **6. b.** *Cor.* V. vi. 5. **7. c.** I dare swear the Lady will v. for the truth of every word of it SHERIDAN. **8.** *Ham.* V. i. 117.

Vouchee (vautʃī·). 1485. [f. prec. + -EE¹.] **1.** *Law.* The person vouched or summoned into court to give warranty of title. **2.** A person cited or appealed to as an authority for some fact or statement, or in evidence of some assertion 1654.

1. *Common v.*; The cryer of the court (who, from being frequently thus vouched, is called the common v.) BLACKSTONE.

Voucher (vau·tʃə.ı), *sb.*¹ 1531. [– AFr. subst. use of OFr. inf. *voucher*; see -ER⁴.] **1.** *Law.* The summoning of a person into court to warrant the title to a property. **2.** *transf.* A piece of evidence; a fact, circumstance, or thing serving to confirm or prove something; a guarantee 1611. **b.** A written document or note, or other material evidence, serving to attest the correctness of accounts or monetary transactions, to prove the delivery of goods or valuables, etc. 1696. **c.** A written warrant or attestation 1796.

1. *V. over*: cf. VOUCH *v.* 1 b. *Double v.*; You shall finde in bookes a recouery..with a double V., and that is when the Vouchee voucheth over COKE. **2.** It has no V. but the Epistles of Phalaris, the very Book that's under debate BENTLEY.

Voucher (vau·tʃə.ı), *sb.*² 1612. [f. VOUCH *v.* + -ER¹.] **1.** One who vouches for the truth or correctness of a fact or statement; an author or literary work serving this purpose. **b.** One who vouches for the good faith or respectability of another, or who undertakes to guarantee some procedure 1667. **c.** *transf.* Of things 1718. †**2.** *Law.* **a.** = VOUCHEE 1. **b.** = VOUCHOR. –1672.

1. They would make him a V. of all their Falshood PENN. **b.** All the great Writers of that Age..stand up together as Vouchers for one another's Reputation ADDISON.

Vouchor. *rare.* 1628. [– AFr., f. *voucher* VOUCH *v.* (cf. sense 1); see -OR 2.] One who calls another into court to warrant a title.

Vouchsafe (vautʃsē·ˡf), *v.* ME. [orig. as two words, f. VOUCH *v.* warrant + SAFE, *adj.* in predic. use, e.g. *He vouchede hyt saufe on us.*] **I.** †**1.** *trans.* To confer or bestow (some thing, favour, or benefit) *on* a person –1671. **2.** To give, grant, or bestow in a gracious or condescending manner. late ME. **b.** To deign or condescend to give (a word, answer, etc.) in reply or by way of friendly notice 1597. †**3. a.** To condescend to engage in (some pursuit) –1667. **b.** To deign to accept –1607. **c.** To be prepared to bear or sustain. SHAKS. †**4.** To acknowledge (a person) in some favourable relationship or manner –1634.

2. Nature indeed vouchsafes, for our delight, The sweet vicissitudes of day and night COWPER. **b.** V. a word, yong sister, but one word SHAKS. **3. a.** Nor other strife with them do I voutsafe MILT. **b.** *Timon* I. i. 152.

II. †**1.** To grant, permit, or allow, as an act of grace or condescension –1639. **2.** To show a gracious readiness or willingness, to condescend or deign, *to* do something ME. Now only *literary.* †**3.** *ellipt.* To grant; to agree graciously; to condescend –1736.

1. *Jul. C.* III. i. 130. **2.** She did not even v. to answer him 1880. **3.** If you pleased, or would v., or condescend, or think proper, I would rather that you would..charge only five per cent. SHERIDAN.

Vouchsafement (vautʃsē·ˡfmėnt). 1628. [f. prec. + -MENT.] **1.** An act of condescension, grace, or favour; a boon, benefit, or blessing. **2.** The action of conferring or granting some boon, favour, advantage, etc. 1666.

‖**Voussoir** (vū·swǫ.ı, -a.ı). ME. [– OFr. *vausoir, vaussoir*, etc., Fr. *voussoir*:– pop. L. **volsorium*, f. **volsum*, L. *volvere* turn. Reintroduced in XVIII.] One of the stones which form part of an arch or vault, usu. having the sides slightly inclined towards each other.

Vow (vau), *sb.* ME. [– AFr. *vou, vu(u*, OFr. *vo, vou* (mod. *vœu*) :– L. *votum* VOTE *sb.*] **1.** A solemn promise made to God, or to any deity or saint, to perform some act or make some gift or sacrifice in return for some special favour; more generally, a solemn engagement, undertaking, or resolve to achieve something or to act in a certain way. **2.** *Eccl.* A solemn engagement to devote oneself to a religious life of a definite nature, such as that of a monastic or conventual order. Freq. in pl.; *to take the vows*, to enter a religious order. late ME. **3.** A solemn promise of fidelity or faithful attachment 1590. **4.** An earnest wish or desire; a prayer; a supplication 1563. **5.** A solemn affirmation or asseveration 1593. †**6.** A votive offering (*rare*) –1700.

1. Holy vows of chastity TENNYSON. The v. of Poverty was turned into a stern reality J. R. GREEN. (The three monastic vows are of poverty, chastity, and obedience.) Phr. *To make, hold, keep, pay a v., to break a v.*; Thou shalt make thy prayer vnto him,..and thou shalt rendre thy vowes BIBLE (Geneva) *Job* 22:27. **3.** They stood beside the altar, and their vows were exchanged 1829. **4.** They haue nothing more in their vowes, then her Maiesties ruine 1600. **5.** *Wint. T.* I. ii. 47.

Vow (vau), *v.*¹ ME. [– (O)Fr. *vouer*, f. *vou* VOW *sb.*] **1.** *trans.* To promise or undertake solemnly, *spec.* by a vow to a deity or saint. **2.** To dedicate, consecrate, or devote *to* some person or service 1526. **3.** To make a solemn resolve or threat to inflict (injury), exact (vengeance), harbour (hatred), etc. 1592. **4.** *intr.* To make a vow or solemn undertaking; to bind oneself by a vow ME.

1. Vowing to do what there is no Use in doing, is trifling with our Creator 1768. Vowing large sacrifice COWPER. To pray the prayer, and v. the vow SCOTT. **2.** He to heaven was vowed WORDSW. **3.** The Empress..could not forbear vowing revenge SWIFT. **4.** It is better that thou shuldest not vowe, then that thou shuldest vowe and not paye it BIBLE (Geneva) *Eccles.* 5:4.

Vow, *v.*² ME. [Aphetic f. AVOW *v.*¹] †**1.** *trans.* To acknowledge, admit –1560. **2.** To affirm or assert solemnly; to asseverate ME. **b.** *I vow*, used to strengthen an assertion 1590. In later use chiefly *U.S.* **c.** To make solemn assertion of (a feeling or quality) 1742.

2. She vowed that it was a delightful ball THACKERAY. **b.** I v., child, you are vastly handsome GOLDSM. **c.** To her again they v. their truth GRAY.

Vowel (vau·ĕl), *sb.* ME. [– OFr. *vouel*, var. of *voiel* masc. (mod. *voyelle* fem.) :– L. *vocalis*, f. *vox, voc-* voice, sound + *-alis* -AL¹ 1. Cl.L. had *vocalis* fem. sb. (sc. *littera* letter) in Cicero, Quintilian.] A sound produced by the vibrations of the vocal cords; a letter or character representing such a sound (as *a, e, i*, etc.).

At meetings young men should be Mutes, and old men Vowels 1657. A v. may be defined as voice (voiced breath) modified by some definite configuration of the super-glottal passages, but without audible friction (which would make it into a consonant) SWEET.

attrib. and *Comb.*: **v.-point,** a sign used to indicate a vowel in certain (esp. the Semitic) alphabets; also as *v. trans.* to supply with points to indicate vowels.

Vowel (vau·ĕl), *v.* 1597. [f. prec.] †**1. a.** *intr.* To utter the vowels in singing. **b.** *trans.* To sing with vowel-articulation. –1646. †**2.** *trans.* To convert into a vowel; to vocalize 1611. **3.** To supply with vowels or vowel-points 1681. †**4.** *slang.* To pay (a creditor) with an I O U. –1796.

Vowelism (vau·ĕliz'm). 1842. [f. VOWEL *sb.* + -ISM.] A system of vowel-sounds; articulation in respect of vowels.

Vowelize (vau·ĕləiz), *v.* 1816. [f. as prec. + -IZE.] **1.** *trans.* To modify or produce by means of vowel-sounds. **2.** To render vocalic 1867. **3.** To supply with vowel-points or signs representing vowels 1883.

Vowelled (vau·ĕld), *ppl. a.* 1662. [f. VOWEL *sb.* or *v.* + -ED.] Of language or words: Supplied or provided with vowels, esp. to an unusual extent. **b.** Having vowels of a specified kind or quality 1783.

Vower (vau·əɹ). 1546. [f. Vow *v.* + -ER[1].] One who makes a vow, or has taken vows.

Vowess (vau·ės). Now *Hist.* or *arch.* 1506. [f. as prec. + -ESS[1].] **1.** A woman, *esp.* a widow, who has taken a vow of chastity for the remainder of her life. **2.** A nun 1533.

†**Vow·son.** ME. [Aphetic f. *avowson* ADVOWSON.] Advowson, patronage –1570.

‖**Vox** (vǫks). 1550. [L., 'voice'.] **1.** *Vox populi*, the voice of the people; expressed general opinion; common talk or rumour. **2.** *V. angelica, v. humana*, varieties of organ-stops imitative of vocal sounds 1726.

Voyage (voi·ėdʒ), *sb.* [ME. *ve(i)age, vaiage, viage* – AFr., OFr. *veiage, voiage*, etc. (mod. *voyage*) :– L. *viaticum* money or provisions for a journey, in late L. journey; see VIATICUM, -AGE.] **1.** An act of travelling (†or transit), a journey (†or passage), by which one goes from one place to another. Now *rare*. †**b.** A pilgrimage –1518. †**2.** A journey or expedition undertaken with a military purpose; a warlike enterprise or undertaking –1686. †**3.** An enterprise of a private character (in early use implying the making of a journey) –1611. **4.** A journey by sea or water from one place to another (usu. to some distant place or country); a course or spell of sailing or navigation, *spec.* one in which a return is made to the starting-point; a cruise ME. **b.** A flight through the air (or through space); *esp.* a trip in a balloon or airship 1667. **5.** Used *fig.* (in senses 1 or 4) to denote the course of human life (or some part of it) or the fate of persons after death. late ME. **6.** A written account of a voyage 1587.

1. The utmost extent of her voyages [from home] had been about two and a half miles COBBETT. **2.** †*V. royal*, an expedition undertaken by a king in person. **4. b.** So stears the prudent Crane Her annual Voiage, born on Windes MILT. **5.** *Jul. C.* IV. iii. 220.

Voyage (voi·ėdʒ), *v.* 1477. [– Fr. *voyager* or f. prec.] **1.** *intr.* To journey by land; to travel. Now *rare*. **2.** To go by sea; to sail or cruise; to make a voyage or voyages 1604. **b.** *transf.* of things: To move through the water or air 1834. **3.** *trans.* To cross or travel over; to traverse; to sail over or on 1667.

2. *fig.* His..silent face, The marble index of a mind for ever Voyaging through strange seas of Thought, alone WORDSW. **b.** Grand clouds still voyaged in the sky STEVENSON. **3.** Like far-off music, voyaging the breeze COLERIDGE.

Voyageable (voi·ėdʒăb'l), *a.* 1819. [f. prec. + -ABLE.] That can be sailed over; navigable.

Voyager (voi·ėdʒəɹ). 1477. [– OFr. *veiaigier, voiagier* (mod. *voyageur*) f. *veiage*, etc. + *-ier* -ER[2] 2, or f. VOYAGE *v.* + -ER[1].] **1.** One who journeys; a traveller by land. **2.** One who goes upon or takes part in a voyage or voyages by sea; a navigator 1622.

‖**Voyageur** (vwayaʒö̆r). 1809. [Fr.; see prec.] In Canada, a man employed by the fur companies in carrying goods to and from the trading posts on the lakes and rivers; a Canadian boatman.

Vraic (vrēⁱk). 1610. [– Fr. dial. *vraic*, var. of *vrec, vrac* – MLG., Du. *wrak* WRACK *sb.*[2] 3. Cf. VAREC.] A seaweed found in the Channel Islands, used for fuel and manure.

‖**Vraisemblance** (vręsaṅblāṅs). 1831. [Fr., f. *vrai* true; see VERY, SEMBLANCE.] **1.** Verisimilitude. **2.** A representation, picture 1853.

Vril. 1871. [Arbitrary invention.] A mysterious force discovered by the imaginary people described in Bulwer-Lytton's *The Coming Race* (1871).

‖**Vrouw, vrow** (vrau). 1620. [Du. *vrouw* (= G. *frau*). Cf. FROW.] A (Dutch) woman, matron, goodwife.

Vug (vɒg). 1818. [– Cornish *vooga.*] *Cornish mining.* A cavity in a rock; a cave, a hollow. Hence **Vu·ggy** *a.* full of cavities.

Vulcan (vɒ·lkăn). 1513. [– L. *Vulcanus.*] **I. 1.** *Rom. Myth.* The god of fire and of metal-working, corresponding to the Greek Hephæstus; the lame son of Jupiter and Juno, and the husband of Venus. **b.** *fig.* A lame slow-moving person 1682. **2.** *transf.* A blacksmith; an iron-worker 1638. **3.** A planet supposed to have its orbit between the Sun and Mercury 1870.

2. His Sire, the blear-ey'd V. of a Shop DRYDEN.

II. †**1.** A volcano –1707. **2.** Fire; a fire. Chiefly *poet.* 1674.

Vulcanian (vɒlkēⁱ·niăn), *a.* 1602. [f. L. *Vulcanius*, f. *Vulcanus* VULCAN; see -IAN.] **1.** Of, pertaining to, characteristic of, or associated with Vulcan. **b.** Fashioned or forged by Vulcan 1603. **2.** Sprung from or related to Vulcan 1630. **3.** Volcanic 1656. **4.** = PLUTONIAN *a.* 2. 1840.

Vulcanic (vɒlkæ·nik), *a.* 1774. [In sense 1 – Fr. *vulcanique* = *volcanique*. In sense 2 f. L. *Vulcanus* VULCAN + -IC.] **1.** = VOLCANIC *a.* 2 b. **2.** (With initial capital.) Of, belonging to, or having the character of Vulcan 1807. **b.** Of or pertaining to fire; fiery 1866.

Vulcanicity (vɒlkăni·sĭti). 1873. [f. prec. + -ITY.] **1.** = VOLCANICITY. **2.** The study of volcanic action 1879.

Vulcanism (vɒ·lkăniz'm). 1877. [– Fr. *vulcanisme*, var. of *volcanisme.*] Volcanic action or condition.

Vulcanist (vɒ·lkănist). 1593. [In early use f. VULCAN + -IST. In sense 2 – Fr. *vulcaniste*, var. of *volcaniste.*] †**1.** One who works by fire; *spec.* an alchemist, a blacksmith –1603. **2.** = VOLCANIST 1. 1802.

Vulcanite (vɒ·lkănəit). 1836. [f. VULCAN + -ITE[1] 4a.] †**1.** Pyroxene –1840. **2.** A preparation of india-rubber and sulphur hardened by exposure to intense heat; ebonite 1860. **b.** *attrib.* Made of vulcanite 1866.

Vulcanization (vɒlkănəizēⁱ·ʃən). 1846. [f. next + -ATION.] The method or process of treating crude india-rubber with sulphur and subjecting it to intense heat, by means of which it is rendered more durable and made adaptable for various purposes.

Vulcanize (vɒ·lkănəiz), *v.* 1827. [f. VULCAN + -IZE.] **1.** *trans.* To commit to the flames (*rare*). **2.** To subject (india-rubber, etc.) to the process of vulcanization 1846. **3.** *intr.* To undergo vulcanization 1890. Hence **Vu·lcanizer,** one who or that which vulcanizes; *esp.* the apparatus used in vulcanizing india-rubber.

Vulcano·logy. 1858. [f. *vulcan-* as in VULCANIC, etc. + -LOGY.] The science or scientific study of volcanoes. So **Vulcanolo·gical** *a.* **Vulcano·logist.**

Vulgar (vɒ·lgăɹ), *sb.* late ME. [absol. use of next, depending on similar uses of med.L. *vulgaris (vulgare* vulgar tongue, vernacular, *vulgares* common people) and (O)Fr. (*le vulgaire* the common herd), etc.] †**1.** The common language of a country; the vernacular –1665. **2.** †**a.** *pl.* Persons belonging to the ordinary or common class of the community –1678. **b.** A person not reckoned as belonging to good society 1763. **3.** *The v.*, the common people 1590. †**4.** *pl.* Sentences or passages in English to be translated into Latin as a school-exercise –1612. †**5.** = VULGATE *sb.* 1 b. –1711.

1. Translations into the v. 1611. **2. a.** For these vile vulgars are extreamly proud CHAPMAN. **b.** A Mr. Brereton (a sad v.) 1767.

Vulgar (vɒ·lgăɹ), *a.* late ME. [– L. *vulgaris*, f. *vulgus* the common people; see -AR[1].] **I. 1.** Employed in common or ordinary reckoning of time, distance, etc.; esp., in later use, *v. era*, the ordinary Christian era. **b.** *V. fraction*: see FRACTION *sb.* 5. 1674. †**c.** *V. arithmetic*, ordinary arithmetic as opp. to *decimal* –1728. **2.** In common or general use; common, customary, ordinary. late ME. †**b.** Used to designate the Vulgate version of the Bible –1823. **3.** Of language or speech: Ordinary, vernacular. Now *arch.* 1513. **b.** Qualifying the name of the language 1483. **4.** Of words or names: Employed in ordinary speech; common, familiar 1676. **5.** Common or customary in respect of the use or understanding of language, words, or ideas 1553. **6.** Commonly current or prevalent, generally or widely disseminated, as a matter of knowledge, assertion, or opinion 1549. **7.** Of or pertaining to the common people 1597.

2. The v. Method of Grammar-Schools LOCKE. **b.** The v. Latine interpretation, of the olde Testament 1583. **3.** To be instructed in their Duties in the known or v. Tongue STEELE. **b.** This in v. English may be called a corner 1766. **5.** By a Month, in the v. way of speaking, is meant 30 Days 1696. **6.** The v. cry against the Dutch MACAULAY. This mode of interpreting Scripture is fatal to the v. notion of its verbal inspiration M. ARNOLD. One of the vulgarest fallacies of statecraft 1879. **7.** An habitation giddy and vnsure Hath he that buildeth on the v. heart SHAKS.

II. 1. Of persons: Belonging to the ordinary or common class in the community; plebeian 1530. **2.** Of the common or usual kind; of an ordinary commonplace character 1555. **3.** Of an ordinary unartificial type; not refined or advanced beyond the common 1580. †**4.** Common in respect of use or association –1602. **5.** Having a common and offensively mean character; coarsely commonplace; lacking in refinement or good taste. 1643. Now the only sense in ordinary colloq. use.

1. Superior to the v. Herd PRIOR. **2.** Copper mettall, adorned with v. precious stones 1617. Yet shall he mount,..Beyond the limits of a v. fate GRAY. **4.** Be thou familiar; but by no meanes v. SHAKS. **5.** The mean malice of the same V. Scribler MARVELL. A coarse, v. spirit KINGLAKE. His features were v., his lips thick and coarse 1846. The v. sort of trade which is carried on by lending money JOWETT. Mean little houses and v. streets 1905. Hence **Vu·lgar-ly** *adv.*, **-ness** (now *rare* or *Obs.*).

Vulgarian (vɒlgēᵊ·riăn), *a.* and *sb.* 1650. [f. prec. + -IAN.] **A.** *adj.* = VULGAR *a.* **B.** *sb.* A vulgar person; freq. a well-to-do or rich person of vulgar manners 1804.

Vulgarism (vɒ·lgăriz'm). 1644. [f. VULGAR *a.* + -ISM.] †**1.** A common or ordinary expression. **2.** A vulgar phrase or expression; a colloquialism of a low or unrefined character 1746. **3.** Vulgarity; a vulgar action, practice, habit, etc. 1749.

2. She leads him and his mother (to use a v.) a devil of a life MRS. SHELLEY.

Vulgarity (vɒlgæ·rĭti). 1579. [– late L. *vulgaritas* commonness, the mass or multitude, f. *vulgaris* + *-itas* -ITY; later, f. VULGAR + -ITY.] †**1.** The commonalty; the common people –1659. †**b.** The ordinary sort or run (*of* a class, etc.) –1681. †**2.** The quality of being usual, ordinary, or commonplace; an instance of this –1716. **3.** The quality of being vulgar, unrefined, or coarse; an instance of this 1774.

3. The ignorant zealotry and sordid v. of the leaders of the day! COLERIDGE.

Vulgarization (vɒlgărəizēⁱ·ʃən). 1656. [f. next + -ATION.] **1.** The action of making usual or common; the process of rendering familiar or popular. **2.** The action or process of rendering coarse or unrefined 1819.

Vulgarize (vɒ·lgărəiz), *v.* 1605. [f. VULGAR *a.* + -IZE.] **1.** *intr.* To act in a vulgar manner; to become vulgar. **2.** *trans.* To make common or popular; to reduce to the level of something usual or ordinary 1709. **3.** To make vulgar or commonplace; to debase, degrade 1756.

3. They vulgarise and degrade whatever is interesting or sacred to the mind HAZLITT.

Vulgate (vɒ·lgĕt), *a.* and *sb.* 1609. [– late L. *vulgata* (sc. *editio* edition, *lectio* reading), *vulgatus* (sc. *textus* text), fem. and masc. pa. pples. of L. *vulgare* make public or common, f. *vulgus* common people; see -ATE[2].] **A.** *adj.* **1.** In common use as a version of the Bible (or portion of this); occurring in one of these versions. **2.** Forming (part of) the common or usual version of a literary work 1861. **B.** *sb.* with *the*. **1. a.** The old Italic version of the Bible, preceding that of St. Jerome 1728. **b.** The Latin version of the Bible made by St. Jerome (completed in 405) 1728. **c.** The usual or received text or version of the Bible or of some portion of this 1815. **d.** with *a* and *pl.* An edition of the Vulgate 1865. **2.** The ordinary reading in a text; the ordinary text of a work or author 1861. **3.** Common or colloquial speech 1855.

‖**Vulgo** (vɒ·lgo), *adv.* 1623. [L. adv., abl. of *vulgus* (next).] Commonly, popularly.

‖**Vulgus**[1] (vɒ·lgŏs). 1687. [L.] The common people; the ordinary ruck.

‖**Vulgus**[2] (vɒ·lgŏs). 1857. [alt. of *vulgars* (VULGAR *sb.* 4), tr. mod.L. *vulgaria*, subst. use of n. pl. of L. *vulgaris*, used as the title of Latin–English phrase-books by J.

Anwykyll (1483), W. Horman (1519), and R. Whitington (1520); the ending was perh. assim. to GRADUS.] In some public schools, a short set of Latin verses on a given subject.

Vulnerable (vɒ·lnĕrăb'l), *a.* 1605. [– late L. *vulnerabilis* wounding, f. *vulnerare*; see VULNERATE *v.*, -ABLE.] †**1.** Having power to wound; wounding (*rare*) –1609. **2.** That may be wounded; susceptible of receiving wounds or physical injury 1605. **b.** *fig.* Open to attack or injury of a non-physical nature 1678. **3.** Of places, etc.: Open to attack or assault by armed forces; liable to be taken or entered in this way 1790. **b.** *Contract Bridge.* Of a side: That has won one game, and is therefore liable to heavier 'penalties' if its 'contract' is not fulfilled 1927.

1. To throw the V. and Ineuitable darte 1609. **2.** Let fall thy blade on v. Crests, I beare a charmed Life SHAKS. **b.** Yet even calumny is sagacious enough to discover and to attack the most v. part GIBBON. **3.** Every v. point was guarded 1800. She felt herself v. in Ireland, and on the Scottish border MOTLEY. Hence **Vulnerabi·lity, Vu·lnerableness,** the quality or state of being v. **Vu·lnerably** *adv.*

Vulnerary (vɒ·lnĕrări), *a.* and *sb.* 1599. [– L. *vulnerarius*, f. *vulnus, vulner-* wound; see -ARY.] **A.** *adj.* **1.** Useful in healing wounds; curative in respect of external injuries. **2.** Causing a wound or wounds; wounding 1615.

1. Let him drinck a vulnerarye potione 1599. The Flowers are v.; the Seed pectoral 1712.

B. *sb.* Any preparation, plant, or drug used in the cure of wounds 1601.

†**Vu·lnerate,** *v.* 1599. [– *vulnerat-*, pa. ppl. stem of L. *vulnerare*, f. *vulnus, vulner-* wound; see -ATE³.] *trans.* To wound. Also *Her.* –1750. So †**Vulnera·tion,** the action of wounding; the fact of being wounded –1688.

Vulpanser (vɒ·lpænsəɹ). 1706. [mod.L., f. *vulpes* fox + *anser* goose, after Gr. χηναλώπηξ.] *Ornith.* The sheldrake (*Anas tadorna*).

Vulpic (vɒ·lpik), *a.* 1886. [f. L. *vulpina* + -IC.] *Chem.* In *v. acid*, an acid occurring in the lichen *Cetraria vulpina*, and extracted from this or obtained artificially.

Vulpicidal (vɒlpisəi·dăl), *a.* Also **vulpe-.** 1826. [f. next + -AL¹ 1.] Committing or taking part in, connected with, or of the nature of vulpicide.

Vulpicide¹ (vɒ·lpisəid). Also **vulpe-.** 1826. [f. L. *vulpes* fox + -CIDE 1.] One who kills a fox otherwise than by hunting it with hounds.

Vu·lpicide². Also **vulpe-.** 1873. [f. as prec. + -CIDE 2.] The act of killing a fox otherwise than by hunting it with hounds.

Vulpine (vɒ·lpəin), *a.* 1628. [– L. *vulpinus*, f. *vulpes* fox; see -INE¹.] **1.** Characteristic of a fox; similar to that of a fox. **2.** Resembling a fox; *spec.* in *V. Opossum* or *Phalanger* 1789. **b.** *fig.* Cunning, sly 1830. **3.** Consisting of foxes 1849. **4.** Of or pertaining to a fox or foxes 1854. Hence **Vu·lpinism,** foxy character.

Vulpinite (vɒ·lpinəit). 1823. [f. *Vulpino*, (*Volpino*), near Bergamo in Lombardy + -ITE¹ 2 b.] *Min.* A granular variety of anhydrite.

Vulture (vɒ·ltiŭɹ, -tʃəɹ). late ME. [– AFr. *vultur*, OFr. *voltour* (mod. *vautour*) :– L. *vulturius*, f. *vultur, voltur.*] **1.** One of a number of large birds of prey of the order *Raptores* which feed almost entirely upon carrion and have the head and neck altogether or almost featherless. (The American vultures belong to different genera from those of the Old World.) **b.** With distinguishing terms 1575. **c.** *King of the vultures*, the king-v. (*Sarcorhamphus papa*) 1743. **2.** *fig.* Something which preys upon a person, the mind, etc., after the manner of a vulture; *esp.* a consuming or torturing passion 1582. **b.** A person of a vile and rapacious disposition 1603. **3.** Either of two northern constellations, dist. as the *falling v.* = LYRA 2, and *flying v.* = EAGLE *sb.* 4. 1638.

1. As when a Vultur on Imaus bred..flies toward the Springs Of Ganges or Hydaspes MILT. *attrib.* Victorious Wrong, with v. scream, Salutes the rising sun SHELLEY. **2.** The vulturs of the mind. Disdainful Anger, pallid Fear, And Shame GRAY. **b.** They sent for the vultures of physic—I was bled copiously 1828.

Vulturine (vɒ·ltiŭrəin), *a.* 1647. [– L. *vulturinus*, f. *vultur*; see prec., -INE¹.] **1.** Of or belonging to the vulture tribe; resembling a vulture. **2.** Of or pertaining to a vulture or vultures; characteristic of or like that of a vulture 1656.

2. The v. nose which smells a carrion in every rosebed KINGSLEY.

Vulturish (vɒ·ltiŭriʃ), *a.* 1826. [f. VULTURE *sb.* + -ISH¹.] Somewhat vulture-like.

Vulturous (vɒ·ltiŭrəs), *a.* 1623. [f. as prec. + -OUS.] Resembling a vulture or that of a vulture; ravenous.

‖**Vulva** (vɒ·lvă). 1548. [L. *vulva, volva* womb, matrix.] **1.** *Anat.* The external organ of generation in the female; *esp.* the opening or orifice of that organ. **2.** *Conch.* An impression behind the umbones of Venus-shells 1840. Hence **Vu·lval, Vu·lvar** *adjs.* of or belonging to the v.

‖**Vulvitis** (vɒlvəi·tis). 1859. [f. VULVA + -ITIS.] *Path.* Inflammation of the vulva.

Vulvo- (vɒ·lvo), comb. form on Gr. models (see -O-) of L. *vulva* VULVA, in *v.-uterine, -vaginal*, etc.

Vum (vɒm), *v.* *U.S. colloq.* 1785. [Alteration of Vow *v.*²] *intr.* To vow, swear.

W

W (dɒ·b'lˌyū), the 23rd letter of the modern English alphabet, is an addition to the ancient Roman alphabet, having originated from a ligatured doubling of the Roman letter represented by the U and V of modern alphabets. The English sound represented by *w*, a gutturally-modified bilabial voiced spirant, acoustically almost identical with the devocalised (*u*) or (u) which was the sound orig. expressed by the Roman U or V as a consonant-symbol, was at first usu. written *uu*; but in the 8th c. this sign began to be superseded by the Runic character ƿ (*wyn*, Kentish *wen*). In the 11th c. the ligatured form was introduced into England by Norman scribes, and ƿ finally went out of use about A.D. 1300.

In OE. the sound (w) occurred initially not only before vowels but also before (l) and (r); the combination *wl* became obs. in the 15th c., and *wr*, though still written, is now pronounced (r) in standard English. OE. had also the initial combination (hw): see WH.

The chief etymological sources of Eng. (w) are (1) OE. (w), repr. Indo-Eur. *w, ghʷ, kw, kʷ*; (2) ON. (w) of the same origin; (3) OFr. (w), later becoming (gw) and finally (g), except in north-eastern Fr. dialects. The sound also occurs in words of L. origin containing the combinations *qu* (kw) and *su* (sw), as *question, persuade*, and in a few Fr. words, as *reservoir* (-vwāɹ).

As a consonant symbol, the letter always denotes (w), but in a few words it has ceased to be pronounced (as in *answer, sword, two*, and in the combination *wr*). In the unstressed second element of a compound, (w) tends to be elided in colloquial speech; this pronunciation is in some words a mere vulgarism (marked by spellings like *allus* for *always*) but in *Norwich* and some other place-names in *-wich* and in the nautical terms *forward* (*forrard*), *gunwale* it is the only one regarded as correct.

In ME. a new (w) arose from the development of intervocalic or final (ɣ), as in *bowe* :– *boȝe* :– OE. *boga* BOW *sb.*¹; but this sound has not survived as a consonant, since every (w) after a stressed vowel became a *u*-glide, the terminal element of a diphthong. In modern spelling *aw, ew, ow* are phonetically equivalent to *au, eu, ou*, though *ow* now never stands for (ū) except in the surname Cowper; the choice between *u* and *w* is mainly arbitrary, but at the end of a word *w*, not *u*, is used almost invariably.

In south-eastern dialects (w) is regularly substituted for (v), and many writers of the first half of the 19th c. attribute to the Cockney dialect the habit of misusing (w) for (v), and also the (probably merely occasional) reverse substitution of (v) for (w) on all occasions.

A mispronunciation of (w) for (v), in some persons due to a physical defect, has sometimes been a fashionable affectation.

1. The letter, its sound or name 1465. **2.** The letter considered with regard to its shape 1798. **3.** Abbrevs. W. = various personal names, as William, Winifred; †W. (*Calendar*) = Whitsunday; W. = West (W.C., the West Central postal district of London); W (*Chem.*) = tungsten (mod.L. *wolframium*); W. (Electr.) = watt; W.C. = water-closet; W.I. = West Indies; W.S. (*Scotland*) = Writer to the Signet.

Wa, obs. f. WAY, WOE.

Wa', Sc. f. WALL *sb.*¹

Waac (wæk). 1917. A member of the *W*omen's *A*rmy *A*uxiliary *C*orps.

Wabble: see WOBBLE.

Wacke (wæ·kə). 1796. [– G. *wacke* (MHG. *wacke* large stone, OHG. *wacko* pebble), miner's word adopted by the geologist Werner.] *Geol.* A sandstone-like rock, resulting from the decomposition of basaltic rocks *in situ*.

Wad (wǫd), *sb.*¹ 1540. [Obscurely rel. to Du. *watten* (whence G. *watte*), Fr. *ouate*, It. *ovatta* padding, cotton-wool, Sp. *bata* dressing-gown, which has been referred to Arab. *baṭn* belly.] **1.** A bundle of hay or straw; esp. a small bundle of hay, peas, beans, etc., made at the time of cutting or reaping. Now *dial.* 1573. **2.** A small bundle of a soft, flexible material; esp. for use as a plug, pad, or rubber 1580. **b.** Something rolled up tightly, as a roll of banknotes. Chiefly *U.S.* 1778. †**3.** = WADDING 2. –1761. **4.** A plug of tow, cloth, etc., a disc of felt, etc., to retain the powder and shot in position in charging a gun or cartridge 1667.

1. Where he encradled was In simple cratch, wrapt in a w. of hay SPENSER.

Comb.: **w. hook,** (*a*) a spiral tool for withdrawing wads or charges from guns; (*b*) *Mining*, a tool 'for removing fragments from the bottom of deep boreholes'.

Wad (wǫd), *sb.*² 1614. [Of unkn. origin.] **1.** *local.* Plumbago or black lead. **2.** An impure earthy ore of manganese 1783.

Wad (wǫd), *v.* 1579. [f. WAD *sb.*¹] **I. 1.** To lay up (the cut haulm of beans, peas, etc.) in bundles 1677. **2.** To press (loose or fibrous material) into a small compass or a compact mass; *U.S.* to roll up tightly 1675. **II. 1.** To put a wad in (a gun, cartridge) 1579. **2.** To line, fill out, pad, as with wadding; to quilt 1759. **3.** To plug (the ears) with wads 1876.

2. You say your prayers in carved stalls wadded with velvet cushions THACKERAY. Hence **Wa·dded** *ppl. a.* lined with wadding.

Wadable, wadeable (wēⁱ·dăb'l), *a.* 1611. [f. WADE *v.* + -ABLE.] That can be waded.

Wadding (wǫ·diŋ), *vbl. sb.* 1627. [f. WAD *sb.* and *v.* + -ING¹.] The action of WAD *v.* Also, *concr.*: **1.** Any soft, pliable material from which gun-wads are made; also, a wad. **2.** Any loose fibrous material for use as a padding, stuffing, quilting, etc. Now chiefly, cotton wool formed into a fleecy layer. 1734.

2. The seat, with plenteous w. stuff'd COWPER.

Waddle (wǫ·d'l), *sb.* 1691. [f. next.] The action of waddling; a waddling gait.

That must be my sweet Duckling—I know her by her pretty W. in her Gate 1691.

Waddle (wǫ·d'l), *v.* 1592. [perh. frequent. of WADE *v.*; see -LE.] To walk with short steps, swaying alternately from one leg to the other, as is done by a stout short-legged person; also said of animals, esp. of ducks or geese. **b.** *transf.* said of inanimate things 1728. †**c.** *Stock Exch. slang.* To become a 'lame duck' (DUCK *sb.*¹ 6) –1834.

Next a fat Author wadled into view 1681. **b.** Like bias to the bowl, Which, as more pond'rous, made its aim more true, Obliquely wadling to the mark in view POPE.

Waddy (wǫ·di). *Austral.* 1814. [perh. native word, but possibly alteration of Eng. *wood.*] An aboriginal war club.

Wade (wēⁱd), *v.* [OE. *wadan* = OFris. *wada*, MDu., MLG. *waden*, OHG. *watan* (G. *waten* wk.), ON. *vaða* :– Gmc. **waðan* go, go through; f. IE. **wădh-*, repr. by L. *vādere* go, *vadare* wade through, *vadum* ford. The orig. str. inflexion became obs. in XVI.] †1. *intr.* To go, proceed (physically or in thought, etc.) –1709. 2. To walk through water or any liquid or soft substance which impedes motion ME. 3. *transf.* Of the sun or moon: To move (apparently) *through* clouds or mist. Chiefly *Sc.* and *north.* late ME. 4. *trans.* To walk through (water, etc.) ME. 5. To cause (a horse) to walk through water 1838.

1. Farewell,..Steepy wayes by which I waded 1648. I have sufficiently waded in this various Doctrine 1653. 2. A rill of water, through which we were compelled to w. as high as the knee BORROW. Phr. *To w. in,* to make a vigorous attack on one's opponent. *To w. into,* to assail energetically.

Wader (wēⁱ·dəɹ). 1673. [f. prec. + -ER¹.] 1. One who wades; *esp.* as the distinctive appellation of those long-legged birds (as the heron, plover, snipe, etc.) which wade in shallow water. 2. *pl.* Waterproof boots reaching above the knee, used by anglers, etc., for wading 1841.

Wadge, variant of WODGE.

‖**Wadi, wady** (wā·di). 1839. [Arab. *al-wādī.*] In some Arabic-speaking countries, a ravine or valley which in the rainy season becomes a watercourse; the stream running through such a ravine.

Wadmal (wǫ·dmăl). late ME. [– ON. *vaðmál,* prob. for **váðmál,* f. *váð* cloth, WEED *sb.*² + *mál* measure (see MEAL *sb.*³).] A kind of woollen cloth. a. In England, a coarse woollen material. *Obs.* exc. in *wadmiltilt.* b. *Hist.* A woollen fabric woven in Orkney and Shetland 1572. c. A woollen fabric worn by country people in Scandinavia and Iceland 1682.

Comb.: **wadmiltilt,** a kind of tarpaulin covering for artillery stores.

Wadset (wǫ·dset), *sb. Sc. obsol.* 1449. [f. next.] 1. *Sc. Law.* The conveyance of land in satisfaction of or as security for a debt, the debtor having the right to recover the lands on payment of the debt. (Cf. MORTGAGE *sb.*) 2. A thing pledged 1796.

Wa·dset, *v.* Chiefly *Sc. obsol.* ME. [Sc. form of ME. *wedset,* f. WED *sb.* + SET *v.*] To put in pledge; to pawn, mortgage. Hence **Wa·dsetter,** *Sc.* a mortgagor (*rare*); a mortgagee.

Wae, obs. or dial. form of WOE.

Wafer (wēⁱ·fəɹ), *sb.* late ME. [– AFr. *wafre* (whence AL. *wafra* XIII), var. of ONFr. *waufre,* (O)Fr. *gaufre* (see GOFFER) – MLG. *wāfel* WAFFLE.] 1. A very light thin crisp cake, baked between wafer-irons; formerly often eaten with wine, now chiefly with ices. 2. The thin disc of unleavened bread used at the Eucharist in the Western Church 1559. 3. A small disc of flour mixed with gum, or of gelatine or the like, used for sealing letters, attaching papers, or receiving the impression of a seal 1635. 4. *Med.* A cachet made of paste, for the administration of a powder 1887.

1. A womans oathes are wafers, breake with making 1625. 2. The adoration of the Sacrament, in the Countrey where they knocke and kneele to a W., is a popishe pollicie 1570.

Combs.: †**w.-cake** = sense 1, 2; also *fig.* as a type of fragility; **-iron,** an apparatus for baking wafers. Hence **Wa·fer** *v. trans.* to fasten or seal with a w. **Wa·ferer,** a maker or seller of wafers. **Wa·ferish, Wa·fery** *adjs.* like a w., extremely thin or fragile.

Wafery (wēⁱ·fəri), *sb.* 1455. [– AFr. *wafrie* (whence AL. *wafria* XV), f. *wafre* WAFER *sb.*] A room or building in which wafers or thin cakes are made; the department of the royal household occupied with the making of wafers.

Waff (waf), *v.* Chiefly *north.* 1513. [var. of WAVE *v.*] 1. *trans.* To cause (something) to move to and fro. b. *intr.* To wave to and fro; to flutter in the wind 1834. 2. To produce a current of air by waving something to and fro 1688.

Waffle (wǫ·f'l). *U.S.* 1808. [– Du. *wafel,* early *waefel* = MLG. *wāfel* (see WAFER).] A kind of batter-cake, baked in a waffle-iron, and eaten hot with butter or molasses.

Comb.: **w.-iron,** an iron utensil for baking waffles over a fire.

Waft (waft, wǫft), *sb.* 1542. [app. noun of action f. WAFT *v.*¹ and ².] 1. A taste or flavour, esp. an ill taste; a scent or odour passing through the air or carried on the breeze. 2. A current or rush of air; a breath of wind 1607. b. A sound carried by the breeze 1697. c. A puff (of smoke or vapour) 1896. †3. An act of transporting or a passage over water –1786. 4. An act of waving; a waving movement 1652. 5. *Naut.* A flag, etc. hoisted as a signal; the act of displaying such a signal 1613.

1. The Strongest Sort of Smells are best in a weft, a farre off BACON. 2. *fig.* Tost too and fro with wafts of appetite 1607. 5. We..saw her make a W. with her Antient, as a Signal for the Boat to come on Board DE FOE.

Waft (waft, wǫft), *v.*¹ 1513. [Back-formation f. WAFTER.] †1. *trans.* To convey –1670. 2. To convey safely by water; to carry *over* or *across* a river, sea, etc. Now *poet.* 1593. †b. *intr.* To sail *about, off,* etc. –1814. 3. *trans.* Of the wind: To propel (a vessel), convey (a navigator or passenger) safely 1653. 4. To carry or send (something, esp. a sound, scent, etc.) through the air or through space 1704. b. To carry in flight: said chiefly of angels 1718. c. *fig.* To transport, as by magic or in imagination 1781. 5. *intr.* To pass through the air or through space; to float upon the wind 1664. b. Of the breeze: To blow softly 1804. 6. *trans.* To drive or carry *away* by producing a current of air 1839.

2. Away with her, and w. her hence to France SHAKS. b. Satan..Wafts on the calmer wave by dubious light And like a weather beaten Vessel holds Gladly the Port MILT. 3. In vain you tell your parting Lover You wish fair winds may w. Him over PRIOR. 5. And now the Shouts w. near the Cittadel DRYDEN. Hence **Wa·ftage,** the action of wafting; conveyance across water (occas. the Styx) by ship or boat; passage through the air; the action or power of propulsion of the wind or breeze.

†**Waft,** *v.*² 1578. [app. alteration of WAFF *v.*] 1. *trans.* To wave (the hand or something held in the hand), esp. as a signal; to signal to (a person, etc.) thus –1719. b. To move (something) *aside* with a wave of the hand. COWPER. 2. To turn (the eyes) aside. SHAKS.

†**Wa·fter.** 1482. [In XV *waughter* – LG., Du. *wachter,* f. *wachten* guard.] 1. An armed vessel employed as a convoy –1670. 2. The commander of a convoying vessel –1622.

Wafture (wa·ftiŭɹ, wǫft-). 1601. [f. WAFT *v.*² and *v.*¹ + -URE.] 1. The action or an act of waving (the hand or something held in the hand). b. The waving (of a wing or wings) 1790. 2. The action of wafting; propulsion by air or current 1755.

1. You answer'd not, but with an angry wafter of your hand, Gaue signe to me to leaue you SHAKS.

Wag (wæg), *sb.*¹ 1553. [prob. shortening of †*waghalter* (of which †*wagstring* and †*wagwith* were vars.) one who is likely to swing in the hangman's noose, gallows-bird XVI. See WAG *v.*, HALTER *sb.*¹] †1. A mischievous boy (often as a term of endearment); in wider application, a youth, young man, 'fellow' –1672. 2. 'Any one ludicrously mischievous; a merry droll' (J.); a habitual joker 1584. 3. *To play (the) wag*: to play truant (*slang*) 1851.

1. But I prythee sweet Wag, shall there be Gallowes standing in England when thou art King? SHAKS. 2. Phr. *To play the wag*; Hauing wit enough..to plaie the wagge 1604.

Wag (wæg), *v.* [ME. *waggen,* iterative formation on OE. *wagian* totter, sway, ME. *waȝe, waw(e* = MLG., MDu. *wagen,* OHG. *wagōn,* ON. *vaga.*] I. *intr.* 1. To be in motion; to stir, move. Now *colloq.* (chiefly w. neg.) to stir, move one's limbs. 2. To oscillate, shake, or sway alternately in opposite directions. late ME. 3. Of a limb, etc.: To be moved briskly from side to side 1484. b. Of the tongue, †lips: To move briskly in animated talk: often with implication of foolish or indiscreet speech 1590. †4. To move, budge *from* a place –1730. 5. To go, depart, be off. Now *colloq.* 1594. b. To travel or make one's way 1684. 6. *slang.* To play truant 1848.

1. Driven to fly with her heavie burden with which she is scarce able to w. 1636. 3. It is a common proverbe, it is mery in hall when beardes wagges all 1550. 5. *Merry W.* I. iii. 7. b. They made a pretty good shift to wagg along BUNYAN. Provb. phr. *How the world wags,* how affairs are going. *To let the world w.* (*as it will*), to regard the course of events with unconcern.

II. *trans.* 1. To brandish (a weapon). Also, to wave (something) defiantly or as a signal, etc. *Obs.* exc. *joc.* ME. 2. To move (a limb or part of the body) to and fro, up and down, from side to side, etc.: usu. implying rapid and repeated movement. late ME. b. (Chiefly in neg. context.) To stir (a limb, finger, etc.) Now *colloq.* 1596. c. To shake (the head) ME. d. To move (the tongue, †lips) in animated speech: esp. with implication of indiscretion or malignity 1569. e. Of an animal: To move (its tail) from side to side. late ME.

1. While there's one Scottish hand that can w. a claymore, sir SCOTT. 2. b. I most positively declined to ask him or anyone to w. a finger to get me there 1898. d. Every one who owed him grudge would eagerly begin to w. his tongue 1871. Hence **Wag** *sb.*² an act of wagging; power or disposition to wag.

Wage (wēⁱdʒ), *sb.* ME. [– AFr., ONFr. *wage* (AL. *vagium, wagium*) = OFr. *guage,* (also mod.) *gage* = Gmc. **waðjam*; see GAGE *sb.*¹, and for the Gmc. collaterals, WED *v.*] †1. = GAGE *sb.*¹ 1 –1590. 2. A payment to a person for service rendered; now esp. the amount paid periodically for the labour or service of a workman or servant. Freq. *pl.* (after Fr. *gages*). ME. b. *fig.* Reward, recompense. late ME.

2. The produce of labour constitutes the natural recompence or wages of labour ADAM SMITH. b. The wagis of synne is deth WYCLIF *Rom.* 6:22

attrib. and *Comb.,* as *w.-earner, -slave*; **wage(s-fund,** *Pol. Econ.* that part of the capital of a community which is available for paying wages; **wage(s-sheet,** the list of wages paid by an employer of labour; **w.-worker** (*U.S.*), a wage-earner. Hence **Wa·geless** *a.* that does not earn or receive wages.

Wage (wēⁱdʒ), *v.* [– AFr. *wager,* ONFr. *wagier, waigier* = OFr. *guagier* (mod. *gager*), f. *guage*; see prec.] I. To gage, pledge. 1. *trans.* To give as a pledge or security –1585. 2. *spec.* in *Law.* Now only *Hist.* a. *To w. battle*: To pledge oneself to judicial combat 1568. b. *To w. one's* (or *the*) *law,* to defend an action by 'wager of law'; erron. to go to law 1455. †3. To put to hazard, venture; *esp.* to stake, wager, bet –1825.

3. I would w. a shilling that the pedestrian outstripped the equestrian travellers FIELDING. Their lives have been freely waged and wasted SCOTT.

II. †1. To engage or employ for wages; to hire, spec. for military service –1662. 2. To pay wages to. Now *rare* or *Obs.* late ME.

1. *fig.* I seem'd his Follower, not Partner; and He wadg'd me with his Countenance, as if I had bin Mercenary SHAKS.

III. To carry on (war, a contest) 1456. Hence **Waged** *ppl. a.* hired for or paid by wages; †of soldiers, mercenary.

‖**Wagenboom** (vā·ɣ'nbōm). *S. Afr.* Also **vaboom.** 1822. [Du., f. *wagen* WAGGON + *boom* tree.] A tree (*Protea grandiflora*), the wood of which is used for making waggon-wheels.

Wager (wēⁱ·dʒəɹ), *sb.* ME. [– AFr. *wageure,* f. *wager* WAGE *v.* In branch II perh. f. WAGE *v.* + -ER⁴.] I. 1. Something (esp. a sum of money) laid down and hazarded on the issue of an uncertain event; a stake. Now *rare* exc. in phr. *to lay, win, lose, a w.* 2. An agreement or contract under which each of the parties promises to give money or its equivalent to the other according to the issue of an uncertain event 1548. b. A contest for a prize 1615. 3. The subject of a bet or bets 1586.

1. Most men..Will back their own opinions with a w. BYRON. 2. Wee'le make a solemne w. on your cunnings SHAKS.

II. *Law* (now *Hist.*). a. *W. of law*: an offer to make oath of innocence of non-indebtedness, to be supported by the oaths of eleven compurgators 1521. b. *W. of battle*: a challenge by a defendant to decide his guilt or innocence by single combat 1625.

Comb.: **w.-boat,** a light racing sculling-boat used in contests between single scullers; **-insurance, -policy,** an insurance policy in which the insurer has no insurable interest in the thing insured.

Wager (wēⁱ·dʒəɹ), *v.* 1602. [f. prec.] 1. *trans.* To stake or hazard (something of value) on the issue of an uncertain event or on some question to be decided 1611. b. To venture on the issue of a contest 1819. **2.** *intr.* To offer or lay a wager, to make a bet 1602.

1. *Cymb.* v. v. 182. **2.** I'll w. that your stopping here to-night would please him better than it would please me DICKENS.

Waggery (wæ·gəri). 1594. [f. WAG *sb.*[1] + -ERY.] **1.** The action or disposition of a wag; drollery; in early use chiefly, practical joking. **2.** A waggish action or speech; in early use, a practical joke 1604.

1. So good a fellow, so full of fun and w.! 1824.

Waggish (wæ·giʃ), *a.* 1589. [f. as prec. + -ISH[1].] **1.** Of a person: Having the qualities of a wag. †Also, wanton, loose. 1590. **2.** Pertaining to or characteristic of a wag. Of an act, etc.: Done in a spirit of waggery. 1589. Hence **Wa·ggish-ly** *adv.*, **-ness.**

Waggle (wæ·g'l), *v.* 1586. [Frequentative of WAG *v.*; see -LE and cf. (M)LG., Du. *waggelen* stagger, totter, which may be the immed. source. Cf. WIGGLE.] **1.** *trans.* **a.** To move (anything held or fixed at one end) to and fro with short quick motions; *esp.* to shake (any movable part of the body) 1594. **b.** *absol. Golf.* To swing the club-head to and fro over the ball in the line of the intended stroke 1897. **2.** *intr.* **a.** With advs. or advb. expressions: To shake or wobble while in motion; to waddle 1611. **b.** Of things held or fixed at one end: To move backwards and forwards with short quick motions 1706.

1. She hinted, she sighed, she waggled her head at me THACKERAY. Hence **Wa·ggle** *sb.* the action or an act of waggling; *spec.* in *Golf.* **Wa·ggly** *a.* waggling, unsteady.

Waggon, wagon (wæ·gən), *sb.* 1523. [Early forms *wagan, wag(h)en* – Du. *wagen*, †*waghen* = OE. *wæġn* WAIN.] **1.** A strong four-wheeled vehicle designed for the transport of heavy goods. **b.** *transf.* The constellation CHARLES'S WAIN 1867. †**2.** A carriage of any kind for the conveyance of persons, their luggage, etc. Also *poet.* a triumphal car, car of state. –1638. **3.** An open four-wheeled vehicle built for carrying hay, corn, etc., consisting of a long body furnished with 'shellboards' 1573. **4.** A covered vehicle for the regular conveyance of commodities and passengers by road. (Now only *colonial* and *U.S.*) 1615. **5. a.** *Mining.* A truck used to convey minerals along the roadways of a mine or from the mine to the place of shipment 1649. **b.** An open truck or closed van for the transport of goods on a railway. †Formerly applied to the open carriages for conveying passengers at the lowest fares. 1756. **6.** *U.S.* A light four-wheeled vehicle used for various business purposes and for pleasure 1837. **7.** A covered four-wheeled vehicle used as a living-house by gipsies, travelling showmen, etc. 1851. **8.** Short for *dinner-w., tea-w.* 1906.

2. *Tit. A.* v. ii. 51. **4.** The two London waggons came in with sixteen and fourteen horses 1776.

Comb.: **w.-bed** *U.S.*, the body of a w.; the bottom of the body; **-ceiling,** a boarded roof of the Tudor period, of either semicircular or polygonal section; **-drift** *S. Afr.*, a passage for waggons across a river; **-head** *Arch.* a cylindrical ceiling, roof, or vault; **-load,** as much as a w. can carry; **-road,** a road for the passage of waggons; spec. in *Coal-mining*, a prepared road or railway for the haulage of waggons; **-train** *Mil.*, a train, collection, or service of transport waggons; also, a train of waggons used by colonial settlers; **-tree** = WAGENBOOM; **-vault** = *w.-head*; **-way** = *w.-road.* Hence **Wa·ggonful. Wa·ggonry,** (*rare*) conveyance or transport by w.

Waggon, wagon (wæ·gən), *v.* 1606. [f. prec.] **1.** *intr.* To travel in a waggon, transport goods by waggon. Chiefly *U.S.* **2.** *trans.* To put into a waggon for conveyance 1649. **3.** *U.S.* To transport (goods) in a waggon or waggons 1755.

Waggonage, wagonage (wæ·gənėdʒ). Now *U.S.* 1609. [f. WAGGON *sb.* or *v.* + -AGE.] Conveyance or transport by waggon; money paid for this.

Waggoner, wagoner[1] (wæ·gənəɹ). 1544. [– Du. *wagenaar*, †*waghenaer*; see WAGGON *sb.*, -ER[1].] **1.** One who has charge of a waggon as driver. **b.** Used as the designation of a particular class of farm servant, whose special duties include the driving of a waggon 1790. †**2.** The driver of a chariot, a charioteer; freq. applied to Phoebus or to Phaethon –1638. **3. a.** The northern constellation AURIGA 1607. †**b.** Applied to the constellation Boötes, viewed as the driver of 'Charles's Wain' –1697.

2. Her W., a smal gray-coated Gnat SHAKS. **3. b.** By this the Northerne wagoner had set His seuenfold teme behind the stedfast starre SPENSER.

Waggoner, wagoner[2] (wæ·gənəɹ). *Obs.* exc. *Hist.* 1687. [Anglicized form of the Du. surname *Waghenaer.*] *orig.* The atlas of charts, *Spieghel der Zeevaerdt*, published by Lucas Janssen Waghenaer in 1584. Hence *gen.* a book of charts for nautical use.

Waggonette, wagonette (wægəne·t). 1858. [f. WAGGON *sb.* + -ETTE.] A four-wheeled carriage, made open or with a removable cover and furnished with a seat or bench at each side facing inwards and with one or two seats arranged crosswise in front.

Wagnerian (vāgnī°·riăn), *a.* and *sb.* 1873. [-IAN.] **A.** *adj.* Of or pertaining to the German operatic composer Richard Wagner (1813–83), his music and theories of musical and dramatic composition. **B.** *sb.* An admirer or adherent of Wagner 1882. So **Wagnere·sque** *a.* resembling the style of Wagner. **Wa·gnerism,** the influence or cult of Wagner. **Wa·gnerist, Wa·gnerite** = B.

‖**Wagon-lit** (vagoṅlī). 1884. [Fr.; *wagon* railway coach + *lit* bed.] A sleeping coach on a Continental train.

Wagtail (wæ·gtē[i]l). 1510. [f. WAG *v.* + TAIL *sb.*[1]] **1.** A small bird belonging to the genus *Motacilla* or family *Motacillidæ*, so called from the continual characteristic wagging motion of the tail. In Great Britain chiefly applied to *M. lugubris*, the *pied w.*, called also *water w.* **b.** With qualifying words, indicating native country, colour, habits, etc., as *grey, Siberian, white, winter w.* 1668. **2.** Applied to other birds, e.g. *U.S.* a water-thrush, *Seiurus nævius* or *S. motacilla* 1868. †**3.** *transf.* A familiar or contemptuous epithet applied to a man or young woman; *esp.* a contemptuous term for a profligate or inconstant woman; hence, a harlot –1783.

1. I..had my spirit as full of life as a wagtayle 1604. **3.** *Lear* II. ii. 73.

Wahabi, Wahabee (wăhā·bi). 1807. [– Arab. *wahhābī*, f. *wahhāb.*] A follower of Abd-el-Wahhab, a Moslem reformer (1691–1787) whose sect flourishes in central Arabia.

Wahoo (wăhū·). 1860. [N. Amer. Indian.] The N. Amer. shrub *Euonymus atropurpureus.*

Waif (wē[i]f), *sb.*[1] (and *a.*) late ME. [– AFr. *waif, weif* (AL. *waivium, weyvium*), var. of ONFr. *gaif*, fem. *gaive*, prob. of Scand. origin (cf. ON. *veif* something wavering or flapping, rel. to *veifa* wave.] **A.** *sb.* **1.** *Law.* A piece of property which is found ownerless and which, if unclaimed within a fixed period after due notice given, falls to the lord of the manor; freq. in *w. and stray.* **2.** *transf.* and *fig.*, *esp.* a person who is without home or friends; one who lives uncared-for; an outcast; an unowned or neglected child 1624.

1. Prowling about the shore after the waifs of the storm KINGSLEY. **2.** They are the waifs and strays, and cast-aways of society 1862.

B. *attrib.* and as *adj.* (indicating lost property, a strayed animal, etc.) 1609.

A Home for W. Boys 1898.

Waif (wē[i]f), *sb.*[2] 1530. [perh. – ON. *veif*; see prec.] A small flag used as a signal. Now *Naut.*

Waif (wē[i]f), *sb.*[3] 1854. [Cf. Sc. *waff*, f. WAFT *v.*] Something borne or driven by the wind; a puff (of smoke), a streak (of cloud).

Wail (wē[i]l), *sb.* late ME. [f. next.] **1.** The action of wailing; esp. sound of lamentation for the dead. **2.** A cry of pain or grief, esp. if loud and prolonged 1863. **3.** *transf.* A sound resembling a cry of pain 1825.

2. *fig.* A long w. of anguish was rising from the persecuted all over France 1867. **3.** The w. Of plover, or the pipe of quail 1858.

Wail (wē[i]l), *v.* ME. [– ON. **weila* (cf. *veilan* wailing), f. *vei* int. = OE. *wā* WOE; the recorded ON. vb. is *væ̆la*, f. *væ̆* int.] **1.** *intr.* To express pain or sorrow by prolonged piteous cries. **b.** To cry piteously *for* (something desired) 1573. **2.** *transf.* Of birds, the wind, etc.: To give forth mournful sounds 1595. **3.** To utter persistent and bitter lamentations or complaints; to say lamentingly ME. **4.** To grieve bitterly. late ME. **5.** *trans.* To bewail, lament, deplore (sin, misfortune, suffering); to mourn bitterly for (the dead). Now *poet.* or *rhet.* late ME.

1. My Mother weeping: my Father wayling: my Sister crying SHAKS. **b.** I heard 'em w. for Bread GRAY. **3.** 'I wish I was dead,' wailed the poor creature 1894. **5.** Yet I must not,..but wayle his fall, Who I my selfe struck downe SHAKS. They neither esteemed him while he was liuing, nor wailed him at all, after that he was dead 1631. Hence **Wai·ler,** one who wails; *spec.* a professional mourner. **Wai·ling** *ppl. a.*, **-ly** *adv.*

Wailful (wē[i]·lfŭl), *a.* Chiefly *poet.* 1544. [f. WAIL *sb.* + -FUL.] **1.** Having the character of a wail, expressive of pain or sorrow; resembling a wail, plaintive. **2.** Full of lamentation, sorrowful 1579. **b.** *transf.* Of animals, etc.: Producing plaintive sounds 1818. †**3.** That is to be bewailed, lamentable –1620.

1. The w. sweetness of the violin 1899. **2. b.** A w. gnat KEATS. **3.** Woe and wailefull miserie SPENSER. Hence **Wai·lfully** *adv.*

Wailing (wē[i]·liŋ), *vbl. sb.* ME. [f. WAIL *v.* + -ING[1].] The action of the verb.

attrib.: **w. place, wall,** *spec.* in *Jews' W. Place*, part of the Solomonic wall in Jerusalem where the Jews assemble to lament the destruction of the Temple.

Wain (wē[i]n), *sb.* [OE. *wæġ(e)n, wǣn* waggon = OFris. *wein*, OLFrankish *reidiwagan*, (M)LG., Du. *wagen*, OHG. *wagan* (G. *wagen*), ON. *vagn* cart, barrow :– Gmc. **waȝnaz* or **weȝnaz* :– IE. **wogh*- **wegh*- carry; cf. WEIGH *v.*, WAY *sb.*] **1.** A large open vehicle, usu. four-wheeled, drawn by horses or oxen, and used for carrying heavy loads, esp. of agricultural produce. Now chiefly *dial.* or *poet.* **b.** *poet.* A car or chariot. Chiefly *fig.* or in mythological use. ME. **2.** In full CHARLES'S WAIN: The group of seven bright stars in the Great Bear. *Lesser W.*, the similar group of stars in the Little Bear. OE.

1. From the sun-burnt hay-field, homeward creeps The loaded w. COWPER. **b.** Fresche Appollo with his golden Wayn LYDG. Hence †**Wain** *v. trans.* to transport in a w. **Wai·ner,** the driver of a w. (*rare*). **Wai·nman,** a wainer; †the constellation Boötes. **Wai·nwright,** a waggon-builder.

Wainscot (wē[i]·nskǫt, we·n-), *sb.* ME. [– MLG. *wagenschot*, presumably f. *wagen* WAGGON + *schot* (?) boarding, planking (cf. *bokenschot* superior beechwood); the first element of this comp. is of doubtful identity.] **1.** A superior quality of foreign oak imported from Russia, Germany, and Holland, chiefly used for fine panel-work; logs, planks, or boarding of this oak. Now *techn.* **2.** Panel-work of oak or other wood, lining or used to line the walls of a room 1548. **3.** *attrib.* passing into *adj.* Made of wainscot; (of a room) lined with wainscot panelling; †resembling wainscot in hardness or colour 1575.

1. *fig.* This kind of men haue faces of wainscote 1630. Hence **Wai·nscot** *v. trans.* to line (a wall etc.) with wooden panel-work, or *transf.* with panels of other materials. **Wai·nscot(t)ing** *vbl. sb.* the action or process of lining a room with w.; *concr.* panelling of w.

Waist (wē[i]st). [Late ME. *wast, waast*, believed to repr. OE. **wæst*, for **weahst*, corresp. to ON. **wahstur*, Goth. *wahstus* growth, size, f. Gmc. **waxs*- grow, WAX *v.*[1]] **1.** The portion of the trunk of the human body that is between the ribs and the hip-bones; the middle section of the body, normally slender in comparison with the parts above and below it. **b.** Applied to the corresponding part in an insect 1713. **2.** †**a.** A girdle –1611. **b.** The part of a garment that covers the waist; the narrowed part of a garment corresponding to the narrowing of the body at the waist (but sometimes, in accordance with fashion, worn higher or lower than the position of this) 1650. **c.** The part of a garment between the shoulders and the narrowed part 1607. **d.** A bodice, blouse. Chiefly *U.S.* 1816. **3.** *Naut.* The middle part of the upper deck of a ship, between the quarter-deck and the forecastle 1495. **4.** Applied to the narrowed part of an object which is smaller in breadth or girth near the middle than at the extremities; esp. of a bell, a violin or similar instrument, a boot or shoe 1612. †**5.** Affectedly used for: Middle (of day or night) –1651.

1. Young Virgins..who..strive..by streight-lacing themselves, to attaine unto a wand-like smalnesse of waste 1650. **2. a.** *John* II. i. 217. **5.** *Ham.* I. ii. 198.

attrib. and *Comb.*: **w.-band,** a band fitting about the w., *esp.* one forming the upper part of a garment (skirt, pair of trousers, etc.) and serving to stiffen or maintain it; **-boat,** one carried in the w. of a ship; **-cloth,** †(*a*) *pl.* coloured cloths hung about the upper works of a ship as an adornment or to screen men stationed there; (*b*) a loin-cloth worn by natives of hot climates. Hence **Wai·sted** *a.* having a w. (usu. of specified size or form, as *long-w.*, *short-w.*). **Wai·ster,** a man stationed in the w. of a ship. **Wai·sting** *vbl. sb.* (*U.S.*) material for waists (sense 2 d). **Wai·stless** *a.*

Waistcoat (wē^{i}s(t)ko^{u}t; *colloq.* or *vulgar* we·skit, -kət). 1519. [f. prec. + COAT *sb.*] A garment covering the upper part of the body down to the waist: **1.** A garment (in early use often elaborate and costly) forming part of ordinary male attire, worn under a coat or jacket, and intended to be partly exposed to view when in wear. †**b.** A plainer and less costly garment, usu. of knitted wool, worn chiefly for additional warmth –1711. †**2.** A short (woollen) garment worn next the skin –1806. **3.** †**a.** A short garment, often elaborate and costly, worn by women about the upper part of the body (usu. underneath an outer gown, but so as to be seen) –1711. **b.** A woman's garment or dress-front designed in imitation of a man's waistcoat 1711. †**c.** A short (sleeveless) under-garment; a camisole –1785.

1. Phr. *Under one's w.*, in one's breast; We Irish have good warm hearts under our waistcoats 1859. *transf.* A woodpecker with black wings, a white w., and a crimson crest 1898. Hence **Wai·stcoated** *a.* **Waistcoatee·r,** a low-class prostitute (*Obs.* exc. *Hist.*). **Wai·stcoating,** a textile fabric made esp. for men's waistcoats.

Wait (wē^{i}t), *sb.* ME. [Partly – ONFr. *wait, wet, f. *waitier* (see WAIT *v.*) and *waite.* The word adopted from Fr. has coalesced with an Engl. formation on WAIT *v.*] **I.** The action of WAIT *v.* **1.** In phrases with the general sense: To lurk in ambush. **2. a.** (*Day's*) *w.*: the duty of keeping guard by day performed by the warders of the Tower 1694. **b.** The period of attendance at court of a lord- or lady-in-waiting 1884. **3.** The state or condition of waiting 1873. **4.** A period of waiting; spec. *Theatr.*, the time of waiting between the acts of a play, etc. 1855.

1. †*To sit in w.*; *to lie* (†*lay*) *in w.* *To lay w.*, †*lay one's w.*; They layed w. for him and murdered him 1597. **4.** The waits between the acts being very much longer than the acts themselves DICKENS.

II. A person who watches or waits. †**1.** A watchman; a scout, spy –1802. **2.** *pl.* †**a.** A small body of wind instrumentalists maintained by a city or town at the public charge –1764. **b.** A band of musicians and singers who perambulate the streets by night at Christmas and the New Year playing and singing carols, etc., for gratuities 1773.

1. At the last..he came to a Castel and there he herd the waytes vpon the wallys MALORY.

Wait (wē^{i}t), *v.* ME. [– ONFr. *waitier*, var. of OFr. *guaitier* (mod. *guetter* watch for) – Gmc. *waxtan, f. *wak- WAKE *v.*] †**1.** *trans.* To watch, observe constantly; esp. to watch with hostile intent; to spy upon, lie in wait for –1597. †**2.** *intr.* To keep watch, be watchful; to act as a watchman –1605. **3.** *trans.* To look forward to (esp. with desire or apprehension); to continue in expectation of. Now somewhat *rare* and superseded by AWAIT *v.* late ME. **b.** *intr.* Chiefly *to w. for* = 3. 1577. **c.** To remain for a time without something expected or promised 1550. **4.** *trans.* To continue stationary or quiescent, in expectation of (a person or thing, an event). Now *rare*; superseded by *w. for* and AWAIT *v.* late ME. **b.** *transf.* Of things: To remain in readiness for, to await 1745. **5.** *intr.* or *absol.* Often *to w. for.* **a.** To remain in a place, defer one's departure until something happens. late ME. **b.** To defer action until some event has taken place; to delay *to do* something 1633. **c.** Of a thing: = 4 b; also, to remain for a while neglected 1838. **d.** quasi-*trans.* To postpone (a meal) in expectation of the arrival of some one (*colloq.*) 1838. **6.** To be in readiness to receive orders; hence, to be in attendance as a servant. Chiefly const. *on.* 1526. **b.** To serve as an attendant at table 1568. †**c.** quasi-*trans.* *To w. attendance*: to remain in attendance –1607. †**7.** To attend or escort –1816.

2. Where be these Warders, that they w. not here? SHAKS. **3. c.** He would agree to w. for his money 1897. **4.** Phr. *To w. one's* (or *the*) *time, hour, opportunity*, etc., to defer action until a fitting season or opportunity presents itself. **b.** Better mansions w. the just, prepar'd above the sky 1745. **5. a.** The old adage, 'time and tide w. for no man' DICKENS. Phr. *To w. about*, to linger expectantly, 'hang about' where something is likely to happen (*colloq.*); also (chiefly *U.S.*) *to w. around.* *To w. on*, (*a*) *Sc.* to linger about a place; also, to linger in expectation of death; (*b*) *Hawking*, of a falcon, to soar in circles above the falconer, waiting for the game to be flushed. *To w. up*, to defer going to bed in expectation of some one or something. *To w. and see*, to wait the course of events (recently often used with allusion to Mr. H. H. Asquith's answers to many questions in parliament during the war of 1914–18). **d.** It's a trying thing waiting supper for lovers DICKENS. **6. b.** Phr. *To w. at table*; She had not prudence enough to hold her tongue before the servants, while they waited at table JANE AUSTEN.

With preps. **Wait for** —. (See 3 b, 5.) **W. of** —. †**a.** = *w. on* e, f. **b.** = *w. for.* Now *dial.* **W. on** or **upon** —. †**a.** To observe, watch; to lie in wait for. †**b.** To await, expect with desire or anxiety. †**c.** In Bible phrase, to place one's hope in (God). **d.** To attend as or in the manner of a servant to the personal requirements of. *To w. on hand and foot*: see HAND *sb.* **e.** To accompany on one's way (as a mark of respect or to render service or assistance): to escort (now *rare*). **f.** To call upon with the intention of showing respect, asking a favour, or the like. **g.** Of things: To accompany; to be associated with. *literary.*

Wai·t-a-bit. Also **wait-a-while.** 1785. [tr. S.Afr. Du. *wacht-een-beetje.*] Usu. *attrib.* with *thorn*, etc. Any of various S. African plants and shrubs, with joc. ref. to their hooked and clinging thorns; e.g. various species of *mimosa.* Also applied to plants of a similar character in other parts of the world.

Waiter (wē^{i}·təɹ). late ME. [f. WAIT *v.* + -ER^{1}.] **I.** †**1.** One who watches or is on the look-out –1687. **2.** †**a.** *Sc.* A watchman at the city gates –1818. **b.** A warder of the Tower of London 1551. **c.** An officer in the employ of the Customs. *Obs.* exc. *Hist.* 1473. **II.** One who waits expectant of some event, opportunity, etc. 1592.

W. upon Providence, †*time*, one who awaits the turn of events when required by duty or honour to come to a personal decision.

III. †**1.** One who visits or pays court to a superior –1611. †**2.** One whose office or privilege it is to attend upon a superior –1714. **3.** A man (rarely a woman) of lower rank employed as a household servant: *esp.* a servant whose particular duty it is to wait at table. *Obs.* exc. *U.S.* 1483. **4.** A man who waits upon the guests (*esp.* at table), at inns, eating-houses, etc. Also, a man hired for a similar purpose on special occasions in a private household. 1663.

2. Gentlemen Wayters of the Court 1630. Ministers about holy things, and waiters at God's altar 1711. **4.** The sum is six pounds, and be pleased to remember the Waiters 1663.

IV. 1. A salver, small tray 1738. †**2.** = DUMB-WAITER 2. –1861.

Waiting (wē^{i}·tiŋ), *vbl. sb.* ME. [-ING^{1}.] The action of WAIT *v.* in various senses, *esp.* **a.** Remaining stationary or quiescent in expectation of something. **b.** Attendance *upon* a superior; official attendance at court; one's period or term of such attendance 1560.

a. *In w.*, (predic.), remaining in one place or condition so as to be ready for some expected event; The coach was in w. 1760. **b.** See LADY-, LORD-*in-w.*

Comb.: **w. game,** applied to the tactics of a player who abstains from attempting to secure advantages in the earlier part of the game, with a view to more effective action at a later stage; also *fig.*; **w. list,** a list of persons waiting for appointments, etc.; **-room,** a room set apart for those who are obliged to wait (now *esp.* in a railway-station; also at a doctor's or dentist's).

Waiting (wē^{i}·tiŋ), *ppl. a.* 1538. [-ING^{2}.] **1.** That waits upon or attends to another. Often hyphened to the qualified sb., as in *w.-gentlewoman, -lady.* **2.** That waits for some person or thing; expectant 1654.

1. W.-maid, a superior female servant in personal attendance on a lady. **W.-woman** (now *arch.*), a female servant or personal attendant.

Waitress (wē^{i}·très). 1834. [f. WAITER + -ESS^{1}.] A woman who waits upon the guests at a hotel, restaurant, etc. Also, one hired for similar duties (on special occasions) in a private household.

Waive (wē^{i}v), *v.* Also freq. †**wave.** ME. [– AFr. *weyver* (whence AL. *waiviare, weiviare*) = var. of OFr. *gaiver, guesver* make a 'waif' of, abandon, f. *gaif* WAIF *sb.*^{1}] **1.** *trans. Law.* To outlaw (a woman). *Hist.* **2.** *Law.* To abandon (stolen goods). *Hist.* 1531. †**3.** To abandon, relinquish, desert, forsake –1817. **4. a.** *Law.* To relinquish (a right, claim, or contention) either by express declaration or by some intentional act which by law is equivalent to this 1469. **b.** To give up (a privilege, right, claim, etc.); to forbear to claim or demand 1625. **c.** To forbear persistence in (an action, etc.); to refrain from pressing (an objection, etc.) 1681. **d.** To dispense with (formality, ceremony, etiquette) 1781. **5.** To evade (doing something); to shun, avoid 1440. †**6.** To avoid acceptance of, reject (an offer, something offered); to decline (an honour) –1753. †**7.** To neglect, ignore, overlook –1713. **8.** To refrain from applying or enforcing (a rule, law); to make an exception to 1665. **9.** To abstain from entering upon (an action, discussion, etc.). Often with some notion of reserving for a future opportunity: To allow to stand over, put aside for the present. 1650. †**b.** To refrain from dealing with in statement or narrative –1742. ¶**10.** [Confused with WAVE *v.*] To put *aside, away, off* with or as with a wave of the hand 1832.

3. For this Reason, he hoped, the Hon. Gentleman would..wave the Motion he had made 1736. He once entertained a desire of taking a tour to Scythia; but waved it 1787. **4. b.** Congreve waved his title to dramatic reputation and desired to be considered only as a gentleman JOHNSON. **5.** The most effectual mode of solving all difficulties and waiving all discussions SCOTT. There appears to be no concealment on the part of the officers in thus waiving the exercise of their duty HAWTHORNE. **9. b.** To wave therefore a circumstance, which..is not greatly material FIELDING.

Waiver (wē^{i}·vəɹ). 1628. [– AFr. *weyver*, subst. use of *weyver* WAIVE *v.*; see -ER^{4}.] *Law.* The action or an act of waiving.

W. clause, a clause in the prospectus of a joint-stock company, by which the subscribers are made to contract themselves out of the provision of the Companies Act requiring the prospectus to contain certain particulars respecting the contracts made with the promoters.

Wakari (wăkā·ri). 1909. [Native name.] A S. Amer. monkey of the genus *Cacajao.*

Wake (wē^{i}k), *sb.*^{1} [OE. *wacu (only in *nihtwacu* night-watch), corresp. to MLG., MDu. *wake* (Du. *waak*), OHG. *wahha* (G. *wache*) watch, watching, wakefulness, ON. *vaka* watch, vigil, eve; rel. to WAKE *v.* Partly a new formation in ME. f. WAKE *v.* Sense 4 prob. – ON. *vaka* (cf. *Jónsvaka* St. John's Eve, Midsummer festivities.] **1.** The state of wakefulness, *esp.* during normal hours of sleep; †the act of awaking. *Obs.* exc. in *sleep and w.* †**2.** Abstinence from sleep practised as a religious observance: often coupled with *fasting.* Also, an instance of this. –1641. **3.** The watching (*esp.* by night) of relatives and friends beside the body of a dead person; the drinking, feasting, and other observances incidental to this. Now chiefly *Anglo-Irish* or with ref. to Irish custom. late ME. **4. a.** The vigil or eve of a festival and the observances belonging to this: also, a festival. *Obs.* exc. *dial.* 1550. **b.** The local annual festival of an English parish, observed (orig. on the feast of the patron saint of the church, but now usu. on some particular Sunday and the two or three days, or the week, following) as an occasion for making holiday, village sports, etc. Now only *dial.* (chiefly northern and west midland) and usu. *pl.* with sing. meaning and construction. ME.

1. Making such difference betwixt W. and Sleepe, As is the difference betwixt Day and Night SHAKS. **4. a.** Their Wakes and Vigils, in all riot and excesse of eating and drinking 1620. **b.** Every town had its fair, every village its w. THACKERAY. *transf.* The Wood-Nymphs..Their merry wakes and pastimes keep MILTON.

Wake (wēik), *sb.*[2] 1547. [prob. – MLG. *wake* – ON. **vaku* (*vǫk*), *vaka* hole or opening in ice, perh. orig. one made for itself by a vessel (whence also Du. *wak*, and G. *wake* hole or channel in ice); the sense 'vessel's track' is rare and local outside Eng.] **1.** The track left on the water's surface by a ship. **2.** *transf.* Anything compared to the wake of a vessel, as the disturbance caused by a body swimming in water, the air-currents behind a body in flight, etc. 1711. **3.** A course that a ship has taken, or is to take 1595.

1. The foaming w. far widening as we go CLOUGH. Phr. *To fetch* (*get, get into, have*) *the w. of* (a pursued vessel), to get so close to her as to be able to see and steer by her wake. **In the w. of:** (*a*) *Naut.*, immediately behind, and (properly) in the actual track made by a vessel; also *transf.*, in the direct line aft from (any object, etc. on a ship), in the line of sight of (an observed object), in the line of recoil of (a gun); (*b*) *transf.* and *fig.*, following close behind, in the train or track of; following as a result or consequence. **2.** Morn in the white w. of the morning star Came furrowing all the orient into gold TENNYSON. Outside it's merry in the wind's w. ROSSETTI. They had left a wide, discoloured w. upon the snow STEVENSON. **3.** They were..quite out of the w. of the Bermudas DE FOE.

Wake (wēik), *v.* Pa. t. **woke** (wōuk), **waked** (wēikt); pa. pple. **woken.** OE. [(i) OE. str. vb. **wacan* (only in pa. t. *wōc*), corresp. to ON. **vaca* (repr. by pa. pple. *vakinn* awake); (ii) OE. wk. vb. *wacian* = OFris. *wakia*, OS. *wakon*, OHG. *wahhēn*, *-ōn* (G. *wachen*) :– Gmc. **wakǣjan*, **wakōjan*, f. **wak-* (see also WATCH *v.*) :– IE. **wog-* **weg-* be lively or active (see VEGETABLE, VIGOUR, VIGIL).] **I.** To remain awake. **1.** *intr.* To be or remain awake. Also, to be still up and about (at night). Now *rare* exc. in pres. pple. and ppl. adj. †**b.** To sit up late for pleasure or revelry –1602. **c.** with advb. obj. *the night, a night* (poet). Also quasi-*trans.* with complement. 1480. **2.** To keep watch while others sleep, be on guard at night. Now only *dial.*, to sit up at night *with* a (sick) person. ME. **3.** To stay awake or pass the night in prayer; to keep vigil in church, in the presence of a corpse, etc. *Obs.* exc. *dial.* OE. **4.** *trans.* To watch or guard (one who sleeps, etc.); to keep watch upon or over. *Obs.* exc. *dial.* ME. **b.** To hold a wake over. Now *dial.* ME.

1. They cannot..be waking at this late hour DICKENS. Phr. *To keep* (†*hold*) *waking*, to prevent from sleeping; to keep watchful or on the alert; This confusion of my Thoughts kept me waking all Night DE FOE. **b.** I could w. a winter night For the sake o' somebody BURNS. **2.** You promised to w. with me the night before my wedding C. BRONTË.

II. To come out of the state of sleep or unconsciousness; to be roused from sleep. Often with *up*. ME. **b.** *transf.* and *fig.*, esp. of inanimate things. Of persons: To become animated, alert, or lively; to throw off lethargy. Of conditions, etc.: To be stirred up or aroused. 1450. **c.** *To w.* (*up*) *to*, to become conscious or aware of 1836.

I..have almost ever since woke at that hour and fancied it morning NEWMAN. **b.** W. vp, w. vp, & be stronge: O thou arme of the Lorde COVERDALE *Isa.* 51:9. Truths that w., To perish never WORDSW. The sleeping zephyrs woke 1814. **c.** The Church..had woke up to the sense of her true position 1863.

III. 1. *trans.* To rouse from sleep or unconsciousness. Also with *up*. late ME. **2.** To rouse to action, activity, or liveliness. Also with *up*. late ME. **3.** To raise, stir up (war, strife, woe, etc.); to arouse, excite (an activity, emotion); to evoke (a sound, echo, etc.) ME.

1. Phr. *To w. snakes* (U.S. slang), to cause trouble or disturbance. **2.** Hands, that..might have..wak'd to extasy the living lyre GRAY. **3.** To w. and wage a danger profitlesse SHAKS. Every melody that wakes the echoes 1889. Hence **Wa·king** *vbl. sb.*

‖**Wakeel** (wăkī·l). *India.* 1803. [var. of VAKEEL.] = VAKEEL 1, 2.

Wakeful (wēi·kfŭl), *a.* 1549. [f. WAKE *v.* + -FUL.] **1.** Keeping awake, esp. while others sleep. **2.** Habitually keeping awake; *fig.* keeping on the alert, vigilant, watchful 1550. **3.** Unable to sleep, restless 1675. **4.** Marked by want of sleep 1628. **5.** Said of dreams, or what is normally characteristic of sleep: Waking 1638. †**6.** Rousing (one) from sleep. MILT.

1. The w. Bird Sings darkling, and in shadiest Covert hid Tunes her nocturnal Note MILT. **2.** W. jealousy GRAY. **4.** They..pass the w. Night in Feasts and Play DRYDEN. **5.** In sort of w. swoon, perplex'd she lay KEATS. A w. doze TENNYSON. Hence **Wa·keful-ly** *adv.*, **-ness.**

Wakeman (wēi·kmæ̆n). *Obs.* exc. *arch.* ME. [f. WAKE *sb.*[1] + MAN *sb.* Survives as a surname.] A watchman.

In the borough of Ripon. **a.** In the 15–16th c. one of a class of municipal officers whose duties included attendance on the shrine of St. Wilfred. **b.** The title, until 1604, of the chief magistrate of the borough 1478.

Waken (wēi·k'n), *v.* [– ON. *vakna* wake up = OE. *wæcnan*, Goth. *gawaknan*, f. Gmc. **wak-* (see WAKE *v.*) + *-n-* suffix of inchoative verbs of state; see -EN[5].] **I.** *intr.* **1.** To cease to sleep; to become awake. Const. *from, out of*, etc. Also with *up*. ME. **b.** *transf.* and *fig.*, of inanimate things, etc. OE. **c.** Of a person: To become lively or animated 1825. †**2.** To remain awake, keep watch or vigil. BUNYAN.

1. An he sleeps in this damp hole, he'll maybe wauken nae mair SCOTT. **b.** It was then a great calm,..and afterwards the wind wakened 1634.

II. *trans.* **1.** To rouse (a person or animal) from sleep or unconsciousness. Also with *up*. ME. **2.** To rouse to activity, to stir up, excite. Also with *up*. late ME. **3.** To raise, stir up (war, wind, etc.); to kindle (fire, flame); to arouse, excite (an activity, emotion); to evoke (sound). ME. **4.** *Scots Law.* To revive (a process) which, after calling a summons, has been allowed to 'sleep' for a year and a day 1560.

1. *fig.* Your sleepie thoughts, Which here we w. to our Countries good SHAKS. **3.** Speake to that Lion Lord, w. his anger 1616. Hence **Wa·kened** (wēi·kənd), **Wa·kening** *ppl. adjs.* **Wa·kener**, a person or thing that wakens or arouses. **Wa·kening** *vbl. sb.*

Wakerife (wēi·krəif), *a. Sc.* and *north.* 1480. [f. WAKE *v.* + RIFE *a.*] Wakeful, vigilant.

Wa·ke-ro:bin. 1530. [Of unkn. origin.] **1.** The plant *Arum maculatum*, also commonly called cuckoo-pint, lords-and-ladies, etc. **2.** In U.S. applied (*a*) to certain araceous plants, esp. *Peltandra undulata*, arrow-arum; (*b*) to liliaceous plants of the genus *Trillium* 1711. **3.** In the West Indies and tropical America, applied to certain araceous plants of either of the genera *Anthurium* (tail-flower) and *Philodendron* 1864.

Waking (wēi·kiŋ), *ppl. a.* ME. [-ING[2].] **1.** That is awake or keeps watch. **2.** Pertaining to or characteristic of one who is awake 1567.

2. A w. vision WALPOLE.

‖**Wakon** (wēi·kən). 1778. [– Dakota *wakaŋ*, subst. use of adj. 'spiritual, sacred, consecrated'.] = MANITOU.

Walach, Wallach (wǫ·lăk). 1786. [See VLACH.] = VLACH.

Walachian, Wallachian (wǫlēi·kiăn), *sb.* and *a.* 1603. [f. *Walachia*, one of the two principalities which united to form the kingdom of Rumania + -AN.] **A.** *sb.* **1.** = prec. Also, a native of Walachia. **b.** A Walachian sheep 1837. **2.** The language spoken by the Walachians 1864. **B.** *adj.* Of or pertaining to Walachia or the Walachians 1791.

Walcheren (va·lχərən). 1810. [The name of a Dutch island at the mouth of the Scheldt.] Used in comb., as *W. ague, fever.*

Waldenses (wǫlde·nsīz), *sb. pl.* 1537. [– med.L. *Waldenses*, app. f. *Waldensis*, a var. form of the cognomen of Peter Waldo. Cf. VAUDOIS.] *Eccl. Hist.* The adherents of a religious sect which originated in the south of France about 1170 through the preaching of Peter Waldo. Hence **Walde·nsian** *a.* and *sb.* of or pertaining to (a member of) the sect of the W.

Wale (wēil), *sb.*[1] [Late OE. *walu* ridge of land, etc., weal = LG. *wāle* weal, ON. *vala* knuckle, rel. to WEAL *sb.*[2] Cf. CHANNEL *sb.*[2], GUNWALE.] **1.** = WEAL *sb.*[2] **2.** *Textile-manuf.* A ridge or raised line in a textile fabric; also *collect.* with epithet, as indicating the texture of a particular fabric 1583. **3.** *Naut.* **a.** The gunwale of a boat ME. **b.** *pl.* The horizontal planks or timbers, broader and thicker than the rest, which extend along a ship's sides, at different heights, from stem to stern; also *sing.*, each of such timbers ME. **4.** Each of the horizontal timbers connecting and bracing the piles of a dam 1754. **5.** *Basket-making.* Each of the horizontal bands round the body of a basket composed of rods intertwined as a finishing-off course 1907.

Comb.: **w.-piece** = 4; **w.-streak** = 3a. Hence **Wa·ling** = sense 4; also *collect.*

Wale (wēil) *sb.*[2] *Sc.* and *north.* ME. [– ON. *val*, corresp. to OHG. *wala* (G. *wahl*), f. Gmc. base **wal-* **wel-*; see WILL *v.*] **1.** The action or an act of choosing; choice. **2.** That which is chosen or selected as the best; the choicest individual kind, etc. 1513.

Wale (wēil) *v.*[1] *Sc.* and *north.* ME. [f. prec.] **1.** *trans.* To choose, select, pick out, sort. Also with *out, through.* **b.** *Coal-mining.* To clean (coal) by picking out the refuse by hand 1860. **2.** *intr.* To make choice. late ME.

1. He wales a portion with judicious care BURNS.

Wale (wēil), *v.*[2] late ME. [f. WALE *sb.*[1]] **1.** *trans.* To mark (the flesh) with wales or weals. **2.** To fasten or protect with a wale 1909. **3. a.** *Mil.* To weave or wattle (a gabion, hurdle) 1842. **b.** *Basket-making.* To intertwine (rods) in making a wale; to supply (a basket) with a wale 1907.

Waler (wēi·ləɹ). *India.* 1849. [f. *Wales* (for New South Wales) + -ER[1].] A horse imported from Australia, esp. from New South Wales.

Walhalla, var. VALHALLA.

‖**Wali** (wā·lī). 1811. [Arab. *al-wālī* ruler, commander.] = VALI.

Walk (wǫk), *sb.* late ME. [f. next.] **I.** Action or manner of walking. **1.** An act or spell of walking or going on foot from place to place; *esp.* a short journey on foot taken for exercise or pleasure. **2.** A procession, ceremonial perambulation. Now *dial.* 1563. **3.** An act of walking as dist. from other more rapid modes of locomotion on foot; the slowest gait of a horse, etc.; a walking pace 1601. **b.** A walking race 1887. **4.** A manner of walking; *esp.* the distinctive manner of walking of an individual 1656. **5.** *fig.* **a.** In religious language (see WALK *v.*[1] 4 a): Manner of behaviour, conduct of life 1586. †**b.** A course of conduct –1786.

1. Phr. *To take a* (*one's*) *w.* **3.** The horses were never suffered to go off a w. 1788. Exchanging her faltering w. for a good, swift, steady run DICKENS. **4.** By her graceful W., the Queen of Love is known DRYDEN.

II. Place or path for walking. †**1.** The usual place of walking, the haunt or resort (of a person or animal). late ME. **2.** A place prepared or set apart for walking. **a.** In a church or other public building: An ambulatory; a place where people can walk, as a cloister, aisle, etc.; *esp.* in the Royal Exchange, each of the portions of the ambulatory formerly allotted to different classes of merchants; designated by special names, as *East India, Virginia*, etc. *w.* 1530. **b.** An avenue bordered by trees 1596. **c.** A broad path in a garden or pleasure-ground. Also *U.S.*, a foot-walk, side-walk. 1533. **d.** A public promenade in or near a town 1840. **e.** The circular pavement on which a mill-horse walks in driving the mill 1734. **f.** A rope-walk 1794. **3.** A tract of forest land comprised in the circuit regularly perambulated by a superintending officer; a division of a forest placed in the charge of a forester, ranger, or keeper 1541. **b.** *West Indian.* A plantation 1793. **4. a.** A fowl-run 1538. **b.** The place in which a game-cock is kept 1615. **5.** Land, or a tract of land, used for the pasture of animals, esp. sheep. *Obs.* exc. in SHEEPWALK. 1549. **6.** A farm, cottage, etc. to which a young hound is sent in order to get accustomed to a variety of surroundings 1735. **7.** The 'beat' round, or circuit of an itinerating official, tradesman, etc. 1703. **8.** A distance or length of way to be walked; *esp.* such a distance as defined by a specified length of time spent in walking 1562. **9.** A course or circuit which may be chosen for walking 1617.

1. *transf.* Far as the solar w. or milky way POPE. 4. b. *Cock of the w.* (fig.), a person whose supremacy in his own circle is undisputed. 6. Phr. *At w. To put, send, to w.*; When about ten or twelve weeks old puppies are sent out to w. 1881. 8. 'A cheerful musical home in a select private family, residing within ten minutes' w. of'—everywhere DICKENS. 9. One of the sweetest walks in Matlock 1757.

III. Department of action. **1.** A department of action; a particular branch or variety of some specified activity 1759. **2.** *W. of life* (more rarely *w. in life*): **a.** A social grade, station of life, rank 1752. **b.** A trade, profession, or occupation 1848. **3.** = 2 a and b (*rare*) 1836.

3. Children in the lower ranks were beginning to choose chimney-sweeping as their particular walk DICKENS.

Comb.: **w.-clerk,** a banker's clerk whose duty it is to collect payment of cheques in a particular district. Hence **Wa·lksman,** an officer charged with the care of a certain length of the banks of a river or canal.

Walk (wǭk), *v.*[1] Pa. t. and pa. pple. **walked** (wǭkt). [OE. *wealcan* roll, toss, corresp. to (M)LG., (M)Du. *walken* full, work (felt), cudgel, drub, ON. *valka* drag about, torment, refl. wallow; f. Gmc. **walk-*, of unkn. origin.] **I.** *intr.* †**1.** To go from place to place; to journey, wander. Also of things, to circulate, pass from hand to hand; to move, be in motion. –1815. †**2.** To go about in public, live, move (in a place or region) –1559. **b.** With complementary adj. or phrase: = Go *v.* I. 6. Now *rare* or *Obs.* 1604. **3.** To travel or move about on foot ME. **b.** with cognate obj.; also with advb. accus. of distance. 1460. **c.** In express or implied contrast with *ride*. Also colloq. *to w. it*. 1668. **d.** More explicitly, *to w. on foot*. late ME. **e.** With advs. *in, up*, and const. *into*, the use of this vb. instead of the indefinite *come* or *go* sometimes implies an additional notion of absence of pausing or hesitation ME. **f.** To move about or go from place to place on foot for the sake of exercise, pleasure, or pastime; to take a walk or walks ME. **g.** *To w. (out) with, to w. together*: in rustic use, said of a young man and young woman 'keeping company' with a view to marriage 1876. **h.** quasi-*trans.* with complementary adj., adv., or phrase 1669. **i.** *Naut.* (*trans.*) To turn (the capstan) by walking round it; to haul by walking round the capstan or by walking away with a rope 1836. **4.** *fig. intr.* **a.** Chiefly in religious use, after Bible examples: To conduct oneself, behave (ill or well, etc.). *To w. with God* (Gen. 5:22), interpreted to mean 'to lead a godly life', or to have intimate communion with God. 1526. **b.** To direct one's conduct *by, after* a rule, etc. 1581. **5. a.** Of human beings or other bipeds: to progress by alternate movements of the legs, so that one of the feet is always on the ground 1762. **b.** Of a horse or other quadruped: To advance by a gait in which there are always two feet on the ground, and during a part of the step three or (in slow walking) four feet: opp. to *amble, trot, gallop*, etc. 1681. **c.** *trans.* To go through (a dance) at a walk 1810. **6.** *intr.* To go away. Now only *colloq.*, to go away perforce; also *slang*, to die. 1460. †**b.** *transf.* Of animals and things: To be stolen, carried off; to be got rid of –1611. **c.** With *off*: To depart suddenly or abruptly. *To w. off with*, to carry away as a prize or plunder. 1604. **7.** Of a ghost, fiend, etc.: To be seen walking, to appear. Of a dead person: To 'come back' as a ghost. ME. **8.** To walk about or perform other actions as a somnambulist. *rare* exc. in phr. *to w. in one's sleep*. 1605. **9.** To go on foot in procession; also, to go in a regular circuit or to and fro over a prescribed track in the course of official duty. Also with cognate accus., as in *to w. one's round(s*, etc., said esp. of a sentinel. 1594. **b.** *Oxford University.* (*a*) Of a proctor or pro-proctor: To perambulate the streets at night, in the exercise of his function. (*b*) Of the proctors: To march to and fro in the Convocation House, as part of the ceremony of conferring degrees. 1530. **10. W. into —.** (*slang* or *colloq.*) **a.** To make a vigorous attack upon 1794. **b.** To assail with invective or reproof 1859. **c.** To eat or drink heartily of 1837. **d.** To make large inroads on (one's stock of anything) 1859.

1. Ther was brybes walking, money makynge, makynge of handes LATIMER. Ever as she went, her toung did walke In foule reproch SPENSER. A wonderfull erroneous obseruation that walketh about BACON. 3. *To w. with* (a stick), to use it as a partial support in walking. *To w. on crutches*, to support oneself by crutches in walking. *To w. upon air*, to be in an exultant state of mind. c. We alighted and walked up all the hills DICKENS. e. 'Will you w. into my parlour?' said the Spider to the Fly 1834. g. A certain young woman I'm walking out with 1902. i. The men..walked the anchor up to the bows MARRYAT. j. *To w. out*, to go on strike. 5. a. *To w. through* (a dance) = sense 5 c. b. *To w. over* (*the course*), of a horse, to go over the course at a walking pace, as as to be accounted the winner of a race in which there is no opposition; *transf.* and *fig.* to win a race or other contest with little or no effort. *To w. round* (U.S. colloq.), to beat easily. 7. I am thy Father's Spirit Doom'd for a certaine terme to walke the night SHAKS. Everybody knows that it's an awful thing for a dead man to *w.* 1882. 10. b. He walks into us..as if it were our faults 1861. c. He..with most voracious swallow Walks into my mutton chops 1871.

II. *trans.* **1.** To go over or traverse on foot ME. **b.** To walk on or along (a road) 1530. **2.** To walk about upon (the ground, etc.). So *Naut.*, of an officer, *to w. the deck, the quarter-deck*. 1634. **3.** To walk along (a line); to perambulate (a boundary) 1602. †**4.** To attend, frequent (the exchange, a market) –1750. **b.** *To w. the hospitals* (*a hospital*), to receive regular clinical instruction and assist in surgical work 1781. **5.** *Shooting.* To start (game-birds) by beating up the ground with pointers or setters. Usu. *to w. up*. 1873.

1. b. *To w. the street(s*: see STREET *sb.* 2. 2. The dear might of him, that walk'd the waves MILT. *To w. the plank*: see PLANK *sb.* 3. *To w. the chalk* (slang), to walk along a chalked line (as a proof of being sober). *To w. one's chalks* (slang): see CHALK *sb.*

III. Causative uses. **1.** To lead, drive, or ride (a horse) at a walk; to exercise (a horse, dog) by causing it to walk 1470. **2.** To cause or induce (a person) to walk; to conduct on a walk 1630. **b.** To force to walk (by holding the arms or pushing before one). Also, to help to walk. 1809. **3. a.** To take charge of (a puppy) 'at walk' 1845. **b.** To keep (a game-cock) in a 'walk' 1854. **4.** *Cribbage.* To cheat by moving one's own pegs forward, or those of one's opponents back 1803.

Comb.: **w.-around** (*a*) *Colonial*, a kind of rotary mill turned by oxen; (*b*) *U.S.*, among Negroes, a dance in which the performers go round in a large circle; music for such a dance; **-mill,** a mechanical contrivance, the driving power of which is furnished by the walking of a horse; **-on** *Theatr.*, a walking-on part (see WALKING *vbl. sb.* 1 a); **-out,** a strike of workmen.

Walk (wǭk), *v.*[2] Now only *dial.* and *Hist.* late ME. [– (M)LG., (M)Du. *walken* (see prec.); perh. partly from WALKER *sb.*[2]] *trans.* = FULL *v.*[2] 1.

Comb.: **w.-mill** a fulling mill (now *rare*). Hence **Walked** (wǭkt) *ppl. a.* (*a*) of cloth, etc., fulled; (*b*) felted, matted (now *dial.* and *Hist.*).

Walker (wǭ·kəɹ), *sb.*[1] late ME. [f. WALK *v.*[1] + -ER[1].] **1.** One who walks; *esp.* with the construction of the vb. in various senses, e.g. One who walks *in* (a place), *about*. **2.** A person (or animal) that journeys or goes about on foot 1578. **b.** One who takes part in walking-matches 1778. **3.** One who acts in a particular manner or pursues a certain line of conduct. Now *rare* or *Obs.* 1680. **4.** *Sport.* One who 'walks up' partridges 1913. **5.** A bird, insect, etc. characterized by walking, as dist. from other modes of progression. Also, a stick-insect. 1658.

2. She was an excellent w. 1880. 3. Cast out of the..Communion of the Faithful as disorderly Walkers 1716.

Walker (wǭkəɹ), *sb.*[2] *Obs.* or *dial.* [OE. *wealcere*, (M)LG., (M)Du. *walker*, OHG. *walkāri* (G. *walker*); see WALK *v.*[1], -ER[1].] One who fulls cloth, a fuller.

attrib. **walker('s earth, clay** (now *dial.*) = FULLER'S *earth.*

Walker (wǭ·kəɹ), *int.* More fully **Hookey Walker.** 1811. [Always written with initial capital; prob. a use of the surname *Walker*.] An exclamation expressive of incredulity.

Walkerite[1] (wǭ·kərəit). 1830. [f. the proper name *Walker* + -ITE[1] 1.] A member of an extreme Calvinistic sect founded in Ireland by John Walker (1768–1833).

Walkerite[2] (wǭ·kərəit). [Named by Heddle 1880, after Prof. John *Walker* (1731–1803) who discovered it; see -ITE[1] 2 b.] *Min.* = PECTOLITE.

Walking (wǭ·kiŋ), *vbl. sb.* late ME. [f. WALK *v.*[1] + -ING[1].] **1.** The action or an act of the verb. **a.** The action of moving on the feet at any pace short of breaking into a run or trot. Also, the manner or style in which a person walks. **b.** *fig.* Manner of conducting or behaving oneself. late ME. **c.** The action of a somnambulist 1605. **d.** The action of appearing as a ghost 1727. **2.** A walk or journey on foot, the distance covered in a certain time 1542. **3.** The condition of a path or road for walking on 1631.

1. a. *attrib.* The 'w.-out' habits of the servant girls 1905. *W.-on part* Theatr., one in which the actor is required only to 'walk on' to the stage, without speaking. 3. Empty heads and tongues a-talking Make the rough road easy w. HOUSMAN.

attrib. and *Comb.*, as *w.-match, -race, -shoe, -tour*; **w.-day,** a day on which school-children walk in procession; **-rapier, -sword,** (now *Hist.*) a rapier or sword such as was worn by gentlemen in civil life.

Walking (wǭ·kiŋ), *ppl. a.* late ME. [-ING[2].] **1.** Moving about from place to place, travelling; †vagrant. Now only with implication of sense 2. **b.** Going about from place to place 1663. **2.** That travels or goes about on foot at a walk 1697. **3.** Theatr. *W. gentleman*, an actor who plays a 'walking-on' part. Similarly *w. lady*. 1815. **4.** That goes about in the semblance of a human being. Often in fig. or similative expressions; e.g. *w. corpse, dictionary, encyclopædia, library* 1605. **5.** Of a spectre: That 'walks' or appears 1607. **6.** Of a bird: That walks, as dist. from one that hops. *W. tyrant*, a South Amer. flycatcher, *Machetornis rixosa*. 1837. **7.** *W. fern*, a club-moss 1829.

Comb.: **w.-leaf,** (*a*) an Amer. evergreen fern *Camptosorus rhizophyllus*; (*b*) a phasmid insect belonging to the genus *Phyllium* or some related genus; also *w.-leaf insect*.

Wa·lking-stick. 1580. [WALKING *vbl. sb.*] **1.** A stick or short staff carried in the hand when walking. **2.** = *Stick-insect* (STICK *sb.*[1]). Also *w.-s. insect*. 1760.

2. The walking-sticks..resembling the twig upon which they rest 1885.

Comb.: **w. palm,** an Australian palm, *Bacularia monostachya*, used for making walking-sticks.

Wa·lk-o:ver. 1838. [f. phr. *walk over*; see WALK *v.*[1] I. 5 b.] A race in which through absence of competitors the winner has merely to 'walk over'; in extended use, a contest in which through the inferiority of his competitors the winner has virtually no opposition. **b.** *transf.* Anything that is easy to accomplish 1902.

Walksman. See WALK *sb.*

Walkyrie (wǫlki·ri). [repr. OE. *wælcyriġe*, f. *wæl* WALE *sb.*[2] + **cur-*, ablaut-root of *ċēosan* CHOOSE *v.*] = VALKYRIE.

Wall (wǭl), *sb.*[1] [OE. *wall* (WS. *weall*), corresp. to OFris., OS., (M)LG., (M)Du. *wal* – L. *vallum* rampart, orig. palisading, f. *vallus* stake.] **I. 1.** A rampart of earth, stone, or other material constructed for defensive purposes. **b.** An embankment to hold back the water of a river or the sea ME. **2.** A defensive structure enclosing a city, castle, etc. Chiefly *pl.*, fortifications. OE. **b.** *Her.* A representation of an embattled wall used as a bearing 1688. **3.** *fig.* **a.** Applied to a person or thing that serves as a defence. late ME. **b.** Applied to the sea, the navy, or shipping (as Britain's external defence). late ME. **4.** An enclosing structure composed of bricks, stones, or similar materials laid in courses; each of the sides and vertical divisions of a building; an enclosing structure round a garden, yard, or other property; also, each of the portions between the angles of such a structure OE. **b.** The inner side of a footpath or pavement; the side next the wall 1606. **c.** (*a*) In phr. *at the w.*, designating a species of football peculiar to Eton played against a wall. (*b*) Applied to each of the players who form the 'bully' or scrimmage against the wall. 1864. **5.** *fig.* Something which is a barrier or impediment to intellectual, moral, spiritual or social union or intercourse ME. **6.** A wall considered with regard to its surface. **a.** The interior wall of an apartment OE. **b.** A garden- or house-wall upon which fruit-trees and flowering trees are trained 1699.

1. The Great W. of China 1850. **2.** *Within the walls*: within the ancient boundaries (of a city) as dist. from the suburbs; hence *fig.* within the limits (of the Church, †Christendom, etc.) **3. a.** It is Aiax the strong, Who is best hope, defence and w., that to the Greeks belong 1581. **b.** *Wooden walls*: see WOODEN *a.* **4.** Four gray walls, and four gray towers, Overlook a space of flowers TENNYSON. *Hollow w.*, a w. built with an interior cavity or composed of hollow bricks. Prov. *Walls have ears*: see EAR *sb.*[1] 4. **b.** A rev'rend sire..Shov'd from the w. perhaps, or rudely press'd By his own son POPE. **5.** A w. of tradition, which may not be broken through RUSKIN. **6. a.** In the mean time, the Preacher speaks to the bare walls 1639. **b.** Grapes, long ling'ring on my only w. POPE. *fig.* Women grow on the sunny side of the w. TROLLOPE.

II. *transf.* **1.** Something that resembles a wall in appearance; a perpendicular surface forming an enclosure or barrier 1697. **2.** Something that confines or encloses; chiefly *pl.*, the containing sides of a vessel, the vertical sides of a tent, and the like 1594. **3.** *Mining.* The coating or crust of a lode or vein; also, the side of a mine next to this 1728. **4.** *Engraving.* A border of wax surrounding the plate, to contain the aquafortis 1797. **5.** *Anat.* and *Zool.* The membranous investment or lining tissue (of any organ or cavity of the body, or of a tumour or the like). Also *Bot.* the cellulose membrane (of a cell). 1677. **b.** The outer horny covering of the foot of a horse 1830.

1. The black w. of forest 1859. A w. of water 1859. **2.** Within this w. of flesh There is a soule counts thee her Creditor SHAKS.

Phrases: *To go to the w.* (†*walls*): (*a*) to give way, succumb in a conflict or struggle; (*b*) of a business, etc., to give precedence (to something else); (*c*) to fail in business. Prov. *The weakest goes* (*must go*) *to the w. To send to the w.*, to thrust aside into a position of neglect. *To drive* (*push*) *to the w.*, to drive to the last extremity. *With one's back to the w.*, hard-pressed, struggling against odds. *To give a person the w.*, to allow a person the right or privilege of walking next the w. as the cleaner and safer side of a pavement, etc.; so *to have, take, the w.* (*of* a person). †*To lie* (*lay*) *by the w.* (or *walls*), to lie on one side, remain idle or useless; of a ship, to lie up (in dock or harbour). (*To be able*) *to see*, etc. *through* or *into a* (*brick, mud, stone*) *w.*, to have great keenness of perception or understanding. *To turn one's face to the w.*, said of a person on his deathbed conscious of the approach of the end (app. after 2 Kings 20: 2, Isa. 38: 2).

attrib. and *Comb.*: **w. box,** a postal collecting box affixed to a w. as dist. from a pillar-box; **-fruit,** fruit grown against a w.; **-game,** the Eton game of football played 'at the w.'; **-plate,** a timber placed horizontally on or in a w., to form a support for joists or rafters; **-stone,** a stone for building; also, masonry; stone suitable for building. **b.** In the names of animals frequenting or living in walls: **-bird** (*dial.*), the Spotted Flycatcher; **-brown,** a common British butterfly *Satyrus megæra.*

Wall (wǫl), *sb.*[2] 1834. *Naut.* Short for WALL-KNOT. Hence **Wall** *v.*[4] *trans.* to make a wall-knot on (a rope).

Wall (wǭl), *sb.*[3] 1884. = LABLAB.

Wall, *v.*[1] *Obs.* exc. *dial.* [OE. *weallan* (intr.) corresp. to OFris. *walla*, OS., OHG. *wallan* boil, gush forth :- WGmc. **wallan.* The trans. use does not occur in OE., and may be descended from OE. *wællan* WELL *v.*] †To boil -1450. **b.** *absol.* To boil brine in salt-making 1600. Hence **Wa·ller**[2], in the Cheshire salt-works, a brine-boiler.

Wall (wǭl), *v.*[2] [OE. **weallian* (only in pa. pple. *ġeweallod*), f. *weall* WALL *sb.*[1]] **1.** *trans.* To furnish with a wall or walls. Also with *about, round, up,* etc. **b.** To line (a well, cistern) with a wall 1707. **2.** *transf.* and *fig.* To enclose, defend, bound, or divide, as with a wall, or as a wall does. late ME. **b.** To form the sides of (a room) like walls: to line the walls of (an apartment) 1832. **3.** To shut up (a person or thing) within walls; to build *up* or entomb in a wall 1530. **4.** To close (a gate or other aperture) with or as with a wall. Chiefly with *up.* 1503. **5.** To build (stone) into a wall 1621. **6.** *absol.* or *intr.* To construct a wall or walls 1588.

1. *To w. in*, to enclose with a wall. *To w. off, out*, to shut off or out with a wall. **2.** A Lady wal'd about with Diamonds SHAKS. A canyon..was here walled across by a dump of rolling stones STEVENSON. **b.** The rest of the room was walled from the floor to the roof with books 1832. **4.** Some of the windows had been walled up DICKENS.

Wall (wǭl), *v.*[3] Now only *U.S.* [MSc. *wawle* :- **waȝle*, rel. to the first element in WALL-EYED.] *trans.* To roll (the eyes). Also *absol.* and *intr.* of the eyes.

Wallaba (wǫ·lăbă). 1825. [perh. – native name.] A large South Amer. timber-tree, *Eperua falcata.*

Wallaby (wǫ·lăbi). 1828. [Native Australian *wolabă.*] A kangaroo belonging to any of the small species of the genus *Macropus* or of the genera *Onychogale* (Nail-tailed W.), *Petrogale* (Rock W.), *Lagorchestes* (Hare W.) and *Lagostrophus* (Banded W.). **b.** *pl.* Australians 1908.

On the w. track, hence *on the w.*, on tramp.

Wallah (wǫ·lā). *India.* 1776. [– Hindi *-wālā*, suffix, expressing relation, forming adjs. and sbs.; Europeans have commonly apprehended it as a sb. = 'man', 'fellow'.] **a.** In certain Hindi or Hindustani words adopted in Anglo-Indian use, as *howdah-w.*, an elephant accustomed to carry a howdah, *jungle-w.*, man of the jungle, *lootie-w.*, a member of a band of looties or robbers, *punkah-w.*, etc. **b.** Used as sb. with Eng. word prefixed attrib., as in *box-w.* (BOX *sb.*[2]), *competition-w.* (COMPETITION) 1785. **c.** Short for *competition-w.* 1863.

Wallaroo (wǫlărū·). 1827. [Native Australian *wolarū.*] A large species of kangaroo, *Macropus robustus*; in Queensland and New South Wales chiefly the black variety.

Walled (wǭld), *ppl. a.* OE. [f. WALL *v.*[2] + -ED[1].] **1.** Furnished with or as with a wall; enclosed with a wall. **2.** With advs. *W.-up*, closed or blocked up with masonry. *W.-in*, *-up*, entombed in a wall. 1826. **3.** *Anat.* and *Zool.* Furnished with a 'wall' or investing structure: chiefly in parasynthetic formations 1875.

1. Twelue Cities, and seuen w. Townes of strength SHAKS. A..large walled-in garden 1826.

Waller[1] (wǭ·ləɹ). 1440. [f. WALL *v.*[2] + -ER[1].] A builder of walls.

Waller[2]. See WALL *v.*[1]

Wallerian (wǫlī³·riăn), *a.* 1877. [f. the name of A. V. *Waller* (1816–70) + -IAN.] *Physiol.* Of or pertaining to Waller, or to the kind of degeneration of nerve fibres discovered by him.

Wallet (wǫ·lėt). late ME. [prob. – AFr. **walet*, the base of which may have been Gmc. **wall-* roll (see WELL *sb.* and *v.*) with which some connect OE. *weallian* = MLG. *wallen*, OHG. *wallōn* (G. *wallen*) go on pilgrimage.] **1.** A bag for holding provisions, clothing, etc., esp. on a journey; a pilgrim's scrip, a pedlar's pack, or the like. **b.** *spec.* A bag having the opening in the middle and a receptacle at each end 1528. **c.** A beggar's bag 1546. **2.** A flat bag, usu. of leather closed by a flap fastened with a button or clasp, or secured by a band; *esp.* a pocket-book for holding paper money without folding, or documents. Orig. *U.S.* 1845.

1. With her scanty wardrobe packed up in a w., she set out on her journey on foot GOLDSM. *transf. Temp.* III. iii. 46. **c.** *fig.* Time hath (my lorde) a w. at his backe Wherein he puts almes for obliuion SHAKS.

Wall eye, wall-eye (wǭ·l,əi·, wǭ·l,əi). 1523. [Back-formation from next.] An eye the iris of which is whitish, streaked, parti-coloured, or different in hue from the other eye, or which has a divergent squint.

Wall-eyed (wǭl,əid; stress var.), *a.* [XIV *wawil|eȝed, waugle eghed* – ON. *vagleygr*, f. **vagl* (surviving in Icel. *vagl* film over the eye, Sw. *vagel* sty on the eye) + *-eygr* -eyed, f. *auga* EYE; see -ED[2].] **1.** Having one or both eyes of an excessively light colour, so that the iris is hardly distinguishable from the white. Also, in ME. and in mod. dialects, having parti-coloured eyes, eyes of different colour, or a divergent squint. †**2.** app. = Having glaring eyes -1613. **3.** *U.S.* Of fishes: Having large prominent eyes 1868.

1. Vulgar opinion has decided that a w. horse is never subject to blindness 1831. *transf.* A little, pale, w., woe-begone, inn DICKENS. **2.** Wall-ey'd wrath, or staring rage SHAKS.

Wallflower (wǭ·l,flau:əɹ). 1578. [f. WALL *sb.*[1]] **1.** A plant of the cruciferous genus *Cheiranthus*, esp. *C. cheiri*, growing wild on old walls, on rocks, etc., and cultivated in gardens for its fragrant flowers. Also called GILLYFLOWER. **b.** Applied to plants of other genera 1804. **2.** *colloq.* A lady who keeps her seat at the side of a room during dancing, usu. because she cannot find a partner 1820.

1. b. *Native w.*, the Tasmanian plant *Pultenæa subumbrosa*; also, in Australia, one of the poison-bushes, *Gastrolobium grandiflorum. Western w.*, any of certain Amer. species of *Erysimum.*

Wa·lling, *vbl. sb.* late ME. [f. WALL *v.*[2] + -ING[1].] **1.** The action of the verb; the making of walls, furnishing with a wall. Also with advs. 1450. **2.** *concr.* Wall-work; also, walls collectively; also, the materials of which a wall is made. late ME.

Wall-knot (wǭ·lnǫt), **wale-knot** (wē¹·l-nǫt). 1627. [rel. obscurely to Norw., Sw. *valknut*, Da. *valknude* double knot, secure knot.] A secure knot made on the end of a rope by unlaying and intertwining the strands.

Walloon (wǭlū·n), *sb.* and *a.* 1530. [– Fr. *Wallon* – med. L. *Wallo, -ōn-*, f. Gmc. **walxaz* foreign. Cf. WELSH, -OON.] **A.** *sb.* **1.** A man or woman of the race, of Gaulish origin and speaking a French dialect, which forms the chief portion of the population of the south-eastern provinces of Belgium 1567. **2.** The language or dialect of the Walloons 1642. **B.** *adj.* Pertaining to the Walloons 1530.

Wallop (wǫ·ləp), *sb.* ME. [– ONFr. *walop*, var. of (O)Fr. *galop*, f. the verb; see next.] †**1.** A horse's gallop -1489. **2.** *dial.* (esp. *Sc.*) and *colloq.* A violent, heavy, clumsy, noisy movement of the body 1820. **b.** Used *quasi-advb.* with vbs. of motion to represent the noise of such movements 1540. **3.** *colloq.* and *joc.* A heavy resounding blow; a whack. Also (in boxing slang) the capacity to deliver such a blow 1823.

2. b. Souple Tam Gaed w. ower the stile 1885. **3.** His opponent..has a prodigious 'w.', but no great amount of skill 1914.

Wallop (wǫ·ləp), *v.* late ME. [– ONFr. *waloper*, var. of (O)Fr. *galoper*, f. Frankish **wala hlaupan*, i.e. *wala* 'well', *hlaupan* run, LEAP.] †**1.** *intr.* To gallop -1721. **2.** To boil violently and with a noisy bubbling 1579. **3.** To make violent heavy movements (accompanied by noise); to flounder, plunge. *colloq.* and *dial.* 1715. **4.** To dangle, flap, wobble. *colloq.* and *dial.* 1822. **5.** *trans.* To beat soundly, belabour, thrash. *colloq.* 1825.

3. The gallop of a cow or a cart-horse is a good specimen of wallopping 1825.

Wallow (wǫ·lo[u]), *sb.* 1591. [f. next.] **1.** The act of wallowing or rolling in mud or filth. Also *concr.*, the filth in which swine wallow. **b.** A mud-hole or dust-hole formed by the wallowing of a buffalo, elephant, or rhinoceros 1841. **2.** †**a.** A rolling walk or gait. DRYDEN. **b.** The roll or swell of the sea. *poet.* 1868.

Wallow (wǫ·lo[u]), *v.* [OE. *walwian* :- WGmc. **walwōjan*, rel. to *wielwan* trans. roll = Goth. *af-, at-, faur|walwjan*; f. Gmc. **walw- *welw-* :- IE. **wolw- *welw-*, repr. by L. *volvere* roll.] **I.** *intr.* **1.** Of a person or animal: To roll about, toss or tumble from side to side, while lying down or stretched out. Now *rare* exc. as in 2. **b.** To move about heavily or clumsily; to go along with a rolling or floundering gait 1570. **2.** To roll about, or lie prostrate and relaxed in or upon some liquid, viscous, or yielding substance (e.g. mire, water, sand). Often implying sensual enjoyment or indifference to defilement. OE. **3.** Of a ship: To roll from side to side ME. **4.** Of the sea, waves: To roll, surge. Of wind: To blow gustily. Of a liquid, smoke, etc.: To spout, gush; to surge *up.* late ME.

1. b. Toads..shrugged and wallowed up from their torpid beds 1845. **2.** Part huge of bulk Wallowing unweildie, enormous in thir Gate Tempest the Ocean MILT. *fig.* The godly..shall not w. in their sinnes *Ecclus.* 23: 12. I wallowed in sloth and voluptuous ease DE FOE. A man that wallows in gold and silver WESLEY. I mean to w. in strawberries and cream 1887.

†**II.** *trans.* **1.** To cause (a rounded object) to

roll on the ground; to trundle –1662. **2.** To cause (a person or animal) to roll or toss about; to cause to lie prostrate or immersed (*in* something) –1673.

2. Gird thee with sackcloth, and wallowe thy selfe in ashes *Jer.* 6:26. Hence **Wa·llower,** a person or animal that wallows; *Mech.* a trundle, lantern-wheel.

Wa·ll-pa:per. 1858. Paper, freq. printed in ornamental designs, used for covering the interior walls of buildings.

Wallsend (wǫ·lzend, wǭ:lze·nd). 1827. The name of a town in Northumberland, used *attrib.* (and *ellipt.* as *sb.*), orig. as the designation of coal from a local seam, subseq. as the trade name for coal of a certain quality.

Wallwort (wǫ·lwɒɹt). [OE. *wealhwyrt*, f. *wealh* foreigner + *wyrt* WORT¹.] The caprifoliaceous plant *Sambucus ebulus*, also called Dwarf Elder, Danewort, Danes' Blood, etc. It has a nauseous taste and an offensive odour, and was formerly valued as a styptic.

Walnut (wǫ·lnɒt). [Late OE. *walh-hnutu*, corresp. to MLG. *wallnut* (whence (M)HG. *walnuss*), MDu. *walnote* (Du. *walnoot*), ON. *walhnot* :– Gmc. formation, prob. orig. of the LDu. area, on **waχlaz* foreign and **χnut-* NUT.] **1.** The nut of the common walnut-tree, *Juglans regia*, consisting of a two-lobed seed (the edible kernel) enclosed in a spheroidal shell covered with a green fleshy husk. **2.** The nut-bearing tree *Juglans regia*. Also applied to other species of *Juglans* and related genera. 1600. In U.S. = SHAGBARK 2. **b.** With defining adj. **Common W.,** *Juglans regia*, called in the U.S. **English W. Black W.,** the American species, *Juglans nigra.* **Grey** or **White W.:** see BUTTERNUT 1. 1754. **3.** The wood of the walnut-tree 1585.

1. In after-dinner talk, Across the walnuts and the wine TENNYSON. *Oil of walnuts*, the essential oil expressed from the kernels of walnuts. **3.** Dust-proof cases of solid w. shaped in the best style of the art 1868.

attrib. and *Comb.*: **w.-brown,** the brown colour produced by the application of w.-juice to the skin; **-juice,** the juice expressed from the green husk of the w., used as a brown stain for the skin; **-tree,** the tree that bears walnuts (*Prov.* A woman, asse, and walnut-tree, the more you beat the better be 1639).

Wa·lnut-shell. 1523. **1.** The hard shell enclosing the seed of the walnut; either of the boat-shaped halves of this. **2.** *transf.* Applied to a boat, as a hyperbolical expression for extreme lightness and fragility 1614.

Walrus (wǫ·lrɒs). 1655. [prob. – Du. *walrus, -ros*, alt., after *walvisch* 'whale-fish', by inversion of the elements of such forms as OE. *horshwæl*, ON. *hrosshvalr* ('horse-whale'), but the mutual relations are obscure.] The sea-horse, or morse (*Trichechus rosmarus*), a carnivorous pinniped marine mammal allied to the *Phocidæ* (seals) and *Otariidæ* (sea-lions), and chiefly distinguished by two tusks (exserted upper canine teeth). It inhabits the Arctic seas.

attrib. and *Comb.*, as *w.-beef, -hide, -ivory.*

†**Walt,** *a.* 1539. [OE. **wealt*, found only in *unwealt* steady; cogn. w. WALLOW. Cf. *walt, walter* vbs. (dial.), to roll, overturn, etc.] *Naut.* Of a ship: Unsteady –1769. So **Walty** (wǫ·lti) *a.* 1702.

Waltonian (wǫltōᵘ·niăn), *a.* and *sb.* 1830. [f. name of Izaac *Walton*, author of *The Compleat Angler* (1653); see -IAN.] **A.** *adj.* Of or pertaining to Izaac Walton. **B.** *sb.* A disciple of Walton, an angler 1832.

Waltz (wǭls, †wǭlts), *sb.* 1781. [– G. *walzer*, f. *walzen* to roll, revolve, waltz.] **1.** A dance performed to music in triple time by couples who swing round and round in the same direction with smooth and even steps, moving on as they gyrate. **2.** A piece of music to accompany this dance 1816.

1. *W.*,..the name of a riotous and indecent German dance 1825. **2.** The band..played a w. 1837.

Waltz (wǭls, †wǭlts), *v.* 1794. [f. prec., or directly – G. *walzen*: see prec.] *intr.* To dance a waltz. Also, to be addicted to or practised in the waltz. **b.** quasi-*trans.*: To move (a person, oneself) as in a waltz 1853.

transf. With a fair wind she waltzed beautifully round the coast 1900. **b.** He seized me and waltzed me around the little dining-room 1883. Hence **Wa·ltzing,** *vbl. sb.* and *ppl. a.*; *waltzing-mouse* = WALTZER (*b*). **Wa·ltzer,** (*a*) one who dances waltzes; (*b*) one of a breed of domesticated mice which have the habit of spinning round rapidly.

Waly (wǭ·li, wēⁱ·li), *int. Sc.* and *north.* 1724. [perh. cognate with WOE, WELLAWAY.] An exclamation of sorrow.

O w., w. up the bank, And w., w. down the brae 1724.

Wamara (wămā·ră). 1840. [Native name.] The brown ebony of British Guiana.

Wambais. *Obs.* exc. *Hist.* 1761. [– OFr. *wambais*; see GAMBESON.] = GAMBESON.

Wamble (wǫ·mb'l, wæ·mb'l), *sb.* Now *colloq.* or *dial.* 1603. [f. next.] **1.** A rolling or uneasiness in the stomach; a feeling of nausea. **2.** An unsteady movement (of a person or thing); a roll of the body; a rolling or staggering gait 1825.

Wamble (wǫ·mb'l, wæ·mb'l), *v.* Now *dial.* late ME. [In branch I perh. corresp. to Da. *vamle* feel nausea, f. Gmc. root **wem-, wam-* (cf. L. *vomere*, Gr. ἐμεῖν); with branch II cf. Norw. *vamla, vamra* stagger, etc.] **I.** *intr.* †**a.** To be qualmish, feel nausea –1500. **b.** Of the stomach or its contents: To be felt to roll about (in nausea) 1518.

fig. The pains o' love'll work and wommle in the inside of ye like a knot o' adders! 1898.

II. 1. To turn and twist the body about, roll or wriggle about, roll over and over. late ME. **2.** To roll about in walking; to go with an unsteady gait 1611. **b.** Of things: To move unsteadily, stagger, reel 1589.

2. b. His feet wambling one over the other like those of a mummer's bear 1896. Hence **Wa·mbling** *vbl. sb.* and *ppl. a.*, **-ly** *adv.* **Wa·mbly** *a.* affected with nausea; shaky, tottering, unsteady.

Wame (wēⁱm). *Sc.* and *north.* late ME. [Northern form of WOMB.] **1.** The belly, abdomen. **b.** The womb, uterus. late ME. †**2.** In the 17th c. the word seems to have been adopted (in the forms *wem(b, weamb*) in southern use as a joc. substitute for 'belly' –1764.

1. *transf.* In a wreath o' snaw, or in the w. o' a wave, what signifies how the auld gaberlunzie dies? SCOTT. **2.** If not their Purse, their Wems they fill 1691. Hence **Wa·meful** = BELLY-FUL.

Wampee (wǫmpī·). 1830. [– Chinese *hwang-pi* 'yellow skin'.] The fruit of an Asiatic tree *Clausena wampi*, also, the tree itself.

Wampum (wǫ·mpɒ̆m). 1636. [Shortening of next, falsely analysed as *wampam* + *peag*.] **1.** Cylindrical beads made from the ends of shells rubbed down, polished, and threaded on strings; used among N. Amer. Indians as currency, for ornament, and (as a substitute for writing) for mnemonic and symbolic purposes, according to the arrangement of the beads. **2.** Short for *w.-snake.*

1. *transf.* He arrayed himself in the w. and war-paint proper for such engagements as manufactured by Mr. Poole, of Saville Row 1890.

Comb.: **w. snake,** a colubrid snake, *Farancia abacura* of the southern U.S.

Wampumpeag (wǫ·mpɒ̆mpīg). Now *rare.* 1631. [Adopted from the northerly dials. of the Algonquin language, f. *wap* white (cf. WAPITI) + *umpe* string + pl. suffix *-ag.*] = prec.

Wamus (wæ·mɒs). *U.S.* 1805. [– Du. *wammes*, contracted f. *wambuis* – OFr. *wambois* WAMBAIS, GAMBESON.] In southern and western U.S., a warm knitted jacket resembling a cardigan.

Wan (wǫn), *a.* [OE. *wann* dark, gloomy, black; of unknown origin.] †**1.** Lacking light, or lustre; dark-hued, gloomy, dark –1591. **b.** *esp.* in conventional application in poetry to the sea (waves, etc.) or other waters. (In recent use, prob. always with some ref. to sense 3.) OE. †**2.** Of an unwholesome colour; livid, leaden-hued: applied *esp.* to wounds, corpses, etc. –1655. **3.** Pallid, faded, sickly; unusually or unhealthily pale ME. **b.** Applied to the (light of) heavenly bodies, etc.: Faint, sickly, partially obscured 1601. **4.** *absol.* (quasi-*sb.*) Wan hue, wanness. *poet.* 1821.

1. With vysage w. As swarte as tan SKELTON. **3.** As pale and w. as ashes was his looke SPENSER. *A w. smile*, a faint or forced smile (as of one sick or unhappy). **b.** The blasted Starrs lookt w. MILT. **4.** Melissa, tinged with w. from lack of sleep TENNYSON. Hence **Wan** *v.* to grow or make pale (*rare*). **Wa·n-ly** *adv.*, **-ness.**

Wan- (wǫn), a prefix expressing privation or negation (approximately equivalent to UN-¹ or MIS-), repr. OE. *wan-*. A similar prefix appears in most Germanic langs. Most of the surviving words formed with this prefix are *Sc.* and *north.*; as **Wanchancy,** *a.* unlucky, dangerous; eerie, uncanny. **Wan-thriven,** *a.* ill-developed, stunted in growth, etc.

Wand (wǫnd). ME. [– ON. **wandur* (*vǫndr*) = Goth. *wandus* :– **wanduz* (not in WGmc.), prob. f. **wand-* **wend-* turn, WEND.] **1.** A straight slender stick. Now *Sc.* and *dial.* **b.** As a type of slenderness or straightness 1508. †**c.** A light walking-stick, cane –1762. **d.** A stick used as a pointer 1589. **2.** A young shoot, a slender stem of a shrub or tree, a sapling. *Obs.* exc. *poet.* and *dial.* ME. **3.** A young shoot of willow cut to be used in basket-making, wattled buildings, or the like. Now *Sc.* and *dial.* ME. **4.** A stick or switch for urging on a horse. *Obs.* exc. *dial.* late ME. **5.** A rod or staff borne as a sign of office; esp. a tall slender rod of white wood, sometimes of ebony or silver, carried erect by an officer of the royal household or of a court of justice, by a verger or beadle, etc. late ME. **b.** Applied to the *caduceus* of Hermes or Mercury. late ME. †**6.** A measuring rod –1829. **7.** A magic rod; the staff used in enchantments by a fairy or a magician. late ME. **8.** A fishing-rod. Now chiefly *Sc.* 1565.

1. Looke you, she is as white as a lilly, and as small as a w. SHAKS. **2.** The stem bends like a hazel w. 1919. **4.** Fodder, a w., and burdens are for the asse *Ecclus.* 33:24. **7.** If a good fairy had built the house for me with a wave of her w. DICKENS.

Comb.: **w.-bearer,** one who carries a w. in a procession, etc., as a sign of office; *spec.* as a title of certain honorary lay officials of St Paul's Cathedral, London. Hence **Wa·ndsman,** an official who carries a w.; a verger of a cathedral.

Wander (wǫ·ndəɹ), *v.* [OE. *wandrian* = OFris. *wondria*, MLG., MDu. *wanderen* :– WGmc. **wandrōjan*, f. **wand-* **wend-* WEND; see -ER⁵.] **I.** *intr.* **1.** Of persons, etc.: To move hither and thither without fixed course or certain aim; to go idly or restlessly about. Also with adv., as *about, up and down.* **b.** quasi-*trans.* with cognate obj. *poet.* ME. **c.** To go or take one's way casually or without predetermined route; to go *to* a place by a devious and leisurely course. Also with *forth, out.* 1596. **2.** Of an inanimate thing: To travel, move, or be carried about in an uncertain course; to stray OE. **b.** Of rumours, etc.: To be in circulation 1547. **c.** Of the eyes: To turn this way and that; to rove. Hence, of the vision: To pass (idly or restlessly) from one point to another. 1574. **d.** Of the mind, thoughts, desires, etc.: To move (hither and thither) uncontrolled. late ME. **e.** Of rivers, roads, etc.: To pursue a devious or winding course; to meander 1742. **3.** To deviate from a given path, or determined course; to stray from one's home or company, or from protection or control 1500. **b.** *fig.* or in fig. context: Of persons (also of thoughts, desires, etc. personified): To turn aside from a purpose, from a determined course of conduct, or train of thought; to pass out of the control of reason or conscience; to fall into error (moral or intellectual), etc. OE. **4.** To be unsettled, or incoherent, in mind, purpose, etc. Hence, later, to be temporarily disordered in mind; to be delirious; to ramble, rave. late ME.

1. With Caine go w. through the shade of night SHAKS. Multitudes wandering about they knew not whither, in quest they knew not of what JOHNSON. *fig.* Not in Fancy's maze he wander'd long, But stoop'd to Truth POPE. **2.** In some, the gout wanders through the whole body 1764. **b.** There was no evidence..: but strange whispers wandered about the camp MACAULAY. **c.** Their eyes wandered over the glorious scene 1794. **d.** Thoughts that w. through Eternity MILT. **3.** If the Moone should w. from her beaten way HOOKER. **b.** Madam, you w. from the goode We ayme at SHAKS. **4.** They said he was wandering in his head yesterday DICKENS.

II. *trans.* **1.** To roam over, in, through (a place). Now only *poet.* 1573. **2.** To cause to wander, lead astray; also *fig.* to confuse in mind, bewilder. Chiefly *colloq.* or *joc.* 1897.

1. She wandred many a wood, and measurd many a vale SPENSER. Hence **Wa·nder** *sb.* an act of wandering. **Wa·ndered** *ppl. a.* that has wandered; astray; bewildered. late ME.

Wanderer (wǫ·ndərəɹ). 1440. [f. prec. + -ER[1].] **1.** A person or thing that is wandering, or that has long wandered. **b.** as tr. L. *planeta* or Gr. πλανήτης: A wandering star, planet 1614. **c.** *Hist.* One of the Covenanters who left their homes to follow their dispossessed ministers in 1669. -1724. **2.** *Zool.* As tr. various mod.L. terms of classification; a bird of the group *Vagatores* in Macgillivray's system; one of the wandering spiders (*Vacabundæ*) 1837.

Wandering (wǫ·ndəriŋ), *vbl. sb.* ME. [f. as prec. + -ING[1].] **1.** Travelling from place to place or from country to country without settled route or destination; roaming. late ME. **b.** Of inanimate things: Devious movement from place to place 1827. **c.** Of the eyes: Irregular turning this way and that 1818. **d.** Of the mind, thoughts, etc.: Aimless passing from object to object ME. **2.** Deviation from the right or intended path or direction, straying, aberration 1711. **3.** Disordered action of the mind due to illness; delirium; in *pl.*, delirious fancies, esp. as expressed in speech 1837.

Wandering (wǫ·ndəriŋ), *ppl. a.* OE. [f. as prec. + -ING[2].] **1.** That moves from place to place or from country to country without readily apparent purpose; roving; vagrant. **b.** Of primitive peoples, etc.: Nomadic, migratory. Frequently tr. scientific L. *errans, vagus*, etc. late ME. **2.** Of things: Travelling (or carried) along in an uncertain or frequently changing direction 1590. **b.** Of the mind, thoughts, etc.: Not directed by reason or fixed purpose; random; wanton 1450. **c.** Of the eyes: Roving, restless 1578. **d.** Of the moon or stars (*esp.* tr. L. *planeta*, or Gr. πλανήτης): Not fixed, having a separate individual motion 1526. **e.** Of plants: Trailing; sending out long tendrils or runners 1590. **f.** *W. fire* or *light*, will-o'-the-wisp 1666. **g.** *Phys.* and *Path.* Of diseases, pains, etc.: Moving from one part of the body to another (without clearly ascertained cause). Also (in recent use), *W. cells*: amœboid cells. 1585. **h.** Of roads, rivers, etc.: Winding, meandering. Also *transf.* (*Phys.*) as the distinctive epithet of a particular pair of nerves (after mod.L. *nervi vagi*). 1667. **3.** Deviating from the proper or determined course; †*fig.* disloyal 1600. **4.** Characterized by wandering 1582.

1. To sie that thair be no w. persones efter the hour of ten 1607. **The W. Jew,** a legendary personage who (according to a popular belief first mentioned in the 13th c.), for having insulted Our Lord on his way to the Cross, was condemned to wander over the earth without rest until the Day of Judgement. **2.** O cuckoo, shall I call thee Bird, Or but a w. Voice? WORDSW. **e.** *W. Jew, Sailor(s, Jenny, Willie*, popular names of certain plants. **f.** *fig.* How often..This chance of noble deeds will come and go Unchallenged, while ye follow w. fires Lost in the quagmire! TENNYSON. Hence **Wa·ndering-ly** *adv.*, **-ness.**

‖**Wanderlust** (va·ndərlust, wǫ·ndəɹlɒst). 1902. [G.] Eager desire or fondness for wandering or travelling.

Wanderoo (wǫndərū·). 1681. [– Sinhalese *wanderu* monkey.] A name properly belonging to the langur monkeys (genus *Semnopithecus*), inhabiting Ceylon, but until recently almost always misapplied, after Buffon, to the Lion-tailed Macaque of Malabar.

Wa·nder-year. 1895. [f. WANDER *v.*, after G. *wanderjahr* a year spent in travel for the purpose of perfecting one's skill and knowledge after the completion of apprenticeship.] A year of wandering or travel (usu. with more or less direct ref. to German usage).

Wandoo (wǫndū·). 1884. [Native Australian.] The White Gum-tree (*Eucalyptus redunca*) of Western Australia.

Wane (wēⁱn), *sb.*[1] [OE. *wana, wan* want, lack; cf. Du. *wan* leakage, etc., Goth. *wan* lack.] †**1.** Decrease in size. –late ME. **2.** The waning or gradual decrease of the visible illuminated area on the moon. Now *rare* exc. in phrases *on, upon* the *w.*, *in* (*the, her, its*) *w.* 1548. **b.** The period characterized by the waning of the moon, *esp.* regarded as a favourable, or unfavourable, time for various (usu. agricultural) operations 1563. **3.** Gradual decrease or decline in splendour, power, importance, or the like, esp. as following on the culmination of a process of gradual increase; the declining period (of a person's life, an institution, etc.). late ME.

2. b. In Suffolk it is considered unlucky to kill a pig in the w. of the moon 1866. **3.** The day was in its w., and still..she slept on DICKENS. It is quite possible that his power may be on the w. 1885.

Wane (wēⁱn), *sb.*[2] 1662. [– LDu. *wan-*, G. *wahn-* in *wahnholz, wahnkante*; see WAN-.] The bevelled edge left on a plank (by reason of one face being narrower than the other), or the imperfect angles of a rough-hewn log (the section of which is thus octagonal). Hence **Waney** (wēⁱ·ni) *a.* [cf. G. *wahnig*].

Wane (wēⁱn), *v.* [OE. *wanian* lessen (intr. and trans.) = OFris. *wonia*, OS. *wanon*, OHG. *wanōn, wanēn*, ON. *vana*, Goth. **wanan* (cf. *wanains* loss) :– Gmc. **wanōjan* **wanǣjan*, f. **wana-* lacking, f. IE. **wā̆-*, repr. also by L. *vānus* vain.] **1.** *intr.* To decrease in size or extent; to dwindle. Now *rare.* †**b.** To grow less in quantity or volume. Of the sea, water: To subside, ebb. –1815. **2.** Of the moon: To undergo the periodical decrease in the extent of its visible illuminated portion, characteristic of the second half of the lunation OE. **3.** Of light, luminous objects, colour, etc.: To decrease in brilliance or splendour; to become faint or dim OE. **4.** Of a person, etc.: To decline in power, importance, prosperity, or renown OE. **5.** Of qualities, activities, feelings, etc.: To become gradually less in degree, to decline in intensity ME. **6.** Of a period of time: To draw to its close (usu. with some notion of sense 3 or 5) 1590.

2. But oh, methinkes, how slow This old Moon wanes SHAKS. **3.** The light waned without, it grew dusk DICKENS. **4.** Plato..had seen the Athenian empire..wax and w. JOWETT.

Wangle (wæ·ŋg'l), *v. slang* and *colloq.* 1888. [perh. based on WAGGLE and dial. *wankle* unsteady, unconstant, precarious, under the infl. of a vague sense of phonetic symbolism.] *trans.* To accomplish (something) in an irregular way by scheming or contrivance; to bring about or obtain by indirect or insidious means; to manipulate, 'fake' (an account, report, prices, etc.); also, to influence or induce (a person) to do something. Also *intr.* Hence **Wa·ngle** *sb.*

Wangun (wæ·ŋgŏn). *U.S.* 1848. [Shortened f. Montagnais Indian *atawangan*, f. *atawan* buy or sell.] A receptacle for small supplies or a reserve stock; *esp.*, a boat or chest containing outfit supplies for a lumber camp; also, stores.

Wa·nhope. *Obs.* exc. *arch.* ME. [f. WAN- + HOPE *sb.*[1]] Hopelessness, despair.

Waning (wēⁱ·niŋ), *vbl. sb.* OE. [f. WANE *v.* + -ING[1].] **1.** Decrease or diminution in magnitude, importance, etc. **2.** Of the moon; Periodical decrease in apparent size; the half of the lunar month in which this takes place OE. †**3.** Decline (of life); concluding part (of a period) –1594.

Wa·ning, *ppl. a.* OE. [f. WANE *v.* + -ING[2].] That wanes or is on the wane. **1.** Of the moon. **2.** Decreasing or declining in power, importance, etc. 1596. **3.** Of light, or a luminary: Declining in lustre 1700. **b.** Of the day: Drawing to a close 1767. **4.** Becoming scanty, running short. Now *rare.* 1632.

2. *Tam. Shr.* Induct. ii. 65.

Wanion, wannion (wǫ·nyən). *Obs.* exc. *arch.* 1549. [An altered form of obs. *waniand* waning (moon), used in phr. *in the* (*wild*) *waniand* in an unlucky hour, (hence) with a vengeance.] **a.** *In a w.*, later *with a* (*wild*) *w.*: with a plague, with a vengeance. **b.** *A* (*wild*) *w. on, a w. to*: May a curse or plague light on (a person, etc.)! 1570.

a. Come away, or Ile fetch'th with a w. SHAKS. **b.** I'll teach you to take place of Tradesmens Wives with a wannion to you DRYDEN.

Want (wǫnt), *sb.* ME. [– ON. *vant*, n. of *vanr* adj. (= OE. *wana*, ME. *wane*) lacking, missing, also quasi-sb. In later Eng. usage often directly f. WANT *v.*] **1.** Deficiency, shortage, lack (*of* something desirable or necessary). **2.** The state of lacking the necessaries of life; penury. Also, the condition of lacking food; starvation. ME. †**b.** Straits, circumstances of want, hardship, etc. –1731. †**3.** The fact that a person (*rarely* a thing) is not present; absence –1831. **4.** A condition marked by the lack of some necessary thing; need; also, an instance of this; hence quasi-*concr.*, something needed or desired. Freq. *pl.* 1578.

1. Three votes of w. of confidence 1859. *For* (occas. *by, from, in, through*) *w. of*, because of the absence or deficiency of; Many, for W. of Wit, shall sell their Freehold for Tobacco-pipes and red Petticoats 1608. **2.** *To come to w.*, to be reduced to penury. Prov. *Wilful waste makes woeful w.* **4.** I would..Supplie your present wants SHAKS. Still by the pillow of the unconscious sufferer, still anticipating his every w. DICKENS. Phr. *A* (*long-*)*felt w.*: something of which the want has (long) been felt. *In w. of*, in need of; not having, or having in insufficient measure. *In no w. of*, having abundantly. Provb. phr. *Then W. must be your master*, used in refusing a demand expressed by 'I want —'. Hence **Wa·ntless** *a.*

Want (wǫnt), *v.* ME. [– ON. *vanta* be lacking, lack: cf. prec. and WANE *v.*] **1.** *intr.* To be lacking or missing; not to be forthcoming; to be deficient in quantity or degree. Now *rare arch.* †**b.** To be lacking to complete a certain total or achieve a result. Const. *of* or with neg. clause. –1768. **2.** *trans.* To lack; to be destitute of or deficient in. Now *rare*, exc. with obj. a desirable quality or attribute. ME. **b.** To come short by (so much) of completing a certain total or attaining a certain result. Now chiefly *impers.* in telling the time of day. late ME. †**c.** To be deprived of, to lose –1724. **d.** *Wanting* (pres. pple.): deprived of, without; lacking, less, minus. *Obs.* exc. *Sc.* 1536. **e.** To go or do without. *Obs.* exc. *dial.* 1562. **3.** *intr.* †**a.** To be in want of something implied by the context, or of the necessaries of life –1684. **b.** *To w. for* (chiefly in neg. context): to suffer from the want of; to be ill-provided with; in later use also, to be lacking in (some quality). *To w. for nothing*, to have no lack of any of the necessaries or comforts of life. 1607. **4.** *trans.* To suffer the want of; to need, require; to stand in need of (something salutary, but often not desired) 1470. **b.** With *vbl. sb.* or *inf.* (esp. *pass.*) as obj. (now chiefly *colloq.*). *It wants doing* (dial. *to be done*), it needs doing, should be done. 1563. **5.** To desire, wish for 1706. **b.** To desire, with *accusative* and *inf.* Also *U.S.*, with clause as object. 1845. **c.** To wish to see or speak to (a person); to desire the presence or assistance of (for a specified purpose). Freq. *pass.* 1760. **d.** *Wanted* (pa. pple.): colloq. or joc. ellipsis for *wanted by the police.* 1812.

1. In France there neuer wanted discontented Persons, who would joyn with his Forces 1648. **2.** Some hae meat, and canna eat, And some wad eat that w. it BURNS. **b.** 'Wants a few minutes of five o'clock, sir' DICKENS. It only wants five minutes to dinner TROLLOPE. **d.** What a wearie way From Rauenspurgh to Cottshold will be found.., wanting your companie SHAKS. **e.** A worthless old play-fellow of mine, whose company I would rather w. than have SCOTT. **4.** Man wants but little here below, Nor wants that little long GOLDSM. **b.** 'Your hair wants cutting', said the Hatter L. CARROLL. **5.** *What does he w. with* (dial. and U.S. *of*) (a certain person or thing)? = What is his object in dealing with (the person)?, why should he care to possess (the thing)? Hence **Wa·nted** *ppl. a.*, *esp.* of a person, sought for by the police (also *absol.* as *sb.*). **Wa·nter,** one who is deficient in something; one who is in need or desirous of something; (*dial.*) one who seeks a husband or wife.

Wanting (wǫ·ntiŋ), *pres. pple.* and *ppl. a.* ME. [f. prec. + -ING[2].] **A.** *pres. pple.* (only predic.). **1.** That is absent or lacking; not forthcoming, not supplied or provided. †**2.** Needful, requisite –1802. **3.** That lacks, or is without something. Usu. const. †*of, in.* 1592. **4.** Mentally defective, weak-minded (*dial.*) 1877.

1. Were our Teares w. to this Funerall SHAKS. *To be w. to*: to fail to help or satisfy; to prove unequal to. *To be w. to oneself*, to fail to do justice to oneself (*arch.*). **3.** Thou art weighed in the balances, and art found w. *Dan.* 5:27. England is not w. in a Learned Nobility DRYDEN.

B. *ppl. a.* (in attrib. use). **1.** Absent, lacking, missing 1573. †**2.** Deficient, lacking; esp. lacking in money or necessaries of life; needy 1616.

Wanton (wǫ·ntən), *a.* and *sb.* [ME. *wantowen*, f. WAN- + *towen*, OE. *togen*, pa. pple. of *tēon* discipline, train; see TEE *v.*¹] **A.** *adj.* †**1.** Undisciplined, ungoverned; unmanageable, rebellious –1697. **b.** Said of boys, with mixture of sense 4; often (after Shakespeare) with ref. to childish cruelty 1605. **2.** Lascivious, unchaste, lewd. late ME. **3.** (Chiefly *poet.*) of young animals: Frisky, frolicsome. Of moving objects, viewed as if endowed with life: Sportive, impelled by caprice or fancy, unrestrained. 1565. †**4.** 'Spoiled', petulant (of children); hence self-indulgent, luxurious –1835. †**b.** Said of money or wealth, as tempting to extravagance or luxury –1770. †**5.** Insolent in triumph or prosperity; merciless –1764. **b.** Of cruelty, injury, etc.: Unprovoked and reckless of justice or compassion; arbitrary, gratuitous 1651. **6.** Profuse in growth, luxuriant, rank (*poet.*) 1590. †**7.** Of speech, etc.: Unrestrained, extravagant, impetuous –1759.

1. b. *Lear* IV. i. 38. **5. b.** W. and superfluous insults JOHNSON. Protecting beasts against the w. cruelty of men MACAULAY. **6.** *Mids. N.* II. i. 99. Where w. Ivy twines POPE. **7.** How does your Tongue grow w. in her Praise! ADDISON.

B. *sb.* †**1.** A person, esp. a child, spoiled by over-indulgence and excessive leniency –1656. †**2.** A sportive or roguish person, child, animal, etc. –1812. **3.** A lascivious or lewd person 1540.

Phr. *To play the w.*: to dally, trifle; †to behave lewdly or lasciviously. Hence **Wa·ntonize** *v. intr. arch.* to play the w.

Wanton (wǫ·ntən), *v.* 1582. [f. prec.] **1.** *intr.* To sport amorously 1588. **b.** To play sportively, heedlessly, or idly, to gambol 1582. **c.** To go idly or heedlessly *up and down, over, through*, etc. 1682. **2.** To run into excesses or extravagances of conduct, language, thought, etc. 1631. **b.** *transf.* Of a garden, plant: To flourish profusely or extravagantly 1800. **3.** To deal carelessly or wastefully (*with* property, etc.). Also *trans.* with *away*, to dissipate (life, time, resources). 1646.

1. b. Dancing Leaves, that wanton'd in the Wind DRYDEN. **2.** Wantoning on venison and champagne KINGSLEY. *fig.* A Wilderness of sweets; for Nature here Wantoned as in her prime MILT.

Wantonly (wǫ·ntənli), *adv.* late ME. [f. WANTON *a.* + -LY².] **a.** Lewdly, lasciviously. **b.** Sportively, lightheartedly. **c.** Recklessly, unadvisedly; without regard for consequences; wilfully.

Wantonness (wǫ·ntən,nės). ME. [f. WANTON *a.* + -NESS.] **1.** The quality of being wanton. **2.** An instance of wantonness; a caprice, whim 1630. †**3.** As the name of an allegorical personage in a morality play; also *transf.* 1506.

Wa·nt-wit. 1448. [f. WANT *v.* + WIT *sb.*] One who lacks wit or sense.

Wanze (wǫnz), *v. Obs.* or *dial.* [OE. *wansian*, f. *wane* wanting.] *trans.* and *intr.* To diminish; to decrease; to waste.

Wap (wǫp), *sb. Obs.* exc. *dial.* late ME. [Belongs to next.] **1.** A blow, knock, thump. **2.** *Sc.* A sudden storm 1818. **3.** A shake, flap; a sweeping or tossing movement 1663.

Wap (wǫp), *v.* Now *dial.* late ME. [Origin obsc.; cf. SWAP *v.* and WHOP *v.*] **1.** *trans.* To throw quickly or with violence. **2.** *intr.* To strike, knock *upon*; to strike *through*. late ME.

‖**Wapacut** (wǫ·păkɒt). 1785. [Amer. Indian.] A large white spotted owl, believed to be the snowy owl, *Nyctea scandiaca*.

Wapentake (wǫ·p-, wæ·p'ntēⁱk). [Late OE. *wǣpen(ȝe)tæc* – ON. *vápnatak*, f. *vápna*, gen. pl. of *vápn* WEAPON + *tak* act of taking, f. *taka* TAKE *v.* The evolution of the Eng. sense from that of the ON. word, 'vote or consent expressed by waving or brandishing weapons', can only be conjectured.] A subdivision of certain English shires, corresponding to the 'hundred' of other counties. **b.** The judicial court of such a subdivision. late ME.

The shires which have divisions so termed are Yorkshire, Derbyshire, Notts, Lincolnshire, Northamptonshire, and Leicestershire, all of which have a large Danish element in the population.

Wapiti (wǫ·piti). 1817. [– Cree *wapitik* (Shawnee *wahpetee*) lit. 'white deer'.] The North Amer. stag or elk, *Cervus canadensis*. Also attrib., *w. deer, stag*.

Wappato(o (wǫ·păto, -ū). *U.S.* 1807. [– Chinook Jargon *wappatoo* – Cree *wapatowa* 'white mushroom'.] The tubers of the plant *Sagittaria variabilis*, used for food by Indians.

Wappens(c)haw (wæ·p'nʃǭ). Also **weapon-.** *Sc.* 1503. [f. *wapen* WEAPON + *schaw* SHOW *sb.*; prob. orig. a shortening of next.] **1.** *Hist.* = next. **2.** A volunteer rifle-meeting 1868. **b.** *S. Africa.* Used to render Du. *wapenschouwing*, applied by the Boers to a rifle-shooting competition 1899.

Wappens(c)hawing (wæ·p'nʃǭ,iŋ). Also **weapon-.** *Sc. Hist.* 1624. [f. *wapen* WEAPON + *schawing* SHOWING *vbl. sb.*; = Du. *wapenschouwing*.] A periodical muster or review of the men under arms within a particular lordship or district.

War (wǭɹ), *sb.* [Late OE. *werre* – AFr., ONFr. *werre*, var. of (O)Fr. *guerre*:– Frankish (or WGmc.) *werra*, rel. to OHG. *werra* confusion, discord, strife, OS., OHG. *werran* bring into confusion (G. *wirren* confuse, perplex); f. base repr. by WORSE *a.*] **1.** Hostile contention by means of armed forces, carried on between nations, states, or rulers, or between parties in the same nation or state; the employment of armed forces against a foreign power or against an opposing party in the state. Formerly freq. *pl.* in sing. sense. **b.** *transf.* and *fig.* Applied *poet.* or *rhet.* to any kind of active hostility or contention between living beings, or of conflict between opposing forces or principles ME. **2.** A contest between armed forces carried on in a campaign or series of campaigns. (Often with identifying word or phrase, as in *the Trojan war, the Wars of the Roses, the Thirty Years' War.*) ME. †**3.** Actual fighting; a battle, engagement (chiefly *poet.*) –1827. **4.** The kind of operations by which the contention of armed forces is carried on; fighting as a department of activity, as a profession, or as an art. ME. **5.** *concr.* Used *poet.* for: †**a.** Instruments of war, munitions –1713. †**b.** Soldiers in fighting array –1822.

1. *W. to the knife*: see KNIFE *sb.* 1 b. *Open w.*, avowed active hostility. Phr. *To have been in the wars* (colloq.), to show marks of injury or of rough usage. *At (open) w.*, †*wars*, engaged in w. *To go to w.*, to enter on hostilities. *To go to the war(s* (arch.), to go abroad as a soldier. *To make w.* **b.** Such railing eloquence and w. of words POPE. **2.** *Holy w.*, a war waged in a religious cause: applied e.g. to the Crusades. *Sacred W.* [= Gr. ἱερὸς πόλεμος], in *Gr. Hist.*, the designation of two wars waged by the Amphictyonic Council against Phocis in punishment of alleged sacrilege.

attrib. and *Comb.*: **w.-baby,** one born during a war while the father is on active service; **-correspondent,** a journalist engaged by a newspaper to send home first-hand descriptions of a campaign; **warcraft,** cunning and skill in warfare; w.-vessels collectively; **-cry,** a cry uttered by a body of fighters to encourage each other in a charge, etc. (also *fig.*); **-dance,** a dance performed by savage tribes before a warlike excursion or to celebrate a victory; **-dog,** a dog trained for use in w.; also *fig.*, a fierce warrior; **-game** = KRIEGSPIEL; **-horse,** a powerful horse ridden in w. by a knight or trooper; also, a veteran soldier or politician; **-kettle,** among North Amer. Indians, a kettle which was set on the fire as part of the ceremony of inaugurating a w.; **-lord,** a military commander; often used to render *Kriegsherr* as a title of the German Emperors; **-man,** a fighting-man, warrior (now *rare*); **-monger,** †(*a*) a mercenary soldier; (*b*) one who seeks to bring about w.; **-note,** a musical summons to w.; **-paint,** among North Amer. Indians, paint applied to the face and body before going into battle; *colloq.*, one's best clothes and finery; **w. savings certificate:** see SAVINGS; **-song,** a song inciting to w., or celebrating martial deeds; **-worn** *a.* wasted, etc. by w.

War, waur (wār, wǭr), *a.* and *adv. Sc.* and *north.* ME. [– ON. *verre* adj., *verr* adv.; see WORSE *a.* and *adv.*] = WORSE *a.* and *adv.* Hence **War** *v.*² *trans.* to worst; to surpass.

War (wǭɹ), *v.*¹ ME. [f. WAR *sb.*¹, partly after OFr. *werreier* WARRAY *v.*] **1.** *intr.* To make or carry on war; to fight. Now only *literary*. **b.** To serve as a soldier 1535. **2.** *fig.* Of persons: To contend, fight with immaterial weapons. Of things, forces, etc.: To be in strong opposition. ME.

2. Carnal desires which warre against the soule BIBLE (Rheims) 1 *Pet.* 2:11. So **Wa·rrer,** †one who engages in warfare –1482; one who wars or contends (*against* something) 1836. **Wa·rring** *vbl. sb.*

Waratah (wǫ·rătā). 1793. [Native Australian name.] **1.** Any Australian shrub of the genus *Telopea*, esp. *T. speciosissima* and *T. oreades*, which bear crimson or scarlet flowers in terminal clusters; also, the flower. **2.** In full *w. camellia*: a variety of the camellia 1824.

Warble (wǭ·ɹb'l), *sb.*¹ late ME. [– ONFr. (esp. Picard) *werble*, f. *werbler*; see WARBLE *v.*¹] *orig.* A tune or melody performed on an instrument or sung; subseq. (influenced by WARBLE *v.*¹), the action or an act of warbling; gentle and melodious singing, esp. of birds. **b.** Manner of warbling 1547. **c.** *collect.* The united sound of bird-songs 1776.

Warble (wǭ·ɹb'l), *sb.*² 1585. [Origin obsc. Cf. WARNEL.] **1.** Usually *pl.* A small hard tumour, caused by the pressure of the saddle on a horse's back 1607. **2.** A small tumour or swelling on the back of cattle, deer, etc., produced by the larva of a gad-fly 1585. **3.** In full *w.-fly*: The gadfly or its larva which produces 'warbles' 1808. Hence **Wa·rbled** *a.* of hides: injured by warbles.

Warble (wǭ·ɹb'l), *v.*¹ 1530. [– ONFr. (esp. Picard) *werbler*, *werbloier* trill, sing (of birds) – Frankish *hwirbilōn* whirl, trill; cf. OHG. *wirbil* whirlwind (G. *wirbel*).] **1.** *intr.* To modulate the voice in singing; to sing with trills and quavers. In later use (influenced by sense 3), to sing softly and sweetly, in a birdlike manner. **b.** *poet.* Of a small stream: To make melody as it flows 1579. **2.** *trans.* To sing with quavering trills and runs, to carol 1576. **b.** To express or celebrate in song or verse 1591. **3.** *intr.* Of birds: To sing clearly and sweetly 1606.

2. The Sky-lark warbles high His trembling thrilling ecstasy GRAY. **b.** You..w. out your groans with uncommon elegance JOHNSON. Hence **Wa·rbling** *vbl. sb.* soft and melodious singing. **Wa·rbling** *ppl. a.* that warbles; occas. in specific names of birds, as the Warbling Flycatcher, *Vireo gilvus*.

Warble (wǭ·ɹb'l), *v.*² 1486. [Origin obsc.] *Falconry.* (*trans.*) To cross (the wings) together over the back after 'rousing' and 'mantling'.

Warbler (wǭ·ɹbləɹ). 1611. [f. WARBLE *v.*¹ + -ER¹.] **1.** One who warbles or sings; a singer, songster. **2. a.** In the Old World: Any of the numerous small plain-coloured singing-birds of the family *Sylviidæ*, including the blackcap, whitethroat, and others having names in which *w.* is the second element, as *garden-w.*, REED-WARBLER, etc. 1733. **b.** In America: One of the small, usu. bright-coloured, birds, with little power of song, of the family *Mniotiltidæ* 1783. **c.** In Australia and New Zealand: A bird of the genera *Gerygone, Malurus*, and others 1790. **3.** *Sc.* A group of grace-notes on the bagpipe 1875. **4.** *The W.*: the title of a song-book 1760.

Ward (wǭɹd), *sb.* [OE. *weard* = MLG. *warde*, OHG. *warta* watch (G. *warte* watch-tower); ON. *varða, varði* cairn :– Gmc. **warðō*, f. **warð-*, extension of **war-* be on guard; see WARE *v.*¹; reinforced in ME. by ONFr. *warde* = (O)Fr. *garde* GUARD *sb.*] **I.** Action of watching or guarding. **1.** The action or function of a watchman, sentinel, or the like; look-out, watch, guard; also, surveillance. **2.** Guardianship, keeping, control (now *rare*); *spec.* guardianship of a child, a minor, or other person legally incapable of conducting his affairs. Also, the condition of being subject to a guardian. ME. **b.** *Feudal Law.* The control and use of the lands of a deceased tenant by knight-service, and the guardianship of the infant heir, which belonged to the superior until the heir attained his majority ME. **c.** *Court of Wards*: a court established by Hen. VIII (and abolished in

1660) for the trial of causes relating to wardships. Also, in British India, a court which deals with cases pertaining to the property of minors. 1560. **3.** Care or charge of a prisoner; the condition of being a prisoner. Now *rare.* ME.

1. Phr. *To hold, keep w. Watch and w.*: see WATCH *sb.* II. 2. **2. b.** *All's Well*, I. i. 5. **c.** Called also *Court of Wards and Liveries. Master of the Wards (and Liveries)*, the presiding judge of the Court of Wards. **3.** *Free w.*: see FREE *a.*

II. A person 'in ward'. **1.** A minor under the control of a guardian; *transf.* one who is under the protection or control of another. late ME. †**2.** An orphan under age –1592.

1. *W. in chancery, w. of court*, a minor for whom a guardian has been appointed by the Court of Chancery, or who has become directly subject to the authority of that Court.

III. Defence. **1.** *Fencing.* A defensive posture or movement; a mode of parrying 1586. †**b.** Defence, protection, shelter –1697. **2.** *Scots Law.* Tenure by military service. Also, a payment in commutation of military service; more explicitly *taxed w.* Now *Hist.* 1508.

IV. A body of guards. **1.** A company of watchmen or guards. Now *rare.* OE. †**2.** A garrison –1660. †**3.** One of the three main divisions of an army –1656.

3. The fore-w. foremost, the battell in the middest, the rere-w. hindermost, ech w. hauing his troope of horssemen HOLINSHED.

V. Place for guarding. **1.** In a fortress: The circuit of the walls of a castle; the ground between two encircling walls. *Obs.* exc. *arch.* late ME. **2.** †**a.** A prison. **b.** Each of the divisions or separate departments of a prison. ME. **3.** An apartment or division in a hospital or lunatic asylum, containing a certain number of beds, or allocated to a particular class of patients 1749. **4.** An administrative division of a borough or city; orig. a district under the jurisdiction of an alderman; now usu., a district which elects its own Town Councillors. late ME. **5.** One of the administrative districts into which Cumberland, Northumberland, and some Scottish counties are divided. late ME.

3. He was lodged in the Fever W. 1758. **4.** *Meas. for M.* II. i. 281.

VI. An appliance for guarding. **a.** Each of the ridges projecting from the inside plate of a lock, serving to prevent the passage of any key the bit of which is not provided with incisions of corresponding form and size 1440. **b.** Each of the incisions in the bit of a key, corresponding to the 'wards' of the lock. late ME.

Comb.: **wardcorn** (*Feudal Law*), a periodical payment of corn in commutation of military service; **w.-maid,** a maidservant who performs the menial offices of a hospital w.; **-penny** (*Feudal Law*), a rent paid to the superior in commutation of military service; **-woman** (*arch.*), a woman in charge of her mistress's wardrobe. Also, with *genitive*, **wardsman,** an inmate appointed to supervise his w. in a prison or workhouse. Hence **Wa·rdable** *a.* liable to pay castle-guard.

Ward (wǭɹd), *v.* [OE. *weardian* = OFris. *wardia*, OS. *wardon*, OHG. *wartēn* (G. *warten* nurse, look after), ON. *varða* :– Gmc. **wardōjan*, *-ǣjan*, f. *wardō* WARD *sb.*; reinforced in ME. by ONFr. *warder*, var. of (O)Fr. *garder* GUARD *v.*] **1.** *trans.* To guard, stand guard over; to defend, protect. *arch.* or *obsol.* Also †*intr.* (*absol.*), to keep guard. **2.** With *in, off, up*: To enclose, hem in, shut off (esp. for safety or protection). *rare.* 1586. **3.** To parry, fend off, turn aside (a blow, attack, weapon, etc.). Now usu. with *off.* 1571. **b.** *absol.* or *intr.* To parry blows; to stand on the defensive in a combat. *Obs.* or *arch.* late ME. **4.** *trans.* To avert, keep off (harm, danger, etc.) 1586. †**5.** To take up a position of defence, take precautions *against* –1755. **6.** *trans.* To place (a patient) in a particular hospital ward; to lodge (a vagrant) in a 'casual ward' 1879. **7.** Of a dog: To line or cover (a bitch) 1781.

1. S. Michels Mount..That wardes the Westerne coste SPENSER. *To watch and w.* see WATCH *v.* I. 6, II. 2. **2.** The machinery not warded off or guarded in any way DICKENS. **3. b.** A Nation..redier to strike than w. LYLY. **5.** Regard must be had..to w. against the bleak Northwind 1726.

-ward *suffix*, OE. *-weard*, primarily forming adjs. with the sense 'having a specified direction' :– Gmc. **-warda-*, f. **ward-*, var. of **werþ-* :– pre-Teut. **wert-* (L. *vertere*) turn.

1. The suffix, usu. denoting direction of movement, was orig. appended only to local advs., and in OE., was still confined to this use. **2.** The adjs. in *-weard*, like the corresponding words in other Teut. langs., admitted of being used advb. in the accus. (OE. *-weard*) or in the gen. (OE. *-weardes* -WARDS) of the neut. sing. On the analogy of the older advs. with this suffix, there were formed in ME. several compounds in which *-weard* was added to advs., esp. to compound advs. of phrasal origin, as in *abackward, adownward, awayward* (which were soon displaced by the aphetic forms *backward, downward, wayward*). **3.** In OE. the adv. *tōweard* was also used as a prep., with the sense 'in the direction leading to', and in early ME. †*fromward* acquired a similar use. Later there are isolated examples of this development of function in some other advs. in *-ward* (e.g. *inward, onward*). **4.** In OE. the suffix was sometimes attached to a phrase consisting of a sb. or pronoun governed by a prep. The description of this type of expression (represented by the obs. or arch. forms 'to heavenward(s', 'to the city ward(s', 'to us-ward'), as a 'tmesis' of the preps. *toward(s*, †*fromward(s*, is not historically correct. **5.** On the analogy of the advb. compounds originating from the omission of *to* (e.g. *heavenward* adv. from *to heavenward*), the suffix has in the mod. Eng. period been added freely to sbs. to form advs. expressing direction, aspect, or tendency. From the 16th c. onwards there has been a growing disposition to use the advs. in *-ward* as adjs.; in the 19th c. or the last years of the 18th c. several new adjs. of this formation appear for the first time: e.g. *earthward, Godward, skyward*; these, however, have been confined to literary use.

Warden[1] (wǭ·ɹd'n). ME. [– AFr., ONFr. *wardein*, var. of OFr. *g(u)arden* GUARDIAN.] **1.** One who has the care of something specified; a keeper. *Obs.* exc. *poet.* **b.** A gatekeeper, porter, sentinel. Now *rare.* ME. †**2.** = GUARDIAN 2. –1700. **3.** A regent or viceroy appointed to rule a country in the king's absence or minority. *Obs.* exc. *Hist.* ME. **b.** The governor of a town, province, or district; the commander of a fortress. *Obs.* exc. *Hist.* in the title *W. of the Marches.* ME. **4.** In certain guilds, esp. in the Livery Companies of the City of London: A member of the governing body under the authority of the Master or the Prime W. late ME. **b.** *Freemasonry.* Either of two officers (called *Senior* and *Junior W.*) in a symbolic lodge, whose duty it is to assist the Worshipful Master 1723. **5.** The superintendent of a harbour, market, or the like 1538. **6.** = CHURCHWARDEN 1. late ME. **b.** *transf.* Applied to an official with similar functions in a Jewish synagogue 1879. **7.** In the titles of officers holding positions of trust under the Crown. **a.** (*Lord*) *W. of the Cinque Ports*: see CINQUE PORTS. 1435. **b.** *W. of the Mint*: until 1823 the title of the chief officer of the Mint 1463. **c.** (*Lord*) *W. of the Stanneries*: an officer appointed by the Duke of Cornwall to preside over the mining parliaments of Cornwall 1485. **d.** *W. of the Standards*: an officer of the Board of Trade having the custody of the standards of weight and measure 1878. **8.** The title given to the head or presiding officer of certain colleges and schools, hospitals, etc. 1575. **9.** An officer to whose custody prisoners are committed; the governor of a prison, esp. in the old title *W. of the Fleet* (*Prison*) ME. **10.** A member of a committee appointed to take charge of the repair and make regulations for the use of a bridge, a highway, etc. 1486. **11.** *U.S.* (and earlier in colonial use). The officer who presides at ward-meetings or elections 1763. **12.** *Canada.* The head of a county council 1873. **13.** *Australia.* The government official, with magisterial powers, in charge of a goldfield 1861.

1. b. Female wardens made a fit outpost for this palace of many women STEVENSON. **5.** *Fire-w.* (U.S.): see FIRE *sb.* 5. *Fish-w.* (U.S.) an official in charge of fisheries. *Game w.*, an officer having the superintendence of the game of a particular locality. **6.** Rival candidates for the office of the people's w. 1914. **8.** I'll..talke as superciliously, and walke As stately, as the W. of a colledge 1632.

attrib.: **w.-court** (*Hist.*), a court held by the W. of the Marches. Hence **Wa·rdency,** the position of a w.; the sphere or district in which a w. exercises his functions. **Wa·rdenry,** the office or position of w.; the jurisdiction of, or district under the care of, a W. of the Marches. **Wa·rdenship,** the office or position of a w.

Warden[2] (wǭrd'n). late ME. [Of unkn. origin.] An old variety of baking pear.

attrib. and *Comb.*, as *w.-pear, -pie, -tree.*

Warder (wǭ·ɹdəɹ), *sb.*[1] late ME. [– AFr. *wardere, wardour*, f. OFr. *warder*; see WARD *v.*, -ER[2] 3, -OUR.] **1.** A soldier or other person set to guard an entrance; also, a watchman on a tower. **2.** An official in charge of prisoners in a jail 1855.

1. Late wardours in the Tower of London 1679. *fig.* Memorie, the W. of the Braine SHAKS. Hence **Wa·rder** *v. trans.* to provide with a w. or sentinel. **Wa·rdership,** the office or position of w.; the carrying out of the duties of a w.

Warder (wǭ·ɹdər), *sb.*[2] 1440. [Reduced form of next.] In early use: A staff or wand. Later, the baton or truncheon carried as a symbol of office, etc., esp. as used to give the signal for the commencement or cessation of hostilities in a battle or tournament.

Wa·rderer. *Obs.* exc. *Hist.* late ME. [perh. orig. joc. use of †*warderere* look out behind (Ch.) – AFr. **ware derere*, i.e. *ware* look out (see WARE *v.*[1]) + *derere* (mod. *derrière*) behind.] A warder or truncheon.

Wardian (wǭ·ɹdiăn), *a.* 1842. [f. the name of the inventor, N.B. *Ward* + -IAN.] In *W. case*, a close-fitting case with glass sides and top for growing small ferns and other moisture-loving plants.

Warding (wǭ·ɹdiŋ), *vbl. sb.* late ME. [f. WARD *v.* + -ING[1].] **1.** The action of guarding (a place); the action or duty of keeping guard. **2.** *Sc.* Imprisonment 1497. **3.** The fashioning of the wards of keys, in *w. file* 1846.

1. *Watching and w.*; see WATCHING *vbl. sb.* 1 b. **2.** He was put under w. for a time SCOTT. **3.** A thin flat file called a 'w. file' 1881.

Wardmote (wǭ·ɹdmoᵘt). late ME. [f. WARD *sb.* + *mote* MOOT *sb.*] A meeting of the citizens of a ward; esp. in the City of London, a meeting of the liverymen of a ward under the presidency of the alderman.

attrib.: **w. inquest, quest,** (*a*) a judicial inquiry made by a w.; (*b*) the body of men composing a w.

Wardour-street (wǭ·ɹdəɹ,strīt). The name of a street in London, once mainly occupied by dealers in antique and imitation-antique furniture. Used *attrib.* in *W. English*, applied to the pseudo-archaic diction affected by some writers, esp. of historical novels 1888.

Wardress (wǭ·ɹdrės). 1878. [f. WARDER *sb.*[1] + -ESS[1].] A female warder in a prison.

Wardrobe (wǭ·ɹd,roᵘb). late ME. [– ONFr. *warderobe*, var. of (O)Fr. *garderobe*, f. *garder* (GUARD *v.*, WARD *v.*) + *robe* ROBE *sb.* See GARDEROBE.] †**1.** A room in which wearing apparel was kept; esp. a room adjoining the sleeping apartment; hence, a dressing-room –1859. **b.** A room in which theatrical costumes and properties are kept 1711. **c.** A movable closed cupboard, fitted with hooks or pegs, often also with shelves or movable trays and drawers, in which wearing apparel is kept; esp. as a piece of bedroom furniture 1794. **2.** The office or department of a royal or noble household charged with the care of the wearing apparel. late ME. **3.** A person's stock of wearing apparel. late ME.

1. *transf.* France appears to be the w. of the world 1754. **c.** Their intellectual w...has few whole pieces in it LAMB. **2.** The Lady of the Strachy, married the yeoman of the wardrob SHAKS. **3.** *transf.* Flowers, that their gay wardrop wear MILT.

attrib. and *Comb.*: **w. bedstead,** a bedstead adapted to fold up into a w.; **w. book,** a book in which the accounts of a w. were kept; **w. dealer,** a dealer in second-hand clothes; **w. master, mistress,** one who has charge of the professional w. of an actor or actress or of a theatrical company; **-room** = 1 b; **-trunk,** a trunk designed to stand on end and serve as a wardrobe. Hence **Wa·rdrober** (now *Hist.*), an officer of a royal household who had charge of the robes, wearing apparel, etc. late ME.

Wa·rd-room. 1801. [WARD *sb.*] **1.** The mess-cabin of naval commissioned officers above the rank of sub-lieutenant; hence, the commissioned officers as a body. **2.** = GUARDROOM 1853.

-wards, *suffix*, OE. *-weardes*, corresp. to OS., MLG. *-wardes*, OHG., MHG. *-wartes*, the ending of the neut. gen. sing. (used advb.) of adjs. in Gmc. **-warda-*; see -WARD.

1. The history of *-wards* as an advb. suffix is identical with that of *-ward*; beside every adv. in *-ward* there has existed (at least potentially) a parallel formation in *-wards*, and vice versa. The two forms are so nearly synonymous that the choice between them is mostly determined by some notion of euphony in the particular context. Where, however, the meaning to be expressed includes the notion of manner as well as direction of movement, *-wards* is required, as in 'to walk backwards'. In other instances the distinction seems to be that *-wards* is used when the adv. is meant to express a definite direction in contrast with other directions: thus we say 'it is moving *forwards* if it is moving at all', but 'to come forward', not 'forwards'. **2.** In OE. the suffix *-weardes*, like *-weard*, was added to phrases containing the preps. *tō* and *wið* (see -WARD 4). In *to..ward(s, from..ward(s*, the two forms of the suffix were formerly equally common, but *-wards* now survives only in dialects.

To Troyewardes CHAUCER. To me-wards HERRICK. The nobles come peoplewards THACKERAY. He was growing downwards, brutewards 1893.

Wardship (wǭ·ɹdʃip). 1454. [f. WARD *sb.* + -SHIP.] **1.** The office or position of a guardian; *spec.* in *Feudal law*, the guardianship and custody of the person and lands of a minor with all profits accruing during his minority. **2.** The state or condition of being a ward; *spec.* in *Feudal law*, the condition of being under guardianship as a minor 1549.

1. This is the master-piece of a modern politician,..how the puny Law may be brought under the w. and controul of lust and will MILT.

Ware (wēᵊɹ), *sb.*[1] *Sc.* and *dial.* [OE. *wār*, corresp. to NFris. *wier* sea-weed, pond-weed, whence prob. Du. *wier*; repr. Gmc. **wairam*, f. **wai-* **wi-* bind; see WIRE *sb.*] Seaweed; *esp.* large drift seaweed used as manure. In *Scots Law*, the right of gathering seaweed on the shore. Also SEAWARE.

Ware (wēᵊɹ), *sb.*[2] [OE. *waru* = OFris. *ware, were*, MLG., MDu. *ware* (Du. *waar*), ON. *vara* :– Gmc. **warō*, perh. orig. 'object of care', and f. **war-* (see next).] **1.** *collect. sing.* or *pl.* Articles of merchandise or manufacture; the things which a merchant, tradesman, or pedlar has to sell; goods, commodities. **b.** An article of merchandise, a saleable commodity (*rare*) 1881. **2.** With defining word, as *dye-, grocery-, peltry-ware*. Also HARDWARE, HOLLOW-WARE, IRONWARE, SMALL-WARE(S, etc. late ME. **3.** *spec.* **a.** Vessels, etc., made of baked clay. Chiefly with defining word, as BROWN-, CHINA-, DELF-, GLASS-*ware*: see these words, and EARTHENWARE, STONE-WARE 1761. †**b.** Textile fabrics –1748. **c.** The spat of oysters in its third year 1877. **4.** *transf.* and *fig.* ME. **b.** Applied *joc.* to women 1558. **c.** *The hale w.* (Sc.): the whole number, quantity, or amount 1563.

1. *pl.* A capricious man of fashion might sometimes prefer foreign wares, merely because they were foreign, to cheaper and better goods..made at home ADAM SMITH. **3. b.** Euerything he wore was substantial honest, home-spun w. ADDISON. **4.** There is nothing immodest..in the advertisement of a man's literary wares 1865.

Ware (wēᵊɹ), *a. arch.* [OE. *wær*, also *ġewær* = OS. *war*, OHG. *giwar* (G. *gewahr*), Goth. **wars* (pl. *warai*) :– Gmc. *(*ʒa*)*waraz*, f. **war-* **wer-* observe, take care; see WARE *v.*[1]] *predic.* **1.** = AWARE *a.* 2. **2.** Prepared, on one's guard, vigilant, cautious. OE. **3.** Careful or cautious in avoiding. Const. *of.* late ME. **4.** Prudent, sagacious, cunning, skilled. Frequently coupled with *wise*. OE.

1. Thou speak'st wiser then thou art w. of SHAKS. **2.** They shall find him w. an' wakin', as they found him long ago! 1897. **3.** 'Be ye waure o' judgin' the Almichty' 1868.

Ware (wēᵊɹ), *v.*[1] [OE. *warian* = OFris. *waria*, OS. *waron*, OHG. *bi|warōn* beware, ON. *vara*, f. **war-* (see prec.); in ME. coalescing with ONFr. *warer* (mod. *garer*), f. Gmc.] †**1.** *intr.* To give heed, take care, be on one's guard; esp. *imper.*, as a warning cry, a call to animals, and in hunting –1825. **b.** with clause. *Obs.* and *arch.* OE. **2.** *trans.* To beware of, guard against; to avoid, shun. Chiefly in imper. = look out for! *arch.* OE. **b.** In hunting and in cries to animals, as *w. hawk* (fig. = look out for police, detectives, etc.), *w. horse*, etc. Now chiefly in *w. wheat* (= don't ride over it), *w. holes*, *w. wire*. Occas. pron. (wǭɹ). 1529.

1. W. there, roome for Sir Adam Prickeshaft DEKKER. **b.** W. what you do B. JONS.

Ware (wēᵊɹ), *v.*[2] Now *Sc.* and *dial.* late ME. [– ON. *verja* invest (money), lay out.] *trans.* To spend, lay out (money, goods). Const. *in, on, upon.*

fig. There would be little love wared on the matter SCOTT.

Warehouse (wēᵊ·ɹhaus), *sb.* ME. [f. WARE *sb.*[2] + HOUSE *sb.* Cf. Du. *warenhuis*, G. *warenhaus*.] A building or part of a building used for the storage of merchandise; the building in which a wholesale dealer keeps his stock of goods for sale; a building in which furniture or other property may be stored; a government building (more fully BONDED *w.*) where goods are kept in bond. †**b.** Used as a more dignified synonym for 'shop' –1857. **c.** In a printing office, the department responsible for printed work and 'white' paper 1888.

transf. The kidney-pie man has just walked away with his w. on his arm DICKENS.

attrib.: **w.-room,** storage in a w.

Warehouse (wēᵊ·ɹhaus), *v.* 1799. [f. prec.] *trans.* To deposit or secure (goods, furniture, bonded wares) in a warehouse. Hence **Wa·rehousing** *vbl. sb.*, the depositing goods, etc., in a warehouse; also, money paid for the accommodation of a warehouse.

Warehouseman (wēᵊ·ɹhausmĕn, wēᵊ·rəsmĕn). 1635. [f. WAREHOUSE *sb.* + MAN *sb.*] **1.** A man employed in or having the charge of a warehouse. **2.** A wholesale merchant (esp. a trader in textile materials) who has a warehouse for the storing of merchandise 1677. **b.** *Italian w.*: see ITALIAN *a.*

Wa·reless, *a. arch.* 1562. [f. †*ware* care, heed + -LESS.] **1.** Unwary, incautious. **2.** Unguarded, unconscious (*of* danger) 1562.

Wa·rely, *adv. Obs.* or *arch.* [OE. *wærliċe*; see WARE *a.*, -LY[2].] Watchfully, cautiously; prudently.

Warfare (wǭ·ɹfeᵊɹ), *sb.* 1456. [f. WAR *sb.* + FARE *sb.*[1]] *orig.* A going to war, in phrases, as †*to go a w.*; now, the action of carrying on in war; the act or state of conflict.

The Philistines gathered their armies together for w. 1 *Sam.* 28:1. Hence †**Wa·rfare** *v. intr.* to wage war, take part in war.

†**Wa·riangle.** OE. [Of unkn. origin.] The shrike.

Warily (wēᵊ·rili), *adv.* 1552. [f. WARY *a.* + -LY[2].] In a wary manner, cautiously, †watchfully.

Wariness (wēᵊ·rinės). 1552. [f. as prec. + -NESS.] The quality of being wary; cautiousness, circumspection.

†**Wa·rison.** ME. [– ONFr. *warison*, var. of OFr. *garison*; see GARRISON *sb.*] **1.** A gift bestowed by a superior; a reward –1572. ¶**2.** Misused by Scott for: A note of assault.

1. Mynstrells, playe vp for your waryson And well quyt it schall bee 1460. **2.** Straight they sound their w. And storm and spoil thy garrison SCOTT.

Wark, obs. and dial. f. WORK.

Warlike (wǭ·ɹləik), *a.* late ME. [f. WAR *sb.* + -LIKE.] **1.** Naturally disposed to warfare or fighting; skilled in war, martial; valiant; bellicose 1470. †**2.** Equipped for fighting or war –1711. **3.** Of or pertaining to war 1560. **4.** Of or belonging to a warrior (*poet.*) 1551.

1. The w. sound Of Trumpets loud and Clarions MILT. **2.** A Pyrate of very Warlicke appointment SHAKS. **3.** Thirtie Carts loaden with Munition, carriages, and other w. utensils 1652.

Warlock (wǭ·ɹlǫk). [OE. *wǣrloga* = OS. *wārlogo*; f. OE. *wǣr* covenant + **log*, wk. base of *lēogan* LIE *v.*[2] The mod. forms with final -(*c*)*k* are Sc. in origin.] †**1.** The Devil; Satan –1568. **2.** One in league with the Devil and so possessing occult and evil powers; a sorcerer, wizard; the male equivalent of *witch*. *Sc.* and *n. dial.* late ME. **b.** *Sc.* A magician, conjurer 1721. **3.** *attrib.* or as *adj.* That is a warlock. late ME. **b.** Pertaining to a warlock or warlocks 1786.

2. The gipsy..sneaks out at night with the bats and the owls,—So do Witches and Warlocks, Ghosts, Goblins, and Ghouls BARHAM. Hence **Wa·rlockry** (*Obs.* or *arch.*), the practice of magic; wizardry.

Warm (wǭɹm), *a.* (and *sb.*[1]) [OE. *wearm* = OFris., OS. *warm*, OHG. *war(a)m* (Du., G. *warm*), ON. *varmr* :– Gmc. **warmaz* (cf. Goth. *warmjan* to warm), with var. **werm-* prob. to be referred to IE. **ghworm-* **ghwerm-*, repr. by L. *formus* warm, Gr. θερμός hot, Skr. *gharmás* heat.] **A.** *adj.* **1.** Having a fairly high temperature; affording or giving out a considerable degree of heat (less than that indicated by *hot*). **2.** Of the body, the blood, etc.: Having the degree of heat natural to the living organism OE. **b.** Of persons: Glowing with exertion or exercise, with eating and drinking, etc. Of exercise: Strenuous enough to raise one's temperature. 1606. **c.** Applied to tears, kisses (combining the literal idea of bodily warmth with that of affection), etc. late ME. **3.** Of clothing, etc.: Made of material which retains heat in the body ME. **4.** Of a drug or edible: Producing a sensation of heat in the body 1737. **5.** Of a scent or trail: Fresh, strong 1713. **6.** Of the person chosen to seek or guess, in children's games: Near the object sought; on the verge of finding or guessing 1860. †**7.** Comfortably settled (*in* a seat, office); securely established *in* (possession of) –1809. **8.** Comfortably off, well to do. Now chiefly *colloq.* 1571. **9.** Of fighting, etc.: Vigorously conducted. Of a combatant: Dangerous to tackle. Of a locality: Dangerous to live in. 1627. **10.** Of persons, controversy, the passions, etc.: Ardent, zealous, keen; prone to excitement, impulsive. Now somewhat *rare*. late ME. **11.** Hot-tempered, angry 1547. **12.** Full of love, gratitude, etc.; very cordial or tender 1480. **13.** Characterized by, of the nature of, or prone to sexual desire; amorous 1592. **14.** Of fancy, ideas, etc.: Ardent, lively, glowing 1668. **b.** Of imaginative composition: Indelicate in its appeal to sexual emotion 1814. **15.** Of colour: Suggestive of warmth 1764.

1. Promise me to take a little something w. before you go to bed DICKENS. *fig. To keep a seat* or *place w.*, to occupy it temporarily for another. **2.** A fur'd gowne to keepe him warme SHAKS. **c.** In Winter with warme teares Ile melt the snow SHAKS. **3.** W. clothing for the poor 1917. **7.** The conquering King was scarce w. in his Throne 1647. **8.** A w. man; a fellow who will cut up well MACAULAY. **9.** Phr. *W. work*, hot fighting. *To make it* (or *things*) *w. for* (a person), to attack or 'go for' him. A *w. reception*, a vigorous onslaught or resistance: a demonstration of hostile feeling. **12.** My warmest vows of constancy GOLDSM. A very w. friendship DICKENS. They were now w. friends 1891.

B. *absol.* and *sb.*[1] **1.** That which is warm; warmth (*rare*) ME. **2.** *British* (*Service*) *w.*, a warm short overcoat worn especially by officers of the army 1901.

Comb.: **w. bath,** a bath of w. water (often as medical treatment); **-blooded** *a.*, having w. blood; *spec.* of mammals and birds, which have a uniform high temperature; **-hearted** *a.*, having a w. heart; of a generous and affectionate nature; **-house,** a kind of hot-house; **w. water,** water heated to a degree considerably below boiling-point; the seas of warmer regions as opposed to the Arctic Ocean; **w. with** *colloq.*, (spirits) mixed with hot water and sugar. Hence **Wa·rmish** *a.* somewhat w. **Wa·rm-ly** *adv.*, **-ness** (now *rare*).

Warm (wǭɹm), *adv.* [OE. *wearme*, f. the adj.] Warmly; so as to be warm.

Warm (wǭɹm), *v.* [Two formations: (i) OE. **wierman, werman, wirman* trans. = OS. *wermian* (Du. *warmen*), OHG. *wermen* (G. *wärmen*), ON. *verma*, Goth. *warmjan* :– Gmc. **warmjan*; (ii) OE. *wearmian* intr. = OHG. *war(a)mēn* (early mod.G. *warmen*) :– **warmǣjan*.] **I. 1.** *trans.* To make (the body, etc.) warm by approach to a fire, by exercise, clothing, etc.; to impart warmth to. **2.** *fig.* To inspire with affection or kindly feelings; to render eager or zealous; †to exhort to valour; †to provoke (temper). Of drink: To excite, stimulate. 1526. **3.** To make (a material object or substance) warm; to heat moderately OE. **b.** To impart warmth of colour to 1853. **4.** To heat (a building, a room) to a moderate temperature 1858. †**5.** To inaugurate (a new house) by a feast or entertainment –1800. †**6.** *Mil.* To throw (an enemy) into commotion by a cannonade –1720. **7.** *dial.* To beat, flog 1824.

1. Warming themselves in the sun 1798. The blood that warms an English yeoman 1896. *absol.* There shall not be a coale to w. at *Isa.* 47: 14. **2.** It will w. my heart to witness the happiness of those friends who are dearest to me DICKENS. Anne, who is so difficult to w. up to bare satisfaction point 1857. **3.** *To w. up* (U.S. *to w. over*), to make warm again (cooked food that has become cold). Also *fig.*; All the old anti-Turk abuse was warmed up again 1876. **7.** Take out your strap and w. him 1853.

II. *intr.* **1.** To be raised in temperature OE. **b.** Of colour: To become 'warmer' or more ruddy 1831. **2.** To become affectionate, kindly, or genial (*to, towards* a person). late ME. **3.** To become eager, animated, or enthusiastic. Also with *up*. 1749.

2. Your Grace's heart wad w. to the tartan SCOTT. **3.** *To w.* (*up*) *to*, to acquire zest for, 'put one's back into'. Hence **Warm** *sb.*[2] an act of warming or state of becoming warm (somewhat *colloq.*). **Wa·rmer,** a person who warms (*poet.*); a contrivance for warming (usu. with defining word prefixed, as *foot-, plate-w.*). **Wa·rming,** *vbl. sb.* the action of making warm, the state of becoming warm; (*dial.*) a thrashing, trouncing; also *attrib.* **Wa·rming** *ppl. a.* **Wa·rmish** *a.* somewhat warm.

Wa·rming-pan. 1573. **1.** A long-handled covered pan of metal (usu. of brass) to contain live coals, etc., formerly in common use for warming beds. **2.** *Hist.* With allusion to the story that James II's son, afterwards called the Old Pretender, was a supposititious child introduced into the Queen's bed in a warming-pan 1689. **3.** *slang.* A person who temporarily holds a place or employment until the intended occupant is ready to take it. 1846.

2. Our immortal deliverer from papists and pretenders, and wooden shoes and warming pans SCOTT. **3.** A *locum tenens* (ecclesiasticè, a w.) was wanted for a Yorkshire living 1846.

Warmth (wǭɹmþ). ME. [OE. **wiermþu*, **wærmþu* = MLG. *wermede* (Du. *warmte*), MHG. *wermede* (G. †*wärmte*) :- WGmc. **warmiþō*; see WARM *a.*, -TH[1].] **1.** A moderately hot or pleasantly heated state of the atmosphere; a temperate heat radiating from the sun, a fire, etc. **2.** The natural heat of a living body; vital heat 1592. **3.** A moderate degree of heat inherent or produced in a substance or liquid 1748. **4.** An excited or fervent state of the feelings; strength or glow of feeling; ardour, enthusiasm; heartiness 1596. **b.** A heated state of the temper approaching anger; the expression or exhibition of this 1710. **5.** A glowing hue; *spec.* in *Painting*, a glowing effect produced by the use of warm colours 1717.

2. No w., no breath shall testifie thou liuest SHAKS. **4.** The matter was taken up with unexpected w. 1893. **5.** Titian's w. divine POPE. His skin had a truly Spanish w. and intensity of colouring 1834. Hence **Wa·rmthless** *a.* (*rare*) devoid of warmth.

Warn (wǭɹn), *v.*[1] [OE. *war(e)nian, wearnian* = MLG. *warnen*, OHG. *warnōn, warnēn* (G. *warnen*) :- WGmc. **warnōjan, -ǣjan*, f. **war-* be cautious; see WARE *a.*] **1.** *trans.* To give timely notice to (a person) of impending danger or misfortune. **2.** To put (a person) on his guard, to caution *against* some person or thing as dangerous ME. **3.** To give (a person) cautionary notice or advice with regard to actions or conduct OE. **4.** To inform, notify. Now only in restricted use, to notify of something requiring attention. ME. **b.** To give previous notice to ME. **c.** *absol.* or *intr.* Of a clock: To make the clicking or whirring noise which indicates that it is about to strike. *dial.* 1846. **5.** To notify of something commanded; to order under penalties. late ME. **b.** To notify (a person) to go *from, out of* (a place), *away* 1592. **6.** To summon (a person *to* a duty, place, etc.). In later use chiefly, To summon officially; to command the attendance of. Now only *Mil.* ME.

1. They say it often comes to w. people of their death MRS. RADCLIFFE. **3.** *absol.* A perfect Woman, nobly planned, To w., to comfort, and command WORDSW. I w. you not to do so; I w. you to read what I have written 1852. **4.** The broker did not w. us of the arrival of the vessel 1886. **b.** But I w. you I will call again very soon 1866. **5.** He had warn'd them from the Seas DRYDEN. His royal summons warn'd the land, That all..Should instant take the spear SCOTT. *To w. off*, to notify (a person) to keep at a distance, or to keep *off* (private ground). *To w. off* (*the course*) (Racing), to prohibit (a defaulter against the laws of the Jockey Club) from riding or running horses at meetings under its jurisdiction. **6.** *Rich. III*, I. iii. 39. Officers and soldiers are warned for guard 1802. Hence **Wa·rner,** one who warns or gives warning to others; *transf.* esp. a mechanical device for giving warning.

†**Warn,** *v.*[2] [Two formations: (i) OE. *wiernan* = OFris. *werna*, OS. *wernian*, OHG. *wernen*, ON. *verna* :- Gmc. **warnjan*; (ii) OE. *wearnian* (by confusion with WARN *v.*[1]), = OFris. *warna*, ON. *varna* :- Gmc. **warnōjan*; both f. Gmc. **warnō* (OE. *wearn*), f. base **wer-* **war-* obstruct, defend.] *trans.* To refuse, deny, forbid; to prevent, hinder, restrain –1611.

Warnel (wǭ·ɹnĕl). Now *dial.* [OE. *wernæġel*, perh. f. **wearh* pus + *næġel* NAIL *sb.*] = WARBLE *sb.*[2] 2, 3.

Warning (wǭ·ɹniŋ), *vbl. sb.* [OE. *war(e)nung, wearning*, f. *war(e)nian, wearnian* WARN *v.*[1]; see -ING[1].] †**1.** Taking heed, precaution –1590. **2.** Previous intimation or threat of impending evil or danger; a portent of coming evil OE. **3.** Advice to beware of a person or thing; cautionary advice against imprudent or vicious action, etc. OE. **b.** A deterrent example 1613. **4.** Previous notice of an event whether good or bad ME. **b.** In some clocks, the rattling or whirring noise which precedes the striking 1775. **5.** Notice of the termination of a business relation given by one of the parties to the other; esp. by a landlord to a tenant, a master to a servant, etc., or vice versa. late ME. †**6.** Intimation, notification of a fact or a present occurrence –1821.

2. Phr. *To give w.* (*to*); Looke to thy selfe; I gyue thee fayre w. 1600. †*Scarborough w.*: see SCARBOROUGH. **3.** A wyse man wil receaue warnynge, but a foole wil sooner be smytten in the face COVERDALE *Prov.* 10:8. *To take w.*, to alter one's course of action when warned of its danger. **b.** Such a man is a spectacle and a w. to us all 1857. **4.** *Tam. Shr.* IV. iv. 60. An Angel gave the Blessed Virgin three days w. of her Death 1701. **5.** Mary Dishley gave her mistress w.: no fault to find with her place, but wanted a change 1872.

Comb.: **w.-bell,** (*a*) a bell for giving alarm of fire or invasion; (*b*) a bell announcing the imminent departure of a vessel; **-gun,** a gun sounded as an alarm or announcement; **-lever,** *Horology*, the lever that sets in motion the w.-wheel; **-piece,** (*a*) = *w.-gun*; (*b*) *Horology*, the piece that 'warns' that the clock is about to strike; **w.-pipe,** an overflow pipe serving to show when a cistern is too full; **w.-wheel,** *Horology*, the wheel that produces the 'warning'.

Warning (wǭ·ɹniŋ), *ppl. a.* 1552. [f. as prec. + -ING[2].] That warns, in senses of the verb; *spec.* in *Biol.* of coloration or other distinctive marks found in caterpillars, etc. Hence **Wa·rningly** *adv.*

Wa·r O:ffice. 1721. **a.** The department of the British Government, presided over by the Secretary of State for War, which is charged with the administration of the Army; the building in which the business of this department is carried on. **b.** *U.S.* The War Department.

Warp (wǭɹp), *sb.* [OE. *wearp*, with Continental equivalents, f. base of WARP *v.* Some later senses are from the vb.] **1.** *Weaving.* The threads which are extended lengthwise in the loom, usu. twisted harder than the weft or woof, with which these threads are crossed to form the web or piece. **2.** *Naut.* A rope or light hawser attached at one end to some fixed object, used in hauling or in moving a ship from one place to another in a harbour, road, or river ME. **b.** *Trawl-fishing.* A rope attached to a net 1835. **c.** *Whaling.* A rope fastened to a harpoon 1897. **3.** A tale of four (occas. three or a couple) esp. used of fish and oysters. late ME. **4.** Alluvial sediment deposited by water; silt 1698. **b.** A bed or layer of this 1678. **5.** A twist or bending, esp. in wood not properly dried; also, the state of being warped or twisted 1679. **6.** *fig.* A perversion or perverse inclination of the mind; a mental twist 1764.

1. *fig.* Sorrow is..the..woof which is woven into the w. of life 1849. **4.** The tide is let in at high water to deposit the w. 1805. **5.** A w. in the glass made him look as if he had taken poison 1871.

attrib. and *Comb.*: (sense 1) *w.-twist, -yarn*; (sense 2) *w.-anchor, -rope*; **w.-beam,** the roller on which the w. is wound; **-lace,** a kind of lace having threads so placed as to resemble the w. of a fabric; **-wire,** one of the lengthwise wires in a wire-loom.

Warp (wǭɹp), *v.* [OE. *weorpan* (the ordinary vb. for 'cast, throw') = OS. *werpan*, OHG. *werfan* (Du. *werpen*, G. *werfen*), ON. *verpa*, Goth. *wairpan*; Gmc. str. vb., becoming wk. in Eng. XIV; f. base **werp-*, **warp-* with no known cogns.] †**I.** *trans.* To cast, throw, fling –1513. **II. 1.** To bend, curve, or twist (an object) out of shape; *spec.* to curve (timber) by the application of steam; also, to distort, contort (the body or a limb, the features). late ME. **2.** *intr.* To become bent, twisted, or uneven, by shrinkage or contraction: *esp.* said of timber 1440. **3.** *trans.* To cause to shrink, shrivel, corrugate (*rare*) 1600. **b.** *intr.* To shrink or shrivel, become contracted or winkled (*rare*) 1579. **4.** *trans.* To pervert, distort (the mind, judgement, principles, etc.); to turn (*aside*) from rectitude or the straight path. Also const. *from, out of, to, into.* 1599. **5.** To distort, wrest, misinterpret (a fact, account, etc.) 1717. **6.** To turn aside (a moving body) from its path or orbit. Also, to deflect (one's journey). *rare.* 1725. †**7.** *intr.* To turn from the straight path; to deviate, swerve, go astray –1817.

2. Old wood seldom warps in the wetting SCOTT. **3.** *A.Y.L.* II. vii. 187. **b.** The Fames of Shakespear and of Ben Must w., before my nobler fire To their regardless Tombs retire TUTCHIN. **4.** I have no private considerations to w. me in this controversy ADDISON. By the present mode of education we are forcibly warped from the bias of nature GOLDSM. **5.** Warping the Scriptures into Erastianism SCOTT. **7.** *Meas. for M.* I. i. 15.

III. 1. *trans.* To arrange (threads, yarn) so as to form a warp; to wind on a warp-beam 1598. **2.** *Rope-making.* To stretch (yarn) into lengths to be tarred 1815. †**3.** To twist, entwine, insert (something *into* something else) –1822. **4.** *Angling.* To fasten (the materials of an artificial fly) to the hook 1676.

3. Those strings of pearl, which you fret me by warping into my tresses SCOTT.

IV. 1. *Naut.* To move (a ship) along by hauling on a 'warp'. Also *absol.* and *intr.* of a ship: To move by warping. 1513. **2.** *intr.* To progress slowly or with effort by using the hands as well as the feet. Also *refl.* 1796. **3.** To float or whirl through the air. Chiefly *poet.* 1565.

1. Phr. *To w. one's way.* **2.** The first mate.. warping himself from one belaying-pin to another 1859.

V. 1. *trans.* To choke *up* (a channel) with alluvial deposit. Also *intr.*, to become choked *up.* 1745. **2.** To cover (land) by natural or artificial flooding, with a deposit of alluvial soil 1799. Hence **Warped** *ppl. a.* bent, contorted, or twisted out of shape; enriched with alluvial warp. **Wa·rper,** one who winds yarn in preparation for weaving; one who lays the warp for the weaver.

Wa·r-path. 1768. Among North Amer. Indians: The path or route taken by a warlike expedition.

To be or *go on the w.*, to go to war, be out for scalps; also *transf.* and *fig.*

Wa·rping, *vbl. sb.* 1440. [f. WARP *v.* + -ING[1].] **1.** The action of preparing a warp for weaving. **2.** The action of moving a ship from one place to another by means of warps 1513. **3.** The process of flooding low-lying land near a tidal river so that the muddy alluvium may be deposited when the water is withdrawn 1799. **4.** The action of twisting or bending, or the fact of becoming twisted or bent; an instance of this 1440. **5.** *Carpentry.* A strengthening brace 1833. **6.** *Angling.* The wound thread which attaches the artificial fly to the hook 1676.

4. *fig.* The w. of opinion which the bias of patriotism causes SPENCER.

‖**Warracoori** (wǫrăkū·ᵊri). 1858. [Native name.] The wood of the white cedar of Demarara.

Warrandice (wǫ·răndis). Chiefly *Sc.* 1466. [– AFr. *warandise*, var. of *warantise*; see WARRANTISE, -ICE.] **a.** A guarantee, an undertaking to secure another against risk. Chiefly in *Scots Law*; now only as a literary archaism 1488. **b.** *spec.* in *Scots Law.* The obligation to indemnify the grantee or purchaser of land if an evictive or paramount claim should be established against the lands through defect of title 1466.

a. I'se be caution for them—I'se give you my personal w. SCOTT.

Warrant (wǫ·rănt), *sb.*[1] [ME. *warant, warand* = ONFr. *warant*, var. of OFr. *guarant, -and* (mod. *garant*) – Frankish *werĕnd* (= OHG. *werĕnt*), f. *gi|werĕn*, G. *gewähren* = OFris. *wera* be surety for, guarantee.] **I.** †**1.** A protector, defender –1829. †**2.** A guarantor, surety (*Sc.*); assurance, pledge, guaranty –1828. **3.** One who is answerable for a fact or statement; an authoritative witness ME. †**4.** One whose command justifies an action –1821. **5.** Command or permission of a superior which frees the doer of an act from blame or legal responsibility; authorization, sanction ME. **b.** A token or evidence of authorization. late ME. **6.** Justifying reason or ground for an action, belief, or feeling 1576.

1. I will be thy warrand for a year and a day SCOTT. **2.** *Rich. II*, IV. 235. *To take w. on oneself*, to pledge oneself. **4.** Use axe and lever, Master Foster—I will be your w. SCOTT. **5. b.** Fayth is willing to obey, as soone as it seeth a Warrand 1635. **6.** Good intentions are no w. for irregular actions 1703. Phr. †*Of w.*, warranted. †*Out of w.*, unlawful, unwarranted.

II. 1. A writing issued by the sovereign, an officer of state, or an administrative body, authorizing those to whom it is addressed to perform some act 1513. **2.** A writ or order issued by some executive authority, empowering a ministerial officer to make an arrest, a seizure, or a search, to execute a judicial sentence, etc. 1450. **3.** A writing which authorizes one person to pay or deliver, and another to receive, a sum of money. late ME. †**4.** A voucher, certificate –1598. **5.** A form of receipt given to a person who has deposited goods in a warehouse, by assignment of which the title to the goods is transferred 1825. **6.** *Mil.* and *Naval.* An official certificate of appointment issued to an officer of lower rank than a commissioned officer 1786. **b.** Short for WARRANT OFFICER 1706. **7.** *W. of attorney* = letter, power of attorney (see ATTORNEY *sb.*[2]) 1512.

2. There's a w. out against me, and I must fly 1859. *General w.*, a w. for the apprehension of the persons suspected of an offence, no individual being named or particularly described.

Comb.: **w. holder**, a tradesman who has written authority to supply goods to the household of the king or a member of the royal family.

Warrant (wǫ·rănt), *sb.*[2] *Mining.* 1847. [Of unkn. origin.] Under-clay.

Warrant (wǫ·rănt), *v.* [ME. *warent(e, warant, war(r)and* – OFr. *warantir, warandir*, vars. of *g(u)arantir, -andir*; a common Rom. formation on the sb.; see WARRANT *sb.*[1]] †**1.** *trans.* To keep safe from danger, to protect –1600. **2.** *Law.* To guarantee the security of (land, possessions *to* a person); to give warranty of (title); to give warranty of title to (a person). late ME. **3.** To guarantee (goods, etc.) to be of the quality, quantity, etc. specified. late ME. **b.** To promise under guarantees 1849. **4.** To guarantee as true, make oneself answerable for (a statement) ME. †**b.** To promise or predict as certain. Also, of a thing: To be a sure presage of. –1821. **5.** To give (a person) assurance of a fact. Chiefly in *I (I'll) w. you*, used colloq. = 'I'll be bound'. 1520. **6.** To attest the truth or authenticity of; to authenticate. †Also with clause as obj. or with obj. and complement. 1591. †**7.** To furnish (a person) with a guarantee or assurance –1597. **8.** To guarantee the security or immunity of (a person or thing). Now *rare.* 1530. **9.** To give (a person) warrant or authority, authorize (*to* do something); to authorize, sanction (a course of action, a payment, etc.) 1579. **10.** Of things: To furnish good and sufficient grounds for (a course of action); to justify (a person *in* or *to* a course of action) 1654.

1. Hym I beseche to kepe and waraunt thee.. from evyl CAXTON. **3.** The manuscript sermons of a clergyman lately deceased, all warranted originals, and never printed FIELDING. One French roll rasped, one egg new laid (or warranted to be) DICKENS. **4.** I will w. her a good Huswife BUNYAN. *I w., I will w.*, often used *colloq.* as a mere expression of strong belief = 'I'll be bound'; I w. she kissed thee DE FOE. Some chapel where she comforts herself with brimstone doctrine, I w. DICKENS. **b.** My fainting words doe w. death SHAKS. **5.** ¶ *I w. me* (orig. quasi-*arch.*) = 'I w.' (see 4). **6.** A thousand oathes..W. me welcome to my Protheus SHAKS. **9.** The Lord warrants us to suspect the inconstant 1642. **10.** We are not warranted in referring our sensations to a cause MILL. Hence **Wa·rranted** *ppl. a.* allowed by law or authority; sanctioned; furnished with a legal or official warrant. **Wa:rrantee·**, (*Law*) the person to whom a warranty is given.

Warrantable (wǫ·răntăb'l), *a.* 1581. [f. prec. + -ABLE.] **1.** That may be authorized, sanctioned, or permitted; justifiable 1597. †**2.** That may be guaranteed as good, true, genuine, or the like; praiseworthy, acceptable –1821. **3.** That can be legally guaranteed 1876. **4.** *Venery.* Applied to a stag which is of an age to be hunted (5 or 6 years) 1677.

2. Grave and w. personages LAMB. Hence **Wa·rrantableness** 1586. **Wa·rrantably** *adv.*

Warranter (wǫ·răntəɹ). 1583. [f. WARRANT *v.* + -ER[1].] One who warrants or guarantees. **b.** *Law* = WARRANTOR 1706.

Warrantise (wǫ·răntəiz). *arch.* ME. [– OFr. *warentise*, f. *warentir* WARRANT *v.* See WARRANDICE, -ISE[2].] **1.** *Law.* = WARRANTY 1 a; often in *clause of w.* **2.** *gen.* The action of warranting; the state or fact of being guaranteed. Also *predic.*, of a thing or person that serves as a guarantee or security. ME. **3.** Authorization, permission, sanction 1580.

2. Breake vp the Gates, Ile be your warrantize SHAKS. **3.** *Ham.* V. i. 250.

Wa·rrant o:fficer. 1693. **1.** An officer of the army or navy who holds office by warrant, as dist. from a commissioned officer. (In the army, the warrant officers are now intermediate in rank between the commissioned and the non-commissioned officers.) **2.** An officer whose duty it is to serve warrants 1895.

Warrantor (wǫ·răntǭɹ, wǫrăntǭ·ɹ). 1685. [f. WARRANT *v.* + -OR 2.] *Law.* One who gives warranty.

Warranty (wǫ·rănti). ME. [– AFr. *warantie*, var. of *garantie*; see GUARANTY.] **1.** *Law.* An act of warranting: in certain specific applications. **a.** A covenant (either expressed by a *clause of w.* or implied) annexed to a conveyance of real estate, by which the vendor warrants the security of the title conveyed. **b.** An undertaking, express or implied, given by one of the parties to a contract to the other, that he will be answerable for the truth of some statement incidental to the contract; esp. an assurance given by the seller of goods that he will be answerable for their possession of some quality attributed to them 1543. **c.** In a contract for insurance, an engagement by the assured that certain statements are true or that certain conditions shall be fulfilled 1817. **2.** *transf.* A guarantee, an assurance. Now *dial.* 1555. **3.** Formal or official sanction; authorization = WARRANT *sb.*[1] I. 5. Now *rare.* 1591. **4.** Justifying reason, ground (*for* an action or belief) 1836. **5.** Substantiating evidence or witness 1561.

1. a. *Covenant of w.* (U.S.) corresp. to English 'covenant for quiet enjoyment'. **3.** From your loue I haue a warrantie To vnburthen all my plots and purposes SHAKS. **4.** The smallest civility was sufficient w. for the opening of an acquaintanceship 1877.

†**Warray**, *v.* [ME. *werreye* – OFr. *werreier*, var. of *guerreier* (mod. *-oyer*) f. *guerre* WAR *sb.*] **1.** *trans.* To make war upon, ravage by war –1768. **2.** *intr.* To make war –1600.

1. With this she oft hath Villainy warray'd 1768.

War(r)ee (wǫ·ri). 1684. [Of unkn. origin.] The white-lipped peccary, *Dicotyles labiatus*, native to Central and South America.

Warren (wǫ·rĕn, -ən). late ME. [– AFr., ONFr. *warenne*, var. of (O)Fr. *garenne* game-park, now esp. rabbit-warren – Gaulish **varrenna* area marked off by palisading, f. **varros* post (cf. Ir. *farr* pillar, post), evidenced in Gaulish place-names.] **1.** A piece of land enclosed and preserved for breeding game. *Obs.* exc. *Hist.* **2.** *spec.* A piece of land appropriated to the breeding of rabbits (formerly also of hares). More fully *rabbit-w., cony-w., hare-w.* Now usu. a piece of uncultivated ground in which rabbits breed wild in burrows. late ME. **3.** The inhabitants of a warren; *transf.* any collection of small animals 1607. **4.** A building, etc., likened to a rabbit-warren; †a brothel; a building or number of buildings densely populated by poor tenants 1649. †**5.** An old name for the site of Woolwich Arsenal. Hence *gen.* –1805.

1. As melancholy as a Lodge in a W. SHAKS. †(*Free*) *w.*, a right of keeping or hunting *beasts* and *fowls of w.* **4.** A large passenger steamer..is..an amazing w. of passages 1919.

Warrener (wǫ·rĕnəɹ, -ənər). ME. [– AFr. *warener* (= ONFr. *warennier*, (O)Fr. *garennier*), f. *warenne* WARREN; see -ER[2] 2.] **1. a.** An officer employed to watch over the game in a park or preserve. *Obs.* exc. *Hist.* **b.** A servant who has the charge of a rabbit-warren. **2.** One who owns or rents a warren 1846.

Warrigal (wǫ·rigăl), *sb.* (and *a.*) *Austral.* Also **warragal.** 1852. [Native Australian word, recorded as *warregal, wor-re-gal, worrikul*, etc.] **A.** *sb.* **1.** = DINGO. **2.** A wild Australian aboriginal 1890. **3.** A wild or untamed Australian horse 1881. **B.** *adj.* Wild 1890.

Warring (wǭ·riŋ), *ppl. a.* 1608. [f. WAR *v.*[1] + -ING[2].] **1.** That makes or carries on war; that contends in warfare 1702. **2.** *fig.* Engaged in strife, contending; *esp.* with plural subject, mutually contending, discordant 1608.

1. W. nations BYRON. **2.** All the w. Winds that sweep the Skies DRYDEN. W. Passions 1703. What means this senseless din of w. tongues? 1883.

Warrior (wǫ·riəɹ). [ME. *werre(y)our* – ONFr. *werreior, werreieur*, var. of OFr. *guerreieor* (mod. *guerroyeur*), f. *werreier, guerreier*; see WARRAY, -ER[2] 3, -OR 2.] **1.** One whose occupation is warfare; a fighting man; in eulogistic sense, a valiant or an experienced man of war. Now chiefly *poet.* and *rhet.*, exc. as applied to the fighting men and heroes of past ages and of uncivilized peoples. **b.** occas. applied to a woman. late ME. **c.** *transf.* Applied to an animal 1697. **2.** (*Bloody*) *w.*: (*local*) the wallflower, *Cheiranthus cheiri* 1825. **3.** A South Amer. humming-bird of the genus *Oxypogon* 1861. **4.** *Black w.*, an Amer. bird of prey, *Buteo harlani* 1884.

1. Then should al captaines..be tendre ouer there poore warriours and base souldiours 1551. *The Unknown W.*, a member of one of the fighting forces (army, navy, or air force) who was buried in Westminster Abbey on 11 Nov. 1920, as the representative of all members of the British Empire who lost their lives in the war of 1914–18. *Warrior's belt*, three bright stars in the constellation Orion. **b.** *Oth.* II. i. 184.

attrib.: (*a*) quasi-adj., belonging to or characteristic of a w., martial, as *w.-blood, hymn, laurel, lay, spirit, trumpet*; (*b*) appositive, that is a w., as *w.-angel, chief, dame, god, guest, king, love, maid, queen, son, steed*; consisting of warriors, as *w.-host, -train*; (*c*) similative, as *w.-like* adj. and adv., *-wise* adv. Hence **Wa·rrioress**, a female w. 1594.

Warsaw (wǭ·ɹsǭ). *U.S.* 1884. [An attempt to pronounce the Sp. name *guasa.*] **a.** The American fish guasa, *Garrupa nigrita*. **b.** The jew-fish, *Promicrops itaiara*.

Warship, war-ship (wǭ·ɹʃip).· 1533. [f. WAR *sb.* + SHIP *sb.*] A ship armed and manned for war.

Warsle (wa·rs'l), *v. Sc.* and *north.* ME. [Metathetic form of WRESTLE *v.* Cf. WORSLE.] *intr.* and *trans.* = WRESTLE *v.*

1. Ye'll soon hae poets o' the Scottish nation, Will..w. Time, and lay him on his back BURNS. Hence **Wa·rsle** *sb.*, a struggle; a wrestling bout 1792. **Wa·rsler**, a wrestler.

Wart (wǭɹt). [OE. *wearte* = OFris. *warte, worte*, OS. *warta*, OHG. *warza* (Du. *wrat*, G. *warze*), ON. *varta* :– Gmc. **wartōn.*] **1.** A small, round, dry, tough excrescence on the skin; especially common on the hands of young persons. Also applied to other small excrescences on animals, etc. **b.** = CONDYLOMA 1552. **c.** A normal callosity on the legs of a horse, ass, etc. 1523. **2.** *Bot.* A rounded protuberance or excrescence on the surface of a plant 1793. **3.** *transf.* and *fig.* (from sense 1). A relatively small or disfiguring protuberance 1602. **4.** *Mil. colloq.* A very young subaltern 1894.

1. Vp on the cope right of his nose he hade A werte CHAUCER. An unhealthy-looking boy, with warts all over his hands DICKENS. **3.** *Ham.* V. i. 306. You will not deny you are..A nuisance, a w., a blot, a stain upon the face of nature! 1792.

attrib. and *Comb.*: **w.-biter** [= G. *warzenbeisser*], a grasshopper (*Gryllus verrucivorus*) supposed to destroy warts by biting them; **-cress**, the genus *Senebiera*; **-hog**, a swine of the African genus

Phacochœrus, having w.-like excrescences on the face; **-snake,** a colubriform snake of the family *Acrochordidæ*, having w.-like scales; **-weed** = WARTWORT. Hence **Wa·rted** *a.* covered with warts (*rare*); *Bot., Zool.*, etc. verrucose.

Warth. *Obs.* exc. *dial.* [OE. *waroþ*, etc., corresp. to MLG. *werde, -er*, OHG. *werid* (G. *wert, werder* island).] A shore, strand; in mod. use 'a flat meadow, esp. one close to a stream; a stretch of coast' (*Eng. Dial. Dict.*).

Wa·r-time. late ME. The time when war is being waged.

These war times were hard, and everything was dear C. BRONTË. *attrib.* A W. Journal 1915.

Wartwort (wǭ·ɹtˌwɒɹt). late ME. [f. WART + WORT¹.] A name for *Euphorbia helioscopia*, *E. peplus* and *E. peplis* (Sea Wartwort), the juice of these plants being used to cure warts. Also applied to other plants, as *Chelidonium majus* and *Senebiera coronopus*.

Warty (wǭ·ɹti), *a.* 1483. [f. WART + -Y¹.] **1.** Afflicted with warts on the skin. **2.** Chiefly *Zool., Bot.*, etc. Having wart-like excrescences or protuberances 1693. **3.** Of the nature of or resembling a wart 1762. **4.** *fig.* Rocky, rough 1648.

1. Freckled, wartie, and wodden-faced wenches CAMDEN. **2.** Tall, w., black-boled trees 1894.

War-whoop (wǭ·ɹˌhūp). 1761. The cry or yell of Amer. Indians and other savage peoples on rushing into battle.

transf. The accustomed maternal warwhoop. BYRON.

Warwickite (wǫ·rikəit). 1838. [f. *Warwick*, New York, where it was found; see -ITE¹ 2 b.] *Min.* A borotitanate of magnesium and iron in dark-brown acicular crystals.

Wa·r-wolf. 1610. **1.** *Hist.* A kind of siege engine. †**2.** A fierce warrior. SCOTT.

Wary (wēᵊ·ri), *a.* 1552. [f. WARE *a.* + -Y¹.] **1.** Given to caution, habitually on one's guard against danger, deception, or mistake; circumspect. **2.** On one's guard, cautious, careful 1575. **3.** Of action, behaviour, etc.: Proceeding from or characterized by caution 1557. †**4.** Careful in expenditure, thrifty –1812.

1. A w. man he is in Grammar; very nice as to Solæcism or Barbarism DRYDEN. W. old alligators KINGSLEY. **2.** The day is broke, be w., looke about SHAKS. Thus men cannot be too w. what they inscribe on Tombs FULLER. To be very cautious and w. in the choice of our words 1680. A tradesman ought to be very w. of taking too much credit 1745. **3.** I shall keep a w. eye upon all that passes 1794. **4.** I have, by leading a very w. Life, laid up a little Money STEELE.

†**Wary,** *v.* [OE. *wierġan, wærġan* curse, corresp. to OS. *waragean*, OHG. *gawergen*, Goth. *gawargjan* condemn :– Gmc. **warȝjan*, f. **warȝaz* whence OE. *wearg* felon.] *trans.* and *intr.* To curse –1746.

Was (wǫz), *sb.* ME. [pa. t. sing. of BE *v.*] What was; something past.

If the 'w.' is hard to face, how much harder the 'might have been' 1876.

Was (wǫz, wəz), 1st. and 3rd. pers. sing. pa. t. of BE *v.*

Wash (wǫʃ), *sb.* 1440. [f. WASH *v.*] **I.** Act of washing. **1.** An act or process of washing or cleansing with water 1663. **b.** An act of washing oneself, esp. of washing one's hands and face 1825. **2.** An act, spell, or task of washing clothes, etc.; the process of washing undergone by clothes or the like; *concr.* the quantity of clothes or other textile articles washed (or set apart to be washed) on one occasion 1704. **3.** A washing with some liquid for the purpose of producing a particular effect; a liquid preparation used or intended to be used in this manner 1626. **4.** A thin coat of water-colour or distemper spread over a wall or similar surface; a preparation used for this purpose (cf. WHITEWASH) 1698. **b.** *Water-colour Painting.* A broad thin layer of colour laid on by a continuous movement of the brush 1597. **5.** A solution applied to metals for producing an appearance of gold or silver 1697.

1. b. What we really did want was a w. and a brush up 1912. **2.** The family w... flutters gracefully in the breeze 1889. (*To be lost, damaged*, etc.) *in the w.*, in course of being washed. *At the w.*, of clothes, etc., sent away or set aside to be washed. **3.** Essences, powders, pastes, washes for the hair, washes for the skin, recal the days of one's grandmothers 1859. *Black, yellow w.*, various liquid preparations of mercury for application to ulcers or to the skin in eruptive diseases. *White w.*, dilute liquor of subacetate of lead. **4.** *transf.* One broad w. of shadow STEVENSON.

II. Washing movement of water. **1.** The washing of the waves upon the shore; surging movement of the sea or other water 1579. **b.** A surge raised by the passage of a vessel 1883. **c.** The sound of the surge of water 1845. **d.** Wear or attrition due to the action of waves 1791. **2.** A sandbank or tract of land alternately covered and exposed by the sea 1440. **b.** A low-lying tract of ground, often flooded, and interspersed with shallow pools and marshes 1483. **c.** *Western U.S.* The dry bed or portion of the bed of a winter torrent 1894. **3.** A tract of shallow water, a lagoon. Also, a shallow pool or runnel formed by the overflow of a river; a stream running across a road. 1530.

1. The long w. of Australasian seas TENNYSON. **2.** †*The Washes*, applied *spec.* to the fordable portion of the estuary between Lincolnshire and Norfolk; hence as a name for the estuary itself, now called *The W.*

III. 1. Waste water discharged after use in washing; liquid refuse. Now *rare.* 1440. **2.** *Sc.* and *north.* Stale urine 1480. **3.** Kitchen swill or brewery refuse as food for swine; HOGWASH, PIG-WASH. 1585.

3. *Rich. III*, V. ii. 9.

IV. Matter washed away or deposited by running water; alluvial deposit 1707. **b.** *Mining.* A formation of gravel, etc. over an abraded coal seam 1888. **V.** Soil from which gold (or diamonds) can be extracted by washing 1875. **VI.** Watery infusion or mixture. **1.** Orig., the partially fermented wort remaining after ale or beer has been brewed from it. In later use, malt or other fermentable substance or mixture of substances steeped in water to undergo fermentation preparatory to distillation. 1700. **2.** Washy or vapid liquor. Also *fig.*, vapid discourse or writing. 1548.

2. Coffee; not the vile and vapid w. which is usually made in England 1819.

VII. Senses of doubtful origin. **1.** A measure for oysters and whelks 1481. **2.** The underground den of a beaver or a bear 1809. **3.** *slang.* **a.** *Printers.* An act of 'washing' 1841. **b.** *Stock Exch.* A fictitious sale of securities by a broker who has a commission from an intending buyer and also from an intending seller, and who simply transfers from the one account to the other, the difference going to his own profit 1891.

Comb.: **w.-basket**, a basket for clothes sent to the w.; **-day**, the day for the washing of clothes in a household; **-drawing**, the method of water-colour drawing in which washes of colour are extensively used; a picture produced by this method; **-land**, a tract of land periodically overflowed by a river; **-linen**, linen sent to the w.; **-plain**, a tract of land formed by alluvial deposits.

†**Wash,** *a.* 1548. [perh. f. WASH *v.*] Washy, weak, tender –1639.

Wash (wǫʃ), *v.* Pa. t. and pa. pple. **washed** (wǫʃt). [OE. *wæsćan, wasćan, waxan* = OS. *wascan* (Du. *wasschen*), OHG. *wascan* (G. *waschen*), ON. *vaska* (wk.) :– Gmc. orig. str. vb. **waskan* :– **watskan*, f. **wat-* WATER *sb.* The strong forms seldom occur exc. dial. after XVI.] **I.** To cleanse by means of water. Also with compl. adj., *to w. white, clean.* **1.** *trans.* To cleanse, remove the dirt from (something) by affusion of or immersion in water. **2.** To cleanse (soiled clothes, etc.) by rubbing in water, with soap or some equivalent. Also *to w. clean, white.* OE. **b.** *absol.* To wash clothes (as an occupation or as part of one's household duties) 1591. **c.** *trans.* To wash clothes for (a customer or lodger). *dial.* 1795. **d.** *absol.* To have one's clothes washed. *joc.* DICKENS. **e.** *trans.* Of water, etc.: To have the property of cleansing (clothes) easily and well (*rare*) 1697. **f.** *intr.* Of a fabric, a dye: To bear cleansing with soap and water without damage to colour or texture 1765. **g.** *fig.* (*colloq.*) To bear trial or investigation, stand the test. Chiefly in phr. (*it*) *won't w.* 1849. **h.** *pass.* or *intr.* with *out.* To lose colour in the wash. Hence *fig.* to lose all vigour or freshness. 1848. **3.** To cleanse (the body or part of it) with water ME. **b.** Said of the water as agent. late ME. **c.** Of a cat, etc.: To cleanse (itself, its face) by licking and rubbing with its paw 1661. **d.** *refl.* and *intr.* To cleanse one's body or (often) merely one's face and hands, with water ME. **e.** To cleanse, rinse (the mouth, etc.) with a douche or medicinal application 1538. **f.** Said with ref. to baptism ME. **g.** *fig.* To cleanse *from* the stain of sin ME. **4.** To flush or drench (a substance) with water or other liquid, in order to remove impurities or to dissolve out some component 1650. **b.** Of running water, rain, etc.: To pass over (a surface) so as to carry off adherent matter 1523.

1. Take cockles at a full moon and w. 'em 1764. Prov. †*To w. a wall of loam, a brick or tile*, to labour in vain. *To w. out*, to cleanse the interior of (a vessel). *To w. up*, to w. (table utensils) after a meal; also *absol.* *To w. down*, to wash from top to bottom or from end to end 1877. **2.** *To w. one's dirty linen at home, in public* (said *fig.* with ref. to domestic quarrels or grievances). *To w. out*, to rinse so as to remove soap, etc. from the web of the stuff. **b.** What wilt thou do to the Germans, who w. scarce twice in a year? 1671. Goes out charing and washing by the day DICKENS. **c.** That'd be nigh enough for me to w. 'im an' mend 'im 1895. **f.** Only eighteenpence a yard, ma'am, and warranted to w. 1883. **h.** I'm quite washed out and unfit for anything 1886. **3.** Keep your Temper, w. your Face, and go to Bed STEELE. Prov. *To w. an Ethiop, a blackamoor* (*white*); *to w. an ass's head* (or *ears*), to labour in vain. Phr. *To w. one's hands of*, to disown responsibility for, refuse to have any further connection with (orig. an allusion to Pilate's washing his hands; see *Matt.* 27:24). *To w. one's hands*, to rub the hands together, in imitation of the act of washing them. **d.** No Earl is to w. with a Duke without the Dukes Permission 1694. **f.** The Anabaptist washt and washt, and shrunk in the washing 1653. **g.** Washed in the blood of the Lamb 1874.

II. To subject to the action of water or other liquid. **1.** To bathe, lave (the body, limbs, etc.) with water or other liquid ME. **b.** To moisten (the throat) with wine. late ME. †**c.** *intr.* for *refl.* To use cosmetic washes –1693. †**2.** To plunge, bathe (a person) in a river or lake –1660. †**b.** *refl.* To bathe –1775. **c.** *intr.* for *refl.* To bathe. *Obs.* exc. of animals. late ME. **3.** To wet or moisten thoroughly; to saturate with water (esp. rain) or other liquid; to sprinkle or pour water upon ME. **b.** To form *in* holes by running or dropping water; to form (a hole or depression) by such erosion 1766. †**4.** To sweat (coin) by the application of acids –1643. **5.** To cover or smear (a surface) with a liquid; to cover (a wall, etc.) with pigment mixed with water or watery liquid, to whitewash, colour-wash; *Water-colour Painting*, to cover with a broad layer of colour by a continuous movement of the brush; to depict by this means; to lay (colour) in washes 1604. **b.** *transf.* in *pass.* in Natural History, said of surfaces that appear to have a superficial layer of colour spread over them 1844. **c.** To cover *with* a film of metal deposited from a solution 1792. **6.** *Mining.* To agitate in water, or to pass a stream of water through (metalliferous earth) in order to separate the metallic particles. Also *absol.* 1543.

1. †*To w. the eyes* (joc.); to clear or sharpen the sight of the eyes with strong drink; His eyes washed with only a single cup of canary SCOTT. **b.** †*To w. one's brain, head*, etc., as jocular expressions for wine-drinking; *Ant. & Cl.* II. vii. 105. **2. b.** He went but forth to w. him in the Hellespont, and being taken with the crampe, was droun'd SHAKS. **3.** Reyn shal thee wassche, and sonne shal thee drye CHAUCER. Morning Roses newly washt with dew SHAKS. He, a marble to her teares, is washed with them, but relents not SHAKS. **5. c.** Any of the current Coin which shall have been gilt, silvered, washed, coloured, or cased over 1861.

III. Of a sea or river: To flow over or past (the sand, shore, coast); to beat upon (walls, cliffs, etc.); to touch, adjoin (a town, country, etc.). Also of a river: To pass through, 'water' (a country). ME. **b.** *intr.* Of waves: To sweep *over* a surface; to break or surge *against* (the shore, etc.); to break *in.* Also used by onomatopœia to suggest the sound of moving water. 1774.

The land By Danube wash'd 1814. *transf.* Great spaces washed with sun KIPLING. **b.** I heard the ripple washing in the reeds TENNYSON.

IV. 1. *trans.* To remove (dirt, a stain, colouring, etc.) by the application of water or other liquid. Chiefly with adv., as *away*, *out*, *off*. ME. **b.** *transf.* and *fig.* To blot out, obliterate, cancel. late ME. **c.** *intr.* with *out*. Of colouring matter: To disappear from a fabric when washed 1755. **2.** trans. *To w. down*: to swallow liquor along with or after (solid food), in order to assist deglutition or digestion 1600. **3.** Of waves, running water, etc.: To remove, dislodge, carry away. late ME. **b.** To separate (metallic particles) by treating the containing earth with water 1555. †**c.** Of a hard surface: To beat *off* waves, etc. DRYDEN. **d.** *intr.* To be carried away or detached by moving water 1590. **4.** To be tossed about, to be carried or driven along, by waves, etc. 1623. **5.** *Rowing*. trans. To steer so as to impede (a competitor) by the 'wash' of one's own boat 1865.

1. *fig.* Nor Tears, that w. out Sin, can w. out Shame PRIOR. **b.** This Wilford..thirsts to w. out the insult he has received in blood 1850. **2.** In this one draught I w. my sorrow downe 1600. **3.** What wilt thou w. him from his graue with teares? SHAKS.

V. *Mech.* With *off*: to cut to a slope or bevel 1833. **VI.** *slang.* **a.** *Printing.* To punish or 'rag' (a fellow-workman for telling falsehoods) by hammering on his desk 1841. **b.** *Stockbroking.* To subject (stock) to a 'wash' 1895.

attrib. and *Comb.*: **w.-ball,** a ball of soap used for washing the hands and face, and for shaving (now *rare*); **-basin,** a w.-hand basin (now chiefly *U.S.*); **-bottle,** *Chem.* (*a*) a bottle containing liquid through which gases may be passed for purification; (*b*) a bottle with a mouthpiece and issue tube, for directing a stream of liquid on to a substance or utensil to be washed; **-bowl,** †(*a*) a w.-hand basin; **-day** = WASHING-*day*; **-dirt** *Mining*, auriferous soil or gravel to be submitted to washing; **-gourd,** the loofah; **-kitchen,** a kitchen used for washing clothes; **-leather,** a soft kind of leather, usu. of split sheepskin, dressed to imitate chamois leather; also *attrib.*, made of w.-leather; *Path.* of eruptions resembling w.-leather in appearance; **-man,** (*a*) = WASHERMAN; (*b*) a workman employed in applying the w. of tin in the manufacture of tinplate; **-mill,** (*a*) in *Brickmaking*, etc., a machine for washing clay or materials for cement; (*b*) in *Leather Manuf.*, a machine for washing skins after unhairing by the application of lime; **-pool,** a pool for washing sheep; **-room,** *U.S.* a lavatory; **-stand,** a w.-hand stand; **-strake** *Naut.* = WASHBOARD 1; **-trough** *Mining*, a trough in which ore is washed; **-tub,** a tub in which clothes are washed; **-water,** water for washing or that has been used for washing; **-woman,** (now *U.S.*) = WASHERWOMAN. Hence **Wa·shable** *a.* that can be washed without damage to texture or colour. **Washabi·lity. Wa·shery,** a place at which the washing of coal, ore, wool, etc. is carried on.

Wa·shaway. *Colonial.* 1893. [f. vbl. phr. *to wash away.*] The removal by flood of a portion of a hillside; the destruction of a portion of railway or road track by flood; a hole or breach produced by the washing away of soil.

Wa·sh-bear. *U.S.* 1891. [f. WASH *v.* In G. *waschbär*, a transl. of *Ursus lotor* (Linn.); cf. WASHER[1] 4 b.] The racoon.

Wa·shboard. 1742. [f. WASH *sb.*] **1.** *Naut.* A board on the side of a boat, or the sill of a lower-deck port, to prevent the sea breaking over. **2.** *dial.* A skirting-board 1828. **3.** *U.S.* A hardwood board, with a fluted surface or covered with corrugated zinc, on which clothes are rubbed in washing 1882.

Wa·shbrew. *dial.* 1620. [f. WASH *sb.* or *v.*] Oatmeal boiled to a stiff jelly.

Washed (wǫʃt), *ppl. a.* 1575. [f. WASH *v.* + -ED[1].] **1.** Cleansed by rubbing in water or other liquid; treated with water or other liquid so as to remove impurities or soluble matter, etc. †**b.** Of coin: Sweated –1711. **c.** Covered with a coating of precious metal 1772. **d.** Having the tints produced by colour laid on in 'washes' 1770. **2. W. out,** of a fabric, dye, etc.: That has faded, or lost freshness, in the wash 1837. **b.** *fig.* Lacking in colour, animation, vigour, etc. 1850.

Washen (wǫ·ʃ'n), *ppl. a. arch.* and *dial.* 1483. [str. pa. pple. of WASH *v.*] Washed.

Washer (wǫ·ʃəɹ), *sb.*[1] ME. [f. WASH *v.* + -ER[1].] **1.** One who washes 1450. **2.** One who sweats coin –1771. **3.** One whose occupation or profession is the cleansing of materials, vessels, etc.; †a launderer or laundress 1515. **b.** One who washes sheep before shearing 1520. **c.** One who washes (ore, etc.) as a mining operation 1531. **4. a.** A popular name of the wagtail, *Motacilla lugubris* (cf. Fr. *lavandière*) ME. **b.** The racoon 1891. **5.** An apparatus for washing; a washing-machine used in various industries, e.g. for washing rags in paper-making, or for washing domestic linen, photographic plates or prints, etc. 1808. **6.** A cock or outlet valve of a water-supplying pipe; the outlet valve of a basin, cistern, etc., to which a waste-pipe is attached 1596.

Comb.: **w.-wife** (*Sc.*) = WASHERWOMAN.

Washer (wǫ·ʃəɹ), *sb.*[2] ME. [Of unkn. origin.] A perforated annular disc or flattened ring of metal, leather, etc., placed between two surfaces subject to rotative friction, to relieve friction and prevent lateral motion and unsteadiness. **b.** An annular disc of leather, rubber, or other material placed between the flanges of abutting water-pipes, beneath the plunger of a screw-down water-tap, etc., to prevent leakage 1850. **c.** A bearing-plate of iron placed under the nut of a bolt or tie-rod 1821. Hence **Wa·sher** *v. trans.* to furnish with a w.

Wa·sherman. 1715. [f. WASHER *sb.*[1] + MAN *sb.*] A man whose occupation is the washing of clothes. (Chiefly designating the Chinese laundryman of the U.S. and the Asiatic native washer of clothes.)

Wa·sherwoman. 1632. [f. WASHER *sb.*[1] + WOMAN.] **1.** A woman whose occupation is the washing of dirty linen; one who takes in washing. **2.** = WASHER *sb.*[1] 4 a. 1817.

1. *Washerwoman's fingers, hand*, a condition of the hands, characteristic of cholera, resembling the wrinkling of the skin produced in the hands of washerwomen by the action of soap and soda. *Washerwoman's itch, scall*, a form of eczema incident to the hands of washerwomen.

Wa·sh-hand, *a.* 1759. [f. WASH *v.*] Intended for use in washing the hands. Only in certain combs. (sometimes hyphened or written continuously as single words): *w. basin*, a basin for washing the hands; *w. stand*, a piece of furniture for holding the w. basin, ewer, soap-dish, etc.; *w. table*, a table serving the purpose of a w. stand.

Wash-house (wǫ·ʃhaus). 1577. [f. WASH *v.* + HOUSE *sb.*] **a.** An outbuilding or apartment used for washing clothes. **b.** A building in which goods are washed in the process of bleaching, or calico printing 1701. **c.** *U.S.* A laundry 1873. **d.** A building, provided with suitable accommodation, at which the public may wash clothes 1846.

Washiness (wǫ·ʃinės). 1631. [f. WASHY *a.* + -NESS.] The quality or state of being washy.

The w. of the following line is only surpassed by that of the two which succeed it 1814.

Washing (wǫ·ʃiŋ), *vbl. sb.* ME. [f. WASH *v.* + -ING[1].] **I.** The action of WASH *v.* **1.** The action or an act of cleansing by water, or of laving or bathing with water or other liquid. Also *fig.* with ref. to spiritual or moral purification. *W. up*: the washing of table utensils after a meal. **b.** A ceremonial ablution ME. **c.** *spec.* = 'washing of clothes', esp. as one of the regular requirements of a person or household 1480. **d.** In chemical and mining operations 1600. **e.** With advs. *away, off, out, up* 1612. **2.** *Painting.* The action of laying on a thin coat of colour. Also *w. in.* 1650. **3.** Sweating of coin by means of acids. late ME. **4.** Surging, overflowing (of waves); the action of moving water in carrying off loose matter 1471. **5.** *Printers' slang.* See WASH *v.* VI. 1825.

1. Abstention from w. was a common form of asceticism 1911. **b.** Their pilgrimages to Idols, their shauings and their washings 1606. **c.** Meat, drink, w., and lodging 1765. †*At* (*the*) *w.* = 'at the wash.'

II. *Concr.* **1.** *pl.* (formerly also *sing.*) The liquid that has been used to wash something; matter removed when something is washed ME. **b.** Matter carried away by rain or running water; metal obtained by washing ore or soil 1604. **c.** Places containing soil from which gold or diamonds are obtained by washing 1865. **2.** Clothes newly washed or set apart to be washed 1854.

Comb.: **w.-bill,** a statement of laundry charges; **-book,** a book in which a person's laundry-charges are entered; **-crystals,** crystallized soda used for washing clothes, etc.; **-day,** the day on which the dirty clothes of a household are washed; **-machine,** a machine for washing clothes, etc.

Wa·shing, *ppl. a.* 1560. [f. WASH *v.* + -ING[2].] **1.** That washes; *spec.* of a garment, a textile fabric: That will admit of being washed without injury to colour or texture. †**2.** Of a blow: = SWASHING *ppl. a.* 2. –1625. **3.** *W. bear, racoon* = WASH-BEAR 1891.

Wa·sh-out. 1876. [f. vbl. phr. *to w. out.*] **1.** An act of washing out a cistern, etc.; a pipe or other appliance for doing this 1877. **2.** *Mining.* A place where a portion of coal or ironstone seam has been carried away by a stream, a deposit of sandstone being left in its place 1876. **3.** The removal by flood of a portion of a hillside; a hole or breach in a railway or road track caused by flood or erosion. Orig. (and chiefly) *U.S.* 1883. **4.** *slang.* A disappointing failure, a 'sell' 1902.

Wa·sh-pot. 1535. [f. WASH *v.*] †**1.** A servant employed to wash pots; *spec.* the designation of a servant employed at the Inns of Court –1816. **2.** A vessel for washing one's hands. *Obs.* exc. *fig.* in allusion to Ps. 60:8. 1535. **3.** A vessel containing melted tin, into which iron plates are plunged to be converted into tinplate 1839. **4.** A vessel used in separating silver from lead 1879.

2. Moab is my washpotte, ouer Edom wil I stretch out my shue COVERDALE *Ps.* 60:8.

Wa·sh-up. 1884. [f. vbl. phr. *to wash up.*] **1.** = *washing up.* **2.** *Mining.* The washing of a collected quantity of ore; the quantity of gold that has been obtained by washing 1890.

Wash-up, joc. or vulgar f. WORSHIP *sb.*

Washy (wǫ·ʃi), *a.* 1566. [f. WASH *sb.* or *v.* + -Y[1].] †**1.** Having too much moisture, water-logged. Of wind or weather: Bringing moisture or rain. –1726. **2.** Of food, drink, etc.: Too much diluted, weak, sloppy, thin. Hence *fig.* of literary style, productions, etc. 1615. **3.** Of colour, painting, etc.: Lacking body, weak, pale 1639. **4.** Of the stomach: Having an accumulation of liquid and undigested food; relaxed 1622. **5.** Of a horse or cow: Poor in quality or condition; esp. liable to sweat or scour after slight exertion 1639. **6.** Of a person: Lacking strength or stamina; weak, feeble, insipid; = WISHY-WASHY. Now *rare* or *Obs.* 1631.

1. The washie Oose MILT. **2.** Other persons' w. opinions GEO. ELIOT. **3.** Sir Joshua's w. Virtues WALPOLE. Blue eyes like hers..look so mild and gentle and w. 1886. **6.** What w. Rogues are here, are these the Sons of Beef, and English Beer? 1719.

Wasn't (wǫ·z'nt), colloq. contraction of *was not.*

Wasp (wǫsp). [OE. *wæsp, wæps, wæfs*, corresp. to OS. *wepsia, wespa, wasp*, OHG. *wafsa, wefsa* (G. *wespe*), MLG. *wepse, wespe* :– WGmc. **wabis-*, **waps-* :– IE. **wobhes-*, **wops-*, usu. taken to be f. **webh-* **wobh-* WEAVE *v.*[1], with ref. to the weblike construction of the insect's nest.] **1.** In pop. lang., any insect of the genus *Vespa*; chiefly applied to *V. vulgaris*, the Common W., and other species not readily distinguishable from this; sometimes taken to include the hornet, *V. crabro*. The obvious characteristics of the genus are the alternate rings of black and yellow on the abdomen, the narrow stalk or petiole by which the abdomen is attached to the thorax, and the formidable sting (peculiar to the females and the workers). In scientific lang. applied gen. to two divisions of hymenopterous insects, the Diploptera or true wasps, and the Fossores or digger wasps. **2.** *fig.* **a.** Applied to persons characterized by irascibility and persistent petty malignity 1508. **b.** Something that irritates or offends one 1588. **3.** An artificial fly for salmon fishing (made to imitate the appearance of a w.) 1867. **4.** *Conchol.* A variety of cowry 1815.

1. Angry as a waspe HEYWOOD. Then the wasps arrived. They killed three in the jam alone. 1905. **2.** *Tam. Shr.* II. i. 210. I raised a nest of holy wasps and hornets about my ears 1721. **b.** *Hen. VIII*, III. ii. 55.

attrib. and *Comb.*, as *w.-sting*, etc.: **w.-bee,** a bee of the genus *Nomada*, a cuckoo-bee; **-beetle,** a beetle of the genus *Clytus*, esp. *C. arietis*; **-fly,** a syrphid fly somewhat resembling a hornet;

also = sense 3; **-paper,** the paper-like material, produced by mastication, of which wasps' nests are made; **-waist,** a very slender waist, *esp.* one produced by tight-lacing; so **w.-waisted** *a.* **b.** with genit.: **wasp's nest,** the nest of a w., often used *fig.* like *hornet's nest.* Hence **Wa·spy** *a.* wasp-like; abounding in wasps.

Waspish (wǫ·spiʃ), *a.* 1566. [f. prec. + -ISH[1].] Pertaining to or resembling a wasp or some characteristic of it; *esp.* quick to resent any trifling affront; irascible, petulantly spiteful.

If I be w., best beware my sting SHAKS. W., dogmatical, over-bearing fellows 1861. Hence **Wa·spish-ly** *adv.*, **-ness.**

Wassail (wæ·s'l, wǫ·s'l, -e^{i}l), *sb.* Now only *arch.* and *Hist.* [ME. *wæs hæil, wassayl* – ON. *ves heill* 'be in good health', corresp. to OE. *wes hāl* (see HALE *a.*).] **1.** A salutation used when presenting a cup of wine to a guest, or drinking the health of a person, the reply being DRINK-HAIL. **2.** The liquor in which healths were drunk; esp. the spiced ale used in Twelfth-night and Christmas-eve celebrations ME. **3.** †A custom formerly observed on Twelfth-night and New-Year's eve of drinking healths from the w.-bowl –1661; a carousal, riotous festivity, revelling 1602. †**4.** A carol or song sung by wassailers –1650.

2. The Wassell well spiced, about shall go round 1661. *Wine and w.* (now *arch.*, echoing Shaks.), *vaguely*, strong drink in abundance; *Macb.* I. vii. 64. **3.** The King doth wake to night, and takes his rouse, Keepes wassels SHAKS. Merry Eastcheap, that ancient region of wit and w. 1820.

attrib. and *Comb.*, as *w.-candle, -singer*, etc.; **w.-bowl, -cup,** a large bowl or cup in which w. was made, and from which healths were drunk; also the liquor contained in the bowl. Hence **Wa·ssailry,** carousing, revelry (*rare*) 1814.

Wassail (wæ·s'l, wǫ·s'l, -e^{i}l), *v.* ME. [f. prec.] **1.** *intr.* To 'keep wassail'; to sit carousing and health-drinking. **2.** *trans.* (*local.*) To drink to (fruit-trees, cattle) in wassail, in order to ensure their thriving 1648.

2. The old Christmas custom of wassailing the apple-trees 1895. Hence **Wa·ssailer,** one who takes part in riotous festivities; a reveller; one who takes part in Twelfth-night or Christmastide 'wassailing'. **Wa·ssailing** *vbl. sb.* the action of the vb.; carousing; the action of going from house to house at Christmas-time, singing a song expressive of good wishes for Christmas and the coming year, usu. with the addition of carols or other songs.

Wast (wǫst, wəst). *arch.* and *poet.* 2nd pers. sing. pa. t. of BE *v.*

Wastage (wē^{i}·stėdʒ). 1756. [f. WASTE *v.* + -AGE.] **1. a.** Loss or diminution by use, decay, leakage or the like 1756. **b.** The action of spending uselessly or using wastefully; loss incurred by wastefulness 1885. **2.** The product of wear or decay, waste 1898. **3.** *Sc.* A ruined or deserted place; also, a waste piece of ground 1823.

Waste (wē^{i}st), *sb.* ME. [– ONFr. *wast(e* var. of OFr. *guast(e, gast(e*, partly repr. L. *vastum*, n. of *vastus* waste, desert, partly f. *waster* WASTE *v.*] **I.** Waste or desert land. **1.** Uninhabited (or sparsely inhabited) and uncultivated country; a wild and desolate region, a wilderness; also *transf.*, applied e.g. to the ocean or to land covered with snow. **2.** A piece of land not cultivated or used for any purpose, and producing little or no herbage or wood. In legal use *spec.* a piece of such land not in any man's occupation, but lying common. late ME. †**3.** A devastated region –1697. **4.** *Coal-mining.* A disused working 1695.

1. Satan..in the emptier w., resembling Air, Weighs his spread wings MILT. Tartary's extended W. PRIOR. *fig.* A dreary w. of cold potatoes, looking as eatable as Stonehenge DICKENS. **3.** They shall build the olde wastes, they shall raise vp the former desolations *Isa.* 61:4.

II. Action or process of wasting. **1.** Useless expenditure or consumption, squandering (*of* money, time, etc.); †the consumption or using up of material, resources, etc. ME. **b.** An instance or example of wasting 1612. **c.** A profusion, lavish abundance *of* something 1725. **2.** Destruction or devastation caused by war, floods, fire, etc. Now *rare* or *Obs.* 1560. †**b.** *pl.* Ravages –1738. †**c.** *concr.* Something wasted or destroyed –1640. **3.** *Law.* 'Any unauthorized act of a tenant for a freehold estate not of inheritance, or for any lesser interest, which tends to the destruction of the tenement, or otherwise to the injury of the inheritance' (F. Pollock) ME. **4.** Gradual loss or diminution from use, wear and tear, decay or natural process; *spec.* with ref. to animal tissues and structures; (now *dial.*) a wasting of the body by disease. Now somewhat *rare.* late ME.

1. The clocke vpbraides me with the w. of time SHAKS. These insulting Words, this w. of Breath DRYDEN. *Prov.* Hast maketh w. 1546. Phr. †*To make w.*, to be wasteful. †*In w.*, in vain, to no purpose. *To run to w.*, to flow away so as to be wasted; *fig.* of wealth, powers, etc., to be wasted. *To go to w.*, to be wasted. *To cut to w.*, lit. to cut (cloth) in a wasteful manner; *fig.* (*slang*) to apportion (time) wastefully. **b.** Prefaces..are great wastes of time BACON. **c.** And there the garden yields a w. of flow'rs POPE. **2. b.** Pleas'd with the Work of thy own Hands, Thou dost the Wastes of Time repair WESLEY. **c.** Then of thy beauty do I question make That thou among the wastes of time must goe SHAKS. **4.** Sudden W. made upon Fat Persons by violent Fevers 1695. Her mother went off in a w. 1878.

III. Waste matter, refuse. **1.** Refuse matter; the useless by-products of any industrial process; material or manufactured articles so damaged as to be useless or unsaleable. late ME. **b.** = COTTON-*waste* 1886. **c.** *Printing*, etc. The surplus sheets of a work 1785. **2.** A pipe, conduit, or other contrivance for carrying off waste matter or surplus water, steam, etc. 1707.

Combs.: **w.-basket** (now chiefly *U.S.*) = WASTE-PAPER *basket*; **-land,** land in its natural, uncultivated state; **-man** *Mining*, a man whose duty is to inspect the w., and to secure the proper ventilation of the mine; **-pipe** = III. 2; **-way** *U.S.*, a channel for the passage of waste water; †**-yard,** app. a yard for the reception of odds and ends of little value. Hence **Wa·steless** *a.* without diminution, unwasting. **Wa·sty** *a.* liable to waste from deterioration; *U.S.*, that resembles cotton-w.

Waste (wē^{i}st), *a.* ME. [– ONFr. *wast*, var. of *g(u)ast* :– Rom. **wasto*, repr. L. *vastus* (see prec.).] **1.** Of land: **a.** Uncultivated and uninhabited or sparsely inhabited. Sometimes with stronger implication: Incapable of habitation or cultivation; barren, desert. **b.** In weaker sense: Not applied to any purpose; not utilized for cultivation or building. late ME. †**2.** Of former places of habitation or cultivation, buildings, etc.: Devastated, ruinous –1823. †**3.** Of speech, thought, or action: Profitless, serving no purpose –1598. †**b.** Superfluous, needless –1618. †**4.** Spare, unoccupied, unused –1772. **5.** Of materials, etc.: Eliminated or thrown aside as worthless after the completion of a process; refuse. Of manufactured articles: Rejected as defective; also, produced in excess of what can be used. 1450.

1. Eden rais'd in the wast Wilderness MILT. *fig.* This w. weary of life 1825. *To lie w.*, to remain in an uncultivated or ruinous condition. *To lay w.*, to devastate, ravage (land, buildings); I will lay thy cities w., and thou shalt be desolate *Ezek.* 35:4. **4.** Shee took penne and inke and in those wast leaues wrote a most Godly and learned exhortation 1615. I was locked up and confined in a w. room 1772. **5.** The duty of the kidneys is to filter w. matters from the blood as it circulates through them 1908. *W. water*, superfluous water, or water that has served its purpose, allowed to run away. *W. steam*, the superfluous steam discharged from a boiler, or the spent steam discharged from the cylinder of a steam-engine.

Comb.: **w.-book** *Book-keeping*, a rough account-book (now little used) in which entries are made of all transactions at the time of their occurrence, to be 'posted' afterwards in the more formal books.

Waste (wē^{i}st), *v.* ME. [– ONFr. *waster*, var. of *g(u)aster* :– Rom. **wastare*, for L. *vastare*, f. *vastus*; see prec.] **I.** *trans.* **1.** To lay waste, devastate, ruin (a land, town, its inhabitants, etc.). **2.** *Law.* To destroy, injure, damage (property); to cause to deteriorate in value 1450. **3.** To consume, use up, wear away, exhaust by gradual loss; to consume or destroy (a person, etc.) by decay or disease; to emaciate, enfeeble ME. †**b.** To destroy, put an end to (something immaterial, e.g. sin, sorrow) –1689. †**4.** To diminish or consume the livelihood of, impoverish (a person) –1727. †**b.** To spend, diminish one's store of (money, etc.); to spend, pass (time); to get over (a distance in travelling) –1764. **5.** To spend, consume, employ uselessly, unprofitably or without adequate return; to make prodigal or improvident use of; to squander ME. **b.** *pass.* (without distinct ref. to an agent). To fail to be appreciated; to make no impression; to have no opportunities for displaying useful qualities 1898. **c.** To fail to take advantage of (an opportunity) 1836. **d.** To cause or allow (a substance, etc.) to be used unprofitably or lost 1826.

1. *absol.* For now I see Peace to corrupt no less then Warr to w. MILT. **3.** To..wast huge stones with little water drops SHAKS. Would he were wasted, Marrow, Bones, and all SHAKS. **b.** The pryde off Iordane is waisted awaye COVERDALE *Zech.* 11:3. **4. b.** I like this place, And willingly could w. my time in it SHAKS. The Goddess wasts her Days In joyous Songs DRYDEN. **5.** The yonger sonne..wasted his substance with riotous liuing *Luke* 15:13. Full many a flower is born to blush unseen, And w. its sweetness on the desert air GRAY. To w. a great deal of time in novel-reading 1881. *To w. words, breath*, to speak to no purpose; similarly *to w. paper, space.* **b.** Two such amusing liars as we were utterly wasted on after-dinner oratory 1898.

II. *intr.* **1.** To lose strength, health, or vitality; to lose flesh, pine, decay. Also with *away.* ME. **b.** *Sport.* To reduce one's weight by training. Also *refl.* 1763. **2.** To be used up or worn away; to lose substance or volume by gradual loss or wear or decay; to be consumed or spent. late ME. †**3.** Of time: To pass away, be spent –1847.

1. Shall I wasting in Dispaire, Dye because a Womans faire? 1622. **2.** Euphues had rather shrinke in the wetting then wast in the wearing LYLY. Hence **Wa·stable** *a.* liable to be wasted, subject to waste; also in *Law*, said of things in respect of which a tenant may be chargeable with waste. **Wa·sting** *vbl. sb.* the action of the vb.; *ppl. a.* that wastes.

Wasteful (wē^{i}·stfŭl), *a.* late ME. [f. WASTE *sb.* + -FUL.] **1.** That causes devastation, desolation or ruin; that destroys or lays waste. †**2.** Useless, worthless, vain; unused –1577. **3.** Of a place: Desolate; unfrequented, uninhabited. *Obs.* exc. *arch.* and *poet.* 1572. **4.** Addicted to waste; given to useless or excessive expenditure. Of expenditure, etc.: Characterized by waste or extravagance. 1451. **5.** That wastes, consumes or expends unprofitably. Const. *of.* 1587. **6.** That causes bodily waste or decay. Now *rare.* 1600.

1. Wastefull vengeance SHAKS. **3.** The Throne Of Chaos, and his dark Pavilion spread Wide on the w. Deep MILT. W. Tartarus BRIDGES. **6.** Leane and w. Learnings SHAKS. This w. excess of grief 1824. Hence **Wa·steful-ly** *adv.*, **-ness.**

Wastel (wǫ·st'l). *Obs.* exc. *Hist.* ME. [– ONFr. *wastel*, var. of OFr. *guastel* (mod. *gâteau* cake), prob. of Gmc. origin.] **1.** Bread made of the finest flour; a cake or loaf of this bread. **2.** *Her.* = TORTEAU 1. 1486.

Wasteness (wē^{i}·stnės). late ME. [f. WASTE *a.* + -NESS.] **1.** †**a.** Desolation, destruction, ruin. (Chiefly *biblical.*) –1863. **b.** The state of lying waste, being uncultivated or barren 1608. **2.** An uninhabited or unfrequented region or place. *Obs.* exc. *dial.* 1500.

1. a. Desolacion shal remayne in the cities, and the gates shalbe smytten with waistnesse COVERDALE *Isa.* 24:12.

Wa·ste-pa·per. 1585. Paper cast aside as spoiled, superfluous, or useless for its original purpose.

The securities..proved to be little better than waste paper 1905.

attrib.: **w.-basket,** a basket into which waste paper is thrown.

Waster[1] (wē^{i}·stəɹ). ME. [orig. – AFr. *wastere, -our*, f. *waster* WASTE *v.* (see -ER[2] 3). This coalesced with later formation on WASTE *v.* + -ER[1].] **I. 1.** One who lives in idleness and extravagance; a squanderer, spendthrift. Now chiefly with some notion of sense II, a 'ne'er-do-well'. **b.** One who, or something which wastefully dissipates or consumes (something specified). late ME. **2.** One who lays waste, despoils or plunders. late ME. **3.** The designation of a class of thieves mentioned in a statute of Edw. III. *Obs.* exc. *arch.* 1543. **4.** An animal, etc. that is wasting away or losing flesh, or that will not fatten. late ME. **5.** Something which causes or allows waste or loss of material 1788. **b.** *Path.* = COMEDO 1899.

1. Ye will think I am turned w., for I wear clean hose and shoon every day SCOTT. Here was a wretched invertebrate fellow, an absolute 'w.' 1904. **b.** Building and marrying of children are great wasters 1611. **4.** *A bad w.*, said of a jockey who has difficulty in 'wasting'. **5.** Oft on the wick there hangs a w., Which makes the candle burn the faster 1788.

II. Something rejected as waste. **a.** An article of faulty or inferior manufacture 1800. **b.** An animal, etc., which is not good enough to be kept for breeding purposes 1722.

†**Wa·ster²**. 1455. [Of unkn. origin.] **1.** A wooden foil used in sword-exercise and fencing; a cudgel, staff, club –1661. **2.** Fencing with a 'waster'; single-stick –1636.

Waster³ (wēⁱ·stəɹ). *Sc.* 1580. [Altered f. synonymous *wawsper*, infl. by synonymous LEISTER.] A fishing-spear.

Wastrel (wēⁱ·strĕl), *sb.* and *a.* 1589. [f. WASTE *v.* + -REL.] **A.** *sb.* **1.** In Cornwall, a tract of waste land; now only, a strip of roadside waste. **2.** *dial.* = WASTER¹ II. 1790. **3.** An idle, worthless, disreputable person 1847. **b.** A street arab 1877. **4.** A wasteful person, a spendthrift 1887. **B.** *adj.* **1.** Of manufactured articles: Waste, rejected as imperfect 1790. **2.** Of an animal: Feeble, lacking strength or vigour 1880. **3.** Spendthrift 1894.

Wat¹ (wǫt). *Obs.* exc. *dial.* 1500. [prob. a use of *Wat*, short for *Walter*.] A hare.

‖**Wat²** (wat). 1871. [Siamese.] A Siamese Buddhist temple.

Watap, wattap (wǫ·tæp). 1789. [Narragansett Indian *wattap* root of a tree.] Thread or fibre from the roots of the spruce fir, used by Indians for weaving, sewing, etc.

Watch (wǫtʃ), *sb.* [OE. *wæćće*, f. stem of **wæććan* (see next). In some later uses directly from the vb.] **I.** Wakefulness, vigil. †**1.** The state of being awake; going without sleep –1631. †**2.** Watching as a devotional exercise or religious observance; an act or instance of this. *Obs.* exc. in *w.-night.* –1526. †**b.** A wake or revel held on St. John the Baptist's (Midsummer) Eve (23 June) –1592. **c.** A 'wake' over a dead person (*rare*) ME. **3.** The action or a continued act of watching; a keeping awake and vigilant for the purpose of attending, guarding, or the like OE. **4.** [tr. L. *vigilia*, Gr. φυλακή, Heb. *'ašmōreṯ*.] Each of the (three, four, or five) periods into which the night was anciently divided OE.

1. *Ham.* II. ii. 148. **4.** And about the fourth w. of the night, he commeth vnto them, walking vpon the Sea *Mark* 6:48. *The watches of the night*, now often rhet. = 'the night-time'.

II. Action of watching or observing. **1.** The action or an act of watching or observing with continuous attention; a continued look-out, as of a sentinel or guard, late ME. **b.** The duty, post, or office of watchman or sentinel. *Obs.* exc. in Bible phr. *to stand upon one's w.* 1535. **c.** Surveillance *over* a person 1611. **2.** *W. and ward*, the performance of the duty of a watchman or sentinel, esp. as a feudal obligation. Now only a rhetorical and more emphatic synonym of *w.* in sense II. 1. late ME. †**3.** The action of keeping guard and maintaining order in the streets, esp. during the night, performed by a picked body of the community –1878. †**4.** A lying in wait, an ambush –1653. **5.** One who watches; a look-out man. late ME. **b.** *Cricket.* A fieldsman; also a fielding position. (*Winchester Coll.*) 1836. **6.** One who watches, or those who watch, for purposes of guarding and protecting life and property, and the like; *esp.* before the introduction of the new Police, a watchman or body of watchmen, who patrolled and guarded the streets of a town, proclaimed the hour, etc. 1539. **7.** A sentinel; also, the body of soldiers constituting the guard of a camp, town, etc. *Obs.* exc. *Hist.* late ME. **8.** In the early 18th c., the designation of certain companies of irregular troops in the Highlands 1739.

1. Vse carefull W., chuse trusty Centinels SHAKS. Phr. *to keep* (*a, the*) *w., to set a w. On, upon* (*the*) *w.*, on the look out, exercising vigilance. **b.** As I did stand my w. vpon the Hill I look'd toward Byrnane SHAKS. **c.** Am I a sea, or a whale, that thou settest a w. ouer me? *Job* 7:12. **6.** The Sherife and all the W. are at the doore: they are come to search the House SHAKS. **8.** *Black W.*, a name given (from the dark-coloured tartan worn by them) to some companies of irregular Highland troops raised *c* 1729–30, and afterwards embodied as the 42nd Regiment, which still retains the name.

III. Naut. uses. **1.** That period of time for which each of the divisions of a ship's company alternately remains on deck; usu. four hours, with the exception of the DOG-WATCHES 1585. **b.** A sailor's turn or period of duty 1725. **2.** That part, usu. one half, of the officers and crew, who together attend to the working of a vessel during a 'watch' 1626. **b.** *W. and w.*, the arrangement by which the two halves of a ship's crew take duty alternately every four hours 1780.

1. (One's) *w. below, off*, the time one is off duty. **2.** 'The grub's horrid', said both watches 1913.

IV. A timepiece. **1.** †**a.** A dial or clock-face; the circle of figures on a dial –1672. †**b.** The going-part of a clock –1816. **2.** A small timepiece with a spring-driven movement, and of a size to be carried in the pocket 1588. **b.** A chronometer as used on board ship 1778. **3.** A trial-piece of glass, pottery, copper, etc. put in a furnace and taken out again, to enable the workman to judge of the degree of heating, etc. [app. a mistranslation of Fr. *montre*, in this application used in the sense of 'show-piece'.] 1606.

1. a. *Rich. II*, v. v. 52. **2.** Dictionaries are like watches, the worst is better than none, and the best cannot be expected to go quite true JOHNSON.

attrib. and *Comb.*: **w.-bell,** (*a*) a bell on which the half-hourly periods in each w. are struck on board ship; (*b*) a bell rung at the setting and relief of a military w., or to sound an alarm; **-boat,** a boat on patrol-duty; **-box,** a small structure to shelter a person on w.; a small wooden shelter resembling a sentry-box, but furnished with a seat and half-door, used by a municipal watchman (now only *Colonial*); **-bracelet,** a bracelet carrying a wrist-watch; †**-candle,** = *watching-candle*; **-case,** a hinged case or cover of an old-fashioned w. enclosing the w. proper; now, the metal cover enclosing the works of a w.; **-chain,** a metal chain used as a w.-guard; **w. committee,** the committee of a borough council which deals with all matters pertaining to the policing and public lighting of the borough; **-cry,** the periodical cry of a watchman; *fig.* = WATCHWORD 3 b; **-dog,** a dog kept to guard a house, etc., and give warning of the approach of intruders; **-fire,** a fire maintained during the night as a signal or for the use of a party or person on w.; **-guard,** a chain, cord, ribbon, or the like used to secure a w. when it is worn on the person; **-house,** (*a*) a house in which a w. or guard is stationed; (*b*) a house used as a station for municipal night-watchmen (now only *U.S.* and *Colonial*); **-light** = NIGHTLIGHT 2 b; **-night,** orig. a religious service extending over midnight held monthly by Wesleyan Methodists; in later use a service held on New Year's eve, lasting until midnight; also the night on which the service is held; **-oil,** a highly refined lubricating oil used for watches and clocks; **-spring,** the mainspring of a w.; also (without article) as a material; **-stand,** a small case or stand in or upon which a w. may be placed so that its face may be seen; **-wheel,** the balance-wheel of the 'w.-work' of a clock. Hence **Wa·tchless** *a.*, keeping no w.; unwatched, unguarded; not having or possessing a watch (IV. 2).

Watch (wǫtʃ), *v.* Pa. t. and pa. pple. **watched** (wǫtʃt). [OE. **wæććan* (only in pr. pple. *wæććende*), a doublet of *wacian* WAKE *v.*, repr. WGer. **wakǣjan* (OHG. *wahhên*).] **I.** *intr.* †**1.** To be or remain awake –1667. **b.** To remain awake *with* a sick person or at his bedside 1691. **2.** To remain awake for purposes of devotion; to keep vigil OE. **3.** To be on the alert, to be vigilant; to be on one's guard ME. **4.** To be on the look out; to keep a person or thing in sight, so as to be aware of any movement or change. late ME. **b.** To be on the watch for opportunities *to do* something. late ME. **c.** To be on the watch *for* (something expected) 1831. **5. W. over** —. To exercise protecting care over 1526. **6.** To fulfil the duty of a watchman, sentinel, or guard. late ME. **b.** Of a sailor: To be on duty during a watch 1799.

1. Sleepest thou? Couldest not thou w. one houre? W. ye and pray. *Mark* 14:38, 39. **4.** To w. as the cat for the mous 1547. They watch'd what the end would be TENNYSON. *To w. after*, to follow with one's looks (*rare*). *To w. out* (Cricket), = FIELD *v.* 5; (orig. *U.S. colloq.*) to look out, be on one's guard. **5.** There is a Providence..that watches over innocence and folly GIBBON. **6.** †*To w. and ward*, to keep 'watch and ward'. **b.** Each man watches four hours, and rests eight 1820.

II. *trans.* †**1.** To keep under surveillance; to set an armed watch upon –1579. **b.** To guard (a dead body, goods) 1450. †**2.** To guard against attack; to provide with a body of guards or armed watchmen; to serve as a guard to. Also *to w. and ward.* –1819. **3.** To keep (a person or thing) in view in order to observe any actions, movements, or changes that may occur 1515. **4.** To keep in mental view; to keep oneself informed about 1675. **b.** To be on the alert to avail oneself of (opportunities, etc.); to be vigilant to choose (one's time for action) 1578. **c.** Of a barrister: To attend the trial of (a case) in order to note and act upon any point that may arise to affect the interests of a client who is not a party in the litigation 1890. **5.** To exercise protecting vigilance over; to tend (a flock); to sit up beside (a sick person); to keep watch beside (a dead body) 1526. †**6.** To do (a person a good or bad turn) –1705. **7.** To provide (a town) with watchmen; *pass.* to be policed *by* a specified body of men 1806. **8.** *Falconry.* To prevent (a hawk) from sleeping, in order to tame it 1575.

3. Didn't I w. him into Codger's commercial boarding-house, and w. him out, and w. him home to his hotel DICKENS. **4.** Youth should w. joys, and shoot 'em as they flie DRYDEN. The natural jealousy of the Spaniards watched every naval enterprise of Englishmen 1868. **5.** While Shepherds watch'd their Flocks by Night 1700. **8.** *Tam. Shr.* IV. i. 198. Hence †**Wa·tchment** (*rare*), a task of watching.

Watcher (wǫ·tʃəɹ). 1525. [f. WATCH *v.* + -ER¹.] One who watches or keeps watch; *spec.* (*a*) one who watches by a sick bed, or by the dead; (*b*) a watchman, guard, sentry; (*c*) as the title of a class of angels, or of angels generally [tr. Aramaic *'īr* one who is wakeful].

Beholde, a w. (euen an holy angel) came downe from heauen COVERDALE *Dan.* 4:13. An eye like mine A lidless w. of the public weal TENNYSON.

Watchet (wǫ·tʃėt), *sb.* and *a.* *Obs.* or *arch.* late ME. [In XIV *wachet*, etc., app. – ONFr. *watchet* (XV), earlier *waschet* (XII), in AL. *waschetum* (XIII); of unkn. origin.] **A.** *sb.* **1.** A light blue colour; cloth or garments of this colour. **2.** In full *w. fly*: A fly used by anglers; an artificial fly made to imitate this 1700. **B.** *adj.* Light blue, sky-blue; sometimes prefixed to *blue* as a qualifying term 1496.

Watchful (wǫ·tʃfŭl), *a.* 1548. [f. WATCH *sb.* + -FUL.] **1.** Wakeful, sleepless; accustomed to keeping awake. Of time: Passed in wakefulness. *arch.* **2.** Engaged in or accustomed to watching or close observation; vigilant 1601. **3.** Characterized by vigilance; in which one must be vigilant 1582.

1. W. nights and laborious days 1878. **2.** A w. mamma and governess in chaperonage 1882. **3.** The souldier may not moue from watchfull sted SPENSER. Keeping w. guard HAWTHORNE. Hence **Wa·tchful-ly** *adv.* 1538, **-ness.**

Wa·tch-glass. 1637. [WATCH *sb.*] †**1.** A sand-glass or hour-glass used to measure the time of keeping watch, esp. on board ship –1769. **2.** A thin piece of glass, usu. concavo-convex in form, fitted into the case of a watch over the dial-plate 1773. **b.** as a receptacle for small objects or portions of material to be subjected to scientific observation 1757.

Watching (wǫ·tʃiŋ), *vbl. sb.* late ME. [-ING¹.] **1.** The action of WATCH *v.*; an act or instance of this. **b.** Sc. *W. and warding*: see WATCH *v.* I. 6, II. 2. 1579. **2.** The state or condition of being awake, wakefulness; an instance of this 1550.

Comb.: **w. brief,** a brief instructing counsel to 'watch' a case; **w. candle,** a candle used at the 'watching' of a shrine or a corpse.

Wa·tchma:ker. 1630. One whose trade it is to make watches. So **Wa·tchma:king** *vbl. sb.*

Watchman (wǫ·tʃmæ̆n). late ME. [f. WATCH *sb.* + MAN *sb.*] **1.** A member of a military guard, a sentinel or sentry; a look-out. (Now *rare* exc. with allusion to Bible uses.) †**2.** One who keeps vigil; one who watches over or guards a person or thing –1628. †**b.** Applied to angels –1613. **3.** One of a body of men formerly appointed to keep watch and ward in all towns from sunset to sunrise;

later, a constable of the watch who, before the Police Act of 1839, patrolled the streets by night to safeguard life and property. late ME. **4.** A man employed to guard private property, a building, etc., esp. during the night 1600. **5.** The dor-beetle, *Geotrupes stercorarius* 1864.

1. Excepte the Lorde kepe the cite, the w. waketh but in vayne COVERDALE *Ps.* 126:1. **2.** 1 *Hen. VI*, III. i. 66. **3.** A face..that had just as much play of expression as a watchman's rattle DICKENS.

Wa·tch-tow:er. 1544. [WATCH *sb.*] **1.** A tower or station from which observation is kept of the approach of danger; a look-out station. †**2.** A pharos or lighthouse –1804.

1. *fig.* Morning sought Her eastern w. SHELLEY.

Watchword (wǭ·tʃwɒ̄ɹd). late ME. [WATCH *sb.*] **1.** *Mil.* A word or short phrase used as a password. *Obs.* in techn. use. †**b.** The call of a sentinel on his rounds –1797. †**2.** A preconcerted signal to begin an attack –1834. **3.** A password used among members of the same sect, society, etc. *Obs.* or *arch.* 1534. **b.** A word or phrase used as embodying the guiding principle or rule of action of a party or individual 1738. †**4.** A cautionary word or speech –1761.

2. *transf.* Which giues the watch word to his hand ful soon, To draw the clowd that hides the siluer Moon SHAKS. **3.** Classical quotations are the watchwords of scholars, by which they distinguish each other from the ignorant and the illiterate SYD. SMITH. **b.** When the rude rabble's watchword was—destroy COWPER.

Watchwork (wǭ·tʃwɒɹk). 1667. [WATCH *sb.*] That part of the movement of a timepiece which is concerned with the measuring of the hours, as distinguished from the 'clockwork' or striking part; also the 'works' or parts composing the movement of a watch.

Water (wǭ·təɹ), *sb.* [OE. *wæter* = OFris. *weter*, OS. *watar*, OHG. *wazzar* (Du. *water*, G. *wasser*) :- WGmc. **watar* (ON. *vatn*, Goth. *wato*, gen. *watins*, show a var. with *n*-formative), f. Gmc. **wat-* :- IE. **wod-*, repr. by OSl., Russ. *vodá* (cf. VODKA); the var. **wed-* is repr. by WET *a.*, the var. **ud-* by L. *unda* wave, Gr. ὕδωρ, Skr. *uddn* water.] **I. 1.** The liquid of which seas, lakes, and rivers are composed, and which falls as rain and issues from springs. When pure, it is transparent, colourless (except as seen in large quantity, when it has a blue tint), tasteless, and inodorous. **b.** With various qualifying words, as *ice-w.*, RAIN-W., etc. **c.** Considered as antagonistic to fire. late ME. **d.** As supplied for domestic needs, esp. as distributed through pipes to the houses of a district 1535. **2.** As a drink, as satisfying thirst, or as necessary aliment for animals and plants OE. **3.** As used for dilution of liquors OE. **b.** *fig.* (*Stock Exch.*) Fictitious capital created by the 'watering' of the stock of a trading company 1883. **4.** As used for washing, steeping, boiling, etc. OE. **b.** Each of the quantities of water used successively in a gradual process of washing ME. **5.** Water of a mineral spring or a collection of mineral springs used medicinally for bathing or for drinking, or both. Freq. *pl.* with *the.* 1542. **6.** Water regarded as collected in seas, lakes, etc., or as flowing in rivers or streams. (The pl. is often used instead of the sing., esp. with ref. to flowing water or water moving in waves.) OE. **b.** *Hunting*, etc. Streams or ditches which a horse is required to leap 1860. **7.** Quantity or depth of water, as sufficient or insufficient for navigation 1546. **b.** With prefixed adj., a particular state of the tide; see HIGH W., LOW W. late ME. **8.** Water received into a boat or ship through a leak, or by the breaking of the waves over the sides. late ME. **9.** As an enveloping or covering medium; in various phrases. late ME. **10.** A body of water on the surface of the earth. (In sense 'a stream, river', now chiefly *Sc.* and *north.*) OE. **11.** *pl.* Floods: esp. in phr. *the waters are out.* 1523.

1. W., w., every where, Nor any drop to drink COLERIDGE. All else..runs off them like w. off a duck's back 1871. Phr. *To write on* or *in w.*, to fail to leave abiding record of (something). (To spend money) *like w.*, profusely, recklessly. **d.** *To cut off, turn on the w.* **2.** *Bread and w.*, the type of extreme hard fare, as of a prisoner or penitent. *W. bewitched* (colloq.), excessively diluted liquor; now chiefly, very weak tea. **3.** *Brandy-and-w.*, *whisky-and-w.*, etc.; hence joc. in nonce-combs.; The weak Addison-and-w. of the 'Mirror' 1882. **5.** It is..very long, Mr. Pickwick, since you drank the waters DICKENS. A wine-glass of Orezza w. after breakfast every morning 1879. **6.** Thy waye was in the see, and thy pathes in the great waters COVERDALE *Ps.* 77:19. *fig.* Therfore she loves to fish in troubled Waters 1628. Phrases. *Deep waters* (after *Ps.* 69:2, 14), grave distresses and anxieties; also difficult or dangerous affairs. *To make a hole in the w.* (slang), to commit suicide by drowning. *By w.*, by ship or boat on the sea or a lake or river or canal. *On* or *upon the w.*, on the sea, in naval employments or enterprises. *Across, over, on this side the w., to cross the w.*, across, etc. the sea; (in London *the w.* in such phrases is often = the Thames). *The king over the w.*: see OVER *prep.* IV. 4. *To take (the) w.*, (*a*) to enter the sea, or lake, or river, and begin to swim; (*b*) to embark, take ship; (*c*) *U.S.* 'to abandon one's position'; (*d*) of a ship, to be launched. **7.** *To draw* (so much) *w.*: see DRAW *v.* I. 11. **8.** *To make w., take (in) w.*, to leak, or to admit or 'ship' w. over the side, etc. **9.** *Under w.*, below the surface of w.; (of land) flooded, submerged; hence *fig.* unsuccessful in life; also (*Sc.*) in debt. *Above w.*, above the surface of the w.; also *fig.*, esp. in *to keep one's head above w.*, to avoid ruin by a continued struggle. **10.** By the waters of Babilon we sat downe and wepte COVERDALE *Ps.* 137:1. The winters..are seldom severe enough to freeze any considerable w. BURKE. Within a little [we] found ourselves crossing the w. of Leith 1793. On one side lay the Ocean, and on one Lay a great w., and the moon was full TENNYSON.

II. The substance of which the liquid 'water' is one form among several; the chemical compound of two volumes of hydrogen and one of oxygen (formula H_2O); in ancient speculation regarded as one of the four (or later, five) elements of which all bodies are composed. OE. **III.** A liquid resembling (and usu. containing) water. **1.** An aqueous decoction, infusion, or tincture, used medicinally or as a cosmetic or perfume ME. **b.** With defining word, applied to liquid preparations of various kinds (see LAVENDER-W., LIME-W., SODA-W., etc.). late ME. **2.** Used to denote various watery liquids found in the human or animal body, either normally or in disease 1533. **b.** The fluid contained in the amniotic cavity (*liquor amnii*); now usu. *pl.* 1688. **c.** Tears. late ME. **d.** Saliva; now only, flow of saliva provoked by appetite 1598. **3.** *esp.* Urine. late ME. **4.** Applied to vegetable juices 1585.

2. *W. on the brain, in the head*, hydrocephalus. **c.** A dexterous rap on the nose..which brought the w. into his eyes DICKENS. **3.** *To make w.*, to urinate. *To pass w.*, to void urine (usu. with ref. to obstruction or the absence of it).

IV. The transparency and lustre characteristic of a diamond or a pearl 1607.

The three highest grades of quality in diamonds were formerly known as the *first*, *second*, and *third w.*; the phrase *of the first w.* survives in pop. use as a designation of the finest quality O. E. D. *fig. Of the first* (occas. *purest, finest*) *w.*, orig., of the highest excellence or purity; now only with the sense 'out-and-out', 'thorough-paced'.

attrib. and *Comb.*, as *w.-biscuit, -brook, -broth, -bucket, -cask, -cock, -diet, -drainage, -gauge, -pole, -pool, -pump, -sprite, -supply, -tap, -trough, -turbine*, etc.; *w.-cooled* adj.; also (designating substances which harden under water) *w.-cement, -lime, -mortar.*

Comb.: **a. w. authority,** a municipal body administering a system of w.-supply; **-balance,** a machine for raising loads to a height by the weight of w.; **-ballast,** cisterns filled with w., placed in the hold of a vessel to serve as ballast; **-bearing** *a.* producing w., not arid; *Geol.* through which w. percolates; **W. Board,** an administrative body having control of the supply of w. to a town or district; **-boot,** a boot intended for those who have to stand or walk in w.; **-bound** *a.* of macadam roads: solidified by watering and rolling; **-breather,** any animal capable of breathing in w. (by means of gills); **-cell,** each of the cells in the walls of the stomach of the camel, in which w. is stored; **-company,** a commercial association for the purpose of supplying w. to a town or district; **-diviner,** one who finds subterranean springs or supplies of w. by means of a divining-rod; **-doctor,** (*a*) = W.-CASTER; (*b*) a hydropathist; **-finder** = *w.-diviner*; **-gilding,** the process of gilding metal surfaces by applying liquid amalgam, the mercury being afterwards removed by evaporation; so **-gilt** *a.*; **-head,** the head or source of a stream; **-jacket,** a casing containing w., placed about something to prevent its becoming unduly heated or chilled; hence **-jacketed** *ppl. a.*; **-jump,** a place where a horse is required to leap a stream or ditch; **-knot,** a knot used in joining together lengths of fishing-line; **-lead** (līd), (*a*) a mill-lead; (*b*) an open channel through an ice-field; †**-leader,** one who carts w. for sale; **-leaf** *Arch.*, an ornament used on capitals, supposed to represent the leaf of some w.-plant; **-mouth,** (*Sc.*), the mouth of a river; **-organ,** the hydraulicon or hydraulic organ; **-parting** = WATERSHED 1; **-pistol,** a weapon constructed to discharge a sudden jet of w. or other liquid; **-plane,** an aeroplane that can rise from or alight on water; a hydroplane; **-plate,** a plate with a receptacle underneath for hot w. to keep the food warm; **-power,** the power of moving or falling w. employed to drive machinery; **-quake,** a seismic disturbance in the sea; **-rate,** a rate or tax levied by a municipality or a w.-company for the supply of w.; **-spaniel,** a variety of spaniel, much used for retrieving w.-fowl; **-splash,** a shallow stream or ford crossing a road; **-stone,** a nodule of chalcedony having an internal cavity containing w.; **-tower,** (*a*) a tower serving as a reservoir to deliver w. at a required head; (*b*) a long iron tube, carried vertically on a wheeled frame, for discharging w. to extinguish fires in the upper stories of buildings; **-waggon,** *U.S.* = W.-CART; also *slang* in phr. *on the w.-waggon* = teetotal; **-worn** *a.* (chiefly *Geol.*), worn or corroded by the action of w.

b. Prefixed to names of animals to denote species inhabiting the w.: **w.-bear,** a sloth-animalcule; **-beetle,** a beetle of the group *Hydradephaga*; **-boatman,** a w.-bug of either of the families *Notonectidæ* or *Corixidæ*; **- buffalo,** the common domestic Indian buffalo, *Bos bubalus* or *Bubalus buffelus*; **-bug,** (*a*) any heteropterous insect of aquatic habit; (*b*) *U.S.* the cockroach, *Blatta orientalis*; **-flea,** any of the small crustaceans that hop like fleas; **-fly,** a fly that frequents w. and the w.-side; **-lawyer** *joc.*, a shark; **-mole** *Austral.*, the ornithorhyncus or duck-bill; **-mouse,** the w.-vole; **-rail,** a bird, *Rallus aquaticus*, having a general resemblance to the landrail; **-scorpion,** an aquatic bug of the family *Nepidæ*; **-serpent, -snake,** any snake that inhabits or frequents the w.; **-vole,** the common w.-rat, *Arvicola amphibius*; **-worm,** any aquatic annelid.

c. Denoting vegetable growths that live in w., as *w.-plant, -reed*, etc.; also **w.-blob** *dial.*, a name for the marsh-marigold and similar plants; **-elder,** the guelder-rose; **-flag,** the yellow flag, *Iris pseudacorus*; **-oak,** a hard coarse-grained oak, *Quercus aquatica*, of the southern U.S.; also applied to certain Australian trees of the genera *Casuarina* and *Callistemon*; **-parsley,** name for *Sium latifolium* or other aquatic umbellifers; **-parsnip,** name for aquatic umbelliferous plants of the genus *Sium*, esp. *S. latifolium*; **-plantain,** the plant *Alisma plantago*, with leaves somewhat like those of the plantain, growing in ditches, etc.; **-violet,** the feather-foil, *Hottonia palustri.*

d. *Med.* Designating specific ailments, eruptions, etc., as *w.-blister*; also **w.-blebs,** pemphigus; **-pox,** chicken-pox.

Water (wǭ·təɹ), *v.* [OE. *wæterian*, f. *wæter* WATER *sb.*] **I.** *trans.* **1.** To give a drink of water to (an animal, esp. a horse on a journey); also, to take (cattle) to the water to drink. **2.** To furnish with a supply of water OE. **3.** To supply water as aliment to (a plant, crop, etc.), esp. by pouring or sprinkling with a watering-can, hose, or the like; to pour or sprinkle water on (soil) OE. **b.** To supply (land, crops) with water by flooding or by means of irrigation-channels; to irrigate 1555. **4.** Of a river, etc.; To supply water to (land, etc.). Now chiefly passive. OE. **5.** *To w.* (something) *with one's tears*; to make wet or moist with copious and continued weeping. *Obs.* or *arch.* Also †said of the tears. ME. †**6.** To soak in or with water, to steep in a liquor –1675. **b.** To sprinkle or drench (a road, pavement, etc.) with water, in order to lay the dust 1662. **c.** To sprinkle or drench (a material) with water in order to moisten it or with a solution to impregnate it 1474. **d.** *To w. one's clay*, to take liquid refreshment 1769. **7.** To add water to as a diluent or solvent, thereby increasing the bulk and reducing the strength. late ME. **a. To w. down.** To reduce the strength of (liquor) by dilution; *fig.* to weaken the force or strength of (language) by addition or alteration; to reduce in efficacy or potency 1850. **b.** *Comm.* To increase in nominal amount (the stock or capital of a trading company) by the creation of fictitious stock 1870. **8.** To produce a moiré or wavy lustrous finish on (silk or other textile fabrics) by sprinkling them with water and passing them through a calender 1450.

1. *Cymb.* II. iii. 23. **2.** Lord Hood has gone to w.

the Fleet NELSON. In a campaign like this..It should be easy to w. troops at fixed intervals 1898. 3. *fig.* The Apostles..planted this Faith.. and watred it with their blood 1672. 4. That pleasant district..which is watered by the river Don SCOTT. 7. Tea twice watered with a good deal of sugar in it 1902.

II. *intr.* **1.** Of the eyes: To fill and run with moisture; to flow with tears ME. **2.** Of the mouth, also (now *Sc.*) of the teeth: To secrete abundant saliva in the anticipation of appetizing food or delicacies 1530. **3.** Of a ship, ship's company, etc.: To take on board a fresh store of water 1557. **4.** To drink water; to obtain water to drink 1607.

1. *Mids. N.* III. i. 200. The smoke..got into the Captain's eyes, and made them blink and w. DICKENS. 2. He sees no green cheese but his mouth waters after it 1639. 4. Cattle were watering in a lake 1839. Hence **Wa·tered** *ppl. a. spec.* of silk, etc., having a wavy lustrous damask-like pattern or finish; of steel, damascened. **Wa·terer,** one who waters (plants, etc.); one who is sent ashore to obtain fresh water for a ship's company; one who supplies animals with drinking-water.

Wa·ter-bag. 1638. A bag of skin or leather used for holding or carrying water, esp. one used in Eastern countries for transporting and distributing water.

Wa·ter bai:lage. 1669. [See BAILAGE.] A duty or tax levied on all goods brought into or carried out of the Port of London.

Wa·ter-bai:liff. late ME. †**1.** An officer in various port towns, charged with the enforcement of shipping regulations, the collection of customs, and the like –1871. **2.** An official responsible for the enforcement of by-laws relating to fishing-waters 1667. **b.** A river-policeman employed to prevent poaching, etc. 1860.

Wa·ter-bath. 1824. **1.** *Chem.* A vessel containing water heated to a given temperature in or over which preparations are placed in suitable vessels to be digested, evaporated, or dried. **2.** A bath of water, as dist. from a vapour-bath 1891.

Wa·ter-bea:rer. late ME. One who carries water; *spec.* one whose employment is to carry water from a spring, etc. for domestic use.

Wa·ter-bed. 1791. **1.** A stratum through which water percolates. **2.** A water-tight mattress partly filled with water, designed to serve as a bed for an invalid, esp. for the prevention of bed-sores 1853. **3.** *Anat.* The cavity between the arachnoidea and pia mater containing cerebrospinal fluid, upon which the brain rests 1899.

‖**Waterbok** (wǭ·təɹbǫk). 1850. [Du., f. *water* WATER + *bok* BUCK *sb.*[1]] = WATERBUCK.

Wa·ter-borne, *a.* 1558. [BORNE *ppl. a.*] **1.** Of a boat: Supported by the water so as to be clear of the bottom upon which it has rested; afloat 1608. **2.** Of goods: **a.** Carried or transported by water. Hence of traffic, commerce. 1702. **b.** Put aboard a vessel for shipment 1558. **3.** Of disease: Propagated by the use of contaminated drinking-w. 1892.

Wa·ter bo:ttle. 1591. **1.** A vessel of leather or skin used in certain countries to convey water for domestic use. **2.** A bottle to hold drinking-water. **a.** One placed on the table for use at meals or in a bedroom 1825. **b.** A kind of flask used by soldiers and travellers 1889.

Wa·ter-break. 1806. Broken water; a piece of broken water.

Wa·ter-buck. 1850. [Anglicized f. WATERBOK.] A species of antelope, *Cobus ellipsiprymnus*, found in watered districts in central South Africa; an animal of this species. Sometimes applied to other species.

Wa·ter-butt. 1833. A large open-headed cask set up on end to receive the rain-water from a roof. **b.** Contempt. epithet for a teetotaller 1898.

Wa·ter-can. late ME. **1.** A portable vessel (in mod. use, of tin-plate or other metal) for holding or conveying water. **2.** The yellow water-lily, *Nuphar lutea*, so called from the shape of the seed-vessels. Also, the white water-lily, *Nymphæa alba.* 1622.

Wa·ter-ca:rriage. 1536. **1.** Conveyance or transportation by water. **b.** Carrying away (of sewage) by water 1873. **2.** Means or facilities for transporting by water 1727.

Wa·ter-ca:rrier. 1764. **1.** One who transports goods, etc. by water, not by land. **2.** A man (or animal) that carries water; *esp.* in oriental countries, the native who supplies an establishment or a number of troops with water 1787. **3.** A tank or other vessel for carrying water 1854.

Wa·ter-cart. 1707. A cart, usu. a barrel or tank on wheels, carrying water; chiefly, an apparatus of this kind intended for watering the streets, the receptacle being fitted with an arrangement by which the water escapes through a number of small holes or is forced through a nozzle, as the vehicle goes along.

†**Water-caster.** 1603. [See CAST *v.* VI.] One who practises inspection of patients' urine as a means of diagnosis; latterly, used as = quack –1828.

Wa·ter-clock. 1601. [CLOCK *sb.*[1]] An instrument actuated by water for the measurement of time.

Wa·ter-clo:set. 1755. A small room fitted up to serve as a privy, and furnished with water-supply to flush the pan and discharge its contents into a waste-pipe below. Abbreviated W.C., w.c.

Wa·ter-co:lour. 1596. **1.** A pigment for which water and not oil is used as a solvent. Usu. in *pl.* **2.** A picture painted with water-colours 1854. **3.** The art or method of painting with water-colours 1843. **4.** *attrib.*, as *w. drawing, painting*, etc. 1698. Hence **Wa·ter-co:lourist,** one who paints in water-colours.

Wa·tercourse. 1510. **1.** A stream of water, a river or brook; also, an artificial channel for the conveyance of water. **2.** The bed or channel of a river or stream 1566.

1. They shall spring vp..as willowes by the water courses *Isa.* 44:4.

Wa·ter-cress. ME. [See CRESS. Cf. AL. *cresso aquaticus* (XII), MLG., MDu., *waterkerse.*] **1.** The hardy perennial, *Nasturtium officinale* (family *Cruciferæ*), found in abundance near springs and in small running streams, and now widely cultivated for use as a salad. *sing.* and *pl.* **2.** Applied (chiefly as booknames) to some other cruciferous plants, esp. *Cardamine amara, C. pratensis*; also to *Helioscadium nodiflorum.* late ME.

1. Watercresses doth cure tothe ache 1528. He loved..his brook with its water-cresses LONGF. I grew in my stream, some Watercress 1881.

Wa·ter-cure. 1842. [CURE *sb.*[1] 4; after G. *wasserkur.*] A method or course of medical treatment by means of water.

Wa·ter-dog. ME. **1.** A dog bred for or trained to the water; esp. one trained to retrieve water-fowl. Formerly as a specific name, the barbet or poodle imported from the Continent. **2.** A man thoroughly at home on or in the water; a sailor; a good swimmer 1674. **3.** A name for various animals. †**a.** The otter –1856. **b.** *U.S.* One of the various species of salamanders, *esp.* the hellbender or the mud-puppy 1859.

Wa·ter-dri:nker. 1440. **1.** A drinker of water, one who drinks water in preference to wine or other liquors; now usu. *spec.* a total abstainer. **2.** One who drinks the 'waters' at a spa 1707. So **Wa·ter-dri:nking** *vbl. sb.*; *ppl. a.* that drinks water and abstains from stronger liquors.

Wa·ter-drop. 1593. **1.** A drop or globule of water. Usu. *pl.* **2.** A tear, tear-drop 1605.

1. When water drops haue worne the Stones of Troy SHAKS. 2. Let not womens weapons, water drops, Staine my mans cheekes SHAKS.

Wa·ter-e:ngine. 1677. †**1.** A fire-engine –1864. **2.** An engine to raise water; a water-pumping engine 1685. **3.** An engine driven by water-power 1858.

Waterfall (wǭ·təɹfǭl). late ME. [f. WATER *sb.* + FALL *sb.*; OE. had *wætergefeall.*] **1.** A more or less perpendicular descent of water from a height over a ledge of rock or precipice; a cascade, cataract. **2.** Such an inclination of the ground as will facilitate the fall or drainage of water 1522. †**3.** A swift stream tumbling in a rocky bed, a rapid –1748. **4.** *Coal-mining.* A special 'head' of water to be turned down a pit-shaft when needed 1797. **5.** (orig. *U.S.*) A chignon; also, a wave of hair falling down the neck below the chignon or net 1866.

3. To..steep In wholsom Water-falls the woolly Sheep DRYDEN. 5. The young lady that affects waterfalls, the Grecian bend, or the kangaroo hop 1875.

Wa·ter-flood. [OE. *wæterflōd.*] **1.** A moving flood or overflowing of water; a tempestuous sea. **2.** A body or mass of water in flood. late ME.

1. The Lord stilleth the water floude COVERDALE *Ps.* 29:10.

Waterfowl (wǭ·təɹfaul). ME. [f. WATER *sb.* + FOWL *sb.*] Any bird that frequents the water, or inhabits the margin of lakes, rivers, seas, etc.; in mod. use chiefly applied to the larger kinds of swimming birds, esp. those which are regarded as game. Often *collect. sing.* for *pl.*

Wa·ter-front. orig. *US.* 1856. Land or buildings abutting on a river, a lake, the sea, etc.; the frontage of a town on the water-side.

Wa·ter-fu:rrow, *sb.* OE. A deep furrow made for conducting water from the ground and keeping it dry. Hence **Wa·ter-fu:rrow** *v. trans.* to make water-furrows in (land).

Wa·ter-gall. Now *dial.* 1594. [See GALL *sb.*[2]] A secondary or imperfectly-formed rainbow; also applied to various other phenomena in the clouds that are believed to portend rain.

Wa·ter-gas. 1851. **1.** A gas made by forcing steam over incandescent carbon; used as fuel, and when carburetted as an illuminator. **2.** Water in the form of vapour 1881.

Wa·ter-gate. late ME. [GATE *sb.*[1]] †**1.** A sluice or floodgate –1755. **2.** A gate (of a town, a castle, etc.) giving access to the waterside. late ME. **3.** A place through which water-traffic passes 1893.

Wa·ter-glass. 1612. **1.** A water-clock or clepsydra 1661. †**2.** A glass finger-bowl –1784. **3.** A glass vessel to contain water; esp. such a vessel intended for keeping plants in water 1612. **4.** An instrument for making observations beneath the surface of water, consisting of a bucket with a glass bottom 1848. **5.** An aqueous solution of silicate of soda or potash (or of both). which solidifies when exposed to the air. It is used as a vehicle for fresco-painting, for pickling eggs, etc. 1859.

Wa·ter-gruel. late ME. **1.** Thin gruel made with water instead of milk. †**2.** *fig.* as the type of what is insipid. Chiefly *attrib.* (quasi-*adj.*), namby-pamby. –1811.

2. A pretty, sweet, smiling, flexible, insipid, w. girl 1784.

Wa·ter-ha:mmer. 1805. **1.** An instrument used to illustrate the fact that in a vacuum liquids and solids fall at the same rate. (It consists of a hermetically sealed tube exhausted of air and partly filled with water. When the tube is quickly reversed the water falls on the end with a noise like that of a hammer.) **2.** *Hydraulics.* The concussion or sound of concussion of water in a pipe when its flow is suddenly stopped, or when live steam is admitted 1891. **b.** Path. *W. pulse*, a jerky pulse with a full expansion, followed by a sudden collapse 1899.

Wa·ter-hen. 1529. Any of the various ralline birds, esp. the MOOR-HEN, *Gallinula chloropus.* **b.** *W. hackle*, an artificial fly made of the hackle feathers of the w. 1837.

Wa·ter-hole. 1679. A hole or depression in which water collects, a pond or pool; a reservoir. *Obs.* exc. *dial.* and *Colonial.* **b.** A cavity in the bed of a river, esp., in Colonial use, one that retains water when the river itself is dry 1792.

Wa·ter-horse. late ME. †**1.** The hippopotamus –1642. **2.** A fabled water-spirit appearing in the form of a horse 1800.

Wa·ter-ice. 1818. **1.** A confection of water and sugar, flavoured and frozen. **2.** Ice formed by the freezing of water, not by the compacting of snow 1882.

Watering (wǭ·təriŋ), *vbl. sb.* OE. [f. WATER *v.* + -ING[1].] **I.** The action of the verb WATER; an instance of this. **1.** The action or an act of pouring or sprinkling water on plants, crops, or the soil. **2.** The action or an act of soaking or steeping in water or of impregnating with a liquor. late ME. **3.** The application of water to a road, etc., in order to lay the dust 1673. **4.** The action of giving drinking-water to cattle, etc.; also, the action (of an animal) of going to the water to drink 1440. **5.** The action of procuring fresh water for a ship 1613. **6.** The action or process of giving a 'watered' appearance to the surface of a material 1665. **7.** Dilution with water 1888. **8.** Dilution of the capital of a trading company 1884. **9.** Running (of the eyes); filling with tears. late ME. **10.** Salivation of the teeth, mouth, or 'chops' induced by the thought or anticipation of appetizing food 1601. †**11.** Taking the waters –1765.

4. *transf.* 1 *Hen. IV*, II. iv. 17. **7.** Six drops to the half-pint seems a sinful w. of grog 1896.

II. *concr.* **1.** A ditch for draining a marsh; the tract drained by such a ditch 1790. **2.** The wavy variegated appearance given to silk, metal, etc. 1670.

Comb.: **w.-can** = WATERING-POT 1; **-cart** = WATER-CART; †**-house**, an inn or public house where coachmen may obtain water for their horses and refreshment for themselves.

Wa·tering-pla:ce. 1440. **1.** A place in a river or lake where animals come or are brought to drink; also, a pool or trough prepared for the use of cattle and horses. **2.** A place where a ship's company goes to fill the ship's casks with fresh water 1613. **b.** *gen.* A place where a supply of water can be obtained 1621. **3.** [See prec. 11.] A resort of fashionable or holiday visitants, either for drinking or bathing in the waters of a mineral spring, or for sea-bathing 1757.

Wa·tering-po:t. 1580. **1.** A portable vessel for watering plants; now usu. of tinned iron, and furnished with a long tubular spout, often ending with a rose for scattering the water. **2.** *Zool.* A mollusc of the genus *Aspergillum*, so named from the shape of its shell 1815.

Wa·terish, *a.* 1542. [f. WATER *sb.* + -ISH[1].] **1.** Resembling water in appearance or sensible properties 1583. **2.** Containing excess of water. Of liquids: Dilute, thin, poor. Of solids: Loose in texture, not firm or compact. 1542. **3.** Of weather, air, mist: Charged with water, watery 1650. **4.** Of light or of luminous bodies: Dimmed by watery vapour 1607.

2. *fig.* Out of a w. and queasy conscience MILT. **4.** The w. moonlight 1845.

Wa·ter-lane. 1872. **1.** *dial.* A green lane with a stream running along it. **2.** A narrow passage of open water, e.g. between masses of reeds or between lines of shipping 1883.

Waterless (wǭ·təɹlės), *a.* [OE. *wæterlēas*; see WATER *sb.*, -LESS.] Destitute of water; containing no water; unsupplied with water.

Wa·ter-level. 1563. **1.** A levelling instrument in which water is used instead of alcohol. **2.** *Mining.* A road driven on the strike of a seam to carry off water 1698. **3.** The plane below which the rock or soil is saturated with water; the situation of this plane 1839. **4.** The horizontal surface of still water. Also, the position of the surface of water. 1860.

Wa·ter-lily. 1549. The common name for many aquatic plants with large flowers, belonging to the family *Nymphæaceæ*. In England chiefly applied to the white water-lily *Nymphæa alba*, and the yellow water-lily *Nuphar lutea*. **b.** Applied to aquatic plants of other orders 1653.

Wa·ter-line. 1625. **1.** *Naut.* The line of floatation of a ship; the line supposed to be described on the hull by the surface of the water when a ship is afloat. Often = LOAD-WATERLINE. **2.** *Shipbuilding.* Any one of certain structural lines of a ship, parallel with the surface of the water which represent the contour of the hull at various heights above the keel 1750. **3.** = WATER-LEVEL 3. 1849. **4.** The outline of a coast 1791. **5.** A linear watermark in paper 1847.

Waterlog (wǭ·təɹlǫg), *v.* 1779. [app. f. WATER *sb.* + LOG *v.*[1] (in the sense of 'to reduce to a log-like condition').] **1.** *trans.* To render (a ship, etc.) unmanageable by flooding with water. **2.** To saturate with water so as to render inert 1868.

Waterlogged (wǭ·təɹlǫgd), *ppl. a.* 1769. [f. prec. + -ED[1].] **1.** Of a ship, boat: Flooded with water so as to become impaired in buoyancy, heavy, and unmanageable. **2.** Of floating bodies: Saturated with water so as to be deprived of buoyance 1832. **3.** Suffering from, deteriorated or rendered unserviceable by, excessive saturation with water 1829.

1. *transf.* That water-logged country called Holland 1840. **3.** W. mines 1895. Rotten water-logged earth 1897.

Waterloo (wǭtəɹlū·). 1816. The battle fought outside the village of Waterloo, near Brussels, on June 18, 1815, in which Napoleon was finally defeated. Hence, something which is a 'settler'; a decisive and final contest; chiefly in phr. *to meet one's W.*

Waterman (wǭ·təɹmĕn). late ME. [f. WATER *sb.* + MAN *sb.*] †**1.** A seaman, mariner –1682. **2.** A man working on a boat or among boats, *esp.* a boatman who plies for hire on a river, etc. 1458. **b.** *colloq.* One having a (good) knowledge of boating, etc. 1912. **3.** A man employed in the supply or distribution of water; *e.g.* a water-carrier, a turncock or fireman; *esp.* an attendant at cabstands whose duty was to water the horses 1705. Hence **Wa·termanship,** the art of a w.; skill in rowing or managing boats, etc.

Wa·ter-mark, wa·termark, *sb.* 1678. [MARK *sb.*[1]] **1.** The line (whether actually marked or not) forming the limit to which the tide, or the water of a river, well, etc., has risen or usu. rises. Cf. HIGH-WATER *mark*, LOW-WATER *mark*. **2.** A mark left by a flood 1822. **3.** The line showing the draught of a ship 1764. **4.** A distinguishing mark or device impressed in the substance of a sheet of paper during manufacture, usu. barely noticeable except when the sheet is held up against the light 1708. **b.** The metal design from which the impression is made 1854. Hence **Wa·ter-mark** *v. trans.* to mark or stamp with a w.; to embody as a w.

Wa·ter-meadow. 1733. A meadow periodically overflowed by a stream.

Wa·ter-measure. 1465. A kind of measurement formerly used for coal, salt, etc., sold on board vessels in port or in the river.

Wa·ter-melon. 1615. [So called from the abundance of watery juice.] A kind of gourd, *Citrullus vulgaris*.

Wa·ter-mill. late ME. **1.** A corn-mill whose machinery is driven by water. **2.** A water-wheel or a machine driven by a water-wheel 1580.

Wa·ter-mint. 1542. Any aquatic plant of the labiate genus *Mentha*; chiefly the Bergamot Mint (*Mentha aquatica*) or the Brook-mint (*M. hirsuta*).

Wa·ter-nymph. late ME. **1.** A nymph inhabiting or presiding over water; a naiad. **2.** A water-lily of the genus *Nymphæa* 1866.

Water of Ayr. 1805. The name of the river at the mouth of which the town of Ayr stands. Used *attrib.* in *Water of Ayr stone*, a kind of stone found on its banks, used for whetstones and for polishing.

Water of life. late ME. **1.** *fig.* A drink which gives life or immortality to the drinker. **2.** A name for brandy or whisky; tr. med.L. *aqua vitæ*, Fr. *eau-de-vie*. rare. 1576.

Wa·ter-pipe. late ME. **1.** A pipe through which water is conducted. **2.** A hookah, narghile, or kalian 1824.

1. One depe calleth another because of yͤ noyse of thy water pipes *Ps.* 42:8 (Great Bible): see note s. v. WATER-SPOUT.

Wa·ter-pot. late ME. **1.** A vessel, usu. of earthenware, for holding water. **b.** *Astr.* The portion of the zodiacal constellation Aquarius which is figured as a vase or urn 1546. **2.** = WATERING-POT 1. 1530. **3.** = WATERING-POT 2. 1815.

Waterproof (wǭ·təɹprūf), *a.* and *sb.* 1736. [See PROOF *a.* 1 b.] **A.** *adj.* Impervious to water; capable of resisting the deleterious action of water.

Neat w. travelling suits 1871. *fig.* Tears were not the things to find their way to Mr. Bumble's soul; his heart was w. DICKENS.

B. *sb.* A fabric or garment rendered impervious to water by treatment with india-rubber or the like 1799. Hence **Wa·terproof** *v. trans.* to make w. **Wa·terproofed** (-prūft) *ppl. a.* **Wa·ter-proofing** *vbl. sb.* the action or process of making materials, etc. w.; material with which a substance is made w.

Wa·ter-rat. 1552. **1.** An aquatic rodent of the family *Muridæ*; in British use, the water-vole, *Arvicola amphibius*. In the U.S. applied to the MUSK-RAT, and in Australia to the genus *Hydromys*. **2.** *fig.* A water-thief, pirate. Also contempt., a sailor, boatman, or the like. 1596.

Watershed (wǭ·təɹʃed). 1803. [f. WATER *sb.* + SHED *sb.*[1], after G. *wasserscheide*, which became common in scientific use *c* 1800.] **1.** The line separating the waters flowing into different rivers or river basins; a narrow elevated tract of ground between two drainage areas. **2.** *loosely.* **a.** The slope down which the water flows from a watershed. 1839. **b.** The whole gathering ground of a river system 1874. **3.** A structure for throwing off water 1881.

Wa·tershoot. 1625. [See SHOOT *sb.* 5.] **1.** †**a.** Outflow of drainage water from land, water carried off by drainage –1721. **b.** A gutter or channel for the overflow of water 1819. **2.** An artificial cascade contrived for the amusement or exercise of 'shooting the rapids' in a boat or by swimming 1900.

Wa·terside. late ME. **1.** The side or brink of water; the bank or margin of the sea, or of a river, stream, or lake. **2.** The side towards the water 1868.

Water-souchy (-sū·tʃi, -sū·ʃi). 1731. [– Du. *waterzootje*, f. *water* WATER *sb.* + *zootje*, *zoodje* boiling (of fish).] Fish (prop. perch) boiled and served in its own liquor.

Wa·ter-spout, wa·terspout. late ME. **1.** A spout, pipe, or nozzle, through which water is discharged; also †a squirt, syringe. **2.** *Meteorol.* A gyrating column of mist, spray, and water, produced by the action of a whirlwind on a portion of the sea and the clouds immediately above it 1738. **b.** A sudden and violent fall of rain; a cloudburst 1779.

In Ps. 42:7 (version of 1611), the word is now commonly apprehended as an example of sense 2; it was, however, probably intended as a metaphorical use of sense 1.

Wa·ter-spring. 1440. = SPRING *sb.*[1] I. 2. Now chiefly in echoes of the Bible.

Wa·ter-stream. Now *rare.* [Late OE. *wæterstrēam.*] A stream or current of water; a river or brook; †a flood.

Wa·ter-table. late ME. [See TABLE *sb.* IV. 2, 3.] **1.** *Arch.* **a.** The sloping top of a plinth. **b.** A projecting ledge or moulding sloping on the top, set along the side of a wall so as to throw off rain. **2.** A channel or gutter on each side of or across a road 1707. **3.** A window-ledge or sill in a ship or railway carriage 1883. **4.** = WATER-LEVEL 3. 1879. Hence **Wa·ter-tabling** *Arch.*, water-tables collectively; a line of water-tables.

Watertight (wǭ·təɹtəit), *a.* late ME. [See TIGHT *a.* 2.] **1.** So closely constructed or fitted that water cannot leak through. **b.** *fig.* 1647. **2.** As *sb. pl.* Watertight boots 1880.

1. *W. compartment*, each of the many compartments, with w. partitions, into which the interior of a large ship is now usu. divided for safety; hence often *fig.*

Wa·ter-wa·gtail. 1611. **1.** The common pied wagtail, *Motacilla lugubris*. Also applied with distinctive epithet to other species. **2.** *U.S.* A bird of the Amer. genus *Seiurus* 1865.

Wa·ter-wave. 1560. **1.** A wave of water. **2.** A wave in the hair produced by **W.-waving,** a method of waving the hair with w. 1882.

Wa·ter-way. 1440. **1.** A channel for the escape or passage of water. **2.** *Naut.* A long piece of timber, hollowed in the middle, serving as a channel for carrying off water from the deck of a ship 1635. **3.** A route for travel or transport by water; a river, canal, or a portion of a sea or lake, viewed as a medium of transit 1858. **4.** The breadth of a navigable watercourse; esp. the breadth allowed for the watercourse of a canal or the like passing under a bridge or tunnel 1739. **5.** An opening for the passage of vessels, esp. entering and leaving a harbour, the fairway 1883. **6.** The full-open passage area in a cock or valve 1744.

Wa·ter-weed. 1842. Any aquatic plant with inconspicuous flowers; spec. the Amer.

weed *Elodea canadensis*, common in Eng. waters.

Wa·ter-wheel. late ME. **1.** A wheel designed to drive machinery with water as the motive power. **2.** A wheel for raising water by means of buckets or boxes fitted on its circumference 1639. †**3.** A paddle-wheel –1822.

Wa·ter-witch. 1680. **1.** A witch inhabiting the water. **2.** *U.S.* A name for several water-birds noted for their quickness in diving 1789. **3.** *U.S.* = WATER-*diviner* 1859.

Waterwork (wǭ·təɹwɒ̄ɹk). 1443. [f. WATER *sb.* + WORK *sb.*] †**1.** A structure built in the water or serving as a receptacle for water or a defence against the force of water –1791. **2.** †**a.** A system of machinery for raising, conveying, or distributing water –1775. **b.** *collect. pl.* (Sometimes construed as sing.) The machinery, buildings, and engineering constructions, used for the purpose of supplying a town, etc., with water distributed through pipes 1621. †**3.** Any contrivance for producing a pleasing spectacle by means of water in motion; an ornamental fountain or cascade –1779. **b.** *transf.* Chiefly in joc. ref. to shedding of tears or making water 1647. **4.** An operation or department of labour concerned with hydraulic engineering, irrigation, or the like. Now *rare.* 1564.

Watery (wǭ·təri), *a.* OE. [f. WATER *sb.* + -Y[1].] **1.** Of land or soil: Full of water; moist, plashy. **b.** Of clouds; Full of moisture which is ready to fall as rain. Also of wind, etc. late ME. **c.** *transf.* Covered with or permeated by water; set or built in the water 1593. **2.** Resembling water in consistence; thin, fluid OE. **3.** Having the appearance of water; resembling water in colour. Of colour: Looking as if diluted with water. late ME. **4.** Of the nature of water 1477. **b.** applied to the rainbow. *poet.* 1600. **c.** Of a chemical solution, etc.: Made with water, aqueous 1826. **5.** Consisting of water. Chiefly *poet.* or *rhet.* 1535. **6.** Of, belonging to, or connected with the water; aquatic. Now *rare.* late ME. **7.** Of food: Containing too much moisture; tasting too much like water 1440. **8.** Of the eyes: Suffused with tears, tearful; exuding moisture, as a result of weakness or disease in the lachrymal glands 1447. **9.** Of the skin, etc.: Exuding or suffused with a humour or moisture resembling water. late ME. **10.** *fig.* Of thought, feeling, expression, etc.: Vapid, washy, poor, thin ME.

1. c. The Lark now leaves his watry Nest DAVENANT. **3.** A w. sunbeam SCOTT. **5.** *W. grave*, †*tomb*, (*a*) the place in which a person lies drowned; (*b*) death by drowning; A youth..was rescued from the w. grave 1802; similarly *w. death.* **6.** W. Neptune SHAKS. The sev'ral sorts of watry Fowls, That swim the Seas, or haunt the standing Pools DRYDEN. Swithin..the w. saint 1818. **7.** W. soup for beggars 1871. **10.** A w. but harmless story of London society 1904.

Watt (wǫt). 1882. [f. name of James *Watt* (1736–1819), the inventor of the modern steam-engine.] *Physics.* A unit of activity or power (used chiefly with ref. to electricity), corresponding to the rate of work represented by a current of one ampère under a pressure of one volt.

Comb.: **w.-hour,** the work done by one w. in one hour; **wattmeter,** an instrument for measuring electric energy. Hence **Wa·ttless** *a.*

Watteau (wǫ·to[u], ‖vato). 1833. The name of Antoine *Watteau* (1684–1721), a French painter, used *attrib.* in *W. school*, *W.-like* adj.; also in designations of articles of female costume similar to those represented in Watteau's pictures, as *W. bodice, hat.* Hence **Wa·tteauish** *a.* resembling the style of Watteau.

Wattle (wǫ·t'l), *sb.*[1] [OE. *watul*, of uncertain origin, but app. cogn. with *wætla* bandage for a wound.] **I. 1.** *pl.* and *collect. sing.* Rods or stakes, interlaced with twigs or branches of trees, used to make fences, walls, and roofs. Also, rods and branches of trees collected for this purpose. **2.** *dial.* A hurdle 1640. **3.** *dial.* A wand, rod 1570.

1. *W. and daub*, interwoven twigs plastered with clay or mud, as a building material for huts, etc.

II. *Australian.* [orig. *w.-tree*, from the use of the long pliant branches for making wattled fences, etc.] The common name in Australia for indigenous trees of the genus *Acacia*. Also with defining word indicating the particular species, as *Black, Silver W.* 1810.

Wattle (wǫ·t'l), *sb.*[2] 1513. [Of unkn. origin.] **1.** A fleshy lobe (usu. bright-coloured) pendent from the head or neck of certain birds, as the domestic fowl, the turkey, etc. **2.** A flap of skin pendent from the throat or neck of some swine. Also, a similar excrescence on the jaws of sheep or goats, and *joc.* of human beings 1570. **3.** A fleshy appendage hanging from the mouths of some fishes; a barb 1655. Hence **Wa·ttled** *a.* of a bird, having wattles or a w.; in *Heraldry*, having the wattles of a specified tincture distinct from that of the body.

Wattle (wǫ·t'l), *v.* late ME. [f. WATTLE *sb.*[1]] **1.** *trans.* To construct (a building, fence, etc.) of wattle. **2.** To interlace (boughs, twigs, etc.) so as to form wattle-work 1486. **3.** To bind together (posts, laths, etc.) with interlaced osiers, twigs, or flexible branches 1602. Hence **Wa·ttled** *ppl. a.* constructed of wattle; interlaced. **Wa·ttling** *vbl. sb.* (*a*) an assemblage of rods or laths interlaced with twigs, osiers, or the like, serving as the material of a wattled wall, fence, etc.; (*b*) boughs and twigs for use in wattle-work.

Wave (wē[i]v), *sb.* 1526. [alt., by assoc. with WAVE *v.*, of ME. †*wawe*, earlier *waȝe* (see WAW[1]). In branch II. a new formation from the verb.] **I. 1.** A movement in the sea or other collection of water, by which a portion of the water rises above the normal level and then subsides, at the same time travelling over the surface; a moving ridge or swell of water between two depressions; one of the long ridges or rollers which, in the shallower parts of the sea, follow each other at regular intervals, and successively break on the shore. **b.** *poet.* Used in collect. sing. for 'water', 'sea' 1588. **2.** *transf.* **a.** An undulatory movement, or one of an intermittent series of movements, of something passing over or on a surface or through the air 1810. **b.** A forward movement of a large body of persons (chiefly invaders or immigrants overrunning a country, or soldiers advancing to an attack), who either recede and return after an interval, or are followed after a time by another body of persons repeating the same movement 1852. **c.** A long convex strip of land between two long broad hollows; also occas. a rounded ridge of sand or snow 1788. **3.** *fig.* and in fig. context 1548. **4.** An undulating conformation; each of the undulations of such a conformation 1547. **5. a.** *Physics.* Each of those rhythmic alternations of disturbance and recovery of configuration in successively contiguous portions of a body or medium, by which a state of motion travels in some direction without corresponding progressive movement of the particles successively affected 1832. **b.** *Meteorol.* A change of atmospheric pressure or temperature, consisting of gradual rise and fall or fall and rise, taking place successively at successive points in some particular line of direction on the earth's surface. (In pop. lang., a 'heat-wave', etc. denotes a spell of abnormal heat, etc., which is assumed to be travelling over the country in a particular direction) 1843. **c.** *Seismology.* A seismic disturbance of the crust or surface of the earth, travelling continuously for a certain distance 1862. **d.** *Physics* (see quots.) 1851. **6.** A book-name of certain geometrid moths 1819.

2. a. The..waves of wheat, That ripple round the lonely grange TENNYSON. **b.** Europe was peopled by several successive migrations, or.. waves of population, all flowing from one point in the east 1852. They send forward w. after w. of men, regardless of the punishment 1915. **3.** Man, on the dubious waves of error toss'd COWPER. A w. of militarism sweeps through the nation 1915. **4.** Freedom's northern wind will take all the w. out of your hair 1886. **5. a.** Examples are the waves in the surface of water, the waves of the air which convey sound, and the waves of the ether which are concerned in the transmission of light, heat, and electricity. O.E.D. *Hertzian waves*, a class of ether-waves (discovered by the German physicist Heinrich Hertz in 1888) similar to light waves but of much greater w.-length. **d.** *W. of contraction*, the onward contraction of a muscle from the point where the stimulus is applied. *W. of stimulation*, the (hypothetical) impulse of molecular vibration travelling along a nerve from the point at which it is stimulated.

II. An act of waving. **1.** A motion to and fro of the hand or of something held in the hand, used as a signal or as an expressive sign 1688. **2.** A swaying to and fro 1648. **3.** An act of waving the hair.

attrib. and *Comb.*: **w.-front** *Physics*, the continuous lines or surface including all the waves or radiatory emissions which are in the same phase; **-length** (*a*) the distance from crest to crest or from hollow to hollow of a wave of water or other liquid; (*b*) the distance between two successive points of maximum compression or maximum rarefaction in sound-waves; (*c*) the distance between points in the same phase on two successive heat, light, electro-magnetic, or other waves; *esp.* the length of electro-magnetic wave employed by a broadcasting station; also *fig.*; **-line,** (*a*) *Shipbuilding*, an outline recommended by some naval architects for the hull of a vessel as facilitating movement through the waves; (*b*) *Physics*, the path of a w. of light, sound, etc.; also, the graphic representation of the path. Hence **Wa·veless** *a.* having no waves, not agitated or disturbed by waves. **Wa·velet,** a little w., a ripple.

Wave (wē[i]v), *v.* [Not certainly continuous with OE. *wafian* make a movement to and fro with the hands, corresp. to MHG. *waben* wave, undulate, f. Gmc. **wab-* as in WAVER *v.*] **I.** To move to and fro or up and down. **1.** *intr.* Of a thing having a free end: To move to and fro, shake or sway in the air by the action of the wind or breeze. late ME. **b.** *trans.* Of the wind, etc.: To cause (a thing) to sway or move to and fro 1602. †**2.** *intr.* To move to and fro restlessly or uncertainly; to waver; also, to hover –1728. †**3.** To be restless in mind; to vacillate, waver –1796. **4.** Of water: To move in waves, undulate; also *transf.* of a crowd 1530. **b.** Of a field of corn, etc.: To undulate like the waves of the sea 1667. †**5.** To make a movement to and fro (with the hands). OE. only. †**6.** To make motions (with the uplifted hands or something held in the hands) by way of signal –1644. †**b.** *trans.* To signal to (a person) –1627. †**7.** *trans.* and *intr.* To move to and fro or up and down regularly or rhythmically –1808. **8.** *trans.* To move through the air with a sweeping gesture (the uplifted or extended arm or hand, or something held in the hand), often as a sign of greeting or farewell, or as an expression of exultation; usu. implying repeated movements. Said also (chiefly *poet.*) of impersonal things personified 1607. **b.** To brandish (a weapon) 1601. **c.** *intr.* (for *pass.*) To be moved to and fro 1605. **9.** To signify (something) by a wave of the hand or arm 1810. **b.** To motion (a person, etc.) *aside, away, off*, etc.; also with preps. *from, to*, etc. 1840. **c.** *intr.* To make a sign by a wave of the hand 1803.

1. A stately Ship..Sails fill'd, and streamers waving MILT. **3.** *Cor.* II. ii. 19. **4. b.** Fair waved the golden corn In Canaan's pleasant land 1851. **7.** At last,..thrice his head thus wauing vp and downe, He rais'd a sigh SHAKS. Colours that change whene'er they w. their wings POPE. **8.** Maidens w. Their 'kerchiefs, and old women weep for joy COWPER. Cypresses that seldom w. their boughs SHELLEY.

II. [from WAVE *sb.*] **1.** *trans.* To ornament with an undulating design; to make wavy in outline 1547. **2.** *intr.* To undulate in form or outline 1789.

1. Hair that has been waved by hot irons till it is broken and irregular 1909.

Comb., in the names of the several offerings which, according to the Levitical law, were 'waved' by the priest when presented in sacrifice, as **wavebread, -breast, -loaf, -offering, -sheaf.** Hence **Waved** (wē[i]vd) *ppl. a.* having the form of waves, presenting a wavy outline or appearance, having wavy markings or a wavy texture; held aloft and moved to and fro. **Wa·ver** *sb.*[2] one who waves or causes to wave; an implement for making the hair wavy; *Printing*, an inking roller which has a waving motion, because placed diagonally in the machine.

Wa·ve-like, *a.* and *adv.* 1685. [f. WAVE *sb.* + -LIKE.] **A.** *adj.* Resembling a wave, or what pertains to a wave. **B.** *adv.* After the manner of a wave or waves 1872.

Wavellite (wē[i]·vělǝit). 1805. [Named 1805

after Dr. W. *Wavel* its discoverer; see -ITE[1] 2 b.] *Min.* Hydrous phosphate of aluminium, found in globular aggregates with a radiated structure.

Waver (wē^{i}·vəɹ), *sb.*[1] 1555. [Origin obsc.; perh. f. WAIVE *v.*, in the sense 'to leave untouched'.] A young tree left standing when the surrounding wood is felled.

Waver (wē^{i}·vəɹ), *v.* [– ON. *vafra* move unsteadily, flicker (Norw. *vavra* go to and fro, stagger) = MHG. *waberen* (G. *wabern*) move about, frequent. f. Gmc. **wab-*; cf. WAVE *v.*, -ER[5].] **1.** *intr.* To sway to and fro, as if in danger of falling; to reel, stagger, totter. Now *rare.* late ME. **2.** To swing or wave in the air; to float or flutter 1440. **3.** To exhibit doubt or indecision; to change or vary; to fluctuate or vacillate (*between*); to become unsteady, flinch, give way ME. **4.** Of things (or a person as an unconscious agent): To change, vary, fluctuate 1490. **5.** Of the voice, the eye, etc. (or a person in respect of these): To become unsteady; to shake, tremble, falter 1621. **6.** Of light, shade, objects seen indistinctly: To flicker, quiver 1664.

3. Vertue that wavers is not vertue MILT. The line wavered and broke 1915. Hence **Wa·ver** *sb.*[3] the act or condition of wavering. **Wa·verer,** one who wavers. **Wa·vering** *vbl. sb.* and *ppl. a.*; hence **Wa·veringly** *adv.* **Wa·very** *a.* characterized by wavering or fluttering; tremulous, unsteady 1820.

Wavey (wē^{i}·vi). 1795. [var. of WAWA.] A northern (Amer.) goose of the genus *Chen*, esp. the common w., *C. hyperboreus*.

Wavy (wē^{i}·vi), *a.* 1562. [f. WAVE *sb.* or *v.* + -Y[1].] **1.** Full of waves, abounding in waves, billowy 1593. **2.** *transf.* Said of the air, clouds, etc. 1586. **3.** *fig.* Fluctuating, wavering, changing 1795. **4.** Moving to and fro or up and down with a wave-like motion 1700. **b.** Of movements: Taking place in undulating curves, sinuous 1836. **5.** Rising and falling gently in a succession of waves and hollows; forming an undulating line or a series of wave-like curves 1701. **b.** *Bot.* and *Zool.* Undulate, sinuate; having undulate or sinuate markings 1832. **c.** *Her.* = UNDEE 1562. **d.** Of a dog (short for *w.-coated*): Having the coat in waves, not curly 1884.

2. *W. breathing, respiration* (Path.), respiration in which the inspiratory, and sometimes the expiratory, sounds are broken into two or more separate parts. 4. Let her glad Vallies smile with w. Corn PRIOR. 5. Her dark hair flowed behind, w. but uncurled 1858. A fine w. chalk down 1891. **c.** *Barry w.*, of the field, divided into waving bands of generally horizontal direction. Hence **Wa·vi-ly** *adv.*, **-ness.**

†**Waw**[1]. [ME. *waȝe*, related to OE. *wagian* to wave, shake, totter. Cf. WAG *v.*, WAVE *v.*] A wave –1600.

‖**Waw**[2], **wau.** 1832. The 6th letter in the Hebrew and the corresponding letter in the Arabic and other Semitic alphabets.

‖**Wawa** (wē^{i}·wă). 1768. [– Cree *wehweh*, Ojibwa *wēwe* goose. Cf. WAVEY.] An Amer.-Indian name for the wild goose.

Wax (wæks), *sb.*[1] [OE. *wæx, weax* = OFris. *wax*, OS., OHG. *wahs* (Du. *was*, G. *wachs*), ON. *vax* :– Gmc. **waχsam.*] **1.** A substance (also distinctively called BEESWAX) produced by bees and used by them as the material of the honeycomb; when slightly warmed it is readily moulded into any shape. **2.** Beeswax as melted down, bleached, or otherwise prepared for some special purpose in the arts, in medicine, or in manufactures OE. **b.** As used for the coating of writing tablets 1533. **c.** A particular variety of wax. Usu. with adj., as *white, yellow w.* 1545. **d.** An object made of wax; a wax candle; a figure or model in wax 1844. **3.** In fig. and similative uses, referring to the easy fusibility of wax, its softness, adhesiveness, etc. OE. **4.** = SEALING-WAX OE. **b.** With designation of colour 1485. **5.** Any of a class of substances, found in nature in greater or less purity, including beeswax and other compounds resembling it in general properties and (more or less) in chemical composition. **a.** A vegetable product obtained from various trees and plants 1799. **b.** A substance resembling beeswax secreted or produced by various species of scale-insects 1802. **c.** A mineral product somewhat resembling beeswax 1838. **d.** *gen.* 1866. **6.** = EARWAX 1706. **7.** A thick resinous composition used by shoemakers for rubbing their thread. More fully *cobblers', shoemakers' wax.* 1622. **8.** *U.S.* A thick syrup produced by boiling down the sap of the sugar-maple tree 1845. **9.** *attrib.* (quasi-*adj.*) = composed of or modelled in w. 1585.

2. Effigies. .Curiously done in W. to the Life 1702. The Art of Painting in Wax 1787. 3. I'll work her as I go, I know shee's w. 1612. His heart was. .W. to receive, and marble to retain BYRON. Phr. *Close, tight, neat as w.*; *to stick like w.*; *to fit like w. Man, lad of w.*, used as a term of emphatic commendation (now *arch.* and *dial.*). 5. **c.** *Fossil, mineral w.* = OZOCERITE. *Paraffin w.*: see PARAFFIN *sb.*

Comb.: **w.-berry,** (*a*) the fruit of plants of the genus *Myrica*, esp. *M. cerifera*; also, the plant itself; (*b*) = *Symphoricarpus racemosus*; **-bill,** any one of numerous small birds of the *Ploceidæ* or Weaver-bird family, whose bills have a waxy appearance; **-billed** *a.*, having a bill resembling sealing-w.; **-cloth,** cloth coated with w. as a protection from wet; **w. doll,** (*a*) a doll with head and bust (often also the limbs) of w.; (*b*) *pl.* = FUMITORY; **-end,** thread coated with cobblers' w., used by shoemakers; hence **-ended** *a.*, bound with w.-ends; **-flower,** (*a*) an imitation flower made of w.; (*b*) the genus *Hoya*; (*c*) *Clusia insignis* of British Guiana; (*d*) *Stephanotis floribunda*; **-leather,** leather 'waxed' or finished on the 'flesh' side; **-light,** a candle, taper, or night-light made of w.; **-maker,** a worker-bee that makes w.; **-myrtle** = *w.-berry* (*a*); **-plant,** any one of various plants either yielding a vegetable w. or having a waxy appearance; esp. *Myrica cerifera*, any species of *Hoya*, and *Monotropa uniflora*; **w. tablet,** a board coated with w., to be written on with a stylus; **w. taper,** a taper made of w.; **-tree,** any of various trees yielding vegetable w.; esp. *Myrica cerifera* of N. America, the privet, *Ligustrum lucidum*, of China, the genus *Vismia* of S. America, the varnish-tree of S. America, *Elæagia utilis*, the Japanese shrub *Rhus succedanea.*

Wax (wæks), *sb.*[2] *colloq.* or *slang.* 1854. [perh. evolved from a usage such as *wax wroth* (WAX *v.*).] Angry feeling; a fit of anger; chiefly *to be in a w.*

I used to rush out in a frightful state of w., and show a leg 1854.

Wax (wæks), *v.*[1] Now chiefly *literary* or *arch.* Pa. t. and pa. pple. **waxed** (wækst); pa. pple. also **waxen.** [OE. *weaxan* = OFris. *waxa*, OS., OHG. *wahsan* (Du. *wassen*, G. *wachsen*), ON. *vaxa*, Goth. *wahsjan* :– Gmc. str. vb. f. **waχs-* :– IE. **woks- *aweks- *auks- *uks-* repr. by Gr. αὐξάνειν increase, L. *augēre*, Skr. *ukš* grow, and Gmc. *auk-* in OE. *ēacian* EKE *v.*] **I.** To grow, increase. (Opp. to *wane.*) **1.** *intr.* To increase gradually in size and strength; to grow, develop. *arch.* and *dial.* **2.** To advance *in* power, importance, prosperity, etc. OE. **3.** Of inanimate things: To increase in size, quantity, volume, intensity, etc. OE. **4.** Of the moon: To undergo the periodical increase in the extent of its visible illuminated portion, characteristic of the first half of the lunation OE. **5.** Of a quality, state of things, activity, etc.: To become gradually greater or more striking; to increase in potency or intensity OE.

1. There wex. .euery holsum spice CHAUCER. Thy bairn waxes fast, she's taller ivery time I see her 1889. 2. *Cor.* II. ii. 103. A democratic party. . was waxing in size and strength 1873. 3. The river, which I observed to be somewhat waxen SCOTT. Glaciers. .w. and wane in some mysterious manner 1884. 4. States thrive or wither, as moons w. and wane COWPER.

II. With complement: To change by growth or increase; to turn, become, grow ME.

When her sonne to mans estate did wex SPENSER. What? Art thou like the Adder waxen deafe? SHAKS. It was now waxing towards morning 1831. Mr. Chuckster waxed wroth at this answer DICKENS. As time waxed on 1870.

Wax (wæks), *v.*[2] late ME. [f. WAX *sb.*[1]] **1.** *trans.* To cover with a layer of wax; to dress with wax; to polish or stiffen with a dressing of wax. †**2.** To stop up (an aperture) with or as with wax –1709. **3.** *Leather-manuf.* To dress (a skin) with a mixture of lamp-black, oil, etc. 1885.

1. As a Shoemaker waxeth his thread 1615. The elegant ignoramus whose sole accomplishments consist in parting his hair, waxing his moustaches, and smoking a meerschaum 1863. Hence **Waxed** (wækst) *ppl. a.* coated with a layer of wax; polished or stiffened with wax; dressed or saturated with wax, e.g. for water-proofing; of a skin, dressed on the flesh side with a mixture of lamp-black and oil.

Wax candle. OE. A candle made of wax.

Wa·x-cha:ndler. late ME. [CHANDLER 2.] One whose trade is to make or sell wax candles.

Waxen (wæ·ks'n), *a.* [OE. *wexen*, superseded by a new formation f. WAX *sb.*[1] + -EN[4].] **1.** Made of wax. **2.** *transf.* and *fig.* As if made of wax (with ref. to its softness, impressibility or fusibility, or to the smooth and lustrous surface of things modelled in wax) 1591. **3.** Covered or coated with wax, loaded with wax 1590.

1. *W. image*, spec. an effigy in wax representing a person whom it was desired to injure by witchcraft; The W.-Image being found and broken,. . the King did. .recover 1685. 2. For men haue marble, women w. mindes SHAKS. His rosy neck, and w. arms 1743. W. paleness 1853.

Comb.: **w.-chatterer,** the Bohemian waxwing, *Ampelis garrulus.*

†**Wa·xen,** *v.* 1540. [An unexpl. var. for WAX *v.*[1]] = WAX *v.*[1] –1647. (See O.E.D.)

Wa·x-shot. *Obs.* exc. *Hist.* 1550. [f. WAX *sb.*[1] + SHOT *sb.*[1]] A customary payment made for the maintenance of lights in churches.

Waxwing (wæ·ksˌwiŋ). 1817. A passerine bird of the genus *Ampelis* (*Bombycilla*), esp. *A. garrulus*, the Bohemian w.

Waxwork (wæ·ksˌwɒɹk). 1697. **1.** Work executed in wax; *esp.* modelling in wax; an object modelled in wax; usu. applied to life-size effigies of persons, with head, hands, and bust of wax, coloured and clothed to look like life. **2.** An exhibition of wax figures representing celebrated or notorious characters; also, the place of exhibition. Now *pl.* 1796. **3.** *U.S.* The climbing bitter-sweet, *Celastrus scandens*; so called from the waxy scarlet aril of the fruit 1856.

1. I've seen wax-work quite like life DICKENS. *attrib.* and *Comb.*, as *w.-figure, -show*, etc. So **Wa·x-wo:rker,** a worker in wax; *spec.* a bee that makes wax. **Wa·x-wo:rking** *a.* making wax.

Waxy (wæ·ksi), *a.*[1] 1596. [f. WAX *sb.*[1] + -Y[1].] **1.** Having the nature or distinctive properties of wax; *fig.* of a person, etc., soft, plastic, impressionable like wax. **2.** Resembling wax in colour or consistence; (of a quality) like that of wax 1835. **b.** *Med.* Affected with amyloid degeneration 1845. Hence **Wa·xi-ly** *adv.*, **-ness.**

Waxy (wæ·ksi), *a.*[2] *colloq.* or *slang.* 1853. [f. WAX *sb.*[2] + -Y[1].] Angry, 'in a wax'.

Way (wē^{i}), *sb.* [OE. *weġ* = OFris. *wei, wī*, OS., OHG. *weg* (Du., G. *weg*), ON. *vegr*, Goth. *wigs* :– Gmc. **weʒaz*, f. **weʒ-* move, journey, carry (see WEIGH *v.*, WAIN *sb.*), repr. also by L. *vehere* carry.] **I.** Road, path. **1.** A track prepared or available for travelling along; a road, street, lane, or path. **b.** A road considered with ref. to the condition of its surface, etc. OE. **c.** A place of passage, e.g. an opening made through a crowd, a door or gate, etc. ME. **d.** *Railways.* See PERMANENT *w.*, SIX-FOOT *w.*, etc. **2.** *pl.* Parallel wooden planks or balks for heavy loads, ships, etc. to slide upon 1639. **b.** *Mech.* Parallel sills forming a track for the slides of the uprights of a planing machine, the carriage of a lathe, or the like 1869.

1. Broad on the left before him lay, For many a mile, the Roman w. SCOTT. *Beside, over, across the w., the other side of the w.*, etc.; He called out to a gentleman on the opposite side of the w. DICKENS. For the most part, no English creature ever does see farther than over the w. RUSKIN. *transf.* The Via lactea, or 'milky w.', which the peasantry of the North frequently designate 'the w.' 1844. *fig.* But in the beaten w. of friendship, What make you at Elsonower? SHAKS. **b.** The weather was cold, the ways dirty and dangerous 1663. **d.** *Line of w.*, a track formed by a pair of rails.

II. Course of travel or movement. **1.** A line or course of travel or progression by which a place may be reached, or along which a person or thing may pass OE. **2.** Course or line of actual movement. late ME. **3.** *gen.* Opportunity for passage or advance; absence of obstruction; hence *fig.* freedom of action, scope, opportunity. late ME. **b.** In legal documents sometimes = RIGHT OF W. 1766. **4.** Travel or motion along a particular route or in a particular direction OE. **b.** *Naut.* Progress (of a ship or boat) through the water; rate of progress, velocity 1663. **5.** Distance travelled or to be travelled along a particular route OE. **6.** Direction of motion, relative position, or aspect. Chiefly in advb. phr., as *this w.* (= hitherwards), *my w.* (= towards me, into my neighbourhood), *that w.*, *which w.*, *all ways*, etc. ME.

1. Mr. Bourne..asked if I were going his w. 1856. *fig.* That go the Primrose w. to th' euerlasting Bonfire SHAKS. *Prov.* There be mo waies to the wood than one HEYWOOD. The Longest w. about is the nearest W. Home 1661. Phrases. *To hold, keep* (a certain) *w.*, to follow it without deviation. *To know one's w. about*, to know how to get from place to place in a neighbourhood; *fig.* to know how to act in any emergency, to possess wide experience of the ways of the world, esp. with derogatory implication. †*There lies your w.*, please to go away. *To go the wrong w.*, of food or drink, to go into the windpipe instead of the gullet when being swallowed. *W. of the Cross* (= eccl. L. *Via Crucis*), a series of (fourteen) images or pictures representing the 'Stations of the Cross' (STATION *sb.* IV. 3), ranged round the interior of a church, or on the road to or in the vicinity of a church or shrine, esp. as used as an object of devotion; hence, a series of devotions used in connection with the Stations. **2.** The weie of an egle in heuene,..the weie of a ship in the myd se WYCLIF *Prov.* 30:19. The series of parallel paths hewn out by the rocker on a mezzotint is technically termed a *w.* 1891. **3.** Phr. *To give w.*, *make w.*; also *Way!* (= 'make w.'). **4.** *To take* (a place, etc.) *in one's w.*, to visit in the course of one's journey; We may take Chatsworth in our w. 1777. *To go, wend one's w.*, (now *arch.*) almost = to go away; Then she railed on me, and I went my w. BUNYAN. *Go, come your* (*thy*) *w.* (see also IV), now *dial.*; Go your w. for a simpleton, and say no more about the matter 1772. *To go the w. of all the earth* (Josh. 23:14, 1 Kings 2:2), to die; so (by confusion with other Bible passages) *the w. of all flesh* (sometimes used to mean the experience common to all men in their passage through life), *of all living*; I heard that Don Rodrigo had gone the w. of all flesh 1809. *To force, push, squeeze*, etc., *one's w.*, to effect a forward movement by the action denoted by the verb; to accompany one's advance by the specified action; The plowman homeward plods his weary w. GRAY. *To hold, keep one's w.*, to travel without interruption; *fig.* to 'keep going'. **b.** *transf.* A..short dark man came into the room with so much w. upon him, that he was within a foot of Clennam before he could stop DICKENS. **5.** Long w. he traveiled before he heard of ought SPENSER. The village..is not a great w. off 1882. (*By*) *a long w.*, fig., qualifying a comparative, = 'far' (better, etc.). †*A great w.*, to a great extent; I..Thinke him a great w. foole SHAKS. *All the way from —— to ——* (U.S.), expressing the lower and upper limits of value, number, etc. **6.** *fig.* *Lear* III. iv. 21. *The other w. about, round*, conversely, vice versa. *One w. or* (*the*) *other*, *either w.*

III. Course of life or action, means, manner. **1.** A path or course of life; the activities and fortunes of a person; a prescribed course of life or conduct OE. **b.** *pl.* Habits of life, esp. with regard to moral conduct OE. **c.** *The w.* or *ways of God*, the course of God's providence OE. **2.** A course of action ME. †**b.** (One's) best or most advisable course. SHAKS. **3.** A course of action; a device, expedient method, or means by which some end may be attained. Sometimes coupled with MEAN *sb.*; see WAYS AND MEANS. ME. **4.** Manner in which something is done or takes place; method of performing an action or operation OE. **b.** advb. phrases without prep. (now *rare*) ME. **5.** In advb. phrases like (*in*) *all ways*, (*in*) *any w.*, etc., the sense of 'manner' passes into that of: An aspect, feature, or respect; a point or particular of comparison 1598. **6.** A condition regarded as hopeful or the contrary (usu. with qualifying adj.) 1467. **7.** Kind, sort, description. Now only in phr. *in the w. of*, of the nature of, belonging to the class of; so *in the — w.* 1647. **8.** Kind of occupation, work, or business 1690. **9.** *In a great, small w.*, (living) on a large or small scale of income and expenditure 1750. **10.** The customary or usual manner of acting or behaving 1613. **b.** *pl.* Customary modes of behaviour; usages 1742. **11.** A Habitual or characteristic manner of action, expression, or the like 1709.

1. They kept the noiseless tenor of their w. GRAY. *The W.*, in the Acts of the Apostles, the Christian religion. **2.** He told me that I went the wrong w. to work SMOLLETT. *To have* (*get*, etc.) *one's* (*own*) *w.*, to be allowed to follow or to enforce on others the course of action on which one is resolved; hence *to love, be fond of one's own w.* **3.** Mr. Huxley..can see but one w. of arriving at truth; which he calls experience 1892. Prov. *Where there's a will there's a w.* **4.** After dinner we rode in like way two miles MORYSON. There are several Ways of making Sauce for a Pig 1747. *The humid, moist*, or *wet w.*, *the dry w.*, (Fr. *voie humide, voie sèche*), Chem. and Assaying, processes distinguished by the presence or absence of liquid. *In his* (*her*, etc.) *w.*, appended to expressions of praise, implying that the praise is to be understood in a limited sense appropriate to the object; so *in a w.* *W. of thinking*, a set of opinions or principles characteristic of a party or sect. *W. of living, life*, habits with regard to food, habitation, etc. *To have everything one's own w.*, *to have it all one's own w.*, to have one's wishes carried out; to meet with no resistance or opposition. *No two ways about it*, there can be no doubt of the fact. *It is always the w. with* (*him*), (he) always acts so. **b.** Without..his being any manner of ways connected in it 1705. I..hope she will..allow them to be happy their own way JOHNSON. **5.** A teetotaler, however admirable in other ways, is not the fit person to edit Burns 1893. **6.** *In the family w.*: see FAMILY (Phr.). *To be in a w.*, to be in a state of mental distress or anxiety. **7.** I should want for nothing in the bread and water w.! 1809. **8.** It was a new house, but did a tremendous business in the fig and sponge w. THACKERAY. **9.** Contractors and builders in a large w. of business 1864. **10.** Even so Sir, 'tis the w. of the World CONGREVE. **11.** *It is* (*only*) *his w.*, often said of some perverse or annoying habit of behaviour which the friends of the person guilty of it are accustomed to regard with toleration; And all that's madly wild, or oddly gay, We call it only pretty Fanny's w. PARNELL. (Parnell's phr. is often used allus.) *To have a w. with one*, to have a persuasive manner.

IV. Ways (orig. genitive) used as sing. OE.

To go, come one's ways (now *dial.*); Go thy ways for a true Pattern of the Vanity, Impertinence,..and Ostentation of thy Country FARQUHAR. *A good, great, little, long ways* (now only *dial.* and *U.S.*).

Phrases. **Have w.** †**a.** To be allowed liberty of action SHAKS. **b.** Of feelings, etc.: To find vent. **Make w. a.** To open a passage (*for*, †*to*), remove obstacles to progress. **b.** To move from one's place so as to allow a person to pass. **c.** To leave a place vacant *for* a successor or substitute. **d.** To make progress on a journey or voyage. **Make one's (its) w. a.** To travel or proceed in an intended direction or to a certain place. *To make the best of one's w.*, to go as quickly as one can. **b.** To make progress in one's career; to advance in wealth, station, etc., by one's own efforts. **c.** Of a thing: to travel, make progress; of an opinion, etc., to gain acceptance. **Pay one's (its) w.** To succeed in paying one's expenses as they arise, without incurring debts. Of a business undertaking: To be self-supporting. **See one's w.** To have a view of the portion of the road or route immediately before one, so as to be able to avoid wandering or stumbling; hence *fig.*, now often (chiefly with neg.) to feel justified in deciding *to do* something. **Take one's w.** To set out on a journey; to journey, travel.

By the w. a. Along or near the road by which one travels. **b.** In the course of one's walk or journey; *fig.* incidentally, in passing, as a side-topic. **c.** Used parenthetically to apologize for introducing a new topic, a casual remark, or the like. **d.** As a by-work, as a subordinate piece of work. †**e.** Indirectly. SHAKS. **By w. of —.** †**a.** By means of, through the medium of. **b.** As an instance or a mode of; in the capacity or with the function of. **c.** Followed by gerund, used *predic.* with the sense: In the habit of (doing something); also, usu., making a profession of, having a reputation for (being or doing so-and-so). *colloq.* **d.** = VIA *prep.* **In the** (etc.) **w.** (see also III. senses 7–9). **a.** (Usu. *in one's w.*) On or along the road by which one travels; so as to be met, encountered, or observed. **b.** *fig.* in phr. *to come, fall, lie*, etc., *in* (one's) *w.*, to be met with in one's experience, to come within (one's) range of possible observation, attainment, etc. So *to lay, put, throw in* (a person's) *w.* **c.** In such a position or of such a nature as to obstruct, impede, or be an annoyance. **d.** Within reach or call, at hand; in a place where things are going on or where one can be found readily. Now *rare.* **e.** *Once in a w.*, on a single (rare or exceptional) occasion; as a solitary or rare instance. Also *for once in a w.* **In the way of —.** (See also III. 7.) †**a.** = *By w. of* b. **b.** By means of. Now *rare.* **c.** In the course or routine of. †**d.** When one is concerned with. SHAKS. **e.** *To be in the w. of*, to be likely to do or obtain (something), to have a good chance of (doing or attaining something). So *to put* (a person) *in the w. of.* Also with *to* and inf. †**f.** *In* (*the*) *w. of marriage, in w. to marriage*, with a view to matrimony. **On the** or **one's w.** On, or in the course of, a journey. *To be well on one's w.*, to have made some progress; also *fig.* **Out of the w.** (See also OUT-OF-THE-W.) **a.** Away from the road by which one is travelling; off the track or proper route. **b.** With *of* or possessive. Away from the path in which a person or thing is moving; in a position where one does not meet or impede another; out of reach of, not in danger from. *Out of harm's w.*: see HARM *sb.* 1. **c.** *To go out of one's w. to* (do something), to do something which the circumstances do not call for or invite. **d.** *To put* (a person) *out of his w.*: to disturb, inconvenience, trouble; often *refl.* to submit to inconvenience or bother for the sake of others. **e.** Away from the resort or society or other persons; in a position remote or inconvenient to get at. **f.** Away from an obstructive position. **g.** *To put out of the w.*, to make away with, kill. *Out of the w.*, no longer alive. **h.** *predic.* as adj.: Beside the mark, out of place; odd, bizarre. **Under w.** *Naut.* [– Du. *onderweg.*] Having begun to move through the water. Often spelt *under weigh*: see WEIGH *sb.*[2] Also *transf.* and *fig.* beginning to advance or make progress.

Comb.: **w.-board,** *Mining* and *Geol.*, any thin layer or bed of rock, clay, etc. separating thicker strata; **-leave,** permission to make and use a way for conveying coal from the pit-head across a person's land; the rent paid for such permission; the way or road constructed for the purpose; permission to carry telephone wires over buildings, drains or water-pipes across private land, etc.; also, the rent or charge for such permission; **-man,** a workman employed on the permanent w. of a railway, a plate-layer; **-mark,** any object which serves as a guide to the traveller; **w. passenger,** *U.S.*, a passenger picked up or set down at a stage or station intermediate between the main stopping-places; **-station,** *U.S.*, an intermediate station on a railway route, a wayside station; **-wise** *a. dial.* and *U.S.*, of a horse, familiar with the roads he is required to travel; also *fig.* of persons; **-wort,** a name for the pimpernel. Hence **Way·less** *a.* having no way or road; trackless, pathless; **-ness.**

Way (wē^{i}), *adv.* Now *Sc.*, *north.*, and *U.S.* ME. [Aphetic f. AWAY.] **1.** = AWAY *adv.* **2.** *esp.* At or to a (great) distance, far 1849. Hence **W.-off** *a.* distant. **W.-back** *U.S. slang*, in phr. *from w.-back*, from a remote or rural district; hence attrib. and quasi-adj.

Way (wē^{i}), *int.* 1836. [Cf. Wo *int.*] A call to a horse to stop.

-way (wē^{i}), as terminal element of advs., is identical with WAY *sb.* Cf. -WAYS.

1. Phrases consisting of the sb. qualified by an adj. are often used advb., and some of the combinations thus used have come to be apprehended as single words, and to be so pronounced and written; e.g. *anyway, someway*; *broadway, crossway, straightway.* **2.** The few advs. f. sb. + *-way* are genuine compounds; *edgeway, endway, sideway*, etc., are not older than the 16th c. These words may also be used as adjs.

Way·-bill. 1791. **1.** A list of passengers booked for seats in a stage-coach or other public vehicle for places on the road. Also, a detailed statement of goods entrusted to a public carrier for delivery. **2.** A list of places to be visited on a journey. **3.** *U.S.* A label attached to an article in transport to indicate its destination, etc. 1887. **4.** A kind of pass by producing which a man 'on the road' can obtain relief at certain stages of his journey. So *w. system.* 1893. Hence **Way·-bill** *v. U.S. trans.* to enter (goods) on a w.

Waybread, waybred (wē^{i}·bred). [OE. *weġbrǣde, -brāde*, corresp. to OS. *wegabrēda*, OHG. *wegabreita* (G. *wegbreit* masc., *wegebreite* fem.), WGmc. comp. of WAY *sb.* and *braiðja, f. *braið- BROAD *a.* 'the broad-leaved plant of the roadside(s)'.] = PLANTAIN[1] 1. Also *water w.* = water plantain: see PLANTAIN[1] 2.

Wayfare (wē^{i}·fe^{ə}ɹ), *sb. arch.* late ME. [f. WAY *sb.* + FARE *sb.*[1], after WAYFARING *a.*] Wayfaring, travelling.

Wayfare (wē^{i}·fe^{ə}ɹ), *v.* Now *rare* and *arch.* 1547. [Back-formation from WAYFARING *sb.*] *intr.* To journey or travel, esp. on foot.

Wayfarer (wē^{i}·fē^{ə}:rəɹ). 1440. [f. WAY *sb.* + *farer* (f. FARE *v.*[1]).] A traveller by road, esp. one who journeys on foot. **b.** *Wayfarer's-tree*, the hobble-bush. *U.S.* 1858.

Wayfaring (wē^{i}·fē^{ə}:riŋ), *vbl. sb. arch.* 1536. [f. WAY *sb.* + *faring* vbl. sb. f. FARE *v.*[1], after next.] Journeying, travelling; an instance of this.

fig. This earthly waifaring 1561. That I may dare, in w., To stammer where old Chaucer used to sing KEATS.

Wayfaring (wē^{i}·fē^{ə}:riŋ), *ppl. a. arch.* [OE. *weġfarende*, f. *weġ* WAY *sb.* + pres. pple. of *faran* FARE *v.*[1]] Travelling or journeying by road. Usu. *w. man*, a traveller by road.

Isa. 35:8.

Way·fa:ring-tree:. 1597. [Short for *way-*

faring man's tree; cf. *traveller's joy*.] **1.** The tall shrub *Viburnum lantana*, growing wild in hedges and underwood. **2.** *U.S.* The hobble-bush 1814.

Waygoose. Now *dial.* or *Obs.* 1683. [Earlier form of WAYZGOOSE.] = WAYZGOOSE.

Waylay (wēⁱlēⁱ·), *v.* Pa. t. and pa. pple. **waylaid** (wēⁱlēⁱ·d). 1513. [f. WAY *sb.* + LAY *v.*¹, after MLG., MDu. *wegelāgen*, f. *wegelage* :– OS., OHG. **wega lāga* besetting of ways.] **1.** *trans.* To lie in wait for with evil or hostile intent; to seize or attack in the way. **b.** To intercept and seize (a thing in transit) 1599. **2.** *transf.* To wait for and accost (a person) in the way; to stop (a person) in order to converse with him 1612. †**3.** To impede or intercept; to block the path or progress of –1688. †**4.** To beset or blockade (a road, position, etc.) with an armed force of the like –1828.

1. *fig.* The..Miseries, which way-lay our Passage through the World JOHNSON. **2.** I have held it the first principle of manners not to w. people RUSKIN.

†**Wayment,** *v.* late ME. [– OFr. *waimenter, guaimenter*, f. *wai, guai* alas, prob. after *lamenter* lament.] *intr.* To lament, wail; to sorrow bitterly –1861.

-ways, terminal element of advs., was orig. a use of the genitive of WAY *sb.*

1. Many phrases consisting of the genitive of *way* qualified by an adj. were formerly used advb., and later apprehended as one word; see ALWAYS, OTHERWAYS, etc. On the analogy of these were subsequently formed *anyways, crossways, longways, straightways*, etc. **2.** In advs. f. sb. + *-ways*, as *endways, lengthways, sideways*, the general sense is 'in a specified direction'. **3.** Most advs. in *-ways* have synonyms in -WAY, and often also in -WISE, which is often preferred to *-ways* or *-way* because it is supposed to be the more 'correct' form. **4.** The combs. of *-ways*, except SIDEWAYS, are hardly ever used as adjs.

Ways and means. late ME. Formerly also †**means and ways. 1.** The methods and resources which are at a person's disposal for effecting some object. **2.** *spec.* In *Legislation*: Methods of procuring funds or supplies for the current expenditure of the state 1644. **b.** Pecuniary resources in general 1738.

2. *Committee of Ways and Means*, (*a*) a committee of the whole House of Commons, which sits to consider the budget (see BUDGET 4); (*b*) *U.S.*, a standing committee of the House of Representatives, to which are referred bills dealing with revenue, tariff, etc.

Way·side. late ME. The side of a road or path; the land bordering either side of the way. **b.** *attrib.* passing into *adj.* Of or pertaining to the w.; situated on, growing by, etc., the w. 1817.

Wayward (wēⁱ·wə̆ɹd), *a.* Not now in colloq. use. late ME. [Aphetic f. AWAYWARD.] **1.** Disposed to go counter to the wishes or advice of others or to what is reasonable; wrong-headed, intractable, self-willed, perverse. **2.** Capriciously wilful; conforming to no fixed rule or principle of conduct; erratic 1533.

1. A! thou generacioun vnbyleeful and weiward WYCLIF *Matt.* 17:16. Pericles Is now againe thwarting thy w. seas SHAKS. Mutt'ring his w. fancies GRAY. Hence **Way·ward-ly** *adv.*, **-ness.**

Waywarden (wēⁱ·wǭɹd'n). 1776. [f. WAY *sb.* + WARDEN¹.] A person (later, one of a board) elected to supervise the highways of a parish or district.

Way-wiser (wēⁱ·wəi:zəɹ). Now *Hist.* 1651. [Formed after G. *wegweiser*, f. *weg* WAY *sb.* + *weiser*, agent-n. f. *weisen* show.] An instrument for measuring and indicating a distance travelled by road.

Waywode (wēⁱ·wōᵘd). Now *Hist.* 1661. [var. of VAIVODE, repr. an early Magyar form of a common Slavonic title.] = VOIVODE. Hence **Way·wodeship,** the province or district ruled by a w.

Way·-worn, *a.* 1777. Worn or wearied by travel.

Wayzgoose (wēⁱ·zgūs). 1731. [Earlier WAYGOOSE. The first element is of unkn. origin, and there is no evidence that the second is to be identified with GOOSE *sb.*] orig. An entertainment given by a master-printer to his workmen in August, marking the beginning of the season of working by candle-light. Later, an annual festivity held in summer by the employees of a printing establishment, consisting of a dinner and (usu.) an excursion into the country.

‖**Wazir** (wăzīᵊ·ɹ). 1715. [Arab. *wazīr*; see VIZIER.] = VIZIER 1.

We (wī, wi), *pron.* [OE. *wĕ*, corresp. to OFris. *wī*, OS. *wī, wē*, OHG. *wir* (Du. *wij*, G. *wir*), ON. *vér, vær*, Goth. *weis*. These forms repr. more than one Gmc. type; Goth. *weis* repr. Gmc. **wīz* :– **weis*, extension (with pl. *-s*) of **wei*, repr. also by Skr. *vayám*, Av. *vaēm*; other forms may repr. **wĭz*, of doubtful origin; Tokh. has *was*; dual OE. *wit* = OS. *wit*, ON. *vit*, Goth. *wit*, has a parallel in Lith. *vèdu*. For the obl. cases see OUR, US.] **1.** The pronoun of the first person plural nominative, denoting the speaker and one or more other persons whom he associates with himself as the subject of the sentence. **b.** Used confidentially or playfully to mean the person addressed, with whose interests the speaker thus identifies himself. **c.** Used indefinitely in general statements in which the speaker or writer includes those whom he addresses, his contemporaries, or the like OE. **2.** Used by a single person to denote himself: **a.** by a sovereign or ruler OE. **b.** by a speaker or writer (e.g. in editorial or unsigned articles in newspapers or other periodicals), in order to secure an impersonal style and tone OE. **c.** Hence joc. as quasi-*sb.*: The editor of a periodical; the periodical itself 1853. **3.** Used for the accusative *us* (now *local*) 1500.

1. Vppon the texte whee sware, both I and my wiffe 1460. Put we our quarell to the will of heauen SHAKS. When shall we three meet againe? SHAKS. We, Your Majesty's most dutiful and loyal subjects, the Commons of the United Kingdom..in Parliament assembled 1918. **b.** Well, Jane, and how are we this morning? 1884. **c.** There is nothing which we receive with so much Reluctance as Advice ADDISON. What do we, as a nation, care about books? RUSKIN. **2. b.** There is a mysterious authority in the plural *we*, which no single name..can acquire 1807. **3.** You must ride On horseback after we COWPER.

Weak (wīk), *a.* [ME. *wayke* – ON. *veikr* (**weikr*) = OE. *wāc* weak, slothful, pliant, insignificant, mean (ME. *wōke*), OS. *wēk*, OHG. *weih* (Du. *week*, G. *weich* soft) :– Gmc. **waikaz*, f. **waik-* **wīk-* yield, give way.] **1.** Wanting in moral strength for endurance or resistance; lacking fortitude or courage, strength of purpose or will. late ME. **b.** Used to render Gr. ἀσθενής, ἀσθενῶν, applied by St. Paul (esp. in Rom. 14 and 1 Cor. 8) to believers whose scruples, though unsound, should be treated with tenderness, lest they should be led into acts condemned by their conscience. Hence allus. in *weaker brethren*. 1526. **c.** Of features, expression, tears, etc.: Indicating weakness; of persons, etc., deficient in power to control emotion; unduly swayed by grief, compassion, or affection 1768. **2.** Wanting in strength and skill as a combatant; deficient in numbers, resources, etc.; relatively deficient in fighting power as shown by the result of the contest ME. **b.** Wanting in or exhibiting want of skill in a game, sport, contest, etc. 1827. **3.** Deficient in bodily or muscular strength; esp. of a child or woman, inferior in respect of physical strength ME. **4.** Deficient in bodily vigour through age, sickness, privation, etc.; wanting in strength of the vital functions of the body ME. **5.** Constitutionally feeble; not vigorous or robust in health 1523. **6.** Of bodily organs or their functions: Deficient in functional strength 1480. **7.** Of the mind or mental faculties: Deficient in power. late ME. **b.** Lacking force of intellect or strength of mind; easily deceived; feeble (*in* one's intellect, the head, etc.). late ME. **8.** Of a person, his qualities, productions, etc.: Inefficient, ill-qualified. late ME. **9.** Wanting in power or authority over others. late ME. **b.** Of power, strength, authority, etc. late ME. **10. a.** *Card-playing.* Of a hand, suit, etc.: Not of a commanding nature or value. Of a player; Ill-provided with commanding cards (*in* a specified suit). 1680. **b.** Of money or stock: Insufficient to meet a demand or to carry on operations. Similarly of a holder of stock. 1875. **11.** Not strong or energetic in action; lacking in force or power ME. **12.** Wanting in effectiveness; not convincing 1538. †**13.** Of a thing: Of little account or worth –1822. **14.** Having less than the full or proper amount of a specific ingredient. Of an infusion: Over diluted. 1597. **15.** Wanting in material strength, unsound, insecure. late ME. **16.** Wanting in solidity or firmness; of a texture: easily broken, fragile 1581. **17.** Not strongly marked; faint 1585. **18.** *Comm.* Of market prices, commodities, etc.: Having a downward tendency; not firm 1856. **19.** *Phonetics* and *Prosody.* Of a sound or syllable: Pronounced with less force than the adjacent sound or sounds; unstressed. Of stress: Having relatively little force. Of the cæsura: Falling after a short syllable. 1637. **20.** *Philol.* (Opp. to STRONG *a.* 21). **a.** Of Germanic nouns and adjs.: Belonging to any of the declensions in which the stem in Primitive Germanic ended in *-n* 1841. **b.** Of Germanic verbs: Forming the preterite by means of a suffix 1841. **c.** In Greek grammar, applied to the sigmatic or 'first' aorist 1875. **d.** In Sanskrit grammar, the designation of the reduced stems of nouns, and of the cases in which the reduced stem occurs 1863. **e.** In Hebrew and Syriac grammar, applied to certain consonants and to verbs which have any of these in the root 1874. **f.** Applied to the ablaut-grade which results from absence of stress 1888.

1. The spirite ys willynge but the flesshe is weeke TINDALE *Matt.* 26:41. Disraeli, in a w. moment, offered him office again 1878. **c.** You must have a w. spot in your heart for him 1886. **2. b.** The Surrey bowling was w. 1862. Seek for the w. spot in the batsman's defence 1891. **3.** *The weaker vessel*, in 1 Pet. 3:7 said of the wife as compared with the husband; hence occas. *joc.* = wife. **5.** Stake and bind up the weakest Plants 1696. Laws to prevent the education of w. children 1772. **6.** My weake stomacke SHAKS. A woman of w. nerves 1825. **7. b.** By these means w. men are often deceived by others 1736. **8.** My w. oratorie SHAKS. The weakest Part of a very w. Book 1713. W. to perform, though mighty to pretend COWPER. **11.** My loue is strengthned, though more weake in seeming SHAKS. A w. Pulse 1707. If these terms are w., or ambiguous 1771. W., sad voices CRABBE. **12.** My w. endeavours to amuse you 1741. Justin..is..a w. authority for any disputed historical fact 1863. **14.** A little brandy and water, not too w. 1891. **15.** The strength of the chain is in the weakest link 1885. *W. side* (of a fortified place), a side unsound in its defences; also *fig.*; The Love of Mutton was his W. side 1692. *W. point*, the point of feature where a thing is defective or unsound; a (moral or intellectual) failing or weakness. **19.** *W. ending*, the occurrence of an unstressed or proclitic monosyllable in the normally stressed place at the end of an iambic line.

Comb.: **w.-headed** *a.*, lacking strength of mind or purpose; **-hearted** *a.*, faint-hearted, tender-hearted; **-sighted** *a.*, having w. sight. Hence **Wea·kish** *a.* somewhat w.

Weaken (wī·k'n), *v.* 1530. [f. prec. + -EN⁵.] **I.** *trans.* To make weak or weaker. **1.** To lessen the physical strength or vigour of; to lessen the functional vigour of (the mind, etc.). Now *rare.* 1536. **3.** To lessen (authority, credit, etc.) 1530. **4.** To reduce the strength of (a body of men) in numbers or fighting power; to render (a position) less secure 1560. **5.** To render weaker in resources, authority, power, or the like 1568. **6.** To render less efficacious 1606. **7.** To render (a material thing) less strong 1827. **8.** To reduce the intensity of (a colour, sound, fire) 1683. **b.** *Phonetics.* To reduce in force or intensity of utterance 1863. **9.** *Card-games.* To lessen the strength of (one's hand, etc.) 1742. **10.** To render (market prices, a market) less firm 1875.

6. *Tr. & Cr.* I. iii. 195. Another fragment of the true cross..weakened in virtue, doubtless, by sojourning with infidels SCOTT. **7.** This weakened the central tower, which fell with a crash 1914.

II. *intr.* To grow or become weak or weaker 1541. **b.** (orig. *U.S.*) To take a less firm attitude; to give way 1876.

Weakfish (wī·kfiʃ). *U.S.* 1838. [– Du. †*weekvisch*, f. *week* soft + *visch* fish.] A marine sciænoid food-fish of the genus *Cynoscion*, esp. *C. regalis*, the sea-trout of the Atlantic.

Weak-kneed (stress var.), *a.* 1870. Having

weak knees; chiefly *fig.* wanting in resolution or determination.

Weakling (wī·kliŋ). 1557. [f. WEAK *a.* + -LING[1]; first used by Tindale after G. *weichling* (Luther).] **1.** A person or animal that lacks physical strength or is weak in health or constitution 1576. **2.** One who is weak in character or intellect 1577. **3.** *appos.* or as *adj.* Weak, feeble 1557.

Weakly (wī·kli), *a.* 1577. [f. WEAK *a.* + -LY[1].] **1.** Weak in constitution, not strong or robust, delicate. **2.** Characterized by moral weakness 1890. Hence **Wea·kliness,** w. quality.

Weakly (wī·kli), *adv.* late ME. [-LY[2].] **1.** With little force or strength. **2.** With slight defensive strength 1582. **3.** Sparsely, meagrely, slightly. Now *rare.* 1605. **4.** With weakness of mind or character 1610. **5.** Inefficiently 1663. **6.** With little force of argument 1662.

Weak-minded, *a.* 1782. **1.** Having a weak mind; lacking strength of purpose. Of actions, etc.: Indicating weakness of mind. **2.** Mentally deficient; half-witted 1883.

1. It is my misfortune to be w. I can't say 'no' to people. 1863. Hence **Wea:kmi·ndedness.**

Weakness (wī·knės). ME. [f. WEAK *a.* + -NESS.] **1.** The quality or condition of being weak. **2. a.** A weak point, a circumstance of disadvantage 1597. **b.** An infirmity of character, a failing 1645. **†c.** A weakened bodily condition; an attack of faintness –1756. **3.** An unreasonable or self-indulgent liking or inclination *for* (a person or thing) 1712. **b.** quasi-*concr.* Something for which one has an unreasonable liking 1822.

2. a. The brakes of the Britannia cars have always been their w. 1914. **c.** *Ham.* II. ii. 148. **3. b.** Fashion and whiskers have been my weaknesses, and I don't care who knows it DICKENS.

Weal (wīl), *sb.*[1] [OE. *wela* = OS. *welo* (cf. OHG. *wela, wola* adv.) :– WGmc. **welon,* f. **wel-*; see WELL *adv.*] **†1.** Wealth, riches, possessions –1838. **2.** Welfare, well-being; happiness, prosperity (often contrasted with *woe*) OE. **3.** *contextually.* The welfare of a country or community; the general good. Now *arch.* 1444.

2. For the w. of Michael's soul SCOTT. In w. and woe I have ever had the true sympathy of all my people Q. VICTORIA. Hence **†Weal-public** [after Fr. *le bien public,* L. *bonum publicum*], the general good of the community; public welfare or interest; also, a state, community, commonwealth.

Weal (wīl), *sb.*[2] 1821. [var. of WALE *sb.*[1] infl. by WHEAL *sb.*] The mark or ridge raised on the flesh by the blow of a rod, lash, etc.

Weal (wīl), *v.* 1722. [var. of WALE *v.*[2] by confusion with WHEAL *v.*] = WALE *v.*[2] 1.

Weald (wīld). Also **†wild.** [OE. *weald,* WS. var. of Anglian *wald* WOLD; normally repr. by ME. *weld,* the present *weald* being a reversion to the OE. *weald,* due to Lambarde.] **1.** The tract of country, formerly wooded, including the portions of Sussex, Kent, and Surrey which lie between the North and South Downs. **2.** A wooded district or an open country; a wold (now only *poet.*) 1544.

1. A native of the Wild of Kent, which is none of the most polite parts of the world 1801.

attrib. and *Comb.*: **W. clay,** the upper stratum of the Wealden formation immediately above the 'Hastings sand'; **W. saurian** = HYLÆOSAURUS.

Wealden (wī·ldən), *a.* and *sb.* 1828. [f. WEALD + -EN[4]. The use of the suffix -EN[4] is arbitrary.] **A.** *adj.* **1.** Of or pertaining to the geological formation known as the Wealden (see B). **2.** Of or pertaining to the Weald 1870.

1. *W. lizard* = HYLÆOSAURUS.

B. *sb. Geol.* A formation or series of estuarine and freshwater deposits of Lower Cretaceous age, extensively developed in the Weald 1828.

Wealth (welþ). [ME. *welþe,* f. WELL *adv.* or WEAL *sb.*[1] + -TH[1], on the analogy of *health.*] **1.** The condition of being happy and prosperous; well-being. *Obs.* exc. *arch.* **†b.** Chiefly *pl.* An instance or kind of prosperity; a felicity, blessing –1652. **2.** Prosperity consisting in abundance of possessions; riches, affluence ME. **b.** Abundance of possessions or of valuable products, as characteristic of a people, country, or region; the collective riches of a people or country 1666. **c.** said of a specific commodity as the chief source of a country's riches 1645. **3.** *Economics.* A collective term for those things the abundant possession of which constitutes riches, or 'wealth' in the popular sense 1821. **4.** Plenty, abundance, profusion (*of* what is specified) 1596.

1. *Merch. V.* v. 249. **2.** *fig.* No time more..prolific of intellectual w. HAZLITT. **b.** An Inquiry into the Nature and Causes of the W. of Nations A. SMITH. Not for all the w. of India would he have given up his lamb to that young wolf TROLLOPE. **3.** W..., all useful or agreeable things which possess exchangeable value MILL. **4.** Dark Italian eyes, and a w. of deep black hair 1894. Hence **Wea·lthful** *a.* (now *rare*) abounding in w. ME. **Wea·lthless** *a.* without w.; having no money.

Wealthy (we·lþi), *a.* late ME. [f. prec. + -Y[1].] **1.** Having wealth or abundant means at command; opulent; prosperous, flourishing. **2.** Rich *in* some possession or advantage; plentifully furnished with something 1601. **†3.** Of great worth or value –1746.

1. The southern provinces, the most fertile and wealthiest of the kingdom SOUTHEY. *Prov.* Earely to bed and earely to rise, makes a man healthy, w., and wise 1639. Hence **†Wea·lthi-ly** *adv.*, **†-ness.**

Wean (wīn, wēn), *sb. Sc.* and *n. dial.* 1692. **(wie-one).** [Contraction of *wee ane*; see WEE *a.* and ONE.] A young child.

Wean (wīn), *v.* [OE. *wenian* accustom, wean = OFris. *wenna,* OS. *wennian* (Du. *wennen*), OHG. *gi|wennen* (G. *entwöhnen*), ON. *venja* :– Gmc. **wanjan,* f. **wanaz* accustomed; see WONT, WON *v.*] **1.** *trans.* To accustom (a child or young animal) to the loss of its mother's milk; to cause to cease to be suckled. **2.** *fig.* To detach or alienate *from* some accustomed object of pursuit or enjoyment; to reconcile by degrees to the privation of something 1526.

2. A long continuance of ill health has weaned me from the world 1741. A love of secular learning from which Edmund found it hard to w. himself 1874.

Weanling (wī·nliŋ), *sb.* and *a.* 1532. [f. prec. + -LING[1].] **A.** *sb.* A young child or animal newly weaned. **B.** *adj.* Recently weaned 1637.

Weapon (we·pən, we·p'n), *sb.* [OE. *wǣp(e)n* = OFris. *wēpen,* OS. *wāpan* (Du. *wapen*), OHG. *waf(f)an* (G. *waffe*), ON. *vápn,* Goth. **wēpn* (in pl. *wēpna*) :– Gmc. **wǣpnam,* of unkn. origin.] An instrument of any kind used in warfare or combat to attack and overcome an enemy. **b.** *transf.* Any part of the body (esp. of a bird or beast) which is or may be used as a means of attack or defence, as a claw, horn, or the like 1635.

fig. Let not womens weapons, water drops, Staine my mans cheekes SHAKS. So voluble a w. is the tongue POPE. *†At all, any weapons,* with weapons of any kind. (To challenge, fight, etc., an adversary) *at, with, his own w.* or *weapons,* i.e. with such as he is expert in; chiefly *fig.* Hence **Wea·ponless** *a.* without a w.; unarmed; of an animal, without natural means of attack or defence OE.

Weapon (we·pən, we·p'n), *v.* Now *rare* exc. in pa. pple. [OE. *wǣpnian,* f. *wǣpen* WEAPON *sb.*] *trans.* To furnish with weapons or a weapon; to arm. Hence **Wea·poned** *ppl. a.*

Wear (wēᵊɹ), *sb.* 1464. [f. next.] **I. 1.** The action of wearing or carrying on the person (an article of clothing, an ornament, or the like); the condition or fact of being worn or carried upon the person. **2.** What one wears or should wear; the thing or things worn or proper to be worn in a particular period or on a particular occasion 1570. **3. a.** Capacity for being worn or for further advantageous use 1699. **b.** Advantage of continued wearing 1836.

1. A charming coat for restaurant w. 1912. *The worse for w.,* deteriorated through wearing. *To be in w.*: *(a)* of a garment, etc., to be actually on the person of the wearer; also, to be (still) habitually worn by a person, not to have been discarded; *(b)* of a kind or style of garment, etc., to be worn by people generally; to be in vogue or fashion. **2.** Motley's the onely weare SHAKS. **3. a.** The shoe that has still w. in it 1881.

II. The process or condition of being worn or gradually reduced in bulk or impaired in quality by friction, exposure, etc.; loss or diminution of substance or deterioration of quality due to these causes 1666.

W. and tear, wearing or damage due to ordinary usage; deterioration in the condition of a thing through constant use or service; (a common formula in leases and similar documents); also *transf.* and *fig.*; Unequal to the w. and tear of daily life DICKENS.

III. The anterior surface of the lower part of the mouth of a carpenter's plane 1850.

Wear (wēᵊɹ), *v.*[1] Pa. t. **wore** (wōᵊɹ); pa. pple. **worn** (wǭɹn). [OE. *werian* = OS. *werian,* OHG. *werien,* ON. *verja,* Goth. *wasjan* clothe :– Gmc. wk. vb. **wazjan,* f. **was-*, var. of Gmc. and IE. **wes-* repr. also by ON. *vest* cloak, L. *vestis* clothing. The change from the wk. to the str. conj., due to analogy with *bear, tear,* etc., began in XIV.] **I. 1.** *trans.* To carry or bear on one's body or on some part of it, for covering, warmth, ornament, etc.; to be dressed in. **b.** To dress oneself habitually or at a particular season in (a material, garment) of a particular sort or fashion. Also *pass.,* of the material or garment. ME. **2.** To bear or carry (arms, also a stick or cane) OE. **3.** To allow (one's hair, beard) to grow in a specified fashion, or as opposed to shaving or to the use of a wig ME. **4.** Of a ship (or its commander): To fly (a flag, colours) 1558. **5.** *transf.* To bear or possess as a member or part of the body 1513. **6.** To exhibit or present (a particular look, expression, etc.) 1611. **7.** *fig.* To carry about with one in one's heart, mind, or memory; to have as a quality or attribute; to bear (a name, title) 1586. **b.** To possess and enjoy as one's own 1573.

1. Miss McFlimsey..was in utter despair, Because she had nothing whatever to w.! 1857. **b.** When the Court went into mourning, she always wore black THACKERAY. **3.** The Officers, Petty Officers, and Seamen of the Fleet are not to w. moustaches or beards 1862. **5.** *A.Y.L.* II. i. 14. **7.** *Ham.* III. ii. 77. I shame To weare a Heart so white SHAKS. **b.** *To win and w.* (a lady as one's wife).

Phrases. *To w. a crown, diadem, palm, the purple,* etc., to hold the dignity or office of which the ornament is a symbol. *†To w. the horn(s,* to be a cuckold. *To w. one's heart on one's sleeve*: see HEART *sb.* *To w. the breeches*: see BREECH *sb.* *To w. the willow*: see WILLOW *sb.*

II. To waste, damage, or destroy by use. **1.** To waste and impair (a material) gradually by use or attrition. Also with adv., as *away, out,* and with pred. extension, as *to w. smooth.* late ME. **2.** To sap the strength or energy of (a person, his faculties, etc.) by toil, age, grief etc. (Chiefly with adv., as *away, out,* or advb. phr.) 1508. **3.** *fig.* with object a quality, condition, etc.: To cause to weaken, diminish, or disappear gradually. late ME. **4.** To form or produce by attrition 1597.

1. All the linnen is quite worne out 1647. She would w. a gown to rags, because he had once liked it THACKERAY. **2.** You that haue worne your eyes almost out in the seruice SHAKS. She tells you that her patience is quite wore out 1729. **3.** *To w. down,* to blunt the force of and overcome by steady resistance or counter-attack.

III. *intr.* To suffer waste or decay by use or by lapse of time (usu. with adv. or advb. phr.) ME.

All thyng weareth save the grace of God 1530. My Suit begins to w. out 1687. In a little Time.. the Fear of their Coming wore off DE FOE. A Man had better w. out than rust out 1720.

IV. To last or hold out in use or with the lapse of time; to resist (well or ill) the attrition or waste of use and age; also, to stand the test of experience, criticism, etc. 1568.

I..chose my wife, as she did her wedding-gown, not for a fine glossy surface, but such qualities as would w. well GOLDSM. How are you, Minns? 'Pon my soul you w. capitally! DICKENS.

V. In ref. to time, change, etc. **1.** In *pa. pple.* of time, a period of time: Past, spent, passed away. Now chiefly *poet.* late ME. **2.** *trans.* To spend, pass (one's time, a period of time). Chiefly *poet.* Also with adv., as *away, out.* 1535. **3.** *intr.* Of time, a period of time: To pass on or advance gradually to its conclusion; to pass away 1597. **4. a.** To pass gradually *into* (a condition, etc.) 1555. **b.** *trans.* To bring (a person) gradually *into* (a habit or disposition) 1690.

1. Winter is worne that was the flowers bale 1547. **2.** We wore away a good part of the night in ..drinking 1809. **3.** The daye began to weare awaye TINDALE *Luke* 9:12. Away I say, time weares SHAKS.

VI. With ref. to movement in space. **1.** *intr.* Chiefly *Sc.* To go, proceed, advance (usu. of a slow or gradual movement); with adv. or advb. phr. indicating direction 1470. **2.** *Sc.* To conduct (sheep or cattle) to the fold or other enclosure 1724. Hence **Wea·rable** *a.* capable of being worn; fit or suitable to be worn; also as *sb.* (chiefly *pl.*) a wearable commodity, an article of clothing. **Wea·ring** *ppl. a.* exhausting, tiring; that gradually destroys or impairs by continued use or attrition; that is undergoing wear by continued use or attrition.

Wear (wēᵊɹ), *v.*[2] Pa. t. and pa. pple. **wore.** 1614. [Of unkn. origin.] *Naut.* **1.** *intr.* Of a ship: To come round on the other tack by turning the head away from the wind (opp. to *tack*). **2.** *trans.* To put (a ship) about, bringing her stern to windward 1719.

Weariful (wīᵊ·riful), *a.* 1454. [f. WEARY *v.* + -FUL.] **1.** That causes weariness; that tires one's endurance or patience. **2.** Full of weariness; utterly fatigued 1862.

Weariless (wīᵊ·rilės), *a.* late ME. [f. as prec. + -LESS.] That does not weary or become weary.

Weariness (wīᵊ·rinės). OE. [f. WEARY *a.* + -NESS.] **1.** Weary condition, extreme tiredness or fatigue. **2.** Tedium or distaste induced by monotonous or uncongenial conditions or occupations; tiredness *of* a course of action, a state of things, etc. 1526. **3.** Something that wearies 1560.

2. A man would die..only vpon a wearinesse to do the same thing, so oft ouer and ouer BACON. **3.** There is none end in making manie bokes: and muche readinge is a wearines of the flesh BIBLE (Genev.) *Eccles.* 12:12.

Wearing (wēᵊ·riŋ), *vbl. sb.* ME. [f. WEAR *v.*[1] + -ING[1].] †**1.** The fact or habit of being clothed in a particular way; kind or style of clothing; also *concr.* what a person wears or might wear –1690. **2.** The action of carrying on the body (an article of dress, an ornament, or the like). Also *attrib.* in *w. apparel, w. gear,* articles of clothing collectively. late ME. **3.** The condition or process of being continuously in wear or use 1546. **4.** The action of wearing, or the process of being worn, by continuous use or exposure 1473. **5.** Passing, elapsing (of a period of time). *rare.* 1876.

1. Giue me my nightly w., and adieu SHAKS. **2.** The opposition..wished..to make the crown of England not worth the w. MACAULAY. **3.** *In (the) w., (the) worse for w.*

Wearisome (wīᵊ·risŏm), *a.* 1450. [f. WEARY *v.* and *a.* + -SOME[1].] **1.** Causing weariness through monotony, or the continuance of uncongenial conditions; tedious. **2.** Causing weariness from bodily or mental exhaustion or protracted pain. Now somewhat *rare.* 1594.

1. This w. murder-mongering 1891. **2.** The w. gallery stairs 1883. Hence **Wea·risome-ly** *adv.*, **-ness.**

Weary (wīᵊ·ri), *a.* [OE. *wērig, wǣrig,* corresp. to OS. *sīðwōrig* weary (with journey), OHG. *wuarag* drunk :- WGmc. **wōriʒa,* **woraʒa.*] **I. 1.** Having the feeling of loss of strength, languor, and need for rest, produced by continued exertion (physical or mental), endurance of severe pain, or wakefulness; tired, fatigued. Now usu., Intensely tired, worn out with fatigue. **2.** Discontented at the continuance or continued recurrence *of* something, and desiring its cessation; having one's patience, tolerance, zeal, or energy exhausted ME. **b.** Tired *of* (a person) 1472. **3.** Depressed and dispirited through trouble, anxiety, disappointment, etc. OE.

1. Come vnto me all ye that are wearie and laden N.T. (Genev.) *Matt.* 11:28. W. with his Toyl DRYDEN. *W. Willie:* see TIRED *ppl. a. absol.* There the wearie be at rest *Job* 3:17. **2.** Brethren be not w. in well doynge TINDALE 2 *Thess.* 3:13. I grew w. of the sea SWIFT. **b.** I am w. of her TENNYSON. **3.** So wearie with Disasters, tugg'd with Fortune SHAKS.

II. Causing weariness. **1.** Fatiguing, toilsome, exhausting. (Sometimes indistinguishable from sense 2.) ME. **2.** Irksome, wearisome, tedious; burdensome to the spirit 1465. †**b.** Of a speaker, etc.: Tedious, wearisome –1603. **3.** *Sc.* and *north.* Sad, sorrowful, hard to endure 1785. **b.** *Sc.* Tiresome, 'wretched'; in phr. *weary fa',* etc., a curse on 1785.

1. It was w. work with any tool but the hatchet 1832. **2. b.** *Meas. for M.* I. v. 25. **3.** A w. lot is thine SCOTT. Hence **Wea·rily** *adv.*

Weary (wīᵊ·ri), *v.* [OE. *wēr(i)ġian* intr., and *ġewēriġian* trans., f. *wēriġ* WEARY *a.*] **I.** *intr.* To grow weary.

I had not ridden four miles when one of the horses wearyed 1686. She..wearied of passing all her time by herself 1782. Diligence which never wearies 1829. I was beginning to w. for a letter from you 1856.

II. *trans.* To make weary OE.

I will wearie you then no longer with idle talking SHAKS. A mighty curtal axe, which would have wearied the arm of any other than Cœur de Lion SCOTT. He..wearied Heaven and every saint with prayers..for the prolongation of his life SCOTT. **Wea·rying** *ppl. a.* that causes fatigue, weariness, tedium, or ennui.

Weasand (wī·zănd). Now chiefly *dial.* [OE. *wāsend,* corresp. to OFris. *wāsanda, -enda,* OS. *wāsend(i,* OHG. *weisant;* app. a WGmc. pr. ppl. formation. The mod. *weasand* may repr. an OE. **wǣsend.*] **1.** The œsophagus or gullet. **2.** The trachea or windpipe. late ME. **3.** The throat generally 1450.

3. There thou maist braine him..Or cut his wezand with thy knife SHAKS.

Weasel (wī·z'l). [OE. *wesule, wesle, weosule* = MLG. *wesel, wezel,* OHG. *wisula* (G. *wiesel*) :- WGmc. **wisula,* of unkn. origin.] **1.** A carnivorous animal (*Putorius nivalis*), the smallest European species of the genus (of the family *Mustelidæ*) which includes the polecat, stoat, etc. **b.** Confused with the STOAT, sometimes called *ermine w., white w.* 1607. **2.** Applied to various animals of the family *Mustelidæ,* or having some resemblance to the weasel 1771. **3.** *U.S.* Nickname for a native of S. Carolina 1875.

2. *Four-toed w.* = SURICATE. *Malacca w.* = RASSE. *Mexican w.* = KINKAJOU. **4.** *attrib.* **w.-word** (*U.S.*), a word which destroys the force of a statement, as a weasel ruins an egg by sucking out its contents. Hence **Wea·sel** *v.*, to deprive of its meaning by using weasel-words. **Weaselly** (wī·z'li) *a.* weasel-like.

Weather (we·ðəɹ), *sb.* [OE. *weder* = OFris. *wedar,* OS. *wedar,* OHG. *wetar* (Du. *weer,* G. *wetter*), ON. *veðr* :- Gmc. **weðram* :- either **wedhrom* or **wetróm;* prob. f. *wē-* WIND *sb.*[1] For the change of d to ð (shown XV) cf. *father, gather,* etc.] **1.** The condition of the atmosphere (at a given place and time) with respect to heat or cold, presence or absence of rain, etc. **b.** *pl.* Kinds of weather. Now *rare* exc. in phr. (*in*) *all weathers.* OE. **c.** With unfavourable implication: Adverse, unpleasant, hurtful, or destructive condition of the atmosphere; rain, frost, etc. as destructive agents ME. **d.** Violent wind accompanied by heavy rain or agitation of the waves (now *dial.* and *Naut.*) OE. †**e.** What falls from the clouds; rain, snow, etc. late ME. **2.** *Naut.* The direction in which the wind is blowing. late ME. **3.** The angle (more fully *angle of w.*) which the sails of a windmill make with the perpendicular to the axis 1759.

1. In Autumne when the whether is milde and pleasant 1578. The conversation began about the w. 1779. *Wind and w.:* see WIND *sb.* †*To make fair w.*, to be conciliatory, make a show of friendliness, goodness, etc. *In the w.*, in an exposed situation, unprotected from rain, cold, wind, etc. *Under the w.* (orig. *U.S.*), indisposed, not quite well. *W. permitting,* often appended to an announcement (e.g. of the sailing of a vessel) to indicate that it is conditional on the weather being favourable. *Clerk of the w.*, an imaginary functionary humorously supposed to control the w. **c.** *To make good, bad,* etc. *w. of it,* (of a ship) to behave well or ill in a storm. *fig.* The..muddle-headed, making heavy w. of the simplest tasks 1915. **2.** *To drive with the w.*, to drift with the wind and waves. *To have the w. of,* to be to windward of (another ship).

attrib. and *Comb.*, as *w.-chart, forecast, report,* etc.; **w.-bitt,** *Naut.* an extra turn of the cable about the bitts in bad w.; also *v. trans.* to give this extra turn to (the cable); †**-bitten,** nipped, gnawed, or worn by the weather; **-bound** *a.*, detained by bad w.; prevented by stress of w. from sailing, travelling, etc.; **-brained** = W.-HEADED; **-breeder,** a day of exceptionally sunny and calm w., pop. supposed to presage a coming storm; **-cloth,** *Naut.* a covering of canvas or tarpaulin used as a protection against the w., or against wind and spray; **-driven,** driven by stormy w.; **-fend** *v. trans.*, to defend from the w., to shelter (SHAKS.); **-gall** = WATERGALL; **-gleam, -glim** *Sc.* and *north.*, clear sky near a dark horizon; **-house,** a toy hygroscope in the form of a small house with figures of a man and woman standing in two porches; by the varying torsion of a string the man comes out of his porch in wet w., and the woman out of hers in dry; **-moulding,** *Arch.* a drip-stone; **-proof** *a.*, impervious to the w.; **-prophet,** one who foretells the w.; one who is w.-wise; **-side,** the side (e.g. of a building, a tree) that is most exposed to injury from w.; **-stain,** a stain or discolouration caused by the w.; **-tiled** *a.*, covered with overlapping tiles; so **-tiling.**

b. *Naut.* in the sense 'situated on the side which is turned towards the wind; windward', as *w.-beam, -port, -quarter, -tack,* etc.; **w.-bow,** the bow that is turned towards the wind; hence as *v. trans.* to turn the w.-bow to; **-gage, -gauge,** (see GAUGE *sb.* I. 5); **-helm,** a tendency in a ship under sail to come too near the wind; **-side,** the windward side.

Weather (we·ðəɹ), *v.* late ME. [f. prec.] **1.** *trans.* To subject to the beneficial action of the wind and sun; to air. **2.** *trans.* and *intr.* To change by exposure to the weather; to wear away, disintegrate, discolour, under atmospheric influences 1757. **3.** *Naut.* **a.** *trans.* To sail to the windward of (a point or headland, another ship, etc.) 1595. **b.** *fig.* To get safely round; to get the better of 1626. **c.** intr. *To w. on* or *upon,* to gain upon in a windward direction; also *fig.*, to get the advantage of 1595. **4.** *trans.* **a.** *Naut.* To withstand and come safely through (a storm) 1655. **b.** *gen.* To pass through and survive (severe weather) 1680. †**c.** To take shelter from (a storm) –1798. **5.** To set (the sails of a windmill) at the proper angle to obtain the maximum effect of the wind-force 1745. **6.** *Arch.* To slope or bevel (a surface) so as to throw off the rain; to furnish (a wall, buttress) with a weathering 1833.

1. It shall be well done to w. your garmentes in Marche for feare of mothes 1530. **2.** The face of the limestone is hollowed out and weathered LYELL. **3. b.** That soule which is but neare destruction, may w. that mischiefe DONNE. **4. a.** *fig.* He weathered out the Raign of Queen Mary FULLER. The Government..could not have weathered the session 1834. **b.** I began..to fear I should never be able to w. out the winter in so lonely a dwelling COWPER.

Wea·ther-bea:ten, *pa. pple.* and *ppl. a.* 1530. **1.** Beaten or buffeted by wind and rain; that has been exposed to severe weather 1560. **2. a.** Of things: Worn, defaced, or damaged by exposure to the weather 1547. **b.** Of persons, etc.: Bronzed, coarsened, hardened by exposure to all kinds of weather 1530.

2. a. Pancras Church..old and wetherbeaten 1593. **b.** Two weatherbeaten old seamen MACAULAY.

Wea·therboard. 1539. **1.** One of a series of boards nailed horizontally, with overlapping edges, as an outside covering for walls. **b.** A board laid over builders' work or material as a protection 1851. **2.** A board placed sloping over a window or other opening to throw off or keep out rain 1568. **3.** *Naut.* The windward side of a ship 1625. Hence **Wea·therboard** *v. trans.* to nail weatherboards upon (a wall or roof). **Wea·therboa:rding** *vbl. sb.* the covering of a building with weatherboards; *concr.* weatherboards collectively.

Wea·thercock, *sb.* ME. **1.** A vane in the form of a cock, which turns with its head to the wind. Also *gen.*, a vane of any form. Often as a symbol of mutability or fickleness; also *fig.* of persons or things. **2.** *attrib.* and *appos.*, passing into *adj.* = changeable, inconstant 1680.

1. As a wedercok, that turneth his face With every wind CHAUCER. **2.** The wavering and w. resolutions of men 1680. Hence **Wea·thercock** *v. trans.* to provide with a w.; to serve as a w. for.

Weathered (we·ðəɹd), *ppl. a.* 1879. [f. WEATHER *v.* + -ED[1].] **1.** Worn, stained, or seasoned by the weather or by atmospheric influences. Chiefly *Geol.* **2.** Of a crop of grain or hay: Deteriorated by too long exposure to the elements 1875. **3.** *Arch.* Made sloping, so as to prevent the lodgement of water; furnished with a weathering 1840.

Wea·ther-eye. 1839. [app. a joc. use of WEATHER *sb.* used *attrib.*] In fig. phrases, as *to keep one's w. open,* to be watchful and alert, keep one's wits about one.

Wea·ther-glass. 1626. †**1.** A kind of thermometer used to ascertain the temperature of the air, and also to prognosticate changes in the weather –1720. **2.** A barometer 1695.

2. *Poor Man's, Shepherd's W.*, the scarlet pimpernel, *Anagallis arvensis* (from its closing its flowers before rain).

†**Weather-headed,** *ppl. a.* 1652. [prob. f. WETHER.] Light-headed, foolish –1822.

Weathering (we·ðəriŋ), *vbl. sb.* ME. [In sense 1 repr. OE. *wederung*, f. *wed(e)rian*; in late uses f. WEATHER *v.* + -ING¹.] †**1.** Weather conditions; (good or bad) weather –1565. **2.** The action of the atmospheric agencies or elements on substances exposed to them; the discoloration, disintegration, etc., resulting from this action 1665. **3.** *Naut.* The action of passing (an object) on the windward side 1878. **4.** *Arch.* A projecting course on the face of a wall, serving to throw off rain-water; a sloped 'set-off' of a wall or buttress; the inclination or slope given to a surface in order to prevent the lodgement of water 1739.

Weatherly (we·ðəɹli), *a.* 1729. *Naut.* Of a sailing-vessel: Able to sail close to the wind without drifting to leeward. Hence **Wea·therliness.**

Weatherology (weðərǫ·lŏdʒi). 1823. [f. WEATHER *sb.* + -LOGY.] The science and study of the weather and its phenomena.

Weather-wise (we·ðəɹwəiz), *a.* late ME. [f. WEATHER *sb.* + WISE *a.*] Skilled in prognostics of the weather. So **Wea·ther-wi:sdom** 1822.

Weave (wīv), *sb.* 1581. [f. next.] †**1.** Something that has been woven, a woven fabric –1646. **2.** A particular method or pattern of weaving 1888.

Weave (wīv), *v.*¹ Pa. t. **wove** (wōᵘv); pa. ppl. **wo·ven.** [OE. *wefan* = OFris. *weva*, (M)LG., (M)Du. *weven*, OHG. *weban* (G. *weben*), ON. *vefa* :– Gmc. **weban*, f. Gmc. **web-* **wab-* :– IE. **webh-* **wobh-* **ubh-*, repr. also by Gr. ὑφή, ὕφος web, ὑφαίνειν weave, Skr. *ūrṇavābhis* spider, lit. 'wool-weaver'.] **1.** *trans.* To form or fabricate (a stuff or material) by interlacing yarns or other filaments of a particular substance in a continuous web; to manufacture in a loom by crossing the threads or yarns called the warp and the weft. Also with obj. the web itself, a garment made up of such a stuff or material. **b.** *fig.* To contrive, fabricate, or construct (a mental product) with elaborate care. late ME. **c.** To form (e.g. a basket, a wreath) by interlacing rods or twigs, flowers, etc. late ME. **2.** *absol.* or *intr.* To practise weaving; to work with a loom OE. **3.** *trans.* Of a spider, insect: To spin (a web, a cocoon) ME. **4.** To form a texture with (threads, filaments, strips of some material); to interlace or interwine so as to form a fabric 1538. **b.** To entwine or wreathe together 1578. **5.** To cause to move in a devious course; to direct (one's steps) in a devious or intricate course, as in dancing 1650. **b.** To go through the intricate movements of (a dance) 1792.

1. O what a tangled web we w., When first we practise to deceive! SCOTT. **b.** I had already woven a little romance..in my imagination 1819. The evil arts of brewing charms and weaving spells 1876. **3.** 2 *Hen. VI*, III. i. 340. **4.** *fig.* Untruth is so maliciously weaved with truth 1545. Put the melody in the bass,..and w. in a new melody with it in the upper part 1875.

Weave, *v.*² 1593. [prob. continuation of ME. †*weve* (XIII) move from place to place, wave, brandish, var. of †*waive* – ON. *veifa*, corresp. to (M)Du. *weiven*, OHG. *-weiben* :– Gmc. **weibjan*, rel. ult. to L. *vibrare* VIBRATE.] **1.** *intr.* To move repeatedly from side to side; to sway the body alternately to one side and the other; to pursue a devious course 1596. **2.** *trans.* To make a signal to (a ship or its occupants) by waving a flag or something used as a substitute 1593. **3.** *Pugilism.* To creep close into (one's opponent) before delivering one's blow 1818.

Weaver¹ (wī·vəɹ). late ME. [f. WEAVE *v.*¹ + -ER¹.] **1.** One who weaves textile fabrics; a workman or workwoman whose occupation is weaving. **2.** (Also *w.-bird.*) One of numerous Asiatic or African tropical birds of the family *Ploceidæ*, so called from the elaborately interwoven nests that many of them build 1828. **3.** = WHIRLIGIG *sb.* 4. 1864.

1. *fig.* Sedentary weavers of long tales Give me the fidgets COWPER.

Comb., with possessive, as **weaver's knot,** a sheetbend or single bend, used for joining threads in weaving.

Wea·ver². 1847. [f. WEAVE *v.*² + -ER¹.] A horse that 'weaves' or rolls the neck and body from side to side.

Weazen (wī·z'n), *a.* 1765. Altered f. WIZEN *a.* Hence **Wea·zeny** *a.* somewhat w.

Weazen (wī·z'n), *v.* 1821. [Altered f. WIZEN *v.*] *intr.* To shrink, shrivel. Hence **Wea·zened** *ppl. a.*

Web (web), *sb.* [OE. *web(b*, corresp. to OFris. *webb*, OS. *webbi* (MDu. *webbe*, Du. *web*), OHG. *wappi*, *weppi*, ON. *vefr* :– Gmc. **wabjam*, *-jaz*, f. *wab-*; see WEAVE *v.*¹] **I. 1.** A woven fabric; *spec.* a whole piece of cloth in process of being woven or after it comes from the loom. Also *collect.*, woven stuff. **b.** *transf.* and *fig.* Something likened to a woven fabric; also, the texture of such a fabric 1599. **c.** Used for WARP 1538. **2.** An article made of woven stuff. Also *collect.* woven stuff of a particular material or pattern. (Now chiefly literary or *arch.*) OE. **3.** A band of material woven strongly without pile. Also *collect.* = WEBBING. ME. **b.** *attrib.* (and *Comb.*) Made of webbing 1844. **4.** A cobweb. Also applied to the filmy textures spun by some caterpillars. ME. **b.** = COBWEB 1 b. 1877. **c.** *fig.* esp. (*a*) a subtly-woven snare or entanglement; (*b*) something flimsy and unsubstantial 1574. **5.** *Paper-making.* **a.** An endless wire-cloth working on rollers and carrying the pulp. **b.** A large sheet or roll of paper made in this way. 1825.

1. b. The webbe of our life is of a mingled yarne, good and ill together SHAKS. The w. of diplomatic negotiation and court-intrigue 1860. **4. c.** Entangled in a w. of crime and guilt 1859.

II. 1. A tissue or membrane in an animal body or in a plant; also applied to similar pathological formations ME. **b.** The omentum or caul of cattle 1808. †**2.** A thin white film or opacity growing over the eye –1827. **3.** The membrane or fold of skin which connects the digits of an animal; esp. that which connects the toes of an aquatic bird or beast, forming a palmate foot 1576. **b.** *Path.* An extension of the normal fold which occurs as a congenital malformation in the human hand or foot 1866. **4.** The series of barbs on each side of the shaft of a bird's feather; the vane or vexillum 1713.

2. †*Pin and w.*: a disease of the eye, perh. characterized by a pin-like spot and a film.

III. †**1.** A sheet of lead, such as is used for roofing and for coffins –1852. **2.** The piece of bent iron which forms a horseshoe 1587. **3. a.** The thin sharp part of the coulter of a plough 1784. **b.** The detachable long narrow blade of a frame-saw or fret-saw 1831. **4.** The bit of a key; also, each of the 'steps' or incisions in this 1773. **5.** The vertical plate which connects the upper and lower laterally-extending plates in a beam or girder 1851. **b.** The upright portion between the tread and the bottom flange of a rail 1838. **c.** The arm of a crank, connecting the shaft and the wrist 1875. **d.** The thinner part of an anvil, between the head and the base 1874. **6.** The basket-work of a gabion 1852.

Comb.: **w.-fingered** *a.*, having the fingers united for a considerable part of their length by a fold of skin; also, applied to a fish, *Prionotus carolinus* or *palmipes*; **-machine, (-perfecting) press,** a printing machine which is automatically supplied with paper from a roll or w.; **-printing,** printing on a w.-press; **-saw,** a frame-saw; **-toed** *a.*, w.-footed; **-worm** *U.S.*, any of various lepidopterous larvæ which are more or less gregarious and spin large webs in which they feed or rest. Hence **Webbed** (webd) *ppl. a.* furnished with a w. or connecting membrane; *esp.* of the feet of certain birds; covered with or as with cobweb. **We·bby** *a.* consisting of w.; resembling w. or a w.; of the digits, palmated.

Web (web), *v.* [In sense 1 OE. *webbian*, f. WEB *sb.* In other senses f. WEB *sb.*] †**1.** *trans.* To weave (a fabric) in the loom –1892. **2.** To cover with a (spider's) web, or something resembling this 1853. **b.** To stretch threads of spider's web across (a micrometer, etc.) 1883. **3.** To entangle or envelop in or as in a (spider's) web 1864. **4.** To connect (fingers, toes, etc.) with a web or membrane 1774.

We·b-beam. OE. [Cf. OHG. *weppi-boum* liciatorium.] The roller in a loom on which the web is wound as it is woven.

Webbing (we·biŋ), *vbl. sb.* 1440. [f. WEB *v.* + -ING¹.] †**1.** The action or process of weaving –1657. **2.** *concr.* A woven material 1754. **b.** Woven material in the form of a strong wide band, used by upholsterers, etc. 1794. **3.** = PALMATION *concr.* Also *Path.*, a webbed state of the fingers or toes. 1872.

Weberian (wībīᵊ·riăn), *a.* 1849. [f. name of E. H. *Weber* (1795–1833), a German anatomist + -IAN.] *W. corpuscle, organ*, a tubular vesicle in the prostatic portion of the urethra. *W. ossicles*, a chain of small bones between the ear and the air-bladder in certain fishes; *W. apparatus*, the set of structures which connect the air-bladder with the ear.

We·b-foot. 1765. [See WEB *sb.* II. 3.] **1.** A foot with webbed toes. Also, the condition of being web-footed. **2.** †**a.** A nickname for a dweller in the Fens. **b.** A native of the State of Oregon (so called on account of the moist climate) 1873. So **We·b-foo:ted** *a.* having web-feet 1681.

Webster (we·bstəɹ). *Obs.* exc. *Hist.* [OE. *webbestre*, fem. of *webba* weaver; see -STER.] A weaver: **a.** as the designation of a woman; **b.** extended, or applied *spec.*, to a male weaver.

Websterite (we·bstərəit). 1823. [f. name of T. *Webster*, who discovered it; see -ITE¹ 2 b.] *Min.* = ALUMINITE.

Wed (wed), *sb. Obs.* exc. *dial.* [OE. *wedd*, corresp. to OFris. *wedd*, OS. *weddi* (Du. *wedde*), OHG. *wetti* (G. *wette*), ON. *veð*, Goth. *wadi* :– Gmc. **waðjam*, rel. to L. *vas, vad-* surety. See GAGE *sb.*¹, WAGE *sb.*] **1.** A pledge, something deposited as security for a payment or the fulfilment of an obligation; occas., a hostage. **2.** A stake in a game or wager ME.

Wed (wed), *v.* Pa. t. and pa. pple. **wedded** (*dial.* **wed**). [OE. *weddian* covenant, marry, bind in wedlock = OFris. *weddia*, MLG. *wedden*, OHG. *wettōn* (G. *wetten*) pledge, wager, ON. *veðja* pledge, Goth. *gawadjōn* espouse :– Gmc. **waðjōjan*, f. **waðjam* (see prec.).] **1.** *trans.* To wager, stake. *Obs.* exc. *Sc.* and *north.* late ME. **2.** *orig.* To make (a woman) one's wife by the giving of a pledge or earnest; hence, to take in marriage; to become the husband or wife of (a person) by participating in a prescribed ceremony or formal act OE. **3.** To bind (the contracting parties) in wedlock; to conduct the marriage ceremony for OE. **4.** *pass.* To be joined in wedlock; to be married *to*, †*with*, †*unto* (a husband or wife) ME. **5.** *intr.* To enter into the matrimonial state; to take a wife or husband ME. **6.** *trans.* To unite as in marriage. late ME.

2. With thys ring I thee w. *Bk. Com. Prayer.* **3.** The sayd incumbent shuld..burye, wedde, and christen wythin the sayd chappell 1546. **6.** The quene was wedded to her awne opinion 1548. A book in which matter and manner are wedded as in few other books of the same kind 1887.

Wedded (we·dėd), *ppl. a.* OE. [f. prec. + -ED¹.] **1.** Joined in wedlock; living in the married state. **2.** Of or pertaining to marriage or to married persons 1592. **3.** Obstinately attached (to a habit, opinion, etc.) 1579.

1. My lawful, w. wife 1798. **2.** *Rom. & Jul.* I. v. 137 (Fo.).

Wedding (we·diŋ), *vbl. sb.* OE. [f. WED *v.* + -ING¹.] **1.** The action of marrying; marriage, espousal. **2.** The performance of the marriage-rite; the ceremony of a marriage, with its attendant festivities ME.

2. *Penny w.*: see PENNY. *Silver w.*, the 25th anniversary of a w. (see SILVER *sb.*). *Golden w.*, the 50th anniversary. *Diamond w.*, the 60th anniversary.

attrib., as *w.-bell, -dress, -feast, -guest, journey*; **w.-breakfast,** the entertainment given to the wedding-guests after the marriage-ceremony and before the departure for the honeymoon; **-cake,** a large rich cake, covered with icing and decorated with sugar ornaments, cut and distributed to the guests at the w.-feast or sent in small portions to absent friends; **-garment,** usu. *fig.* (with ref. to *Matt.* 22:11–12); **-march,** a march (Mendelssohn's, if not otherwise specified) composed for performance at a w.; **-ring,** a ring placed by the bridegroom on the third finger of the bride's left hand as part of the marriage ceremony.

Wedge (wedʒ), *sb.* [OE. *weċġ* = OS. *weggi,* OHG. *weggi, wecki* (Du. *wegge,* G. *weck, -e* wedge-shaped piece of cake, etc.), MLG., MDu. *wigge* (Du. *wigge* wedge, piece of cake), ON. *veggr* :– Gmc. **waʒjaz.*] **1.** A piece of wood, metal, or other hard material, thick at one end and tapering to a thin edge at the other; chiefly used as a tool operated by percussion applied to the thick end, for splitting wood, etc., dilating a fissure or cavity, tightening or securing some part of a structure, and other similar purposes. Hence, in *Mechanics,* the type of simple machine of which this is an example, and which includes also knives, chisels, etc.; now regarded as a variety of the inclined plane. **b.** *Grafting.* (*a*) A peg to keep the cleft open. (*b*) The tongue or tapered end of a scion or stock. 1523. **c.** *Arch.* A voussoir 1726. †**2.** An ingot of gold, silver, etc. –1719. **b.** *Cant.* Silver, whether money or plate 1725. **3.** *transf.* **a.** A formation of troops tapering to the front or van, in order to cleave a way through an opposing force. Now more widely of a body of people. 1614. **b.** The V-shaped formation adopted by a number of geese or other wild-fowl when flying 1869. **c.** *gen.* Something in the form of a wedge; a wedge-shaped part or piece of anything 1821. **d.** *Meteorol.* A narrow w.-shaped area of high pressure between two adjacent cyclonic systems; also, the representation of this on a weather-chart 1887. **e.** The wedge-shaped stroke in cuneiform characters 1821. **4.** *Geom.* **a.** A triangular prism. **b.** A simple solid formed by cutting a triangular prism by any two planes. 1710. **5.** *Her.* A charge consisting of an isosceles triangle with a very acute angle at its vertex 1716.

1. *The thin end of the w.,* fig. a small beginning which it is hoped or feared may lead to something greater. **3. c.** A pot of the real draught stout, and..wedges of cheese DICKENS.

Comb.: **w.-bill,** a bird with a w.-shaped bill; **-shaped** *a.,* shaped like a w., cuneiform; *Bot.* and *Zool.* = CUNEATE *a.*; **-shell,** a marine bivalve, belonging to *Donax* or allied genera; **-tailed** *a.,* having a w.-shaped tail; used *spec.* in the names of birds, as the w.-tailed gull, *Rhodostethia rosea.* Hence **We·dgewise** *adv.* after the manner or in the form of a w.

Wedge (wedʒ), *v.*[1] 1440. [f. prec.] **1.** *trans.* To tighten, fasten tight by driving in a wedge or wedges. Also with *in, on, up.* **2.** To cleave or split by driving in a wedge 1530. **b.** To split *off,* force *apart, asunder,* or *open,* by driving in a wedge 1853. **3.** *transf.* To drive, push, or squeeze (an object) into something where it is held fast; to fix firmly by driving in, or by pressing tight 1513. **4.** To pack or crowd (a number of persons or animals) in close formation, or in a limited space 1720.

2. My heart, As wedged with a sigh, would riue in twaine SHAKS. **3.** *fig. Cor.* II. iii. 30. Hence **We·dging** *vbl. sb.* the action of driving in a wedge or wedges; *Geol.* the jutting *out* or flaking *off* (of rock, etc.), as if by the operation of a wedge.

Wedge (wedʒ), *v.*[2] 1686. [Of unkn. origin.] *trans.* To cut (wet clay) into masses and work them by kneading and throwing down, in order to expel air-bubbles.

Wedgwood (we·dʒwud). 1787. [Proper name.] **1.** Used *attrib.* to designate the pottery made by Josiah Wedgwood (1730–95) and his successors at Etruria, Staffs. **b.** Used to designate the blue colour which is characteristic of Wedgwood ware 1900. **c.** as *sb.* = Wedgwood pottery or ware 1863. **2.** Designating the scale of temperature used in the pyrometer invented by Josiah Wedgwood for testing the heat of kilns 1807.

Wedgy (we·dʒi), *a. rare.* 1799. [f. WEDGE *sb.* + -Y[1].] Resembling a wedge; shaped like a wedge.

Wedlock (we·dlǫk). [Late OE. *wedlāc,* f. *wed* pledge (WED *sb.*) + *-lāc* -LOCK.] †**1.** The marriage vow or obligation –1611. **2.** The condition of being married; marriage as a state of life or as an institution; matrimonial relationship. Now only in literary or legal use. ME. **b.** *Born in, out of w.,* said distinctively of legitimate or illegitimate offspring ME. **c.** A matrimonial union; a married life. late ME. †**3.** A wife –1690.

1. *Oth.* v. ii. 142. **3.** The most true constant lover of his w. FLETCHER.

Wednesday (we·nzde[i], -di, we·d'nzde[i]). [ME. *wednesdei* (XIII), corresp. to OFris. *wēnsdei,* repl. OE. *wōdnesdæġ* = OFris. *wōnsdei,* MLG. *wōdensdach* (Du. *woensdag*), ON. *óðinsdagr* 'day of Odin', tr. late L. *Mercurii dies* 'day of the planet Mercury'.] The fourth day of the week. Also *attrib.* **b.** In names of certain days of the ecclesiastical calendar, as ASH WEDNESDAY. Also *Good W., Holy W., Spy W.* (Anglo-Ir.), the W. before Easter.

Wee (wī), *sb.* and *a.* orig. *Sc.* [Northern ME. *wei,* repr. Angl. *wēġ(e* = WS. *wǣġ(e*; see WEIGH *sb.*[1]] **A.** *sb.* In early use almost always *a little w.,* later also *a w.* (chiefly as advb. acc.) **1. a.** To a small extent, in a small degree 1513. **b.** Qualifying an adj. or an adv.: Somewhat, rather 1816. **2.** A short time ME.

1. a. I have been drinking a wi, and I believe the Devil was in me 1793. **2.** Bide a w.—bide a w.; you southrons are aye in sic a hurry SCOTT.

B. *adj.* Extremely small, tiny 1450. **b.** *A w. bit*: = 'a wee'. Often quasi-*adj.* and quasi-*adv.* 1661. **c.** *The w. folk,* the fairies 1819. **d.** *The W. Free Kirk,* a nickname given to the minority of the Free Church of Scotland which stood apart when the main body amalgamated with the United Presbyterian Church to form the United Free Church in 1900. Hence *W. Frees,* members of the 'W. Free' church. 1904.

Weed (wīd), *sb.*[1] [OE. *wēod* = OS. *wiod,* rel. to OHG. *wiota* fern; of unkn. origin.] **1.** A herbaceous plant not valued for use or beauty, growing wild and rank, and regarded as cumbering the ground or hindering the growth of superior vegetation. **b.** A plant that grows wild in fresh or salt water. Cf. PONDWEED, SEAWEED, WATERWEED. 1538. **c.** Used, with defining word, to form the names of wild plants, as BINDWEED, DUCKWEED, KNAPWEED, etc. **2.** *gen.* Any herb or small plant. Chiefly *poet.* OE. **b.** Applied to a shrub or tree, *esp.* to a large tree, on account of its abundance in a district 1697. **3.** *spec.* Tobacco 1606. **b.** A cigar or cheroot. *colloq.* 1847. **4.** *fig.* An unprofitable, troublesome, or noxious growth. late ME. **5.** *slang.* **a.** A poor, leggy, loosely-built horse 1845. **b.** A lank delicate person without muscle or stamina 1869.

1. They bid thee crop a w., thou pluckst a flower SHAKS. In the garden there was not a w. to be seen DICKENS. Prov. *Ill weeds grow apace.* **2. b.** The elm..is still known as the 'Warwickshire w.' 1890. **4.** *Oth.* IV. ii. 67.

Comb.: **w.-killer,** a preparation of arsenic used for killing weeds. Hence **Wee·dery,** weeds collectively; also, a place where weeds abound. **Wee·dling,** a small w.; a slight, weakly person.

Weed (wīd), *sb.*[2] *arch.* exc. in sense 6 b. OE. [ME. *wēde,* repr. (1) OE. *wǣd* = OFris. *wēd,* OS. *wād* (in Du. *lijnwaad*), OHG. *wāt,* ON. *váð, vóð* :– Gmc. **wǣðiz*; (2) OE. *wǣde, ġewǣde* = OFris. *wēde,* OS. *wādi, giwādi* (Du. *gewaad*), OHG. *giwāti* :– Gmc. **ʒawǣðjam,* of disputed origin.] **1.** An article of apparel; a garment. **2.** *collect. sing.* Clothing, raiment, dress OE. **3.** *transf.* and *fig.* ME. **4.** Used contextually for: Defensive covering, armour, mail ME. **5.** A garment, or garb, distinctive of a person's sex, profession, or state of life ME. **6.** With defining word: A black garment worn in token of bereavement. Also, a scarf or band of crape worn by a mourner. 1536. **b.** *spec.* The deep mourning worn by a widow. Now always *pl.* 1595.

2. Deposed..for apparelling himselfe in such weede as was not decent for the dignity and order of priesthood 1576. **3.** There the snake throwes her enammel'd skinne, W. wide enough to rap a Fairy in SHAKS. **5.** They who to be sure of Paradise Dying put on the weeds of Dominic MILT. This poor gown,..this beggar-woman's w. TENNYSON. **6. b.** An afflicted Widow in her Mourning-Weeds ADDISON.

Weed (wīd), *v.* [OE. *wēodian* = OS. *wiodon* (M)LG. *weden,* (M)Du. *wieden*; f. *wēod* WEED *sb.*[1]] **1.** *intr.* (or *absol.*) To clear the ground of weeds; to pull up weeds. **2.** *trans.* To free (land, a crop, plant) from weeds ME. **3.** To remove (weeds) from land, esp. from cultivated land or from a crop. Also with *out, up.* late ME. **b.** *fig.* To eradicate (errors, faults, etc.); to remove (things or persons) as noxious or useless 1526. **4.** To clear *away* (plants, not necessarily noxious or useless); to take *out* (plants or trees) to prevent overcrowding; to thin (a crop). 1543. **b.** *transf.* To remove (inferior or superfluous individuals) from a company, herd, etc.; also with *out* 1863.

2. *fig.* Prouided that you w. your better iudgements Of all opinion that growes ranke in them SHAKS. **3. b.** Those who are so active to w. out the prejudices of education BERKELEY. **4.** The Flowers of the Forest are weeded away 1760. **b.** All her old society (excepting such as she had judiciously weeded out) 1889. Hence **Wee·der,** an implement used to eradicate weeds, a person employed to remove weeds from a crop, land, etc.; an extirpator (of weeds).

Wee·d-hook. OE. [f. WEED *sb.*[1] + HOOK *sb.*] A hook for cutting away weeds. Also **Wee·ding-hook** ME.

Weedy (wī·di), *a.*[1] late ME. [f. WEED *sb.*[1] + -Y[1].] **1.** Full of, abounding, or overgrown with weeds. **2.** Of the nature of or resembling a weed; made or consisting of weeds 1602. **3.** *colloq.* **a.** Of animals, esp. horses and hounds: Lean, leggy, loose-bodied, and lacking in strength and mettle 1800. **b.** Of persons: Unhealthily thin and tall; lanky and wanting physical vigour 1852.

2. When downe the w. Trophies, and her selfe, Fell in the weeping Brooke SHAKS.

Weedy (wī·di), *a.*[2] 1848. [f. WEED *sb.*[2] + -Y[1].] Wearing widow's 'weeds'; clad in mourning.

I think there was some compromise in the cap; but otherwise she was as w. as in the early days of her mourning DICKENS.

Week (wīk), *sb.* [OE. *wice, wicu* = OFris. *wike,* OS. *-wika* in *crūcewika* Holy Week (Du. *week*), OHG. *wehha, wohha* (G. *woche*), ON. *vika,* Goth. *wikō* (rend. τάξις 'order') :– Gmc. **wikōn,* prob. orig. 'succession, series', and rel. to L. **vix, vic-*; see VICE *prep.,* VICE-.] **1.** The cycle of seven days, recognized in the calendar of the Jews and thence adopted in the calendars of Christian, Moslem, and various other peoples; a single period of this cycle, beginning with the day traditionally fixed as the first of the week. **b.** With prefixed word, denoting some particular week of the year OE. **2.** A space of seven days, irrespective of the time from which it is reckoned OE. **b.** Seven days as a term for periodical payments (of wages, rent, or the like), or as a unit of reckoning for time of work or service. late ME. **c.** Used vaguely for an indefinite time. late ME. **d. Feast of weeks** *Heb. Antiq.* [tr. Heb. *ḥag šāḇū'ōṯ*] = PENTECOST 1. late ME. **3.** The six working days, as opp. to Sunday; the period from Monday to Saturday inclusive OE.

1. b. In Cristemesse wike 1450. Being the Tuesday in Easter w. 1622. **2.** She was within six weeks of seventeen 1856. There came a w. of rain 1865. **b.** In two days..the week's rent would be due 1882. A week's notice 1886. **c.** *A w. or two,* a moderate space of time. *Weeks,* a time which is felt as long; He *did* feel the same, Elinor—for weeks and weeks he felt it J. AUSTEN. **3.** *Ham.* I. i. 76.

Phrases. *A w.,* every w., weekly; A good woman ..that fasted .iij. tymes a woke 1450. *This day, tomorrow, Monday,* etc. *w.,* seven days before or after the day specified. *Yesterday, Monday,* etc., *was a w.* (dial.), seven days before the day mentioned. †*To be in by the w.,* to be ensnared, caught; *fig.* to be deeply in love. *Too late a week,* joc. understatement for 'far too late'; *A.Y.L.* II. iii. 74. *A w. of Sundays,* seven Sundays or weeks as repr. a long time. *To knock* (a person) *into the middle of next w.,* to give (him) a decisive blow, to punish severely.

Comb.: **w.-long** *a.* continuing for a w.; **-night,** a night in the w. other than Sunday night; also *attrib.*; **-old** *a.,* that has lived or lasted a w.

Week (wīk), *int.* 1588. Imitation of the squeak of a pig or mouse.

Weekday (wī·kde[i]). [OE. *wicdæġ,* f. *wicu* WEEK.] †**1.** A day of the week –1456. **2.** A day of the week other than Sunday 1546.

2. A hard-working man on week-days, and a preacher on Sundays 1860. *attrib.* Week-day services GEO. ELIOT.

Week-end (stress var.). 1878. **a.** (with *a* and *pl.*). The holiday period at the end of a week's work, usu. extending from Saturday noon or Friday night to Monday morning

1879. **b.** The period from Saturday to Monday during which business is suspended and shops are closed 1878.

a. They had evidently taken the house for week-ends 1892. *attrib.* W. tickets 1887. Hence **Week-end** *v. intr.* to spend a w. holiday.

Weekly (wī·kli), *a.* and *sb.* 1489. [f. WEEK *sb.* + -LY[1].] **A.** *adj.* That occurs, is done, made, given, etc. once a week. **b.** With a personal designation: Performing some action, or employed in some capacity, once a week; that has a contract by the week 1712.

The w. charge in this establishment..is three dollars DICKENS. *W. tenancy*, one determinable at the end of any week. **b.** *W. tenant*, one paying rent by the week, and subject to removal at a week's notice.

B. *sb.* A newspaper or review published once in each week 1846.

A new literary W. of high pretensions 1863.

Weekly (wī·kli), *adv.* 1465. [f. WEEK *sb.* + -LY[2].] In each or every week; week by week. Usu., once in seven days.

Wee·k-work. *Hist.* [OE. *wicweorc*, f. *wic(u* WEEK + *weorc* WORK *sb.*] In Old English Law, work done for the lord by the tenant so many days a week.

Weel[1] (wīl). *Sc.* and *north.* [OE. *wǣl* = MDu. *wael*, MLG. *wēl*.] A deep pool; a deep place in a river or the sea; a whirlpool or eddy.

Weel[2] (wīl). ME. [OE. *wile-* (in *wile-wise*), reduced form of *wiliȝe* WILLY *sb.*[1]] **1.** A wicker trap for catching fish, esp. eels. **b.** *Her.* A conventional representation of such a fish-trap, borne as a charge 1688. **2.** A basket, *esp.* one in which fish are kept. late ME.

Weem (wīm). 1792. [– early Gael. *uaim* cavern.] Applied in Scotland to a cave or underground dwelling-place used by early inhabitants of the country.

Ween (wīn), *v. Obs.* exc. *arch.* [OE. *wēnan* = OFris. *wēna*, OS. *wānian* (Du. *wanen* fancy, imagine), OHG. *wan(n)ēn* (G. *wähnen* suppose wrongly), ON. *vǣna*, Goth. *wēnjan* hope :– Gmc. *wǣnjan, f. *wǣniz hope, etc. (OE. *wēn*).] **1.** *trans.* To think, surmise, suppose, conceive, believe, consider. **b.** used parenthetically (esp. in *I w.*) ME. **2.** In regard to what is future or contingent; To expect, anticipate, count on; to think possible or likely OE. †**3.** *intr.* with *of*, *for*: To dream of, look for, expect –1613.

1. *absol.* I know you better than ye wene MALORY. **b.** Nor turnd I weene Adam from his fair Spouse MILT. A stalwart knight, I w., was he BARHAM. **2.** Weening in his pride to make the land nauigable 2 *Macc.* 5:21. **3.** *Hen. VIII*, v. i. 136.

Weeny (wī·ni), *a. dial.* and *colloq.* 1790. [f. WEE, with ending imitated from TINY, TEENY *a.*[2]] Very small, tiny.

Such a little tiny w. pill can never cure such a great big headache 1833.

Weep (wīp), *sb.* ME. [f. next.] †**1.** Weeping, lamentation –1545. **b.** A fit or bout of weeping 1836. **2.** An exudation, percolation, or sweating of moisture 1838.

Weep (wīp), *v.* Pa. t. and pa. pple. **wept.** [OE. *wēpan*, corresp. to OFris. *wēpa* cry aloud, OS. *wōpian* bewail, OHG. *wuofan*, ON. *œpa* scream, shout, Goth. *wōpjan*, f. Gmc. *wōp-; without cogns., prob. of imit. origin.] **I.** *intr.* **1.** To manifest the combination of bodily symptoms (instinctive cries or moans, sobs, and shedding of tears) which is the natural expression of painful (and sometimes of intensely pleasurable) emotion; also, and in mod. use chiefly, to shed tears (more or less silently). **b.** Said of animals. late ME. **c.** Const. *for*, *over*, †*on* (a person or thing regretted or commiserated), *for* (the emotion that prompts weeping). Also with *to* and inf., or a *that*-clause. OE. **2.** Of the eyes: To shed tears 1567. **b.** *fig.* of the heart ME. **3.** *transf.* Of things: To shed water or moisture in drops; to exude drops of moisture. late ME. **b.** To issue in drops; to trickle or fall as tears 1596. **c.** Of a boiler, etc.: To allow small drops of water to percolate or trickle through 1869. **d.** Of a sore, etc.: To exude a serous fluid 1882. **4.** Of a tree: To droop its branches 1764.

1. I am a foole To weepe at what I am glad of SHAKS. I could have wept like a child 1860. It is a sight to make the angels w. 1889. Phr. *To w. one's fill.* **b.** Þeise serpentes [crocodiles] slen men & þei eten hem wepynge MAUNDEV. **c.** Weepe thou for me in France; I, for thee heere SHAKS. Faire Daffadills, we w. to see You haste away so soone HERRICK. She embrac'd him, and for joy Tenderly wept MILT. **3.** The sky ceased to w. 1854. **4.** The Willow weeping o'er the fatal wave 1764.

II. *trans.* **1.** To shed tears over; to lament with tears OE. **2.** To let fall from the eyes, to shed (tears) ME. **b.** *fig.* Of the heart, or a wound: *To w.* (*tears of*) *blood* 1592. **c.** To declare, express, utter with lamentation. *rare* (chiefly *poet.*) 1599. **3.** quasi-*trans.* with adv. or compl. **a.** in phrases expressing excessive or prolonged weeping; esp. *to w. out one's eyes* or *heart* ME. **b.** To bring into a specified state or condition by weeping 1591. **c.** with advs. 1590. **4.** To shed (water or moisture) in drops; to exude 1634.

1. Now they 'gin to weepe The Mischiefe they haue done B. JONSON. **2.** When we vowe to weepe seas SHAKS. *To w. crocodile tears*, to feign grief (see CROCODILE 2). †*To w. millstones*, said of a hard-hearted person. **3. b** She wept her true eyes blind for such a one TENNYSON. Phil wept herself to sleep 1891. **c.** *To w.* (a thing) *back*, to recover it by weeping. *To w. out*, to remove, put out, extinguish, by weeping; also, to expend (one's life) in weeping. *To w. down*, to w. until the setting of (the sun). *To w. away*: (*a*) to spend, consume in tears and lamentation; (*b*) to remove or wash *away* with tears of commiseration. **4.** Groves whose rich Trees wept odorous Gumms and Balme MILT.

Weeper (wī·pəɹ). late ME. [f. prec. + -ER[1].] **1.** One who weeps or sheds tears, *esp.* one who is constantly weeping. **b.** *spec.* A hired mourner at a death-bed or funeral. late ME. **c.** One of a number of little images in niches on a funeral monument, representing mourners 1656. **d.** *Church Hist.* One of the lowest class of penitents (προσκλαίοντες, *flentes*) in the early Eastern Church 1841. **2.** The Capuchin monkey (*Cebus capucinus*) of S. America 1781. **3.** A conventional badge of mourning. Usu. *pl.* **a.** A strip of white linen or muslin formerly worn on the cuff of a man's sleeve (cf. Fr. *pleureuse*) 1724. **b.** A broad white cuff worn by widows 1755. **c.** A long black hat-band formerly worn by men 1832. **d.** The long black crape veil of a widow 1860. **4.** Usu. *pl.* Long flowing side-whiskers as worn by 'Lord Dundreary' in the play *Our American Cousin* 1894. **5.** A hole or pipe in a wall for the escape of dripping water 1890.

Weeping (wī·piŋ), *vbl. sb.* ME. [f. as prec. + -ING[1].] The action of the vb. in various senses; an instance of this.

Comb.: **w.-hole**, an opening through which moisture percolates; **-ripe** *a.*, ready to weep.

Weeping (wī·piŋ), *ppl. a.* OE. [f. as prec. + -ING[2].] **1.** That weeps. **2.** Tearful, lachrymose; accompanied with or expressed by weeping OE. **3.** Falling or issuing in drops like tears. Now *rare.* ·1686. **4.** Exuding moisture; (of soil), oozing, swampy 1550. **b.** *Path.* Of the eyes: Running, watering. Also of diseased tissues or structures from which moisture exudes. 1580. **5.** Of climate, skies, etc.: Dripping, rainy 1597. **6.** Applied to trees (less usu. to other plants) the branches of which arch over and hang down drooping. Chiefly in distinctive names of particular species or varieties. 1606.

4. b. *W. eczema*, a variety of eczema characterized by abundant exudation. **6.** *W. oak*, the Californian white oak, *Quercus lobata*; also, a cultivated variety of the English oak, *Quercus robur*. Hence **Wee·pingly** *adv.*

Weeping Cross. 1564. A place-name occurring in several English counties, presumably indicating the site of a stone cross formerly known by this designation.

Provb. phr. *To come home by Weeping Cross*, to suffer grievous disappointment or failure.

Weeping willow. 1731. [See WEEPING *ppl. a.* 6. Cf. Fr. *saule pleureur.*] A species of willow, *Salix babylonica*, having long and slender pendulous branches, cultivated in Europe as an ornamental tree and regarded as symbolical of mourning.

Weepy (wī·pi), *a.* 1825. [f. WEEP *v.* + -Y[1].] **1.** Inclined to weep or shed tears, tearful 1863. **2.** *dial.* Exuding moisture, damp, oozy 1825.

Weeshy (wī·ʃi), *a. Anglo-Irish.* 1830. [Origin obsc. Cf. WEE *a.*] Very small, tiny.

Weet (wīt), *v.*[1] *arch.* 1547. [repr. ME. *wēte(n*, var. f. *wite(n* WIT *v.* Frequent as a literary archaism in XVI and XVII.] **a.** *trans.* To know (a fact, the answer to a question). **b.** *intr.* To know of something.

Weet (wīt), *int.* and *v.*[2] 1852. [imit.] **A.** *int.* An imitation of the cry of certain small birds. **B.** *v. intr.* Of a bird: To chirp or twitter.

Weetless (wī·tlės), *a. arch.* 1579. [f. WEET *v.*[1] + -LESS (Spenser).] Unknowing, unconscious. Also, †meaningless.

Weet-weet, *int.* and *sb.*[1] 1808. [imit.] **A.** *int.* (wī·tˌwī·t). An imitation of the cry of certain birds, esp. the sandpiper and chaffinch. Also *sb.* as the name for this cry. **B.** *sb.* (wī·t-wīt). The sandpiper 1852.

‖**Weet-weet** (wī·tˌwīt), *sb.*[2] 1878. [Native Australian.] An Australian toy, consisting of a head and a stem, and so constructed as to be capable of being thrown to a great distance.

Weever (wī·vəɹ). 1622. [perh. orig. *wiver* – transf. use of OFr. (NE.) *wivre* serpent, dragon, var. of *guivre* :– L. *vipera* VIPER.] A fish of the genus *Trachinus* or family *Trachinidæ* (esp. *T. draco* the Greater, and *T. vipera* the Lesser W.), having sharp dorsal and opercular spines with which they can inflict painful wounds.

Weevil (wī·vil). OE. [Late ME. *wevyl*, prob. – MLG. *wevel* = OE. *wifel* beetle, OS. *goldwivil* glow-worm, OHG. *wibil*, *wipil* beetle, chafer, ON. **vifill* (in *tordýfill* dung-beetle :– Gmc. *webilaz, f. *web- *wǣb- move briskly (see WAVE *v.*, or *web- WEAVE *v.*[1]).] In OE., a beetle of any kind; in later use, any beetle classed under the group *Rhyncophora*, the larvæ of which, and sometimes the beetles themselves, are destructive by boring into grain, nuts, the bark of trees, etc.; *esp.* a beetle belonging to any species of the family *Curculionidæ*, the true weevils. Hence **Wee·vily** *a.* infested with weevils.

Weft[1] (weft). [OE. *wefta*, *weft*, corresp. to ON. *veptr*, *vipta* weft, MHG. *wift* fine thread :– Gmc. *wefton, *weftaz, *weftiz, f. *web- WEAVE *v.*[1]] **1.** *Weaving.* The threads that cross from side to side of a web, at right angles to the warp threads with which they are interlaced. **b.** The strips of cane, palm-leaf, etc. used as the filling, in weaving baskets, mats, etc. 1845. **2.** Yarn to be used for the weft-threads 1795. **3.** That which is spun or woven. late ME. **4.** *transf.* A layer of closely interwoven hyphæ produced in certain fungi 1875. **5.** A streak of cloud; a thin layer of smoke or mist 1822. Hence **We·ftage**, the arrangement of the threads of a woven fabric. **We·fted** *a.* composed of interwoven hyphæ.

†**Weft**[2]. 1579. Variant or perversion of WAIF *sb.*[1] –1838.

Wegotism (wī·gŏtiz'm). 1797. [joc. f. WE *pron.* and EGOTISM.] An obtrusive and too frequent use of the first person plural by a speaker or writer.

Wehee (wihī·), *int.*, *sb.*, *v. Obs.* exc. *dial.* late ME. [imit.] **A.** *int.* A conventional representation of the sound uttered by horses. **B.** *sb.* An utterance of this sound; a whinny or neigh. late ME. †**C.** *v. intr.* To neigh or whinny, as a horse does –1847.

Weierstrassian (vəiːəɹstrā·siăn), *a.* 1878. [f. name of Karl W. *Weierstrass* (1815–97), a German mathematician + -IAN.] *Math.* Pertaining to or invented by Weierstrass, esp. *W. function.*

‖**Weigel(i)a** (wəidʒī·lă, -ī·liă). 1846. [mod. L., f. name of C. E. *Weigel* (1748–1831), a German physician; see -A 2, -IA[1].] *Bot.* A genus of caprifoliaceous shrubs from China and Japan cultivated for its flowers; a plant of this genus.

Weigh (wē[i]), *sb.*[1] *Obs.* exc. *dial.* [OE. *wǣġ*, *wǣġe* balance, weight (see WEY), corresp. to OS., OHG. *wāga* (Du. *waag*, G. *wage*), ON. *vág* :– Gmc. *wǣȝō, *wǣȝōn, f. *wǣȝ-; see WEIGH *v.*] **A** balance, pair of scales. †**a.** *sing.* –1450. **b.** *pl.* (sometimes construed as *sing.*). Now *dial.* OE.

Weigh (wē[i]), *sb.*[2] 1785. In *under w.*, common var. of *under way*, from erron.

association with the phr. 'to weigh anchor'. See WAY *sb.*

Weigh (wē^{i}), *v.* [OE. *weġan* = OFris. *wega*, *weia* move, weigh, OS. *wegan* (Du. *wegen*) weigh, OHG. *wegan* move, shake, weigh (G. *bewegen* move), ON. *vega* lift, weigh, Goth. **wigan* in pa. pple. *gawigans* shaken :– Gmc. **weʒan*, f. **weʒ-* **waʒ-* **wǣʒ-* :– IE. **wegh-* **wogh-* **wēgh-*, repr. also by Gr. *Ϝοχος*, *ὄχος* vehicle, L. *vehere* convey. Rel. are WAG *v.*, WAGGON, WAIN.] **I.** To bear, carry; to heave up, lift. †**1.** *trans.* To bear from one place to another; to carry, transport. –late ME. **2.** *Naut.* To heave up (a ship's anchor) from the ground, before sailing. Now usu. *to w. anchor.* ME. **b.** *absol.* = to w. anchor. Hence, to sail (*from*, *out of* a port, etc.). 1513. **3.** To raise (a sunk ship, gun, etc.) from the bottom of the water. Also with *up*. 1500. **II.** To balance in the scales; to ascertain the weight of. **1.** *trans.* To ascertain the exact heaviness of (an object or substance) by balancing it in a pair of scales or on a steelyard, against a counterpoise of known amount. Also *absol.* OE. **b.** In Horse-racing. *To weigh out, in*: to take the weight of (a jockey) respectively before and after a race 1890. **2.** To measure a definite quantity of (a substance) on the scales. Usu. with *out*: To portion out (a quantity measured by weight) from a larger mass; to apportion (such a quantity) *to* (a person or persons). late ME. **3.** *intr.* in *Horse-racing.* Of a jockey: To take his place in the scales, in order that his declared weight may be verified by the clerk. *To w. out, in*, to do this before and after a race. 1805. **b.** Hence *To w. in with*: to introduce or produce (something that is additional or extra). *colloq.* 1885. **4.** *trans.* To hold (an object) in the hand (or hands) in order to observe or estimate its weight; to balance an object in the hand as if estimating its weight 1540. **5.** *fig.* To estimate, assess the value of (a person, quality, etc.) as if by placing in the scales ME. **b.** To balance *with* or *against* (another object regarded as a counterpoise) in order to a comparative estimate 1513. **6.** To consider (a fact, circumstance, statement, etc.) in order to assess its value or importance; to balance in the mind with a view to choice or preference. late ME. **b.** To ponder and examine the force of (words or expressions) ME. **c.** with object-cl. Now *rare.* 1526. **d.** *To w. up*, to appraise, form an estimate of (a person). *colloq.* 1894. †**7.** To esteem, value, think highly of; to ascribe value or importance to. Often with negative: (Not) to care for or regard. Also with adj. compl. –1681.

3. *To w. in*, also of boxers before a fight, or in gen. use. **5.** Not waiyng our merites, but pardonyng our offences *Bk. Com. Prayer.* **b.** Weighing anxiously prudence against sentiment LAMB. **6.** I weighed the consequences on both sides as fairly as I could FIELDING. The jurymen..little accustomed to w. evidence MACAULAY. **b.** *To w. one's words*, to speak deliberately and in calculated terms. **c.** Let any one w. well what it is to translate such a collection of documents 1841. **7.** All that she so deare did way, Thenceforth she left SPENSER. You waigh me not, O that's you care not for me SHAKS.

III. To have heaviness or weight. **1.** *intr.* To have a greater or less degree of heaviness, as measured by the scales. **a.** To be equal to or balance (a specified weight) in the scales OE. **b.** with adv. or pred. adj. ME. **2.** *fig.* ME. †**b.** *To w. with*, to counterpoise in power, value, etc.; to be of equal value or importance with –1656. **c.** *To w. against*, to counterbalance, countervail. late ME. **d.** quasi-*trans.* To equal (something else) in weight or value 1583. **3.** *intr.* To be of (much or little) value or account; to have influence *with* (a person) when he is forming an estimate or judgement. late ME.

2. For synne is not lyȝt, but it is hevy, and weythe the more than lede 1440. **b.** *Timon* I. i. 146. **d.** The heads of all thy Brother-Cardinals.. Weigh'd not a haire of his SHAKS. **3.** In truth, their testimonie did little w. with me EVELYN.

IV. To affect, or be affected, by weight. **1.** trans. *To w. down*: to draw, force, or bend down by pressure of weight; *fig.* to depress, oppress, lie heavy on ME. **2.** Of an object set in the scales (with *down*, *up*): To turn the scale when weighed against (something else); to outweigh, cause to rise in the scale. Also *to w. down* (the balance or scale). late ME. **3.** *intr.* with *on* or *upon*. Of a thought, feeling, etc.: To lie heavy upon, depress (a person, his spirits, etc.) 1775.

1. Weighed down by this habitual Sorrow of Heart ADDISON. The people were weighed down by an insufferable taxation 1857. **2.** *Rich. II*, III. iv. 89. One Whig shall w. down ten Tories SWIFT. **3.** While care weighs on your brow KEATS. Something seemed to w. upon her spirits LYTTON.

Comb.: **w.-beam**, a balance or steelyard; **-box**, (*a*) one of a set of boxes, used in 'drawing' wool, in which the wool is more accurately weighed; (*b*) a w.-house; **-house**, a public building to which commodities are brought to be weighed; **-lock** *U.S.*, a canal-lock at which barges are weighed and their tonnage settled; **-man**, in a colliery, one who weighs the tubs of coal as they leave the cage at the pit-mouth; **-master**, the official in charge of a w.-house or public scales; **-out**, the verification of a jockey's declared weight before a race. Hence **Wei·ghable** *a.* that can be weighed; heavy enough to be weighed in scales. †**Wei·ghage**, a duty or toll paid for the weighing of goods. **Wei·gher**, a person employed to weigh commodities; an official appointed to w. or supervise weighing, to test weights, etc.

Wei·gh-bridge. 1796. A platform scale, flush with the road, for weighing vehicles, cattle, etc.

Weighing (wē^{i}·iŋ), *vbl. sb.* late ME. [f. WEIGH *v.* + -ING[1].] The action of WEIGH *v.*

Comb.: **w.-engine**, **-machine**, an apparatus (e.g. a combination of levers, a spring-balance) for weighing heavy bodies.

Weighment (wē^{i}·mĕnt). *India.* 1878. [f. WEIGH *v.* + -MENT, after *measurement.*] The action of weighing (commodities).

Wei·gh-scale. orig. *north.* ME. [– Du. *waagschaal* or MLG. *wageschale.* In recent use perh. a new formation.] The pan of a balance; *pl.* a pair of scales.

Weight (wē^{i}t), *sb.* [OE. *wiht*, *ġewiht*, corresp. to OFris. *wicht*, MDu. *wicht*, *ghewichte* (Du. *wicht*, *gewicht*, G. *gewicht*), ON. *vétt*, *vætt* :– Gmc. *-wextiz* and **ʒawextjam*, f. **weʒ-* (see WEIGH *v.*) + -T[1]. The mod. vowel is mainly due to the verb.] **I.** Measurement of quantity by means of weighing; quantity as determined in this way. **1.** *By w.*: as determined by weighing. **2.** Assoc. with *measure* and *number*, esp. in fig. expressions referring to due proportion ME. **3.** Ponderability, as a general property of material substances; relative heaviness. late ME. **b.** Impetus (of a heavy falling body; also of a blow). late ME. **4.** The amount which an article of given price or value ought to weigh. late ME. **5.** Ponderable matter; that which weighs 1663.

3. As clocks to w. their nimble motion owe, The wheels above urg'd by the load below POPE. *fig.* I would rather be knock'd down By w. of argument than w. of fist WOLCOT. **4.** It was near two ounces more than w. in a pound DE FOE. To see if the money he was going to pay was w. 1850. *Short w.*: see SHORT *a.* III. 1. Phr. *In w.*, added to adjs. such as *heavy*, *light*, etc. **5.** Overcharged with W. laid upon them 1755.

II. An amount determined or determinable by weighing. **1.** A portion or quantity weighing a definite amount. Often preceded by an expression indicating the amount. Abbrev. *wt.* OE. **2.** *Its*, *his*, etc. *w. in* or *of gold*, *silver*, etc.: a quantity of gold, silver, etc. of the same weight. Chiefly in hyperbolical statements of value. ME. **3.** The amount that something weighs; the quantity of a portion of matter as measured by the amount of its downward force due to gravitation. late ME. **4.** A heavy mass; usu., something heavy that is lifted or carried; a burden. late ME. **5.** *spec.* **a.** In horse-racing or riding: The amount (expressed in stones and pounds) which the jockey or rider is expected or required to weigh or which the mount can without difficulty carry 1692. **b.** Without article 1734. **c.** *Boxing.* A match between boxers of a particular weight 1914.

3. The w. of an hayre will turne the Scales betweene their Haber-de-pois SHAKS. *fig.* We have seen such a system fall by its own w. 1794. People round us were not pulling their w. 1921. Phr. *Atomic w.* (Chem.), the relative w. of the atom of any element. *Live w.*: see LIVE *a.* 7. **4.** The greater weighte that is cast on, the soner it breakes 1562. The simplest form of work is the raising of a w. TYNDALL. **5. b.** He carries w.! he rides a race! COWPER.

III. *fig.* **1.** A burden (of responsibility, obligation, years, etc.). late ME. **2. a.** The force of an onslaught or encounter in the field; pressure exerted by numbers 1500. **b.** *To feel the w. of*, to suffer from (by receiving a heavy blow or undergoing severe pressure) 1553. **3.** Importance, moment, claim to consideration 1521. **4.** Persuasive or convincing power (of utterances, arguments, evidence); impressiveness (of matter or speech) 1534. **5.** Weightiest or heaviest part; greatest stress or severity; preponderance, superior amount on one side or the other of a question 1568. **6.** Influence or authority (of a person) due to character, position, wealth, or the like 1710.

1. The w. of seventy Winters prest him down DRYDEN. For my Part, I had a W. taken off from my Heart DE FOE. **2. b.** He that ones wincheth shall fele the waite of my fiste 1553. **3.** Obedience ..due to them in matters of small weight 1583. The objection is of w. BURKE. **5.** A new trial on the ground..that the verdict was against the w. of evidence 1883.

Phrases. *To lay w. upon*, to attach importance or value to. *To have w.*, to make an impression on, weigh *with* (those who judge a matter); to be recognized as valid or important; so *to carry w.* *To give* (full, due) *w. to*, to allow its proper force; to treat as valid or important.

IV. A standard of quantity determined by or employed in weighing. **1.** †**a.** A standard of weight. late ME. **b.** With qualifying word, as in *troy*, *avoirdupois w.*: Any of the systems used for stating the weight of a quantity of matter 1500. **2.** A unit or denomination of ponderable quantity ME. **b.** In pl. and coupled with *measures.* late ME. **3.** A piece of metal or other substance, weighing a known amount and identical with one of the units or with a multiple or aliquot part of a unit in some recognized scale ME. **b.** *Athletics.* A heavy lump of stone or ball of metal, which is thrown from one hand placed close to the shoulder: chiefly in *putting the w.* 1865. **4.** A block or lump of metal or other heavy substance, or a heavy object, used to pull or press down something, to give an impulse to machinery (e.g. in a clock), to act as a counterpoise, or the like. late ME.

2. b. Certaine brief Tables of English waights, and Measures 1596.

attrib. and *Comb.*: **w.-clock**, a clock operated by weights; **-plate**, a plate on which articles are set to be weighed in a weighing-machine. Hence **Wei·ghtless** *a.* without w., having comparatively little w.

Weight (wē^{i}t), *v.* 1647. [f. prec.] †**1.** *trans.* To oppress the mind; also *pass.*, to be oppressed in mind or spirit –1728. **2.** To load with a weight; to supply with an additional weight; to make weighty 1747. **b.** *techn.* To add weight to (an inferior commodity) by the admixture or use of an adulterant 1862. **c.** *Statistics.* To multiply the components of (an average) by compensating factors 1901. **3.** To assign to (a horse) the weight he must carry in a handicap race 1846. Hence **Wei·ghting** *vbl. sb.* the action of the vb.; *concr.* something used as a weight to press down, steady, or balance.

Weighty (wē^{i}·ti), *a.* 1489. [f. WEIGHT *sb.* + -Y[1].] **I. 1.** Of a considerable or appreciable weight; that weighs a good deal, heavy 1500. **b.** Of persons or animals: Of more than the usual size, large or bulky of body 1581. **c.** Of great weight in proportion to its bulk, of high specific gravity 1585. **2.** Bearing down heavily as if weighted or of great weight; falling with force or violence 1583.

1. c. It look'd like a fungus, but was w. like metall EVELYN. **2.** [I]..Prest the sinking sands With w. steps POPE.

II. 1. a. Of great gravity or significance; highly important, serious, grave, momentous 1489. **b.** Of a substantial or solid nature; ranking high in respect of importance or value 1558. **2. a.** Of an argument, etc.: Producing a powerful effect; adapted to influence or convince 1560. **b.** Of persons: Having great authority or influence; important in respect of position, views, or utterance 1662. **3.** Hard to bear or endure without failing or giving way; oppressive; burdensome 1540. †**b.** Rigorous, severe. SHAKS. †**4.** Expressing seriousness or gravity, earnest, solemn –1677.

1. a. 1 *Hen. VI*, II. i. 62. **b.** Were they weightie Treatises? NASHE. **2. b.** There is not any necessity that men should aim at being important and w. in every sentence they speak 1729. 4. *Hen. VIII*, Prol. I. 2. Hence **Wei·ghti-ly** *adv.*, **-ness.**

Weir (wīᵊɹ), *sb.* [OE. *wer*, corresp. to OS. *werr*, MLG., MHG. *wer*, *were* (LG. *wēr*, *wēre*, G. *wehr*); f. OE. *werian* defend, dam up.] **1.** A barrier or dam to restrain water, *esp.* one placed across a river or canal in order to raise or divert the water for driving a mill wheel; now gen., a dam constructed on the reaches of a canal or navigable river to retain the water and regulate its flow. **2.** A fence or enclosure of stakes made in a river, harbour, etc., for taking or preserving fish OE. **b.** A weel for catching fish 1611. **3.** A pond or pool. *Obs.* exc. *dial.* ME. **4.** *local.* A fence or embankment to prevent the encroachment of a river or sea-sand, or to turn the course of a stream 1599.

attrib. and *Comb.*: **w.-hatch**, the flood-gate or sluice of a w.; **w. house**, a trap for salmon at a salmon w. Hence **Weir** *v. trans.* (usu. in pa. pple.) to provide with a w. **Wei·ring** *vbl. sb.* the constructing of a w. or weirs; *concr.* materials used for making a weir.

Weird (wīᵊɹd), *sb.* Now *Sc.* or *arch.* [OE. *wyrd* = OS. *wurd*, OHG. *wurt*, ON. *urðr*, f. wk. grade of **werþ-* **warþ-* **wurþ-* become; see WORTH *v.*] **1.** The principle, power, or agency by which events are predetermined; fate, destiny. **2.** *pl.* The Fates OE. **b.** One pretending or supposed to have the power to foresee and to control future events 1625. **3.** That which is destined or fated to happen to a particular person, etc.; one's appointed lot or fortune, destiny OE. **b.** *spec.* An evil fate inflicted by supernatural power, esp. by way of retribution 1874. **4. a.** A happening, event, occurrence OE. **b.** That which is destined or fated to happen; predetermined events collectively 1470. **c.** A supernatural or marvellous occurrence or tale 1814.

2. b. With this green nettle And cross of metal I witches and wierds defy 1899. **3.** My w. maun be fulfilled SCOTT. *To dree one's w.*: see DREE *v.* 1. **4. a.** Prov. *After word comes w.*, the mention of a thing is followed by its occurrence or appearance. Hence **Wei·rdly** *a. Sc.* (*a*) favoured by fate, prosperous; (*b*) pertaining to or suggestive of witchcraft or the supernatural.

Weird (wīᵊɹd), *a.* late ME. [orig. attrib. use of prec. in *weird sisters* (see sense 1).] **1.** Having the power to control the fate or destiny of men; claiming such power. Orig. in *the W. Sisters* = †(*a*) the Fates; (*b*) the witches in Shakespeare's *Macbeth.* **2.** Partaking of or suggestive of the supernatural; of a mysterious or unearthly character; uncanny 1817. **3.** Of strange or unusual appearance, odd-looking 1815. **4.** Out of the ordinary course, strange, unusual; hence, odd, fantastic 1820.

2. Awakened by a w. and unearthly moaning 1876. **3.** Mutable As shapes in the w. clouds SHELLEY. **4.** A w. belief..that no one could count the stones of Stonehenge twice, and make the same number of them DICKENS. Hence **Wei·rdish** *a.* somewhat w. **Wei·rd-ly** *adv.*, **-ness.**

Weird (wīᵊɹd), *v. Sc.* and †*north.* ME. [f. WEIRD *sb.*] **1.** *trans.* To preordain by the decree of fate; esp. in *pass.* to be destined or divinely appointed *to.* **2.** To assign to (a person) as his fate, destiny, or lot 1550.

Weism (wi·iz'm). 1800. [f. WE *pron.* + -ISM, after EGOISM.] The too frequent use of 'we' (see WE *pron.* 2 b) by a speaker or writer.

Weismannian (vəi·smæniăn), *a.* and *sb.* 1903. [f. as next + -IAN.] **A.** *adj.* Of or pertaining to Weismann or his biological theory. **B.** *sb.* One who accepts the theory of Weismannism.

Weismannism (vəi·smăniz'm). 1894. [f. name *Weismann* + -ISM.] The theory of evolution and heredity propounded by the German biologist, August Weismann, esp. in regard to the continuity of the germ-plasm and the non-transmission of acquired characteristics.

Weissite (vəi·səit). 1836. [f. name of C. S. *Weiss*, German crystallographer + -ITE¹ 2 b.] *Min.* An altered form of iolite.

Weka (we·ka, wē¹·kă, wi·kă). 1845. [Maori, so named from its cry.] Either of the flightless rails, *Ocydromus australis* and *O. brachypterus* of New Zealand.

Welcome (we·lkŏm), *sb.*¹, *int.*, and *a.* [orig. OE. *wilcuma* (f. *wil-* desire, pleasure + *cuma* comer), with later alteration of first element to *wel-* WELL *adv.* under influence of OFr. *bien venu* (or ON. *velkominn*).] †**A.** *sb.* One whose coming is pleasing or desirable; an acceptable person or thing. OE. only. **B.** *predic.*, passing into *adj.* **1.** Of a person: Acceptable as a visitor, companion, etc.; also in phr. *to make* (a person) *w.* OE. **b.** *attrib.* 1579. **2.** Of a thing: Acceptable, agreeable, pleasing ME. **b.** *attrib.* 1577. **3.** Freely permitted or allowed, cordially invited (*to* do or have something) ME.

1. The oftner they come to him, the welcomer they are 1667. **b.** They..with full Mirth receive the w. Guest PRIOR. **2.** Praise is not so w. to the Idler as quiet JOHNSON. **b.** He hath brought vs smooth and w. newes SHAKS. **3.** You're very w. to pass another night here DICKENS. *And w.*, added to a statement to imply: and he is (you are, etc.) freely permitted or cordially invited to do so, to have it, or the like; And if this be done, let them judge and w. 1755.

C. Used in the vocative as a form of address to a visitor or guest; hence as *int.*, serving as an expression of good will or pleasure at the coming of a person OE.

To bid, wish (a person) *w.* (*home*), to tell him that he is gladly received (*home*, as a guest, etc.). Hence **We·lcome-ly** *adv.*, **-ness.**

Welcome (we·lkŏm), *sb.*² 1525. [f. prec. or next.] **1.** An assurance to a visitor or stranger that he is welcome; a pleasant or hearty greeting or reception given to a person on arrival. **b.** *transf.* (esp. with *adjs.*). A greeting or reception of an unpleasant or unsatisfactory nature 1548. **2.** *W. home*: entertainment provided to celebrate the return home of a person; also, expressions of greeting made at a person's homecoming 1530. **3.** Hearty or hospitable reception of a stranger or guest 1590. **4.** A welcoming salute 1615.

1. And to thee, and thy Company, I bid A hearty w. SHAKS. *To outstay* or *overstay one's w.*, to remain in a place longer than one is desired. **b.** We met but with a cold w. 1725. **3.** Small cheere and great w., makes a merrie feast SHAKS.

Welcome (we·lkŏm), *v.* [orig. OE. *wilcumian*, f. *wilcuma* WELCOME *sb.*¹, with later alteration of the first element, as in the noun.] **1.** *trans.* To greet (a person) with 'welcome!'; to receive gladly and hospitably; to make welcome. Also const. *to, into* (a place), and with advs. of place, as *back*; esp. *to w. home.* **2.** To greet or receive *with* (or *by*) something (esp. of an unpleasant nature) 1590. **3.** To greet heartily or with pleasure (the return of a person, the occurrence of an event, etc.) 1697.

1. I know no cause Why I should w. such a guest as greefe SHAKS. Your wiues shall w. home the Conquerors SHAKS. **2.** If you return..you will be welcomed by a brace of bullets 1791. Hence **We·lcomer**, one who, or something which, welcomes or greets (a person or thing). **We·lcoming** *ppl. a.* that welcomes or gives a welcome.

Weld (weld), *sb.*¹ [Late ME. *welde*, repr. OE. **wealde*, **walde* = (M)LG. †*walde*, MDu. *woude* (Du. *wouw*), poss. rel. to WEALD, WOLD.] The plant *Reseda luteola*, which yields a yellow dye. Also, the dye obtained from this plant.

Weld (weld), *sb.*² 1831. [f. next.] **1.** A joining or joint made by welding. **2.** The act, process, or result of welding; the state or fact of being welded 1862. Hence **We·ldless** *a.* made without a w.

Weld (weld), *v.* 1599. [var. of WELL *v.* (q.v. sense 2), prob. after Sw. *välle*; the *-d* appears to have come from the pa. t. and pa. pple.] **1.** *intr.* To undergo junction by welding; to admit of being welded. **2.** *trans.* To soften by heat and join together (pieces of metal, esp. iron or iron and steel) in a solid mass, by hammering or by pressure; to forge (an article) by this method 1677.

2. A steel blade welded to a wrought-iron socket 1880. Hence **We·ldable** *a.* capable of being welded; so **Weldabi·lity. We·lder**, one who welds; *spec.* a smith employed exclusively in welding.

Welding (we·ldiŋ), *vbl. sb.* 1603. [f. prec. + -ING¹.] The action of the vb. WELD; the process of joining with a weld. **b.** Capacity for uniting under the operation of heat and pressure 1825.

Comb.: **w. heat**, the degree of heat to which iron is brought for w.; **w. point**, degree of heat requisite for w.; **w. powder**, a flux used in w.

Welfare (we·lfeᵊɹ), *sb.* ME. [f. the verbal phr. *wel fare* (WELL *adv.* II. 3, FARE *v.*¹ 8), prob. after ON. *velferð.*] The state or condition of doing or being well; good fortune, happiness, or well-being (of a person, community, or thing); prosperity.

One continued Series of Actions, for the W. of the People 1718. Her first wish in life is for your happiness and w. 1838.

Comb. in sense 'concerned with or devoted to the w.' (of workers, etc.), as *w. policy, work, -worker.*

†**We·lfare,** *vbl. phr.* 1534. [f. as prec. Cf. FAREWELL.] The optative phr. *well fare* (you, it, etc.) = 'May it go well with', 'good luck to' –1672.

‖**Weli, -y** (we·li). 1819. [– Arab. *walī* friend (of God), saint.] **1.** A Moslem saint. **2.** The tomb or shrine of a saint 1838.

Welk (welk), *v. Obs.* exc. *dial.* [prob. of LDu. origin (cf. (M)LG., (M)Du. *welken*).] **1.** *intr.* Of a flower, plant, etc.: To lose freshness or greenness; to wilt, wither, fade. **2.** *trans.* To cause to fade or wither 1579. Hence **Welked** *ppl. a.*

Welkin (we·lkin). [OE. *weolcen, wolc(e)n*, corresp. to OFris. *wolken, wulken*, OS., OHG. *wolkan* (Du. *wolk*, G. *wolke*).] †**1.** A cloud –ME. **2.** The apparent arch or vault of heaven overhead; the sky, the firmament. (In later use chiefly *poet.* and *dial.*) ME. **3.** The upper atmosphere; the region of the air in which the clouds float, birds fly, etc. late ME.

2. *By the w.*; This villanous poetrie will vndoe you, by the w. B. JONSON. *To make the w. ring, to rend the w.*, etc., said of loud sounds; Making the w. ring with the music of their deep-toned notes SURTEES.

Well (wel), *sb.* [OE. (Anglian) *wella* (WS. **wiella*, etc.), corresp. to OHG. *wella* (G. *welle*) wave, ON. *vella* boiling heat, ebullition, f. Gmc. **wall-*; see WALL *v.*¹, WELL *v.*] **1.** A spring of water rising to the surface of the earth and forming a small pool or flowing in a spring. Now *arch.* or *dial.* **b.** A spring of water supposed to be of miraculous origin or to have supernatural healing powers; also, a medicinal or mineral spring OE. **c.** *pl.* A place where medicinal springs exist; a watering-place or spa (cf. the place-name *Wells*) 1673. **2.** *transf.* and *fig.* **a.** In allusive contexts directly suggestive of the nature or uses of a spring OE. **b.** That from which something springs or arises; a source or origin OE. **c.** Applied to persons regarded as a source or abundant manifestation of some quality or virtue ME. **d.** A whirlpool 1654. **3.** A pit dug in the ground to obtain a supply of spring-water; *spec.* a vertical excavation, usu. circular in form and lined with masonry, sunk to such a depth as to penetrate a water-bearing stratum OE. **4.** *Naut.* **a.** A vertical shaft protecting the pump below the lower (or upper) deck in a ship's hold 1611. **b.** A cistern or tank in a fishing-boat, in which the catch of fish is preserved alive 1614. **5.** A shaft or pit bored or dug in the ground. In various specific uses. **a.** An excavation for the storage of ice 1681. **b.** A shaft sunk to obtain oil, brine, gas, etc. 1799. **c.** A shaft to carry water through a retentive to a porous stratum or to a drain 1856. **d.** A hollow cylinder or shaft of masonry sunk and filled in solid to form a foundation 1885. **6. a.** The central open space, from roof to basement, of a winding, spiral, or elliptical staircase; the open space in which a lift operates 1700. **b.** The space on the floor of a law-court where the solicitors sit 1853. **c.** A deep narrow space formed by the surrounding walls of a building or buildings, serving for the access of light and air 1859. **7.** In *Ship-* and *Boat-building*, applied to various vertical apertures 1874. **8. a.** A box-like receptacle in the body of a vehicle, for articles of luggage 1783. **b.** A deep receptacle at the bottom of a piece of furniture, esp. of one fitted with trays, drawers, etc. 1841. **9.** A hole or cavity containing or to contain a liquid. **a.** The water-tank at the base of a shot-tower, into which the drops of melted lead fall 1851. **b.** A cavity at the bottom of a furnace, into which the molten metal falls 1864. **c.** A sunk receptacle for a liquid, as ink (*ink-w.*), etc. 1873.

1. **b.** Where meete we?..At Saint Gregories w. SHAKS. **2. a.** O sleep,..Holding unto our lips thy goblet filled Out of Oblivion's w. LONGF. **b.** Understandyng is a w. of life vnto him that hath it BIBLE (Great) *Prov.* 16:22. **c.** Dan Chaucer, w. of English vndefyled SPENSER. **3.** No: 'tis not so deepe as a w., nor so wide as a Church doore, but 'tis inough SHAKS. *fig.* With ioy shall yee draw water out of the wels of saluation *Isaiah* 12:3. Provb. phr. If Truth, as Democritus fansied, lies at the bottom of a deep W. 1691. 'He's as deep as a w.' 1860. *A w. of a* (place), like a w., as being damp and cold, or deep and dark; The veriest old w. of a shivering best-parlour that ever was seen DICKENS. **4. a.** *To sound the w.*, to ascertain, by means of a sounding-rod, the depth of water in the hold.

Comb.: **w.-beam,** the wooden beam or roller over which the rope of a w.-bucket runs; **-boat,** a fishing boat provided with a w.; **-bucket,** a bucket used to draw water from a w. by means of a rope and pulley or windlass; **-curb,** the stone border round the mouth of a w.; **-deck,** an open space on the main deck of a ship, lying at a lower level between the forecastle and poop; **-dish,** a meat-dish with a depression at one end as a receptacle for gravy; **-drain** *Agric.*, a drain for wet land with a boring through which the water rises to be carried off by the drain; **-grate,** a grate in which the fire burns on the hearth, receiving its air supply from below; **-house,** a small building or room enclosing a w. and its apparatus; **-staircase, -stairs, -stairway,** a winding or geometrical staircase with a w. or open centre; **-trap,** a depression in a drain, in which water lies and prevents the escape of foul air; **-water,** water issuing, or drawn, from a w. or spring.

Well (wel), *a.* (*predic.*). ME. [Arising from WELL *adv.* in impers. use of sense II. 3.] **1.** In a state of good fortune, welfare, or happiness –1825. **2.** In favour, in good standing or estimation, on good terms *with* (a person) ME. **b.** *spec.* On terms of intimate friendship or familiarity *with* (a woman) 1704. **3.** = WELL OFF 1 c. Now *rare* exc. in *w. to do, w. off.* late ME. **b.** = WELL OFF 1 a. Now *rare.* 1440. **4.** In a sound or undamaged state; *spec.* in marine insurance, of a vessel 1450. **5.** Sound in health; free or recovered from sickness or infirmity 1555. **b.** *attrib.*, esp. with *man.* Now only *U.S.* 1628. **c.** *absol.* (as pl.) Those who are sound in health 1676. **d.** Of a person's health or spirits: Sound, good. Of sickness: Cured. 1712. **6.** In phr. (*It is*) *w.* (*that*) or *to*: **a.** Advisable, desirable, to be recommended 1475. **b.** Fortunate, lucky; forming a matter for satisfaction or thankfulness 1665. **c.** *As w...if* or *that*, in preceding senses 1753. **7.** Of a state of things, an undertaking, etc.: Satisfactory; of such a nature or in such a condition as to meet with approval. Also, formerly, of material things. late ME. **8.** Good; of a character or quality to which no exception can be taken. *arch.* or *Obs.* 1661. **9.** †**a.** Of good or satisfactory appearance –1748. **b.** *W. to see, to be seen*: good to look upon, comely (*rare*) 1804. **10.** In concessive use, followed by an objection or contrary view expressed or implied 1560.

1. O w. were wee in the daies of Queene Elizabeth 1595. **2.** Good reasons for standing w. with his neighbours 1883. **3.** *To leave* (a person) *w., to be w. left*, to leave or be left w. off by devise or inheritance. **b.** Apparently they found themselves very w. as they were M. ARNOLD. **5.** Where young Adonis oft reposes, Waxing w. of his deep wound MILT. *Not w.* = UNWELL *a. W. day*, a day on which one is free from sickness, esp. from an attack of an intermittent disorder. **d.** He had.. determined, if his cold was w. enough, to ride over to Snailswell SURTEES. **6. a.** 'Twer w., It were done quickly SHAKS. **c.** I think it would be as w. if John was to go off..this afternoon 1801. **7.** Though it is vastly w. to be here for a few weeks, we would not live here for millions J. AUSTEN. *Prov.* All is w. that endes well HEYWOOD. *To let* (or *leave*) *w. alone*, to refrain from trying to make better that which is already w. *All's w.*, a sentry's reply when he has received the password in answer to his challenge. **8.** No weakness,..or blame, nothing but w. and fair MILT. **10.** *It is all very w.*, it is right and proper in itself or under certain circumstances; Written contracts are all very w., but if the contractor stops payment—where are you? RUSKIN. *He* (*it, etc.*) *is all very w., is w. enough*, there is no fault to be found with him, it, etc. *W. and good* (without vb.); 'If you like to bow and scrape to rich people, w. and good', I said 1888.

Well (wel), *v.* Now only *literary* or *dial.* [OE. *wællan, wellan* (WS. *wiellan, wyllan*) boil, melt, causative vb. f. *weallan*, WALL *v.*[1] Cf. (M)LG., (M)Du. *wellen*, ON. *vella* :– Gmc. *walljan.* The form is appropriate only to the trans. senses; in the intr. it has taken the place of the orig. str. verb WALL *v.*] †**1.** *trans.* To boil –1450. †**2.** To liquefy (metal) by heat; to cast, found –1570. **b.** To weld. *Obs.* exc. *dial.* late ME. **3.** *intr.* To boil. Also with *up.* late ME. **4.** Of liquids, esp. of a well or spring of water: To rise (*up*) to the surface (of the earth) and flow in a copious stream. late ME. **5.** Of tears: To rise (*up*) to the eyes in a copious flood. late ME. **6.** Of blood or corrupt matter: To flow from the body, a wound, or sore. late ME. **7.** *fig.* To spring or originate; to issue or flow *forth* or *out* ME. **8.** *trans.* Of a spring, etc.: To pour forth (water, etc.). late ME.

4. *transf.* What sweet sounds from her fast-closed lips are welling KINGSLEY. Smoke welled slowly through the leaves 1895. *To w. over*: (*lit.* and *fig.*) to overflow; His heart welled over with joy 1883. **8.** *fig.* Mary welle of mercy, wellyng euer pite 1425.

Well (wel), *adv.* [OE. *wel(l* = OFris., OS. (Du.) *wel*, ON. *vel*; also with advb. suffix (and vowel-variation) OS. *wela, wala, wola*, OHG. *wela, wola* (G. *wohl*), Goth. *waila*; prob. f. IE. **wel-* **wol-*; see WILL *v.*[1] Cf. WEAL *sb.*[1]] **I. 1.** In accordance with a good or high standard of conduct or morality; in a way which is morally good. **b.** Satisfactorily in respect of conduct or action OE. **2.** In such a manner as to constitute good treatment or confer a benefit; kindly, considerately; in a kind and friendly manner; with favour or welcome OE. **b.** With equanimity or good nature; without resentment. Chiefly with *take.* 1753. **3.** With courage and spirit; gallantly, bravely. ME.

1. b. Ye swear that ye w. and trulie shall serve our Sovraigne Lord the King 1534. **2.** We grete you wele 1483. Each man desireth to bee w. thought of 1576. His forward voyce now is to speake w. of his friend SHAKS. He was w. receiv'd at Court 1706. At least I meant w. 1729. We wished the man w. DICKENS. *To deserve w. of*, to be entitled to gratitude or good treatment from.

II. 1. Faithfully; heedfully, carefully, attentively OE. **2.** In a way appropriate to the facts or circumstances; fittingly, properly OE. **3.** Prosperously, successfully, fortunately, happily; without harm or accident OE. **4. a.** In a state of plenty or comfort OE. **b.** Satisfactorily or excellently in respect of health or recovery from illness: usu. with *do.* 1440. **5.** With good reason; as a natural result or consequence OE. **6.** Without difficulty or hindrance; readily, easily OE. **b.** Denoting the possibility or likelihood of an occurrence or fact. late ME. **c.** In negative or comparative clauses 1523.

1. Take him and looke w. to him, and doe him no harme *Jer.* 39:12. After thinking the matter w. over, we have determined not to compete 1873. **2.** This is wel sayd, saide Morgan le fay MALORY. I think it will do very w. RICHARDSON. *To do w.*, to act prudently or sensibly; You will do w. to keep a watchful eye over..Villiams SMOLLETT. **3.** What a father doth to marie his daughter wel, is to give her a great portion 1604. In Iudah things went w. 2 *Chron.* 12:12. Blessing ourselves that we had come off so w. SMOLLETT. All went w. as far as the foot of the ice-fall 1899. Formerly freq. in impers. construction †*Well is me* (etc.): I (etc.) am fortunate or happy. Wel is me that I haue mette with you MALORY. **4. a.** He would be able to live w. and good all his days 1874. **b.** A fine child, and the Queen doing w. 1841. **5.** Back to the Thicket slunk The guiltie Serpent, and w. might MILT. A regulation of which the legality might w. be questioned MACAULAY. **6.** Nor were the refugees such as a country can w. spare MACAULAY. **b.** This was as strong a case as could w. come before the Court 1818. **c.** He can praise a sharp remark before it is w. out of another's mouth JOWETT.

III. 1. Effectively; successfully as regards result or progress OE. **2.** In a manner, or to an extent, approaching thoroughness or completeness OE. **3.** Used as an intensive to strengthen the idea implied in the verb, or to denote that the action, etc., indicated by it attains a high point or degree. Similarly with pa. pples. OE. **4.** Clearly, definitely, without any doubt or uncertainty ME. **b.** Intimately, familiarly; closely, in detail ME. **5.** In a skilful or expert manner OE. **b.** In a sufficient or satisfactory manner ME. **c.** With good appearance or effect; elegantly ME.

1. The printer gets on w. with my History SOUTHEY. **2.** The market here is not very w. supplied 1799. **3.** Wel loued he garleek, oynons, and eek lekes CHAUCER. W. instructed in sciences 1538. Many moo..had w. deserued to be whipped UDALL. Your plainnesse and your shortnesse please me w. SHAKS. I am neither w. litter'd, nor w. provender'd..nor indeed w. anything'd 1639. The twain had got on very w. together 1877. **4.** The parties know perfectly w...what are the points in dispute 1895. **b.** He being w. known to us all STEELE. **5. b.** She appears moping, but eats very w. 1855. **c.** Carrying my six feet w. 1898.

IV. As an intensive with adjs., numerals, advs., etc. OE.

They were wel at peace, when I did leaue 'em SHAKS. A seemely..tree, and w. worth the hauing 1612. Nor w. alive nor wholly dead they were DRYDEN. You are w. able to settle this affair STEELE. The Captain stood w. to the westward, to run inside the Bermudas 1840. She held her head w. up 1883.

V. 1. As w. as: a. In as good, efficient, satisfactory (etc.) a way or manner as. late ME. **b.** To the same extent, in the same degree, as much, as. late ME. **c.** With weakened force, passing into the sense of 'both..and', 'not only..but also'. late ME. **d.** Used to denote the inclusion of one thing or class with another 1449. **2. As w.: a.** Also, in addition; in the same way ME. **b.** With *may, might*, etc., implying the equivalence or equal result of one action in comparison with another 1440. **3.** With qualifying adv. prefixed, as *too w., pretty w.* OE. **b.** *W. enough*: sufficiently well, adequately. late ME.

2. b. He thought he might as w. strive to promote his own ends 1870. **3. b.** The vulgar translation is known welinough 1585.

VI. Employed without construction to introduce a remark or statement, sometimes implying that the speaker accepts a situation, etc., already expressed or indicated, or desires to qualify this in some way, but frequently used merely as a preliminary or resumptive word OE. **b.** *sb.* An instance of this use of the word 1866.

W., my boy, what have you brought us from the fair? GOLDSM. W., and what of that? 1826. *W., w.*, denoting surprise, resignation, or acquiescence; W., w., you may banter as long as you please STEELE. *Very w.*, denoting agreement, approval, or acquiescence. *W. then*, introducing a conclusion or further statement, or implying that one can naturally be drawn or made.

Comb.: *Well* is extensively employed in comb. with various parts of the vb., esp. the past and present pples., and in parasynthetic adjs. ending in *-ed*. In modern practice the latter are regularly hyphened. The more important are entered as Main words; the following illustrate the wider extent of the use with some indications of date; *well-aimed* CHAPMAN, *-aired* SCOTT, *-apaid* (= satisfied) ME. and mod. dial., *-apparelled* SHAKS., *-applied* SIDNEY, *-appointed* COVERDALE, *-approved* SPENSER, *-armed* ME., *-arrayed* CHAUCER, *-attested* GLANVILL, *-behaved* SHAKS., *-bodied* 1481, *-built* CHAPMAN, *-clad* CAXTON, *-concerted* POPE, *-conducted* 1749, *-considered* 1769, *-covered* 1697, *-cultivated* CONGREVE, *-cut* COWLEY, *-defined* NEWTON, *-deserved, -directed* SIDNEY, *-disciplined* 1595, *-dressed* 1576, *-earned* THOMSON, *-educated* SHAKS., *-endowed* LOCKE, *-established* 1709, *-featured* 1500, *-fed* CHAUCER, *-filled* CHAPMAN, *-flavoured* 1771, *-formed* 1520, *-framed* SIDNEY, *-furnished* 1474, *-governed* late ME., *-horsed* late ME., *-inclined* SIDNEY, *-informed* 1440, *-instructed* 1553, *-intended* SIDNEY, *-intentioned* 1598, *-kept* late ME., *-learned* 1426, *-lettered* ME., *-limbed* LYDG., *-looked* PEPYS, *-looking* STEELE, *-managed* 1665, *-manned* 1450, *-marked* 1797, *-matched* DRYDEN, *-minded* SIR T. MORE, *-mounted* SHAKS., *-mouthed* late ME., *-natured* 1561, *-ordered* SHAKS., *-placed* CHAPMAN, *-pleased* LYDG., *-polished* CHAPMAN, *-practised* SPENSER, *-prepared* SPENSER, *-proportioned* CHAUCER, *-proved* PECOCK, *-regulated, -seasoned* 1583, *-shaped* ME., *-shapen* late ME., *-skilled* SHAFTESB., *-remembered* 1482, *-rooted* CHAPMAN, UDALL, *-sounding* ME., *-spread* 1577, *-stocked* MILTON, *-stored* 1591, *-tasted* COWLEY, *-taught* CHAUCER, *-timbered* SPENSER, *-toned* 1460, *-trained* CHAPMAN, *-trimmed* 1667, *-tuned* COVERDALE, *-watered* 1450, *-weighed* SIDNEY, *-won* SHAKS., *-woven* SPENSER, *-written* 1598.

Such compounds carry even stress (or strong secondary stress on *well-*) when used predicatively, but *well-* bears the main stress in attributive positions.

Well(-)acquai·nted, *ppl. a.* 1565. †**1.** Familiarly known (to others) –1590. **2.** Having a good acquaintance *with* a person or thing; familiar *with.* Also without const. 1728.

1. *Com. Err.* IV. iii. 2. 2. Time was when Love and I were well acquainted W. S. GILBERT.

Welladay (we·lădē¹·), *int.* (*sb.*) Now *arch.* and *dial.* 1570. [Altered f. WELLAWAY, by substitution of DAY, as in *lackaday.*] **A.** *int.* An exclam. expressing sorrow or lamentation; = alas! **b.** redupl. *wella, welladay* 1805. **B.** *sb.* The utterance of this; lamentation, a lament 1582.

Well(-)advi·sed, *ppl. a.* (In mod. use chiefly *predic.*) late ME. **1.** Of persons: Prudent, wary, circumspect. **b.** In one's right mind, sane. SHAKS. **2.** Of actions, etc.: Based on wise counsel or careful consideration 1470.

Well(-)affe·cted, *ppl. a.* 1563. **1.** Favourably disposed, inclined to be favourable or friendly; *spec.* well-disposed towards existing authority, loyal. **2.** Adroitly assumed or simulated 1907.

Well-anea·r, *int. Obs.* exc. *dial.* 1600. [app. altered f. WELLAWAY by substitution of ANEAR.] Alas, alack-a-day!

Wellaway (we·lăwē¹·), *int.* and *sb. arch.* [OE. *weġ lā weġ, wei lā wei,* alteration of *wā lā wā* by substitution of OScand. **wei* for OE. *wā* (see WOE).] **A.** *int.* An exclam. of sorrow or lamentation. **B.** *sb.* The utterance of this; hence, lamentation, a lament ME.

Well-ba·lanced, *ppl. a.* 1629. **1.** Exactly poised or equilibrated. **2.** Having an orderly or harmonious disposition of parts 1859. **3.** Having or betokening a good balance of the mental faculties; sane and sensible; not flighty or eccentric 1861.

Well-being (we·l₁bī·iŋ, we·l₁bī:iŋ), *vbl. sb.* 1613. [Cf. Fr. *bien-être*, Du. *welzijn*, G. *wohlsein.*] The state of being or doing well in life; happy, healthy, or prosperous condition; welfare. **b.** Satisfactory condition (of a thing) 1702.

Most healthy persons feel..a sense of w. after a meal 1883. **b.** His loudly-expressed anxiety.. respecting the..w. of the two bags, the leather hat-box, and the brown-paper parcel DICKENS.

Well-belo·ved, *ppl. a.* and *sb.* late ME. [Cf. Fr. *bien-aimé*, med.L. *bene dilectus.*] **A.** *ppl. a.* **1.** Dearly loved, greatly beloved. **2.** In letters, etc., of a sovereign or lord, prefixed to the names or designations of the persons addressed or referred to. Usu. '(right) trusty and w.' late ME. **B.** *sb.* A dearly loved one. late ME.

A bundle of myrrhe is my welbeloued vnto me *S. of S.* 1:13.

Well(-)born, *ppl. a.* OE. [Cf. Du. *welgeboren*, G. *wohlgeboren* (MHG. *wolgeborn*).] **1.** Of good birth or lineage, of gentle blood. **b.** *absol.* 1787. **2.** [after Fr. *bien-né.*] Having the personal qualities naturally associated with good birth; noble in nature or character 1450.

Well-breathed (-brīðd, -breþt), *a.* 1470. [See BREATHED *ppl. a.* 1.] Sound or strong of wind; exercised so as to be in good wind; not out of breath.

Well-bred, *ppl. a.* 1597. **1.** Of good family and upbringing. Usu., displaying good breeding; having refined manners; courteous in speech and behaviour. **b.** of speech, behaviour, etc. 1699. **2.** Of animals: Of good breed or stock 1815.

Well(-)cho·sen, *ppl. a.* 1586. Carefully or happily selected; esp. of words or language.

A w. Library 1697. The Conversation of a well chosen Friend ADDISON. A w. epithet 1828.

Well-condi·tioned, *a.* 1482. **1.** Of good disposition, morals, or behaviour; right-minded. **2.** Having a good physical condition; being in a sound, healthy, or satisfactory state; *spec.* in *Surg.*, of a wound, etc. 1613. **3.** Established on good terms or conditions 1645.

Well(-)conne·cted, *ppl. a.* 1734. **1.** Linked together in good order or sequence; exhibiting proper sequence or coherence of thought. **2.** Of good family and connections. Also *absol.* 1840.

Well(-)conte·nt, *a. arch.* 1440. Highly pleased, gratified, or satisfied. So **Well-conte·nted** *ppl. a.* 1555.

We·ll-cress. Now *dial.* [OE. *wyllecærse*; see WELL *sb.* and CRESS.] Water-cress, *Nasturtium officinale.*

†Well-dese·rver. 1617. One who deserves well (*of* another) –1709.

Well-dispo·sed, *ppl. a.* late ME. **†1.** In good physical condition; healthy –1716. **2.** Suitably or skilfully placed, arranged, or adjusted 1470. **3.** Of good disposition; *esp.* disposed to be friendly or favourable 1455.

We·ll-doing (we:l₁dū·iŋ), *vbl. sb.* late ME. **1.** The action or practice of doing good; virtuous life and behaviour. **2.** Thriving condition; health, prosperity, success. late ME.

1. Brethren be not weary in well doynge TINDALE 2 *Thess.* 3:13. So **We:ll-do·er. We·ll-do:ing** *ppl. a.* that does good or well; diligent in performance of work or duty; well-behaved ME.

Well(-)done (we·l₁dʌ·n), *ppl. a.* 1449. **1.** Skilfully or rightly performed or executed. **b.** as exclam., expressing approval of what some one has done 1460. **c.** quasi-*sb.* The utterance of this, as an expression of commendation 1628. **2.** Of meat: Thoroughly cooked 1846.

1. *Twel. N.* I. v. 253. **b.** Well done, my dear boy! —O bravo! SMOLLETT.

Welled (weld), *ppl. a.* 1848. [f. WELL *sb.* + -ED².] **1.** Having a well or hollow in the surface. **2.** Having a tank or cistern in which fish are carried or preserved alive 1864.

Welleresque (welərе·sk), **Wellerian** (wеlīᵊ·riăn), *adjs.* 1868. [See -ESQUE, -IAN.] Typical or reminiscent of Sam Weller or his father, two celebrated characters in Dickens's *Pickwick Papers.* So **We·llerism,** a speech or expression employed by or typical of either of these characters.

Well-fa·voured, *a.* late ME. Handsome or attractive in appearance, good-looking. Hence **†Well-fa·vouredly** *adv.* in a w. manner; *iron.*, in ref. to punishment, etc.: severely, soundly. **Well-fa·vouredness.** *Obs.* or *rare.*

Well(-)found, *ppl. a.* 1601. **†1.** Of tried goodness, merit, or value –1887. **2.** Fully furnished or equipped 1793.

1. *All's Well* II. i. 105.

Well(-)fou·nded, *ppl. a.* late ME. Built on a good and solid base; esp. of a belief, statement, etc.: Having a foundation in fact; based on good or sure grounds or reasons.

Well-groomed (grūmd), *ppl. a.* 1886. **a.** *lit.* of a horse 1890. **b.** of persons: Neat and trim, with hair, skin, etc. carefully tended 1886.

Well-grou·nded, *ppl. a.* late ME. Of immaterial things: Based on good grounds; having a good basis or foundation.

No man..can be w. in any branch of learning, who has not been at one of our famous Universities RICHARDSON. To determine whether our fears are w. 1888.

Well-grown, *ppl. a.* 1597. Showing satisfactory or adequate growth.

We·ll-head. ME. [WELL *sb.*] **1.** The place at which a spring breaks out of the ground; the head-spring or source of a stream or river. **b.** *Sc.* A spring in a marsh or morass 1816. **2.** *fig.* The chief source or fountain-head of anything 1542. **3.** The top of a draw-well; also, a more or less elaborate structure erected over this 1613.

We·ll-hole. 1680. [WELL *sb.*] **1. a.** An opening through a floor or series of floors, for staircase, chimney-stack, or for the admission of light, etc. **b.** The space round which the stairs of a winding staircase turn 1823. **c.** A vertical passage-way (for machinery, a lift, etc.); a shaft 1841. **2.** The compartment at the lower end of a ship's pump 1774.

Well-hung, *ppl. a.* 1611. **1. a.** Furnished with large pendent organs (*rare*). **b.** Decorated with rich hangings or tapestry (*rare*) 1667. **2.** Of the tongue: Working readily and freely; glib, fluent 1678. **3.** Suspended or attached so as to hang well 1762. **4.** Of meat or game: Hung up for a sufficient time 1877.

Wellington (we·liŋtən). 1817. [Named after Arthur, first Duke of *Wellington* (1769–1852).] **1.** *attrib.* **a.** *W. boot* = sense 2. 1818. **b.** Used to designate other articles of clothing, as *W. coat, hat, trousers* 1818. **2.** In military use, a high boot covering the knee in front and cut away behind. Also, a somewhat shorter boot worn under the trousers. More recently, a waterproof rubber boot reaching to the knee and worn by women, girls, and children as a protection against rain, etc. 1817. **3.** A variety of cooking apple, large, roundish, and with yellowish white flesh 1821.

Wellingtonia (weliŋtōᵘ·niă). 1853. [f. prec. + -IA¹.] The pop. name in England of *Sequoia* (*Wellingtonia*) *gigantea*, a large coniferous tree, native to California.

Wellingtonian (weliŋtōᵘ·niăn), *a.* 1854. [f. as prec. + -IAN.] Belonging to or characteristic of the Duke of Wellington.

Well-knit, *ppl. a.* 1445. **1.** Firmly conjoined or compacted; closely linked or connected. **2.** Of a person, his frame: Strongly and compactly built, not loose-jointed 1588.

Well(-)known, *ppl. a.* 1470. **1.** Known to many, widely or generally known. **2.** Intimately or thoroughly known 1590.

Well-li·king, *ppl. a. arch.* ME. In good condition and of lusty appearance; thriving, healthy and plump.

They..shalbe fat and wel lyking *Bible* (Great) Ps. 92:13.

Well-lined, *ppl. a.* 1562. Furnished with a good lining. **b.** *spec.* Of a purse: Full of money 1820.

Well-made, *ppl. a.* ME. **1.** Of a person or animal: Well-proportioned, of good build. **2.** Of things: Skilfully fabricated, constructed, or contrived 1530.

Well-ma·nnered, *a.* late ME. **1.** Of good morals –1597. **2.** Having good manners, courteous 1547.

Well-mea·ning, *ppl. a.* late ME. Having or actuated by good intentions; animated by a kindly purpose or friendly disposition.

'Tis the fault of many a w. Man, to be officious in a wrong place DRYDEN.

Well-meant, *ppl. a.* 1476. Rightly, honestly, or kindly intended; said or done with good intention.

Well-near, *adv. Obs.* exc. *dial.* [Early ME. *wel-ner*, f. WELL *adv.* + NEAR *adv.*²] = WELL-NIGH.

Wellness (we·lnės). 1654. [f. WELL *a.* + -NESS.] The state of being w. or in good health.

Well(-)nigh (we·l₁nəi), *adv.* [OE. *wel nēah*, f. WELL *adv.* + NIGH *adv.*] Very nearly, almost wholly or entirely.

Well off, *adv.* and *a.* 1733. **1.** *predic.*, normally without hyphen: **a.** Favourably circumstanced, fortunately situated. **b.** Well provided, having no lack 1800. *esp.* **c.** In easy circumstances, well-to-do 1849. **2.** *attrib.* or *adj.* (with hyphen). In sense 1 c. Also *absol.* 1884.

1. **a.** She was a silly little thing, and did not know when she was well off 1865. **b.** We are well-off for wild-flowers here MEREDITH. **c.** He was rich (or at least certainly well off) 1889.

Well-oiled, *ppl. a.* 1740. Sufficiently lubricated; also *fig.* smoothly expressed; *slang*, in liquor.

I was courteous, every phrase well-oil'd TENNYSON.

Well-prese·rved, *ppl. a.* 1854. (Often used to describe elderly persons who carry their years well.)

Well(-)read, *ppl. a.* 1596. **1.** Well-informed in reading, learned *in* (a subject); also *gen.*, versed or skilled (*in*). **2.** Of a book: Read in a proper, attentive, or profitable way 1865.

Well(-)seen, *ppl. a.* ME. **†1.** Well provided or furnished –1450. **2.** Skilled, versed, proficient *in* (some subject or affair). *arch.* 1528. **†3.** Plainly visible, evident –1725.

Well(-)set, *ppl. a.* ME. **1.** Skilfully, fittingly, or happily placed, arranged, or adjusted. late ME. **2.** Of a person, etc.: Strongly built, firmly knit ME. **b.** Now usu. *well set-up* 1867. **3.** *Cricket.* Said of a batsman who is playing the bowling with ease, and seems unlikely to get out 1880.

Well-spent, *ppl. a.* 1534. **1.** Of time, life: Passed profitably and virtuously. **2.** Expended judiciously or to advantage 1749.

Well(-)spo·ken, *ppl. a.* 1440. **1.** Of a person: Gifted with good or ready speech; courteous and refined in speech. **2.** Of words: Spoken well or with propriety 1592. **3.** With *of*: Favourably mentioned –1538.

We·ll-spring. [OE. *welsprynġ*, f. WELL *sb.* + SPRING *sb.*¹] The source or headspring of a stream; a fountain-head; *fig.* a source of perennial emanation or supply.

Well-te·mpered, *ppl. a.* 1422. †**1.** Having a good bodily constitution –1716. **b.** †Having a well-balanced mental temperament; good-tempered. †**2.** Of climate: Temperate –1628. **3.** Of metal, clay, etc.: Properly tempered 1597.

Well-thought, *ppl. a.* 1579. In comb. with a prep. or adv., as *of, on, upon, out.*

Well-timed, *ppl. a.* 1635. **1.** Occurring, done, or made at a good or fitting time; timely, opportune. **2.** Actuated in regular time or at the right moment 1697.

Well-to-do·, *adj. phr.* 1825. [See WELL *a.* 3.] **1.** Possessed of a competency; in easy circumstances; thriving, prosperous. Also *well to do in the world.* **b.** *transf.* Indicative of easy circumstances, prosperous-looking 1863. **2.** Of an animal or plant: Thriving 1875.

1. It is only idle and w. people who kill themselves 1850. For Corsicans they were w. 1874. *absol.* He has strayed into the paradise of the w. 1851.

Well to live, *adj. phr.* Now *rare. Sc.* and *U.S.* 1579. [See WELL *a.* 3.] Prosperous, well-to-do. **b.** Partly intoxicated 1619.

Well to pass, *adj. phr.* Now *Sc.* 1610. [See WELL *a.* 3.] Well off, well to do.

Well-tried, *ppl. a.* 1449. Often tried or tested with good result; thoroughly tried.

Well-turned, *ppl. a.* 1616. [TURN *v.* II.] **1.** Skilfully turned or rounded 1725. **2.** Of the body, etc.: Symmetrically shaped or rounded 1616. **3.** Of speech: Neatly finished, felicitously expressed 1623.

Well-wa·rranted, *ppl. a.* 1603. Authorized, guaranteed, or approved by good warrant.

Well-wi·lled, *a.* late ME. Now *Sc.* and *north.* Kindly or favourably disposed (*to*).

We·ll-wi·ller. Now *rare.* 1448. One who bears good will or wishes well (to another, a cause, etc.); one who is disposed to be kind or friendly; †one who is addicted or devoted *to* a study. So **We·ll-wi·lling** *a.* (now *rare* or *dial.*) wishing well to another; disposed to be kind or friendly; loyal, well-affected OE.

We·ll-wi·sher. 1590. One who wishes well to another, a cause, etc. So **Well-wish** (now *rare*), an act of wishing well to another; a good wish. **Well-wi·shing** *vbl. sb.* and *ppl. a.*

Well-worn, *ppl. a.* 1621. **1.** Much worn or used; *fig.* trite, hackneyed. **2.** Becomingly carried or displayed 1814.

Well-wrought, *ppl. a.* ME. Well made or fashioned, skilfully constructed or put together. **b.** Of immaterial things, esp. literary or musical composition 1460.

Welsh (welʃ), *a.* and *sb.* [OE. (Angl., Kent.) *Wēlisć, Wǣlisć,* (WS.) *Wīlisć, Wȳlisć,* **Wīelisć,* corresp. to OHG. *wal(a)hisc, walesc* (G. *wälsch, welsch*) Roman, Italian, French, Du. *waalsch* WALLOON, ON. *valskr* Gaulish, French; f. OE. *Walh, Wealh,* corresp. to OHG. *Wal(a)h,* ON. **Valr,* pl. *Valir* :– Gmc. **walχaz* foreign (Celtic or Roman), pl. *-ōs* – L. *Volcæ* name of a Celtic people, of unkn. origin. Cf. WALACH, VLACH.] **A.** *adj.* **1. a.** *orig.* Belonging to the native British population of England in contrast to the Anglo-Saxons. *Hist.* **b.** In later use, belonging to Wales by birth and descent; forming (part of) the native population of Wales. **2.** Of things: Pertaining to Wales or its inhabitants, †or to the British race in Anglo-Saxon times OE. **3.** As the designation of the language of the Welsh people; written or spoken in the Welsh language; of or belonging to the language or literature of Wales 1547.

2. The Pump-room.. crowded like a W. fair SMOLLETT. Yesterday I returned from my Welch journey JOHNSON. Provb. phr. As long as a W. pedigree 1661.

B. *sb.* (Elliptical uses of the adj.) **1. a.** *pl.* The Britons as dist. from the Anglo-Saxons. *Obs.* exc. *Hist.* OE. **b.** The inhabitants or natives of Wales ME. **2.** The Welsh language OE. **b.** *transf.* A strange language; speech that one does not understand 1648. **3.** Short for: Welsh coal 1898.

Collocations: **a.** in the names of various products of, and commodities obtained from, Wales, as **W. coal,** coal obtained from the South Wales coal-fields; anthracite; **W. dresser,** a kind of dresser orig. made on the borders of Staffordshire and Shropshire; **W. flannel,** a heavy variety of flannel with a bluish tinge, made from Welsh fleeces; **W. mutton,** mutton obtained from a small breed of sheep pastured on the W. mountains, highly esteemed for the delicacy of its flavour. **b.** in the names of plants, beasts, insects, etc. indigenous to or found chiefly in Wales, as *W. cattle, pony*; **W. poppy,** a perennial poppy of the genus *Meconopsis.* **c.** in other collocations: **W. ambassador,** the cuckoo; **W. mile,** a distance of a mile and more; a long and tedious mile (chiefly provb.); **W. niece,** a first cousin; **W. onion** = CHIBOL 1; **W. wig,** a worsted cap.

Welsh (welʃ), *v.* 1857. [Of unkn. origin.] *Racing. trans.* To swindle (a person) out of money laid as a bet; also *absol.* or *intr.*

Welsher (we·lʃəɹ). 1860. [f. prec. + -ER[1].] A book-maker at a race-meeting, who takes money for a bet, and absconds or refuses to pay if he loses.

Welsh harp. 1637. Applied spec. to the triple-strung harp; also called *Welsh triple harp.*

†**Welsh hook.** 1593. A bill-hook; a weapon of this form –1694.

Welshman (we·lʃmæ̆n). OE. [f. WELSH *a.* + MAN *sb.*] **1.** †**a.** A native Briton. **b.** A native of Wales. **2.** *U.S.* Applied locally to the black bass (*Micropterus*) and other fishes 1714. So **We·lshwoman,** a woman of Welsh nationality 1442.

Welsh rabbit. 1725. A dish consisting of cheese and a little butter melted and mixed together, with seasoning, the whole being stirred until it is creamy, and then poured over buttered toast.

Welsh rarebit. 1785. [Etymologizing alteration of prec.] = prec.

Welshry (we·lʃri). 1603. [f. WELSH *a.* + -RY; cf. AL. *Wallescheria,* etc. (XIII).] **1.** That part of a town or county (inhabited by English and Welsh) which is appropriated to the Celtic population, as dist. from the ENGLISHRY. **2.** Welsh origin or nationality 1894.

Welt (welt), *sb.* late ME. [The co-existence of forms *walt* and *welt* suggests OE. **wealt,* with Angl. var. **walt,* but the ult. origin is unknown.] **1.** *Shoemaking.* A strip of leather placed between and sewn to the edge of the sole and the turned-in edge of the upper in soling a boot or shoe. **2.** A narrow strip of material put on the edge of a garment, etc., as a border, binding, or hem; a frill, fringe, or trimming 1506. **3.** †A narrow ridge, a raised stripe; spec. in *Nat. Hist.* (now *rare*) 1578. **b.** A ridge in the flesh, esp. the mark of a healed wound; a seam 1800. **4.** In various techn. applications, as a flange on a horseshoe, a strip or fillet laid over a seam or joint or placed in an angle to secure or strengthen it, the ribbed border of a piece of knitting 1770. **5.** A stroke with a lash or pliant stick; also, a heavy blow with the fist 1863. Hence **We·lted** *ppl. a.* furnished with a w. **We·lter** *sb.*[2] a worker who makes or inserts the w. (in a manufactured article). **We·lting** *vbl. sb.* (often *concr.* an edging, a border).

Welt (welt), *v.* 1483. [f. prec.] **1.** *trans.* To furnish (shoes) with welts; to repair or renew the welts of. **2.** To border, hem, or ornament (a garment) with welts or strips of material. Now *rare* or *Obs.* 1489. **3.** *techn.* **a.** To bind with strips or a strip of leather 1795. **b.** *Plumbing.* To join (the ends of a pipe, etc.) by turning the edges one over the other and pressing them together 1888. **4.** To beat, thrash (chiefly *dial.*) 1823.

Welter (we·ltəɹ), *sb.*[1] 1596. [f. WELTER *v.*] **1.** A state of confusion, upheaval, or turmoil. **2.** The rolling, tossing, or tumbling (of the sea or waves) 1849. **3.** A surging or confused mass: **a.** Of material things, persons, etc. 1857; **b.** Of immaterial things 1851.

Welter (we·ltəɹ), *sb.*[3] 1804. [Origin obsc.] **1.** A heavy-weight horseman or pugilist. **b.** *Horse-racing.* Used *attrib.* with the meaning 'for heavy-weight riders', as *w. handicap.* Also *ellipt.* (= w. race, etc.) 1843. **2.** Something exceptionally big or heavy of its kind. *colloq.* and *dial.* 1865.

Welter (we·ltəɹ), *v.* ME. [– MLG., MDu. *welteren.*] *intr.* **1.** To roll or twist the body; to turn or tumble about; to writhe, to wriggle. Now *rare* or *Obs.* **b.** To roll about (*in* the mire, etc.). Now *rare* or *Obs.* 1530. **c.** To roll or lie prostrate (*in* one's blood); hence (hyperbolically) to be soaked with blood or gore; also *fig.* of a nation, etc. Now only *poet.* 1590. **2.** *fig.* **a.** = WALLOW *v.* **2.** *fig.* (now *rare*) 1535. **b.** To be sunk or deeply involved *in* 1629. **c.** *transf.* of inanimate things 1847. **3.** Of a ship, a dead body: To roll to and fro, be tossed about (on the waves); to roll or tumble about (in water). late ME. **4.** To roll down in a stream; to flow. late ME. **5.** Of waves, water: To roll; to toss and tumble; to surge. Now only *poet.* late ME. **b.** *transf.* of a mass of persons or things: To be in a state of turmoil or confusion 1837. **6.** To go with a heavy rolling gait; to flounder 1595.

1. c. Down dropt the Hero, welt'ring in his Gore 1744. **2. a.** Numbers of them lay senslesse and weltring in wine 1611. Those that w. in sin TENNYSON. **3.** He must not flote upon his watry bear Unwept, and w. to the parching wind MILT.

Welter weight. 1825. [WELTER *sb.*[3]] **1.** †**a.** Heavy weight (of a horseman). **b.** A heavy-weight rider 1850. **c.** *Horse-racing.* An extra weight sometimes imposed in addition to weight for age 1880. **2.** A boxer or wrestler whose weight is from 10 st. 7 to 9 st. 9. 1896.

Wem (wem). Now *arch.* or *dial.* [ME., substituted for OE. *wam(m, wom(m,* under the influence of †*wem* vb. (OE. *wemmam*).] **1.** Moral defilement; stain (of sin). *Obs.* exc. *arch.* **2.** Material blemish, defect, injury, or stain. Now *dial.* ME. **3.** Bodily blemish, disfigurement, or defect; also, the mark of a bodily injury, a scar. *arch.* ME.

Wen[1] (wen). [OE. *wen(n, wæn(n* = Du. *wen,* prob. rel. to MLG. *wene,* LG. *wehne* tumour, wart; of unkn. origin.] **1.** †**a.** A lump or protuberance on the body, a wart. **b.** *Path.* A sebaceous cystic tumour under the skin, occurring chiefly on the head. **c.** Applied to the swelling on the throat characteristic of goitre 1530. **d.** An excrescence or tumour on the body of a horse 1559. †**e.** An excrescence on a tree –1791. **f.** *transf.* and *fig.* (occas. applied *spec.* to London) 1597. †**2.** A spot, blemish, stain –1593.

1. f. 2 *Hen. IV,* II. ii. 115. But what is to be the fate of the great w. of all? The monster, called.. 'the metropolis of the empire'? COBBETT. Hence **We·nny** *a.* of the nature of or similar to a w.; afflicted with wens.

Wen[2] (wen). [Kentish var. of OE. *wyn.*] The name of the OE. runic letter ƿ (= w) and of the manuscript form of this (ƿ) in Old and early Middle English.

Wench (wenʃ), *sb.* [ME. *wenche,* clipped form of *wenchel,* OE. *wenćel* :– **waŋkil,* perh. rel. to *wancol* (dial. *wankle*) unsteady, inconstant. For the loss of final syll. cf. EVE *sb.,* GAME *sb.,* MUCH.] **1. a.** A girl, maid, young woman; a female child. Now *dial.* **b.** A girl of the rustic or working class 1575. **c.** As a familiar or endearing form of address. Now only *dial.* or *arch.* 1581. **2.** A wanton woman; a mistress. *Obs.* exc. *arch.* late ME. **3.** A female servant, maid-servant. late ME. **b.** *U.S.* A coloured female servant. *colloq.* 1765.

1. a. Prythee how many Boyes and Wenches must I haue SHAKS. **b.** She was but a milkmaide, and a plaine cuntrie w. 1575. **2.** I am a gentil womman and no wenche CHAUCER.

Wench (wenʃ), *v. Obs.* exc. *arch.* 1599. [f. prec.] *intr.* To associate with common women. Hence **We·ncher. We·nching** *ppl. a.* that habitually associates with common women.

Wend (wend), *sb.* 1786. [– G. *Wende,* pl. *Wenden* (= OE. *Winedas, Weonodland,* OHG. *Winida,* ON. *Vindr*), of unkn. origin.] A member of the Slavonic race now inhabiting Lusatia in the east of Saxony, but formerly extending over northern Germany; a Sorb.

Wend (wend), *v.* Pa. t. and pa. pple. **wended,** †**went.** [OE. *wendan* = OFris. *wenda,* OS. *wendian,* OHG. *wentan* (Du., G. *wenden*), ON. *venda,* Goth. *wandjan* :– Gmc. causative of **windan* WIND *v.*[1]] **I.** *trans.* and *refl.* **1.** †**a.** To alter the position or direction of; to turn (something) round or over –1450. **b.** *Naut.* To turn (a ship's bow or head) to the opposite tack 1556. †2. *refl.* To turn, direct, or betake (oneself) –1635. **II.** *intr.* †**1.** *Naut.* Of a ship: To turn her head about –1704. †**2.** To turn from one condition or form to another; to change *to* or *into* –1579. **3.** To go off, away, or out; to depart. Now *arch.* OE. **4.** To go forward, proceed; to journey, travel; to take one's way. Now *arch.* ME. **5.** *transf.* and *fig.* of things: To move, flow, run (in a specified course or direction) ME. **6.** With advb. acc., esp. *way*: To go or journey in a certain way or direction. Now only *to w. one's way*, a phr. revived *c* 1800. ME.

2. Must not the world w. in his commun course From good to badd, and from badde to worse? SPENSER. **4.** Whither away w. you so late? 1635.

Wendic (we·ndik), *a.* and *sb.* 1861. [f. WEND *sb.* + -IC.] **A.** *adj.* Of or pertaining to the Wends. **B.** *sb.* The language of the Wends, Sorabian.

Wendish (we·ndiʃ), *a.* and *sb.* 1614. [f. as prec. + -ISH, or – G. *Wendisch.*] **A.** *adj.* Of or pertaining to the Wends. **B.** *sb.* The language of the Wends, esp. the Sorabian tongue spoken in Saxony 1617.

Wenlock (we·nlǫk). 1834. Name of a town in Shropshire, used attrib. in **W. formation, group,** a formation of upper Silurian age, typically developed near W. Also **W. limestone, shale, slate.**

Wensleydale (we·nslidēᶦl). Name of a district of the North Riding of Yorkshire, used *attrib.*, and hence *ellipt.* as sb., to designate **a.** A breed of long-woolled sheep orig. raised there; **b.** A local variety of blue-mould cheese.

Went (went). *Obs.* exc. *dial.* ME. [Related to WEND *v.*] A course, path, way, or passage.

Went, orig. pa. t. (and pa. pple.) of WEND *v.*; now used as the pa. t. of GO *v.*

Wentletrap (we·nt'ltræp). 1758. [– Du. *wenteltrap* winding stair, spiral shell.] A marine shell of the genus *Scalaria* or family *Scalariidæ*, esp. *S. pretiosa*.

Were (wīᵊɹ). *Hist.* 1607. [OE. *were* (whence AL. *wera* XII), abbr. of *wer(e)ġild* WERGELD.] = WERGELD.

Were (wē̆ɹ), pa. t. pl. of BE *v.*

Were- (wīᵊɹ). The first element of WEREWOLF used in comb., chiefly with names of animals, to indicate a human being imagined to be transformed into a beast; as *w.-bear*, etc.

Werewolf, werwolf (wīᵊ·ɹ-, wǭ·ɹwulf). Also *Sc.* **warwolf.** [Late OE. *werewulf* = LG. *werwulf*, (M)Du. *weerwolf*, MHG. *werwolf* (G. *wer-, wehrwolf*). The first element is doubtful, but it has been identified with OE. *wer* (= L. *vir*) man.] A person who (according to mediæval mythology) was transformed or was capable of transforming himself at times into a wolf.

Wergeld (wǭ·ɹgeld), **-gild.** *Hist.* ME. [OE. *werġeld*, WS. *-ġild*, in AL. *weregildum* (XII); f. *wer* man + *ġield* YIELD *sb.*] In ancient Teut. and OE. law, the price set upon a man according to his rank, paid by way of compensation or fine in cases of homicide and certain other crimes to free the offender from further obligation or punishment.

Wernerian (wəɹnīᵊ·riăn), *a.* and *sb.* 1811. [See -IAN.] **A.** *adj.* Of or relating to A. G. *Werner* (1750–1817), a German mineralogist and geologist, who advocated the theory of the aqueous origin of rocks; agreeing with Werner's system or theory. **B.** *sb.* A supporter of Werner's theory; a Neptunian 1815.

Wernerite (wǭ·ɹnərəit). 1811. [f. name of A. G. *Werner* (see prec.) + -ITE¹ 2 b.] *Min.* Silicate of aluminium and calcium, the most important member of the scapolite group.

Werowance (we·rowɑns). 1588. [Amer.-Indian.] A chief of the Indians of Virginia and Maryland in old colonial days.

Wertherian (vəɹtīᵊ·riăn), *a.* 1831. [f. G. *Werther*, hero of Goethe's romance 'Die Leiden des jungen Werther' (1774) + -IAN.] Morbidly sentimental and melancholy. So **Wertherism** (vǭ·ɹtəriz'm), morbid sentimentality.

Werwolf: see WEREWOLF.

Wesleyan (we·sliăn, we·zliăn, wezlī·ăn), *a.* and *sb.* 1771. [f. name of John *Wesley* (1703–1791), originator of Methodism + -AN.] **A.** *adj.* Of or pertaining to Wesley or his teachings; belonging to the Wesleyans as a religious organization.

W. Methodist, a member of the society of Methodists as constituted by John Wesley; also *attrib.* passing into *adj.*, of or pertaining to the W. Methodists as an organization. *W. Methodism*, the religious principles, practice, and organization of the W. Methodists.

B. *sb.* A follower of John Wesley; a W. Methodist 1791. Hence **We·sleyanized** *pa. pple.* affected by Wesleyanism.

Wesleyanism (see prec.). 1774. [f. prec. + -ISM.] The system of Arminian theology introduced and taught by John Wesley; the doctrines and church polity of the Wesleyans; Wesleyan Methodism. So **We·sleyism.**

West (west), *adv., sb.* and *a.* [OE. *west* = OFris., OS., OHG. (Du., G.) *west*, ON. *vestr* :– Gmc. **westaz*, f. IE. **wes-*, repr. also in Gr. ἕσπερος, L. *vesper.*] **A.** *adv.* Towards or in the direction of that part of the horizon where the sun sets. **1. a.** With ref. to movement, extension, or direction. **b.** (*a*) *To go w.*, of the sun; also *fig.* to die, perish, disappear. late ME. (*b*) To America, or to the Western States 1839. **2.** With ref. to a place or location OE. **3.** With modifying addition, as *w. by south*, etc. 1577.

1. b. (*a*) All the Lewis guns gone w. 1919. **2.** The Kenet ryseth. . v or vj miles w. of Marleborow 1577. A nice little flat somewhere, not too far w. 1905.

B. 1. quasi-*sb.* = C. ME. **2.** *By w.* †**a.** In the w.; on the w. side –1596. **b.** *Naut.* Indicating certain points of the compass (see BY *prep.* 1 d). late ME.

1. East is East, and W. is W., and never the twain shall meet KIPLING.

C. *sb.* (usu. with *the*). **1.** That one of the four cardinal points which lies opposite the east and at right angles to the north and south; that part of the horizon or of the sky which is near the place of the sun's setting ME. **b.** That quarter which with regard to the speaker or some particular place lies in a westerly direction 1537. **2.** *spec.* **a.** The western part of the world. Now usu., Europe and America as dist. from Asia ME. **b.** The western portion of the Roman world after its division into two empires in A.D. 395. 1577. **3.** The western part of a country, region, or area; *spec.* **a.** of England, Great Britain, Scotland, or Ireland. late ME. **b.** The western states of N. America. (Sometimes dist. as *the Far, Middle W.*) 1829. **c.** The western part *of* a specified country, etc. 1613. **d.** The W. End of London 1823. **4.** *Ch. Hist.* The Catholic Church in the Western Roman Empire and countries adjacent to it; the Roman or Latin church 1586. **5.** The w. wind 1604.

1. Pikes. . never bite more freely, than when the Wind is in the W. 1712. **b.** A Sunny hill. . Back'd on the North and W. by a thick wood MILT. **2. a.** Once did She hold the gorgeous east in fee; And was the safeguard of the w. WORDSW. **5.** As roses, when the warm W. blows, Break to full flower SWINBURNE.

D. *adj.* **1.** Lying towards the w.; situated at or in the w.; western, westerly. late ME. **b.** Of western Europe, as opp. to the east; *esp.* belonging to the Roman or Latin church. Now *rare* or *Obs.* 1553. **c.** Of or pertaining to the w. 1572. **2.** With proper names: **a.**. Denoting the western part of a country, district, etc., or the more westerly of two places having the same name 1470. **b.** Denoting the western division of a race, nation, or people 1561. **c.** With sbs. and adjs. derived from the names of countries, districts, or peoples 1614. **3.** *Eccl.* Situated in or at that part of a church (normally the actual w.) which is farthest from the altar or high altar. late ME. **4.** Facing to the w. 1593.

2. a. The mountainous district of the W. Riding of Yorkshire 1811. **c.** The W. African River Shrew 1877.

Comb.: **w.-bound** *a.* (orig. *U.S.*), travelling to the w. or in a westerly direction; connected with travel in this direction; **-central** *a.* (abbrev. W.C.), belonging to the western half of the central postal division of London; **-land** (chiefly *Sc.*), the western part of a country, *esp.* the W. of Scotland; also *attrib.*; **w. wind,** the (or a) wind blowing from the w.

West (west), *v. poet.* or *rhet.* late ME. [f. prec.] *intr.* To move towards the west. Chiefly of the sun: To draw near to the west, to sink in the west.

West country. late ME. [WEST *a.*] The western part of any country; the district or region towards the west; *spec.* of England or of Scotland. Sometimes *spec.* the south-western counties (Somerset, Devon, etc.) of England.

attrib. Zome honest plain West-Country-mon 1678. A west-country whig frae Kilmarnock SCOTT.

We:st e·nd. [OE. *westende.* In later use f. WEST *a.*] **1.** The western quarter, district, end, or extremity. **2.** *spec. The West End*, that part of London lying westward of Charing Cross and Regent St. and including the fashionable shopping district, Mayfair, and the Parks; also, those living within this area 1807. **3.** *transf.* The fashionable or aristocratic quarter of a town or other place 1823.

Wester (we·stəɹ), *v.* late ME. [f. WEST *adv.* + -ER⁵.] **1.** *intr.* Of the sun, moon, or a star: To travel westward in its course; to draw near the west. **2.** Of the wind: To shift to the west 1580.

Westering (we·stəriŋ), *ppl. a.* 1637. [f. prec. + -ING².] **1.** That declines from the meridian towards the west (chiefly of the sun when it is nearing the western horizon). **2.** That moves in a westward direction. Of the wind: That shifts to the west. 1747.

1. Earthward he slopes again his w. wheels COWPER. Hills. . illumined by the w. sun SOUTHEY.

Westerly (we·stəɹli), *a.* and *sb.* 1577. [f. *wester* adj. + -LY¹.] **A.** *adj.* **1.** Coming from the west. **2.** Situated in or towards the west 1577. **3.** Situated near the western horizon 1801. **4.** Extending towards the west; facing the west. Of motion, etc.: Directed towards the west or the western horizon. 1637.

1. A fine gentle westerlie sea winde blowing 1690. **3.** Till over the w. heaven The shadows of evening had spread SOUTHEY.

B. *sb. pl.* The prevailing w. winds found in certain latitudes 1876.

Westerly (we·stəɹli), *adv.* 1625. [f. as prec. + -LY².] **1.** In a westward direction; towards the west. **2.** (Blowing) from the west 1708.

We·stermost, *a.* 1555. Now *rare* or *Obs.* [f. *wester* adj. (OE. *westra* lying towards the west) + -MOST.] = WESTERNMOST.

Western (we·stəɹn), *a.* and *sb.* [OE. *westerne* adj., f. *west* WEST *adv.*; cf. OS., OHG. *westrōni*. Cf. EASTERN.] **A.** *adj.* **1.** Coming from the west. **2.** Dwelling in the west; *spec.* living or originating in the 'West country' or south-western counties OE. **b.** Of or belonging to the south-western counties 1545. **3.** Having a position relatively west; lying towards or in the west. late ME. **b.** Of or belonging to the west; found or produced in the west 1590. **c.** In the specific names of animals or plants 1784. **4.** Of or pertaining to the Western or European countries as dist. from the Eastern or Oriental 1600. **b.** Of, belonging to, connected with, or characteristic of the Western Church 1699. **5.** With *States*: Constituting the more westerly of the United States of America 1829. **b.** Of or belonging to the W. States 1834. **6.** Directed towards the west; facing westward 1589. **7.** *fig.* Of a person's life or days: Declining 1615. **8.** Hinder, posterior 1829.

1. A westerne milde, and pretty whispering gale 1613. An amazing strong w. current NELSON. **3.** The Sun begins to guild the westerne skie SHAKS. *W. hemisphere*, the hemisphere containing America. **4.** *W. Church*, the Latin as dist. from the Greek or Eastern Church. *W. Empire*, the more westerly of the two parts into which the Roman Empire was divided in 395 A.D.; so *W. emperor*, etc.

B. *sb.* **1.** A member of a Western race; a native or inhabitant of the west, as dist. from an Oriental or Asiatic 1708. **2.** A member of the W. or Latin Church 1860. **3.** *U.S.* An inhabitant or native of the W. States 1846. Hence **We·sternism,** an idiom or expression peculiar to the W. States of America; W. characteristics, practices, etc. 1884.

Westerner (we·stəɹnəɹ). 1837. [f. prec. + -ER¹.] **1.** An inhabitant or native of the Western States of America. **2.** One belonging to a western race, as dist. from an Oriental 1910.

Westernize (we·stəɹnəiz), *v.* 1842. [f. as

prec. + -IZE.] *trans.* To make western in character; esp. to make (an Oriental race or country) Western in ideas, institutions, etc.

We·sternmost, *a.* 1703. [f. as prec. + -MOST.] Farthest towards the west; most westerly.

Westfalite (we·stfăləit). 1896. [– G. *Westfalit*, f. *Westfalisch* WESTPHALIAN, in the name of the original manufacturing company; see -ITE¹ 4 a.] An explosive compound, of which the principal ingredient is ammonium nitrate.

West I·ndia. 1555. †**1.** = WEST INDIES –1648. **2.** *attrib.* Of, pertaining to, or connected with the West Indies 1656.

2. *West India Islands*, the islands lying between N. and S. America.

West-I·ndiaman. 1689. [f. prec. 2.] A vessel engaged in the West India trade.

West I·ndian, *sb.* and *a.* 1584. [f. WEST INDIA + -AN.] **A.** *sb.* †**a.** *pl.* The original inhabitants of the West Indies –1658. **b.** An inhabitant or native of the West Indies, of European origin or descent 1661. **B.** *adj.* Of, pertaining to, situated in, or connected with the West Indies 1611. **b.** In specific names, as *West Indian pike* 1781.

West I·ndies. 1555. [f. WEST *a.* + INDIES.] †**a.** The parts of America first discovered by Columbus and other early navigators. **b.** The West India Islands.

Westing (we·stiŋ), *vbl. sb.* 1628. [f. WEST *adv.* or *v.* + -ING¹.] **1.** *Naut.* The net distance made by a vessel towards the west. **2.** Direction towards the west 1825. **3.** Of winds: The fact of blowing from or shifting to the west 1860.

Westland (we·stlænd). Chiefly *Sc.* 1470. Also **-lin.** [WEST *a.*] The western part of a country. Also *attrib.*

Westminster (we·sᵗmi:nstəɹ). 1549. The name of the City of Westminster in London, the Abbey of St. Peter on the north bank of the Thames, the Palace which was superseded by the Houses of Parliament (hence *allus.* for parliamentary life or politics), the Hall used as a court of justice and for the assembly of divines held in 1643 (hence of the Confession drawn up by them), or to St. Peter's College. **b.** An alumnus of St. Peter's College, W.

West-north-west, *adv.* late ME. In or from the direction situated between west and north-west. Also as *sb.* and *adj.*

Westphalia (westfē¹·liă). 1650. [med.L., f. OHG. *Westfalo* an inhabitant of the district of *Westfalen.*] The name of a province of western Germany lying between Hanover and Rhenish Prussia, used *attrib.* with *bacon, gammon*, or *ham.* Hence **Westpha·lian** *a.* of, belonging to, or connected with W.; *sb.* a native or inhabitant of W. 1604.

Westralian (westrē¹·liăn), *a.* and *sb.* 1896. [f. *Westralia*, telegraphic abbrev. of *Western Australia* + -AN.] **A.** *adj.* Of or pertaining to West Australia. **B.** *sb.* A native or inhabitant of West Australia; *pl.* West Australian mining shares 1896.

West Saxon, *sb.* and *a. Hist.* late ME. [f. WEST *a.* + SAXON *sb.* and *a.*, after OE. *Westseaxan* pl.] **A.** *sb.* **1.** *pl.* The division of the Saxons in England occupying the area south of the Thames and westward from Surrey and Sussex; also *sing.* an individual belonging to this group or area. **2.** The dialect of Old English spoken by the West Saxons 1844. **B.** *adj.* Of, pertaining to, or characteristic of the West Saxons or their speech 1570.

West-south-west, *adv.* late ME. In or from the direction situated midway between west and south-west. Also as *sb.* and *adj.*

Westward (we·stwəɹd), *adv., sb.*, and *a.* [OE. *westweard*, f. WEST *adv.* + -WARD.] **A.** *adv.* **1.** Towards the west; in a westerly direction. **2.** quasi-*sb.* = B. 1697.

1. W. there are people. . whose king hath but one eie HOLLAND. W. to the Sea the Sun declin'd DRYDEN.

B. *sb.* That direction or part which lies to the west of a place, etc. 1652. **C.** *adj.* Having a westerly situation or direction; lying, facing, moving, etc., towards the west 1872. Hence **We·stwardly** *a.* blowing from the w.; moving w.; situated to the w.; *adv.* in or to the w.; in a westerly direction.

We·stwards, *adv.* and *sb.* 1540. [See prec., -WARDS.] **A.** *adv.* = prec. A. 1. **B.** *sb.* = prec. B. Now *rare.* 1574.

Wet (wet), *sb.* [OE. *wǣt* (subst. use of *wǣt* WET *a.*), whence ME. *wēt*, etc., with vowel shortened since XVI after the adj.; partly – OE. *wǣta* sb.] **1.** Moisture; liquid or moist substance. **2.** Rainy or damp weather ME. **b.** Atmospheric moisture precipitated as rain, mist, or dew ME. **c.** Rain, water, or damp regarded as deleterious or detrimental. Also, standing water which collects in pools, or makes the ground muddy. late ME. **d.** (With *pl.*) A burst, storm, or downpour of rain 1440. **3.** Liquor, drink. In mod. use only *slang*. OE. **b.** A drink or draught of some alcoholic beverage; a glass of liquor 1719. **4.** One who is in favour of the sale and consumption of alcoholic liquor; an anti-prohibitionist 1906. **5.** An incompetent or futile person. *slang.*

1. The floor of the staircase was covered with w. and slime 1897. **2.** This distempered messenger of w., The manie colour'd Iris SHAKS. Make haste in out of the w. DICKENS. **c.** All our rations. . being . . saturated with w. 1858. **3.** *Heavy w.*, malt liquor.

Wet (wet), *a.* [From XIV repr. pa. pple. of WET *v.*, repl. *wēt* (mod. dial. *weet*) in standard Eng., from OE. *wǣt, wēt* = OFris. *wēt*, ON. *vátr*, a word of the Anglo-Frisian and Scand. groups, based on the lengthened stem of WATER.] **1.** Consisting of moisture, liquid. Chiefly as a pleonastic rhetorical epithet of water or tears. **2.** Rainy OE. **3.** Of land or soil: Holding water, saturated with water OE. **b.** Of a crop: Grown in a moist or watery soil 1885. **4.** Made damp or moist by exposure to the elements or by falling in water; sprinkled, covered, or permeated with rain, dew, etc. OE. **b.** With prefixed intensive pple., as *wringing, dripping w.* 1500. **5. a.** Suffused with tears; moist with weeping or with being wept upon ME. **b.** Moist or damp with perspiration. late ME. **6.** Made moist or damp by dipping in, or sprinkling or smearing with, water or other liquid. late ME. **7.** Of timber: Full of sap, unseasoned. late ME. **8.** Of paint, varnish, ink: Not yet dry, sticky, liable to smudge 1519. **9.** *Fort.* Of a ditch: Containing water 1590. **10.** Of fish: **a.** Cured with salt or brine 1580. **b.** Fresh, not dried 1851. **11.** Of confections: Preserved in syrup; of a syrupy nature. Of surgical or natural history specimens: Bottled in spirits. 1612. †**12.** Of measure: Used for liquid articles –1638. **13.** *Med.* **a.** Designating certain diseases which are characterized by moist secretions 1565. **b.** Designating various modes of hydropathic treatment, as in *w. compress, pack* 1843. **14.** *colloq.* **a.** Primed with liquor; more or less intoxicated 1704. **b.** Addicted to drink (*dial.* or *slang*) 1700. **c.** *transf.* 1592. **15.** *colloq.* Of a Quaker: Not very strict in the observances of his sect 1700. **16. a.** Consisting of alcoholic liquor; concerned with the sale and consumption of alcoholic liquor 1779. **b.** *U.S.* Permitting the sale of alcoholic liquor; opposed to the prohibition of the liquor traffic 1888. **17.** Designating various technical processes or operations 1800. **18.** *Naut.* Of a vessel: Liable to ship water over the bows or gunwale 1832.

2. Upon Thursday which was a wete day 1461. The wettest spot in England being near Seathwaite in Cumberland 1877. *transf.* Scotland was evidently bent on giving us a w. welcome 1872. 4. I hate to get w. 1861. Mad as a w. hen because I refuse to take his word for it 1918. *W. through, to the skin*, having one's clothes completely saturated. **6.** *W. from the press*, freq. of new-printed matter (newspapers or books). †*With a w. finger*, easily, with little effort. *To come with a w. sail*, to make swift progress, like a ship with sails wetted in order to keep close to the wind. **14. c.** Some of us had a w. night of it, last night 1905. **16. b.** Like a cow-hand with three month's pay hitting a w. town 1919.

Collocations and *Comb.*: **w. bob,** a boy at Eton who devotes himself to boating; **-bulb,** applied to that one of the two thermometers of a psychrometer the bulb of which is covered with muslin, which is wetted at the time of observation; **w. dock:** see DOCK *sb.*³ 4; **w. fly** *Angling*, a fly allowed to sink under the surface of the water; **w. meter,** a gas-meter in which the gas passes through a body of water; **w. plate** *Photogr.*, a sensitized collodion plate exposed in the camera while the collodion is moist; **-shod** *a.* (now *dial.*) having the feet wet. Hence **We·t-ly** *adv.*, **-ness** (OE.). **We·ttish** *a.* somewhat w.

Wet (wet), *v.* Pa. t. **wet, wetted.** [OE. *wǣtan*, f. *wǣt* WET *a.*] **I.** *trans.* **1.** To make (an object) humid or moist by the application of water or other liquid; to moisten, sprinkle, drench, bathe *with* (water, etc.); to dip, soak *in.* **2.** To suffuse with tears, bedew with weeping. Also said of the tears. OE. **3.** To make moist or damp by exposure to rain, by a fall into water, or the like ME. **4.** To get (oneself, one's body or clothes, also another person or object) moist or damp by contact with, or immersion in, water or other liquid ME. **b.** To void urine in (one's bed, clothes) 1767. **5. a.** *To w.* (one's) *whistle, weasand*, etc., to take a drink. late ME. **b.** *To w. the other eye*, to drink one glass after another 1745. **c.** *absol.* To drink alcoholic liquor; to 'liquor *up*' 1840. **d.** *trans.* To accompany (solid or dry food) with liquor 1878. **6.** To celebrate by drinking; to have a drink over 1687. **7. a.** To steep or soak (grain) in water in order to convert it into malt 1695. **b.** To infuse (tea) by pouring boiling water on the leaves. *dial.* 1905.

2. Who wets my graue, can be no friend of mine B. JONSON. **3.** *To wet through, to the skin*, to drench the clothes of (a person); I had been w. to the skin in the afternoon 1775. *To w. one's line*, to start fishing, to fish. *To w. down*, to damp (sails, paper, embers) with water. *To w. out* (Dyeing), to soak in water **6.** He was as Drunk as a Chaplain of the Army upon wetting his Commission 1687.

II. *intr.* **1.** To become wet. Also *to w. through.* ME. **2.** To rain, drizzle. *dial.* 1740. **3.** *Naut.* Of a vessel: To ship water 1875. Hence **We·tter** one who wets; *spec.* one who damps paper to be used in printing.

Wet blanket. 1662. **1.** A blanket that has been drenched in water; esp. one used for quenching a conflagration. **2.** *fig.* **a.** Something that acts as a damper to activity, enthusiasm, or cheerfulness 1810. **b.** A person who has a depressing or dispiriting effect on those around him 1857. Hence **Wet-bla·nket** *v. trans.* to throw a damper on, discourage, depress.

2. b. She would spoil the whole evening: she is such a w.

Wether (we·ðəɹ). [OE. *weþer* = OFris. **wether*, OS. *withar* (Du. *weer*), OHG. *widar* (G. *widder*), ON. *veðr* ram, Goth. *wiþrus* lamb :– Gmc. **weþruz*, of disputed origin.] **1.** A male sheep, a ram; *esp.* a castrated ram. **b.** *transf.* of a man; *spec.* a eunuch 1548. **2.** *Grey wethers*, boulders of hard sand-stone found lying on the surface of the Downs in Wiltshire and Devonshire 1661. **3.** *Comm.* The fleece obtained from the second or any subsequent shearing of a sheep 1879.

1. b. I am a tainted Weather of the flock Meetest for death SHAKS.

Comb.: **w.-gammon,** a leg of mutton; **w.-head,** a sheep's head; *fig.* a stupid person; **w. hog,** a male sheep before its first shearing; **w. sheep** = sense 1.

Wet nurse, we·t-nurse, *sb.* 1620. A woman who is hired to suckle and nurse another woman's child. Cf. DRY-NURSE. Hence **We·t-nurse** *v. trans.* to serve as wet-nurse to; *fig.* to treat tenderly or take under special care, as if helpless.

We've, contracted f. *we have.*

Wey (wē¹). [OE. *wǣġ, wǣġe* balance, weight; see WEIGH *sb.*¹] A standard of dry-goods weight used for cheese, wool, salt, coal, corn, etc., varying greatly with different commodities.

Weymouth (wē¹·məþ). 1766. [Title of the first Lord *Weymouth*, by whom the tree was extensively planted after its introduction to England in 1705.] *W. pine*, the Amer. white pine, *Pinus strobus.*

Wh, a consonantal digraph, normally represents initial *hw* in words of OE. origin; in words of other origin its occurrence may be due to analogy; it sometimes varies with *h* or simple *w*; e.g. *whoop* and *hoop, whelked* and *welked.* Historically OE. initial *hw* represents Gmc. *hw*, under which Indo-European q^w and *kw* were levelled. The normal OE. spelling *hw* was generally preserved in ME. till late in the 13th c.; the modern spelling *wh* is first found in regular use in the *Ormulum.*

In OE. the pronunciation symbolized by *hw* was probably in the earliest periods a voiced bilabial consonant preceded by a breath. This was developed in two different directions: (1) it was reduced to a simple voiced consonant (w); (2) by the influence of the accompanying breath, the voiced (w) became unvoiced. The first of these pronunciations (w) is now universal in English dialect speech except in the four northernmost counties and north Yorkshire, and is that prevailing among educated speakers. The second pronunciation, denoted in this dictionary by the conventional symbol (hw), is general in Scotland, Ireland, and America, and is used by a large proportion of educated speakers in England, either from social or educational tradition, or from a preference for what is considered a careful or correct pronunciation.

The symbol (hw) is used systematically in this Dictionary in the pronunc. of words beginning with *wh*.

Whack (hwæk), *sb. colloq.* 1737. [perh. alt. of THWACK *sb.* Cf. Sc. WHANG *sb.*[1], var. of *thwang* THONG.] **1.** A vigorous stroke with a stick or the like; a heavy resounding blow; also, the sound of this. **2.** A portion, share, allowance; *esp.* a full share, a large portion or amount 1785. **3.** As *int.* or *adv.*: With a w. (in sense 1) 1812.

1. *To have* or *take a w. at* (orig. *U.S.*), to make an attempt or attack upon. **2.** Phr. *To get, have, take one's w. Out of w.*, not in proper condition; disordered.

Whack (hwæk), *v. colloq.* 1719. [Goes with prec. Cf. THWACK *v.*] **1.** *trans.* To beat or strike vigorously, as with a stick, to thrash 1721. **b.** *fig.* To beat in a contest 1877. **2.** *transf.* and *fig.* Substituted for 'put', 'bring', 'get', etc., with implication of vigorous or violent action 1719. **3.** To share, divide (*up*) 1812. Hence **Wha·cking** *vbl. sb.*

Whacker (hwæ·kəɹ). *colloq.* 1823. [f. prec. + -ER[1].] **1. a.** A heavy blow. *dial.* **b.** A driver of animals, a drover. *U.S.* 1880. **2.** Anything abnormally large of its kind; *esp.* a 'thumping' lie; a 'whopper' 1825. So **Wha·cking** *ppl. a.* that is a w.; 'thumping', 'whopping'; often quasi-*adv.* in *whacking big, great.*

Whale (hwēil), *sb.* [OE. *hwæl* = OHG. *wal* (mod. *walfisch*), ON. *hvalr*. The present form reflects obl. cases of OE. *hwæl* which is itself repr. by †*whall* (XIV–XVII), and is parallel to *all*, AWL, *small*.] **1.** Any of the larger fish-like marine mammals of the order *Cetacea*, which have fore-limbs like fins and a tail with horizontal flukes, and are hunted for their oil and whale-bone; in wider (scientific) use, any cetacean of the groups *Mystacoceti* or whalebone-whales, and *Odontoceti* or toothed whales. **b.** With specific names 1755. **2.** Applied to the 'great fish' which swallowed Jonah (*Jonah* 1:17) OE. **3.** *transf.* An object resembling a w.; *Astron.* (with cap.) the constellation *Cetus* 1551.

1. *allus.* Amid a shoal of minnows they..pose as authoritative whales 1914. fig. phr. *A w. on*, having a great capacity or appetite for, very good at or keen on. *A w. of* (colloq., orig. U.S.), 'no end of'. *Very like a w.*, used in ironical assent to an absurd statement (after Shaks. *Ham.* III. ii. 399). **b.** **Right w.**, a whalebone-w., esp. of the genus *Balæna*.

attrib. and *Comb.*: **w.-bird,** any of various birds which inhabit the places where whales are found, or which feed on their oil or offal; (*a*) a petrel of the genus *Prion* or *Procellaria*; (*b*) the turnstone; (*c*) the red or grey phalarope; (*d*) the ivory gull; **-boat,** (*a*) a long carvel-built boat, sharp at both ends, and steered with a rudder or an oar, used in w.-fishing; (*b*) a boat of this kind carried by a large ship as a life-boat; †**-fin,** whalebone, formerly supposed to be the fin of the w.; **-fisher** = WHALER 1; **-fishery; -fishing,** the occupation of taking whales, whaling; **-man** = WHALER 1, 2; **-oil,** oil from w.-blubber; **-shark** (*a*) a very large shark, *Rhinodon typicus*; (*b*) the BASKING-*shark*. Hence **Whale** *v.*[1] *intr.* to engage in w.-fishing.

Whale *v.*[2] Now *U.S. colloq.* 1790. [Of unkn. origin.] **1.** *trans.* To beat, flog, thrash. **2.** *transf. intr.* To do something implied by the context continuously or vehemently 1897. Hence **Wha·ling** *vbl. sb.*[2] (*dial.* and *U.S.*) beating, thrashing.

Whaleback (hwēi·lbæk). 1886. [f. WHALE *sb.* + BACK *sb.*] **1.** = TURTLE-BACK 1. **2.** A kind of steam vessel having a spoon bow and the main decks covered in and rounded over, suggesting the back of a whale 1891. **3.** *Geol.* A large mound of the shape of the back of a whale 1893. **4.** *attrib.* or as *adj.* Furnished with a w.; of the shape of the back of a whale 1891. Hence **Wha·le-backed** (-bækt) *a.* shaped like a whale's back 1879.

Whalebone (hwēi·lbōun). ME. †**1.** Ivory from the walrus or some similar animal confused with the whale; chiefly in phr. *white as whale's bone* –1848. **2.** The elastic horny substance which grows in a series of thin parallel plates in the upper jaw of certain whales in place of teeth; baleen 1604. **3.** A strip of w., esp. used as stiffening in woman's stays, dresses, etc. 1601. **b.** A riding-whip of w. 1842. **4.** *attrib.* as *adj.* Stiffened with strips of w.; made of or containing w.; *fig.* 'stiff', affected 1601.

1. *L.L.L.* V. ii. 332. **2.** A female who is thus invested in W. is sufficiently secured against the Approaches of an ill-bred Fellow ADDISON. **4.** A few words in defence of sacks, long waists, and w. stays MARIA EDGEWORTH.

attrib. and *Comb.*: **w.-tree,** an Australian urticaceous tree, *Pseudomorus brunoniana*; **-whale,** a whale of the family *Balænidæ*, having plates of w. developed from the palate instead of teeth. Hence **Wha·leboned** *pa. pple.* and *ppl. a.* stiffened with w.

Whaler (hwēi·ləɹ). 1684. [f. WHALE *sb.* or *v.*[1] + -ER[1].] **1.** A person engaged in whaling; a whale-catcher. **2. a.** A vessel used in whaling. **b.** = WHALE-BOAT b. 1806. **3.** Anything unusually large of its kind; a 'whacker', 'whopper'. *U.S. slang.* 1860.

Whalery (hwēi·ləri). 1683. [f. WHALE *sb.* + -ERY.] The industry of whale-fishing, or the establishment for carrying it on.

Whaling (hwēi·liŋ), *vbl. sb.*[1] 1716. [f. WHALE *sb.* or *v.*[1] + -ING[1].] The action, practice, or business of catching whales. Also *attrib.* or as *ppl. a.*, as *w. ship, voyage.*

Whang (hwæŋ), *sb.*[1] *Sc.* and *dial.* 1536. [var. of *thwang* THONG.] **1.** = THONG *sb.* **2.** A large or thick slice, esp. of cheese, bread, etc. 1684. So **Whang** *v.*[1] *trans.* to beat as with a thong, to lash; *gen.* to beat, strike, or knock violently.

Whang, *sb.*[2] Chiefly *dial.* 1824. [imit.] A resounding blow or stroke, or the sound of such a blow; a bang. So **Whang** *v.*[2] *intr.* to make a loud resounding noise, as of a heavy blow or explosion; also used advb.

Whangee (hwæŋgī·). 1813. [Chinese *huang* bamboo sprouts too old for eating.] A cane made of the stem of one or other species of *Phyllostachys*, Chinese and Japanese plants allied to and resembling bamboos. Also *w.-cane.*

‖**Whare** (hwā·re, hwǫ·ri, wǫ·ri). Also **ware, wharry.** 1833. [Maori *whare, ware* house.] A Maori hut or native dwelling.

Wharf (hwǭɹf), *sb. Pl.* **wharfs** (hwǭɹfs), **wharves** (hwǭɹvz). [Late OE. *hwearf*, *w(e)arf*, corresp. to MLG. *warf, werf* mole, dam, wharf (whence Du. *werf* shipyard, G. *werft* wharf, shipyard).] **1.** A substantial structure of timber, stone, etc. built along the water's edge, so that ships may lie alongside for loading and unloading. **2.** †**a.** An embankment, mole, or dam –1601. **b.** †The bank of a river; also, a gravel or sandbank 1602. **c.** A place raised or otherwise marked out on which anything is deposited for subsequent removal to another place 1725.

2. b. *Ant. & Cl.* II. ii. 218.

atttrib. and *Comb.*: **w.-boat,** (*a*) *U.S.* a boat supporting a platform and moored at a bank, used as a w.; (*b*) a boat employed about a w.; **-rat,** (*a*) the common brown rat, *Mus decumanus*, which infests wharfs; (*b*) a man or boy who loafs about wharfs, often with the intention of stealing (*slang*). Hence **Wha·rfless** *a.* having no w.

Wharf (hwǭɹf), *v.* 1569. [f. prec.] †**1.** *trans.* To strengthen with a wall of timber or stone –1793. **2.** To discharge at a wharf 1629. **3.** To accommodate (vessels) at a wharf 1902. **4.** *intr.* To come to wharf 1891.

Wharfage (hwǭ·ɹfėdʒ). 1469. [f. WHARF *sb.* + -AGE; in AL. *wharfagium* XIII.] **1.** The provision of or accommodation at a wharf; the stowage of goods on a wharf; the loading and unloading at a wharf. **2.** The charge or dues exacted for the use of a wharf 1535. **3.** Wharf accommodation 1807.

Wharfe (hwǭɹf). 1888. Short for **Wharfedale** (*machine*), a cylindrical printing machine made in Wharfedale in Yorkshire.

Wharfing (hwǭ·ɹfiŋ). 1691. [f. WHARF *sb.* + -ING[1].] A structure in the form of a wharf; materials of which a wharf is constructed.

Wharfinger (hwǭ·ɹfindʒəɹ). 1552. [alt. (cf. HARBINGER, MESSENGER) of **wharfager*, f. WHARFAGE + -ER[1].] An owner or manager of a wharf.

Wharl (hwāɹl), *v.* late ME. [Imitative.] = BURR *v.* 1. Hence **Wharl** *sb.* **Wha·rl-er, -ing.**

Wharrow (hwæ·rou). Now *dial.* 1519. By-form of WHARVE. Also attrib. *w.-spindle.*

Whartonian (hwǭɹtōu·niăn), *a.* 1840. [-IAN.] *Anat.* Discovered or described by Thomas *Wharton*, English anatomist (1610–73).

Wharve (hwǭɹv). [OE. *hweorfa*, corresp. to OS. *hwervo*, OHG. *hwerbo*, f. *hweorfan*, etc. turn, f. Gmc. **χwerƀ-* **χwarƀ-* turn. Cf. WHIRL.] The whorl of a spindle.

What (hwǫt), *pron., a., adv., conj., int.* (*sb.*). [OE. *hwæt* = OFris. *hwet*, OS. *hwat* (Du. *wat*), OHG. *hwaz, waz* (G. *was*), ON. *hvat*, Goth. *hwa* :– Gmc. **χwat* :– IE. **qʷod* (cf. L. *quod*), n. of **qʷos* WHO.] **A.** Interrogative and allied uses. **I.** *pron.* *In direct questions. **1.** As the ordinary interrogative pronoun of neuter gender; orig. sing., in later use also pl.: used of a thing or things. **2.** Of a person (or persons) in predic. use: formerly gen., in ref. to name or identity; in later use only in ref. to nature, character, function, or the like OE. **3.** In rhetorical questions, implying an emphatic contrary assertion OE. **b.** *predic.*, quasi-*adj.* Of what account, consequence, value, or force? OE. **4. a.** With ellipsis, esp. of the remainder of the question; hence (*colloq.*) short for 'What did you say?' or 'What is it?' ME. **b.** Substituted for a word or phr, of which explanation is asked 1676. **c.** As an interrogative expletive, usu. at the end of a sentence, esp. in recent trivial or affected colloq. use 1785. **In dependent clauses. **5.** In indirect questions, and clauses of similar meaning: corresp. to the direct use in 1. OE. **6.** Of a person, in predic. use OE. ***Various special uses. **7.** With intensive additions, as *w. the deuce (devil, dickens), w. in the name of.., w. in the world, on earth*, etc. late ME. **8.** Of quantity, amount, or price: How much, how many. So of the time of day, in *what's o'clock, what's the time.* OE. **9.** *W. for* (introducing a clause); Sc. and n. dial; now in polite colloq. use, only *W...for*, or *W. for?*: For w. purpose, With w. object? Why, Wherefore? ME. **b.** When subordinated *w...for* comes to mean 'the reason why' 1714. **c.** As sb. phr. (slang) in *to give* (one) *w. for*, to inflict severe pain or chastisement 1873. **10.** As indefinite final alternative in a disjunctive question. Chiefly *colloq.* 1766.

1. W. is your broders name? MALORY. W. do you meane by Catholike Religion? 1582. Odd people? and in w. are we so very odd? MISS BURNEY. **2.** W. are these which are arayed in longe whyte garmentes? TINDALE *Rev.* 7:13. W. were they? They were..atheists COWPER. **3.** W. cannot Praise effect in Mighty Minds? DRYDEN. Give a young woman admiration, and w. more can she wish for? 1780. **b.** What's death? You'll love me yet! BROWNING. W. would your assertion be against mine? 1885. **4. b.** 'Your chummage ticket will be on twenty-seven, in the third.'..'My w., did you say?' DICKENS. **c.** Goodbye, Miss Thornton, awfully jolly evening—w.? 1906. **5.** Demaunding of them w. the matter was 1568. More money than he knew w. to do with 1883. **6.** And knowing w. I am, I know w. she shall be SHAKS. Who or w. he was,..no one ever cared to inquire 1854. **9.** W. for should I burn a' my..bukies? 1760. W. are you staring..like that for? 1879. **10.** Have you supposed me dead or w.? 1842.

Phrases. *W. if* (†*W. and, W. an(d if)*..? W. is or would be the case if..? What does it matter if..? etc.; often = 'Suppose..', 'Supposing..'. *W. of..?* w. is to be said of..? What comes of or follows from..? etc. *W. then?* What happens or would happen in that case? W. of that?; so *W. next? W. though..?* W. happens or would happen in view of the fact that..? (implying some opposition between the circumstance mentioned and the possible one implied); also *absol.*, W. if it is (or were) so? W. does it matter? †*W. lack you? W. do you lack?* a salesman's cry; hence as an appelation for an itinerant vendor or pedlar. *W. say you* (*W. do you say*) *to..? W. think you* (*W. do you think*) *of*..? Are you inclined for..? How would you like..? *To know what's what.*, to have a good judgement or apprehension, to know what is fitting or profitable. *To know w. it is*, to apprehend w. it implies or may involve; hence, to have had experience of it; Though I am always serious, I do not know w. it is to be melancholy ADDISON. *I('ll) tell you w.* (†*I know w.*, †*wot you w.*), used to emphasize or call special attention to what is said (= let me tell you), or (*mod. colloq.*) in making a proposal.

Phrases used as sbs. *I know* (or *wot*) *not w.*, *Lord* or *God knows w.* (cf. L. *nescio quid*, Fr. *je ne sais quoi*), something unknown or only vaguely apprehended or suggested; so..*and I don't know w. all* (colloq.) = '..and all sorts of things besides'. *You know w.*, something that need not be specified.

II. *adj.* **1.** As the ordinary interrogative adj., used of a thing or things, a person or persons, in direct questions ME. **b.** In rhetorical questions, implying a contrary assertion. late ME. **2.** In indirect questions, and dependent clauses of similar meaning ME. **3.** In ref. to quality or character: = W. kind of (= L. *qualis*) ME. **4.** In ref. to quantity or amount: How much, how many. late ME. **5.** In predic. use, corresp. to a predic. adj. in a direct statement: usu. referring to quality. = of what kind, character, or disposition ME. **6.** In parasynthetic compounds, as *w.-fashioned* adj. (= of w. fashion). So *w. countryman* (= a man of w. country). 1559.

1. W. impossible matter wil he make easy next? SHAKS. W. good would it do? 1880. **b.** W. hope of refuge, or retreat, or aid? SHELLEY. **2.** *I know not w.*, *Heaven knows w.*, used as adj. phr. = some unknown or undefined.., some..or other; There was present..I knowe not w. poetical preacher 1635. **3.** Þou..askist w. life this man hath had 1445. **4.** Pray thee w. money hast thou brought? 1820. **5.** I see you w. you are, you are too proud SHAKS.

III. *adv.* †**1.** For w. cause or reason? For w. end or purpose? –1677. **2.** In w. way? In w. respect? How? *Obs.* or *arch.* ME. **b.** To w. extent or degree? How much? late ME. **3.** As a mere sign of interrogation, introducing a question. *Obs.* exc. *dial.* OE.

1. W. sit we then projecting Peace and Warr? MILT. **2.** But alas, w. can I helpe you? COVERDALE *Baruch* 4:17. **b.** W. shal it profit vs if we sleen oure brother? WYCLIF *Gen.* 37:26. **3.** *Rom. & Jul.* I. v. 57.

B. Exclamatory and allied uses. **I.** *int.* **1.** As an exclam. of surprise or astonishment (sometimes mixed with indignation) ME. **b.** With intensive additions, esp. in *What ho!* late ME. **2.** Used to hail, summon, or call the attention of a person. *arch.* and *dial.* late ME.

1. W.! no go-to-meeting clothes? 1886. **b.** W. the deuyll! can ye agre no better? SKELTON. **3.** W. ho, thou iollye shepheards swayne, Come vp the hyll to me SPENSER. *Rom. & Jul.* I. iii. 3, 4.

II. *adj.* Used to express the surprising or striking nature of the thing(s or person(s denoted by the sb.; in *sing.* now always followed by indef. art., exc. with sb. in collective or abstract sense ME. **b.** In dependent clauses, after vbs. of thinking or perceiving ME.

W. a piece of worke is a man! SHAKS. W. shocking times we live in! 1798. **b.** You cannot imagine w. a parcel of cheating brutes the work people here are 1708.

C. Relative and allied uses. **I.** *pron.* **1.** That which, the thing which ME. **b.** In ref. to a prec. sb., esp. after *but, except, than, like*, etc., with quasi-adj. force: The one which; chiefly as *pl.* those which 1597. **2. a.** So much (or many) as, as much as 1646. **b.** Such as; the kind of thing (or person) that 1658. **c.** Expressing parallel relation or correspondence 1673. **3. a.** In a parenthetic phr. (chiefly with *call*) qualifying a following word or phr.; equivalent to an adj. phr., or to a following phr. with *as* 1697. **b.** Introducing a prefatory (usu. parenthetic) qualifying clause, equivalent to a following clause with *which* 1697. **4.** = WHATEVER 2 a. ME. **5.** *But w.* (after a negative expressed or implied): except w. (or who); which (or who)..not 1596. **b.** *loosely* as conj. phr.: But that, that..not *colloq.* 1662. **6.** Redundantly after *than* introducing a clause. *dial.* or *vulgar.* 1818. **7.** As simple relative (*sing.* or *pl.*): Which (or who); that. Now *dial.* or *vulgar.* ME.

1. He..abetted them in w. they did MILT. **b.** *The Usurper*, which is no good play, though better than w. I saw yesterday PEPYS. All fevers, except w. are called nervous 1824. **2. a.** Their service was six biscuits a-piece, and w. they pleased of burnt claret PEPYS. **c.** Intellect is to the mind w. sight is to the body BERKELEY. **3. a.** I..am still w. men call young 1856. **b.** She wore, what was then..unusual, a coat, vest, and hat resembling those of a man SCOTT. **4.** Twelfe Night, Or w. you will SHAKS. It may have been murdered, for w. I can tell SCOTT. *W. else*, orig. ellipt. = whatever else there may be; hence, anything else, anything and everything; 3 *Hen. VI*, III. i. 51. **5.** Padua affords nothing but w. is kinde SHAKS. **b.** Not but w. many changes had been wrought 1894. **7.** To tell that w. ye see needs not SPENSER. Long Forster, w. walked to Colne and back before breakfast 1842.

II. *adj.* **1.** That (or those)..which (or who); such..as; so much (or many)..as ME. **2.** Any..which (or who), any..that. Now only in certain collocations. late ME. **b.** Followed by *ever, so, soever, somever* (now only, exc. with *soever*, immediately following: see WHATEVER, etc.) ME. **c.** Usu. with *soever*, in indef. (non-relative) sense: = WHATEVER 4. 1597. **3.** *W. time*, as conj. phr.: At the time at which; when; whenever ME.

1. I will peece out the comfort with what addition I can SHAKS. **2.** Spirits..Assume w. sexes and w. shapes they please POPE. **c.** I loue thee not a Iarre o' th' Clock, behind W. Lady she her Lord SHAKS. Things of w. Nature or Value soever 1736.

D. Indefinite (non-relative) uses. †**I.** *pron.* Something; anything; only OE. exc. in phrases in which *w.* is qualified by a quantitative or identifying word –1596.

They..gaue him for to feed Such homely w., as serues the simple clowne SPENSER.

II. *adv.* or *conj.* Introducing (*a*) each, or (*b*) only the first, of two or more alternative or coordinate words or phrases. Now *rare.* ME. **b.** Introducing advb. phrases formed with preps., implying 'in consequence of, on account of; in view of, considering' ME.

(*a*) Seven Children at the least (w. Male w. Female) were brought forth 1693. (*b*) They rode so long w. night and day 1523. **b.** W. with hunting, fishing,..and bad weather, the progress..was..slow 1867.

E. Substantival nonce-uses. **1.** The question 'W.?', 'W. is it?', or the like, or the answer to such question; the essence or substance of the thing in question 1656. **2.** A something 1654. **3.** An instance of the exclam. 'What!' 1779.

1. My lady will know all the w. and the why 1844. **2.** We are not seeking a W.; we are seeking a Whom 1903.

What-d'ye-call-'em, -her, -him, -it (hwǫ·tdyə-, wǫ·tʃəkǭləm, etc.) *colloq.* 1639. An appellation for a thing or person whose name the speaker forgets, does not know or wish to mention, or thinks not worth mentioning. Also in contracted forms, as **†whatd'ecalt, †what-sha-callum**, etc.; so **what-ye** (or **-you**) **-call** (**-it**, etc.).

There is no What 's-his-name but Thingummy, and What-you-may-call-it is his prophet! DICKENS.

Whatever (hwǫtˌe·vəɹ), *pron.* and *a.* Also *poet.* **whate'er** (hwǫtˌēə·ɹ). ME. [WHAT C. II. 2 b.] **1.** *interrog.* (prop. as two words.) Emphatic extension of *what*, implying perplexity or surprise. Now *colloq.* **2.** As compound relative. **a.** *pron.* Anything at all which, anything that; sometimes (esp. *poet.*), all that, everything that. late ME. **b.** *adj.* Any..at all which (or who), any..that; occas. (*poet.*), all or every..that. late ME. **3.** Introducing a qualifying dependent clause, often with vb. in subjunctive: **a.** *pron.* = 'No matter what'; frequently = 'Notwithstanding anything that' ME. **b.** *adj.* 1561. **4.** As indefinite adj. or pron., with loss of the relative force: Any (thing)..at all. late ME.

1. W. can you want to emigrate for? 1880. **2. a.** Being mou'd he strikes, whatere is in his way SHAKS. **3. a.** Take no repulse, what euer she doth say SHAKS. W. the defects of American universities may be, they disseminate no prejudices DICKENS. **b.** Money, in w. hands, will confer power JOHNSON. **4.** If thence he scape into what ever world, Or unknown Region MILT. I know nothing w. of Mr. Jellyby DICKENS.

What-like, *interrog. a. arch.* and *dial.* 1821. [orig. Sc., f. WHAT *pron.* + LIKE *a.*, as in '*What is he like*?', after SUCH-LIKE.] Of what appearance or aspect. (Usu. predic.)

Whatman (hwǫ·tmăn). 1880. [From the name of the maker.] In full *W. paper*: A kind of paper used for drawings, engravings, etc.

Whatness (hwǫ·tnės). 1611. [f. WHAT *pron.* + -NESS; tr. med.L. *quidditas.*] = QUIDDITY 1.

What(-)not (hwǫ·tnǫt). 1540. [prop. ellipt. interrog. phr.] **1.** Usu. as two words (hwǫ·t nǫ·t): Anything whatever; everything; 'all sorts of things'; now only as final item of an enumeration: = various things besides. **b.** A thing or person that may be variously named or described (*rare*) 1602. **2.** An article of furniture consisting of an open stand with shelves one above another, for keeping or displaying various objects 1808.

1. *Tam. Shr.* V. ii. 110. Fencing, dam-making, cattle-droving, what not 1890.

What's-his-name (hwǫ·tsʰiznēⁱm). *colloq.* 1697. Substituted for the name of a man or boy (loosely, of a thing) which the speaker forgets, does not know, or is unwilling to mention. So **What's-her-name, What's-its-name, What's-your-name**; also in ambiguous form, **Whatsename.**

Whatso (hwǫ·tsoᵘ), *pron.* and *a. arch.*, chiefly *poet.* [ME. *what so, what se*, reduced f. OE. *swā hwæt swā*.] = WHATEVER 2 a, b, 3a, b, 4.

Whatsoever (hwǫ·tsoᵘe·vəɹ), *poet.* **whatsoe'er** (hwǫtsoᵘēə·ɹ), *pron.* and *a.* ME. [f. prec. + EVER *adv.*] = WHATEVER 2 a, b, 3 a, b, 4 (as adj.). †**b.** *pron.* Whoever –1628.

W. ye axe in my name, that will I do TINDALE. *John* 14:13. W. thyngs are true, w. thyngs are honest,..those same haue ye in youre minde TINDALE *Phil.* 4:8. I woll not be dyspleased what so euer thou sayest 1533. In w. shape he lurk, of whom Thou telst MILT. In every circumstance of government and legislation w. 1792. **b.** *Twel. N.* I. iii. 124.

Whatsomever (hwǫtsǒme·vəɹ), *pron.* and *a. Obs.* exc. *dial.* ME. [f. WHAT *pron.* + SOMEVER; see -SOME³.] = WHATEVER 2 a, b, 3 a, b, 4 (as adj.). †**b.** = prec. b. –1601.

b. What somere he is He's brauely taken heere SHAKS.

Whaup (hwǭp, hwāp). 1538. *Sc.* and *north.* [perh. for **whalp*, and allied to OE. *huilpe* :– **χwalpjō*, f. **χwalp-*, **χwelp-*, a stem imitative of the bird's cry.] The larger curlew, *Numenius arquata.*

Wheal (hwīl), *sb.* 1808. [var. of WALE *sb.*¹ 1 due to assoc. with †*wheal* suppurate, OE. *hwelian*; cf. WHELK².] **a.** = WEAL *sb.*² 1811. **b.** *Med.* A flat, usu. circular, hard elevation of the skin, esp. that characteristic of urticaria 1808. **c.** *gen.* A ridge 1855. So **Wheal** *v. trans.* to mark with wales or weals 1698.

Wheat (hwīt). [OE. *hwǣte* = OS. *hwēti* (Du. *weit*), OHG. *weizi* (also *weizzi*, whence G. *weizen*), ON. *hveiti*, Goth. *hwaiteis* :– Gmc. **χwaitjaz*, f. var. of **χwit-* WHITE.] **1.** The grain of a cereal (see sense 2), furnishing a meal or flour which constitutes the chief breadstuff in temperate countries. **2.** The cereal plant (closely related to barley and rye) which yields this grain, esp. common wheat, *Triticum vulgare* (*sativum*). OE. **3.** *pl.* Wheat-plants; crops of wheat; kinds of wheat 1795.

2. When wheate is greene, when hauthorne buds appeare SHAKS.

attrib. and *Comb.*, as *w.-bread, -crop, -flour, -harvest*; **w.-corn,** a grain of w.; **-duck,** the Amer. widgeon, *Mareca americana*, found in flocks in w.-fields; **-grass,** any of various species of the genus *Triticum*, esp. couch-grass, *T. repens*; **-land,** land on which w. is grown, or suitable for growing w. on.

Wheatear¹ (hwī·tˌiᵊɹ). late ME. [EAR *sb.*²] An ear of wheat.

Wheatear² (hwī·tˌiᵊɹ). 1591. [app. orig. *wheatears* for **whiteeres*, f. *whit-* WHITE *a.* + *eeres, ers* ARSE, in allusion to the bird's white rump.] A small passerine bird, *Saxicola œnanthe*, widely distributed over the Old World, having a bluish-grey back, white belly, rump, and upper tail-coverts, and blackish wings.

Wheaten (hwī·t'n), *a.* Now *rare.* [OE. *hwǣten*; see -EN⁴.] **1.** Composed of the grain or flour of wheat. **2.** Of or belonging to wheat as a plant; made of the stalks or straw of wheat OE.

Wheatmeal (hwī·tmīl). [OE. *hwǣtemelu*; see MEAL *sb.*¹] Meal or flour of wheat.

Wheatstone (hwī·tstən). 1872. [Called after Sir Charles *Wheatstone*.] Short for

Wheatstone('s bridge: an apparatus for measuring electrical resistances.

Wheedle (hwī·d'l), *v.* 1661. [prob. a canting term, perh. – G. *wedeln* fawn (upon), cringe or crouch (to), f. *wedel* tail, fan.] **1.** *trans.* To entice or persuade by coaxing or cajolery; to bring into a specified condition by such action. **2.** To do (a person) *out of* a thing, or to get (a thing) *out of* a person, by such action 1670. **3.** *absol.* or *intr.* To use soft flattering words; (of an animal) to fawn 1664.

1. Smooth words he had to w. simple souls WORDSW. How to w. a man into ordering something he doesn't want DICKENS. Hence **Whee·dle** *sb.* (now *rare*) an act or instance of wheedling, wheedling speech; †a wheedler.

Wheel (hwīl), *sb.* [OE. *hwēol, hwēogol, hweowol* = (M)LG. *wēl*, (M)Du. *wiel*, ON. *hjól, hvél* :– Gmc. *χwe(ʒ)ula, *χweχula :– IE. *qʷeqʷlo-, repr. by Skr. *cakrá-* circle, wheel, Gr. κύκλος CYCLE, redupl. of *qʷelo- *qʷolo move around, repr. by Gr. πόλος axis, L. *colus* distaff.] **I.** A circular frame of wood, metal, or other hard substance (sometimes in the form of a solid disc, but usu. of a ring (*rim* or *felloe*) with spokes radiating from the central part or *nave*) attached or capable of being attached at its centre to an axle around which it revolves. **a.** In a vehicle, etc., each of two or more such appliances which support it and, by rolling upon the ground or other surface, enable it to move along with the least possible friction. **b.** *gen.*, in machinery or mechanical apparatus of any kind OE. **c.** With prefixed defining words indicating kind, use, etc., as COG-W., DRIVING-W., FLY-W., etc.

a. *At* or *in the w.*, of horses, next to the carriage, in the place of the wheelers. *On the w., on wheels*, riding in wheeled vehicles. **b.** Some wheels were taken off. .so the Clock was spoild 1616. *W. and axle*, one of the mechanical powers (see POWER III. 2). **c.** *Fifth w.*; see FIFTH *a.* *Idle w.*: see IDLE *a.* 5.

II. A wheel or wheel-like structure, or an instrument or appliance having a wheel as its essential part, used for some specific purpose. **1.** A large wheel, or a contrivance resembling one, used as an instrument of torture or punishment OE. **2.** Various mechanical contrivances. **a.** The revolving part of a turning-lathe, or of a potter's lathe. late ME. **b.** = MILL-W. late ME. **c.** = SPINNING-W. 1467. **d.** = TREAD-W.; also, a treadmill 1623. **e.** = PERAMBULATOR 2. 1696. **f.** = GRINDING-*w.* 1707. **g.** *Naut.*, etc. = STEERING-*w.* 1743. **h.** = PADDLE-W. 1842. **3.** In full *w. of fortune* = LOTTERY-*w.* 1698. **4. a.** A rotatory firework in the form of a w. 1629. **b.** *W. of colour* = CHROMATROPE 1877. **c.** *W. of life* = ZOETROPE 1872. **5.** orig. and esp. *U.S.* A bicycle or tricycle; also, the practice of riding on one, cycling 1884.

1. *To break on the w.*: see BREAK *v.* II. 1.

III. Something resembling a w. **1.** An object having the form or figure of a w.; a circle, or something circular OE. **2.** The celestial sphere or firmament, or one of the spheres of the planets, etc. in the ancient astronomy, regarded as revolving like a w. *Obs.* or only *fig.* ME. **3.** *techn.* One of the wards of a lock, which are rotated by the key 1784. **IV.** *fig.*, *allus.*, etc. **1. a.** The w. which Fortune is fabled to turn, an emblem of mutability OE. **b.** With allusion to the wheels of the chariot of the Sun. *poet.* 1557. **2.** In direct fig. use from I. 1, esp. in ref. to the course or sequence of events, procedure, the passage of time ME. **3.** With allusion to sense I. 1 b, denoting a constituent part of something figured as a machine 1625. **4.** *fig.* A reiterated or recurring course of actions, events, or time; an endless round or cycle ME. **5.** A movement like that of a w. **a.** A movement in a circular or curved course; a revolution 1604. **b.** A movement about an axis or centre; *spec.* (*Mil.*) such a movement of a rank or body of troops about a pivot (PIVOT *sb.* 2) 1660. **6.** *Prosody.* A set of short lines forming the concluding part of a stanza, usu. five in number (also *bob and w.*) 1838.

1. Turn, Fortune, turn thy w. and lower the proud TENNYSON. **2.** To oyl the Wheels of Mens utmost Endeavours 1675. *On wheels*, with rapid and continuous movement or action; *to go* or *run on wheels*, to go smoothly or swiftly, make good progress; (joc., of a clock) to go too fast or irregularly. **3.** *Wheels within wheels* (after *Ezek.* 1:16), a complexity of forces or influences; a complication of motives, designs, plots, etc. **5.** Satan. .Throws his steep flight in many an Aerie wheele MILT.

Comb. **w.-animal, -animalcule** = ROTIFER; **-back,** a back resembling a w., characteristic of chairs made by Hepplewhite about 1775; **-base,** the distance between the points of contact of the front and back wheels of a vehicle with the ground or a rail; **-carriage,** a carriage moving on wheels, a wheeled vehicle; also as part of a machine; **-chair,** a chair with wheels, *esp.* a Bath chair; **-guard,** (*a*) a circular guard on a sword or dagger; (*b*) a guard to protect a w. (or adjacent parts) from dirt or injury; **-horse,** a horse harnessed between the shafts of a vehicle, next to the wheels, as dist. from a *leader*; **-house,** (*a*) a structure enclosing a large w.; *spec.* a pilot-house; (*b*) a building in which cart-wheels are stored; **-lock,** a form of gun-lock in which the powder was fired by the friction of a small w. against a piece of iron pyrites; **-man,** (*a*) a man who attends to a w.; *U.S.* a helmsman; (*b*) a man who rides a bicycle or tricycle (*colloq.*); **-pit,** a space enclosed by masonry for a large w. to turn in; **-tracery,** tracery radiating from a centre, as in a **w.-window,** a circular window with mullions radiating from the centre like the spokes of a w.; **-work,** a set of connected wheels forming part of a machine or mechanical contrivance. Hence **Whee·lage** (*Hist.*) a toll paid for the passage of a wheeled vehicle; cost of carriage in a wheeled vehicle. **Wheeled** (hwīld, *poet.* hwī·lėd) *a.* furnished with a w. or wheels; effected on wheels or by wheeled vehicles. **Whee·ly** *a. rare*, of or pertaining to a w.

Wheel, *v.* ME. [f. prec.] **I.** To move like a wheel. **1.** *intr.* To turn or revolve about an axis or centre, like a wheel on its axle; to rotate, to whirl. **b.** To reel, as from giddiness; to be affected with giddiness 1593. **2.** *trans.* To turn (something) on or as on a wheel; to cause to revolve about an axis, or to move in a circle or cycle. late ME. **3.** *intr. Mil.* Of a rank or body of troops: To turn, with a movement like that of the spokes of a wheel, about a pivot (PIVOT *sb.* 2), so as to change front 1579. **b.** *trans.* To cause to turn in this way 1634. **4.** *intr.* To turn so as to face in a different direction; to turn round or aside, esp. quickly or suddenly 1639. **b.** *trans.* To cause to turn round or aside 1805. **5.** *intr.* To move like a point in the circumference of a wheel; to move in a circle, spiral, or similar curve. *poet.* 1600. **b.** *trans.* To cause (something) to move in this way; to perform (a movement), trace (a course) in this way. *poet.* 1725. **6.** *intr.* To roll along like a wheel (*rare*) 1667.

4. *fig.* Who had wheeled from his Loyalty during the War 1663. **5.** The gulls that w. and dip around me DICKENS. **b.** Save where the beetle wheels his droning flight GRAY.

II. To move on or by means of wheels. **1.** *trans.* To convey in a wheeled vehicle or on a chair, etc. moving on wheels 1601. **2.** *intr.* To travel in or drive a wheeled vehicle; to go along on wheels, as a vehicle 1721. **3.** *trans.* To push or draw (something) on wheels 1784.

3. The other man. .had a bad puncture and was wheeling his machine 1896.

III. 1. *trans.* To make like a wheel; to give a circular or curved form to (*rare*) 1656. **2.** To furnish with a wheel or wheels 1661.

Wheelbarrow (hwī·lbæːrōᵘ). ME. [See BARROW *sb.*³] A barrow or shallow open box mounted between two shafts that receive the axle of a wheel at the front ends, the rear ends being shaped into handles and having legs on which it rests; also, a similar contrivance with more than one wheel.

Wheeler (hwī·ləɹ). 1497. [f. WHEEL *sb.* and *v.* + -ER¹.] **1.** A wheelwright. **2.** A wheel-horse or other draught-animal in the same position 1813. **3.** Something, as a vehicle, boat, etc., furnished with a wheel or wheels; chiefly in comb., as FOUR-W. 1886. **4.** One who wheels a vehicle, or conveys something in a wheeled vehicle 1683. **5.** *Mil.* The man at the outermost end of the rank in wheeling 1798.

Wheelerite (hwī·lərəit). 1874. [f. name of Lieut. G. M. *Wheeler*, of the U.S. Army; see -ITE¹ 2 b.] *Min.* A yellowish fossil resin occurring in lignite in the cretaceous strata of New Mexico.

Wheelwright (hwī·lrəit). ME. [See WRIGHT.] A man who makes wheels and wheeled vehicles.

Ween (hwīn), *a.* and *sb. Sc.* and *n. dial.* late ME. [repr. OE. *hwêne* in some degree, instr. case of *hwōn* a few.] (A) few.

Wheep (hwīp). 1891. [imit.] A long-drawn sound of a steel weapon drawn from its sheath.

Wheeze (hwīz), *sb.* 1834. [f. next.] **1.** An act of wheezing; a whistling sound caused by difficult breathing; *transf.* a sound resembling this. **2.** orig. *Theatr. slang.* A joke or comic gag introduced into a performance by a clown or comedian; hence (*slang* or *colloq.*) a catch phrase constantly repeated; a trick or dodge frequently used 1864.

Wheeze (hwīz), *v.* 1460. [prob. – ON. *hvæsa* to hiss. (Not conn. w. OE. *hwōsan* to cough, dial. *hoose*.)] **1.** *intr.* To breathe hard with a whistling sound from dryness or obstruction in the throat, as in asthma. **b.** *transf.* To make a similar sound 1854. **2.** *trans.* To utter with a sound of wheezing 1849. Hence **Whee·zer** one who wheezes; *esp.* a broken-winded horse.

Wheezy (hwī·zi), *a.* 1818. [f. WHEEZE *sb.* + -Y¹.] Characterized by wheezing; resembling a wheeze. Also *transf.*

A lean, w. old clock 1859.

Whelk¹ (hwelk). [OE. *weoloc, wioloc*; cf. WFlem. *willok, wullok*. The sp. with *wh-* (XV) is perh. due to assoc. with next.] A marine gasteropod mollusc of the genus *Buccinum*, having a turbinate shell, esp. *B. undatum*, much used for food.

Whelk² (hwelk). [Late OE. *hwylca*, rel. to ME. *whele* pustule, OE. *hwelian* suppurate. See WHEAL *sb.*] **1.** A pustule, pimple. **2.** Used by confusion for WEAL *sb.*² 1761.

1. His face is all bubukles and whelkes SHAKS.

Whelked, welked (hwelkt, welkt), *ppl. a.* 1560. [f. WHELK¹ + -ED².] **1.** Formed like a whelk; twisted, convoluted, or ridged like the shell of a whelk. **2.** Marked with ridges on the flesh; waled, wealed 1727.

Whelm (hwelm), *sb.* 1576. [f. next.] **1.** A wooden drain-pipe; orig. a tree-trunk halved vertically, hollowed, and turned with the concavity downwards to form an arched water-course. Now *dial.* **2.** The overwhelming surge of waters *poet.* 1842.

Whelm (hwelm), *v.* [ME. *whelme*, repr. OE. **hwelman*, parallel to synon. OE. *hwylfan*, mod. dial. *whelve*.] **1.** *trans.* To turn (a hollow vessel) upside down, or *over* or *upon* something so as to cover it. Now *dial.* **b.** To throw (something) over violently or in a heap upon something else, esp. so as to cover or to crush or smother it 1624. †**2.** *intr.* (*poet.*) To come or pass over something so as to cover it –1700. **3.** *trans.* **a.** To cover completely with water or other fluid so as to ruin or destroy; to submerge, drown 1555. **b.** To bury under a load of earth, snow, or the like 1555. **4.** *transf.* To engulf or bear down like a flood, storm, avalanche, etc.; hence, to involve in destruction or ruin 1553.

2. The Waves whelm'd over him DRYDEN. **3. a.** *Merry W.* II. ii. 143. **4.** Sorrow whelm'd his soul COWPER.

Whelp (hwelp), *sb.* [OE. *hwelp* = OS. *hwelp* (Du. *welp*), OHG. *hwelf*, (also mod.) *welf*, ON. *hvelpr*; a Gmc. word of which no cogns. are known.] **1.** The young of the dog. (Now mostly superseded by *puppy*.) **2.** The young of various wild animals, *esp.* and now only (chiefly as a literary archaism) of such as the lion, tiger, bear, and wolf, to the young of which the name *cub* is usu. applied OE. **3. a.** Applied to the offspring or young of a noxious creature or being ME. **b.** An ill-conditioned or low fellow; later, a saucy or impertinent young fellow, a 'puppy' ME. **4.** *Naut.* One of the longitudinal projections on the barrel of a capstan or the drum of a windlass ME.

2. *fig.* 1 *Hen. IV*, III. iii. 167. **3. a.** The Son,. . A frekelld whelpe, hagborne SHAKS.

Whelp (hwelp), *v.* ME. [f. prec.] **1.** *trans.* To bring forth (a whelp or whelps). **b.** *transf.* and *fig.* To bring forth: often *contempt.* 1581. **2.** *intr.* To bring forth whelps. late ME.

1. b. Having whelped a prologue with great pains COWPER.

When (hwen), *adv.* (*conj.*, *sb.*) [OE. *hwenne, hwænne*, beside *hwanne, hwonne*, corresp. to OFris. *hwanne, hwenne* until, if, OS. *hwan(na* when, OHG. *wenne, wanne* (G. *wenn* if, *wann* when), Goth. *hwan* when, how, advb. deriv. of the interrog. base **χwa-* WHO, WHAT, as THEN, THAN of the demonstr. **þa* THE, THAT; cf. Av. *kəm* how, L. *quom, cum* when, OIr. *can*, W. *pan* when.] **I.** *interrog.* **1.** In a direct question: At what time? on what occasion? Sometimes passing into the sense: In what case or circumstances? †**b.** *ellipt.* as exclam. of impatience –1623. **2.** In a dependent question or clause: At what time; on what occasion; in what case or circumstances. Also *ellipt.* OE. **3.** After a prep.: = What time? (Cf. Fr. *depuis quand*, G. *seit wann.*) ME.

2. To know w. to speake, and w. to be silent 1676. I haven't seen such food I don't know w. 1888. *Say w.*, colloq. formula used by a person pouring out a drink for another, to ask him to say when he shall stop. **3.** Since w. have you missed her? 1861.

II. Relative and conjunctive uses. **1.** As compound relative, or as correlative to *then* (implied and sometimes expressed): At the (or a) time at which: on the (or an) occasion on which OE. **2.** Introducing a clause as the object of a verb, or (later) governed by a prep.: = The or a time at which OE. **3.** As simple relative: At which time, on which occasion; and then. Sometimes implying suddenness: = and just then, and at that moment. OE. **b.** quasi-*pron.* after a prep.: = which time ME. **4.** With *time, day*, etc. as antecedent: = at or on which ME. **5.** With the notion of time weakened or modified: In the, or any, case or circumstances in which ME. **b.** As simple relative: In which case; whereupon 1803. **6. a.** It being the case that, considering that, since ME. **b.** While on the other hand, whereas ME.

1. W. I begin, I wil also make an end BIBLE (Geneva) 1 *Sam.* 3:12. I could not say Amen, W. they did say God blesse vs SHAKS. W. God will, all winds bring raine 1639. **2.** Expecting w. our turn shall come to die MORRIS. **3. b.** Till w., thou Charmer of my Soul, Farewel 1712. **4.** In A somer sesun whon softe was þe sonne LANGL. **5.** Most confident, w. palpably most wrong COWPER. **6. a.** What's the good of my pretending to stand out, w. I can't help myself? DICKENS. **b.** You rub the sore, W. you should bring the plaister SHAKS.

III. as *sb.* The time at which something happens (or did or will happen); also *vaguely*, Time, duration 1616.

The *hows* and *whens* of life STERNE.

Whenas, when as (hwen,æ·z, hwe·n æ̆z). *adv., conj. arch.* late ME. [f. prec. + AS *adv.*] **1.** = WHEN II. 1, 5. **2. a.** = WHEN II. 6 a. 1551. **b.** = WHEN II. 6 b. 1578.

1. Subjects must vail, w. their Sov'raigne's by 1638. **2. b.** So Iudas kist his master, And cried all haile, whenas he meant all harme SHAKS.

Whence (hwens), *adv., conj. (sb.)* [ME. *whannes, whennes*, f. (+ -S suffix) *whanne, whenne*, OE. *hwanon(e* = OS. *hwanan(a*, OHG. *(h)wanana, (h)wanān*; cf. HENCE, THENCE.] **I.** *interrog.* in direct and indirect questions. (Now repl. in colloq. use by *where..from.*) **1.** From what place? **2.** *gen.* and *transf.* From what source, origin, or cause? ME. **II.** Relative or conjunctive uses. **1.** From which place; from or out of which. late ME. †**b.** as *compound relative*: From where. SHAKS. **2.** *gen.* and *transf.* From which source or origin; from which cause; from which fact or circumstance 1568.

1. Let me alone that I may take comfort a litle, Before I goe w. I shall not returne *Job* 10:21. **b.** *All's Well* III. ii. 124.

III. as *sb.* That from which something comes or arises; place of origin; source 1832. Hence **Whencesoe·ver, -soe'er, Whence·ver** *advs.* and *conjs.* from whatever place or source; wherever..from.

Whenever (hwene·vəɹ), *adv., conj.* Also *poet.* **whene'er** (hwenēə·ɹ). late ME. [f. WHEN + EVER *adv.*] **1.** At any time when; every time that, as often as; at whatever time, no matter when. Also, in any or every case in which. **2.** As soon as. Now *Sc.* and *Irish.* 1655. **3.** As interrog. adv., emphatic extension of *when*. (prop. two words.) Now *colloq.* 1713.

Whenso (hwe·nsoᵘ), *adv., conj. arch.* [ME., repr. OE. **swā hwanne swā.*] = WHENEVER 1.

Whensoever (hwensoᵘe·vəɹ), *adv., conj.* Also *poet.* **whensoe'er** (-ēə·ɹ). ME. [f. prec. + EVER *adv.*] = WHENEVER 1. **b.** *ellipt.* At any time 1604.

b. *Ham.* v. ii. 210. So **Whensome·ver** (now *dial.* or *vulgar*).

Where (hwēəɹ), *adv.* and *conj.* [OE. *hwǣr*, beside *hwār* and *hwāra*, corresp. to OFris. *hwēr*, OS. *hwār* (Du. *waar*), OHG. *(h)wār, wā* (G. *wo*), ON. *hvar*, Goth. *hwar*; Gmc. derivs. of **χwa-* WHO, WHAT, as HERE is of **χi-* HE and THERE of **þa-* THE.] **I.** *interrog.* **1.** In or at what place (region, country, etc.)? **b.** colloq. *W...from?* = whence? *w...to?* = whither? 1760. **2.** In what position or situation? At what point or stage? In what passage or part? In what particular? In what? also (contextually, with *get*, etc.) From what source? ME. **3.** To what place? Now, in ordinary use, replacing WHITHER. OE. **4.** In rhetorical questions having the effect of emphatic negations OE.

1. My dearest Edith,..w. on earth have you been? DICKENS. You come from no one knows w.; you live no one knows how 1882. *Lo, see, look, behold w.* (he comes) = Here *or* there (he comes)! *arch.* **b.** I must go.., but w. to? 1760. **2.** That is all very well; but w. do I come in? 1908. **3.** Unconscionable dogs! W. do they expect to go when they die? 1809. **4.** W. would be the good of..quarrelling over it? DICKENS.

II. Relative and conjunctive uses. **1.** as compound relative, or as correlative to *there*: In or at the (or a) place in or at which; at the part at which ME. **b.** To the (or a) place in or at which. late ME. **2.** Introducing a clause as obj. of a vb. or prep., or as predicate: = a or the place in (or to) which ME. **3.** as simple relative: In or at which; in or at which place; and there ME. **4.** (In or to the place) to which; whither ME. **5.** In, or to, any (or every) place in, or to, which; wherever ME. **6.** as compound rel.: **a.** In the passage or part (of a writing) in which; at or to the point or stage at which. late ME. **b.** In a or the case in which; in the circumstances, position, or condition in which; in that respect in which. late ME. **c.** †A case in which; †a person to whom; the point or particular in which ME. **7.** as simple rel.: In or at which; and there; †whereupon. late ME.

1. Wher God buildes a church, the deuill builds a chappell 1583. **b.** Me seemes I see them going W. mulberies are growing 1586. **2.** Within about twenty paces of w. we were sitting GOLDSM. **3.** Russet Lawns, and Fallows Gray, W. the nibling flocks do stray MILT. Th' unhappy climes, w. Spring was never known DRYDEN. **4.** He is in heauen, w. thou shalt neuer come SHAKS. **5.** W. he arriues, he moues All hearts against vs SHAKS. Go w. you like DICKENS. **6. a.** I marked the booke w. there is a passage full of treason 1661. **b.** We cannot be easy w. we are not safe 1766. Thee know'st we canna love just w. other folks 'ud have us GEO. ELIOT. **c.** *Cymb.* II. iv. 111. **7.** The Yorkshire Tragedy, a play..w. a Rake..throws his wife down stairs SCOTT. The precise spot w. confidence merges into conceit 1887.

III. 1. With preceding qualifying words, forming advb. phrases: In or at (one, another, etc.) place. (Chiefly in compounds: see ANYWHERE, ELSEWHERE, etc.) 1508. **2.** As *sb.* Place, locality; now *esp.* the place at which the thing spoken of is or happens 1443.

Comb. with advs. and preps.: **wherea·fter,** after which (now *formal* or *arch.*); **whereane·nt** (chiefly *Sc.*), anent or concerning which; **whereaway,** whither, in what direction; **wherefro·m** (now *formal* or *arch.*), from which, whence; **whereinsoe·ver** (now *formal* or *arch.*), in whatever matter, respect, etc.; **wherei·nto** (*arch.*), into which; **whereou·t** (*arch.*), out of which, out from which; **whereu·nder** (*arch.*), under which; **whereunti·l** (*dial.*), **whereunto** (now *formal* or *arch.*), unto what? unto which. Hence **Whe·reness,** the condition, quality, or fact of being w. it is; position, location, *ubi*.

Whereabout (hwēə·răbaut: stress var.), *interrog.* and *rel. adv., sb.* ME. [f. WHERE *adv.* + ABOUT *prep.*] **1.** *interrog.* About where? In or near what place, part, situation, or position? Now *rare.* †**2.** *interrog.* and *rel.* About, concerning, or in regard to what or which –1653. **3.** As *sb.* With possessive or *of*: The place in or near which a person or thing is; (approximate) position or situation. Now repl. by next. 2. 1605.

Whe·reabou·ts (stress var.), *adv., sb.* 1450. [f. prec. + advb. *-s.*] **1.** *interrog.* = prec. 1. **2.** as *sb.* (hwēə·răbauts). = prec. 3. 1795.

2. The prisoner..succeeded in concealing his w. 1903.

Whereas (hweəræ·z), *rel. adv., conj. (sb.)* [See AS VI. 5.] †**I.** As rel. adv. or advb. phr. = WHERE II. 1, 3–7. –1868. **II.** As illative or adversative conj. **1.** In view or consideration of the fact that; forasmuch as, inasmuch as. (Chiefly, now only, introducing a preamble or recital in a formal document.) late ME. **2.** Introducing a statement of fact in contrast or opposition to that expressed by the principal clause 1535.

2. His father, whom he had always imagined to be a gentleman; w. he was only a sergeant in a Line regiment 1882.

III. as *sb.* A statement introduced by 'w.'; the preamble of a formal document 1795.

Whereat (hweəræ·t), *adv.* Now *formal* or *arch.* ME. [f. WHERE + AT *prep.*] **1.** *interrog.*: At what? *rare.* **2.** *rel.* At which. late ME.

1. W. are you offended? JOHNSON. **2.** W. his speech he thus renews MILT. The spot w. the Squire kept..watch 1891.

Whereby (hweəɹbəi·), *adv.* ME. [f. WHERE + BY *prep.*] **I.** *interrog.* **a.** By, beside, or near what? In what direction? **b.** By what means? how? **II.** *rel.* **1.** By means of or by the agency of which; according to which, in the matter of which, etc. ME. **2.** In consequence of, as a result of, or owing to which; wherefore. *Obs.* exc. *dial.* late ME. †**b.** Upon which, whereupon. *dial.* –1748. **3.** Beside or near which; along, through, or over which. Now *rare.* ME.

2. 1 *Hen. IV*, v. i. 67. **b.** 2 *Hen. IV*, II. i. 104.

Wherefore (hwēə·ɹfo̜ɹ), **wherefor** (hweəɹfo̜·ɹ), *adv. (sb.)* ME. [FOR *prep.*] **I.** *interrog.* **1.** For what? *esp.* For what purpose or end? **2.** For what cause? On what account? Why? ME.

1. W. was I borne? SHAKS. **2.** You..ran away..without leaving me word why or w. 1809.

II. *rel.* **1.** (Now *wherefo·r*). For which ME. **2.** On account of or because of which; in consequence of which. *arch.* ME. **3.** (Now always *whe·refore.*) Introducing a clause expressing a consequence or inference from what has just been stated. ME.

1. Peace to this meeting, w. we are met SHAKS. **2.** The causes wherfore this playe was founden 1474. **3.** And ryght forth said geffray, 'I chalenge the, wherfor deffende the' 1500.

III. as *sb.* A question beginning with *wherefore*, or (more usu.) the answer to such question; cause, reason 1590.

They *will* have the why and the w., and will take nothing for granted DICKENS.

Wherein (hweəri·n), *adv.* Now *formal* or *arch.* ME. [IN *prep.*] **I.** *interrog.* In what (thing, matter, respect, etc.)?

To what can I be useful, w. serve My Nation? MILT.

II. *rel.* **1.** In which (place, material, etc.); where. late ME. **b.** In, at, during, or in the course of which (time) 1535. **2.** In which (matter, action, condition, etc.); in respect of which. late ME.

1. b. The yeares wherin we haue suffred aduersite COVERDALE *Ps.* 89:15. **2.** He taketh from him his harnes wherein he trusted TINDALE *Luke* 11:22.

Whereof (hweərǫ·v, -ǫ·f), *adv.* Now *formal* or *arch.* ME. [OF *prep.*] **I.** *interrog.* Of what.

To know..how this World..first began, When, and w. created MILT.

II. *rel.* **1.** From or out of which ME. **b.** Of which material substance ME. **2.** For, by reason of, on account of; wherefore ME. †**3.** By means of which, with which, whereby, wherewith –1607. **4.** About or concerning which; in regard to or in respect of which ME. **5.** Of which or whom, in *obj., poss.*, and *partitive* senses. late ME.

2. The Lorde hath done greate thynges for vs.. wherof we reioyse BIBLE (Great) *Ps.* 126:3. **3.** *Timon* IV. iii. 194. **4.** Thys newe doctrine wher off thou speakest TINDALE *Acts* 17:19. **5.** In wittenesse qwherof I haue set to myn seele 1469. The greene sowre Ringlets..W. the Ewe not bites SHAKS.

Whereon (hweərǫ·n), *adv.* Now *formal* or *arch.* ME. [ON *prep.*] **I.** *interrog.* On what?

W. do you looke? SHAKS.

II. *rel.* On which. **1.** Of local position ME. **2.** Of time, esp. with antecedent *day* 1588. **3.** Of immediately subsequent or consequent action. (Now usu. WHEREUPON.) 1597. **4.** Of motion or direction to or towards ME. **5.** In ref. to the object of an action, feeling, etc. ME.

2. On that day at noone, w. he sayes, I shall yeeld vp my Crowne SHAKS. **4.** His triple-colour'd Bow, w. to look And call to mind his Cov'nant MILT. 5. *Wint. T.* I. i. 2.

Whereso (hwēᵊ·ɹsoᵘ), *adv., conj. arch.* [ME., repr. OE. *swā hwǣr swā*.] = WHEREVER 2–5.

Wheresoever (hwēᵊɹsoᵘe·vəɹ), *adv., conj.* Now *formal* or *arch.* Also *poet.* **wheresoe'er** (-ēᵊ·ɹ). ME. [f. prec. + EVER.] = WHEREVER 2–5. So **Wheresome·ver** (*Obs.* exc. *dial.*).

Wherethrough (hweᵊɹþrū·), *adv.* Now *formal* or *arch.* ME. [THROUGH *prep.*] Through which. **1.** In ref. to movement or direction in space, etc., or to duration in time. **2.** By means of which, whereby, wherewith. Now *rare* or *Obs.* ME. **3.** By reason of which, on account of which; in consequence of which, whereby, whence (as result or inference); *rarely* = by whom ME.

Whereto (hweᵊɹtu·), *adv.* Now *formal* or *arch.* ME. [TO *prep.*] **I.** *interrog.* **1.** To what? In what direction, Whither? †**2.** To what end? For what reason? –1790.

2. W. serues mercy, But to confront the visage of Offence? SHAKS.

II. *rel.* To which ME.

I hold an old accustom'd Feast, W. I haue inuited many a Guest SHAKS.

Whereupon (hwēᵊrŏpǫ·n), *adv.* Now *arch.* or *formal* exc. in sense II. 3. ME. [UPON *prep.*] **I.** *interrog.* = WHEREON I; †At what? Upon what ground? Wherefore? **II.** *rel.* **1.** = WHEREON II. 1. late ME. **2.** Upon which as a basis of action, argument, etc. 1521. †**b.** (with clause as antecedent.) On which account, for which reason, wherefore –1674. **3.** Upon (the occurrence or occasion of) which; immediately after and in consequence of which 1461. **4.** About, as to, or concerning which. Now *rare.* 1533. **5.** = WHEREON II. 4, 5. 1560.

2. b. *Wint. T.* IV. iv. 763. **3.** Last month I receiv'd my fortune..; w. I have taken a house in one of the principal streets DE FOE. **4.** *Hen. VIII,* II. iv. 201. **5.** The desire of their eyes, and that w. they set their minds *Ezek.* 24:25.

Wherever (hweᵊre·vəɹ). Also *poet.* **where'er** (-ēᵊ·ɹ), *adv., conj.* ME. [EVER *adv.*] **1.** *interrog.* An emphatic extension of *where?* implying perplexity or surprise. Now *colloq.* **2.** *rel.* At (or to) any place at which ME. **b.** *ellipt.* At any place whatever, at some place or other. Now *rare* or *Obs.* 1667. **3.** To (or at) any place to which; whithersoever. late ME. **4.** introducing a qualifying dependent clause, often with vb. in subjunctive: In (or to) whatever place; no matter where. late ME. **5.** *gen.* or *fig.* In any case, condition, or circumstances in which 1600.

2. To Oxford, or where ere these Traitors are SHAKS. **4.** W. they come from,..they have perform'd very well 1703. **5.** W. there is genius there is pride GOLDSM.

Wherewith (hweᵊɹwi·ð, -wi·þ), *adv.* (*sb.*) Now *formal* or *arch.* ME. [WITH *prep.*] **I.** *interrog.* With what? **II.** *rel.* With which. **1.** By means of which; whereby ME. **b.** With ellipsis of antecedent, or as compound relative: That, or something, with which; the means by which ME. **2.** With which as cause or occasion; on account of or by reason of which; by the agency or effect of which. late ME. **3.** Along with or together with which; against which; in addition to or besides which. late ME. **b.** With which occurrence, act, etc.; whereat, whereupon 1533.

Wherewithal (hwēᵊɹwiðǭ·l), *adv.* (*sb.*) 1535. [WITHAL.] **I.** *interrog.* = prec. I. *arch.*

Wherewithall shall wee be clothed? *Matt.* 6:31.

II. *rel.* = prec. II. 1. *arch.* 1578. **b.** = prec. II. 1 b. 1583. **c.** Preceded by the definite (rarely the indefinite) article: (*a*) followed by inf. with *to* = means by which, resources with which (*to do* something) 1809; (*b*) with ellipsis of inf. (chiefly *colloq.*), thus becoming a *sb.* = means, *esp.* pecuniary means 1809.

b. My husband and I cannot live by Love..; we must have w. DRYDEN. He had not w. to buy a coat FIELDING. **c.** The design comprised a harbour..but the w. failed 1861.

Wherret (hwe·rĕt), *v.* Now *rare.* 1599. [perh. imit.] *trans.* To give a blow or slap to. So **Whe·rret** *sb.* a sharp blow; esp. a box on the ear or slap on the face 1577.

Wherry (hwe·ri), *sb.* 1443. [Of unkn. origin.] **1.** A light rowing-boat used chiefly on rivers to carry passengers and goods. **2.** *local.* A large boat of the barge kind 1589. **3.** *local.* A large four-wheeled dray or cart without sides 1881. Hence **Whe·rry** *v. trans.* to carry in or as in a w. **Whe·rryman,** a man employed on a wherry (sense 1 and 2).

Whet (hwet), *sb.* 1628. [f. next.] **1.** An act of sharpening; *transf.* the interval between two sharpenings of a scythe, etc.; *fig.* an occasion, turn. Now *dial.* **2.** *fig.* Something that incites or stimulates desire; an incitement or inducement to action 1698. **b.** Something that whets the appetite; *esp.* an appetizer in the form of a small draught of liquor; a dram, a drink (cf. WET *sb.* 4 b) 1688.

2. b. I have seen turnips..not as a dessert, but by way of *hors d'œuvres*, or whets SMOLLETT.

Whet (hwet), *v.* [OE. *hwettan* = (M)LG., (M)Du. *wetten,* OHG. *wezzan* (G. *wetzen*), ON. *hvetja,* Goth. *gahwatjan* :– Gmc. **χwatjan,* f. **χwattaz* sharp (OE. *hwæt* quick, active, brave).] **1.** *trans.* To sharpen, put a sharp edge or point upon. **b.** *absol.*; also *fig.* to get ready for an attack (like a boar whetting his tusks). late ME. †**2.** *fig.* To incite, instigate, egg or urge *on to* or *to do* something –1761. **3.** To sharpen, render (more) acute, keen, or eager (a person's wits, appetite, interest, etc.). late ME. **4.** *To w. one's whistle,* to clear the throat or vice by taking a drink 1674.

1. Like an ill Mower, that mowes on still, and neuer whets his Syth BACON. The eagle whets his beak BYRON. Hence **Whe·tter,** *spec.* (from sense 4) a habitual drinker of whets; a dram-drinker.

Whether (hwe·ðəɹ), *pron., adj., conj.* (*sb.*) [OE. *hweþer,* beside *hwæþer,* corresp. to OFris. *hwed(d)er,* OS. *hweðar,* OHG. (*h*)*wedar* (G. *weder* neither), ON. *hvaðarr,* Goth. *hwaþar* :– Gmc. **χwa-,* **χweþaraz,* f. **χwa-* **χwe-* who + compar. suffix as in OTHER; see -THER.] **I.** *pron.* and *adj. Obs., arch.,* or *dial.* **1.** Which of the two. (In direct and indirect questions.) **2.** In generalized or indef. sense: Whichever of the two: (*a*) as *compound rel.*; (*b*) introducing a qualifying clause: No matter which of the two ME.

1. What children.., and how many, Of w. sex 1598. W. doest thou professe thy selfe, a knaue, or a foole? SHAKS. I am troubled With the toothach, or with love, I know not w. MASSINGER.

II. *conj.* **1.** As an interrogative particle introducing a disjunctive direct question, expressing doubt between alternatives: usu. with correl. *or. Obs.* or *rare arch.* OE. **2.** Introducing a disjunctive dependent question or its equivalent expressing doubt, choice, etc. between alternatives: usu. with correlative *or.* Sometimes repeated after (or without) *or* before the second or later alternative. OE. **3.** By suppression of the second alternative, *whether* comes to introduce a simple dependent question, and = IF II. OE. **4.** Introducing a disjunctive clause (usu. with correl. *or*) having a qualifying or conditional force: *w...or* = in either of the cases mentioned ME. **b.** With ellipsis in both alternatives: often virtually equivalent to *either* ME. **5.** *W. or no* (*not*). **a.** as *conj. phr.* introducing a dependent interrog. clause 1650. **b.** Introducing a qualifying clause 1665. **c.** *ellipt.* as *adv. phr.* In any case, at all events 1784. **6.** as *sb.* (*nonce-use*) 1827.

1. *Merch. V.* III. ii. 117. **2.** W. this be, Or be not, I'le not sweare SHAKS. **3.** A loud chearful Voice enquiring w. the Philosopher was at Home ADDISON. **4.** Ye shal abyde w. ye will or nyll MALORY. **b.** This, I say, w. right or wrong 1732.

Whetstone (hwe·tstoᵘn). [OE. *hwetstān,* f. WHET *v.* + STONE *sb.*] **1.** A shaped stone used for giving a smooth edge to cutting tools when they have been ground. **b.** Any hard fine-grained rock of which whetstones are made; hone-stone 1578. **2.** *allus.* and *fig.*: freq. in allusion to the former custom of hanging a w. round the neck of a liar. late ME. *Obs.* or *dial.*

2. Wits w., want 1618. He serves for nothing but a mere W. of your Ill-humour 1763. *To lie for the w.,* to be a great liar.

Whew (hwiū, hiū), *sb.* 1513. [imit.] **1.** A sound as of whistling or of something rushing through the air; *spec.* the cry of the plover. **2.** An utterance of the interjection *whew!* 1751. **3.** (Also *w.-duck*) = WHEWER 1804. So **Whew** *v.*[1] *intr.* to whistle; to utter the interjection *whew!* 1475. **Whe·wer** (*dial.*) the female widgeon, *Mareca penelope.*

Whew (hwiū, hiū), *int.* late ME. [imit.] An exclam. of the nature of a whistle uttered by a person as a sign of astonishment, disgust, dismay, etc.

Whewellite (hiū·ĕləit). 1852. [f. name of Professor William *Whewell* (1794–1866) + -ITE[1] 2 b.] *Min.* Calcium oxalate, occurring in colourless or white monoclinic crystals.

Whey (hwēⁱ). [OE. *hwæġ, hweġ* = OFris. **wei,* MDu. *wey* (Du. *wei*) :– Anglo-Frisian and LG. **χwaja-,* rel. by gradation to MLG. *huy, hoie,* Du. *hui* whey :– **χwuja.*] The serum or watery part of milk which remains after the separation of the curd by coagulation, esp. in the manufacture of cheese.

W. of butter, butter milk; *alum w.,* w. formed in the coagulation of milk by powdered alum; *celery, mustard, sack, wine w.,* names of beverages or medicinal drinks.

Comb.: **w.-butter,** butter made from w. or from **w.-cream,** the cream remaining in the w. after the curd has been removed; **-face,** a person having a pale face; so **w.-faced** *a.* Hence **Wheyey** (hwē·i) *a.* of the nature of w.; consisting of, containing, or resembling w. **Whey·ish** *a.,* having the nature or quality of w.; like or resembling w.

Which (hwitʃ), *a.* and *pron.* [OE. *hwilć* = OS. (*h*)*wilik,* MLG., MDu. *wilk,* ON. *hvílíkr,* Goth. *hwileiks*; Gmc. formation on **χwa-* **χwe-* (see WHO) and **likam* body, form; see LICH and cf. EACH, SUCH.] **I.** *interrog.* **1.** †**a.** *adj.* = WHAT A. II. 1, 2. **b.** *pron.* = WHAT A. I. 1, 6. *Obs.* exc. as joc. substitute for *what.* OE. **2.** *adj.* and *pron.* Expressing a request for selection from a definite number: What one (or ones) of a (stated or implied) set of persons, things, or alternatives OE. **3.** *adj.* and *pron.* Repeated (in prec. sense): **a.** In each of two (or more) separate clauses, usu. connected by a conj. OE. **b.** In the same clause, in abbreviated expressions, esp. *w. is w.*; also with another interrog., as *who is to have w.* ME.

1. *L. L. L.* IV. i. 105. **b.** 'I want a so-and-so' he says..'A w.?' says the Captain DICKENS. **2.** I know on w. syde my bread is buttred 1562. Of these two I doe not know w. to prefer 1601. W. way shall i flie? MILT. But w. is it to be? Fight or make friends? STEVENSON. **3. b.** To see w. went best with w. 1881. Phr. (joc.) *To tell tother from w.,* to distinguish between (two things or people).

II. *rel.* **1.** *adj.* The ordinary relative adj. ME. **2.** *pron.* Introducing an additional statement about the antecedent, the sense of the principal clause being complete without the relative clause ME. **3.** Introducing a clause defining or restricting the antecedent and thus completing the sense (= THAT *rel. pron.* I. 1) ME. **4.** Used of persons. Now only *dial.* exc. of people in a body ME. **b.** Still regularly used of a person in ref. to character, function, or the like 1645. **5.** Rarely used after an antecedent to which the ordinary correlative is *as* ME. †**6.** as compound *rel. pron.* That which, one which, something that ME. **7.** *adj.* or *pron.* Any (person or thing) that, whatever; usu., now always, with limitation of reference, as in I. 2. OE. **8. The w.** *arch.* as *adj.* (= II. 1), or *pron.* (= II. 2, 3). ME. †**b.** Of persons: = II. 4. –1606. **9.** (as *pron.* or *adj.*) With pleonastic personal pronoun or equivalent in the latter part of the relative clause, referring to the antecedent, *which* thus serving merely to link the clauses together. late ME. ¶**b.** Hence, in vulgar use, without any antecedent as a mere connective or introductory particle 1723. ¶**10.** In sylleptic construction, e.g. as obj. of two different verbs or of a prep. and a verb, etc.; giving the effect of ellipsis of a personal pronoun 1687. **11.** Preceded by *and* 1579. ¶**b.** In erroneous or illogical use, either *and* or *which* being superfluous 1606.

1. It rain'd all Night and all Day,..during w. time the Ship broke in pieces DE FOE. **2.** A letter ..qwych I send yow a copy of 1451. I spy'd a small Piece of a Rope, w. I wondered I did not see at first DE FOE. We have no Methodists settled amongst us, w. is very fortunate 1787. A similar experiment, w. was soon discontinued 1875. W. when he saw, thither full fast ran he 1883. **3.** This is the path w. leads to death J. H. NEWMAN. A bar upon w. the sea breaks 1839. **4.** Euery one heares that, w. can distinguish sound SHAKS. I am all the Subiects that you haue, W. first was min owne King SHAKS. **b.** He was not quite the craven..w. she thought him J. H. NEWMAN. **5.** There is not any argument so absurd w. is not daily received BENTHAM. **6.** I am [illegible] fellow, and w. is more, an officer, and w. is more, a housholder SHAKS. **7.** W. waye I flie is Hell; my self am Hell MILT. Place it w. way they would, it could not be prevented from shewing 1844. **9.** The history of myself, w., I could not die in peace unless I left it as a legacy to the world STERNE. **b.** If anything 'appens to you—w. God be between you and 'arm—I'll look after the kids 1905. **10.** A quality..w., if we could obtain, would add nothing to our honour 1741. **11. b.** This is their Due, and w. ought to be rendered to them by all people G. WHITE.

Whichever (hwitʃ,e·vəɹ), *a.* and *pron.* late ME. [orig. two words, WHICH and EVER *adv.*] **1.** As compound relative: Any or either (of a definite set of persons or things, expressed or implied); that one (or those) who or which. **2.** Introducing a qualifying dependent clause: Whether one or another (of a definite set); no matter which 1690. So **Whichsoe·ver** *pron. arch.* 1450.

Whicker (hwi·kəɹ), *v. dial.* and *U.S.* 1656. [Imitative. Cf. NICKER *v.*, SNICKER *v.*, SNIGGER *v.*] **1.** *intr.* To utter a half-suppressed laugh; to snigger, titter. **2.** Of a horse: To whinny 1808. So **Whi·cker** *sb.* a snigger; a whinny.

Whid (hwid). 1567. [Possibly dial. development of OE. *cwide* speech.] **1.** A word. *Cant.* **2.** A lie, fib, *Sc.* 1791.

Whidah, whydah (hwi·dă). 1781 [Name of a town in Dahomey, West Africa.] **1.** In full *w.-bird*, alteration of WIDOW-BIRD 1783. **2. W. goat,** a West African goat, *Capra reversa.* **W. thrush,** *Pholidauges leucogaster.* 1781.

Whiff (hwif), *sb.*[1] 1591. [Of imitative formation.] **I. 1.** A slight puff or gust of wind, a breath. **b.** *transf.* and *fig.* A 'breath', 'blast', 'burst' 1644. **2.** An inhalation of tobacco smoke; smoke so inhaled 1599. **3.** A wave of waft of (usu. unsavoury) odour 1668. **4.** A puff of smoke or vapour, esp. of tobacco-smoke 1714. **b.** *transf.* A small cheroot 1881. **5.** A puffing or whistling sound, as of a puff or gust of wind through a small opening; a short or gentle whistle 1712. **b.** A discharge of shot or explosive 1837.

1. b. The whiffe of every new pamphlet MILT. **3.** *fig.* Apologising for some whiffs of orthodoxy which Voltaire scented MORLEY.

II. A flag hoisted as a signal 1693. **III.** A light kind of outrigged boat for one sculler, used on the Thames 1859.

Whiff, *sb.*[2] 1713. [perh. same word as prec.] A name for various flat-fishes or flounders, as the sail-fluke, *Rhombus megastoma*, the smear-dab, *Pleuronectes microcephalus.*

Whiff, *v.*[1] 1591. [f. WHIFF *sb.*[1]] **1.** *intr.* To blow with a whiff or slight blast; to move with or make the sound of this. **b.** *trans.* To utter with a whiff or puff of air 1765. **2.** To drive or carry (*off, away*, etc.) by or as by a whiff 1601. **b.** *intr.* To move with or as with a puff of air 1686. **3.** *trans.* To puff out tobacco-smoke from a pipe, etc.; hence, to smoke. Also *absol.* or *intr.* 1602. **4.** *trans.* To inhale, sniff; also *intr.* to smell, sniff 1635.

Whiff, *v.*[2] 1836. [perh. same as prec.] *Angling. intr.* To angle for mackerel, etc. from a swiftly moving boat with a hand-line towing the bait near the surface. Hence **Whi·ffing** *vbl. sb.*

Whiffle (hwi·f'l), *v.* 1568. [f. WHIFF *v.*[1] + -LE.] **1.** *intr.* To blow in puffs or slight gusts; hence, to veer or shift *about* (of the wind or a ship). **2.** *trans.* To blow or drive with or as with a puff of air. Often *fig.* 1641. **3.** *intr.* To move lightly as if blown by a puff of air; to flicker or flutter as if stirred by the wind. Often *fig.* 1662. **4.** To make a light whistling sound; *trans.* to utter with such a sound 1832. So **Whi·ffle** *sb.* an act of whiffling; a slight blast of air; a veering *round.* Hence **Whi·ffling** *ppl. a.* that whiffles; inconstant, shifting, evasive; trifling, paltry, insignificant.

Whiffler[1] (hwi·fləɹ). *Obs.* exc. *Hist.* 1539. [f. *wifle* javelin, battle-axe, OE. *wifel*, f. Gmc. **wib-* (cf. ON. *vifr* sword) :– IE. **wip-* wave, swing; see -ER[1].] One of a body of attendants armed with a javelin, battle-axe, sword, or staff, and wearing a chain, employed to keep the way clear for a procession or at some public spectacle. **b.** *transf.* A swaggerer, braggadocio 1581.

Whiffler[2] (hwi·fləɹ). 1617. [f. WHIFFLE *v.* + -ER[1].] †**1.** A smoker of tobacco –1836. **2.** A trifler; an insignificant or contemptible fellow; also, a shifty or evasive person 1659.

Whig (hwig), *sb.*[1] Now *Sc.* and *dial.* 1528. [Of unascertained origin, but presumably rel. to WHEY.] Variously applied to (*a*) sour milk or cream, (*b*) whey, (*c*) buttermilk, (*d*) a beverage consisting of whey fermented and flavoured with herbs.

Whig (hwig), *sb.*[2] and *a.* 1657. [prob. shortening of WHIGGAMORE.] **1.** An adherent of the Presbyterian cause in Scotland in the seventeenth century. *Hist.* **2.** Applied to the Exclusioners who opposed the succession of James, Duke of York, to the Crown, on the ground of his being a Roman Catholic. *Hist.* 1679. **3.** Hence, from 1689, an adherent of one of the two great parliamentary parties in England. (Opp. to TORY; later superseded by *Liberal.*) 1702. **4.** *Amer. Hist.* **a.** An American colonist who supported the American War of Independence 1768. **b.** A member of a party formed in 1834 from a fusion of the National Republicans and other elements opposed to the Democrats; it was succeeded in 1856 by the Republican party 1834.

1. I am as sorry to see a man day, even a whigue, as any of themselfs CLAVERHOUSE. **3.** All that opposed the Court came in contempt to be called Whiggs BURNET. I have always said, the first W. was the Devil JOHNSON.

B. *adj.* That is a W.; of, pertaining to, or characteristic of a W. or Whigs; holding the opinions or principles of a W. 1681. Hence **Whig** *v. trans.* to behave like a W. towards; *intr.* to play the W. **Whi·ggish** *a.* having something of the character of a W., inclined to Whiggism (usu. *hostile* or *contempt.*); *transf.* liberal, 'broad'; **Whi·ggish-ly** *adv.*, **-ness.**

Whiggamore (hwi·gămōᵊɹ). *Hist.* 1649. [Sc. *whiggamaire, -mer, wiggomer*, f. *whig* drive + MARE[1], the expedition against Edinburgh in 1648 being called 'the whiggamore raid'.] One of a body of insurgents of the West of Scotland who in 1648 marched on Edinburgh; later (*contempt.*) = WHIG *sb.*[2] 1.

Whiggery (hwi·gəri). 1682. [f. WHIG *sb.*[2] + -ERY.] Whig principles or practice; Whiggism. (Mostly *hostile* or *contempt.*)

Whiggism (hwi·giz'm). 1666. [f. WHIG *sb.*[2] + -ISM.] The principles, tenets, or methods of the Whigs; moderate or antiquated Liberalism.

While (hwəil), *sb.* [OE. *hwīl* = OFris. *hwīle*, OS. *hwīl(a* time, OHG. *(h)wīla* point or period of time (Du. *wijl*, G. *weile*), ON. *hvíla* bed, Goth. *hweila* time :– Gmc. **χwīlō*. The base is IE. **qwi-*, repr. also by L. *quies* QUIET, *tranquillus* TRANQUIL.] **I. 1.** A portion of time considered with respect to its duration. Now almost always in certain connections (see below). **b.** With adj. expressing quantity, as *good, great, little, short*, etc.: forming esp. advb. phr. = for a (long, etc.) time OE. **2.** *spec.* The time spent (connoting the trouble taken or labour performed) in doing something. Now only in phr. *worth the w.* (now rare or arch.), *worth* one's *w.*, *worth w.*: often = worth doing, profitable, advantageous. ME.

1. *A w.* (*a*) as sb. phr., a time, esp. a short or moderate time; contextually = a considerable time, some time, as in *quite a w.* (colloq.); (*b*) as adv. phr. = for a (short or moderate) time. *Once in a w.*: see ONCE. *That* or *this w.* (now only with *all* preceding); I haue this w. with leaden thoughts beene prest SHAKS. *The w.*: (*a*) as advb. phr., during the time, meanwhile; (*b*) followed by conj. †*the* or *that*, and later with ellipsis = WHILE *conj.* 1 (*arch.*). *All the w.*, during the whole time (that). **2.** It is worth w. being a soldier in Ireland 1842. *To make it worth* (a person's) *w.*, to give (him) sufficient recompense.

II. Time at which something happens or is done; occasion. *Obs.* exc. *arch.* or *dial.* OE. **b.** In exclams. of grief. Chiefly *poet. Obs.* or *arch.* late ME. **c.** With pl. *At whiles*, at times, sometimes, at intervals. *Between whiles*: see BETWEEN-WHILES. 1540.

There are whiles..when ye are altogether too..Whiggish to be company for a gentleman like me STEVENSON. †*One w.*, at one time, on one occasion, in one case (usu. opp. to *another w.*). **b.** God helpe the w., a bad world I say SHAKS.

While (hwəil), *adv., conj.* (*prep.*) [As adv., OE. *hwīle*, accus. of *hwīl* WHILE *sb.*; as conj., abbr. of OE. phr. *þā hwīle þe* during the time that.] †**A.** *adv.* At a time or times; *esp.* at one time..at another time; now..then –1632. **B.** *conj.* (or in *conj. phr.*) and *prep.* **1.** *W.* (*that*): during the time that ME. **b.** (*a*) During the whole, or until the end, of the time that ME.; (*b*) within, or before the end of, the time that ME. **c.** During which time; and meanwhile. late ME. **2.** *transf.* **a.** As long as, so long as (implying 'provided that', 'if only'). late ME. **b.** At the same time that; *adversatively*, when on the contrary or the other hand; *concessively*, it being granted that; occas. nearly = although 1588. **c.** At the same time that, in addition to the fact that; often = and at the same time, and besides 1860. **3.** Up to the time that; till, until. Now *dial.* (chiefly *north.*) ME. **b.** as *prep.* Up to (a time), up to the time of; until. Now *dial.* (chiefly *north.*) 1450.

1. b. (*a*) She told her 'w. there was life there was hope' FIELDING. (*b*) Lett ws be mery wyll we be here! 1450. **c.** Moses sate reading, w. I taught the little ones GOLDSM. **2. b.** W. they deny a Deity, they assert other things on far less reason 1662. **c.** The walls..are decorated with white enamelled panelling, w. the frieze and ceiling are in modelled plaster 1904. **3.** They drank of the byshopis wyne Quhill they culde drynk ne mair 1813. **b.** W. then, God be with you SHAKS.

While (hwəil), *v.* 1635. [f. WHILE *sb.*] *trans.* To cause (time) to pass without wearisomeness; to pass or get through (a vacant time), esp. by some idle or trivial occupation. Usu. with *away*. Also, to beguile (sorrow, pain). **b.** *intr.* Of time: To pass tediously. Now *dial.* 1712.

Whilere (hwəil,ēᵊ·ɹ), *adv. arch.* OE. [orig. two words, WHILE *adv.* and ERE.] = EREWHILE.

That cursed wight, from whom I scapt whyleare SPENSER.

Whiles (hwəilz), *sb.* (*advb. gen.*) *conj.* (*prep.*), *adv. Obs.* or *arch.* ME. [orig. in advb. and conj. phr., as *sume-hwiles* SOMEWHILE(S, *oðerhwiles* OTHERWHILE(S, formed with advb. -S on *sumhwile, oðerhwile.*] **I.** †**1.** In advb. phrases: e.g. *that w.*, at or during that time; *long w.*, for a long while –1654. **2.** *The w.*, advb. and conj. phr. = *the while* (WHILE *sb.* 2.) ME.

2. We wyll walke vp and downe..the whyles 1540.

II. 1. *conj.* = WHILE *conj.* 1. ME. †**b.** *transf.* = WHILE *conj.* 2. –1665. †**2.** *conj.* and *prep.* Till, until –1601. **3.** *adv.* = WHILE *adv.* 1. (In mod. use apprehended as sb. pl.) Chiefly *Sc.* 1480.

1. Fyghte ye, my myrry men, whyllys ye may 1465. **2.** *Twel. N.* IV. iii. 29. **3.** She took w. fits of distraction 1722. W. whispering, w. lying still STEVENSON.

Whillywha (hwi·lihwā, -ǭ), *sb. Sc.* 1680. [Of unkn. origin.] **1.** A wheedling or insinuating person; a flattering deceiver. **2.** Wheedling speech, cajolery 1816. So **Whi·llywha, Whi·lly** *vbs. trans.* to take in or persuade by flattery; to wheedle, cajole.

Whilom (hwəi·lŏm), *adv.* (*adj.*) *Obs.* or *arch.* [OE. *hwīlum*, dat. pl. of WHILE *sb.*] †**1.** At times –1600. **2.** At some past time; once upon a time ME. **b.** as *adj.* That existed, or was such, at a former time; former 1452.

2. b. Mexico..that w. dependency of the Spanish Crown 1868.

Whilst (hwəilst), *adv.* and *conj.* late ME. [f. WHILES + *-t* as in *amongst, amidst.*] **1. a.** In advb. phr. *the w.* (obs. or rare arch.), also as simple adv. (obs. exc. dial.): During that time, meanwhile. **b.** *The w.*, conj. phr.: During the time that, while. *Obs.* or *rare arch.* late ME. **2.** *conj.* = WHILE *conj.* 1, b, c. late ME. **3.** *transf.* = WHILE *conj.* 2 a, b, c. 1548. **4.** *conj.* Till, until. *Obs.* exc. *dial.* 1520.

Whim (hwim), *sb.* 1678. [Of unkn. origin; cf. synon. WHIMSY, WHIM-WHAM.] **I.** †**1.** A fanciful or fantastic creation; a whimsical object –1821. †**b.** A whimsical fellow. ADDISON. **2.** A capricious notion or fancy; a fantastic or freakish idea 1697. **b.** *gen.* Capricious humour or disposition of mind 1721.

2. The scheme was no w. of the moment 1832.

II. A machine, used esp. for raising ore or water from a mine, consisting of a vertical shaft with one or more radiating arms to which a horse or horses, etc. may be yoked and by which it may be turned 1738. Hence **Whim** *v. trans.* to desire capriciously, to have an odd fancy for; *intr.* of the head: to be giddy (now *dial.*). **Whi·mmy** *a.* of the nature of a w.; full of whims.

Whimberry (hwi·mbĕri). *local.* OE. [Assimilated f. *whinberry*, alteration of *winberry* (OE. *wīnberige*), by assoc. w. WHIN¹.] The bilberry or whortleberry.

Whimbrel (hwi·mbrĕl). 1530. [f. dial. *whimp* (XVI) or WHIMPER, on account of the bird's cry; for the ending cf. DOTTEREL.] Applied to various small species of curlew, esp. *Numenius phæopus*.

Whimper (hwi·mpəɹ), *sb.* 1700. [f. next.] A feeble, broken cry, as of a child about to burst into tears; a fretful cry. **b.** A similar cry of dogs, etc. 1810.

Whimper (hwi·mpəɹ), *v.* 1513. [Extension of dial. *whimp* (XVI), of imit. origin; see -ER⁵.] **1.** *intr.* To utter a feeble, whining, broken cry, as a child about to burst into tears; to make a low complaining sound. **b.** *trans.* To utter or express in a whimper 1784. **2.** *intr.* Of an animal, esp. a dog: To utter a feeble querulous cry 1576. **3.** Of running water or the wind: To make a continuous plaintive murmur 1795.

1. The poore boye whympereth a lytell, but he dare nat wepe for his lyfe 1530. *fig.* The great Grecian youth, Who whimper'd for more worlds to conquer 1815. Hence **Whi·mperer.**

Whimsical (hwi·mzikăl), *a.* (*sb.*) 1653. [f. WHIMS(Y + -ICAL.] **1.** Full of, subject to, or characterized by a whim or whims; actuated by or depending upon whim or caprice. **2.** Characterized by deviation from the ordinary as if determined by mere caprice; fantastic, fanciful; freakish 1675. **†b.** Subject to uncertainty –1748.

1. One Sir Roger de Coverley, a w. Country Knight ADDISON. **2.** The Germans are w. animals in their appearance 1826. **b.** Must the bread of Life be ground only by the winde of every Doctrine? and whimsicall Wind-Mills? 1654.

B. *sb.* (in *pl.*) A cant name for a section of the Tories in the reign of Queen Anne 1714. Hence **Whimsica·lity,** the quality or state of being w.; oddity, fantasticalness. **Whi·msical-ly** *adv.*, **-ness.**

Whimsy, whimsey (hwi·mzi), *sb.* 1605. [Related to next as *flimsy* to *flim-flam*.] **I. †1.** Dizziness, vertigo –1656. **2.** = WHIM *sb.* I. 2. 1605. **b.** = WHIM *sb.* I. 2 b. *arch.* 1680. **3.** = WHIM *sb.* I. 1. 1712.

2. Those vain Attempts of Flying, and Whimsies of passing to the Moon 1713.

II. = WHIM *sb.* II. *local.* 1789. Hence **Whimsy-whamsy** = next 2.

Whim-wham (hwi·mˌhwæm). 1529. [Reduplicating formation with vowel-variation resembling that in *flim-flam*, *jim-jam*; the origin is unknown.] **1.** A fanciful or fantastic object; *fig.* a trifle; in early use chiefly, a trifling ornament of dress, a trinket. **2.** A fantastic notion, odd fancy 1580.

1. I have spent 700 pounds..for her to learn music and whim-whams 1808. **2.** Such blind vnreasonable whimwhams 1588.

Whin¹ (hwin). late ME. [prob. of Scand. origin; cf. Sw. *hven*, ODa. *hvine*, *hvinegræs*, *-strå*, Norw. *hvine*, applied to certain grasses.] **1.** The common furze or gorse, *Ulex europæus*. (Often *collect. pl.* and *sing.*) **2.** Applied to other prickly or thorny shrubs, as rest-harrow and buckthorn; also to heather 1530. **3.** With distinctive additions, in local names of various prickly shrubs. late ME.

3. Cammock, Lady-, Land-w. = *petty w.* (*a*). **Heather-, Moor-, Moss-, Needle-w.** = *petty w.* (*b*). **Petty w.,** (*a*) the rest-harrow, *Ononis arvensis*; (*b*) the needle-furze, *Genista anglica*. Hence **Whi·n-bush,** a furze-bush.

Whin² (hwin). *Sc.* and *n. dial.* ME. [Of unkn. origin.] = WHINSTONE.

Comb.: **w.-rock,** whinstone; **w.-sill,** a sill or layer of whinstone; also, whinstone.

Whinchat (hwi·nˌtʃæt). 1678. [f. WHIN¹ + CHAT *sb.*²] A small European bird, *Pratincola rubetra*, closely allied to the stonechat.

Whine (hwəin), *sb.* 1633. [f. next.] An act of whining; a low somewhat shrill protracted cry, usu. expressive of pain or distress; a suppressed nasal tone, as of feeble, mean, or undignified complaint; a complaint uttered in this tone.

A peevish w. in his voice like a beaten schoolboy HAZLITT.

Whine (hwəin), *v.* [OE. *hwīnan* (once of the droning flight of an arrow); ME. *hwyne*, *whyne* of persons; cogn. with ON. *hvina* whizz, whistle in the air; a wk. grade of the imit. base is repr. by ON. *hvinr* whizzing and late OE. *hwinsian* (see WHINGE *v.*).] **1.** *intr.* Of persons, also of animals, esp. dogs: To utter a low somewhat shrill protracted sound or cry, usu. expressive of pain or distress; to cry in a subdued plaintive tone ME. **2.** To utter complaints in a low querulous tone; to complain in a feeble, mean, or undignified way 1530. **3.** *trans.* **a.** To cause to pass *away* by whining; to waste in whining 1607. **b.** To utter in a whining tone 1698.

1. Yet canne thys peuyshe gyrl neuer ceace whining and pulyng for fear SIR T. MORE. Thrice the brinded Cat hath mew'd..Thrice, and once the Hedge-Pigge whin'd SHAKS. The bullets.. whined through the air 1901. **3. a.** *Cor.* V. vi. 98. Hence **Whi·ner,** a person or animal that whines. **Whi·ning** *ppl. a.*, **-ly** *adv.*

Whing (hwiŋ), *int.* and *sb.* 1912. [imit.] A word expressing a high-pitched ringing sound.

Whing (hwiŋ), *v.* 1882. [imit.] *trans.* and *intr.* To move with great force or impetus.

Whinge (hwindʒ), *v. Sc.* and *n. dial.* 1513. [north. form of late OE. *hwinsian* = OHG. *win(i)sōn* (whence G. *winseln*) :– Gmc. **χwinisōjan*; see WHINE *v.*] *intr.* To whine. Hence **Whinge** *sb.* a whine 1500.

Whinger (hwi·ŋᵊəɹ, hwi·ndʒəɹ). Chiefly *Sc. Obs.* exc. *Hist.* 1540. Sc. form of WHINYARD.

Whinner (hwi·nəɹ), *v. local.* 1700. [Frequentative of WHINE *v.*; see -ER⁵.] *intr.* To whine (feebly). Also as *sb.*

Whinny (hwi·ni), *sb.* 1823. [f. WHINNY *v.*] An act of whinnying; the sound of this.

Whinny (hwi·ni), *a.* 1482. [f. WHIN *sb.*¹ + -Y¹.] Covered or abounding with whins or furze-bushes.

Whinny (hwi·ni), *v.* 1530. [Imitative; cf. earlier *whine*, *whrinny*, and L. *hinnire*.] **1.** *intr.* Of a horse: To neigh, esp. in a low or gentle way; also occas. of other animals or of inanimate objects. **2.** *trans.* To utter with a whinnying sound; to express by whinnying 1815.

Whinstone (hwi·nstoᵘn). 1513. [f. WHIN² + STONE *sb.*] A name for various very hard dark-coloured rocks or stones, as greenstone, basalt, chert, or quartzose sandstone. **b.** A boulder or slab of this rock 1585.

b. Despair..such as would have melted the heart of a whinstane SCOTT.

Whiny (hwəi·ni), *a.* 1854. [f. WHINE *sb.* or *v.* + -Y¹.] Characterized by whining; disposed to whine; fretful.

Whinyard (hwi·nyăɹd). Now *Hist.* 1478. [Earlier forms are *whyneherd*, *whyn(e)ard*, of obscure formation; for the ending cf. *daggard* (DAGGER), PONIARD. The Sc. form is WHINGER.] A short-sword, a hanger.

Whip (hwip), *sb.* ME. [Partly f. next, partly – (M)LG. *wippe*, *wip* quick movement, leap, etc.] **I. 1.** An instrument for flogging or beating, consisting either of a rigid rod or stick with a lash of cord, leather, etc. attached, or of a flexible switch with or without a lash, used for driving horses, chastising human beings, spinning a top, and other purposes. **b.** *transf.* The occupation or art of driving horses; coachmanship 1792. **2.** An object resembling a whip; a slender flexible branch of a plant, a switch; a collection or growth of such branches 1585. **3.** A blow or stroke with or as with a whip; a lash, stripe. Now only *Sc.* late ME. **4.** One who wields a driving-whip; a driver of horses. (Usu. with descriptive adj. or phr. expressing skill or style.) 1775. **5.** *Hunting.* = WHIPPER-IN 1. 1848. **6.** (orig. *whipper-in*.) A member of a particular party in Parliament whose duty it is to secure the attendance of members of that party on the occasion of an important division 1853. **7. a.** The action of 'whipping *up*' the members of a party for a Parliamentary division, or any body of persons for some united action 1828. **b.** A call or appeal to a number of persons for contributions to a sum or fund; now esp. *w.-round* (for some object of charity) 1861. **c.** The written appeal issued by a Parliament 'whip' to summon the members of his party 1879. **8.** A preparation of whipped cream, eggs, or the like 1756. **9.** A movement as of a whip or switch; *spec.* a slight bending movement produced by sudden strain, as in a piece of mechanism 1889.

1. *fig.* And I forsooth in loue, I that haue beene loues whip! SHAKS. Phr. *W. and spur* (advb. usu. with *ride*), at one's utmost speed, at a furious pace. *W. behind!*, a cry to the driver of a horse vehicle calling his attention to the presence of some one riding on the back of the vehicle without his knowledge. **3.** *Ham.* III. i. 70. **4.** You're a wery good w., and can do what you like with your horses DICKENS.

II. †a. A sudden, brisk, or hasty movement; a start –1631. **b.** *Fencing.* A thrust in which the blade slides along the adversary's blade 1771. **III.** Something moved briskly. **†1.** *Naut.* = WHIPSTAFF 2. –1625. **2.** Each of the arms carrying the sails in a windmill 1759. **3.** A simple kind of tackle or pulley, consisting of a single block with a rope rove through it (*single w.*); used on board ship, etc., for hoisting, esp. light objects 1769.

2. *Double w.*, *w. on w.*, *w. and runner*, a standing block and running block, the 'fall' of the former being attached to the latter. *W. and derry* = WHIPSY-DERRY.

IV. 1. *Needlework.* An overcast stitch (see WHIP *v.* III. 2); the portion of the stuff between such stitches 1592. **2.** *Weaving.* (See quot.) 1825.

2. In the weaving of ribands and other ornamental works, many extraneous substances, totally unconnected with the warp or weft, are thrown in...These..are..denominated whips. 1825.

Whip, *v.* [ME. *(h)wippen*, prob. – (M)LG., (M)Du. *wippen* swing, vacillate, leap, f. Gmc. **wip-* move quickly, repr. also in Du. *wipplank* see-saw, *wipstaart* wagtail. Chronological relations and sense-developments are obscure.] **I.** To move briskly. **1.** *intr.* **†a.** To flap violently with the wings. ME. only. **b.** *gen.* To make a sudden brisk movement; to move hastily or nimbly (almost always with advb. extension) 1440. **2.** *trans.* To move (something) suddenly or briskly; to take, pull, strike, etc. with a sudden vigorous movement or action; *fig.* to 'come *out* with', utter suddenly. Almost always with advb. extension. late ME. **b.** *slang.* To drink quickly, 'toss off' (usu. with *off* or *up*) 1600. **c.** To make *up* quickly or hastily 1611. **†3.** *slang.* To run *through* with a sword thrust –1842. **4.** *Fencing. intr.* To make a thrust in which the blade slides along the opponent's blade. Also *trans.* with the blade as obj. 1771. **5.** *Naut.*, etc. *trans.* To hoist or lower with a whip 1769.

1. b. I whipt behind the Arras SHAKS. **2.** He.. leapes behind me, whippes my purse away 1600.

II. To use a whip, strike with a whip. **1.** To strike or beat with or as with a whip. **a.** To punish or chastise with a whip or rod; to scourge. Also *loosely*, to beat (esp. a child) with the hand or otherwise; to spank. late ME. **b.** To drive *away*, *out*, etc. with a whip 1567. **c.** To drive or urge on (a horse, etc.) with strokes of a whip. Also (occas.) *absol.* 1587. **d.** Hunting. *W. in*: to drive (hounds) with the whip back into the pack so as to prevent them from straying; *absol.* to act as whipper-in. *W. off*: to drive (the hounds) with the whip away from the chase; *absol.* to give over the chase. 1739. **e.** To spin (a top) by striking it with a whip 1588. **2.** To beat up into a froth (eggs, cream, etc.) with a fork, spoon, or other instrument; to prepare (a fancy dish) in this way 1673. **3.** *Angling.* To cast the line upon the water with a movement like the stroke of a whip; to draw a fly or other bait along the surface by such a movement; *intr.*, or *trans.* with the bait or (usu.) the water as obj. 1653. **4.** *trans.* To strike like a whip, lash; to move or drive in this way 1699. **b.** *intr.* To lash; also, to bend or spring like a whip or switch 1872. **5.** *trans.* To bring, get, render, make or produce by whipping 1635. **6.** *fig.* To vex, afflict, torment; to punish, chastise; to administer severe reproof or satire to 1530. **†b.** esp. *imper.* as a mild execration: = 'confound', 'hang' –1872. **7.** To overcome, vanquish; to surpass, outdo. Now *U.S. colloq.* 1571. **8.** To urge, incite, rouse; to revive 1573. **9.** (orig. *fig.* from II. 1 d.) To summon to attend, as the members of a party for a division in Parliament. Const. *in, up*; also simply or *absol.* 1769. †**10.** *pa. pple.* Streaked, striped. (After Fr. *fouetté*.) –1721.

1. She deserves to be whipped, and sent to bed THACKERAY. **b.** For whipping dogges from ye churche 1567. **e.** Thou disputes like an Infant: goe w. thy Gigge SHAKS. **6. b.** W. me such honest knaues SHAKS. **7.** The British can w. the whole airth, and we can w. the British 1836.

Phrases. *To w. the cat* (chiefly *dial.* or *techn. colloq.*), †(*a*) to get drunk; (*b*) to work as an itinerant tailor, carpenter, etc. at private houses by the day; (*c*) to play a practical joke; (*d*) to practise extreme parsimony; (*e*) to shirk work on Monday; (*f*) to win all the tricks at whist. *To w. the devil* (or *the old gentleman*) *round the post* (U.S. *around the stump*): to accomplish by underhand or roundabout means what cannot be done openly or directly.

III. To bind round or over. **1.** *trans.* To overlay (a rope, string, or other object) with cord, thread, or the like wound closely and regularly round and round. Also, to bind (cord, etc.) in this way round something. 1440. **b.** To fasten or 'seize' by binding in this way 1760. **2.** *Needlework.* **a.** To sew over and over; to overcast. **b.** To draw into gathers, as a frill, by a combination of overcast and running stitch. 1592.

†**Whip,** *int.* and *adv.* 1460. [The vb.-stem used as int. and adv.] Suddenly, forthwith, in a trice; quick! presto! –1806.

Whip- in combination.

1. Combs. of the sb.: as *w.-leather, -maker, -mark, -smacking*; *w.-shaped, -wielding* adjs.; **w.-beam,** the white-beam; **-bird,** an Australian bird (*Psodophes crepitans*) with a note resembling the crack of a whip; **-crane,** a crane with a 'whip' for hoisting; **-crop,** local name for several trees whose stems are used for w.-stocks, as the white-beam (*Pyrus aria*); **-fish,** a chætodont fish, *Heniochus macrolepidotus*, having a dorsal spine elongated into a filament like a w.-lash; **-handle** = *w.-stock*; **-line** (*a*) = WHIPCORD 1; (*b*) the rope of a 'whip' (WHIP *sb.* III. 3); **-man,** a driver of horses; *dial.* a carter; **-master,** a master who uses the whip; a flogger; **-net,** techn. name of a simple kind of network; **-ray,** a fish of the family *Trygonidæ*, having a long slender flexible tail resembling the lash of a whip; a sting-ray; **-scorpion,** an arachnid of the genus *Thelyphonus* or some allied genus having a long slender abdomen like a w.-lash; **-snake,** name for various serpents of long slender form like a w.-lash, as *Masticophis flagelliformis* of N. America, *Hoplocephalus flagellum* of Australia; **-socket,** a socket fixed to the dash-board of a vehicle to hold the butt-end of a whip; **-stalk** (*dial.*), **-stick, -stock,** the stick or staff to which the lash of a whip is attached; the handle of a whip; **-tail,** name used (simply or attrib.) for any one of various animals having a long slender tail like a w.-lash; **-worm,** a parasitic nematoid worm of the genus *Trichocephalus*, consisting of a stout posterior and slender anterior part, like a w.-stock with a lash.

2. The vb.-stem in comb. **a.** with second element in objective relation: **w.-belly (-vengeance),** *slang*, weak thin beer or other liquor; **-cat,** a workman who 'whips the cat' (see WHIP *v.* II). **b.** in attrib. relation to second element: †**w.-gig** = *w.-top*; **-rod,** a fishing-rod whipped or wound round with twine; **-sillabub,** whipped sillabub; **-top** = WHIPPING-*top*.

Whipcord (hwi·pkǭɹd). ME. [prob. f. WHIP *v.* III, with later association of WHIP *sb.* I.] **1.** A thin tough kind of hempen cord, of which whip-lashes or the ends of them are made. **b.** A piece of this material, as a whip-lash or its extremity 1500. **c.** *attrib.* Tough as w. 1879. **2.** *transf.* **a.** A kind of catgut 1880. **b.** A close-woven ribbed worsted material used for dresses, riding-breeches, etc. 1897. **3.** Applied (simply or attrib.) to **a.** species of willow with very flexible shoots, as *Salix purpurea* or *S. vitellina*; **b.** species of seaweed with long slender fronds, as *Chorda filum* or *Chordaria flagelliformis* 1812.

1. He looks as hard as iron, and tough as w. 1861.

Whi·p-gra:fting. 1657. [f. WHIP *v.* I. 2.] *Hort.* (See quot.)

The old-fashioned system of 'w.'. The stock is headed down and cut on one side only to receive the scion, which is cut with a long splice-cut and partially cleft or notched 1878.

Whip-hand (hwi·phæ·nd). 1680. [f. WHIP *sb.* I. 1.] **1.** The hand in which the whip is held in driving or riding; the driver's or rider's right hand 1809. **2.** fig. phr. *To have the w. of*: to have the advantage or upper hand of, control. Hence in similar phr. 1680.

†**Whi·p-jack.** 1556. [app. f. WHIP *v.* II. + JACK *sb.*[1]] A vagabond or beggar who pretends to be a distressed sailor –1753.

Whi·p-lash. 1573. [f. WHIP *sb.* I. 1 + LASH *sb.*[1] 2.] **1.** The lash of a whip. **2.** *transf.* An object resembling the lash of a whip, as the *vibraculum* of certain polyzoans; *spec.* a species of seaweed with long narrow fronds 1850.

1. *fig.* The sharp w. of furious voices in the room below 1915.

Whippable (hwi·păb'l), *a.* 1853. [f. WHIP *v.* II. 1 + -ABLE.] Liable to be whipped.

Whipper (hwi·pəɹ). 1552. [f. WHIP *v.* + -ER[1].] One who or that which whips. **1.** One who beats or chastises with (or as with) a whip; *spec.* an official who inflicts whipping as a legal punishment. †**b.** = FLAGELLANT A. 1. –1782. **2.** A workman who hoists coal with a 'whip' 1835. **3.** One who runs the coloured thread along the edge of a blanket 1881.

Whipper-i·n. 1739. [f. phr. *to whip in*; see WHIP *v.* II. 1 d.] **1.** A huntsman's assistant who keeps the hounds from straying by driving them back into the pack with a whip. **b.** In the game of hare and hounds, a runner whose business it is to keep the hounds in order 1855. **c.** *Racing slang.* The horse last in a race or at any given moment of a race 1892. **2.** = WHIP *sb.* I. 6. *Obs.* exc. *Hist.* 1771.

Whi·pper-sna:pper. 1674. [app. jingling extension of **whip-snapper* a cracker of whips, on the model of the earlier *snipper-snapper*.] A diminutive or insignificant person, *esp.* a sprightly or impertinent young fellow.

Whippet (hwi·pėt). 1550. [prob. f. †*whippet* vb. move briskly, i.e. *whip it*, intr. use with *it* of WHIP *v.*] **1.** A lively young woman; a light wench; now *dial.* a nimble, diminutive, or puny person. **2.** A small breed of dog; now *spec.* a cross between a greyhound and a terrier or spaniel, used for coursing and racing, esp. in the north of England 1610. **b.** *transf. Mil.* A light kind of 'tank' used in the last year of the war of 1914–18.

Whipping (hwi·piŋ), *vbl. sb.* 1540. [f. WHIP *v.* + -ING[1].] The action of WHIP *v.* in various senses.

attrib. and *Comb.*: †**w.-cheer** (*joc.*), flogging, flagellation; **-post,** a post set up, usu. in a public place, to which offenders are or were tied to be whipped; so **-cart, -house; -top,** a top spun by whipping.

Whi·pping, *ppl. a.* 1530. [f. WHIP *v.* + -ING[2].] That whips. **1.** Moving briskly or nimbly; acting vigorously or violently; characterized by such movement or action. **2.** Beating with or as with a whip; flogging; lashing 1598.

2. *W. Tom*, a man who whips others or flagellates himself.

Whi·pping-boy. 1647. A boy educated together with a young prince or royal personage, and flogged in his stead when he committed a fault that was considered to deserve flogging; hence *allus.*

Whippletree (hwi·p'ltrī). 1733. [The first element is app. f. WHIP.] = SWINGLETREE 2.

Whi·p-poor-wi·ll. 1747. [imit., from the bird's note.] Popular name in U.S. and Canada for a species of Goatsucker, *Antrostomus* (*Caprimulgus*) *vociferus*.

Whippy (hwi·pi), *a.* 1867. [f. WHIP *sb.* + -Y[1].] Resembling a whip; *esp.* bending like a whip, flexible, springy.

Whip-saw (hwi·pˌsǭ), *sb.* 1538. [f. WHIP *sb.* or *v.* + SAW *sb.*[1]] **a.** A long narrow two-handed saw. **b.** A frame-saw with a narrow blade, used esp. for curved work 1875. **c.** *fig.* (cf. the verb). Hence **Whi·p-saw** *v. intr.* to work a w.; *trans.* to cut with a w.; *fig.* (*U.S. slang*) to have or get the advantage of in two ways; *spec.* at cards. **Whi·p-saw:yer, -saw:ing** *vbl. sb.*

Whipstaff (hwi·pˌstɑf). 1599. [STAFF *sb.*[1]] **1.** The handle of a whip. †**2.** A handle attached to the tiller, formerly used in small ships –1769.

Whipster (hwi·pstəɹ). 1589. [app. f. WHIP *v.* + -STER.] **1.** A vague term of reproach, contempt, or the like. **a.** A lively, smart, reckless, violent, or mischievous person. *Obs.* or *dial.* **b.** A wanton or licentious person, a debauchee. *Obs.* or *dial.* 1593. **c.** A slight, insignificant, or contemptible person. (Often with the epithet *puny*, after Shaks.) 1604. **2.** One who wields a whip: **a.** a driver of horses; **b.** one addicted to whipping or flogging –1825.

1. **c.** I am not valiant neither: But euery Punie w. gets my Sword SHAKS.

Whip-stitch (hwi·pˌstitʃ), *sb.* (*adv.*) 1640. [f. WHIP *sb.* + STITCH *sb.*] **1.** = WHIP *sb.* IV. 1. †**2.** As *adv.* or *int.* expressing sudden movement or action *slang* or *colloq.* –1706.

1. Phr. (*At*) *every w.*, at short or frequent intervals (*dial.* and *U.S.*). Hence **Whi·p-stitch** *v. trans.* to sew with a w.

Whi·psy-de:rry. 1865. [app. connected w. WHIP *sb.* III. 2 and DERRICK *sb.*] A contrivance for hoisting (esp. ore in shallow mines), consisting of a derrick with a 'whip' attached, and worked by a horse or horses.

Whip-tom-kelly. 1756. [Imitative, from the bird's note.] Popular name for the Red-eyed Greenlet or 'Flycatcher' (*Vireo olivaceus* or *Vireosylvia olivacia*) of eastern N. America, and the Black-whiskered Greenlet (*Vireo barbatulus* or *Vireosylvia calidris*) of the W. Indies.

Whirl (hwɔ̃ɹl), *sb.* late ME. [Partly – (M)LG., (M)Du. *wervel* †spindle, etc. (corresp. to OHG. *wirbil*, G. *wirbel*), or ON. *hvirfill* circle, etc. :– Gmc. **χwerƀilaz*, f. **χwerƀ- *χwarƀ-* turn. Cf. WHARVE.] **I. 1.** The fly-wheel or pulley of a spindle. **b.** *Rope-making.* A cylindrical piece of wood furnished with a hook on which the ends of the fibre are hung in spinning 1794. **2.** *Bot.* and *Zool.* = WHORL 2. 1713. **3.** *Conch.* = WHORL 3. 1681. **4.** = WHORL 4. 1862. **5.** *Angling.* A spinning bait 1888.

II. 1. The action or an act of whirling; (swift) rotatory or circling movement; a (rapid) turn, as of a wheel, around an axis or centre 1480. **2.** Something, as a body of water or air, in (rapid) circling motion, or the part at which this takes place; an eddy, a vortex 1547. **3.** Swift or violent movement, as of something hurled or flung, or of a wheeled vehicle, etc.; rapid course; rush; *transf.* and *fig.* Confused and hurried activity of any kind 1552. **b.** A confused, distracted, or dizzy state of mind or feeling 1707.

3. The w. of dissipation 1780. **b.** His head was in a complete w. 1854. Hence **Whi·rl-about,** the action of whirling about; something that whirls about; *attrib.* characterized by whirling about. **Whi·rly** *a.* (*rare*) characterized by whirling or rotatory movement.

Whirl (hwɔ̃ɹl), *v.* ME. [– ON. *hvirfla* turn about, whirl, rel. to *hvirfill* (see prec.).] **1.** *intr.* To move in a circle or similar curve; to circle, circulate; more vaguely, to move *about* in various directions, esp. with rapidity or force; to be in commotion. **2.** To turn, esp. swiftly, around an axis, like a wheel; to spin. late ME. **b.** To turn round or aside quickly 1861. **3.** *trans.* To cause to rotate or revolve, esp. swiftly or forcibly; to move (something) around an axis, or in a circle or the like. late ME. **4.** *intr.* To move along swiftly or as if on wheels; *gen.* to go swiftly or impetuously, rush or sweep along. late ME. **5.** *trans.* To drive (a wheeled vehicle) or convey in a wheeled vehicle swiftly; *gen.* to drive or carry along impetuously, as a strong wind or stream (now only with implication of circular movement). late ME. **6.** To throw or cast with violence, hurl (esp. with rotatory movement, as from a sling). Also *absol.* 1440. **7.** *intr.* To be affected with giddiness; to reel: usu. (now only) of the head or brain 1561. †**b.** *trans.* To affect with giddiness, to put in a whirl or tumult –1829.

1. This world is not certeine ne stable, But whirlyng a bowte and mutable 1475. **2.** Fortunes wheele, Howe constantly it whyrleth styll about 1563. **4.** *Tit. A.* v. ii. 49. **5.** The winds begin to rise..; The last red leaf is whirl'd away TENNYSON. **7. b.** I am giddy: expectation whirles me round SHAKS. Hence **Whi·rler,** one who or that which whirls; a revolving piece of mechanism, as a potter's whirling-table, etc.

Whirl-, the sb. or vb. stem in Comb.

†**Whi·rlbat, who·rlbat.** 1565. [alt. of earlier HURLBAT; cf. HURTLEBERRY, WHORTLEBERRY.] = CESTUS[2] –1700.

Whi·rl-blast. 1798. [app. a Cumberland dial. wd., for which Wordsworth is the earliest literary authority.] A whirlwind, hurricane.

Whi·rlicote. *Obs.* exc. *Hist.* late ME. [Form doubtful; app. orig. *whirlecole*, f. WHIRL *v.*; recorded by Stow in the form *whirlicote*, whence its later use.] A coach, carriage.

Whirligig (hwə̄·ɹligig), *sb.* 1440. [orig. two words, f. WHIRL- and WHIRLY- + GIG *sb.*[1]] **1.** Name of various toys that are whirled, twirled, or spun round; *spec.* †(*a*) a top or teetotum; (*b*) a small spindle turned by means of a string; (*c*) a toy with four arms like windmill-sails, which whirl round when it is moved through the air. **2.** Applied to various mechanical contrivances having a whirling or rotatory movement; *spec.* a roundabout or merry-go-round 1477. **3.** *gen.* and *fig.* in various applications: (*a*) Something that is continually whirling, or in constant activity of any kind; (*b*) circling course, revolution (of time or events); (*c*) an antic; (*d*) a circling movement, a whirl 1589. **b.** A fickle, inconstant, giddy, or flighty person 1602. **4.** A water-beetle of the family *Gyrinidæ*, esp. the common species *Gyrinus natator*, found in large numbers circling rapidly over the surface of the water in ponds and ditches 1713. **5.** *advb.* Like a w.; with rapid circling movement 1598.

3. And thus the whirlegigge of time brings in his reuenges SHAKS. *attrib.* That intoxicating, inflammatory, and w. dance, the waltz 1807. Hence **Whi·rligig** *v. intr.* to turn like a w.; to whirl or spin round.

Whirling (hwə̄·ɹliŋ), *ppl. a.* late ME. [f. WHIRL *v.* + -ING[2].] That whirls, in various senses of the verb.

fig. These are but wild and wherling words, my Lord SHAKS.

Collocations: **w. blue, dun,** artificial flies used in angling; **w. plant,** the 'telegraph-plant', *Desmodium gyrans*; **-table,** (*a*) a machine consisting essentially of a table contrived to revolve rapidly, used for experiments or demonstrations in dynamics, etc.; (*b*) a horizontally rotating disc in a potter's lathe, carrying a mould which shapes the inside of a plate or other circular piece of ware. Hence **Whi·rlingly** *adv.*

†Whi·rlpit. 1570. [f. WHIRL- + PIT *sb.*[1]] = next –1724.

Whirlpool (hwə̄·ɹlpūl). 1529. [f. WHIRL- + POOL *sb.*[1]] A place in, or part of, a river, the sea, or any expanse of water where there is constant (and usu. rapid) circular movement; a (large and violent) eddy or vortex 1530. **b.** *fig.* esp. a destructive or absorbing agency by which something is figured as engulfed or swallowed up; a scene of confused and turbulent activity 1529.

b. In yᵉ deepest whoorlpools of aduersities, faith may hold vs vp 1571. The Whirl-pool of Poetry suck'd me in, and I fell a Rhiming 1704.

Whirlwig (hwə̄·ɹlwig). 1816. = WHIRLIGIG 4.

Whirlwind (hwə̄·ɹlwind). ME. [– ON. *hvirfilwindr*; see WHIRL-, WIND *sb.*] **1.** A whirling or rotating wind; a body of air moving rapidly in a circular or upward spiral course around a vertical or slightly inclined axis which has also a progressive motion over the surface of land or water. **2.** *transf.* and *fig.* Something rushing impetuously like a whirlwind; a violent or destructive agency; a confused and tumultuous process or condition. late ME.

2. Mr. Pickwick concluded amidst a w. of applause DICKENS. Phr. *To sow the wind and reap the w.* (Hos. 8:7), to indulge in reckless wickedness or folly, and suffer the disastrous consequences.

Whirly-, obs. or dial. var. of WHIRL-, as **†whirly-pool, -wind** = WHIRLPOOL, -WIND.

Whirr, whir (hwə̄ɹ), *sb.* late ME. [Goes with next.] **†1.** Violent or rapid movement, rush, hurry; the force or impetus of such movement –1553. **†b.** *fig.* Commotion of mind or feeling; a mental or nervous shock –1728. **2.** A continuous vibratory sound, such as that made by the rapid fluttering of a bird's or insect's wings, by a wheel turning swiftly, or by a body rushing through the air 1677.

2. A w. of unseen wings SOUTHEY.

Whirr, whir, *v.* (*adv.*, *int.*) late ME. [prob. first of Scand. origin (cf. Da. *hvirre*, Norw. *kvirra*, Sw. dial. *hvirra*, which are perh. assim. forms of ON. **hvirfa*, repr. the base of *hvirfill*, *hvirfla* WHIRL; reinforced later by echoism.] **1.** *trans.* **†a.** To throw or cast with violence and noise –1605. **b.** To carry or hurry along, to move or stir, with a rushing or vibratory sound (now *causal* from 2) 1608. **2.** *intr.* To move swiftly in some way with a continuous vibratory sound, as various birds, rapidly revolving wheels, etc. late ME. **3.** To make or emit a vibratory sound 1804. **b.** *dial.* To snarl or growl; to purr 1706. **4.** The vb.-stem as *int.* or *adv.*, expressing a sudden or rapid movement with vibratory sound 1600.

1. b. *Per.* IV. i. 21. **3.** Grasshoppers whirring in the grass STEVENSON.

Whish (hwiʃ), *sb.*, *int.*[2] 1808. [f. next.] A soft sibilant sound, as of something moving rapidly through the air or over the surface of water. Also as *int.*

Whish (hwiʃ), *v.* 1518. [imit.] **1.** *intr.* To utter the syllable 'whish' or a sound resembling it; *trans.* to drive or chase by crying 'whish!' **2.** To make a soft sibilant sound of this kind; as a body rushing through air or water, the wind among the trees, etc. 1540.

Whish, *int.*[1] Now *dial.* 1635. [A natural utterance. Cf. WHIST *int.*] = Hush!

Whisht (hwiʃt), *sb.* 1553. [f. WHISHT *int.*] **1.** An utterance of 'whisht!' to enjoin silence. **2.** Silence; in phr. *to hold one's w.*, to keep silence. *Sc.* 1785.

Whisht (hwiʃt), *a.* Now *dial.* 1570. [Variant of WHIST *a.*] Silent, still, hushed. Hence **Whi·shtly** *adv.* 1548.

Whisht (hwiʃt), *int.* Now *dial.* late ME. [A natural utterance. Cf. HUSHT *int.*, WHIST *int.*] An exclamation enjoining silence: Hush! Hence **Whisht** *v.* (*dial.*) *intr.* to be silent; *trans.* to silence, hush.

Whisk (hwisk), *sb.*[1] late ME. [orig. *wisk*, *wysk*; partly f. WHISK *v.*, partly – ON. *visk* wisp.] **I.** A brief rapid sweeping movement; a light stroke of a brush or other sweeping implement.

fig. The whiske of one of his Epigrams 1644. *With a w., in a w.*, in an instant, in a flash.

II. 1. A neckerchief worn by women in the latter half of the 17th c. *Obs.* exc. *Hist.* 1654. **2.** A small instrument, usu. made of wire, for beating up eggs, cream, or the like 1666. **3.** A bundle or tuft of hairs, feathers, etc. fixed on a handle, used for brushing or dusting 1729. **b.** A slender hair-like or bristle-like part or appendage, as those on the tails of certain insects 1618. **c.** The panicle or other part of certain plants used for making into brushes or brooms; *esp.* the panicle of the common millet or 'broomcorn' (*Sorghum vulgare*); hence, the plant itself 1757. **d.** A small bunch or tuft 1845. **4.** A mechanical appliance having a whisking movement: **a.** A kind of winnowing-machine. **b.** A machine for winding yarn. **c.** A cooper's plane for levelling the chimes of casks. 1813.

1. My wife..brought her a white w. and put it on PEPYS.

attrib. and *Comb.*: **w. broom** = sense II. 3; **w. seed,** millet seed.

Whisk, *sb.*[2] *Obs.* or *dial.* 1621. [perh. f. next.] The earlier name of the card-game now called whist.

Whisk, *v.* (*adv.*, *int.*) 1480. [orig. Sc.; prob. of Scand. origin; cf. Sw. *viska* whisk (off), Da. *viske.*] **1.** *intr.* To move with a light rapid sweeping motion; to make a single sudden movement of this kind; to move about or travel swiftly or briskly. **b.** as *adv.* or *int.* With a whisk, or sudden light movement 1750. **2.** *trans.* To move (something) *about*, *away*, etc. with a light sweeping motion 1513. **b.** in ref. to rapid travel 1694. **3.** To brush or sweep lightly and rapidly from a surface, esp. with a light instrument, as a feather or small brush 1621. **4.** To beat or whip with a rod of twigs or the like. *Obs.* in *gen.* sense: now, to beat up (eggs, cream, or the like) with a light rapid movement by means of a whisk 1530.

2. The squirrel..there whisks his brush, and perks his ears COWPER. **3.** The beadle..whisked the crumbs off his knees DICKENS. **4.** Whites of Eggs beat up and whisk'd 'till it stand all in froth 1710.

Whisker (hwi·skəɹ). late ME. [f. WHISK *v.* + -ER[1].] **1.** Something that whisks or is used for whisking; applied to various objects, as a fan, a bunch of feathers used as a brush. *Obs.* or *dial.* **2.** *slang* or *colloq.* Something great or excessive; esp. a great lie. Now *rare* or *Obs.* 1668. **3.** The hair that grows on an adult man's face; formerly commonly applied to the *moustache*, and sometimes to (or including) the *beard*; now restricted to that on the cheeks or sides of the face. **a.** *pl.*: usu. collective 1600. **b.** *sing.*: formerly, a moustache; now, the hair on one side of the face; also *collect.* 1706. **4.** Each of a set of projecting hairs or bristles growing on the upper lip or about the mouth of certain animals; also applied to a similar set of feathers in certain birds 1678. **5.** *Naut.* Each of two spars extending laterally on each side of the bowsprit, for spreading the guys of the jib-boom 1844. **b.** A lever for exploding a torpedo 1880.

3. a. A tall fellow, with..very thick bushy whiskers meeting under his chin DICKENS. Hence **Whi·skered** *a.* having whiskers; *spec.* as a descriptive appellation of particular species of animals, as *whiskered auk, tern.* **Whi·skerless** *a.* **Whis·kery** *a.* having large whiskers.

Whiskey: see WHISKY.

Whiskied (hwi·skid), *a. rare.* 1850. [f. WHISKY *sb.*[1] + -ED[2].] Saturated or tainted with whisky.

Whiskified (hwi·skifəid), *a.* 1802. [f. WHISKY *sb.*[1]; see -FY.] Affected by excessive drinking of whisky.

Whisky, whiskey (hwi·ski), *sb.*[1] 1715. [Short for †*whiskybae*, var. USQUEBAUGH. In mod. trade usage, Scotch *whisky* and Irish *whiskey* are thus distinguished in spelling.] A spirituous liquor distilled orig. in Ireland and Scotland, and in the British Islands still chiefly, from malted barley, in U.S. chiefly from maize or rye. With *a* and *pl.*, a drink of whisky

W.-and-milk, -soda, -water, mixed or diluted drinks. He..went home..for his whiskey-and-water DICKENS.

attrib. and *Comb.*, as *w.-punch, -still, -toddy*; **w. insurrection, rebellion** *U.S. Hist.*, an outbreak in Pennsylvania in 1794 against an excise duty on spirits; **w. ring** *U.S. Hist.*, a combination of distillers and revenue officers formed in 1872 to defraud the government of part of the tax on spirits; **-straight** *U.S. slang*, whisky without water.

Whisky, whiskey, *sb.*[2] 1769. [f. WHISK *v.* + -Y[1], from its swift movement.] A kind of light two-wheeled one-horse carriage, used in England and America in the late 18th and early 19th c.

Whi·sky, *a. rare.* 1782. [f. WHISK *v.* + -Y[1].] Light and lively, flighty.

Whisky jack (hwi·skiˌdʒæk). 1772. [Altered f. next by substitution of *jack* for *john.*] Popular name for the Common Grey Jay of Canada, *Perisoreus canadensis.*

Whisky john (hwi·skiˌdʒǫn). 1772. [alt., with assim. to JOHN of N. Amer. Indian name (Cree *wiskatjan*, Montagnais *wishkutshan*).] = prec.

Whisper (hwi·spəɹ), *sb.* 1596. [f. next.] **1.** An act or the action of whispering; the low non-resonant quality of voice which characterizes this 1608. **b.** *Phonetics.* Speech or vocal sound without vibration of the vocal cords and with contraction of the glottis 1856. **c.** A whispered word, phrase, or speech 1599. **2.** A secret or slight utterance, mention, or report; a suggestion, insinuation, hint; with negative, the slightest mention, the 'least word' 1596. **3.** *fig.* A soft rustling sound resembling or suggesting that of a whispering voice 1637. **4.** *attrib.* Uttered in a whisper 1626.

1. Secrets which he always communicates in a w. JOHNSON. *Stage w.*: see STAGE *sb.* **c.** *Hen. V*, IV. Chor. 7. **2.** At least the w. goes so SHAKS. No one raises even a w. of reproach against Peel 1827.

Whisper (hwi·spəɹ), *v.* [OE. *hwisprian* = early Flem. *wisperen*, G. *wispern* (of LG. origin), f. Gmc. imit. base **χwis-*, whence also synon. MLG., MDu. *wispelen*, OHG. *(h)wispalōn* (G. *wispeln*), ON. *hviskra*, *hvisla*; cf. dial. *whister* (XIV), OE. *hwǣstrian.*] **1.** *intr.* To speak softly 'under one's breath', i.e. without the resonant tone produced by vibration of the vocal cords; to talk or converse in this way, esp. in the ear of another, for the sake of secrecy. **2.** *trans.* To say, tell, communicate, utter, or express by whispering 1588. **3.** To address in a whisper; to tell, inform, bid, or ask in a whisper 1540. **4. a.** *intr.* To speak or converse quietly or secretly about something (usu. implying hostility, malice, etc.); also (with negative) to speak ever so slightly, to say 'the least thing' about something 1515. **b.** *trans.* To say, report, or utter quietly, secretly, or confidentially; also (with negative), to say the least word of 1562. **c.** with *adv.* or *advb. phr.* To bring *into* or *out of* something, or to take *away* by secret (esp. malicious or slanderous) speech 1631. **5.** *intr. fig.* To make a soft rustling sound resembling or suggesting a whisper 1653. **6.** *trans. fig.* To suggest secretly to the mind; also, to express or communicate by a soft rustling sound 1640. **b.** With the person, etc. as obj. 1605.

2. What did you w. in your Ladies eare? SHAKS. **3.** Miss Jane..whispered her sister to observe how jealous Mr. Cheggs was DICKENS. **4. a.** All myne enemyes w. together agaynst me BIBLE (Great) *Ps.* 41:7. **b.** This newes was first wispered here the 19th November. 1628. Some vague rumour.. which had been whispered abroad DICKENS. **5.** No tree is heard to w., bird to sing GRAY. **6. b.** What devil whispered thee to marry such a woman? 1761. Hence **Whi·spered** *ppl. a.* **Whi·spering** *ppl. a.* that whispers; uttered in a whisper; reporting something secretly or confidentially; **-ly** *adv.*

Whisperer (hwi·spərəɹ). 1547. [f. prec. + -ER[1].] One who whispers. **1.** One who speaks in a whisper 1567. **b.** An appellation for certain horse-breakers, said to have obtained obedience by whispering to the horses 1810. **2.** One who communicates something quietly or secretly; *esp.* a secret slanderer or talebearer 1547.

Whispering (hwi·spəriŋ), *vbl. sb.* OE. [f. as prec. + -ING[1].] The action of WHISPER *vb.* in various senses.

Foule whisp'rings are abroad SHAKS. The Gazings and Whisperings of the Ladies and Gentlemen RICHARDSON. The w. of the leaves,.. and the plashing of the fountains SCOTT. The whisperings of her womanly nature..caused her to shrink from any unmaidenly action MRS. GASKELL.

attrib.: **w.-gallery,** a gallery or dome, usu. of circular or elliptical plan, in which a whisper or other faint sound at one point can be heard by reflexion at a distant point where the direct sound is inaudible.

Whist (hwist), *sb.*[1] *Irish.* 1897. [f. WHIST *v.* or *int.*; cf. WHISHT *sb.*] Silence: in phr. *to hold one's w.*, to keep silence.

Whist (hwist), *sb.*[2] 1663. [Altered f. WHISK *sb.*[2]] A game of cards played (ordinarily) by four persons each having a *hand* of 13 cards; one of the suits is *trumps* (see TRUMP *sb.*[2] 1); the players play in rotation, each four successive cards played constituting a *trick*, in which each player after the leader must follow suit if he holds a card of the suit led, otherwise may discard or trump; points are scored according to the number of tricks won and sometimes also by *honours* or highest trumps held by each pair of partners.

Dummy w.: see DUMMY *sb.* 2. *Duplicate w.*, a form in which the hands played are preserved and played again by the opposing partners. *Long w.*, a form in which the score is ten points with honours counting. *Short w.*, the form now usual in England, in which the score is five points with honours counting.

attrib. and *Comb.*, as *w.-club, -party, -player*; **w.-drive,** a party of progressive w. (see PROGRESSIVE *a.* 2 b) usu. played for prizes.

Whist (hwist), *a. arch.* and *dial.* late ME. [f. WHIST *int.*] Silent, quiet, hushed; free from noise or disturbance. (Usu. predic.) **b.** Keeping silence in relation to something; saying nothing about the matter 1577.

Curtsied when you haue, and kist the wilde waues w. SHAKS. **b.** The Heybrooks were w. folks about their concerns 1880. Hence **Whi·stly** *adv.*

Whist, *v.* Pa. t. and pple. **whi·sted, whist.** 1541. [f. next.] **1.** *intr.* To become or be silent, keep silence. *arch.* and *dial.* 1547. †**2.** *trans.* To put to silence; to hush –1602.

Whist (hwist), *int.* Now *dial.* late ME. [A natural utterance; cf. WHISHT *int.*] An exclam. to command silence: Hush!

Whistle (hwi·s'l), *sb.* [OE. *hwistle, wistle*, rel. to *hwistlian* (see next).] **1.** A tubular wind instrument of wood, metal, or other hard substance, having a more or less shrill tone; a shrill pipe. **2.** *colloq.* A joc. name for the mouth or throat as used in speaking or singing. late ME. **3.** An act of whistling; the sound of this, esp. as a call or signal to a person or animal, or as an expression of surprise or astonishment. Also, the act of sounding or the sound made by a whistle or pipe. 1447. **b.** *fig.* or in fig. phrases: Call, summons 1529. **c.** The clear shrill voice or note of a bird or of certain other animals 1784. **d.** Any similar sound, as of wind blowing through trees, etc. 1648.

1. Boatswain with your w. command the Saylors to the upper deck 1610. The w. sounded, and the train began..to glide out of the station 1898. *Penny w., tin w.*, a musical toy, usu. of tin and pierced with six holes. *As clean, clear, dry as a w.*; A first rate shot;..head taken off as clean as a w. 1849. †*Box* or (Sc.) *kist of whistles*: a contemptuous phr. for a church organ. *To pay (too dear) for one's w.*, to pay more for something than it is worth. **2.** *To wet* (erron. *whet*) *one's w.*, to take a drink (esp. of alcoholic liquor). **3. b.** Ready to run at every mans w. 1639. Phr. (*Not*) *worth a w.*; I haue beene worth the w. SHAKS.

Whistle (hwi·s'l), *v.* [OE. *hwistlian, wistlian*, corresp. to ON. *hvísla* whisper, MSw. *hvisla*, Sw. *vissla* whistle, Da. *hvisle* hiss, f. Gmc. imit. base **χwis-* (see WHISPER *v.*).] **I. 1.** *intr.* To utter a clear, more or less shrill sound or note by forcing the breath through the narrow opening formed by contracting the lips; esp. as a call or signal, also as an expression of derision, etc., later more usu. of surprise or astonishment; also, to utter a melody or tune consisting of a succession of such notes, esp. by way of idle diversion. **2.** To utter a clear shrill sound, note, or song, as various birds and certain other animals; to pipe OE. **3.** To produce a shrill sound of this kind in any way, esp. by rapid movement, as the wind, a missile, etc. 1480. **b.** To rustle shrilly, as silk or other stiff fabric. *Obs.* or *dial.* 1633. **4.** To blow or sound a whistle; to sound as a whistle 1530. **5.** *trans.* To produce or utter by whistling, as a tune or melody; to express by whistling 1530. **6.** To shoot or drive with a whistling sound 1697. **b.** To make (one's way) with whistling 1853.

1. He whistled thrice for his little foot-page SCOTT. Richard, whistling to the dog, led the way 1905. *To w. for a wind*, in ref. to the common superstitious practice among sailors; The more we whistled for the wind The more it did not blow HOOD. **3.** The wind whistled through the cracked walls DICKENS. **b.** Brave Glorie puffing by In silks that whistled G. HERBERT. **5.** Those tunes.. that he heard the Car-men w. SHAKS.

II. 1. a. To call, summon, bring, or get by or as by whistling 1486. **b.** (With *away, off*, etc.) To send or dismiss by whistling (esp. as a term of falconry); also *fig.* to cast off or abandon lightly: so *to w. down the wind* (the hawk being usu. cast off against the wind in pursuit of prey, but with the wind when turned loose) 1555. **2.** *To go w.*: to go and do what one will, to occupy oneself idly or to no purpose (esp. in phrases expressing contemptuous dismissal, or the like). *To w. for*: to seek, await, or expect in vain, to go without. *colloq.* 1513. †**3.** *intr.* and *trans.* To speak, tell, or utter secretly; to give secret information, turn informer –1815.

1. b. *Oth.* III. iii. 262. Having accepted my love you cannot w. me down the wind as though I were of no account TROLLOPE. **2.** This being done, let the Law goe w. SHAKS. She..rode off, telling him he might w. for his money 1882. **3.** *Wint. T.* IV. iv. 248.

Whistler (hwi·s'ləɹ). [OE. *hwistlere*, f. *hwistlian* WHISTLE *v.*; see -ER[1].] A person, animal, or thing that whistles. **1. a.** One who sounds or plays upon a whistle or pipe. Now *rare.* **b.** One who whistles with the lips 1440. **c.** A keeper of a 'whistling-shop' 1821. **2. a.** A bird that whistles: applied locally to various species; also *spec.* used of some nocturnal bird having a whistling note believed to be of ill omen 1590. **b.** (tr. Canadian Fr. *siffleur.*) A large species of marmot, *Arctomys pruinosus*, found in mountainous parts of N. America 1820. **c.** A broken-winded horse that breathes hard with a shrill sound 1824. **3.** Something that makes a whistling sound 1812.

2. a. The W. shrill, that who so heares, doth dy SPENSER.

Whistling (hwi·s'liŋ), *vbl. sb.* [OE. *hwistlung*, f. *hwistlian* WHISTLE *v.*; see -ING[1].] The action of the vb. WHISTLE, in various senses.

attrib.: **w. post,** a post beside a railway-line, on passing which the engine-whistle is sounded; **-shop** *slang*, a room in a prison in which spirits were secretly sold without a licence (a signal being given by whistling to escape detection).

Whi·stling, *ppl. a.* late ME. [f. WHISTLE *v.* + -ING[2].] That whistles, in various senses.

To dance our ringlets to the w. Winde SHAKS. *Prov.* A w. woman and a crowing hen Is neither fit for God nor men.

W. buoy, a buoy fitted with a whistle which is automatically sounded by the movement of the waves; **w. dick,** any of various species of thrush, esp. of the Australian genus *Colluricincla*; **w. duck,** various species of duck, as the golden-eye and the widgeon; **w. marmot** = WHISTLER 2 b; **w. thrush,** local name for the song-thrush.

Whit (hwit), *sb.*[1] Now *arch.* or *literary.* 1480. [Early mod.E. *whyt, wyt*, app. an alteration of *wight* in *no wight, little wight* (see WIGHT *sb.*); the sp. *wh-* is unexpl.] A very small or the least portion or amount; a particle, jot; freq. in phrases used advb., esp. with negative expressed or implied.

Every w., the whole. *Never a w., not a w.*, none at all. *A w.*, to a very small extent, very little; *any w., one w.*, to the least amount, in the least degree; *every w.*, completely, thoroughly, quite (in late use almost always with *as* in comparisons of equality); I have written..a whole cartload of things, every w. as good as this 1672. *Never, not* (etc.) *a w., no w.*, not in the least, not at all; You don't seem one w. the happier at this SHERIDAN.

Whit, *int.* (*adv.*), *sb.*[2], *v.* 1833. [Imitative.] A word expressing a shrill abrupt sound, as of a bird's chirp, etc.

White (hwəit), *sb.* OE. [absol. uses of WHITE *a.*] **1.** The translucent viscous fluid surrounding the yolk of an egg, which becomes white when coagulated (usu. in full, *the w. of an egg*, pl. *whites of eggs*, or, as a substance, *w.* or *the w. of egg*). **2.** The white part (sclerotic coat) of the eyeball, surrounding the coloured iris (usu. in full, *the w. of the eye*). late ME. **3.** The white or light-coloured part of some substance or structure, as flesh, wood, etc. late ME. **4.** *Archery.* **a.** The white target usu. placed on the butt. *arch.* or *Hist.* 1456. **b.** In modern practice, a circular band of white on the target, or each of two such bands (*inner* and *outer w.*); hence, a shot that hits this 1687. **5. a.** *Printing.* The blank space in certain letters or types; a space left blank between words or lines 1594. **b.** *Drawing*, etc. *pl.* White or blank parts 1892. **6.** White cloth or textile fabric: applied *spec.* to various particular kinds; often in *pl.* ME. **7.** White clothing or array; usu. in phr. *in w.* ME. **b.** *pl.* White garments or vestments; *spec.* (*a*) surplices worn by clergymen, choristers, etc. (now chiefly *Hist.*); (*b*) white trousers or breeches 1622. **8.** = BLANK *sb.* 1. *Hist.* 1716. **9.** White wine. late ME. **10.** An animal of a species, breed, or variety distinguished by a white colour (chiefly as a fancier's abbrev.) 1530. **11.** A white man; a person of a race distinguished by light complexion 1671. **12.** Either of the white balls in billiards 1856. **13. a.** Applied variously to any white body or substance 1540. **b.** As a specific name (chiefly in *pl.*) for various manufactured articles and products of a white colour; as pins, sugar, flour, etc. 1690. **14.** *pl.* Pop. name for leucorrhœa 1572. **15.** White colour or hue; white coloration or appearance. Sometimes semi-*concr.* OE. **b.** Whiteness or fairness of complexion ME. **16.** A white pigment; often with defining word denoting a particular kind, as *Chinese, flake, Spanish w.*, etc. 1546. **17.** A member of any one of certain political parties (from the colour of the badge worn) 1680. **18.** Short for *white squadron* 1704. **19.** The player who holds the white pieces at chess or any similar game 1750.

2. Phr. *To turn up the whites of one's eyes* (usu., in affected devotion, but also in death, in astonishment, horror, etc.). **4. a.** *fig.* 'Twas I wonne the wager, though you hit the w. SHAKS. **5. b.** If a plate is over-exposed..the whites will be muddy, and the blacks lacking in richness 1892. **11.** *Poor whites* = 'poor white folks' (see next 4). **13. a.** †*To spit w.*, to eject frothy-white sputum from a dry mouth. **15.** Provb. phr. *To call w. black, to turn w. into black.* **b.** Varying her Cheeks by Turns, with w. and red DRYDEN.

Phrases. *In black and w.*: see BLACK *a.* *In the w.*, said of cloth in an undyed state; hence of manufactured articles generally in an unfinished state.

White (hwəit), *a.* [OE. *hwīt* = OFris., OS. *hwīt*, OHG. (*h*)*wīʒ* (G. *weiss*), ON. *hvítr*, Goth. *hweits* :- Gmc. **χwītaz* :- IE. **kwitnos*, *kwidnos.] **1.** Of the colour of snow or milk; having that colour produced by reflection, transmission, or emission of all kinds of light in the proportion in which they exist in the complete visible spectrum, without sensible absorption, being thus fully luminous and devoid of any distinctive hue. **b.** Of the colour of the hair or beard in old age; also *transf.* white-haired, hoary ME. **2. a.** Of a light or pale colour: applied to things of various indefinite hues approaching white, esp. dull or pale shades of yellow OE. **b.** Of metal, or objects made of metal, of a light grey colour and lustrous appearance OE. **c.** Colourless, uncoloured, as glass or other transparent substance OE. **d.** Blank, not written or printed upon 1466. **3.** Of or in ref. to the skin or complexion: Light in colour, fair. Now *rare.* or *Obs.* OE. **4.** Applied to those races of men (chiefly European or of European extraction) characterized by light complexion 1604. **b.** *slang* or *colloq.* (orig. *U.S.*) Honourable; square-dealing 1877. **5.** Pale, pallid, esp. from fear or other emotion. Also in allusive phrases expressing cowardice, and *transf.* (as in *w. rage*). 1508. **6. a.** Clothed or arrayed in white; *spec.* belonging to an eccl. order distinguished by wearing a white habit ME. **b.** Regarded as specially associated with royalist and legitimist causes (as in the white flag of the Bourbons); hence applied in recent times to certain constitutional or anti-revolutionary parties and the policy for which they stand (cf. RED *a.* I. 9 b) 1749. **7.** *fig.* Morally or spiritually pure or stainless; spotless, innocent OE. **b.** Free from malignity or evil intent; innocent, harmless, esp. as opp. to something characterized as *black*: chiefly in phr. *w. lie* (LIE *sb.*[1] 1), *w. magic* (MAGIC *sb.* 1) 1651. **8.** Chiefly of times and seasons: Propitious; auspicious, happy. Now *rare.* 1629. †**9.** Highly prized, precious; dear, beloved –1821. (see WHITE BOY 1). †**10.** Specious, plausible –1825.

1. *As w. as* (or *whiter than*) *snow, milk, a lily*, etc.; I am as w. as driven snow compared to some blackguards 1885. **3.** Fair be their wives, right lovesom, w. and small DUNBAR. **4.** The W. Australia policy—the determination to keep Australia w. 1921. *Poor w. folks* or *trash*, a contemptuous name given in America by negroes to white people of no substance. **b.** As w. a man as I ever knew 1877. **5.** I shame to weare a Heart so w. SHAKS. She is as w. as a sheet 1866. *To bleed* (a person, etc.) *w.*, to drain completely of resources. **6. b.** Boswell, in the year 1745,..wore a w. cockade, and prayed for King James. JOHNSON.

Special collocations and Combs.: **w. ash,** a species or variety of ash with light-coloured wood; hence (*colloq.*) an oar; **w. bonnet** [BONNET *sb.* 7.], a fictitious bidder at an auction; **w.-book** [tr. med.L. *liber albus*], a book of official records or reports bound in white; **w. brass,** an alloy of copper and zinc, containing a large proportion of the latter; **w. bread,** bread of a light colour, made from fine wheaten flour, as dist. from *brown bread*; **w. corpuscle,** a colourless blood-corpuscle, a leucocyte; **-ear,** a gasteropod resembling, or having some part resembling, a w. ear; e.g. one of the family *Vanicoridæ*, having a w.-ribbed shell with a wide opening; **w. elephant** (see ELEPHANT 1); **w. ensign,** an ensign (ENSIGN 5) with a white ground; **-face,** a name for Hereford cattle; **w. feather** (see FEATHER *sb.* 1); **-fellow,** applied by Australian natives to a w. man; **w. flag,** (*a*) a flag of a w. colour displayed in token of peaceful intention, desire for parley, or surrender; (*b*) the national flag of France before the Revolution; **w. flux,** leucorrhœa; **-heart** (in full *w.-heart cherry*), a light-coloured variety of cultivated cherry; **W. House,** pop. name for the official residence of the President of the U.S. at Washington; **w. iron,** (*a*) tinned iron, tin-plate; (*b*) cast iron of a silvery colour containing a large proportion of carbon; **w. lead,** a compound of lead carbonate and hydrated oxide of lead, much used as a w. pigment; *w. lead ore*, native carbonate of lead, cerusite; **w. letter** *Printing*, occasional name for the (now) ordinary or 'roman' style of type, as dist. from BLACK-LETTER; **w. lie** (see 7 b); **w. matter,** the fibrous matter of the brain and spinal cord, as dist. from the *grey matter*; **w. metal,** applied to various alloys of a light grey colour; **w. monk,** a Cistercian monk, so called from the colour of his habit of undyed wool; **w. mouse,** (*a*) an albino variety or fancy breed of the common house mouse; (*b*) the collared lemming, *Cuniculus torquatus*; **w. night** (tr. Fr. *nuit blanche*), a sleepless night; **w. note** *Mus.*, a note with an open head, as a semibreve or minim; **w. paper,** (*a*) paper of a w. colour; (*b*) *techn.* blank paper, not written or printed upon; (*c*) an official document printed on w. paper; **w. plague,** tuberculosis; **w. point,** a moth (*Leucania albipuncta*) having a w. dot on each forewing; **-pot,** a dish made (chiefly in Devonshire) of milk or cream boiled with eggs, flour, spices, etc.; so **w. pudding; w. rose,** the emblem, and hence a designation, of the House of York in the Wars of the Roses; also adopted by the Jacobites in the 18th c.; **W. Russian,** (*a*) a Russian of the stock inhabiting the western part of Russia; (*b*) the dialect of these; **w. sale,** a sale of linen (LINEN *sb.* 3) and the like; **w. sauce,** a sauce made with flour, milk, and butter, seasoned or sweetened and used as a dressing for food; **w. scourge,** tuberculosis; **w. sheet,** in phr. referring to the performance of penance in a sheet; **-skin,** a w. man (cf. *redskin*); **w. slave,** a w. person who is or is treated like a slave; freq. attrib. in *w.-slave traffic*, so **w. slaver, w. slavery** (*spec.* in ref. to prostitution); **w. squadron,** one of the three squadrons into which the Royal Navy was formerly divided; **w. squall** (see SQUALL *sb.*[3] 1 c); **-stocking,** one who wears w. stockings; occas. applied to a horse with w. legs; **w. stone,** in provb. phr. *to mark with a w. stone*, to reckon as specially fortunate or happy (in allusion to the use of a w. stone among the ancients as a memorial of a fortunate event); **-tip,** an artificial fly; **w. vine,** (*a*) the common bryony, *Bryonia dioica*; (*b*) traveller's-joy, *Clematis vitalba*; **-weed,** name in N. America for the ox-eye daisy (*Chrysanthemum leucanthemum*); **w. wheat,** wheat with w. or light-coloured grain; **w.-wing,** local name for (*a*) the chaffinch; (*b*) *U.S.* the w.-winged scoter, *Œdemia fusca deglandi*; (*c*) *w.-wing dove*, a dove of the genus *Melopelia*; **w. wings,** (*a*) sails; (*b*) (*U.S.*) a person, esp. a street sweeper, wearing a white uniform; **w. witch,** a witch (or wizard) who uses witchcraft for beneficent purposes: cf. WHITE *a.* 7 b; **-wood,** any of various trees with w. or light-coloured wood, as the N. Amer. tulip-tree, the W. Indian wild cinnamon, etc.; also, the wood.

Parasynthetic Combs., as *w.-armed, -handed, -hatted, -lipped, -whiskered*, etc.; **w.-blooded,** having light-coloured or colourless blood, without red corpuscles, as most invertebrates; **-eyed,** having w. eyes; having the iris of the eye white, or having w. plumage round the eyes; **-haired,** having w. hair, esp. from age; also, covered with w. hairs or down, as a plant; **-winged,** having w. wings; often in specific names of birds having the wings wholly or partly w. Hence **Whi·te-ly** *adv.* so as to be or appear w.; with a w. colour or aspect.

White (hwəit), *v.* [OE. *hwītian*, f. *hwīt* WHITE *a.*] †**1.** *intr.* To become white –1471. †**2.** *trans.* To make white –1721. **b.** *spec.* To cover or coat with white; to whitewash. Now *rare.* ME. †**c.** To bleach; to blanch –1714. **d.** *Printing.* To space *out* (matter) with 'white'.

White ant: see ANT.

Whitebait (hwəi·tbeⁱt). 1758. [f. WHITE *a.* + BAIT *sb.*; so called from its former use as bait.] A small silvery-white fish (the fry of various fishes, chiefly the herring and sprat), caught in large numbers in the estuary of the Thames and elsewhere, and esteemed as a delicacy. **b.** Applied to other small fishes in different parts of the world resembling this and used as food 1882.

Whitebeam (hwəi·tbīm). 1705. [perh. alt. of WHITTEN on the anal. of *quicken* and *quickbeam*.] A small tree, *Pyrus aria*, having large leaves with white silky hairs on the under side.

Whitebeard (hwəi·tbīᵊɹd). 1450. **1.** An old man with a white beard. **2.** *Australia.* The plant *Styphelia ericoides*, from the white hairs on the corolla 1898.

White boy, whi·teboy. 1599. †**1.** A favourite, pet, or darling boy: a term of endearment for a boy or (usu.) man –1821. **2.** (usu. with capital.) Adopted by or applied to the members of various illegal, rebellious, or riotous associations 1644; *spec.* in *Irish Hist.* a member of a secret agrarian association formed in 1761. Hence **Whi·teboyism,** the principles or practices of the Irish Whiteboys.

Whitecap, white-cap (hwəi·tkæp). 1668. [CAP *sb.*[1]] **1.** Any of several birds having a white or light-coloured patch on the head. **2.** *pl.* Local name for species of mushroom 1818. **3.** A white-capped or crested wave; a breaker 1773. **4.** A person wearing a white cap; *spec.* one of a self-constituted body in the U.S. who commit outrages upon persons under the pretence of regulating public morals 1891.

Whitechapel (hwəi·tˌtʃæ:p'l). 1700. [Name of a district in the East End of London.] **1. a.** In various slang uses, mostly *attrib.* (see quots.) **b.** *attrib.* or *absol.* Applied to certain irregular or unskilful methods of play in whist and billiards *colloq.* 1755. **2.** In full *W. cart*, a kind of light two-wheeled spring-cart 1842. **3.** as *adj.* Low, vulgar 1901.

1. a. *W. beau*, who dresses with a needle and thread, and undresses with a knife 1785. A 'W. shave' (..which is, in fact, whitening, judiciously applied to the jaws with the palm of the hand) DICKENS. **b.** Avoid the hateful 'W.', *i.e.* the lead from a single card 1899.

Whi·tecoat. 1555. **1.** A soldier wearing a white or light-coloured coat. *Hist.* **b.** An Austrian soldier 1861. **2.** A young seal, having a coat of white fur; also, the fur itself 1792.

White-collar. *U.S.* 1921. Applied *attrib.* to persons engaged in non-manual work, or to the occupations of these; 'black-coated'.

Whited (hwəi·tėd), *ppl. a.* Now *rare* or *arch.* ME. [f. WHITE *v.* + -ED[1].] **1.** Covered or coated with white; *spec.* plastered over with white, whitewashed; now chiefly in biblical phr. *w. sepulchre* (Matt. 23:27) used *allus.* **2.** Whitened by deprivation of colour; also, peeled so as to expose the white interior 1529.

Whitefieldian, Whitfieldian (hwəi·t-, hwi·tfīldiăn), *sb.* and *a.* 1744. [f. proper name *Whitefield* or *Whitfield* + -IAN.] **A.** *sb.* A follower of George Whitefield; a Calvinistic Methodist. **B.** *adj.* Of or belonging to George Whitefield or the Whitefieldians. So **Whi·t(e)fieldism. Whi·t(e)fieldite,** a W.

Whitefish (hwəi·tfiʃ). 1461. **1.** A general name for fishes of a white or light colour, as cod, haddock, whiting, etc. **2.** The Great Sturgeon (= BELUGA 1); the White Whale (= BELUGA 2) 1662. **3.** Any fish of the genus *Coregonus* (family *Salmonidæ*), found in the lakes of N. America, and valued as food 1748. Hence **Whi·tefisher,** one who catches white fish (sense 1). **Whi·tefishery, -fishing.**

Whitefoot (hwəi·tfut). 1753. [Cf. OE. *hwītfōt* adj.] **1.** *Farriery.* A white marking on a horse's foot; also, a horse with such a mark. **2.** Collector's name for a species of moth 1832. **3.** *Hist.* A member of a secret society in Ireland who committed murders and outrages about 1832.

White friar. late ME. [WHITE *a.* 6 a.] **1.** A Carmelite friar (whose habit is distinguished by a white cloak and scapular). Also, loosely, a Premonstratensian. Hence in *pl.*, the quarters of these friars, in London or elsewhere 1561.

Whi·teha·ll. 1827. Any of the government offices situated in Whitehall, London; *fig.* the British government generally.

Whitehead (hwəi·thed), *a.* and *sb.*[1] 1577. **A.** *adj.* = WHITE-HEADED (*rare*). **B.** *sb.* **1.** Any of various species of birds having the head (wholly or partly) white 1686. **2.** A West Indian feverfew, *Parthenium hysterophorus* 1864.

Whitehead, *sb.*[2] 1884. A kind of torpedo, invented by Robert Whitehead.

White-headed (hwəi·the:dėd), *a.* 1525. **1.** Of an animal: Having the head (wholly or partly) white; having white hair, plumage, etc. on the head. **2.** Of a person: White-haired; also, flaxen-haired 1815. **b.** with *boy*: Favourite, darling. *Irish colloq.* 1820. **3.** Of a wave: White-capped, white-crested; also of a sea covered with such waves 1897.

White heat. 1710. [HEAT *sb.* 1 c.] That degree of heat or temperature at which metals and some other bodies radiate white light; the state of being white-hot. **b.** *fig.* A state of intense emotion 1839.

White horse. 1647. **1.** The figure of a white horse; freq. used for an inn-sign, and hence as the name of an inn. **2.** The W. Indian shrub *Portlandia grandiflora* (family *Rubiaceæ*), with large white flowers 1866. **3.** A tough sinewy substance lying between the upper jaw and junk of a sperm whale 1874.

White-hot (stress var.), *a.* 1820. Heated to such a degree as to radiate white light; at white heat.

White lime, white-lime, *sb.* Now *rare* or *Obs.* 1528. [LIME *sb.*[1]] Lime mixed with water as a coating for walls, etc.; whitewash. So **Whi·telime** *v.* (*Obs.* or *dial.*) *trans.* to coat or cover with white lime, to whitewash ME.

White line, white-line, *sb.* 1598. **1.** *Anat.* **a.** (tr. L. *linea alba.*) A longitudinal band of tendinous tissue extending from the sternum to the pubis. **b.** A whitish band in the pelvic fascia extending from the symphysis pubis to the spine of the ischium. **2.** *Printing.* A line left blank between two lines of type 1683. **3. a.** = BOBBIN *sb.* 2. 1824. **b.** An untarred 'line' or rope 1867. **c.** A line of white paint on the surface of a road used as a mark for the regulation of traffic 1927. So **White-line** *v. trans.* to mark with white lines.

White-livered (-livəɹd), *a.* 1549. Having (according to an old notion) a light-coloured liver, supposed to be due to a deficiency of bile or 'choler', and hence of vigour, spirit, or courage; feeble-spirited, cowardly, dastardly.
A double-faced, w., sneaking spy DICKENS.

Whitely (hwəi·tli), *a.* Now only *Sc.* late ME. [f. WHITE *a.* + -LY[1].] Whitish; pale; light-complexioned.
A whitly wanton, with a veluet brow, With two pitch bals..for eyes SHAKS.

White man. 1691. †**1.** A man clothed in white –1693. **2.** A man belonging to a race having naturally light-coloured skin or complexion: chiefly applied to those of European extraction 1695. **b.** orig. *U.S. slang.* A man of honourable character such as one associates with a European 1883.

White meat, whi·temeat. *Obs.* exc. *dial.* late ME. **a.** *collect. sing.* or *pl.* Foods prepared from milk; dairy produce (occas. including eggs.) **b.** *pl.* Certain white or light-coloured flesh foods, as chicken, etc. 1752.

Whiten (hwəi·t'n), *v.* ME. [f. WHITE *a.* + -EN[5].] **1.** *trans.* To make or render white; to impart a white colour or appearance to. **b.** To cover, coat, or overspread with something white; *spec.* to whitewash; to coat (metal) with tin; to tin. late ME. **c.** To make white by depriving of the natural colour; to blanch; to bleach 1693. **d.** *fig.* To free or clear from evil, guilt, or the like; also, to give a specious appearance to 1440. **2.** *intr.* To become or turn white; to assume a white colour or aspect; *vaguely,* to appear white 1633. **b.** To turn pale, esp. from fear or other emotion 1783.
1. b. Sails unnumber'd w. all the stream 1719. **2.** Willows w., aspens quiver,..By the island in the river TENNYSON. Hence **Whi·tener,** one who whitens, *spec.* a person employed in bleaching or other whitening process; a thing that whitens, *spec.* an agent used for bleaching, etc.

Whiteness (hwəi·tnės). [OE. *hwītnes.*] The quality or condition of being white; white colour or appearance. **b.** Of the human skin or face: †(*a*) Fairness of complexion; (*b*) Paleness, pallor. late ME. **c.** quasi-*concr.* A white substance or part of something 1560. **d.** Purity, stainless character or quality 1555.

Whitening (hwəi·t'niŋ), *vbl. sb.* 1601. [f. WHITEN *v.* + -ING[1].] **1.** The action or process of making white; bleaching, whitewashing, tinning, etc. Also, the fact or process of becoming white. **2.** *concr.* = WHITING *vbl. sb.* II. 1710.

Whitesmith[1] (hwəi·tˌsmiþ). ME. [Cf. WHITE *a.* 2 b, and BLACKSMITH.] **a.** A worker in 'white iron', a tinsmith. **b.** One who polishes or finishes metal goods, as dist. from one who forges them; also, more widely, a worker in metals.

Whi·tesmith[2]. 1860. [f. WHITE *a.* + surname of Sir William Sidney *Smith* (1764–1840).] A variety of gooseberry with white fruit.

White staff. *Pl.* **-staves.** 1581. [STAFF *sb.*[1] 6.] **1.** A white rod or wand carried as a symbol of office by certain officials, as the steward of the king's household; hence, the office held by these. **2.** An official who carries a white staff 1601.
attrib.: **white staff officer** = sense 2. So **White stick.**

White-tail (hwəi·tˌteⁱl). 1611. [TAIL *sb.*[1]] **1.** = WHEATEAR[2]. *Obs.* or *dial.* **2.** The white-tailed deer (*Cariacus virginianus*), a common N. Amer. species, having the under side of the tail white 1888.

Whitethorn (hwəi·tþǭɹn). ME. [After L. *alba spina.*] The common hawthorn, *Cratægus oxyacantha*: so called from the lighter colour of its bark as compared with that of the BLACKTHORN.

Whitethroat (hwəi·tþrōᵘt), *sb.* (*a.*) 1676. **1.** Any of several species of warbler (*Sylvia*), esp. the common w., *S. cinerea*, and the lesser w., *S. curruca*. **2.** The white-throated sparrow of N. America, *Zonotrichia albicollis* 1889. **B.** *adj.* White-throated. *W. warbler* = sense 1 above. 1876.

Whitewash (hwəi·tˌwǫʃ), *sb.* 1689. [f. the vb.] †**1.** A cosmetic wash used for imparting a light colour to the skin –1764. **2.** A liquid composition of lime and water, or of whiting, size, and water, for whitening walls, ceilings, etc. 1697. **3.** *fig.* Something that conceals faults or gives a fair appearance 1865. **4.** An act of 'whitewashing', as of a bankrupt; also (*U.S. colloq.*) a victory at baseball or other game in which the opponents fail to score 1851.
3. The w. of diplomacy 1885. **4.** The Report is a fairly comprehensive w. of everybody concerned 1920.

Whi·tewash, *v.* 1591. [f. WHITE *sb.* 16 + WASH *v.* II. 5.] **1.** *trans.* To plaster over (a wall, etc.) with a white composition; to cover or coat with whitewash. Also *absol.* **b.** *intr.* To become coated with a white efflorescence: see next b. 1889. **2.** *fig.* To give a fair appearance to; to cover up, conceal, or gloss over the faults or blemishes of 1762. **b.** *spec.* To clear (a bankrupt or insolvent) by judicial process from liability for his debts. Also with the debts, etc. as obj., and *intr.* for *pass.* to go through the bankruptcy court. 1762. **3.** In *Baseball* and other games: To beat (the opponents) so that they fail to score. *U.S. colloq.* 1884.
1. To w. a church is..a profanity 1834. **2. b.** If I'm dunned, I w. THACKERAY. Hence **Whi·tewa:sher,** one who or that which whitewashes; *slang* or *colloq.* a final glass of white wine taken after dinner.

Whitewashing (hwəi·tˌwǫːʃiŋ), *vbl. sb.* 1663. [f. prec. + -ING[1].] The action or process of coating with whitewash; also *fig.* **b.** The production of a white efflorescence (saltpetre rot) on a brick wall 1889.
I think the book an altogether foolish..book..having but one object, the w. of James KINGSLEY. *attrib.* We allege that no assets have been recovered, and that this is a w. case 1890.

White water. 1586. **1.** Shallow or shoal water; water with breakers or foam, as in shallows or rapids. **2.** Water mixed with oatmeal or bran, as a medicinal drink for horses 1737.

Whitey: see WHITY *a.*

White wine. ME. [WHITE *a.* 2 a.] Any light-coloured transparent wine: a general designation for wines of various colours from pale yellow to amber, in contradistinction to *red wine.*
attrib.: **white wine vinegar,** vinegar made from white wine; **white wine whey,** a medicinal drink consisting of white wine and whey.

Whither (hwi·ðəɹ), *adv.* (*sb.*) Now only *arch.* or *literary.* [OE. *hwider*, f. Gmc. **χwi-* (see WHICH); for the suffix, cf. HITHER, THITHER.] **I.** *interrog.* **1.** To what place? **2.** *gen.* or *fig.* To what result, condition, action, cause? OE.
1. W. will you go? and what can you do? DE FOE. Wandering they knew not w. DICKENS. **2.** Thou tedious varlet, w. tends This putrid stuff? 1746.
II. *rel.* **1. a.** as compound relative: To the place to (or in) which OE. **b.** as simple relative: To which place; after a noun of place = to which; also with ellipsis = a place to which. late ME. **2.** To (or in) any place to which; whithersoever ME.
1. a. And whother the head went thither must the bodye folow 1535. **b.** He which..is a fugitive, may have..w. to escape BIBLE (Douay) *Deut.* 19:3. Dined at Melville Castle, w. I went through a snow-storm SCOTT. **2.** I haue hyred this shyppe ..to sayle whyder as me lyst 1523.
B. as *sb.* (*nonce-use.*) Place or state to which a person or thing moves or tends 1875.

Whi·therso, *adv. arch.* [ME. *hwiderse*, repr. OE. *swā hwider swā.*] = next.

Whithersoever (hwiːðəɹsoᵘe·vəɹ), *adv.* ME. [f. prec. + EVER *adv.*] To whatever place. **a.** To (or in) any place to which. **b.** Whether to one place or another; no matter to what place 1583.

Whitherto (hwiðəɹtū·, hwi·ðəɹtu), *adv.* Now *rare* or *Obs.* 1549. [f. WHITHER *adv.* + To *prep.*] To what place, result, etc.? to what? whither?

Whitherward (hwi·ðəɹwǭɹd), *adv.* (*sb.*) *arch.* ME. [f. WHITHER *adv.* + -WARD.] **1.** *interrog.* Towards or to what place? Whither? Also *fig.* or *gen.* Towards what? **2.** *rel.* **a.** as compound relative: Towards the place that; usu., towards any place that, whithersoever ME. **b.** as simple relative: Towards which. late ME.

Whiting (hwəi·tiŋ), *sb.* late ME. [– (M)Du. *wijting*; see WHITE *a.*, -ING[3].] A gadoid fish of the genus *Merlangus*, a small fish with pearly-white flesh, highly esteemed as food. **b.** Locally applied to fishes of other genera: (*a*) some freshwater fish found in Wales; (*b*) *U.S.*, a fish of the genus *Menticirrus*; also applied to the silver hake, and the menhaden; (*c*) in Australia, a fish of the genus *Sillago* 1587.
Comb., in names of fishes resembling the w., as **w. perch** (*Perca alburnus*); *w.* POLLACK, *w.* POUT; **w. salmon** (*Salmo phinoc*).

Whiting (hwəi·tiŋ), *vbl. sb.* 1440. [f. WHITE *v.* + -ING[1].] †**I.** The action or process of making white; whitening; **a.** by covering or coating with white; **b.** by depriving of colour –1683. **II.** *concr.* A preparation of finely powdered chalk, used for whitewashing, etc. 1440.

Whitish (hwəi·tiʃ), *a.* late ME. [f. WHITE *a.* + -ISH[1].] **1.** Somewhat white; of a colour inclining to or approaching white. **2.** Qualifying other adjs. (or sbs.) of colour, indicating a pale or light tint of the colour specified 1653. Hence **Whi·tishness.**

Whitleather (hwi·tleːðəɹ). late ME. [f. WHITE *a.* + LEATHER *sb.*] **1.** Leather of a white or light colour and soft pliant consistence, prepared by dressing with alum and salt, so as to retain the natural colour. **b.** In comparisons, or as a type of toughness, elasticity, softness, etc. 1605. **2.** = PAXWAX 1713.

Whi·tley Cou·ncil. 1923. [f. the name of J. H. *Whitley*, chairman of the committee of 1916 which recommended the setting up of such councils.] A council of representatives of employers and workers for discussing and settling industrial relations and conditions. Hence **Whi·tleyism,** the use of such methods.

Whitling (hwi·tliŋ). *Sc.* and *north.* 1597. [f. WHITE *a.* + -LING[1].] A fish of the salmon family; app. the young of the bull-trout.

Whitlow (hwi·tloᵘ). late ME. [orig. *whitflaw*, *-flow*, i.e. WHITE *a.* + FLAW *sb.*[1] breach, fissure; but the similarity of the first syll. to Du. *fijt*, †*vijt*, LG. *fit*, suggests a poss. alien origin; the alt. to *whitlow* (XV) and †*whitblow* (XVI) is not accounted for.] = PARONYCHIA 1.
attrib.: **w.-grass,** book-name for *Saxifraga tridactylites*, rue-leaved w.-grass, and *Draba* (*Erophila*) *verna*, formerly reputed to cure whitlows; **-wort,** a plant of the genus *Paronychia*, formerly reputed to cure whitlows.

Whitneyite (hwi·tniˌəit). 1861. [f. the name of J. D. *Whitney*, an Amer. geologist; see -ITE[1] 2 b.] *Min.* A native arsenide of copper, of a reddish-white colour, found in America.

Whitsun (hwi·tsŏn). [ME. *w(h)itsone(n*, the first two elements of WHIT SUNDAY, analysed as *Whitsun Day.*] **1.** Used attrib. to denote something belonging to, connected with, or occurring on Whit Sunday or at Whitsuntide. **2.** *sb.* Short for WHITSUNTIDE (*rare*) 1849.
1. W. ale *Hist.*, a parish festival formerly held at Whitsuntide, marked by feasting, sports, and merrymaking; **W. week,** the week beginning with Whit Sunday, Whit-week.

Whit Sunday, Whitsunday (hwi·t sʊ·ndi, hwi·tsŏndeⁱ). [Late OE. *Hwīta Sunnandæġ* lit. 'white Sunday'. The epithet 'white' is generally taken to refer to the ancient custom of the wearing of white baptismal robes by the newly-baptized at the feast of Pentecost.] **1.** The seventh Sunday after Easter, observed as a festival of the Christian Church in commemoration of the descent of the Holy Spirit upon the Apostles on the Day of Pentecost. **2.** (In form *Whitsunday*, or *Whitsun Day.*) One of the Scottish quarter-days or term-days, ordinárily May 15th, but in certain cases May 26th (= May 15th, Old Style) or May 28th. 1450. So **Whit Monday, Whit Tuesday,** the Monday and Tuesday following Whit Sunday; also (in occas. recent use) *W. Saturday*, the day before Whit Sunday. **W.-week,** the week beginning with Whit Sunday.

Whitsuntide (hwi·tsŏntəid). ME. [f. WHITSUN + TIDE *sb.*] The season of Whit Sunday; Whit Sunday and the days immediately following.

Tis Whitson-tyde, and we must frolick it MARSTON.

Whittawer (hwi·tǭəɹ). Now *Hist.* or *dial.* ME. [f. WHITE *a.* + TAWER.] One who taws skins into WHITLEATHER. In mod. dial., a saddler, harness-maker.

Whitten (hwi·t'n). *dial.* ME. [In full *w.-tree*, repr. OE. *hwītingtrēow*, f. *hwīting* (f. as WHITING *sb.*) + *trēow* tree.] The water elder or wild guelder-rose (*Viburnum opulus*), and the wayfaring-tree (*V. lantana*). Also (by confusion with *whicken* QUICKEN *sb.*[1]), the mountain-ash (*Pyrus aucuparia*), and some allied plants.

Whittle (hwi·t'l), *sb.*[1] Now *dial.* [OE. *hwītel*, corresp. to ON. *hvītill* white bed-cover, f. *hwīt* WHITE *a.* + -LE.] †**a.** A cloak, mantle. †**b.** A blanket. **c.** A baby's woollen napkin or flannel petticoat. **d.** A shawl or wrap.

Whittle (hwi·t'l), *sb.*[2] Now *dial.* late ME. [Variant of *thwittle*, f. *thwite* (OE. *þwītan* shave off, cogn. with *ġeþwit* chip, ON. *þveita* small axe, *þveit(i* cut-off piece); see -LE.] A knife, esp. one of a large size, as a carving-knife; also, a clasp-knife.

†**Whittle,** *v.*[1] 1530. [Of unkn. origin.] *trans.* To ply with drink, to make drunk, intoxicate –1694.

Whittle (hwi·t'l), *v.*[2] 1552. [f. WHITTLE *sb.*[2]] **1.** *trans.* To cut thin slices or shavings from the surface of (a stick, etc.); to dress or pare with a knife; to reduce or sharpen by doing this. Also *absol.* or *intr.* **b.** *transf.* To wear away or reduce by a process analogous to paring 1736. **2.** *fig.* To reduce or make smaller by successive abstractions; to diminish the amount, force, or importance of; to take *away* by degrees, so as to reduce to nothing 1746. **3.** To make or shape by whittling; to carve 1848.

1. Cambyses..whitling a sticke to passe away the time 1614.

Whitworth (hwi·twǒɹþ). 1858. In full, *W. gun* or *rifle*: A form of rifle invented by Sir Joseph Whitworth (1854), having a hexagonal bore with a rapid twist, and firing an elongated shot.

W. metal or *steel*, a specially strong make of steel cast under hydraulic pressure, used for ordnance.

Whity, whitey (hwəi·ti), *a.* (*adv.*) 1593. [f. WHITE *a.* + -Y[1].] = WHITISH. **b.** *esp.* (quasi-*adv.*) with other adjs. (or *adj.* with sbs.) of colour 1856.

b. The insipid w.-grey bread of towns DE QUINCEY.

Whi·ty-brow·n, *a.* (*sb.*) 1777. [prec. b.] **1.** Of a brown colour inclining to white; whitish brown: most commonly of paper. As *sb.* (prop. two words) a whitish brown; *ellipt.* = w. paper. **2.** *fig.* Neither one thing nor another, neutral, half-and-half 1892.

Whizgig (hwi·zgig). *Obs.* or *U.S.* 1848. [f. WHIZ(Z + GIG *sb.*[1]] An object that whizzes round, as a revolving humming toy.

Whizz, whiz (hwiz), *sb.* 1620. [f. next.] **1.** An act, or the action, of whizzing; a sibilant sound between a hiss and a buzz; a swift movement producing such a sound. **2.** *U.S. slang.* An agreement, 'bargain' 1869.

1. Their shot would go by their ears with a W. BUNYAN. **2.** They said,..Let us sleep here..And each..said, It is a whiz' MARK TWAIN'.

Whizz, whiz, *v.* 1547. [imit.] **1.** *intr.* To make a sound as of a body rushing through the air; of trees, to rustle; of a burning or hot object, to hiss, sizzle. Now *dial.* **2.** To move swiftly with or as with such a sound 1591. **b.** *fig.* To have a sensation of such a sound 1797. **3.** *trans.* To cause to whizz; to hurl, shoot, or convey with a whizz; *spec.* to dry by centrifugal force in a rapidly revolving apparatus 1836.

2. *Jul. C.* II. i. 44. **b.** Reading makes my head whiz DARWIN. Hence **Whi·zzer,** something that whizzes; *spec.* (*a*) a toy that whizzes when whirled round; (*b*) a machine for drying articles by the centrifugal force of rapid revolution. **Whi·zzing,** *vbl. sb.* and *ppl. a.* **Whi·zzy** *a.* (*rare*) characterized by whizzing; *dial.* dizzy, giddy.

Whizz, whiz (hwiz), *int.* 1812. An exclam. imitating a whizzing sound; also *advb.* = with a whizz. **b.** *Comb.* **whi·zz-bang** *colloq.*, the shell of a small-calibre high-velocity German gun 1915.

Who (hū, unstressed hu), *pron.* (*sb.*) Infl. WHOM, WHOSE, q.v. [OE. *hwǎ*, corresp. to OFris. *hwǎ*, OS. *hwē*, *hwie*, OHG. (*h*)*wer* (Du. *wie*, G. *wer*), OSw. *ho*, ODa. *hwa* (Da. *hvo*), Goth. *hwas* :– Gmc. **χwas* **χwes* :– IE. **q^{w}os* **q^{w}es*, parallel to **q^{w}i-* (cf. L. *quis*).] **I.** *interrog.* **1.** As the ordinary interrogative pronoun, in the nominative singular or plural, used of a person or persons. **b.** With intensive additions, as *w. the devil*, etc. 1470. **c.** In pregnant or emphatic sense, referring to a person's origin, character, position, or the like. late ME. **d.** Substituted for the name of a person in asking for an explanation 1749. **2.** In rhetorical questions, suggesting or implying an emphatic contrary assertion OE. **3.** In a dependent question or clause of similar meaning OE. ¶**4.** Used ungrammatically for the objective WHOM (common in colloq. use as obj. of a vb., or of a prep. following the end of a clause) 1450.

1. c. Jesus I knowe, and Paul I knowe: but w. are ye? TINDALE *Acts* 19:15. W. is the Lord that I should obey him? *Exod.* 5:2. **d.** 'My Lord Fellamar.' 'My Lord w.?' FIELDING. **2.** W. stands if freedom fall? KIPLING. *W. would..?* = No one would... *W. would not..?* = Any one would... *W. knows..?* = No one knows... *W. but..?* = no one but, no one else than... Then came brave Glorie puffing by, In silks that whistled, w. but he! 1633. **3.** They throng w. should buy first SHAKS. Did he know w. I was? 1677.

Phrases. *W. is w.*, w. is one and w. is the other; w. each of a number of persons is, or what position each holds. †*W. and w. are* (or *who's*) *together*, w. is allied with or engaged to whom. *Who's W.*, the title of a reference manual of contemporary biography first issued in 1849. *I know not* (mod. *I don't know*) *w.*, *Lord knows w.*, etc., some person or persons unknown, or of unknown origin, status, etc.; so *and I don't know w. all* (colloq. rare) = 'and various other persons unspecified'. *W. not*, any one whatever, any one and every one (now rare or obs.). *Who's-afraid* adj. phr., defiant, swaggering; A vagabondish who's-afraid sort of bearing DICKENS.

II. *rel.* **1.** As compound relative in the nominative in general or indefinite sense: Any one that. *arch.* or *literary.* ME. †**b.** = WHOEVER 2 –1556. **2. As who** (freq. followed by *would* or *should*): as or like one who; hence, as if one. *arch.* late ME. **b.** With the vb. *say*: (*a*) †*as w. saith* or *say*, as they say, as the saying is –1611; (*b*) *as w. should say* (arch.). late ME. **3.** As compound relative, of persons (less freq. a person): The persons (or person) that. *arch.* (Chiefly a latinism; esp. in 'There are w...' = L. *Sunt qui..*) 1596. **4.** As simple relative (of a person or persons), introducing a clause defining or restricting the antecedent and thus completing the sense ME. **5.** As simple relative introducing an additional statement about the antecedent; thus sometimes = 'and he (she, they)' 1466. **6. a.** With antecedent denoting or connoting a number of persons collectively: usu. with pl. concord 1593. **b.** Used in ref. to an animal (or animals) or an inanimate thing (or things): usu. with personification or implication of personality 1585. ¶**7.** In irregular constructions: **a.** with pleonastic personal pronoun in the relative clause, *who* thus becoming a mere link between the clauses; **b.** preceded by redundant *and* 1523. ¶**8.** Used ungrammatically for the objective WHOM (still common colloq. in indefinite sense, = *whomsoever*) ME.

1. W. that holdeth ageynst it we wille slee hym MALORY. Be good, sweet maid, and let w. can be clever KINGSLEY. **2. b.** They command Regard, as w. should say, We are your Defenders 1717. **3.** *Macb.* I. iii. 109. **4.** A man w. hath anie honestie in him SHAKS. **5.** I should do Brutus wrong, and Cassius wrong, Who (you all know) are Honourable men SHAKS. Scots, wha hae wi' Wallace bled BURNS. **7. a.** *Tit. A.* III. i. 37.

III. Substantival nonce-uses. **a.** A person, indefinitely or abstractly; a 'some one' 1654. **b.** with *the*: The question 'who?' 1771.

Who (wō^u), *int.* 1450. [Variant of HO *int.*[2]] Stop! esp. as a call to a horse = next 2.

Whoa (wō^u), *int.* 1623. [Variant of prec.] †**1.** *W. ho ho*, used to call attention from a distance. SHAKS. **2.** A word of command to a horse or other draught-animal to stop or stand still; hence used joc. to a person as a command to stop or desist 1849.

Whoever (hu,e·vəɹ), *pron.* Also (*poet.*) **whoe'er** (-ē^ə·ɹ). ME. [orig. two words, WHO *pron.* and EVER *adv.*] **I. 1.** As compound relative, or with correlative in principal clause: Whatever person or persons; any one who, any who. **2.** Introducing a qualifying clause with conditional or disjunctive force: If any one at all; whether one person or another; no matter who 1500. ¶**3.** Used for the objective: Any one whom; whomsoever 1592.

2. W. you may be, sir,..I am deeply grateful to you DICKENS. **3.** Who ere you find attach SHAKS.

II. *interrog.* An emphatic extension of *who*, implying perplexity or surprise (prop. written as two words). *colloq.* 1875.

Who ever would have thought it? 1875.

Whole (hō^{u}l), *a.*, *sb.*, *adv.* [OE. *hāl* (and *ġehāl*) = OFris., OS. *hēl* (Du. *heel* and *geheel*), (O)HG. *heil*, ON. *heill*, Goth. *hails*, *gahails* :– Gmc. *(*ʒa*)*χailaz*. The sp. with *wh-*, corresp. to a widespread dial. pron. with w, appeared in XV.] **A.** *adj.* **I.** In good condition, sound. **1.** Of a man or animal, the body, limbs, skin: Uninjured, unwounded, unhurt; (contextually) recovered from injury or a wound; †(of a wound) healed. *arch.* **2.** Of inanimate objects: Free from damage or defect; uninjured, unbroken, intact ME. **3.** In good health; free from disease; healthy; (contextually) restored to health, recovered from disease. *arch.* OE.

1. Phr. *As w. as a fish* (*a trout*); They are both as w. as fish SHAKS. *In* (or *with*) *a w. skin*, uninjured. **2.** *Hen. V*, III. ii. 37. **3.** Goo in peace, and be w. off thy plage TINDALE *Mark* 5:34. *fig.* My life is yet w. within me COVERDALE 2 *Sam.* 1:9.

II. Complete, total. **1.** Having all its parts or elements; having its complete or entire extent or magnitude ME. **b.** Containing all its proper or essential constituents; of milk, unskimmed 1794. **2.** The full or total amount of; all, all of. (Only attrib., and now always preceding the sb.) OE. †**b.** In phr. *w. and some*, 'the whole lot', all; in all, altogether –1566. **c.** With rhetorical emphasis, implying an unusually large quantity or number 1628. **3.** Not divided into parts or particles; undivided, entire OE. **b.** *Math.* Of a number: Denoting a complete and undivided thing or a set of such things; integral, not fractional. late ME. **4.** Constituting the total amount, without admixture of anything different; full, unmixed, pure: often opp. to *half*. late ME. **b.** *Bookbinding.* Forming the whole of the cover, as *w. calf* 1839.

2. The roare Of a w. heard of Lyons SHAKS. The ..captain,..upon whom they fix Their w. attention COWPER. The w...manner of looking at things alters 1845. **b.** Sitting..W. days and nights 1664. W. towns..were left in ruins MACAULAY. **3.** One pint of w. oatmeal 1756. Apples..baked w. in a dish 1842. **4.** *W. blood*: see BLOOD *sb.* III. 2; so *w. brother*, *sister*, a brother or sister of the w. blood. *W. holiday*, a day the w. of which is observed as a holiday.

B. *sb.* **1.** The full, complete, or total amount; the assemblage of all the parts, elements, or individuals (*of*). late ME. **b.** In a charade, *my w.* denoted the complete word of which the syllables, called *my first*, *my second*, etc., are the parts 1789. **2.** Something made up of parts in combination or mutual connection; a complex unity or system 1697.

1. The good of the w.,..is the same with the good of all its parts JOHNSON. Thicken with flour, and pour the w. on the deer when roasted 1853. **2.** The complex w. which we call Civilization 1865.

Phrases. **As a w.,** as a complete thing; as a unity; in its entirety, all together. **In (the) w.,** (*a*) to the full amount, in full, entirely, completely; (*b*) in total amount, all together, in all (now *rare*). **On** or **upon the w.,** (*a*) on the basis of the affair as a w., all things considered; hence †(*b*) as the upshot, or summing up, of the whole matter, as a final result, ultimately; (*c*) in respect of the w., notwithstanding exceptions in detail; for the most part; The clergy were regarded as, on the w., a plebeian class MACAULAY.

C. *adv.* Wholly, entirely, fully, perfectly. *Obs.* exc. in nonce-use in explicit or implied opposition to *half.* ME.

The ills thou dost are w. thine own COWLEY. Laying a half-dirty cloth upon a w.-dirty deal table SCOTT.

Special collocations and Combs., etc.: **w.-bred** *a.* of pure breed; **w. cloth,** a piece of cloth of the full size as manufactured; also *fig.* esp. in phr. *cut* (etc.) *out of the w. cloth*; now esp. (*U.S. colloq.* or *slang*) of a statement wholly fabricated or false; **-colour, -coloured** *adjs.*, of the same colour throughout; **-feather,** a variety of pigeon having all the feathers of one colour; so **w.-feathered** *a.*; **-footed** *a.*, †having 'whole' feet, i.e. with the toes united, web-footed, solid-footed; treading with the w. foot on the ground, not lightly or on tiptoe; **-hearted** *a.*, having one's w. heart in something (orig. and chiefly *U.S.*); done with one's w. heart, thoroughly earnest or sincere; **w. hog,** in slang phr. *to go the w. hog* (see HOG *sb.*[1]); hence *w.-hogger, -hoggery,* etc.; **-hoofed** *a.*, having undivided hoofs; **-length** *a.*, (*a*) of a portrait, etc., representing the w. human figure, usu. standing; also *ellipt.* as *sb.*; (*b*) *gen.* exhibited at full length; **w. meal,** meal or flour made from the w. grain of wheat, etc. (occas. including the bran); **-minded** *a.* giving one's w. mind to something, completely interested; **w. note** *Mus.*, a semibreve, as the longest note in ordinary use (now *U.S.*); **w. plate** *Photogr.*, see PLATE *sb.* I. 5 c; **-souled** *a.*, (orig. *U.S.*) = *w.-hearted*; **-time** *a.*, occupying the w. of some particular time, esp. of the working time; (of a person) employed during the w. time; **-timer** = FULL-TIMER. Hence **Who·leness,** the quality or condition of being w.

Wholesale (hōᵘ·lseᶦl), *sb.*, *a.*, *adv.* late ME. **I. 1.** orig. two words, in phr. *by whole sale,* now usu. ellipt. as adv., qualifying *buy, sell,* etc.: In large quantities, in gross (opp. to *by retail*). **2.** *fig.* In a large way, in large numbers or amount, in abundance, indiscriminately 1601.

2. They..throw contempt upon it by w. 1741. Homer never allows distinguished Greeks to fall w. by the Trojan sword 1869.

II. *attrib.* or *adj.* **1. a.** Selling a commodity by w. 1645. **b.** Pertaining to sale in gross; used for a commodity sold by w. 1724. **2.** *fig.* Having an extensive application; unlimited or indiscriminate in range; doing something, or done, profusely or in great quantities 1642.

1. a. A w. Dealer in Silks and Ribbons ADDISON. **2.** A w. admirer of our legal solemnities DICKENS. A w. creation of peers for the purpose of obtaining a majority 1863. Hence **Who·lesaler,** one who sells goods w., a w. dealer.

Wholesome (hōᵘ·lsŏm), *a.* (*sb.*) ME. [OE. **hālsum,* corresp. to OHG. *heilsam,* ON. *heilsamr*; see WHOLE *a.* and -SOME[1].] **1.** Conducive to well-being in general, esp. of mind or character; tending or calculated to do good; beneficial, salutary. **2.** Promoting or conducive to health; health-giving or health-preserving; salubrious. late ME. †**b.** Having the property of restoring health; curative, medicinal –1651. **3.** Sound in (physical or moral) condition or constitution; free from disease or taint; healthy. Now *rare.* 1533. **b.** *transf.* of a quality, condition, place, etc. 1604.

1. To enjoy better air, keep better hours, and employ herself in quieter and wholesomer pleasures SOUTHEY. **2.** Abrecockes..are lesse then the other peches and are holsummer for the stomack 1562. **3.** A plump rosy-cheeked w. apple-faced young woman DICKENS. **b.** In wholsome Wisedome He might not but refuse you SHAKS.

B. as *sb.* in *pl.* Wholesome things 1731. Hence **Who·lesome-ly** *adv.*, **-ness.**

Wholly (hōᵘ·lli, hōᵘ·li), *adv.* [ME. *hol(l)iche, iholliche,* repr. OE. **(ʒe)hālliče*; see WHOLE *a.* and -LY[2]. The normal development *holly* (hǫ·li), which survives in some dials., was generally superseded by a form influenced by *hǭl* WHOLE, whence the present pronunc. The current sp. *wholly* derives from ME. *holliche,* and has superseded the once frequent *wholely, wholy.*] **1.** As a whole, in its entirety, in full, throughout, all of it (now *rare*). **2.** Completely, entirely, to the full extent; altogether, thoroughly, quite ME. **b.** Entirely, so as to exclude everything else; hence practically = exclusively, solely, only. late ME.

1. *Non omnis moriar,* I shall not w. die 1681. **2.** Sleepe hath ceiz'd me w. SHAKS. We were w. at a loss what to do 1833. **b.** A creature w. given to brawls and wine TENNYSON.

Whom (hūm), *pron.* [repr. formally OE. *hwām,* later variant of *hwǣm* (:– **hwaimi*), dat. of *hwā* WHO, *hwæt* WHAT. In its usage, *whom* combines the functions of OE. *hwǣm* and OE. *hwone, hwane, hwæne,* acc. masc. of *hwā.*] The objective case of WHO: no longer current in unstudied colloquial speech. ¶**b.** Used for the nominative WHO, esp. (in later use only) when taken as obj. of a vb. of which the whole clause is really the obj. 1467. ¶**c.** In irregular constructions. (*a*) With pleonastic personal pronoun; often also with anacoluthon, *whom* serving as apparent obj. to a vb. whose real obj. is a dependent clause of which the pron. is subj.; (*b*) preceded by redundant *and* 1556.

To w. lesse is forgiuen, the same doeth lesse loue TINDALE *Luke* 7:47. W. shall I sende, and who wilbe oure messaunger? COVERDALE *Isa.* 6:8. Chose you this daye w. ye wyll serue COVERDALE *Josh.* 24:15. W. he wolde, he set vp: & w. he list, he put downe COVERDALE *Dan.* 5:19. This is the man, w. I spake to the of BIBLE (Great) 1 *Sam.* 9:17. I..am come to see of w. such noise Hath walk'd about MILT. For w. in the world do you think that I was kept so long kicking my heels? 1780. 'W. the gods love die young' was said of yore BYRON. **b.** Tel me in sadnes whome she is you loue SHAKS. **c.** Let him be w. he will 1603.

Whomever (hūme·vəɹ), *pron.* Also (*poet.*) **whome'er** (-ēᵊɹ). *literary.* ME. [orig. two words WHOM and EVER *adv.*] The objective case of WHOEVER. (Less frequent than WHOMSOEVER.)

Whomso (hū·msoᵘ), *pron. arch.*, chiefly *poet.* [Early ME. *swa hwam swa*; see WHOM and SO *adv.*] = next.

Whomsoever (hūmsoᵘe·vəɹ), *pron.*; also (*poet.*) **whomsoe'er** (-ēᵊ·ɹ). *literary.* 1450. The objective case of WHOSOEVER. ¶**b.** Used for WHOSOEVER, chiefly by attraction to the case of the unexpressed antecedent 1560.

b. They shall not be impeded by w. it may be RUSKIN.

Whoo (hwū), *int.* 1608. [Variant of HOO *int.*] An exclam. of surprise, grief, or other emotion; *occas.* an imitation of an owl's hoot. So **Whoo** *sb.* an utterance of this, or a similar sound. **Whoo** *v. intr.* to utter this sound.

Whoof (hwūf, hwuf), *int.* (*sb.*, *v.*) 1766. Imitation of a gruff abrupt cry or noise; as *vb.* to utter such a cry.

Whoop (hūp), *sb.* 1600. [f. WHOOP *int.* Cf. HOOP *sb.*[2]] **1.** An act of whooping; a cry of 'whoop!', or a shout or call resembling this; *spec.* as used in hunting, esp. at the death of the game, or by N. Amer. Indians, etc. as a signal or war-cry. **b.** The characteristic sonorous inspiration following a fit of coughing in whooping-cough 1873. **2.** A form of the game of hide-and-seek 1798.

Whoop (hūp), *v.* late ME. [Parallel w. next. Cf. HOOP *v.*[2]] **1.** *intr.* To utter a cry of 'whoop!' or a loud vocal sound resembling this; to shout (as in summons, exultation, defiance, or mere excitement). **b.** *trans.* with obj. of cognate meaning, or indef. *it*: To utter with a whoop; to express by whooping 1576. **c.** with adv. or advb. phr: To bring, summon, or urge by or with whooping. late ME. **d.** To shout at, hoot (a person). *rare.* 1690. **e.** *U.S.* To increase or raise 1896. **2.** *intr.* To hoot, as an owl. Also *trans.* 1658. **3.** To utter the 'whoop' in whooping-cough 1887.

1. With that the shepheard whoop'd for ioy DRAYTON. **2.** Owls whooping after Sunset..foreshews a fair day to ensue 1658. Hence **Whoo·per,** a person or animal that whoops; *spec.* the wild or whistling swan, *Cygnus musicus* (*ferus*). **Whoo·ping** *ppl. a.* that whoops; esp. in **whooping crane,** the large white crane of America, *Grus americana,* **whooping swan,** the whooper.

Whoop (hūp), *int.* 1568. [A natural exclam.] An exclam., or representation of a shout or cry, expressing excitement, etc.

W. Iugge I loue thee SHAKS. Whop Sir, thought I, and what ado's here? 1691.

Whoopee (hū·pi), *int.* orig. *U.S.* 1845. An exclam. accompanying or inviting to hilarious enjoyment; also *sb.*, esp. in *to make w.*, to have a good time, go on the razzle-dazzle.

Whooping-cough (hū·piŋ,kǫf). 1739. The now prevalent spelling of HOOPING-COUGH.

Whoosh (hwūʃ, hwuʃ), *v.* 1856. [Imitative.] *intr.* To utter or emit a dull soft sibilant sound, like that of something rushing through the air. So **Whoosh** *sb.* a sound of this nature.

Who(o)-whoop (hŭhū·p), *int.* and *sb.* 1611. The shout of the huntsmen at the death of the game. Hence **Whoo-whoo·p** *v.* to utter this cry.

Whop (hwǫp), *v.* (*adv.*) late ME. [Variant of WAP *v.*] **1.** *trans.* To cast, pull out, etc. violently; to take or put suddenly. *dial.* **2.** To strike with heavy blows; to beat soundly, flog. *colloq.* or *vulgar.* 1575. **b.** *fig.* To overcome, vanquish, defeat utterly; hence, to surpass or excel greatly. *colloq.* or *vulgar* 1836. **3.** The vb.-stem used as *adv.*: With a 'whop'; with a sudden movement or impact 1812.

2. Ain't nobody to be whopped for takin' this here liberty, sir? DICKENS. **b.** Nelson, as was a British General and wopped the French 1865. Hence **Whop** *sb.* an act of whopping; a heavy blow or impact (*colloq.* or *vulgar*). **Who·pping** *vbl. sb.* the action of the vb.; a severe beating or flogging.

Whopper (hwǫ·pəɹ). *colloq.* or *vulgar.* 1785. [f. prec. + -ER[1].] Something uncommonly large of its kind; a very big thing, animal, or person. **b.** *spec.* A great lie, a monstrous falsehood 1791.

b. Better to get a licking than to tell a w. 1870.

Who·pping, *ppl. a. colloq.* or *vulgar.* 1625. [f. as prec. + -ING[2].] That whops; usu. *fig.* that is a 'whopper'; abnormally large or great; 'thumping'.

Whore (hōᵊɹ), *sb.* [Late OE. *hōre,* corresp. to (M)LG. *hore,* MDu. *hoere* (Du. *hoer*), OHG. *huora* (G. *hure*), ON. *hóra* :– Gmc. **xōrōn,* f. base repr. also by ON. *hórr,* Goth. *hōrs* adulterer; the IE. base **qār-* appears in L. *cārus* dear. For *wh-* cf. WHOLE. The normally developed pronunc. (hūᵊɹ) remains in local use.] **1.** A woman who prostitutes herself for hire; a prostitute, harlot. **b.** More gen.: An unchaste or lewd woman; a fornicatress or adulteress; occas. applied opprobriously to a concubine or kept mistress; also, with distinguishing epithet, to a catamite. ME. **2.** *fig.*; *spec.* in bibl. use, applied to a corrupt or idolatrous community, and hence in controversial use, esp. in phr. *the w. of Babylon,* to the Church of Rome (in allusion to Rev. 17:1, 5, etc.). late ME.

1. *Whore's bird* (also dial. *wosbird*), prop., the child of a w.; but usu. as a mere vulgar term of abuse or reprobation. **b.** *To play the w.* (of a woman) to commit fornication or adultery.

Comb.: †**w.-house,** a brothel; †**-hunt** *v. intr.* to go after whores, practise fornication; **-master** (*Obs.* or *arch.*), a whoremonger.

Whore, *v.* 1583. [f. prec.] **1.** *intr.* To have to do with a whore or whores; to commit whoredom; (of a woman) to play the whore. †**2.** *trans.* To make a whore of; to debauch (a woman) –1740. Hence **Who·ring** *vbl. sb.* the action of the vb.; also *fig.*, *spec.* in bibl. use: chiefly in phr. *to go a whoring.*

Whoredom (hōᵊ·ɹdəm). *arch.* ME. [prob. – ON. *hórdómr* = OFris. *hōrdōm*; see -DOM.] **1.** The practice of playing the whore or of intercourse with whores; illicit sexual indulgence in general. **b.** *pl.* Acts of sexual immorality ME. **2.** *fig.*, *esp.* in bibl. and religious use, applied to idolatry or other form of unfaithfulness to the true God. late ME.

Whoremonger (hōᵊ·ɹmɒ:ŋgəɹ). *arch.* 1526. [f. WHORE *sb.* + MONGER.] One who has dealings with whores; one who practises whoredom; a fornicator. So **Who·re-mo:nging,** the practice of a w.

Whoreson (hōᵊ·ɹsən). *Obs.* or *arch.* ME. [f. WHORE *sb.* + SON *sb.*, after AFr. *fiz a putain.*] prop. The son of a whore, but commonly used as a coarse term of reprobation, abuse, or contempt; occas. even of jocular familiarity. **b.** *attrib.*: commonly as a coarsely abusive epithet, applied to a person or thing; also sometimes expressing humorous familiarity or commendation.

Whorish (hōᵊ·riʃ), *a.* Now *rare* or *Obs.* 1535. [f. WHORE *sb.* + -ISH[1].] **1.** Having the character of a whore; addicted to whoredom; lewd, unchaste 1560. **b.** Belonging to or characteristic of a whore; lewd, unchaste 1552. **2.** *fig.*, esp. in religious and controversial use (often = idolatrous) 1535. Hence **Who·rish-ly** *adv.*, **-ness.**

Whorl (hwǭɹl, hwǭɹl). 1440. [Earliest forms *wharwyl, whorwil,* of E. Anglian or north. provenance; prob. vars. of *wherwille,*

WHIRL, infl. by †*wharve* turn, WHARVE *sb.* and Du. †*worvel*, var. of *wervel*.] **1.** A small fly-wheel fixed on the spindle of a spinning-wheel to maintain or regulate the speed; a small pulley by which the spindle is driven in a spinning-machine. **2.** *Bot.* A set of members, as leaves, flowers, or parts of the flower, springing from the stem or axis at the same level and encircling it. Also in *Zool.* a set of parts or structures similarly arranged. 1578. **3.** *Conch.* and *Anat.* Each of the turns, coils, or convolutions of a spiral shell, or of any spiral structure 1828. **4.** *gen.* A convolution, coil, curl (esp. of something whirling, or suggesting a whirling movement) 1592.

3. See what a lovely shell, Small and pure as a pearl,..With delicate spire and w. TENNYSON.

Comb.: **w.-flower,** a plant of the genus *Morina* (family *Dipsacaceæ*), having the flowers in dense whorls; **-grass,** a grass of the genus *Catabrosa*. Hence **Whorled** (hwǭɹld) *a.* having or arranged in a w. or whorls; verticillate; convoluted, turbinate.

Whort (hwɒ̄ɹt). *dial.* 1578. [South-western dial. f. HURT *sb.*[3]] = WHORTLEBERRY.

Whortle (hwɒ̄·ɹt'l). 1597. [Short for WHORTLEBERRY.] = next.

Whortleberry (hwɒ̄·ɹtl'lbĕri). 1578. [South-western dial. f. HURTLEBERRY; now the usual book-name. For the sp. with *wh-* cf. (dial.) *whoam* home, WHOLE, WHORE.] The blue-black fruit of the dwarf shrub *Vaccinium myrtillus*, or the plant itself; the BILBERRY. Also extended to the genus *Vaccinium* as a whole (excepting the species called CRANBERRY, *V. oxycoccos* and *V. macrocarpon*).

Bear's w., the Bearberry, *Arctostaphylos uvaursi*. **Bog w.,** *Vaccinium uliginosum*. **Red w.,** *V. vitis-idæa*. **Victorian w.,** *Wittsteinia vacciniacea* a shrub allied to *Vaccinium*, found in Victoria.

Whory (hōᵊ·ri), *a. rare.* 1862. [f. WHORE *sb.* + -Y[1].] = WHORISH.

Whose (hūz), *pron.* [Early ME. *hwās*, *hwōs* (XII–XIII), alt., by assim. to *hwā*, *hwō* WHO, *hwām* WHOM, of *hwas*, *hwes*, OE. *hwæs* gen. of masc. *hwā* and n. *hwæt* WHAT, in interrog. use only :- **χwasa*.] The genitive case of WHO (and in OE. of the neuter WHAT). Used, in all senses, either before a sb. as a possessive adj., or *absol.*: in the latter case chiefly *interrog.* as predicate. In ref. to things now usu. replaced by *of which*, exc. where this would produce an intolerably clumsy form.

I could a Tale vnfold, w. lightest word Would harrow vp thy soule SHAKS. Arrest me? at w. sute? 1607. The man w. these are *Gen.* 38:25. Any thing w. loss they can so easily supply 1754. Fishermen, who's humanity he had occasion to remember GOLDSM. I cheer a dead man's sweetheart, Never ask me w. HOUSMAN. So **Whosesoever** (hūzsoᵘe·vəɹ) *pron. arch.* whatever person's; of whomsoever.

Whoso (hū·soᵘ), *pron. arch.* [ME. *hwa swa*, *hwa se*, reduced form of OE. *swā hwā swā*; see SO *adv.*] = WHOEVER 1, 2.

W. eats thereof, forthwith attains Wisdom MILT.

Whosoever (hūsoᵘe·vəɹ), *pron.* Also *poet.* **whosoe'er** (-ēᵊ·ɹ). ME. [f. prec. + EVER *adv.*] **1.** = WHOEVER 1. **2.** = WHOEVER 2; also formerly = 'if any one' ME. **3.** With loss of relative force: Any one at all. Now *rare* or *Obs.* 1583. **b.** qualifying a preceding sb. or *any*: now usu. replaced by WHATEVER 1586.

1. Let w. wyll, take of the water of lyfe fre TINDALE *Rev.* 22:17. **2.** Margaret my name, and daughter to a King,..who so ere thou art SHAKS. **3. b.** Gentlemen, and curteous Readers whosoeuer 1586.

†**Whosome,** *pron.* ME. [f. WHO + -SOME[3] *adv.*] = WHOEVER 1, 2. –late ME.

Whosomever (hūsɒ̆mˌe·vəɹ), *pron. Obs.* or *dial.* late ME. [f. prec. + EVER *adv.*] = WHOEVER.

Who some euer you take him to be, he is Aiax SHAKS.

Whuff (hwɒf), *v.* 1896. [imit.; cf. WHOOF.] *intr.* To make a sound as of a forcible blast of breath or wind; *trans.* to utter with such a sound.

Why (hwəi), *adv.*, *sb.*, *int.* [OE. *hwī*, *hwȳ*, instr. case of *hwæt* WHAT, governed by *tō* or *for* (whence †*forwhy* why, because), or simply as adv., corresp. to OS. *hwī*, ON. *hví* :- Gmc. **χwī* :- IE. **qʷei*, loc. of **qʷo-* WHO, WHAT (cf. Doric πεῖ where).] **I. 1.** In a direct question: For what reason? From what cause or motive? For what purpose? Wherefore? **b.** Implying or suggesting a negative assertion (= 'there is no reason why..'); hence often expressing a protest or objection OE. **c.** With ellipsis of the remainder of the sentence, or of all except the principal word or words (esp. when emphatic); also with simple inf. (= 'W. should one..?'). late ME. **2.** In an indirect question or dependent clause of similar meaning OE. **3.** With intensive additions: see DEVIL *sb.*, DICKENS, etc. 1475. **4.** With a negative particle immediately following OE.

1. W. don't you learn Italian? 1883. **b.** Whie should our faults at home be spred abroad? 1608. W., w. was I born to undergo such unmerited misfortunes? THACKERAY. **c.** W. so Cold, and w. so Coy? VANBRUGH. But w. prolong the tale? WORDSW. **2.** I dare give him no counsell, and I will tell you w. 1581. **3.** W. in the name of all patience should you work so hard as this? 1860. **4.** You can't marry me? W. not? When I offer you a fortune? 1882.

II. As relative: On account of which, because of which, for which. Usu., now almost always, after *reason*. Also *ellipt.* ME. **b.** Introducing a subject or predicative clause: = 'the reason w.' 1605.

Reasons w. Catholiques refuse to go to Church 1581. I'll have my Earl, as well as She, or know the Reason w. PRIOR. **b.** And this is w. I sojourn here KEATS.

III. as *sb.* (pl. *whys*). **a.** Reason, cause (now only with conscious allusion to the interrogative use) ME. **b.** A question beginning with (or consisting of) the word 'Why?'; a question as to the reason of something; hence, a problem, an enigma 1532. **c.** Conjoined with *wherefore* similarly used 1590.

a. As may perchance be done for sum gude quhy 1560. The when, and the how, and the w. of the surrender SOUTHEY. **c.** The savage is no authority on the w. and wherefore of his customs 1911.

IV. Used interjectionally before a sentence or clause. **a.** As an expression of surprise (sometimes only momentary or slight, sometimes involving protest), either in reply to a remark or question, or on perceiving something unexpected 1519. **b.** Emphasizing or calling more or less abrupt attention to the statement following, in opposition to a possible or vaguely apprehended doubt or objection 1545. †**c.** As an emphasized call or summons, expressing some degree of impatience. SHAKS. †**d.** *W., so!* an expression of content, acquiescence, or relief –1826.

a. *Bene.* Doo not you loue me? *Beat.* W. no, no more then reason SHAKS. W., I believe I've been asleep! 1893. **b.** Take an honest woman from her husband! w., it is intollerable 1596. If you will have Caesar for your master, w. have him GOLDSM. Not a doubt... W., it stands to reason. 1882. **c.** *Rom. & Jul.* IV. v. 2, 3. **d.** *Macb.* III. iv. 107.

V. For w.: a. *interrog.* For what reason; **b.** *rel.* For which reason, wherefore; **c.** *conj.* For the reason that, because, for. *Obs.*, *arch.*, or *dial.* (Now commonly apprehended as the adv. *why* with a redundant *for* prefixed.) OE.

As for what he was like I cannot tell,..for w. I never saw un SCOTT. Hence **Whye·ver** *adv.* for whatever reason. †**Why-for, why for** *advb.* and *conj. phr.*

Why-not (hwəi·nǫt). 1611. [The phr. *why not?* used as sb.] An argument of the form 'why not?', which attempts to leave the opponent without a reply.

Wibble-wobble (wi·b'lwǫ·b'l). *colloq.* 1847. Reduplication of WOBBLE. So **Wi·bbly-wo·bbly** *a.* characterized by 'wibbling and wobbling', unsteady.

Wich, wych (witʃ, *locally* wəitʃ). *local.* 1601. [app. a differentiated variant of WICK *sb.*[2] Cf. the place-names (of salt-making towns) *Droitwich* (formerly *Wich*), *Nantwich*, *Northwich*; cf. *ditch* and *dike* (OE. *dīć*), *lich* and *lyke* (OE. *līć*).] A salt-works, salt-pit, or brine-spring, in the salt-manufacturing district of Cheshire and neighbouring parts; *pl.* the salt-making towns of these parts.

Comb.: **w.-house,** a building in which brine is evaporated for making salt; **-man,** a man employed in salt-making; **-waller,** a salt-boiler.

Wick[1] (wik). [OE. *wēoc* (in *candelwēoc*), *wēoce*, corresp. to MDu. *wiecke* (Du. *wiek*), MLG. *wēke*, OHG. *wiohha* (G. *wieche*), of unkn. origin. For the vocalism cf. SICK.] The bundle of fibre, now usu. loosely twisted or woven cotton, in a lamp, candle, or taper (formerly also in a torch), immersed or enclosed except at one end in the oil or grease, which it absorbs and draws up on being kindled at the free end, so as to maintain the flame. **b.** Without article = WICKING. late ME. **c.** Used as a tent or dressing in surgery 1658.

Wick[2] (wik). Now only *local.* [OE. *wīc* = OFris. *wīk*, OS. *wīc* (Du. *wijk* quarter, district, ward), OHG. *wīh* (G. in *weichbild* municipal area), Goth. *weihs* village; prob. Gmc. – L. *vicus* row of houses, street, village, cogn. with Gr. οἶκος house. Survives locally and in BAILIWICK.] †**1.** An abode, dwelling, dwelling-place –ME. **2.** A town, village, or hamlet. *Obs.* or *dial.* (Surviving as an element of place-names in forms *-wich*, *-wick*.) OE. **3.** A farm; *spec.* a dairy farm: Now *local.* OE.

-wick, *suffix*, shortened form of †*wike* (OE. *wīce*) office, function of an official, as in BAILIFFWICK, BAILIWICK, SHERIFFWICK.

Wicked (wi·kĕd), *a.*[1] (*sb.*, *adv.*) ME. [f. ME. *wicke*, *wikke* (which survives as dial. *wick*) + -ED[2]. Cf. WRETCHED.] **I. 1.** Bad in moral character, disposition, or conduct; practising or disposed to practise evil; morally depraved. **2.** Bad, in various senses. Freq. in ME.; later chiefly *dial.*, or *colloq.* as a conscious metaphor (now often joc.) from sense 1, = 'very or excessively bad', 'beastly'. **a.** In ref. to character or action: Cruel, severe, fierce. Of animals: Savage, vicious ME. **b.** Actually or potentially harmful, destructive, or pernicious; baleful ME. **c.** Of bad quality; poor, vile, 'sorry' ME. **3.** In weakened sense, usu. more or less joc.: Malicious; mischievous, sly 1600.

1. The Divine Vengeance on a W. World 1696. Vice increases, and men grow daily more and more w. BERKELEY. 'Yes, hang it' (said Sir Pitt, only, he used, dear, a much wickeder word) THACKERAY. **2. b.** *Temp.* I. ii. 321. It was a w. country for fever 1895. **3.** That same w. Bastard of Venus,..that blinde rascally boy SHAKS.

II. *absol.* or as *sb.* **a.** *absol.* in *pl.* sense: Wicked persons. (Usu., now always, with *the*.) ME. **b.** *absol.* or as *sb.* in *sing.* sense: A wicked person. *Obs.* or *rare arch.* 1484.

b. Let the w. forsake his waies BIBLE (Geneva) *Isa.* 55:7.

III. as *adv.* Wickedly; fiercely, savagely, furiously; 'cruelly', 'terribly'. late ME.

Yesterday was..a w. hot day 1663. A hungry louse bites w. sair HOGG. Hence **Wi·cked-ly** *adv.*; **-ness,** the quality of being w.; w. action or conduct; a piece of wickedness, a w. act or proceeding.

Wicked (wikt), *a.*[2] 1507. [f. WICK[1] + -ED[2].] Furnished with or having a wick or wicks; usu. in comb., as *two-w.*

Wicker (wi·kəɹ), *sb.* ME. [Of E. Scand. origin (cf. Sw. *viker*, Da. *viger* willow), f. base of Sw. *vika* bend (cf. OE. *wīcan* give way, collapse, and WEAK).] **1.** A pliant twig or small rod, usu. of willow, esp. as used for making baskets and various other objects; an osier. Chiefly in *pl.* late ME. **2.** (without *pl.*) Wickers collectively, or as plaited together; wickerwork ME. **3.** A basket, cradle, chair, etc. of wicker 1646. **4. a.** *attrib.* Made or consisting of wicker, as a basket, chair, etc.; also, covered with or encased in wicker, as a bottle 1502. **b.** *W. wings*, attributed to various sinister creatures 1637.

4. b. The Goblin plys his w. wings CONGREVE. Hence **Wi·cker** *v. trans.* to furnish, fit, cover, or enclose with w. **Wi·ckered** (-əɹd) *a.* encased in w.; made of w. **Wi·ckerwork,** work consisting of wickers; a structure of flexible twigs or the like plaited together; basket-work.

Wicket (wi·kĕt). ME. [– AFr., ONFr. *wiket* = (O)Fr. *guichet*, usu. referred to the Gmc. base appearing in ON. *vikja* move, turn (Sw. *vika*, Da. *vige*).] **1.** A small door or gate made in or placed beside a large one, for ingress and egress when the large one is closed; also, any small gate for foot-passengers, as at the entrance of a field. **2.** *Cricket.* A set of three sticks called *stumps*, fixed upright in the ground, and surmounted by two small pieces of wood called *bails*, forming the structure at which the bowler aims the ball, and at which (in front and a little to one side of it) the batsman stands to defend it with the bat 1733. **b.** In various expressions referring to a batsman's tenure of the wicket, or that part of an innings during which some particular batsman is (or might be) 'in', i.e. at the wicket 1738. **c.** *transf.* The ground between and about the wickets, esp. in respect of its condition; the pitch 1862. **3.** *U.S. Croquet.* A hoop 1868. **4.** In various techn. senses, as (*a*) a small gate or valve for emptying the chamber of a canal-lock, etc.; (*b*) one of a set of gratings in the form of which the lead is made up in the manufacture of white lead 1875.

2. *Single w.*, a form of cricket in which there is only one w., and therefore only one batsman 'in' at a time. *Double w.*, the ordinary form, in which there are two wickets placed 22 yards apart, between which the two batsmen run. *To keep w.*, to act as w.-keeper. **b.** *To take* so many *wickets* (said of a bowler), to put so many batsmen 'out'. *Three wickets* (or *third w.*) *down*, three men having been put out. *The sixth w. fell for 75* = the sixth batsman was put out after 75 runs had been made in the innings. *To win by eight wickets*, i.e. by exceeding the opponents' full score of runs with eight wickets yet to 'fall' (= with two men 'not out' and seven not having been 'in' in the innings). **c.** The w. did not seem to play particularly well 1881. The English eleven commenced batting on a perfect w. 1884.

attrib. and *Comb.*: **w.-gate** = sense 1; **-keep** (*colloq.*), **-keeper** *Cricket*, a player stationed behind the w. to stop the ball if it passes by, and if possible to put the batsman 'out' by 'stumping' or 'catching'.

Wicking (wi·kiŋ). 1873. [f. WICK[1] + -ING[1].] Material for making wicks; cord or tape of cotton or other fibre, to be cut into lengths for wicks.

Wickyup (wi·ki,ɒp). *U.S.* 1857. [Amer. Indian (Menominee *wikiop*, Saki *wekeab*); perh. a variant of *wikiwam* WIGWAM.] A rude hut consisting of a frame covered with brushwood or the like, used by nomadic tribes in the west and south-west. Hence extended to any small hut or shanty.

Wicopy (wi·kŏpi). 1778. [Amer. Indian (Cree *wikupiy*).] **a.** The leatherwood or moosewood of N. America, *Dirca palustris*; also the basswood, *Tilia americana*. **b.** An Amer. name for species of willow-herb (*Epilobium*): distinctively *Indian* or *herb w.*

Widdershins: see WITHERSHINS.

Widdy (wi·di). Chiefly *Sc.* 1450. [Sc. and n. dial. var. of WITHY.] **1.** A band or rope, prop. one made of intertwined osiers or the like 1470. **2.** A rope for hanging, a halter; freq. *allus.* 1450.

Wide (wəid), *sb.* ME. [absol. use of next.] **1.** †**a.** The open sea. ME. only. **b.** A wide, extensive, or open space *poet.* 1833. **2.** *Cricket.* [Short for *wide ball.*] A ball bowled wide of the wicket, counting one against the bowler's side 1850. **3.** *The w.* (short for 'the wide world') in slang. phr., as *done, whacked to the w.*, utterly done up; *broke to the w.*, completely broke.

Wide (wəid), *a.* [OE. *wīd* = OFris., OS. *wīd*, OHG. *wīt* (Du. *wijd*, G. *weit*), ON. *víðr* :- Gmc. **wīdaz*, of unkn. origin.] **I. 1.** Having great extent (esp. horizontally); vast, spacious, extensive. *Obs.* exc. as generalized use of II. 1. **b.** as a conventional epithet of words denoting an extensive area, esp. the earth and the sea (*poet.* and *rhet.*); as an epithet of *world*, sometimes implying contrast to the privacy or security of one's own home or country OE. **c.** Of a garment, etc.: Capacious; large and loose. *Obs.* exc. *dial.* in *w. coat*, a greatcoat. ME. **2.** *transf.* Extending over or affecting a large space or region; far-reaching. Chiefly *poet.* OE. **3.** *fig.* Having a large range; extensive, largely inclusive; (of a word or term) having a large extent of meaning 1534. **b.** Of views or opinions, or *transf.* of a person: = BROAD *a.* 10. 1824.

1. *A.Y.L.* II. vii. 137. **b.** I shall be turn'd a drift to the w. World DE FOE. **c.** And there the Snake throwes her enammel'd skinne, Weed w. enough to wrap a Fairy in SHAKS. **3.** A definition of art w. enough to include all its varieties of aim RUSKIN. His w. knowledge of ethnography 1865.

II. 1. Having great extent from side to side; large across, or in transverse measurement (now dist. from *broad* in so far as it tends to be restricted to applications in which actual mensuration is possible, and in which there is no implication of superficial extent) OE. **b.** *transf.* of the lateral boundaries: Having a wide space between, far apart 1840. **2.** Having a specified or particular transverse measurement indicated by a numerical quantity or by a comparison; (so much) across OE. **3.** Opened widely, expanded; of the arms, stretched widely apart. (Now superseded in general use by *w. open.*) 1508. **b.** *Phonetics.* Of a vowel-sound: Pronounced with the tongue relaxed, or with a wider opening between it and some other part of the mouth than the corresponding *narrow* vowel 1867.

2. 'Tis not so deepe as a well, nor so w. as a Church doore SHAKS. A Bed-chamber..Thirty foot w. 1663.

III. 1. Extending far between limits; existing between two things which are far apart, *lit.* or *fig.* 1589. †**2.** Situated a great way off, distant, far -1854. **b.** *fig.* Far, far apart (in nature, views, etc.); not in accordance, disagreeing, different. Const. *from, of.* Now *rare.* 1542. **3.** Deviating from the aim, or from the direct or proper course; missing the mark or the way. **a.** *lit.*; *spec.* in *Cricket*, of a ball bowled too far aside from the wicket for the batsman to strike it 1588. **b.** *fig.* (*a*) without prep. (now *rare*): often = Astray in opinion or belief, mistaken 1561. (*b*) Const. *of, from* (now rare or obs.): esp. in phr. *w. of the mark* 1566. **4. a.** Going beyond bounds of restraint, propriety, or virtue; loose, immoral. Now *colloq.* or *slang.* 1574. **b.** Going beyond bounds of moderation; excessive, immoderate 1858. **c.** *slang.* Wide-awake, shrewd 1887.

1. The w. difference 'Twixt Amorous, and Villanous SHAKS. *To give a w. berth to*, to keep well away from, steer quite clear of. **3. b.** *Lear* IV. vii. 50. **4. a.** W. females in pink 1902. **c.** Well, she was tipsy; but she was very 'w.' 1891.

Comb.: *w.-brimmed* adj.; **w.-angle** *a.*, applied to a lens of short focus, the field of which extends through a w. angle, used for photographing at short range; **-eyed** *a.*, having w. eyes; usu., having the eyes wide open, gazing intently; **-watered,** having a w. expanse of water; watered over a w. extent; bordered or traversed by w. waters.

Wide (wəid), *adv.* [OE. *wīde*, advb. f. *wīd* WIDE *a.*] Widely. **1.** Over or through a large space or region; so as to affect many or various persons or places. Chiefly *poet.* (exc. as in b). **b.** in phr. *far and w.* (rarely *w. and far*); †*w. and side* OE. **2.** With a large space or spaces between; at a wide interval or intervals; far apart or asunder OE. **b.** Of a horse: With the legs apart: opp. to NEAR *adv.*[2] I. 10. 1680. **c.** Loosely asunder; so as not to remain close or in contact 1784. **3.** With a wide or broad opening; esp. with *open* vb. or adj. = fully; with *fling, fly*, etc. = *wide open* OE. **4.** At (to, from) a (great, or specified) distance; far, far away, far off. Now only *dial.* OE. **5.** At a distance to one side; aside from the aim, or from the direct or proper course 1534.

1. There..W. roams the Russian exile THOMSON. **b.** They scoured the country far and w. 1862. **2. c.** Shaking w. thy yellow hair SHELLEY. **3.** This is a strange repose, to be asleepe With eyes w. open SHAKS. The doors were flung w. 1895. **5.** Is my Lord well, that he doth speake so w.? SHAKS. You hurt not me, Your anger flies so w. FLETCHER. A..ball..pitched a little w. of the off stump 1833.

Wi·de awa·ke, *adj. phr.*, **wi·de-awake,** *a.* and *sb.* 1818. [f. prec. + AWAKE *pred. a.*] **A.** *adj.* (or *adj. phr.*) **1.** Awake with the eyes wide open; full awake (usu. *predic.*). **2.** *fig.* Thoroughly vigilant or on the alert; fully aware of what is going on or of what it is best to do; sharp-witted, knowing (*colloq.*, orig. *slang*) 1833. **3.** Applied joc. to a soft felt hat with broad brim and low crown: app. so called as having no 'nap'. Now usu. *absol.* as *sb.* 1841.

2. Our governor's wide awake, he is..He knows what's o'clock DICKENS.

B. *sb.* **1.** A 'wide-awake' hat 1837. **2.** A sailor's name for the Sooty Tern (*Sterna fuliginosa* and allied species) from its cry 1881. Hence **Wide-awa·keness,** the state or character of being wide awake.

Widely (wəi·dli), *adv.* 1663. [f. WIDE *a.* + -LY[2].] **1.** Over or through a wide area; in or to various places 1697. **2.** Over a wide range; in relation to many or various things, subjects, etc. 1695. **3.** With or at a wide interval; far apart; to a considerable width 1663. **4.** To a large extent, greatly, far 1688.

Wide-mouthed (-mauðd, -mauþt), *a.* 1593. **1.** Having a wide mouth 1611. **2.** Having the mouth wide open: (*a*) loud-spoken; (*b*) voracious.

Widen (wəi·d'n), *v.* 1607. [f. WIDE *a.* + -EN[5].] †**1.** *trans.* To open wide, set wide open -1627. **2.** To make wide or wider 1669. **3.** *intr.* To become wide or wider 1650.

1. *Cor.* I. iv. 44. **2.** I would cleanse, w., and deepen the river Stort 1785. The society is widening its scheme of operations 1885. **3.** A reall quarrell widening 1650. The streamlet widens into a pond 1920. Hence **Wi·dener,** one who or that which widens; *spec.* a drill constructed to bore a hole of greater diameter than its own.

Wideness (wəi·dnės). OE. Also **widness** (*Obs.* or *dial.*). [f. WIDE *a.* + -NESS.] Width: **a.** Large extension, vastness (in later use only as transf. use of c) ME.; **b.** Transverse measurement, breadth OE. (in standard Eng. replaced by WIDTH); **c.** Large transverse measurement 1548. **d.** *concr.* A wide space or expanse. **e.** Largeness of range, wide reach 1551.

Wide-open, *a.* 1610. [WIDE *adv.* 3.] **1.** Open to a wide extent. **2.** *U.S.* Free from limitations or restrictions; also, characterized by overt law-breaking 1902.

Wide-spread, *a.* 1705. [f. WIDE *adv.* + *spread*, pa. pple. of SPREAD *v.*] **1.** Extended over or occupying a wide space; broad in spatial extent 1735. **2.** Distributed over a wide region; extensively or generally diffused 1705.

Wide-spreading, *a.* 1591. **1.** Extending over a wide space. **2.** Extending to many places or persons, far-reaching 1766.

†**Wide-where,** *adv. Obs.* exc. *rare arch.* ME. [f. WIDE *adv.* + WHERE *adv.*] In or to various places, widely, far and wide; in or to a distant place, far away -1906.

Widgeon, wigeon (wi·dʒən). 1513. [perh. f. echoic base **wi-*, after PIGEON *sb.*; parallel formations of later date are Fr. *vigeon, vingeon, gingeon, digeon.*] **1.** A wild duck of the genus *Mareca*, esp. *M. penelope* of Europe and Northern Asia. (Collective pl. in later use usu. *widgeon.*) **b.** Applied locally to various wild ducks of other genera, as *Anas fusca*, the Redheaded W. 1668. †**2.** Of a person, in allusion to the supposed stupidity of the bird: A fool, simpleton, ninny -1741.

attrib. and *Comb.*: **w.-grass, -weed,** (*local*) the grass-wrack, *Zostera marina.*

Widish (wəi·diʃ), *a.* 1780. [f. WIDE *a.* + -ISH[1].] Somewhat wide.

Widow (wi·do[u]), *sb.*[1] [OE. *widewe, wuduwe* = OFris. *widwe*, OS. *widowa*, OHG. *wituwa* (Du. *weduwe, weef*, G. *witwe*), Goth. *widuwō*, adj. formation of IE. range, **widhewo*, repr. by Skr. *vidhawā* widow, Gr. ἠ(F)ίθε(F)ος unmarried man, L. *viduus* bereft, void, widowed.] **1.** A woman whose husband is dead (and who has not married again). **b.** Prefixed as a title to the name. Now chiefly *dial.* or *vulgar.* 1576. **c.** In extended sense: A wife separated from or deserted by her husband; esp. in colloq. or dial. phr. *a w. bewitched*; see also GRASS WIDOW 2. 1461. **d.** *Eccl.* One of a class or order of devout or consecrated widows in the Early Church 1572. **e.** *transf.* A female animal, esp. a hen bird, that has lost its mate ME. **2. a.** A bird of the subfamily *Viduinæ*. **b.** Collector's name for a geometrid moth, *Cidaria luctuata*; also *mourning w.* **c.** *Mournful* or *mourning w.*, pop. names of certain plants with dusky flowers. 1747. **3.** *colloq.* or *slang.* **a.** An extra hand dealt to the table in certain card-games. **b.** *The w.*: champagne. [From 'Veuve Cliquot', the name of a firm of wine merchants.] 1891.

1. Take example by your father, my boy, and be wery careful o' widders DICKENS. **c.** Has Mr. Balfour never heard of the Golf Widow? 1908.

Comb.: as *w. lady, woman* (arch. or dial.), etc.; **w.-duck,** a species of tree-duck, *Dendrocygna viduata*; **-finch** = W.-BIRD; **w. right,** that part of a deceased husband's estate to which a w. has a right. **b.** with genitive: **widow's cruse,** an inexhaustible source of supply (after 1 *Kings* 17:14); **widow's lock,** a lock or tuft of hair growing apart from the rest, supposed to presage early widowhood; **widow's mite,** a small money contribution (in allusion to *Mark* 12:43); **widow's**

peak (see PEAK *sb.*[2] I. 1 b, and cf. *widow's lock*); **widow's weeds,** the mourning apparel of a w.

Widow, *sb.*[2] *Obs.* exc. *dial.* [OE. *widewa*, masc. corresp. to *widewe* WIDOW *sb.*[1]] = WIDOWER.

Wi·dow, *v.* ME. [f. WIDOW *sb.*[1] or [2].] **1.** *trans.* To make a widow (*rarely*, a widower) of; to bereave of one's husband (or wife). Most commonly in *pa. pple.* **b.** *fig.* To deprive *of* a valuable or highly prized possession; to bereave. Usu. in *pa. pple.* 1595. †**2.** To survive as a widow, become the widow of. SHAKS. †**3.** To endow with a widow's right. SHAKS.

Wi·dow-bird. 1772. [Representing L. generic name *Vidua* (widow).] A bird of the genus *Vidua* or subfamily *Viduinæ* of the family *Ploceidæ* (Weaver-birds), found in various parts of Africa; so called from the prevailingly black plumage of the males. (Cf. WHIDAH.)

Widowed (wi·do^{u}d), *ppl. a.* 1600. [f. WIDOW *sb.*[1] or [2] or *v.* + -ED.] **1.** Made or become a widow (or widower). Also of an animal, esp. a bird: Bereaved of its mate. **2.** *fig.* Deprived of a partner, friend, companion, or mate; bereaved; hence, deserted, desolate, solitary 1633. **b.** Of an elm: Not 'mated' with a vine; conversely of the vine. (After L. *ulmus* and *vitis vidua.*) 1743.

1. *transf.* Sleepelesse she spent in her now widow'd bed..the night that followed 1627.

Widower (wi·do^{u}əɹ). late ME. [f. WIDOW *sb.*[1] + -ER[1].] **1.** A man whose wife is dead (and who has not married again); a husband bereaved of his wife. †**2.** One of an ecclesiastical class or order of men corresp. to the order of 'widows' –1610. Hence **Wi·dowerhoo:d** [after WIDOWHOOD], the condition of a w., or the time during which a man is a w.

Widowhood (wi·do^{u}hud). [OE. *widewanhād*, f. gen. of WIDOW *sb.*[1] or [2] + *-hād* -HOOD.] **1.** The state or condition of a widow or widower, or (contextually) the time during which one is a widow or widower; also *transf.* of an animal, esp. a bird. †**2.** An estate settled on a widow, a widow's right. SHAKS.

1. In my wedowhode, afore I maried this gentilwoman 1528. Lucretia..in the deep weeds of w. 1846.

Wi·dow-wail. 1597. **a.** The shrub Mezereon (*Daphne mezereum*) or other species of *Daphne*. **b.** A shrub of the genus *Cneorum* (family *Simarubaceæ*), esp. *C. tricoccum*, a dwarf shrub with evergreen leaves and pink sweet scented flowers, found in Spain and the south of France.

Width (widþ, witþ). 1627. [A literary formation of the 17th century, taking the place of *widness* WIDENESS. 'A low word' (J.).] **1.** Extent across or from side to side; transverse dimension; *occas.* extent of opening, distance apart (of the two parts of something). **2.** Large extent across, or in general 1697. **3.** *concr.* = BREADTH 2. 1876. Hence **Wi·dthless** *a.* having no (great) w., narrow. **Wi·dthways, -wise** *adv.* in the direction of the w., transversely.

Wield (wīld), *v.* [ME. *wēlde*, repr. (1) str. vb. OE. *wealdan* = OS. *waldan*, OHG. *waltan* (G. *walten*), ON. *valda*, Goth. *waldan*, and (2) wk. vb. OE. *wieldan*, f. mutated form of **walð-*.] †**1.** *trans.* To rule or reign over, govern, command. *Obs.* exc. as merged in 4. –1633. †**2.** To have at command or disposal, hold, own, possess; to have the advantage of, enjoy –1603. **3.** To direct the movement or action of, to control; to use, have the use of, as a bodily member or faculty; *gen.* to deal with, have to do with; to deal with successfully. *Obs.* or *dial.* exc. as in 4. OE. †**b.** To express, utter –1635. **4.** To use or handle with skill and effect; to manage, ply (a weapon, tool, or instrument, now always one held or carried in the hand) OE. **b.** To exercise (power, authority, influence) 1612. **c.** To use after the fashion of a tool or weapon for the performance of something 1601.

3. b. *Lear* I. i. 56. **4.** Monstrouse cudgells..as bigge as the partie is well able to wild 1603. *To w. a* or *the sceptre* (and similar phrases), to exercise supreme authority, to reign or rule (also *fig.*). **c.** A trained soldier wielding a graphic and powerful pen 1882. Who could w. such scathing invective? 1918. Hence **Wie·lder,** one who wields.

Wieldy (wī·ldi), *a.* late ME. [f. prec. + -Y[1].] **1.** Capable of easily 'wielding' one's body or limbs, or a weapon, etc.; vigorous, active, nimble. *Obs.* exc. *dial.* **2.** Easily wielded, controlled, or handled; manageable, handy. [In later use a back-formation from *unwieldy.*] 1583.

1. So fressh so yong so weldy semed he CHAUCER.

Wife (wəif). *Pl.* **wives** (wəivz). [OE. *wīf* = OFris., OS. *wīf* (Du. *wijf*), OHG. *wīp* (G. *weib* woman), ON. *víf*; of unkn. origin; not extant in Goth., which has *qinō* 'mulier', QUEAN, and *qēns* 'uxor', QUEEN.] **1.** A woman: formerly in general sense; in later use restricted to a woman of humble rank, esp. one engaged in the sale of some commodity. Now *dial.*, exc. with prefixed descriptive word, esp. in compounds such as FISHWIFE, etc. **b.** Qualified by *old*, esp. in the phr. *old wives' tale*: see OLD WIFE 1. OE. **2.** A woman joined to a man by marriage; a married woman OE. **b.** *transf.* The female of a pair of the lower animals; the mate of a male animal. late ME. **3.** The mistress of a household; the hostess or landlady of an inn. *Obs.* exc. as surviving in GOODWIFE 1, HOUSEWIFE 1. late ME. **4.** Collector's name for a moth, *Catocala nupta*, also called Willow Red Underwing 1832.

1. Where ginger-bread wives have a scanty sale KEATS. **2.** He was still on the look-out for a w. with money DICKENS. Phrases. *To w.*, for a w., to be one's w. *To take a w.*, to marry (somewhat *arch.*). †*To have to w.*, to have as one's w., be the husband of. *All the world and his w.* (joc. colloq.), all men and women, everybody: usu. hyperbolically for a large and miscellaneous company of people of both sexes. *W. of the left hand*: see LEFT HAND. Hence **Wi·fedom** = WIFEHOOD 1, 2; also, wives collectively, married women as a class. **Wi·feless** *a.* having no wife; unmarried, celibate.

Wifehood (wəi·fhud). late ME. [f. prec. + -HOOD.] **1.** The position or condition of a wife; married state (of a woman). **2.** The character of or befitting a wife; wifeliness. late ME.

Wifelike (wəi·f,ləik), *a.* and *adv.* 1598. [f. as prec. + -LIKE.] **A.** *adj.* Resembling, or having the character of, a wife; characteristic of or befitting a wife 1613. **B.** *adv.* In the manner of a wife 1598.

Wifely (wəi·f,li), *a.* [OE. *wīflić*; see -LY[1].] †**1.** Of or pertaining to a woman or women; womanly (*rare* exc. OE.) –1533. **2.** Pertaining to, characteristic of, or befitting a wife OE. **3.** Having the character befitting a wife; such as a wife should be 1633.

2. A picture of w. patience 1863. **3.** A w. wife, a motherly mother, and above all, a lady 1853. Hence **Wi·feliness,** w. character or quality.

Wifie (wəi·fi). 1825. [f. WIFE *sb.* + -IE, -Y[6].] Little wife: used as a term of endearment.

Wifish (wəi·fiʃ), *a.* 1535. [f. WIFE *sb.* + -ISH[1].] †**1.** Belonging to or characteristic of a woman; womanly; womanish –1560. **2.** Belonging to or characteristic of, having the character of, a wife 1616.

Wig (wig), *sb.*[1] Now *dial.* late ME. [– MLG., MDu. *wigge* wedge, wedge-shaped cake; see WEDGE.] A kind of bun or small cake made of fine flour.

Home to the only Lenten supper I have had of wiggs and ale PEPYS.

Wig, *sb.*[2] 1675. [Shortening of PERIWIG, as WINKLE of PERIWINKLE[2].] **1.** An artificial covering of hair for the head, worn to conceal baldness or to cover the inadequacy of the natural hair, as part of professional, ceremonial, or formerly of fashionable, costume (as still by judges and barristers), or as a disguise (as by actors on the stage). **b.** Applied joc. to a (natural) head of hair, esp. of a child. **2.** *transf.* A person who wears a wig (professionally); a dignitary. *colloq.* 1828. (Cf. BIGWIG.) **3.** *techn.* The coarse hair on the shoulders of a full-grown male fur-seal; the seal itself when bearing this 1830. **4.** A severe rebuke or scolding; an act of WIGGING. *slang* or *colloq.* 1804.

1. The disappearance of the bishops' wigs, which he said had done more harm to the church than anything else! GLADSTONE. Phr. *Dash my wig(s* (colloq.), a mild imprecation. *My wig(s!* (colloq.), a trivial expression of surprise, etc. *Wigs on the green*, a colloquial expression (orig. Irish) for coming to blows or sharp altercation (wigs being liable to fall or be pulled off in a fray).

attrib. and *Comb.*: **w.-block,** a rounded block for placing a w. upon when being made or not in use; **-tail,** (*a*) a bird of the tropics, from its long tail-feathers; (*b*) the tail of a w.; **-sumach, -tree,** the Venetian sumach (*Rhus. cotinus*), from its hairy inflorescence. Hence **Wi·gdom,** judges or lawyers as a body. **Wigged** (wigd) *a.* furnished with or wearing a w. **Wi·ggery,** wigs collectively, the practice of wearing a w.; used by Carlyle for empty formality (in legal proceedings), 'red tape'. **Wi·ggy** *a.* wearing, or distinguished by, a w., bewigged. **Wi·gless** *a.* destitute of a w., not wearing a w. †**Wi·gsby** [-BY 2] *joc. slang* or *colloq.*, a person wearing a w.

Wig, *v.* 1826. [f. prec.] **1.** *trans.* To supply with a wig; to put a w. upon; *spec.* to provide with wigs in preparation for a theatrical performance. **2.** To rebuke or censure severely, scold, rate. *slang* or *colloq.* 1829.

Wigging (wi·giŋ), *vbl. sb.* *slang* or *colloq.* 1813. [f. WIG *sb.*[2] 4 + -ING[1].] A severe rebuke, reproof or reprimand; a scolding.

Wiggle (wi·g'l), *v.* Now *colloq.* or *dial.* ME. [– (M)LG., (M)Du. *wiggelen*, frequent. (see -LE) of **wig-*, repr. by LG. *wiggen* and Eng. dial. *wig*; cf. *wag*, *waggle*, and WRIGGLE.] **1.** *intr.* To move to and fro or from side to side irregularly and lightly; to walk with such a movement, to stagger, reel; to go or move sinuously, to wriggle. **2.** *trans.* To move (something) in this way; also *refl.* 1685. Hence **Wi·ggle** *sb.* an act of 'wiggling'.

Wiggle-waggle (wi·g'l,wæ:g'l), *v.* *colloq.* 1825. Redupl. form combining WIGGLE *v.* and WAGGLE *v.*, emphasizing the alternation of movement. *trans.* or *intr.* So **Wiggle-waggle** *a.* that 'wiggle-waggles'; *fig.* vacillating 1778.

Wiggly (wi·gli), *a.* *colloq.* 1903. [f. WIGGLE *v.* or *sb.* + -Y[1].] Characterized by or suggestive of 'wiggling'; (in ref. to form) having small irregular undulations. Also in redupl. form **Wi·ggly-wa:ggly.**

Wight (wəit), *sb.* *arch.* [OE. *wiht*, corresp. (with variation of gender and meaning) to OS. *wiht*, (M)LG., (M)Du. *wicht*, OHG. *wiht* (G. *wicht*), ON. *vættr* fem., Goth. *waihts* fem.; ult. connections uncertain.] †**1.** A living being; a creature –1587. **b.** orig. and chiefly with (good or bad) epithet, applied to supernatural, preternatural, or unearthly beings. *Obs.* or *rare arch.* OE. **2.** A human being, man or woman, person. Now *arch.* or *dial.* (often implying contempt or commiseration). ME. †**3.** In advb. phrases, qualified by *no*, *any*, *a little*, or the like: (A certain) amount; for (any, a little, etc.) time or distance –1470.

1. b. These were the good wights (fairies) dwelling in the court of Elfland SCOTT. **2.** Of fayre Elisa be your siluer song, that blessed w. SPENSER. The unlucky w...is doomed 1869.

Wight (wəit), *a.* (*adv.*) *arch.* and *dial.* ME. [– ON. *vigt*, n. of *vigr* of fighting age, skilled in arms, cogn. with OE. *wīġ* battle, conflict, *wiġa* warrior, based on IE. **wik-* **wīk-*, repr. by L. *vincere*, *vic-*. For similar adoptions of ON. neuters in *-t* see SCANT *a.*, THWART *a.*, WANT *sb.*] **1.** Of persons, actions, etc.: Strong and courageous, esp. in warfare; having or showing prowess; valiant, doughty, bold. **2.** Strong, vigorous, robust, stalwart; exercising strength, energetic ME. **3.** Moving briskly or rapidly; active, agile; swift, fleet. late ME.

1. Where is Robin Hood, and yᵉ w. Scarlet? 1601. **3.** Mount thee on the wightest steed SCOTT.

B. *adv.* Actively, nimbly, energetically; quickly, rapidly ME. Hence **Wi·ght-ly** *adv.* (*arch.* and *dial.*); **-ness** (*Obs.* or *arch.*).

Wig-wag (wi·g,wæg), *v.* *colloq.* or *techn.* 1846. [Reduplicated formation; cf. *wiggle-waggle*, *zig-zag*.] *trans.* and *intr.* To move lightly to and fro, to wag; *esp.* to wave a flag or other object to and fro in signalling; to signal in this way. Also as *adv.* = with a to-and-fro movement. So **Wi·g-wag** *sb.* 1582.

Wigwam (wi·gwæm, -wǫm). 1628. [– Ojibwa *wigwaum*, *wigiwam*, var. of Algonquin *weekuwom*, *wikiwam* lit. 'their house'.] A lodge, cabin, tent, or hut of the N. Amer. Indian tribes of the region of the Great Lakes and eastward, formed of bark, matting, or hides stretched over a frame of poles converging at the top. **b.** Extended to similar structures among native tribes in other parts of the world 1743. **c.** Applied *joc.* to a house or dwelling in general 1818.

Wild (wəild), *a.* and *sb.* [OE. *wilde* = OFris. *wilde*, OS., OHG. *wildi* (Du., G. *wild*), ON. *villr*, Goth. *wilþeis* :– Gmc. **wilþijaz.*] **A.** *adj.* **I. 1.** Of an animal: Living in a state of nature; not tame, not domesticated (freq. in names of particular species or varieties, for which see the sbs.). **2.** Of a plant (or flower): Growing in a state of nature; not cultivated (freq. in names of particular species or varieties, for which see the sbs.) OE. **3.** Produced or yielded by wild animals or plants; sometimes, having the characteristic (usu. inferior) quality of such productions ME. **b.** *Mining.* Applied to impure or inferior minerals or ores 1778. **4.** Of a place or region: Uncultivated or uninhabited; hence, waste, desert, desolate OE. **b.** *transf.* Belonging to or characteristic of a wild region; of or in a wilderness 1690. **5.** Of persons (or their attributes): Uncivilized; savage; uncultured, rude; also, not accepting the constituted government, rebellious ME.

1. Eight Wilde-Boares rosted whole SHAKS. **2.** I know a banke where the wilde time blowes SHAKS. With woodbine and w. roses mantled o'er COWPER. *attrib. phr.* A young lady with a w.-rose complexion 1890. **3.** Their flesh is hot and unsauorie, and hath a wilde tast 1600. **4.** The scenery was w. without being grand 1849. **5.** When w. in woods the noble Savage ran DRYDEN. The 'slim' ways of the w. Boer 1901.

II. 1. Not under or not submitting to control or restraint; taking or disposed to take one's own way; uncontrolled OE. **b.** Shy; *esp.* of game, afraid of or avoiding the pursuer 1594. **2.** *spec.* Not submitting to moral control; taking one's own way in defiance of moral obligation or authority OE. **b.** Giving way to sexual passion; also, licentious, dissolute, loose ME. **3.** Fierce, savage; furious, violent, cruel ME. **4.** Of the sea, the weather, etc.: Violently agitated, rough, stormy; hence *fig.* or *gen.* Full of disturbance or confusion, tumultuous, turbulent ME. **b.** Of vocal sounds: Loud and unrestrained 1549. **5.** Of feelings or their expression: Highly excited or agitated; passionately vehement or impetuous 1594. **6.** Of persons: **a.** Extremely irritated or vexed; angry, 'furious' 1653. **b.** Passionately or excitedly desirous *to do* something 1797. **c.** Elated, enthusiastic, 'raving' 1868. **7.** Not having control of one's mental faculties; demented, out of one's wits; hence, extremely foolish or unreasonable ME. **b.** Of the eyes or look: Having an expression of distraction 1592. **8.** Of actions, statements, etc.: Going beyond prudent or reasonable limits; rashly or inconsiderately venturesome; fantastically unreasonable 1515. **9.** Artless, free, unconventional or romantic in style; having a somewhat barbaric character 1632. **b.** Of strange aspect; fantastic in appearance 1605. **10.** Aimed wide of the mark or at random; random: usu. *advb.* at random, astray 1810.

1. Depriving Cupid's wing of some w. feathers SCOTT. The children w. in the streets, the mother a destitute widow DICKENS. Phr. *To run w.*: (*a*) of an animal or plant, to live in or revert to a state of nature, not under domestication or cultivation; (*b*) of a person; He had a bold spirit, and he ran a little w., and went for a soldier DICKENS. **b.** *Much Ado* III. i. 35. **2.** I am afraid he has turned out very w. JANE AUSTEN. **b.** If a young man is w., and must run after women and bad company JOHNSON. **5.** A fit of w. weeping 1885. **6. c.** She had accepted me, and I was w. with joy 1891. **7.** Her misery had actually drove her w. DICKENS. **8.** This vnheedfull, desperate, wilde aduenture SHAKS. **9.** If..sweetest Shakespear fancies childe, Warble his native Wood-notes wilde MILT. **10.** The Chinese shells..'went wild' 1895.

Special collocations: **w. beast,** orig. in sense I. 1, now always with mixture of sense II. 3; also *attrib.*, as in *w. beast show*, etc.; **w. boar:** see BOAR *sb.* c; **w. horse,** a horse not domesticated or broken in; esp. in phr., referring to a mode of punishment or torture, *to draw with w. horses*, and hence joc. with negative; **w. Irish,** the less civilized Irish; formerly, those not subject to English rule.

B. *sb.* †**1.** A wild animal, or wild animals collectively; *spec.* a beast, or beasts, of the chase; game –1599. **2.** A wild or waste place; a waste, wilderness. Now mostly *rhet.* or *poet.* 1637. **b.** *pl.* (Chiefly in *the wilds of* a specified region.) 1596.

2. *transf.* A lighthouse o'er the w. of dreary waves SHELLEY. **b.** *fig.* Striving to cut a new road through the wilds of jurisprudence 1832. Hence **Wi·ldish** *a.* somewhat w., inclining to wildness. **Wi·ldling** = WILDING A. 2, 3. **Wi·ld-ly** *adv.*, **-ness.**

Wi·ldbore. *local.* 1784. [Of unkn. origin.] A stout and closely woven unglazed tammy.

Wild cat. late ME. [Cf. WILD DEER.] **1.** The European wild species of cat, *Felis catus*; also applied to other wild animals of the cat tribe, esp. in U.S. to species of lynx. **2.** *fig.* Applied to a savage, ill-tempered, or spiteful person, esp. a woman 1573. **3.** *fig.* **a.** One who forms a rash project, or engages in a risky enterprise. **b.** An unsound business undertaking, as a 'wild-cat bank'. Chiefly *U.S. colloq.* 1812. **4.** *attrib.* (usu. with hyphen). *fig.* Applied to banks in the western United States which fraudulently issued notes with little or no capital, or to their notes or transactions; hence extended to unsound, risky, or illicit business enterprises generally; and more widely to reckless or rash undertakings, statements, etc. 1838.

2. But will you woo this Wilde-cat? SHAKS. Hence **Wild-catter, -catting,** one who engages, the action of engaging, in a 'wild-cat' business or enterprise.

Wild deer. OE. [In sense 1 OE. *wil(d)-dēor*, *wildedēor*, alteration of **wildor*, pl. *wildru*.] †**1.** A wild animal –ME. **2.** Deer in a wild state 1748.

‖**Wildebeest** (vi·ldəbēst). 1838. [S. African Du., f. *wild* WILD *a.* + *beest* BEAST *sb.*] The gnu.

Wilder (wi·ldəɹ), *v. arch.* (now chiefly *poet.*) 1613. [Of unkn. origin; perh. extracted from WILDERNESS, but cf. MDu. *verwildern*, and BEWILDER, which is, however, of later appearance.] **1.** *trans.* To cause to lose one's way, as in a wild or unknown place; to lead or drive astray; also *refl.* **b.** *fig.*; *esp.* to render at a loss how to act or what to think; to perplex, bewilder 1642. **2.** *intr.* To lose one's way, go astray, stray; to be bewildered 1658.

1. Young Actæon, wilder'd in the wood ADDISON. **b.** You shall be left wildred with strange Revelations 1654. Hence **Wi·ldered** (wi·ldəɹd) *ppl. a.* straying, 'lost'; perplexed, bewildered; of a place, etc., pathless, wild. **Wi·ldering** *ppl. a.* that 'wilders'.

Wilderness (wi·ldəɹnės). ME. [OE. *wild-(d)ēornes*; f. *wild(d)ēor* WILD DEER + -NESS. Cf. (M)Du., G. *wildernis*.] **1. a.** (without article) Wild or uncultivated land. **b.** A wild or uncultivated region or tract of land, uninhabited, or inhabited only by wild animals ME. **c.** A piece of ground in a large garden or park, planted with trees, and laid out in an ornamental or fantastic style, often in the form of a maze or labyrinth 1644. **2.** *transf.* or *gen.* A waste or desolate region of any kind, e.g. of open sea 1588. **3.** *fig.* Something figured as a region of a wild or desolate character, in which one wanders or loses one's way; in religious use applied to the present world or life as contrasted with heaven or the future life ME. **b.** Rhetorically applied to a building, town, etc., which is regarded as 'desolate' or in which one is lonely or 'lost' 1842. **4.** A mingled, confused, or vast assemblage or collection *of* persons or things (usu. coloured by other senses) 1588. †**5.** Wildness, uncultivated condition –1667. †**b.** *fig.* Wildness of character. SHAKS.

2. Inuiron'd with a wildernesse of Sea SHAKS. **3.** As I walk'd through the w. of this world BUNYAN. **4.** I would not haue giuen it for a wildernesse of Monkies SHAKS. **5. b.** *Meas. for M.* III. i. 142.

Wild-fire, wildfire (wəi·ldfəiᵊɹ). OE. †**1.** Furious or destructive fire; a conflagration –1634. **2.** *spec.* **a.** Will-o'-the-wisp, *ignis fatuus* 1663. **b.** Lightning; *esp.* sheet lightning without audible thunder, 'summer lightning' 1795. **3.** A composition of highly inflammable substances, readily ignited and very difficult to extinguish, used in warfare, etc. ME. **4.** A name for erysipelas and various inflammatory eruptive diseases, esp. those in which the eruption spreads from one part to another OE. **5.** *fig.* or in fig. allusions, in ref. to a destructive agency, etc. ME.

5. The wilde-fire of my Passions burnèd me 1612. *Like w.*, with immense rapidity and effect; very swiftly and forcibly; The report..spread like w. through the town DISRAELI.

Wi·ld-fowl. (Also as one word, or as two.) OE. A wild bird, or (usu.) wild birds collectively; chiefly applied to those caught for food, game birds. **b.** *joc.* misapplied to a wild beast; hence *allus.* 1590.

b. There is not a more fearefull wilde foule then your Lyon liuing SHAKS.

Wild goose. OE. **1.** Any wild bird of the goose kind; in Britain usu. the greylag (*Anser ferus* or *cinereus*), in N. America the Canada goose (*Bernicla canadensis*). **2.** *fig.* **a.** Used of or in ref. to a flighty or foolish person. **b.** *Eng. Hist.* (*pl.*) A nickname for the Irish Jacobites who went over to the Continent on the abdication of James II and later. 1592. **3.** *attrib.* [after next 2.] Wild, fantastic, very foolish or risky 1770.

3. Gone away upon some wild-goose errand, seeking his fortune DICKENS.

Wild goo·se chase. 1592. †**1.** A kind of horse-race in which the second or any succeeding horse had to follow accurately the course of the leader, like a flight of wild geese –1685. **2.** *fig.* An erratic course taken by one person (or thing) and followed (or that may be followed) by another; in later use apprehended as 'a pursuit of something as unlikely to be caught as the wild goose' (J.); a foolish, fruitless, or hopeless quest 1592.

2. Don't let me think..you will set out upon every wild-goose chase, sticking to nothing H. WALPOLE.

Wilding (wəi·ldiŋ), *sb.* and *a.* 1525. [f. WILD *a.* + -ING³.] **A.** *sb.* **1.** A wild apple or apple-tree; a crab-apple or crab-tree. **2.** *gen.* A wild plant, flower, or fruit 1577. **3.** A wild animal (*rare*) 1897. **4.** *fig.* (applied to a person or thing) 1621. **B.** *attrib.* or *adj.* **1.** Applied to a crab-apple or crab-tree 1538. **2.** Of a plant, etc.: Growing wild. Chiefly *poet.* 1697.

2. *fig.* That growth of w. art 1884.

Wild man. ME. [Cf. ON. *villumaðr*.] **1.** A man who is wild. **a.** A man of savage, fierce, uncultured, or unruly nature or character. **b.** A man of an uncivilized race or tribe; a savage, or one reverted to a savage state ME. **c.** *pl.* The extremists of a political party, profession, etc. 1923. **2.** The orang-outang: also *wild man of the woods* 1791.

Wildwood (wəi·ld,wud). Now chiefly *poet.* OE. [orig. two words, WILD *a.* and WOOD *sb.*] A forest of natural growth, or one allowed to grow naturally; an uncultivated or unfrequented wood.

attrib. When With wild wood-leaues & weeds, I ha' strew'd his graue SHAKS.

Wile (wəil), *sb.* [Early ME. *wīl*, evidenced first from Scandinavianized areas and therefore poss. – ON. **wihl-* (*vél*) craft, artifice, rel. to *véla* defraud.] **1.** A crafty, cunning, or deceitful trick; a sly, insidious, or underhand artifice; a stratagem, ruse, Chiefly *pl.* (in *sing.* now *arch.* or *poet.*). †**b.** Without implication of deceit: A subtle contrivance; a skilful device or scheme –1830. **c.** In lighter sense: An amorous or playful trick; a piece of sportive cunning or artfulness 1600. **d.** *spec.* A cunning turn or other trick of the hare to escape the hunters 1691. **2.** Deceit or deceitfulness; craft, cunning, subtlety. Now *rare.* late ME.

1. The wiles by which its members are lured..to their goal 1888. **c.** Haste thee nymph, and bring with thee..Quips and Cranks, and wanton Wiles, Nods, and Becks, and Wreathed Smiles MILT.

Wile, *v.* late ME. [f. WILE *sb.*, or aphetic f. *biwile* (XIII–XIV).] **1.** *trans.* To bring, draw, or get by a wile; to lead, induce, or obtain by craft or cunning. **2.** (as substitute for WHILE *v.*) To divert attention pleasantly from (something tedious); to charm *away*; *esp.* to cause (time) to pass *away* pleasantly or insensibly 1796.

1. She talk'd, she smil'd, my heart she wil'd BURNS. She could neither be driven nor wiled into the parish kirk STEVENSON. **2.** I was reading a book..to w. the time away DICKENS.

Wilful (wi·lfŭl), *a.* (*adv.*, *sb.*) ME. [f. WILL *sb.*¹ + -FUL.] **1.** Asserting or disposed to assert one's own will against persuasion, instruction, or command; governed by will without regard to reason; obstinately self-willed or perverse. †**2.** Willing; consenting; ready to comply with a request, desire, or requirement -1598. †3. Proceeding from the will; done or suffered of one's own free will or choice; voluntary -1687. **4.** Done on purpose or wittingly; purposed, deliberate, intentional. (Chiefly, now always, in bad sense, of a blameworthy action; freq. implying 'perverse, obstinate'.) Also *transf.* of the agent. ME.

1. The seid Henry is sklanderus and a wylfull person and wyll not be ordered but after his owne wyll 1529. **2.** *Merry W.* III. ii. 44. **3.** Amazed to see Contempt of wealth, and w. poverty DRYDEN. **4.** Wylfull murtherers, whom God commaundeth to be taken from the aulter 1548. *Prov.* Wilful waste makes woeful want.

†**B.** as *adv.* = WILFULLY 3, 4. -1611.

Since from thee going, he went wilfull slow SHAKS.

C. as *sb.* A wilful person; *rarely*, a wilful act 1819. Hence **Wi·lfulness.**

Wilfully (wi·lfŭli), *adv.* [Late OE. *wilfullīće*; see prec., -LY².] †**1.** Willingly, readily; patiently, submissively -1513. †**2.** Of one's own free will, of one's own accord, voluntarily -1705. †**b.** According to one's own will; at will, freely -1600. **3.** Purposely, on purpose, intentionally, deliberately. Chiefly, now always, in bad sense; occas. implying 'maliciously'. late ME. **4.** In a self-willed manner; perversely, obstinately, stubbornly 1586.

2. Martyrs are to die willingly but not w. FULLER. **3.** For those that set houses on fire w., they are smoked to death 1617.

Wilga (wi·lgă). 1889. [Native name in New South Wales.] An Australian tree of the rutaceous genus *Geijera*, esp. *G. parviflora*.

Wilily (wəi·lili), *adv.* late ME. [f. WILY *a.* + -LY².] In a wily manner; craftily, cunningly, by stratagem.

Wiliness (wəi·linės). 1450. [f. as prec. + -NESS.] The quality or character of being wily; craftiness, cunning, guile.

Will (wil), *sb.*¹ [OE. *willa* = OFris. *willa*, OS. *willio*, OHG. *willo*, *willio* (Du. *wil*, G. *wille*), ON. *vili* (gen. *vilja*), Goth. *wilja* :- Gmc. **wiljon* :- **weljon*, f. **wel-* be pleasing (see WELL *adv.*).] **I. 1.** Desire, wish, longing; inclination, disposition (*to do* something). Now coloured by or merged in sense II. 1. **b.** An inclination *to do* something, as contrasted with power or opportunity 1594. †**2.** *spec.* Carnal desire or appetite -1603 **3.** *transf.* That which one desires, (one's) 'desire'. Now *arch.* or *poet.* OE. **b.** A desire or wish as expressed in a request; hence (contextually) the expression of a wish, a request. *arch.* or *dial.* ME.

1. b. They desired the power; and want not the w., to do us an ill turn 1667. **2.** *Meas. for M.* II. iv. 164. **3.** Would'st haue me weepe? why now thou hast thy w. SHAKS. A lad that lives and has his w. Is worth a dozen dead HOUSMAN. **b.** *Ant. & Cl.* I. ii. 7. *What's your w.?* (now *arch.* or *dial.*, esp. *Sc.*), What do you want? What do you wish me to do?

II. 1. The action of willing or choosing to do something; the movement or attitude of the mind which is directed with conscious intention to (and, normally, issues immediately in) some action, physical or mental OE. †**b.** Intention, purpose, determination -1712. **c.** *W. to* with sb. or inf. (after G. *wille zu*) 1823. **2.** The power or capacity of willing; power of choice in regard to action OE. **3.** Intention or determination that something shall be done by another or others, or shall happen or take place; (contextually) an expression or embodiment of such intention or determination OE. **b.** Intent, purport (of a document). late ME. **4.** Qualified by possessive: That which one wills should be done; one's 'pleasure' OE.

1. c. Wherever I found living matter I found w. unto power 1896. The triumph of the w. to live 1908. **2.** All is not lost; the unconquerable W.,.. And courage never to submit or yield MILT. A girl of high spirit and strong w. 1907. *A w. of one's own*, implying a strong or self-assertive w., and hence used as a euphemism for 'wilfulness'. **3.** Is it your w. Claudio shall die to morrow? SHAKS. Such was the w. of Heav'n MILT. My w. is law TENNYSON. **4.** Direct me, if it be your w., where great Auffidius lies SHAKS. If then he wreak on me his wicked w. GRAY.

III. A person's formal declaration (usu. in writing) of his intention as to the disposal of his property or other matters to be performed after his death; commonly *transf.* the document in which such intention is expressed. late ME.

She threw her w. into the fire JOHNSON. To make the gentleman's last w. and testament STERNE.

Phrases. *Good w.*, *ill w.*, see GOODWILL, ILL WILL. *With the best w.* (*in the world*); With the best w. we found it impossible to eat anything 1857. *To take the w. for the deed*; The reasonable will accept the w. for the deed 1661. *Where there's a w. there's a way* (WAY *sb.*¹ 13). See also FREE WILL. **Against** (one's) **w.** In opposition to (one's own) inclination or liking, unwillingly; in opposition to (another's) choice, intention, or desire. **At** (one's) **w. a.** According to one's volition or choice; as (when, where) one will. **b.** In readiness to be dealt with as one will; at one's command or disposal. **c.** In ref. to an estate held during the owner's or lessor's pleasure, from which the tenant may be ousted at any time; chiefly in phr. *estate, tenant*, etc. *at w.* †**By** (one's) **w.** With one's consent, or of one's own free will, willingly; according to one's desire. **Of** (one's) **w.** Of one's own accord, spontaneously, voluntarily. (Now only with poss. and *own*, e.g. 'He did it of his own (free) w.') **With** (one's) **w.** †**a.** Intentionally; willingly; voluntarily. **b.** *With a w.*, with determination, resolutely, energetically. Hence **Willed** (wild) *a.* having a w. of a specified kind: chiefly in *comb.*, as SELF-WILLED; having the w. directed to some (specified) action. **Wi·ll-less** *a.* not having 'a w. of one's own'; not involving exercise of the w.; destitute of the faculty of volition.

Will, *sb.*² Abbrev. form of the Christian name *William*. **b.** *dial.* = WILL-O'-THE-WISP 1718.

Will, *sb.*³ 1677. [f. WILL *v.*¹] **a.** An utterance of the verb 'will'; a determination expressed by this. **b.** The verb 'will' as used in contradistinction to 'shall.'

Will *a. Sc.* and *dial.* [- ON. *villr* WILD.] Astray; 'lost'; perplexed.

Will (wil), *v.*¹ *Pres. t.* 1st and 3rd pers. sing.; pl. **will**; 2nd sing. **wilt** (*arch.*). *Pa. t.* **would** (wud). Abbreviated (colloq.) forms: **'ll** = *will*, esp. after prons., e.g. *I'll* (†*Ile*), *they'll* (†*theile*); **'lt** = *wilt*; **'ld, 'd** = *would*, esp. after prons., e.g. †*I'ld*, *I'd*, *we'd*; **won't** (wōᵘnt) = †*wonnot* for †*wol not*. [OE. **willan*, *wyllan* = OFris. *willa*, OS. *willian* (Du. *willen*), ON. *vilja*, Goth. *wiljan* :- Gmc. **wel(l)jan*, parallel with Gmc. **wal(l)jan*, repr. by OFris. *wella*, OHG. *wellen* (G. *wollen*), ON. *velja*, Goth. *waljan* choose; based on IE. **wol-* **wel-* (cf. L. *velle*, *volo*).] **I.** *The present tense* **will.** †**1.** *trans.* Desire, wish for, have a mind to (something); sometimes implying 'intend, purpose' -1734. †**b.** with neg. = have no desire for, do not wish for, often implying 'refuse, decline' -1606. **2.** with obj. clause: Desire, wish; sometimes implying also 'intend, purpose' (that something be done or happen). *Obs.* or *arch.* OE. †**3.** Denoting expression (usu. authoritative) of a wish or intention: Determine, decree, give order (*that* something be done) -1682. **b.** *spec.* in a direction or instruction in one's will or testament; hence, to direct by will OE. †**c.** *fig.* of an abstract thing: Demands, requires -1597. **4.** Desire to, wish to, have a mind to (do something); often implying intention. *Obs.* or *arch.*, or merged in other senses. OE. **5.** In relation to another's desire, etc., or to an obligation of some kind: Am (is, are) disposed or willing to consent to OE. **b.** In 2nd person, interrog., or in a dependent clause after *beg* or the like, expressing a request (usu. courteous; with emphasis, impatient) ME. **6.** Expressing voluntary action, or conscious intention directed to the doing of what is expressed by the principal verb (without emphasis as in 9, and without temporal ref. as in 10) OE. **7.** Expressing natural disposition to do something, and hence habitual action: Has the habit of -ing; is addicted or accustomed to -ing; habitually does; sometimes connoting 'may be expected to' OE. **8.** Expressing potentiality, etc.: Can, may, is capable of -ing; is (large) enough or sufficient to. late ME. **9.** *emphatically.* Is fully determined to; insists on or persists in -ing. Also *fig.* = must inevitably, is sure to. 1611. **b.** In phr. of ironical or critical force referring to another's assertion or opinion. Now *arch.* exc. in *w. have it.* 1591. **10.** *As auxiliary of the future tense* with implication of intention or volition. **a.** In 1st pers.: *occas.* = intend to, mean to OE. **b.** In 2nd and 3rd pers., in questions or indirect statements OE. **11.** With neg.: commonly = refuse or decline to; *emphatically* insist on or persist in not -ing OE. **12.** In 1st pers., expressing immediate intention: = 'I am now going to', 'I proceed at once to'. With neg., used with *say* or the like: *I w. not* = 'I do not venture so far as to'. ME. **b.** In 1st pers. pl., expressing a proposal = 'let us' ME. **13.** In 2nd and 3rd pers., as auxiliary expressing mere futurity, forming (with pres. inf.) the future, and (with pf. inf.) the future pf. tense OE. **b.** As auxiliary of future substituted for the imper. in mild injunctions or requests 1824. **14.** As auxiliary of future expressing a contingent event, or a result to be expected, in a supposed case or under particular conditions OE. **b.** Expressing a voluntary act or choice in a supposed case, or a conditional promise or undertaking: esp. in asseverations (e.g. *I w. die sooner than..*, *I'll be hanged if..*). late ME. **c.** Expressing a determinate or necessary consequence (without the notion of futurity). late ME. **d.** With the notion of futurity obscured or lost: = w. prove or turn out to; may be supposed to, presumably does. Hence (chiefly *Sc.* and *n. dial.*) in estimates of amount, etc., the future becoming equivalent to a present with qualification: e.g. *it w. be..* = I think it is.., it is about... 1450. **15.** Used where *shall* is now the normal auxiliary; since 17th c. chiefly in Scottish, Irish, provincial, or extra-British use OE. **16.** *absol.* or with ellipsis of obj. clause as in 2: = sense I. 4-6. OE. **17.** With ellipsis of a verb of motion. *arch.* OE. **18.** With ellipsis of active inf. to be supplied from the context; also with generalized ellipsis, and with *so* or *that* (now usu. at the beginning of the sentence) substituted for the omitted inf. phr. OE. **b.** In a qualifying phr. with relative, equivalent to a phr. with indef. relative in *-ever*: e.g. *shout as loud as you w.* = 'however loud you (choose to) shout'. late ME. **19.** In a disjunctive qualifying clause or phr. (usu. parenthetical), as *whether he w. or no, w. he nill he*, etc. late ME.

1. (*title*) Twelfe Night, Or what you w. SHAKS. **b.** Ile no Swaggerers;..shut the doore, there comes no Swaggerers heere SHAKS. **3. b.** I wyll that Rose Plandon shall haue x marc 1504. **c.** 2 *Hen. IV*, IV. i. 157. **4.** Sen now al men wilbe theologis 1562. **5. b.** O, O, O,..O, w. you have done! HARDY. **7.** Crabs move sideling, Lobsters w. swim swiftly backward SIR T. BROWNE. **8.** My periwig is arrived,..my head w. only go into the first half of it COWPER. **9.** Fate's such a shrewish thing, She w. be mistris CHAPMAN. An impulse which w. vent itself in some form or other 1845. **b.** The Rosie-cross Philosophers, Whom you w. have to be but Sorcerers 1664. **10. a.** I haue both glorified it, and w. glorify it agayne BIBLE (Great) *John* 12:28. **b.** Her..sonne..Swears he will shoote no more SHAKS. **11.** I cannot, I wo'not sit down at Table with her RICHARDSON. **12.** My host (whom I w. call Mr. Newman) 1856. **b.** We w. forget Mistress Dods for the present, if you please SCOTT. **13.** They w. probably return this day fortnight COWPER. **b.** In your intercourse with their chiefs,..you w. take care to give no offence to their natural presumption SCOTT. **14.** *Lear* III. vi. 85. You'll be surprised when you find how easy it is 1882. **b.** I'll take you five children from London, who shall cuff five Highland children JOHNSON. **c.** Then ioyn the Points *A* and *f* with a Right-line, and it w. form the Angle requir'd 1709. **d.** What lights w. those out to the northward be? M. ARNOLD. This word we have only once heard, and that w. be twenty years ago 1876. **15.** Perchance I w. be there as soone as you SHAKS. I expect we w. have some good singing SCOTT. **16.** *If you w.*, sometimes = 'if you choose or prefer to call it so'; Very savage! monstrous! if you w. RUSKIN. *If God w.*, *God willing*, if it be the will of God, 'D.V.' **17.** Ile to my booke SHAKS. **18.** Wilt thou haue thys woman to thy wedded wyfe..? I w. *Bk. Com. Prayer.* I hope it may do you some good, as it won't me RUSKIN. Prov. He that w. not when he may, When he would he shall haue nay 1562. **b.** *Come what w.* = 'whatever may come'; Well, come what w., Ile tarry at home SHAKS. *Be that as it w.* = 'however that may be'.

II. *The pa. t.* **would** *with temporal function.* **1.** Desired, wished for, wished; often implying 'intended'. With †simple obj., with obj. cl. or acc. and inf. *Obs.* or *rare arch.* OE. **2.** Wished to; often implying 'intended to'. *Obs.* or *arch.* exc. in dependence on a vb. in pa. time. OE. **3.** Was (were) willing to, consented to; chose to. Now only in dependence on a vb. in pa. time. OE. **b.** In a dependent clause after an expression of request, command, or the like, where the principal vb. is in pa. time. Now *rare*. ME. **4.** Was (were) accustomed to; used to OE. **5.** Was capable of –ing; could (usu. in relative cl.). late ME. **6.** Was determined to; insisted on or persisted in –ing 1706. **7.** In indirect reports, usu. in 3rd pers., of past utterances, etc.; in the 1st pers. (now) implying intention OE. **8.** With neg., commonly denoting refusal ME. **9.** Forming (with pres. inf.) the auxiliary of the 'anterior future' or 'future in the past', and (with pf. inf.) of the 'anterior future perfect', in the 2nd and 3rd pers. OE. **b.** without notion of futurity: Probably or presumably did 1857. **10.** Used where *should* is now the normal auxiliary (cf. I. 15) 1760. **11.** Elliptical and quasi-elliptical uses as in I. 16–19. Now *rare* or *Obs.* exc. with ellipsis of active inf. to be supplied from the context, or in disjunctive qualifying clauses OE.

1. Heauen would that shee these gifts should haue SHAKS. When we would no Pardon, they laboured to punish us 1643. **2.** Certaine, which would be counted pillars of the State A.V. *Transl. Pref.* **3.** I said you would be all right in a few days if you would only hold on 1884. **4.** There..His listless length at noontide would he stretch GRAY. **8.** Editors and publishers..would have none of it 1918. **9.** This he protested to be true, as he would answer before God 1582. **10.** My aunt did not expect that I would be plucked in any examination 1870. **11.** Look where you would, some exquisite form glided..through the throng DICKENS. I wanted Mr. Meyers to come with us but he wouldn't 1882.

III. *The pa. t.* **would** *with modal function.* **1.** with simple obj.: Could or might desire; should like. *Obs.* or *rare arch.* **2.** with obj. cl., with vb. in past subj. (*arch.* exc. in *would rather* or *sooner*), or with acc. and inf. Hence (*arch.*) with ellipsis of 1st pers. pron. as an expression of longing; also, by confusion with 3, in the form *(I) would to God* ME. **3.** *Would God* = 'O that God would', as an expression of earnest desire or longing. *Obs.* or *rare arch.* late ME. **4.** The past subj. used with potential or conditional force as a softening of the pres. indic. in sense I. 4: Could or should wish to; should like, wish, or desire to. *arch.* or *dial.* exc. in *would have* = should like or wish (a person or thing) to be or to do something OE. **b.** Am (is, are) disposed or inclined to; often (in 1st pers. sing.) = 'wish to..if I may'. late ME. **5.** In the apodosis of a conditional sentence (expressed or implied), forming the auxiliary of the periphrastic past subj. with implication of intention or volition: = 'should choose or be willing to' ME. **b.** *I would* (sc. 'if I were you') often = 'I advise or recommend you to'. So *I wouldn't* = 'I advise you not to'. 1591. **c.** *Would you..?* = 'Will you, please..? 1607. **6.** In the apodosis of a conditional sentence (expressed or implied), in the 2nd or 3rd pers., forming the auxiliary of the simple 'conditional mood', expressing merely a possibility or contingency in the supposed case OE. **b.** With the hypothetical notion obscured, the 'conditional mood' becoming a qualification of the pres. indic. expressing some degree of hesitation or uncertainty 1449. **c.** Used in the 1st pers. instead of the normal auxiliary *should* 1448. **7.** In a question or indirect statement in the 2nd or 3rd pers., where *should* would be used in the corresponding direct statement in the 1st. late ME. **8.** In a conditional (or equivalent) clause with implication of intention or volition: = 'choose to', 'were willing to' OE. **b.** With inversion of subj., expressing desire or longing 1593. **9.** In a noun-clause expressing the object of desire, advice, or request 1555. **10.** Elliptical and quasi-elliptical uses, as in I. 16–19. ME.

1. But, in a word, what would you with me? BYRON. **2.** I am wearie of this Moone; would he would change SHAKS. I am not mad, I would to heauen I were SHAKS. Would to God that we had peace! 1777. **4.** I would not..be thought to share Mr. St. John's extreme scepticism 1869. **b.** I would..humbly propose to the ladies, to be good-humoured 1779. *Would say* = 'intend to say, mean'. *Would have* = 'is inclined to believe or assert (something *to be* so-and-so)'. **5.** I wouldn't do such a thing here, sir..upon my word and honour, I wouldn't DICKENS. **6. b.** *It would seem* = 'it almost or somewhat seems'. *One would think* = 'one is inclined to think'; You'd think she'd get off her luxurious pillows for once 1882. **c.** He makes everything turn out exactly as we would wish it COLERIDGE. **7.** Would you believe it, Sir, my daughter Elizabeth..said it was fanatical to find fault with card-playing on Sunday 1779. Would you like to see it? 1886. **8. b.** O wad some Pow'r the giftie gie us To see oursels as others see us! BURNS. **9.** I wish the lady would favour us with something more than a side-front SHERIDAN. **10.** Who so mounted hyher than he shold he falleth lower than he wold CAXTON. Letting I dare not, wait vpon I would SHAKS.

IV. Followed by *to* with inf., esp. after an intervening word or words; now the regular constr. only with pres. pple. *willing* ME.

†**V.** Pa. pple. **would**: chiefly in sense I. 6 = wished, chosen –1633.

Many tymes he myghte haue had her and he had wold MALORY. If hee had would, he might easily ..occupied the Monarchy 1633.

VI. Conjoined with NILL *v.* **1.** *absol.* or *intr.* **a.** In disjunctive qualifying phr., as *whether he w. or nill*, willingly or unwillingly; voluntarily or compulsorily. *Obs.* or *rare arch.* OE. **b.** esp. with inversion of subj. (usu. a pron.), as *w. I (or) nill I (he, etc.)*; occas. vaguely = 'one way or another', 'in any case'. Now chiefly in WILLY-NILLY. OE. **2.** (Always inflected *willeth* (*wills*), *willed*; thus prop. belonging to WILL *v.*[2]) **a.** *trans.* To desire, have a mind to, choose (as opp. to *nill* = 'refuse); to determine by the will (as opp. to *nill* = 'negative', 'prevent') 1585. **b.** *absol.* or *intr.* 1577.

Will (wil), *v.*[2] Pres. t. 3rd pers. sing. **wills, willeth** (*arch.*); pa. t. and pple. **willed** (wild). [OE. *willian* = OHG. *willōn*; f. WILL *sb.*[1]] **1.** *trans.* = prec. I. 1, 2, 4. *Obs.* or *rare arch.* **b.** with NILL: see prec. VI. **2. a.** To direct by one's will or testament (*that* something be done, or something *to be* done) OE. **b.** To dispose of by will; to bequeath or devise 1460. **3.** To determine by the will; to aim at effecting by exercise of the will; to set the mind with conscious intention to the performance or occurrence of something OE. **b.** *intr.* To exercise the will; to perform the mental act of volition 1582. **c.** *trans.* To control (another person), or induce (another) *to do* something, by the mere exercise of one's will, as in hypnotism 1882. **4.** To express or communicate one's will or wish with regard to something. **a.** To enjoin; to decree, ordain. *Obs.* or *arch.* ME. †**b.** To pray, request, entreat –1690. †**c.** *fig.* of a thing: To require, demand –1667.

2. b. Was it not enough that I should have been willed away, like a horse? DICKENS. **3.** If I *w.* to move my Arm, it is presently moved 1710. All shall be as God wills CARLYLE. **4. a.** It is common with Princes..to w. contradictories BACON. Willing and requiring all Officers and men to obey you NELSON. **c.** *Cor.* II. iii. 125. Hence **Willed** (wild) *ppl. a.* disposed of by will or testament; determined by the will; controlled by another's will.

Willemite (wi·lĕməit). 1850. [– Du. *willemit* (A. Levy, 1829), f. *Willem* William I of the Netherlands; see -ITE[1] 2 b.] *Min.* Native silicate of zinc, found in masses or crystals of various colours from light greenish-yellow to flesh-red.

Willet (wi·lĕt). 1862. [From its cry, *pill-will-willet*.] A N. Amer. bird of the snipe family, *Symphemia semipalmata*.

William (wi·lyăm). 1597. A common masculine personal name, used in the names of certain species of pinks and other flowers: now only in SWEET-WILLIAM. ¶*W. pear*: see WILLIAMS.

Williamite (wi·lyămait). 1689. [f. the name *William* + -ITE[1] 1.] A supporter of William of Orange (King William III): opp. to JACOBITE *sb.*[4]

Williams (wi·lyămz). 1814. In full, *Williams'*, *Williams's* (erron. *William*) *Bon Chrétien*: A very juicy variety of the Bon Chrétien pear (see BON *a.*), so called from the name of its first distributor in England.

Williamsite (wi·lyămzəit). 1833. [f. the surname *Williams* + -ITE[1] 1.] **1.** A follower of Roger Williams, an Amer. colonist of the 17th c. **2.** *Min.* An impure variety of serpentine, named after L. W. Williams, an Amer. mineralogist 1848.

Willing (wi·liŋ), *ppl. a.* ME. [OE. **willende*, in *selfwillende*, *unwillende*, *willendlīce* WILLINGLY, etc.; f. WILL *v.*[1] + -ING[2].] †**1.** Wishing, wishful, desirous –1825. **2.** Having a ready will; disposed to consent or comply; ready to do (what is specified or implied) without reluctance; *spec.* disposed to do what is required, ready to be of use or service ME. **b.** *transf.* Given, rendered, offered, performed, assumed, borne, or undergone willingly 1568. **c.** *fig.* of things: Compliant, yielding; (of the wind) favourable 1500. **d.** *advb.* Willingly, consentingly, without reluctance. Now *rare* or *Obs.* 1578. †**3.** That is so, or is done or borne, of one's own will; voluntary, intentional –1613. **4.** Exercising or capable of exercising the will, volitional; conveying impulses of the will 1875.

2. He snatch'd the w. Goddess to his Arms DRYDEN. The king was willinger to comply with anything than this DE FOE. Barkis is willin' DICKENS. *W. horse* (in provb. phrases), applied to one who is w. to work or to take trouble. **d.** *W. (or) nilling* (arch.), with or against one's will, willy-nilly. **3.** The willing'st sinne I euer yet committed SHAKS.

Comb., as *w.-hearted*, *-minded* adjs. Hence **Wi·lling-ly** *adv.*, **-ness.**

Williwaw (wi·liwǭ). 1842. [Of unkn. origin.] A sailor's name for a sudden violent squall, orig. in the Straits of Magellan.

Willock (wi·lək). *local.* 1631. [f. WILL *sb.*[2] + -OCK.] The GUILLEMOT; also, the puffin and the razor-bill.

Will-o'-the-wisp (wi·lədəwi·sp). 1608. [orig. **Will with the wisp**; see WILL *sb.*[2] and WISP *sb.* Cf. JACK-O'-LANTERN, and, for the second element, G. *irrwisch* (XVI) lit. 'wander-wisp'.] **1.** = IGNIS FATUUS; *fig.* a thing (rarely a person) that deludes or misleads by means of fugitive appearances. **2.** An alga, *Nostoc commune*, so called from the inexplicable suddenness of its appearance 1866.

1. Wenches..Use to call me Willy Wispe 1628. To play Will in the Wisp with Men of Honour VANBRUGH. Those Wills-o-the-wisp, the Reviewers 1806. *attrib.* A fluttering, shadowy, will-o-the-wisp style 1860.

Willow (wi·lo[u]), *sb.* [OE. *weliģ* = OS. *wilgia*, (M)LG. *wilge*, Du. *wilg*; the form history is obscure, the change of vowel may be due to assoc. with WILLY *sb.*[1]; the precursor of the present form, *wilwe*, appears in XIV.] **I. 1.** Any plant of the genus *Salix*, which consists of trees and shrubs of various sizes, growing for the most part by the side of watercourses, characterized by very pliant branches and long narrow drooping leaves. **b.** The wood or osiers of any tree of this genus 1489. **c.** Taken as a symbol of grief for unrequited love or the loss of a mate; esp. in phr. *to wear (the) w.*, *the w. garland*, or *the green w.*: to grieve for the loss of a loved one 1584. **2.** With qualification, denoting a particular species or variety of the genus *Salix*, and extended to plants of other genera having some resemblance to the w. 1548.

1. By the rushy-fringed bank, Where grows the W. and the Osier dank MILT. (*allus.*, with ref. to pliability) Burleigh..was of the w., and not of the oak MACAULAY. *Bat w.*, a species of willow from which cricket-bats are made. **c.** In such a night Stood Dido with a W. in her hand Vpon the wilde sea bankes SHAKS. **2.** ALMOND, GOAT, GROUND, WEEPING *w.*, etc.: see these wds. *Bay, flowering, French, Persian w.*, the WILLOW-HERB, *Epilobium angustifolium*.

II. 1. = WILLY[1] 3. 1835. **2.** A cricket-bat (made of willow-wood). Similarly, the bat at baseball. 1866.

attrib. and *Comb.*: **w. bay,** *Salix pentandra*; **-earth,** compost made of rotten w.-branches; **-grouse,** the common ptarmigan of N. America, *Lagopus albus*; **-lark,** the sedge-warbler; **-leaf,** a leaf of the w.-tree, or a figure resembling this; *pl.* the luminous filaments of the sun's surface; **w. myrtle,** a myrtaceous w.-leaved tree (*Agonis flexuosa*) of Western Australia; **w. pattern,** a design in blue, upon domestic crockery originated by Thomas Turner in the late 18th c., having w.-trees as a prominent feature; so **w. ware; -tree** = sense 1; **-warbler, -wren,** a small bird, *Sylvia trochilus*. **b.** In several names of insects or their larvæ which infest willows, as **w.-beauty** (*Boarmia rhomboidaria*), **-butterfly, -caterpillar, -fly, -worm.** Hence **Wi·llow** *v. trans.* to put (cotton, etc.) through a w. (sense II. 1). **Wi·llowed** (-o[u]d) *a.* bordered or grown with willows. **Wi·llower,** one who tends a w. (sense II. 1). **Wi·llowish** *a.* resembling that of a w., esp. in ref. to the colour of w.-leaves; like a w., *fig.* of a pliant character (*rare*).

Wi·llow-herb. 1578. [So named from the resemblance of the leaves to the willow's.] **1.** Yellow Loosestrife, *Lysimachia vulgaris.* **2.** Any plant of the genus *Epilobium*, esp. *E. angustifolium* and *hirsutum* 1578. **3.** *Spiked* or *Purple-spiked W.*: Purple Loosestrife, *Lythrum salicaria* 1578. **4.** In full *Hooded W.*: *Scutellaria galericulata* or *S. minor* 1597.

Willowy (wi·loᵘi), *a.* 1766. [f. WILLOW *sb.* + -Y¹.] **1.** Bordered, shaded, or clad with willows. **2.** Resembling a willow in its flexible or drooping gracefulness 1791. **3.** Suggesting the sound of willows agitated by the wind 1895.

2. A fragile form, With a w. droop MRS. HEMANS.

Wi·ll-wo:rship. 1549. [f. WILL *sb.*¹ + WORSHIP *sb.*, rendering Gr. ἐθελοθρησκεία (Col. 2:23).] Worship according to one's own will or fancy, or imposed by human will without divine authority.

Willy, willey (wi·li), *sb.*¹ [OE. *wiliġe, wiliġa*; see WEEL², WILLOW *sb.*] **1.** A basket. *dial.* **2.** *local.* A fish-trap 1602. **3.** A revolving machine of a conical or cylindrical shape armed internally with spikes for opening and cleaning wool, cotton, and flax 1835. Hence **Wi·ll(e)y** *v. trans.* to treat with the w. **Wi·ll(e)yer,** one who tends a w.

Willy *sb.*², **Willie** (wi·li). 1849. [Pet form of the name *William.*] Applied locally to various animals; e.g. the guillemot.

attrib.: **w.-goat,** a he-goat (= BILLY-GOAT); **-wagtail,** (*a*) the water-wagtail; (*b*) in Australia, the black-and-white fantail, *Rhipidura tricolor.*

Willy-nilly (wi·li ni·li), *adv.* and *a.* 1608. [= *will I, nill I* (*he, ye*); see WILL *v.*¹ VI.] **A.** *adv.* Whether it be with or against the will of the person or persons concerned; whether one likes it or not; *nolens volens.*

Carrying her off and marrying her willy nilly at Gretna Green 1884.

B. *adj.* **1.** That is such, or that takes place, whether one will or no 1877. ¶**2.** *erron.* Undecided, shilly-shally 1883.

Willy-willy (wi·liwi·li). *Austral.* 1894. [Native name.] A cyclonic storm or tornado.

Wilsome (wi·lsǝ̆m), *a. Obs.* exc. *dial.* ME. [– ON. *villusamr*, f. *villr* WILL *a.* + *-samr* -SOME¹.] **1.** Desert, dreary. **2.** Erring, perplexed. **3.** Wilful, obstinate.

Wilt (wilt), *sb.* 1855. [f. next.] The action or an act of wilting; *spec.* (also *w. disease*) any fungous disease of plants which is characterized by wilting.

Wilt (wilt), *v.* 1691. [orig. dial. (in early XIX largely U.S.); perh. alteration of *wilk* WELK *v.*] **1.** *intr.* Of plants or their parts: To become limp or flaccid, through heat or drought. **b.** *transf.* and *gen.* To become limp; to lose energy or vigour; to become dispirited or nerveless 1787. **2.** *trans.* To cause to become limp; to deprive of stiffness, energy, vigour, or spirit 1809.

1. b. The major..pale as death; and wiltin' away, like a cabbage leaf, in the hot sun 1825.

Wilt, 2nd pers. sing. pres. ind. of WILL *v.*¹

Wilton (wi·ltǝn). 1773. Name of a town in the south of Wiltshire, noted for the manufacture of carpets; applied to †(*a*) a kind of cloth, (*b*) a carpet of which the manufacture resembles that of a Brussels carpet but differing in having the rib cut so as to produce a velvet pile.

Wiltshire (wi·ltʃǝɹ). 1794. Name of an English county, applied to (*a*) a breed of sheep, (*b*) a kind of 'smoked' bacon, (*c*) a kind of cheese (also **Wilts**).

Wily (wəi·li), *a.* ME. [f. WILE *sb.* + -Y¹.] Full of or characterized by wiles; crafty, cunning, sly, artful.

The serpent that was moost w. of alle othere beestes CHAUCER. The w. suttleties and refluxes of mans thoughts MILT. Here w. Jesuits simple Quakers meet CRABBE.

Comb.: **w. beguile,** also freq. in jingling form **w. beguily**: orig. in phr. *to play w. beguile oneself*, to act wilily in such a way as to be oneself beguiled; hence as sb. phr. (*a*) a person who acts thus, or (simply) who acts wilily or craftily; (*b*) an act of this kind, or (simply) a w. act or action.

Wimble (wi·mb'l), *sb.* Now *dial.* or *techn.* ME. [– AFr. *wimble, var. of *guimble, whence ME. *gymble* and *gimlet.*] **1.** A gimlet. **2.** An auger; also, a brace. late ME. **3.** An instrument for boring in soft ground or for extracting rubbish from a bore-hole in mining 1692. Hence **Wi·mble** *v.* (*Obs.* exc. *dial.*) *trans.* to pierce with or as with a w., to make (a hole) with a w.; *intr.* to bore *into*; chiefly *fig.*, to penetrate or insinuate oneself *into.*

Wimble (wi·mb'l), *a. dial.* 1579. [app. a northern word taken up by Spencer; immed. source unknown.] Active, nimble.

Wimple (wi·mp'l), *sb.* [Late OE. *wimpel* = OFris., (M)LG., (M)Du. *wimpel*, OS. *wimpal*, OHG. *winfila* (G. *wimpel* streamer, pennon), ON. *vimpill.*] **I.** A garment of linen or silk formerly worn by women, so folded as to envelop the head, chin, and sides of the face, and neck: now retained in the dress of nuns. **II. 1.** A fold or wrinkle; a turn, winding, or twist; a ripple or rippling in a stream 1513. **2.** A crafty turn or twist; a wile. *Sc.* 1638. Hence **Wi·mpler,** a maker of wimples (*Obs.* exc. *Hist.*).

Wi·mple, *v.* ME. [f. prec.] **I. 1.** *trans.* To envelop in a wimple; loosely, to veil. **2.** *fig.* To veil, cover. late ME. **3.** *pass.* and *intr.* To fall in folds 1590.

1. Al wayes she was wympeld that no man myȝt see her vysage MALORY. **3.** A vele, that wimpled was full low SPENSER.

II. 1. *intr.* Of a stream: To meander, twist and turn; also, to ripple. Chiefly *Sc.* 1721. **2.** To move shiftily or unsteadily 1819.

Wimpled (wi·mpl'd), *ppl. a.* 1579. [f. WIMPLE *v.* or *sb.* + -ED.] **1.** Enveloped in or wearing a wimple; hence, veiled, *occas.* blindfolded. **2.** Arranged or falling in folds like a wimple; hence, wrinkled; rippled 1599. **3.** *fig.* Involved, intricate. *Sc.* 1722.

1. This w., whyning, purblinde waiward Boy SHAKS.

Win (win), *sb.*¹ [OE. *win(n* labour, strife, conflict. The modern senses are from WIN *v.*] **I.** †**1.** Strife, contention; tumult, disturbance, agitation –ME. †**2.** Gain, acquisition, profit; also, advantage, benefit –1535. **II.** *colloq.* **1.** A victory in a game or contest 1862. **2.** A gain; *pl.* gains, winnings 1891.

1. I was real pleased with the w., for lots of my pals had backed Actea 1894.

†**Win,** *sb.*² [OE. *wynn*, corresp. to OS. *wunnia*, OHG. *wunja* (G. *wonne*), f. Gmc. *wun-; see WISH *v.* and cf. WINSOME.] Joy, pleasure, bliss, or a source of this –1700. (See also WEN².)

Win, *sb.*³ *slang.* 1567. [Of unkn. origin.] A penny.

Win (win), *v.* Pa. t. and pple. **won** (wɒn). [OE. *winnan* = OFris. *winna*, OS. *winnan* suffer, win, OHG. *winnan* contend, *gewinnan* gain by labour (G. *gewinnen* earn, gain, produce), ON. *vinna*, Goth. (*ga*)*winnan* suffer; ult. origin unknown.] †**1.** *intr.* To work, labour; to strive, contend, fight –ME. †**2.** *trans.* To conquer, subdue, defeat, vanquish –1610. **3.** To be victorious in (a contest of any kind). Also *to w. the day, the field.* ME. **4.** *absol.* or *intr.* To overcome one's adversary, opponent, or competitor; to be victorious, gain the victory (now chiefly in sports or games of skill) ME. **5.** *trans.* To subdue and take possession of; to seize, capture, take (a place). *arch.* ME. **b.** To seize, capture, take as spoil; to capture, take captive (a person). *Obs.* exc. in euphemistic slang, to steal. ME. **c.** *Cards.* (*a*) To be of higher value than, to 'beat' (another card, hand, suit); (*b*) to gain possession of, take (a trick) 1680. **6.** To get, obtain, acquire; *esp.* to get as something profitable or desired; to gain, procure. **a.** with material obj. *Obs.* or *arch.* ME. **b.** with immaterial obj., or *gen.* OE. **7.** *spec.* **a.** To obtain (a woman) as a wife or 'lady' by action or effort of some kind: usu. with implication of gaining her affection and consent ME. **b.** To gain by effort or competition, as a prize or reward, or in gaming or betting, as a wager, etc. Also *absol.* ME. **c.** To get by labour, to earn (now *dial.*); †to get as profit, to gain ME. **d.** To get, gather (crops or other produce); to gather in, harvest. Now *dial.* late ME. **e.** To get or extract (coal, or other mineral) from the mine, pit, or quarry; also, to sink a shaft or make an excavation so as to reach (a seam of coal or vein of ore) and prepare it for working 1447. †**f.** To gain (ground) *upon*; to gain (time) –1717. **8.** To overcome the unwillingness or indifference of; to attract, allure; to prevail upon; to gain the affection or allegiance of. Also with adv. or prep., as *away, over, to, from*, etc., and with *to* and inf. (*arch.*). ME. **9.** *intr.* with *upon, on.* †**a.** To gain an advantage over, get the better of; to gain or encroach upon –1791. **b.** To gain influence over; to prevail with; to gain the favour or engage the affections of (esp. gradually or increasingly). Also with *affection, esteem*, or the like as obj. 1601. **10.** *trans.* To reach, attain, arrive at; *occas.* to get at, get hold of (an object); to overtake (a person); to be in time for, 'catch'. *arch.* 1471. **11.** *intr.* To make or find one's way; also, to arrive at or come to some place, etc. Formerly chiefly *Sc.* and *n. dial.* ME. **b.** In ref. to a desired end, a condition, experience, proceeding, etc.: with various preps. and advs. ME. **c.** with adj. as compl.: = GET *v.* V. 3. 1886. **12.** *intr.* with *to* and inf.: To succeed in doing (what is denoted by the vb.); to contrive *to do* something. Now *Sc.* and *dial.* ME. **13.** *trans.* To succeed in bringing, putting, etc. *Obs.* or *arch.* ME.

3. Won the toss—first innings—seven o'clock a.m. DICKENS. **4.** 2 *Hen. IV*, I. i. 132. Now freq. with *out* (cf. 11 b). orig. *U.S.* **5.** He that will Fraunce wynne must with Scotlánde firste begyn 1548. **6. b.** *To w. confidence, esteem, fame, love, praise, respect*; I am glad to have won your confidence DICKENS. *To w. the* (or *a*) *victory*, to be victorious. *To w. one's way*, to make or find one's way, succeed in getting somewhere. **7. a.** Faint heart never won faire lady 1639. *To w. and wear*: see WEAR *v.*¹ I. 7 b. **b.** Frank took dummy; and I won sixpence DICKENS. **8.** The worst temper of minds are wonne 1653. She could not w. him.. to any conversation J. AUSTEN. **10.** And if they once may w. the bridge, What hope to save the town? MACAULAY. **11.** The Germans never won through to the Channel ports 1923. *To w. up*, to get up, get up on one's feet; to get on horseback, mount. **b.** *To w. by..*, to escape, avoid. *To w. out* or *through*, to come out successfully, succeed in attaining one's end. **c.** To w. free from every form and observance 1886.

Wince (wins), *sb.*¹ 1612. [f. WINCE *v.*¹] **1.** A kick. Now *dial.* **2.** An involuntary, shrinking movement 1865.

Wince (wins), *sb.*² 1688. [Variant of WINCH *sb.*] **1.** = WINCH *sb.* 1, 2. **2.** *Dyeing.* A reel or roller placed over the division between two vats so that a fabric spread upon it may be let down into one or the other 1839. Hence **Wince** *v.*² *trans.* to immerse or pass through a vat by means of a w. **Wi·ncer,** one who tends a w.

Wince (wins), *v.*¹ ME. [– AFr. *wencir, var. of OFr. *guenchir* turn aside, avoid; see WINCH *v.*¹] **1.** *intr.* To kick restlessly from impatience or pain. Now *dial.* **2.** To start or make an involuntary shrinking movement in consequence of or in order to avoid pain, or when alarmed or suddenly affected 1748.

1. Wynsynge she was as is a ioly colt CHAUCER. Let the galld iade w. SHAKS.

Wincey (wi·nsi). 1808. [orig. Sc.; app. alteration of *woolsey* in LINSEY-WOOLSEY, through the medium of the assimilated form *linsey-winsey.] A very durable cloth having a linen warp and a woollen weft.

Winch (winʃ), *sb.* [Late OE. *winċe* :– Gmc. *wiŋkjōn :– *weŋk- WINK *v.*] **1.** A reel, roller, or pulley. **b.** *spec.* An angler's reel 1662. **c.** *Naut.* A small machine used for making ropes and spun-yarn 1640. **2.** The cranked handle by means of which the axis of a revolving machine is turned 1660. **3.** A hoisting or hauling apparatus consisting essentially of a horizontal drum round which a rope passes, and a crank by which it is turned 1577. **b.** In the navigation of the river Thames, a revolving apparatus at the riverside, round which a rope was wound to haul craft through difficult places; a toll levied for the use of this 1623. **4.** *Dyeing.* = WINCE *sb.*² 2. 1791.

Winch (winʃ), *v.*¹ *Obs.* exc. *dial.* ME. [– AFr. *wencier, -ir = OFr. *guenchier* (see WINCE *v.*¹) :– Gmc. *weŋkjan :– *waŋkjan; see WINK *v.*] **1.** *intr.* To start back or away, recoil, flinch; to wince. †**b.** *fig.* To recoil in fear or disgust (*at*) –1709. †**2.** = WINCE *v.*¹ 1. –1718.

Winch, *v.*² 1529. [f. WINCH *sb.*] **1.** *trans.* To hoist or draw *up*, etc. with or as with a winch. **2.** *Dyeing.* = WINCE *v.*² 1831.

Winchester (wi·nˌtʃėstəɹ). 1550. [Proper name.] **I.** The name of a city in Hampshire, the capital of Wessex and later of the Anglo-Saxon kingdom: used *attrib.* in specific designations.

W. measure, dry and liquid measures the standards of which were orig. deposited at Winchester. So *W. bushel, gallon, quart*, for which *W.* is used for short (in druggists' use = W. quart). *W. goose*: see GOOSE *sb.* 3.

II. The name of Oliver F. *Winchester* (1810–1880), an American manufacturer, used as the designation of a breech-loading rifle having a tubular magazine under the barrel and a horizontal bolt operated by a lever on the underside of the stock 1871.

Wind (wind, *poet.* also waind), *sb.*[1] [OE. *wind* = OFris., OS. *wind*, OHG. *wint* (Du., G. *wind*), ON. *vindr*, Goth. *winds* :– Gmc. **windaz*, based on IE. pr. pple. **went-*, whence L. *ventus* wind. The normal development is (waind), as in *hind, rind*; (wind) became current in polite speech in XVIII; the short vowel is prob. due to the influence of *windy*, where it is normal.] **I. 1.** Air in motion; a state of movement in the air; a current of air, of any degree of force perceptible to the senses, occurring naturally in the atmosphere, usu. parallel to the surface of the ground. **2.** With specific ref. to the direction from which it blows; usu. qualified by the name of a point of the compass, or in *pl.* by a numeral, esp. *four* (hence sometimes *transf.* = points of the compass, directions) OE. **3.** In ref. to navigation, as the means of propulsion of a sailing-vessel OE. **b.** *Naut.* in various expressions referring to the direction or position of the wind in relation to the ship; hence also *allus.* late ME. **4.** As conveying scent, esp. the scent of a person or animal in hunting, etc. ME. **5.** In alliterative conjunction with *weather*: now always *w. and weather* ME. **6.** As a thing devoid of sense or perception, or that is unaffected by what one does to it: in phrases usu. expressing futile action or effort ME. **7.** As a type of violence or fury, swiftness, freedom, or unrestrainable character, mutability or fickleness, lightness or emptiness. late ME.

1. Hither the winds blow, here the spring-tide roar MARLOWE. There was just such a w. and just such a fall of snow, a good many years back DICKENS. Not a breath of w. crossed the heavens 1849. *fig.* Lady Petherwin crashed out of the room in a w. of indignation HARDY. **2.** O, wild West W., thou breath of Autumn's being SHELLEY. The cousins disperse to the four winds of heaven DICKENS. **3.** I set up my sail, the w. being fair SWIFT. **b.** *To gain, get, take the w. of*, to get to windward of (another ship) so as to intercept the w.; so *to give, have the w. of. To take the w. out of the sails of* (fig.), to deprive of the means of progress, put a check upon the action of, put at a disadvantage. **4.** *To take, have, get, gain the w. of*, to scent or detect by or as by the w. *To keep the w.*, to keep the game on the windward side so as to scent it, or so that it does not scent one; Hee knowes the Game, how true hee keepes the winde? SHAKS. *Within w. of*, near enough to be detected by. **6.** This I tell her, but talk to the winds SWIFT. **7.** About the wood, goe swifter then the winde SHAKS. Thou shalt be as free As mountaine windes SHAKS.

II. *transf.* **1.** Air in general, as a substance or 'element'. *Obs.* exc. in *w. and water*. ME. **2.** 'Air' or gas in the stomach or intestines; flatus OE. **3.** Air inhaled and exhaled by the lungs. *Obs.* exc. as coloured by c. OE. **b.** Breath as used in speaking; hence *transf.* speech, talk. *Obs.* or *arch.* (exc. as implied in LONG-WINDED 2). ME. **c.** Easy or regular breathing; power or capacity of breathing; condition with regard to respiration. Now only in sporting phrases. ME. (*b*) in ref. to diseased or disordered breathing in horses 1523. **d.** *transf.* (*Pugilistic slang*). That part of the body in front of the stomach a blow upon which takes away the breath by checking the action of the diaphragm 1823. **4.** Air as used for 'blowing' or sounding a musical instrument (*w.-instrument*) such as a horn, trumpet, flute, etc., or an organ-pipe. late ME. **b.** *transf.* The wind-instruments of an orchestra (or their players) collectively, as dist. from the 'strings' and 'percussion' 1876. **5.** A blast of air artificially produced, *e.g.* by bellows; the rush of air caused by a rapidly moving body 1556.

1. *Between* (or *betwixt*) *w. and water* (Naut.), referring to that part of ship's side which is sometimes above water and sometimes submerged, in which part a shot is peculiarly dangerous. *W. and water line*, the part of a ship's side between w. and water. *To break w.*, to discharge flatus from the stomach or bowels. *To get the w. up* (slang), to get into a state of alarm or 'funk'. **3.** She..fetches her winde so short, as if she were fraid with a sprite SHAKS. **b.** *Com. Err.* I. ii. 53. **c.** *Second w.*, a condition of regular breathing regained after breathlessness during long-continued exertion. *W. and limb, limb and w.*: see LIMB *sb.*[1] 2. (*b*) A very handsome English coach-horse (a little touched in the w.) 1777. **4.** Heaving a long sigh, like w. in a trombone G. B. SHAW. **5.** He was knocked down by the w. of the shell 1804.

III. *fig.* and *allus.* **1.** Applied to something empty, vain, trifling, or unsubstantial, as empty talk, vain imagination or conceit ME. **2.** In provb. and other expressions, figuring or denoting a force or agency that drives or carries along or that strikes upon some person or thing OE. **b.** In expressions referring to a tendency, turn, or condition of affairs. late ME. **3. a.** *To get* or *take w.*: to be revealed or divulged, become known. Now *rare.* 1667. **b.** *To get w. of*, to receive information or a hint of. Hence, in recent use, *w.* = a hint or slight intimation (*of*). 1809.

1. I hope the Lord has let some of the w. out of you, that I thought was in you when first I knew you 1779. Hard words..are but w. SCOTT. Is Society become wholly a bag of w., then, ballasted by guineas? CARLYLE. **2.** *What w. blows you here? It's an ill w. that blows nobody good. To sow the w. and reap the whirlwind*: see WHIRLWIND 2. *To raise the w.*: see RAISE *v.* I. 7. **b.** *To know which way the w. blows. The w. has changed.* †*Is the w. in that corner? To sail with every* (*shift of*) *w.*, to turn every change of circumstances to one's advantage.

With preps. **Before the w.:** said of a ship sailing directly with the w.; also *fig.* **By the w.** (*Naut.*): as near as possible to the direction from which the w. is blowing. **Down (the) w.:** in the direction in which the w. is blowing; along the course of the w. Also *down-w.* (attrib.), situated in this direction, 'lee'. **In the w.: a.** In (or into) the direction from which the w. is blowing; to windward. **b.** *fig.* So as to be 'scented' or perceived (or so as to 'scent' or perceive something). **c.** *predic.* Happening or ready to happen; astir, afoot; (of a person or thing) as the subject of what is going on, 'in the business'. **d.** *To hang in the w.*: to remain in suspense or indecision. **e.** *Naut. slang* (predic.). Intoxicated; the worse for liquor: usu. with qualification, esp. *three sheets in the w.* **Into the w.:** into or towards the direction from which the w. is blowing; so as to face the w. **Near the w.:** nearly in the direction from which the w. is blowing; hence *fig.* nearly up to the possible or permissible limit. **Off the w.** (*Naut.*): away from the w. **On a** (less commonly **the**) **w.** (*Naut.*): towards or close to the direction from which the w. is blowing. **To the w.: a.** *Naut.* Towards the direction from which the w. is blowing. *Close to the w.*, very nearly in this direction. **b.** *To fling, give*, etc. *to the winds* (fig.): to cast away, reject utterly. **Under the w.:** on the side away from the w.; *spec.* in a position of shelter from the w.; under the lee of something. Chiefly *Naut.* and *dial.* **Up (the) w.:** in the direction contrary to that in which the w. is blowing; against the w. **With the w.:** in the direction in which the w. is blowing.

Comb.: **w.-ball,** an inflated ball; a game played with such a ball by striking it with the fist; **-band,** a band of w.-instruments, as a military band; **-belt,** a belt of trees planted for protection from the w.; **-blown** *a.*, blown up or inflated; blown along or about; blown upon by (the) w.; **-break,** something, esp. a row of trees, used to break the force of the w. (chiefly *U.S.*); **-chest,** an air-tight chest or box in an organ or similar instrument, which is filled with w. from the bellows, and from which the w. is admitted to the pipes or reeds; **-driven** *a.*, driven, carried, or impelled by the w.; †**-gun** = AIR-*gun*; **-hole,** (*a*) an opening in brickwork for the passage of air; (*b*) the hole in the lower board of a pair of bellows; (*c*) a ventilating shaft in a mine; (*d*) each of the openings in the sound-board of an organ, through which w. is admitted to the pipes; **-jammer** *U.S. slang*, a sailing vessel; **-porch,** a chamber constructed on the inner side of a doorway to keep the w. out; **-pump,** a pump driven by a w.-wheel; **-rode** *a. Naut.*, swung by the w., as a ship riding at anchor; **-screen,** a screen for protection from the w., now esp. in front of the driver's seat on a motor-car; **-suck** *v.*, *intr.* of a horse, to have the vice of noisily drawing in and swallowing air; **-sucker,** a horse addicted to w.-sucking; **-tight** *a.*, solidly constructed to keep out w.; also of a vessel = AIR-*tight*; **-wheel,** a wheel turned by the w. to drive some mechanism, as in a windmill or w.-pump.

Wind (waind), *sb.*[2] late ME. [Partly – MDu., MLG. *winde* windlass; partly f. WIND *v.*[1]] **1.** An apparatus for winding, a winch or windlass. *Obs.* exc. *dial.* **2.** An act or instance of winding; curved or twisted form; *techn.* bend or twist, esp. in phr. *out of w.*, not twisted 1825.

Wind (waind), *v.*[1] Pa. t. and pple. **wound** (waund). [OE. *windan* = OFris. *winda*, OS. *windan* (Du., G. *winden*), ON. *vinda*, Goth. *-windan* :– Gmc. **windan*, rel. to **wand-* in WANDER *v.*, WEND *v.*] †**1.** *intr.* To go on one's way, take oneself; to proceed, go –1608. **2.** *trans.* To wield (a weapon, an implement). *Obs.* or *dial.* OE. **3.** *intr.* To turn this way and that; to writhe. *Obs.* exc. *dial.* OE. †**4.** *trans.* To put into a curved or twisted form or state; to bend –1624. **b.** *intr.* To take or have a bent form; now only *dial.* or *techn.* of a board, door, etc., to be twisted. late ME. **5. a.** *refl.* = 6 a, b. *arch.* ME. **b.** *trans.* To turn; to cause to move in a curve. *arch.* ME. **6. a.** *intr.* To move in a curve; to turn, esp. in a specified direction. *Obs.* exc. as in b, c. late ME. **b.** To move along in a sinuous course; to go or travel *along, up, down*, etc. a path or road which turns this way and that 1682. **c.** *transf.* Of a line, road, or the like: To have a curved (esp. a sinuous) course; to lie or extend in a curve or succession of curves 1555. **d.** with advb. acc., or *trans.* with obj. (*one's* or *its*) *way*, etc. 1667. **e.** *trans.* To traverse in a curved or sinuous course. *arch.* 1648. **7.** *Naut.* **a.** *intr.* Of a ship: To turn in some direction, e.g. to swing round when at anchor; to lie with her head towards a particular point of the compass. **b.** *trans.* To turn (a vessel) about, or in some particular direction. 1613. **8.** To turn or deflect in a particular direction; *esp.* to turn or lead (a person) according to one's will; also *to turn and w.* Now *rare* or *Obs.* late ME. †**b.** To draw, bring, or involve (a person) *in*, attract *into*, by alluring or enticing methods –1655. **9.** *intr.* To pursue a devious, circuitous, or intricate course in argument, statement, or conduct; to use circumlocution or subtle terms of argument. *arch.* late ME. **10.** *intr.* and *refl.* †**a.** With *out*: To extricate or disentangle oneself from a state of confinement or embarrassment –1667. **b.** With *in, into*: To insinuate oneself 1548. **11.** *trans.* To turn or pass (something) around something else so as to encircle or enclose it and be in contact with it; to turn, twist, or wrap (something) *about, round*, or *upon* something else ME. **12.** To put (thread, tape, or the like) in coils or convolutions around something, as a reel, or upon itself, so as to form it into a compact mass (hank, skein, ball, etc.). Also with *from* or *off*, to undo the coils of (thread, etc.) by rotating the object on which they are wound; to unwind. ME. **13.** To encircle *with* or enclose in something passed round and in contact; now only of binding a thing *round* with tape, wire, or the like ME. **b.** *spec.* To wrap (a corpse) in a shroud or *winding-sheet*; to shroud. *Obs.* exc. *dial.* ME. **c.** Chiefly in pa. pple. and *fig.*: To involve, entangle ME. **14.** *intr.* To turn so as to encircle and lie in contact with something else; to twist or coil *about, around*, or *upon* something. So *to w. off*, to unwind. 1575. †**15.** *trans.* To plait, wreathe, weave –1601. **16.** To haul or hoist by turning a winch, windlass, or the like, around which a rope or chain is passed. **a.** *gen.* late ME. **b.** *Naut.* To move or warp (the ship), by hauling, as on a capstan or windlass. Also *absol.* or *intr.* 1515. **c.** *Mining.* To hoist (coal, etc.) to the surface 1883. **17.** To set (a watch, clock, or other mechanism) in order for going by turning an axis with a key or other device so as to coil the spring tighter or draw up the weights 1601. **b.** *fig.* To exalt or 'screw up' *to* a certain pitch 1635.

1. But winde away, bee gone I say SHAKS. **6. b.** The lowing herd wind slowly o'er the lea GRAY. **d.** He..windes..his oblique way Amongst innumerable Starrs MILT. **8.** He can w. the proud Earl to his will SCOTT. **9.** *Merch. V.* I. i. 154. **10. b.** Of your having..wound yourself..almost into his confidence DICKENS. **11.** *To w.* (a person, etc.) *round one's* (*little*) *finger*, to make him do anything. **13.** Her twin brother couldn't w. up a top for his life DICKENS. **b.** She had winded a many of them in her time 1860.

W. up.: **a.** *trans.* To draw up or hoist with a winch or the like. †**b.** *fig.* To involve, implicate. **c.** †(*a*) To coil, roll, or fold up; to furl; (*b*) to coil (thread, etc.) into a compact mass: chiefly in phr. †*to w. up a bottom, one's bottoms*, usu. *fig.* to sum up, conclude. **d.** †(*a*) To sum up; (*b*) to bring to a close or conclusion; to form the conclusion of, be the final event in; (*c*) to bring (an affair) to a final settlement; *spec.* to arrange and adjust the affairs of (a company or business concern) on its dissolution; (*d*) *absol.* or *intr.* to bring the proceeding to a close; to conclude *with* something. **e.** = 17 a. **f.** *fig.* To set in readiness for action; to raise (feeling) to a high degree; now usu., to put into a state of tension or intensity of feeling, etc.; to excite.

Wind (wind, wəind), *v.*[2] Pa. t. and pple. **winded.** late ME. [f. WIND *sb.*[1]] **I.** *trans.* To get the wind of; to perceive (an animal, a person, or thing) by the scent conveyed by the wind. **b.** *intr.* Of an animal: To sniff in order to scent or on scenting something. late ME. **c.** *fig.* (*trans.*) To perceive by some subtle indication; to smell or nose *out* 1583.

They had winded two lions 1850. **c.** No nose to.. winde out all your tricks 1611.

II. 1. *trans.* To expose to the wind or air; to air. late ME. **b.** *intr.* To become tainted by exposure to air; *trans.* to taint by such exposure (*dial.*) 1842. **2.** *trans.* (usu. wəind). To sound by forcing the breath through, to blow (a wind-instrument, esp. a horn). Often with pa. t. and pple. *wound.* 1586. **b.** To blow (a blast, call, or note) on a horn, etc. 1599. **c.** To supply (an organ-pipe) with wind at a particular pressure 1879. **3.** To deprive of 'wind' or breath, put out of breath 1811.

2. Where the Beetle winds His small but sullen Horn COLLINS. **b.** *Much Ado* I. i. 243. **3.** Parkes was very faint, and apparently quite winded 1811.

Windage (wi·ndėdʒ). 1710. [f. WIND *sb.*[1] + -AGE.] **1.** An allowance of space (for expansion of gas in firing) between the inner wall of a fire-arm and the shot or shell with which it is charged. **2.** Allowance made (esp. in shooting) for deflexion from the direct course by the wind; such deflexion itself 1867. **3.** = WIND *sb.*[1] II. 5; also, the friction of the air upon a moving part of a machine 1889.

Wind-bag, windbag (wi·ndbæg). 1470. [f. WIND *sb.*[1] + BAG *sb.*] **1.** A bag containing 'wind' or air, as the bag of a bagpipe, the lungs, the chest or body considered as a receptacle of breath (now only *joc.*). **2.** *fig.* (*contempt.*) An empty pretender, or something pretentious but unsubstantial; *esp.* a voluble and senseless talker 1827.

Wi·nd-bound, *a.* [f. WIND *sb.*[1] + BOUND *ppl. a.*[2]] Detained by contrary winds.

Winded (wi·ndėd), *a.* 1440. [f. WIND *sb.*[1] + -ED[2].] Having wind, i.e. (usu.) breath, of a specified kind or in a specified condition; chiefly in parasynthetic combs., as LONG-W., SHORT-W.

Wi·nded, *ppl. a.* 1595. [f. WIND *v.*[2] + -ED[1].] **1.** (wi·ndėd) Exposed to or spoilt by wind or air. **2.** (wəi·ndėd) Blown, as a wind-instrument 1622. **3.** (wi·ndėd) Put out of breath, blown 1597.

Wind-egg (wi·nd,eg). late ME. [f. WIND *sb.*[1] + EGG *sb.*] An imperfect or unproductive egg, esp. one with a soft shell.

Winder[1] (wəi·ndəɹ). 1552. [f. WIND *v.*[1] + -ER[1].] A person or thing that winds, in various senses. **1.** One who turns or manages a winch or windlass, esp. at a mine 1747. **2.** An operative employed in winding wool, etc. 1552. **3.** One who winds a clock or other mechanism 1823. **4.** An apparatus (of various kinds) for winding something, or upon which something is wound or coiled 1585. **5.** A key for winding a jack, clock, or other mechanism 1606. **6.** A winding step in a staircase: usu. in *pl.*, opp. to *flyers* 1667.

Wi·nder[2]. 1611. [f. WIND *v.*[2] + -ER[1].] **1.** (wəi·ndəɹ). One who blows a wind-instrument. **2.** (wi·ndəɹ). Something that takes one's breath away; a blow that 'knocks the wind' out of one; run or other exertion that puts one out of breath *colloq.* 1825.

Windfall (wi·ndfǫl). 1464. [perh. of foreign origin; cf. MHG. *wintval.*] **1.** Something blown down by the wind, or the fall of something so blown down: **a.** a tree or branch, or a number of trees or branches; *spec.* (chiefly *U.S.*) a heap or tract of fallen trees blown down by a tornado; **b.** fruit from a tree or bush (*rarely* flowers). 1592. **2.** *fig.* A casual or unexpected acquisition or advantage 1542.

2. This man..by these windfalles and unexpected cheats became very wealthy HOLLAND. So **Wi·ndfallen** *a.* blown down by the wind.

Wi·nd-flow:er. 1551. [Turner's rendering of L. *anemone*, Gr. ἀνεμώνη. Cf. (M)HG. *windblume.*] The wood-anemone (*Anemone nemorosa*), or any plant or flower of the genus *Anemone.* **b.** A species of gentian 1866.

Windgall[1] (wi·ndgǫl). 1523. [f. WIND *sb.*[1] + GALL *sb.*[2]] A soft tumour on either side of a horse's leg just above the fetlock, caused by distension of the synovial bursa. Hence **Wi·ndgalled** *a.* affected with a w. or windgalls.

Wi·nd-gall[2]. 1840. [f. as prec.; cf. G. *windgalle, -gelle* and see WATERGALL.] = WEATHER-*gall.*

Wi·nd-gauge. 1774. [f. WIND *sb.*[1] + GAUGE.] **1.** = ANEMOMETER 1. **2.** A graduated attachment to the sights of a gun, to enable allowance to be made for the effect of the wind on the projectile 1862. **3.** = ANEMOMETER 2. 1876.

Windhover (wi·ndhǫ:vəɹ, -hɒ:vəɹ). 1674. [f. WIND *sb.*[1] + HOVER *v.*] A name for the kestrel, from its habit of hovering in the air with its head to the wind.

Windily (wi·ndili), *adv.* 1866. [f. WINDY *a.* + -LY[2].] In a windy manner; as if driven or agitated by the wind.

Windiness (wi·ndinės). 1450. [f. WINDY *a.* + -NESS.] **1.** Windy condition of the atmosphere; prevalence of windy weather 1687. **2.** Flatulence. Now *rare.* 1450. **b.** Quality of causing or tendency to cause 'wind'. Now *rare.* 1576. **3.** *fig.* 'Airiness', emptiness, want of substance; inflated or verbose style 1614.

Winding (wəi·ndiŋ), *vbl. sb.* OE. [f. WIND *v.*[1] + -ING[1].] **I.** The action of WIND *v.*[1], or the resulting condition. **1.** Motion in a curve; sinuous progress or movement. late ME. **2.** *fig.* Turning this way and that in thought or conduct; usu. *pl.* devious or intricate motions; tortuous or crooked ways or dealings 1621. **3.** *Carpentry*, etc. Condition of being twisted; chiefly in phr. *out of w.* = *out of wind* (WIND *sb.*[2] 2); *in w.*, twisted 1711. **4.** The action of twining a flexible object round another or itself, *esp.* the coiling or twining of thread, silk, etc. late ME. **5.** Hoisting or hauling by means of a winch, windlass, or the like 1440. **6.** Usu. with *up*, of a clock or other mechanism 1630. **7.** *W. up*, conclusion, finish; now usu. the bringing to an end the activities of a business concern 1560. **II.** That which winds or is wound. **1.** An object that winds or is wound round; a coil or coiled object OE. **2.** A curved, sinuous, or meandering line, path, or the like; esp. *pl.* meanderings, twists and turns. late ME. **3.** A flexible rod or withy. *Obs.* or *dial.* late ME.

1. To nurse the Saplings tall, and curl the grove With Ringlets quaint, and wanton windings wove MILT. **2.** I..follow'd long The windings of the stream COWPER.

Winding (wəi·ndiŋ), *ppl. a.* 1530. [f. WIND *v.*[1] + -ING[2].] That winds, in various senses. **a.** That follows a sinuous course or is full of bends and turns; esp. of a staircase: Spiral. **b.** Of a narrative: Circuitous, rambling 1887. Hence **Wi·nding-ly** *adv.*, **-ness.**

Winding-sheet (wəi·ndiŋʃīt). late ME. [f. WINDING *vbl. sb.* + SHEET *sb.*[1]] **1.** A sheet in which a corpse is wrapped for burial. **2.** A mass of solidified drippings of grease clinging to the side of a candle, resembling a sheet folded in creases, and regarded as an omen of death or calamity 1708.

1. A thousand Coarses, some standing bolt upright in their knotted winding sheetes DEKKER **2.** She..sees..gifts in her finger-nails, letters and winding-sheets in the candle 1824.

Wi·nd-i:nstrument. 1582. (Often as two words.) A musical instrument played by means of 'wind', supplied either by the breath of the player or by bellows: most commonly applied to portable instruments of this kind, such as those used in an orchestra. (Strictly, applied to instruments whose sounds are produced by vibration of air in a pipe or tube, or in a number of pipes; but usu. also including those sounding by vibration of reeds.)

Windlass (wi·ndlăs), *sb.*[1] late ME. [Presumably obsc. alt. of †*windas* – AFr. *windas* (AL. *windasius* XII) = OFr. *guindas* – ON. *vindáss*, f. *vinda* WIND *v.*[1] + *áss* pole.] A mechanical contrivance working on the principle of the wheel and axle, on a horizontal axis; consisting of a roller or beam, resting on supports, round which a rope or chain is wound, and used for various purposes, as on board ship for weighing the anchor, for raising a bucket from a well, etc.

attrib.; **w.-bar,** any of a set of bars inserted in holes in a ship's w. by which it is turned; **w.-bitt, -chock,** each of the supports of a ship's w. Hence **Wi·ndlass** *v.*[2] *trans.* to hoist or haul with a w.

†**Windlass,** *sb.*[2] 1530. [alt. of †*wanlace* – AFr. *wanelace* XII–XIV (AL. *wanelassum* XIV), of unkn. origin.] **1.** A circuit made to intercept the game in hunting; *gen.* a circuit, circuitous movement –1602, **2.** *fig.* A circuitous course of action; a crafty device –1734.

2. *Ham.* II. i. 65. Hence †**Windlass** *v.*[1] *trans.* to decoy or ensnare; *intr.* to make a circuit, to act circuitously or craftily –1660.

Windle (wi·nd'l). [OE. *windel* basket, f. *windan* WIND *v.*[1] + -LE 1. Cf. AL. *windellus* (XIII) measure of meal.] **1.** A basket. Now *dial.* **2.** A measure of corn and other commodities; of wheat, usu. about 3 bushels. *local.* ME.

Windless (wi·nd,lės), *a.* late ME. [f. WIND *sb.*[1] + -LESS.] **1.** Breathless, out of breath. Now *rare.* **2.** Free from wind; not exposed to or stirred by the wind, in or upon which no wind blows 1591. Hence **Wi·ndless-ly** *adv.*, **-ness.**

Windlestraw (wi·nd'l,strǫ). *Sc.* and *dial.* [OE. *windelstrēaw*, f. *windel* WINDLE + *strēaw* STRAW *sb.*] **1.** A dry thin withered stalk of grass, such as is left standing after the flower or seed is shed. **2.** Any of various long-stalked species of grass, as *Cynosurus cristatus* (dog's-tail grass), *Lolium perenne* (rye-grass), and *Agrostis spicaventi* OE.

1. *fig.* He grippit me..and drew his windlestrae of a sword 1895.

Windmill (wi·ndmil, wi·nmil). ME. [f. WIND *sb.*[1] + MILL *sb.*[1]] **1.** A mill the machinery of which is driven by the wind acting upon sails, used (chiefly in flat districts) for grinding corn, pumping water, etc. **2.** A figure of a windmill; a sign or character resembling this, as a cross or asterisk. Now *rare* or *Obs.* late ME. **3. a.** A model of a windmill. **b.** A toy consisting of a cross-shaped piece of card or other light substance fixed at the end of a stick so as to revolve like the sails of a windmill when moved through the air. 1557. **4.** *fig.* and *allus.* †**a.** A fanciful notion, a crotchet –1749. **b.** In allusions to the story of Don Quixote tilting at windmills under the delusion that they were giants 1644. **c.** *To fling (throw) one's cap over the w.* [= Fr. *jeter son bonnet par-dessus les moulins*]: to act recklessly and defiantly, fly in the face of convention 1885.

4. a. Thy head is full of Windemils 1622.

Comb.: **w. aero(plane** = AUTOGIRO; **w.-cap,** the upper story of a w. when made movable so as to turn the sails to the wind; **w. plant** = TELEGRAPH-*plant*; **-pump,** a wind-pump.

Window (wi·ndo[u]), *sb.* [ME. *windoȝe* – ON. *vindauga*, f. *vindr* WIND *sb.*[1] + *auga* EYE *sb.*[1]] **1.** An opening in a wall or side of a building, ship, or carriage, to admit light or air, or both, and to afford a view of what is outside or inside; now usu. fitted with sheets of glass, horn, mica, etc., a frame containing a pane or panes of glass, or glazed sashes. **2.** *transf.* A window space or opening; *esp.* in phr. *in the w.*, now chiefly with ref. to the exhibition of notices, advertisements, etc., or the display of goods (as in a shop-w.) ME. **3.** Applied to openings, resembling or likened to a window in shape or function, e.g. *pl.* a pattern of squares made with sugar on bread and butter; soap-bubbles blown between the finger and thumb. late ME. **b.** *Windows of heaven*: openings in the sky through which rain was thought to pour. late ME. **c.** *Anat.* = FENESTRA 1. 1615. **4.** *fig.* Applied to the senses or organs of sense, esp. the eyes, regarded as inlets or outlets to or from the mind or soul ME. **b.** *fig.* and in allusive or provb. expressions. late ME.

1. At the chekker hous windo 1583. Storied Windows richly dight MILT. 2. *To dress a w.*: cf. *w.-dresser, -dressing.* 3. A large..lamp, having side windows 1892. 4. The eyes..are the windowes of the minde 1544. b. *To throw the house out at (the) w.* [= Fr. *jeter la maison par la fenêtre*], to make a great commotion, turn everything topsy-turvy. *To come in by the w.* [= Fr. *entrer par la fenêtre*], to come in stealthily.

Comb.: **w.-box,** a box placed outside a w., in which ornamental plants are cultivated; **-cleaner,** a person whose business it is to clean windows; **-dresser,** one whose business it is to arrange and display goods to the best advantage in a shop-w.; **-dressing,** (*a*) the dressing of a w. with goods attractively displayed; (*b*) *fig.* a display made in such a way as to give a falsely favourable impression of the facts; *esp.* the arrangement of a balance-sheet so as to suggest that the business concerned is more prosperous than it is; **-envelope,** an envelope with an opening or transparent 'panel' in the front through which the address is visible; **w. gardening,** the cultivation of plants in w. spaces or on w.-sills; **-mirror,** a mirror fixed outside a w. and adjustable so as to reflect the image of objects in the street; **-pane; -seat,** a seat fixed under a w. or windows, often upholstered; **-sill** = SILL^1 2; **-tax,** a duty levied upon windows, imposed in 1695 and abolished in 1851. Hence †**Wi·ndow** *v.* (*rare*) *trans.* to furnish with windows or w.-like openings; to place in a w. **Wi·ndowless** *a.* not having or furnished with windows.

Windowed (wi·ndo^{u}d), *ppl. a.* 1483. [f. prec. + -ED^2.] **1.** Furnished with or having windows. Also with prefixed word in comb. **2.** Having decorative openings 1483. **3.** Full of holes. (In later use echoing Shaks.) 1605.

3. Your lop'd, and window'd raggedness SHAKS.

Windpipe (wi·ndpəip, wəi·ndpəip). 1530. [f. WIND *sb.*^{1} + PIPE *sb.*^{1}] **1.** = TRACHEA 1 a. **2.** An artificial pipe or tube for conducting a blast or air (*rare*) 1688.

Wind-rose (wi·nd,ro^{u}z). 1597. [f. as prec. + ROSE *sb.*; in sense 2, after G. *windrose.*] **1. a.** The 'bastard wild poppy', *Argemone mexicana*, or the common wild poppy, *Papaver rhœas*; **b.** the violet horned poppy, *Rœmeria hybrida*. **2.** *Meteorol.* A diagram indicating the relative frequency, force, etc. of the winds from the various points of the compass at some given place 1846.

Windrow (wi·nd,ro^u), *sb.* 1523. [f. WIND *sb.*^{1} + ROW *sb.*^{1}] A row in which mown grass or hay is laid before being made up into heaps or cocks, in which sods, peats, etc. are set up to be dried by the wind, or in which dead branches, etc. are gathered to be burnt. Hence **Wi·ndrow** *v. trans.* to set or lay in windrows.

Windsail (wi·ndsē^{i}l). 1725. [f. WIND *sb.*^{1} + SAIL *sb.*^{1}] **1.** *Naut.* A long wide tube or funnel of sail-cloth used for ventilating a ship 1741. **2.** A sail of a windmill 1725.

Wind-shake (wi·ndʃē^{i}k). 1545. [f. WIND *sb.*^{1} + SHAKE *sb.* II. 1.] A flaw or crack in timber, supposed to be due to a strain caused by the force of the wind.

Wind-shaken (wi·ndʃē^i:k'n), *ppl. a.* 1550. [f. WIND *sb.*^{1} + *shaken*, pa. pple. of SHAKE *v.*] **1.** Shaken or agitated by the wind. **2.** Of timber: Affected with wind-shake 1565. So †**Wi·nd-shaked** *ppl. a.* (*rare*) = sense 1.

Windsor (wi·nzəɹ). Name of a town in Berkshire, on the right bank of the Thames, at which is W. Castle, a royal residence. **1.** *attrib.* in names of various things now or formerly obtained, made, etc. at or near W., or of persons connected with W. Castle 1473. **2.** Short for *W. bean, brick, soap* 1786.

1. **W. bean,** the common broad bean; **W. brick,** a kind of red fire-resisting brick formerly made at Hedgerley, near W.; **W. chair,** a kind of wooden chair with the back formed of upright rod-like pieces surmounted by a cross-piece, and often with arms; **W. herald,** an officer whose duties are now performed by the Garter King of Arms; **W. knight,** one of a body of military pensioners residing within the precincts of W. Castle; **W. soap,** a kind of toilet soap, usu. brown; **W. tie** (*U.S.*), a kind of broad silk necktie, tied in a double bow; **W. uniform,** a uniform introduced by King George III, worn on certain occasions at W. Castle by members of the royal household.

Wind-up (wəi·nd,ʌp), *sb.* and *a.* 1573. [f. the phr. *to wind up.*] **A.** *sb.* The action of 'winding-up', or something that 'winds up' or concludes a course of action, etc.; close, conclusion; final settlement; closing act or proceeding. **B.** *adj.* **1.** Constructed to be wound up 1784. **2.** Forming the conclusion of something; concluding, closing 1843.

Windward (wi·nd,wǭɹd), quasi-*sb.* in *phr.*, *a.*, and *adv.* 1549. [f. WIND *sb.*^{1} + -WARD.] **A.** Phr. *To (the) w.*, to the w. side or direction.

To get to w. of (fig.), to gain an advantage over. *To keep to w. of*, to keep out of the reach of.

B. *adj.* **1.** Having a direction towards, *i.e.* opposite to that of, the wind; moving against the wind 1627. **b.** = WEATHERLY *a.* 1895. **2.** Situated towards the direction from which the wind blows; facing the wind. *W. tide*, a tide running contrary to the direction of the wind. 1687. **C.** *adv.* Towards the wind, to w. 1690. Hence **Wi·ndwardly** *a.* = B 1 b, 2. So **Wi·ndwards** = A.

Windy (wi·ndi), *a.* [OE. *windiġ*; see WIND *sb.*^{1} and -Y^1.] **I. 1.** Consisting of wind; of or pertaining to (the) wind; indicating or suggesting wind. **b.** Produced, or actuated, by 'wind' or compressed air: said of a wind-instrument, or its music 1841. **2. a.** Of places, etc.: Full of, exposed to, or blown upon or through by the wind OE. **b.** Of times, conditions, etc.: Characterized by wind, in which wind is frequent or prevalent; accompanied by (much) wind OE. **c.** Situated towards the wind, windward 1599. **3.** Resembling the wind in storminess, quality of sound, swiftness, etc. OE. **4. a.** = FLATULENT 3. OE. **b.** = FLATULENT 2. late ME.

1. March, departed with his w. rage 1602. 2. a. The w. tall elm-tree TENNYSON. c. Phr. *On the w. side of* (fig.): out of reach of, away from, clear of (in modern use echoing SHAKS.); Still you keepe o' the windie side of the Law: good. SHAKS.

II. *fig.* **1.** Having 'nothing in it', intangible, empty, vain, trifling, worthless 1593. **2. a.** Of speech or discourse: Verbose; violent, vehement; empty and high-sounding; extravagant. late ME. **b.** Of a speaker or writer: Full of talk or verbiage, long-winded; violent or extravagant in utterance, bragging, boastful 1513. **3.** †**a.** That 'puffs one up'; inducing pride or vain-glory –1784. **b.** 'Puffed up'; inflated with, or showing, pride or vain conceit. Now *Sc. colloq.* 1603. **4.** Apt to 'get the wind up'; 'funky'. *slang.* 1916.

1. The Prince of Wales had some w. projects of encouraging literature..and the arts THACKERAY. 2. a. The w. speeches made at..political meetings 1886.

Wine (wəin), *sb.* [OE. *wīn* = OFris., OS., OHG. *wīn* (Du. *wijn*, G. *wein*), ON. *vín*, Goth. *wein* :– Gmc. **wīnam* – L. *vīnum*, **wīnom* (whence also the Balto-Slavic and Celtic words), prob. borrowed with Gr. οἶνος, etc. from a common Mediterranean source.] **1.** The fermented juice of the grape used as a beverage. **b.** As one of the elements in the Eucharist OE. **c.** Regarded as the usual accompaniment of dessert 1824. **2.** In wider use, usu. with qualifying word: A fermented liquor made from the juice of other fruits, or from grain, flowers, the sap of various trees, etc.: sometimes called *made w.* late ME. **3.** *Pharmacy.* A solution of a medicinal substance (denoted by a qualifying word) in wine; a medicated wine 1652. **4.** A wine-party, esp. of undergraduates 1860. **5.** *Spirit(s) of w.*, alcohol, rectified spirit; *oil of w.*, œnanthic ester; also, a heavy oily liquid (*heavy oil of w.*) consisting of etherin, etherol, and ethyl sulphate 1646. **6.** *pl.* Short for: Wine-glasses 1848.

1. Wyne to make glad yᵉ herte of man COVERDALE *Ps.* 103[4]: 15. The Sons Of Belial, flown with insolence and w. MILT. The..W. and Spirit Merchant 1828. *fig. Macb.* II. iii. 100. Phrases. *In w.*: in a state of intoxication with w.; in one's cups. *To take w.*, to drink w. *with* another person in a ceremonial manner, esp. as a token of friendship or regard. Provb. phrases. *New w. in old bottles* (see *Matt.* 9:17). *To look on the w. when it is red* (see *Prov.* 23:31). *Good w. needs no (ivy) bush* (see BUSH *sb.*^{1} 5). *When w. is in, wit* (or *truth*) *is out. W. and women*; Those two maine plagues and common dotages of humane kind, W. & Women BURTON. c. In after-dinner talk Across the walnuts and the w. TENNYSON. 2. *The w. of the country*: prop., the wine made in a particular locality for local consumption; usu. *transf.* the alcoholic beverage most drunk in a particular country. 3. W. of Ipecacuanha 1811.

attrib. and *Comb.*: **w.-bibber** (now *literary*). [Coverdale's rendering in *Prov.* 23:20, *Matt.* 11:19 of Luther's (*wein*)*säufer*], a tippler, a drunkard; **-biscuit,** a small light biscuit served with w.; **-card** [G. *weinkarte*], a list of the wines that may be obtained at a restaurant; **-cellar,** a cellar used for storing w.; **-cooler,** a vessel in which bottles of w. can be immersed in ice or iced liquid; **-dark** *a.*, of the colour of deep-red w.; used esp. to render Gr. οἴνοψ as an epithet of the sea; **-fly,** any fly the larva of which lives in w.; **-glass,** a small drinking-glass for w.; **-grape,** *U.S.* a grape from which w. is made; **-grower,** one who cultivates vines for the production of w.; **-lees,** the sediment deposited in a vessel containing w.; **-measure,** the standard of liquid measure used for w.; **-party,** a party, the chief object of which is to drink w.; **-sap,** a large red Amer. winter apple; **-sour,** a small acid variety of plum; **-taster,** (*a*) one who judges the quality of w. by tasting; (*b*) an instrument for drawing a small sample of w. from a cask; **-vat,** a w.-press; **-vault(s,** (*a*) a vault in which w. is stored; (*b*) a pretentious name for a public-house; **-vinegar,** vinegar made from w., as opp. to *malt vinegar.* Hence **Wine** *v. intr.* to take w., esp. at an undergraduates' w.-party (*colloq.*) 1829; *trans.* to entertain to w.: usu. in jingling phr. *dine and w.* (colloq.) 1862. **Wi·neless** *a.* lacking or destitute of w.

Wineberry (wəi·nbe:ri). [OE. *winberiġe*; f. WINE *sb.* + BERRY *sb.*^{1}] †**1.** A grape –1562. **2.** Applied formerly or now locally to various berries, e.g. †the bilberry; *dial.* the currant, the gooseberry. late ME.

Wi·ne-house. 1607. [Cf. OE. *wīnhūs.*] A public-house where wine is drunk. Now chiefly *Hist.* or with particular local reference. **2.** A house that deals in wine; a firm of wine-merchants 1834.

Wi·ne-press. 1526. [f. WINE *sb.* + PRESS *sb.*^{1} III. 2.] A press in which the juice is extracted from the grapes in the manufacture of wine. Also *fig.*, esp. with ref. to *Isa.* 63:3, *Rev.* 14:19, 20, 19:15.

He must Tread the w. alone, calling no God-fearing man his friend FROUDE.

Winery (wəi·nəri). orig. *U.S.* 1882. [f. WINE *sb.*^{1} + -ERY.] An establishment for making wine.

Wing (wiŋ), *sb.* ME. [First in pl. *wenge(n, -es* – ON. *vængir*, acc. *vengi*, pl. of *vængr* wing of a bird, aisle, repl. OE. *feþra* wings, pl. of *feþer* FEATHER, and *fiþere.*] **I. 1.** Each of the organs of flight of any flying animal, as a bird, bat, or insect. **b.** The wing of a bird, used as food. Also, the shoulder of a hare or rabbit. 1470. **c.** The wing of a bird (usu. of a hen, goose, or turkey) used as a brush 1573. **d.** A figure or imitation of a wing (e.g. on an angler's artificial fly) 1552. **2. a.** Attributed to supernatural beings, as angels, demons, etc., and to fabulous creatures, as dragons, etc. ME. **b.** Attributed to inanimate or abstract things represented as flying, or as carrying one swiftly along (esp. in phr. *on the wings of*). late ME. **3.** *transf.* and *fig.* **a.** Power or means of flight, or of action figured as flight; action or manner of flying ME. **b.** In biblical and derived expressions referring to a mother bird's use of her wings for the protection of her young; thus virtually = protecting care ME. **4.** *transf.* †**a.** In phr. *of* (such-and-such) *w.*, = kind or description of bird (usu. *fig.*) –1630. **b.** Qualified by a restrictive word, or in techn. phr., = bird or birds 1601. **c.** A flock (of plover) 1805.

1. b. Something light for supper—the w. of a roasted fowl DICKENS. 2. b. Thou..goest vpon the wynges of the wynde COVERDALE *Ps.* 103[4]:3. 3. a. The self same place where hee First lighted from his Wing MILT. b. Under the shelter of her aunt's w. 1883. Give w. to your desires, and let 'em fly DRYDEN.

II. 1. An appliance or appendage resembling or analogous to a wing in form or function ME. **2.** A lateral part or appendage: in various connections, as an outlying portion of a space or region, the mudguard of a motor vehicle, each of two side pieces at the top of an arm-chair against which the head may be rested. late ME. **3.** Either of the two divisions (*right w.*, *left w.*) on each side of the main body of an army or fleet in battle array; also each of the two divisions of a regiment, a division of the Royal Air Force (so *w. commander*, etc.) late ME. **b.** *Football*, etc. The position of the forwards on either side of the centre; a player or players occupying this position (so *w. forward*, etc.) 1889. **c.** A section of a party, holding views deviating in one direction or the other from those generally held 1879. **4.** One of a pair of lateral projecting pieces of a garment on or near the shoulder, as of a doublet; also, a side-flap of a cap, etc. late ME. **5. a.** A subordinate part of a building on one side of the main or central part 1523. **b.** *Theatr.* Each of the side-scenes on the stage; also (usu. *pl.*) the space at each side of the stage where these stand 1790. **6.** *Anat.* = ALA 1. 1650. **7.** *Bot.* **a.** Each of the two lateral petals of a papilionaceous flower 1776. **b.** A thin membranous appendage of a seed or fruit, serving for its dispersal by the wind; a thin lateral projection extending along a stem 1776.

1. Your Argosies..with their wouen wings SHAKS. Wind milles..hauing ten wings a piece 1609. Being unable to swim he had made use of a pair of swimming wings 1908. Aeroplanes..depend for their support in the air upon the spread of surfaces which are..called wings..or planes 1910. *Wings*, in the Royal Air Force, a certificate of ability to pilot an aeroplane, the badge representing a pair of wings.

Phrases. **On** or **upon the w.: a.** *lit.* Flying, in flight. **b.** *fig.* (*a*) Moving or travelling swiftly or briskly; astir, active. (*b*) Going off or away; ready to start or depart. **c.** *On the wings of*: see I. 2 b. **On wings:** going with light steps as one in a joyously exalted mood. **Under** (..) **w.:** *Under the w. of, under —'s w.*, under the protection, care, or patronage of. †**Make w.:** to make one's way by flying, to fly. **Take w.: a.** Of a bird, etc.: To take flight, begin flying. **b.** *fig.* To 'take flight', take one's departure, make off. **W.-and-w.:** (of a ship) sailing before the wind with the foresail hauled over one side and the mainsail over the other.

Comb.: **w.-case,** each of the structures (modified fore-wings) which cover the functional wings in certain insects, as the *elytra* of beetles and the *tegmina* of *Orthoptera*; **-covert,** any one of the small feathers overlying the flight-feathers of a bird's w.; **-fish,** (*a*) = PTERICHTHYS; (*b*) a flying-fish, esp. of the genus *Prionotus*; **w. rib,** the end rib of a loin of beef; **-shell,** any of several kinds of molluscs having the shell or some part of it resembling a w., as the genus *Pinna*; also, a w.-snail; **-snail** = PTEROPOD; **-spread,** (*a*) the extent of a bird's wings when spread; (*b*) the surface or area of an aeroplane's wings; **-tip,** (*a*) the tip of the w. of a bird, bat, or insect; (*b*) the outer end of the 'wing' of an aeroplane. Hence **Wi·nger** *Football*, a player on the (right or left) w.; in the Rugby game, a forward whose place is on the 'wing' in the back row of the scrum.

Wing, *v.* 1486. [f. prec.] **I.** †**1.** *trans.* To carve (a quail or partridge) –1804. **2.** *intr.* (†occas. *refl.*) To use one's wings, take flight, fly. *poet.* or *rhet.* 1611. **b.** In pa. pple. = flying, on the wing. *Obs.* or *arch.* 1591. **3.** *trans.* **a.** To fly through, upon, or across; to traverse by flying 1605. **b.** With cognate obj. 1697. **4.** To put wings upon, to furnish or fit with wings for flying; to feather (an arrow) 1616. **b.** *fig.* To 'give wings to'; to give speed or swift motion to; to speed, hasten 1599. **5.** To convey by or as by means of wings; to carry through the air as if flying; to waft 1628. **6.** To send flying, let fly (as a missile); to send off swiftly, to dart 1718. **7.** To shoot (a bird) in the wing, so as to disable it from flying without killing it; *transf.* to wound (a person, etc.) with a shot in the arm or shoulder, or some other not vital part 1802.

2. b. *Cymb.* IV. ii. 348. **3. a.** The Crowes and Choughes, that w. the midway ayre SHAKS. **4. b.** The Thunder, Wing'd with red Lightning and impetuous rage MILT. **7.** *transf.* One aeroplane was winged by Russian soldiery 1914.

II. †**a.** *Mil.* To furnish (a force) *with* additional troops on the wings; also of such troops, to form the wings of –1699. **b.** To furnish with side parts or projections, as a building, etc. 1700.

Winged (wi·ŋėd, *less freq.* wiŋd), *a.* late ME. [f. WING *sb.* + -ED².] **1.** Having wings, as a bird, bat, insect, supernatural or mythical being, etc.; represented or figured with wings. **b.** *poet.* Applied to a ship with sails set 1586. †**c.** Full of wings; crowded with flying birds. MILT. **2.** Furnished with or having a wing or wings, i.e. lateral part(s, appendage(s, or projection(s 1597. **3.** *Bot.*, etc. **a.** Having lateral processes or appendages, as a stem, seed, fruit, etc. 1776. **b.** in names of plants dist. by having w. stems or other parts 1650. **4.** *fig.* Capable of or performing some movement or action figured as flight; flying or passing swiftly, swift, rapid 1513. **b.** *esp.* of words or speech (rendering or imitating the Homeric phr. ἔπεα πτερόεντα) 1616.

1. c. Th'earth cumber'd, and the wing'd air dark't with plumes MILT. **3. b. W. elm,** a small N. Amer. species of elm (*Ulmus alata*) with corky w. branches. **W. pea,** a plant of the S. European genus *Tetragonolobus* (now included in *Lotus*), having four-w. pods. **4.** Oswald leaves her with w. heels to make his arrangements 1877.

Wi·ngless, *a.* 1591. [f. WING *sb.* + -LESS.] Having no wings; also, having rudimentary wings, as an apteryx.

Winglet (wi·ŋlėt). 1611. [f. WING *sb.* + -LET.] **1.** A little wing. **2. a.** *Entom.* A small appendage at the base of each wing or wing-sheath, as in certain flies and beetles, or on each side of the rostrum in certain weevils. **b.** *Ornith.* A process on the terminal joint of a bird's wing, having small feathers 1816. **3.** A small wing-like appendage on some article of dress 1611.

Wingy (wi·ŋi), *a.* 1596. [f. WING *sb.* + -Y¹.] †**1.** Of, pertaining to, or resembling a wing or wings –1694. **2.** Having wings, winged (*poet.*); having large or conspicuous wings 1566. **3.** *fig.* Capable of 'flight', soaring, aspiring; eluding grasp or comprehension 1643.

Winish (wəi·niʃ), *a.* Now *rare.* 1540. [f. WINE *sb.* + -ISH¹.] Having the quality or nature of wine; resembling wine.

Wink (wiŋk), *sb.* ME. [f. WINK *v.*] **1.** A closing of the eyes for sleep; a (short) spell of sleep, a nap. *rare* exc. in phr. (*not*) *a w.* (*of sleep*). **2.** A glance or significant movement of the eye (often accompanied by a nod) expressing command, assent, invitation, or the like. *Obs.* exc. in prov. *A nod's as good as a w. to a blind horse*, and phr. *to tip, give*, or *get the w.* 1500. **3.** *transf.* **a.** A moment of time, as being that occupied by a glance of the eyes 1585. **b.** (*Not*) *a w.*: (not) the slightest amount 1596. **4.** A nictitation of the eyelid; a blink 1611. **5.** An act of winking (see WINK *v.* 6) 1837.

1. *Temp.* II. i. 285. I will go to-bed; but not one W., I fear, shall I get this Night RICHARDSON. *Forty winks* (colloq.) a brief sleep, a short nap. **2.** He gave me the w. that the lady was a friend of his 1872. **3. a.** *In a w.*, in a trice. **b.** Ambition cannot pierce a winke beyond SHAKS. **5.** A knowing w. or a sarcastic smile 1891.

Wink (wiŋk), *v.* [OE. *wincian* = OS. *wincon* (MLG., MDu. *winken*), rel. to OHG. *winchan* (G. *winken*) move sideways, stagger, nod, f. Gmc. **wiŋk-* (**weŋk-*) **waŋk-* :– IE. **weŋg-* **woŋg-* move sideways or from side to side, whence also WINCE *v.*¹, WINCH *v.*¹] **1.** *intr.* To close one's eyes –1816. **b.** Said of the eyes: To close. *Obs.* or *rare arch.* ME. **2.** To open and shut one's eyes momentarily and involuntarily; to blink, nictitate ME. **b.** Said of the eyes or eyelids: To blink. Now *rare.* 1661. **c.** Of a light, etc.: To emit quick intermittent flashes; to twinkle. (Now assoc. with sense 6.) 1591. **3.** To have the eyes closed in sleep; to sleep –1649. **4.** To 'shut one's eyes' to something faulty, wrong, or improper; to be complaisant. (Now *rare* exc. with *at.*) 1480. **5.** To give a significant glance, as of command, direction, or invitation –1835. †**b.** *trans.* To bring into a specified state by a glance or nod –1728. **6.** *intr.* To close one eye momentarily, in a flippant or frivolous manner, esp. to convey intimate information or to express good-humoured interest 1837. **7.** *trans.* To close (an eye, the eyes) for a moment 1838. **b.** *To w. away*: to remove (tears) by blinking one's eyes 1876. **c.** To give (a signal), express (a message), etc. by means of flashlights 1918.

1. *Cymb.* V. iv. 194. **2. c.** A beaker..With beaded bubbles winking at the brim KEATS. **3.** *Temp.* II. i. 216. **4. W. at: a.** To 'shut one's eyes to' (an offence, fault, impropriety or irregularity), to connive at. **b.** To disregard, overlook, pass unnoticed (now *rare* or *Obs.*). **c.** To be complaisant with (an offending or contumacious person); to connive at the doings of. **5.** Davis winked to his friends that it was all right 1819. Winking at me not to take any notice 1821. Hence **Wi·nker,** one who winks (*rare*); *pl.* applied to the eyes or eyelashes (now *dial.* or *slang*); *pl.* = BLINKER 2 b. **Wi·nking** *ppl. a.* that winks; **-ly** *adv.*

Winking (wi·ŋkiŋ), *vbl. sb.* ME. [f. prec. + -ING¹.] The action of WINK *v.*

Like w., in a flash, in a twinkling; very rapidly or suddenly. So, *as easy as w.*

Winkle (wi·ŋk'l). 1585. Shortened from PERIWINKLE². (Cf. *wig* f. *periwig.*)

A typical family..lives..on a nutriment of winkles and gin 1899. Hence **Wi·nkler,** one who gathers winkles. **Wi·nkling** *gerund* and *vbl. sb.*

Winnable (wi·năb'l), *a.* 1544. [f. WIN *v.* + -ABLE.] Capable of being won, in various senses.

Winner (wi·nəɹ). ME. [f. WIN *v.* + -ER¹.] One who or that which wins, in various senses; *spec.* a horse, dog, etc. that wins a race; a winning shot; in recent slang, a thing that scores a success.

I'd ridden seven great winners before I was eighteen 1859.

Winning (wi·niŋ), *vbl. sb.* ME. [f. WIN *v.* + -ING¹.] The action of WIN *v.*; *concr.* something won. **1.** Conquest, capture, taking (of a place). **2.** The action of gaining, getting, or obtaining; acquisition ME. **3.** *concr.* That which is won; a thing or amount obtained or gained; gain, profit. Now *rare* or *Obs.* exc. as in 4. ME. **4.** *pl.* Things or sums gained, gains, profits; earnings (*obs.* or *dial.*); in mod. use chiefly applied to money won by gaming or betting. late ME. **5.** *spec.* Getting, gathering, taking (of produce, coal, stone, etc.) 1473. **6.** Gaining of a person's affection or allegiance; also with *over.* late ME.

attrib.: **w.-gallery** *Tennis*, the last gallery on the hazard-side of a tennis-court; **-post,** a post set up at the goal of a race-course, the racer who first passes it being the winner.

Wi·nning, *ppl. a.* 1592. [f. WIN *v.* + -ING².] That wins. **1.** Gaining or resulting in victory or superiority in a contest or competition; victorious. **2.** Persuasive (now *rare* or *obs.*); alluring, attractive, 'taking' 1596.

1. *W. hazard*: see HAZARD *sb.* 6 b. *W. stroke*, a stroke that gains a point in a game, or one by which the game is won. **2.** The W. Air, the Bewitching Glance, the Amorous Smirk 1700. Hence **Wi·nning-ly** *adv.*, **-ness.**

Winnow (wi·noᵘ), *v.* [OE. *windwian*, f. *wind* WIND *sb.*¹ The form *window* survives dial.] **1.** *trans.* To expose (grain or other substances) to the wind or to a current of air so that the lighter particles (as chaff or other refuse matter) are separated or blown away; to clear of refuse material by this method. Also *absol.* or *intr.* **b.** *fig.* To subject to a process likened to the winnowing of grain, in order to separate the various parts or elements, esp. the good from the bad; hence, to clear of worthless or inferior elements. late ME. **2. a.** To separate or drive off (lighter or refuse particles) by the process described in 1; also *fig.* OE. **b.** To separate (the valuable part *from* the worthless); now esp. with *out*, to extract, select, or obtain (something desirable) by such separation 1611. **c.** To waft, diffuse. *poet.* 1764. **3.** *transf.* **a.** To beat (the air) with or as with wings; to flap (the wings), to wave (the fins); also *intr.* 1579. **b.** Of the air, etc.: *trans.* To fan with a breeze. *intr.* To blow fitfully or in gusts. 1796.

2. a. Do but w. their chaffe from their wheat, ye shall see their great heape shrink MILT. **3. a.** He..with quick Fann Winnows the buxom Air MILT. **b.** Falling snows that w. by CLARE. Hence **Wi·nnow** *sb.* a contrivance for winnowing grain; an act of winnowing or a motion resembling it. **Wi·nnower,** one who winnows; an apparatus for winnowing, a winnowing-machine. **Wi·nnowing** *vbl. sb.* also in combs., esp. in names of appliances for winnowing, as *w.-fan, -machine, -sheet.*

Winsome (wi·nsŏm), *a.* [OE. *wynsum*, f. *wyn(n* WIN *sb.*² + *-sum* -SOME¹.] †**1.** Pleasant, delightful, agreeable –ME. **2.** [In the mod. lit. lang. from north. dial.] Pleasing or attractive in appearance, handsome, comely; of attractive nature or disposition, of winning character or manners 1677. Hence **Wi·nsome-ly** *adv.*, **-ness.**

Winter (wi·ntəɹ), *sb.*¹ [OE. *winter* = OFris. *winter*, OS., OHG. *wintar* (Du., G. *winter*), ON. *vetr*, earlier *vettr, vittr*, Goth. *wintrus* :– Gmc. **wentrus*, prob. nasalized var. of IE. base **wed-* **wod-* be wet (see WATER, WET *a.*).] **1.** The fourth and coldest season of the year, coming between autumn and spring; reckoned astronomically from the winter solstice to the vernal equinox, i.e. in the northern hemisphere from the 22nd of December to the 20th of March; pop. comprising the months of December, January, and February; also often in contradistinction to *summer*, the colder half of the year. **b.** With ref. to the chilling or injurious effect of winter, esp. on plants; *transf.* a period resembling winter, wintry or cold weather OE. **c.** *fig.* and *allus.*, esp. in ref. to old age, or to a time or state of affliction or distress 1590. **2.** Put for 'year': nearly always *pl.* with a numeral; often in expressions referring to a person's age; now *poet.* or *rhet.*, chiefly in ref. to advanced age or to a protracted period of hardship or misfortune OE. **3.** *attrib.* passing into *adj.* **a.** = Of, pertaining to, or characteristic of winter; adapted or appropriate to, used or occupied in, winter; existing, appearing, flourishing, or performed in winter OE. **b.** The possessive *winter's* is similarly used, chiefly with *day, night, morning, evening* OE. **c.** Applied to autumn-sown crops that stand through the winter; also to fruits that ripen late, or keep well until or during winter; *spec.* in names of late-ripening apples, pears, etc. late ME. **d.** *fig.*; †occas. = Old, aged 1593.

1. God bless us in the spring, after this green w. LAUD. Store of fire-wood for the w. DICKENS. **c.** Now is the W. of our Discontent, Made glorious Summer by this Son of Yorke SHAKS. **2.** I knew a man Of eightie winters 1612. **3. a.** W.-flies, all Anglers know,..are as useful as an Almanack out of date WALTON. Black Velvet Scarfs..are a handsome W.-wear GAY. The w.-sleep..of hibernating animals 1836. **d.** The tasteless, dry embrace Of a stale virgin with a w. face POPE.

Comb.: **w. bud** *Zool.*, a statoblast (formed at the approach of, or quiescent during, w.); **-fallow** *sb.* a lying fallow, or land that lies fallow, during the w.; *v. trans.* to lay (land) fallow during the w.; **-feed** *v. trans.* to feed or maintain (animals, etc.) during w.; **w. garden,** (*a*) a garden of plants that flourish in w., as evergreens; (*b*) a greenhouse or conservatory in which plants are kept flourishing in w.; **-long** *a.* as tediously long as w.; *adv.* through a whole w.; **w. ova,** eggs produced by certain invertebrates at the approach of w.; **-pride,** the condition of being w.-proud; **-proud** *a.* (of wheat or other crops) too luxuriant in w.; **w. quarters,** (*a*) the place occupied by troops, or by members of an expedition, during the w. (between two campaigns or periods of activity or travel); (*b*) the place in which certain animals find shelter during the w.; **-rot,** a disease incident to sheep in the w.; **w. solstice,** the time at which the sun reaches the w. tropic, i.e. in the northern hemisphere the tropic of Capricorn, in the southern the tropic of Cancer; the middle of the w. half of the year; **-tide** (*arch.*) = *w.-time*; **-time,** the season of w. **b.** In names of animals and plants that are active or flourish in w. or in the w. half of the year, or of late-ripening fruits: **w. berry,** any of several N. Amer. species of holly with berries, usu. scarlet, which persist through the w., esp. *Ilex verticillata* and *I. lævigata*; **-bloom,** (*a*) a late-flowering species of *Azalea*; (*b*) the Amer. witch-hazel, *Hamamelis virginica*, which blossoms late in autumn and ripens its fruit the following year; **-bunting,** the snow bunting; **w. corn,** corn sown in w., or in autumn and remaining in the ground through the w.; **-cress,** any of the cruciferous herbs of the genus *Barbarea*, the leaves of which were formerly used as a w. salad; **w. grape,** an Amer. species of grape-vine, *Vitis cordifolia*; **w. queening,** a late-ripening variety of apple, which keeps well through the w.; **w. rocket,** the common w.-cress, *Barbarea vulgaris*; **w. snipe,** the purple sandpiper or rock-snipe, *Tringa striata* or *maritima*; **w. strawberry** = ARBUTUS. Hence **Wi·nterish** *a.* (somewhat) winterly or wintry. **Wi·nterless** *a.* having no w.; free from or not experiencing w. **Wi·nterling,** a yearling 1825.

Wi·nter, *sb.*² 1683. [Of unkn. origin.] In a hand-printing press, a block of wood about nine inches broad by nine deep, supporting the carriage and having a tenon at each end to fit into corresponding mortices in the cheeks.

Wi·nter, *v.* late ME. [f. WINTER *sb.*¹ after L. *hiemare, hibernare.*] **1.** *intr.* To pass or spend the winter; to stay or reside (at a specific place) during the winter; (of animals) to find or be provided with food and shelter in the winter. **2.** *trans.* To keep or maintain during winter; *esp.* to provide (animals) with food and shelter in winter 1440. **3.** To affect like winter, subject to wintry conditions; to chill, freeze. Chiefly *fig.* 1622. Hence **Wi·nterer,** one who spends the winter in a specified place; *spec.* a servant of the Hudson's Bay Company who was employed in the far interior of N. America 1801.

Winterbourne (wi·ntəɹbōᵊɹn). [OE. *winterburna*, f. WINTER *sb.*¹ + *burna* BURN *sb.*¹, BOURNE *sb.*¹] An intermittent stream, such as those found in chalk and limestone districts, which flows only in winter or at long intervals.

Winter cherry. 1548. **1.** Any of several plants of the nightshade family (*Solanaceæ*) with cherry-like fruit which is ripe in winter; also, the fruit itself. **a.** = ALKEKENGI; also applied to other species of *Physalis*, as the Cape Gooseberry, *P. edulis.* **b.** Applied to species of *Solanum* with cherry-like fruit, as *S. pseudo-capsicum*, also called Jerusalem Cherry 1629. **2.** Applied to species of *Cardiospermum* (family *Sapindaceæ*), having fruit enclosed in an inflated calyx like that of *Physalis*; esp. *C. halicacabum*, also called Balloon Vine 1597.

Winter day. [OE. *winterdæġ.*] A day in winter. (More commonly **winter's day.**)

Wintered (wi·ntəɹd), *a.* [OE. *ġewintred*, f. *ġe-* Y- + *winter* WINTER *sb.*¹ + *-ed* -ED².] †**1.** Having lived through or experienced many winters or years; aged; veteran –1599. **2.** Exposed to the influence of winter; subjected to wintry conditions; chilled or blasted by winter ME. †**3.** Adapted for or used in winter. SHAKS.

1. W. souldiers vs'd to conquering KYD. **3.** *A.Y.L.* III. ii. 111.

Wintergreen (wi·ntəɹ,grīn). 1548. [After Du. *wintergroen*, G. *wintergrün.*] **1.** Name for various plants of low growth or creeping habit whose leaves remain green in winter. **a.** Any plant of the genus *Pyrola*, esp. *P. minor*, a woodland plant with roundish drooping white flowers. Also applied to plants of the allied genus *Chimaphila*, as *C. maculata* (Spotted W.). **b.** The N. Amer. plant *Gaultheria procumbens* (Aromatic, Creeping, or Spring W.), bearing drooping white flowers and edible scarlet berries 1778. **c. Chickweed W.,** either species of *Trientalis* (*T. europæa* or *americana*), woodland plants of high latitudes or altitudes 1760. **d. Flowering W.,** the Fringed Milkwort of N. America, *Polygala paucifolia* 1856. **2.** Usu. *pl.* (with hyphen, or as two words). An evergreen. *rare* or *Obs.* 1681. **3.** (With hyphen, or as two words.) Green vegetables for winter use 1846.

1. b. *Oil of w., w. oil*, a heavy volatile oil obtained from the leaves of *Gaultheria procumbens*, used as an aromatic stimulant, and for flavouring confectionery, etc.

Wi·nter-house. [OE. *winterhūs.*] A house for winter occupation.

Winterly (wi·ntəɹli), *a.* [OE. *winterlić*, f. WINTER *sb.*¹ + -LY¹; in mod. use a new formation.] **1.** Of, belonging to, or occurring in winter. **2.** Having the character of or characteristic of winter; wintry 1611.

2. *fig. Cymb.* III. iv. 13.

Winter's bark. 1622. [= mod. L. *cortex Winteranus*, named from its discoverer, Captain William *Winter*, who accompanied Francis Drake to the Magellan Straits in 1578.] **a.** The pungent aromatic bark of *Drimys winteri*, used as a stimulant tonic and antiscorbutic; also called **Winter's cinnamon. b.** Extended to other medicinal barks, as that of the W. Indian whitewood or wild cinnamon, *Canella alba.* **c.** Any of the trees themselves.

Wintry (wi·ntri), *a.* [OE. *wintriġ*, f. WINTER *sb.*¹ + -Y¹; in mod. use a new formation.] **1.** Of or pertaining to winter; occurring, existing, or found in winter; adapted or suitable for winter. Now *rare* or merged in 2. **2.** Having the quality of winter; of such a kind as occurs in winter; characteristic of winter 1590. **3.** Exposed or subject to the effect or influence of winter; chilled or blasted by winter 1697. **4.** *fig.* esp. (*a*) Aged, infirm or withered from age; (*b*) devoid of fervour or affection, 'cold'; (*c*) destitute of warmth or brightness, dreary 1633.

1. The w. Misleto DRYDEN. **3.** The w. top of giant Lebanon HEBER. **4.** (**b**) A somewhat w. welcome 1895. Hence **Wi·ntri-ly** *adv.*, **-ness.**

Winy, winey (wəi·ni), *a.* late ME. [f. WINE *sb.* + -Y¹.] **1.** Of, belonging to, or characteristic of wine; having the nature or properties of wine; *occas.* producing wine; vinous. **2. a.** Accompanied by the drinking of wine (*rare*) 1586. **b.** Affected by or due to (excessive) consumption of wine 1594.

1. Ful of a redde wynie sappe or iuyce 1578. **2. b.** If their w. wits must needs be working NASHE.

Winze (winz). 1757. [perh. derived from WIND *sb.*²] *Mining.* A shaft or an inclined passage sunk from one level to another, but not rising to the surface.

Wipe (wəip), *sb.* 1550. [f. next.] **1.** An act of wiping 1642. **2.** A slashing blow; a sweeping cut; a swipe 1550. †**b.** *transf.* A mark as of a blow or lash; a scar. SHAKS. **3.** *fig.* A cutting remark; a sarcastic reproof or rebuff; a jeer 1596. **4.** *slang.* A handkerchief 1789. **5.** = WIPER 4. 1884.

1. A brush to give the gemman a w. down 1822. **2.** The cove used to fetch me a w. over the knuckles with his stick 1851. **4.** Three boys brought in for prigging of wipes 1800.

Wipe (wəip), *v.* [OE. *wīpian*, corresp. formally to OHG. *wīfan* wind round, Goth. *weipan* crown (cf. *waips* wreath); rel. to the forms given under WHIP.] **1.** *trans.* To rub (something) gently with a soft cloth or the like, or *on* something, so as to clear its surface of dust, dirt, moisture, etc.; to clean or dry in this way. **2.** To remove or clear away (moisture, dust, etc.) from something by the action described in 1. OE. **3.** To apply or spread a soft or liquid substance over the surface of a body by rubbing it on with a cloth, pad, or the like (with the substance or the body as obj.); *spec.* in *Plumbing*, to apply solder by this method so as to unite and finish off a joint 1799. †**4.** *fig.* To deprive, rob, defraud, do out of some possession or advantage –1746. **5.** To clear away, remove: usu. with adv. (*away, off, out*). **a:** To remove the guilt, blame, or dishonour of; to clear a person, or oneself, of (a charge or imputation). late ME. **b.** To destroy the trace of, obliterate; to destroy the effect or value of, bring to naught 1564. **c.** To do away with, put an end to, annihilate. Now always with *out.* 1538. **d.** *spec.* To put all to death, destroy completely (a body of persons); usu. with *out.* 1577. **e.** With *off*, †*out*: To cancel (an account or score); to discharge, pay off (a debt) 1667. **6.** To strike, beat, or attack with blows, or with mockery, rebuke, or the like. Now *dial.* or *slang.* 1523. **7.** *intr.* for *pass.* To be rubbed *away*, removed, obliterated, etc. ME.

1. Wiping his lips, after having finished his draught SCOTT. Stopping on the mat to w. his shoes all round DICKENS. *fig.* I..wyll wype out Ierusalem, euen as one wypeth a platter COVERDALE 2 *Kings* 21:13. **5. b.** *Wint. T.* IV. ii. 11. The anxiety wiped away from his face as if by magic 1898. **d.** A tragedy which wiped out an entire crew 1898.

Phrases. *To w.* a person's *eye* (slang or colloq.): (*a*) to get the better of, 'score off'; (*b*) to 'give a black eye to'. *To w. one's boots on*, to inflict the utmost indignity upon. *To w. the floor with*, to 'bring to the ground' utterly, inflict a crushing defeat on.

Wiper (wəi·pəɹ). 1552. [f. prec. + -ER¹.] **1.** A person who wipes; *spec.* in various industries, a workman employed in wiping something clean or dry. **2.** A cloth or other appliance used for wiping; *slang*, a handkerchief (cf. WIPE *sb.* 4) 1587. **b.** See *screen-w.* s.v. SCREEN *sb.* **3.** One who or that which strikes or assails. *slang.* 1611. **4.** In machinery, a projecting piece fixed on a rotating or oscillating part, as an axle or wheel, and periodically communicating movement by a rubbing action to some other part; a cam, eccentric, or tappet 1796.

Wiping (wəi·piŋ), *vbl. sb.* late ME. [f. as prec. + -ING¹.] The action of WIPE *v.*

Comb. **w.-rod, -stick,** a rod fitted with a piece of cloth or tow for cleaning out the bore of a gun.

Wire (wəiᵊɹ), *sb.* [OE. *wīr*, corresp. to MLG. *wire* (LG. *wir*), ON. **virr* in *vira virki* filigree work, rel. to OHG. *wiara* (ornament of) finest gold; prob. f. base **wi-* of L. *viēre* plait, weave (cf. WITHE *sb.*).] **I.** Metal wrought into the form of a slender rod or thread, formerly by hammering, now by the operation of wire-drawing. **b.** used as fencing; esp. *barbed* (earlier *barb*) *w.*: A fencing wire composed of two or more strands twisted together, with barbs or short spikes fastened a few inches apart in the strands; also, the fencing or defence so constructed 1876.

Gold wir ME. Shakt his long lockes, colourd like copper-w. SPENSER. **b.** I was in hopes that a country like the Bicester..would be free of such an enemy as w. 1876.

II. ***1.** A piece, length, or line of wire used for various purposes OE. **b.** *spec.* One of the fine platinum cross-wires fixed horizontally and vertically at the focus of a telescope 1774. **c.** connecting a bell with the bell-pull or -push 1837. **2.** A line of wire used as a conductor of electric current 1747. **b.** *spec.* The line of wire connecting the transmitting and receiving instruments of a telegraph or telephone; *transf.* the telegraphic system (e.g. *by w.*). Also (*colloq.*) a telegraphic message, a telegram. 1854. **Senses used mainly in pl. or collect. sing. **3.** Metallic strings (of a musical instrument). late ME. **4.** Metallic bars (of a cage) 1656. **5.** *Croquet.* The iron hoops through which the balls are driven. 1868. **6.** The metallic lines by which puppets are worked 1607.

2. *Live w.*, a w. charged with electricity; *fig.* (*colloq.*) an energetic or vigorously active person. **3.** Apollo sings To th' touch of golden wires MILT. **6.** Phr. *To pull (the) wires* (cf. WIRE-PULLER); A demagogue..may..pull the wires of a President whom he has put into the chair 1888. *To be on wires* (fig.), to be in a state of nervous excitement or jumpiness.

III. Network or framework of wire. **a.** Wirework; now usu., wire netting 1547. †**b.** A frame of wire (*a*) to support the hair, (*b*) to support the ruff. –1690. **c.** *Paper-making.* Woven brass wire-cloth 1700. **d.** A snare for hares or rabbits 1749.

a. In the middle of this garden was a cupola made of wyre, supported by slender pillars of brick EVELYN.

IV. 1. Something resembling wire or a wire; e.g. a long thin plant-stem, as a strawberry runner; a cylindrical piece of native silver 1601. **2.** *pl.* Applied to hairs, or rays, as resembling shining wires (*poet.* and *rhet.*). Now *rare.* 1589. **3.** *slang.* A pickpocket (from the practice of extracting handkerchiefs from pockets with a piece of wire) 1851. **4.** Short for: **a.** Wire rope or cable 1882. **b.** Wire-haired fox terrier 1892.

Comb.: **w. bar,** a bar of copper cast into a suitable form for drawing into w.; **w. bridge,** (*a*) a suspension bridge supported by wires; (*b*) a kind of electric bridge furnished with a w. and a graduated scale; **-cutter,** nippers or pliers for cutting w.; also, a man employed to cut w., e.g. in war operations; **w. edge,** the turned-over strips of metal produced on the edge of a cutting tool by faulty grinding or honing; **w. entanglement** *Mil.*, an abatis of (barbed) w. stretched over the ground in order to impede the advance of an enemy; **-glass,** sheet glass in which w. netting is embedded; **-hair,** a wire-haired terrier; **-haired,** *a.* having a rough coat of a hard and wiry texture, esp. designating a kind of fox-terrier as dist. from the smooth-haired variety; **-mark** *Paper-making*, (*a*) *pl.*, the faint lines made by the impression of the wires of the mould in the substance of laid paper; (*b*) = WATERMARK 4; **w. saw,** a kind of saw of which the cutting-part is made of w.; **w. silver,** native silver found in w.-shaped pieces; **-walker,** an acrobat who performs feats on a w. rope.

Wire (wəiᵊɹ), *v.* ME. [f. prec.] †**1.** *trans.* To adorn with (gold) wire. ME. only. **2.** To fasten, join, or fit with a wire or wires; *spec.* to secure (the cork of a bottle, the bottle itself) with wire. late ME. **b.** To furnish with a wire support; to stiffen with wire 1834. **c.** To fence with wire: chiefly *to w. in*, to enclose with a wire fence 1691. **d.** To strengthen or protect with (barbed) wire 1881. **e.** To furnish with electric wires 1892. **3.** To catch or trap in a wire snare 1749. **4.** *Croquet.* To place (one's own or an opponent's ball) so that a hoop intervenes between it and its object; also with the player as obj. Chiefly *pass.* 1866. **5.** To send (a message) 'over the wires', to telegraph; also *absol.* or *intr.*; *transf.* to send a telegraph message to. *colloq.* 1859. **6.** intr. *To w. in*, to get to work with a will, to apply oneself energetically to something; *to w. into* (a meal, etc.) to set about it with avidity. *colloq.* or *slang.* 1865.

4. Red..has wired the player for all the balls 1874. **5.** I am going to w. my broker fellow to buy a couple of thousand Bs and Cs 1876.

Wired (wəiᵊɹd), *ppl. a.* late ME. [f. WIRE *sb.* or *v.* + -ED.] **1.** Supported, strengthened, or stiffened with wire. **2.** Furnished with or consisting of a wire fence or netting for confinement or protection 1748. **3.** Fastened or secured with wire 1798.

1. A lovely bouquet..—not a nasty w. affair, but just a lot of loose flowers 1885. **3.** *W. on*, designating a kind of tyre which is secured to the wheel-rim by means of wire.

Wire-draw (wəiᵊ·ɹ₁drǭ), *v.* Now *rare.* 1598. [Back-formation from next.] **1.** *trans.* To draw out (metal) into wire 1666. **2.** *transf.* To draw out (a material thing) to an elongated form; to stretch, elongate 1598. **b.** To cause (steam or water) to pass through a small aperture, thereby diminishing its pressure 1744. **3.** *fig.* **a.** To protract excessively, spin out 1598. **b.** To draw out to an extreme tenuity; to reduce to a subtle fineness 1660. **c.** To strain, force, or wrest by subtle argument or the like 1610. †**d.** To draw, get, induce, extract, etc. by some subtle device –1748.

3. c. Do not wrest, and wiredraw, and colour my words WESLEY.

Wire-drawer (wəiᵊ·ɹ₁drǭːəɹ). ME. [f. WIRE *sb.* + DRAWER.] One who draws metal into wire; one who practises or is skilled in wire-drawing. So **Wi·re-dra:wing** *vbl. sb.*

Wire-drawn (wəiᵊ·ɹ₁drǭn), *ppl. a.* 1603. [pa. pple. of WIRE-DRAW *v.*] **1.** Drawn out to a great length or with subtle ingenuity; fine-spun. **2.** Of steam, water: see WIRE-DRAW *v.* 2 b. 1744. **3.** *nonce-uses.* Attenuated; 'weak'; 'thin' 1856.

1. The..w. distinctions..of the Schoolmen BERKELEY.

Wi·re-grass. 1793. [f. WIRE *sb.* + GRASS *sb.*] A name for various grasses or grass-like plants having wiry stems. **1.** *U.S.* The British flat-stemmed meadow-grass, *Poa compressa*, or the annual grass *Elusine indica*, naturalized in N. America. **2.** One of several other plants, as the West Indian *Paspale filiforme*, the Australian *Tetrarrhena juncea*, the N. Amer. *Sporobolus junceus* and species of *Aristida* 1824.

Wireless (wəiᵊ·ɹ₁lės), *a.* (*sb.*) 1894. [f. WIRE *sb.* + -LESS.] Without a wire or wires; spec. *Electr.* dispensing with the use of a conducting wire. **b.** as *sb.* Short for *w. telegraphy, telephony, message, apparatus, receiver* 1904.

W. telegraphy, a system of telegraphy in which no conducting wire is used between the transmitting and receiving stations, the signals or messages being transmitted through space by means of electric waves; so *w. telegraph, telephone, telephony.* Hence **Wi·reless** *v. intr.* to send a message by w.; *trans.* to send (a message) or inform (a person) by w. 1899.

Wire-puller (wəiᵊ·ɹ₁puːləɹ). orig. *U.S.* 1848. [See WIRE *sb.* II. 6 and PULL *v.* II. 3.] One who 'pulls the wires'; one who works secretly to further the interests of a person or party; *esp.* a politician or political agent who privately influences and directs others. Hence **Wi·re-pull** *v. trans.* to actuate or promote by wire-pulling. **Wi·re-pu:lling** *vbl. sb.* and *ppl. a.*

Wirework (wəiᵊ·ɹwɒ̄ɹk). 1587. **1.** The making of wire; work done in or with wire; fabrics or objects made of wire. **2.** *pl.* An establishment where wire is made or where wire goods are manufactured 1598.

Wire-worker (wəiᵊ·ɹwɒ̄ːɹkəɹ). 1670. **1.** An artisan who works in wire. **2.** One who pulls the wires of a puppet-show 1843. **3.** *U.S.* = WIRE-PULLER 1835.

Wireworm (wəiᵊ·ɹwɒ̄ɹm). 1790. **1.** The slender hard-skinned larva of any of the click-beetles (family *Elateridæ*), which is destructive to the roots of plants; also applied to similar larvæ, *esp.* the leather-jacket grub of the crane-fly. **2.** A myriapod, esp. one belonging to the genus *Iulus*; a millepede 1875.

Wi·re-wove, *ppl. a.* 1799. [f. WIRE *sb.* + *wove*, pa. pple. of WEAVE *v.*] **1.** Denoting a very fine kind of paper used chiefly for letter-paper. **2.** Made of woven wire 1888.

Wirra (wi·rə), *int. Irish.* 1839. [Preceded by *oh*, = Ir. *a muire.*] An exclam. of sorrow or lament.

Wiry (wəiᵊ·ri), *a.* 1588. [f. WIRE *sb.* + -Y¹.] **1.** Made or consisting of wire; in the form of wire. **2.** Resembling wire in form and consistence: said esp. of hair (hence of a dog's coat), grass, stems of plants 1595. **b.** *Med.* Of the pulse: Small and tense 1801. **3.** Of sound: Produced by or as by the plucking or vibration of a wire; (of a voice) thin and metallic 1819. **4.** Of a person or animal: Lean, tough, and sinewy. Hence *fig.* of personal attributes. 1808.

1. Her yeolow locks, like wyrie golde, About her shoulders careleslie downe trailing SPENSER. **4.** Mrs. Blimber..was a lady of great suavity, and a w. figure DICKENS.

†**Wis,** *v.*¹ [OE. *wissian*, f. *wis* certain (cf. IWIS *adv.*); a late formation after synon. *wisian* WISE *v.*¹] *trans.* To make (a thing) known; to direct, guide, instruct (a person) –1550.

Wis (wis), *v.*² *pseudo-arch.* 1606. orig. in *I wis* for IWIS *adv.*, erron. taken as = 'I know'; hence occas. as a synonym of 'know' in other parts of the verb, being apprehended as the present of *wist*, pa. t. of WIT *v.*¹

Where my morning haunts are he wisses not MILT.

Wisdom (wi·zdəm). [OE. *wīsdōm* = OFris., OS. *wīsdōm*, OHG. *wīstuom* (G. *weistum* legal sentence, precedent), ON. *visdómr*; see WISE *a.*, -DOM.] The quality or character of being wise, or something in which this is exhibited. **1.** Capacity of judging rightly in matters relating to life and conduct; soundness of judgement in the choice of means and ends; sometimes, less strictly, sound sense, esp. in practical affairs: opp. to *folly.* **b.** as one of the manifestations of the divine nature in Jesus Christ; hence used as a title of the Second Person of the Trinity (*the W. of the Father*); also occas. applied to God or the Trinity OE. **c.** Contextually, usu. predic. with following inf.: = a wise thing to do; also with *a* and *pl.*, a wise action or proceeding. *arch.* late ME. **d.** *pl.* as attribute of a number of persons: hence, with possessive, as a title of dignity or respect, esp. for the members of a deliberative assembly; also, less commonly, in *sing.* of a single person. Now *joc.* late ME. **2.** Knowledge (esp. of a high or abstruse kind); learning, erudition, in early use often = philosophy, science. Now only *Hist.* OE. **3.** Wise discourse or teaching; with *a* and *pl.*, a wise saying or precept. Now *rare* or *arch.* ME. **b.** In the titles of two books of the Apocrypha, viz. *The W. of Solomon* (often abbrev. *W.* or *The Book of W.*), and *The W. of Jesus the son of Sirach* (commonly called *Ecclesiasticus*). late ME. †**4.** Sanity, 'reason'. SHAKS.

1. The feare of the Lorde is the begynnynge of wysdome COVERDALE *Prov.* 9:10. **c.** Till then, 'tis wisdome to conceale our meaning SHAKS. **d.** Even folly..freely on your Wisdom cracks her jokes WOLCOT. **2.** Moses was learned in all maner off w. of the Egipcians TINDALE *Acts* 7:22. **4.** *Meas. for M.* IV. iv. 5.

Wisdom tooth. 1848. [usu. pl.; orig. *teeth of wisdom*, rendering L. *dentes sapientiæ* = Arab. *'aḍrāsu-lḥikmi*, after Gr. σωφρονιστῆρες; so called as not appearing till the attainment of years of discretion.] The hindmost molar tooth on each side of both upper and lower jaws in man, usu. 'cut' about the age of twenty. Often in phr. *to cut one's wisdom teeth*, to attain to wisdom or discretion.

Wise (wəiz), *sb.*¹ *arch.* [OE. *wīse*, corresp. to OFris. *wīs*, OS. *wīsa* (Du. *wijze*), OHG. *wīsa*, *wīs* manner, custom, tune (G. *weise*), ON. *visa* stanza, **vis* in *ǫðruvis* otherwise :– Gmc. **wīsōn*, **wīsō*, f. **wit-* WIT *v.*; for the sense-development cf. Gr. εἶδος form, shape, kind, state of things, course of action; see -WISE.] †**I.** Manner, mode, fashion, style; *spec.* habitual manner of action, habit, custom –1572. **II.** OE. *wise* was used in various kinds of advb. expressions meaning 'in such-and-such a manner, way, or respect', in which it was qualified by an adj. or a sb. with or without a governing prep. Several of these, with similarly-formed later ones, have survived as simple words, e.g. *crosswise, likewise, no-wise, otherwise.* The free use of *wise* in such expressions, apart from the established simple words, is now only arch. (Cf. -WAYS.) **1. a.** With demonstr., interrog., or indef. adj. in an oblique case, e.g. OE. *ōðre wīsan* OTHERWISE. **b.** With general adjs., forming an equiv. of -LY², e.g. †*humble wise.* **2. a.** With prep. (orig. *on*, later *in*), and demonstr., interrog., or indef. adj., as *on nāne* *wīsan* NOWISE. **b.** With general adjs., e.g. *in like wise* (see LIKEWISE), in *gentle wise.* **3.** With prep. and sb. in comb. with *wise*, e.g. OE. *on scipwīsan* like a ship, ME. *on crosse wyse* (see CROSSWISE), *in maiden wise.* **b.** without prep., e.g. *festoon-wise.*

The nyghtes longe Encressen double wise the peynes stronge CHAUCER. I will. . that ye be wel bisene in the richest wyse MALORY. Are we better then they? No in no wyse TINDALE *Rom.* 3:9. Humble w. To thee my sighes in verse I sacrifise 1592. Let them tie upon a stick, posie w., a little piece of sponge 1631. Whilst things stand this w. with me 1649. The Houses, that can no w. afford above one Garden EVELYN. Geraldine, in maiden w.,. . turned her from Sir Leoline COLERIDGE. Timothy or Titus-wise 1876.

Wise (wəiz), *a.* (*sb.*², *adv.*) [OE. *wīs* = OFris., OS., OHG. *wīs*(*i* (Du. *wijs*, G. *weise*), ON. *víss*, Goth. *-weis* :- Gmc. **wīsaz* :- **wittos*, f. IE. **weid-* (see WIT *v.*¹) + ppl. suffix **-tos*. The pronunc. with *z* comes from the obl. forms.] **1.** Having or exercising sound judgement or discernment; having the ability to perceive and adopt the best means for accomplishing an end; characterized by good sense and prudence: opp. to *foolish.* **b.** Of action, speech, personal attributes, etc.: Proceeding from, indicating, or suggesting sound judgement or good sense; sage OE. **2.** †Skilled, expert; *spec.* skilled in magic or hidden arts. Now only *dial.* OE. **3.** Having knowledge; well-informed; learned. *Obs.* exc. as in b. OE. **b.** Informed or aware *of* something specified or implied. Now only in such phrases as *none the wiser, as w. as before* = knowing no more than before (i.e., usu., nothing) about the matter. ME. (*b*) U.S. colloq. *To be* (or *get*) *w. to*, to be (or become) aware of; *to put* (a person) *w.* (*to*), to inform (of), enlighten (concerning) 1901. **4.** In one's right mind, sane. Now *Sc.* and *dial.* ME. **5.** *absol.* or as *sb. pl.* Wise men or persons: now always with *the* OE. **b.** The compar. *wiser* as sb. (with pl. *wisers*): One who is wiser; usu. with possessive, (one's) superior in wisdom. Now *rare.* ME. **6.** Used as *adv.* = WISELY. In later use only in compar. *rare.* late ME.

1. Fyve of them were folysshe, and fyve were wyse TINDALE *Matt.* 25:2. W. to frustrate all our plots and wiles MILT. The w. Ant her wintry Store provides DRYDEN. *Provb. phr.* It is a w. Father that knowes his owne childe SHAKS. The proverb of being w. behind the time 1717. **b.** Full of w. sawes, and moderne instances SHAKS. By a w. dispensation of Providence MACAULAY. **3.** Where ignorance is bliss, 'Tis folly to be w. GRAY. **4.** *Oth.* IV. i. 245. **5.** A *word to the w.* (*is enough*): = VERBUM SAP. **b.** Of þi wysers lern bettyr gouernaunce 1447. **6.** Thou speakst wiser then thou art ware of SHAKS. Hence **Wi·se-ly** *adv.* [OE. *wīslīće*] with wisdom, sagacity, or good sense; †carefully; †skilfully; **-ness** (*rare*).

Wise (wəiz), *v.*¹ *Obs.* exc. *Sc.* and *n. dial.* [OE. *wīsian* = OFris. *wīsa*, OS. *wīsian* (Du. *wijzen*), OHG. *wīsen* (G. *weisen*), ON. *vísa*, Goth. *fullaweisjan* πείθειν; f. **wīsaz* WISE *a.* Cf. WIS *v.*¹] **1.** *trans.* To show the way to (a person); to guide, direct. **2.** To direct the course or movement of; to move in some direction or into some position; to convey, conduct ME. **3.** To show, point out (the way). late ME.

Wise (wəiz), *v.*² 1919. [f. WISE *a.* 3 b (*b*).] *To w. up* (U.S. slang) *trans.* and *intr.*: to 'get wise'; to 'put wise'.

- wise; see WISE *sb.*¹ II.

Wiseacre (wəi·zēⁱ:kəɹ). 1595. [- (with unexpl. assim. to *acre*) MDu. *wijssegher* soothsayer, prob. - (with assim. to *segghen* say) OHG. *wīssago*, alt., by assoc. with *wīs* WISE *a.* + *sagen* SAY, of *wīzago* = OE. *wīteġa* prophet, f. **wit-* WIT.] **1.** One who thinks himself or wishes to be thought wise; a foolish person with an air of wisdom. **2.** A wise or learned person. (Usu. *contempt.*) 1753.

Wise crack. *U.S. slang.* 1924. A smart sententious saying; a clever witticism So **Wi·se-crack** *v. intr.*, **-cracker, -cracking** *vbl. sb.*

Wisehead (wəi·zhed). 1756. [f. WISE *a.* + HEAD *sb.*] One who has a wise head; always *iron.* one who fancies himself wise, a wiseacre.

Wise man. OE. **1.** *gen.* A man who is wise; a discreet or prudent man. (Often opp. to *fool.*) **b.** Applied *iron.* to a fool or simpleton, as in *the wise men of Gotham* (see GOTHAM 1) 1526. **2.** *spec.* **a.** A man deeply versed in some subject of study, or in studies generally; a learned man, sage. Now *rare* or *arch.* OE. †**b.** A man who utters wise sayings or maxims; *esp.* as a title for any of the writers of the Jewish 'Wisdom Literature' -1750. **3.** A man versed or skilled in hidden arts, as magic, witchcraft, and the like; *spec.* applied to the three Oriental astrologers or Magi who came to worship the infant Jesus. In general senses now *dial.* or *vulgar.* late ME.

1. *Worldly wiseman*: see WORLDLY. **2.** *The seven wise men* = the seven sages: see SAGE *sb.*² B. **b.** There is no new thing vnder the Sunne, saith the wiseman 1611. So **Wise woman,** a woman skilled in magic or hidden arts; a witch, sorceress; *esp.* a harmless or beneficent one, who deals in charms against disease, etc. (now *dial.* or *arch.*).

Wisent (wī·zěnt). 1866. [- G. *wisent*; see BISON.] *Antiq.* The aurochs.

Wish (wiʃ), *sb.* ME. [f. next.] **1.** An instance of wishing; a feeling in the mind directed towards something which one believes would give satisfaction if attained, possessed, or realized. **2.** A desire expressed in words, or the expression of such; sometimes nearly = 'request' 1513. **b.** *spec.* An expression of desire for another's welfare: often as a farewell greeting. Usu., now always, in *pl.* 1593. **c.** An imprecation; a malediction. *Obs.* or *dial.* 1592. **3.** *transf.* An object of desire; what one wishes or wishes for ME.

1. Thy w. was Father (Harry) to that thought SHAKS. *Prov.* If Wishes were Horses, Beggars would ride 1721. Phr. *To one's w.*, as one wishes; *esp.* to the full extent of one's desire (now *rare* or *Obs.*). **2. b.** Take from my mouth, the w. of happy yeares SHAKS. **3.** *Two Gent.* IV. ii. 93.

Comb.: **w. bone** = MERRYTHOUGHT.

Wish (wiʃ), *v.* [OE. *wȳśćan* = MLG. *wünschen*, MDu. *wonscen, wunscen*, OHG. *wunsken* (G. *wünschen*), ON. *œskja* :- Gmc. **wunskjan*, f. **wunskon*, *-ō* (OE. *wūsć*, OHG. *wunsc* (G. *wunsch*), ON. *ósk* wish), f. **wun-* **wen-* **wan-* (see WEEN *v.*, WONT *ppl. a.*); cf. Skr. *vāñcā, vāñc* wish.] **1.** *trans.* To have or feel a wish for; to desire: with various const.; with simple obj. now *dial.* **2.** *intr.* To have or feel a wish; in early use often, to long, yearn ME. **b.** *trans.* with cognate obj. late ME. **3.** *trans.* To express a wish for; to say that one wishes. . ; *spec.* to imprecate, invoke (an evil or curse) OE. **4.** *spec.* To desire (something, usu. good) for or on behalf of a person, etc.: esp. in formulæ of greeting or expressions of goodwill; hence, to express such a wish for, esp. as a formal greeting OE. **b.** To desire, or express a desire for, the welfare or misfortune of (a person); only in *evil wished*, ILL-WISH *v.*, *well-wished* 1577. **5.** In expressions of desire for something to be done by another, thus conveying a request; hence, to request, entreat; formerly sometimes, to bid, command 1533. **6.** To recommend (a person) *to* another, or *to* a place, etc. *Obs.* or *dial.* 1596.

1. I am as well nowe, I thanke God, as I could wysshe 1530. 'Tis a consummation Deuoutly to be wish'd SHAKS. I neuer wish'd to see you sorry, now I trust I shall SHAKS. Kings for such a Tomb would w. to die MILT. He is certainly bewitched: I w. the old hag upon the green has done him no mischief 1756. Heigh ho! I w. I was drunk—but I have nothing but this damned barley-water BYRON. I wished both magazine and review at the bottom of the sea LAMB. Would you w. a little more hot water, ma'am? DICKENS. **2.** Having nothing to do and nothing to w. for, she naturally imagined she must be very ill DICKENS. **3.** *Rich. III*, I. iii. 218. **4.** We w. you good lucke in the name of the Lorde COVERDALE *Ps.* 129:8. I w. Jane Fairfax very well; but she tires me to death JANE AUSTEN. **5.** There is another thing I w. you to notice specially RUSKIN. Hence **Wi·shable** *a.* (*rare*). **Wished** (wiʃt, *poet.* wi·ʃěd) *ppl. a.*; **-ly** *adv.* (*rare* or *Obs.*). **Wi·sher. Wi·shing** *ppl. a.*

Wishful (wi·ʃfŭl), *a.* 1523. [f. WISH *sb.* + -FUL.] †**1.** Such as is or is to be wished; desirable; desired -1645. **2. a.** Of the eye or look, feeling, etc.: Full of desire; longing, wistful. *Obs.* or *dial.* 1593. **b.** Of a person: Possessed by a wish for something specified or implied; wishing, desirous. Now *rare* in literary prose. 1733.

2. a. To greet mine owne Land with my wishfull sight SHAKS. Hence **Wi·shful-ly** *adv.*, **-ness.**

Wishing (wi·ʃiŋ), *vbl. sb.* ME. [f. WISH *v.* + -ING¹.] The action of WISH *v.*; an instance of this.

attrib. and *Comb.* in many designations of objects supposed to be capable of magically conferring the fulfilment of one's wishes, as *w.-cap, -gate, -well.*

Wishmay (wi·ʃmeⁱ). 1863. [transl. ON. *óskmær*, f. *ósk* wish + *mær* MAY *sb.*¹] A Valkyrie.

Wisht (wiʃt), *a.* Chiefly *s. w. dial.* 1800. [Of unkn. origin.] **1.** Dreary, dismal; melancholy 1829. **2.** Uncanny, eerie, weird 1800. **3.** Sickly, wan 1868.

Wishtonwish (wi·ʃtənwiʃ). 1806. [Imitative, from the cry of the animal.] Native name for the prairie-dog of N. America.

Wish-wash (wi·ʃ,wǫʃ). 1786. [redupl. formation from WASH *sb.* (III.3); cf. synon. *swish-swash* (XVI).] **1.** A contemptuous name for weak, insipid or unsubstantial drink (or liquid food). **2.** *fig.* Wishy-washy talk or writing 1842. Hence †**Wi·sh-wa:shy** *a.* = next.

Wishy-washy (wi·ʃi,wǫ:ʃi), *a.* (*int.*) 1693. [redupl. formation on WASHY *a.*; cf. -Y¹.] **1.** Of drink (or liquid food): Weak and insipid, sloppy 1791. **2.** *fig.* **a.** Feeble or poor in constitution, condition, or aspect; weakly, sickly. Now *rare* or *Obs.* 1703. **b.** Feeble or poor in quality or character; unsubstantial, 'milk-and-watery'. †Also rarely as *int.* = pish! tush! 1693.

1. Their w., watery wine 1898. **2. b.** Isabel painted w. looking flowers on Bristol-board from Nature 1865. Hence **Wi·shy-wa:shiness.**

Wisp (wisp), *sb.* ME. [Cf. WFris. *wisp* wisp, twig, handful of straw; for synon. var. see WHISK *sb.*¹] **1.** A handful, bunch, or small bundle (of hay, straw, grass, etc.). **b.** Used to wipe something dry or clean; now chiefly to rub down a horse. late ME. **c.** in various special uses, e.g. as an ale-house sign; hung outside a house as a sign of the plague; as a plug, strainer or wad 1508. **2.** A twisted band, esp. of hay or straw; a ring or wreath of twisted material, used as a pad. late ME. †**b.** A twist or figure of straw for a scold to rail at -1698. **3.** A bunch or twisted bundle of hay or straw, used for burning as a torch, etc. late ME. **b.** A WILL-O'-THE-W. In recent use *poet.* 1618. **4.** *transf.* and *allus.* **a.** A twist of paper 1597. **b.** A heap or bundle (of clothes) 1736. **c.** A thin, narrow, filmy, or slight piece, fragment, or portion (*of* something) 1836. **d.** A small broom; a whisk 1875.

2. b. 3 *Hen. VI*, II. ii. 144. **4. c.** A rusty black neckerchief with a red border, tied in a narrow w. round his neck DICKENS. A thin w. of smoke on the horizon 1919.

Wisp (wisp), *v.* 1598. [f. prec.] **1.** *trans.* To rub (an animal, esp. a horse) *down* or *over* with a wisp. **2.** To twist into or as a wisp; *dial.* to rumple 1753. **3.** *intr.* To pass *away*, as a wisp of vapour 1883.

Wispish (wi·spiʃ), *a.* 1896. [f. WISP *sb.* + -ISH¹.] Of the nature of or resembling a wisp.

Wispy (wi·spi), *a.* 1717. [f. WISP *sb.* + -Y¹.] Consisting of or resembling a wisp or wisps.

Wist (wist), *v. pseudo-arch.* 1508. [Partly from *I wist*, for IWIS (see WIS *v.*²), partly erron. use of pa. t. *wist* of WIT *v.*¹] To know.

Wist, pa. t. of WIT *v.*¹

Wistaria (wistēᵊ·riă). Also **wisteria** (-Iᵊ·riă). 1842. [mod.L., f. name of Caspar *Wistar* (or *Wister*) 1761-1818, Amer. anatomist; named by T. Nuttall in 1818; see -IA¹.] Any plant of the leguminous genus *Wistaria*, native to N. America, Japan, and China, the species of which are hardy, climbing, deciduous shrubs bearing racemes of blue-lilac papilionaceous flowers.

Wistful (wi·stfŭl), *a.* 1613. [app. f. WISTLY *adv.* In early use chiefly poet. with reminiscence of *wishful.*] †**1.** Closely attentive, intent -1711. **2.** Expectantly or yearningly eager, watchful, or intent; mournfully expectant or longing. (Chiefly in ref. to the look.) 1714. Hence **Wi·stfulness.**

Wistfully (wi·stfŭli), *adv.* 1663. [f. prec. + -LY².] †**1.** Attentively, intently -1833. **2.**

With expectant or yearning eagerness; with mournful expectancy or longing 1663.

Wistiti (wi·stiti). 1774. [– Fr. *ouistiti* (imitative); named by Buffon from the cry of the animal.] A S. American monkey of the family *Hapalidæ*; a marmoset, esp. the Common Marmoset, *Hapale jacchus*.

†**Wi·stly,** *adv.* 1500. [var. of WHISHTLY silently + -FUL, and assoc. with WISHFUL and (dial.) *wishly* steadfastly (XVI).] With close attention; intently (occas. with implication of WISTFULLY 2).

Wit (wit), *sb.* [OE. *wit(t*, more frequently *ġewit(t*, corresp. to OFris. OS. *wit*, OHG. *wizzi* (Du. *weet*, G. *witz*), ON. *vit*, Goth. *unwiti* ignorance, f. **wit-* (see WIT *v.*[1]).] **I.** Denoting a faculty (or the person possessing it). †**1.** The seat of consciousness or thought, the mind –1660. **2.** The faculty of thinking and reasoning in general; mental capacity, intellect, reason. *arch.* (now esp. in phr. *the w. of man* = human understanding). OE. **b.** Often denoting indifferently the faculty or the person possessing it, and hence sometimes used definitely for the person in respect of this faculty. Usu. in pl., of a number of persons. *arch.* 1536. **c.** Phr. *At one's wit's end*: utterly perplexed; at a loss what to think or what to do. So *to bring (drive) to one's wit's end.* late ME. †**d.** *W., whither wilt thou?*: phr. addressed to a person who is letting his tongue run away with him –1637. †**3.** = SENSE *sb.* 1, 7. Also *common w.* = COMMON SENSE 1. –1592. **b.** *Five wits*: usu., the five (bodily) senses; often vaguely, the perceptions or mental faculties generally. *Obs.* or *rare arch.* ME. **c.** *pl.* Mental faculties, intellectual powers. late ME. **4.** The understanding or mental faculties in respect of their condition; chiefly = 'right mind', 'senses', sanity. **a.** *sing.* (*Obs.* or *dial.*) OE. **b.** *pl.* = SENSE *sb.* I. 9: esp. in phr. *in* or *out of one's wits* ME.

1. If a mans w. be wandring, let him study the Mathematiks BACON. **2. b.** A schole for the training up of young wits HOLLAND. **d.** *A.Y.L.* IV. i. 167. **3. b.** Alone and warming his five wits, The white owl in the belfry sits TENNYSON. **c.** *To have one's wits about one*, to have one's mental powers in full exercise, to be mentally alert. *To live by one's wits*, to get one's living by clever or (now esp.) crafty devices, without any settled occupation. **4. a.** *In (one's right) w.*, sane, of sound mind. *Out of (one's) w.*, insane, out of one's mind. **b.** The governor..was frightened out of his wits MACAULAY.

II. Denoting a quality (or the possessor of it). **1.** Good or great mental capacity; genius, talent, cleverness; mental quickness or sharpness, acumen. *arch.* ME. †**b.** Practical talent or cleverness; skill, ingenuity –1726. **2.** Wisdom, good judgement, discretion. *Obs.* exc. in phr. like *to have the w. to.* ME. **3.** Quickness of intellect or liveliness of fancy, with capacity of apt expression; talent for saying brilliant or sparkling things, esp. in an amusing way. *arch.* 1579. **4.** That quality of speech or writing which consists in the apt association of thought and expression, calculated to surprise and delight by its unexpectedness; later always with ref. to the utterance of brilliant or sparkling things in an amusing way 1542. **5.** (*transf.* from II. 1.) A person of great mental ability; a learned, clever, or intellectual person; a man of talent or intellect. *arch.* or *Hist.* 1470. **6.** (*transf.* from II. 3.) A person of lively fancy, who has the faculty of saying smart or brilliant things, now always so as to amuse; a witty person 1692.

1. *Meas. for M.* II. i. 282. **b.** It..spake the praises of the workmans w. SPENSER. **2.** Since Breuitie is the Soule of Wit,..I will be breefe SHAKS. **3.** Men of all sorts take a pride to gird at mee:..I am not onely witty in my selfe, but the cause that w. is in other men SHAKS. **4.** W.; which is a just mixture of Reason and Extravagance 1693. True W. is Nature to advantage dress'd, What oft was thought, but ne'er so well express'd POPE. A species of minor w., which is much used,..I mean Raillery CHESTERF. **5.** There goes an Author! One of the Wits! 1638. **6.** Uncle Bill..is evidently the w. of the party DICKENS. Hence **Wit** *v.*[2] (in nonce-uses) (*a*) *intr.* with *it*, to play the w.; (*b*) *trans.* as a meaningless repetition of the word just used, by way of a vague threat; (*c*) to call (a person) a w., attribute w. to.

Wit, *v. arch.* exc. in *to wit.* Pres. t. **wot;** pa. t. and pple. **wist.** [OE. *witan* = OFris. *wita*, OS. *witan*, OHG. *wizzan* (Du. *weten*, G. *wissen*), ON. *vita*, Goth. *witan*, f. Gmc. **wait-* **wīt-* :– IE. **woid-* **weid-* **wid-* whence Skr. *véda* (cf. VEDA), Gr. οἶδα, ἴδμεν, know, L. *vidēre* see.] **1.** *trans.* To have cognizance or knowledge of; to be aware of; to know (as a fact or an existing thing). **2.** *intr.* with *of*: To be aware of (as existing, or as happening or having happened); to know of ME. †**3.** Passing into the sense: To become aware of, gain knowledge of, get or come to know; to find out; to be informed of, learn. *trans.* and *absol.* or *intr.* with *of.* –1795. **4.** *trans.* with *to* and *inf.*: To know how, be able ME. †**5.** In imper. = 'be assured', and later in monitory formulæ and polite phrases = 'you must know', 'allow me to inform you' –1608. **6.** To recognize; to distinguish, discern, detect. *Obs.* or *rare arch.* ME.

1. For aught I woot, he was of Dertemouthe CHAUCER. Hee never wist the matter to bee haynous 1571. As witting I no other comfort haue SHAKS. Whether they speak Gaelic or no I wotna SCOTT. **3.** O Lassie, are ye sleepin yet, Or are ye waukin, I wad w.? BURNS. **4.** Fear wist not to evade, as Love wist to pursue F. THOMPSON. **5.** Please you w.: The Epitaph is for Marina writ SHAKS.

Phrases. †**Do to w.** To cause (a person) to know, make known to. **Let w.** To let (a person) know (a thing); to inform (one), or to make (something) known; to disclose, reveal. *Obs.* exc. *dial.* **To w.:** †**a.** *It is to w.*: it is to be observed, noted, or ascertained. †**b.** *That is to w.* = AFr. *cestasavoir*, L. *scilicet*, *videlicet*; occas. = *id est.* **c.** *To w.*: (*a*) 'To be sure', truly, indeed (*Obs.* or *rare arch.*). (*b*) That is, namely, *scilicet.* **God wot:** God knows.

Witan (wi·tăn). *Hist.* 1807. [OE. *witan*, pl. of *wita* wise man, councillor, f. base of *witan* WIT *v.*] The members of the national council of Anglo-Saxon times; the council itself.

Witch (witʃ), *sb.*[1] Now *dial.* [OE. *wiċċa* masc.; see next.] A man who practises witchcraft or magic; a magician, sorcerer, wizard.

Witch (witʃ), *sb.*[2] [OE. *wiċċe* fem., corresp. to *wiċċa* (prec.), rel. to *wiċċian* WITCH *v.*] **1.** A female magician; sorceress; in later use, *esp.* a woman supposed to have dealings with the devil or evil spirits and to be able by their co-operation to perform supernatural acts. **2.** *fig.* **a.** *gen.* 1659. **b.** (*a*) A young woman or girl of bewitching aspect or manners 1740. (*b*) *Old w.*: a contemptuous appellation for a malevolent or repulsive-looking old woman. late ME. **3.** Applied to various animals and objects. **a.** The stormy petrel 1784. **b.** A kind of snail 1815. **c.** In a loom: = DOBBY 3. 1883. **d.** *W. of Agnesi* (Math.): a plane curve named after M. G. Agnesi (1718–99) of the university of Bologna 1875.

1. *The w. is in it*, it is bewitched. *As nervous as a w.*: a New England phr., applied to a very restless person. **2. b.** (*a*) For my part I find every woman a w. LYTTON. (*b*) A lusti galaunt that weddithe an olde wiche LYDG.

Comb.: **w.-bell(s**, *Sc.* the harebell, *Campanula rotundifolia*; **-finder,** one formerly employed to search for and obtain evidence against witches; **-fire** = CORPOSANT; **-grass,** *U.S.* (*a*) *Panicum capillare*, a weed-grass found throughout the U.S.; (*b*) couch-grass, *Triticum* (*Agropyrum*) *repens*; **-hat,** a hat with a conical crown and flat brim, represented as worn by witches; **-lock** = W. KNOT 1; **-mark,** a mark on the body, supposed by w.-finders to denote that its possessor was a w.; **-monger,** one who has dealings with witches, or who believes in witchcraft; **-weed,** *S. Afr.* a parasitic plant, *Striga lutea.*

Combs. with *witch's, witches'*: **witch's bells,** the foxglove; **witches' besom, broom,** a bushy tuft developed on the branches of trees by a fungus; **witches' bridle,** an iron collar and gag formerly used as an instrument of torture in Scottish w.-trials; **witches' butter,** pop. name for certain gelatinous algæ and fungi, esp. *Tremella nostoc*; **witches' Sabbath** = SABBATH 3.

Witch, wych (witʃ), *sb.*[3] [OE. *wiċe* and *wiċ*, app. f. Gmc. *wīk-* bend; cf. WEAK.] Applied gen. or vaguely to various trees having pliant branches: *esp.* †**a.** the WYCH ELM; **b.** (now *dial.*) the mountain ash, *Pyrus aucuparia.* Also *attrib.*; **w. alder,** a w. hazel with alder-like leaves, *Fothergilla alnifolia*, native to Virginia and N. Carolina.

Witch (witʃ), *sb.*[4] *local.* 1879. [Of unkn. origin.] The flat-fish *Pleuronectes cynoglossus*, resembling the lemon sole.

Witch (witʃ), *v.* [OE. *wiċċian*, corresp. to (M)LG. *wikken*, *wicken* (agent-noun *wikker*, n. of action *wikkerie*), the source of which is unknown. In later senses, prob. aphetic from *bewitch.*] †**1.** *intr.* To practise witchcraft; to use sorcery or enchantment –1623. **2.** *trans.* = BEWITCH *v.* 1. ME. **b.** (with prep. or adv.) To bring, draw, put, or change by witchcraft 1597. **3.** *fig.* = BEWITCH *v.* 2. 1590.

2. Thou art a W...and diddest procure Mother Bale to w. the Cattell of J. S. 1647. **3.** 1 *Hen. IV*, IV. i. 110. Hence **Wi·tching** *vbl. sb.* the use or practice of witchcraft OE.

Witchcraft (wi·tʃ,kraft). [OE. *wiċċe-cræft*, f. *wiċċa*, *wiċċe* WITCH *sb.*[1] and [2] + *cræft* CRAFT *sb.*] **1.** The practices of a witch or witches; the exercise of supernatural power supposed to be possessed by persons in league with the devil or evil spirits. **b.** *pl.* Acts or instances of this; magic arts OE. **2.** *fig.* Power or influence like that of a magician; bewitching or fascinating attraction or charm 1599.

1. The Sickness is more than natural, and W. is to be feared 1671. **2.** You haue Witch-craft in your Lippes, Kate. SHAKS.

Wi·tch-do:ctor. 1718. One who professes to cure disease and to counteract witchcraft by magic arts. **b.** A magician among African tribes, esp. Kaffirs, whose business it is to detect witches, and to counteract the effects of magic 1836.

Witchen (wi·tʃĕn). Now *dial.* 1594. [f. WITCH *sb.*[3] + -EN[4].] **1.** In full *w. elm*: = WYCH ELM. **2.** The mountain ash, *Pyrus aucuparia* 1664.

Witchery (wi·tʃəri). 1546. [f. WITCH *sb.*[2] or *v.* + -ERY.] **1.** The use or practice of witchcraft. **b.** *pl.* Deeds of witchcraft 1591. **2.** *fig.* Charming or fascinating power or influence 1582.

2. He never felt The w. of the soft blue sky! WORDSW.

Witchetty (wi·tʃĕti). *Austral.* 1891. [Native name.] The larva of some species of longicorn beetles, used as food by Australian natives.

Wi·tch ha:zel, wy·ch ha:zel. 1541. [WITCH *sb.*[3]] **1.** = WYCH ELM. Also, the hornbeam. **2.** A N. Amer. shrub, *Hamamelis virginica*; also, an extract of the leaves and bark of this shrub, used as an astringent remedy 1760.

Witching (wi·tʃiŋ), *ppl. a.* late ME. [f. WITCH *v.* + -ING[2].] **1.** That casts a spell; enchanting, bewitching. **2.** *transf.* Of or belonging to witchcraft; concerned with the practice of witchcraft or sorcery 1584. **b.** *spec.* Of time: Belonging or appropriate to the deeds of witches and witchcraft, and hence to supposed supernatural occurrences. (In later use echoing Shaks.) 1602. **3.** *fig.* 'Bewitching', fascinating 1600. **b.** *advb.* Bewitchingly 1821.

2. b. 'Tis now the verie w. time of night, When Churchyards yawne, and Hell it selfe breaths out Contagion to this world SHAKS.

Wi·tch knot. 1598. **1.** A tangled knot of hair supposed to be made by witches. **2.** = *witches' besom* (see WITCH *sb.*[2]) 1806.

Wite, wyte (wəit), *sb. Obs.* exc. *Hist.* and *n. dial.* [OE. *wīte* = OFris. *wīte*, OS. *wīti*, OHG. *wīzzi*, ON. *víti* punishment, based on a var. of **wit-* know; see WIT *v.*[1]] †**1. a.** Punishment, penalty; pain inflicted in punishment or torture, *esp.* the torments of hell –ME. **b.** In Anglo-Saxon law, a fine imposed for certain offences or privileges; often as second element in compounds, as BLOODWITE. Now *Hist.* OE. **2.** Blame, reproach; blameworthiness, fault. Now *Sc.* and *n. dial.* ME.

Wite, wyte (wəit), *v. Obs.* exc. *Sc.* and *n. dial.* [OE. *wītan* (see ATWITE *v.*), corresp. to OFris. *wīta*, OS. *wītan*, OHG. *wīzan* (*fráweitan* avenge), ON. *víta* punish, Goth. *-weitan* (*fraweitan* avenge), rel. to prec.] **1.** *trans.* To impute the guilt or lay the blame of (something) to or upon a person (his action, conduct, or character) or a thing, condition, or event. **2.** To impute the guilt or fault to, blame (a person) OE. **3.** To lay the fault or blame upon (a thing) ME.

Witenagemot (wi·tĕnăgĕmōᵘ:t, *popularly* witĕnæ·gĕmǫt). *Hist.* [OE. *witena ġemōt* assembly of wise men; see WITAN, GEMOT(E, MOOT.] The assembly of the WITAN, the national council of Anglo-Saxon times; *transf.* of modern parliaments or other deliberative assemblies.

Wi·tereden. *Hist.* [OE. *witerǣden*, f. *wite* WITE *sb.* + *rǣden* -RED.] A fine (erron. explained by antiquaries as a royal imposition or aid).

With (wiþ), *sb.* 1708. [perh. corruption of WIDTH.] A partition between flues in a chimney stack.

With (wið; *chiefly north.* wiþ), *prep.* [OE. *wiþ* = OFris. *with*, OS. *wið*, prob. shortening of Gmc. prep. repr. by OE. *wiþer*; see WITHER *a.* and *adv.*] **I.** Denoting opposition and derived notions. †**1.** In a position opposite to; over against –ME. **b.** In exchange, return, or payment for. *Obs.* exc. *dial.* OE. **2.** Of conflict, rivalry, and the like: In opposition to, adversely to. (Still the normal prep. with such words as *battle, compete, vie,* and phrases like *go to law, at odds,* but now assoc. with or merged in other senses.) OE. **3.** †**a.** Towards, in the direction of. OE. only. **b.** Near or close to, against, alongside. Now only *Naut.* with words denoting proximity. OE.

2. Let us go and have t'other Brush w. them DE FOE. **3. b.** A man..saw..some dark troubled object close in w. the land DICKENS.

II. Denoting personal relation, agreement, association, union, addition. **1.** After words denoting speech or other verbal communication between persons (with the person as obj.) OE. **b.** Followed by refl. pron., in ref. to soliloquy, consideration, etc. *arch.* 1530. **2. a.** After words expressing transaction or dealing between persons (with the person as obj.) OE. **b.** After words expressing conduct or feeling towards (a person, etc.). Now sometimes repl. by other preps., e.g. envious *of.* OE. **3.** In the matter of, in regard to, concerning; in regard to the condition or fortune of OE. **b.** After an adv. or phr. with ellipsis of or equivalent to a vb., usu. imper.: e.g. *away w. it* = 'take it away'. late ME. **c.** In phr. *w. reference, regard,* or *respect to*: concerning, anent, respecting. **4.** In the opinion, view, or estimation of; 'in the sight of' OE. **5.** In the practice or experience of, in the life or conduct of; sometimes *spec.* in the language or statement of, according to. (With pl. obj. = AMONG A. 5.) ME. **b.** After words expressing influence or the like 1573. **6.** Following words expressing comparison, likeness, equality, or identity. (Sometimes varying with or now replaced by *to.*) OE. **7.** Following words expressing agreement, conformity, sympathy, and the like OE. **b.** By extension, after words expressing disagreement 1646. **8.** On the side or party of; in favour of; on behalf of ME. **b.** In ref. to wind, tide, etc.: Favourable to, in a favourable direction for 1647. **9.** In the same way as; as — does or did, is or was, etc.; like ME. **b.** Followed by *the* and a superlative used *absol.*: As well or thoroughly as; (as) one of, 'among': forming advb. phrases denoting 'to the full or fullest extent', '(nearly) as — as any or as possible' ME. **10.** Expressing simultaneous occurrence and association. **a.** At the same time as; on the occurrence of (and because of); at, on, upon ME. **b.** Followed by a sb. or pron., forming a phr. = a clause with *when* in which the vb. is identical with that in the principal clause; e.g. *to rise w. the lark*, i.e. when the lark rises (= early in the morning). late ME. **c.** In the course or duration of, in process of, 'in' (time, etc.) 1440. **d.** After words denoting change or variation: At the same rate as; in proportion to, according to 1697. **11.** Expressing agreement or accordance, esp. in opinion or statement 1456. **12.** In the same direction as; along the course of: opp. to AGAINST III. 1. 1489. **13.** Following words expressing accompaniment or addition, as *associate, connect, join, marry, share, unite* vbs.; *connection, company, contact* sbs.; *together* adv. OE. **b.** Following words expressing acquaintance or familiarity ME. **c.** By extension, following words expressing separation, as *break, part* ME. **14.** Expressing association or participation in some act, proceeding, or experience; *spec.* = acting on the same side as (another lawyer) in an action at law ME. **15. a.** (with such vbs. as *bring, take, come, go*) Followed by a sb. or (most commonly) pron. denoting the person (vessel, etc.) that leads, conveys, or carries a person or thing, thus having it in charge ME. **b.** In the possession, keeping, care, or charge of (a person); in the hands of ME. **c.** In the nature or character of; as a quality or attribute of. Now chiefly after *way.* late ME. **16.** In the company, society, or presence of ME. **b.** *spec.* At the house of, or in the same house or meeting-place as; in the household, retinue, or service of; on a visit to, being the guest of ME. **c.** *fig.* in ref. to an abstract thing: *to be w.*, to accompany, 'attend'. Also in ref. to God. ME. †**d.** *To be w.*, used in menace, etc. = to be avenged on, chastise, be even with –1825. **17.** Having in one's hold, keeping, or charge; having within its compass, limits, area, etc.; leading, bringing, carrying, wearing, etc. ME. **b.** In phr. *w. child, w. young,* etc., said of a pregnant woman or animal ME. **c.** In phr. *w. costs, w. damages*: in early use = 'in possession of', 'having as awarded'; later, in ref. to the verdict = 'accompanied by an order to the losing party to pay' 1466. **18.** Accompanied by; having as an addition; having in one's company. Often = 'and in addition', 'and besides', or simply 'and'. ME. **b.** Comprising in the whole number or total; including ME. **c.** Having the advantage of (favourable wind, weather, etc.) 1536. **19.** Expressing association, conjunction, or connection in thought, action, or condition. late ME. **20.** Expressing collocation in space 1480. **b.** Expressing mixture or combination of material substances. late ME. (*b*) *ellipt.* in slang use, in ref. to liquor = mixed with sugar, having sugar added; usu. in phr. *hot* (*warm*) or *cold w.* 1835. **21.** Having, possessing; having in or upon it, containing, bearing ME. **22.** Indicating a quality or attribute of the action spoken of: forming phrases equivalent to advs., e.g. *w. one accord* = unanimously. Similarly after an adj., in phr. expressing a particular kind or degree of the quality denoted by the adj. ME. **23.** Indicating a feeling, purpose, or other mental state accompanying the action spoken of ME. **b.** In expressions of devotion, affection, or gratitude accompanying what is said or written, esp. by way of greeting 1454. **24.** Indicating an attribute, quality, or condition of the person or thing spoken of: Having, possessing, characterized by 1450. **b.** Still having; without loss of or detriment to; consistently with 1440. (*b*) Though having; notwithstanding, in spite of. (Usu. followed by *all* qualifying the sb.) ME. **25.** Indicating an accompanying or attendant circumstance, or a result following from the action expressed by the verb ME. **26.** Indicating something granted, received, or assumed: often with conditional implication, as in *w. your permission* = 'if you will allow me'. late ME. **27.** Followed by a sb. denoting some alteration or modification, or something imposed in the way of a demand or requirement: e.g. *exception, proviso, qualification* 1450. **28. a.** Followed by a sb. denoting misfortune or evil, in imprecations and intensive phrases: now usu. *w. a vengeance* (in intensive sense) ME. **b.** Introducing a refrain (often meaningless) in a poem or ballad. late ME. **29.** In various preceding senses, followed by object and complement ME.

1. White handed Mistris, one sweet word w. thee SHAKS. **2. a.** All who had business to transact w. him 1838. **b.** Be opposite w. a kinsman, surly w. seruants SHAKS. **3.** We tooke more Cod then we knew what to doe w. 1624. **4.** Juan stood well both w. Ins and Outs BYRON. **5.** It is an accustom'd action w. her, to seeme thus washing her hands SHAKS. **6.** A sniveling Gentleman of not half the sense w. the late poor spirited Dick Cromwell 1710. **7.** Spain..on friendly terms with France 1796. **b.** Impossibilities and things inconsistent w. truth SIR T. BROWNE. **8.** He that is nat w. me, is aȝeinus me WYCLIF *Matt.* 12:30. Shakespeare was of us, Milton was for us, Burns, Shelley, were w. us BROWNING. **9.** Whether we should love everybody w. Tolstoy, or spare nobody w. Nietzsche 1905. **b.** At your age..I could have wept w. the best TENNYSON. **10.** *W. that*, when (and, often because) that occurred, thereupon; saying or having just said that. *W. this*, hereupon. **c.** Mans labours and skill wil faile w. yeeres 1611. **d.** The probability of an error diminishes w. its magnitude 1838. **11.** *To be w.*, to be of the same opinion as, to agree with; Ah, it's a fine dance—I'm w. you there STEVENSON. **12.** W. the Grain of the wood 1678. **13. b.** He is..a man of sorrows, and acquainted w. griefe *Isa.* 53:3. **c.** *To break w.* = to break off connection w.; It cannot be The Volsces dare breake w. vs SHAKS. **14.** I will..for the future be merry w. the Vulgar STEELE. **15. a.** Ten poundes..To carie in your pursse about w. ye 1596. **b.** The 'burden of proof' lies w. the accusers 1828. **c.** He had such an honest way w. him 1711. **16.** I have no one to go w. 1914. *Face to face w.*, looking in the face of, confronting. *W. God*, in heaven. **c.** Luck, my lads, be w. you still HOUSMAN. **d.** *Mids. N.* III. ii. 403. **17.** A tall..Man,..w. Ruffles and a light bag Wig 1722. **c.** A verdict ..for the plaintiff, w. one pound eleven shillings and sixpence damages 1775. **18.** Imprisonment w. or without hard labour 1911. **b.** 'What's the terms?'..'Five guineas a week, ma'am, w. attendance.' DICKENS. **19.** *One* (*day*, etc.) *w. another*; see ONE IV. 3; One week w. another she earned about half-a-crown 1784. **20.** The aristocracy dare not ask the professors to dinner for fear lest..they should wear green ties w. their dress clothes 1914. **21.** A Man with a sour rivell'd Face ADDISON. **22.** I look'd vpon her with a souldiers eie SHAKS. **23.** A land of exile, visited with reluctance and quitted w. delight MACAULAY. **b.** Here: take George his hat and stick w. my compliments 1898. **24.** She had a tongue with a tang SHAKS. In a cool sweat, w. a low pulse 1776. **b.** He vnnethis gatt away w. his life 1440. (*b*) England, w. all thy faults, I love thee still COWPER. **25.** The frosty silence..w. which it is received 1806. **26.** Another gentleman ..collars that glass of punch, without a 'w. your leave', or 'by your leave' DICKENS.

III. Denoting instrumentality, causation, or agency. **1.** Indicating the means or instrument of any kind of action: By means of, by the use of ME. **b.** Formerly used in many cases where *by* is now the usual or only construction, e.g. with obj. a person, or an action ME. **c.** Used where other preps. are now usual, as *at* (a charge or cost), *on* or *upon* (food, etc.) ME. †**d.** In ref. to procreation: = BY *prep.* 5. –1714. **e.** After *begin* or *end* and words of like sense. late ME. **2.** After words of furnishing, filling, covering, and the like ME. **3.** In consequence of, as a result of, by the action of; because of ME. **4.** After a passive verb or participle, indicating the principal agent. *Obs.* exc. *dial.* ME.

1. They build w. vnburnt clay 1634. The people w. a shout Rifted the Air MILT. **b.** W. all this the King was convinced 1715. **c.** You shall fast a Weeke w. Branne and water SHAKS. **d.** I had but two children w. my wife 1709. **e.** We may close her national history w. the seventeenth century RUSKIN. 'Middle' begins with 'm' 1887. *To begin w.*, to take what is mentioned or indicated as one's starting-point; To begyne w., we shall interdyte the lond 1550. **2.** Her wombe then rich w. my yong squire SHAKS. **3.** Went they not quickly, I should die w. laughing SHAKS. Now glow'd the Firmament W. living Saphirs MILT. None shall tax me with base Perjury DRYDEN. Men and horses..nearly spent w. toil 1839. *It is pouring w. rain* = rain is pouring. *Dripping w. dew*, having dew dripping from it. **4.** He was torne to pieces w. a Beare SHAKS. This island is inhabited..w. monkies and myself 1727.

With-, repr. OE. *wiþ-* used as a prefix to vbs. (and derived sbs.) with the meanings (1) away, back, as in OE. *wiþgān*; so WITHDRAW, WITHHOLD; (2) away from one, as in several OE. vbs. meaning 'reject, refuse', *wiþcēosan, wiþsacan*; (3) against, in opposition, as in OE. *wiþhabban* to resist, *wiþstandan* WITHSTAND *v.*

Withal (wiðǭ·l), *adv.* and *prep. arch.* ME. [prop. two words, orig. *with al(le*; ultimately superseding earlier *mid alle* (MID *prep.*[1]).] **A.** *adv.* **1.** Along with the rest; in addition; moreover; as well. **b.** Contextually: 'At the same time'; notwithstanding, nevertheless 1596. **2.** = THEREWITH 1 c, 2. ME.

1. b. He confessed that his master was rather severe, but w. a very good man 1859. **2.** *To begin w.* = to begin with (see WITH *prep.* III. 1 e); I wyll (to begyn w.) shew you what repentance is 1553.

B. *prep.* Substituted for WITH *prep.* in postposition, esp. at the end of a relative clause or its equivalent or of a direct or indirect question, governing a relative or an interrogative ME.

Ile tel you who Time ambles withall, who Time trots w.,..and who he stands stil withall SHAKS.

Withamite (wi·ðəməit). 1825. [f. the name of its discoverer, H. *Witham*; see -ITE[1] 2b.] *Min.* A red or reddish-yellow variety of epidote, found at Glencoe in Scotland.

Withdraw (wiðdrǭ·, wiþdrǭ·), *v.* Pa. t. **withdrew** (-drū·), pa. pple. **withdrawn** (-drǭ·n). ME. [f. WITH- (1) + DRAW *v.*] **I.** *trans.* **1.** To take back or away (something that has been given, allowed, possessed, experienced, or enjoyed). **2.** To draw back, take away, remove (a thing) *from* its place or position ME. **b.** To take (one's eyes, etc.) off something 1477. **c.** To remove (money) *from* capital, or *from* a bank or other place of deposit 1776. **d.** To draw (a veil, curtain, etc.) back or aside; to draw back (a bolt). Now *rare.* 1797. **3.** To remove *from* the scope of an inquiry, *from* a particular category, or the like 1725. **b.** To take back, retract (one's words, an expression). Often *absol.* in imper., in parliamentary procedure, to demand the withdrawal by a member of an expression or statement. 1793. **c.** To refrain from proceeding with or prosecuting (a course of action, etc.); to cease to support or present (a candidate, etc.) 1781. **4.** To draw away, deflect, divert (a person, his mind, etc.) *from* an object, pursuit, etc. Now *rare.* ME. **5.** To remove (a person) *from* a position; to cause to retire or recede; *spec.* to cause (a force, troops) to retire *from* a position, an engagement 1450. **b.** *Law.* To remove (a juror) from the panel in order to put an end to the proceedings 1676.

1. They..said they'd w. their subscriptions from the hounds SURTEES. **2.** In prosperous days They swarm, but in adverse w. their head MILTON. **3. b.** Burke got up twice, but..nothing was heard but *W., w.* 1793. **c.** Amendment, by leave, withdrawn 1880. **4.** With how contrarious thoughts am I withdrawne GREENE. **5.** Walter Scape was withdrawn from Eton THACKERAY.

II. *refl.* Now *rare* or *arch.* **1.** To remove oneself *from* a place or position. ME. **2.** To remove oneself *from* a condition, sphere, society, etc. ME.

1. W. your selues, and leaue vs here alone SHAKS.

III. *intr.* **1.** To go away, depart, or retire *from* a place or position, *from* some one's presence, to another room or a private place, etc. ME. **b.** Of combatants, troops, etc.: To retire *from* the field of battle or any contest, or *from* an advanced position ME. **2.** To draw away *from* a person; to remove oneself or retire *from* a society or community, etc.; to retire from participation in or pursuit of something. late ME.

1. Sophia now took the first Opportunity of withdrawing with the Ladies FIELDING. **2.** Withdrawing into his own soul 1911. So **Withdrau·ght** (*obs.* exc. *arch.*) withdrawal; †a place of withdrawal; a sewer, a privy (now *local*). **Withdraw·** *sb.* withdrawal, removal. **Withdraw·able** *a.* capable of being withdrawn. **Withdraw·er,** *spec.* in *Sc. Church Hist.* one who did not conform to the established church in the 17th century. **Withdraw·ment** (now *rare*) = WITHDRAWAL. **Withdraw·n** *ppl. a.* in various senses; occas. secluded; also, of mental state, detached.

Withdrawal (wiðdrǭ·ăl, wiþ-). 1824. [f. prec. + -AL[1] 2. (Superseding the earlier WITHDRAWMENT.)] **1.** The act of taking back or away what has been held, occupied, or enjoyed 1839. **b.** The removal of money or securities from a bank or other place of deposit 1861. **2.** The act of withdrawing a person or thing *from* a place or position, *esp.* the removal of troops by way of retreat 1838. **3.** The retraction of a statement, proposal, etc. 1835. **4.** The act of retiring or retreating *from* a place or position 1824.

Withdrawing (wiðdrǭ·iŋ, wiþ-), *vbl. sb.* ME. [f. WITHDRAW *v.* + -ING[1].] The action of WITHDRAW *v.* in various senses.

attrib.: †**w.-chamber, -room** (*arch.* or *Hist.*), a room to withdraw to; = DRAWING ROOM 1.

Withe, with (wiþ, wið, waið), *sb.* [OE. *wiþþe* = OFris. *withthe*, MDu. *wisse* (Du. *wis*), OHG. *wit, withi, wid, widi*, ON. *við, viðja*; cf. Goth. *kunawida* bonds; :- Gmc. **wiþōn*, **wiþi*, f. base **weit-* **wit-*, f. **wi-* as in WIRE; cf. WITHY.] **1.** A band, tie, or shackle consisting of a tough, flexible twig or branch, as of willow or osier, or of several twisted together; such a twig or branch used for binding or tying, and occas. for plaiting. **b.** *gen.* A pliant twig or bough 1817. **c.** With allusion to the story of Samson in *Judges* 16:7. 1835. †**2.** A halter, prop. one made with withes –1694. **3.** A willow. Now *dial.* ME. **b.** The creeping plant *Heliotropium fruticosum*, of Jamaica, the stems of which are used for making baskets 1657. **4.** Applied to various iron implements resembling a withe in some respect 1688.

1. If they binde me with seuen greene withs, that were neuer dried, then shall I be weake *Judges* 16:7. Hence **Withe** *v.* (now *dial.* and *U.S.*) *trans.* to twist like a w.; to bind with a w. or withes; *U.S.* to take (deer) with a noose made of withes.

Wither (wi·ðəɹ), *sb.* 1652. [f. WITHER *v.*] †**1.** A disease of cows –1722. **2.** *Tea-manuf.* The process of withering 1897.

Wi·ther, *a.* and *adv.* *Obs.* or *dial.* [OE. *wiþer* adv. or adj., related to *wiþer* prep. = OS. *withar*, OHG. *widar*, ON. *viðr*, Goth. *wiþra*; f. Indo-Eur. **wi-* denoting separation or division + comp. suffix *-tero-* -THER *suff.*] **A.** *adj.* **1.** Hostile, adverse; fierce. †**2.** Contrary, opposite; wrong (side) –1450. †**B.** *adv.* Hostilely; perversely, fiercely –ME.

Wither (wi·ðəɹ), *v.* late ME. [app. var. of WEATHER *v.*, ult. differentiated for certain senses.] **1.** *intr.* Of a plant: To become dry and shrivel up. **2.** Of other animate things: To become dried up or shrivelled; to lose vigour from lack of animal moisture; to pine or fade *away.* late ME. **3.** *fig.* Of persons, or of inanimate and immaterial things: To lose vigour or freshness, to pine *away*, languish, fade, fall into decay 1508. **4.** *Tea-manuf.* (*trans.*) To dry (tea-leaf) before roasting. Also *absol.* Also *intr.* of the leaf. 1753. **5.** To cause (a plant, flower, etc.) to dry up and shrivel 1555. **6.** To cause (the body or the physical powers) to become wasted or decayed; to cause to shrink, become wrinkled, or lose freshness 1599. **7.** *fig.* To destroy the vitality or vigour of; to cause to decline, decay, or waste; now somewhat *rare* exc. in hyperbolical use, to blight or paralyse with a look of scorn or the like 1590.

1. Like a neglected rose, It withers on the stalk MILT. **2.** Now I wax old,..As muk apon mold I widder away 1460. **3.** An honest gentellman witheringe in pouerty 1647. **6.** Age cannot w. her SHAKS. **7.** Like to a Step-dame, or a Dowager, Long withering out a yong mans reuennew SHAKS. Dr. Slammer..withering the company with a look DICKENS.

Withered (wi·ðəɹd), *ppl. a.* 1470. [f. prec. + -ED[1].] **1.** Of a plant, fruit, etc.: Shrivelled or shrunken through lack of moisture, and so deprived of its natural colour, freshness, or bloom; hence of fields, etc., and *gen.*: Dried up, arid. **2.** Of men or the lower animals: Physically shrunken, shrivelled, wasted, or decayed 1500. **b.** Of the body, or parts of it: Shrivelled or shrunken, esp. by the wasting of disease or age. Formerly, and now *colloq.* or *dial.*, often applied to a paralysed limb 1513. **3.** *fig.* Deprived of or having lost vigour, freshness, or 'bloom'; shrunken and decayed 1561.

2. b. There was a man which had a widdred honde TINDALE *Mark* 3:1. **3.** The curse of the wither'd heart SCOTT. Hence **Wi·thered-ly** *adv.*, **-ness.**

Witherite (wi·ðərəit). 1794. [f. name of W. *Withering*, who first described and analysed it in 1784; see -ITE[1] 2 b.] *Min.* Native barium carbonate.

Withernam (wi·ðəɹnăm). *Law.* Now *Hist.* ME. [Law-French (whence AL. *withernamium* XIII), app. – ON. *viðrnám*, f. *viðr* WITHER *adv.* + *nām* NAAM.] *Law.* In an action of replevin, the reprisal of other goods in lieu of those taken by a first distress and eloigned; also, the writ (*capias in w.*) commanding the sheriff to take the reprisal. **b.** A process of distress (or arrest) for debt, formerly current in the Cinque Ports (and other towns) ME.

Withers (wi·ðəɹz), *sb. pl.*, occas. *sing.* **wither.** 1580. [app. a reduced form of *widersome* or *-sone*, f. *wider* WITHER *adv.* + an obsc. element; cf. G. *widerrist*, f. *wider* WITHER *adv.* + *rist* WRIST.] In a horse, the highest part of the back, lying between the shoulder-blades. Also, the corresponding part in some other animals, as the ox. (Often in fig. use, esp. after Shaks. with allusion to the 'wringing' of a horse's withers.)

Let the gall'd iade winch: our w. are vnrung SHAKS.

Withershins, widdershins (wi·ðəɹ-, wi·dəɹʃinz), *adv. dial.* (chiefly *Sc.*) 1513. [– MLG. *weddersin(ne)s* – MHG. *widersinnes*, f. *wider* WITHER *adv.* + gen. of *sin* way, direction. In sense 2 assoc. with SUN *sb.*] †**1.** In a direction opposite to the usual; the wrong way –1721. **2.** In a direction contrary to the apparent course of the sun (considered as unlucky or causing disaster) 1545.

Withhold (wiðhōᵘ·ld, wiþ-), *v.* Pa. t. and pa. pple. **withheld.** ME. [See WITH- (1) and HOLD *v.* The pa. pple. **withholden** was still freq. in XIX.] **1.** *trans.* To keep *from* doing something; to hold back, restrain. **b.** *refl.* To restrain oneself ME. †**c.** *intr.* To refrain *from*; occas. const. inf., or *trans.* with gerund –1817. **2.** To keep back; to keep in one's possession (what belongs to, is due to, or is desired by another); to refrain from granting or giving ME. †**3.** To detain; to keep in bondage, in custody, or under control –1714.

1. What cause with-holds you then to mourne for him? SHAKS. Had not some awe of the company.. withheld his rage FIELDING. **2.** From such an inference, I must..w. my assent 1794. [Parliament's] acknowledged power to give or to w. supplies 1861. Hence **Withhe·ld, -ho·lden** (*arch.*) *ppl. adjs.* kept or held back. **Withho·lder.**

Within (wiðiˑn), *adv.*, *prep.* (*adj.*) [Late OE. *wiþinnan*, f. *wiþ* WITH *prep.* + *innan* INNE, the second element being assim. to IN *adv.* in ME.] **A.** *adv.* **1.** In the inner part or interior, or on the inner side (of a receptacle or other material thing). **b.** In the interior of the body or some part of it ME. **c.** In this writing or document; herein. *Obs.* exc. *techn.* late ME. **2. a.** In the limits of, or in the inner part of, a space or region, esp. a city or country ME. **b.** In (or into) the house or dwelling, indoors; also, in the inner part of the house, in an inner chamber; *Theatr.* (esp. in stage-directions) behind the scenes ME. **3.** *fig.* In the inward being; in the mind, soul, or heart; inwardly OE. **4.** Preceded by *from*, in various senses 1489.

1. b. Why should a man whose bloud is warme w., Sit like his Grandsire, cut in Alabaster? SHAKS. **2. b.** Apartments furnished for a single gentleman. Inquire w. DICKENS. **3.** Be suche wiþ-ynne, as ȝe outward seme 1421.

B. *prep.* **1.** In the inner part or interior of, inside of. (*a*) as a mere synonym of IN *prep.* I. 1 (*arch.*) ME. (*b*) with emphasis on the restriction or confinement by limits or boundaries: In the limits of, not outside or beyond ME. **b.** In (an enclosure or enclosing boundary); so as to be included, contained, surrounded, or confined by. late ME. (*b*) Appended to names of places lying within a certain boundary or area, as *Bishopsgate W.* (i.e. w. the walls of London) 1598. **c.** On the inner (esp. landward) side of; further in than. Now *rare* or *Obs.* 1743. **d.** *transf.* In the membership of (a class, society, etc.); (in predicate) included in, forming a part of 1697. **2.** To the interior of; into. *Obs.* or *arch.* ME. †**3.** In or into the midst of, among, with; *spec.* in the house of –1609. **4.** *transf. W. onself* (*itself*, etc.): (*a*) so as to be self-contained or independent (now *dial.*) 1518; †(*b*) in self-command or self-control –1606; (*c*) without external supply or aid (now *dial.*) 1738; (*d*) not beyond one's normal capacity of exertion; without strain 1737. **5.** *fig.* In the (inner) being, soul, or mind of OE. **6.** In the limits of (a period of time); most usu., before the end of, after not more than; also, since the beginning of; *gen.* in the course of, during ME. †**b.** (without ref. to limits) At some time during –1651. **7.** Not beyond or above (a specified or implied amount or degree); so as not to exceed or surpass; *esp.* in expressions of a small difference or margin of error from a larger amount: = with a difference of not more than (so much) above or, usu., below. late ME. **b.** Not beyond or outside (a specified distance); nearer or not farther away than 1440. **8.** In expressions referring to the physical range of some action or perception: Not beyond, not farther than the extent of: as *w. reach*, near enough to reach, or to be reached 1533. **b.** Inside the guard, defence, or point of; *Fencing*, on the inside of (one's sword, arm, etc.). Now *rare* or *Obs.* 1565. **9.** *fig.* In the extent of (something abstract figured as a region, or as having extension); *esp.* in the scope or sphere of action of (authority, knowledge, a law, etc.) 1493.

1. (*a*) Her head leaning on one side w. her hand STERNE. **b.** *W. board* (Naut.), in the inside of a ship. (*b*) The united parishes of Saint Simon Without, and Saint Walker W. DICKENS. **2.** I would Haue suncke the Sea w. the Earth SHAKS. **5.** *W. oneself*, spec. (after *say, think*, etc.) = in thought, mentally, without outward expression. **6.** The Hours w. which Marriages may be lawfully solemnized 1918. **b.** *Hen. V*, I. ii. 60. **7.** She has a tall Daughter w. a Fortnight of Fifteen STEELE. Determined to live w. my income 1783. **8.** *W. call*, near enough to hear a call. *W. sight* or *hearing*, near enough to see or hear, to be seen or heard. **b.** Some get w. him, take his sword away SHAKS. **9.** A written warranty w. the meaning of the above section 1891.

C. *adj.* That is within; †(of a letter or document) enclosed (*rare*) 1748.

†Withi·n-doo:r, *adv. phr.* (*a.*) 1579. = next –1821.

Speak within door, 'do not clamour so as to be heard beyond the house' (J.).

Withi·n(-)doors, *adv. phr.* (*adj., sb.*) *arch.* 1581. In (or into) the house. **b.** (with hyphen) †*attrib.* or as *adj.* = INDOOR 1; also as *sb.* that which is, or those who are, indoors 1612.

Withi·nside, *adv., prep.* Now *arch.* or *dial.* 1595. [f. WITHIN + SIDE *sb.*[1], after *inside*.] **A.** *adv.* **1.** On the inner side. **2.** In (or to) the inner part or interior (*of*) 1598. **B.** *prep.* = INSIDE *prep.* 1686. So **Withi·nsides** *adv.* (*arch.* or *dial.*) 1891.

Without (wiðau·t), *adv., prep., conj.* [Late OE. *wiþūtan*, f. *wiþ* WITH *prep.* + *ūtan* from the outside.] **A.** *adv.* Outside: opp. to WITHIN *adv.* Now only *literary* and somewhat *arch.* **1.** On the outside or outer surface (of a material thing); externally. **2.** Outside (or out of) the place mentioned or implied; *esp.* outside the house or room; out of doors OE. **b.** *transf.* Outside of a class, body, or community; in an alien or foreign community. (Now only in echoes of 1 *Cor.* 5:12.) ME. **3.** *fig.* and *gen.* Outside of the inward being, soul, or mind; with regard to external actions or circumstances; sometimes, in outward appearance as opp. to inward reality OE. **4.** Preceded by *from*; in above senses. late ME.

2. b. *Those* (*that are*) *w.* = 'outsiders'. **3.** Then you will be at ease w. and at peace within 1832.

B. *prep.* **I.** Outside of, beyond: opp. to WITHIN *prep.* Now only *literary* or *arch.* **1.** Outside of, on or at the outside of, in the space external to (a space, receptacle, enclosing boundary, etc.) OE. **b.** (with verb of motion). So as to be outside of, out of. *Obs.* or *arch.* OE. **c.** On the outer side of; further out than; beyond 1623. **2.** *transf.* and *fig.* Outside of, not in the limits of, external(ly to OE. **†3.** Beyond the extent of, outside the range of (some action or perception); beyond the scope of sphere of action of –1809. **4.** Used *absol.* by ellipsis of obj., in opposition to *within* (or *in*) prep. ME.

1. The church of S[t]. Agnes w. the City BERKELEY. **3.** Conjectures of things w. our knowledge 1676. **4.** Placez within the shire of Couentre & withoute 1480.

II. Expressing absence, privation, or negation: opp. to WITH *prep.* II. **1.** With absence of; not with the presence or addition of; not having with it or with one, not accompanied by (a thing or person) ME. **2.** In a state of not possessing (a part, an advantage, a possession of any kind); in want of, destitute of, lacking ME. **b.** Not with (something that might be given or obtained); not getting or receiving, or having got or received ME. **c.** In the construction of certain verbs: see Do *v.* V. 6, Go *v.* VI. 1458. **3.** With no use, employment, or action of (an instrument, means, etc.): with no action or agency of (a person); *esp.* with no co-operation of, or support from ME. **4.** (with obj. an abstract thing, as a quality, action, etc.): **a.** (depending on or referring to a verb). With absence or lack of, or freedom from; often forming phrases equivalent to neg. advs., e.g. *w. end* = endlessly, *w. success* = unsuccessfully, etc. ME. **b.** (depending on or referring to a sb.) Characterized by absence of, lacking or free from: often forming phrases equivalent to neg. adjs., e.g. *w. end* = endless, etc. ME. **c.** With no possibility of; so, or such, as not to admit of ME. **5.** Followed by a gerund or vbl. sb. in *-ing*: = 'so as not to' or 'and not' with the corresp. vb., or 'not' with the pres. pple. ME. **b.** By ellipsis of the gerund: Not counting, leaving out of account. *colloq.* 1871. **6.** With conditional implication (mostly with neg., expressed or implied): If one have (or had) not, if there be (or were) not, in the absence of, in default of ME. **7.** With ellipsis of the obj. Now *colloq.* (exc. in contrast with *with*). late ME. **b.** *slang.* in ref. to liquor: Not mixed with sugar 1835. **8.** Qualified by a negative: *not w.* = not lacking, with or having some (implying or suggesting a somewhat slight or not very great amount) 1596.

1. There is no fyre w. some smoke 1546. If you can live w. me 1877. **2.** I do believe you are better w. the money GEO. ELIOT. **b.** They are all Guilty of Felony, w. Benefit of the Clergy 1723. **3.** Imprisoned for burying a Catholic w. a minister 1592. Withouten wind, withouten tide, She steddies with upright keel COLERIDGE. *W. book*: without authority; also lit. without the aid of a book, from memory, by rote; hence (with hyphen) attrib. or as adj., recited w. book or from memory; Weele haue..no withoutbooke Prologue faintly spoke After the Prompter SHAKS. **4.** I hope I may say it w. vanity 1779. He..let her go w. a word 1881. **c.** These wounds..are w. cure JOHNSON. **5.** I can hardly stir abroad w. catching cold 1734. **b.** My father has enough to do to keep the rest, w. me GEO. ELIOT. **6.** Noþer man ne womman schulde be punsched wiþ oute gilt 1387. **7.** You must have given him some encouragement... A man wouldn't offer to lend a lady his opera-glasses w. 1898.

C. *conj.* (or in *conj. phr.*) **1.** The prep. governing a clause introduced by *that*, so that *w. that* becomes a conjunctional phr. **a.** Without its being the case that. Now *rare* or *Obs.* 1450. **†b.** *W. that* (or *this*) *that*: legal phr. introducing an exception, *spec.* in pleading [tr. law-Fr. *sans ceo que*], a form, obs. since 1852, whereby a defendant asserted special matter of exception or justification against the plaintiff's claim while reserving his denial of the whole cause of action –1824. **2.** Hence, by omission of *that*, simply as a conjunction: If..not, except, unless. In later use *colloq.* or *arch.*, and now chiefly *illiterate*. late ME.

2. I'm but a working woman, and cannot live w. I gets my due 1814.

†Withou·t doo:r, *adv. phr.* (*adj.*) ME. = next –1739. **b.** *attrib.* or as *adj.* = OUT-DOOR *a.*; also *transf.* or *fig.* –1611.

Withou·t doo:rs, *adv. phr.* (*adj.*) *Obs.* or *rare arch.* 1617. **1.** Out of doors, outside the house, in the open air. **2.** *transf.* and *fig.* Outside the community (family, nation, etc.) 1697. **3.** *attrib.* or as *adj.* = prec. b. 1654.

Withou·tside, *adv.* and *prep.* Now *rare* or *Obs.* 1578. [f. WITHOUT + SIDE *sb.*[1], after *outside*.] **A.** *adv.* **1.** On the outer side or surface. **2.** In (or to) the place or space without 1700. **3. W. of,** *prep. phr.* = *outside of* 1638. **B.** *prep.* = A. 3. 1686.

Withstand (wiðstæ·nd, wiþ-), *v.* Pa. t. and pa. pple. **withstood.** [OE. *wiþstandan*; see WITH-.] **1.** *trans.* To stand or maintain one's or its position against; to offer resistance to: often with implication that the resistance is successful or effectual. **b.** To resist the attraction, influence or cogency of; occas. to abstain from (doing something) 1725. **2.** To stand in the way of; to oppose or hinder the performance, operation, or progress of. *Obs.* or merged in 1. late ME. **3.** *intr.* To offer resistance or opposition OE.

1. To w. your enemyes in tyme of nede 1434. And sturdy strokes he did w. 1558. Rage must be withstood SHAKS. **2.** I hope you will not w. your own preferment FIELDING.

Withwind (wi·þwəind). Now *dial.* [OE. *wiþowinde, wiþe-*, f. *wiþo-, wiþe-* (related to WITHE) + *winde* WIND *sb.*[2]] Bindweed, *Convolvulus arvensis* or *C. sepium*; also *C. soldanella* (Sea W.). Applied also to other climbing plants, e.g. dodder, smilax.

Withy (wi·ði). [OE. *wiþig* (cf. OHG. *wīda* (G. *weide*), ON. *víðir* willow); see WITHE.] **1.** A willow of any species: sometime *spec.* the osier willow, *Salix viminalis*. **b.** With qualification, applied to various species of willow. late ME. **2.** A flexible branch of a willow, esp. as used for tying or binding, as a halter, etc.; any similar flexible branch or twig; a leash, hoop, or the like made of a w. late ME.

Withywind (wi·ðiwəind). Now *dial.* 1578. [Alteration of WITHWIND, after prec.] = WITHWIND.

Witless (wi·tlės), *a.* Now only *literary* and somewhat *arch.* [OE. *witlēas*; see WIT *sb.* and -LESS.] **1.** Lacking wisdom or sense; not guided by reason; foolish, heedless ME. **2.** Mentally deficient or deranged; crazy, out of one's wits OE. **3.** Deficient in understanding; having undeveloped or imperfect intellectual power; stupid, dull-witted 1562. **b.** Not understanding (something specified or implied); inapprehensive 1614. **4.** Not knowing; unaware, unconscious *of* 1584. **5.** Devoid of wit (*rare*) 1753.

1. I was witlesse, wanton, fond, and yong 1559. **4.** Guiltlesse and witlesse of the crime 1597. **5.** Solemn dinners,..and w. tea-parties 1859. Hence **Wi·tless-ly** *adv.*, **-ness.**

Witling (wi·tliŋ). 1693. [f. WIT *sb.* + -LING[1] 2.] A petty wit; one who fancies himself a wit; one who utters light or feeble witticisms.

‖**Witloof** (wi·tlōf). 1885. [Du. lit. 'white leaf'.] = CHICORY.

Witness (wi·tnės), *sb.* [OE. *witnes*, f. *wit* WIT *sb.* + *-nes* -NESS.] **†1.** Knowledge, understanding, wisdom –1482. **2.** Attestation of a fact, event, or statement; testimony, evidence OE. **b.** Applied to the inward testimony of the conscience; after 2 *Cor.* 1:12. ME. **3.** Testimony by signature, oath, etc. Chiefly in phr. *in w. of, whereof*, etc. ME. **4.** One who gives evidence in relation to matters of fact under inquiry; *spec.* one who gives or is legally qualified to give evidence upon oath or affirmation in a court of justice or judicial inquiry OE. **5.** One who is called on, selected, or appointed to be present at a transaction, so as to be able to testify to its having taken place; *spec.* one who is present at the execution of a document and subscribes it in attestation thereof (*attesting* or *subscribing w.*) ME. **†b.** A sponsor or god-parent at baptism (orig. in Puritan use) –1837. **6.** One who is or was present and is able to testify from personal observation; one present as a spectator or auditor ME. **b.** In asseverative formulæ, in which a deity or a person is invoked as one who is cognizant of a fact; as *God is my w. that*... Chiefly in phr. *to call* or *take to w.*: to call upon or appeal to as one's surety; to swear by. ME. **7.** *fig.* Something that furnishes evidence or proof of the thing or fact mentioned; an evidential mark or sign, a token ME. **b.** Introducing a name, designation, phrase, or clause denoting a person or thing that furnishes evidence of the fact or exemplifies the statement. (After L. *teste*.., Fr. *témoin*..) ME. **c.** *spec.* In textual criticism, a manuscript or an early version which is regarded as evidence of authority for the text. (Usu. in *pl.*) 1853. **8.** One who testifies for Christ or the Christian faith, esp. by death; a martyr. *Obs.* exc. as literal rendering of Gr. *μάρτυς* MARTYR. late ME.

2. b. May we with..the witnesse of a good conscience, pursue him with any further reuenge? SHAKS. **3.** In witnesse whereof I have hereunto set my hand and seal 1658. **4.** False witnesses are much cheaper than in Christendom 1718. *transf.* Well, let my Deeds be witnesse of my worth SHAKS. *Hostile w.*, one who gives evidence adverse to the party by whom he is called. *Ultroneous w.*, see ULTRONEOUS b. **6.** No man might haue accesse to him, nor speake w[t] him without a witnesse 1560. I..stood the helpless w. of thy fate POPE. **b.** The tall boy..called those about him to w. that he had only shouted in a whisper DICKENS. **7. b.** Nature oftentimes recompenceth deform'd bodies with excellent wits. Witnesse Æsop. FULLER. And novels (w. ev'ry month's review) Belie their name, and offer nothing new COWPER.

Phrases. *In w.*, as a testimony or piece of evidence (*rare* or *Obs.* exc. as in 3). *To bear w.*, (said prop. of a person, a book, etc.) to give oral or written testimony or evidence; hence *fig.* to furnish or constitute evidence or proof. *To bear* (one) *w.*, to corroborate one's statement or be a witness of one's action. †*To take w. of*, to call or take to w. (see 6 b). *With a w.*, with clear evidence, without a doubt, 'and no mistake' (*Obs.* or *rare arch.*). *attrib.* and *Comb.*: **w. action,** an action in which witnesses are summoned, as dist. from one in which only matters of law are argued; **-box,** an enclosed space in which a w. is placed while giving evidence; **-stand** *U.S.*, the place where a w. is stationed while giving evidence.

Witness (wi·tnės), *v.* ME. [f. prec.] **1.** *trans.* To bear witness to (a fact or statement); to furnish oral or written evidence of. **b.** *transf.* Of a document: To furnish formally attested evidence of 1474. **c.** *fig.* To furnish evidence or proof of; to be a sign or mark of, betoken. late ME. †**d.** To give evidence of by one's behaviour; to make evident –1728. **e.** To show forth evidence of or as to (an object of allegiance) by faithful speech or conduct; to be a witness for. Now *rare* or *Obs.* 1526. **2.** *intr.* To bear oral or written witness; to testify. Now usu. with *to* or *against*. ME. **3.** *trans.* **a.** To give formal or sworn evidence of (a fact, etc.); to depose in evidence. Now *rare*. ME. **b.** To attest formally by signature; to sign (a document) as a witness of its execution. Also *absol.* ME. **c.** To be formally present as a witness of (a transaction). late ME. **4.** (*transf.* from 3 c.) To be a witness, spectator or auditor of (something of interest, importance, or special concern); to experience by personal (esp. ocular) observation; to see with one's own eyes. (In loose writing often used merely as a synonym of 'see'.) 1582. **b.** *fig.* Of a place, time, etc.: To be associated with (a fact or event); to be the scene or setting of; to 'see' 1785.

1. c. Thy face, and thy behauiour, Which..Witnesse good bringing vp SHAKS. And there it stands unto this day To w. if I lie MACAULAY. **4.** Never did I w. a more melancholy scene of devastation SOUTHEY. Large crowds witnessed their departure, but no demonstration occurred 1912. **b.** These fertile plains..once witnessed the defeat and death of a Gothic monarch 1813. Hence **Wi·tnessable,** *a.* (*rare*) that may be witnessed. **Wi·tnesser** (now *rare*), one who witnesses, a witness.

Witney (wi·tni). 1716. A heavy loose woollen material with a nap, manufactured and made up into blankets at Witney, a town in Oxfordshire; also, formerly, a kind of cloth or coating made there. Also *attrib.*, esp. in *W. blanket*.

Witted (wi·tėd), *a.* late ME. [f. WIT *sb.* + -ED[2].] Having wit or wits (of a specified quality or amount): in parasynthetic comb. with an adj., as *dull-*, HALF-WITTED, *quick-*, *sharp-*, *slow-w.*

A quick-w. though not whole-w. lad 1904.

Wittichenite (wi·tikĕnəit). 1868. [– G. *wittichenit*, f. *Wittichen* in Baden, where found; see -ITE[1] 2 b.] *Min.* Native sulphide of bismuth and copper.

Witticism (wi·tisiz'm). 1677. [irreg. f. WITTY, after *criticism* (Dryden).] A piece of wit; a witty saying or remark. In earlier use often *contempt.*, or applied esp. to a joke made at another's expense, a jeer.

Maternal witticisms upon his uncouth appearance MARIA EDGEWORTH. Hence **Wi·tticize** *v. intr.*, to utter witticisms.

Wittily (wi·tili), *adv.* ME. [f. WITTY *a.* + -LY[2].] †**1.** Intelligently, cleverly; wisely discreetly, sensibly –1825. **2.** In a manner characterized by wit; in a cleverly amusing way; with smart jocosity 1553.

1. W. wicked SIR T. BROWNE. Dr. Pritchard.. preached..very allegorically..yet very gravely and wittily EVELYN. **2.** In conversation w. pleasant, and pleasantly gamesome SIDNEY.

Wittiness (wi·tinės). 1533. [f. WITTY *a.* + -NESS.] The quality or character of being witty.

Witting (wi·tiŋ), *vbl. sb. Obs.* exc. *dial.* late ME. [Partly (in forms †*witand*, †*wetand*) – ON. *vitand* in phr. *at minni, várri* (etc.) *vitand* to my, our (etc.) knowledge; partly f. WIT *v.*[1] + -ING[1].] **1.** The fact of knowing or being aware of something; knowledge, cognizance. Most freq. in phr. *at*, *by* (*etc.*) *one's w.* (cf. OFr. *a son escient*): to one's knowledge, as one knows. **2.** Knowledge obtained or (esp.) communicated; information, tidings; notice, warning. Chiefly in *to get* or *have w.* late ME.

Wi·tting, *ppl. a.* late ME. [f. WIT *v.*[1] + -ING[2].] **a.** *advb.* = WITTINGLY. **b.** Chiefly *predic.*: Aware, cognizant 1500. **c.** Conscious as an agent; that is consciously what the sb. denotes 1678. **d.** *transf.* of the action: Done consciously (and so with responsibility), deliberate 1553.

a. No man wyttyng and wyllyng wyl hurt hymselfe 1538. **d.** The notion of w. and wilful vice 1879.

Wittingite (wi·tiŋəit). 1868. [– G. *wittingit*, f. *Wittingi* in Finland; see -ITE[1] 2 b.] *Min.* A variety of neotocite.

Wittingly (wi·tiŋli), *adv.* ME. [f. WITTING *ppl. a.* + -LY[2].] With knowledge or awareness of what one is doing: knowingly, consciously; often implying 'designedly, deliberately'.

Wittol (wi·təl). *Obs.* or *arch.* [Late ME. *wetewold*, app. formed after *cokewold* CUCKOLD, with substitution of *wete* WIT *v.*[1] for the first part of the word.] **1.** A man who is aware of and complaisant about the infidelity of his wife; a contented cuckold. **b.** *transf.* (app. with pun on *wit-all.*) One who has little sense; a half-witted person 1588. **2.** *attrib.* That is a wittol; pertaining to or characteristic of a wittol; *transf.* half-witted 1604.

1. *Merry W.* II. ii. 313. Hence **Wi·ttolly** *a.* having the character, or characteristic, of a w.

Witty (wi·ti), *a.* [OE. *wit(t)iġ*, f. WIT *sb.* + -Y[1].] †**1.** Having wisdom, wise –1611. **2.** clever; skilful, capable. *Obs.* exc. *dial.* OE. †**b.** Crafty, cunning, wily, artful –1706. †**3.** *transf.* Showing or demanding intellectual ability; (later, esp. of discourse) clever, ingenious, or subtle in conception or expression –1700. †**b.** Skilfully devised for an evil purpose; (of torment, etc.) ingeniously contrived –1686. †**4.** *transf.* Showing, or springing from, good judgement or discernment; wise, discreet –1710. **5.** Possessing wit; capable of or given to saying (or writing) brilliant or sparkling things, esp. in an amusing way 1590. †**b.** Sharply critical, censorious, sarcastic –1748. **6.** Of speech or writing: Characterized by or full of wit; cleverly amusing, smartly facetious or jocular; †sarcastic 1588.

2. Iudges ought to be more Learned, then Wittie BACON. **b.** *Much Ado* IV. ii. 27. **3.** I wisedome dwell with prudence, and find out knowledge of w. inuentions *Prov.* 8:12. The Fallacies that are often concealed in florid, witty or involved Discourses LOCKE. **5.** I know a wench of excellent discourse, Prettie and wittie SHAKS. **b.** My Mother..says, I am too w.; Anglicè, too pert RICHARDSON. **6.** He told the wittiest stories in the world without omitting anything in them but the point LYTTON.

Witwall (wi·twǫl). Now *dial.* 1544. [– early mod. G. †*wittewal(e* (now *wiedewal*) = MLG. *wedewale* (early Flem. *widewael*), f. *wede* WOOD *sb.* + **wale* of obscure origin. Cf. WOODWALL.] †**1.** The Golden Oriole, *Oriolus galbula* –1678. **2.** The Green Woodpecker, *Gecinus viridis*, or the Greater Spotted Woodpecker, *Dendrocopus major* 1668.

Wive (wəiv), *v.* [OE. (*ġe*)*wīfian* = MLG., MDu. *wīven*; f. *wīf* WIFE.] **1.** *intr.* To take a wife, get married, marry. **2.** To be a wife, act as a wife (*rare*) 1583. **3.** *trans.* To take to wife, make one's wife, wed (a woman); *pa. pple.* made or become a wife, married (*to* a man) 1592. **4.** To furnish with a wife, obtain a wife for: chiefly in *pa. pple.* married (of a man). *Obs.* or *arch.* 1513. **5.** To become the wife of, marry (a man). *Obs.* or *arch.* 1621.

1. Ther as myn herte is set ther wol I wyue CHAUCER. **3.** It is no vulgar nature I have wived MEREDITH. **4.** 2 *Hen. IV*, I. ii. 61. Hence **Wi·ving** *vbl. sb.* taking a wife, marrying, marriage.

Wivern, var. sp. of WYVERN.

Wiwi[1] (wī·wī). 1842. [Maori, = 'rushes'.] A New Zealand rush used to make an outer covering for the roof and walls of a house.

Wi-wi[2] (wī·wī). *Austral. slang.* 1845. [– Fr. *oui, oui* yes, yes, taken as typical of the French language.] A Frenchman; as *pl.*, the French.

Wizard (wi·zəɹd), *sb.* and *a.* late ME. [Earliest forms *wis(e)ard, wissard*; f. ME. *wis* WISE *a.* + -ARD; the pronunc. with ĭ and z follows *wisdom.*] **A.** *sb.* †**1.** A philosopher, sage. Often *contempt.* –1841. **2.** A man who is skilled in occult arts; in later use, a man who practises witchcraft 1550. **b.** *transf.* and *fig.*: *esp.* a man who 'does wonders' in his profession; in recent use often trivially applied to an expert 1620. **c.** A witch-doctor or medicine-man 1845.

1. Therefore the antique wisards well inuented, That Venus of the fomy sea was bred SPENSER. **2.** The Star-led Wisards haste with odours sweet MILT. I call myself a w. as well; but that's only the polite term for conjurer 1851. **b.** *The W. of the North*, Sir Walter Scott.

B. *adj.* **1.** Having the powers or properties of a wizard; hence *gen.* having magical or witching power or influence 1579. **2.** Of, pertaining to, or associated with wizards or wizardry; hence *gen.* magic, enchanted, bewitched 1638.

2. Nor on the shaggy top of Mona high, Nor yet where Deva spreads her wisard stream MILT. Hence **Wi·zard** *v.* (*rare*) to practise wizardry upon, to bewitch. **Wi·zardly** *a.* (now *rare*) of, pertaining to, characteristic of, or resembling a w. or wizardry.

Wizardry (wi·zəɹdri). 1583. [f. WIZARD *sb.* + -RY.] **1.** The art or practice of a wizard or wizards; wizardly or magic skill; witchcraft. **2.** *fig.* 'Magical' or 'bewitching' art, power, or influence 1884.

Wizen (wi·z'n), *a.* 1786. [Clipped f. WIZENED.] = WIZENED 2.

Wizen (wi·z'n), *v.* [OE. *wisnian*, corresp. to OHG. *wesanēn*, ON. *visna*, f. Gmc. **wis-*, repr. by L. *viescere* wither.] **1.** *intr.* Of plants: To dry up, shrivel, wither. Also *transf.* of persons, their features, etc. **2.** *trans.* To cause to wither or shrivel. *Sc.* 1513.

Wizened (wi·z'nd), *a.* 1513. orig. *Sc.* and *north.* [f. prec. + -ED[1].] **1.** Of plants, foliage, etc.: Dried up, withered, shrivelled. **2.** Of persons or animals, their features, etc.: Shrunken and dried up, thin and shrivelled 1513.

1. The w. pomegranate HAWTHORNE. **2.** A w. old hen instead of the plump pullet you look for MEREDITH. *transf.* A w. old city hidden among the hills 1905.

Wo (wōᵘ), *int.* 1588. [var. of WHO *int.*] **1.** In *wo ho, wo ho ho, wo ha ho*: a falconer's call to a hawk; also *allus.* **2.** A call to a horse to stop. Also used in conjunction with other interjections, as *wo-back, wo-ho.* 1787.

2. I pulled very hard, and cried out, Wo! but he wouldn't: and on I went galloping for the dear life THACKERAY. Hence **Wo** *v. intr.* to call 'wo' to a horse.

Woa (wōᵘ), *int.* 1840. [var. of WHOA *int.*] = prec. 2. Hence **Woa** *v.* to stop (*trans.* and *intr.*) with the call of 'woa'.

Woad (wōᵘd), *sb.* [OE. *wād* = OFris. *wēd*, MLG., MDu. *wēt*, *weede*, OHG. *weit* (Du. *weede*, G. *waid*) :– WGmc. **waida*, **waisda* (whence med.L. *waida*, *waisdo*, *-da*, Fr. *guède*).] **1.** A blue dye-stuff prepared from the leaves of *Isatis tinctoria* powdered and fermented: now generally superseded by indigo. **2.** The plant *Isatis tinctoria*, formerly extensively cultivated for the blue colouring matter furnished by it; sometimes called *Dyer's* or *Garden W.* Also applied to other species of *Isatis*. OE. **b. Wild W.,** the plant *Reseda luteola* 1578.

1. Al the Britons doe dye themselves wyth woade, which setteth a blewish color uppon them 1563.

Comb.: †**w.-ashes,** (*a*) the ashes of burnt wine-lees, used by dyers; (*b*) the ashes of burnt wood used to make a lye. Hence **Woad** *v. trans.* to dye, colour, or stain with w., sometimes (in dyeing) as a ground for another colour; to treat with w., in dyeing. **Woa·der** (*rare*), a dyer with w.; a cultivator of w.

Wobble, wabble (wǫ·b'l), *sb.* 1699. [f. next.] The action or an act of wobbling; an unsteady rocky motion or movement. **b.** *pl.* (*Austral.*) A disease in cattle caused by eating the leaves of the palm-tree 1895.

Wobble, wabble (wǫ·b'l), *v.* 1657. [corresp. to LG. *wabbeln*, ON. *vafla* (synon. with *vafra* WAVER *v.*), f. Gmc. base **wab-*; see WAVE *v.*, WAVER *v.*, -LE.] **1.** *intr.* Of a person or animal: To move from side to side unsteadily or with uncertain direction. **b.** Of a piece of mechanism, a top, a missile, etc. 1677. **c.** To shake or quiver like a jelly or fleshy body 1748. **d.** To move unsteadily from side to side or backwards and forwards (without progression) 1858. **2.** *fig.* To hesitate or waver between different opinions or courses of action; to be inclined to favour first one side and then the other 1884. **3.** *trans.* To cause to move unsteadily from side to side 1831.

1. Such a figure *I* never saw on a horse!..bumping when she trots, and wobbling when she canters 1856. **c.** Her chin wobbled pathetically 1875.

Comb.: **w.-saw,** a circular saw mounted askew on its spindle so as to cut a groove wider than its own thickness. Hence **Wo·bbler,** one who or that which wobbles. **Wo·bbly** *a.* inclined to w.

Wodenism (wō^{u}·dəniz'm). *rare.* 1891. [f. *Woden* (see ODINISM) + -ISM.] Odinism.

Wodge (wǫdʒ). *dial.* and *colloq.* 1860. Also **wadge.** [Expressive alt. of WEDGE *sb.*] A lumpy bundle or mass. Hence **Wo·dgy** *a.*

Woe (wō^{u}), *int.*, *adv.*, *sb.*, *a.* [Com. IE. interjection, used as a natural exclam. of lament; OE. *wā* (also *wǣ*), corresp. to OFris., OS., MLG. *wē*, (M)Du. *wee*, OHG. *wē* (G. *weh*), ON. *vei*, *væ*, Goth. *wai*, and Gr. *οὐαί, οὐά, οᾶ*, L. *væ*, Lett. *wai*, W. *gwæ*. Cf. WAIL *v.* WELLAWAY.] **A.** *int.* and *adv.* **I.** As an exclam. of grief or lamentation: = Alas! *arch.* **II.** Construed with dat. or its equivalent. **1.** In prophetic or denunciatory utterances, as *w. be to us* = may affliction or distress light upon us; *w. is him* = cursed is he. *Obs.* or *arch.* OE. **2.** In merely declaratory statements of the type of ME. *him is* (*full*) *wo* = he is (much) distressed or grieved. *Obs.* exc. in *w. is me*: I am distressed, afflicted, unfortunate, grieved (now *arch.* and *dial.*). OE. **3.** *W. worth*: may evil befall or light upon; a curse upon: freq. in phr. *w. worth the day*, (*the while, the time*). *arch.* ME. **b.** Similarly, *W. betide you* (etc.): In mod. use colloq. = You (etc.) will get into trouble (if..). late ME. **4.** Without vb. OE. †**5.** *To do* or *work* (a person) *w.*: to inflict distress or trouble upon; to do harm to OE.

1. W. is him whose bed is made in hell 1636. **3.** Then they all wept again, and cryed out: Oh, Wo worth the day BUNYAN. *W. worth me!* used occas. = *W. is me.* **4.** Then w. mine eyes vnlesse they beautie see GREENE. Now wae to thee, thou cruel lord, A bluidy man I trow thou be BURNS.

B. *sb.* **1.** A condition of misery, affliction, or distress; misfortune, trouble. *poet.* or *rhet.* ME. **b.** in conjunction with *weal* ME. **c.** In particularized use: chiefly *pl.*, Misfortunes, troubles, griefs. late ME. **2.** Sorrow, grief, anguish (as a state of mind or feeling). *Obs.* or merged in 1. ME. **3.** An utterance of the word 'woe' in denunciation; an anathema, curse. late ME.

1. The Fruit Of that Forbidden Tree, whose mortal tast Brought Death into the World, and all our w. MILT. **c.** One w. makes another w. seeme lesse DRAYTON. **3.** The wo denounced against our original mother SCOTT.

C. *adj.* (orig. and chiefly predic.) **1.** Grieved, wretched, miserable, sorrowful. *Obs.* exc. *Sc.* and *n. dial.* ME. **b.** attrib. *Obs.* or *dial.* 1670. †**2.** Of an event, situation, etc.: Woeful, miserable, 'sorry' –1795.

1. An' mony a time my heart's been wae BURNS. Poor Queen!..I was wae to look at her, wae to think of her MRS. CARLYLE. She was not there, and my heart is w. R. BRIDGES. **b.** I am a w. woman this heavy day 1778. **2.** Oh! woe it is to think So many men shall never see the sun Go down! SOUTHEY.

Woe-begone (wō^{u}·bĭgǫn), *a.* (*sb.*) ME. [From constructions in which an object is governed by a compound tense of BEGO *v.* (q.v., sense 4), as *me is woe begone* = woe has beset me.] **1.** 'Beset with woe'; oppressed with misfortune, distress, sorrow, or grief. *Obs.* or *arch.* **2.** Of persons in respect of their looks, manner, etc.: Exhibiting or betraying a state of distress, misery, anguish, or grief 1802. **b.** as *sb.* A w. creature 1879.

1. Euen such a man, so faint, so spiritlesse, So dull, so dead in looke, so woe-be-gone SHAKS. **2.** A poor mendicant..old and woebegone LOCKHART. *transf.* It was the most woebegone excavation..you ever saw 1862.

Woeful (wō^{u}·fŭl), *a.* ME. [f. WOE *sb.* + -FUL. (Revived or newly formed *c* 1750.)] **1.** Full of woe; afflicted with sorrow, distress, or misfortune; sorrowful, mournful. **2.** Of times, places, etc.: Fraught with woe, affliction, or misery; miserable ME. **3.** In weakened or trivial senses: Such as to excite commiseration or dissatisfaction; 'grievous'; 'pitiful', 'deplorable', 'wretched' 1619. **4.** In comb. with another adj., as *w.-wan*; also advb. = woefully 1750.

1. A w. wight was he 1802. **2.** The wofulest anniversary in the whole year HAWTHORNE. **3.** What woful stuff this madrigal would be POPE. So **Woe·fulness. Woe·some** (*Sc.* **waesome**) *a.* woeful.

Woefully (wō^{u}·fŭli), *adv.* 1390. [f. prec. + -LY².] **1.** Miserably; mournfully, sadly. *arch.* **2.** Grievously, deplorably, 'sadly' 1648.

2. Thou hast once wofully, irreparably deceived me GOLDSM.

Woggle (wǫ·g'l), *v.* 1648. Variant of WAGGLE *v.*

Wogul, vogul (w-, vō^{u}·gul). 1780. [Russian *vogúl*, G. *Wogul*, etc.] One of a tribe of the Ugrian stock inhabiting Tobolsk and Perm.

Woke, pa. t. and pa. pple. of WAKE *v.*

Wo·ken, *ppl. a. rare.* 1649. [pa. pple. of WAKE *v.*] Awakened.

Wold (wō^{u}ld). [OE. (Anglian) *wald*, WS. *weald* (see WEALD) = OFris., OS., OHG. *wald* (Du. *woud*, G. *wald*) forest, ON. *vǫllr* untilled field, plain :– Gmc. **walþus*, perh. cogn. with WILD. After the early XVI it fell out of gen. use and was restricted to names of particular areas (e.g. Yorkshire Wolds), prob. once thickly wooded, whence it was generalized in literary use (sense 3) after *c*1600.] †**1.** Forest, forest and; wooded upland –1450. †**2.** A hill, down –1513. **3.** A piece of open country; a plain; in later use chiefly, an elevated tract of open country or moorland; also *collect. pl.* or *sing.* rolling uplands ME. **4.** Used in specific designations of certain hilly tracts in England, viz. the hill country of the East and North Ridings (*Yorkshire Wolds*), the Cotswold district, the hilly districts of Leicestershire and Lincolnshire 1472.

3. Swithold footed thrice the old SHAKS. On they went, through wild and over w. SCOTT. The long pure line of the rising w. 1905.

Wolf (wulf), *sb. Pl.* **wolves** (wulvz). [OE. *wulf* = OFris. *wolf*, OS. *wulf*, OHG. *wolf* (Du., G. *wolf*), ON. *ulfr*, Goth. *wulfs* :– Gmc. **wulfaz* :– IE. **wlqwos*, repr. also by L. *lupus*, Gr. *λύκος*, Skr. *vṛ́kas*.] **1.** A somewhat large canine animal (*Canis lupus*) found in Europe, Asia, and N. America, hunting in packs, and noted for its fierceness and rapacity. Also applied, with or without defining word, to various other species of *Canis* resembling or allied to this. **b.** In comparisons, with allusion to the fierceness or rapacity of the beast OE. **2.** A figure or representation of a wolf 1562. **b.** *Astron.* The constellation *Lupus* 1551. **3.** Applied to other animals in some way resembling wolves. **a.** (*a*) In S. Africa, a hyena; (*b*) a Tasmanian marsupial, *Thylacinus cynocephalus* 1812. **b.** A name for various voracious fishes (after Gr. *λύκος*, L. *lupus*) 1555. **c.** A name for various destructive insect larvæ, esp. that of the w.-moth, which infests granaries 1682. **4.** A person or being having the character of a wolf; one of a cruel, ferocious, or rapacious disposition OE. †**b.** Applied to a person, etc., that should be hunted down like a wolf –1638. **5.** As a type of a destructive or 'devouring' agency, esp. hunger or famine; often in such phrases as *to keep the w. from the door* (now always = to ward off hunger or starvation) 1470. **b.** Applied to a ravenous appetite or craving for food 1576. **6.** A name for certain malignant or erosive diseases in men and animals; *esp* = LUPUS 1. *Obs.* or *dial.* 1559. **7.** A name for apparatus of various kinds. †**a.** An ancient military engine with sharp teeth, employed for grasping battering-rams used by beseigers –1632. **b.** A kind of fishing-net 1725. **c.** *Textile Manuf.* A willow or willy 1875. **8.** *Mus.* [after G. *wolf*] **a.** 'The harsh howling sound of certain chords on keyed instruments, particularly the organ, when tuned by any form of unequal temperament' (Grove); a chord or interval characterized by such a sound 1788. **b.** In instruments of the viol class, a harsh sound due to faulty vibration in certain notes 1876.

1. The wolves howled from the prairies LONGF. **b.** Hog in sloth, Foxe in stealth, Wolfe in greedinesse SHAKS. The Assyrian came down like the w. on the fold BYRON. **3. b.** The Pike..is called the Wolfe of the water 1634. **4. b.** 3 *Hen. VI*, II. iv. 13. **5.** That Hee or Shee should have wherewith to support both,..at least to keep the Woolf from the door, otherwise 'twere a meer madnes to marry 1645.

Phrases. *To cry w.*, to raise a false alarm (in allusion to the fable of the shepherd boy who deluded people with false cries of 'Wolf!'). *To keep the w. from the door*: see 5. *A w. in a lamb's skin, in sheep's clothing*, etc., a person who conceals malicious intentions under an appearance of gentleness or friendliness (in allusion to *Matt.* 7: 15). *To see* or *have seen a w.* [= Gr. *λύκον ἰδεῖν*, etc.], to be tongue-tied (from the old belief that a man on seeing a w. lost his voice). *To wake a sleeping w.*, to invite trouble or disturbance.

attrib. and *Comb.* as *w. cub, -hunter, pack*; **w.-berry,** a N. Amer. shrub, *Symphoricarpus occidentalis*, allied to the snowberry; **-fish,** a large and voracious sea-fish, *Anarrhichas lupus*, having numerous sharp teeth and edible flesh; also applied to other fishes of the same genus; **-moth,** a moth, *Tinea granella*, infesting granaries; **-skin,** the skin or pelt of a w.; a garment, etc. made of this; **-spider,** a spider of the family *Lycosidæ*, which hunts after and springs upon its prey. **b.** Combs. with genitive: **wolf's claw,** club-moss.

Wolf (wulf), *v.* 1862. [f. prec.] **1.** *trans.* To eat like a wolf; to devour ravenously. **2.** To delude with false alarms 1910.

1. [She] used to w. her food with her fingers 1862.

Wo·lf-dog. 1652. **1.** Any of several large varieties of dog formerly kept for hunting wolves, *esp.* the Irish greyhound or wolf-hound. **2.** A cross of a domestic dog and a wolf 1736. **3.** *Alsatian w.*, the official name originally adopted by the Kennel Club for the German sheep-dog or shepherd-dog (*deutscher schäferhund*) 1924.

Wolffian (vǫ·lfiăn, wu·lfiăn), *a.* 1844. [f. name of K. F. *Wolff* (1733–94), German embryologist + -IAN.] *Anat.* and *Zool.* In *W. body*, the mesonephron or primitive kidney; either of the two renal organs of the embryo of vertebrates; so *W. duct*.

Wolf-hound. 1823. = WOLF-DOG 1.

Russian w. (or borzoi), a slender type with silky, usu. white, hair. *Irish w.*, a heavy type, resembling the deerhound, with a hard wiry coat.

Wolfian (vǫ·lfiăn, wu·lfiăn), *a.*¹ and *sb.*¹ 1791. [f. name of Christian *Wolf* or *Wolff* (1679–1754), German philosopher + -IAN.] **A.** *adj.* Pertaining to the philosophical system of Wolf, which was an eclectic adaptation of Leibnitzianism and scholasticism. **B.** *sb.* An adherent of this system.

Wo·lfian (see prec.) *a.*² and *sb.*² 1875. [f. name of F. A. *Wolf* (1759–1824). German philologist + -IAN.] **A.** *adj.* Of or pertaining to F. A. Wolf or his theory regarding the Homeric poems. **B.** *sb.* One who accepts this theory.

Wolfish (wu·lfiʃ), *a.* 1570. [f. WOLF *sb.* + -ISH¹.] **1.** Of or pertaining to a wolf or wolves. †**b.** Abounding in wolves. COLLINS. **2.** Characteristic of, befitting, or resembling that of a wolf 1674. **3.** Resembling a wolf, wolf-like 1775. **b.** Ravenously hungry. *U.S. colloq.* 1848.

2. The eyes of the three men, with a fierce and w. glare LYTTON. Hence **Wo·lfish-ly** *adv.*, **-ness.**

Wo·lfling. ME. [f. WOLF *sb.* + -LING¹.] A young or little wolf.

Wolfram (wu·lfrăm, vǫ·lfrăm). 1757. [– G. *wolfram*, gen. assumed to be an old miner's name, f. *wolf* WOLF + *rahm* cream or MHG. *rām* soot. Presumably orig. a pejorative term ('a kind of mock tin', 1757) with ref. to its inferiority compared with the tin which it accompanies; cf. *cobalt, nickel.*] **1.** *Min.* A native tungstate of iron and manganese. **2.** The metal tungsten, obtained from this 1845.

attrib.: **w. lamp, -steel** = TUNGSTEN *lamp, steel*; **-ochre** = TUNGSTITE.

Wolf's-bane (wu·lfsbē^{i}n), †**wolfbane.** 1548. [f. gen. of WOLF *sb.* + BANE *sb.*, rendering mod.L. *lycoctonum* – Gr. *λυκοκτόνον*, f. *λύκος* WOLF + *κτον-* (*κτεν-*) slay.] A plant of the genus *Aconitum*, esp. *A. lycoctonum*, with dull yellow flowers, occurring in mountainous regions in Europe. Also applied to *Arnica montana* (*winter w.*), and to the winter aconite, *Eranthis hyemalis*.

Wo·lf's-head, wolf-head. OE. **1.** The head of a wolf; a figure of this, e.g. as a heraldic bearing. **2.** *Old English Law.* A cry for the pursuit of an outlaw as one to be hunted down like a wolf; *transf.* an outlaw ME.

Wo·lfskin. late ME. The skin or pelt of a wolf, or a garment made of this.

Wo·lf's-milk. 1575. [Cf. LG. *wulfsmelk*, MHG. *wolfmilch* (G. *wolfs-*).] **1.** The sun-spurge, *Euphorbia helioscopia*, having an acrid milky juice. **2.** The milk of a wolf 1847.

Wollastonite (wu·lǝstǝnǝit). 1823. [f. name of W. H. *Wollaston* (1766–1828), chemist and physicist + -ITE^1 2 b.] *Min.* Native metasilicate of calcium; tabular spar.

Wolve (wulv), *v.* 1702. [f. inflexional stem of WOLF *sb.*] **1.** *intr.* (also with *it*). To behave like a wolf, play the wolf. **2.** Of an organ: To give forth a hollow wailing sound like the howl of a wolf, from deficient wind-supply 1864. So **Wo·lver** (*rare*), one who behaves like a wolf, a ravenous or savage creature; one who searches or hunts for wolves 1593.

Wolverene, -ine (wu·lvǝrīn). 1574. [Obscurely f. inflexional stem of WOLF *sb.*] **1.** The glutton (*Gulo luscus*), now esp. the N. Amer. variety. **2.** The fur of the wolverene 1596. **3.** A nickname for an inhabitant of Michigan. So *W. State*, Michigan. 1835.

†**Wo·lvish,** *a.* late ME. [f. *wolv-*, inflexional stem of WOLF *sb.* + -ISH^1.] = WOLFISH –1817.

The w. howl BLAKE. If superstition and despotism have been suffered to let in their woolvish sheep COLERIDGE.

Woman (wu·măn), *sb. Pl.* **women** (wi·mėn). [OE. *wifmon(n, -man(n*, pl. *wifmen(n*, f. *wif* woman, WIFE + *mon(n* MAN *sb.* A formation peculiar to English and not extant in the earliest period of OE., the primitive words being *wif* WIFE and *cwene* QUEAN. In the mod. period five pronuncs. of the sing. have been current: wu·măn, wū·măn, wɒ·măn, u·măn, ɒ·măn. The last four are now only in vulgar or dial. use; (u·măn) was in educated use in the early 19th c. The standard sing. form represents a divergence (due to the rounding influence of w) from the normal phonetic development, which is preserved in the (wi-) of the pl.] **1.** An adult female human being. **b.** *generically* without article: The female human being; the female sex. Hence gen. *woman's* = womanly, female, feminine. OE. **c.** *pl.* in pregnant use with ref. to (irregular) intercourse with women ME. **d.** As a mode of address. Now (exc. *dial.*) used chiefly derogatorily or joc. ME. **e.** With allusion to qualities attributed to the female sex, as mutability, proneness to tears, or physical weakness; also to their position of inferiority or subjection. late ME. **f.** (Now always with *the*.) The essential qualities of a woman; womanly characteristics; *occas.* the feminine side or aspect 1611. **g.** In contrast, explicit or implicit, with 'lady' 1788. †**h.** In the 16th and 17th cc. freq. with play on a pseudo-etymol. association with *woe* –1653. **2.** A female servant, *esp.* a lady's maid or personal attendant. Often *pl.* OE. **3.** †**a.** A lady-love, mistress. **b.** A kept mistress, paramour. ME. **4.** A wife. Now only *dial.* and *U.S.* 1450. **5.** The reverse of a coin, in ref. to the figure of Britannia upon it 1785.

1. I saw women acte, a thing that I neuer saw before 1611. A perfect W., nobly planned, To warn, to comfort, and command WORDSW. A girl she was not, but a w. of at least nine and twenty 1889. Provbs. A woman, asse, and walnut-tree, the more you beat, the better be 1639. Three Women make a Market 1659. *Little w.*, a female child; also, an affectionate or playful form of address to a girl or young w., esp. one in whom womanly qualities are conspicuous. *New w.* (Hist.), a w. of 'advanced' views, advocating the independence of her sex and defying convention. **b.** W. is the glory of all created existence:—But you, madam, are *more* than w.! RICHARDSON. **c.** Aboue all thynges let hym keepe hym self from Women 1577. **e.** Frailty, thy name is w. SHAKS. Don't make such a fuss; you're as bad as a w. 1850. **f.** Teach her to subdue The w. in her nature 1834. **g.** Defendant pleaded. . that the person described as a w. was in fact a lady 1847. **h.** A woman! As who saith, woe to the man! 1546. **2.** In Town I visit none but the Women of Quality FIELDING. From Mrs. Crouch, ma'am, her Grace's w. 1898. **4.** *Merry W.* II. ii. 305.

attrib. and *Comb.*, simple attrib. or appos. = 'feminine', 'womanly', 'female', as *w. friend, guard, helper, slave, wit*; **w.-boat** = *women's boat*; **-grown** *a.*, that has become a w.; **w. movement,** the movement for the emancipation of women, or the recognition and extension of women's rights; **-suffrage,** the right of women to vote in public affairs. **b.** Comb. with *woman's, women, women's*: **woman's, women's-boat,** a boat to be used by women only = OOMIAK; **women's courses** = CATAMENIA; **·women-house,** *Sc.* a building set apart for women only; **woman's man,** a lady's man, a gallant. Hence **Wo·mandom,** the realm of women, womankind. **Wo·manfully** *adv.* (after *manfully*) with womanly courage or perseverence; like a w. of spirit. †**Wo·manhead** = WOMANHOOD. **Wo·manism,** advocacy of or enthusiasm for the rights, achievements, etc. of women. **Woma·nity** (after *humanity*) *rare*, the normal disposition or character of womankind. **Wo·manless** *a.* without a w. or women; having or containing no women. **Wo·manness** (*rare*), womanliness.

Woman (wu·măn), *v.* 1595. [f. prec.] †**1.** Nonce-uses. **a.** *intr.* To become woman-like; with *it*, to behave as a woman. **b.** *trans.* To make like a woman in weakness or subservience. **c.** *pa. pple.* Accompanied by a woman. –1613. **2.** *trans.* To furnish or provide with women; to equip with a staff of women. (After MAN *v.*) 1706. **3.** To address (contemptuously) as 'woman': see prec. 1 d. 1740.

3. She call'd her another time Fat-face and woman'd her most violently RICHARDSON.

Wo·man-child. *Pl.* **wo·men-chi:ldren.** *arch.* 1558. A female child.

Wo·man-ha:ter. 1607. One who hates women, a misogynist.

Womanhood (wu·mănhud). late ME. [-HOOD.] **1.** The state or condition of being a woman. **b.** The state of being a grown woman; the period of life succeeding to girlhood 1608. **2.** The disposition, character, or qualities natural to a woman or womankind; womanliness. late ME. **3.** Women collectively, womankind 1523.

1. She. ., contrarie to Gods lawe, and the honest estate of w., was clothed in mans apparell 1568.

Womanish (wu·măniʃ), *a.* late ME. [-ISH^1 2.] **1.** Of or belonging to a woman or women; used or done by women. Now *rare*. **2.** Characteristic of or proper to a woman or women; womanly, feminine. late ME. **b.** In derogatory use. late ME. **3.** Resembling a woman, womanlike: in later use chiefly derogatory. late ME.

1. Spinning, weaving, and the like w. chares 1624. **2. b.** Her questions. . wer like to be but friuolous & womannish 1532. Hence **Wo·manish-ly** *adv.*, **-ness.**

Womanize (wu·mănǝiz), *v.* 1593. [f. WOMAN *sb.* + -IZE.] **1.** *trans.* To make a woman of (a man); *gen.* to render effeminate. †**2.** *intr.* To become womanlike; to behave like a woman –1736. **3.** To consort illicitly with women (*colloq.*) 1893. Hence **Wo·manizer,** one who goes after or consorts illicitly with women.

Womankind (wu·mănkǝind). late ME. [f. WOMAN *sb.* + KIND *sb.*] **1.** The female part of the human race; women in general. **2.** The women of a family, household, company, country, etc.; (one's) women-folk 1573. †**3.** A female human being; a woman –1823.

1. I do admire Of w. but one COWPER. **2.** The persecution which his w. had inflicted upon him THACKERAY.

Womanlike (wu·mănlǝik), *a.* and *adv.* 1440. [f. WOMAN *sb.* + -LIKE.] **A.** *adj.* Like, resembling, or characteristic of a woman or women; in derogatory use, womanish, effeminate. **B.** *adv.* In a manner characteristic of women, after the fashion of women; like a woman 1440.

Looking, w., straight on to the purpose she had in view 1857.

Wo·manliness. 1538. [f. next + -NESS.] The quality of being womanly; womanly character.

Womanly (wu·mănli), *a.* ME. [f. WOMAN *sb.* + -LY^1.] **1.** Possessing the attributes proper to a woman; having the qualities (as of gentleness, devotion, etc.) characteristic of women; also said of these qualities or of actions which exhibit them. late ME. **b.** In derogatory use, with ref. to the bad qualitie attributed to women ME. **2.** Having the character of, befitting or characteristic of, a woman as contrasted with a girl 1709. **3.** Belonging or proper to the female sex 1863.

1. b. Has she baffled me by some piece of w. jugglery? 1862. **2.** A very little girl. . wearing a w. sort of bonnet much too large for her DICKENS.

Wo·manly, *adv. Obs.* or *arch.* ME. [f. as prec.; see -LY^2.] In a womanly manner; like a woman.

Wo·man-se:rvant. 1529. A female servant.

Woman's rights. Also **women's rights.** 1840. The rights claimed by women of equal privileges and opportunities with men. Hence **Woman's (women's) righter,** a believer in or supporter of woman's rights.

Womb (wūm), *sb.* [OE. *wamb, womb* = OFris., MLG., MDu. *wamme* (Du. *wam*), OHG. *wamba, wampa* (G. *wamme*, dial. *wampe*), ON. *vǫmb*, Goth. *wamba*; of unkn. origin.] †**1.** = BELLY. **a.** The abdomen –1684. **b.** The stomach (as the receptacle of food) –1756. **2.** The uterus OE. **3.** *transf.* A hollow space or cavity, or something conceived as such (*e.g.* the depth of night) OE. **4.** *fig.* A place or medium of conception and development; a place or point of origin and growth 1593.

1. a. 2 *Hen. IV*, IV. iii. 25. **3.** Yee sootie coursers of the night, Hurrie your chariot into hels black wombe MARSTON. **4.** Some vnborne sorrow, ripe in fortunes wombe SHAKS. Hence **Womb** *v. trans.* to enclose as in a w. **Wombed** (wūmd) *a.* having a w. or belly (of a specified kind). **Womby** (wū·mi) *a.* (*rare*) having a w.-like cavity; hollow.

Wombat (wǫ·mbæt). 1798. [Native Australian name.] Any of the burrowing marsupials of the genus *Phascolomys*, native to S. Australia and Tasmania, characterized by a thick heavy body, short legs, and a general resemblance to a small bear.

Womenfolk (wi·mėnfōᵘk). 1833. [f. pl. of WOMAN *sb.* + FOLK.] **a.** Women collectively, womankind. Now *dial.* **b.** The women of a household, a party, or the like: *dial.* the female servants.

Womenkind (wi·mėnkǝind). late ME. [f. as prec. + KIND *sb.*] **1.** = WOMANKIND 1. **2.** = WOMANKIND 2. 1648.

1. This behaviour disgusted Mr. Bousfield with w. 1889. **2.** The old gentleman evidently took a secret pride in his w. 1852.

Won, wone (wɒn, wōᵘn), *v. Obs.* exc. *Sc.* and *n. dial.*, and *arch.* [OE. *wunian* dwell, continue, be accustomed or used = OFris. *wunia, wonia*, OS. *wunon, wonon*, OHG. *wonēn* (Du. *wonen*, G. *wohnen*), ON. *una*, Goth. **wunan* :- Gmc. **wunōjan*, **wunǣjan*, f. **wun-* **wen-* **wan-* (see WEAN *v.*, WEEN *v.*, WIN *sb.*^{2}, WISH *v.*).] **I. 1.** *intr.* To stay habitually, dwell, live (in a place or with some one). †**2.** To continue to be, remain; to have existence, live –1633. †**3.** *trans.* To dwell in, inhabit –1600. †**II.** *intr.* To be accustomed or used *to do* something –1642.

To be wont: see WONT *pa. pple.*

Won (wɒn), *ppl. a.* 1500. Pa. pple. of WIN *v.*

A w. battle SCOTT.

Wonder (wɒndǝɹ), *sb.* [OE. *wundor* = OFris. *wunder*, OS. *wundar*, OHG. *wuntar* (Du. *wonder*, G. *wunder*), ON. *undr*; of unkn. origin.] **I.** Something that causes astonishment. **1.** A marvellous object; a marvel, prodigy. **b.** Marvellous character or quality; marvels collectively ME. **c.** (*transf.* from II. 1.) The object of astonishment (usu. implying profound admiration) for a particular country, age, or the like 1591. **d.** A marvellous specimen or example (*of* something) 1721. **e.** *U.S.* = CRULLER 1848. **2.** A deed performed or an event brought about by miraculous or supernatural power; a miracle. *arch.* OE. †**b.** An extraordinary natural occurrence, esp. when regarded as supernatural or taken as an omen or portent. Chiefly *pl.* –1681. **3.** A marvellous act or achievement ME. **4.** *gen.* An astonishing occurrence, event, or fact; a wonderful thing ME.

1. *The seven wonders of the world* (= L. *septem mira, miracula*, or *spectacula*), the seven monuments regarded as the most remarkable structures of ancient times. *Nine days' w.*: see NINE *a.* **b.** Great things and full of w. in our eares MILT. **c.** She's the w. of the Court, And talke oth' Towne 1639. *World's w.*, the Marvel of Peru. **2.** *To do* or *work wonders*, to perform miracles. **3.** *To work, do* or *perform wonders*, to do marvellous acts or bring about marvellous results; hence *gen.* to do surprising things; Inspired by your Ladyship's approbation, my steward has really done wonders DISRAELI. **4.** Bee you in the Parke about midnight, . . and you shall see wonders SHAKS.

Phrases. *To a w.*, marvellously, wonderfully, marvellously well. (*Obs.* or *arch.*) *It is* (*was, were,* etc.) *no w.*, it is (etc.) not surprising; usu. with dependent *that-* or *if-* clause. Also, without vb., *No w. that, if*, or *though*; similarly *Small w. that* (etc.), *what w. if..?* Also interjectionally in (*and*) *no w.!, and what w.! The w. is..*, what is surprising is... *For a w.*, as an instance of a surprising fact; strange to say. *In the name of w.*, used with an interrogative word to give emphasis to a question.

II. 1. The emotion excited by the perception of something novel and unexpected, or inexplicable; astonishment mingled with perplexity or bewildered curiosity. Also, the state of mind in which this emotion exists. ME. †**b.** Profound admiration –1607. **2.** [f. WONDER *v.* 2.] A state of wondering (*whether*, etc.). *rare.* 1853.

1. Satan..Looks down with w. at the sudden view Of all this world at once MILT. **b.** *Macb.* I. iii. 92.

III. *attrib.* and *Comb.*, as *w.-book, -child, -story, -world; w.-loving, -struck* adjs.; *w.-monger* 1552.

†**Wo·nder,** *a.* ME. [repr. OE. *wundor* WONDER *sb.* in compounds, as *wundorcræft* marvellous skill or power.] Wonderful, wondrous, marvellous –1590.

Wonder (wɒ·ndəɹ), *v.* [OE. *wundrian*, f. WONDER *sb.*] **1.** *intr.* To feel or be affected with wonder; to be struck with surprise or astonishment, to marvel. Also *occas.* to express wonder in speech. **2.** Usu. with clause: To ask oneself in wonderment; to feel some doubt or curiosity (*how, whether, why*, etc.); to be desirous to know or learn ME. †**3.** *trans.* To regard with wonder; to marvel at –1821. **b.** impers. pass. *It is to be wondered* = it is to be wondered at. Now *rare* or *Obs.* 1654.

1. That to hymself..he seme a stoute felow and one to be wondered at 1549. I w. of this being heere together SHAKS. I w. that you will still be talking, signior Benedicke, no body markes you SHAKS. I w. at you RICHARDSON. He wondered to hear a Man of his Sense talk after that Manner ADDISON. *I shouldn't w.* (colloq.), I should not be surprised (*if*, etc.). **2.** *I w.!*, colloq. exclam. expressing doubt, incredulity, or reserve of judgement. Hence **Wo·ndering** *vbl. sb.* and *ppl. a.*, **-ly** *adv.*

Wo·nder, *adv. Obs.* or *arch.* (in later use *Sc.*) ME. [Partly OE. *wundor* WONDER *sb.* in compounds; partly OE. *wundrum*, advb. dat. pl. of *wundor*.] Wondrously, marvellously; exceedingly, very.

Wonderful (wɒ·ndəɹfŭl), *a.*, (*sb.*), and *adv.* [Late OE. *wunderfull*, f. WONDER *sb.* + -FUL.] **A.** *adj.* Full of wonder; such as to excite wonder or astonishment; marvellous; sometimes used trivially, = surprisingly large, fine, excellent, etc. **b.** *The w.*: that which is wonderful. †Also *sb. pl.* wonderful things. 1727.

Whereof ensued unto me..a wonderfull payne in my stomacke 1596. There be three things which are too wonderfull for me; yea foure, which I know not *Prov.* 30:18. He trimmed his whiskers, and put on a w. waistcoat 1880.

B. *adv.* Wonderfully. Now *dial.* late ME. Hence **Wo·nderful-ly** *adv.*, **-ness.**

Wonderland (wɒ·ndəɹlænd). 1790. [f. WONDER *sb.* + LAND *sb.*] **a.** An imaginary realm of wonder and faery. **b.** A country, realm, or domain which is full of wonders or marvels.

a. Alice's Adventures in Wonderland 'LEWIS CARROLL'. **b.** The w. of molecular physics 1903.

Wonderment (wɒ·ndəɹmĕnt). Chiefly *literary.* 1535. [f. WONDER *v.* + -MENT.] **1.** The or a state of wonder. **b.** An expression of wonder: chiefly in *to make a w.*, to express wonder 1553. **2.** An object of or matter for wonder; a wonderful thing 1542. **b.** A wonderful example or instance (*of* something) 1606. **3.** Wonderful quality 1596.

1. Whom all..gazd vpon with gaping w. SPENSER. **2.** It's a w. to me..how you got us off 1841.

†**Wo·nders,** *a.* and *adv.* ME. [gen. of WONDER *sb.*; a Scand. idiom: cf. MSw. *unders.*] = WONDROUS *a.* and *adv.* –1602.

Wo·nder-work. [OE. *wundorweorc*, f. WONDER *sb.* + WORK *sb.* In mod. use a new formation.] **1.** A marvellous or miraculous act; a miracle. **2.** A wonderful work or structure ME. **3.** Marvellous work or workmanship 1513.

2. Wonder-works of God and Nature's hand BYRON.

Wo·nder-wo:rker. 1599. [f. WONDER *sb.* + WORKER.] One who performs wonders; *esp.* a worker of miracles; a thaumaturge.

That he may be accounted a stupendious W., a Creatour of his Creatour HY. MORE. So **Wo·nder-wo:rking** *ppl. a.*

Wondrous (wɒ·ndrəs), *a.* and *adv. literary.* 1500. [Alteration of WONDERS *a.* by substitution of suffix -OUS, after *marvellous.*] Wonderful.

A faire young man, Of w. beautie SPENSER. Some of Serpent kinde W. in length and corpulence MILT.

B. *adv.* In a wondrous manner; to a wonderful degree 1557.

They tell me she is grown w. pretty RICHARDSON. Hence **Wo·ndrous-ly** *adv.*, **-ness.**

†**Wone,** *sb.*[1] [ME. *wune, wōne*, aphetic f. OE. *ġewuna*, corresp. to OS. *giwono*, OHG. *giwona*, f. Gmc. **ʒa-* Y- + **wun-* WON *v.*] **1.** Habit, custom –1562. **2.** A dwelling-place, abode; *spec.* this world –1748.

†**Wone,** *sb.*[2] ME. [midl. and southern var. of ME. *wāne*, which is prob. – ON. *ván* hope, expectation; derived (with lengthened vowel) f. Gmc. **wan-* (see WON *v.*), var. of **wǣn-* (see WEEN, WISH *v.*).] A dwelling place; a country –1570.

†**Wone,** *sb.*[3] ME. [app. – ON. *ván*; see prec.] **I.** Hope, expectation; opinion, belief –1583. **II.** Resources, abundance, wealth –1570.

Wone, *v.*: see WON *v.*

‖**Wonga-wonga** (wǫ·ŋgăwǫ·ŋgă). *Austral.* 1827. [Native name.] An Australian pigeon, *Leucosarcia picata.*

Wonky (wǫ·ŋki), *a. slang.* 1925. [Fanciful.] Shaky; ailing.

Wo·nning, wo·ning, *vbl. sb. Obs., dial.*, or *arch.* [OE. *wunung*, f. *wunian* WON *v.*; see -ING[1].] **1.** The action or state of dwelling or abiding. **2.** A place of habitation, dwelling-place OE. **3.** A dwelling-house or dwelling-room, dwelling, habitation OE.

Wont (wōᵘnt; *now chiefly U.S.* wɒnt), *sb. arch.* 1530. [Of doubtful origin; perh. due to a conflation of *it is my wone* (WONE *sb.*[1]) and *I am wont* (WONT *pa. pple.* and *ppl. a.*).] Habitual or customary usage, custom, habit.

As merry as that fellow Joyce could make us with his mad talking, after the old w. PEPYS. *Use and w.*: see USE *sb.* II. 3.

Wont (wōᵘnt; *now chiefly U.S.* wɒnt), *v. arch.* 1440. [f. WONT *pa. pple.* or back-formation from WONTED.] **1.** *trans.* To make (a person, etc.) accustomed or used *to.* **b.** *refl.* (rarely *intr.* for *refl.*) 1603. **2.** *intr.* To be wont or accustomed; to be in the habit of (doing that which is expressed by the inf.) 1547.

2. Talbot is taken, whom we w. to feare SHAKS. To bouze old Wine, mad Pindar wonted 1700.

Wont (wōᵘnt; *now chiefly U.S.* wɒnt), *pa. pple.* and *ppl. a.* [OE. *ġewunod*, pa. pple. of *ġewunian* WON *v.*] **A.** *pa. pple.* †**1.** Accustomed, used *to*, familiar *with* –1520. **2.** Conjugated with the verb 'to be' and const. inf.: Accustomed, used; in the habit of (doing something). Also without inf. OE. **b.** Conjugated with the verb 'to have': in *had w.*, had been accustomed. Now *rare.* 1594.

2. He was wonte to boste, brage, and to brace SKELTON. The longer your letters were the more they were woont to please mee 1647. All is going on as it was w. DICKENS.

†**B.** *ppl. a.* = WONTED B. –1596.

Won't (wōᵘnt), colloq. contraction of *wol(l not* = *will not.* Also as *sb.* = refusal.

Wonted (wōᵘ·ntĕd; *now chiefly U.S.* wɒ·ntĕd), *pa. pple.* and *ppl. a.* late ME. [Either f. WONT *sb.* + -ED[2], or an extension of WONT *pa. pple.* + -ED[1].] **A.** *pa. pple.* †**1.** = WONT *pa. pple.* 2. –1612. **2.** = WONT *pa. pple.* 1. Now *U.S.* 1610. **b.** *absol.* Made familiar with one's environment. Now *U.S.* 1610.

2. She was w. to the Place, she said, and would not Remove 1692.

B. *ppl. a.* Accustomed, customary, usual. Now *arch.* or *U.S.* late ME.

E'en in our Ashes live their w. Fires GRAY. Hence **Wo·nted-ly,** *adv.* (now *rare* or *Obs.*), **-ness** (*rare*).

Woo (wū), *v.* Now *literary.* [Late OE. *wōgian* intr. (also, trans., *āwōgian*), of unkn. origin.] **I.** *intr.* (or *absol.*) **1.** To solicit or sue a woman in love; to court, make love. **2.** To make solicitation or entreaty; to sue *for* 1615.

1. To wo is a pleasure in a young man, a fault in an old 1670.

II. *trans.* **1.** To sue to or solicit (a woman) in love, esp. with a view to marriage; to court ME. **2.** To move or invite by alluring means; to entreat or solicit alluringly. late ME. **3.** To sue for or solicit the possession or achievement of; hence *fig.* to 'court', 'invite', 'tempt' 1440.

1. Wooe hir, win hir, and weare hir LYLY. See that you come Not to wooe honour, but to wed it SHAKS. **2.** I..will w. my pillow For thoughts more tranquil BYRON.

Wood (wud), *sb.* [OE. *wudu*, later form of *widu, wiodu* = OHG. *witu*, ON. *viðr* :– Gmc. **widuz*, rel. to OIr. *fid* tree, wood, Gael. *fiodh*, W. *gwȳdd* trees.] **I.** †**1.** A tree –ME. **2.** A collection of trees growing more or less thickly together (esp. naturally, as dist. from a *plantation*), of considerable extent, usu. larger than a *grove* or *copse* (but including these), and smaller than a *forest*; a piece of ground covered with trees OE. **b.** *Woods and Forests*, more fully *Woods, Forests, and Land Revenues*, a department of the Civil Service 1803. **3.** Without article: Wooded country, woodland; trees collectively (growing together). Now *rare* exc. as in BRUSHWOOD 2, UNDERWOOD. OE. **4.** *transf.* and *fig.* A collection or crowd of spears or the like (suggesting the trees of a wood); *gen.* a collection, crowd, 'forest'. (After L. *silva.*) Now *rare* or *Obs.* 1584.

4. In such a w. of words MILT.

Phrases, etc. †*In a w.*, in a difficulty, trouble, or perplexity; at a loss. *Out of the w.* (U.S. *woods*), clear or free from difficulties. *Man of the woods* = ORANG-OUTANG. *Not to see the w. for the trees*, to lose the view of the whole in the multitude of details.

II. 1. The substance of which the roots, trunks, and branches of trees or shrubs consist; trunks or other parts of trees collectively (whether growing or cut down ready for use) OE. **b.** as prepared for and used in arts and crafts ME. **c.** as used for fuel; firewood OE. **d.** *Hort.* The substance forming the head of a tree or shrub; branch-wood; in a fruit-tree, primarily leaf-bearing, as dist. from fruit-bearing, branches 1523. **e.** In bibl. use, as the material of an idol or image 1535. **f.** *spec.* (*Hort.* and *Bot.*) The hard compact fibrous substance lying between the bark outside and the pith within 1600. **g.** A particular kind of wood; freq. *pl.* kinds of wood 1580. **h.** In echoes of the L. proverb *Ne e quovis ligno Mercurius fiat*; hence the 'material' of which a person is 'made' 1594. (Cf. Gr. ὕλη HYLE.) **2.** Something made of wood: *spec.* **a.** The wooden part, as the shaft of a spear 1683. **b.** The cask or barrel as a receptacle for liquor, as opp. to the bottle 1826. **c.** *slang.* The pulpit 1854. **d.** The wooden wind-instruments in an orchestra collectively (also called *the w.-wind*) 1879. **e.** Each of the bowls in the game of bowls 1884.

1. c. Heape on muche w.: kindle the fyre BIBLE (Geneva) *Ezek.* 24:10. **e.** The Heathen, in his blindness, Bows down to wood and stone! HEBER. **h.** I know better than most men of what w. a minister is made DISRAELI. **2. b.** Ordinary clarets from the w. 1882. Phrases. *W. of Jerusalem*, a variety of pear. *W. of life* = GUAIACUM.

III. a. *attrib.* or as *adj.* Made or consisting of wood, wooden 1538. **b.** *attrib.* in sense I. 2 or 3. OE. **c.** attrib. uses and comb. of pl. (sense I. 2) *U.S.* 1849. (Cf. WOODSMAN.)

a. Fower woodd bottels, one lether bottle 1578. The..Sap of thir W.-fewel burning on the fire MILT. **b.** Begin these w. birds but to couple now? SHAKS. **c.** Bands of woods-creatures 1902.

Comb.: **w.-alcohol** = WOOD-SPIRIT 2; **-ash, -ashes,** the ash or ashes of burnt wood; **-bill,** an implement used for cutting w., etc.; **-block,** a block of w., *esp.* one on which a design is cut for printing from; **-borer,** *esp.* any one of certain insects and other invertebrates which make perforations in w.; **-carving,** the ornamental carving of wooden utensils, furniture, etc.; **-coal,** (*a*) charcoal obtained from w.; (*b*) = LIGNITE; **-engraver,** (*a*) one who engraves on w.; (*b*) any of various species of N. Amer. w.-boring beetles, esp. *Xyleborus cælatus*; **-engraving,** the process or art of engraving on w. or of making woodcuts; *concr.* a woodcut; **-gum** = XYLAN; **-house,** a house, shed, or room in which w. is stored; **-knife,** a dagger or short sword used by huntsmen for cutting up the game, or gen. as a weapon (*Obs.* or *Hist.*); **-monger,** a dealer in wood; a timber-merchant, or (*esp.*) a seller of w. for fuel (now *rare* exc. *Hist.*); **-note,** a natural untrained musical note or song like that of a wild bird in a w. (in later use echoing Milton); **-oil,** any of several oils or oily substances, obtained from various trees;

(*a*) the East Indian *Dipterocarpus alatus* and other species; (*b*) the East Indian Satin-wood, *Chloroxylon swietenia*; (*c*) (called also *tung-oil*) the seeds of the Chinese Oil-tree or Varnish-tree, *Aleurites cordata* (the *tung-tree*), used chiefly for varnishing woodwork; **-pulp,** a pulp made by mechanical or chemical disintegration of w.-fibre, and used for making paper; **-ranger** *U.S.*, one who ranges woods; a scout or sharpshooter in Amer. armies; **-reeve,** the steward or overseer of a w. or forest; **†-shaw,** a thicket; **-spell** *U.S.*, a spell or turn of work at piling or storing w. for fuel; **-sugar** = XYLOSE; **-vinegar,** vinegar or crude acetic acid obtained by distillation of w.; **-wind,** the wooden wind-instruments in an orchestra collectively; **-wool,** fine shavings of w., usu. pine-w., used as a surgical dressing and for various other purposes; **-yard,** a yard or enclosure in which w. is chopped, sawn, or stored, esp. for use as fuel. **b.** In names of animals, chiefly birds and insects, that live in woods or trees, or that live, bore, or burrow in w., as **w.-ant,** (*a*) a large ant, *Formica rufa*, living in woods; (*b*) a termite or white ant, which burrows in w., **-dove** = W.-PIGEON; **-duck,** a species of duck inhabiting woods, *esp.* the N. Amer. summer duck *Æx sponsa*, and the Australian *Bernicla jubata*; **-frog,** a species of frog found in woods, as the N. Amer. *Rana sylvatica*; **-grouse,** (*a*) the capercailye *Tetrao urogallus*; (*b*) the spotted Canada grouse, *Canace* (*Dendragapus*) *canadensis*, or allied species; **-lark,** a species of lark (*Alauda arborea*) which perches on trees; dist. from the skylark by having a shorter tail, more variegated plumage, and a different song; **-warbler,** (*a*) the w.-wren, *Phylloscopus sibilatrix*; (*b*) a general name for the Amer. warblers, esp. those of the genus *Dendrœca*. **c.** In names of plants or their products (usu. designating particular species) growing in woods, as **w. anemone,** the common wild anemone, *A. nemorosa*, abundant in woods; **-lily,** (*a*) the lily-of-the-valley, *Convallaria majalis*; (*b*) the common winter-green, *Pyrola minor*; (*c*) any plant of the N. Amer. genus *Trillium*; **-rush,** any plant of the genus *Luzula* (prop. the sylvan species, as *L. sylvatica*), comprising grass-like herbs allied to the rushes, with clusters of chaffy brown flowers; **-sage,** a common name for the W. Germander (*Teucrium scorodonia*), a labiate herb with dull greenish-yellow flowers, and leaves having a heavy aromatic smell like sage. Hence **Woo·dish** *a.* somewhat woody; †sylvan. **Woo·dlet** (*rare*), a little w.

Wood, *a.* (*adv.*) *Obs.* exc. *dial.* or *rare arch.* [OE. *wōd* = OHG. *wuot*, ON. *ōðr*, Goth. *wōþs* possessed by a devil, f. Gmc. *wōð-* :- IE. **wāt-*, repr. also by L. *vates* seer, poet, OIr. *fáith* poet.] **1.** Out of one's mind, insane, lunatic. **b.** Of a dog or other beast: Rabid OE. **2.** Going beyond all reasonable bounds; extremely rash or reckless, wild; vehemently excited OE. **a.** Extremely fierce or violent, ferocious; irascible, passionate ME. **b.** Violently angry or irritated; enraged, furious ME.

1. The folk in Lunnon are a' clean wud about this bit job SCOTT. **2. b.** Heere am I, and w. within this wood, Because I cannot meet my Hermia SHAKS.

†B. *adv.* Madly, frantically, furiously (chiefly in *wood wroth*) –1601. Hence (*Obs.* or *dial.*) **Woo·d-ly** *adv.*, **-ness.**

Wood (wud), *v.* 1538. [f. WOOD *sb.*] **I. †1.** *trans.* To surround with a wood or trees; *refl.* and *intr.* to hide or take refuge in a wood –1645. **2.** *trans.* To cover (land) with trees; to convert into woodland (cf. WOODED *ppl. a.*) 1807. **II. a.** *trans.* To supply with wood for fuel; to load (a vessel) with wood 1628. **b.** *intr.* To take in a supply of wood for fuel 1630.

Woodbine[1] (wu·dbəin), **woodbind** (-bəind). [OE. *wudubind(e*, f. *wudu* WOOD *sb.* + root of BIND *v.* For the loss of final *d* cf. *line, rine* for *lind, rind.*] **1.** A name for various plants of a climbing habit; in early use (later only *dial.*), convolvulus and ivy; now chiefly (*U.S.*), the Virginia Creeper, *Ampelopsis quinquefolia*, and the West Indian *Ipomœa tuberosa* (Spanish W.). **2.** *esp.* The common honeysuckle, *Lonicera periclymenum*; also extended to other species, as the N. Amer. *L. grata* ME.

2. I know a banke where the wilde time blowes, . . Quite ouer-canoped with luscious w. SHAKS. Hence **Woo·dbined** (-bəind) *a.* overgrown or adorned with w.

Woo·dbine[2]. 1915. A cigarette of the *Wild Woodbine* brand.

Woodbury (wu·dbəri). 1869. The name of Walter Bentley *Woodbury* (1834–1885), used attrib. in designation of processes connected with photography invented by him; esp. **Woo·dburyty:pe,** a process in which a design on a film of gelatine, obtained from a photographic negative, is transferred by heavy pressure to a metal plate from which it may be printed; a print thus produced.

Woodchat (wu·d,tʃæt). 1705. [First found in a posthumous work of Ray's, where it appears to be for **woodcat*, a literal rendering of G. *waldkatze* or *-kater*.] A species of shrike, *Lanius rutilus* (*rufus*, or *auriculatus*), a rare summer visitor to England; also called *w.-shrike*.

Woodchuck (wu·d,tʃɒk). 1689. [Alteration, by association with WOOD *sb.*, of Amer. Indian name (cf. Cree *wuchak, otchock*).] A common N. Amer. species of marmot, *Arctomys monax*, of a large stout form, which burrows in the ground and hibernates in winter.

Woodcock (wu·dkǫk). [Late OE. *wudu-, wudecoc(c*, f. WOOD *sb.* + COCK *sb.*[1]] **1.** A common European migratory bird, *Scolopax rusticula*, allied to the snipe, having a long bill, large eyes, and variegated plumage, and much esteemed as food. Also, the allied *Philohela minor* of N. America. **2.** *allus.* (from the ease with which the w. is taken in a snare or net), in ref. to capture by some trickery, or as a type of gullibility or folly; hence applied to a person: A fool, simpleton, dupe. *Obs.* or *arch.* late ME. **3.** *transf.* **a.** = *w. shell* 1815. **b.** A variety of apple 1700. **c.** *Scotch w.*, a savoury dish of eggs, anchovy, etc. 1879.

2. *Twel. N.* II. v. 92.

attrib. and *Comb.*: **w. clay** = *w. soil*; **-shell,** one of several species of *Murex* having a long spout resembling a woodcock's bill; **-snipe,** the great snipe, *Scolopax major*; **w. soil,** a loose soil consisting of a mixture of clay and gravel.

Woodcraft (wu·dkraft). Also *U.S.* **woodscraft.** late ME. (revived or re-formed by Scott). [f. WOOD *sb.* + CRAFT *sb.*] **1.** Skill in or skilled practice of matters pertaining to woods or forests, esp. (in early use) to the chase; now (chiefly *U.S.* and *Colonial*) esp. such knowledge of forest conditions as enables one to maintain oneself or make one's way. **2.** Skill in woodwork, or in constructing something of wood 1833.

Woodcut (wu·dkɒt). 1662. [f. WOOD *sb.* + CUT *sb.*[2] IV. 4.] A design cut in relief on a block of wood, for printing from; a print or impression obtained from this.

Wood-cutter (wu·dkɒ:təɹ). 1774. **1.** One who cuts wood; one who cuts down trees, or cuts off their branches, for the wood. **2.** A maker of woodcuts, a wood-engraver 1821. So **Woo·d-cu:tting** *sb.* 1722.

Wooded (wu·dėd), *ppl. a.* 1605. [f. WOOD *sb.* or *v.* + -ED.] Furnished with wood or woods; abounding in woods or forests.

Wooden (wu·d'n), *a.* 1538. [f. WOOD *sb.* + -EN[4].] **1.** Made or consisting of wood. **b.** *transf.*: Made or produced by means of wood; dull or dead, as the sound of wood when struck; relating to or occupied with wood; hard and stiff like wood 1606. **2.** *fig.* Having some quality likened to the hard dry consistence of wood, or to its inferior value as compared with precious metal or the like. **a.** Expressionless, spiritless; dull and inert; stiff and lifeless 1566. **b.** Mentally dull; insensitive; unintelligent, blockish 1586. **†c.** Of inferior character, poor, worthless –1719.

1. b. *Tr. & Cr.* I. iii. 155. **2. a.** He wyll neuer blush, he hath a wodden face 1566. **b.** When people have w. heads. .it can't be helped GEO. ELIOT.

Collocations: **†w. cut** = WOODCUT; **†w. dagger,** the dagger of lath worn by Vice in the old moralities; **w. horse,** (*a*) a ship (*Obs.* or *arch.*); (*b*) an instrument of punishment, chiefly military, formerly in use; (*c*) the w. figure of a horse (ἵππος δουράτεος, *Odyssey* VIII. 492, 512) in which the Greek invaders were concealed at the siege of Troy; (*d*) a w. structure in a gymnasium, for vaulting exercise; **w. leg,** an artificial leg made of wood; **w. pear,** an Australian tree, *Xylomelum pyriforme*, bearing hard pear-shaped seed-vessels; **w. shoe,** a shoe made of wood, as the French sabot; in the 18th c. pop. taken as typical of the miserable condition of the French peasantry; **w. spoon,** a spoon made of wood; *spec.* one presented by custom at Cambridge to the lowest of those taking honours in the Mathematical Tripos; hence, this position in the examination, or the person who takes it; **w. tongue,** an infectious disease in horses and cattle, in which the tongue is enlarged and hardened; **w. walls** (after ξύλινον τεῖχος, Herodotus vii. 141), ships or shipping, as a defensive force; **w. wedding** *U.S.*, the fifth anniversary of one's wedding, on which it is appropriate to give presents made of wood.

Comb. as *w.-faced, -featured* adjs.; **w.-head,** a blockhead; **w.-headed** *a.* blockish, stupid. Hence **Woo·den-ly** *adv.*, **-ness.**

Woo·d-hen. ME. **1.** A female woodcock. Now *rare*. **2.** Any flightless rail of the genus *Ocydromus*, of New Zealand and other Pacific islands; = WEKA. 1773.

Woodhouse: see WOODWOSE.

Woodiness (wu·dinės). 1601. [f. WOODY *a.* + -NESS.] The quality or condition of being woody. **1.** Woody texture, consistence, or appearance. **2.** The condition of being full of woods or forests; prevalence or abundance of woodland 1796.

Woo·d-kern(e. *Hist.* 1548. [tr. Ir. *ceithearnach* (KERN *sb.*[1]), *coille* (wood).] An Irish outlaw or robber haunting woods or wild country; such outlaws collectively.

Woodland (wu·dlǣnd). [OE. *wuduland.*] Land covered with wood, i.e. with trees; a wooded region or piece of ground. **b.** *attrib.* Of or pertaining to w.; used, situated, dwelling, or growing in w.; consisting of or containing w.; sylvan ME.

What is now the W. in Warwickshire, was heretofore part of a larger. .Forest, called Arden SELDEN. **b.** I am a w. fellow sir, that alwaies loued a great fire SHAKS. Hence **Woo·dlander,** an inhabitant of the w. 1774.

Wood-louse (wu·dlaus). *Pl.* **wood-lice** (-ləis). 1611. **1.** A small isopod crustacean of the sub-order *Oniscoidea*; esp. the common wood-louse, *Armadillidium*, found in old wood, under stones, etc., and having the property of rolling itself up into a ball. **2.** Locally or occas. applied to various other small invertebrates found in woodwork or in woods, or resembling the crustacean described in 1, as a white ant or termite, various insects of the family *Psocidæ*, etc. 1666.

Woodman[1] (wu·dmǎn). *Pl.* **-men.** ME. [f. WOOD *sb.* Cf. WOODSMAN.] **1.** One who hunts game in a wood or forest; a huntsman. *Obs.* or *arch.* **2.** One who looks after the trees in a wood or forest; one who fells or lops trees for timber or fuel; also, one who provides or purveys wood. late ME. **†3.** = WOODWOSE –1780. **4.** A workman who makes something of wood, esp. the woodwork of a carriage 1879.

1. *Merry W.* V. v. 30. *fig.* Has the old Cupid, your Father, chosen well for you? is he a good W.? DRYDEN. **2.** Spare, w., spare the beechen tree CAMPBELL.

†Woo·dman[2]. ME. [WOOD *a.*] A madman, lunatic, maniac –1512.

Woo·d-nymph. 1577. **1.** A nymph of the woods; a dryad or hamadryad. **2. a.** Any of certain species of humming-bird, esp. of the genus *Thalurania*. **b.** Collectors' name for moths of the genus *Eudryas* 1861.

1. By dimpled Brook, and Fountain brim, The Wood-Nymphs deckt with Daisies trim, Their merry wakes and pastimes keep MILT.

‖**Woodoo** (wudū·). 1794. [Turkish *wazū*.] The minor ablution of the Moslems.

Woodpecker (wu·dpe:kəɹ). 1530. [f WOOD *sb.* + PECK *v.*[1] + -ER[1]. Cf. Gr. δρυ(ο)κολάπτης, δρυοκόπος.] A bird of the family *Picidæ*, esp. of the sub-family *Picinæ*, usu. having variegated plumage of bright contrasted colours; characterized by their habit of pecking the trunks and branches of trees in search of insects. **b.** With defining words, denoting various species 1668.

b. The three British species are the Green W. (*Gecinus viridis*), the Pied or Greater Spotted W. (*Dendrocopus major*), and the Barred or Lesser Spotted W. (*D. minor*).

Woo·d-pi:geon. 1668. Any of the species of pigeon that live in woods, as the stock-dove, *Columba œnas*, and (now esp.) the ring-dove *C. palumbus*.

Woodruff (wu·drɒf). [OE. *wudurofe*, f. *wudu* WOOD *sb.* + **rōfe*, **rife*, of unkn. meaning.] A low-growing rubiaceous herb (*Asperula odorata*) found in woods in Britain and Europe generally, with clusters of small white flowers, and strongly sweet-scented leaves in whorls. **B.** Extended to other species of *Asperula* 1597.

A-way is huere [= their] wynter wo, when woderove springeth 1310.

Wood-sear, -seer, -sere (wu·dsīᵊɹ). *Obs.* or *dial.* 1573. [perh. f. WOOD *sb.* + SERE *a.*] **1.** A frothy exudation on plants, produced by an insect; cuckoo-spit; also, the insect itself 1585. **2.** The season in which a tree or shrub will decay or die if its wood be cut 1573. **3.** *attrib.* or *adj.* Applied to loose, spongy ground. *local.* 1670.

Woodshock (wu·dʃǫk). 1829. [app. popular alteration of a native form of WOODCHUCK.] A N. Amer. species of marten or its fur, = PEKAN.

Woodside (wu·dsəid). ME. The side or edge of a wood.

By or *under the* or *a w.* = beside a wood; I would have been glad to have lived under my w., to have kept a flock of sheep, rather than undertaken such a government as this CROMWELL.

Woodsman (wu·dzmæn). *Pl.* **-men.** Chiefly *U.S.* 1688. [f. *woods*, pl. of WOOD *sb.* Cf. BACKWOODSMAN.] A man who inhabits, frequents, or ranges the woods, as a huntsman, wood-cutter, etc.; one acquainted with or accustomed to the woods.

Woo·dso:rrel. 1525. [Englishing of *sorrel de boys*, superseding WOOD-SOUR (see SORREL *sb.*[1] 3); so called from the sour taste of the leaves, resembling that of sorrel.] The common name of *Oxalis acetosella*, a low-growing woodland plant having delicate trifoliate leaves and small white flowers streaked with purple, appearing in spring. **b.** Applied with defining words to other species of *Oxalis*; also in the W. Indies to species of *Begonia* 1770.

†**Woo·d-sour.** late ME. [f. WOOD *sb.* + SOUR *sb.*, corresp. to ON. *skógarsúra* (*skóg* wood, *súra* sorrel).] = prec. –1597.

Woo·d-spi:rit. 1842. [f. WOOD *sb.* + SPIRIT *sb.*] **1.** *Myth.* A spirit or imaginary being, fabled to dwell in or haunt woods 1845. **2.** Crude methyl alcohol obtained from wood by destructive distillation 1842.

Woodspite (wu·dspəit). Now *dial.* 1555. [f. WOOD *sb.* + SPEIGHT.] A woodpecker; *esp.* the Green Woodpecker, *Gecinus viridis*.

Woodsy (wu·dzi), *a.* *U.S.* 1861. [irreg. f. *woods*, pl. of WOOD *sb.* + -Y[1]; formed thus for distinction from *woody*.] Of, pertaining to, characteristic or suggestive of the woods; sylvan.

Woodwall (wu·dwǫl). Now *dial.* [ME. *wodewale* – or cogn. with MLG. *wedewale*; see WITWALL. For sense 2 cf. HICKWALL.] †**1.** A singing bird, the Golden Oriole, *Oriolus galbula*, which has a loud flute-like whistle –1667. **2.** A woodpecker; *esp.* the Green Woodpecker, *Gecinus viridis* 1489.

1. Nyghtyngales, Alpes, fynches, and wodewales, That in her swete song deliten CHAUCER.

Woodward (wu·dwǭɹd). *Hist.* [Late OE. *wuduweard*, f. WOOD *sb.* + WARD *sb.*[1] Survives as a surname.] The keeper of a wood; an officer of a wood or forest, having charge of the growing timber. **b.** As the title of an officer of the 'Ancient Order of Foresters' 1886.

Woodwax (wu·dwæks). *Obs.* or *dial.* [OE. *wuduweaxe*, f. *wudu* WOOD *sb.* + **weaxe*, app. f. Gmc. **wahs-* WAX *v.*[1]] = next.

Woodwaxen (wu·dwæ:ksən). late ME. [app. oblique case of OE. *wuduweaxe* (*wuduweaxan*) taken as nom. See prec.] The plant dyer's broom or greenweed, *Genista tinctoria*.

Woodwork, wood-work (wu·dwɔɹk). 1650. **1.** †**a.** An article made of wood, or such articles collectively –1792. **b.** (without *pl.*) Work in wood; *esp.* those parts or details of a manufactured object or artificial structure which are made of wood; the wooden part *of* something 1684. **2.** Work done in wood, as carpentry 1913.

1. a. I give vnto my sonne..all my plate,..hangings, wood worke, houshold stuffe, and furniture 1650. Hence **Woo·dwo:rker,** (*a*) a worker in wood, one who makes things of wood; (*b*) a machine for working in wood.

Woo·dwose, woo·dhouse. *Obs.* (exc. *Hist.*). [Late OE. *wudewāsa*, f. *wudu* WOOD *sb.* + **wāsa*, of obsc. origin.] A wild man of the woods; a savage; a satyr, faun; a person dressed to represent such a being in a pageant. **b.** A figure of such a being, as a decoration, a heraldic bearing or supporter, etc. ME.

Woody (wu·di), *a.* late ME. [f. WOOD *sb.* + -Y[1].] **I. 1.** Covered or overgrown with wood; having a growth of trees or shrubs; wooded. †**2.** Belonging to, inhabiting, or growing in woods or woodland; sylvan –1655. **b.** Of, pertaining to, or situated in a wood 1721.

2. A grassie hillock..With woodie primroses befreckled 1610.

II. 1. Of the nature of or consisting of wood; of or belonging to the wood as a constituent part of the plant; ligneous 1597. **b.** Of a plant: Of which wood is a constituent part; forming wood; having the stem and branches of wood; *spec.* in distinctive names of particular species, as *w. nightshade* 1578. **c.** Resembling wood; having the texture or consistence of wood 1791. **2.** Pertaining to or characteristic of wood; resembling that of wood 1830. **b.** Having a dull sound like that of wood when struck 1875.

1. b. *W. plant*, a tree or shrub, as dist. from a *herb*. Hence **Woo·diness.**

Wooer (wū·əɹ). [OE. *wōgere*, f. *wōgian* WOO *v.* + -ER[1].] One who woos (a woman); a suitor.

Woof (wūf), *sb.*[1] [OE. *ōwef*, alt. of *ōwebb* (see ABB, WEB) after *wefan* WEAVE; ME. *oof* became *woof* partly by assoc. in the phr. *warp and (w)oof*.] **1.** = WEFT[1] 1. **2.** Thread used to make the woof 1540. **3.** A woven fabric, esp. as being of a particular texture; also, the texture of a fabric 1674.

1. *fig.* Where euery English thread is ouercast with a thicke woollen woofe of strange wordes 1627. 3. Flames dart their glare o'er midnight's sable w. SCOTT. Hence **Woof** *v.*[1] (*rare*) to arrange (threads) so as to form a w.; to weave. **Woo·fed** (wūft, *poet.* wūfėd) *ppl. a.* woven; *fig.* intricate. **Woo·fy** *a.* (*rare*) resembling a w. or woven fabric; of dense texture.

Woof (wuf), *int.*, *sb.*[2] and *v.*[2] 1804. Imitation of a gruff abrupt bark of a dog. (Cf. WHOOF.)

Wooing (wū·iŋ), *vbl. sb.* OE. [f. WOO *v.* + -ING[1].] The action of WOO *v.*; amorous solicitation, courtship.

Hys vnaduised wowyng, hasty louyng and to spedy mariage 1548. What? Michael Cassio, That came a woing with you? SHAKS. *Prov.* Happy is the woing, that is not long in doing 1670.

Wooing (wū·iŋ), *ppl. a.* late ME. [f. as prec. + -ING[2].] That woos. **a.** That solicits in love; courting, as a lover. **b.** *fig.* Alluring, enticing 1549. Hence **Woo·ingly** *adv.*

Wool (wul), *sb.* [OE. *wull* = OFris. *wolle*, *ulle*, MLG., MDu. *wulle*, *wolle*, OHG. *wolla* (Du. *wol*, G. *wolle*), ON. *ull*, Goth. *wulla* :– Gmc. **wullō* :– IE. **wlnā*, whence Skr. *ūrnā*, L. *lāna*, beside *vellus* (:– **welnos*) fleece.] **1.** The fine soft curly hair forming the fleecy coat of the domesticated sheep (and similar animals), characterized by its property of felting (due to the imbricated surface of the filaments) and used chiefly in a prepared state for making cloth; freq., the material in a prepared state as a commodity. **b.** The fleece or complete woolly covering of a sheep, etc. late ME. **c.** The short soft underhair or down forming part of the coat of certain hairy or furry animals 1605. **2.** Applied to substances resembling sheep's wool. **a.** A downy substance or fibre found on certain trees and plants; also, the thick furry hair of some insects or larvæ. late ME. **b.** Any fine fibrous substance naturally or artifically produced 1599. **c.** The short crisp curly hair of a Negro. Also *gen.* (joc.), the hair of the head. 1697. **3.** Woollen clothing or material ME. **b.** The nap of a woollen fabric 1563. **c.** Twisted woollen yarn used for knitting and mending garments 1840. **4.** A quantity or supply, or a particular kind or class, of wool. Chiefly in *pl.* late ME.

1. *Spanish* or *oriental w.*, w. treated with a dye, used as a cosmetic; I am ashamed to tell you that we are indebted to Spanish W. for many of our masculine ruddy complexions 1755. Phr. *Against the w.*, contrary to the direction in which w. naturally lies, the wrong way. *To draw, pull, the w. over* (a person's) *eyes*, to hoodwink, deceive (orig. *U.S.*). *To dye in the w.*, to dye the w. before spinning; *fig.* in *pass.* to be thoroughly imbued; *dyed in the w.* (chiefly *U.S.*), thoroughgoing, out-and-out. *Great* (or *much*) *cry and little w.* (etc.), much talk or clamour with insignificant results. **b.** *Out of the w.*, shorn. **c.** Eye of Newt, and Toe of Frogge, Wooll of Bat, and Tongue of Dogge SHAKS. **2. c.** 'Keep your w. on', don't get angry BARRÈRE & LELAND *Dict. Slang.*

Comb.: *w. blanket, mattress, tax*; *w.-cleaner, -dresser, -grower, -monger, -picker, -washer*; *w.-lined* adj.; **w.-bearer,** an animal that bears w., *esp.* a sheep; **-card,** an instrument used in carding w.; **-comb,** the toothed instrument used in carding wool by hand; later also, a machine to perform the same operation; **-comber,** one who combs or cards wool; **-fat** (*a*) = SUINT; (*b*) = LANOLIN; **-fell** = *w.-skin* (*Hist.*); **-needle,** a blunt needle used for w.-work; **-packer,** one who makes up packages of w. for transport or sale; also, a machine for packing w.; **-shed,** *Austral.*, the large building at a sheep-station in which shearing and w.-packing are done; **-skin,** a sheepskin with the fleece on it; **-sorter,** a sorter of w.; *wool-sorter's disease*, anthrax; **-winder,** one who 'winds' or packs up fleeces for transport or sale.

Wool (wul), *v.* 1660. [f. prec.] †**1.** *trans.* To coat or line with wool. **2.** *U.S. slang.* To pull the 'wool' or hair of (a person) in sport or (esp.) in anger 1854.

Woold (wūld), *sb.* [Late ME. *wole* (Sandahl, 1358–9); cf. MDu. *woelreep* 'woolding-rope'; (see next.] **a.** *Naut.* = WOOLDING. **b.** *attrib.* in *w. cord, rope*, binding cord or rope.

Woold (wūld), *v.* 1616. [Earliest form *wole*, implied in *wolynge* (XV; see next) – MLG. *wōlen*, MDu. *woelen* 'premere, constringere, torquere' Kilian (Du. *woelen* woold a mast).] *trans.* (*Naut.*) To wind rope or chain round (a mast or the like) to strengthen it where it is broken, or where it is fished or scarfed. Also said of the rope. **b.** *gen.* To wrap or bind round 1775. Hence **Woo·lder,** †*Naut.* a woold rope; *Rope-making*, a stick used as a lever in woolding; also, a workman operating this.

Woolding (wū·ldiŋ), *vbl. sb.* late ME. [Earliest forms *wol(l)yng* (XV), *wooling* (XVI), prob. – MLG. **wōling*, MDu. **woeling*, f. MLG. *wōlen*, etc.; see prec., -ING[1].] **1.** The action of binding an object tightly with cord; esp. *Naut.* of winding rope or chain round a mast or yard, to support it where it is fished or broken 1440. **2.** *concr.* A wrapping, swathing; esp. *Naut.* (often *pl.*) the rope or chain used in woolding a mast, spar, etc. late ME.

Woo·l-ga:thering, *vbl. sb.* and *gerund.* 1553. **1.** The action of gathering fragments of wool torn from sheep by bushes, etc. 1581. **2.** In fig. phr. *to go* (*run, be*) *w.*, to indulge in wandering fancies or purposeless thinking; to be in a dreamy or absent-minded state 1553. **b.** Hence, Indulgence in idle imagining or aimless speculation 1607.

2. Hackyng & hemmyng as though our wittes and our senses were a woll gatheryng 1553. So **Woo·l-ga:thering** *a.* indulging in wandering thoughts or idle fancies.

Woollen (wu·lėn, wu·lən), *a.* and *sb.* Also (now *U.S.*) **woolen.** [Late OE. *wullen*, f. *wull* WOOL *sb.* + -EN[4].] **A.** *adj.* **1.** Made of or manufactured from wool. †**2.** Wearing woollen clothing, (*a*) as a mark of penance; (*b*) as a mark of poor or lowly status –1607.

2. *Cor.* III. ii. 9.

B. *sb.* Cloth or other fabric made of wool or chiefly of wool. Now *rare*. ME. **b.** *pl.* Woollen cloths or clothes 1800.

†*To lie in the w.*, to sleep with a blanket next to one; I could not endure a husband with a beard on his face, I had rather lie in the w. SHAKS. *To be buried in w.*, to have a w. shroud, as required by the Act of 18 and 19 Chas. II for the encouragement of the w. manufacture.

Woo·llen-dra:per. Now *Hist.* 1554. [f. prec. sb. + DRAPER *sb.*] A dealer in woollen goods.

Woolliness (wu·linės). 1597. [f. WOOLLY *a.* + -NESS.] The quality or condition of being woolly, in various senses; also *concr.* a woolly substance.

Woolly (wu·li), *a.* (*sb.*) 1578. [f. WOOL *sb.* + -Y[1].] **1.** Consisting of wool. Also *transf.* relating to wool; containing wool (or sheep) 1591. **2.** Of the nature, texture, or appearance of wool; resembling wool 1586. **b.** Having a soft and clinging texture; said esp. of edible things which are consequently unpleasant to the palate 1687. **3.** Having a natural covering of wool, wool-bearing 1596. **b.** Having hair resembling wool: applied esp. to Negroes 1767. **c.** In specific names of animals, often rendering L. *lanatus*, *laniger* 1781. **d.** *Wild and w.*, orig. applied to the Far West of the U.S., on account of its rude and uncivilized character.

hence *gen.* barbarous, lacking culture 1891. **4.** Of parts of plants: Covered with a pubescence resembling wool; downy, lanate, tomentose 1578. **b.** In specific names of plants, often rendering L. *lanatus* or *tomentosus* 1597. **5.** *gen.* Having a wool-like texture, surface, or covering 1796. **6.** *transf.* and *fig.* Lacking in definiteness or incisiveness; confused and hazy; lacking in clearness or definition 1815.

1. Silent was the flock in w. fold KEATS. **3. b.** It was a large, w. poodle, snowy white 1886. **c. W. bear** *colloq.* (esp. *children's*), a large hairy caterpillar, esp. the larva of the tiger-moth. **4. b. W. butt,** Australian name for species of *Eucalyptus*, esp. *E. longifolia*. **6.** Pusey's w. mind 1865. A drawing to look into, but rather w. at a few paces off 1884.

B. *sb.* A woollen garment or covering; now esp. *pl.*, garments or wraps knitted of (fleecy) wool 1865.

Woo·lly-head. 1859. A person with woolly hair, *esp.* a Negro; hence, a nickname for an abolitionist in America.

Woolly-headed, *a.* 1650. Having a woolly head: **a.** in specific names of plants; **b.** Woolly-haired 1708; **c.** *fig.* Dull-witted 1883.

Woo·lman. Now chiefly *Hist.* late ME. A dealer in wool; a wool-merchant.

Woo·l-pack. ME. [PACK *sb.*[1]] **1.** A large bag into which a quantity of wool or of fleeces is packed for carriage or sale. †**b.** = next 2. –1710. **2.** *transf.* Something resembling a wool-pack. †**a.** A large mass of white water –1733. **b.** orig. *w. cloud*: A fleecy cumulus cloud. Chiefly *pl.* (or *collect. sing.*). 1648.

Woolsack (wu·lsæk). ME. [SACK *sb.*[1]] **1.** A large package or bale of wool. **b.** Applied *joc.* to a corpulent person. SHAKS. **2.** A seat made of a bag of wool for the use of judges when summoned to attend the House of Lords (in recent practice only at the opening of Parliament); also, the usual seat of the Lord Chancellor in the House of Lords, made of a large square bag of wool without back or arms and covered with cloth. Often *allus.* with ref. to the position of the Lord Chancellor as the highest judicial officer; hence, *the w.*, the Lord-Chancellorship. 1577.

She drags her husband on to the w., or pushes him into parliament 1862.

‖**Woolsaw** (wu·lsǭ). 1757. [Mosquito *wulasha.*] Among people of African descent in Central America, an evil spirit or demon.

Woolsey (wu·lzi), *a. rare.* 1839. [f. WOOL *sb.* + *-sey* derived from LINSEY-WOOLSEY.] Woolly; woollen.

Woo·l-sta:ple. 1593. [STAPLE *sb.*[2]] A market appointed for the sale of wool. So **Woo·l-sta:pler,** a merchant who buys wool from the producer, grades it, and sells it to the manufacturer.

†**Woo·lward,** *a.* [ME. *wolleward*, prob. alteration of **wollewerd*, from OE. **wullwerd*, f. *wull* WOOL *sb.* + *-werd, -wered* wearing, clothed (in), f. stem of *werian* WEAR *v.*[1]] Wearing wool next the skin, esp. as a penance: chiefly in *to go w.* –1822.

The naked truth of it is, I haue no shirt, I go w. for penance SHAKS. To walk wool-ward in winter SCOTT.

Woolwich (wu·lidʒ). 1794. The name of a town in Kent, used attrib., esp. to designate productions of its old dockyard and the Royal Arsenal, as *W. gun, hulk*; *W. infant*, a joc. name for certain heavy guns.

Woo·l-work. 1475. †**1.** Working in wool; manufacture of woollen goods –1630. **2.** Needlework executed in wool usu. on a canvas foundation. Also, knitted wool fabric 1871. So **Woo·l-wo:rker,** one who works in wool. late ME.

Woomera (wū·mərǎ). *Austral.* 1817. [Native name.] A throwing-stick used by Australian aboriginals. Also = next.

Woomerang (wū·məræŋ). *Austral.* 1849. [Native name. Cf. BOOMERANG.] A missile club used by Australian aboriginals.

Woon (wūn). 1800. [Burmese *wun.*] A Burmese administrative officer.

Woorali, wourali (wurā·li). 1769. [See CURARE.] A S. Amer. climbing plant, *Strychnos toxifera*, from the root of which one of the ingredients of the poison CURARE is obtained; also, the poison itself.

Wootz (wūts). 1795. [app. orig. misprint for *wook*, repr. Canarese *ukku* (pron. with initial *w*) steel.] A crucible steel made in southern India by fusing magnetic iron ore with carbonaceous matter.

Woozy (wū·zi), *a. U.S. slang.* 1897. [Of unkn. origin.] Fuddled with drink; hence, muzzy.

Wop (wǫp). *U.S. slang.* 1916. [Of unkn. origin.] A Mid- or South-European (esp. Italian) immigrant in the United States of America.

Worcester (wu·stəɹ). 1551. The name of the county town of Worcestershire, used *attrib.* to designate articles originating there, e.g. †a fine cloth, (now chiefly) a kind of China ware; also *ellipt.*

W. sauce = Worcestershire sauce (see next).

Worcestershire (wu·stəɹʃəɹ, -ʃiᵊɹ). 1686. The name of an English county: *attrib.* in *W. sauce*, a sauce made in Worcester; also *ellipt.*

Word (wɔ̄ɹd), *sb.* [OE. *word* = OFris., OS. *word* (Du. *woord*), (O)HG. *wort*, ON. *orð*, Goth. *waurd* :– Gmc. **wordam*, cogn. with Gr. Ϝερέω I shall say, L. *verbum* word.] **I.** Speech, utterance, verbal expression. **1.** *collect. pl.* Things said, or something said; speech, discourse, utterance; *esp.* with possessive, what the person mentioned says or said; (one's) form of expression or language. **b.** *spec.* The text of a song or other vocal composition, as dist. from the music; also, the text of an actor's part 1450. **2.** *sing.* Something said; a speech or utterance *arch.* OE. **b.** with negative expressed or implied, or with *every*: Any or the least utterance, statement, or fragment of speech OE. **c.** *A w.*: a (short or slight) utterance or statement; a brief speech or conversation; similarly *a w. or two* 1485. **d.** *spec.* Something said on behalf of another; esp. in such phrases as *to speak a (good) w. for* 1540. **e.** *spec.* A watchword or password 1533. †**3.** *abstr.* or *collect. sing.* Speech, speaking: often as dist. from writing, esp. in phr. *by w.*; also, the faculty of speech –1728. **4.** *sing.* and *pl.* Speech, verbal expression, in contrast with action or thought OE. **5.** *pl.* orig. in various phr. denoting verbal contention or altercation, e.g. †*to be* or *fall at words*, etc., now chiefly *to have words (with)*; hence *words* = contentious or violent talk between persons; altercation 1462. **6.** *sing.* (without article). Report, tidings, news, information OE. **b.** Common report or statement, rumour. Now *rare* or *Obs.* OE. **7.** A command, order, bidding; a request OE. **8.** A promise, undertaking. Almost always with possessive. late ME. **9.** With possessive: Assertion, affirmation, declaration, assurance; esp. as involving the veracity or good faith of the person who makes it 1601. **10. a.** An utterance or declaration in the form of a phrase or sentence. *arch.* OE. **b.** A pithy or sententious utterance; a saying; a maxim, proverb. Now *rare* exc. in BYWORD 1, NAYWORD 2, *household w.* late ME. †**c.** A significant phrase or short sentence inscribed upon something –1630. **11.** Religious and theological uses; often more fully *word of God* (or *the Lord*), *God's word*, freq. with cap. **a.** A divine communication, command, or proclamation, as one made to or through a prophet or inspired person; *esp.* the message of the gospel OE. **b.** The Bible, or some part or passage of it, as embodying a divine communication 1553. **c.** *The W.* (*of God, of the Father*), *the Eternal W.*, etc., as a title of Jesus Christ: = LOGOS. OE.

1. Words can't describe the figures the women dress here 1813. I have no words..to express the very great thanks which I..owe you 1878. *In these, other,* etc. *words*, in (such-and-such) language. *To give words to, to put into words*, to express by means of language. *Beyond words*, incapable of being expressed in language, unutterable. **b.** Songs without words (tr. G. *Lieder ohne Worte*). **2.** At this worde which he coupled with an othe, came I in FOXE. He bless'd the bread, but vanish'd at the w. COWPER. **b.** They never heard a w. of English DE FOE. **c.** To speake a worde in season to him that is wearie *Isa.* 50:4. **e.** *To give the w.*: (*a*) to utter the password in answer to a sentinel's challenge; (*b*) to inform officers or men of the password to be used. **4.** Thy actions to thy words accord MILT. **5.** High words passed between them. They parted in passion. RICHARDSON. My old man said he was a blood-sucker, and that led to words 1913. **6.** Bid you Alexas Bring me w., how tall she is SHAKS. Send me W...whether he has so great an Estate STEELE. **b.** W. gae'd she was nae canny 1718. **7.** In my time a father's w. was law TENNYSON. *To say the w.*, to give the order, say 'go' or the like; Say the w., Ile have him by the eares HEYWOOD. **8.** Having solemnly pledged his w...not to attempt anything against the government MACAULAY. *To be as good as one's w.*, to keep one's promise. *A man of his w.*, one who keeps his promises. **9.** I give you my w. that my brother did not leave a shilling to his son THACKERAY. **10. a.** The hopelesse w., of Neuer to returne, Breath I against thee SHAKS. **c.** And round about the wreath this w. was writ, *Burnt I do burne* SPENSER. **11. b.** *Merry W.* III. i. 44.

II. An element of speech: A combination of vocal sounds, or one such sound, used in a language to express an idea (e.g. to denote a thing, attribute, or relation), and constituting an ultimate minimal element of speech having a meaning as such; a vocable OE. **b.** †(*a*) A name, title, appellation. (*b*) A term, expression. OE. **c.** A written (engraved, printed, etc.) character or set of characters representing this OE. **d.** In contrast with the thing or idea signified 1450. **e.** *The w.* (predicatively): the right word for the thing, the proper expression; hence contextually denoting or indicating the thing spoken of, esp. the business in hand (*colloq.*) 1596.

Sometimes with ref. to the writing of a word as an indivisible unit, e.g. *as one or a single w., as two words* O.E.D.

d. A business of words only, and ideas not concerned in it 1782. **e.** Come Sir, are you ready for death?..Hanging is the w., Sir. SHAKS. Contempt? Why, damsel, when I think of man, Contempt is not the w. 1885.

Phrases. **At a** or **one w.: a.** Upon the utterance of a single w.; without more ado; at once, forthwith. **b.** In short, briefly, in a word. *Obs.* exc. *arch.* or *dial.* *To take* a person *at his w.*, to accept what he says and act accordingly. **In a w.** In a simple or short, (esp. comprehensive) statement or phrase; briefly, in short. **In so many words** (tr. L. *totidem verbis*), lit. in precisely that number of words; in those very words. **On** or **upon one's w.: a.** On the security of, or as bound by, one's promise or affirmation; hence as an asseveration, *on, upon my w.* = Assuredly, truly, indeed. **b.** (with ellipsis of prep.) *My w.!* as an ejaculation of surprise (*colloq.* or *vulgar*). **A w. and a blow.** A brief utterance of anger or defiance, followed immediately by the delivery of a blow, as the beginning of a fight; hence in ref. to hasty or sudden action of any kind. **W. of command.** A w. or short phrase uttered by an officer to a body of soldiers as an order for some particular movement or evolution. **W. of honour.** An affirmation or promise by which one pledges one's honour or good faith. **By w. of mouth.** By speaking, as dist. from writing or other method of expression; orally. Hence *w.-of-mouth* attrib., oral. **W. for w.** In the exact or (in ref. to translation) precisely corresponding words; verbatim. Also *attrib.* **Fair words.** Pleasant or attractive speech (usu. implying deceitfulness or insincerity). **Of few words.** Not given to much or lengthy speaking; taciturn. **Good w.** A friendly, favourable, or laudatory utterance; something said on behalf of or in commendation of a person or thing. *To give* (a person) *a good w.*, to speak well of. *To say* or *speak a good w. for*, (*spec.*) to recommend to the favour of another. *Half a w.*, a very short utterance, a slight fragment of speech or conversation. **Last w.: a.** The final utterance in a conversation or (esp.) dispute. **b.** *pl.* The latest utterance of a person before death. *The Seven Last Words*, the seven utterances of Jesus Christ on the Cross. **c.** The final or conclusive statement, after which there is no more to be said; hence *transf.* the final achievement, the latest thing. **Of many words.** Given to much or lengthy speaking, loquacious, verbose.

Make words. with neg.: (Not) to say anything (more) about a matter. **Take (up) the w.** To begin speaking, esp. immediately after or instead of some one else. **b.** *To take* (a person's) *w.*, to accept his statement or assertion as true or trustworthy: usu. with *for*, esp. in the phr. *take my w. for it* = I can assure you, you may be sure, believe me.

Comb.: *w.-order, -stock*; *w.-building, -formation*; **w.-blind** *a. Path.*, affected with **w.-blindness,** inability to understand written or printed words when seen, owing to disease of the visual w.-centre; **-centre,** *Anat.* each of certain centres in the brain which govern the perception and use of words (spoken or written); **-deaf** *a. Path.*, affected with **w.-deafness,** inability to understand words when heard, owing to disease of the auditory w.-centre; **-hoard,** literal rendering of OE. *wordhord* treasure of speech; **-lore,** (*a*) the study of words and their history; (*b*) the doctrine of the forms and formation of words, morphology (= G. *wortlehre*); **-man,** a man who deals with or has command of words; a master of language; **-monger,** *contempt.* one who deals in words, esp. in strange or pedantic words, or in empty words without sense; **-paint,** *v. trans.* to 'paint' in words, describe vividly; so **-painter, -painting; -perfect,** *a.* knowing perfectly every w. of one's lesson, part, etc.; **-picture,** a vivid description in words, presenting the object to the mind like a picture; **w. square,** a set of words of the same number of letters to be arranged in a square so as to read the same horizontally or vertically; a puzzle in which such a set of words has to be guessed.

Word (wɒ̄ɹd), *v.* ME. [f. prec.] **1.** *intr.* To utter words; to speak, talk. *Obs.* or *arch.* **b.** *To w. it*: to talk, esp. excessively or violently; to have (high) words *with*. *Obs.* or *dial.* 1612. **2.** *trans.* To utter in words, say, speak (occas. as dist. from singing). *Obs.* or *arch.* late ME. †**3. a.** To ply or urge with words. SHAKS. **b.** To bring by the use of words (into or out of a specified condition, etc.) –1716. **4.** To express in or put into words; to compose, draw up. *Obs.* exc. as in b. –1831. **b.** esp. with ref. to the kind of language or form of words used 1619. **c.** *nonce-use.* To represent as in words. SHAKS.

3. a. *Ant. & Cl.* v. ii. 191. **4.** Songs of Mourning ... Worded by Tho. Campion. 1613. **b.** 'Tis in reality one and the same question, only differently worded 1701.

Word-book (wɒ̄·ɹdbuk). 1598. [f. WORD *sb.* + BOOK *sb.*; in sense 1 cf. G. *wörterbuch*, Icel. *orðabók*, etc.] **1.** A book containing a list of words (as of the vocabulary of a language, a book, an art, or science) arranged in alphabetical or other systematic order. (Often implying less elaboration or fullness than *dictionary* or *lexicon*.) **2.** The 'book of the words' or libretto of a musical composition 1878.

Worded (wɒ̄·ɹdėd), *ppl. a.* 1606. [f. WORD *sb.* or *v.* + -ED.] **1.** Formed into words; expressed in or put into words (*rare*). **b.** Qualified by an adv.: Expressed in a particular kind of language or form of words; phrased in such-and-such a manner 1848.

Wordily (wɒ̄·ɹdili), *adv.* 1522. [f. WORDY *a.* + -LY².] In a wordy manner or style, with excess or abundance of words; verbosely. So **Wo·rdiness,** verbosity.

Wording (wɒ̄·ɹdiŋ), *vbl. sb.* 1564. [f. WORD *v.* or *sb.* + -ING¹.] **1.** Speaking, talking, utterance. *Obs.* or *arch.* 1604. †**2.** Angry or abusive speech: 'having words' –1614. **3.** The action of putting or condition of being put into words; composition or expression in language, esp. in ref. to the words used; mode of speech, form of words 1649. **4.** A set of written words, an inscription (*rare*) 1908.

3. Things for which no w. can be found KEATS. I entreat the attention of the jury to the w. of this document DICKENS.

Wordless (wɒ̄·ɹdlės), *a.* ME. [f. WORD *sb.* + -LESS.] **1.** Inexpressible in words; unspeakable, unutterable. *Obs.* or merged in 2. **2.** Not expressed in words; unspoken, unuttered 1500. **3.** Not uttering a word; silent, speechless 1500. **b.** Lacking the faculty or power of speech 1648. **c.** Lacking words for expression 1881. **4.** Not accompanied by words; (of a play) acted without words 1598.

2. So sat she joylesse down in wordlesse grief complaining 1633. Hence **Wo·rdless-ly** *adv.*, **-ness.**

Wordsworthian (wɒ̄ɹdzwɒ̄·ɹðiăn, -wɒ̄·ɹþiăn), *sb.* and *a.* 1815. [f. the name of the English poet William *Wordsworth* (1770–1850) + -IAN.] **A.** *sb.* An admirer or imitator of Wordsworth, or a student of his works. **B.** *adj.* Of, belonging to, or characteristic of Wordsworth; (of a poem) composed by or in the style of Wordsworth.

Wordy (wɒ̄·ɹdi), *a.* [Late OE. *wordiġ*, f. WORD *sb.* + *-iġ* -Y¹.] **1.** Full of or abounding in words. **a.** Of speech or writing: Consisting of or containing many words; verbose. **b.** Of persons: Using an excess of words; *occas.* garrulous, talkative. late ME. †**2.** Skilled in the use of words (*rare*) –1680. **3.** Consisting or expressed in words; of words; verbal. Now chiefly in phr. *w. war*(*fare*). 1627.

1. To deal in w. Compliment Is much against the Plainness of my Nature 1713. **3.** All that w. tempest for a girl COWPER.

Work (wɒ̄ɹk), *sb.* [OE. *weorc, werc, worc, wurc* = OFris., OS. *werk*, OHG. *werah, werc* (Du., G. *werk*), ON. *verk* :- Gmc. **werkam* :- IE. **wergon*, whence also Gr. (ϝ)ἔργον.] **I. 1.** Something that is or was done; what a person does or did; an act, deed, proceeding, business; *pl.* actions, doings (often *collect.*) *arch.* or *literary* in gen. sense. **b.** *Theol.* (*pl.*) Moral actions considered in relation to justification: usu. as contrasted with *faith* or *grace*. late ME. **2.** Something to be done, or something to do; occupation, business, task, function OE. **b.** *Cricket, Rowing*, etc. What a batsman, an oarsman, etc. has to do, esp. with ref. to the points at which his force is to be applied 1851. **3. a.** Action (of a person or thing) of a particular kind: in various connections 1440. **b.** *Cricket*. Deflexion of the ball after touching the ground, resulting from the spin or twist imparted to it by the bowler 1846. **4.** Action involving effort or exertion directed to a definite end, esp. as a means of gaining one's livelihood; (one's) regular occupation or employment OE. **b.** *gen.* in ref. to any action requiring effort or difficult to do 1518. **c.** *spec.* The labour done in making something, as dist. from the material used (in ref. to the cost) 1737. **d.** Exercise or practice in a sport or game; also, exertion or movement proper to a particular sport, game, or exercise 1856. **5.** A particular piece or act of labour; a task, job. Also *gen.* something difficult to do. *Obs.* or *arch.* OE. **6. a.** Trouble, affliction; in later use, disturbance, fuss. **b.** Pain, ache. *dial.* OE. **7.** *Math.* The process of or an operation in calculation; a process of calculation written out in full. Now *rare* or *Obs.* 1557. **8.** *Physics* and *Mech.* The operation of a force in producing movement or other physical change, esp. as a definitely measurable quantity 1855.

1. Their workes are workes of iniquitie BIBLE (Genev.) *Isa.* 59:6. It is a damned, and a bloody worke SHAKS. I have another W. of Charity upon my hands,..to reform an extravagant Husband 1703. *The w. of..*, a proceeding occupying (a stated length of time); All this was..but the w. of a few minutes 1834. So *a w. of time*, a proceeding which takes a long time. **2.** Fie vpon this quiet life, I want worke SHAKS. Euerie bodies worke is no bodies worke 1611. **3. a.** *To do its w.* (of a thing, in ref. to result), to produce its effect; The brandy-and-water had done its w. DICKENS. **4.** Doinge certen Iobbes of woorke 1557. I do all the w. of the house DICKENS. **b.** It was hard w. rowing, for the wind was against him 1902. **7.** Take a few Examples without their W. at large 1709.

II. 1. With possessive: The product of the operation or labour *of* a person or other agent; creation, handiwork. Also vaguely, the result of one's labour, something accomplished. OE. **b.** The result of the action or operation of some person or thing; (one's) 'doing'; the device or invention *of* some one. late ME. **2.** A thing made; a manufactured article or object; a structure or apparatus of some kind, esp. one forming part of a larger thing. Now chiefly in gen. sense with qualification, esp. in compounds like BRICKWORK, FIREWORK, etc. OE. †**3.** An architectural or engineering structure; a building, edifice –1667. **b.** *pl.* Architectural or engineering operations 1700. **4.** *spec.* (*Mil.*) A fortified building; a defensive structure, fortification; any one of the several parts of such a structure OE. **5.** A literary or musical composition (viewed in relation to its author or composer); often *pl.* and *collect. sing.*, (a person's) writings or compositions as a whole ME. **6.** A product of any of the fine arts (in relation to the artist), as a painting, a statue, etc.: in the phr. *a w. of art* including literary or musical works, and connoting high artistic quality. 1531. †**7.** Make, workmanship; *esp.* ornamental workmanship –1795. **8.** The operation of making a textile fabric or (more often) something consisting of such fabric, as weaving or (usu.) sewing, knitting, or the like; *esp.* any of the lighter occupations of this kind, as a distinctively feminine occupation; also *concr.*, the fabric or the thing made of it, esp. while being made or operated upon. late ME. **9.** An excavation in the earth, made for the purpose of obtaining metals or minerals; a mine. *Obs.* exc. = WORKING *vbl. sb.* II. 1475. **10.** *pl.* An establishment where some industrial labour, esp. manufacture, is carried on, including the whole of the buildings and machinery used. Now commonly construed as sing. (in earlier use also sing. in form) 1581. **11.** A set of parts forming a machine or piece of mechanism: orig. *sing.*, esp. as the second element of compounds; as an independent word now only *pl.*, the internal mechanism of a clock or watch 1628.

1. We all are the worke of thy hondes COVERDALE *Isa.* 64:8. **b.** Other Hereticks..condemned Marriage as the W. of the Devil 1753. **3. b.** *Clerk of the Works*, an officer who superintends the erection of buildings, etc. **5.** A man who publishes his Works in a Volume ADDISON. **6.** They breake downe all yᵉ carued worcke therof BIBLE (Great) *Ps.* 74:6. **10.** We went to see..silk works 1748. **11.** He took to pieces the eight-day clock..under pretence of cleaning the works DICKENS.

Phrases. **At w.: a.** Occupied with labour; engaged in a task; working, esp. at one's regular occupation. **b.** *gen.* Occupied in some action or process; actively engaged; operating. **In w.** In regular occupation. **Of w.**—*of all w.*, employed in all kinds of w., esp. in a household: chiefly in *maid-of-all-w.*; hence allus. **Out of w.** Having no w. to do, unemployed, workless. Also *attrib.*, or as *sb.* **To go to w.** To proceed to some action (expressed or implied); to commence operations. So *to fall to w.* **To set to w.: a.** *trans.* To set (a person, the faculties, etc.) to a task, or to do something; *refl.* to set about doing something. **b.** *intr.* for *refl.* **To cut out w.** *for* (a person). To prepare work to be done by him, to give him something to do; now only in *to have* (*all*) *one's w. cut out* (colloq.), to have as much as one can manage to do. **To make w.: a.** (also *to make a w.*) To work havoc or confusion; hence, to make a to-do or fuss. **b.** *To make w. for*, to give (a person, etc.) something to do. **c.** with qualifying adj., as *to make good, short*, etc. *w.* (*of* or *with*) a person or thing, to do the business, or deal with the person or thing, well, shortly, etc.; often with special implication, as *to make short w. of*, to destroy or put an end to quickly. **Good w.** A morally commendable or virtuous act (also colloq. as *int.* in commendation of some action or performance); *esp.* an act of piety; usu. *pl.* such acts done in obedience to divine law, or as the fruits of faith or godliness. *Prov.* Many hondys makyn lygth worke. ME. All w. and no play, makes Jack a dull boy 1659.

attrib. and *Comb.*, as *w.-girl, -place, -room*, etc.; **w.-bag, -basket,** a bag, or basket, to contain implements and materials for needlework; **-bench,** a bench, with accessories, at which mechanics work; **-box,** a box to contain instruments and materials for needlework; **-hand,** (*a*) a person employed by another to do w.; (*b*) with defining adj., as *a good w.-hand*, one who is a 'good hand' at w., a capable worker; **-mate,** fellow-labourer; **-shy** *a.*, shy of or disinclined for w., lazy; **-table,** a table for supporting working materials and tools; *esp.* a small table with compartments and drawers, and sometimes with a well for needlework; **-train,** a train of waggons or trucks for conveying materials for construction or repair of a railway, etc.

Work (wɒ̄ɹk), *v.* Pa. t. and pple. **worked** (wɒ̄ɹkt), *arch.* and *techn.* **wrought** (rǭt). [(1) OE. *wyrćan* (*worhte, ġeworht*) :- Gmc. **wurkjan*, **wurht-*; (2) OE. (Mercian) *wircan* :- Gmc. **werkjan*, **warht-* (**wurht-*); (3) late OE. *wercan, weorc*(*e*)*an*, partly after the sb. The Indo-Eur. base **worg- werg- wr̥g-* appears in Gr. ἔρδω, ῥέζω I do, perf. ἔοργα, ὄργανον ORGAN, ὄργιον ORGY. The normal descendant of OE. *wyrcan* would be **worch*; the substitution of *k* was due mainly to the sb. The new pa. t. and pa. pple. *worked* has supplanted the original *wrought* in most senses.] **I.** *trans.* **1.** To do, perform, practise (a deed, course of action, task, process, etc.). Now *arch.*; chiefly with cogn. obj., or in such phr. as *to w. a miracle, to w. wonders*. **b.** To do (something evil or harmful). *arch.* OE. **2.** To perform, carry out, execute (a person's will, advice, etc.). *Obs.* or *arch.* OE. **3.** To produce by (or as by) labour or exertion; to make; to fashion. *Obs.* or *arch.* in gen. sense; often, now usu., implying artistic or ornamental workmanship. OE. **b.** Said of God: To create. Also in *pass. Obs.* or *rare arch.* OE. **c.** To construct, build (a house, wall, etc.). *Obs.* or *rare arch.* OE. **d.** const. *of*, rarely *out of* (the material or constituents); also *in* (some material), usu. implying artistic or ornamental workmanship. (Now almost always in pa. pple. *wrought*.) OE. †**4.** To compose (a book or writing), to write –1746. **5.** To make (a 'web' or textile fabric), to weave; to make (something consisting of such fabric) by means of needlework, to sew or knit; to embroider ME. **6.** To make (an image or figure); to delineate, paint, draw, or carve; also, to represent by an image, portray. *Obs.* or *arch.* exc. in special connections. ME. †**7.** To cause to be.., make, render; to bring into a specified state; also, to make or create in the form of –1639. **8.** To make, form, or fashion *into* something; to make up 1538. **9.** To put in, insert, incorporate, esp. in the way of construction or composition 1663. **b.** To graft (*on* a stock) 1658. **10.** To effect, bring about, bring to pass; to cause, produce ME. †**11.** To act in order to or so as to effect (something); to plan, contrive; to manage (a business or proceeding) –1667. **12.** To bestow labour or effort upon; to operate upon: *esp.* **a.** To till, cultivate (land) OE. **b.** To get (stone or slate from a quarry, ore or coal from a mine, etc.) by labour; also with the quarry, etc. as obj. ME. **c.** To manipulate (a substance) so as to bring it into the required condition; *esp.* to knead, press, etc. (a plastic substance), or to mix or incorporate (such substances) together by this means. late ME. **d.** To shape (stone, metal, or other hard substance) by cutting or other process; also, to beat out or shape (metal) by hammering 1665. **e.** *colloq.* or *slang.* To go through or about (a place) for the purposes of one's business or occupation; to carry on some operation in; *spec.* of a hound, of an itinerant vendor, beggar, etc., of a clergyman, and of a canvasser 1834. **f.** *slang.* To deal with in some way; to get, or to get rid of, esp. by artifice 1839. **g.** To operate upon so as to get into some state or convert into something else; *refl.* with *compl. adj.* to go through some process so as to become 1594. **13.** *Math.*, etc. = *w. out* 1593. **14. a.** To act upon the mind or will of; to influence, induce, persuade (esp. by subtle or insidious means); to bring into a particular mental state, etc. 1595. **b.** To act upon the feelings of; to stir, move, incite 1605. **c.** Of medicine: To take effect upon 1712. **d.** To practise on, hoax, cheat. *U.S.* 1892. **15.** To move (something) into or out of some position, or with alternating movement (to and fro, etc.): usu. with some implication of force exerted against resistance or impediment 1617. **16.** To direct or manage the movement of; to guide or drive in a particular course; *spec.*, *Naut.* to direct the movement of (a ship) by management of the sails and rudder 1667. **17.** *refl.* To make one's (or its) way 1576. **18.** with *way*, etc. as obj. 1713. **19.** To set or compel (a person, animal, etc.) to work; to employ or use in work 1445. **b.** To bring or get into some condition by labour or exertion 1628. **20.** To set in action, cause to act; to exercise (a faculty, etc.); to actuate, operate, manage. late ME. **b.** In fig. or allusive phrases expressing cunning management or manœuvring, as *to w. the oracle, the ropes* 1859.

1. She worcketh knittinge of stockings 1600. **b.** Depart from me, ye that worke iniquity *Matt.* 7:23. **5.** Now she vnweaues the web that she hath wrought SHAKS. I'm going to w. Mr. Laurence a pair of slippers 1868. **7.** *Hen. VIII*, II. ii. 47. **9.** Those occasional Dissertations, which he has wrought into the Body of his History STEELE. **10.** He wirkis sorrow to himsell DUNBAR. The ravages that confinement and sorrow had worked upon him 1831. **11.** To w. in close design, by fraud or guile What force effected not MILT. **12.** *To w. one's passage* (etc.), to pay for one's passage on board ship by working during the voyage. **e.** A professional beggar, who 'works' seventy or eighty streets in a few hours 1897. **14. b.** My dull Braine was wrought with things forgotten SHAKS. Endeavouring to w. herself into a state of resentment DICKENS. **16.** Having no Sails to w. the Ship with DE FOE. **17.** The women worked themselves into the centre of the crowd DICKENS. **19.** Whether it was right to w. little boys and girls in the mills, longer than from six o'clock in the morning to six o'clock in the evening 1841. **b.** She worked herself to death DICKENS. Richard said that he would w. his fingers to the bone for Ada. DICKENS. **20.** They are..dead dolls, wooden, worked with wires KINGSLEY.

II. *intr.* **1.** To do something, or to do things generally; to conduct oneself, behave, 'do'. *Obs.* or *arch.* OE. **2.** To act for a purpose or so as to gain an end; to plot, contrive. *arch.* OE. **3.** Of a thing: To do something; to perform a function, or produce an effect; *esp.* to act in the desired way, do what is required; to be practicable or effectual, to succeed ME. **b.** Of a machine or apparatus: To perform its proper function; to act, operate 1610. **c.** Of a part of mechanism: To have its proper action or movement in relation to another part with which it is in contact 1770. **4.** To do something involving effort (of body or mind); to exert oneself for a definite purpose, esp. in order to produce something or effect some useful result, to gain one's livelihood OE. **b.** const. *at, on* or *upon* (a material object, a subject of study or literary treatment, an occupation, etc.) ME. **5.** To exert oneself in order to accomplish something or gain some end (expressed by context) ME. **6.** To do one's ordinary business; to pursue a regular occupation. Also more widely, to do something for a definite end, to engage in some systematic occupation. (Often coinciding with II. 4.) ME. **b.** const. *in* the material upon which labour is expended in some business or manufacture 1471. **c.** *spec.* of sporting dogs 1832. **7.** To perform the work proper or incidental to one's business or avocation. *Obs.* exc. as in b. ME. **b.** Said esp. of the performance of artistic work or the practice of an artist 1539. **8.** *Math.*, etc. To proceed (in a particular way) in calculation; to go through the process of solving a problem. late ME. **9.** Of a substance: To behave in a particular way while being worked 1489. **10.** To operate *upon* (physically, mentally, or morally), produce an effect upon; to take effect *on*, affect, influence. late ME. **b.** To ache (Now north. dial. chiefly in the form *wark* from OE. *wærcan.*) late ME. **11.** Of liquor: To ferment 1570. **12.** To go or move along, or in a particular course; to make one's (or its) way; now usu., to make way slowly, laboriously, with some exertion or difficulty, or in an indirect course. late ME. **b.** To make one's (or its) way slowly or with effort through something. late ME. **c.** *Naut.* Of a sailing vessel: To sail in a particular course, to make sail; *esp.* to beat to windward, to tack 1633. **d.** To proceed in a particular direction in some operation 1877. **13.** To move restlessly, violently, or convulsively; to be in a state of agitation or commotion; to toss, seethe; *Naut.* of a ship, to strain or 'labour' so that the fastenings become slack; so of an engine or carriage 1581. **14.** With complement: To move irregularly or unsteadily so as to become out of gear 1770.

1. *All's Well* IV. ii. 29. **2.** Without the King's assent or knowledge, You wrought to be a Legate SHAKS. **3.** All thynges worke for the best [A.V. worke together for good] vnto them that love god TINDALE *Rom.* 8:28. Lady Lufton was beginning to fear that her plan would not w. TROLLOPE. **c.** The four bevelled nuts w. into the bevelled wheels..and so turn them 1825. **4.** For men must w., and women must weep KINGSLEY. **b.** Vulcan working at the Anvil PRIOR. How hard some folks do w. at what they call pleasure 1840. **5.** 1 *Hen. VI*, III. iii. 27. **6.** Rude Mechanicals, That worke for bread vpon Athenian stals SHAKS. **7. b.** *Timon* I. i. 200. **10.** He toke poison..but..it would not worke vpon hym UDALL. She.. worked on his feelings by pretending to be ill MACAULAY. **12. d.** The paper hanger generally works from left to right 1877. **13.** With his face all working with sorrow STEVENSON. **14.** The anchor on the lee bow had worked loose 1840.

With advs. **W. in.: a.** *trans.* To insert, introduce, incorporate. **b.** *intr.* To make one's (or its) way in. **W. off.: a.** *trans.* To print off (as from a plate); esp. to print in final form, so as to be ready for publication or distribution. **b.** To perpetrate, 'play off'. **c.** To take off or away by a gradual process; to get rid of, disburden oneself of, free oneself from, by some continuous action or effort. **d.** To finish working at; to dispose of and get done with. **e.** To put to death; to hang (*slang*). **W. out.: a.** *trans.* To bring, fetch, or get out by some process or course of action; to get rid of. **b.** *intr.* To make its way out, esp. from being embedded or enclosed in something. **c.** *trans.* To work (a mine, etc.) until it yields no more. **d.** To discharge (a debt or obligation) by labour instead of a money payment. **e.** To bring about, effect, produce, or procure (a result) by labour or effort; to carry out, accomplish (a plan or purpose). **f.** To go through a process of calculation or consideration so as to arrive at the solution of (a problem or question), to solve; also, to reckon out, calculate. **g.** *intr.* for *pass.*: (*a*) of a course of events, narrative, etc.: To proceed so as to issue in a particular result; (*b*) with *at*, of a quantity: To amount to (so much) when reckoned up, to 'come to'. **h.** To bring to a fuller or finished state; to develop, elaborate. **W. up.:** †**a.** *trans.* To build up, construct (a wall, etc.). **b.** *intr.* To make one's (or its) way up, esp. against impediment or indirectly; to ascend, advance. **c.** *trans.* To stir up, mix, or compound, as a plastic substance. **d.** To make up (material) *into* something by labour; also, to bring into some condition, esp. so as to be ready for use. **e.** *gen.*, or in ref. to something immaterial; To make up, develop, expand, enlarge (*to* or *into* something). **f.** To bring by labour or effort *to* or *into* a higher state or condition. **g.** To make up, form, construct, produce (something material or immaterial): with special ref. to the process, or to the labour, etc. expended upon it. **h.** *Naut.* To set to or keep at needless and disagreeable hard work as a punishment. **i.** To 'get up' (a subject) by mental labour; to master by research. **j.** To bring by effort, or by some influence, into a particular state of mind or feeling, esp. one of strong emotion; to induce or persuade by effort *to do* something; to put into a state of excitement, excite, agitate. Also *refl.* **k.** *intr.* To be gradually stirred up or excited. Hence **Worked** (wɔ̄ɹkt) *ppl. a.* in senses of the vb.; *esp.* executed or ornamented with needlework, engraving, or the like.

Workable (wɔ̄·ɹkăb'l), *a.* 1545. [f. prec. + -ABLE.] **1.** Of substances or materials: That can be worked, fashioned, or manipulated for use; said also of the state in which they are capable of being worked. **2.** That can be worked, managed, or conducted, as a contrivance, establishment, institution, etc. 1756. **b.** of a plan, system, scheme, or the like 1865.

2. The only w. boat of the Lord Hood was manned 1881. Hence **Workabi·lity. Wo·rkableness.**

Workaday, work-a-day (wɔ̄·ɹkădeⁱ), *sb.* and *a.* [ME. *werkedai* (trisyllabic) XI, of uncertain origin, perh. after *sunnedei* SUNDAY, the later *workyday* being after *holiday*, with *workaday* quite late.] **A.** *sb.* A day on which work is ordinarily done (dist. from *holiday*); a working-day. *Obs.* or *dial.* **B.** *attrib.* passing into *adj.* Belonging to or characteristic of a work-day or its occupations; characterized by a regular succession or round of tasks and employments; of ordinary humdrum everyday life: freq. in phr. *this w. world* 1554.

Prythee tel her but a worky day Fortune SHAKS. We cannot long indulge in day-dreams in this w. world 1859.

Work-day (wɔ̄·ɹkdeⁱ), *sb.* and *a.* late ME. [OE. *weorcdæǵ* does not seem to have survived; ME. *werkday* is prob. a new formation.] **A.** *sb.* A day on which work is ordinarily performed; a week-day. **B.** *attrib.* passing into *adj.* Belonging to or characteristic of a work-day; performed, worn, etc. on a work-day 1500.

My woorkday gowne..thre woorkday aprens, one workday band 1622.

Worker (wɔ̄·ɹkəɹ). late ME. [f. WORK *v.* + -ER¹.] **1.** One who makes, produces, or contrives. †**a.** Applied to God as maker or creator –1602. **b.** An author, producer, contriver, or doer. *arch.* late ME. **c.** *transf.* of things ME. **2.** One who works or does work of any kind; esp. one who works *in* a certain medium, *at* a specified trade, etc. or in a certain position or status (often denoted by prefixed sb., etc., as *cloth-w.*, *iron-w.*; *brain-w.*, *hand-w.*). late ME. **b.** In emphatic use, esp. as opp. to *idler*, or the like 1628. **c.** One who is employed for a wage, esp. in manual or industrial work; now often in the language of social economics, a 'producer of wealth', as opp. to *capitalist* 1848. **d.** Of animals: (*a*) A horse, dog, etc. that works (well) 1844. (*b*) The neuter or undeveloped female of certain social hymenopterous or other insects, as ants and bees, which supplies food and performs other services for the community 1747. **e.** *U.S. Politics.* One of a class of political agents or partisans subordinate to a 'boss' 1888. **3.** Applied to apparatus or pieces of machinery, as (*a*) one of the small card-covered cylinders in a carding-machine; (*b*) *pl.* in pillow lace-making, the bobbins that are worked across a pattern, etc. 1594. **4.** With advs., as *w.-up* 1656.

2. b. The distinction between workers and idlers, as between knaves and honest men RUSKIN.

attrib., as *w.-ant*, *-bee*: **w. bobbin** = 3 (*b*); **w. card** = 3 (*a*).

Workfolk (wɒ̄·ɹkfōᵘk). 1475. [FOLK *sb.*] = WORK-PEOPLE, *esp.* farm labourers.

Workful (wɒ̄·ɹkfŭl), *a.* ME. [f. WORK *sb.* + -FUL.] †**1.** Active, operative –1674. **2.** Full of (hard) work; hard-working 1854. Hence **Wo·rkfulness,** †activity; laborious activity.

Workhouse (wɒ̄·ɹkhaus). [Late OE. *weorchūs*; f. WORK *sb.* + HOUSE *sb.*[1]] **1.** A house, shop, or room in which work is regularly performed; a workshop or factory. *Obs.* or *Hist.* **2.** *spec.* orig. A house established for the provision of work for the unemployed poor of a parish; later, an institution, administered by Guardians of the Poor, in which paupers are lodged and the able-bodied set to work. (Formerly †*house of work*, †*working-house*, †*house of industry*; see also POORHOUSE, UNION 9 b.) 1652. **3.** A prison or house of correction for petty offenders. *U.S.* 1888.

2. Most well-regulated Bridewells are Paradises compared to the Oxford Work-house 1797.

Working (wɒ̄·ɹkiŋ), *vbl. sb.* ME. [f. WORK *v.* + -ING[1].] The action of WORK *v.*; the result of this. **I. 1.** Performance of work or labour; †also, that which is done, work. †**2.** Performance, execution, achievement (of some particular work or action) –1693. †**3.** Making, construction; handiwork, workmanship –1726. **4.** The action of operating or performing work upon something; manipulation, management; exploitation (of a mine, etc.) 1450. **b.** The carrying on or putting into operation (of a scheme, system, legislation, etc.) 1832. **5.** Action, operation. **a.** Of a person; esp. *collect. sing.* and *pl.* actions, doings, deeds. late ME. **b.** Of a drug, medicine, etc. late ME. **c.** Of the mind, conscience, etc. Often *pl.* 1588. **d.** The conduct or operations collectively of a factory, vessel, or the like 1873. **6.** Influential operation; influence; also, the result or effect of operation or influence. late ME. **7.** Mathematical calculation; now chiefly, the statement of the operations involved in solving a mathematical problem. late ME. **8.** Fermentation of liquor 1565. **9.** Restless movement of water (esp. the sea); straining of a ship, vehicle, etc. so as to loosen the fittings 1582. **b.** Involuntary movement of the face or mouth, esp. due to emotion 1800. **10.** The proper action or movement of a piece of mechanism or the like 1645. **11.** Gradual movement or progress (as against resistance) 1683.

5. b. After my physicks w. 1648. **c.** I am sicke with w. of my thoughts SHAKS. **6.** The w. of clerical prejudice in..a liberal mind 1861. **7.** A knowledge of mathematics may be gained without the perpetual w. of examples 1873. **10.** The workings of his lungs pumped great jets of blood out KINGSLEY.

II. *concr.* A place in which mineral is or has been worked; a mining excavation 1766. **III.** With advs., as *w.-off*, *-together*, *-up* 1623.

attrib. and *Comb.*: *w. hour(s*; *w. capital, expenses*; **w. drawing,** usu. pl., the drawings made of the plan, etc. of a building from which the workmen carry out the construction of the work; †**-house,** = WORKHOUSE; **w. load,** the maximum load that a member in a machine or other structure is designed to bear; **w. order,** a condition in which a machine, system, etc. works (well, badly, etc.); **w. room,** (*a*) space in which one may work, room for the performance of work; (*b*) a work-room.

Working (wɒ̄·ɹkiŋ), *ppl. a.* late ME. [-ING[2].] That works. **1.** Of a person, etc.: Active, operative; energetic. *Obs.* or *arch.* †**b.** Of a thing: Operative, effective –1709. **2.** That works or labours; *esp.* that works for an employer in a manual or industrial occupation 1639. **b.** In contrast with: (*a*) 'master', 'managing', etc., in designations of trade or occupation; (*b*) 'sleeping', in ref. to partners in a firm 1708. **c.** Mil. *W. party*: a party of men detailed for a special piece of work outside their ordinary duties 1744. **d.** Of horses and cattle: Employed in work, esp. in agricultural work 1613. **e.** Of a bee or ant: That is a 'worker' 1766. **3.** Of the sea, etc.: Agitated, tossing. *poet.* 1581. **4.** Of the features: Moving involuntarily or convulsively, esp. as the result of emotion 1753. **5.** Of an organism, piece of machinery, etc.: That performs its function (esp. in a specified manner); that 'goes' (as opp. to being stationary) 1608. **b.** *Naut.* applied to certain sails 1882. **6. a.** Of a majority: Sufficient to secure the passing of measures 1858. **b.** Of a theory, etc.: That provides a basis upon which to work 1849.

1. b. Things..Sad, high, and w., full of State and Woe SHAKS. **4.** The w. lip was loosened; and the tears came streaming forth DICKENS. **5.** But are you flesh and bloud? Haue you a w. pulse, and are no Fairie? SHAKS. **6. a.** A w. majority of about a hundred in the House of Commons 1858. **b.** No one asks more of Evolution at present than permission to use it as a w. theory 1894.

Wo·rking(-)cla·ss. Chiefly pl. **wo·rking cla·sses.** 1813. [f. prec.] The grade or grades of society comprising those who are employed to work for wages in manual or industrial occupations. **b.** *attrib.*, as *w. family, vote*, etc. 1869.

What are termed *the* working-classes, as if the only workers were those who wrought with their hands 1844.

Wo·rking(-)day:. 1478. [f. WORKING *vbl. sb.* + DAY *sb.*] **1.** A work-day. **b.** *attrib.* or as *adj.* 1533. **2.** The portion of a day devoted to work or allotted to labour as a day's work 1875.

1. They quite forgot the days, and knew not a Sunday from a w. any longer DE FOE. **2.** Leaving the length of the working day unchanged 1875.

Wo·rking-ma·n. 1816. A man of the working classes; a man employed to work for a wage, esp. in a manual or industrial occupation. So **Wo·rking-wo·man.**

The word 'working-man' was held to include a clerk or small shopkeeper, or anyone whose total income did not exceed £150 a year 1896.

Workless (wɒ̄·ɹklės), *a.* 1484. [f. WORK *sb.* + -LESS.] **1.** Doing no work; inactive, idle. *Obs.* or *arch.* **2.** Unprovided with work; out of work, unemployed. Often *absol.* with *the.* 1848. Hence **Wo·rklessness.**

Workman (wɒ·ɹkmæ̆n). *Pl.* **workmen.** [OE. *weorcmann.*] **1.** A man engaged to do work or (usu.) manual labour, esp. one employed upon some particular piece of work; often (contextually) a skilled worker. **b.** Connoting a class or grade, or in correlation with 'employer', 'capitalist', or the like 1704. **2.** A skilled or expert craftsman. *Obs.* exc. in *Glassmaking*, the first man of a 'chair'. 1478. **b.** *transf.*; e.g. applied to a rider, esp. in hunting, who manages his horse well or is conversant with the technique of the field; also to a horse that takes its fences well, etc. 1832. **3.** One who works or practises his craft or art (in some specified manner) 1484.

2. b. The Squire having hit off his fox like a w. 1832. **3.** Never had ill workemen good tooles 1633. Hence **Wo·rkmanly** *a.* and *adv.* = WORKMANLIKE 1467.

Workmanlike (wɒ̄·ɹkmæ̆nləik), *adv.* and *a.* 1447. [See -LIKE.] **A.** *adv.* In a manner or style characteristic of a good workman.

To be all plastered over with lyme and hayer workeman lyke 1618.

B. *adj.* **1.** Of or pertaining to a workman; characteristic of or suitable to a workman (*rare*) 1663. **2.** Characteristic of or resembling (that of) a good workman 1739.

2. To compleat the intended Bridge..in a..w. Manner 1739. Two very workmanlike little horses 1878.

Workmanship (wɒ̄·ɹkmæ̆nʃip). late ME. [f. WORKMAN + -SHIP.] †**1.** The performance or execution of work or a work; work, labour –1818. †**2.** Action, agency, operation –1641. **3.** That which is wrought or made by a workman or craftsman; (a person's) work. Also *transf.* something produced: *arch.* exc. as in *piece of w.* 1523. **4.** Skill or cunning as a workman; craftsmanship as exhibited in a piece of work 1529.

3. A little Hut,..the W...of some Indian 1751. There's no denying she's a rare bit o' w. GEO. ELIOT. **4.** Idiots admire in things the Beauty of their Materials, but Artists that of the Workmanship BOYLE.

Wo·rk-ma:ster. Now *rare.* 1533. A master workman; an overseer or employer of workmen. **b.** *fig.*: esp. applied to God as creator and ruler; rarely of a thing 1535. So **Wo·rk-mi:stress,** only *fig.*, chiefly of Nature.

Workpeople (wɒ̄·ɹkpī:p'l). 1708. [WORK *sb.*] People employed in manual or industrial labour for a wage; workmen and (or) workwomen.

Workshop (wɒ̄·ɹkʃɒp). 1562. [f. WORK *sb.* + SHOP *sb.* 3.] A room, apartment, or building in which manual or industrial work is carried on.

transf. England..the w. for the world DISRAELI.

Workwoman (wɒ̄·ɹkwu:măn). 1530. [f. after *workman.*] A woman who works; a female worker; †a woman who does needlework.

Worky (wɒ̄·ɹki). *U.S.* 1833. [f. WORK *sb.* + -Y[6].] A worker or operative; one of the working class.

World (wɒ̄ɹld). [OE. *weorold, worold, world* = OFris. *wrald, warld*, OS. *wėrold* (Du. *wereld*), OHG. *weralt* (G. *welt*), ON. *verǫld*; a formation peculiar to Gmc. f. **weraz* man (OE., OS., OHG. *wer*, cogn. with L. *vir*) + **ald-* age (cf. OLD), the etymol. meaning being, therefore, 'age' or 'life of man'.] **I.** Human existence; a period of this. **1. a.** Chiefly *This w.*, *the w.*: the earthly state of human existence; this present life. **b.** *The other, another, the next, a better w., the w. to come* or *to be*: the future state, the life after death. Sometimes viewed as the 'realm' of departed spirits. OE. **c.** *gen.* A state of (present or future) existence ME. **2.** The pursuits and interests of this present life; *esp.*, in religious use, the least worthy of these; temporal or mundane affairs OE. **3.** The affairs and conditions of life; chiefly in phr., esp. with the verb *go*, as *how the w. goes*, how events shape themselves, etc.; also *to let the w. wag* OE. †**b.** State of human affairs, state of things; hence, season of time as marked by the state of affairs –1614. **4.** Secular (or lay) life and interests, as dist. from religious (or clerical); also, secular (or lay) people OE. **b.** In the Society of Friends applied to those outside their own body 1648. †**c.** *To go to the w., to be* (a man, woman) *of the w.*, to be married –1601. **d.** In biblical and religious use: Those who are concerned only with the interests and pleasures of this life or with temporal or mundane things; the worldly and irreligious. late ME. †**5.** An age or (long) period of time in earthly or human existence or history; *pl.* ages –1674. **b.** A period or age of human history characterized by certain conditions or indicated by the character or those living in it. *Obs.* exc. as coloured by III. 3. 1530. **6.** *W. without* (ME. *abuten* or *buten*) *end*, earlier also †*in world(s of world(s*, etc. (tr. eccl.L. *in secula seculorum, in seculum seculi*): for ever and ever, for all time, through eternity. Later used hyperbolically: Endlessly, eternally. Hence as *adj. phr.* = perpetual, everlasting, eternal; and as *subst. phr.* = eternal existence, endlessness, eternity. ME.

1. She was too good for this w. and for me, and she died six weeks before our marriage-day DICKENS. *To the world's end*, as long as human things shall last, to the end of time; similarly *as long as the* or *this w. lasts, in this w. To bring into the w.*, to give birth to. *To come into* (or *to*) *the w.*, to be born; *fig.* (of a book) to be published. *To go* or *depart out of this w.*, to die. **c.** Both the worlds I giue to negligence, Let come what comes SHAKS. **2.** The w. is too much with us WORDSW. **3.** Some must watch, while some must sleepe; So runnes the w. away SHAKS. How 's the w. used you since this morning? DICKENS. *How goes the w. with* (a person), how are his affairs. *As the* (or *this*) *w. goes*, as things are, considering the state of affairs. **b.** This is no w. To play with Mammets SHAKS. **4.** How happy is the blameless Vestal's lot! The w. forgetting, by the w. forgot POPE. Having resigned the situation I held in the w. 1888. **d.** The W. with fruitless Pain Seek Happiness below WESLEY. **5.** *Tr. & Cr.* III. ii. 180. **6.** A time me thinkes too short, To make a w.-without-end bargaine in SHAKS.

II. The earth or a region of it; the universe or a part of it. **1.** The earth and all created things upon it; the terraqueous globe and its inhabitants OE. **b.** In generalized sense, usu. qualified by *a.* 1676. **c.** *pl.* Used hyperbolically for: 'a great quantity'; often advb. 'a great deal', 'infinitely'. (*a*) pl. *Not..for worlds*, not on any account; (*b*) sing. *Not for* (*all*) *the w., not for anything in the w.* 1586. **2.** Any part of the universe considered as an entity, as *lower* or *nether w.*, Hades or hell, less freq. the earth; UNDERWORLD ME. **b.** A planet or other heavenly body, esp. one viewed as inhabited 1713. **3.** The material universe as an ordered system; the system of created things; the cosmos ME. **4.** The sphere within which one's interests are bound up or one's activities find scope; (one's) sphere of action or thought 1586. **5.** A section or part of the earth at large, as a place of inhabitation or settlement 1555. **6.** A division of created things; *esp.* each of the three primary divisions of natural objects (the animal, vegetable, and mineral kingdoms) 1695. **7.** A group or system of things or beings associated by common characteristics (denoted by a qualifying word or phr.), or considered as constituting a unity 1673.

1. The W. was all before them, where to choose Thir place of rest, and Providence thir guide MILT. *Citizen of the w.*: see CITIZEN 2. *Universal w.*: see UNIVERSAL *a.* 4; cf. VARSAL. *Wide w.*: see WIDE *a.* I. 1 b. Phr. (chiefly *fig.*) with *go round*; Their fame it shall last while the w. goes round BURNS; It's Love that makes the w. go round! W. S. GILBERT. *The world's end*, the farthest limit of the earth (chiefly hyperbolical). **b.** Each thinks a W. too little for his sway DRYDEN. **c.** Nor doth this wood lacke worlds of company SHAKS. I'm sure I wouldn't stand in his way for worlds 1874. **4.** [His] w. was a narrow one, consisting as it did of himself and his bank-book 1898. **5.** *New W.*, a continent or country discovered or colonized at a comparatively late period, esp. the continents of America, as dist. from the *Old W.*, or the continents of the Eastern Hemisphere, esp. Europe and Asia, as being known before the discovery of America. **7.** Then, all the w. of waters sleeps again COWPER. The Outdoor W.: or, Young Collector's Handbook 1893.

III. The inhabitants of the earth, or a section of them. **1.** The human race; the whole of mankind; human society OE. **2.** The body of living persons in general; society at large, 'people'; often with ref. to its judgement or opinion 1603. **3.** Usu. with qualification: A particular division, section, or generation of the earth's inhabitants or human society, with ref. to the time or place of their existence or to their interests or pursuits. late ME. **4.** Human society considered in relation to its activities, difficulties, and the like; hence, the ways, practices, or customs of the people among whom one lives; the occupations and interests of society at large 1449. **b.** with ref. to social status or worldly fortune 1687. **5.** High or fashionable society. More explicitly *the w. of fashion, the great w.*, etc. 1673.

1. *Against the w.*, in opposition to or in the face of all mankind; hence, against all opposition. †*World's shame, shame of the w.*, universal or public disgrace. **2.** There are all sorts of stories of the Lord High Admiral, and the w. says he is mad 1828. **3.** A gentleman well known in the theatrical w. SHERIDAN. The whole w. of ruffiandom 1882. Theodosius left the Roman w. in peace 1890. **4.** Olde folkes you know, haue discretion,..and know the w. SHAKS. He was a perfect child in the world's ways 1882. *To begin the w.*, to begin to take an active part in the affairs of life; to start one's career. **b.** Indications of the good gentleman's having gone down in the w. of late DICKENS. **5.** To know the w.! a modern phrase For visits, ombre, balls, and plays SWIFT.

Phrases. **A world: a.** A vast quantity, an 'infinity'; sometimes more emphatically *a whole w. of.* **b.** Used advb.: Infinitely, vastly (*arch.*). †**c.** *It is a w.*, it is a great thing, it is a marvel. **The w.: a.** *In the w.*, on earth, in existence; (*a*) as an intensive phr. after a superlative or *all, no, nothing*, etc.; (*b*) intensifying an interrogative, as *how, why, what in the w...?* †**b.** *Of the w. = in the w.* **c.** *Of (all) the w.*, out of the whole w. above all others. **d.** *To think the w. of*, to have the highest possible opinion of or regard for. **e.** See MAN OF THE W. So *woman of the w.*, a woman who is experienced in the ways of life or the conventions of society. **f.** Living the secular as opposed to the religious life. **All the w.: a.** The whole of the inhabited globe; the entire earth (or universe). **b.** (= Fr. *tout le monde.*) Everybody in existence; in narrower sense, everybody in the community, the public. *Against all the w.*, in opposition to or competition with everybody. *All the w. and his wife*: see WIFE 2. **c.** Everybody in fashionable society; everybody of account. **d.** Everything in existence: often in intensive emotional use = All that is of value or account *to* a person, something supremely precious. **e.** *For all the w.*, in regard to or taking into consideration everything in the w.; hence, in every respect, exactly (like, etc.). **The whole w.** = *all the w.* a, b.

attrib. and *Comb.* in simple attrib., objective, and advb. uses (sometimes echoing German compounds), as *w. sadness, -sorrow*; *w.-famous, -renowned, -weary*, adjs.; often passing into adj., with the meaning 'of or pertaining to the whole w., world-wide, universal', as *w.-commerce, -empire, -war*; also **w.-history** [G. *weltgeschichte*], history embracing the events of the whole w.; **-old** *a.* [G. *weltalt*] as old as the world; **-policy, -politics** [G. *weltpolitik*], a policy or politics based upon considerations affecting the w. as a whole; **-ruler,** a ruler of the (known) w.; **w.('s series** *Baseball*, a series of games to decide the professional championship of the U.S.; **-soul** [G. *weltgeist, -seele*], the animating principle which informs the physical world; **-state,** (*a*) a state comprising the whole w.; (*b*) a state possessing w.-power. Hence **Wo·rldish** *a.* (*rare*) of or belonging to this w., worldly. **Wo·rldless** *a.* (*rare*) not having a w. to live in; not containing a w. or worlds; free from the w., unworldly.

Worldliness (wɒ̄·ɹldlinės). late ME. [f. WORLDLY *a.* + -NESS.] The condition of being worldly; devotion to worldly affairs to the neglect of religious duties or spiritual needs; love of the world and its pleasures.

Worldling (wɒ̄·ɹldliŋ). 1549. [f. WORLD + -LING¹.] **1.** One who is devoted to the interests and pleasures of the world; a worldly or worldly-minded person. †**2. a.** A 'citizen of the world', cosmopolite. **b.** An inhabitant of the world. –1816.

1. The various pretexts under which Worldlings delude themselves and neglect the welfare of their Souls 1844.

Worldly (wɒ̄·ɹldli), *a.* [OE. *woruldlić*; see -LY¹.] **1.** Of or belonging to this world (as dist. from the other world); earthly, mundane. †**2.** Of, belonging to, or connected with this world and its inhabitants; earthly, human, mortal –1674. †**3.** Of or belonging to the world (as dist. from the church or the cloister); secular –1658. **4.** Devoted to the world and its pursuits ME.

1. With al my w. Goodes I thee endowe *Bk. Com. Prayer, Matrimony.* Too much a child in w. matters DICKENS. **4.** W. prelatis ful of coueitise symonye & heresie WYCLIF.

Comb.: **w.-minded** *a.*, having a w. mind, having the thoughts set upon the things of this world.

Worldly (wɒ̄·ɹldli), *adv.* ME. [f. after prec. + -LY².] In a worldly manner; with a worldly intent or disposition.

Worldly-wise (stress variable), *a.* late ME. Wise in a worldly manner or in worldly affairs; *transf.* of actions or conduct.

Worldly wiseman, a w. man; now only with allusion to the character so named in Bunyan's *Pilgrim's Progress.*

Wo·rld-power. 1866. [After G. *weltmacht.*] **1.** The power of 'this world' (as dist. from the spiritual world); secular power. **2.** Any of the powers (nations, empires) that dominate the world 1901.

2. The foundation of England's greatness as a w. 1904.

Worldward (wɒ̄·ɹldwǫ̈ɹd), *adv.* (*a.*) 1583. [f. WORLD + -WARD.] **1.** (orig. *To the w.*) In regard to the world; in worldly respects. **2.** Towards or in the direction of the world 1642. **B.** *adj.* Directed towards or facing the world 1857.

World-wide (stress variable), *a.* 1632. [f. WORLD + WIDE *a.*] 'As wide as the world'; extending over or covering the whole world.

Worm (wɒ̄ɹm), *sb.* [OE. *wyrm*, later *wurm*, corresp. to OFris. *wirm*, OS., (O)HG. *wurm* (Du. *worm*), ON. *ormr* serpent, Goth. *waurms* :– Gmc. **wurmiz* and **wurmaz*, rel. to L. *vermis* worm, Gr. *ῥόμος, ῥόμοξ* wood-worm.] **I. 1.** A serpent, snake, dragon. Now only *arch.* †**2.** Any animal that creeps or crawls; a reptile, an insect –1820. **3.** A member of the genus *Lumbricus*; a slender, creeping, naked, limbless animal, usu. brown or reddish, with a soft body divided into a series of segments; an earthworm. More widely, any annelid. OE. **4.** Any endoparasitic helminth breeding in the living body of men and other animals. Usu. *pl.* Also, the disease or disorder constituted by the presence of these parasites. OE. **5.** The larva of an insect; a maggot, grub, or caterpillar, esp. one that feeds on and destroys flesh, fruit, leaves, textile fabrics, and the like. Also collect. *the w.*, as a destructive pest. OE. **b.** The larva or grub of many kinds of beetles, destructive to trees, timber, furniture, etc. OE. **c.** *contextually.* A silkworm OE. **6.** A maggot, or, in popular belief, an earthworm, supposed to eat dead bodies in the grave OE. **b.** *fig.* as one of the pains of Hell (*Mark* 9:48, Isa. 66:24) OE. **7.** †**a.** A tick or mite breeding in the hand, foot, or other part of the body –1605. **b.** *pop.* = COMEDO 1730. **8.** An earthworm, or a larva: **a.** as the food of birds ME. **b.** as bait for fish ME. **9.** A name for various long slender crustaceans and molluscs (e.g. *Teredo navalis*, the ship-w.) which destroy timber by boring. Also collect. *the w.*, as a destructive pest. 1621.

1. Hast thou the pretty worme of Nylus there, That killes and paines not? SHAKS. **3.** Prov. *Tread on a w. and it will turn*, i.e. even the humblest will resent extreme ill-treatment; also, *even a w. will turn*, etc. See also DEW-W., EARTH-WORM, SAND-*w.*, etc. **4.** See ROUND-W., TAPE-WORM, etc. **5.** She..let concealment like a worme i'th budde Feede on her damaske cheeke SHAKS. See also BOOK-W., CADDIS-*w.*, PALMER-W., etc. **6.** Men haue died from time to time, and wormes haue eaten them SHAKS. *Worm's* or *worms' meat*, said of a man's dead body, or of man as mortal; also, *food* or *meat for worms*. **7. a.** *Rom. & Jul.* I. iv. 65.

II. 1. *fig.* A human being likened to a worm or reptile as an object of contempt, scorn, or pity; an abject miserable creature OE. †**b.** With qualification expressing tenderness, playfulness, or commiseration –1626. **2.** *fig.* A grief or passion that preys stealthily on a man's heart or torments his conscience (like a worm in a dead body or a maggot in food); esp. the gnawing pain of remorse OE. †**b.** A whim or 'maggot' in the brain; a streak of insanity –1705. **3.** *The w.*: formerly a pop. name for various ailments supposed to be caused by the working of a 'worm'. †**a.** Colic. *Sc.* –1654. **b.** Toothache. *Sc. Obs.* or *rare.* 1583.

1. Sith that wickide worme, Wiclyf..began to sowe the seed of cisme in the erthe 1402. **b.** *Temp.* III. i. 31. **2.** The Worme of Conscience still begnaw thy Soule SHAKS.

III. 1. A small vermiform ligament or tendon in a dog's tongue, often cut out when the animal is young, as a supposed safeguard against rabies 1530. **b.** A tendon in a dog's tail, often cut or pulled out when the tail is being docked 1877. **2.** An artificial or natural object resembling an earthworm 1702. **b.** *pl.* The coiled pods of *Astragalus hamosus* 1849. **3.** As the name of various implements of spiral form (supposed to resemble the sinuous shape and movement of an earthworm). **a.** A screw fixed on the end of a rod, used for withdrawing the charge or wad from a muzzle-loading gun 1591. **b.** The thread or spiral ridge of a male screw 1677. **c.** The spiral of a female or hollow screw 1725. **d.** An endless or tangent screw the thread of which gears with the teeth of a toothed wheel (or similar device) 1729. **e.** A long spiral or coiled tube connected with the head of a still, in which the vapour is condensed 1641. **f.** A spiral heating flue in a furnace or coiled steam pipe in a boiler 1758. **g.** A spring or strip of metal of spiral shape 1724.

attrib. and *Comb.*: **w.-bark,** the anthelmintic bark of the W. Indian cabbage-tree, *Andira inermis*; **-cast,** the convoluted mass of mould thrown up by an earthworm on the surface of the soil after passing through the worm's body; **-eater,** a bird or other creature that feeds on worms; *spec.* the W.-eating Warbler, *Helminthotherus vermivorus* of the eastern U.S.; **-grass,** the Pinkroot, *Spigelia marilandica*, of the Southern U.S., used as a vermifuge; **-hole,** a hole made by a burrowing worm or insect in wood, fruit, books, etc.; **-shell,** the twisted shell or tube of a marine annelid or mollusc, as *Serpula* and *Vermetus*; **-snake,** any of various small harmless snakes, as *Typhlops nigrescens* and *Carphophis amœna*; **-spring,** a spiral spring. Hence **Wo·rmless** *a.* (*rare*) free from or destitute of worms. **Wo·rm-like** *a.* resembling a w., vermiform; *adv.* after the manner of a w. **Wo·rmling,** a small w. chiefly *fig.*, a poor despicable creature.

Worm (wɒ̄ɹm), *v.* 1564. [f. prec.] **I. 1.** *intr.* To hunt for or catch worms 1576. **2.** *trans.* To cause to be eaten by worms; to devour, as a burrowing worm does. Chiefly *pass.*, to be eaten by worms. 1604. **II. 1.** To extract the 'worm' or lytta from the tongue of (a dog) as a safeguard against madness 1575. **b.** *transf.* and *fig.* (as a remedy for madness, a ribald tongue, or greediness) 1564. **2.** To rid (plants, esp. tobacco) of 'worms' or grubs 1624.

1. b. He is such a froward testy old fellow, he should be Wormed like a mad dog SHADWELL.

III. †**1.** To pry into the secrets of (a person); to play the spy upon –1807. **2.** *To w.* (a person) *out of*: to deprive or dispossess of (property, etc.) by underhand dealing. Now *rare* or *Obs.* 1617. **3.** *To w. out*: to thrust out, get rid of, by subtle and persistent pressure or undermining 1594. **4.** *To w. out*: to extract (information, a secret, etc.) by insidious questioning 1715. **5.** *intr.* To move or progress sinuously like a worm; also *transf.* of things. Usu. with adv. 1610. **b.** *refl.* in same sense 1865. **c.** With advb. acc. as *to w. one's way* 1822. **6.** *fig.* To make one's way insidiously like a worm *into* (a person's confidence, secret affairs, etc.); to burrow *in* so as to hurt or destroy 1627. **b.** *refl.* To insinuate oneself *into* (a person's favour or confidence, a desirable position, etc.) 1711. **7.** *trans.* with predicate-extension: To move (an object) *off*, *down*, etc. by a gradual tortuous propulsion or dragging 1861.

4. Old Wood knew all her history...He had wormed it out of her, day by day THACKERAY. **6.** Vse subtle and crafty men, they will search, and skrew, and worme into busines of difficulty 1639. **b.** W. yourself into her secrets DICKENS.

IV. 1. To make a screw-thread on 1598. **2.** *Naut.* To wind spun-yarn or small rope spirally round (a rope or cable) so as to fill up the grooves between the strands and render the surface smooth 1644. **3.** To remove the charge or wad from (a gun) by means of a worm 1802. Hence **Wormed** (wɒ̄ɹmd) *ppl. a.* eaten into or bored by worms, infested with worms; formed with a screw-thread; furnished with a (specified) number of screw-threads. **Wo·rmer.**

Wo·rm-ea:ten, *pa. pple.* and *ppl. a.* late ME. Eaten into by a worm or worms. **b.** *transf.* Applied to organic tissue which is indented with small holes 1592. **c.** *fig.* (of persons and things). Decayed, decrepit; antiquated, outworn 1575.

Smircht w. tapestrie SHAKS. **c.** That worme-eaten name of Liberall..it's a name of the old fashion DEKKER.

Wo·rm-ea:ting, *ppl. a.* 1817. That eats worms for food.

W. Warbler, the bird *Helminthotherus vermivorus* of the eastern U.S.

Wormian (wǭ·ɹmiăn), *a.* 1831. [– mod.L. *(ossa) Wormiana*, f. the name of the Danish physician Olaus *Worm* (1588–1654); see -IAN.] *Anat.* The designation of small bones of irregular shape, freq. found in the sutures of the skull.

Wormseed (wɒ̄·ɹmsīd). late ME. [WORM *sb.* I. 4.] **1.** Any of various plants considered to have anthelmintic properties, e.g. swine's fennel or sulphurwort, *Peucedanum officinale*; *Erysimum cheiranthoides* (Treacle or English W.); *Chenopodium anthelminticum* and *Ambrina anthelmintica* (American W.); *Halogeton tamariscifolium* (Spanish W.). **2.** The dried flower-heads of one or other of these plants, used as an anthelmintic 1502. **3.** The eggs of the silkworm moth 1733.

Wormwood (wɒ̄·ɹmwud). late ME. [alt., by assim. of the second syll. to WOOD, of late ME. *wormod*, OE. *wormōd* (corresp. to MLG. *wormōde*, OHG. *wormuota*), alt. by assim. to WORM of OE. *wermōd* = OS. *wer(i)moda*, OHG. *wer(i)muota* (G. †*wermuth*; cf. VERMOUTH); of unkn. origin.] **1.** The plant *Artemisia absinthium*, proverbial for its bitter taste. **b.** With qualifying word, designating species of *Artemisia* and some similar plants 1548. **c.** *Salt of w.*, an impure carbonate of potash, obtained from the ashes of w. 1617. **2.** *fig.* An emblem or type of what is bitter and grievous to the soul 1535. **3.** Used as a name or specific epithet for certain moths 1832. **4.** Short for *w. ale* 1843. **5.** *fig.* attrib., passing into adj. = bitter, tart, unpleasant to experience 1593.

1.b. Pontic, Roman w., *Artemisia pontica* or *A. absinthium*; **Sea w.**, *A. maritima*; **Tree w.**, *A. arborescens* of the Mediterranean; **Wild w.**, *Parthenium hysterophorus*. **2.** *To be w.* (or *gall and w.*), to be acutely mortifying or vexing (*to* a person). **5.** Thy secret pleasure turnes to open shame,..Thy sugred tongue to bitter w. tast SHAKS.

attrib. and *Comb.*: **w.-ale, -beer**, ale or beer in which w. is infused; **w. water, wine**, a cordial prepared (like absinthe or vermouth) from w.

Wormy (wɒ̄·ɹmi), *a.* late ME. [f. WORM *sb.* + -Y[1].] **1.** Attacked, gnawed, or bored by worms and grubs; worm-eaten. **b.** *fig.* = WORM-EATEN c. (*rare*) 1611. **2.** Of the body, etc.: Infested or affected with worms, itch-mites, etc. 1599. **3.** Of soil, the grave, etc.: Infested with worms, full of worms 1590. **4.** Resembling a worm; worm-like 1545. **b.** *fig.* Grovelling; earthy; crooked, tortuous 1640. **5.** Of or pertaining to worms. *poet.* 1801.

3. Damned spirits all,..Alreadie to their wormie beds are gone SHAKS. **4.** Long w. feelers instead of fins 1888.

Worn (wǭɹn, wōᵊɹn), *ppl. a.* 1508. [pa. pple. of WEAR *v.*[1]] **1.** Impaired by wear, use, or exposure; showing the results of use or attrition. **b.** *fig.* Of words or ideas: Hackneyed, trite 1569. **2.** Wasted, enfeebled, or exhausted by toil, exposure, age, anxiety, or ill-health; showing signs of such enfeeblement 1508. †**3.** Of time, a period: Past, spent. SHAKS. **4.** With adv. **a.** *W.-down* = 1, 2. 1814. **b.** *W.-in*, ingrained by attrition or exposure to weather 1883.

2. The President..looked somewhat w. and anxious, and well he might DICKENS. **3.** *Wint. T.* v. i. 142.

Worn-out, *ppl. a.* 1593. **1.** Injured, damaged, defaced by wear, attrition, or exposure, esp. to such a degree as to be no longer of use or service 1612. **2.** Utterly exhausted and wasted in strength or vitality 1700. **3.** Of ideas, etc.: Hackneyed by use, trite, stale, out of fashion. Of institutions: Effete. 1713. †**4.** Of time: Past, departed. SHAKS.

1. The w. carpets and old-fashioned chairs TROLLOPE. **2.** Every w. Preacher shall receive, if he wants it, at least ten pounds a-year WESLEY. **3.** The House of Lords..was an effete and w. institution 1882. **4.** This patterne of the worne-out age SHAKS.

Worricow (wɒ·rikau). *Sc.* 1711. [f. WORRY *v.* + COW *sb.*[2]] A scarecrow; a hobgoblin. Also *transf.* of persons.

Worried (wɒ·rid), *ppl. a.* 1559. [f. WORRY *v.*; see -ED[1].] In senses of WORRY *v.*

'I don't mean that', said Mrs. Boffin, with a w. look DICKENS.

Worrier (wɒ·riəɹ). 1536. [f. WORRY *v.* + -ER[1].] **1.** An animal that kills or injures others by biting and rough treatment. **2.** One who harasses or persecutes another 1712. **3.** One who causes distress of mind to another; also, one who gives way to anxiety or mental disquietude 1891.

Worriment (wɒ·rimĕnt). Chiefly *U.S.* 1855. [f. WORRY *v.* + -MENT.] The act of worrying or causing anxiety; the state of being worried or troubled in mind. Also, something that harasses or causes worry.

Worrisome (wɒ·risɒ̆m), *a.* 1869. *dial.* [f. WORRY *sb.* or *v.* + -SOME[1].] Apt to cause worry or distress; given to worrying.

Worrit (wɒ·rit), *sb. dial.* and *vulgar.* 1836. [f. next.] A state of worry or mental distress; a fretting care or anxiety. Also, a person that worries others or himself.

Worrit (wɒ·rit), *v. dial.* and *vulgar.* 1818. [app. vulgar alteration of WORRY *v.*; but cf. dial. *wherrit* (1762), *werrit* (1825), of app. different origin.] **1.** *trans.* To worry, distress, vex, pester. **2.** *intr.* To give way to worry; to experience or display mental disquietude, impatience, etc. 1854.

1. Don't w. your poor mother DICKENS. It will worret you to death, Lucy; *that* I can see GEO. ELIOT.

Worry (wɒ·ri), *sb.* 1804. [f. next.] **1.** A troubled state of mind arising from the frets and cares of life; harassing anxiety or solicitude. **b.** An instance or case of this; a cause of or matter for anxiety; *pl.* cares, solicitudes 1813. **2.** The act of biting and shaking an animal so as to injure or kill it. (Properly of hounds when they seize their quarry.) 1847.

1. It is not the work that kills, but 'w.' 1879. **b.** Delicious spot to come and repose in from the cares and worries of life LEVER.

Worry (wɒ·ri), *v.* Pa. t. and pple. **worried.** [OE. *wyrġan* = OFris. *wergia* kill, MLG., MDu. *worgen*, OHG. *wurgan* (Du. *wurgen*, G. *würgen*) :– WGmc. **wurzjan*.] †**1.** *trans.* To strangle (a person or animal) –1606. †**2.** To choke (a person or animal) with a mouthful of food –1779. **3.** To seize by the throat with the teeth and tear or lacerate; to kill or injure by biting and shaking. Said e.g. of dogs or wolves attacking sheep, or of hounds when they seize their quarry. late ME. **b.** *transf.* To bite at or upon (an object); to kiss or hug vehemently 1567. **c.** *intr.* To pull or tear *at* (an object) with the teeth 1882. **d.** *trans.* To devour. Chiefly *north.* ME. **4.** *trans.* To harass by rough or severe treatment, by repeated aggression or attack; to assail with hostile or menacing speech 1553. **b.** *transf.* With adv. or advb. phr.: To get or bring into a specified condition by harassing treatment, persistent aggression, or dogged effort 1727. **c.** To irritate (an animal) by a repetition of feigned attacks, etc. 1807. **d.** *U.S.* To afflict with physical fatigue or distress 1828. **5.** To vex, distress, or persecute by inconsiderate or importunate behaviour; to plague or pester with reiterated demands, requests, or the like 1671. **6.** To cause distress of mind to; to afflict with mental trouble or agitation; to make anxious and ill at ease. Freq. *refl.* or *pass.* 1822. **b.** in pa. pple., denoting a state of mind 1863. **c.** *intr.* (for *refl.*) To give way to anxiety or mental disquietude 1860. **7.** With advb. extension. **a.** To advance or progress by a harassing or dogged effort; to force or work one's way *through* 1699. **b.** To get *through* (a business, piece of work) by persistent effort or struggle 1873.

3. She bit me..She worried me like a tigress C. BRONTË. **4.** Thus she worries him out of his senses 1678. **b.** Worrying out a knotty point in the 'Original Hebrew' 1894. **5.** You w. me to death with your chattering DICKENS. They won't really do anything but w. you with questions 1927. **6. c.** When she can find nothing to do, then she worries 1861. *I should w.* (U.S. colloq.), it does not trouble me at all. **7. b.** *To w. along* (orig. U.S.), to contrive to live, 'keep going', in the teeth of trials or difficulties. Hence **Wo·rrying** *vbl. sb.* and *ppl. a.*

Worse (wɒ̄ɹs), *a.* and *sb.* [OE. adj. *wiersa*, *wyrsa* = OFris. *werra*, *wirra*, OS. *wirsa*, OHG. *wirsiro*, ON. *verri* (:– **wersi*), Goth. *wairsiza* :– Gmc. **wersizon*, f. **wers-*, found also in OS., OHG. *werran* (cf. WAR); see -ER[3].]

A. *adj.* Used as the comparative of BAD, EVIL, ILL, or as the opposite of BETTER. **1.** More reprehensible morally; more wicked, depraved, or vicious; more cruel, unkind, or ill-conditioned. **2.** More harmful, painful, grievous, unpleasant, unlucky, etc. OE. **b.** More unattractive; more unsuitable or unfitting; more faulty, incorrect, etc. 1640. **c.** With agent-noun: More unskilful or inefficient. Also, more addicted to some (specified) bad habit. 1719. **3.** Less good, not so good, inferior; of lower quality or value OE. **4.** *predic.* **a.** Of persons: Less fortunate, less well off; in less favourable circumstances or position *for* (some person or thing that causes deterioration or loss) OE. **b.** Less well in health, physical condition, or spirits OE. **c.** Of things: In less good condition; showing signs of damage, deterioration, or loss of quality ME. **5.** *Comb.*, as *w.-natured*, *-tempered* adjs. 1648.

1. Three Iudasses, each one thrice w. then Iudas SHAKS. I only hope and trust he wasn't a w. liver than we think of GEO. ELIOT. **2.** Come, you drop that stick or it'll be w. for you DICKENS. No very good news; but then it might be w. GEO. ELIOT. **b.** She has bad Features, and a w. Complexion SWIFT. **3.** *To be w. than one's word*, to fail to carry out or act up to what one has promised. *W. half*, corresp. to *better half* (HALF *sb.* II. 2). **4. a.** To make fayre promyse, what are ye the w.? SKELTON. Nobody seem'd one penny the w.! BARHAM. **b.** He was at first very ill, then got better; he is now w. 1776. *The w. for*, overcome or intoxicated by (liquor, drink). **c.** Blue satin shoes and sandals (a *leettle* the w. for wear) DICKENS. *It would be none the w. for*, it would be improved by (colloq.). *W. and w.*, w. in an increasing degree, progressively w.

B. *absol.* or as *sb.* Chiefly ellipt. or absol. uses. **1.** A person that is less good, virtuous, kindly, etc. ME. **2.** Something worse; a greater degree of badness OE. **b.** *To do w.*: to behave more wickedly, badly, foolishly, etc. ME. **c.** What is less good or precious or valuable 1586. **d.** Used as an alternative or addition to an unfavourable epithet or characterization = something worse still: usu. *or w.*, *and w.* late ME.

1. I feare there will a w. come in his place SHAKS. **2.** You had better take yourself off peaceably, before w. comes of it 1864. **d.** I might say more of this, but it might be thought curiosity or worse WALTON.

Phrases. *For better, for w.*, also *for better or (for)*

w.: used where an issue is doubtful or beyond human control; I N. take the N. to my wedded wif to haue and to holde fro this day forward for bettere for wers for richere for pouerer 1500. *For the w.*: chiefly used to indicate the result of a change in condition or quality, fortune, or circumstances. *From bad to w.*; Thus will this latter, as the former World, Still tend from bad to w. MILT. *The w.*, the losing or less desirable part (in a contest, or the like); disadvantage. *To have the w.*, to be worsted or defeated in a contest; also *gen.* to have the disadvantage in a comparison with another. †*To put to the w.*, to defeat, worst, discomfit.

Worse (wɒ̄ɹs), *v. Obs.* exc. in nonce-use. [OE. *wyrsian*, f. *wyrsa* WORSE *a.*] **1.** *intr.* To become or grow worse, deteriorate. **2.** *trans.* To make worse, impair, injure, blemish ME.

Worse (wɒ̄ɹs), *adv.* [OE. *wiers* = OS., OHG. *wirs*, ON. *verr*, Goth. *wairs*; see WORSE *a.*] **1.** More badly or wickedly; more censurably or foolishly in regard to conduct. **b.** More severely, hardly, harshly, etc. ME. **c.** More carelessly, faultily, imperfectly, etc. ME. **2.** More unfortunately, unluckily, or unhappily OE. **3. a.** As an intensive, with verbs of hurting, hearing, hating, etc.: More greatly, severely, or intensely; in a greater degree 1596. **b.** With a verb of liking, loving, pleasing, etc.: In a lesser or lower degree, less well. Similarly *w. at ease*, less well at ease. OE. **4.** *W. than*, used before an adj. (sb., vb.) as a form of perjorative comparison ME. **5.** Used parenthetically or continuatively to introduce an additional clause or sentence containing a further and stronger instance of action which incurs reprobation 1784.

1. I judg'd a man of sense could scarce do w. Than caper in the morris-dance of verse COWPER. **b.** You are sure you won't think the w. of me, if I tell it? 1881. **c.** I may put all the good I have ever got by you in my eyes, and see never the w. FIELDING. **2.** With ruin upon ruin, rout on rout, Confusion w. confounded MILT. *W. off*, in w. circumstances. less happily or fortunately situated. *To go w. with*, to be the worse for (a person). Prov. *To go further, and fare w.* **4.** Brutish Villaine; w. then brutish SHAKS. He.. chose to w. than waste his opportunities and his talents 1897. **5.** They stir us up against our kind; And worse, against ourselves WORDSW.

Worsement (wɒ̄·ɹsmĕnt). 1884. [f. WORSE *v.* + -MENT, after *betterment.*] Deterioration and depreciation of real property caused by the action of persons outside without the owner's consent.

Worsen (wɒ̄·ɹs'n), *v.* ME. [f. WORSE *a.* + -EN[5]. Cf. LESSEN *v.* Common in dialect, and reintroduced to literature *c* 1800–1830 by writers like Southey and De Quincey.] **1.** *trans.* To make worse; to impair, vitiate, cause to deteriorate. **b.** *spec.* To inflict loss upon (a person, locality) in respect of real property (see prec.) 1894. **c.** To represent (a thing) as worse than it is; to depreciate 1885. **d.** *refl.* To make oneself worse or (*dial.*) worse off 1828. **2.** *intr.* To become worse, deteriorate 1795.

1. Life..is not worsened by being long 1647. **2.** I am still much engaged with my sick friend; and sorry am I to add that he worsens daily WORDSW.

Worsen (wɒ̄·ɹs'n). 1634. dial. or illiterate alteration of WORSE (perh. arising f. *worse'n* = *worse than*).

It stinket..w. than ony brimstone 1634.

Worseness (wɒ̄·ɹsnės). late ME. [-NESS.] The quality or condition of being worse.

Worser (wɒ̄·ɹsəɹ), *a.* and *adv.* 1495. [A double comparative, f. WORSE *a.* + -ER[3]. Cf. *lesser.*] **A.** *adj.* = WORSE *a.* **b.** *absol.* and *ellipt.* 1586.

Chang'd to a w. shape thou canst not be SHAKS. You might ha' made a w. guess than that, old feller DICKENS.

B. *adv.* = WORSE *adv.* 1560.

Oth. IV. i. 105. Your poor dear wife as you uses w. nor a dog DICKENS. Also **Wo·rserer,** a further extension (joc. or vulgar) of WORSER; e.g. *wusserer and wusserer* 1752.

Worship (wɒ̄·ɹʃip), *sb.* [OE. *weorþsćipe*, f. *weorþ* WORTH *a.* + *-sćipe* -SHIP. Formation peculiar to Eng.] **I. 1.** The condition (in a person) of deserving or being held in esteem or repute; honour, renown; good name, credit. *Obs.* exc. *arch.* **2.** The condition of holding a prominent place or rank; dignity, importance, high standing or degree. *arch.* OE. †**b.** With *a* and *pl.* A distinction or dignity; a position of honour or high place –1606. **3.** *Man, gentleman*, etc., *of w.*: a person of repute and standing. *arch.* ME. **4.** With *your* or *his*: A title of honour used in addressing or speaking to a person of note. In later use *spec.* as the title of a magistrate 1548.

1. †*To win* (*one's*) *w.*, to gain honour or renown. **2.** She was as fine as Fi'pence; but truly, I thought there was more Cost than W. SWIFT. **b.** *Lear* I. iv. 288. **4.** What does your w. know about farming? LAMB. This here's Pickvick, your washup DICKENS.

II. †**1.** Respect or honour shown to a person or thing –1610. **2.** Reverence or veneration paid to a being or power regarded as supernatural or divine; the action or practice of displaying this by appropriate acts, rites, or ceremonies ME. **b.** *transf.* Veneration similar to that paid to a deity 1838. **3.** With *a* and *pl.* A form or type of veneration or adoration 1604.

1. †*To do* (a person) *w.*, to show honour or pay respect or homage to. **2.** *Place of w.*: see PLACE *sb.* Hence **Wo·rshipless** *a.* not practising w.; unworshipped.

Worship (wɒ̄·ɹʃip), *v.* [Early ME., f. prec.] **1.** *trans.* To honour or revere as a supernatural being or power or as a holy thing; to adore with appropriate acts, rites, or ceremonies. **b.** *transf.* To regard with extreme respect or devotion; to 'adore' 1720. **c.** *absol.* To engage in worship; to perform or take part in the act of worship 1703. †**2.** *trans.* To honour; to regard or treat with honour or respect; to salute, bow down to –1737. †**3.** To invest with or raise to honour or repute; to confer honour or dignity upon –1601.

1. I come from Ierusalem, where I have worshypd the holy grave CAXTON. **b.** I worshipped the very ground she walked on! 1856. Hence **Wo·rshipable** *a.* †entitled to honour or respect, worshipful; capable of being worshipped. **Wo·rshipper,** one who worships; one engaged in, or taking part in, divine worship; *transf.* one who regards a person or thing with feelings akin to worship.

Worshipful (wɒ̄·ɹʃipfŭl), *a.* (*sb.*) ME. [f. WORSHIP *sb.* + -FUL.] **1.** Of things: Notable or outstanding in respect of some (good) quality or property; imposing; reputable, honourable. *arch.* **2.** Of persons: Distinguished in respect of character or rank; entitled to honour or respect on this account. *arch.* ME. **3. a.** As an honorific title for persons or bodies of distinguished rank or importance: now restricted to justices of the peace, aldermen, recorders, the London city companies, and freemasons' lodges and their masters. *Right w.* is applied to mayors, and the sheriffs, aldermen, and recorder of London. late ME. **b.** Used in forms of address, as *w. sir*, (*right*) *w. master*, etc. late ME. **c.** *absol.* (chiefly pl.) or as *sb.* In later use *spec.* a magistrate 1450. **4.** Imbued with the spirit of worship or veneration 1809. **5.** Deserving or capable of being worshipped; worshipable 1872.

3. a. The Master and Wardens of the W. Company of Mercers 1768. **b.** Ryght wyrshypfull and my ryght tendre modre, I recommaunde me to yow 1473. Hence **Wo·rshipful-ly** *adv.* (now *rare*), **-ness.**

Wo·rsle, *v.* 1513. *Sc.* and *north.* var. of WARSLE *v.*

Worst (wɒ̄ɹst), *a.* and *sb.* [OE. *wierresta*, *wyrresta* = OFris. *wersta*, OS. *wirsista*, OHG. *-isto*, ON. *verstr* :– Gmc. **wersistaz*, f. **wers-*; see WORSE *a.*, -EST.] **A.** *adj.* Used as the superlative of the adjs. *bad*, *evil*, or *ill*. **1.** Most bad or evil in regard to moral character or behaviour; also qualifying an agent-noun or the like. **2.** Most grievous, painful, unlucky, or unpleasant OE. **b.** Hardest, most difficult to deal with. late ME. **c.** U.S. colloq. phr. *the w. kind*; also used advb. = most severely, most thoroughly; so *the w. way* 1839. **3.** Most wanting in the good qualities required or expected; least good, valuable, desirable, or successful; least considerable or important ME. †**4.** *predic.* Most unfortunate or badly off 1603.

1. His worst fault is that he is giuen to prayer SHAKS. My w. enemies..never accused me of being meek DICKENS. **2.** They ought to be every one of them put to the w. of Deaths DE FOE. **b.** The best things are w. to come by 1639. **3.** One of that class..who, with the best intentions, have made the w. citizens LYTTON. **4.** *Lear* IV. i. 2.

B. *sb.* (absol. uses of the adj.) **1.** *The w.*: one who is or those who are most objectionable, or least estimable in moral character, behaviour, etc. 1606. **2.** What is most objectionable or deplorable in regard to morals, taste, etc. late ME. **3.** What is most grievous, unlucky, painful; a state of things that is most undesirable or most to be dreaded. late ME. **b.** A course of action ill-advised in the highest degree 1568. **c.** The worst part, degree, or phase *of* 1615. **4.** What is least good in quality or least valuable; the most inferior kind. late ME. **5.** The harshest view or judgment; as *to speak* or *think the w.* (*of* a person or thing) 1586. **6.** Defeat in a contest 1460.

2. Do you know the w. of your father? DICKENS. **3.** I am prepared for the w. LYTTON. *The w. is*, the most unfortunate thing or circumstance is (*that*..). Also, *the w. of* (something), *the w. of it is*, etc. *If the w. comes to the w.*, if things fall out as badly as possible or conceivable. **6.** †*To put to the w.*, to defeat, overcome. *To have the w.*, to be defeated.

Phrases. *At* (*the*) *w.*: (*a*) in the most evil or undesirable state that can be; at the greatest disadvantage; (*b*) even on the most unfavourable view, estimate, or surmise. (*To do*) *the w.* or *one's w.*, the utmost evil or harm possible. *To make the w. of*, to regard or represent in the most unfavourable light.

Worst (wɒ̄ɹst), *v.* 1602. [f. WORST *a.*] †**1.** *trans.* To make worse, impair, damage, inflict loss upon –1783. †**b.** *intr.* To grow worse, deteriorate (*rare*) –1815. **2.** *trans.* To defeat, overcome, get the better of (an adversary) in a fight or battle 1636. **b.** To defeat in argument, in a suit, attempt, etc.; to outdo, prove better than 1651.

1. b. Anne haggard, Mary coarse, every face in the neighbourhood worsting JANE AUSTEN. **2. b.** Johnson could not brook appearing to be worsted in argument BOSWELL. Hence **Worsted** (wɒ̄·ɹstėd) *ppl. a.*

Worst (wɒ̄ɹst), *adv.* [OE. *wyrrest*, *wyrst* = ON. *verst*; cf. WORST *a.*] In a manner or to a degree that is most (or extemely) bad or evil. **b.** With a vb. of liking, loving, pleasing, etc.: Least well, least OE.

Worsted (wu·stėd), *sb.* ME. [From the name of a parish in Norfolk, orig. (OE.) *Wurðestede*, now written *Worstead*; in AL. *pannus* (XIII), in AFr. *drap, de Wurthstede.*] **1.** A woollen fabric or stuff made from well-twisted yarn spun of long-staple wool combed to lay the fibres parallel. **b.** with *pl.* A particular variety of this fabric ME. **2.** A closely twisted yarn made of long-staple wool in which the fibres are arranged to lie parallel to each other. Later, a fine and soft woollen yarn used for knitting and embroidery. 1465. **3.** *attrib.* or *adj.* Made of worsted or worsted yarn; often in specific names of fabrics or materials, as *w. braid, damask*, etc. late ME.

†**Wo·rsum.** Survived in 19th c. in north. dial. [OE. *worsm*, *wursm*, var. of more usual *worms*, *wurms*, app. rel. to *wyrm* WORM *sb.*] Pus.

Wort[1] (wɒ̄ɹt). [OE. *wyrt* root, plant = OS. *wurt*, (O)HG. *wurz*, ON. *urt*, Goth. *waurts*; the base is rel. to that of ROOT *sb.*] **1.** A plant, herb, or vegetable used for food or medicine; often = pot-herb. *arch.* exc. as second element of various plant-names, as *colewort*, *liverwort*. †**2.** Any plant of the cabbage kind (genus *Brassica*); colewort –1755.

Wort[2] (wɒ̄ɹt). [OE. *wyrt* = OS. *wurtja* spicery, (M)HG. *würze* spice, brewer's wort; f. the same base as that of prec.] **1.** The infusion of malt or other grain which after fermentation becomes beer (or may be used for the distillation of spirits). **2.** An infusion or decoction of malt formerly used in the treatment of ulcers, of scurvy, and other diseases 1694.

Worth (wɒ̄ɹþ), *sb.*[1] [OE. *worþ*, *weorþ*, *wurþ* = OFris. *werth*, OS. *werð*, OHG. *werd* (G. *wert*), ON. *verð*, Goth. *wairþ*; subst. use of WORTH *a.*] **1.** Pecuniary value; †price; †money. **b.** The equivalent *of* a specified sum or amount (cf. HALFPENNYWORTH, PENNYWORTH, SHILLINGSWORTH). OE. **2.** The relative value of a thing in respect of its qualities or of the estimation in which it is held ME. **b.** High or outstanding value, excellence. *Obs.* or *arch.* 1617. **3.** The character or standing of a person in respect of moral and intellectual qualities; *esp.* high personal merit or attainments 1591. **4.** The position or standing of a person in respect of property; hence *concr.* possessions, property, means. *Obs.* or *arch.* 1592.

1. Some poverty-stricken legatee,..selling his chance..for a twelth part of its w. DICKENS. **2.** The w. of man's homage to God 1877. **3.** He was a iust Prince, full of w. and magnanimitie 1615. How hard for real w. to gain its price! YOUNG. **4.** They are but beggers that can count their w. SHAKS.

Phrases. *Of great, little, no,* etc. *w.*; Euerie day Men of great w. resorted to this forrest SHAKS. *Of w.*, of high merit or excellence. †*To take at, of,* or *to w.*, *to take, bear, have in (good) w.*; *to take well in w.*: to take at its true value, take in good part, be content with.

Worth (wǒɹþ), *sb.*² *Hist.* 1575. [Used mainly as extracted from place-names containing it as final element, e.g. *Kenilworth.* OE. *worþ* = OS. *wurð* soil, MLG. *wurt, wort* homestead; of unkn. origin.] An enclosed place; a homestead.

Worth (wǒɹþ), *a.* [OE. *worþ, weorþ, wurþ* = OFris. *werth*, OS. *werð*, MDu. *waert, wert,* OHG. *werd* (Du. *waard*, G. *wert*), ON. *verðr*, Goth. *wairþs*; Gmc. adj. of doubtful etym.] Almost always (now only) *predic.*, or following the sb. as part of a qualifying phrase. **I. 1.** Of the value of a specified amount or sum; equivalent to (something) in material value. **b.** Of (such-and-such) value *to* a person 1484. **c.** In contemptuous comparisons ME. **2.** Of material value; capable of being estimated in terms of money or some other material standard. *arch.* ME. **b.** Of value in other than material respects. *arch.* ME. **3.** Of a specified or certain value in other than material respects ME. **4.** Of standing in respect of possessions, property, or income; possessed of, owning: usu. with specification of the sum 1460.

1. There is a fayre Diamond, what is it w.? 1605. It is esteem'd w. its weight in Gold ADDISON. **c.** She knewe it to be but a feigned & peinted mattre & not woorth two strawes 1548. Manufacturers, and meagre mechanicks? fellows not w. powder and shot 1776. **2. b.** Little w. is woman's beauty, So oft an image dumb we see 1871. **3.** I thought an howers rest w. a Kings ransome 1617. *As much as..is w.*; It is as much as my Life is w., if she should think we were intimate STEELE. *For all one* or *it is w.* (orig. U.S.): to the utmost of one's or its powers or possibilities; to the fullest extent. Prov. *A bird in the hand is w. two in the bush.* **4.** I shall be w. Fifty thousand Pound STEELE.

II. 1. Deserving or worthy of the bestowal or expenditure of (something) OE. **2.** Sufficiently valuable or important to be an equivalent or good return for (something). late ME. **b.** With vbl. sb., or a noun having the force of a vbl. sb., as obj. 1540.

1. The captain..is not w. his salt MARRYAT. **2.** To reign is w. ambition though in Hell MILT. **b.** An Ass like this was w. the stealing! WORDSW. 'They are not w. your notice', said the dismal man DICKENS. Is Life w. living? 1877. *W. it* (colloq.), having a value or importance commensurate with what is expended upon it, WORTH-WHILE.

Worth (wǒɹþ), *v. Obs.* exc. *arch.* [OE. *weorþan, wurþan* = OFris. *wertha*, OS. *werðan*, OHG. *werdan* (Du. *worden*, G. *werden*), ON. *verða*, Goth. *wairþan* :- Gmc. **werþan*, f. IE. **wert-*, whence L. *vertere*, earlier *vortere* turn, Skr. *vártate* turns, passes on, takes place. Cf. WEIRD *sb.*] **1.** *intr.* To come to be, come to pass, happen; in subjunctive, expressing a wish for something to happen to one. **2.** To become, come to be OE. **b.** To become *of* (= happen to, betide). late ME.

1. Phr. *Woe w.*, †*well w.*, followed by a noun or pronoun orig. in the dative = May evil or good betide; Woo worthe the oure that euer I was made in! 1440. Woe w. the chase, woe w. the day! SCOTT.

Worthful (wǒ·ɹþfŭl), *a.* [OE. *weorþ-, wurþful*, f. *weorþ* WORTH *sb.*¹ In later use app. re-formed in XVI–XVII and again in XIX.] **1.** Of persons: Honourable; meriting respect or reverence; full of worth or merit. **2.** Having worth or value; valuable, precious ME.

Worthily (wǒ·ɹðili), *adv.* ME. [f. WORTHY *a.* + -LY².] †**1.** With due dignity, pomp, or splendour –1522. **2.** In a manner befitting one of high standing or character; in accordance with one's own dignity or personal worth. late ME. **3.** According to desert or merit; deservedly, justly, rightly ME. **b.** Fittingly (in respect of subject or matter) 1553. **4.** With due devotion or reverence; in a fitting spirit; also, with real desert by reason of faith or good life ME.

2. An incident of a life w. spent 1858. **4.** The vertue and efficacie of this Sacrament duely and worthely received 1565. So **Wo·rthiness,** the character or quality of being worthy ME.

Worthless (wǒ·ɹþlės), *a.* 1588. [f. WORTH *sb.*¹ + -LESS.] **1.** Of things, etc.: Destitute of (material) worth; having no intrinsic value. **2.** Of persons: Lacking worth or merit; contemptible, despicable 1591. †**3.** Unworthy *of* –1639.

2. Am I then doom'd to fall..for a w. woman? ADDISON. A w. adventurer, whose only recommendation was that he was a Papist MACAULAY. **3.** A peeuish School-boy, worthles of such Honor SHAKS. Hence **Wo·rthless-ly** *adv.*, **-ness.**

Worth-while, *a.* 1884. Chiefly *predic.* [See WHILE *sb.* I. 2.] That is worth while; of sufficient value or importance.

Worthy (wǒ·ɹði), *a., adv., sb.* [ME. *wurþi, worþi*, f. WORTH *sb.*¹ + -Y¹; superseding OE. *wurþe*, etc., WORTH *a.*] **A.** *adj.* **I. 1.** Of things: Having worth; possessed of value or importance; valuable; excellent. *arch.* **2.** Of persons: Distinguished by good qualities; entitled to honour or respect on this account. Now often with patronizing implication (e.g. *She's a very w. woman*). ME. **b.** *absol.* in sing. or pl. sense. late ME. **c.** Of mind or character: Having a high moral standard 1753. †**3.** Of things: Honourable; held in honour or esteem –1721. **4.** Of sufficient worth or value; appropriate, fitting, suitable ME. †**b.** Deserved; merited by default or wrong-doing, condign –1622. **5.** Of persons: Possessed of sufficient worth, desert, or merit 1552. **b.** Of actions, etc.: Adequate or suitable in respect of moral excellence or noble aims 1563.

1. Cows and Oxen are w. Beasts, and in great request with the Husbandman 1669. **2.** A small collection of your late dear and w. Pastor's sermons 1758. **c.** Such as are styled, in the cant term of the day, men of w. characters WESLEY. **4. b.** He has much w. blame laid vpon him SHAKS. **5.** A w. successor to Mr. Russell Lowell 1885.

II. 1. Of sufficient merit, excellence, or desert *to* be or have something, or †*for* (some purpose) ME. **2.** Deserving *of* something by reason of merit or excellence; also with ellipsis of *of* ME. **3.** Deserving or meriting by fault or wrong-doing ME. **4.** Corresponding to the worth of; appropriate or suitable (to), fit (for). Const. noun as obj. (now *arch.* and *rare*), or *of.* ME.

1. He is as w. for an Empresse loue, As meet to be an Emperors Councellor SHAKS. The only knowledge w. to be called knowledge JOWETT. **2.** Be w. me, as I am w. you DRYDEN. 'Twere matter W. the hearing WORDSW. **3.** Thou arte w. to be hanged 1508. **4.** The stern joy which warriors feel In foemen w. of their steel SCOTT.

B. *adv.* or quasi-*adv.* Worthily; in a manner worthy *of* (something). *Obs.* or *poet.* late ME.

C. *sb.* **1.** A distinguished or eminent person; esp. a man of courage or of noble character. late ME. **b.** *spec.* A hero of antiquity 1552. **c.** Applied colloq. or joc. to any person, esp. one having a marked personality 1751. †**2.** A thing of worth or value. SHAKS.

1. b. *The Nine Worthies*: nine famous personages of ancient and mediæval history and legend; the number is composed of three Jews (Joshua, David, and Judas Maccabæus), three Gentiles (Hector, Alexander, and Julius Cæsar), and three Christians (Arthur, Charlemagne, and Godfrey of Bouillon). Hence †**Worthy** *v. trans.* to render, or hold, w. (*of* something); to raise to honour or distinction –1624.

-worthy, the adj. as a second element in a number of compounds, of which only a few are in regular use, as *blame-, note-, praise-, seaworthy* (so *airworthy*). The earliest examples replace compounds of OE. *-wyrþe*.

Wortle (wǒ·ɹt'l). late ME. [Of unkn. origin.] An implement used in drawing wire or lead-pipe.

Wot (wǫt), *v. arch.* ME. [New formation due to the carrying over of the pret.-pres. stem *wot* of WIT *v.*¹ into other parts of the verb.] To know.

He she wots of remained here..expecting to see her SCOTT. There are more dangers around than you w. of 1841.

Wou·bit, oo·bit. *dial.* [ME. *wolbode, -bede*, app. f. *wol* WOOL *sb.* with obscure second element.] A hairy caterpillar; a woolly bear.

Wough¹ (wōᵘ, wǭ). *Obs.* exc. *dial.* [OE. *wāg* (also *wǣġ*), *wāh* = OFris. *wach*, OS. *wēg*, rel. to Goth. *waddjus*, ON. *veggr*.] **1.** A wall of a house; a partition. **2.** *Mining.* The side of a vein 1653.

Wough² (wuf). 1824. [Imitative. Cf. WHOOF, WOOF, WUFF.] The bark of a dog, etc.

Would (wud). late ME. [pa. t. subj. of WILL *v.*¹ used subst.] The feeling or expression of a conditional or undecided desire or intention. **b.** With *the*, denoting desire or intention in contrast to duty or necessity 1753.

Would-be (wu·dbi), *a.* and *sb.* ME. [The phrase *would be* used attrib. and absol.] **A.** *adj.* Of persons: That would be; wishing to be; posing as. **b.** Of things: Intended to be what is denoted by the sb. 1839. **c.** With following adj., forming a hyphened phr. 1826. **B.** *sb.* One who fain would be (something specified or implied) 1605.

Would-have-been, *a.* 1744. [The verbal phrase used attrib.] That would have liked to be, that aimed at being (something specified).

Woulfe (wulf). 1800. [The surname of Peter *Woulfe* (? 1727–1803), a London chemist.] *Woulfe's apparatus*, a series of glass receivers (called *Woulfe's bottles*), formerly used in distillation.

Wound (wūnd), *sb.* [OE. *wund* = OFris. *wunde, wund*, OS. *wunda*, OHG. *wunta* (Du. *wond*, G. *wunde*), ON. *und*; ult. origin unknown. The normal mod. pronunc. would be (waund); cf. WOUNDY, ZOUNDS.] **1.** A hurt caused by the laceration or separation of the tissues of the body by a hard or sharp instrument, a bullet, etc.; an external injury. **b.** esp. in *the (Five) Wounds* of Christ ME. **c.** Used as an oath or strong exclam., as *By Christ's wounds, Wounds of God*, etc. (see SWOUNDS, ZOUNDS, WOUNDS) ME. **2.** *transf.* An incision, abrasion, or other injury due to external violence, in any part of a tree or plant 1574. **b.** In other transf. uses 1667. **3.** *Surgery.* An incision or opening made by a surgical operator 1668. **4.** Something which causes a wound 1715.

1. *fig.* She..Pours balm into the bleeding lover's wounds POPE. The wounds of honour never close 1744. **2. b.** Her rash hand..Forth reaching to the Fruit, she pluck'd, she eat: Earth felt the w. MILT.

Combs.: **w.-cork,** a protective layer formed on a damaged trunk or branch of a plant or tree; **-fungus,** a fungus which grows on the injured part of a plant; **-stripe,** a stripe of gold braid worn by a wounded soldier on the left sleeve, vertically, above the cuff; **-weed** = WOUNDWORT. Hence **Wou·ndless** *a.* unwounded; †invulnerable; harmless.

Wound (wūnd), *v.* [OE. *wundian*, f. *wund* WOUND *sb.*] **1.** *trans.* To inflict a wound on (a person, the body, etc.) by means of a weapon; to injure intentionally in such a way as to cut or tear the flesh: freq. in pass. Also said of the weapon, etc. **2.** *fig.* To injure, inflict pain or hurt upon, in a manner comparable to the infliction of a wound; in later use *esp.* to pain or grieve deeply ME. **b.** Used to express the effect of harsh or disagreeable sounds upon the ear 1669. **3.** *absol.* or *intr.* To inflict a wound or wounds; to do harm, hurt, or injury (physically or otherwise); to impair in any way OE. **4.** *transf.* To pierce or cut as if to wound; to damage in this way ME. **b.** *fig.* Of wine: To overpower (*rare*) 1613.

1. An honest Man that has been wounded in the Queen's Service ADDISON. **2.** *A. Y. L.* v. ii. 25. Moore's vanity was easily wounded at any time 1884. **4.** When she would with sharpe needle w. The Cambricke SHAKS. Hence **Wou·nded** *ppl. a.* **Wou·ndedly** *adv.* in a wounded manner, as though wounded. **Wou·nder. Wou·nding** *vbl. sb.* and *ppl. a.*

Wound (waund), pa. t. and pa. pple. of WIND *v.*¹

Woundily (wau·ndili), *adv. Obs.* exc. *arch.* 1706. [f. WOUNDY *a.* + -LY².] Excessively, extremely, dreadfully.

I own I 's w. afraid of dead men 1796.

Wounds (waundz), *int. Obs.* exc. *arch.* 1610. [ellipt. for *God's wounds*; see WOUND *sb.* 1 c. Cf. OONS, ZOUNDS.] Used as an oath or asseveration.

Wound-up (wau·nd,ʊp), *a.* 1837. [f.

wound. pa. pple. of WIND *v.*[1] + UP *adv.*] That has undergone winding-up.

Woundwort (wū·ndwɒ̄ɹt). 1548. [f. WOUND *sb.* + WORT *sb.*[1], after Du. *wondkruid*, G. *wundkraut.*] A popular name for various plants, from their use in healing wounds, *esp.* (*a*) one of the species of *Stachys*; (*b*) the golden-rod, *Solidago virgaurea*; (*c*) the kidney-vetch, *Anthyllis vulneraria*; (*d*) the comfrey, *Symphytum officinale*.

Woundy (wau·ndi), *adv.* and *a.* 1621. [f. WOUNDS *int.* + -Y[1]. Cf. *bloody.*] **A.** *adv.* Very, extremely, excessively.

He was w. angry when I gav'n that wipe CONGREVE.

B. *adj.* Very great; extreme 1681.

He flew into a w. passion 1794.

Wove (wōᵘv), *ppl. a.* and *sb.* 1710. [var. of WOVEN.] **1.** = next. **b.** *W. mould*, the particular kind of mould used in making w. paper (see 2) 1839. **2.** Of paper: Made on a mould of closely woven wire 1809. **b.** *absol.* or as *sb.* Paper so made 1859.

Woven (wōᵘ·v'n), *ppl. a.* 1470. [pa. pple. of WEAVE *v.*[1]] **1.** That has undergone the process of weaving; formed or fabricated by weaving. **2.** Formed by interlacing or intertwining after the manner of weaving 1590. **3.** Interlaced, intertwined; wreathed 1815.

2. Soone after comes the cruell Sarazin, In wouen maile all armed warily SPENSER. **3.** The kiss, The w. arms TENNYSON.

Wow (wau), *sb.* 1811. [Imitative.] A bark or similar sound; a cat's howl. So **Wow** *v. intr.* to howl; to waul.

Wow (wau), *int.* and *sb.*[2] *Sc.* and *U.S.* 1513. An exclamation of surprise, admiration, aversion, or commiseration. **b.** phr. *It's a wow* (U.S.), used to express admiration or approval 1927.

Wowser (wau·zəɹ). *Austral.* 1909. [Of unkn. origin.] A Puritanical enthusiast or fanatic.

‖**Wow-wow** (wau·wau). 1827. [– Malay *wauwau*, Javanese *wawa*, imitative of the animal's cry.] The silver gibbon of Java, *Hylobates leuciscus*; also *H. agilis*.

Wr- (r), a consonantal combination occurring initially in a number of words (freq. implying twisting or distortion), the earlier of which usu. have cognates with the same initial sounds in the older Germanic langs. The combination was regularly preserved in Gothic, OS., OFris., and OE., but in OHG. and ON. was reduced to *r*.

In English, signs of the dropping of the *w* in pronunciation begin to appear about the middle of the 15th cent., and become common in the 16th cent. In standard English the *w* was finally dropped in the 17th cent.; it has remained (though now *obsol.*) in Scottish, and in some south-western dialects is represented by *v*, which is also regular in north-eastern Scottish.

Wrack (ræk), *sb.*[1] [OE. *wræc*, f. gradation-var. of *wrecan* WREAK *v.*] **I. 1.** Retributive punishment; vengeance, revenge; later also, active enmity, persecution. *Obs.* exc. *arch.* or *poet.* **2.** Damage, disaster, or injury to a person, state, etc., by reason of force, outrage, or violence. late ME. **3.** A disastrous change in a state or condition of affairs; wreck, ruin. late ME. †**b.** The ruin, downfall, or overthrow of a person or persons –1699.

1. *fig.* Hath he not lost much wealth by w. of sea? SHAKS. **2.** Phr. *To bring, go, put, run to w.* (*and ruin*). Cf. RACK *sb.*[4] **3.** *All's Well* III. v. 24.

II. †**1.** An instance of causing or suffering wreck, ruin, destruction, etc. –1632. †**b.** A means or cause of subversion, overthrow, or downfall –1682. **2.** A thing or person in an impaired, wrecked, or shattered condition 1586. **b.** That which remains after the operation of any destructive action or agency; a vestige or trace left by some subversive cause 1602.

1. b. And thus I feare at last, Humes Knauerie will be the Duchesse Wracke SHAKS. **2. b.** I am a poore, poore orphant—a weake, weake childe. The w. of splitted fortune. MARSTON.

Wrack (ræk), *sb.*[2] late ME. [– MDu. *wrak* (= MLG. *wrak, wrack*, whence G. *wrack*), corresp. to OE. *wræc* WRACK *sb.*[1]; cf. VAREC(H.] **1.** A wrecked ship or other vessel. Now *dial.* **b.** Remnants of or goods from a wrecked vessel, esp. as driven or cast ashore; wreckage. *arch.* late ME. **2.** = SHIPWRECK *sb.* 2. *rare* or *Obs.* 1579. **3.** Marine vegetation, seaweed or the like, cast ashore by the waves or growing on the tidal sea-shore 1513. **b.** Weeds, rubbish, etc., floating on or washed down or ashore by a river, pond, or the like 1598. **c.** Field-weeds, roots of couch-grass or the like, esp. as loosened from the soil to be collected for burning 1715.

1. b. As rich . . As is the Owse and bottome of the Sea With sunken Wrack SHAKS. Hence **Wra·ckful** *a.* (now *rare arch.*) causing shipwreck, causing destruction or devastation, subject to or attended by harm, injury, etc.

Wrack (ræk), *sb.*[3] 1472. [– (M)LG. or Du. *wrak.*] **1.** That which is of an inferior, poor, or worthless quality; waste material; rubbish. Now *rare*. **2.** An inferior grade of flax 1879.

†*World's w.* (Sc.): earthly 'dross'; worldly possessions.

Wrack (ræk), *v.* Now *arch.* or *dial.* 1470. [f. WRACK *sb.*[2]] †**1.** *intr.* To suffer or undergo shipwreck –1632. **2.** *trans.* To wreck; to ruin or cast ashore by shipwreck: chiefly *pass.* 1562. **3.** To cause the ruin, downfall, or subversion of (a person, etc.); to ruin, overthrow 1564. **b.** To render useless by breaking, etc.; to injure or spoil severely; to destroy 1587. **4.** *intr.* To undergo ruin or subversion 1586.

3. b. Eightie odde yeeres of sorrow haue I seene, And each howres ioy wrackt with a weeke of teene SHAKS. Hence **Wracked** (rækt) *ppl. a.*

Wraith (rēⁱþ). orig. *Sc.* 1513. [Of unkn. origin.] **1.** An apparition or spectre of a dead person; a phantom or ghost. **b.** An immaterial or spectral appearance of a living being, freq. regarded as portending that person's death 1513. **2.** A water-spirit 1742. **3.** An appearance or configuration suggestive of a wraith or spectre 1882.

1. b. The shape of the warning w. haunts the mountaineer 1838.

Wrangle (ræ·ŋg'l), *sb.* 1547. [f. next.] **1.** An angry dispute or noisy quarrel; an altercation or bitter disputation. **2.** Without article: The action of wrangling; angry altercation or argument 1797.

1. The disgraceful wrangles of the religious newspapers 1859.

Wrangle (ræ·ŋg'l), *v.* late ME. [prob. of LDu. origin; cf. LG., G. dial. *wrangeln* wrestle, etc., frequent. of (M)LG. *wrangen*, rel. to *ringen*; see WRING *v.*] **1.** *intr.* To dispute angrily and noisily; to bicker. **2.** To argue or debate; to engage in controversy; †to dispute or discuss publicly, as at a university, for or against a thesis, etc. 1570. †**3.** *trans.* To argue *out* (a case, dispute, etc.) –1728. **4.** To influence (a person) by wrangling or contention; to argue *out of* a possession, etc. 1633. **5.** *Western U.S.* To take charge of (horses) 1903.

1. Wrangling about trifles 1746. **4.** To w. the Church of England out of a good possession 1658.

Wrangler (ræ·ŋgləɹ). 1515. [f. prec. + -ER[1].] **1.** One who wrangles or quarrels; an angry or noisy disputer or arguer. **b.** One who engages in argument, debate, or controversy 1561. **c.** One who has been placed in the first class in the mathematical tripos at Cambridge University 1750. **2.** *Western U.S.* One who is in charge of a string of horses or ponies on a stock-farm 1888. Hence **Wra·nglership,** the position or rank of a w. at Camb. Univ.

Wrap (ræp), *sb.* 1460. [f. next.] **1. a.** A wrapper or covering. **b.** A blanket, rug, or the like for laying over or drawing about the person when travelling, resting, etc. 1861. **2.** A loose garment or article of feminine dress used to wrap about the person; a shawl, scarf, or the like 1827. **b.** An additional outer garment worn as a protection against cold, wind, and weather, etc. Usu. *pl.* = outdoor garments. 1817.

1. b. We have heard . . Livingstone . . say that at night no w. could equal the beard 1861. **2. b.** I was taking off my wraps, and making ready to go up stairs 1855.

Wrap (ræp), *v.* ME. [Of unkn. origin; cf. the earlier BEWRAP *v.*, also BELAP *v.*, LAP *v.*[2] with var. *wlappe.*] **1.** *trans.* To cover, enwrap, or swathe (a person or part of the body) with a cloth or the like; now *esp.* to envelop or enshroud in a garment: freq. with *up*; esp. *pass.* = attired in warm or protective clothing. **b.** *absol.* for *refl.* 1848. **2.** To cover or envelop (an object) by winding or folding something round or about it, esp. so as to protect from injury, loss, etc. late ME. **3.** To envelop or enclose *in* a surrounding medium, as flames, water, etc. late ME. **b.** To clasp, embrace 1588. **4.** To envelop or implicate (a person, etc.) *in* some (esp. prejudicial) condition of things, as sin, trouble, sorrow, etc. late ME. **b.** To involve or enfold (a person, etc.) *in* some soothing or tranquillizing state or influence. Freq. *pass.* late ME. **5.** To involve or enfold (a subject or matter) so as to obscure or disguise the true or full nature of it. late ME. **6.** Of qualities, etc.: To invest or environ (a person, etc.); encompass *in* some condition. late ME. **b.** To form a wrap or covering for (a person or thing); to clothe; to veil 1602. **c.** Of flames, etc.: To spread or extend around, about, or over (something); to surround, encompass 1656.

1. Are you well wrapped up? . . It's a desperate sharp night DICKENS. **2.** We can't be kept in bandboxes and wrapped in cotton wool all our lives 1890. **4.** It is a Man wrapped in woe 1659. **b.** The house is wrapped in slumbers DICKENS. **5.** The religion of the Egyptians . . was all mystery, wrapt in obscurity 1770. Without troubling to w. up his resolve in smooth-sounding words 1897. See also WRAPPED. **6. b.** Cauld's the clay, That wraps my Highland Mary! BURNS.

II. 1. To wind or fold up or together, as a pliant or flexible object; to roll or gather up in successive layers ME. **2.** To fold, wind, or roll (a covering, garment, or the like) about a person, etc.; to arrange or dispose (a wrapping, etc.) so as to cover or envelop. late ME. **b.** To twist or coil (a pliable or flexible substance, etc.) *round, about,* or *on* something 1523. **3.** *intr.* for *refl.* To twine, encircle, or wreathe *round* or *about* something 1608. **b.** Of a garment, etc.: To extend *over* something so as to cover it, or form a lap 1798.

2. Wrapping my plaid around me, I wandered up towards Charmoz 1860. **b.** Again she wrapped her arms about me RICHARDSON. Hence **Wra·ppage,** that which wraps, enfolds, or covers; a wrap or outer covering; a wrapper; something wrapped up, a package 1827.

Wrap-, the vb. stem in comb. with a sb. or adv., in the sense 'that which wraps or is wrapped about', as **w. tobacco** (also *ellipt.*) = WRAPPER *sb.* 4.

Wrapped (ræpt), *pa. pple.* and *ppl. a.* Formerly often **wrapt.** late ME. [f. WRAP *v.* + -ED[1].] **I.** In senses of the vb.: Covered, enwrapped; (with *up*) involved, complicated; etc. **II.** In predic. use. **1.** Deeply interested or absorbed *in*. Often with *up*. 1548. **b.** *W.* (*up*) *in*, entirely associated or bound up with, involved in 1648. **2.** Absorbed or engrossed *in* thought. (Cf. RAPT *pa. pple.* 4.) 1601.

1. b. His young Wife (in whom all his Happiness was wrapt up) ADDISON. **2.** Wrapt in a pleasing fit of melancholy MILT. As if wrapt in prayer or meditation GEO. ELIOT.

Wrapper (ræ·pəɹ), *sb.* 1460. [f. WRAP *v.* + -ER[1].] **1.** That in which anything is wrapped; a piece of fabric or other material forming a wrapping; esp. in later use, a protective covering for a parcel or the like. **b.** A detachable outer paper cover of a book, etc., intended to protect the print, boards, or binding 1806. **c.** A covering to protect and compact a newspaper or the like when sent by post, etc. 1846. **d.** A dust sheet 1848. **2.** A head-dress wrapped about the head (*rare*) 1548. **b.** A shawl, mantle, etc., for wearing about the person. Now *rare*. 1782. **3.** A garment, esp. for indoor wear, designed for loosely enveloping the whole (or nearly the whole) figure; a loose robe or gown. Now chiefly *U.S.* 1734. **b.** An article of dress, esp. for men, intended to wrap about or fit loosely over the person; also, an overall. Now *dial.* 1799. **4.** Tobacco-leaf of a superior grade used for the outer covering of cigars or of plug tobacco; a covering made of this. Chiefly *U.S.* 1688. **b.** *U.S.* A cigar 1849. **5.** *Bot.* In fungi, = VOLVA 1796. **6.** One who wraps or packs up anything; *spec.* one whose occupation is wrapping parcels 1591.

3. His wife . . had just risen—or so it seemed, for she wore a rose-colored w. 1883. **6.** Women &

Girls as Lacquerers. . Press Women, & Wrappers-up 1866. Hence **Wra·pper** *v. trans.* to enclose or envelop in a w., cover *up* in or as in a w. **Wra·p-pering,** coarse fabric used or designed for wrapping or covering; a wrap or wrapper.

Wrapping (ræ·piŋ), *vbl. sb.* late ME. [f. WRAP *v.* + -ING[1].] **1.** The action of covering with or enveloping in a wrap or wrapper 1440. **2.** Something used or designed for enveloping or wrapping up; a wrap or covering. late ME. **b.** An article of dress enveloping the figure; a loose or warm outer garment 1635.

2. Tearing the paper wrappings off the big box of sweeties 1894. **b.** A gentleman in the coach who. . looked very large in a quantity of wrappings DICKENS.

Comb.: †**w.-gown,** a nightgown; **-paper,** a special make of strong paper for packing or wrapping up parcels.

Wrap-rascal (ræ·p,ra:skăl). 1716. Now *arch.* or *dial.* [f. WRAP *v.* + RASCAL *sb.* 3.] A loose overcoat or greatcoat; a surtout.

Wrasse (ræs). 1672. [– Cornish *wrach*, mutated f. *gwrach* = Welsh *gwrach* wrasse, old woman (cf. OLD WIFE 3).] **1.** Any species belonging to the acanthopterygian family *Labridæ*, esp. of the genus *Labrus* of bony, thick-lipped marine fishes; e.g. the ballan, *Labrus maculatus*, or *L. mixtus*, found on the British coasts. **b.** With distinguishing epithet, as *cook, rainbow, striped w.*, etc. 1769. **2.** Without article: Wrasses collectively 1750.

Wrath (rǭþ, *U.S.* and *Sc.* rāþ), *sb.* [OE. *wrǣþþu*, f. *wrāþ* WROTH *a.* + -*iþō -TH[1].] **1.** Vehement or violent anger; intense exasperation or resentment; deep indignation. **b.** The righteous indignation (of God or a deity) OE. **c.** *transf.* Violence or extreme force of a natural agency, regarded as hostile to mankind or growth 1579. **2.** An instance of deep or violent anger; a fit or spell of ire or fierce indignation ME. †**3.** Impetuous ardour, rage, or fury –1601. **4.** Anger displayed in action; the manifestation of anger or fury, esp. by way of retributory punishment; vengeance OE. †**5.** An act done in anger or indignation –1754.

1. Upon every triffle they shall be provoked to W. 1691. When he had respectfully suffered her w. to vent itself, he made apologies MME. D'ARBLAY. **b.** As when the w. of Jove Speaks thunder MILT. **c.** Thou barrein ground, whome winters w. hath wasted SPENSER. **2.** *Temp.* III. iii. 79. **3.** They are in the verie w. of loue, and they will together SHAKS. **4.** Remembre that the w. shall not be longe in tarienge COVERDALE *Ecclus.* 7:16. The wrauth Of stern Achilles on his Foe MILT. Phr. (orig. biblical). *The w. of God, the day of w.*

Wrath (rǭþ), *a.* Somewhat *rare.* 1535. [var. of WROTH *a.*, infl. by association with prec.] = WROTH *a.*

Wrathful (rǭ·þfŭl), *a.* ME. [f. WRATH *sb.* + -FUL.] **1.** Harbouring wrath; full of anger; enraged, incensed. Also *transf.* of things. **2.** Marked or characterized by, expressive of, or of the nature of wrath or anger. late ME.

1. The wrathfull Skies SHAKS. The Bees, a w. Race DRYDEN. Hence **Wra·thful-ly** *adv.*, **-ness.**

Wrathy (rǭ·þi, *U.S.* rā·þi), *a.* orig. and chiefly *U.S.* 1828. [f. WRATH *sb.* + -Y[1].] Feeling or inclined to wrath; wrathful, incensed. Also *transf.* of things. **b.** Marked or characterized by wrath; expressing or evincing deep anger or indignation 1873.

†**Wray,** *v.* [OE. *wrēgan* accuse = OFris. *wrēia*, OS. *wrōgian*, OHG. *ruogen* (G. *rügen*), ON. *rægja* :- Gmc. **wrōʒjan* (in Goth. *wrōhjan*), of unkn. origin.] **1.** *trans.* To accuse, denounce –1450. **2.** = BEWRAY *v.* 2, 3, 4. –1587.

Wreak (rīk), *sb.* Now *arch.* or *Obs.* ME. [Northern form of ME. *wreche* (OE. *wrǣc*) vengeance; in later use prob. substituted for this under the influence of the vb.] **1.** Hurt or harm done from vindictive motives; vengeance, revenge. †**2.** An instance of taking revenge or exacting retribution –1626. †**3.** Harm, injury, damage –1600.

2. Where mortall wreakes their blis may not remoue SPENSER. Hence **Wrea·kless** *a. rare,* unpunished, unavenged.

Wreak (rīk), *v* [OE. *wrecan* = OFris. *wreka*, OS. *wrekan*, OHG. *rehhan* (Du. *wreken*, G. *rächen*), ON. *reka*, Goth. *wrikan* persecute :- Gmc. **wrekan*, f. **wrek-* (cf. **wrak-* s.v. WRETCH) :- IE. **wreg-*, prob. cogn. with L. *urgēre* URGE Gr. εἴργειν shut up.] **I. 1.** *trans.* To give vent or expression to, exercise or gratify (wrath, anger, etc.); to vent. **b.** *refl.* Of a passion, feeling, etc.: To give expression to (itself); to find utterance or free course 1590. **c.** To bestow or spend *on* a person, etc.; to expend (*rare*) 1586. †**2.** To punish or chastise; to visit with retributive punishment –1683.

1. The more to wreake his wrath, the King spoyled many Religious houses of their goodes HOLINSHED. I wreaked my Resentment upon the innocent Cause of my Disgraces SMOLLETT.

II. 1. To avenge (a person) OE. †**b.** To revenge (a person) *of* a wrong, injury, etc. –1591. **2.** *refl.* and (now arch. or obs.) *pass.* To take vengeance. **3.** *trans.* To take vengeance or inflict retributive punishment for; to avenge or revenge (a wrong, harm, or injury) OE. †**4.** To visit (a fault, misdeed) with punishment –1610. **5.** To inflict (vengeance, etc.) *on* or *upon* a person; to execute or carry out by way of punishment or revenge 1489. **b.** To cause or effect (harm, damage, etc.) 1817. **c.** To inflict or deliver (a blow, etc.) 1817.

1. To wreake the Loue I bore my Cozin, Vpon his body that hath slaughter'd him SHAKS. **2.** He micht hae spared my lady's life, And wreakit himsell on me! *Ballad, Capt. Car.* **5.** Resolv'd. . To w. his Vengeance, and to cure her Love DRYDEN. Hence **Wrea·ker** (now *arch.* and *rare*), an avenger.

Wreakful (rī·kfŭl), *a.* 1531. [f. WREAK *sb.* + -FUL.] **1.** Given or addicted to revenge; vengeful. **b.** *transf.* Of natural agencies 1561. **2.** Marked or characterized by desire for revenge; of the nature of vengeance or retribution 1532.

Wreath (rīþ). *Pl.* **wreaths** (rīðz). [OE. *wriþa*, f. wk. grade of *wrīþan* WRITHE *v.*] **I. 1.** Something wound, wreathed, or coiled into a circular shape or form; a twisted or wreathed band, fillet, or the like. **b.** A ring, band, or circlet of (usu. precious) metal, etc., esp. for wearing as an ornament OE. **c.** *Her.* A representation of a ring or circlet used as a bearing; *spec.* the circular fillet or twisted band by which the crest is joined to the helmet 1478. **2.** Something resembling or comparable to a twisted or circular band; *esp.* a coil of a spiral column of smoke, steam, or the like 1667. **b.** A bank or drift of snow. Orig. and chiefly *Sc.* 1725. **3.** Each of the turns, convolutions, or coils of a ringed or spiral structure; a whirl, whorl 1641. **b.** *Conch.* A member of the genus *Turbo*; a turbinated shell; a turbinate 1777. **4.** A twist, coil, or winding (of some material thing or natural growth); a sinuosity 1589. **5.** A curve in the handrail or string of a geometrical stair 1814.

2. Clouds began To darken all the Hill, and smoak to rowl In duskie wreathes MILT.

II. A chaplet or garland of flowers, leaves, or the like, esp. worn or awarded as a mark of distinction, honour, etc., or laid upon a grave, etc. 1450. **b.** A trailing cluster of flowers, tendrils, etc. 1610. **c.** As the title of a book comprising a collection of short literary pieces 1753. **d.** A representation of a wreath in decorative work, metal, stone, etc. 1847.

A Crown, Golden in shew, is but a w. of thorns MILT.

Comb.: **w. shell** = I. 3 b; **-wort,** the early purple orchis, *Orchis mascula.* Hence **Wrea·thless** *a.* having no w. **Wrea·thlet,** a small w.

Wreathe (rīð), *v.* 1530. [Partly back formation from *wrethen* WREATHEN *ppl. a.* partly f. WREATH *sb.*] **I. 1.** *trans.* To twist or coil (something); to form into a coil or coils 1535. **b.** To wind or turn (some pliant object) about or over something; to form or adjust as a wreath or encircling coil 1530. **2.** To surround or invest with or as with something twisted or turned; to encircle or surround with a wreath or garland; to adorn with or as with a wreath; to form a wreath about (something) 1558. **3.** To unite (two or more things) by twining or twisting together; to entwine, intertwine 1553. **b.** To combine (several things into one structure) by interweaving; to form or make by intertwining 1547. **4.** To arrange or dispose flowers, etc., in the form of a wreath; to fashion (flowers, etc.) into a garland or chaplet 1595.

1. An adder Wreathed up in fatal folds SHAKS. **b.** An ill-adjusted turban. . wreathed around their sunburnt brows WORDSW. **2.** With Laurels wreath your posts, And strow with Flow'rs the Pavement DRYDEN. Each flower that wreath'd the dewy locks of Spring COLERIDGE. **3.** Enter Andrugio and Antonio wreathed together MARSTON. **4.** The Garland wreath'd for Eve MILT.

II. †**a.** To strain or turn forcibly round or to one side; to wring, wrench, or wrest –1737. **b.** To twist, turn, or contort (the body, limbs, etc.); to writhe 1642. **c.** To alter (the features, etc.) *in, into,* or *to* a smile, etc. 1813.

b. Even in death their lips are wreathed with fear SHELLEY.

III. *intr.* **1.** To undergo writhing, twisting, or deviation; to bend, turn, or coil 1584. **2.** To assume the form of or circle in the manner of a wreath 1776.

2. The flames of fire shall round him w. 1776. Hence **Wreathed** (rīðd) *ppl. a.* **Wrea·thing** *vbl. sb.* the action of twisting or contorting, or of entwining or intertwining; an instance of this; *concr.* something wreathed or twisted.

Wreathen (rī·ð'n), *ppl. a.* [Late ME. *wrēðen*, var. of *wriðen*, pa. pple. of *wrīðen* WRITHE *v.*] **1.** Wreathed; contorted, twisted. **2.** Entwined, intertwined 1611.

Wreathy (rī·þi), *a.* 1644. [f. WREATH *sb.* + -Y[1].] **1.** Of the form of a wreath; marked or characterized by convolution, twisting, or twining. **2.** Decked with a wreath 1697. **3.** Of the nature of, forming, or constituting a wreath or garland 1718.

Wreck (rek), *sb.* ME. [– AFr. *wrec*, etc. – ON. **wrek* (Norw., Icel. *rek*), f. **wrekan* drive; see WREAK *v.*, VAREC(H).] **I. 1.** *Law.* That which is cast ashore by the sea in tidal waters; *esp.* goods or cargo from a wrecked, stranded, or foundered vessel. **2.** A vessel broken, destroyed, or totally disabled by being driven on rocks, cast ashore, or stranded; a wrecked or helpless ship 1500. **3. a.** *Law.* A piece or article of wreckage. Freq. *pl.* 1570. **b.** Without article: = WRECKAGE 2. 1744. **4.** That which remains *of* something that has suffered ruin, demolishment, waste, etc. 1713. **5.** That which is in a state of ruin; anything that is broken down or has undergone wrecking, shattering, or dilapidation 1814. **b.** A person of undermined, shattered, or ruined constitution 1795. ¶**6.** = WRACK *sb.*[1] II. 2 b. 1787.

1. A warrant against 11 Britton men for riotously taking a whale and other wrecke 1666. **2.** The ship. . struck upon a reef of rocks. ., and shortly became a total w. 1805. **3. b.** Several chests, broken masts, and other pieces of w. floating in the sea 1744. **4.** As Mamma surveyed the w. of luncheon 1854. The Republican party was formed . . out of the wrecks of the Whig party 1888. **5. b.** I was a nervous w. 1899. I feel a perfect w. 1901. **6.** These ruins soon left not a w. behind SHELLEY.

II. 1. The disabling or destruction of a vessel by any disaster or accident of navigation; = SHIPWRECK *sb.* 2. 1463. **2.** The action of subverting or overthrowing an established order of things, etc., or of wrecking or breaking apart; the fact of being brought to disaster or wrecked; destruction, downfall, demolition 1577.

1. A range of rocks, the terrible scene of many a disastrous w. 1809. **2.** Books, which. . may. . perish only in the general W. of Nature ADDISON. The w. of their ancient liberties PRESCOTT. Phr. *To go to w. (and ruin)*; cf. RACK *sb.*[4]

Wreck (rek), *v.*[1] late ME. [f. prec.] †**1.** *trans.* To cast on shore –1821. **2.** To cause the wreck of (a vessel). Chiefly *pass.* 1570. **b.** To make or cause (a person) to suffer or undergo shipwreck; also, to cause the loss of (goods or cargo) by shipwreck. Chiefly *pass.* 1617. **3.** To cause or bring about the ruin or destruction of (a structure, etc.) as by violence or misuse; to shatter, ruin, destroy 1510. **b.** To cause or bring about the subversion or overthrow of (some condition or order of things) 1749. **c.** To frustrate or thwart; to prevent the passing of (a measure, etc.) 1855. **4.** To bring (a person) to ruin or disaster 1590. **b.** To shatter (a person's health, constitution, or nerves) by sickness, hardship, or the like: usu. *pass.* 1850. **5.** *intr.* To suffer or undergo shipwreck 1671. **6.** To seize or collect wreck or wreckage; to search *for* wreck 1843.

2. The shallop of my peace is wrecked on Beauty's shore 1845. **3. b.** Their want of tact and judgment has wrecked the party 1826. **4. b.** I wonder your nervous system isn't completely wrecked KIPLING. **5.** Honour, glory, and popular praise; Rocks whereon greatest men have oftest wreck'd MILT.

†**Wreck**, *v.*[2] 1570. [Late var. of WREAK *v.*] = WREAK *v.* –1793.

Wreckage (re·kėdʒ). 1837. [f. WRECK *v.*[1] + -AGE.] **1.** The action or process of wrecking; the fact of being wrecked. **2.** Fragments or remains of a shattered or wrecked vessel; wreck 1846. **3.** Material of or from a wrecked or shattered structure; a ruined fabric, building, etc. 1874. **b.** *fig.* Persons whose lives have been wrecked or who have failed to maintain a position in society 1883.

3. The venerable w. of a feudal keep 1894.

Wrecker[1] (re·kəɹ). 1820. [f. WRECK *v.*[1] + -ER[1].] One who causes shipwreck, esp. for purposes of plunder by showing luring lights or false signals; a person who makes a business of watching for and plundering wrecked vessels; *transf.* one who destroys machinery or the like. **b.** One who wrecks or ruins a structure, institution, etc.; one who successfully obstructs the passing of a measure, etc. 1882.

Wrecker[2] (re·kəɹ). orig. and chiefly *U.S.* 1804. [f. WRECK *sb.* + -ER[1].] **1.** A person engaged in salvaging wrecked or endangered vessels or cargo; a salvager, salvor. **2.** A ship or vessel employed in salvaging sunk, wrecked, or stranded vessels 1864. **Wre·cking** *vbl. sb.*

Wren[1] (ren). [OE. *wrenna*, obscurely related to OHG. *wrendo, wrendilo*, Icel. *rindill.*] **1.** Any species of small dentirostral passerine birds belonging to the genus *Troglodytes*, esp. the common w. (jenny- or kitty-w.), *T. parvulus*, native to Europe. **2.** Applied, esp. with distinguishing term, to various other small birds of the family *Troglodytidæ* or *Sylviidæ*, resembling the common w. in appearance or habits; esp. the gold-crest, *Regulus cristatus* 1674. **b.** Applied to various Australasian species of w.-like birds 1848.

1. Thus the fable tells us, that the w. mounted as high as the eagle, by getting upon his back ADDISON.

Comb.: **w.-boys,** in Ireland, a party of boys or young men, carrying a decorated holly-bush with a w. or wrens hanging from it, who go about on St. Stephen's day singing verses; **w. song,** the song sung by the w.-boys.

Wren[2] (ren). 1918. A member of the *W*omen's *R*oyal *N*aval *S*ervice.

Wrench (renʃ), *sb.* 1530. [f. next.] **1.** An act of wrenching or the fact of being wrenched; a twisting or putting aside, awry, or out of shape. **b.** A sudden or sharp twist or jerk causing pain or injury to a limb, person, etc. 1530. **c.** An instance of this in horses 1578. **d.** *fig.* A parting or separation causing painful or violent emotion; pain or anguish resulting from separation 1849. **e.** *Mech.* A system made up of a force and a couple in a plane perpendicular to it 1876. †**2.** A sharp turn, bend, or deflexion –1654. **b.** *Coursing.* A turning or bringing round of the hare at less than a right angle 1615. **3.** A strained or wrested meaning; a forced or false interpretation 1603. **4.** A mechanical screw 1552. **b.** A tool or implement consisting essentially of a metal bar with jaws adapted for catching or gripping a bolt-head, nut, etc., to turn it; a screw-key, screw-wrench, or spanner 1794. **c.** *Surg.* Applied to various instruments having adjustable jaws, *spec.* one for gripping a deformed foot to be rectified by torsion 1895.

Wrench (renʃ), *v.* [Late OE. *wrenćan* = OHG. *renchen* (G. *renken*), of unkn. origin.] **I.** †**1.** *intr.* To perform or undergo a quick or forcible turning or twisting motion; to turn or writhe –1716. **2.** *Coursing.* Of a hare, etc.: To veer or come round at less than a right angle 1576.

II. *trans.* **1.** To twist or turn forcibly or with effort; to jerk or pull with a violent twist ME. **b.** To tighten with or as with a wrench 1577. **2.** To injure or pain (a person, the limbs, etc.) by undue straining or stretching; to rick, sprain, strain 1530. **b.** To affect with severe pain, suffering, or anguish; to distress or pain greatly 1798. **3.** To pull or draw with a wrench or twist; to twist or wrest out; to force, turn, etc., by a twisting movement 1582. **b.** To seize or take forcibly 1605. **4.** To twist, alter, or change from the right or true form, application, or import 1549. **5.** *Coursing.* To divert, turn, or bring round (a hare, etc.) at less than a right angle 1622. **6.** *absol.* To pull or tug (*at* something) with a turn or twist 1697.

1. b. *fig.* For thy Reuenge W. vp thy power to th' highest SHAKS. **2.** You wrenched your foot against a stone, and were forced to stay SWIFT. **3.** W. his Sword from him SHAKS. He went up to the door, wrenched off the fastenings 1825. Hence **Wre·ncher,** a machine or instrument for wrenching or wringing (*rare*); one who or that which wrenches or twists.

Wrest (rest), *sb.*[1] ME. [f. the vb.] **1.** The action of twisting or writhing; a twist, wrench; a tug or violent pull. **2.** An implement for tuning certain wire-stringed instruments, as the harp or spinet; a tuning-key. Now *arch.* late ME.

Comb.: **w.-pin,** the peg round which the ends of the strings or wires of certain musical instruments are coiled, a tuning-pin; **-plank,** the board in a piano in which the w.-pins are fixed.

Wrest, *sb.*[2] Now *dial.* 1653. [Variant spelling of dial. *reest* (OE. *rēost*), by association w. prec.] *Agric.* A piece of iron (†or wood) fastened beneath the mould-board in certain ploughs. **b.** A mould-board.

Wrest (rest), *v.* [OE. *wrǣstan* = ON. **wreista* (ONorw., Icel. *reista*, MDa. *vreste*, Da. *vriste*) :- **wraistjan*; cf. WRIST.] **1.** *trans.* To subject (something) to a twisting movement; to turn or twist. **2.** To pull, pluck, drag away, or detach (a person or thing) with a wrench or twist; to twist, tear, or wrench out, etc. ME. †**3.** To turn or dispose (some one, his heart) to a person or thing; to incline or influence (a person, etc.) *to* do something –1618. **4.** To usurp, arrogate, or take by force (power, lands, etc.) from another or others; to assume forcibly (a dignity or office). late ME. **b.** To obtain or gain (money, information, etc.) by extortion, persistency, or strong persuasion; to wring 1565. **5.** To strain or overstrain the meaning or bearing of (a writing, passage, word, etc.); to twist, pervert 1533. **b.** To put a wrong construction on the words or purport of (a writer); to interpret perversely 1555. **6.** To turn or deflect (a matter, etc.); to divert *to* some different (esp. undue or improper) purpose, end, etc. 1524. **b.** To deflect (the law, etc.) from its proper course or interpretation; to misapply, pervert 1530. †**7.** *intr.* To struggle or contend *against* something –1594. †**8.** To force a way (*out*), make way with effort, find egress –1590.

2. You w. the Bolt from Heav'ns avenging Hand PRIOR. **4.** I had wrested from fortune her favours and smiles 1890. **b.** Did not she..reveal The secret wrested from me? MILT. **5.** You try to w. Scripture and history to your own use KINGSLEY. **6. b.** The law was generally supposed to be wrested, in order to prolong their imprisonment HUME.

Wrestle (re·s'l), *sb.* 1593. [f. next.] **1.** The action of wrestling or struggling; the fact of having wrestled. **2.** A struggle between two persons, each trying to throw the other by grasping his body or limbs; also, a wrestling-match 1670. **b.** *fig.* A struggle or contest 1850.

2. b. The body politic..straining every nerve in a w. for life or death MACAULAY.

Wrestle (re·s'l), *v.* [OE. **wrǣstlian* (implied in late OE. *wrǣstlung* 'palestram'), corresp. to LDu. repr. by NFris. *wrassele*, MLG. *worstelen, wrostelen*, (M)Du. *worstelen*, OE. *wraxlian*, OFris. *wrāxlia*, perh. f. **wrasc-*, dial. *wrasle*.] **I.** *intr.* **1.** To strive with strength and skill to throw a person to the ground by grappling with him; to endeavour to overpower another, esp. in a contest governed by fixed rules, by grasping his body or limbs and tripping or overbalancing him. **b.** To struggle (*with* something) after the manner of wrestling 1589. **2.** To contend or struggle in hostility or opposition (*with* or *against* another or others) ME. **b.** *fig.* To strive or labour (*with* or *against* difficulties, personal feelings, etc.) ME. **c.** To strive earnestly (*with* God) in prayer 1612. **3. a.** To labour, toil, or exert oneself; to strive (*for* something); to tussle. late ME. **b.** To engage strenuously in argument, debate, or controversy 1450. **c.** To busy, occupy, or concern oneself closely or earnestly *with* a subject, etc. 1454. **4.** To twist or writhe about; to wriggle, move sinuously. late ME. **b.** To move or proceed with effort or toil; to struggle *out* (*of*) or *through* some place or condition 1591.

1. A handsome sum of money has been subscribed to be wrestled for 1811. He challenges all comers to w. with him 1856. Learnin' her son to box..and wrastle 1896. **b.** I must w. here with death 1844. **2. b.** I had to w. with my self-respect DICKENS. **3. b.** Hosius doth w. maruelously about the word 1565. **c.** After wrestling with French history or German poetry 1905.

II. *trans.* **1.** To engage in (a wrestling-bout or match). late ME. **2. a.** To contend with (a person) in wrestling; to overcome by wrestling 1818. **b.** *Western U.S.* To throw (a calf, etc.) for branding 1888.

1. Wilt thou w. a fall with me? SCOTT. **2. a.** A stout girl of twenty, strong enough to w. any man 1881.

Phr. *W. down,* to put down by wrestling or striving. *W. out,* to go through, perform, or execute with effort. Hence **Wre·stler** [OE. *wrǣstlere*].

Wrestling (re·sliŋ), *vbl. sb.* [OE. *wrǣstlung* (see prec.); f. prec. + -ING[1].] **1.** The action or exercise of two persons grappling or gripping in a contest of strength and adroitness, each endeavouring to throw the other by tripping or overbalancing him; the fact of contending or throwing in this manner. **b.** With *the.* The sport of grappling and throwing; a contest in wrestling; a w.-match ME. **c.** With *a* and *pl.* A w.-bout or match ME. **2.** The action of striving or contending; maintenance of resistance, opposition, or strife OE. **b.** The action of striving earnestly in prayer; an instance of this 1722.

attrib. and *Comb.*, as *w. bout, -match*; **w. school,** *Gr. Antiq.* = PALÆSTRA.

Wretch (retʃ), *sb.* and *a.* [OE. *wrećća* = OS. *wrekkio* (applied to the Magi), OHG. (*w*)*recch*(*e*)*o* exile, adventurer, knight errant (MHG., G. *recke* warrior, hero, dial. giant) :- WGmc. **wrakjo*, f. **wrak-* (see WREAK *v.*).] **A.** *sb.* †**1.** One driven out of or away from his native country; an exile –1450. **2.** One who is sunk in deep distress, sorrow, misfortune, or poverty; a miserable, unhappy, or unfortunate person OE. **b.** Applied to animals ME. **c.** A person or little creature. (Used as a term of playful depreciation, or to denote slight commiseration or pity.) 1450. **3.** A vile, sorry, or despicable person; one of opprobrious or reprehensible character; a mean or contemptible creature OE. **b.** Used without serious imputation of bad qualities; *a w. of a,* a miserable 1688.

2. Poore wretches, which (were it not for your charity) would perish in your streetes 1623. Poor w., I pity thee SHELLEY. **c.** Excellent w.: Perdition catch my Soule But I do loue thee SHAKS. **3.** W.!..look back upon a mis-spent Life DE FOE. The wickedness of the w. who would import a cargo of spirituous liquors into the..Society Islands 1805. **b.** A w. of a pedant who knows all about tetrameters 1847.

†**B.** *adj.* = next 1, 2. –1596.

Wretched (re·tʃėd), *a.* ME. [irreg. f. WRETCH *sb.* + -ED[2]. Cf. WICKED.] **1.** Living in a state of misery, poverty, or degradation; very miserable or unhappy. **b.** *absol.* late ME. **2.** Of conditions, etc.: Marked or distinguished by misery or unhappiness; attended by distress, discomfort, or sorrow ME. **b.** Of weather etc.: Causing discomfort; very unpleasant or uncomfortable 1711. **3.** Distinguished by base, vile, or unworthy character or quality; contemptible ME. **b.** Of a poor, mean, or paltry character; mean, sorry, trifling. late ME. **4.** Contemptible in character or quality; despicable; hateful. late ME. **5.** Poor in ability, capacity, character, etc. 1482.

1. We are no Spinsters; nor..So w. as you take us 1622. **b.** Who might be your mother That you insult, exult,..Ouer the w.? SHAKS. **2.** Myserabul penury and wrechyd pouerty 1538. **3.** The thing was clearly some w. court intrigue 1868. **b.** Their lean and flashy songs Grate on their scrannel Pipes of w. straw MILT.

Wretchedly (re·tʃėdli), *adv.* ME. [f. prec. + -LY[2].] In a wretched manner. **1.** In a miserable or unhappy fashion; miserably. **b.** In a way suggestive of indisposition or bad health 1728. **2.** So as to cause or involve in misery, distress, or discomfort ME. **3.** To a distressing, vexing, or unsatisfactory degree; deplorably, very badly 1546. **4.** In an inexpert, unsatisfactory, or crude manner; inefficiently, very poorly 1677.

1. b. Methinks I look so w. to-day! YOUNG. 3. Miss Berry..looking w. ill 1810. 4. A statue of Coilus in wood, w. carved EVELYN. So **Wre·tchedness.**

†**Wretchless** (re·tʃlės), *a.* 1598. [erron. form of *retchless*, obs. var. of RECKLESS *a.*] = RECKLESS *a.* 1, 2, 3 –1853. So **Wre·tchlessness** (now *arch.*).

Wretchock (re·tʃək). Now *dial.* 1529. [f. WRETCH *sb.* + -OCK.] The smallest or weakest of a brood, etc.; a diminutive person, little wretch.

Wrick, var. of RICK *sb.*[2], *v.*[2]

Wried (rəid), *ppl. a. arch.* 1576. [f. WRY *v.* + -ED[1].] That has undergone contortion or twisting; writhed, contorted.

Wriggle (ri·g'l), *sb.* 1709. [f. next.] **1.** A quick writhing movement or flexion of the body, etc. **b.** A sinuous or tortuous formation, marking, etc.; a wriggling or meandering course 1825. **2.** *local.* The sand-eel or sand-launce 1816.

Wriggle (ri·g'l), *v.* 1495. [–(M)LG. (= Du.) *wriggelen*, frequent. of *wriggen*; see -LE and cf. WIGGLE.] **1.** *intr.* To twist or turn about with short writhing movements; to move sinuously; to writhe, squirm, wiggle. **2.** To move, proceed, or go with a writhing or worming movement 1602. **b.** To flow or run sinuously; to meander 1640. **3.** To advance, 'creep' or get *in*, to insinuate oneself *into* favour, place, etc., by wheedling or ingratiation; to get *out of*, escape *from* (a condition or position by evasion, mean artifice, or contrivance) 1598. **4.** *trans.* To cause to writhe, twist, or bend tortuously; to move or turn writhingly or with quick jerks 1573. **b.** To bring into a specified state, form, etc., by writhing or twisting 1677. **5.** To introduce, insert, or bring *in* (something) by wriggling; to insinuate (*into* something) 1599. **b.** To insinuate or introduce (a person) gradually (*into* favour, office, etc.), esp. by subtle or shifty means 1670. **c.** To make (one's way) by sinuous motion 1863. **6.** To form in a tortuous or sinuous manner 1760.

1. His nose at the same time wriggling with most portentous agitation 1831. 2. Truth..forbids us to riggle into her sacred presence through by-paths WARBURTON. 3. He wriggled out of his bargain 1858. 4. The wretched Patient cannot lie down..wrigling his body all manner of ways 1684. 5. b. While he was wriggling himself into my favour SWIFT. Hence **Wri·ggler**, one who or that which wriggles; one who makes his way by subtle, ingratiating, or underhand means. **Wri·ggly** *a.* given to wriggling.

Wright (rəit). [OE. *wryhta* metathetic var. of *wyrhta* = OFris. *wrichta*, OS. *wurhtio*, OHG. *wurhto* :– WGmc. **wurhtjo*, f. **wurk*- WORK *v.*] **1.** An artificer or handicraftsman; *esp.* a constructive workman. Now *arch.* or *dial.* **2.** One who works in wood; a carpenter, a joiner. See also CARTWRIGHT, SHIPWRIGHT, WAINWRIGHT, WHEELWRIGHT. ME.

Wring (riŋ), *sb.*[1] Now *dial.* [OE. *wringe*, f. *wringan* WRING *v.*] **1.** A cider-press or wine-press. **2.** A cheese-press 1670.

attrib.: **w.-house**, the house or shed where a cider- or cheese-w. is kept.

Wring (riŋ), *sb.*[2] 1460. [f. next.] **1.** The act of wringing, twisting, or writhing; an instance of this. **b.** The action of squeezing, pressing, or clasping; a squeeze or clasp of the hand 1599. **2.** A sharp or griping pain, esp. in the intestines 1500.

1. She gave the shirt..a vicious w. 1889.

Wring (riŋ), *v.* Pa. t. and pa. pple. **wrung** (rɒŋ). [OE. *wringen* = OS. -*wringan* (MLG., Du. *wringen*); WGmc. str. vb. f. base **wreŋg*-, rel. to **wraŋg*- WRONG *a.*] **I.** *trans.* **1.** To press, squeeze, or twist (a moist substance, juicy fruit, etc.), esp. so as to drain or make dry. **b.** To strain (juice, moisture, etc.) from a moist or wet substance by squeezing or torsion OE. **c.** *transf.* To force (tears) *out of* the eye, *from* a person, etc. late ME. **2.** To twist, writhe, or wrest (a person or thing); to force (a limb, etc.) *round* or *about* so as to cause a sprain or pain OE. **b.** To contract or contort (the features, etc.); to screw, distort, turn awry ME. **3.** To twist (a wet garment, cloth, etc.) in the hands, so as to force out water; also in recent use, to pass through a wringer ME. **b.** To clasp and twist (the hands or fingers) together, esp. in token or by reason of distress or pain ME. **4.** Of a shoe or boot: To press painfully upon (the foot, toe, etc.); to hurt (a person) in this way. Also *absol.* late ME. **5.** To cause anguish or distress to (a person, his heart, etc.); to vex, distress, rack. late ME. **b.** To affect (a person, etc.) with bodily pain, hurt, or damage (sometimes *spec.* by torsion or pressure). Now *dial.* or *arch.* (after Shaks.) 1520. †**c.** To distress or afflict (a person) by exaction, severity, etc.; to oppress, keep down –1742. **6.** To wrench or wrest out of position or relation; to cause to change place by turning or twisting ME. **b.** To bring out (words, etc.) with effort ME. **7.** To acquire or gain (money, property, a right, etc.) by exaction or extortion ME. **b.** To exact, extort, or draw (an admission, consent, etc.) *from* or *out of* a person, etc. 1444. **8.** To press, clasp, or shake (a person's hand); to press (a person) *by* the hand; to shake hands with 1534. **9. a.** To subject (something) to a writhing, wresting, or turning movement; to press, drive, or impel in this way ME. †**b.** To strain the purport or meaning of (a writing, words, etc.) –1645. **c.** To wreathe, twist, or coil (something flexible); to wind or dispose in coils 1585.

1. b. A laundress wringing water out of a piece of linen EVELYN. 2. I shall w. that Budd's neck if he comes in my way 1881. b. When pain and anguish w. the brow SCOTT. 3. b. Persons in violent grief w. their hands MAR. EDGEWORTH. 4. Provb. phr. *To know where the shoe wrings* (*one*), cf. PINCH *v.* 1 b. 5. b. *fig.* The poore Iade is wrung in the withers SHAKS. 6. I'll wring his calf's head off his body STEVENSON. 7. The fields which the usurer has wrung from the orphan 1868. b. I wrung a promise from him he would try YOUNG. 9. a. It is a hint That wrings mine eyes too 't SHAKS.

With advs. **W. down.** To force, squeeze, or press down. †**W. in.** To insert, insinuate, or bring in with or as with a twisting movement. **W. off.** To wrest or force off by twisting or turning round. **W. out. a.** To force out (moisture) by or as by twisting; to squeeze out. **b.** To strain (a wet fabric, etc.) with a twisting motion, so as to press out most of the moisture. Also const. *of* (the liquid). **c.** To express or bring out with effort. **d.** To obtain or draw (something) from another by pressure, application, or art; to extract, elicit. **W. up.**: **a.** To squeeze, press, or compact by torsion; to twist or screw up. **b.** *Mining.* In pass., of a lode: To become diminished or dwindled.

II. *intr.* **1.** To be engaged in, to perform the action of, writhing or twisting; *esp.* of the hands. late ME. **2.** To twist the body in struggling or striving *with* or *against* something; to contend, labour, or endeavour earnestly 1470. **b.** To twist, turn, or struggle in pain or anguish; to writhe 1485. †**c.** To suffer or undergo grief, pain, punishment, etc. (*for* something) –1882.

Wringer (ri·ŋəɹ). ME. [f. prec. + -ER[1].] **1.** An exactor, extortioner; an oppressor. **2.** One who wrings clothes or the like after washing; one whose occupation consists in wringing 1598. **3.** A wringing-machine 1799. **4.** A device for wringing hot fomentations before application 1884.

Wringing (ri·ŋiŋ), *vbl. sb.* ME. [f. as prec. + -ING[1].] The action of the verb WRING in various senses; the fact of being wrung.

attrib.: **w. machine**, a machine for wringing clothes, etc., after washing. So **Wri·nging** *ppl. a.*

Wrinkle (ri·ŋk'l), *sb.* late ME. [In early use (sense 1) repr. the rare OE. pa. ppl. form *ġewrinclod* winding (as a ditch), of which no infin. is recorded.] **I.** †**1.** A sinuous or tortuous movement, formation, etc. –1513. **2.** A crease, fold, or ridge caused by the folding, puckering, or contraction of a fabric, cloth, or other pliant substance. late ME. **b.** A slight narrow ridge or depression on a surface; a longitudinal mark; a corrugation 1523. **3.** A small fold or crease of the skin, esp. due to age, care, displeasure, etc. late ME. **b.** A ripple or ruffle on the surface of water; a wavelet. Chiefly *poet.* 1633. **4.** *fig.* A moral stain or blemish. late ME. **5.** *Anat.*, *Zool.*, *Bot.* = RUGA 1545.

2. With their hosen hanging about their heels, ful of wrinckles 1594. b. *transf.* Every point and w. in the headland 1849. 3. The calm..forehead that had as yet no w. of age or care 1877. 4. A glorious congregacion with oute spot or wrynckle TINDALE *Eph.* 5:27.

II. †**1.** A crooked or tortuous action; a trick or wile –1579. **2.** *colloq.* A clever or adroit expedient or trick; a happy device; a 'dodge' 1817. **b.** A piece or item of useful information, knowledge, or advice; a helpful or valuable hint; a 'tip' 1818.

2. He could put her up to a w. or two 1817. Hence **Wri·nkly** *a.* full of or marked with wrinkles; creased, puckered.

Wrinkle (ri·ŋk'l), *v.* 1528. [f. WRINKLE *sb.*] **1.** *intr.* To suffer or undergo contraction or puckering into wrinkles or small folds; to become corrugated. **b.** Of persons, the face, etc.: To become creased or puckered; to assume or undergo marking with wrinkles, creases, or lines; also, to crease *into* smiles, etc. 1530. **2.** *trans.* To form or cause corrugations, wrinkles, or folds in or on (a surface, etc.); to corrugate 1611. **b.** To contract or draw (the skin, countenance, etc.) into creases or wrinkles 1566. **c.** To screw up (the eyes) 1840. **3.** To manifest (something) in or by facial wrinkles 1586.

1. b. The finest Skin wrinkles in a few Years ADDISON. 2. b. *fig.* A Grecian Queen, whose youth & freshnesse Wrinkles Apolloes SHAKS.

Wrinkled (ri·ŋk'ld), *a.* late ME. [f. WRINKLE *sb.* + -ED[2], but in sense 1 (Lydg.) repr. the rare OE. pple. *ġewrinclod*; see WRINKLE *sb.*] †**1.** Formed or disposed in convolutions, sinuosities, or windings –1587. **2.** Having, distinguished by, or formed into wrinkles, corrugations, or creases 1523. **3.** Of persons, the face, etc.: Marked with small folds, wrinkles, or furrows; creased, lined, furrowed 1529. **b.** Marked or characterized by wrinkles 1576. **4.** *Bot.*, *Anat.*, *Zool.* Marked by rugæ or wrinkles; rugose; freq. in specific names 1563.

2. Every Ribbon was w., and every Part of her Garments in Curl ADDISON. 3. I am..crabbed, wringkled, olde 1616. The w. face of antiquity CLARENDON. So **Wri·nkling** *vbl. sb.* the action or fact of becoming w.; *concr.* a series or collection of wrinkles, a w. surface, formation, etc.

Wrist (rist). [OE. *wrist*, corresp. to OFris. *wrist*, *wirst*, (M)LG. *wrist*, (M)HG. *rist* wrist, instep, withers, ON. *rist* instep :– Gmc. **wristiz*, prob. f. **wrīð*-, f. wk. grade of the base of WRITHE.] **1.** *Anat.* That part of the human frame between the fore-arm and the metacarpus; the joint by which the hand is united to the fore-arm; the carpus or radio-carpal joint of primates. (Cf. HAND-WRIST.) **b.** *transf.* That part of a garment, sleeve, or glove which covers the wrist 1828. **2.** The ankle; the instep. Usu. *w. of the foot.* (Cf. G. and ON. *rist.*) Now *dial.* 1530. **3.** A part or joint analogous or answering to the wrist in man: **a.** The carpus or carpal joint in birds 1843. **b.** The knee or knee-joint in the fore-legs of animals 1843. **c.** In some spinous fishes, an elongation of the carpal bones, to the extremity of which the pectoral fin is attached 1840. **4.** *Mech.* A pin or stud projecting from the side of a wheel, crank, etc., to which a connecting-rod is attached 1864.

Comb.: **w.-bone**, any of the small bones of the w.; a carpal bone; **-drop**, *Path.* an affection marked by inability to extend the hand and fingers, resulting from paralysis of the fore-arm extensor muscles; **w. jerk**, *Path.* spasmodic contraction of the muscles of the hand, produced by sudden backward pressure; **-joint**, the radio-carpal articulation or joint; **-pin**, *Mech.* = sense 4; **-watch**, a small watch worn in a wristlet or strap around the w. Hence **Wri·sted** *a.* having a (specified kind of) w.; carried on the w.

Wristband (ri·sbænd, ri·zbǎnd). 1571. [f. WRIST + BAND *sb.*[1]] **1.** The band or part of a sleeve (esp. of a shirt-sleeve) which covers or fastens about the wrist; a cuff or sleeve-band. **2.** A bracelet or wristlet 1585. **b.** A band for shackling the wrist 1884. **3.** A bandage for fastening round the wrist 1663.

Wristlet (ri·stlėt). 1851. [f. WRIST + -LET.] **1. a.** A bracelet. **b.** A handcuff 1881. **c.** A small strap for wearing on the wrist. Also *attrib.*, in *w. watch* = wrist-watch. 1891. **2.** An ornamental band or covering for the wrist 1851.

Writ (rit). [OE. *writ* = OHG. *riʒ* stroke, written character (G. *riss*, as in *umriss* outline), ON. *rit* writing, writ, letter, Goth. *writs* pen-stroke, f. **writ*- **wrīt*- WRITE.] **1.** Something written, penned, or recorded in writing. Now *rare.* †**b.** A written work, a book –1687. **c.** *spec.* Sacred writings collectively, the Bible or Holy Scriptures: freq.

in *Holy* or *Sacred W.* OE. †**d.** A written communication, letter –1592. **2. a.** Without article. That which is written; written record ME. **b.** Written command, order, or authority. late ME. **3.** A formal writing or paper of any kind; a legal document or instrument OE. **b.** *Law.* A written command, precept, or formal order issued by a court, directing or enjoining the person or persons to whom it is addressed to do or refrain from doing some act specified therein. late ME. **c.** *spec.* A document issued by the crown conveying a summons to a spiritual or temporal lord to attend Parliament, or directing a sheriff to hold an election of a member or members of Parliament. late ME. †**4.** WRITING *vbl. sb.* I. 5. –1684.

1. c. *transf.* At Tarsus, where each man Thinks all is w. he speken can *Per.* II. Prol. 12. **3. b.** Writts are out for me, to apprehend me 1602.

Writable (rəi·tăb'l), *a.* 1782. [f. WRITE *v.* + -ABLE.] **1.** That may be written; capable of being reduced to or set down in writing. **2.** Suitable for writing with 1844.

Writative (rəi·tătiv), *a. rare.* 1736. [f. as prec. + -ATIVE, after *talkative.*] **1.** Disposed to write; given or addicted to writing. **2.** Marked by inclination or addiction to writing 1746.

Write (rəit), *sb.*[1] Chiefly *Sc.* ME. [var. of WRIT *sb.* after WRITE *v.*, or directly f. the vb.] †**1.** = WRIT *sb.* 1. –1762. †**2.** *Holy W.* = WRIT *sb.* 1 c. –1567. †**b.** = WRIT *sb.* 2. –1825. †**3.** = WRIT *sb.* 3 b. –1550. **4.** *Sc.* Handwriting; manner or style of calligraphy 1614.

4. *Hand of w.*, handwriting, style of writing.

Write, *sb.*[2] 1752. [f. the vb.] *W. -off*, a cancellation in or by writing. *W.-up*, a written account or description commending or praising a person or thing (orig. and chiefly *U.S.*).

Write (rəit), *v.* Pa. t. **wrote** (rō^u^t). Pa. pple. **written** (ri·t'n); from 16th to 18th c., later dial. or illiterate **wrote**. [OE. *wrītan* = OFris. *wrīta* score, write, OS. *wrītan* cut, write, OHG. *rīzan* tear, draw (G. *reissen* sketch, tear, pull, drag), ON. *rita* score, write :- Gmc. **wrītan*, of unkn. origin. The sense-development is due to the earliest forms of inscribed symbols being made on stone and wood with sharp tools.] **I.** *trans.* **1.** †**a.** To score, outline, or draw the figure of (something) –1590. **b.** To form (letters, symbols, words, etc.) by carving, engraving, or incision; to record in this way OE. **c.** *transf.* To impress or stamp marks indicating (some condition or quality) *on, in,* or *over* a person, etc. 1603. **2.** To form or delineate (a letter, symbol, ideogram, etc.) on paper or the like with a pen, pencil, brush, etc. OE. **b.** To enter or record (a name); to mention (a person) in this way ME. **3. a.** To set down in writing; to express or present (words, etc.) in written form. Also said of the pen, etc. OE. **b.** To form by painting or the like; to paint (a sign, etc.). late ME. **c.** Of a manuscript, etc.: To bear or exhibit in writing 1607. **d.** To print by means of a typewriter; to typewrite 1883. **4.** To state or relate in writing; to draw up or frame a written statement of (circumstances, events, etc.) OE. **b.** To convey (tidings, information, etc.) by letter; to send (a message) in writing. late ME. **c.** To decree, ordain, or enjoin in writing 1560. **5. a.** To give a written account or enumeration of; to describe or depict in writing OE. **b.** To treat of (a subject, theme, etc.) in writing OE. **c.** To give expression to (one's feelings, thoughts, etc.) by means of writing ME. **6.** To compose and set down on paper (a literary composition, narrative, verse, etc.); to put into or produce in literary form, to bring out (a book or literary work) as an author OE. **b.** To compose and set down (music, a melody, etc.) in notes 1672. **7.** To pen (a document, etc.); to put into proper written form; to draft or draw up OE. **b.** To pen (a letter, note, etc.); to communicate with a person by (letter, etc.) OE. **c.** To fill in (a cheque) 1837. **8.** To describe or designate (a person) in writing as something; to set down in a particular class. late ME. **b.** *refl.* To name (oneself) in writing; to sign 1821. **c.** To bring or reduce (a person, etc.) to a specified state by writing. Freq. *refl.* 1735. **9.** To spell (a word, name, etc.) in a specified or particular manner in writing ME. **10.** To cover, fill, or mark (a paper, etc.) with writing ME. **11. a.** To employ or be able to employ (a particular language) in writing ME. **b.** To employ (a name, word, etc.) in designating oneself 1591. **12.** To execute (a particular style of handwriting). late ME.

1. b. fig. *To w. in the dust, in sand, water, the wind*, etc., with ref. to absence of abiding record; Here lies one whose name was writ in water KEATS. **c.** Duty is written all over him 1899. **2. b.** To hae your name Wrote in the bonny book of fame 1772. **3.** *Writ (written) large*, penned or exhibited in large characters (chiefly *fig.*). **4. b.** She writes me..what conflicts she had endur'd EVELYN. You will.. w. me word how it looks 1850. **e.** = UNDERWRITE *v.* 2. b. 1882. **5. a.** If I could w. the beauty of your eyes SHAKS. **b.** The Difficulties of writing History 1711. **c.** I did w. my mind plainly to you 1524. **6.** Some-body had written a Book against the 'Squire ADDISON. **7.** A lawyer.. to w. her last will SMOLLETT. **8.** The Author Writes himself a Church-of-England-Man 1687. *fig.* Nature had writ him villain on his face DICKENS. *To w. oneself man*, etc., to arrive at man's (or woman's) estate; to attain manhood, or a specified age. **c.** That no man was ever written out of reputation, but by himself WARBURTON. **9.** Many words written alike are differently pronounced JOHNSON. **11. b.** †*To w. man* = to w. oneself man (see 8). **12.** 2 *Hen. VI*, IV. ii. 100.

With advs. **W. down.: a.** To put or set down in writing. **b.** To overcome or suppress, to disparage or depreciate, by writing; to w. in disparagement of. **c.** *refl.* To diminish or destroy one's literary reputation by inferior writing. **d.** To reduce (an account, assets, etc.) to a lower amount in writing. **W. in.** To insert (a fact, statement, etc.) in writing. **W. off. a.** To note the deduction of (money) in an account or financial statement; now *spec.* to record the cancelling of (a sum, as a bad debt, etc.). **b.** To compose (a letter, etc.) with facility or expedition. **W. out. a.** To make a (fair or perfect) transcription or written copy of (something, a rough draft, etc.); also, to transcribe in full or detail, as from brief notes or shorthand. **b.** *refl.* To exhaust one's resources or stock of ideas by excessive writing. **W. over.: a.** To rewrite. **b.** To cover the whole or remaining surface of (a book, etc.) with writing. **W. up: a.** To put in writing a full account, statement, or record of (something); to give an elaborate description of, describe fully; to pen or write in full or detail. **b.** To form, trace, or place (something) in writing in an elevated position. **c.** To commend (something) to notice or favour by appreciative writing; to laud by way of advertisement. **d.** To bring (a journal, report, etc.) up to date, or down to the latest event, fact, or transaction; to complete some record in writing.

b. *W.-down, -off, -up* are also used as sbs.

II. *intr.* **1.** To inscribe letters *in, on,* or *upon* a hard or plastic surface by scoring, tracing, engraving, etc. OE. **2.** To engage in or perform the action of writing (esp. with pen and ink); to produce (a specified kind of) writing. Also said of the pen, etc. OE. **b.** To depict or paint on glass, etc. 1854. **c.** To typewrite 1875. **3.** To perform the action of composing and putting on paper; to practise literary composition; to engage in authorship or literary work ME. **b.** To compose music, a melody, etc. 1672. **4.** To compose a letter, note, etc.; to communicate information, etc. by writing; to conduct epistolary correspondence ME. **b.** With preps., e.g. *to*, or indirect personal obj. OE. **5.** To follow or practise writing as a profession or occupation. late ME. **6.** To spell words in writing; to represent words, etc. orthographically 1620.

2. My having at last found a Pen that writes GRAY. *transf.* The Moving Finger writes; and, having writ, Moves on FITZGERALD. **3.** A gentleman who had wrote for the stage SMOLLETT. I should be sorry to w. down to their comprehension 1809. **4.** He wrote to request my aid 1842. Tell Mary she hasn't written for an age 1890. **b.** Wrote me, and write you (merchant's language) PEGGE. Ferrers wrote to a friend of his 1888.

Writer (rəi·təɹ). [OE. *wrītere*, f. *wrītan* WRITE *v.* + -ER[1].] **1.** A person who can write; one who practises or performs writing; occas., one who writes in a specified manner. **b.** A sign-writer 1837. **2.** One whose business or occupation consists in writing; a functionary, officer, etc., who performs clerical or secretarial duties OE. **b.** Sc. *W. to the Signet* (abbrev. *W.S.*), orig., a clerk in the Secretary of State's office, who prepared writs to pass the royal signet; now, one of an ancient society of law-agents who conduct cases before the Court of Session, and have the exclusive privilege of preparing crown writs, charters, etc. 1488. **c.** *Sc.* An attorney or law-agent; an ordinary legal practitioner in country towns 1540. **d.** A clerk in the service of the former East India Company. Now *Hist.* 1676. **3.** One who writes, compiles, or produces a literary composition; a literary man or author OE. **b.** One who is writing 1578. **c.** A composer of music 1688. **4.** A make of paint-brush 1884. **5.** A pen, etc. that writes in a specified manner 1907.

1. *Writer's cramp, (palsy, paralysis)*, a form of cramp or spasm affecting certain muscles of the hand and fingers essential to writing, and resulting from excessive use of these. **3.** I saw the other day in an American w. a humorous account 1859. **b.** *The (present) w.*, the w. hereof; The present Writer's belief on this subject 1895. Hence **Wri·tership**, the office or position of a w. in the service of the East India Company (now *Hist.*); the office or employment of a clerk.

Writhe (rəið), *sb.* 1513. [f. next.] †**1.** Something twisted, wreathed, or formed into a circular shape –1569. **b.** A curled or twisted formation; a wreath or twist 1857. **2.** An act of writhing; a contortion 1611.

Writhe (rəið), *v.* [OE. *wrīþan* = OHG. *rīdan*, ON. *rīða*, rel. to WREATHE.] **I.** *trans.* **1.** To twist or coil (something); to fashion into coils or folds; to bend or distort by twisting. †**2.** To unite, combine, or make compact by twisting, entwining, or interweaving; to intertwine –1671. †**3.** To turn or wrench round or to a side; to wring –1713. **4.** To subject (the body, limbs, etc.) to a contorting or twisting movement; to twist, contort. late ME. **b.** To distort (the face, etc.) 1480. **c.** To utter or speak *out* with a writhe 1889. **d.** To make or pursue (its way) by writhing 1867. **5.** To twist or wrench (something) out of place, position, or relation. late ME.

4. Then Satan first knew pain, And writh'd him to and fro convolv'd MILT. **5.** She writhed herself free 1859.

II. *intr.* **1.** To move or stir in a turning or sinuous manner; to twist about ME. **b.** To contort the body, limbs, etc., as from agony, emotion, or stimulation; to twist *under* or *with* pain, distress, etc. late ME. **2.** To change place or position, to turn, move, or go, with a writhing or twisting motion ME.

1. Human wrecks, writhing in anguish 1890. **b.** *fig.* His heart writhing with hatred 1846. Hence **Wri·thing** *vbl. sb.*

Writhen (ri·ð'n), *ppl. a.* ME. [pa. pple. of prec.] **1.** Subjected to writhing, twisting, or turning; contorted. **2.** Combined, made by, or subjected to twining or plaiting OE. **3.** Disposed or arranged in coils, folds, or windings; formed or fashioned by or as by coiling 1542.

1. 'Till, with a w. Mouth,.. He tastes the bitter Morsel 1708. The w. elder spreads its creamy bloom 1850.

Writhled (ri·ð'ld), *a. Obs.* exc. *arch.* 1565. [app. f. stem of WRITHE *v.* (see -LE 3); but perh. an alteration of RIVELLED *a.*] Wrinkled, shrivelled, withered.

Writing (rəi·tiŋ), *vbl. sb.* ME. [f. WRITE *v.* + -ING[1].] **I. 1.** The action of one who writes, in various senses. **2.** The art or practice of penmanship or handwriting 1440. **b.** Style, form, or method of fashioning letters or other conventional signs (esp. in handwriting or penmanship); the 'hand' or HANDWRITING of a particular person 1440. **3.** The action of composing and committing to manuscript; literary composition or production. late ME. **b.** Style or manner of composition or literary expression 1509. **c.** The composition of music 1782. †**4.** Spelling, orthography –1728. **5.** The state or condition of having been written or penned; written form. late ME.

1. *At this (present) w.*, at the time of writing this. **2.** The three R's—Reading, Writing, and Rithmetic 1828. **b.** It was his awne propir hand and writting 1476. **3. b.** Fine w. is, next to fine doing, the top thing in the world KEATS. **5.** The author's agreement..is in w. 1887.

II. 1. That which is in a written (now also typewritten) state or form; written information, composition, or production ME. **2.**

A written composition; freq. *pl.*, the work or works of an author or group of authors; literary productions ME. **b.** *The* (*sacred* or *holy*) *writings*, the Scriptures ME. **3. a.** A written document, note, etc.; a letter or missive 1456. **b.** A written paper or instrument, having force in law; a deed, bond, agreement, or the like 1448. **4.** Wording or lettering scored, engraved, or impressed on a surface; an inscription. late ME. **5.** Words, letters, etc. embodied in written (or type-written) form; written lettering ME.

3. b. The Lawyers finished the Writings..and they were married STEELE. **4.** The width between the lines of w. 1899.

Comb.: **w.-board,** a board on which to rest the paper while writing; **-book,** (*a*) a blank book in which to write, a book containing or consisting of w.-paper; (*b*) a copy-book; **-case,** a portable case for holding writing requisites, and providing a surface to write on; **-centre,** a physical centre in the brain which controls the action of writing; **-desk,** (*a*) a desk used or designed for writing on; such a desk fitted with conveniences for holding writing materials, papers, etc.; (*b*) a portable w.-case which on being opened forms a desk or surface for writing on; **-ink,** ink or writing-fluid prepared or suitable for writing with the pen; **-master,** (*a*) a teacher of w., penmanship, or calligraphy: (*b*) the yellow-hammer, *Emberiza citrinella*; **-paper,** a special kind of paper, usu. with a smooth surface and sized, for w. upon; now *esp.*, notepaper; **-pen,** a pen suitable or adapted for w.; **-school,** †(*a*) a school in which w. is taught; (*b*) at Oxford University, a room used or set apart for written examinations.

Wri·ting-ta:ble. 1526. [f. prec. + TABLE *sb.*] †**1.** A small thin tablet, sheet, or plate of wood, ivory, or other material for writing (esp. notes or memoranda) upon –1829. †**2.** = ESCRITOIRE –1722. **3.** A table used, suitable, or adapted for writing on, having usu. drawers and other accessories or conveniences 1833.

Written (ri·t'n), *ppl. a.* ME. [pa. pple. of WRITE *v.*] **1.** That is composed, recorded, preserved, or mentioned in writing; committed to writing; also, that is in writing (as opp. to *oral* or *printed*); manuscript. **b.** Of laws: Reduced to or established by writing; formulated in documents, codes, or printed works ME. **2. a.** That is inscribed or carved upon 1440. **b.** Bearing, inscribed or covered with, writing 1580. †**3.** *W. hand*, cursive form of writing; a form of running hand –1849. **4.** Of letters, etc.: Traced or formed with the pen, pencil, etc. 1582. **5.** That has been written *to*, *about*, *down*, *out*, or *up* 1748.

1. He will consent to accept a w. apology DICKENS. **2. b.** A flat bundle of w. Papers 1692. **3.** We appoint him our Secretary for he can read w. hand 1764.

Wrizzled (ri·z'ld), *a.* Now *dial.* 1590. [perh. var. of WRITHLED *a.*] Marked with creases, wrinkles, or corrugations; wrinkled, shrivelled.

Wrong (rǫŋ), *sb.* OE. [Substantival use of next.] **I. 1.** That which is morally unjust, unfair, amiss, or improper; the negation of equity, goodness, or rectitude. (Freq. contrasted w. *right*.) **2.** Unjust action or conduct; evil or damage inflicted or received; injustice, unfairness ME. **b.** *Law.* Violation, transgression, or infringement of law; invasion of right to the damage or prejudice of another or others. orig. *Sc.* ME. †**3.** Claim, possession, or seizure that is unjustifiable or unwarranted on legal or moral grounds –1590. **b.** In the phr. *by*, *in*, †*of* (..) *w.* ME. **4.** With poss. pron. or genitive: †**a.** Injustice, harm, or evil inflicted upon another or others –1642. **b.** Injury, hurt, harm, or prejudice received or sustained by a person or persons. late ME. **5.** Physical hurt or harm caused to or sustained by some thing or person. late ME. **6.** *The w.*, that which is wrong; absence of right or fairness; unjust or wrongful action ME. **7.** The fact or position of acting unjustly or indefensibly; the state of being wrong in respect of attitude, procedure, or belief ME.

1. They put no difference betuix wrang and right 1578. **2.** Expos'd To daily fraud, contempt, abuse and w. MILT. *To do* (a person or thing) *w.*, to act unjustly or unfairly *to*. **4. a.** Loue knowes it is a greater griefe To beare loues w., then hates knowne iniury SHAKS. **b.** Wail, for the world's w.! SHELLEY. **6.** If the w. has been wholly on one side PALEY. **7.** Phr. *To be* or *put in the w.*; He had now put himself in the w. MACAULAY.

II. A wrongful, unjust, or unfair action; an injury received or inflicted; a mischief OE. **b.** *Law.* An invasion of right to the damage, harm, or prejudice of another or others; a violation of law or statute. late ME.

As thou lou'st me, do him not that w. SHAKS. Beare not hatred to thy neighbour for euery w. *Ecclus.* 10:6. Trees bent their Heads to hear him sing his Wrongs DRYDEN. The Earl deeply resented the w. done to himself SCOTT.

Wrong (rǫŋ), *a.* and *adv.* [Late OE. *wrang*, *wrong* = ON. **wrangr*, *rangr* awry, unjust (MSw. *vranger*, Sw. *vrång*, (M)Da. *vrang*) = MLG. *wrangh* sour, tart, MDu. *wrangh* bitter, hostile, Du. *wrang* acid, rel. to WRING.] **A.** *adj.* †**I.** Having a crooked or curved course, form, or direction; twisted or bent in shape or contour –1613. **II. 1.** Of actions, etc.: Deviating from equity, justice, or goodness; not morally right or equitable. ME. **2.** Of persons: Doing or prone to do that which is evil, noxious, or unjust; opprobrious, vicious ME. †**b.** Actively opposed; antagonistic (*rare*). **3.** Not in conformity with some standard, rule, or principle; contrary to or at variance with what one approves or regards as right ME. **b.** Not in consonance with facts or truth; incorrect, false, mistaken. late ME. **c.** Of belief, etc.: Partaking of or based on error; erroneous. late ME. **4.** Not right or satisfactory in state or order; in unsatisfactory or bad condition; amiss. late ME. **5.** Not adapted, according, or answering to intention, requirement, or purpose; not proper, fitting, or appropriate. late ME. **b.** *Typog.* Not of the proper size, character, or face. Freq. in *w. fount* (abbrev. *w. f.*). 1771. **6.** Of a way, course, etc.: Leading in or having a trend or aspect to a direction other than one intends, desires, or expects. late ME. **7. W. side. a.** That side of a thing, a fabric, etc., which lies or is normally turned inward, downward, or away from one; the side opposite to the usual or principal, the reverse surface 1511. **b.** The side, party, or principle of which one disapproves 1649. **c.** The disadvantageous, undesirable, or unsafe side *of* some place, object, etc. 1719. **8.** Of persons, etc.: **a.** Judging, believing, or acting contrary to the facts of the case; mistaken, in error 1693. **b.** Not normal or sound *in the head*, etc. (*dial.* or *colloq.*) 1765.

1. There is nothing..morally w. in a strike 1878. It was very w. of him to make such a request 1879. **2.** It don't make black white, 'cause I'm a w. 'un 1896. **3. b.** Her watch..being seldom more than twenty minutes w., either way 1871. **4.** You see, ..it might put us w. with our son-in-law DICKENS. *What's w. with* (mod. colloq.), what objection is there to, why not have (etc.)? **5.** You are barking up the w. tree, Johnson 1833. Does he want.. money?..He's come to the w. shop for that. DICKENS. *The w. end*, the end, extremity, or limit less adapted, suitable, or proper for a required or particular purpose; This was..beginning at the w. end 1809. See also STICK *sb.*[1] Phr. **6.** *To go the w. way*, of food, etc.; see WAY *sb.* II. 1. *The* (or *a*) *w. way*, the way or method least conducive to a desired end or purpose; advb., in a contrary or opposite direction or position to the proper or usual one. **7.** Advb. phr. (*The*) *w. side out, before*; My sicke Foole Rodorigo, Whom Loue hath turn'd almost the w. side out SHAKS. *To laugh on the w. side of one's face, mouth*: see LAUGH *v.* 1. *On the w. side of the blanket*: see BLANKET *sb.* 2. *On the w. side of*, older than (a specified age). *To get out of bed* (*on*) *the w. side*, with allusion to the supposed disturbing effect on one's temper. **c.** The poor meagre home in a dingy street; the w. side of Oxford Street 1893.

B. *adv.* **1.** In a direction differing from the right or true one; by an erroneous course or way; astray ME. **2.** Not in accordance with good morals or a just standard of actions; in a manner contrary to equity or uprightness ME. **3.** Out of accordance or consistence with facts or the truth of the case; mistakenly, erroneously; incorrectly ME. **4.** Not in the right or proper way; improperly, unduly, amiss ME. **b.** Out of proper order or due place 1573.

1. Lock-a-daisy, my masters, you're come a deadly deal w.! GOLDSM. **3.** You took my meaning w. 1681. In spite of her care..she guessed w. THACKERAY. **To go w.: a.** To take a wrong way, road, or course; to go astray: freq. *fig.* **b.** To deviate or depart from moral rectitude or integrity, to take to evil courses; also, to fall from virtue. **c.** To happen amiss or unfortunately; to issue or result unsuccessfully or unprosperously. **d.** To get out of gear or working order; (of a clock, etc.) to fail to keep correct time. **e.** To fail in some undertaking or enterprise, or in the general conduct of life. Hence **Wro·ngness.**

Wrong (rǫŋ), *v.* ME. [f. prec.] **1.** *trans.* To do wrong or injury to (a person); to treat with injustice, prejudice, or harshness. **b.** To violate or do violence to; to treat unfairly or without due respect 1449. **2.** To deprive or dispossess (a person) wrongfully *of* something; to cheat, defraud 1484. **3.** To do injustice to (a person) by statement, imputation, opinion, etc.; to discredit or dishonour by word or thought 1594. †**4.** To impair or injure the quality or substance of (something); to mar, spoil –1784. **5.** *Naut.* To outsail (another vessel); to outdo or surpass in sailing 1685.

2. Ask anybody..whether I have ever wronged them of a farthing DICKENS. **3.** He says that the Duke of York is suspected..; but that he do know that he is wronged therein PEPYS. Hence **Wro·nger.**

Wrong-doer (rǫ·ŋdū·əɹ). late ME. [f. WRONG *sb.* + DOER.] **1.** One who commits wrongful, unjust, or blameworthy acts; one who transgresses or offends against the moral law. **2.** *Law.* One who is guilty of a wrong, tort, or trespass; a law-breaker 1501. So **Wro:ng-do·ing** *vbl. sb.*

Wrongful (rǫ·ŋfŭl), *a.* ME. [f. WRONG *sb.* + -FUL.] **1.** Full of wrong, injustice, or injury; marked or characterized by wrong, unfairness, or violation of equity. **b.** Of actions: Performed, executed, or done unjustly, unfairly, or harmfully ME. †**2.** That commits wrong; that does wrong or injustice *to* (or *against*) another –1614. **3. a.** That is contrary to law, statute, or established rule; unlawful, illegal. late ME. **b.** Holding office, possession, etc., unlawfully or illegally; having no legal right or claim 1567.

1. He regarded slavery simply as an unnatural and w. accident 1879. **2.** Mighty wrongfull foes, Who do evill for good SIDNEY. Hence **Wro·ngful-ly** *adv.*, **-ness.**

Wrong-headed (stress variable), *a.* 1732. [f. WRONG *a.*] **1.** Having a perverse judgement or intellect; persistent or obstinate in erroneous opinion. **2.** Marked or characterized by perversity of judgement 1735. So **Wro·ng-head** *sb.* a w. person; *adj.* wrong-headed 1729. **Wrong-hea·ded-ly** *adv.*, **-ness.**

Wrongly (rǫ·ŋli), *adv.* ME. [-LY[2].] **1.** Unfittingly, improperly. **b.** Inaccurately, incorrectly 1633. **c.** By mistake or misapprehension 1755. **2.** Unfairly, wrongfully ME.

Wrongous (rǫ·ŋəs), *a.* Now *Sc.* (and *n. dial.*) [Early ME. *wrangwis*, f. *wrang* WRONG *a.* + *-wis*, after *rihtwis* RIGHTEOUS *a.*] †**1.** Of persons: Acting wrongfully, inequitably, or unjustly –1625. **2.** = WRONGFUL *a.* 1, 1 b. ME. **3.** Not right or justifiable in nature or application; unfitting, unsuitable ME. **4.** *Scots Law.* Contrary to law; unlawful, illegal 1671. Hence **Wro·ngously** *adv.*

Wroot, original form of ROOT *v.*[2]

Wroth (rōᵘþ, rǫþ), *a.* [OE. *wrāþ* = OFris. *wrēth*, OS. *wrēð* (Du. *wreed* cruel), OHG. *reid*, ON. *reiðr*, f. Gmc. **wraiþ-* **wrīþ-* WRITHE.] **1.** Stirred to wrath; very angry or indignant; wrathful, incensed. †**2.** Of animals: Of a fierce or violent nature; enraged –1526. **b.** *transf.* Of the wind, sea, etc.: Moved to a state of turmoil or commotion; violent, stormy. *poet.* late ME.

1. When the kyng hearde that, he was w. TINDALE *Matt.* 22:7. Then got Sir Lancelot suddenly to horse, W. at himself TENNYSON. Why should not Heaven be w.? TENNYSON. **2. b.** The most holy heart of the deep sea, Late w. now full of quiet SWINBURNE. Hence **Wro·thful** *a.* (*Obs.* or *arch.*) = WRATHFUL *a.* 1. **Wro·thy** *a.* wrathful, angry 1422.

Wrought (rǭt), *ppl. a.* [ME. *wroȝt*, metathetic var. of *worȝt*, *worht*, pa. pple. of WORK *v.*] Worked into shape or condition. †**1.** Created, shaped, moulded. –late ME. **b.** That is made or constructed by means of labour or art; fashioned, formed. late ME. **c.** Shaped, fashioned, or finished from the rough or crude material; cut 1560. **2. a.** Of textile materials, esp. silk: Manufactured; spun 1463. **b.** Decorated or ornamented, as with needlework: embellished, embroidered 1455. **c.** Of articles: Made, manufactured, or prepared for use or commerce 1580. **3. a.** Of metals: Beaten out or shaped with the hammer or other tools 1535. **b.** *W. iron*, slag-bearing malleable iron 1703. **c.** Of metal-work: Made by hammering or hand-work (in contrast to *cast*) 1807.

1. b. Handsomely chased and w. silver garlands 1890. **2. b.** The old Tapestry Hangings and W. Bed pulled down 1711. **3. b.** Great old w.-iron gates 1885.

With advs. *W.-off*, worked off; printed. *W.-up*, stirred up, excited or stimulated.

Wrung (rɒŋ), *ppl. a.* late ME. [pa. pple. of WRING *v.*] **1.** Subjected to wringing, twisting, or squeezing; pressed, squeezed. **2.** That has suffered or undergone distress, grief, or pain; racked, distressed 1730. **b.** Marked by distress, worry, or pain 1862.

2. The refuge of many a w. and broken heart 1841.

Wry (rəi), *a.* and *adv.* 1523. [f. WRY *v.*[2]] **A.** *adj.* **1.** Of the features, neck, etc.: Abnormally deflected, bent, or turned to one side; distorted. **b.** Temporarily twisted, contorted, or writhed by reason or in manifestation of disrelish, disgust, or the like 1598. **c.** Of a smile, etc.: Made with a twisting of the features expressing dislike or distaste 1883. **2.** That has undergone twisting, contortion, or deflexion; twisted, crooked, bent 1552. **b.** Deflected from a straight course; inclined or turned to one side 1587. **3.** Of words, thoughts, etc.: Contrary to that which is right, fitting, or just; cross, ill-natured 1599. **b.** Wrested; perverted; distorted 1663. **4.** Marked or characterized by perversion, unfairness, or injustice 1561.

1. With faire black eyes and haire, and a w. nose B. JONSON. **b.** Physic to be quickly swallowed with w. face 1876. He..shook his head with a w. smile 1883. **2. b.** A w. step COWPER. *W. look*, one expressive of displeasure or dislike.

B. *adv.* In an oblique manner, course, or direction; awry 1575.

Comb.: **w.-faced** *a.*, having the face out of line with the neck and chest; also, that has or makes a w. face; **-mouth** *U.S.*, (*a*) one or other fish belonging to the genus *Cryptacanthodes* of blennioid fishes; (*b*) the electric ray or torpedo; *attrib.* = *w.-mouthed* (*a*); **-mouthed** *a.* (*a*) having a w. mouth; (*b*) marked or characterized by contortion of the mouth. Hence **Wry·-ly** *adv.*, **-ness.**

Wry (rəi), *v.*[1] *Obs.* exc. *dial.* [OE. *wrēon.* Cf. BEWRY *v.*[1]] To cover, veil, conceal.

Wry (rəi), *v.*[2] [OE. *wrīgian* strive, go forward, tend, in ME. deviate, swerve, contort = OFris. *wrīgia* bend, stoop; cf. AWRY, WRIGGLE.] **I.** *intr.* †**1.** To have a particular or specified tendency, disposition, or inclination –1581. †**2.** Of persons: To move or go, to swerve or turn *aside, away*, etc.; *fig.* to deviate or swerve from the right or proper course; to go wrong –1634. **3.** To contort the limbs, features, etc., as from pain or agony; to writhe ME.

2. How many Must murther Wiues much better then themselues For wrying but a little? SHAKS.

II. *trans.* †**1.** To deflect or divert (a person or thing) from some course or in some direction –1650. **2.** To twist or turn (the body, neck, etc.) round or about; to contort, wring, wrench 1460. **b.** To twist out of shape, form, or relationship; to pull, contort, make wry 1586. **3.** To twist or distort (the face or mouth), esp. so as to manifest disgust or distaste 1510.

3. I made my eyes to roll, and wrayed my face in a frightful manner 1779. She wried her mouth to a smile 1898.

Wryneck (rəi·nek). 1585. [f. WRY *a.* + NECK *sb.*] **1.** One or other species of the genus *Iynx* of small migratory scansorial picoid birds; esp. the common species, *I. torquilla*, distinguished by its habit of writhing the neck and head. **2. a.** One who has a wry neck 1607. **b.** *attrib.* = next 2. 1586. **3.** *Path.* = TORTICOLLIS 1753.

Wry-necked (stress var.), *a.* 1596. [f. as prec. + -ED[2].] **1.** Having a wry or crooked neck. **2.** Affected with distortion of the neck; having wryneck 1608.

1. The vile squealing of the wry-neckt Fife SHAKS.

Wuff (wɒf). 1824. [Cf. *waff, woof, wough.*] A dog's low suppressed bark. Also as vb.

Wulfenite (wu·lfĕnəit). 1849. [– G. *wulfenit*, f. F. X. von *Wulfen* (1728–1805), Austrian scientist + -ITE[1] 2 b.] *Min.* Native molybdate of lead, found in brilliant-coloured crystals; called also *yellow lead ore*.

Wurley (wɔ̄·ɹli). *Austral.* 1847. [Native word.] An aboriginal's hut.

Wurtzite (wūᵊ·ɹtsəit). 1868. [f. C. A. *Wurtz* (1817–84), a French chemist + -ITE[1] 2 b.] *Min.* Native zinc sulphide.

Wyandotte (wəi·ăndǫt). 1884. [f. name of an Iroquoian tribe of N. Amer. Indians.] One of a handsome breed of medium-sized domestic fowls.

Wych elm, witch elm (wi·tʃ,elm). 1626. [f. WITCH *sb.*[3] + ELM; cf. WITCHEN.] A species of elm, *Ulmus montana*, having broader leaves and more spreading branches than the common elm; the witch hazel; also, the wood of this.

Wyclif(f)ian (wikli·fiăn), *sb.* and *a.* 1570. [In XVI–XVII *Wicleuian* – AL. *Wyclivianus* (XIV), with later assim. to *Wyclif*.] †**A.** *sb.* = WYCLIFFITE A –1717. **B.** *adj.* Of, pertaining to, or characterizing the teaching of Wyclif or his followers 1720.

Wyclif(f)ism (wi·klifiz'm). 1675. [f. *Wyclif* + -ISM; cf. next.] The religious doctrines or tenets advocated or propagated by Wyclif or held by his followers. So **Wy·clif(f)ist** *sb.* and *a.* = next.

Wyclif(f)ite (wi·klifəit), *sb.* and *a.* Also **Wic-.** 1580. [f. *Wyclif* + -ITE[1] 1; cf. med. L., AL. *Wyclefista* (XIV).] **A.** *sb.* One who held or propagated the religious tenets or doctrines of Wyclif; a follower of Wyclif. **B.** *adj.* **1.** Of, pertaining to, written or made by Wyclif or his followers 1843. **2.** That is a follower of Wyclif; holding, advocating, or propagating the religious views of Wyclif and his school 1875.

Wykehamical (wikæ·mikăl), *a.* 1758. [See next and -AL[1] 1.] **1.** Of or pertaining to Winchester College, or the pupils or staff of this. **2.** That is or has been a pupil of, or connected with, Winchester College 1844.

Wykehamist (wi·kămist), *sb.* and *a.* 1758. [– mod.L. *Wykehamista*, f. name of William of *Wykeham* (1324–1404), Bishop of Winchester and founder of Winchester College.] **A.** *sb.* One who is or has been a pupil at Winchester College. **B.** *adj.* = prec. 1. 1805.

Wynd (wəind). Chiefly *Sc.* and *n. dial.* late ME. [app. f. the stem of WIND *v.*[1] (cf. OE. *ġewind* spiral, etc.).] A narrow street or passage turning off from a main thoroughfare; a narrow cross-street.

Wyvern (wəi·vəɹn), also **wivern.** 1610. [alt. of †*wyver* (XIII) – OFr. *wivre* (also mod.) *guivre* :– L. *vipera* VIPER; for the excrescent *n* cf. BITTERN.] **1.** *Her.* A representation of a chimerical animal imagined as a winged dragon with two feet like those of an eagle, and a serpent-like barbed tail. **b.** An image or figure of this monster 1863. **2.** Such a monster conceived as having a real existence 1700.

2. Lakes which..Blaze like a w. flying round the sun BROWNING.

X

X (eks), pl. **X's**, *Xs* (e·ksėz), the 24th letter of the modern and 21st of the ancient Roman alphabet, corresp. to Gr. X, representing (ks) in the Chalcidian alphabet.

Most English words with initial *x* (pronounced as *z*) are of Gr. origin; but in a few (as *xebec, Xerez*) *x* represents the early Spanish *x*, now *j*. In OE. *x* was used medially and finally as a variant spelling of *cs* (as in *āxian* = *ācsian, āscian* to ASK, *fixas* pl. of *fisc* FISH.) Some East Anglian texts of the 14th c. have *x* for initial *sh, sch*, as in *xal* shall. In early forms of some oriental words *x-* stands for *sh-* (or *s-*), as *xerif* SHEREEF. Temporary uses of *x* are seen e.g. in obsolete spellings of ACCESS (*axes, axis*), EXCELLENT (*exelent*), EXCITE (*exite*); cf. the forms *pox* (= pocks), which has survived, and *sox* (= socks), which has been adopted in trade use.

Phonetically, the normal value of *x* is (ks), as in *axis, excuse*; but the prefix *ex-* followed by a vowel or *h*, is usu. pronounced (ėgz) if the stress is not on the prefix, but (eks) if *ex-* is stressed; so *exact* (ėgzæ·kt), *exhort* (ėgzǭ·ɹt), but *exile* (e·ksəil). The same general principle governs the pronunciation of *anxious* (æ·ŋkʃəs), *anxiety* (aŋgzəi·ėti), *luxury* (lɒ·kʃəri), *luxurious* (lɒgzūᵊ·riəs). In all words having initial *x*, (gz) is reduced to (z), e.g. *Xerxes* (zɔ̄·ɹksīz), *xylophone* (zəi·lŏfōᵘn).

I. The letter or its sound. **b.** The letter considered with regard to its shape; chiefly *attrib.* and *Comb.* Hence identified with a cross. *X's and O's*, the game of noughts and crosses (see NOUGHT 3 b). **c.** Denoting serial order.

II. Symbolic uses. **1.** The Roman numeral symbol for ten; so xx = 20, xxx = 30. OE. **b.** U.S. colloq. *X, XX*, a ten-, twenty-dollar note 1837. **2.** In *Algebra* and *Higher Math.* used as the symbol for an unknown or variable quantity (or for the first of such quantities, the others being denoted by *y, z*, etc.); *spec.* the sign for an abscissa 1660. Hence *allus.* for something unknown or undetermined. 1859. See also X RAYS. **b.** Used *attrib.* as an indeterminate numeral adjective = 'an unknown number of'. Chiefly *joc.* 1848. **c.** Put for a person's name when unknown or left undetermined 1797. **d.** In wireless telegraphy: A discharge of atmospheric electricity causing irregular signals, atmospherics 1906. **3.** In designations of brands of malt liquor, XX or double X denotes a medium quality; XXX or treble X the strongest quality. Also in the marking of qualities of tin-plate. 1827. **4.** XYZ: used to denote some thing or person unknown or undetermined 1808.

III. *Abbreviations.* **1.** In writing the name *Christ*, esp. in abbreviations, X represents the first letter of Gr. XPICTOC, and XP or xp the first two letters (kəi·rǫᵘ). Hence in early times Xp̄, in modern times Xt, X[t], and X, are used as abbreviations of the syllable *Christ*, alone or in derivatives, thus *Xtian(ity)* = CHRISTIAN(ITY); *Xmas* = CHRISTMAS. **2.** For *ex* or a word with initial *ex-*: **a.** *slang. X's* (e·ksėz), expenses 1894. **b.** Stock Exchange. *xd* = ex dividend (see Ex 2 b) 1885. Hence **X** *v. trans.*, to supply with x's in place of types that are wanting 1849.

Xanth- (zænþ), = XANTHO- in derivatives and compounds before a suffix or second element beginning with a vowel.

Xa·nthate, *Chem.* a salt of xanthic acid. **Xa·nthein** (-i,in), *Chem.* the water-soluble part of the yellow colouring-matter of flowers. ‖**Xanthelasma** (-æ·zmă) [Gr. ἔλασμα metal plate], *Path.* = XANTHOMA. **Xa·nthic** *a.*, (*a*) *Chem.* in *xanthic oxide*, earlier name for XANTHINE; *xanthic acid*, a complex acid, $C_3H_6OS_2$, many of whose salts are yellow; (*b*) *Bot.* applied to a series of flower-colours of which the type is yellow. **Xa·nthin,** (*a*) *Chem.* a yellow colouring-matter obtained from madder; (*b*) the insoluble part of the yellow colouring-matter of flowers. **Xa·nthine** (-əin), a substance ($C_5H_4N_4O_2$) allied to uric acid found in animal organs and secretions, and forming a lemon-yellow compound with nitric acid. **Xa·nthite,** *Min.* a variety of vesuvianite occurring in yellowish crystals. ‖**Xantho·ma** [Gr. -ωμα, cf. *sarcoma*], *Path.* a skin-affection characterized by the growth of yellowish patches or tubercles; hence **Xantho·matous** (-ōᵘ-) *a.* **Xantho·psia, Xa·nthopsy** [Gr. ὄψις sight], *Path.* yellow vision. **Xantho·psin** [as prec.], *Chem.* yellow pigment of the retina. ‖**Xantho·sis** [-OSIS], *Path.* yellow discoloration as in cancerous tumours. **Xa·nthous** *a.*, *Ethnol.* characterized by yellowish hair and light complexion; also said of the hair, etc.

Xanthian (zæ·nþiăn), *a.* (*sb.*). 1685. [f. *Xanthus* + -IAN.] Of, pertaining to (or an inhabitant of) Xanthus, an ancient town in Asia Minor; *spec.* of the marbles found near it.

Xantho- (zæ·nþo), repr. Gr. ξανθο-, comb. form of ξανθός yellow, in many terms chiefly of chemistry, botany, pathology, and mineralogy.

Xanthoca·rpous *a.* [Gr. καρπός fruit], *Bot.* having yellow fruit. ‖**Xanthochroi** (-ǫ·kro,əi, -ōᵘ·kroi) *sb. pl.* [mod.L., app. meant as f. Gr. ξανθός yellow + ὠχρός pale], *Anthrop.* in Huxley's classification of the varieties of mankind, a subdivision of the *Leiotrichi* or smooth-haired class, having light-coloured hair and pale complexion; **Xanthochro·ic, Xanthochroid** (-ōᵘ·kroid), **Xanthochrooid** (-ǫ·kro,oid), **Xanthochroous** (-ǫ·kro,əs), **Xanthochrous** (-ōᵘ·krəs), *adjs.* **Xanthochroism** (-ǫ·kro,iz'm), *Ornith.* abnormal replacement of another colour by yellow in the plumage of certain birds. **Xanthocy·anopsy, -cya·nopy** [Gr. κύανος blue + *ὄψις, ὠπή* sight], *Path.* colour-blindness, in which yellow and blue are the only colours discerned. **Xanthode·rm(i)a,** [Gr. *δέρμα* skin], *Path.* yellowness of skin. **Xa·nthodont, Xanthodo·ntous** *adjs.* [Gr. *ὀδούς, ὀδοντ-* tooth], *Zool.* (of rodents) yellow-toothed. **Xa·nthogen,** *Chem.* the hypothetical radical of xanthic acid. ‖**Xanthome·lanoi** *sb. pl.* [mod.L.; cf. MELANOI], *Anthropol.* in Huxley's classification, a subdivision of the *Leiotrichi* or smooth-haired class of mankind, having black hair and yellowy-brown, or olive complexion; hence **Xanthome·lanous** *a.* **Xanthopa·thia, Xantho·pathy** [-PATHY], *Path.* yellow discoloration of the skin. **Xa·nthophyll** [Gr. *φύλλον* leaf], *Chem.* the yellow pigment of autumn leaves. **Xanthophy·llite,** *Min.* a micaceous mineral, a species of seybertite, occurring in yellowish crusts or implanted globules in talcose schist. ‖**Xanthorrhœa** (zænþorī·ă) [Gr. *ῥοία* flow], *Bot.* a genus of Australian liliaceous plants, some of which yield a yellow resin. **Xanthospe·rmous** *a.* [Gr. *σπέρμα* seed], *Bot.* with yellow seeds. ‖**Xantho·xylon, -um** [Gr. *ξύλον* wood], *Bot.* a large genus of trees and shrubs of the family *Rutaceae*, yielding various products, esp. pungent and aromatic drugs and condiments: hence **Xantho·xyl,** a plant of the genus; **Xanthoxyla·ceous** *a.*

Xantippe (zænti·pi). 1596. [prop. *Xanthippe*, Gr. *Ξανθίππη*.] The wife of Socrates; *allus.*, a shrewish wife.

As curst and shrow'd As Socrates Zentippe SHAKS.

Xebec (zī·bek, zĭbe·k). 1756. [alt., after Sp. †*xabeque* (now *jabeque*), of CHEBEC.] A small three-masted (orig. two-masted) Mediterranean ship, lateen-rigged but with some square sails, used formerly as a war-ship and now as a merchant ship.

Xeme (zīm). 1836. [– arbitrary mod.L. *Xema*.] *Ornith.* A bird of the genus *Xema*; a fork-tailed gull.

‖**Xenia** (zī·niă). 1899. [mod.L. – Gr. *ξενία* state of a guest, f. *ξένος* guest; see -IA[1].] *Bot.* A supposed direct action or influence of foreign pollen upon the seed or fruit which is pollinated.

‖**Xenium** (zī·niŏm); usu. in pl. **xe·nia.** 1706. [L. – Gr. *ξένιον*, subst. use of n. of *ξένιος* pertaining to a guest, f. *ξένος* guest.] *Gr.* and *Rom. Antiq.* A present (esp. of table delicacies) given to a guest or stranger; *transf.* in mediæval usage, an offering made (occas. compulsorily) by subjects to their prince on the occasion of his passing through their estates.

Xeno- (ze·no, zėnǫ·), before a vowel **xen-,** repr. Gr. *ξενο-, ξεν-*, comb. form of *ξένος* strange, foreign, stranger, guest, used in various scientific and other terms.

Xenaca·nthine (-ăkæ·nþəin) *a.* (*sb*) [Gr. *ἄκανθα* spine], *Zool.* (a fish) of an extinct selachian order with long slender spines. **Xena·rthral** *a.* [Gr. *ἄρθρον* joint], *Zool.* having peculiar accessory articulations in the vertebræ, as the Amer. edentates. **Xenobiosis** (-bəiō^u·sis) [Gr. *βίωσις* manner of life], *Zool.* a symbiosis of two colonies of ants of different species, living together but not interbreeding. ‖**Xenodochium** (-dǫ·kiŏm) [Gr. *δέχεσθαι* receive], a hostel, guest-house, esp. in a monastery. **Xeno·gamy** [Gr. *γάμος* marriage], *Bot.* cross-fertilization. **Xenoge·nesis,** *Biol.* production of offspring permanently unlike the parent; so **Xenogene·tic, Xenoge·nic** *adjs.* **Xe·nolite** [-LITE], *Min.* a silicate of aluminium. **Xenomo·rphic** *a.* [Gr. *μορφή* form], *Geol.* applied to mineral constituents of a rock having an abnormal form in consequence of the pressure of other constituents. **Xeno·phoran** *a.* [Gr. *-φορος* -carrying], *Zool.* belonging or allied to the genus *Xenophora* of gasteropod molluscs distinguished by the habit of cementing foreign bodies to their shells. **Xe·nurine** [Gr. *οὐρά* tail], *Zool. a.* belonging to the genus *Xenurus* of armadillos, having the tail nearly naked; *sb.* an armadillo of this genus, a kabassou.

Xenon (ze·nǫn). 1898. [– Gr. *ξένον*, n. of *ξένος* strange.] *Chem.* A heavy inert gaseous element present in minute quantity in the atmosphere. Symbol Xe or X.

Xenophontean, -ian (zenŏfǫ·ntiăn), *a.* 1593. [f. Gr. *Ξενοφῶν, -ῶντος* Xenophon, an ancient Greek historian and biographer (*c* 444–354 B.C.) + -EAN, -IAN.] Pertaining to, characteristic of, or resembling (that of) Xenophon. So **Xenopho·ntic** *a.* 1822.

Xenotime (ze·notəim). 1844. [Named 1832, as if f. Gr. *ξένος* strange + *τιμή* honour; 'but app. in error for **kenotime* f. Gr. *κενός* empty, vain.] *Min.* A native phosphate of yttrium.

Beudant named the species *xenotime*.., but in the next line gives the derivation '*κενος*, vain, et *τιμή*, honneur', as if the word were *kenotime*, and adds..that this name is intended to recall the fact that the mineral was erroneously supposed by Berzelius..to contain a new metal DANA.

‖**Xeranthemum** (ziᵊræ·nþĭmŏm). 1741. [mod.L. (Tournefort, 1700), f. Gr. *ξηρός* dry + *ἄνθεμον* blossom.] *Bot.* A genus of composites having flower-heads with purplish or whitish dry chaffy bracts; a plant of this genus; one kind of the plants commonly called *everlasting* or *immortelle*.

‖**Xerasia** (ziᵊrē^i·ziă). 1706. [– Gr. *ξηρασία* dryness.] *Path.* Excessive dryness of the hair.

Xeres (ze·rės, zīᵊ·rėz). 1661. Name of an Andalusian town famous for its wine; in full, *X. sack, wine,* = SHERRIS, SHERRY.

Xeriff (ze·rif, zīᵊ·rif), var. of SHEREEF.

Xero- (zīᵊ·ro), before a vowel **xer-,** repr. Gr. *ξηρο- ξηρ-*, comb. form of *ξηρός* dry, in scientific and technical terms.

Xerode·rm(i)a [Gr. *δέρμα* skin], *Path.* a disease characterized by excessive dryness of the skin; hence **Xeroderma·tic, -de·rmatous, -de·rmic** *adjs.* **Xero·ma,** *Path.*, abnormal dryness of some parts; *spec.* = XEROPHTHALMIA; hence **Xero·matous** *a.* **Xero·phagy** [– Gr. *ξηροφαγία*; see -PHAGY], the eating of dry food, esp. as a form of fasting practised in the early church. **Xero·philous** *a.* [Gr. *-φιλος* -loving], *Bot.* adapted to dry conditions: so **Xe·rophil(e,** a xerophilous plant; **Xero·phily,** the condition or character of being xerophilous. **Xerophtha·lmia,** *Path.* inflammation of the conjunctiva of the eye with abnormal dryness and corrugation. **Xe·rophyte** [Gr *φυτόν* plant], *Bot.* = *xerophil*; so **Xerophy·tic** *a.*, **Xero·phytism. Xero·sis** [-OSIS], *Path.* = XEROMA; *spec.* = *xeroderma*; so **Xero·tic** *a.*

Xiphias (zi·fiæ̆s). 1667. [L. – Gr. *ξιφίας*, f. *ξίφος* sword.] **1.** A swordfish, esp. *X. gladius*; the genus of fishes to which this belongs, characterized by having the upper jaw prolonged into a sword-like weapon. **2.** *Astron.* A southern constellation, also called Dorado or the Swordfish 1728. Hence **Xi·phioid** *a.* resembling or allied to the genus *X.*; *sb.* a xiphioid fish.

Xiphi-, xipho- (zi·fi, zi·fo), comb. form. of Gr. *ξίφος* sword in terms of *Anat.* and *Zool.*

‖**Xiphipla·stron** (pl. **-a**), each of the hindmost pair of lateral plates in the plastron of a turtle; hence **Xiphipla·stral** *a.*; *sb.* a xiphiplastron. **Xiphiste·rnal,** *a.* belonging to or constituting the xiphisternum; *sb.* a xiphisternal part or appendage. **Xiphiste·rnum** [STERNUM], the cartilaginous or bony process ending the sternum (in man, the xiphoid cartilage); also = *xiphiplastron*. ‖**Xipho·pagus** [Gr. *πάγος* something firmly fixed], a twin monster united by a band extending downwards from the xiphoid cartilage, as in the case of the Siamese twins; hence **Xipho·pagous** *a.* **Xiphosu·ran** [irreg. f. Gr. *οὐρά* tail], *Zool. a.* belonging to the arachnid order *Xiphosura*, including the king-crab with a long sharp telson; *sb.* an arachnid of this order; so **Xi·phosure,** a xiphosuran.

Xiphoid (zi·foid), *a.* (*sb.*) 1746. [– Gr. *ξιφοειδής*, f. *ξίφος* sword; see -OID.] *Anat.* Sword-shaped; applied to the bony or cartilaginous process at the lower or posterior end of the sternum in man and other animals, and to a projecting bone at the back of the head in the cormorants and related birds.

Xmas, earlier also **X't-, Xst-.** 1551. Common abbrev. in writing of CHRISTMAS; see X III. 1. Sometimes vulgarly pronounced (e·ksmæ̆s).

Xoanon (zō^u·ănǫn). *Pl.* **-a.** 1706. [Gr. *ξόανον*, rel. to *ξεῖν* carve.] *Gr. Antiq.* A primitive rudely-carved image (orig. wooden), esp. of a deity.

Xonotlite (zonǫ·tləit). Also **xonaltite.** 1868. [f. *Xonotla*, a village in Puebla, Mexico, where found; see -ITE[1] 2 b.] *Min.* A hard massive hydrated silicate of calcium.

X rays (eks rē^iz), *sb. pl.* Also **X-rays.** 1896. [tr. G. *x-strahlen*, the name given by the discoverer, Prof. Röntgen, expressing the fact that their essential nature is unknown; see X II. 2.] A form of radiation capable of penetrating many substances impervious to light, and of affecting a sensitized plate and producing shadow-photographs of objects enclosed within opaque bodies; they produce phosphorescence, fluorescence, and electrical effects, and have a curative effect in certain skin diseases; much used in recent surgical and medical practice. Also called *Röntgen rays.* **b.** *attrib.* and *Comb.* (in sing. form *X-ray*), as *X-ray examination, photograph* 1897. Hence **X-ray** (e:ksrē^i·) *v. trans.* to examine or treat with X rays. So **X-radia·tion.**

Xylan (zəi·læn). 1894. [f. XYLO- + -AN I. 2.] *Chem.* A gelatinous compound contained in wood, also called *tree-gum, wood-gum.*

Xylem (zəi·lem). 1875. [f. Gr. *ξύλον* wood; cf. PHLOEM.] *Bot.* Collective name for the cells, vessels, and fibres forming the harder portion of the fibrovascular tissue; the wood.

Xylite (zəi·ləit). 1843. [– G. *xylit*, f. Gr. *ξύλον* wood; see -ITE[1] 2 b.] **1.** *Chem.* A volatile liquid obtained from wood-spirit. **2.** *Min.* An impure silicate of iron, occurring in brown fibrous masses resembling asbestos or 'mountain-wood' 1850.

Xylo- (zəi·lo), before a vowel **xyl-,** repr. Gr. *ξυλο-, ξυλ-*, comb. form of *ξύλον* wood, in scientific and technical terms.

Xy·lene [-ENE], *Chem.* a mixture of three isomeric hydrocarbons, obtained as a volatile colourless liquid from wood-spirit or coal-naphtha; any one of these three; dimethylbenzene; also called *xylol*; hence **Xy·lic** *a.* in *xylic acid*, dimethylbenzoic acid. **Xy·lidine** [-ID[4], -INE[5]], *Chem.* (*a*) an amine-derivative of xylene, homologous with aniline, used in the preparation of artificial dyes; (*b*) = *xyloidin*. ‖**Xyloba·lsamum** [– Gr. *ξυλοβάλσαμον*; see BALSAM], the fragrant wood of the tree *Balsamodendron gileadense*, which yields OPOBALSAMUM or Balm of Gilead. **Xylo·copid** *a.* [Gr. *-κοπος* -cutting] *a.*, *Entom.* belonging or related to the genus *Xylocopa*, comprising the carpenter-bees. **Xylo·graphy** [– Fr. *xylographie*; see -GRAPHY], wood-engraving, esp. of the early period or of a primitive kind; printing from wood-blocks as distinct from type; so **Xy·lograph,** *sb.* a wood-engraving; *v. trans.* to produce by xylography; **Xylo·grapher, -graphist**; **Xylogra·phic, -al** *adjs.*; **Xylogra·phically** *adv.* **Xyloi·din, -ine** [-OID, -IN[1]], *Chem.* an explosive substance obtained by treating starch or vegetable fibre with nitric acid. **Xy·lol** = *xylene*. **Xylo·phagous** [Gr. *-φαγος* eating] *a.*, *Zool.* wood-eating, destructive to wood (of larvæ, etc.); so **Xylo·phagan** *a.* (*sb.*), (a member) of the *Xylophaga* or *Xylophagi*, various groups of insects with wood-devouring larvæ. **Xylo·philan** *a.* (*sb.*), (a beetle) of the group *Xylophili* of beetles, which live in decayed wood; so **Xylo·philous** *a.* living or growing in or on wood, as an insect or a fungus. **Xylo·stein** (-tĭin) [Gr. *ὀστέον* bone, -IN[1]], *Chem.* a poisonous bitter substance found in the berries of the fly-honeysuckle, *Lonicera xylosteum.* **Xy·lotil(e** (-təil, -til), [Gr. *τίλος* down], *Min.* an asbestos-like mineral called also *mountain-wood.* **Xylo·tomous** [Gr. *-τομος* cutting], *a.* cutting or boring wood (of insects). **Xy:lotypogra·phic** *a.*, printed from wooden blocks or types.

Xylonite (zəi·lŏnəit). 1869. [Early form *xyloinite*, irreg. f. XYLOIDIN + -ITE[1] 4.] A proprietary name for CELLULOID.

Xylophone (zəi·lŏfō^un). 1866. [f. XYLO- + -PHONE.] A musical instrument consisting of a graduated series of flat wooden bars, played by striking with a small hammer or rubbing with rosined gloves.

Xylose (zəi·lo^us). 1894. [f. XYLO- + -OSE[2].] *Chem.* A colourless carbohydrate, $C_5H_{10}O_5$, obtained by the action of sulphuric acid on xylan; wood-sugar.

Xylyl (zəi·lil). 1862. [f. XYL- + -YL.] *Chem.* The hypothetical radical of xylene.

Xyrid (zəiᵊ·rid). 1846. [– mod.L. *Xyris, Xyrid* – Gr. *ξυρίς* species of iris with sharp-edged leaves, f. *ξύρον* razor; see -ID[2].] *Bot.* A plant of the monocotyledonous family *Xyridaceæ*, typified by the genus *Xyris*, sedge-like herbs having flowers with three coloured petals; chiefly N. Amer. and tropical. So **Xyridaceous** (ziridē^i·ʃəs) *a.* belonging to the *Xyridaceæ*.

‖**Xyster** (zi·stəɹ). 1684. [mod.L. – Gr. *ξυστήρ*, f. *ξύειν* scrape.] *Surg.* An instrument for scraping bones.

‖**Xystus** (zi·stŏs). *Pl.* **xysti** (-əi). Also anglicized **xyst.** 1664. [L. – Gr. *ξυστός* (also *-όν*), f. *ξύειν* scrape.] In ancient Greece, a long covered portico or court for athletic exercises; in ancient Rome, an open colonnade, or walk planted with trees, used for recreation and conversation.

Y

Y (wəi), pl. Y's, *Ys* (wəiz), the 25th letter of the modern and the 23rd of the ancient Roman alphabet, repr. ult. Greek Y, Υ (u psilon), a differentiated form of the primitive V which has given also U and V. The Latin alphabet adopted first the V form for the sounds (*u*) and (w), and later the Y form for the Υ of borrowed Greek words. The French and German names for y (*i grec, ipsilon*) preserve the fact of its Greek origin. The English name *wy* (wəi) is of obscure origin.

In early OE. the letter expressed the *i/j*-mutation of *u*; its forms varied from those resembling Gr. Υ to ƿ, the latter prevailing in ME. and becoming identical with debased forms of þ, whence the y^e, y^t, etc., for *the, that*, etc., which continued to be extensively employed in manuscript in the 17th and 18th centuries; y^e is still often used pseudo-archaically or jocularly, and vulgarly pronounced as *ye*. In later (West-Saxon) OE. *y* was written alternatively for *i*, e.g. as repr. older *ie*; and as its function of expressing rounded *i* (*ü, ǖ*) was taken over by *u* in imitation of French usage, it became ultimately a possible substitute for vocalic *i* in any position. This use had become established by the middle of the 13th century, and thenceforward *y* served as a convenient means of breaking up an ambiguous series of minims produced by a succession of *i, u, n, m*, as *nym, myn*, for *nim, min*, etc. This free use of *y* continued long after the introduction of printing, but usage has now restored *i*, except (1) in final *i*-sounds of all but alien words (as in *fly, family, daily, destroy*); (2) for Greek upsilon (as in *hymn*); (3) in verb-inflexions before *i* (as in *lying*); (4) in plurals of nouns in *-ay, -ey, -oy* (as in *rays, alleys, boys, moneys*, but also *monies*). Particular usages, not falling under these categories, are the use of *y* to distinguish *dye* from *die*, and the fluctuation between *tire* and *tyre*, *flyer* and *flier*, *siphon* and *syphon*, *silva* and *sylva*, etc.

As a consonant, *y* represents the voiced palatal spirant (y), which was one of the values of the obsolete letter ȝ (see YOGH); *y* began to occur as a variant of ȝ in this use about 1250.

Pronunciation. The vocalic sounds now normally expressed by *y* are:—(1) i, as in h*y*mn (him), sill*y* (si·li); (2) əi, as in m*y* (məi), den*y* (dǐnəi·); (3) $əi^ə$, as in l*y*re ($ləi^ə$ɹ); (4) ɔ̄, as in m*y*rtle (mɔ̄·ɹt'l); (5) ə as in sat*y*r (sæ·təɹ). With other vowels it forms combinations having special values:—*ay* (final) = e^i, as in l*ay* ($l\bar{e}^i$), essay ($e·se^i$), = əi in *aye* (əi), = ī in qu*ay* (kī), = e in s*ay*s (sez); *ey* = $\bar{e}^i$, as in obe*y* ($ob\bar{e}^i$·), = i, as in alle*y* (æ·li), = əi in *eye* (əi) and its derivatives, = $\bar{e}^ə$ in *ey*re ($\bar{e}^ə$ɹ); *oy* = oi, as in b*oy* (boi); *uy* (*rare*) = əi in b*uy* (bəi), g*uy* (gəi).

1. The letter. OE. **b.** Used for the Greek Υ (*u psilon*), esp. as a Pythagorean symbol. late ME. **2.** The letter considered with regard to its shape; a figure or marking of this shape. Also comb. *Y-shaped* adj. 1513. **3.** A Y-shaped contrivance or piece of apparatus, *esp.* a forked support for a telescope, theodolite, etc. Also *attrib.*, as *Y bearing*; **Y branch,** a piece of piping with a branch at an acute angle to the main; **Y cross,** (*a*) a y-shaped ornament on ecclesiastical vestments, (*b*) a piece of piping diverging into three; **Y level,** the common spirit-level, used with a telescope, etc. resting on Y's; **Y track,** a piece of railway line at right angles to the main line, and connected with it by two switches in opposite directions, for reversing an engine or car. Also in names of natural structures, as *Y cartilage*. 1793. **b.** As a name for various moths of the genus *Plusia*, having markings resembling the letter Y 1775. **4.** *Math.* Used to denote the second of a set of unknown or variable quantities (cf. X II. 1 b); *spec.* in Analytical Geometry the symbol for an ordinate 1728. **5.** Used in abstract reasoning (usu. in connection with X) for the name of a person or thing. Also *Y.Z.*, as initials of an anonymous person (cf. X). 1765. **6.** Denoting serial order. **7.** *Abbreviations*. y. = year(s); Y = Yttrium; Y.M.C.A., Y.W.C.A. = Young Men's (Women's) Christian Association; also colloq. abbrev. YM (wəiˌe·m), YW (wəiˌdɒ·b'lyu).

Y- *prefix* represents OE. *ġe-* :— Gmc. **ʒa-* (G., Du. *ge-*), perh. identical w. L. *co-, com-* (cf. OE. *ġemǣne*, L. *communis*). The original (physical) meaning 'with', 'together', yielded the notions of (1) association, and hence of suitability or appropriateness, and (2) collectivity, the final stage being (3) a perfective, completive, or intensive notion evolved in some measure from each of the others. Its use as a prefix of pa. pples. is an instance of the latter meaning. The prefix survives in such archaic pa. pples. as YCLEPT and YCLAD, and in a disguised form in the first syllables of ALIKE, AWARE, AFFORD, ENOUGH, AMONG, q.v.; HANDIWORK (OE. *handġeweorc*), EITHER (OE. *ǣġhwæðer*) also contain it. Its use as a mark of the pa. pple. continued regularly in southern ME. into the 15th c., and, in the form *a-*, is not yet extinct in south-western dialects. The OE. *ġe-* was succeeded first by *ie-, i-*, and later by *y-*, which, being adopted by Spenser and his imitators in their archaistic forms, has remained the accepted spelling in such use.

-y *suffix*[1] descends from the OE. adj. suffix *-iġ* :— Gmc. **-īʒa-*, and **-aʒa-*. With sbs. ending in *y, -ey* it takes the form *-ey*, e.g. *clayey*; sbs. ending in mute *e* preceded by a vowel retain the *-e* (as in *gluey*); in other cases there may be variation, as *homey, homy, nosey, nosy*.

1. The general sense of the suffix is 'having the qualities of' or 'full of' that which is denoted by the sb. to which it is added, as *icy* = (1) of the nature of or having the coldness, hardness, etc. of ice; (2) full of or covered with ice. Such adjs. were numerous in OE., and large additions were made at particular periods, esp. in the 14th c. (as *angry, hearty, milky, naughty*) and 16th c. (as *frothy, dirty, healthy, saucy*). Later formations tend to be colloquial, undignified, or trivial, as *bumpy, hammy, messy, oniony*. A sense 'addicted to', as in *booky, doggy, horsy*, is of modern growth. **2.** Some monosyllabic adjs. were extended by means of this suffix as early as the 15th c., apparently with the design of giving them a more adjectival appearance; so *chilly, dusky, paly, vasty*. Similarly *slippery*, f. *slipper*. The majority of such words arose in the 16th and 17th cc. The suffix has not infrequently come to express the same notion as *-ish*, particularly with colour-epithets, and esp. when these are used quasi-advb., as *greeny-blue*. **3.** From the 13th c. the suffix has been added to verb-stems to express the meaning 'inclined or apt to' do something, or 'giving occasion to' a certain action; e.g. *blowy, drowsy, sticky*. **4.** From the early years of the 19th c. the suffix has been used in nonce-words, connoting characteristics which call for condemnation as *beery, catty, fuggy*.

-y *suffix*[2], represents the OE. infin. ending *-ian* (:— **-ōjan*, whence also OS. *-ōian, -ōn*, OHG., Goth. *-ōn*), and **-ǣjan* (whence OHG. *-ēn*) of the second class of weak verbs, surviving in Somerset, Devon, and Dorset, as the infin. ending of any verb used intransitively.

-y *suffix*[3] represents, through Fr. *-ie*, the Com. Romanic *-ia* = L. *-ĭa* (Gr. *-ια, -εια*). Many English words in *-y*, such as *glory, history, victory*, were adopted from AFr., which preferred learned adoptions in *-ie* of L. nouns in *-ĭa* to the popular or semi-popular OFr. forms in *-e*. This suffix has never been in English a prolific formative, but the correspondence of adjs. in *-ic* and *-ous* to sbs. in *-y* has made possible in modern times the formation after Gr. types of such words as *brachycephaly, synchrony* from *brachycephalic, synchronous*. The suffix also constitutes the final element of a great number of compound suffixes, e.g. -ACY, -CY, -ERY, -GRAPHY, -LATRY, -LOGY, -PATHY, -PHILY, -RY, -TOMY.

-y *suffix*[4] represents (first through AFr. forms in *-ie*) L. *-ium* as appended to vbl. roots to denote an act; so *remedy* (L. *remedium*, f. *mederi* heal); *colloquy, perjury, subsidy* are similarly from L. originals. The suffix has not been independently used in English, except, perhaps helped by the false analogy of -RY, in *expiry* and *inquiry*, and in *entreaty*, f. *entreat* vb. on the analogy of *treat, treaty*.

-y *suffix*[5] represents AFr., OFr. *-e, -ee*, mod. Fr. *-é, -ée* :— L. *-atu-, -ata-* (see -ATE[1], -ATE[2]). **a.** In sbs. = -ATE[1]; as in (i) COUNTY, Fr. *comté*, L. *comitatus*, DUCHY, etc. (ii) ARMY, Fr. *armée*, L. *armata*. **b.** In adjs. = -ATE[2]; as in *easy*, OFr. *aisié*; chiefly in heraldic terms, *as barry lozengy*; also with var. in *-é*, as *tenné, tenny*; *wavy* (after *undy*) is a rare instance of an analogical use of *-y* with a native word.

-y *suffix*[6], **-ie,** forming pet names and familiar diminutives. The spelling varies, sometimes in the same word, but with a tendency to *-y* in proper names (as in BILLY, TOMMY, *Fanny*, but with many exceptions) and transferred applications of these (as JEMMY, DICKY, JENNY, PEGGY, but CHARLEY, CHARLIE), and to *-ie* (after Sc. usage) in general hypocoristic forms (*laddie, dearie*). The earliest appearance of the suffix is in Scottish pet forms of proper names, c1400, many of which have survived as Sc. surnames, e.g. *Christie, Pirrie, Ritchie, Jamieson*. *Bookie* for *bookmaker* (1885) shows an extension of the type; cf. *nighty* for *nightdress*, *undies* for *underclothes*, *frillies* f. *frill*, *movie, talkie*.

Yabber (yæ·bəɹ), *sb. Austral.* 1874. [Native Austral. *yabba*.] Speech, language, applied to the speech of the Australian aborigines. So **Ya·bber** *v. trans.* and *intr.* to talk.

‖**Yaboo** (yabū·). 1753. [Hindustani = Persian *yābū*.] One of a breed of large ponies or small stout horses in Afghanistan, Persia, and adjacent countries.

‖**Yacca** (yæ·kă). 1843. [Native name.] A W. Indian evergreen tree (*Podocarpus coriacea* or *P. purdieana*), or its wood, used in cabinet-work, etc.

Yacht (yǫt), *sb.* 1557. [– early mod.Du. *jaghte* = *jaghtschip* fast piratical ship, f. *jag(h)t* hunting, f. *jagen* hunt.] A light fast-sailing ship, in early use esp. for the conveyance of royal or other important persons; later, a vessel, usu. light and comparatively small, for cruising, now esp. one built and rigged for racing. 1886.

I sailed this morning with his Majesty in one of his Yatchts EVELYN.

attrib. and *Comb.*, as *y.-club, -race, -squadron*; **Ya·chtsman** 1862, **-woman.** Hence **Yacht** *v. intr.* to cruise or race in a yacht; **Ya·chting** *vbl. sb.* and *ppl. a.* 1836.

Yaffingale (yæ·fiŋgē[i]l). *south.* and *s.w. dial.* 1609. [imit., with termination modelled on *nightingale*.] = next.

Yaffle (yæ·f'l). *dial.* 1792. [imit. of its laughing cry.] The green woodpecker.

Yager (yē[i]·gəɹ). 1804. [Anglicized spelling of G. *jäger* JÄGER.] = JÄGER 1, 2. **b.** *U.S.* A rifle 1840.

Yah (yā), *int.* 1812. [imit.] An exclamation of disgust, aversion, or malicious defiance.

Yah!..Never thinking of anybody but yourself DICKENS.

Yah, in pseudo-phonetic representations (*y.! y.!*) of the House of Commons ejaculation *Hear! hear!* 1886.

Yahoo (yahū·). 1726. A name invented by Swift in *Gulliver's Travels* for an imaginary race of brutes having the form of men; hence *transf.* and *allus.*, a human being of degraded or bestial type.

attrib.: Some Corruptions of my Y. Nature have revived in me SWIFT. Hence **Yahoo·ism.**

Yahveh, -vism, etc., **-weh,** etc.: see JEHOVAH, JAHVISM.

Yair, yare (yē[ə]ɹ). *Sc.* and *n. dial.* [OE. *ġear* (in comb. *mylenġear* mill-yair).] An enclosure extending into a tideway, for catching fish; a fishgarth.

Yak (yæk, yāk). 1799. [Tibetan *γyag*.] A silky-haired bovine animal (*Poephagus grunniens*), found wild and domesticated in Tibet and other high regions of central Asia.

Yale (yē[i]l). late ME. [– L. *eale* (Pliny).] A fabulous beast with horns and tusks; used *Her.*

Yale lock. 1882. [f. name of Linus *Yale* (1821–68), a locksmith of New England.] Proprietary name for a type of cylinder lock.

Yam (yæm). 1588. [– Pg. *inhame* or Sp. †*iñame* (mod. *ñame*), whence Fr. *igname*; ult. source unkn.] **1.** The starchy tuberous root of various species of *Dioscorea*, taking the place in tropical and subtropical countries of the potato; also, any plant of the genus *Dioscorea*, comprising twining herbs or shrubs with spikes of small inconspicuous flowers. **2.** Applied to †(*a*) the mangrove; (*b*) varieties of the common potato, cultivated in

Scotland; (*c*) a variety of the sweet potato (*Batatas edulis*) largely eaten by Negroes in America 1753.

1. Chinese or **Japanese Y.**, *D. Batatas.* **Coco Y.** = Cocco. **Common Y.**, *D. sativa.* **Granada** or **Guinea Y.**, *D. bulbifera.* **Indian Y.**, *D. trifida.* **Long Y.**, of Australia, *D. transversa.* **Native Y.**, applied to Australian species of *Ipomœa* with edible tubers. **Red, White, Negro Country, Winged Y.**, *D. alata.* **Round Y.**, (*a*) a species with a round tuber; (*b*) the Burdekin Vine of Australia, *Vitis* (*Cissus*) *opaca.* **Wild Y.**, *D. villosa* of N. America, also called *colic-root*; also applied to other plants.

attrib. and *Comb.*: **yam-bean,** either of two tropical leguminous plants with edible pods and tubers, *Pachyrrhizus* (*Dolichos*) *tuberosus* and *angulatus*; **y. potato,** = 2 (*b*); **y.-stick,** a long sharp stick used by Australian natives for digging and as a weapon; **y.-stock,** a nickname for an inhabitant of St. Helena; **y.-vine,** (*a*) a species of y., *Dioscorea bulbifera*; (*b*) the 'vine' or climbing stem of the y.-plant.

Yammer (yæ·məɹ), *v. Obs.* exc. *Sc.* and *dial.* 1481. [Alteration (after MDu., MLG. *jammeren*) of ME. *ȝomer* :- OE. *ġeōmrian*, f. *ġeōmor* sorrowful.] **1.** *intr.* To lament, mourn; to utter cries of lamentation or distress, to wail. **b.** To murmur, complain, grumble; also *trans.* 1786. **2.** To make a loud, unpleasant noise or outcry 1513. Hence **Ya·mmer** *sb.* the action or an act of 'yammering'; a wail; a loud outcry; lamentation, complaint.

‖**Yamstchick** (yæ·mstʃik). 1753. [Russ. *yamshchik.*] The driver of a post-horse.

‖**Yamun, yamen** (yā·mɒn). 1827. [Chinese *ya* official residence, office + *mun* gate.] A mandarin's office or official residence; hence, any department of the Chinese public service, as the *tsung li y.*, or Chinese 'foreign office'.

Yank (yæŋk), *sb.*[1] (*a.*) 1778. Colloq. abbrev. of YANKEE.

As clever at a trick as a Y. 1886.

Yank (yæŋk), *v. dial.* and *U.S.* 1822. [Of unkn. origin.] **1.** *trans.* To pull with a jerk; to jerk or twitch vigorously 1848. **2.** *intr.* To pull or jerk vigorously; *fig.* to be vigorously active 1822. Hence **Yank** *sb.*[2], a sharp stroke (*Sc.*); a jerk, tug (*U.S.*) 1818.

Yankee (yæ·ŋki), *sb.* and *a.* 1758. [Origin unknown. None of the several attempts that have been made to establish the etymology are convincing. As a surname or nickname with Dutch associations *Yank(e)y*, *Yankee* is recorded as early as 1683, and may be based on Du. *Jan* John and intended as a dim. form (= *Jantje*).] **A.** *sb.* **1. a.** *U.S.* A nickname for a New-Englander, or an inhabitant or native of the northern States generally; during the War of Secession applied by the Confederates to the soldiers of the Federal army. **b.** In English use: A native or inhabitant of the U.S., an American 1784. **2.** The New England dialect; *loosely*, American English 1772. **3.** pl. *Stock Exch. slang.* American stocks or securities 1887.

1. Our hero being a New-Englander by birth, has a right to the epithet of Yankey; a name of derision 1765. **b.** I..am determined not to suffer the Yankies to come where the ship is NELSON.

B. *adj.* That is a Yankee; pertaining to or characteristic of Yankees (often connoting cleverness, cunning, or cold calculation); of or pertaining to the United States, American 1781.

Comb., etc.: **Y. Doodle,** a popular air of the U.S., considered to be characteristically national; also, a Y.; **Ya·nkeeland,** New England, the United States of America; **Y. notions,** small wares or useful articles made in New England or the northern States; **Y. State,** a nickname for Ohio. Hence **Ya·nkeedom** = YANKEELAND; Yankees collectively. **Ya·nkeefied** *ppl. a.*; **Ya·nkeeish** *a.* Americanized or as of Americans. **Ya·nkeeism,** Y. character or style, a Y. idiom. **Ya·nkeeize** *v. trans.* to give a Y. character to.

Yanolite (yæ·noləit). 1850. [– Fr. *yanolithe*, perh. f. Gr. ἴανθος violet; see -LITE.] *Min.* = AXINITE.

‖**Yaourt** (yā·uɹt). 1819. [Turk. *yoğurt* (with quiescent *ğ*).] = YOGURT.

Yap (yæp), *v.* 1668. [imit.] **1.** *intr.* To bark sharply, as a small dog. **2.** *transf.* To speak snappishly 1864. So **Yap** *sb.* a short sharp bark or cry. **Ya·pping** *vbl. sb.* and *ppl. a.*

Yapo(c)k (yæ·pǫk). 1827. [f. *Oyapok*, name of a river between French Guiana and Brazil.] The S. Amer. water opossum, *Chironectes variegatus.*

Yapon, yaupon (yǭ·pǫn). 1712. [North Carolina.] An evergreen shrub or small tree (*Ilex cassine* or *vomitoria*) of Southern U.S.; a decoction of the leaves (*y. tea*) is used as an emetic and purgative.

Yapp (yæp). 1882. [Name of a London bookseller for whom first made about 1860.] A style of bookbinding in limp leather with overlapping edges or flaps. Hence **Yapped** (yæpt) *a.*

Yarak (yæ·ræk). 1855. [perh. Pers. *yārakī* strength.] Falconry. *In y.*, (of a hawk) in condition for hunting.

Yarborough (yā·ɹbŏrə). 1900. [Said to be so called because an Earl of Yarborough used to bet 1,000 to 1 against its occurrence.] *Cards.* In whist and bridge, a hand which contains no card above a nine.

Yard (yāɹd), *sb.*[1] [OE. *ġeard* fence, enclosure, courtyard, dwelling, region (as in *middanġeard* the earth, *ortġeard* ORCHARD). Corresponds, with variation of declension, to OFris. *garda*, OS. *gardo*, OHG. *gart*, *garto* (Du. *gaard*, G. *garten* garden), ON. *garðr*, Goth. *gards* house, *garda* enclosure, stall :- Gmc. **ȝardaz*, *-on*, rel. to OSl. *gradŭ* city, garden, Russ. *gorod* town. Cf. GARDEN.] **1.** A comparatively small uncultivated area attached to a building or enclosed by it; esp. such an area surrounded by walls or buildings within the precincts of a castle, house, inn, etc. (Cf. *back-y.*, *inn-y.*, *stable-y.*) **b.** *spec.* (*a*) *Sc. pl.* a school playground 1808; (*b*) = COURT *sb.*[1] I. 3 (esp. in proper names) 1851. **c.** = CHURCHYARD 1791. **d.** An enclosure attached to a prison, in which the prisoners take exercise 1777. **e.** *The Yard*, short for *Scotland Yard*, the chief London police office 1888. **2.** An enclosure forming a pen for cattle or poultry, a storing place for hay, or the like, belonging to a farm-house, or surrounded by farm-buildings ME. **3.** A garden. Now *dial.* and *U.S.*, a kitchen- or cottage-garden ME. **4. a.** An enclosure devoted to some work or business; cf. *brickyard*, DOCKYARD, etc. late ME. **b.** The space used for storing rolling-stock, making up trains, etc., adjacent to a railway station or terminus; also, an enclosure in which cabs, trams, etc. are kept when not in use 1827. **5.** *U.S.* and *Canada.* = MOOSE-YARD 1829.

attrib. and *Comb.*: **y.-dog,** a watch-dog kept in the y.; **-money,** fees payable by cab-hirers to stablemen, etc., on returning them to the y.

Yard (yāɹd), *sb.*[2] [OE. *ġerd*, (WS.) **ġierd*, *ġird*, *ġyrd* = OFris. *jerde*, OS. *gerdia* switch, *segalgerd* sail-yard (Du. *gard* twig, rod), OHG. *gart(e)a*, *gerta* (G. *gerte*) :- WGmc. **ȝazdjo*, f. Gmc. **ȝazdaz* GAD *sb.*[1]] †**1.** A branch, twig, shoot –1450. †**2.** A staff, stick –1538. †**3.** A stick or rod used as an instrument for administering strokes –1450. †**b.** *fig.* A means or instrument of punishment; hence, chastisement –1530. †**4.** A wand, rod, or staff of office –1470. **5.** *Naut.* A spar slung at its centre from, and forward of, a mast and serving to support and extend a square sail OE. †**6.** A measuring-rod; *spec.* a yard-measure –1751. **7.** A unit of linear measure of 16½ ft. (but varying locally); a rod, pole, or perch. Now *local.* OE. **8.** The standard unit of English long measure, equal to three feet or thirty-six inches. Also the corresponding measure of area (*square y.* = 9 sq. ft.) or of solidity (*cubic y.* = 27 cub. ft.). In *Building*, used as a measure of lime, mortar, stone, etc. late ME. **b.** Vaguely, hyperbolically, or fig. late ME. **9. a.** In full *y. of land* = YARDLAND OE. **b.** A quarter of an acre, a rood 1450. †**10.** The virile member, penis –1884.

6. *fig.* We imagine God to be lyke ourselues, & we measure him by our owne y. 1583. **8.** Phrases. *Y. of ale, wine*, a long slender glass and its contents. *Y. of clay*, a long clay pipe. *Y. of satin* (slang), a glass of gin. *Y. of tin*, a coachman's horn. **b.** He could talk by the y. of what little he did know 1869.

Yard, *v.*[1] *Colonial* and *U.S.* 1828. [f. YARD *sb.*[1]] **1.** *trans.* To enclose (cattle, etc.) or store (wood) in a yard. **2.** *intr.* Of moose, etc.: To resort to winter quarters (see MOOSE-YARD) 1852.

Yard, *v.*[2] [f. YARD *sb.*[2], used to render Manx *slattys*, f. *slat* rod, wand of authority.] *trans.* In the Isle of Man, to summon for hiring.

Yardage[1] (yā·ɹdėdʒ). 1889. [f. YARD *sb.*[1] + -AGE.] The use of or charge for a yard for storing, etc.

Ya·rdage[2]. 1877. [f. YARD *sb.*[2] + -AGE.] **1.** The cutting of coal at a fixed rate per yard. **2.** The aggregate number of yards; amount reckoned in yards 1900.

Ya·rd-arm. 1553. [f. YARD *sb.*[2] 5 + ARM *sb.*[1] II. 3.] *Naut.* Either end of a yard; *esp.* that part which is outside the sheave-hole; often used for the yard as a whole. **b.** in ref. to hanging or ducking a person from the extremity of a yard as a punishment 1553.

Y. and (or *to*) *y.*, said of two ships so near that their yard-arms touch or cross.

Yardland (yā·ɹdlæ̆nd). 1450. [= *yard of land*, OE. *ġyrd landes*; see YARD *sb.*[2] 9 a.] An area of land, usu. of 30 acres, but varying locally: commonly taken as = a fourth of a hide.

Yardman[1] (yā·ɹdmæ̆n). 1825. [YARD *sb.*[1]] A man in charge of or employed in a yard.

Ya·rdman[2]. 1886. [YARD *sb.*[2]] *Naut. Royal, upper*, etc. *y.*, a sailor occupied on the royal yards, the upper yards, etc.

Ya·rd-mea·sure. 1831. [YARD *sb.*[2]] A rod, bar, or tape for measuring by the yard (but not necessarily restricted to that length).

Yardsman (yā·ɹdzmæ̆n). 1872. [f. gen. of YARD *sb.*[1]] = YARDMAN[1]. So **Ya·rdswoman** 1817.

Yardstick (yā·ɹdstik). orig. *U.S.* 1828. [YARD *sb.*[2]] A three-foot measuring-rod. Often *fig.* = a standard of comparison.

Ya·rd-wand. late ME. [YARD *sb.*[2]] A 3-ft. measuring-rod.

Yare (yēᵊɹ), *a.* and *adv. arch.* and *dial.* [OE. *ġearu* = OS. *garu*, *-o* (Du. *gaar* done, dressed, clever), OHG. *garo* (G. *gar* ready, prepared, adv. quite), ON. *gǫrr*, *gorv* -ready-made, prompt, skilled :- Gmc. **ȝarwu* (cf. GAR *v.*).] **A.** *adj.* **1.** Ready, prepared OE. **2.** Brisk, quick ME. **b.** Of a ship: Responsive to the helm. late ME.

1. The gunner held his linstock y. SCOTT. **2.** A halter'd necke, which do's the Hangman thanke, For being y. about him SHAKS.

B. *adv.* †Quickly, promptly –1513. **b.** As exclam.: = QUICK! esp. in nautical use. *arch.* 1606.

b. Cheerely my harts: y., y.: Take in the toppe-sale SHAKS.

Ya·rely, *adv. arch.* [OE. *ġearoliċe*; see YARE *a.* and -LY[2].] Promptly, briskly.

Come y. my mates DRYDEN.

Yark. See YERK.

Yarl. See JARL.

Yarmouth (yā·ɹməþ). 1614. Name of a fishing town on the Norfolk coast; used *attrib.* in *Y. bloater*, a slightly salted and smoked herring; also *transf.* a native of Y.

Yarn (yāɹn), *sb.* [OE. *ġearn* = MDu. *gaern* (Du. *garen*), OHG., G., ON. *garn*, prob. f. base repr. also by **ȝarnō* in ON. *gǫrn*, pl. *garnar* guts, and **ȝarnjo-* in OE. *miċġern* etc. entrail fat, suet.] **1.** *orig.* Spun fibre, as of wool, flax, silk, cotton; now usu., fibre spun and prepared for use in weaving, knitting, etc. **b.** In Rope-making, one of the threads composing a strand, or these threads collectively 1627. **2.** *To spin a y.* (*fig.*, orig. *Naut. slang*), to tell a tale. Hence, *yarn* = a (long) tale, esp. a marvellous or incredible one 1812.

1. *fig.* The webbe of our life, is of a mingled yarne, good and ill together SHAKS. **2.** Come, spin us a good y., father MARRYAT.

attrib. and *Comb.*: **y.-beam** *Weaving*, the roller on which y. is wound; **-spinner,** one who spins y. or who 'spins a y.'; **-wind, -windle,** an appliance for winding a skein of y. into a ball (*obs.* exc. *dial.*). Hence **Yarn** *v.* colloq. *intr.* 'to spin a y.', tell a story.

Yarrow (yæ·roᵘ). [OE. *ġearwe*, corresp. to MDu. *garwe*, *gherwe* (Du. *gerwe*), OHG. *gar(a)wa* (G. *schafgarbe*); WGmc., of unkn. origin.] The composite herb *Achillea millefolium* or MILFOIL, common on waste land, with finely divided bipinnate leaves and close flat flower-clusters of a somewhat dull white, often varying to pink or crimson. **b.** **Soldier's Y.**, *Stratiotes aloides.* **Water Y.**, any of various water-plants with finely divided leaves, as *Ranunculus aquatilis* and *Hottonia palustris*.

‖**Yashmak** (yæ·ʃmæk). 1844. [Arab. *yašmaḳ*, Turk. *yaşmak*.] The double veil concealing the lower part of the face, worn by Moslem women in public.

Yataghan (yæ·tăgæn). 1819. [Turk. *yātāğan*.] A sword of Moslem countries, having a handle without a guard and often a double-curved blade.

Yate (yēⁱt). 1830. [Native name.] Either of two species of gum-tree (*Eucalyptus cornuta* and *E. occidentalis*), of S.W. Australia, with tough wood; also, the wood itself.

Yaud (yǭd, yād). *Sc.* and *north.* 1500. [– ON. *jalda*.] A mare, an old mare; a worn-out horse (assoc. w. JADE).

‖**Yava** (yā·vă). 1804. Variant of KAVA. Cf. AVA.

Yaw (yǭ), *sb.*[1] 1546. [Related to YAW *v.*] *Naut.* An act of yawing; a movement of deviation from the direct course, as from bad steering.

The boat took a sudden y. or sheer, which canted me overboard SMEATON.

Yaw, *sb.*[2] 1679. [Back-formation from YAWS apprehended as pl.] Each of the spots of eruption in yaws. **b.** As attrib. form of YAWS: **y.-house,** a hospital for persons affected with yaws; **y.-weed,** the shrub *Morinda royoc*, used in the West Indies as a remedy for yaws.

Yaw, *v.* 1584. [Of unkn. origin.] **1.** *Naut. intr.* Of a vessel: To deviate temporarily from the straight course, as through faulty or unsteady steering. **2.** *trans.* To cause to yaw 1746.

1. *transf.* I shot ahead, and yawed a little—caught a peep at her through her veil MARRYAT.

Yaw-haw (yǭ·hǭ), *sb.* and *v.* 1836. [Imitative.] = GUFFAW.

Yawl (yǭl), *sb.*[1] 1670. [– (M)LG. *jolle* or Du. *jol*; ult. origin unkn. Cf. JOLLY-BOAT.] **1.** A ship's boat resembling a pinnace, but smaller, usu. with four or six oars. **2.** A small sailing-boat of the cutter class, with a jigger 1684. **3.** A small fishing-boat 1670.

Yawl, *v.* Now *dial.* late ME. [Parallel to YOWL with vowel-variation; cf. LG. *jaulen* (of cats).] *intr.* and *trans.* To cry out loudly from pain, grief, or distress; to howl, scream, bawl: also said of the howling of dogs, the 'wauling' of cats, etc. Hence **Yawl** *sb.*[2], a howl, scream, yell.

Yawn (yǭn), *sb.* 1602. [f. next.] **1.** Something that yawns; a gaping aperture; *esp.* a chasm, abyss. **2.** The or an act of yawning. **a.** Gaping 1697. **b.** Involuntary opening of the mouth, as from drowsiness 1706.

1. Spaces of fire, and all the y. of hell KEATS. **2. b.** Our salutation is a Y. and a Stretch STEELE.

Yawn, *v.* [spec. symbolic alt. of ME. *ȝone*, which with *ȝene* repr. OE. *ġeonian*, var. of *ġinian* = OHG. *ginōn, -ēn*, MDu. *ghēnen*, rel. to synon. OE. *gānian* (see GANE *v.*) and *ġinan*.] †**1.** *intr.* To open the mouth wide voluntarily, esp. in order to swallow or devour something; to gape. Said also of the mouth. –1603. **2.** To lie, stand, or be wide open, as a chasm, gap, etc.; to have or form a wide opening, gap, or chasm OE. **3.** To show fatigue, drowsiness, or boredom by making (usu. involuntarily) a prolonged inspiration with the mouth wide open and the lower jaw dropped. late ME. **b.** *trans.* To say or utter with a yawn. Also with cognate obj. 1718. **c.** To open the mouth wide from surprise or the like, to gape. *Obs.* exc. *dial.* 1604. **d.** To bring into some position or condition by or to the accompaniment of yawning 1742. **4.** *intr.* To open wide as a mouth; to form a chasm; to gape 1599. **5.** *trans.* To make, produce, or afford by opening wide. *rare.* 1605.

1. Crocodiles lyinge in the sande, and yanyng to take the heate of the soonne 1555. **2.** The gashes That bloodily did yawne vpon his face SHAKS. **3.** The audience yawned through the play THACKERAY. **c.** *Oth.* v. ii. 101. **d.** Who y. away their existence in the assemblies of London 1817. **4.** Graues yawne and yeelde your dead SHAKS. Hence **Yaw·ner,** one who yawns; something that yawns, a wide ditch.

Yawning (yǭ·niŋ), *ppl. a.* OE. [f. prec. + -ING[2].] That yawns. **b.** *transf.* Characterized by or producing yawning; drowsy, soporific 1575.

b. The shard-borne Beetle, with his drowsie hums, Hath rung Nights y. Peale SHAKS. Hence **Yaw·ningly** *adv.*

Yawny (yǭ·ni), *a.* 1805. [f. YAWN *sb.* or *v.* + -Y[1].] Inclined to or provocative of yawning.

Yawp, yaup (yǭp), *v.* Chiefly *dial.* late ME. [imit. Cf. YAP, YELP *v.*] To utter a strident call; to yelp, as a dog; to cry harshly or querulously, as a bird. Hence **Yawp, yaup** *sb.* a harsh, hoarse, or querulous cry, esp. of a bird; *fig.* speech or utterance likened to this.

Yaws (yǭz). 1679. [So *jas* in Guiana; identity with synon. *pians* pl. (Fr. *pian*, Sp., Pg. *epian, pian* – Guarani *pià*) has been suggested, through Negro jargon.] A contagious disease of Negroes, characterized by raspberry-like tubercles on the skin; also called *frambœsia*. Hence **Yaw·y** *a.*

Yaw-yaw (yǭ·yǭ·), *v.* 1854. [imit.] *intr.* To talk affectedly.

They liked fine gentlemen..and they yaw-yawed in their speech like them DICKENS.

†**Yble·nt,** *pa. pple.*[1] ME. [Y- 3, BLEND *v.*[1]] Blinded; dazed –1590.

The eye of reason was with rage y. SPENSER.

†**Yble·nt,** *pa. pple.*[2] late ME. [Y- 3, BLEND *v.*[2]] Mingled –1748.

†**Ybo·rn,** *pa. pple.* OE. [Y- 6, BORN *pa. pple.*] **1.** Born –1755. **2.** Borne –1642.

†**Ybre·nt,** *pa. pple.* ME. [Y- 3 + *brent*, pa. pple. of BURN *v.*[1]] Burnt –1767.

With feverish Thirste y. 1767.

Yclad (iklæ·d), *pa. pple. arch.* ME. [Y- 3, CLAD *pa. pple.*] Clothed.

Spring y. in grassy dye BYRON.

Yclept (ikle·pt), **ycleped** (iklī·pt, *poet.* iklī·pėd), *pa. pple. arch.* [OE. *ġecleopod*, pa. pple. of *cleopian, clipian* call; see Y- 3, CLEPE *v.*] Called (so-and-so), named, styled. (A frequent poetic or serio-comic archaism.)

But com thou Goddes fair and free, In Heav'n ycleap'd Euphrosyne MILT. The sweet wood yclept sassafras LAMB.

Ye (yī, yi), *pers. pron. 2nd pers. nom.* (*obj.*), *pl.* (*sing.*). Now *arch.*, *poet.*, or *dial.*, in ordinary use replaced by YOU. [OE. *ġē* = OFris. *jī*, OS. *gi, ge* (Du. *gij*), OHG. *ir* (G. *ihr*), ON *ér* (:– *jēr*), analogically modified forms (after the 1st pers. pron., e.g. OE. *ġe* after *we*, OHG. *ir* after *wir*, ON. *ér* after *vér*) of Gmc. **juz*, accented *jūz*, repr. by Goth. *jūs*, f. *ju-* (with pl. ending); see YOU, YOUR.] **1.** As the nom. or voc. pl. of THOU, used in addressing a number of persons OE. **b.** In apposition with a following sb. in the vocative. late ME. **2.** Used instead of *thou* in addressing a single person (orig. as a sign of respect or deference) ME. **3.** Used instead of *you* as obj. sing. or pl. 1449.

1. Ye [*1st Pr. Bk.* 1549 You] that do truly and earnestly repent you of your sins *Bk. Com. Pr.* 1662. But ye at home, ye bore the brunt BRIDGES. **b.** Ye holy Angels bright 1681. **2.** Good lord, ye created & made our fader Adam CAXTON. 'Damsel', he said, 'ye be not all to blame' TENNYSON. **3.** As I haue made ye one Lords, one remaine SHAKS.

Ye, ye, graphic var. *þe, þ*ᵉ THE; see Y.

Yea (yēⁱ), *adv.* (*sb.*). Now *dial.* and *arch.* [OE. *ġē*, (WS.) *ġēa*, corresp. to OFris. *gē, jē*, OS., OHG. *jā* (Du., G. *ja*), ON. *já*, Goth. *ja, jai*; ult. Gmc. **ja*, **je*, which was variously modified through stress or emotional emphasis.] **A.** *adv.* A word used to express affirmation or assent: now ordinarily replaced by YES. **1.** = YES 1, 2, 3, 4. †**2.** Even, truly, verily –1581. **3.** Introducing a question or remark in reply to a statement, etc., expressing either vague assent or (more commonly) opposition or objection: = 'indeed?'; 'Well', 'well then' ME.

1. Thei..seiden to hym, ȝoure maister payeth nat tribute? And he seith, ȝhe WYCLIF *Matt.* 17:23. He asked whether our countrey had warres? I answered him y. 1611. Some of them use improper, yea, indecent, expressions in prayer WESLEY. *To say y.*, to answer in the affirmative; hence, to give assent; They praed them to say.. playnly ye or nay 1440. **2.** They fell a chydynge.. Ye, dyd they so? SKELTON. Y., is it come to this? SHAKS.

B. *sb.* **1.** An utterance of the word 'yea'; an affirmative reply or statement; an expression of assent ME. **b.** Affirmation, assurance, certainty, absolute truth. late ME. **2.** An affirmative vote; a person who votes in the affirmative. Usu. *pl.* Still in use in U.S. Congress. 1657. **3.** *Yea and nay* (or *no*): positive and negative statement (or command); affirmation and denial; *occas.*, shilly-shally. late ME. **b.** *By yea and nay*, a substitute for an oath 1588.

1. Let youre ye be ye, and youre naye naye TINDALE *James* 5:12. Their No should be as welcome unto him as their Yea 1611. **b.** Love God. This is the Everlasting Yea. CARLYLE. **2.** If one fifth of a quorum demand a call of yeas and nays, this is taken BRYCE. **3.** These two went on, With yea and nay, and pro and con PRIOR. *attrib.* One of your water-gruel, yea-and-nay good boys 1781. **b.** He swore by yea and nay He would have no denial 1661.

Comb.: **y.-forsooth** *a.*, addicted to saying yea forsooth' in the way of superficial assent; **-word,** a word of assent. Hence **Yea** *v. intr.* to say y.; to reply affirmatively.

Yean (yīn), *v. arch.* and *dial.* late ME. [repr. OE. **ġeēanian* (rel. to *ġeēan* pregnant), f. *ġe-* Y- + *ēanian* EAN *v.*] **1.** *trans.* Of a ewe: To bring forth (a lamb); also said of goats. **2.** *intr.* To bring forth young, as a sheep 1548.

Yeanling (yī·nliŋ). *arch.* 1637. [f. prec. + -LING[1].] A young lamb or kid. **b.** appositive or as *adj.* That is a y., young or new-born: esp. of a lamb.

Year (yīᵊɹ). [OE. (Anglian) *ġēr*, (WS.) *ġēar* = OFris. *jār, jēr*, OS. *jār, gēr* (Du. *jaar*), OHG. *jār* (G. *jahr*), ON. *ár*, Goth. *jēr* :– Gmc. **jǣram*, f. IE. base **jēr-* **jōr-*, repr. also by Avestic *yāre* year, Gr. ὥρα season (whence L. *hora* hour), etc.] **1.** The time occupied by the sun in its apparent passage through the signs of the zodiac; the period of the earth's revolution round the sun, forming a natural unit of time (nearly = 365¼ days); hence, a space of time approximately equal to this in any conventional practical reckoning OE. **b.** Following and qualifying a date: = a year before or after...1533. **c.** In ref. to the duration of some (usu. painful) experience, as a term of imprisonment, etc. ME. **d.** *pl.* with numeral, expressing a person's age ME. **2. a.** With qualifying words, denoting periods differing in length according to the manner in which they are computed in some scientific or conventional reckoning, as *anomalistic, astronomical, canicular, civil, embolismic, equinoctial, Gregorian, Julian, lunar, lunisolar, natural, sidereal, solar, Sothic, tropical, vague year.* **b.** *transf.* Applied to a very long period or cycle. late ME. **c.** The period of a planet's revolution round the sun (*planetary y.*) 1728. **3.** A space of time, of the length stated in sense 1, with fixed limits. **a.** *esp.* Such a space of time as reckoned in a calendar and denoted by a number in a particular era; also called the *civil y.*; in the ordinary or Roman calendar beginning on 1st Jan., divided into twelve months, and having 365 (or 366) days OE. **b.** Such a space of time, with limits not necessarily coinciding with those of the civil year, forming a division of a period (or the whole period) of office, study, etc., or taken between definite dates for some special purpose, e.g. taxation, etc. OE. **c.** Such a space of time as arranged for religious observance in the Christian Church, beginning with Advent. late ME. **4.** The round of the seasons. late ME. **5.** *pl.* Age (of a person) OE. **b.** Maturity; old age (esp. in phr. *in years* = old, aged). Now *arch.* or *poet.* 1579. **6.** *pl.* Times; a spell of time, one's time or period of life ME. **b.** Chiefly *pl.* A very long time, 'ages' 1692.

1. He will last you some eight yeare SHAKS. **b.** On the day y. on which he had received our Lord's servants into his house 1873. **c.** If he was not careful she could get him fifteen years 1901. **d.** A nurse of ninety years TENNYSON. **2. b.** *Cynic y.*: see CYNIC *a.* 3. *Great y.* (Gr. μέγας ἐνιαυτός), the period (variously reckoned) after which all the heavenly bodies were supposed to return to their original positions; also called *Platonic y.* **c.** According to the Neptunian calendar, it is only thirty-six years since the creation of Adam 1870. **3.** Dr. Pauli..gives the day and the month, without remembering to add the y. 1861. *Y. of Christ, of our Lord, of grace*, a particular year of the Christian era (denoted by a number following). **b.** The relative positions which the boys of each y. had occupied in the school 1848. **c.** The first Sunday in Advent was not always the beginning of the liturgical y. 1875. **4.** Shatter your leaves before the mellowing y. MILT. The varying y. with blade and sheaf Clothes and reclothes the happy plains TENNYSON. **5.** Vane, young in yeares, but in sage counsell old MILT. **6.** The state of painting in this country of late years H. WALPOLE. **b.** We live years of emotion in a few weeks THACKERAY.

Phrases. **A y., every y.,** *per annum.* **Y. after y., y. by y., from y. to y.,** through a succession of years; every y. successively. **Y. in (and) y. out,** as each y. begins and until it ends; continually throughout the y. (and through successive years). **Y. and day** (*Law*) a period constituting a term for some purposes, in order to ensure the completion of a full y.

Year-book (yīᵊ·ɹbuk). 1588. **1.** *pl.* The books of reports of cases in the English law-courts published annually during several periods from the reign of Edw. II to that of Hen. VIII. **2.** A book published annually and containing the latest information for the year; an annual on its subject 1710.

Yearling (yīᵊ·ɹliŋ), *sb.* and *a.* 1465. [f. YEAR + -LING[1].] **A.** *sb.* **1.** An animal a year old, or in its second year (esp. a sheep, calf, or foal). **b.** *transf.* The fleece of a y. sheep 1888. **2.** A plant a year old; *spec.* applied to hops of the previous year's growth 1849. **B.** *adj.* A year old; in its second year; of the previous year's growth 1528.

Yea·r-long, *a.* 1813. [f. YEAR + LONG *a.*[1]; cf. OE. *ġēarlanges* adv. for a year.] Lasting for a year; lasting for years in succession; *occas.*, age-long.

Through y. hours of hope and woe 1871. The year-long alliance between philosophy and theology 1886.

Yearly (yīᵊ·ɹli), *a.* [OE. *ġēarlić*; see YEAR and -LY[1].] †**1.** Of the year; belonging or relating to a year (*rare*) –1811. **2.** Of or in each year; happening, etc., once a year; annual OE.

1. The varietie..of the yearely seasons PURCHAS.

Yea·rly, *adv.* [OE. *ġēarlīće* see YEAR and -LY[2].] Every year, once a year, annually.

He gave y. great sums in charity 1715.

Yearn (yɔ̄ɹn), *v.*[1] [OE. *ġiernan* = OS. *ġernean*, *ġirnean*, ON. *girna*, Goth. *gairnjan* :– Gmc. *ʒ*ernjan*, f. *ʒ*ernaz*, repr. by OE. *ġeorn* eager, OHG. *gern* (G. *gern* willingly).] †**1.** *trans.* To long for –1568. **2.** *intr.* To have a longing: **a.** Const. inf. with *to* OE. **b.** Const. *after*, *for*. †*to*, *towards*. Also *absol.* OE. †**3.** Of hounds: To give tongue –1680. **4.** To express yearning or strong desire; also *trans.* to utter in an emotional voice 1816. **5.** To be deeply moved, esp. with pity or tenderness 1500. †**6.** *trans.* To move to compassion –1641.

2. a. The child yearned to be out of doors DICKENS. **b.** His heart yearned after the damsel W. IRVING. **4.** The music, yearning like a God in pain KEATS. The faces of thy ministers Yearned pale with bitter ecstasy ROSSETTI. The kind of voice..in which..actresses y. out passages from 'The Cenci' 1894. **5.** Her bowelles yerned vpon her sonne BIBLE (Great) 1 *Kings* 3:26. Her Heart yearns towards you ADDISON. **6.** She laments Sir for it, that it would yern your heart to see it SHAKS. Hence **Yearn** *sb.* a yearning. **Yea·rner. Yea·rnful** *a.* mournful. **Yea·rning** *vbl. sb.*[1] the action of the vb., an instance of this; *ppl. a.* that yearns; **-ly** *adv.*

Yearn (yɔ̄ɹn), *v.*[2] Chiefly *Sc.* and *n. dial.* late ME. [poss. dial. var. of EARN *v.*[2] (XVII) with initial *y*-glide, but the chronology creates a difficulty.] **a.** *intr.* To coagulate, curdle. **b.** *trans.* To curdle (milk); to make (cheese) of curdled milk. Hence **Yea·rning** *vbl. sb.*[2] rennet.

Yea·r-old, *a.* and *sb.* 1539. **A.** *adj.* A year old 1767. **B.** *sb.* A yearling 1539.

Year's mind, yea·r-mind. [OE. *ġēar-ġemynd*; see YEAR, MIND *sb.* 4 b.] The commemoration of a deceased person by requiem services on the first or on each anniversary of his death or funeral.

The 'Year's Mind' of her late Majesty Queen Victoria 1902.

Yeast (yīst); *formerly and now dial.* **yest,** *sb.* [OE. (Anglian) **ġest*, WS. **ġiest* (late *ġist*), corresp. to MLG. *gest* dregs, dirt, MDu. *ghist*, *ghest* (Du. *gist*, *gest* yeast), MHG. *jist*, etc. (G. *gischt* sea-foam) yeast, froth, ON. *jǫstr*, rel. to OHG. *jesan*, *gesan* ferment, Gr. ζεῖν boil, ζεστός boiled.] **1.** A yellowish substance produced by the propagation of a fungus (*Saccharomyces cerevisiæ*) as a froth (*top* or *surface y.*) or sediment (*bottom*, *under*, or *sediment y.*) during the alcoholic fermentation of malt worts and other saccharine fluids, and used in making beer, leavening bread, and medicinally. **b.** *fig.* = LEAVEN *sb.* 2 a. 1760. **2.** *transf.* Foam or froth 1611.

1. b. The best of men have but a portion of good in them—a kind of spiritual y. KEATS.

attrib. and *Comb.*: **y.-cake,** y. drained and pressed for keeping; also a cake resembling a dough-cake; **-plant,** any plant of the genus *Saccharomyces*, esp. *S. cerevisiæ*. Hence **Yeast** *v. intr.* to ferment, to form froth (*rare*).

Yeasty (yī·sti), *a.* 1598. [f. prec. + -Y[1].] **1.** Of, full of, or like yeast 1599. **2.** *fig.* In a ferment; acting like leaven; turbid and restless; light and superficial 1598. **3.** *transf.* Frothy, foamy 1605. Hence **Yea·stily** *adv.* **Yea·stiness.**

Yegg (yeg). *U.S.* 1903. [Said to be a surname.] A burglar or safe-breaker. So **Ye·ggman.**

Yeld (yeld), *a.* (*sb.*) *Sc.* and *n. dial.* [Late OE. **ġielde*, *ġelde*, corresp. to MLG., OHG. *galt* (G. *gelt*), ON. *geldr*; cf. GELD *a.* and *v.*[1]] **A.** *adj.* **1.** Of an animal: Barren; that has missed having her young, or is not old enough to bear. **2.** Of cattle: Not yielding milk 1670. **3.** *transf.* Unproductive 1721. **B.** *sb.* A barren cow or ewe; a hind that is not pregnant 1856.

‖**Yelek** (ye·lek). 1836. [Turk.; cf. JELICK.] A long vest worn by Turkish women.

Yelk: see YOLK.

Yell (yel), *sb.* late ME. [f. next] An act of yelling; a sharp loud outcry. **b.** *U.S.* The distinctive cheer used by the students of any particular college. 1889.

Once or twice the Indian y. was given 1841.

Yell, *v.* [OE. (Anglian) *ġellan*, (WS.) *ġiellan* = MLG., MDu. *ghellen*, OHG. *gellan* (Du. *ghillen*, G. *gellen*), ON. *gjalla*, f.Gmc. *ʒ*el-* *ʒ*al-*, whence also OE., OHG. *galan*, ON. *gala* sing, cry out; see GALE *v.*[1], NIGHTINGALE.] **1.** *intr.* To utter a loud strident cry, esp. from some strong or sudden emotion, as rage, horror, or agony ME. **b.** Of some birds and beasts; To emit a strident cry, either as their natural utterance or when hurt or from rage OE. **2.** *trans.* To utter with a yell ME.

1. She yelled out on seeing him SCOTT. **b.** The Dogges did y. SHAKS. **2.** Yelling their uncouth dirge BYRON.

Yelloch (ye·ləχ), *sb.* and *v.* *Sc.* 1513. [app. f. prec. with symbolic ending.] = YELL *sb.* and *v.*

Yellow (ye·loᵘ), *a.* and *sb.* [OE. *ġeolu*, *-o* = OS. *gelo*, (M)LG. *geel*, MDu. *gel(e)u*, *geel*, OHG. *gelo* (Du. *geel*, G. *gelb*) :– WGmc. **gelwa* :– IE. **ghelwo-*, rel. to L. *helvus*, Gr. χλόος. Cf. GALL *sb.*[1], GOLD *sb.*] **A.** *adj.* **1.** Of the colour of gold, butter, yolk of egg, etc.; constituting the most luminous primary colour, occurring in the spectrum between green and orange. **b.** Of the complexion in age or disease; also as the colour of faded leaves, ripe corn, or old paper; hence *allus.* OE. **c.** Having a naturally yellow skin or complexion, as the people of the Mongolian races; hence = MONGOLIAN A. 2. 1834. **d.** Applied to naval captains retired as rear admirals in H.M. Fleet without being attached to a particular squadron (red, white, or blue) 1788. **e.** *transf.* Dressed in yellow 1848. †**2.** *fig.* Jealous –1858. **3.** Applied to newspapers (or writers of newspaper articles) of a recklessly or unscrupulously sensational character (orig. *U.S.*: from a picture in the *New York World*, 1895, with the central figure in a yellow dress) 1898.

1. This Pardoner hadde heer as yelow as wex CHAUCER. **b.** *Macb.* V. iii. 23. **c.** *The y. peril*, a supposed danger of a destructive invasion of Europe by Asiatic peoples. **2.** Your y. humour interprets this to be too much familiarity 1665. Phr. †*To wear y. hose* or *stockings*, to be jealous. **b.** Craven, cowardly 1896.

B. *sb.* **1.** The colour described in A. 1, or a pigment, fabric, or stuff of this colour ME. **b.** With qualifying words, denoting shades of the colour, as *brass-*, *primrose-*, *sulphur-y.*, or various pigments and dyes, as *aniline*, *Naples y.*, etc., for which see the first element 1532. **2.** A yellow object, substance, part, etc., as the yolk of an egg, sulphur, a kind of turnip, etc. 1738. **b.** A particular yellow species or variety of bird, butterfly, or moth 1816. **3.** A member of a yellow race, a Mongolian. Only *pl.* 1808. **4.** As the colour of a party badge; hence *transf.* a member of a party whose colour is yellow 1755. **5.** A 'yellow' newspaper (see A. 3) 1898. **6.** In specialized uses of the pl. in sing. sense: **a.** (*The*) *yellows*, jaundice, esp. in beasts 1561. †**b.** (*The*) *yellows*, jealousy –1638. **c.** (*The*) *yellows*, a disease of wheat or of peach-trees (*peach-yellows*) 1771. **d.** *Yellows*, a name for certain plants yielding a yellow dye, as *Genista tinctoria* and *Reseda luteola*; *dial.*, the yellow-flowered wild mustard and the wild cabbage 1601.

1. Elms, whose fallen leaves have made the road one y. 1824. **c.** Cowardice; meanness (cf. A. 2 b) 1896.

Collocations and *Combs.*: **y. admiral** (see A. 1 d); **-ammer,** see YELLOW-HAMMER; **y. atrophy,** atrophy and y. discoloration of the liver with jaundice; **-back,** a cheap y.-backed (esp. French) novel; **y. bark,** any kind of Peruvian bark of a y. colour; **-beak** = BEJAN; **-belly,** a frog; *transf.* a native of the fens; a kind of tortoise, or its shell; western *U.S.* a Mexican or half-caste; any of various fishes having the underparts y.; **y. berries,** the fruit of *Rhamnus infectorius* and other species, yielding a y. die; **-bill,** any of various birds with a y. bill, as the Amer. scoter; **-bird,** any of several birds having y. plumage; now esp. the N. Amer. goldfinch, *Chrysomitris* (*Spinus*, *Carduelis*) *tristis*, and the N. Amer. summer warbler (*summer y.-bird*), *Dendrœca æstiva*; **-boy** (*slang*; now *rare* or *Obs.*), a gold coin, a guinea or sovereign; **y. cartilage,** *Anat.* cartilage containing *y. fibres*; **-cup,** a buttercup; **y. deal,** the wood of the Scotch fir, *Pinus sylvestris*; **y. earth,** a yellowish clay, coloured by iron, used as a pigment; **y. fever,** a highly fatal infectious febrile disease of hot climates, characterized by vomiting, constipation, jaundice, etc.; **y. fibre,** *Anat.* one of the elastic fibres of a y. colour occurring in certain tissues; **-fin,** any of various fishes with y. fins; **-fish,** any of various fishes with y. coloration; now esp. a species of rock-trout, *Pleurogrammus* (*Hexagrammus*) *monopterygius*, of the coast of Alaska; **y. flag,** one displayed on a ship as a signal of infectious disease or quarantine; **Y. George** (see GEORGE II. 2); **y. gum,** jaundice in infants, characterized by yellowness of the gums; **y. jack** *slang* = *y. fever*; **-jacket,** *U.S. colloq.* a wasp or hornet; **y. metal,** an alloy of two parts of copper and one of zinc, used for sheathing vessels; **y. ore,** copper pyrites; **-pate,** the yellow-hammer; **y. peril** (see A. 1 c); **y. plague,** jaundice; **ye·llowplush,** plush of a y. colour, as worn by footmen; hence *transf. joc.*, a footman; **y. press** (see A. 3); **-rattle** (see RATTLE *sb.* I. 3 a); **-root,** (the root of) two N. Amer. ranunculaceous plants, *Hydrastis canadensis* (*Canadian y.-root* or *golden seal*) and *Xanthorrhiza apiifolia* (*shrub y.-root*), yielding y. dyes, and used as tonics; **Y. Sally,** a species of stone-fly used as a bait by anglers; **yellowseed,** *Lepidium campestre*, mithridate mustard (pepperwort); **y. sickness,** jaundice; **y. soap,** a common soap made of tallow, rosin, and soda; **y. spot,** *Anat.* a yellowish circular depression in the middle of the retina, being the region of most distinct vision; **yellowtail,** (*a*) any of various fishes, chiefly of N. America and Australasia, as species of *Serviola*, *Caranx*, and *Latris*; (*b*) collector's name for a species of moth, also called *gold-tail*; **y. ware,** y. earthenware or stoneware; **-weed,** (*a*) *dial.* dyer's-weed, *Reseda luteola*; (*b*) common ragwort, *Senecio jacobæa*; (*c*) *U.S.* various species of golden-rod (*Solidago*); **-wood,** any of various trees and shrubs having y. wood, or the wood of any of these; **-wort,** y. centaury. Hence **Ye·llow-ly** (*rare*) *adv.*, **-ness. Ye·llowy** *a.* = YELLOWISH.

Ye·llow, *v.* OE. [f. YELLOW *a.*] **1.** *intr.* To become yellow. **2.** *trans.* To make yellow 1598. **b.** *Naut. colloq.* To make a 'yellow admiral' of (see YELLOW A. 1 d) 1747.

Yellow dog. *U.S.* 1840. **1.** A mongrel dog or cur, of a yellow or yellowish colour. **2.** *fig.* A person or thing of no account or of a low type 1903. **b.** *attrib.*; applied *spec.* to organizations, etc. opposed to trade-unionism 1902.

Ye·llow-ha·mmer, -a·mmer. 1556. Also **Ye·llow ham** 1544, now *dial.* [The source of (*h*)*ammer* may be OE. *amore* 'scorellus' (unidentified), with possible conflation with *hama* covering, feathers, there being a syn. in dial. *yellowham* (XVI); there are numerous Continental names of birds which contain an element meaning 'yellow' or 'gold'.] A species of bunting, *Emberiza citrinella*, with yellow head, throat, and under parts. **b.** *U.S.* The golden-winged woodpecker, *Colaptes auratus* 1857.

Ye·llowish, *a.* late ME. [-ISH[1].] Somewhat yellow. Hence **Ye·llowishness.**

Yelm (yelm), *sb. dial.* [OE. *ġielm, ġelm, ġilm, ġylm.*] A bundle of straw laid straight for thatching. **Yelm** *v.* (*dial.*) *trans.* and *intr.*

Yelp (yelp), *sb.* [OE. *ġielp*, etc. vainglory, pride = OS. *gelp*, OHG. *gelph, gelf*, ON. *gjalp*; see next.] †**1.** Boasting. –late ME. **2.** A dog's shrill bark of excitement or distress 1500.

2. *transf.* How is it that we hear the loudest yelps for liberty among the drivers of negroes? JOHNSON.

Yelp (yelp), *v.* [OE. *ġielpan, ġelpan, ġilpan* = MHG *gelfen, gelpfen*, f. echoic base otherwise repr. in OS. *galpon* (LG. *galpen*); cf. GALP *v.*, YAWP *v.*] †**1.** To boast –late ME. †**2.** To cry aloud; to sing shrilly –1549. **3.** *intr.* To utter a yelp or yelps 1553. **4.** *fig.* To complain, whine 1706. **5.** *trans.* To express yelpingly 1654.

Hence **Ye·lping** *vbl. sb.* and *ppl. a.*

Yelper (ye·lpəɹ). ME. [f. prec. + -ER[1].] †**1.** A boaster. ME. only. **2.** An animal or person that yelps; e.g. a whelp; the avocet (*local*), a young partridge 1673. **b.** *slang.* A town-crier 1725. **3.** *contempt.* A speaker or writer whose utterance is compared to a dog's yelp 1673.

3. In the house of commons he was the terror of that species of orators called the Yelpers SCOTT.

Yelt (yelt.) *dial.* [Late OE. *ġilte* = MLG. *gelte* spayed sow :– **ʒaltjōn*; see GILT *sb.*[2]] A young sow.

‖**Yen** (yen). 1875. [Japanese – Chin. *yüan* round, dollar.] A gold or silver coin, the monetary unit of Japan since 1871, formerly of about the value of the U.S. dollar, now of about two shillings. Also *collect.* as *pl.*

Yengees (ye·ŋgīz), *pl.* 1819. Stated to be a N. Amer. Indian corruption of *English*, applied to the people of New England.

Yeoman (yōᵘ·măn). *Pl.* **yeomen** (yōᵘ·mĕn). [ME. *ʒoman, ʒuman, ʒeman, ʒiman*, prob. reduced forms of *ʒong-, ʒung-, ʒeng-, ʒing-man*, i.e. *youngman*, which was similarly used in ME.] **1.** A servant or attendant in a royal or noble household, usu. ranking between a sergeant and a groom or between a squire and a page. **b.** An attendant or assistant to an official, etc. late ME. **c.** *Yeoman('s) service*, good, efficient, or useful service 1602. **2.** With *of* (or *for*), in official titles, as *y. of the cellar, revels, robes, wardrobe, y. for the household* ME.; also in burlesque titles, as *y. of the cord*, hangman 1640. **b.** *Y. of the Guard*, a member of the sovereign's body-guard, instituted at the accession of Henry VII 1485. *Y. extraordinary* (*of the Guard*), any of the warders of the Tower 1552. **c.** In the British and U.S. navies, an inferior officer in charge of stores, as *y. of the signals, engineer's y.* 1669. **3.** Appositive in the titles of various attendants and officials, as *y. bedel, farrier, pricker, usher.* late ME. **4.** A man owning and cultivating a small estate; a freeholder under the rank of gentleman; *loosely*, a countryman of respectable standing, a farmer. late ME. **5.** A yeoman (as in 4) serving as a (foot) soldier. Now *arch.* or *Hist.* late ME. **b.** *spec.* A member of the (Imperial) Yeomanry (see YEOMANRY 2) 1798.

1. Knyʒt. squiere, ʒomon & page 1420. The kyng callyd vpon hys knyghtes squyers and yemen MALORY. **b.** The senior Sheriff's y. read Her Majesty's writ 1861. **c.** I once did hold it..A basenesse to write faire; ..but Sir now, It did me Yeomans seruice SHAKS. **2.** William Pratte, Yoman for the King's mouth 1455. Extraordinary Y.: see BEEFEATERS 2. **3.** The Yeomen Ushers of Devotion MILT. **4.** Yeoman: which worde now signifieth among vs, a man well at ease and hauing honestlie to liue, and yet not a gentleman 1577. My father was a Yoman, and had no landes of his owne, onlye he had a farme LATIMER. Those only who rent..are, properly speaking, farmers. Those who till their own land are yeomen COBBETT.

Yeomanly (yōᵘ·mănli), *a.* 1576. [f. prec. + -LY[1].] **1.** Having the rank or the character of a yeoman. **2.** Of, characteristic of, or befitting a yeoman; sturdy; homely 1626.

Yeo·manly, *adv.* ME. [f. as prec. + -LY[2].] In a yeomanly manner.

Wel koude he dresse his takel yemanly CHAUCER.

Yeomanry (yōᵘ·mănri). late ME. [f. YEOMAN + -RY.] **1.** The body of small landed proprietors; yeomen collectively. **b.** *Hist.* The freemen of a livery company 1497. **2.** A British volunteer cavalry force first embodied in 1794 and consisting chiefly of men of the yeomanry class or status. 1794.

Imperial Y., a corps recruited for service in the South African War (1899–1902) from the y., the volunteers, and civilians; the title was subsequently extended to the original y. and was retained till 1908.

Yeowoman (yōᵘ·wu:măn). *Pl.* **yeowomen** (-wi:mĕn). 1852. [After YEOMAN.] A woman having the rank or position of a yeoman.

Yep, *dial.* (esp. *U.S.*) pron. of YES. Cf. NOPE[2].

-yer, *suffix*, var. of -IER, esp. after *w*, as *bowyer, lawyer, sawyer.*

‖**Yerba-maté** (yə̄·ɹbă mæ·te). Also simply **yerba** (**yerva**). 1818. [Sp. *yerba* herb + *mate* MATÉ.] = MATÉ 2.

‖**Yercum** (yə̄·ɹkŏm). 1826. [Tamil.] Either of two East Indian shrubs, *Calotropis gigantea* and *C. procera*, or the fibre of their bark, used medicinally.

Yerk, yark (yə̄ɹk, yāɹk), *v.* Now *Sc.* and *dial.* [Late ME. *yerk* (XV), first as a technical term in bootmaking; prob. in part phonetically symbolic; cf. the largely synonymous JERK *v.*[1], FIRK *v.*] **1.** In shoe-making: *intr.* To draw stitches tight, to twitch; *trans.* to sew (leather, etc.) thus. **2.** *trans.* To strike smartly, esp. with a rod or whip 1520. **b.** To crack (a whip) 1566. **3.** *fig.* To lash, beat (as with sharp words or treatment) 1593. **b.** *intr.* To carp *at* 1621. **4.** *trans.* To push or pull suddenly; to jerk 1568. **5.** To fling out (the heels, etc.), *intr.* to lash or strike *out* with the heels, to kick 1565.

1. His hands and feet are yerked as tight as cords can be drawn SCOTT. **2.** Like as the carter.. yerketh his horsse with the whyp COVERDALE. **3.** Aye, Satan! does that y. ye? KEATS. **5.** Their wounded steeds..Yerke out their armed heeles at their dead masters SHAKS. Hence **Yerk, yark,** *sb.* a smart blow; a horse's kick; a jerk 1509.

Yerva: see YERBA.

Yes (yes), *adv.* (*sb.*). [Peculiar to English. OE. *ġēse, ġīse, ġȳse*, prob. for **ġīese*, f. **ġīa sīe* 'yea, may it be (so)'; formerly used spec. in response to a neg. question.] A word used to express an affirmative reply to a question, statement, command, etc. **A.** *adv.* **1.** In answer to a question not involving a negative; = 'It is so'. (Formerly usu. more emphatic than *yea* or *aye*; in later use taking the place of these.) **2. a.** In answer to a question involving a negative. (Formerly regularly used thus, and as in b, in distinction from *yea*; the distinction became obsolete soon after 1600 (but is retained in the 1611 transl. of the Bible), and since then *yes* has been the ordinary affirmative particle in reply to any question positive or negative.) OE. **b.** In contradiction of or opposition to a negative statement expressed or implied, or a negative command or request. (Now usu. accompanied by a short asseverative phr. echoing the preceding statement.) ME. **3.** Expressing assent to a command, request, proposal, or summons ME. **b.** Expressing assent to a statement or implication. late ME. **c.** In iron. assent, or conceding something as true but irrelevant or immaterial; often *Yes, but* or impatiently *Yes, yes* 1596. **d.** (Usu. interrog.) Inviting a speaker to repeat, confirm, or amplify what he has said, or expressing provisional acceptance of a statement 1842. **4.** Used to emphasize or strengthen the speaker's own preceding statement 1598. ¶*O yes*: see OYEZ.

1. Þanne þe kyng com, and þe pope axede of hym ʒif he hadde i-holde his oth..Þe kyng..seide 'ʒis al at þe fulle' TREVISA. *To say y.*, to assent, comply; *spec.* to accept a proposal of marriage. *Yes and No*, a round game, in which questions are asked which must be answered only by one of these words. **2.** Myn hertes greef, mote I not wepe? O yis. 1400. **b.** Knowest hym ought? *Lamaunt.* Yhe, dame, parde. *Raisoun.* Nay, nay. *Lamaunt.* Yhis, I. 1400. **3. c.** *Jew.*: May I speake with Anthonio? *Bass.* If it please you to dine with vs. *Jew.* Yes, to smell porke. SHAKS. 'It was the *best* butter.'..'Yes, but some crumbs must have got in as well.' 'L. CARROLL'. **d.** My landlady's daughter..Says 'Yes?' when you tell her anything. O. W. HOLMES. **4.** 'The race of Dermid, whose children murdered—yes,' she added, with a wild shriek, 'murdered your mother's fathers' SCOTT.

B. *sb.* (*Pl. yes's, yeses.*) An utterance of the word 'yes'; an affirmative reply, or expression of assent 1712. **Yes** *v. intr.* to say 'yes' 1820.

attrib. **Yes-man** (*U.S. slang*), a person who agrees with everything that is said to him.

Yester (ye·stəɹ), *a. poet.* 1577. [The first element of *yesterday*, etc. treated as a separate word.] Of yesterday.

Yester-, in comb. or as prefix = immediately preceding the present, last; in *y.-afternoon, -age, -noon, -week*; YESTEREVE, etc.

Yesterday (ye·stəɹdeᶦ, -di), *adv.* and *sb.* [OE. *ġeostran, ġiestran dæġ*, having one Gmc. parallel in Gothic (once) *gistradagis* tomorrow, the other langs. having only the simplex: OHG. *gestaron, gesterēn* (G. *gestern*), MLG. *ghist(e)ren*, Du. *gisteren.* Of IE. extent (exc. Balto-Sl.), the Gmc. forms showing the addition of compar. *-ter-* (cf. L. *hesternus* of yesterday) to the stem of Gr. *χθές*, Skr. *hyás*, L. *heri* yesterday.] **A.** *adv.* **1.** On the day immediately preceding the present day. Also, in reported speech, on the day before. **2.** *transf.* Not long ago, recently. late ME.

1. He..was to dine, as y., with the Frasers JANE AUSTEN. **2.** Towns that y. were hamlets 1856. Provb. phr. *Not born y.*, too old to be gulled.

B. *sb.* **1.** The day next before this; also *pl.* past days OE. **2.** *transf.* Time not long past. late ME. **3.** *attrib.* with times of the day: *y. afternoon, evening, morning, night, noon* sbs. or advs. 1654.

1. Did you receive my yesterday's note? BYRON. **2.** Lo, all our pomp of y. Is one with Nineveh and Tyre! KIPLING. So **Yestere·ve** *adv.* and *sb.* (*poet.*) 1603 = y. evening. **Yester-e·ven, -e'en** (-ĭ·n) *arch.* and *dial.* late ME. **Yester-e·vening** *adv.* and *sb. arch.* 1715 (in) the evening of y. **Yester-mo·rn** *adv.* and *sb.* (*poet.*) 1702. **Yester-mo·rning** *adv.* and *sb.* (*arch.* and *dial.*) (in) the morning of y. 1654.

Yesternight (yestəɹnəi·t), *adv.* and *sb.* Chiefly *dial.* and *arch.* [OE., f. *ġystran* (see YESTERDAY) + *niht* NIGHT *sb.*] **A.** *adv.* On the night of yesterday, last night. **B.** *sb.* The night last post 1513.

Yester-year (yestəɹyīᵊɹ). 1870. [D. G. Rossetti's rendering of Villon's *antan.*] Last year.

Yestreen (yestrī·n), *adv.* and *sb.* Chiefly *Sc.* and *poet.* late ME. [MSc. *ʒystrewin* = *ʒystir-* YESTER- + *ewin* EVEN *sb.*, in XVI contr. to *ʒistrene*; taken up by English writers in XVIII.] **A.** *adv.* On the evening of yesterday. **B.** *sb.* Yesterday evening 1816.

Yet, *v. dial.* [OE. *ġēotan* = OHG. *giozan* (G. *giessen*), ON. *gjóta*, Goth. *giutan* :– Gmc. **geut-* **gaut-* **gut-*, rel. to L. *fundere, fudi* pour.] To pour, shed; to cast (metal, a metal object).

Yet (yet), *adv.* and *conj.* [OE. *ġīet, ġīeta* = OFris. *iēta, ēta, ita*, of unkn. origin, like the synon. OE. *ġēn, ġēna.*] **A.** *adv.* **1.** In addition, or in continuation; besides; moreover. With numerals, etc. = 'more', as *y. a, y. one* = 'another', 'one more'. Now *arch.* exc. with *again* or *once more.* **b.** Used to strengthen a comparative: Even, still OE. **c.** Emphasizing *nor*: *nor y.* = and also not ME. **2.** Temporal uses: **a.** Now (or then) as before; still OE. **b.** Followed by an inf. referring to the future and thus implying incompleteness 1659. **c.** Up to this (or that) time; thus far; with a superlative, *only*, etc., = at any time up to now (or then) OE. **d.** By this (or that) time, so soon as this (or that). Usu. in questions to which the negative answer would be *not y.* ME. **e.** *Ere yet*, before the coming of the time when. *arch.* 1643. **f.** *Not* or *never yet*, not by this (or that) time, not up to now (or then): implying the possibility of subsequent change OE. **g.** With neg. following. *Obs.* or *arch.* exc. when preceded by *even* or *as.* OE. **h.** At some future time; hereafter; before all is over; after all, even now OE. **i.** Even now (though not till now); sometimes implying 'while there is still time' OE. **j.** Henceforth (or thenceforth). Usu., now only, with words denoting time; often replaceable by 'to come'. OE. **k.** *As y.*, hitherto, up to this time. late ME.

1. Yet once more, O ye Laurels..I com to pluck your Berries MILT. **b.** I purpose to dive y. more deeply into the depth of my Text 1626. **c.** I.. founde noo faute in this man..No nor yett

Herode TINDALE *Luke* 23:15. **2. a.** While her Beauty was y. in all its Height and Bloom ADDISON. Till you have finish'd these that are y. unprinted POPE. **c.** This is the queerest thing y.! SCOTT. **d.** Haue you enquir'd y. who pick'd my Pocket? SHAKS. **e.** Ere y. from Orleans to the war we went SOUTHEY. **f.** The tyme of fygges was not y. BIBLE (Great) *Mark* 11:13. **g.** Even y. not quite finished MOORE. **h.** He sees that he may y. be happy GOLDSM. **i.** Cum ȝytt, and thou schalt fynde Myne endlys mercy and grace SKELTON. **j.** There are yet xl. dayes, and then shal Niniue be ouerthrowen COVERDALE *Jonah* 3:4. **k.** I failled neuere of my trouthe as yit CHAUCER. As yet the Duke professed himself a member of the Anglican Church MACAULAY.

B. *conj. adv.* or *conj.* For all that, nevertheless, but. Sometimes preceded by *and* or *but*; sometimes strengthened by *nevertheless*, etc.; often correlative to *though*, etc. ME.

Oftymes we doo many thynges that we wene it be for the best & y. peraduenture hit torneth to the werst MALORY. Though his belief be true, y. the very truth he holds, becomes his heresie MILT. The splendid y. useless imagery SCOTT.

Yew (yū). [OE. *īw*, *ēow*, corresp. with cons.-alternation and variation in gender to OE. *ī(o)h*, *ēoh*, OS. *īh*, MLG., MDu. *iwe*, *īewe*, *uwe*, OHG. *īwu*, *īwa*, etc. (G. *eibe*), ON. *ýr* (chiefly 'bow') :- Gmc. **īχwaz*, **īȝwaz*, **īχwō*, **īȝwō*, with parallel forms in Celtic and Balto-Sl.] **1.** A tree of the genus *Taxus*, esp. the common y. of Europe and Asia, *T. baccata*, having heavy coniferous elastic wood, dark foliage, and red berries; often planted in churchyards and associated with mourning. **b.** The wood of this tree, esp. as the material of bows. late ME. **c.** Branches or sprigs of the tree, esp. as signs of mourning 1450. **2.** A bow of yew-wood 1598.

1. Beneath a Bow'r for sorrow made,..Of the black Yew's unlucky green COWLEY. **b.** Ewe of all other thynges, is that, wherof perfite shootyng woulde haue a bowe made ASCHAM. **c.** My shrowd of white, stuck all with Ew SHAKS. **2.** To send the arrow from the twanging Y. PRIOR. *attrib.* **y.-tree.** late ME. Hence **Yew·en** *a.* (*arch.*) of y.-wood or y.-trees 1563.

Yex (yeks), **yesk** (yesk), *v.* Now *Sc.* and *dial.* [OE. *ġeocsian*, *ġiscian*, corresp. to OHG. *gescōn*; of imitative origin.] †**1.** *intr.* To sob –1629. **2.** To hiccup. late ME. **3.** *trans.* To belch forth. late ME. So **Yex, yesk** *sb.* †a sob; a hiccup or the hiccups.

Yezidi, -dee (ye·zidi). 1818. [Of disputed origin.] One of a religious sect found in Kurdistan, Armenia and the Caucasus, which, while believing in a Supreme God, regards the Devil with reverential fear.

†**Yfere**, *adv.* ME. [prob. a predic. use of pl. of *yfere* sb., OE. *ġefēra* companion, f. *faran* go; see Y-, FERE *sb.*[1]] In company, together.

O goodly golden chaine, wherewith yfere The vertues linked are in louely wize SPENSER.

Yggdrasil (i·gdrăsil). [ON. *yg(g)drasill* (app. f. *Yggr*, name of Odin + *drasill* horse).] *Myth.* In later Scand. mythology, the great tree whose branches and roots extend through the universe and support it.

Yiddish (yi·diʃ), *sb.* (*a.*) 1886. [Anglicization of G. *jüdisch* (*deutsch*) Jewish (-German).] The language used by Jews in Europe and America, consisting mainly of German (orig. from the Middle Rhine area) with admixture of Balto-Slavic or Hebrew words and written in Hebrew characters. So **Yid** *U.S. slang.*, a Jew. **Yi·ddisher**, a y.-speaking Jew.

Yield (yīld), *sb.* [In senses 1, 2 OE. *ġield* payment, f. base of Gmc. **ȝelđan* (see next); in 3, f. the verb.] †**1.** Payment, a sum paid or exacted –1582. †**b.** Payment for loss or injury, compensation –1500. **2.** Recompense; retribution. ME. only. **3.** The action of yielding crops or other products; *esp.* produce 1440. **b.** The amount obtained from an investment, undertaking, tax, etc. 1877.

3. The yong plants ought daily to be plucked vp from the old, for feare of hindring the yeeld of the old 1563.

Yield (yīld), *v.* [OE. (non-WS.) *ġeldan*, (WS.) *-ġieldan* = OFris. *gelda*, *ielda*, OS. *geldan*, OHG. *geltan* (Du. *gelden*, G. *gelten*), ON. *gjalda*, Goth. *-gildan* :- Gmc. **ȝelđan* pay, requite, further cogns. of which are doubtful.] †**1.** To give in payment, render as due (money, a debt, tribute, etc.) –1652. **2.** To give (service, obedience, thanks, etc.) as due or of right, or as demanded or required. Now somewhat *arch.* OE. †**3.** To repay; to restore –1552. †**4.** To give in return for something received, to render, return (a benefit, injury, etc.) –1586. **5.** To return (an answer, greeting, or the like). Now only, to vouchsafe (an assent) *to*. ME. †**6.** With personal obj. (orig. dat.; occas. with *to*): To reward, requite, repay. Now *arch.* OE. **7.** To give forth from its own substance by a natural process or in return for cultivation or labour; to produce, bear, put forth (fruit, seed, minerals, vegetation, etc.) Now chiefly *arch.* or *poet.* ME. **b.** To furnish (a produce of so much) ME. **c.** *absol.* To bear produce ME. **8.** †**a.** To deliver, present, offer –1807. **b.** To give as a favour; to grant, accord ME. **c.** To give forth, emit, discharge. *Obs.* exc. as a weakened use of other senses. 1450. **9.** To supply for use, furnish, afford 1548. **b.** To give rise to, occasion (a state or feeling). Now *rare* 1576. **c.** To produce as profit, bring in 1573. **10.** To give up, hand over, surrender, relinquish (a place, possession, advantage, opinion, point). *arch.* or *poet.* ME. **b.** *To y. up the ghost*, *life*, etc., to die ME. **11.** *refl.* To give oneself *up*, surrender, submit, as to a conqueror. Now *rare.* ME. **12.** *intr.* To give oneself up, surrender, submit (as overcome in fight) ME. **b.** To give way, be subjected, submit 1576. **c.** To be inferior *to*. Now *rare.* 1604. **13.** To comply, give consent *to* persuasion, entreaty, etc.; to comply, submit 1500. †**b.** To consent (*to do* something, *that* something should be done, etc.) –1814. **14.** *trans.* To admit, confess: †**a.** with compl. adj. or adj. phr. –1744. †**b.** with clause or acc. and inf. –1703. **c.** With simple obj. Now *rare.* 1571. **15.** *intr.* To give way under some natural or mechanical force, so as to collapse, bend, stretch, crack, etc. 1552. **b.** To submit *to* some physical action or agent (e.g. pressure, friction, heat) so as to be affected by it 1794.

3. Yeld eftesones a thinge receiued, or taken 1552. **4.** It with kinde nevere stod A man to yelden evil for good GOWER. **6.** Tend me to night two houres, I aske no more, And the Gods yeeld you for't SHAKS. **7.** For want of seede, land yeeldeth weede 1573. **8. b.** To y. him loue she doth deny SPENSER. The King yielded the citizens the right of justice 1874. **9.** The narrow valley..yielded fresh pasturage W. IRVING. **b.** Curved forms and winding movements y. of themselves a certain satisfaction 1855. **10.** The besieged did yeeld the place to the Queene 1617. Constantius, yielding to fear what he denied to justice NEWMAN. **b.** He..yeelded vp the ghost, and was gathered vnto his people *Gen.* 49:33. **11.** I yelde my self prisoner to you 1560. **12.** England shall couch downe in feare, and yeeld SHAKS. **b.** The night has yielded to the morn SCOTT. **c.** Their mutton yields to ours SWIFT. **13.** I haue yeelded vnto those of my freindes which pressed me in the matter HAKLUYT. **b.** How hast thou yeelded to transgress The strict forbiddance? MILT. **14. a.** ȝeldynge him self gylty, and cryenge him mercy 1400.

Comb.: **y.-capacity**, capacity for producing; **-point**, the degree of force at which a particular substance, etc. begins to yield (see 15). Hence **Yie·lder**, one who or that which yields or produces, now esp. with qualifying word referring to the amount or quality of the produce.

Yie·lding, *ppl. a.* ME. [f. prec. + -ING[2].] †**1.** Indebted. ME. only. †**2.** Productive, fertile –1777. **3.** Submissive, compliant, unresisting 1578. **4.** Not rigid, giving way to pressure or other physical force 1577. Hence **Yie·ldingly** *adv.*, **-ness.**

Yike (yəik), *sb.* 1891. [imit.] An imitation of the cry of the woodpecker. So **Yike** *v.* 1889.

Yill, Sc. var. of ALE.

Yite (yəit). *dial.* 1812. [Of unkn. origin.] The yellow-hammer.

-yl (il, əil), a terminal element of chemical terms, – Fr. *-yle*, f. Gr. ὕλη wood, substance, used for 'chemical principle, radical'. It is used in forming the names of radicals compounded of two or three elements in various atomic proportions, which behave in combination like simple elements and are the constant bases of series of compounds; the majority are compounds of carbon and hydrogen, either alone, as *amyl*, *ethyl*, or with oxygen, as *acetyl*.

Ylang-ylang (ī·læŋ ī·læŋ). 1876. [Tagalog *álang-ilang*.] A Malaysian tree (*Cananġium odoratum*) with fragrant greenish-yellow flowers; hence, the perfume distilled from these.

Yo (yōu), *int.* late ME. An exclamation of incitement, warning, etc. In nautical use = YOHO.

Yod (yǫd, yōud). 1735. **1.** The name of the tenth (the smallest) letter in the Hebrew alphabet. **2.** *Philol.* The consonantal *i* = (y), the front voiced open consonant, denoted in prehistoric forms by *j*. Cf. IOTA, JOT.

†**Yode, yede**, *v.* [Early ME. *ȝeode*, *ȝede*, var. of *eode*, *ede* (OE. *ēode*).] Past tense of GO *v.* –1808.

So forth they yode, and forward softly paced SPENSER. In other pace than forth he yode, Returned Lord Marmion SCOTT.

Yodel (yōu·dĕl), *v.* Also **jodel.** 1830. [– G. *jodeln*.] *intr.* To sing or warble with interchange of falsetto and the natural voice, in the manner of Swiss and Tyrolese mountaineers. **b.** *trans.* To utter (a song, refrain) thus. Hence **Yo·del, jo·del** *sb.* a melody or musical phrase sung thus. **Yo·del(l)er.**

Yoga (yōu·gă). 1820. [Hind., Skr. *yoga* lit. union, YOKE.] In Hindu philosophy, union with the Supreme Spirit; a system of ascetic practice, abstract meditation, and mental concentration, pursued as a method of obtaining this.

Yogh (yǫg, yoʏ). Also **ȝok**, etc. ME. The name of the ME. letter ȝ; see G, Y.

‖**Yogi** (yōu·gi). 1619. [Hind. *yogī* (Skr. *yogin*), f. YOGA.] An Indian devotee practising YOGA. So **Yo·gism, Yo·geeism**, the system of yoga.

‖**Yogurt** (yōu·guəɹt). 1625. [Turkish *yoġurt*. Cf. YAOURT.] A sour semi-solid food made from fermented milk, orig. in Turkey and other countries of the Levant.

Yo-heave-ho (yōu hī·vhōu), *int.* (*sb.*) Also **yeo-**. 1803. [See YO *int.* and HEAVE HO.] A sailor's accompaniment to hauling and heaving motions.

Yohi·mbenine, Yohi·mbine. 1898. [See def. and -INE[5].] *Chem.* Either of two colourless alkaloids obtained from the bark and leaves of a W. African tree, the *yohimbé*.

Yoho, yo-ho (yŏhōu·), *int.* 1769. [See YO *int.*, HO *int.*[3]] An exclamation (orig. *Naut.*) used to call attention; also occas. used like YO-HEAVE-HO. Hence **Yoho·** *v. intr.* to shout 'yoho!'

Yoi, *int.* 1826. A huntsman's cry to encourage the hounds.

Yoicks (yoiks), *int.* 1774. [app. related to HYKE *int.* (*hike hallow*, *hyke a Bewmont*, Turberville).] A fox-hunting cry urging on the hounds; also *gen.* as an exclam. of excitement or exultation. Hence **Yoicks, yoick** *v. int.* to cry 'y.!'; *trans.* to urge on with this cry.

‖**Yojan** (yōu·dʒăn), **yojana** (yōu·dʒănă). *India.* 1784. [Hindi *yójan*, Skr. *yójana* yoking, distance travelled at one time without unyoking, f. *yóga*; see next.] A measure of distance, varying locally from about four to ten miles.

Yoke (yōuk), *sb.* [OE. *ġeoc* = OS. *juc*, OHG. *joh* (Du. *juk*, G. *joch*), ON. *ok*, Goth. *juk* :- Gmc. **jukam* :- IE. **jugom*, corresp. to L. *jugum*, Gr. ζυγόν, Skr. *yugám*, f. **jug-*, repr. also by L. *jungere* join, Gr. ζευγνύναι, Skr. YOGA.] **1.** A contrivance by which two oxen or other beasts are coupled together for drawing a plough or vehicle; usu. a curved bar of wood fitted with 'bows' or hoops at each end which are passed round the beasts' necks, and having an attachment in the middle for the trace or chain OE. **b.** A similar appliance anciently placed on the neck of a captive or conquered enemy; a symbol of this, consisting of three spears arranged as an arch beneath which vanquished enemies were forced to pass by the ancient Romans and others OE. **2.** A wooden frame fixed on an animal's neck to prevent it from breaking through or leaping over a hedge, fence, etc. 1573. **3.** A frame fitted to the neck and shoulders of a person for carrying a pair of pails, baskets, etc. 1618. **b.** A part of a garment, made to fit the shoulders (or the hips), and supporting the depending parts 1882. **4.** Applied to various objects resembling the yoke of a plough. late ME. **b.** *Naut.* A board or bar fixed transversely to the head of the rudder, and having two ropes (*y.-lines*) attached for steering 1625. **5.** *transf.* A pair of animals, esp. oxen, that are or may be coupled by a yoke (in this sense the pl. after a numeral is freq. *yoke*) OE. **6.** A quarter of a SULING, about 50 or 60 acres; hence, later applied vaguely to small manors OE. **7.** *fig.* or in fig. phrases denoting servitude, subjection, restraint, etc. OE. **b.** Co-operation, union; the marriage bond. late ME.

1. In time the sauage Bull doth beare the yoake SHAKS. **b.** His army was routed, and passed under the y. 1875. **2.** I have..seen a number of hens all wearing yokes 1886. **3.** The speaker, who had been carrying a pair of pails on a y. HARDY. **5.** A deep well whence they draw water, with a wheel turned round by a y. of Bulls 1660. A M. yock oxen COVERDALE *Job* 42:12. [A.V. a thousand yoke of oxen.] **7.** He brouȝte alle þe kynges þat were nyh hym under his ȝok TREVISA. **b.** We haue byn ioyned togyther with the y. of holy matrimonie 1555.

Comb.: **y.-band,** a band for fastening the y. to the pole; **-elm,** the hornbeam, the wood of which is used for yokes; **-fellow,** a person 'yoked' or associated with another; a fellow-worker, *spec.* a husband or wife, spouse; **-mate** (now *rare*), a y.-fellow.

Yoke, *v.* [OE. *ġeocian*, f. *ġeoc* YOKE *sb.*] **1.** *trans.* To put a yoke on (draught beasts); to couple with a yoke OE. **2.** To attach (a draught-animal) *to* a plough or vehicle; to 'put in', 'put to'. late ME. **b.** With the plough or vehicle as object 1568. **c.** *fig.* To set (a person, force, etc.) to work; to harness 1606. **3.** To fasten a yoke round the neck of (a hog, etc.) 1530. **4.** To suspend (a heavy bell) on a yoke 1701. **5.** To bring into or hold in subjection or servitude; to subjugate, oppress. Now *rare* or *Obs.* ME. **6.** *fig.* To. join, link, couple, connect ME. **b.** With ref. to marriage; only in *pa. pple.* 1604. **7.** *intr.* (for *refl.*), To consort, to be associated or matched. Now *rare.* 1500.

1. It was cautioned in the Law not to yoake an Oxe, and an Asse together 1641. **2.** Lions have been yoked to the chariots of conquerors GOLDSM. **b.** Without his license the pleugh cannot be yoked 1638. **c.** It is by wisdom and knowledge that the Forces of Nature ..are yoked to service 1867. **3.** You muste y. your hogge, for he ronneth thorowe every hedge PALSGR. **5.** But foul effeminacy held me yok't Her Bond-slave MILT. **6.** Oh then,..my Name Be yoak'd with his, that did betray the Best SHAKS. **b.** He that is yoaked with a wife must not put her away 1632. **7.** 'Twere pittie, to sunder them, That yoake so well together SHAKS. Hence **Yo·keless** *a.* (*rare*) used as tr. L. *absque jugo* 'without yoke', Jerome's explanation of *b'li-yasal* BELIAL. **Yo·king** *vbl. sb.*; *spec.* a spell of work at the plough or with a cart, etc., done at a stretch.

Yokel (yōᵘ·k'l). 1812. [perh. a fig. application of dial. *yokel* green woodpecker, yellowhammer.] A countryman, rustic; a country bumpkin.

Yokohama (yōᵘkohā·mă). 1882. The name of a city in Japan, used as a specific epithet of a breed of fowls, etc.; also as *sb.* (*ellipt.*).

Yo·ldring, ye·ldring. *Sc.* and *north. dial.* 1790. [var. of earlier †*yowlring*, f. *yowlo(w* YELLOW + RING *sb.*] A yellow-hammer.

Yolk¹, yelk (yōᵘk, *formerly* yelk). [OE. *ġeoloca, ġeolca*, f. *ġeolu* YELLOW. The sp. *yelk*, still found in techn. and scientific works, is otherwise now rare.] **1.** The yellow internal part of an egg, surrounded by the 'white' or albumen, and serving as nourishment for the young before it is hatched. **b.** *Biol.* Extended to the part in any animal ovum that nourishes the embryo (*nutritive* or *food-y*) and to the protoplasmic substance from which the embryo is developed (*formative* or *germ-y.*) 1835. †**2.** *fig.* Centre; innermost part, 'core' –1730. **3.** (Also *y. of egg*) A gasteropod of the genus *Nerita*, from the appearance of its shell 1796. **4.** A rounded opaque or semi-opaque part in window-glass 1808.

An Addle-egg with double Yoalk 1666. Beat up the yolks of three eggs MRS. HAYWOOD. The leather is..soaked in liquor made of the yelks of eggs 1884.

attrib. and *Comb.*: **y.-bag, -sac,** the sac or vesicle enclosing the y., esp. when attached to the umbilicus, as an organ of nutrition; it is connected with the embryo by the **y.-duct** or **y.-stalk; y.-cleavage,** the division of the (formative) y. as the initial process in the development of the embryo. Hence **Yolked** (yōᵘkt) *ppl. a.* (chiefly in comb., as *double-y.*). **Yo·lkless** *a.*

Yolk² (yōᵘk). 1607. [repr. OE. **eowoca*, see YOLKY *a.*²; cf. Flem. *ieke*, whence Sc. *eik.*] The greasy substance secreted by the sebaceous glands in the skin of a sheep, which serves to moisten and soften the wool; also called *suint*, *wool-oil*, and *lanolin*.

Yolky (yōᵘ·ki), *a.*¹ 1528. [f. YOLK¹ + Y¹.] Like, of, or abounding in (egg) yolk.

Yolky (yōᵘ·ki), *a.*² [OE. *eowociġ*, f. **eowoca*; see YOLK², -Y¹.] Containing 'yolk'; greasy with yolk, as unwashed wool.

Yon (yǫn), *dem. a.*, *pron.* and *dem. adv.* [OE. *ġeon*, corresp., with variation of vowels, to OFris. *jen(a, -e*, MLG. *gene*, MDu. *ghens*, OHG. *jenēr* (G. *jener* that one), Goth. *jains* that; there is a parallel series of forms without cons. initial, viz. OHG. *enēr*, ON. *enn, inn* (def. art.), cogn. with Gr. ἔνη day after tomorrow, ἔνιοι some, Skr. *āna-* this one.] **A.** *adj.* That, those; applied chiefly to what is visible but not close: = 'that' (those)..over there'. *arch.* and *dial.* **B.** *pron.* The adj. used *absol.*: = 'That *or* those' (over there). Now only *Sc.* and *dial.* ME. **C.** *dem. adv.* = YONDER *adv. Obs.* exc. *dial.* 1475. **b.** *Hither and y.*, hither and thither, this way and that. *dial.* 1787.

A. Because of his being of this or this, or that, or y., or of that other Religion 1652. **B.** Was y. the messenger? SCOTT. **C.** But..with thee bring, Him that y. soars on golden wing MILT. **b.** She swayed hither and y. 1836.

Yond (yǫnd), *a.*, *pron.*, *prep.*, and *adv. Obs.* exc. *dial.* [OE. *ġeond* (*iand*), which enters into some 35 comps., corresp. to MLG. *gent, genten, jint*, LG. *gunt, gunten*, early Flem. *ghins*, Du. *ginds*, Goth. *jaind* thither; cf. BEYOND, AYOND.] **A.** *adj.* †**1.** Qualifying *half, side*, or the like. The farther, 'the other' –1623. **2.** = prec. A. ME. **B.** *pron.* That or those person(s) or thing(s) ME. **C.** *prep.* †**1.** Over, throughout, across –ME. **2.** On (or to) the farther side of, beyond. Now *poet.* or *Sc.* late ME. **D.** *adv.* = YONDER *adv.* Now *dial.* OE.

A. 1. To y. side o' th' riuer lies a wall WEBSTER. **2.** Y. same Starre that's Westward from the Pole SHAKS. **B.** Who is yonde that for the dothe call? SKELTON. **C. 1.** He..sette tweyne and tweyne to gon ȝond al þe world to prechen vchon 1320. **2.** Thou God of grace,..y. whome we can not roaue Or raunge aright 1579. **D.** Say what thou see'st y. SHAKS.

Yonder (yǫ·ndəɹ), *adv.*, *a.*, and *pron.* Now only *literary* and somewhat *arch.* or *dial.* [ME. *ȝonder* (beside *ȝender*), corresp. to OS. *gendra* (adj.), WFris. *ginder* (adj.) on this side, MDu. *ghinder, gunder* (Du. *ginder*), Goth. *jaindrē*.] **A.** *adv.* At or in that place; there: usu. implying that the object spoken of is at some distance but within sight; over there, away there. **b.** To that place, thither ME. **c.** *Here* (*hither*) *and y.*, here and there, to and fro. late ME.

But, as I live, y. comes Moses GOLDSM. **b.** As for me and the childe, we wyl go y. COVERDALE.

B. *adj.* **1.** With *the*. Farther, more distant, 'other'. late ME. **2.** That is yonder. late ME.

1. O she was fair as a beech in May With the sun on the y. side MEREDITH. **2.** Y. bank hath choice of Sun or shade MILT.

C. *pron. sing.* or *pl.* = YON *pron.* Now *dial.* late ME.

An inquiry whether 'y. was a lad or a lass' 1880.

Yondmost (yǫ·ndməst), *a. Sc.* 1608. [f. YOND *a.* + -MOST.] Farthest, extreme, uttermost.

‖**Yoni** (yōᵘ·ni). 1799. [Skr.] A figure or symbol of the female organ of generation as an object of veneration among Hindus and others.

Yonside (yǫ·nsəid), *sb.*, *adv.* and *prep.* Now *dial.* and *literary*. 1535. [f. YON *a.* + SIDE *sb.*; cf. INSIDE, OUTSIDE; thus LG. *gunsiet, -syts*, G. *jenseits*.] **A.** *sb.* The farther side. **B.** *adv.* On the farther side (*of*) 1681. **C.** *prep.* Beyond 1856.

Yoop (yūp), *sb.* and *int.* 1848. A word expressing the sound made by convulsive sobbing.

Yore (yōᵊɹ), *adv. arch.* [OE. *ġeāra, ġeāre, ġeāro*, advb. formations of obsc. origin.] †**1.** A long time ago, of old –1613. †**2.** Formerly, before –1574. †**3.** For a long time (past, or *rarely* to come) –1522. **4. Of yore: a.** *advb.* Of old, anciently, formerly. late ME. **b.** as *adj.*: Ancient, former 1598.

4. a. A form, not now gymnastic as of y. COWPER. **b.** This is altogether different from the village politics of y. COLERIDGE.

York (yǭɹk), *sb.* [OE. *Eoforwic*, ME. *Everwik, Yerk, York* – L. *Eboracum* + *wīc* dwelling.] **1.** The name of the capital of Yorkshire, used attrib. in names of things originating from or peculiar to York or Yorkshire, as *Y. ham, tan* 1794. **b.** Short for *Yorkshire cabbage* 1823. **2.** *attrib.* Pertaining to the royal house of York; *spec.* = YORKIST 1 b. late ME. **3.** One of the heralds of the College of Arms 1630.

1. Y. paving, paving with Yorkshire stone. **Y. pitch** (of a plane) an angle of the iron of 50°; hence **Y.-pitched** *a.* **2. Y. pence** copper coins of the reign of Henry VI.

York (yǭɹk), *v.* 1888. [Back-formation f. YORKER².] *Cricket. trans.* To bowl (a batsman) out or strike (the wicket) with a yorker.

Yorker¹ (yǭ·ɹkəɹ). 1599. [f. YORK *sb.* + -ER¹.] **1.** An inhabitant of York or Yorkshire. **2.** An inhabitant or soldier of New York 1776.

Yorker² (yǭ·ɹkəɹ). 1870. [prob. f. YORK *sb.* + -ER¹, as being introduced by Yorkshire players.] *Cricket.* A ball that pitches directly beneath the bat.

Yorkish (yǭ·ɹkiʃ), *a. rare.* 1548. [f. YORK *sb.* + -ISH¹.] = next 1 b.

Yorkist (yǭ·ɹkist), *sb.* (*a.*) 1601. [f. YORK *sb.* (see below) + -IST.] **1.** An adherent of the royal house of York, which descended from Lionel, Duke of Clarence, and Edmund, Duke of York, third and fifth sons of Edward III; or one of the party (whose emblem was the white rose) which supported this family in the Wars of the Roses. **b.** as *adj.* 1823. **2.** A supporter of the claim of James, Duke of York, to succeed his brother, Charles II. 1681.

Yorkshire (yǭ·ɹkʃəɹ, -ʃiᵊɹ). 1683. [f. YORK *sb.* + SHIRE.] The largest of the counties of England. **1.** *attrib.* Of, made or grown or used in, characteristic of Yorkshire. **2.** *allus.*, esp. with ref. to the bargaining skill, cunning, or sharp practices attributed to Yorkshire people. Phr. *To come* or *put Y. on* (a person), to dupe or overreach (him). 1620. **3.** *ellipt.* as the designation of thick coarse cloth made in Yorkshire, a breed of canary, (pl.) soldiers of a Yorkshire regiment; also, short for *Y. dialect*, etc. 1726.

1. *Y. ale, cabbage, grit* (GRIT *sb.*¹ 2), *kidney* (potato), *stone, tyke* (TYKE 3); **Y. pudding,** a batter-pudding cooked under a joint of meat or in meat juice. **Y. terrier,** one of a small shaggy breed. Hence **Yorkshireman** (yǭ·ɹkʃəɹmæ̆n), a man of Y.

You (yū, yŭ), *pers. pron., 2nd pers. obj.* (*nom.*), *pl.* (*sing.*). [OE. *ēow, ēow* (also *ēowic*, Northumb. *iuih*) = OFris. *ju*, OS. *ju* (Du. *u*), OHG. dat. *iu, eu*, acc. *iuwih, iuh* (G. *euch*) :– WGmc. **iwwi(z*, paralleled by **izwiz* in ON. *yðr*, Goth. *izwis*. See THOU. Orig. restricted to acc. and dat. pl. uses, *you* gradually replaced *ye* as nom. pl. in XIV–XV, and also by extension of the deferential plural (see YE) came into general use for *thou* and *thee*; it is now, in ordinary use, the 2nd pers. pron. for any number and case.] **1.** As *pl.* The persons or things addressed: **a.** As direct or indirect obj. of a vb., or as obj. of a prep. **b.** As *refl. pron.* Yourselves. *arch.* OE. **c.** As *nom.* = YE ME. **d.** As *vocative*, chiefly in apposition with a sb. following 1569. **e.** In apposition with a sb., a numeral, *all*, or *both* ME. **2.** As sing., used in addressing a person (or thing); orig. as a mark of respect, later *gen.* **a.** As direct or ind. obj. of a vb., or obj. of a prep.: Thee ME. **b.** As *refl. pron.* Thyself, yourself. *arch.* late ME. **c.** As *nom.* replacing THOU. late ME. **d.** As *vocative*, chiefly in apposition with a sb. following; in reproach or contempt often repeated after the sb. 1500. **3.** Any hearer or reader, any one concerned 1577. **b.** Used with no definite meaning as indirect obj. ('ethic dative') 1590. **4.** Qualified by a preceding adj. 1600. **5.** As *sb.*: **a.** The word as used in addressing a person or persons 1645. **b.** The person (or such a person as the one) addressed 1700.

1. a. I graunte you leue, seyth what yow semyth 1400. Ryght trusty & wele-beloued, we grete yewe wele 1482. I will..make y. both friends 1607. You have killed me between y. 1896. **b.** Home y. idle Creatures, get y. home SHAKS. **c.** What ye rede, se you practise it in lyfe and dede 1526. Do y. assure us that y. are all sound men? DE FOE. **d.** Farwell y. Ladies of the Court 1569. **e.** If y. men durst not vndertake it.. women would 1596. *You-all* (U.S.) = YOU (as sing. or plur.) 1919. **2. a.** Myn lord,..þis ringe, þat I yu present now, Me gafe a pilgram to gyf ȝow 1375. Unto you that bene a member of chirche 1455. Hold, woman, hold!..the dog will not do y. harm SCOTT. **b.** Pray set it downe, and rest y...Pray now rest your selfe. SHAKS. **c.** 'Syr Gye', he seyde,..'To morowe schall yow weddyd bee.' late ME. Old year, y. shall not go TENNYSON. **d.** Fie, fie, y. counterfeit, y. puppet, y. SHAKS. **3.** Nay more, y. shall haue Atheists striue to get Disciples BACON. Y. can talk a mob into anything RUSKIN. **b.** I will roare y. as gently as any Sucking Doue SHAKS. **5. a.** Several Sober Reasons against Hat-Honour, Titular Respects, Y. to a Single Person PENN. **b.** If your flesh and blood be new, You'll be no more the former y. SWIFT.

Phrasal combs.: **y.-be-damned** *a.*, addicted to saying 'y. be damned!'; contemptuously overbearing; **y.-know-what,** used instead of the name of something which it is needless or undesirable to specify. Hence **You** *v. trans.* to address (a person) as 'you' (instead of 'thou').

Young (yɒŋ). *a.* (*sb.*) See also YOUNGER, YOUNGEST. [OE. *ġ(e)ong, ġung,* later *iung* = OFris., OS. *jung,* OHG. *junc* (Du. *jong,* G. *jung*), ON. *ungr,* Goth. *juggs* :- Gmc. **juŋgaz,* contr. of **juwuŋgaz* :- IE. **juwŋkós,* repr. by Skr. *juvaçás,* youthful, L. *juvencus* young bull.] **A.** *adj.* **1.** That has lived a relatively short time; not mature or fully developed; youthful: opp. to OLD *a.* I. 1. **b.** Used to distinguish the younger of two persons of the same name or title in a family (esp. a son from his father) ME. **2.** *transf.* Belonging or pertaining to a young person or persons, or to youth OE. **3.** Having the characteristics of young persons, or of youth; *esp.* having the vigour or freshness of youth 1513. **4.** That has newly or not long since entered upon some course of action, or having the character of such a one; newly or recently initiated; 'raw' OE. **5.** Of a thing: That is in an early stage or phase; lately begun, formed, introduced, etc.; not far advanced; recent, new. late ME. **b.** Applied to the moon in the early part of the lunar month, soon after 'new moon'. late ME. **6.** *fig.* Small, diminutive, miniature, not full-sized. Now *colloq.* and *joc.* 1550.

1. Philip..died y. before his Father 1617. That they might..set a meet example to the *y. folk* SCOTT. The heart wood is..of a darker colour than the soft or y. wood 1842. The expression 'y. person' means a person under eighteen years of age who is no longer a child *Act* 8 & 9 *Geo. V,* c. 39, § 48. *Y. one,* a young person; *pl.* offspring, progeny; *y. 'un* (colloq.) = YOUNGSTER. See also YOUNG LADY, YOUNG MAN, YOUNG WOMAN. **b.** The chief leaders, Nathaniel Fynes and y. Sir H. Vane CLARENDON. **2.** Hauyng a yonge and a lusty courage,..he set on hys enemyes 1548. A remnant of my y. days 1852. **3.** To se the a quene wyll make vs yonge agayne 1513. Mr. Gresham was y. for his age TROLLOPE. **4.** I was but y. at the work DE FOE. We are still so y. in the study of Nature 1796. **5.** A little yonge yellowe bearde 1569. *Rom.* Is the day so y.? *Ben.* But new strooke nine SHAKS. A severe tax on a y. concern not earning profits 1913. **6.** Such a weapon is really a y. cannon 1885.

B. *absol.* or as *sb.* **1.** *absol.* in pl. sense (with def. art., or in *y. and old, old and y.*): Young people OE. **2.** Young animals collectively in relation to the parent; offspring 1484. **b.** Phr. *With* (also *in*) *y.*, of a female animal: Pregnant 1535.

1. Thus there was killing of yong and old 2 *Macc.* 5:13. That Vigour which the Y. possess STEELE. **2.** The brindled lioness led forth her y. SHELLEY.

Collocations and *Comb.*: **a.** (with the names of countries, etc., in the designations of political parties chiefly composed of y. men, as **Y. England,** name assumed by a group of Tory politicians in the early part of the reign of Queen Victoria (hence **Y.-Englander, Y.-Englandism**); **Y. Europe,** the republican agitators of various countries (*Y. France, Y. Italy,* etc.) working together after the July revolution (1830) in France; **Y. Ireland,** Irish agitators of 1840–50. **Y. Pretender** (see PRETENDER 1 c); **Y. Turk,** a member of a party of Turkish agitators which brought about the revolution of 1908. (Such phrases may also be used in gen. sense, as *Y. England* = the typical young Englishman, or the rising generation of Englishmen.) **b. y.-eyed** *a.* having the bright or lively eyes of a y. person; **y.-old,** vigorous or young in disposition in spite of age; **y. thing,** said playfully or indulgently of a child or woman. Hence **Youngish** *a.* somewhat y. **Young-like** *a.* resembling one that is y.

Younger (yɒ·ŋgəɹ), *a.* (*sb.*) OE. [f. YOUNG *a.* + -ER³. (The normal mutated OE. *ġyngra, ġingra* did not survive.)] The comparative of YOUNG *a.* **1.** Of less age: opp. to ELDER *a.*, OLDER. Also *absol.* or as *sb.* **b.** Used after a person's name for distinction from an older person of the same name. Chiefly *Sc.* late ME. **c.** Belonging to the earlier part of life, earlier 1578. **2.** Less advanced in practice or experience, later, more recent 1593. **b.** *Y. hand,* at cards, the second player in a two-handed game 1744.

1. It is fit that the yonger obey the elder 1612. Not many a moon his y. TENNYSON. The y. brother may not marry the elder brother's widows 1897. **c.** To shake all cares and busines of our state, Confirming them on yonger yeares SHAKS. **2.** The y. the science, the smaller will be the amount of known facts 1874.

Youngest (yɒ·ŋgést), *a.* OE. [f. YOUNG *a.* + -EST. (The normal mutated OE. form *ġyngest, ġingest* did not survive.)] The superlative degree of YOUNG *a.*: opp. to ELDEST, OLDEST, in uses corresp. to those of prec. **b.** *Y. hand,* at cards, the last player, or the last except the dealer 1680.

Young lady. late ME. **1.** A young woman, usu. unmarried, of superior social position: formerly often used to connote the primness, etc. attributed to these. (Now, exc. in old-fashioned polite use or as playfully applied to a girl, only applied, with the intention of avoiding the implications of *young woman,* to female shop assistants or clerks of good appearance and manners.) **2.** A fiancée. *vulgar* or *joc.* 1896.

1. Young Lady Wanted, with good experience, as Book-keeper 1920.

Youngling (yɒ·ŋliŋ). *arch.* [OE. *ġeongling;* see YOUNG, -LING¹.] **1.** A young person. †**b.** A beginner, novice, tiro –1682. **2.** A young animal ME. **3.** A young plant, sapling; a young shoot or blossom of a plant 1559. **4.** *attrib.* That is a 'youngling'; youthful; pertaining to or characteristic of a 'youngling', juvenile. late ME.

1. Like as a yongling that to schoole is set QUARLES. **b.** Younglynges in the feith UDALL. **2.** The linnet..was bringing out her younglings 1772. **3.** Masses of precipitous ruin, overgrown with the younglings of the forest SHELLEY. **4.** The y. Cottagers retire to rest BURNS.

Youngly (yɒ·ŋli), *adv.* Now *rare.* 1530. [f. YOUNG *a.* + -LY².] **1.** In youth 1559. **2.** In a youthful way 1530.

Young man. late OE. **1.** One in early manhood. Also applied playfully to a boy. **b.** A youth employed by a tradesman, etc. 1751. **2.** A lover; a fiancé. *vulgar* or *joc.* 1851.

Youngness (yɒ·ŋnės). 1510. [f. YOUNG *a.* + -NESS.] The state or quality of being young; youthfulness 1528. †**b.** The time when one is young, one's youth –1579.

Youngster (yɒ·ŋstəɹ). Chiefly *colloq.* 1589. [f. YOUNG *a.* + -STER, suggested by YOUNKER.] **1.** A young person, *esp.* a young man: now usu. connoting inexperience or immaturity. **2.** Familiarly applied to a boy or junior seaman on board ship; also to a junior officer in the army or navy 1608. **3.** A child, *esp.* a boy. *colloq.* 1732. **4.** A young animal 1849.

Young woman. late OE. **1.** One in early womanhood. Also applied playfully to a girl. **2.** A female sweetheart; a fiancée. *vulgar* or *joc.* 1858.

Younker (yɒ·ŋkəɹ). 1505. [– MDu. *jonckher* = *jonc* YOUNG + *hēre* lord; cf. JUNKER.] †**1.** A young nobleman or gentleman (orig. Dutch or German) –1645. **2.** A young man, in early use *esp.* a gay or fashionable young man 1513. †**b.** = YOUNGSTER 2 –1818. **3.** A child. Now *rare.* 1601.

Your (yūᵊɹ, *usu. unemphatic* yŭɹ, yǒɹ), *poss. pron.* and *a.* [(i) OE. *ēower,* usu. in partitive sense, gen. of *ġē* YE, corresp. to OFris. *iuwer,* OS. *iuwar,* OHG. *iuwēr* (G. *euer*); cf. ON. *yðr,* Goth. *izwara;* (ii) OE. *ēower* masc. and n., *ēowru* fem., poss. adj. corresp. to OHG. *iuwar* (G. *euer*); cf. ON. *yð(v)arr,* Goth. *izwar.*] †**1.** As genit. of the 2nd pers. pron.: Of you (*pl.*, in partitive sense). late ME. **2.** As poss. pron. and adj. of the 2nd pers.: Of or belonging to you, that you have. **a.** as poss. pl., referring to a number of persons addressed OE. **b.** as poss. sing., referring to one person addressed ME. **c.** In titles of honour substituted for *you* in addressing a person (or persons) of high rank, as *y. Excellency, y. Honour, y. Majesty.* late ME. **d.** Qualifying a sb. denoting the speaker or writer himself, esp. in the subscription of a letter. late ME. †**3.** *absol.* or as *pron.* = YOURS. –1625. **4.** Used more or less vaguely of something which the person(s) addressed may be expected to possess, or to have to do with in some way ME. **b.** Without definite meaning, or vaguely implying 'that you know of': often expressing contempt 1568. **5.** As poss. of the indef. pron. (YOU 3) One's, any one's 1598.

2. b. 'Madame, mercy,' quod I 'me liketh wel ȝowre wordes' LANGL. **d.** Yoʳ loving Father Charles R. CHAS. I. **3.** For ye are myne and i am y. 1400. **4.** The most ancient of all histories, you will read in y. Bible 1773. **b.** There is not a more fearefull wilde foule then y. Lyon liuing SHAKS. I hate y. accomplished women FITZGERALD. **5.** Here there is no living without them [curtains], one whole side of y. house being glass 1708.

Yourn (yūᵊɹn), *poss. pron. dial.* late ME. [f. prec. + *-n* as in HERN, HISN, OURN.] = next.

Yours (yūᵊɹz), *poss. pron.* ME. Also (now illiterate) **your's.** [f. YOUR + *-s* as in HERS, OURS.] The absol. form of YOUR, used when no sb. follows: That or those belonging to you. **1.** *predic.* late ME. **b.** In the subscription of a letter, often qualified by an adv. or advb. phr. late ME. **c.** = Your affair or task 1841. **2.** Standing for *your* and a sb. to be supplied from the context ME. **b.** Those who belong to you; your relations or friends: chiefly in *you and yours* ME. **c.** = Your letter, the letter from you. (Now chiefly commercial.) 1536. **3.** Used instead of *your* before another possessive, etc., qualifying the same sb. Now *rare* or *Obs.* 1534. **4.** *Of yours,* that is yours, belonging to you ME.

1. b. *Y. truly,* etc., *joc.* for 'I' or 'me', 'myself'; The verdict will be 'Guilty..' against y. truly 1860. **c.** Be it your's to help him 1841. **4.** She hath that Ring of y. SHAKS.

Yourself (yuᵊɹse·lf), *pron.* [ME. *ȝour selfe, ȝour selven;* see SELF.] The emphatic and reflexive pronoun corresp. to *you* (now only in sing. sense). **b.** In pregnant sense: Your being or personality; also, you as you are in your natural or normal condition 1590. **c.** Used as simple subject, with the vb. either in the pl. or in the 3rd pers. sing. late ME.

Ye proude galants that thus your selfe disguise 1509. Here is a Table of Latitudes..and the way to calculate it your self 1669. Not one of them equals y. or Southey 1807. **b.** What euill starre On you hath frownd,..That of your selfe ye thus berobbed are SPENSER. You will soon come to y. again FIELDING. **c.** Madam, your selfe is not exempt from this SHAKS. Conversation is but carving; Carve for all, y. is starving SWIFT.

Yourselves (yuᵊɹse·lvz), *pron. pl.* 1526. [f. prec. with pl. inflexion.] The emphatic and reflexive pronoun corresp. to *you* in pl. sense: replacing the earlier *yourself.*

‖**Yourt** (yūᵊɹt). 1784. [= Russ. *yurta,* through Fr. *yourte* or G. *jurte.*] A semi-subterranean native hut of northern and central Asia, usu. formed of timber covered with earth or turf.

Youth (yūþ). [OE. *ġeoguþ,* (late) *iuguþ* = OFris. *jogethe,* OS. *juguð* (Du. *jeugd*), OHG. *jugund* (G. *jugend*) :- WGmc. **juȝunþ-,* alt. of **juwunþ-* (cf. L. *juventa, -tus,* Goth. *junda*), f. **ȝuwuŋ-* YOUNG; see -TH¹.] **1.** The fact or state of being young; youngness. **b.** *fig.* Newness, recentness 1596. **2.** The early part of life, esp. the period between childhood and adult age OE. **b.** *transf.* and *fig.* Early stage of existence 1602. **3.** A quality or condition characteristic of the young; e.g. freshness, vigour, wantonness, rashness, youthful appearance OE. **4.** Personified, or vaguely denoting any young person or persons. late ME. **5.** Young people, the young. Now always construed as *pl.* OE. **6.** A young person; *esp.* a young man between boyhood and mature age ME.

1. b. If that the y. of my new interest here Have

power to bid you welcome SHAKS. **2.** The ymaginacion of mans hert is euell, euen from the very y. of him COVERDALE *Gen.* 8:21. **3.** Though..that youthe of wytte haue made hym to defye the kynge LD. BERNERS. **4.** We haue an olde prouerbe y. wil haue his course LYLY. **4.** Now all the Y. of England are on fire SHAKS. **6.** Profitable to bee read of all godly and vertuous Youthes of both sexe 1580.

Youthful (yū·pfŭl), *a.* 1561. [f. YOUTH + -FUL.] **1.** That is still young 1590. **2.** *transf.* Juvenile; of, characteristic of, or suitable for youth or the young 1561. **3.** *fig.* In the early stage, new; having the freshness or vigour of youth 1588.

1. The y. Socrates JOWETT. **2.** In a very y. costume DICKENS. **3.** The larger stature..of men in those youthfull times and age of the world PURCHAS. Hence **You·thful-ly** *adv.*, **-ness.**

Youthhead (yū·þhed). Chiefly *Sc.* ME. [f. YOUTH + -HEAD.] = YOUTH 1, 2, 5.

Youthhood (yū·þhud). Now *rare* or *arch.* [OE. *ġeoguþhād*; see YOUTH and -HOOD.] = YOUTH 1, 2, 3, 5.

Youthly (yū·þli), *a.* Now *rare.* [OE. *ġeoguþlić*; see YOUTH and -LY¹.] = YOUTHFUL 1, 2.

Youthy (yū·þi), *a.* Now *rare.* 1712. [f. YOUTH + -Y¹.] Having or affecting youth.

A withered beauty who persists in looking y. SCOTT. Hence **You·thily** *adv.*, **You·thiness.**

Youward(s, in phr. *to y.*: see -WARDS.

Yow (yau), *int.* 1820. [Imitative.] Representing the cry of a cat or dog; also as *sb.* and *vb.* (redupl. *yow-yow*).

Yowl (yaul), *v.* [imit.; cf. YAWL *v.*, and dial. *gawl* (ON. *gaula*), G. *johlen*.] **1.** *intr.* To utter loud wailing cries; to howl. **2.** *trans.* To utter with a yowl 1842. Hence **Yowl** *sb.* an act of yowling; a prolonged loud cry, now esp. of a dog or cat.

Yo-yo (yǭᵘ·yo). 1932. [Of unkn. origin.] A toy resembling the old BANDALORE. Also as vb.

Ypight (ipəi·t), *pa. pple. arch.* ME. [f. Y- + *pight*, obs. pa. pple. of PITCH *v.*¹] Set, pitched.

Far underneath a craggy cliff y. SPENSER.

Ypocras: see HIPPOCRAS.

Ypsiliform (ipsi·lifǭɹm), *a.* 1886. [f. *ypsilon* = UPSILON + -FORM.] Shaped like the Greek letter upsilon; Y-shaped.

Yt, yᵗ, graphic var. *that*; see Y.

Ytter (i·təɹ). 1805. *Min.* The first element of *Ytterby* (see next) used attrib. = combined with *yttria*, *yttrious*.

Ytterbite (i·təɹbəit). 1839. [Named from *Ytterby* in Sweden, where found; see -ITE¹ 2 b.] *Min.* = GADOLINITE. So **Ytterbia** (itə·ɹbiă) *Chem.*, oxide of ytterbium. **Ytte·rbic** *a.* containing ytterbium. **Ytte·rbium,** a rare metallic element occurring in gadolinite, etc.

Ytterite (i·tərəit). 1849. [f. *Ytter(by* (see prec.) + ITE¹ 2 b.] *Min.* = GADOLINITE.

Yttria (i·triă). 1800. [mod.L., f. *Ytterby*; see prec., -IA.] *Chem.* Sesquioxide of yttrium (Y_2O_3), obtained as a white earth from gadolinite and other rare minerals.

Yttrium (i·triɒ̆m). 1822. [mod.L., f. prec.; see -IUM.] *Chem.* A rare metal of the cerium group, the base of yttria. Symbol Y. Hence **Yttrialite** (i·triăləit) *Min.*, a silicate of thorium and the yttrium metals. **Y·ttric** *a.* related to or containing y. **Yttri·ferous** *a.* containing y. **Y·ttrious** *a.* pertaining to or containing yttria. **Yttrite** (i·trəit) *Min.*, = GADOLINITE.

Yttro- *Min.*, comb. form of YTTRIUM.

Yuan (yū·ăn). The monetary unit of China since 1933, superseding the TAEL.

Yucca (yɒ·kă), **yuca** (yū·kă). 1555. [Of Carib origin.] **1.** (usu. *yuca.*) The common name in S. and Central America for the CASSAVA. **2.** Any plant of the N.-Amer. liliaceous genus *Yucca*, characterized by a woody stem, crown of sword-like leaves, and a spike of white bell-shaped flowers 1664.

attrib. and *Comb.*: **y.-borer,** (*a*) a N.-Amer. moth, *Megathymus yuccæ*, whose larva bores into y.-roots; (*b*) a Californian weevil, *Yuccaborus frontalis*; **y.-moth,** a tineid moth of the genus *Pronuba*, esp. *P. yuccasella*: **-tree,** any arborescent species of Y.

Yuffrouw (yu·frau). 1494. [– early mod. Du. *jongvrouw*, later *juffrouw*, *juffer*, f. *jong* YOUNG + *vrouw* woman. Cf. EUPHROE, UFER.] **1.** A young lady, girl 1589. **2.** *Naut.* = EUPHROE.

‖**Yuft** (yɒft). 1799. [Russ. *yuft'*.] Russia leather.

‖**Yug** (yug), **yuga** (yu·gă). 1784. [Hindi *yug*, Skr. *yugá-* YOKE, an age of the world.] In Hindu cosmology, any of the four ages in the duration of the world, the four ages comprising 4,320,000 years and constituting a *Mahāyuga*.

Yugoslav: see JUGOSLAV.

Yuke (yuk), *v. Sc.* and *n. dial.* 1551. [app. alt. of ME. *ȝeke*, *ȝike* (see ITCH *v.*¹), prob. after MDu. *jeuken*.] To itch. **Yu·ky** *a.*, itching.

‖**Yulan** (yū·lăn). 1822. [Chinese, f. *yu* a gem + *lan* plant.] A Chinese species of magnolia, *Magnolia conspicua*.

Yule (yūl). [OE. *ġēol*, earlier *ġeo(h)ol*, *ġeh(h)ol*; also *ġēola* Christmas Day, corresp. to ON. *jól* pl. heathen feast lasting twelve days, (later) Christmas; rel. to OE. (Anglian) *ġiuli* December and January (Bede) = ON. *ýlir* month beginning on the second day of the week falling within November 10–17, Goth. *jiuleis* in *fruma jiuleis* November; ult. origin unkn.] †**1.** December or January –ME. **2.** Christmas and its festivities (still the name in *Sc.* and *north. dial.*; now a literary archaism in England) OE. †**3.** An exclam. of joy or revelry at Christmas –1853.

2. The kynge is now deed sithe Martin-masse, and fro hens to yoole is but litill space 1450. At Ewle we wonten, gambole, daunce, to carrole, and to sing 1589. Ye ken a green Y. makes a fat kirk-yard SCOTT. The merry merry bells of Y. TENNYSON.

attrib. and *Comb.*: **y.-day** (chiefly *Sc.*), Christmas day; **-even** (*Sc.*), Christmas Eve; **-log,** a large log burnt on the hearth at Christmas; **-song** (*dial.*), a Christmas carol.

Ywrought (irǭ·t), *pa. pple. arch.* [See Y-, WROUGHT.] Wrought, worked.

A plesaunt herber, wel y-wrought *a*1500.

Z

Z (zed), the twenty-sixth and last letter of the English alphabet, the twenty-third of the later Roman, and seventh of the earlier Roman, Greek, and Phœnician alphabets, derives its form from Phœnician and ancient Hebrew ⵊ Z Z.

Z was used in OE. in alien words, and in certain loan-words, with the value (ts), which is preserved in and indicated by the spelling of mod. *assets* (AFr. *asetz*, OFr. *asez* enough) and *Fitz-* (AFr. *fiz* = *fius*, *fils*, L. *filius*); but by the end of the 13th c. it is found with its modern value (voiced *s*) in some words, and by the end of the 14th was in general use with that value. Similarity between the tailed *z* and *ȝ* led to confusion in MSS. from 1300, and in the typography of early Scottish printers, who represented the two sounds (y) and (z) by the same characters; this confusion has led to the general mispronunciation by Englishmen of *capercailzie* (kē·lyi) and proper names such as *Dalziel* (diye·l), *Mackenzie*, *Menzies* (mi·ŋis).

The letter has been called in England by other names besides *zed*, of which *izzard*, *ezod*, *uzzard*, *zad*, survive in dialects, and *zee* is the general U.S. form. Initially and medially *z* occurs largely in words of Greek or Oriental origin, and in this dictionary the spelling of the suffix derived ultimately from Gr. -ίζειν has been normalized throughout as -IZE. In other classes of words the use of *z* has been determined by various circumstances, e.g. the immediate source of the word, as in *bronze*, or the desirability of an unambiguous or distinctive spelling, as in *ooze*, *prize*; but the difficulty of writing the character rapidly and intelligibly has told against an extensive use of it instead of *s* to represent the sound (z).

Z is normally employed to denote (z), the blade-open-voice consonant, the voiced analogue of (s). In the combination *-zure* in *azure* it denotes (ʒ).

1. The letter, or its sound OE. **2.** As a shape or figure; a Z-shaped object or figure. Also *attrib.*, as *Z-bar* (see ZED 2), *-iron*, *-crank*. 1680. **3.** As the last letter of the alphabet; hence *allus.* for 'end', esp. in phr. *from A to Z*, from beginning to end 1819. **4.** Used (usu. repeated) to represent a buzzing sound 1852. **5.** *Math.* Used as a symbol for the third unknown or variable quantity (cf. X, Y) 1660. **6.** Used abstractly for the name of a person or thing 1755. **7.** Denoting serial order 1842.

‖**Zabra** (þa·bră, zā·bră). 1523. [Sp.] A small vessel used off the coasts of Spain and Portugal.

Zaffre, zaffer (zæ̆·fəɹ). 1662. [– It. *zaffera* (Neri) or its source (O)Fr. *safre*.] An impure oxide of cobalt, used in preparing smalt and as blue colouring-matter (cobalt blue) for pottery, glass, etc.

†**Zagai·e, -ay·e.** 1590. [– Fr. *zagaie*, earlier †*azagaie*, see ASSAGAI.] = ASSAGAI –1869.

Zalambdodont (zălæ·mdǒdǫnt), *a.* 1885. [f. Gr. ζα- intensive prefix + λάμβδα lambda + ὀδούς, ὀδοντ- tooth.] *Zool.* Belonging to the *Zalambdodonta*, insectivorous mammals having short molar teeth with a single Λ- or V-shaped ridge.

‖**Zamang** (zæ·mæŋ). 1819. [Native name.] A giant mimosa (*Pithecolobium saman*) of tropical S. America, having a vast spreading head of branches.

‖**Zamarra** (þama·rra). 1842. [Sp.] A sheepskin jacket worn by Spaniards.

Zambo (zæ·mbo). 1819. [Sp.; see SAMBO.] **1.** = SAMBO 1. **2.** A species of American monkey 1851.

‖**Zambra** (þa·mbra, zæ·mbră). 1670. [Sp.] A Spanish or Moorish dance.

‖**Zamia** (zē̆·miă). 1819. [mod.L. (Linn., 1767), due to a misreading of *azaniæ* (in Pliny) pine-nuts which open on the tree.] *Bot.* A genus of cycadaceous palm-like plants, of tropical and subtropical N. America, the W. Indies, and S. Africa, having fern-like leaves and oblong cones; a plant of this genus.

‖**Zamorin** (zæ·mǒrin). *India.* 1582. [– Pg. *samorim*, *ça-* – Malayalam *sāmūri*.] 'The title for many centuries of the Hindu Sovereign of Calicut and the country round' (Yule).

Zander (zæ·ndəɹ). 1854. [– G. *zander*; in mod.L. *sandra* (Cuvier).] A common European species of pike-perch, *Stizostedion lucioperca* (*Lucioperca sandra*).

Zany (zē̆·ni), *sb.* 1588. [– Fr. *zani*, or its source It. *zani*, *zanni*, orig. Venetian and Lombardic form of *Gianni* = *Giovanni* John, name of the servants who act as clowns in the *commedia dell' arte*.] **1.** A clown's or mountebank's comic assistant; a merry-andrew, jack-pudding; occas. vaguely, a professional jester or buffoon in general. *Hist.* or *arch.* 1588. **2.** An attendant; an underling, parasite. Now *rare.* 1601. **b.** One who plays the fool for the amusement, or so as to be the laughing-stock, of others. Now *rare* or *Obs.* 1606. **c.** A fool, simpleton, 'idiot'. *dial.* 1784.

1. Hee's like a *Zani* to a Tumbler, That tries tricks after him to make men laugh B. JONS. **2.** Pitt and his z. Beckford quarrelled H. WALPOLE. **c.** The printers are awful zanies, they print erasures and corrections too TENNYSON. Hence **Za·ny** *v.* (*Obs.* or *rare arch.*) *trans.* to play the z. to, to imitate poorly or awkwardly; hence *gen.* to mimic. **Za·nyism.**

‖**Zaptieh** (zæ·ptie). 1869. [Turk. *zabtiye* gendarmerie, gendarme, f. Arab. *ḍābiṭ* an officer.] A Turkish policeman.

Zarathustrian (zæræ̆þu·striăn), *a.* and *sb.* 1871. [f. *Zarathustra*, Old Iranian f. *Zoroaster*.] = ZOROASTRIAN.

Zaratite (zæ·rătəit). 1858. [– Sp. *zaratita* (Casares, 1851), f. the name of Señor *Zarate*; see -ITE¹ 2 b.] *Min.* A green hydrous carbonate of nickel.

‖**Zariba** (zărī·bă), *sb.* 1849. [Arab. *zarība* pen or enclosure for cattle.] In the Sudan, an enclosure, usu. of thorn-bushes, for defence against enemies or wild beasts; a fenced camp.

We employed ourselves..in cutting thorn

branches, and constructing a zareeba 1867. Hence **Zari·ba** *v. trans.* to enclose with a z.; *intr.* to make a z.

‖**Zayat** (zā·yăt). 1823. [Burmese.] A public hall for meetings or shelter.

‖**Zea** (zī·ă). 1577. [L. (and mod.L.) *zea* (Pliny) – Gr. ζειά.] †**1.** Spelt –1611. **2.** *Bot.* Adopted by Linnæus as the name of a genus of graminaceous plants, comprising one species, *Z. mays* (occas. anglicized as *z. maize*), maize 1787.

Zeal (zīl). [Late ME. *zele* – L. (esp. eccl.L.) *zelus* – Gr. ζῆλος.] **1.** In biblical language, tr. L. *zelus*, denoting ardent feeling (taking the form of love, wrath, 'jealousy', or righteous indignation). †**2.** Eager desire; longing –1697. **3.** Ardour in the pursuit of an end or in favour of a person or cause; active enthusiasm. Const. *for*. 1520.

1. He brought an honger vpon them and in his zele he made them few in nombre COVERDALE *Ecclus.* 48:2. **2.** This doth inferre the zeale I had to see him SHAKS. **3.** He joined with his drinking propensities a great z. for the Episcopal Church 1860. Hence **Zea·lful, Zea·lless** *adjs.*

Zealander (zī·lændəɹ). 1573. [f. *Zealand* = Du. *Zeeland* + -ER¹.] A native or inhabitant of Zealand in the Netherlands.

See also NEW ZEALANDER.

Zealot (ze·lət). 1537. [– eccl.L. *zelotes* – Gr. ζηλωτής, f. ζηλοῦν be zealous, f. ζῆλος ZEAL.] **1.** A member of a Jewish sect which was bitterly opposed to the Roman domination of Palestine and inspired the fanatical resistance which led to the destruction of Jerusalem in A.D. 70. **2.** A zealous person (*for* a cause, etc.); esp. one who is carried away by excess of zeal; a fanatical enthusiast 1638.

2. The true Z. whom God approveth, namely, He whose Spirit is in Fervency and not in Shew 1638. The queen [Elizabeth] was as a mark for the pistol or dagger of every z. HALLAM. Hence **Zea·lotry,** action or feeling characteristic of a zealot; an instance of this 1656.

Zealous (ze·ləs), *a.* 1535. [– med.L. **zelosus* (cf. *gelositas* XIV), f. *zelus*; see ZEAL, -OUS. Cf. Fr. †*zéleux*.] **1.** Full of or incited by zeal; fervent; actively enthusiastic. Const. *for*. (In the 17th cent. occas. connoting puritanical zeal.) **2.** Eagerly desirous 1605. Hence **Zea·lous-ly** *adv.*, **-ness** (now *rare*).

Zebra (zī·bră, ze·bră). 1600. [– It. or Pg. *zebra*, of Congolese origin. Cf. Fr. *zèbre*, Sp. *cebra*.] **1.** A S. African equine quadruped (*Equus* or *Hippotigris z.*), of a whitish ground-colour striped all over with black bars; noted for its wildness and swiftness. Also applied to other species of *Hippotigris*, or occas. to the whole subgenus, comprising all the striped species of African wild horses. **2.** *transf.* Applied to things having zebra-like stripes, as a kind of agate, a striped shawl, scarf, or the like 1811.

attrib. and *Comb.*: **z. fish,** an Australian fish, *Neotephrœops z.*; **z. opossum,** = THYLACINE; **-poison,** the S. African tree, *Euphorbia arborea*, with poisonous milky juice; **-wolf** = THYLACINE; **-wood,** any of several kinds of ornamentally-striped wood used in cabinet-making.

Zebu (zī·biu). 1774. [– Fr. *zébu* (Buffon); of unkn. origin.] The small humped ox, *Bos indicus*, domesticated in India, China, Japan, and parts of Africa.

Zecchin (ze·kin). 1575. [– It. *zecchino*, f. *zecca* the mint at Venice = Sp. *seca* – Arab. *sikka* coin.] = SEQUIN 1.

‖**Zechstein** (ze·kstəin). 1823. [G., lit. mine-stone.] *Geol.* A limestone stratum of the Permian system in Germany; also extended to the series of rocks containing this, forming the upper division of the Permian.

Zed. late ME. [– (O)Fr. *zède* (= Sp., It. *zeta*) – late L. *zeta* – Gr. ζῆτα.] **1.** Name of the letter Z. **2.** *Zed* (*-bar*), a metal bar of Z-shaped cross-section 1891.

1. *allus.* Thou whoreson Zed, thou vnnecessary Letter *Lear* II. ii. 69.

Zedoary (ze·doări). 1475. [– med.L. *zedoarium* – Pers. *zidwār*.] The aromatic tuberous root of one or more E. Indian species of *Curcuma*, used as a drug, having properties resembling those of ginger; the plant itself. *Yellow z.*, = CASSUMUNAR.

Zee (zī). 1677. A name, esp. now in U.S., of the letter Z.

Zeilanite (zəi·lănəit). 1851. [– G. *zeilanit*, f. *Zeilan* CEYLON; see -ITE¹ 2 b.] *Min.* = CEYLONITE.

Zein (zī·in). 1822. [f. ZEA + -IN¹.] *Chem.* A protein found in maize, analogous to gluten.

‖**Zeitgeist** (tsai·tgaist). 1884. [G., f. *zeit* time + *geist* spirit.] The thought or feeling peculiar to a generation or period.

Zel. 1817. [Turk. *zil*.] A kind of cymbal.

Zelator (ze·lătǫɹ). 1460. [– Fr. *zélateur* (XV) or its source, eccl. L. *zelator*, f. *zelare* be zealous; see -ATOR.] **1.** A zealous defender or supporter (*rare*). **2.** = ZEALOT 1, 2. (*rare*) 1644. **3.** A sister in a religious community with the duty of admonishing the mother superior or other members of the community when necessary 1851. So (in sense 3) **Ze·latrice** (-tris), **Ze·latrix.**

Zelotic, zealotic (zīlǫ·tik), *a.* 1657. [– Gr. ζηλωτικός, f. ζηλωτής ZEALOT; see -IC.] Of or like a zealot. So **Ze(a)·lotism,** zealotry.

Zeme, zemi (zī·mi). 1613. [Carib *cemi*.] An idol or tutelary spirit worshipped by the aborigines of the W. Indian islands. Hence **Ze·meism. Zemei·stic** *a.*

Zemindar (zĕmī·ndaɹ). *India.* 1683. [Hind. – Pers. *zamīndār*, f. *zamin* earth + *dār* holder.] Formerly, a collector of the revenue from land held by a number of cultivators; now, a native who holds land for which he pays revenue direct to the British government. Hence **Zemi·ndarship.**

Zemindary (zĕmī·ndări). *India.* 1757. [Hind. – Pers. *zamīndārī*, f. *zamīndār* (see prec.).] **1.** The system of holding lands and farming revenue by means of zemindars; the office or jurisdiction of a zemindar. **2.** The territory administered by a zemindar 1764.

‖**Zemni** (ze·mni). 1785. [Short for Russ. dial. *shchenók zemnói* 'puppy of earth'.] The blind mole-rat, *Spalax typhlus*.

Zemstvo (ze·mstvo). 1865. [Russ., f. *zemlyá* land.] An elective provincial council in Russia for purposes of local government.

Zenana (zĕnā·nă). 1761. [Hind. *zenāna* – Pers. *zanāna*, f. *zan* rel. to Gr. γυνή woman.] **1.** In India and Persia, the women's apartments; an E. Indian harem. **2.** (Also *z.-cloth*.) A light thin dress-fabric 1900. **3.** *attrib.*, esp. of Christian missionary work among native Indian women 1810.

Zend (zend). 1700. [– Fr. *zend* (used as the name of the language by Anquetil du Perron, 1771), abstracted from *Avesta-va-Zend*, i.e. Avesta with interpretation. See next.] **1.** = next 1715. **2.** The language of the Avesta: also called *Avestic* and *Old Bactrian*, forming with Old Persian the Iranian group of Indo-European languages 1700. Hence **Ze·ndic, Ze·ndish** *adjs.* **Ze·ndist,** one versed in Z.

Zend-Avesta (zendăve·stă). 1630. [alt. of Pers. *zand(a) vastā, zandastā* (= *Avestā-va-Zend*, see prec.), in which *Zend* was erron. taken for an attrib. element denoting the language of the books.] The sacred writings of the Parsees, usu. attributed to Zoroaster.

Zendic (ze·ndik). 1842. [– Arab. *zindīk*, from Pers. *zandīk* fire-worshipper.] In the East, a disbeliever in revealed religion or a practiser of heretical magic. Hence **Ze·ndicism,** the belief of a z. 1697.

Zenick (zī·nik). Also **-ik.** 1843. [– Fr. *zénik*.] The African suricate.

Zenith (ze·niþ, zī·niþ). [Late ME. *cenyth, senith, cinit* – OFr. *cenit* (mod. *zénith*) or med.L. *cenit* (also *zenith*) XIII, obscurely – Arab. *samt* in *samt-al-ra's* 'path over the head'; cf. AZIMUTH.] **1.** The point of the sky directly overhead; the upper pole of the horizon. †**b.** *transf.* Course towards the zenith. MILT. **c.** *Magnetic z.*, the point of the sky directly above the magnetic pole of the earth 1885. **2.** *loosely.* The upper region of the sky; the highest or culminating point of a heavenly body 1631. **3.** *fig.* Highest point or state, climax, acme 1610.

1. The stars..near the z. shine with a steady light TYNDALL. **2.** The conscious Moon, now in her Z. SWIFT. **3.** The hand of God, whereby all Estates arise to their Z. and verticall points SIR T. BROWNE.

attrib. and *Comb.*: **z. distance,** the angular distance of a heavenly body from the z. (the complement of its *altitude*); **z. sweep,** a series of observations of the sky passing through the z. Hence **Ze·nithal** *a.*

Zenonian (zīnōᵘ·niăn), *a.* and *sb.* 1843. [f. L. *Zeno, Zenon*, Gr. Ζήνων + -IAN.] **A.** *adj.* (*a*) Of or pertaining to Zeno of Elea, a philosopher of the 5th century B.C., and author of a disproof of the possibility of motion. (*b*) Of or pertaining to Zeno of Citium (*c*300 B.C.), the founder of the Stoic philosophy. **B.** *sb.* A follower of (esp. the Stoic) Zeno; a Stoic. So **Zenonic** (zīnǫ·nik) *a.* **Zenonism** (zī·nŏniz'm), Stoicism.

Zeolite (zī·ŏləit). 1777. [– Sw., G., etc. *zeolit*, f. Gr. ζεῖν boil + λίθος -LITE.] *Min.* Generic name for a group of hydrous silicates in which the bases are alumina and the alkalies and alkaline earths; generally characterized by swelling up and fusing to a glass or enamel under the blowpipe; commonly found in the cavities of igneous rocks. Hence **Zeolitic** (-i·tik) *a.*

Zep, colloq. abbrev. of ZEPPELIN.

Zephyr (ze·fəɹ). Also **zephyrus,** †**zefferus.** [In XVI – Fr. *zéphyr* (Marot) or L. *zephyrus* – Gr. ζέφυρος; preceded by late OE. *zefferus* and ME. *zephirus* direct from Latin.] **1.** The west wind, esp. as personified, or the god of the west wind. **2.** A mild soft gentle breeze or wind 1611. **3. a.** A shawl, coat, shirt, etc., of light gauzy material 1774. **b.** A fine light cotton dress-material, having the colours woven into the fabric 1849. **4.** A butterfly of the genus *Zephyrus*. **5.** A (French) Algerian light-infantryman 1854.

1. Zephirus..with his swete breeth CHAUCER. Zephir with Aurora playing MILT. **2.** The zephyrs breathed softly from the south 1883. Hence **Zephyre·an, Zephy·rian, Ze·phyrous, Ze·phyry** *adjs.*

Zephyranth (ze·firænþ). 1845. [– mod.L. *Zephyranthes*, f. Gr. ζέφυρος + ἄνθος flower: with allusion to the waving flower-stalks.] A plant of the genus *Zephyranthes*.

Zeppelin (ze·pəlin). 1900. [f. name of the German Count F. von *Zeppelin*.] A dirigible airship of the type constructed by Count Zeppelin in 1900. Often colloq. abbrev. *Zep(p*. Hence **Ze·ppelin** *v. trans.* to bomb from a Z.

Zerda (zō·ɹdă). 1781. [So called by the 'Moors'.] = FENNEC.

Zereba, -iba, var. ff. ZARIBA.

Zero (zīᵊ·ro). *Pl.* **zeros** (-oᵘz). 1604. [– Fr. *zéro* or its source It. *zero* – Sp. *zero* (mod. *cero*) – Arab. *ṣifr* CIPHER.] **1.** The symbol 0, 'nought'. Now *rare*. **b.** The compartment numbered 0 on a roulette table 1859. **2.** The point marked 0 on a graduated scale, from which the reckoning begins; esp. in a thermometer or other measuring instrument 1795. **3.** The temperature or degree of heat reckoned as zero in any thermometric scale, e.g. the freezing point of water in Centigrade 1800. **4.** Nought or nothing reckoned as a number denoted by the figure 0, and constituting the starting-point of the series of natural numbers; the total absence of quantity considered as a quantity (in *Alg.*, etc. as intermediate between positive and negative quantities); hence = 'none at all' 1823. **b.** In the theory of functions, a value of a variable for which a function vanishes 1893. **5.** *fig.* A person or thing of no account; a 'cipher', nonentity 1813. **6.** *fig.* The lowest point; vanishing-point; nullity 1820. **b.** The starting-point of a process or reckoning 1849.

3. *Absolute z.*, the lowest temperature possible in the nature of things, at which the molecular motion which constitutes heat would cease; the z. of absolute temperature reckoned as –273.16° C. **4.** Dante's direct acquaintance with Plato may be reckoned at z. LOWELL. **5.** The other gentlemen are zeros MARIA EDGEWORTH. **6.** My courage sinks to z. HOOD. **b.** He..makes 1788 his z. of human history 1866.

attrib., as *z. line, point* (sense 2), *z. value* (sense 4), *z. weather* (sense 3); **z. creep,** spontaneous displacement of the z.-point on a graduated scale; **z. hour** *Mil.*, the hour at which an attack or operation is timed to begin; *fig.* the moment at which any ordeal is to begin; the hour at which the lowest value of anything is reached or recorded; **z. magnet,** a magnet for adjusting the z., e.g. of a galvanometer; **z. mark, post,** a mark or post from which road distances are measured.

The coming of the z. hour of 3.30 in the morning 1917.

Zerumbet (zīrɒ·mbet). 1555. [– Pg. –

Hind., Pers. *zerumbād*.] An E. Indian plant (or its aromatic root) of the genus *Curcuma*, yielding a tonic drug.

Zest (zest), *sb.* 1674. [– Fr. *zeste*, †*zest*, *zec* 'the thicke skin..whereby the kernell of a wall-nut is divided' (Cotgr.), orange or lemon peel; of unkn. origin.] **1.** Orange or lemon peel used as a flavouring or for preserving. Now *rare* or *Obs.* **2.** *fig.* Something that gives savour, relish, or piquancy; piquant quality 1709. **3.** Keen relish or enjoyment displayed in speech or action; gusto, appetite or strong inclination (*for*) 1791. **4.** *transf.* An appetizer or appetizing food; also, a relish, a piquant flavour 1835.

1. To prepare lemon-juice you must first carefully remove the z. and then the white part 1800. **2.** The sense that, perhaps, it was imprudent to take a cab or drink a bottle of wine added a z. to those enjoyments THACKERAY. **3.** She went to a lying-in or a laying-out with equal z. DICKENS. **4.** Private zests and flavours on a side-table DICKENS. Hence **Zest** *v. trans.* to flavour with 'z.'; to add a relish to; to give a piquant quality to. **Ze·stful** *a.*, **-ly** *adv.*, **-ness.**

Zeta (zī·tă). 1840. [Gr. ζῆτα the letter Z, ζ.] The sixth letter of the Greek alphabet, used *attrib.* in **z.-function** *Math.*, one of a set of functions (denoted by Z or ζ prefixed to the variable) connected with elliptic integrals.

Zetetic (zīte·tik), *a.* and *sb.* *rare.* 1645. [– Gr. ζητητικός, f. ζητεῖν seek; see -IC.] **A.** *adj.* Investigating; proceeding by inquiry.

This was called the Zetetick Philosophy, from its continual enquiry after Truth 1660.

B. *sb.* **1.** (*sing.* or *pl.*) Investigation, scientific inquiry 1679. **2.** An inquirer; *spec.* an adherent of the ancient Greek sceptic school of philosophy 1660.

2. The ancient Pyrrhonists were called Zetetics or seekers 1838. Hence **Zete·tically** *adv.*

‖**Zeuglodon** (ziū·glodǫn). 1839. [mod.L. (Owen, 1839), f. Gr. ζεύγλη strap or loop of a yoke + ὀδούς, ὀδοντ- tooth.] *Palæont.* A genus of extinct Eocene cetaceans. Hence **Zeu·glodont** *sb.* and *a.* (a cetacean) of this genus. **Zeuglodo·ntoid** *a.* and *sb.* having the characters of this genus; (a cetacean) of the family *Zeuglodontidæ*.

‖**Zeugma** (ziū·gmă). 1586. [L. *zeugma* – Gr. ζεῦγμα yoking, f. ζευγνύναι vb. rel. to ζυγόν yoke.] *Gram.* and *Rhet.* A figure by which a single word is made to refer to two or more words in the sentence; esp. when applying in sense to only one of them, or applying to them in different senses. (Example: *She came in a flood of tears and a Bath chair.*) Hence **Zeugma·tic** *a.* **Zeugma·tically** *adv.*

Zeunerite (zoi·nərəit). 1873. [f. name of Gustav *Zeuner* of Freiberg, Saxony; see -ITE[1] 2 b.] *Min.* A hydrous arseniate of uranium and copper, occurring in bright-green crystals.

‖**Zeus** (ziūs). 1706. [Gr. Ζεύς, related to L. *Jovis*; see JOVE.] **1.** *Myth.* The supreme deity of the ancient Greeks 1839. **2.** *Ichth.* A genus of spiny-finned fishes, including the John Dory, *Z. faber*, anciently sacred to Zeus 1706.

Zeuxite (ziū·ksəit). 1836. [f. Gr. ζεῦξις yoking, joining, tr. 'unity' in *Huel Unity*, name of the mine where found.] *Min.* A variety of tourmaline.

‖**Zho** (ʒōᵘ). 1841. [Tibetan *mdso*.] A hybrid animal, bred from the yak bull and a common cow, used for domestic purposes in northern India. Also called ‖**Zo·bo, zo·bu** [with masc. affix *-bo*]. So **Zho·mo,** a female zho.

Zibeline (zi·bĕlin, -əin). 1585. [– Fr. *zibeline*, deriv. of Slav. word rel. to Russ. *sóbol'* SABLE *sb.*[1]] **1.** The sable. **2.** The fur of the sable 1869. **3.** (In full *z. cloth.*) A soft woollen dress-material with a slightly furry surface 1892.

Zibet (zi·bĕt). 1594. [– med.L. *zibethum*; see CIVET *sb.*[1]] Variant of CIVET, esp. the Asiatic species.

Ziczac (zi·kzæk). Also **siksak, sagsag, sicsac, zi(c)kza(c)k.** 1844. [ult. – Arab. *zakzāk*, *saksak*.] An Egyptian plover, *Pluvianus ægyptius*, which warns the crocodile of approaching danger; perhaps identical with TROCHILUS[1].

Zigan, var. TZIGANE.

Zigzag (zi·gzæg), *sb.*, *a.*, *adv.* 1712. [Earliest forms *ziczac*, *zig-zac* – Fr. *zigzag*, †*ziczac* – G. *zickzack*, of symbolic formation suggesting alternation of direction, applied first to fortifications.] **A.** *sb.* **1.** A series of short lines inclined at angles in alternate directions; a line or course having sharp turns of this kind; *concr.* something characterized by such lines or turns. **b.** Chiefly in *pl.*: Each of the such lines or turns 1728. **c.** *fig.* 1781. **2.** A road or path turning sharply at angles in alternate directions esp. so as to reduce the gradient on a steep slope 1728. **b.** *Fortif.* An attacking trench dug in zigzag to prevent enfilading 1733. **c.** *Arch.* A chevron-moulding 1814. **d.** A shell, or a moth, with zigzag marking 1815.

1. The hieroglyphic use of the z., for water, by the Egyptians RUSKIN. **b.** A winding road, which forms thirteen zig-zags 1775. **c.** The little zigzags of embarrassment JANE AUSTEN.

B. *adj.* **1.** Having the form of a z.; turning sharply at angles in alternate directions; characterized by such turns 1750. **b.** *Bot.* Applied to the stem of a plant, or to a plant having such a stem 1796. **2.** Chiefly *Nat. Hist.* Having z. markings 1785.

1. The chevron-work (or zig-zag moulding) GRAY. Flashes of forked, or zig-zag lightning 1767. Up from the lake a z. path will creep WORDSW. *fig.* All the brood of zig-zag politicians 1863.

C. *adv.* In a zigzag manner or direction 1730.

It may go straight forward, or zig-zag 1846. Hence **Zi·gzag** *v. intr.* to go or move in a z. course, to have a z. direction; *trans.* to give a z. form or motion to 1777. **Zi·gzagged** *ppl. a.* 1774: **Zi·gzagging** *vbl. sb.* and *ppl. a.*; **Zi·gzaggery,** z. course or proceeding 1760; **Zi·gzaggy** *a.* 1845.

‖**Zikkurat, ziggurat** (zi·kŭrăt, zi·g-). 1877. [Assyrian *ziqquratu* height, pinnacle.] A staged tower in which each storey is smaller than that below it; an Assyrian or Babylonian temple-tower.

‖**Zillah** (zi·lă). 1800. [Hind. *ḍilah* division.] An administrative district in British India. Hence **Zi·lladar,** the collector of a zillah.

‖**Zimb** (zimb). 1790. [Amharic.] An Abyssinian dipterous insect allied to the tsetse.

Zinc (ziŋk), *sb.* 1651. [– G. *zink*, †*zinken* (of unkn. origin), whence also Fr. *zinc*, †*zin*, Sp. *zinc*, It. *zinco*, etc.] A hard brittle bluish-white metal (commercially called SPELTER), malleable and ductile between 200° and 250° F., obtained from various ores (BLENDE, CALAMINE, SMITHSONITE, ZINCITE), and used for roofing, for 'galvanizing' iron, etc., and as a component in alloys, esp. with copper in BRASS. Chemical symbol Zn; atomic weight 65. **b.** (with *pl.*). A plate of zinc used as the electropositive metal in a voltaic battery 1876.

attrib. and *Comb.*, as *z. filings, wire*; *z. lotion, ointment*; *z. carbonate, oxide*; *z. etching*; *z. lined, roofed* adjs. **z.-blende,** native zinc sulphide, blende; **-bloom,** hydrous carbonate of zinc; **-dust,** z. in the form of a fine powder, used as a deoxidizing agent and as a paint; **-grey,** (*a*) z.-dust obtained by grinding in oil, used as a preservative paint for ironwork; (*b*) a colour resembling that of z.; **-powder,** = *z.-dust*; **-spinel,** = GAHNITE; **-white,** oxide of z. used as a white paint. Hence **Zinc** *v. trans.* to coat or treat with z. or some compound of z. **Zi·ncate** *Chem.*, a compound of zincic oxide with the oxide of a more electropositive metal. **Zincic** (zi·ŋkik) *a.* of, pertaining to, or containing z. **Zinciferous** (ziŋki·fĕrəs) *a.* producing z. **Zi·ncify** *v. trans.* to coat or impregnate with z. **Zincite** (zi·ŋkəit) *Min.*, red oxide of z., red z. ore. **Zi·ncous** *a. Chem.* and *Electr.* pertaining to or of the nature of zinc; having the affinity of z.; relatively electropositive.

‖**Zincalo** (zi·ŋkălo), *fem.* **-ala.** *Pl.* **-ali, -ale.** 1842. [Cf. ZINGANO.] The name by which the Gitanos or gipsies of Spain call themselves.

Zinco (zi·ŋko). 1887. Abbreviation of ZINCOGRAPH. Also, a zincographic plate or block.

Zinco-, comb. form of mod.L. *zincum* ZINC, in names of chemical compounds of zinc and another element or radical, as *z.-sulphate*. Also **Zincolysis** (ziŋkǫ·lisis), decomposition by an electric current, electrolysis. **Zincolyte** (zi·ŋkoləit), a substance so decomposed, an electrolyte. **Zincopo·lar** *a.*, having the polarity of a zincode. **Zi·ncotype** = ZINCOGRAPH.

Zincode (zi·ŋkoᵘd). 1839. [f. ZINC *sb.*, after ANODE.] *Electr.* = ZINC *sb.* b.

Zincography (ziŋkǫ·grăfi). 1834. [f. ZINCO- + -GRAPHY.] The art or process of engraving or etching designs on zinc, or of printing from such designs. Hence **Zi·ncograph** *sb.* a design or print produced by z.; *v. trans.* to engrave or print by z. **Zinco·grapher,** an engraver on zinc. **Zincogra·phic** *a.*

Zincoid (zi·ŋkoid). 1842. [f. ZINC *sb.* + -OID.] = ZINCODE.

Zinfandel (zi·nfăndel). 1896. A red or white dry Californian wine.

‖**Zingano** (zi·ŋgăno), *fem.* **-ana.** *Pl.* **-ani, -e.** 1581. [It., = Gr. Ἀθίγγανοι, an oriental people. See next.] = next.

‖**Zingaro** (zi·ŋgăro), *fem.* **-ara.** *Pl.* **-ari, -e.** 1617. [It., alt. of prec.] A gipsy; also *attrib.* or as *adj.*

‖**Zingel** (tsi·ŋgəl). 1803. [G.] Any fish of the percoid genus *Aspro*; esp. *A. zingel* of the Danube.

Zingiberaceous (zi:ndʒibĕrēⁱ·ʃəs), *a.* 1846. [f. mod.L. *Zingiberaceæ*; see GINGER *sb.* and -ACEOUS.] *Bot.* Belonging to the family *Zingiberaceæ* of monocotyledonous plants, typified by the genus *Zingiber* (GINGER).

‖**Zinke** (zi·ŋkĭ, tsi·ŋkĕ). 1776. [G.] A cornet-like musical instrument, formerly common in Europe; a loud reed-stop in an organ.

Zinked, pa. t. and pa. pple. of ZINC *v.*

Zinkenite (zi·ŋkĕnəit). 1835. [– G. *zinkenit*, named from J. K. L. *Zincken*.] *Min.* A steel-grey sulphide of antimony and lead.

Zinkiferous, -ify, -ing, -ite. See ZINC.

Zinky (zi·ŋki), *a.* 1757. [f. ZINC *sb.* + -Y[1].] Pertaining to or containing zinc.

‖**Zinnia** (zi·niă). 1767. [mod.L. (Linn., 1763), f. name of J. G. *Zinn*, German botanist; see -IA[1].] *Bot.* A plant of the Amer. composite genus *Zinnia*, extensively cultivated for the beauty of its flowers.

Zinnwaldite (zi·nwǫldəit). 1861. [– G. *zinnwaldit*, f. *Zinnwald* in Bohemia; see -ITE[1] 2 b.] *Min.* A kind of mica containing lithium and iron.

Zion (zəi·ən). OE. [– eccl.L. *Sion*, Gr. Σεών, Σειών – Hebr. *ṣîyôn*.] One of the hills of Jerusalem, on which the city of David was built, and which became the centre of Jewish life and worship; hence, the house of God, Israel, the Jewish religion, the Christian Church, Heaven, a place of worship. Hence **Zi·onism,** a movement aiming at the reestablishment of the Jewish nation in Palestine 1896; so **Zi·onist** *sb.* and *a.* **Zi·onward(s** *adv.* usu. *fig.* = heavenwards.

Zip (zip). *colloq.* 1875. [Imitative.] **1.** A light sharp sound as of a bullet in flight or of the tearing of canvas or the like; movement accompanied by such a sound. **2.** *fig.* Energy, impetus, 'go' 1900. **3.** *attrib.* in the trade name of a slide fastener, a device by which an opening is closed by the interlocking of metal strips placed on adjacent edges 1925. (Also **Zi·pper.**) Hence **Zip** *v. intr.*, to make a zip-like sound.

Ziphioid (zi·fi,oid), *a.* and *sb.* 1870. [f. mod.L. *Ziphius* (Cuvier, 1834), erron. for *Xiphius* – Gr. ξίφιος, var. of ξιφίας XIPHIAS swordfish; see -OID.] *Zool.* **A.** *adj.* Resembling or allied to the genus *Ziphius* of whales. **B.** *sb.* A z. whale. So **Zi·phiiform** *a.*

Zippeite (zi·pĭ,əit). 1854. [– G. *zippeit* (Haidinger, 1845), named after F. X. M. *Zippe*, German mineralogist; see -ITE[1] 2 b.] *Min.* A sulphate of uranium, occurring in small yellow needles.

Zircon (zɔ̄·ɹkǫn). 1794. [– G. *zirkon*; see JARGON *sb.*[2] Cf. Fr. *zircone*.] *Min.* A native silicate of zirconium, occurring in tetragonal crystals of various colours some of which, are used as gems. Hence **Zi·rconate,** a salt of zirconic acid. **Zirconia** (-kōᵘ·niă), a white earth, zirconium dioxide, ZrO_2, used in incandescent burners. **Zirconian** (-kōᵘ·niăn), **Zirconic** (-kǫ·nik) *adjs.* of, pertaining to, or like z.; containing zirconia or zirconium; **Zircon(i)o-, zirco-,** comb. ff. in names of zirconium compounds, as **Zi:rcon(i)oflu·oride.** **Zi·rconite,** a greyish or brownish variety of z. **Zirconium** (-kōᵘ·niŏm), a metallic element obtained from z. as a black powder or in greyish crystals; symbol Zr.

Zither (zi·þəɹ). 1850. [– G. *zither* CITHER, CITHERN.] An Austrian musical instrument having from thirty to forty strings let into the lower rim of a shallow resonance-box, and played by striking with the fingers and thumb. So **Zi·thern.**

‖**Zizania** (zi-, zəizēⁱ·niă). 1829. [mod.L. fem. sing. = eccl.L. n. pl. – Gr. ζιζάνιά pl. darnel.] *Bot.* (Any aquatic grass of) the genus *Zizania*, esp. *Z. aquatica* (Canada, Indian, water, or wild rice). Also †**Zizany,** tares ME.

Zizel (zi·zĕl). 1785. [– G. *ziesel.*] The ground-squirrel, *Spermophilus citillus.*

‖**Zizyphus** (zi·zifŏs). 1440. [L. – Gr. ζίζυφος.] *Bot.* A plant of the genus *Zizyphus*, comprising spiny shrubs or trees of the buckthorn family, various species of which bear an edible fruit called JUJUBE. Also †**Zi·zypha,** the fruit itself, = JUJUBE 1. 1546.

Zoantharian (zōᵘæn þēᵊ·riăn), *a.* and *sb.* 1887. [f. mod.L. *Zoantharia*, n. pl., f. Gr. ζῷον animal + ἄνθος flower; see -ARY¹, -AN.] *Zool.* (A member) of the *Zoantharia*, one of the main divisions of *Actinozoa*, comprising the sea-anemones and other (often flower-like) animals, usu. with simple tentacles and parts arranged in sixes. So **Zoa·nthid,** a member of the zoantharian family *Zoanthidæ.* **Zoa·nthodeme** (-dīm) [Gr. δέμα bundle], a compound organism formed of coherent z. zooids or polyps. **Zoa·nthoid** *a.* of or like the zoanthids.

Zoanthropy (zoᵘæ·nþrŏpi). 1856. [f. ZOO-, ZO-, after CYNANTHROPY and LYCANTHROPY (XVI).] *Path.* A form of mania in which a man imagines himself to be a beast. Hence **Zoanthropic** (-ǫ·pik) *a.*

‖**Zoarium** (zoᵘēᵊ·riŏm). 1880. [app. extracted f. (earlier) *polyzoarium*: see POLYZOARY.] *Zool.* The supporting structure of a colony of polyps; also, the colony or compound organism as a whole.

Zobo: see ZHO.

Zodiac (zōᵘ·diæk). late ME. [– (O)Fr. *zodiaque* – L. *zodiacus* (Cicero) – Gr. ζῳδιακός (sc. κύκλος the circle of the figures or signs, ὁ τῶν ζῳδίων κύκλος), f. ζῴδιον sculptured figure (of an animal), sign of the zodiac, dim. of ζῷον animal; see -AC.] **1.** *Astr.* A belt of the celestial sphere extending 8 or 9 degrees on each side of the ecliptic, within which the apparent motions of the sun, moon, and principal planets take place; it is divided into twelve equal parts called *signs.* **b.** *Signs of the z.*: the twelve equal parts of the zodiac, through one of which the sun passes in each month; they are named after the twelve constellations (Aries, Taurus, Gemini, Cancer, Leo, Virgo, Libra, Scorpio, Sagittarius, Capricornus, Aquarius, Pisces) with which at a former epoch they severally coincided approximately 1532. **c.** *Z. of the moon, a planet*, etc.: that belt of the heavens to which its apparent motion is confined 1704. **2.** A representation of the zodiac. late ME. **3.** *transf.* (*a*) Recurrent series, round, course. (*b*) Compass, range. (*c*) Set of twelve. 1560.

1. Thus Phœbus through the Zodiack takes his way POPE.

Zodiacal (zodəi·ăkăl), *a.* 1576. [– Fr. *zodiacal*, f. *zodiaque*; see prec., -AL¹ 1.] Of, pertaining to or situated in the zodiac. **b.** *Z. light*: a tract of nebulous light sometimes visible before sunrise or after sunset extending along the zodiac on each side of the sun in the form of an elongated ellipse 1734.

‖**Zoea** (zoᵢī·ă). *Pl.* **zoeæ** (zoᵢī·i). 1828. [mod.L. *zoe, zoea* (Bosc, 1802), the first form – Gr. ζωή life, the second an extension of it + -A 2.] *Zool.* A larval stage of development in crustaceans, esp. decapods, usu. characterized by one or more spines on the carapace and rudimentary thoracic and abdominal limbs. Hence **Zoeal** (zoᵢī·ăl) *a.*

Zoetrope (zōᵘ·ĭtroᵘp). 1869. [irreg. f. Gr. ζωή life + -τροπος turning.] The 'wheel of life', a mechanical toy consisting of a revolving cylinder in which the effect of motion is produced by pictures on the inner surface of successive positions of a moving object, viewed through slits in the circumference.

Zoic (zōᵘ·ik), *a.* 1863. [prob. extracted from AZOIC.] Showing traces of life; *Geol.* containing organic remains.

Zoilus (zōᵘ·ilŏs). 1567. [L. – Gr. Ζωΐλος, the grammarian and critic of Homer.] A censorious, malignant, or envious critic. Hence **Zo·ilism,** carping criticism like that of Zoilus. **Zo·ilist.**

Zoisite (zoi·səit). 1805. [– G. *zoisit*, named from Baron von *Zois*; see -ITE¹ 2 b.] *Min.* A native silicate of alumina and lime, occurring in orthorhombic prismatic crystals.

Zoism (zōᵘ·iz'm). 1843. [f. Gr. ζωή life + -ISM.] The doctrine that life depends on a peculiar vital principle, and is not a mere resultant of combined forces; esp. in connection with animal magnetism. So **Zo·ist. Zoi·stic** *a.*

Zolaism (zōᵘ·lăᵢiz'm). 1882. [f. name of Émile *Zola* (1840–1902), French novelist + -ISM.] Excessively realistic treatment of the coarser sides of life, as in Zola's novels. So **Zolaesque** (-e·sk) *a.* characteristic of or resembling the style of Zola.

‖**Zollverein** (tsǫ·lfərəin). 1843. [G., f. *zoll* TOLL *sb.*¹ + *verein* union.] A union of states for free trade among themselves and uniform customs rates against others; orig. between certain states of the German empire, later including all the states; hence *gen.* of other countries.

‖**Zolotnik** (zolotni·k). 1783. [Russ., f. *zóloto* gold.] A Russian unit of weight, $\frac{1}{96}$ of the funt or Russian pound.

‖**Zona** (zōᵘ·nă). 1706. [L., = ZONE.] **1.** *Archæol.* A girdle 1800. **2.** In Latin medical or anatomical terms, as **z. ignea** [= fiery girdle], also simply z., the disease shingles; **z. pellucida,** the transparent cell-wall of the ovum in Mammalia.

Zonal (zōᵘ·năl), *a.* 1867. [f. ZONE *sb.* + -AL¹ 1.] **1.** Characterized by or arranged in zones; of the nature of or forming a zone 1873. **b.** Of varieties of pelargonium: Having the leaves marked with zones of colour 1868. **2.** *Math.* and *Cryst.* Relating to a zone or zones of a sphere or of a crystalline form 1867. **3.** Pertaining or relating to, involving, or constituting a 'zone' or 'zones' 1882. Hence **Zona·lity,** z. character or distribution. **Zo·nally** *adv.*

Zone (zōᵘn), *sb.* 1500. [– (O)Fr. *zone* or L. *zona* girdle – Gr. ζώνη.] **1.** *Geog.*, etc. Each of the five 'belts' or encircling regions, differing in climate, into which the tropics of Cancer and Capricorn and the arctic and antarctic circles divide the surface of the earth; viz. the *torrid* (†*burning*) *z.* between the tropics, the (north and south) *temperate zones* extending from the tropics to the polar circles, and the *frigid* (†*frozen*) *zones* (arctic and antarctic) within the polar circles. **b.** Any region extending round the earth and comprised between definite limits, e.g. between two parallels of latitude. Also applied to a similar region in the heavens or on the surface of a planet, etc. 1559. **2.** A region or tract of the world, esp. in relation ot its climate 1599. **b.** A limited area distinguished from those adjacent by some quality or condition, freq. indicated by a defining word or phrase 1822. **3.** A girdle or belt, as a part of dress. Chiefly *poet.* Hence, any encircling band. 1608. **b.** *Astron.* The girdle of Orion 1599. **4.** A circumscribing or enclosing ring, band, or line 1591. **b.** A band or stripe of colour, etc. extending around something or over any surface or area; freq. one of a number of concentric or alternate markings of this kind 1752. **5.** *Astr.* A region of the sky comprised between definite limits 1795. **6.** *Anat.*, *Zool.*, *Bot.* A growth or structure surrounding some part in the form of a ring or cylinder; also, a region or area of some special character extending around or over some part 1811. **7.** *Geol.* and *Physical Geog.* A region comprised between definite limits, as of depth or height, and distinguished by special characters 1829. **8.** *Math.* The part of the surface of a solid of revolution contained between two planes perpendicular to the axis 1795. **b.** *Cryst.* A series of faces extending round a crystal and having their lines of intersection parallel 1868.

1. The Sun, with Rays directly darting down, Fires all beneath, and fries the middle Z. DRYDEN. **b.** We have, extending entirely around the earth, two zones of perpetual winds 1860. **2.** We may.. in some milde Z. Dwell not unvisited of Heav'ns fair Light Secure MILT. **b.** All extensions should be performed before entering within the fire z. 1873. **3.** Shall these course hands untie The sacred Z. of thy Virginitie? QUARLES. **4.** Tentacles disposed in a z. around the mouth 1856. **b.** All such white marbles as are marked with green-coloured zones 1816.

attrib. and *Comb.*, as *z.-like* adj.; **z.-plate,** a glass plate with concentric rings alternately opaque and clear, for focusing light; **z. system,** division of a country into regions for railway travel, etc., travellers paying according to the number of zones traversed; so **z.-tariff; z. time,** the local time for any longitude as opposed to Greenwich time.

Hence **Zo·nary** *a.* having the form of a z. or girdle. **Zonate** (zōᵘ·neⁱt), **Zo·nated** *adjs.* marked with rings or bands of colour. **Zona·tion,** distribution in zones; also, formation of zones or concentric layers.

Zone, *v.* 1792. [f. prec.] **1.** *trans.* To furnish with or encircle like a zone or girdle 1795. **2.** *Nat. Hist.* To mark with zones, rings, or bands of colour. Only in *pa. pple.* 1792. **3.** To distribute or arrange in zones 1904.

Zoned (zōᵘnd), *a.* 1718. [f. ZONE *sb.* or *v.* + -ED.] **1.** Wearing a zone or girdle. Hence, virgin, chaste. **2.** Characterized by or arranged naturally in zones, rings, or bands; marked with zones of colour 1792. **3.** Arranged according to zones or definite regions 1795.

Zonite (zōᵘ·nəit). 1860. [– mod.L. *Zonites*, f. L. *zona* ZONE *sb.*; see -ITE¹ 3.] **1.** A snail of the genus *Zonites.* **2.** Any of the body-rings of a segmented animal, as an annelid 1880.

Zono- (zōᵘno), repr. Gr. ζωνο-, comb. form of ζώνη ZONE *sb.*, occurring in a few scientific and technical words; **Zonociliate** (-si·liĕt) *a.* *Zool.*, having a circlet of cilia. **Zo:noplace·ntal** *a.* *Zool.*, having a zonary placenta.

Zonule (zōᵘ·niul). 1831. [– mod.L. *zonula*, dim. of L. *zona* ZONE *sb.*; see -ULE.] *Anat.* A little zone: *spec.* the ring-shaped suspensory ligament of the crystalline lens (*z. of Zinn*). Hence **Zo·nular** *a.* pertaining to or forming a z. or little zone; *spec.* belonging to or affecting the z. of Zinn.

Zonure (zōᵘ·niuᵊɹ). 1883. [– mod.L. *Zonurus*, f. Gr. ζώνη ZONE + οὐρά tail.] *Zool.* A lizard of the genus *Zonurus*, having rings of spiny scales on the tail.

Zoo (zū). *colloq.* 1847. [First three letters of ZOOLOGICAL taken as one syllable.] The Zoological Gardens in London; also, any similar collection of animals elsewhere.

Zoo- (zōᵘ·o, zoᵢǫ·), before a vowel properly **zo-,** repr. Gr. ζῳο-, comb. form of ζῷον animal, occurring in numerous scientific and technical terms; occas. denoting the power of spontaneous movement.

‖**Zo·ocarp** [Gr. καρπός fruit], a zoospore. **Zooche·mistry,** the chemistry of animal bodies; so **Zooche·mical** *a.* **Zo·oculture** = *zootechny*; so **Zoocu·ltural** *a.* **Zo:odyna·mics,** the dynamics of animal bodies. ‖**Zoœcium** (zoᵢī·ʃⁱŏm) [Gr. οἶκος house], the thickened and hardened part of the cuticle of each polyp in a colony of Polyzoa, forming a cell or sheath in which it is lodged. **Zo·ogamete,** a motile gamete. **Zooge·nic** *a.*, produced from animals; *Geol.* applied to formations of animal origin. **Zo:ogeo·graphy,** the geographical distribution of animals; hence **Zo:o-geo·grapher, Zo:ogeogra·phical** *a.*, **-ally** *adv.* **Zo:ogeo·logy,** that branch of geology which deals with fossil animal remains; **-lo·gical** *a.*, **-o·logist.** ‖**Zooglœa** (-glī·ă) [Gr. γλοιά glue], a gelatinous mass of bacteria; hence **Zooglœ·ic** *a.* ‖**Zo:ogoni·dium,** pl. **-ia,** a motile gonidium. **Zoo·graphy** (now *rare*), descriptive zoology 1593; hence **Zoo·grapher, -gra·phic, -al** *adjs.*, **-ally** *adv.* **Zoogyroscope** (-dʒəiᵉ·rŏ-), a revolving glass cylinder enabling successive photographs of an animal to be thrown on a screen as continuous motion. **Zoo·latry** [-LATRY], the worship of animals. **Zo·olite,** a fossil animal or animal substance. **Zooma·gnetism,** animal magnetism. **Zo·omancy** [Gr. μαντεία], divination by observing the actions of animals. **Zo:omecha·nics,** = *zoodynamics*; hence **Zo:omecha·nical** *a.* **Zo:onoso·logy** [Gr. νόσος disease], the study of the diseases of animals. **Zoo·phagous** *a.* [Gr. -φαγος -eating], feeding on animals; carnivorous. **Zo·ophile,** a zoophilous plant; a zoophilist. **Zoo·philist** [Gr. -φιλος -loving], a lover of animals; an opponent of cruelty to animals, *spec.* an anti-vivisectionist. **Zoo·philous** *a.*, loving animals; also (*Bot.*) applied to plants whose seeds are disseminated by animal agency. **Zoophy·sics,** the study of physics in relation to animal bodies; so

Zoophy·sical *a.* **Zo:ophysio·logy,** animal physiology. **Zoopla·nkton,** floating animal organisms collectively. **Zoopra·xiscope** [Gr. πρᾶξις action], a form of zoogyroscope. **Zoo·scopy,** a species of hallucination in which imaginary animal forms are seen, as in delirium tremens; so **Zoosco·pic** *a.* **Zoo·sophy,** the knowledge or study of animals. **Zo·osperm,** (*a*) a spermatozoon, (*b*) a zoospore; hence **Zo:osperma·tic** *a.* **Zo·ospore,** a motile spore, swarm-spore, occurring in some Algæ, Fungi, and Protozoa. **Zo:ospora·ngium,** a receptacle containing zoospores. **Zoo·sporous** *a.*, producing, of the nature of, or affected by zoospores. **Zo·otaxy** [Gr. τάξις arrangement], zoological classification, a systematic zoology. **Zo·otechny** [Gr. τέχνη art], the art of rearing and using animals for any purpose; so **Zoote·chnic** *a.*, **Zoote·chnics** *sb.* **Zoo·theism,** the attribution of deity to animals; so **Zoothei·stic** *a.* **Zo·otype,** an animal, or figure of one, used as the type of a deity, as in Egyptian hieroglyphics. **Zootypic** (-ti·pik) *a.*, pertaining to the animal type or types.

Zooid (zōᵘ·oid). 1851. [f. Gr. ζῷον animal + -OID.] *Biol.* Something that resembles an animal (but is not one in the strict or full sense): now chiefly restricted to an animal arising from another by asexual reproduction, i.e. gemmation or fission; *spec.* each of the distinct beings which make up a compound or 'colonial' animal organism, and often have different forms and functions, thus more or less corresponding to the various organs in the higher animals.
The sexual z. is developed from the asexual, either directly by metamorphosis, or indirectly by gemmation or fission, thus giving rise to an Alternation of Generations 1888. Hence **Zo,oi·dal** *a.* **Zo,oidio·gamous** *a.* characterized by or of the nature of fertilization by the union of a motile cell with another cell.

Zookers (zu·kəɹz), *int. Obs.* or *arch.* and *dial.* 1620. [Short for *gadzwookers*; cf. next.] = next.

Zooks (zuks), *int. Obs.* or *arch.* and *dial.* 1634. [Short for *gadzooks* (GAD *sb.*⁵ 3).] An exclam. or minced oath, expressing vexation, surprise, or other emotion.

Zoological (zōᵘ,ǒlǫ·dʒikăl, *popularly* zū-lǫ·dʒ-), *a.* 1815. [f. ZOOLOGY + -ICAL.] Pertaining or relating to zoology; belonging or devoted to the scientific study of animals. **b.** *transf.* (freq. *joc.*) Animal 1855.
Z. Garden(s, the grounds of the London Z. Society in which its collection of wild animals is housed; hence *gen.* a garden or park in which wild animals are kept for public exhibition. **b.** One of the apartments has a zoological papering on the walls DICKENS. So **Zo,olo·gic** *a.* (*rare*) 1810. **Zo,olo·gically** *adv.*

Zoologist (zo,ǫ·lǒdʒist). 1663. [f. mod.L. *zoologia* + -IST.] One versed in zoology.

Zoologize (zo,ǫlǒdʒəiz), *v.* 1861. [f. next or prec.; see -IZE.] *intr.* To study zoology practically; to examine animals zoologically; *trans.* to explore or study zoologically.

Zoology (zo,ǫ·lǒdʒi). 1669. [– mod.L. *zoologia* (Sperling), mod.Gr. ζῳολογία (Schröder), f. Gr. ζῷον animal; see ZOO-, -LOGY.] The science which treats of animals, one of the two branches (*z.* and *botany*) of Natural History or Biology, and itself divided into ornithology, ichthyology, entomology, etc.; also, a treatise on, or system of, this science. So **Zoo·loger** (*rare*) = *zoologist* 1663.

Zoom (zūm), *v.* 1886. [imit.] **1.** *intr.* To make a continuous low-pitched buzzing sound. **2.** *Aircraft slang.* To rise very steeply after flying horizontally at a low level 1917.

Zoomorph (zōᵘ·omǭɹf). 1895. [f. Gr. ζῷον animal + μορφή shape.] A zoomorphic design or figure.

Zoomorphic (zōᵘomǭ·ɹfik), *a.* 1872. [f. as prec. + -IC.] **1.** Representing or imitating animal forms, as in decorative art. **2.** Attributing the form or nature of an animal to something, esp. to a deity or superhuman being 1880. **b.** Having, or represented as having, the form of an animal 1886.

Zoomorphism (zōᵘ·omǭɹfiz'm). 1840. [f. as prec. + -ISM, after ANTHROPOMORPHISM. Cf. Fr. *zoomorphisme.*] **1.** Attribution of animal form or nature to a deity or superhuman being. **2.** Imitation or representation of animal forms in decorative art or symbolism 1879.

‖**Zoon** (zōᵘ·ǫn). *Pl.* **zoa** (zōᵘ·ă). 1864. [mod.L. – Gr. ζῷον animal.] *Biol.* An organism scientifically regarded as a complete animal, whether consisting of a single being as in the higher animals, or a number of zooids as in the various 'persons' that make up a 'colonial' animal.

Zoophyte (zōᵘ·ǒfəit). 1621. [– Fr. *zoophyte* (Rabelais) – mod.L. *zoophyton* – Gr. ζῳόφυτον (Aristotle), f. ζῷον animal; see ZOO-, -PHYTE.] Any of the various animals of low organization formerly classed as intermediate between animals and plants, resembling the latter in being usu. fixed and in having a branched or radiating structure: as crinoids, sea-anemones, corals, sponges. So **Zo·ophytal, Zoophytic** (-fi·tik), *adjs.* **Zo:ophyto·graphy,** description of zoophytes. **Zo:ophyto·logy,** the department of zoology which treats of zoophytes; so **Zo:ophytolo·gical** *a.*

Zootomy (zo,ǫ·tǒmi). 1663. [– mod.L. *zootomia* (M.A. Severinus, 1645), prob. after late L. *anatomia* ANATOMY; see ZOO-, -TOMY.] The anatomy of animals; the dissection of animal bodies; in mod. use *esp.* comparative anatomy. So **Zooto·mic, -ical** *adjs.*, **-ically** *adv.* **Zoo·tomist,** a dissector of animal bodies, a comparative anatomist.

‖**Zophorus** (zōᵘ·fǒrǒs), **zoophorus** (zo,ǫ·fǒrǒs). 1563. [L. (Vitruvius) – Gr. ζῳ(ο)φόρος, f. ζῷον animal + -φορος -bearing.] *Anc. Arch.* A frieze bearing figures of men and animals carved in relief.

‖**Zopilote** (zōᵘ·piloᵘt). 1787. [Sp. – Mex. *azopilotl.*] A vulture of the family *Cathartidæ*, esp. the Amer. carrion vulture or turkey-buzzard, *Cathartes aura.*

Zoril (zǫ·ril). Also **zo·rille, zori·llo.** 1774. [– Fr. *sorille* – Sp. *zorrilla, -illo*, dim. of *zorro* ZORRO.] An animal of the African genus *Zorilla*, allied to the skunks; also applied to some Central and S. Amer. skunks.

Zoroastrian (zǫroæ·striăn), *a.* and *sb.* 1743. [f. L. *Zoroastres* – Gr. Ζωροάστρης – Zend *Zarathustra*; see -IAN.] **A.** *adj.* Of or pertaining to Zoroaster or his dualistic religious system. **B.** *sb.* A follower of Zoroaster; a Parsee 1811. Hence **Zoroa·strianism.**

‖**Zorro** (þo·rro, zǫ·ro). 1838. [Sp., = fox.] The S. Amer. fox-wolf. Also **Zorri·no,** a kind of skunk, or its fur.

‖**Zoster** (zǫ·stəɹ). 1706. [L. – Gr. ζωστήρ girdle.] **1.** The disease shingles, *Herpes zoster.* **2.** *Gr. Antiq.* A belt or girdle, esp. as worn by men 1824.

‖**Zostera** (zǫstīᵊ·ră). 1819. [mod.L. (Linn.), f. Gr. ζωστήρ; see prec., -A 2.] *Bot.* A marine plant of the genus *Zostera*, esp. grasswrack, *Z. marina.*

‖**Zosterops** (zǫ·stěrǫps). 1867. [mod.L. (Vigors and Horsefield, 1827), f. Gr. ζωστήρ girdle + ὤψ eye.] *Ornith.* Any small bird of the tropical and sub-tropical genus so named, characterized by a ring of white feathers round the eye; a silver-eye or white-eye.

Zouave (zuā·v). 1848. [– Fr. *zouave*, f. native name *Zouaoua.*] **1.** One of a body of French light infantry, orig. recruited from the Algerian Kabyle tribe of Zouaoua, but afterwards composed of selected French soldiers, formerly retaining the Oriental uniform. **b.** (Also *Pontifical* or *Papal Z.*) One of a French corps organized at Rome in 1860 for the defence of the Pope, and disbanded after 11 years. 1864. **c.** Applied to certain Northern volunteers in the American civil war (1861–5) 1865. **2.** In full *z. jacket, bodice*: A woman's short embroidered jacket or bodice, resembling the jacket of the Z. uniform 1859.

Zounds (zaundz), *int. Obs.* or *arch.* 1600. A euphemistic abbrev. of *by God's wounds* used in oaths and asseverations. See 's.

Zubr (zūbr). 1847. [Russ.] The European bison or aurochs.

‖**Zucchetto** (tsuke·to). 1853. [Incorrect but usual form for It. *zucchetta*, dim. of *zucca* gourd, the head.] The skull-cap of an ecclesiastic.

Zulu (zū·lu), *sb.* and *a.* 1824. [Native name.] **1.** Also *Z.-Kaffir.* (A member) of a warlike S. African race of blacks of a type resembling the Kaffir, and inhabiting Natal. **2.** Applied to the language spoken by the Zulus 1850. **3.** An artificial fly used in angling 1898.

Zumbooruk (zʊ·mburʊk). 1825. [– Hind. *zambūrak*, f. Pers. *zambūr* bee.] A small swivel-gun, esp. one mounted on the back of a camel.

Zunyite (zū·nyəit). 1885. [f. *Zuñi*, name of a mine in Colorado + -ITE¹ 2 b.] *Min.* A fluosilicate of aluminium.

Zurlite (zǖ·ɹləit). 1826. [f. name of Signor *Zurlo* of Naples + -ITE¹ 2 b.] *Min.* A white or green variety of melilite.

‖**Zwanziger** (tsva·ntsigəɹ). 1828. [G., f. *zwanzig* twenty.] An Austrian silver coin, equivalent to twenty kreutzers.

Zwieselite (tsvī·zěləit). 1861. [– G *zwieselit* (Breithaupt, 1841), f. *Zwiesel* in Bavaria; see -ITE¹ 2 b.] *Min.* A clove-brown variety of triplite.

Zwinglian (zwi·ngliăn, tsvi·-), *sb.* and *a.* 1532. [f. *Zwingli* (see below) + -AN.] **A.** *sb.* A follower of Ulrich Zwingli (1484–1531), the Swiss religious reformer. **B.** *adj.* Of or pertaining to Ulrich Zwingli or his doctrine, esp. concerning the Eucharist 1565. Hence **Zwi·nglianism.**

Zygadite (zi·gădəit). 1861. [– G. *zygadit*, f. Gr. ζυγάδην in pairs, f. ζυγόν yoke.] *Min.* A variety of albite occurring in reddish or yellowish-white tabular twin crystals.

‖**Zygæna** (zəidʒī·nă). 1683. [mod.L. – Gr. ζύγαινα.] **a.** *Ichth.* Any fish of the genus formerly so named (now *Sphyrna*), comprising the hammer-headed sharks. **b.** *Entom.* A genus of moths (also called *Anthrocera*), comprising the burnet-moths 1837.

Zygal (zəi·găl), *a.* 1886. [f. ZYGON + -AL¹ 1.] *Anat.* Pertaining to or having a zygon.

‖**Zygantrum** (zəigæ·ntrǒm, zig-). *Pl.* **-antra.** 1854. [mod.L., f. Gr. ζυγόν yoke + ἄντρον cave.] *Anat.* A double cavity on the posterior side of the neural arch of each ordinary vertebra in serpents and some lizards, into which the *zygosphene* of the next vertebra fits.

‖**Zygapophysis** (zəigăpǫ·fisis, zig-). *Pl.* **-physes** (fisīz). 1854. [mod.L., f. Gr. ζυγόν yoke + ἀπόφυσις APOPHYSIS.] *Anat.* and *Zool.* A lateral process on the neural arch of a vertebra articulating with the corresponding process of the next vertebra. Hence **Zygapophysial** (-ăpoti·ziăl) *a.*

Zygite (zəi·dʒəit). 1888. [– Gr. ζυγίτης, f. ζυγόν; see ZYGON 2, -ITE¹ 1.] *Gr. Antiq.* A rower in the upper tier of a bireme or the middle tier of a trireme; cf. THALAMITE, THRANITE.

Zygnemaceous (zignīmēⁱ·ʃəs), *a.* 1887. [f. mod.L. *Zygnemaceæ*, f. *Zygnema* (Kützing, 1843), irreg. f. Gr. ζυγόν yoke + νῆμα thread; see -ACEOUS.] *Bot.* Belonging to the family *Zygnemaceæ* of filamentous freshwater algæ, which propagate by conjugation. So **Zygnemid** (zignī·mid), a member of this order.

Zygo- (zəi·go, zi·go), before a vowel properly **zyg-**, repr. Gr. ζυγο-, comb. form of ζυγόν yoke; occurring in various scientific terms (in *Biol.* freq. with ref. to *zygosis* as a method of reproduction).
Zygobranchiate (-æ·ŋki,ět) *a.* and *sb.* (a gasteropod mollusc) having paired (right and left) gills. **Zygoda·ctyl** *a.*, having the toes arranged in pairs; yoke-toed; *sb.* a yoke-toed bird; so **Zygodacty·lic, Zygoda·ctylous** *adjs.* **Zy·godont** [Gr. ὀδούς, ὀδοντ- tooth] *a.*, of a molar tooth, having an even number of cusps arranged in pairs; of an animal, having such molar teeth. **Zygomo·rphic, Zygomo·rphous** *adjs.* [Gr. μορφή form] *Bot.*, of a flower, symmetrical about a single plane, divisible into similar lateral halves in only one way. **Zygophylla·ceous** [Gr. φύλλον leaf] *a.* *Bot.*, belonging to the family *Zygophyllaceæ*, typified by the genus *Zygophyllum* (bean-capers). **Zy·gophyte** (-fəit) [Gr. φυτόν plant], a plant which reproduces by conjugation. **Zygopleu·ra** [Gr. πλευρά side] *sb. pl. Morphology*, organic forms having bilateral symmetry, with either two or four antimeres; hence **Zygopleu·ral** *a.* **Zygo·pterid** [Gr. πτερόν wing] *sb.* and *a.*, (a member) of the *Zygoptera*, a division of dragon-flies, having all the wings nearly or quite equal in size. **Zy·gosperm,** = *zygospore.* **Zy·gosphere,** either of the two conjugating cells or gametes forming a zygospore. **Zy·gospore,** a germ-cell arising from the fusion of two similar cells (gametes), as in certain Algæ and Fungi. **Zygozo·ospore,** a motile zygospore.

‖**Zygoma** (zəigōu·mă, zig-). *Pl.* **-o·mata, -o·mas.** 1684. [– Gr. ζύγωμα, f. ζυγόν yoke; see -OMA.] *Anat.* The bony arch on each side of the skull in vertebrates, consisting of the malar or jugal bone (cheekbone) and its connections, and joining the facial to the cranial bones; also, some part of this arch, as the malar bone itself, or either of the two processes by which the cheekbone and the temporal bone articulate. So **Zygomatic** (-æ·tik) *a.* pertaining to, forming part of, or articulating with the zygoma; *sb.* a zygomatic muscle or bone. **Zygoma·tico-, zygo·mato-,** comb. forms of ZYGOMATIC, ZYGOMA.

‖**Zygon** (zəi·gǫn). *Pl.* **zyga** (zəi·gă). 1886. [– Gr. ζυγόν yoke.] *Anat.* The bar or stem connecting the two branches of an H-shaped fissure (*zygal fissure*) of the brain.

‖**Zygosis** (zəigōu·sis, zig-). 1880. [mod.L. – Gr. ζύγωσις, f. ζυγοῦν to yoke, f. ζυγόν yoke; see -OSIS.] *Biol.* = CONJUGATION 5.

Zygosphene (zəi·gosfīn, zi·g-). 1854. [f. Gr. ζυγόν yoke + σφήν wedge.] *Anat.* and *Zool.* A double wedge-shaped projection on the anterior side of the neural arch of each ordinary vertebra in serpents and some lizards, which fits into the *zygantrum* of the next vertebra.

Zygote (zəi·gout). 1891. [– Gr. ζυγωτός yoked, f. ζυγοῦν to yoke.] *Biol.* A germ-cell resulting from the union of two reproductive cells or gametes; also *attrib.* or as *adj.* Hence **Zygotic** (-ǫ·tik) *a.* pertaining to or of the nature of a zygote; produced or characterized by zygosis. **Zygo·toblast** [-BLAST], one of a number of germ-cells or sporozoites produced by budding from a zygotomere. **Zygo·tomere** [Gr. μέρος part], one of a number of cells formed by segmentation of a zygote in the malaria parasite or other *Sporozoa*.

Zymase (zəi·meis). 1875. [– Fr. *zymase* Béchamp), f. Gr. ζύμη leaven; see -ASE.] *Biochem.* Any of a group of enzymes which convert glucose into carbon dioxide and water or into alcohol and carbon dioxide according as oxygen is present or absent.

Zyme (zəim). 1882. [– Gr. ζύμη leaven.] The substance causing a zymotic disease.

Zymo- (zəi·mo), before a vowel **zym-**, comb. form repr. Gr. ζύμη leaven, used in the general sense 'ferment'.

Zymogen (zəi·modʒen) *Biol. Chem.*, a substance formed in an organism and producing a ferment; so **Zymogene·tic, Zymoge·nic** *adjs.* **Zym-o·logy,** the science of ferments and their action; so **Zymolo·gical** *a.*, **Zymo·logist. Zymo·lysis** [Gr. λύσις loosening], decomposition by means of a (esp. an unorganized) ferment; so **Zymoly·tic** *a.* **Zymo·meter,** an instrument measuring the degree of fermentation of a fermenting liquor. **Zy·mophyte** [Gr. φυτόν plant], a vegetable organism which causes fermentation. **Zy·motechny,** the art of fermentation; so **Zymote·chnic, -ical,** *adjs.*; **Zymote·chnics, Zy:motechno·logy,** the scientific study of the principles of zymotechny.

‖**Zymosis** (zəimōu·sis). *Pl.* **-oses** (-sīz). 1842. [mod.L. – Gr. ζύμωσις fermentation, f. ζύμη leaven; see -OSIS.] Fermentation; *spec.* the morbid process, regarded as analogous to or involving fermentation, which constitutes a zymotic disease.

Zymotic (zəimǫ·tik), *a.* (*sb.*) 1842. [– Gr. ζυμωτικός causing fermentation; see prec., -OTIC.] **A.** *adj.* A general epithet for infectious diseases, orig. because regarded as being caused by a process analogous to fermentation; pertaining to this theory of disease; causing such disease. **b.** Fermentative 1874. **c.** *transf.* Containing putrefactive germs 1881. **B.** *sb.* A zymotic disease 1842. Hence **Zymo·tically** *adv.*

Zymurgy (zəi·mɒɹdʒi). 1868. [f. Gr. ζύμη leaven + *-urgy* as in *metallurgy*, *thaumaturgy*. Cf. Gr. ζυμουργός maker of leaven.] The practice or art of fermentation, as in wine-making, brewing, distilling, etc.

ADDENDA

These addenda consist of (1) words not recorded in the body of the dictionary, and (2) further senses and constructions of words already treated. Additions of the latter kind, being arranged as appendages to existing articles, are readily distinguished by the absence of pronunciation, grammatical description, and etymology from the independent articles dealing with new words.

Words in the range A–G are drawn mainly from Volume I of *A Supplement to the Oxford English Dictionary* (1972). The letters H–Z in these addenda are based on the material in the *O.E.D.* files that will in due course be included in Volumes II and III of the *Supplement to the O.E.D.*

References to other entries in the dictionary are in CAPITALS, preceded by * for entries in these addenda.

The entries here shown were prepared by members of the O.E.D. department under the general direction of the Chief Editor, R. W. Burchfield, and in particular by the following: A. J. Augarde, M. W. Grose, A. M. Hughes, Miss S. Raphael, and Dr. J. B. Sykes. A first draft of some of the entries was prepared by Mrs. J. Coulson, Mrs. J. E. A. Field, Miss G. A. Rathbone, and Mrs. A. Wallace-Hadrill.

A.
I. *attrib.* Shaped like the letter A, as in *A-tent*.
II. 6. Designating a first-class road.
III. A = adult, designating cinema films suitable for adult audiences; A = advanced, as in *A level*; A = ampere; A = amalgamated, associated; Å, A = Ångstrom; A = atom(ic), as in *A-bomb*; A = auxiliary; A.A., Automobile Association, anti-aircraft; A.A.A., Amateur Athletic Association; A.C., A/C, aircraftman; A.D.C., aide-de-camp; A.F., a.f., audio frequency; A.I. (D., H.), artificial insemination (by donor, husband); A.L.(S.), autograph letter (signed); A.R.P., air-raid precautions; Å.U., A.U., Ångstrom unit; A.W.O.L., absent without leave.

‖**Aasvogel** (ā·sfōugəl). 1838. [S.-Afr. Du., f. *aas* carrion + *vogel* bird, FOWL.] A South African vulture, *Gyps kolbii*.

Aberdeen (æbəɹdī·n), name of a city and county in Scotland; **A. Angus,** a breed of polled black beef cattle 1862; **A. terrier,** a rough variety of Scotch terrier 1880. The adj. is **Aberdonian** (æbəɹdōu·niăn) 1670 [f. med.L. *Aberdonia*].

Abo (æ·bo). *Austral. slang.* 1922. [Shortened f. ABORIGINAL.] An Australian Aboriginal. Also *attrib.*

Aboard, *adv.* and *prep.* **A. 1. b.** On or on to a railway train, aircraft, etc. (orig. *U.S.*) 1856. Phr. *All aboard*, call to warn passengers to board a ship, aircraft, etc. 1838.

Abominable, *a.* **A. Snowman:** see *YETI.

Abort, *v.* **1. b.** *fig.* To bring to a premature or fruitless termination; *spec.* in *Aeronautics.* Also *intr.* 1614.

About-face. 1918. [Shortened f. RIGHT ABOUT *face*.] **a.** An instance of facing about. **b.** A complete reversal of principles, policy, or opinion 1934.

Above, *prep.*
3. Phr. *A. oneself*, in a more high-spirited, uncontrolled, or overweening state than the normal; out of hand.

Abrasive (ăbrēi·siv, -ziv), *a.* and *sb.* 1853. [f. ABRASE *v.* + -IVE.] **A.** *adj.* (In Dict. s.v. ABRASE *v.*) Also *fig.* 1875. **B.** *sb.* An abrasive agent 1853.

Abreaction (æbriæ·kʃən). 1912. [f. AB- + REACTION, after G. *abreagierung*.] *Psychiatry.* The liberation by revival and expression of the emotion associated with a repressed memory, instinct, etc.

Abroad. C. *sb.* Everywhere or anywhere that is outside one's own country 1895.
'Frogs,' he would say, 'are slightly better than Huns or Wops, but a. is unutterably bloody and foreigners are fiends' 1945.

Abseil (æ·bzəil, -sēil), *v.* 1941. [– G. *abseilen*, f. *ab* down + *seil* rope.] *Mountaineering. intr.* To descend a steep face by sliding down a doubled rope. Also as *sb.* 1933.

Absolute, *a.*
a. magnitude: see *MAGNITUDE; **a. pitch,** the pitch of a note as determined by its frequency; ability to recognize or reproduce any note within the range of the ear or the voice; **a. temperature,** temperature measured from a. zero (in degrees centigrade or Fahrenheit); **a. value** *Math.*, of a real number, its value irrespective of sign; of any complex number $a + ib$, the positive square root of $a^2 + b^2$; **a. zero:** see ZERO 3.

Abstract, *a.* **4.** In the fine arts, characterized by lack of, or freedom from, representational qualities 1915.
Two of his abstract pictures have been deliberately hung sideways..at the Tate Gallery 1952.
Abstra·ctionism, the pursuit or cult of abstraction in art.

Academic. A. 5. Conforming too rigidly to the methods or principles of an academy (esp. of the fine arts) 1889.

Accelerate, *v.* **1. b.** *spec.* To increase the speed of (a vehicle or its engine); also *absol.* 1902.

Accelerator. c. *Physics.* A large apparatus for producing charged atomic or sub-atomic particles and accelerating them to high energies by means of electric or electromagnetic fields 1931.

Acceptor. (See after ACCEPT *v.*) **2.** *Chem.* and *Physics.* An atom or molecule capable of receiving an electron pair from another atom, so forming a co-ordinate bond with it; in a semiconductor, an impurity atom that has a lower valency than the majority of atoms and can receive an electron from the valency band; cf. *DONOR 2. 1907.

Accessory. B. *sb.* **1.** *spec.* (usu. *pl.*), any of the smaller articles (as shoes, gloves, etc.) of a woman's dress 1896.

Accident.
Comb.: **a.-prone** *a.*, predisposed or likely to cause or attract an accident.

Accommodation.
a. address, an address used only or primarily for convenience of correspondence, esp. one adopted to conceal the addressee's whereabouts; **a. ladder,** a ladder up a ship's side for use in entering or leaving small boats; **a. road,** a road constructed to give access to land or property not adjoining a public road.

Acculturation (ăkʌltiŭrēi·ʃən). 1880. [f. AC- *pref.* + CULTURE + -ATION.] *Anthrop.* The adoption and assimilation of an alien culture or some of its traits.
Hence **Accu·lturate, Accu·lturize** *vbs.*
Acculturation comprehends those phenomena which result when groups of individuals having different cultures come into continuous first-hand contact, with subsequent changes in the original culture patterns of either or both groups 1936.

Accumulator. **3. b.** A form of betting in which the amount won on one event is staked on a subsequent event 1923.

Ace. **1. b.** Substitute: In lawn-tennis, etc., an unreturnable stroke, esp. a service that the opponent fails to touch; the point scored by this 1889. **2. b.** Also (chiefly *U.S.*), a person outstanding in any activity or occupation; also *attrib.* 1919.

Acetate. **2.** Synthetic material (e.g. textile fibre or fabric, plastic) made from cellulose acetate; freq. *attrib.* 1920.

A. rayons burn more slowly than other rayons 1926.

Acetyl. **Acetylcholine** (æ:sītil-, ăsī:til,-kōu·līn), the acetyl ester of choline, a compound synthesized at the end of certain nerve fibres and released when a nerve impulse reaches it, thereby transmitting the impulse to the next nerve fibre (at a synapse) or to the muscle fibre (at a neuromuscular junction) 1906.

Acheulian (ăʃi·ū·liăn), *a.* 1894. [– Fr. *acheuléen* (G. de Mortillet, 1873).] *Archæol.* Of or belonging to the Palæolithic period so called, named from the site at Saint-Acheul, near Amiens.

Achilles (ăki·līz). 1810. [L. form of Gr. Ἀχιλλεύς.] *Achilles' heel, heel of Achilles*: the only vulnerable spot. *Achilles' tendon* = TENDON *of Achilles.*

Acid. **B.** *sb.* **b.** = *LSD 1966.

Also *attrib.* and *Comb.*, as *a. trip*, etc.; **a.-head,** one who takes LSD.

Ack (æk). 1898. Arbitrary syllable formerly used for *a* in telephone communications and in oral transliterations of code messages.

ack-ack (= *A.A.*), anti-aircraft (gunfire, regiment, etc.); **a. emma** (= *a.m.*), ante meridiem; air mechanic.

Acoustic, *a.* **1. b.** Applied to any device or material designed to reduce noise; sound-absorbent 1924.

An acoustic tile that is many times as absorbent as the usual masonry surfaces 1924.

a. mine, an underwater mine designed to explode when triggered by sound waves from a ship's engines or propellers.

Acronym (æ·krŏnim). 1943. [f. ACRO- + *-onym* after HOMONYM.] A word formed from the initial letters of other words, as *ANZAC, *LASER[2].

Across, *adv.*

3. Phr. *To come a.* (*with*): *colloq.*, orig. *U.S.*, to hand over, contribute (money, information, etc.). *To get* or *come a.*: see GET *v.* VII. *To put a.*: to put over (see PUT *v.*[1] IV).

Acrylic (-i·lik), *a.* Also applied to synthetic substances made by polymerizing a. acid or derivatives of it, as *a. fibre, plastic, resin*; made of acrylic plastic. Also as *sb.*

Dresses in Courtelle, the first British a. fibre 1958.

Actinomycetes (æ:ktinomaisī·tīz), *sb. pl.* 1916. [f. ACTINO- + MYCETES.] *Biol.* Micro-organisms belonging to the order Actinomycetales; filamentous bacteria.

Action.

attrib. **a. painting,** a form of painting in which the paint is applied by the spontaneous or random action of the artist; **a. stations,** positions in a ship, etc., to be taken up when going into action or proceeding to a manœuvre.

Activate, *v.* Delete † and add: *Esp.* = ACTUATE *v.* 3, 4. **b.** To make (a substance, a molecule, an organism, etc.) active or more active (esp. in various technical senses); to increase the activity of 1858. So **Activa·tion, A·ctivator.**

Activated carbon, charcoal, carbon, esp. charcoal, which has been treated to make it more adsorbent; **activated sludge,** aerated sewage containing aerobic bacteria.

Active, *a.*

A. list: see LIST *sb.*[5] **A. service:** see SERVICE[1] II. 6.

Ad (æd), colloq. abbrev. of ADVERTISEMENT and *advertising* 1841.

Also *attrib.* and *Comb.*, as *ad-man*, *ADMASS. Like all successful ad-men he has come to believe quite uncritically in what he sells 1933.

Adam[2] (æ·dăm). 1872. The surname of the brothers Robert (1728–92) and James (1730–94) *Adam*, used to designate buildings, furniture, etc., designed by them. Also **Adams.**

Adamant. **B.** *adj.* Unshakeable, inflexible.

Adapt, *v.* **3.** *intr.* To become adapted (*to*) 1956.

Birds certainly a...particularly well to the suburban community 1962.

Addicted, *ppl. a.* **3. b.** Dependent on the continued taking of some drug; characterized by addiction (sense *2b) *to.*

Addiction. **2. b.** The condition in which a person is dependent on the continued taking of some drug, the deprivation of which causes adverse effects including an uncontrolled craving for it.

Addiction to alcohol occurs in some individuals who drink excessively 1970.

Addictive (ădi·ktiv), *a.* 1939. [f. ADDICT *v.* + -IVE.] (Of drugs, etc.) tending to cause addiction.

Additive, *a.* **B.** *sb.* A substance added in small quantities to impart specific qualities to the resulting product 1945.

Adélie (ăde·li). Also **Adelie.** 1907. The name of *Adélie* Land in the Antarctic, used *attrib.* or *ellipt.* of a kind of penguin (*Pygoscelis adeliæ*) found there.

Adenine (æ·dėnīn). Also **-in.** 1885. [–G. *adenin* (A. Kossel, 1885), f. Gr. ἀδήν gland: see -INE[5].] *Biochem.* A crystalline base, $C_5H_5N_5$, found esp. in certain glands and as a constituent of nucleic acids, being paired with thymine in double-stranded DNA.

Ad lib. (æ:dli·b). 1811. **A.** *adv. phr.* See AD LIBITUM. **B.** *adj.* orig. *U.S.* Extemporized, improvised, spontaneous 1925. Also as *sb.* Hence **A:d-li·b** *v.* (orig. *U.S.*), to speak extempore, improvise (words, etc.), esp. in the course of a stage or broadcast performance 1919.

When Jones got lost back stage, I had to ad-lib. . until he came on 1929.

Ad-man: see *AD.

Admass (æ·dmæs). 1955. [f. *AD + MASS *sb.*[2]] That section of the community which is readily influenced by mass publicity, advertising, etc.

Admin. (æ̆dmi·n), colloq. abbrev. of ADMINISTRATION 1942.

‖**Ad nauseam** (æd nǭ·sīæm), *advb. phr.* 1647. [L., 'to sickness'.] To a sickening extent.

Adsorption. Substitute for def.: The process by which atoms or molecules are attracted to the exposed surface of a solid or liquid and adhere to it, covering it with a very thin layer. Hence **Adso·rb** *v.*, to collect or attract by adsorption. **Adso·rbate,** the material that is adsorbed. **Adso·rbent,** the material or body that adsorbs.

Advance, *sb.*

a. copy, a copy of a book sent out in advance of publication.

Advert (æ·dvəɹt), *sb.* 1860. Colloq. abbrev. of ADVERTISEMENT.

Aerobe. So **Aerobic** (-ōu·bik) *a.* 1884.

Aerofoil (ēə·rŏfoil). 1907. [f. AERO- + FOIL *sb.*[1]] A structure (e.g. a rudder or wing of an aircraft) designed to give rise to a force (other than drag) when moving through the air.

Aerosol (ēə·rŏsǫl). 1923. [f. AERO- + SOL[5].] **1.** A colloidal suspension of liquid or solid particles in a gas. **2.** A substance packed under pressure in a container with a device for releasing the substance in the form of an aerosol; a container of this kind 1944.

Aerospace (ēə·rŏspēˡs). 1958. [SPACE *sb.* II. 4.] The earth's atmosphere and the regions beyond it. Also *attrib.*

Affiliate, *a.* Also as *sb.*, an affiliated organization, company, etc. 1879.

Afghan (æ·fgæn), *a.* and *sb.* 1798. Pertaining to, a native of, Afghanistan.

A. hound, a swift hunting dog of the Near East, having thick silky hair.

‖**Aficionado** (ăfiþionā·ðo; anglicized as ăfisiŏnā·do). Pl. **-os.** 1845. [Sp., = amateur.] A devotee of bull-fighting; by extension an ardent follower of any hobby or activity.

This sham fight is despised by the *torero* and *aficionado* 1845. The *aficionados* of science fiction and golf 1957.

African.

Comb.: **A. violet** = *SAINTPAULIA.

Africana (æfrikā·nă, -ēˡ·nă). 1908. [f. *Africa* + *-ANA.] Books, documents, etc., relating to or concerned with, or objects peculiar to or connected with Africa, especially Southern Africa.

Afrikaner (æfrikā·nəɹ). 1801. [Afrikaans, earlier (Cape) Du. *Afrikaander*, f. *Afrikaan* sb., African + *-d)er*, pers. suff. modelled on termination of *Hollander* Dutchman.] **1.** An Afrikaans-speaking white South African, esp. one of Dutch descent. (Replacing AFRICANDER.) 1824. **2.** *Bot.* An iridaceous South African flower belonging to any of various species of *Gladiolus* or *Homoglossum.*

Afro- (æ·fro), comb. form of L. *Afer*, pl. *Afri* African, as in **Afro-A·sian** *a.*, pertaining to the countries of Africa and Asia together.

Afrormosia (æfrǫɹmōu·ziă). 1920. [mod. L. (H. Harms, 1906), f. *AFRO- + mod. L. *Ormosia*, a genus of trees.] A North and West African tree of the leguminous genus *Afrormosia*, esp. *A. laxiflora* and *A. elata*; the wood of this tree.

A consumers' paradise of transistor radio sets, electric food mixers, and a. coffee tables 1960.

A·fter-care. 1854. [AFTER-, CARE *sb.*[1]] Care or attention given after a course of medical treatment, a term of imprisonment, etc.

Agapanthus (ægăpæ·nþŏs). 1789. [mod. L. (C. L. L'Héritier de Brutelle, 1788), f. Gr. ἀγάπη love + ἄνθος flower.] A perennial herb of the genus so called, which is native to South Africa, belongs to the family Liliaceæ, and is cultivated for its large umbels of blue or white flowers.

Age, *v.* Also, of a substance or a thing, to undergo certain definite changes in its properties that are the natural consequence of the passage of time; freq. as **Ageing** *vbl. sb.* Also *trans.*, to produce such changes, esp. by artificial means, in.

‖**Agent provocateur** (aʒaṅ provokatŏr). 1877. [Fr., 'provocative agent'.] An agent employed to induce or incite a suspected person or group to commit an incriminating act.

Aid, *sb.* **1. b.** phr. *In a. of*: in support of (a cause or charity) 1837. Hence, *fig.* and *colloq.* (presumably having its origin in the freq. use of the phr. in appealing for the public support of a cause), about, concerned with 1935.

3. b. *spec.* Anything, esp. a device or apparatus, by which assistance is given in performing an operation or fulfilling a function; esp. with defining word, as *hearing aid, navigational aid, visual aid* 1924.

1. b. A Benefit will take place in A. of the Funds of the New Alms Houses 1837. 'That's your disillusioned expression, Fox,' said Alleyn. 'What's it in a. of?' 1935.

‖**Aide-mémoire** (ēˡ·dmemwāɹ, ‖ędmemwār). 1846. [Fr., f. *aider* to AID + *mémoire* MEMORY.] An aid to the memory; in diplomatic use, a memorandum.

Aileron (ēˡ·lĕrǫn). 1909. [– Fr. *aileron*, dim. of *aile* (:– L. *ala*) wing.] A movable aerofoil used to maintain or restore the balance of an aircraft in flight, usu. a hinged flap in the trailing edge of a wing.

Air, *sb.* **I. 1. b.** The air considered as a medium for the transmission of radio waves 1927. **3. b.** The air considered as a medium for the operation of aircraft.

1. b. *On the a.*: (being) broadcast by radio or television; so *off the a.* **3. b.** *By a.*: by air transport.

Comb.: **a. arm,** that branch of the armed forces which fights in the air; **a.-borne** *a.*, carried through the air; (of aircraft) that is in the air; (of troops) carried by aircraft; **a.-bus,** a short- to medium-range subsonic aircraft designed to carry a large number of passengers relatively cheaply; **a.-conditioning,** the process of cleaning air and controlling its temperature and humidity before it enters a room, building, etc.; so **a.-conditioned** *a.*; **a.-cooled** *a.*, cooled by means of a current of air; **a.-corridor,** a route to which aircraft are restricted; **a.-cushion,** (*b*) a body of air serving to provide support; esp. *attrib.* in **a.-cushion vehicle,** a hovercraft; **a.-drop,** the landing of troops or supplies by parachute; **airfield,** an area of land where aircraft are accommodated and maintained, and may take off or land; **a. hostess,** a stewardess in a passenger aircraft; **a.-lift,** transportation of supplies or troops by aircraft; **a.-lock,** (*a*) = LOCK *sb.*[2] II.4; a similar chamber in a submarine, spacecraft, etc.; (*b*) a stoppage of the flow of liquid in a pump or pipe by a bubble of air; **airmail,** mail conveyed by air; **a.-pocket,** a local atmospheric condition which causes an aircraft to lose height suddenly; **a. power,** power of defensive and offensive action dependent upon a supply of aircraft, missiles, etc.; **a.-raid,** also *attrib.*, as *a.-raid precautions, shelter, warning*; **airscrew,** the driving screw of an aircraft, a propeller; **a.-sea rescue,** applied to a branch of the R.A.F. whose task is to rescue airmen and passengers from the sea, and to such operations; **a.-sick** *a.*, sick from the motion of an aircraft; **a. space,** the air above a country, esp. considered as subject to its jurisdiction; **a. speed,** the speed of an aircraft, or of anything flying, in relation to the air through which it is moving; **a.-strip,** a strip of land prepared for the taking off and landing of aircraft; **a. terminal,** the town office of an air-line, equipped for the reception of passengers; **air-to-air** *a.*, from one aircraft to another.

Air, *v.* 4. Also, to expose (an opinion, etc.) to public view, to make public 1879.

A chance of airing some of his pet theories 1879.

Aircraft. Pl. **aircraft.** For 1907 read 1850 and substitute for def.: A flying machine; now usually used of aeroplanes, helicopters, etc., as distinct from balloons and airships.

Comb.: **a.-carrier,** a ship that carries and serves as a base for aircraft; **aircraftman,** the lowest non-commissioned rank in the Royal Air Force; so **aircraftwoman.**

Airport (ēᵊ·ɹpōᵊɹt). 1919. [PORT *sb.*¹, in transf. use of sense 2.] An aerodrome, esp. with customs facilities, to which aircraft resort to take on board or set down passengers, or load and unload freight.

Aisle. 3. c. A passage-way between rows of seats in a building other than a church (esp. a theatre or cinema), or in a train, etc. 1755.

Alarm, *sb.* **II. 1.** *Alarms* (or *alarums*) *and excursions*: a stage direction occurring in varying forms in Shakes. *Hen. VI* and *Rich. III*; now used playfully for: skirmishing, confused fighting, sudden divagations, and the like 1891.

Albanian (ælbē¹·niǎn), *a.* and *sb.* 1596. [f. med.L. *Albania*, med.Gr. Ἀλβανία + -AN.] **A.** *adj.* Of or pertaining to Albania, a country of the western part of the Balkan peninsula. **B.** *sb.* A native or inhabitant of Albania 1596. **b.** The language of the Albanian people 1813.

Albion (æ·lbiən). *poet.* or *rhet.* OE. [L. *Albion* (Gr. Ἀλουίων Ptolemy, Ἀλβίων), – Celtic **Albiō(n)-*, referred to **albho-* (L. *albus* white), with ref. to the white cliffs of Dover.] Great Britain.

Perfidious A., rendering F. *la perfide Albion*, a rhetorical expression for 'Britain', with ref. to her alleged treacherous policy towards foreigners 1841.

Alcoholic, *a.* **B.** *sb.* One who suffers from alcoholism; also, one who is addicted to alcohol 1891.

Aldrin (æ·ldrin). 1949. [f. the name of K. *Ald(e)r* (1902–58), German chemist + -IN¹.] A crystalline solid that is a chlorinated cyclic hydrocarbon, $C_{12}H_8Cl_6$, and is used as an insecticide.

Aleck: see *SMART *a.*

Alembicated (ăle·mbikē¹tėd), *ppl. a.* 1786. [f. ALEMBIC + -ATE³ + -ED¹.] Of literary style, ideas, etc., over-refined, over-subtilized, as if by repeated distillation. So **Alembica·tion.**

Alert (ălɔ̄·ɹt), *v.* 1868. [f. the adj.] *trans.* To put on the alert, to rouse to vigilance.

Algol (æ·lgǫl). Also **ALGOL.** 1959. [f. *algo(rithmic* (see *ALGORITHM) + initial letter of *language.*] *Computers.* A programming language used chiefly for mathematical and scientific calculations.

Algonquian, -kian (ælgǫ·ŋkiǎn, -ŋkwiǎn), *a.* and *sb.* 1885. [f. *Algonquin*, name of a N. Amer. Indian people; see -IAN.] **A.** *adj.* Of or pertaining to a large group, which includes the Algonquins, of tribes speaking languages or dialects belonging to the most widespread family of N. American Indian languages. **B.** *sb.* **1.** The Algonquian family of languages; an Algonquian language 1891. **2.** An Algonquian Indian 1900.

Algorithm (æ·lgŏriđ'm). 1699. [var. of ALGORISM due to confusion with Gr. ἀριθμός number.] **1.** Algorism. **2.** A procedure or set of rules for calculation or problem-solving, now esp. with a computer 1938. Hence **Algori·thmic** *a.*

Alibi, *sb.* **b.** orig. *U.S.* A plea of innocence; a pretext, an excuse 1912. Hence **Alibi** *v.*

Alicyclic (ælisəi·klik), *a.* 1891. [– G. *alicyclisch* (E. Bamberger, 1889), f. *ali phatisch* *ALIPHATIC + *cyclisch* (now *zyklisch*) CYCLIC.] *Chem.* Combining the properties of aliphatic and cyclic compounds; cyclic but not containing a benzene ring or similar structure.

Alienation. 1. b. [tr. G. *verfremdung* (Brecht).] The effect, regarded by some playwrights as desirable or essential, of preventing the emotional involvement of the audience with the events or characters on the stage 1949.

Aliphatic (ælifæ·tik), *a.* 1889. [f. Gr. ἄλειφαρ, ἀλειφατ- fat (so named from the structure of the fatty acids) + -IC.]. *Chem.* Applied to organic compounds having an open-chain structure (i.e. one with no rings).

All. A. 7. b. In scoring at games, denoting that both sides have made the stated score; *love all* = neither side has scored 1742.

All- in comb. **a. clear,** a signal giving information that there is no (further) danger; **a.-electric** *a.*, using only electric power; **a. in** *a.*, exhausted; **a.-in** *a.*, inclusive of all; in *Wrestling*, without restrictions; **a. right:** see RIGHT *a.* II.11, RIGHT *adv.* III.2; **a.-sorts,** a mixture of all or many kinds, esp. (*liquorice a.-sorts*) of sweets containing liquorice; **a.-star** *a.*, in which all the performers, etc., are stars; **a. there:** see THERE *adv.*; **a.-time** *a.*, of a record level or figure, etc., for all time up to the present (orig. *U.S.*); **a.-up weight,** the total weight of an aircraft in the air, including fuel, crew, passengers, and cargo; so **a. up** *adv.*

Allergy (æ·ləɹdʒi). 1911. [– G. *allergie* (von Pirquet, 1906), f. Gr. ἄλλος other, different + ἐργεια (known only in ἐνέργεια ENERGY), used for 'reactivity'; see -Y³.] *Path.* The altered degree of susceptibility of a body produced by a sensitizing dosage or exposure to some foreign material; more widely, abnormal sensitivity to the action of a particular foreign material, as certain foods, pollens, etc. Also *fig.* Hence **A·llergen** [after *ANTIGEN], a substance producing a.; **Alle·rgic** *a.*, characterized by or pertaining to a., or an a.; const. *to*; (*colloq.*) antipathetic *to.*

Alley-way (æ·liwē¹). orig. *U.S.* 1788. [f. ALLEY + WAY *sb.*] A narrow passage-way.

Allomorph (æ·lomǭɹf). 1948. [f. Gr. ἄλλος other, different + *MORPH(EME.] *Philol.* A morphemic alternant; one of two or more morphs making up a morpheme. Hence **Allomo·rphic** *a.*

Allophone (æ·lofōᵘn). 1938. [f. Gr. ἄλλος other, different + PHONE(ME.] *Philol.* Any of the variants making up a single phoneme. Hence **Allopho·nic** *a.*

All out, *adv.* Delete † and add: **2.** Using or involving all one's (or its) strength or resources; 'fully extended'; at top speed 1895. Hence as *adj. phr.*

All over, *adv.* **3. b.** Covering every part, esp. of ornamental patterns or designs 1859.

Allure, *sb.*¹ Delete † and add: **b.** [– Fr. *allure.*] Personal charm or power of attraction 1901.

Alpha-numeric (æ:lfǎ,niume·rik), *a.* Also **alpha-numerical.** 1955. [f. ALPHA(BET *sb.* + NUMERIC(AL *a.*] *Computers.* Consisting of or employing both letters and numerals.

Also, *adv.*

2. *A. ran*, applied to horses in a race which are not placed; *fig.* an unsuccessful competitor, an inferior person or thing 1896.

Alstrœmeria (ælströmĭᵊ·riǎ). 1791. [mod. L. (Linnæus, 1762), f. the name of Baron Clas *Alstrœmer* (1736–96), Swedish naturalist: see -IA¹.] A plant of the large genus so called, belonging to the family Amaryllidaceæ, native to South America, and including several species cultivated in gardens or greenhouses.

Alternator (ǭ·ltəɹnē¹tǭɹ). 1892. [f. ALTERNATE *v.* + -OR 2.] *Electr.* An electric generator that gives an alternating current.

Altimeter. 2. (*usu.* æ·ltimitəɹ). An instrument for measuring the altitude, esp. of an aircraft 1918.

Altogether. C. *sb.* **b.** *The a.* (colloq.), the nude 1894.

I have sat for the 'a.' to several other people DU MAURIER.

Alumnus. Also, a graduate or former student (chiefly *U.S.*) 1696.

Ambi- (æmbi), repr. L. *ambi-*, both, on both sides, comb. form of *ambo* both.

Ambience (æ·mbiěns). 1889. [f. AMBIENT: see -ENCE. Cf. Fr. *ambiance.*] Environment, surroundings; atmosphere.

Ambivalence (æmbi·vǎlěns). 1912. [– G. *ambivalenz* (Bleuler), f. *AMBI-, after EQUIVALENCE.] The coexistence in one person of contradictory emotions or attitudes towards a person or thing; the quality of being ambivalent; contradiction, ambiguity.

Ambivalent (æmbi·vǎlěnt), *a.* 1916. [f. prec., after EQUIVALENT.] Having either or both of two contrary or parallel values, qualities, or meanings; entertaining contrary emotions towards the same person or thing; ambiguous, equivocal. Hence **Ambi·valently** *adv.*

Ambulance. 2. b. A vehicle for conveying sick, injured, or disabled persons 1922.

Americium (æměri·siǒm, -ʃiǒm). 1946. [f. *Americ(a* + -IUM.] A radioactive silvery-white metallic element produced artificially. Symbol Am; atomic number 95.

Amerind (æ·měrind), **Amerindian** (æměri·ndiǎn), *sbs.* and *adjs.* 1900. Contractions of *American Indian.*

Amharic (æmhæ·rik), *a.* and *sb.* 1813. [f. *Amhara*, name of a province of Ethiopia + -IC.] **A.** *adj.* Of or pertaining to Amhara, its people, or its language. **B.** *sb.* The language of Amhara, the principal language of modern Ethiopia 1836.

Amino- (ǎmī·no), *Chem.*, combining form of AMINE, used *spec.* in names of compounds containing the group $—NH_2$ combined with a non-acid radical.

A.-acid, any of numerous simple organic compounds that contain a basic amino group and an acidic carboxyl group, certain of which are important as essential constituents of proteins.

Ammo (æ·mo). Slang abbrev. of AMMUNITION (used esp. of ammunition for small arms). Also *attrib.* 1917.

Amœbic (ǎmī·bik), *a.* 1891. [f. AMŒB)A + -IC.] Pertaining to, of the nature of, or caused by an amœba or amœbæ.

Amp. 1886. [abbrev.] = AMPÈRE.

Ampelopsis (æmpėlǫ·psis). 1807. [mod. L. (L. C. M. Richard, 1803), f. Gr. ἄμπελος vine + ὄψις appearance.] A climbing plant of the genus so called, which belongs to the vine family and formerly included the Virginia Creeper (now transferred to the genus *Parthenocissus*).

Amphetamine (æmfe·tǎmīn, -in). 1938. [f. *a*lpha-*m*ethyl-*ph*en*et*hyl*amine.*] A synthetic drug used as a stimulant for the central nervous system.

A., popularly known as an ingredient of 'pep pills' 1955.

Amphibian, *a.* (Of a vehicle) able to operate both on land and in water; *sb.* an amphibian tank or other vehicle 1920.

Amplify, *v.* **1. b.** *Electr.* To increase the strength of (a current, signal, etc.) 1915.

Amplitude. 6. b. *Electr.* The maximum departure of the value of an alternating current or voltage from the average value 1895.

A. modulation (in *Radio*), modulation of a wave by variation of its a.; abbrev. *A.M.*

Ampoule (æ·mpūl). 1907. [– Fr. – L. AMPULLA.] A small sealed (glass) vessel containing sterilized materials for injection.

Amputee (æmpiutī·). 1910. [f. AMPUT(ATE *v.* + -EE¹.] One who has lost a limb, etc., by amputation.

Amytal (æ·mitæl, -ǎl). 1926. [Proprietary name, f. AMY(L², another name for the pentyl radical + **Barbi)tal*, from which Amytal differs in having one of the two ethyl groups replaced by a pentyl group.] *Pharm.* Amylobarbitone, a barbiturate used, often as the sodium salt, as a sedative and hypnotic; both it and the sodium salt are white, odourless powders with a bitter taste.

Here's some sodium amytal. One of these capsules will calm him down STEINBECK.

-ana (ā·nǎ, ē¹·nǎ), *suffix.* [See ANA.] Appended to proper names to form collective substantives with the general meaning of 'books, documents, and the like relating to or concerned with, a place or person', as *Africana, Americana, Victoriana.*

Anabolism (ǎnæ·bŏliz'm). 1886. [f. Gr.

ἀναβολή ascent, f. ἀναβάλλειν throw upwards, f. ἀνά ANA- + βάλλειν throw; see -ISM.] *Biol.* Constructive metabolism, in which new, more complex substances (such as constituents of body tissues) are synthesized from simpler ones, usually with the consumption of energy. So **Anabo·lic** *a.*

Anaerobe (ænēᵊ·rōᵘb, -ē·ərōᵘb, æ·nēᵊrōᵘb). 1884. [– Fr. *anaérobie* adj. (Pasteur, 1863) anaerobic (later also as sb.), f. AN- 10 + *aérobie* aerobic. The English sb. is modelled on MICROBE.] A micro-organism which requires, or can live in, the absence of free oxygen. So **Anaerobic** (-ōᵘ·bic) *a.*, of, pertaining to, or of the nature of an anaerobe; not involving free oxygen.

Glycolysis does not involve a consumption of oxygen, and is therefore an anaerobic process 1970.

Analogue. **3. Analogue computer,** a computer which operates with numbers represented by some physically measurable quantity, such as length, voltage, etc. Also *a. device, machine,* etc. 1946.

Analysis. **1. b.** *In the last* (*final, ultimate*) *a.* [after Fr. *en dernière analyse*]: at the conclusion of the investigation or examination involved, all things duly considered and weighed 1791. **9.** = PSYCHO-ANALYSIS 1907.

Anaphora. **b.** *Gram.* The use of a word which refers to, or is a substitute for, a preceding word or group of words 1933. Hence **Anapho·ric** *a.*

Anaphylaxis (æ:năfilæ·ksis). 1907. [mod. L., – Fr. *anaphylaxie* (Portier & Richet 1902), f. ANA- + Gr. φύλαξις guarding. Cf. *prophylaxis.*] *Med.* Extreme sensitivity to the re-introduction of an antigen. Hence **A:naphyla·ctic** *a.*

Anaptyxis (ænăpti·ksis). 1895. [mod.L., – Gr. ἀνάπτυξις unfolding.] *Phonetics.* The development of a vowel between two consonants. So **Anapty·ctic** *a.* 1885.

Anarchy. **1. b.** A theoretical state of society in which there is no governing person or body, but each individual has absolute liberty 1850.

A:nastigma·tic, *a.* 1890. [f. AN- 10 + ASTIGMATIC *a.*; cf. G. *anastigmatisch.*] Not astigmatic: applied to a compound lens for correcting astigmatic aberration. So **Ana-sti·gmat** [G.], an a. lens or system of lenses.

And, *conj.*¹ **B. I. 3. c.** *and/or*: formula denoting that the items joined by it are to be taken either together or as alternatives 1855.

The Press has rather plumped for the scholar as writer, and/or as bibliophile 1959.

Androgen (æ·ndrodʒĕn). 1936. [f. Gr. ἀνδρο-, comb. form of ἀνήρ man, male + -GEN.] *Physiol.* Any sex hormone or other substance which in a male mammal will produce or maintain the secondary sex characteristics. Hence **Androge·nic** *a.*

Angel. **6.** *slang* (orig. *U.S.*). A financial backer of an enterprise, esp. one who supports a theatrical production 1891. **7.** An unexplained mark on a radar screen 1947.

Angle, *sb.*² **1. b.** Used for: The point or direction from which one views or approaches an object, circumstance, event, subject of inquiry, etc.; hence (loosely), aspect. Also (in full *camera a.*), the direction or viewpoint from which a photograph, film scene, etc., is taken 1872.

Mr. Lewis turns the figure round and allows us to view it from every possible a. 1922.

A:nglo-Fri·sian, *sb.* and *a.* 1877. [f. ANGLO- + FRISIAN.] **A.** *adj.* **1.** Pertaining to both English and Frisian. **2.** In the use of H. Sweet and some later writers: pertaining to a subdivision of the West Germanic branch of the Germanic group of languages, the hypothetical parent language of Anglo-Saxon and Old Frisian 1907. **B.** *sb.* In senses of the *adj.*

Anglophile (æ·ŋglofəil), *a.* and *sb.* 1867. [See ANGLO-, -PHIL.] **A.** *adj.* Friendly to England or to what is English. **B.** *sb.* One who is friendly to England 1883.

Anglophone (æ·ŋglofōᵘn), *sb.* and *a.* 1900. [f. ANGLO- + Gr. φωνή voice.] **A.** *sb.* An English-speaking person. **B.** *adj.* English-speaking.

Angora. **1.** Also applied to a variety of rabbit having long fine white fur and pink eyes, and to its fur or a yarn or fabric made from it. Also ellipt. as *sb.*

‖**Angst** (æŋst). 1944. [G.] Anxiety, anguish, neurotic fear; guilt, remorse.

A. may take the form of remorse about the past, guilt about the present, anxiety about the future 1944.

Animated, *ppl. a.* **1. b.** Cinematographic; (of cinema cartoons) given the appearance of motion 1897.

Animation. **1. c.** The production of motion pictures; now usu., the technique or process by which apparent movement is given on film to inanimate drawings or objects 1912.

Anodize (æ·nŏdəiz), *v.* 1931. [f. ANOD(E + -IZE.] *trans.* To give (aluminium or one of its alloys) a protective coating of aluminium oxide by making it the anode in a process of electrolysis.

Anomy. Restrict † to sense in Dict. and add: **2.** Also commonly in French form **anomie.** [Fr. (Durkheim *Suicide,* 1897).] Absence of accepted social standards or values; the state or condition of an individual or society lacking such standards 1933.

Anopheles (ănǫ·fĭlīz). 1899. [mod.L. (J. W. Meigen, 1818), – Gr. ἀνωφελής unprofitable, useless.] *Ent.* A mosquito of the genus so called, which includes species that carry the parasites causing malaria and other diseases.

Hence **Ano·pheline** *sb.* and *a.*, a mosquito belonging to this or a closely related genus; of or pertaining to an insect of this type.

Anorak (æ·nŏræk). 1924. [Greenland Eskimo.] A weatherproof jacket of skin or cloth, with hood attached.

Anorexy. Now usu. as **Anorexia. A. nervosa,** a condition in which loss of appetite due to severe emotional disturbance results in emaciation.

Another. **1.** *You're a.*: colloq. phr. primarily used in retorting a charge upon the person who makes it (cf. TU QUOQUE); hence humorously as a vaguely contemptuous (often meaningless) retort 1553. **3.** *A. place*: a traditional phr. used by members of parliament in referring to the other House, i.e. the House of Lords or the House of Commons 1789.

1. 'Sir,' said Mr. Tupman, 'you're a fellow.' 'Sir,' said Mr. Pickwick, 'you're a.' DICKENS.

Anoxic (ănǫ·ksik), *a.* 1920. [f. AN- 10 + OX- + -IC.] *Med.* Characterized by or causing a deficiency of oxygen. So **Ano·xia** [-IA¹], a deficiency of oxygen in the tissues.

‖**Anschluss** (æ·nʃlus). 1924. [G., 'addition, annexation, union', f. *anschliessen* join, annex.] Annexation, *spec.* of Austria to Germany.

Answer, *v.* **II. 1. b.** *To a. back*: to reply where silence or acquiescence would be proper; to retort or reply impertinently 1904. **8.** Also, *to a. the door* 1866.

Ante (æ·ntĭ), *sb.* 1838. [– L. *ante* before.] In poker, a stake put up by a player (usu. the eldest hand) before drawing new cards; *transf.* cash, esp. cash required or paid in advance. Hence **Ante** *v. trans.* to put up (an ante); *transf.* to bet, stake; also, to pay *off, up.*

Ante-post (æ·ntĭ,pōᵘst), *a.* 1902. [f. ANTE- + POST *sb.*¹] *Horse-racing.* Of bets or betting: made, taking place, before the numbers of the runners are displayed on the board.

Anti-, *prefix*¹. As a living formative prefix *anti-* has been extraordinarily productive in the 20th century, and it is now freely used to form sbs. and adjs., esp. denoting: (an agent, device, product, etc.) that inhibits, limits, or counteracts a condition, effect, etc.; affording protection from or used in defence against; (that is) the opposite, reverse, or negation of. **anti-clockwise** = COUNTER-CLOCKWISE; **a.-freeze,** a chemical agent added to water to lower its freezing-point; **anti-g** *a.*, designed to counteract the effects of high acceleration (as *anti-g suit*); **a.-gravity,** a fictitious or hypothetical force that opposes or counteracts the force of gravity; also (*colloq.*) **anti-grav**; **a.-hero,** one who is the opposite or reverse of a hero; esp. a chief character in a poem, play, or story who is totally unlike a conventional hero; **a.-histamine** *a.*, that counteracts the effect of histamine; *sb.* a drug having this property, used esp. in the treatment of some allergies; **a.-matter,** (hypothetical) matter composed of a.-particles; **a.-novel, -play,** etc., a form of art or literature opposed to the basic conventions of the form in question or to the form itself; **a.-particle,** an elementary particle of the same mass as a given particle but having an opposite electric charge or a magnetic moment equal in magnitude but opposite in direction; **a.-personnel** *a.*, of bombs, etc., designed to kill or injure human beings; **a.-tank** *a.*, used in defence against tanks.

Antibiotic, *a.* **2.** [– Fr. *antibiotique* (P. Vuillemin, 1890).] Injurious to or destructive of living matter, esp. micro-organisms 1894.

B. *sb.* A substance, esp. one produced by a mould or other micro-organism, capable of destroying, or inhibiting the growth of, bacteria or other micro-organisms 1944. So **Antibio·sis,** a condition of antagonism between life-forms, esp. micro-organisms.

Anti-convulsant (æ:nti,kŏnvʌ·lsănt), *a.* and *sb.* 1910. [ANTI-¹ 3.] **A.** *adj.* That retards or prevents convulsions. **B.** *sb.* A substance that is antagonistic to convulsions 1943.

Antigen (æ·ntidʒĕn). 1908. [– G. *antigen,* f. *anti(körper* ANTIBODY + -GEN.] *Biochem.* A foreign substance which, when introduced into the body, stimulates the production of an antibody. Hence **Antige·nic** *a.*, **-ically** *adv.* **Antigeni·city,** antigenic property or condition.

Anti-Semitism (æntise·mitiz'm, -sī·məit-iz'm). 1881. [f. ANTI- + SEMITE + -ISM.] Theory, action, or practice directed against the Jews. Hence **Anti-Se·mite. Anti-Semi·tic** *a.*

Anti-social, *a.* **2.** Also, of persons, actions, etc.: devoid of or antagonistic to normal social instincts or practices 1889. Hence **Anti-so·cially** *adv.*, in an anti-social manner, against the interests of society as a whole.

Anzac (æ·nzæk). 1915. A word made up from the initial letters of *Australian and New Zealand Army Corps,* used colloq. for a member of that corps; later gen. pertaining to Australia and New Zealand together. *A. Day*: 25 April 1915, when A. troops landed in the Gallipoli Peninsula; an anniversary of this day.

‖**Apartheid** (ăpā·ɹthēⁱt). 1947. [Afrikaans, f. Du. *apart* (– Fr. *à part* APART) + *heid* -HOOD.] Segregation of the inhabitants of European descent from those of non-European descent in S. Africa. Also *transf.* and *fig.*

Apartment. **1. b.** A set of rooms forming one dwelling in a building containing a number of these. Chiefly *U.S.* 1874. Also *attrib.*, as *a. building, hotel, house.*

‖**Apologia** (æpŏlōᵘ·dʒiă). 1784. [L. – Gr. ἀπολογία speech in defence.] A written defence or justification of the opinions or conduct of a writer, speaker, etc.

The currency of the word is largely derived from J. H. Newman's *Apologia pro vita sua,* 1864.

Apolune (æ·po,lⁱūn). 1960. [f. APO- + *lune* (f. L. *luna* moon), after *apogee.*] The point at which a body in orbit round the moon is most distant from its centre.

Apperceive (æpəɹsī·v), *v.* Delete † and add: **2.** *Psychol.* To be or become conscious of perceiving; to comprehend (something perceived) by a mental act which unites and assimilates the perception to a mass of ideas already possessed 1876. So **Apperce·ption. Apperce·ptive** *a.*

Apport, *sb.* Transfer †*Obs.* to senses 1 and 2 and add: **3.** usu. *pl.* A material object produced, professedly by occult means, at a spiritualist séance, etc. 1894.

Approach, *sb.* **1. b.** *Golf.* The play or stroke by which a player reaches the putting-green or approaches the hole 1879.

Approved, *ppl. a.*

a. school, a place of training for boys or girls who have been found guilty of offences or exposed to moral danger 1932.

Apron, *sb.* **4. g.** A flat area, usu. with a hard surface, where aircraft may conveniently stand for repairs or loading; a similar area in front of a garage 1925.

Aqualung (æ·kwălʌŋ). 1950. [f. L. *aqua* water + LUNG.] A portable apparatus enabling a diver to breathe under water, consisting of cylinders of compressed air, usu. carried on the back, which supply air through a water-tight face-mask. Hence **A·qualung** *v. intr.*, to use an a.

Aquaplane (æ·kwăplēⁱn). 1914. [f. L. *aqua* water + PLANE *sb.*³] A flat board on which a person can ride standing, which when towed behind a speedboat rises partly out of the water and skims along the surface. Hence **A·quaplane** *v. intr.*, to ride on an a.; *transf.*, of a vehicle or aircraft, or its wheels, to skid over a wet surface on a thin film of water.

Arabesque. B. *sb.* **3.** *Ballet.* A pose in which the performer stands on one foot with one arm extended in front and the other leg and arm extended behind in line with the body and parallel with the floor 1830.

Arbitrary, *a.* (*sb.*) **5. b.** *Typogr.* A character used to supplement the letters and accents of an ordinary fount of type; orig. *a. character* 1890.

Arc, *sb.*

5. a.-welding, welding in which the heat required for fusion is produced by an arc (e.g. between the metal to be welded and an electrode).

Arc (ăɹk), *v.* Pa. t. **arced** (ăɹkt). 1893. [f. ARC *sb.* 5.] *intr.* To form an electric arc.

Armour. 6. b. Also, the protective metal covering of a vehicle or aircraft. **c.** Armoured vehicles collectively 1944.

Armoured *ppl. a.* Also, of military vehicles, aircraft, etc., or of military forces, warfare.

Around. B. *prep.* **4. b.** Of time, amount, etc.: something near, about. *U.S.* 1888.

Arrestable (ăre·stăb'l), *a.* 1555. [– OFr. *a(r)restable*, f. *a(r)rester*: see ARREST *v.* and -ABLE.] Liable to be arrested.

a. disease, a disease that can be prevented from getting worse; **a. offence** *Law*, an offence for which a person can be arrested without a warrant.

Arrester. 2. A contrivance for bringing an aircraft to rest when it alights on an aircraft-carrier. Usu. *attrib.* 1926.

Arrive, *v.* **7. b.** [after Fr. *arriver.*] To be successful, establish one's position or reputation 1889. So ‖**Arriviste** (arivist), one who is bent on succeeding or making a good position for himself 1901.

Artefact (ā·ɹtĭfækt). Also **arti-.** 1821. [f. L. *arte*, abl. of *ars* ART + *factum* FACT.] **1.** A thing made by human art; an artificial product; *Archæol.* a product of aboriginal art as dist. from natural remains. **2.** In scientific use, a spurious product or effect that is introduced by the experimental procedure or is due to some other extraneous agency 1908.

Arteriosclerosis (aɹtīᵊrioskliᵊrōᵘ·sis). 1886. [f. ARTERIO- + SCLEROSIS.] *Path.* Abnormal thickening and hardening of the walls of the arteries, occurring chiefly in old age. Hence **Arte:rioscler·o·tic** *a.* and *sb.*

Articulate, *a.* **3. b.** Able to speak articulately; capable of giving esp. ready and fluent verbal expression to emotions, ideas, etc. 1937.

The more a. of our young rebels claim that sexual freedom is essential 1965. So **Arti·culacy.**

Arti·culated, *ppl. a.* [See -ED¹.] Applied to various kinds of vehicle in which elements are joined in a flexible (i.e. non-rigid) arrangement 1923.

a. locomotive, one with one or two sets of driving wheels mounted as a large bogie that can rotate with respect to the rest of the locomotive; **a. lorry,** a lorry made up of two separable parts joined so as to allow one to swivel with respect to the other; also (*slang*) **artic; a. train,** one in which the ends of adjoining coaches are supported on a common bogie.

Artificial, *a.*

Comb.: **a. fertilizer,** a chemical fertilizer; **a. horizon,** also, a gyroscopic instrument used in an aircraft to indicate its attitude in relation to the horizon; **a. insemination,** injection of semen into the uterus by other than natural means (abbrev. *A.I.*); **a. kidney,** an apparatus that performs the functions of a human kidney in place of a damaged organ; **a. respiration,** a manual or mechanical procedure designed to restore or initiate the natural function of breathing.

‖**Art nouveau** (ār nūvo). 1899. [Fr., 'new art'.] A style of art developed in the last decade of the 19th century, characterized by flowing lines and curves and by the free use of ornament based on organic or foliate forms.

Arty (ā·ɹti), *a.* 1901. [f. ART *sb.* + -Y¹.] Of artistic pretensions; also applied to persons who wish to be regarded as artistic in taste, dress, etc. (*joc. colloq.*). So **a·rty-(and-)crafty** *a.*

As, *adv.* **VIII. 1.** *As for, as to*: in respect of, with regard to. *As from*, (*U.S.*) *as of*: (in formal dating) from, after.

Ascend, *v.*

Asce·nder, one who or that which ascends; esp., *Typogr.*, etc., an ascending stroke, a stroke extending above the body of a letter 1934.

Ascomycetes (æ:skoməisī·tīz), *sb. pl.* 1857. [f. ASCO- + MYCETES.] *Bot.* A class of higher fungi, distinguished by the possession of an Ascus; see *Ascomycetal, Ascomycetous* (s.v. ASCO-).

Ascorbic (ăskǭ·ɹbik), *a.* 1933. [f. A- 14 + SCORB(UT)IC *a.*] *A. acid*: vitamin C, the antiscorbutic vitamin.

Asdic (æ·zdik). 1939. [f. initials of *Anti-submarine detection investigation committee.*] = *SONAR.

Asepsis (ēⁱse·psis). 1892. [f. A- 14 + SEPSIS.] Absence of micro-organisms likely to cause infection; procedures or treatment aimed at preventing septic infection.

Ashkenazim (æʃkĭnā·zīm), *sb. pl.* 1839. [With Heb. pl. suffix *-īm* f. *Ashkenaz*, name of a son of Gomer and great-grandson of Noah (Gen. 10:3), taken as the progenitor of one of the nations of the world (cf. 'the kingdoms of Ararat, Minni, and Ashchenaz', Jer. 51:27.] Jews of middle and northern Europe as distinguished from Sephardim or Jews of Spain and Portugal. Hence **Ashkena·zic** *a.*

Asian. In recent official use superseding *Asiatic* because of the alleged depreciatory implication of the latter term.

Ask, *v.* **IV. 6.** *To a. for trouble* or the like; also (*slang* or *colloq.*) *for it*: to act in such a way as to bring trouble upon oneself, to give provocation 1902.

Asking, *vbl. sb. attrib.* **a. price,** the price that is asked for a thing. Cf. sense 3.

I..gave the a. Price for every thing I bought 1755.

Aslib (æ·zlib). 1926. [f. the initials.] The Association of Special Libraries and Information Bureaux, set up to facilitate the co-ordination of information, etc.

Assemble, *v.*¹ **1. b.** To put together (the separately manufactured parts of a composite machine or mechanical appliance; also with the machine as obj. 1852. So **Assembly;** often *attrib.*, as *a. line, room, shop, worker.*

Assignment. 5. b. A task assigned to one; a commission (orig. *U.S.*) 1848.

Assimilate, *v.* **I. 1. b.** *pass.* (Philol.) Of a sound: to become identical with or similar in some respect *to* another sound in the same or a contiguous word. Also *intr.* 1854. So **Assimila·tion,** the process of becoming or fact of being assimilated.

Assistant. B. *sb.* **3. d.** A shop assistant (see *SHOP *sb.*) 1853.

Association. 9. *Ecology.* A group of associated plants within a formation 1900.

Astatine (æ·stătīn). 1947. [f. Gr. ἄστατος unstable (f. ἀ- (A- 14) + στατός standing) + -INE⁵.] A radioactive element that can be produced artificially, all the isotopes of which have a half-life of a few hours or less; the heaviest of the halogens. Symbol At; atomic number 85.

Astilbe (ăsti·lbi). 1843. [mod.L. (F. Buchanan-Hamilton, 1825), f. Gr. ἀ- (A- 14) + στίλβη, fem. of στίλβος glittering.] A perennial plant of the genus so called, belonging to the family Saxifragaceæ, native to the Far East, and bearing panicles of small flowers.

Astral, *a.* **1. b.** Pertaining to or consisting of a supersensible substance considered to be next above the sensible world in refinement and held to pervade all space 1877. *A. body*, the ethereal counterpart of a human or animal body 1881.

Astro-.

A·strodome, a transparent dome on the top of the fuselage of an aircraft from within which astronomical observations may be made. **A.-fix,** the determination of an aircraft's position by observation of the stars. **A.-hatch** = **Astrodome.*

Astronau·tics [– Fr. *astronautique* (J. H. H. Boëx-Borel, 1927)], the branch of science and engineering concerned with travel beyond the earth's atmosphere; so **A·stronaut,** one who travels in space. **Astrophy·sics,** that branch of astronomy which treats of the physical (and chemical) properties of the celestial bodies.

Astronomical, *a.* **b.** Of figures, measurements, etc.: similar in magnitude to those used in astronomy, immense 1899.

The odds against a poor person becoming a millionaire are of a. magnitude SHAW.

At, *prep.* **I. 14.** With verbs of speaking, implying indirect attack aimed *at* as opp. to direct address *to* a person 1711.

Mrs. Parsons talked *to* Miss Littleton and *at* her better half DICKENS.

Ataractic, ataraxic (ætăræ·ktik, -æ·ksik), *a.* 1941. [*-actic* f. Gr. ἀτάρακτος not disturbed + -IC; *-axic* f. Gr. ἀταραξία impassiveness, calmness (see ATARAXY).] **1.** Calm, serene. **2.** *Pharm.* Of a drug: inducing calmness, tranquillizing (without being hypnotic). As *sb.*, such a drug 1955.

Atcha, atchoo, var. forms of *ATISHOO.

-ate¹. 1. d. On the analogy of *distillate, filtrate, precipitate*, etc., other sbs. in *-ate* are formed on a vb. stem to denote the product of some kind of operation, as *eluate, homogenate*, etc.

Athematic (æþ-, ēⁱþīmæ·tik), *a.* 1894. [f. A- 14 + THEMATIC.] *Gram.* Of verb-forms: having no thematic vowel, having suffixes attached immediately to the stem.

Atishoo (ăti·ʃū), *int.* and *sb.* 1878. A representation of the characteristic noises accompanying a sneeze.

Atlantic, *a.* **1. b.** Of or pertaining to countries bordering on the Atlantic Ocean, now esp. with reference to their political alliances 1776. **c.** Transatlantic 1839. **d.** Applied to one of the successive periods of vegetation in the post-glacial period 1876.

Atom. Loosely used *attrib.* for *atomic* (see next), as in *a. bomb, a. scientist* 1945.

The effect of the a. bomb on Japan 1947.

Atomic, *a.* **1, 2.** Now *spec.* applied to the energy released by the fission of heavy atomic nuclei or the fusion of light nuclei, to apparatus, machines, etc., utilizing such energy or used in its production, and to weapons deriving their destructive power from its sudden release; also to research and researchers in atomic energy, structure, etc., and loosely to the age characterized by the various applications of atomic energy.

Comb.: **a. number,** (of a chemical element) the number of unit positive charges carried by the nucleus of its atom, being the physical property which determines the position of the element in the periodic table; symbol *Z*; **a. weight,** (after the adoption of carbon as a standard) the ratio between the weight of one atom of the element and $\frac{1}{12}$ of the weight of an atom of carbon 12.

Attested (ăte·stėd), *ppl. a.* 1934. [f. ATTEST *v.* + -ED¹.] Of cattle, milk: officially approved as free from disease.

Attitude. 2. b. The orientation of an aircraft or spacecraft in relation to some reference line(s) (e.g. its direction from the observer or its line of motion) 1910. **4. b.** = *Attitude of mind* (ATTITUDE 4) 1873.

Atto- (æ·to), *prefix.* 1963. [f. Da., Norw. *atten* eighteen + -O-, after *kilo-, micro-*, etc.] Prefixed to the names of units to form the names of units 10^{18} times smaller (i.e. one million million millionth part of them). Abbrev. a.

Atypical (æ-, ēⁱti·pikăl), *a.* 1885. [f. A- 14 + TYPICAL *a.*] Not typical; not conformable to the ordinary type. Hence **Aty·pically** *adv.*

Aubrietia (ǭbrī·ʃⁱă) Also very freq. in erron. form **aubretia.** 1829. [mod.L., – *Aubrieta* (M. Adanson, 1763), f. the name of Claude *Aubriet* (1668–1743), French botanist: see -IA¹.] The common name of a member of the genus *Aubrieta* of spring-flowering dwarf perennial plants belonging to the family Cruciferæ.

Aubrieta is the original spelling of the generic name but the form Aubrietia has been so generally used that it has come into common speech and we retain that form as the common name. R. Hort. Soc. *Dict. Gardening* 1951.

‖**Au courant** (o kuraṅ). 1762. [Fr., 'in the

(regular) course (of events)'.] Acquainted with what is going on: const. *with, of.*

Audile (ǭ·dəil), *a.* and *sb.* 1886. [irreg. f. L. *audire* hear + -ILE. Cf. TACTILE *a.*] **A.** *adj.* Pertaining to or involving hearing 1897. **B.** *sb.* A person to whom auditory images are more prominent than motile or visual images 1886.

Audio- (ǭ·dio), comb. form f. L. *audire* hear + -O-. Also in independent use as a quasi-sb. used *attrib.*

a.-frequency, a frequency capable of being perceived aurally; **a. typing, typist,** typing, one who types, directly from material previously recorded; **a.-visual** *a.*, of or pertaining to both hearing and sight: applied esp. to mechanical aids to teaching.

Audition, *sb.* **1. b.** Also, a trial performance by any performer (as a dancer, etc). Hence **Audition** *v. trans.*, to give an audition to (a performer); also *absol.*, to hold auditions.

Au gratin: see *GRATIN.

Auguste (au·gust). 1910. [Adopted in Fr. spelling *auguste*, f. G. *august* (*der dumme August* circus clown).] A type of circus clown.

He was called an 'auguste', and wore ill-fitting ordinary clothes. .and a large bulbous red nose 1950.

Au pair. Now esp. of a young girl receiving instruction in the language of a foreign country in return for esp. domestic services. Also as *sb.*, and *attrib.* in *au pair girl*, etc.

Aurignacian (ǭrinyē¹·ʃ¹ăn, -ign-), *a.* 1914. [– Fr. *Aurignacien* (H. Breuil, 1906).] Of or belonging to an Upper Palæolithic period characterized by flint implements of the type found in the Aurignac cave in the Pyrenees and by the earliest examples of cave art.

Aussie (ǭ·zi, ǫzi, -s-), *sb.* and *a.* 1918. [f. first syllable of *Australia* + -IE.] **a.** (An) Australian. **b.** Australia 1918.

Australopithecus (ǭstrā:lopi·pĭkŏs). [mod. L. (R. A. Dart, 1925), f. L. *australis* southern + Gr. πίθηκος ape.] A small-brained fossil hominid of the genus so called, which includes several species found in Africa. Hence **Austra:lopi·thecine** *sb* and *a.*, a member of the Australopithecinæ, a sub-family of the Hominidæ sometimes used to separate A. from more recent hominids; of, pertaining to, or resembling A.

In their cranial features the members of the *Australopithecus* group neatly split the differences between ape and man, but the consensus of opinion is that, on the whole, they must be considered as men...The australopithecine were small in stature A. S. ROMER.

Autism (ǭ·tiz'm). 1912. [– mod.L. *autismus* (Bleuler), f. Gr. αὐτός self + -ISM.] *Psychol.* A condition in which a person is morbidly self-absorbed and out of contact with reality. Hence **Auti·stic** *a.*

Auto-.

au·toclave, (*b*) a vessel for carrying out chemical reactions at high temperatures under pressure; an apparatus for sterilizing by steam at high pressure; **autodida·ctic** *a.*, self-taught; acquired by teaching oneself; **a.-ero·ticism, -e·rotism,** erotism not resulting from any external stimulus; **a.-ero·tic** *a.*; **autotomy** (ǭtǫ·tŏmi), the casting off by some animals of a part or parts of the body, esp. as a reflex action.

b. au·to(-)pilot = **automatic pilot*.

c. au·tocycle, a vehicle resembling a bicycle, propelled by a motor.

Automat (ǭ·tŏmæt). *U.S.* 1903. [– G. – Fr. *automate.*] A self-service restaurant in which food is obtained from compartments by the insertion of a coin or token.

Automatic, *a.* **2. b.** Of a firearm: furnished with mechanism for successively and continuously loading, firing, and ejecting cartridges as long as ammunition is supplied; also *sb.* = *a. pistol* 1902. **c.** Of a telephone exchange or system: operated by automatic switches 1879.

Comb.: **a. pilot,** a device in an aircraft for maintaining a set course or height; **a. transmission,** an automatic gear-changing system in a motor vehicle (so *a. gear*, etc.); **a. writing,** in Spiritualism, writing produced without the conscious agency of the writer.

Automation (ǭtŏmē¹·ʃən). 1948. [irreg. f. AUTOMATIC *a.* + -ATION.] Automatic control of a manufacturing process through a number of successive stages; the application of automatic control to any manufacturing plant, branch of industry, etc.; also, the use of mechanical or electronic devices to replace human labour. So **Au·tomate** *v. trans.*, to apply automation to; to convert to (largely) automatic operation.

Automatism. 4. Any action performed automatically or not controlled by the conscious mind; the performance of such actions or the mental state in which they may occur 1884.

Auxin (ǭ·ksin). 1934. [– G. *auxin* (A. J. Haagen-Smit, 1931), f. Gr. αὔξειν to increase + -IN¹.] *Biochem.* Any of numerous compounds that cause the elongation of plant cells in shoots and (with cytokinins) control the growth and development of a plant.

Avalanche (æ·vălɑnʃ), *v.* 1872. [f. the sb.] *intr.* To descend in or like an avalanche; *trans.* to carry by or as by an avalanche. Also *fig.*

Avant-.

avant-garde, also, the pioneers or innovators in any art in a particular period 1910; **avant-ga·rdism, -ga·rdist(e).**

Avestic (ăve·stik), *a.* and *sb.* 1888. [f. *Avesta* (see ZEND-AVESTA) + -IC.] (Pertaining to) the language of the Avesta, called also *Zend* and *Old Bactrian*.

Avitaminosis (ē¹vi:tăminō^u·sis). 1914. [mod.L., f. A- 14 + VITAMIN + -OSIS.] *Path.* A condition resulting from a deficiency of one or more vitamins.

Away, *adv.* **III. 3. b.** In reference to games or matches played away from the home ground. Also *adj.* (as *a. game, win*) and quasi-*sb.*; an away match or (esp.) win. 1893.

Axiology (æksiǫ·lŏdʒi). 1908. [f. Gr. ἀξία worth, value + -LOGY.] *Philos.* The theory or doctrine of values. Hence **A:xiolo·gical** *a.*, **Axio·logist.**

Axon (æ·ksǫn). 1848. [mod.L. – Gr. ἄξων axis.] *Anat.* † **a.** The axis of a vertebrate body –1884. **b.** A process of a nerve cell that is usu. single and long (in contrast to the dendrites) and in most cases carries outgoing nerve impulses.

B.

III. B, BB, BBB, black, double-, treble-black (of pencil lead); B.A.O.R., British Army of the Rhine; B.C.G., Bacillus Calmette-Guérin (used as an anti-tuberculosis vaccine); B.E.A., B.O.A.C., British European (Overseas) Airways (Corporation); B.E.M., British Empire Medal; B.F., bloody fool; b.h.p., brake horsepower; B.M., British Museum; B.M.A., British Medical Association; B.O., body odour; B.P., British Pharmacopœia; B.R., British Rail(ways); B.S.T., British Standard Time; b.t.m., bottom.

Babbitt² (bæ·bit). *U.S. colloq.* 1923. A type of materialistic self-satisfied business man conforming to the standards of his set: generalized from Sinclair Lewis's novel *Babbitt* (1922). Hence **Ba·bbittry.**

Baby, *sb.* **1. b.** *transf.* The junior member of a family, group of persons, etc. **c.** A girl, girl-friend, young woman (*slang*, orig. *U.S.*) 1839. **d.** A person (*slang*) 1899. **e.** phr. *To carry* or *hold the b.*, to be saddled with an unwelcome responsibility. *To empty*, etc., *the b. out with the bathwater*, to reject the essential with the inessential.

Comb.: **b.-sitter,** a person who is at hand to look after a young child or children in the absence of the parents. So **b.-sit** *v.*

Bach (bætʃ), *sb.* 1855. [Shortened f. BACHELOR 4.] **1.** orig. *U.S.* A bachelor, esp. in phrase *to keep b.*, to live as a bachelor. **2.** *N.Z.* A makeshift hut, usu. one in which a man lives alone and fends for himself; now esp. a small week-end or holiday house 1927.

Bach (bætʃ), *v.* orig. *U.S.* 1870. [f. prec.] *intr.* To live as a bachelor, doing one's own cooking and housekeeping (usu. of a man).

Bachelor. 4. b. *transf.* One of the young male fur-seals which are kept away from the breeding-grounds by the adult bulls 1874.

attrib.: **b. girl, woman** orig. *U.S.*, an unmarried woman who lives independently.

Bacillary, *a.* **2.** (bă·siläri). Of, pertaining to, or caused by bacilli 1884.

Back *sb.*¹

II. *Back-to-back*, advb. phr. used attrib., esp. of houses built in a continuous terrace divided along its length so that there is no communication between the two façades.

Back-.

b.-boiler, a boiler behind a domestic fire or cooking-range; **b.-cloth, -drop,** a cloth, usu. painted, hung at the back of a stage as part of the scenery or to conceal the area behind; **b. country,** the country lying in or towards the rear of a settled district; **b.-date** *v.* = ANTEDATE *v.* 1, 2; also, to render an agreement, etc., retroactively valid from a given date (const. *to*); **b.-lighting** *Photogr.*, lighting coming from behind the subject; **b.-marker,** one who starts from 'scratch' or has the least favourable handicap in a race; **b. number,** a number of a periodical earlier than the current one; hence *colloq.*, one who or a thing which is out of date, behind the times, or useless; **b.-pack** (chiefly *U.S.*), a pack, *spec.* one consisting of a folded parachute, carried on the back; **b.-pedalling** *Bicycling*, the action of pressing down upon the rising pedal (on a bicycle without a free wheel), in order to check the movement of the wheel; *fig.* the checking of a forward movement, the reversing of an action; hence **b.-pedal** *v.*; **b. projection,** projection on to a translucent screen from the rear, as a means of providing still or moving background to a scene, etc.; **b. room,** a room at the back of a house or other building; *spec.* a room or premises where (esp. secret) research, etc., is carried out; applied *attrib.*, esp in *backroom boy(s*, to one who works or wields influence 'behind the scenes'.

Back bench. 1874. [BACK *a.* 1, BENCH *sb.* 3.] Any of the benches in the House of Commons or similar assembly occupied by members not entitled to places in the front benches on either side; also *attrib.* Hence **Ba:ck-be·ncher,** a member who occupies a seat on the back benches.

Mr. Baldwin filled the modest rôle of a back-bencher in the House for many years 1923.

Back blocks, ba·ckblocks, *sb. pl. Austral.* and *N.Z.* 1872. [f. BACK *a.* 1 + *BLOCK *sb.* 10 c.] Land in the remote and sparsely inhabited interior. Also *attrib.* or as *adj.* Hence **Ba·ck-blocker,** one who lives in the back blocks.

Back-fire, *v.* 1886. [f. BACK-FIRE *sb.* or back-formation from *Back-firing* vbl. sb.] **1.** *intr. N. Amer.* To light a fire ahead of an advancing prairie-fire in order to deprive it of fuel. **2.** Of an internal-combustion engine or its fuel: to ignite or explode prematurely 1902. Also *transf.*, e.g. of a firearm. Also *fig.* of plans, etc., to go disastrously wrong.

Background. 1. b. Education, experience, training, social conditions, and other factors regarded as forming the setting of a person, period, movement, etc., or making an important contribution to the understanding of a problem 1854. **c.** Music, sound-effects, etc., subordinated to or accompanying some activity, esp. music as an accompaniment to a cinema film, broadcast programme, etc. 1928. **3.** *Radio, Electr.*, etc. Adventitious signals or other sounds in the reception or recording of sound 1927. **b.** *Physics.* Radiation arising from cosmic rays and other natural sources 1930.

1.b. A charming girl lacking only the 'b.' that wealth makes possible 1923.

attrib., as *b. music, reading*, etc.; **b. heater,** a radiator, etc., supplying a constant level of warmth that can be supplemented at need by other means.

Back-lash. 2. *fig.* After-effects; excessive or violent reaction 1921.

Back-log. *fig.* Also, arrears 1932.

Back seat. 1832. [BACK *a.*, BACK-.] A seat at the back of a hall, etc.; hence *colloq.* a position of inferiority or comparative obscurity (orig. U.S. in phr. *to take a b. s.*).

b.-s. driver, a passenger in the rear seat of a car who gives unsolicited directions to the driver; also *fig.*

Back stage, backstage, *sb.* and *adv.* 1898. [f. BACK *a* + STAGE *sb.*] The rear part of a stage; the part of a theatre behind the stage; *adv.* up-stage; behind the scenes.

Backstroke. b. *Swimming.* A stroke used in swimming on the back 1876.

Back-up. Chiefly *U.S.* Also **backup.** 1952. [BACK *v.* 2]. A stand-by, reserve. Also *attrib.*

Nearby was Glenn's backup pilot 1962.

Backwoodsman. b. A member of the House of Lords who rarely attends meetings of that body, but is prepared on occasion to assert his political rights 1909.

Bacteriological, *a.*

b. warfare, the deliberate use of bacteria to spread disease in the enemy.

Badian (bē̆ⁱ·diăn), *sb.*[2] and *a.* Also **Bajan, Bajun** (bē̆ⁱ·dʒən). 1910. [Shortened from *BARBADIAN.] = *BARBADIAN.

Baffle, *sb.* **5.** More widely, any shielding structure or device for deflecting or regulating the passage of a fluid or deflecting or absorbing radiation.

Bag. *sb.* **1. b.** *fig.* A distinctive style or category esp. in playing jazz or similar music. *slang* (orig. *U.S.*). 1962. **13.** *slang.* A disparaging term for a woman, esp. one who is unattractive or elderly; = BAGGAGE 6. 1924.

Comb.: **bagwash,** the rough unfinished washing of clothes; a laundry that undertakes such rough washing; the bag of clothes to be washed.

Bagel (bē̆ⁱ·g'l). 1932. [– Yiddish *beygel.*] A hard ring-shaped salty bread roll.

Bailey bridge (bē̆ⁱ·li). 1944. [f. name of the designer, D. C. *Bailey* (1901–), English engineer.] A lattice-steel bridge designed for rapid assembly from prefabricated standard parts, used esp. in military operations.

A Bailey bridge more than 1,000 ft. long has been built over the Chindwin near Kalewa 1944.

Balance, *sb.* **16. b.** *On b.* (earlier *upon the b.*): balancing one thing with another, taking all things into consideration 1843. **19.** Also in gen. use: *The b.*, what is left, the rest, the remainder (recorded from late 18th cent. in Amer. use).

Phr. **B. of nature:** a state of equilibrium in nature produced by the interaction of living organisms; ecological b. **B. of payments:** the difference of value between payments into and out of a country.

Bale, *v*[3]. *To b. out*: (of an airman) to make a descent by parachute from an aircraft 1930. Usu. so spelt, as if the action were that of letting a bundle fall through a trapdoor; but also as *bail*, as if a use of BAIL *v.*[3]

Ball, *sb.*[1] **13. b.** pl. *vulg.* The testicles; *fig.* nonsense, freq. as interj.; hence phr. *to make a balls of*, to muddle, make a mess of; also *balls-up*, confusion, muddle. ME.

attrib.: **b. pen** or **b. point pen,** one of which the writing point is a minute ball moistened from a reservoir of viscous ink; **b. turret,** a spherical gun turret that projects from the body of an aircraft.

Ball, *sb.*[2] **3.** *slang.* A very enjoyable time 1945.

Balloon.

b. barrage, a defence against hostile aircraft consisting of a connected system of balloons carrying wire cables reaching to the ground; **b. tyre,** a low-pressure pneumatic tyre of large section.

Baloney, boloney (bălōᵘ·ni, bŏlōᵘ·ni). *slang* (orig. *U.S.*). 1928. [perh. alt. f. BOLOGNA (sausage).] Humbug, nonsense.

Balsa. 2. A tree of tropical America, *Ochroma lagopus*; also, the wood of this tree, used for its extreme lightness 1866.

Balto-Slavic (bǫltoslæ·vik), *a.* and *sb.* 1896. [f. *Balto-*, used as comb. form of *Baltic* + SLAVIC.] Designation of the group of Indo-European languages comprising the Baltic branch (Lithuanian, Lettish, and Old Prussian) and the Slavonic branch (Russian, Polish, Czech, etc.). Also **Ba:lto-Slavo·nic.**

Band, *sb.*[2] **12.** *Electr.* A range of frequencies or wavelengths between given limits 1922.

Comb.: **b. width,** the interval separating the limits of a band.

Band, *sb.*[3] **4. b.** Phr. *When the b. begins to play*: when matters become serious or exciting 1890. *To beat the b.*: lit. so as to drown the noise made by the b.; hence, to surpass or beat some stated or implied project 1897.

Comb.: **b.-wagon** *U.S.*, the wagon carrying the band at the head of a procession; *to be on the b.-w.*, fig. to be in the forefront of an enterprise; also *to climb on the b.-w.*

Bang, *adv. colloq.* 1828. [See BANG *v.*[1] 6, and cf. SLAM-BANG.] Thoroughly, completely, exactly. **b.** *b. on*, exactly on. Used as *adj.*, exactly right, excellent 1936.

Banger (bæ·ŋəɹ). 1919. [f. BANG *v.*[1] + -ER.[1]] **a.** A sausage, esp. in phr. *bangers and mash*, a dish of sausages and mashed potatoes. **b.** A decrepit motor vehicle.

Bank, *sb.*[3] **7.** *transf.* A store of things for future use; *spec.* of blood for transfusion, tissue for grafting, etc. So *blood b., eye b.* 1938.

Comb.: **b.-account,** an account with a b.; **b.-robber,** one who robs a b.

Banner, *sb.* **6.** *U.S.* A banner as a distinction, used esp. *attrib.* (orig. in *b. county, state*) 1840; hence as *adj.*, pre-eminent, supreme. **b.** A headline in large type, esp. one running right across the page of a newspaper (orig. *U.S.*) 1913.

The *Daily Herald* came out with a huge b. headline, in letters half an inch high, on its opening page 1952.

Bantu (bæ·ntu, bæntū·), *a.* and *sb.* 1862. [In certain Bantu dialects, pl. of *-ntu* man.] **A.** *adj.* Of or pertaining to an extensive group of negroid peoples inhabiting the equatorial and southern region of Africa, and of the languages spoken by them. **B.** *sb. ellipt.* as *pl.* Bantu people. **b.** Any of the languages spoken by them.

Bar (bāɹ), *sb.*[4] 1903. [– Gr. βάρος weight.] **1.** A unit of pressure equivalent to one dyne per square centimetre. **2.** *Meteorol.* A unit of barometric pressure equivalent to one million dynes per square centimetre (corresponding to the pressure of 750.1 mm. of mercury at 0°C. in latitude 45° at sea level) 1910. So **Mi·llibar,** a thousandth of a bar (sense 2) (the unit usually used).

Barathea (bæră̄þī·a). 1862. [Origin unkn.] A cloth of fine texture made of wool, wool and silk, etc.

Barbadian (baɹbē̆ⁱ·diăn), *a.* and *sb.* 1732. [f. BARBAD(OES + -IAN.] **A.** *adj.* Of or pertaining to Barbados or its inhabitants 1741. **B.** *sb.* An inhabitant of Barbados.

Barbecue, *sb.* **3.** Now also an entertainment where steaks, chops, etc., are cooked in the open air. Also as *vb.*

Barbiturate (baɹbi·tiŭrĕt, -ēⁱt, bāɹbitiūᵊ·rĕt). 1928. [f. *BARBITUR(IC *a.* + -ATE[1] 1 c.] *Chem.* A salt of barbituric acid; any of the group of hypnotic or sedative substances derived from barbituric acid. Also *attrib.*

The pathologist's view was that the overdose of b. she had taken would have proved fatal 1963.

Barbituric (bāɹbitiūᵊ·rik), *a.* 1866. [– Fr. *barbiturique*, f. G. *barbitur(säure)*, f. *Barbara*, woman's name.] Chem. *B. acid*: a crystalline acid, $C_4H_4N_2O_3$, from which many important hypnotic and sedative drugs are derived; malonyl urea. Hence **Ba·rbitone,** name in the British Pharmacopœia of VERONAL; formerly in U.S. Pharmacopeia as **Ba·rbital.**

Bargain, *sb.* **3.** *esp.* An article of which the price is professedly reduced for the purpose of a special sale in a shop or stores; also *attrib.* and *Comb.* designating persons and things associated with the practice of offering goods for sale in this way, e.g. *b. counter, -day, -hunter, -hunting, -price, -sale*; **b. basement,** the basement floor of a store devoted to the display of bargains; also *transf.* and *fig.*

Barium.

attrib.: **b. meal,** a mixture containing barium sulphate, opaque to X-rays, that is swallowed before radiological examination of the alimentary tract.

Bar-mitzvah (bāɹ,mi·tsvā). *Judaism.* 1861. [Heb., lit. 'son of commandment, man of duty'.] **a.** A Jewish boy who has reached the age of thirteen, regarded as the age of religious responsibility. **b.** The 'confirmation' ceremony in a synagogue on this occasion. Also *attrib.*

Barn, *sb.* **2.** [Said to have originated in the phrase '*as big as a barn*'.] In nuclear physics, 10^{-24} sq. cm., a unit of area used in the measurement of the cross-section of a nucleus 1947.

Barney. c. A noisy dispute or altercation. Also *Austral.* and *N.Z.* 1864.

Barnstorm (bā·ɹnstǫɹm), *v.* 1883. [f. BARN *sb.* + STORM *v.* 5.] *intr.* **1.** *Theatr.* To tour (rural districts), giving popular theatrical performances (formerly often in barns). **2.** *U.S.* To make a rapid tour holding meetings for propaganda or election purposes 1896.

1. I have dreamed of a threadbare barnstorming actor, and he was a national symbol AUDEN & ISHERWOOD.

Baron. 8. orig. *U.S.* A great merchant in a particular commodity, an industrial or commercial 'magnate' 1818.

The 'money barons' were using the whole of their influence to restrict the raising of money for national development 1932.

Barrage. 2. Also *transf.* and *fig.* 1917.

Comb.: **b. balloon,** one forming part of a **balloon barrage.*

Barrier. 4. b. Freq. with defining word; *sound b.*, the excessive resistance which air offers to objects travelling at speeds approaching or not greatly exceeding that of sound, and which has to be overcome before greater speed can be achieved.

Comb.: **b. cream,** a protective cream for the skin.

Baryon (bæ·riǫn, bēᵊ·riǫn). 1953. [f. Gr. βαρύς heavy + *-ON.] *Nuclear Physics.* Any of the sub-atomic particles with a half-integral spin and a mass equal to or greater than the mass of the proton or neutron.

Base, *sb.*[1] **18.** *Electr.* The middle portion of a transistor, which is in contact with both the other regions (the emitter and the collector) and differs from them in conductivity type 1948.

Basenji (băse·ndʒi). 1933. [Bantu.] An African breed of smallish hunting dog, native to the inner Congo regions, which rarely barks.

Bash (bæʃ), *sb.* 1805. [f. BASH *v.*[2]] A heavy blow. (Orig. *Sc.*, now in gen. use.)

Phr. *To have a b. (at)*, to attempt.

Come on..have a b. You can translate the first word anyway I. MURDOCH.

Basic, *a.* **1. b.** That is or constitutes a starting-point in a scale of remuneration or the like, as *b. wage, working-day* 1922. **c.** Applied to a limited 'essential' vocabulary in any language, spec. **B. English,** a vocabulary of 850 English words selected by C. K. Ogden, of Cambridge, and intended for use as a medium of international communication 1929. **2. d. b. slag,** slag from the basic process of manufacturing steel, used as a fertilizer when finely ground 1888.

Basically (bē̆ⁱ·sikăli), *adv.* 1903. [f. BASIC *a.*: see -ICALLY.] As a basic or fundamental principle, condition, matter, etc.; essentially.

Bastard, *sb.* **1. b.** Used vulgarly as a term of abuse for a man, and, with weakened force, as the equivalent of 'fellow', 'chap', also trivially for 'thing' 1830.

'We've knocked the b. off' (reported remark of Sir Edmund Hillary after his ascent of Mount Everest in 1953).

Bat, *sb.*[1] Phr. *To have bats in the belfry*: to be crazy or eccentric 1901. Hence **Bats** as adj. in predic. use = BATTY *a.* 2.

Batho- (bæþo), **Bathy-** (bæþi), comb. forms respectively of Gr. βάθος depth and βαθύς deep, in various techn. terms, e.g. **ba·tho-, ba·thylith** [see -LITH], a very large body of intrusive igneous rock that has no detectable lower limit; **batho·-, bathy·-meter** [see -METER], an instrument used for deep-water soundings; **bathophilous** (băþǫ·filəs), adapted to life in deep water.

Bathyscaph(e) (bæ·þiskæf). 1947. [– Fr. *bathyscaphe* (Piccard), f. *BATHY- + Gr. σκάφος ship.] A vessel constructed for deep-sea diving and exploration. Also **Ba·thysphere.**

The new bathysphere in which Prof. Auguste Piccard, the Swiss scientist, will try to descend more than two miles into the Mediterranean 1953.

Batik (bæ·tik, bătī·k). 1880. [Javanese, lit. 'painted'.] The Javanese method of executing designs on textiles by covering the material with wax in a pattern, dyeing the parts left exposed, and then removing the wax; the material so dyed. Also *attrib.* passing into *adj.*: of, or ornamented with, batik work; loosely, characterized by a fantastic colour-pattern.

Battery. 13. A series of hutches, cages, or nesting-boxes in which laying hens are confined for intensive laying or poultry reared and fattened; later extended to denote accommodation for fattening cattle 1931. Freq. *attrib.*, as *b. hen, system.*

Battle, *sb.*

b.-dress, a soldier's uniform consisting of tunic and trousers, often with ankle-leggings.

Battle-axe. 3. *Archæol.* A type of prehistoric stone weapon; hence applied *attrib.* to a neolithic culture characterized by this weapon 1859. **4.** *fig.* A formidable or domineering woman. orig. *U.S. slang*, now *colloq.* 1896.

Bauhaus (bau·haus). 1923. [G., lit. 'architecture house', f. *bau* building + *haus* house.] The name of a school of design founded in Weimar, Germany, in 1919 by Walter Gropius (1883–1969); used for the principles or traditions characteristic of the Bauhaus.

The Bauhaus became in Germany the focussing point of the new creative forces accepting the challenge of the time and technical progress 1932.

Bazooka (băzū·kă). orig. *U.S.* 1935. [Cf. U.S. *bazoo* trumpet.] **1.** A crude pipe-shaped musical instrument. **2.** A tubular anti-tank rocket-launcher 1943.

Beach, *sb.*

b.-head [illogically formed after *bridge-head*], a fortified position of troops landed on a beach.

Beach-la-mar (bīt∫ˌlamā·ɹ). 1911. [Alteration, by association with Pg. *bicho do mar*, of BÊCHE-DE-MER *English* (quasi 'English spoken by bêche-de-mer fishermen').] The commercial jargon English used in the Western Pacific.

Beacon, *sb.* **3.** See *BELISHA *beacon.* **6. b.** *Aeronaut.* A light placed at or near an aerodrome for the guidance of pilots 1918. **c.** A radio transmitter enabling pilots to fix their position 1919.

Beaker. 1. c. *Archæol.* A type of tall wide-mouthed vessel found in the graves of a people who came to Britain from Central Europe in the early Bronze Age: hence *attrib.*, as *b.-folk, people* 1902.

Beam, *sb.* **15. c.** *Aeronaut.* A directional radio transmission used to guide aircraft or missiles 1927. Freq. *attrib.*, as *b. approach.*

Phr. *To be on the b., off the b.*: to be on (off) the course indicated by a radio beam; also *fig.*

Béarnaise (bēˈăɹnēⁱ·z, ‖bearnę̄z). 1877. [Fr., fem. of *béarnais* of Béarn, a region of south-western France.] *B. sauce*, also in Fr. form *sauce béarnaise*, a rich white sauce flavoured with herbs.

Beat generation. 1952. [perh. BEAT *ppl. a.* with infl. fr. BEAT *sb.*[1] 4, but see quot.] A term first applied to a group of young artists, writers, etc., in San Francisco and later to others adopting their unconventional dress, habits, and attitudes as a means of self-expression and social protest.

'The Beat Generation is basically a religious generation.' In another interview Kerouac amplified 'Beat means beatitude, not beat up.' 1958.

Beatnik (bī·tnik). 1958. [See *BEAT GENERATION; -NIK as in *SPUTNIK infl. by Yiddish *-NIK.] One of the beat generation.

Beaufort scale (bōᵘ·fǒɹt). 1858. [Devised by Admiral Sir Francis *Beaufort* (1774–1857).] *Meteorol.* A series of numbers from 0 to 12 indicating the strength of the wind from a calm to a hurricane.

South-westerly winds between force 5 and force 6 on the Beaufort scale meant rigorous yachting conditions 1961.

Beautician (biūti·∫ăn). orig. *U.S.* 1924. [irreg. f. BEAUTY; cf. *MORTICIAN.] One who runs a beauty parlour, a beauty specialist.

Bebop (bī·bǫp). orig. *U.S.* Also **bop.** 1945. A development of jazz, begun in the U.S., characterized by complex harmony, dissonant chords, and highly syncopated rhythm. Hence **Be·bopper.**

Bedlington (be·dliŋtən). 1867. [Named after *Bedlington* in Northumberland.] In full *B. terrier*: a short-haired terrier characterized by a narrow head, short body, and longish legs.

Bed-sitting-room. 1892. [f. BED(ROOM) + SITTING-*room.*] A room used as both living and sleeping quarters. Also abbrev. **bed-sitter** and **bed-sit.**

Beef, *v.* 1860. [f. BEEF *sb.*] **1.** *trans.* To apply raw beef to (a bruise) 1870. **2.** *U.S. slang.* To put more muscle into; to strengthen 1860. **3.** To slaughter (an ox, etc.) for beef 1869. **4.** *intr.* To complain, grumble, protest. *slang.* 1888.

Behavioural (bǐˌhēⁱ·vyərăl), *a.* 1927. [f. BEHAVIOUR + -AL[1].] Concerned with, or forming part of, behaviour. Hence **Beha·viourally** *adv.*

Behaviourism (bǐˌhēⁱ·vyəriz'm). 1913. [f. BEHAVIOUR + -ISM.] *Psychol.* A theory and method of psychological investigation based on the study and analysis of behaviour. Hence **Beha·viourist,** one who practises this method; also *attrib.* **Behaviouri·stic** *a.*, **-i·stically** *adv.*

Beigel, var. *BAGEL.

Bel (bel). 1929. [f. the name of A. G. *Bell* (1847–1922), inventor of the telephone.] A unit equivalent to ten *DECIBELS (the unit usually used).

Belay, *v.* **3. b.** *Climbing.* To secure a rope round a spike of rock 1910. Hence **Belay** *sb.*, the position so secured or the point providing it 1908.

Belisha (bǐlī·∫ă). Surname of Leslie Hore-*Belisha*, Minister of Transport 1931–7.

B. beacon, a post about seven feet high surmounted by a flashing amber-coloured globe and erected on the pavement at each end of officially recognized pedestrian crossings.

Bell, *sb.*[1] **1.** colloq. phr. *To ring the b.*: to carry off the prize; to be the best of a lot: in allusion to the ringing of the bell attached to a strength-testing machine. *To ring a b.*: to call up the memory of or suggest an earlier occurrence of the thing referred to.

Belly, *sb.*

Comb.: **b.-dance,** an erotic oriental dance performed by women, involving abdominal contortions; **b.-flop** *colloq.*, (of a swimmer) a dive that brings one's body flat on the water; **b.-landing,** the crash-landing of an aircraft on the under surface of the fuselage without the use of the under-carriage; **b.-laugh** *colloq.*, a deep, unrestrained laugh.

Bellyache (be·liēⁱk), *v.* 1888. [f. *belly-ache* (see BELLY *sb. Comb.*)] *intr. slang.* (orig. *U.S.*). To whimper, whine, grizzle, complain querulously.

I reckon there's enough to complain about these days if a fellow wants to belly-ache some E. CALDWELL.

Belt, *sb.* **3. b.** In a machine gun, a length of woven fabric or of metal plates pinned together, fitted with cartridges, and revolving on the feed-block 1902. **5. d.** A zone or district, usu. with defining term denoting the principal product or characteristic, as **Bible b., green b.* 1869.

Bend, *sb.*[4] **6.** *pl.* The severe pains in joints and limbs experienced by a person when the pressure on him drops rapidly (as when a deep-sea diver surfaces too quickly) 1894.

Benefit, *sb.* **4. e.** A performance, as of a play, a game, a concert, or the like, the proceeds from which go to a particular player or company 1802. **f.** That which a person is entitled to under the National Insurance Act of 1911, etc., or as a member of a benefit (or friendly) society 1875.

Benny (be·ni). orig. *U.S.* 1955. Slang abbrev. of *BENZEDRINE.

Bent, *ppl. a.* **5.** *fig.* In various slang uses: **a.** Dishonest (cf. CROOKED) 1914. **b.** Illegal; stolen (orig. *U.S.*) 1930. **c.** Perverted, spoiled; *spec.* homosexual 1930.

Benzedrine (be·nzėdrīn). 1933. [Proprietary term, f. BENZO- + *EPH)EDRINE.] A preparation of amphetamine used medicinally by inhalation to relieve respiratory congestion and in tablet form to lessen fatigue.

Béret. Now usu. **beret** (be·rēⁱ). **b.** A hat resembling the Basque cap, worn by men and women; also forming part of many British service and other uniforms 1827.

Berk (bɔ̄ɹk). *slang.* Also **birk, burk.** 1936. [abbrev. of *Berkeley* (or *Berkshire*) *Hunt*, rhyming slang for *cunt.*] A fool.

Berkelium (bəɹkī·liŏm, bɔ̄·ɹkliŏm). 1950. [mod.L., f. *Berkeley*, California, where the element was first made + -IUM.] *Chem.* A metallic radioactive element not occurring in nature but made artificially. Symbol Bk; atomic number 97.

Bermuda.

Comb.: **B. rig,** a rig for a yacht, carrying a tall, tapering main-sail; **B. shorts,** knee-length shorts; also *ellipt.* as *Bermudas.*

Berserk. Also pronounced (bəɹsɔ̄·ɹk, bəɹzɔ̄·ɹk). Now usu. as *adj.*, frenzied, furiously or madly violent. Esp. in phr. *To go b.*

Bespoke (bǐˌspōᵘ·k), *ppl. a.* 1755. [See BESPEAK *v.*] Made to order, as distinguished from READY-MADE. Also said of the maker.

Bible.

Comb.: **B. belt** [*BELT *sb.* 5 d], a designation of those parts of the United States reputed to be fanatically puritan or fundamentalist.

Bid, *sb.* phr. *To make a b. for*: to make an attempt to obtain, try to get. Hence the simple sb. is freq. used, esp. in journalese, for: an attempt to secure or win something. **2.** *Card-playing.* The statement of an undertaking which a player makes; *spec.* in *Bridge*, an announcement of the number of tricks in a specified suit or 'no-trumps' by which a player proposes to beat his opponents 1880.

Biff (bif), *v. slang.* 1888. [Imitative.] *trans.* To hit, strike. Also *to biff* (a person) *one.* Hence **Biff** *sb.*, a blow, whack 1889.

Bifocal (bəifōᵘ·kăl), *a.* and *sb.* orig. *U.S.* 1888. [BI-[2].] **A.** *adj.* Designating spectacles in which each lens has two portions of different focal lengths. **B.** *sb. pl.* Bifocal spectacles 1899.

Big, a. 3. d. colloq. phr. *To get, grow*, etc., *too b. for one's boots* (*breeches, trousers*): to become conceited, put on airs.

B. Brother, after the head of state in G. Orwell's novel *1984*, any apparently benevolent but ruthlessly omnipotent authority; **b. bud,** a disease of plants caused by a gall-mite; **b. bug** [see BUG *sb.* 1 b] orig. *U.S.*, a person of importance, great man; **b. business** orig. *U.S.*, (those in control of) large mercantile organizations or transactions collectively; **b. end,** the end of the connecting-rod that encircles the crank-pin in an internal combustion engine; **b. noise** (see NOISE *sb. phr.*); **b. shot** *U.S. slang*, a prominent member of an organization, e.g. a notorious gangster; **b. smoke,** (*a*) *Austral.*, Aboriginal name for a town; (*b*) London; **b. stick** [STICK *sb.*[1] 4] orig. *U.S.*, a display of force; **b. top** orig. *U.S.*, the main tent of a circus; a circus in general.

Bikini (bikī·ni). 1948. Name of one of the Marshall Islands, in the Pacific Ocean, which was used, in 1946, as the locale of an atomic bomb test: applied to a scanty two-piece beach garment for women.

Bilateral, *a.* **b.** *spec.* Pertaining to or concerning two countries (only), esp. of the trade and financial agreements made between them. **c.** *Education.* Of a secondary school or its educational system: providing two or three possible types of course 1947.

Bilharzia (bilhā·ɹziă). 1859. [mod.L. (T. S. Cobbold, 1859), f. the name of T. *Bilharz* (1825–62), German physician.] A genus of trematode worms parasitic in human beings, esp. in Egypt and other parts of Africa. **b.** By extension, the disease caused by the worm, also called **Bilharzia·sis** 1889.

Billabong (bi·lăbǫŋ). *Austral.* 1865. [– *Billibang*, Aboriginal name of Bell River, f. *billa* water + *bang* of uncertain meaning.] A branch or effluent of a river forming a backwater.

Once a jolly swagman camped by a billabong *Waltzing Matilda.*

Billy, delete **c.** and substitute next.

Billy[2] (bi·li). *Austral.* and *N.Z.* 1839. [perh. f. Austral. Aboriginal *billa* river, water (cf. *BILLABONG).] A tin can with a lid, used as container and cooking pot, esp. for making tea.

Comb.: **b.-can** (also in Eng. use) = *billy*; **b. tea,** tea made in a billy.

Binary. A. *adj.*

b. digit, one of the two digits (conventionally 0 and 1) in a BINARY *scale*; a bit (*BIT *sb.*[4]); **b. fission,** the division of a cell or organism into two.

Bind, *v.* **14.** *slang. trans.* To bore, weary 1929. **15.** *slang. intr.* To complain, grumble 1943. Also *sb.*

Bingo[2] (bi·ŋgo). 1936. [Origin unkn.; perh. first as exclam.] A gambling game, a development of LOTTO, often played in public halls, etc., for prizes. So **Bi·ngo** *interj.*, the cry made by the winner.

Binomial. A. *adj.* **1.**

B. expansion, an expansion of a power of a binomial; the coefficients in it are *b. coefficients.*

B. *sb.* **2.** The two-part Latin name of a plant or animal 1945.

Bio-. Biodegra·dable *a.*, susceptible to the decomposing action of living organisms; so **Bi:odegradabi·lity. Bi:olumine·scence,** the emission of light by living organisms. **Biometry,** (*b*) the application of statistics to biology, esp. to the study of resemblances between organisms; also called **Biome·trics** so **Biome·tric, -ical** *adjs.*; **Bi:ometri·cian, -me·tricist. Biophy·sics,** the science dealing with the mechanical and electrical properties of the parts of living organisms; so **Biophy·sical** *a.*, **-phy·sicist. Biosy·n-thesis,** the production of a chemical substance by a living organism; so **Biosynthe·-tic** *a.*

Biochemical (bəiǒke·mikăl), *a.* 1867. [f. BIO- + CHEMICAL *a.*, after G. *biochemisch.*] Of or pertaining to biochemistry. Hence **Bioche·mically** *adv.*

Biochemistry (bəiǒke·mistri). 1881. [f. BIO- + CHEMISTRY, after *biochemical.*] The science dealing with the substances present in living organisms and with their relation to each other and to the life of the organism; biological or physiological chemistry. So **Bioche·mist,** one versed in biochemistry.

Biocœnosis (bəioˌsīnōᵘ·sis). Also **bio-cenose, biocœnose.** 1883. [mod.L. (K. Möbius, 1877), f. BIO- + Gr. κοίνωσις sharing.] *Ecology.* An association of organisms forming a biotic community; the relationship that exists between such organisms. Hence **Biocœno·logy,** the study of b.; **Biocœno·tic** *a.*

Biological, *a.*

Comb.: **b. clock,** an innate mechanism that regulates various cyclic and rhythmic activities of an organism; **b. control,** the use of natural predators to subdue a living pest; **b. warfare,** the use in war of harmful toxins, germs, etc.

Biopsy (bəi·ǫpsi, bəiˌǫ·psi). 1895. [– Fr. *biopsie*, f. Gr. βίος life + ὄψις sight. After NECROPSY.] Examination of tissues, etc., taken from the living body for diagnostic purposes.

Bioscope (bəi·ǒskōᵘp). 1812. [f. BIO- + -SCOPE.] † **1.** (In Dict. s.v. BIO-.) –1824. **2.** An earlier form of cinematograph; retained in South Africa as the usual term for a cinema or a moving film 1897. Hence **Biosco·pic** *a.*

Biosphere (bəi·ǒsfīᵊɹ). 1899. [– G. *biosphäre* (E. Suess 1875), f. BIO- + SPHERE.] The regions of the earth's crust and atmosphere that are occupied by living organisms; occas., the living organisms themselves; also *transf.*

Bipa:rtisa·n, *a.* 1909. [BI-².] Of, representing, or composed of members of, two (political or other) parties.

Bird.

Comb.: **b.-strike,** a collision between birds and aircraft; **b.-watcher,** one who observes the ways of birds; so **b.-watching** *vbl. sb.*

Biro (bəiᵊ·ro). 1947. [f. the name of László *Biró* the Hungarian inventor.] The proprietary name of a particular make of ball-point pen: also (with lower-case initial) applied loosely to any ball-point pen.

Bit, *sb.*⁴ 1948. [abbrev. of *BINARY *digit.*] A unit of information derived from a choice between two equally probable alternatives or 'events'; such a unit stored electronically in a computer.

Existing electronic computers can store, in their normal memories, up to about one million bits 1957.

Bite, *sb.* **1. c.** *Dentistry.* The bringing together of the teeth in occlusion 1848. **d.** *fig.* Incisiveness, pungency; point or cogency of style, language, etc. 1899.

Black, *a.* **2. b.** Of coffee: without milk 1796. **7. c.** Macabre 1963. **8. b.** Performed by 'blackleg' labour; boycotted by trade unions during a dispute 1927.

Comb.: **B. and Tans,** pop. name for an armed force specially recruited to combat the Sinn-Feiners in 1921, so named from the mixture of constabulary and military uniforms worn by them; **b. belt,** the belt worn by one who has attained a certain degree of proficiency at Judo; a person qualified to wear such a belt; **b. body,** a body or surface that absorbs all radiation falling upon it; **b. box** orig. R.A.F. *slang*, a navigational instrument, later a flight recorder, or by extension any intricate automatic apparatus; **b. market,** unauthorized dealing in commodities that are rationed or of which the supply is otherwise restricted; hence **b. marketeer; B. Muslim,** a member of an American Negro sect, established in 1931, which preaches a form of Islam and proposes principally the separation of Negroes and Whites; **B. Panther,** a member of an American Negro organization which adopts a militant attitude to the promotion of the Negro cause; **b. power,** power for black people; used as a slogan in connection with Negro civil rights; **b. spot,** (*a*) any of several plant diseases usually caused by fungi, esp. a disease of roses, caused by the fungus *Diplocarpon rosæ*, which produces black blotches on the leaves; (*b*) a place or area of trouble, anxiety, or danger; esp. a dangerous section of a road.

Black, *v.* **2. b.** *To b. out*: to obscure or obliterate with black material, fog, or the like; to extinguish the lights on a stage during a performance; to prevent the emission of light from buildings and to minimize street lighting as a precaution against observation by hostile aircraft (*trans.* and *intr.*) 1921. **c.** *To b. out* (*intr.*), to be temporarily blinded or lose consciousness as a result of an interruption to the blood supply to the brain, esp. in flying, on acceleration or a sharp turn 1940. **3. b.** *trans.* To declare to be 'black' (*BLACK *a.* 8 b).

Black-out (blæ·kaut). 1913. [f. *BLACK *v.* 2 b, c.] **1.** *Theatr.* The darkening of a stage during a performance. **2.** The action of extinguishing or obscuring lights as a precaution against air-raids, etc.; the resultant darkness; the material used to obscure the lights; also *attrib.* and *transf.* 1935. **3.** Temporary loss of consciousness; in flying, temporary blindness resulting from an interruption to the blood supply to the brain during acceleration or a sharp turn 1940.

Blah (blā). *colloq.* (orig. *U.S.*). 1918. [Imitative.] Nonsense, humbug; insincere or pretentious talk or writing.

Blanket, *sb.* **5.** *attrib.* passing into *adj.* Covering all cases, inclusive (orig. *U.S.*) 1886.

Once we lose faith in the blanket formula of education..we can turn our attention to the vital matter of developing individuals 1930.

Blast, *sb.* **7. b.** A sudden momentary increase in pressure that travels through the air as a destructive wave from a large explosion; usu. as *b. wave* 1852.

Blast, *v.* **4. b.** *intr.* Of a rocket: to take *off*, to be launched into space 1951.

Comb.: **b.-off,** the launching of a rocket.

Blatant, *a.* **2. b.** Palpably prominent or obvious 1889.

The transactions were more than open: they were b. W. S. CHURCHILL. Clad in a suit of blatant check A. E. COPPARD.

Bleed, *v.* **II.** *trans.* **3.** To make the printed area extend to the edge of a page, either accidentally in trimming or by design in printing; used with the printed area or the edge as obj. Also *intr.*, to extend to the edge of the page. Also with *off* 1835. **4.** To allow liquid or gas to escape from a closed system by means of a valve, cock, etc.; used with the fluid or the system as obj. 1889.

Bleep (blīp). 1953. [imit.] A thin high-pitched piping sound, *spec.* that of a radio signal. Also as vb.

Science 'fiction' has become fact. Those eerie 'bleeps' from outer space tell us that 1957.

Blimp (blimp). 1916. [Of uncertain origin.] **1.** A small non-rigid airship consisting of a gas-bag with the fuselage of an aeroplane slung underneath; in the 1939–45 war the name was applied to a barrage balloon. **2.** (*Colonel*) *Blimp*: a character invented by David Low (1891–1963), cartoonist and caricaturist, and pictured as an obese, pompous-looking elderly figure voicing reactionary opinions 1934. Hence *transf.*, a person of this type.

Blind, *a.* **1. d.** Blind-drunk 1630. **e.** Applied to flying and aerial bombing executed by means of instruments without direct observation or visual identification 1919. **f.** In Poker, as *adv.*, *to go b.*: to put up a blind (see *BLIND *sb.* 6); hence, *to go* (a specified stake) *b.*; fig. *to go it b.*, to act without previous investigation of the circumstances, plunge without regard to the risks involved 1840. **8. b.** Of a corner or other feature where the road or course ahead is concealed from view, as *b. corner*, *b. fence* 1927. **9. b.** *Cookery.* Of a pastry case, baked without a filling. Also as *adv.* 1943.

Comb.: **b. date,** an assignation with a previously unseen partner; also, the person so met; **b. spot** *transf.* and *fig.*, a limited area where vision, judgement, etc., fails; **b.-stamped,** (of book-covers) stamped without colour or gold leaf (cf. *blind-blocking*, *-tooling*).

Blind, *sb.* **6.** In Poker, a stake put up by a player before seeing his cards 1857. **7.** [f. *BLIND *a.* 1 d.] A drunken bout or orgy, binge 1917.

Blind, *v.* **6.** *slang.* To proceed blindly or recklessly 1923.

Blinding along the Brighton road at fifty miles an hour 1928.

Blip (blip). 1894. [imit.] **1.** Any sudden brisk blow or twitch; a quick popping sound. **2.** A small elongated mark displayed on a radar screen 1945.

Blitz (blits). 1939. [Shortening of next.] An attack or offensive launched suddenly with great violence with the object of reducing the defences immediately; *spec.* an air-raid or a series of them conducted in this way. Also **Blitz** *v. trans.*, to attack in this way; to hit, blast, etc., by an air-raid. **Blitzed** (blitst) *ppl. a.*

Emergency kitchens for people 'blitzed' out of their homes 1942.

Blitzkrieg (bli·tskrīg, ‖-krīk). 1939. [G., 'lightning-war'.] See prec.

The complete failure of the Soviet B. [on Finland] 1940.

‖**Bloc** (blǫk). 1903. [Fr.; see BLOCK *sb.*] In Continental politics, a combination of parties of divergent views which supports the government in power; also *transf.*, a combination of groups or nations formed to foster a particular interest.

The Soviet Union has been..forming a compact and well-organized political and economic *bloc* 1946.

Block, *sb.* **10. c.** *Austral.* and *N.Z.* Each of the large lots into which land for settlers is divided by the government; any large area of land 1840.

Comb.: **b.-buster** [see *BUSTER], an aerial bomb of a type designed to wreck a block of buildings; **b. capital,** a capital letter written or printed without serifs; **b. (-storage) heater,** a heating unit that accumulates heat during the night and gives it off during the day.

Block, *v.* **4. b.** *Finance.* To restrict the use or conversion of (currency or other assets) 1932. Hence **Blocked** *ppl. a.*

Blood, *sb.* **I. 1. b.** (*You cannot get*) *b. out of a stone*, i.e. sympathy from the hard-hearted or money from the avaricious. **3. c.** *B. and thunder*, bloodshed and violence, used *attrib.* in *b.-and-thunder book, tale*, etc., one describing or relating the exploits of men of violence or desperadoes 1852; also (orig. *U.S.*) abbrev. to *blood* (esp. in pl.), e.g. *b. books*, (*penny*) *b-s* 1897. **d.** *B. and iron* [tr. G. *blut und eisen*], military force as opp. to diplomacy, esp. in *the man of b. and iron*, Prince Bismarck, Prussian statesman 1869.

Comb.: **b.-bank,** a place where a supply of blood for transfusion is stored; **b.-brother,** (*a*) a brother by birth; (*b*) one who has been bound to another by a ceremonial mingling of blood; **b. count,** (the determination of) the number of blood cells contained in a given volume of blood; **b. donor,** one who gives blood for transfusion; **b. group,** one of the genetically determined types into which human blood may be divided on the basis of its compatibility with the blood of other individuals; **b. orange,** a variety of orange having the pulp streaked with red; **b.-poisoning,** a morbid condition of the blood; **b. pressure,** the pressure of circulating blood, esp. in the systemic arteries; **b. sports,** sports involving the killing of animals, esp. those of the chase; **bloodstock** [see III. 5], thoroughbred horses collectively; **b.-stream,** the blood circulating through the human system; **b. test,** a test performed on the blood; **b. transfusion** = TRANSFUSION 2.

Bloody-minded, *a.* 1584. [BLOODY *a.*] **1.** Bloodthirsty, cruel. **2.** Perverse, cantankerous; perversely obstructive 1935.

2. The building unions..have never been as bloody-minded about demarcation as the ship-builders and others 1959.

Bloom, *v.*¹ **7.** To apply a thin, transparent coating to (a lens) in order to reduce surface reflection; chiefly as **Bloomed** *ppl. a.*, **-ing** *vbl. sb.* 1943.

Blotto (blǫ·to), *a. slang.* 1917. [Origin unknown.] Fuddled with drink, intoxicated.

Blow, *v.*¹. **I. 8. c.** *slang.* To lay out or get through (money) extravagantly; to squander 1874. **10. c.** *slang* (orig. *U.S.*). To leave (hurriedly) 1912.

II. 1. d. *colloq.* (orig. *U.S.*). To play jazz (on) 1949. **7. b.** *Photogr. To b. up*: to enlarge (a photograph, etc.). *colloq.* 1930. **10. b.** *Electr.* Of a fuse: to melt under an excessive current; also *trans.*, to cause (a fuse) to melt 1902.

9. *To b. one's top*: to lose control of oneself. *To b.* (a person's) *mind*: to induce hallucinatory experiences in (a person) by means of drugs, esp. LSD; hence *transf.*, to shock or excite (a person).

Blow-.

b.-lamp, b.-torch, a small burner that uses the pressure of air or another gas to produce a fierce flame that may be directed on a selected spot; **b.-up** *colloq.*, a photographic enlargement.

Blower¹. **3. b.** *colloq.* A speaking-tube or telephone 1922.

Blue, *a.* **3. b.** Of affairs, etc.: dismal, unpromising, depressing 1833. **c.** Of musical tone: characteristic of the *BLUES 1919.

b. It's a b. look out, Master 1833. **c.** The 'blue notes' and 'flattened chords'..which provide sensations in jazz 1969.

Comb.: **b. baby,** an infant suffering from congenital cyanosis; **b. bag,** a barrister's (orig. a solicitor's) brief-bag of blue stuff; **b. chip** orig. *U.S.*, a high-value poker counter; *transf.*, a Stock Exchange investment considered to be fairly reliable, though not entirely without risk; **b. pencil,** a blue 'lead pencil' as used in marking corrections, obliterations, and the like; hence **b.-pencil** *v. trans.*, to mark, score through, or obliterate with a blue pencil: to make cuts in, censor; **b.-print,** a photographic print composed of white lines on a blue ground or vice versa, used for making copies of plans and designs; *fig.* a plan, scheme; **b.-vinn(e)y,** a blue-mould cheese made in Dorset.

Blue (blū), *v.*² 1846. [Origin unkn.] *trans.* To spend lavishly or improvidently; = *BLOW *v.*¹ I. 8 c.

Blue grass, blue-grass. Chiefly *U.S.* 1751. [BLUE *a. Comb.* 1 b.] A field-grass (*Poa pratensis* or *P. compressa*) characteristic especially of Kentucky and Virginia. **b.** The region of the blue grass, spec. the state of Kentucky 1872. Also *attrib.* or as *adj.*, of Kentucky and esp. its folk-music and horses 1772.

Blues (blūz). orig. *U.S.* 1912. [See BLUE *sb.* ad fin.] A melody of a mournful and haunting character, originating among the Negroes of the Southern U.S., freq. in a twelve-bar sequence using many 'blue' notes.

Bobby-dazzler (bǫ·biˌdæ·zləɹ). orig. and chiefly *dial.* 1866. Something striking or excellent; a strikingly dressed person.

Bobby pin. *U.S.* 1936. [Origin unknown.] A kind of sprung hair-pin or small clip, orig. for use with bobbed hair.

Bo·bby sock. orig. *U.S.* 1943. [Origin unknown.] (Usu. in pl. **bobby socks, sox.**) Socks reaching just above the ankle, esp. those worn by girls in their teens. Hence **Bo·bby-soxer,** an adolescent girl, esp. one in her early teens, wearing bobby socks.

Boffin (bǫ·fin). *slang.* 1941. [Origin unkn.] **1.** An 'elderly' naval officer. **2.** One engaged in scientific or technical research 1945.

2. The man from Farnborough. Everybody calls them boffins...Because they behave like boffins, I suppose 1948.

Bohunk (bōᵘ·hʌŋk). *N. Amer. slang.* 1903. [app. f. BO(HEMIAN + *-hunk*, alt. of HUNG(ARIAN.] A Hungarian; an immigrant from central or south-eastern Europe, esp. one of inferior class; hence a rough fellow, a lout.

Boiler.

Comb.: **b. suit,** a one-piece suit of overalls worn to protect the clothing.

Bolero. 2. A short jacket coming barely to the waist, worn by men in Spain. Also, a similar garment worn by women 1892.

Boloney, var. *BALONEY.

Bomb, *sb.* **2.** In modern use: a case filled with explosive, inflammable material, poison gas, or smoke, etc., fired from a gun, dropped from aircraft, or thrown or placed by hand 1914. **b.** *spec.* The atomic or hydrogen bomb 1945. **c.** *slang.* A success, esp. in entertainment 1954. **d.** *slang.* A large sum of money 1958.

Comb.: *b.-aimer*; **b. bay,** a compartment in an aircraft to hold bombs; **b.-disposal,** the removal and detonation of unexploded bombs; **b.-proof** *a.* (see PROOF *a.* 1 b); **b.-sight,** a device in an aircraft for the aiming of bombs; **b.-site,** an open space in a town left after the destruction of buildings by aerial bombing.

Bombard, *v.* **2. b.** *Physics.* To subject to a stream of ions or sub-atomic particles 1907.

Bombe (bonb). 1892. [Fr.: see BOMB *sb.*] A conical or cup-shaped confection, freq. frozen.

Claret and *tournedos*; a *b. surprise* BETJEMAN.

Bomber (bǫ·məɹ). 1915. [f. BOMB *sb.* or *v.* + -ER¹.] **1.** One who throws a bomb, one of a bombing party. **2.** An aircraft used for bombing 1917. Hence *B. Command*, an organization of bomber aircraft forming part of the Royal Air Force. **3.** *U.S. slang.* A marijuana cigarette 1952. **b.** *slang.* A barbiturate drug 1962.

Bonce. 2. *slang.* The head 1889.

Bond, *sb.*¹ **9. d.** *Chem.* A linkage by which one atom is joined to another 1884.

Bongo¹ (bǫ·ŋgo). 1861. [Cf. Bangi *mbangani*, Lingala *mongu*.] In full *b. antelope.* A Central African forest antelope, *Taurotragus eurycerus.*

Bongo² (bǫ·ŋgo). 1920. [Amer. Sp.] In full *b. drum.* One of a pair of small (Cuban) drums, usu. held between the knees and played with the fingers.

Bonkers (bǫ·ŋkəɹz), *a. slang.* 1948. [Origin unkn.] Mad, 'crackers'.

‖**Bonsai** (bǫ·nsəi, bōᵘ·nsəi). 1950. [Jap.] A Japanese potted plant, esp. a tree, intentionally dwarfed; the method of cultivating such a plant.

Booby, *sb.*

b. trap, (also) *Mil. colloq.*, a harmless-looking object concealing an explosive charge, designed to go off if the object is disturbed. Hence **b.-trap** *v. trans.*

The enemy left..'booby-traps' to blow a man to bits 1918. Doors and windows are easily booby-trapped 1943.

Boogie-woogie (bū·giˌwū·gi). orig. *U.S.* 1928. [Origin unkn.] A style of playing blues (usu. on the piano) marked by a persistent bass rhythm.

Book, *sb.*

b. club, a society which produces books for its members; **b. match,** one of a set of tear-off matches, sold in packets hinged at one end like a book; **b. token,** a voucher exchangeable at a bookseller's for a book or books; **b. value,** the value of a commodity as shown by a firm's books, as distinguished from its market value.

Boolean (bū·liăn), *a.* Also **Boolian.** 1851. [f. the proper name *Boole* + -AN.] Of or pertaining to the work of George *Boole* (1815–64), English mathematician and logician; **B. algebra,** a kind of algebra applicable to problems in logic and the manipulation of sets.

Boondock (bū·ndǫk). *U.S. slang.* 1944. [– Tagalog *bundok* mountain.] Rough country; an isolated or wild region. Usu. in *pl.*

Booster. b. *Electr.* A device for amplifying signals received from a distant point and relaying them 1935. **c.** *Aeronaut.* An auxiliary engine or rocket, esp. one used to give initial speed to a rocket or missile 1944. **d.** *Med.* A dose or injection that increases or prolongs the effectiveness of an earlier one 1950.

attrib. in all senses, as *b. dose, rocket.*

Boot, *sb.*³ **4. c.** The luggage compartment of a motor vehicle 1933.

Phr. *To give* (a person) *the b.*: to dismiss; so *to get the b.*

Boot, *v.*² **4.** To kick (a person) 1877.

Bop (bǫp). orig. *U.S.* 1948. = *BEBOP. Hence **Bo·pper. Bo·pster.**

‖**Borsch, bortsch** (bǭɹʃ, bǭɹtʃ). 1884. [Russ. *borshch* (borʃtʃ).] A Russian soup containing beetroot and other vegetables.

Boson (bōᵘ·zǫn). 1947. [f. the name of S. N. *Bose* (b. 1894), Indian physicist + *-ON.] *Nuclear Physics.* Any particle which has zero or integral spin and does not obey the exclusion principle.

Boss (bǫs), *v.*³ *dial.* and *slang.* 1887. [Cf. *BOSS-EYED *a.*] *trans.* To miss or bungle (a shot); *gen.*, to make a mess of. Hence **Boss** *sb.*⁶ (*b. shot*), a bungled shot 1890.

Bossa nova (bǫ·să nōᵘ·vă). 1962. [Pg. *bossa* tendency + *nova* new.] A style of Brazilian music related to the samba; a dance performed to this music.

Boss-eyed, *a. dial.* and *slang.* 1860. [Cf. Boss *v.*³] Squint-eyed, cross-eyed. Also *fig.*, oblique, crooked.

Bottle, *sb.*²

b.-neck, (also) a restricted or crowded condition which causes obstruction or delay of production; **b. party,** a party to which each guest contributes a bottle of wine, or other drinks.

Bottom.

Comb.: **b. drawer,** lit. the lowest drawer of a chest of drawers, etc., in which a woman stores clothes, linen, etc., in preparation for her marriage.

‖**Bouclé** (bukle), *a.* 1895. [Fr., = buckled, curled.] Of fabric: covered with numerous small loops or curls of thread. Hence as *sb.*, a yarn of looped or curled ply; bouclé fabric.

Bounce, *v.* **6. b.** Of a cheque: to be returned to the drawer because there are insufficient funds to meet it 1927. **7. b.** To eject summarily. Chiefly *U.S. colloq.* 1877.

Bouncer. 4. Someone engaged to eject undesirable persons from a club, dance-hall, etc. *colloq.* (orig. *U.S.*). 1865.

Bourbon. 4. Whisky of a kind originally made in Bourbon County, Kentucky; a glass of this whisky. orig. *U.S.* 1846.

Bourgeois, *sb.*¹ and *a.* **A.** *sb.* **2.** Used *disparagingly.* **a.** In communist or socialist writings: anyone judged to be an exploiter of the proletariat 1883. **b.** A socially or æsthetically conventional person 1930.

B. *adj.* **2.** Resembling the middle classes in way of thinking, appearance, etc. Also used *disparagingly*: selfishly materialistic or conventionally respectable and unimaginative 1764. **3.** Capitalistic, non-communist; esp. used *disparagingly* 1850.

2. The old b. morality SHAW. **3.** Powder and cosmetics are banned..as attributes of 'b. decay' KOESTLER.

Boutique (butī·k). 1767. [– Fr. *boutique*; see BODEGA.] A small shop; in modern use *spec.* a small shop or department selling ready-made fashionable clothes, etc.

Box, *sb.*²

Comb.: **b.-camera,** a very simple camera of a box shape; **b.-car** *U.S.*, a large closed-in railway goods wagon; **b.-girder,** a hollow girder of square or rectangular section; **b. junction,** a road junction with a grid of yellow lines painted on the road forbidding the road-user to enter the junction area until his exit is clear; **b.-kite,** a toy kite having the form of a box; also = **b.-kite aeroplane,** an early form of biplane in which the arrangement of the wings resembled a box-kite; **b.-office,** the office at a theatre or other place of public entertainment where tickets of admission are sold; *ellipt.* used of the financial success of a show; **b.-spanner,** a spanner with a socket-head at one or both ends which fits over the nut, etc., to be turned.

Boxer³ (bǫ·ksəɹ). 1934. [G., – Eng. BOXER².] A smooth-coated, square-built, fawn or brindle breed of dog of the bulldog type, originating in Germany.

Bra (brā). 1936. Colloq. abbrev. of BRASSIÈRE.

Brachiate (bræ·kiˌēⁱt), *v.* 1899. [f. BRACHI(UM + -ATE³.] *intr.* Of apes: to move by using the arms to swing from branch to branch. Hence **Bra·chiating** *ppl. a.* and *vbl. sb.* **Brachia·tion,** the act of brachiating. **Bra·chiator,** an animal that brachiates.

Bracket, *sb.* **5. b.** The (specified) distance between a pair of shots fired, one beyond the target and one short of it, in order to find the range for artillery 1899. So **Bracket** *v.* 3. To drop shot beyond (the target) and short of it. **c.** A range within a classified series, as *age b., income b.* 1880.

5. b. The German gun had got its b. 1916.

Bradshaw (bræ·dʃǭ). 1847. Colloq. designation of 'Bradshaw's Railway Guide' (1839–1961), a timetable of all railway trains in Great Britain, originally issued in Manchester by George *Bradshaw* (1801–53). Also *transf.* and *fig.*

Brain, *sb.* **2. b.** An electronic device that performs complicated operations similar to those of the human brain 1934. **3. b.** *colloq.* A clever person; *the brains*: the 'mastermind' 1914.

Comb.: **b.-child** *colloq.*, the product of a person's mind, an invention; **b. drain** *colloq.*, the emigration of highly trained or qualified persons; **b.-storm,** (*a*) (see STORM *sb.* I. 4); (*b*) *U.S.* a concerted attack on a problem by amassing rapidly a number of spontaneous ideas which are then discussed; **B. Trust** *U.S.*, a group of experts appointed to advise and direct policy; **Brains Trust,** a group of persons chosen to give their impromptu views on topics of current or general interest; **brainwashing,** clearing or purging the mind of established ideas by persistent suggestion and indoctrination; **b.-wave,** (*a*) a hypothetical telepathic vibration; (*b*) (usu. in *pl.*) a measurable electrical impulse in the brain; (*c*) *colloq.* [in Dict.].

Bramley (bræ·mli). 1900. [f. the name of M. *Bramley*, an English butcher, in whose garden at Southwell, Notts., this apple is said to have been first grown *c.*1850.] A large green variety of cooking apple; in full *B.('s) seedling.*

Brash, *a.*[2] Latterly in general colloq. use, in imitation of U.S. currency. Other U.S. senses are: **b.** Rough, harsh 1868. **c.** Active, quick 1884. Hence **Bra·shly** *adv.*, **Bra·shness.**

Brass, *sb.* **1.** *transf.*, 'Brass hats' collectively *slang* (orig. *U.S.*) 1899.

attrib.: **b. hat** *slang*, an officer of high rank in one of the services, so called from the gilt insignia on his cap; **b. tacks** (see TACK *sb.*[1] I. 2).

‖**Brasserie** (brasəri). 1864. [Fr., orig. = brewery.] A beer saloon, usually one in which food is served.

Bread, *sb.* **5. b.** *slang* (orig. *U.S.*). Money 1952.

Break, *v.* **IV. 1. b.** To solve (a code or cipher); to decipher 1928.

Phr. *To b. even*, to emerge from a transaction, enterprise, etc., with balancing gains and losses (orig. *U.S.*).

Break, *sb.*[1] **1. b.** With adverbs, expressing the action of the corresponding verbal combinations, as *BREAK-AWAY, *BREAK-DOWN, **Break-out. 5. c.** A short interval between lessons in the middle of morning or afternoon school. Also *transf.* 1861. **d.** A mistake, blunder (*U.S.*) 1884. **6. b.** In jazz, a short solo or improvised phrase (orig. *U.S.*) 1926. **9.** A stroke of fortune or chance, as *even, lucky b.* (orig. *U.S.*) 1911.

Break-away (brēⁱ·kăwēⁱ). 1885. [f. phr. *to break away*: see BREAK *v.*] Severance; the act of breaking away or getting free; spec.: **a.** *Athletics* (*Running*). A premature start. **b.** *Boxing.* The separating of the combatants after a spell of in-fighting. **c.** *Football.* A sudden rush of a player or players with the ball towards the opponents' goal (esp. after a period of pressure). Also *attrib.* or as *adj.*, that breaks away or has broken away.

B. unions were condemned by . . the Minister of Labour 1951. The 'b.' province of Katanga 1961.

Break-down. Now usu. as one word. **1. b.** A failure of (esp. mental) health; *spec.* a *nervous b.* (see *NERVOUS *a.*) 1858. **c.** Chemical or physical decomposition; also *attrib.*, as *b. product* 1928. **d.** Analysis or classification (of statistics, etc.) 1936.

Brea·k-through, breakthrough. 1918. [f. phr. *to break through*: cf. G. *durchbruch.*] An act of breaking through a barrier of any kind; *spec.* the making of a breach in the enemy's lines; *fig.* a significant advance in knowledge, achievement, etc.

Breast, *sb.*

Comb.: **b.-fed** *a.* (of infants), nourished at the mother's b.; so *b.-feeding*; opp. to *bottle-fed, -feeding*; **b.-stroke** *Swimming*, a stroke in which the breast is squarely opposed to the water, the arms are pushed forward and outwards in a wide arc, and the legs perform a frog-like action.

Breathalyser (bre·pălaizəɹ). Also **-zer** (chiefly *U.S.*). 1960. [f. BREATH + AN)-ALYSER, -ZER.] An instrument for measuring the amount of alcohol in a person's breath.

Breather. 2. b. A short rest in which to recover breath; a breathing-space 1901.

Breeder. 2. A nuclear reactor that can produce more fissile material than it consumes. Also *b. reactor* 1948.

Breeze, *sb.*[3]

Comb.: **b.-block,** a light-weight building-block made of **b.-concrete,** concrete made from b., sand, and cement.

Breeze, *v.* **2.** *colloq.* (orig. *U.S.*). To move or proceed briskly 1907. So *to b. in.*

Bremsstrahlung (bre·mzʃtrālun). 1944. [G., lit. 'braking radiation', f. *bremsen* to brake + *strahlung* radiation.] *Physics.* Electromagnetic radiation emitted by a charged particle when it is suddenly slowed down by an electric field (usu. an electron passing through the field of an atomic nucleus).

Bren (bren). 1937. [f. *Brno*, town in Czechoslovakia, where it was orig. made + first syll. of *Enfield*, town in Middlesex, England, seat of a small-arms factory.] In full *B. gun.* A type of light machine-gun.

Bridge, *sb.*[1]

Comb.: **b.-head,** latterly extended to cover any military position established in the face of the enemy, e.g. by a landing force.

British troops established a bridgehead of considerable width 1944.

Bridge, *sb.*[2] Now usu. = *auction b., contract b.*, in which the declarer's partner is dummy.

Brie (brī). 1848. A kind of soft cheese, made in *Brie*, an agricultural district in the north of France.

Brief, *sb.* **9.** *pl.* Very short knickers or trunks 1934.

Brief, *v.*[2] **3. b.** To give instructions or information to 1866.

Bring-and-buy, *adj. phr.* 1932. Descriptive of a charity bazaar or stall to which people bring objects for sale and buy those brought by others.

Brink. 5. *spec.* The verge of war. Hence **Bri·nkmanship,** the art of advancing to the very brink of war but not engaging in it 1956. Also *transf.* and *fig.*

Anglo-French 'brinkmanship' over Suez had failed to stop at the brink 1958.

Bristol. 4. *pl.* (with lower-case initial). *Rhyming slang.* [ellipt. for *Bristol Cities* = titties.] The breasts 1961.

Broad. B. *sb.* **6.** *slang* (orig. and chiefly *U.S.*). A woman; *spec.* a prostitute 1914.

Comb.: **b.-brow** *colloq.*, a person of broad tastes or interests; **broadloom** *a.*, applied to a carpet woven in broad widths; also *absol.*; **b.-mindedness,** the condition of being liberal or tolerant in thought or opinion; **b.-spectrum** *a.*, of a drug, effective over a wide range of diseases or microorganisms.

Broad-leaved, *a.* **2.** *Forestry. B. tree*, an angiosperm tree which produces a timber classified as hardwood 1905.

Broderie anglaise (brodri anglęz). 1852. [Fr., = English embroidery.] Open embroidery on linen, cambric, etc.; cloth so embroidered.

Broiler.[1] **2.** Now normally a chicken reared in close confinement in a broiler house. Also *attrib.* and *transf.*

The continued spread of b. houses, the buildings for rearing chickens 1959. A state of affairs which seems to be treating these old people [in hospitals] as if they were b. fowls 1966.

Brolly (brǫ·li). *colloq.* 1874. Clipped and altered form of UMBRELLA 2. **b.** *slang.* A parachute 1934.

Brouhaha (brū·hāhā). 1890. [Fr.] A commotion; hubbub, uproar.

Brown, *v.* **3.** *To be browned off*: to be bored or 'fed up' (*slang*) 1938.

Brucellosis (brūselōᵘ·sis). 1930. [mod.L., f. *Brucell(a* (f. the name of Sir David Bruce, Scottish physician, 1855–1931) + -OSIS.] *Path.* A disease caused by organisms of the genus *Brucella*; occurring in man also called Malta fever, undulant fever, etc., and in cattle, contagious abortion.

Brumby, brumbie (brɒ·mbi). *Austral.* 1880. [Origin unkn.] A wild or unbroken horse.

Brunch (brɒntʃ). orig. *University slang.* 1896. [A 'portmanteau' word f. BR(EAKFAST and L)UNCH.] A single meal taken late in the morning and intended to combine breakfast with lunch.

Brush, *sb.*[1]

Comb.: **b.-fire,** a fire in an area of brushwood or scrub; *attrib.*, as **b.-fire war,** a war on a small scale.

Brush, *v.*[2] **1. b.** *To b. up*, to brighten up by brushing; also *fig.* to refresh one's acquaintance with a thing *a* 1600. Hence **Bru·sh-up,** the action or process of brushing up. **3. b.** *To b. off*, fig., to rebuff, dismiss (a person) 1941. So **Bru·sh-off,** a rebuff, dismissal. orig. *U.S.*

Bryophyte (brəi·ŏfəit). 1878. [f. mod.L. *Bryophyta* (A. Braun, 1864). f. Gr. βρύον moss + φυτόν plant.] *Bot.* A member of the division Bryophyta of non-flowering plants, which includes mosses and liverworts.

Bubble, *sb.*

Comb.: **b. bath,** a bath prepared with a foaming toilet preparation; **b. car,** a miniature motor-car with a transparent domed top; **b. chamber,** a container of superheated liquid for the detection of ionizing particles.

Bubbly, *a. B. water* (slang), champagne; also simply *bubbly* (as *sb.*).

Buchmanism (bu·k-, bɒ·kmăniz'm). 1928. [f. name of Frank *Buchman* (1878–1961), the founder + -ISM.] The religious tenets and practice propagated by Buchman in the Oxford Group Movement, the adherents of which work by means of groups of persons who are encouraged to make 'total recall' of their past, to 'share' this with others, and so to become 'changed'. So **Bu·chmanite** *a.* and *sb.*

Buck (bɒk), *sb.*[7] *U.S. slang.* 1856. [Origin obscure.] A dollar.

Buck (bɒk), *sb.*[8] orig. *U.S.* 1865. [Origin obscure.] In Poker, any article placed in the pool with the chips. *To pass the b. to* (fig.): to make a scapegoat of, shift responsibility to.

Buckshee (bɒ·kʃī, bɒkʃī·), *sb.* and *a.* orig. *Army slang.* 1916. [Alteration of BAKSHEESH.] **A.** *sb.* Something extra, free, or to spare; an allowance above the usual amount. **B.** *adj.* Free; spare, extra. Hence as *adv.*

Bud (bɒd), *sb.*[2] *U.S. colloq.* 1851. [Childish or colloq. pronunc. of BROTHER, or abbrev. of next.] Brother: used chiefly as a form of address.

Buddy (bɒ·di), *sb. colloq.* (orig. *U.S.*). 1850. [perh. an alteration of BROTHER (cf. prec.), or a variant of BUTTY.] Brother; companion, friend; freq. as a form of address.

Budget. 4. b. Applied to the domestic accounts of a family or individual 1854. Also *attrib.* or quasi-*adj.*, suitable for someone of limited means; cheap.

Budgie (bɒ·dʒi) 1936. Colloq. abbrev. of BUDGERIGAR.

Buffer, *sb.*[2] **b.** *Chem.* A substance or mixture of substances (usu. a weak acid or base and its salt) which stabilizes the degree of acidity or alkalinity; a solution containing this. Freq. *attrib.*, as *b. action, base, solution* 1914. **d.** *Computers.* A memory device that is used to compensate for differences in the rates at which data pass through different devices; freq. *attrib.*, as *b. memory, store* 1948.

Bug, *sb.*[2] **3.** Various *slang* uses. **a.** orig. *U.S.* An enthusiast; also, a craze or obsession 1841. **b.** orig. *U.S.* A defect or fault that prevents normal operation 1889. **c.** *Schoolboys' slang.* A boy; usu. with defining word, as *day-b.* 1909. **d.** A microbe or germ; also, a disease; in *pl.*, bacteriology or biology 1919. **e.** *U.S.* A burglar-alarm system 1925. **f.** orig. *U.S.* A concealed microphone or a device for tapping a telephone line 1946.

Bug, *v.*[1] 1869. [f. BUG *sb.*[2]] **1.** *trans.* and *intr.* To clear (plants, etc.) of insects; to look for insects. **2.** *trans.* To equip with an alarm system or a concealed microphone 1919. So **Bugged** *ppl. a.* **3.** *slang* (orig. and chiefly *U.S.*). To annoy, irritate 1949.

Bug, *v.*[2] *U.S. colloq.* 1877. [Origin uncertain.] Of the eyes: to bulge *out.*

Comb.: **b.-eyed** *a.*, having bulging eyes.

Bugger, *v.* **2.** *coarse slang.* **a.** = DAMN *v.* 5 1794. **b.** To mess *up*; to ruin, spoil 1923. **c.** *intr.* With *off*: to go away, depart 1922. **d.** With *about*: to potter about; to act ineffectually; also const. *around* 1929.

Build, *v.* **1.** Phr. *To b. in*: to incorporate in the structure of a house, car, etc. Hence **built-in** *a.*, forming part of the structure; *fig.* inherent 1933. **4.** *To b. up*: to bring together the elements necessary to constitute or establish (a thing); to collect and organize men and materials for (also *absol.*).

The desire to 'build-up' the figure of the Leader (*El Caudillo*) in the approved Fascist style 1939. Hence **Bui·ld-up** *sb.*

Bui·lt-up, *a.* 1829. [See prec.] **1.** Constructed of separately prepared parts which are afterwards joined together. **2.** Covered or closed in with buildings, as *b. area* 1853. **3.** Raised, as *b. shoes.*

Bulge, *sb.* **2. b.** Phr. *To have the b. on*: to have the advantage over (*slang*, orig. *U.S.*) 1841. **c.** A bulging part of a military front; a salient 1927. **d.** A temporary increase in volume or numbers, esp. of schoolchildren after the 1914–18 and 1939–45 wars 1930.

Bull, *sb.*[4] **3.** *slang* (orig. *U.S.*). Trivial, insincere, or untruthful talk or writing; nonsense 1914. **4.** *slang* (orig. *Services*'). Unnecessary routine tasks or ceremonial; 'spit-and-polish' 1941.

Bulldoze, *v.*

b.-dozer, (also) a heavy caterpillar tractor fitted with a broad steel blade in front, used for removing obstacles, levelling uneven surfaces, etc.

Bum, *sb.*[3] *slang* (orig. and chiefly *U.S.*). 1864. [prob. short for BUMMER.] A lazy and dissolute person; an habitual loafer or tramp.

Bum, *v.*[4] *U.S. colloq.* 1863. [?Back-formation from BUMMER.] **1.** *intr.* To wander *around* idly. **2.** *trans.* To beg; to obtain by begging 1863. **b.** To travel on (a train) without a ticket 1896; so *to bum one's way*: to make one's way by begging; to hitch-hike.

Bumble-puppy. c. A game in which a ball slung to a post is struck with a racket by each player in opposite directions, the object being to wind the string entirely round the post 1900.

Bumf (bɒmf). *slang.* 1889. [Short for *bumfodder* (BUM *sb.*[1]).] Toilet paper; hence, paper (esp. with contemptuous implication), documents collectively.

Bummaree. 2. A licensed meat porter at Smithfield market 1954.

Bump, *v.*[1] **1. b.** *To b. off*: to remove by violence, to kill. *slang* (orig. *U.S.*). 1910.

Bumper, *sb.*[1] **2.** esp. in attrib. use = exceptionally full or abundant 1864. **5. b.** A log, bar, etc., used as a fender or shock-absorber 1867; *spec.* a metal bar attached to either end of a motor vehicle to protect it in the event of a collision 1926. **6.** One who or a thing which bumps; an operative employed in bumping; *Cricket*, a bumping ball 1855.

Comb.: **b.-to-b.** *adv.* and *a.*, (of cars) very close together.

Bung, *v.*[2] *slang* (orig. *dial.*). 1825. [imit.] *trans.* To throw (violently); to send; to put forcibly. Also *fig.*

Bunker. 5. A military dug-out; a reinforced concrete shelter 1939.

Bunny.[2] **b.** In full *bunny girl*. A night-club hostess dressed in a costume partly imitative of a rabbit 1960.

Bunyip (bɒ·nyip). 1848. The Aboriginal name of a fabulous monster inhabiting the rushy swamps and lagoons in the interior of Australia. †**b.** *transf.* An impostor –1853.

Burger (bɔ̄·ɹgəɹ). A familiar shortening of *HAMBURGER. 2. Also used as a terminal element on the analogy of *HAMBURGER as if formed upon HAM *sb.*[1] 2 + *-burger*, meaning a particular item of food served inside a roll, as *cheese-burger, egg-burger, steak-burger.* Chiefly *U.S.* 1939.

Burlesque. B. *sb.* **3.** *U.S.* A variety show, frequently featuring strip-tease 1870.

Burn, *sb.*[2] **1. b.** *Astronautics.* The provision of thrust by the engine of a spacecraft 1965.

Bus, *sb.* **1. b.** Phr. *To miss the b.*: (fig.) to lose an opportunity, fail in an undertaking or attempt (*slang*) 1915. **2.** *colloq.* **a.** An aeroplane 1910. **b.** A motor car 1921.

attrib., as *b. company, conductor* (CONDUCTOR 3): **b.-bar, -conductor** *Electr.*, a system of conductors in a generating station on which all the power of all the generators is collected for distribution or, in a receiving station, on which the power from the generating station is received for distribution; **busman,** the driver of a bus; *busman's holiday*, leisure time spent in occupations of the same nature as those in which one engages for a living; **b.-stop,** a place where a bus makes a regular halt.

Bus, *v.* **2.** *trans.* To transport (people) by bus, esp. in order to encourage or achieve racial integration 1961. Hence **Bus(s)ed** *ppl. a.* **Bu·s(s)ing** (*U.S.*).

Bush, *sb.*[1]

Comb.: **b.-baby,** an African lemur of the genus *Galago*; **b. shirt,** a loose-fitting light shirt worn by men in hot climates; **b. telegraph,** (*hist.*) Australian bushrangers' confederates disseminating information about the movements of the police; (now) rapid spreading of information, or of a rumour, etc.

Bushido (bū·ʃido). 1898. [Jap., 'way of a soldier or knight'.] In feudal Japan, the ethical code of the Samurai or military knighthood.

Business.

Comb.: **b. end,** the functional end of a tool or object; **b. hours,** normal working hours; **b. man,** one who engages in trade or commerce. Phrases. *B. as usual*: things will proceed in spite of disturbing circumstances. *B. is b.*: there is an agreed code in affairs of commerce. *Like nobody's b.* (*colloq.*): beyond the normal range (of a person's capacity); in no ordinary way.

Busker (bɒ·skəɹ). 1857. [f. BUSK *v.*[2] + -ER[1].] An itinerant musician or actor, esp. one who plays music or entertains in the street.

Buster. 3. As the second element of an objective compound, e.g. **dam-b.,** wrecker of a dam; in familiar designations of guns, bombs, etc., e.g. *BLOCK-*buster*; **tank-b.,** a gun or an aircraft powerful enough to 'knock out' a tank.

Butane (biū·tēⁱn). 1875. [f. BUT(YL + -ANE.] *Chem.* A paraffin hydrocarbon, C_4H_{10}, of which there are two isomers, both colourless gases present in natural gas and petroleum, and sold in cylinders as a liquid under pressure for domestic heating and lighting purposes.

Butch (butʃ), *sb. slang* (orig. *U.S.*). 1941. [Origin unknown, but perh. abbrev. of BUTCHER *sb.*] A tough youth or man; a lesbian of masculine appearance or behaviour. Also *attrib.* In the U.S. also applied to a type of short hair-cut.

Bu·tty, *sb.*[2] *north. dial.* Also **buttie.** 1855. [f. BUTT(ER *sb.*[1] + -Y[6].] A slice of bread and butter. Also *jam b.*

Buy, *sb.* orig. *U.S.* 1879. [f. BUY *v.*] A purchase, bargain.

I believe it's a good b.! 1911. Because each of these prams had some drawbacks, we do not choose a Best Buy 1964.

Buzz, *sb.*[1] **1. b.** *Phonetics.* A voiced hiss 1877. **c.** *spec.* The buzzing sound made by a telephone. Hence, a telephone call (*slang*) 1913.

Comb.: **b.-bomb** *colloq.*, a flying bomb; **b.-saw** *U.S.*, a circular saw.

Buzz, *v.*[1] **6. b.** *Phonetics.* To pronounce as or with a b. 1877. **7.** To telephone or signal (a call, etc.) by the 'buzzer'. *To b. off*: to ring off (RING *v.*[2] II. 5 d). Also *intr.* of a message: to come *in* by the buzzer 1914. **b.** To go *off* or *away* quickly (*slang*) 1914. **8.** To throw swiftly or forcibly (*colloq.*) 1890. **9.** Of a pilot of aircraft: to fly fast and close to 1941.

Buzzer. 4. An electric mechanism for producing an intermittent current and a buzzing sound or series of sounds: used chiefly as a call or signal 1884.

Bwana (bwā·na). 1878. [Swahili.] As a term of address (formerly used) in Africa, = 'master', 'sir'.

By. B. *adv.* **1. By and large. a.** *Naut.* To the wind and off it 1669. **b.** *To take..by and large*: to regard in a general aspect, without entering into details; (also, without *take*) everything considered, on the whole 1706.

They soon find out one another's rate of sailing, by and large 1833. Taking it 'by and large', as the sailors say, we had a pleasant..run 1869. The virtue of sound broadcasting was that, by and large, the content mattered more than anything else 1955.

Byssinosis (bisinōᵘ·sis). 1890. [mod.L., f. Gr. βύσσινος made of BYSSUS + -OSIS.] *Path.* A chronic lung disease caused by the inhalation of cotton dust. Hence **Byssino·tic** *a.* and *sb.*

Byte (bəit). 1964. [Arbitrary, prob. influenced by *BIT *sb.*[4] and BITE *sb.*] *Computers.* A group of eight consecutive bits operated on as a unit.

C.

III. 3. C.B., confined to barracks (as a punishment in the army); C.B.E., Commander of the Order of the British Empire; C.B.(W.), chemical and biological (warfare); C.G.S., centimetre-gramme-second; C.I.D., Committee of Imperial Defence, Criminal Investigation Department; C.O., Commanding Officer, Colonial Office, conscientious objector; C.O.D., cash on delivery; C.P., Communist Party; CS (*gas*) [initials of B. B. Corson and R. W. Stoughton, who discovered its irritant properties], an irritating solid substance used as a fine powder in riot control, etc.; C.S.E., Certificate of Secondary Education; C.S.M., company sergeant-major.

Cab, *sb.*[3] **1.** Applied also to motor-driven vehicles (see TAXI-CAB).

The c.-without-a-horse 1899.

Cabinet, *sb.*

III.5. c. pudding, a pudding made of bread or cake, dried fruit, eggs, and milk, usu. served with a sauce.

Cable, *sb.*

Comb.: **c.-stitch,** a stitch in knitting and embroidery that produces a rope-like pattern.

Cabotage. b. (The reservation to a country of) the air-traffic within its territory 1933.

Cabriole (kæ·briōᵘl). **1. b.** = CAPRIOLE *sb.* 1; *spec.* in *Ballet*, a springing step in which one leg is extended and the second leg is brought up to the first 1805. **4. c. leg,** a form of curved leg, frequent in Queen Anne and Chippendale furniture, so called from its resemblance to the front leg of a leaping or capering quadruped 1888.

Cack-handed (kæ:kˌhæ·ndėd), *a. dial.* or *colloq.* 1854. Left-handed; ham-handed, clumsy.

An insanely slothful or c. publican 1961. He saw the [hockey] ball going the wrong side of him..'Just thought I'd try a bit of your c. stuff' 1967.

Cadre. 3. (A member of) a group working to promote the interests of the Communist Party 1930.

Caerphilly (kēᵊɹfi·li). 1901. [Name of a town in S. Wales.] A mild cheese (originally) made in Caerphilly.

Café. Also written **cafe** and vulgarly or jocularly pronounced (kēⁱf) or (kæf).

Cafeteria (kæfėtiᵊ·riă). orig. *U.S.* 1839. [Amer. Sp. *cafeteria* coffee-shop.] A coffee-house; (now) a self-service restaurant.

Caftan. 2. A wide-sleeved, loose-fitting shirt or dress worn in Western countries 1965.

Cagey (kēⁱ·dʒi), *a. colloq.* (orig. *U.S.*). 1909. [Origin unkn.] Reticent, wary, reluctant to commit oneself. Hence **Ca·gily** *adv.* **Ca·geyness, Ca·giness,** the state or quality of being cagey.

Cahoot. Freq. *pl.*, esp. in phr. *in cahoot(s)* (*with*) (orig. *U.S.*): in league or partnership (with).

Cake, *sb.* Phr. *A piece of c.*: something easy or pleasant (*colloq.*) 1936.

I was in Crete, and that was a piece of c. compared with the bridgehead at Arnhem 1944.

Comb.: **c.-mix,** the prepared ingredients of a cake sold ready for cooking; **c.-walk,** (*a*) among American Negroes, a competition in stylish walking; (*b*) a dance modelled on this; (*c*) *fig.* something easy.

Calamity.

Comb.: *c.-howler, -prophet*; **C. Jane,** the nickname of Martha Jane Burke (*née* Canary) (?1852–1903), a famous American horse-rider and markswoman, applied to a prophet of disaster.

Calandria (kălæ·ndriă). 1929. [Sp., lit. 'lark (bird); calander'.] A closed cylindrical vessel with a number of tubes passing through it, used as a heat exchanger in an evaporator or (in some nuclear reactors) to separate a liquid moderator from the fuel rods and coolant.

Californium (kælifǭ·ɹniŏm). 1950. [f. the name of the University of *California*, where it was discovered + -IUM.] An artificial transuranic element, all the isotopes of which are radioactive. Atomic number 98; symbol Cf.

Call, *v.* **I. 8.** To communicate with (a person) by radio or telephone 1889.

C. off. b. To cancel (an engagement, etc.).

Call, *sb.* **1. b.** A summons or communication by telephone 1878.

Comb.: **c.-box,** a telephone-booth; **c.-girl,** a prostitute who makes appointments by telephone; **c.-sign** *Radio*, a conventional sign used at the beginning of a transmitted message to identify the sender.

Calque (kælk). 1937. [Fr., 'tracing', f. *calquer* to trace (a design, etc.), – It. *calcare*, – L. *calcāre* to tread.] *Philol.* The translated imitation of a meaning, as *foot* in measurement after Latin *pes*. Also as vb.

Calvados (kæ·lvădǫs). 1906. [Name of a department in Normandy, France.] A spirit distilled from cider; apple-jack.

Calypso (kăli·pso). 1934. [Origin unkn.] A West Indian song in African rhythm, freq. improvised to comment on a topic of current interest.

Camber, *sb.* **1. b.** The transverse arch of the surface of a road 1905. **c.** The curvature of the wings of an aircraft 1910.

Cambridge (kē¹·mbridʒ). The name of a university town in England, used *attrib.*, as **C. blue,** a light blue.

Camembert (kæ·manbēəɹ). 1878. [Name of a village near Argentan, France.] A rich soft cheese made (originally) in the vicinity of C.

Cameo. 2. A short literary sketch or portrait; a small outstanding character part in a play, etc.; freq. *attrib.* 1851.

Camera. 3. c. *Television.* The apparatus which forms the image and converts it into electrical impulses 1928.

Comb.: **c.-man,** one who uses or operates a camera professionally; **c.-shy** *a.*, fearful or diffident about being photographed or filmed.

Camford (kæ·mfǒɹd). 1850. [f. *CAM(BRIDGE + OX)FORD.] = *OXBRIDGE.

Camp (kæmp), *a. slang.* 1909. [Origin unkn.] Ostentatious, affected, theatrical; effeminate or homosexual; pertaining to or characteristic of homosexuals. So as *sb.*, 'camp' behaviour, mannerisms, etc. Also as *v. trans.*, to make (something) 'camp'; *intr.*, to be 'camp' or behave in a 'camp' manner.

Hearty naval commanders or jolly colonels acquired the 'camp' manners of calling everything from Joan of Arc to Merlin 'lots of fun' C. BEATON. The cute little dirty chuckle and the well-timed 'camp' gesture have made stage and audience indistinguishable from any would-be-smart cocktail-party 1959.

Can, *sb.* Slang phr. *to carry* (or *take*) *the c.* (*back*): to bear the responsibility, take the blame 1929.

It's always my fault, everything's my fault. I always carry the bloody c. back J. BRAINE.

Can, *v.*³ **2.** To record on disc, tape, or film (freq. as **canned** *ppl. a.*) 1904.

We'll export canned music to the Latins 'O. HENRY'.

Canada¹.

Comb.: **C. goose,** the common wild goose of N. America, *Branta canadensis*, frequently kept on ornamental lakes in England.

Canalize, *v.* **2.** *fig.* To lead in a desired direction, so as to control or regulate 1922.

Canapé (kæ·năpi). 1890. [Fr.] A piece of bread or toast, etc., on which small savouries are served.

Canasta (kănæ·stă). 1948. [Sp., 'basket'.] A card game, of Uruguayan origin, in which two packs are used with four jokers, combining features of rummy and pinochle (*canasta* is also the name of a meld having a high bonus value).

Candela (kændī·lă). 1950. [L.: see CANDLE.] A unit of luminous intensity.

The c. is the luminous intensity, in the perpendicular direction, of a surface of 1/600 000 square metre of a black body at the temperature of freezing platinum under a pressure of 101 325 newtons per square metre 1968.

Candid, *a.* **4. b.** Of a photograph or photography: unposed, informal; so **c. camera,** a small camera for taking informal photographs 1929. Also as *sb.*, an unposed photograph.

Candle.

Comb.: **c.-wick,** *spec.* (a soft yarn used to make) a tufted material.

Candy, *sb.*¹

Comb.: **c.-floss,** a confection of fluffy spun sugar; also *transf.* and *attrib.*

Cannibalize (kæ·nibăləiz), *v.* 1943. [f. CANNIBAL + -IZE.] *trans.* To take parts from (a machine, etc.) to make up deficiencies in another.

Capacitor (kăpæ·sitǫɹ). 1926. [f. CAPACIT(Y + -OR 2.] *Electr.* A device consisting of two conductors separated by an insulating medium, used for its capacitance; a condenser.

Capacity. 1. b. *Electr.* The ability of a device to hold a charge of static electricity on conductors at different potentials; the value of this, measured by the ratio of the charge on one of the conductors to their difference in potential; = CAPACITANCE 1777. **2.** *spec.* The largest audience that a theatre, etc., can hold; freq. *attrib.* or as *adj.*

Cape, *sb.*³

Comb.: **C. Coloured** *a.*, of or designating the Coloured or brown population group of the Cape Province in S. Africa; *sb.*, a person (or the people) of this group.

‖**Cappuccino** (kapʊtʃī·no). 1948. [It., see CAPUCHIN.] Coffee with milk, freq. topped with white foam.

Capsule, *sb.* **8.** A small, freq. detachable, pressurized compartment of an aircraft or space vehicle 1954.

Caption. 4. Now usu. the title below an illustration.

Carcinogen (kāɹsi·nŏdʒĕn). 1936. [f. CARCINO(MA + -GEN.] *Path.* A substance or agent that produces cancer. So **Ca:rcinoge·nesis. Ca:rcinoge·nic** *a.* **Ca:rcinogeni·city.**

Card, *sb.*² **1. b.** *colloq.* A 'character', an eccentric. **4. b.** A c. held by a delegate at a (trade-union) meeting or conference indicating the number of members he represents 1902. **c.** *pl.* An employee's documents held by his employer 1929.

Phr. *To have a c.* (or *cards*) *up one's sleeve*: to have a plan, resources, etc., in reserve. *To lay, put* (or *play with*) (*all*) *one's cards on the table*: to 'show one's cards', to reveal one's resources.

Comb.: **c.-carrying** *a.*, being a member of a specified organization.

The most dangerous Communists in the nation today are not the open, avowed, c.-carrying party members 1948.

Cardan (kā·ɹdăn). 1902. [Name of *Cardan* (Geronimo *Cardano*, 1501–76, Italian mathematician.]

c. joint, a universal joint; **c. shaft,** a shaft having a universal joint at one or both ends for transmitting motion from one shaft to another not in a direct line with it.

Cardboard. *attrib.* (*fig.*) Unsubstantial, unreal 1893.

The c. family that has become larger than life 1952.

Cardio-. Ca·rdiogram, the tracing made by a cardiograph. **Ca·rdio-va·scular** *a.*, relating to both the heart and the blood-vessels.

Care, *v.* **3.** Phr. (*I*, etc.) *couldn't c. less*: (I am, etc.) completely uninterested or indifferent 1946.

Career, *sb.* **4.**

Also *attrib.*, as **c. diplomat,** one whose profession is diplomacy; **c. girl, woman,** a woman who pursues a profession.

Careerist (kărīə·rist). 1910. [f. CAREER *sb.* + -IST.] One who is mainly intent on the furtherance of his career. So **Caree·rism.**

Carioca (kæriōᵘ·kă). 1830. [Pg.] **1.** A native of Rio de Janeiro. **2.** A type of dance, originating in Brazil, or its music 1934.

Carnet (kā·ɹne). 1897. [Fr.] **1.** A notebook. **2.** A permit issued to an aviator, motorist, or camper 1926.

Carotene (kæ·rǒtīn). Also **-in.** 1861. [– G. *carotin* (H. Wackenroder, 1831), f. L. *carota* CARROT + -ENE, -IN¹.] *Chem.* An orange or red pigment, $C_{40}H_{56}$, present in several isomeric forms in plants (notably carrots) and some animal tissues, and important as a source of vitamin A. Hence **Ca·rotenoid,** any of a group of plant and animal pigments related to carotene.

Vitamin A..is one half of a c. molecule and is formed from c. in the intestinal wall of animals 1951.

Carousel. 2. Chiefly *U.S.* A merry-go-round, roundabout 1673. **3.** *U.S.* A conveyor carrying objects in a horizontal circuit 1961.

Carrel(l (kæ·rəl). 1919. [var. CAROL *sb.* 5.] A private cubicle provided in a library for use by a reader.

Carrier. 7. *Physics.* A charged particle, atom, etc. 1901; *spec.* any of the mobile electrons or holes in a semiconductor 1939. **8.** An aircraft-carrier 1917. **9.** *Genetics.* An individual that has a recessive gene and so can pass a hereditary characteristic on to a descendant although not itself showing it 1933.

Carry, *v.* **I. 13.** *intr.* Of sound: to travel or be heard at a distance 1896.

III. C. on. f. To continue what one is doing; to proceed to carry out instructions.

In verbal phrases used subst.: **c.-on,** fuss, excitement; **c.-over,** on the Stock Exchange: postponement of payment of an account until the next settling-day; the amount so kept over; also *transf.*, something remaining or transferred forward.

Cartel, *sb.* **4.** After G. *kartell*: in Germany, an association of business houses for the regulation of output, prices, etc.; the businesses so combined; a trust, syndicate; later *gen.* 1902. **b.** *Hist.* The coalition of German Conservatives and National Liberals in 1887 for the support of each other's candidates; also used for similar combinations in other countries.

Cartoon, *sb.* **2.** Now usu. a humorous or topical drawing (of any size) in a newspaper, etc. **b.** *Cinemat.* A film made from a series of animated drawings 1916.

Cartridge. 3. a. *Photogr.* A spool of film in a cylindrical light-proof container designed for daylight loading 1918. **b.** = *CASSETTE 2 c 1960. **4.** A unit that fits at the end of the pick-up arm of a record player and contains the stylus and the device that converts its motion into electrical signals 1941.

Casbah: see *KASBAH.

Cascara. 2. pop. pronounced (kæskā·ră). In full *cascara sagrada*: a preparation of the bark of Californian buckthorn, *Rhamnus purshiana*, used as a laxative 1879.

Case, *sb.*¹ *In case*: **e.** Esp. in *just in case*, orig. with aposiopesis, *in case* —, to indicate an unspecified apprehension of accident.

A London policeman directing the traffic at a busy point in Paris, with a French traffic constable standing by, just in case 1951.

Comb.: **c.-book,** a book containing records of cases treated by a doctor, etc.; also *transf.* and *fig.*; **c.-history,** the record of a case in medicine, psychiatry, etc.; **c.-load,** the number of cases that a doctor, social worker, etc., is concerned with at any one time; **c.-work,** social work carried out by the study of individual persons or groups; hence **c.-worker.**

Case, *v.*² **4.** *slang* (orig. *U.S.*). To examine, inspect, size up beforehand; esp. in phr. *to c. the joint*, to study the layout of premises before robbing them 1915.

Cash, *v.*² **C. in,** (*a*) *U.S. colloq.*, to settle accounts; (*b*) *U.S. slang*, to die; (*c*) orig. *U.S.*, to make a profit *on*, to take advantage of (an opportunity, etc.).

Casino. 4. A building for gambling, often with other amenities 1851. (Now the usual sense.)

Casserole. 1. b. A dish cooked and served in a casserole.

Cassette. 2. b. A container for a spool of film or for an X-ray plate or film 1934. **c.** A closed container of magnetic tape with both supply and take-up spools, for insertion into a suitable tape recorder 1960.

Casual, *a.* **6. b.** Of clothes: suitable for informal wear 1939. Also as *sb.*, freq. *pl.* 1941.

Cat, *sb.*¹ **I. 1. b.** *slang* (orig. *U.S.*). An expert in, or enthusiast for, jazz; hence, a man, fellow 1932.

Comb.: **c.-burglar,** a burglar who enters by extraordinarily skilful feats of climbing; **c.-lick** *colloq.*, a perfunctory wash; **cat's pyjamas** *slang* (orig. *U.S.*), the acme of excellence; **c.-suit,** an all-in-one garment reaching from neck to feet; **catwalk,** a narrow footway or platform; **cat's whisker,** (*a*) a fine adjustable wire in a crystal wireless receiver; (*b*) *pl. slang* (orig. *U.S.*) = **cat's pyjamas.*

Catabolism. 1889. = KATABOLISM.

‖**Catalogue raisonné** (katalog rẹzone) 1784. [Fr.] A descriptive catalogue arranged according to subjects; a classified or methodical list.

Catalyse (kæ·tăləiz), *v.* Also **†kata-, -lyze.** 1890. [f. CATALYSIS, after *analyse, analysis.*] *Chem.* To increase the rate of (a reaction or process) by catalytic action; to produce by catalysis; also *fig.*

Catalyst (kæ·tălist). 1902. [f. CATALYSIS, after *analyst, analysis.*] *Chem.* A substance which when present in small amounts increases the rate of a chemical reaction but is chemically unchanged by it; a catalytic agent; also *fig.*

Catalytic, *a.* Also *fig.* Also **c. cracking,** the cracking of heavy oils by a process involving the use of a catalyst; so **c. cracker,** an apparatus for this; abbrev. **cat cracker, cracking.**

Catamaran. 1. Also, a sailing boat with twin hulls placed side by side.

Catch, *sb.*[1] **7. b.** A concealed disadvantage; an unforeseen difficulty or awkwardness, a 'snag' 1855. **8. b.** A person matrimonially desirable on account of wealth or position 1749.

Catch-.

c.-phrase, a phrase caught up and repeated; cf. CATCHWORD 3.

'Can't believe a word you read' had long been becoming a kind of c. in the army 1922.

Cathode.

Comb.: **c. ray(s),** a beam of electrons emitted by the cathode of an electron tube under the action of an electric field; **c.-ray oscilloscope, oscillograph,** an oscilloscope or oscillograph using a c.-ray tube as indicator; **c.-ray tube,** an electron tube in which a controlled beam of electrons is directed on to a fluorescent screen to produce a visible effect.

Cat's-eye. 4. One of the chain of light-reflecting studs used to demarcate traffic lanes on roads at night 1940.

Cattleya (kæ·tliă). 1828. [mod.L. (J. Lindley, 1824), f. the name of W. *Cattley*, English patron of botany.] An epiphytal orchid of the genus so called, native to Central America and Brazil.

Cauliflower, *sb.*

Comb.: **c. cheese,** a dish of which the principal ingredients are cauliflower and cheese; **c. ear,** an ear (as of a boxer) thickened and distorted by blows.

Cease fire, cease-fire. 1859. [CEASE *v.*, FIRE *sb.* 14.] **a.** *Mil.* The command to cease firing; formerly *cease firing* and simply *cease* (1847). **b.** A cessation of shooting or fighting; an armistice 1918.

Ceilidh (kē̆ⁱ·li). 1875. [Irish.] In Scotland and Ireland: **a.** An evening visit, a friendly social call. **b.** A session of traditional music, storytelling, or dancing.

Cell. III. 3. A small group of people working within a larger organization as a nucleus of political, esp. revolutionary, activity 1925.

Cellophane (se·lŏfēⁱn). 1912. [f. CELL(ULOSE + -O- + *-phane* as in DIAPHANE.] Proprietary term for a transparent material made from regenerated cellulose and used as a wrapping.

Celluloid. b. *transf.* Films; the 'cinema' 1934. Also *attrib.* or as *adj.*, (*a*) made of celluloid 1871; (*b*) of or pertaining to films; *fig.*, synthetic, unreal 1922.

The celluloid hero flashed his impartial smile across the screen 1922.

Celsius (se·lsiŏs). 1797. The name of Anders *Celsius* (1701–44), Swedish astronomer, used to designate the centigrade temperature-scale (see CENTIGRADE *a.*).

Celtic, *a.* Often pronounced (ke·ltik).

C. fringe, (the land of) the Scots, Welsh, Irish, and Cornish, regarded as occupying the fringe or outlying edge of the British Isles; **C. twilight,** W. B. Yeats's title for his collection of stories, etc., based on Irish folk-tales; hence, the atmosphere of the folk-lore of Celtic Britain, esp. Ireland.

Central, *a.* **4.** *C. heating*: a system of heating a building by hot water, steam, or air conveyed through pipes from a c. source, or by any other method which simultaneously heats several rooms 1906.

Ceramic, *a.* (*sb.*) **1. b.** Of or pertaining to ceramics; that is a ceramic (sense *B. 2). **B.** *sb.* **1.** *pl.* (See sense 2 in Dict.) **b.** (Usu. *sing.*) Products of the c. art; pottery. **2.** Any non-metallic inorganic solid for which high temperatures are generally required in its fabrication or manufacture.

Cereal, *sb.* **b.** An article of food (*esp.* a breakfast dish) made from a cereal 1899. orig. *U.S.*

Clarissa looked so sweet eating her cereals A. THIRKELL.

Cermet (sō·ɹmet). 1950. [f. CER(AMIC *sb.* + MET(AL *sb.*] Any of a group of solid materials composed of a ceramic and a metal in intimate combination and useful for their good mechanical properties at very high temperatures.

Certify, *v.* **2. b.** To declare (a person) officially insane 1877. So **Ce·rtified** *ppl. a.*

Cha-cha (tʃā·tʃā), **cha-cha-cha** (tʃaːtʃatʃā·). 1954. [Amer. Sp. *cha-cha-cha.*] A type of ballroom dance to Latin-American rhythm; also, the music for this dance. Hence as *v. intr.*

Chagas'(s) disease (tʃā·gās). 1912. [f. the name of C. *Chagas* (1879–1934), Brazilian physician.] A form of sleeping sickness endemic in S. and Central America and in Africa, caused by the parasite *Trypanosoma cruzi* and transmitted by certain blood-sucking bugs.

Chain, *sb.*

Comb.: **c. reaction,** a chemical or nuclear reaction forming intermediate products which react with the original substance and are repeatedly renewed; also *fig.*; **c.-smoker** [tr. G. *kettenraucher*], one who smokes cigarettes or cigars in unbroken succession; **c. store** orig. *U.S.*, one of a series of stores belonging to one firm and dealing in the same class of goods.

Chair, *sb.*[1] **1. b.** *The (electric) c.*: the chair in which a condemned criminal is placed for electrocution. *U.S.* 1889.

Chalone (kēⁱ·lōᵘn, kæ·-). 1914. [– Gr. χαλῶν, pres. pple. of χαλᾶν to slacken, after *hormone.*] *Physiol.* †**a.** A hormone that inhibits rather than stimulates. **b.** Any of various substances that are thought to inhibit, and so control, cell division in the tissue in which they are produced 1962. Hence **Chalo·nic** *a.*

Champion, *sb.*[1] *attrib.* passing into *adj.* (also *adv.*). Excellent(ly). *colloq.* and *dial.*

'He cried c.,' said a proud Yorkshireman 1923.

Chance, *v.* **4.** *To c. one's arm*: to perform an action in the face of probable failure, take one's chance of success (*colloq.*) 1889.

Channel, *sb.*[1] **II. 3.** A circuit for the transmission of a signal in telecommunications 1848. **b.** A band of frequencies of sufficient width for the transmission of a radio or television signal; also, a television service using a particular band 1928.

Char, *sb.*[1] Also (*colloq.*) short for CHARWOMAN 1906.

Char (tʃāɹ), *sb.*[5] *slang.* 1919. [var. CHA.] Tea.

Charcoal, *sb.*

Comb.: **c. biscuit,** a biscuit containing wood-charcoal to aid the digestion; **c. grey,** a dark grey pigment made from charcoal; a dark grey colour (also simply *charcoal*).

Charisma (kări·zmă). Pl. **-ata.** 1641. [See CHARISM.] **a.** = CHARISM. **b.** A gift or power of leadership or authority 1947.

Charleston (tʃā·ɹlstən, -lz-). orig. *U.S.* 1923. [Name of a county and city in S. Carolina, U.S.] A ballroom dance characterized by side kicks from the knee. Hence as *v. intr.*

Charley, Charlie. 4. *slang.* A fool 1946. **5.** *U.S. Services' slang.* The North Vietnamese or Vietcong; a North Vietnamese or Vietcong soldier 1965.

Charollais, Charolais (ʃæ·rolēⁱ, ‖ʃarole). 1893. The name of a region of eastern France, used to designate a breed of large white cattle.

Chart, *sb.* **2. b.** *spec.* A list of the gramophone records or tunes that are most popular at a particular time 1963.

Charter, *sb.* **2. b.** Used *attrib.* of or pertaining to an aircraft hired by contract for a particular purpose 1922.

Chaser[1]. **4.** = CHASSE[2]; a small quantity of water, etc., taken after spirits, etc. 1897.

Chastity.

Comb.: **c. belt,** a belt designed to prevent a woman from having sexual intercourse; also *fig.*

A traffic plan which enclosed Oxford in, so to speak, a c. belt 1960.

Château. 2. A French vineyard, usu. in the neighbourhood of a c. 1754. Hence **c.-bottled** *a.*, bottled at the vineyard.

Check-.

c.-list, a list of names, titles, etc., so arranged as to form a ready means of reference or verification; **c.-out,** (*a*) the act of recording one's departure from a hotel, factory, etc.; (*b*) a desk at which payment is made in a self-service shop; **c.-point,** a place where the movement of traffic, pedestrians, etc., is checked; **c.-up,** a careful or detailed examination or scrutiny; *spec.* a medical examination.

Cheese, *sb.*[1]

Comb.: **c.-cake,** (*b*) *slang* (orig. *U.S.*), display of the female form in the interest of sex-appeal; female sexual attractiveness.

Tabloid and Heartsmen go after 'cheesecake'—leg-pictures of sporty females 1934.

Cheesed (tʃīzd), *pred. a. slang.* 1941. [Origin unkn.] Disgruntled, exasperated, 'fed up'; freq. *c. off.*

Chelate (kī·lēⁱt), *a.* and *sb.* 1920. [f. CHEL(A[1] + -ATE[2].] *Chem.* **A.** *adj.* Applied to an organic group or compound that is attached at two or more points to a central metal ion, and also to the compound so formed. **B.** *sb.* A c. compound.

Chelsea (tʃe·lsi). The name of a district of London on the north bank of the Thames, used *attrib.* in the names of articles associated with it: **C. boots,** elastic-sided boots 1962; **C. bun,** a kind of rolled currant-bun originally made in C. 1741; **C. porcelain,** a kind made there in the 18th century 1754.

Chemical, *a.*

c. warfare, that in which chemicals (other than explosives) are used, as gases, smoke, incendiary compounds.

Che:milumine·scence. 1905. [– G. *chemilumineszenz* (M. Trautz, 1905): see LUMINESCENT *a.*] Emission of light accompanying a chemical reaction, as in the oxidation of yellow phosphorus. So **Che:milumine·scent** *a.*

Chemin de fer (ʃəmæ̃n də fę̄r). 1891. [Fr., 'road of iron', railway.] A form of baccarat. Whence colloq. **Chemmy** (ʃe·mi) 1923.

Chemo- (ke·mo), used as comb. form of CHEMICAL, as in **Che:mokine·sis,** increased activity of an organism induced by a chemical substance 1900.

Chemotherapy (ke:moþe·răpi). 1910. [– G. *chemotherapie* (Ehrlich), f. *CHEMO- + THERAPY.] *Med.* The treatment of disease, esp. of parasitic infections or cancer, by means of chemicals that act selectively on micro-organisms or malignant tissue. Also **Che:motherapeu·tics.** Hence **Che:motherapeu·tic(al)** *adjs.*

‖**Cheongsam** (tʃiǫ·ŋsæ·m). 1957. [Chinese.] A garment worn by Chinese women: a dress with a high collar and a split skirt.

Chest, *sb.*[1] Colloq. phrases. *To get* (something) *off one's c.*: to relieve one's mind by making a statement or confession about (it). *To play* (*cards, a thing,* etc.) *close to one's c.*: to be cautious or secretive about (something).

Chesty (tʃe·sti), *a.* 1900. [f. CHEST *sb.*[1] 4 + -Y[1].] **1.** *U.S. slang.* Conceited and self-assertive. **2. a.** *colloq.* Inclined to or symptomatic of weakness or disease of the chest 1930. **b.** *colloq.* Of a woman: having prominent breasts 1955. Hence **Che·stily** *adv.* **Che·stiness.**

Chew, *v.* Slang phr. *To c. the rag* or *fat*: to discuss a matter, esp. complainingly; to talk.

‖**Chez** (ʃe), *prep.* 1740. [Fr.] Used with (French) personal pronoun or proper name: at the house or home of.

I thought it might not be very restful chez Dave 1954.

Chicane, *sb.* **4.** A disguised or artificial construction, esp. a barricaded ramp, in motor racing 1955.

Chicano (tʃikā·no, ʃi-). 1947. [f. Sp. *mejicano* Mexican, f. *Méjico* Mexico.] An American of Mexican descent: used esp. in political contexts, e.g. *C. power.*

Chichi (ʃī·ʃī·), *sb.* and *a.* 1908. [Fr.] **A.** *sb.* Fuss(iness); pretentiousness. **B.** *adj.* Fussy, affected, over-elaborate 1932.

Chick, *sb.*[1] **2. b.** *slang* (orig. *U.S.*). A girl; a young woman 1927.

Chicken. 3. Also (*slang*) quasi-*adj.*, cowardly 1941; (*to play*) *chicken*: (to engage in) a game of physical hazard which tests the courage. Hence as *v. intr.*, to back *out* because of cowardice 1943.

Comb.: **c.-feed** *colloq.* (orig. *U.S.*), food for chickens; *fig.* anything of little importance, esp. a trifling sum of money.

Chi-hike (tʃəiˈ,həiˑk), *sb. slang.* Also **chi-ike, chy-**; *Austral.* and *N.Z.* (with pronunc. tʃəiˑæk) **chiack, chyack,** etc. 1859. The shouting of 'chi-hike' as a salute; hence, a noisy demonstration; jeering, banter, cheek. Hence as *v. trans.*, to cheer or jeer at; also *absol.* or *intr.*, to make a noisy demonstration 1874.

Chihuahua (tʃiwāˑwă, ʃi-). 1858. [Name of a city and state in Mexico.] A breed of very small smooth-haired dog which originated in Mexico.

Chincherinchee: see *CHINKERINCHEE.

Chindit (tʃiˑndit). 1943. [– Burmese *chinthé*, a mythological creature.] A member of an Allied force fighting during the 1939–45 war behind the Japanese lines in Burma.

Chinese, *a.* **2. C. cabbage,** one of two brassicas, *B. pekinensis* or *B. chinensis*; **C. gooseberry,** the N.Z. name for the plant and fruit of *Actinidia chinensis*, a deciduous fruiting vine; **C. lantern,** *Physalis alkekengi*, a plant of the family Solanaceæ, grown for the decorative effect of the orange-coloured, inflated calyx.

Chinkerinchee (tʃiːnkərintʃī). *S. Afr.* Also **chincherinchee.** 1793. [Said to be imitative from the squeaky sound produced when two flower-stalks are rubbed together.] A popular name for the liliaceous bulbous plant *Ornithogalum thyrsoides*, bearing white to golden-yellow flowers in a dense 12- to 30-flowered raceme.

A recognized American name for the flowering bulb *Ornithogalum* is *chinkerinchee* (as I saw it first) or *chincherinchee* (as I see it nowadays) 1964.

Chionodoxa (kəiŏnodǫˑksă). 1879. [mod.L. (E. P. Boissier, 1844), f. Gr. χιών snow + δόξα glory.] A plant of the genus so called, belonging to the family Liliaceæ, native to the Eastern Mediterranean region and Asia Minor, and cultivated for its early blue flowers.

Chip, *sb.*[1] **1. b.** Usu. *pl.* A fried piece of potato, usu. oblong in shape 1859. **c.** *Electronics.* A tiny square of semiconducting material made to take the place of a large number of conventional circuit components 1962.

Colloq. phrases. *A c. off the old block*: a son resembling his father. *A c. on one's shoulder*: something carried as a challenge; hence, a display of defiance or ill-humour; a grudge, grievance. *To have had one's chips*: to be beaten, killed, etc. *(When) the chips are down*: (when) it comes to the point.

He was a man with a c. on his shoulder. Everyone seemed in a conspiracy to slight or injure him W. S. MAUGHAM. When the chips are down a man shows what he really is 1949.

Comb.: **c.-board,** a type of pasteboard made by compressing waste paper or wood refuse; **c.-shot,** a short lofted shot in golf, football, etc.

Chipolata (tʃipŏlāˑtă). 1877. [Fr. – It. *cipollata* dish with onions, f. *cipolla* onion.] A small spicy sausage.

Chi-rho (kəi rōᵘ). (1611, Florio), 1868. The first two letters of Gr. ΧΡΙϹΤΟϹ CHRIST, often joined in a monogram ☧ and used to symbolize the name.

Choc (tʃǫk). 1874. Colloq. abbrev. of CHOCOLATE *sb.* (*a.*).

Choke, *sb.*[1] **6.** *Electr.* (also *c.-coil, choking coil*). An inductance coil, an inductor 1893. **7.** A valve which controls the flow of air through the air-intake of a carburettor 1926.

Choke, *v. To c. off*: to put a stop to or get rid of (someone) as if by throttling, as bulldogs are made to loosen their hold by throttling them; to deter, discourage (forcibly).

Choosey, choosy (tʃūˑzi), *a.* orig. *U.S.* 1862. [f. CHOOSE *v.* + -Y[1].] Disposed to be particular in one's choice. Hence **Chooˑsiness.**

Chordate (kǭˑɹdēⁱt), *a.* and *sb.* 1889. [– mod.L. *Chordata*, f. L. *chorda* CHORD *sb.*[1], with termination as in VERTEBRATA, etc.] Belonging to, having the characteristics of, or a member of, the Chordata, a phylum of animals having a well-developed notochord at some stage in their lives.

Chow. 2. *slang.* (derogatory, chiefly *Austral.*) A Chinaman 1872. **3.** *Pidgin-English* and *slang.* Food, or a meal 1886.

Chow mein (tʃau mēⁱn). 1903. [Chinese, lit. fried flour.] Fried noodles served with a thick sauce or stew composed of chopped meat, vegetables, etc.

Christiania (kristiāˑniă). 1905. [Former name of the capital of Norway, now Oslo.] A swing in skiing, used to stop short. Abbrev. **Chriˑstie.**

Christian Science. 1863. A theory of the nature of disease, a system of therapeutic practice, and a religious sect, founded on principles formulated by Mrs. M. B. G. Eddy of Concord, New Hampshire, U.S.A. Hence **Christian Scientist,** an adherent of, one who practises, Christian Science.

Chromatogram (kromæˑtogræm). 1922. [– G. *chromatogramm* (M. Tswett, 1906): see -GRAM.] *Chem.* The result of a chromatographic separation: either a series of zones or spots or a graphical record.

Chromatograph (kromæˑtograf), *sb.* 1958. [-GRAPH.] *Chem.* An apparatus for producing a chromatogram.

Chromaˑtograph, *v.* 1956. [f. prec. *sb.* or as back-formation from next.] *Chem.* To separate or analyse by chromatography.

Chromatography. 2. *Chem.* [– G. *chromatographie* (M. Tswett, 1906).] Any technique for separating a mixture into its components by utilizing differences in their rate of travel when the mixture is carried by a liquid or gas through or over some (solid or liquid) medium that selectively adsorbs or otherwise interacts with the different components, thereby causing them to become separated into distinct zones or spots (sometimes coloured) 1937. So **Chromatograˑphic, -ical** *adjs.* **Chromatograˑphically** *adv.*

Chug (tʃɒg), *sb.* orig. *U.S.* 1866. [imit.] A plunging, muffled, or explosive sound. Also repeated. Hence as *v. intr.*, to make or proceed with such a sound 1896.

Churinga (tʃŭriˑŋgă). *Anthropol.* Also **tjurunga.** Pl. **-a, -as.** 1899. [Australian Aboriginal word.] A sacred object, an amulet.

CinemaScope (siˑnĭmăskōᵘp). Also **Cinemascope.** 1953. [f. CINEMA + -SCOPE.] The proprietary name of a form of cinema film using a very wide screen.

‖**Cinéma-vérité** (sinema,verite). Also **cinema-verité, ciné-vérité.** 1963. [Fr.] A film or films which have the appearance of real life; documentary films collectively.

Cinerama (sinĕrāˑmă). 1951. [f. CINE- + *-rama*, after PANORAMA.] The proprietary name of a cinema film projected on a wide curved screen by three projectors.

Cinnamon. *Comb.*: **c. bear,** the American black bear, *Ursus americanus*, in its cinnamon phase; **c. fern,** a large North American fern, *Osmunda cinnamomea*, having brown fronds when young; **c. rose,** *Rosa cinnamomea*, a red rose with a scent of cinnamon; **c. toast,** buttered toast spread with a mixture of sugar and cinnamon.

Circadian (sŏɹkēⁱˑdiăn), *a.* 1959. [irreg. f. L. *circa* about + *dies* day + -AN.] Designating a physiological activity or property which fluctuates or recurs with a period of approximately twenty-four hours, or the rhythm of such an activity.

Circs (sɔ̄ɹks), colloq. abbrev. of pl. of CIRCUMSTANCE *sb.* 1883.

Circuitry (sɔ̄ˑɹkitri). 1946. [f. CIRCUIT *sb.* + -RY.] The plan or components of an electric circuit; a system of such circuits.

Ciˑrcumcircle. 1885. [CIRCUM-.] *Geom.* A circle which passes through the vertices of a triangle or polygon.

Circus. 2. b. *colloq.* (orig. *U.S.*). A disturbance, uproar, or lively display 1869. **c.** *slang.* A group of aircraft or their pilots engaged in spectacular flying 1917.

Cis-. 2. *Chem.* Applied to a compound or molecular structure in which two carbon atoms joined by a double bond or forming part of a ring have attached to them identical atoms or groups that lie on the same side of the plane containing the two carbon atoms; also used *attrib.* as an independent word 1888.

Citify (siˑtifəi), *v.* Also **cityfy.** 1828. [f. CITY + -FY.] *trans.* To give the characteristics of a city. Freq. as **citified** *ppl. a.*

Citronella (sitrŏneˑlă). 1858. [mod.L., with dim. suffix as in NIGELLA.] A fragrant Asian grass, *Cymbopogon nardus*, which yields an oil used in perfumery and as an insect repellant; also, the oil itself.

City.

Comb.: **c. page,** the page of a newspaper which deals with financial and business matters; **c. slicker** orig. *U.S.*, a smart and plausible rogue; a smartly dressed or sophisticated city-dweller; **c.-state,** a city which is also an independent sovereign state.

Civil, *a.*

c. defence, the organization and training of civilians for the preservation of lives and property during and after air raids, etc.; **c. disobedience,** refusal to obey a government's laws, etc., as part of a political campaign; **c. rights,** the rights of each citizen to liberty, equality, etc.; *spec.* in the U.S., the rights of Negroes as citizens.

Civvy (siˑvi), *sb.* and *a. colloq.* 1889. Short for CIVILIAN as *sb.* and *a.*; *pl.* civilian clothes. *C. street*, civilian life.

When I get back to c. street I'll never moan about my job again 1943.

Clade (klēⁱd), *sb.*[2] 1957. [f. Gr. κλάδος branch.] *Biol.* A group of organisms evolved from a common ancestor. Hence **Cladiˑstic** *a.*

Cladogenesis results in the formation of delimitable monophyletic units, which may be called clades J. S. HUXLEY.

Clanger (klæˑŋəɹ). *slang.* 1948. [f. CLANG *v.* + -ER[1].] A mistake.

I have boobed dreadfully, old boy. Apparently a carnation with gongs is a terrible c. 1959.

Class, *sb.* **2. b.** *colloq.* Distinction, high quality; *no c.*, of low or no quality, inferior. Also *attrib.* or quasi-*adj.*, high-class 1874.

Classified (klæˑsifəid), *ppl. a.* 1889. [f. CLASSIFY *v.*] **a.** Arranged in classes; also as *sb. pl.*, c. advertisements. **b.** Of a road: graded according to its relative importance 1935. **c.** Classed as secret for reasons of national security 1944.

Classless (klaˑslės), *a.* 1878. [f. CLASS *sb.* + -LESS.] Having or belonging to no class; designating or pertaining to a society without distinctions of social class. Hence **Claˑsslessness.**

The Socialist movement..is based on the conviction of the desirability of a c. society 1937.

Clean, *a.* **3. b.** Of a nuclear weapon: producing relatively little fall-out 1956. **4. b.** *spec.* Free from obscenity or indelicacy 1867.

Colloq. phrases. *To make a c. job (of it)*: to do something thoroughly. *To come c.*: to confess, to make a clean breast of it.

Clean, *v. To c. up*: to bring (something) up to a certain standard of cleanness; to clean or clear; hence in various *colloq.* and *slang* uses (orig. *U.S.*): (*a*) *trans.* to acquire as gain or profit; *intr.*, to make a large profit; (*b*) *trans.* to beat or vanquish; (*c*) to clear (a place, etc.) of harmful elements or persons.

Clear, *a., adv.*, and *sb. Comb.*: **c.-way, clearway,** an unobstructed route or passage; *spec.* a road on which vehicles must not park or wait.

Clearance. 2. b. orig. *U.S.* Approval, permission; *spec.* permission (from the control-tower) to land or take off in an aircraft 1944. **c.** orig. *U.S.* The clearing of a person for work involving matters of (national) security 1948.

Clearing, *vbl. sb.*

Comb.: **c.-bank,** a bank that is a member of a clearing-house; **c.-hospital,** a field hospital for the temporary treatment of sick and wounded.

Clementine (kleˑmĕntīn), *sb.* 1926. [Fr. *clémentine* (L. Trabut, 1902), f. personal name *Clément*.] A variety of small orange originally produced by an accidental hybrid of the tangerine and the sour orange.

Clerihew (kleˑrihiū). 1928. [Name of Edmund *Clerihew* Bentley (1875–1956).] A short comic or nonsensical verse, professedly biographical, of two couplets differing in length.

Cleˑver-cleˑver, *a.* 1896. [Reduplic. CLEVER *a.*] Anxious to be considered clever; excessively clever.

Cliff.
Comb.: **c.-hanger** orig. *U.S.*, a film, story, play, etc., in which suspense is a main element; also *transf.*

Climate, *sb.* **3. b.** *fig.* The mental, moral, etc., environment or attitude of a body of people in respect of some aspect of life, policy, etc., esp. in *c. of opinion* or *thought* 1661.

We have reached a 'climate' of opinion where figures rule BAGEHOT 1866.

Climax, *sb.* **3. b.** *Ecology.* The point at which a plant-community reaches a state of equilibrium with its environment 1915. **c.** A sexual orgasm 1918.

Cline (kləin), *sb.* 1938. [f. Gr. κλίνειν to slope, bend.] *Biol.* A graded series of characters or differences in form within a species or other group of related organisms. Also *transf.* in *Linguistics.*

Some special term seems desirable to direct attention to variation within groups, and I propose the word *cline*, meaning a gradation in measurable characters J. S. HUXLEY.

Clinical, *a.* **3.** Coldly detached and dispassionate, like a medical report; bare and functional, like a hospital 1928.

Clip, *sb.*[1]
Comb.: **clipboard,** a board bearing a spring-clip at one end for holding papers, etc.; **c.-on** *a.*, that is fitted into position with a clip.

Clip, *sb.*[2] **5.** *colloq.* A (specified) speed; a rapid motion *a* 1867.

Clip-joint (kli·pdʒoint). *slang* (orig. *U.S.*). 1933. [f. CLIP *v.*[2] (in U.S. slang sense 'to swindle') + JOINT *sb.* III.] A club, bar, etc., charging exorbitant prices.

Cloak-room. 2. = LAVATORY 4. Also abbrev. *cloaks* 1953.

Clo·bber, *sb.*[2] *slang.* 1879. [Origin unkn.] **a.** Clothes. **b.** Equipment; 'gear'; rubbish 1890.

Clo·bber, *v. slang.* 1944. [Origin unkn.] *trans.* To hit, thrash, 'beat up', shoot down; to criticize severely.

Cloche. 1. Now, a translucent plant-cover of any shape or size.

Clock, *sb.*[1] **2. b.** A dial or meter for registering speed, mileage, etc. 1930.
Comb.: **c.-watcher,** one who takes care not to exceed minimum working hours; so **c.-watching.**

Clone (klō^{u}n), *sb.* 1903. [– Gr. κλών twig, slip.] *Biol.* **a.** A group of cultivated plants the individuals of which are transplanted parts of one original seedling or stock. **b.** More widely, any group of cells or organisms produced asexually from a single sexually produced ancestor. Hence **Clo·nal** *a.* **Clo·nally** *adv.*

Clone (klō^{u}n), *v.* 1959. [f. prec.] *trans.* To grow or obtain a c. from; to produce (organisms) that are collectively a c. So **Cloned** *ppl. a.*, produced by cloning.

Close, *a.* **II. 2.**
c. call or **shave,** a 'near thing'; a narrow escape. orig. *U.S.*

Closed, *ppl. a.*
Comb.: **c. book,** something unknown or uncomprehended; **c. circuit,** an unbroken circuit, *spec.* of television transmitted by wire to the receiver and not broadcast; **c. society,** a society characterized by its rigid structure and beliefs; one having little contact with other peoples; **c. system,** a self-contained, unalterable system (of ideas, etc.); a material system in which the total mass or energy remains constant.

Close-up (klō^{u}·sɒp). orig. *U.S.* 1913. [f. CLOSE *adv.* + UP *adv.*[2]] A photograph, or cinema or television shot, taken at short range so as to magnify detail; also *transf.* and *fig.*

Cloud, *sb.*
Comb.: **c. chamber,** a chamber (originally designed for experiments on cloud formation) in which a gas can be made supersaturated with water vapour, so that the paths of ionizing particles passing through it are rendered visible by the condensation along them; **c.-seeding:** see *SEED *v.*

Cloud-cuckoo-land or **-town.** 1824. [tr. Gr. Νεφελοκοκκυγία, f. νεφέλη cloud + κόκκυξ cuckoo.] The name of the realm in Aristophanes' *Birds* (l. 819) built by the birds to separate the gods from mankind; also allusively: a fanciful or ideal realm or domain.

Clouded (klau·dėd), *ppl. a.* 1599. [f. CLOUD *sb.* or *v.* + -ED[1].] **1.** Covered by clouds; situated in the clouds. **2.** Marked with stripes, spots, or veins of colour, as in *C. leopard, tiger*, a large, mainly arboreal, species of the cat family, *Neofelis nebulosa*, of southern Asia 1879.

Clue. *spec.* (*a*) A piece of evidence useful in the detection of a crime 1886; (*b*) in a crossword puzzle, a sentence or phrase serving to indicate a word or words to be inserted 1914.

Colloq. phr. *Not to have a c.*: to be ignorant or incompetent.

How valuable such sociological inquiries could be to local authorities, who usually haven't a c. 1957.

Coach, *sb.* **1. b.** A single-decker bus 1923.
Comb.: **c.-built** *a.*, of a motor body: built of wood or on a wooden framework; **c.-work,** the bodywork of a motor-vehicle or railway coach.

Coarse, *a.* **1. b.** Designating any freshwater fish except the Salmonidæ (or game-fish); so *c. fisherman, fishing* 1895.

Coat, *sb.*
Comb.: **c.-hanger,** a piece of wood, metal, or plastic on which a coat, etc., may be hung; **c.-tail,** the tail (TAIL *sb.*[1] 3) of a coat; *to climb on, hang on to*, etc. (a person's) *c.-tails* (orig. *U.S.*): to attach oneself to another to gain some undeserved benefit.

Coaxial, *a.* Delete *Math.*
Comb.: **c. cable,** a c. line, or a cable containing several of them (usu. along with conductors to supply repeaters and other equipment); **c. line,** a transmission line made up of a wire inside a flexible cylindrical conductor and separated from it by an insulating material, used esp. for carrying television signals and in multiplex telephony; also *ellipt.*

Cobber (kǫ·bəɹ). *Austral.* and *N.Z. colloq.* 1895. [perh. f. dial. *cob* to take a liking to.] A companion, mate, friend.

Cobbler. 1. b. [Rhyming slang from *cobbler's* (or *cobblers'*) *awl(s)*.] A ball; esp. in *pl.*, 'balls', testicles; nonsense, rubbish 1934.

Cobol (kō^{u}·bǫl). Also **COBOL.** 1960. [f. the initial letters of *C*ommon *B*usiness *O*riented *L*anguage.] *Computers.* A programming language using standardized English terms and designed for use in business operations.

Coca-Cola (kō^{u}·kă,kō^{u}·lă). 1887. Trade name of a popular American soft drink.

Co-ca·rcinogen. 1938. [CO-.] A substance that increases the carcinogenic effect of some other substance but is not itself carcinogenic. So **Co:-carcinoge·nic** *a.*

Coccidiosis (kǫ·ksidiō^{u}·sis). 1892. [f. *COCCIDI(UM 2 + -OSIS.] A disease of birds and mammals caused by the presence of coccidia.

Nine hens had died..and it was given out that they had died of c. G. ORWELL.

Coccidium. 2. *Zool.* Formerly the name of a genus of protozoan internal parasites (R. Leuckart, 1879); now a parasite of this kind belonging to the order Coccidia, which causes disease in mammals and birds 1886.

Coccus. 3. Any bacterium with a spherical or nearly spherical shape 1883. So **Coccal** (kǫ·kăl), **Coccoid** (kǫ·koid) *adjs.*

Cockpit. 3. In the fuselage of an aircraft, or in a spacecraft, the space occupied by a pilot, observer, astronaut, or (formerly) a passenger 1914. **c.** The space in a racing car occupied by the driver 1935.

Cocktail. 3. b. A preparation of food, usu. served at the beginning of a meal; freq. with the main ingredient prefixed, as *fruit, lobster, prawn c.* 1928.
Comb.: **c. dress,** a dress suitable for wearing at a c. party; **c. party,** a party at which cocktails are served, usu. with other drinks, snacks, etc.; **c. stick,** a small pointed stick on which sausages, onions, etc., are served at c. parties.

Cock-up, cockup. 5. *slang.* A blunder, a confused situation 1948.

Cocoon. 2. A coating applied to metal equipment, esp. surplus military apparatus, to prevent corrosion 1948. So as *v. trans.*, to coat with a protective layer 1947.

Code, *sb.* **4. b.** Any system of symbols and rules for expressing data or instructions in a form usable by a computer or other equipment for processing or transmitting data 1946. Also in extended uses in *Biol.* and *Linguistics.*

Code, *v.* Restrict *rare* to sense in Dict. **b.** To put (a message, data, etc.) into the form indicated by a code 1898. So **Co·ded** *ppl. a.*

I'm going to c. that cable GALSWORTHY.

Codon (kō^{u}·dǫn). 1963. [f. CODE *v.* + *-ON.] *Biochem.* A sequence of three consecutive nucleotides in a polynucleotide molecule that determines, in accordance with the genetic code, which amino-acid shall be inserted at any given position in a polypeptide chain.

Codswallop (kǫ·dzwǫlǫ̆p). *slang.* 1963. [Origin unkn.] Nonsense, drivel.

Cœlacanth, *sb.* (Specimens of this fish found in modern times have been systematically named *Latimeria chalumnæ.*) Also **Cœlaca·nthid** [-ID[2]] *attrib.* or *adj.*

The almost static coelacanths with their notorious single living representative *Latimeria* 1966.

Coexistence. b. *spec.* Peaceful existence side by side of states professing different ideologies 1954.

Coffee.
Comb.: **c. bar,** a bar at which coffee is sold as a beverage; **c. stall,** a movable structure in which coffee and other light refreshments are sold; **c. table,** a low occasional table for serving coffee; **c.-table book,** a large book with lavish illustrations.

Coherent, *a.* (*sb.*) **5.** *Physics.* Producing or involving waves between which there is a definite phase relationship. Of light: consisting of waves that are all in phase with one another 1902.

Cohort. 3. b. In demography, a group of persons having a common statistical characteristic, esp. that of being born in the same year 1944.

Coil, *sb.*[2] **4. b.** An intra-uterine contraceptive device of flexible material shaped into a spiral 1931.

Coitus.
c. interruptus, coition in which the penis is withdrawn from the vagina before ejaculation 1900.

Coke, *sb.*[2] orig. *U.S.* 1908. Slang abbrev. of COCAINE.

Coke, *sb.*[3] orig. *U.S.* 1909. A registered trade-mark of the Coca-Cola Company, = *COCA-COLA.

Cold, *a.*
Comb.: **c. cream,** a cooling creamy unguent for the skin; **c. front** *Meteorol.*, the forward boundary of a mass of advancing cold air; **c. table,** (a table bearing dishes of) cold food; **c. turkey,** (*a*) *U.S. slang*, matter-of-fact plainness; freq. *attrib.* or used as *adv.*; (*b*) *slang* (orig. *U.S.*), the immediate withdrawal from a habit, esp. from the taking of drugs, as opposed to a gradual withdrawal; also *attrib.* and used as *adv.*

Drug addicts are given what is called the 'cold turkey' treatment 1921. The only honorable way..was to go at it 'cold turkey' 1967. The patient is expected to break his antiwar reading habit cold-turkey 1967. One day I walked cold turkey into a meeting where the engineers were worrying about two electrical switches 1970.

Collaborate *v.*, **Collaboration, Collaborator.** *spec.* Applied to traitorous co-operation with the enemy 1940. So **Collabora·tionist** *sb.* and *a.*

Collage (kǫlā·ʒ). 1919. [Fr., lit. 'pasting'.] An abstract form of art in which photographs, pieces of paper, string, etc., are placed in juxtaposition and glued to the pictorial surface; such a work of art.

Collect, *v.* **1. b.** orig. *U.S.* Used as imper., adv., or adj. to indicate that something sent is to be paid for by the recipient or that a telephone call is to be paid for by the person called 1893. **c.** To retrieve or 'pick up' from a place of deposit 1896.

Collective, *a.* **2. b.**
c. bargain, bargaining, agreement on terms of employment fixed between employer and an organized body of employees; **c. farm,** a farm, esp. in the U.S.S.R., run by a group of people in co-operation; **c. security,** a system by which international peace and security are maintained by an association of nations; **c. unconscious,** that part of the unconscious mind which derives from ancestral experience.

Collectivization (kǫ̆le:ktivəizē^{i}·ʃən). 1890. [f. COLLECTIVE *a.* + -IZATION.] Organization in accordance with the principles of collectivism. So **Colle·ctivize** *v. trans.* **Colle·ctivized** *ppl. a.*

Collector. 1. b. *Electr.* One of the three regions of a transistor, into which most of the carriers pass from the base 1948.

Collins (kǫ·linz). 1904. A letter of thanks

for entertainment or hospitality, sent by a departed guest: named after William *Collins* in Jane Austen's *Pride & Prejudice* xxii.

Collision.
Comb.: **c. course,** a course that will end in collision; also *fig.*

Colobus (kǫ·lŏbʊ̆s). 1835. [mod.L. (J. C. W. Illiger, 1811), f. Gr. κολοβός docked.] A member of a genus of African monkeys so called, distinguished by their shortened thumbs.

Colonic (kōᵘlǫ·nik), *a.* 1906. [f. COLON¹ + -IC.] Of or affecting the colon.

Colostomy (kōᵘlǫ·stŏmi). 1888. [f. Gr. κόλον COLON¹ + στόμα mouth + -Y³.] *Surg.* The operation of making an opening into the colon through the abdominal wall.

Colour, color, *sb.*
Comb.: **c. bar,** legal or social distinction between 'whites' and coloured people; so *c. prejudice, problem, question*; **c. code,** a guide or code using certain colours as a standard method of identification; **c. magazine** or **supplement,** a supplement in a newspaper, etc., containing coloured illustrations; **c. scheme,** (*a*) an arrangement of colours following a thought-out design; (*b*) a scheme of protective coloration (of animals or birds).

Colourful (kʌ·ləɹfŭl), *a.* 1889. [f. COLOUR *sb.* + -FUL 1.] Full of colour; of bright and varied colour. Also *fig.*, full of interest, excitement, etc.

Columnist (kǫ·lə̆mnist, -mist). orig. *U.S.* 1920. [f. COLUMN *sb.* 2 + -IST.] One who writes a regular column or feature in a newspaper, etc.

Combination. 10. The series of movements required to open a **c. lock,** a lock which can be opened only by performing a certain c. of movements 1845.

Combine, *sb.*
Comb.: **c. harvester,** a machine which performs various harvesting functions (as cutting and threshing) simultaneously; also *ellipt.*, and as *combined harvester.*

Combo (kǫ·mbo). *slang.* 1926. [f. COMBINATION.] **1.** *Austral.* A white man who lives with an Aboriginal woman. **2.** *U.S.* Combination, partnership 1929. **3.** orig. *U.S.* A small instrumental band 1935.

Comb-out (kōᵘ·maut). 1919. [f. phr. *comb out*: see COMB *v.* 4.] An act of combing or clearing out.

Come, *v.* **VI. 4. c.** *colloq.* Due or deservedly falling *to* one; esp. in phr. *to have it coming* (*to one*): to be about to suffer (deservedly) 1793.

VII. 2. Colloq. phr. *C. off it*: (usu. in *imp.*) don't go on like that, stop trying to fool me!

VIII. C. again. b. An off-hand slang equivalent of 'what did you say?', 'I beg your pardon'.

Comedian. 2. b. A comic entertainer; also *transf.* 1898.

Come-hither (kʌ:mhi·ðəɹ). *colloq.* 1900. [f. COME *v.* + HITHER *adv.*] An invitation to approach; enticement. Freq. *attrib.*
Courage and c. eyes AUDEN.

Co·me-on. *slang* (orig. *U.S.*). 1898. [f. phr. *to come on* (COME *v.* VIII).] **1.** A swindler or his victim. **2.** An inducement, enticement 1902.

Come-u·ppance, comeuppance. orig. *dial.* 1859. [f. phr. *to come up* (COME *v.* VIII) + -ANCE.] One's deserts.
She's bound to get her c. one day 1957.

Command, *sb.*
Comb.: **c. module,** a module in a spacecraft containing the crew and the main controls; **c. paper,** a paper laid before Parliament, etc., by c. of the Crown; **c. performance,** a theatrical, musical, etc., performance given by royal c.; **c. post,** the headquarters of a military unit.

Commando. 2. A member of a specially trained unit of shock troops; also *attrib.*, *transf.*, and *fig.* 1940.
Plans should be studied to land secretly by night on the islands and kill or capture the invaders. This is exactly one of the exploits for which the Commandos would be suited W. S. CHURCHILL. Two South Vietnamese drivers..apparently helped a Viet Cong commando squad invade the embassy grounds 1968.

‖**Commedia dell'arte** (kŏme·diă del ă·rte). 1877. [It., lit. 'comedy of art'.] Improvised popular comedy as played in Italian theatres from the 16th to early 18th centuries with actors representing stock characters.

Commie (kǫ·mi). Also **Commy.** 1940. [See -IE. Cf. *CONCHIE.] Slang abbrev. of COMMUNIST.

Commissioner. 1. d. *C. for Oaths,* a solicitor authorized to administer oaths to persons making affidavits.

Common, *a.*
Phrases: **c. cold,** an infection of the upper respiratory tract accompanied by catarrh, coughing, etc.; **c. market:** see *MARKET *sb.*

Common law.
Comb.: **common-law marriage,** one agreed upon between the parties but without an ecclesiastical or civic ceremony; so *common-law wife.*

Commonwealth. 6. In full *British C.* (*of Nations*). The association of Great Britain and certain former dominions or colonies, together with her and their dependencies 1917.

Communication.
Comb.: **c.-cord,** a cord, etc., by which passengers in a railway train may signal to the guard or driver; **c. theory,** the study and theory of the means whereby information is conveyed, e.g. in language.
The train ground to a standstill. Obviously, someone had pulled the c. cord 1936.

Community. II. 4. *spec.* in *Ecology.* A group of plants or animals growing or living together in natural conditions or found inhabiting a restricted area 1883.

Commute, *v.* **4. b.** Also, more generally, to travel daily or regularly to and from one's place of work (by any means of conveyance) 1889.

Compact (kǫ·mpækt), *sb.*² Restrict † to senses in Dict. and add: **2.** A small case for compressed face-powder, rouge, etc. 1921.

Compassionate, *a.* **1. b.** Granted out of compassion, without legal or other obligation, as *c. allowance, c. leave* 1830.

Compelling, *ppl. a.* 1606. [f. COMPEL *v.* + -ING².] **a.** That compels. **b.** Of a person, his words, etc.: irresistible; demanding attention or respect 1901.

Compiler. b. *Computers.* A routine for translating a program into a machine-coded form 1953.

Complement, *sb.* **I. 5. b.** *Biochem.* A group of proteins in the blood which by combining with an antigen–antibody complex can cause the lysis of antigens such as bacteria or red blood cells 1900. Also *Comb.*, as **c.-fixation,** the removal of c. from solution by combination with an antigen–antibody complex.

Complex, *sb.* **c.** *Chem.* A substance formed by the combination of molecules of simpler substances 1895.

Composite, *a.* and *sb.* **B.** *sb.* **2. b.** A material made from two or more physically different constituents each of which largely retains its original structure and identity 1959.
Carbon-fibre composites having resinous matrices 1966.

Comprehensive, *a.* **1. b.** Designating a secondary school or a system of education which provides for children of all levels of intellectual and other ability; also *ellipt.* as *sb.*, a school of this kind 1947.

Compression. 1. b. The reduction in volume of the mixture of fuel and air drawn into the cylinder of an internal-combustion engine 1887.
Comb.: **c. ratio,** the ratio of the maximum to the minimum volume in the cylinder of an internal-combustion engine.

Compulsion. 2. *Psychol.* An insistent impulse to behave in a certain way 1913. Also *attrib.*, as *c. neurosis* 1909.

Compulsive, *a.* **3.** *Psychol.* Acting from or related to a compulsion 1902. **b.** Of a book, etc.: holding one's attention, as if by a compulsion 1961.

Computer. 2. A calculating-machine; *esp.* an automatic electronic device for performing mathematical or other operations; freq. with defining word prefixed, as *analogue, digital, electronic computer* 1897. Hence **Compu·terize** *v.*, to prepare for operation by, or to operate by means of, a c. **Compu:teriza·tion.** Also *attrib.* and *Comb.*, as *c.-controlled, c.-generated* adjs.

Comrade. b. *spec.* Used by socialists and communists as a prefix to the surname or as a term of address; hence, a (fellow-)socialist or communist 1884.

Con (kǫn). orig. *U.S.* 1889. Short for CONFIDENCE in attrib. use, as *c. game, man, talk*; also *ellipt.*, a confidence trick, a swindle. Hence as *v. trans.*, to persuade, trick, swindle.

Concentration. *Comb.*: **c. camp,** also, a camp for the detention of political prisoners, internees, etc., esp. as organized by the Nazi regime in Germany before and during the war of 1939–45.

Conchie, conchy (kǫ·nʃi), slang abbrev. of **conscientious objector* 1917. See -IE.

Concrete. A. *adj.* **7. c. music,** music constructed by the arrangement of various recorded sounds into a sequence; **c. poetry,** poetry which depends to a larger degree than usual upon the physical shape or pattern of the printed material.

Condition, *v.* **9.** To bring to a desired state or condition 1850. **b.** To teach or accustom (a person or animal) to adopt certain habits, attitudes, etc.; to establish a conditioned reflex in 1909.

Conditioned, *ppl. a.* **4. c. reflex,** a reflex or reflex action which through habit or training has been induced to follow a particular stimulus 1906.

Condom (kǫ·ndǫm). *c*1706. [Origin unkn.] A contraceptive sheath.

Conga (kǫ·ŋgă). 1935. [Amer. Sp., – Sp. *conga*, fem. of *congo* of or pertaining to the Congo.] A Latin-American dance usu. performed by several people in single file and consisting of three steps forward followed by a kick.
Comb.: **c. drum,** a tall, narrow, low-toned drum usu. played with the hands.

Conk, *v.*¹ *slang.* 1821. [f. CONK *sb.*] *trans.* To punch on the nose; to hit.

Conk (kǫŋk), *v.*² *colloq.* 1918. [Origin unkn.] *intr.* To give *out*, fail or show signs of failing.

Conning, *vbl. sb.*²
c.-tower, also, a superstructure on a submarine containing the periscope and from which steering, firing, etc., are directed when the submarine is on the surface.

Conscientious, *a.* **1. b.**
c. objector, one who refuses to conform to the requirements of a public enactment on the plea of conscientious scruple; esp. such an objector to military service 1899.

Conservationist (kǫnsəɹvēⁱ·ʃənist). 1870. [f. CONSERVATION + -IST.] One who advocates conservation, esp. of natural resources and amenities. Also *attrib.* or as *adj.*

Consociation. 5. *Ecology.* A subdivision of an association of plants or animals, dominated by a single species 1905.

Console, *sb.* **2. b.** orig. *U.S.* A cabinet for a gramophone, television set, etc. 1926. **3. b.** A desk, cabinet, etc., incorporating a number of switches, dials, or other controls; a control panel 1944.

Consortium. Delete ‖ and add: Now commonly with pronunc. (kǫ̆nsǭ·ɹtiǒm). Pl. **consortia.** Now more specifically, an association of business, banking, or manufacturing organizations.

Conspicuous, *a.* **3.** Designating expenditure on or consumption of luxuries on a lavish scale 1899.

Construct (kǫ·nstrǒkt), *sb.* 1871. [f. CONSTRUCT *v.*] **1.** *Linguistics.* A group of words forming a phrase, as distinct from a compound. **2.** *Psychol.* An object of perception or thought, formed by a combination of present with past sense-impressions; *gen.*, anything constructed, esp. by the mind 1890.

Consumer.
Comb.: **c. durable,** an article for domestic use which does not need to be rapidly replaced by the purchaser; **c. goods,** things which directly satisfy human needs and desires, *e.g.* food and clothing; **c. research,** investigation of the habits, motivation, etc., of the buying public; **c. resistance,** the unwillingness of a potential buyer.

Contact, *sb.* **1. b.** The touching or uniting of points or surfaces of conductors to permit the flow of electric current; also, a device for effecting this; in *Aeronaut.* used as *int.* for a signal to a person about to swing an aircraft propeller that the ignition system is switched on 1913. **4.** A person exposed to infection by

proximity to someone suffering from an infectious disease 1901. **b.** orig. *U.S. colloq.* Someone who can be called upon for assistance, information, etc.; an acquaintance or connection, esp. in business 1931.
Comb.: **c. lens,** a lens worn in c. with the eyeball to correct faulty vision.

Contact, *v.* Delete *rare, techn.* and add: *trans.* to get in touch with (a person) 1929.

Container. *spec.* A large standardized receptacle for the transport of freight; also *attrib.* Hence **Contai·nerize** *v. trans.*, to pack into, or transport by means of, containers.

Containment. Delete *rare* and add: *spec.* the action or policy of confining (an enemy) to a particular area 1947.

Continental, *a.*
Comb.: **c. drift,** the postulated movement of continents, by which those existing today are thought to have reached their present position after having originally formed a single land-mass.

Contingency.
Also *attrib.*, as **c. fund,** one set aside for conditional or incidental expenses; **c. plan,** a plan made contingent upon an uncertain event.

Continuity. 4. A detailed scenario for a cinema film; also, the maintenance of consistency or a continuous flow of action in successive shots of a film; also, (the use of) linking material in a radio broadcast 1921. Also *attrib.*

Contract, *v.* **2. b.** *To c. out*: to make an arrangement not to participate under certain conditions; to refuse to take part. Conversely *to c. in.* 1894.

Contrast, *sb.* **2. b.** The degree of differentiation between different tones in a photographic negative or print or in a television picture 1911. So **Co·ntrasty** *a.*, exhibiting (strong) contrasts; (of a photograph, etc.) having marked differentiation of tones.

Control, *sb.* **3. b.** In motor racing, etc., a section of road over which speed is controlled; also, a point where contesting cars are halted for examination and repairs 1900. **c.** The apparatus by means of which a machine is controlled during operation; freq. *pl.* 1908. **d.** A means adopted for the regulation of prices, consumption of goods, etc. 1935. **4. b.** *Spiritualism.* A spirit who controls the words and actions of a medium in a trance.
Comb.: **c. panel,** a board, panel, etc., on which are mounted switches, dials, etc., for the remote control of electrical or other apparatus; **c. tower,** a tower or other elevated building from which aircraft pilots are directed by radio.

Conurbation (kǫnɔ̆ɹbēⁱ·ʃən). 1915. [f. CON- + L. *urbs, urb-* city + -ATION.] A aggregation of urban areas.

Convector (kǫ̆nve·ktǫɹ). 1907. [f. CONVECTION: see -OR 2.] An appliance that warms a room by convection. Also *attrib.*, esp. in *c. heater.*

Convenience, *sb.* **5. b.** *spec.* A (public) lavatory, a water-closet 1841. **6.** *attrib.*, in sense 'designed for convenience, used when convenient', esp. in *c. food* 1961.

Conventional, *a.* **4. b.** Of weapons, etc.: other than nuclear; of war: fought without nuclear weapons; of power stations, etc.: using other than nuclear energy 1955.

Convertible, *a.* **3. b.** orig. *U.S.* Of a car: having a top that may be folded back or removed; also as *sb.*, such a car 1916. **4. b.** Of currency: that can be freely converted into gold or dollars at a fixed price 1911.

Conveyer.
Comb.: **c. belt,** an endless belt of rubber, canvas, etc., running over rollers or the like, on which objects or material can be conveyed; also *attrib.* and *fig.*

Convulsant (kǫ̆nvɒ·lsănt), *a.* and *sb.* 1879. [– Fr. *convulsant*, pr. pple. of *convulser* CONVULSE.] **A.** *adj.* Producing convulsions. **B.** *sb.* A substance that produces convulsions.

Cool, *a.* **4. b.** *colloq.* (orig. *U.S.*). Of jazz music: restrained or relaxed in style; also applied to the performer; hence, characteristic of those who favour such music; unemotional; also used as a general term of approval 1947. Hence as *sb.*, composure, relaxedness; also as *v.*, esp. in phr. *to c. it*, to calm down, 'take it easy'.

Coolabah, coolibah (kū·lăbă, -lĭb-). *Austral.* 1887. [Aboriginal.] Any of several Australian gum-trees, esp. *Eucalyptus microtheca.*

Coolant (kū·lănt). 1930. [f. COOL *v.* + -ANT.] A cooling agent; esp. (*a*) a fluid applied to a cutting-tool to cool it and lessen friction; (*b*) a cooling medium in an internal-combustion engine or the like.

Cooling, *vbl. sb.*
Comb.: **c. tower,** a structure in which water heated in some industrial process is cooled for re-use.

Coon. 2. c. *slang* (derogatory). A Negro 1862.

Coon-can (kū·n,kæ·n). 1889. [– Sp. *con quién* with whom?] A card-game, originating in Mexico, the main object of which is to secure sequences.

Cop (kǫp), *sb.*[5] *slang.* 1886. [f. COP *v.*[2]] **1.** Capture; chiefly in phr. *a fair c.* **2.** Catch, acquisition; usu. with neg.: *no c., not much c.*, of little or no value or use 1902.

Cop, *v.*[2] **b.** *To c. it*: to be punished, get into trouble; also, to die 1884. **c.** *slang.* To drop *out*; to escape or avoid involvement 1942. So **co·p-out** *sb.*, an escape; a cowardly compromise or evasion.

Cope, *v.*[2] **2. b.** *absol.* To deal (competently) with a situation or problem (*colloq.*) 1934.

Copy, *sb.* **6. b.** That which lends itself to interesting narration in a book, newspaper, etc.; material for a story 1886.
Comb.: **c.-cat** *colloq.*, someone who copies another; **c. desk** *U.S.*, the desk where copy is edited for printing; **c.-typist,** one who makes typewritten copies of documents, etc.; **c.-writer,** a writer of copy for the press, *spec.* of advertising copy.

Core, *sb.*[1] **5. b.** *Electr.* A mass of iron for increasing the magnetic field of a surrounding coil, as in an electromagnet 1849; hence, a unit of magnetic material in a computer in which two directions of magnetization represent 0 and 1; also *attrib.*, as *c. memory, store* 1950. **c.** That part of a nuclear reactor which contains the fissile material 1949.
5. b. Tiny rings of magnetic material, called 'cores' 1955.

Corgi (kǭ·ɹgi). Also **corgy.** 1926. [W.] A small short-legged dog of Welsh origin.
The Queen, with a firm hand on the leash for a reluctant corgi, arriving at Euston station 1970.

Corn, *sb.*[1] **3. b.** *colloq.* (orig. *U.S.*). Something 'corny' (see *CORNY *a.*[1] 1 b); *spec.* old-fashioned or inferior music 1936.

Corner, *v.* **6.** Of a vehicle, horse, etc.: to go round a corner 1909.

Corny, *a.*[1] **1. b.** *colloq.* Rustic or unsophisticated; old-fashioned, trite, or inferior 1932.

Corona[1]. **8.** *Electr.* A luminous appearance in the gas surrounding a conductor when the electric field at its surface is strong enough to ionize the gas but not strong enough to cause a spark 1906. Also *attrib.*, as **c. discharge,** the discharge causing a c.

Corona[2] (kŏrōᵘ·nă). 1887. [From the proprietary name *La Corona* (Sp.) the crown.] A well-known brand of Havana cigar.

Coronary, *a.* **3.** Also, pertaining to or affecting the coronary artery of the heart, as *c. thrombosis* 1930. Also *ellipt.* = c. artery, thrombosis, etc.
Pa was carried off by a c. about ten years ago 1957.

Corridor. 4. c. A passage in a railway carriage upon which all the compartments open; also *attrib.* 1892.

Cortisone (kǭ·ɹtizōᵘn). 1949. [f. 17-dehydroxy-11-dehydro*corticosterone*, its chemical name, f. DE- + HYDROXY- + HYDRO- + *corticosterone* (f. *cortico-*, comb. form of CORTEX + STER(OL + -ONE).] *Biochem.* A steroid hormone, $C_{21}H_{28}O_5$, produced in the adrenal cortex and prepared synthetically for use as an anti-inflammatory and anti-allergic agent in rheumatoid arthritis and other conditions.

Cosh (kǫʃ), *sb.*[1] *slang.* 1869. [Origin unkn.] A stout stick, bludgeon, or truncheon. Also *attrib.* Hence as *v. trans.*, to strike with a c.

Cosh (kǫsĕⁱ·tʃ, kǫʃ), *sb.*[2] *Math.* 1873. Abbrev. of *hyperbolic cosine.* Cf. SINH.

Cosmetic. A. *adj.* **b.** Of surgery or prosthetic devices: that improves or modifies the appearance 1926.

Cosmic, *a.* **3. b. c. rays,** high-energy radiations with great penetrative power which are incident on the earth from all directions and originate in space (*primary radiation*) or are produced in the upper atmosphere by the primary radiation (*secondary radiation*) 1925. So **c. radiation.**
The highest-energy c.-ray particles may be of extragalactic origin 1967.

Cosmonaut (kǫ·zmŏnǭt). 1959. [f. COSMO- + Gr. ναύτης sailor; cf. *ASTRONAUT.] A traveller in space; an astronaut (esp. Russian).
Tass said..both cosmonauts reported that everything was working normally 1970.

Co·sting, *vbl. sb.* 1884. [f. COST *v.* + -ING[1].] (Estimation of) the cost of production. Also *attrib.*

Costume, *sb.*
Comb.: **c. jewellery** orig. *U.S.*, showy artificial jewellery; **c. play,** etc., one in which historical costumes are worn.

‖**Couchette** (kuʃet). 1920. [Fr.] A Continental railway carriage in which the seats are convertible into sleeping-berths; such a berth.

Count, *sb.*[1] **1. b.** *Boxing.* The counting of ten seconds, the limit of time allowed to a fallen boxer to rise and resume the fight or accept defeat; *out for the c.*: defeated; *to take the (full) c.*: to be defeated 1902.

Cou·nt-down, cou·ntdown. orig. *U.S.* 1953. [f. COUNT *sb.*[1] and *v.* + DOWN *adv.*] The action of counting in reverse, from a given number to zero, to mark the seconds, etc., before an explosion, the launching of a missile, etc. Also *transf.* and *fig.*

Counter, *sb.*[3] **4. b.** Phr. *Under the c.*: used with reference to illegal or clandestine transactions 1926.

Country.
Comb.: **c.-and-western,** a type of music originating in the southern and western United States, consisting mainly of rural or cowboy songs; also *ellipt.* as *country*; **c. club** orig. *U.S.*, a social or recreational club in or near the country.

Coupon. c. A form, part of a printed advertisement, etc., entitling the holder to a gift or discount, or designed to be filled up and sent to the advertiser for information, goods, etc., or as an entry-form for a competition 1906. **d.** A ticket entitling the holder to a ration of food, etc. 1918.

Courgette (kūᵊɹʒe·t). 1931. [Fr.] A variety of small vegetable marrow.

Court, *sb.*[1]
Comb.: **c. shoe,** a woman's light, low-cut shoe.

Courtly, *a.* **2. b.**
c. love, a highly conventionalized medieval system of chivalric love and etiquette developed by the troubadours of southern France and extensively employed in European literature from the 12th century throughout the medieval period 1896.

‖**Couture** (kutür). 1908. [Fr., sewing, dressmaking.] Fashionable dressmaking or design; used as a collective term for the designers or makers of women's fashionable clothes, or the clothes made by them. Also *attrib.*

Covalency (kōᵘ,vēⁱlĕnsi). 1919. [Co-.] *Chem.* The linking of two atoms by a bond in which they share a pair of electrons; the number of electrons in an atom that go to form such a bond. Also **Cova·lence.** Hence **Cova·lent** *a.* **Cova·lently** *adv.*

Cover, *v.*[1] **III. 1. b.** orig. *U.S.* To report (an event, etc.) for a newspaper or the like; to investigate, etc., as a reporter 1893.

Cover, *sb.*[1] **2. b.** Protection from attack; a force providing such protection 1802.
Comb.: **c. charge,** a charge for service added to the basic charge in a restaurant; **c.-girl** orig. *U.S.*, a young woman whose picture appears on the front c. of a magazine; **c. note,** a note which declares the holder to have a current insurance policy.

Coverage (kɒ·vərĕdʒ). orig. *U.S.* 1912. [f. COVER *v.*[1] + -AGE.] The act or fact of covering; the area, range, number, etc., that is covered by something; *spec.* the risks covered by an insurance policy; the area within range of a radio or television transmitter; the extent of reporting news.

Cow, *sb.* **1. b.** A woman, esp. one who is coarse, unpleasant, etc. 1696. **c.** *Austral.* and *N.Z. slang.* An objectionable person or thing, a distasteful situation, etc. 1891.

Crack, *sb.* **I. 1. b.** *colloq.* (orig. *U.S.*) An attempt; esp. in phr. *to have a c.* (*at* something) 1836. **4. b.** *colloq.* (orig. *U.S.*). A sharp or cutting remark; = WISE CRACK 1896.

Crack, *v.* **II. 1. b.** Delete † and add: esp. to decipher (a code). **7. b.** To decompose (heavy oils such as petroleum) by the application of heat and pressure alone or by means of a catalyst so as to produce lighter hydrocarbons 1868.

Cra·ckerjack, *sb.* and *a.* *colloq.* (orig. *U.S.*). 1895. [A fanciful formation upon CRACK *v.* or CRACKER.] **A.** *sb.* **1.** Something exceptionally fine; someone very skilful. **2.** *U.S.* Proprietary term for a sweetmeat made of popcorn and syrup 1902. **B.** *adj.* Exceptionally fine or good 1910.

Crackers (kræ·kəɹz), *pred. a. slang.* 1928. [f. CRACKER; cf. CRACKED *ppl. a.* 5.] Crazy, mad; infatuated.

Crackpot (kræ·kˌpǫt). *colloq.* 1883. [For *cracked-pot*: i.e. CRACKED *ppl. a.* + POT *sb.*[1] 1.] A crazy person, a crank. Also *attrib.*

Craft, *sb.* **8. b.** Any sailing or floating vessel 1775.

Crap, *sb.*[1] So **Cra·ppy** *a.*, soiled; rubbishy, worthless.

Crash, *sb.*[1]

Comb.: **c. barrier,** a barrier erected to halt an aircraft, car, etc., that goes off its intended course; **c.-helmet,** a helmet worn to protect the head; **c. landing,** a landing involving damage to the aircraft; so (back-formation) **c.-land** *v. intr.*; **c. pad,** (*a*) a shock-absorbing pad; (*b*) *slang*, a place to sleep, esp. for a single night or in an emergency.

Also *attrib.*, passing into *adj.* Undertaken with rapidity or intensive effort; organized for an emergency.

A 'crash' job, that is, a job to be done with all possible speed 1952.

Crazy, *a.* **3. c.** *slang* (orig. *U.S.*). Of music, esp. jazz: unrestrained, exciting; hence as a general term of approbation 1927.

Cream, *v.* **6.** To work (butter and sugar, etc.) into a creamy consistency 1889. **7.** To treat (the skin) with a cosmetic cream 1921.

Create, *v.* **5.** *intr.* To make a fuss, 'go on' *about* something (*slang*) 1919.

Credibility.

Comb.: **c. gap** orig. *U.S.*, a disinclination to believe a person, statement, etc., esp. an official statement; a disparity between facts and what is said or written about them.

Credit, *sb.* **13.** An acknowledgement of authorship, performance, direction, etc., esp. at the beginning or end of a film, broadcast, etc.; freq. *pl.* and *attrib.* 1914.

Comb.: **c. card** orig. *U.S.*, a card issued by an organization authorizing a named person to draw on its account or to make purchases on credit; **c. squeeze,** the restriction of financial credit facilities through banks, etc.

Creek, *sb.* **6.** Slang phr. *Up the c.*: (*a*) in trouble or difficulties; *spec.* pregnant; (*b*) crazy, eccentric 1941.

Creep, *sb.* **1. b.** *slang.* A sycophantic, despicable, or stupid person *a* 1876.

Crème (krẹm, krēⁱm). Also **crême.** *a* 1821. [Fr., = CREAM *sb.*[2]] **1.** A name for various syrupy liqueurs, as **c. de cacao, c. de menthe** (peppermint). **b.** = CREAM *sb.*[2] 2a. So **c. brûlée,** one topped with caramelized sugar; **c. caramel,** one coated with caramel; **c. renversée,** one turned out of a mould 1845. **2.** Phr. *C. de la c.*: the élite, the pick of society 1848.

Crêpe. 2. In full *crêpe rubber.* Indiarubber rolled into thin corrugated sheets 1907. **3.** A small, thin pancake; **c. Suzette,** a pancake served in a hot sauce, often containing a liqueur 1922.

Comb.: **c. paper,** a thin crinkled paper.

Crew, *sb.* **3.** Also, the persons manning an aircraft or spacecraft 1917.

Comb.: **c. (hair-)cut** orig. *U.S.*, a closely cropped hair-style for men (app. first adopted by boat crews at Harvard and Yale Universities).

Crew (krū), *v.* 1935. [f. the sb.] *trans.* and *intr.* To act as (a member of a) crew of a ship, aircraft, etc.

‖**Crime passionnel** (krīm pasyonẹl). Also **crime passionel.** 1919. [Fr.] A crime due to passion; *spec.* a murder resulting from jealousy.

Crisp, *sb.* **4.** In full *potato crisp.* A thin sliver of potato fried until crisp and eaten cold; usu. *pl.* 1929.

Critical, *a.* **7. b.** *Nuclear Physics.* Of a nuclear reactor: maintaining a self-sustaining chain-reaction; esp. in phr. *to go c.*: to reach the stage of maintaining such a reaction 1949.

6. critical path, the most important sequence of stages in an operation, determining the time needed for the whole operation. **7. b. c. mass** or **size,** the minimum quantity of fissile material required to sustain a chain-reaction.

Croak, *v.* **4.** *intr.* To die (*slang*) 1812. **b.** *trans.* To kill, murder (*dial.* or *slang*) 1823.

Croc[2], colloq. abbrev. of CROCODILE 1884.

Cro-Magnon (kromæ·nyoṅ, kromæ·gnǫn). Also **Cromagnon.** 1869. Name of a hill in the Dordogne department of France where human skeletons were found in Upper Palæolithic deposits, applied, chiefly *attrib.*, to a type of Palæolithic man.

Crook, *sb.* and *a.* **B.** *adj.* **2.** *Austral.* and *N.Z.* **a.** Of things; out of order, unsatisfactory 1898. **b.** Dishonest, unscrupulous, 'crooked' 1911. **c.** Irritable, bad-tempered, angry; esp. in phr. *to go c.* (*at* or *on*), to become angry (*at*), to lose one's temper (with) 1911. **d.** Ailing, out of sorts; injured, disabled 1916.

a. You know how the old wagon is c. in water 1968. **b.** They said it [*sc.* pulling a race-horse] was a c. business right through F. SARGESON. **c.** If Phoebe's gone c. at you..she's had some good reason for it 1933. **d.** She's crook. It looks like the milk fever P. WHITE.

Cross-. B.

c.-check *v. trans.*, (*a*) *Ice Hockey*, to obstruct by holding one's stick across an opponent; (*b*) to check by an alternative method of verification; so as *sb.*; **c.-connect** *v. trans.*, to interchange the connections of (electric wires); **c.-ply** *a.*, denoting a tyre in which the layers of fabric are laid with the cords at right angles across one another; also *ellipt.* as *sb.*; **c.-section,** a section formed by a transverse cut; a piece so cut or a drawing, etc., of it; *spec.* in *Physics*, the apparent area of a particle, etc., as representing the probability of a specified interaction with another particle, etc.; *fig.*, a representative sample or an examination of this; **c.-talk,** (*b*) altercation; repartee.

Cross-road. 2. b. *fig.* (usu. *pl.*). A critical turning-point 1795.

Christianity at the cross roads 1924.

‖**Croûton** (krū·toṅ). 1806. [Fr., f. *croûte* CRUST *sb.*] A small piece of toasted or fried bread used in soups and to garnish stewed dishes and minces.

Crowd, *sb.*[3] **1. b.** *spec.* A collection of actors playing the part of a crowd; also *attrib.* 1899.

Crown, *sb.* **III. 1. b.**

C. and Anchor, a gambling game played with dice marked with crowns, anchors, and the four card-suits, on a board similarly marked 1880.

V. *Comb.*: **c.-court,** now, a local court higher than a magistrates' court; **c. of thorns (starfish),** a poisonous starfish, *Acanthaster planci* or *A. ellisi.*

Crud. 2. *slang* (orig. *U.S.*). **a.** An undesirable person or thing; nonsense, rubbish 1940. **b.** A real or imaginary disease 1945. **c.** An undesirable impurity, deposit, etc. 1950.

Crumb, *sb.* **2. b.** *slang* (orig. *U.S.*). A filthy, objectionable, or insignificant person 1918.

Crumble, *sb.* **b.** Food, such as bread or a mixture of flour and fat, in the form of crumbs; a dish made from such crumbs with fruit, as *apple c.* 1947.

Crumbs (krɒmz), *int.* Also **by crum(s), by crumbs.** 1892. [In phr. *by crum(s)*, a disguised oath.] An exclamation of consternation or dismay.

Crummy, *a.* **5.** *slang.* Rubbishy, dirty, inferior 1859.

Crumpet. 4. *slang.* Women regarded collectively as a means of sexual gratification 1936.

Crunch, *sb.* **b.** A crisis; a decisive event, confrontation, etc. 1939.

When it came to the c. de Fleury wasn't to be relied on 1963.

Crush, *sb.* **2. b.** *slang* (orig. *U.S.*). A person with whom one is enamoured; an infatuation; esp. in *to have* or *get a c. on*: to be infatuated with (someone) 1884.

Comb.: **c. bar,** a bar used during intervals in a theatre; **c. barrier,** a barrier erected to restrain a crowd.

Cryo- (krəiˌo), combining form of Gr. κρύος frost, icy cold (cf. KRYO-); as in **Cry·ostat,** an apparatus for maintaining a very low temperature. **Cryosu·rgery,** surgery using instruments that produce intense cold locally.

Cryogenic (krəiodʒe·nik), *a.* 1902. [f. *CRYO- + *-GENIC.] Of of pertaining to the production or use of very low temperatures. So **Cryoge·nics,** that branch of physics which deals with the production of very low temperatures and their effects on matter.

Cubicle. Now, any small partitioned space.

Cubism (kiū·biz'm). 1911. [– Fr. *cubisme*, f. *cube* CUBE *sb.*] A style in art in which objects are so presented as to give the effect of an assemblage of geometrical figures. So **Cu·bist** *sb.* and *a.*

Cuckoo (ku·kū), *a. slang* (orig. *U.S.*). 1918. [f. the sb.] Crazy.

Cuff, *sb.*[1] **2.** Colloq. (orig. *U.S.*) phr. *Off the c.*: extempore, unrehearsed; also *attrib.* (with hyphens) 1938. **b.** Chiefly *U.S.* The turn-up on a trouser leg 1911.

Comb.: **c.-link,** a device for fastening a shirt-cuff.

Cuisenaire (kwīzĕnēᵊ·ɹ). 1954. Name of a Belgian educationalist, Georges Cuisenaire, used *attrib.* or in the poss. to designate (one of) a set of wooden rods of different length and colour according to the number they represent, used in the teaching of arithmetic.

Culotte (kiulǫ·t, ‖külot). 1842. [Fr., = knee-breeches; cf. SANSCULOTTE.] **1.** Knee-breeches. **2.** (Usu. in *pl.*) A divided skirt. Also *attrib.* 1911. **3.** The soft hair on the back of the forelegs of a dog 1928.

Cultivar (kɒ·ltivāɹ). 1923. [f. CULTI(VATED *ppl. a.* + VAR(IETY 5 b.] *Hort.* A variety that has arisen in cultivation.

I now propose another name, cultivar, for a botanical variety, or for a race subordinate to species, that has originated and persisted under cultivation L. H. BAILEY.

Cunnilingus (kɒ:nili·ŋgɒs). 1887. [– L. *cunnilingus* (Martial) one who licks the vulva, f. *cunnus* female pudenda + *-lingus* (*lingere* to lick).] Oral stimulation of the vulva or clitoris.

Cup, *sb.* Colloq. phrases: (*a*) *c. of tea*: a specified type of person; (*b*) *one's c. of tea*: what interests or suits one; (*c*) *a different c. of tea*: something altogether different.

Miss Prentice..seems to be a very unpleasant c. of tea N. MARSH. Freddy..stood..regarding the heavy-laden altar and the exotic clusters of coloured lamps hung round it, [and] said, 'It's not really my c. of tea, you know.' M. SPARK. London in wartime..is a very different c. of tea from Winchester 1946.

Cuppa (kɒ·pă). 1925. Colloq. form of *cup o'*, *cup of.* Also used *ellipt.* for *cup of tea.*

Cure, *sb.*[1] **8.** The process of vulcanizing rubber or curing plastic; also (with qualifying adj.), the degree of hardness produced 1902.

Fine Hard C. Para Rubber 1909.

Cure, *v.* **8.** To vulcanize (rubber); to harden (plastic) or otherwise improve physical properties during manufacture; to harden (concrete) 1853. **b.** *intr.* To undergo vulcanization 1922.

Curettage (kiure·tāʒ). 1897. [Fr.: see CURETTE and -AGE.] *Surg.* The application of the curette; scraping or cleaning by means of a curette.

Curfew. 1. c. A restriction imposed upon the movements of the inhabitants of an area for a specified period 1939.

Curie (kiūᵊ·ri, ‖küri). 1910. [Named in honour of Pierre *Curie* (1859–1906), co-discoverer of radium.] A unit of radioactivity equal to $3{\cdot}7 \times 10^{10}$ disintegrations per second; *loosely*, a quantity of any radioactive substance in which there is this degree of radioactivity.

A single 1000 MWe reactor will..accumulate in its fuel many thousands of millions of curies of fission products 1970.

Curium (kiūᵊ·riɒm). 1946. [mod.L., f. the surname of Pierre and Marie *Curie*: see -IUM.] An artificial, highly radioactive metallic element of the actinide series. Symbol Cm; atomic number 96.

Curriculum. c. vitæ, the course of one's life; a brief account of one's career 1902.

Cursus. d. The regular varying cadences which mark the end of sentences and phrases, esp. in Greek and Latin prose 1904.

Curtain, *sb.* **2. b.** *slang.* In *pl.* (occas. in *sing.*) the end 1912. **3. b.** *Mil.* (In full *c. of fire, c. fire.*) A concentration of rapid and continuous artillery or machine-gun fire, etc., on a designated line or area 1916. **c.** Short for **iron curtain*; also in similar metaphors, esp. implying restriction of information 1945.

Curvaceous (kɒɹvēⁱ·ʃəs), *a. colloq.* (orig. *U.S.*). 1936. [f. CURVE *sb.* + -ACEOUS.] Curving, full of curves; *spec.* of a well-rounded female figure.

Cusec. Abbreviation used by engineers of '*cu*bic feet per *sec*ond' 1913.

Custard.
Comb.: **c. pie,** a pie containing custard; commonly used as a missile in broad comedy, hence used *attrib.* or allusively to denote comedy of this type; **c. powder,** a preparation in powder form for making custard by mixing it with milk.

Custom, *sb.*
Comb.: **c.-built, -made** *adjs.*, built or made to order or to measure.

Cut, *v.* Phr. *To c. a corner* or *corners*: to pass round a corner or corners as closely as possible; *fig.*, to pursue an economical or easy but hazardous course of action.
Comb. (with adverbs): **C. in. b.** *spec.* To drive a motor-vehicle closely between two others; to overtake and move sharply in front of another vehicle. **c.** *spec.* To supersede a partner during a dance.

Cut-away, *a.* (*sb.*). **2.** Applied to a model or drawing of a piece of apparatus, etc., in which part is cut away to reveal the interior 1946.

Cutie (kiū·ti). *slang* (orig. *U.S.*). Also **cutey.** 1768. [f. CUTE *a.* + -IE.] A cute person; esp. an attractive young woman.

Cut-out. c. Something cut out; *spec.* a piece of paper, etc., cut out in a certain design 1905.

Cutthroat, cut-throat. 6. Used *attrib.* or *ellipt.* of a razor consisting of a blade set in a handle, as distinguished from a safety-razor 1932.

Cwm (kum). 1853. [W. *cwm* (cf. COOMB²).] A valley; in *Physical Geogr.*, a bowl-shaped hollow partly enclosed by steep walls lying at the head of a valley or on a mountain slope and formed originally by a glacier; a cirque.

Cybernation (səibəɹnēⁱ·ʃən). 1962. [f. CYBERN(ETICS *sb. pl.* + -ATION.] The theory, practice, or condition of control by machines. Hence (as a back-formation) **Cy·bernate** *v. trans.*, to control in this manner.

Cybernetics (səibəɹne·tiks), *sb. pl.* const. as *sing.* 1948. [f. Gr. κυβερνήτης steersman (f. κυβερνᾶν to steer, GOVERN) + -ICS.] The theory or study of control and communication in living organisms or machines. Hence **Cyberne·tic** *a.* Also **Cyberneti·cian, Cyberne·ticist,** an expert in c.

Cyclic, *a.* **6.** *Chem.* Of a compound: having a molecular structure that contains one or more rings of atoms 1898.

Cyclorama. 2. *Theatr.* A large backcloth or wall, used esp. to represent the sky 1915.

Cyclotron (səi·klǒtrǫn). 1935. [f. CYCLO- + *-TRON.] *Physics.* An apparatus for accelerating charged particles by subjecting them repeatedly to an electric field as they revolve in orbits of increasing diameter in a constant magnetic field.

Cyto-. Cy·tochrome, any of several related compounds, present in the cells of most aerobic organisms, which are important in cell respiration. **Cytogene·tics,** the study of cytology and genetics in relation to each other, esp. of chromosomes as the constituents of cells that determine hereditary properties. **Cytogene·tic, -ical** *adjs.* **Cytogene·tically** *adv.* **Cytogene·ticist. Cytokinin** (-kəi·nin), any of numerous compounds which promote cell division and inhibit ageing in higher plants and (with auxins) control their growth and development. **Cy·tosine** (-īn), a crystalline base, $C_4H_5N_3O$, that is one of the constituents of nucleic acids and is paired with guanine in double-stranded DNA.

D.
III. D. = dimensional, as 3-D, 3 D, three-dimensional; D.A., District Attorney (*U.S.*); D.D.T., *d*ichloro*d*iphenyl*t*richloroethane, an insecticide; D.J., dinner-jacket, disc-jockey; DNA, de(s)oxyribonucleic acid; *D notice*, Defence notice, an official notice giving guidance to the press, broadcasting authorites, etc., about matters which, in the interests of national security, should not be publicly disclosed; D.O.A., dead on arrival (at hospital, etc.); D.P., displaced person; D. Phil., Doctor of Philosophy.

‖**Dacha** (dæ·tʃă). Also **datcha, datsha.** Pl. **da(t)chas, datche.** 1896. [Russ. *dácha*, pl. *dáchi*, lit. 'act of payment'.] In Russia, a small country house for summer use.

Dada² (da·da). 1920. [Fr. (*être sur son dada* to ride one's hobby-horse); title of a review which appeared at Zurich first in 1916.] Applied to an international artistic movement repudiating tradition and reason, and intended to outrage. Hence **Da·daism. Da·daist(e** *sb.* and *a.*

Dagga (dæ·gă, ‖da·χa). *S. Afr.* Also **dacca, dacha, dacka, dakha, dak(k)a.** 1670. [Afrikaans, f. Hottentot *dachab.*] Hemp, *Cannabis sativa*, used as a narcotic. Also applied to any indigenous plant of the genus *Leonotis.*

Dah (dā). Also **dao, dha.** 1832. [Burmese.] A short heavy sword used esp. in Burma.

Daily, *sb.* **b.** A domestic cleaner or servant who does not live on the premises 1933.

Daiquiri (dəi·kiri, dæ·k-). Also **daquiri.** 1920. [Name of district in Cuba.] A cocktail containing rum, lime, etc.

Dalton¹ (dǭ·ltən). 1920. Name of the high school (at *Dalton*, Mass., U.S.A.) in which the educational plan so named (devised by Miss Helen Parkhurst) was first adopted in 1920: it divides up work into 'assignments' for the pupils to carry through on their own.

Dalton² (dǭ·ltən). 1938. [Name of John *Dalton* (see DALTONIAN), to whom the concept of atomic weights is due.] Chiefly *Biochem.* A name for the atomic mass unit ($\frac{1}{12}$ of the mass of an atom of carbon 12); freq. used to express molecular weight (which being a ratio is a pure number and requires no unit).

Da·mping, *vbl. sb.* of DAMP *v.*
d. off, the decay of seedlings or cuttings due to excessive damp.

Dan⁴ (dæn). 1941. [Jap.] In Judo, a degree of proficiency; the holder of such a qualification.

Dandy, *sb.¹* (and *a.*). **B. 2.** *colloq.* (orig. *U.S.*). Splendid, first-rate; freq. in phr. *fine and dandy* 1794.

Danger, *sb.*
Comb.: **d. money,** payment made beyond basic wages for dangerous work; also *fig.*

Danthonia (dænþōᵘ·niă). 1863. [mod.L. (de Candolle & Lamarck, 1805), f. the name of Étienne *Danthoine*, XIX Fr. botanist + -IA¹.] A grass of a large genus of tufted perennial pasture grasses, chiefly of Australia and N.Z.

Dartmoor (dā·ɹtmūᵊɹ, -mōᵊɹ). 1831. Name of a district in Devonshire, applied *attrib.* (also *ellipt.*) to special breeds of ponies and sheep produced there.

Darwin (dā·ɹwin). 1889. The name of Charles *Darwin* (see DARWINIAN *a.* (*sb.*) 2), used *attrib.* (also *ellipt.*) to designate a race of tulips with tall stems and large self-coloured flowers.

Dash, *sb.¹* **6. c.** One of the two signals (the other being the dot) which in various combinations make up the letters of the Morse alphabet 1859.

Data processing: see s.v. *DATUM.

Date, *sb.²*
Comb.: **d.-line,** also, a line, or part of one, giving the date of issue of a newspaper or the date (and usu. the place of origin) of a dispatch, letter, etc.; hence as *v.* (usu. in pa. pple. *d.-lined*).

Date, *v.* **2.** Also (*colloq.*), to mark as being of a certain date or period; to render outdated. Also *intr.*, to be, or bear evidence of being, old-fashioned; freq. **da·ted** *ppl. a.* **b.** *trans.* To make or have an appointment (with) someone, esp. regularly; freq. in *pass.*; also *intr.* and with *up* (*colloq.*, orig. *U.S.*).

Datum. b. *pl.* The quantities, characters, or symbols on which operations are performed by computers and other automatic equipment and which may be stored or transmitted as electrical signals, records on punched cards, etc. 1946. **2.** *pl.* Facts, esp. numerical facts, collected together for reference or information 1899. ¶Used in pl. form with sing. construction.
b. Data..is transmitted from the satellite to Fairbanks in Alaska and from there..to Oxford for initial processing 1970. **2.** He took out a patent but some of the data is missing 1963.
Comb. of *data*: **d. processing,** the performance by automatic means of any operations on empirical data (e.g. classification, analysis, calculation).

Day, *sb.* Colloq. phrases. *One of those days*: a day of misfortune. *To call it a d.*: to consider that one has done a day's work; *fig.*, to rest content, leave off.
Comb.: **d. release,** a system whereby employers allow employees days off from work for education; also *attrib.*

D-Day (dī·dēⁱ). Also **D Day, D-day.** 1918. [*D* for *day.*] The military code-name for a day fixed for the beginning of an operation; *spec.* the day (6 June 1944) of the Allied invasion of German-occupied France. Also *transf.*, of non-military undertakings; later also used for *decimalization day* (e.g. in Britain 15 Feb. 1971, when decimal currency came into official use).

De. 2. *de rigueur*, strictly or rigorously obligatory.

Dead, *a.* (*sb.*, *adv.*). **C. 2. d.-end,** also *fig.*, a policy, etc., that leads nowhere; also *attrib.* or as *adj.*, (*a*) that leads nowhere; (*b*) **d.-end kid,** a tough young person; **d. loss,** a complete loss; freq. *colloq.*, a person or thing that is totally worthless or unsuccessful; **d.-pan** *a.* and *sb.* orig. *U.S.*, (a face that is) expressionless or impassive; a person with such a face; hence as *adv.*, with a d.-pan face; in a d.-pan manner.

Dead-line. 2. b. orig. *U.S.* A time-limit 1920.

Dead man.
Dead man's handle, in an electric train, a handle that must be held in position for the current to pass, so that the train is automatically brought to a standstill should the driver release his grasp through illness or accident.

Deal, *sb.²* **3. b.** *colloq.* (orig. *U.S.*). *A bad, raw,* or *rough d.*: harsh or unfair treatment. *A fair* or *square d.*: equitable treatment. **c.** *new d., New D.*: a new improved arrangement; *spec.* the programme of social and economic reform in the United States planned by the Roosevelt administration of 1932 onwards; also *transf.* and *attrib.* orig. *U.S.*. **d.** *colloq.* (orig. *U.S.*). *Big d.*: an important business transaction; something important; freq. as an ironical exclamation.

Death.
Comb.: **d.-wish,** a conscious or unconscious wish for the death of oneself or another; also *fig.*

Debag (dībæ·g), *v. slang.* 1914. [f. DE- II. 2 a + BAG *sb.* 12.] *trans.* To remove the trousers from (someone).

Debrief (dībrī·f), *v. colloq.* 1945. [f. DE- II. 1 + BRIEF *v.²*] *trans.* To obtain information from (a person) on the completion of a mission. Usu. *pass.* So **Debrie·fing** *vbl. sb.*

Debug (dībʊ·g), *v.* 1945. [f. DE- II. 2 a + BUG *sb.²*] **1.** *trans.* To remove faults from (a machine, system, etc.). **2.** = *DELOUSE *v.* 1960.

Decarbonize, *v.* **b.** To remove carbon deposit from (an internal-combustion engine) 1915.

Decathlon (dekæ·þlǫn). 1912. [f. Gr. δέκα ten + ἆθλον contest.] In the modern Olympic games, a composite contest of ten events.

Decay, *sb.* **2. b.** *Physics.* The gradual decrease in the radioactivity of a substance; hence, the spontaneous transformation of a nucleus or sub-atomic particle into one or more other nuclei or particles 1897. **c.** A progressive diminution in the amplitude of an oscillation 1906.
2. b. The d. of the neutron into a proton, an electron, and an antineutrino 1968.

Decay, *v.* **I. 1. b.** Of an oscillation: gradually to decrease in amplitude. Also said of the amplitude 1879. **c.** *Physics.* Of

radioactivity: gradually to diminish in intensity. Of a substance: to suffer a gradual decrease in its radioactive power. Hence, of a radioactive substance, or a nucleus or sub-atomic particle: to change *into* one or more other substances, particles, etc. 1900.
1. c. Uranium X does not d. into a stable product 1962.

Decibel (de·sibel). 1928. [f. DECI- + *BEL.] The usual unit (equal to one tenth of a bel) used in comparing two power levels in an electrical communication circuit, or the intensities of two sounds; freq. used to express a single power level or sound intensity relative to some reference level (stated or understood). Abbrev. db.
Two power levels P_1 and P_2 differ by N decibels, where $N = 10 \log_{10} (P_1/P_2)$.

Deck, *sb.*[1] **3. c.** *Aeronaut. slang.* The ground 1925. **d.** The surface of a tape recorder above which the tape moves, together with its motor and other apparatus, the whole being built as a single unit; more fully *tape d.*; also, the corresponding part of a system for playing gramophone records 1949.

Deck, *sb.*[2]: see *DEKKO.

Declassify (dīklæ·sifəi), *v.* 1865. [f. DE- II. 1 + CLASSIFY *v.*] *trans.* To remove from a class or classes; *spec.* to remove (information, etc.) from the category of being 'classified' (see *CLASSIFIED *ppl. a.* c).

Decoke (dīkōᵘ·k), *v. colloq.* 1928. [f. DE- II. 2 a + COKE *sb.*] *trans.* = *DECARBONIZE *v.* b. Also *transf.* Hence **Deco·king** *vbl. sb.*

Decompression.
Comb.: **d. chamber,** a chamber in which pressure is reduced to, or below, that of the atmosphere; **d. sickness,** sickness resulting from the effects of too rapid d.

Decontaminate (dīkǭntæ·minēⁱt), *v.* 1936. [f. DE- II. 1 + CONTAMINATE *v.*] *trans.* To remove (the risk of) contamination from (a person, area, etc.). So **Decontamina·tion.**

Decrypt (dīkri·pt), *v.* 1936. [f. DE- II. 1 + *crypt* as in CRYPTOGRAM; cf. It. *decriptare.*] *trans.* To decipher or decode (a cryptogram).

Dedicated (de·dikēⁱtėd), *ppl. a.* c1600. [f. DEDICATE *v.* + -ED[1].] Sacredly, solemnly, or formally devoted. **b.** Of a person: devoted to his aims or his vocation 1944.

Deductivism (dīdɒ·ktiviz'm). 1908. [f. DEDUCTIVE *a.* + -ISM.] *Philos.* The preference for, use of, or belief in the superiority of, deductive as opposed to inductive methods. So **Dedu·ctivist** *sb.* and *a.*

Dee-jay, deejay (dīdʒē·). *slang* (orig. *U.S.*). 1955. [pronunc. of *D.J.* (see *D. III).] A disc-jockey.

Deep, *a.*
Comb.: **d.-breathing,** the act of breathing deeply as a form of physical exercise; **d. space,** the regions of space that are either well outside the earth's atmosphere or beyond the solar system; **d. therapy,** the treatment of disease by short-wave X-rays.

Deep-freeze, deep freeze. orig. *U.S.* 1941. [f. DEEP *a.* + FREEZE *sb.*] (The registered American trade-name of) a type of refrigerator capable of rapid freezing; also *transf.* and *fig.* Hence **Deep-freeze** *v. trans.*, to subject to a deep-freeze process; also *fig.*

De-escalation (dī,eskălēⁱ·ʃən). orig. *U.S.* 1964. [f. DE- II. 2 + *ESCALATION.] The reversal of escalation. So **De-e·scalate** *v. trans.* and *intr.*

Defect, *v.* **2.** *spec.* To desert *to* a Communist country from a non-Communist country, or *vice versa* 1955.

Defective. A. 1. b. *spec.* Mentally defective 1898. **B. 1. b.** A mentally defective person 1899.

Defence, defense, *sb.* **II. 1. b.** *Psychol.* Behaviour the object of which is to seek to protect an organism from real or apparent danger. Also *attrib.*, esp. in *d. mechanism* 1909.

Deficiency.
Comb.: **d. disease,** disease caused by the lack of an essential or important substance in the diet.

Definition. 5. b. *spec.* The degree of distinctness of the details in a photograph, film, television picture, etc. 1889.

Deflate, *v.* **1. b.** To reduce the size, importance, reputation, etc., of (a person or thing). Also *intr.*, to 'climb down', lose spirit or confidence 1912.

Deflationary (dīflēⁱ·ʃənări), *a.* 1920. [f. DEFLATION + -ARY[1].] Of, pertaining to, or tending to deflation.

Defrost (dīfrǫ·st), *v.* 1895. [f. DE- II. 2 a + FROST *sb.*] *trans.* To unfreeze; *spec.* (*a*) to unfreeze (frozen meat, etc.); (*b*) to clear the frost from (the interior of a refrigerator, etc.). Also *absol.* and *intr.* So **Defro·sted** *ppl. a.* **Defro·sting** *vbl. sb.*

Degauss (dīgau·s, dīgǭ·s), *v.* 1940. [f. DE- II. 2 + GAUSS.] *trans.* To protect (a ship) against magnetic mines by encircling it with an electrically charged cable so as to demagnetize it; hence *gen.*, to remove unwanted magnetism from.
It is wise to d. the heads prior to each recording session 1960.

Degenerate (dĭdʒe·nĕrĕt), *sb.* 1555. [subst. use of the adj.] One who has lost or become deficient in the qualities considered proper to the race; a person of debased or perverted physical or mental constitution.

Degrease (dīgrī·s), *v.* 1889. [f. DE- II. 2 a + GREASE *sb.*] *trans.* To remove grease or fat from.

Dehydrate, *v.* **1. b.** *spec.* To remove the water from (foods), so as to preserve them and reduce their bulk 1921.

De-ice (dī,əi·s), *v.* 1935. [f. DE- II. 2 a + ICE *sb.*] *trans.* To remove, or prevent the formation of, ice on (parts of an aircraft, etc.). So **De-i·cer. De-i·cing** *ppl. a.* and *vbl. sb.*

Déjà vu (deʒa vü·). 1903. [Fr., = already seen.] A feeling, usu. illusory, of having previously experienced a present situation.

Dekko (de·ko). *slang* (orig. *Army*). 1894. [– Hind. *dekho*, imper. of *dekhnā* to look.] A look. Also as *vb.*, to look (at). (Earlier *deck.*)

Delicatessen (de:likăte·sən). orig. *U.S.* 1889. [G. *delikatessen*, Du. *delicatessen*, – Fr. *délicatesse* (see DELICATESSE).] Delicacies or relishes for the table; food ready to be eaten; also *attrib.* **b.** A shop selling such food.

Delouse (dīlau·s), *v.* 1919. [f. DE- II. 2 a + LOUSE *sb.*] *trans.* To clear of lice. Also *transf.* and *fig.*

Delta.
Comb.: **d. wing,** a type of triangular swept-back aeroplane wing; so **d.-winged** *adj.*

Delusion. 2. b. *Delusions of grandeur*: a false belief that one's personality or status is more important than it is. Also *fig.* 1909.

Demantoid (dimæ·ntoid). 1892. [– G. *demantoid.*] *Min.* A green kind of garnet with a brilliant lustre.

Demarcation. b. Used *attrib.* to denote a dispute, rule, etc., concerning the precise scope and kind of work laid down by trade unions for their members in their rules, a dispute occurring between two unions where such rules appear to conflict.

‖**Dementia præcox** (dīme·nʃiă prī·kǫks). 1899. [mod.L. (A. Pick, 1891), f. DEMENTIA + L. *præcox* (see PRECOCIOUS *a.*).] *Med.* = SCHIZOPHRENIA.

Demilitarize (dīmi·litărəiz), *v.* 1883. [f. DE- II. 1 + MILITARY *a.* + -IZE.] *trans.* To take away military organization or forces from; to place (a state) under an obligation not to maintain armed forces in a specified region. Hence **Demi:litariza·tion. Demi·litarized** *ppl. a.*

Demineralization (dīmi:nĕrălaizēⁱ·ʃən). 1903. [f. DE- II + MINERALIZATION.] The removal of salts, esp. from sea or brackish water; also, any abnormal loss of salts from the body.

‖**Demi-pension** (dəmi,pãnsyoñ). 1951. [Fr.] The price of bed, breakfast, and one other meal at a (French) hotel, etc.

Demister (dīmi·stəɹ). 1939. [f. DE- II + MIST *sb.*[1] + -ER[1].] A device for clearing mist from the windscreen, etc., of a motor vehicle, etc. So **Demi·st** *v.* **Demi·sting** *ppl. a.* and *vbl. sb.*

Demi-tasse (dəmi,tas, de·mitæs). Chiefly *U.S.* 1842. [Fr., lit. 'half-cup'.] A small coffee-cup; its contents. Also *attrib.* and as *adv.*

Demo (de·mo). 1936. Colloq. abbrev. of DEMONSTRATION.

Demob (dīmǫ·b), *sb.* and *v.* 1920. Colloq. abbrev. of DEMOBILIZATION and DEMOBILIZE *v.* Also *attrib.*, as in **d. suit,** a suit issued to a soldier, etc., upon demobilization.

Demote (dīmōᵘ·t), *v.* orig. *U.S.* 1893. [f. DE- II. 1 + *-mote* of PROMOTE.] *trans.* To reduce to a lower rank or class. Hence **Demo·tion.**

Denationalize, *v.* **2.** To transfer (an industry) from national to private ownership. Also *intr.* 1921.

Denazify (dīnā·tsifəi), *v.* 1944. [f. DE- II + NAZI + -FY.] *trans.* To (attempt to) detach (Nazis or their adherents) from Nazi allegiance or connection; also *transf.* Hence **Denazifica·tion.**

Dendrite. 3. *Anat.* Any of one or more processes from a nerve cell which are typically short and extensively branched and conduct impulses towards the cell body 1893.

Dendrochronology (de:ndro,krono·lŏdʒi). 1928. [f. DENDRO- + CHRONOLOGY.] The science of arranging past events chronologically by the comparative study of the annual growth rings in (ancient) wood. Hence **De:ndrochronolo·gical** *a.*, **-lo·gically** *adv.* **De:ndrochrono·logist.**

Denial. 5. *Bridge.* A bid of another suit in order to show weakness in the suit bid by one's partner 1916.

Denim. Also *pl.*, overalls or trousers made of d.

Denominator. 2. *Common d.*: (the lowest) multiple of the denominators of two or more fractions; also *fig.*

Densitometer (densitǫ·mĭtəɹ). 1901. [f. DENSIT(Y + -OMETER.] *Photogr.* An instrument for the measurement of photographic density.

Dentex (de·nteks). 1836. [mod.L. (G. Cuvier, 1815), f. L. *dentex, dentix* a kind of marine fish.] The common name of a sea bream, *Dentex dentex*, found in the Mediterranean and along the N. African Atlantic coast.

Denu·clearize, *v.* 1958. [f. DE- II. 1 + NUCLEAR *a.* + -IZE; cf. *DEMILITARIZE *v.*] *trans.* To remove nuclear armaments from. Chiefly as *ppl. a.*, esp. with *zone*. So **De:nucleariza·tion.**

Deoxy- (di,ǫksi), *prefix.* 1871. [f. DE- + OXY-.] *Chem.* A prefix used in forming the names of compounds, indicating the loss of one or more atoms of oxygen; = DESOXY- (which is less common).

Deo:xyribonu·cleic a·cid. Also **desoxy-.** 1931. [f. *DEOXYRIBO(SE + *NUCLEIC *a.*] *Biochem.* A generic term for any of the nucleic acids yielding deoxyribose on hydrolysis, which occur chiefly in chromosomes and some viruses and are important as the carriers of genetic information required for synthesizing more DNA and also RNA. Abbrev. DNA.

Deoxyri·bose. Also **desoxy-.** 1931. [f. *DEOXY-, DESOXY- + *RIBOSE.] *Biochem.* Any sugar derived from ribose by the replacement of a hydroxyl group by a hydrogen atom.

Dependability (dĭpendăbi·lĭti). 1901. [f. DEPENDABLE *a.*: see -ILITY.] The quality of being dependable; reliability.

Depersonalization (dīpɔ̄:ɹsənălaizēⁱ·ʃən). 1904. [f. DEPERSONALIZE *v.* + -ATION.] The deprivation of personality; *spec.* in *Psychol.*, a morbid state involving a loss of the sense of personal identity and a feeling of the strangeness or unreality of one's own words and actions.

Deportee (dīpōᵊɹtī·). 1895. [f. DEPORT *v.* + -EE[1].] One who is or has been deported; *spec.* in Indian use, = DÉTENU.

Depressed, *ppl. a.* **4. b.**
d. area, an area of economic depression 1928.

Depression. 4. a. spec. *the Depression*: the financial and industrial 'slump' of 1929 and subsequent years. **5.** Also, as a sign of a psychiatric disorder or a component of a psychosis 1905.

Depressive, *a.* **b.** Involving or characterized by depression as a psychiatric illness

1905. Hence as *sb.*, one who suffers from this condition.

Depre·ssurize, *v.* 1944. [f. DE- II. 1 + *PRESSURIZE *v.*] *trans.* To cause an appreciable drop in the pressure of the gas inside (a container, etc.). So **Depre·ssurized** *ppl. a.*

Deproletarianize (dīːprōᵘlĭtēᵊ·riănəiz), *v.* Also **deproletarize.** 1954. [f. DE- II. 1 + *PROLETARIANIZE *v.*] *trans.* To free of proletarian qualities; to cause to lose proletarian nature. Also *absol.*

Depth. 1. 3. b. *in depth*: profoundly; with deep insight or penetration. Hence (hyphenated) as an attrib. phr.

‖**Déraciné** (derasine), *a.* 1921. [Fr.: see DERACINATE *v.*] 'Uprooted' from one's (national or social) environment. Also as *sb.*

Derby. 4. Denoting a variety of porcelain made at Derby, *esp.* a soft-paste procelain made from *c*1750.

Derequisition (dīrekwizi·ʃən), *v.* 1945. [f. DE- II. 1 + REQUISITION *v.*] *trans.* To convey (requisitioned land, etc.) to its original owner. Hence as *sb.*

Derestri·ct, *v.* 1935. [DE- II. 1 + RESTRICT *v.*] *trans.* To remove restrictions from; *spec.* to remove a speed limit on traffic in (a specified road, area, etc.). So **Derestri·cted** *ppl. a.* **Derestri·ction.**

Derisive, *a.* **b.** That causes derision; ridiculous; ridiculously small 1896.

Derisory, *a.* **b.** = prec. 1923.

Both rejected the present rate offer as 'd.' 1971.

Dermabrasion (dəːɹmăbrēⁱ·ʒən). 1954. [f. DERM + ABRASION.] *Surg.* The removal of superficial layers of the skin with a rapidly revolving abrasive tool.

Deːrmatogly·phics. 1926. [f. DERMATO- app. after *hieroglyphics*: see -IC 2.] The science or study of skin markings or patterns, esp. those of the fingers, hands, and feet; also, such skin markings themselves. Hence **Deːrmatogly·phic** *a.* **Deːrmatogly·phically** *adv.*

Derrick. 2. c. orig. *U.S.* A structure erected over a deep-bored well, esp. an oil-well, to support the drilling apparatus 1861.

Derris (de·ris). 1890. [mod.L. (J. de Loureiro, 1790) – Gr. δέρρις leather covering.] A liquid or powder prepared from the root of species of the genus *Derris* of woody vines, used as an insecticide. Also *attrib.*

Derv (dəɹv). 1948. [f. the initial letters of *diesel-engined road vehicle.*] Diesel oil for road vehicles. Also *attrib.*

Desalinate (dīsæ·linēⁱt), *v.* 1949. [f. DE- II. 1 + SALINE *a.* and *sb.* + -ATE³.] *trans.* To remove salt from. Hence **Desa·linated** *ppl. a.* **Desalina·tion.**

Descriptive, *a.* **b.** *Linguistics.* Describing the structure of a language at a given time, avoiding comparisons with other languages or other historical phases, and free from social valuations 1927.

Desegregate (dīse·grĭgēⁱt), *v.* 1952. [f. DE- II. 1 + SEGREGATE *v.*] *trans.* To reunite (persons, classes, etc.) hitherto segregated; esp. (orig. *U.S.*) to abolish racial segregation in schools, etc. So **Desegrega·tion.**

Despecialize (dīspe·ʃăləiz), *v.* 1896. [f. DE- II. 1 + SPECIALIZE.] *trans.* To eliminate as a specialist or specialized vocation, subject, etc. **b.** *intr.* To pass from a specialized to a general condition. Hence **Despecializa·tion.**

De-Stalinize (dīˌstā·linəiz), *v.* 1957. [f. DE- II. 1 + *Stalin* (adopted name of Iosif Vissarionovich Dzhugashvili (1879–1953), head of government of the Soviet Union) + -IZE.] *intr.* To counteract the excesses of Stalinism or the influence of Stalin, as by reversing or amending his policies, etc.; also *trans.*, to affect in some way by **De-Staliniza·tion.** So **De-Sta·linized** *ppl. a.* **De-Sta·linizer. De-Sta·linizing** *vbl. sb.*

Destruct (dĭstrʊ·kt), *v.* Chiefly *U.S.* 1958. [In mod. use a back-formation from DESTRUCTION. An isolated 17th c. use f. L. *destruct-*, ppl. stem of *destruere* to destroy, is known: see O.E.D.] *trans.* To destroy (a rocket) by pre-arranged means. Also as *sb.*, destruction in this way.

Detainee (dĭtēⁱnī·). 1928. [f. DETAIN *v.* + -EE¹.] A person detained in custody, usu. on political grounds.

Detention.

Comb.: **d. barrack,** a military prison; **d. camp,** a camp in which aliens, etc., are detained; **d. centre,** an institution in which young offenders are detained for short periods.

Detergent. B. *sb.* Now esp., any of various synthetic substances soluble in or miscible with water and differing from soap in not combining with the salts present esp. in hard water; also, any of various oil-soluble substances that hold dirt in suspension in lubricating oils.

Deterrence. *spec.* The reduction of the likelihood of war by the fear that nuclear weapons will be used against an aggressor 1955.

Deterrent. B. *sb. spec.* The nuclear weapons of any one country or alliance; freq. *the (great) d.* 1954.

‖**Deus ex machina** (dī·ʊs eks mæ·kĭnā). 1697. [mod.L., lit. 'god from the *machina*' (by which gods were suspended above the stage in the Greek theatre): cf. MACHINE *sb.* 6.] A power, event, person, or thing that comes in the nick of time to solve a difficulty.

Deuterium (diūtīᵊ·riʊ̆m). 1933. [mod.L., f. Gr. δεύτερος second + -IUM.] *Chem.* One of the isotopes of hydrogen, differing from the commonest isotope in having a neutron as well as a proton in the nucleus and present to about 1 part in 6000 in naturally occurring hydrogen; also called *heavy hydrogen.* So **Deu·teron** [*-ON], the nucleus of an atom of d., consisting of a proton and a neutron in combination.

Deutsche mark, Deutschemark (doi·tʃəmāːɹk). Also **Deutschmark.** 1948. [G. 'German mark'.] The monetary unit of the German Federal Republic, instituted in June 1948. Abbrev. *D.M.* or *D-mark.*

Devaluation. *spec.* The reduction of the official value of a currency in terms of gold or of another currency 1921.

Devastating (de·văstēⁱtiŋ), *ppl. a.* 1634. [f. DEVASTATE *v.* + -ING².] That devastates; freq. *fig.*, esp. in trivial or hyperbolical use: very effective, surprising, or upsetting. Hence **De·vastatingly** *adv.*

Develop, *v.* **3. b.** To realize the potentialities of (a site, estate, etc.) by laying it out, building, etc.; to convert (a tract of land) to a new purpose 1890.

Development. 3. b. The act or process of developing (see *DEVELOP *v.* 3 b) a site, etc.; also, a developed tract of land 1885. Freq. *attrib.*, esp. in *d. area, work.*

Deviance (dī·viăns). 1944. [f. DEVIANT *ppl. a.* + -ANCE.] Deviant state, quality, or behaviour.

Deviant (dī·viănt), *sb.* 1927. [f. the ppl. adj.] **a.** Something that deviates from normal. **b.** = next 1928.

Deviate (dī·viĕt), *sb.* 1912. [f. the vb.] A person who deviates, esp. from normal social, etc., standards or behaviour; *spec.* a sexual pervert.

Deviation. 3. a. *spec.* Departure or divergence from the principles or policies of a government or political party, used esp. of such actions in a Communist society. So **Devia·tionism. Devia·tionist** *sb.* and *a.*

Devon. 1834. The name of a county in the south-west of England, used *attrib.* or as *sb.* to designate (*a*) a breed of cattle; (*b*) a breed of sheep.

Dewar, dewar (diū·əɹ). 1899. The name of Sir James *Dewar* (1842–1923), British physicist and chemist, used *attrib.* or *absol.* to designate a double-walled vessel, usu. of glass or copper, having the space between the walls empty of air to prevent conduction and convection of heat to and from the inner container. Cf. *vacuum-flask s.v.* VACUUM.

Dewey (diū·i). 1879. The name of Melvil *Dewey* (1851–1931), American librarian, used *attrib.* to designate a decimal system of library classification developed by him.

Deːxamphe·tamine. 1952. [f. DEX(TRO- + *AMPHETAMINE.] *Pharm.* The dextro-rotatory form of amphetamine, used as the sulphate and phosphate and having more marked effects than amphetamine sulphate.

Dexedrine (de·ksĕdrīn). 1942. [prob. f. DEX(TRO- + *-edrine* as in *BENZEDRINE.] *Pharm.* Proprietary name of a preparation of dexamphetamine sulphate.

Brain stimulants such as caffeine and D. ('pep pill' ingredient) 1955.

Dharma (dā·ɹmă). Also **dhamma, dharm, dharmma, dherma, dhurm.** 1796. [Skr., = decree, custom.] In India, social or caste custom; right behaviour; law; *esp.* in Buddhism and Hinduism: moral law, truth.

‖**Diable au corps** (diablokǭr). 1895. [Fr., lit. 'devil in the body'.] Restless or inexhaustible energy; devilment.

Diachronic (dəiăkrǫ·nik), *a.* 1857. [f. Gr. διά DIA- + χρόνος time + -IC.] **1.** *rare.* Lasting through time, or during the existing period. **2.** *Linguistics.* [tr. Fr. *diachronique* (Saussure, *a* 1913).] Pertaining to or designating linguistic study concerned with the historical development of a language; historical, as opposed to descriptive or synchronic. Also *transf.* 1927. Hence **Diachro·nically** *adv.* **Dia·chrony.**

Dial, *sb.* **4. b.** *slang.* A person's face 1811. **6. b.** On a telephone, a circular plate marked with letters, numbers, etc., above which is a disc which can be rotated by means of finger-holes to make connection with another telephone 1879.

Dialectical, *a.* **b. d. materialism,** the theory propagated by Karl Marx and Friedrich Engels according to which political events or social phenomena are to be interpreted as a conflict of social forces (the 'class struggle') produced by economic causes, and history is to be interpreted as a series of contradictions and their solutions (the thesis, antithesis, and synthesis of Hegelian philosophy) 1927.

Dialling, *vbl. sb.*

Comb.: **d. tone,** the sound produced by a telephone indicating that the line is in order and dialling can commence.

Dialogue, *sb.* **1. b.** In *Politics*, a discussion between the representatives of two nations, groups, etc.; hence *gen.*, valuable discussion or communication 1953.

Diaphragm, *sb.* **II. 1. b.** A thin rubber or plastic contraceptive cap which fits over the cervix 1933.

Dicey (dəi·si), *a. slang* (orig. *Air Force*). 1950. [f. DICE *sb.* + -Y¹.] Dangerous; uncertain, unreliable.

Diddums (di·dəmz), *sb.* and *int.* Also **didums.** 1893. [= *did 'em*, i.e. 'did they (tease you, etc.)?', with addition of plural *-s.*] An expression of commiseration, or a meaningless term of address, used to a child or jocularly to an adult.

Didgeridoo (diːdʒĕrĭdū·). Also **didjeridoo, didjeridu,** etc. 1924. [Imitative.] A musical instrument of the Australian Aborigines, consisting of a long hollow tube which is blown into to produce a resonant sound.

Die·-cast, *v.* 1909. [f. DIE *sb.* II. 2 + CAST IX.] *trans.* To make by casting hot metal in a metal mould. So **Die·cast** *ppl. a.* **Die·-casting** *vbl. sb.*, the action of the vb.; *concr.*, a casting produced from a mould.

Dieldrin (dī·ldrin). 1949. [f. the name of O. *Diels* (1876–1954), German chemist + *-drin*, after *ALDRIN.] A crystalline solid, $C_{12}H_8Cl_6O$, chemically a derivative of aldrin, which is light brown in commercial preparations and is used as an insecticide.

Diesel. Also *ellipt.*, a d. engine; a locomotive, motor vehicle, etc., driven by a d. engine (also *attrib.*).

Comb.: **d.-electric** *a.*, driven by electric motors powered by current from a generator, which in turn is driven by a d. engine; also *ellipt.*, a d.-electric engine, locomotive, or vehicle; **d. oil,** a heavy oil used as fuel in d. engines.

Differential. B. *sb.* **3. b.** The difference in wages between one class of workmen and another, or between one industry, etc., and another; a difference in prices of similar products, etc. 1941. **4.** A d. gear, *spec.* of a motor vehicle 1902.

Diffractometer (difrækto̜·mĭtəɹ). 1909. [f. DIFFRACT *v.* + -OMETER.] An instrument for measuring diffraction; esp. one used in diffraction analysis in crystallography.

Dig, *v.* II. 4. b. *slang* (orig. *U.S.*). To understand, appreciate, like; to look at or listen to; to experience. Also *intr.* 1935.

D. out. a. Also *fig.*, to obtain by search or effort.

Dig, *sb.* **1. b.** *colloq.* An archæological excavation 1896.

Digest, *sb.* **1. b.** *spec.* A periodical composed wholly or mainly of condensed versions of articles, stories, etc., previously published elsewhere 1922.

Digger. 2. d. *colloq.* An Australian or New Zealander; freq. as a term of address 1917.

Digital. A. *adj.* **4.** Of, pertaining to, or using digits (DIGIT *sb.* 3); *spec.* applied to a computer which operates on data in the form of digits or similar discrete elements 1938.

‖**Diktat** (di·ktæt). 1933. [– G. *diktat* DICTATE *sb.*] **a.** A severe settlement or decision, esp. a dictated peace; used *spec.* with reference to the Treaty of Versailles of 1919. **b.** A dictate, decree, or command.

Dim. A. 3. b. Of a person: not 'bright' intellectually; somewhat stupid and dull 1892.

Comb.: **d.-wit** *colloq.* (orig. *U.S.*), a stupid or slow-witted person; hence *d.-witted* adj.; *d.-wittedness.*

Diminished, *ppl. a.* **1. b. d. responsibility**, a state of mental disturbance or abnormality recognized in law as a ground for exempting a person from full liability for criminal behaviour 1957.

Dim-out (di·maut). 1942. [f. phr. *to dim out.*] A reduction in the brightness of lighting; *e.g.* in a theatre, the ending of a scene, etc., by a slow diminution of lighting. Also *transf.* and *attrib.*

Ding-dong. B. *sb.* **1. b.** *fig.* Esp. (*a*) a heated argument; (*b*) a tumultuous party or gathering. *colloq.*

Dinkum (di·ŋkŏm). *dial.* and *colloq.* (chiefly *Austral.* and *N.Z.*). Also **dincum.** 1888. [Origin unkn.] **A.** *sb.* **1.** Work, esp. hard work. **2.** The truth 1916. †**3.** An Australian. **B.** *adj.* Honest, genuine, real; as *adv.*, honestly; *d. oil*, the honest truth 1894.

Dinoflagellate (dəinoflæ·dʒĕlēⁱt). 1889. [f. mod.L. *Dinoflagellata* (O. Bütschli, 1885), f. Gr. δῖνος whirling + L. *flagellum* FLAGELLUM + -ATE².] *Biol.* A member of the subclass Dinoflagellata, which includes protistans having two flagella. Also *attrib.* or as *adj.*

Diode (dəi·ōᵘd). 1919. [f. DI-² + ELECTR)ODE.] *Electronics.* **a.** A thermionic valve of the simplest kind, with just two electrodes (cathode and anode). Also *d. valve.* **b.** A simple semiconductor device with two terminals which, like a d. valve, rectifies an alternating current. Also *crystal* or *semiconductor d.*

Dip, *v.* I. **5. b.** To lower (the beams of the headlights of a vehicle) 1922. Also *absol.*

Dip, *sb.* **1. b.** *Pros.* An unstressed element in a line of alliterative verse 1894. (G. *senkung.*) Cf. *LIFT *sb.*² 5.

Comb.: **d.-stick**, a rod for measuring the depth of liquid; **d.-switch**, a switch that dips the beams of a vehicle's headlights.

Diploid. B. *adj.* [– G. *diploid* (E. Strasburger, 1905): see *-PLOID.] *Biol.* Of a cell or its nucleus: having two homologous sets of chromosomes, one from each parent, each containing the haploid number of chromosomes. Of an organism: having d. somatic cells 1908. Also as *sb.*, a d. organism. Hence **Di·ploidy**, d. condition.

A normal plant is known as a d., each cell containing twice the number of chromosomes that are basic to that plant 1970.

Dipole (dəi·pōᵘl). 1912. [f. DI-² + POLE *sb.*²] **1.** A pair of non-coincident equal and opposite electric charges or magnetic poles (usu. close together); something having such charges or poles, esp. a molecule, atomic particle, etc. **2.** *Radio.* An aerial consisting either of two metal rods mounted close together in line or of a single rod, with the electrical connection made to the centre of the aerial and a total length usu. about half the wavelength to be transmitted or received; also *d. aerial* or *antenna* 1929.

1. D. moment, the product of the distance between the two charges or poles and the magnitude of either of them; the electric or magnetic moment of a d.

Direct, *v.* **5. b.** *trans.* and *intr.* To supervise and control the making of a film, play, etc. 1913. **6. c.** To assign (workers) to a particular industry or employment 1943.

Direct, *a.* and *adv.* **A.** *adj.*

Phr. **d. grant**, a grant of money paid directly to a school from public funds; freq. *attrib.*; **d. method**, a method of teaching a foreign language through conversation, reading, etc., in the language itself without using the pupil's native language; **d. voice** *Spiritualism*, speech said to emanate directly from a disembodied spirit without using a medium.

Direction. 1. b. The action or technique of directing a film, play, etc. 1938.

Comb.: **d.-finder**, a receiving device that determines from which direction radio waves come to it.

Directive, *a.* (*sb.*). **4. b.** A general instruction how to proceed or act 1902.

Director. 1. d. One who directs a film, play, etc. orig. *U.S.* 1911.

‖**Dirigisme** (diriʒiz'm). Also **dirigism.** 1951. [Fr., f. *diriger* to direct.] The policy of state direction and control in economic and social matters. Also *transf.*

Dirndl (dɔ̄·ɹnd'l). 1937. [G. dial., dim. of *dirne* girl; cf. G. *dirndlkleid* peasant dress.] A style of woman's dress imitating Alpine peasant costume with bodice and full skirt; also **d. skirt**, a full skirt with a tight waistband.

Dirty, *a.*

Phr. **d. dog** *slang*, a despicable, untrustworthy, or lascivious person; **d. word**, (*a*) a vulgar or 'smutty' word; (*b*) a word made disreputable by what are regarded as its discreditable associations.

Disaffiliate (disăfi·liēⁱt), *v.* 1870. [f. DIS- II. 1. + AFFILIATE *v.*] *trans.* To undo the affiliation of; to detach. Hence **Disaffilia·tion.**

Disco (di·sko). orig. *U.S.* 1964. Colloq. abbrev. of *DISCOTHÈQUE.

Discography (diskǫ·grăfi). 1935. [f. DISC + -OGRAPHY.] A catalogue raisonné of gramophone recordings; also, the study of recordings. Hence **Disco·grapher. Discogra·phical** *a.*

Discothèque, -theque (di·skŏtek). 1954. [– Fr. *discothèque*, after BIBLIOTHÈQUE.] A club, etc., where recorded music is played for dancing.

Discrimination. 1. b. *spec.* The making of distinctions prejudicial to people of a different race or colour from oneself; racial d. 1866.

Dish, *sb.* **2. b.** *transf.* and *fig. spec.* An attractive person, esp. a woman. Now *colloq.* 1599.

Dishy (di·ʃi), *a. slang.* 1961. [f. *DISH *sb.* 2 b + -Y¹.] Very attractive.

Disincentive (disinse·ntiv). 1946. [DIS- 9.] A source of discouragement, esp. to economic progress. Also as *adj.*

Disinfla·tion. 1880. [DIS- 9.] The reversal of inflation; *spec.* of monetary inflation. Hence **Disinfla·tionary** *a.*

Disintegrate, *v.* **1. c.** To cause (a substance or an atom or nucleus) to undergo nuclear disintegration 1920. **2. b.** Of a nucleus or particle, or a radioactive substance: to undergo disintegration (see next); to decay (*DECAY *v.* I. 1 c) 1904.

Disintegration. In *Nuclear Physics*, a process which a nucleus may undergo, spontaneously or under bombardment, in which it emits one or more particles and becomes a nucleus of a different element or isotope, or else splits up into two or more smaller nuclei; also, the decay of a subatomic particle 1903.

The d. of elements by high velocity protons COCKROFT & WALTON.

Disinterested, *ppl. a.* **1.** Delete ?*Obs.* (Often regarded as a loose use.)

Disk, disc. (The latter is now the usual British form.) **2. b.** A device used in **d. parking**, a parking scheme for vehicles whereby the driver must display on his vehicle a d. or card showing the time he arrived or the time he must leave a parking area, or both times.

Comb.: **d.-jockey** orig. *U.S. slang*, a person who introduces gramophone records for broadcasting; hence as *v. intr.*

Displaced (displēⁱ·st), *ppl. a.* 1571. [f. DISPLACE *v.* + -ED¹.] Removed from his or its place; spec. **d. person**, one removed from his home country by military or political pressure 1944.

Disposable, *a.* **3.** Applied to an article designed to be thrown away after use 1943. Hence *absol.* as *sb.*

Dissociated (disōᵘ·ʃi,ĕⁱtėd), *ppl. a.* 1611. [f. DISSOCIATE *v.* + -ED¹.] **a.** Separated or severed. **b.** *Psychol.* Characterized by the disjunction of associated mental connections or the disaggregation of consciousness 1890.

Dissociation. 3. *Psychol.* The process or result of breaking up associations of ideas 1890. **b.** The disintegration of personality 1897.

Distortion. 4. *Electr.* A change in the wave-form of a signal when it is amplified transmitted, etc., usually impairing the quality of reproduction (e.g. of sound by a radio) 1887.

Disto·rtionless *a.*, not producing any d.; not affected by d.

Ditch, *v.* **5. b.** *slang* (orig. *U.S.*). To defeat, frustrate; to discard, jilt 1899. **c.** *trans.* and *intr.* (*slang*). To bring (an aircraft) down into the sea in an emergency 1941.

Divan. 3. b. A low bed or couch with no back or ends; also **d.-bed** 1840.

Dive, *v.* I. **1. b.** *Aeronaut.* To descend precipitously with increasing speed 1908. Also as *sb.*, a precipitate descent 1914. Hence **d.-bomb** *v. trans.*, to attack with bombs at a low level after diving; so **d.-bomber, d.-bombing.**

Diversion. 1. b. An alternative route bypassing a road that is temporarily closed 1955.

Divvy (di·vi). Also **divi.** 1872. Colloq. abbrev. of DIVIDEND. Hence as *v.*, to divide *up.*

Dobermann (dōᵘ·bəɹmæ̆n). 1917. [Name of Ludwig *Dobermann*, 19th-cent. German dog-breeder.] In full *D. Pinscher.* A kind of German hound with a smooth coat and docked tail.

Dock, *v.*² **1. b.** To join (a spacecraft) to another in space; also *intr.*, to become joined. Const. *with.* Freq. **docking** *vbl. sb.* 1960.

Doctor, *sb.* Colloq. phrases. *What the d. ordered*: something beneficial or desirable. *You are* (freq. *you're*) *the doctor*: you are the expert; it is for you to decide.

Doctor, *v.* **2. b.** To castrate (an animal) 1902.

Documentary, *a.* **4.** Factual, realistic; applied esp. to a film, etc., that depicts real happenings. Also *ellipt.* as *sb.* 1930.

Dodecaphonic (dōᵘ·dekăfǫ·nik), *a.* 1950. [f. DODECA- + PHONIC *a.*] *Mus.* Designating or pertaining to a system of music devised by Arnold Schönberg, based on the twelve chromatic notes of the octave arranged in a chosen order, without regard for the conventional key-system. Hence **Dodecaphonism, -onist, -ony.**

Dodgem (dǫ·dʒĕm). Also **Dodge-Em**, and with small initial(s). 1921. [f. DODGE *v.* 4 + 'EM.] Esp. in *pl.*, a fairground amusement consisting of a number of small electrically-powered cars steered about in an enclosure. Also *attrib.*, as *d. car.*

Dodgy, *a.* Also (*colloq.*) of things: difficult, tricky.

Dog, *sb.* **1. e.** *The dogs*: greyhound racing; a greyhound race meeting (*colloq.*) 1927.

Comb. **a. d.-collar**, (*a*) a collar for a dog's neck; (*b*) a close-fitting collar worn by a man or woman; *spec.* a clerical collar; **d.-fight**, (*a*) a fight between dogs; (*b*) a general disturbance or mêlée; *spec.* a 'scrap' between aircraft; **d.-house**, a house or kennel for a dog; slang phr. *in the d.-house*, in disgrace; **d.-paddle** *colloq.*, a stroke, or way of swimming, like a dog's.

b. dog's body, (*b*) *colloq.* a junior person, esp. one to whom menial tasks are given; a drudge.

Do-good (dū·gud). 1654. [f. phr. *to do good.*] One who does good; *spec.* a well-meaning but unrealistic philanthropist or reformer. Also *attrib.* or as *adj.* So **Do-goo·der.**

Do:-it-yourse·lf. 1952. [See Do *v.* 9 and YOURSELF *pron.*] The action or practice of doing work of any kind by oneself, esp. one's own household repairs, etc. Also *transf.* and *fig.* Freq. *attrib.*

‖**Dolce vita** (doltʃe vītă, dǫ:ltʃi vī·tă). 1961. [It., lit. 'sweet life'.] A life of luxury, pleasure, and self-indulgence. (Freq. preceded by *the* or *la.*)

Dollar.

Comb.: **d. area,** the area comprising countries where the American dollar is used as currency or as a basis for exchange; **d. gap,** the excess of a country's (*spec.* Britain's) receipts or imports from the U.S. or other countries in the dollar area over its payments or exports to those countries; **d. spot,** a discoloured patch caused by disease, as on an animal or a lawn; the disease itself.

Dolly, *sb.*[1] **4. e.** orig. *U.S.* A small platform on wheels or rollers used as a conveyance; *spec.* a mobile platform for a film- or television-camera 1901.

Comb.: **d.-bag** = *DOROTHY BAG; **d. mixture,** tiny coloured sweets of various shapes; also *fig.*

Domain, *sb.* **4.** *Physics.* In ferromagnetic materials, a region which behaves as an elementary magnet, all the atoms or ions in the region having their permanent magnetic moment aligned in the same direction 1926.

Domino. 3. c. *fig.* Used, freq. *attrib.*, of a theory that a political event or development in one country, etc., will lead to its occurrence in others; also *transf.* 1954.

By the 'd. theory', once a lead has been given, others may be encouraged 1971.

Donkey.

Comb.: **d. jacket,** a thick jacket worn, orig. by workmen, as a protection against wet, etc.; **d.-work,** the hard or unattractive part of an undertaking.

‖**Donnée** (done). Also **donné.** 1876. [Fr., fem. pa. pple. of *donner* to give.] The subject, theme, or motif of a story, play, etc.; a basic fact, assumption, etc.

Donor. *spec.* = **blood donor*; also, a person or animal, alive or dead, from whom an organ or tissue is removed for surgical transplantation; in artificial insemination, one from whom semen is obtained. **2.** *Chem.* and *Physics.* An atom, molecule, etc., that loses a constituent part to something else; *esp.* (*a*) an atom, etc., that forms a bond with another by sharing a pair of its valency electrons with it; (*b*) in a semiconductor, an impurity atom that has a higher valency than the majority of the atoms and can give up a valency electron to the conduction band of the crystal 1927.

Doodle, *sb.* **2.** An aimless scrawl made by a person while his mind is more or less otherwise applied 1937. So as *v. intr.*; also *fig.*, to idle. Also **Doo·dler. Doo·dling** *vbl. sb.* and *ppl. a.*

Comb.: **d.-bug,** (*a*) *U.S.* a tiger-beetle, or the larva of this or various other insects; (*b*) a German pilotless plane or flying bomb of the war of 1939–45.

Dopa (dōᵘ·pă). 1917. [– G. *dopa* (B. Bloch, 1917), f. the initial letters of the formative elements of *dioxyphenylalanine*, a former name of the compound.] *Chem.* and *Biochem.* 3,4-Dihydroxyphenylalanine, $C_9H_{11}NO_4$, an amino-acid which in man is formed from tyrosine in the nerves and adrenal medulla and gives rise to noradrenaline and tyrosine.

During the past decade a new approach to Parkinsonism has evolved, culminating in the introduction of L-dopa 1970. Hence **Do·pamine,** a compound, $C_8H_{11}NO_2$, formed from d. in the body and found esp. in nervous and peripheral tissue.

Dope, *sb.* **5.** *colloq.* (orig. *dial.*). A stupid person, a fool 1851. Also (*U.S. slang*), a person under the influence of, or addicted to, some drug 1948.

Comb.: **d.-pedlar** (also **-peddler**), **-runner,** a seller of illicit drugs.

Dope, *v.* (See in Dict. after DOPE *sb.*) **b.** *Electr.* To add an impurity to (a semiconductor) to produce a desired electrical characteristic; freq. as **Doped** *ppl. a.*, **Do·ping** *vbl. sb.* 1955. Hence **Dopant** (dōᵘ·pănt) [-ANT], the substance used for this.

Doppler (dǫ·pləɪ). The name of C. J. *Doppler* (1803–1853), Austrian mathematician and physicist, used *attrib.* or in the possessive to designate an effect first explained by him, phenomena related to it or caused by it, and equipment utilizing it 1871.

D. effect, the effect on sound, light, or other waves of relative motion between their source and the observer: the observed frequency is higher (lower) when one is moving toward (away from) the other.

A D. radar unit is used to obtain a running record of the speed of guided missiles 1959.

Dormitory. 1. b. A small town, or a suburb of a large town, containing residences of those who work in the metropolitan area 1923. Freq. *attrib.*

Do·rothy bag. 1907. [f. the female proper name *Dorothy.*] A woman's handbag gathered at the top by a drawstring.

Dose, *sb.* **1. b.** A given quantity of X-rays or other ionizing radiation, esp. considered in relation to a person receiving it; a quantity of ionizing radiation received or absorbed at one time or over a specified period 1912.

Dot, *sb.*[1] **5. e.** *Telegraphy.* (See *DASH *sb.*[1] 6 c.) 1838.

Dotted, *ppl. a.* **1. b.** *D. line,* a line of dots or small dashes; *spec.* (on a document) one to indicate the space left for signature (and therefore acceptance of its terms); hence *to sign on the d. line*: to agree fully or formally.

Double, *a.* (*adv.*).

Comb.: **d.-glazing,** (the fixing of) two layers of glass in a window to reduce the transmission of heat, sound, etc.; **d. helix,** a pair of parallel helices intertwined about a common axis: the postulated structure of the DNA molecule; **d. standard,** a rule or principle applied more strictly to one group of people than to another; **d.-take** orig. *U.S.*, a delayed reaction to a situation, sight of a person, etc., following an earlier inappropriate reaction; **d.-talk** orig. *U.S.*, (*a*) deliberately unintelligible speech; (*b*) ambiguous or deceitful language; **doublethink,** the mental capacity to accept as valid two contrary opinions or beliefs.

C. 1. d.-jointed, having joints that permit abnormal flexibility of parts of the body.

2. a. d.-blind, applied to a test conducted by one person on another in which some information about the test is concealed from both the tester and the subject.

3. d.-park *v. trans.* and *intr.*, to place (a vehicle) parallel to another vehicle parked near the side of the road; so **d.-parking.**

Douglas (dɒ·glăs). 1856. [The name of David *Douglas* (1798–1834), Scottish botanist.] In full *Douglas fir, pine,* or *spruce.* A large coniferous tree, *Pseudotsuga menziesii* or the blue *P. glauca,* native to western North America.

Douroucouli (dūrukū·li). Also **dorou-couli, douracouli, douro(u)coli.** 1842. [– S. Amer. Indian name.] A South or Central American monkey of the genus *Aotus*, characterized by large staring eyes, long non-prehensile tails, and nocturnal habits; = *owl-monkey.*

Dove, *sb.* **2. b.** *Polit.* One who advocates negotiations, reduction of the scale of military operations, etc., as a means of preventing or terminating a military conflict, as opposed to a 'hawk', who advocates a hard-line or warlike policy 1962.

Down, *adv.* Phrase. **d. under** *adv.*, at the antipodes; in Australia, New Zealand, etc. 1899.

Down, *v.* **1.** *To d. tools*: to cease working. Hence *d.-tools* is used attrib. to designate such action. Also *fig.* 1898.

Down-grade, *v.* 1930. [f. the sb.] *trans.* To lower in grade, rank, status, etc. So **Down-grading** *vbl. sb.*

Down's syndrome. 1961. [Named after J. L. H. *Down* (1828–96), English physician.] = *MONGOLISM.

Draft, *sb.* **2.** *spec.* in *U.S.* Conscription. Freq. *attrib.* and *Comb.*

Draft, *v.* **1. a.** *spec.* in *U.S.* To conscript. Hence **Draftee·**, a conscript.

Drag, *v.* **1.** Phr. *To d. one's feet* (orig. U.S.): to delay or hold back deliberately.

Drag, *sb.* **3. d.** *spec.* An annoying or boring person or thing. **e.** *slang.* Feminine attire worn by a man 1870. **6. b.** The force resisting the motion of a body through a gas or liquid 1909.

Drain, *sb.* **1.** Colloq. phr. *To go down the d.*: to disappear, vanish, get lost.

Dramamine (dræ·mămīn). 1949. [Proprietary term.] *Pharm.* An antihistamine compound, taken to prevent nausea.

Dress, *sb.*

Comb.: **d. rehearsal,** a rehearsal of a play in costume, esp. the final rehearsal before the first public performance; also *transf.* and *fig.*

Dressage (dre·sāʒ). 1936. [Fr., lit. 'training', f. *dresser* to train.] The training of a horse in obedience and deportment; the execution by a horse of precise movements in response to its rider. Also *attrib.* and *fig.*

Drinamyl (dri·nămil). 1950. [f. D(EXT)R(O- + *AMPHETAM)IN(E + AMYL[2].] *Pharm.* The proprietary name of a preparation of dexamphetamine and amylobarbitone, used as a stimulant.

Drip, *sb.* **2. b.** *Med.* The continuous slow introduction of fluid into the body (esp. intravenously) involving its passage drop by drop through a chamber; also, the fluid so introduced or a device for this 1933. **3. b.** *slang.* A stupid, feeble, or dull person 1932.

Drip-dry (dri·pdrəi·), *v. intr.* 1953. Of certain synthetic or chemically treated fabrics: to dry when hung up to drip without subsequently requiring ironing; also *trans.*, to dry (a garment) thus. Hence as *adj.* and *sb.* Also *transf.* and *fig.*

Drive-in (drəi·vin), *a.* and *sb.* orig. *U.S.* 1930. [f. DRIVE *v.* I. 4.] (Designating) a restaurant, cinema, etc., into or up to which a customer can drive his car.

Drogue. 3. A cone of fabric open at both ends with a hoop at the larger end, used for various purposes: e.g. (*a*) towed behind an aircraft as a target or a brake; (*b*) as a small parachute in an ejection-seat mechanism or on a spacecraft during re-entry; (*c*) to indicate the direction of the wind 1919.

Drop, *v.* **D. out,** *spec.* to 'opt out' from society.

Drop-out. Also **dropout.** 1882. [f. DROP *v.*] **1.** *Rugby Football.* A drop-kick made from within the defending players' twenty-five-yard line in order to restart play after the ball has gone dead. **2.** *colloq.* (orig. *U.S.*). A person who 'drops out', esp. from a course of study or from society; also, the act of withdrawing 1930. **3.** *Photogr.* (A half-tone negative or positive having) an area from which highlight dots have been eliminated 1948. **4.** (A flaw in recording tape causing) a momentary drop in the amplitude of a recorded signal 1955.

Drosophila (drǫsǫ·filă). 1829. [mod.L. (C. F. Fallén, 1823), f. Gr. δρόσος dew + φίλος loving.] *Ent.* A fruit-fly of the genus so called, much used as an experimental subject in the study of genetics.

Dry, *a.* **3.**

Comb.: **b. d.-clean** *v. trans.* and *intr.*, to clean (clothes, etc.) without using water; also *transf.* **c. d. cell,** a voltaic cell in which the electrolyte is contained in an absorbent material or is in the form of a paste, thus preventing spilling of the contents; **d. run,** (*a*) *U.S.* a dry creek or arroyo; (*b*) *colloq.* (orig. *U.S.*) a rehearsal.

Dual, *a.* **3.**

Phrases. **d. carriageway,** a road with separate carriageways, divided by a central strip, for up and down vehicular traffic; **d. control,** control exercised by two parties or persons jointly; the duplication of an aircraft's or motor vehicle's controls for instructional purposes; freq. *attrib.*, **d.-purpose** *a.*, serving two purposes.

Dub, *v.*[4] 1929. [Shortened form of DOUBLE *v.*] *trans.* To provide an alternative sound track to (a film or television broadcast), esp. a translation from a foreign language; to mix (various sound tracks) into a single track; to transfer (recorded sound) on to a new record.

Dublin (dɒ·blin). The name of the capital of the Republic of Ireland, used *attrib.* in **Dublin (Bay) prawn,** the Norway lobster, *Nephrops norvegicus*; = *SCAMPI.

Dude. 2. Chiefly *U.S.* A visitor to the west of the U.S., esp. one who spends his holidays on a ranch; a tenderfoot 1883. So **d. ranch,** a ranch which provides entertainment for paying guests and tourists.

Duff (dɒf), *a. colloq.* 1889. [f. DUFF *sb.*[2]] Worthless, spurious, bad.

Duffel, duffle. (The more common form is now **duffle.**)

Comb.: **d. bag** orig. *U.S.*, a cylindrical canvas bag; **d. coat,** a coat made of d.; *spec.* a short coat with a hood and fastened at the front with toggles.

Dump, *sb.*[4] **2. b.** *colloq.* (orig. *U.S.*). A place, building, etc.: usu. as a pejorative or contemptuous term 1899.

Dunk (dʌŋk), *v.* orig *U.S.* 1919. [Pennsylvanian G. *dunke* to dip (cf. G. *tunken*).] *trans.* To dip (bread, cake, etc.) into a beverage or other liquid. Also *absol.*, *transf.*, and *fig.*

Dunno (dʌ·no, dŏnōᵘ·), also **dunno(w),** etc., colloq. forms of (*I*) *do not* (or *don't*) *know* 1842.

Duplex (diū·pleks), *sb.* orig. *U.S.* 1922. [f. the adj.] A house or other building so divided that it forms two dwelling-places; also, one of the dwellings. Also *attrib.* or *adj.*

Dust, *sb.*

Comb.: **d.-bowl** orig. *U.S.*, a region subject to drought where the wind has eroded the soil and made the land unproductive; **d.-up** *colloq.*, a fight, disturbance; **d.-wrapper** = *d.-cover.*

Dutch. A. 4. *D. lunch, party, supper, treat* (orig. *U.S.*), one at which each person contributes his or her own share; hence *advb.*, with each person paying for his own share. **D. barn,** a barn consisting of a roof supported on poles; **D. elm disease,** a fungous disease of elms, caused by *Ceratocystis ulmi.*

The D. Elm Disease..was first observed in Holland in September, 1919. *Gardeners' Chronicle* 1927.

Dye-line, dyeline (dəi·ləin). 1951. [f. DYE *sb.* + LINE *sb.*] A method of photographic copying using paper or film impregnated or coated with a diazo compound; also, a print or copy prepared by this process. Freq. *attrib.*

-dyne (dəin), *suffix*, repr. Gr. δύναμις power, used in the formation of scientific (esp. electrical) terms

Dyslexia (disle·ksiă). 1888. [– G. *dyslexie* (R. Berlin, 1883), f. DYS- + Gr. λέξις speaking.] Difficulty in reading as a mental or neurological disorder; *spec.* = *word-blindness.* Hence **Dysle·ctic, -le·xic** *adjs.* and *sbs.*

Dysprosium (disprōᵘ·ziŏm). 1886. [mod. L. (L. de Boisbaudran 1886), f. Gr. δυσπρόσιτος difficult of access + -IUM.] *Chem.* A paramagnetic metallic element of the lanthanide series, present in yttria-rich minerals and forming yellowish-green salts in which it is trivalent. Symbol Dy; atomic number 66.

E.

III. E.C.T., electro-convulsive therapy; E.D.C., European Defence Community; E.D.D., English Dialect Dictionary; E.E.C., European Economic Community (see *common market*, *MARKET *sb.*); E.E.G., electro-encephalogram; E.E.T.S., Early English Text Society; E.F.T.A., European Free Trade Association; E.L.D.O., European Launcher Development Organization; E.N.S.A. (see *ENSA); E.N.T., ear, nose, and throat; E.P., extended-play (record); E.P.N.S., electro-plated nickel silver; E.R., East Riding, Edwardus Rex, Elizabetha Regina; E.S.N., e.s.n., educationally subnormal; E.S.P., extra-sensory perception; E.V.A., extra-vehicular activity (activity outside a spacecraft). See also *E-BOAT.

Each, *a.* **1. c. each way,** a racing term denoting that a horse has been backed for a win and a place 1869.

Eager, *a.*

Comb.: **e. beaver** *colloq.* (orig. *U.S.*), a glutton for work; an over-zealous or officious person. Also *attrib.*

Earful (īᵊ·ɹful). *colloq.* 1917. [f. EAR *sb.*[1] + -FUL 2.] As much (talk) as one's ears can take in at one time; a strong reprimand.

She got one of the hottest earfuls I ever heard L. A. G. STRONG.

Easter.

attrib. **E. egg,** now commonly an imitation egg, esp. one made of chocolate.

Easy. A. *adj.*

Comb.: **e. rider** (*U.S. slang*), (*a*) a sexually satisfying lover; (*b*) a guitar.

Eatery (ī·tĕri). *colloq.* (orig. *U.S.*). 1901. [f. EAT + -ERY.] An eating-house.

‖**Eau.**

E.-de-Nil, a pale green colour supposed to resemble that of the river Nile.

E-boat (ī·bōᵘt). Used, esp. in the war of 1939–45, as an abbrev. for an enemy torpedo-boat 1940.

Echoic (ekōᵘ·ik), *a.* 1880 (J. A. H. Murray). [f. ECHO *sb.* + -IC.] Of the nature of an echo: applied to words that echo the sound which they are intended to denote or symbolize.

E·cho-sounding, *vbl. sb.* 1923. [f. ECHO *sb.* + SOUNDING *vbl. sb.*[2]] The action or process of ascertaining the depth of water or of an object below a ship by measuring the time taken for a transmitted sound signal to be returned as an echo. Hence **Echo-sounder,** a device used for this.

ECHO virus (e·kōᵘ vəi·rŏs). Also **echo-virus.** 1955. [f. the initials of *e*nteric *c*ytopathogenic *h*uman *o*rphan: 'orphan' because when first discovered there was no disease of which they were known to be the cause.] *Med.* Any of a group of enteroviruses which may produce symptoms resembling those of the common cold, mild meningitis, or (rarely) poliomyelitis, but which are sometimes also found in healthy persons.

‖**Echt** (exʸt), *a.* 1916. [G., real, true, genuine.] Authentic, genuine, typical. Also as *adv.*

Those passages in his letters which are *echt*-Coleridge do not belong at all to letter-writing 1956.

Econometric (īkǫnome·trik), *a.* and *sb. pl.* 1933. [f. ECONO(MY + METRIC(AL *a.*[1] 2.] *Econ.* **A.** *adj.* Of, relating to, or characterized by the application of mathematics to economic data or theories. **B.** *sb. pl.* The branch of economics concerned with the application of mathematical techniques to economic data. Hence **Eco:nometri·cian.**

Economic. A. *adj.* **2. b.** *spec.* Utilitarian in practice or use, with reference to the satisfaction of man's material needs, as *e. botany, e. geography, e. zoology* 1861.

Economy. I. 3. b. The cheapest class of air travel.

Comb.: **e.-size,** a size (freq. large) that is said to be economically advantageous to the consumer.

Ecosystem (ī·kosistĕm, e·ko-). 1935. [f. *eco-* as in ECOLOGY + SYSTEM.] *Ecology.* The plants and animals of a particular habitat, together with the environment influenced by their presence.

Ecto-.

E·ctomorph, a person with an innate lean body-build. **Ectoplasm,** (*b*) a viscous substance which is supposed by some to emanate from the body of a spiritualistic medium, and to develop into a human form or face.

Ed., abbrev. of *edited (by), edition, editor.*

Edam (ī·dăm). 1836. In full *Edam cheese*: a cheese originally made at Edam, near Amsterdam, and distinguished by its red rind and spherical shape.

Edaphic (ĭdæ·fik), *a.* 1900. [– G. *edaphisch* (A. F. W. Schimper, 1898), f. Gr. ἔδαφος floor + -IC.] *Ecology.* Pertaining to, produced by, or influenced by the soil.

Edge, *sb.* **2.** *On e.*, (also) in an excited, irritable, or nervous state 1872.

Edgy, *a.* **3.** Having the nerves on edge 1837.

Edh, Eth (eð). Name of the Anglo-Saxon and Old Icelandic letter Đ, ð 1846.

Edit, *v.* **2. d.** To prepare (a film) for the cinema, or (recordings) for broadcasting, etc. 1917.

Editor. 2. b. A person in charge of a particular section of a newspaper 1843. **c.** The literary manager of a publishing house, or head of one of its publishing departments 1915. **d.** One who cuts and edits a film 1917.

Eel-worm. 1890. [f. EEL + WORM *sb.*] A nematode worm, esp. one parasitic on plants.

Eff (ef), *v.* 1943. [Variant of EF, name of the letter F, euphemistically representing FUCK *v.*] Used as a milder alternative to the full word *fuck*, esp. in phr. *e. off.* Hence **E·ffing** *vbl. sb.* and *ppl. a.*

Efficiency. 3. The ratio of useful work performed to the total energy expended or heat taken in. 1855.

attrib. **e. apartment** *N. Amer.*, one with limited facilities for washing and cooking; **e. bar,** a restriction of salary to a maximum figure which may be increased only when satisfactory evidence of efficiency has been produced; **e. expert** *U.S.*, one who examines the efficiency of industrial or commercial organization or production.

Effluent. B. *sb.* **c.** Waste discharged from an industrial works 1930.

Effort. 2. b. Often used somewhat trivially for any kind of achievement, artefact, or result of activity.

Companies who have extensive development efforts under way. The government recognizes the benefits of a broadbased space e. 1967.

Effusive, *a.* **1. b.** *Geol.* Of an igneous rock: having solidified after being poured out on the earth's surface while molten 1888.

Egg, *sb.* **3. b.** *slang.* A bomb, a mine 1917.

Special comb.: **e.-and-spoon race,** a race in which the competitors carry an egg in a spoon; **e.-bread** *U.S.*, bread made of the meal of Indian corn, eggs, etc.; **e.-cosy,** a cover to keep a boiled egg warm; **e.-timer,** a device for timing the cooking of an egg; **e.-tooth,** a tooth-like protuberance in an embryo bird or reptile which is used to crack the egg and is cast off after hatching; **e.-white,** the white of an egg.

E·gg-head, egghead. *colloq.* (orig. *U.S.*). 1952. [f. EGG *sb.* + HEAD *sb.*] An intellectual; a 'highbrow'. Also *attrib.*

Mr. Stevenson..said..'Eggheads of the world, unite–you have nothing to lose but your yolks.' 1954.

Ego. 2. In speech: I, the speaker, esp. in claiming an object, as a response to *quis* 1913. **3.** Self-esteem, egotism, self-importance 1891. **4.** *Psychol.* That part of the mind which is most conscious of self; *spec.* in the work of Freud that part which, acted upon by both the id and the super-ego (ego-ideal), mediates with the environment 1894.

Egocentric (egose·ntrik), *a.* 1900. [f. EGO + CENTRE *sb.*, after *geocentric*, etc.] Centred in the ego, (pop.) self-centred, egoistic.

Eidetic (əide·tik), *a.* 1924. [– G. *eidetisch* (E. R. Jaensch), f. Gr. εἰδητικός, f. εἶδος form.] *Psychol.* Applied to an image that revives an optical impression with hallucinatory clearness, to the faculty of seeing such images, and to a person having this faculty. Also as *sb.*, (*a*) one who sees such images; (*b*) *pl.*, the theory of e. or perceptual images. Hence **Eide·tically** *adv.*, as an e. image.

Eigen- (əi·gən). G. *eigen* OWN, proper, peculiar, characteristic, used in adoptions or partial translations of G. compounds in *Math.* and *Physics*, as *Eigenfrequency, Eigenstate.* **Ei·genvalue,** one of those special values of a parameter in a differential equation for which the equation has a solution.

Einsteinium (əinʃtəi·niŏm, -st-). 1955. [mod.L., f. the name of Albert *Einstein* (1879–1955), German physicist and mathematician + -IUM.] *Chem.* An artificially produced transuranic element, all the isotopes of which are radioactive. Symbol Es; atomic number 99.

Either. B. *Either-or*: indicating a necessary or unavoidable choice between alternatives.

Too much rigid logic of the black-and-white either-or variety 1953.

Ejection. 1. c. *Aeronaut.* The mechanically contrived 'baling out' of a pilot from an aircraft or spacecraft 1945. Also *attrib.*, as **e. seat,** a seat on which this is effected.

Ejector.

2. e. seat = **ejection seat.*

Eka- (ī·kă), *prefix.* 1889. [– Skr. *eka* one.] *Chem.* Used (orig. by Mendeleev) to denote a predicted element that should occupy the next lower position to that so qualified in the same group in the periodic system.

Ekistics (ĭki·stiks). 1959. [f. mod. Gr. ἡ οἰκιστική, f. Gr. οἰκιστικός relating to settlement, f. οἰκίζειν to settle (a colony), f. οἶκος house, dwelling.] A name given by C. A. Doxiadis to the study of human settlements. Hence **Eki·stic** *a.* **Ekisti·cian** (–ʃăn), one who studies or is versed in e.

‖**Élan vital** (elaṅ vītal). 1907. [Fr.: see ÉLAN.] In the philosophy of Henri Bergson (1859–1941), a vital impulse or life force, of which we are aware intuitively; any mysterious vital principle.

Elastomer (ĭlæ·stŏməɹ). 1939. [f. ELAST(IC *a.* + *-omer* as in ISOMER.] Any of various synthetic rubbers or plastics resembling rubber. Hence **Elastome·ric** *a.*

Elective, *a.* and *sb.* **A.** *adj.* **3. b.** orig. *U.S.* Of college or high-school studies:

Subject to the student's choice; optional 1847. **4.** Revived in medical use: optional, not urgent. **B.** *sb.* **2.** *U.S.* An optional subject or course of study in a college or university 1850.

Electra (ĭle·ktră). In ancient Gr. tragedy, name of the daughter of Agamemnon and Clytemnestra responsible for the murder of the latter, used *attrib.* in *E. complex*, a term used by psychoanalysts to denote a daughter's feelings of attraction towards her father and hostility towards her mother 1913.

Electric, *a.*

Comb.: **e. blanket,** a blanket warmed electrically; **e. chair** (see *CHAIR *sb.*¹ 1 b); **e. fence,** a fence, often consisting of a single strand of wire, charged with electricity; **e. guitar,** a guitar in which the sound from the plucked strings is electronically amplified; **e. organ,** (*a*) *Zool.*, in certain fishes, the organ that produces an electric shock; (*b*) *Mus.*, an organ with an electric action.

Electro-.

Ele:ctroca·rdiogram *Med.* [– G. *elektrocardiogramm* (W. Einthoven, 1894)], a record of the variation in electric potential in the body produced by the beating of the heart. **Ele:ctroca·rdiograph,** an instrument for registering electrocardiograms; hence **Ele:ctrocardiogra·phic** *a.*, **-cardio·graphy. Ele:ctrochroma·togram,** a chromatogram produced by **Ele:ctrochromato·graphy** [– Fr. *électrochromatographie* (H. Lecoq, 1944)], chromatography in which the migration of the components of a mixture takes place under the influence of a constant electric field; hence **Ele:ctrochromatogra·phic** *a.* **Ele:ctro-convu·lsive** *a.*, of or involving a convulsive response to electric shock treatment, spec. *electroconvulsive therapy* (abbrev. *E.C.T.*), used in treating mental disease. **Ele:ctro-ence·phalogram** (occas. **Electrence·phalogram**) *Med.* [– G. *elektrenkephalogramm* (H. Berger, 1929)], a record of the electrical activity of the brain; abbrev. *E.E.G.* **Ele:ctro-ence·phalograph,** an instrument for registering an electro-encephalogram; hence **Ele:ctro-encephalo·grapher, -ist, -y** *sbs.*, **Ele:ctro-encephalogra·phic** *a.* **Ele:ctrophoresis** (-fŏrī·sis) [Gr. φόρησις being carried], the migration towards an electrode of particles in a colloidal suspension under the influence of an electric field, esp. as used to separate the constituents in a mixture; hence **Ele:ctrophoretic** *a.*, **-phore·tically** *adv.*

Electron².

Comb.: **e. gun,** a device for producing a narrow beam of electrons; **e. lens,** (a device for producing) an electric and/or magnetic field that acts on a beam of electrons as an ordinary lens does on a beam of light; **e. microscope,** an instrument for producing images of much greater magnification and resolution than is possible with an ordinary microscope by the use of a beam of electrons controlled by a system of e. lenses; **e. multiplier,** a device for increasing the strength of a small current of electrons by utilizing the emission of further electrons when one strikes an electrode at a higher potential than the emitting electrode; **e. optics,** the study of the influence of electric and magnetic fields on a beam of electrons; so *electron-optical* adj.; **e. tube,** a sealed tube, either evacuated or containing gas at low pressure, in which a current of electrons passes between electrodes; **e. volt,** a unit of energy used in connection with atomic and sub-atomic phenomena, equal to the energy acquired by an e. when accelerated through a potential of one volt.

Electronic (ĭlek-, elektrǫ·nik), *a.* 1902. [f. ELECTRON² + -IC.] **1.** Of or pertaining to an electron or electrons. **2.** Of or pertaining to electronics; operated by the methods of electronics; *spec.* (of music) produced by such means, without pipes, strings, etc.; (of an instrument) producing such music 1930. Hence **Electro·nically** *adv.*, by e. means.

Comb.: **e. brain,** pop. term for **e. computer,** a computer operated electronically; **e. flash,** a flash produced by an electrical discharge in a gas-filled tube.

Electronics (ĭlek-, elektrǫ·niks), *sb. pl.* const. as *sing.* 1910. [f. prec.: see -IC 2.] The study and application of phenomena associated with the movement of electrons in such devices as the thermionic valve, cathode-ray tube, and transistor.

Element, *sb.* **I. 4. c.** A length of resistance wire that becomes hot with the passage of current in an electric fire, cooker, etc.; the wire together with its immediate support or container 1906. **5. b.** *Math.* and *Logic.* Any of the entities of which a set is composed; any entity that satisfies the criterion or criteria used to define a set 1901.

Elementary.

6. e. particle *Physics*, any of a number of particles much smaller than an atom and not known to be composed of simpler particles: e.g. the proton, the electron, and the mesons.

Eleven. A. *adj.* **2. b.** *E. o'clock* (U.S. and dial.), *e. hours* (Sc.), a refreshment taken about 11 o'clock 1808. So (orig. dial.) **Ele·vens(es)** 1819.

C. *Comb.*: **e.-plus,** the age at which pupils leave Junior schools; also, an examination then taken before entering one of the various types of Senior school.

Eleventh. Phr. **E. hour,** the hour preceding midnight, as symbolizing the last available opportunity. Also *attrib.*

In response to John's eleventh-hour prayers 1897. An eleventh-hour alteration 1904. The dark eleventh hour Draws on and sees us sold To every evil power We fought against of old KIPLING.

Elsan (e·lsæn). 1939. [appar. f. initials of *E*phraim *L*ouis Jackson, a chemical manufacturer + SAN(ITATION.] The proprietary name for a make of lavatory in which the sludge is disposed of by chemical means.

Eluate (e·liu,ĕt). 1934. [f. L. *eluere* to wash out + *-ATE¹ 1 d.] The solution obtained in elution.

Eluent (e·liu,ĕnt). Also **-ant.** 1941. [f. L. *eluens, -ent-*, pres. pple. of *eluere* to wash out: see -ENT, -ANT.] A fluid used to elute adsorbed material.

Elute, *v.* Revived [after G. *eluieren*] in the sense: to wash (adsorbed matter) away from the substance that has adsorbed it 1934. Hence **Elu·ted** *ppl. a.*

Elution. In later use, the removal of adsorbed matter. (Cf. prec.)

Eluvial, *a.* **2.** *Soil Sci.* Applied to a layer of soil from which material has been removed by eluviation 1928.

Eluviate (ĭliū·viēⁱt), *v.* 1926. [f. ELUVI(UM + -ATE³.] *Soil Sci.* To undergo eluviation. Usu. in pa. pple. or as **elu·viated** *ppl. a.*

Eluviation (ĭliuviēⁱ·ʃən). 1928. [f. prec.: see -ATION.] *Soil Sci.* The lateral or vertical movement of material in solution or suspension through the soil.

Embri·ttle, *v.* 1902. [f. EM- + BRITTLE *a.*] *trans.* To render brittle. Hence **Embri·ttlement,** the process of rendering or becoming brittle.

‖**Éminence grise** (eminaṅs grīz). 1838. [Fr., = grey eminence: see EMINENCE II. 2.] A term orig. applied to Père Joseph (1577–1638), the confidential agent of Cardinal Richelieu; now extended to describe one who wields real though not titular control.

Emitter. b. *Electr.* One of the three regions of a transistor, from which come most of the carriers passing into the base 1948.

Emma (e·mă), used for *m* in telephone communications and oral transliteration of messages in code 1891. Cf. *ACK.

Emment(h)al (e·məntāl). Also **-t(h)aler** (-tālər). 1902. [– G. *Emmentaler* (formerly *-thaler*), f. *Emmental*, a region in Switzerland.] In full *Emmental* (etc.) *cheese*. A Swiss cheese containing numerous holes.

Empathy (e·mpăþi). 1904. [– Gr. ἐμπάθεια affection (f. ἐμ- EM-, in, into + παθ- (see SYMPATHY)), tr. G. *einfühlung* (T. Lipps, 1903).] *Psychol.* and *Æsthetics.* The power of projecting one's personality into (and so fully comprehending) the object of contemplation. Hence **Empathe·tic, Empa·thic** *adjs.*, of, relating to, or involving e.; having e. *to* or *with* something or someone. **Empathe·tically, Empa·thically** *advs.* Also **E·mpathize** *v. trans.* and *intr.*, to treat with, or use, e.

Emperor.

Comb.: **e. penguin,** the largest member of the penguin family, *Aptenodytes forsteri*.

Empire, *sb.* *The E.*: (*c*) the rule of Napoleon Bonaparte as Emperor of the French, 1804–14, or the period of this 1830. *E.* is used attrib. to denote styles of furniture, etc., characteristic of this period 1810.

Empty. B. *sb.* Also, an empty bottle.

Emu. Now the usual spelling of EMEU.

En.

en attendant, in the meantime; **en brosse,** of hair: cut short, giving a bristly effect; **en clair,** in ordinary language (not in cipher); **en face,** facing forward, opposite; **en fête,** in festival array, keeping holiday; **en grand seigneur,** like a lord; **en grande tenue,** in full dress; **en pantoufles,** at ease; **en pointe(s)** *Ballet*, on the extremity of the toe(s); **en poste,** of a diplomat: in an official position; **en revanche,** in return; **en ventre sa mère** [legal Fr.], in the womb, unborn.

Enabling, *ppl. a.*

e. act, (*a*) *U.S.* an act making legal something that is otherwise unlawful 1856; an act of 1906 prescribing the conditions in which a territory may be admitted into the United States; (*b*) *gen.* an enactment empowering a person, corporation, etc., to take certain action.

Let Congress pass an e. act for that Territory 1873.

Enantiodromia (enæ:nti,odrōᵘ·mia). 1917. [– Gr. ἐναντιοδρομία running in contrary ways, f. ἐναντίος opposite + δρόμος running.] The process by which something becomes its opposite, and the subsequent interaction of the two: applied esp. to the adoption by an individual or by a community, etc., of a set of beliefs, etc., opposite to those held at an earlier stage.

Enantiomorph (enæ·nti,omǫɹf). 1885. [– G. *enantiomorph* (C. F. Naumann, 1856), f. Gr. ἐναντίος opposite + μορφή form.] Chiefly *Cryst.* and *Chem.* A form which is related to another as an object is to its image in a mirror; a mirror image. Hence **Enantiomo·rphic, -ous** *adjs.* **Enantiomo·rphism, -mo·rphy,** the condition or property of being enantiomorphous.

Encode (enkōᵘ·d), *v.* 1919. [EN-¹ + CODE *sb.*] *trans.* To translate into cipher or code. Hence **Enco·ding** *vbl. sb.* Also **Enco·der,** someone or something that encodes.

End, *sb.*

Comb.: **e. game,** the last phase of a game at Chess, Bridge, etc.

Endo-.

Endomorph, (*b*) a person with an innate soft round body-build. **Endothe·rmic** *a.* *Chem.* [– Fr. *endothermique* (M. Berthelot, 1879)], attended with the absorption of heat; (of a compound) absorbing heat on formation.

Endorse, *v.* **1. b.** To make an entry of an offence on (a licence, e.g. of a publican or motorist) 1902.

Endowment.

e. assurance, insurance, life insurance by which an e. or fixed sum is paid to the insured person at a specified date, or to his representatives on his death, if that occurs before.

Engaged, *ppl. a.* **3.** *Telephony.* Of a number or line: in use; of a person: telephoning. Hence *e. signal, -test, -tone* 1891.

‖**Enosis** (enōᵘ·sis, e·nŏsis). 1948. [mod.Gr. ἕνωσις, f. εἰς, ἐν- one.] The (proposed) union of Cyprus with Greece.

Enrich, *v.* **5. b.** To increase the proportion of some substance in (a mixture) 1921.

enriched uranium: uranium in which the proportion of the fissile isotope uranium 235 has been increased.

Ensa (e·nsă). Also **E.N.S.A., ENSA.** 1939. [f. the initials of *E*ntertainments *N*ational *S*ervice *A*ssociation.] An organization established in 1939 to arrange entertainments for the services during the war of 1939–45.

Entanglement. 3. *Mil.* An extensive barrier arranged so as to obstruct an enemy's movements; an abatis formed of trees and branches or an obstruction consisting of stakes and barbed wire 1834.

Enterovirus (e·ntĕro,vaiᵊ:rŏs). 1957. [f. ENTERO- + VIRUS.] *Med.* Any of a group of RNA viruses which primarily infect the lymphoid tissue of the alimentary tract but may also affect the nervous system or other tissue.

‖**Entrecôte** (aṅtrəkōt). 1841. [Fr., 'between-rib'.] A boned steak cut off the sirloin.

Entrepreneurial (ăntrʼpreniūᵊ·riăl), *a.* 1922. [f. ENTREPRENEUR + -IAL.] Of or pertaining to an entrepreneur or entrepreneurs.

Entropy. 2. *Communication theory.* A logarithmic function of the probabilities of occurrence of the symbols from which a message or language is composed, representing the average amount of information carried by each symbol 1948.

Envi:ronme·ntal, *a.* 1887. [f. ENVIRONMENT + -AL¹.] Of or pertaining to environments or the environment. Hence **Environme·ntally** *adv.*, with reference to or by means of (one's or the) environment.

Pesticides, which..constitute such an important contribution to e. pollution 1967.

Environme·ntalist. 1916. [f. prec. + -IST.] One who believes that environment is the primary influence on the development of a person or community; *spec.* a Lamarckian; also, one who is concerned with the preservation of the environment (e.g. from pollution). Also *attrib.* or as *adj.* So **Environme·ntalism,** the e. theory. **Envi:ronmentali·stic** *a.*

The age-long dispute between the hereditarians and the environmentalists 1940. The project to build a supersonic transport has run into renewed complaints from the environmentalists 1970.

Envision (envi·ʒən), *v.* 1921. [f. EN-¹ + VISION *sb.*] *trans.* To see or foresee as in a vision; to envisage; to visualize.

E.O.K.A., EOKA, Eoka (ēˈōᵘ·kă). 1955. [f. the initials of mod.Gr. Ἐθνική Ὀργάνωσις Κυπριακοῦ Ἀγῶνος National Organization of Cypriot Struggle.] The name of a Greek-Cypriot movement seeking union of Cyprus with Greece.

Eolith (ī·oliþ). 1895. [f. EO- + -LITH, after *neolith.*] *Archæol.* The name given to certain flints which have been claimed to be the earliest traces of human handiwork, but whose origin is much disputed.

Eolithic (ī,oli·þik), *a.* 1890. [– Fr. *éolithique* (de Mortillet, 1883), f. EO- after *neolithic, palæolithic.*] *Archæol.* Of, pertaining to, or designating the earliest age of man that is represented by the use of worked flint implements. Also *absol.*

‖**Épée** (*epe*). 1889. [Fr., 'sword'.] The sharp-pointed sword used in duelling and (blunted) in fencing.

Ephedrine (e·fĕdrin). Also **-in.** 1889. [f. *Ephedra*, name of a genus of shrubs (f. Gr. ἐφέδρα sitting upon) + -INE⁵.] *Pharm.* An alkaloid, $C_{10}H_{15}NO$, which occurs in certain species of *Ephedra* and is made synthetically, and which resembles adrenaline in its effects on the body.

E. has been used successfully in the treatment of..hay fever and other allergic conditions 1967.

Epinephrine (epine·frin). Also **-in.** 1899. [f. EPI- + Gr. νεφρός kidney + -INE⁵.] *Pharm.* = ADRENALIN.

Adrenaline..is called e. in the United States Pharmacopoeia 1963.

Epistemic (episte·mik, -ī·mik), *a.* 1922. [f. Gr. ἐπιστήμη knowledge + -IC.] *Philos.* Of or relating to knowledge or degree of acceptance. Hence **Episte·mically** *adv.*

The Experience Philosophy arranges judgements in an 'epistemic order' K. BRITTON.

Epitaxy (epitæ·ksi, e·pitæksi). Also in mod.L. form **epitaxis.** 1931. [– Fr. *épitaxie* (L. Royer, 1928), f. Gr. ἐπί upon + τάξις arrangement: see -Y³.] The growth of crystals on a crystalline substrate that determines their orientation; the orientation of crystals so grown. Hence **Epita·xial** *a.*, grown by, characterized by, or resulting from e. **Epita·xially** *adv.*

Epoxide (ĭpǫ·ksəid). 1930. [f. EPI- + OXIDE.] *Chem.* A compound with a molecular structure containing an oxygen atom and two carbon atoms linked together in a ring.

e. resin = *epoxy resin.

Epoxy (ĭpǫ·ksi), *prefix* and quasi-*adj.* 1916. [f. EPI- + OXY-.] **A.** *prefix.* A formative element in the names of epoxides, as *epoxyethane.* **B.** As quasi-*adj.* Pertaining to or derived from an epoxide; containing the ring structure characteristic of an epoxide.

e. resin, any of various chemically resistant synthetic resins which are made by polymerizing an epoxide with a phenol derivative, are converted into a thermosetting form by the addition of a hardening agent, and have good adhesive and insulating properties.

Epsilon (epsəi·lǫn). ME. [Gr. ἒ ψιλόν, lit. 'bare e', i.e. 'e and nothing else'.] Name of the fifth letter (E, ε) of the Greek alphabet. Used in *Astr.* to denote the fifth brightest star in a constellation.

Equiprobable (īkwi,prǫ·băb'l), *a.* 1921. [f. EQUI- + PROBABLE *a.*] *Logic.* Equally probable. Hence **Equiprobabi·lity,** the characteristic of being equally probable.

Erase, *v.* **1. b.** *trans.* To remove recorded signals from a magnetic medium, esp. magnetic tape: used with the medium or the signals as obj. 1945. Hence **Era·se** *sb.*, the action of erasing tape; usu. *attrib.*

Comb.: **e. head,** the head on a tape recorder used to erase tape.

Ergative (ə̄·ɹgătiv) *a.* 1943. [f. Gr. ἐργάτης workman + -IVE.] *Gram.* In full *ergative case.* A term used of languages such as Eskimo, Basque, and some others, where the subject noun of an intransitive verb and the object noun of a transitive verb have the same case, to designate this case.

Ergonomics (əɹgǒnǫ·miks). 1950. [f. Gr. ἔργον work, after *economics.*] The scientific study of the efficiency of man in his working environment. Hence **Ergono·mic** *a.*, of or pertaining to ergonomics. **Ergono·mically** *adv.* Also **Ergo·nomist,** one who is skilled in e.

Erigeron. Restrict † to sense in Dict. and add: **2.** (Linnæus, 1737). A hardy herbaceous plant bearing daisy-like flowers and belonging to the large genus so called, of the family Compositæ 1815.

Ernie (ə̄·ɹni). 1956. [f. *e*lectronic *r*andom *n*umber *i*ndicator *e*quipment.] Name given to the device for drawing the prize-winning numbers of premium bonds.

Eros. 1. b. *spec.* In Freudian Psychology: the urge towards self-preservation and sexual pleasure 1922.

Erotica (erǫ·tikă). 1854. [– Gr. ἐρωτικά neut. pl. of ἐρωτικός amatory.] Matters of love; erotic literature or art.

Erotogenic (ėrōᵘtodʒe·nik), *a.* 1909. [f. Gr. ἔρως, ἐρωτ- love + *-GENIC.] Producing sexual pleasure.

Ersatz (ə̄·ɹzæts, ‖ę·rzats). 1875. [G., 'compensation, replacement'.] A substitute or imitation, usu. inferior to the real article. Also *attrib.* or as *adj.*

Mr. Shaw and Mr. Wells are also much occupied with religion and *E.-religion* T. S. ELIOT.

Eryngium (ĭri·ndʒiŏm). 1548. [mod.L., f. L. *eryngion*, – Gr. ἠρύγγιον: see ERYNGO.] A hardy herbaceous perennial plant of the genus so called, belonging to the family Umbelliferæ, and bearing blue or white thistle-like flowers; SEA-HOLLY.

Escalate (e·skălēˈt), *v.* 1922. [Back-formation f. ESCALATOR.] **1. a.** *trans.* To climb or reach by means of an escalator. **b.** *intr.* To travel on an escalator. **2.** *fig.* (*trans.* and *intr.*) To increase or develop by successive stages; *spec.* to develop from 'conventional' warfare into nuclear warfare 1959. Hence **Escala·tion** (used only in sense 2 of the vb.).

Escalope (e·skălōᵘp). 1828. [Cf. Fr. *escalope* (XIX): see ESCALLOP.] Thin slices of boneless meat (occas. of fish) prepared in various ways; *esp.* a special cut of veal taken from the leg.

Escape, *sb.*¹ **1. b.** *fig.* Mental or emotional distraction from the realities of life 1853. Hence **Esca·pism,** the tendency to seek or practice of seeking such distraction.

Comb.: **e. clause,** a clause that allows avoidance of some condition; **e. hatch,** an emergency exit in a ship, submarine, or aircraft; **e. velocity,** a speed sufficient to overcome the gravitational force of a planet.

Escapee (eskēˈpī·). 1875. [f. ESCAPE *v.* + -EE, after Fr. *échappé*, subst. use of pa. pple. of *échapper.*] One who has escaped, e.g. from captivity or confinement; an escaped military or political prisoner.

Escapist (eskēˈ·pist). 1930. [f. ESCAPE *sb.*¹ + -IST.] One who escapes, or tries to escape, from captivity; also *fig.*, esp. one who seeks distraction from reality or from routine activities. Also *attrib.* or as *adj.*

Escapologist (eskēˈpǫ·lŏdʒist, eskăp-). 1926. [f. ESCAP(E *sb.*¹ + -OLOGIST.] A performer trained to extricate himself from knots, handcuffs, confinement in a box, etc. So **Escapo·logy,** the methods and technique of escaping from captivity or danger; the calling of an e.

‖**Escargot** (ęskargo). 1892. [Fr.] *Cookery.* An edible snail.

Escudo (eskiū·do). 1821. [Sp., Pg. :– L. *scutum* shield; cf. ECU.] A Spanish and Portuguese silver coin; a Portuguese monetary unit.

Eskimo (e·skimo). pl. **-os.** 1584. [– Da. *Eskimo*, – Fr. *Esquimaux* pl., corruption of an Amer. Indian word meaning 'eaters of raw flesh'.] **1.** A member of a N. American Indian race inhabiting the Arctic from Greenland to Alaska. **2.** The language of this people 1819. **3.** An E. dog, a 'husky' 1856.

Comb.: **E. dog,** a large, powerful dog used in the Arctic to draw sledges and for hunting; **E. pie** (chiefly *U.S.*), a chocolate-coated bar of ice cream; **E. roll,** in Canoeing, a complete roll-over under the water.

Espresso (espre·so). Also **expresso.** 1945. [It. *caffè espresso*, lit. 'pressed-out coffee'.] Coffee made under steam pressure; the apparatus for making it; a coffee-bar where it is sold.

Esraj (esrā·dʒ). 1921. [Bengali.] An Indian musical instrument with three or four strings, played with a bow, and extra sympathetic strings.

Essence, *sb.* **11.** *Of the e.* (*of*) (cf. Fr. *de l'essence de*): indispensable (to).

Stipulations as to time [not] deemed to be..of the e. of such contracts 1873.

Establishment. II. 2. b. esp. as *The Establishment*: a social group exercising power generally, or within a given field or institution, by virtue of its traditional superiority, and by the use esp. of tacit understandings and often a common mode of speech, and having as a general interest the maintenance of the *status quo.*

By the 'Establishment' I do not mean only the centres of official power—though they are certainly part of it—but rather the whole matrix of official and social relations within which power is exercised H. FAIRLIE.

Estate. 11. b. A housing estate.

Comb.: **e. agent,** a steward or manager of a landed estate; one who conducts business in the sale of houses and land; **e. car,** a light saloon motor vehicle specially constructed or adapted to carry both passengers and goods; **e. duty,** a graduated charge levied by the state on real or personal property at the death of the owner.

Estrogen, U.S. var. *ŒSTROGEN.

Eternity.

attrib. **e. ring,** a finger ring which has a continuous setting of stones.

Ethical, *a.* **4.** *Med.* Of a medicine or drug: advertised only in the professional press, and often available only on prescription 1935.

Ethno- (e·þno), comb. form of Gr. ἔθνο-ς nation. **Ethnobo·tany,** the traditional knowledge and customs of a people concerning plants; the scientific study of such knowledge; hence **E:thnobota·nical** *a.*, **-bo·tanist. Ethnohi·story,** the study of the history of races or cultures; hence **E:thnohisto·rian, -histo·rical** *a.* **E:thnomusico·logy,** the scientific or comparative study of the music of a culture, considered either as a pattern of sounds or as an aspect of socio-cultural behaviour; hence **E:thnomusicolo·gical** *a.*, **-musico·logist.**

Ethology. 4. That branch of Natural History which deals with the actions and habits of animals, and their reaction to their environment; esp. the study of instinctive animal behaviour 1897.

‖**Étude** (*etüd*). 1837. [Fr., 'study'.] A short musical composition, often used as a beginner's exercise.

Eucalypt (yū·kălipt). *Austral.* and *N.Z.* 1877. [shortened f. EUCALYPTUS.] = EUCALYPTUS.

Eunuchoid (yū·nŏkoid), *a.* 1906. [f. EUNUCH + -OID.] Resembling or characteristic of a eunuch. Also as *sb.*, a e. person.

Euphoric (yufǫ·rik), *a.* 1888. [f. next + -IC.] Of or characterized by euphoria; cheerful; also, producing euphoria. Hence **Eupho·rically** *adv.*, cheerfully.

Euphory. (The mod.L. form **Euphoria** (yufō·riă) is now usual.) Esp. (in non-technical use always), an exaggerated sense of well-being; a state of cheerfulness based on over-optimism or over-confidence.

Euro. Now the normal sp. of UROO.

Euro- (yūᵊro), comb. form of *Europe*, in **Euro-African, Euro-American, Euro-Asiatic** *adjs.* **Eurocrat** [-CRAT], a member of the administrative staff of a European organization, esp. the E.E.C. **Euro-dollar,** a U.S. dollar deposited outside the U.S.A. **Eurovision** [after TELEVISION], the co-operative organization of European television stations.

Europium (yūᵊrōᵘ·pið̆m). 1901. [mod.L. (E. Demarçay, 1901), f. *Europe* + -IUM.] *Chem.* A soft metallic element of the lanthanide series that forms salts in which it is bivalent or trivalent. Symbol Eu; atomic number 63.

Eutherian (yuþīᵊ·riăn), *sb.* and *a.* 1880. [f. mod.L. *Eutheria* (T. N. Gill, 1872), f. Gr. εὐ- EU- + θηρία beasts.] **A.** *sb.* A member of the Eutheria, an infraclass which includes the placental mammals. **B.** *adj.* Of or pertaining to this group.

Eutrophic, *a.* **2.** Of a lake: (over-)rich in nutrients and having as a result an excessive growth of algæ and other plants, with depletion of oxygen in the lower layers and consequently a reduction in the animal life 1931. Hence **Eutrophica·tion,** the process of becoming e.

Eutrophy. 2. The state (of a lake) of being eutrophic 1947.

Evacuate, *v.* **7. b.** To remove (inhabitants of an area liable to aerial bombing or other hazards) *to* safer surroundings 1938. So [after Fr. *évacué*] **Evacuee·,** a person so evacuated.

Ever, *adv.* After a superl. used ellipt. for 'that ever was', or the like, e.g. *the biggest e.* (orig. *U.S.*) 1906.

Everest (e·vərest). 1929. [The name of the highest mountain in the world, on the frontier of Nepal and Tibet, f. the name of Sir George *Everest* (1790–1866), Surveyor-General of India.] Used *transf.* to designate the greatest conceivable achievement. Also *attrib.*

Every man has to face his E. some time during his life DUKE OF EDINBURGH.

Everyman (e·v'rimæn). [EVERY *a.*, MAN *sb.*; the name of the leading character in a 15th-c. morality play.] The typical man or ordinary human being, common humanity.

Évolué (evolüe), *sb.* 1953. [Fr., pa. pple. of *évoluer* to evolve.] An African (from a part of Africa formerly Belgian or French) who has been educated on European principles; an African who has adopted European modes of thought. Hence as *adj.*, Europeanized.

Excite, *v.* **6.** *Physics.* To cause (a substance) to emit a characteristic spectrum of radiation; to bring about the emission of (a spectrum) 1913. Hence, to raise (an atom, nucleus, etc.) into a state of higher energy 1921. Freq. as **Exci·ted** *ppl. a.*

Exclave (e·ksklēⁱv). 1888. [f. EX-¹ + EN)-CLAVE *sb.*] A portion of territory separated from the country to which it politically belongs and entirely surrounded by alien dominions; an *enclave* from another viewpoint.

Exclusion.

Comb.: **e. principle** *Physics*, the hypothesis that no two particles of the same kind can exist in states designated by the same quantum number, found to be true for the particles known as fermions.

Exclusive. B. *sb.* **3.** An article, news-item, etc., contributed exclusively to, or published exclusively by, a particular newspaper or periodical 1901.

Ex-dire·ctory, *a.* 1936. [f. EX *prep.* + DIRECTORY *sb.*] Denoting a telephone-number that is not listed in the telephone-directory; also, of a person who has such a telephone-number.

Executive. B. *sb.* **3.** orig. *U.S.* A person holding an e. position in a business organization; a business man 1902.

‖**Exemplum** (egze·mplŏm). Pl. **exempla.** 1890. [L. (see EXAMPLE *sb.*).] An example; *spec.* a moralizing tale or parable; an illustrative story.

‖**Ex gratia** (eks grēⁱ·ʃiă), *adj.* and *adv. phr.* 1769. [L., 'from favour'.] (Done or given) as a favour; *spec.* implying the absence of any legal compulsion.

‖**Ex hypothesi** (eks həipǫ·þisəi), *advb. phr.* 1603. [mod.L.] From or according to the hypothesis; as a result of the assumptions made; supposedly, hypothetically.

Existential, *a.* **3.** *Philos.* Concerned with or relating to existence, esp. human existence as seen from the point of view of existentialism 1937.

Existentialism (egziste·nʃăliz'm). 1941. [– G. *existentialismus* (1919): see EXISTENTIAL, -ISM.] *Philos.* A doctrine that concentrates on the existence of the individual, who, being free and responsible, is held to be what he makes himself by the self-development of his essence through acts of the will (which, in the Christian form of the theory, leads to God). Hence **Existe·ntialist;** also *attrib.*

Exo-.

Exobio·logy, the study of life, or the possibilities of life, on other planets; so **Exobio·logist. Exodo·ntia,** the extraction of teeth; so **Exodo·ntist. E·xosphere,** the outermost layer of the atmosphere, lying beyond the ionosphere. **Exothe·rmal, -ic** *adjs. Chem.* [– Fr. *exothermique* (M. Berthelot, 1879)], attended with the liberation of heat; (of a compound) liberating heat on its formation; so **Exothe·rmally, -the·rmically** *advs.*

Exotic. A. *adj.* **2.** Also, having the attraction of the strange or foreign, glamorous. **c.** orig. *U.S.* Applied to various high-energy fuels, esp. non-hydrocarbon ones, developed orig. for rocket engines; also to certain metals not previously used to a significant extent in technology 1957.

Expanded, *ppl. a.*

e. metal, sheet metal slit and stretched into a lattice, to form screens and to reinforce concrete.

Expectant. A. *adj.* **1.** *E. mother*, a pregnant woman; so (in *joc.* use) *e. father.*

Expellee (ekspelī·). 1947. [f. EXPEL + -EE¹.] One who has been expelled, esp. from his country.

The Trades Union Congress..agreed..that 500,000 D.P.'s and expellees in Germany might be admitted 1947.

Expe·ndable, *a.* Also **expendible.** 1805. [f. EXPEND *v.* + -ABLE.] That may be expended; liable to be wasted, i.e. killed or lost, and so deliberately sacrificed, as in a military operation. Also as *sb.*

In a war anything can be e.—money or gasoline or equipment or most usually men 1942.

Explosion. 4. b. A sudden marked increase or development; esp. *population* c. 1953.

Expo (e·kspo). 1963. [Abbrev. of EXPOSITION.] A large international exhibition; *spec.* the world fair held at Montreal in 1967.

Extended, *ppl. a.* **3. b.** Of a family, etc.: that comprises not only parents and children but also consanguine and conjugal relatives living in proximity 1942.

Extra. C. *sb.* **b.** A person temporarily engaged for a minor part, or to be present during a crowd scene, in a film or play 1777–8. **c.** At a ball, a dance additional to those on the dance-programme 1885.

Extra-.

Extra-curri·cular, outside the normal curriculum. **Extra-ma·rital,** of sexual relationships outside marriage. **Extra-pe·rsonal,** situated or coming from outside a person. **Extra-se·nsory,** (of perception) made by other means than those of the known sense-organs. **Extraso·lar,** outside the solar system. **Extra-vehi·cular,** outside a vehicle; *spec.* denoting activity outside a space-vehicle while it is in flight.

Extramural, *a.* In *Education*, applied to institutions or teaching organized by a university or college for persons other than its resident students 1884.

Extrapolate (ekstræ·pŏlēⁱt), *v.* 1831. [f. EXTRA- + -*polate* of INTERPOLATE *v.*, or as back-formation from EXTRAPOLATION.] †**1.** To remove (a passage) from written matter GLADSTONE (*nonce-use*). **2.** *Math.* To estimate the values of (a function or series) by extrapolation; to extend (a graph) on the basis of points already plotted; freq. *absol.* 1874. Also *intr.* (const. *to*), to reach (a specified value) when extrapolated. **b.** *transf.* To apply (a theory, etc.) to unknown situations on the basis of its relevance to known situations; to infer (conclusions) from observed tendencies; also *absol.* or *intr.* 1905. Hence **Extra·polated** *ppl. a.*

Extraversion. 2. *Psychol.* = *EXTROVERSION 2 1915. So **E·xtravert** *sb.* = EXTROVERT *sb.* **E·xtraverted** *ppl. a.*

Extroversion. 2. *Psychol.* The fact of having, or the tendency to have, one's interests directed exclusively or predominantly towards things outside the self 1920. So **E·xtroverted** *ppl. a.*

Extrude, *v.* **b.** To shape (metal or plastic) by forcing through a die 1913.

Eye, *sb.*¹ **I. 3. d.** *Eyes and no eyes*: used to express the difference between an observant and an unobservant person; so, said of or to one who fails to observe 1795.

Comb.: **e.-bath,** a small vessel for applying lotion, etc., to the eye; **e. rhyme** *Pros.*, a rhyme that is not phonetically exact but makes an appeal to the eye only; **e.-shadow,** a cosmetic for the eyes; **e.-strain,** a strained condition resulting from excessive or improper use of the eyes.

Eyra (əi·ră). 1860. [– Tupi *eirara, irara.*] In full *eyra cat.* A South and Central American wild cat, *Felis yagouaroundi*, in its red phase.

F.

II. 3. F_1, F_2: see **Filial generation.*

III. 8. F.A., Football Association; also = *FANNY ADAMS 2; F.B.I., Federal Bureau of Investigation (*U.S.*); F.C., football club; F.M., f.m., frequency modulation; F.O., Foreign Office.

Fab, colloq. abbrev. of *FABULOUS *a.* 4 b 1961.

Fabergé (fabẹ̄rʒe). 1930. The name of Peter Carl *Fabergé* (1846–1920), a Russian jeweller famed for his small, intricate ornaments, used *attrib.* to designate pieces of his workmanship. Also *transf.* and *fig.*

Fabricate, *v.* **1. b.** To form (a manufacturing material) into the shape required for a finished product; also with the product as obj. 1926.

The rotor blades are fabricated from aluminium alloy sheet 1971.

Fabrication. 1. b. The process of fabricating in the manufacture of finished products (see prec.) 1926.

Fabulous, *a.* **4. b.** Now freq. in trivial use, esp. = 'marvellous', 'terrific' 1959.

Face, *sb.*

Comb.: **2. f.-ache,** (*b*) *slang*, a mournful-looking person; **f.-cloth,** (*b*) a woollen cloth with a smooth napped surface; (*c*) a cloth for washing the f.; **f.-fungus** *colloq.*, hair on a man's face, esp. a beard; **faceless** *a.*, without a f.; anonymous, characterless; **f.-lift,** the operation of *f.-lifting*, in which facial wrinkles are smoothed out; also *transf.* and *fig.*; **f.-man, -worker,** a miner who works at the f.

Facia. 2. The instrument panel of a motor vehicle 1924.

Facial, *a.* **2.** *sb.* orig. *U.S.* Beauty treatment for the face 1914.

‖**Facile princeps** (fæ·silí pri·nseps), *phr.* and *sb.* 1834. [L.] (One who is) easily first; the acknowledged leader or chief.

‖**Façon de parler** (fasoṅdəparle). 1804. [Fr.] A manner of speaking; a mere phrase or formula.

Facsimile. 2. *spec.* (Matter reproduced by) a radio, telegraphic, or other system that scans written, printed, or photographic material and transmits signals used to produce a likeness of the original 1815.

Fact. 3. b. *F. of life*: a (stark) reality of existence; freq. *the facts of life*, spec. as a colloq. euphemism for 'knowledge of human sexual functions' 1854.

Comb.: **f.-finding** *ppl. a.* and *vbl. sb.*, (involved in) the finding out of facts.

Factor. 9. *F. of safety*: the ratio between the load which a structure or material is capable of supporting and the load which it is required to support, or between the stress which causes it to break and the stress which it is required to stand 1858.

Factorization (fæ:ktŏrəizē¹·ʃən). 1886. [f. FACTORIZE *v.* + -ATION.] *Math.* Resolution of a quantity into factors; the product of factors so obtained.

Factory.
Comb.: **f. farm** orig. *U.S.*, a farm organized on industrial lines; **f. ship,** the base ship of a whaling fleet.

Fade, *v.* **2. b.** Of the brakes of a motor vehicle: to lose efficiency 1940. Hence as *sb.*

‖**Fado** (fā·du). 1902. [Pg., lit. 'fate'.] A Portuguese folk-song of melancholy type; also, any of various kinds of dance (music) and song popular in Portugal.

Faff (fæf), *v. dial.* and *colloq.* 1874. [Cf. FAFFLE *v.*] *intr.* To fuss, to dither. Often with *about*. Also as *sb.*, fuss, 'flap'.

Fag (fæg), *sb.*⁴ *slang* (orig. *U.S.*). 1923. = *FAGGOT *sb.* 5 b.

Faggot, fagot, *sb.* **4. b.** Usu. *pl.* A rissole of chopped liver, lights, etc. 1851. **5. b.** *slang* (orig. *U.S.*). A (male) homosexual 1914.

Fagin (fē¹·gin). 1847. The name of a character in Dickens's 'Oliver Twist', a receiver who trained children to be thieves and pickpockets; allus. used for a thief, a trainer of thieves, or a receiver.

Fail, *v.* **I. 4. b.** *To fail safe*: of a mechanical or electrical device, etc., to revert, in the event of failure or breakdown, to a condition involving no danger. Also **f.-safe** *a.* 1948. **III. 4.** *trans.* To be unsuccessful in (an examination) 1906.

Fairy. A. 6. *slang.* A male homosexual 1895.
Comb.: **f.-cycle,** a small bicycle for children; **f. godmother,** a fairy who acts as godmother or protector to a mortal child; also *transf.*, a benefactress; **f. story** = FAIRY-TALE.

‖**Faites vos jeux** (fẹ̄tvoʒö), *int.* 1867. [Fr.] Place your bets (an instruction given by croupiers at roulette).

Fake, *sb.*² **3.** *attrib.* or as *adj.* Spurious, counterfeit 1775.

Fall, *sb.*¹
Comb.: **f. guy** *slang* (orig. *U.S.*), an easy victim; a scapegoat.

Fa·ll-out. 1950. [f. phr. *to fall out.*] Radioactive refuse of a nuclear bomb explosion. Also *transf.* and *fig.*

Familial (fămi·liăl), *a.* 1900. [– Fr. *familial*, f. L. *familia* family + -AL¹.] Of, occurring in, or characteristic of (members of) a family.

Family, *sb.* **6. b.** In *Bot.*, as in *Zool.*, 'f.' is now used for a division of an order, superseding the term 'natural order'.
Comb.: **f. allowance,** an allowance paid by the state (or by an employer) to parents who have a specified number of children; **f. doctor,** a general practitioner; **f. planning,** birth control.

Fan, *sb.*¹
Comb.: **f. dance,** a solo dance in which the performer uses a fan or fans; **f. heater,** a heater containing an electric fan that forces air over an electrically-heated element into a room, etc.

Fan, *sb.*²
Comb.: **f. club,** a group formed by the devotees of some hero, 'star', etc.; **f. mail,** the letters sent to a celebrity by his or her followers.

Fanny Adams (fæ·ni æ·dămz). 1889. [Name of a woman who was murdered *c*1867.] **1.** *Naut. slang.* **a.** Tinned meat. **b.** Stew. **2.** *slang.* Freq. preceded by *sweet*: nothing at all 1919.

Fantastic. A. 7. *colloq.* Excellent, extraordinarily good.

Far East. 1852. [FAR *a.* 1 a, EAST *sb.*] The extreme eastern regions of the Old World, esp. China and Japan.

Far-flung, *a.* 1895. [FAR *adv.* 3 a, pa. pple. of FLING *v.*] 'Flung', i.e. extended, to a great distance.
Lord of our f. battle-line KIPLING.

Far-out, *a.* 1887. [f. FAR *adv.* + OUT *adv.*] **a.** Remote, distant. **b.** orig. *U.S.* Of jazz: of the most progressive kind. More generally, avant-garde, far-fetched; excellent, splendid 1954.

‖**Farruca** (fǣrū·kă). 1931. [Sp., fem. of *farruco* Galician or Asturian, f. *Farruco* nickname of *Francisco* Francis.] A Spanish dance.

Fascist. Also *transf.*, one of a similar body in other countries than Italy; (*loosely*) a person of right-wing authoritarian views. Hence as *adj.* Also **Fasci·stic** *a.*

Fast, *a.*
Comb.: **f. back, fastback,** (*a*) in *Bookbinding*, a back that adheres to the sheets; (*b*) orig. *U.S.*, (a car with) a back that slopes in one continuous line from the top of the car to the rear bumper; **f. buck** orig. *U.S.*, a quickly-earned dollar or profit; **f. lane,** a traffic lane intended for drivers who wish to overtake slower cars; **f. neutron,** a neutron with kinetic energy greater than some arbitrary value, esp. one that has not been slowed down by the action of a moderator after being produced by the fission of a nucleus; so **f. pile, reactor,** a nuclear reactor in which fission is caused primarily by unmoderated neutrons.

Father, *sb.*
Comb.: **f.-figure,** a person having some of the characteristics of a f.; **f.-fixation,** a fixation (*FIXATION 2 d) on one's f.

‖**Faute de mieux** (fot də myö̆). 1766. [Fr.] For want of something better; *attrib.*, used for lack of an alternative.

Fauve (fōᵘv). 1915. [Fr., lit. 'wild beast'.] A member of a movement in painting, chiefly associated with Henri Matisse (1869–1954), which flourished in Paris from 1905, and which is mainly characterized by a vivid use of colour. Also *attrib.* or as *adj.*, and *transf.* Hence (as adj), of a bright or vivid colour. So **Fau·vism. Fau·vist(e),** *sb.* and *a.*
The name was coined by the French art critic Louis Vauxcelles at the Autumn Salon of 1905; coming across a quattrocento-like statue in the midst of works by Matisse and his associates, he remarked, 'Donatello au milieu des fauves!'

‖**Faux-naïf** (fonaif), *sb.* and *a.* 1941. [Fr. *faux* false + NAÏF *a.*] (A person who is) self-consciously or pretendedly artless or naïve.

Fear, *sb.* Phr. *No. f.*: formerly = there is no reason for alarm; now = not likely, certainly not. *Without f. or favour*: impartially.

Feather-bedding, *vbl. sb.* 1921. [f. FEATHER-BED + -ING¹.] (The action of) making comfortable by favourable, esp. economic or financial, treatment; *spec.* the employment of superfluous staff. Hence, as a back-formation, **Feather-bed** *v. trans.*, to provide with advantages. **Feather-bedded** *ppl. a.* **Feather-bedder.**

Fed, *ppl. a.* **b.** Also without *up*, esp. in phrases *f. to the (back) teeth, f. to death.*

‖**Fedayeen** (fedayī·n), *sb. pl.* Also **-yin.** 1955. [colloq. Arab. *fidā'iyīn*, pl. of Class. Arab. *fidā'ī* one who undertakes perilous adventures.] Arab guerrillas operating against the Israelis.

Fedora (fĕdōᵊ·ră) orig. *U.S.* 1895. [f. *Fédora*, title of drama (1882) by Victorien Sardou.] A low soft felt hat with a curled brim and the crown creased lengthways. Also *attrib.*

Feed, *sb.* **6.** *Theatr. slang.* A performer who supplies cues 1929.

Feed, *v.* **6. b.** *trans.* and *intr.* To supply (a performer) with cues 1921. **8. c.** *to f. back*: *trans.* (chiefly in *pass.*), to return (a fraction of an output signal) to an input of the same or a preceding stage of the circuit, device, etc., that produced it; also *transf.*; *intr.* (of a result or effect), to return as feedback; to affect or modify the process that brought it about 1921.
The experience from the teaching of English to foreign learners is feeding back. . to the teaching profession 1964.

Fee·dback, feed-back, *sb.* 1920. [f. FEED *v.* + BACK *adv.*] **a.** *Electr.* The return of a fraction of the output signal from one stage of a circuit, amplifier, etc., to the input of the same or a preceding stage; also, a signal so returned. **b.** *transf.* The modification, adjustment, or control of a process by its result or effect, esp. by a difference between a desired and an actual result; information about the result of a process, experiment, etc.; a response 1943.

‖**Feldscher** (fe·ldʃəɹ). Also **feldschar, feldsher.** 1877. [Russ. *fél'dsher* – G. *feldscher* field surgeon.] In Russia, a person with practical training in medicine and surgery, but without professional medical qualifications; a physician's or surgeon's assistant.

Fellatio (felē¹·ʃio, felā·tio). Also **fellation.** 1887. [mod.L., f. *fellatus*, pa. pple. of L. *fellare* to suck.] A sexual act in which the partner's penis is sucked or licked. Hence **Fella·tor** [L. (Martial)], *fem.* **fella·trix,** the partner who performs such an act. **Fella·te** *v. trans.*, to practise f. on.

Fellow, *sb.*
Comb.: **f.-traveller,** (*a*) one who travels with another; (*b*) one who sympathizes with the Communist movement without being a party member; also *transf.*

Felt, *sb.*¹
Comb.: **f. (-tip, -tipped) pen,** a pen with a felt point, used for labelling, etc.

Femto- (fe·mto), *prefix.* 1961. [f. Da., Norw. *femt-en* fifteen + -O-, after *kilo-*, *micro-*, etc.] Prefixed to the names of units to form the names of units 10^{15} times smaller (i.e. one thousand million millionth part of them). Abbrev. f.

Fender. 2. d. *N. Amer.* = *BUMPER *sb.*¹ 5 b. 1919.

Fenestra. 3. *Surg.* **a.** A perforation in a surgical instrument other than in the handle 1876. **b.** A hole cut by a surgeon in any structure of the body 1941.

Fenestration. 3. *Surg.* The making of a fenestra, esp. into the labyrinth of the ear to restore hearing 1935.

Fermi (fə̄·ɹmi). 1956. [Name of Enrico *Fermi* (1901–54), Italian-born physicist.] A unit of length used in nuclear physics, equal to 10^{-15} m.

Fermion (fə̄·ɹmiǫn). 1947. [f. as prec. + *-ON.] *Nuclear Physics.* Any particle which has a half-integral spin quantum number and obeys the exclusion principle.

Fermium (fə̄·ɹmiǒm). 1955. [f. as prec. + -IUM.] *Chem.* An artificially produced radioactive element. Atomic number 100; symbol Fm.

Ferredoxin (ferėdǫ·ksin). 1962. [f. *fer* (repr. L. *ferrum* iron) + *REDOX + -IN¹.] *Biochem.* Any of certain iron-containing proteins of low redox potential which participate in intracellular electron-transfer processes.

Ferritin (fe·rĭtin). 1937. [– Czech *ferritin* (V. Laufberger, 1934), f. FERRI- after *ferratin* (f. L. *ferratus* containing iron), name previously given to a substance supposed to have similar properties.] *Biochem.* A water-soluble crystalline protein containing trivalent iron that occurs in many animals, esp. in the liver and spleen, and is involved in the storage of iron by the body.

Ferro-. 1. Ferro-ceme·nt [– It. *ferrocemento* (P. L. Nervi, 1951)], a construction material consisting of thin slabs of cement mortar reinforced with a meshwork of steel rods or wires. **Ferroele·ctric** *a.* [after *ferromagnetic*], (of a body or substance) having the property that a lasting electric polarization can be induced or reversed by the application of an electric field; also as *sb.*, a ferroelectric body or substance. So **Ferroele·ctrically** *adv.*, **-electri·city. Ferromagnetic** *a.*, in mod. use distinguished from PARAMAGNETIC, and applied to bodies and substances which, like iron, have a large variable magnetic permeability and exhibit hysteresis; also as *sb.*, a ferromagnetic body or substance. So **Ferroma·gnet,** a ferromagnetic.

2. Fe·rrocene (-sīn) [cyclopentadi*ene*], an orange crystalline compound, $Fe(C_5H_5)_2$ with a molecular structure in which an atom of iron is sandwiched between two identical parallel hydrocarbon rings.

Ferry, *sb.* **3. c.** An aircraft flight for carrying goods or persons from one place to another, esp. one of a series of flights on a regular course; also, the aircraft itself 1917. Also, a module or spacecraft for transporting an astronaut between the surface of a planet and another spacecraft.

Ferry, *v.* **2. c.** To fly (an aircraft, etc.) from one place to another, esp. on some regular route 1921.

‖**Festschrift** (fe·st,ʃrift). Pl. **-en, -s.** 1901. [G., lit. 'festival-writing'.] A collection of writings forming a volume presented to a scholar on the occasion of his attaining a certain age or period in his career.

This volume, a *Festschrift* presented to M. Maritain on his sixtieth birthday, comprises some twenty papers written by American admirers 1943.

Fetish, fetich(e. 1. d. *Psychol.* An object, a non-sexual part of the body, or a particular non-sexual action which, abnormally, serves as the stimulus to sexual desire 1901.

Fetishism, fetichism, (also) a perversion of the sexual instinct (often resulting from earlier repression) in which sexual desire is stimulated by a fetish.

Feud (fiūd), *v.* 1673. [f. FEUD[1].] *intr.* To conduct a feud. Hence **Feu·ding** *ppl. a.* and *vbl. sb.*

Fibonacci (fībona·tʃi). 1891. The name of Leonardo *Fibonacci*, also called Leonardo Pisano (fl. 1200), Tuscan mathematician, used *attrib.* and in the possessive.

Fibonacci('s) numbers: the numbers 1, 1, 2, 3, 5, 8, . ., where every number after the first two is the sum of the two preceding numbers (0 is sometimes included as the first term); *Fibonacci('s) sequence, series*: the series of F. numbers, or any similar series in which each term is an integer equal to the sum of the two preceding terms.

Fibre, *sb.*

Comb.: **f.-board, fibreboard,** (a piece of) board made from compressed wood or other plant fibres; **f. optics,** the study and application of the transmission of images by means of total internal reflection through filaments of glass, transparent plastic, etc.; so *f.-optic* adj.

Fibreglass, fiber-glass. Also **Fiberglas** (U.S. proprietary name). 1937. Any material consisting of glass filaments made into a textile or paper, or embedded in plastic or another substance for use as a construction or insulating material; glass in the form of filaments suitable for such uses. Freq. *attrib.*

Fibrositis (fəibrŏsəi·tis). 1904. [f. mod.L. *fibrosus* FIBROUS + -ITIS.] *Path.* Any painful rheumatic disorder of the white fibrous tissue that is of unknown or uncertain cause; inflammation of white fibrous tissue. So **Fibrosi·tic** *a.*

Fiddle, *sb.* **4. d.** orig. *U.S.* A swindle 1874.

Field, *sb.* **III. 1. b.** Used *attrib.* to denote an investigation, study, etc., carried out on the spot, and not in the laboratory, office, etc.; also denoting a person taking part in such an activity 1789. **c.** *Television.* A set of equally spaced scanning lines extending over the whole picture and produced by a single passage of the spot 1943. **d.** *Computers.* A set of characters in a record, or columns on a punched card, which together represent a single item of information; an item of information that can be so represented 1946.

Field-work. 3. The practical side of research in archæology, linguistics, the social sciences, etc., carried out in the areas concerned, as distinguished from theoretical or laboratory investigation 1922. Hence **Fie·ld-worker.**

Fiesta (fiˌe·stă). 1844. [Sp., feast.] In Spain or Spanish America, a religious festival; any festivity or holiday.

Fifth, *a.*

F. column, orig. the column of supporters which General Mola declared himself to have in Madrid, when he was besieging it in the Spanish civil war in 1936, in addition to the four columns of his army outside the city; hence (allusively), a body of one's supporters in an attacked or occupied foreign country, or of the enemy's supporters in one's own country. Also *transf.* Hence **F.-columnist.**

Fighter. 3. A high-speed aircraft designed for aerial combat 1917. Also **f.-bomber,** an aircraft combining the functions of a f. and a bomber.

Fighting, *vbl. sb.*

Comb.: **f. chance,** an opportunity of succeeding by great effort; **f.-fit** *a.*, fit enough to take part in a fight; **f. fund,** money raised to finance a campaign.

Fijian (fīdʒī·ăn), *sb.* and *a.* Also formerly **Feegeean, Feejeean, Fejean.** 1809. [f. *Fiji*, native name of the principal island of the Fiji archipelago + -AN.] **A.** *sb.* **1.** A native or inhabitant of the Fiji archipelago. **2.** The language of the Fijian people. **B.** *adj.* Of or pertaining to the Fijians 1846.

Filial, *a.*

Comb.: **f. generation** *Biol.*, the offspring of a cross, the first filial (or F_1) generation being the immediate offspring of the organisms selected for crossing, the second filial (or F_2) generation being produced usually by self-fertilization or intercrossing of F_1 individuals, and so on.

Filipino (filipī·no), *sb.* and *a.* Also **Filipina** (-ī·nă) fem. 1898. [Sp., f. (*las Islas*) *Filipinas* the Philippine Islands.] **A.** *sb.* A native or inhabitant of the Philippine islands, esp. one of Spanish or mixed blood. **B.** *adj.* Of or pertaining to Filipinos or the Philippine islands 1900.

Fill, *v.* **IV. 2. b.** *Dentistry.* = STOP *v.* 3 d 1848.

Filling, *vbl. sb.*

Comb.: **f.-station** orig. *U.S.*, a depot for the supply of petrol, oil, etc., to motorists; a petrol station.

Film, *sb.*

7. f.-goer, a frequenter of the cinema; hence **f.-going** *ppl. a.*; **filmset** *v. trans.*, to compose (matter for printing) by projecting images on to photographic film in a photo-composing machine; so **filmset** *ppl. a.*, **filmsetting** *ppl. a.* and *vbl. sb.*; **f. stock,** unexposed film; **f. strip,** a length of film bearing a sequence of still frames.

Filter, *sb.* **4. a.** *Photogr.* A screen to cut out rays which interfere with correct colour-rendering 1900. **b.** In a cigarette: a pad of absorbent material fitted at the unlit end to purify the smoke; also, a cigarette so fitted 1908.

Filter, *v.* **3. b.** Of vehicles: to join another line of traffic at a road junction 1928. **4. b.** *To f. out* (trans.): to separate or prevent the passage of by, or as by, filtering 1917.

Filterable (fi·ltərăb'l), *a.* Also **filtrable.** 1908. [f. FILTER *v.* + -ABLE.] Able to pass through a filter, esp. one that retains bacteria.

Finagle (finēi·g'l), *v. colloq.* (orig. *U.S.*). Also **fin(n)agel, finaygle, phe-.** 1926. [– Eng. dial. *fainaigue* to cheat. See *E.D.D.* and cf. RENEGUE *v.*] *intr.* To use dishonest or devious methods to bring something about; to fiddle. Also *trans.*, to 'wangle', to scheme, to get (something) by trickery. So **Fina·gling** *vbl. sb.*

Final. B. *sb.* **2. d.** The edition of a newspaper that is published latest in the day 1931.

Finalize (fəi·nălәiz), *v.* 1922. [f. FINAL *a.* + -IZE.] *trans.* To complete, put in final form. Also occas. *intr.* Hence **Fi:naliza·tion.**

‖**Fines herbes** (fīnzęrb'), *sb. pl.* 1846. [Fr., lit. 'fine herbs'.] A mixture of herbs used in cooking. Freq. in adj. phr. with *aux*, as *omelette aux fines herbes*, a savoury omelette flavoured with herbs.

Finger, *sb.*

Comb.: **2. f.-nail:** see NAIL *sb.* I. 1 a; **f.-tip,** the tip of a f.; used *attrib.* to indicate length (of a garment), sensitivity (of an object) to pressure, or ornamentation made with the tips of the fingers; so *at one's f.-tips*: ready at hand; *to the* (or *one's*) *f.-tips*: through one's whole body, throughout.

Fink (fiŋk). *slang* (orig. *U.S.*). 1903. [Origin unkn.] A pejorative term of wide application, esp. (*a*) an unpleasant or contemptible person; (*b*) an informer; a detective; (*c*) a strike-breaker. Hence as *v. intr.*, to inform *on.*

Fire-.

2. f.-lighter, (*a*) one who kindles a f.; (*b*) a device for lighting a f.; **f.-power,** the total effectiveness of the fire of guns, missiles, etc., of a military force; **f.-risk,** (*a*) the risk of loss by f.; (*b*) a fire-insurance company's obligation to make good loss by f.; (*c*) property insured against f.; **f.-storm,** (*a*) *poet.*, a storm of f.; (*b*) *spec.* a storm following a conflagration caused by bombs; **f.-walk,** the ceremony of walking barefoot over hot stones; so *f.-walker, -walking*; **f.-watcher,** (*a*) one who tends a f.; (*b*) one engaged in **f.-watching,** watching for and reporting the occurrence or spread of fires, esp. after bombing.

Firing, *vbl. sb.*

Comb.: **f. squad,** (*a*) = *f.-party*, a detachment of men who fire a salute at a military funeral; (*b*) a squad of soldiers detailed to shoot a condemned man.

First. A. *adj.* **I. 1.** Phrases. *The f. thing*: the elements or rudiments, esp. in phr. *not to know the f. thing about.* (*To put* or *do*) *first things first*: (to give) first place to the most important things.

Comb.: **2. f.-day cover,** an envelope bearing, or designed to bear, stamps postmarked on the day when they were first issued; **f. lady,** the most important lady; *spec.* in *U.S.*, the wife of the President; **f. love,** (*a*) the first time one falls in love; (*b*) one's favourite occupation, possession, etc.; **f. name,** a person's first or Christian name; **f. refusal,** an option to buy goods, etc., before they are offered to anyone else; **f. strike,** a first aggressive attack with nuclear weapons; freq. *attrib.*

Fish, *sb.*[1]

Comb.: **2. f. finger,** a small finger-shaped or rectangular section of fish covered with bread crumbs or batter; **f.-net,** used *attrib.* of an open-meshed fabric or garment.

Fissile, *a.* Add pronunc. (fi·səil). **2.** *Nuclear Physics.* Capable of undergoing nuclear fission 1945.

Fission, *sb.* **3.** *Nuclear Physics.* The splitting, either spontaneously or under the impact of another particle, of a heavy nucleus into approximately equal parts, with resulting release of large amounts of energy 1939. Hence **Fi·ssionable** *a.* = *FISSILE *a.* 2. **Fi:ssionabi·lity.**

Fission (fi·ʃən), *v.* 1929. [f. the sb.] **1.** *intr.* To divide into a small number of parts comparable in size. **2.** *trans.* and *intr.* In *Nuclear Physics*: (to cause) to undergo nuclear fission 1947. So **Fi·ssioning** *vbl. sb.* and *ppl. a.*

Fit-up (fi·tɒp). *Theatr. slang.* 1864. [f. phr. *to fit up.*] A stage or other theatrical accessory that can be fitted up for the occasion; hence (in full *f. company*), a travelling theatrical company which carries such objects.

FitzGerald (fitsdʒe·răld). 1905. The name of G. F. *FitzGerald* (1851–1901), Irish physicist, used (freq. with *LORENTZ) *attrib.*

F.(–Lorentz) contraction or **effect:** the contraction of a moving body in a direction parallel to its direction of motion (small except at speeds comparable to that of light).

Fix, *sb.* **3.** (A reliable indication of) the position of a ship, aircraft, etc. 1902. **4.** *slang* (orig. *U.S.*). A dose of a narcotic or other drug 1934.

Fix, *v.* **I. 4. b.** *trans.* Of a plant or micro-organism: to assimilate (the nitrogen or carbon dioxide in the air) by causing it to become combined in a non-gaseous metabolizable form 1850. Hence, to cause (an element, esp. nitrogen) to form a compound as the first step in some biological or industrial process. **c.** To preserve and harden (plant or animal tissue), esp. before microscopic examination 1878.

4. b. Photosynthesis fixes carbon in the leaf 1971.

II. 9. *intr.* and *trans.* To inject (oneself) with a drug; to take drugs (*slang*, orig. *U.S.*) 1938.

Fixate (fi·ksēit), *v.* 1885. [f. L. *fixus* (see FIX *a.*) + -ATE[3].] **1.** *trans.* To fix, render stable. **2.** *intr.* To become fixed 1888. **3.** *trans.* **a.** To concentrate one's gaze on 1889. **b.** *Psychol.* To cause (a component of the libido) to be arrested at an immature stage; to cause (a person) to react automatically to stimuli in terms which relate to a previous strong experience; to establish (such a response). Usu. *pass.* 1926. Hence **Fixa·ted** *ppl. a.*

Fixation. 2. c. The fixing of nitrogen or another substance as part of a biological or industrial process 1850. **d.** *Psychol.* The process or result of *FIXATE *v.* 3 b; an obsession 1910.

Fixer (fi·ksəɹ). 1849. [f. FIX *v.* + -ER[1].] **1.** Something used for fixing (a volatile substance, a photograph, a colour or dye, etc.). **2.** One who fixes; *spec.* one who arranges matters (often illicitly) 1885.

‖**Fladbrod, -bröd** (fla·tbrŏ, flā·brŏ). 1799. [Norw., lit. 'flat bread'.] A type of thin unleavened bread eaten in Norway.

Flagellate, *a.* **B.** *sb.* A microscopic protozoan organism of the class Mastigophora (or Flagellata), characterized by the possession at some stage of its life of one or more flagella that are used for locomotion 1879.

Flak (flæk). 1938. [G., f. the initials of the elements of *flieger abwehr-kanone* 'pilot-defence-gun'.] An anti-aircraft gun or anti-aircraft fire. Also *attrib.*, as **f. jacket,** a protective jacket containing metal strips or plates.

Flake (flēⁱk), *v.*² 1480. [var. FLAG *v.*¹] † **1.** *intr.* = FLAG *v.*¹ *Obs.* **2.** *To f.* (*out*): to faint, fall asleep; so **flaked (out)** *ppl. adj.*, exhausted; asleep, unconscious (*colloq.*) 1942.

Flaky, *a.* **2. b.** *spec.* Of pastry: consisting of thin delicate flakes or layers 1837.

‖**Flambé** (flaṅbe), *a.* 1886. [Fr., pa. pple. of *flamber* to pass through flame.] **1.** Of Chinese porcelain: iridescent as a result of the process of firing or the irregular application of glaze; also as *sb.* **2.** *Cookery.* Covered with spirit and set alight 1914.

Flame, *v.* **1. b.** *To flame out*: of a jet engine, to cease operation through extinction of the flame in the combustion chamber. So *flame-out* sb. 1950.

Flamenco (flăme·ŋko). 1896. [Sp., = FLAMINGO.] A Spanish gipsy style of singing or dancing; a song or dance in this style.

Flammability. Delete †. Revived in mod. use to avoid the possible ambiguity of *inflammability*, in which the prefix *in-* might be taken for a negative (IN-³).

Flannel, *sb.* **1. c.** A piece of flannel (or other fabric) for washing the face, etc., or washing the floor, etc. 1819. **d.** *slang.* Nonsense, 'hot air'; flattery, unnecessary ostentation 1927.

Flannel, *v.* **b.** *slang.* To flatter, curry favour with 1941; so **flannelling** *vbl. sb.*

Flap, *sb.* **1. b.** *colloq.* A state of worry, agitation, or excitement 1916. **4. c.** *Aeronaut.* An aileron 1906.

Flap, *v.* **8.** *intr. colloq.* To speak (anxiously) *about*; to become agitated; to fuss 1910.

Flare, *sb.*¹ **1. b.** *Astr.* A sudden increase in brightness of part of the sun as seen at certain visible and ultra-violet wavelengths (also *solar f.*) 1937. Also, any sudden and short-lived increase in the overall brightness of a star other than the sun 1949.

Comb.: **f. path** *Aeronaut.*, a line of lights to guide aircraft in taking off or coming in to land.

Flash, *sb.*²

Comb.: **f.-back, flashback,** (*a*) a backward flash of flame, etc.; (*b*) in a film, a scene which is a return to a previous action; hence, a revival of the memory of past events; **f.-bulb,** a bulb producing light for a f.-light photograph; **f.-gun,** a device that can be attached to a camera to hold and operate a f.-bulb; **f.-point,** (*b*) *fig.*, a point of climax, indignation, etc.

Flat, *a.*, *adv.*, and *sb.*² **A.** *adj.* **3. b.** Of an amplifier or other electronic device: amplifying, attenuating, or reproducing equally signals of all frequencies (within a certain range). Of the frequency response: uniform 1926. **4. b.** Of paint, lacquer, or varnish: lustreless, not glossy 1896.

Comb.: **f. spin,** a spin in which an aircraft descends in tight circles while not departing greatly from the horizontal; *fig.*, a frenzy of agitation.

B. *adv.* **2. b.** *f. out*: using or involving all one's (or its) strength or resources; at top speed; also as *adj.*

Flatlet (flæ·tlėt). 1925. [f. FLAT *sb.*¹ + -LET.] A small flat, usu. of one or two rooms.

Flea, *sb.*

Comb.: **f. market** *slang* [cf. Fr. *marché aux puces*, in Paris], a street market; **f. pit** *colloq.*, an allegedly verminous place of public assembly, e.g. a cinema.

Fleet, *sb.*² **Fleet Street,** a street in London devoted largely to the production and publication of newspapers and periodicals; hence *allusively*, newspapers generally; journalism 1882.

Flexography (fleksǫ·grăfi). 1952. [f. *flexo-* (f. L. *flexus*, f. *flectere* to bend) + -GRAPHY.] A rotary letterpress printing technique using rubber or plastic plates and aniline inks. So **Flexogra·phic** *a.*

Flexowriter (fle·ksorəitəɹ). Also **flexo-writer.** 1955. The proprietary name of a kind of electric typewriter incorporating a tape-punch and a tape-reader.

Flick, *sb.*¹

Comb.: **f.-knife,** a weapon with the blade held in the handle by a catch which can be released with a flick of the finger.

Flight, *sb.*¹

Comb.: **f. deck,** (*a*) of an aircraft-carrier: the deck on which aircraft take off and land; (*b*) of an aircraft: the part accommodating the pilot, navigator, etc.; **f. path,** the planned course of an aircraft or space vehicle; **f. recorder,** a device which records technical details of an aircraft's flight, to assist investigation in the event of an accident.

Flint, *sb.* **2. b.** A piece of metal used to produce a spark in a cigarette-lighter.

Flip, *sb.*²

Comb.: **f. side,** the reverse, or less important, side of a gramophone record; also *transf.*

Flip, *v.* **4.** *slang* (orig. *U.S.*). In full *to f. one's lid* or *wig.* To go wild, lose one's head 1950.

Flip (flip), *a.* orig. *dial.* 1847. [f. FLIP *v.*] Flippant, glib; nimble; voluble.

Flip-flop (fli·pˌflǫp). 1902. [Reduplication of FLOP; cf. FLIP-FLAP.] **1.** *U.S.* A somersault. **2.** *Electronics.* A switching circuit which in response to a triggering pulse either passes from a stable to an unstable state and back again, or makes a single transition from one of two stable states to the other 1935.

Flipper. **1. b.** A rubber attachment to the foot used for underwater swimming, esp. by frogmen 1945.

Float, *sb.*

Comb.: **f. glass,** glass manufactured by the **f. process,** in which the glass is drawn from the melting tank in a continuous sheet and made to float on molten metal while it hardens.

Floating, *ppl. a.*

Comb.: **f. voter,** a voter who has not attached himself to any political party; so **f. vote,** the vote of such a person; also *collect.*

Flog, *v.* **3.** *slang* (orig. *Mil.*). To sell or offer for sale, orig. illicitly 1919.

Floor, *sb.*

Comb.: **f. show,** an entertainment presented on the floor of a restaurant, night-club, etc.

Flop, *sb.* **3.** *slang.* A failure, collapse, or decline 1893.

Flop, *v.* **2. b.** *slang.* To collapse, fail 1919.

Floribunda (flōᵊribʊ·ndă, flǫ-). 1898. [mod.L., f. *floribundus* flowering freely, f. L. *flos*, *flor-* flower + *-bundus* (as in *moribundus*), influenced in meaning by *abundus* copious.] A plant bearing flowers in dense clusters, *esp.* a type of rose formerly described as a hybrid polyantha. Freq. *attrib.*

Flower, *sb.*

Comb.: **f. children, people,** young people who wear or carry flowers as symbols of peace and love; so **f. power,** the qualities or beliefs of these people.

Fluence² (flū·ĕns), aphæretic form of INFLUENCE *sb.*, occurring esp. in phr. *to put the fluence on* (a person), to apply mysterious, magical, or hypnotic power to (a person) 1909.

Fluff, *sb.*¹ **3.** A mistake, blunder; esp. a mistake made when playing music, etc. 1928.

Fluff, *v.* **5. b.** *trans.* and *intr.* To make a mistake in (something); to bungle; to play (music) wrongly 1884.

Fluidic, *a.* **2.** Designed or operating in accordance with the principles and techniques of fluidics; of or pertaining to fluidics 1965.

Fluidics (fluˌi·diks), *sb. pl.* (const. as sing.). 1965. [f. FLUID: see -IC 2.] A field of technology concerned with using small interacting flows and jets of fluid in systems of tubes, nozzles, and cavities that have few or no moving parts to carry out operations such as amplification and switching.

Fluidize (flū·idəiz), *v.* 1943. [f. FLUID + -IZE.] To cause (a mass of solid particles) to assume fluidity by passing a current of gas, vapour, or liquid upwards through it.

Powder is transferred by pipe..and is fluidized whenever it is necessary to lift it vertically 1965.

Hence **Flu·idized** *ppl. a.* (esp. in *fluidized bed*), **-izing** *ppl. a.* and *vbl. sb.* Also **Flu:idiza·tion.**

Fluoridate (flū·ŏridēⁱt), *v.* 1949. [Back-formation from next.] *trans.* **a.** To add a fluoride or other fluorine compound to (water, toothpaste, etc.). Also *absol.* **b.** To treat (teeth) with a preparation containing a fluoride 1963. Hence **Flu·oridated** *ppl. a.*

Fluoridation (flū:ŏridēⁱ·ʃən). 1904. [f. FLUORIDE + -ATION.] **1.** *Min.* The process by which a mineral absorbs fluorine. **2. a.** The addition of a fluoride or other fluorine compound to drinking-water 1949. **b.** The application of a fluoride to teeth 1963. So **Flu:oridiza·tion** (in sense 2, esp. 2 b).

Flutter, *sb.* **1. c.** A rapid fluctuation in the pitch or loudness of a sound (in sound reproduction usu. the former) 1931.

Flux, *sb.* **II. 7. b.** *Electr.* and *Magn.* (The number of) lines of magnetic induction (*magnetic f.*) or of electric displacement (*electric f.*) 1873.

Fly, *sb.*²

Comb.: **f.-half** *Rugby Football*, the half-back who stands off from the scrum-half; **f.-post** *v. intr.*, to display posters rapidly in unauthorized places; also *trans.*

Fly-by (fləi·bəi). 1953. [f. phr. *to fly by.*] **a.** orig. *U.S.* = *FLY-PAST. **b.** A close approach made by a spacecraft to a celestial body for purposes of observation; a spacecraft that makes such an approach 1960.

An observation f. of Mars 1969.

Flying, *vbl. sb.*

2. f. boat, (*a*) an experimental flying machine built by J. P. Blanchard; (*b*) a boat-shaped car on a merry-go-round; (*c*) a seaplane with a boat-like fuselage; **f. bomb,** a pilotless jet-propelled aircraft with an explosive warhead; **f. doctor,** a doctor who uses an aeroplane for visiting patients in areas remote from his headquarters; **f. saucer,** an unidentified saucer-shaped object reported as appearing in the sky.

Flying, *ppl. a.*

4. f. squad, a detachment of a police force organized for rapid movement; also *transf.*

Fly-over (fləi·ōᵘvəɹ). 1901. [f. phr. *to fly over.*] **1.** A railway or road bridge over another line or road. Also *fig.* **2.** = *FLY-PAST; the passage of an aircraft over an area 1931.

Fly-past (fləi·pɑst). 1914. [f. *to fly past*, after *march-past.*] The action of flying past; a procession of aircraft.

Foam, *sb.* **1. c.** A foaming substance used in fire-fighting 1906. **d.** Rubber or plastic in a cellular mass resembling foam 1937.

Foie gras, foie-gras (fwaˌgra). *colloq.* 1818. Short for *pâté de foie gras*: see PÂTÉ 1.

Folk. **5.** *Ellipt.* for *f.-music* 1963.

Comb.: **f.-music,** music of popular origin or style; **folkway** (usu. *pl.*), traditional behaviour.

Folksy (fōᵘ·ksi), *a.* orig. *U.S.* 1852. [f. pl. of FOLK + -Y¹.] **1.** Sociable; informal, casual. **2.** Having the characteristics of popular art, culture, etc. 1947. Hence **Fo·lksiness.**

Folky (fōᵘ·ki), *a.* 1914. [f. FOLK + -Y¹.] Characteristic of the common people; = *FOLKSY *a.* 2. Hence **Fo·lkiness.**

Follow-up. 1923. [f. phr. *to follow up* (FOLLOW *v.*).] The action of following up; the pursuit or prosecution of something begun or attempted.

‖**Fons et origo** (fǫnz et ŏrəi·go). 1873. [L.] The source and origin (*of*).

Food, *sb.*

Comb.: **f.-chain** *Ecology*, a series of organisms each dependent upon another for food; **f. poisoning,** any illness caused by harmful bacteria or substances in food; **f.-value,** value as food; *spec.* in dietetics, the relative nourishing power assigned to foods.

Foot, *sb.* Phrases. **k.** *My foot!*: colloq. phr. expressing a contemptuous denial. **l.** *On the right f.*: successfully. *On the wrong f.*: unawares, unprepared, unsuccessfully.

Comb.: **f.-loose** *a.* orig. *U.S.*, free to act as one pleases.

Footage (fu·tėdʒ). 1892. [f. FOOT *sb.* + -AGE.] **1.** A piece-work system of paying miners by the running foot of work; the amount paid; also, the amount mined. **2.** The length in feet of cinematographic film 1916.

Football.

Comb.: **f. coupon,** a coupon used in an entry for a football pool; **f. pool,** an organized system of betting on the results of football matches.

Forced, *ppl. a.*

2. f.-choice, used *attrib.* of a question, etc., in which a choice must be made between alternatives; **f. landing,** the unpremeditated landing of an aircraft in an emergency.

‖**Force majeure** (fors maʒœ̄r). 1883. [Fr., lit. 'superior strength'.] Irresistible force or overwhelming power.

It was thought..that the mayor had yielded the town by treachery, but later they learned that it was rather by *force majeure* 1941.

Fore-court. *spec.* The petrol-dispensing part of a filling-station 1958.

Fork, *sb.*

Comb.: **f.-lift (truck,** etc.), a vehicle fitted with a pronged device in front for lifting and carrying goods; **f. supper (-buffet,** etc.), a meal served at a buffet, etc., consisting of food suitable for eating with fork alone, making the provision of set places at table unnecessary.

Formant (fǭ·ɹmănt). *Phonetics.* 1901. [– G. *formant* (Hermann and Matthias, 1894), f. L. *formans, formant-* pres. pple. of *formare* to form: see -ANT.] The characteristic pitch of a vowel-sound; *spec.* one of several characteristic bands of resonance.

Format, *sb.* **b.** A style of arrangement or presentation; a mode of procedure 1955. **c.** *Computers.* A particular arrangement of data or characters in a record, instruction, etc., in a form that can be processed or stored by a computer 1955.

Format (fǭ·ɹmæt), *v.* Pa. t. and pa. pple. **formatted;** pres. pple. **formatting.** 1964. [f. the sb.] *trans.* To arrange or put into a format: used chiefly in connection with *Computers* (see *FORMAT *sb.* c).

Formation. 4. b. The orderly disposition of a number of aircraft in flight 1914.

Former, *sb.*[1] **3.** *Aeronaut.* A transverse structural member 1919.

Formica[2] (fǭɹmai·kă). 1922. The proprietary name of a hard, durable plastic laminate.

Formula. 6. *Motor Racing.* The class or specification of a racing car, usu. expressed in terms of engine capacity 1927. Also *attrib.*

Fort, *sb.* **1.** Phr. *To hold the f.*: to remain at one's post, to 'cope'; to act as a temporary substitute.

Fortran (fǭ·ɹtræn). Also **FORTRAN.** 1956. [f. *for(mula tran(slation.*] *Computers.* A programming language using standardized English terms and algebraic formulæ, used chiefly for scientific and mathematical calculations.

Fossa[2], **foussa** (fǫ·să, fū·să). Also **fosa.** 1838. [Malagasy.] **a.** A mammal (*Cryptoprocta ferox*) related to both cats and civets, which is the largest carnivore found in Madagascar. **b.** *Fossa fossa* (popular names FOSSANE, *foussa,* and *fanaloka*), a monotypic genus of civets also found in Madagascar.

The fact that the generic name of this animal [*Fossa*] is the same as the vernacular name of another Madagascar mammal, the fossa (*Cryptoprocta*) should not lead to confusion as they are distinctly different animals 1964.

Four.

Comb.: **f.-letter** *a.*, consisting of f. letters; applied esp. to any of several monosyllabic English words, referring to the sexual or excretory functions or organs of the human body, that are conventionally excluded from polite use.

Foussa: see *FOSSA[2].

Fox, *sb.*

Comb.: **f.-hole,** a hole in the ground used by a soldier for protection; also *transf.* and *fig.*; **f.-mark,** a brown stain on a print, book, etc.

Frabjous (fræ·bdʒəs), *a.* 1872. A nonsense-word invented by 'Lewis Carroll' (C. L. Dodgson), app. intended to suggest 'fair' and 'joyous'.

Fraction, *sb.* **6.** Any one of the portions, differing in physical or chemical properties, into which a mixture may be separated, esp. by physical means 1857.

Fragmentation.

Comb.: **f. bomb, grenade,** one designed to disintegrate into small fragments on explosion.

Frail (frē̆ⁱl), *sb.*[2] *slang* (chiefly *U.S.*). 1908. [Subst. use of the adj.] A woman.

Frame, *sb.* **II. 3. c.** *F. of reference*: (*a*) (also *frame* simply) a system of co-ordinate axes in relation to which position and motion may be defined; (*b*) a set of standards, beliefs, or assumptions governing thought, behaviour, etc.

III. 4. b. *Cinematography.* One of the separate pictures on a film 1916. **c.** *Television.* A single complete image or picture; formerly also = *FIELD *sb.* III. 1 c 1935.

Comb.: **f.-up** *colloq.* (orig. *U.S.*), an arrangement or plot, esp. with a sinister intent.

Franchise, *sb.* **I. 2. c.** The authorization granted to an individual or group by a company to sell its products or services in a particular area 1959.

Francium (fræ·nsiŏm). 1946. [mod.L. (M. Perey, 1946), f. *France* + -IUM.] *Chem.* A radioactive metallic element that is the heaviest member of the alkali-metal series and is chemically similar to cæsium. Atomic number 87; symbol Fr.

Francophone (fræ·ŋkofōᵘn), *sb.* and *a.* 1900. [f. FRANCO- + Gr. φωνή voice.] **A.** *sb.* A French-speaking person. **B.** *adj.* French-speaking. Hence **Francopho·nia, -pho·nic** *a.*

‖**Franglais** (fraṅglɛ). 1964. [Blend of Fr. *fran(çais* + *an)glais* (M. Rat, 1959).] A corrupt version of the French language produced by the indiscriminate introduction of words and phrases of English and American origin. Also *transf.* and as *adj.*

That awful way French women had on the phone, using idiotic f. phrases like 'because le job' 1969.

Frankenstein (fræ·ŋkənstəin). 1838. The name of the title-character of Mrs. Shelley's romance *Frankenstein* (1818), who constructed a human monster; commonly misused allus. as a name for a monster who terrifies and destroys his creator. Also *attrib.*

Frankfurter (fræ·ŋkfōɹtəɹ). Also **frankfurt.** 1894. [G. *Frankfurter wurst* Frankfurt sausage. Cf. FRANKFORT.] A highly seasoned smoked beef and pork sausage.

Fraternize, *v.* **1. b.** To cultivate friendly relations *with* (troops or inhabitants of an enemy country) 1897. Hence **Fra·ternizing** *vbl. sb.*

Fratting (fræ·tiŋ), *vbl. sb. slang.* 1945. [Short for *FRATERNIZING *vbl. sb.*] The act of the verb *FRATERNIZE 1 b. So **Frat** *v. intr.*, to fraternize. **Frat,** (a woman met by) 'fratting'.

Fraunhofer (frau·nhōᵘfər). 1837. Name of Joseph von *Fraunhofer* (1787–1826), Bavarian physicist; chiefly in *F. lines* (of solar or stellar spectra), *spectrum.*

Freak, *sb.*[1] **4. c.** One who 'freaks out'; a social nonconformist; a drug addict; also *transf.* 1967.

Freak, *v.* **3.** *To f. (out)*: to undergo an intense emotional experience; to become stimulated or wild, esp. under the influence of drugs. Also *trans.*, to cause (a person) to be aroused or stimulated 1965. Hence **F.-out** *sb.*, an intense emotional experience; a 'rave-up'.

Freaky (frī·ki), *a.* 1824. [f. FREAK *sb.*[1] + -Y[1].] Freakish; *spec.* characteristic of a freak (*FREAK *sb.*[1] 4 c).

Free, *a.*

Comb.: **c. f. enterprise,** private business free from state control; **f. fall,** movement of a body under no forces other than gravity; **f. kick** *Football,* a kick at the ball in any way the kicker pleases while the opponents are kept at a specified distance; **f. range,** (*a*) *U.S.* free pasturage; (*b*) used esp. *attrib.* of chickens given freedom to range for food; hence of their eggs; **freeway** orig. *U.S.*, a thoroughfare with restricted access; an express highway.

Freedom.

Comb.: **f. fighter,** a member of a resistance movement against the established political system of a country; **f. ride** *U.S.*, an organized ride (in buses, etc.) by people demonstrating against racial segregation; so *f. rider.*

Free-for-all, *a.* and *sb.* orig. *U.S.* 1881. [FREE *a.* II. 6.] **A.** *adj.* Open to all. **B.** *sb.* A fight, etc., in which anyone may take part.

Freeze, *sb. spec.* **b.** The fixing of wages, dividends, military strength, etc., at a certain level or figure 1942. **c.** A cinematographic shot in which the movement is arrested; also **f.-frame, -shot** 1960.

Freeze, *v.* **I. 4. b.** To make oneself suddenly rigid and motionless 1848.

II. 1. d. To fix (wages, prices, etc.) at a stated level; to make (assets, etc.) unrealizable 1922.

Comb.: **f.-drying,** the drying of foodstuffs, blood plasma, etc., by first freezing them and then warming them in a high vacuum; **f.-up,** a period in which land or water is frozen, *esp.* so as to prevent travel; an area so affected; a frozen condition (as of a water-tank, etc.).

Freighter. 4. A freight-carrying aircraft 1920.

French. A. *adj.*

F. blue, (*a*) artificial ultramarine; (*b*) *colloq.* a pill containing amphetamine and a barbiturate; **F. Canadian** *a.* and *sb.*, (of) a Canadian of French ancestry; **F. cricket,** an informal type of cricket without stumps, in which the bowler tries to hit the batsman's legs; **F. letter** *colloq.*, a contraceptive sheath.

Freon (frī·ǫn). 1932. The proprietary name of any of a group of simple compounds of carbon, hydrogen, fluorine and usu. also chlorine or bromine, used esp. as refrigerants and aerosol propellants.

Frequency.

Comb.: **f. modulation** *Electr.*, modulation of a wave by variation of its frequency; abbrev. *F.M.*; **f. response,** the relationship between the output-input ratio of an amplifier, microphone, etc., and the f. of the signal.

Fridge, frig (fridʒ). 1926. Colloq. abbrev. of REFRIGERATOR.

Friesian (frī·ziăn), var. FRISIAN, as the name of a breed of large dairy cattle 1923.

Frig (frig), *v.* late ME. [Origin unkn.] † **1.** *intr.* To move about restlessly. † **2.** *trans.* To rub, chafe *a* 1529. **3.** *trans.* and *intr.* = FUCK *v.* 1598. Hence **Fri·gger. Fri·gging** *vbl. sb.* and *ppl. a.*

Fringe, *sb.*

Comb.: **f. benefit** orig. *U.S.*, a perquisite provided by an employer to supplement a money wage or salary; also *transf.*

Frisk, *v.* **3.** To search (a person or place); esp. to run the hand rapidly over (a person or his clothing), in a search for a concealed weapon, stolen goods, etc. 1789.

Fröbel (frö·bĕl). Also **Froebel.** 1873. The name of F. W. A. *Fröbel* (1782–1852), German teacher, used *attrib.* or in the possessive to designate his system of child education, or a school following this system. Hence **Froebe·lian** *a.* and *sb.* **Froe·belism.**

Frog[1]. **2. b.** = FROGGY *sb.* 2. Also, the French language. Also *attrib.* or as *adj.* 1778.

Comb.: **frogman,** a man wearing a close-fitting suit of rubber or the like, with goggles and flippers, and equipped with a self-contained supply of oxygen to enable him to swim and operate under water.

Frog-march, frog's-march, *v.* 1884. [f. the sb.] *trans.* To subject (a person) to a frog-march; now usu., to hustle (a person) forward after seizing him from behind and pinning his arms together.

Front, *sb.* and *a.* **II. 1. e.** An organized sector of activity, or body of political forces; freq. with defining word prefixed 1919. **3. e.** orig. *U.S.* A person, organization, etc., that serves as a cover for subversive or illegal activities 1905. **f.** *Meteorol.* The boundary or transition zone between two air masses of different temperatures; so **cold, warm f.,** the forward boundary of a mass of advancing cold, or warm, air 1921.

Comb.: **f. line** = FRONT *sb.* II. 1 a; **f. page,** the front outside page of a newspaper; often *attrib.* to indicate an important or striking piece of news; **f.-page** *v. trans.*, to feature on the f. page; **f.-runner** orig. *U.S.*, the leading contestant in a competition.

Frontality (frɒntæ·lĭti). 1905. [f. FRONTAL + -ITY, after Da. *frontalitet.*] A principle in sculpture according to which the figure is carved or moulded as viewed from the full front.

Frug (frɒg, frūg). 1964. [Origin unkn.] A modern dance. Hence as *v. intr.*

Fruit, *sb.*

Comb.: **f.-body,** the part of a fungus that bears the spores and spore-producing organs; **f. machine,** a type of gaming machine; **f. salad,** (*a*) fruits cut up and mixed together; (*b*) *Services' slang,* an array of service ribbons and decorations.

Fuddy-duddy (fɒ·di,dɒ·di). *slang.* 1904. [Origin unkn.] An old-fashioned person; an ineffectual old fogy. Also *attrib.* or as *adj.*

Fuel, *sb.* **3. a.** Food, or a constituent of food, which is utilized by the body to produce energy 1876. **b.** *Nuclear Sci.* (A kind of) material used as a source of energy in a nuclear reactor; material that can support a self-sustaining chain reaction 1946.

Fugue, *sb.* **2.** *Psychiatry.* A flight from one's own identity, often involving travel to some unconsciously desired locality 1901. So **Fu·gal** *a.*

A f. is a combination of amnesia and physical fright 1965.

Führer (fü·rəɹ). Also **Fuehrer.** 1934. [G., leader.] Part of the title (*Führer und Reichskanzler*) assumed by Adolf Hitler as head of the German Reich. Also *transf.* and *attrib.*

Full. A. *adj.*

Comb.: **2. f.-cream** *attrib.*, consisting of, or made from, unskimmed milk; **f. house,** (*a*) an assembly or audience which fills a building; (*b*) *Poker,* a hand containing three of a kind and a pair; **f. time,** the total hours normally allotted to work; freq. *attrib.* and advb., esp. in sense 'that occupies all one's time, that engages one to the exclusion of other activities'.

Fun, *sb.* **3.** *attrib.* passing into *adj.* with the sense 'amusing, entertaining, enjoyable'. **b.** *Comb.*: **f. fair,** a fair devoted to amusements and side-shows.

Funeral. B. *sb.* **1.** Phr. *One's funeral*: one's affair or concern (often with an implication of unpleasant consequences). orig. *U.S. slang.*

Funk, *sb.*[2] **2.** *slang* (orig. *U.S.*). Music that is 'funky' 1959.

Funkia (fʌ·ŋkiă). Also **funckia.** 1839. [mod.L. (K. Sprengel, 1817), f. the name of H. C. *Funck* (1771–1839), Prussian botanist + -IA[1].] A member of the genus of liliaceous plants from Japan once so named, but now called *Hosta*, having racemes of white or lilac drooping bell-shaped flowers; a plantain-lily.

Funky, *a.*[2] 1784. [f. FUNK *sb.*[2]] **1.** Mouldy, musty, evil-smelling. **2.** *slang* (orig. *U.S.*). Of jazz or similar music: down-to-earth and uncomplicated; also *transf.*, 'swinging', fashionable 1954.

Furan (fiūᵊ·ræn). Also **-ane.** 1894. [abbrev. of *FURFURAN.] *Chem.* **a.** A colourless liquid with an ethereal odour, the molecule of which is a heterocyclic five-membered ring, $(CH)_4O$. **b.** Any derivative of f. that contains a f. ring.
Comb.: **f. resin,** any of various resins that are polymers of a f.; **f. ring,** a ring of four carbon atoms and one oxygen atom.

Furfural (fɔ̄·ɹfiūræl). 1879. [f. FURFUR(OL + *-al* of *aldehyde.*] *Chem.* = FURFUROL. Also called **Furfura·ldehyde.**

Furfuran (fɔ̄·ɹfiūræn). Also **-ane.** 1877. [– G. *furfuran* (A. Baeyer, 1877), f. FURFUR(OL + *-an.*] *Chem.* = *FURAN.

‖**Furoshiki** (furǫ·ʃiki). 1891. [Jap.] A square of fabric, usually silk, used by the Japanese as a wrapping for small bundles.

Further, *a.* **2. f. education,** formal education organized for adults, or for young people who have left school.

Fuse (fiūz), *v.*[3] 1914. [f. FUSE *sb.*[4]] *trans.* To provide with a fuse (FUSE *sb.*[4]). Hence **Fused** *ppl. a.*

Fusion. 3. c. *Nuclear Sci.* The formation of a heavier, more complex nucleus by the union of two or more lighter ones, usu. accompanied by the release of large amounts of energy 1947.

Futurology (fiūtiŭrǫ·lŏdʒi, -tʃər-). 1946. [f. FUTURE *sb.* + -OLOGY.] The forecasting of the future on a systematic basis. Hence **Futuro·logist.**

Fuzz (fʌz), *sb.*[3] *slang* (orig. *U.S.*). 1929. [Origin unkn.] A policeman or detective; freq. *collect.*, the police.

G.
III. = General, in G.H.Q. (headquarters), G.P. (practitioner), G.P.I. (paralysis of the insane), G.P.O. (post office). Also G.B., Great Britain; G.C.E., General Certificate of Education; G.M.T., Greenwich mean time; G.N.P., gross national product; G.W.(R.), Great Western (Railway).

Gadolinium (gædoli·niŏm). 1886. [mod.L. (J. C. G. de Marignac, 1886), f. GADOLIN(ITE (in which it occurs) + -IUM.] *Chem.* A metallic element of the lanthanide series, similar to steel in appearance and strongly magnetic below room temperature. Atomic number 64; symbol Gd.

Gag, *sb.*[1] **2. b.** A joke; a humorous remark, action, etc. Freq. *attrib.* 1863.

Gaga (gā·gā, gæ·gă), *a. slang.* Also **ga-ga.** 1920. [– Fr. *gaga* senile (person).] Senile; 'dotty', mad; fatuous.

Galley. 5. b. A galley-proof 1890.

Gallica (gæ·likă). 1848. [f. L. *Gallicus* GALLIC *a.*[1]] A species of rose, *Rosa gallica*; a plant or a flower of a variety of this species.

Gallup (gæ·lŏp). 1940. The name of the American statistician George Horace *Gallup* (born 1901), used *attrib.* (chiefly in *G. poll*) to denote a type of public-opinion poll (*POLL *sb.*[1] II. 2 d).

Game, *sb.* **4. c.** *The Game*: also, (*a*) *slang*, thieving, housebreaking; (*b*) *slang*, prostitution; (*c*) a form of charades.

Gamesmanship (gēi·mzmænʃip). 1947. [f. GAME *sb.* + *-manship* as in SPORTSMANSHIP.] Skill in winning games, esp. by barely legitimate means. So **Ga·mesman.**
The theory & practice of gamesmanship or the art of winning games without actually cheating S. POTTER.

Gamma. 5. Used as a symbol or designation in science. **a.** The third in a series, e.g. of alloys of copper and zinc (*g. brass*), or of crystalline forms of iron (*g. iron*, stable from 910°C to 1403°C). **b.** The contrast of a photographic print or television picture (strictly, compared with that of the original scene) 1903. **c.** A unit of magnetic field strength (10^{-5} oersted) or of mass (10^{-6} gramme) 1903. **6.** *Ellipt.* for *g. rays* or *radiation*, as in *g. counter, emitter*, etc. 1929.
5. c. The lunar magnetic field is no bigger than two gammas 1967. **6.** Radioactivity was measured in a well-type g. counter 1971.

Gammy (gæ·mi), *a. dial.* and *slang.* 1839. [dial. equivalent of GAMY *a.*] † **1.** Bad. **2.** Lame; disabled 1879.

Gang, *sb.*
Comb.: **g.-bang** *slang* (orig. *U.S.*), an occasion on which several men have sexual intercourse one after another with one woman; **gangland** orig. *U.S.*, the domain of gangsters; gangs or gangsters collectively.

Gangling (gæ·ŋgliŋ), *a.* 1808. [Of unkn. origin.] Of straggling growth; loosely built, lanky.

Garden, *sb.* Phrases. *Everything in the g. is lovely*: the situation is perfectly satisfactory; all is well. *To cultivate one's g.*: to attend to one's own affairs. *To lead* (someone) *up the g.* (*-path*): to lead on, entice; mislead, deceive.

Garn (gāɹn), *int.* 1886. Colloq. (chiefly Cockney) pronunc. of *go on* (see *Go on* j s.v. GO *v.* VII), often expressing disbelief or ridicule of a statement.

Garrya (gæ·riă). 1834. [mod.L. (D. Douglas, 1834), f. the name of N. *Garry* (1781–1856), an officer of the Hudson's Bay Company.] An evergreen shrub of the genus so called, esp. *G. elliptica*, which is native to California and Oregon, and cultivated for the ornamental catkins it bears during the winter.

Gas, *sb.*[1] **5.** *slang* (orig. *U.S.*). Something or someone that is very pleasing, exciting, impressive, etc.; freq. *a gas* 1957.
Comb.: **2. g. chamber,** a chamber containing gas; *spec.* one of the chambers used by the Germans in the 1939–45 war for killing groups of human beings by gas-poisoning; **g. gangrene,** a rapidly spreading form of gangrene marked by the evolution of gas; **g.-turbine,** a turbine powered by gas; an internal-combustion engine in which compressed air is heated by combustion with fuel, and the expansion of the resulting hot gases powers a turbine.

Gat[2] (gæt). *slang* (orig. *U.S.*). Also **gatt.** 1904. [Short for GATLING.] A revolver or other gun.

Gate, *sb.*[1] **6. d.** The mechanism in a cinematographic camera or projector that holds each frame momentarily behind the lens 1909.

Gâteau (gæ·to, ‖gato). 1845. [Fr.] **a.** Meat, fish, etc., served in the form of a cake. **b.** A large rich cake, often filled with cream and highly decorated.

Gauleiter (gau·ləitəɹ). 1936. [G.] An official controlling a district under Nazi rule; also *transf.* and *fig.*

Gay. A. 2. b. *slang.* Of a person: homosexual. Of a place: frequented by homosexuals 1935.

Gazoomph (găzu·mf), *v. slang.* Also **gasumph, gazump(h), gezumph.** 1928. [Origin uncertain.] *trans.* and *intr.* To swindle; *spec.* (normally spelt *gazump*) to raise the price of a house, etc., after accepting an offer but before the contracts are exchanged. Also as *sb.*, a swindle. Hence **Gazoo·mpher. Gazoo·mphing** *vbl. sb.*

Gear, *sb.* **II. 1. c.** Slang phr. *That's* (or *it's*) *the g.*: an expression of approval. Hence as *adj.*, good, excellent. Also as *int.* 1925.

Gear, *v.* **4. a.** Also *fig.*, to adjust or coordinate; *spec.* to adapt (something) *to* a particular system, situation, etc.; freq. in *pass.*

Gee (dʒī), *int.*[2] orig. *U.S.* 1895. [prob. a shortening of *Jesus!* (or *Jerusalem!*).] An exclamation of surprise or enthusiasm; also used simply for emphasis. So **Geewhi·llickins, gee whi·zz** *ints.*

Geezer (gī·zəɹ). *slang.* Also **geeser, geyser.** 1885. [dial. pronunc. of GUISER.] A person, esp. as a derisive term for an elderly person; a chap, fellow.

‖**Gefüllte fish** (gĕfi·ltə fiʃ). Also **gefil(l)te, gefu(el)lte, gefülte fish** or **fisch.** 1892. [Yiddish, – G. *gefüllt* stuffed, f. *füllen* FILL *v.*] A Jewish dish of stewed or baked stuffed fish or fish-cakes, boiled in a broth.

Geiger (-Müller) counter (gəi·gəɹ mülər). 1924. [f. name of Hans *Geiger* (1882–1945), German physicist.] An instrument for detecting and counting ionizing radiation, used esp. for measuring radioactivity; it consists essentially of a wire anode surrounded by a cylindrical cathode in a chamber containing gas at low pressure. Also *fig.*

Geissler tube (gəi·sləɹ). Also †**Geissler's tube.** 1863. [f. name of Heinrich *Geissler* (1814–79), German physicist.] A sealed glass tube containing gas at low pressure and a pair of electrodes between which a luminous discharge may be produced.
Modified forms of G. tubes..have become familiar..as luminous signs or fluorescent tube lamps 1966.

Gelada (dʒe·lădă). 1843. [Native name.] In full *g. baboon.* An Ethiopian baboon, *Theropithecus gelada*, characterized by a heavy mane in the adult male, and by a tufted tail.

Gemmology (dʒemǫ·lŏdʒi). 1811. [f. L. *gemma* GEM *sb.* + -OLOGY.] The science or study of gems. Hence **Gemmo·logist.**

Gen (dʒen). *slang* (orig. *Services'*). 1940. [perh. abbrev. of *general* in phr. 'for the general information of all ranks', or possibly from part of the words *genuine* or *intelligence.*] Information; facts. Also *attrib.* Hence as *v. intr.*, to learn quickly; *trans.* to inform (const. *up*).

Genetic, *a.* **4.** Of or pertaining to genetics or genes 1908.
g. code, the system by which nucleic acid molecules store g. information, now known to operate with triplets of the constituent nucleotides read in sequence along the molecule. So **Genetical** *a.* in same sense. **Genetically** *adv.*, (also) by the agency of genes; according to genetics.

Geneticist (dʒéne·tĭsist). 1913. [f. GENETICS + -IST.] An expert in or student of genetics.

-genic (dʒe·nik), *suffix.* [f. -GEN + -IC.] Forming adjs. with the meaning (*a*) 'producing, causing', as in *carcino-, hallucinogenic*; (*b*) 'produced by, originating in', as in *radiogenic* (sense *2).

Genotype[1] (dʒe·nŏtəip). 1897. [f. Gr. γένος GENUS + -TYPE (C. Schuchert, 1897).] *Biol.* The type-species of a genus.
The International Commission (Paris, 1948) recommends that the term g. not be used because of possible confusion with the same word as used in genetics 1953.

Genotype[2] (dʒe·nŏtəip). 1910. [– G. *genotypus* (W. Johannsen, 1909), f. *gen* GENE: see -O-, -TYPE.] *Biol.* Genetic constitution; the sum-total of the genes in an individual or group. Hence **Genoty·pic(al)** *adjs.*, **-ty·pically** *adv.*

Gent, *sb.* **b.** *pl.* = *GENTLEMAN 4 d (*colloq.*) 1938.

Genteelism (dʒentī·liz'm). 1908. [f. GENTEEL *a.* + -ISM.] Genteel behaviour or characteristics; (the use of) a genteel word or euphemism.

Gentleman. 4. d. *pl.* A public convenience for male persons. Freq. *gentlemen's*, and with capital initial 1929.
Over on that platform's the general waiting-room,..and over there's the Gentlemen's 1933.

Geo-.
Geoma·gnetism, the study of the magnetic properties of the earth and related phenomena; so **Geomagne·tic** *a.*, **-magne·tically** *adv.* **Geosta·tionary** *a.*, of, pertaining to, or designating an artificial satellite that revolves round the earth in one day and so remains above a fixed point on its surface.

Geochemistry (dʒīˌoke·mistri). 1903. [f. GEO- + CHEMISTRY.] The study of the chemical composition of the earth. So **Geoche·mical** *a.* **Geoche·mically** *adv.* **Geoche·mist.**

Geomorphology (dʒīˌomǭɹfǫ·lǒdʒi). 1893. [f. GEO- + MORPHOLOGY.] The branch of geology dealing with the origin, evolution, and configuration of the natural features of the earth's surface. So **Ge:omorpholo·gical** *a.*, **-lo·gically** *adv.* **Geomorpho·logist.**

Geordie. 2. d. A native or inhabitant of Tyneside 1866.

George. II. 5. a. Colloq. phr. (orig. *U.S.*). *Let G. do it*: let someone else do the work or take the responsibility 1910. **b.** Used as a familiar form of address to a stranger; *spec.* in Services' slang: (*a*) an airman; (*b*) an automatic pilot 1925.

Comb.: **G. Cross, G. Medal,** decorations for gallantry in civilian life instituted by King George VI.

Georgian, *a.*[1] **1. b.** Belonging to or characteristic of the reign of George V (1910–36) or VI (1936–52); *spec.* of poetry or poets of the first years of George V's reign 1910.

Geriatrics (dʒeriˌæ·triks). 1909. [f. Gr. γῆρας old age + ἰατρικός (see IATRIC *a.*), after *PÆDIATRICS.] The branch of medicine, or of social science, dealing with the health of old people. Hence **Geria·tric** *a.* **Geriatri·cian.**

Gerontology (dʒe:rǫ̆ntǫ·lǒdʒi). 1903. [f. Gr. γέρων, γεροντ- old man + -OLOGY.] The scientific study of old age and of the process of ageing. Hence **Gero:ntolo·gical** *a.* **Ge:ronto·logist.**

Gestalt (gəʃta·lt). 1922. [G., 'form, shape'.] *Psychol.* Something which, as an object of perception, forms a specific whole incapable of expression simply in terms of its parts. Freq. attrib., as *g. psychology, theory.*

Gestapo (gĕstā·po, ge-). 1934. [G., f. the initial letters of *Ge*heime *Sta*ats-*Po*lizei, Secret State-Police.] The secret police of the Nazi regime in Germany. Also *transf.*

Get, *v.* **6. b.** *colloq.* (orig. *U.S.*). To understand (a person or statement). Also *absol.* 1907. **c.** *colloq.* To notice, look at (a person, esp. one who is conceited or laughable); usu. *imper.* 1958. **14. b.** *colloq.* (orig. *U.S.*). To worry, annoy 1867. **c.** *colloq.* To enthral, attract, obsess 1913.

VII. G. together. a. *trans.* To collect or gather together (persons or things); to organize or harmonize. **b.** *intr.* To meet, confer; to agree.

Get-out. *colloq.* 1838. [f. *Get out* s.v. GET *v.* VII.] **1.** Phr. *As* or *like* (*all*) *g.*: used to indicate a high degree of something. **2.** An escape from a difficult position; an evasion 1899. **3.** *Theatr.* The total weekly cost of a production 1952.

Get-rich-quick, *a.* orig. *U.S.* 1904. Characterized by attempts at, or hopes of, acquiring wealth rapidly.

Ge·t-toge:ther. *colloq.* (orig. *U.S.*). 1911. [See *GET *v.* VII.] A meeting, gathering; an informal party.

Get-up. 3. *colloq.* (orig. *U.S.*). Energy, enterprise, determination. Also *get-up-and-get, get-up-and-go,* etc. 1841.

Gherao (gerau·). 1967. [f. Hind. *gherna* to surround, besiege.] A form of harassment in labour disputes in India and Pakistan, whereby workers detain their employers or managers on the premises. Hence as *v. trans.*, to detain (a person) in this manner.

Ghetto. 2. *transf.* and *fig.* A quarter in a city, etc., esp. a thickly populated slum area, inhabited by a minority group or groups; an isolated or segregated group, community, or area 1892.

Ghost, *sb.* **1). c.** A displaced repeated image on a television screen caused by a duplicate signal travelling by a longer path 1927.

Comb.: **g. town** orig. *U.S.*, a town partially or completely devoid of inhabitants; **g. train,** (*a*) a railway train run unofficially; (*b*) a train at a fun fair that travels through dark tunnels in which there are ghost-like effects; (*c*) a train run at night to keep the track clear of snow or severe frost; **g. writer** orig. *U.S.* = sense 11 in Dict.; hence **g.-write** *v. trans.* and *intr.*

Ghost, *v.* **4.** *trans.* and *intr.* To write (something) as a ghost writer 1922.

G.I. (dʒī·ˌəi, dʒīˌəi·). 1928. **1.** Abbrev. of *galvanized iron.* **2.** Abbrev. of *government* (or *general*) *issue*, used *attrib.* of things provided for or associated with American servicemen 1936. **G.I. bride,** a foreign woman married by an American serviceman while he is on duty abroad. Hence as *sb.*, a U.S. serviceman.

Giantism (dʒəi·ăntiz'm). 1639. [f. GIANT *sb.* + -ISM.] **a.** The quality, state, or practices of a giant or giants. **b.** Abnormal development in size. Also *transf.* and *fig.* 1885. Cf. *GIGANTISM.

Gibber (gi·bəɹ), *sb.*[3] *Austral.* 1834. [Aboriginal word.] A large stone; a boulder.

Gibberellin (dʒibəre·lin). 1939. [f. mod.L. *Gibberella* (generic name of the fungus from which it was first isolated), dim. of the generic name *Gibbera*, f. L. *gibber* hump: see -IN[1].] Any of numerous chemically related compounds (e.g. *gibberellic acid*, $C_{18}H_{21}O_4COOH$) which are present in many higher plants as growth regulators, with characteristic effects that include elongation of the stem and other parts and the promotion of germination and flowering.

The gibberellins are used to stimulate swelling of..grapes and tomato 1961.

Gig (gig), *sb.*[4] *colloq.* 1926. [Origin unkn.] An engagement for a musician or musicians playing jazz, dance-music, etc., esp. for one evening only; also, the place of such a performance. Also *transf.* and *attrib.* Hence as *v. intr.*, to do a 'gig' or 'gigs'; freq. *to g. around.*

Giga- (dʒ-, gəi·gă; dʒ-, gi·gă), *prefix.* 1951. An arbitrary deriv. of Gr. γίγας giant, prefixed to the names of units to form the names of units 1000 million times greater; as *gigahertz* = 10^9 hertz. Abbrev. G.

Gigantism (dʒəi·gæntiz'm). 1885. [f. L. *gigas, gigant-* + -ISM.] *Biol.* Abnormal or monstrous size, *spec.* **a.** In man, excessive size due to an increase in the supply of growth hormone. **b.** In plants, excessive size due to polyploidy 1927. Also *fig.* Cf. *GIANTISM.

Gigas (dʒəi·găs), *a.* 1915. [– L. *gigas*: see GIANT.] *Bot.* Of or designating a polyploid form of a plant which is larger and more vigorous than the normal form.

The leaf, or any other part of a g. plant, contains not only larger cells than the wild type, but also more of them 1970.

Gila (hī·lă). 1877. [Name of a river in New Mexico and Arizona.] *G. monster*, a large venomous lizard, *Heloderma suspectum.*

Gimmick (gi·mik). orig. *U.S. slang.* 1926. [Origin unkn.] A gadget; a tricky or ingenious device, idea, etc., esp. one adopted to attract attention or publicity. Hence **Gi·mmick** *v. trans.*, to provide with a g., to alter or tamper with. **Gi·mmick(e)ry,** the use of gimmicks; gimmicks collectively. **Gi·mmicky** *a.*, employing or characterized by gimmicks.

Gin (dʒin), *sb.*[3] *Austral.* Also **ginn, jin.** 1798. [Aboriginal word.] A female Australian Aboriginal.

Gippy (dʒi·pi). *slang.* Also **gippo, gypo, gyppie, gyppo, gyppy.** *a* 1889. [f. GIP(SY *sb.* + -Y[6], infl. by EGYPTIAN.] **1.** An Egyptian, esp. a native Egyptian soldier. Also *attrib.* or as *adj.* So **g. tummy,** diarrhœa suffered by visitors to hot countries. **2.** A gypsy. Also *attrib.* or as *adj.* 1902.

Girdle, *sb.*[1] **1. b.** orig. *U.S.* = CORSET 2. 1925.

Girl, *sb.* **4. g. Friday,** a resourceful young woman assistant; **g. friend, g.-friend,** a female friend; *spec.* a sweetheart, a man's favourite female companion.

Giro[2] (dʒəi·ro). 1896. [G. – It. *giro* circulation (of money).] A system whereby credits are transferred between banks, post offices, etc.; *spec.* a British Post Office system for the banking and transfer of money. Freq. *attrib.*

Git (git). *slang.* 1946. [var. GET *sb.*] In contemptuous use: a worthless person.

Give-away (gi·văwēⁱ). *colloq.* (orig. *U.S.*). Also **give away, giveaway.** 1872. [f. phr. *to give away* (GIVE *v.* XV. 3).] **1.** The act of giving something away; the thing so given; *spec.* (*a*) a game in which the object is to lose points, etc.; (*b*) a very low price for goods; (*c*) a radio or television programme or the like in which prizes are given. Freq. *attrib.* **2.** An inadvertent betrayal or revelation 1882.

Glagolitic (glægǒli·tik), *a.* 1861. [– mod.L. *glagoliticus*, f. Serbo-Croatian *glagolica*, f. *glagól* word.] Epithet of the ancient Slavonic alphabet, still retained in the service-books of the Roman Catholics of the Slavonic rite.

Glamour, *sb.* **2. b.** *colloq.* (orig. *U.S.*). Attractiveness; physical allure, esp. feminine beauty; freq. *attrib.* as *g. boy, girl* 1935. Hence **Gla·mo(u)rize** *v. trans.* (orig. *U.S.*), to make glamorous or attractive.

Glandular, *a.*

Comb.: **g. fever,** an acute disease, esp. of young adults, characterized by fever, swelling of the lymph nodes and leucocytosis.

Glass fibre. 1824. **a.** An individual filament of glass, of any length. **b.** (Also *glass-fibre, glassfibre.*) Glass in the form of such filaments; any material made from them, as a textile woven from them or a plastic containing them as reinforcement: = *FIBREGLASS 1882.

Glass-house. 2. b. *slang.* A military prison or guard-room 1925.

Glide, *sb.* **1. b.** *Cricket.* A stroke by which the ball is deflected towards long leg by the turned blade of the bat 1888.

Glissando (glisæ·ndo). Pl. **glissandi.** 1873. [Italianized form of Fr. *glissant*, gerund and pres. pple. of *glisser* to slide.] *Mus.* = PORTAMENTO.

Glitch (glitʃ). *slang.* 1962. [Origin unkn.] A surge of current or a spurious electrical signal; a brief irregularity in function or behaviour; a hitch or snag.

Gloire de Dijon (glwār də dīʒoṅ). 1845. [Fr., lit. 'glory of Dijon'.] A yellow hybrid tea rose.

A new variety exhibited last year in Paris, raised at Dijon, and called Gloire de Dijon, is a great acquisition 1854.

Glomerular (glǫme·rŭlăɹ), *a.* 1885. [f. GLOMERUL(E + -AR[1].] Of, pertaining to, or affecting the glomeruli of the kidneys.

Glottal, *a.* *G. catch* or *stop*: a sound produced by the sudden opening or shutting of the glottis with an emission of breath or voice 1877.

Go (gōᵘ), *sb.*[2] Also **Goh, I-go.** 1890. [Jap.] A Japanese board game of territorial possession.

Go (gōᵘ), *a. colloq.* (orig. *U.S.*). 1951. [f. the vb.] **1.** Functioning properly; ready and prepared; esp. of devices in spacecraft. **2.** Fashionable, modern, progressive 1962.

Goalie (gōᵘ·li). Also **-ee.** 1921. [f. GOAL + -IE.] A goal-keeper.

Gobbledygook (gǫ·b'ldigu:k, -gū:k). orig. *U.S.* Also **gobbledegook.** 1944. [prob. repr. a turkey-cock's gobble.] Official, professional, or pretentious verbiage or jargon.

Godetia (gǒdī·ʃiă). 1840. [mod.L. (E. Spach, 1835), f. the name of C. H. *Godet* (1797–1879), Swiss botanist.] A hardy annual plant of the genus so called, native to North America, and bearing cup-shaped flowers in racemes or spikes.

Go-go (gōᵘ·gōᵘ), *a* 1962. [redupl. of GO *sb.* or *v.*] Fashionable, 'swinging', unrestrained; *spec.* designating a lively dance, dancer, or music. Also **Go-go(-go)** *sb.*, continuous movement or activity.

Go-kart (gōᵘ·kāɹt). 1959. [Commercial adaptation of GO-CART.] A small racing car consisting of a chassis mounted on four wheels and powered by a light engine.

Gold.

Comb.: **g. brick, g.-brick,** (*a*) a brick-shaped piece of g.; (*b*) *slang* (orig. *U.S.*), a brick that appears to be made of g.; something only superficially valuable; (*c*) *U.S. slang*, a shirker; **g.-digger,** (*a*) one who digs for g.; (*b*) *slang* (orig. *U.S.*), a woman who attaches herself to a man merely for gain.

Golden, *a.*

5. g. mean, also = **g. section*; **g. section** [earliest known use of this name or its foreign equivalents is 1835 (as G. *goldene Schnitt*), though the proportion has been known since the 4th c. B.C.], the proportion obtained by dividing a line into two parts so that the ratio of the whole to the larger part is the same as the larger part to the smaller, viz. $\frac{1}{2}(\sqrt{5} + 1)$:1, or 1·61803....

Golf, *sb.*

Comb.: **g.-ball,** (*a*) a ball used in golf; (*b*) *colloq.*, a ball in certain kinds of electric typewriter on which all the type is mounted and which is caused to move to present the required symbol to the paper; **g.-widow,** a woman whose husband spends much of his spare time playing golf.

Gollop (gǫ·lǫp), *v. dial.* and *colloq.* Also **gollup.** 1823. [perh. extended form of GULP *v.*, infl. by GOBBLE *v.*[1]] *trans.* To swallow greedily or hastily; also *fig.* Hence as *sb.*, a greedy or hasty gulp.

Gonadotrophic (gōᵘ:nădotrōᵘ·fik), **-tropic** (-trōᵘ·pik, -trǫ·pik), *a.* 1931. [f. GONAD + -O- + Gr. τροφικός (f. τροφή nourishment) or τροπικός (f. τροπή turning).] *Physiol.* Regulating the activity of the gonads; of or pertaining to gonadotrophins. So **Go:nadotro·phin, -tro·pin,** any of several g. hormones that originate in the pituitary or the placenta.

Goo (gū). *slang* (orig. *U.S.*). 1911. [Of obscure origin but perh. f. BURGOO.] A viscid or sticky substance. Also *fig.* Hence **Goo·ey** *a.*

Goof. 2. A mistake 1955.

Comb.: **g.-ball,** (*a*) (a tablet of) any of various drugs, *spec.* marijuana; (*b*) a stupid person.

Goof (gūf), *v. slang.* 1932. [f. the sb.] **1.** *intr.* **a.** To spend time idly or foolishly. **b.** To make a mistake 1941. **2.** *trans.* To take a stupefying dose of (a drug) 1944. **3.** To bungle, mess *up* (something) 1960. Hence **Goo·fer,** a bungler.

Googol (gū·gǫl). 1940. [Arbitrary name.] A fanciful name (not in formal use) for ten raised to the hundredth power (10^{100}). Also **Goo·golplex** [cf. *-plex* in *multiplex, complex*], a name for ten raised to the power of a googol.

Gook (gūk, guk). *slang* (orig. and chiefly *U.S.*). 1935. [Origin unkn.] A term of contempt for a foreigner; *spec.* a coloured inhabitant of (south-)east Asia or elsewhere.

Goon (gūn). *slang.* 1921. [perh. f. dial. *gooney* a booby, but more immediately from the name of a subhuman creature called Alice the *Goon* in a cartoon series by E. C. Segar, American cartoonist.] **1.** orig. *U.S.* A stolid, dull, or stupid person. **2.** orig. *U.S.* A person hired to terrorize workers; a thug 1938. **3.** A guard in a German prisoner-of-war camp 1945. **4.** A member of the cast of the British radio series *The Goon Show*, noted for its crazy humour 1951. Also *attrib.* and *Comb.* Hence **Goo·nery** *sb.* **Goo·nish** *a.*

Gormless (gǭ·ɹmlės), *a.* orig. *dial.* Also **gaumless, gawmless.** *c* 1746. [f. dial. *gaum* understanding + -LESS.] Lacking understanding or discernment; stupid. Hence **Gorm,** a fool. **Go·rmlessness.**

Go-slow (gōᵘslōᵘ·). 1930. [f. GO *v.* + SLOW *adv.*] A form of industrial protest in which employees work at a deliberately slow pace. Also *attrib.*

Gouda (gau·dă, gū·dă). 1885. A flat round cheese orig. made at Gouda in Holland.

‖**Goum** (gūm). 1845. [Fr. – Arab. *gūm*, dial. var. *ḳaum* band, troop.] (A member of) a group of North African tribesmen or soldiers.

Gourami (gūᵊ·rămi, gūᵊrā·mi). Also **goramy, gouramy.** 1878. [– Mal. *gurāmi.*] A large freshwater food fish, *Osphronemus goramy*, of the family Anabantidæ, native to south-east Asia; also, any of various smaller members of the family, freq. kept in aquaria.

Goy (goi). Pl. **goyim, goys.** Fem. **goyah.** 1835. [Heb. *gōy* people, nation.] A Jewish designation for a non-Jew, a Gentile. Hence **Goy·ish** *a.*

Grade, *sb.* **9. d.** *To make the g.*: to reach the proper standard (orig. *U.S.*) 1912.

‖**Gramdan** (grāmdā·n, græ·mdæn). 1957. [Hindi, f. *grām-a* village + *dān* gift.] In India, (a movement for) the free gift of a village for the benefit of the community.

Grandiflora (græ:ndiflōᵊ·ră), *a.* 1901. [– mod.L. *grandiflora* a specific epithet often used in the names of large-flowered plants, f. L. *grandis* great + FLORA.] Bearing large flowers.

We, the unholy innocents, study the bulb catalogue and order one dozen paper-white G. Narcissus 1938.

‖**Grand mal** (grañ mal). 1842. [Fr., 'great sickness'.] General convulsive epilepsy with loss of consciousness; epilepsis gravior. Cf. **petit mal.*

Granny Smith. 1895. [f. the name of Maria Ann *Smith* ('Granny Smith'), d. 1870.] An Australasian variety of apple, which is bright green and suitable for eating raw or cooked.

Grape-vine. 2. a. Also, the route by which a rumour or piece of (secret) information is passed.

Grass, *sb.* **1. b.** *slang* (orig. *U.S.*). Marijuana, used as a drug 1943. **11.** *slang.* A police informer 1932.

Comb.: **g. root,** the fundamental level; the source or origin; *spec.* (orig. *U.S.*) the rank-and-file of the electorate or of a political party; freq. *pl.* and *attrib.*

Grass, *v.* **7.** *trans.* and *intr.* (*slang*). To betray (someone); to inform the police about (someone) 1936.

Graticule. 2. A transparent plate or cell bearing a grid, cross-wire, or scale, designed to be used with an optical instrument or cathode-ray oscilloscope for the purpose of positioning, measuring, or counting objects in the field of view; the grid, etc., on such a plate 1914.

Gratin. *spec.* The light crust on such dishes, now usu. made of breadcrumbs or grated cheese browned in the oven or under the grill; **au g.** *a.* and *sb.*, (a dish) cooked in this way.

Graves (grāv). 1605. [Fr. (pl.), name for gravelly sandy parts of the Bordeaux country.] A wine of the Graves district.

Gravy. 2. b. *slang* (orig. *U.S.*). Money easily acquired; an unearned or unexpected bonus. Hence *To ride* (or *board*) *the g. train* (or *boat*): to obtain easy financial success 1910.

Grease, *sb.*

Comb.: **g.-gun,** a device for pumping g. into bearings; **g.-paint,** a composition used by actors in painting their faces; **g.-proof** *a.*, impermeable to g.

Greaser. 2. b. An objectionable person; a sycophant 1900. **c.** Term applied to long-haired youths who, as members of a group or gang, habitually ride about on motor-cycles 1964.

Green. A. I. 1. b. Used of lights and signals on a road, railway, etc., to indicate that traffic is free to proceed 1883. Hence fig. phr. (*to give*) *the g. light*: (to give) permission to proceed. **c.** *To have g. fingers* or *a g. thumb*, to be unusually successful in making plants grow 1934.

Comb.: **g. belt,** an officially designated belt of open countryside where development is severely restricted, usu. enclosing a built-up area.

II. 2. b.

g. mamba, a venomous African snake *Dendraspis angusticeps* or *D. viridis*; **g. monkey,** the West African race of the grass monkey, *Cercopithecus æthiops*; formerly used for several other monkeys with greenish fur; **g. pigeon,** a pigeon of the genus *Treron*, widely distributed in Africa south of the Sahara and southern Asia.

Gremlin (gre·mlin). orig. *R.A.F. slang.* 1941. [Origin unkn., but prob. formed by analogy with GOBLIN.] A mischievous sprite imagined as the cause of mishaps to aircraft; hence, an embodiment of mischance in other activities.

Grenadine[3] (grenădī·n). 1896. [– Fr. (*sirop de*) *grenadine*, f. *grenade* GRENADE[1].] A syrup made from pomegranates (or other fruit).

Grey Squirrel. 1674. A common squirrel of the United States (*Sciurus carolinensis*), which was introduced to Europe in the late 19th century.

In America Grey Squirrel is prized game animal, in British Isles regarded as forest pest 1964.

Grid. 5. Also applied to any other network consisting of two series of regularly spaced lines crossing one another at right angles.

Griff (grif), *sb.*[5] *slang.* 1891. [Shortened form of next.] A tip; news; reliable information.

Griffin[4] (gri·fin). *slang.* 1889. [Origin unkn.] A tip (in betting, etc.); a signal, hint.

Gri·zzle, *v.*[2] *local.* 1746. [Origin unkn.] **1.** *intr.* To grin, snarl. **2.** To fret, cry in a whining or whimpering fashion 1842.

Groove, *sb.* **2. b.** *spec.* The spiral cut in a gramophone record (earlier, in a phonograph cylinder) which forms the path for the needle 1902. **4. b.** *In the g.* = *GROOVY *a.* 3. Hence *g.* is used to mean: a style of playing jazz or similar music, esp. one that is good; one's predilection or favourite style; something excellent 1932. *slang* (orig. *U.S.*).

Groove, *v.* **5.** *intr.* To be 'in the groove'; to dance or listen *to* music with pleasure; hence, to get on well *with* someone; to make love. Also *trans.*, to play (music) swingingly; to please (someone) 1935. *slang* (orig. *U.S.*).

Groovy (grū·vi), *a.* 1853. [f. GROOVE *sb.* + -Y[1].] **1.** Pertaining to or resembling a groove. **2.** *fig. colloq.* Tending to get into a rut 1882. **3.** *slang* (orig. *U.S.*). Playing, or capable of playing, jazz or similar music brilliantly or easily; appreciative of such music, sophisticated; hence generally, excellent 1937.

Gross, *a.* and *sb.*[3] **A. II. 2. c. gross national product,** the total value of all goods produced and services provided in a country during one year.

Grotty (grǫ·ti), *a. slang.* 1964. [f. GROT(ESQUE *a.* + -Y[1].] Unpleasant, dirty, nasty, etc.: a general term of disapproval.

Ground, *sb.*

Comb.: **2. g. cover,** the plants covering the surface of the earth, esp., in horticulture, plants whose low, spreading habit of growth smothers weeds; **g. rule,** (*a*) *Sport*, a rule devised for a particular ground; (*b*) a basic principle; **g.-sheet,** a waterproof sheet for spreading on the ground as a protection against damp.

Group, *sb.* **3. b.** One of the constituent bodies of the (*Oxford*) *Group(s) Movement* or *Oxford Group*, a religious movement brought from America to England in 1921 by Frank Buchman, characterized by the 'sharing' of personal problems by groups 1928. Hence **Grou·per. Grou·pism. Grou·pist.**

Groupie (grū·pi). 1943. [f. GROUP *sb.* + -IE.] **1.** *R.A.F. slang.* Short for *group captain.* **2.** Also *groupy.* A female follower of a popular musical group or groups 1967.

Growing, *vbl. sb.*

Comb.: **g.-on,** the cultivating of seedlings, the breeding of young chicks, etc., to maturity or full size; **g. season,** the season when rainfall and temperature permit plants to grow.

Growler. 4. A small iceberg 1912.

G string (dʒī·striŋ). 1831. **1.** *Mus.* A string tuned to G on a stringed instrument. **2.** Also **G-string, gee-string. a.** A loincloth, or the string supporting this, worn by American Indians, etc. 1878. **b.** A similar piece of material worn by show-girls, striptease artists, etc. 1936.

Guarani (gwā·rănī). Also **Guarany.** 1797. [Sp.] **1.** One of the main divisions of Tupi-Guarani, a family of South American Indian languages; a speaker of one of these languages. Also *attrib.* or as *adj.* **2.** The currency unit of Paraguay, consisting of 100 centimos 1943.

Guayule (gwəiˌū·li, hwəiˌū·li). 1906. [Amer. Sp., f. Nahuatl *cuauhuli.*] A silver-leaved shrub, *Parthenium argentatum*, of the family Compositæ, native to northern Mexico and adjacent parts of Texas, formerly cultivated as the source of a type of rubber; also, the rubber produced from this plant.

Guesstimate (ge·stimět), *sb.* orig. *U.S.* Also **guestimate.** 1936. [f. GUESS *sb.* + ESTIMATE *sb.*] An estimate which is based on both guess-work and reasoning. Hence as *v. trans.* and *intr.*

Guff (gɒf). 1825. [imit.; cf. Norw. dial. *gufs* puff of wind, *guffa* to blow softly.] **1.** A puff, whiff. **2.** *slang* (orig. *U.S.*). Nonsense, 'stuff' 1888.

Guide, *sb.*

Comb.: **2. g. dog,** a dog trained to lead blind people.

Guided (gəi·dėd), *a.* 1909. [f. GUIDE *sb.* + -ED[2].] **1.** Accompanied by a guide. **2.** Of weapons: operating by remote control or as directed by equipment carried in the weapon 1945.

Guinea-pig. **1. b.** A person or thing used like a g. as the subject of an experiment 1920.

Gullah (gɒ·lă), *a.* and *sb.* *U.S.* Also **Golla, Goolah.** 1739. [perh. a shortening of *Angola*, or f. the *Golas*, a Liberian group of tribes.] (Designating) a Negro or Negroes living on the sea-islands and tide-water coastline of South Carolina and Georgia, and their dialect.

Gun, *v.* **2. b.** *To g. for*: to shoot for; to go in search of (someone) with a gun; to seek to kill or harm 1888.

Guppy (gɒ·pi). 1925. [f. the name of R. J. L. *Guppy*, a Trinidad clergyman, used as the specific epithet in *Gerardinus guppyi* (A. Günther, 1866), the name used when the fish was first described.] A small fish, *Lebistes reticulatus*, originally from the West Indies, freq. kept in aquaria.

Gurkha (gūᵊ·ɹkă). Also **Ghoorka, Ghorkha, Ghurka, Goork(h)a.** 1811. A member of one of the dominant races of Nepal, of Hindu descent and Sanskritic speech, and especially famous for prowess in fighting. Also *attrib.*

Guru. Now the usual spelling. Also in gen. or trivial use: an influential teacher; a mentor.

Gut, *sb.* **1. d.** Used *attrib.* or quasi-*adj.*, of an issue, question, etc.: fundamental; of a reaction: instinctive and emotional rather than rational 1964.

Colloq. phrases. *To bust* (or *rupture*) *a g.*: to make a great effort. *To sweat* (or *work*) *one's guts out*: to work extremely hard. *To hate* (someone's) *guts*: to dislike (a person) intensely. *To have* (someone's) *guts for garters* (a hyperbolical threat).

Gutsy (gɒ·tsi), *a.* Also **gutsey, gutzy.** 1803. [f. *guts* (GUT *sb.* 1) + -Y[1].] **1.** orig. *Sc.* Greedy, voracious. **2.** Tough, spirited, courageous 1893.

Gym. Also *attrib.*, as **g.-slip, -tunic,** a schoolgirl's sleeveless, usu. belted, garment reaching from shoulder to thigh.

Gyp[1]. **3.** orig. *U.S.* A swindle 1914. Hence as *v. trans.*, to cheat, trick 1889.

Gypsophila (dʒipsǫ·filă). 1771. [mod.L. (Linnæus, 1751), f. Gr. γύψος chalk + φίλος loving.] A member of the genus of herbs so called, belonging to the family Caryophyllaceæ and bearing small pink or white flowers in panicles.

Gyro (dʒəiᵊro). 1910. Colloq. abbrev. of (*a*) GYROSCOPE, (*b*) *Gyro-compass*.

Comb.: **g.-pilot,** a gyro-compass used to steer a vessel or an aircraft without human agency; **g.-stabilizer,** a gyroscopic device for maintaining the equilibrium of a vessel; *g.-stabilized* adj.

Gyro-.

Gy·rocopter [after *helicopter*], a kind of helicopter; now *spec.* a small, light, single-seater one. **Gy·rofrequency,** the frequency with which a charged particle spirals about the lines of force of a magnetic field through which it is passing. **Gy·roplane** = *Gyrocopter.

Gyromagnetic (dʒəiᵊ:romæ̆gne·tik), *a.* 1922. [f. *GYRO, GYRO- + MAGNETIC.] **1.** *Physics.* Of or pertaining to the interdependence of the angular momentum of a spinning charged particle and its resulting magnetic moment. **2.** Applied to a type of compass in which a magnetic compass automatically corrects the gradual deviations of a directional gyroscope, which in turn provides the compass reading 1946.

H.

III. h. = hot, as h. & c., hot and cold (water); H-*bomb*, hydrogen bomb; H. E., His Excellency, high explosive; H.F., high frequency; H.M.I., Her (His) Majesty's Inspector (of Schools); H.M.S.O., Her (His) Majesty's Stationery Office; H.N.C., Higher National Certificate; H.P., hire purchase; H.Q., Headquarters; Hz, hertz.

Habit, *sb.* **III. 2. d.** *Psychol.* An automatic reaction to a specific situation 1859. **e.** *colloq.* (orig. *U.S.*). The practice of taking drugs 1887.

Hadron (hæ·drǫn). 1962. [f. Gr. ἁδρός thick, bulky + *-ON; first used in Russ. (as *adron*).] *Physics.* Any strongly interacting sub-atomic particle. Hence **Hadro·nic** *a.*

Hæm, heme (hīm). 1925. [– Gr. αἷμα blood or f. HÆM(OGLOBIN.] *Biochem.* A red compound, $C_{34}H_{32}N_4O_4Fe$, that is the non-protein constituent of hæmoglobin; also, any of various iron-containing compounds that are constituents of some proteins and have a similar structure. Freq. *attrib.*

‖**Haiku** (həi·ku). 1899. [Jap.] A form of Japanese verse consisting of three lines of five, seven, and five syllables respectively; an English imitation of this.

Hair, *sb.*

Colloq. phr. *In one's h.*: being a nuisance or encumbrance; in one's way; opp. *out of one's h.* *To let one's h. down*: to throw off reserve. *To get by the short hairs*: to have complete control over.

Comb.: **h. crack,** a fine short crack in metal; **h.-piece,** a length of false h. used to augment the natural h.; **h.-raising** *a.*, capable of causing the h. to stand on end through fear or excitement; **h.-style,** a particular way of dressing the h.

Hair-do (hēᵊ·ɹdū). 1932. [f. HAIR *sb.* + DO *sb.*] **a.** orig. *U.S.* A way or style of dressing the hair. **b.** A cutting and setting of the hair.

Hairy, *a.* **4.** *slang.* Difficult, unpleasant, crude, clumsy 1848.

Half-. I.

Comb.: **h.-integral** *a.*, equal to half an odd integer.

II.

Comb.: **h.-blue,** colours awarded to a player or competitor chosen as a second choice to a full blue, or to a representative in minor sports; a player so distinguished; **h.-landing,** a landing half-way up a flight of stairs; **h. nelson** *Wrestling*, a hold in which one arm is thrust from the back under the corresponding arm of the opponent and the hand placed on the back of his neck; **h. shot** *Golf*, a shot played with something less than a full swing; **h.-staff** *U.S.*, half-mast; **h.-title,** (*b*) the title of a section of a book printed on the recto of the leaf preceding it.

Ha·lf-life. 1909. The time in which a physical property or parameter, esp. radioactivity, decreases by a half.

Half-tone. **3.** *Printing.* A photo-mechanical illustration printed from a block in which the continuous tones of the original are represented by dots of varying size; this process 1894.

Halide (hēⁱ·ləid). 1876. [f. HAL(OGEN + -IDE.] *Chem.* Any compound consisting of a halogen combined with another element or radical.

Hallstatt (ha·lʃtat). 1866. [Name of a village in Upper Austria, where the remains were discovered.] *Archæol.* Denoting finds representing a phase of the early Iron Age.

Hallucinogen (hæ̆lⁱ¹ū·sinodʒen). 1955. [f. HALLUCIN(ATION + -O- + -GEN.] A drug which causes hallucinations. Hence **Hallu:cinoge·nic** *a.*, causing hallucinations.

Ham, *sb.*[1] **3.** *slang* (orig. *U.S.*). An inexpert performer; an ineffective or over-emphatic actor; an inexpert or over-theatrical performance 1882. Hence **Ham** *a.*, self-consciously theatrical. **Ham** *v.*, to over-act. **4.** *slang.* An amateur radio operator 1922.

Comb.: **h.-fisted, -footed, -handed** *adjs.*, clumsy, awkward.

Hamamelis (hæmămī·lis). 1743. [mod.L. (J. F. Gronovius, 1739) – Gr. ἀμαμηλίς medlar.] A shrub or small tree belonging to the genus so called, which is native to eastern Asia and eastern North America and includes the common witch hazel, *H. virginiana*, whose leaves and bark yield a medicinal extract.

Hamburger (hæ·mbɒ̄ɹgəɹ). 1616. [G.] **1.** A native or inhabitant of the German town of Hamburg. **2.** (Freq. w. lower-case initial.) A fried cake of chopped beef served between two halves of a toasted bun 1889.

Hammer, *sb.*

Comb.: **h. lock** *Wrestling*, a position in which a wrestler is held with one arm bent behind his back.

Hammy (hæ·mi), *a.* 1861. [f. HAM *sb.*[1] + -Y[1].] **1.** Characterized by the presence of ham; resembling ham. **2.** *slang.* Of, pertaining to, or characteristic of ham actors or acting 1929.

Hand, *v.* **1.** *To h. off* (Rugby football), to push (a tackler) off with the hand 1897. **4.** *To h. it to*: to acknowledge the superiority of (orig. *U.S.*) 1916.

Handedness (hæ·ndėdnės). 1921. [f. HANDED *a.* + -NESS.] The tendency to, or a preference for, the use of either the right or the left hand.

The left hemisphere is usually dominant for speech regardless of the h. of the individual 1961.

Ha·nd-out. 1882. [f. HAND *v.* + OUT *adv.*] **1.** What is handed out, e.g. alms (orig. *U.S.*). **2.** Matter handed out to the newspaper press 1929.

Hang-over. **b.** Unpleasant after-effects of dissipation (*slang*) 1904.

Ha·ng-up. *slang.* 1959. Drawback; difficulty; fixation.

Hanky (hæ·ŋki). 1895 (*handky*). Familiar colloquialism for HANDKERCHIEF (hæ·ŋkəɹtʃif); see -Y[6].

Hanuman (hɒnumā·n). Also **hoonoomaun, huniman.** 1814. [Hind., Hindi.] **1.** *Hindu Mythol.* Proper name of a semi-divine monkey-like creature. **2.** An Indian monkey, *Presbytis entellus*, venerated by Hindus 1843.

Hapax legomenon (hæ·pæks lėgǫ·mĕnǫn). Pl. **hapax legomena.** Also simply **hapax.** 1654. [Gr. ἅπαξ λεγόμενον thing once said.] A word or form of which only one instance is recorded.

Haploid (hæ·ploid), *a.* 1908. [– G. *haploid* (E. Strasburger, 1905), f. Gr. ἁπλόος single + εἶδος form.] *Biol.* Of a cell or its nucleus: having a single set of unpaired chromosomes, as in a gamete. Of an organism: having h. somatic cells. Also as *sb.*, a h. organism. Cf. *DIPLOID, etc.

Happen, *v.* **1. b.** With a vague subject (e.g. *anything, something*), said of some serious thing (e.g. death) coming *to* a person 1795.

If anything happens to me, recollect that death is a debt we must all pay LD. NELSON.

Happening, *vbl. sb.* **2.** An improvised or spontaneous theatrical or pseudo-theatrical entertainment 1962.

Happy, *a.* **4.** *Happy ship*, a ship on which the crew work together harmoniously; also *transf.* of the conduct of any organization; **b.** As the second element of a compound (orig. *U.S. colloq.*): in a state of excitement or nervousness, in respect of the object, event, use, or practice of the action, etc., denoted by the first element; e.g. *bomb-h.*, *slap-h.*, *trigger-h.*

4. A branch or a department may be a theoretical monstrosity and yet be a 'h. ship'; and traditionally a 'h. ship' is the only efficient ship 1950.

Hard, *a.* **I. 1. b.** Of a lawn-tennis court: made of asphalt or other h. material 1889. **III. 2. d.** Of a drug that is taken non-medicinally: addictive and seriously harmful to health with continued use 1967. **6.** Of ionizing radiation: having great penetrating power 1902.

Comb.: **h. copy,** a legible permanent record of matter stored on microfilm, magnetic tape, etc., which cannot normally be consulted directly; **h. core,** (*a*) heavy material forming the foundation of a road, etc.; (*b*) *fig.*, an irreducible nucleus or residuum; **h. cover,** a stiff binding case (on a book); chiefly *attrib.*; **h. currency,** one not likely to depreciate suddenly or fluctuate greatly in value; **h. hat,** (*a*) a bowler hat; (*b*) a safety helmet; **h. landing** (see *LANDING *vbl. sb.* 1 d); **h.-line** *attrib.*, adhering unwaveringly to a hard or firm policy; **h.-lying money,** for *h.-line money* (see LINE *sb.*[2] I. 6); **h. pad,** a form of distemper in dogs; **h. sell,** aggressive salesmanship or advertising; **h. shoulder,** land hardened and laid down for vehicles to get safely off the running lanes of a motorway in an emergency.

Ha·rdboard. 1929. [BOARD *sb.* 3.] A type of stiff board made from wood-pulp fibre and used as a substitute for wood.

Hardware. **b.** Weapons 1865. **c.** The physical components of a system or device as opposed to the procedures required for its operation. Opp. *SOFTWARE. 1953.

Hare, *v.*[2] 1893. [f. HARE *sb.*] *intr.* †**a.** To double like a hare. **b.** To run or move with great speed 1908.

Harewood (hēᵊ·ɹwud). Also **hairwood, air-wood** (8 **aire-**); and simply 7 **ayer, ayre.** 1664. [– dial. G. *aehre, ehre*, prob. f. Friulian, etc., *ayar, ayer, aire* :– Rom. **acre* = L. *acer* maple.] Stained sycamore wood, used by cabinet-makers.

Harijan (hæ·ridʒăn). 1931. [Skr., 'person devoted to the god Vishnu', f. *Hari* Vishnu

+ *jana* person.] The name given by Gandhi to an Untouchable in India. Also as *adj.*

Harris (hæ·ris). 1894. The name of the southern part of the Island of Lewis with Harris in the Outer Hebrides, used to designate the hand-woven tweed produced by the inhabitants of this region.

Hassle, -el (hæ·s'l). *colloq.* 1945. [Eng. and U.S. dial.] A quarrel, argument, fuss. Also as *v. intr.*, to quarrel, argue.

Hatch, *sb.*[1] **2. d.** An opening or door in an aircraft or spacecraft 1948.

‖**Haut, haute.** Fr. High (class), in borrowed phrases, as: **Haute couture** (ot kutür), high fashion; the leading dressmakers and dressmaking establishments collectively. **Haute cuisine** (ot kwizīn), high-class (French) cooking. **Haute école** (ot ekol), the more difficult feats of horsemanship. **Haute vulgarisation** (ot vulgarizasioṅ), successful popularization of abstruse or complex matters.

Have, *v.* **III. 1. b.** To possess sexually; to have sexual intercourse with 1594.

Colloq. phr. *To h. had it*: to have (had one's chance and) missed it; to have had enough. *To h. it* (or *nothing*) *on*: to have the (or no) advantage over. *To h. it* (*so*) *good*: to possess (so many) advantages. *To h. on*: to puzzle intentionally; to tease.

Have-not (hæ·vnǫt). 1836. [HAVE *v.*, NOT *adv.*] One who has no possessions, or very few in comparison with others; esp. of those nations that are considered not to have a due share of territory or material resources (1919).

The Rich and the Poor—the Havenots and the Haves LYTTON. They contemplate a World-Federation when the international League of the Have-Nots has conquered all the Haves J. L. GARVIN.

Hawk, *sb.*[1] **2. b.** *Polit.* (See *DOVE *sb.* 2 b.)

Haymaker. 4. A swinging blow or punch (*slang*) 1912.

Head, *sb.* **I. 7. d.** A drug-addict or drug-taker. Freq. with defining word prefixed, as *HOPHEAD, etc. 1911. **II. 4. b.** A device for converting electrical signals into mechanical movements (in disc recording) or variations in magnetization (on magnetic tape), and *vice versa* 1951. **14. b.** A seamen's latrine (in the ship's bows). Often *pl.* 1748.

Headache. 3. *transf.* A troublesome or annoying thing; a trouble, trial (*slang* or *colloq.*); orig. *U.S.* 1934.

Headline. 2. d. A heading in large letters in a newspaper; *pl.* the summary of a news broadcast 1867 (orig. *U.S.*). *To make* or *hit the headlines*: to be news of the first importance.

Head-on, *adv.* and *a.* orig. *U.S.* **A.** *adv.* (*head-o·n*) With the head or front pointed directly towards something 1840. **B.** *adj.* (*hea·d-on*) Involving the direct meeting of the front of a vehicle with another object 1903.

Health. Phr. *Not for one's h.* (orig. *U.S.*): for one's material advantage or interest.

Comb.: **h. centre,** a local headquarters of medical services; **h. food,** food chosen for its dietary or h.-giving properties; **h. physics,** that branch of radiology which is concerned with the h. of those working with radioactive material.

Hearty, *a.* (*adv.*) and *sb.* **C.** *sb.* **b.** *Univ. slang.* An athletic non-studious man 1925.

Heat, *sb.* **8. c.** *slang* (orig. *U.S.*). In various interconnected senses, as (*a*) a gun (? as an instrument of 'heat'), also *heater*; (*b*) in phr. *to turn on the heat*: to use a gun; hence *fig.*, *to turn the heat on*: to apply pressure; (*c*) involvement with or pursuit by the police 1928.

Comb.: **h. exchanger,** a device used to transfer heat from one medium to another; **h.-pump,** a heat-engine working in reverse, using energy supplied to it to transfer heat from a colder to a hotter place; **h. sink,** a device used to carry away unwanted heat.

Heater. 2. Also, a gun (see *HEAT *sb.* 8 c).

Heath Robinson (hīþ rǫ·binsǫn). 1917. [f. the name of the humorous artist W. *Heath Robinson* (1872–1944).] Used *attrib.* or *ellipt.* of any absurdly ingenious device of the kind illustrated by this artist.

Heavy, *a.*[1] **I. 5. c.** *Physics.* Distinguished by having a greater than the usual mass: applied to certain isotopes and to compounds containing them, as *h. hydrogen, water* 1930. **III. 2. b.** Of amatory relationships: intense 1952. **V. 4. b.** Of newspapers, etc.: serious 1875. **c.** In Jazz and popular music, used in various senses: serious; important; loud, forceful, etc. 1937.

Hebe. 4. *Bot.* [mod.L. (P. Commerson, 1789).] A member of a large genus of shrubs so called, mostly native to New Zealand and formerly included in the genus *Veronica* 1921.

The hebes, as the shrubby veronicas are now called 1961.

Heck[2] (hek). *dial.* and *U.S.* 1887. Euphemistic alteration of HELL.

One h. of a messenger E. POUND.

Hedge, *sb.*

h. hop, the action of an airman in flying at low levels so as to suggest hopping over hedges.

Heebie-jeebies (hī:bi,dʒī·biz), *sb. pl. slang* (orig. *U.S.*). 1924. A dance resembling the blues; also, *fig.* the 'blues', the 'jim-jams'.

Heel (hīl), *sb.*[3] *slang* (orig. *U.S.*). 1914. [Of doubtful origin: perh. f. HEEL *sb.*[1]] An untrustworthy person, a rotter.

He was a h. and she's well rid of him L. P. HARTLEY.

Heel (hīl), *v.*[3] 1857. [Corruption of earlier HELE, HEAL *v.*] With *in* = HELE *v.* Hence **Hee·ling-i·n** *vbl. sb.*

Heist (həist). *U.S. slang.* 1927. [repr. U.S. local pronunc. of HOIST *sb.* and *v.*] A hold-up, a robbery. Also as *v. trans.*, to hold up, rob. Hence **Hei·ster,** a robber, a hijacker.

HeLa (hē·,lā). 1953. [f. the name, *He*len *La*ne, of the patient from whom the original tissue was taken.] Used *attrib.* to designate a strain of human epithelial cells maintained in tissue culture and derived originally from tissue from a carcinoma of the cervix. Occas. *absol.*

Heliport (he·lipǭᵊɹt). 1948. [f. HELI-, after *AIRPORT.] A landing-place for helicopters.

Hell, *sb.*

Slang phr. *To give* (a person) *h.*: to give him 'a bad time'. *To knock, blast*, etc., *h. out of*: to pound heavily. *Like h.*: (*a*) recklessly, desperately; very much; (*b*) *ironically*, not at all, on the contrary.

Comb.: **hell's angel,** name given, orig. in the 1950s in the U.S., to a member of a group of awless, usually leather-jacketed, motor-cyclists notorious for their disturbances of civil order in California.

Heme: see *HÆM.

Henge (hendʒ). 1932. [f. STONE)HENGE.] A term for a monument more or less akin to the stone circle of Stonehenge. Also *attrib.*

Henry (he·nri). Pl. **henries, henrys.** 1893. [Name of Joseph *Henry* (1797–1878), American physicist.] *Electr.* A unit of inductance (now incorporated in the S.I.), equal to the inductance of a closed circuit in which an e.m.f. of one volt is produced by a current changing at the rate of one ampere per second.

Hep (hep), *a. slang* (orig. *U.S.*). 1908. [Of unknown origin.] Well-informed, knowledgeable, 'wise *to*', up-to-date; smart, stylish. Hence as *sb.*, the state of being 'hep'; as *vb.*, to pep *up*. Also **Hepped** *ppl. a.* (often with *up*); *to be hepped on*, to be enthusiastic about. Cf. next.

Hep-cat (he·pkæt). *slang* (orig. *U.S.*). 1938. [f. *HEP *a* + *CAT *sb.*[1] I. 1. b.] An addict of jazz, swing music, etc.; one who is 'hep'; = *HIPSTER[1].

Herbicide (hə̄·ɹbisəid). 1899. [f. L. *herba* grass, green crops + -I- + -CIDE.] Any substance that is toxic to some or all plants and is used to destroy unwanted vegetation. (Orig. a proprietary name.) Hence **Herbici·dal** *a.*

Hereford (he·rĭfǭɹd). 1805. The name of the county town of Herefordshire, an English county on the Welsh border, used to designate a breed of cattle originating there. Also **He·refordshire** 1789.

‖**Herrenvolk** (hę̄·rənfǫlk, -fōᵘk). 1941. [G., 'master-race'.] The Nazi conception of the German people as born to mastery. Also *transf.* as an appellation of other 'superior' groups. Also *attrib.* or as *adj.*

Forms of warfare which, according to the German view, should be the strict monopoly of the *Herrenvolk* W. S. CHURCHILL.

Hertz (hə̄ɹts, ‖hę̄rts). 1928. [See HERTZIAN *a.*] A unit of frequency, now incorporated into the S.I., equal to one cycle per second.

Het (het), *pa. pple.* late ME. [pa. pple. of HEAT *v.*] Heated; orig. *dial.* and *U.S.* (with *up*: excited).

Hetero-.

He·terograft, a graft taken from an individual of a different species from that of the recipient. **Heteropolar** *a.*, (*b*) applied to an electric generator in which the armature conductor passes north and south poles alternately; (*c*) *Chem.*, formed by ions of opposite sign, between which there is electrostatic attraction; ionic. **He:tero-tra·nsplant** *sb.*, a heterograft. **He:tero-transpla·nt** *v. trans.*, to transplant from one individual to another of a different species; so **He:terotransplanta·tion.**

Heterocyclic (hetĕrosəi·klik), *a.* 1895. [f. HETERO- + CYCLIC *a.*] **1.** *Bot.* = HETEROMEROUS *a.* 2. **2.** *Chem.* Containing or designating a ring composed of more than one kind of atom 1899. Also as *sb.*, a h. compound. Hence **He·terocycle,** a h. ring or compound.

Heterosexual (he:tĕrose·ksiuăl), *a.* 1892. [f. HETERO-, after *homosexual.*] Involving, related to, or characterized by a sexual propensity for the opposite sex; of or involving sexual activity between individuals of opposite sex. Also as *sb.*, a h. individual. Hence **He:terosexua·lity,** the condition of being h.

Heterosis (hetĕrōᵘ·sis). 1914. [– late Gr. ἑτέρωσις alteration, f. ἕτερος different.] *Genetics.* The tendency of cross-breeding to produce an individual with a greater hardiness and capacity for growth than either of the parents. Hence **Hetero·tic** *a.*

Heuristic, *a.* **1. b.** *Computers.* Proceeding by trial and error: used of a method of problem-solving in which the next step depends on an evaluation of progress made towards a solution 1962. Hence **Heuri·stically** *adv.* Also **Heuristics** *sb. pl.* (const. as *sing.*), the study and use of h. techniques in data processing.

Hex (heks), *v.* Chiefly *U.S.* 1830. [– Pennsylvanian G. *hexe*, f. G. *hexen.*] *intr.* To practise witchcraft. Also *trans.*, to bewitch, to cast a spell on.

Hex (heks), *sb.* Chiefly *U.S.* 1856. [Pennsylvanian G. – G. *hexe.*] **1.** A witch. Also *transf.*, a witch-like female. **2.** A magic spell or curse 1909.

Hexa-.

Hexachlo·rophane, a white crystalline powder, $CH_2(C_6HCl_3OH)_2$, used as a disinfectant; also (*U.S.*) **-phene.**

Hexode. B. *sb.* *Radio.* [– G. *hexode.*] A valve with six electrodes 1933. Also *attrib.* or as *adj.*

Hide, *sb.*[3] **3.** A place of concealment for the observation of wild animals 1864.

Hide, *v.*[1]

h.-out orig. *U.S. colloq.*, a hiding-place (f. phr. *to h. out*: to go into hiding). So **Hi·dy-hole, hidey-hole** (həi·dihōᵘl) orig. *Sc.* [Alteration of *hiding-hole.*]

Hi-fi (həi·fəi·). 1950. Colloq. abbrev. of *HIGH-FIDELITY.

High, *a.* **II. 12. b.** Under the influence of a drug or drugs 1934.

Comb.: **2. h. camp,** 'camp' (see *CAMP *a.*) of a sophisticated kind; **h.-key** *Photogr.*, consisting of light tones; **h. life,** a W. African dance; **h. polymer,** a polymer with a high molecular weight; **h.-ranking** *a.*, of high rank, senior; **h.-rise** *a.*, of a building: tall, multi-storey; **h.-tensile,** used *attrib.* of metals possessing great tensile strength; **h. wire,** a high tight-rope.

B. *sb.* **1. c.** An area of high barometric pressure. Also *transf.* 1878. **d.** *slang.* A euphoric state induced by the taking of a drug or drugs 1961.

High altar. late ME. [HIGH *a.* II. 3.] The principal altar of a church.

High-fide·lity. 1934. [FIDELITY 2.] The property of equipment used in the recording and reproduction of sound, of producing little distortion in the signal, so that the sound produced bears as close a resemblance as possible to the original. Also *attrib.*

Highlight (həi·ləit), *v.* 1934. [f. HIGH LIGHT.] *trans.* To bring into prominence, to 'feature', to draw attention to.

Thursday's polling is unlikely to h. any notable national trends 1965.

High-up (hǝi·ʌp), *a. colloq.* 1868. In a high or exalted position, chiefly *fig.* (cf. HIGH *a.* II. 1); hence as *sb.*, an exalted personage. So **Hi·gher-up** *sb.*

Hijack, hi-jack (hǝi·dʒæk), *v.* orig. *U.S.* Also formerly **high-jack.** 1923. [Origin unknown.] *trans.* To steal (contraband or stolen goods) in transit; to hold up and commandeer (a vehicle and its load) in transit; to seize (an aeroplane) in flight and force the pilot to fly to a new destination. So **Hi·jacking** *vbl. sb.* and *ppl. a.* Also **Hi·jack** *sb.*, an instance of hijacking. **Hi·jacker** (in Dict.).

Hike, *sb.* orig. *dial.* and *U.S.* 1865. [f. HIKE *v.*] A vigorous walk; a tramp.

Hi·ll-bi·lly. Chiefly *U.S.* 1900. [f. HILL *sb.* + BILLY.] **1.** A rustic, esp. from the backwoods or mountains. Also *attrib.* and *transf.* **2.** A type of American folk music. Also *attrib.* 1924.

Hip (hip), *a. slang* (orig. *U.S.*). 1904. [Of unknown origin.] = *HEP *a.* Hence **Hip** *v. trans.*, to render 'hip', to inform. **Hipped** *ppl. a.*, well-informed; fond of. **Hi·p-cat** = *HEP-CAT. **Hi·pness,** the condition or quality of being 'hip'.

Hippeastrum (hipǐæ·strǒm). 1821. [mod. L. (W. Herbert, 1821), f. Gr. ἱππεύς horseman, knight + ἄστρον star.] A member of the genus of South American bulbous plants so named, belonging to the family Amaryllidaceæ; the knight's star lily.

Hippie, hippy (hi·pi), *sb.* and *a. slang* (orig. *U.S.*). 1953. [f. *HIP *a.* + -Y[6].] **A.** *sb.* A hipster; a person, usually exotically dressed, who is, or appears to be, given to the use of hallucinogenic drugs; a beatnik. **B.** *adj.* Of, pertaining to, or characteristic of hippies 1959.

Hippocratic, *a. H. oath*, an oath comprising the obligations and professional conduct of physicians, taken by those entering upon medical practice.

Hipster[1] (hi·pstǝɹ). *slang* (orig. *U.S.*). 1946. [f. *HIP *a.* + -STER.] One who is 'hip'; a hip- (or hep-) cat; also *attrib.* Hence **Hi·psterism,** the condition or fact of being a hipster; the characteristics of hipsters.

Hipster[2] (hi·pstǝɹ). 1962. [f. HIP *sb.*[1] + -STER.] Used esp. *attrib.*: of, or pertaining to, a garment, e.g. a skirt or trousers, that extends from the hips rather than the waist. In *pl.*: such a pair of trousers.

Hire, *sb.*

Comb.: **h.-car,** a car available for hire; **h.-purchase,** a system by which a hired thing becomes the hirer's property after a certain number of payments.

Histamine (hi·stămīn, -in). 1913. [f. ἱστός (see HISTO-) + AMINE.] *Biochem.* A simple base, $C_3H_3N_2{\cdot}(CH_2)_2{\cdot}NH_2$, present in all body tissues and responsible for certain allergic reactions.

Histo-.

Hi:stopatho·logy, (the study of) the changes in tissues associated with a disease or disorder; so **Hi:stopatholo·gic, -lo·gical** *adjs.* **Hi:stopatho·logist.**

Histogram (hi·stǒgræm). 1891. [f. Gr. ἱστός mast + -GRAM.] A diagram in which columns represent the frequency with which some quantity has values within different ranges.

Historicism (histǫ·risiz'm). 1901. [f. HISTORIC *a.* + -ISM; tr. Gr. *historismus.*] **1.** The theory that all social and cultural phenomena are relative and historically determined, and hence are only to be understood in their historical context *a*1902. **2.** The belief that historical change occurs in accordance with laws, so that the course of history may be predicted but cannot be altered by human will 1901. **3.** A tendency in philosophy to see historical development as the most fundamental aspect of human existence 1939. **4.** Excessive regard for the institutions and values of the past; *spec.* in *Archit.*, the use of historical styles in design 1939. Hence **Histo·ricist.**

Hit, *sb.* **4. c.** A popular success in public entertainment 1811.

Comb.: **h. parade,** a programme or grouping of 'hits'; **h. tune,** a tune that proves popular.

Hitch-hike (hi·tʃ,hǝik), *v.* orig. *U.S.* 1923. [f. HITCH *v.* 3. + HIKE *v.*] *intr.* To travel by means of lifts in vehicles. Hence as *sb.*, such a journey. Also **Hi·tch-hiker,** one who hitch-hikes. **Hi·tch-hiking** *vbl. sb.*

Kids When their imagination bids Hitch-hike a thousand miles to find the Hesperides that's on their mind AUDEN.

Hitler (hi·tlǝɹ). 1930. [Name of Adolf *Hitler* (1889–1945), Chancellor of the German Reich and leader of the National Socialist Party.] One who embodies the characteristics of Hitler. Also *attrib.* and *Comb.* Hence **Hi·tlerism,** the political principles or policy of the Nazi party in Germany. **Hi·tlerite,** a follower of Hitler.

Hive, *v.* **4.** *To hive off*: to swarm off like bees; esp. to break away from, to separate from, a group 1902. Also *trans.*, to remove from a group, a large unit, etc.; to make separate.

Hock (hǫk), *sb.*[5] *slang.* 1859. [– Du. *hok* hutch, prison, credit, debt.] *In h.*: (*a*) in the act (of gambling), (*b*) in prison, (*c*) in pawn, (*d*) in debt.

Comb.: **h.-shop,** a pawnshop.

Holdfast. B. 4. b. *Bot.* An organ of attachment developed by some algæ 1841.

Holding, *vbl. sb.* **II. 1.** See also *small h.* s.v. SMALL *a.* ad fin.

Hole, *sb.* **I. 6.** *Physics.* A position from which an electron is absent; *esp.* one in a semiconductor that may be regarded as a mobile particle having mass and a positive charge 1930.

Hollandaise (hǫlăndē^i^z, ‖olandẹ̄z). 1841. [Fr., fem. of *hollandais* Dutch, f. *Hollande* Holland.] In full *H. sauce.* A creamy sauce made of butter, egg-yolks, vinegar, etc., served with fish or vegetables.

Holmium (hō^u^·lmiǒm). 1879. [mod.L. (P. T. Cleve, 1879), f. *Holmia*, latinized name of Stockholm: see -IUM.] *Chem.* A silvery, relatively soft metallic element of the lanthanide series which forms a series of strongly paramagnetic salts in which it is trivalent. Atomic number 67; symbol Ho.

Holocene (hǫ·losīn), *a.* 1897. [– Fr. *holocène*, f. HOLO- + Gr. καινός recent, after *Eocene*, etc.] Of, pertaining to, or designating the most recent geological epoch, which began approximately 10,000 years ago and still continues. Also *absol.*

Hologram (hǫ·logræm). 1949. [f. HOLO- + -GRAM.] *Physics.* A pattern produced when light (or other radiation) reflected, diffracted, or transmitted by an object placed in a coherent beam (e.g. from a laser) is allowed to interfere with the undiffracted beam; a photographic plate or film containing such a pattern.

When suitably illuminated, a photographic h. produces a two- or three-dimensional image of the original (two- or three-dimensional) object.

Holograph (hǫ·logrɑf), *v.* 1968. [Back-formation from *HOLOGRAPHY, after *photograph, telegraph* vbs.] *trans.* To record as a hologram.

Holography. 2. *Physics.* [After *HOLOGRAM.] The process or science of producing and using holograms 1964. Hence **Holographic** *a.* in corresponding sense. Also **Hologra·phically** *adv.*, by means of h., in a holographic manner.

Holotype (hǫ·lotǝip). 1897. [f. HOLO- + -TYPE.] *Biol.* A specimen chosen as the basis of the first description of a new species.

As long as a h. is extant, it automatically fixes the application of the name concerned 1966.

Holy, *a.* colloq. phr. *holier-than-thou*: characterized by an attitude of superior sanctity.

We didn't want a preachy 'holier-than-thou' lecture 1950.

Home, *v.* **4.** *intr.* Of a vessel, aircraft, etc.: to be guided to its destination by the use of a landmark or by means of a radio beam, etc. Freq. const. *on.* 1920.

Home Guard. a. *U.S.* A member of a local volunteer force 1861. **b.** The Territorial Forces of England 1909; in the war of 1939–1945 applied to the Local Defence Volunteers organized for the defence of the country.

Homing, *vbl. sb.* **2.** Used *attrib.* of automatic devices for guiding aircraft, missiles, etc.

Homo (hō^u^·mo), *sb.*[2] and *a.* 1929. Colloq. shortening of HOMOSEXUAL *a.* (*sb.*).

Homo-.

Ho·mograft, a graft taken from another individual of the same species as the recipient. **Homopolar** *a.*, (*b*) applied to electric generators in which the direction of the flux does not alternate with relation to the armature conductor(s), so that a direct current is generated without the use of commutators; (*c*) *Chem.* [– G. *homöopolar* (R. Abegg, 1906)], formed by or arising out of the sharing of electrons between neutral atoms; covalent. **Homotra·nsplant** *sb.*, a homograft. **Ho:motranspla·nt** *v. trans.*, to transplant from one individual to another of the same species; so **Ho:motransplanta·tion.**

Homogenize (hǒmǫ·dʒǐnǝiz), *v.* 1886. [f. HOMOGEN(EOUS *a.* + -IZE.] *trans.* To render homogeneous or similar; to unite into a single whole of uniform composition; also *fig. Spec.* **a.** To subject (milk) to a process by which the fat globules are broken up and distributed throughout the liquid, so that they have no tendency to collect into a cream 1904. **b.** To prepare a suspension of cell fragments and constituents from (tissue) by physical treatment in a liquid medium 1936. So **Homo·genized** *ppl. a.* **Homo·genizing** *vbl. sb.* and *ppl. a.* **Homo·genizer,** a machine or apparatus for homogenizing some kind of material. Also **Homo·genization,** the process of making or becoming homogeneous; also, uniformity of composition.

Honey, *sb.*

Comb.: **h.-fungus,** *Armillaria mellea*, a fungus causing a root disease in trees and shrubs, shown by honey-coloured toadstools around them and black threads attached to their roots.

Honey-dew. 4. In full *h. melon.* A cultivar of the musk melon, *Cucumis melo*, which has a smooth ivory or pale yellow skin and sweet greenish flesh 1916.

Honey-pot. 3. In full *h. ant.* An ant belonging to one of several genera in which some of the workers become distended with surplus food, which is regurgitated when it is needed 1880.

Honky-tonk (hǫ·ŋkitǫŋk). *U.S. slang.* 1924. [Origin unknown.] **1.** A tawdry drinking-saloon, dance-hall, or gambling-house; a night-club. Also *attrib.* or quasi-*adj.* **2.** Ragtime music as played in honky-tonks 1933. Also *attrib.* or quasi-*adj.*, as **h. piano,** an out-of-tune or tinny-sounding piano.

Hood (hud), *sb.*[2] *slang* (orig. *U.S.*). 1930. [f. HOOD(LUM.] A gangster.

Hoodoo. 3. A malignant spell; a thing that causes ill-luck; also *attrib.* 1881.

Hooey (hū·i). *U.S. slang.* 1924. [Origin unknown.] Nonsense, humbug.

Hook, *sb.* **10. b.** [f. HOOK *v.* 8d.] *Boxing.* A swinging blow with the elbow bent 1898.

Comb.: **h. worm,** a parasitic nematode worm of the family Ancylostomatidæ, which infests man, other mammals, or birds, using hook-like organs to attach itself to the host's intestinal lining.

Hook, *v.* **4. b.** *pass.* To be addicted to; to be captivated by. Freq. const. *on.* 1925.

Hooker[1]. **2.** *U.S. slang.* A prostitute 1845. **3.** *Rugby Football.* A player in the centre of the front row of the scrum, who endeavours to secure the ball by hooking it 1906.

Hookey, hooky (hu·ki). *U.S.* [Origin unknown.] **1.** *To play h.*: to play truant 1848. **2.** *Blind h.*: a gambling game at cards, in which players make guesses concerning the bottom card of each packet into which the pack of cards is divided 1840.

Hook-up (hu·kʌp). orig. *U.S. colloq.* 1903. [f. phr. *hook up*, HOOK *v.* 4.] A combination of apparatus, etc., esp. of broadcasting equipment; *gen.* a connection, an alliance.

Hoop, *sb.*[1] **1. b.** A hoop, often with paper stretched across it, through which acrobats, etc. leap 1793. *To go* (*put*) *through the hoop*(*s*: to undergo (subject to) an ordeal or trial 1919.

Hooray (hurē^i·), var. HURRAY (HURRAH).

Hoover (hū·vəɹ). 1927. A vacuum cleaner manufactured by *Hoover* Ltd. Also *loosely* applied to any vacuum cleaner. Hence **Hoover** *v. trans.*, to clean with a H.

Hop (hǫp), *sb.*[3] *slang* (chiefly *U.S.*). 1887. [Origin obscure.] A narcotic drug; *spec.* opium.

Hopefully, *adv.* Now also (orig. *U.S.*) in sense 'it is hoped (that)' (cf. G. *hoffentlich*) 1932.

Hophead (hǫ·phed). *slang* (orig. and chiefly *U.S.*). 1911. [f. *HOP *sb.*[3] + *HEAD *sb.* I. 7 d.] An opium-smoker; a drug-addict.

Hopped (hǫpt), *a.*[2] *U.S. slang.* 1923. [f. *HOP *sb.*[3] + -ED.] Chiefly with *up.* **1.** Excited, enthusiastic; angry. **2.** Stimulated by, or under the influence of, a narcotic drug 1924. Hence (as a back-formation) **hop up** *v.*, to stimulate with drugs.

Hoppus (hǫ·pŏs). 1894. The name of Edward *Hoppus*, 18th-c. English surveyor, used *attrib.* and in the possessive to designate a method of measuring the cubic content of round timber used in the British Commonwealth, and tabulated by him in 1736; it involves multiplying the length by the square of the quarter-girth.

H. foot, a name for the 'cubic foot' as arrived at by this method, equal to 1.27 true cubic feet.

Hormone. Also **Hormonal** (hǭɹmōᵘ·năl, hǭ·ɹmŏnăl), *a.* (Now the usual adj.)

Horse, *sb.*

Comb.: **2. c. h. mushroom,** a species of edible mushroom, *Agaricus arvensis*, larger and coarser than the common mushroom.

Hortensia (hǫɹte·nsiă). 1799. [mod.L. (P. Commerson, 1789), f. *Hortense*, adopted Christian name of the wife of J. A. Lepaute (1720–*c*1787), French clockmaker.] A variety of the common hydrangea, *H. macrophylla* var. *hortensia.*

Hospitalize (hǫ·spitălaiz), *v.* 1901. [f. HOSPITAL *sb.* + -IZE.] *trans.* To place or accommodate in a hospital. Hence **Ho:spitaliza·tion,** confinement to, or accommodation in, a hospital.

Hosta (hǫ·stă). 1938. [mod.L. (L. Trattinick, 1812), f. the name of N. T. *Host* (1761–1834), Austrian physician.] A plant of the genus so named (formerly called *FUNKIA), native to Japan and eastern Asia and belonging to the family Liliaceæ; a plantain-lily.

Hostess. 2. b. A woman employed to entertain customers at a night-club, etc.; a prostitute 1933. **c.** = **air hostess*; also, a woman similarly employed on a train 1936.

Hot, *a.* **2.** Colloq. phr. *H. under the collar*: feeling anger or resentment (cf. 5, 6). **6. c.** (Of a hit, etc.) difficult to deal with 1882; (of a competitor) strongly expected or fancied to win. **7. d.** Also applied to jazz or similar music with a marked beat and strong emotional appeal; also to the performer; opp. *COOL *a.* 4 b. **e.** Of property: stolen, *spec.* easily identifiable and so difficult to dispose of 1834. **f.** Radioactive 1942.

Comb.: **h. line,** a direct exclusive communication channel between two points; *spec.* between Washington and Moscow; also *attrib.* and *fig.*; **h. money,** capital which is transferred from one country to another for short-term gain; **h. rod,** a motor vehicle specially modified to give high power and speed; **h. seat,** (*a*) an electric chair; (*b*) a situation involving embarrassment or onerous responsibilities; (*c*) an ejection seat in an aircraft; **h. war,** an open war involving active hostilities.

House, *sb.*[1] **4. b.** *The H.*, Christ Church, Oxford: from the Latin title *Ædes Christi* 'House of Christ'. **d.** *To keep a h.*: to ensure that there is always a sufficient attendance of members in the House of Commons to form a quorum and to secure support for the chosen speakers of a party. Also *to make a h.* (see MAKE *v.* II. 7). **g.** Also, a performance at a particular time in a theatre, e.g. *first, second h.* **10.** *Mil. slang.* A variant of lotto 1900. (Also **Housie** hau·si.)

Comb.: **h. arrest,** detention in one's house in protective custody; **h.-proud** *a.*, (of a woman) giving intense or excessive attention to the upkeep and outward appearance of the house.

Housekeeping. 3. Those operations of a computer, organization, etc., which make its work possible but do not directly constitute its performance 1958. Freq. *attrib.*

Housing, *sb.*[1] **6. d.** A rigid case or cover that encloses and protects a mechanism or piece of apparatus 1889.

Hovercraft (hǫ·vəɹkraft). Pl. **-craft.** 1959. [f. HOVER *v.* + CRAFT *sb.*] A vehicle or craft that can be supported by a cushion of air ejected downwards against a surface close below it, and can in principle travel over any relatively smooth surface without significant contact with it.

My wife and I tried to find a name and settled for the not altogether appropriate word 'Hovercraft'. C. S. COCKERELL.

How, *adv.* **II.** *And h.!*: excl. used to indicate that the effect of something is difficult to describe = and no mistake, very much so! (*U.S. slang*) 1932. *Here's h.!*: a familiar toasting formula 1890.

Hoyle[2] (hoil). Name of Edmond *Hoyle* (1672–1769), author of several works on card-games (the earliest, on whist, dated 1742); often cited typically for an authority.

Hubby (hʋ·bi), *sb.* 1688. Familiar colloquialism for HUSBAND; see -Y[6].

‖**Hubris** (hiū·bris). 1884. [– Gr. ὕβρις.] Presumption, orig. towards the gods; pride, excessive self-confidence.

Huddle, *sb.* **4.** A close or secret conference (*colloq.*) 1929.

Hula (hū·lă). 1886. [Hawaiian.] An orig. Hawaiian dance; the music accompanying this dance. Also *Hu·la-hu·la.* Hence **Hula** *v. intr.*

Comb.: **h. hoop,** a child's hoop adapted for spinning round the body with movements akin to those of the h.; **h. skirt,** a long grass skirt.

Human, *a.* **4. b.** Belonging or relating to man as distinguished from the lower animals, machinery and mechanism, or mere objects or events 1847.

Comb.: **h. engineering,** (the study of) the management of labour in industry, and esp. of the relationship between operatives and machines.

Humanism. 3. b. A theory of the life of man in the world as a responsible being behaving independently of any revelation or of preternatural powers.

Humoral, *a.* **1. b.** Also (in mod. use), contained in or involving the blood or other body fluid, esp. as distinct from cells.

Hunt, *sb.*[2] **4.** A hunting or oscillatory motion 1920.

Hunt, *v.* **8.** *intr.* To run alternately faster and more slowly than the desired speed; to oscillate to an undesirable extent *about* a desired position or state. Freq. as **Hu·nting** *vbl. sb.* 1880.

Hydrofoil (həi·drofoil). 1920. [f. HYDRO- + FOIL *sb.*[1], after *aerofoil.*] **1.** A structure designed to generate a force (other than drag) when moving through a liquid; *spec.* a thin structure attached underneath a vessel by means of which its hull is lifted clear of the water at speed 1920. **2.** A vessel fitted with hydrofoils 1959. **3.** *attrib.*, as *h. boat, ship* 1950.

Hydrogen.

Comb.: **h. bomb,** an extremely powerful bomb in which the energy released is derived from the fusion of h. nuclei in an uncontrolled chain reaction.

Hydroponics (həi:dropǫ·niks). 1937. [f. HYDRO- + Gr. πόνος work: see -IC 2.] The process of growing plants without soil, in beds of sand, gravel, or similar supporting material, flooded with nutrient solutions. Hence **Hydropo·nic** *a.* **Hydropo·nicist,** one who practises h.

'H.', which was suggested by Dr. W. A. Setchell, of the University of California, appears to convey the desired meaning better than any of a number of words considered W. F. GERICKE.

Hype (həip), *v. slang* (orig. *U.S.*). 1931. [Of unknown origin.] *trans.* To cheat, to 'short-change'; to build *up* something; to boost; to excite. Hence **Hype** *sb.*, a confidence trick; a publicity stunt. **Hy·ping** *vbl. sb.* and *ppl. a.*

Hyper-.

Hy·pergol [– G. *hypergol*, app. f. Gr. ἔργον work + -OL 3], a hypergolic rocket propellant. **Hypergo·lic** *a.*, igniting spontaneously on contact with an oxidant or another propellant. **Hyperse·nsitive** *a.*, abnormally or excessively sensitive; so **Hyperse·nsitiveness,** a h. condition. **Hy·persensiti·vity,** hypersensitiveness, esp. of the body in allergic conditions. **Hyperte·nsion,** abnormally high tension; *spec.* in *Med.*, abnormally high pressure of arterial blood; so **Hyperte·nsive** *a.*, having h.; acting to increase the blood pressure.

Hypermarket (həi·pəɹmāɹkėt). 1971. [tr. Fr. *hypermarché*, f. HYPER- + *marché* market.] A very large self-service store, usu. situated outside a town, with an extensive car park, and selling a wide range of goods.

Hyperon (həi·pĕrǫn). 1954. [app. f. HYPER- + *-ON.] *Nuclear Physics.* Any of a group of unstable sub-atomic particles that includes all the baryons except the proton and neutron.

Hypersonic (həipəɹsǫ·nik), *a.* 1946. [f. HYPER- + *SONIC *a.*, after *supersonic, ultrasonic.*] **1.** Pertaining to, involving, capable of, or designating speeds significantly greater than the speed of sound, esp. speeds greater than five times it. **2.** Of sound waves or vibrations: having a frequency greater than 1000 million Hz (or thereabouts) 1959.

Hypo-.

Hypote·nsion, abnormally low tension; *spec.* in *Med.*, abnormally low pressure of arterial blood; so **Hypote·nsive** *a.*, having h.; acting to lower the blood pressure. **Hypothe·rmia** [Gr. θέρμη heat] *Med.*, the condition of having a depressed body temperature.

Hypoxia (həipǫ·ksiă). 1946. [f. HYP- + OX- + -IA[1].] *Med.* A deficiency of oxygen in the tissues or in inspired air. Hence **Hypo·xic** *a.*, characterized by or causing h.

I.

Abbrevs.: I.B.A., Independent Broadcasting Authority; I.C.B.M., intercontinental ballistic missile; I.C.I., Imperial Chemical Industries; *i.e.*, *id est*; I.P.A., International Phonetic Alphabet (or Association); I.Q., intelligence quotient; I.R.A., Irish Republican Army; I.T.A., Independent Television Authority; i.t.a., initial teaching alphabet; I.T.V., Independent Television; I.U.(C.)D., intra-uterine (contraceptive) device.

Iatrogenic (əiˌætroˌdʒe·nik), *a.* 1927. [f. IATRO- + *-GENIC.] *Med.* Of a disease or disorder: induced by a physician or surgeon through his diagnosis or treatment.

Icaco (ikā·ko). 1756. [– Sp. *icaco, hicaco*, f. Taino *hikako.*] A shrub or small tree, *Chrysobalanus icaco*, of the family Rosaceæ, native to tropical America and the West Indies; the fruit of this tree. Also called COCO-PLUM.

Ice, *sb.*

Comb.: **i. cube,** a cube of ice formed in an ice-tray; **i.-pack,** (*b*) a pack (PACK *sb.*[1] 8) containing ice, usu. applied to the head; **i.-tray,** a tray in a refrigerator in which ice is made.

Ichabod (i·kăbǫd). 1901. Name given by Eli's daughter-in-law to her son; used as an excl. of regret, in allusion to 1 Sam. 4:21 (She named the child Ichabod, saying, 'The glory is departed from Israel').

Icing, *vbl. sb.*

Comb.: **i. sugar,** finely powdered sugar for icing cakes, etc.

Id[2] (id). 1924. [L. *id* it, as tr. G. *es* (Groddeck, 1923).] *Psychol.* The inherited instinctive impulses of the individual, forming an unconscious part of the mind.

Idea, *sb.* **I.**

4. Phr. *The big i.*: the grand scheme; usu. ironical in phr. *what's the big idea?* orig. *U.S.*

‖**Idée reçue** (*ide rəsü*). 1937. [Fr.] A generally accepted notion or opinion.

Ideology. 3. More particularly, the ideas forming the basis of a political theory or system.

Idle, *v.* **1. b.** Of an engine: to run at a low speed, without performing any work; also with *over* 1931.

‖**Ikebana** (iki*bā*·nă). 1903. [Jap., lit. 'living flowers'.] The art of Japanese flower arrangement in which flowers are displayed according to strict rules, sometimes in conjunction with other natural objects, informal arrangements designed to be viewed from one side only.

Illawarra (ilăwǫ·ră). 1884. The name of a district in New South Wales, used *attrib.* in the names of plants and animals connected with it: (*a*) **I. ash,** a small tree, *Elæocarpus cyaneus*; **I. mountain pine,** a cypress pine, *Callitris cupressiformis*; (*b*) **I. (dairy, milking) shorthorn,** a local breed of cattle.

Illuvial (ilˈū·viăl), *a.* 1928. [f. L. *illuvies* overflowing + -AL[1].] *Soil Sci.* Applied to a layer of soil in which material has been deposited by illuviation.

Illuviation (ilˈūviēˈ·ʃən). 1928. [f. L. *illuvies* overflowing + -ATION.] *Soil Sci.* The deposition of material in a layer of soil by water that carries it in solution or suspension from a higher layer.

Image, *sb.* **5.** *spec.* A concept or impression, created in the minds of the public, of a particular person, institution, product, etc.

Imbalance (imbæ·lăns). 1900. [f. IM-[2] + BALANCE *sb.*] Lack of balance; disproportion.

Immersion.

5. i. heater, an electric heating apparatus fitted in a hot-water tank, etc.

Immunology (imiunǫ·lŏdʒi). 1916. [f. IMMUN(ITY + -OLOGY.] The branch of medicine dealing with resistance to infection in man and animals (whether natural, acquired, or induced). Hence **Immu:nolo·gic** (chiefly *U.S.*), **-lo·gical** *adjs.*, **-lo·gically** *adv.* (all also stressed *i:mmuno-*). **Immuno·logist.** So **Immu·no-,** used as comb. form in related terms, as *immunochemistry* (so *-chemical*, etc.), *-therapy*.

Impala (impā·lă, -pæ·lă). 1875. [Zulu.] A South African antelope, *Æpyceros melampus*. Cf. PALLAH.

Imperfect, *a.* **II. 4. b.** Of a pleomorphic fungus: describing the stage of the life-cycle in which asexual spores or no spores at all are produced 1895.

‖**Imponderabilia** (impǫ:ndərăbi·liă). 1933. [neut. pl. of mod.L. *imponderabilis* imponderable.] Imponderable things.

Importune, *v.* **3. b.** *spec.* To solicit for an immoral purpose 1847.

Impressionism. 4. A style of musical composition expressing subjective impressions, moods, etc., through subtle and changing harmonies and timbres 1889.

Impressionist. 2. An exponent of impressionism in music 1908. Also *attrib.* or as *adj.*

Imprint, *v.* **5.** Of an animal or thing: to become established as an object of recognition or trust in the behaviour pattern of (an animal): see *IMPRINTING *vbl. sb.* Usu. as pa. pple. **Impri·nted,** and const. *by* or *on*.

Ducks, and dogs raised by humans, may be imprinted by them 1967.

Imprinting (impri·ntiŋ), *vbl. sb.* late ME. [f. IMPRINT *v.* + -ING[1].] The action of imprinting. **b.** *Psychol.* The establishment of a behaviour pattern of recognition and trust, usu. directed at its own species, during a critical period of susceptibility in a (young) social animal, esp. in birds 1937.

I. data suggest that in birds early experiences before or during a critical period can influence social attachment in a relatively permanent fashion 1970.

In, *sb.* **3.** *colloq.* (orig. *U.S.*). An introduction to, or influence with, someone of fame or authority 1929.

In, *a.* **2.** Fashionable, sophisticated; esoteric 1960.

In, *adv.* (*a.*)

Phrases. **In on.** Participating in; being one of (a group); being in possession of knowledge concerning (something).

In, L. *prep.*

21. in vitro (in vī·tro) ['in glass'] *Biol.*, in a test tube, culture dish, etc.; hence, outside a living organism 1900. **22. in vivo** (in vī·vo) ['in the living (subject)'] *Biol.*, within a living organism 1901.

-in, *suffix*[3], the adv. IN, originally (*U.S.*) designating a communal act of protest, as *SIT-IN; subsequently indicating any group action or large gathering for some purpose, as *be-in, fish-in, love-in, pray-in, study-in,* *TEACH-IN, *walk-in*.

Ina·ctivate, *v.* 1913. [IN-[3].] *trans.* To render inactive or inoperative. So **Inactiva·tion.**

Incentive. B. *sb.* **b.** A payment or concession to encourage harder work. Also *attrib.* or as *adj.* 1943.

Incinerator (insi·nĕrēˈtəɹ). 1883. [Agent-n. in L. form f. INCINERATE *v.* See -OR 2.] One who or that which incinerates; *spec.* an apparatus for burning substances to ashes.

Include, *v.* **3. b.** *To i.* (someone) *out*: to exclude. *colloq.* or *joc.* (orig. *U.S.*). 1937.

‖**Incommunicado** (i:nkǫmˈiūnikā·do), *a.* Also **incomunicado.** 1844. [Sp. *incomunicado*, f. *incomunicar* to deprive of communication.] Having no communication with other persons; in solitary confinement.

Indic (i·ndik), *a.* 1877. [– L. *Indicus* – Gr. Ἰνδικός INDIAN.] Indian; *spec.* designating or pertaining to a branch of the Indo-European languages comprising Sanskrit and its modern descendants.

Indulge, *v.* **II. 3.** (Without prep.) To gratify a desire, appetite, etc.; *spec.* (*colloq.*) to partake (too) freely of intoxicants *a* 1717.

Industrial. A. *adj.* **I. Revolution,** the rapid development of industry in Britain in the late 18th and early 19th centuries; also *transf.*

Industry. 5. b. *Archæol.* (A technique of working revealed by) implements, etc., found at an archæological site 1911. **c.** *colloq.* Preceded by a personal name, etc.: the study of, or work on, a particular subject 1965.

Ineducable (ine·diŭkăb'l), *a.* 1884. [IN-[3].] Incapable of being educated. Hence **Ine:ducabi·lity.**

Inertia.

Comb.: **i. reel,** a reel which enables a safety-belt rolled around it to be self-adjusting; **i. selling,** the supply of goods to persons who have not requested them, in the hope that the recipients will not take the necessary action to refuse them.

Infantile, *a.* **i. paralysis** = POLIOMYELITIS.

Inferiority.

Comb.: **i. complex,** generalized and unrealistic feelings of inadequacy caused by a person's reactions to actual or supposed inferiority in one sphere, sometimes compensated for by aggressive self-assertion; *colloq.*, exaggerated feelings of personal inadequacy.

Information.

Comb.: **i. retrieval,** the tracing of information stored in books, computers, or other collections of reference material; **i. theory,** the quantitative study, by means of the theory of probability and other mathematical techniques, of the coding and transmission of signals or information.

Infra-red, *a.* 1881. [INFRA-.] **a.** The epithet of electromagnetic radiation which has a wavelength between that of red light (approximately 0.8 micron) and that of the shortest microwaves (approximately 1000 microns, or 1 mm.); it is invisible, and most of the radiation from bodies below red heat is emitted in this form. **b.** Involving, using, or relating to such radiation.

b. Infra-red photography 1929, cookers 1959, astronomy 1968.

Infrastructure (i·nfrăstrɒktiŭɹ). 1927. [– Fr., f. INFRA- + STRUCTURE *sb.*] A collective term for the subordinate parts of an undertaking; substructure; *spec.* the permanent installations forming a basis for military operations.

Inhibiter, -or. 2. (Spelt *-or*.) Something that inhibits; *esp.* a substance whose presence prevents some chemical reaction from taking place 1902.

Inhibition. 4. *Psychol.* A voluntary or involuntary restraint or check that prevents the direct expression of an instinctive impulse; also *colloq.* in looser use, an inner hindrance to conduct or activity 1889.

Initial.

A. *adj.* **1. initial teaching alphabet,** a 44-letter phonetic alphabet devised by Sir James Pitman to assist the teaching of reading and writing.

Injun (i·ndʒən). 1812. Colloq. and U.S. dial. form of INDIAN *sb.* 2. Freq. in phr. *honest I.*: honour bright.

Innards (i·nəɹdz), *sb. pl.* 1825. Dial., vulgar, or jocular pronunc. of *inwards* (see INWARD *sb.* 1), = entrails, stomach. Also *transf.* and *fig.*

Inner, *a.* **1.**

i. space, (*a*) the regions between the earth and outer space; (*b*) the regions below the surface of the sea; (*c*) the part of one's mind or personality that is not normally experienced or within one's consciousness; **i. tube,** in a pneumatic tyre, a tube, inside the cover, which is inflated with air.

Innumeracy (iniū·mĕrăsi). 1959. [f. IN-[3] + *NUMERACY.] The quality or state of being innumerate.

Innumerate (iniū·mĕrĕt), *a.* 1959. [f. IN-[3] + *NUMERATE *a.*] Unacquainted with the basic principles of mathematics and science Also as *sb.*, one who is innumerate.

Inoperable (inǫ·pĕrăb'l), *a.* 1886. [– Fr. *inopérable*; see IN-[3] and OPERABLE.] That cannot be operated (upon).

Input, *sb.* **3.** A place or point where energy, information, etc., is supplied to or enters a system 1931.

Input, *v.* Restrict † to sense in Dict. **3.** (Stressed *i·nput*.) *Computers.* To supply (data, a program, etc.) *to* a computer; to put in or *into* 1964. Pa. pple. **I·nput** or **I·nputted.**

Inseminate, *v.* **b.** To impregnate with semen, spec. by artificial means 1923. So **Insemina·tion, Inse·minator.**

Inside. C. *adv.* **2. b.** *slang.* In prison 1888.

Insomniac (insǫ·mniˌæk). 1909. [f. INSOMNIA + -AC.] One affected with insomnia. Also *attrib.* or as *adj.*

Instant, *a.* (*adv.*) **4. b.** Of a processed food: that can be prepared for use immediately, e.g. *instant* (soluble) *coffee.* Also *transf.* 1914.

Instantiate (instæ·nʃiēˈt), *v.* [f. L. *instantia* INSTANCE *sb.* + -ATE[3].] *trans.* To represent by an instance. So **Instantiation** (instænʃiēˈ·ʃən), representation by an instance.

Everything about the universal which distinguishes its instantiation in one case from its instantiation in another must be itself particular... This universal is clearly not instantiated by either apple 1951.

Instar (i·nstāɹ), *sb.* 1895. [L., = form, figure, likeness (L. H. Fischer, 1853).] Any stage between ecdyses in the life-cycle of an insect. Also *attrib.* and *fig.*

Instinctual (insti·ŋktiuăl), *a.* 1928. [f. INSTINCT, after *context, -ual.*] Of or pertaining to, involving or depending upon, instinct.

Instruction. 4. c. *Computers.* An expression in a program that defines an operation or results in its being performed 1950.

Integrate, *v.* **2. b.** To bring (members of different racial groups, etc.) into equal membership of a society or system; to cease to segregate (racially). Also *intr.* 1949.

2. integrated circuit *Electronics*, a small unit or package, often no larger than a button, which is made as a single indivisible structure (such as a chip) and is electrically equivalent to a conventional circuit of many separate components.

Integration. 1. b. The action or result of *INTEGRATE *v.* 2 b. 1940.

Intelligence, *sb.*

Comb.: **i. quotient,** a number intended to express the ratio of a given person's intelligence to the average for his age-group, which is fixed at 100; so *i. test*.

Intensive, *a.* (*sb.*) **5. b.** Suffixed to sbs. to form adjs. with the sense 'intensively using the thing specified', as *capital-i., labour-i.* 1957. **6. i. care,** medical treatment which keeps a patient under special concentrated observation; freq. *attrib.*

Interceptor. *spec.* An aeroplane having the task of intercepting enemy raiders 1930.

Intercom (i·ntəɹkǫm). *colloq.* 1940. [abbrev.] A system of intercommunication by radio or telephone.

I:nterdiscipli·nary, *a.* 1956. [INTER- II. 2 c.] Of, or carried on between, different branches of learning.

Interface (i·ntəɹfēˈs). 1882. [f. INTER- II. 1 a + FACE *sb.*] **1.** A surface separating two portions of matter or space and forming their common boundary. **2.** *transf.* A place or region, or a piece of equipment, where interaction occurs between two systems, organizations, processes, or persons 1962.

2. The i. between physics and music is of direct relevance to..the psychological effects of hearing 1970. All it needed was an i. between customer and..manufacturer 1971.

Interferometry (i:ntəɹfĕrǫ·mĕtri). 1911. [f. INTERFEROMETER: see -METRY.] The use of the interferometer; the measurement of interference phenomena by means of that instrument. Hence **I:nterferome·tric** *a.*

Interferon (intəɹfī°·rǫn). 1957. [f. INTERFER(E *v.*² + *-on.*] *Biol.* A protein released by an animal cell, usu. in response to the entry of a virus, which has the property of inhibiting the development of viruses in the animal (or in others of the same species).

Interior.
Comb.: **i. decoration,** the design and decoration of the inside of a building or room; so *i. decorating, decorator*; **i. monologue,** a form of writing which represents the inner thoughts of a character; **i.-sprung** *a.*, with springs inside.

Intermediate, *sb.* **3.** *Chem.* A compound which after being produced by one reaction participates in another; *esp.* one manufactured from naturally occurring materials for use in the synthesis of dyes, plastics, or other substances 1926.

Interplanetary, *a.* Also, existing between planets; pertaining to travel between planets.

Interpol (i·ntəɹpǫl). 1923. [abbrev. of *Inter*national *pol*ice.] The International Criminal Police Commission, with headquarters in Paris.

Into, *prep.* **III. 2.** *colloq.* Interested or involved in; knowledgeable about 1969.
First I was i. Zen, then I was i. peace, then I was i. love, then I was i. freedom, then I was i. religion. Now I'm i. money 1971.

Intro, colloq. abbrev. of INTRODUCTION.

Intruder. 3. An aircraft over enemy territory. Also *attrib.* 1941.

Invisible, *a.*
1. invisible exports, imports, items not appearing in returns of exported or imported goods but for which payment is accepted from, or made to, another country; **i. mending,** repairs so carefully executed on clothing, etc., that no trace of the repair can be seen.

Invoice, *v.* **b.** To send an invoice to.
Invoice me on despatch of the volume at the special pre-publication price of 6 guineas. *Mod.*

Ionosphere (əi,ǫ·nǒsfī°ɹ). 1929. [f. ION + -O- + SPHERE *sb.*] A layer of the atmosphere, beginning at a height of 30 to 50 miles, which contains many ions and free electrons and is able to reflect radio waves. Hence **Ionosphe·ric** *a.*

Ipsilateral (ipsilæ·tĕrăl), *a.* 1913. [irreg. f. L. *ipse* self + LATERAL.] Belonging to or occurring on the same side of the body.

‖**Ipsissima verba** (ipsi·simă vɔ̄·ɹbă). 1807. [L.] The very identical words.

Iraqi (irā·ki). Also formerly **Iraki.** 1777. [Arab., f. *Iraq* (see def.) + *-ī* adj. suffix.] An inhabitant of Iraq, proclaimed 23 Aug. 1921 as the official name of Mesopotamia. Also *attrib.* or as *adj.* Hence **Ira·qian.**

Iroko (irōᵘ·ko). 1909. [Ibo.] A tree of the genus *Chlorophora*, either *C. regia*, which grows in West Africa, or *C. excelsa*, which is found throughout the central part of the continent; also, the timber of these trees.
The rich brown colour and partridge-wing figure of i. render it especially suitable for use in panelling 1934.

Iron, *sb.*¹
Comb.: **2. i. curtain,** in a theatre, a curtain of iron which can be lowered between the stage and the auditorium; hence *fig.*, any impenetrable barrier, *spec.* the barrier to the passage of information, etc., at the limit of the Soviet sphere of influence; **i. lung,** an iron case fitted over a patient's chest for prolonged artificial respiration; **i. ration,** an emergency ration of tinned or concentrated food; also *fig.*

Irradiate, *v.* **1. c.** To subject to the action of some kind of radiation (as X-rays, ultraviolet light, or neutrons) 1903.
Food can be preserved for long periods if irradiated 1957.

Irradiation. III. The action or process of irradiating something; exposure to radiation 1903.
Therapeutic i. of the pelvic region would..involve considerable risk to an embryo 1957.

Ischæmia (iskī·miă). 1866. [mod.L., f. Gr. ἰσχαιμος (f. ἴσχειν keep back, staunch + αἷμα blood) + -IA¹.] *Med.* A reduction in the supply of blood to part of the body. Hence **Ischæ·mic** *a.*

Isle of Wight (əiləvwəi·t). 1908. Name of an island off the coast of Hampshire, used to designate a disease (in full, *I. of W. disease*) of bees caused by the parasitic mite *Acarapis woodsi*, first found there in 1905; later called *acarine disease.*

Isolationist (əisŏlēⁱ·ʃənist). 1899. [See -IST.] One who favours a policy of (political or national) isolation. So **Isola·tionism.**

Isometric, *a.* **4.** *Physiol.* Of the action of a muscle: developing tension while the muscle is prevented from contracting; also, of or pertaining to isometrics 1900.

Isometrics (əisome·triks), *sb. pl.* orig. *U.S.* 1962. [f. prec.: see -IC 2.] A system of stationary physical exercises which involve pitting one set of muscles against another or against an unyielding object.

Isotonic (əisotǫ·nik), *a.* 1898. [f. Gr. ἰσότονος (f. ἴσος equal + τόνος TONE *sb.*) + -IC.] **1.** Having the same osmotic pressure. **2.** *Physiol.* Of the action of a muscle: taking place while the muscle is allowed to contract normally under its own tension 1900.

It, *pron.* **I. 1. e.** In children's games, the player who has to catch the others. **II. 1. c.** *colloq.* Sexual intercourse.

Itsy-bitsy (i:tsibi·tsi), *a.* *colloq.* (orig. *U.S.*). Also **itty-bitty.** 1938. [Childish reduplic. LITTLE *a.*, infl. by BIT *sb.*²] Tiny, insubstantial.

Ivory.
Comb.: **i. tower** [tr. Fr. *tour d'ivoire* (used by Sainte-Beuve concerning Alfred de Vigny)], a condition or position of seclusion from the world, or withdrawal from the harsh realities of life.

J.

Jab, *sb.* *spec.* A hypodermic injection 1914.

Jack, *sb.*¹
Comb.: **jackpot,** (*b*) any large prize, as from a lottery or a gambling machine; often, a prize that accumulates until it is won 1920. Phr. *to hit the j.*: to have an extraordinary stroke of luck.

Jack-knife. 1. b. Applied to actions resembling that of the knife: (*a*) *Swimming*, a kind of dive executed by first doubling up and then straightening the body before entering the water 1922. (*b*) The accidental folding up of an articulated vehicle. Also as *v. intr.*

Jaffa (dʒæ·fă). 1881. [mod. (Arabic) name of *Joppa*, ancient seaport of Palestine, now in Israel.] In full *J. orange.* An oval thick-skinned variety of orange first cultivated near Jaffa, and later introduced to other parts of Israel and suitable regions elsewhere.

Jalopy (dʒălǫ·pi). orig. *U.S.* 1929. [Of unknown origin.] A battered old motor vehicle.
And in jalopies there migrates A rootless tribe from windblown states AUDEN.

Jam, *sb.*¹ **a.** *transf.* An awkward situation, fix (*slang*). **c.** A group improvisation by jazz musicians 1929. Also *attrib.* as *j. session.*
Comb.: **j.-packed** *a. colloq.*, very full.

Janeite (dʒēⁱ·nəit). 1896. [f. *Jane*, Christian name of Jane Austen (1775–1817), English novelist + -ITE¹ 1.] A devotee of Jane Austen and her writings.
Now Dr. Chapman places 'Janeites' even more deeply in his debt 1934.

Java. J. man, the fossil hominid *Homo erectus* (formerly *Pithecanthropus erectus*), whose remains were first found by E. Dubois in Java in 1891. *ellipt.* = J. coffee 1850; in *U.S. slang*, any coffee.
Cheesecake is very popular in some circles, and goes very good with j. D. RUNYON.

Jean. 2. c. *pl.* Trousers made of this material 1846.

Jeep (dʒīp). orig. *U.S.* 1941. [f. the initials *G.P.* (dʒī pī) '*general purposes*', prob. infl. by Eugene the *Jeep*, name of an animal in the U.S. comic strip 'Popeye' by E. C. Segar.] A small, sturdy, four-wheel-drive army vehicle; a similar vehicle in non-military use.

Jehovah.
Comb.: **Jehovah's Witness,** a member of a fundamentalist millenary sect, which refuses to acknowledge the claims of the State when these are in conflict with the principles of the sect.

Jelly, *sb.* **2. d.** Slang abbrev. of GELIGNITE 1941.

Jerry, *sb.* **5.** By association with *German* used (orig. by the British Army) in the wars of 1914–18 and 1939–45 as a joc. designation of the German soldier.

Jerrycan, jerrican. 1943. [f. *JERRY *sb.* 5 + CAN *sb.*] A large can for petrol or water, of a type originally supplied to the German army.

Jet, *sb.*³ **4. b.** [ellipt. use.] A j. plane 1944; a j. engine 1948.
Comb. (very numerous in connection with j. propulsion and j. planes): **j. engine,** one utilizing j. propulsion to provide forward thrust, esp. an aircraft engine that ejects hot compressed air and exhaust gases; so *j.-engined* adj.; **j. plane** (also *j. aircraft*, etc.), one powered by a j. engine; **j. propulsion,** the backward ejection of a high-speed j. of gas (or liquid) as a source of propulsive power, esp. for aircraft; so *j.-propelled* adj. (also *fig.*, very fast); **j. set,** a social *élite* whose life is characterized by frequent air journeys from one 'event' to another; **j. stream,** (*a*) *Meteorol.*, a strong wind confined to a narrow region of the atmosphere, esp. one in the upper troposphere in middle latitudes; (*b*) the j. ejected by a j. engine.

Jet (dʒet), *v.*³ 1951. [f. *JET *sb.*³ 4 b.] *intr.* To travel by jet plane.

‖**Jeunesse dorée** (ʒönęs dore). 1837. [Fr., 'gilded youth'.] Orig. in France, a group of fashionable counter-revolutionaries; later, young men of wealth and fashion.

Jig, *sb.* **6. d.** *Engin.* An appliance that holds a piece of work and guides the tools operating upon it 1913.

Jigger, *sb.*¹ **5. a.** An illicit distillery 1824. **b.** orig. *U.S.* A drink of spirits, a dram; also a small glass holding such a measure 1836.

Jim Crow. 2. A Negro 1835. **b.** Used, often *attrib.*, to indicate racial discrimination in the United States 1842. Hence **Jim Crow·ism,** racial discrimination.
The Uncle Tom presidents of the captive Jim Crow colleges 1960.

Jink, *v.* **2. b.** To make a tricky turn in Rugby football 1914.

Jinx (dʒiŋks). orig. *U.S.* 1911. [perh. var. spelling of JYNX (in the sense 'charm, spell').] A person or thing that brings bad luck. Hence **Jinx** *v.*, to cast a spell on, bring bad luck.

Jitter (dʒi·təɹ), *v.* orig. *U.S.* 1931. [Of unknown origin.] *intr.* To be nervous, act nervously. *Comb.* **Ji·tterbug,** (*a*) a person who dances to hot-rhythm music; (*b*) a nervous person. So **Ji·tters** *sb. pl.*, extreme nervousness; **Ji·ttery** *a.* [-Y¹], nervy, jumpy.

Jive (dʒəiv), *sb.* orig. *U.S. slang.* 1928. [Origin uncertain.] **1.** Talk, esp. misleading talk; hence anything false, worthless, or misleading. **2.** Jazz, esp. a type of fast, lively jazz; 'swing' 1928. **b.** Lively and uninhibited dancing to dance-music or jazz 1943. Hence **Jive** *v.* **1.** To mislead; to talk nonsense. **2.** To play 'jive'; to dance the 'jive'. **Ji·ver. Ji·ving** *vbl. sb.*

Job, *sb.*¹ **1. b.** *Thieves' slang.* A crime 1722. **c.** The product of work, esp. well done 1923. **4. b.** A paid position of employment 1861. Hence **Jo·bless** *a.*, out of work, unemployed.
Phr. *to have a j. to do something*: to find it hard; *out of a j.*: unemployed.

Jock (dʒǫk). 1508. [Sc. var. of the name JACK.] **1.** By-form for *John*; a man, esp. of the people. **b.** *Army slang.* A Scottish soldier 1931. **2.** A countryman, rustic 1568.

Jodhpur (dʒǫ·dpŭɹ). 1899. [Name of a town in Rajasthan, India.] *pl.* A kind of riding-breeches tight from knee to ankle.

‖**Joie de vivre** (ʒwa də vīvr). 1901. [Fr., 'joy of living'.] A feeling of healthy enjoyment of life.

‖**Jolie laide** (ʒoli lę̄d). 1894. [Fr., fem. sing. of *joli* pretty + *laid* ugly.] A girl who is attractive in spite of not being pretty.
One was a beauty or a *jolie-laide* and that was that N. MITFORD.

Jonathan. b. An American variety of dessert apple 1842.

Jordanian (dʒǫɹdēⁱ·niăn), *a.* 1951. [-IAN.] Of or pertaining to the territory of Jordan. Also *sb.*, a native or inhabitant of Jordan.
The refugees..aided by Jordanian and Egyptian officials 1953.

Jotter (under JOT *v.*²). Also, a small pad

or notebook used for jotting down notes, memoranda, etc.

Judder (dʒʌ·dəɹ), *v.* 1931. [imit., cf. SHUDDER *v.*] *intr.* To shake violently, esp. of the mechanism in cars, cameras, etc.; also of the voice in singing, to oscillate between greater and less intensity. Hence **Ju·dder** *sb.*, an instance of such shaking.

Judo (dʒū·do). 1892. [Jap., f. *jiu, jū* (– Chinese *jou* soft) + *dō* (– Chinese *tao* way).] A form of ju-jitsu.

Judo is a way of learning to control yourself and your opponent 1972. The first j. club in England was founded in 1918 in London 1972.

Juke (dʒūk). orig. *U.S. slang.* 1936. [prob. f. Gullah *juke, joog* disorderly, wicked.] A road-house or brothel.

Comb.: **j.-box**, a machine that automatically plays selected gramophone records when a coin is inserted.

Jumbo. b. In full *j. jet.* A large jet aircraft having room for several hundred passengers 1964.

Jump, *v.*

Phr. **I.** *To j. on* (or *down*) *someone's throat*: to reprimand or contradict fiercely; *to j. to it*: to make an energetic start upon something. **II.** *To j. ship*: of a seaman, to desert before his contract expires; *to j. the gun*: to anticipate the starting-gun in a race; also *fig.*; *to j. the queue*: to push forward out of one's turn; *to j. the rails*: of a train or tram, to leave the line.

Jump-.

j.-bid, in Contract Bridge, a bid of more than is necessary; **j.-cut** *Cinematogr.*, the excision of the middle portion of a shot, producing discontinuity of action; **j.-off,** in *Show-jumping*, the final round for tied contestants; **j. suit** a one-piece garment for the whole body, combining jumper and trousers.

Ju·mped-up, *a.* 1835. [f. pa. pple. of JUMP *v.* + UP *adv.*[1]] That has newly or suddenly risen in status or importance; upstart.

Junction. 2. b. *Electronics.* A transition zone between two regions in a semiconductor that have conduction mainly by electrons and by holes respectively 1949. Freq. *attrib.*, as *j. diode, transistor.*

Jungle. 2. c. A scene of ruthless competition, struggle, or exploitation; esp. with qualification, as *blackboard j.* in schools, *concrete j.* in cities.

Junk, *sb.*[2] **6.** *slang.* A narcotic drug, esp. heroin 1925. Hence **Ju·nkie,** a drug-addict.

Comb.: **j.-shop,** also a shop selling second-hand goods of low value; *derog.* an antique shop.

Juvenile.

1. j. delinquent, an offender below the age of legal responsibility; hence **j. delinquency.**

K.

IV. c. K.C.V.O., Knight Commander of the (Royal) Victorian Order. **e.** kc/s = kilocycles per second; kl. = kilolitre; kW = kilowatt. **f.** K.D., knocked down; K.E., kinetic energy; K.O., knock-out, knocked out; KWIC, KWOC, key word in, out of, context.

‖**Kabuki** (kăbū·ki). 1899. [Jap., f. *ka* song + *bu* dance + *ki* art, skill.] A traditional popular form of Japanese drama which employs highly stylized song, mime, and dance in addition to acting, and in which all the parts are played by males.

Kamikaze (kæmikā·zi). 1945. [Jap., lit. 'divine wind', f. *kami* KAMI + *kaze* wind.] In the war of 1939–45, a Japanese 'suicide plane'; an aircraft containing explosives deliberately crashed on its target. Also *attrib.* (as *k. pilot*), *transf.* and *fig.*

‖**Kampong** (kæ·mpɒŋ). 1844. [Malay; see COMPOUND *sb.*[2]] A Malay village; an enclosure or compound.

Kangaroo.

Comb.: **k. court** orig. *U.S.*, an improperly constituted court having no legal standing.

Kangaroo-rat. 2. *U.S.* A rodent of the genus *Dipodomys*, native to the south-western United States and Mexico, so called because it travels with kangaroo-like jumps, rather than at a run 1867.

Kaon (kē[i]·ɒn). 1962. [f. *ka-* (representing the pronunc. of the letter *K*) + *-ON.] *Nuclear Physics.* Any of a group of mesons having a mass several times that of the pions and non-zero 'strangeness'; a K-meson.

Karabiner (karăbī·nəɹ). 1933. [– G. *karabiner (haken)* carbine(-swivel).] *Mountaineering.* A coupling device consisting of a metal oval or D-shaped link with a gate protected against accidental opening.

Karate (kărā·ti). 1955. [Jap., lit. 'empty hand'.] A Japanese system of unarmed combat in which hands, feet, etc., are used as weapons.

Karst (kāɹst). 1894. [Name (*the K.*) of a high barren limestone region of this type south of Ljubljana in N.W. Yugoslavia.] *Physical Geogr.* Any region with predominantly underground drainage and numerous abrupt ridges, fissures, sink-holes, and caverns caused by solution of the rock (usu. limestone). Usu. *attrib.* Hence **Ka·rstic** *a.* **Ka·rstland,** a karstic region.

Kart: see *GO-KART.

Karyotype (kæ·riotəip), *sb.* 1929. [f. KARYO- + -TYPE.] *Biol.* The character of a cell nucleus as determined by the number, size, shape, etc., of all its chromosomes; a systematized representation of the chromosomes in a diagram or photograph. Hence **Karyoty·pic** *a.*

Karyotype (kæ·riotəip), *v.* 1966. [f. prec. sb.] *trans.* To determine the karyotype of. Hence **Ka·ryotyped** *ppl. a.*, **-typing** *vbl. sb.*

Kasbah, casbah (kæ·zbā). 1895. [– Fr. *casbah* – Arab. *ḳaṣba, ḳaṣaba* citadel.] The Arab quarter round the citadel of Algiers; a similar quarter in other towns of northern Africa.

Kazoo (kăzū·). 1884. orig. *U.S.* [app. with some ref. to the sound.] A toy musical instrument composed of a tube with a membrane- or gauze-covered hole, which vibrates with a harsh sound when sung into.

Kelvin (ke·lvin). 1892. [Name of Sir William Thomson, Lord *Kelvin* (1824–1907), British physicist and inventor.] **1.** A name proposed for the kilowatt-hour, but little used. **2.** Used *attrib.* to designate the thermodynamic scale of absolute temperature in which temperature intervals are the same as in the centigrade scale 1922. **b.** (Formerly *degree Kelvin*, symbol °K; now simply *kelvin*, symbol K.) A degree of the K. scale, now incorporated into the S.I. and defined as 1/273.16 of the temperature of the triple point of water 1930.

Kenyapithecus (ke·nyăpi·þīkɒs, -piþī·kɒs). 1961. [mod.L., (1961), f. *Kenya* + Gr. πίθηκος ape.] A fossil hominid of the genus so called, first discovered in Kenya in 1961 by L. S. B. Leakey; sometimes included in the genus *Ramapithecus.*

Dr. Leakey..endeavours to show..that his *Kenyapithecus* hominids are quite distinct from the ancestors of apes living at the same time 1967.

Key, *sb.*[1]

Comb.: **k. punch,** a keyboard-operated perforator for cards or paper tape; also as *v. trans.*, to produce or transcribe by the use of a k. punch; **k. stroke,** a depression of a k. on a keyboard, usu. as a measure of work done; **k. word,** (*a*) a word serving as a k. to a cipher; (*b*) a significant word, esp. (in information retrieval) one in the title of an article, etc.

Key, *v.* **5.** To actuate or operate the key or keys of a telegraph, typewriter, etc.; to produce or transcribe by this means 1921.

Keyboard (kī·bōəɹd), *v.* 1961. [f. the sb.] *trans.* To produce or transcribe by the use of the keyboard of a typewriter, composing machine, etc.

Keynesian (kē[i]·nziăn), *a.* and *sb.* 1937. [f. Lord *Keynes* (1883–1946), British economist + -IAN.] **A.** *adj.* Of, pertaining to, or following the theories of Keynes. **B.** *sb.* An adherent of Keynes's economic theories.

Key-note. b. *attrib.*, as *key-note address* or *speech* (orig. *U.S.*), a speech designed to set the prevailing tone for a conference, etc.; often used at political rallies merely to arouse enthusiasm or unity. Hence **Key·note** *v. trans.*, to express the prevailing tone or idea of (something); to address as a k. speaker; so **Key·noter.**

‖**Kibbutz** (kibu·ts). Pl. **-im** (-ī·m). 1946. [f. mod. Heb. *qibbūs* gathering.] A communal farming settlement in Israel. So **Kibbu·tznik,** a member of a kibbutz.

Kibitzer (ki·bitsəɹ, kibi·tsəɹ). orig. *U.S. slang.* 1928. [– Yiddish *kibitser*, f. G. *kiebitz* pewit.] A busybody, an officious meddler; orig., an onlooker at cards, esp. one who offered unwanted advice.

Kick-, KICK *sb.*[1] or KICK *v.* used in *Comb.*: **ki·ckback,** (*a*) the action or an instance of kicking back; a recoil; (*b*) a payment made to a person who has made possible or facilitated a transaction, appointment, etc.; **k.-pleat,** a pleat in a narrow skirt to allow freedom of movement; **k.-start, -starter,** a device for starting an internal combustion engine, esp. on a motorcycle, by a downward thrust on a pedal; hence *k.-start v.*; **k.-turn** *Skiing*, a form of standing turn.

Kikuyu (kikū·yū). 1890. [Native name.] An agricultural Negroid tribe of Kenya; a member of this tribe. Also, the language of the Kikuyus.

Kill, *v.* **7.** *fig.* To destroy, eliminate, obliterate, remove; *esp.* to remove or not use (a newspaper 'story'), to switch off (a light on a stage or film set) 1903.

Killing, *vbl. sb.* **1. b.** *transf.* A great or notable success or victory, esp. financial; a successful coup 1888.

Comb.: **k.-bottle,** a bottle containing poisonous vapour, used for killing insects collected as specimens.

Kinetic, *a.*

Comb.: **k. art,** art which depends upon movement for its effect.

King, *sb.*

Comb.: **2. k.-size(d),** *a.*, larger than the normal, very large (esp. of cigarettes).

Kinin (kəi·nin). 1954. [f. Gr. κινεῖν to move + -IN[1].] *Biochem.* **1.** Any of a group of peptides formed in the blood in response to injury and causing sensations of pain; some occur in the venom of wasps, snakes, etc. **2.** = *CYTOKININ 1956.

Kinky, *a.* **3.** Perverted, *spec.* homosexual; suggestive of sexual perversion; bizarre 1959.

Kiosk. (Now usu. with pronunc. kī·ǫsk.) **2. b.** A telephone call-box 1928.

Kit, *v.* **2.** To supply with kit or a kit; to equip, fit *out* or *up*, with a kit 1945.

Kitsch (kitʃ). 1926. [G.] Art or *objets d'art* characterized by worthless pretentiousness; the qualities associated with such art or artefacts. Hence **Ki·tschy** *a.*

Kiwi. 2. *colloq.* A nickname for a New Zealander 1918.

Klein bottle (kləin). 1941. [f. the name of Felix *Klein* (1849–1925), German mathematician.] A closed one-sided surface obtained by passing the neck of a bottle through its side and joining its end to a hole in the base.

Klieg (klīg). Also **kleig.** 1925. [f. the name of two brothers, A. T. and J. H. *Kliegl*, who invented it in the U.S.] In full *K. light.* A kind of powerful lamp used in film-making.

Klystron (kləi·strɒn). 1939. [f. Gr. κλύζειν (stem κλυσ-) wash or break over + *-TRON.] *Electronics.* An electron tube for amplifying or generating microwaves in which a beam of electrons is passed through a gap in a cavity resonator across which is applied a high-frequency voltage, so that the electrons collect into bunches and on reaching a second gap induce a (larger) high-frequency voltage across it. Also *attrib.*, as *k. oscillator, tube.*

Knitwear (ni·twē[ə]ɹ). 1925. [f. *knit* ppl. adj. + WEAR *sb.*] Knitted articles of clothing.

Knock, *sb.*[1] **1. b.** *Knock for knock*: applied to an agreement between insurers that each will pay his own assured without regard to the question of liability 1906. **2.** *Cricket.* A spell of batting; an innings. *colloq.* 1900. **3.** A knocking or thumping sound in an engine 1903.

Knock-out. A. *adj.* **c.** Applied to a tournament or other competition in which the defeated competitors in each round are eliminated 1897.

‖**Kolkhoz** (kǫ·lkǫz). 1932. [Russ., f. *kol(lektivnoe khoz(yaĭstvo* collective farm.] A collective farm in the U.S.S.R.

Kookaburra (ku·kăbɒ:ră). *Austral.* 1862. [Native name.] A native kingfisher, *Dacelo novæguineæ*, noted for its loud discordant cry; the laughing jackass.

Kraft (krɑft). 1907. [– G. *kraft* strength, in *kraftpapier*, etc.] A strong smooth brown wrapping-paper made from unbleached soda pulp.

Kremlin. b. *The K.*, (used for) the Government of the U.S.S.R. 1933. Hence **Kremlino·logy,** the study and analysis of the Soviet Government and its policies. **Kremlino·logist,** such an analyst.

Krill (kril). 1911. [f. Norw. *kril*, very small fish.] The planktonic crustaceans which are found in dense concentrations in polar seas, where they serve as food for some fishes and whales.

Kromesky (krome·ski, krǫ·meski). 1861. [app. alt. of Russ. *krómochka* dim. of *kromá* slice of bread.] A croquette made of minced meat or fish rolled in bacon and fried.

‖**Kulak** (kᴵū·læk). 1886. [Russ., 'fist, tight-fisted person'.] A well-to-do Russian peasant; under the Soviet régime, a peasant-proprietor working for his own profit.

Kumquat (kɒ·mkwǫt). [See CUMQUAT.] **1.** A small orange-like citrus fruit from a tree of the genus *Fortunella*, native to southern China and Malaysia and cultivated elsewhere; = CUMQUAT. **2.** *Austral.* A very small native citrus fruit, *Eremocitrus glauca*, or its tree; also called *desert lemon* 1889.

Kwashiorkor (kwǫʃiˌǫ·ɹkǭɹ). 1935. [Native name in Ghana.] *Path.* A disease that is caused by insufficient dietary protein and chiefly affects young children in tropical regions, producing diarrhœa, œdema, partial loss of pigmentation, desquamation, and stunted growth, and leading in severe cases to death.

L.

III. L on a plate or card affixed to a motor vehicle indicating that the driver is a learner; L.E.M., lunar excursion module; L.F., low frequency; L.M., lunar module; L.P., long playing (record); low pressure; L.P.G., liquefied petroleum gas; L.S.D., lysergic acid diethylamide; L.S.E., London School of Economics; L.T., low tension.

Label, *v.* **2.** To replace (one of the atoms in a molecule) by an atom of another isotope of the same element which is radioactive or which differs in mass, so that the path taken by it may be followed (e.g. in the body or a chemical reaction); to treat (a molecule or a substance) in this way 1937.

Labour, *sb.* **2. c.** The labouring classes as a political force, party, or organization; representatives of these, e.g. in parliament, considered as a body. Also *attrib.* passing into *adj.*: belonging to the Labour Party or holding opinions favourable to their (political) claims or aspirations. 1870.

Lachrymator (læ·krimēⁱtǭɹ). Also **lacri-.** 1922. [f. *lachrymat-* (in LACHRYMATORY, etc.) + -OR².] A gas that makes the eyes water; a tear-gas.

Ladder, *sb.* **2.** Delete 'recently' and add '1838' after 'stocking'.

Ladin (lædī·n). 1879. [Romansh; – L. *Latinus* LATIN.] The Rhæto-Romanic language spoken in the Engadine in Switzerland.

Lady, *sb.* **4. c.** *pl.* A public convenience for female persons 1918. Freq. *ladies'*, and with capital initial. (Cf. *GENTLEMAN 4d.)

Lallans (læ·lănz). 1785. [Sc. var. of *Lowlands* (see LOWLAND A. 2).] Lowland Scottish; the vernacular speech of the Lowlands of Scotland, latterly in respect of its status as a literary language.

They..spak their thochts in plain braid L. BURNS. Thochts anent L. prose 1947.

Lamé (la·me). 1924. [Fr.] Gold or silver thread; fabric containing such thread.

Laminate (læ·minĕt), *sb.* 1944. [subst. use of the adj.] A laminated structure or material, as: **a.** a more or less rigid material made by bonding together under pressure layers of plastic or of resin-impregnated paper or cloth; **b.** a fabric or a flexible packaging material consisting of two or more layers held together by an adhesive.

Land, *sb.*

Comb.: **l. grant** *U.S.*, a grant of public land; **l.-grant college** *U.S.*, a state college supported by a grant of public land under the Morrill Land Grant Act of 1862; **l.-mine,** (*a*) an explosive mine used on land; (*b*) pop., a parachute mine.

Land, *v.* **I. 1. b.** To place (an aircraft, passengers, etc.) on the ground again; to bring to earth from the air 1918.

Landing, *vbl. sb.* **I. 1. d.** The (or an) action of coming to or alighting upon the ground after flying through the air or through space 1909.

Hard l., an uncontrolled l. in which the craft is destroyed; **soft l.**, one in which the craft is brought down safely.

Comb.: **l. beam** *Aeronaut.*, a radio beam for guiding aircraft coming in to land; **l. craft,** a boat designed to put troops and equipment ashore on a beach; **l. gear,** the retractable undercarriage of an aircraft; **l. strip** = *air-strip.

Landscape (læ·ndskēⁱp), *v.* 1934. [f. LANDSCAPE-*gardening*.] *trans.* To improve by landscape-gardening.

Lane. II. 1. b. A strip of road marked out for a single line of vehicles 1926.

Lane discipline...Do not wander from lane to lane 1966.

Sea, air l., a route commonly followed by sea or air traffic.

Language, *sb.* **1. c.** *Computers.* Any system of symbols and rules devised for writing programs 1956.

Comb.: **l. laboratory,** a class-room equipped with tape recorders, etc., where foreign languages are learnt by means of repeated oral practice.

Langur (lɒ·ŋgūᵊɹ). 1826. [Hindi; cf. Skr. *lāṅgūlin* tailed.] A southern Asian monkey of the genus *Presbytis*.

Lanthanide (læ·nþănəid). 1926. [f. LANTHAN(UM + -IDE.] *Chem.* Any element of the l. series.

l. series, the series of elements with an atomic number between 57 (lanthanum) and 71 (lutetium), inclusive, all of which are metals with similar chemical properties occupying a single position in the periodic table and occurring together in gadolinite, samarskite, and certain other minerals; (yttrium, at. no. 39, is sometimes included); also called *rare-earth elements*.

Lapse, *sb.*

Comb.: **l. rate** *Meteorol.*, the rate of fall of temperature with height.

Large, *a.*, etc. **C.** *sb.*

At l.: (also) in full, in unabridged form.

A Chronicle at l. and meere History of the affayres of England 1569. The whole volume of the Statutes at l. 1587. Trials at L. (A. Thistlewood) 1817.

Laryngeal, *a.* **B.** *sb. Philology.* A hypothetical phonetic element of a laryngeal quality supposed to have existed in Proto-Indo-European and to have left traces in the vocalic features of extant Indo-European languages.

I reconstruct in terms of the so-called 'laryngeal theory', here, however, without committing myself to the number of laryngeals necessarily to be assumed at a given time 1952.

Lase (lēⁱz), *v.* 1962. [Back-formation from next.] *intr.* Of a substance or an atom: to undergo the physical processes (of excitation and stimulated emission) employed in the laser; to function as the working substance of a laser. Of an apparatus: to operate as a laser.

Different dyes l. at different wavelengths 1969.

Laser² (lēⁱ·zəɹ). 1960. [f. the initial letters of '*l*ight *a*mplification by the *s*timulated *e*mission of *r*adiation', after the earlier *MASER.] A device that emits a very intense, narrow, parallel beam of highly monochromatic and coherent light (or infra-red radiation), either continuously or in pulses, and operates by using light to stimulate the emission of more light of the same wavelength and phase by atoms that have been excited by some means; an optical maser.

La·sh-up. 1898. [f. phr. *lash up*; see LASH *v.*² 2.] A makeshift, a hastily improvised apparatus, structure, etc.

Last, *a.*

1. *L. across*: a children's game in which each tries to be the last to cross a road safely in front of an approaching vehicle.

Latin, *a.* **4. a.** *L. square*, a square conceived as consisting of n letters, a, b, c,.., n, arranged in a square lattice of n^2 compartments in such a way that no letter occurs twice in the same row or in the same column. **b.** *L. American*: of or pertaining to, or a national of, *L. America*, the designation of those parts of Central and South America in which Spanish or Portuguese is the dominant language.

Launch, *sb.*¹ **5. l. pad** = *launching pad.

Launcher (lǭ·ntʃəɹ). 1824. [f. LAUNCH *v.* + -ER¹.] **1.** One who launches (in any sense). **2.** A device or structure that launches something; *spec.* (*a*) a structure that holds a rocket or missile during launching; (*b*) a rocket from which a satellite is released into orbit 1944.

Launching, *vbl. sb.*

Comb.: **l. pad,** the area on which a rocket stands for launching; also *fig.*; also *l. platform, site*, etc.

Launderette (lǭndəre·t). 1949. [f. LAUNDER *v.* + -ETTE.] An establishment providing washing machines for the use of customers.

Lawrencium (lǒre·nsiǒm). 1961. [f. the name of Ernest O. *Lawrence* (1901–58), U.S. physicist + -IUM.] *Chem.* An artificially produced transuranic element, the longest-lived isotope of which has a half-life of just under a minute. Atomic number 103; symbol Lw.

Lay, *v.* **VII.**

L. on. h. Also *fig.*, to organize a supply, as of food, drink, entertainment, etc.

Layabout (lēⁱ·ăbɑut). 1932. [f. LAY *v.* + ABOUT *adv.*] An habitual loafer or tramp.

Lay-by. 1. c. An area adjoining a road where vehicles may park without interfering with the traffic 1939.

L-dopa, the lævo-rotatory form of *DOPA.

Lead, *sb.*¹

Comb.: **l. tetraethyl** (see *tetraethyl lead*).

Leading, *ppl. a.*

Comb.: **l. edge,** (*a*) the forward edge of the blade of a screw-propeller; (*b*) the foremost edge of a wing, tailplane, or other part of an aircraft; (*c*) *Electr.*, the part of a pulse in which the amplitude first increases.

League, *sb.*² **1. c.** orig. *U.S.* A group of sports clubs competing for a championship, esp. in football. Also *attrib.* and *fig.* 1879.

Comb.: **l. table,** a list of the members of a league in ranking order.

Leak, *v.* **4.** Delete † and add: *spec.* to allow the disclosure of (secret information) 1916.

‖**Lebensraum** (lē·bənzraum). 1939. [G., f. genit. of *leben* life + *raum* space, ROOM.] The area claimed by the Germans for their due development (now *Hist.*); also *transf.*

Left-wing (see LEFT A. 2); frequent in attrib. use in politics, as *l. element, member, view* 1922. Hence **Le:ft-wi·ngism.**

Le:ft-wi·nger. 1891. [f. prec. + -ER¹.] **1.** A player on the left wing in games. **2.** A left-wing politician 1924.

Leg, *sb.* **II. 7. b.** In various extended uses, as: a stage in a relay race, a flight, or other journey.

Comb.: **l.-man,** a roving assistant, *esp.* a news-gathering journalist.

Legal, *a.*

1. *l. aid*, financial assistance granted officially to a litigator.

Legionnaire (līdʒənēᵊ·ɹ). 1927. [– Fr. *légionnaire*, f. *légion* LEGION 1 b.] A member of the American, British, Foreign, or other Legion.

Lei (lēⁱ). 1909. [Hawaiian.] A Polynesian garland of flowers.

Length, *etc.* Add to pronuncs. (leŋkþ), (le·ŋkþ'n), etc.

Comb.: **l.-man,** a railway employee charged with the maintenance of a section of the permanent way.

Leninism (le·niniz'm). 1919. [f. *Lenin*, assumed name of Vladimir Ilyich Ulianov (1870–1924), a leader in the Russian Revolution of 1917.] The principles or policy of Lenin.

Lenition (lĭni·ʃən). 1913. [f. L. *lenis* smooth + -ITION, after G. *lenierung*.] *Philol.* The soft mutation in Welsh; the aspiration in Irish. So **Lenited** (lĭ·nəitĕd) *a.*, having been subjected to lenition; also **U·nlenited** *a.*

Continental scholars use 'Lenition' as a term embracing the Welsh 'soft mutation' and the corresponding Irish 'aspiration' 1913.

Leotard (lī·ŏtāɹd). 1934. [Name of J. *Léotard* (1830–70), Fr. trapeze artist.] A close-fitting one-piece garment worn by acrobats and dancers.

Lepton[2] (le·ptǫn). 1948. [f. Gr. λεπτός slight + *-ON.] *Nuclear Physics.* Any of the subatomic particles that do not participate in the strong interaction and have a mass less than that of a nucleon and a half-integral spin.
These, the leptons, consist of the electron, the muon, two types of..neutrino..and the antiparticles of these four 1967.

Lesbian, *a.* **2.** Also applied to a woman who is homosexual. **B.** *sb.* A female homosexual, a sapphist 1925. Hence **Le·sbianism.**

Leucotomy (lⁱukǫ·tŏmi). 1942. [f. Gr. λευκός white + -TOMY.] *Surg.* Incision into the frontal lobe of the brain. Hence **Leu·cotome** [-TOME[1]], an instrument designed for this. **Leuco·tomize** *v. trans.*, to perform l. on.

Level, *sb.* **I. 2. b.** *On the l.*: (in a) fair, honest, or straightforward (way); honestly speaking (*colloq.*) 1875. **4.** Also, a plane or status in respect of rank or authority, e.g. *consultation at cabinet l., action taken at the highest l., a system of high-l. consultations.*
How long it takes to get even a simple low-l. decision 1952.

Levis (lī·vəiz). orig. *U.S.* 1935. [f. name of the original manufacturer, *Levi* Strauss, of U.S.A.] A type of (orig. blue) denim jeans or bibless overalls, with rivets to reinforce stress-points, patented and produced by Levi Strauss in the 1860s.

Lexis (le·ksis). 1960. [– Gr. λέξις word.] Words, vocabulary.
The priority of l. over morphology in preparing the way for machine translation was taken for granted 1960.

Ley (lēⁱ), var. of LEA *sb.*[2], established in agriculturists' use, e.g. *l.-farming.*

Liaise (liēⁱ·z), *v.* orig. *Services' slang.* 1943. [Back-formation from LIAISON.] *intr.* To make liaison *with* or *between.*

Lib (lib), colloq. abbrev. of LIBERAL, LIBERATION.

Liberate, *v.* **b.** In the language of the war of 1939–45, to free (an occupied country) of the enemy; also *ironically*, to subject to a new tyranny. **c.** To loot (property). So **Liberation.**

Liberty, *sb.*[1]
Comb.: **l. boat** *Naut.*, a boat carrying liberty men; **l. ship,** a type of prefabricated freighter built in the U.S. in the war of 1939–45.

Liberty (li·bəɹti), *sb.*[2] 1888. The name of a London drapery firm, Messrs. *Liberty* and Co., used *attrib.* to designate materials, styles, colours, etc., characteristic of fabrics or articles sold by them.

Libido (libī·do, libəi·do). 1913. [L., 'desire, lust'.] In psycho-analytic theory, psychic drive or energy, esp. that associated with the sexual instinct.

Lickety-split (li:kəti,spli·t), *adv.* orig. *U.S.* 1859. At full speed, 'full lick', headlong.

‖**Lido** (lī·do, ləi·do). 1930. [Venetian It. *lido* :– L. *litus* shore.] Name of a beach resort near Venice, used gen. for: a public open-air swimming-pool.

Life, *sb.* Phr. *Not on your l.*: not on any account, by no means. (*You*) *bet your l.*: you can be sure. *To save one's l.*: for the life of one. *Such is l.*: an expression signifying acquiescence in whatever happens. *Life-and-death* attrib. phr.: involving life and death, vitally important.

Lift, *sb.*[2] **I. 1. c.** Transport by air (cf. **air-lift*); a number of persons or an amount of supplies so transported 1942.
The United Kingdom will provide the troop-lift, troops..and shipping..Transports..with a lift of 52,000 men 1942.
5. *Pros.* An element of high intensity in an alliterative measure, marked by stress or tone 1894. (G. *hebung.*) Cf. *DIP *sb.* 1 b.

Li·ft-off, *attrib. phr.* and *sb.* [f. vbl. phr. *to lift off* (LIFT *v.* 1).] **A.** *attrib. phr.* Removable simply by lifting 1907. **B.** *sb.* [After *take-off, blast-off.*] The vertical take-off of a spacecraft or rocket; the time at which it begins to leave the ground 1961.
A. Box, with l. lid 1907. **B.** From l. at Cape Kennedy..to splash-down in the Pacific 1967.

Liger (ləi·gəɹ). 1938. [f. LI(ON + TI)GER]. The offspring of a lion and a tigress.

Light, *sb.*
5. *Mil. Lights out*: the last bugle-call of the day, being the signal for all lights to be put out.
Comb.: **l. pen,** a photo-electric device used for communication with a computer by means of a cathode-ray tube; **l. show,** a display of changing coloured lights for entertainment.

Lighter, *sb.*[2] **b.** *spec.* An instrument for producing a light, consisting usu. of a reservoir containing fuel which is ignited by friction of a steel wheel on a flint 1895.

Limb, *sb.*[1]
4. a. Phr. *Out on a l.*: at a disadvantage; in a dangerous or minority position. orig. *U.S.*

Limburger (li·mbǖ:ɹgəɹ). 1887. [Du.] A soft, strong-smelling cheese first made in the province of Limburg, Belgium.

Lime-juicer (ləi·mdʒū:səɹ). 1859. [f. *lime juice* (LIME *sb.*[2]) + -ER[1].] **a.** *Austral.* One who has lately made a voyage from England. **b.** *U.S.* A British sailor or ship, so called because in the British Navy the consumption of lime juice was at one time enforced 1884. Hence *abbrev.* **Li·mey,** a British sailor; an Englishman (*U.S.*).

Limnology (limnǫ·lŏdʒi). 1893. [f. Gr. λίμνη lake + -OLOGY.] The study of lakes and other bodies of fresh water. Hence **Limnolo·gical** *a.* **Limno·logist.**

Limp, *v.* **b.** Of a ship, etc.: to proceed slowly and with difficulty because of damage 1920.

Lindane (li·ndēⁱn). 1949. [f. the name of T. van der *Linden* (b. 1884), Dutch chemist + -ANE.] The gamma isomer of benzene hexachloride used as an insecticide; it is a colourless crystalline compound that is toxic to mammals but relatively harmless to plant life.

Linear, *a.*
Comb.: **Linear A,** the earlier of two related forms of writing discovered at Knossos in Crete by Sir A. J. Evans, 1894–1901; **Linear B,** the later form, found also on the mainland of Greece, and now shown to be a syllabary imperfectly adapted to the writing of Mycenæan Greek.

Li·nk-up. The act or result of linking up (see LINK *v.* 3) 1945.

Lip, *sb.* **II. 2.**
Comb.: **lipstick:** also as *v. trans.*, to apply l. to.

Lipid (li·pid). Also **-ide.** 1925. [– Fr. *lipide* (G. Bertrand, 1923), f. Gr. λίπος fat + -IDE.] *Chem.* Any of the fats or fat-like substances, comprising esters of the higher aliphatic acids and related compounds. Also **Li·poid** (used synonymously or, formerly, to denote a fat-like substance in distinction to a fat).

Liquidate, *v.* **6.** [After Russ. *likvidirovat'.*] To put an end to, abolish, stamp out, wipe out, kill 1930. So **Liquidation.**

List, *v.*[4]
1. c. *listed building*, one protected from demolition or major alteration by being included in an official list of buildings of architectural or historical importance.

Lit, *ppl. a. L.-up*, rather drunk (*slang*) 1921.

Litho-.

Li·thosphere, the earth's crust; occas. used for the whole earth (in distinction to the hydrosphere and the atmosphere); so **Lithosphe·ric** *a.*

Live, *v.*
8, 9. Phr. *To l. and let l.*, used to typify an attitude or policy of independence combined with tolerance; so *l.-and-let-l.* in attrib. use. *To l. it up*, to live gaily and extravagantly.
A live-and-let-live individualism 1947.

Liver[1].
Comb.: **l. sausage** [tr. G. *leberwurst*], a soft sausage filled with cooked liver, or a mixture of liver and pork, with various seasonings.

Livid, *a.* **b.** Furiously angry, as if pale with rage (*colloq.*) 1918.

Load, *sb.*
Comb.: **l.-shedding,** reduction of the supply of electric current over a specific area, esp. with a view to adjustment of consumption.

Loaded, *ppl. a.* **1. d.** Charged with a hidden implication, as a *l. question* 1942. **3. b.** *slang* (orig. *U.S.*). Rich 1949.

Loading, *vbl. sb.* **4.** The (maximum) current or power taken by an electrical appliance 1951.

Loan, *sb.*[1]
Comb.: **l.-translation** [after G. *lehnübersetzung*], = *CALQUE.

Lobectomy (lobe·ktŏmi). 1932. [f. LOB(E + -ECTOMY.] *Surg.* The excision of a lobe of some organ, esp. of a lung or the brain.

Lobotomy (lobǫ·tŏmi). 1938. [f. LOB(E + -O- + -TOMY.] *Surg.* = *LEUCOTOMY. Hence **Lobo·tomize** *v. trans.*, to perform l. on.
Schizophrenia is no longer a standard reason for performing any kind of lobotomy 1972.

Local, *sb.*[2] **2.** *The l.*: the public house in the immediate neighbourhood (*colloq.*) 1934.

Location. Delete 'Now chiefly *U.S.*' and add: **7.** *Cinematogr.* A place outside the studio where a film is made 1908.

Loco (lō^u·ko), *a.* *slang* (orig. *U.S.*). 1887. [Sp.; cf. LOCO[1].] Insane, crazy, 'cracked'.

Lodging, *vbl. sb.*
Comb.: **l. turn,** an occasion or period for which a railway employee or a vehicle driver has to lodge at his place of destination before returning to his place of departure.

Logical, *a.*
1. l. positivism *Philos.*, a form of positivism in which symbolic logic is applied (cf. G. *logistischer positivismus*, Åke Petzäll), originating in 'der Wiener Kreis'. Hence **l. positivist.**

Lolly (lǫ·li). *slang.* 1943. [Short for LOLLIPOP.] Money.

London.
L. plane, a hybrid of *Platanus occidentalis* and *P. orientalis*, often planted as a street tree.

Loner (lō^u·nəɹ). orig. *U.S.* 1951. [f. LONE *a.* + -ER[1].] A person who avoids company, an individualist.

Long, *a.*
Phr. *l. in the tooth*: see TOOTH.
Comb.: **l. arm,** a pole fitted with a hook, shears, etc., for lifting objects, cutting branches, etc., at or to a height beyond the ordinary reach of the arm; **l.-day** *a.*, of a plant: needing a long daily period of light before flowering; **l. distance,** applied to a telephone service between distant places; **l.-haired** *a.*, having the hair longer than normal; artistic, intellectual, non-conformist; **l. letter** *Typogr.*, a letter carrying a 'long mark'; **l. pull** (see PULL *sb.* I. 2 f); **l.-short (story),** a short story of more than an average length; **l. shot,** a wild guess; *Cinematogr.*, a shot which includes figures or scenery at a distance; **l. suit** (SUIT *sb.* V. 3), the suit of which one holds the longest run of cards; *fig.* one's speciality, a thing in which one excels, **l.-term,** used attrib. of a plan, policy, or the like designed to meet the circumstances of a long time ahead.

‖**Longueur** (loṅgǖr). 1821. [Fr., 'length'.] An over-lengthy tedious passage in a book, etc.; a long tedious stretch (of time).
Unnecessary longueurs which disfigure the narrative 1887.

Loo (lū), *sb.*[3] *colloq.* 1940. [Origin unknown.] A water-closet.

Loop, *sb.*[1] **2.b.** = *COIL *sb.*[2] 4 b. 1965.

Loopy, *a.* **3.** *slang.* Crazy, 'cracked' 1929.

Loose, *a.*
l. change, an amount of money kept or left in one's pocket, etc., for casual use (orig. *U.S.*).

Lorentz (lǭre·nts). 1910. The name of H. A. *Lorentz* (1853–1928), Dutch physicist, used *attrib.* **L. contraction** = **FitzGerald contraction.* **L. transformation:** the set of equations which in the special theory of relativity relate the space and time coordinates of one frame of reference to those of another moving uniformly with respect to the first.

Loud-hai·ler. 1943. [LOUD *a.* + HAIL *v.*[2] 2 + -ER[1].] A megaphone, especially as used at sea.

Loupe (lūp). 1891. [Fr.] A watchmaker's magnifying glass.

Lousy, *a.* **2. b.** 'Swarming' *with*; abundantly supplied *with* (money, etc.) *slang* (orig. *U.S.*) 1850.

Love-hate. 1937. An intense emotion embracing both love and hate. Used esp. *attrib.*, as *l. complex, l. relationship.*

Lo·vely, *sb.* 1933. [f. the adj.] A woman or girl of glamorous loveliness, esp. one who takes part in an entertainment or 'show'.

Luck.
Phrases: *Just my l.* (ironical exclamation). *No such l.*: unfortunately not. *With l.*: if all goes well. *You never know your l.*: you may be lucky.

‖**Luftwaffe** (lu·ftvafə, -wafə). 1936. [G., 'air-arm'.] The German air force.

Lumber, *sb.*[1]
Comb.: **l.-jack,** a man who fells trees or prepares them for the N. American timber trade.

Lunar. A. *adj.*
1. lunar (excursion) module, a module designed to take an astronaut from an orbiting spacecraft to the moon's surface and back.

Lunch, *sb.*
Comb.: **l.-hour,** the mid-day break from work.

Lutetium (l[i]ūtī·ʃ[i]ŏm). Also **lutecium.** 1907. [– Fr. *lutécium* (G. Urbain, 1907) – L. *Lutetia,* Roman name of Paris + -IUM.] A rare metallic element that is the heaviest member of the lanthanide series and forms colourless salts in which it is trivalent. Atomic number 71; symbol Lu.

Lux (lɒks). 1892. [L., 'light'.] *Physics.* A unit of illumination, now incorporated into the S.I., equal to one lumen per square metre; i.e. the illumination of a surface all of which is at a distance of one metre from a uniform point source of light of one candela (formerly, one candle-power) intensity.

Luxury. 7. *attrib.* **a.** Concerning the inessentials or superfluities of a comfortable life, as *l. duty, l. tax, l. trade* 1905. **b.** Especially comfortable and expensive, as *l. flat, l. liner* 1931.

Lysergic (ləisə̄·ɹdʒik), *a.* 1934. [f. *lys* (in HYDROLYSIS) + ERG(OT + -IC.] *Chem. L. acid*: **a.** a crystalline compound, $C_{16}H_{16}N_2O_2$, related to indole, the dextrorotatory isomer of which is produced by the hydrolysis of ergot alkaloids; **b.** used *ellipt.* for *l. acid diethylamide* 1954.
b. The creation of experimental psychoses with l. acid 1955.
Comb.: **l. acid diethylamide,** the diethylamide of l. acid, an extremely powerful synthetic hallucinogen that can produce profound changes in perception and mood and has been used in psychiatric treatment, usu. as the water-soluble tartrate, a colourless odourless powder; abbrev. *LSD.*

M.
III. M. = motorway; m. = million. Also M.I., Military Intelligence; M.I.R.V., multiple independently targeted re-entry vehicle (a type of missile); M.K.S., metre-kilogramme-second; M.O., medical officer; M.O.T., Ministry of Transport; M.P., military police(man); m.p.g., miles per gallon; m.p.h., miles per hour; M.T.B., motor torpedo boat.

McCoy (məkoi·). *colloq.* 1883. [Origin uncertain.] *The real M.*: the real thing, the genuine article.

Mach (māk, mæk). 1937. [Name of E. *Mach* (1838–1916), Austrian physicist.] *M. number,* the ratio of the speed of a fluid, or of a body (esp. an aircraft) in a fluid, to the speed of sound at the same point; *M. one, two,* etc., a speed corresponding to a M. number of one, two, etc.
It was diving at round about M. unity, and the wings came off N. SHUTE.

Macrobiotic. A. *adj.* **2.** Designating or pertaining to a diet or food intended to prolong life, comprising pure vegetable foods, brown rice, etc. 1967. Hence **Macrobio·tics** *sb. pl.,* the use or theory of such a diet.

Ma·cro-mo:lecule. 1886. [MACRO- b.] *Chem.* A molecule containing a very large number of atoms; a polymeric molecule. Hence **Macro-mole·cular** *a.*

Mae West (mē[i] we·st). *slang* (orig. *R.A.F.*). 1940. [Professional name of an American film actress and entertainer.] An airman's inflatable life-saving jacket.

Magnetic, *a.*
1. M. tape, tape (now usu. of plastic) coated or impregnated with a magnetic substance for use as a recording medium.

Magneto-. In wider use as comb. form of *magnetic, magnetism,* etc.
M.-che·mistry, the branch of science concerned with the relation between magnetism and chemical phenomena, molecular and atomic structure, etc.; hence **M.-che·mical** *a.* **Magne·topause,** the outer limit of the magnetosphere. **Magne·tosphere,** the region surrounding the earth in which its magnetic field is effective. **Magnetostri·ction,** a dependence of the state of strain of a body (and hence its dimensions) on its state of magnetization; hence **Magnetostri·ctive** *a.*

Magne:tohydrodyna·mic, *a.* 1943. [f. *MAGNETO- (from *electromagnet*) + HYDRODYNAMIC *a.*] *Physics.* Of, relating to, or involving an electrically conducting fluid (as a plasma or molten metal) acted on by a magnetic field. Abbrev. MHD.
As the term 'electromagnetic-hydrodynamic waves' is somewhat complicated, it may be convenient to call the phenomenon 'magneto-hydrodynamic' waves H. ALFVÉN. Hence **Magne:tohydrodyna·mics** *sb. pl.* (const. as *sing.*), the study of m. phenomena.

Magneton (mæ·gnetǫn). 1914. [– Fr. *magnéton* (P. Weiss, 1912), f. *magnétique* magnetic + *-on* (in *electron*).] *Physics.* Any of several units of magnetic moment used in dealing with the magnetic properties of atoms, molecules, etc.

Magnetron (mæ·gnétrǫn). 1924. [f. MAGNET + *-TRON.] *Electronics.* An electron tube in which the flow of electrons is controlled by an externally applied magnetic field, used for amplifying or generating microwaves. Also *attrib.,* as *m. oscillator, tube.*

Magnitude. 3. *Absolute m.,* a measure of the intrinsic luminosity of a star, equal to the apparent m. it would have if at a standard distance of ten parsecs.

Mail, *sb.*[3]
Comb.: **m.-order** orig. *U.S.,* an order for goods that is sent to a business house by post; also *attrib.*

Main, *a.*
8. m. line, also (*slang,* orig. *U.S.*), a principal vein, into which drugs can readily be injected; hence **m.-line** *v. trans.* and *intr.,* to inject (a drug) into a vein; **m.-liner,** a person who does this; **m. stream,** the principal stream or current (of a river, etc.); also *transf.* and *fig.,* the prevailing direction of opinion, fashion, etc.; also *attrib.,* spec. designating a type of jazz that is neither 'traditional' nor 'modern'.

Make, *v.* **VIII. 2. b.** *To m. do*: to manage *with* (what is available, esp. an inferior substitute). Also *absol.,* esp. in *to m. do and mend*: to use a temporary expedient 1927. **5.** *slang* (orig. *U.S.*). To win the affection of (someone); *spec.* to persuade (someone) to consent to sexual intercourse; to seduce 1926.

Make-up. 2. b. Cosmetics, etc., used by actors in making up or by women generally 1886.

Malarkey (mălā·ɹki). *slang* (orig. *U.S.*). Also **malarky, mullarkey.** 1930. [Origin unkn.] Humbug, nonsense.

Malathion (mælăþəi·ǫ̆n). 1953. [Manufactured from diethyl *male*ate (an ester of MALEIC acid) and a *thio*-acid (see s.v. THIO-).] An organophosphorus insecticide which is relatively harmless to plants and mammals; in commercial preparations it is a brownish liquid with a strong smell of garlic.

‖**Mal de mer** (mal də mę̄r). 1778. [Fr., 'malady of sea'.] Sea-sickness.

Mamba (mæ·mbă). 1882. [– Zulu *m'namba.*] A venomous southern African snake of the genus *Dendroaspis.*

Mambo (mæ·mbo). 1948. [Amer. Sp., prob. from Haitian.] A Latin-American dance, or its music, resembling the rumba.

Man, *sb.*
Comb.: With a period of time, as **man-day, -hour, -week, -year,** a day, hour, etc., of a man's work.

Mana (mā·nă). 1843. [Maori.] Power in general, authority, prestige; *spec.* supernatural or magical power or influence.

‖**Mañana** (mæn[y]ā·nă), *adv.* and *sb.* 1845. [Sp.] Tomorrow. Often taken as a synonym for easy-going procrastination as found in Spanish-speaking countries: the indefinite future.

Mandala (mæ·ndălă). 1882. [– Skr. *máṇḍala* disc, circle.] A symbolic circular figure found in many cultures as a religious symbol; *spec.* in *Jungian Psychol.,* an image of such a circle visualized in dreams and symbolizing the dreamer's striving for unity of self and completeness.

Manhattan (mænhæ·tăn). 1890. [Name of the island on which the older part of New York is situated.] A cocktail made of vermouth and whisky with a dash of bitters.

Manic (mæ·nik), *a.* 1902. [f. MANIA: see -IC.] Pertaining to or affected with mania; hence as *sb.,* a person affected with mania.
Comb.: **m.-depressive** *a.,* characterized by alternating periods of elation and mental depression; also as *sb.*

Manœuvrable (mănū·vrăb'l), *a.* 1928. [fr MANŒUVRE *v.* + -ABLE.] Of an aircraft, moto. vehicle, etc.: capable of being (easily) manœuvred. Hence **Manœuvrabi·lity.**

Manor. 3. c. A police district; a local unit of police administration. Also *transf.* 1924.

-manship, *suff.* [f. MAN *sb.* + -SHIP, after CRAFTSMANSHIP, SPORTSMANSHIP, etc.] Added to sb. (occas. vb.), denotes skill in a subject or activity, esp. so deployed as to disconcert a rival or opponent, as in *BRINKMANSHIP, *GAMESMANSHIP, *lifemanship,* **one-upmanship.*

Mantle, *sb.* **7.** The part of the interior of the earth which lies below the thin outer crust and extends approximately 1,800 miles towards the centre, differing from the region beneath in its solidity and rigidity and in its composition 1940.

Mao (mau). 1967. The name of *Mao* Tse-Tung (born 1893), Chairman of the Central Committee of the Chinese Communist Party, used *attrib.* to denote a style of clothing based on that worn in Communist China, as *M. cap, collar, jacket, trousers.* So **Mao·ism,** the Communist theories of Mao Tse-Tung. **Mao·ist,** a follower of these theories; also as *adj.*

Maquette (mæke·t). 1903. [Fr. – It. *machietta* speck, dim. of *macchia* spot, f. *macchiare* to spot, stain :– L. *maculare*; cf. MACULATE.] A sculptor's small preliminary model in wax, clay, etc. Also *transf.* and *fig.*

‖**Maquillage** (maki[y]āʒ). 1892. [Fr., f. *maquiller* :– OFr. *masquiller* to stain, alt. of OFr. *mascurer* to darken.] The action of applying make-up; also, make-up, cosmetics.

Maquis (ma·ki). 1858. [Fr., 'brushwood, scrub' – Corsican It. *macchia* thicket – L. *macula* spot.] **a.** The dense scrub characteristic of certain Mediterranean coastal regions, esp. Corsica, often used as a refuge by fugitives. **b.** A secret army of patriots in France during the German occupation in the 1939–45 war. Also *transf.* and *attrib.* 1944.

Maraca (măræ·kă). Also **maracca.** 1928. [Pg. *maracá,* prob. f. Tupi.] Usu. *pl.*: a Latin-American percussion instrument consisting of a gourd, etc., containing beans, beads, etc., and shaken (usu. in pairs) to produce a rattling sound.

Marathon. Also *transf.* and *fig.*
The House of Commons finally went home.. after sitting through a marathon session of 20 hours and 20 minutes 1951.

‖**Mare**[3] (mā·re, mā·ri, mæ·ri). Pl. **maria** (mā·riă). 1895. [L., 'sea': first used, in the 17th c., in proper names of the various regions.] *Astr.* Any of the extensive areas of flat land on the surface of the moon, which appear dark in the telescope and were once thought to be seas.

Marge[2] (māɹdʒ). 1922. Colloq. abbrev. of MARGARINE.

Maria, pl. of *MARE[3].

Marijuana (mærihwā·nă). Also **-huana.** 1894. [Amer. Sp.] The hemp plant, *Cannabis sativa,* as prepared or used for ingestion, usu. by smoking, as an intoxicating and hallucinogenic drug; usu. applied to a crude preparation of the dried leaves, flowering tops, and stem of the plant.
His eyes were as wide and pained as the eyes of one who smokes m. J. STEINBECK. M., otherwise cannabis..and about a hundred other names,.. has not yet become in this country a popular way of escape from the worries of normal life 1939.

Marina. 2. orig. *U.S.* A dock or basin with moorings for yachts and other small craft 1934.

Mark, *sb.*[1] **III. 5. b.** Also, followed by a numeral, a particular design of a weapon, piece of equipment, or the like.
Enfield Revolver Pistol, Mark II 1888.

Marker. 5. A flare, object, etc., used as a guide to an aircraft pilot seeking a particular area or the like 1936.

Market, *sb.*
6. *Black m.*: see *BLACK *a. Buyer's m.*: a state of trade in favour of the buyer; so *seller's m.*

Common m.: a customs union, *spec.* the European Economic Community.
Comb.: **m. research,** the systematic investigation of factors affecting the sale of particular goods.

Ma·rk-up. 1920. [f. phr. *to mark up*: see MARK *v.*] The amount added by a retailer to the cost-price of goods to cover overhead charges and provide profits.

Marmite (mā·ɹmīt, mā·ɹmait). 1918. [Fr.] **1.** An earthenware cooking vessel; a stockpot. **2.** The proprietary term for an extract made from fresh brewer's yeast 1920.

Martini[2] (māɹtī·ni). 1894. [Origin uncertain; perh. from the name *Martini* and Rossi, Italian purveyors of a type of vermouth.] A cocktail made from gin and French vermouth, etc.; **dry M.,** such a cocktail containing more gin than vermouth, with orange bitters added.

Mascon (mæ·skǫn). 1968. [f. *mass concentration.*] *Astr.* One of the concentrations of denser material thought to exist under some lunar maria, discovered as a result of the variations they produce in the speed of an orbiting satellite.

Maser (mē[i]·zəɹ). 1955. [f. the initial letters of '*m*icrowave *a*mplification by the *s*timulated *e*mission of *r*adiation'.] Any device in which the stimulated emission of radiation by excited atoms, molecules, etc., is utilized to amplify or generate electromagnetic radiation that is highly monochromatic; *esp.* one used as a very sensitive low-noise amplifier of microwaves. (A m. that operates in the visible region of the spectrum is usu. called a *LASER[2].)

Mass, *sb.*[2]
Comb.: **d. m. medium** (usu. in pl. *m. media*), a medium of communication (such as radio, television, or newspapers) that reaches a large number of people; **m. number** *Nuclear Physics*, the total number of protons and neutrons in an atomic nucleus; **m. radiography,** radiography of the chests of a large number of people by a quick routine method; **m. spectrograph** *Physics*, an instrument in which a beam of ions is passed in a vacuum through an electric and a magnetic field on to a photographic plate, so that their masses may be determined from the deflections they undergo; **m. spectrometer** *Physics*, a similar instrument in which the ions are detected electrically rather than photographically.

Ma·ster-mi·nd. 1720. [MASTER *sb.*[1] V.] **1.** An outstanding or commanding mind or intellect. Also applied to the possessor of such a mind, and *transf.* **2.** *spec.* Such a mind, or person, directing a criminal enterprise 1873. Hence as *v. trans.*, to be the master-mind behind (an enterprise, a crime, etc.); to plan and direct.

Match, *sb.*[1]
Comb.: **m.-point,** the state of a game when one side needs only one point to win the m.; the point itself; in *Bridge*, a unit used in scoring in tournament play.

Matelot (mæ·tlo). *slang.* 1909. [Fr.; cf. MATLO(W.] A sailor.

Maternity. 3. m. home, premises to be used for the reception and delivery of pregnant women or of women immediately after childbirth.

Mathematical. A. *adj.* **1. m. model**: see *MODEL *sb.* I. 2 c.

Matilda (mǎti·ldǎ). *Austral. slang.* 1893. [A female Christian name.] A bushman's bundle or swag. So *to walk* or *waltz M.*: to carry one's swag, to travel the road.

Matrilineal (mætrili·nǐǎl), *a.* 1904. [f. L. *mater, matr-* mother + LINEAL *a.*] Of, pertaining to, or based on (kinship with) the mother or the female line; recognizing kinship with and descent through females only. So **Matrili·neage,** matrilineal lineage. **Ma·triliny,** the observance of matrilineal descent and kinship.

Matrilocal (mætrilō[u]·kǎl), *a.* 1906. [f. L. *mater, matr-* mother + LOCAL *a.*] Applied to a system of marriage among primitive peoples, where a husband moves to his wife's local group.

‖**Mauvais quart d'heure** (move kārdǿr). 1871. [Fr., lit. 'bad quarter of an hour.] A short but unpleasant experience, interview, etc.

Maxi-, comb. f. MAXIMUM, denoting things that are very large or long of their kind, as *maxi-coat, maxi-skirt*, etc. Hence **Maxi** *sb.*, such a coat, skirt, etc.

Mayday[2] (mē[i]·dē[i]). 1927. [Phonetic repr. of Fr. *m'aider* imper. inf. 'help me!'.] An international radio-telephone signal of distress. Also *transf.*

Mean, *sb.* **II. 4. means test,** an official inquiry into an applicant's private resources, determining or limiting a financial grant or allowance.

Meanie, meany (mī·ni). *colloq.* 1928. [f. MEAN *a.*[1] + -IE, -Y[6].] A mean person.

Meaningful (mī·niŋfŭl), *a.* 1852. [f. MEANING *vbl. sb.* + -FUL.] Full of meaning or expression; having a meaning, comprehensible. Hence **Mea·ningfully** *adv.*

Medium. A. *sb.* **5. b.** A means of communication; *spec.* = **mass medium*; freq. *pl.* 1880.

Mega-. b. Me·gadeath, the death of a million persons, as a unit in calculating the effect of warfare. **Me·gaton,** a unit of explosive power equivalent to that of a million tons of T.N.T.

Megalopolis (megǎlǫ·pǒlis). 1832. [f. MEGALO- + Gr. πόλις city.] A great city, or its way of life. So **Megalopo·litan** *a.* and *sb.*

Meiosis. 2. *Cytology.* The process of nuclear division by which the diploid number of chromosomes is halved to the haploid number, so offsetting the subsequent doubling of chromosomes at fertilization 1905.

Melamine. Substitute pronunc. (me·lǎmīn). **2.** M. resin, or plastic derived from it 1943.
Tough new plastic tableware is made of m. 1958.
Comb.: **m. resin,** any of the synthetic resins made from m. and formaldehyde or some other aldehyde.

Meld (meld), *v.*[2] orig. and chiefly *U.S.* 1939. [perh. f. MELT *v.* + WELD *v.*] *trans.* and *intr.* To merge, blend; to combine, incorporate.

Memory. 2. b. *Computers.* A device in which data or instructions may be stored and from which they may be retrieved when required; freq. *attrib.*, as *m. bank, circuit*, etc. 1946.
There are four kinds of 'm.' in the Eniac 1946.

Mendelevium (mendělī·vǐǒm). 1955. [f. the name of D. I. *Mendeleev* (1834–1907), Russian chemist + -IUM.] *Chem.* An artificially produced transuranic element, the longest-lived isotope of which has a half-life of two months. Atomic number 101; symbol Md (formerly Mv).

Mental, *a.*[1] **1. b.** *colloq.* Mentally defective; insane 1927.
Comb.: **m. age,** the degree of a person's mental development, expressed as the age at which it is attained by an average person; **m. cruelty,** the infliction of suffering on the mind of another person, esp. as constituting grounds for legal separation or divorce.

Mercy. *attrib.* passing into *adj.* (orig. *U.S.*). Administered or performed out of m. or pity in order to put a suffering person out of pain or distress, as *m. killing* (so *m. killer*), *murder*, etc. 1930.

Meritocracy (meritǫ·krǎsi). 1958. [f. MERIT *sb.* + -OCRACY.] Government by persons selected on the basis of merit in a competitive educational system.
The rise of the m. (*title*) M. YOUNG 1958.

Mescal. 2. a. Any of several plants of the genus *Agave*, esp. *A. americana* 1831. **b.** A small desert cactus, *Lophophora williamsii*, also called *peyote*, found in the south-western U.S. and Mexico 1885.
Comb.: **m. buttons,** the dried sliced fruit of *L. williamsii*, used for its intoxicating and hallucinogenic properties. Hence **Me·scaline** (occas. **-in**), the alkaloid that is the active principle of m. buttons, possessing effects similar to those of LSD but much less strongly.
The soul is transported to its far-off destination by the aid of. . mescalin A. HUXLEY.

Mesic (mī·zik, me·zik), *a.* 1952. [f. *MES(ON + -IC.] *Nuclear Physics.* = *MESONIC *a.*

Meso-.

Me·somorph, a person with an innate muscular body-build. **Me·sosphere,** the region of the atmosphere extending from the top of the stratosphere (at a height of either 12–15 miles or 30–35 miles) to a height of about 50 miles, where the temperature stops decreasing with height and starts to increase.

Meson (mī·zǫn, me·zǫn). 1939. [Alteration of the earlier name *MESOTRON: see *-ON.] *Nuclear Physics.* Any of a group of unstable sub-atomic particles (first found in cosmic rays) that are intermediate in mass between an electron and a proton; the name is now commonly restricted to such particles that are strongly interacting and have zero or integral spin (cf. *MUON), certain of which occur in atomic nuclei as transmitters of the binding force between the nucleons.
High-energy cosmic ray collisions produce a shower of secondary particles, principally kaons (*K* mesons) and pions (pi mesons) 1971. Hence **Meso·nic** *a.*

Mesotron (mī·zotrǫn). *rare* or *Obs.* 1938. [f. Gr. μέσος middle (adj.) + *-TRON.] *Nuclear Physics.* The name orig. given to the *MESON.

Messenger.
Comb.: **m. RNA,** RNA which carries genetic information stored in a gene to a ribosome, where it determines what particular protein is synthesized; abbrev. mRNA.

Met, colloq. abbrev. of METEOROLOGICAL *a.* or *Meteorological Office* 1940.

Metalanguage (me·tǎlæŋgwédʒ). 1936. [See META- 1.] A language used to discuss the nature or properties of an 'object' language; a system of propositions about other propositions. So **Metalingui·stic** *a.* and *sb. pl.*

Metastable, *a.* Read: Applied to a state of equilibrium that is stable only with respect to certain (small) disturbances; also, passing to another state so slowly as to appear stable. Hence **Me:tastabi·lity,** the property or state of being m.

Methadone (me·pǎdō[u]n). orig. *U.S.* Also **-on** (-ǫn). 1947. [f. 6-*dimethylamino*-4,4-*diphenyl*-3-*heptan*one, the systematic chemical name.] *Pharm.* A powerful synthetic analgesic, similar to morphine in its properties, which is used (as the hydrochloride) as a substitute drug in the treatment of morphine and heroin addicts.

Methamphetamine (mepæmfe·tǎmīn, -in). 1949. [f. METH(YL + *AMPHETAMINE.] *Pharm.* A methyl derivative of amphetamine, used in the form of the hydrochloride, a white crystalline compound, as a stimulant of the central nervous system; its effects resemble those of amphetamine but are more rapid in onset and longer lasting.

Methedrine (me·pědrin, -īn). 1939. [f. METH(YL + *BENZ)EDRINE.] *Pharm.* A proprietary name for methamphetamine hydrochloride.

Method. I. 2. b. *Theatr.* A theory and practice of acting in which the actor seeks to identify himself closely with the part he plays; freq. *attrib.* 1956.

Meths (meps). Also **meth.** Colloq. abbrev. of *methylated spirit* 1933.

Metricate (me·trikē[i]t), *v.* 1965. [f. METRIC *a.*[2] + -ATE[3].] *trans.* and *intr.* To change, convert, or adapt to the metric system of weights and measures. Hence **Me·tricated** *ppl. a.*
The encouragement of the use of 'metricated' products 1972.

Metrication (metrikē[i]·ʃən). 1965. [f. METRIC *a.*[2] + -ATION.] The process of converting to the metric system of weights and measures; the adoption of the metric system.
The m. of large sections of British industry will soon be an accomplished fact 1969.

Metricize (me·trisəiz), *v.* 1873. [f. METRIC *a.*[2] + -IZE.] *trans.* To adapt to the metric system of weights and measures.

Mickey (mi·ki). *slang.* Also **micky.** 1952. [Origin uncertain.] *To take the m.* (*out of*) (someone): to act in a satirical, disrespectful, or teasing manner (towards). Hence **Mi·ckey-take** *v. intr.* **Mi·ckey-taking** *vbl. sb.* and *ppl. a.*

Mickey Finn (mi:ki fi·n). *slang* (orig. *U.S.*). Also **Mickey, Mickey Flynn.** 1929. [Origin uncertain.] A strong alcoholic drink; a drink adulterated with a narcotic substance, usu. with the intention of stupefying someone; also *transf.* and *fig.*

Micro-. 1. Mi·crocircuit *Electronics*, an integrated circuit or other minute circuit. **Mi:crocli:mate,** the climate of a small area or of the immediate surroundings of an organism. **Mi:cro-electro·nics,** the branch of technology concerned with the design, manufacture, and use of microcircuits; so **Mi:cro-electro·nic** *a.* **Mi·crogroove,** a very narrow groove on a gramophone record; a record having such grooves. **Mi:crominiaturiza·tion,** the development or use of techniques for making electronic components and devices of greatly reduced size.

b. Prefixed to a sb. to indicate a reduction in size by microphotography. **Mi:crocard,** the proprietary name for an opaque card bearing microphotographs of a portion of a book, periodical, etc. **Mi·crodot,** a photograph, esp. of printed or written matter, reduced to the size of a dot. **Mi·crofiche** (-fīʃ). [Fr. *fiche* index card], a small flat piece of film containing microphotographs of about sixty pages of a book, periodical, etc. **Mi·crofilm** *sb.*, (a length of) photographic film containing microphotographs of a book, periodical, etc.; hence as *v. trans.*, to record in this way.

2. Mi·crograph, a photograph taken with the aid of a microscope so as to obtain great enlargement.

Microphone. 3. An instrument designed to convert sound waves impinging upon it into corresponding variations in voltage or current, which may then be amplified or transmitted for reconversion into sound (as in broadcasting and the telephone); *esp.* one made as an independent unit (colloq. abbrev. *mike*) 1929.

Microwave (məi·krowēⁱv). 1931. An electromagnetic wave with a wavelength between about 1 mm. and 30 cm. (the figures vary somewhat). Freq. *attrib.* or *pl.*

Micrurgy (məi·krɒ̈ɹdʒi). 1928. [f. MICRO- + *-urgy* (Gr. -ουργία work).] The manipulation, injection, etc., of individual cells under a microscope.

Middle. A. *adj.*

Special collocations. **m.-brow,** (*a*) *sb.* a person of average or moderate cultural interests; (*b*) *adj.* claiming to be or regarded as only moderately intellectual; **m. game** *Chess*, the central phase of play between the opening and the end game; **m.-of-the-road** *phr.*, often used *attrib.* of a person or course of action: moderate, avoiding extremes.

Middle East. 1902. [MIDDLE *a.*, EAST *sb.*] The countries lying between the Near and Far East, esp. Egypt and Iran and the countries between them.

Midi-, comb. f. MID *a.*, MIDDLE, in imitation of *MAXI- and *MINI-, denoting garments longer than mini- but shorter than maxi-. Hence **Midi** *sb.*, such a garment.

Milk, *sb.*

4. *M. of magnesia*: a proprietary name for a white suspension of magnesium hydroxide in water, taken as an antacid.

Comb.: **m. bar,** a place where drinks made from m., etc., are sold; **m. chocolate,** eating chocolate made with m.; **m. shake,** a drink made of m., flavouring, etc., mixed by shaking.

‖**Mille-feuille** (milföy). 1895. [Fr., lit. 'thousand leaves'.] A rich pastry consisting of layers of puff pastry split and filled with jam, cream, etc.

Minded, *ppl. a.* **3. b.** Now commonly with prefixed *sb.*, as *air-m.*, *car-m.*

Mine, *sb.* **3.** Also, a receptacle containing explosive placed in or on the ground as a weapon of war.

Comb.: **m. detector,** an instrument that indicates the presence of mines; **m. field,** an area sown with mines.

Minestrone (ministrōᵘ·ni). 1891. [It.] A thick soup containing vegetables and rice or pasta.

Ming (miŋ). 1671. [Chinese.] The name of a dynasty that ruled in China from 1368 to 1644; a member of this dynasty. Also, the Chinese porcelain of this period. Also *attrib.*

Mini (mi·ni). 1964. [See next.] **a.** Shortened f. *minicar*. **b.** Shortened f. *miniskirt* 1966.

Mini-, comb. f. MINIATURE *a.*, denoting things that are very small of their kind, as *minibus, minicar, miniskirt*.

Miniature. B. *adj.* Also, designed on a small scale; smaller than normal.

Miniaturize (mi·nit-, mi·niătiŭrəiz), *v.* 1950. [f. MINIATURE + -IZE.] *trans.* To produce in a smaller version; to render small. Hence **Mi·niaturized** *ppl. a.* **Mi:niaturiza·tion.**

There has been a general move to m. radio components 1950. The pages fall open easily,..four of the original appearing in each page of the miniaturized volumes 1971.

Minority. 3. b. A small group of people separated from the rest of the community by a difference in race, religion, language, etc. 1930.

Minute, *sb.* **I. 1. d.** The distance that can be travelled in a minute 1886.

Only twenty minutes from the station R. CAMPBELL.

Misfit, *sb.* **b.** A person unsuited to his environment, work, etc. 1903.

Mishit (mishi·t), *sb.* 1882. Also erron. **miss-.** [MIS-¹ 4.] A faulty or bad hit. Hence **Mishi·t** *v. trans.*

Miss, *sb.*¹ **III. 1.** *To give* (a thing) *a m.*: to pass by, leave alone (*colloq.*) 1918.

Miss (mis), *sb.*⁴ Also **mis.** 1897. Colloq. shortening of MISCARRIAGE 3.

Missile. B. *sb.* **1. b.** *Mil.* A destructive projectile that during part or all of its course is self-propelling and directed by remote control or automatically 1945.

Mission, *sb.* **2. b.** orig. *U.S.* A military operation or project; esp. the dispatch of an aircraft or spacecraft on an operational flight; also *transf.* and *attrib.* 1929.

Mitochondrion (məitokǫ·ndriŏn). Pl. **mitochondria.** 1911. [mod.L. (C. Benda, 1898), f. Gr. μίτος thread + χονδρίον, dim. of χόνδρος granule.] *Cytology.* An organelle present in the cytoplasm of most cells and containing enzymes necessary for various metabolic processes. Hence **Mitocho·ndrial** *a.*

Mix, *sb.* Also, a mixture; the proportion of materials in a mixture; also *transf.* and *fig.*; *spec.* (*a*) the action of *MIX *v.* 6; (*b*) the ingredients prepared for making a cake, etc.

Mix, *v.* **1. a.** *To m. one's drinks*: to drink different kinds of alcoholic liquor in succession. **4. c.** Colloq. phr. *To m. in* or *it*: to start fighting; to fight. **6.** *trans.* and *intr.* To cause (a cinematographic or television picture) to merge gradually with, or be replaced by, another picture; in sound recording, to combine (different sounds) 1922.

Mixed, *ppl. a.* **2.** *M. up*: involved, tangled; (mentally) confused, unbalanced, neurotic. orig. *U.S.*

Mi·x-up. 1898. [f. phr. *to mix up.*] A muddle, confusion.

Mobile (mōᵘ·bəil), *sb.*³ 1949. [subst. use of MOBILE *a.*] A form of decoration consisting usu. of abstract designs in metal, plastic, etc., contrived (as by suspension) so as to be mobile.

Möbius, Moebius (mö·biŭs). 1909. The name of A. F. *Möbius* (1790–1868), German mathematician, used, now always *attrib.*, to designate a surface having only one side and one edge, formed by twisting one end of a rectangular strip through 180° and joining it to the other end; so *M. strip*, etc.

Mobster (mǫ·bstəɹ). orig. *U.S. slang.* 1917. [f. MOB *sb.*¹ 5 + -STER.] A member of a group of criminals; a gangster.

Mock-up (mǫ·kɒp). 1920. [f. MOCK *v.* + UP, after *make-up, set-up.*] An experimental model (often full-sized) of a projected ship, aircraft, etc.

Mod (mǫd), *sb.* 1960. [abbrev. of MODERN *a.* or MODERNIST.] A teenager who is characterized by his sophistication and tidiness; freq. contrasted with *ROCKER 5. Also *attrib.* or as *adj.*

The beaches of England have become arenas for rival gangs of..motorcycle-riding Rockers..and ..motorscooter-riding Mods 1964.

Mode. II. 1. b. *Statistics.* That value of a variate of which the instances are most numerous 1895.

Model, *sb.* **I. 2. c.** A simplified or idealized description of a system, situation, or process, often in mathematical terms (so *mathematical m.*), devised to facilitate calculations and predictions 1949.

Forrester has designed a m. of the world system to try to discover the long term effects of pollution and overpopulation. The m., processed through a computer, predicts a variety of different futures 1971.

Moderator. 6. c. *Nuclear Physics.* A substance used in a nuclear reactor to slow down the neutrons produced by fission 1945.

Modulate, *v.* **5.** *trans. Telecommunications.* To vary the amplitude or some other characteristic of (a wave) in accordance with the variations of a second wave of lower frequency 1908.

Modulation. 7. *Telecommunications.* The process of modulating a wave in order to impress a signal upon it (see prec.) 1919.

Module. 4. b. *Archit.* A unit of measurement, multiples of which are used to fix the dimensions of building components, facilitating their co-ordination 1936. **5.** One of a series of production units standardized to facilitate assembly or replacement, as in buildings and in electronic and mechanical systems 1955. **6.** A separable section of a spacecraft that can operate as an independent unit 1961.

5. The vast majority of tuner-amplifiers are now transistored, the designs being based on printed circuit boards or 'modules' 1970. Our housing needs in the next nine years must be met with factory-built modules, assembled on site 1971. **6.** As additional modules are placed in orbit and docked with the first m., some could be devoted to specialized activities 1970.

Moebius: see *MÖBIUS.

Mogul. 2. c. A powerful or wealthy business-man 1934.

Mohorovičić discontinuity (mohorōᵘ·vitʃitʃ). 1953. [f. the name of A. *Mohorovičić* (1857–1936), Yugoslav seismologist.] The discontinuity between the earth's crust and the mantle which is believed to exist at a depth of about seven miles under the ocean beds and 20–25 miles under the continents. Also known as the **Moho** (mōᵘ·ho).

Moisturize (moi·stiŭrəi:z), *v.* 1943. [f. MOISTURE *sb.* + -IZE.] *trans.* To render moist, esp. of a cosmetic applied to the skin. Hence **Moi·sturi:zer,** a cosmetic having this effect.

Mole (mōᵘl), *sb.*⁶ Also **mol** (formerly as an alternative spelling, now usu. as an abbrev.). 1902. [– G. *mol* (W. Ostwald), f. *molekül* MOLECULE.] *Physical Chem.* That amount of a particular substance having a mass in grammes numerically the same as the molecular weight; now defined equivalently in the S.I. as that amount which contains as many elementary entities (atoms, molecules, etc.) as there are atoms in 0.012 kg. of carbon 12. Hence **Mo·lar** *a.*

Molotov (mǫ·lŏtǫf). 1940. Name of Vyacheslav Mikhailovich *Molotov*, People's Minister for Foreign Affairs, U.S.S.R., 1939–49, in: *M. bread-basket*, a container carrying high explosive and scattering incendiary bombs; *M. cocktail*, an incendiary hand-grenade.

Moment.

1. *M. of truth*: the time of the final sword-thrust in a bull-fight (Sp. *el momento de la verdad*); *transf.*, a crisis or turning-point; a testing situation.

Mongol. A. *sb.* **2.** A person afflicted with mongolism 1866.

Mongolism (mǫ·ŋgŏliz'm). 1922. [f. MONGOL + -ISM.] A type of congenital mental deficiency accompanied by a physical resemblance to the Mongolians.

Monicker (mǫ·nikəɹ). *slang.* Also **monacer, moniker, monniker.** 1851. [Origin unkn.] A name.

Monitor, *sb.* **3. b.** One who is appointed to listen to and report on foreign broadcasts 1939. **c.** (Also *m. screen.*) A television receiver used to verify the picture being transmitted during broadcasting 1944.

Monitor, *v.* (See s.v. MONITOR *sb.*) **2. a.** To regulate the strength of (a signal) during recording or transmission 1929. **b.** To listen to and report on (foreign radio broadcasts) 1939. **c.** In extended use: to keep under observation, to measure or test at intervals, esp. for the purpose of regulation or control 1947.

Mono (mǫ·no), *a.* 1959. Colloq. abbrev. of *MONOPHONIC *a.* 2. Also as *sb.*, monophonic recording or reproduction.

Monolith. A. *sb.* **2.** A person or thing resembling a monolith; esp. a monolithic organization, government, etc. 1934.

Monolithic, *a.* **2.** Resembling a monolith; massive, immovable; esp. applied to organizations, governments, etc., which are autocratic or monopolistic 1922. Hence **Monoli·thically** *adv.*

Monophonic (mǫnŏfǫ·nik), *a.* 1885. [f. MONO- + Gr. φωνή sound + -IC.] **1.** *Mus.* = HOMOPHONIC *a.* **2.** Of sound broadcasts, gramophone records, etc.: involving only a single channel, so that all the sound appears to the listener to come from a single source.

Monotone. A. *adj.* **2.** *Math.* = *MONOTONIC *a.* 2. 1905.

Monotonic, *a.* **2.** *Math.* Of a function, series, quantity, etc.: either never increasing or never decreasing 1901. So **Mo:notoni·city,** the property of being m.

Montage (mǫ·ntāʒ). 1929. [Fr., f. *monter* to MOUNT.] **1.** *Cinema, T.V.* The selection and arrangement of separate shots as a consecutive whole. **2.** The production of a composite picture by superimposing several different pictures or pictorial elements; a picture so produced 1938.

Montessori (mǫntésōᵊ·ri). 1912. Name of the Italian educationalist Dr. Maria *Montessori* (1870–1952), designating a system of educating the young through natural activities without direct control.

Moon, *sb.*
Comb.: **m.-craft, -probe,** a spacecraft travelling to or round the m.; **m.-shot,** (the launching of) a m.-probe; an attempt to send a spacecraft to the m.

Moonlighting, *vbl. sb.* **1. b.** The practice of doing another job, generally at night, besides one's main employment 1957.

Moonquake (mū·nkwēⁱk). 1959. [f. MOON *sb.* + QUAKE *sb.*, after *earthquake*.] A tremor of the moon's surface.

Moped (mōᵘ·ped). 1956. [Sw., f. *trampcykel med motor och pedaler*.] A motorized pedal cycle.

Moral, *a.* **7. a.** *Moral Rearmament*: the Oxford Group Movement (see *GROUP *sb.* 3 b) or its beliefs; = *BUCHMANISM. **b. moral support,** support or help the effect of which is psychological rather than physical.

Mores (mōᵊ·rīz). 1907. [L., pl. of *mos* manner, custom.] The customs, habits, or moral assumptions of a community, etc.

Morpheme (mǫ·ɹfīm). 1925. [– Fr. *morphème*, f. Gr. μορφή form, after *phonème* PHONEME.] *Philol.* A morphological element considered in respect of its functional relations in a linguistic system; the smallest meaningful morphological unit of language.

Mortician (mǫɹti·ʃăn). *U.S.* 1895. [f. L. *mors, mort-* death + -ICIAN.] An undertaker; one who arranges funerals.

Motel (mōᵘte·l). orig. *U.S.* 1932. [Blend of MOTOR and HOTEL.] A roadside hotel for motorists.

Moth, *sb.*
Comb.: **m.-ball,** a ball of naphthalene, etc., used among stored fabrics to repel moths; also *fig.*, esp. in phr. *to put* (something) *in m.-balls*: to store away; to put out of use or action for a long time; hence **m.-ball** *v. trans.*; **m.-proof** *a.*, resistant to damage by moths; also as *v. trans.*

Mother, *sb.*[1]
Comb.: **m.-fucker** *coarse slang* (orig. *U.S.*), a despicable or unpleasant person; also ellipt. **mother;** hence **m.-fucking** *ppl. a.*

Motion, *sb.* **3.** Phr. *To go through the motions*: to simulate the gestures or movements used in a particular action; also *fig.*, to pretend, counterfeit, do something only superficially.

Motivate (mōᵘ·tivēⁱt), *v.* 1863. [f. MOTIVE *sb.* + -ATE[3], after Fr. *motiver*, G. *motivieren*.] *trans.* To furnish with a motive; to cause (someone) to act in a particular way. Hence **Motiva·tion. Motiva·tional** *a.*

‖**Mot juste** (moʒüst). 1915. [Fr., *mot* word, *juste* exact.] The precisely appropriate expression.

Motorcade (mōᵘ·təɹkēⁱd). orig. *U.S.* 1924. [f. MOTOR, after CAVALCADE.] A procession of motor vehicles.

Motorway (mōᵘ·təɹwēⁱ). 1937. [f. MOTOR *sb.* 5 + WAY *sb.* 1.] A highway specially designed and regulated for use by fast motor vehicles.

Mountie (mau·nti). *colloq.* Also **Mounty.** 1924. [f. MOUNTED *ppl. a.* + -IE, -Y[6].] A member of the Royal Canadian Mounted Police.

Mousetrap. *Attrib.* in **m.-cheese,** cheese such as is used as bait in mousetraps; *joc.* (also with ellipsis of *cheese*), the cheapest household cheese.

Mug, *sb.*[3] Phr. *A mug's game*: a senseless or unprofitable activity.

Mug, *v.*[2] **2.** *trans.* To thrash, beat up; to strangle; to rob with violence. Also *intr.* 1846. Hence **Mu·gger**[2]. **Mu·gging** *vbl. sb.*

Mule[2]. **2. b.** A heelless slipper 1922.

Multiplex. A. *adj.* **3.** *Telecommunications.* Involving the simultaneous transmission of several independent signals or programmes over a single wire or channel 1909. Hence **Mu·ltiplex** *v. trans.*, to transmit in this way.

Multiversity (mɒltivə̄·ɹsiti). orig. *U.S.* 1963. [f. MULTI- + UNI)VERSITY.] A large university comprising many different departments and activities.

Mumbo Jumbo. 2. b. Obscure or meaningless talk or writing; nonsense 1896.

Mu-meson (miū:mī·zǫn, -me·zǫn). 1953. [f. *mu*, name of the Gr. letter μ (used as a symbol for the particle) + *MESON.] *Nuclear Physics.* The original name for the *MUON.

Muon (miū·ǫn). 1953. [f. *MU(-MESON + *-ON.] *Nuclear Physics.* An unstable lepton (orig. called a meson) that has properties similar to those of the electron except that its mass is 207 times greater.

Muscle, *sb.*
Comb.: **m.-bound** *a.*, having the muscles stiff and enlarged, esp. owing to excessive exercise; also *fig.*

Muscular, *a.* **1. muscular dystrophy** [DYS- + Gr. τροφή nourishment], any of a group of hereditary disorders (or these disorders collectively) marked by the progressive wasting and weakening of some muscles.

Mushroom, *sb.*
Comb.: **m. cloud,** a m.-shaped cloud above the site of a nuclear explosion.

Mushroom, *v.* **d.** *intr.* To rise like a mushroom; to expand or increase rapidly 1937. Hence **Mu·shrooming** *vbl. sb.* and *ppl. a.*

Musical, *a.* (and *sb.*) **A.** *adj.* **4.**
m. comedy (or **farce**), a light dramatic piece, consisting of dialogue, songs, and dancing, connected by a slight plot.
B. *sb.* **2.** A film or theatrical piece (not opera) of which music is an essential element 1939.

Musicology (miūzikǫ·lŏdʒi). 1919. [– Fr. *musicologie*; or f. MUSIC + -OLOGY.] The study of music, other than technique of performance or composition. Hence **Musico·gical** *a.* **Musico·logist.**

Muskeg (mɒ·skeg). 1775. [Cree Indian.] A level swampy or boggy area in regions of Canada.

Must, *sb.*[3] **b.** *colloq.* Something that must be done, possessed, considered, etc.; a necessity 1941. Also *attrib.* or as *adj.*
'Inside' [*sc.* a book on prison life] is a m. for people who care 1953.

Mutagen (miū·tădʒĕn). 1953. [f. MUTA(-TION + -GEN.] An agent that causes mutation in an organism. Hence **Mutage·nic** *a.* **Mutageni·city,** the property of being a m. **Mutage·nesis,** the production or origination of mutations.

Mycorrhiza (məi:korəi·ză). *Pl.* **-æ** (-ī). 1895. [mod.L. (A. B. Frank, 1885), f. MYCO- + Gr. ῥίζα root.] *Bot.* A symbiotic or slightly pathogenic fungus growing in association with the roots of a plant. Hence **Mycorrhi·zal** *a.*

Mycotrophy (məikǫ·trŏfi). 1927. [– G. *mykotrophie* (R. Falck, 1923), f. MYCO- + Gr. τροφή nourishment.] *Bot.* The state of certain plants which have mycorrhizæ growing in association with their roots, possibly as an aid in the assimilation of nutrients. Hence **Mycotro·phic** *a.*

Mystique (mistī·k). 1940. [Fr. *mystique* MYSTIC.] The atmosphere of mystery and veneration investing some doctrines, arts, professions, or personages; any professional skill or technique which mystifies and impresses the layman.
The 'mystique' built up around him [*sc.* Stalin] has become a genuine outlet for the Russian religious instinct 1951.

Myxomatosis (mi:ksŏmătōᵘ·sis). 1927. [mod.L., f. MYXOMA (pl. -MATA) + -OSIS.] A virus disease of rabbits, characterized by the presence of myxomata.
As a means of eliminating the rabbit, the Commonwealth Scientific and Industrial Research Organisation is now experimenting with m. 1952.

N

N.A.A.F.I., NAAFI, Naffy (næ·fi). 1927. The Navy, Army, and Air Force Institutes; a canteen, etc., organized by them.
The NAAFI Is a sort of caafi Where soldiers are rude About the food 1959.

Nagana (năgā·nă). 1895. [– Zulu *nakane.*] A parasitic disease of domesticated animals in Africa, characterized by anæmia and caused by *Trypanosoma brucei*, which is spread by tsetse flies.

Name, *sb.*
Colloq. phr. *The n. of the game*: the object or essence of an action, agent, etc.
Comb.: **n.-calling,** abusive language, mere abuse; **n.-dropping,** familiar mention of the names of distinguished people in order to imply one's own importance.

Nance, nancy (næns, næ·nsi). Also **nancy-boy.** 1904. [orig. *Miss Nancy*; f. pet-forms of the female name *Ann.*] An effeminate man or boy; a homosexual. Also as *adj.* Hence **Na·ncified** *ppl. a.*

Nannoplankton (næ·noplæŋktǫn). 1912. [G. (H. Lohmann, 1909), f. *nanno-* used as comb. f. of L. *nanus* dwarf + PLANKTON.] *Biol.* The smallest forms of plankton.

Nano- (næ·no-, nēⁱ·no-, nā·no-), *prefix.* 1951. [f. L. *nanus*, Gr. νᾶνος a dwarf + -O-, after *kilo-, micro-*, etc.] Prefixed to the names of units to form the names of units 10^9 times smaller (i.e. one thousand millionth part of them); as *nanosecond* = 10^{-9} second. Abbrev. n.

Nap, *sb.*[3] **2. c.** A tip that a horse, etc., is certain to win; a horse so tipped 1895. Hence **Nap** *v.*[4] *trans.*, to tip as a certain winner.

Napa: see *NAPPA.

Napalm (nēⁱ·pām), *sb.* orig. *U.S.* 1946. [f. *NA(PHTHENIC *a.* + PALM(ITIC *a.*] **a.** A thickening agent consisting of aluminium derivatives of naphthenic acids and those of the fatty acids of coconut oil. **b.** A thixotropic gel consisting of n. and petrol, used in flame throwers and incendiary bombs; jellied petrol. Also *attrib.*, as *n. bomb.*

Napalm (nēⁱ·pām), *v.* 1952. [f. prec. sb.] *trans.* To attack or destroy with napalm bombs.

Naphthene (næ·fþīn). 1884. [f. NAPHTH(A + -ENE.] *Chem.* Any saturated cyclic hydrocarbon.

Naphthenic (næfþī·nik), *a.* 1884. [f. prec. + -IC.] **1.** *n. acid* (Chem.): any of the carboxylic acids obtained in the refining of petroleum; *esp.* an alicyclic carboxylic acid. Also, an unspecified mixture of these acids. **2.** Of or pertaining to the naphthenes 1931.

Nappa, napa (næ·pă). 1897. [f. *Napa*, name of a county and town in California.] Leather prepared from sheep- or goat-skin by a special tawing process. Also *attrib.*

Nappy (næ·pi), *sb.*[2] *colloq.* 1927. [f. NAP(KIN + -Y[6].] A baby's napkin.

Narcolepsy (nā·ɹkŏlepsi). 1888. [f. *narco-* as in NARCOTIC + *-lepsy* as in EPILEPSY.] *Path.* A condition characterized by irresistible, usu. brief, attacks of sleep. Hence **Narcole·ptic** *sb.*, one with this condition.

Narrow. A. *adj.*
1. *n. boat,* a canal boat, *spec.* one not exceeding 7 feet in width and 72 feet in length.

Nasty, *a.* **3.** Colloq. phr. *a n. piece* (or *bit*) *of work*: an unpleasant or contemptible person.

Natch (nætʃ), *adv.* 1945. Colloq. (orig. *U.S.*) shortening of *NATURALLY *adv.* b.

National, *a.* and *sb.* **A.** *adj.*
Spec. collocations: **n. grid,** (*a*) the network of high-voltage electricity lines that interconnects the major power stations and distribution centres in Great Britain; (*b*) the metric co-ordinate system, based on a point west of the Isles of Scilly, used in the Ordnance Survey maps; **N. Health Service,** the British system, initiated by the N. Insurance Act of 1946, providing a national medical service financed by taxation; **n. park,** an area of countryside, often of particular beauty, which is protected by strict control of building and land use; **N. Trust,** a trust for the preservation of places of historic interest or natural beauty in England, Wales, and N. Ireland, incorporated in 1907 and supported by endowment and private subscription.
B. *sb.* **3.** Any person regarded as a member of a specified nation, without respect to domicile or status 1904.

N.A.T.O., Nato (nēⁱ·to). 1949. [Acronym.] The North Atlantic Treaty Organization, an alliance of certain European nations with the United States and Canada.

Natter (næ·təɹ), *v. colloq.* (orig. *Sc.* and *n. dial.*). 1804. [Of imit. origin; cf. LG. *gnatteren.*] *intr.* To grumble, scold, nag; to chatter, chat. Hence as *sb.*, grumbling, nagging talk; aimless chatter; a chat, talk.

Natural, *sb.* **I. 3.** A person naturally endowed *for* (a role, etc.); one having natural gifts or talents; also, a thing with qualities that make it particularly suitable *for* some purpose 1934.

Natural, *a.* **I.**
6. c. n. gas, inflammable gas occurring underground, consisting chiefly of methane and other simple paraffins and often found associated with petroleum.

Naturally, *adv.* **b.** As a natural result or consequence; as might be expected; of course 1641.

Navicert (næ·visəɹt), *sb.* 1923. [f. L. *navis* ship + *cert-* of CERTIFICATE *sb.*] A consular certificate granted to a neutral ship testifying that her cargo is correctly described according to the manifest. Hence as *v. trans.*, to authorize with a n.

Nazi. Hence **Na·zidom, Na·zify** *v. trans.*, **-fication, Na·z(i)ism.**

Near, *a.*
6. n. miss, a shot that only just misses a target; **n. thing,** something barely effected; a narrow escape.

Neck, *sb.*[1] **II.**
Phr. *To stick one's n. out*: to expose oneself to danger, reprisal, criticism, etc.

Necrophily (ne̍krǫ·fili). 1897. [f. Gr. νεκρός dead body + -PHILY; see -PHILOUS.] A morbid, esp. erotic, attraction to corpses. Also **Necrophi·lia, Necro·philism.** So **Ne:crophili·stic** *a.*

Needle, *sb.* **I. 3. d.** In gramophones, etc., the stylus used in recording or playing 1902.
Comb.: **n. contest, fight, match,** a contest, etc., that arouses much interest and excitement.

Negritude (nī·gritiud). Also **négritude.** 1960. [— Fr. *négritude* NIGRITUDE.] The quality or characteristic of being a Negro; the affirmation of the value of Negro or African culture, identity, etc.

Nembutal (ne·mbiutæl). 1931. [f. *Na,* symbol for sodium + initial letters of the elements of 5-*e*thyl-5-(1-*m*ethyl*but*yl) barbiturate, the systematic name + *-al* (as in *barbital*).] *Pharm.* A proprietary name for pentobarbitone sodium, a barbiturate used as a hypnotic and an anticonvulsant. Also, a capsule of N.

Neo-. 2. Ne:o-colo·nialism, the acquisition or retention of influence over other countries, esp. one's former colonies, often by economic or political measures; so **ne:o-colo·nial** *a.*, **ne:o-colo·nialist** *a.* and *sb.*

Neon. Add: It is an element belonging to the group of inert gases, with neither colour, smell, nor taste, and it gives an orange-red glow when subjected to an electric discharge at low pressure. Atomic number 10; symbol Ne.
Comb.: **n. lamp, light, tube,** a lamp, etc., in which the light is produced by an electric discharge in a mixture of gases, predominantly n.; **n. sign,** a coloured advertising sign using n. tubes.

Neoprene (nī·ǒprīn). 1937. [f. NEO- + *-prene* (in *chloroprene, isoprene*), perh. f. PR(OPYL + -ENE.] Any of various synthetic rubber-like substances made by polymerizing chloroprene, CH_2:CCl·CH:CH_2, and useful for their resistance to oil, heat, and weathering and their higher strength than natural rubber.

Neoteny (niˌǫ·tĭni). 1894. [— G. *neotenie* (J. C. E. Kollman, 1884), f. NEO- + Gr. τείνειν to extend.] *Zool.* The retention of juvenile characteristics in an adult animal; sexual maturity in a larval form. So **Neote·nic, Neo·tenous** *adjs.*

Neptunium (neptiū·niǒm). 1945. [f. NEPTUNE, name of the planet next beyond Uranus (as n. is the element next after uranium): see -IUM.] *Chem.* A transuranic element formed when uranium is bombarded with neutrons and occurring naturally in trace amounts, the longest-lived isotope having a half-life of 2¼ million years. Atomic number 93; symbol Np.

Nerine (nīrəi·ni). 1820. [mod.L. (W. Herbert, 1820), f. L. *Nerine* (Virg. *Ecl.* vii. 37), Gr. Νηρεΐς a water nymph.] A bulbous plant of the genus so called, belonging to the family Amaryllidaceæ and native to South Africa.

Nerve, *sb.* **II. 1. d.** *War of nerves*: a campaign against an enemy consisting of intimidation, propaganda intended to undermine morale, or the like 1939.
The British public..did not allow the 'war of nerves' organized by the Nazi Government to interfere..with its August holiday *Ann. Register for* 1939.
Comb.: **n. gas,** any poisonous gas that affects the nervous system.

Nervous, *a.*
7. b. n. breakdown, (a case of) neurasthenia; any severe or incapacitating nervous disorder.

Network (ne·twǒɹk), *v.* 1957. [f. the sb.] *trans.* To broadcast simultaneously from two or more radio stations or on two or more television channels. Hence **Ne·tworked** *ppl. a.* **Ne·tworking** *vbl. sb.*
The new companies..operate within a networking system still dominated by Granada, ATV and..Thames 1968.

Neutrino (niūtrī·no). 1934. [— It. *neutrino* (E. Fermi, 1933), f. *neutro* NEUTER, neutral + *-ino,* dim. suffix.] *Nuclear Physics.* Either of two stable, uncharged sub-atomic particles (associated respectively with the electron and the muon) which have zero or negligible mass and an extremely low probability of interaction with matter.

Neutron.
Comb.: **n. star** *Astr.*, a hypothetical extremely dense kind of star composed predominantly of neutrons, with a mass similar to that of the sun but a diameter of only a few miles; cf. *PULSAR.

Never, *adv.* **II. never-never** *a. colloq.*, denoting a system of paying for articles by periodic instalments over an extended period; also *ellipt.* as *sb.*

New, *a.* and *sb.* **A.** *adj.*
I. 1. a. n. town (freq. **N. Town**), any of several British towns designed as a completely new unit.
5. n. wave = *NOUVELLE VAGUE.

Newly, *adv.*
Comb.: **newly-wed, newlywed,** a person recently married.

New Orleans (niu: ǭɹlī·ănz). 1935. The name of a city in Louisiana, U.S.A., used *attrib.* or *absol.* to designate a style of jazz which originated there.

News. 3. b. *The n.*: a regularly broadcast n. programme 1925.
Comb.: **n. bulletin,** a collection of items of news, etc., esp. for broadcasting; **newscast,** a radio or television broadcast of news; so **newscaster, -casting; n. cinema, theatre,** a cinema theatre showing only newsreels and other short films.

News-letter. Also, a periodical sent out by post to subscribers, members of an organization, etc.

Newspeak (niū·spīk). 1949. [f. NEW *a.* + SPEAK *v.*] The name of the artificial language used for official communications in George Orwell's novel *1984.*

Newton (niū·tən). 1924. [Named after Sir Isaac *Newton* (see NEWTONIAN).] *Physics.* The unit of force in the metre-kilogramme-second system (and now in the S.I.): the force that would give a mass of one kilogramme an acceleration of one metre per second per second; 100,000 dynes (approximately the weight of 102 gm. or 3·6 oz.). Abbrev. N.

Newtown (niū·taun). 1760. [Name of a town in Long Island, U.S.A.] In full *Newtown pippin.* An American variety of dessert apple, with green skin and crisp white flesh.

Niacin (nəi·ăsin). 1942. [f. *NI(COTINIC *a.* + AC(ID + -IN[1].] Nicotinic acid (or its amide).

Nick, *sb.*[1] **III. 4.** Colloq. phr. (orig. *dial.*) *in good n.*: in good condition 1905.

Nicotinic (nikǒti·nik), *a.* 1890. [f. NICOTIN(E + -IC.] *N. acid* (Chem. and Biochem.): a white crystalline pyridine derivative, $C_5H_4N{\cdot}COOH$, which is formed when nicotine is oxidized and is one of the B group of vitamins (its deficiency in humans causing pellagra). Also called *NIACIN.

Night, *sb.*
Comb.: **2. n.-life,** urban entertainments open to pleasure-seekers at n.; hence **n.-lifer.**

-nik (nik), *suffix,* from Russian (cf. *SPUTNIK) and Yiddish, appended to sbs. and adjs. to denote a person involved in or associated with the thing or quality specified, as *beatnik, folknik, nogoodnik, peacenik.*

Nim (nim), *sb.* 1901. [Origin uncertain: perh. suggested by NIM *v.* or G. *nimm* (imper. of *nehmen* to take).] A game in which two players alternately take one or more objects from any one of several heaps, the aim being to compel one's opponent to take the last remaining object (or, sometimes, to take it oneself).

Nip (nip), *sb.*[3] and *a.* 1942. Slang abbrev. of NIPPONESE *sb.* and *a.*

Nipponese (nipǫnī·z), *sb.* and *a.* 1931. [f. *Nippon,* name of the main island of Japan: see -ESE.] (A) Japanese. So **Nippo·nian** *a.*

Nissen (ni·sən). 1917. [Name of the inventor, Lt.-Col. Peter Norman *Nissen* (1871–1930).] **N. hut,** a tunnel-shaped hut made of corrugated iron with a cement floor.

Nit. 2. Delete †. Now esp., a stupid or incompetent person.

Nitty-gritty (ni:tigri·ti). *slang* (orig. *U.S.*). 1963. [Origin uncertain.] The realities or basic facts of a problem, situation, etc.; the heart of the matter. Also *attrib.* or as *adj.*

Nitwit (ni·twit). *colloq.* 1928. [perh. f. NIT + WIT *sb.*] A stupid person. Hence **Ni·twitted** *a.*

Nix[2] (niks). *slang.* 1789. [— G. dial. and colloq. *nix,* for *nichts* nothing.] Nothing.

No, *a.* **I.**
1. *No trumps*: at Bridge, a declaration or bid involving playing without a trump suit.

No: see *NOH.

Nobelium (nobī·liǒm). 1957. [f. the name of A. B. *Nobel* (1833–96), Swedish inventor + -IUM.] *Chem.* An artificially produced transuranic element, the longest-lived isotope of which has a half-life of 3 minutes. Atomic number 102; symbol No.

Nod, *sb.*
1. Colloq. phr. *On the n.*: with a merely formal assent.

Noh, No (nōᵘ), *sb.* 1871. [Jap.] The traditional Japanese drama evolved from the rites of Shinto worship and substantially unchanged since the 15th c.; the oldest form of drama in Japan. Freq. *attrib.*
The music to my Noh play *The Dreaming of the Bones* W. B. YEATS. A course on the *No* dramas of Japan 1958.

Noise, *sb.* **3.** *Noises off*: sounds, usu. loud or confused, produced off the stage but heard by the audience at the performance of a play; also *allus.* **b.** In scientific use, a collective term (used without *a*) for: fluctuations or disturbances (usu. irregular) which are not part of a wanted signal or which interfere with its intelligibility 1930.
3. b. A radar echo which may otherwise be hidden by 'n.' is rendered visible 1966. The distortions produced in one's handwriting in a moving train can be attributed to 'n.' 1968.

Non-.
1. *non-aggression*; *non-fiction*; *non-violence*; *non-zero*. Also *spec.*, intended to be but not (*n.-event*). 2. *non-driver*; *non-smoker* = one who does not smoke; also, a railway-carriage, etc., in which smoking is not permitted; *non-starter*. 3. *non-ferrous*; *non-nuclear*; *non-operational*; *non-U*. 5. *non-iron* fabric, etc.; *non-stick*. 6. *non-playing*. b. *non-profit-making*.

Noradrenaline (nǭrædre·nălin, -ædrī·n-ălin). Also **-in.** 1932. [f. *nor-*, prefix (f. NORMAL *a.*) denoting loss of a methyl or methylene group + ADRENALIN.] An amine, $(HO)_2C_6H_3{\cdot}CHOH{\cdot}CH_2NH_2$, related to adrenaline, having a hydrogen atom in place of the methyl group; *spec.* the lævorotatory form, produced by the adrenal medulla and at sympathetic nerve endings and serving to raise the blood pressure.

Norfolk Island. The name of a South Pacific island, used *attrib.* to designate the **Norfolk (Island) pine,** *Araucaria excelsa*, which is native to the island 1834.
The Norfolk Island pine..is much planted in the Mediterranean regions 1957.

Nose, *sb.* **I.**
Colloq. phr. *To keep one's n. clean*: to behave properly, keep out of trouble, mind one's own business.
Comb.: **n.-cone,** the cone-shaped nose of a rocket or the like.

Nosh (nǫʃ), *v. slang.* 1957. [Yiddish; cf. G. *naschen* to nibble, eat on the sly.] *trans.* and *intr.* To eat or drink, esp. to have a small snack between meals. Hence as *sb.*, a snack; food or drink. **No·sh-up,** a meal; a good feed.

Nostalgia. b. *transf.* Regret or sorrowful longing *for* the conditions of a past age; regretful or wistful memory or recall of an earlier time 1920. So **Nosta·lgic** *a.*
We rarely find a strong nostalgic sense of tradition 1949. N. for one's childhood does not necessarily mean that the childhood was a happy one 1959. N.'s all right, but it's not what it was 1971.

Nothing. A. *sb.* **8.** *colloq.* (orig. *U.S.*). Used *attrib.* or as *adj.*: of no importance, insignificant, trivial 1961.

Notional, *a.* **4.** *Gram.* Of verbs: principal as opposed to auxiliary 1933.

‖**Nouveau riche** (nuvorīʃ). 1828. [Fr., f. *nouveau* new, *riche* rich.] One who has recently attained to wealth; usu. with connotation of ostentation or vulgar show. Also *attrib.* or as *adj.*

‖**Nouvelle vague** (nuvẹl vag). 1961. [Fr., f. *nouvelle* (fem.) new + *vague* wave.] A new movement or trend; *spec.* one in film-making originating in France in the early 1960s.

Novella (nŏve·lă). 1902. [It. (see NOVEL *sb.*).] A short novel or narrative.

Nuclear, *a.* **1. b. nuclear family,** a family comprising a father, a mother, and children; opp. **extended family*. **2. b.** Of or pertaining to the, or an, atomic nucleus, or reactions of atomic nuclei; *spec.* used like *ATOMIC, q.v. 1917.
2. b. N. bomb 1945, energy 1931, -powered 1949, reactor 1945, weapon 1948; **n. disarmament,** the renunciation or abandonment of n. weapons; **n. fission** = *FISSION *sb.* 3.

Nucleic (niuklī·ik, -ē¹·ik, niū·klī,ik), *a.* 1893. [f. NUCLE(US + -IC.] *N. acid* (Biochem.): either of two kinds (DNA and RNA) of acid that are present in some form in all cells and have a molecular structure in which many nucleotide molecules are linked together in a long chain.

Nucleon (niū·kliǫn). 1942. [f. NUCLE(AR, -US + *-ON.] *Nuclear Physics.* A proton or neutron; a particle of which these may be regarded as two different states.

Nucleonic (niūkliǫ·nik), *a.* 1947. [Partly f. prec. + -IC, partly a back-formation from next.] Of or pertaining to the nucleon or nucleonics.

Nucleonics (niūkliǫ·niks), *sb. pl.* (const. as *sing.*). 1945. [app. f. NUCLE(AR *a.* + *ELECTR)ONICS *sb. pl.*] The branch of science and technology concerned with nucleons and the atomic nucleus, esp. with the practical applications of nuclear phenomena and associated techniques.

Nucleoside (niū·kliŏsəid). 1911. [f. NUCLEO- + -OS(E² + -IDE.] *Biochem.* Any compound in which a sugar (usu. ribose or deoxyribose) is linked to a heterocyclic base.

Nucleotide (niū·kliŏtəid). 1911. [f. NUCLEO- + *t* + -IDE.] *Biochem.* Any compound in which a phosphate group is linked to the sugar of a nucleoside.

Nucleus. 3. b. *spec.* The dense central portion, enclosed by a membrane and containing the genetic material, of nearly all living cells. **4.** *Physics.* The positively charged central constituent, consisting in general of protons and neutrons, of the atom, comprising nearly all its mass but occupying only a very small part of its volume 1912.

Nuclide (niū·kləid). 1947. [f. NUCL(EUS + *-ide* (f. Gr. εἶδος form, kind).] *Nuclear Physics.* A particular kind of atom, as defined by the number of protons and the number of neutrons in the nucleus. Hence **Nuclidic** (-i·dik), *a.*

Nudism (niū·diz'm). 1931. [f. NUDE + -ISM.] The principles or practice of nudists.

Nuff, 'nuff (nɒf). 1841. Colloq. (orig. *U.S.*) shortening of ENOUGH; esp. in phr. *N. said*: enough has been said, that's all right, agreed.

Numbat (nɒ·mbæt). 1923. [Native name.] A small marsupial belonging to either species of the genus *Myrmecobius*, found in southern and south-western Australia; called also the *banded* or *marsupial ant-eater*.
The N. resembles a squirrel, being about the same size, and having a long bushy tail 1965.

Number, *sb.* **I. 5. d.** A song or musical item in a concert, etc. 1885. **e.** *colloq.* A person or thing; esp. (*a*) an article of apparel; (*b*) an attractive woman; (*c*) a job 1894.
Comb.: **n.-plate,** a plate bearing a number, esp. that on a registered vehicle.

Numeracy (niū·mĕrăsi). 1959. [f. next + -ACY, after *literacy*.] The quality or state of being numerate.

Numerate (niū·mĕrĕt), *a.* 1959. [f. L. *numerus* number + -ATE², after *literate*.] Acquainted with the basic principles of mathematics and science.
It should be possible to make scientists literate and arts men 'n.' 1960.

Numerology (niūmĕrǫ·lŏdʒi). 1932. [f. L. *numerus* number + -OLOGY.] Divination by numbers; the study of the esoteric meaning of numbers. So **Numerolo·gical** *a.* **Numero·logist.**

Numinous (niū·minəs), *a.* 1647. [f. L. *numen, numin-* NUMEN + -OUS.] Of or pertaining to a numen; divine, spiritual; revealing or suggesting the presence of a god; inspiring awe and reverence.

Nunatak (nɒ·nătæk). 1882. [Eskimo.] A peak of rock projecting from the surface of an ice-cap, orig. in Greenland.

Nursery.
Comb.: **n.-slopes,** in a skiing-resort, those slopes considered most suitable for beginners.

Nut, *sb.* **I. 5. b.** *pl.* (*a*) Used as a derisive retort 1931. (*b*) *adj.* Crazy 1914. **7.** *slang* (orig. *U.S.*). A lunatic; a crank 1914.

Nutty, *a.* **3. b.** *slang.* Crazy 1901.

Nylon (nəi·lǫn). 1938. [Invented word, with *-on* suggested by *rayon, cotton*.] Any of the thermoplastics that are wholly synthetic polymeric amides, many of which are tough, lightweight, and resistant to heat and chemicals, may be produced as filaments, bristles, or sheets and as moulded objects, and are widely used for textile fabrics and industrially; *esp.* nylon 66, made from adipic acid and hexamethylenediamine. Freq. *attrib.* **2.** *pl.* N. stockings 1941. **3.** Fabric or cloth made from n. yarn; freq. *attrib.* or as *adj.* 1958.
1. Fabrics manufactured of N. artificial fibre 1941. **3.** Men who had n. shirts and terylene suits before those fabrics got into Marks and Spencer's 1958.

Nymphet (ni·mfet). 1612. [f. NYMPH + -ET.] **a.** A young or little nymph. **b.** A nymph-like or sexually attractive young girl 1955.

Nympho (ni·mfo). 1935. Colloq. abbrev. of NYMPHOMANIAC *a.* and *sb.*

O.
II. O.A.P., old age pension(er); O.A.S., Organization of American States; O.A.U., Organization of African Unity; O.E.C.D., Organization for European Co-operation and Development (formerly O.E.E.C.); O.E.E.C., Organization for European Economic Co-operation; O.H.M.S., on His (Her) Majesty's service; O Level, Ordinary Level (of the G.C.E. examination); O.P., Order of Preachers, Ordo Prædicatorum (i.e. Dominicans); O/S, outsize; O.U. (A.C., etc.), Oxford University (Athletic Club, etc.); O.U.D.S., Oxford University Dramatic Society; O.U.P., Oxford University Press.

Obeche (obī·tʃi). 1934. [Nigerian name.] A West African tree, *Triplochiton scleroxylon*, or the light-coloured timber obtained from it.

Object, *sb.*
Comb.: **o. language,** a language being referred to or investigated in terms of another language (known as the metalanguage).

‖**Objet d'art** (ǫbʒe dār). 1866. [Fr., lit. 'object of art'.] A small article of artistic value or design. Also *objet de vertu*.

‖**Objet trouvé** (ǫbʒe trūve). Pl. **objets trouvés.** 1940. [Fr., lit. 'found object'.] An object found or picked up at random and put forward as a work of art or a collector's piece. Also *transf.* and *attrib.*
The exhibition of objets trouvés—broken bicycles, mangled hurricane lamps and mouldering frying-pans 1959.

Obscene, *a.* **2. b.** *transf.* Repulsive, highly offensive (*colloq.*) 1936.
That diversity of o. knick knacks 1936.

Occlude, *v.*
occluded front *Meteorol.*, the system of adjoining fronts that results from occlusion.

Occlusion. 4. *Meteorol.* The overtaking of the warm front of a depression by the cold front, so that the body of warm air between them is forced upwards off the earth's surface by two wedges of cold air; an occluded front 1922.

Occlusive (ŏklū·siv), *sb.* 1920. [f. *occlus-*, pa. ppl. stem of L. *occludere*; see OCCLUDE, -IVE.] *Phonetics.* A mute consonant.

Occupational, *a.*
Comb.: **o. disease,** a disease to which a particular occupation renders a person particularly liable; **o. therapy,** an activity, mental or physical, prescribed as an aid to recovery from disease and injury; so *o. therapist*.

Octane.
Comb.: **o. number,** a number indicating the anti-knock properties of a motor or aviation fuel, equal (for numbers below 100) to the percentage by volume of iso-octane in an iso-octane/normal heptane mixture of equivalent performance.

Odd, *a.* (*sb.*) and *adv.*
Comb.: **o.-even** *Nuclear Physics*, applied to a nucleus containing an o. number of protons and an even number of neutrons; similarly **odd-odd.**

Oersted (ɔ̄·ɹsted). 1903. [Named after H. C. *Oersted* (1777–1851), Danish physicist.] *Physics.* † **a.** The unit of reluctance in the C.G.S. system. **b.** The unit of magnetic field strength in the C.G.S. system, defined as the field strength at the centre of a plane circular coil of one turn carrying a current of $5/\pi$ (approximately 1.59) amperes; $1000/4\pi$ (approximately 79.6) amp./m. 1930.

Œstrogen (ī·strŏdʒĕn). Also (*U.S.*) **estro-.** 1928. [f. ŒSTR(US + -O- + -GEN.] *Physiol.* Any sex hormone or other substance which in a female mammal will produce or maintain the secondary sex characteristics and can initiate certain bodily changes associated with the menstrual or œstrous cycle.
The principal ovarian hormones..fall into three broad functional categories, oestrogens, progestagens and androgens 1968. Hence **Œstroge·nic** *a.*, of the nature of, having the properties of, an œstrogen.

Ofay (ōᵘ·fē¹). *slang* (chiefly *U.S. Blacks*). 1925. [Origin unknown.] A white person. Also *attrib.*

Off, *prep.* **II. 1.**
Comb.: **o.-beat** *a.* (*Jazz*), not coinciding with the musical beat; *fig.* unconventional, unusual; **o.-key** *a.*, out of tune; also *fig.*; **o.-peak** *a.*, away from the peak (PEAK *sb.*² II. d); **o.-stage** *a.* and *adv.*, not on the stage; invisible to the audience; also *ellipt.*, as in phr. *noises off*, sounds from off the stage; **o.-street** *a.*, not on the street.

Off-, *prefix.*
5. With adjs., esp. of colour, with the sense 'verging on, not quite': as in *off-white, off-black*.

Offensive, *sb.* **b.** *transf.* Aggressive action or movement directed to any end, e.g. *peace offensive* 1943.

Office, *sb.*
8. o.-block, a large building designed to contain offices.

Off-line (stress variable), *adj.* and *adv.* 1962. [f. OFF *prep.* II + LINE *sb.*[2]] *Computers.* Not *ON-LINE; other than on-line.

O·ff-putting, *ppl. a. colloq.* 1941. [See *put off* e.] Repellent, antipathetic.

Oil, *sb.* **6.** *Austral.* and *N.Z. slang.* Information, news, the facts of the matter, esp. in phr. **dinkum oil.* 1919.

Okay, = O.K.

Old, *a.*

C. *Comb.*: **o. boy, girl,** a former pupil (of a school); **o. hat,** outdated; **o. school tie,** the neck-tie of characteristic pattern as worn by former members of a particular (public) school; used symbolically to denote extreme loyalty to a traditional mode of thought or behaviour.

Oleum (ōu·liŏm). 1919. [L., 'oil'.] *Chem.* Fuming sulphuric acid: concentrated sulphuric acid containing excess sulphur trioxide in solution.

Oligopoly (ǫligǫ·pŏli). 1933. [f. OLIGO- + Gr. πωλεῖν to sell, after MONOPOLY.] A state of limited competition when a market is shared by a small number of producers or sellers. Hence **Oligo·polist. Oligo:poli·stic** *a.*

Ombudsman (ǫ·mbudzmæn). 1959. [Sw., 'solicitor, representative'.] An official appointed to investigate complaints by individuals against maladministration by public authorities; *spec.* in U.K., the Parliamentary Commissioner for Administration.

On, *adv.* **13. e.** *To be on to*: to be aware of (the intentions of). orig. *U.S.* 1888.

-on, *suffix*, the ending of ION (and of *anion, cation*). **1.** *Physics.* Used (first in ELECTRON[2]) in the names of sub-atomic particles, as *meson, neutron.* **b.** Used in the names of quanta, as *graviton, phonon.* **2.** *Biol.* Used in molecular biology in the names of some entities conceived of as units, as *cistron, codon.*

Onco-.

Oncoge·nic, Onco·genous *adjs.*, tumour-producing; so **O:ncogeni·city.**

One, *numeral a.*, etc.

Comb.: **2. o.-armed bandit** orig. *U.S.*, a coin- or token-operated gambling machine operated by pulling down a handle; **o.-off** *a.*, applied to an article, product, etc., of which only o. is made; also *transf.*, not repeated, unique; also as *sb.*; **o.-time pad,** a pad containing several ciphers each of which is used once only; **o.-track** *a.*, (of a mind) that is concentrated on only one line of thought or action; **o.-up** *a.*, a move ahead, scoring a point higher; **o.-upmanship** *colloq.*, the art of keeping one-up (see *-MANSHIP).

Onion, *sb.*

Comb.: **o.-domed, -spired** *adjs.*, having a bulbous cupola of characteristic Russian design.

Phr. *To know one's onions* (? orig. *U.S. slang*): to be well-informed, not easily fooled.

On-line (stress variable), *adj.* and *adv.* 1961. [f. ON *prep.* + LINE *sb.*[2]] *Computers.* **A.** *adj.* (Usu. stressed *o·n-line.*) Directly connected, so that a computer receives an input from or sends an output to a peripheral device, process, etc., as soon as it is produced; carried out while so connected or under direct computer control. **B.** *adv.* (Usu. *on-li·ne.*) While connected to a computer; under direct computer control.

If. .each payslip is printed immediately after it is calculated, we use the term o. processing 1964. It was found. .using the 250 ft. dish telescope connected to an o. computer 1968. The sorter is designed to operate o. with the 3600. 1971.

Op. (ǫp), abbrev. of (1) OPERATION 6, 7, (2) OPUS, (3) OPERATOR (e.g. *wireless op.*), (4) OPTICAL (e.g. *op. art*).

Open, *a.*

Comb.: **c. o.-and-shut** *a. colloq.*, of a (legal) case which is perfectly straightforward; **o. cheque,** one that is not crossed; **o.-ended** *a.*, permitting an indefinite range of answers, interpretation, etc.; **o.-heart** *a.*, having the heart opened surgically while the circulation is made to by-pass it; **o.-plan** *Archit.*, a design using few or no interior walls; also *attrib.*; **o. prison,** one in which locking up and security precautions are reduced to a minimum; **o. secret,** a fact that is generally known though purporting to be secret; **o. society,** one characterized by an absence of an over-rigid structure and beliefs; opposed to a 'closed' tribal or totalitarian society.

Open, *v.*

O. out. f. *trans.* and *intr.* To open the throttle of a motor vehicle, accelerate. **O. up. c.** *intr.* To begin firing *on, upon.*

Operational research. Also **operation(s research.** 1943. [f. OPERATIONAL *a.* + RESEARCH *sb.* 2.] A method of scientifically based investigation to provide a quantitative basis for management decisions (orig. for military planning). Abbrev. O.R., OR.

Operative, *a.* **2.** *spec.* In legal use, applied to those words in a deed which express the intention to effect the transaction concerned.

Something to prevent that should be put into the o. part of the treaty 1951.

Opinion, *sb.*

2. o. poll, the assessment of the o. of all, or of a section of, the general public by questioning a random or representative sample.

Opposite, *prep.* **b.** *To play o.*: to have (a specified actor or actress) as one's leading man or lady 1936.

Opt, *v.*

Phr. *To o. out of*: to choose not to do or participate in (something); also *absol.*

Optical art. 1963. [f. OPTICAL *a.* as in *optical illusion*; cf. *pop art*, s.v. *POP *a.*] An abstract art form using contrasting colours, often black and white, to create optical illusions, often involving motion. Abbrev. **op art.**

Orange, *sb.*[1]

Comb.: **o.-stick,** a thin stick esp. of o.-tree wood with the ends shaped for manicuring the finger-nails.

Orbit, *sb.* **2. c.** The state of being or moving in an orbit; so phr. *in o., into o.* 1958.

Orbit (ǭ·ɹbit), *v.* 1949. [f. the sb.] **1.** *trans.* To revolve round in an orbit. **2.** *intr.* To move in an orbit (*round* a planet, *above* or *over* a region) 1952. **b.** To fly in a circle 1952. **3.** *trans.* To put, send, or place in orbit 1958. Hence **O·rbiting** *ppl. a.* Also **O·rbiter,** a spacecraft in orbit or intended to go into orbit.

Order, *sb.* **I. 4. b.** Phr. *o. of magnitude*: approximate size or number in a scale in which equal steps correspond to a fixed multiplying factor (usu. taken as 10); a range between one power of ten and the next 1897. Also *ellipt.*, in phr. *of* (occas. *in* or *on*) *the o. of*: of the o. of magnitude of; *loosely*, approximately 1903.

The accuracy of spectroscopic measurements (of the o. of one in a million) 1927. Concentrations. . in the o. of 1 per cent 1947. A reliable measure of electron density. .over four orders of magnitude (say 10^{14}—10^{18} cm^{-3}) 1971.

IV. 2. *o. to view*: a requisition from a house or estate agent to an occupier to allow a client to inspect his premises.

Oregano (ǫrēgā·no). 1771. [Sp. and Amer. Sp. var. of ORIGANUM.] Dried wild marjoram, *Origanum vulgare*, or the dried leaves of a small shrub of the genus *Lippia*, esp. *L. graveolens*; both are used as seasonings for food, the latter having a stronger flavour.

Oregon (ǫ·règǫn). The name of an American state, used *attrib.* in the names of plants found there, as **O. pine,** *Pseudotsuga menziesii*, the *DOUGLAS *fir* 1845.

Organelle (ǭɹgăne·l). Also **-ella** (*rare*). 1920. [mod.L. *organella*; see ORGAN *sb.*, -EL[2].] *Cytology.* Any of various specialized structures within the cytoplasm of a cell.

Orienteering (ōᵊriĕntīᵊ·riŋ). 1964. [– Sw. *orientering.*] The competitive sport of navigating on foot across rough country with the aid of map and compass.

Origami (ǫrigā·mi). 1960. [Jap.] The Japanese art of folding paper into intricate designs.

Original, *a.* **4. o. print,** a print made directly from a master image on wood, stone, metal, etc., which is executed by the artist himself, printed by him or under his supervision and, in recent times, usually signed by him.

Orogenic (ǫ:rodʒe·nik), *a.* 1886. [f. Gr. ὄρος mountain + *-GENIC.] Forming mountains; concerned in the formation of mountains. So **Oroge·nesis, Oro·geny,** (a period of) mountain-building.

Orthodontia, Orthodontics (ǭ:ɹþodǫ·ntiă, -iks). 1890. [f. ORTHO- + Gr. ὀδούς, ὀδοντ- tooth + -IA[1], -ICS.] *Med.* The branch of dentistry concerned with the treatment and prevention of irregularities of the teeth and jaws. Hence **Orthodo·ntic** *a.* **Orthodo·ntist.**

Orthoptic, *a.* **3.** *Med.* Relating to or concerned with the correct or normal use of the eyes 1892. Hence **Ortho·ptics** [-IC 2], the theory or practice of remedial measures for the ocular muscles. **Ortho·ptist,** an expert in o. training.

Oscar (ǫ·skăɹ). 1936. [Arbitrary use of the Christian name.] Any of a number of statuettes awarded by the Academy of Motion Picture Arts and Sciences, of Hollywood, U.S.A., for excellence in acting, directing, etc.; also used *loosely* of similar awards.

Ostensive, *a.*

1. o. definition *Philos.*, the definition of a term by indicating or demonstrating what is signified.

Ostinato (ǫstinā·to). 1876. [It., 'obstinate'.] *Mus.* A melodic figure which is repeated throughout a piece of music or a section of it. Cf. BASSO *ostinato*, GROUND-*bass.*

Oto-.

O:tolaryngo·logy, the branch of medicine concerned with the ears and the larynx. **O:torhi:nolaryngo·logy,** the branch of medicine concerned with the ears, nose, and larynx.

Out, *sb.* **7.** A way out, way of escape 1845.

Out, *adv.* **I. 6. c.** *Boxing.* Unable to put up a defence, e.g. *out for the count* (i.e. the counting of seconds from one to ten). **II. 1. d.** *To be o. for*: to have one's interests or energies directed to, be intent on (orig. *U.S.*) 1889.

Outlet. 1. b. A market (for goods) 1919.

Output. 1. c. *Electr.* The power, current, or voltage delivered by a circuit or apparatus. Freq. *attrib.* 1902. **2.** A place or point where energy, information, etc., is taken from or leaves a system 1937.

Outsize, *sb.* and *a.* 1883. [OUT *a.* 4, SIZE *sb.*[1]] **A.** *sb.* A person or thing larger than the normal, *esp.* a ready-made article of dress larger than a standard size. **B.** *adj.* Larger than the average or stock size.

fig. Our own age is so inured to the monstrous and o. in destruction 1944.

Outsma·rt, *v.* 1926. [f. OUT *adv.* C. II. 4 + SMART *a.*] *trans.* To outwit, be smarter than.

Ouzo (ū·zo). 1898. [mod. Gr.] A Greek spirit flavoured with aniseed.

Two glasses of *ouzo* and a saucer of sunflower seeds for supper 1937.

Oven, *sb.*

Comb.: **ovenware,** dishes that can be used for baking in the oven.

Over, *adv.* **I. 2. b.** Phr. *That is* (someone) *all o.*: exactly what one might expect of him or her 1916.

II. 4. b. *Radio Telephony.* Used by a speaker to indicate that he has finished transmitting and the other person can begin 1926.

Over, *prep.* **I. 1.** *O. one's head*: without consulting or informing one. **II. 3. e.** *To be all o.* (a person): to ply with attentions.

Over-all, overall, *adj. phr.* As a fully-developed adj.: that which includes or covers all features or aspects; inclusive of everybody and/or everything 1937.

Overall Report of the U.S. Strategic Bombing Survey 1945. A small over-all scale reduction has been applied to each map 1951. The deficiency can be made up only by increasing the overall supply of women teachers 1953.

Overdrive (ōu·vəɹdrəiv). 1934. [OVER- II. 8 b.] In a motor vehicle, a mechanism that permits the propeller shaft to turn more rapidly than the output shaft of the gear-box, so providing a gear ratio higher than that of the direct drive (the usual top gear) and in some cases correspondingly increased ratios for other gears. Also *fig.*

Overkill (ōu·vəɹkil). 1958. [OVER- II. 8 b.] A theoretical measurement of any excess over a capacity to destroy an enemy completely; greater (capacity for) destruction than is necessary. Also *attrib.*

Overpass (ōu·vəɹpas), *sb.* 1934. [OVER- I. 4.] A road that crosses another by a bridge.

O:ver-si·mplify, *v.* 1936. [OVER- II. 6.] *trans.* To state (a problem) in terms that are too simple and so distort it.

Overspill (ōu·vəɹspil). 1944. [OVER- II. 8 b.] Excess town population that needs rehousing in a new area.

Oversteer (ōu·vəɹstīᵊɹ), *sb.* 1957. [OVER- II. 8 b.] A tendency in a motor vehicle to increase the sharpness of the turn when made to deviate from the straight. Also as *v. intr.*, to have this tendency.

Overtone, *sb.* **2.** *fig.* Applied to literature, esp. poetry, chiefly in pl.: what is suggested or implied by the sound or meaning of the words 1912.

Ovonic (ovǫ·nik), *a.* 1968. [f. *ov-* (in the name of Stanford R. *Ov*shinsky (b. 1922), the American physicist and industrialist who discovered the property) + *-onic* (in *electronic*).] *Electronics.* Pertaining to, involving, or utilizing the property of certain amorphous semiconductors of making a rapid, reversible transition from a non-conducting to a conducting state on the application of an electric field stronger than some minimum value.

O. switches have a number of unique characteristics 1970. Hence **Ovo·nics** *sb. pl.* (const. as *sing.*) [-IC 2], the study and application of o. effects and devices.

Oxbridge (ǫ·ksbridʒ). 1849. Short for '*Ox*ford and Cam*bridge*': a name used to designate the universities of Oxford and of Cambridge; the characteristics common to both, esp. as distinct from other universities in the British Isles. Also *attrib.* Cf. *CAMFORD.

Oxford.

O. accent, a style of pronouncing English popularly supposed to be particularly characteristic of members of the University of Oxford and to be marked by affected utterance; **O. bags,** a style of trousers very wide at the ankles; **O. blue,** a dark shade of blue; **O. group (movement), O. groups:** see *GROUP *sb.* 3 b.

Oxygen.

Comb.: **b. o. tent,** a cover which may be placed over a patient's head and shoulders to form an enclosure through which air enriched with o. may be passed.

Oxytocin (ǫksitōᵘ·sin). 1928. [f. OXYTOC(IC *a.* + -IN¹.] *Physiol.* A hormone found in the posterior lobe of the pituitary body in mammals that stimulates the contraction of the uterus and the ejection of milk and is made synthetically for use in inducing labour and controlling bleeding after delivery.

P.

II. p. = (decimal) pence, penny; P.A., public-address (system); P.A.Y.E., pay-as-you-earn; P.D.Q., pretty damn(ed) quick; P.E., physical education; P.G., paying guest; P.M., Prime Minister, Provost Marshal; P.O.W., prisoner of war; P.P.E., philosophy, politics, and economics; P.R.(o), public relations (officer); p.s.i., pounds per square inch; P.T.A., parent-teacher association; P.V.C., polyvinyl chloride. Also *PH.

Pace, *sb.*

Comb.: **p.-maker,** (*b*) the region of the heart in vertebrates where the contraction of each beat begins; (*c*) a device for providing electrical impulses that will control the beat of a weak or defective heart.

Pachinko (pătʃi·ŋko). 1953. [Jap.] A variety of pin-ball popular in Japan.

Pack, *sb.*¹ **8. b.** The application to a part of the body of a medicinal or cosmetic substance; a substance so applied or intended for such application 1900.

Pack, *v.*¹ **I. 1. d.** *To p. up*: to retire from a contest, active life, etc.; to stop 1925. **6. c.** *To p.* (something) *up* (or *in*): to stop doing (something), esp. talking or misbehaving; freq. in phr. *p. it up* (or *in*) 1942.

Package. 3. b. orig. *U.S.* A combination or collection of interdependent or related items 1931. Also *attrib.*, as **p. deal,** a transaction or proposal the parts or items of which are regarded as inseparably bound up together; **p. holiday, tour,** one in which all arrangements are the responsibility of agents.

Packet, *sb.* **1. c.** *slang.* A considerable sum of money; a load (*lit.* and *fig.*); to *catch, cop, stop a p.*, to be (mortally) hit by a bullet, etc. 1917.

Pad, *sb.*³ **I. 1. b.** *slang* (orig. *U.S.*). A bed; hence, a lodging, a place to sleep; one's residence 1935. **3. d.** = **launching pad* 1953.

Pædiatric (pīdi,æ·trik), *a.* Also **ped-.** 1893. [f. PÆD(O- + IATRIC *a.*] Of, pertaining to, or concerned with pædiatrics. So **Pædiatrician** (-tri·ʃăn). **Pædia·trics** *sb. pl.* (const. as *sing.*), the branch of medical science dealing with the study of childhood and the diseases of children.

Paella (pa,e·lă). 1929. [Cat. *paella* – OFr. *paele* (mod. *poêle*) :– L. *patella* pan, dish.] A Spanish dish of rice with chicken, shell-fish, vegetables, etc., cooked and served in a large, shallow pan.

Pakeha (pā·kėhā). 1817. The Maori word used in N.Z. for a white man.

Palais (‖palę, pæ·lē¹). 1928. = PALAIS DE DANSE.

Palatogram (pæ·lătogræm). 1902. [f. PALATO- + -GRAM.] A drawing or diagram recording the areas of contact between tongue and palate in the production of a speech-sound.

Pallet². 8. A portable tray or platform used, esp. in conjunction with a fork lift truck, for moving or stacking heavy loads 1921.

Palomino (pælomī·no). 1914. [Amer. Sp., – Sp. *palomino* young pigeon, f. *paloma* dove, pigeon, f. L. *palumbes, palumba.*] A cream-coloured horse with light mane and tail, belonging to a variety so called, originating in the south-western U.S.A.

Palynology (pæ:linǫ·lŏdʒi). 1944. [f. Gr. παλύνειν sprinkle (cf. πάλη fine meal = L. *pollen*) + -OLOGY.] The study of the structure and dispersal of pollen grains and other spores, as indicators of plant geography, fossils used in dating geological formations or archæological remains, taxonomic characteristics of plants, or causative agents of allergic reactions. Hence **Palynolo·gical** *a.* **Palyno·logist,** a student of p.

Pan, *v.*¹ **6.** *trans.* orig. *U.S. colloq.* To criticize harshly; to disparage 1922.

Pan (pæn), *v.*³ 1934. [abbrev. of PANORAMA used as vb.] *trans.* To swing (a cine or television camera) horizontally in order to produce a panoramic effect or follow a moving object. Also *intr.* or *absol.* Hence **Pa·nning** *vbl. sb.*

Panache. 2. *fig.* Display, swagger (*colloq.*) 1900.

Panda. 2. The giant panda, *Ailuropoda melanoleuca*, a large black-and-white bear-like mammal, native to central China 1926. **3.** *colloq.* In full *p. car.* A police patrol-car, so called from its broad white stripe resembling the markings of the giant panda 1966.

Panel, *sb.* **II. 4. b.** A list or group of persons regarded as experts who are or may be called upon to advise, judge, take part in a discussion or contest, etc.; a group of people assembled for a particular purpose; freq. of those taking part in a public, esp. broadcast, performance 1933. **III. 2. c.** One of the shaped sections of a parachute 1930. **IV. c.** A board or other surface carrying the instruments, gauges, controls, switches, etc., of a machine, etc.; a control or instrument panel 1940.

Comb.: **p.-beater,** one whose occupation is beating out the metal panels of motor vehicles; **p.-game,** a 'quiz' or similar game played before an audience by a small group of people; **p.-pin,** a thin wire nail with a very small head, nearly invisible when driven below the surface; **p.-wall,** (*a*) a division between two panels in a coal-mine; (*b*) a wall in a building that does not bear any structural weight. Hence **Pa·nel(l)ist,** a member of a radio or television panel (sense *II. 4 b).

Pansy. 2. *colloq.* An effeminate man; a homosexual. Also as *adj.* 1929.

Pantihose (pæ·ntihōᵘz). Also **panty-hose.** 1967. [f. PANTI(ES + HOSE *sb.*] = *TIGHTS *sb. pl.* c.

Panto-.

Pantograph, (*b*) (from the resemblance in shape), a jointed framework on the top of an electric locomotive that conveys the current from the overhead wires.

‖**Panzer** (pæ·nzəɹ, ‖pa·ntsər). 1939. [G., 'mail, coat of mail'.] Properly used *attrib.* = armoured, as *p. forces, p. division*; also *sb. pl.* = *p. forces.*

Papillon (păpi·lyǫn). 1924. [Fr., 'butterfly'.] A breed of toy dog related to the spaniel, having ears that suggest the form of a butterfly.

The P. or Butterfly dog was first introduced into England in any number in 1923. 1927.

Para-¹.

3. Paralingui·stics, the study of gestures accompanying verbal communication. **Parami·litary** *a.*, having a function or status ancillary to that of military forces, though not professedly a military unit. **Parano·rmal** *a.*, lying outside the range of normal scientific investigation, etc. **Parapsycho·logy,** the science or study of mental phenomena which lie outside the sphere of orthodox psychology; so **parapsycholo·gical** *a.*

Paracetamol (pærăse·tămǫl, -sī·t-). 1957. [f. *para-acetylaminophenol.*] *Pharm.* A white crystalline powder with mild analgesic and antipyretic properties; a tablet containing this substance.

Parachute, *sb. attrib.* '(To be) dropped by parachute', as *p. flare, mine, troops. P. troops* is contr. to **Pa·ratroops,** whence **Pa·ratrooper,** one of these.

Paradiddle (pæ·rădid'l). 1934. [imit.] A basic drum roll, produced by the drumsticks beating alternately.

Paramagnetic, *a.* In mod. use restricted to those bodies and substances which have a magnetic permeability slightly greater than one, i.e. are only weakly magnetic (cf. *FERROMAGNETIC *a.*); also as *sb.*, a p. body or substance.

Parameter. 3. A distinguishing or defining characteristic or feature, esp. one that may be measured or quantified 1962.

Paranoid (pæ·rănoid), *a.* 1904. [irreg. f. PARANOIA + -OID.] Resembling, characterized by, or characteristic of, paranoia. Hence as *sb.*

Paraquat (pæ·răkwǫt). 1962. [f. PARA-¹ 2 b + QUAT(ERNARY *a.*, the bond between the two pyridyl groups being in the *para* position with respect to their quaternary nitrogen atom.] Any salt, esp. the dichloride or dimethylsulphate, of the 1,1′-dimethyl-4, 4′-bipyridylium ion, a quick-acting contact herbicide that is rendered inactive by the soil.

Parent, *sb.*

Comb.: **p.-teacher association,** an organization to promote good relations between teachers and the parents of schoolchildren.

Parfait (pā·ɹfē¹). 1906. [– Fr. *parfait* sb., absolute use of *parfait* PERFECT *a.*] A rich iced pudding of whipped cream, eggs, etc.; also, ice cream, fruit, syrup, whipped cream, etc., arranged in layers and served in a tall glass.

Parka (pā·ɹkă). 1890. [Aleutian.] An outer garment or long jacket with a hood attached, made of skins and worn by Eskimos; a similar garment, usu. of wind-proof fabric, worn by mountaineers, skiers, etc.

Parking, *vbl. sb.*

Comb.: **p. meter,** a coin-operated meter which registers the time allowed for a vehicle to be parked.

Parkinson¹ (pā·ɹkinsǫn). 1924. [The name of James *Parkinson* (d. 1824), English surgeon and palæontologist.]

P.'s disease: a chronic, progressive disorder of the central nervous system that produces tremor, rigidity of the limbs, and slowness of movement; shaking palsy. So **Parkinso·nian** *a.*¹ **Pa·rkinsonism¹.**

Parkinson² (pā·ɹkinsǫn). 1955. The name of Cyril Northcote *Parkinson* (born 1909), used in the possessive to denote the 'law' that work expands to fill the time available for its completion. Also *transf.* Hence **Parkinso·nian** *a.*² **Pa·rkinsonism².**

Parliamentary, *a.*

2. *P. Commissioner for Administration*: see *OMBUDSMAN.

‖**Partita** (paɹtī·tă). *Pl.* **-te.** 1895. [It.] *Mus.* A variation; a suite.

Party, *sb.*

Comb.: **p. line,** (*a*) a policy adopted by a political party; (*b*) a telephone line which is shared by two or more subscribers.

Pascal (pæ·skăl). 1956. [Named after Blaise *Pascal* (1623–62), French scientist and philosopher.] *Physics.* The unit of pressure in the metre-kilogramme-second system (and now in the S.I.), equal to one newton per square metre (approximately 0.000,145 p.s.i. or 9.9 × 10^{-6} atmosphere). Abbrev. Pa.

Pass, *sb.*² **I. 5.** *Cards.* The act of declining or being unable to take one's turn to play, bid, etc. 1927.

IV. 1. c. *colloq.* (orig. *U.S.*). An amorous advance; esp. in phr. *to make a p. at* (someone) 1928.

Men seldom make passes At girls who wear glasses DOROTHY PARKER.

Pass, *v.*
With preps. and advs. **P. out,** also, to become unconscious; to die. **P. up** *colloq.* (orig. *U.S.*), to refuse to have further dealings with; to give up, abandon.

Pasta (pæ·stă). 1883. [It., = paste.] A generic name for various forms of Italian dough mixtures or pastes, such as macaroni, spaghetti, and ravioli.

Pastedown (pēⁱ·stdaun). 1895. [f. PASTE *v.* + DOWN *adv.*] An outer blank leaf of a book pasted on to the cover; a piece of paper or parchment from a manuscript or printed book pasted on the inside of the binding of a book for the protection of an end leaf.

Pastel.[2] **3.** Also *attrib.* or as *adj.*, of colour: soft, subdued.

Patch, *sb.*[1] **3.** *To strike a bad p.*: to have a period of bad luck.
Comb.: **p. pocket,** a pocket consisting of a piece of cloth sewn on like a patch.

Patent, *a.* **I. 3. c.** Applied to proprietary foods and medicines 1871.

Patio. 1. b. A paved area adjoining a house 1961.

Patrilineal (pætrili·niăl), *a.* 1904. [f. L. *pater, patr-* father + LINEAL *a.*] Of, pertaining to, or based on (kinship with) the father or the male line; recognizing kinship with and descent through males only.

Patrilocal (pætrilōᵘ·kăl), *a.* 1906. [f. L. *pater, patr-* father + LOCAL *a.*] Applied to a system of marriage among primitive peoples, where a wife moves to her husband's local group.

Pay, *v.*[1]
6. Phr. *To put paid to*: to settle the affair of (*colloq.*).
p.-as-you-earn, applied to a method of collecting income tax by deducting at the source as the income is earned.

Pay-.
1. p.-bed, a bed in a hospital for the use of which payment is made; **p.-load, payload,** (*a*) the load carried by a lorry, aircraft, etc.; (*b*) the weight of explosive carried by a missile; **p.-off** *slang,* (*a*) an act of paying or being paid; (*b*) the climax, conclusion, final result; retribution.

Peanut.
Comb.: **p. butter,** a buttery paste made from ground roasted peanuts.

Peck, *sb.*[2]
Comb.: **p. order** = *PECKING *order.*

Pecking (pe·kiŋ), *vbl. sb.* ME. [f. PECK *v.*[1] + -ING[1].] The action of PECK *v.*[1]; **p. order** *Zool.* [tr. G. *hackliste* (T. J. Schjelderup-Ebbe, 1922)], a social hierarchy, first observed in domestic hens and later in groups of other animals. Also *transf.* and *fig.*
The fat little bantam hen, who proved first in the pecking order. . quickly asserted herself 1972.

Pediatric, -ician, -ics, vars. *PÆDIATRIC, etc.

Peep, *v.*[2]
Comb.: **p.-toe(d)** *a.*, designating a type of shoe which allows the toes to be seen.

Peg, *sb.*[1]
1. Phr. *Off the p.*: said of (the purchase of) ready-made clothes from the peg on which they hang in a shop.

Peg, *v.* **I. 1. c.** Similarly, to fix (payments, e.g. wages) at a certain figure or level.

Pelican. II. 4. In full *p. crossing.* A type of pedestrian crossing marked by traffic lights 1966.
The Pelican (PEdestrian LIght CONtrolled) crossing will show a green signal to a driver until a pedestrian presses the button to start the signal sequence 1969.

Pen, *sb.*[2]
Comb.: **p.-friend,** a friend with whom one has exchanged letters but whom one has not met in person.

Penicillin (penisi·lin). 1929. [f. mod.L. *Penicillium,* generic name of the mould in which it was first found, f. L. *penicillum, penicillus* painter's brush, PENCIL: see -IN[1].] Any of a group of chemically related antibiotics, some of which are organic acids produced naturally by the growth of various moulds of the genera *Penicillium* and *Aspergillus,* while others are acids, salts, or esters prepared synthetically from these; they are active against many bacteria while being almost completely harmless to man.
To avoid the repetition of the rather cumbersome phrase 'Mould broth filtrate', the name 'p.' will be used A. FLEMING. There are a number of naturally occurring penicillins, with somewhat different medical effectiveness 1947. Hence **Penici·llinase** [-ASE], an enzyme produced by some bacteria that breaks down p., so rendering it inactive.

Pentagon. B. *sb.* **2. The Pentagon:** a pentagonal building in Washington, D.C., the headquarters of the U.S. Department of Defense; used allusively for U.S. military leaders 1957.

Penthouse. 1. d. A separate flat, house, etc., situated on the roof of a tall building 1955. Also *attrib.*

Pep.
Comb.: **p.-pill,** a pill containing a stimulant; **p.-talk,** a talk or speech designed to invigorate or encourage the hearer(s).
Hence **Pep** *v. trans.*, to fill with energy or vigour, to ginger *up.* **Pe·ppy** *a.*, full of pep.

Peptide (pe·ptəid). 1906. [– G. *peptid,* back-formation from *polypeptid* *POLYPEPTIDE.] *Biochem.* Any compound in which two or more amino-acids are linked together in a linear sequence, the carboxyl group of each acid being joined to the amino group of the next with the elimination of a molecule of water, so forming a *p. bond* or *linkage,* —CO·NH—.

Perfect, *a.* **II. 5. b.** Of a pleomorphic fungus, describing the stage of the life-cycle in which sexual spores are formed 1891.

Perilune (pe·rilᵘūn). 1960. [f. PERI- + *lune* (f. L. *luna* moon), after *perigee.*] *Astronautics.* The point at which a body in orbit round the moon is closest to its centre.

Periodic, *a.*[1]
2. p. table *Chem.*, a table or diagram of the elements illustrating the p. law.

Peripheral, *a.* **2.** *Computers.* Applied to equipment that is used in conjunction with a computer without being an integral part of it, and to operations involving such equipment. Also as *sb.*, a p. device 1962.

Perk (pɔ̄ɹk), *sb.* 1887. Colloq. abbrev. of PERQUISITE 3. Usu. *pl.*

Permafrost (pɔ̄·ɹmăfrǫst). 1946. [f. PERMA(NENT *a.* + FROST *sb.*] Subsoil that is at a temperature of less than 0°C throughout the year, as in Arctic regions.
The heated pipeline would be laid for several hundred miles. . where the p. may reach as much as 500 metres depth 1971.

Permissive, *a.* **1.** *spec.* Tolerant, liberal, allowing freedom, esp. in sexual matters; freq. in phr. *p. society.* Hence as *sb.*, a p. person.

Persian. A.
2. P. lamb, the silky tightly curled black or brown fur of the young of the karakul, a central Asian breed of sheep.

Persona. 3. The aspect of personality corresponding to the attitude of the moment 1914.

Personality. 3. b. An exceptionally gifted or well-known person; a celebrity 1889.

Perspex (pɔ̄·ɹspeks). 1937. [irreg. f. *perspect-,* ppl. stem of L. *perspicere* look through, f. PER-[1] I. 1 + *specere* look (at).] The proprietary name of a tough transparent acrylic thermoplastic that is much lighter than glass and does not splinter.

Pesticide (pe·stisəid). 1943. [f. L. *pestis* PEST + -CIDE 1.] A substance for destroying pests, esp. insects.

Pet, *v.*[1] **b.** *intr.* To have erotic physical contact with another person by kissing, caressing, and sexually arousing 1925.

Petit, *a.* (*sb.*) **6. p. four** [Fr., lit. 'small oven'], a very small fancy cake, biscuit, or sweet; **p. mal** [Fr., 'little sickness'], epilepsy in which the seizures are mild and very brief, with only momentary confusion or unconsciousness and without general convulsions or other manifestations; also *attrib.*

Petrochemical (pe:troke·mikăl), *a.* and *sb.* 1942. [f. next, after *chemistry, chemical.*] **A.** *adj.* Of or pertaining to petrochemistry (in either sense) or petrochemicals. **B.** *sb.* Any substance obtained or derived from petroleum on an industrial scale 1942.

Petrochemistry (pe:troke·mistri). 1937. [f. PETRO- (in sense 2 repr. *petroleum*) + CHEMISTRY.] **1.** The chemistry of the compositions and formation of rocks. **2.** The chemistry of petroleum and its refining and processing 1942.

Peyote (peyōᵘ·te). Also **peyotl.** 1892. [Amer. Sp. – Nahuatl *peyotl.*] **1.** A cactus of the genus *Lophophora,* esp. *L. williamsii,* found in desert areas of the south-western United States and northern Mexico. **2.** A preparation of part of this plant as a drug 1953.
Comb.: **p. button** = *MESCAL *button.* Hence **Pe·yotism,** a religious cult of American Indians in which p. is taken sacramentally.

pH, pH (pīˌēⁱtʃ). 1909. [Devised in G. by S. P. L. Sörensen (1909), f. *p,* repr. G. *potenz* power + *H,* symbol for hydrogen.] *Chem.* A measure of the acidity or alkalinity of a solution, defined as the logarithm to the base 10 of the reciprocal of the effective concentration of hydrogen ions (in moles per litre).
A solution has a *p*H of less or more than 7 according as it is acidic or alkaline.

Phase (fēⁱz), *v.* 1959. [f. PHASE *sb.*] *trans.* To carry out (a programme, operation, etc.) in phases or stages; so *p. out*: to eliminate gradually. Hence **Pha·se-out** *sb.*

Phatic (fæ·tik), *a.* 1923. [– Gr. φατός spoken, f. φάναι speak, say; see -IC.] In **p. communion,** the use of speech, as in greetings, etc., to convey general sociability rather than communicate specific meaning.

Phenoba·rbitone. 1938. [See PHEN-, *BARBITONE.] A barbiturate, 5-ethyl-5-phenylbarbituric acid, used as a sedative and hypnotic and as an anticonvulsant.

Phenotype (fī·notəip). 1911. [– G. *phaenotypus* (now *phäno-*) (W. Johannsen, 1909), f. Gr. φαινο- showing + -TYPE.] *Biol.* The sum-total of the observable or detectable characteristics of an individual or group, as determined by its genotype and by environmental factors. Hence **Phenoty·pic(al)** *adjs.*, **-ty·pically** *adv.*

Pheromone (fe·romōᵘn). 1959. [f. Gr. φέρειν convey + -O- + ὁρμῶν, pres. pple. of ὁρμᾶν urge on (after *hormone*).] *Biol.* Any substance that is secreted and released by an animal and causes a specific response when detected by another animal of the same (or a closely related) species.
The social organisation of honey bee colonies depends on a p., a chemical produced by the queen 1965. Hence **Pheromo·nal** *a.*

Philadelphus (filăde·lfŏs). [mod.L. (C. Bauhin, 1623) – Gr. φιλάδελφον.] A member of a genus of deciduous shrubs so called, which includes *P. coronarius,* the mock-orange or syringa.

Phillumenist (filⁱū·mĕnist). 1943. [f. PHIL- + L. *lumen* light + -IST.] A collector of match-box labels. Hence **Phillu·meny.**

Phon (fǫn). 1933. [– Gr. φωνή sound.] *Physics.* A unit of loudness (strictly, loudness level), defined so that the loudness in phons of any sound is numerically equal to the intensity in decibels of a pure 1000 Hz tone judged to be equally loud.

Phoneme. (The variants of a phoneme as conditioned by differences of enunciation or articulation (e.g. the point and flat varieties of *l,* the trilled and uvular varieties of *r*) are normally represented by the same symbol, or an accepted equivalent, and do not constitute distinctions between words otherwise identical.) Hence **Phonematic** (-æ·tik), **Phonemic** (-ī·mik) *adjs.* **Phone·micist,** a student of phonemes.

Phoney (fōᵘ·ni), *sb. slang.* Also **phony.** 1905. [f. the adj.] A phoney person or thing.

Phonon (fōᵘ·nǫn). 1932. [f. Gr. φωνή sound + *-ON.] *Physics.* A quantum of sound or elastic vibrations.

Phosphor, *sb.* **2.** Revived [following use in G. by Lenard & Klatt, 1904] in the sense: any synthetic substance having fluorescent or phosphorescent properties 1910.

Photo-.
1. Pho·tocell, a photo-electric cell. **2. Pho·tocompose** *v. trans.*, **Pho·tocomposition,** = *filmset, filmsetting* (s.v. *FILM *sb.* 7). **Pho·tocopy** *sb.*, a document produced by photography that can serve as a copy of a document from which it was made; hence as *v. trans.* **P.-finish,** the finish of a race in which competitors are so close that the result has to be determined by reference to a photograph of the situation. **Pho·toset** *v. trans.* and *ppl. a.*, **Pho·tosetting**

ppl. a. and *vbl. sb.* = *filmset, filmsetting* (s.v. *FILM *sb.* 7).

Photo-electric, *a.*

b. p. cell, any device that depends for its operation on the changes in its electrical properties produced by light or other electromagnetic radiation.

Physio-. Phy:siothe·rapy, the treatment of disease or deformity by physical means, such as exercises, massage, or heat. Hence **Phy:siothe·rapist.**

Pianistic (piăni·stik), *a.* 1881. [f. PIANIST + -IC.] Of or pertaining to a pianist; adapted for playing on a piano.

The same 12-bar pattern. .serves as a basis for the 'Boogie-Woogie', a typically p. species 1950.

Pick, *v.*[1] **VII.**

P. up. i. Also (*colloq.*), to make the acquaintance of (someone) casually and informally, *e.g.* in the street.

Pickled, *ppl. a.* **2.** *slang.* Drunk 1912.

Pick-up, *sb.* (*a.*) **d.** *colloq.* A man or woman 'picked up' (see *PICK *v.*[1] VII) 1895. **e.** orig. *U.S.* A small truck or lorry for collecting and delivering goods, etc. Also *attrib.*, as *p. truck* 1932.

Pico- (pī·ko-, pəi·ko-), *prefix.* 1926. [– Sp. *pico* beak, peak, little bit.] Prefixed to the names of units to form the names of units 10^{12} times smaller (i.e. one million millionth part of them); as *picofarad* = 10^{-12} farad. Abbrev. p.

Pidgin, pigeon. 2. *One's p.*: one's particular concern 1925.

Pie, *sb.*[2]

3. Slang phr. *P. in the sky*: a prospect, often illusory, of future happiness, esp. as a reward for virtue or suffering on earth.

Piezo-electri·city (pəi,ī·zo,i-). 1895. [f. Gr. πιέζειν to press + -O- + ELECTRICITY.] Electricity resulting from pressure, as in certain crystals. So **Pie:zo-ele·ctric** *a.*, having the property of becoming polarized when subjected to pressure; of or pertaining to p.

Pig, *sb.*[1] **I. 5. b.** *slang.* A policeman 1811.

Comb.: **p. Latin,** a made-up jargon; *spec.* one in which the first consonant or consonant-clusters of a word is transferred to the end and followed by *ay.*

Piggy (pi·gi). 1799. [f. PIG *sb.*[1] + -Y[6].] A little pig.

Comb.: **p. bank,** a hollow pig-shaped pot with a slit in the back, in which money can be saved.

Pile, *sb.*[2] **6.** More fully *atomic p.*: a nuclear reactor (see *REACTOR 3 b) 1945.

Pill, *sb.*[2] **1. a.** spec. *The pill,* an oral contraceptive 1960.

Pilot, *sb.* Used *attrib.* or quasi-*adj.* to denote a project, scheme, apparatus, etc., that is experimental or exploratory.

Pi-meson (pəi:mī·zǫn, -me·zǫn). 1953. [f. PI *sb.* (π being the symbol for the particle) + *MESON.] *Nuclear Physics.* = *PION.

Pin, *sb.*

Comb.: **pin-ball, pinball** orig. *U.S.*, a game resembling bagatelle, in which small metal balls are propelled across a sloping surface towards targets which indicate the score when they are hit; freq. *attrib.*; **p.-point,** the point of a p.; usu. *fig.*, as a type of something extremely small or sharp; hence as *v. trans.*, to indicate or determine precisely; **p.-table,** a table on which pinball is played.

Pincers, *sb. pl.*

Comb.: **pincer movement,** an operation involving the convergence of two forces on an enemy position like the jaws of a pair of pincers.

Pinta (pəi·ntă). *colloq.* 1960. [colloq. pronunc. of *pint of.*] A pint of milk, beer, etc.

Pin-up (pi·nʌp). *colloq.* (orig. *U.S.*). 1941. [f. phr. *to pin up.*] A picture, esp. of a beautiful woman, pinned up on a wall, post, etc.; an attractive or favoured person. Freq. *attrib.*

Pion (pəi·ǫn). 1953. [f. *PI(-MESON + *-ON.] *Nuclear Physics.* Any of a group of mesons which have a mass approximately 270 times that of the electron and zero 'strangeness'; a pi-meson.

Pip, *sb.*[5] 1933. [imit.] A high-pitched momentary sound.

The six 'pips' of the time-signal 1938.

Pipe, *v.*[1] **IV.** *To p. down*: to be less insistent or confident; to be quiet (*colloq.*).

Pipe-line. Also *transf.* and *fig.*, esp. a direct channel of supply, information, etc.; *in the p.*: in the process of being, or waiting to be, effected or dealt with.

Piranha (pirā·nʸă). 1869. [Pg., f. Tupi *piranya*, var. of *piraya* scissors.] A voracious South American fresh-water fish of the genus *Serrasalmus*; = PERAI.

Piss, *v.* **1. b.** To rain hard; freq. const. *down* 1950. **4. To p. off.** *slang.* **a.** *intr.* To go away, depart. **b.** *trans.* To annoy, depress.

Pissed (pist), *ppl. a. slang.* 1937. [f. PISS *v.*] **1.** Intoxicated, drunk. **2.** Fed up, depressed, annoyed; freq. *p. off* 1946.

‖**Pissoir** (pĭswār). 1919. [Fr.] A public urinal.

‖**Piste** (pĭst). 1929. [Fr., running track, race-track.] A ski-trail of compacted snow.

Pit, *sb.* **I. 1. g.** In full *inspection p.* A sunken place where vehicles can be inspected or repaired from below 1907. **h.** Usu. *pl.* The part of a motor-racing course where cars are repaired, refuelled, etc. 1914.

Pixilated (pi·ksilēⁱtėd), *ppl. a.* orig. *U.S. dial.* Also **pixillated.** 1886. [var. PIXY-LED *a.*] **a.** = PIXY-LED *a.*; enchanted, confused, insane. **b.** Tipsy, drunk 1958.

Pizza (pī·tsă). 1935. [It., = pie.] An open pie made from dough or pastry covered with a spiced mixture of tomatoes, cheese, anchovies, etc.

Planck's constant (plæŋks). Also **Planck constant.** 1918. [Named after the German physicist, Max *Planck* (1858–1947).] *Physics.* One of the fundamental physical constants (symbol h), relating the energy E of a quantum of electromagnetic radiation to its frequency ν according to the equation $E = h\nu$; approximately 6.63×10^{-34} joule-second.

Planning (plæ·niŋ), *vbl. sb.* 1748. [f. PLAN *v.* + -ING[1].] The action of PLAN *v.*, *spec.* the organization of the lay-out or design of buildings, the development of land, etc. Also *attrib.*, as **p. blight,** an adverse effect on property values, resulting from long-term development plans; **p. permission,** official permission to erect a building, develop a site, etc.

Plasma. 5. *Physics.* A gas (usually at a very high temperature) composed of positive ions and free electrons in approximately equal numbers; orig. applied by I. Langmuir to the region of an electric discharge in a rarefied gas in which there were equal numbers of ions and electrons (as well as un-ionized molecules) 1928.

The stable p. reaches the high temperatures, of the order of 5 million deg. K., necessary for producing thermonuclear reactions 1958.

Plaster, *sb.*

Comb.: **p. board, plasterboard,** board containing a plaster core, used for walling, ceilings, etc.

Plastered (pla·stəɹd), *ppl. a.* late ME. [f. PLASTER *v.* + -ED[1].] **1.** Covered with, or formed of, plaster. **2.** *slang.* Drunk, intoxicated 1912.

Plastic, *a.* **II. 2. p. bomb,** a bomb containing p. explosive, i.e. explosive that can be shaped by hand.

IV. [deriving from the sb. used attrib.] Made of p.; of the nature of a p., or containing p. as an essential constituent 1938.

P. wood 1938. Pre-cooked hamburgers. .in their little frozen transparent p. bags 1957. P. flowers 1961.

B. *sb.* Any of a large and varied class of wholly or partly synthetic substances which are organic in composition and polymeric in structure and may be given a permanent shape by moulding, extrusion, or other means during manufacture or use. Also used generically (without *a* and *pl.*): material of this kind 1909. **b.** Used *attrib.* in *pl.*, often to avoid possible confusion with branches I and II of the adj. 1935.

b. New plastics materials such as bakelite 1944. Tools with plastics handles 1958.

Plate, *sb.* **III.**

Colloq. phrases. *On a p.*: ready to be taken without asking or seeking. *On one's plate*: for one to deal with or consider.

Platinum.

Comb.: **p. blonde** orig. *U.S.*, a woman with silvery-blonde hair.

Play, *sb.*

Comb.: **p.-back, playback,** the reproduction of sound or pictures from magnetic tape, film, etc.; **p.-boy, playboy,** a pleasure-loving man, usu. irresponsible and often wealthy; **p. group,** a group of children who play together under adult supervision, usu. at a regular time and place; **p.-pen,** an enclosure in which a young child may play in safety.

Play, *v.* **II. 4. b.** *To p.* (someone) *up*: to tease, irritate 1924. **III. 1. c.** *To p. ball* (*with*): to act fairly or co-operate (with) 1903. **IV. 2. b.** *To p. by ear*: (*a*) to play (something) without the aid of written music 1674; (*b*) to proceed step by step according to results; to act instinctively 1961. **VI. 8.** *To p. up*: to make the most of, exploit 1926. Similarly *to p. down.*

Pleb (pleb). 1865. Slang abbrev. of PLEBEIAN *sb.* b. (See also PLEBE 2.)

-ploid. The terminal element of *HAPLOID, used in forming other adjs. describing the number of chromosome sets in a cell or in the somatic cells of an organism; as *diploid, triploid, polyploid,* etc.

Plonk (plǫŋk), *int.*, *sb.*[1], and *v. colloq.* 1903. [imit.] = PLUNK *int.*, *sb.*, *v.*

Plonk (plǫŋk), *sb.*[2] orig. *Austral. slang.* 1919. [perh. f. prec., or modification of Fr. *vin blanc* white wine.] Cheap or inferior wine.

Plough, *v.*

Phrases. *To p. back*: to bury (grass, vegetation) in the soil by ploughing; *fig.* to invest (earnings or profits) in the business in which they have been made. *To p. a lonely furrow*: to carry on alone.

Plug, *sb.* **7.** A device for facilitating the safe connection of a lead to a voltage source or electrical appliance, consisting of an insulated casing with metal pins that may be inserted into a suitable socket 1936.

Plug, *v.* **1. c.** *to p. in* (trans.): to connect (an electrical appliance or apparatus) to a voltage source by inserting a plug into a socket 1939. **4. c.** *trans.* To endeavour to popularize (a song, etc.) by having it performed often; to present over and over again for advertisement 1927. Hence as *sb.*, an advertisement, publicity.

Plummet (plʌ·mėt), *v.* 1626. [f. the sb.] †**1.** *trans.* To fathom, sound. †**2.** To draw (a vertical line) by means of a plummet 1711. **3.** *intr.* To fish with a line weighted with a plummet. **4.** To plunge, fall rapidly downwards 1939.

Plush. 4. *colloq.* Used as *adj.*: stylish, luxurious 1934. Also **Plushy** *a.*, in same sense.

Pluto (plū·to). 1930. [– L. *Pluto*, Gr. Πλούτων, name of the god of the underworld, brother of Jupiter and Neptune.] *Astr.* A planet of the solar system lying beyond the orbit of Neptune, discovered in 1930 and visible only through large telescopes.

Plutonium (plūtōᵘ·niŏm). 1945. [f. prec. (as plutonium is the element next after neptunium): see -IUM.] *Chem.* A transuranic element formed indirectly from uranium in nuclear reactors and occurring naturally in trace amounts; the longest-lived isotope (plutonium 239) has a half-life of 24,000 years and is fissile, being produced for use in nuclear weapons and as fuel. Atomic number 94; symbol Pu.

Pneumo-.

Pneu:moconiosis (-kōᵘni,ōᵘ·sis) [Gr. κόνι-ς dust + -OSIS], any condition of the lungs that results from inhalation of dust, esp. chronic fibrosis as an occupational disease of coal miners or other workers.

Pocket, *sb.* **5. f.** An isolated area occupied by troops in a battlefield; the troops themselves. Also *transf.* 1918. **8. b. p. battleship,** a ship equipped and armoured like a battleship but on a small scale.

Po-faced (pōᵘ·fēⁱst), *a. colloq.* 1934. [prob. f. Po.] Solemn-faced.

Pohutukawa (pohū:tūkā·wă). *N.Z.* 1835. [Maori.] A New Zealand evergreen tree, *Metrosideros excelsa*, which bears brilliant crimson flowers; also called, locally, *Christmas tree.*

Poinciana (poinsĭ,ā·nă). 1829. [mod.L. (Tournefort, 1700), f. the name of M. de *Poinci*, 17th-cent. governor of the Antilles.] A tropical tree of the genus once so called, but now included in the genera *Cæsalpinia* and *Delonix*; esp. *D. regia*, the flamboyante, which bears scarlet flowers.

Point, *sb.*[1] **A. V. 4. b.** A proposition or contention; a subject suitable for discussion; so *to make a p.*: to prove a contention, to attain a goal 1809. Cf. sense B. IV a.

Phr. *P. of no return*: the stage at which one can no longer turn back or alter one's course; also *fig.*

Poison, *sb.* **2. b.** Colloq. phr. *One's p.*: one's favourite drink 1866.

Comb.: **p. pen,** (the practice of) an anonymous writer of malignant, libellous, or scurrilous letters; freq. *attrib.*

Police, *sb.*

Comb.: **p. dog,** a dog trained and used by p. to track criminals; **p. state,** a state regulated by means of a national p. having supervision and control of the activities of citizens.

Polio (pōᵘ·lio). 1931. Colloq. abbrev. of POLIOMYELITIS.

Politico (pǒli·tiko). 1630. [Sp., sb. use of the adj. (POLITIC).] A politician (sense 2 b).

Polka, *sb.*[1]

Comb.: **p.-dot,** a round dot or spot as one of a regular series forming a pattern on a textile fabric, etc.; also *attrib.*

Poll, *sb.*[1] **II. 2. d.** An assessment of public opinion made by ascertaining the opinions of a representative selection of the people; cf. **Gallup poll* 1940. Hence **Po·llster,** one who organizes a p.

Pollen, *sb.*

Comb.: **p. analysis** = *PALYNOLOGY; **p. count,** an index of the quantity of p. in the air, published as a warning to those allergic to it.

Pollution. 1. *spec.* The contamination or defilement of man's environment.

Poly-.

2. a. Polye·ster [ESTER], any polymer in which the units are linked by the group —CO·O—; also (*a*) (more fully *polyester fibre*), a man-made fibre consisting of a polyester; (*b*) (more fully *polyester resin*), any of numerous synthetic resins or plastics consisting of or made from a polyester, different kinds of which are used as fibres or films, in paint, and as moulding materials or reinforced plastics. **Polye·thylene,** a polymer of ethylene; *esp.* = *POLYTHENE. **Polysty·rene** [*styrene*, another name for STYROL, STYROLENE], a hard, colourless thermoplastic that is a polymer of styrene and is used as a moulding material, a rigid foam, and in sheet form. **Polyurethane** (-yū·rĕþēⁱn, -yure·þēⁱn) [URETHANE], any of various synthetic resins or plastics consisting of or made from polymers with the units linked by the group —NH·CO·O—, and used esp. as foams or coatings. **Po:lyvinyl chlo·ride** [VINYL], any polymer of vinyl chloride; also, any of various thermoplastics consisting of or made from such a polymer, produced in a wide variety of forms and characterized esp. by their toughness, chemical inertness, and electrical resistivity.

Polypeptide (pǫlipe·ptəid). 1903. [– G. *polypeptid* (E. Fischer, 1903), f. POLY- 2 a + G. *pepton* PEPTONE + *-id*.] *Biochem.* Any peptide in which the number of amino-acids that go to make up the molecule is not small, but which is not so large as to be regarded as a protein.

The p. chain, the backbone of the protein molecule, was found to be coiled in a helix-like spiral spring 1961.

Polyploid (pǫ·liploid), *a.* 1920. [G. (H. Winkler, 1916): see POLY- and *-PLOID.] *Biol.* Of a cell or its nucleus: having more than two sets of chromosomes, each set containing the haploid number. Of an organism: having p. somatic cells. Hence **Po·lyploidy,** p. condition.

The p. plant..is 'larger in all its parts' 1970.

Polythene (pǫ·liþīn). 1939. [contr. of *polyethylene*.] A tough, light, translucent thermoplastic made by polymerizing ethylene and used esp. for moulded and extruded articles and as film for packaging.

Pommy. Also *N.Z.* Also **Pom, Po·mmie.**

Ponce (pǫns), *sb.* orig. *slang.* 1861. [perh. f. POUNCE *v.*] A man who lives off a prostitute's earnings; a prostitute's protector; a pimp; also as a vague term of abuse. Hence as *v. intr.*, to act as, or behave like, a p.; to live *on* the earnings of a prostitute; to move *about* languidly, effeminately, etc.

Pong (pǫŋ), *sb. colloq.* 1925. [Origin uncertain.] An unpleasant smell, a stink. Also as *v. intr.*, to smell unpleasant.

Pony, *sb.*

Comb.: **p.-tail,** the hair (of a woman) worn hanging from the back of the head like a pony's tail.

Poof (puf, pūf), *sb. colloq.* Also **pooff, poove, pouf(f), pouve, puff.** *c* 1860. [Cf. PUFF *sb.* 7.] An effeminate man; a male homosexual. Also as *adj.*

Pool, *sb.*[2] **4. c.** = **football pool*; freq. *pl.* 1939. **5. b.** A common stock of a commodity or the like; a group of people or things available to an organization 1917.

Poop (pūp), *v.*[3] *colloq.* (orig. *U.S.*). 1932. [Origin unkn.] *trans.* To exhaust, wear out. Freq. **Pooped** (pūpt) *ppl. a.*, exhausted; also *pooped out.*

Pop (pǫp), *a.* 1934. Colloq. abbrev. of POPULAR *a.* So as *sb.*, something popular; *spec.* (*a*) a popular concert (see POP *sb.*[2]) 1862; (*b*) a popular tune, record, etc. 1935; (*c*) popular music generally 1957; (*d*) popular culture 1962.

Special Comb.: **p. art,** art that derives its images, style, etc., from popular culture and the mass media.

Popular, *a.*

2. *P. front* [tr. Sp. *frente popular*, whence Fr. *front populaire*]: a political party or organized group representing left-wing elements 1936.

Porn (pǭɹn). 1962. Colloq. abbrev. of PORNOGRAPHY. So **Po·rno,** (*a*) *adj.* pornographic; (*b*) *sb.* pornography.

Positron (pǫ·zitrǫn). 1933. [f. POSI(TIVE + *-TRON.] *Nuclear Physics.* The antiparticle of the electron, having the same mass and a numerically equal but positive charge.

Possible. B. *sb.* **3.** A possible candidate, winner, member, etc. 1915.

Post, *sb.*[2]

Comb.: **p.-code, postcode,** a group of letters and figures appended to a postal address to facilitate the sorting of mail.

Pot, *sb.*[1] **1. h.** *colloq.* = POT-BELLY 1; a paunch 1936.

Pot (pǫt), *sb.*[4] *slang* (orig. *U.S.*). 1951. [prob. f. Mexican Sp. *potiguaya*, but perh. f. POT *sb.*[1] or POD *sb.*[2]] = *MARIJUANA.

Pot, *v.* **II. 5.** *colloq.* To put (a child) on a chamber-pot 1948.

Potato.

Comb.: **p. crisp** (see *CRISP *sb.* 4).

Potential, *sb.* **3. b.** *fig.* The resources that can be employed for an undertaking 1943.

Pot-hole. 1. Hence **Po·t-holer,** one who explores pot-holes. **Po·t-holing** *vbl. sb.*

Potty (pǫ·ti), *sb. colloq.* 1942. [f. POT *sb.*[1] + -Y[6].] A chamber-pot, esp. for a child.

Power, *sb.*

Comb.: **p.-dive,** (of aircraft) a dive made without shutting off the motor power; also as vb.; **p. politics** [tr. G. *machtpolitik*], international policy based on or backed by the threat of force.

Praseodymium (prēⁱ:ziŏdi·miŏm). 1885. [– G. *praseodym* (C. A. von Welsbach, 1885), f. Gr. πράσιος leek-green (f. πράσον leek) + G. *di-dym* DIDYMIUM: see -IUM. Named in allusion to the colour of its salts and its isolation, with neodymium, from the supposed element didymium.] *Chem.* An element of the lanthanide series similar to iron in appearance, the only naturally occurring isotope of which is present in cerium-rich minerals. Atomic number 59; symbol Pr.

Pre-. A.

I. Pre-cast *a.*, of concrete: that is cast in blocks before being used in construction. **Pre-igni·tion,** premature ignition in an internal-combustion engine. **Pre-sele·ctive** *a.*, of a gear: that can be selected and set in advance; so *pre-sele·ctor*. **Pre-stressed** *a.*, of concrete: strengthened by the introduction of stretched wires or the like.

Precinct, *sb.* **4.** A district in a town where traffic is prohibited, esp. to allow pedestrians to shop in safety 1943.

Precision. *attrib.* Designed for or concerned with precise work or action, as *p. bombing, machine, tool.*

Pre-emptive, *a.*

p. bid, in Bridge, a bid made with the expectation that it is high enough to prevent opponents from bidding normally and so obtaining adequate information.

Prefab (prī·fæb), *a.* and *sb.* 1942. Colloq. abbrev. of **prefabricated (house).*

Prefabricate (prīfæ·brikēⁱt), *v.* 1932. [f. PRE- A. I. 1 + FABRICATE *v.*] *trans.* To manufacture the component parts of (a building or other structure) in preparation for their assembly on a site. Also *fig.* So **Prefa·bricated** *ppl. a.* **Pre:fabrica·tion.**

Premium.

Comb.: **p. bond,** a government bond not bearing interest but with the periodical chance of a cash prize.

Presidium (prĭsi·diŏm). 1924. [Russ. *prezidium* – L. *præsidium* garrison, f. *præsidēre* (see PRESIDE *v.*).] The presiding body or standing committee in a Communist organization.

Press, *sb.*[1]

Comb.: **b. p. conference,** a prearranged interview given to journalists by a celebrity, etc.

Press-up (pre·sʌp). 1947. [f. PRESS *v.*[1] + UP *adv.*] An exercise in which the body is raised from a prone position by pressing down on the hands until the arms are straightened. Usu. *pl.*

Pressure, *sb.*

Comb.: **p. cooker,** an apparatus for cooking under high p. at high temperature; **p. group,** a group or body of people which exerts p. upon the legislature, public policy, etc., by concerted agitation, propaganda, and the like; **p. mine,** a mine that is detonated by p.

Pressure (pre·ʃiŭɹ, pre·ʃəɹ), *v.* orig. *U.S.* 1939. [f. the sb.] *trans.* To put pressure on; to coerce or persuade.

Pressurize (pre·ʃərəiz), *v.* 1938. [f. PRESSURE *sb.* + -IZE.] *trans.* To produce or maintain pressure artificially in (a container, closed space, etc., or a fluid); *spec.* to maintain normal atmospheric pressure in (an aircraft) during a high-altitude flight. So **Pre·ssurized** *ppl. a.* **Pre:ssuriza·tion.**

The sodium-cooled reactor..on the submarine USS *Seawolf* has been replaced by a pressurized-water reactor 1966. Before re-entry, the camera and payload section were sealed and pressurized to two atmospheres 1970.

Prestige. 2. b. *attrib.* or quasi-*adj.* Having, conferring, or pertaining to prestige 1929. Hence **Presti·geful** *a.*, having or conferring prestige.

Prestigious, *a.* **2.** Having or manifesting prestige; renowned and influential 1934.

Preview (prī·viū), *sb.* 1855. [f. PRE- A. I. 2 + VIEW *sb.*; cf. REVIEW *sb.*] **1.** Foresight, prevision. **2.** A previous view or inspection; *spec.* a viewing of a picture, film, etc., before it can be seen by the public 1882. Hence as *v. trans.*, to view (a film, etc.) at a p.

Pricey (prəi·si), *a. colloq.* Also **pricy.** 1933. [f. PRICE *sb.* + -Y[1].] Expensive.

Prime, *v.*[1] **3. c.** To pour water into (a pump) to assist its power of suction and so bring up water 1882.

Print, *v.*

Printed circuit, an electric circuit in which wires are replaced by thin conducting strips on a flat sheet of some insulating material, usu. mass-produced by a method that involves 'printing' a pattern on to the sheet.

Pri·nt-out. 1961. [f. vbl. phr. *to print out.*] (A sheet or strip of) printed matter produced by a computer or other automatic apparatus; the production of such matter.

Everyone should be entitled to a p. of the information in the data bank in regard to him 1969. The drafting and p. of leases, wills and forms 1971.

Priority. 3. Also *gen.* An interest having a prior claim to consideration; often with qualification, as *first p., top p.*

Prissy (pri·si), *a.* orig. *U.S.* 1905. [perh. blend of PRIM *a.* and SISSY.] Prim, prudish, girlish.

Private. A. *adj.*

1. d. p. eye, a detective who is engaged privately and works independently of any police force. **3. b. p. enterprise,** a privately owned business concern or activity, not under state control; such concerns collectively.

Pro.[1]

3. pro forma invoice, an invoice sent to a purchaser in advance of the ordered goods, so that formalities may be completed.

Probe, *sb.* **4.** *Astronautics.* An unmanned spacecraft on an exploratory flight and having instruments for transmitting information about its surroundings 1953.

Procedural (prŏsī·diŭrăl), *a.* 1919. [f. PROCEDURE + -AL[1].] Pertaining to, concerning, or involving procedure.

Prof (prǫf). 1838. Colloq. abbrev. of PROFESSOR.

Profiterole (prŏfi·tĕrōᵘl). 1515. [Fr., f. *profit* PROFIT *sb.* + *-erole* dim. suffix.] A type of cake or other kind of cooked food; *spec.* a small hollow ball of choux pastry which may be filled with a sweet or savoury mixture.

Progesterone (prodʒe·stěrōᵘn). 1935. [Blend of *PROGEST(IN and *luteosterone* (f. LUTEO-, repr. *corpus luteum* + STER(OL + -ONE), names previously given to the hormone.] *Physiol.* A steroid sex hormone produced in the *corpus luteum* that is involved in maintaining pregnancy and is used in the treatment of some menstrual disturbances.

P. inhibits ovulation during pregnancy 1967.

Progestin (prodʒe·stin). 1930. [f. PRO-² 1 + GEST(ATION + -IN¹.] *Physiol.* **a.** Progesterone, now esp. a preparation of it with unspecified purity. **b.** A progestogen, esp. a synthetic one.

Progestogen (prodʒe·stǒdʒěn). 1941. [f. as prec. + -O- + -GEN.] *Physiol.* Any sex hormone or other substance that resembles progesterone in its physiological effects.

Most oral contraceptives contain both a p. and an oestrogen 1968. Hence **Progestoge·nic** *a.*

Program, programme. 2. c. *Computers.* A fully explicit series of instructions which when fed into a computer will automatically direct its operation in carrying out a specific task 1946. Also as *v. trans.*, to supply (a computer) with a p.; to cause (a computer) *to* do something by this means; also, to express as or in a p. Hence **Pro·gramming** *vbl. sb.*, the operation of programming a computer; also, the writing or preparation of programs. **Pro·grammer**, a person who does this.

The spelling *program* is generally preferred in this sense (for both sb. and vb.).

Prole (prōᵘl), *a.* and *sb.* 1938. Colloq. abbrev. of PROLETARIAN *a.* and *sb.*

Proletarianize (prōᵘlītēᵊ·riănəiz), *v.* 1887. [f. PROLETARIAN *a.* + -IZE.] *trans.* To render proletarian. Hence **Pro:letarianiza·tion.** Also **Proletariza·tion.**

Proliferate, *v.* **1. c.** *gen.* To increase vastly in numbers, grow prolifically 1926. Also **Proliferation** in corresp. sense.

Promethium (promī·þiǒm). 1948. [f. PROMETH(EUS + -IUM; orig. *prometheum.*] *Chem.* A radioactive element of the lanthanide series that is formed as a fission product in nuclear reactors but is not known to occur naturally, the longest-lived isotope having a half-life of 18 years. Atomic number 61; symbol Pm.

Promote, *v.* **I. 2. c.** orig. *U.S.* To further the sale of (an article) by promotion (see next) 1930.

Promotion. 2. c. orig. *U.S.* The encouragement of the sale of an article by advertising, etc.; publicity, advertising; an occasion, etc., on which an article is publicized 1925.

Prop (prǫp), *sb.*⁶ 1918. Colloq. abbrev. of PROPELLER (sense 2).

Propellent, *a.* and *sb.* As sb. usu. spelt **propellant. B.** *sb.* **b.** A substance which reacts with another in a rocket engine to provide the thrust 1930.

A propellant can be either fuel or oxidizer 1957.

Proportional, *a.*

2. p. representation, a method of parliamentary representation designed to allow the various political parties to be represented in proportion to their size and characterized by the use of the transferable vote, i.e. the filling up of seats, where a quota is not secured by first choices, by the transference of votes from second choices, and so on.

Proposition (prǫpǒzi·ʃən), *v. colloq.* (orig. *U.S.*). 1924. [f. the sb.] *trans.* To make a proposition to; *spec.* to suggest sexual intercourse to (someone).

Prosopography (prǫsoᵘpǫ·grăfi). 1577. [– mod.L. *prosopographia*, f. Gr. πρόσωπον face, countenance, person; see -GRAPHY.] Description of an individual's personality and career. Hence **Prosopo·grapher. Prosopogra·phical** *a.*

Prostaglandin (prǫstăglæ·ndin). 1936. [– G. *prostaglandin* (U.S. von Euler, 1935), f. G. *prosta(ta* or Eng. PROSTA(TE *sb.* (*a.*) + GLAND² + -IN¹.] *Biochem.* Any of a group of closely related cyclic fatty acids which occur in seminal fluid and many tissues in mammals and have numerous marked physiological effects (notably the contraction of smooth muscle, esp. that of the uterus).

Prosthetic, *a.* **3.** *Biochem.* Applied to a non-protein group forming part of or combined with a protein 1910. **B.** *sb. pl.* (const. as *sing.*) = PROSTHESIS 2. 1911.

Protactinium (prōᵘtækti·niǒm). Also **protoactinium.** 1919. [– G. *protactinium* (Hahn and Meitner, 1918), f. PROT(O- + ACTINIUM: so named because the principal isotope produces actinium by radioactive decay.] *Chem.* A hard radioactive metallic element of which the longest-lived isotope (half-life 34,000 years) is formed by radioactive decay in uranium ores. Atomic number 91; symbol Pa.

Protection: 1. c. orig. *U.S.* Freedom from molestation obtained by paying money to a criminal who threatens violence or retribution if payment is not made. Freq. *attrib.*, as *p. money, racket* 1903.

Protective, *a.*

1. p. custody, detention, detention of a person supposedly for his own protection.

Protium (prōᵘ·tiǒm). 1933. [mod.L., f. PROT(O- + -IUM.] *Chem.* The common isotope of hydrogen, as distinct from the heavy isotopes deuterium and tritium.

Protocol, *sb.* **4. b.** Rigid prescription or observance of precedence and deference to rank as in diplomatic and military services; official etiquette and formality 1945.

Provo (prōᵘ·vo). 1966. [abbrev. of Fr. *provocateur* one who provokes.] A member of a Dutch group of anarchist agitators whose policy is to provoke the authorities.

Psephology (sefǫ·lǒdʒi). 1952. [f. Gr. ψῆφος pebble + -LOGY.] The study of trends in voting or elections. Hence **Psepholo·gical** *a.* **Psepho·logist.**

Pseud (siūd), *a.* and *sb. colloq.* 1962. [abbrev. of PSEUDO, PSEUDO-.] **A.** *adj.* Fake; pretentious or affected, esp. about intellectual or social matters or accomplishments. **B.** *sb.* A 'pseud' person 1964.

Psi (səi). 1934. [The 23rd letter of the Gr. alphabet, written ψ.] Parapsychological factors or faculties collectively, including telepathy and precognition. Freq. *attrib.*

Psilocybin (səilǒsəi·bin). 1958. [f. *Psilocybe* (see def.) (f. PSILO- + Gr. κύβη head) + -IN¹.] *Chem.* A hallucinogenic indole derivative present in various Mexican mushrooms of the genus *Psilocybe*, esp. *P. mexicana*, and producing effects similar to those of LSD but less strongly and for a shorter period.

Psychedelic (səikĕdī·lik, -e·lik), *a.* Also occas. **psychodelic.** 1957. [irreg. f. Gr. ψυχή PSYCHE + δῆλος clear, manifest: see -IC.] Expanding the mind's awareness: used esp. of certain hallucinogenic drugs and their effects. Also as *sb.*, a drug of this kind. Hence **Psychede·lia**, p. drugs, articles, etc.

Psycho-.

Psy:chosoma·tic *a.*, of or pertaining to phenomena, esp. diseases, that are both physiological and psychological. **Psychosu·rgery,** brain surgery as a means of treating mental or emotional disorders. **Psychothe·rapy,** the treatment of mental or emotional disorders by psychological means.

Psychotic (səikǫ·tik), *a.* and *sb.* 1895. [f. PSYCHOSIS: see -OTIC.] **A.** *adj.* Of the nature of or resulting from a psychosis; suffering from a psychosis. **B.** *sb.* A p. person 1915.

Public. A. *adj.* **I.**

1. p.-address system, a system of microphones, loudspeakers, etc., whereby a speaker, musician, or the like may be heard by an audience; **p. relations,** (the establishment or maintenance of) relations, esp. a good relationship, between an organization, firm, etc., and the general public; also *attrib.* as *p.-relations officer.*

Publicize (pɒ·blisəiz), *v.* 1928. [f. PUBLIC *a.* + -IZE.] *trans.* To bring to public notice; to advertise.

Puerperal, *a.*

Comb.: **p. fever** or **sepsis,** fever following parturition, due to infection in the uterus, sometimes with septicæmia or local inflammation.

Pull, *v.* **II. 1. b.** *U.S.* To draw (a revolver or pistol) for the purpose of firing 1883.

P. in, out. *intr.* To draw into, out of (a position). **P. round.** *intr.* To recover from sickness, a swoon, etc.

III. 4. b. Colloq. phr. *To p. one's punches* [PUNCH *sb.*²]: to use less than the force of which one is capable, hold oneself in.

Pull-.

1. p.-in, an entry, recess, etc., where a vehicle may pull in; **p.-out,** a folded leaf or plate in a book that can be pulled out for reference; **p.-up,** a house of call, where travellers may pull up.

Pulp, *sb.* **4.** orig. *U.S.* Used, freq. *attrib.*, to designate a book or magazine made from poor-quality paper and containing chiefly sensational stories, articles, etc. 1931.

Pulsar (pɒ·lsāɹ). 1968. [f. *pulsating star*, after *quasar.*] *Astr.* A cosmic source of radio signals that pulsate with great regularity at intervals of the order of one second or less; now thought to be a rapidly rotating neutron star.

Pump, *sb.*¹

Comb.: **p.-priming,** the stimulation of commerce or economy by means of investment; also *attrib.* or as *ppl. adj.*

Punch, *sb.*²

Comb.: **p.-drunk** *a.*, stupefied through being severely or repeatedly punched; (*gen*). dazed, groggy; **p.-line,** the final line in a joke, speech, etc., when the point is made forcefully; **p.-up,** a fist-fight, brawl.

Punchy (pɒ·ntʃi), *a.*² 1930. [f. PUNCH *sb.*² + -Y¹.] **1.** Full of punch or vigour. **2.** *colloq.* (orig. *U.S.*). Punch-drunk 1937.

Punk². 1. b. *slang* (orig. *U.S.*). Anything worthless; rubbish, nonsense. Also as *adj.* 1896. **c.** *slang* (orig. *U.S.*). An insignificant, mean, or unpleasant person (cf. PUNK¹); *spec.* a homosexual 1917.

Puppy, *sb.*

Comb.: **p. fat,** temporary fatness in children and adolescents.

Purée. Also, the thick paste produced when cooked fruit, vegetables, etc., are sieved.

Purge, *v.* **3.** *spec.* (in more recent use) To dismiss or expel from a party or community as being suspected of disloyalty or deviation. Similarly *sb.*, an act of purging.

Purple, *a.* and *sb.*

Comb.: **p. heart,** (*a*) (with capital initials) a medal awarded to U.S. servicemen wounded in action; (*b*) a tablet of the drug Drinamyl, so called from its colour and shape.

Push, *sb.* **1. d.** Slang phr. *To give (get) the p.*, to dismiss (be dismissed) 1899.

Push, *v.* **II. 6. c.** To sell (drugs) illegally. Also *intr.* 1938. **8.** *To be pushing* (a specified age): to be nearly (that age) 1953.

Push-.

p.-button war, a war carried on by means of guided missiles whose flight is controlled by pushing a button; **p.-over** orig. *U.S. slang*, a pugilist who is easily pushed over; *fig.* a thing easily overcome.

Pusher. 2. *slang* (orig. *U.S.*). An illegal seller of drugs 1948.

Pushy (pu·ʃi), *a. colloq.* (orig. *U.S.*). 1936. [f. PUSH *sb.*¹ or *v.* + -Y¹.] Self-assertive, esp. in an unpleasant way.

Put, *v.*¹ **IV. P. on. 1.** To deceive, play a joke on (someone).

Put-on (pu·tǫn), *sb. colloq.* 1937. [f. prec.] A deception, pretence, hoax.

‖**Putsch** (putʃ). 1920. [Swiss G., 'thrust, blow'.] A revolutionary attempt.

Pyknic (pi·kniķ), *a.* Also **pycnic.** 1925. [f. Gr. πυκνός thick + -IC.] Designating or pertaining to a type of physique characterized by short limbs and a rounded face and body.

Q.

II. 2. *Mil.* as *adj.* = Pertaining to the duties of a quarter-master, as *Q. side, Q. work.*

Quadriplegia (kwǫdriplī·dʒ¹ă). 1940. [mod. L., f. QUADRI- + Gr. πληγή blow, stroke + -IA¹.] *Path.* Paralysis of both arms and both legs.

Quadriplegic (kwǫdriplī·dʒik), *sb.* and *a.* 1959. [f. prec. + -IC.] **A.** *sb.* A q. person. **B.** *adj.* Affected with quadriplegia 1962.

Quark (kwāɹk). 1964. [Named by M. Gell-Mann (*Physics Lett.* VIII. 214) in allusion to 'three *quarks* for Muster Mark' (Joyce

Finnegans Wake II. iv).] *Physics.* Any of the three hypothetical particles conceived of as making up in different combinations many of the known 'elementary' (sub-atomic) particles and carrying a fractional electric charge.

Quarter, *sb.*
Comb.: **q.-light,** a side-window in the body of a closed carriage or motor vehicle.

Quartile. B. *sb.* **2.** *Statistics.* Any of the three values of a variable that divide a classification based on its value into four groups of equal size; any of the groups so produced 1901.

Quasar (kwē¹·sāɹ, -zāɹ). 1964. [f. *quasi-stellar.*] *Astr.* Any of numerous celestial objects that give a star-like image on a photograph and have a spectrum which is unusually bright towards the ultra-violet and shows a large red shift, usu. taken to indicate great remoteness and immense power.
Many quasars are from 50 to 100 times brighter than entire galaxies 1971.

Quechua, Quichua (ke·tʃwă, ki·tʃwă). Also **Kechua, K(h)etschua, Kichua.** 1840. [Sp. forms (*Que-*, *Qui-*) based on a native name.] (An Indian of) a tribe of this name inhabiting areas of Peru; also, their language, Incan. Hence **Que·chuan, Qui·chuan** *a.* and *sb.*

Queen, *sb.* **9.** *slang.* A male homosexual 1929. So **Quee·nie.**

Queensberry (kwī·nzbĕri). 1895. Name of the eighth Marquis of *Queensberry,* under whose supervision a code of laws for boxing (*Q. Rules*) was drawn up in 1867, which governs all boxing contests in Great Britain. Also *transf.*

Queer, *a.*¹ used as *sb. slang.* A homosexual 1935.

Question, *sb.*
Comb.: **q.-master,** the chairman of a radio quiz. Also *transf.*

Quiche (kīʃ). 1960. [Fr.] An uncovered pastry case containing a sweet or savoury filling.
A q. is a flat open tart 1960.

Quick, *a.* **III. 7. b.** *A q. one*: a q. drink 1945.
The studied taste that could refuse The golf-house quick one and the rector's tea AUDEN.
Comb.: **q. lunch,** a lunch designed to be served and eaten quickly; **q. trick** *Bridge,* a card that should take a trick in the first or second round of the suit; an ace or king; the trick so taken.

Quick-free·ze, *v.* 1930. [f. QUICK *adv.* + FREEZE *v.*] *trans.* To freeze (food) by a quick process that preserves the cell-structure and flavour. Hence **Quick-fro·zen** *ppl. a.*

Quickie (kwi·ki). 1927. [f. QUICK *a.* + -IE, -Y⁶.] A thing hastily done, made up, or performed, esp. a film so produced.
The primary objective of the Board of Trade was the complete extirpation of the 'quota quickie' 1936.

Quisling (kwi·zliŋ). 1940. Surname of Major Vidkun *Quisling* (1887–1945), a Norwegian who collaborated with the Germans when they invaded Norway in 1940, used allusively for: a collaborationist, traitor to one's country. Hence **Qui·slingite** [-ITE¹]. **Quisle** (kwi·z'l) *v. joc.*, to play the q.

Quiz, *sb.*² **b.** A form of entertainment in which a series of questions is put to a team, e.g. *Round-Britain q., Transatlantic q.* 1938.

Quote, *sb.* **2. b.** Also used in dictation, etc., as a quasi-vb. to introduce quoted words. Cf. *UNQUOTE.
Don't go around saying Quote I don't mind being a grampa but I hate being married to a gramma Unquote OGDEN NASH.

R.
II. 2. a. R.A.C., Royal Armoured Corps, Royal Automobile Club; R.A.D.A., Royal Academy of Dramatic Art; R. & B., rhythm-and-blues; R. & D., research and development; R.D.C., Rural District Council; Rh, Rhesus; RNA., ribonucleic acid; r.p.m., revolutions per minute; R.T., radio telegraphy, telephony.

Rabbit, *sb.*
Comb.: **r.-punch,** a blow on the nape of the neck.

Rabble, *sb.*¹
Comb.: **r.-rouser,** one who stirs up the people to agitate for social or political change.

Race, *sb.*²
Comb.: **r. relations,** the relations between different races inhabiting one country; **r.-riot,** an outbreak of violence and disorder resulting from racial antagonism.

Racemate. b. A racemic mixture 1936.

Racemic, *a.* **b.** Composed of the dextro- and lævorotatory isomers of a compound in equal molecular proportions, and therefore optically inactive 1897.

Racialism (rē¹·ʃ¹ăliz'm). 1907. [f. RACIAL *a.* + -ISM.] Belief in the superiority of a particular race; antagonism between different races of men. Hence **Ra·cialist** *a.* and *sb.*

Racism (rē¹·siz'm). 1936. [f. RACE *sb.*² + -ISM; cf. Fr. *racisme.*] The theory that distinctive human characteristics, abilities, etc., are determined by race; also, = *RACIALISM. Hence **Ra·cist** *a.* and *sb.*

Rad² (ræd). 1955. [f. RAD(IATION.] The unit of absorbed dose of ionizing radiation, corresponding to 0.01 joule per kilogramme of absorbing material (100 ergs per gramme).

Radar (rē¹·dāɹ). orig. *U.S.* 1942. [f. *radio detection and ranging.*] A system for detecting the presence of an object or ascertaining its position or motion by transmitting a beam of short radio waves and detecting or measuring their return after being reflected; (an) apparatus used for this. Freq. *attrib.*
'R.', the device for detecting enemy aircraft and ships 1943. [He] complained..that police r. speed traps were 'un-British' when he was fined.. for speeding 1962.

Radial, *a.* and *sb.* **A.** *adj.* **2. radial (-ply)** *a.*, denoting a tyre in which the layers of fabric are laid in a straight line without crossing and in which the tread is strengthened with layers around the circumference; also *ellipt.* as *sb.*

Radiation. 1. b. More generally (usu. *sing.*), any form of energy transmitted as waves or by particles.
Comb.: **r. sickness,** illness caused by exposure to ionizing radiation.

Radio, *sb.*
Comb.: **r. astronomy,** a branch of astronomy in which celestial objects are studied by means of the r. waves they emit; so *r. astronomer*; also *r.-astrono·mical* adj.; **r. car,** a car equipped for r. communication; **r. star** *Astr.*, any discrete source of r. waves beyond the solar system (rarely a star); **r. telescope** *Astr.*, an apparatus for detecting and recording radio waves from a small area of the sky, consisting essentially of a large sensitive aerial together with a receiver and recording equipment.

Radio-. 2. Ra:dio-ca·rbon, radioactive carbon; *esp.* the isotope carbon 14, which is present in living matter and decays at a fixed rate following death or lignification, and is measured by archæologists to determine the date of ancient organic material. **Radio-i·sotope,** a radioactive isotope; similarly *radio-cobalt, -element,* etc. **Radiothe·rapy,** the treatment of disease by X-rays or radioactive substances; so **Radiothe·rapist;** also **Ra:diotherapeu·tic** *a.*, **-ics. 3.** [RADIO *sb.* used as prefix.] Relating to or involving radio or radio waves. **Ra·dio-frequency,** a frequency in the range used for telecommunication, greater than the highest audio-frequency and less than that of the shortest infra-red waves (i.e. between about 10^4 Hz and 10^{11} Hz); freq. *attrib.* **Ra:dioloca·tion,** the determination of the position or course of ships, aircraft, etc., by radar. **Radiopho·nic** *a.*, pertaining to or designating synthetic sound produced by electronic means and the use of tape recorders, usually for use in broadcasting in conjunction with conventional material. **Ra·diosonde** (-sǫnd) [– G. *radiosonde* (P. Moltchanoff, 1931), f. *sonde* probe, sounding-line], a small instrument that may be sent aloft (e.g. by means of a balloon) to transmit radio signals indicating the pressure, temperature, and humidity at different heights.

Radiogenic (rē¹diodʒe·nik), *a.* 1931. [f. RADIO- + *-GENIC.] **1.** [*RADIO- 3, after *photogenic.*] Well suited for broadcasting by radio; providing an attractive subject for a radio broadcast. **2.** [RADIO- 2, *-GENIC b.] Produced by or resulting from radioactive decay 1940. Hence **Radioge·nically** *adv.*, by means of radioactive decay.

Radiogram² (rē¹·diogræm). 1932. [f. *RADIO- 3 + GRAM(OPHONE.] A radio and (electric) gramophone combined.

Rag, *sb.*¹
Comb.: **r. book,** a children's book made of untearable cloth; **r. trade** *colloq.*, the business of designing, making, and selling clothes.

Rag, *sb.*³ Now often a parade, carnival, etc., held by students to raise money for charity.

Raga (rā·gă). 1788. [Skr.] In Hindu music, a pattern of notes which provides the basis for improvisation.

Rail, *sb.*²
Comb.: **r.-head, railhead,** (*a*) the farthest point reached by a railway; (*b*) a point on a railway from which goods are transported by road.

Rain, *sb.*
Comb.: **r.-check** (or **-cheque**) orig. *U.S.*, a ticket given to spectators at a baseball match providing for admission at a later date if the game is interrupted by rain; also *transf.* and *fig.*; **r. stone,** a pebble used in rain-making ceremonies by primitive peoples.

Rain forest. 1903. [tr. G. *regenwald* (A. F. W. Schimper, 1898).] A luxuriant type of forest characteristic of wet, tropical regions.

Rake-off (rē¹·kǫf). *colloq.* (orig. *U.S.*). 1891. [f. phr. *to rake off* (RAKE *v.*¹).] A share of profits, commission.

Rally, *sb.*¹ **5.** A competitive event over public roads for motorists or motor-cyclists 1955.

Raman (rā·măn, rămā·n). 1931. Name of Sir C. V. *Raman* (1888–1970), Indian physicist, used *attrib.*
R. effect, the change in the frequency of some of the light scattered by the molecules of a medium by an amount characteristic of the scattering molecules; **R. spectrum,** the set of new spectral lines produced in light by the R. effect; so *R. lines, spectroscopy,* etc.

Ram-jet (ræ·mˌdʒet). 1945. [f. RAM *sb.*¹ or *v.* + JET *sb.*³] *Aeronaut.* A type of jet engine without moving parts, the air being drawn in and compressed solely as a result of its motion.

Rand, *sb.* **4.** (rănt). [S. Afr. Du. *rand* edge, rim.] **a.** In South Africa, the ridge of high ground each side of a river 1891. **b.** The unit of South African currency, divided into 100 cents 1961.

Random. B. *adj.* **1. b.** *Statistics.* Governed by or involving equal chances for each of the actual or hypothetical items in a population; produced or obtained by a r. process (and therefore completely unpredictable in detail) 1898.

Randomize (ræ·ndəməiz), *v.* 1936. [f. prec. + -IZE.] *trans.* To arrange (items) or determine (a sequence) according to a random process; to employ random selection or sampling in (an experiment, procedure, etc.). Hence **Ra·ndomized** *ppl. a.* Also **Ra:ndomiza·tion.**

Randy (ræ·ndi), *a.* (and *sb.*) 1698. [perh. f. RAND *v.*] **1.** *Sc.* Rude, aggressive; noisy and coarse. **2.** *dial.* Boisterous, disorderly, unmanageable 1787. **b.** orig. *dial.* Lustful, lewd; eager for sexual intercourse or gratification 1847. Hence as *sb.*, a r. person.

Rangatira (ræŋgăti·ră). *N.Z.* 1820. [Maori.] A Maori chief (male or female); a noble person.

Range, *sb.*¹
Comb.: **r.-finder,** an instrument for determining the distance of an object to be photographed, fired at, etc.

Rap, *sb.*¹ **2.** *slang* (orig. *U.S.*). A rebuke; blame; an accusation or punishment for a crime; esp. in phr. *to take the r.*, to take the blame or punishment, to suffer the consequences 1777.

Rap, *v.*¹ **3. c.** *intr.* To talk 1968. *slang* (orig. *U.S.*). Hence as *sb.*, a conversation.

Rara avis. Also of things: a very unusual or exceptional occurrence.
A perfect day with us is something of a *r. a.* 1884.

Rare, *a.*¹ **5. r. earth** *Chem.*, an oxide of an element of the **lanthanide series*; also (*loosely*) = *LANTHANIDE.

Raster (ræ·stəɹ). 1934. [– G. *raster* screen, f. L. *rastrum* rake (f. *radere* scrape).] A pattern of scanning lines making up (or corresponding to) a picture on a cathode-ray tube.

Rat, *sb.*
Comb.: **ratbag** *slang* (chiefly *Austral.* and *N.Z.*), an eccentric person; an unpleasant person, troublemaker; **r. race** orig. *U.S.*, a ruthless competitive struggle.

Ratatouille (ratatūiʸ). 1950. [Fr. dial.] A Provençal ragout of vegetables, usually including sweet peppers, onions, tomatoes, and aubergines.

Rating, *vbl. sb.*[1] **3.** orig. *U.S.* The popularity of a radio or television broadcast, assessed by the estimated size of its audience. Also *transf.* 1940.

Rave, *sb.*[2] **2.** *colloq.* An enthusiastic review 1936. Also *attrib.*, as *r. review.* **b.** *slang.* A party, esp. one that is lively and exciting; also *transf.* and *fig.* Also *r.-up.* 1960.

Ravioli (rævi*ō*ᵘ·li). 1841. [It.] A dish consisting of small pasta cases each containing a savoury filling of forcemeat, cheese, or spinach.

Razzmatazz (ræ:zmătæ·z). *colloq.* (orig. *U.S.*). Also **razamatazz, razmataz, razzamataz(z), razz-ma-tazz.** 1900. [prob. alteration of RAZZLE-DAZZLE.] = RAZZLE-DAZZLE; also, something out of date, sentimental, or insincere, *spec.* old-fashioned jazz; humbug, nonsense. Also *attrib.* or as *adj.*

Reaction. 3. b. In pop. use, the mental or moral response to a statement, event, etc.

Reactor. 3. A vessel or apparatus, esp. one in an industrial plant, in which substances are made to react 1943. **b.** More fully *atomic* or *nuclear r.*: an apparatus or structure in which fissile material can be made to undergo a controlled, self-sustaining nuclear reaction 1946.

Read, *v.* **I. 4. f.** *Computers.* To copy or extract data stored on (magnetic tape, a punched card, etc.); (also *r. out*) to copy, extract, or transfer (data) 1953.
The length of time required to r. information from or store information into one of the..12-bit memory locations 1964. The card or tape is then 'read' 1964. On each orbit the storage system reads out the information to a ground station 1968. So **Rea·d-out** *sb.*, the process of reading data; an apparatus for doing this; a display of data.

Readership. 2. orig. *U.S.* Readers collectively, *esp.* the number of regular readers of a newspaper or periodical; circulation 1923.

‖**Realpolitik** (reā:lpoli*t*ī·k). 1914. [G.] Practical politics; politics concerned with realities, material needs, etc., rather than with morals or ideals.

Rear, *sb.* (and *a.*[1])
Comb.: **r.-lamp, -light,** a (usu. red) lamp or light at the rear of a vehicle; **r.-view mirror,** a mirror enabling the driver of a vehicle to see traffic, etc., behind him.

Recall, *sb.* **3.** The act of remembering; the revival of past experiences 1934. Esp. in phr. *total r.*, the ability to recall the past in great detail.

Recap (rī·kæp). 1952. Shortening (orig. *U.S.*) of RECAPITULATE, -ATION.

Recce (re·*k*i). 1942. Slang (orig. *Mil.*) shortening of RECONNAISSANCE, RECONNOITRE.

Receiving, *vbl. sb.* and *ppl. a.* Colloq. phr. *To be at* (or *on*) *the r. end*: to be the recipient *of* (something, esp. something unpleasant); to bear the brunt.

Reception.
Comb.: **r. room,** a room available or suitable for the reception of guests.

Recession. 2. b. *spec.* A temporary decline or setback in economic activity or prosperity 1930.

Recondi·tion, *v.* 1920. [RE- 5 a.] *trans.* To restore to a proper, habitable, or usable condition. Hence **Recondi·tioned** *ppl. a.* **Recondi·tioning** *vbl. sb.*

Record, *sb.* **II. 2.**
e. Phr. *Off the r.*: unofficial(ly), secret(ly). *For the r.*: official(ly), formal(ly), for the sake of having the facts recorded or known.
IV. r. player, a device for playing gramophone records. Hence **Reco·rding** *vbl. sb.*, the action or result of the vb. RECORD; *spec.* (the making of) a gramophone record.

Recycle (rīsəi·k'l), *v.* 1934. [RE- 5 a.] *trans.* To return to a previous stage of a cyclic process; *esp.* to convert (waste) into material that can be used again.
Systems which r. urine and waste water into drinkable water 1960. Hence **Recy·cling** *vbl. sb.*

Red, *a.* and *sb.* **A. II.**
Comb.: **c. r. brick,** a building-brick that is r. in colour; used *attrib.* to denote a building made of such bricks, esp. a modern university (in contrast with the stone-built ancient universities); also *collect.* (freq. as one word, with capital initial), such universities in general; **r. carpet,** (*a*) a species of moth, *Xanthorhoë munitata*; (*b*) a red-coloured carpet, esp. a long narrow one that is placed outside an entrance for an important visitor to walk upon; freq. *fig.* and *attrib.* to denote ceremonious and hospitable treatment accorded to a visitor, guest, etc.; **r. shift** *Astr.*, a displacement of spectral lines in the light from some celestial objects towards the red end of the spectrum, usu. interpreted as due to movement away from the observer; so **r.-shift** *v. trans.*

Redeploy (rī:dėploi·), *v.* 1945. [RE- 5 a.] *trans.* To send (troops, workers, etc.) to a new place or task. Also *absol.* or *intr.* So **Redeplo·yment.**

Rediffusion (rī:difiū·ʒən). 1927. [f. RE- + DIFFUSION.] The broadcasting of a radio or television programme by a person, company, etc., which did not make the programme; *spec.* the transmission of such programmes on an independent line network.

Redox (re·-, rī·dǫks). 1930. [f. RED(UCTION + OX(IDATION.] *Chem.* Oxidation-reduction: usu. *attrib.*, indicating (some connection with) a reversible oxidation and reduction, or a simultaneous oxidation and reduction.

Redundant, *a.* **1. c.** Of an employee or his post: (liable to be dispensed with because) considered no longer necessary 1928.

Reefer[2] (rī·fəɹ). 1931. [f. REEF *sb.*[1] (in the generalized sense of 'something rolled') + -ER[1].] A marijuana cigarette.

Ref (ref), colloq. abbrev. of (*a*) REFERENCE *sb.* 1901; (*b*) REFEREE *sb.* 1937.

Referent. A. *sb.* **3.** That which is symbolized by a linguistic sign or word 1923.

Refresher.
attrib.: **r. course,** also, a course serving as a review of material previously studied or to instruct a person in new developments, techniques, etc.

Refuel (rī:fiū·ėl), *v.* 1930. [RE- 5 a.] *trans.* To refill the tank of (an oil- or petrol-consuming machine).

Reggae (re·gēⁱ). 1969. [West Indian.] A kind of music of West Indian origin with a strongly accented off-beat.

Rehabilitate, *v.* **2. b.** To restore (a disabled person, a criminal, etc.) to some degree of independence by appropriate training 1941.

Reich. Also, a period or stage of the German Empire: *the First R.*, the Holy Roman Empire, A.D. 962–1806; *the Second R.*, 1871–1918; *the Third R.*, the Nazi régime, 1933–1945.

Rejection.
Comb.: **r. slip,** a formal notice sent by an editor or publisher with a rejected MS.

Rejig (rīdʒi·g), *v.* 1948. [f. RE- 5 c + JIG *sb.* 6.] *trans.* To re-equip or re-arrange (a factory, etc.). Also *fig.*

Relegation. 1. c. The transference of a football team to a lower division of the Football League 1928. So **Relegate** *v. trans.*

Relief[1].
Comb.: **r. road** = BY-PASS 2.

Remote, *a.* **3. a. r. control,** control of the operation of a device, apparatus, etc., from a distance, as by a switchboard, radio signals, etc.

Re:orienta·tion. 1920. [RE- 5 a.] A change of outlook; re-adjustment.

Rep[4] (rep). 1909. Colloq. abbrev. of REPRESENTATIVE *sb.*

Rep[5] (rep). 1925. Colloq. abbrev. of REPERTORY (occas. of REPERTOIRE). Also, a repertory theatre.

Repeat, *sb.* **4.** *Broadcasting.* A repetition of a programme which has already been broadcast 1937.

Repeat, *v.* **I. 1. b.** Used in radio-communication, dictation, etc., to emphasize an important part of the message; also *transf.* 1943.
'The Horse's Mouth' is not, repeat not, about the race track 1959.

Repellent. B. *sb.* **3.** A preparation that repels insects or the like 1926.

Repertory. 3. Also, theatrical presentation in which different plays are performed by one company; a company presenting such plays; r. theatres collectively.

‖**Répétiteur** (repe*t*i*t*ǫ̈r). Also **repetiteur.** 1941. [Fr.] A tutor or coach of musicians, esp. opera-singers.

Reportage. Also, the reporting of events for the press, esp. with reference to style.

Reportedly (rǐpō°·ɹtėdli), *adv.* 1901. [f. pa. pple. of REPORT *v.* + -LY[2].] According to report.

Reprography (rǐprǫ·grăfi). 1961. [f. REPRO(DUCE *v.* + -GRAPHY.] The production of copies of documents, by photographic or other means; the study of methods used in such production. Hence **Reprogra·phic** *a.*

Research, *v.* **a.** Delete 'Now *rare* or *Obs.*'

Reserpine (rǐsə̄·ɹpīn). 1952. [– G. *reserpin* (J. M. Müller et al., 1952), f. R*auwolfia serpentina* (with inserted *e*) + -INE[5].] *Pharm.* An alkaloid obtained from the roots of some shrubs and trees of the genus *Rauwolfia*, used in the treatment of hypertension and as a tranquillizer in cases of mental or emotional disorder.

Reservation. I. 3. c. orig. *U.S.* The engaging of a seat, room, place, etc., in advance; a seat, etc., so reserved 1906.

Reserve, *sb.* **I. 1. b.** *spec.* (In reference to joint stock companies) that part of the profit which is not distributed to shareholders, but is added to the capital of the company. (*Hidden r.*: part of the profit concealed in the balance sheet by the device of assessing the value of assets below its true level). (In reference to banks) that part of the assets held in the form of cash, i.e. gold, coin, notes, or a deposit with the central bank. (In reference to central banks) that part of the assets held in the form of gold or foreign exchange.

Reshuffle (rī∫ɒ·f'l). 1922. [RE- 4.] A re-arrangement; *spec.* of posts within a government or cabinet. Hence as *v. trans.* Also **Reshu·ffling** *vbl. sb.*

Resin, *sb.* **3.** Usu. with qualifying adj. or sb., esp. *synthetic*: any of a large and varied class of synthetic organic compounds (solid or liquid) that are made by polymerization, are thermosetting or thermoplastic, and are used esp. as plastics or their chief ingredients; also, a substance made by chemically modifying a natural resin or polymer 1923.

Resistance. 1. b. [After Fr. *Résistance.*] An underground organization in a conquered country, engaged in opposing the occupying forces; *spec.* the French organization of this type in the war of 1939–45.

Resistor (rǐzi·stəɹ). 1930. [f. RESIST *v.* + -OR 2.] *Electr.* = RESISTANCE 4 b.

Respirator. 3. *Med.* An apparatus for maintaining artificial respiration 1949.

Restrictive, *a.* and *sb.* **A.** *adj.*
3. r. practice, an arrangement in industry and trade which restricts or controls competition between firms; an arrangement by a group of workers to control output or restrict the entry of new workers.

Restru·cture, *v.* 1951. [f. RE- 5 c + STRUCTURE *sb.*] *trans.* To give a new structure to; to rebuild, re-arrange. So **Restru·cturing** *vbl. sb.*

Retarded (rǐtā·ɹdėd), *ppl. a.* 1810. [pa. pple. of RETARD *v.*] That is or has been kept back or delayed; now often with respect to education or mental development.

Rethink (rī·þiŋk), *v.* *a* 1700. [RE- 5 a.] *trans.* To consider afresh, esp. with a view to making changes. Also *intr.* Hence as *sb.*, a re-assessment. Hence **Rethi·nking** *vbl. sb.*

Retoo·l, *v.* 1940. [f. RE- 5 c + TOOL *sb.*] *trans.* To equip (a factory, etc.) with new tools. Hence **Retoo·ling** *vbl. sb.*

Re·tread, *v.* 1908. [f. RE- 5 c + TREAD *sb.*] *trans.* To furnish (a tyre) with a fresh tread. Hence as *sb.*, a tyre renovated thus. Also **Retrea·ding** *vbl. sb.*

Retro-. a. Re·tro-rocket, a rocket on a satellite, spacecraft, etc., that points in the forward direction, so that it slows the craft down when fired.

Retsina, rezina (retsī·nă). 1948. [mod. Gr.] A resin-flavoured Greek wine.

Reva·mp, *v.* 1859. [RE- 5 a.] *trans.* To vamp or patch up again; to renovate, revise, improve.

Reverse, *v.* **8. c.**

Phr. *To reverse the charge(s)*: to charge the recipient with the cost of a telephone-call 1927.

Revisionism (rĭvi·ʒəniz'm). 1921. [f. REVISION + -ISM.] A scheme or policy of revision; *spec.* the revision or modification of Marxist-Leninist doctrine or policies.

Revisionist. 1. b. *spec.* An adherent of revisionism (see prec.). Also as *adj.* 1935.

Rhenium (rī·niŏm). 1925. [mod.L. (Berg and Tacke, 1925), f. L. *Rhenus* Rhine (river) + -IUM.] *Chem.* A very dense, refractory, metallic element of the manganese group, obtained from molybdenite ores. Atomic number 75; symbol Re.

Rheology (rĭ,ǫ·lŏdʒi). 1931. [f. RHEO- + -LOGY.] The science dealing with the flow and deformation of matter. Hence **Rheolo·gical** *a.* **Rheo·logist.**

Rhesus. 2. *Med.* [Named from its having been discovered in the R. monkey.] *R. factor* (abbrev. *Rh*): a set of related antigens, naturally occurring antibodies to which are rare, and which are present in the blood of many mammals; they constitute one of the two principal systems of blood groups, the other being the ABO system; so *Rh antigen, system,* etc. *Rh-positive* (*negative*) adjs.: having (not having) the most important of these antigens 1941.

Comb.: **R. baby**, an infant with a hæmolytic disorder as a result of incompatibility between its own blood (Rh-positive) and that of its mother (Rh-negative).

In Britain, five persons out of six are classed as R. positive 1961.

Rhode Island (rōᵘ:d əi·lănd). 1902. The name of a North American state, used *attrib.* to designate a variety of fowl first introduced there (in full *Rhode Island Red*).

Rhubarb. 2. c. The word 'rhubarb' as repeated by actors to give the impression of murmurous hubbub or conversation; hence allusively 1934.

Rhumba, var. *RUMBA.

Rhyme, *v.* Hence **Rhy·ming** *ppl. a.* and *vbl. sb.* spec. **rhyming dictionary**, a dictionary in which words are arranged according to the correspondence of their terminal sounds; **rhyming slang**, slang in which a word is replaced by a word or phrase that rhymes with it.

Rhythm. II.

Comb.: **r.-and-blues**, a type of popular music (orig. among American Negroes) characterized by the use of blues themes and a strong r.; **r. method**, a method of birth control depending upon continence during the period of female ovulation; **r. section**, the part of a dance- or jazz-band whose main function is to supply the r., usu. consisting of piano, double-bass, and drums, sometimes with a guitar or other instruments.

Ria (rī·ă). 1898. [– Sp. *ria* estuary.] *Physical Geogr.* A long narrow inlet that becomes deeper and broader towards the sea, formed by the partial submergence of a river valley.

Rib, *v.* **3.** *colloq.* To make fun of, tease; to deceive, trick 1930.

Ribbon, *sb.*

Comb.: **5. r. microphone**, a microphone in which the electrical signal is generated by a thin strip of metal mounted between the poles of a magnet.

Riboflavin (rəiboflē¹·vin). Also **-ine.** 1935. [f. *RIBO(SE + *flavin(e* (f. L. *flavus* yellow + -IN¹, -INE⁵).] *Biochem.* Vitamin B_2, a yellow pigment present in many foods (esp. milk, liver, and green vegetables), deficiency of which leads to poor growth and deterioration of the skin.

Ribonucleic (rəiboniū·klī,ik, -niuklī·ik, -ē·ik), *a.* 1931. [f. *RIBO(SE + *NUCLEIC *a.*] *Ribonucleic acid* (Biochem.): a generic term for any of the nucleic acids yielding ribose on hydrolysis; they occur chiefly in the cytoplasm of cells, where they direct the synthesis of proteins, and in some viruses, where they also store the genetic information. Abbrev. RNA.

Ribose (rəi·bōᵘz). 1892. [– G. *ribose*, f. *ribonsäure* (both E. Fischer, 1891) + -OSE²; *ribon* formed arbitrarily by rearrangement of some of the letters of *arabinose*, name of the related sugar from which Fischer prepared ribose.] *Chem.* One of the four sugars with the formula $CHO(CHOH)_3CH_2OH$, the D- (lævorotatory) isomer of which is a constituent of many nucleosides and several vitamins and enzymes.

Ribosome (rəi·bŏsōᵘm). 1958. [f. *RIBO-(NUCLEIC + Gr. σῶμα body.] *Cytology.* One of the minute particles of RNA and protein in the cytoplasm of a cell where amino-acids are linked together to form protein molecules. Hence **Riboso·mal** *a.*

Rich. A. *adj.* **8. c.** Of the mixture in an internal-combustion engine: containing more than the normal proportion of fuel 1917.

Rickettsia (rike·tsiă). 1922. [mod.L. (H. da Rocha-Lima, 1916), f. name of H. T. *Ricketts* (1871–1910), Amer. pathologist, + -IA¹.] A parasitic micro-organism of the genus so called, causing typhus and other fevers in man and certain other mammals. Hence **Ricke·ttsial** *a.*

The rickettsiæ are primarily intestinal parasites of arthropod blood-sucking insects..but some half-dozen species have become adapted to invade the animal body and cause disease 1951.

Ride, *sb.* **1. a.** Slang phr. (orig. *U.S.*) *to take* (a person) *for a ride*: (*a*) to take (a person) away in a motor vehicle in order to murder him; (*b*) to deceive, hoax.

Ride, *v.* **II. 6.** Colloq. phr. (orig. *U.S.*) *to let* (something) *ride*: to leave alone; to allow to take its natural course.

Riesling (rī·sliŋ). 1836. [G.] The name of the variety of grape used for making white wine in Alsace, Austria, Germany, Hungary, and Yugoslavia; the wine itself.

Riff (rif), *sb.* 1935. [Origin unkn.] *Mus.* A short repeated phrase, esp. in jazz and similar music. Hence as *v. intr.*, to play such phrases. Also **Ri·ffing** *vbl. sb.*

Riffle, *v.* **3. b.** To flick through (the pages of a book) 1922.

Rift, *sb.*¹

Comb.: **r.-valley**, a valley with steep parallel walls, formed by the subsidence of a part of the earth's crust; a depression in the earth's surface bounded by faults.

Right, *sb.*¹ **IV. 1. c.** Now in general use for parties or people of conservative principles.

Right, *adv.* **II. 3. c.** Colloq. phr. (orig. *U.S.*) *Right on*: used as an exclamation of approval 1970.

Shouting 'Right on!'—the rallying cry of black militants 1972.

Rightist (rəi·tist), *sb.* and *a.* 1937. [f. RIGHT *sb.*¹ IV. 1 c + -IST.] **A.** *sb.* An adherent of the political 'right'. **B.** *adj.* Of or pertaining to the political 'right' 1938.

Ring, *sb.*¹ **II.** Colloq. phr. *To make* or *run rings round*: to outdo in achievement, production, or performance; be greatly superior to.

Comb.: **r. circuit**, a circuit in a building on the principle of the r. main, enabling any number of power points to be served by a single fuse in the supply to the r.; **r. main**, an electric main in which the cable forms a closed r., so that each consumer has an alternative path for supply in the event of a failure.

Ring, *sb.*² **3. b.** *colloq.* A telephone-call 1930.

Ring, *v.*² **II. 5. b.** *spec.* To call (a person) on the telephone; also *absol.*

Rinse, *sb.* **2.** A tinting solution for the hair, esp. *blue r.* 1941.

Rip, *sb.*²

Comb.: **r.-cord**, a cord that is pulled to release a parachute.

Rip, *v.* **I. 5.** Slang phr. (orig. U.S.) *To r. off*: to defraud or exploit (someone); to steal (something) 1970. So **r.-off**, a swindle; exploitation.

Rip-roaring (ri·prōᵊ:riŋ), *a.* orig. *U.S. slang.* 1830. [f. RIP *sb.*², *v.* + pres. pple. of ROAR *v.*] Riotously vigorous, wildly noisy. So **Rip-roa·rious** *a.*

Risk, *sb.* **1.** Phr. *At r.*: exposed to a r.; in danger.

‖**Ritardando** (rĭtāɹdæ·ndo). 1811. [It.] *Mus.* A direction indicating a gradual reduction of speed. Cf. RALLENTANDO.

‖**Rite de passage** (rĭt də pasāʒ). 1934. [Fr.] *Social Anthrop.* The ritual observed at the entrance upon different phases in the life of an individual.

‖**Ritenuto** (rĭtenu·to, -ˈuto). 1828. [It.] *Mus.* A direction indicating an immediate reduction of speed.

Ritzy (ri·tsi), *a.* *colloq.* (orig. *U.S.*). 1923. [f. the name of César *Ritz* (1850–1918), owner of several luxurious hotels bearing his name.] High-class, 'posh', luxurious; ostentatiously smart.

River, *sb.*¹ **1. a.** Colloq. phr. (orig. *U.S.*) *To sell* (a person) *down the river*: (*a*) to sell into slavery, esp. into a worse form of slavery; (*b*) to defraud, swindle; to betray.

Riviera (riviēᵊ·ră, pop. riviᵊ·ră). 1852. [It., 'sea-shore'.] With *the*: The maritime region of the departments of Alpes Maritimes (France) and Liguria (Italy); *transf.* applied to regions having a similar climate and scenery, e.g. *The Cornish Riviera.*

Road, *sb.*

Comb.: **r.-block**, a barrier or obstruction on a r., set up by the army or police; also *fig.*; **r. fund**, a fund established by the Roads Act of 1920 to meet provisions for roads; **r.-holding**, the ability of a car to retain its stability; **r.-house**, a house beside a r. where refreshments, lodging, etc., are provided for motorists or other travellers.

Robe, *sb.* **1. a.** *spec.* A dressing-gown.

Rock, *sb.*¹ **1. c.** *slang* (orig. *U.S.*). A jewel, esp. a diamond. Freq. *pl.* 1908. **d.** *colloq.* (orig. *U.S.*). An ice-cube. Usu. *pl.*, esp. in phr. *on the rocks*: (of a drink) served with ice 1951.

Rock (rǫk), *sb.*³ 1823. [f. ROCK *v.*] **1.** The action of ROCK *v.* **2.** orig. *U.S.* A rocking or swinging type of music; *spec.* (in full *rock and roll* or *rock 'n' roll*), a type of popular dance-music characterized by a heavy beat and simple melodies, often with elements of the 'blues'; also, dancing suited to this music 1946.

Rocker. 5. A teenager of a type characterized by liking 'rock and roll' (see *ROCK *sb.*³ 2), riding a motor-cycle, and wearing a leather jacket; freq. contrasted with *MOD *sb.* 1963.

Rocket, *sb.*² **b.** Any elongated device or craft (as a flying bomb, a missile, a spacecraft) in which a r. engine is the means of propulsion 1920. **c.** More fully *r. engine, r. motor.* An engine operated on the principle of the pyrotechnic r., providing thrust by the same method as a jet engine but independently of the surrounding air 1931. So *r. propulsion, r.-propelled* adj. **2.** *slang.* A severe reprimand 1941.

Rocket, *v.* **2. c.** Of prices, etc.: to 'soar' to a great height 1934.

Rocketeer (rǫkĕtīᵊ·ɹ). 1935. [f. ROCKET *sb.*² + -EER.] One who experiments or works with rockets; a rocket expert.

Rocketry (rǫ·kĕtri). 1934. [f. ROCKET *sb.*² + -RY.] The science or employment of rockets or rocket propulsion.

Roger, *sb.* **3.** In signalling code used for the letter R; in radio-telephony used to mean 'your message has been received and understood'. Also *transf.* 1941.

Roger (rǫ·dʒəɹ), *v. slang.* Also **rodger.** 1711. ['From the name of Roger, frequently given to a bull' (Grose).] *trans.* and *intr.* To copulate (with).

Roll, *v.* **II. 11. d.** Of an aircraft: to turn on its longitudinal axis 1918.

Comb.: **roll-on**, (*a*) an elasticated corset that is put on by rolling it upwards; (*b*) a liquid preparation, such as a deodorant, that is applied from a bottle topped with a revolving ball or the like.

Roller, *sb.*¹ **I. 9.** A kind of hair-curler 1782. **10.** Usu. *paint-roller.* A cylindrical device for applying paint to a flat surface 1955.

Comb.: **r.-coaster** orig. *U.S.*, a switchback at a place of amusement; also *attrib.* and *fig.*

Rollmops (rōᵘ·lmǫps). Also **rollmop.** 1933. [G.] A rolled fillet of herring, flavoured with sliced onions, spices, etc., and pickled in brine.

‖**Romaji** (rōᵘ·madʒi). 1903. [Jap.] A Roman alphabet used for the transliteration of Japanese.

‖**Ronggeng** (rǫ·ŋgeŋ). 1817. [Malay.] Formerly, a dancing-girl in Malaysia; now, a form of popular dancing, often accompanied by singing. Also *attrib.*

‖**Ronin** (rōᵘ·nin). 1871. [Jap.] In feudal Japan, a lordless wandering samurai; an outlaw. Now, (*transf.*) a student who has failed a university (entrance) examination.
The well.., where the Rōnins washed the head of the foe on whom they had taken vengeance, still exists 1891. High school students who fail the university exam and are waiting to try again are called *ronin* 1970.

Röntgen. 2. The unit of exposure to ionizing radiation, equal to the quantity of radiation that gives rise to ions carrying a total charge of 2·58 coulombs per kilogramme of air (regardless of sign). Abbrev. r. 1934.
Large populations should not be exposed to a dosage exceeding 0.03 roentgens a week 1955.

Rope, *v.* **1. d.** *intr.* In phr. *r. down, up*, to climb down or up using a rope 1920.

Ropy, *a.* **3.** *colloq.* Also **ropey.** Of poor quality, inferior, bad 1942.

Rorschach (rǭ·ɹʃāx). 1934. The name of Hermann *Rorschach* (1884–1922), Swiss psychiatrist, used *attrib.* to designate a psychological test devised by him, in which a standard set of ink blots of different shapes and colours is presented one at a time to a subject with the request that he should describe what they suggest or resemble. Also *absol.*

‖**Rosé** (roze), *a.* and *sb.* 1897. [Fr., = 'pink'.] (Designating) a light pink wine.

Round, *sb.*¹ **I. 5. a.** *In the r.*: (*fig.*) with all the features or elements fully displayed; see also **theatre-in-the-round*.

Rouseabout (rau·zăbaut). 1746. [f. ROUSE *v.*] **1.** *dial.* A rough, bustling person. **2.** *Austral. and N.Z.* (rau·s-). An odd-job man on a sheep-station, farm, etc. 1861.

Rozzer (rǫ·zəɹ). *slang.* 1893. [Origin unkn.] A policeman.

Rubber, *sb.*¹
Comb.: **r.-stamp,** a r. device that is inked and pressed on a surface to reproduce an imprint; also *fig.*, one who or that which reproduces, endorses, or carries out something mechanically; hence as *v. trans.*, to approve (a policy, etc.) perfunctorily.

Rubberized (rɒ·bəraizd). *ppl. a.* 1918. [f. RUBBER *sb.* + -IZE + -ED¹.] Treated or coated with rubber.

Ruckus (rɒ·kəs). orig. *U.S.* Also **rucus.** 1907. [Cf. RUCTION and RUMPUS.] A ruction, rumpus.

Rudbeckia (rɒdbe·kiă). 1759. [mod.L. (Linnæus, 1735), f. the name of Olof *Rudbeck* (1660–1740), Swedish botanist; see -IA.] A perennial herb of the genus so called, native to North America, and bearing yellow composite flowers with dark centres.

Rugby.
Comb.: **Rugby League,** a type of rugby football played mainly by professionals in teams of thirteen, as distinct from **Rugby Union,** which is played only by amateurs, in teams of fifteen.

Rumba (rɒ·mbă). Also **rhumba.** 1923. [Amer. Sp.] A Cuban Negro dance; a ballroom dance imitative of this, or the music for it. Hence as *v. intr.*, to dance the r.

Rumble, *sb.* **4.** *U.S. slang.* A gang-fight, esp. a pre-arranged one 1958.

Run, *sb.* **III. 8. c.** *R.-of-the-mill*: an ordinary or average specimen or series of products; freq. *attrib.* or quasi-*adj.*, ordinary, average.

Runcible (rɒ·nsib'l), *a.* 1871. [Presumably fanciful alteration of ROUNCIVAL, which has been used in many senses of obscure origin and connection.] Used by Edward Lear as a nonsense word (*r. cat, r. hat, r. spoon*) and established in **r. spoon,** a kind of fork used for pickles, etc., curved like a spoon and having three broad prongs of which one has a sharp edge.

Run-down, *ppl. a.* **5.** Decayed, declined from prosperity 1930.

Runny (rɒ·ni), *a.* 1817. [f. RUN *v.* + -Y¹.] Tending to run or flow; excessively fluid.

Runway. 4. A prepared track on an airfield for aircraft to use in taking off and landing 1923.

Ruritania (rūᵊritēⁱ·niă). [Name of the scene of Anthony Hope's novels 'The Prisoner of Zenda' (1894) and 'Rupert of Hentzau' (1898); f. L. *rus, ruri* country + *-tania*, as in *Lusitania*.] An imaginary kingdom of Central Europe: used typically for a scene of court romance and intrigue in a modern setting, or for a petty state. Hence **Rurita·nian** *a.* and *sb.*
The somewhat silly Ruritanian gambols of our imagination G. B. SHAW.

Rush, *sb.*² **6.** *Cinemat. pl.* The first prints of film resulting from a period of shooting 1927. *colloq.* (orig. *U.S.*). **7.** Used *attrib.* or quasi-*adj.* to denote something done or produced with the least possible delay, as *r. edition, job, work* 1901.

Russian. B. *adj.* **1. b.** *R. roulette*, an act of bravado in which a revolver with one of its chambers loaded is held to the head and fired; also *fig.*

Rustle, *v.* **4. c.** *To r. up*: to forage around for; to find, provide, prepare. *colloq.* (orig. *U.S.*) *a* 1846.

‖**Ryokan** (ryōᵘ·kăn). 1969. [Jap.] A traditional Japanese inn or hostelry.

S.
Abbreviations: S.A., sex appeal; S.A.E., stamped addressed envelope; SALT, strategic arms limitation talks; S.C., special constable; S.C.M., Student Christian Movement; S.C.R., Senior Common (Combination) Room; S.F., science fiction; S.I., Fr. *Système International (d'Unités)*, 'International System (of Units)', a system of physical units (together with a set of prefixes indicating multiplication or division by a power of ten) based on the metre, kilogramme, second, ampere, kelvin, candela, and mole as independent basic units, with each of the derived units defined in terms of the basic units without any multiplying factor; S.P.Q.R., (*a*) L. *Senatus Populusque Romanus*, 'the senate and people of Rome'; (*b*) *joc.*, small profits, quick returns; S.S., G. *Schutz Staffel* 'protection squad' (Nazi Black Guards); S.T.C., short title catalogue; S.T.D., subscriber trunk dialling; S.W.G., s.w.g., standard wire gauge.

Saccadic (săkæ·dik), *a.* 1934. [f. Fr. *saccade* jerk, violent pull (f. OFr. *saquer, sachier* to pull, draw) + -IC.] Applied to the very brief, rapid movement of the eye from one position of rest to another, whether voluntary (as in reading) or involuntary (as when a point is fixated). So **Saccade** (săkā·d), a single movement of this kind.

Sacred, *a.*
3. s. cow, an idea or institution held to be immune from questioning or criticism.

‖**Sadhu** (sā·du). 1845. [Skr., 'holy man'.] In India, a holy man or sage.

Safety.
attrib.: **s. belt,** a strap that secures the occupant to the seat of an aircraft, motor vehicle, etc.; **s. film,** slow-burning film specially prepared for cinematographic work; **s. glass,** laminated or toughened glass unlikely to splinter or shatter; **s. man,** a man engaged to guard a temporarily disused pit in readiness for the resumption of work.

Saga. 3. A series of stories dealing with the history of a family; e.g. 'The Forsyte Saga' of John Galsworthy 1918. **4.** A long and involved story 1942.

Sailplane (sēⁱ·l,plēⁱn). 1922. [f. SAIL *sb.*¹ + PLANE *sb.*³] *Aeronaut.* A kind of glider designed for soaring. Hence **Sai·lplane** *v. intr.*, to fly in a s.

Saintpaulia (sĕntpǭ·liă). 1895. [mod.L. (H. Wendland, 1893), f. the name of Baron Walter von *Saint Paul* (1860–1910), who discovered the first specimens.] A blue-flowered perennial herb of the genus so called, native to tropical Africa, but often grown as a house plant elsewhere; also called *African violet*.

Sale, *sb.*
Comb.: **sales engineer,** a salesman with technical knowledge of his goods and their market; **sales resistance,** the unwillingness of the prospective customer to be overcome by salesmanship; **sales talk,** persuasive rhetoric designed to promote the s. of goods or, *transf.*, the acceptance of an idea.

Salk vaccine (sǫlk-). 1955. [Named after Jonas E. *Salk* (b. 1914), the American scientist who developed it.] *Med.* The first vaccine developed against poliomyelitis, containing polio viruses killed with formaldehyde.

Salmonella (sælmŏne·lă). 1913. [mod.L. (J. Lignières, 1900), f. the name of D. E. *Salmon* (1850–1914), Amer. veterinary surgeon.] *Bacteriol.* A pathogenic bacterium of the genus so called, which includes species causing food poisoning in man and various diseases in domestic animals. Hence **Salmonello·sis,** an infection produced by a type of s.

Salon. 4. An establishment in which the trade of a beauty specialist or hairdresser is carried on 1913.

Samba (sæ·mbă). 1885. [Pg., of Afr. origin.] A Brazilian Negro dance; a ballroom dance imitative of this. Hence **Sa·mba** *v. intr.*, to dance the s.

‖**Samfu** (sa·mfū). Also **samfoo.** 1955. [Cantonese.] A suit consisting of jacket and trousers worn by Chinese women, particularly in Malaysia and Hong Kong.

Sanction, *sb.* **8.** *Polit.* An economic or military action taken by one or more states against another state as a coercive measure 1919. Hence **Sanctionee·r,** one who advocates sanctions.
Such widely advocated and little thought-out 'sanctions' as the outlawry and economic boycott of a recalcitrant nation G. B. SHAW.

Sand, *sb.*
Comb.: **s.-groper** *Austral.*, a pioneer at the time of the gold-rush; *joc.*, a Western Australian; **s.-pit,** also, a pit filled with s. for children to play in.

Sandwich, *sb.*
Comb.: **s. course,** a course of higher education in which periods of practical training in industry alternate with periods of study at a college or university.

Sanitary, *a.*
1. b. s. towel, an absorbent pad for use during menstruation.

Sapele (săpī·li). 1914. [West Afr. name.] A West African tree of the genus *Entandrophragma*, esp. *E. cylindricum*, or its hard, mahogany-like timber.

‖**Sashimi** (sæ·ʃimi). 1880. [Jap.] A Japanese dish consisting of fresh fish served raw in thin slices elegantly garnished.

Sastruga (sæstrū·gă). Usu. as pl. **sastrugi** (-i). 1840. [– Russ. *zastrúga* small ridge, furrow, f. *zastrugát'* (begin to) plane, smooth, f. *strug* plane (*sb.*²).] A ridge of hard snow, usu. one of a parallel series, formed by the action of the wind on level areas in polar regions.

Satellite. 1. b. A state nominally independent but politically dominated by a powerful neighbour 1949. **2. b.** A man-made body designed to orbit the earth or another planet 1936.
Comb.: **s. town,** a small town built near a larger one to house excess population.

‖**Satrangi** (sătrɒ·ndʒi). Also **sitringee.** 1621. [Bengali, f. Skr. *caturaṅga* chess (played by four).] An Indian cotton carpet.

Satsuma. 2. A variety of mandarin orange, originally grown in Japan 1881.

Saturate, *v.* **4. c.** To bomb (a target) from the air so thoroughly that the anti-aircraft defences are rendered powerless 1942. So **Saturation.**
A 'saturation shelling' of advanced enemy positions 1951.

‖**Satyagraha** (satyā·graha). 1921. [Skr., f. *satya* true, sincere, *āgraha* obstinacy.] Passive resistance, esp. as used in India under the leadership of M. K. Gandhi (1869–1948).

Sauna (sau·nă, sǭ·nă). 1936. [Finnish.] A Finnish steam bath; the building in which this is taken.

Sax² (sæks). Colloq. abbrev. of SAXOPHONE.

Say, *v.*¹ **1.** Phrases. *Says you*: dial. or vulgar for *you say*; cf. *SEZ. *To s. a few words*: to make a short (usu. extempore) speech 1930.
Arrah, why, says you, couldn't he manage it? JOYCE.

Scads (skædz), *sb. pl.* *U.S. colloq.* 1809. [Origin unkn.] **a.** Dollars, money. **b.** 'Lots' 'heaps' 1869.

Scampi (skæ·mpi), *sb. pl.* 1930. [It., pl. of *scampo*.] Dublin Bay prawns, *Nephrops norvegicus*; a dish of these.

Scan, *v.* **7. b.** Of a beam or detector: systematically to traverse (a particular area) in order to extract information 1950.
The photographs are scanned point by point by a photoelectric device 1969.

Scanner (skæ·nəɹ). 1557. [f. SCAN *v.* + -ER¹.] **1.** One who examines critically. **2.** One who scans verse 1800. **3.** An apparatus or detector that scans (sense 7, *7b) or directs a beam used in scanning 1929.
3. The radar s. continuously sweeps the sky 1965.

Scanties (skæ·ntiz), *sb. pl. colloq.* 1928. [f. SCANT *a.*, after *frillies* (1900), *panties* (1926).] Short panties.

Scarper (skā·ɹpəɹ), *v. slang.* Also **scapa.** 1844. [prob. f. It. *scappare* to escape; from the war of 1914–18 infl. by Cockney rhyming slang *Scapa Flow* to go.] *intr.* To escape, run away.

Scat (skæt), *sb.*² 1929. [prob. imit.] In Jazz: a wordless song in which the voice is used as a musical instrument. Also *attrib.*, and as *vb.*, to sing s.

Scatty (skæ·ti), *a.* 1911. [f. *scatt*er-brained + -Y¹.] Scatter-brained, crazy.

Scene. II. 1. c. *slang.* An area of action in real life; a way of life 1931.
I decided I wanted to play jazz more than any other s. 1966.

Schedule, *v.* **1. b.** To include (a building) in a list of those to be preserved and protected for architectural and historic reasons 1921.

Schistosomiasis (ʃi-, skistosōməi·ăsis). 1913. [f. mod.L. *Schistosoma*, name of a genus of worms (= *BILHARZIA), f. Gr. σχιστό-ς divided + σῶμα body: see -ASIS.] *Med.* = *BILHARZIASIS.

Schizo (ski·tso). 1952. Colloq. abbrev. of *schizophrenic* (adj. and sb.).

Schizoid (ski·tsoid), *a.* and *sb.* 1925. [f. SCHIZO(PHRENIA + -OID.] **A.** *adj.* Tending towards or resembling (that of) schizophrenia or a schizophrenic. **B.** *sb.* A s. person.

Schlieren (ʃlīᵊ·rən). 1934. [G., pl. of *schliere* streak.] Used *attrib.* to designate techniques and equipment for producing patterns of light corresponding to the variations in refractive index and density in a transparent medium, esp. a gas, by utilizing their deflecting effect on light rays passing through it.

Schmaltz (ʃmǫlts). Also **schmalz.** 1937. [Yiddish, f. G. *schmalz* dripping.] Sickly sentimentality, esp. in music and literary criticism. Hence **Schma·ltzy** *a.*

Schnauzer (ʃnau·tsəɹ). 1923. [G., f. *schnauze* snout, muzzle.] A German breed of wire-haired terrier; a dog of this breed.

Schnitzel (ʃni·tsəl). 1906. [G., 'slice'.] A veal cutlet, esp. *Wiener* (or *Vienna*) *s.*, one coated with egg and breadcrumbs, fried, and garnished with lemon, anchovy, etc.

Schnorkel (ʃnǭ·ɹkəl), **snorkel** (snǭ·ɹkəl), *sb.* 1944. [– G. *schnorchel*, in same senses.] **1.** A tube that may be extended to project above the surface of the water when a submarine is at periscope depth for air to be drawn in. **2.** A breathing-tube for an underwater swimmer 1953. Hence **S(ch)no·rkel** *v. intr.*, to swim with a s. **S(ch)no·rkelling** *vbl. sb.*

Science fiction. 1933. A genre of fiction in which the story presupposes some scientific discovery or technological innovation not established at the time of writing or deals with effects of a spectacular change in the human environment, the setting being realistically presented but often conjectural; fiction of this kind.

Scientology (səiˌĕntǫ·lŏdʒi). 1954. [f. L. *scientia* knowledge + -LOGY.] A religious system based on the study of knowledge, and seeking to develop the highest potentialities of its members. Hence **Sciento·logist.**

Sci-fi (səi· fəi·). 1955. Colloq. abbrev. of *SCIENCE FICTION (cf. *HI-FI). Also *attrib.*

Scorched, *ppl. a.* **1. b.** *S. earth*: applied to a policy of destroying all means of sustenance or supply in a country that might be of use to an invading enemy 1937.

Score, *sb.* **II. 7. c.** orig. *U.S.* The essential point or crux of a matter, esp. in phr. *to know the s.* 1939.

Score, *v.* **III. 7. c.** *slang* (orig. *U.S.*). To buy or obtain drugs illegally 1926.

Scouse. 2. *slang.* A native of Liverpool; the Liverpool dialect 1959. **B.** *adj. slang.* Of or pertaining to Liverpool 1960.

Scout, *sb.*²
Comb.: **s. car,** a fast armoured vehicle used for reconnaissance and liaison.

Scram (skræm), *v. slang* (orig. *U.S.*). 1928. [perh. shortening of synon. dial. *scramble*.] *intr.* To go away quickly, to be off. Usu. as imper.

Scramble, *sb.* **3.** A type of motor-cycle race on rough and hilly ground 1936.

Scramble, *v.* **1. c.** *trans.* with advs. To deal with in a hasty manner 1869. **4.** To alter the frequencies of the speech of (a transmitted message) in a prearranged manner so as to render it unintelligible to an eavesdropper 1929. **5.** *intr.* Of military aircraft or their pilots: to (hasten to their aircraft and) take off in response to an alert. Freq. imper. 1942.

Scrapie (skrēⁱ·pi). 1914. [f. SCRAPE *v.* + -IE. One of the symptoms is severe itching, which makes the animal rub itself against trees, fences, etc.] A degenerative, usually fatal, disease affecting the central nervous system of sheep.

Scratchy, *a.* **2. b.** *fig.* Inclined to be cattish 1928.

Screen, *sb.* **1. e.** The surface on which moving pictures are projected 1882; *transf.* (usu. with def. art.), moving pictures collectively; *the* cinema, *the* films 1928.
Comb.: **s.-printing,** a printing process akin to stencilling using a screen or ground of fine material (originally silk).

Screen, *v.* **4. b.** *transf.* and *fig.* To subject (a person) to a process that may indicate or reveal possession of a particular undesirable quality or object (as disloyalty, incipient disease, a weapon). orig. *U.S.* 1946.
Electronic equipment at airports to 's.' passengers for weapons 1971.

Screw, *sb.*
Comb.: **s.-ball,** in Baseball, a ball delivered with a spin; *fig.* a crazy person; **s.-top** *a.*, of a jar, bottle etc.: having a lid that screws on.

Screwy, *a.* **4.** Crazy, eccentric; odd, unusual 1887.

Script. 5. b. The text of a broadcast announcement, play, talk, etc. 1931. **6.** An examinee's written answers.
5. b. His characteristic s. of 'Germany speaking' and 'Views on the News' is being read by one of his stooges 1944.
Comb.: **s.-writer,** a writer for films, radio, television, etc.

Scruffy (skrɒ·fi), *a.* 1660. [f. SCRUFF *sb.*¹ + -Y¹.] **1.** In Dict. s.v. SCRUFF *sb.*¹ **2.** Shabby, slovenly, untidy 1925.

Scrumpy (skrɒ·mpi). orig. and chiefly *dial.* 1904. [f. dial. *scrump* something undersized, esp. a small apple, f. *scrump* to shrink, shrivel: cf. Sw., Da. *skrumpen* shrivelled, G. *schrumpfen* to shrivel, crumple.] Rough or home-brewed cider.

Scuba (skⁱū·bă). 1956. [f. initial letters of *self-contained underwater breathing apparatus*.] A form of equipment for underwater swimmers.

Sculduddery, var. *SKULDUGGERY.

Sea.
Comb.: **s. lane** (see *LANE); **s. power,** (*a*) a nation or state having international power or influence on the sea; (*b*) the efficiency of a nation (or of nations) for maritime warfare; *gen.* ability to control and make successful use of the sea.

Seal, *v.*¹ **II. 6.** *To s. off*: to cut off (an area) so that those within it have no escape 1938.

Search, *v.* **3. b.** *S. me!*: used to imply that the speaker has no knowledge of some fact or no idea what course to take (orig. *U.S.*) 1901.

Seat, *sb.*
Comb.: **s.-belt** = **safety belt*; **s.-mile,** a statistical unit denoting one mile travelled by one passenger.

Secondment (sĭkǫ·ndmĕnt). 1897. [f. SECOND *v.*² + -MENT.] The process or state of being seconded.

Secret, *a.*
1. s. agent, a secret service agent; **s. police,** a police force operating in s., esp. to further the political ends of government.

Security. I. 1. b. The safety of a state from covert foreign influence or espionage; scrutiny of persons (e.g. those in government employment) in respect of their reliability 1930. Also *attrib.*, as *s. police*; *s. risk*, a person of doubtful loyalty.

Seed, *sb.* **6.** In sports, a seeded player 1933.

Seed, *v.* **II. 1. b.** To introduce a crystal or small particle into (a supercooled liquid or vapour, or a supersaturated solution) in order to induce condensation or crystallization; *esp.* to treat (a cloud) in this way so as to produce rain 1930.

See-through (sī·þrū), *a.* 1960. [f. *to see through* (SEE *v.*).] Transparent, esp. of clothes and fabrics.

Segmental, *a.* **3.** *Phonetics.* Of or pertaining to units of sound (sound segments) analysed out from the continuum of speech 1942.

Segregate, *v.* **1. b.** To subject (people) to racial segregation; to enforce racial segregation in (a community, institution, etc.) 1930. Freq. as **Se·gregated** *ppl. a.*

Segregation. 1. d. The enforced separation of different racial groups in a country, community, or institution 1934. Hence **Segrega·tionist,** one who advocates or supports racial s.

Seiche (sēⁱʃ). 1839. [Swiss Fr.] An oscillation of a wholly or partly enclosed body of water (e.g. a lake or harbour) as a whole, with a period dependent on the shape and size of the enclosing basin.

Selectivity (sīlekti·vĭti). 1903. [f. SELECTIVE + -ITY.] In Dict. s.v. SELECTIVE *a*; *spec.* in *Radio*, the ability to receive transmissions on one frequency to the exclusion of those on neighbouring frequencies (at any one time).

Selenium.
Comb.: **s. cell,** a photo-electric cell in which s. is the active substance.

Self-. 1. d. *self-doubt.*
The steps that must be taken to meet it will not be clouded by self-doubts 1951.
4. self-sealing (*ppl.*) *a.*, having a device for filling up a hole in the framework or structure caused by shot, etc.

Self-drive (se·lf drəi·v), *a.* 1929. [SELF- 3.] Of a hired vehicle: intended to be driven by the hirer.

Self-employed (-emploi·d), *ppl. a.* 1948. [SELF- 2.] Working as the owner of a business, etc.

Self-se·rvice. 1919. [SELF- 1 a.] *attrib.* Designating a commercial establishment where the customer serves himself, payment being made either to a cashier on the way out or by means of a slot-machine.

Sell, *v.* With advs. **S. out. d.** Hence **s.-out** *sb.*, a commercial success. **e.** To betray, let down. Hence **s.-out** *sb.*, betrayal.

Seller. 1. Phr. *seller's market*, a market where supplies are short and prices high; cf. *MARKET *sb.* 6.

Sellotape (se·lotēⁱp). 1957. The proprietary name of a kind of adhesive, usu. transparent, tape used for mending and joining paper, film, etc. Hence **Se·llotape** *v. trans.*, to stick (together) with this.

Semanteme (sĭmæ·ntīm). 1925. [– Fr. *sémantème*, f. *sémantique* SEMANTIC, after *phonème* PHONEME, *morphème* *MORPHEME.] *Philol.* A linguistic element that expresses or denotes an image or idea.

Semi² (se·mi). 1912. Colloq. abbrev. of *semi-detached house.*

Se:micondu·ctor. 1879. [SEMI- II. 3.] A solid substance (e.g. germanium or silicon) which is a non-conductor of electricity when pure or at a very low temperature but when containing a suitable impurity or at a higher temperature has a conductivity much less than that of most metals but much greater than that of insulators. Also **Se:micondu·cting** *a.* 1787.

Semiotics (sīmiˌǫ·tiks), *sb. pl.* 1897. [– Gr. σημειωτική (*sc.* τέχνη) pertaining to symbols.] That branch of linguistics which deals with signs and symbols and their relation to meaning. Hence **Semio·tic(al** *a.* **Semio·tically** *adv.*

Send, *v.*[1] **2. c.** *slang* (orig. *U.S.*) Of popular music, etc.: to move (a person), to affect (a person) emotionally.

s. up. e. To satirize. Hence **s.-up** *colloq.*, a satire.

Sense, *sb.*

Comb.: **s.-datum,** an element of experience due to the stimulation of a sense organ.

Sensor, *a.* **B.** *sb.* A device that directly responds to some physical property and produces a signal enabling the property to be detected or measured 1958.

‖**Sensum** (se·nsǒm). Pl. **sensa** (se·nsă). 1924. [mod.L., neut. pa. pple. of L. *sentire* feel, perceive (cf. SENTENCE, SENTIMENT).] *Philos.* A sense-datum.

It is only because Russell and Joad *first* knew that there are external objects that they are able to *infer* that there are private sensa 1937.

Separate. C. *sb.* **3.** *pl.* Separate articles of dress suitable for wearing together in various combinations 1945.

Septic, *a.* **b.** Of a tank: in which the decomposition of organic matter in sewage is effected through the agency of anaerobic bacteria 1902.

Sequence. 8. *Cinemat.* A film scene 1929.

Serial, *a.* and *sb.* **A.** *adj.* **2.** *Mus.* Applied to a type of composition using transformations of a fixed series of notes based on a permutation of the twelve tones of the chromatic scale 1947. Hence **Se·rialism,** the practice of this technique. Cf. *DODECAPHONIC, *SERIES II. 9, *TWELVE-TONE.

Anton Webern..adopted Schönberg's s. technique 1960.

Series. II. 9. *Mus.* The permutation of the twelve-tone chromatic scale which is used as the starting-point of a piece of *SERIAL music; also called a tone-row 1930.

The primary function of the s. is that of a sort of 'store of motifs' out of which all the individual elements of the composition are to be developed 1940.

Serigraphy (seri·grăfi). orig. *U.S.* 1946. [irreg. f. L. *sericum* silk (see SERIC *a.*) + -GRAPHY; cf. Fr. *sérigraphie.*] The art or process of printing designs by means of a silk screen. So **Se·rigraph,** a print so made.

Serum.

Comb.: **s. eruption, sickness,** manifestations that sometimes follow upon an injection of serum, as a rash, fever, or swelling of the joints.

Service, *sb.*[1] **V. 4. b.** Provision or supply of what is necessary for the due maintenance of a thing or an operation 1925. Also *attrib.*, as *s. department, depot, station.*

Comb.: **s. area,** (*a*) *Broadcasting*, the area surrounding a transmitter within which satisfactory reception is normally possible; (*b*) an area close to the road where motorists can stop for petrol, oil, etc., and sometimes also obtain refreshment; **s.-bus, -car** *Austral.* and *N.Z.*, a motor-coach; **s. charge,** an additional charge made for services rendered; **s. engineer,** an engineer who maintains and services equipment already in use; **s. module,** a module containing the main engine and power supplies of a spacecraft; **s. road,** a road not intended for through traffic but constructed and situated for the convenience of houses lying off the main road.

Service, *v.* 1893. [f. SERVICE *sb.*[1]] *trans.* To give one's services to, supply with service (*rare*). **b.** To provide service for (a car, etc.) 1935; see *SERVICE *sb.*[1] V. 4. b. Often in *vbl. sb.*

Servo (sǭ·ɹvo). 1926. [First element of *servo-motor, -mechanism.*] A servo-motor or servo-mechanism. So **Se:rvo-assi·sted** *a.*

Se·rvo-me:chanism. 1926. [f. *servo-* (after *servo-motor*) + MECHANISM.] A powered mechanism for controlling the motion of a much larger or more powerful system, usu. automatically in accordance with predetermined criteria. Hence **Se:rvo-mecha·nical** *a.*

Se:squicente·nnial, *a.* and *sb.* orig. *U.S.* 1880. [SESQUI-.] (Pertaining to) a hundred-and-fiftieth anniversary.

Set, *sb.*[1] **I. 4. b.** *Austral.* and *N.Z.* A grudge; esp. in phr. *to have a s. on*, to have a grudge against 1941. **8.** *Psychol.* A predisposition to or preparedness for some response, course of action, or experience 1890. **III. 9.** A 'set scene' (SET *ppl. a.*); the setting, stage furniture, etc., used in a theatre or in film production 1861.

Set, *sb.*[2] **II. 1. b.** A radio or television receiver; now usu. apprehended as short for *radio s., television s.* 1903. **6. b.** *Math.* and *Logic.* A collection of entities ('elements') having some specified property or properties in common 1901.

6. b. s. theory, the branch of mathematics and logic concerned with the study of sets as mere collections, without regard to the nature of their constituent elements.

Set-.

s.-up, (*c*) *colloq.* (orig. *U.S.*), the structure or arrangement of an organization, or the like.

Sex, *sb.* **5.** Sexual activity; *spec.* sexual intercourse, esp. in phr. *to have s.* (*with*) 1952.

Comb.: **a.** In many mod. scientific terms relating to the origin, transmission, and functions of sex, as *sex chromosome, control, determination, factor, hormone, linkage, reversal.* **b. s. change,** apparent sex reversal effected by surgical intervention; **s. life,** sexual experience or habits; the gratification derived from them; **s. maniac,** a person immoderately desirous of sexual gratification; **s. ratio,** the proportion between the number of males in a population and the number of females; **s.-starved** *a.*, deprived of sexual activity.

Sexology (seksǫ·lŏdʒi). 1902. [f. SEX *sb.* + -OLOGY.] Study of the relations of the sexes or of sexual life. Hence **Sexolo·gical** *a.* **Sexo·logist.**

Sexy (se·ksi), *a.* 1928. [f. SEX *sb.* + -Y[1].] **a.** Engrossed in or concerned with sex. **b.** Sexually attractive or provocative 1932. Hence **Se·xiness.**

Sez, phonetic representation of *says* in *says you* (see *SAY *v.*[1]), used joc. as an ironical formula to express incredulity on the part of the speaker (*colloq.*) 1932.

Shag (ʃæg), *v.*[2] *slang.* 1796. [Origin unkn.] *trans.* To copulate with. Also as *ppl. a.* **shagged (out),** tired out, exhausted.

Shaggy, *a.*

1. s. dog story, a lengthy tediously detailed story of an inconsequential series of events, more amusing to the teller than to his audience, or amusing only by its pointlessness.

Sha·ke-out. 1957. [f. SHAKE *v.*] An upheaval or reorganization in which important or radical changes are made.

Sha·ke-up. orig. *U.S.* [f. phr. *shake up*, SHAKE *v.* ad fin.] An act of shaking up or being shaken up, or the result of this: **a.** A hastily or roughly made article 1873. **b.** A thorough or drastic change or rearrangement 1887.

Shalom (ʃalōᵘ·m), *int.* and *sb.* 1962. [Heb., 'peace'.] In Jewish society, a word used as a salutation at meeting or parting.

Shamateur (ʃæ·mătǒɹ, ʃæ·mătiūᵊɹ). 1896. [f. SHAM *a.* + AMATEUR.] In sports, a player who is classed as an amateur, while often making money out of his play like a professional. Hence **Sha·mateurism.**

Shangri-La (variable stress). 1933. [f. the name of a hidden Himalayan valley in the novel (and film) *Lost Horizon* by James Hilton (1933).] A type of imaginary earthly paradise.

Shanty, *sb.*[1]

Comb.: **s. town,** a town or suburb consisting of shanties.

Shape, *sb.* **11.** Also, in wider use, with ref. to condition of health, as *in good, bad,* or *poor s.*

Share, *sb.*[2]

Comb.: **s.-pusher** *colloq.*, one who peddles shares by circular or advertisement instead of selling them on the market.

Shark, *sb.*[1]

Comb.: **s.-skin,** the skin of a shark, shagreen; a heavy, smooth fabric with a dull surface.

Shaver. 4. b. More fully *electric s.* A shaving instrument in which an electric motor drives a set of small shielded blades 1925.

Sheer, *a.* **3.** Also as *sb.*, a sheer or diaphanous textile material; similarly **Semi·-sheer** 1937.

Treat all sheers as you would chiffon 1964.

Sheila (ʃī·lă). *Austral.* and *N.Z. slang.* Also formerly **shaler, sheelah.** 1864. [Early form *shaler* of unknown origin, assim. to the personal name *Sheila.*] A girl; a young woman.

She·ll-out. 1866. [f. phr. *shell out* (see SHELL *v.*).] *Billiards.* The game of pyramids played by three or more persons.

Sherpa (ʃǝ̄·ɹpă). 1847. [Native word.] The name of a Tibetan people living on the southern slopes of the Himalayas; a member of this people. Also as *adj.*

Shish kebab (ʃi·ʃ₍kĕbæb). Also **shish-kabob, shish-kebab, shishkebab.** 1914. [– Turk. *şiş kebabi*, f. *şiş* skewer + *kebab* roast meat.] A dish consisting of pieces of meat roasted or broiled on a skewer; = CABOB 1.

Shock, *sb.*[3]

Comb.: **s. therapy, treatment,** treatment of psychiatric patients in which a coma or convulsions are induced by chemical or electrical means; **s. wave,** a disturbance that travels through a fluid as a narrow region in which the pressure changes abruptly, produced by a sudden and violent disturbance such as an explosion or by a body moving at a speed greater than the local speed of sound.

Shoe, *sb.*

Comb.: **s.-string,** also, a very small sum of money; *attrib.*, financially precarious.

Shoot, *v.* **III. 3. b.** To give vent or utterance to; also *absol.* in imper. (*slang*) say what you have to say, fire away, spit it out 1922. **c.** *intr.* To give oneself a hypodermic injection; *trans.*, to inject (a drug, a person) hypodermically (*slang*) 1914. **IV. 3. b.** *To s. up*: to assail with indiscriminate or continuous shooting (orig. *U.S.*) 1901.

III. 3. b. At shooting the smart stuff, Miss Blakeney has the world well beaten 1930.

Shop, *sb.*

Comb.: **s. assistant,** a salesman or saleswoman in a retail s. or store; **s. floor,** a factory workshop or place of work; the workers there collectively; **shophouse,** a Chinese shop (esp. in Singapore) opening on to the pavement and also used as the residence of the proprietor; **s.-lifter,** a pretended customer who steals goods in a s.; **s.-steward,** a person elected by his fellow-workmen in a factory, etc., or a branch of it as their spokesman on conditions of work, etc.

Shore, *sb.*[1]

Comb.: **s.-based** *a.*, operating from a base on s., as *s.-b. aircraft.*

Short, *a.*

Comb.: **s.-change** *v. trans.* (orig. *U.S.*), to rob by giving insufficient change; hence *gen.*, to cheat; **s.-day** *a.*, of a plant: needing a regular cycle of light and darkness to induce flowering, the length of the dark period being critical; **s.-head** *v. trans.*, to beat by a s. head; **s. list,** a list of selected candidates for a post from which it is intended to make a final selection; hence **s.-list** *v. trans.*, to put on a s. list; **s.-staffed** *a.*, not adequately provided with staff; **s. time,** the condition of working fewer than the regular number of hours per day or days per week.

Short-fall (ʃǭ·ɹtfǭl). *colloq.* 1949. [f. phr. *fall short* (FALL *v.* VII. 2).] A falling short or failure to reach a standard or degree of production.

Shot, *sb.*[1] **I. 4. e.** orig. *U.S.* A hypodermic injection; *s. in the arm* (fig.), (*a*) a drink of alcoholic liquor; (*b*) a stimulant, encouragement 1922. **6.** A dram (of spirits) 1928.

Comb.: **s. noise** *Electronics*, random fluctuations in current due to corresponding fluctuations in the emission of individual electrons in a valve or transistor; so *s. effect.*

Shot-gun, shotgun.

Comb.: **s. marriage** or **wedding** orig. *U.S.*, a forced marriage, *spec.* one necessitated by pregnancy; also *transf.* and *fig.*

Show, *sb.* **II. 8.** In trivial exclam. *Good show!* = an excellent performance or production!, fine!, splendid!

Comb.: **s.-business,** the profession of entertainment, esp. theatrical; also abbrev. *showbiz*; **s.-girl,** an actress whose role is decorative rather than histrionic; **s.-jumping,** the competitive display of horse-jumping; **s.-trial,** a judicial trial organized by a (usu. Communist) government with much publicity.

Showing, *vbl. sb.* **1. b.** The presentation of a film 1947.

Shrink-wrap (ʃri·ŋk₍ræp), *v.* 1957. [f. SHRINK *v.* + WRAP *v.*] *trans.* To protect (an article) by causing the packaging material to contract around it and cling tightly to its surface.

Shrug, *v.* **3.** *To s. off*: to dismiss (something) as unimportant.

Shuttle, *sb.*[1] **6.** *Astronaut.* A space rocket with wings enabling it to land like an aircraft and be used repeatedly 1969.

Comb.: **s. service,** a service of trains, buses, or aircraft to and and fro between two points.

Shy, *a.* **3.** As an element of compds. = frightened (of), averse (to), as GUN-SHY

(1884), *work-s.* (1904); cf. G. *feuerscheu, arbeitscheu.*

Siamese, *a.* and *sb.* **A.** *adj.* **3.** *S. cat,* a cat of a cream- or buff-coloured short-haired breed with dark points and tail and blue eyes 1881. Also *ellipt.* as sb.

Sick, *a.* **II. 4.** Of humour: perverted, finding amusement in misfortune and the macabre 1959. **III. 5. b. s. benefit** (see BENEFIT *sb.* 4 d) 1909.

Sickle.
Comb.: **s. cell,** a s.-shaped (crescentic) red blood cell; freq. *attrib.*, esp. in **s.-cell anæmia,** a severe (often fatal) hereditary form of anæmia, found chiefly among Negroes, in which red blood cells become s.-shaped.

Side, *sb.*[1] **II. 1. sides-to-middle** *adv. phr.*, with the sides and middle changing places, as a sheet cut down the centre and re-sewn thus for strengthening. Also as *vb.*
Comb.: **s.-effect,** *spec.* an effect that a drug has other than the principal one for which it is given; also *transf.*; **s.-road,** a minor or subsidiary road; a road off a main road; **s.-street,** a street lying aside from main streets or roads or through-traffic routes.

Sighting, *vbl. sb.* **1. b.** An instance of seeing something, esp. an aircraft or unidentified flying object 1955.

Sigla. Used esp. for editorial designations of the sources of an edition of a text.

Sign, *sb.* **II. 1.** (*b*) *Theol.* In sacramental ordinances, the outward or visible part which symbolizes the inward or spiritual part 1553. **c.** *Path.* An objective and characteristic indication of a disease 1885.

Sign, *v.*[1] **I. 5.** *spec.* To make an undertaking 1903; also with *up.* **6. c.** Also with *up.*
5. She also signed up for evening classes 1926. **6. c.** Seversky..signed the violinist up for his broadcast 1932.

Si·gnpost, *v.* 1895. [f. the sb.] *trans.* **a.** To provide or equip with signposts. **b.** To indicate (a route), or the road to (a place), by means of a signpost. Also *fig.* Hence **Si·gnposted** *ppl. a.* **Si·gnposting** *vbl. sb.*

Silicone (si·likoᵘn). 1908. [f. SILIC(O- + -ONE.] *Chem.* Orig., the name given to any supposed compound of silicon analogous to the ketones, having a formula RR′SiO (R,R′ being organic radicals); in mod. use, any of a large group of polymeric organic compounds of silicon based on chains or networks of alternating silicon and oxygen atoms, many of these being good electrical insulators with high resistance to the effects of cold, heat, and water and finding uses as liquids, greases, synthetic rubbers, or synthetic resins.

Silk, *sb.*
Comb.: **s.-screen** *attrib.*, of a printing process akin to stencilling, using a silk screen; cf. *SERIGRAPHY.

Si·mulated, *ppl. a.* 1622. [f. SIMULATE *v.* + -ED[1].] **1.** Pretended, feigned. **2.** = IMITATION 5. 1942.

Simulation. 3. The technique of imitating the behaviour of some situation or system (economic, military, mechanical, etc.) by means of an analogous situation, model, or apparatus, either to gain information more conveniently or to train personnel 1948.

Simulator. 2. An apparatus for reproducing the behaviour of some situation or system; *esp.* one that is fitted with the controls of an aircraft, motor vehicle, etc., and gives the illusion to an operator of responding like the real thing 1948.

Singaporean (siŋăpōᵊ·riăn), *a.* and *sb.* 1880. [f. the name of the city (now the republic) of *Singapore* + -AN.] **A.** *adj.* Of or pertaining to Singapore. **B.** *sb.* A native or inhabitant of Singapore 1927.

‖**Singh** (siŋ). 1623. [Hind. – Skr. *sinhá* 'the powerful one', lion.] *India.* A great warrior: title of warrior castes, as Rajputs and Sikhs.

Single, *a.* **II. 3.** (Of a ticket for public transport) valid for one journey only; opp. RETURN. Also as *sb.*

Sino-.
Sinoma·nia, a passion for the Chinese or their beliefs, civilization, etc.; **Si·nophile,** one who approves of the Chinese and their ways; **Si·nophobe** *sb.* and *a.*, (one who is) hostile to the Chinese.

Sinter (si·ntəɹ), *v.* 1871. [f. the sb.] *intr.* Of particles or particulate material: to coalesce into a solid mass under the influence of heat without liquefaction; *trans.*, to cause to s. Freq. as **Si·ntered** *ppl. a.* **Si·ntering** *vbl. sb.*

Sinusitis (səinŏsəi·tis). 1900. [f. SINUS + -ITIS.] *Med.* Inflammation of a sinus, esp. one of the nasal sinuses.

Siren. 5. c. An instrument for giving warning of air-raids; the warning itself 1939.
Comb.: **s. suit,** a one-piece suit of clothes, easily put on or taken off, for use during a night air-raid.

Sit-in (si·tˌin). 1960. [f. SIT *v.* + *-IN *suffix*[3].] The fact or occasion of a number of people occupying and refusing to move from a certain place in protest against activities (thought to be) carried on or originating there.

Sitka (si·tkă). 1884. The name of a town in Alaska, used *attrib.* to denote trees native to the region, esp. **S. cypress,** the yellow cedar, *Chamæcyparis nootkatensis,* and **S. spruce,** *Picea sitchensis,* an important timber tree.

Sitter.
Comb.: **s.-in,** one who sits in with a child or family of children while the parents or guardians are absent.

Situational (sitiuˌēⁱ·ʃənăl), *a.* 1903. [f. SITUATION + -AL[1].] Pertaining to, derived from, or determined by situation. Hence **Situa·tionally** *adv.*

Sixth, *a.*
s. day, Friday (with the Society of Friends); **s. sense,** a supposed faculty by which a person perceives facts and regulates action without the direct use of any of the five senses.

Sixty.
Comb.: **s.-four dollar question,** a difficult and crucial question; orig. from a U.S. radio quiz show, begun in 1942, in which progressively harder questions led up to a prize of $64. Hence (later) **sixty-four thousand dollar question.**

Ski.
Comb.: **s.-bob,** a bicycle-like machine for winter sports, equipped with skis instead of wheels; **s.-lift,** a device for transporting skiers up a mountain side, usually consisting of seats suspended from an overhead cable; **s.-wear,** clothes suitable for persons engaged in skiing.

Skid, *sb.*
Comb.: **s.-pan,** a slippery road surface prepared for drivers to practise the control of skids; **s. road** *U.S.*, the area of a town where loggers spend their leisure; **s. row** [corruption of prec.], an area where the unemployed, down-and-outs, alcoholics, etc., tend to congregate.

Skier (skī·əɹ). 1895. [f. SKI *v.* + -ER[1].] One who uses or travels on skis.

Skiffle (ski·f'l). 1949. [perh. imit. Cf. dial. *skiffle* scuffle.] A kind of folk music played by a group using primarily rhythm instruments, including improvised ones.

Skin, *sb.*
Comb.: **s.-flick** *slang,* a film of an explicitly pornographic nature; **skinhead,** (*a*) *U.S.* a Marine recruit; (*b*) a member of a gang of youths characterized in part by close-cropped hair and violent behaviour.

Skin-dive, *v.* (ski·ndəiv). 1950. [f. SKIN *sb.* + DIVE *v.*] To swim under water without a conventional diving suit, using flippers and an aqualung. Esp. as *vbl. sb.* **Skin-diving.**

Skulduggery (skɒldɒ·gəri). Also **sculdu·ddery.** 1713. [Origin unkn.] **1.** *Sc.* Fornication or adultery. **2.** *Sc.* Obscenity 1821. **3.** orig. *U.S.* Dishonest behaviour, deception 1867.

Sky, *sb.*
Comb.: **s. army, men, troops,** air-borne troops; **s.-diving,** the sport of 'diving' from an aeroplane and falling freely, opening the parachute just in time to land safely; **s. marker,** a parachute flare dropped by a raiding aeroplane to mark the target area.

Skyjack (skəi·dʒæk), *v. slang.* 1959. [f. SKY *sb.* + *HI)JACK.] *trans.* To hijack (an aircraft). So **Sky·jacked** *ppl. a.*, **-jacking** *vbl. sb.* Also **Sky·jacker.**

Sky-·ro:cket, *v.* 1851. [f. the sb.] *intr.* To shoot into the air, rise steeply; esp. *fig.* of prices, sales etc. Also *trans.*, to send up rapidly.

Slant, *v.* **5.** To adapt (esp. writing) to some special need; to present in a biased or unfair way 1939.

Slap, *sb.*
1. Phr. **s. and tickle** *colloq.*, boisterous or knockabout entertainment.
He hoped that the cultural side [of the Festival Gardens] as well as 'the slap and tickle' would be considered 1951.

Slap-happy (slæ·pˌhæ:pi), *a.* 1936. [f. SLAP *sb.* 1 + *HAPPY *a.* 4 b.] **1.** Punch-drunk; dazed, dizzy. **2.** Haphazard; carefree; irresponsible, thoughtless 1940.

Slather (slæ·ðəɹ). 1876. [Origin unkn.] **1.** *U.S. colloq.* usually *pl.*: a large amount. **2.** *Austral.* and *N.Z. slang.* Usually in phr. *open s.*: a free rein, a free-for-all 1916.

Sleazy, *a.* **2.** Shoddy, slatternly 1946.

Sleeve, *sb.* **5.** A drogue towed behind an aircraft 1933. **6.** The cover of a gramophone record 1953. So **s.-note,** a critique of the contents of the record, printed on the s.

Slip, *sb.*[3] **III. 2. b.** Also, in *Aeronaut.*, the corresponding difference for an aircraft propeller, usually expressed as a percentage 1897.

Slip, *v.*[1] **III. 5. b. slipped disc,** a distortion or herniation of an intervertebral disc producing pressure on the roots of spinal nerves.

Slip-. s.-road, a minor or local road giving access to or exit from a more important road.

Slipstream (sli·pˌstrīm). 1916. [f. *SLIP *sb.*[3] III. 2 b + STREAM *sb.*] The current of air or water driven backward by a revolving propeller. Also *fig.*

Slit, *sb.*
Comb.: **s. trench,** a narrow trench made to accommodate a soldier or a weapon.

Slivovitz (sli·vŏvits). 1885. [Serbo-Croat *sljivovica*, f. *sljiva, sliva,* plum.] A Yugoslav plum brandy.

Sloshed (slǫ·ʃt), *ppl. a. colloq.* 1946. [f. SLOSH *v.*] Drunk, tipsy.

Slub (slɒb), *sb.*[2] (See under SLUB *v.*[2]) Also *attrib.*, having an irregular effect given by a warp of uneven thickness.

Slumber, *sb.*
attrib.: **s. wear,** (in shop usage) night-clothes.

Slurry (slɒ·ri). late ME. [Related to dial. *slur* thin or fluid mud.] Thin sloppy mud or cement; any mixture of a liquid, esp. water, with fine solid material.

Smart, *a. S. Aleck* (also *Alec, Alick*): depreciatory expression for a would-be clever person who knows everything about everything 1873. Also *attrib.* orig. *U.S.*

Smashing (smæ·ʃiŋ), *ppl. a. colloq.* 1910. [f. SMASH *v.*[1] + -ING[2].] Overwhelmingly fine, impressive, or the like.

Smear, *sb.* **2. c.** *colloq.* (orig. *U.S.*). An intentionally disparaging rumour or allusive remark; freq. *attrib.*, as *s. campaign, tactics* 1944.

Smear, *v.* **4. c.** *colloq.* (orig. *U.S.*) To sully the reputation or good name of 1936.

Smile, *v.* **I. 1.** Colloq. phr. *To come up smiling*: to recover from a bout in a contest (e.g. boxing) and cheerfully face what is to come.

Smog (smǫg). 1905. [Blend of SMOKE *sb.* + FOG *sb.*] Fog intensified by smoke.

Smoke, *sb.* **2. c.** Slang phr. *The (big) S.*, London 1864. **6. b.** A break in working hours to allow workers to smoke. In Australia and New Zealand **Smoko** (smōᵘ·ko). 1934.

Smorgasbord (smōᵊ·ɹgăsbōᵊ:ɹd), ‖**smörgåsbord** (smö·ɹgǫsbōᵊ:ɹd). 1895. [Sw., f. *smör* butter (cogn. w. SMEAR *sb.*) + *gås* goose + *bord* table.] The Swedish equivalent of hors d'œuvres; a buffet of cold food.

Snafu (snăfū·), *a.* and *sb. U.S. slang* (orig. *Services'*). 1942. [f. initials of *situation normal, all fouled up.*] **A.** *adj.* Chaotic. **B.** *sb.* Utter confusion.

Snap, *v.* **II. 5.** *intr.* (orig. *U.S.*). To move or proceed quickly, as in *to s. into it, out of it* 1918. So *to make it snappy*: to be quick about it.

Snap-. b. s.-fastener, a press-stud. **d. s. decision,** one taken on the spur of the moment.

Snarl, *v.*[1] **2.** *transf.* and *fig.* To confuse and trammel the movement of (*U.S.*).
Heaviest Snowfall in 3 Years Snarls Traffic in

New York 1952. Surprise rail strike snarls midwest 1952. Hence **s.-up**, a confused mass.

Sneak-, (also) *s.-raid, -raider, -raiding.*

Snide, *a.* and *sb.* **A.** *adj.* **2.** orig. *U.S.* Slyly disparaging, sneering 1887.

Snifter. 3. A (small) drink of intoxicating liquor 1848.

Snip, *sb.* **II. 5.** *slang* (orig. *Sporting*). Something easily won; a sure thing, certainty; a bargain 1894.

Snooper (snū·pəɹ). 1891. [f. SNOOP *v.* + -ER [1].] One who pries into people's doings in order to discover infractions of the law or offences of any kind.

Snooperscope (snū·pəɹ,skōᵘp). *U.S.* 1946. [f. *SNOOPER + -SCOPE.] An instrument that produces a visible image of objects obscured by darkness, fog, etc., by emitting infra-red radiation and detecting its reflection with a fluorescent screen.

Snooty (snū·ti), *a. slang.* 1919. [Origin unkn.] Superciliously contemptuous. Hence **Snoo·tily** *adv.*

Snorkel, var. *SCHNORKEL.

Snort (snǫɹt), *sb.* [2] 1944. [Substituted for *SCHNORKEL, SNORKEL *sb.*] = *SCHNORKEL, SNORKEL *sb.* 1. Hence as *v. intr.*, (of a submarine) to be submerged with the schnorkel up.

Snowmobile (snōᵘ·mŏbīl). Chiefly *N. Amer.* 1931. [f. SNOW *sb.* [1] + AUTO)MOBILE.] Any motor vehicle designed for travelling over snow; *spec.* a small, light passenger vehicle supported on skis and a caterpillar track. Hence **Sno·wmobiling** *vbl. sb.*, the sport of travelling in such a vehicle.

So, *adv.* **II. 4.** phr. *So what?*: a retort made to a serious assertion implying that the problem expressed or implicit has no immediate interest or obvious solution.

The tragedy of the 'So what?' generation 1953.

Soap, *sb.*

Comb.: **s. opera** orig. *U.S.*, a radio or television serial of a trivial and sentimental nature, formerly often sponsored (in U.S.A.) by s. companies.

‖**Soba** (sōᵘ·bă). 1910. [Jap.] In Japan, a type of noodle made from buckwheat.

Social, *a.* **7.** *s. science*, the study of human society regarded as a science, frequently taken to include not only sociology but economics, political science, *s. anthropology, s. medicine, s. psychology*, etc. **8.** *s. security*, assistance provided by the State out of taxation for those whose income is inadequate because of unemployment, disability, etc.; *s. worker*, a person trained in s. service.

Socialite (sōᵘ·ʃăləit). orig. *U.S.* 1935. [f. SOCIAL *a.* + -ITE [1].] A person prominent in fashionable society.

Society. II. 4. *Ecology.* A plant community, forming part of a consociation 1905.

Sociolinguistic (sōᵘ:ʃⁱoliŋgwi·stik, sōᵘ·sⁱo-), *a.* (and *sb.*) 1946. [f. SOCIO- + LINGUISTIC.] **A.** *adj.* Of or pertaining to the study of language in its social context. **B.** *sb. pl.* The study of language in relation to social factors.

Sociometry (sōᵘsⁱǫ·mĕtri). 1908. [f. SOCIO- + -METRY.] The study of relationships within a group of people. Hence **socio·metrist**, one who studies such relationships; **sociome·tric** *a.*, of or pertaining to such a study.

Sockeye (sǫ·kəi). 1887. [– Salish Indian *sukai* 'fish of fishes'.] = NERKA.

Soft, *a.* **II. 6. b.** Of a drug that is taken non-medicinally: considered less harmful than the 'hard' drugs and not likely to lead to addiction 1959. **IV. 9.** Of a detergent: biodegradable 1959.

Comb.: **s. landing** *Astronaut.* (see *LANDING *vbl. sb.* 1 d.)

Soften, *v.* **4. b.** To reduce the strength of (a defended position) by bombing or bombardment. Also with *up*, and *transf.* Often in *gerund* or *vbl. sb.* (and attrib., as *softening process*) 1948.

Software (sǫ·ftwēᵊɹ). 1963. [f. SOFT *a.* + WARE *sb.* [2], after *hardware.*] *Computers.* The collection of programs that can be used with a particular kind of computer, esp. the general and routine ones not written for specific tasks and often supplied by the manufacturer. Cf. *HARDWARE c.

‖**Soigné(e** (swa·nʸe), *a.* 1921. [pa. pple. of Fr. *soigner* to care for, f. *soin* care.] Dressed or adorned with great care.

Soil, *sb.* [1]

Comb.: **s. science** = PEDOLOGY.

Solar, *a.*

Comb.: **s. battery, cell,** a photoelectric device designed to convert s. radiation incident upon it into electrical energy; **s. flare:** see *FLARE *sb.* [1] 1 b; **s. wind** *Astron.*, the continuous flow of charged particles from the sun.

Solid-state (stress variable), *attrib. phr.* 1953. [f. SOLID *a.* + STATE *sb.*] **a.** Concerned with the structure and properties of solids, esp. with their explanation in terms of atomic and nuclear physics. **b.** (Employing devices) utilizing the electronic properties of solids (as in transistors and other semiconductor devices, in contrast to the partial vacuum of valves) 1960.

a. S. physics 1953. **b.** S. electronic devices 1968. All silicon s. circuitry, using 20 transistors and 2 diodes 1971.

Solubilize (sǫ·liŭbiləiz), *v.* 1931. [f. SOLUBILITY + -IZE, after *stability, stabilize.*] *trans.* To render soluble or more soluble. Also **So:lubiliza·tion.**

Soluble, *a.*

2. s. glass = WATER-GLASS 5.

Somatotype (sōᵘ·mătotəip), *sb.* 1940. [f. SOMATO- + TYPE *sb.*] Body-build or physique assessed in terms of the extent to which it exhibits the characteristics of each of three extremes (the endomorph, mesomorph, and ectomorph). Hence **So:matoty·pic** *a.*, **-ically** *adv.*

Somatotype (sōᵘ·mătotəip), *v.* 1940. [f. prec. sb.] *trans.* To assess the somatotype of. Hence **So·matoty:ping** *vbl. sb.*

Somatotyping along Sheldonian lines A. HUXLEY.

Some, *indef. pron.* **I. 3.** *And then s.*: and a good deal or a great many in addition (*U.S. slang*) 1914.

Son. 6. d. *U.S.* in the names of societies, e.g. *The Sons of America, of Liberty, of Temperance* 1766.

Sonar (sōᵘ·nāɹ). orig. *U.S.* 1946. [f. initial letters of *sound navigation (and) ranging*, after *radar.*] A system for use under water in which the sound reflected or emitted by an object in the water is used to detect its presence or ascertain its nature, direction, or position; (an) apparatus used for this. Freq. *attrib.*

To conform with the Nato practice, the name Asdic. .has been superseded by the word S., the Admiralty announced yesterday 1963.

Sonde (sǫnd). 1901. [Fr., 'sounding-line, sounding'.] A radiosonde or similar device that is sent aloft to transmit or record information on conditions in the atmosphere. Freq. as a second element in *Combs.*

Sone (sōᵘn). 1936. [– L. *sonus* sound.] A unit of subjective loudness, defined so that the number of sones is proportional to the loudness of a sound, 1 sone being equated with 40 phons.

‖**Son et lumière** (soṅ e lümiḝr). 1958. [Fr., 'sound and light'.] An entertainment given by night outside a historic building in which recorded sound and lighting effects are used to present a dramatic narrative about its history.

Song. 4. b. *Nothing to make a s. about*: nothing to boast of, of slight or no importance. **c.** *s. and dance* (colloq.): a palaver, rigmarole; a commotion 1899 (in *lit.* sense 1628).

Sonic (sǫ·nik), *a.* 1924. [f. L. *sonus* sound + -IC.] **a.** Employing or operated by sound waves. **b.** Of or pertaining to sound; equal to that of (audible) sound 1942.

b. An aircraft reaching s. speed 1950.

Comb.: **s. bang** = *s. boom:* **s. barrier** (see *BARRIER 4 b); **s. boom,** a sudden loud noise heard when the shock wave from an aircraft travelling faster than sound reaches the ears.

Sonnet, *sb.*

Comb.: **s. sequence,** a set of sonnets connected in theme.

Sonobuoy (sōᵘ·noboi). 1946. [f. *sono-*, comb. form of L. *sonus* sound + BUOY *sb.*] A buoy having equipment for detecting underwater sounds and automatically transmitting them by radio.

Son of a bitch. *slang.* Also **son-of-a-bitch, sonofabitch.** 1724. [Cf. SON *sb.* 7 c.] A despicable or hateful man; also, with weakened force, a 'fellow', 'guy'; = *BASTARD 1 b. Also as *int.*, an exclamation of surprise or disgust.

Sophisticate (sŏfi·stikĕt), *sb.* 1924. [f. the ppl. adj.] A sophisticated person.

Sophisticated, *ppl. a.* **2. b.** Of a person: free of naïvety, experienced, worldly-wise; cultured 1895. **c.** Of a thing: such as appeals to s. persons 1915. **4.** Of equipment, techniques, processes, etc.: refined, highly elaborate; employing advanced or complicated techniques; incorporating the latest developments and refinements 1952.

2. b. She preferred smooth s. young men. .who amused and flattered *her* 1957. **c.** S. melodramas in which a glamor is thrown about the underworld 1915. **4.** He represents a. .more s. stage in the evoluation of Pythagorean astronomy 1952. Laser beams. .are useful to scientists as a s. light-source 1970. The High Gothic font was a s. piece of furniture 1970. Hence **Sophi·sticatedly** *adv.*

Sophistication. 5. Sophisticated quality; refinement, subtlety 1951.

Sore, *a.* [1] **II. 4.** Now in U.S. colloq. use: displeased, vexed 1886.

Sorption (sǫ·ɹpʃən). 1909. [Extracted from *absorption* and *adsorption.*] *Physical Chem.* The combined or undifferentiated action of absorption and adsorption.

Sortie. 3. An operational flight by a military aircraft 1941.

Souk (sūk). Also **sôk, sook, suk(h), suq.** 1899. [Arab.] A market or market-place.

Soul, *sb.* **3. c.** The fact or essence of being an American Black. Also *attrib.*, as **s.-brother,** a fellow Black; **s.-food,** the traditional food of U.S. Blacks; **s.-music,** a style of jazz allied to the blues.

Sound, *sb.* [2]

Comb.: **s. barrier** (see *BARRIER 4 b); **s.-effect,** a sound other than speech or music introduced artificially into a film, play, etc.; **s.-track,** the narrow strip along the edge of a cinema film that carries the sound recording.

Soup, *v.* (See under SOUP *sb.*) **2.** To increase the power of (an engine); to supercharge; freq. const. *up.* Also *transf.* and *fig.* So **Souped(-up)** *ppl. a.* **Souping-up** *vbl. sb.* 1921.

Sourpuss (sauᵊ·ɹpus). orig. *U.S.* 1940. [f. SOUR *a.* + U.S. slang *puss* face.] A sour-tempered person.

Sousaphone (sū·zăfōᵘn). [f. name of John Philip *Sousa*, U.S. bandmaster (1854–1932) + *-phone* of SAXOPHONE.] A variety of bass tuba common in brass bands.

Soused (saust), *ppl. a.* 1550. [SOUSE *v.* [1]] **1.** Pickled (*dial.*). **2.** Soaked in liquor 1613; (*mod. slang*) drunk 1902. Cf. *PICKLED *ppl. a.* 2.

Southpaw (sau·þpǭ:). orig. *U.S.* 1892. [f. SOUTH *a.* + PAW *sb.*] **1.** A left-handed baseball pitcher. **2.** A left-handed boxer 1942.

Space, *sb.* **II. 4. b.** Add to def.: *spec.* the universe beyond the earth's atmosphere. In numerous *Combs.*, as *s. flight, sickness, station, suit, travel, vehicle*; **s.-walk** *sb.*, an act or spell of physical activity undertaken by an astronaut in space outside a spacecraft; hence as *v. intr.*; also **s.-walker.**

Comb.: **s.-heater,** a self-contained heater designed to heat the space in which it is situated; hence **s.-heating** *vbl. sb.* and *ppl. a.*

Spa·cecraft. Also **space-craft** and as two words. Pl. **-craft.** 1944. [f. SPACE *sb.* + CRAFT *sb.*] Any vehicle designed to travel in space.

An American attempt to put a 388lb s. into orbit around the moon 1960.

Spa·ceship. Also **space-ship.** 1894. [f. SPACE *sb.* + SHIP *sb.* [1]] A spacecraft; *esp.* one (conceived as) capable of carrying men and of taking off and landing under their control.

Spade, *sb.* [2] **3.** *slang* (orig. *U.S.*). A Negro 1934.

Spam (spæm). 1939. [f. initial and final letters of *spiced ham.*] Proprietary name for a type of tinned meat.

Spastic, *a.* **3.** Of a person: affected with s. paralysis, a condition in which some muscles undergo tonic spasm (sometimes resulting in abnormal posture) and resist passive displacement, so that voluntary movement of the part affected is difficult and poorly coordinated 1903. **B.** *sb.* A s. person 1937.

Special, *a.* **3. b.** *Special Drawing Rights* (abbrev. S.D.R.s): additional drawing rights allocated to member countries of the International Monetary Fund, allowing them extra powers to purchase foreign currency from the Fund.

Speciation (spīsi,ēⁱ·ʃən, spīʃi,ēⁱ·ʃən). 1907. [f. SPECIES + -ATION.] The development of new biological species, or the causes of this process.

Spectrum. 3. b. The entire range of wavelengths (or frequencies) of electromagnetic radiation, from the longest radio waves to the shortest gamma rays, of which the range of visible light is only a small part; also *transf.*, of radiation of other kinds 1929. **c.** *fig.* The (or an) entire range of anything, ordered according to degree, quality, etc.; a gamut 1926.

3. c. A broad s. of opinion, ranging from moderates to extremists 1959. A s. of derivatives is available, ranging from ineffective to extremely powerful inhibitors 1971.

Speed, *sb.* **II. 1.** *At s.* (delete †). **4.** *slang* (orig. *U.S.*). Methamphetamine or one of its salts 1969.

Spee·d-up. 1923. [f. *to speed up*, SPEED *v.* II. 2 d.] Increase of the rate of work, production, movement, etc.

Spiel[1] (spīl). 1824. [See BONSPIEL.] A curling match.

Spiel[2] (spīl, ʃpīl). *slang* (orig. and chiefly *U.S.*). 1896. [– G. *spiel* game, play.] (A) glib or persuasive talk or speech. Hence as *v. trans.* and *intr.*

Spillage (spi·lėdʒ). 1934. [f. SPILL *v.* + -AGE.] That which is spilled; the action of spilling.

Spin-dri·er. 1939. [f. SPIN *v.* + DRIER.] A machine for drying washing in a rapidly rotating drum.

Spin-off (spi·n,ǫf). orig. *U.S.* 1961. [f. SPIN *v.* + OFF *adv.*] An incidental result, esp. an incidental benefit of an industrial or technological process or activity; such results collectively.

Non-stick frying pans used to be the s. which made space research worthwhile 1969.

Spiral, *sb.* **3. f.** A progressive rising movement in which two or more interdependent quantities (as prices and incomes) increase successively by turns 1939.

Spiv (spiv). *slang.* 1934. [Of unkn. origin.] A man who makes a living by his wits without working. (The orig. sense is said to be a bookmaker's runner or assistant.) Hence **Spivvery** (spi·vəri), the characteristic activities of a spiv.

Splash, *sb.* **1. c.** A small quantity of soda-water, etc., added to a glass of spirits 1929.

attrib. Applied to an item in a newspaper or journal set on the page with a wide display, e.g. *a front-page s. story.*

Splash-. s.-down, the alighting of a spacecraft on the sea; hence as *v. intr.*

From launch to s. the Apollo-8 mission went entirely without hitch 1968.

Splinter, *sb.* **1. c.** Applied to a small part that splits off from a group or party 1935.

More marked . . than any net transfer between the major parties was the rejection of their lesser rivals and of the 'splinter groups' 1951.

Split, *ppl. a.*

Special collocations: **s.-level** *Archit.* used *attrib.* of a building in which one room or set of rooms is a fraction of a storey higher or lower than adjoining rooms; **s.-mind** = SCHIZOPHRENIA; **s.-second,** (also, *transf.*) a very brief moment of time.

Spot, *sb.*

Comb.: **s.-check,** a check made on the spot; a test taken at random.

Spread, *sb.* **5. a.** *slang.* Butter 1812. **b.** Jam, paste, etc., for spreading on bread, e.g. *chocolate s.* 1886.

Sputnik (spu·tnik). 1957. [Russ., 'travelling companion, satellite', f. *s* with + *put'* way, journey + *-NIK (agent-suffix).] A Russian artificial satellite.

Square, *sb.* **II. 3. a.** Colloq. phr. *back to* (or *in, on*) *s. one*: back where one started; returning to the beginning. **13.** *slang* (orig. *Jazz*). A person who is old-fashioned or out of touch with modern ways 1938.

Phr. *To be on the s.*, to be a freemason.

Square, *a.* **II. 2. c.** Having the characteristics of a SQUARE (sense *13).

Comb.: **s. dance,** a dance in which the partners are arranged in a square or similar set form, e.g. the lancers, the quadrille; so **s. dancer, s. dancing.**

Squeeze, *sb.* **1. d.** *Economics.* A restriction imposed on borrowing, investment, etc. 1927.

Stack, *v.* **5.** *Aeronaut.* To keep (aircraft) flying over an airport at different heights until they can land 1948.

Staff, *sb.*[1] **I. 6. b.** A token given to an engine-driver on a single-line railway as an authority to proceed over a given section of the line; also *attrib.*, as *s. system* 1902.

Stage, *sb.* **II. 5.** *Electronics.* A single amplifying transistor or valve together with the associated resistors, capacitors, etc. 1920. **6.** Each of two or more sections of a rocket that have their own engines and propellant and fall away in turn as their propellant becomes exhausted 1952.

Staging, *vbl. sb.* **1. a.** Also, the shelves for plants in a greenhouse.

Comb.: **s. area** *Mil.*, the place where troops in transit are assembled prior to moving to their next destination.

Stakhanovite (stăkā·novəit). 1937. [f. name of a Russian coal-miner, A. G. *Stakhanov*, with whom the practice originated + -ITE[1].] A (Russian) worker who is awarded recognition with special privileges for extraordinary output. Also *attrib.* Hence **Stakha·novism,** the efficiency system under which such competition and awards are current.

S. women miners in the Donetz basin are performing four, nine, and eleven norms each 1952.

‖**Stalag** (stā·læg, stæ·læg, ‖ʃtā·lag). 1940. [G., f. *stamm* STEM *sb.*[1] (used for 'of the main stock') + *lager* camp, LEAGUER *sb.*[1] 1.] A German prison camp primarily for non-commissioned officers and privates.

Stalinism (stā·liniz'm). 1927. [f. name of J. V. *Stalin* (Dzhugashvili) (1879–1953), Soviet statesman.] The policy of Stalin in the Soviet government of Russia. Hence **Sta·linist** *a.* and *sb.*

Stand, *v.*

With advs. **S. down. d.** To go off duty; hence **s.-down** *sb.* **S. in. c.** To act as substitute (*for*); hence **s.-in** *sb.*, a person who does this. **S. to.** †**a.** To be present; to set to work, fall to. **b.** *Mil.* To take up a position in preparation for an attack (see To *adv.* 5).

Starch, *sb.*

Comb.: **s.-reduced** *a.*, (of bread, etc.) having less than the normal proportion of starch.

Stardom (stā·ɹdəm). 1865. [f. STAR *sb.* + -DOM.] The status of a theatrical or other star; the realm or sphere of such stars.

Starkers (stā·ɹkəɹz), *a. slang.* 1923. [f. STARK(-NAKED + -ER[6] + *-s.*] = STARK-NAKED *a.*

Starlet. 3. A young film actress who is being prepared for major roles 1922.

Starry, *a.*

3. s.-eyed *a. colloq.*, having the stars (the height of one's ambition) reflected in one's eyes.

Stash (stæʃ), *v. slang.* 1794. [Origin unknown.] **1.** *trans.* and *intr.* To stop, desist from; to leave (a place); to extinguish (a light). **2.** *trans.* To conceal; to put *away*, usu. in a place of safety 1797. Hence **Stashed** (stæʃt) *ppl. a.*, hidden, stored (freq. with *away*).

Stash (stæʃ), *sb. U.S. slang.* 1930. [f. prec.] **1.** A house, dwelling, or hiding-place. **2.** Something concealed, esp. a hidden supply of drugs 1942.

Statal (stēⁱ·tăl), *a.* orig. *U.S.* 1862. [f. STATE *sb.* + -AL[1] 1.] Pertaining to a state or states.

Political citizenship . . s. or national 1862. Three great s. groups [in India] 1949.

Stateless, *a.* **c.** *Polit.* Lacking nationality or citizenship 1902. Hence **Sta·telessness.**

Stately, *a.* **3. s. home,** a large and magnificent house, of a type now often open for the public to view.

The s. homes of England, How beautiful they stand F. D. HEMANS.

Stateside (stēⁱ·tsəid), *a.* and *adv. U.S. colloq.* 1944. [f. STATE *sb.* + SIDE *sb.*[1]] Of the United States; in or towards the United States.

Station, *sb.*

Comb.: **s.-wagon** *U.S.*, a type of covered carriage; in later use (not only in U.S.A.), a sturdy saloon motor vehicle capable of carrying both passengers and goods.

Statism (stēⁱ·tiz'm). 1609. [f. STATE *sb.* + -ISM.] † **1.** Subservience to political expediency in religious matters –1660. † **2.** Political science, statecraft –1620. **3.** Government of a country by the state, as opposed to anarchy 1880. **b.** State administration and control of social and economic affairs 1948.

Status.

Comb.: **s. symbol,** anything considered to show the high social s. of its owner or user.

The vigorous merchandising of goods as s. symbols V. PACKARD.

Stay, *v.*[1]

Comb., f. phr. with advs.: **s.-in,** (of miners) **s.-down, strike,** one in which strikers remain in the place in which they are employed.

Steady, *a.* **B.** *adv.* **d.** *to go steady*: to be regular sweethearts (*with*). *colloq.* (orig. *U.S.*) 1923.

Comb.: **s. state,** an unvarying condition; also *attrib.*

Steam, *sb.*

Comb.: **s. iron,** an electric iron that provides its own supply of steam to the under surface; **s. radio** *colloq.*, radio broadcasting, so called after the coming of television made it seem as old-fashioned as a steam-engine.

Steel, *sb.*

Comb.: **s. band,** a band of West Indian musicians using instruments made from oil-drums; **s. wool** = **wire wool.*

Stegophilist (stegǫ·filist). 1952. [f. Gr. στέγος roof + -PHIL(E + -IST.] One who practises climbing buildings.

Stem, *v.*[1] **4.** *Skiing.* To force the heel of the skis outwards; to check progress by so doing 1924.

Sten (gun). 1942. [f. *S, T*, initials of the inventors + *-en*, as in *BREN.] A type of sub-machine-gun.

Step, *v.* **1.** Phr. *To s. on the gas*: see GAS *sb.*[2]; hence *to s. on it*: to hurry (*colloq.*) 1930.

Stereo[3] (ste·rio, stīᵊ·rio). 1958. *Colloq.* abbrev. of *STEREOPHONIC, -PHONY.

Stereo-isomer (ste:rio-, stīᵊ:rio,əi·soməɹ). 1903. [f. STEREO- + ISOMER.] *Chem.* One of two or more compounds whose molecules consist of identical sequences of atoms and differ only in the spatial orientation of certain atoms. So **Ste:reo-isome·ric** *a.*, **-iso·merism.**

Stereophonic (ste:rio-, stīᵊ:riofǫ·nik), *a.* 1927. [f. STEREO- + PHONIC *a.*] Of sound broadcasts, gramophone records, etc.: involving two (or more) channels, so that particular sounds appear to the listener to come from two or more directions, resulting in increased realism. Hence **Ste:reopho·nically** *adv.* **Stereo·phony.**

Sterling. B. *adj.* **1. b.** Later applied to balances (and debts) repayable in sterling.

Comb.: **s. area,** a group of countries whose currency is tied to the (British) pound s.

Sternutator (stə·ɹniutēⁱtǫɹ). 1922. [f. *sternutat-* (in STERNUTATORY, etc.) + -OR 2.] A substance that causes nasal irritation; esp. a poison gas that causes irritation of the nose and eyes, pain in the chest, and nausea.

Steroid (stīᵊ·roid, ste·roid). 1936. [f. STER)OL + -OID.] *Chem.* Any of a large group of structurally related organic compounds based on three rings of six carbon atoms joined to one of five, including cholesterol and other sterols, the adrenal and sex hormones, and many other compounds with important physiological effects in animals or plants. Also *attrib.* or as *adj.* Hence **Steroi·dal** *a.*

Stevengraph (stī·vəngraf). 1879. [f. the name of the inventor Thomas *Stevens* (1828–1888), a weaver of Coventry, + -GRAPH.] A colourful woven silk picture produced by the firm founded by Stevens.

Stick, *sb.*[1] **II. 6.** A number of aerial bombs released in close succession, or of parachute troops from an aircraft 1940.

Phr. *the sticks*, orig. *U.S. slang*: the country, 'backwoods'.

Sticky, *a.*[2] **1.** Also, covered with adhesive or 'tacky' foreign matter 1870. **2.** *slang.* Extremely disagreeable and painful 1915. **3.** *slang.* Very critical, particular, or captious 1920.
1. s. bomb, a grenade which sticks to the object that it hits. **2.** A s. time in the trenches 1915. [To] come to a s. end 1915.

Stiff, *sb.* **4.** orig. *U.S.* An intractable or incorrigible person 1896.

Stilbœstrol (stilbī·strǒl). Also (*U.S.*) **stilbestrol.** 1938. [f. STILB(ENE + ŒSTR(US + -OL.] *Biochem.* A powerful synthetic œstrogen, $C_{18}H_{20}O_2$, that is active when used as a cream or taken orally; also called *diethylstilbœstrol.*

Stiletto.
Comb.: **s. heel,** a high, sharply pointed heel on a shoe.

Sting, *v.* **2. d.** *pass.* To be heavily charged or involved in expense, be swindled. *colloq.* (orig. *U.S.*) 1903. Also *actively.*

Stinker. 4. *slang.* Something irritating or offensive 1919.

Stirrup, *sb.*
Comb.: **s. pump,** a pump having a foot-plate and fitted with a tube having a nozzle for producing a jet or spray to extinguish a fire or incendiary bombs.

Stochastic, *a.* Restrict 'Now *rare* or *Obs.*' to sense in Dict. and add: **2.** Governed by or proceeding in accordance with the laws of probability 1943.

Stock, *sb.*[1] **B.** *adj.* **4. s. car,** a racing-car with the basic chassis of an ordinary commercial model 1934.

Stockholm (stǫ·khō^{u}m). Name of the capital of Sweden: used *attrib.* in **S. pitch,** pitch yielded by **S. tar,** a variety of tar prepared from resinous pinewood and used in the maintenance of a ship's rigging, etc. 1867.

Stocking, *sb.*
Comb.: **s. mask,** a (nylon) s. pulled over the head and face, worn as a disguise by criminals; **s.-stitch,** a knitting stitch commonly used in stockings, producing a plain smooth surface.

Sto·ckpile, *sb.* 1895. [f. STOCK *sb.*[1] + PILE *sb.*[2]] **1.** *Mining.* A pile of ore built up when the rate of mining exceeds that of disposal, or maintained as a reserve. **2.** *transf.* A reserve store of anything, *spec.* of nuclear weapons: chiefly in political and commercial contexts 1946. Hence **Sto·ckpile** *v. trans.*, to accumulate or keep in a s. **Sto·ckpiling** *vbl. sb.*

Stomp (stǫmp), *sb.* 1924. [U.S. dial., f. STAMP *sb.*] *Jazz.* A lively dance characterized by heavy stamping. Hence **Stomp** *v. intr.*, to dance in this manner.

Stone, *v.* **2. b.** *slang* (orig. *U.S.*). Chiefly as *ppl. a.* or *pa. pple.*: intoxicated, drugged, or stimulated with drink, drugs, etc. 1954.

Stonk (stǫŋk), *v.* 1944. [Cf. dial. *stonk* (game of marbles).] *trans.* To bombard with artillery. Hence as *sb.*

Stonker (stǫ·ŋkəɹ), *v. Austral.* and *N.Z. slang.* 1923. [Origin unkn.] *trans.* To baffle, make useless; to beat. Hence **Sto·nkered** *ppl. a.*, tired, worn out.

Stooge (stūdʒ), *sb. slang* (orig. *U.S.*). 1913. [Of unkn. origin.] A butt, foil, esp. for a comedian; *transf.* a deputy in difficult or strange circumstances. Hence **Stooge** *v. intr.*, to move, travel, esp. to fly *about, around* in aircraft 1942.

Store, *sb.* **9. b.** *Computers.* = *MEMORY 2 b. 1956.

Straddle, *v.* **7. b.** To drop shot or bombs across (a target), beginning on one side or end and finishing on the other 1917. Hence **Straddle** *sb.*, an instance of this action.

Straight, *a.*, etc. **A.** *adj.* **5. c.** *slang.* Of a person: heterosexual.

Strange, *a.* **8. c.** *Nuclear Physics.* Of a sub-atomic particle: having non-zero 'strangeness' 1956.

Strangeness. (See after STRANGELY *adv.*) **2.** *Nuclear Physics.* A quantized property assigned to mesons and baryons that is conserved in strong interactions, a particle with non-zero s. having a relatively long life-time despite being produced by the strong interaction 1956.

Strap, *sb.*
Comb.: **strapwork,** ornamental work representing narrow bands or straps folded, interlaced, etc.

Strategic, *a.* **b.** *S. bombing*: bombing designed to disrupt the enemy's internal economy, to destroy morale, and the like: opp. *tactical bombing.* **c.** Of materials: essential to the provision of munitions of war, as *s. metals, ores.*

Stratosphere. For pronunc. read (stræ·tǒsfīᵊɹ). In current British use the upper limit is raised (being at a height of 30–35 miles instead of at 12–15 miles), so that the s. includes a region in which the temperature increases with height. Hence **Stratosphe·ric** *a.*

Stray, *a.* **3. b.** *colloq.* Occurring or met with casually or unexpectedly, as a *s. customer, instance, remark* 1873.

Stream, *sb.* **7.** Each of several groups of school-children regarded as having similar ability (in relation to their age); often designated *A, B, C,* etc. 1946.
5. Phr. *s. of consciousness,* the conscious reaction of an individual to external events viewed as a continual flow; a method of fiction depicting events through this flow in the mind of a character.

Streaming, *vbl. sb.* **c.** The practice in a school of separating pupils of the same age into streams according to their ability, so that the range of ability in any one class is reduced 1957.

Strep. 1942. Colloq. abbrev. of STREPTOCOCCUS, -COCCAL *a.*

Strine (strəin). 1967. [Alleged Austral. pronunciation of 'Australian'.] A name given to comic transliterations of Australian speech, as *Emma Chisit,* 'How much is it?'

String, *sb.* **II. 1. b.** *colloq.* (orig. *U.S.*). A condition attached *to* an agreement, etc. 1888. **2. c.** The horses in training at a stable.
Comb.: **s. alphabet,** a reading contrivance for the use of the blind by which words are denoted by means of knots of various kinds in a s.

Stringer. 3. d. A longitudinal structural member in an aircraft fuselage or wing 1932.

Strip, *sb.*[2] **1. c.** orig. *U.S.* A row of pictures in a newspaper or magazine portraying some incident or story usu. a humorous one and often involving characters that appear recurrently; esp. *comic s., s. cartoon* 1928.
Comb.: **s. lighting,** lighting in the form of tubular fluorescent lamps; **s. mill,** a mill in which steel slabs are rolled into strips.

Strip, *v.*[1]
Comb.: **s.-tease,** an entertainment in which a woman divests herself of her garments one by one before an audience.

Stripper. 4. A woman who performs in a strip-tease act 1942.

Strobe (strō^{u}b). 1962. [repr. first syllable of STROBOSCOPE, -SCOPIC.] An apparatus for producing *s. lighting,* rapidly flashing bright light; so *s. light.*

Stroganoff (strǫ·gănǫf). 1932. [The name of Count Paul *Stroganoff,* 19th-cent. Russian diplomat.] Applied to a dish of meat sliced into strips and cooked in a sauce containing sour cream, as *beef (bœuf) S.*

Strong, *a.*
Comb.: **b. s. interaction** *Nuclear Physics,* a physical interaction that is effective only between certain sub-atomic particles when very close together (e.g. protons and neutrons in an atomic nucleus), at which distance it is the strongest of the four known kinds of interaction.

Strong-arm, *a.* orig. *U.S.* 1903. [f. STRONG *a.* + ARM *sb.*[1]] Having or showing strength of arm, physically powerful, able to overpower by force.

Strong(-)point. 1922. [tr. G. *feste stellung*; see STRONG *a.* 8, POINT IV. 2.] *Mil.* A specially fortified position in a defence system.
To destroy trenches, 'pill-boxes', strong points 1930.

Structural, *a.*
3. s. linguistics, the study of a language viewed as a system made up of interrelated elements; **s. psychology,** the study of the arrangement and composition of mental states and conscious experiences.

Strudel (strū·d'l). 1924. [G.] A pastry confection, originating in Austria, of very thin paste rolled up with various fillings, as *apple s.* Also *attrib.*, as *s. pastry.*

Studio.
Comb.: **s. couch,** a sofa that can be used as a bed.

Stuff, *sb.* **III. 2.** Phr. (orig. *U.S.*) *To do one's s.*: to perform one's tricks, do what one is required or expected to do. Also *to know one's s.*

Stuffed (stʌft), *ppl. a.*
s. shirt *U.S.*, a man of imposing or self-important exterior but of inferior abilities.
While Pompey was a competent soldier, politically he was to prove pretty much a s. shirt 1942.

Stunt, *sb.*[2]
Comb.: **s. man,** a man employed to double for an actor in performing dangerous stunts.

Sub, *sb.* **6.** = SUBMARINE *sb.* 1917.

Sub, *v.* **1. b.** To act as a substitute, in general senses 1938.

Sub-.
7. b. Su·b-culture *Anthrop.*, a cultural group within a larger culture.

Sub-ato·mic, *a.* 1903. [SUB- 7.] Smaller than or occurring in an atom; relating to such particles or to phenomena involving them. (In use generally = *SUB-NUCLEAR *a.*)

Sub-critical, *a.* 1945. [SUB- 19.] *Nuclear Physics.* Not critical, less than critical (see *CRITICAL *a.* 7 b).

Subliminal, *a.*
s. advertising, advertising that is presented in such a way (e.g. by means of very brief pictures on television) that it is not consciously perceived, although capable of influencing opinion or behaviour.

Sub-machi·ne-gun. 1924. [SUB- 5 b.] A light machine-gun that does not need a mount and fires pistol cartridges.

Sub-mi·niature, *a.* 1947. [SUB- 9.] Even smaller than 'miniature': very much reduced in size.
There are two alternative designs, one using s. valves and the other transistors 1956.

Sub-nu·clear, *a.* 1964. [SUB- 7.] Smaller than or occurring in an atomic nucleus; relating to such particles or to phenomena involving them.

Suborbital, *a.* and *sb.* **A.** *adj.* **2.** *Astronaut.* [SUB- 19.] Not involving or completing an orbit of the earth (or another planet) 1959.

Su·b-song. 1927. [SUB- 5 c.] *Ornith.* A quiet low-pitched type of bird song, distinguished from the full song.

Subsonic (sʌbsǫ·nik), *a.* 1940. [f. SUB- 19 + *SONIC *a.*, after *supersonic.*] Pertaining to, involving, capable of, or designating speeds less than the speed of sound.
S. tunnels 1946. S. speeds of around 600 m.p.h. 1958. Hence **Subso·nically** *adv.*

Sub-sta·ndard, *a.* 1909. [SUB- 19.] Of less than required or normal quality, size, etc.; inferior.

Su·bstitutable, *a.* 1805. [f. SUBSTITUT(E *v.* + -ABLE.] Capable of being substituted. Hence **Su·bstitutabi·lity,** the property of being substitutable.

Subtopia (sʌbtō^{u}·piă). 1955. [f. SUB-(URBAN + U)TOPIA.] Term applied to urban and rural areas disfigured by ill-planned and ugly building development; unsightly suburbs regarded as encroaching upon the natural scene; also *fig.*

Sugar, *sb.*
Comb.: **s.-daddy** *slang* (orig. *U.S.*), an elderly man who lavishes gifts on a young woman.

Suicide, *sb.*[2]
Comb.: **s. club,** (*a*) a club whose members are pledged to commit s.; (*b*) ironical term for units with particularly dangerous missions in war; **s. pact,** an agreement between two persons to commit s. together; **s. pilot, squad,** a pilot or group on a dangerous mission in war.

Suk(h, varr. *SOUK.

‖**Sukiyaki** (su·kiya·ki; also skī·^{y}aki). 1920. [Jap.] A Japanese dish consisting of slices of beef fried with vegetables and sauce and served with rice.

Sulfa, var. *SULPHA.

Sulpha (sʌ·lfă). Also **sulfa.** 1942. [First syllable of *SULPHANILAMIDE.] Pharm. *Sulpha drug,* a sulphonamide drug.

Sulphanilamide (sʌlfăni·lămǝid). Also (*U.S.*) **sulf-.** 1935. [f. *sulphanil(ic* (f. SULPH- + ANILIC *a.*) + AMIDE.] *Chem.* A synthetic colourless crystalline compound, $H_2N{\cdot}C_6H_4{\cdot}SO_2NH_2$, with anti-bacterial properties.

Sulphonamide (sʌlfōᵘ·nămәid). Also (*U.S.*) **sulf-**. 1910. [f. SULPHON(E + AMIDE.] *Chem.* Any organic compound containing the group —SO_2N=; *spec.* any of numerous drugs derived from sulphanilamide that prevent the multiplication of certain pathogenic bacteria.

Summer time. **2.** *Double s. t.*, the standard time, two hours in advance of Greenwich mean time, first adopted in May 1941, ceased in July 1945.

Summit. **4.** *Polit.* Used *attrib.* of the heads of states, as *s. conference*, *s. level* 1955.

‖**Sumo** (sū·mo). 1901. [Jap.] In Japan, a form of wrestling in which a wrestler wins a bout by forcing his opponent out of a circle or by obliging him to touch the ground with any part of his body except his feet; also, a competitor in this sport. Also *attrib.* and *Comb.*

Sump, *sb.* **2. c.** The oil reservoir at the bottom of the crank-case of an internal-combustion engine 1907.

Sun, *sb.*

Comb.: **s.-glasses,** tinted spectacles for protecting the eyes from sunlight or glare; **s.-lamp,** (*a*) a large lamp with a parabolic reflector used in film-making; (*b*) a lamp emitting ultra-violet rays, used esp. for therapeutic purposes and to produce sun-tan artificially.

Sunday.

Comb.: **S. painter,** one who paints purely for pleasure (= Fr. *peintre de dimanche*).

Super, *a.* **3.** *colloq.* Of superlative or exceptional quality 1895.

Superconductivity (s¹ū:pəɹkǫndɒkti·viti). 1913. [f. SUPER- II. 2 + CONDUCTIVITY.] *Physics.* The property, exhibited by some substances at temperatures close to absolute zero, of having zero electrical resistance. Hence **Supercondu·cting, -condu·ctive** *adjs.*, exhibiting s.; perfectly conducting. **Supercondu·ctor,** a substance that becomes superconducting at sufficiently low temperatures.

Super-ego (s¹ūpəɹe·go, -ī·go). 1923. [f. SUPER- II. 3 + EGO.] *Psychol.* In Freudian psychology, the part of the mind that evolves from the ego in infancy and comprises (unconscious) ideals of conduct as well as inhibitions on it; conscience, inner morality.

Superintendent. **A.** *sb.* **1. b.** A police officer above the rank of inspector 1836.

Supermarket (s¹ū·pəɹmā:ɹkėt). orig. *U.S.* 1938. [f. SUPER- II. 2 + MARKET *sb.*] A large self-service store selling foods and some household goods.

Supernova (s¹ūpəɹnōᵘ·vă). Pl. **supernovæ** (-ī), **-novas.** 1934. [f. SUPER- II. 2 + NOVA.] *Astron.* A star that suddenly undergoes an immense increase in brightness as a result of an explosion in which most of its mass is ejected.

A s. will outshine even an entire galaxy for a few days 1972.

Supersonic, *a.* (Sense 1 is now *rare*: cf. *ULTRASONIC *a.*) **B.** *sb. colloq.* A s. aircraft 1962. Hence **Superso·nically** *adv.*

Supply, *sb.* **I. 4.** *In short s.*: of which the s. is short of what is required.

Supply-, SUPPLY *sb.* or *v.* in comb. = (*a*) having charge of or carrying the supplies of an army, etc. as *s. column, officer, ship, train*; (*b*) supplying water, oil, etc. to an apparatus, etc., as *s.-pipe, -pump, -roller* 1840; (*c*) supplying a vacancy, as *s. teacher*.

Suppo·rting, *ppl. a.* 1610. [-ING².] That supports (*spec.* in techn. senses). *S. film*: a less important film presented with the chief item of a programme.

Suppress, *v.* **8.** *Electronics.* To reduce the amplitude of (unwanted frequencies); to counteract (interference) 1929. **b.** To equip with a suppressor for reducing electrical interference 1948.

Supra-segmental (s¹ū·prăˌsegme·ntăl), *a.* 1941. [f. SUPRA- + *SEGMENTAL *a.*] *Phonetics.* Of or pertaining to certain articulatory features of an utterance, esp. length, pitch, and stress.

Supremo (sūpre·mo, sūprī·mo). 1937. [f. Sp. (*generalissimo*) *supremo* supreme general.] A supreme leader or ruler; a man holding the highest military or political authority.

Suq, var. *SOUK.

Sure, *a.* **IV. 1. d.** *S. thing*: a certainty 1836. Also *advb.*, certainly 1896.

Surface, *sb.* **1.** *spec.* The surface of the sea, as in **s. mail,** mail carried by sea (or, in U.S.A., by land), **s. craft, s.-raider, s.-ship** (as opp. to submarine).

Surface, *v.* **3.** *intr.* To come to the surface; also *fig.* 1922.

Surra (sɒ·ră, sū·ră). 1883. [Marathi.] A tropical, febrile disease of horses and other animals, caused by the protozoan parasite *Trypanosoma evansi*.

Surtax. **b.** A graduated tax in addition to income tax on incomes above a certain level 1929.

‖**Sushi** (sū·ʃi). 1893. [Jap.] In Japan, a snack consisting of cold boiled rice flavoured with vinegar and commonly garnished with slices of fish, sea-weed, or cooked egg.

Swag, *sb.*

Comb.: **swagman** *Austral.*, one who carries a swag; a tramp.

Swash, *a.*²

s. plate *Engin.*, a circular plate fixed obliquely at the end of a shaft so as to give a reciprocating motion to a part in contact with it.

Swastika. **2.** This symbol as the emblem of the German Nazi party and régime 1934.

Sweat, *sb.*

Comb.: **s.-shirt,** a kind of thin cotton sweater.

Sweep, *v.*

Comb.: **s.-back,** the angle between the lateral axis and the wing axis of an aeroplane.

Sweet, *a.*

Comb.: **s.-and-sour,** of meat, etc.: dressed in a sauce containing sugar and vinegar.

Swept, *ppl. a.*

Comb.: **s.-back** *Aeronaut.*, (of an aircraft wing) having the axis running backwards at an angle to that of the aircraft; so *s. wing*; **s.-up,** (of hair) brushed up towards the top of the head.

Swim, *v.*

Comb.: **s.-suit,** a bathing costume.

Swing, *sb.* **I. 11.** An easy rhythmic pulse in jazz; *spec.* a type of jazz or dance music, popular in the 1930s and 1940s, characterized by a strong regular rhythm 1937.

Swing, *v.* **15.** *trans.* and *intr.* To play (music) with a buoyant beat 1933.

Swing-. **2. s.-wing,** an aircraft wing that can be moved backwards or forwards; usu. *attrib.*

Swinging, *ppl. a.* **2.** In Jazz music: lively, go-ahead; superlatively good; also *transf.* 1955.

Switch, *sb.* **6.** *fig.* Diversion of activity, effort, or production 1915. Also **Switch-over.**

Switch, *v.* **6. b.** To exchange, esp. of race horses, and of investments 1897. **7. b.** *slang. Switched on*, under the influence of marijuana or other drugs; cf. **turn on*. Hence, in more general sense, aware of all that is considered fashionable and up-to-date; 'hip'.

Swither (swi·ðəɹ), *v. Sc.* 1501. [Origin unkn.] *intr.* To hesitate, be uncertain. Hence **Swi·ther** *sb.* 1719.

Swiz(z (swiz). *slang.* 1932. [Origin unkn.] A swindle.

Symphonic, *a.*

3. s. ballet, a ballet such as may be danced to a symphony; **s. dance,** an orchestral piece in dance rhythm and style but not necessarily intended for dancing.

Synchro- (si·ŋkro), abbrev. of *synchronized, synchronous*, used in combs.

Synchrocyclotron (si:ŋkroˌsəi·klŏtrǫn). 1947. [f. *SYNCHRO- + *CYCLOTRON.] *Physics.* A modification of the cyclotron in which the frequency of the electric field is decreased as the particles gain energy, to allow for their increase in mass, so that higher energies can be achieved.

Synchronic, *a.* Restrict *rare* to senses in Dict. and add: **2.** *Linguistics.* Pertaining to or designating a method of linguistic study concerned with a language at a given time; descriptive as opposed to historical or diachronic 1927.

Synchrotron (si·ŋkrŏtrǫn). 1947. [f. *SYNCHRO- + *-TRON.] *Physics.* A modification of the cyclotron in which the strength of the magnetic field is increased as the particles gain energy, to keep the radius of their path constant (the frequency of the electric field being decreased in addition in the case of a proton s.).

Syncretism. **2.** *Philol.* The merging of two or more case-forms in one 1901.

Synthetic, *a.* **2. b.** Applied *gen.* to substances and preparations simulating a natural product; hence, artificial 1907. **c.** As *sb. pl.*, s. products 1940.

System. **I. 1. c.** The established political or social order 1806.

Comb.: **systems analysis,** the technique of analysing an activity, process, organization, etc., in order to determine how a computer may be employed to achieve the desired end more efficiently or conveniently.

T.

I. 3. b. T-bone, a T-shaped bone; **T-bone steak,** a beef-steak cut from the thin end of the loin, containing a T-bone; **T-shirt,** a short-sleeved shirt so cut that when spread out flat its shape suggests the letter T.

II. 3. T. T., teetotal(ler, tuberculin-tested; T.V.A., Tennessee Valley Authority.

Tab¹**.** **I. 1. c.** *Theatr.* A loop or cord by which stage curtains are hung; hence, a stage curtain 1930.

Tabla (ta·blă). 1865. [Urdu *tabla* – Arab. *ṭabla* drum.] In Indian music, a pair of small drums played with the hands.

Tachism(e (tæ·ʃiz'm). 1956. [Fr. *tachisme*, f. *tache* stain + *isme* -ISM.] = **action painting*.

Tachograph (tæ·kogrɑf). 1968. [f. Gr. τάχος speed + -GRAPH.] A device that may be fitted to a motor vehicle to record automatically its speed and its times of travel.

Tack (tæk), *sb.*⁵ 1940. [Short for TACKLE *sb.* 6.] = TACKLE *sb.* 6. Also *attrib.*, as **t. room,** a room where such tackle is stored.

‖**Tædium vitæ** (tī·diŏm vəi·tī). 1811. [L.] Weariness of life.

Tag, *v.*¹ **1. b.** = *LABEL *v.* 2. 1941.

Tagliatelle, -i (talyate·le, -i). 1919. [It., pl. of *tagliatella, -o*.] A ribbon-shaped variety of pasta.

Taiga (tai·gă). 1888. [Russ.] A region of coniferous forest in northern Russia; hence, a similar region elsewhere.

Tail, *sb.*¹ **2. b.** The rear part of an aircraft 1909. **3. b.** *pl.* (Evening dress with) a tail coat (*colloq.*) 1857. **9.** *slang.* A person who follows or 'shadows' another 1914.

Tail, *v.*¹ **I. 7.** *slang.* To follow or 'shadow' (someone) 1871.

Tailor-made, *a.* **2. c.** Perfectly suited *for* a particular purpose 1958. Hence as *sb.*, (*a*) a tailor-made suit or costume 1899; (*b*) *slang*, a ready-made cigarette (opp. one that the smoker rolls for himself) 1928.

Take, *sb.* **6. b.** A sound recording made in one unbroken session 1926.

Take, *v.* **IV. 6.** Phr. *To have what it takes*: to possess the necessary qualities, esp. those needed for success. orig. *U.S.*

Take-over (tē¹·kōᵘvəɹ). 1930. [f. *to take over* (see TAKE *v.*).] An act of taking over; *spec.* the assumption of control or ownership, esp. of a business concern. Also *attrib.*, as **t. bid,** an attempt or offer to take control of a company.

Tala (ta·lă). 1891. [Skr.] In Indian music, the rhythmic pattern of time and metre.

Talent, *sb.*

Comb.: **t.-scout,** one who seeks out talented people for acting, sports, business, etc.

Talk, *v.* **II.**

3. Phr. *To t. down*: also, to provide (a pilot) with directions that enable him to land, esp. in overcast or emergency conditions. Hence **t.-down** *sb.*

Talking, *vbl. sb.*

Comb.: **t. point,** a topic suitable for or inviting discussion or argument.

Talking, *ppl. a.*

T. book, a recording on disc or tape of the reading of a book, esp. for use by blind people.

Tamboura (tæmbūᵊ·ră). Also **tambur, tambura.** 1891. [– Arab. *ṭanbūra*.] An

Indian musical instrument with four or five strings, used as a drone.

Tam-tam (tæ·mtæm). 1839. [Hindi: see TOM-TOM.] A large metal gong.

Tangy (tæ·ŋi), *a.* Also **tangey.** 1875. [f. TANG *sb.*[1] + -Y[1].] Having a tang or sharp flavour.

Tank, *sb.*[1]

Comb.: **t. farm,** an area used for the storage of petroleum in tanks; **t. farming,** growing plants in tanks of water without soil (cf. *HYDROPONICS).

Tank (tæŋk), *v.* 1863. [f. TANK[1].] **1.** *trans.* To place, store, immerse, etc., in a tank. **2.** *To t.* (*up*). **a.** *intr.* To drink heavily 1899. **b.** *trans.* and *intr.* To refuel (an aircraft, car, etc.) 1933. So **Tanked** *ppl. a.* **Ta·nking** *vbl. sb.*

‖**Tanka**[2] (tæ·ŋkă). 1899. [Jap.] A short Japanese poem of five lines containing a total of thirty-one syllables.

Tanker. 2. An aircraft from which other aircraft are refuelled in the air 1938. **3.** A road vehicle for transporting liquids in bulk 1945.

Tape, *sb.* **2. c.** = **magnetic tape*; also, a recording on t. 1941.

Comb.: **t. recorder,** an apparatus for recording sound, pictures, or other signals on magnetic t. and for reproducing signals so recorded; **t. recording** *vbl. sb.*, the process of recording in this way; *concr.*, a recording so made; so *t.-record* vb. trans., *-recorded* ppl. adj.

Tape, *v.* **4.** *trans.* To record on magnetic tape 1953.

Target, *sb.* **2. d.** A result (*e.g.* a figure, sum of money) aimed at; a goal 1942.

Tarmac. Also, any surface covered with this material; *spec.* that of a runway on an airfield.

Tart (tāɹt), *v. slang.* 1938. [f. TART *sb.*[2]] *trans.* To dress *up* like a 'tart' (TART *sb.*[2]); to dress *up* smartly or showily; also *transf.* and *fig.* So **Ta·rted(-up)** *ppl. a.*

Tartar, *sb.*[2] **B.** *adj.* **t. sauce** (also **tartare sauce**) [Fr. *sauce tartare*], a savoury sauce containing mayonnaise and chopped gherkins, capers, etc.

Tarty (tā·ɹti), *a.* 1929. [f. TART *sb.*[2] + -Y[1].] Resembling or suggestive of a 'tart' (TART *sb.*[2]); gaudy.

Task, *sb.*

attrib. **t. force** *U.S.*, an armed force organized for operations under a unified command.

‖**Tass**[3] (tæs). [f. initials of Russ. *Telegráfnoe Agént·stvo SSSR.*] The telegraphic news agency of the Soviet Union.

‖**Tatami** (tăta·mi). Also (formerly) **tatame(e, tattami.** 1614. [Jap.] A Japanese mat made from rice straw covered with rush matting of a standard size, approx. six feet by three feet, in terms of which the size of Japanese rooms is expressed.

On no account must any form of footwear soil the sacrosanct *tatami* 1965.

Tatty (tæ·ti), *a.* 1513. [app. related in form and sense to OE. *tættec* a rag; cf. TATTER *sb.*[1]] **1.** *Sc.* Of hair: tangled, matted; of an animal or skin: shaggy. **2.** *colloq.* Tattered, shabby, tawdry 1933.

Tea, *sb.* **7.** *slang* (orig. *U.S.*). Marijuana; *spec.* marijuana brewed in hot water to make a drink 1938.

Comb.: **t.-bag,** a small bag holding t.-leaves for infusion; **t.-break,** an interruption of work allowed for drinking t., etc.; **t.-towel,** a cloth for drying washed crockery; **t.-trolley,** a small table on wheels for the conveyance of t.-things.

Teach-in (tī·tʃ,in). orig. *U.S.* 1965. [f. TEACH *v.* + *-IN[3].] A series of lectures and discussions as a means of drawing attention to, or protesting against, some matter of public importance.

Teaching, *vbl. sb.*

Comb.: **t.-machine,** a mechanical device for imparting instruction.

Tear-. t.-away *sb.*, also, a ruffian or hooligan.

Tech (tek). Also **tec.** 1911. Colloq. abbrev. of *technical college, institute,* or *school.*

Technetium (teknī·ʃiŏm). 1947. [mod. L., f. Gr. τεχνητός artificial (f. τέχνη art, craft) + -IUM.] An artificially produced radioactive metallic element similar to rhenium, of which the longest-lived isotope has a half-life of 200,000 years. Atomic number 43; symbol Tc.

Technical, *a.* **2. a. t. college,** a major institution for further education, mainly vocational.

Technicolor (te·knikɒləɹ). orig. *U.S.* Also **-our.** 1917. *Cinemat.* Trade name for a process of colour photography in which the colours are separately but simultaneously recorded and then transferred to a single positive print. Also *transf.*, *fig.*, and *attrib.*

Teddy (te·di). Pet-form of the Christian name *Edward*, used *attrib.* in **T. boy,** colloq. description of a youth who affects a style of dress held to be characteristic of Edward VII's reign 1954. Also **T. girl,** and abbrev. **Ted.**

Teen-age (tī·nē̆ⁱdʒ), *a.* 1921. [f. TEEN(S + AGE *sb.*] Designating, pertaining to, or characteristic of young people in their teens. So **Tee·n-aged** *a.*

Teeny-bopper (tī·nibǫpəɹ). *colloq.* 1967. [f. *teeny*, abbrev. of TEEN-AGER + *BOPPER.] A teen-age girl who follows the latest fashions in clothes, popular music, etc.

Teething, *vbl. sb.*

Comb.: **t.-ring,** a small ring for an infant to bite on while teething; **t. troubles,** initial difficulties in a new venture.

Tektite (te·ktəit). 1909. [– G. *tektit* (F. E. Suess, 1901), f. Gr. τηκτός molten (f. τήκειν make molten) + -ITE[1].] One of the small, roundish, glassy bodies of unknown origin that occur scattered over various parts of the earth.

Tele-. Also as comb. form of TELEVISION.

Te·le-camera, (*a*) a telephotographic camera; (*b*) a television camera. **Te·lecast,** a television broadcast; hence as *v. trans.*; so **Te·lecaster, Te·lecasting** *vbl. sb.* **Telege·nic** *a.* [after PHOTOGENIC *a.* 3], well suited to be shown on television. **Te·leprinter,** a type-printing telegraph. **Te·leprompter** orig. *U.S.*, proprietary name of a device which assists a speaker or actor on television, etc., by unrolling the script, in large print, for him to see. **Te·leview** *v. intr.*, to watch television; so **Te·leviewer; Te·leviewing** *vbl. sb.* and *ppl. a.*

Te:lecommunica·tion. 1932. [– Fr. *télécommunication*: see TELE-.] Communication over long distances by electrical or electromagnetic means; also (usu. *pl.*), the branch of technology concerned with the study and utilization of this.

Telemeter (te·lǐmǐtəɹ, tĕ-, tele·mǐtəɹ), *v.* 1934. [f. the sb.] *trans.* To (take and) transmit (a measurement or reading) to a distant point; also with *back*. Hence **Te·lemetered** *ppl. a.* **Te·lemetering** *vbl. sb.*

Telemetry (tĕ-, tele·mětri). 1885. [f. TELE- + -METRY.] The process or practice of obtaining measurements at a point removed from the place where they are made.

Television. 2. A t. set 1955.

Comb.: **t. set,** an apparatus capable of displaying pictures transmitted by t.

Telex (te·leks), *sb.* 1932. [f. *TELE(*printer* + EX(CHANGE *sb.*] A system of telecommunication by which a subscriber can send messages from his teleprinter to be received on that of any other subscriber.

Telex (te·leks), *v.* 1960. [f. the sb.] *trans.* **a.** To convey or transmit by telex. **b.** To communicate with by telex.

Tell, *v.* **I.**

7. *You're telling me!*: there is no need to tell me, I'm well aware of that (orig. *U.S. colloq.*).

When he declares that 'over-nutrition has its dangers'.. the layman is inclined to reply 'You're telling me' 1954.

Templet[1]. **3.** *Biochem.* A molecule or molecular pattern that determines the sequence in which other molecules are built up into a macromolecule, esp. a nucleic acid or polypeptide 1949.

Tempo. b. *transf.* Rate of movement, activity, or progress 1901.

‖**Tempura** (te·mpura). 1936. [Jap.] A Japanese dish consisting of fish or shellfish, often with vegetables, coated in batter and deep-fried.

Tequila (tekī·lă). 1849. [Name of a district of Mexico.] = PULQUE.

Tera- (te·ră), *prefix.* 1951. [f. Gr. τέρας marvel, monster.] Prefixed to the names of units to form the names of units a million million (10^{12}) times greater. Abbrev. T.

Teratogenic (te:rătodʒe·nik), *a.* 1879. [f. Gr. τέρας, τερατ- marvel, monster + -O- + *-GENIC.] Producing malformation in a fœtus. Hence **Te:ratogeni·city,** t. property. Also **Te·ratogen,** a t. substance.

Terminal, *a.* and *sb.* **A.** *adj.* **3. t. velocity,** the speed which, once attained by a falling body, is not exceeded, because the resistance of the air is equal to the pull of gravity. **B.** *sb.* **1. b.** Any apparatus where data may be supplied to a computer or which presents the output of one in an intelligible form 1969.

Terotechnology (tīᵊ:ro-, te:roteknǫ·lŏdʒi). 1970. [f. Gr. τηρεῖν watch over, take care of + -O- + TECHNOLOGY.] The branch of technology and engineering concerned with the installation, maintenance, and replacement of industrial plant and equipment and with related subjects and practices.

Terrace, *sb.*

Comb.: **t.** (or **terraced**) **house,** one of a row of houses joined by party-walls.

Territory. 6. *Zool.* The area of land secured by an animal or group of animals against others of the same species 1774.

Terylene (te·rǐlīn). 1951. [f. TER(EPHTHALIC *a.* + ETH)YLENE.] The proprietary name of a synthetic polyester made from ethylene glycol and an ester of terephthalic acid, used as a textile fibre.

Tesla. 2. The unit of magnetic induction (flux density) in the S.I., equal to 1 weber/ sq. metre (10,000 gauss). Abbrev. T. 1960.

Test, *sb.*[1]

Comb.: **t. bed,** an engine mounting on which aircraft engines are tested before being accepted for general use; **t. flight,** a flight to determine the performance of an aircraft; **t. pilot,** one who undertakes such a flight.

Testosterone (testǫ·stĕrōᵘn). 1939. [f. TEST(IS[2] + -O- + STER(OL + -ONE.] *Physiol.* A steroid androgen produced in the testes.

Test-tube.

Comb.: **t. baby,** a baby produced by artificial insemination, or a human embryo developing elsewhere than in a mother's body; so *t. child, puppy*, etc.

Tetra-. 2. a. Tetraethyl (te:tră,e·pil) **lead,** a poisonous oily liquid, $(C_2H_5)_4Pb$, that is added to petrol as an anti-knock agent making possible higher compression ratios.

Thalidomide (þăli·dŏməid). 1958. [f. *ph*thal*imido*glu*tari*mide, f. PHTHALIMID(E + -O- + GLUTARI(C *a.* + IMIDE.] A non-barbiturate sedative and hypnotic which in 1961 was found to be teratogenic when taken early in pregnancy, sometimes causing malformation or absence of limbs in the fœtus; **t. baby, child,** one born deformed through the effects of t.

The construction of a body harness for armless t. children 1971.

Theatre.

Comb.: **t.-in-the-round,** the staging of a play on a platform which is completely surrounded by spectators.

Theme, *sb.*

Comb.: **t. song,** a recurrent melody in a musical play, film, etc.

Thermistor (þə̄ɹmi·stəɹ). 1940. [Contraction of *therm(al res)istor.*] *Electr.* A resistor having a resistance that varies greatly with temperature (being smaller when the resistor is hot), enabling it to be used for measurement and control.

Thermo-. The·rmosphere, the region of the atmosphere lying beyond the mesosphere.

Thermocouple (þə̄·ɹmŏkɒp'l). 1890. [f. THERMO- + COUPLE *sb.*] *Electr.* A pair of wires of different metals welded together at one end, so that the thermo-electric e.m.f. generated in a circuit of which they form part may be measured to determine the temperature of the junction.

Thermonuclear (þə̄:ɹmoniū·klĭăɹ), *a.* 1938. [f. THERMO- + NUCLEAR *a.*] Derived from, utilizing, or designating nuclear reactions that occur only at very high temperatures (millions of degrees), viz. fusion of hydrogen or other light nuclei; of or pertaining to weapons utilizing such reactions.

The t. cloud overshadowing the world 1959.

Thermoplastic (þǝ̄ːɹmoplæ·stɪk), *a.* and *sb.* 1883. [f. THERMO- + PLASTIC *a.*] **A.** *adj.* Becoming plastic when heated and rigid when cooled, and capable of being repeatedly reheated and reshaped without loss of properties; made of such a substance. **B.** *sb.* A t. substance 1933.

Thermosetting (þǝ̄ːɹmose·tiŋ), *ppl. a.* 1936. [f. THERMO- + *setting*, pres. pple. of SET *v.*] Undergoing a permanent change in chemical and physical properties on being heated or treated with a suitable agent that results in rigidity unaffected by subsequent heating. Hence **The·rmoset** *a.*, thermosetting; rendered incapable of being softened by heat; *sb.*, a thermoset substance.

Thiamine (þəi·ămīn). Also **-in.** 1939. [f. THI(O- + VIT)AMINE.] *Biochem.* Vitamin B_1, an organic compound containing sulphur, present in meat (esp. pork) and the outer layers of seeds, deficiency of which leads to a deterioration in nerve and muscle tissue and in man causes beriberi.

Thing, *sb.*[1] **I. 3. b.** One's interest, concern, speciality, or talent; esp. in phr. *to do one's (own) t.* 1841.

Phrases. *To have a t. about*: to have an obsession or prejudice about (something). *To make a t. of*: to make an issue of, to get excited about (something).

Think, *sb.*

Comb.: **t.-piece,** a thoughtful piece of writing; *spec.* a general article in a newspaper or periodical, as distinct from a news-item: **t. tank,** (*a*) *U.S. slang*, the brain; (*b*) orig. *U.S.*, a body of highly intelligent people or their place of work; *spec.* a research organization providing advice and ideas on national and commercial problems.

Think, *v.*[2]

T. up, to devise, invent, contrive, or produce by thought or cogitation. (orig. *U.S. colloq.*)

Third. A. *adj.*

Comb.: **t. force** [tr. Fr. *troisième force*], a party, body, etc., that checks any extreme action of, or conflict between, two others; **t. man** *Cricket*, a fielder (or his position) between point and short slip; **T. World,** the underdeveloped countries of Asia, Africa, and Latin America which are not politically aligned with either the Communist or the Western nations.

Thixotropy (þiksǫ·trŏpi). 1927. [f. Gr. θίξις touching + -O- + τροπή turning + -Y[3].] The property exhibited by some gels of becoming fluid when shaken, stirred, etc., and of changing back to a gel when allowed to stand. So **Thixotro·pic** *a.*, exhibiting or pertaining to t.

Three, *a.* and *sb.*

Comb.: **t.-dimensional** *a.*, having, or appearing to have, the t. dimensions of length, breadth, and depth; also *fig.*; abbr. *3-D*; **t.-point landing,** an aircraft landing in which all t. wheels touch the ground simultaneously; **t.-point turn,** a method of turning a vehicle round in a narrow space, whereby the vehicle moves in t. arcs, forwards, backwards, then forwards again; **t.-ring circus,** a circus having t. rings; hence *fig.*, a showy or extravagant spectacle.

Threshold. 2. c. The amount, value, intensity, etc., above which something first becomes operative or some effect or response first occurs 1874.

The absence of a lower t. for the production of mutations by radiation 1959. With a 5 per cent cost of living t. the inflation slows down dramatically if the basic settlements give an earnings rise of significantly less than 11 per cent 1972.

Through, *prep.* and *adv.* **A.** *prep.* **5. c.** Esp. in *U.S.*, up to and including (a specified date, number, etc.), e.g. *Monday t. Thursday, 17th t. 19th July.*

Throughput (þrū·put). 1922. [f. THROUGH *adv.*, after OUTPUT.] An amount of material produced, processed, distributed, etc.

Through-way, throughway (þrū·wē[i]). Also *U.S.* **thruway.** 1934. [f. THROUGH *adv.* + WAY *sb.*] A thoroughfare; *spec.* a motorway.

Throw, *sb.*[2] **II. 3. d.** *colloq.* A 'go' at anything, a chance, venture; freq. in phr. *a throw* preceded by a specified sum of money to denote 'so much a go' or 'so much apiece' 1901.

You have to serve the actor. At a thousand pounds a t. they're very important 1971.

Throw, *v.* **II. 10. b.** *colloq.* (orig. *U.S.*). To give (a party, dance, etc.) 1922. **III. 1. c.** *colloq.* (orig. *U.S.*). To disconcert, upset, confuse; to surprise, amaze 1942.

T. away. d. *Theatr.* To deliver (lines in a play, etc.) in a deliberately off-hand manner.

Throw-. 2. t.-away *a.*, (*a*) disposable, that can be thrown away after use; (*b*) casual, off-hand, unemphasized.

Thrust, *sb.* **I. 3.** (*e*) *Aero-* and *Astronaut.* Forward force produced by the jet of an aircraft or rocket.

Thruway, var. *THROUGH-WAY.

Thulium (þ[i]ū·liǒm). 1879. [mod.L. (P. T. Cleve, 1879), f. THUL(E + -IUM.] A metallic element of the lanthanide series that forms pale green salts in which it is trivalent. Atomic number 69; symbol Tm.

Thumb, *v.*

1. Phr. *To t. one's nose*: to 'make a long nose' (orig. *U.S.*). **5.** orig. *U.S.* To make a request for (a ride in a vehicle) by pointing with a thumb in the direction one wishes to go 1934.

Thymine. Now the usual form of THYMIN.

Tick, *sb.*[1] **1. b.** *colloq.* An unpleasant or despicable person 1631.

Tick, *v.*[1] **2. a.** *To t. over*: (of an internal-combustion engine) to run slowly with the gears disengaged; also *fig.* 1916. **2. c.** *intr.* To function, work; esp. in phr. *what makes one t.*: what motivates one 1942.

Tie, *v.*

T. up. g. Also, to be closely associated or allied *with*; to agree *with*. Also *t. in* in the same senses. Hence **t.-in, t.-up** *sbs.*, a connection, link, relationship.

Tight, *a.*

Comb.: **t.-wad, tightwad** *slang* (orig. *U.S.*), a miserly person.

Tights, *sb. pl.* **c.** A woman's one-piece undergarment of stretch fabric, taking the place of knickers and stockings 1897.

Tigon (təi·gǒn). 1932. [f. TIG(ER + LI)ON.] The offspring of a tiger and a lioness.

Time, *sb.*

Comb.: **t.-and-motion** *attrib.*, concerned with measuring the efficiency of industrial or other operations; **t. bomb,** a bomb designed to explode after a predetermined period of t.; **t.-switch,** a switch that acts automatically at a set t.

Timpani (ti·mpăni), *sb. pl.* 1884. [It., pl. of *timpano* TYMPANUM.] Kettledrums. Hence **Ti·mpanist,** one who plays the kettledrums.

Tin, *sb.*

Comb.: **tin-pan alley** orig. *U.S.*, the world of the composers and publishers of popular music.

Tip, *v.*[5] **2. b.** Slang phr. (orig. *U.S.*). *To t. off*: to give (a person) a warning, hint, information, etc. 1893. Hence **t.-off** *sb.*, a warning, information, etc.

Tissue, *sb.* **6. b.** A piece of soft absorbent paper used as a handkerchief, for drying or cleansing the skin, etc. 1929.

Titfer (ti·tfəɹ). *slang.* Also **titfa, tit-for.** 1930. [Rhyming slang f. *tit for tat* (TIT *sb.*[1] 1).] A hat.

Title, *sb.* **1. b.** *Cinemat.* A caption or sub-title on a film; also, a credit at the beginning or end of a film 1922. **3. c.** A book; a literary work 1898.

Tizzy[2] (ti·zi). *slang.* 1935. [Origin unkn.] A nervous state, a state of agitation; esp. in phr. *all of a t.*, *in a t.* Also shortened to *tizz.*

Tobacco.

Comb.: **t. mosaic virus,** the virus that causes mosaic disease in t. and similar effects in other plants; it is much used as an experimental subject in biochemical research.

Toe, *sb.*

Phr. *To be on one's toes*: to be alert or poised for action.

Comb.: **t.-hold,** (*b*) a small foothold; also *fig.*

Toffee.

Comb.: **t.-apple,** a t.-coated apple on a stick; **t.-nose** *slang*, one who considers himself superior; a snob; so **t.-nosed** *a.*

Together (tǔge·ðəɹ), *a. colloq.* 1968. [f. the adv.] Composed, well organized, controlled.

Togetherness (tǔge·ðəɹnės). 1656. [f. TOGETHER *adv.* + -NESS.] Being together; the quality or fact of unity, closeness; the sense of belonging.

Toilet.

Comb.: **t.-roll,** a roll of t.-paper; **t.-training,** the training of a child to adopt acceptable habits of urination and evacuation of the bowels.

Token, *sb.* **10. b.** A voucher or document that can be exchanged for goods, as *book t.*, *gift t.*, *record t.* 1932.

Used *attrib.* or quasi-*adj.* to denote something small serving as a sample or indication of something larger or more important; hence of something minimal or perfunctory.

Tokenism (tō[u]·kěniz'm). orig. *U.S.* 1962. [f. TOKEN *sb.* + -ISM.] The practice or policy of making merely a token effort or granting only minimal concessions.

‖**Tokonoma** (tō[u]:kǒnō[u]·mă). Also (formerly) **toko, tokko.** 1727. [Jap.] In a Japanese house, a recess or alcove for pictures or other treasured objects.

Tommy gun (tǫ·mi gʊn). orig. *U.S.* 1929. [f. the trade-mark names *Tommy* or *Thompson*, f. the name of General J. T. *Thompson* (1860–1940), its co-inventor.] A type of sub-machine-gun.

Ton[1]. **5.** *slang.* A hundred; *spec.* (*a*) a sum of one hundred pounds 1946; (*b*) a speed of a hundred miles per hour 1954. Also **ton-up,** freq. used *attrib.* to denote people (esp. boys in gangs) who ride motor-cycles at or approaching a hundred miles an hour.

Tone, *sb.*

Comb.: **t.-row** *Mus.* = *SERIES II. 9.

Toneme (tō[u]·nīm). 1924. [f. TONE *sb.*, after PHONEME.] In tone languages, a 'tone phoneme', i.e. a phoneme distinguishable from the nearest phoneme in terms only of pitch or tone. Hence **Tone·mic** *a.*

Tonic, *a.* **2. t. water,** a non-alcoholic carbonated drink; freq. *ellipt.* as *tonic.*

Tonne (tʊn; *occas.* tʊ·ni *for distinction from* 'ton'). 1877. [Fr. *tonne* (see TUN *sb.*).] A metric ton (see TON[1] 4).

Too, *adv.*

T. much, also (orig. *U.S.*) as an expression of delight, praise, or amazement. *Not t.*, not very, only moderately; freq. as an understatement.

Tooth, *sb.* **I. 2. c.** Phr. *To have teeth in it*: to contain stringent provisions or stipulations. So *to put teeth into.*

To 'put teeth' into the Charter of the United Nations 1947.

Top, *sb.*[1] **IV. 5. b.** (*The*) *tops* (used predicatively): a person or thing of supreme quality or standing 1936.

Comb.: **t. brass,** the highest-ranking 'brass hats' (see *BRASS *sb.* 1); **t. flight,** the highest level of achievement, status, etc.; freq. *attrib.*; **t.-secret** *a.*, of the highest secrecy.

Top, *v.*[1] **I. 4.** *slang.* To execute, hang, kill 1718.

Topless, *a.* **1.** Delete *rare* and add: *spec.* of clothes: having no top portion; hence, of a person: wearing a t. garment; bare-breasted.

Topology. 3. *Math.* [– G. *topologie* (J. B. Listing, 1847).] The branch of mathematics concerned with those properties of figures and surfaces which, unlike shape and size, are unchanged by any continuous deformation (i.e. excluding breaking and tearing), and hence with those of abstract 'spaces' (sets composed of points and subsets of points) which are similarly unchanged by certain kinds of transformation 1883. Hence **Topolo·gical** *a.*, **-ally** *adv.* **Topo·logist.**

Torch, *sb.* **1. a.** Now usu, a device consisting of an electric lamp enclosed in a portable case containing a battery; also *electric t.* 1902.

Colloq. phr. *To carry a t.*: to have an infatuation or devotion, often unrequited, *for* someone. orig. *U.S.*

Comb.: **t. singer** orig. *U.S.*, a singer of t. songs; **t. song** orig. *U.S.*, a popular emotional love-song, esp. one sung by women about unrequited love.

‖**Torii** (tǫ·ri,i). Also **tori, torij.** 1727. [Jap.] A ceremonial gateway leading to a Japanese Shintō shrine consisting of two uprights and two cross-pieces of which the lower is straight and the upper curved and projecting.

Toroidal (toroi·dal), *a.* 1889. [f. TOR(US + -OIDAL.] Resembling or pertaining to a torus (sense 4).

Torr (tǭɹ). 1958. [f. the name of *Torricelli* (see TORRICELLIAN *a.*).] *Physics.* A unit of pressure used in measuring partial vacuums, equal to 1/760 of a standard atmosphere (i.e. very nearly the pressure of 1 mm. of mercury); 133·32 newton/sq. metre.

Toss, *sb.*
5. Colloq. phr. *To argue the t.*: to argue or dispute, esp. about a choice between two alternatives.

Toss, *v.*
T. off. c. *refl.* and *intr.* To masturbate.

Tot (tǫt), *sb.*[3] 1873. [Of unkn. origin; cf. earlier *tat* rag, *tatting* 'gathering rags' (1851).] A dust-heap picker's name for a bone; hence, anything worth picking from dustbins, refuse-heaps, etc. Hence **To·tter,** a rag-and-bone collector. **To·tting** *vbl. sb.*, the collection of items of value from among refuse.

Total. A. *adj.*
1. t. war, war in which all available resources are employed and in which civilians are involved as well as the military.

Totalitarian (totælitēə·riăn), *a.* 1937. [f. TOTALITY + -ARIAN.] Of or pertaining to a system of government which permits no rival loyalties or parties. Hence **Totalita·rianism,** t. principles and practices.

Touch, *v.*
T. down. b. *intr.* To alight on the ground from the air; to land. So **t.-down** *sb.*, the action of landing.

‖**Touché** (tuʃe), *int.* 1904. [Fr., pa. pple. of *toucher* to hit.] In *Fencing*, an exclamation used to acknowledge a hit; hence *gen.*, an exclamation recognizing a telling point, just accusation, etc., made by another person.

Tourism. More recently, the management of tours and tourists as a business; the provision of facilities or attractions for tourists; profit from tourists.

Tourist.
Comb.: **t. class,** the inferior or lowest class of accommodation on a liner, train, etc.

Tournedos (tūə·ɹnədo). 1877. [Fr.] A small piece of beef fillet steak for grilling, etc.

Town, *sb.*
Phr. *To go to t.*: to act or work energetically, rapidly, or excitedly.
Comb.: **t. gas,** inflammable gas manufactured and supplied for general domestic and commercial use; **townscape,** *(a)* a picture or view of a town; *(b)* an urban environment.

Trace, *sb.*[1]
Comb.: **t. element,** one present (esp. in the soil), or required, only in minute amounts.

Tracer. 2. b. A radio-isotope used on account of its being readily detected, located, and measured on successive occasions, e.g. when used to label a substance (*LABEL *v.* 2) or attached to an animal 1938.

Track, *sb.* **I. 6. d.** = **sound-track*; also, the groove on a gramophone record; a section of a gramophone record containing one recorded sequence; a strip running lengthwise along magnetic tape and containing one signal at any point along it 1931.
Comb.: **t.-suit,** a suit worn by athletes or the like during their training on the t., etc.

Trad (træd), colloq. abbrev. of TRADITIONAL *a.* or TRADITIONALIST; *spec.* referring to traditional jazz. Also *ellipt.* as *sb.*, traditional jazz 1957.

Trade, *sb.*
Comb.: **t. journal** or **paper,** a periodical containing articles, etc., on a particular trade, business, etc.

Trade, *v.* **8.** So **t.-in** orig. *U.S.*, the action of giving a used commodity in part payment for a new one; also, the commodity so given; also *attrib.* or as *adj.*

Traditional, *a.* **1. a.** *spec.* Denoting a type of jazz of a style which was formed in the earlier years of jazz history.

Traffic, *sb.*
Comb.: **t. lights,** a set of lights (usu. red, amber, and green) used for the automatic control of traffic in a street, e.g. at cross roads; **t. warden,** a person appointed to control the movement of t., esp. the parking of vehicles.

Trafficator (træ·fikēɪtəɹ). 1935. [f. TRAFFIC + -ATOR, after *indicator*.] A device attached to the side of a motor vehicle to be operated so as to show the proposed direction of travel.

Trailer. 3. *Cinemat.* A set of short extracts from a film advertising it in advance. Also *transf.* 1931.

Trailing, *ppl. a.*
Comb.: **t. edge,** *(a)* the rear edge of a wing, tailplane, or other part of an aircraft; *(b) Electr.*, the part of a pulse in which the amplitude diminishes.

Train, *sb.*[1]
Comb.: **t.-spotter,** a collector of locomotive numbers. So **t.-spotting,** the activities of such a person.

Trainee (trē¹nī·). 1841. [f. TRAIN *v.* + -EE.] One who is being trained (for an occupation).

Tram-line. b. *fig.* An immovable rule, principle, etc. 1955. **2.** *pl. colloq.* Either pair of parallel lines bordering the side of a lawn-tennis court, the inner of each pair marking the boundary of the court for 'singles' and the outer for 'doubles' 1937.

Tramp, *sb.* **4. b.** *slang* (orig. *U.S.*). A dissolute woman; a whore 1929.

Trampoline (træ·mpŏlīn). 1928. [– It. *trampolino*, f. *trampoli* stilts.] A sheet of canvas held in a frame by springs, used for acrobatic exercises and displays.

Transceiver (transī·vəɹ). 1943. [f. TRANS(MITTER + RE)CEIVER.] An instrument combining a radio transmitter with a radio receiver.

Transducer (transdiū·səɹ). 1934. [f. L. *transducere* lead across, f. *trans* TRANS- + *ducere* lead: see -ER[1].] Any device by which variations in one quantity (e.g. pressure, brightness) are quantitatively converted into variations in another (e.g. voltage, position).

Transexual, var. *TRANSSEXUAL *a.* and *sb.*

Transfer, *sb.*
Comb.: **transfer RNA,** RNA which becomes attached to an amino-acid molecule in the cytoplasm of a cell and conveys it to a ribosome, where the amino-acid is released to form part of a polypeptide or protein molecule.

Transferrin (transfe·rin). 1959. [f. TRANS- + L. *ferrum* iron + -IN[1].] *Biochem.* Any of several proteins in the blood of different animals that by combining with trivalent iron are responsible for its transport in the body.

Transformation. 1. d. *Linguistics.* 'A method of stating how the structures of many sentences in languages can be generated or explained formally as the result of specific transformations applied to certain basic sentence structures' (R. H. Robins), e.g. *John eats spinach* → *spinach is eaten by John* 1957. So **Transforma·tional** *a.*, designating or pertaining to grammar using such transformations.

Transistor (tranzi·stəɹ). 1948. [f. TRAN(SFER *v.* + *RE)SISTOR.] **1.** A semiconductor device with three electrodes that is analogous to a valve in its electronic functions but differs in being much smaller and more robust, in operating at a lower voltage, and in consuming less power and producing less heat. **2.** A t. radio 1961.
2. The endless croak of a cheap t. BETJEMAN.
Comb.: **t. radio,** a small portable radio having transistors and other solid-state devices in place of valves.

Transi·storized, *a.* 1953. [f. prec. + -IZ(E + -ED[1].] Using transistors (rather than valves).
The compactness of t. equipment 1959. T. ignition and electronic fuel injection 1972.
Also **Transi:storiza·tion,** the use of transistors in electronic apparatus.

Transit, *sb.*
Comb.: **t. camp,** a camp where soldiers, prisoners of war, refugees, etc., are temporarily accommodated before proceeding to their destination.

Transmission.
Comb.: **t. line,** a conductor or set of conductors designed to carry electricity (esp. on a large scale) or electromagnetic waves with minimum loss and distortion.

Transmitter. c. *Physiol.* A substance which is released at the end of a nerve fibre by the arrival of an impulse and, by diffusing across the synapse or neuromuscular junction, effects the transfer of the impulse to another nerve fibre or a muscle fibre 1935.
Enzymes which synthesize t. 1970.

Transonic (tranz,sǫ·nik), *a.* Also **trans-sonic.** 1946. [f. TRANS- + *SONIC *a.*, after *supersonic, ultrasonic*.] Pertaining to, involving, capable of, or designating speeds close to that of sound, at which some of the flow round a body is supersonic and some subsonic and there are characteristic changes in the behaviour of an aircraft.

Transplant, *sb.* **2.** *Surg.* An operation in which an organ is transplanted from one person or animal to another 1968.
Prof. Christian Barnard .. is standing by to carry out his first t. for two years 1971.

Transponder (tranzpǫ·ndəɹ). 1945. [f. TRAN(SMIT *v.* + RE)SPOND *v.* + -ER[1].] A device which on receiving a particular kind of radio signal automatically transmits another signal.

Transport, *sb.*
Comb.: **t. café,** a café providing meals for drivers of (esp. commercial) road-vehicles.

Transsexual (tranz,se·ksiuăl), *a.* and *sb.* Also **transexual.** 1953. [f. TRANS- + SEXUAL *a.*] **A.** *adj.* Having the physical characteristics of one sex and the psychological characteristics of the other. **B.** *sb.* A t. person. So **Tran(s)se·xualism.**

Trans-sonic, var. *TRANSONIC *a.*

Transuranic (transiuræ·nik), *a.* 1935. [f. TRANS- + URANIC *a.*] Of a chemical element: having a higher atomic number than uranium (i.e. 93 or over). Also **Transura·nium** *a.*, in same sense.

Transvestite (tranzve·stəit). 1922. [– G. *transvestit*, f. TRANS- + VEST *v.* + -ITE[1].] A person who dresses in the clothes of the opposite sex. Also *attrib.* or as *adj.* Hence **Transve·stism. Transve·stist** *sb.* and *a.*

Trap, *sb.*[1] **2. b.** *slang.* The mouth; esp. in phr. *shut one's t.* 1776. **4. b.** In greyhound racing, the compartment in which a dog is placed and from which it is released at the start of a race 1928. **10.** *colloq.* A percussion instrument; freq. *pl.* Cf. *t.-drummer* and TRAPS. 1908.

Travel, *sb.*
Comb.: **t.-agent,** one who makes arrangements for travellers; so *t.-agency*; **t.-sickness,** nausea induced by motion; so **t.-sick** *a.*, suffering from t.-sickness.

Traveller.
Comb.: **t.'s cheque,** a cheque for a fixed amount of money, that can be cashed in banks in many countries on the holder's endorsement against his original signature.

Treen, *a.* **B.** *sb.* Small domestic objects made of wood, esp. as antiques 1949.

Trek, *sb.* **d.** *transf.* and *fig.* spec. A movement of people in large numbers from one place to another 1895.
The great holiday t. begins 1953.

Trendy (tre·ndi), *a. colloq.* 1962. [f. TREND *sb.* + -Y[1].] Fashionable, up to date, following the latest trend. Hence as *sb.*, a t. person.

Tribology (trəi-, tribǫ·lŏdʒi). 1966. [f. Gr. τρίβος rubbing + -OLOGY.] The branch of science and technology concerned with interacting surfaces in relative motion, and with related subjects and practices (as friction, lubrication, and the design of bearings). Hence **Tribolo·gical** *a.* **Tribo·logist.**

Trick, *sb.*
Comb.: **t.-cyclist,** also a humorous perversion of PSYCHIATRIST.

Trigger (tri·gəɹ), *v.* 1930. [f. TRIGGER[1].] *trans.* To pull or press (a device such as a trigger); to fire (a gun); freq. *transf.* and *fig.*, to initiate or activate (a force, mechanism, etc.). Freq. const. *off.*

Trimaran (trəi·măræn). 1959. [f. TRI- + CATA)MARAN.] A vessel similar to a catamaran, but with three hulls.

Trip, *sb.*[1] **I. 2. c.** *colloq.* (orig. *U.S.*). An experience induced by a hallucinatory or other drug. Also *transf.* and *fig.* 1959.
Comb.: **t.-wire,** a wire stretched close to the ground to trip up an enemy, etc., freq. one activating a mine or a warning device; also *fig.*

Trip, *v.* **I. 5. b.** *colloq.* To have a 'trip' (see prec., I. 2 c) 1969.

Trishaw (trəi·ʃǭ). Also **trisha.** 1952. [f. TRI- + RICK)SHAW.] In the Far East, a light three-wheeled vehicle propelled by pedalling. Also *attrib.*
I flagged a t. and told the boy to take me to Wing Yan's silk shop 1952. One t. driver pedalled slowly by towards the river front G. GREENE.

Tritium (tri·tiŏm). 1933. [mod.L., f. Gr. τρίτος third + -IUM.] *Chem.* One of the heavy isotopes of hydrogen, differing from the other isotopes in having two neutrons as well as a proton in the nucleus and in being radioactive, and occurring naturally in minute amounts. So **Triton** (trəi·tǫn) [*-ON], the nucleus of an atom of t., consisting of two neutrons and a proton in combination.

Trivia (tri·viă), *sb. pl.* 1902. [mod.L., pl. of. L. *trivium* (see TRIVIUM), infl. in sense by TRIVIAL *a.*] Trivialities.

Troika. 2. A group of three people; *spec.* a three-man administrative council 1954.

‖**Trompe l'œil** (tronplöʸ). 1921. [Fr., lit. 'deceives the eye'.] A style of painting, decoration, or sculpture in which objects represented have the illusion of reality. Also *transf.* and *attrib.*

-tron, *suffix,* the ending of ELECTRON², used in: **1.** The names of some kinds of thermionic valves and other electron tubes, as *klystron, magnetron.* **2.** The names of a few sub-atomic particles, as †*mesotron, positron.* **3.** The names of particle accelerators, as *cyclotron, synchrotron.*

Trouble, *sb.*
Comb.: **t.-maker,** a troublesome person, esp. one who deliberately foments disagreement; **t.-shooter,** (*a*) one who traces and corrects faults in machinery; (*b*) a mediator in diplomatic, industrial, etc., affairs; hence **t.-shoot** *v. trans.* and *intr.*; **t.-shooting** *vbl. sb.*

Trousers, *sb. pl.*
Comb.: **trouser-suit,** a woman's suit consisting of t. and a jacket.

Truffle. 2. A sweet made of a chocolate mixture, freq. flavoured with rum, shaped into a ball and covered with powdered chocolate 1926.

Truth.
Comb.: **t. drug,** a medicinal substance supposed to make people tell the t.

Tsunami (tsunā·mi). 1904. [Jap., f. *tsu* harbour + *nami* waves.] A series of very long, high undulations of the surface of the sea that sometimes results from an underwater earthquake or similar disturbance and may be sufficiently great to inundate coastal regions; freq. misnamed a *tidal wave.*

Tularæmia (tiūlărī·miă). 1921. [f. mod.L. *tularensis* (see def.), f. name of *Tulare* Co., Calif. (where the disease was first observed) + Gr. αἷμα blood + -IA¹.] *Med.* A severe infectious illness of man and domestic animals caused by the bacterium *Pasteurella tularensis,* present in many wild rodents in N. America and elsewhere, and transmitted esp. by blood-sucking insects and by contact.

Tumbler.
Comb.: **t. drier,** a machine that dries washing in a heated rotating drum.

Tupamaro (tupămā·ro). 1969. [f. the names of the Inca leaders *Tupac Amaru I* (died 1571) and *Tupac Amaru II* (died 1781).] A member of a left-wing guerrilla organization in Uruguay.

Turbo-. T.-jet (engine), (an aircraft having) a jet engine in which the jet drives a turbine that powers a compressor to compress the incoming air. **T.-prop** (rarely **-propeller**) **(engine),** (an aircraft having) a jet engine similar to a t.-jet but having a propeller driven by the turbine as well as a compressor.

Turf, *v.* **4.** *trans.* To throw or kick *out* (*slang*) 1888.

Turn, *v.*
T. on. c. *colloq.* (orig. *U.S.*). To interest, excite, arouse, esp. sexually; *spec.* to cause (someone) to start taking drugs. Also *intr.* for *pass.*

Turn-. t.-round, the process of a ship entering port, discharging and loading cargo, and leaving; also *transf.,* of motor transport, etc.

Turn-over. A. *sb.* **5. b.** Change in the labour force at a particular place of work 1940.

Turtle².
Comb.: **t.-neck** *a.* (orig. *U.S.*), denoting a sweater or jersey having a round, rolled neck; hence as *sb.,* a sweater or jersey of this type; so **t.-necked** *a.*

Tutu (tū·tū). 1913. [Fr.] A ballet dancer's short frilly skirt.

Tweeter (twī·təɹ). 1934. [f. TWEET *v.* + -ER¹.] A small loudspeaker designed to reproduce high-frequency signals with fidelity while being relatively unresponsive to those of lower frequency. Cf. *WOOFER.

Twelve.
Comb.: **t.-note, t.-tone** *adjs.* = *DODECAPHONIC *a.*

Twerp (twəɹp). *slang.* Also **twirp.** 1925. [Origin unkn.] A stupid or objectionable person.

Twilight.
Comb.: **t. zone,** (*a*) an area between two distinct regions, having characteristics of both; also *fig.*; (*b*) an urban area of old and deteriorating buildings.

Twin, *a.* and *sb.*
Comb.: **t. beds,** a pair of single beds; **t. set,** a jumper with cardigan.

Twist, *sb.* **III. 1. b.** A dance in which the body is twisted from side to side 1898; *spec.* a dance of this type popular in the early 1960s. **9. c.** Slang phr. *Round the t.*: insane 1960.

Twist, *v.* **IV. 2. b.** To dance the twist (see prec.) 1961.

Two.
Comb.: **e. t.-stroke** *a.,* of an internal-combustion engine: having a power cycle completed in one downward and one upward stroke of the piston; **t.-time** *v. trans. slang* (orig. *U.S.*), to deceive, swindle; hence **t.-timing** *ppl. a.*; **t.-up,** a gambling game played by tossing up t. coins.

Type, *sb.* **6. b.** Used in combination to indicate the general character of something, as *Cheddar-type cheese.* **7. c.** A person of a specified character; hence *colloq.,* a person 1922.
7. c. The Judge's mistress, an ample t. named. Victoria 1942. 'Oh, by the way, do you know these types?' and he introduced the two men with him 1951.
Comb.: **t.-cast** *v. trans.,* to cast (a performer) in a role that accords with his nature; so **t.-casting;** also *transf.* and *fig.*; **t.-face,** the design of, or the image produced by, the surface of a printing type.

Type, *v.* **2. b.** To assign (a person or thing) to a particular class; *spec.* to type-cast 1933.

U.
I. 2. c. U-turn, the turning of a vehicle (without reversing) so that it faces the opposite direction.
II. 1. U = upper-class; U.D.C., Universal Decimal Classification, Urban District Council; U.D.I., unilateral declaration of independence; U.F.O., unidentified flying object; U.H.F., ultra-high frequency; U.N.(O.), United Nations (Organization); U.N.E.S.C.O., United Nations Educational, Scientific, and Cultural Organization; U.P.U., Universal Postal Union; U.V., ultra-violet.

Ugli (ɒ·gli). 1934. [f. UGLY *a.*] A thick-skinned, globular, green and yellow citrus fruit, probably a hybrid of the grapefruit and the tangerine; originally found and cultivated in Jamaica.

‖**Ukiyo-ye** (u·kīyoˌye·). Also **Ukiyo-e, Ukiyo-we.** 1879. [Jap., f. *ukiyo* fleeting world + *e* picture.] A school of Japanese art which produced wood-block prints of subjects taken from the common life of the lower classes treated in a naturalistic style.

Ultrace·ntrifuge. 1924. [f. ULTRA- + CENTRIFUGE *sb.*] A high-speed centrifuge designed for the determination of the rate of sedimentation (and hence the size) of small particles and large molecules in a liquid.

Ultrasonic (ɒltrăsǫ·nik), *a.* and *sb. pl.* 1926. [f. ULTRA- + *SONIC *a.,* after *supersonic.*] **A.** *adj.* Pertaining to, employing, or designating sound waves or vibrations having a frequency beyond the audible range (i.e. greater than 15,000–20,000 Hz). **B.** *sb. pl.* **a.** U. waves 1931. **b.** (const. as *sing.*) The branch of science and technology concerned with the study and use of u. waves 1941.
A. U. echo-location by bats 1958. Hence **Ultraso·nically** *adv.*

Ultrasound (ɒ·ltrăsaund). 1936. [f. ULTRA- + SOUND *sb.*²] Sound of ultrasonic frequency; ultrasonic waves collectively.

U·ltrastructure. 1939. [f. ULTRA- + STRUCTURE *sb.*] *Biol.* Structure of biological material that is visible only under greater magnification than can be obtained with optical microscopy. Hence **Ultrastru·ctural** *a.*

‖**Ulu** (ū·lū). 1878. [Malay.] The head or source of a Malaysian river; jungle or rural country in the heart of the Malaysian peninsula.

Umbrella. 3. Delete † and add: also, patronage; a co-ordinating or unifying agency, organization, etc.

Uncle, *sb.* **2. e. Uncle Tom,** an American Negro who is submissive or servile to white Americans 1945. Also *attrib.* and *transf.*
The first aboriginal Senator . . is labelled an 'Uncle Tom' 1972.

Uncoo·l, *a. slang* (orig. *U.S.*). 1953. [UN-¹ 1.] Not cool (see *COOL *a.* 4 b); unrelaxed; unpleasant, bad.

Under-¹.
I. 2. b. U·nderpass, a road passing under another road or a railway, etc.
IV. a. Underdeve·loped *a.,* inadequately developed; *spec.* (*a*) of a photographic negative: insufficiently developed; (*b*) of a country, etc.: that is below its potential economic level. **Underpri·vileged** *a.,* not enjoying the normal standard of living or rights in a civilized society. **b. U·nder-achie:ver,** a person who achieves less than expected.

Under-².
U·nder-co:ver *a.,* surreptitious, secret, illicit. **U·nder-floo:r** *a.,* of heating: coming from a source beneath the floor.

Undercarriage. b. The landing-gear of an aeroplane 1911.

Undercoat. 4. A coat of paint beneath the topmost coat; also, paint for this purpose 1876.

Underground, *a.* (*sb.*) **B.** *sb.* **4.** A clandestine or secret movement, group, etc., esp. of resistance to the established order 1946. Also *attrib.* or as *adj.*

Understeer (ɒ·ndəɹstīᵊɹ). 1957. [UNDER-¹ IV. b.] A tendency in a motor vehicle to decrease the sharpness of the turn when made to deviate from the straight. Also as *v. intr.,* to have this tendency.

Unflappable (ɒnflæ·păb'l), *a.* 1958. [f. UN-¹ 1 + FLAP *v.* + -ABLE.] Imperturbable; cool in a crisis. So **U:nflappabi·lity.**

Unfu·nny, *a.* 1858. [UN-¹ 1.] Not funny, though intended to amuse.

Uninhi·bited, *ppl. a.* 1880. Not inhibited; unconventional or informal. Hence **Uninhi·bitedly** *adv.*

Unipod (yū·nipǫd). 1935. [f. UNI- + Gr. πούς, ποδ- foot. Cf. TRIPOD.] *Photogr.* A one-legged support for a camera.

Unisex (yū·niseks). 1969. [f. UNI- + SEX *sb.*] A tendency for the two human sexes to adopt each other's characteristics of behaviour, esp. in the matter of dressing alike.

Unit, *sb.* (and *a.*)
3. u. furniture, furniture made in sections, often interchangeable; **u. trust,** a company selling units of investment and offering the benefits of a varied group of securities to the holder of each u.

United, *ppl. a.*
U. Nations, in the war of 1939–45, the nations united against the Axis powers; later an international organization of these and other States on the basis of a charter, April–June 1945.

Unlenited: see *LENITION.

Unperson (ɒ·npəɹsən). 1949. [f. UN-¹ 6 + PERSON *sb.*] A person whose name, or the fact of whose existence, is erased from the knowledge of a group or nation, esp. for political reasons.
Withers, however, was already an *unperson.* He did not exist: he had never existed 'GEORGE ORWELL' *1984.*

Unputdownable (ɒ:nputdau·năb'l), *a.* 1947. [f. UN-¹ 1 + *put down* (see PUT *v.*¹) + -ABLE.] Of a book: so engrossing that the reader cannot put it down; = *COMPULSIVE *a.* 3 b.

U·nquote. 1934. [UN-².] Used in dictation, etc., as a quasi-vb. to indicate that a series of quoted words has ended. Cf. *QUOTE *sb.* 2 b.

Unscra·mble, *v.* 1923. [UN-².] *trans.* To restore from a scrambled state; *spec.* to clarify or interpret (a scrambled message) (see *SCRAMBLE *v.* 4).

Unscri·pted, *a.* 1953. [UN-¹ 3.] Delivered without a prepared script; extempore.

Unsee·ded, *ppl. a.* 1952. [UN-¹ 2.] *Lawn Tennis,* etc. That has not been seeded (SEED *v.* II. 5).

Unsti·ck, *v.* 1706. [UN-².] **1.** *trans.* To remove (something) so that it no longer adheres. **2.** Colloq. phr. *To come unstuck*: to come to grief, fail 1911. **3.** *intr.* Of an aircraft: to take off; freq. *to come* or *get unstuck* 1913. Hence as *sb.*, take-off.

Unstru·ctured, *ppl. a.* 1952. Not structured; having no structure; informal, free.

Unstu·ffy, *a.* 1929. [UN-[1] 1.] **1.** Not stuffy. **2.** Informal, casual 1952.

Unwind, *v.* **3. b.** *colloq.* To relax, become calm 1938.

Unzi·p, *v.* 1939. [UN-[2].] *trans.* To undo (a zip-fastener); to open by undoing a zip. Also *intr.* and *transf.*

Up, *sb.* **2. d.** *On the up-and-up*: (*a*) continually improving; (*b*) on the level, honest. *colloq.* (orig. *U.S.*).

Up, *a.* **3. c.** *colloq.* In Jazz or dance-music, denoting a tempo that is fast 1948.

Up, *v.* **7.** *trans.* To increase, raise (a price, salary, etc.). *colloq.* (orig. *U.S.*). 1934.

Up, *adv.*[1]

Up to-. f. Colloq. phr. *Up-to-the-minute*: up to date, modern, fashionable.

Up, *adv.*[2] **II. 4. f.** Colloq. phr. *Up and coming*: energetic, enterprising, promising. orig. *U.S.* 1848.

Update (ʌpdēⁱ·t), *v.* 1914. [f. UP- III. 1 + DATE *sb.*[2]] *trans.* To bring up to date. So **Upda·ted** *ppl. a.*

Uppity (ʌ·pĭti), *a. colloq.* (orig. *U.S.*). 1881. [Fanciful formation on UP *adv.*[1]] Arrogant, snobbish.

Up-stage, upstage (ʌpstēⁱ·dʒ), *v.* 1933. [f. phr. *up stage* (UP *prep.* 5).] *trans.* To move up stage from (another actor) so that he has to turn his back to the audience; hence *fig.* to overshadow, force into a disadvantageous position.

U·psurge. 1930. [UP- I. 2.] An upward surge; a rise.

Uptight (ʌ·ptəit, ʌptəi·t), *a. colloq.* (orig. *U.S.*). 1962. [f. UP *adv.*[2] + TIGHT *a.*] **1.** Excellent, fine. **2.** Tense, worried, angry, aggressive 1966.

U·pturn, *sb.* 1864. [UP- I. 2.] **1.** An upheaval. **2.** An improvement; an upward trend in commerce, finance, etc. 1930.

Urchin. 7. Used *attrib.* to designate a short style of haircut for women 1951.

Utility. 5. c. Applied to clothes, furniture, etc., made in standardized form in accordance with the official allowance of material; also *transf.* and *fig.* 1942.

V.

I. 2. V.-sign, a sign made by holding up the first and second fingers spread apart, either representing the letter *V* (for *victory*) or as an obscene gesture of contempt.

III. b. V.A.D., Voluntary Aid Detachments; V.A.T., value-added tax; V.D., venereal disease; volunteer decoration; V.H.F., very high frequency; V.I.P., very important person; V.T.O. (L.), vertical take-off (and landing). In V1, V2 (types of flying bomb) = G. *Vergeltungswaffe* 'reprisal weapon'.

Vacuum.

Comb.: **v.-clean** *v. trans.* and *intr.*, to clean by means of a v.-cleaner; so **va·cuum** *v.*, in the same sense.

Valine (vēⁱ·līn). 1907. [f. VAL(ERIC *a.* (in *valeric acid*, of which v. is a simple derivative) + -INE[5].] *Biochem.* A white crystalline amino-acid, $(CH_3)_2CHCH(NH_2)COOH$, that is a constituent of proteins and an essential ingredient of the diet of man and other vertebrates.

Value, *sb.* **II. 2. c.** The quality of a thing considered in respect of its power or validity for a specified purpose or effect, as *news v.* 1892. **d.** *pl.* One's principles or standards; one's judgement of what is valuable or important in life 1921.

Comb.: **v.-added (tax),** (a tax on) the amount by which the v. of an article is increased by each stage in its production.

Van Allen (radiation) belt. 1959. [f. the name of James A. *Van Allen* (b. 1914), American physicist, who discovered these belts.] Either of two regions that partly surround the earth (at heights of about 2,000 and 10,000 miles at the equator) and contain large numbers of high-energy charged particles trapped in the earth's magnetic field. So *V. A. radiation.*

Vapour, *sb*

Comb.: **v.-trail,** a visible trail of condensed water vapour left in the sky by an aircraft.

Varactor (vǎræ·ktəɹ). 1960. [f. *var(ying re)actor.*] *Electronics.* A semiconductor diode whose capacitance depends on the applied voltage.

Variate (vēᵊ·riět), *sb.* 1889. [– pa. pple. of L. *variare* VARY; see -ATE[1] 1.] *Statistics.* A quantity that has a particular numerical value for each specimen or individual of a group; a variable, esp. one whose values occur with a frequency described by some probability function.

Variation. III. 4. b. A solo dance in a classical ballet 1912.

Varna (vā·ɹnǎ). 1876. [Skr., 'colour, class'.] Any of the four main Hindu social groups or castes.

Varve (vāɹv). 1912. [– Sw. *varv* (formerly *hvarf*) turn, layer.] A pair of thin layers of clay and silt of contrasting colour and texture which represents the deposit of a single year (summer and winter) in still water at some time in the past (usu. in a lake formed by a retreating ice-sheet); they have been used to establish a chronology of the late glacial and post-glacial period. Hence **Varved** *ppl. a.*, characterized by such layers.

Vasectomy (văse·ktǒmi). 1899. [f. VAS + Gr. ἐκτομή excision + -Y[3].] *Surg.* Excision of part of each *vas deferens* (the duct in the male along which sperms pass from the testis to the ejaculatory duct).

A v. operation, a once and for all method of contraception, costs about £15 10s. 1970. Hence **Vase·ctomized** *ppl. a.*, having undergone this operation.

Vaso-a·ctive, *a.* 1962. [VASO-.] *Physiol.* Acting upon the blood-vessels, esp. in regard to their constriction and dilatation.

Vasopressin (vēⁱsopre·sin). 1928. [f. VASO- + PRESS(OR + -IN[1].] *Physiol.* Either of two similar hormones, one or other of which is found in the posterior lobe of the pituitary body in mammals; they reduce the release of water into the urine by the kidneys and, when present in large quantities, raise the blood pressure.

Vector, *sb.* **2. b.** *Aeronaut.* The course to be taken by an aircraft 1950. Hence as *v. trans.*, to direct (an aircraft) on a course.

Veg (vedʒ), colloq. abbrev. of *vegetable(s.*

Vegan (vī·gǎn), *sb.* and *a.* 1944. [f. VEG(ETARI)AN *sb.* and *a.*] **A.** *sb.* A strict vegetarian; one who eats no animals or animal products. **B.** *adj.* Of or pertaining to vegans or their principles.

Velocity. 1. b. *Mech.*, etc. A vector quantity equivalent to speed in a particular direction 1883.

Velouté (vəlū·te). 1842. [Fr. *velouté* velvety.] *Cookery.* A basic sauce using white stock added to a cooked mixture of butter and flour, sometimes with added vegetable flavouring.

‖**Vendeuse** (vaṅdǒz). 1913. [Fr.] A saleswoman, esp. in a fashion house.

Vending (ve·ndiŋ), *vbl. sb.* 1666. [f. VEND *v.* + -ING[1].] The action of selling or retailing; now freq. in **v.-machine,** a slot-machine which supplies small articles, refreshments, etc.

Venereology (vĭnīᵊriǫ·lǒdʒi). 1900. [f. L. *venereus* VENEREAL + -OLOGY.] *Med.* The scientific study of venereal diseases. So **Venerǫolo·gical** *a.* **Venereo·logist.**

Ventifact (ve·ntifækt). 1911. [f. L. *ventus* WIND *sb.*[1] + -I- + *factus*, pa. pple. of *facere* make.] A faceted stone shaped or altered by wind-blown sand.

Venturi (ventiūᵊ·ri). 1887. The name of G. B. *Venturi* (1746–1822), It. physicist, used *attrib.* or *absol.* to designate a short straight tube between two tapering sections of larger diameter, so that there is a drop in pressure of a fluid flowing through it, which may be measured to determine the rate of flow or used as a source of suction.

Venusian (veniū·ziǎn), *sb.* and *a.* [f. 1874. VENUS + -IAN.] **A.** *sb.* An inhabitant of the planet Venus. **B.** *adj.* Of or pertaining to the planet Venus 1909.

‖**Verglas** (vęrgla). 1886. [Fr.] A thin coating of ice or sleet.

‖**Verismo** (veri·smo). 1934. [It.] Realism, esp. in opera.

Vernalization (vəːɹnǎləizēⁱ·ʃən). 1933. [Rendering of Russ. *yarovizátsiya* (Whyte and Hudson, 1933), f. VERNAL *a.* + -IZ(E + -ATION.] *Bot.* The process of keeping seed at low temperatures for a time before it is planted, in order to shorten the period of growth before the flowering of the plant. Hence, by back-formation, **Ve·rnalize** *v. trans.*, to treat seed in this way.

Vernier. 2. *Astronaut.* Also *v. engine.* A small auxiliary engine used for changing the velocity, attitude, etc., of a rocket by small amounts 1958.

Vertical. A. *adj.*

Comb.: **v. take-off** *Aeronaut.*, a take-off directly upward; freq. *attrib.*

Veteran. B. *adj.* **3.** *spec.* **v. car,** a car made before the year 1916.

Viable, *a.* Also *transf.* and *fig.*, feasible, workable, capable of being carried out.

Vibes (vəibz). Colloq. abbrev. of *VIBRAPHONE 1942.

Vibraphone (vəi·brǎfōᵘn). 1926. [f. VIBRA(TION, VIBRA(TO, etc. + Gr. φωνή sound.] *Mus.* A percussion instrument consisting of a series of graduated metal bars, beneath which are motor-driven resonators over metal tubes producing a vibrato effect. Hence **Vi·braphonist,** one who plays the v.

Vice, *sb.*[1]

Comb.: **v.-squad** orig. *U.S.*, a subdivision of the police force formed to enforce the laws concerning v.

Vichyssoise (viʃiswa·z). 1941. [Fr., f. *Vichy*, the name of a watering-place.] A creamy leek and potato soup, served chilled.

Victoriana (vi:ktōᵊriā·nǎ), *sb. pl.* 1931. [See *-ANA.] Things dating from, relating to, or characteristic of the reign of Queen Victoria.

Video (vi·dio). 1935. [L. *video* I see.] **a.** *U.S.* Television. **b.** Used *attrib.* and in Combs. to denote a connection with the broadcasting or electronic processing of images, as **v.-frequency,** a frequency in the range employed for the v. signal in television, (viz. a few hertz to several million hertz), esp. one in the higher part of this range; **v. signal,** a signal that contains all the information required for producing the picture in television broadcasting.

a. Coast-to-coast v. network starts operation in the U.S. 1951.

Videotape (vi·diotēⁱp), *sb.* 1953. [f. prec. + TAPE *sb.*] Magnetic tape on which television pictures as well as sound may be, or have been, recorded. Hence **Vi·deotape** *v. trans.*, to record on v. (both picture and sound). **Vi·deotaped** *ppl. a.*

Vienna. V. steak, a rissole made of minced meat and fried.

Vietnamese (vi:ětnǎmī·z), *a.* and *sb.* 1947. [f. *Vietnam* + -ESE.] **A.** *adj.* Of or pertaining to Vietnam, a country on the east of the Indo-Chinese peninsula. **B.** *sb.* A native or inhabitant of Vietnam; freq. *collect.*; also, the language of Vietnam 1952.

‖**Vieux jeu** (vyö ʒö), *adj. phr.* 1896. [Fr.] Old-fashioned, antiquated.

View, *sb.*

Colloq. phr. *To take a dim* (or *poor*) *v. of*: to regard critically or unenthusiastically; to disapprove of.

View, *v.* **2. d.** *trans.* and *intr.* To watch (television) 1935. So **View·ing** *vbl. sb.*

Viewable (viū·ǎb'l), *a.* 1909. [f. VIEW *v.* + -ABLE.] That may be viewed; *spec.* of a television programme: worth watching. So **Viewabi·lity.**

Viewer. 1. b. One who watches television 1935. **3.** An instrument used to look at film transparencies, slides, etc. 1940.

-ville (vil). 1906. [Fr. *ville* town.] A terminal element appended to sbs. or adjs. (freq. *pl.*) to denote: (*a*) a fictitious place; (*b*) a particular quality suggested by the word to which it is appended.

That girl is a winner from Winnersville 1906. No need to feel cubesville (that's worse than being a square) 1961.

Vinaigrette. 3. In full *v. sauce.* A dressing of oil and wine vinegar, sometimes with herbs, used esp. with salads and cold vegetables 1886.

Vintage, *sb.* **1. d.** *transf.* and *fig.* The age or year of a specified thing 1929. Also *attrib.* or as *adj.*, *spec.* (*a*) designating a motor vehicle made between 1916 and 1930 inclusive; (*b*) characterized by maturity, enduring quality, excellence, etc.

Vinyl. 2. Any plastic or synthetic resin that is made by polymerizing a compound containing the v. group (as polyvinyl chloride or polyvinyl acetate) 1939.

Viral (vəiᵊ·răl), *a.* 1950. [f. VIR(US + -AL¹.] Of, pertaining to, or caused by a virus. Hence **Vi·rally** *adv.*, by a virus or viruses.

‖**Virement** (vī·rman, viᵊ·ɹmənt). 1902. [Fr. (e.g. *virement de fonds*), f. *virer* turn (cf. VEER *v.*²); see -MENT.] *Finance.* The application of resources intended for one end to the purposes of another.

Virgule. Also, a short slanting line used to mark the place of line or word division, or an alternative (as *and/or*).

Virology (vəiᵊrǫ·lŏdʒi). 1935. [f. VIR(US + -OLOGY.] The scientific study of viruses and their actions. Hence **Virolo·gical** *a.* **Viro·logist.**

Virus. 2. b. Any of numerous kinds of very simple organisms smaller than bacteria, which consist principally of a strand of nucleic acid within a protein coat, can multiply only inside a living cell, and are responsible for many diseases 1909.

Vision, *sb.* **2. b.** Without article or pl.: power of discerning future conditions in some sphere; sagacity in planning for these 1926. **4. b.** What is seen on a television screen by the viewer 1937.

Visitor.

4. a. visitors' book, a book in which visitors to a house, church, etc., enter their names.

Visor. 5. A flap above a car's windscreen for protection of the driver's eyes against direct sunlight 1925.

Visual, *a.* **6. v. aid,** a visual means, such as a diagram, illustration, film, etc., used as an aid to learning.

Vital, *a.* **4. b.** Also applied *colloq.* to a woman's body measurements, *spec.* those round the bust, waist, and hips; also *transf.* and *fig.*

Vocabulary. 2. b. *transf.* and *fig.* A set of artistic or stylistic forms or techniques; *spec.* the range of set movements used in ballet or dancing 1917.

Vocal, *sb.* **3.** A musical arrangement or performance that includes singing 1934.

Vogue. 6. b. *attrib.* or quasi-*adj.* Fashionable, esp. in *v.-word* 1926.

Voice, *sb.*

Comb.: **v.-over,** narration on a film or television broadcast that is not accompanied by a picture of the person speaking; also, the person whose voice is heard; **v.-print,** a visual record of speech depicting its varying spectral constitution, usu. by means of marks that represent frequency by their height above a base line, duration by their horizontal length, and amplitude by their darkness.

Voyeur (‖vwayǒr, voi·ǒɹ). 1929. [Fr.] One who obtains sexual gratification from looking at the sexual behaviour or the sexual organs of others. Also *transf.* and *fig.* Hence **Voy·eurism.**

W.

3. W.A.A.F., Women's Auxiliary Air Force; W.E.A., Workers' Educational Association; W.E.U., Western European Union; W.H.O., World Health Organization; W.I., Women's Institute; W/O, warrant officer; w.p.b., waste-paper basket; W.R.A.C., Women's Royal Army Corps; W.R.A.F., Women's Royal Air Force; W.R.N.S., Women's Royal Naval Service; W.(R.)V.S., Women's (Royal) Voluntary Service.

Wacky (wæ·ki), *sb.* and *a.* Also **whacky.** 1861. [f. WHACK *sb.* + -Y¹.] **A.** *sb.* orig. *dial.* A fool; a crazy or eccentric person. **B.** *adj.* **1.** *dial.* Left-handed 1905. **2.** *slang* (orig. *U.S.*). Crazy, odd 1936.

Wad, *sb.*¹ **5.** *slang* (orig. *Army*). A bun; a sandwich; something to eat 1919.

Waffle (wǫ·f'l), *sb.*² 1861. [f. next vb.] **1.** *dial.* The bark of a small dog. **2.** Aimless or ignorant talk or writing; gossip 1888.

Waffle (wǫ·f'l), *v.* Also **whaffle.** 1698. [imit.] **1.** *intr.* To yelp. *dial.* **2.** To talk or write aimlessly or ignorantly; to vacillate 1701.

Waggon, *sb.* **1.** *On the w.* = *on the water-w.* (see WATER *sb.*), teetotal 1917.

Wahine (wahī·ne). *N.Z.* Also (formerly) **whinie, wienie.** 1773. [Maori.] A woman, a wife.

Waist.

Comb.: **w.-line, waistline,** the line of the waist, esp. as an indication of a person's fatness; also *transf.*

Walk, *sb.*

Comb.: **walkway** orig. *U.S.* = WALK *sb.* II. 2 c.

Walk, *v.*¹ **I. 3. j.** *To w. out*: to depart suddenly and angrily 1840. **k.** *To w. out on*: to forsake, desert, leave in the lurch (orig. *U.S. slang*) 1896.

Walkabout (wǭ·kăbaut). orig. and chiefly *Austral.* 1907. [Aboriginal pidgin.] A period of wandering in the Australian bush country; esp. in phr. *to go w.* Also *transf.*, *spec.* an informal stroll by a public figure.

Walkie-talkie (wǭ·kitǭ·ki). orig. *U.S.* Also **walky-talky.** 1939. [f. WALK *v.*, TALK *v.* + -IE repeated.] A radio transmitting and receiving set carried on the person to provide two-way communication while perambulating an area.

Walk-out (wǭ·kaut). 1888. [f. *to walk out* (WALK *v.*¹ I. 3 j).] The act of walking out of a place, esp. as a protest or at the start of a strike.

Wall, *sb.*¹ **I. 4. d.** Colloq. phr. (*To drive*) *up the w.*: (to make) mad or furious.

Comb.: **w.-board,** board made from wood-pulp, fibre, or the like, and used for surfacing walls, ceilings, etc.; **w.-to-w.** *a.*, of a carpet: covering the whole floor.

Wallop, *sb.* **4.** *slang.* Beer or other drink 1936.

Wall Street (wǭ·l strīt). 1806. The name of a street in New York City; used *allusively* for the American money-market, financial interests, etc.

‖**Walpurgisnacht** (valpū·ɹgisnaχt). Also **Walpurgis night.** 1822. [G., f. *Walpurgis*, gen. of *Walpurga*, name of an English saint who was a missionary in Germany + *nacht* night.] The witches' sabbath celebrated on the 30th of April, the eve of St. Walpurga's feast; hence *allusively.*

Wankel (wæ-, væ·ŋkĕl). 1967. The name of Felix *Wankel* (b. 1902), German engineer, used *attrib.* or *absol.* to designate a kind of rotary internal-combustion engine he invented that has an eccentrically pivoted shaft rotating continuously in a chamber, the shaft being roughly triangular in cross-section so that the shaft forms with the chamber wall three combustion spaces of varying volume.

War, *sb.*

1. *War of nerves*: the use of hostile propaganda, intimidation, etc., to lower an enemy's morale.

Comb.: **w.-bride,** a woman who gets married during war-time, esp. to a foreigner; **w.-crime,** a crime against international law, committed in war-time; so *w.-criminal*; **w.-head,** the explosive head of a missile, torpedo, etc.; **w. work,** work undertaken in consequence of, or directly concerned with, a war.

Warm, *v.* **II. 1. a.** *To w. up*, to become warmer; *spec.* (*a*) of a radio, engine, etc.: to come to an efficient working temperature; (*b*) of an athlete or the like: to get in suitable condition before a race or other contest. So **w.-up** *sb.*, the act of becoming warmer or warmed up; *spec.* entertainment before a broadcast performance or the like, to set performers and audience at ease.

Wart. 3. Phr. *Warts and all*: including the unpleasant or uncomplimentary parts or features 1930.

Washed, *ppl. a.* **3. W. up** *slang* (orig. *U.S.*), finished, defeated, having failed completely; freq. *all w. up* 1923.

WASP, Wasp². 1963. [f. the initials.] A white Anglo-Saxon Protestant (usu. a contemptuous term).

Watch, *v.* **II. 3.** Colloq. phr. *To w. it*: to be careful; freq. *imper.*

Water, *sb.*

Comb.: **w.-bloom,** the discoloration of the surface of fresh waters, esp. lakes, by the presence of various kinds of algæ; **w.-bus,** a boat, esp. a motor-boat, for conveying passengers; **w.-ski** *sb.*, one of a pair of skis enabling the wearer to skim the surface of w., towed by a motor-boat; hence as *v. intr.*; so *w.-skier,-skiing*; **w.-softener,** an apparatus for softening hard w.

Waterford (wǭ·təɹfŏɹd). 1935. Name of a city in southern Ireland, used *attrib.* to denote a clear and colourless flint-glass.

Wattage (wǫ·tėdʒ). 1909. [f. WATT + -AGE.] Electrical power, or the rating of an electrical appliance, expressed in watts.

Wave, *sb.*

Comb.: **w.-band** = *BAND *sb.*² 12; **w.-form,** the form or shape of a w.; a w. regarded as characterized by a particular shape; **w. mechanics,** a branch of mathematical physics, used esp. for the analysis of atomic and sub-atomic phenomena, in which particles are represented mathematically by differential equations of a form appropriate to waves; so **w.-mechanical** adj.

Waveguide (wēⁱ·vgəid). 1936. [f. WAVE *sb.* + GUIDE *sb.*] A metal tube or other linear structure designed to confine electromagnetic waves within itself and conduct them with minimum loss of energy.

Wa-wa² (wā·wā). orig. *U.S.* 1926. [imit.] A sound such as is made by a brass musical instrument when a mute is moved in and out of the bell; so **wa-wa mute,** a mute used to produce this sound.

Wax, *sb.*¹ **2. e.** *colloq.* (orig. *U.S.*). The material from which gramophone records are made; a gramophone record 1932. Hence as *v. trans.*, to record for the gramophone.

Way, *sb.* **II. 4. a.** Colloq. phr. *On the* (or *one's*) *way out*: about to disappear, fail, or perish.

Way, *adv.* **W.-out** *a. colloq.* (orig. *U.S. slang*), recondite, very unusual, progressive; hence as a general term of commendation = *FAR-OUT *a.* b.

Weak, *a.*

11. w. interaction *Nuclear Physics*, a physical interaction that is effective only on the sub-atomic scale and is very much weaker than the electromagnetic and the strong interactions.

Wear, *v.*¹ **I. 7. c.** *colloq.* To tolerate, accept, agree to (usu. in negative, with *it* as object) 1925.

Weasel, *sb.* **4.** A tracked vehicle capable of travelling over snow, boggy land, etc. 1944.

Weather, *sb.*

Comb.: **wea·therman,** (*a*) a meteorologist; esp. one who broadcasts a w. forecast on radio or television; (*b*) (freq. with capital initial) a member of a violent revolutionary group in the U.S.A.; **w.-ship,** a ship serving as a w.-station; **w.-station,** a meteorological observation post.

Weave, *v.*² **1. b.** To take evasive action in the air (*R.A.F. slang*). Also *transf.* in *to get weaving*, to 'get a move on' 1940.

Web, *sb.*

Comb.: **w. offset,** offset printing on a continuous reel of paper; freq. *attrib.*

Weber (vēⁱ·bəɹ). 1876. [Named after Wilhelm *Weber* (1804–91), German physicist.] †*a.* = COULOMB. †**b.** = AMPÈRE 1881. †**c.** An M.K.S. unit of magnetic induction (flux density), equivalent to 10,000 teslas 1889. **d.** The M.K.S. unit of magnetic flux (now incorporated in the S.I.), equal to 1 volt-second (10^8 C.G.S. units). Abbrev. Wb. 1891.

Wedge, *sb.* **3. f.** Used *attrib.* to designate a wedge-shaped heel or a shoe having such a heel 1939. **6.** *Golf.* An iron club, with a wedge-shaped head, used for approach shots 1951.

Weed, *sb.*¹ **3. c.** *slang* (orig. *U.S.*). Marijuana 1938.

Weepie (wī·pi). *colloq.* Also **weepy.** 1928. [f. WEEP *sb.* or *v.* + -IE.] A sentimental or mournful film, play, etc.

Wee-wee (wī·wī), *v. slang.* Also **wee.** 1930. [Origin unkn.] To urinate. Also as *sb.*, urination; urine.

Weigh, *v. Comb.*: **w.-in,** the action of weighing in a jockey, boxer, etc.; cf senses II. 1 b, 3.

Weight, *sb.* **II. 3.** Colloq. phr. *To throw* (or *chuck*, etc.) *one's w. about*: to assert oneself or one's authority, esp. in an objectionable way.

Weighting, *vbl. sb. spec.* An amount added to a salary for a special reason.

Weightless, *a.* Also (of a body having significant mass), not perceptibly or apparently acted on by gravity. Hence **Wei·ghtlessness.**

Weimaraner (vai·mărānəɹ, waimără·nəɹ). 1943. [G., f. *Weimar*, the name of the town in which the breed was developed + G. suffix *-aner*, as in *Lutheraner*, etc.] A kind of pointer, usually grey, used as a gun dog.

Weirdie (wīə·ɹdi). *dial.* or *colloq.* Also **weirdy.** 1894. [f. WEIRD *a.* + -IE.] A weird person; an eccentric. Also **Wei·rdo.**

Welfare, *sb. spec.* The maintenance of members of a community in a state of well-being and satisfaction, esp. as provided for and organized by legislation or social effort; often *attrib.* as in **w. state,** a country so organized that every member of the community is assured of his due maintenance, with the most advantageous conditions possible for all.

Well, *adv.*

Comb.: **w.-heeled** *a.*, prosperous, wealthy.

Wellsian (we·lziăn), *a.* (and *sb.*) 1912. [f. the name of H. G. *Wells* (1866–1946) + -IAN.] Of, pertaining to, or characteristic of the writings of H. G. Wells, esp. in the anticipation of future conditions. Also as *sb.*, a devotee or follower of H. G. Wells.

‖**Weltanschauung** (ve:ltanʃau·uŋ). 1868. [G., f. *welt* world + *anschauung* view, perception.] A philosophy of life; a conception of the world.

‖**Weltschmerz** (ve·ltʃmēəɹts). 1875. [G., f. *welt* world + *schmerz* pain.] An apathetic or pessimistic outlook on life; depression.

Western, *sb.* **3. b.** orig. *U.S.* A film or novel about the adventures of cowboys, rustlers, etc., in the western parts of N. America 1918.

Wet, *a.* **19.** *colloq.* Of a person: feeble, spiritless, silly 1916.

Comb.: **w.-back, we·tback** *U.S. slang*, an illegal immigrant from Mexico to the U.S.A.; **w.-dream,** an erotic dream accompanied by an orgasm.

Whacky, var. *WACKY *sb.* and *a.*

What. A. Phr. used as sb.: *W. have you*: anything else that there may be or that one can think of.

Wheeler.

Comb.: **w.-dealer** *colloq.* (orig. *U.S.*), a shrewd or scheming person.

Whip-lash.

Comb.: **w. injury,** an injury to a driver resulting from the sudden collision of his vehicle causing his head to move suddenly and violently.

Whirlybird (hwə̄·ɹlibə̄ɹd). *slang* (orig. *U.S.*). 1951. [f. WHIRLY *a.* + BIRD *sb.*] A helicopter.

Whistle, *sb.*

Comb.: **w.-stop** *U.S.*, a small town on a railway line at which trains stop when a signal is given on a whistle; *transf.* applied to organized stops on a (political) candidate's tour of the country.

White, *a.*

Comb.: **w. dwarf** *Astron.*, a small, very dense star of low intrinsic brightness and in the final stage of stellar evolution, all its hydrogen having been consumed; **w. hope** orig. *U.S.*, a person who is expected to be very successful; also *transf.*; **w. noise,** sound or noise in which all frequencies are present with roughly equal energies; **w. spirit,** a distillate of petroleum used as a substitute for turpentine.

White man. Phr. *The w. m.'s burden*: the responsibility of the white for the coloured peoples.

Take up the White Man's burden KIPLING.

Whitey, whity (hwəi·ti), *sb.* 1828. [f. WHITE *a.* + -Y[6].] A white person; also, white people collectively; now usu. derogatory.

Whizz, whiz, *sb.* **3.** Also **wiz** [perh. abbrev. of WIZARD *sb.*] An expert, a marvellous person 1921. *colloq.* (orig. *U.S.*). **4.** *Comb.*: **w.-kid,** a young person who is exceptionally successful, businesslike, etc.

Whodunit (hūdɒ·nit). *colloq.* (orig. *U.S.*). 1930. [repr. pronunc. of *who done it?*, illiterate form of *who did it?*] A mystery or detective story, play, etc.

Whole.

Comb.: **whole-tone** *a.*, of a piece of music, using a scale based on intervals of w. tones, as distinct from the semitones of the normal chromatic scale.

Wilco (wi·lko), *int.* 1948. Abbrev. of '(I) will comply', orig. used in Services' radio communications; hence as a general expression of compliance or agreement.

Wild. A. *adj.* **I. 1. wild-life, wildlife,** wild animals collectively; also *attrib.*

Wild cat.

Comb.: **w. strike,** a sudden unofficial strike.

Will, *sb.*[1]

Comb.: **w.-power,** the power to control one's own actions, etc., by means of one's w.

Willies (wi·liz), *sb. pl. slang* (orig. *U.S.*). 1896. [Origin unkn.] A nervous feeling of discomfort or fear; 'the creeps'; freq. *to give* (someone) *the w.*

Winceyette (wi:nsi,e·t). 1922. [f. WINCEY + -ETTE.] A kind of light-weight napped flannelette used for night-clothes, etc.

Wind, *sb.*[1] **III. 2. b.** *Wind(s) of change*: a force or tendency for reform.

Comb.: **w.-cheater,** a jacket of heavy fabric; an anorak; **w.-shield** chiefly *U.S.* = *w.-screen*; **w.-sock,** a tube of fabric flown from an airport mast to indicate the direction of the w.; **w.-tunnel,** an enclosed chamber or duct through which air may be driven at a known speed, so that its flow round (model) aircraft or other objects may be investigated or the objects themselves tested.

Window, *sb.* **5.** A collective term (app. orig. a code name) for: metal or metal-covered strips released in the atmosphere to interfere with radar detection 1942. **6.** A part of the electromagnetic spectrum to which a body or medium is relatively transparent 1949. **7.** *Astronautics.* A period outside which a planned launch cannot take place if the journey is to be completed, owing to the changing positions of the planets 1968.

5. The crews of these new bomber formations had been cascading W. into the air 1963. **7.** The Soviets availed themselves of the opportunity to launch interplanetary probes when the Venus w. opened in August 1971.

Comb.: **w.-shopping,** looking at displays in shop-windows without buying anything; hence **w.-shop** *v. intr.*, **w.-shopper.**

Winkle (wi·ŋk'l), *v.* 1925. [f. the sb.] *trans.* To extract, eject, get *out* (as a winkle from its shell with a knife).

If they're in the garden we'll wait and w. them out in the morning 1972.

Wino (wəi·no). *slang* (orig. *U.S.*). 1926. [f. WINE + *-o.*] A person addicted to wine; an alcoholic.

Winter, *sb.*[1]

Comb.: **w. sports,** open-air sports such as skating and skiing practised in w.

Winterize (wi·ntərəiz), *v.* 1934. [f. WINTER *sb.* + -IZE.] *trans.* To adapt for operation or use in winter or cold weather. Hence **Wi:nteriza·tion.**

Wipe-out (wəi·paut). 1921. [f. *to wipe out*: WIPE *v.* 5.] **1.** Obliteration of radio signals by other radio signals. **2.** *Surfing.* A fall from one's surf-board 1963.

Wire, *sb.*

Comb.: **w.-tapping,** eavesdropping on telephone conversations; **w. wool,** matted thin wire, used esp. for scouring kitchen utensils.

Wise, *sb.* **II. 3. b.** Revived (orig. *U.S.*) as a formative suffix attached to sbs. (occas. to other parts of speech) in the sense of 'with regard to or in the manner of (the thing specified)'.

And saleswise, the Webster dictionary gained out of all proportion to its rival 1947.

Wise, *a.*

3. b. w.-crack *colloq.* (orig. *U.S.*), a joke, witticism; **w. guy** *colloq.* (orig. *U.S.*), a know-all, a 'smart Aleck'.

Wish, *sb.*

Comb.: **w.-fulfilment,** the gratification of freq. subconscious desires, often through fantasy or by some substitute.

Wishful, *a.* **2. c.** *w. thinking*: an illusory state of mind towards events which is coloured by one's wishes concerning the future 1932.

Witch, *sb.*[2]

Comb.: **w.-hunt,** a search for a w. or witches; also *transf.*, esp. a search for, or persecution of, a person or persons with unacceptable political views.

With, *prep.* **II. 14. b.** Colloq. phr. *W. it*: up to date or progressive; following or knowledgeable about the latest trends, ideas, etc. 1959.

Withdrawal. 1. c. The process of ceasing to take addictive drugs, freq. accompanied by unpleasant physical reactions 1929. Also *attrib.*, as *w. symptoms.*

Wog (wɒg). *slang.* 1929. [Origin unknown.] A contemptuous name for a foreigner, esp. one from a Middle Eastern country.

Wolf, *sb.* **4. c.** A sexually aggressive man; a would-be seducer of women 1848.

Comb.: **w.-whistle** *colloq.*, a whistle from a man expressing admiration for a woman.

Woofer (wu·fəɹ, wū·-). 1940. [f. WOOF *v.*[2] + -ER[1].] A loudspeaker designed to reproduce low-frequency signals with fidelity while being relatively unresponsive to those of higher frequency. Cf. *TWEETER.

Word, *sb.* **II. 2.** *Computers.* The basic unit in terms of which data and instructions are stored and processed in a computer, often equal to a fixed number of bits 1948.

Work, *sb.* **II. 11. b.** Slang phr. (orig. *U.S.*). *The works*: everything; all the available material, information, etc.; freq. *to give* (someone) *the works*: to give or tell everything; *spec.* to kill; also *to get the works.*

Comb.: **w.-camp,** a camp for workers; *spec.* a place where volunteers work for a short period, usu. to help a community or the like; **w.-load,** the amount of w. which an employee, department, etc., is expected to complete; **w.-study,** investigation of the manner in which w. is done, with the aim of improving efficiency, output, etc.

Work, *v.* **II. 4. a.** Phr. *To w. to rule*: to follow pedantically the rules pertaining to one's occupation in order to slow down the work, usu. as a form of protest; so **w.-to-rule** *sb.*

Working, *ppl. a.* **2. c.** *W. party*: also in non-military use, a group of people working on a particular project; *spec.* a committee appointed to advise upon methods of improving efficiency in industry, etc.

World. I. 1. a. Colloq. phr. *out of this w.*: incredibly good, beautiful, etc.; beyond description; also *attrib.*

Worm, *sb.*

Comb.: **worm's-eye view,** a view as seen from below (opp. *bird's-eye view*); also *fig.*

Worry, *sb.*

Comb.: **w. beads,** a string of beads to manipulate with the fingers as a means of occupying one's hands or calming one's nerves.

Worry, *v.* **6. c.** Colloq. phrases: *I should w.*: an ironical phrase disclaiming concern or responsibility; *not to w.*: there is no need to w.; do not w.

Wow (wau), *sb.*[3] 1940. [imit.] In sound reproduction, a fluctuation in pitch that is slow enough to be perceptible as such on sustained notes.

Wow (wau), *v. slang* (orig. *U.S.*). 1926. [f. WOW *int.* and *sb.*[2]] *trans.* To impress or excite greatly: said esp. of an entertainer's effect on his audience.

Wrap, *sb.* **1. c.** *fig.* in *pl.* Concealment, a veil of secrecy; freq. in phr. *under wraps* 1939. *colloq.* (orig. *U.S.*).

Wrap, *v.* **I. 1. c.** *fig. To w. up*: to complete, finish off, settle (something). Also *intr.*, freq. as *imper.*, shut up, be quiet.

Write, *v.* **I. 3. e.** *Computers.* To enter (data) *in* or *on* a store or a storage medium, esp. magnetic tape 1948.

W. off. c. To reckon as lost. Hence **w.-off,** cancellation, amount cancelled, a dead loss.

Writing, *vbl. sb.* **II. 1.** Phr. *The w. on the wall* (with allusion to *Daniel* 5:5 and 25–28): a warning of impending disaster, misfortune, etc.

X.

II. 5. An X-chromosome 1902. **6.** Used to denote a cinema film which is unsuitable for children.

X-chromosome (e·ks-). 1911. [f. *X* used as an arbitrary label.] *Genetics.* A sex-chromosome of which there are two in the somatic cells and one in the gametes of one sex (in man and other mammals, the female), and one in the somatic cells and half the gametes of the other sex. Cf. *Y-CHROMOSOME.

Xenophobia (zenǒfōᵘ·biă). 1919. [See XENO-, -PHOBIA.] Morbid dread or dislike of foreigners. Hence **Xe·nophobe** [see -PHOBE]. **Xenopho·bic** *a.*

Xerography (zīᵊrǫ·grăfi). 1948. [f. XERO- + -GRAPHY, after *photography*.] A process for copying documentary material that does not employ liquids or chemical development of the image, but uses instead an electrically charged surface with the property of retaining a (dark) powder on those parts not exposed to light from the document, so that a permanent copy may be made by placing paper on the surface and fusing the powder to it by heating. Hence **Xerogra·phic** *a.*

Y.

8. A Y-chromosome 1911.

Yang (yæŋ). 1911. [Chin.] In Chinese philosophy, the active, male principle of the universe. Cf. *YIN.

Y-chromosome (wəi·-). 1911. [f. *Y* used as an arbitrary label.] *Genetics.* A sex-chromosome of which there is one in the somatic cells and in half the gametes of one sex (in man and other mammals, the male), and none in those of the other, its presence or absence in the zygote determining (in man and many other species) the sex of the future organism. Cf. *X-CHROMOSOME.

Yeah (yēᵊ), *adv.* orig. *U.S.* 1933. [repr. a casual pronunc. of YES *adv.*] = YES *adv.*; freq. *oh, yeah?* as an expression of incredulity.

Yellow. A. *adj.* **4.** *colloq.* (orig. *U.S.*). Cowardly 1856. Hence as *sb.*, cowardice.

Comb.: **y.-belly,** also, a coward; **y. pages,** a section of a telephone directory printed on y. paper and listing subscribers according to the services or goods they offer; **y. streak** orig. *U.S.*, cowardice.

Yen² (yen). *colloq.* (orig. *U.S.*). 1906. [Chin.] A desire, craving.

Yeti (ye·ti). 1938. Native (Sherpa) name of a hypothetical ape-like animal whose tracks have supposedly been found in snow on the Himalaya mountains; also known as 'the abominable snowman'.

Yin (yin). 1911. [Chin.] In Chinese philosophy, the passive, female principle of the universe. Cf. *YANG.

Yippee (yi·pī), *int.* orig. *U.S.* 1920. [perh. connected with HIP *int.*] An exclamation of delight or excitement.

Yippie (yi·pi). orig. *U.S.*. Also **Yippy,** and with lower-case initial. 1968. [f. the initials of *Youth International Party* + -IE, affected by prec. and by *HIPPIE, HIPPY.] A member of an American group of politically active hippies.

Yob (yǫb). *slang.* 1859. [Back-slang for BOY *sb.*] A boy; *spec.* a lout, hooligan. Also **Yo·bbo.**

Yours, *poss. pron.* **2. d.** Colloq. phr. *What's yours?*: what would you like to drink? 1930.

Youth.

Comb.: **y. club,** a club for young people; **y. hostel,** a lodging specially provided where young travellers or hikers can put up for the night.

Z.

Zabaglione, zabaione (zabalʸō·ne, zabayō·ne). 1906. [It.] An Italian sweet made of egg yolks, sugar, and Marsala, whipped together as they are heated.

‖**Zaibatsu** (zəibæ·tsu). 1937. [Jap.] In Japan, a group of financial and industrial establishments linked together in such a way as to constitute a monopoly; the members of such a financial oligarchy; (since 1947) a cartel, conglomerate.

Zany. 3. *attrib.* passing into *adj.* Characteristic of a z.; mad, comically idiotic 1616.

Zap (zæp), *v.* *slang* (orig. *U.S.*). 1942. [imit.] *trans.* To hit, attack, knock out, kill. Also as *sb.* and *int.*

Zebra.

Comb.: **z. crossing,** a pedestrian street crossing marked by parallel black and white bands on the road surface; also *ellipt.* as *zebra.*

Zen (zen). 1902. [Jap., 'meditation'.] An orig. Japanese and Chinese form of Buddhism which emphasizes the value of meditation and intuition. Also *attrib.*, as *Zen Buddhism, Buddhist.*

Zengakuren (ze:ŋgăkū·rĕn). 1959. [Jap., abbrev. of Zen Nihon Gakusei Jichikai Sorengo = All-Japan Federation of Student Self-Government Association (formed in 1948).] In Japan, an extreme left-wing student movement, noted for its violent interventions in national politics.

Zero (zīᵊ·ro), *v.* 1925. [f. the sb.] *intr.* To set the sights of a gun ready to fire; to take aim on a target; freq. *to z. in on* (a target). Also *transf.* and *fig.*

Zeroth (zīᵊ·rōᵘþ), *a.* 1899. [f. ZERO + -TH².] Coming next in a series before the one conventionally called or referred to as the 'first': the ordinal numeral corresponding to the cardinal zero. (Chiefly in scientific and mathematical use.)

Zing (ziŋ), *v.* *colloq.* (orig. *U.S.*). 1923. [imit.] *intr.* To move swiftly or with a shrill sound. Also as *sb.*, vigour, energy.

Zip, *v.* **2.** To close *up* with a zip fastener; also *refl.*, to put (oneself) into a garment or the like by closing it with a zip fastener 1951.

‖**Zloty** (zlǫ·ti). 1923. [Pol., f. *złoto* gold.] The basic monetary unit of Poland.

Zombie (zǫ·mbi). 1871. [Of West Afr. origin.] **1.** Orig., the snake-deity of voodoo cults in W. Africa, Haiti, and the southern U.S.; hence, a supernatural power which may reanimate dead bodies, or a body so reanimated. **2.** *colloq.* A person resembling a revived corpse; a dull, slow-witted, or apathetic person 1941.

Zoom, *v.* **2. b.** To move or rise quickly 1917. **c.** Of a cinematographic camera: to move quickly from a distant shot to a close-up; also *to z. in* (*on*) 1959.

Zoom (zūm), *sb.* 1917. [f. the vb.] The action of ZOOM *v.*; *spec.* of a cinematographic camera (see prec., 2 c). Also *attrib.*, as **z. lens,** a lens whose focal length and magnification can be changed quickly and smoothly while the image remains in the same plane.

Zoot suit (zū·t sᶦū·t). *colloq.* (orig. *U.S.*). 1939. [Rhyming formation on SUIT *sb.*] A type of men's suit, popular in the 1940s, consisting of a long loose jacket and high-waisted tapering trousers. Hence **Zoo·t-suiter,** one who wears such a suit.

‖**Zori** (zǫ·ri). Also **sori.** 1823. [Jap.] A Japanese straw sandal with a thong between the big toe and the small toes.

Zucchini (zukī·ni), *sb. pl.* *U.S.* 1929. [It., pl. of *zucchino*, dim. of *zucca* gourd, pumpkin.] = *COURGETTE(S.

Zwitterion (tsvi·təɹ,əi:ǒn, zwi-). 1906. [– G. *zwitterion* (F. W. Küster, 1897), f. *zwitter* hybrid (sb.) + *ion* ION.] *Physical Chem.* A molecule or ion that has separate positively and negatively charged groups; a dipolar ion. Hence **Zwitterio·nic** *a.*